W9-BFL-291

Presented

To

From

Date

Shout to the Lord, all the earth let us sing,

Power and majesty, praise to the King

Mountains bow down and the seas will roar,

At the sound of your name

I sing for joy at the work of your hands

Forever I'll love you, forever I'll stand

Nothing compares to the promise I have in You

My Story

I became a believer when I was ______ years old.
This is how:

____

____

____

The following people have supported me in my Christian walk:

____

____

____

They have helped me by:

____

____

____

This Bible verse has blessed me in my walk with God:

____

[I am] confident of this,
that he who began a good work in [me]
will carry it on to completion
until the day of Christ Jesus.

Philippians 1:6

NIV WOMEN of FAITH STUDY BIBLE

NEW INTERNATIONAL VERSION

GENERAL EDITOR
JEAN E. SYSWERDA

GRAND RAPIDS, MICHIGAN 49530

ZONDERVAN™

NIV Women of Faith Study Bible, New International Version ®

Published by Zondervan
Grand Rapids, Michigan 49530, U.S.A.

www.zondervan.com

Library of Congress Catalog Card Number 00-133720

Printed in the United States of America

05 06 07 08 09 10 /RRD-C/ 15 14 13 12 11

You will be pleased to know that a portion of the purchase price of your new NIV Bible has been provided to International Bible Society to help spread the gospel of Jesus Christ around the world!

Contents

Old Testament

New Testament

Weekly Studies Index

Old Testament

New Testament

Character Sketches Index

Old Testament

New Testament

Alphabetical List and Abbreviations

Alphabetical List

The books of the New Testament are in *italic.*

Abbreviations

Genesis *Ge*
Exodus *Ex*
Leviticus *Lev*
Numbers *Nu*
Deuteronomy *Dt*
Joshua *Jos*
Judges *Jdg*
Ruth *Ru*
1 Samuel *1Sa*
2 Samuel *2Sa*
1 Kings *1Ki*
2 Kings *2Ki*
1 Chronicles *1Ch*
2 Chronicles *2Ch*
Ezra *Ezr*
Nehemiah *Neh*
Esther *Est*
Job *Job*
Psalms *Ps*
Proverbs *Pr*
Ecclesiastes *Ecc*
Song of Songs *SS*
Isaiah *Isa*
Jeremiah *Jer*
Lamentations *La*
Ezekiel *Eze*
Daniel *Da*
Hosea *Hos*
Joel *Joel*
Amos *Am*
Obadiah *Ob*
Jonah *Jnh*
Micah *Mic*
Nahum *Na*
Habakkuk *Hab*
Zephaniah *Zep*
Haggai *Hag*
Zechariah *Zec*
Malachi *Mal*
Matthew *Mt*
Mark *Mk*
Luke *Lk*
John *Jn*
Acts *Ac*
Romans *Ro*
1 Corinthians *1Co*
2 Corinthians *2Co*
Galatians *Gal*
Ephesians *Eph*
Philippians *Php*
Colossians *Col*
1 Thessalonians *1Th*
2 Thessalonians *2Th*
1 Timothy *1Ti*
2 Timothy *2Ti*
Titus *Tit*
Philemon *Phm*
Hebrews *Heb*
James *Jas*
1 Peter *1Pe*
2 Peter *2Pe*
1 John *1Jn*
2 John *2Jn*
3 John *3Jn*
Jude *Jude*
Revelation *Rev*

How to Use This Bible

If your day is a typical kind of day, you probably experience both blessings and challenges. The good times are good. But sometimes you wonder, *Do other people go through what I'm going through? How do I know what's right?* God's Word has much to say to you—more than any other resource . . . even your closest friends and family. The *NIV Women of Faith Study Bible* has been written specifically with today's Christian woman in mind. The goal has been to draw out truths of Scripture in a way that highlights the women of Scripture and their situations, that reveals God's will and way, and that helps you consider and comprehend the beautiful truths of the Bible.

Features of the NIV Women of Faith Study Bible

The New International Version of the Bible

The Bible text itself it the most important part of this study Bible. Trusted by many Bible scholars and used by millions, the New International Version is the most read, most trusted translation in the world.

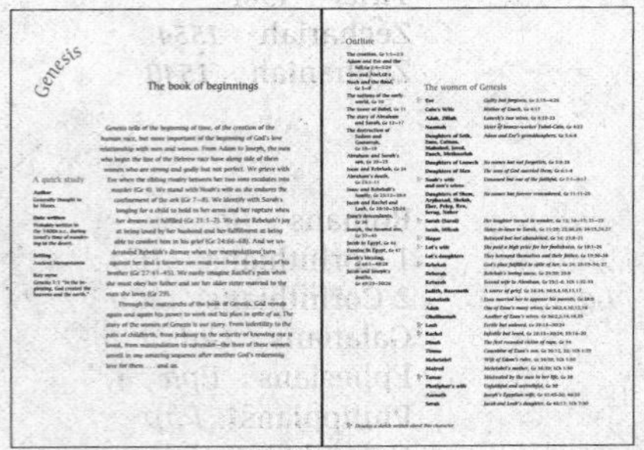

Book Introductions

Each of the Bible's 66 books begins with an introduction that highlights that book's background information, describes the part women played in the book and lists all the women who are found in the book. A basic outline, which will help you understand the book's structure and focus, is also included.

Bible Studies

Fifty-two Bible studies bring you deeper into the Word. With a focus on "Enjoying God," these studies will lead you through reading several Scripture passages and then applying the truths learned to your life. Each study can be used individually or in a group setting.

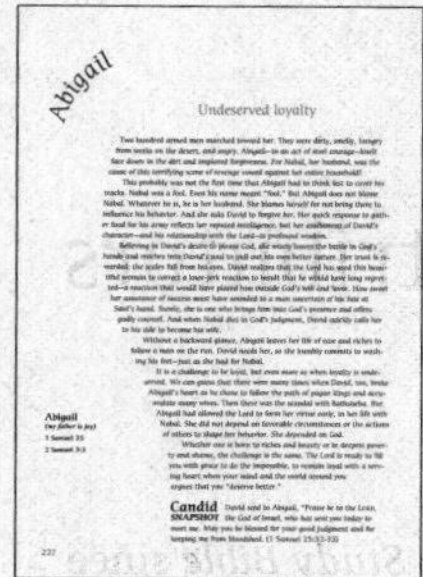

Character Sketches

Located throughout the Old and New Testaments, the character sketches highlight almost 80 of women in the Bible. Examining what their lives may have been like, observing their actions and reactions, then holding them in the light of God's Word will help you in your walk and growth as a woman of faith.

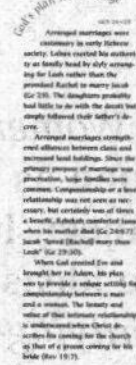

Study Notes

Forming the backbone of the NIV Women of Faith Study Bible are almost 1700 study notes on specific verses and passages of Scripture. These notes reveal background information and supply theological insight—all with the purpose of helping you find God in his Word and enjoy a more intimate walk with him.

Quotes

From 18th century hymn writers to 14th century mystics, from poets to essayists, women have been recording the heart of their Christian journeys for years. In this Bible, women of all ages, throughout all of history, are quoted and wonderful insights from your favorite Women of Faith conference speakers are also included for your encouragement.

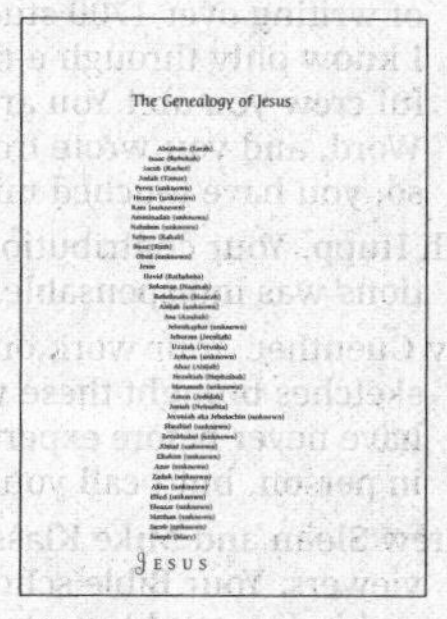

The Women in Jesus' Family Tree

The female ancestors of Jesus form a long line of faithful, God-fearing women whose lives inspire hope and faith. All of the women in Jesus' family line are presented in this feature.

Study Helps

A Bible concordance, a center-column reference system and color maps are included to assist you in your studies.

As you read and study the *NIV Women of Faith Study Bible*, we pray that your knowledge of the truths of Scripture will increase, that the Holy Spirit's work will cause a personal response in your life, and that your walk with God will become closer and more intimate.

Women of Faith helps women grow emotionally, spiritually and relationally. Since 1996, Women of Faith conferences have enjoyed an enthusiastic welcome by more than a million women across the country.

Acknowledgments and Contributors

I have had the privilege of being involved in the work of the *NIV Women of Faith Study Bible* since its beginnings in 1996, first as a publisher at Zondervan Bibles, then as general editor. In November of that year about ten of us gathered to plan and pray over the project. It would take another year for the ideas to really begin to take shape. And another year for those ideas to gel. Now, after hours and hours of planning and writing and designing and checking and *praying*—the *NIV Women of Faith Study Bible* is a reality.

I took on the job of general editor because I think I was and am uniquely equipped to do the job—not *primarily* because of any education or experience or capability—but because *I am you.* I am a wife and mother. I am a Bible reader. I am a Bible student. I go to church and small group studies, and I value what I learn there. I prayerfully approach my friends with my struggles and find help. I cook meals and clean up dishes and write checks and hug my kids and grandkids and go on the occasional vacation and mow the lawn and—well, you know the scene.

There are many who need to be thanked for their involvement in this work. Here they are, in no particular order except the first one, who deserves to be the first and the last.

I thank:

Our God and Savior, Jesus Christ. His presence blesses every part of this work. Without his touch our efforts would be futile.

The people and organization of Women of Faith. Through the written word and conference ministry, they are an inspiration.

My church "care circle" companions. You supported this work with your encouragement and prayers. A special thanks to the prayer warriors in this group. You know who you are.

John, my husband and my best friend. You are my encourager, smiling even when I frowned with the weight of the work.

My editors at Zondervan, Catherine DeVries and Shari TeSlaa. You were gracious and helpful and capably brought the work from average to excellent.

Natalie Block. You willingly jumped beyond what is comfortable for you and took on the enormous task of writing the 52 "Enjoying God" Bible studies. Your sincerity and hard work strengthened me.

The women who willingly and eagerly took on the task of writing over 1700 study notes. Most of you I know only through e-mail. But what a wonderful crew you are! You are fellow students of the Word, and you wrote from your hearts. In doing so, you have touched mine.

Sarah Hupp. Your contribution to the book introductions was indispensable.

Mary Guenther. Your work on the Bible character sketches brought these women to life in a way I have never before experienced. I've never met you in person, but I call you friend.

Andrew Sloan and Mike Klassen, the theological reviewers. Your Bible scholarship was an integral and indispensable part of making this work accessible and, above all, accurate.

Ruth DeJager. Your expertise in planning was essential, not only from a Biblical standpoint but from one of understanding the joys and sorrows of life as a woman of God.

My daughter Holly Grate. Your help at data entry made my work much more pleasant and efficient.

I've been in Christian publishing since the early 1970s and Bible publishing since the early 1980s. I've "done it all." I do not say that out of any sense of pride but to reveal my own inadequacies. As a Bible editor and publisher at Zondervan, I often encouraged a general editor or writer with these blissfully ignorant words: "You can do it! Just get started! We'll help! God will be with you!" never knowing the enormous weight of the blank page when an entire Bible of notes needs to be compiled and edited and checked and rechecked. I humbly apologize.

I now recognize more than ever the need for God's hand and help. I have agonized in prayer, recognizing that this is a work of God, not of a group of people who, though well-versed in Scripture and able writers, are not capable of what only the Holy Spirit can accomplish. So I conclude with the prayer that God will breathe his life into these efforts, that his voice will be heard through ours, and that this *NIV Women of Faith Study Bible* will ignite spiritual growth in you and make you, truly and surely, a woman of faith.

GENERAL EDITOR
Jean E. Syswerda
Best-selling author of *Women of the Bible* (co-authored with Ann Spangler). She is an editorial and publishing consultant and former editor and associate publisher for Zondervan Bibles. While at Zondervan, she was responsible for such best-selling Bibles as the *NIV Women's Devotional Bible*, the *NIV Adventure Bible*, and the *NIV Teen Study Bible*. She and her husband live in Allendale, MI.

ZONDERVAN EDITORS
Catherine DeVries Senior Bible Editor
Shari TeSlaa Editor

BOOK INTRODUCTION SUMMARIES
Sarah M. Hupp
Writer and editor. Author of several books including *God Bless Your Marriage* and *God's Storybook About Jesus*. Sarah enjoys her three pets, two children and one husband of 25 years.

ENJOYING GOD BIBLE STUDIES
Natalie J. Block
Freelance writer and editor. Her desire is that women will experience the intimate love of Jesus through the Word and Spirit's touch. She lives in Belmont, Michigan, with her husband and two teenage daughters.

CHARACTER SKETCHES
Mary E. Guenther
Former manager of book publishing, Promise Keepers. She is a freelance writer living in Nashville with her dog Smoke and a yard full of flowering shrubs. Mary is a mother of two, grandmother of four.

STUDY NOTES

Evelyn Bence Author of *Prayers for Girlfriends and Sisters and Me*, the Women of Faith Bible study *Knowing God's Will*, and the award-winning Biblical novel *Mary's Journal*.

Sally T. Breedlove Pastor's wife, mother of five, two of whom are married. Sally devotes her time to communicating God's heart of love for women through a writing and speaking ministry.

Judith Couchman Author, speaker, seminar leader. Judith writes Bible studies, devotionals and books for women, encouraging them to apply God's truths to their lives. She contributed significantly to the NIV Promises of God Bible. She lives in Colorado.

Tricia Goyer Freelance writer of over 100 articles and co-author of Mealtime Moments.Wife and mother of three, Tricia lives in Montana where she homeschools, teaches children's church, and co-directs a crisis pregnancy center.

Janet Kobobel Grant Former Zondervan editor and managing editor of books at Focus on the Family. Author of four Bible studies in the Women of Faith Bible study series. Janet holds a master's degree in Biblical Studies. She collects cookbooks and even cooks every once in awhile.

Sherry L. Harney Author and co-author of 30 small group study guides and over 100 articles. She is the Director of Children's ministry at her church. Wife and mother to three boys, she lives in Michigan.

Sharon A. Hersh Licensed professional counselor and author of *BRAVEHEARTS: Unlocking the Courage to Love with Abandon*. She and her husband speak for Family Life, a worldwide ministry of Campus Crusade. They live in Littleton, Colorado, with their two children.

Beth Lueders Owns MacBeth Communications, a business specializing in writing and editing. An award-winning journalist, Beth has traveled to 17 countries to report on God's work in the lives of women. Beth writes for numerous publications and is the co-author of *Celebrations of Faith*.

Shari MacDonald Freelance author whose work includes *Our God Reigns: The Stories Behind Your Favorite Praise and Worship Songs* (co-authored with Phil Christensen) and numerous Christian novels. She and her husband, photojournalist Craig Strong, make their home in Oregon.

Traci Mullins President of Eclipse Editorial Services, which provides editing, collaborative writing and consulting services to a wide variety of authors and publishing houses. Former senior editor at Piñon Press and senior acquisitions editor for NavPress, Traci has edited more than 150 books and authored five, including two Bible studies in the Women of Faith Bible study series. Traci lives in Colorado Springs.

Karen O'Connor Retreat speaker, Bible teacher, and award-winning author of *Basket of Blessings, Squeeze the Moment* and other Christian books. Karen is a wife, mother and grandmother living in California.

Paula Rinehart Counselor and author of five books, most recently, *Strong Women, Soft Hearts.* Paula lives with her husband and two children in North Carolina. She has been on staff with The Navigators for 25 years.

Joan C. Webb Bible teacher and author of six books, including the forthcoming workbook, *The Intentional Woman*. International Director of Family to Family, she travels regularly to the Middle East and Central Asia. Joan is a wife, mom and grandma, living in Arizona.

Preface

THE NEW INTERNATIONAL VERSION is a completely new translation of the Holy Bible made by over a hundred scholars working directly from the best available Hebrew, Aramaic and Greek texts. It had its beginning in 1965 when, after several years of exploratory study by committees from the Christian Reformed Church and the National Association of Evangelicals, a group of scholars met at Palos Heights, Illinois, and concurred in the need for a new translation of the Bible in contemporary English. This group, though not made up of official church representatives, was transdenominational. Its conclusion was endorsed by a large number of leaders from many denominations who met in Chicago in 1966.

Responsibility for the new version was delegated by the Palos Heights group to a self-governing body of fifteen, the Committee on Bible Translation, composed for the most part of biblical scholars from colleges, universities and seminaries. In 1967 the New York Bible Society (now the International Bible Society) generously undertook the financial sponsorship of the project—a sponsorship that made it possible to enlist the help of many distinguished scholars. The fact that participants from the United States, Great Britain, Canada, Australia and New Zealand worked together gave the project its international scope. That they were from many denominations—including Anglican, Assemblies of God, Baptist, Brethren, Christian Reformed, Church of Christ, Evangelical Free, Lutheran, Mennonite, Methodist, Nazarene, Presbyterian, Wesleyan and other churches—helped to safeguard the translation from sectarian bias.

How it was made helps to give the New International Version its distinctiveness. The translation of each book was assigned to a team of scholars. Next, one of the Intermediate Editorial Committees revised the initial translation, with constant reference to the Hebrew, Aramaic or Greek. Their work then went to one of the General Editorial Committees, which checked it in detail and made another thorough revision. This revision in turn was carefully reviewed by the Committee on Bible Translation, which made further changes and then released the final version for publication. In this way the entire Bible underwent three revisions, during each of which the translation was examined for its faithfulness to the original languages and for its English style.

All this involved many thousands of hours of research and discussion regarding the meaning of the texts and the precise way of putting them into English. It may well be that no other translation has been made by a more thorough process of review and revision from committee to committee than this one.

From the beginning of the project, the Committee on Bible Translation held to certain goals for the New International Version: that it would be an accurate translation and one that would have clarity and literary quality and so prove suitable for public and private reading, teaching, preaching, memorizing and liturgical use. The Committee also sought to preserve some measure of continuity with the long tradition of translating the Scriptures into English.

In working toward these goals, the translators were united in their commitment to the authority and infallibility of the Bible as God's Word in written form. They believe that it contains the divine answer to the deepest needs of humanity, that it sheds unique light on our path in a dark world, and that it sets forth the way to our eternal well-being.

The first concern of the translators has been the accuracy of the translation and its fidelity to the thought of the biblical writers. They have weighed the significance of the lexical and grammatical details of the Hebrew, Aramaic and Greek texts. At the same time, they have striven for more than a word-for-word translation. Because thought patterns and syntax differ from language to language, faithful communication of the meaning of the writers of the Bible demands frequent modifications in sentence structure and constant regard for the contextual meanings of words.

A sensitive feeling for style does not always accompany scholarship. Accordingly the Committee on Bible Translation submitted the developing version to a number of stylistic consultants. Two of them read every book of both Old and New Testaments twice—once before and once after the last major revision—and made invaluable suggestions. Samples of the translation were tested for clarity and ease of reading by various kinds of people—young and old, highly educated and less well educated, ministers and laymen.

Concern for clear and natural English—that the New International Version should be idiomatic but not idiosyncratic, contemporary but not dated—motivated the translators and consultants. At the same time, they tried to reflect the differing styles of the biblical writers. In view of the international use of English, the translators sought to avoid obvious Americanisms on the one hand and obvious Anglicisms on the other. A British edition reflects the comparatively few differences of significant idiom and of spelling.

As for the traditional pronouns "thou," "thee" and "thine" in reference to the Deity, the translators judged that to use these archaisms (along with the old verb forms such as "doest," "wouldest" and "hadst") would violate accuracy in translation. Neither Hebrew, Aramaic nor Greek uses special pronouns for the persons of the Godhead. A present-day translation is not enhanced by forms that in the time of the King James Version were used in everyday speech, whether referring to God or man.

For the Old Testament the standard Hebrew text, the Masoretic Text as published in the latest editions of Biblia Hebraica, was used throughout. The Dead Sea Scrolls contain material bearing on an earlier stage of the Hebrew text. They were consulted, as were the Samaritan Pentateuch and the ancient scribal traditions relating to textual changes. Sometimes a variant Hebrew reading in the margin of the Masoretic Text was followed instead of the text itself. Such instances, being variants within the Masoretic tradition, are not specified by footnotes. In rare cases, words in the consonantal text were divided differently from the way they appear in the Masoretic Text. Footnotes indicate this. The translators also consulted the more important early versions—the Septuagint; Aquila, Symmachus and Theodotion; the Vulgate; the Syriac Peshitta; the Targums; and for the Psalms the Juxta Hebraica of Jerome. Readings from these versions were occasionally followed where the Masoretic Text seemed doubtful and where accepted principles of textual criticism showed that one or more of these textual witnesses appeared to provide the correct reading. Such instances are footnoted. Sometimes vowel letters and vowel signs did not, in the judgment of the translators, represent the correct vowels for the original consonantal text. Accordingly some words were read with a different set of vowels. These instances are usually not indicated by footnotes.

The Greek text used in translating the New Testament was an eclectic one. No other piece of ancient literature has such an abundance of manuscript witnesses as does the New Testament. Where existing manuscripts differ, the translators made their choice of readings according to accepted principles of New Testament textual criticism. Footnotes call attention to places where there was uncertainty about what the original text was. The best current printed texts of the Greek New Testament were used.

There is a sense in which the work of translation is never wholly finished. This applies to all great literature and uniquely so to the Bible. In 1973 the New Testament in the New International Version was published. Since then, suggestions for corrections and revisions have been received from various sources. The Committee on Bible Translation carefully considered the suggestions and adopted a number of them. These were incorporated in the first printing of the entire Bible in 1978. Additional revisions were made by the Committee on Bible Translation in 1983 and appear in printings after that date.

As in other ancient documents, the precise meaning of the biblical texts is sometimes uncertain. This is more often the case with the Hebrew and Aramaic texts than with the Greek text. Although archaeological and linguistic discoveries in this century aid in understanding difficult passages, some uncertainties remain. The more significant of these have been called to the reader's attention in the footnotes.

In regard to the divine name YHWH, commonly referred to as the Tetragrammaton, the translators adopted the device used in most English versions of rendering that name as "LORD" in capital letters to distinguish it from Adonai, another Hebrew word rendered "Lord," for which small letters are used. Wherever the two names stand together in the Old Testament as a compound name of God, they are rendered "Sovereign LORD."

Because for most readers today the phrases "the LORD of hosts" and "God of hosts" have little meaning, this version renders them "the LORD Almighty" and "God Almighty." These renderings convey the sense of the Hebrew, namely, "he who is sovereign over all the 'hosts' (powers) in heaven and on earth, especially over the 'hosts' (armies) of Israel." For readers unacquainted with Hebrew this does not make clear the distinction between Sabaoth ("hosts" or "Almighty") and Shaddai (which can also be translated "Almighty"), but the latter occurs infrequently and is always footnoted. When Adonai and YHWH Sabaoth occur together, they are rendered "the Lord, the LORD Almighty."

As for other proper nouns, the familiar spellings of the King James Version are generally retained. Names traditionally spelled with "ch," except where it is final, are usually spelled in this translation with "k" or "c," since the biblical languages do not have the sound that "ch" frequently indicates in English—for example, in chant. For well-known names such as Zechariah, however, the traditional spelling has been retained. Variation in the spelling of names in the original languages has usually not been indicated. Where a person or place has two or more different names in the Hebrew, Aramaic or Greek texts, the more familiar one has generally been used, with footnotes where needed.

To achieve clarity the translators sometimes supplied words not in the original texts but required by the context. If there was uncertainty about such material, it is enclosed in brackets. Also for the sake of clarity or style, nouns, including some proper nouns, are sometimes substituted for pronouns, and vice versa. And though the Hebrew writers often shifted back and forth between first, second and third personal pronouns without change of antecedent, this translation often makes them uniform, in accordance with English style and without the use of footnotes.

Poetical passages are printed as poetry, that is, with indentation of lines and with separate stanzas. These are generally designed to reflect the structure of Hebrew poetry. This poetry is normally characterized by parallelism in balanced lines. Most of the poetry in the Bible is in the Old Testament, and scholars differ regarding the scansion of Hebrew lines. The translators determined the stanza divisions for the most part by analysis of the subject matter. The stanzas therefore serve as poetic paragraphs.

As an aid to the reader, italicized sectional headings are inserted in most of the books. They are not to be regarded as part of the NIV text, are not for oral reading, and are not intended to dictate the interpretation of the sections they head.

The footnotes in this version are of several kinds, most of which need no explanation. Those giving alternative translations begin with "Or" and generally introduce the alternative with the last word preceding it in the text, except when it is a single-word alternative; in poetry quoted in a footnote a slant mark indicates a line division. Footnotes introduced by "Or" do not have uniform significance. In some cases two possible translations were considered to have about equal validity. In other cases, though the translators were convinced that the translation in the text was correct, they judged that another interpretation was possible and of sufficient importance to be represented in a footnote.

In the New Testament, footnotes that refer to uncertainty regarding the original text are introduced by "Some manuscripts" or similar expressions. In the Old Testament, evidence for the reading chosen is given first and evidence for the alternative is added after a semicolon (for example: Septuagint; Hebrew father). In such notes the term "Hebrew" refers to the Masoretic Text.

It should be noted that minerals, flora and fauna, architectural details, articles of clothing and jewelry, musical instruments and other articles cannot always be identified with precision. Also measures of capacity in the biblical period are particularly uncertain (see the table of weights and measures following the text).

Like all translations of the Bible, made as they are by imperfect man, this one undoubtedly falls short of its goals. Yet we are grateful to God for the extent to which he has enabled us to realize these goals and for the strength he has given us and our colleagues to complete our task. We offer this version of the Bible to him in whose name and for whose glory it has been made. We pray that it will lead many into a better understanding of the Holy Scriptures and a fuller knowledge of Jesus Christ the incarnate Word, of whom the Scriptures so faithfully testify.

The Committee on Bible Translation

June 1978
(Revised Aug 1983)

Names of the translators and editors may be secured
from the International Bible Society translation sponsors
of the New International Version, 1820 Jet Stream Drive,
Colorado Springs, Colorado 08921-3696 U.S.A

Old Testament

Genesis

The book of beginnings.

Genesis tells of the beginning of time and of the creation of the human race, but, more important, it tells of the beginning of God's love relationship with men and women. From Adam to Joseph, the men who begin the line of the Hebrew race have alongside them women who, though imperfect, are strong and godly.

We grieve with Eve when the sibling rivalry between her two sons escalates into murder (Ge 4:8-12). We empathize with Noah's wife as she endures the confinement of the ark (Ge 7:13–8:14). We identify with Sarah's longing for a child and with her rapture when her dream is fulfilled (Ge 21:1-7). We share Rebekah's joy in the love of her husband and her fulfillment in her ability to comfort him in his grief (Ge 24:66-68). And we feel Rachel's pain when she must obey her father and see her older sister married to the man she loves (Ge 29:22-27).

Through the matriarchs of the book of Genesis, God reveals again and again his power to work out his plan *in spite of us.* The story of the women of Genesis is our story. From infertility to the pain of childbirth, from jealousy to the security of knowing one is loved, from manipulation to surrender—the lives of these women unveil in one amazing sequence after another God's redeeming love for them . . . and for us.

Quick Study

Author
Generally thought to be Moses.

Date Written
Probably written during the 1400s B.C., at the time of Israel's wandering in the desert.

Setting
Ancient Mesopotamia and Egypt.

Key Passage
Genesis 1:1 "In the beginning God created the heavens and the earth."

Outline

- The creation.
  Ge 1:1–2:3
- Adam and Eve and the fall.
  Ge 2:4–3:24
- Cain and Abel.
  Ge 4
- From Adam to Noah.
  Ge 5
- Noah and the flood.
  Ge 6-9
- The nations of the early world.
  Ge 10
- The tower of Babel.
  Ge 11
- Abraham and Sarah.
  Ge 12-17
- The destruction of Sodom and Gomorrah.
  Ge 18-19
- Abraham and Abimelech.
  Ge 20
- Abraham and Sarah's son.
  Ge 21-22
- Sarah's death.
  Ge 23
- Isaac and Rebekah.
  Ge 24
- Abraham's death.
  Ge 25:1-11
- Ishmael's sons.
  Ge 25:12-18
- Isaac and Rebekah's family.
  Ge 25:19–28:9
- Jacob's flight, marriages and return.
  Ge 28:10–35:29
- Esau's descendants.
  Ge 36
- The story of Joseph.
  Ge 37-45
- Jacob in Egypt.
  Ge 46:1–47:12
- Famine in Egypt.
  Ge 47:13-31
- Jacob's blessing.
  Ge 48:1–49:28
- The deaths of Jacob and Joseph.
  Ge 49:29–50:26

The Women of Genesis

⚘ **Eve**	*Guilty but forgiven.* Ge 2:15–4:26 (page 5)
Cain's wife	*Mother of Enoch, after whom a city was named.* Ge 4:17
Adah, Zillah	*Lamech's two wives.* Ge 4:19-23
Naamah	*Sister of bronze-worker Tubal-Cain.* Ge 4:22
Seth's daughters	*Adam and Eve's granddaughters.* Ge 5:6-8
Daughters of Enosh, Kenan, Mahalalel, Jared, Enoch, Methuselah, Lamech	*Names unknown but not forgotten.* Ge 5:9-28
Daughters of men	*Married the sons of God.* Ge 6:1-4
⚘ **Noah's wife and sons' wives**	*Unnamed but among the faithful.* Ge 7:1–9:17 (page 6)
Daughters of Shem, Arphaxad, Shelah, Eber, Peleg, Reu, Serug, Nahor	*Names unknown but forever remembered.* Ge 11:11-25
⚘ **Sarah (Sarai)**	*Her laughter turned to wonder.* Ge 12; 16–18:15; 21-23 (page 67)
Milcah	*Sister-in-law to Sarah.* Ge 11:29; 22:20-23; 24:15,24
⚘ **Hagar**	*Betrayed but not abandoned.* Ge 16; 21:8-21 (page 68)
⚘ **Lot's wife**	*Paid a high price for rebellion.* Ge 19:1-26 (page 135)
Lot's daughters	*Betrayed themselves and their father.* Ge 19:30-38
⚘ **Rebekah**	*God's plan fulfilled in spite of her.* Ge 24; 25:19-34; 27 (page 136)
Deborah	*Rebekah's faithful nurse.* Ge 24:59; 35:8
Keturah	*Second wife to Abraham.* Ge 25:1-6
Judith, Basemath	*A source of grief to their in-laws.* Ge 26:34-35
Mahalath	*Esau married her to appease his parents.* Ge 28:6-9
Adah	*One of Esau's many wives (may be the same as Basemath of Ge 26:34).* Ge 36:2,4,10,12,16
Oholibamah	*Another of Esau's wives (may be the same as Basemath of Ge 26:34).* Ge 36:2,5,14,18,25
⚘ **Leah**	*Fertile but unloved.* Ge 29:15–30:24 (page 199)
⚘ **Rachel**	*Infertile but loved.* Ge 29:15–30:24; 35:16-20 (page 200)
Dinah	*First recorded rape victim.* Ge 34
Timna	*Concubine of Esau's son.* Ge 36:12,22
Mehetabel	*Wife of Edom's ruler.* Ge 36:39
Matred	*Mehetabel's mother.* Ge 36:39
⚘ **Tamar**	*Mistreated by the men in her life.* Ge 38 (page 267)
Potiphar's wife	*Unfaithful and untruthful.* Ge 39
Asenath	*Joseph's Egyptian wife.* Ge 41:45,50; 46:20
Serah	*Jacob and Leah's granddaughter.* Ge 46:17

⚘ Denotes a sketch written about this character

The Beginning

1:1 **1** In the beginning[a] God created the heavens
[a]Jn 1:1-2 [b]Job 38:4; and the earth.[b] [2]Now the earth was[a] formless
Ps 90:2; and empty,[c] darkness was over the surface of
Isa 42:5; 44:24; 45:12, the deep, and the Spirit of God[d] was hover-
18; Ac 17:24; ing over the waters.
Heb 11:3; Rev 4:11 [3] And God said,[e] "Let there be light," and there
was light.[f] [4]God saw that the light was good,
1:2 [c]Jer 4:23 and he separated the light from the darkness.
[d]Ps 104:30 [5]God called the light "day," and the darkness
1:3 he called "night."[g] And there was evening,
[e]Ps 33:6,9; 148:5; and there was morning—the first day.
Heb 11:3 [6]And God said, "Let there be an expanse[h]
[f]2Co 4:6* between the waters to separate water from
water." [7]So God made the expanse and sepa-
1:5 [g]Ps 74:16 rated the water under the expanse from the
water above it.[i] And it was so. [8]God called the
1:6 [h]Jer 10:12 expanse "sky." And there was evening, and
there was morning—the second day.
1:7 [i]Job 38:8-11, [9] And God said, "Let the water under the sky be
16; Ps 148:4 gathered to one place,[j] and let dry ground
appear." And it was so. [10]God called the dry
1:9 [j]Job 38:8-11; ground "land," and the gathered waters he
Ps 104:6-9; called "seas." And God saw that it was good.
Pr 8:29; Jer 5:22; [11]Then God said, "Let the land produce veg-
2Pe 3:5 etation:[k] seed-bearing plants and trees on the
land that bear fruit with seed in it, according
1:11 [k]Ps 65:9-13; to their various kinds." And it was so. [12]The
104:14 land produced vegetation: plants bearing
seed according to their kinds and trees bearing fruit with seed in it according to their
kinds. And God saw that it was good. [13]And
there was evening, and there was morning—
the third day.
1:14 [l]Ps 74:16 [14]And God said, "Let there be lights[l] in the
[m]Jer 10:2 expanse of the sky to separate the day from
[n]Ps 104:19 the night, and let them serve as signs[m] to
mark seasons[n] and days and years, [15]and let
them be lights in the expanse of the sky to
give light on the earth." And it was so. [16]God
1:16 made two great lights—the greater light to
[o]Ps 136:8 [p]Ps 136:9 govern[o] the day and the lesser light to gov-
[q]Job 38:7,31- ern[p] the night. He also made the stars.[q] [17]God
32; Ps 8:3; set them in the expanse of the sky to give
Isa 40:26 light on the earth, [18]to govern the day and the
1:18 [r]Jer 33:20,25 night,[r] and to separate light from darkness.
And God saw that it was good. [19]And there
was evening, and there was morning—the
fourth day.
[20]And God said, "Let the water teem with living
creatures, and let birds fly above the earth
across the expanse of the sky." [21]So God created the great creatures of the sea and every
1:21 living and moving thing with which the
[s]Ps 104:25- water teems,[s] according to their kinds, and
26 every winged bird according to its kind. And
God saw that it was good. [22]God blessed them
and said, "Be fruitful and increase in number

[a] 2 Or possibly *became*

The God of Order

GE 1:1-26

The Bible's opening verses offer us our first glimpse of God. He presents himself as one who brings order from darkness, emptiness and formlessness. He separates light from darkness, sky from water, water from land. He commands his creation to "produce," to "mark" seasons and days and years to "govern" the day and night—all ways of establishing order. One can almost picture a woman coming into a house to find all its contents piled in a single, great heap. She separates the bedroom linens from the kitchen utensils, the living room furniture from the dining room furniture and, in the process, creates a lovely, warm and hospitable place to live. Read Genesis 1:1-26 and underline each word or phrase that shows God bringing order to his "house."

Male and Female

GE 1:27-31

Men and women are both created—intricately, exquisitely—in the image of God. Many have heard that statement and even quoted it. The difficulty arises when defining what being created in God's image actually means. God's image involves the spiritual more than the physical. God is a spiritual being and, as humans created in his image, so are we. The human spirit can commune with God's spirit. Humans created in God's image can exhibit godly characteristics: holiness, righteousness and justice.

The verses that follow (Ge 1:28-30) explain the importance of this image in the creation context. Human beings are uniquely fitted to rule creation as God's image-bearers and as his representatives. Their superior position allows them to use and enjoy the creation but also carries the responsibility to uphold and protect it. Spend a few moments thinking of ways in which you are an image-bearer of the Creator God, then list one way you enjoy the creation and one way you could uphold or protect it.

and fill the water in the seas, and let the birds
increase on the earth."[t] 23 And there was
evening, and there was morning—the fifth
day.
24 And God said, "Let the land produce living creatures according to their kinds: livestock, creatures that move along the ground, and wild
animals, each according to its kind." And it
was so. 25 God made the wild animals[u] according to their kinds, the livestock according to
their kinds, and all the creatures that move
along the ground according to their kinds.
And God saw that it was good.
26 Then God said, "Let us[v] make man in our
image,[w] in our likeness, and let them rule[x]
over the fish of the sea and the birds of the
air, over the livestock, over all the earth,[a] and
over all the creatures that move along the
ground."

27 So God created man in his own image,[y]
in the image of God he created him;
male and female[z] he created them.

28 God blessed them and said to them, "Be
fruitful and increase in number; fill the earth[a]
and subdue it. Rule over the fish of the sea
and the birds of the air and over every living
creature that moves on the ground."
29 Then God said, "I give you every seed-
bearing plant on the face of the whole earth
and every tree that has fruit with seed in it.
They will be yours for food.[b] 30 And to all the
beasts of the earth and all the birds of the air
and all the creatures that move on the
ground—everything that has the breath of life
in it—I give every green plant for food.[c]" And
it was so.
31 God saw all that he had made,[d] and it was
very good.[e] And there was evening, and there
was morning—the sixth day.

2 Thus the heavens and the earth were completed in all their vast array.
2 By the seventh day God had finished the work
he had been doing; so on the seventh day he
rested[b] from all his work.[f] 3 And God blessed
the seventh day and made it holy,[g] because
on it he rested from all the work of creating
that he had done.

Adam and Eve

4 This is the account of the heavens and the
earth when they were created.

When the LORD God made the earth and the
heavens— 5 and no shrub of the field had yet
appeared on the earth[c] and no plant of the field
had yet sprung up,[h] for the LORD God had not sent
rain on the earth[c][i] and there was no man to work

1:22 [t]ver 28; Ge 8:17
1:25 [u]Jer 27:5
1:26 [v]Ps 100:3 [w]Ge 9:6; Jas 3:9 [x]Ps 8:6-8
1:27 [y]1Co 11:7 [z]Ge 5:2; Mt 19:4*; Mk 10:6*
1:28 [a]Ge 9:1,7; Lev 26:9
1:29 [b]Ps 104:14
1:30 [c]Ps 104:14, 27; 145:15
1:31 [d]Ps 104:24 [e]1Ti 4:4
2:2 [f]Ex 20:11; 31:17; Heb 4:4*
2:3 [g]Lev 23:3; Isa 58:13
2:5 [h]Ge 1:11 [i]Ps 65:9-10

[a] 26 Hebrew; Syriac *all the wild animals* [b] 2 Or *ceased*; also in verse 3 [c] 5 Or *land*; also in verse 6

Mother of Discontent

Can the serpent be right? He is so beautiful and seems so wise. Am I missing out on something? Is God holding back something good? Eve entertained the thought. And so began the slide of the human race into chaos, pain and death.

Eve had been blessed with every perfection by a loving Creator. She had a perfect body that was unhampered by disease, deterioration or death. She needed no clothing to protect her in a climate perfect for life. The perfect diet grew around her, just waiting to be plucked. Delight filled her days. Animals had no fear of humans and peacefully shared the wealth of the Garden of Eden. Eve had no need to hide, no need to fear, no need to control, no need to fight.

She had never known loneliness, for Adam was her constant companion and lover. Their attachment was complete and uncomplicated—they were *one.* She was his partner, even in the work that gave their lives purpose. Best of all, Eve knew her Creator intimately, meeting him face-to-face with Adam each day. Perfect—still, Eve wondered . . .

Then she decided: She *would* have that fruit! So Eve accepted the *serpent's* insinuation that God was holding out on her. We—who still live out the consequences—long to cry, "No! Stop!" And in that pivotal crisis of all time, Adam too chose to eat the forbidden fruit. The serpent inserted a tiny wedge of discontent, which—except for the work of Jesus Christ—opened a chasm of perpetual despair.

The perfect love that had permeated the garden no longer existed in the fallen world; the change was immediate. Adam and Eve scrambled to cover their shame; their oneness with God and with each other shattered. Too late, they discovered that they had traded priceless treasures for empty promises.

Beware of discontent. We all face the temptation to believe there is something better out there. When we accept that belief, we scorn the One who gives us our deepest intimacy and security. Life on earth is flawed. Nothing and no one apart from God can satisfy the aching vacuum in us caused by the fall; only Jesus' love can fill the gap between what is and what was meant to be. We can never return to the garden. But believers in Jesus will see him face-to-face in a place better than Eden. Don't you long to be there?

Eve
(life, living)

Genesis 2–3

2 Corinthians 11:3

1 Timothy 2:13–14

Candid SNAPSHOT *When the woman saw that the fruit of the tree was good for food and pleasing to the eye, and also desirable for gaining wisdom, she took some and ate it. She also gave some to her husband, who was with her, and he ate it* (Genesis 3:6).

Noah's Wife

Along for the Ride or Partner in Adventure?

Can you picture the scene? Logs and wood chips are all over the yard; Noah hammers all day on this big boat. He's been at it for years now, and the whole time he has been preaching tales to the neighbors of God's judgment on the earth.

Did Noah's wife truly understand their situation? "The LORD was grieved that he had made man on the earth, and his heart was filled with pain" (Ge 6:6). How tragic! The crown of God's creation—made in his own image, for his glory and his pleasure—gave him only pain and were bringing judgment down on their own heads. Yet—Noah found favor. Noah walked with God, and because of his righteousness, his family was saved from destruction. That included his wife.

Little is written about her. We don't even know her name. We don't know if she opposed Noah or if she helped him significantly. Was she just along for the ride, or was she sharing the work and the achievement?

She had a magnificent opportunity to be an active partner in a great adventure. But perhaps she resented all the extra work Noah's obsession caused. We don't know if she shared his priorities—before it began to rain . . .

It's easy to lose perspective in the day-to-day grind. Are you married to a man you think is overzealous for the Lord? He may be a giant of the faith, like Noah. You need to decide if you will just go along or if you'll be your husband's wholehearted partner in the adventure that is your life together.

Candid SNAPSHOT The LORD then said to Noah, "Go into the ark, you and your whole family, because I have found you righteous in this generation" (Genesis 7:1).

Noah's Wife

Genesis 6:18; 7:1,7,13; 8:16,18

2:7 the ground, 6but streams[a] came up from the earth
[j]Ge 3:19 and watered the whole surface of the ground—
[k]Ps 103:14 7the LORD God formed the man[b] from the dust[j] of
[l]Job 33:4 the ground[k] and breathed into his nostrils the
[m]Ac 17:25 breath[l] of life,[m] and the man became a living
[n]1Co 15:45* being.[n]
8Now the LORD God had planted a garden in the
2:8 east, in Eden;[o] and there he put the man he had
[o]Ge 3:23,24; Isa 51:3 formed. 9And the LORD God made all kinds of trees
grow out of the ground—trees that were pleasing
2:9 to the eye and good for food. In the middle of the
[p]Ge 3:22,24; garden were the tree of life[p] and the tree of the
Rev 2:7; 22:2,14,19 knowledge of good and evil.[q]
[q]Eze 47:12 10A river watering the garden flowed from Eden;
from there it was separated into four headwaters.
11The name of the first is the Pishon; it winds
through the entire land of Havilah, where there is
gold. 12(The gold of that land is good; aromatic
resin[c] and onyx are also there.) 13The name of the
second river is the Gihon; it winds through the
entire land of Cush.[d] 14The name of the third riv-
2:14 er is the Tigris;[r] it runs along the east side of
[r]Da 10:4 Asshur. And the fourth river is the Euphrates.
15The LORD God took the man and put him in
the Garden of Eden to work it and take care of it.
16And the LORD God commanded the man, "You
are free to eat from any tree in the garden; 17but
you must not eat from the tree of the knowledge
2:17 of good and evil, for when you eat of it you will
[s]Dt 30:15, 19; Ro 5:12; surely die."[s]
6:23; 18The LORD God said, "It is not good for the man
Jas 1:15 to be alone. I will make a helper suitable for him."[t]
2:18 19Now the LORD God had formed out of the
[t]1Co 11:9 ground all the beasts of the field[u] and all the birds
2:19 of the air. He brought them to the man to see what
[u]Ps 8:7 he would name them; and whatever the man
[v]Ge 1:24 called each living creature,[v] that was its name.
20So the man gave names to all the livestock, the
birds of the air and all the beasts of the field.
But for Adam[e] no suitable helper was found.
21So the LORD God caused the man to fall into a
deep sleep; and while he was sleeping, he took
one of the man's ribs[f] and closed up the place
2:22 with flesh. 22Then the LORD God made a woman
[w]1Co 11:8,9, from the rib[g][w] he had taken out of the man, and
12 he brought her to the man.
23The man said,

2:23 "This is now bone of my bones
[x]Ge 29:14; and flesh of my flesh;[x]
Eph 5:28-30 she shall be called 'woman,[h]'
2:24 for she was taken out of man."

[y]Mal 2:15
[z]Mt 19:5*; 24For this reason a man will leave his father and
Mk 10:7-8*; 1Co 6:16*; mother and be united[y] to his wife, and they will
Eph 5:31* become one flesh.[z]

[a] 6 Or *mist* [b] 7 The Hebrew for *man (adam)* sounds like and may be related to the Hebrew for *ground (adamah)*; it is also the name *Adam* (see Gen. 2:20). [c] 12 Or *good; pearls* [d] 13 Possibly southeast Mesopotamia [e] 20 Or *the man* [f] 21 Or *took part of the man's side* [g] 22 Or *part* [h] 23 The Hebrew for *woman* sounds like the Hebrew for *man.*

Intimate by Design

GE 2:1-25

Eve is distinctive from all the other creatures God made, including Adam. The birds, animals and Adam are created "out of the ground" (Ge 2:19) or from "dust" (Ge 2:7). But Eve is formed from a part of Adam. The special link between these two shows how God established them to intricately relate to one another. Today, a person can donate an organ that another person might live, and we even transfer bone marrow from one individual to another. But the "transplant" God conducts is much more than a physical sharing. It creates a bond between man and woman that is intended to be emotional, spiritual and intellectual. That is why the story of Eve's creation is followed by the proclamation: "For this reason [because they are made of the same flesh and the same bone] a man will leave his father and mother and be united to his wife" (Ge 2:24). (See character sketch for Eve on page 5.)

Temptation

GE 3:1–6

While these verses portray Satan as a seductive tempter, the Bible's view of temptation goes beyond a person being wooed to do something evil. Instead, temptation is presented as a trial or test in which the individual has the opportunity to display faithfulness and devotion (which is part of the reason God put the tree in the garden). Sadly, Eve fails to reveal loyalty and love. Instead, she is won over by the fruit's appeal, the thought that she doesn't have to live within the parameters God has set for her, and the goal of becoming like God—through disobedience rather than obedience.

The same is true for us today. God challenges us to be "conformed to the likeness of his Son" (Ro 8:29), but when we use distorted means to try to become like God, we distance ourselves from him rather than drawing nearer to him, just as Eve did.

25 The man and his wife were both naked,[a] and
they felt no shame.

The Fall of Man

3 Now the serpent[b] was more crafty than any of
the wild animals the LORD God had made. He
said to the woman, "Did God really say, 'You must
not eat from any tree in the garden'?"
2 The woman said to the serpent, "We may eat
fruit from the trees in the garden, 3 but God did
say, 'You must not eat fruit from the tree that is in
the middle of the garden, and you must not touch
it, or you will die.' "
4 "You will not surely die," the serpent said to
the woman.[c] 5 "For God knows that when you eat
of it your eyes will be opened, and you will be like
God,[d] knowing good and evil."
6 When the woman saw that the fruit of the tree
was good for food and pleasing to the eye, and
also desirable[e] for gaining wisdom, she took some
and ate it. She also gave some to her husband,
who was with her, and he ate it.[f] 7 Then the eyes of
both of them were opened, and they realized they
were naked; so they sewed fig leaves together and
made coverings for themselves.
8 Then the man and his wife heard the sound of
the LORD God as he was walking[g] in the garden in
the cool of the day, and they hid[h] from the LORD
God among the trees of the garden. 9 But the LORD
God called to the man, "Where are you?"
10 He answered, "I heard you in the garden, and
I was afraid because I was naked; so I hid."
11 And he said, "Who told you that you were
naked? Have you eaten from the tree that I commanded you not to eat from?"
12 The man said, "The woman you put here with
me—she gave me some fruit from the tree, and I
ate it."
13 Then the LORD God said to the woman, "What
is this you have done?"
The woman said, "The serpent deceived me,[i]
and I ate."
14 So the LORD God said to the serpent, "Because
you have done this,

"Cursed[j] are you above all the livestock
and all the wild animals!
You will crawl on your belly
and you will eat dust[k]
all the days of your life.
15 And I will put enmity
between you and the woman,
and between your offspring[a][l] and
hers;[m]
he will crush[b] your head,[n]
and you will strike his heel."

16 To the woman he said,

2:25 [a]Ge 3:7,10-11
3:1 [b]2Co 11:3; Rev 12:9; 20:2
3:4 [c]Jn 8:44; 2Co 11:3
3:5 [d]Isa 14:14; Eze 28:2
3:6 [e]Jas 1:14-15; 1Jn 2:16 [f]1Ti 2:14
3:8 [g]Dt 23:14 [h]Job 31:33; Ps 139:7-12; Jer 23:24
3:13 [i]2Co 11:3; 1Ti 2:14
3:14 [j]Dt 28:15-20 [k]Isa 65:25; Mic 7:17
3:15 [l]Jn 8:44; Ac 13:10; 1Jn 3:8 [m]Isa 7:14; Mt 1:23; Rev 12:17 [n]Ro 16:20; Heb 2:14

[a] 15 Or *seed* [b] 15 Or *strike*

Week 1

God's Pursuit of You

Each day in the Garden of Eden is perfect. The soft ground cushions Adam and Eve's bare feet. The dew waters their surroundings to a perfect, lush green. Evenings in the garden are even better—if perfection can be improved on. That's when Adam and Eve walk with God. His presence surpasses the rest of their day and brings them joy and peace.

But this day is different. They hear the "sound of the LORD God" as he walks "in the garden in the cool of the day" (Ge 3:8). But they don't run to meet him. They don't feel the way they used to. They hide because they are filled with *shame,* a new emotion for them.

God is calling you too. Are you running to meet him—or are you hiding from him? Shame can prevent an intimate, personal relationship with God. But it's important to differentiate between *true* shame and *false* shame. You feel true shame if you feel guilty for your sin (and all of us sin). You feel false shame if you feel dirty because another person sinned against you (for example, the shame felt by victims of sexual or spousal abuse or rape). If you have been wounded by someone else's sin, you may feel a sense of shame, but it is not true shame. Bring true shame to the cross of Jesus for forgiveness. Bring false shame into the arms of Jesus for healing (1Pe 2:24).

- Adam and Eve feel shame. What is the root of their shame and guilt (Ge 3:11; Ro 5:12-14)?
- What have you done that causes you to feel shame? What is the root of your shame (Ro 3:10-12)?
- Adam and Eve cover their nakedness (the outward evidence of their shame) with a few flimsy fig leaves (Ge 3:7). What have you done to try to cover your shame? Have your efforts had any impact (Isa 59:2)?
- What has Jesus done to remove your shame (Isa 53:4-6; Ro 6:22-23)?
- Where do you stand with God now (Eph 2:4-7; Heb 4:14-16)?

If your sin seems too great or horrible to be forgiven or if your shame seems so overwhelming that it can't be removed, remember, Jesus loves you so much that he has already taken your sin and shame on himself. He makes you clean from it. Receive his gift and let him wash your shame away.

Enjoying God THROUGH the Word

Read Acts 22:3-21 (pages 1833-34). Paul tells the crowd he had been passionate in his persecution of Jesus' followers. He had thought he was pleasing God by destroying those heretics. At his conversion Paul discovered the truth. By persecuting Jesus' followers, he had been persecuting God. Yet God forgave Paul and used him in a mighty way (Ac 22:14-16).

In spite of your past—no matter what you have done—God loves you and has plans for you (Jer 29:11-14). You can believe him when he says, "I have loved you with an everlasting love; I have drawn you with loving-kindness" (Jer 31:3).

Enjoying God THROUGH Experience

If your shame is for your own sin, write the name of that sin on a sheet of paper. Then with a pencil write the word *shame* in large letters across the paper. Jesus knows what's happened, and he loves you anyway. In prayer, confess your sin and your need for Jesus. In faith, erase the word *shame.* Now write in ink the word *forgiven* across your paper. Remember: "Those who look to him are radiant; their faces are never covered with shame" (Ps 34:5).

Go to page 119 for your next weekly study.

The Curse

GE 3:16

After Adam and Eve disobey God, creation, which had been orderly and without blemish, becomes disorderly and flawed. Eve will experience pain in childbirth, and her "desire" will be for her husband. In the Hebrew language, the word *desire* encompasses much more than the idea of longing. The entire soul or essence of the person is involved. Therefore, this passage suggests that Eve's sense of herself, emotionally and physically, will become dependent on her husband.

Clearly, woman's subordinate position to man is reflected in ancient society. As with all the other curses, this is not an ideal state. We do all we can to ease childbirth pain, and we strive to make working and laboring as efficient and productive as possible. So, too, the ideal in a husband and wife relationship is not to live within the confines of the curse but to live as the equals God created the original pair to be.

"I will greatly increase your pains in
childbearing;
with pain you will give birth to
children. 3:16
Your desire will be for your husband, [o]1Co 11:3;
and he will rule over you.[o]" Eph 5:22

17 To Adam he said, "Because you listened to
your wife and ate from the tree about which I
commanded you, 'You must not eat of it,'

"Cursed[p] is the ground because of you; 3:17
through painful toil you will eat of it [p]Ge 5:29; Ro 8:20-22
all the days of your life.[q] [q]Job 5:7;
18 It will produce thorns and thistles for 14:1;
you, Ecc 2:23
and you will eat the plants of the 3:18
field.[r] [r]Ps 104:14
19 By the sweat of your brow 3:19
you will eat your food[s] [s]2Th 3:10
until you return to the ground, [t]Ge 2:7;
since from it you were taken; Ps 90:3;
for dust you are 104:29; Ecc 12:7
and to dust you will return."[t]

20 Adam[a] named his wife Eve,[b] because she
would become the mother of all the living.
21 The LORD God made garments of skin for
Adam and his wife and clothed them. 22 And the
LORD God said, "The man has now become like
one of us, knowing good and evil. He must not be
allowed to reach out his hand and take also from 3:22
the tree of life[u] and eat, and live forever." 23 So the [u]Rev 22:14
LORD God banished him from the Garden of Eden[v] 3:23
to work the ground[w] from which he had been tak- [v]Ge 2:8 [w]Ge 4:2
en. 24 After he drove the man out, he placed on the 3:24
east side[c] of the Garden of Eden cherubim[x] and a [x]Ex 25:18-22
flaming sword[y] flashing back and forth to guard [y]Ps 104:4
the way to the tree of life.[z] [z]Ge 2:9

Cain and Abel

4 Adam[a] lay with his wife Eve, and she became
pregnant and gave birth to Cain.[d] She said,
"With the help of the LORD I have brought forth[e] a 4:2
man." 2 Later she gave birth to his brother Abel.[a] [a]Lk 11:51
Now Abel kept flocks, and Cain worked the
soil. 3 In the course of time Cain brought some of 4:3
the fruits of the soil as an offering to the LORD.[b] [b]Nu 18:12
4 But Abel brought fat portions[c] from some of the 4:4
firstborn of his flock.[d] The LORD looked with favor [c]Lev 3:16
on Abel and his offering,[e] 5 but on Cain and his [d]Ex 13:2,12
offering he did not look with favor. So Cain was [e]Heb 11:4
very angry, and his face was downcast.
6 Then the LORD said to Cain, "Why are you
angry? Why is your face downcast? 7 If you do
what is right, will you not be accepted? But if you
do not do what is right, sin is crouching at your 4:7
door;[f] it desires to have you, but you must mas- [f]Nu 32:23
ter it.[g]" [g]Ro 6:16

[a] 20,1 Or *The man* [b] 20 *Eve* probably means *living.* [c] 24 Or *placed in front* [d] 1 *Cain* sounds like the Hebrew for *brought forth* or *acquired.* [e] 1 Or *have acquired*

8 Now Cain said to his brother Abel, "Let's go
out to the field."[a] And while they were in the
field, Cain attacked his brother Abel and killed
him.[h]
9 Then the LORD said to Cain, "Where is your
brother Abel?"
"I don't know," he replied. "Am I my brother's
keeper?"
10 The LORD said, "What have you done? Listen!
Your brother's blood cries out to me from the
ground.[i] 11 Now you are under a curse and driven
from the ground, which opened its mouth to
receive your brother's blood from your hand.
12 When you work the ground, it will no longer
yield its crops for you. You will be a restless wanderer on the earth."
13 Cain said to the LORD, "My punishment is
more than I can bear. 14 Today you are driving me
from the land, and I will be hidden from your
presence;[j] I will be a restless wanderer on the
earth, and whoever finds me will kill me."[k]
15 But the LORD said to him, "Not so[b]; if anyone
kills Cain[l], he will suffer vengeance seven times
over.[m]" Then the LORD put a mark on Cain so that
no one who found him would kill him. 16 So Cain
went out from the LORD's presence and lived in
the land of Nod,[c] east of Eden.[n]
17 Cain lay with his wife, and she became pregnant and gave birth to Enoch. Cain was then
building a city, and he named it after his son[o]
Enoch. 18 To Enoch was born Irad, and Irad was
the father of Mehujael, and Mehujael was the
father of Methushael, and Methushael was the
father of Lamech.
19 Lamech married two women, one named
Adah and the other Zillah. 20 Adah gave birth to
Jabal; he was the father of those who live in tents
and raise livestock. 21 His brother's name was
Jubal; he was the father of all who play the harp
and flute. 22 Zillah also had a son, Tubal-Cain, who
forged all kinds of tools out of[d] bronze and iron.
Tubal-Cain's sister was Naamah.
23 Lamech said to his wives,

"Adah and Zillah, listen to me;
wives of Lamech, hear my words.
I have killed[e][p] a man for wounding me,
a young man for injuring me.
24 If Cain is avenged[q] seven times,[r]
then Lamech seventy-seven times."

25 Adam lay with his wife again, and she gave
birth to a son and named him Seth,[f][s] saying, "God
has granted me another child in place of Abel,
since Cain killed him."[t] 26 Seth also had a son, and
he named him Enosh.

4:8 [h]Mt 23:35; 1Jn 3:12
4:10 [i]Ge 9:5; Nu 35:33; Heb 12:24; Rev 6:9-10
4:14 [j]2Ki 17:18; Ps 51:11; 139:7-12; Jer 7:15; 52:3 [k]Ge 9:6; Nu 35:19,21, 27,33
4:15 [l]Eze 9:4,6 [m]ver 24; Ps 79:12
4:16 [n]Ge 2:8
4:17 [o]Ps 49:11
4:23 [p]Ex 20:13; Lev 19:18
4:24 [q]Dt 32:35 [r]ver 15
4:25 [s]Ge 5:3 [t]ver 8

[a] *8* Samaritan Pentateuch, Septuagint, Vulgate and Syriac; Masoretic Text does not have *"Let's go out to the field."*
[b] *15* Septuagint, Vulgate and Syriac; Hebrew *Very well*
[c] *16* *Nod* means *wandering* (see verses 12 and 14).
[d] *22* Or *who instructed all who work in*
[e] *23* Or *I will kill*
[f] *25* *Seth* probably means *granted.*

Motherhood

GE 4:25

Eve soon learns that motherhood brings pain that goes beyond childbirth. Her son Cain murders his brother Abel. Because Cain is then sent into exile, Eve loses not one son, but both sons. God consoles her by giving her another son, Seth, whom Eve views as a gift from God for what must have been an aching heart. Often, even today, in a mother's sorrow God comes alongside her and soothes her pain-filled heart by providing sweet consolation and comfort.

At that time men began to call on[a] the name of
the LORD.[u]

From Adam to Noah

5 This is the written account of Adam's line.

When God created man, he made him in the
likeness of God.[v] 2He created them male and
female[w] and blessed them. And when they were
created, he called them "man.[b]"
3When Adam had lived 130 years, he had a son
in his own likeness, in his own image;[x] and he
named him Seth. 4After Seth was born, Adam lived
800 years and had other sons and daughters. 5Alto-
gether, Adam lived 930 years, and then he died.[y]
6When Seth had lived 105 years, he became the
father[c] of Enosh. 7And after he became the father
of Enosh, Seth lived 807 years and had other sons
and daughters. 8Altogether, Seth lived 912 years,
and then he died.
9When Enosh had lived 90 years, he became the
father of Kenan. 10And after he became the father
of Kenan, Enosh lived 815 years and had other
sons and daughters. 11Altogether, Enosh lived 905
years, and then he died.
12When Kenan had lived 70 years, he became
the father of Mahalalel. 13And after he became the
father of Mahalalel, Kenan lived 840 years and
had other sons and daughters. 14Altogether, Kenan
lived 910 years, and then he died.
15When Mahalalel had lived 65 years, he
became the father of Jared. 16And after he became
the father of Jared, Mahalalel lived 830 years and
had other sons and daughters. 17Altogether, Mahalalel lived 895 years, and then he died.
18When Jared had lived 162 years, he became
the father of Enoch.[z] 19And after he became the
father of Enoch, Jared lived 800 years and had
other sons and daughters. 20Altogether, Jared lived
962 years, and then he died.
21When Enoch had lived 65 years, he became
the father of Methuselah. 22And after he became
the father of Methuselah, Enoch walked with
God[a] 300 years and had other sons and daughters.
23Altogether, Enoch lived 365 years. 24Enoch
walked with God;[b] then he was no more, because
God took him away.[c]
25When Methuselah had lived 187 years, he
became the father of Lamech. 26And after he
became the father of Lamech, Methuselah lived
782 years and had other sons and daughters.
27Altogether, Methuselah lived 969 years, and
then he died.
28When Lamech had lived 182 years, he had a
son. 29He named him Noah[d] and said, "He will
comfort us in the labor and painful toil of our
hands caused by the ground the LORD has cursed.[d]"

[a] 26 Or *to proclaim* [b] 2 Hebrew *adam* [c] 6 *Father* may mean *ancestor*; also in verses 7–26. [d] 29 *Noah* sounds like the Hebrew for *comfort*.

4:26 [u]Ge 12:8; 1Ki 18:24; Ps 116:17; Joel 2:32; Zep 3:9; Ac 2:21; 1Co 1:2
5:1 [v]Ge 1:27; Eph 4:24; Col 3:10
5:2 [w]Ge 1:27; Mt 19:4; Mk 10:6; Gal 3:28
5:3 [x]Ge 1:26; 1Co 15:49
5:5 [y]Ge 3:19
5:18 [z]Jude 1:14
5:22 [a]ver 24; Ge 6:9; 17:1; 48:15; Mic 6:8; Mal 2:6
5:24 [b]ver 22 [c]2Ki 2:1,11; Heb 11:5
5:29 [d]Ge 3:17; Ro 8:20

Since the fall, we all feel a . . . sense of loss, and our relationships are tainted by mistrust and fear. Even in the most happy, fulfilled moments of our lives, we, like Adam and Eve, quietly long for something more . . . Before the fall we had a perfect place on this earth, and now we do not . . . Jesus said, "In my Father's house are many rooms; if it were not so, I would have told you. I am going there to prepare a place for you" (Jn 14:2). That is our hope and our final destination. Until that day we have each other.

Here and now, the only part of eternity that we get to touch is each other. As sons and daughters of Adam and Eve, we tend to live as isolated beings, locked into the invisible walls of our mind. We need to reach beyond our fears because we need each other; right beside us is another soul who longs for home, another soul who can help us discern the signs along life's road, as they give us input and as we reach out to them.

—Sheila Walsh

30 After Noah was born, Lamech lived 595 years
and had other sons and daughters. 31 Altogether,
Lamech lived 777 years, and then he died.
32 After Noah was 500 years old, he became the
father of Shem, Ham and Japheth.

The Flood

6 When men began to increase in number on
6:1 [e]Ge 1:28 the earth[e] and daughters were born to them,
2 the sons of God saw that the daughters of men
were beautiful, and they married any of them they
6:3 chose. 3 Then the LORD said, "My Spirit will not
[f]Isa 57:16 contend with[a] man forever,[f] for he is mortal[b];[g] his
[g]Ps 78:39 days will be a hundred and twenty years."
6:4 4 The Nephilim[h] were on the earth in those
[h]Nu 13:33 days—and also afterward—when the sons of God
went to the daughters of men and had children by
them. They were the heroes of old, men of renown.
5 The LORD saw how great man's wickedness on
6:5 the earth had become, and that every inclination
[i]Ge 8:21; of the thoughts of his heart was only evil all the
Ps 14:1-3 time.[i] 6 The LORD was grieved[j] that he had made
6:6 man on the earth, and his heart was filled with
[j]1Sa 15:11, pain. 7 So the LORD said, "I will wipe mankind,
35; Isa 63:10 whom I have created, from the face of the earth—
men and animals, and creatures that move along
the ground, and birds of the air—for I am grieved
6:8 that I have made them." 8 But Noah found favor in
[k]Ge 19:19; the eyes of the LORD.[k]
Ex 33:12,13,
17; Lk 1:30; 9 This is the account of Noah.
Ac 7:46

6:9 Noah was a righteous man, blameless among
[l]Ge 7:1; the people of his time,[l] and he walked with God.[m]
Eze 14:14, 10 Noah had three sons: Shem, Ham and Japheth.[n]
20; Heb 11:7; 11 Now the earth was corrupt in God's sight and
2Pe 2:5 [m]Ge 5:22 was full of violence.[o] 12 God saw how corrupt the
6:10 earth had become, for all the people on earth had
[n]Ge 5:32 corrupted their ways.[p] 13 So God said to Noah, "I
6:11 am going to put an end to all people, for the earth
[o]Eze 7:23; is filled with violence because of them. I am sure-
8:17 ly going to destroy both them and the earth.[q] 14 So
6:12 make yourself an ark of cypress[c] wood;[r] make
[p]Ps 14:1-3 rooms in it and coat it with pitch[s] inside and out.
6:13 15 This is how you are to build it: The ark is to be
[q]ver 17; 450 feet long, 75 feet wide and 45 feet high.[d]
Eze 7:2-3 16 Make a roof for it and finish[e] the ark to within
6:14 18 inches[f] of the top. Put a door in the side of the
[r]Heb 11:7; ark and make lower, middle and upper decks. 17 I
1Pe 3:20 am going to bring floodwaters on the earth to
[s]Ex 2:3 destroy all life under the heavens, every creature
6:17 that has the breath of life in it. Everything on
[t]Ge 7:4,21- earth will perish.[t] 18 But I will establish my cov-
23; 2Pe 2:5 enant with you,[u] and you will enter the ark[v]—you
6:18 and your sons and your wife and your sons' wives
[u]Ge 9:9-16 [v]Ge 7:1,7,13 with you. 19 You are to bring into the ark two of all

[a] 3 Or *My spirit will not remain in* [b] 3 Or *corrupt*
[c] 14 The meaning of the Hebrew for this word is uncertain.
[d] 15 Hebrew *300 cubits long, 50 cubits wide and 30 cubits high* (about 140 meters long, 23 meters wide and 13.5 meters high)
[e] 16 Or *Make an opening for light by finishing* [f] 16 Hebrew *a cubit* (about 0.5 meter)

But Noah

GE 6:8

The human race veers away from God. Rulers develop harems, signaling sexual dissipation, while "wickedness" (Ge 6:5)—criminal acts that violate the rights of others—and "violence" (Ge 6:11)—acts that intentionally damage others—are rampant. In the midst of this wanton scene stands Noah, who is not only righteous but is also living blamelessly among his neighbors (Ge 6:9). Now, that's a difficult balance when your neighbor is filled with violent thoughts, leading a life of debauchery, and committing crimes against others.

Even more surprising is that Noah isn't in hiding. Instead, 2 Peter 2:5 describes him as "a preacher of righteousness." He is busy telling others that a judgment day is coming. No wonder God is pleased when he sees Noah—in the center of rampant sinfulness—living faithfully, righteously and evangelistically. And no wonder God's Word interrupts its depiction of debauchery to declare, "But Noah" (Ge 6:8).

living creatures, male and female, to keep them **6:20**
alive with you. 20 Two[w] of every kind of bird, of [w]Ge 7:15
every kind of animal and of every kind of creature
that moves along the ground will come to you to
be kept alive. 21 You are to take every kind of food
that is to be eaten and store it away as food for
you and for them."
22 Noah did everything just as God commanded **6:22**
him.[x] [x]Ge 7:5,9,16
7 The LORD then said to Noah, "Go into the ark, **7:1**
you and your whole family,[y] because I have [y]Mt 24:38
found you righteous[z] in this generation. 2 Take [z]Ge 6:9;
with you seven[a] of every kind of clean[a] animal, a Eze 14:14
male and its mate, and two of every kind of **7:2**
unclean animal, a male and its mate, 3 and also [a]ver 8;
seven of every kind of bird, male and female, to Ge 8:20;
keep their various kinds alive throughout the Lev 10:10;
earth. 4 Seven days from now I will send rain on 11:1-47
the earth for forty days and forty nights, and I will
wipe from the face of the earth every living creature I have made."
5 And Noah did all that the LORD commanded **7:5**
him.[b] [b]Ge 6:22
6 Noah was six hundred years old when the
floodwaters came on the earth. 7 And Noah and his
sons and his wife and his sons' wives entered the
ark to escape the waters of the flood. 8 Pairs of
clean and unclean animals, of birds and of all
creatures that move along the ground, 9 male and
female, came to Noah and entered the ark, as God
had commanded Noah. 10 And after the seven days
the floodwaters came on the earth.
11 In the six hundredth year of Noah's life, on the
seventeenth day of the second month—on that **7:11**
day all the springs of the great deep[c] burst forth, [c]Eze 26:19
and the floodgates of the heavens[d] were opened. [d]Ge 8:2
12 And rain fell on the earth forty days and forty **7:12**
nights.[e] [e]ver 4
13 On that very day Noah and his sons, Shem,
Ham and Japheth, together with his wife and the
wives of his three sons, entered the ark. 14 They
had with them every wild animal according to
its kind, all livestock according to their kinds,
every creature that moves along the ground
according to its kind and every bird according to
its kind, everything with wings. 15 Pairs of all
creatures that have the breath of life in them **7:15**
came to Noah and entered the ark.[f] 16 The ani- [f]Ge 6:19
mals going in were male and female of every living thing, as God had commanded Noah. Then
the LORD shut him in.
17 For forty days[g] the flood kept coming on the **7:17**
earth, and as the waters increased they lifted the [g]ver 4
ark high above the earth. 18 The waters rose and
increased greatly on the earth, and the ark floated
on the surface of the water. 19 They rose greatly on
the earth, and all the high mountains under the **7:19**
entire heavens were covered.[h] 20 The waters rose [h]Ps 104:6
and covered the mountains to a depth of more

a 2 Or *seven pairs*; also in verse 3

*T*he Bible says Noah "walked with God" (Ge 6:9). It doesn't say he *talked* with God. Instead the image implies quiet companionship. Noah walked with God—and, no doubt, he listened. He "found favor in the eyes of the LORD" (Ge 6:8). Noah spent time with the Father, and during their time together God spoke to him. And as outrageous as God's instructions may have seemed at the time, Noah set about building an ark. He stepped out with courage to do what he perceived as God's will.

—Barbara Johnson

than twenty feet.[a,b] 21 Every living thing that
moved on the earth perished—birds, livestock,
wild animals, all the creatures that swarm over
the earth, and all mankind.[i] 22 Everything on dry
land that had the breath of life[j] in its nostrils died.
23 Every living thing on the face of the earth was
wiped out; men and animals and the creatures
that move along the ground and the birds of the
air were wiped from the earth.[k] Only Noah was
left, and those with him in the ark.[l]
24 The waters flooded the earth for a hundred
and fifty days.[m]

8 But God remembered[n] Noah and all the wild
animals and the livestock that were with him
in the ark, and he sent a wind over the earth,[o] and
the waters receded. 2 Now the springs of the deep
and the floodgates of the heavens[p] had been closed,
and the rain had stopped falling from the sky. 3 The
water receded steadily from the earth. At the end of
the hundred and fifty days the water had gone
down, 4 and on the seventeenth day of the seventh
month the ark came to rest on the mountains of
Ararat. 5 The waters continued to recede until the
tenth month, and on the first day of the tenth
month the tops of the mountains became visible.
6 After forty days Noah opened the window he
had made in the ark 7 and sent out a raven, and it
kept flying back and forth until the water had
dried up from the earth. 8 Then he sent out a dove
to see if the water had receded from the surface
of the ground. 9 But the dove could find no place to
set its feet because there was water over all the
surface of the earth; so it returned to Noah in the
ark. He reached out his hand and took the dove
and brought it back to himself in the ark. 10 He
waited seven more days and again sent out the
dove from the ark. 11 When the dove returned to
him in the evening, there in its beak was a fresh-
ly plucked olive leaf! Then Noah knew that the
water had receded from the earth. 12 He waited
seven more days and sent the dove out again, but
this time it did not return to him.
13 By the first day of the first month of Noah's
six hundred and first year, the water had dried up
from the earth. Noah then removed the covering
from the ark and saw that the surface of the
ground was dry. 14 By the twenty-seventh day of
the second month the earth was completely dry.
15 Then God said to Noah, 16 "Come out of the
ark, you and your wife and your sons and their
wives.[q] 17 Bring out every kind of living creature
that is with you—the birds, the animals, and all
the creatures that move along the ground—so
they can multiply on the earth and be fruitful and
increase in number upon it."[r]
18 So Noah came out, together with his sons and
his wife and his sons' wives. 19 All the animals
and all the creatures that move along the ground

7:21 [i]Ge 6:7,13
7:22 [j]Ge 1:30
7:23 [k]Mt 24:39; Lk 17:27; 1Pe 3:20; 2Pe 2:5 [l]Heb 11:7
7:24 [m]Ge 8:3
8:1 [n]Ge 9:15; 19:29; Ex 2:24; 1Sa 1:11,19 [o]Ex 14:21
8:2 [p]Ge 7:11
8:16 [q]Ge 7:13
8:17 [r]Ge 1:22

[a] 20 Hebrew *fifteen cubits* (about 6.9 meters) [b] 20 Or *rose more than twenty feet, and the mountains were covered*

A Long, Long Cruise

GE 7:24—8:17

Often we think of the flood as lasting for "forty days" (Ge 7:17), but a closer reading of Scripture reveals that the ark's occupants didn't feel the earth beneath their feet for about a full year (compare Ge 7:11 and Ge 8:13–14). That's a longer cruise than most of us would willingly sign up for. Cabin fever, 150 days of rain or flooding, seasickness, personality conflicts, and wondering about their qualifications to be zookeepers are just some of the battles Noah and his family likely wage during their "cruise." In addition to these factors, the boat's occupants probably experience loneliness, grief over all those who lost their lives in the wash of water, and concern about their own welfare when the flood ends. But the story doesn't end there. Genesis 9 begins with these wonderful words: "God blessed Noah . . ."

Punishment and Love

GE 8:20–22

After releasing all the animals from the ark, Noah's first act is one of thanksgiving. He builds an altar and sacrifices "some of all the clean animals and clean birds" (Ge 8:20). *The aroma of that sacrifice pleases God. His response is one of love and promise. God resolves that from this time on—even though he recognizes that evil will continue in the hearts of human beings—he will never again destroy as he did in the flood. Planting and harvesting, heat, cold, the seasons, and night and day are all reinstated, never to be so devastatingly disrupted again. Our loving Father expresses his faithfulness and love in ways visible to us even today.*

and all the birds—everything that moves on the
earth—came out of the ark, one kind after another.
20 Then Noah built an altar to the LORD[s] and, taking some of all the clean animals and clean[t] birds,
he sacrificed burnt offerings[u] on it. 21 The LORD
smelled the pleasing aroma[v] and said in his heart:
"Never again will I curse the ground[w] because of
man, even though[a] every inclination of his heart
is evil from childhood.[x] And never again will I
destroy all living creatures,[y] as I have done.

22 "As long as the earth endures,
seedtime and harvest,
cold and heat,
summer and winter,
day and night
will never cease."[z]

God's Covenant With Noah

9 Then God blessed Noah and his sons, saying to
them, "Be fruitful and increase in number and
fill the earth.[a] 2 The fear and dread of you will fall
upon all the beasts of the earth and all the birds of
the air, upon every creature that moves along the
ground, and upon all the fish of the sea; they are
given into your hands. 3 Everything that lives and
moves will be food for you.[b] Just as I gave you the
green plants, I now give you everything.
4 "But you must not eat meat that has its
lifeblood still in it.[c] 5 And for your lifeblood I will
surely demand an accounting. I will demand an
accounting from every animal.[d] And from each
man, too, I will demand an accounting for the life
of his fellow man.[e]

6 "Whoever sheds the blood of man,
by man shall his blood be shed;[f]
for in the image of God[g]
has God made man.

7 As for you, be fruitful and increase in number;
multiply on the earth and increase upon it."[h]
8 Then God said to Noah and to his sons with
him: 9 "I now establish my covenant with you[i] and
with your descendants after you 10 and with every
living creature that was with you—the birds, the
livestock and all the wild animals, all those that
came out of the ark with you—every living creature on earth. 11 I establish my covenant[j] with you:
Never again will all life be cut off by the waters of
a flood; never again will there be a flood to
destroy the earth.[k]"
12 And God said, "This is the sign of the covenant[l] I am making between me and you and
every living creature with you, a covenant for all
generations to come: 13 I have set my rainbow in
the clouds, and it will be the sign of the covenant
between me and the earth. 14 Whenever I bring
clouds over the earth and the rainbow appears in
the clouds, 15 I will remember my covenant[m]

8:20 [s]Ge 12:7-8; 13:18; 22:9 [t]Ge 7:8; Lev 11:1-47 [u]Ge 22:2,13; Ex 10:25
8:21 [v]Lev 1:9,13; 2Co 2:15 [w]Ge 3:17 [x]Ge 6:5; Ps 51:5; Jer 17:9 [y]Ge 9:11,15; Isa 54:9
8:22 [z]Ge 1:14; Jer 33:20,25
9:1 [a]Ge 1:22
9:3 [b]Ge 1:29
9:4 [c]Lev 3:17; 17:10-14; Dt 12:16,23-25; 1Sa 14:33
9:5 [d]Ex 21:28-32 [e]Ge 4:10
9:6 [f]Ge 4:14; Ex 21:12,14; Lev 24:17; Mt 26:52 [g]Ge 1:26
9:7 [h]Ge 1:22
9:9 [i]Ge 6:18
9:11 [j]ver 16; Isa 24:5 [k]Ge 8:21; Isa 54:9
9:12 [l]ver 17; Ge 17:11
9:15 [m]Ex 2:24; Lev 26:42,45; Dt 7:9; Eze 16:60

[a] *21* Or *man, for*

between me and you and all living creatures of every kind. Never again will the waters become a flood to destroy all life. [16]Whenever the rainbow appears in the clouds, I will see it and remember the everlasting covenant[n] between God and all living creatures of every kind on the earth."

[17]So God said to Noah, "This is the sign of the covenant[o] I have established between me and all life on the earth."

The Sons of Noah

[18]The sons of Noah who came out of the ark were Shem, Ham and Japheth. (Ham was the father of Canaan.)[p] [19]These were the three sons of Noah, and from them came the people who were scattered over the earth.[q]

[20]Noah, a man of the soil, proceeded[a] to plant a vineyard. [21]When he drank some of its wine, he became drunk and lay uncovered inside his tent. [22]Ham, the father of Canaan, saw his father's nakedness and told his two brothers outside. [23]But Shem and Japheth took a garment and laid it across their shoulders; then they walked in backward and covered their father's nakedness. Their faces were turned the other way so that they would not see their father's nakedness.

[24]When Noah awoke from his wine and found out what his youngest son had done to him, [25]he said,

"Cursed be Canaan![r]
The lowest of slaves
will he be to his brothers.[s]"

[26]He also said,

"Blessed be the LORD, the God of Shem!
May Canaan be the slave of Shem.[b]
[27]May God extend the territory of
Japheth[c];
may Japheth live in the tents of Shem,
and may Canaan be his[d] slave."

[28]After the flood Noah lived 350 years. [29]Altogether, Noah lived 950 years, and then he died.

The Table of Nations

10 This is the account[t] of Shem, Ham and Japheth, Noah's sons, who themselves had sons after the flood.

The Japhethites

[2]The sons[e] of Japheth:
Gomer,[u] Magog,[v] Madai, Javan, Tubal,[w]
Meshech and Tiras.
[3]The sons of Gomer:
Ashkenaz,[x] Riphath and Togarmah.[y]
[4]The sons of Javan:

[a] 20 Or *soil, was the first* [b] 26 Or *be his slave* [c] 27 *Japheth* sounds like the Hebrew for *extend.* [d] 27 Or *their* [e] 2 *Sons* may mean *descendants* or *successors* or *nations;* also in verses 3, 4, 6, 7, 20–23, 29 and 31.

9:16 [n]ver 11; Ge 17:7,13, 19; 2Sa 7:13; 23:5
9:17 [o]ver 12; Ge 17:11
9:18 [p]ver 25-27; Ge 10:6,15
9:19 [q]Ge 10:32
9:25 [r]ver 18 [s]Ge 25:23; Jos 9:23
10:1 [t]Ge 2:4
10:2 [u]Eze 38:6 [v]Eze 38:2; Rev 20:8 [w]Isa 66:19
10:3 [x]Jer 51:27 [y]Eze 27:14; 38:6

God Remembers

GE 9:14–16

Forgetfulness is a problem for us as humans. Because God knows our tendency not to remember his faithfulness and constancy, he has provided a variety of ways to tie a string around our finger. When we see a rainbow, he intends for us to remember his promise never again to wreak massive destruction on the human race or on earth's creatures. In addition, God assures us in Genesis 9:14–16 that the rainbow will serve to remind** him **of his promise to** us**. He is much like a mother who comforts her child by plugging in a night-light, saying it will remind her to come and check on her little one. In actuality, the mother isn't likely to forget her promise. Nor is God. But the night-light and the rainbow serve as a comfort and a reminder to all the parties involved.

We were created for perfection. In fact, we were originally placed in a perfect world. In Eden . . . God's original design for each of us was to live in a state of perfection. We were created for that experience, and we were created for that expectation.

So what happened? Simply put, Eve disobeyed God and convinced Adam to disobey as well, and the consequence of their disobedience was they were banished from Eden. That meant they lost the perfect environment, the perfect experiences and the fulfillment of perfect expectations. The reverberating aftermath of their disobedience is our yearning and questing for that which was lost to us. This, then, is why Jesus said, "In this world you will have trouble" (Jn 16:33). It all started with Adam and Eve . . .

Nothing in life is perfect because perfection was lost in Eden. But the flip side of this negative is fully understanding and accepting that life will never be perfect and neither will any experience or relationship. If we can accept that, we can quit looking for it, blaming others or ourselves because we can't find it, and even come to a place of peace about that loss.

—*Marilyn Meberg*

Elishah, Tarshish,[z] the Kittim and the Rodanim.[a] 5 (From these the maritime peoples
spread out into their territories by their
clans within their nations, each with its
own language.)

The Hamites

6 The sons of Ham:
Cush, Mizraim,[b] Put and Canaan.[a]
7 The sons of Cush:
Seba, Havilah, Sabtah, Raamah and Sabteca.
The sons of Raamah:
Sheba and Dedan.

8 Cush was the father[c] of Nimrod, who grew to be
a mighty warrior on the earth. 9 He was a mighty
hunter before the LORD; that is why it is said, "Like
Nimrod, a mighty hunter before the LORD." 10 The
first centers of his kingdom were Babylon,[b] Erech,
Akkad and Calneh, in[d] Shinar.[e c] 11 From that land
he went to Assyria,[d] where he built Nineveh,[e]
Rehoboth Ir,[f] Calah 12 and Resen, which is between
Nineveh and Calah; that is the great city.

13 Mizraim was the father of
the Ludites, Anamites, Lehabites, Naphtuhites, 14 Pathrusites, Casluhites (from whom the Philistines[f] came) and Caphtorites.
15 Canaan[g] was the father of
Sidon[h] his firstborn,[g] and of the Hittites,[i]
16 Jebusites,[j] Amorites, Girgashites, 17 Hivites,
Arkites, Sinites, 18 Arvadites, Zemarites and Hamathites.

Later the Canaanite[k] clans scattered 19 and the
borders of Canaan[l] reached from Sidon[m] toward
Gerar as far as Gaza, and then toward Sodom,
Gomorrah, Admah and Zeboiim, as far as Lasha.
20 These are the sons of Ham by their clans and
languages, in their territories and nations.

The Semites

21 Sons were also born to Shem, whose older
brother was[h] Japheth; Shem was the ancestor of
all the sons of Eber.[n]

22 The sons of Shem:
Elam,[o] Asshur, Arphaxad,[p] Lud and Aram.
23 The sons of Aram:
Uz,[q] Hul, Gether and Meshech.[i]
24 Arphaxad was the father of[j] Shelah,

10:4 [z]Eze 27:12, 25; Jnh 1:3
10:6 [a]ver 15; Ge 9:18
10:10 [b]Ge 11:9 [c]Ge 11:2
10:11 [d]Ps 83:8; Mic 5:6 [e]Jnh 1:2; 4:11; Na 1:1
10:14 [f]Ge 21:32,34; 26:1,8
10:15 [g]ver 6; Ge 9:18 [h]Eze 28:21 [i]Ge 23:3,20
10:16 [j]1Ch 11:4
10:18 [k]Ge 12:6; Ex 13:11
10:19 [l]Ge 11:31; 13:12; 17:8 [m]ver 15
10:21 [n]ver 24; Nu 24:24
10:22 [o]Jer 49:34 [p]Lk 3:36
10:23 [q]Job 1:1

[a] *4* Some manuscripts of the Masoretic Text and Samaritan Pentateuch (see also Septuagint and 1 Chron. 1:7); most manuscripts of the Masoretic Text *Dodanim* [b] *6* That is, Egypt; also in verse 13 [c] *8* *Father* may mean *ancestor* or *predecessor* or *founder*; also in verses 13, 15, 24 and 26. [d] *10* Or *Erech and Akkad—all of them in* [e] *10* That is, Babylonia [f] *11* Or *Nineveh with its city squares* [g] *15* Or *of the Sidonians, the foremost* [h] *21* Or *Shem, the older brother of* [i] *23* See Septuagint and 1 Chron. 1:17; Hebrew *Mash* [j] *24* Hebrew; Septuagint *father of Cainan, and Cainan was the father of*

10:24 and Shelah the father of Eber.[r]
[r]ver 21 25 Two sons were born to Eber:
One was named Peleg,[a] because in his time
the earth was divided; his brother was
named Joktan.
26 Joktan was the father of
Almodad, Sheleph, Hazarmaveth, Jerah,
27 Hadoram, Uzal, Diklah, 28 Obal, Abimael,
Sheba, 29 Ophir, Havilah and Jobab. All
these were sons of Joktan.

30 The region where they lived stretched from
Mesha toward Sephar, in the eastern hill country.
31 These are the sons of Shem by their clans and
languages, in their territories and nations.
10:32 [s]ver 1 32 These are the clans of Noah's sons,[s] according
[t]Ge 9:19 to their lines of descent, within their nations.
From these the nations spread out over the earth[t]
after the flood.

The Tower of Babel

11 Now the whole world had one language
11:2 and a common speech. 2 As men moved
[u]Ge 10:10 eastward,[b] they found a plain in Shinar[c][u] and settled there.
11:3 3 They said to each other, "Come, let's make
[v]Ex 1:14 [w]Ge 14:10 bricks[v] and bake them thoroughly." They used
brick instead of stone, and tar[w] for mortar. 4 Then
11:4 they said, "Come, let us build ourselves a city,
[x]Dt 1:28; 9:1 with a tower that reaches to the heavens,[x] so that
[y]Ge 6:4 we may make a name[y] for ourselves and not be
[z]Dt 4:27 scattered over the face of the whole earth."[z]
11:5 5 But the LORD came down[a] to see the city and
[a]ver 7; Ge 18:21; the tower that the men were building. 6 The LORD
Ex 3:8; said, "If as one people speaking the same lan-
19:11,18,20 guage they have begun to do this, then nothing
11:7 they plan to do will be impossible for them.
[b]Ge 1:26 7 Come, let us[b] go down and confuse their lan-
[c]Ge 42:23 guage so they will not understand each other."[c]
11:8 8 So the LORD scattered them from there over all
[d]Ge 9:19; the earth,[d] and they stopped building the city.
Lk 1:51 9 That is why it was called Babel[d][e]—because there
11:9 the LORD confused the language of the whole
[e]Ge 10:10 world. From there the LORD scattered them over
the face of the whole earth.

From Shem to Abram

10 This is the account of Shem.

Two years after the flood, when Shem was 100
years old, he became the father[e] of Arphaxad.
11 And after he became the father of Arphaxad,
Shem lived 500 years and had other sons and
daughters.
11:12 12 When Arphaxad had lived 35 years, he
[f]Lk 3:35 became the father of Shelah.[f] 13 And after he

[a] 25 *Peleg* means *division.* [b] 2 Or *from the east*; or *in the east* [c] 2 That is, Babylonia [d] 9 That is, Babylon; *Babel* sounds like the Hebrew for *confused.* [e] 10 *Father* may mean *ancestor*; also in verses 11–25.

A Tower for a God

GE 11:9

We see a play on words here: While the Hebrew word Babel sounds like the Hebrew word balal, which is also found in this verse and means "confusion" or "mixing," the word Babel itself is Hebrew for "Babylon." The Babylonians understood the word Babylon to mean "gate of god." Some scholars believe, based on the history of the area in which the tower was erected, that the builders of the multi-tiered structure were interested in crowning the edifice with a shrine to a pagan god. That would help to explain why the one true God is so offended by the plan, which goes way beyond their professed purpose of attaining renown and unity (Ge 11:4) and instead is fraught with their wayward affection for gods other than the true God. The true God requires no tower nor any such structure to come near to his people. The only thing he asks is a desire on our part to be close to him (Jas 4:8).

Barrenness

GE 11:30

Sarai, whom we later discover is a remarkably beautiful woman (Ge 12:11), is first introduced to the reader as a marked woman, a woman who suffers under the curse of barrenness. Aside from being Abram's wife, her childlessness is the only thing we know about her for many verses. Barrenness in early Eastern culture was considered much more than a matter of regret, much more than a cause for heartache; it was a matter of reproach and a cause for divorce. Therefore, Sarai's relationship to Abram is considered tenuous at best. (See character sketch for Sarai on page 67.)

became the father of Shelah, Arphaxad lived 403
years and had other sons and daughters.[a]
14 When Shelah had lived 30 years, he became
the father of Eber. 15 And after he became the
father of Eber, Shelah lived 403 years and had other sons and daughters.
16 When Eber had lived 34 years, he became the
father of Peleg. 17 And after he became the father of
Peleg, Eber lived 430 years and had other sons
and daughters.
18 When Peleg had lived 30 years, he became the
father of Reu. 19 And after he became the father of
Reu, Peleg lived 209 years and had other sons and
daughters.
20 When Reu had lived 32 years, he became the
father of Serug.[g] 21 And after he became the father
of Serug, Reu lived 207 years and had other sons
and daughters.
22 When Serug had lived 30 years, he became
the father of Nahor. 23 And after he became the
father of Nahor, Serug lived 200 years and had
other sons and daughters.
24 When Nahor had lived 29 years, he became
the father of Terah.[h] 25 And after he became the
father of Terah, Nahor lived 119 years and had
other sons and daughters.
26 After Terah had lived 70 years, he became the
father of Abram,[i] Nahor[j] and Haran.

27 This is the account of Terah.

Terah became the father of Abram, Nahor and
Haran. And Haran became the father of Lot.[k]
28 While his father Terah was still alive, Haran died
in Ur of the Chaldeans,[l] in the land of his birth.
29 Abram and Nahor both married. The name of
Abram's wife was Sarai,[m] and the name of
Nahor's wife was Milcah;[n] she was the daughter
of Haran, the father of both Milcah and Iscah.
30 Now Sarai was barren; she had no children.[o]
31 Terah took his son Abram, his grandson Lot
son of Haran, and his daughter-in-law Sarai, the
wife of his son Abram, and together they set out
from Ur of the Chaldeans[p] to go to Canaan.[q] But
when they came to Haran, they settled there.
32 Terah lived 205 years, and he died in Haran.

The Call of Abram

12 The LORD had said to Abram, "Leave your
country, your people and your father's
household and go to the land I will show you.[r]

2 "I will make you into a great nation[s]
and I will bless you;[t]
I will make your name great,

11:20 [g]Lk 3:35
11:24 [h]Lk 3:34
11:26 [i]Lk 3:34 [j]Jos 24:2
11:27 [k]ver 31; Ge 12:4; 14:12; 19:1; 2Pe 2:7
11:28 [l]ver 31; Ge 15:7
11:29 [m]Ge 17:15 [n]Ge 22:20
11:30 [o]Ge 16:1; 18:11
11:31 [p]Ge 15:7; Ne 9:7; Ac 7:4 [q]Ge 10:19
12:1 [r]Ac 7:3*; Heb 11:8
12:2 [s]Ge 15:5; 17:2,4; 18:18; 22:17; Dt 26:5 [t]Ge 24:1,35

[a] *12,13* Hebrew; Septuagint (see also Luke 3:35, 36 and note at Gen. 10:24) *35 years, he became the father of Cainan. 13 And after he became the father of Cainan, Arphaxad lived 430 years and had other sons and daughters, and then he died. When Cainan had lived 130 years, he became the father of Shelah. And after he became the father of Shelah, Cainan lived 330 years and had other sons and daughters*

and you will be a blessing.
3I will bless those who bless you,
and whoever curses you I will curse;[u]
and all peoples on earth
will be blessed through you.[v]"

4So Abram left, as the LORD had told him; and
Lot went with him. Abram was seventy-five years
old when he set out from Haran.[w] 5He took his
wife Sarai, his nephew Lot, all the possessions
they had accumulated and the people[x] they had
acquired in Haran, and they set out for the land of
Canaan, and they arrived there.
6Abram traveled through the land[y] as far as the
site of the great tree of Moreh[z] at Shechem. At that
time the Canaanites[a] were in the land. 7The LORD
appeared to Abram[b] and said, "To your offspring[a]
I will give this land."[c] So he built an altar there to
the LORD,[d] who had appeared to him.
8From there he went on toward the hills east of
Bethel[e] and pitched his tent, with Bethel on the
west and Ai on the east. There he built an altar to
the LORD and called on the name of the LORD.
9Then Abram set out and continued toward the
Negev.[f]

Abram in Egypt

10Now there was a famine in the land, and
Abram went down to Egypt to live there for a
while because the famine was severe. 11As he was
about to enter Egypt, he said to his wife Sarai, "I
know what a beautiful woman you are. 12When
the Egyptians see you, they will say, 'This is his
wife.' Then they will kill me but will let you live.
13Say you are my sister,[g] so that I will be treated
well for your sake and my life will be spared
because of you."
14When Abram came to Egypt, the Egyptians
saw that she was a very beautiful woman. 15And
when Pharaoh's officials saw her, they praised her
to Pharaoh, and she was taken into his palace.
16He treated Abram well for her sake, and Abram
acquired sheep and cattle, male and female donkeys, menservants and maidservants, and camels.
17But the LORD inflicted serious diseases on
Pharaoh and his household[h] because of Abram's
wife Sarai. 18So Pharaoh summoned Abram.
"What have you done to me?"[i] he said. "Why
didn't you tell me she was your wife? 19Why did
you say, 'She is my sister,' so that I took her to be
my wife? Now then, here is your wife. Take her
and go!" 20Then Pharaoh gave orders about
Abram to his men, and they sent him on his way,
with his wife and everything he had.

Abram and Lot Separate

13 So Abram went up from Egypt to the Negev,[j] with his wife and everything he had,

12:3 [u]Ge 27:29; Ex 23:22; Nu 24:9 [v]Ge 18:18; 22:18; 26:4; Ac 3:25; Gal 3:8*
12:4 [w]Ge 11:31
12:5 [x]Ge 14:14; 17:23
12:6 [y]Heb 11:9 [z]Ge 35:4; Dt 11:30 [a]Ge 10:18
12:7 [b]Ge 17:1; 18:1; Ex 6:3 [c]Ge 13:15, 17; 15:18; 17:8; Ps 105:9-11 [d]Ge 13:4
12:8 [e]Ge 13:3
12:9 [f]Ge 13:1,3
12:13 [g]Ge 20:2; 26:7
12:17 [h]1Ch 16:21
12:18 [i]Ge 20:9; 26:10
13:1 [j]Ge 12:9

[a] 7 Or *seed*

Protecting the Foolish

GE 12:13

Abram makes a decision based on fear rather than faith, and Sarai follows along. We have no idea how willingly Sarai agrees since ancient cultures expected submission and obedience from wives. Certainly it's hard to imagine she realized her choice would result in becoming a concubine in Pharaoh's harem. The consolation for us in this story is that God protects his own, even when they act foolishly. Sometimes we, too, make fear-based decisions rather than faith-based ones, and sometimes we create worse situations for ourselves than the one we feared. But God takes care of us, sometimes going to extraordinary lengths to assure that his plans are not disrupted. In this case, God directs circumstances to protect the future mother of Israel and to preserve his promise to create a great nation through Abram.

A Change of Heart

GE 13:1–18

Abram shows a shift in his heart from previous decisions he has made (Ge 12:11–13). Now, rather than worrying about taking care of himself, he benevolently suggests that Lot choose a site on which to settle. Perhaps his humbling experience in Egypt taught Abram to trust God to take care of him, or perhaps seeing the place where he had first built an altar to God reminded him of God's promises. For whatever reason, Abram shows himself to be a generous man. After Lot selects the choicest property, God once again appears to Abram and assures him that the Lord will give him more land than Abram could possibly imagine—including that which Lot has chosen.

and Lot went with him. 2Abram had become very
wealthy in livestock and in silver and gold.
3From the Negev he went from place to place
until he came to Bethel,[k] to the place between 13:3
Bethel and Ai where his tent had been earlier 4and [k]Ge 12:8
where he had first built an altar.[l] There Abram 13:4
called on the name of the LORD. [l]Ge 12:7
5Now Lot, who was moving about with Abram,
also had flocks and herds and tents. 6But the land
could not support them while they stayed together, for their possessions were so great that they 13:6
were not able to stay together.[m] 7And quarreling[n] [m]Ge 36:7
arose between Abram's herdsmen and the herds- 13:7
men of Lot. The Canaanites and Perizzites were [n]Ge 26:20,21
also living in the land[o] at that time. [o]Ge 12:6
8So Abram said to Lot, "Let's not have any quarreling between you and me,[p] or between your 13:8
herdsmen and mine, for we are brothers.[q] 9Is not [p]Pr 15:18; 20:3
the whole land before you? Let's part company. If [q]Ps 133:1
you go to the left, I'll go to the right; if you go to
the right, I'll go to the left."
10Lot looked up and saw that the whole plain of
the Jordan was well watered, like the garden of 13:10
the LORD,[r] like the land of Egypt, toward Zoar.[s] [r]Ge 2:8-10; Isa 51:3
(This was before the LORD destroyed Sodom and [s]Ge 19:22,30
Gomorrah.)[t] 11So Lot chose for himself the whole [t]Ge 14:8; 19:17-29
plain of the Jordan and set out toward the east.
The two men parted company: 12Abram lived in 13:12
the land of Canaan, while Lot lived among the cit- [u]Ge 19:17, 25,29
ies of the plain[u] and pitched his tents near Sod- [v]Ge 14:12
om.[v] 13Now the men of Sodom were wicked and
were sinning greatly against the LORD.[w] 13:13
14The LORD said to Abram after Lot had parted [w]Ge 18:20; Eze 16:49-50; 2Pe 2:8
from him, "Lift up your eyes from where you are
and look north and south, east and west.[x] 15All 13:14
the land that you see I will give to you and your [x]Ge 28:14; Dt 3:27
offspring[a] forever.[y] 16I will make your offspring
like the dust of the earth, so that if anyone could 13:15
count the dust, then your offspring could be [y]Ge 12:7; Gal 3:16*
counted. 17Go, walk through the length and
breadth of the land,[z] for I am giving it to you." 13:17
18So Abram moved his tents and went to live [z]ver 15; Nu 13:17-25
near the great trees of Mamre[a] at Hebron,[b] where
he built an altar to the LORD.[c] 13:18

[a]Ge 14:13, 24; 18:1 [b]Ge 35:27 [c]Ge 8:20

Abram Rescues Lot

14 At this time Amraphel king of Shinar,[bd] Arioch king of Ellasar, Kedorlaomer king of 14:1
Elam and Tidal king of Goiim 2went to war [d]Ge 10:10
against Bera king of Sodom, Birsha king of 14:2
Gomorrah, Shinab king of Admah, Shemeber king [e]Ge 10:19
of Zeboiim,[e] and the king of Bela (that is, Zoar).[f] [f]Ge 13:10
3All these latter kings joined forces in the Valley of 14:3
Siddim (the Salt Sea[cg]). 4For twelve years they had [g]Nu 34:3,12; Dt 3:17;
been subject to Kedorlaomer, but in the thirteenth Jos 3:16;
year they rebelled. 15:2,5
5In the fourteenth year, Kedorlaomer and the
kings allied with him went out and defeated the

[a] *15* Or *seed;* also in verse 16 [b] *1* That is, Babylonia; also in verse 9 [c] *3* That is, the Dead Sea

Rephaites[h] in Ashteroth Karnaim, the Zuzites in
Ham, the Emites[i] in Shaveh Kiriathaim 6and the
Horites[j] in the hill country of Seir,[k] as far as El
Paran[l] near the desert. 7Then they turned back
and went to En Mishpat (that is, Kadesh), and
they conquered the whole territory of the
Amalekites, as well as the Amorites who were living in Hazazon Tamar.[m]
8Then the king of Sodom, the king of Gomorrah,[n] the king of Admah, the king of Zeboiim[o] and
the king of Bela (that is, Zoar) marched out and
drew up their battle lines in the Valley of Siddim
9against Kedorlaomer king of Elam, Tidal king of
Goiim, Amraphel king of Shinar and Arioch king
of Ellasar—four kings against five. 10Now the Valley of Siddim was full of tar pits, and when the
kings of Sodom and Gomorrah fled, some of the
men fell into them and the rest fled to the hills.[p]
11The four kings seized all the goods of Sodom and
Gomorrah and all their food; then they went away.
12They also carried off Abram's nephew Lot and
his possessions, since he was living in Sodom.
13One who had escaped came and reported this
to Abram the Hebrew. Now Abram was living near
the great trees of Mamre[q] the Amorite, a brother[a]
of Eshcol and Aner, all of whom were allied with
Abram. 14When Abram heard that his relative had
been taken captive, he called out the 318 trained
men born in his household[r] and went in pursuit
as far as Dan.[s] 15During the night Abram divided
his men to attack them and he routed them, pursuing them as far as Hobah, north of Damascus.
16He recovered all the goods and brought back his
relative Lot and his possessions, together with the
women and the other people.
17After Abram returned from defeating Kedorlaomer and the kings allied with him, the king of
Sodom came out to meet him in the Valley of Shaveh (that is, the King's Valley).[t]
18Then Melchizedek[u] king of Salem[b][v] brought
out bread and wine. He was priest of God Most
High, 19and he blessed Abram,[w] saying,

"Blessed be Abram by God Most High,
Creator[c] of heaven and earth.[x]
20And blessed be[d] God Most High,[y]
who delivered your enemies into your
hand."

Then Abram gave him a tenth of everything.[z]
21The king of Sodom said to Abram, "Give me
the people and keep the goods for yourself."
22But Abram said to the king of Sodom, "I have
raised my hand[a] to the LORD, God Most High, Creator of heaven and earth,[b] and have taken an oath
23that I will accept nothing belonging to you,[c] not
even a thread or the thong of a sandal, so that you
will never be able to say, 'I made Abram rich.' 24I
will accept nothing but what my men have eaten

14:5 [h]Ge 15:20; Dt 2:11,20 [i]Dt 2:10
14:6 [j]Dt 2:12,22 [k]Dt 2:1,5,22 [l]Ge 21:21; Nu 10:12
14:7 [m]2Ch 20:2
14:8 [n]Ge 13:10; 19:17-29 [o]Dt 29:23
14:10 [p]Ge 19:17,30
14:13 [q]ver 24; Ge 13:18
14:14 [r]Ge 15:3 [s]Dt 34:1; Jdg 18:29
14:17 [t]2Sa 18:18
14:18 [u]Ps 110:4; Heb 5:6 [v]Ps 76:2; Heb 7:2
14:19 [w]Heb 7:6 [x]ver 22
14:20 [y]Ge 24:27 [z]Ge 28:22; Dt 26:12; Heb 7:4
14:22 [a]Ex 6:8; Da 12:7; Rev 10:5-6 [b]ver 19
14:23 [c]2Ki 5:16

[a] *13* Or *a relative;* or *an ally* [b] *18* That is, Jerusalem
[c] *19* Or *Possessor;* also in verse 22 [d] *20* Or *And praise be to*

Who Are the Hebrews?

GE 14:13

The term *Hebrew* (which in the Hebrew language is *ibri)* is used in various forms 44 times in the Bible, with Genesis 14:13 being the first. The word derives from one of three sources. It might be based on the verb *ebar,* which means "to cross over or beyond." Thus the Hebrews would be "the ones who crossed over" or "the ones from beyond." Or *Hebrew* might be based on genealogies that identify Eber, Noah's great-great-grandson, as an ancestor to Abram and his descendants, thus the "Eberites." Or *Hebrew* might be derived from the term *apiru,* which refers to a diverse group with an inferior social status who lived on the fringes of settled areas. While the Hebrews were not of this lot, they were made up of several Semitic groups, which might have been the common factor giving rise to the term *Hebrew.*

A Signed Contract

GE 15:17

Abram's questions about becoming a father and a man with property are well founded (Ge 15:2,8). He has a barren wife, and everywhere he looks, others are living on the land God has promised him. God seems to recognize that Abram needs more assurance. So the Lord directs Abram to cut a number of animals in half, laying them on the ground with space between each half. This ancient custom was like writing a contract. The individuals involved in the agreement would walk between the animal halves, signifying that a similar fate should be theirs if they broke the contract. When Abram sees the blazing torch move between the pieces, he understands that God is giving his solemn word to fulfill what he has promised. Compare other passages where fire signifies God's presence, for instance, the burning bush (Ex 3:2) and the tongues of fire of Pentecost (Ac 2:3).

and the share that belongs to the men who went
with me—to Aner, Eshcol and Mamre. Let them
have their share."

God's Covenant With Abram

15 After this, the word of the LORD came to
Abram[d] in a vision:

"Do not be afraid,[e] Abram.
I am your shield,[a][f]
your very great reward.[b]"

2But Abram said, "O Sovereign LORD, what can
you give me since I remain childless[g] and the one
who will inherit[c] my estate is Eliezer of Damascus?" 3And Abram said, "You have given me no
children; so a servant[h] in my household will be
my heir."
4Then the word of the LORD came to him: "This
man will not be your heir, but a son coming from
your own body will be your heir.[i]" 5He took him
outside and said, "Look up at the heavens and
count the stars[j]—if indeed you can count them."
Then he said to him, "So shall your offspring be."[k]
6Abram believed the LORD, and he credited it to
him as righteousness.[l]
7He also said to him, "I am the LORD, who
brought you out of Ur of the Chaldeans to give
you this land to take possession of it."
8But Abram said, "O Sovereign LORD, how can I
know[m] that I will gain possession of it?"
9So the LORD said to him, "Bring me a heifer, a
goat and a ram, each three years old, along with a
dove and a young pigeon."
10Abram brought all these to him, cut them in
two and arranged the halves opposite each other;[n]
the birds, however, he did not cut in half.[o] 11Then
birds of prey came down on the carcasses, but
Abram drove them away.
12As the sun was setting, Abram fell into a deep
sleep,[p] and a thick and dreadful darkness came
over him. 13Then the LORD said to him, "Know for
certain that your descendants will be strangers in
a country not their own, and they will be
enslaved[q] and mistreated four hundred years.[r]
14But I will punish the nation they serve as slaves,
and afterward they will come out[s] with great possessions.[t] 15You, however, will go to your fathers
in peace and be buried at a good old age.[u] 16In the
fourth generation your descendants will come
back here, for the sin of the Amorites[v] has not yet
reached its full measure."
17When the sun had set and darkness had fall-
en, a smoking firepot with a blazing torch
appeared and passed between the pieces.[w] 18On
that day the LORD made a covenant with Abram
and said, "To your descendants I give this land,[x]
from the river[d] of Egypt[y] to the great river, the

15:1 [d]Da 10:1 [e]Ge 21:17; 26:24; 46:3; 2Ki 6:16; Ps 27:1; Isa 41:10,13-14 [f]Dt 33:29; 2Sa 22:3,31; Ps 3:3
15:2 [g]Ac 7:5
15:3 [h]Ge 24:2,34
15:4 [i]Gal 4:28
15:5 [j]Ps 147:4; Jer 33:22 [k]Ge 12:2; 22:17; Ex 32:13; Ro 4:18*; Heb 11:12
15:6 [l]Ps 106:31; Ro 4:3*,20-24*; Gal 3:6*; Jas 2:23*
15:8 [m]Lk 1:18
15:10 [n]ver 17; Jer 34:18 [o]Lev 1:17
15:12 [p]Ge 2:21
15:13 [q]Ex 1:11 [r]ver 16; Ex 12:40; Ac 7:6,17
15:14 [s]Ac 7:7* [t]Ex 12:32-38
15:15 [u]Ge 25:8
15:16 [v]1Ki 21:26
15:17 [w]ver 10
15:18 [x]Ge 12:7 [y]Nu 34:5

[a] 1 Or *sovereign* [b] 1 Or *shield; / your reward will be very great* [c] 2 The meaning of the Hebrew for this phrase is uncertain. [d] 18 Or *Wadi*

Euphrates— 19the land of the Kenites, Kenizzites,
Kadmonites, 20Hittites, Perizzites, Rephaites,
21Amorites, Canaanites, Girgashites and Jebusites."

Hagar and Ishmael

16:1 [z]Ge 11:30; Gal 4:24-25 [a]Ge 21:9 **16** Now Sarai, Abram's wife, had borne him no
children.[z] But she had an Egyptian maid-
servant[a] named Hagar; 2so she said to Abram,
16:2 [b]Ge 30:3-4, 9-10 "The LORD has kept me from having children. Go,
sleep with my maidservant; perhaps I can build a
family through her."[b]
Abram agreed to what Sarai said. 3So after
16:3 [c]Ge 12:5 Abram had been living in Canaan[c] ten years, Sarai
his wife took her Egyptian maidservant Hagar and
gave her to her husband to be his wife. 4He slept
with Hagar, and she conceived.
When she knew she was pregnant, she began
to despise her mistress. 5Then Sarai said to
Abram, "You are responsible for the wrong I am
suffering. I put my servant in your arms, and now
that she knows she is pregnant, she despises me.
16:5 [d]Ge 31:53 May the LORD judge between you and me."[d]
6"Your servant is in your hands," Abram said.
"Do with her whatever you think best." Then
Sarai mistreated Hagar; so she fled from her.
16:7 [e]Ge 21:17; 22:11,15; 31:11 [f]Ge 20:1 7The angel of the LORD[e] found Hagar near a
spring in the desert; it was the spring that is
beside the road to Shur.[f] 8And he said, "Hagar, servant of Sarai, where have you come from, and
where are you going?"
"I'm running away from my mistress Sarai,"
she answered.
9Then the angel of the LORD told her, "Go back
to your mistress and submit to her." 10The angel
added, "I will so increase your descendants that
16:10 [g]Ge 13:16; 17:20 they will be too numerous to count."[g]
11The angel of the LORD also said to her:

"You are now with child
  and you will have a son.
You shall name him Ishmael,[a]
16:11 [h]Ex 2:24; 3:7,9   for the LORD has heard of your
    misery.[h]
12He will be a wild donkey of a man;
  his hand will be against everyone
  and everyone's hand against him,
and he will live in hostility
16:12 [i]Ge 25:18   toward[b] all his brothers."[i]

13She gave this name to the LORD who spoke to
her: "You are the God who sees me," for she said,
16:13 [j]Ge 32:30 "I have now seen[c] the One who sees me."[j] 14That
is why the well was called Beer Lahai Roi[d]; it is
still there, between Kadesh and Bered.
16:15 [k]Gal 4:22 15So Hagar bore Abram a son,[k] and Abram gave
the name Ishmael to the son she had borne.

[a] 11 *Ishmael* means *God hears.* [b] 12 Or *live to the east / of*
[c] 13 Or *seen the back of* [d] 14 *Beer Lahai Roi* means *well of the Living One who sees me.*

Protection for Hagar

GE 16:13

Hagar has three strikes against her: she is a woman, a foreigner and a servant. Yet God cares for Hagar and saves her from death in the desert. The Lord himself apparently visits Hagar (Ge 16:13) and asks her two questions: Where are you coming from? And where are you going (Ge 16:8)? Like Hagar, we usually know the answer to the first question but have no idea about the second. The Lord provides her with direction—perhaps not what Hagar desires to hear—and she obeys. In turn, God blesses her with the promise of a strong and free son, who will not have a trouble-free life. But Hagar is blessed in an even greater way: She is the first woman in Scripture, aside from Eve, who sees the Lord himself and receives a promise of blessing and protection directly from him. ***(See character sketch for Hagar on page 68.)***

16 Abram was eighty-six years old when Hagar bore him Ishmael.

The Covenant of Circumcision

17 When Abram was ninety-nine years old, the LORD appeared to him and said, "I am God Almighty[a];[l] walk before me and be blameless.[m] 2 I will confirm my covenant between me and you[n] and will greatly increase your numbers."

3 Abram fell facedown, and God said to him, 4 "As for me, this is my covenant with you:[o] You will be the father of many nations.[p] 5 No longer will you be called Abram[b]; your name will be Abraham,[c][q] for I have made you a father of many nations.[r] 6 I will make you very fruitful;[s] I will make nations of you, and kings will come from you.[t] 7 I will establish my covenant as an everlasting covenant between me and you and your descendants after you for the generations to come, to be your God[u] and the God of your descendants after you.[v] 8 The whole land of Canaan,[w] where you are now an alien,[x] I will give as an everlasting possession to you and your descendants after you;[y] and I will be their God."

9 Then God said to Abraham, "As for you, you must keep my covenant, you and your descendants after you for the generations to come. 10 This is my covenant with you and your descendants after you, the covenant you are to keep: Every male among you shall be circumcised.[z] 11 You are to undergo circumcision,[a] and it will be the sign of the covenant[b] between me and you. 12 For the generations to come every male among you who is eight days old must be circumcised,[c] including those born in your household or bought with money from a foreigner—those who are not your offspring. 13 Whether born in your household or bought with your money, they must be circumcised. My covenant in your flesh is to be an everlasting covenant. 14 Any uncircumcised male, who has not been circumcised in the flesh, will be cut off from his people;[d] he has broken my covenant."

15 God also said to Abraham, "As for Sarai your wife, you are no longer to call her Sarai; her name will be Sarah. 16 I will bless her and will surely give you a son by her.[e] I will bless her so that she will be the mother of nations;[f] kings of peoples will come from her."

17 Abraham fell facedown; he laughed[g] and said to himself, "Will a son be born to a man a hundred years old? Will Sarah bear a child at the age of ninety?" 18 And Abraham said to God, "If only Ishmael might live under your blessing!"

19 Then God said, "Yes, but your wife Sarah will bear you a son,[h] and you will call him Isaac.[d] I will establish my covenant with him[i] as an everlasting covenant for his descendants after him.

17:1 [l]Ge 28:3; Ex 6:3 [m]Dt 18:13
17:2 [n]Ge 15:18
17:4 [o]Ge 15:18 [p]ver 16; Ge 12:2; 35:11; 48:19
17:5 [q]ver 15; Ne 9:7 [r]Ro 4:17*
17:6 [s]Ge 35:11 [t]Mt 1:6
17:7 [u]Ex 29:45,46 [v]Ro 9:8; Gal 3:16
17:8 [w]Ps 105:9,11 [x]Ge 23:4; 28:4; Ex 6:4 [y]Ge 12:7
17:10 [z]ver 23; Ge 21:4; Jn 7:22; Ac 7:8; Ro 4:11
17:11 [a]Ex 12:48; Dt 10:16 [b]Ro 4:11
17:12 [c]Lev 12:3; Lk 2:21
17:14 [d]Ex 4:24-26
17:16 [e]Ge 18:10 [f]Ge 35:11; Gal 4:31
17:17 [g]Ge 18:12; 21:6
17:19 [h]Ge 18:14; 21:2 [i]Ge 26:3

[a] *1* Hebrew *El-Shaddai* [b] *5 Abram* means *exalted father.* [c] *5 Abraham* means *father of many.* [d] *19 Isaac* means *he laughs.*

Sarai's Promise

GE 17:15-16

It's easy to miss the fact that, up to this point, all the parenthood promises Abram has received have made no mention of Sarai. Since in Middle Eastern culture it wasn't unusual for a barren woman to have children who were legally considered hers through a servant, Sarai's involvement of Hagar makes a bit more sense. But mistreating Hagar and sending her away cannot be excused by the servant-owner relationship. Yet each of these actions—giving Hagar to Abram and then mistreating Hagar, resulting in Hagar running away—displays Sarai's agony over feeling excluded from God's plan for Abram. How kind of God to reveal Sarai's upcoming motherhood even after she has failed to respond with faith and graciousness. Once again God remains faithful, not because of his people, but despite them. (See character sketches for Sarai and Hagar on pages 67 and 68.)

20 And as for Ishmael, I have heard you: I will sure-
17:20 ly bless him; I will make him fruitful and will
[j]Ge 16:10 greatly increase his numbers.[j] He will be the
[k]Ge 25:12-16 father of twelve rulers,[k] and I will make him into
[l]Ge 21:18 a great nation.[l] 21 But my covenant I will establish
17:21 with Isaac, whom Sarah will bear to you by this
[m]Ge 21:2 time next year."[m] 22 When he had finished speaking with Abraham, God went up from him.
23 On that very day Abraham took his son Ishmael and all those born in his household or
bought with his money, every male in his household, and circumcised them, as God told him.
24 Abraham was ninety-nine years old when he
17:24 was circumcised,[n] 25 and his son Ishmael was thir-
[n]Ro 4:11 teen; 26 Abraham and his son Ishmael were both
circumcised on that same day. 27 And every male
in Abraham's household, including those born in
his household or bought from a foreigner, was circumcised with him.

The Three Visitors

18:1 **18** The LORD appeared to Abraham near the
[o]Ge 13:18; great trees of Mamre[o] while he was sitting
14:13 at the entrance to his tent in the heat of the day.
18:2 2 Abraham looked up and saw three men[p] standing
[p]ver 16,22; Ge 32:24; nearby. When he saw them, he hurried from the
Jos 5:13; Jdg 13:6-11; entrance of his tent to meet them and bowed low
Heb 13:2 to the ground.
3 He said, "If I have found favor in your eyes, my
lord,[a] do not pass your servant by. 4 Let a little
18:4 water be brought, and then you may all wash
[q]Ge 19:2; your feet[q] and rest under this tree. 5 Let me get you
43:24 something to eat,[r] so you can be refreshed and
18:5 then go on your way—now that you have come
[r]Jdg 13:15 to your servant."
"Very well," they answered, "do as you say."
6 So Abraham hurried into the tent to Sarah.
"Quick," he said, "get three seahs[b] of fine flour
and knead it and bake some bread."
7 Then he ran to the herd and selected a choice,
tender calf and gave it to a servant, who hurried
to prepare it. 8 He then brought some curds and
milk and the calf that had been prepared, and set
18:8 these before them.[s] While they ate, he stood near
[s]Ge 19:3 them under a tree.
9 "Where is your wife Sarah?" they asked him.
"There, in the tent," he said.
10 Then the LORD[c] said, "I will surely return to
18:10 you about this time next year, and Sarah your wife
[t]Ro 9:9* will have a son."[t]
Now Sarah was listening at the entrance to the
tent, which was behind him. 11 Abraham and Sar-
18:11 ah were already old and well advanced in years,[u]
[u]Ge 17:17 [v]Ro 4:19 and Sarah was past the age of childbearing.[v] 12 So
Sarah laughed[w] to herself as she thought, "After I
18:12 am worn out and my master[d][x] is old, will I now
[w]Ge 17:17; 21:6 have this pleasure?"
[x]1Pe 3:6 13 Then the LORD said to Abraham, "Why did

[a] 3 Or *O Lord* [b] 6 That is, probably about 20 quarts (about 22 liters) [c] 10 Hebrew *Then he* [d] 12 Or *husband*

The Reprimand

GE 18:12–15

Why is Sarah reprimanded for laughing at the idea of bearing a child while Abraham, who also found the idea worth a chuckle (Ge 17:17), did not seem to receive the same kind of response from God? Neither of them scores high on the respectful response meter. And neither of them exhibits much faith, focusing instead on the improbability of the promise being fulfilled.

Perhaps the answer lies in what God saw in their hearts. Sarah, when faced with her sarcastic snicker, lies about it rather than confesses it. But Abraham seems to accept that his son will be called Isaac ("he laughs"), as a reminder that he did indeed laugh at God—and would laugh with Sarah in joy when God fulfills his promise. (See character sketch for Sarai on page 67.)

No Limits

GE 18:14

When God asks Abraham, "Is anything too hard for the LORD?" (Ge 18:14), he might well have in mind a future circumstance that will test Abraham's faith. For, as Abraham escorts his visitors on their way, God tells Abraham he intends to destroy Sodom and Gomorrah. This would be like hearing that the town just down the road is about to experience a major disaster—and your closest relative lives there. Apparently Abraham knows that the cities won't pass muster, for he asks God to turn the scales of justice upside down and preserve the cities for the sake of the few good. Abraham's request is one of great faith. He dares to believe that nothing is too hard for God, including saving the many for the few righteous.

Sarah laugh and say, 'Will I really have a child, now that I am old?' [14]Is anything too hard for the LORD?[y] I will return to you at the appointed time next year and Sarah will have a son."

[15]Sarah was afraid, so she lied and said, "I did not laugh."

But he said, "Yes, you did laugh."

Abraham Pleads for Sodom

[16]When the men got up to leave, they looked down toward Sodom, and Abraham walked along with them to see them on their way. [17]Then the LORD said, "Shall I hide from Abraham[z] what I am about to do?[a] [18]Abraham will surely become a great and powerful nation,[b] and all nations on earth will be blessed through him. [19]For I have chosen him, so that he will direct his children[c] and his household after him to keep the way of the LORD[d] by doing what is right and just, so that the LORD will bring about for Abraham what he has promised him."

[20]Then the LORD said, "The outcry against Sodom and Gomorrah is so great and their sin so grievous [21]that I will go down[e] and see if what they have done is as bad as the outcry that has reached me. If not, I will know."

[22]The men turned away and went toward Sodom,[f] but Abraham remained standing before the LORD.[a] [23]Then Abraham approached him and said: "Will you sweep away the righteous with the wicked?[g] [24]What if there are fifty righteous people in the city? Will you really sweep it away and not spare[b] the place for the sake of the fifty righteous people in it?[h] [25]Far be it from you to do such a thing—to kill the righteous with the wicked, treating the righteous and the wicked alike. Far be it from you! Will not the Judge[c] of all the earth do right?"[i]

[26]The LORD said, "If I find fifty righteous people in the city of Sodom, I will spare the whole place for their sake.[j]"

[27]Then Abraham spoke up again: "Now that I have been so bold as to speak to the Lord, though I am nothing but dust and ashes,[k] [28]what if the number of the righteous is five less than fifty? Will you destroy the whole city because of five people?"

"If I find forty-five there," he said, "I will not destroy it."

[29]Once again he spoke to him, "What if only forty are found there?"

He said, "For the sake of forty, I will not do it."

[30]Then he said, "May the Lord not be angry, but let me speak. What if only thirty can be found there?"

He answered, "I will not do it if I find thirty there."

18:14 [y]Jer 32:17, 27; Zec 8:6; Mt 19:26; Lk 1:37; Ro 4:21
18:17 [z]Am 3:7 [a]Ge 19:24
18:18 [b]Gal 3:8*
18:19 [c]Dt 4:9-10; 6:7 [d]Jos 24:15; Eph 6:4
18:21 [e]Ge 11:5
18:22 [f]Ge 19:1
18:23 [g]Nu 16:22
18:24 [h]Jer 5:1
18:25 [i]Job 8:3,20; Ps 58:11; 94:2; Isa 3:10-11; Ro 3:6
18:26 [j]Jer 5:1
18:27 [k]Ge 2:7; 3:19; Job 30:19; 42:6

[a] 22 Masoretic Text; an ancient Hebrew scribal tradition *but the LORD remained standing before Abraham* [b] 24 Or *forgive*; also in verse 26 [c] 25 Or *Ruler*

31Abraham said, "Now that I have been so bold
as to speak to the Lord, what if only twenty can be
found there?"
He said, "For the sake of twenty, I will not
destroy it."
32Then he said, "May the Lord not be angry, but
18:32 [l]Jdg 6:39 let me speak just once more.[l] What if only ten can
[m]Jer 5:1 be found there?"
He answered, "For the sake of ten,[m] I will not
destroy it."
33When the LORD had finished speaking with
Abraham, he left, and Abraham returned home.

Sodom and Gomorrah Destroyed

19:1 **19** The two angels arrived at Sodom[n] in the
[n]Ge 18:22 evening, and Lot was sitting in the gateway
[o]Ge 18:1 of the city.[o] When he saw them, he got up to meet
them and bowed down with his face to the
19:2 ground. 2"My lords," he said, "please turn aside
[p]Ge 18:4; to your servant's house. You can wash your feet[p]
Lk 7:44 and spend the night and then go on your way early in the morning."
"No," they answered, "we will spend the night
in the square."
3But he insisted so strongly that they did go
with him and entered his house. He prepared a
meal for them, baking bread without yeast, and
19:3 they ate.[q] 4Before they had gone to bed, all the
[q]Ge 18:6 men from every part of the city of Sodom—both
young and old—surrounded the house. 5They
called to Lot, "Where are the men who came to
19:5 you tonight? Bring them out to us so that we can
[r]Jdg 19:22; have sex with them."[r]
Isa 3:9; Ro 1:24-27 6Lot went outside to meet them[s] and shut the
door behind him 7and said, "No, my friends. Don't
19:6 do this wicked thing. 8Look, I have two daughters
[s]Jdg 19:23 who have never slept with a man. Let me bring
them out to you, and you can do what you like
19:8 with them. But don't do anything to these men, for
[t]Jdg 19:24 they have come under the protection of my roof."[t]
9"Get out of our way," they replied. And they
19:9 said, "This fellow came here as an alien, and now
[u]Ex 2:14; he wants to play the judge![u] We'll treat you worse
Ac 7:27 than them." They kept bringing pressure on Lot
and moved forward to break down the door.
10But the men inside reached out and pulled Lot
back into the house and shut the door. 11Then they
struck the men who were at the door of the house,
19:11 young and old, with blindness[v] so that they could
[v]Dt 28:28-29; 2Ki 6:18; not find the door.
Ac 13:11 12The two men said to Lot, "Do you have anyone else here—sons-in-law, sons or daughters, or
19:12 anyone else in the city who belongs to you?[w] Get
[w]Ge 7:1 them out of here, 13because we are going to destroy
this place. The outcry to the LORD against its peo-
19:13 ple is so great that he has sent us to destroy it."[x]
[x]1Ch 21:15 14So Lot went out and spoke to his sons-in-law,
who were pledged to marry[a] his daughters. He
said, "Hurry and get out of this place, because the

[a] 14 Or *were married to*

Hospitality

GE 19:8

Hospitality was one of the most highly prized virtues in ancient culture. A man earned a good reputation by welcoming others into his home. Abraham's hospitable ways in Genesis 18 give us an indication of the lengths to which a host would extend himself and his household to welcome guests. Once a guest had eaten in a man's house, the law of Eastern hospitality guaranteed that guest protection, even if it placed the host in peril.

Thus Lot's proposal to hand over his daughters shows his determination to fulfill that law. His proposal also makes a bit more sense when one considers that wives and daughters were, at that time, viewed merely as property. In addition, Lot has lived in a morally deficient community long enough to have acquired a bent sense of rightness. Fortunately, the angels are able rescue themselves—and Lot's family as well.

The Reluctant Refugees

GE 19:16-20

Fortunately Lot has Abraham to plead for his safety because Lot doesn't show much interest in being saved. The angels literally have to pull him and his family out of town. Even then, Lot dickers with the angels, as if moving into the mountains is just too much work. Lot's wife must have been especially reluctant to leave since—after looking back—she is turned into a pillar of salt while the others are rescued. (See character sketch for Lot's wife on page 135.) God's mercy to Lot should truly console us. Even if we're slow to get the point, reluctant to give up what is dangerous to us, and ready to "bargain" God into taking care of us when we don't follow his commands, he often does just that—if a righteous person undertakes for us, which is the explanation Scripture offers for this remarkable rescue in Genesis 19:29.

LORD is about to destroy the city![y]" But his sons-
in-law thought he was joking.[z]
15With the coming of dawn, the angels urged
Lot, saying, "Hurry! Take your wife and your two
daughters who are here, or you will be swept
away[a] when the city is punished.[b]"
16When he hesitated, the men grasped his hand
and the hands of his wife and of his two daughters and led them safely out of the city, for the
LORD was merciful to them. 17As soon as they had
brought them out, one of them said, "Flee for your
lives![c] Don't look back,[d] and don't stop anywhere
in the plain! Flee to the mountains or you will be
swept away!"
18But Lot said to them, "No, my lords,[a] please!
19Your[b] servant has found favor in your[b] eyes, and
you[b] have shown great kindness to me in sparing
my life. But I can't flee to the mountains; this
disaster will overtake me, and I'll die. 20Look, here
is a town near enough to run to, and it is small.
Let me flee to it—it is very small, isn't it? Then
my life will be spared."
21He said to him, "Very well, I will grant this
request too; I will not overthrow the town you
speak of. 22But flee there quickly, because I cannot
do anything until you reach it." (That is why the
town was called Zoar.[c])
23By the time Lot reached Zoar, the sun had
risen over the land. 24Then the LORD rained down
burning sulfur on Sodom and Gomorrah[e]—from
the LORD out of the heavens.[f] 25Thus he overthrew
those cities and the entire plain, including all
those living in the cities—and also the vegetation
in the land.[g] 26But Lot's wife looked back,[h] and
she became a pillar of salt.[i]
27Early the next morning Abraham got up and
returned to the place where he had stood before
the LORD.[j] 28He looked down toward Sodom and
Gomorrah, toward all the land of the plain, and
he saw dense smoke rising from the land, like
smoke from a furnace.[k]
29So when God destroyed the cities of the plain,
he remembered Abraham, and he brought Lot out
of the catastrophe[l] that overthrew the cities where
Lot had lived.

Lot and His Daughters

30Lot and his two daughters left Zoar and settled in the mountains,[m] for he was afraid to stay in
Zoar. He and his two daughters lived in a cave.
31One day the older daughter said to the younger,
"Our father is old, and there is no man around
here to lie with us, as is the custom all over the
earth. 32Let's get our father to drink wine and then
lie with him and preserve our family line through
our father."
33That night they got their father to drink wine,
and the older daughter went in and lay with him.

19:14 [y]Nu 16:21 [z]Ex 9:21; Lk 17:28
19:15 [a]Nu 16:26 [b]Rev 18:4
19:17 [c]Jer 48:6 [d]ver 26
19:24 [e]Dt 29:23; Isa 1:9; 13:19 [f]Lk 17:29; 2Pe 2:6; Jude 7
19:25 [g]Ps 107:34; Eze 16:48
19:26 [h]ver 17 [i]Lk 17:32
19:27 [j]Ge 18:22
19:28 [k]Rev 9:2; 18:9
19:29 [l]2Pe 2:7
19:30 [m]ver 19

[a] *18* Or *No, Lord*; or *No, my lord* [b] *19* The Hebrew is singular. [c] *22* *Zoar* means *small*.

He was not aware of it when she lay down or
when she got up.
34The next day the older daughter said to the
younger, "Last night I lay with my father. Let's get
him to drink wine again tonight, and you go in
and lie with him so we can preserve our family
line through our father." 35So they got their father
to drink wine that night also, and the younger
daughter went and lay with him. Again he was
not aware of it when she lay down or when she
got up.
36So both of Lot's daughters became pregnant
19:37 by their father. 37The older daughter had a son,
[n]Dt 2:9 and she named him Moab[a]; he is the father of the
Moabites[n] of today. 38The younger daughter also
19:38 had a son, and she named him Ben-Ammi[b]; he is
[o]Dt 2:19 the father of the Ammonites[o] of today.

Abraham and Abimelech

20:1 20 Now Abraham moved on from there[p] into
[p]Ge 18:1 the region of the Negev and lived between
[q]Ge 26:1,6, 17 Kadesh and Shur. For a while he stayed in Gerar,[q]
2and there Abraham said of his wife Sarah, "She is
20:2 [r]ver 12; my sister.[r]" Then Abimelech king of Gerar sent for
Ge 12:13; 26:7 Sarah and took her.[s]
[s]Ge 12:15 3But God came to Abimelech in a dream[t] one
night and said to him, "You are as good as dead
20:3 [t]Job 33:15; because of the woman you have taken; she is a
Mt 27:19 married woman."[u]
[u]Ps 105:14 4Now Abimelech had not gone near her, so he
20:4 said, "Lord, will you destroy an innocent
[v]Ge 18:25 nation?[v] 5Did he not say to me, 'She is my sister,'
and didn't she also say, 'He is my brother'? I
have done this with a clear conscience and clean
hands."
6Then God said to him in the dream, "Yes, I
20:6 know you did this with a clear conscience, and so
[w]1Sa 25:26, 34 I have kept[w] you from sinning against me. That is
why I did not let you touch her. 7Now return the
man's wife, for he is a prophet, and he will pray
20:7 for you[x] and you will live. But if you do not return
[x]ver 17; her, you may be sure that you and all yours will
1Sa 7:5; Job 42:8 die."
8Early the next morning Abimelech summoned
all his officials, and when he told them all that
had happened, they were very much afraid. 9Then
Abimelech called Abraham in and said, "What
have you done to us? How have I wronged you
that you have brought such great guilt upon me
and my kingdom? You have done things to me
20:9 that should not be done.[y]" 10And Abimelech asked
[y]Ge 12:18; 26:10; 34:7 Abraham, "What was your reason for doing this?"
20:11 11Abraham replied, "I said to myself, 'There is
[z]Ge 42:18; surely no fear of God[z] in this place, and they will
Ps 36:1 kill me because of my wife.'[a] 12Besides, she really
[a]Ge 12:12; 26:7 is my sister, the daughter of my father though not
of my mother; and she became my wife. 13And
when God had me wander from my father's

[a] 37 *Moab* sounds like the Hebrew for *from father.*
[b] 38 *Ben-Ammi* means *son of my people.*

No coward soul is mine,
No trembler in the world's storm-troubled sphere:
I see Heaven's glories shine,
And faith shines equal, arming me from fear.

—Emily Brontë (1818–1848)

Cutting Apron Strings

GE 21:8

The weaning feast was a great celebration, for it meant the child, who was now two or three years old, was likely to live to adulthood. Since so many babies died before they were weaned, the party became a rite of passage from babyhood (and all the deadly dangers of that stage of life) to childhood. As all mothers know, weaning is not only a time of celebration but also a time of sadness, for the special bond that exists between the baby and the mother is forever altered. Sarah must be feeling much the same—joyous that her son has passed through the first few crucial years, yet sad that she will never hold him at her breast, giving comfort and sustenance, as she had before.

household, I said to her, 'This is how you can
show your love to me: Everywhere we go, say of
me, "He is my brother." ' "
14Then Abimelech brought sheep and cattle and
male and female slaves and gave them to Abra- **20:14**
ham,[b] and he returned Sarah his wife to him. [b]Ge 12:16
15And Abimelech said, "My land is before you; **20:15**
live wherever you like."[c] [c]Ge 13:9
16To Sarah he said, "I am giving your brother a
thousand shekels[a] of silver. This is to cover the
offense against you before all who are with you;
you are completely vindicated." **20:17**
17Then Abraham prayed to God,[d] and God [d]Job 42:9
healed Abimelech, his wife and his slave girls so
they could have children again, 18for the LORD had
closed up every womb in Abimelech's household **20:18**
because of Abraham's wife Sarah.[e] [e]Ge 12:17

The Birth of Isaac

21 Now the LORD was gracious to Sarah[f] as he **21:1**
had said, and the LORD did for Sarah what [f]1Sa 2:21
he had promised.[g] 2Sarah became pregnant and [g]Ge 8:1; 17:16,21;
bore a son[h] to Abraham in his old age,[i] at the very Gal 4:23
time God had promised him. 3Abraham gave the **21:2**
name Isaac[b][j] to the son Sarah bore him. 4When [h]Ge 17:19
his son Isaac was eight days old, Abraham cir- [i]Gal 4:22;
cumcised him,[k] as God commanded him. 5Abra- Heb 11:11
ham was a hundred years old when his son Isaac **21:3**
was born to him. [j]Ge 17:19
6Sarah said, "God has brought me laughter,[l] and **21:4**
everyone who hears about this will laugh with [k]Ge 17:10,
me." 7And she added, "Who would have said to 12; Ac 7:8
Abraham that Sarah would nurse children? Yet I **21:6**
have borne him a son in his old age." [l]Ge 17:17; Isa 54:1

Hagar and Ishmael Sent Away

8The child grew and was weaned, and on the day
Isaac was weaned Abraham held a great feast. 9But
Sarah saw that the son whom Hagar the Egyptian **21:9**
had borne to Abraham[m] was mocking,[n] 10and she [m]Ge 16:15
said to Abraham, "Get rid of that slave woman and [n]Gal 4:29
her son, for that slave woman's son will never **21:10**
share in the inheritance with my son Isaac."[o] [o]Gal 4:30*
11The matter distressed Abraham greatly **21:11**
because it concerned his son.[p] 12But God said to [p]Ge 17:18
him, "Do not be so distressed about the boy and
your maidservant. Listen to whatever Sarah tells
you, because it is through Isaac that your off- **21:12**
spring[c] will be reckoned.[q] 13I will make the son of [q]Ro 9:7*; Heb 11:18*
the maidservant into a nation[r] also, because he is **21:13**
your offspring." [r]ver 18
14Early the next morning Abraham took some
food and a skin of water and gave them to Hagar.
He set them on her shoulders and then sent her
off with the boy. She went on her way and wan- **21:14**
dered in the desert of Beersheba.[s] [s]ver 31,32
15When the water in the skin was gone, she put
the boy under one of the bushes. 16Then she went

[a] *16* That is, about 25 pounds (about 11.5 kilograms)
[b] *3* *Isaac* means *he laughs.* [c] *12* Or *seed*

off and sat down nearby, about a bowshot away,
for she thought, "I cannot watch the boy die." And
as she sat there nearby, she[a] began to sob.
21:17 17God heard the boy crying,[t] and the angel of
tEx 3:7 God called to Hagar from heaven and said to her,
"What is the matter, Hagar? Do not be afraid; God
has heard the boy crying as he lies there. 18Lift the
21:18 boy up and take him by the hand, for I will make
uver 13 him into a great nation.[u]"
21:19 19Then God opened her eyes[v] and she saw a
vNu 22:31 well of water. So she went and filled the skin with
21:20 water and gave the boy a drink.
wGe 26:3,24; 20God was with the boy[w] as he grew up. He
28:15; 39:2, 21,23 lived in the desert and became an archer. 21While
he was living in the Desert of Paran, his mother
21:21 xGe 24:4,38 got a wife for him[x] from Egypt.

The Treaty at Beersheba

22At that time Abimelech and Phicol the commander of his forces said to Abraham, "God is
21:23 yver 31; with you in everything you do. 23Now swear[y] to
Jos 2:12 me here before God that you will not deal falsely
with me or my children or my descendants. Show
to me and the country where you are living as an
alien the same kindness I have shown to you."
24Abraham said, "I swear it."
25Then Abraham complained to Abimelech
about a well of water that Abimelech's servants
21:25 had seized.[z] 26But Abimelech said, "I don't know
zGe 26:15, 18,20-22 who has done this. You did not tell me, and I
heard about it only today."
27So Abraham brought sheep and cattle and
gave them to Abimelech, and the two men made
21:27 a treaty.[a] 28Abraham set apart seven ewe lambs
aGe 26:28,31 from the flock, 29and Abimelech asked Abraham,
"What is the meaning of these seven ewe lambs
you have set apart by themselves?"
30He replied, "Accept these seven lambs from
21:30 my hand as a witness[b] that I dug this well."
bGe 31:44, 47,48,50,52 31So that place was called Beersheba,[bc] because
21:31 the two men swore an oath there.
cGe 26:33 32After the treaty had been made at Beersheba,
Abimelech and Phicol the commander of his
forces returned to the land of the Philistines.
33Abraham planted a tamarisk tree in Beersheba,
21:33 and there he called upon the name of the LORD,[d]
dGe 4:26 eDt 33:27 the Eternal God.[e] 34And Abraham stayed in the
land of the Philistines for a long time.

Abraham Tested

22:1 **22** Some time later God tested[f] Abraham. He
fDt 8:2,16; Heb 11:17; said to him, "Abraham!"
Jas 1:12-13 "Here I am," he replied.
22:2 2Then God said, "Take your son[g], your only
gver 12,16; Jn 3:16; son, Isaac, whom you love, and go to the region of
Heb 11:17; Moriah.[h] Sacrifice him there as a burnt offering
1Jn 4:9 on one of the mountains I will tell you about."
h2Ch 3:1 3Early the next morning Abraham got up and

[a] 16 Hebrew; Septuagint *the child* [b] 31 *Beersheba* can mean *well of seven* or *well of the oath.*

Happy Ending

***H**agar, the pregnant maidservant of Sarah, had fled into the wilderness. She [evidently] just wanted to die. But God sent an angel who found her and told her to go back home, even though it was the hardest place to go. He then predicted that the child born to her would be a wild man who wouldn't get along with anybody.*

Now I don't know about you, but if I were Hagar, that's not exactly what I would have wanted to hear. Hagar's response, however, was to call God a name that had never been used before: The-God-Who-Sees-Me. *And she accepted what he said.*

Yes, our God is the all-knowing One who sees our scars, our secrets, and our strength. Our wounds and shame are his affair, and he knows just how much trouble we can stand. Somehow, the fact that he knows us so well makes a difference. We understand there is a direction and we are part of a bigger picture. From the wildernesses in our lives, the fact that he sees *[us] gives us a reason to carry on.*

—Barbara Johnson

A Happy Ending

GE 22:5

We know Abraham once bargained successfully with God (Ge 18:16–33). Yet when God asks Abraham to kill the son on whom all the promises rest, Abraham offers no objections. He simply goes about the business of completing the task. The three days that Abraham and Isaac travel to reach the appointed spot must have been agonizing for the old father. Yet, throughout the episode, Abraham displays only faith, including telling his servants that he and *Isaac will return after the sacrifice is made. How that could be true, Abraham doesn't know. But Hebrews 11:19 tells us he "reasoned" that God could bring Isaac back to life. Hence Abraham believes the two of them will return and will have an astounding story to tell. He doesn't know the details, but he has seen the happy ending through eyes of faith.*

saddled his donkey. He took with him two of his
servants and his son Isaac. When he had cut
enough wood for the burnt offering, he set out for
the place God had told him about. 4On the third
day Abraham looked up and saw the place in the
distance. 5He said to his servants, "Stay here with
the donkey while I and the boy go over there. We
will worship and then we will come back to you."
6Abraham took the wood for the burnt offering **22:6**
and placed it on his son Isaac,[i] and he himself car- [i]Jn 19:17
ried the fire and the knife. As the two of them
went on together, 7Isaac spoke up and said to his
father Abraham, "Father?"
"Yes, my son?" Abraham replied.
"The fire and wood are here," Isaac said, "but
where is the lamb[j] for the burnt offering?" **22:7**
8Abraham answered, "God himself will provide [j]Lev 1:10
the lamb for the burnt offering, my son." And the
two of them went on together.
9When they reached the place God had told him
about, Abraham built an altar there and arranged
the wood on it. He bound his son Isaac and laid **22:9**
him on the altar,[k] on top of the wood. 10Then he [k]Heb 11:17-
reached out his hand and took the knife to slay 19; Jas 2:21
his son. 11But the angel of the LORD called out to
him from heaven, "Abraham! Abraham!"
"Here I am," he replied.
12"Do not lay a hand on the boy," he said. "Do
not do anything to him. Now I know that you fear **22:12**
God,[l] because you have not withheld from me [l]1Sa 15:22;
your son, your only son.[m]" Jas 2:21-22 [m]ver 2;
13Abraham looked up and there in a thicket he Jn 3:16
saw a ram[a] caught by its horns. He went over and **22:13**
took the ram and sacrificed it as a burnt offering [n]Ro 8:32
instead of his son.[n] 14So Abraham called that place
The LORD Will Provide. And to this day it is said, **22:14**
"On the mountain of the LORD it will be provided.[o]" [o]ver 8
15The angel of the LORD called to Abraham from
heaven a second time 16and said, "I swear by **22:16**
myself,[p] declares the LORD, that because you have [p]Lk 1:73;
done this and have not withheld your son, your Heb 6:13
only son, 17I will surely bless you and make your **22:17**
descendants[q] as numerous as the stars in the sky[r] [q]Heb 6:14* [r]Ge 15:5
and as the sand on the seashore.[s] Your descen- [s]Ge 26:24;
dants will take possession of the cities of their 32:12
enemies,[t] 18and through your offspring[b] all [t]Ge 24:60
nations on earth will be blessed,[u] because you **22:18**
have obeyed me."[v] [u]Ge 12:2,3; Ac 3:25*;
19Then Abraham returned to his servants, and Gal 3:8*
they set off together for Beersheba. And Abraham [v]ver 10
stayed in Beersheba.

Nahor's Sons

20Some time later Abraham was told, "Milcah is
also a mother; she has borne sons to your broth- **22:20**
er Nahor:[w] 21Uz the firstborn, Buz his brother, [w]Ge 11:29
Kemuel (the father of Aram), 22Kesed, Hazo, Pil-

[a] 13 Many manuscripts of the Masoretic Text, Samaritan Pentateuch, Septuagint and Syriac; most manuscripts of the Masoretic Text *a ram behind ⌞him⌟* [b] 18 Or *seed*

22:23 dash, Jidlaph and Bethuel." [23]Bethuel became the
[x]Ge 24:15 father of Rebekah.[x] Milcah bore these eight sons
to Abraham's brother Nahor. [24]His concubine,
whose name was Reumah, also had sons: Tebah,
Gaham, Tahash and Maacah.

The Death of Sarah

23:2 **23** Sarah lived to be a hundred and twenty-sev-
[y]Jos 14:15 en years old. [2]She died at Kiriath Arba[y] (that
[z]ver 19; is, Hebron)[z] in the land of Canaan, and Abraham
Ge 13:18 went to mourn for Sarah and to weep over her.
[3]Then Abraham rose from beside his dead wife
23:4 [a]Ge 17:8; and spoke to the Hittites.[a] He said, [4]"I am an alien
1Ch 29:15; and a stranger[a] among you. Sell me some proper-
Ps 105:12; Heb 11:9,13 ty for a burial site here so I can bury my dead."
[5]The Hittites replied to Abraham, [6]"Sir, listen to
23:6 us. You are a mighty prince[b] among us. Bury your
[b]Ge 14:14-16; 24:35 dead in the choicest of our tombs. None of us will
refuse you his tomb for burying your dead."
[7]Then Abraham rose and bowed down before
the people of the land, the Hittites. [8]He said to
them, "If you are willing to let me bury my dead,
then listen to me and intercede with Ephron son
23:8 of Zohar[c] on my behalf [9]so he will sell me the
[c]Ge 25:9 cave of Machpelah, which belongs to him and is
at the end of his field. Ask him to sell it to me for
the full price as a burial site among you."
[10]Ephron the Hittite was sitting among his peo-
23:10 ple and he replied to Abraham in the hearing of
[d]Ge 34:20- all the Hittites who had come to the gate[d] of his
24; Ru 4:4 city. [11]"No, my lord," he said. "Listen to me; I
23:11 give[be] you the field, and I give[b] you the cave that
[e]2Sa 24:23 is in it. I give[b] it to you in the presence of my people. Bury your dead."
[12]Again Abraham bowed down before the people of the land [13]and he said to Ephron in their
hearing, "Listen to me, if you will. I will pay the
price of the field. Accept it from me so I can bury
my dead there."
[14]Ephron answered Abraham, [15]"Listen to me,
my lord; the land is worth four hundred shekels[c]
23:15 of silver,[f] but what is that between me and you?
[f]Eze 45:12 Bury your dead."
[16]Abraham agreed to Ephron's terms and
weighed out for him the price he had named in
the hearing of the Hittites: four hundred shekels
23:16 of silver,[g] according to the weight current among
[g]Jer 32:9; Zec 11:12 the merchants.
[17]So Ephron's field in Machpelah near
23:17 [h]Ge 25:9; Mamre[h]—both the field and the cave in it, and all
49:30-32; the trees within the borders of the field—was
50:13; deeded [18]to Abraham as his property in the pres-
Ac 7:16 ence of all the Hittites who had come to the gate
of the city. [19]Afterward Abraham buried his wife
Sarah in the cave in the field of Machpelah near
Mamre (which is at Hebron) in the land of

[a] 3 Or *the sons of Heth*; also in verses 5, 7, 10, 16, 18 and 20
[b] 11 Or *sell*   [c] 15 That is, about 10 pounds (about 4.5 kilograms)

Down Payment

GE 23:1-9

God promised Abraham he would inherit vast amounts of land, but a grief-stricken Abraham finds he doesn't own even a plot of land in which to bury his beloved wife. So he buys a cave from one of his neighbors. This cave also becomes the burial site for Abraham, Isaac, Rebekah, Leah and Jacob. But more importantly, the cave and the accompanying field are like a down payment on God's promise to give this land to the self-described "alien" who now lives in the region—not as a citizen, but as a foreigner.

A Resourceful Servant

GE 24:12–14

Abraham's servant, who is probably his chief servant Eliezer (Ge 15:2), shows that he is a resourceful, loyal and spiritual man. Eliezer takes ten camels on his wife-finding mission for Isaac. Since camels are rare, they will immediately communicate that Eliezer belongs to a wealthy man. Eliezer doesn't leave the choice of a wife to chance or to which woman looks the best. Instead, he commits the decision to God, asking that the Lord show kindness to his master Abraham.

Years of watching Abraham react in faith have obviously influenced his servant Eliezer. Without hesitation he goes to God for direction in completing his important task. And God hears his prayer and honors his request, just as he has promised to honor ours if we approach him in faith (Ps 17:6).

Canaan. 20So the field and the cave in it were
deeded[i] to Abraham by the Hittites as a burial site.

Isaac and Rebekah

24 Abraham was now old and well advanced in
years, and the LORD had blessed him in every
way.[j] 2He said to the chief[a] servant in his household, the one in charge of all that he had,[k] "Put
your hand under my thigh.[l] 3I want you to swear
by the LORD, the God of heaven and the God of
earth,[m] that you will not get a wife for my son[n]
from the daughters of the Canaanites,[o] among
whom I am living, 4but will go to my country and
my own relatives[p] and get a wife for my son Isaac."
5The servant asked him, "What if the woman is
unwilling to come back with me to this land?
Shall I then take your son back to the country you
came from?"
6"Make sure that you do not take my son back
there," Abraham said. 7"The LORD, the God of
heaven, who brought me out of my father's
household and my native land and who spoke to
me and promised me on oath, saying, 'To your offspring[b][q] I will give this land'[r]—he will send his
angel before you[s] so that you can get a wife for
my son from there. 8If the woman is unwilling to
come back with you, then you will be released
from this oath of mine. Only do not take my son
back there." 9So the servant put his hand under
the thigh[t] of his master Abraham and swore an
oath to him concerning this matter.
10Then the servant took ten of his master's
camels and left, taking with him all kinds of good
things from his master. He set out for Aram Naharaim[c] and made his way to the town of Nahor.
11He had the camels kneel down near the well[u]
outside the town; it was toward evening, the time
the women go out to draw water.[v]
12Then he prayed, "O LORD, God of my master
Abraham,[w] give me success today, and show kindness to my master Abraham. 13See, I am standing
beside this spring, and the daughters of the townspeople are coming out to draw water. 14May it be
that when I say to a girl, 'Please let down your jar
that I may have a drink,' and she says, 'Drink, and
I'll water your camels too'—let her be the one you
have chosen for your servant Isaac. By this I will
know[x] that you have shown kindness to my
master."
15Before he had finished praying,[y] Rebekah[z]
came out with her jar on her shoulder. She was
the daughter of Bethuel son of Milcah,[a] who was
the wife of Abraham's brother Nahor.[b] 16The girl
was very beautiful,[c] a virgin; no man had ever
lain with her. She went down to the spring, filled
her jar and came up again.
17The servant hurried to meet her and said,
"Please give me a little water from your jar."

23:20 [i]Jer 32:10
24:1 [j]ver 35
24:2 [k]Ge 39:4-6 [l]ver 9; Ge 47:29
24:3 [m]Ge 14:19 [n]Ge 28:1; Dt 7:3 [o]Ge 10:15-19
24:4 [p]Ge 12:1; 28:2
24:7 [q]Gal 3:16* [r]Ge 12:7; 13:15 [s]Ex 23:20,23
24:9 [t]ver 2
24:11 [u]Ex 2:15 [v]ver 13; 1Sa 9:11
24:12 [w]ver 27,42, 48; Ge 26:24; Ex 3:6,15,16
24:14 [x]Jdg 6:17,37
24:15 [y]ver 45 [z]Ge 22:23 [a]Ge 22:20 [b]Ge 11:29
24:16 [c]Ge 26:7

[a] *2* Or *oldest* [b] *7* Or *seed* [c] *10* That is, Northwest Mesopotamia

24:18 18“Drink,[d] my lord,” she said, and quickly low-
dver 14 ered the jar to her hands and gave him a drink.
19After she had given him a drink, she said, “I'll
24:19 draw water for your camels too,[e] until they have
ever 14 finished drinking.” 20So she quickly emptied her
jar into the trough, ran back to the well to draw
more water, and drew enough for all his camels.
21Without saying a word, the man watched her
24:21 closely to learn whether or not the LORD had made
fver 12 his journey successful.[f]
24:22 22When the camels had finished drinking, the
gver 47 man took out a gold nose ring[g] weighing a beka[a]
and two gold bracelets weighing ten shekels.[b]
23Then he asked, “Whose daughter are you?
Please tell me, is there room in your father's
house for us to spend the night?”
24:24 24She answered him, “I am the daughter of
hver 15 Bethuel, the son that Milcah bore to Nahor.[h]”
25And she added, “We have plenty of straw and
fodder, as well as room for you to spend the night.”
24:26 26Then the man bowed down and worshiped
iver 48,52; the LORD,[i] 27saying, “Praise be to the LORD,[j] the
Ex 4:31 God of my master Abraham, who has not aban-
24:27 doned his kindness and faithfulness[k] to my mas-
jEx 18:10; ter. As for me, the LORD has led me on the jour-
Ru 4:14; ney[l] to the house of my master's relatives.”[m]
1Sa 25:32 28The girl ran and told her mother's household
kver 49; about these things. 29Now Rebekah had a brother
Ge 32:10; named Laban,[n] and he hurried out to the man at
Ps 98:3 lver 21 mver 12,48 the spring. 30As soon as he had seen the nose ring,
24:29 and the bracelets on his sister's arms, and had
nver 4; heard Rebekah tell what the man said to her, he
Ge 29:5,12, went out to the man and found him standing by
13 the camels near the spring. 31“Come, you who are
24:31 blessed by the LORD,”[o] he said. “Why are you
oGe 26:29; standing out here? I have prepared the house and
Ru 3:10; Ps 115:15 a place for the camels.”
32So the man went to the house, and the camels
were unloaded. Straw and fodder were brought
24:32 for the camels, and water for him and his men to
pGe 43:24; wash their feet.[p] 33Then food was set before him,
Jdg 19:21 but he said, “I will not eat until I have told you
what I have to say.”
“Then tell us,” ⌊Laban⌋ said.
24:35 34So he said, “I am Abraham's servant. 35The
qver 1 LORD has blessed my master abundantly,[q] and he
rGe 13:2 has become wealthy. He has given him sheep and
cattle, silver and gold, menservants and maidser-
24:36 vants, and camels and donkeys.[r] 36My master's
sGe 21:2,10 wife Sarah has borne him a son in her[c] old age,[s]
tGe 25:5 and he has given him everything he owns.[t] 37And
my master made me swear an oath, and said, ‘You
24:37 uver 3 must not get a wife for my son from the daughters of the Canaanites, in whose land I live,[u] 38but
24:38 go to my father's family and to my own clan, and
vver 4 get a wife for my son.’[v]
24:39 39“Then I asked my master, ‘What if the woman
wver 5 will not come back with me?’[w]

[a] 22 That is, about 1/5 ounce (about 5.5 grams) [b] 22 That is, about 4 ounces (about 110 grams) [c] 36 Or *his*

Thirsty Camels

GE 24:19-20

Rebekah's offer to water Eliezer's camels is no small undertaking. A camel can go for up to 17 days without water and lose 25 percent of its weight by dehydration without suffering ill effects. It can then regain that lost weight in just a short time by drinking as much as 25 gallons of water. All this adds up to serious work for Rebekah, especially if multiplied by ten camels. Rebekah's gesture reveals the generosity, the selflessness and the inner beauty that Eliezer is looking for in a wife for Isaac. (See character sketch for Rebekah on page 136.)

Rebekah's Choice

GE 24:55-58

Surprisingly, in a culture with little regard for women, Rebekah's brother and mother decide they will let Rebekah choose if she will stay with them for ten days before departing with Abraham's servant to become Isaac's bride. Rebekah, who seems to be a spirited, generous-hearted and spontaneous soul, simply says, "I'll go." And so she mounts a camel to travel to a land she has never been to, to marry a man she has never met, most likely never to see her family again.

Her willingness as well as that of her brother and mother reveal an eagerness to follow the Lord's leading, given through Eliezer. She and her family recognize that leading as from the Lord and move without question or argument—a beautiful exhibition of submission to God's direction.

40"He replied, 'The LORD, before whom I have
walked, will send his angel with you[x] and make
your journey a success, so that you can get a wife
for my son from my own clan and from my
father's family. 41Then, when you go to my clan,
you will be released from my oath even if they
refuse to give her to you—you will be released
from my oath.'[y]
42"When I came to the spring today, I said,
'O LORD, God of my master Abraham, if you will,
please grant success[z] to the journey on which I
have come. 43See, I am standing beside this
spring;[a] if a maiden comes out to draw water and
I say to her, "Please let me drink a little water
from your jar,"[b] 44and if she says to me, "Drink,
and I'll draw water for your camels too," let her
be the one the LORD has chosen for my master's
son.'
45"Before I finished praying in my heart,[c]
Rebekah came out, with her jar on her shoulder.[d]
She went down to the spring and drew water, and
I said to her, 'Please give me a drink.'[e]
46"She quickly lowered her jar from her shoulder and said, 'Drink, and I'll water your camels
too.'[f] So I drank, and she watered the camels also.
47"I asked her, 'Whose daughter are you?'[g]
"She said, 'The daughter of Bethuel son of
Nahor, whom Milcah bore to him.'[h]
"Then I put the ring in her nose and the
bracelets on her arms,[i] 48and I bowed down and
worshiped the LORD.[j] I praised the LORD, the God
of my master Abraham, who had led me on the
right road to get the granddaughter of my master's
brother for his son.[k] 49Now if you will show kindness and faithfulness[l] to my master, tell me; and if
not, tell me, so I may know which way to turn."
50Laban and Bethuel answered, "This is from
the LORD;[m] we can say nothing to you one way or
the other.[n] 51Here is Rebekah; take her and go, and
let her become the wife of your master's son, as
the LORD has directed."
52When Abraham's servant heard what they
said, he bowed down to the ground before the
LORD.[o] 53Then the servant brought out gold and
silver jewelry and articles of clothing and gave
them to Rebekah; he also gave costly gifts[p] to her
brother and to her mother. 54Then he and the men
who were with him ate and drank and spent the
night there.
When they got up the next morning, he said,
"Send me on my way[q] to my master."
55But her brother and her mother replied, "Let
the girl remain with us ten days or so; then you[a]
may go."
56But he said to them, "Do not detain me, now
that the LORD has granted success to my journey.
Send me on my way so I may go to my master."
57Then they said, "Let's call the girl and ask her

24:40 [x]ver 7
24:41 [y]ver 8
24:42 [z]ver 12
24:43 [a]ver 13 [b]ver 14
24:45 [c]1Sa 1:13 [d]ver 15 [e]ver 17
24:46 [f]ver 18-19
24:47 [g]ver 23 [h]ver 24 [i]Eze 16:11-12
24:48 [j]ver 26 [k]ver 27
24:49 [l]Ge 47:29; Jos 2:14
24:50 [m]Ps 118:23 [n]Ge 31:7,24, 29,42
24:52 [o]ver 26
24:53 [p]ver 10,22
24:54 [q]ver 56,59

[a] 55 Or *she*

about it." 58So they called Rebekah and asked her,
"Will you go with this man?"
"I will go," she said.
24:59 59So they sent their sister Rebekah on her way,
rGe 35:8 along with her nurse[r] and Abraham's servant and
his men. 60And they blessed Rebekah and said to
her,

"Our sister, may you increase
24:60 sGe 17:16 to thousands upon thousands;[s]
tGe 22:17 may your offspring possess
the gates of their enemies."[t]

61Then Rebekah and her maids got ready and
mounted their camels and went back with the
24:62 man. So the servant took Rebekah and left.
uGe 16:14; 62Now Isaac had come from Beer Lahai Roi,[u] for
25:11 he was living in the Negev.[v] 63He went out to the
vGe 20:1 field one evening to meditate,[a][w] and as he looked
24:63 up, he saw camels approaching. 64Rebekah also
wPs 1:2; 77:12; looked up and saw Isaac. She got down from her
119:15,27, camel 65and asked the servant, "Who is that man
48,97,148; in the field coming to meet us?"
143:5; 145:5 "He is my master," the servant answered. So
she took her veil and covered herself.
66Then the servant told Isaac all he had done.
67Isaac brought her into the tent of his mother Sar-
24:67 ah, and he married Rebekah.[x] So she became his
xGe 25:20 yGe 29:18,20 wife, and he loved her;[y] and Isaac was comforted
zGe 23:1-2 after his mother's death.[z]

The Death of Abraham

25 Abraham took[b] another wife, whose name
25:2 was Keturah. 2She bore him Zimran, Jok-
a1Ch 1:32,33 shan, Medan, Midian, Ishbak and Shuah.[a] 3Jok-
shan was the father of Sheba and Dedan; the
descendants of Dedan were the Asshurites, the
Letushites and the Leummites. 4The sons of Midian were Ephah, Epher, Hanoch, Abida and Elda-
25:5 ah. All these were descendants of Keturah.
bGe 24:36 5Abraham left everything he owned to Isaac.[b]
25:6 6But while he was still living, he gave gifts to the
cGe 22:24 sons of his concubines[c] and sent them away from
dGe 21:10,14 his son Isaac[d] to the land of the east.
7Altogether, Abraham lived a hundred and sev-
25:8 enty-five years. 8Then Abraham breathed his last
eGe 15:15 fver 17; and died at a good old age,[e] an old man and full of
Ge 35:29; years; and he was gathered to his people.[f] 9His
49:29,33 sons Isaac and Ishmael buried him[g] in the cave of
25:9 Machpelah near Mamre, in the field of Ephron son
gGe 35:29 of Zohar the Hittite,[h] 10the field Abraham had
hGe 50:13 bought from the Hittites.[c][i] There Abraham was
25:10 buried with his wife Sarah. 11After Abraham's
iGe 23:16 death, God blessed his son Isaac, who then lived
25:11 jGe 16:14 near Beer Lahai Roi.[j]

Ishmael's Sons

12This is the account of Abraham's son Ishmael,

[a] 63 The meaning of the Hebrew for this word is uncertain.
[b] 1 Or *had taken* [c] 10 Or *the sons of Heth*

A Sweet Marriage

GE 24:67

Isaac and Rebekah's marriage relationship is written of simply, yet sweetly. Isaac immediately accepts Rebekah when his father's servant presents her. He takes her as his wife, he loves her and she comforts him over the loss of his mother. Most of today's marriages have more favorable beginnings than this one—two strangers meeting and marrying. However, their example of intimacy is one many married couples admire and desire.

An Earthbound Marriage

GE 25:21

Although God clearly brings Isaac and Rebekah together in marriage, their relationship isn't without difficulties. During the first 20 years of their marriage, Rebekah remains infertile. Isaac has reason, considering his own miraculous birth, to believe God can enable a barren woman to have children. So Isaac prays to the Lord "on behalf of his wife." What a beautiful, caring statement of Isaac's love and concern for Rebekah, which says much about the spiritual intimacy they shared.

whom Sarah's maidservant, Hagar[k] the Egyptian,
bore to Abraham.[l]

13These are the names of the sons of Ishmael,
listed in the order of their birth: Nebaioth the firstborn of Ishmael, Kedar, Adbeel, Mibsam, 14Mish-
ma, Dumah, Massa, 15Hadad, Tema, Jetur,
Naphish and Kedemah. 16These were the sons of
Ishmael, and these are the names of the twelve
tribal rulers[m] according to their settlements and
camps. 17Altogether, Ishmael lived a hundred and
thirty-seven years. He breathed his last and died,
and he was gathered to his people.[n] 18His descendants settled in the area from Havilah to Shur,
near the border of Egypt, as you go toward
Asshur. And they lived in hostility toward[a] all
their brothers.[o]

Jacob and Esau

19This is the account of Abraham's son Isaac.

Abraham became the father of Isaac, 20and
Isaac was forty years old[p] when he married
Rebekah[q] daughter of Bethuel the Aramean from
Paddan Aram[b] and sister of Laban[r] the Aramean.
21Isaac prayed to the LORD on behalf of his wife,
because she was barren. The LORD answered his
prayer,[s] and his wife Rebekah became pregnant.
22The babies jostled each other within her, and
she said, "Why is this happening to me?" So she
went to inquire of the LORD.[t]
23The LORD said to her,

"Two nations[u] are in your womb,
and two peoples from within you will
be separated;
one people will be stronger than the
other,
and the older will serve the younger.[v]"

24When the time came for her to give birth,
there were twin boys in her womb. 25The first to
come out was red, and his whole body was like a
hairy garment;[w] so they named him Esau.[c] 26After
this, his brother came out, with his hand grasping Esau's heel;[x] so he was named Jacob.[d][y] Isaac
was sixty years old when Rebekah gave birth to
them.

27The boys grew up, and Esau became a skillful hunter, a man of the open country,[z] while
Jacob was a quiet man, staying among the tents.
28Isaac, who had a taste for wild game,[a] loved
Esau, but Rebekah loved Jacob.[b]

29Once when Jacob was cooking some stew,
Esau came in from the open country, famished.
30He said to Jacob, "Quick, let me have some of
that red stew! I'm famished!" (That is why he was
also called Edom.[e])

25:12 [k]Ge 16:1 [l]Ge 16:15
25:16 [m]Ge 17:20
25:17 [n]ver 8
25:18 [o]Ge 16:12
25:20 [p]ver 26; Ge 26:34 [q]Ge 24:67 [r]Ge 24:29
25:21 [s]1Ch 5:20; 2Ch 33:13; Ezr 8:23; Ps 127:3; Ro 9:10
25:22 [t]1Sa 9:9; 10:22
25:23 [u]Ge 17:4 [v]Ge 27:29, 40; Mal 1:3; Ro 9:11-12*
25:25 [w]Ge 27:11
25:26 [x]Hos 12:3 [y]Ge 27:36
25:27 [z]Ge 27:3,5
25:28 [a]Ge 27:19 [b]Ge 27:6

[a] *18* Or *lived to the east of* [b] *20* That is, Northwest Mesopotamia [c] *25* *Esau* may mean *hairy*; he was also called Edom, which means *red.* [d] *26* *Jacob* means *he grasps the heel* (figuratively, *he deceives*). [e] *30* *Edom* means *red.*

[31]Jacob replied, "First sell me your birthright."
[32]"Look, I am about to die," Esau said. "What
good is the birthright to me?"
25:33 [33]But Jacob said, "Swear to me first." So he
[c]Ge 27:36; swore an oath to him, selling his birthright[c] to
Heb 12:16 Jacob.
[34]Then Jacob gave Esau some bread and some
lentil stew. He ate and drank, and then got up and
left.
So Esau despised his birthright.

Isaac and Abimelech

26:1 **26** Now there was a famine in the land[d]—
[d]Ge 12:10 besides the earlier famine of Abraham's
[e]Ge 20:1 time—and Isaac went to Abimelech king of the
26:2 Philistines in Gerar.[e] [2]The LORD appeared[f] to Isaac
[f]Ge 12:7; 17:1; 18:1 and said, "Do not go down to Egypt; live in the
[g]Ge 12:1 land where I tell you to live.[g] [3]Stay in this land for
26:3 a while,[h] and I will be with you and will bless
[h]Ge 20:1; 28:15 you.[i] For to you and your descendants I will give
[i]Ge 12:2; all these lands[j] and will confirm the oath I swore
22:16-18 to your father Abraham. [4]I will make your descen-
[j]Ge 12:7; 13:15; 15:18 dants as numerous as the stars in the sky[k] and
will give them all these lands, and through your
26:4 offspring[a] all nations on earth will be blessed,[l]
[k]Ge 15:5; 22:17; [5]because Abraham obeyed me[m] and kept my
Ex 32:13 requirements, my commands, my decrees and my
[l]Ge 12:3; 22:18; laws." [6]So Isaac stayed in Gerar.
Gal 3:8 [7]When the men of that place asked him about
26:5 his wife, he said, "She is my sister,[n]" because he
[m]Ge 22:16 was afraid to say, "She is my wife." He thought,
"The men of this place might kill me on account
26:7 of Rebekah, because she is beautiful."
[n]Ge 12:13; 20:2,12; [8]When Isaac had been there a long time, Abim-
Pr 29:25 elech king of the Philistines looked down from a
window and saw Isaac caressing his wife Rebekah. [9]So Abimelech summoned Isaac and said,
"She is really your wife! Why did you say, 'She is
my sister'?"
Isaac answered him, "Because I thought I might
lose my life on account of her."
26:10 [10]Then Abimelech said, "What is this you have
[o]Ge 20:9 done to us?[o] One of the men might well have slept
with your wife, and you would have brought guilt
upon us."
26:11 [11]So Abimelech gave orders to all the people:
[p]Ps 105:15 "Anyone who molests[p] this man or his wife shall
26:12 surely be put to death."
[q]ver 3; Job 42:12 [12]Isaac planted crops in that land and the same
year reaped a hundredfold, because the LORD
26:13 blessed him.[q] [13]The man became rich, and his
[r]Pr 10:22 wealth continued to grow until he became very
26:14 wealthy.[r] [14]He had so many flocks and herds and
[s]Ge 24:36 [t]Ge 37:11 servants[s] that the Philistines envied him.[t] [15]So all
26:15 the wells[u] that his father's servants had dug in the
[u]Ge 21:30 time of his father Abraham, the Philistines
[v]Ge 21:25 stopped up,[v] filling them with earth.
[16]Then Abimelech said to Isaac, "Move away
26:16 [w]Ex 1:9 from us; you have become too powerful for us.[w]"

Family Conflict

GE 25:29-34

Jacob and Esau are about as opposite as twins can be. They go their separate ways each day—Esau off to hunt and Jacob to spend his time by the tents. The two boys bring conflict to their parents as well, with Isaac drawn to Esau, the hunter; and Rebekah to Jacob, a quieter boy. Considering this disunity, it comes as no surprise when Jacob, younger by minutes than his twin brother, Esau, seeks the birthright, the right of the firstborn son. The eldest son generally received the greatest inheritance as well as the privileges and responsibilities of family leadership. Esau holds this position lightly while Jacob covets it. Perhaps this situation is just the one Jacob has been looking for in order to supplant his brother as holder of the birthright, as his name suggests. (Jacob is a play on the Hebrew word for "heel"—"he takes by the heel" or "supplants" or "deceives.")

[a] 4 Or *seed*

A Disappointing Choice

GE 26:34–35

Old Testament Hebrew parents chose wives for their sons. Sometimes the young man did the choosing and his parents, the negotiating. And sometimes the girl was asked whether she consented. But rarely did a man marry against his parents' wishes, as Esau does. Abraham had placed such importance on Isaac marrying a Hebrew that Abraham had sent his servant back to their homeland to find a bride for Isaac. So, too, Isaac and Rebekah desire their sons to choose Hebrew wives. Wives became members of their husbands' families. But such a transition entailed much more than moving to their husband's home. It also involved transferring allegiance to the new family. The cultural and spiritual differences between Esau's wives and their in-laws causes hardship for all involved. Once again, Esau makes a hasty choice rather than a good one—a choice that suggests he does not value his cultural or spiritual heritage.

17 So Isaac moved away from there and encamped in the Valley of Gerar and settled there.
18 Isaac reopened the wells[x] that had been dug in
the time of his father Abraham, which the Philistines had stopped up after Abraham died, and he
gave them the same names his father had given
them.
19 Isaac's servants dug in the valley and discovered a well of fresh water there. 20 But the herdsmen of Gerar quarreled with Isaac's herdsmen
and said, "The water is ours!"[y] So he named the
well Esek,[a] because they disputed with him.
21 Then they dug another well, but they quarreled
over that one also; so he named it Sitnah.[b] 22 He
moved on from there and dug another well, and
no one quarreled over it. He named it Rehoboth,[c]
saying, "Now the LORD has given us room and we
will flourish[z] in the land."
23 From there he went up to Beersheba. 24 That
night the LORD appeared to him and said, "I am
the God of your father Abraham.[a] Do not be
afraid,[b] for I am with you; I will bless you and will
increase the number of your descendants[c] for the
sake of my servant Abraham."[d]
25 Isaac built an altar[e] there and called on the
name of the LORD. There he pitched his tent, and
there his servants dug a well.
26 Meanwhile, Abimelech had come to him from
Gerar, with Ahuzzath his personal adviser and
Phicol the commander of his forces.[f] 27 Isaac asked
them, "Why have you come to me, since you were
hostile to me and sent me away?[g]"
28 They answered, "We saw clearly that the LORD
was with you;[h] so we said, 'There ought to be a
sworn agreement between us'—between us and
you. Let us make a treaty with you 29 that you will
do us no harm, just as we did not molest you but
always treated you well and sent you away in
peace. And now you are blessed by the LORD."[i]
30 Isaac then made a feast[j] for them, and they ate
and drank. 31 Early the next morning the men
swore an oath[k] to each other. Then Isaac sent
them on their way, and they left him in peace.
32 That day Isaac's servants came and told him
about the well they had dug. They said, "We've
found water!" 33 He called it Shibah,[d] and to this
day the name of the town has been Beersheba.[e][l]
34 When Esau was forty years old,[m] he married
Judith daughter of Beeri the Hittite, and also Basemath daughter of Elon the Hittite.[n] 35 They were a
source of grief to Isaac and Rebekah.[o]

Jacob Gets Isaac's Blessing

27 When Isaac was old and his eyes were so
weak that he could no longer see,[p] he called
for Esau his older son[q] and said to him, "My son."

26:18 [x]Ge 21:30
26:20 [y]Ge 21:25
26:22 [z]Ge 17:6; Ex 1:7
26:24 [a]Ge 24:12; Ex 3:6 [b]Ge 15:1 [c]ver 4 [d]Ge 17:7
26:25 [e]Ge 12:7,8; 13:4,18; Ps 116:17
26:26 [f]Ge 21:22
26:27 [g]ver 16
26:28 [h]Ge 21:22
26:29 [i]Ge 24:31; Ps 115:15
26:30 [j]Ge 19:3
26:31 [k]Ge 21:31
26:33 [l]Ge 21:14
26:34 [m]Ge 25:20 [n]Ge 28:9; 36:2
26:35 [o]Ge 27:46
27:1 [p]Ge 48:10; 1Sa 3:2 [q]Ge 25:25

[a] 20 *Esek* means *dispute.* [b] 21 *Sitnah* means *opposition.* [c] 22 *Rehoboth* means *room.* [d] 33 *Shibah* can mean *oath* or *seven.* [e] 33 *Beersheba* can mean *well of the oath* or *well of seven.*

"Here I am," he answered.
27:2 2 Isaac said, "I am now an old man and don't
rGe 47:29 know the day of my death.[r] 3 Now then, get your
27:3 weapons—your quiver and bow—and go out to
sGe 25:27 the open country[s] to hunt some wild game for me.
27:4 4 Prepare me the kind of tasty food I like and bring
tver 10,25, it to me to eat, so that I may give you my blessing[t]
31; Ge 49:28; before I die."
Dt 33:1; 5 Now Rebekah was listening as Isaac spoke to
Heb 11:20 his son Esau. When Esau left for the open country
to hunt game and bring it back, 6 Rebekah said to
27:6 her son Jacob,[u] "Look, I overheard your father say
uGe 25:28 to your brother Esau, 7 'Bring me some game and
prepare me some tasty food to eat, so that I may
give you my blessing in the presence of the LORD
before I die.' 8 Now, my son, listen carefully and
27:8 do what I tell you:[v] 9 Go out to the flock and bring
vver 13,43 me two choice young goats, so I can prepare some
tasty food for your father, just the way he likes it.
10 Then take it to your father to eat, so that he may
give you his blessing before he dies."
11 Jacob said to Rebekah his mother, "But my
27:11 brother Esau is a hairy man,[w] and I'm a man with
wGe 25:25 smooth skin. 12 What if my father touches me?[x] I
27:12 would appear to be tricking him and would bring
xver 22 down a curse on myself rather than a blessing."
13 His mother said to him, "My son, let the curse
27:13 fall on me.[y] Just do what I say;[z] go and get them
yMt 27:25 for me."
zver 8 14 So he went and got them and brought them to
his mother, and she prepared some tasty food, just
the way his father liked it. 15 Then Rebekah took
27:15 the best clothes[a] of Esau her older son, which she
aver 27 had in the house, and put them on her younger
son Jacob. 16 She also covered his hands and the
smooth part of his neck with the goatskins.
17 Then she handed to her son Jacob the tasty food
and the bread she had made.
18 He went to his father and said, "My father."
"Yes, my son," he answered. "Who is it?"
19 Jacob said to his father, "I am Esau your firstborn. I have done as you told me. Please sit up
and eat some of my game so that you may give
27:19 me your blessing."[b]
bver 4 20 Isaac asked his son, "How did you find it so
quickly, my son?"
27:20 "The LORD your God gave me success,"[c] he
cGe 24:12 replied.
21 Then Isaac said to Jacob, "Come near so I can
27:21 touch you,[d] my son, to know whether you really
dver 12 are my son Esau or not."
22 Jacob went close to his father Isaac, who
touched him and said, "The voice is the voice of
Jacob, but the hands are the hands of Esau." 23 He
did not recognize him, for his hands were hairy
27:23 like those of his brother Esau;[e] so he blessed him.
ever 16 24 "Are you really my son Esau?" he asked.
"I am," he replied.
25 Then he said, "My son, bring me some of your
27:25 game to eat, so that I may give you my blessing."[f]
fver 4 Jacob brought it to him and he ate; and he

Betrayal

GE 27:5-10

Deathbed blessings had legal force in the Near East. Rebekah wants her favorite son Jacob to receive this blessing rather than her son Esau, a rough hunter who is indifferent to his heritage and has married foreign women she doesn't approve of. Her mind probably returns to God's promise, given before the twins were born, that Esau would serve his brother (Ge 25:23). She perhaps even uses God's promise as a rationale for taking matters into her own hands. Through her actions Rebekah creates dangerous animosity between the two brothers, betrays her husband and one of her sons, and ends up sending her favorite son into exile to save his life. How often do we, too, grab hold of what we believe God wants to accomplish and use it to manipulate other people, rather than allow God space to work his will, in his timing and in his way?

brought some wine and he drank. 26 Then his
father Isaac said to him, "Come here, my son, and
kiss me."
27 So he went to him and kissed him[g]. When
Isaac caught the smell of his clothes,[h] he blessed
him and said,

> "Ah, the smell of my son
> is like the smell of a field
> that the LORD has blessed.[i]
> 28 May God give you of heaven's dew[j]
> and of earth's richness[k]—
> an abundance of grain and new wine.[l]
> 29 May nations serve you
> and peoples bow down to you.[m]
> Be lord over your brothers,
> and may the sons of your mother bow
> down to you.[n]
> May those who curse you be cursed
> and those who bless you be blessed.[o]"

30 After Isaac finished blessing him and Jacob
had scarcely left his father's presence, his brother
Esau came in from hunting. 31 He too prepared
some tasty food and brought it to his father. Then
he said to him, "My father, sit up and eat some of
my game, so that you may give me your blessing."[p]
32 His father Isaac asked him, "Who are you?"[q]
"I am your son," he answered, "your firstborn,
Esau."
33 Isaac trembled violently and said, "Who was
it, then, that hunted game and brought it to me? I
ate it just before you came and I blessed him—
and indeed he will be blessed![r]"
34 When Esau heard his father's words, he burst
out with a loud and bitter cry[s] and said to his
father, "Bless me—me too, my father!"
35 But he said, "Your brother came deceitfully[t]
and took your blessing."
36 Esau said, "Isn't he rightly named Jacob[a]?[u] He
has deceived me these two times: He took my
birthright,[v] and now he's taken my blessing!"
Then he asked, "Haven't you reserved any blessing for me?"
37 Isaac answered Esau, "I have made him lord
over you and have made all his relatives his servants, and I have sustained him with grain and
new wine.[w] So what can I possibly do for you, my
son?"
38 Esau said to his father, "Do you have only one
blessing, my father? Bless me too, my father!"
Then Esau wept aloud.[x]
39 His father Isaac answered him,

> "Your dwelling will be
> away from the earth's richness,
> away from the dew[y] of heaven above.
> 40 You will live by the sword
> and you will serve[z] your brother.[a]

[a] 36 *Jacob* means *he grasps the heel* (figuratively, *he deceives*).

27:27 [g]Heb 11:20 [h]SS 4:11 [i]Ps 65:9-13
27:28 [j]Dt 33:13 [k]ver 39 [l]Ge 45:18; Nu 18:12; Dt 33:28
27:29 [m]Isa 45:14, 23; 49:7,23 [n]Ge 9:25; 25:23; 37:7 [o]Ge 12:3; Nu 24:9; Zep 2:8
27:31 [p]ver 4
27:32 [q]ver 18
27:33 [r]ver 29; Ge 28:3,4; Ro 11:29
27:34 [s]Heb 12:17
27:35 [t]Jer 9:4; 12:6
27:36 [u]Ge 25:26 [v]Ge 25:33
27:37 [w]ver 28
27:38 [x]Heb 12:17
27:39 [y]ver 28
27:40 [z]2Sa 8:14 [a]Ge 25:23

Such are His mercy and goodness that, even when we are engaged in our worldly pastimes and businesses and pleasures and hagglings, when we are falling into sins and rising from them again . . . in spite of all that, this Lord of ours is so anxious that we should desire Him and strive after His companionship that He calls us ceaselessly, time after time, to approach Him; and this voice of His is so sweet.

—Teresa of Avila (1515–1582)

27:40 But when you grow restless,
[b]2Ki 8:20-22 you will throw his yoke
from off your neck.[b]"

Jacob Flees to Laban

27:41 [41]Esau held a grudge[c] against Jacob[d] because of
[c]Ge 37:4 [d]Ge 32:11 the blessing his father had given him. He said to
[e]Ge 50:4,10 himself, "The days of mourning[e] for my father are
[f]Ob 1:10 near; then I will kill my brother Jacob."[f]
[42]When Rebekah was told what her older son
Esau had said, she sent for her younger son Jacob
and said to him, "Your brother Esau is consoling
27:43 himself with the thought of killing you. [43]Now
[g]ver 8 then, my son, do what I say:[g] Flee at once to my
[h]Ge 24:29 brother Laban[h] in Haran.[i] [44]Stay with him for a
[i]Ge 11:31 while[j] until your brother's fury subsides. [45]When
27:44 your brother is no longer angry with you and for-
[j]Ge 31:38,41 gets what you did to him,[k] I'll send word for you
27:45 to come back from there. Why should I lose both
[k]ver 35 of you in one day?"
[46]Then Rebekah said to Isaac, "I'm disgusted
with living because of these Hittite women. If
Jacob takes a wife from among the women of this
27:46 land, from Hittite women like these, my life will
[l]Ge 26:35 not be worth living."[l]

28:1 **28** So Isaac called for Jacob and blessed[a] him
[m]Ge 24:3 and commanded him: "Do not marry a
28:2 Canaanite woman.[m] [2]Go at once to Paddan Aram,[b]
[n]Ge 25:20 to the house of your mother's father Bethuel.[n]
Take a wife for yourself there, from among the
28:3 daughters of Laban, your mother's brother. [3]May
[o]Ge 17:1 God Almighty[c][o] bless you and make you fruitful[p]
[p]Ge 17:6 and increase your numbers until you become a
community of peoples. [4]May he give you and your
28:4 descendants the blessing given to Abraham,[q] so
[q]Ge 12:2,3 that you may take possession of the land where
[r]Ge 17:8 you now live as an alien,[r] the land God gave to
28:5 Abraham." [5]Then Isaac sent Jacob on his way, and
[s]Hos 12:12 he went to Paddan Aram,[s] to Laban son of Bethu-
[t]Ge 24:29 el the Aramean, the brother of Rebekah,[t] who was
the mother of Jacob and Esau.
[6]Now Esau learned that Isaac had blessed Jacob
and had sent him to Paddan Aram to take a wife
from there, and that when he blessed him he com-
28:6 manded him, "Do not marry a Canaanite wom-
[u]ver 1 an,"[u] [7]and that Jacob had obeyed his father and
28:8 mother and had gone to Paddan Aram. [8]Esau then
[v]Ge 24:3 realized how displeasing the Canaanite women[v]
[w]Ge 26:35 were to his father Isaac;[w] [9]so he went to Ishmael
28:9 and married Mahalath, the sister of Nebaioth[x] and
[x]Ge 25:13 daughter of Ishmael son of Abraham, in addition
[y]Ge 26:34 to the wives he already had.[y]

Jacob's Dream at Bethel

28:10 [10]Jacob left Beersheba and set out for Haran.[z]
[z]Ge 11:31 [11]When he reached a certain place, he stopped for
the night because the sun had set. Taking one of
the stones there, he put it under his head and lay

[a] *1* Or *greeted* [b] *2* That is, Northwest Mesopotamia; also in verses 5, 6 and 7 [c] *3* Hebrew *El-Shaddai*

No Easy Fix

GE 28:6-9

Esau slowly comprehends how reprehensible his parents find his marriages to Hittite women. *In an attempt to one-up Jacob, who journeys to his relatives to acquire an appropriate wife,* the elder brother turns to Ishmael, Isaac's brother, to obtain *an acceptable wife for himself.* But it was too late. *By marrying the Hittite women,* Esau's clumsy choices had pushed him further away from his parents and from the core of his spiritual heritage. *As you look over Genesis 25:29-34 and Genesis 26:34-35, circle each decision or response* Esau makes that indicates a lack of understanding of what is valuable. *Ask God to help you see if any of your choices reflect the same spiritual blindness.*

This hymn by Sarah Fuller Flower Adams is traditionally thought to be the hymn of comfort played by the orchestra as the Titanic sank.

Nearer My God to Thee

Nearer, my God, to Thee, nearer to Thee!
E'en though it be a cross that raiseth me,
Still all my song shall be, nearer, my God, to Thee.
Nearer, my God, to Thee,
Nearer to Thee!

Though like the wanderer, the sun gone down,
Darkness be over me, my rest a stone.
Yet in my dreams I'd be nearer, my God, to Thee.

Then, with my waking thoughts bright with Thy praise,
Out of my stony griefs Bethel I'll raise;
So by my woes to be nearer, my God, to Thee.

Or, if on joyful wing cleaving the sky,
Sun, moon, and stars forgot, upward I'll fly,
Still all my song shall be, nearer, my God, to Thee.

There in my Father's home, safe and at rest,
There in my Savior's love, perfectly blest;
Age after age to be, nearer, my God, to Thee.

—*Sarah Fuller Flower Adams* (1805–1848)

down to sleep. 12He had a dream[a] in which he saw
a stairway[a] resting on the earth, with its top reaching to heaven, and the angels of God were ascending and descending on it.[b] 13There above it[b] stood
the LORD,[c] and he said: "I am the LORD, the God of
your father Abraham and the God of Isaac.[d] I will
give you and your descendants the land[e] on which
you are lying. 14Your descendants will be like the
dust of the earth, and you[f] will spread out to the
west and to the east, to the north and to the south.[g]
All peoples on earth will be blessed through you
and your offspring.[h] 15I am with you[i] and will
watch over you[j] wherever you go, and I will bring
you back to this land. I will not leave you[k] until I
have done what I have promised you."[l]
16When Jacob awoke from his sleep, he
thought, "Surely the LORD is in this place, and I
was not aware of it." 17He was afraid and said,
"How awesome is this place![m] This is none other
than the house of God; this is the gate of heaven."
18Early the next morning Jacob took the stone he
had placed under his head and set it up as a pillar[n]
and poured oil on top of it.[o] 19He called that place
Bethel,[c] though the city used to be called Luz.[p]
20Then Jacob made a vow,[q] saying, "If God will
be with me and will watch over me[r] on this journey I am taking and will give me food to eat and
clothes to wear 21so that I return safely[s] to my
father's house, then the LORD[d] will be my God[t]
22and[e] this stone that I have set up as a pillar will
be God's house,[u] and of all that you give me I will
give you a tenth.[v]"

Jacob Arrives in Paddan Aram

29 Then Jacob continued on his journey and
came to the land of the eastern peoples.[w]
2There he saw a well in the field, with three flocks
of sheep lying near it because the flocks were
watered from that well. The stone over the mouth
of the well was large. 3When all the flocks were
gathered there, the shepherds would roll the stone
away from the well's mouth and water the sheep.
Then they would return the stone to its place over
the mouth of the well.
4Jacob asked the shepherds, "My brothers,
where are you from?"
"We're from Haran,[x]" they replied.
5He said to them, "Do you know Laban,
Nahor's grandson?"
"Yes, we know him," they answered.
6Then Jacob asked them, "Is he well?"
"Yes, he is," they said, "and here comes his
daughter Rachel with the sheep."
7"Look," he said, "the sun is still high; it is not
time for the flocks to be gathered. Water the sheep
and take them back to pasture."

28:12 [a]Ge 20:3 [b]Jn 1:51
28:13 [c]Ge 12:7; 35:7,9; 48:3 [d]Ge 26:24 [e]Ge 13:15; 35:12
28:14 [f]Ge 26:4 [g]Ge 13:14 [h]Ge 12:3; 18:18; 22:18; Gal 3:8
28:15 [i]Ge 26:3; 48:21 [j]Nu 6:24; Ps 121:5,7-8 [k]Dt 31:6,8 [l]Nu 23:19
28:17 [m]Ex 3:5; Jos 5:15
28:18 [n]Ge 35:14 [o]Lev 8:11
28:19 [p]Jdg 1:23,26
28:20 [q]Ge 31:13; Jdg 11:30; 2Sa 15:8 [r]ver 15
28:21 [s]Jdg 11:31 [t]Dt 26:17
28:22 [u]Ge 35:7,14 [v]Ge 14:20; Lev 27:30
29:1 [w]Jdg 6:3,33
29:4 [x]Ge 28:10

[a] 12 Or *ladder* [b] 13 Or *There beside him* [c] 19 *Bethel* means *house of God.* [d] 20,21 Or *Since God . . . father's house, the LORD* [e] 21,22 Or *house, and the LORD will be my God, 22then*

8"We can't," they replied, "until all the flocks
are gathered and the stone has been rolled away
from the mouth of the well. Then we will water
the sheep."
9While he was still talking with them, Rachel
29:9 came with her father's sheep,[y] for she was a shep-
[y]Ex 2:16 herdess. 10When Jacob saw Rachel daughter of
Laban, his mother's brother, and Laban's sheep,
29:10 he went over and rolled the stone away from the
[z]Ex 2:17 mouth of the well and watered his uncle's sheep.[z]
29:11 11Then Jacob kissed Rachel and began to weep
[a]Ge 33:4 aloud.[a] 12He had told Rachel that he was a rela-
29:12 tive[b] of her father and a son of Rebekah. So she
[b]Ge 13:8; 14:14,16 ran and told her father.[c]
[c]Ge 24:28 13As soon as Laban[d] heard the news about
Jacob, his sister's son, he hurried to meet him. He
29:13 [d]Ge 24:29 embraced him and kissed him and brought him
to his home, and there Jacob told him all these
29:14 things. 14Then Laban said to him, "You are my
[e]Ge 2:23; Jdg 9:2; 2Sa 19:12-13 own flesh and blood."[e]

Jacob Marries Leah and Rachel

After Jacob had stayed with him for a whole
month, 15Laban said to him, "Just because you are
a relative of mine, should you work for me for
nothing? Tell me what your wages should be."
16Now Laban had two daughters; the name of
the older was Leah, and the name of the younger
was Rachel. 17Leah had weak[a] eyes, but Rachel
was lovely in form, and beautiful. 18Jacob was in
love with Rachel and said, "I'll work for you sev-
29:18 en years in return for your younger daughter
[f]Hos 12:12 Rachel."[f]
19Laban said, "It's better that I give her to you
than to some other man. Stay here with me." 20So
Jacob served seven years to get Rachel, but they
29:20 seemed like only a few days to him because of his
[g]SS 8:7; Hos 12:12 love for her.[g]
21Then Jacob said to Laban, "Give me my wife.
29:21 My time is completed, and I want to lie with
[h]Jdg 15:1 her.[h]"
22So Laban brought together all the people of
29:22 [i]Jdg 14:10; Jn 2:1-2 the place and gave a feast.[i] 23But when evening
came, he took his daughter Leah and gave her to
Jacob, and Jacob lay with her. 24And Laban gave
his servant girl Zilpah to his daughter as her
maidservant.
25When morning came, there was Leah! So
Jacob said to Laban, "What is this you have done
29:25 to me?[j] I served you for Rachel, didn't I? Why
[j]Ge 12:18 [k]Ge 27:36 have you deceived me?[k]"
26Laban replied, "It is not our custom here to
give the younger daughter in marriage before the
29:27 older one. 27Finish this daughter's bridal week;[l]
[l]Jdg 14:12 then we will give you the younger one also, in
return for another seven years of work."
28And Jacob did so. He finished the week with
Leah, and then Laban gave him his daughter
Rachel to be his wife. 29Laban gave his servant girl

[a] *17* Or *delicate*

Marriage Customs

GE 29:16-30

During Bible times most marriages began somewhat like they do today, with a betrothal or engagement period followed by a wedding ceremony. The betrothal involved choosing a spouse and exchanging gifts. In Jacob's case, his commitment to work seven years is his gift. In turn, Laban gives each of his daughters a servant. Laban claims a local custom requires that the elder daughter be married first, but no evidence of such a custom exists.

The wedding generally involved a procession of the bridegroom and his friends to the bride's house, where a wedding feast followed. The parents and friends blessed the couple, and the bride's father drew up a written contract of marital faithfulness, which the witnesses to the wedding signed. The parents then escorted the couple into a nuptial room, and the newlyweds were prayed over. Afterward, they were left to consummate their marriage, while the wedding festivities continued for a week.

What's in a Name?

GE 29:31–30:13

Hebrews often named their children after physical characteristics or special events. Thus Leah chooses names for her children that mark her marital hopes and fears. Some scholars believe the names show her movement from longing for Jacob's love to resignation. Others see the names as displaying Leah's spiritual progress. Considering the "reproductive battles" Leah and Rachel engage in, with the rancor and jealousy and maidservant pawns involved, the latter interpretation seems somewhat unlikely. Spend a few moments reading these passages, underlining each of Leah's children's names and reviewing the meanings of those names in the NIV footnotes. Draw your own conclusions about her reasons for choosing these names. (See character sketch for Leah on page 199.)

Bilhah[m] to his daughter Rachel as her maidser-
vant.[n] 30Jacob lay with Rachel also, and he loved
Rachel more than Leah.[o] And he worked for
Laban another seven years.[p]

Jacob's Children

31When the LORD saw that Leah was not loved,[q]
he opened her womb,[r] but Rachel was barren.
32Leah became pregnant and gave birth to a son.
She named him Reuben,[a] for she said, "It is
because the LORD has seen my misery.[s] Surely my
husband will love me now."
33She conceived again, and when she gave birth
to a son she said, "Because the LORD heard that I
am not loved, he gave me this one too." So she
named him Simeon.[b t]
34Again she conceived, and when she gave birth
to a son she said, "Now at last my husband will
become attached to me,[u] because I have borne
him three sons." So he was named Levi.[c v]
35She conceived again, and when she gave birth
to a son she said, "This time I will praise the
LORD." So she named him Judah.[d w] Then she
stopped having children.

30 When Rachel saw that she was not bearing
Jacob any children,[x] she became jealous of
her sister.[y] So she said to Jacob, "Give me children, or I'll die!"
2Jacob became angry with her and said, "Am I
in the place of God, who has kept you from having children?"[z]
3Then she said, "Here is Bilhah, my maidservant. Sleep with her so that she can bear children
for me and that through her I too can build a
family."[a]
4So she gave him her servant Bilhah as a wife.[b]
Jacob slept with her,[c] 5and she became pregnant
and bore him a son. 6Then Rachel said, "God has
vindicated me;[d] he has listened to my plea and
given me a son." Because of this she named him
Dan.[e e]
7Rachel's servant Bilhah conceived again and
bore Jacob a second son. 8Then Rachel said, "I
have had a great struggle with my sister, and I
have won."[f] So she named him Naphtali.[f g]
9When Leah saw that she had stopped having
children, she took her maidservant Zilpah and
gave her to Jacob as a wife.[h] 10Leah's servant Zilpah bore Jacob a son. 11Then Leah said, "What
good fortune!"[g] So she named him Gad.[h i]
12Leah's servant Zilpah bore Jacob a second son.
13Then Leah said, "How happy I am! The women
will call me[j] happy."[k] So she named him Asher.[i l]

29:29 [m]Ge 30:3 [n]Ge 16:1
29:30 [o]ver 16 [p]Ge 31:41
29:31 [q]Dt 21:15-17 [r]Ge 11:30; 30:1; Ps 127:3
29:32 [s]Ge 16:11; 31:42; Ex 4:31; Dt 26:7; Ps 25:18
29:33 [t]Ge 34:25; 49:5
29:34 [u]Ge 30:20; 1Sa 1:2-4 [v]Ge 49:5-7
29:35 [w]Ge 49:8; Mt 1:2-3
30:1 [x]Ge 29:31; 1Sa 1:5-6 [y]Lev 18:18
30:2 [z]Ge 16:2; 20:18; 29:31
30:3 [a]Ge 16:2
30:4 [b]ver 9,18 [c]Ge 16:3-4
30:6 [d]Ps 35:24; 43:1; La 3:59 [e]Ge 49:16-17
30:8 [f]Hos 12:3-4 [g]Ge 49:21
30:9 [h]ver 4
30:11 [i]Ge 49:19
30:13 [j]Ps 127:3 [k]Pr 31:28; Lk 1:48 [l]Ge 49:20

[a] 32 *Reuben* sounds like the Hebrew for *he has seen my misery*; the name means *see, a son.* [b] 33 *Simeon* probably means *one who hears.* [c] 34 *Levi* sounds like and may be derived from the Hebrew for *attached.* [d] 35 *Judah* sounds like and may be derived from the Hebrew for *praise.*
[e] 6 *Dan* here means *he has vindicated.* [f] 8 *Naphtali* means *my struggle.* [g] 11 Or *"A troop is coming!"* [h] 11 *Gad* can mean *good fortune* or *a troop.* [i] 13 *Asher* means *happy.*

14 During wheat harvest, Reuben went out into
30:14 [m]SS 7:13 the fields and found some mandrake plants,[m]
which he brought to his mother Leah. Rachel said
to Leah, "Please give me some of your son's
mandrakes."
30:15 [n]Nu 16:9,13 15 But she said to her, "Wasn't it enough[n] that
you took away my husband? Will you take my
son's mandrakes too?"
"Very well," Rachel said, "he can sleep with you
tonight in return for your son's mandrakes."
16 So when Jacob came in from the fields that
evening, Leah went out to meet him. "You must
sleep with me," she said. "I have hired you with
my son's mandrakes." So he slept with her that
night.
30:17 [o]Ge 25:21 17 God listened to Leah,[o] and she became pregnant and bore Jacob a fifth son. 18 Then Leah said,
30:18 "God has rewarded me for giving my maidservant
[p]Ge 49:14 to my husband." So she named him Issachar.[a][p]
19 Leah conceived again and bore Jacob a sixth
son. 20 Then Leah said, "God has presented me
30:20 with a precious gift. This time my husband will
[q]Ge 35:23; treat me with honor, because I have borne him six
49:13; Mt 4:13 sons." So she named him Zebulun.[b][q]
21 Some time later she gave birth to a daughter
30:22 [r]Ge 8:1; and named her Dinah.
1Sa 1:19-20 22 Then God remembered Rachel;[r] he listened to
[s]Ge 29:31 her and opened her womb.[s] 23 She became preg-
30:23 nant and gave birth to a son[t] and said, "God has
[t]ver 6 [u]Isa 4:1; taken away my disgrace."[u] 24 She named him
Lk 1:25 Joseph,[c][v] and said, "May the LORD add to me
another son."[w]

30:24 [v]Ge 35:24;

Jacob's Flocks Increase

37:2; 39:1; 49:22-26 25 After Rachel gave birth to Joseph, Jacob said
[w]Ge 35:17 to Laban, "Send me on my way[x] so I can go back
30:25 [x]Ge 24:54 to my own homeland. 26 Give me my wives and
30:26 children, for whom I have served you,[y] and I will
[y]Ge 29:20, be on my way. You know how much work I've
30; done for you."
Hos 12:12 27 But Laban said to him, "If I have found favor
30:27 in your eyes, please stay. I have learned by div-
[z]Ge 26:24; ination that[d] the LORD has blessed me because of
39:3,5 you."[z] 28 He added, "Name your wages,[a] and I will
30:28 pay them."
[a]Ge 29:15 29 Jacob said to him, "You know how I have
worked for you[b] and how your livestock has fared
30:29 [b]Ge 31:6 under my care.[c] 30 The little you had before I came
[c]Ge 31:38-40 has increased greatly, and the LORD has blessed
30:30 you wherever I have been. But now, when may I
[d]1Ti 5:8 do something for my own household?[d]"
31 "What shall I give you?" he asked.
"Don't give me anything," Jacob replied. "But if
you will do this one thing for me, I will go on tending your flocks and watching over them: 32 Let me
go through all your flocks today and remove from
them every speckled or spotted sheep, every dark-

[a] *18 Issachar* sounds like the Hebrew for *reward.*
[b] *20 Zebulun* probably means *honor.* [c] *24 Joseph* means *may he add.* [d] *27* Or possibly *have become rich and*

The Plant of Love

GE 30:14-16

The mandrake, also called the "love apple," is a fragrant, flowering plant that grows in the desert. The roots of the potato-like plant look something like the lower part of the human body and are purported to have aphrodisiac properties that stimulate conception. This usage still survives in the Holy Land. Actually, the mandrake is slightly poisonous, may cause vomiting, and has a narcotic effect. When Reuben supplies the plant to his mother, he reveals his awareness of the keen competition between Leah and Rachel for Jacob's love and for the position of the first wife, which they seem to assume will be the status of the wife who produces the most sons. Their willingness to bargain over a root, trading it for their husband's attentions, reveals the extent to which they will go in order to gain his love. Ironically, neither comes away satisfied, and the very husband whose love they seek becomes a mere object in their competition. *(See character sketches for Leah and Rachel on pages 199 and 200.)*

colored lamb and every spotted or speckled goat.[e]
They will be my wages. 33 And my honesty will testify for me in the future, whenever you check on
the wages you have paid me. Any goat in my possession that is not speckled or spotted, or any lamb
that is not dark-colored, will be considered stolen."

34 "Agreed," said Laban. "Let it be as you have
said." 35 That same day he removed all the male
goats that were streaked or spotted, and all the
speckled or spotted female goats (all that had
white on them) and all the dark-colored lambs,
and he placed them in the care of his sons.[f] 36 Then
he put a three-day journey between himself and
Jacob, while Jacob continued to tend the rest of
Laban's flocks.

37 Jacob, however, took fresh-cut branches from
poplar, almond and plane trees and made white
stripes on them by peeling the bark and exposing
the white inner wood of the branches. 38 Then he
placed the peeled branches in all the watering
troughs, so that they would be directly in front of
the flocks when they came to drink. When the
flocks were in heat and came to drink, 39 they mat-
ed in front of the branches. And they bore young
that were streaked or speckled or spotted. 40 Jacob
set apart the young of the flock by themselves, but
made the rest face the streaked and dark-colored
animals that belonged to Laban. Thus he made
separate flocks for himself and did not put them
with Laban's animals. 41 Whenever the stronger
females were in heat, Jacob would place the
branches in the troughs in front of the animals so
they would mate near the branches, 42 but if the
animals were weak, he would not place them
there. So the weak animals went to Laban and the
strong ones to Jacob. 43 In this way the man grew
exceedingly prosperous and came to own large
flocks, and maidservants and menservants, and
camels and donkeys.[g]

Jacob Flees From Laban

31 Jacob heard that Laban's sons were saying,
"Jacob has taken everything our father
owned and has gained all this wealth from what
belonged to our father." 2 And Jacob noticed that
Laban's attitude toward him was not what it had
been.

3 Then the LORD said to Jacob, "Go back[h] to the
land of your fathers and to your relatives, and I
will be with you."[i]

4 So Jacob sent word to Rachel and Leah to come
out to the fields where his flocks were. 5 He said to
them, "I see that your father's attitude toward me
is not what it was before, but the God of my father
has been with me.[j] 6 You know that I've worked
for your father with all my strength,[k] 7 yet your
father has cheated me by changing my wages ten
times.[l] However, God has not allowed him to
harm me.[m] 8 If he said, 'The speckled ones will be
your wages,' then all the flocks gave birth to
speckled young; and if he said, 'The streaked ones

30:32 [e]Ge 31:8,12
30:35 [f]Ge 31:1
30:43 [g]ver 30; Ge 12:16; 13:2; 24:35; 26:13-14
31:3 [h]ver 13; Ge 32:9 [i]Ge 21:22; 26:3; 28:15
31:5 [j]Ge 21:22; 26:3
31:6 [k]Ge 30:29
31:7 [l]ver 41; Job 19:3 [m]ver 52; Ps 37:28; 105:14

Granny used to say, when things got hectic and she didn't know what to do, "God's got a ram in the bush." She meant that we don't have to worry or be stressed when we don't see a way to meet our need because God does see and has provided a solution. He never leaves us without a ram in the bush. Abraham can testify to that.

—Thelma Wells

31:8 will be your wages,'[n] then all the flocks bore
[n]Ge 30:32 streaked young. [9]So God has taken away your
31:9 father's livestock and has given them to me.[o]
[o]ver 1,16; Ge 30:42 [10]"In breeding season I once had a dream in
which I looked up and saw that the male goats
mating with the flock were streaked, speckled or
31:11 [p]Ge 16:7; spotted. [11]The angel of God[p] said to me in the
48:16 dream, 'Jacob.' I answered, 'Here I am.' [12]And he
said, 'Look up and see that all the male goats mating with the flock are streaked, speckled or spot-
31:12 ted, for I have seen all that Laban has been doing
[q]Ex 3:7 to you.[q] [13]I am the God of Bethel,[r] where you
31:13 anointed a pillar and where you made a vow to
[r]Ge 28:10-22 me. Now leave this land at once and go back to
[s]ver 3; Ge 32:9 your native land.[s]' "
[14]Then Rachel and Leah replied, "Do we still
have any share in the inheritance of our father's
estate? [15]Does he not regard us as foreigners? Not
only has he sold us, but he has used up what was
31:15 [t]Ge 29:20 paid for us.[t] [16]Surely all the wealth that God took
away from our father belongs to us and our chil-
dren. So do whatever God has told you."
[17]Then Jacob put his children and his wives on
camels, [18]and he drove all his livestock ahead of
31:18 [u]Ge 35:27 him, along with all the goods he had accumulat-
[v]Ge 10:19 ed in Paddan Aram,[a] to go to his father Isaac[u] in
31:19 the land of Canaan.[v]
[w]ver 30,32, 34-35; [19]When Laban had gone to shear his sheep,
Ge 35:2; Rachel stole her father's household gods.[w] [20]More-
Jdg 17:5; 1Sa 19:13; over, Jacob deceived[x] Laban the Aramean by not
Hos 3:4 telling him he was running away.[y] [21]So he fled
with all he had, and crossing the River,[b] he head-
31:20 ed for the hill country of Gilead.[z]
[x]Ge 27:36 [y]ver 27

Laban Pursues Jacob

31:21 [z]Ge 37:25 [22]On the third day Laban was told that Jacob
had fled. [23]Taking his relatives with him, he pursued Jacob for seven days and caught up with him
in the hill country of Gilead. [24]Then God came to
Laban the Aramean in a dream at night and said
31:24 [a]Ge 20:3; to him,[a] "Be careful not to say anything to Jacob,
Job 33:15 [b]Ge 24:50 either good or bad."[b]
[25]Jacob had pitched his tent in the hill country
of Gilead when Laban overtook him, and Laban
and his relatives camped there too. [26]Then Laban
31:26 said to Jacob, "What have you done? You've
[c]Ge 27:36 deceived me,[c] and you've carried off my daugh-
[d]1Sa 30:2-3 ters like captives in war.[d] [27]Why did you run off
secretly and deceive me? Why didn't you tell me,
31:27 so I could send you away with joy and singing to
[e]Ex 15:20 [f]Ge 4:21 the music of tambourines[e] and harps?[f] [28]You
didn't even let me kiss my grandchildren and my
31:28 [g]ver 55 daughters good-by.[g] You have done a foolish
31:29 thing. [29]I have the power to harm you;[h] but last
[h]ver 7 night the God of your father[i] said to me, 'Be care-
[i]ver 53 ful not to say anything to Jacob, either good or
bad.' [30]Now you have gone off because you longed

[a] *18* That is, Northwest Mesopotamia [b] *21* That is, the Euphrates

Idols

GE 31:19

Two possible explanations exist for why Rachel steals her father's household gods. One is that she has not freed herself from the Mesopotamian religious environment in which she grew up. But an equally likely explanation, especially in light of Rachel and Leah's belief that their father has not provided an inheritance for them (Ge 31:14-16), is that these objects are of legal, as well as religious, significance. In ancient law, if a woman's husband possessed these idols, he inherited his father-in-law's property. This would explain why the materialistic Laban makes a fresh agreement with Jacob when Laban fails to recover the household gods (Ge 31:48-55). His concern is for protecting his property. The entire episode reveals how entangled all involved still are in the culture of their time.

Menstrual Period

GE 31:35

Laban seems to accept Rachel's explanation of physical discomfort from her period as a reason to remain seated. Whether she is actually suffering from menstrual discomfort or is lying about it remains a mystery. Her excuse does, however, prevent the discovery of her theft of her father's household gods.

Later, in Leviticus, the law specifies that a woman, as well as anything she sits on, is ceremonially unclean during her period (Lev 15:19–23); but this law was not yet instituted when Laban confronted Rachel.

to return to your father's house. But why did you
steal my gods?[j]"
31 Jacob answered Laban, "I was afraid, because
I thought you would take your daughters away
from me by force. 32 But if you find anyone who
has your gods, he shall not live.[k] In the presence
of our relatives, see for yourself whether there is
anything of yours here with me; and if so, take
it." Now Jacob did not know that Rachel had
stolen the gods.
33 So Laban went into Jacob's tent and into
Leah's tent and into the tent of the two maidservants, but he found nothing. After he came out of
Leah's tent, he entered Rachel's tent. 34 Now
Rachel had taken the household gods and put
them inside her camel's saddle and was sitting on
them. Laban searched[l] through everything in the
tent but found nothing.
35 Rachel said to her father, "Don't be angry, my
lord, that I cannot stand up in your presence;[m] I'm
having my period." So he searched but could not
find the household gods.
36 Jacob was angry and took Laban to task.
"What is my crime?" he asked Laban. "What sin
have I committed that you hunt me down? 37 Now
that you have searched through all my goods,
what have you found that belongs to your household? Put it here in front of your relatives[n] and
mine, and let them judge between the two of us.
38 "I have been with you for twenty years now.
Your sheep and goats have not miscarried, nor
have I eaten rams from your flocks. 39 I did not
bring you animals torn by wild beasts; I bore the
loss myself. And you demanded payment from me
for whatever was stolen by day or night.[o] 40 This
was my situation: The heat consumed me in the
daytime and the cold at night, and sleep fled from
my eyes. 41 It was like this for the twenty years I
was in your household. I worked for you fourteen
years for your two daughters[p] and six years for
your flocks, and you changed my wages ten
times.[q] 42 If the God of my father,[r] the God of Abraham and the Fear of Isaac,[s] had not been with
me,[t] you would surely have sent me away empty-
handed. But God has seen my hardship and the
toil of my hands,[u] and last night he rebuked you."
43 Laban answered Jacob, "The women are my
daughters, the children are my children, and the
flocks are my flocks. All you see is mine. Yet what
can I do today about these daughters of mine, or
about the children they have borne? 44 Come now,
let's make a covenant,[v] you and I, and let it serve
as a witness between us."[w]
45 So Jacob took a stone and set it up as a pillar.[x]
46 He said to his relatives, "Gather some stones."
So they took stones and piled them in a heap, and
they ate there by the heap. 47 Laban called it Jegar
Sahadutha,[a] and Jacob called it Galeed.[b]

31:30 [j]ver 19; Jdg 18:24
31:32 [k]Ge 44:9
31:34 [l]ver 37; Ge 44:12
31:35 [m]Ex 20:12; Lev 19:3,32
31:37 [n]ver 23
31:39 [o]Ex 22:13
31:41 [p]Ge 29:30 [q]ver 7
31:42 [r]ver 5; Ex 3:15; 1Ch 12:17 [s]ver 53; Isa 8:13 [t]Ps 124:1-2 [u]Ge 29:32
31:44 [v]Ge 21:27; 26:28 [w]Jos 24:27
31:45 [x]Ge 28:18

[a] 47 The Aramaic *Jegar Sahadutha* means *witness heap.*
[b] 47 The Hebrew *Galeed* means *witness heap.*

48 Laban said, "This heap is a witness between you and me today." That is why it was called Galeed. 49 It was also called Mizpah,[a][y] because he said, "May the LORD keep watch between you and me when we are away from each other. 50 If you mistreat my daughters or if you take any wives besides my daughters, even though no one is with us, remember that God is a witness[z] between you and me."

51 Laban also said to Jacob, "Here is this heap, and here is this pillar[a] I have set up between you and me. 52 This heap is a witness, and this pillar is a witness,[b] that I will not go past this heap to your side to harm you and that you will not go past this heap and pillar to my side to harm me.[c] 53 May the God of Abraham[d] and the God of Nahor, the God of their father, judge between us."[e]

So Jacob took an oath[f] in the name of the Fear of his father Isaac.[g] 54 He offered a sacrifice there in the hill country and invited his relatives to a meal. After they had eaten, they spent the night there.

55 Early the next morning Laban kissed his grandchildren and his daughters[h] and blessed them. Then he left and returned home.[i]

Jacob Prepares to Meet Esau

32 Jacob also went on his way, and the angels of God[j] met him. 2 When Jacob saw them, he said, "This is the camp of God!"[k] So he named that place Mahanaim.[b][l]

3 Jacob sent messengers ahead of him to his brother Esau[m] in the land of Seir, the country of Edom.[n] 4 He instructed them: "This is what you are to say to my master Esau: 'Your servant Jacob says, I have been staying with Laban and have remained there till now. 5 I have cattle and donkeys, sheep and goats, menservants and maidservants.[o] Now I am sending this message to my lord, that I may find favor in your eyes.[p]' "

6 When the messengers returned to Jacob, they said, "We went to your brother Esau, and now he is coming to meet you, and four hundred men are with him."[q]

7 In great fear[r] and distress Jacob divided the people who were with him into two groups,[c] and the flocks and herds and camels as well. 8 He thought, "If Esau comes and attacks one group,[d] the group[d] that is left may escape."

9 Then Jacob prayed, "O God of my father Abraham, God of my father Isaac,[s] O LORD, who said to me, 'Go back to your country and your relatives, and I will make you prosper,'[t] 10 I am unworthy of all the kindness and faithfulness[u] you have shown your servant. I had only my staff when I crossed this Jordan, but now I have become two groups. 11 Save me, I pray, from the hand of my brother Esau, for I am afraid he will come and attack me,[v] and also the mothers with their children.[w] 12 But

31:49 [y]Jdg 11:29; 1Sa 7:5-6
31:50 [z]Jer 29:23; 42:5
31:51 [a]Ge 28:18
31:52 [b]Ge 21:30 [c]ver 7; Ge 26:29
31:53 [d]Ge 28:13 [e]Ge 16:5 [f]Ge 21:23,27 [g]ver 42
31:55 [h]ver 28 [i]Ge 18:33; 30:25
32:1 [j]Ge 16:11; 2Ki 6:16-17; Ps 34:7; 91:11; Heb 1:14
32:2 [k]Ge 28:17 [l]2Sa 2:8,29
32:3 [m]Ge 27:41-42 [n]Ge 25:30; 36:8,9
32:5 [o]Ge 12:16; 30:43 [p]Ge 33:8,10, 15
32:6 [q]Ge 33:1
32:7 [r]ver 11
32:9 [s]Ge 28:13; 31:42 [t]Ge 31:13
32:10 [u]Ge 24:27
32:11 [v]Ps 59:2 [w]Ge 27:41

[a] 49 *Mizpah* means *watchtower.* [b] 2 *Mahanaim* means *two camps.* [c] 7 Or *camps;* also in verse 10 [d] 8 Or *camp*

An Oath of the Fathers

GE 31:53

Laban reminds Jacob that they are branches of the same family tree when he mentions that Abraham and Nahor have the same God. Abraham and Nahor were brothers. Laban is Nahor's grandson, and Jacob is Abraham's grandson. Jacob, in response, takes an oath (to fulfill his part of their newly struck bargain) in the name of the Fear of his father Isaac. Fear *here refers to God and is also used in verse 42. Sometimes the Bible uses the word* fear *to refer to an allegiance to God that implies profound respect and awe. When Jacob uses* Fear *as a name for God, he is speaking of the One whom Isaac worships in awe and wonder. Thus the two men, who certainly have no reason to depend on each other's word, pledge in the name of their mutual God to keep their newly agreed upon contract.*

Wrestling With God

GE 32:22-32

Jacob, whose name means "supplanter" or "deceiver," manipulates circumstances to his benefit whenever possible. But one night, with his family and belongings in danger, he lives in dread of the next day, when he will encounter his brother, Esau, 20 years after having stolen their father's blessing. During this vulnerable time, Jacob wrestles with a supernatural being, whom he declares is God. How like Jacob, the striver, not to give up. He wrestles with God until dawn, at which time God shows his superiority by dislocating Jacob's hip.

Jacob, who has been afraid to face his brother, faces God and discovers that losing can be a good thing. He realizes that God has shown him mercy by sparing his life. To make sure the humbled Jacob doesn't forget the experience, God gives Jacob a new name and a limp. When we "wrestle" with God in the midst of difficult and disheartening circumstances, we, too, may find the experience transforming—and humbling.

you have said, 'I will surely make you prosper and will make your descendants like the sand[x] of the sea, which cannot be counted.[y]' "

13 He spent the night there, and from what he had with him he selected a gift[z] for his brother Esau: 14 two hundred female goats and twenty male goats, two hundred ewes and twenty rams, 15 thirty female camels with their young, forty cows and ten bulls, and twenty female donkeys and ten male donkeys. 16 He put them in the care of his servants, each herd by itself, and said to his servants, "Go ahead of me, and keep some space between the herds."

17 He instructed the one in the lead: "When my brother Esau meets you and asks, 'To whom do you belong, and where are you going, and who owns all these animals in front of you?' 18 then you are to say, 'They belong to your servant[a] Jacob. They are a gift sent to my lord Esau, and he is coming behind us.' "

19 He also instructed the second, the third and all the others who followed the herds: "You are to say the same thing to Esau when you meet him. 20 And be sure to say, 'Your servant Jacob is coming behind us.' " For he thought, "I will pacify him with these gifts I am sending on ahead; later, when I see him, perhaps he will receive me."[b] 21 So Jacob's gifts went on ahead of him, but he himself spent the night in the camp.

Jacob Wrestles With God

22 That night Jacob got up and took his two wives, his two maidservants and his eleven sons and crossed the ford of the Jabbok.[c] 23 After he had sent them across the stream, he sent over all his possessions. 24 So Jacob was left alone, and a man[d] wrestled with him till daybreak. 25 When the man saw that he could not overpower him, he touched the socket of Jacob's hip[e] so that his hip was wrenched as he wrestled with the man. 26 Then the man said, "Let me go, for it is daybreak."

But Jacob replied, "I will not let you go unless you bless me."[f]

27 The man asked him, "What is your name?"

"Jacob," he answered.

28 Then the man said, "Your name will no longer be Jacob, but Israel,[a][g] because you have struggled with God and with men and have overcome."

29 Jacob said, "Please tell me your name."[h]

But he replied, "Why do you ask my name?"[i] Then he blessed[j] him there.

30 So Jacob called the place Peniel,[b] saying, "It is because I saw God face to face,[k] and yet my life was spared."

31 The sun rose above him as he passed Peniel,[c] and he was limping because of his hip. 32 Therefore to this day the Israelites do not eat the tendon attached to the socket of the hip, because the socket of Jacob's hip was touched near the tendon.

32:12 [x]Ge 22:17 [y]Ge 28:13-15; Hos 1:10; Ro 9:27
32:13 [z]Ge 43:11, 15,25,26; Pr 18:16
32:18 [a]Ge 18:3
32:20 [b]Ge 33:10; Pr 21:14
32:22 [c]Dt 2:37; 3:16; Jos 12:2
32:24 [d]Ge 18:2
32:25 [e]ver 32
32:26 [f]Hos 12:4
32:28 [g]Ge 17:5; 35:10; 1Ki 18:31
32:29 [h]Jdg 13:17 [i]Jdg 13:18 [j]Ge 35:9
32:30 [k]Ge 16:13; Ex 24:11; Nu 12:8; Jdg 6:22; 13:22

[a] *28 Israel* means *he struggles with God.* [b] *30 Peniel* means *face of God.* [c] *31* Hebrew *Penuel,* a variant of *Peniel*

Jacob Meets Esau

33:1 **33** Jacob looked up and there was Esau, com-
[l]Ge 32:6 ing with his four hundred men;[l] so he
divided the children among Leah, Rachel and the
two maidservants. 2He put the maidservants and
their children in front, Leah and her children next,
and Rachel and Joseph in the rear. 3He himself
33:3 [m]Ge 18:2; went on ahead and bowed down to the ground[m]
42:6 seven times as he approached his brother.
4But Esau ran to meet Jacob and embraced him;
33:4 he threw his arms around his neck and kissed
[n]Ge 45:14-15 him. And they wept.[n] 5Then Esau looked up and
saw the women and children. "Who are these
with you?" he asked.
33:5 Jacob answered, "They are the children God has
[o]Ge 48:9; graciously given your servant.[o]"
Ps 127:3; 6Then the maidservants and their children
Isa 8:18 approached and bowed down. 7Next, Leah and her
children came and bowed down. Last of all came
Joseph and Rachel, and they too bowed down.
8Esau asked, "What do you mean by all these
33:8 droves I met?"[p]
[p]Ge 32:14-16 "To find favor in your eyes, my lord,"[q] he said.
[q]Ge 24:9; 9But Esau said, "I already have plenty, my
32:5 brother. Keep what you have for yourself."
10"No, please!" said Jacob. "If I have found favor
33:10 in your eyes, accept this gift from me. For to see
[r]Ge 16:13 your face is like seeing the face of God,[r] now that
[s]Ge 32:20 you have received me favorably.[s] 11Please accept
33:11 the present[t] that was brought to you, for God has
[t]1Sa 25:27 been gracious to me[u] and I have all I need." And
[u]Ge 30:43 because Jacob insisted, Esau accepted it.
12Then Esau said, "Let us be on our way; I'll
accompany you."
13But Jacob said to him, "My lord knows that
the children are tender and that I must care for
the ewes and cows that are nursing their young. If
they are driven hard just one day, all the animals
will die. 14So let my lord go on ahead of his servant, while I move along slowly at the pace of the
33:14 droves before me and that of the children, until I
[v]Ge 32:3 come to my lord in Seir.[v]"
33:15 15Esau said, "Then let me leave some of my men
[w]Ge 34:11; with you."
47:25; "But why do that?" Jacob asked. "Just let me
Ru 2:13 find favor in the eyes of my lord."[w]
33:17 16So that day Esau started on his way back to
[x]Jos 13:27; Seir. 17Jacob, however, went to Succoth,[x] where
Jdg 8:5,6,8, 14-16; he built a place for himself and made shelters for
Ps 60:6 his livestock. That is why the place is called
33:18 Succoth.[a]
[y]Ge 25:20; 18After Jacob came from Paddan Aram,[b][y] he
28:2 [z]Jos 24:1; arrived safely at the[c] city of Shechem[z] in Canaan
Jdg 9:1 and camped within sight of the city. 19For a hun-
33:19 dred pieces of silver,[d] he bought from the sons of
[a]Jos 24:32 Hamor, the father of Shechem,[a] the plot of

[a] 17 *Succoth* means *shelters.* [b] 18 That is, Northwest Mesopotamia [c] 18 Or *arrived at Shalem, a* [d] 19 Hebrew *hundred kesitahs*; a kesitah was a unit of money of unknown weight and value.

A Gracious Exchange

GE 33:10-11

Jacob, in response to Esau's gracious welcome, remarks that seeing Esau's face is like seeing God's. Probably Jacob is remembering how, just the night before, he had seen God's face, and it, too, was gracious. Newly humbled, Jacob seems amazed to receive mercy not only from God but also from his brother, a sibling with whom he has never gotten along. In Genesis 33:11, when Jacob offers a gift of livestock to Esau, the Hebrew word for present *can also be translated "blessing." Perhaps Jacob is saying, "In this small way, let me bless you in payment for our father's blessing, which I stole from you." This scene's colors are painted from the palette of forgiveness and mercy and remind us that, regardless of how we might have been wronged or wrong another, it is possible to give and receive forgiveness and even to be loving and gracious to the other person.*

ground[b] where he pitched his tent. [20]There he set
up an altar and called it El Elohe Israel.[a]

33:19 [b]Jn 4:5

Rape

GE 34:1-2

Dinah's brothers speak of her rape as "a disgraceful thing in Israel" (Ge 34:7), which is ***an expression meaning the crime affects the whole community. Apparently no laws governed such a crime, and some ancient laws even allowed a man to obtain a wife through forcible sexual relations.*** **The thread that runs through the fabric of this story is the tragedy of what happens to Dinah. She is taken from Shechem's home when her brothers attack the city. She is there** ***because, having been raped, she is now considered unavailable to any other man and is waiting there for the arranged wedding to take place. Her brothers' acts of vengeance do nothing to help her,*** **but instead put the entire Hebrew community in danger (Ge 34:30). While Scripture never tells us what happens to Dinah, we know she is left with no possibility of** ***marriage, no identity, no social status—and probably much pain and anguish.***

Dinah and the Shechemites

34 Now Dinah,[c] the daughter Leah had borne
to Jacob, went out to visit the women of the
land. [2]When Shechem son of Hamor the Hivite,
the ruler of that area, saw her, he took her and
violated her. [3]His heart was drawn to Dinah
daughter of Jacob, and he loved the girl and spoke
tenderly to her. [4]And Shechem said to his father
Hamor, "Get me this girl as my wife."
[5]When Jacob heard that his daughter Dinah
had been defiled, his sons were in the fields with
his livestock; so he kept quiet about it until they
came home.
[6]Then Shechem's father Hamor went out to talk
with Jacob.[d] [7]Now Jacob's sons had come in from
the fields as soon as they heard what had happened. They were filled with grief and fury,
because Shechem had done a disgraceful thing in[b]
Israel[e] by lying with Jacob's daughter—a thing
that should not be done.[f]
[8]But Hamor said to them, "My son Shechem
has his heart set on your daughter. Please give her
to him as his wife. [9]Intermarry with us; give us
your daughters and take our daughters for yourselves. [10]You can settle among us;[g] the land is
open to you.[h] Live in it, trade[c] in it,[i] and acquire
property in it."
[11]Then Shechem said to Dinah's father and
brothers, "Let me find favor in your eyes, and I
will give you whatever you ask. [12]Make the price
for the bride[j] and the gift I am to bring as great as
you like, and I'll pay whatever you ask me. Only
give me the girl as my wife."
[13]Because their sister Dinah had been defiled,
Jacob's sons replied deceitfully as they spoke to
Shechem and his father Hamor. [14]They said to
them, "We can't do such a thing; we can't give
our sister to a man who is not circumcised.[k] That
would be a disgrace to us. [15]We will give our consent to you on one condition only: that you
become like us by circumcising all your males.[l]
[16]Then we will give you our daughters and take
your daughters for ourselves. We'll settle among
you and become one people with you. [17]But if you
will not agree to be circumcised, we'll take our
sister[d] and go."
[18]Their proposal seemed good to Hamor and his
son Shechem. [19]The young man, who was the
most honored of all his father's household, lost no
time in doing what they said, because he was
delighted with Jacob's daughter.[m] [20]So Hamor and
his son Shechem went to the gate of their city[n] to
speak to their fellow townsmen. [21]"These men are
friendly toward us," they said. "Let them live in

34:1 [c]Ge 30:21
34:6 [d]Jdg 14:2-5
34:7 [e]Dt 22:21; Jdg 20:6; 2Sa 13:12 [f]Jos 7:15
34:10 [g]Ge 47:6,27 [h]Ge 13:9; 20:15 [i]Ge 42:34
34:12 [j]Ex 22:16; Dt 22:29; 1Sa 18:25
34:14 [k]Ge 17:14; Jdg 14:3
34:15 [l]Ex 12:48
34:19 [m]ver 3
34:20 [n]Ru 4:1; 2Sa 15:2

[a] *20 El Elohe Israel* can mean *God, the God of Israel* or *mighty is the God of Israel.* [b] *7* Or *against* [c] *10* Or *move about freely*; also in verse 21 [d] *17* Hebrew *daughter*

our land and trade in it; the land has plenty of room for them. We can marry their daughters and they can marry ours. [22]But the men will consent to live with us as one people only on the condition that our males be circumcised, as they themselves are. [23]Won't their livestock, their property and all their other animals become ours? So let us give our consent to them, and they will settle among us."

[24]All the men who went out of the city gate[o] agreed with Hamor and his son Shechem, and every male in the city was circumcised.

[25]Three days later, while all of them were still in pain, two of Jacob's sons, Simeon and Levi, Dinah's brothers, took their swords[p] and attacked the unsuspecting city, killing every male.[q] [26]They put Hamor and his son Shechem to the sword and took Dinah from Shechem's house and left. [27]The sons of Jacob came upon the dead bodies and looted the city where[a] their sister had been defiled. [28]They seized their flocks and herds and donkeys and everything else of theirs in the city and out in the fields. [29]They carried off all their wealth and all their women and children, taking as plunder everything in the houses.

[30]Then Jacob said to Simeon and Levi, "You have brought trouble on me by making me a stench[r] to the Canaanites and Perizzites, the people living in this land.[s] We are few in number,[t] and if they join forces against me and attack me, I and my household will be destroyed."

[31]But they replied, "Should he have treated our sister like a prostitute?"

Jacob Returns to Bethel

35 Then God said to Jacob, "Go up to Bethel[u] and settle there, and build an altar there to God, who appeared to you when you were fleeing from your brother Esau."[v]

[2]So Jacob said to his household[w] and to all who were with him, "Get rid of the foreign gods[x] you have with you, and purify yourselves and change your clothes.[y] [3]Then come, let us go up to Bethel, where I will build an altar to God, who answered me in the day of my distress[z] and who has been with me wherever I have gone.[a]" [4]So they gave Jacob all the foreign gods they had and the rings in their ears, and Jacob buried them under the oak at Shechem.[b] [5]Then they set out, and the terror of God[c] fell upon the towns all around them so that no one pursued them.

[6]Jacob and all the people with him came to Luz[d] (that is, Bethel) in the land of Canaan. [7]There he built an altar, and he called the place El Bethel,[b] because it was there that God revealed himself to him[e] when he was fleeing from his brother.

[8]Now Deborah, Rebekah's nurse,[f] died and was buried under the oak below Bethel. So it was named Allon Bacuth.[c]

34:24 [o]Ge 23:10
34:25 [p]Ge 49:5 [q]Ge 49:7
34:30 [r]Ex 5:21; 1Sa 13:4 [s]Ge 13:7 [t]Ge 46:27; 1Ch 16:19; Ps 105:12
35:1 [u]Ge 28:19 [v]Ge 27:43
35:2 [w]Ge 18:19; Jos 24:15 [x]Ge 31:19 [y]Ex 19:10,14
35:3 [z]Ge 32:7 [a]Ge 28:15, 20-22; 31:3, 42
35:4 [b]Jos 24:25-26
35:5 [c]Ex 15:16; 23:27; Jos 2:9
35:6 [d]Ge 28:19; 48:3
35:7 [e]Ge 28:13
35:8 [f]Ge 24:59

[a] 27 Or *because* [b] 7 *El Bethel* means *God of Bethel.*
[c] 8 *Allon Bacuth* means *oak of weeping.*

Cleaning House

GE 35:1-3

These verses describe preparation for a pilgrimage to the place where, 20 years before, God had appeared to Jacob as he fled from his brother after stealing their father's blessing (Ge 28:19-22). Jacob wants to be sure everything is right between his household and God; therefore, each person is to go through a purification process—physically and spiritually. They are to change their clothes and get rid of any foreign gods. Rachel may still have had the household gods she had stolen from her father (Ge 31:19). Also, the hostages Jacob's sons had taken from Shechem after Dinah's rape (Ge 34:29) may have had gods with them. Such a pilgrimage—even just a mental one—to the place where God has met us in the past can provide reassurance of God's continued presence in our lives. And a little housekeeping of the soul prepares us to meet God, ready for his blessing.

Life Rhythm

GE 35:17-18

Life for women in this early Biblical era generally flowed like this: A woman married as a teenager, then bore one or more children and died young, often in childbirth. The mortality rate for infants and mothers was very high, with some Egyptian records indicating that 90 percent of babies died in their first month. The primitive and isolated environment forced many women to give birth alone or with the help of often-inexperienced female family members. Rachel's specific difficulty is not described, however, her experience is extremely painful; her situation, pitiful; and her sorrow, deep. With her final breath she names the son she will never see: Ben-Oni, meaning "son of my trouble." Though a wealthy woman for her time, Rachel, like many today, was not spared her share of heartache. Neither family nor wealth nor the love of a man can satisfy the deepest longings of a woman's heart. That role belongs only to God.

9After Jacob returned from Paddan Aram,[a] God
appeared to him again and blessed him.[g] 10God
said to him, "Your name is Jacob,[b] but you will no
longer be called Jacob; your name will be Israel.[c]"[h] So he named him Israel.
11And God said to him, "I am God Almighty[d];[i]
be fruitful and increase in number. A nation[j] and
a community of nations will come from you, and
kings will come from your body.[k] 12The land I
gave to Abraham and Isaac I also give to you, and
I will give this land to your descendants after
you.[l]"[m] 13Then God went up from him[n] at the
place where he had talked with him.
14Jacob set up a stone pillar at the place where
God had talked with him, and he poured out a
drink offering on it; he also poured oil on it.[o]
15Jacob called the place where God had talked
with him Bethel.[e][p]

The Deaths of Rachel and Isaac

16Then they moved on from Bethel. While they
were still some distance from Ephrath, Rachel
began to give birth and had great difficulty. 17And
as she was having great difficulty in childbirth,
the midwife said to her, "Don't be afraid, for you
have another son."[q] 18As she breathed her last—
for she was dying—she named her son Ben-Oni.[f]
But his father named him Benjamin.[g]
19So Rachel died and was buried on the way to
Ephrath (that is, Bethlehem[r]). 20Over her tomb
Jacob set up a pillar, and to this day that pillar
marks Rachel's tomb.[s]
21Israel moved on again and pitched his tent
beyond Migdal Eder. 22While Israel was living in
that region, Reuben went in and slept with his
father's concubine[t] Bilhah,[u] and Israel heard of it.

Jacob had twelve sons:

23The sons of Leah:
Reuben the firstborn[v] of Jacob,
Simeon, Levi, Judah,[w] Issachar and
Zebulun.[x]
24The sons of Rachel:
Joseph[y] and Benjamin.[z]
25The sons of Rachel's maidservant Bilhah:
Dan and Naphtali.[a]
26The sons of Leah's maidservant Zilpah:
Gad[b] and Asher.[c]
These were the sons of Jacob, who were born
to him in Paddan Aram.

27Jacob came home to his father Isaac in Mamre,[d] near Kiriath Arba[e] (that is, Hebron), where
Abraham and Isaac had stayed. 28Isaac lived a
hundred and eighty years.[f] 29Then he breathed his
last and died and was gathered to his people,[g] old

35:9 [g]Ge 32:29
35:10 [h]Ge 17:5
35:11 [i]Ge 17:1; Ex 6:3 [j]Ge 28:3; 48:4 [k]Ge 17:6
35:12 [l]Ge 13:15; 28:13 [m]Ge 12:7; 26:3
35:13 [n]Ge 17:22
35:14 [o]Ge 28:18
35:15 [p]Ge 28:19
35:17 [q]Ge 30:24
35:19 [r]Ge 48:7; Ru 1:1,19; Mic 5:2; Mt 2:16
35:20 [s]1Sa 10:2
35:22 [t]Ge 49:4; 1Ch 5:1 [u]Ge 29:29; Lev 18:8
35:23 [v]Ge 46:8 [w]Ge 29:35 [x]Ge 30:20
35:24 [y]Ge 30:24 [z]ver 18
35:25 [a]Ge 30:8
35:26 [b]Ge 30:11 [c]Ge 30:13
35:27 [d]Ge 13:18; 18:1 [e]Jos 14:15
35:28 [f]Ge 25:7,20
35:29 [g]Ge 25:8; 49:33

[a] 9 That is, Northwest Mesopotamia; also in verse 26
[b] 10 *Jacob* means *he grasps the heel* (figuratively, *he deceives*).
[c] 10 *Israel* means *he struggles with God.* [d] 11 Hebrew *El-Shaddai* [e] 15 *Bethel* means *house of God.* [f] 18 *Ben-Oni* means *son of my trouble.* [g] 18 *Benjamin* means *son of my right hand.*

35:29 [h]Ge 15:15 and full of years.[h] And his sons Esau and Jacob
[i]Ge 25:9 buried him.[i]

Esau's Descendants

36:1 [j]Ge 25:30 **36** This is the account of Esau (that is, Edom).[j]

36:2 2 Esau took his wives from the women of
[k]Ge 28:8-9 Canaan:[k] Adah daughter of Elon the Hittite,[l]
[l]Ge 26:34 and Oholibamah daughter of Anah[m] and
[m]ver 25 granddaughter of Zibeon the Hivite— 3 also
Basemath daughter of Ishmael and sister of
Nebaioth.
36:4 4 Adah bore Eliphaz to Esau, Basemath bore
[n]1Ch 1:35 Reuel,[n] 5 and Oholibamah bore Jeush, Jalam
and Korah. These were the sons of Esau, who
were born to him in Canaan.
6 Esau took his wives and sons and daughters and all the members of his household, as
well as his livestock and all his other animals
and all the goods he had acquired in
36:6 [o]Ge 12:5 Canaan,[o] and moved to a land some distance
from his brother Jacob. 7 Their possessions
were too great for them to remain together;
the land where they were staying could not
36:7 support them both because of their live-
[p]Ge 13:6; 17:8; 28:4 stock.[p] 8 So Esau[q] (that is, Edom) settled in
the hill country of Seir.[r]
36:8 [q]Dt 2:4 9 This is the account of Esau the father of the
[r]Ge 32:3 Edomites in the hill country of Seir.

10 These are the names of Esau's sons:
Eliphaz, the son of Esau's wife Adah, and
Reuel, the son of Esau's wife Basemath.
36:11 [s]ver 15-16; 11 The sons of Eliphaz:[s]
Job 2:11 Teman,[t] Omar, Zepho, Gatam and Kenaz.
[t]Am 1:12; 12 Esau's son Eliphaz also had a concubine
Hab 3:3 named Timna, who bore him Amalek.[u]
36:12 These were grandsons of Esau's wife
[u]Ex 17:8,16; Adah.[v]
Nu 24:20; 13 The sons of Reuel:
1Sa 15:2 [v]ver 16 Nahath, Zerah, Shammah and Mizzah.
These were grandsons of Esau's wife
Basemath.
14 The sons of Esau's wife Oholibamah daughter of Anah and granddaughter of Zibeon,
whom she bore to Esau:
Jeush, Jalam and Korah.
36:15 [w]Ex 15:15 15 These were the chiefs[w] among Esau's
[x]Job 2:11 descendants:
The sons of Eliphaz the firstborn of Esau:
Chiefs Teman,[x] Omar, Zepho, Kenaz,
36:16 16 Korah,[a] Gatam and Amalek. These were
[y]ver 12 the chiefs descended from Eliphaz in
Edom; they were grandsons of Adah.[y]
36:17 17 The sons of Esau's son Reuel:[z]
[z]1Ch 1:37 Chiefs Nahath, Zerah, Shammah and Mizzah. These were the chiefs descended from

[a] *16* Masoretic Text; Samaritan Pentateuch (see also Gen. 36:11 and 1 Chron. 1:36) does not have *Korah.*

Limited Resources

GE 36:7

The land on which Esau and Jacob are dependent is arid, which creates the challenge for those who have livestock of finding water and food for grazing. Because Jacob is a man wealthy in livestock (see Ge 32:13–15 for what he gives as a gift to his brother), and Esau apparently has a fair share of animals as well, they have to keep their livestock sufficiently separated so that the land and water can sustain their herds. Often a herd that has grown too large is spread over a bigger area. A base camp is set up, and various herders take portions of the herd elsewhere for a season, returning when the grazing in the original area has improved.

Reuel in Edom; they were grandsons of
Esau's wife Basemath.
18 The sons of Esau's wife Oholibamah:
Chiefs Jeush, Jalam and Korah. These were
the chiefs descended from Esau's wife
Oholibamah daughter of Anah.
19 These were the sons of Esau (that is, Edom),[a]
and these were their chiefs.

20 These were the sons of Seir the Horite,[b] who
were living in the region:
Lotan, Shobal, Zibeon, Anah, 21 Dishon,
Ezer and Dishan. These sons of Seir in
Edom were Horite chiefs.
22 The sons of Lotan:
Hori and Homam.[a] Timna was Lotan's
sister.
23 The sons of Shobal:
Alvan, Manahath, Ebal, Shepho and
Onam.
24 The sons of Zibeon:
Aiah and Anah. This is the Anah who discovered the hot springs[b] in the desert while
he was grazing the donkeys of his father
Zibeon.
25 The children of Anah:
Dishon and Oholibamah daughter of Anah.
26 The sons of Dishon[c]:
Hemdan, Eshban, Ithran and Keran.
27 The sons of Ezer:
Bilhan, Zaavan and Akan.
28 The sons of Dishan:
Uz and Aran.
29 These were the Horite chiefs:
Lotan, Shobal, Zibeon, Anah, 30 Dishon,
Ezer and Dishan. These were the Horite
chiefs, according to their divisions, in the
land of Seir.

The Rulers of Edom

31 These were the kings who reigned in Edom
before any Israelite king[c] reigned[d]:
32 Bela son of Beor became king of Edom. His
city was named Dinhabah.
33 When Bela died, Jobab son of Zerah from
Bozrah[d] succeeded him as king.
34 When Jobab died, Husham from the land of
the Temanites[e] succeeded him as king.
35 When Husham died, Hadad son of Bedad,
who defeated Midian in the country of
Moab,[f] succeeded him as king. His city was
named Avith.
36 When Hadad died, Samlah from Masrekah
succeeded him as king.
37 When Samlah died, Shaul from Rehoboth on
the river[e] succeeded him as king.

36:19 [a]Ge 25:30
36:20 [b]Ge 14:6; Dt 2:12,22; 1Ch 1:38
36:31 [c]Ge 17:6; 1Ch 1:43
36:33 [d]Jer 49:13, 22
36:34 [e]Eze 25:13
36:35 [f]Ge 19:37; Nu 22:1; Dt 1:5; Ru 1:1,6

[a] *22* Hebrew *Hemam,* a variant of *Homam* (see 1 Chron. 1:39)
[b] *24* Vulgate; Syriac *discovered water;* the meaning of the Hebrew for this word is uncertain.
[c] *26* Hebrew *Dishan,* a variant of *Dishon*
[d] *31* Or *before an Israelite king reigned over them*
[e] *37* Possibly the Euphrates

We are loved passionately by God. And I don't know why. It is a mystery, and it must remain a mystery. To understand it is to dismiss it . . . If we discovered that God loved us because we were smart, then we would try to do everything we could to be smarter so he would love us more. If we met someone smarter than we are, we would fall into despair. We couldn't believe God would love us if we weren't the smartest. So I don't think God will ever let us know the reason that he loves us as passionately as he does. I don't have a clue why God loves me. But I believe in the core of my being that he does. So I surrender to it. I stop fighting it. I cease trying to figure it out. I collapse on it.

—Nicole Johnson

38 When Shaul died, Baal-Hanan son of Acbor
succeeded him as king.
39 When Baal-Hanan son of Acbor died, Hadad[a]
succeeded him as king. His city was named
Pau, and his wife's name was Mehetabel
daughter of Matred, the daughter of Me-
Zahab.

40 These were the chiefs descended from Esau,
by name, according to their clans and regions:
Timna, Alvah, Jetheth, 41 Oholibamah,
Elah, Pinon, 42 Kenaz, Teman, Mibzar,
43 Magdiel and Iram. These were the chiefs
of Edom, according to their settlements in
the land they occupied.

This was Esau the father of the Edomites.

Joseph's Dreams

37 Jacob lived in the land where his father had
stayed,[g] the land of Canaan.[h]

2 This is the account of Jacob.

Joseph, a young man of seventeen, was tending
the flocks[i] with his brothers, the sons of Bilhah[j]
and the sons of Zilpah,[k] his father's wives, and he
brought their father a bad report[l] about them.
3 Now Israel loved Joseph more than any of his
other sons,[m] because he had been born to him in
his old age;[n] and he made a richly ornamented[b]
robe[o] for him. 4 When his brothers saw that their
father loved him more than any of them, they hated him[p] and could not speak a kind word to him.
5 Joseph had a dream,[q] and when he told it to
his brothers, they hated him all the more. 6 He said
to them, "Listen to this dream I had: 7 We were
binding sheaves of grain out in the field when
suddenly my sheaf rose and stood upright, while
your sheaves gathered around mine and bowed
down to it."[r]
8 His brothers said to him, "Do you intend to
reign over us? Will you actually rule us?"[s] And
they hated him all the more because of his dream
and what he had said.
9 Then he had another dream, and he told it to
his brothers. "Listen," he said, "I had another
dream, and this time the sun and moon and
eleven stars were bowing down to me."
10 When he told his father as well as his brothers,[t] his father rebuked him and said, "What is
this dream you had? Will your mother and I and
your brothers actually come and bow down to the
ground before you?"[u] 11 His brothers were jealous
of him,[v] but his father kept the matter in mind.[w]

Joseph Sold by His Brothers

12 Now his brothers had gone to graze their

37:1 [g]Ge 17:8 [h]Ge 10:19
37:2 [i]Ps 78:71 [j]Ge 35:25 [k]Ge 35:26 [l]1Sa 2:24
37:3 [m]Ge 25:28 [n]Ge 44:20 [o]2Sa 13:18-19
37:4 [p]Ge 27:41; 49:22-23; Ac 7:9
37:5 [q]Ge 20:3; 28:12
37:7 [r]Ge 42:6,9; 43:26,28; 44:14; 50:18
37:8 [s]Ge 49:26
37:10 [t]ver 5 [u]ver 7; Ge 27:29
37:11 [v]Ac 7:9 [w]Lk 2:19,51

[a] *39* Many manuscripts of the Masoretic Text, Samaritan Pentateuch and Syriac (see also 1 Chron. 1:50); most manuscripts of the Masoretic Text *Hadar* [b] *3* The meaning of the Hebrew for *richly ornamented* is uncertain; also in verses 23 and 32.

Favoritism

GE 37:2-11

Joseph comes across as a spoiled teenager with an inflated sense of self-importance. His father favors him, which makes his brothers jealous, and God favors him, which upsets his father. We can all hope that, should we be given special treatment, we would be gracious enough and wise enough to know how to respond to it. Just think what might have happened if Joseph had suggested his father make splendid coats for his brothers similar to the one he had received, or if he had turned down the coat and insisted his father wear it.

Write out a new version of this story, choosing an option that didn't seem to occur to Joseph. Then remember that despite what appears to have been Joseph's early failings, his trials in Egypt taught him to obey God. And these events were God's way of bringing about famine relief for Jacob's family and preserving the nation that would eventually produce the Savior of the world.

Big Brother

GE 37:21-22

Why does Reuben speak up to protect his little brother? Reuben, as the oldest son, will be held responsible if anything happens to Joseph, and he may be trying to prevent his father's anger from landing squarely on him. Also, Reuben already has fallen from his father's good graces by sleeping with one of his father's concubines (Ge 35:22). Another slipup and Reuben may see his inheritance dribbling through his fingers. It is also possible that Reuben hopes he might make up for his sexual indiscretion by rescuing Joseph and taking the credit for saving his life. However, all this comes to naught when Reuben's brothers sell young Joseph to some traders. Reuben goes along with their deception rather than risk his father's anger at Joseph's disappearance. Their hatred and deception come back to haunt them when, years later, they face Joseph in Egypt (Ge 42:22).

father's flocks near Shechem, 13and Israel said to Joseph, "As you know, your brothers are grazing the flocks near Shechem. Come, I am going to send you to them."

"Very well," he replied.

14So he said to him, "Go and see if all is well with your brothers and with the flocks, and bring word back to me." Then he sent him off from the Valley of Hebron.[x]

When Joseph arrived at Shechem, 15a man found him wandering around in the fields and asked him, "What are you looking for?"

16He replied, "I'm looking for my brothers. Can you tell me where they are grazing their flocks?"

17"They have moved on from here," the man answered. "I heard them say, 'Let's go to Dothan.[y]' "

So Joseph went after his brothers and found them near Dothan. 18But they saw him in the distance, and before he reached them, they plotted to kill him.[z]

19"Here comes that dreamer!" they said to each other. 20"Come now, let's kill him and throw him into one of these cisterns[a] and say that a ferocious animal devoured him. Then we'll see what comes of his dreams."[b]

21When Reuben heard this, he tried to rescue him from their hands. "Let's not take his life," he said.[c] 22"Don't shed any blood. Throw him into this cistern here in the desert, but don't lay a hand on him." Reuben said this to rescue him from them and take him back to his father.

23So when Joseph came to his brothers, they stripped him of his robe—the richly ornamented robe he was wearing— 24and they took him and threw him into the cistern.[d] Now the cistern was empty; there was no water in it.

25As they sat down to eat their meal, they looked up and saw a caravan of Ishmaelites coming from Gilead. Their camels were loaded with spices, balm and myrrh,[e] and they were on their way to take them down to Egypt.[f]

26Judah said to his brothers, "What will we gain if we kill our brother and cover up his blood?[g] 27Come, let's sell him to the Ishmaelites and not lay our hands on him; after all, he is our brother,[h] our own flesh and blood." His brothers agreed.

28So when the Midianite[i] merchants came by, his brothers pulled Joseph up out of the cistern and sold him for twenty shekels[a] of silver to the Ishmaelites, who took him to Egypt.[j]

29When Reuben returned to the cistern and saw that Joseph was not there, he tore his clothes.[k] 30He went back to his brothers and said, "The boy isn't there! Where can I turn now?"[l]

31Then they got Joseph's robe,[m] slaughtered a goat and dipped the robe in the blood. 32They took the ornamented robe back to their father and said,

37:14 [x]Ge 13:18; 35:27
37:17 [y]2Ki 6:13
37:18 [z]1Sa 19:1; Mk 14:1; Ac 23:12
37:20 [a]Jer 38:6,9 [b]Ge 50:20
37:21 [c]Ge 42:22
37:24 [d]Jer 41:7
37:25 [e]Ge 43:11 [f]ver 28
37:26 [g]ver 20; Ge 4:10
37:27 [h]Ge 42:21
37:28 [i]Ge 25:2; Jdg 6:1-3 [j]Ge 45:4-5; Ps 105:17; Ac 7:9
37:29 [k]ver 34; Ge 44:13; Job 1:20
37:30 [l]ver 22; Ge 42:13,36
37:31 [m]ver 3,23

[a] *28* That is, about 8 ounces (about 0.2 kilogram)

"We found this. Examine it to see whether it is
your son's robe."
33 He recognized it and said, "It is my son's robe!
37:33 [n]ver 20 [o]Ge 44:20,28 Some ferocious animal[n] has devoured him. Joseph
has surely been torn to pieces."[o]
34 Then Jacob tore his clothes,[p] put on sackcloth[q]
37:34 [p]ver 29 [q]2Sa 3:31 [r]Ge 50:3,10,11 and mourned for his son many days.[r] 35 All his
sons and daughters came to comfort him, but he
refused to be comforted. "No," he said, "in mourning will I go down to the grave[a][s] to my son." So
37:35 [s]Ge 42:38; 44:22,29,31 his father wept for him.
36 Meanwhile, the Midianites[b] sold Joseph in
Egypt to Potiphar, one of Pharaoh's officials, the
37:36 [t]Ge 39:1 captain of the guard.[t]

Judah and Tamar

38 At that time, Judah left his brothers and
went down to stay with a man of Adullam
38:2 [u]1Ch 2:3 named Hirah. 2 There Judah met the daughter of a
Canaanite man named Shua.[u] He married her and
38:3 [v]ver 6; Ge 46:12; Nu 26:19 lay with her; 3 she became pregnant and gave birth
to a son, who was named Er.[v] 4 She conceived
again and gave birth to a son and named him
Onan. 5 She gave birth to still another son and
named him Shelah. It was at Kezib that she gave
birth to him.
6 Judah got a wife for Er, his firstborn, and her
name was Tamar. 7 But Er, Judah's firstborn, was
38:7 [w]ver 10; Ge 46:12; 1Ch 2:3 wicked in the LORD's sight; so the LORD put him to
death.[w]
8 Then Judah said to Onan, "Lie with your
brother's wife and fulfill your duty to her as a
38:8 [x]Dt 25:5-6; Mt 22:24-28 brother-in-law to produce offspring for your
brother."[x] 9 But Onan knew that the offspring
would not be his; so whenever he lay with his
brother's wife, he spilled his semen on the ground
to keep from producing offspring for his brother.
38:10 [y]Ge 46:12; Dt 25:7-10 10 What he did was wicked in the LORD's sight; so
he put him to death also.[y]
11 Judah then said to his daughter-in-law Tamar,
38:11 [z]Ru 1:13 "Live as a widow in your father's house until my
son Shelah grows up."[z] For he thought, "He may
die too, just like his brothers." So Tamar went to
live in her father's house.
12 After a long time Judah's wife, the daughter of
Shua, died. When Judah had recovered from his
38:12 [a]ver 14; Jos 15:10,57 grief, he went up to Timnah,[a] to the men who
were shearing his sheep, and his friend Hirah the
Adullamite went with him.
13 When Tamar was told, "Your father-in-law is
on his way to Timnah to shear his sheep," 14 she
took off her widow's clothes, covered herself with
a veil to disguise herself, and then sat down at the
entrance to Enaim, which is on the road to Tim-
38:14 [b]ver 11 nah. For she saw that, though Shelah[b] had now
grown up, she had not been given to him as his
wife.

[a] 35 Hebrew *Sheol* [b] 36 Samaritan Pentateuch, Septuagint, Vulgate and Syriac (see also verse 28); Masoretic Text *Medanites*

Heirs

GE 38:8-10

In the ancient world the custom of levirate marriage ensured that a dead man's line of descendants would continue. The dead man's brother was required to marry the widow, and the first male child born from this marriage was considered her former husband's child and heir. Since having an heir who would continue the family name was a prime purpose for marriage, such a procedure was of utmost importance and provided a way to care for widows as well. The care of the widow and her dead husband's property also fell to the brother, a responsibility that at times made the law unpopular.

The widow herself had some rights in these cases and could bring before the elders a brother-in-law who refused to fulfill his legal responsibility. If he continued to refuse, she could remove his sandal and spit in his face, a procedure designed, obviously, to humiliate him and perhaps prevent such a lack of responsibility.

Right and Wrong

GE 38:26

How can the word *righteous* be applied to Tamar, who uses an act of prostitution to secure her future? While her behavior is shocking, consider Judah's: He lives separated from his family, marries a Canaanite, hires a prostitute, fails to keep the law that has been established to protect widows, and then decrees Tamar should be burned—for a sin she committed with him! Neither the young widow nor her father-in-law fits the current understanding of the word *righteous*, which suggests "right standing with God." But amazingly, both find their way into the ancestry of Christ! These two seriously flawed individuals are listed in Matthew 1:3 among Jesus' ancestors—beautiful proof that God doesn't wait until his people are perfect or have it all together before fulfilling his plans. (See character sketch for Tamar on page 267.)

15 When Judah saw her, he thought she was a
prostitute, for she had covered her face. 16 Not realizing that she was his daughter-in-law,[c] he went
over to her by the roadside and said, "Come now,
let me sleep with you."
"And what will you give me to sleep with you?"
she asked.
17 "I'll send you a young goat[d] from my flock,"
he said.
"Will you give me something as a pledge[e] until
you send it?" she asked.
18 He said, "What pledge should I give you?"
"Your seal[f] and its cord, and the staff in your
hand," she answered. So he gave them to her and
slept with her, and she became pregnant by him.
19 After she left, she took off her veil and put on
her widow's clothes[g] again.
20 Meanwhile Judah sent the young goat by his
friend the Adullamite in order to get his pledge
back from the woman, but he did not find her.
21 He asked the men who lived there, "Where is the
shrine prostitute[h] who was beside the road at
Enaim?"
"There hasn't been any shrine prostitute here,"
they said.
22 So he went back to Judah and said, "I didn't
find her. Besides, the men who lived there said,
'There hasn't been any shrine prostitute here.' "
23 Then Judah said, "Let her keep what she has,
or we will become a laughingstock. After all, I did
send her this young goat, but you didn't find her."
24 About three months later Judah was told,
"Your daughter-in-law Tamar is guilty of prostitution, and as a result she is now pregnant."
Judah said, "Bring her out and have her burned
to death!"[i]
25 As she was being brought out, she sent a message to her father-in-law. "I am pregnant by the
man who owns these," she said. And she added,
"See if you recognize whose seal and cord and
staff these are."[j]
26 Judah recognized them and said, "She is more
righteous than I,[k] since I wouldn't give her to my
son Shelah.[l]" And he did not sleep with her again.
27 When the time came for her to give birth,
there were twin boys in her womb.[m] 28 As she was
giving birth, one of them put out his hand; so the
midwife took a scarlet thread and tied it on his
wrist and said, "This one came out first." 29 But
when he drew back his hand, his brother came
out, and she said, "So this is how you have broken
out!" And he was named Perez.[a n] 30 Then his
brother, who had the scarlet thread on his wrist,
came out and he was given the name Zerah.[b o]

Joseph and Potiphar's Wife

39 Now Joseph had been taken down to Egypt.
Potiphar, an Egyptian who was one of Phar-

38:16 [c]Lev 18:15; 20:12
38:17 [d]Eze 16:33 [e]ver 20
38:18 [f]ver 25
38:19 [g]ver 14
38:21 [h]Lev 19:29; Hos 4:14
38:24 [i]Lev 21:9; Dt 22:21,22
38:25 [j]ver 18
38:26 [k]1Sa 24:17 [l]ver 11
38:27 [m]Ge 25:24
38:29 [n]Ge 46:12; Nu 26:20,21; Ru 4:12,18; 1Ch 2:4; Mt 1:3
38:30 [o]1Ch 2:4

[a] 29 *Perez* means *breaking out.* [b] 30 *Zerah* can mean *scarlet* or *brightness.*

aoh's officials, the captain of the guard,[p] bought
him from the Ishmaelites who had taken him
there.[q]
2The LORD was with Joseph[r] and he prospered,
and he lived in the house of his Egyptian master.
3When his master saw that the LORD was with him[s]
and that the LORD gave him success in everything
he did,[t] 4Joseph found favor in his eyes and became
his attendant. Potiphar put him in charge of his
household, and he entrusted to his care everything
he owned.[u] 5From the time he put him in charge of
his household and of all that he owned, the LORD
blessed the household of the Egyptian because of
Joseph.[v] The blessing of the LORD was on everything Potiphar had, both in the house and in the
field. 6So he left in Joseph's care everything he had;
with Joseph in charge, he did not concern himself
with anything except the food he ate.
Now Joseph was well-built and handsome,[w]
7and after a while his master's wife took notice of
Joseph and said, "Come to bed with me!"[x]
8But he refused.[y] "With me in charge," he told
her, "my master does not concern himself with
anything in the house; everything he owns he has
entrusted to my care. 9No one is greater in this
house than I am.[z] My master has withheld nothing from me except you, because you are his wife.
How then could I do such a wicked thing and sin
against God?"[a] 10And though she spoke to Joseph
day after day, he refused to go to bed with her or
even be with her.
11One day he went into the house to attend to
his duties, and none of the household servants
was inside. 12She caught him by his cloak[b] and
said, "Come to bed with me!" But he left his cloak
in her hand and ran out of the house.
13When she saw that he had left his cloak in her
hand and had run out of the house, 14she called
her household servants. "Look," she said to them,
"this Hebrew has been brought to us to make
sport of us! He came in here to sleep with me, but
I screamed.[c] 15When he heard me scream for help,
he left his cloak beside me and ran out of the
house."
16She kept his cloak beside her until his master
came home. 17Then she told him this story:[d] "That
Hebrew slave you brought us came to me to make
sport of me. 18But as soon as I screamed for help, he
left his cloak beside me and ran out of the house."
19When his master heard the story his wife told
him, saying, "This is how your slave treated me,"
he burned with anger.[e] 20Joseph's master took
him and put him in prison,[f] the place where the
king's prisoners were confined.
But while Joseph was there in the prison, 21the
LORD was with him; he showed him kindness and
granted him favor in the eyes of the prison warden.[g] 22So the warden put Joseph in charge of all
those held in the prison, and he was made responsible for all that was done there.[h] 23The warden
paid no attention to anything under Joseph's care,

39:1 [p]Ge 37:36 [q]Ge 37:25; Ps 105:17
39:2 [r]Ge 21:20, 22; Ac 7:9
39:3 [s]Ge 21:22; 26:28 [t]Ps 1:3
39:4 [u]ver 8,22; Ge 24:2
39:5 [v]Ge 26:24; 30:27
39:6 [w]1Sa 16:12
39:7 [x]2Sa 13:11; Pr 7:15-18
39:8 [y]Pr 6:23-24
39:9 [z]Ge 41:33,40 [a]Ge 20:6; 42:18; 2Sa 12:13
39:12 [b]Pr 7:13
39:14 [c]Dt 22:24,27
39:17 [d]Ex 23:1,7; Ps 101:5
39:19 [e]Pr 6:34
39:20 [f]Ge 40:3; Ps 105:18
39:21 [g]Ex 3:21
39:22 [h]ver 4

The Seduction

GE 39:11-15

Potiphar's wife's attempt to seduce Joseph was probably not unusual. Bored Egyptian "housewives" may have at times turned to "well-built and handsome" (Ge 39:6) servants to provide them with a little "diversion." Some commentators suggest that Potiphar's position was that of captain of the executioners. If that is the case, Joseph is fortunate to escape from this incident with his life.

More important, Joseph comes away with his honor and morals intact, in stark contrast to his brother's behavior just one chapter before. Joseph recognizes that there are more than just himself and a wayward wife involved in this incident. Such an act is a sin not only against the husband, Potiphar, but also—and ultimately—against God.

Dreams GE 40:8

In only two story cycles in Scripture is a dream interpreter needed: Joseph's and Daniel's (Da 2:27–28; 4:4–8). And in both of these instances, the dreamers are not Israelites. All examples of Israelite dreams are understood by the dreamers themselves. If one compares the "dream" literature of the Babylonians and Egyptians with that of the Bible, the Hebrews were noticeably less preoccupied with dream interpretation than were either the Babylonians or the Egyptians. Instead, the Hebrews considered hearing directly from God a superior method of communication.

because the LORD was with Joseph and gave him 39:23
success in whatever he did.[i] [i]ver 3

The Cupbearer and the Baker

40 Some time later, the cupbearer[j] and the bak- 40:1 [j]Ne 1:11
er of the king of Egypt offended their master,
the king of Egypt. 2Pharaoh was angry[k] with his 40:2 [k]Pr 16:14,15
two officials, the chief cupbearer and the chief
baker, 3and put them in custody in the house of 40:3
the captain of the guard,[l] in the same prison where [l]Ge 39:20
Joseph was confined. 4The captain of the guard 40:4
assigned them to Joseph,[m] and he attended them. [m]Ge 39:4
After they had been in custody for some time,
5each of the two men—the cupbearer and the baker of the king of Egypt, who were being held in
prison—had a dream the same night, and each 40:5
dream had a meaning of its own.[n] [n]Ge 41:11
6When Joseph came to them the next morning,
he saw that they were dejected. 7So he asked
Pharaoh's officials who were in custody with him
in his master's house, "Why are your faces so sad 40:7
today?"[o] [o]Ne 2:2
8"We both had dreams," they answered, "but 40:8
there is no one to interpret them."[p] [p]Ge 41:8,15
Then Joseph said to them, "Do not interpreta- [q]Ge 41:16;
tions belong to God?[q] Tell me your dreams." Da 2:22,28,
9So the chief cupbearer told Joseph his dream. 47
He said to him, "In my dream I saw a vine in front
of me, 10and on the vine were three branches. As
soon as it budded, it blossomed, and its clusters
ripened into grapes. 11Pharaoh's cup was in my
hand, and I took the grapes, squeezed them into
Pharaoh's cup and put the cup in his hand." 40:12
12"This is what it means,[r]" Joseph said to him. [r]Ge 41:12,
"The three branches are three days. 13Within three 15,25;
days Pharaoh will lift up your head and restore Da 2:36;
you to your position, and you will put Pharaoh's 4:19
cup in his hand, just as you used to do when you
were his cupbearer. 14But when all goes well with 40:14
you, remember me[s] and show me kindness;[t] men- [s]Lk 23:42
tion me to Pharaoh and get me out of this prison. [t]Jos 2:12;
15For I was forcibly carried off from the land of the 1Sa 20:14,
Hebrews,[u] and even here I have done nothing to 42; 1Ki 2:7
deserve being put in a dungeon." 40:15
16When the chief baker saw that Joseph had [u]Ge 37:26-28
given a favorable interpretation, he said to Joseph,
"I too had a dream: On my head were three baskets of bread.[a] 17In the top basket were all kinds of
baked goods for Pharaoh, but the birds were eating them out of the basket on my head."
18"This is what it means," Joseph said. "The 40:18
three baskets are three days.[v] 19Within three days [v]ver 12
Pharaoh will lift off your head[w] and hang you on 40:19
a tree.[b] And the birds will eat away your flesh." [w]ver 13
20Now the third day was Pharaoh's birthday,[x] 40:20
and he gave a feast for all his officials.[y] He lifted [x]Mt 14:6-10
up the heads of the chief cupbearer and the chief [y]Mk 6:21
baker in the presence of his officials: 21He restored
the chief cupbearer to his position, so that he once

[a] 16 Or *three wicker baskets* [b] 19 Or *and impale you on a pole*

Sarai (Sarah)

Surely You Jest

"Are you pregnant yet?" How the question must have pierced Sarai each month. The shame of barrenness was intensified by Abram's visible disappointment. Couldn't he see how much *she* had suffered through the years? Even her plan for an heir through Hagar had backfired. Sarai was out of ideas and long past the age for having children. Yet Abram persisted in his desire for a son. He said that God had promised him offspring as numberless as the stars!

Sarai loved Abram. He was a faithful husband and more than a good provider. But he was so *restless*, always looking for more from life. She had gone with him from one place to another, each time leaving people and things she had grown to love. Then there was the day Abram told her that God had changed his name to "Abraham," and hers to "Sarah." He said God told him that she would be the mother of nations! What next?

She laughed when she overheard a stranger say she would bear Abraham's child (Ge 18:10-15). Preposterous! But her doubt turned to fear when the stranger confronted her by asking, "Is anything too hard for the LORD?" (Ge 18:14). The text doesn't tell us so, but we'd like to believe that Sarah acknowledged her bitterness, which extended even to the Lord himself, that she decided to stop doubting and to stop trying to be in control. She gave the Lord room to work a miracle in her life, and Abraham's dream became Sarah's dream.

A year later, Isaac was born—to Sarah's great delight. The text says, "God was *gracious* to Sarah"—God gave her a child without regard to what *she* did. Her laugh of doubt was turned to laughter of joy.

Even our lack of faith doesn't prevent God from keeping his promises and accomplishing what he plans. God is bigger than the weaknesses of men and of women. First Peter 3:6 says, "You are [Sarah's] daughters if you do what is right and do not give way to fear." The goal is to trust, and the power to trust is from the Lord.

Sarai, Sarah
(princess)

Genesis 11:29–12:20; 16:1-8; 17:15–18:15; 20:1–21:12; 23:1-19; 25:10; 49:31

Isaiah 51:2

Romans 4:19; 9:9

Galatians 4:21-31

Hebrews 11:11

1 Peter 3:5-6

Candid SNAPSHOT Sarah said, "God has brought me laughter, and everyone who hears about this will laugh with me." And she added, "Who would have said to Abraham that Sarah would nurse children? Yet I have borne him a son in his old age" (Ge 21:6-7).

Hagar

The Other Woman

The searing desert sun bore down on Hagar as she considered her desperate state. How had it come to this? Where was God now? Not only were she and Ishmael out of water, but they had also been cast out of their family. As a discarded concubine, her choices were all too few. Alone and abandoned in the desert, she was certain she and her son would die.

Then an angel called from heaven: "Do not be afraid; God has heard the boy crying as he lies there . . ." (Ge 21:17), and Hagar suddenly saw a well of water. This sign of God's continued hand in her life must have given Hagar renewed hope.

Seventeen years earlier, "The One who sees me" (Ge 16:13)—the name Hagar had given God at that time—sent Hagar back to Sarai. Hagar had been heading back to Egypt—to her old life, her old ways, her own people—when God intervened. When Hagar heard the voice of God, she obeyed and returned—as Sarah's servant, not Abraham's concubine. There she would raise her son and perhaps grow in her knowledge of God.

Using a concubine to bear an heir was a common practice in pagan cultures. But surely Abraham must have known in his heart that this was the wrong way to gain the heir God had promised. His actions made victims of Hagar and Ishmael. For when their home became a battlefield and a choice was required, Abraham's commitment to Sarah and Isaac took precedence over Hagar and Ishmael. But God saw beyond the actions of his chosen couple and compassionately took care of Hagar and Ishmael.

When the circumstances of life overwhelm, when we feel like we've been treated unfairly, we can be sure that we serve a "God who sees." He knows our circumstances, and he sees what others have done to us. Just as he watched over Hagar, he watches over us, with compassion and a plan for our future. He is not only a God who sees, he is a God who acts and a God who can be trusted.

Hagar
(flight)

Genesis 16; 21:9-21; 25:12

Galatians 4:21-31

Candid SNAPSHOT So after Abram had been living in Canaan ten years, Sarai his wife took her Egyptian maidservant Hagar and gave her to her husband to be his wife. He slept with Hagar, and she conceived. When she knew she was pregnant, she began to despise her mistress (Genesis 16:3-4).

40:21 again put the cup into Pharaoh's hand,[z] 22but he
[z]ver 13 hanged[a] the chief baker,[a] just as Joseph had said
40:22 to them in his interpretation.[b]
[a]ver 19 23The chief cupbearer, however, did not remem-
[b]Ps 105:19 ber Joseph; he forgot him.[c]

40:23
[c]Job 19:14;
Ecc 9:15

Pharaoh's Dreams

41:1 41 When two full years had passed, Pharaoh
[d]Ge 20:3 had a dream:[d] He was standing by the Nile,
2when out of the river there came up seven cows,
41:2 sleek and fat,[e] and they grazed among the reeds.[f]
[e]ver 26 3After them, seven other cows, ugly and gaunt,
[f]Isa 19:6 came up out of the Nile and stood beside those on
the riverbank. 4And the cows that were ugly and
gaunt ate up the seven sleek, fat cows. Then Pharaoh woke up.
5He fell asleep again and had a second dream:
Seven heads of grain, healthy and good, were
growing on a single stalk. 6After them, seven other heads of grain sprouted—thin and scorched by
the east wind. 7The thin heads of grain swallowed
up the seven healthy, full heads. Then Pharaoh
41:8 woke up; it had been a dream.
[g]Da 2:1,3; 8In the morning his mind was troubled,[g] so he
4:5,19 sent for all the magicians[h] and wise men of Egypt.
[h]Ex 7:11,22; Pharaoh told them his dreams, but no one could
Da 1:20; 2:2, interpret them for him.
27; 4:7 9Then the chief cupbearer said to Pharaoh,
41:10 "Today I am reminded of my shortcomings.
[i]Ge 40:2 10Pharaoh was once angry with his servants,[i] and
[j]Ge 39:20 he imprisoned me and the chief baker in the
house of the captain of the guard.[j] 11Each of us
41:11 had a dream the same night, and each dream had
[k]Ge 40:5 a meaning of its own.[k] 12Now a young Hebrew
was there with us, a servant of the captain of the
guard. We told him our dreams, and he interpret-
41:12 ed them for us, giving each man the interpreta-
[l]Ge 40:12 tion of his dream.[l] 13And things turned out exact-
41:13 ly as he interpreted them to us: I was restored to
[m]Ge 40:22 my position, and the other man was hanged.[a][m]"
41:14 14So Pharaoh sent for Joseph, and he was quick-
[n]Ps 105:20; ly brought from the dungeon.[n] When he had
Da 2:25 shaved and changed his clothes, he came before
Pharaoh.
15Pharaoh said to Joseph, "I had a dream, and
no one can interpret it. But I have heard it said of
41:15 you that when you hear a dream you can inter-
[o]Da 5:16 pret it."[o]
41:16 16"I cannot do it," Joseph replied to Pharaoh,
[p]Ge 40:8; "but God will give Pharaoh the answer he desires."[p]
Da 2:30; 17Then Pharaoh said to Joseph, "In my dream I
Ac 3:12; was standing on the bank of the Nile, 18when out
2Co 3:5 of the river there came up seven cows, fat and
sleek, and they grazed among the reeds. 19After
them, seven other cows came up—scrawny and
very ugly and lean. I had never seen such ugly
cows in all the land of Egypt. 20The lean, ugly
cows ate up the seven fat cows that came up first.
21But even after they ate them, no one could tell

Only God

GE 41:16

Joseph's humble response to Pharaoh's request for an interpretation of his dreams stands in sharp contrast to the seemingly flaunting pronouncements of his dreams to his brothers (Ge 37:5-11). As he stands before Pharaoh, Joseph says, "I can't interpret dreams, but God has the answers." And even as Joseph explains the dreams to Pharaoh, Joseph keeps reminding the ruler that these dreams are messages from God. Circle each time God is mentioned by Joseph in Genesis 41:16-32.

Now turn back to Joseph's announcements of his dreams in Genesis 37:5-11. How many times does he mention God? Circle each time he uses pronouns that refer to himself. The lesson here is obvious, isn't it? It took slavery and humbling circumstances for Joseph to discover that all he was, all he is, all he will be are not products of his own character or doing but come only from God.

[a] *22,13* Or *impaled*

The Region's Breadbasket

GE 41:27

Egypt, like much of the Middle East, is made up of vast deserts. But it is blessed with one thing the other land around it doesn't have—the Nile River. The Nile provides water and fertile soil from silt deposits, making Egypt a granary for those in more famine-prone lands. When a drought occurs in other countries, no large, natural bodies of water exist to serve as sources of irrigation, thus famines can develop quickly with the failure of even one year's crops. Egypt, on the other hand, has rich soil, which makes the land more productive in a good year, and it has the Nile to provide water in harsh years. But Pharaoh's dream reveals a scenario the Egyptians aren't prepared for. They, too, will experience crop failures—for seven years in a row; but with God's intervention through Pharaoh's dreams and Joseph's interpretations, the Egyptians, as well as God's people the Israelites, will survive.

that they had done so; they looked just as ugly as before. Then I woke up.

22“In my dreams I also saw seven heads of grain, full and good, growing on a single stalk. 23After them, seven other heads sprouted—withered and thin and scorched by the east wind. 24The thin heads of grain swallowed up the seven good heads. I told this to the magicians, but none could explain it to me.[q]”

25Then Joseph said to Pharaoh, “The dreams of Pharaoh are one and the same. God has revealed to Pharaoh what he is about to do.[r] 26The seven good cows[s] are seven years, and the seven good heads of grain are seven years; it is one and the same dream. 27The seven lean, ugly cows that came up afterward are seven years, and so are the seven worthless heads of grain scorched by the east wind: They are seven years of famine.[t]

28“It is just as I said to Pharaoh: God has shown Pharaoh what he is about to do. 29Seven years of great abundance[u] are coming throughout the land of Egypt, 30but seven years of famine[v] will follow them. Then all the abundance in Egypt will be forgotten, and the famine will ravage the land.[w] 31The abundance in the land will not be remembered, because the famine that follows it will be so severe. 32The reason the dream was given to Pharaoh in two forms is that the matter has been firmly decided[x] by God, and God will do it soon.

33“And now let Pharaoh look for a discerning and wise man[y] and put him in charge of the land of Egypt. 34Let Pharaoh appoint commissioners over the land to take a fifth[z] of the harvest of Egypt during the seven years of abundance.[a] 35They should collect all the food of these good years that are coming and store up the grain under the authority of Pharaoh, to be kept in the cities for food.[b] 36This food should be held in reserve for the country, to be used during the seven years of famine that will come upon Egypt,[c] so that the country may not be ruined by the famine.”

37The plan seemed good to Pharaoh and to all his officials.[d] 38So Pharaoh asked them, “Can we find anyone like this man, one in whom is the spirit of God[a]?”[e]

39Then Pharaoh said to Joseph, “Since God has made all this known to you, there is no one so discerning and wise as you. 40You shall be in charge of my palace, and all my people are to submit to your orders.[f] Only with respect to the throne will I be greater than you.”

Joseph in Charge of Egypt

41So Pharaoh said to Joseph, “I hereby put you in charge of the whole land of Egypt.”[g] 42Then Pharaoh took his signet ring[h] from his finger and put it on Joseph's finger. He dressed him in robes of fine linen and put a gold chain around his neck.[i] 43He had him ride in a chariot as his sec-

41:24 [q]ver 8
41:25 [r]Da 2:45
41:26 [s]ver 2
41:27 [t]Ge 12:10; 2Ki 8:1
41:29 [u]ver 47
41:30 [v]ver 54; Ge 47:13 [w]ver 56
41:32 [x]Nu 23:19; Isa 46:10-11
41:33 [y]ver 39
41:34 [z]1Sa 8:15 [a]ver 48
41:35 [b]ver 48
41:36 [c]ver 56
41:37 [d]Ge 45:16
41:38 [e]Nu 27:18; Job 32:8; Da 4:8-9,18; 5:11,14
41:40 [f]Ps 105:21-22; Ac 7:10
41:41 [g]Ge 42:6; Da 6:3
41:42 [h]Est 3:10 [i]Da 5:7,16, 29

[a] 38 Or *of the gods*

ond-in-command,[a] and men shouted before him,
41:43 [j]Est 6:9 "Make way[b]!"[j] Thus he put him in charge of the
whole land of Egypt.
44 Then Pharaoh said to Joseph, "I am Pharaoh,
but without your word no one will lift hand or
41:44 [k]Ps 105:22 foot in all Egypt."[k] 45 Pharaoh gave Joseph the
name Zaphenath-Paneah and gave him Asenath
41:45 [l]ver 50; Ge 46:20,27 daughter of Potiphera, priest of On,[c] to be his
wife.[l] And Joseph went throughout the land of
Egypt.
41:46 [m]Ge 37:2 46 Joseph was thirty years old[m] when he entered
[n]1Sa 16:21; Da 1:19 the service[n] of Pharaoh king of Egypt. And Joseph
went out from Pharaoh's presence and traveled
throughout Egypt. 47 During the seven years of
abundance the land produced plentifully. 48 Joseph
collected all the food produced in those seven
years of abundance in Egypt and stored it in the
cities. In each city he put the food grown in the
fields surrounding it. 49 Joseph stored up huge
quantities of grain, like the sand of the sea; it was
so much that he stopped keeping records because
it was beyond measure.
50 Before the years of famine came, two sons
41:50 [o]Ge 46:20; 48:5 were born to Joseph by Asenath daughter of
Potiphera, priest of On.[o] 51 Joseph named his firstborn[p] Manasseh[d] and said, "It is because God has
41:51 [p]Ge 48:14, 18,20 made me forget all my trouble and all my father's
household." 52 The second son he named Ephra-
im[e][q] and said, "It is because God has made me
41:52 [q]Ge 48:1,5; 50:23 fruitful[r] in the land of my suffering."
[r]Ge 17:6; 28:3; 49:22 53 The seven years of abundance in Egypt came
to an end, 54 and the seven years of famine began,[s]
just as Joseph had said. There was famine in all
41:54 [s]ver 30; Ps 105:11; Ac 7:11 the other lands, but in the whole land of Egypt
there was food. 55 When all Egypt began to feel the
famine,[t] the people cried to Pharaoh for food.
41:55 [t]Dt 32:24 Then Pharaoh told all the Egyptians, "Go to
[u]ver 41 Joseph and do what he tells you."[u]
56 When the famine had spread over the whole
41:56 [v]Ge 12:10 country, Joseph opened the storehouses and sold
grain to the Egyptians, for the famine[v] was severe
41:57 [w]Ge 42:5; 47:15 throughout Egypt. 57 And all the countries came to
Egypt to buy grain from Joseph,[w] because the
famine was severe in all the world.

Joseph's Brothers Go to Egypt

42:1 [x]Ac 7:12 **42** When Jacob learned that there was grain in
Egypt,[x] he said to his sons, "Why do you
just keep looking at each other?" 2 He continued,
"I have heard that there is grain in Egypt. Go
42:2 [y]Ge 43:8 down there and buy some for us, so that we may
live and not die."[y]
3 Then ten of Joseph's brothers went down to
buy grain from Egypt. 4 But Jacob did not send
Benjamin, Joseph's brother, with the others,
because he was afraid that harm might come to

[a] 43 Or *in the chariot of his second-in-command;* or *in his second chariot* [b] 43 Or *Bow down* [c] 45 That is, Heliopolis; also in verse 50 [d] 51 *Manasseh* sounds like and may be derived from the Hebrew for *forget.* [e] 52 *Ephraim* sounds like the Hebrew for *twice fruitful.*

A Good Marriage?

GE 41:44–45

With Joseph's new position, his name is changed to indicate how thoroughly he is accepted as an Egyptian, and he is given a bride, the daughter of a priest of On, the sun god. Because the sun plays a crucial role in agriculture, the wealthy, powerful priests of On are significant participants in the ruler's court. This passage casts no shadow on Joseph's taking of Asenath as his wife. Instead, the chapter portrays this as a season of contentment for Joseph. He has risen to a position of great power; he has been freed after being a slave and a prisoner for 13 years; and he has two sons, whose names indicate that Joseph has moved beyond the wrongs done to him in the past (see Ge 41:51–52 and NIV footnotes). Now he looks back on those events and sees God's hand far more clearly than he sees his brothers'.

Brotherly Love

GE 42:21-24

More than 20 years have passed since Joseph was sold into slavery; so it's no wonder his brothers don't recognize him, especially considering his powerful position. Joseph now has a chance to exact retribution for his brothers' vicious treatment. Instead, he tests them to see how they will respond. And what pops out of their mouths? Guilt over the evil actions they committed against their younger brother. They even recall the way he pleaded for his life.

But retribution is not at all what Joseph has in mind. His tearful response clearly reveals that he has already forgiven them. Joseph is no longer the brash youth of 20 years before. He is now a powerful, though gentle and understanding, ruler. And 20 years of guilt have transformed his brothers also. They are no longer vindictive or jealous but have examined their consciences and recognize their guilt.

him.[z] 5 So Israel's sons were among those who
went to buy grain,[a] for the famine was in the land
of Canaan also.[b]
6 Now Joseph was the governor of the land,[c] the
one who sold grain to all its people. So when
Joseph's brothers arrived, they bowed down to
him with their faces to the ground.[d] 7 As soon as
Joseph saw his brothers, he recognized them, but
he pretended to be a stranger and spoke harshly to
them.[e] "Where do you come from?" he asked.
"From the land of Canaan," they replied, "to
buy food."
8 Although Joseph recognized his brothers, they
did not recognize him.[f] 9 Then he remembered his
dreams[g] about them and said to them, "You are
spies! You have come to see where our land is
unprotected."
10 "No, my lord," they answered. "Your servants
have come to buy food. 11 We are all the sons of one
man. Your servants are honest men, not spies."
12 "No!" he said to them. "You have come to see
where our land is unprotected."
13 But they replied, "Your servants were twelve
brothers, the sons of one man, who lives in the
land of Canaan. The youngest is now with our
father, and one is no more."[h]
14 Joseph said to them, "It is just as I told you:
You are spies! 15 And this is how you will be tested: As surely as Pharaoh lives,[i] you will not leave
this place unless your youngest brother comes
here. 16 Send one of your number to get your
brother; the rest of you will be kept in prison, so
that your words may be tested to see if you are
telling the truth.[j] If you are not, then as surely as
Pharaoh lives, you are spies!" 17 And he put them
all in custody[k] for three days.
18 On the third day, Joseph said to them, "Do this
and you will live, for I fear God:[l] 19 If you are honest men, let one of your brothers stay here in
prison, while the rest of you go and take grain
back for your starving households. 20 But you must
bring your youngest brother to me,[m] so that your
words may be verified and that you may not die."
This they proceeded to do.
21 They said to one another, "Surely we are being
punished because of our brother.[n] We saw how
distressed he was when he pleaded with us for his
life, but we would not listen; that's why this distress[o] has come upon us."
22 Reuben replied, "Didn't I tell you not to sin
against the boy?[p] But you wouldn't listen! Now
we must give an accounting[q] for his blood."[r]
23 They did not realize that Joseph could understand them, since he was using an interpreter.
24 He turned away from them and began to
weep, but then turned back and spoke to them
again. He had Simeon taken from them and
bound before their eyes.[s]
25 Joseph gave orders to fill their bags with
grain,[t] to put each man's silver back in his sack,[u]
and to give them provisions for their journey.[v]

42:4 [z]ver 38
42:5 [a]Ge 41:57 [b]Ge 12:10; Ac 7:11
42:6 [c]Ge 41:41 [d]Ge 37:7-10
42:7 [e]ver 30
42:8 [f]Ge 37:2
42:9 [g]Ge 37:7
42:13 [h]Ge 37:30, 33; 44:20
42:15 [i]1Sa 17:55
42:16 [j]ver 11
42:17 [k]Ge 40:4
42:18 [l]Ge 20:11; Lev 25:43
42:20 [m]ver 15,34; Ge 43:5; 44:23
42:21 [n]Ge 37:26-28 [o]Hos 5:15
42:22 [p]Ge 37:21-22 [q]Ge 9:5 [r]1Ki 2:32; 2Ch 24:22; Ps 9:12
42:24 [s]ver 13; Ge 43:14,23; 45:14-15
42:25 [t]Ge 43:2 [u]Ge 44:1,8 [v]Ro 12:17, 20-21

After this was done for them, [26]they loaded their
grain on their donkeys and left.
[27]At the place where they stopped for the night
one of them opened his sack to get feed for his
donkey, and he saw his silver in the mouth of his
42:27 sack.[w] [28]"My silver has been returned," he said to
[w]Ge 43:21-22 his brothers. "Here it is in my sack."
Their hearts sank and they turned to each oth-
42:28 er trembling and said, "What is this that God has
[x]Ge 43:23 done to us?"[x]
[29]When they came to their father Jacob in the
land of Canaan, they told him all that had happened to them. They said, [30]"The man who is lord
42:30 over the land spoke harshly to us[y] and treated us
[y]ver 7 as though we were spying on the land. [31]But we
said to him, 'We are honest men; we are not
42:31 spies.[z] [32]We were twelve brothers, sons of one
[z]ver 11 father. One is no more, and the youngest is now
with our father in Canaan.'
[33]"Then the man who is lord over the land said
to us, 'This is how I will know whether you are
honest men: Leave one of your brothers here with
me, and take food for your starving households
42:33 and go.[a] [34]But bring your youngest brother to me
[a]ver 19,20 so I will know that you are not spies but honest
men. Then I will give your brother back to you,
42:34 and you can trade[a] in the land.[b]' "
[b]Ge 34:10 [35]As they were emptying their sacks, there in
each man's sack was his pouch of silver! When
they and their father saw the money pouches,
42:35 they were frightened.[c] [36]Their father Jacob said to
[c]Ge 43:12, 15,18 them, "You have deprived me of my children.
Joseph is no more and Simeon is no more, and
42:36 now you want to take Benjamin.[d] Everything is
[d]Ge 43:14 against me!"
[37]Then Reuben said to his father, "You may put
both of my sons to death if I do not bring him
back to you. Entrust him to my care, and I will
bring him back."
[38]But Jacob said, "My son will not go down
42:38 [e]Ge 37:33 there with you; his brother is dead[e] and he is the
[f]ver 4 only one left. If harm comes to him[f] on the jour-
[g]Ge 37:35 ney you are taking, you will bring my gray head
[h]Ge 44:29,34 down to the grave[b][g] in sorrow.[h]"

The Second Journey to Egypt

43:1 **43** Now the famine was still severe in the land.[i]
[i]Ge 12:10; [2]So when they had eaten all the grain they
41:56-57 had brought from Egypt, their father said to them,
"Go back and buy us a little more food."
[3]But Judah said to him, "The man warned us
solemnly, 'You will not see my face again unless
43:3 your brother is with you.'[j] [4]If you will send our
[j]Ge 42:15; 44:23 brother along with us, we will go down and buy
food for you. [5]But if you will not send him, we
will not go down, because the man said to us,
43:5 'You will not see my face again unless your broth-
[k]Ge 42:15; er is with you.[k]' "
2Sa 3:13 [6]Israel asked, "Why did you bring this trouble

Everything Is Against Me!

GE 42:36

How many times have we felt like joining Jacob in lamenting that the gales of life are blowing unremittingly against us? Jacob focuses on the losses he has experienced and the losses yet to come—one son dead, two more doomed to die. He doesn't know that God is about to unveil amazing news: The "dead" son is alive and wants to reunite the family! Jacob doesn't recognize the strong winds as "trade winds" that are about to blow more joy than he could imagine into his life. We, too, can easily develop a victim mentality and read disaster into every new development in our lives. Even when times are bad, which they certainly are for Jacob as he watches his family starving in the famine, God can bring change as suddenly as, well, as a stiff wind can bring a change in the weather.

[a]34 Or *move about freely* [b]38 Hebrew *Sheol*

on me by telling the man you had another
brother?"
7 They replied, "The man questioned us closely
about ourselves and our family. 'Is your father still
living?'[l] he asked us. 'Do you have another brother?'[m] We simply answered his questions. How
were we to know he would say, 'Bring your brother down here'?"
8 Then Judah said to Israel his father, "Send the
boy along with me and we will go at once, so that
we and you and our children may live and not
die.[n] 9 I myself will guarantee his safety; you can
hold me personally responsible for him. If I do not
bring him back to you and set him here before
you, I will bear the blame before you all my life.[o]
10 As it is, if we had not delayed, we could have
gone and returned twice."
11 Then their father Israel said to them, "If it
must be, then do this: Put some of the best products of the land in your bags and take them down
to the man as a gift[p]—a little balm[q] and a little
honey, some spices[r] and myrrh, some pistachio
nuts and almonds. 12 Take double the amount of
silver with you, for you must return the silver that
was put back into the mouths of your sacks.[s] Perhaps it was a mistake. 13 Take your brother also
and go back to the man at once. 14 And may God
Almighty[a][t] grant you mercy before the man so
that he will let your other brother and Benjamin
come back with you.[u] As for me, if I am bereaved,
I am bereaved."[v]
15 So the men took the gifts and double the
amount of silver, and Benjamin also. They hurried[w] down to Egypt and presented themselves[x] to
Joseph. 16 When Joseph saw Benjamin with them,
he said to the steward of his house,[y] "Take these
men to my house, slaughter an animal and prepare dinner;[z] they are to eat with me at noon."
17 The man did as Joseph told him and took the
men to Joseph's house. 18 Now the men were
frightened[a] when they were taken to his house.
They thought, "We were brought here because of
the silver that was put back into our sacks the first
time. He wants to attack us and overpower us and
seize us as slaves and take our donkeys."
19 So they went up to Joseph's steward and
spoke to him at the entrance to the house.
20 "Please, sir," they said, "we came down here the
first time to buy food.[b] 21 But at the place where
we stopped for the night we opened our sacks and
each of us found his silver—the exact weight—in
the mouth of his sack. So we have brought it back
with us.[c] 22 We have also brought additional silver
with us to buy food. We don't know who put our
silver in our sacks."
23 "It's all right," he said. "Don't be afraid. Your
God, the God of your father, has given you treasure in your sacks;[d] I received your silver." Then
he brought Simeon out to them.[e]

43:7 [l]ver 27 [m]Ge 42:13
43:8 [n]Ge 42:2; Ps 33:18-19
43:9 [o]Ge 42:37; 44:32; Phm 1:18-19
43:11 [p]Ge 32:20; Pr 18:16 [q]Ge 37:25; Jer 8:22 [r]1Ki 10:2
43:12 [s]Ge 42:25
43:14 [t]Ge 17:1; 28:3; 35:11 [u]Ge 42:24 [v]Est 4:16
43:15 [w]Ge 45:9,13 [x]Ge 47:2,7
43:16 [y]Ge 44:1,4, 12 [z]ver 31; Lk 15:23
43:18 [a]Ge 42:35
43:20 [b]Ge 42:3
43:21 [c]ver 15; Ge 42:27,35
43:23 [d]Ge 42:28 [e]Ge 42:24

[a] 14 Hebrew *El-Shaddai*

The most satisfying love is to be loved in spite of being known. Don't we relax into a state of contentment when we no longer have to wear a mask, the function of which is to imply we are more "precious" than we really are sometimes? We can toss the mask and allow ourselves to be seen even when we are unlovable. When we experience being loved in spite of our unlovableness, we've discovered what love is. When we can return that accepting love, we experience a most compelling reciprocity.

And that, incidentally, is the way Jesus loves us. He knows our history, and he knows the sin in that history. Yet because of the unconditional love he feels for his children, when we confess our sin, he forgives us and receives us without condemnation.

—Marilyn Meberg

24 The steward took the men into Joseph's
43:24 [f]ver 16 house,[f] gave them water to wash their feet[g] and
[g]Ge 18:4; provided fodder for their donkeys. 25 They prepared
24:32 their gifts for Joseph's arrival at noon, because
they had heard that they were to eat there.
26 When Joseph came home, they presented to
43:26 him the gifts[h] they had brought into the house,
[h]Mt 2:11 [i]Ge 37:7,10 and they bowed down before him to the ground.[i]
27 He asked them how they were, and then he said,
"How is your aged father you told me about? Is he
43:27 [j]ver 7 still living?"[j]
28 They replied, "Your servant our father is still
alive and well." And they bowed low to pay him
43:28 [k]Ge 37:7 honor.[k]
29 As he looked about and saw his brother Benja-
43:29 min, his own mother's son, he asked, "Is this your
[l]Ge 42:13 [m]Nu 6:25; youngest brother, the one you told me about?"[l] And
Ps 67:1 he said, "God be gracious to you,[m] my son."
30 Deeply moved[n] at the sight of his brother, Joseph
43:30 hurried out and looked for a place to weep. He
[n]Jn 11:33,38 [o]Ge 42:24; went into his private room and wept[o] there.
45:2,14,15; 31 After he had washed his face, he came out
46:29 and, controlling himself,[p] said, "Serve the food."
43:31 32 They served him by himself, the brothers by
[p]Ge 45:1 themselves, and the Egyptians who ate with him
by themselves, because Egyptians could not eat
43:32 [q]Gal 2:12 with Hebrews,[q] for that is detestable to Egyptians.[r]
[r]Ge 46:34; 33 The men had been seated before him in the
Ex 8:26 order of their ages, from the firstborn to the
youngest; and they looked at each other in astonishment. 34 When portions were served to them
43:34 from Joseph's table, Benjamin's portion was five
[s]Ge 37:3; times as much as anyone else's.[s] So they feasted
45:22 and drank freely with him.

A Silver Cup in a Sack

44 Now Joseph gave these instructions to the
steward of his house: "Fill the men's sacks
with as much food as they can carry, and put each
44:1 [t]Ge 42:25 man's silver in the mouth of his sack.[t] 2 Then put
my cup, the silver one, in the mouth of the
youngest one's sack, along with the silver for his
grain." And he did as Joseph said.
3 As morning dawned, the men were sent on
their way with their donkeys. 4 They had not gone
far from the city when Joseph said to his steward,
"Go after those men at once, and when you catch
44:4 up with them, say to them, 'Why have you repaid
[u]Ps 35:12 good with evil?[u] 5 Isn't this the cup my master
44:5 drinks from and also uses for divination?[v] This is
[v]Ge 30:27; a wicked thing you have done.' "
Dt 18:10-14 6 When he caught up with them, he repeated
these words to them. 7 But they said to him, "Why
does my lord say such things? Far be it from your
servants to do anything like that! 8 We even
44:8 brought back to you from the land of Canaan the
[w]Ge 42:25; silver we found inside the mouths of our sacks.[w]
43:21 So why would we steal silver or gold from your
master's house? 9 If any of your servants is found
44:9 to have it, he will die;[x] and the rest of us will
[x]Ge 31:32 become my lord's slaves."

Eating Habits

GE 43:32

The Egyptians eat separately from the Hebrews because Hebrews are deemed ritualistically unclean (the word *detestable* refers to this type of uncleanness) since they don't worship the same gods as the Egyptians. The Egyptians also have certain constraints on what they may eat, and they want to avoid violating various ritual restrictions on food. The situation is similar to the New Testament Jewish restriction requiring separation from Gentiles.

Sibling Unrivals

GE 44:18

Leah and Rachel's children inherited their mothers' rivalry. Just as the two women battled each other for Jacob's love and attention, so also their children live in rancor with each other, maneuvering to find favor with Jacob. Yet Judah (the fourth son of Leah) sets all that aside as he pleads that Benjamin (the only remaining child of Rachel) not be retained as a slave by Joseph. In our families today as well, longstanding rivalries can be set aside, sometimes by just one person being willing to step forward and say, "Let's not be rivals but be riveted together in the bonds of family."

10"Very well, then," he said, "let it be as you say.
Whoever is found to have it will become my slave;
the rest of you will be free from blame."
11Each of them quickly lowered his sack to the
ground and opened it. 12Then the steward proceeded to search, beginning with the oldest and
ending with the youngest. And the cup was found
in Benjamin's sack.[y] 13At this, they tore their
clothes.[z] Then they all loaded their donkeys and
returned to the city.
14Joseph was still in the house when Judah and
his brothers came in, and they threw themselves
to the ground before him.[a] 15Joseph said to them,
"What is this you have done? Don't you know that
a man like me can find things out by divination?[b]"
16"What can we say to my lord?" Judah replied.
"What can we say? How can we prove our innocence? God has uncovered your servants' guilt.
We are now my lord's slaves[c]—we ourselves and
the one who was found to have the cup.[d]"
17But Joseph said, "Far be it from me to do such
a thing! Only the man who was found to have the
cup will become my slave. The rest of you, go
back to your father in peace."
18Then Judah went up to him and said: "Please,
my lord, let your servant speak a word to my lord.
Do not be angry[e] with your servant, though you
are equal to Pharaoh himself. 19My lord asked his
servants, 'Do you have a father or a brother?'[f]
20And we answered, 'We have an aged father, and
there is a young son born to him in his old age.[g]
His brother is dead,[h] and he is the only one of his
mother's sons left, and his father loves him.'[i]
21"Then you said to your servants, 'Bring him
down to me so I can see him for myself.'[j] 22And
we said to my lord, 'The boy cannot leave his
father; if he leaves him, his father will die.'[k] 23But
you told your servants, 'Unless your youngest
brother comes down with you, you will not see
my face again.'[l] 24When we went back to your servant my father, we told him what my lord had
said.
25"Then our father said, 'Go back and buy a little more food.'[m] 26But we said, 'We cannot go
down. Only if our youngest brother is with us will
we go. We cannot see the man's face unless our
youngest brother is with us.'
27"Your servant my father said to us, 'You know
that my wife bore me two sons.[n] 28One of them
went away from me, and I said, "He has surely
been torn to pieces."[o] And I have not seen him
since. 29If you take this one from me too and harm
comes to him, you will bring my gray head down
to the grave[a] in misery.'[p]
30"So now, if the boy is not with us when I go
back to your servant my father and if my father,
whose life is closely bound up with the boy's life,[q]
31sees that the boy isn't there, he will die. Your servants will bring the gray head of our father down

44:12 [y]ver 2
44:13 [z]Ge 37:29; Nu 14:6; 2Sa 1:11
44:14 [a]Ge 37:7, 10
44:15 [b]ver 5; Ge 30:27
44:16 [c]ver 9; Ge 43:18 [d]ver 2
44:18 [e]Ge 18:30; Ex 32:22
44:19 [f]Ge 43:7
44:20 [g]Ge 37:3 [h]Ge 37:33 [i]Ge 42:13
44:21 [j]Ge 42:15
44:22 [k]Ge 37:35
44:23 [l]Ge 43:5
44:25 [m]Ge 43:2
44:27 [n]Ge 46:19
44:28 [o]Ge 37:33
44:29 [p]Ge 42:38
44:30 [q]1Sa 18:1

[a] 29 Hebrew *Sheol*; also in verse 31

to the grave in sorrow. 32Your servant guaranteed
the boy's safety to my father. I said, 'If I do not
bring him back to you, I will bear the blame
44:32 rGe 43:9 before you, my father, all my life!'[r]
33"Now then, please let your servant remain
44:33 sGe 43:18 here as my lord's slave[s] in place of the boy,[t] and
tJn 15:13 let the boy return with his brothers. 34How can I
go back to my father if the boy is not with me?
44:34 No! Do not let me see the misery that would come
uEst 8:6 upon my father."[u]

Joseph Makes Himself Known

45 Then Joseph could no longer control him-
45:1 vGe 43:31 self[v] before all his attendants, and he cried
out, "Have everyone leave my presence!" So there
45:2 was no one with Joseph when he made himself
wGe 29:11 known to his brothers. 2And he wept[w] so loudly
xver 16; that the Egyptians heard him, and Pharaoh's
Ge 46:29 household heard about it.[x]
3Joseph said to his brothers, "I am Joseph! Is
my father still living?"[y] But his brothers were not
45:3 yAc 7:13 able to answer him,[z] because they were terrified
zver 15 at his presence.
4Then Joseph said to his brothers, "Come close
45:4 aGe 37:28 to me." When they had done so, he said, "I am
your brother Joseph, the one you sold into Egypt![a]
45:5 5And now, do not be distressed[b] and do not be
bGe 42:21 angry with yourselves for selling me here,[c]
cGe 42:22 dver 7-8; because it was to save lives that God sent me
Ge 50:20; ahead of you.[d] 6For two years now there has been
Ps 105:17 famine in the land, and for the next five years
there will not be plowing and reaping. 7But God
45:7 sent me ahead of you to preserve for you a rem-
e2Ki 19:4,30, 31; Isa 10:20, nant[e] on earth and to save your lives by a great
21; Mic 4:7; deliverance.[a][f]
Zep 2:7 fEx 15:2; 8"So then, it was not you who sent me here, but
Est 4:14; God. He made me father[g] to Pharaoh, lord of his
Isa 25:9 entire household and ruler of all Egypt.[h] 9Now
hurry back to my father and say to him, 'This is
45:8 gJdg 17:10 what your son Joseph says: God has made me lord
hGe 41:41 of all Egypt. Come down to me; don't delay.[i] 10You
45:9 shall live in the region of Goshen[j] and be near
iGe 43:10 me—you, your children and grandchildren, your
flocks and herds, and all you have. 11I will provide
45:10 jGe 46:28, for you there,[k] because five years of famine are
34; 7:1 still to come. Otherwise you and your household
45:11 and all who belong to you will become destitute.'
kGe 47:12 12"You can see for yourselves, and so can my
brother Benjamin, that it is really I who am speaking to you. 13Tell my father about all the honor
accorded me in Egypt and about everything you
45:13 have seen. And bring my father down here
lAc 7:14 quickly.[l]"
14Then he threw his arms around his brother
Benjamin and wept, and Benjamin embraced him,
45:15 weeping. 15And he kissed[m] all his brothers and
mLk 15:20 nver 3 wept over them. Afterward his brothers talked
with him.[n]
16When the news reached Pharaoh's palace that

[a] 7 Or *save you as a great band of survivors*

Transformed

GE 44:33–45:3

Judah shows how he has been transformed from the brother who was willing to kill Joseph or sell him into slavery and from the son who was willing to lie to his father by telling him his favorite son was dead. Judah is now the brother who is willing to go into slavery to save his brother from such a fate and now the son who cannot bear the thought of having to tell his father he has lost the last of Rachel's children. After Judah's request to take Benjamin's place, Joseph realizes how changed his brothers are. And he breaks into great sobs, revealing his true identity. Judah's sacrificial love provides Joseph with the right moment to be vulnerable as well. That is how vulnerability tends to work: If one person can speak from the heart, the other is likely to respond in kind.

Quarrelsome Ways

GE 45:24

Joseph's farewell admonition to his brothers not to quarrel reveals his recognition that they will be tempted to blame each other for the past. He knows they will now have to face their father with the truth about Joseph and their treatment of him (Ge 45:26–27). Their long-standing deceptive and contentious habits will now have to give way to honesty and forthrightness with their father, which itself might be a cause for arguments between them. The beauty of this story is that God can use even cruel acts like these for his good purposes. The lesson of the story is that dishonorable deeds are not quickly mended nor easily forgotten.

Joseph's brothers had come,[o] Pharaoh and all his
officials were pleased. 17 Pharaoh said to Joseph,
"Tell your brothers, 'Do this: Load your animals
and return to the land of Canaan, 18 and bring your
father and your families back to me. I will give
you the best of the land of Egypt[p] and you can
enjoy the fat of the land.'[q]

19 "You are also directed to tell them, 'Do this:
Take some carts[r] from Egypt for your children and
your wives, and get your father and come. 20 Never mind about your belongings, because the best
of all Egypt will be yours.' "

21 So the sons of Israel did this. Joseph gave
them carts, as Pharaoh had commanded, and he
also gave them provisions for their journey.[s] 22 To
each of them he gave new clothing, but to Benjamin he gave three hundred shekels[a] of silver and
five sets of clothes.[t] 23 And this is what he sent to
his father: ten donkeys loaded with the best things
of Egypt, and ten female donkeys loaded with
grain and bread and other provisions for his journey. 24 Then he sent his brothers away, and as they
were leaving he said to them, "Don't quarrel on
the way!"[u]

25 So they went up out of Egypt and came to
their father Jacob in the land of Canaan. 26 They
told him, "Joseph is still alive! In fact, he is ruler
of all Egypt." Jacob was stunned; he did not
believe them.[v] 27 But when they told him everything Joseph had said to them, and when he saw
the carts[w] Joseph had sent to carry him back, the
spirit of their father Jacob revived. 28 And Israel
said, "I'm convinced! My son Joseph is still alive.
I will go and see him before I die."

Jacob Goes to Egypt

46 So Israel set out with all that was his, and
when he reached Beersheba,[x] he offered
sacrifices to the God of his father Isaac.[y]

2 And God spoke to Israel in a vision at night[z]
and said, "Jacob! Jacob!"

"Here I am,"[a] he replied.

3 "I am God, the God of your father,"[b] he said.
"Do not be afraid to go down to Egypt, for I will
make you into a great nation[c] there.[d] 4 I will go
down to Egypt with you, and I will surely bring
you back again.[e] And Joseph's own hand will
close your eyes.[f]"

5 Then Jacob left Beersheba, and Israel's sons
took their father Jacob and their children and
their wives in the carts[g] that Pharaoh had sent to
transport him. 6 They also took with them their
livestock and the possessions they had acquired
in Canaan, and Jacob and all his offspring went
to Egypt.[h] 7 He took with him to Egypt his sons
and grandsons and his daughters and granddaughters—all his offspring.[i]

45:16 [o]Ac 7:13
45:18 [p]Ge 27:28; 46:34; 47:6, 11,27; Nu 18:12,29 [q]Ps 37:19
45:19 [r]Ge 46:5
45:21 [s]Ge 42:25
45:22 [t]Ge 37:3; 43:34
45:24 [u]Ge 42:21-22
45:26 [v]Ge 44:28
45:27 [w]ver 19
46:1 [x]Ge 21:14; 28:10 [y]Ge 26:24; 28:13; 31:42
46:2 [z]Ge 15:1; Job 33:14-15 [a]Ge 22:1; 31:11
46:3 [b]Ge 28:13 [c]Ge 12:2; Dt 26:5 [d]Ex 1:7
46:4 [e]Ge 28:15; 48:21; Ex 3:8 [f]Ge 50:1,24
46:5 [g]Ge 45:19
46:6 [h]Dt 26:5; Jos 24:4; Ps 105:23; Isa 52:4; Ac 7:15
46:7 [i]Ge 45:10

[a] *22* That is, about 7 1/2 pounds (about 3.5 kilograms)

8These are the names of the sons of Israel[j]
(Jacob and his descendants) who went to Egypt:

Reuben the firstborn of Jacob.
9The sons of Reuben:[k]
Hanoch, Pallu, Hezron and Carmi.
10The sons of Simeon:[l]
Jemuel,[m] Jamin, Ohad, Jakin, Zohar and
Shaul the son of a Canaanite woman.
11The sons of Levi:[n]
Gershon, Kohath and Merari.
12The sons of Judah:[o]
Er, Onan, Shelah, Perez and Zerah (but Er
and Onan had died in the land of Canaan).
The sons of Perez:[p]
Hezron and Hamul.
13The sons of Issachar:[q]
Tola, Puah,[a][r] Jashub[b] and Shimron.
14The sons of Zebulun:[s]
Sered, Elon and Jahleel.
15These were the sons Leah bore to Jacob in
Paddan Aram,[c] besides his daughter Dinah. These
sons and daughters of his were thirty-three in all.

16The sons of Gad:[t]
Zephon,[d][u] Haggi, Shuni, Ezbon, Eri, Arodi
and Areli.
17The sons of Asher:[v]
Imnah, Ishvah, Ishvi and Beriah.
Their sister was Serah.
The sons of Beriah:
Heber and Malkiel.
18These were the children born to Jacob by Zil-
pah,[w] whom Laban had given to his daughter
Leah[x]—sixteen in all.

19The sons of Jacob's wife Rachel:
Joseph and Benjamin.[y] 20In Egypt, Manas-
seh[z] and Ephraim[a] were born to Joseph by
Asenath daughter of Potiphera, priest of
On.[e]
21The sons of Benjamin:[b]
Bela, Beker, Ashbel, Gera, Naaman, Ehi,
Rosh, Muppim, Huppim and Ard.
22These were the sons of Rachel who were born
to Jacob—fourteen in all.

23The son of Dan:
Hushim.
24The sons of Naphtali:
Jahziel, Guni, Jezer and Shillem.
25These were the sons born to Jacob by Bilhah,[c]
whom Laban had given to his daughter Rachel[d]—
seven in all.

26All those who went to Egypt with Jacob—
those who were his direct descendants, not count-

46:8 [j]Ex 1:1; Nu 26:4
46:9 [k]1Ch 5:3
46:10 [l]Ge 29:33; Nu 26:14 [m]Ex 6:15
46:11 [n]Ge 29:34; Nu 3:17
46:12 [o]Ge 29:35 [p]1Ch 2:5; Mt 1:3
46:13 [q]Ge 30:18 [r]1Ch 7:1
46:14 [s]Ge 30:20
46:16 [t]Ge 30:11 [u]Nu 26:15
46:17 [v]Ge 30:13; 1Ch 7:30-31
46:18 [w]Ge 30:10 [x]Ge 29:24
46:19 [y]Ge 44:27
46:20 [z]Ge 41:51 [a]Ge 41:52
46:21 [b]Nu 26:38-41; 1Ch 7:6-12; 8:1
46:25 [c]Ge 30:8 [d]Ge 29:29

[a] *13* Samaritan Pentateuch and Syriac (see also 1 Chron. 7:1); Masoretic Text *Puvah* [b] *13* Samaritan Pentateuch and some Septuagint manuscripts (see also Num. 26:24 and 1 Chron. 7:1); Masoretic Text *Iob* [c] *15* That is, Northwest Mesopotamia [d] *16* Samaritan Pentateuch and Septuagint (see also Num. 26:15); Masoretic Text *Ziphion*
[e] *20* That is, Heliopolis

Wherever we find ourselves employed, whenever we have a job to do, uniform principles should apply that create a balanced life. Our job should be one where our labor produces dignity, self-respect and an attitude of happy diligence. We need to stop looking at work as simply a means of earning a living and start realizing it is one of the elemental ingredients of making a life!

—Luci Swindoll

Detestable Shepherds

GE 46:33–34

Perhaps Joseph's claim that shepherds were detestable referred to shepherds being ritually unclean and therefore unable to participate in religious rites. The word *detestable* can suggest religious avoidance.

Because of this "uncleanness," the Egyptians did not want to live near the Hebrews. Therefore, Joseph wisely puts his family in a somewhat isolated area of Egypt, which also helps to keep them separate and culturally distinct from Egyptians. God, through Joseph, continues to protect and keep a people for himself, separate from the rest of the world's peoples, a nation that will become—and still remains today—a focus of world events.

ing his sons' wives—numbered sixty-six persons.[e]
27 With the two sons[a] who had been born to
Joseph in Egypt, the members of Jacob's family,
which went to Egypt, were seventy[b] in all.[f]

28 Now Jacob sent Judah ahead of him to Joseph
to get directions to Goshen.[g] When they arrived
in the region of Goshen, 29 Joseph had his chariot
made ready and went to Goshen to meet his father
Israel. As soon as Joseph appeared before him, he
threw his arms around his father[c] and wept for a
long time.[h]

30 Israel said to Joseph, "Now I am ready to die,
since I have seen for myself that you are still
alive."

31 Then Joseph said to his brothers and to his
father's household, "I will go up and speak to
Pharaoh and will say to him, 'My brothers and my
father's household, who were living in the land
of Canaan, have come to me.[i] 32 The men are shepherds; they tend livestock, and they have brought
along their flocks and herds and everything they
own.' 33 When Pharaoh calls you in and asks,
'What is your occupation?'[j] 34 you should answer,
'Your servants have tended livestock from our
boyhood on, just as our fathers did.' Then you will
be allowed to settle in the region of Goshen,[k] for
all shepherds are detestable to the Egyptians.[l]"

47

Joseph went and told Pharaoh, "My father
and brothers, with their flocks and herds
and everything they own, have come from the
land of Canaan and are now in Goshen."[m] 2 He
chose five of his brothers and presented them
before Pharaoh.

3 Pharaoh asked the brothers, "What is your
occupation?"[n]

"Your servants are shepherds," they replied to
Pharaoh, "just as our fathers were." 4 They also
said to him, "We have come to live here awhile,[o]
because the famine is severe in Canaan[p] and your
servants' flocks have no pasture. So now, please
let your servants settle in Goshen."[q]

5 Pharaoh said to Joseph, "Your father and your
brothers have come to you, 6 and the land of Egypt
is before you; settle your father and your brothers
in the best part of the land.[r] Let them live in
Goshen. And if you know of any among them
with special ability,[s] put them in charge of my
own livestock."

7 Then Joseph brought his father Jacob in and
presented him before Pharaoh. After Jacob
blessed[d] Pharaoh,[t] 8 Pharaoh asked him, "How old
are you?"

9 And Jacob said to Pharaoh, "The years of my
pilgrimage are a hundred and thirty.[u] My years
have been few and difficult,[v] and they do not
equal the years of the pilgrimage of my fathers.[w]"

46:26 [e]ver 5-7; Ex 1:5; Dt 10:22
46:27 [f]Ac 7:14
46:28 [g]Ge 45:10
46:29 [h]Ge 45:14-15; Lk 15:20
46:31 [i]Ge 47:1
46:33 [j]Ge 47:3
46:34 [k]Ge 45:10 [l]Ge 43:32; Ex 8:26
47:1 [m]Ge 46:31
47:3 [n]Ge 46:33
47:4 [o]Ge 15:13; Dt 26:5 [p]Ge 43:1 [q]Ge 46:34
47:6 [r]Ge 45:18 [s]Ex 18:21,25
47:7 [t]ver 10; 2Sa 14:22
47:9 [u]Ge 25:7 [v]Heb 11:9,13 [w]Ge 35:28

[a] *27* Hebrew; Septuagint *the nine children* [b] *27* Hebrew (see also Exodus 1:5 and footnote); Septuagint (see also Acts 7:14) *seventy-five* [c] *29* Hebrew *around him* [d] *7* Or *greeted*

47:10 10 Then Jacob blessed[a] Pharaoh[x] and went out
[x]ver 7 from his presence.
11 So Joseph settled his father and his brothers
47:11 in Egypt and gave them property in the best part
[y]Ex 1:11; of the land, the district of Rameses,[y] as Pharaoh
12:37 directed. 12 Joseph also provided his father and his
47:12 brothers and all his father's household with food,
[z]Ge 45:11 according to the number of their children.[z]

Joseph and the Famine

13 There was no food, however, in the whole
region because the famine was severe; both Egypt
47:13 and Canaan wasted away because of the famine.[a]
[a]Ge 41:30; 14 Joseph collected all the money that was to be
Ac 7:11 found in Egypt and Canaan in payment for the
grain they were buying, and he brought it to Phar-
47:14 aoh's palace.[b] 15 When the money of the people of
[b]Ge 41:56 Egypt and Canaan was gone, all Egypt came to
47:15 Joseph and said, "Give us food. Why should we
[c]ver 19; die before your eyes?[c] Our money is used up."
Ex 16:3 16 "Then bring your livestock," said Joseph. "I
will sell you food in exchange for your livestock,
since your money is gone." 17 So they brought their
livestock to Joseph, and he gave them food in
47:17 exchange for their horses,[d] their sheep and goats,
[d]Ex 14:9 their cattle and donkeys. And he brought them
through that year with food in exchange for all
their livestock.
18 When that year was over, they came to him
the following year and said, "We cannot hide from
our lord the fact that since our money is gone and
our livestock belongs to you, there is nothing left
for our lord except our bodies and our land.
19 Why should we perish before your eyes—we
and our land as well? Buy us and our land in
exchange for food, and we with our land will be
in bondage to Pharaoh. Give us seed so that we
may live and not die, and that the land may not
become desolate."
20 So Joseph bought all the land in Egypt for
Pharaoh. The Egyptians, one and all, sold their
fields, because the famine was too severe for
them. The land became Pharaoh's, 21 and Joseph
reduced the people to servitude,[b] from one end of
Egypt to the other. 22 However, he did not buy the
land of the priests, because they received a regular allotment from Pharaoh and had food enough
47:22 from the allotment[e] Pharaoh gave them. That is
[e]Dt 14:28-29; why they did not sell their land.
Ezr 7:24 23 Joseph said to the people, "Now that I have
bought you and your land today for Pharaoh, here
is seed for you so you can plant the ground. 24 But
47:24 when the crop comes in, give a fifth[f] of it to Phar-
[f]Ge 41:34 aoh. The other four-fifths you may keep as seed
for the fields and as food for yourselves and your
households and your children."
25 "You have saved our lives," they said. "May

[a] *10* Or *said farewell to* [b] *21* Samaritan Pentateuch and Septuagint (see also Vulgate); Masoretic Text *and he moved the people into the cities*

Annie Sherwood Hawks wrote the words to this song at a time of peace and serenity, overwhelmed by her need and love for the Lord. She was later comforted by the words of her own hymn when her husband died.

I Need Thee Every Hour

I need Thee every hour, most
gracious Lord;
No tender voice like Thine can peace
afford.

I need Thee, O I need Thee;
Every hour I need Thee;
O bless me now, my Savior,
I come to Thee.

I need Thee every hour, stay Thou
nearby;
Temptations lose their power when
Thou art nigh.

I need Thee every hour, in joy or
pain;
Come quickly and abide, or life is in
vain.

I need Thee every hour; teach me
Thy will;
And Thy rich promises in me fulfill.

I need Thee every hour, most Holy
One;
O make me Thine indeed, Thou
blessèd Son.

—Annie Sherwood Hawks (1836-1918)

Home Away From Home

GE 47:27

The Israelites' move to Egypt plays a significant role in their relationship with God. As Joseph acknowledges in Genesis 45:7, God engineers their relocation to preserve them not only from famine but also from the corrupting influence of the Canaanites, whom they have been living among. And they had been a ragtag family, divided among themselves, until the reunion with Joseph forces them into a cohesive unit that faces the guilt of the past and is now ready to press toward the future, together. Through these circumstances God fulfills his promise to Abraham, saving this "remnant" from which he will build a nation.

we find favor in the eyes of our lord;[g] we will be in bondage to Pharaoh."

26 So Joseph established it as a law concerning land in Egypt—still in force today—that a fifth of the produce belongs to Pharaoh. It was only the land of the priests that did not become Pharaoh's.[h]

27 Now the Israelites settled in Egypt in the region of Goshen. They acquired property there and were fruitful and increased greatly in number.[i]

28 Jacob lived in Egypt[j] seventeen years, and the years of his life were a hundred and forty-seven. 29 When the time drew near for Israel to die,[k] he called for his son Joseph and said to him, "If I have found favor in your eyes, put your hand under my thigh[l] and promise that you will show me kindness and faithfulness.[m] Do not bury me in Egypt, 30 but when I rest with my fathers, carry me out of Egypt and bury me where they are buried."[n]

"I will do as you say," he said.

31 "Swear to me,"[o] he said. Then Joseph swore to him,[p] and Israel worshiped as he leaned on the top of his staff.[a][q]

Manasseh and Ephraim

48 Some time later Joseph was told, "Your father is ill." So he took his two sons Manasseh and Ephraim[r] along with him. 2 When Jacob was told, "Your son Joseph has come to you," Israel rallied his strength and sat up on the bed.

3 Jacob said to Joseph, "God Almighty[b] appeared to me at Luz[s] in the land of Canaan, and there he blessed me[t] 4 and said to me, 'I am going to make you fruitful and will increase your numbers.[u] I will make you a community of peoples, and I will give this land as an everlasting possession to your descendants after you.'

5 "Now then, your two sons born to you in Egypt[v] before I came to you here will be reckoned as mine; Ephraim and Manasseh will be mine,[w] just as Reuben and Simeon are mine. 6 Any children born to you after them will be yours; in the territory they inherit they will be reckoned under the names of their brothers. 7 As I was returning from Paddan,[c] to my sorrow Rachel died in the land of Canaan while we were still on the way, a little distance from Ephrath. So I buried her there beside the road to Ephrath" (that is, Bethlehem).[x]

8 When Israel saw the sons of Joseph, he asked, "Who are these?"

9 "They are the sons God has given me here,"[y] Joseph said to his father.

Then Israel said, "Bring them to me so I may bless[z] them."

10 Now Israel's eyes were failing because of old age, and he could hardly see.[a] So Joseph brought

47:25 [g]Ge 32:5
47:26 [h]ver 22
47:27 [i]Ge 17:6; 46:3; Ex 1:7
47:28 [j]Ps 105:23
47:29 [k]Dt 31:14 [l]Ge 24:2 [m]Ge 24:49
47:30 [n]Ge 49:29-32; 50:5,13; Ac 7:15-16
47:31 [o]Ge 21:23 [p]Ge 24:3 [q]Heb 11:21 *fn* 1Ki 1:47
48:1 [r]Ge 41:52
48:3 [s]Ge 28:19 [t]Ge 28:13; 35:9-12
48:4 [u]Ge 17:6
48:5 [v]Ge 41:50-52; 46:20 [w]1Ch 5:1; Jos 14:4
48:7 [x]Ge 35:19
48:9 [y]Ge 33:5 [z]Ge 27:4
48:10 [a]Ge 27:1

[a] 31 Or *Israel bowed down at the head of his bed* [b] 3 Hebrew *El-Shaddai* [c] 7 That is, Northwest Mesopotamia

48:10 his sons close to him, and his father kissed them[b]
[b]Ge 27:27 and embraced them.
11 Israel said to Joseph, "I never expected to see
48:11 your face again, and now God has allowed me to
[c]Ge 50:23; see your children too."[c]
Ps 128:6 12 Then Joseph removed them from Israel's
knees and bowed down with his face to the
ground. 13 And Joseph took both of them, Ephraim
48:13 on his right toward Israel's left hand and Manas-
[d]Ps 110:1 seh on his left toward Israel's right hand,[d] and
brought them close to him. 14 But Israel reached
out his right hand and put it on Ephraim's head,
though he was the younger, and crossing his
48:14 arms, he put his left hand on Manasseh's head,
[e]Ge 41:51 even though Manasseh was the firstborn.[e]
48:15 15 Then he blessed[f] Joseph and said,

[f]Ge 17:1 "May the God before whom my fathers
[g]Ge 49:24 Abraham and Isaac walked,
the God who has been my shepherd[g]
all my life to this day,
16 the Angel who has delivered me from all
harm
48:16 —may he bless these boys.[h]
[h]Heb 11:21 May they be called by my name
[i]Ge 28:13 and the names of my fathers Abraham
and Isaac,[i]
and may they increase greatly
upon the earth."

17 When Joseph saw his father placing his right
48:17 hand on Ephraim's head[j] he was displeased; so he
[j]ver 14 took hold of his father's hand to move it from
Ephraim's head to Manasseh's head. 18 Joseph said
to him, "No, my father, this one is the firstborn;
put your right hand on his head."
19 But his father refused and said, "I know, my
son, I know. He too will become a people, and he
48:19 too will become great.[k] Nevertheless, his younger
[k]Ge 17:20 brother will be greater than he,[l] and his descen-
[l]Ge 25:23 dants will become a group of nations." 20 He
blessed them that day and said,

48:20 "In your[a] name will Israel pronounce
[m]Nu 2:18 this blessing:
[n]Nu 2:20; 'May God make you like Ephraim[m]
Ru 4:11 and Manasseh.[n]' "

48:21 So he put Ephraim ahead of Manasseh.
[o]Ge 26:3; 21 Then Israel said to Joseph, "I am about to die,
46:4 but God will be with you[b][o] and take you[b] back to
[p]Ge 28:13; the land of your[b] fathers.[p] 22 And to you, as one
50:24 who is over your brothers,[q] I give the ridge of
48:22 land[c][r] I took from the Amorites with my sword
[q]Ge 37:8 and my bow."
[r]Jos 24:32;
Jn 4:5

[a] *20* The Hebrew is singular. [b] *21* The Hebrew is plural.
[c] *22* Or *And to you I give one portion more than to your brothers—the portion*

Mixed-Up Blessing

GE 48:13-20

For four generations the younger brother receives the family blessing: Isaac, rather than Ishmael; Jacob, rather than Esau; Joseph, rather than Reuben; and Ephraim, rather than Manasseh. In this way God reminds his people that reliance on custom does not force God's hand. Instead, he will choose whom he will—and often his choice is the individual we humans would not have selected. Blessing is not a right but a privilege, just as grace isn't granted through following legalistic rituals but because of God's unstinting love.

Creation is filled with stunning variety and exquisite beauty. The delicate, intricate and fragile as well as the strong, mighty and powerful testify sweetly to the richness of the Creator. It is crucial that we attend not only to the needs of the human beings that inhabit this earth, but also to the preservation of the countless creatures that contribute to the beauty and balance of our God-given environment. I need to be reminded that "in wisdom" he made them all, and a part of my reverencing him is my reverencing all the earth's creatures: humans, animals, flowers, trees and . . . butterflies.

—Marilyn Meberg

Jacob Blesses His Sons

49 Then Jacob called for his sons and said:
"Gather around so I can tell you what will
happen to you in days to come.[s]

2 "Assemble and listen, sons of Jacob;
listen to your father Israel.[t]

3 "Reuben, you are my firstborn,[u]
my might, the first sign of my strength,[v]
excelling in honor, excelling in power.
4 Turbulent as the waters,[w] you will no longer excel,
for you went up onto your father's bed,
onto my couch and defiled it.[x]

5 "Simeon and Levi are brothers—
their swords[a] are weapons of violence.[y]
6 Let me not enter their council,
let me not join their assembly,[z]
for they have killed men in their anger[a]
and hamstrung oxen as they pleased.
7 Cursed be their anger, so fierce,
and their fury, so cruel!
I will scatter them in Jacob
and disperse them in Israel.[b]

8 "Judah,[b] your brothers will praise you;
your hand will be on the neck of your enemies;
your father's sons will bow down to you.[c]
9 You are a lion's[d] cub, O Judah;[e]
you return from the prey, my son.
Like a lion he crouches and lies down,
like a lioness—who dares to rouse him?
10 The scepter will not depart from Judah,[f]
nor the ruler's staff from between his feet,
until he comes to whom it belongs[c]
and the obedience of the nations is his.[g]
11 He will tether his donkey to a vine,
his colt to the choicest branch;
he will wash his garments in wine,
his robes in the blood of grapes.
12 His eyes will be darker than wine,
his teeth whiter than milk.[d]

13 "Zebulun[h] will live by the seashore
and become a haven for ships;
his border will extend toward Sidon.

14 "Issachar[i] is a rawboned[e] donkey

49:1 [s]Nu 24:14; Jer 23:20
49:2 [t]Ps 34:11
49:3 [u]Ge 29:32 [v]Dt 21:17; Ps 78:51
49:4 [w]Isa 57:20 [x]Ge 35:22; Dt 27:20
49:5 [y]Ge 34:25; Pr 4:17
49:6 [z]Pr 1:15; Eph 5:11 [a]Ge 34:26
49:7 [b]Jos 19:1,9; 21:1-42
49:8 [c]Dt 33:7; 1Ch 5:2
49:9 [d]Nu 24:9; Eze 19:5; Mic 5:8 [e]Rev 5:5
49:10 [f]Nu 24:17, 19; Ps 60:7 [g]Ps 2:9; Isa 42:1,4
49:13 [h]Ge 30:20; Dt 33:18-19; Jos 19:10-11
49:14 [i]Ge 30:18

[a] 5 The meaning of the Hebrew for this word is uncertain. [b] 8 *Judah* sounds like and may be derived from the Hebrew for *praise.* [c] 10 Or *until Shiloh comes*; or *until he comes to whom tribute belongs* [d] 12 Or *will be dull from wine, / his teeth white from milk* [e] 14 Or *strong*

lying down between two saddlebags.[a]
15 When he sees how good is his resting place
and how pleasant is his land,
he will bend his shoulder to the burden
and submit to forced labor.

49:16 [j]Ge 30:6; Dt 33:22; Jdg 18:26-27
16 "Dan[b][j] will provide justice for his people
as one of the tribes of Israel.
49:17 [k]Jdg 18:27
17 Dan[k] will be a serpent by the roadside,
a viper along the path,
that bites the horse's heels
so that its rider tumbles backward.

49:18 [l]Ps 119:166, 174
18 "I look for your deliverance, O LORD.[l]

49:19 [m]Ge 30:11; Dt 33:20; 1Ch 5:18
19 "Gad[c][m] will be attacked by a band of raiders,
but he will attack them at their heels.

49:20 [n]Ge 30:13; Dt 33:24
20 "Asher's[n] food will be rich;
he will provide delicacies fit for a king.

49:21 [o]Ge 30:8; Dt 33:23
21 "Naphtali[o] is a doe set free
that bears beautiful fawns.[d]

49:22 [p]Ge 30:24; Dt 33:13-17
22 "Joseph[p] is a fruitful vine,
a fruitful vine near a spring,
whose branches climb over a wall.[e]
49:23 [q]Ge 37:24
23 With bitterness archers attacked him;
they shot at him with hostility.[q]
49:24 [r]Ps 18:34 [s]Ps 132:2,5; Isa 1:24; 41:10 [t]Isa 28:16
24 But his bow remained steady,
his strong arms[r] stayed[f] limber,
because of the hand of the Mighty One of Jacob,[s]
because of the Shepherd, the Rock of Israel,[t]
49:25 [u]Ge 28:13 [v]Ge 27:28
25 because of your father's God,[u] who helps you,
because of the Almighty,[g] who blesses you
with blessings of the heavens above,
blessings of the deep that lies below,[v]
blessings of the breast and womb.
26 Your father's blessings are greater
than the blessings of the ancient mountains,
49:26 [w]Dt 33:15-16
than[h] the bounty of the age-old hills.
Let all these rest on the head of Joseph,
on the brow of the prince among[i] his brothers.[w]

49:27 [x]Ge 35:18; Jdg 20:12-13
27 "Benjamin[x] is a ravenous wolf;
in the morning he devours the prey,
in the evening he divides the plunder."

[a] 14 Or *campfires* [b] 16 *Dan* here means *he provides justice.* [c] 19 *Gad* can mean *attack* and *band of raiders.* [d] 21 Or *free; / he utters beautiful words* [e] 22 Or *Joseph is a wild colt, / a wild colt near a spring, / a wild donkey on a terraced hill* [f] 23,24 Or *archers will attack . . . will shoot . . . will remain . . . will stay* [g] 25 Hebrew *Shaddai* [h] 26 Or *of my progenitors, / as great as* [i] 26 Or *the one separated from*

The Tribes of Israel

GE 49:28

The Israelites are descended from Jacob's 12 sons, each being the ancestor of the tribe named after him. After Joseph's brothers move to Egypt, their families increase, and they become the people of Israel, literally the "sons of Israel" since Jacob had been renamed Israel when he wrestled with God (Ge 32:28). When the Israelites take possession of the promised land, each tribe is assigned specific territory. The Bible, however, does not always refer to exactly 12 tribes. For example, sometimes Joseph's two sons, Ephraim and Manasseh, are listed as separate tribes, and sometimes Simeon or Levi is not listed. Levi became the priestly line for the Israelites and therefore was seen as distinct from the other tribes, and the tribe of Simeon was eventually absorbed into the tribe of Judah.

Burial Choices

GE 49:29–32

Leah, who competes with her sister, Rachel, for Jacob's attention for much of her life, at last has Jacob's companionship—she is buried with him. Jacob makes it clear that he wants to be buried in the cave that his grandfather Abraham purchased from the Hittites to bury Sarah. This plot of land is God's down payment on his promise to give Abraham's descendants the land of Canaan; so the cave carries the significance of that promise as well as being like the family's "mausoleum." Jacob makes a point of saying that Abraham and Isaac are buried there with their wives, and he wishes to lie next to his wife, Leah, who was already buried in the cave. Rachel is not buried there because she died during childbirth while the family was traveling on a spiritual pilgrimage near Bethlehem (Ge 35:19).

28 All these are the twelve tribes of Israel, and
this is what their father said to them when he
blessed them, giving each the blessing appropriate
to him.

The Death of Jacob

29 Then he gave them these instructions:[y] "I am
about to be gathered to my people.[z] Bury me with
my fathers[a] in the cave in the field of Ephron the
Hittite, 30 the cave in the field of Machpelah,[b] near
Mamre in Canaan, which Abraham bought as a
burial place from Ephron the Hittite, along with
the field.[c] 31 There Abraham[d] and his wife Sarah[e]
were buried, there Isaac and his wife Rebekah[f]
were buried, and there I buried Leah. 32 The field
and the cave in it were bought from the Hittites.[a]"
33 When Jacob had finished giving instructions
to his sons, he drew his feet up into the bed,
breathed his last and was gathered to his people.[g]
50 Joseph threw himself upon his father and
wept over him and kissed him.[h] 2 Then
Joseph directed the physicians in his service to
embalm his father Israel. So the physicians
embalmed him,[i] 3 taking a full forty days, for that
was the time required for embalming. And the
Egyptians mourned for him seventy days.[j]
4 When the days of mourning had passed,
Joseph said to Pharaoh's court, "If I have found
favor in your eyes, speak to Pharaoh for me. Tell
him, 5 'My father made me swear an oath[k] and
said, "I am about to die; bury me in the tomb I
dug for myself[l] in the land of Canaan."[m] Now let
me go up and bury my father; then I will return.' "
6 Pharaoh said, "Go up and bury your father, as
he made you swear to do."
7 So Joseph went up to bury his father. All Pharaoh's
officials accompanied him—the dignitaries
of his court and all the dignitaries of Egypt—
8 besides all the members of Joseph's household
and his brothers and those belonging to his
father's household. Only their children and their
flocks and herds were left in Goshen. 9 Chariots
and horsemen[b] also went up with him. It was a
very large company.
10 When they reached the threshing floor of
Atad, near the Jordan, they lamented loudly and
bitterly;[n] and there Joseph observed a seven-day
period[o] of mourning for his father. 11 When the
Canaanites who lived there saw the mourning at
the threshing floor of Atad, they said, "The Egyptians
are holding a solemn ceremony of mourning."
That is why that place near the Jordan is
called Abel Mizraim.[c]
12 So Jacob's sons did as he had commanded
them: 13 They carried him to the land of Canaan
and buried him in the cave in the field of Machpelah,
near Mamre, which Abraham had bought
as a burial place from Ephron the Hittite, along

49:29 [y]Ge 50:16 [z]Ge 25:8 [a]Ge 15:15; 47:30; 50:13
49:30 [b]Ge 23:9 [c]Ge 23:20
49:31 [d]Ge 25:9 [e]Ge 23:19 [f]Ge 35:29
49:33 [g]ver 29; Ge 25:8; Ac 7:15
50:1 [h]Ge 46:4
50:2 [i]ver 26; 2Ch 16:14
50:3 [j]Ge 37:34; Nu 20:29; Dt 34:8
50:5 [k]Ge 47:31 [l]2Ch 16:14; Isa 22:16 [m]Ge 47:31
50:10 [n]2Sa 1:17; Ac 8:2 [o]1Sa 31:13; Job 2:13

[a] 32 Or *the sons of Heth* [b] 9 Or *charioteers* [c] 11 *Abel Mizraim* means *mourning of the Egyptians.*

with the field.[p] 14 After burying his father, Joseph returned to Egypt, together with his brothers and all the others who had gone with him to bury his father.

Joseph Reassures His Brothers

15 When Joseph's brothers saw that their father was dead, they said, "What if Joseph holds a grudge against us and pays us back for all the wrongs we did to him?"[q] 16 So they sent word to Joseph, saying, "Your father left these instructions before he died: 17 'This is what you are to say to Joseph: I ask you to forgive your brothers the sins and the wrongs they committed in treating you so badly.' Now please forgive the sins of the servants of the God of your father." When their message came to him, Joseph wept.

18 His brothers then came and threw themselves down before him.[r] "We are your slaves,"[s] they said.

19 But Joseph said to them, "Don't be afraid. Am I in the place of God?[t] 20 You intended to harm me,[u] but God intended[v] it for good[w] to accomplish what is now being done, the saving of many lives.[x] 21 So then, don't be afraid. I will provide for you and your children.[y]" And he reassured them and spoke kindly to them.

The Death of Joseph

22 Joseph stayed in Egypt, along with all his father's family. He lived a hundred and ten years[z] 23 and saw the third generation[a] of Ephraim's children. Also the children of Makir[b] son of Manasseh were placed at birth on Joseph's knees.[a]

24 Then Joseph said to his brothers, "I am about to die.[c] But God will surely come to your aid[d] and take you up out of this land to the land[e] he promised on oath to Abraham, Isaac and Jacob."[f] 25 And Joseph made the sons of Israel swear an oath and said, "God will surely come to your aid, and then you must carry my bones up from this place."[g]

26 So Joseph died at the age of a hundred and ten. And after they embalmed him,[h] he was placed in a coffin in Egypt.

50:13 [p]Ge 23:20; Ac 7:16
50:15 [q]Ge 37:28; 42:21-22
50:18 [r]Ge 37:7 [s]Ge 43:18
50:19 [t]Ro 12:19; Heb 10:30
50:20 [u]Ge 37:20 [v]Mic 4:11-12 [w]Ro 8:28 [x]Ge 45:5
50:21 [y]Ge 45:11; 47:12
50:22 [z]Ge 25:7; Jos 24:29
50:23 [a]Job 42:16 [b]Nu 32:39, 40
50:24 [c]Ge 48:21 [d]Ex 3:16-17 [e]Ge 15:14 [f]Ge 12:7; 26:3; 28:13; 35:12
50:25 [g]Ge 47:29-30; Ex 13:19; Jos 24:32; Heb 11:22
50:26 [h]ver 2

A Remembrance

GE 50:24–26

Joseph's deathbed wish that he be buried in the promised land is a statement of his steadfast belief that God will bring his people out of Egypt and back to Canaan. In fact, Joseph leaves as a legacy of that promise his very body! In the hundreds of years during which the Israelites are slaves to the Egyptians, Joseph's embalmed body reminds them that someday they will have their own land. And when that day comes, they will take Joseph's coffin with them and place his body to rest—at last—in that land of milk and honey. And that's exactly what happens (Ex 13:19). So the book of Genesis ends with a reminder that whatever tomorrow holds, even a long day of slavery, that day will end and another day, a day of fulfilled promises, will follow.

[a] *23* That is, were counted as his

Exodus

From slavery to deliverance.

The book of Exodus revolves around the deliverance of God's people from slavery in Egypt and the establishment of God's covenant with them at Sinai. Woven throughout the epic adventures of Exodus are glimpses of women whose lives influenced a nation. Jochebed (Ex 6:20) models the resourcefulness of a mother in crisis as she seeks to save her son from certain death (Ex 2:1-4). Pharaoh's daughter unknowingly becomes a part of Israel's deliverance when she shows compassion to an abandoned baby (Ex 2:5-10). While her husband Moses stands in the limelight of leadership, Zipporah's behind-the-scenes strength provides support for the one God has chosen to lead Israel (Ex 4:18-26).

Exodus traces God's deliverance of his people (Ex 7-14), instilling hope in later generations when troubles overwhelm. We sing and dance for joy with Miriam and Moses after the crossing of the Red Sea (Ex 15:1-21). The establishment of the Sabbath and of the Israelite festivals reveals the benefits of rest and the joy to be found in celebration (Ex 23:10-19). We watch as the Israelites use their creative skills and give sacrificially in order to construct a tent of worship in the Sinai desert (Ex 25-28).

Ultimately the story of Exodus is the story of a relationship—a relationship with a God who never stops working through his people or listening to their prayers. That same God is our God today—ever present, ever faithful, never failing.

Quick Study

Author
Generally thought to be Moses.

Date Written
Probably written during the 1400s B.C., at the time of Israel's wandering in the desert.

Setting
Egypt and the area around Mount Sinai.

Key Passage
Exodus 15:13 "In your unfailing love you will lead the people you have redeemed. In your strength you will guide them to your holy dwelling."

Outline

The Israelites as slaves.
Ex 1

Moses' birth and call to leadership.
Ex 2-4

Israelite misery and the promise of deliverance.
Ex 5:1–6:27

Ten plagues.
Ex 6:28–11:10

The Passover.
Ex 12:1–13:16

Crossing the Red Sea.
Ex 13:17–14:31

A celebration by Moses and Miriam.
Ex 15:1-21

Provision of water and food.
Ex 15:22–17:7

To Mount Sinai.
Ex 17:8–18:27

Moses meets God on the mountain.
Ex 19

God's law.
Ex 20-24

The tabernacle and the priesthood.
Ex 25-31

The golden calf.
Ex 32:1–33:6

The tent of meeting.
Ex 33:7-11

Moses and the glory of the Lord.
Ex 33:12-23

New stone tablets.
Ex 34:1-28

Moses' radiant face.
Ex 34:29-35

Regulations, tabernacle instructions and inspection, tabernacle setup.
Ex 35:1–40:33

God's glory.
Ex 40:34-38

The Women of Exodus

♀ **Puah, Shiphrah**	*Brave midwives who honored God, not Pharaoh.* Ex 1:15-20 (page 268)
♀ **Jochebed**	*Her desperate actions saved her son's life.* Ex 2:1-10; 6:20 (page 329)
♀ **Pharaoh's daughter**	*Defied her father's decree.* Ex 2:5-10 (page 330)
Zipporah	*Moses' Midianite wife.* Ex 2:21-22; 4:18-26
♀ **Miriam**	*Moses' sister; fellow leader; prophetess; poet.* Ex 2:1-9; 15:1-21 (page 401)
♀ **Generous and skilled women**	*Freely gave of themselves and their gifts.* Ex 35:20-29 (page 402)

♀ Denotes a sketch written about this character

Fearing God

EX 1:15–19

As Exodus opens, we see the Egyptian leaders fearful of the growing strength of God's people (Ex 1:9–10). Attempting to thwart this perceived threat against their national security, they take three measures (Ex 1:11–14,15–16,22). The Israelites comply with the rigorous demand for greater productivity, but when the order comes to kill their male babies at birth, the midwives resist.

Midwives may have been childless women who were readily available to help other women deliver. Delivery stool *literally means "two stones." As women gave birth, they sat on two stones, or on a support placed between them. Shiphrah and Puah are probably leaders of groups of midwives. Fearing God, not the king, they either delay their arrival in order to miss the births or they in some way protect the baby boys from death. God blesses their courageous faith by giving them the greatest honor a woman of that culture could experience: families of their own. (See character sketches for Shiphrah and Puah on page 268.)*

The Israelites Oppressed

1 These are the names of the sons of Israel[a] who
went to Egypt with Jacob, each with his family: 2Reuben, Simeon, Levi and Judah; 3Issachar,
Zebulun and Benjamin; 4Dan and Naphtali; Gad
and Asher. 5The descendants of Jacob numbered
seventy[a] in all;[b] Joseph was already in Egypt.
6Now Joseph and all his brothers and all that
generation died,[c] 7but the Israelites were fruitful
and multiplied greatly and became exceedingly
numerous,[d] so that the land was filled with them.
8Then a new king, who did not know about
Joseph, came to power in Egypt. 9"Look," he said
to his people, "the Israelites have become much
too numerous[e] for us. 10Come, we must deal
shrewdly[f] with them or they will become even
more numerous and, if war breaks out, will join
our enemies, fight against us and leave the
country."[g]
11So they put slave masters[h] over them to
oppress them with forced labor,[i] and they built
Pithom and Rameses[j] as store cities[k] for Pharaoh.
12But the more they were oppressed, the more
they multiplied and spread; so the Egyptians came
to dread the Israelites 13and worked them ruthlessly.[l] 14They made their lives bitter with hard
labor in brick and mortar and with all kinds of
work in the fields; in all their hard labor the Egyptians used them ruthlessly.[m]
15The king of Egypt said to the Hebrew midwives, whose names were Shiphrah and Puah,
16"When you help the Hebrew women in childbirth and observe them on the delivery stool, if it
is a boy, kill him; but if it is a girl, let her live."
17The midwives, however, feared[n] God and did not
do what the king of Egypt had told them to do;[o]
they let the boys live. 18Then the king of Egypt
summoned the midwives and asked them, "Why
have you done this? Why have you let the boys
live?"
19The midwives answered Pharaoh, "Hebrew
women are not like Egyptian women; they are
vigorous and give birth before the midwives
arrive."[p]
20So God was kind to the midwives[q] and the
people increased and became even more numerous. 21And because the midwives feared God, he
gave them families[r] of their own.
22Then Pharaoh gave this order to all his people: "Every boy that is born[b] you must throw into
the Nile, but let every girl live."[s]

The Birth of Moses

2 Now a man of the house of Levi married a
Levite woman,[t] 2and she became pregnant and
gave birth to a son. When she saw that he was a

1:1 [a]Ge 46:8
1:5 [b]Ge 46:26
1:6 [c]Ge 50:26
1:7 [d]Ge 46:3; Dt 26:5; Ac 7:17
1:9 [e]Ps 105:24-25
1:10 [f]Ps 83:3 [g]Ac 7:17-19
1:11 [h]Ex 3:7 [i]Ge 15:13; Ex 2:11; 5:4; 6:6-7 [j]Ge 47:11 [k]1Ki 9:19; 2Ch 8:4
1:13 [l]Dt 4:20
1:14 [m]Ex 2:23; 6:9; Nu 20:15; Ps 81:6; Ac 7:19
1:17 [n]ver 21; Pr 16:6 [o]Da 3:16-18; Ac 4:18-20; 5:29
1:19 [p]Jos 2:4-6; 2Sa 17:20
1:20 [q]ver 12; Pr 11:18; Isa 3:10
1:21 [r]1Sa 2:35; 2Sa 7:11,27-29; 1Ki 11:38
1:22 [s]Ac 7:19
2:1 [t]Ex 6:20; Nu 26:59

[a] 5 Masoretic Text (see also Gen. 46:27); Dead Sea Scrolls and Septuagint (see also Acts 7:14 and note at Gen. 46:27) *seventy-five* [b] 22 Masoretic Text; Samaritan Pentateuch, Septuagint and Targums *born to the Hebrews*

2:2 [u]Ac 7:20; Heb 11:23 fine child, she hid him for three months.[u] 3But
when she could hide him no longer, she got a
papyrus basket for him and coated it with tar and
pitch. Then she placed the child in it and put it
among the reeds along the bank of the Nile. 4His
2:4 [v]Ex 15:20; Nu 26:59 sister[v] stood at a distance to see what would happen to him.

5Then Pharaoh's daughter went down to the
2:5 [w]Ex 7:15; 8:20 Nile to bathe, and her attendants were walking
along the river bank.[w] She saw the basket among
the reeds and sent her slave girl to get it. 6She
opened it and saw the baby. He was crying, and
she felt sorry for him. "This is one of the Hebrew
babies," she said.

7Then his sister asked Pharaoh's daughter,
"Shall I go and get one of the Hebrew women to
nurse the baby for you?"

8"Yes, go," she answered. And the girl went and
got the baby's mother. 9Pharaoh's daughter said
to her, "Take this baby and nurse him for me, and
I will pay you." So the woman took the baby and
nursed him. 10When the child grew older, she took
him to Pharaoh's daughter and he became her
son. She named him Moses,[a] saying, "I drew him
out of the water."

Moses Flees to Midian

11One day, after Moses had grown up, he went
2:11 [x]Ac 7:23; Heb 11:24-26 out to where his own people[x] were and watched
them at their hard labor. He saw an Egyptian beat-
ing a Hebrew, one of his own people. 12Glancing
this way and that and seeing no one, he killed the
Egyptian and hid him in the sand. 13The next day
he went out and saw two Hebrews fighting. He
asked the one in the wrong, "Why are you hitting
2:13 [y]Ac 7:26 your fellow Hebrew?"[y]

14The man said, "Who made you ruler and judge
2:14 [z]Ac 7:27* over us?[z] Are you thinking of killing me as you
killed the Egyptian?" Then Moses was afraid and
thought, "What I did must have become known."

15When Pharaoh heard of this, he tried to kill
2:15 [a]Ac 7:29; Heb 11:27 Moses, but Moses fled from Pharaoh and went to
live in Midian,[a] where he sat down by a well.
16Now a priest of Midian[b] had seven daughters, and
2:16 [b]Ex 3:1 [c]Ge 24:11 they came to draw water[c] and fill the troughs to
water their father's flock. 17Some shepherds came
along and drove them away, but Moses got up and
2:17 [d]Ge 29:10 came to their rescue and watered their flock.[d]

18When the girls returned to Reuel[e] their father,
2:18 [e]Nu 10:29 he asked them, "Why have you returned so early
today?"

19They answered, "An Egyptian rescued us from
the shepherds. He even drew water for us and
watered the flock."

20"And where is he?" he asked his daughters.
"Why did you leave him? Invite him to have
2:20 [f]Ge 31:54 something to eat."[f]

21Moses agreed to stay with the man, who gave
2:21 [g]Ex 18:2 his daughter Zipporah[g] to Moses in marriage.

[a] 10 *Moses* sounds like the Hebrew for *draw out.*

A Special Child

EX 2:2-3

Sensing that their child is special (see Ac 7:20; Heb 11:23), Moses' mother, Jochebed, and father, Amram (Ex 6:20), are determined to protect him from death, regardless of the king's orders. Instead of fear leading to inertia, their faith leads them to action. In an attempt to ensure that her child is delivered into the hands of someone who will care for him, Jochebed makes a basket boat out of papyrus. This ten-foot-tall reed flourished along the Nile River. The reed's interior was used for making papyrus paper, and it could also be woven into a basket. Jochebed uses tar and pitch to make the vessel seaworthy, places her precious baby in it, then floats it along the riverbank among the reeds. She is, perhaps, hoping that the women from the royal palace who bathe there will take pity on her little son. (See character sketch for Pharaoh's daughter on page 330.)

A Dramatic Turn

EX 2:24

In Exodus 2:24 the story of the Israelites begins its dramatic turn from oppression, fear and slavery in Egypt to a miraculous deliverance by God. God's intervention in their plight is more than an act of compassion. It is also an act of faithfulness. God had made promises to Israel's patriarchs—to Abraham (Ge 12:1-3; 15:18-21; 17:3-8), to Isaac (Ge 17:21; 26:24) and to Jacob (Ge 35:10-12). The time has come for God to do what he has vowed.

The text says God "remembered his covenant." That does not mean that God had forgotten his promises and now, suddenly, recalls them. His timetable for fulfilling his promises is perfect. During the time of their oppression, God had multiplied his people. Now he will make them into a nation, give them a land of their own and bless them. Just as in our lives, God sees everything (Pr 5:21) and keeps his promises. Yet he is not bound to any timetable we set, but only to his own perfect timing.

22Zipporah gave birth to a son, and Moses named
him Gershom,[a] saying, "I have become an alien[h]
in a foreign land."
23During that long period,[i] the king of Egypt
died. The Israelites groaned in their slavery and
cried out, and their cry[j] for help because of their
slavery went up to God. 24God heard their groaning and he remembered his covenant[k] with Abraham, with Isaac and with Jacob. 25So God looked
on the Israelites and was concerned[l] about them.

Moses and the Burning Bush

3 Now Moses was tending the flock of Jethro[m]
his father-in-law, the priest of Midian, and he
led the flock to the far side of the desert and came
to Horeb,[n] the mountain[o] of God. 2There the angel
of the LORD[p] appeared to him in flames of fire from
within a bush.[q] Moses saw that though the bush
was on fire it did not burn up. 3So Moses thought,
"I will go over and see this strange sight—why the
bush does not burn up."
4When the LORD saw that he had gone over to
look, God called to him from within the bush,
"Moses! Moses!"
And Moses said, "Here I am."
5"Do not come any closer," God said. "Take off
your sandals, for the place where you are standing
is holy ground."[r] 6Then he said, "I am the God of
your father, the God of Abraham, the God of Isaac
and the God of Jacob."[s] At this, Moses hid his face,
because he was afraid to look at God.
7The LORD said, "I have indeed seen the misery
of my people in Egypt. I have heard them crying
out because of their slave drivers, and I am concerned[t] about their suffering. 8So I have come
down[u] to rescue them from the hand of the Egyptians and to bring them up out of that land into a
good and spacious land, a land flowing with milk
and honey[v]—the home of the Canaanites, Hittites,
Amorites, Perizzites, Hivites and Jebusites.[w] 9And
now the cry of the Israelites has reached me, and
I have seen the way the Egyptians are oppressing[x]
them. 10So now, go. I am sending you to Pharaoh
to bring my people the Israelites out of Egypt."[y]
11But Moses said to God, "Who am I,[z] that I
should go to Pharaoh and bring the Israelites out
of Egypt?"
12And God said, "I will be with you.[a] And this
will be the sign to you that it is I who have sent
you: When you have brought the people out of
Egypt, you[b] will worship God on this mountain."
13Moses said to God, "Suppose I go to the Israelites and say to them, 'The God of your fathers
has sent me to you,' and they ask me, 'What is his
name?' Then what shall I tell them?"
14God said to Moses, "I AM WHO I AM.[c] This is
what you are to say to the Israelites: 'I AM[b] has
sent me to you.' "

[a] 22 *Gershom* sounds like the Hebrew for *an alien there.*
[b] 12 The Hebrew is plural. [c] 14 Or *I WILL BE WHAT I WILL BE*

2:22 [h]Ex 18:3-4; Heb 11:13
2:23 [i]Ac 7:30 [j]Ex 3:7,9; Dt 26:7; Jas 5:4
2:24 [k]Ex 6:5; Ps 105:10,42
2:25 [l]Ex 3:7; 4:31
3:1 [m]Ex 2:18 [n]1Ki 19:8 [o]Ex 18:5
3:2 [p]Ge 16:7 [q]Dt 33:16; Mk 12:26; Ac 7:30
3:5 [r]Ge 28:17; Jos 5:15; Ac 7:33*
3:6 [s]Ex 4:5; Mt 22:32*; Mk 12:26*; Lk 20:37*; Ac 7:32*
3:7 [t]Ex 2:25
3:8 [u]Ge 50:24 [v]ver 17; Ex 13:5; Dt 1:25 [w]Ge 15:18-21
3:9 [x]Ex 1:14; 2:23
3:10 [y]Mic 6:4
3:11 [z]Ex 6:12,30; 1Sa 18:18
3:12 [a]Ge 31:3; Jos 1:5; Ro 8:31
3:14 [b]Ex 6:2-3; Jn 8:58; Heb 13:8

3:15 15 God also said to Moses, "Say to the Israelites,
[c]Ps 135:13; 'The LORD,[a] the God of your fathers—the God of
Hos 12:5 Abraham, the God of Isaac and the God of Jacob—
has sent me to you.' This is my name[c] forever, the
name by which I am to be remembered from gen-
3:16 eration to generation.
[d]Ex 4:29 16 "Go, assemble the elders[d] of Israel and say to
them, 'The LORD, the God of your fathers—the
God of Abraham, Isaac and Jacob—appeared to
me and said: I have watched over you and have
seen what has been done to you in Egypt. 17 And I
3:17 have promised to bring you up out of your mis-
[e]Ge 15:16; ery in Egypt[e] into the land of the Canaanites, Hit-
Jos 24:11 tites, Amorites, Perizzites, Hivites and Jebusites—
3:18 a land flowing with milk and honey.'
[f]Ex 4:1,8,31 18 "The elders of Israel will listen[f] to you. Then
[g]Ex 5:1,3 you and the elders are to go to the king of Egypt
and say to him, 'The LORD, the God of the
Hebrews, has met with us. Let us take a three-day
journey into the desert to offer sacrifices[g] to the
3:19 LORD our God.' 19 But I know that the king of Egypt
[h]Ex 4:21; 5:2 will not let you go unless a mighty hand[h] compels
3:20 him. 20 So I will stretch out my hand[i] and strike
[i]Ex 6:1,6; 9:15 the Egyptians with all the wonders[j] that I will per-
[j]Dt 6:22; form among them. After that, he will let you go.[k]
Ne 9:10; Ac 7:36 21 "And I will make the Egyptians favorably dis-
[k]Ex 12:31-33 posed[l] toward this people, so that when you leave
3:21 you will not go empty-handed.[m] 22 Every woman is
[l]Ex 12:36 to ask her neighbor and any woman living in her
[m]Ps 105:37 house for articles of silver and gold[n] and for cloth-
3:22 ing, which you will put on your sons and daugh-
[n]Ex 11:2 ters. And so you will plunder[o] the Egyptians."
[o]Eze 39:10

Signs for Moses

4:1 **4** Moses answered, "What if they do not believe
[p]Ex 3:18; me or listen[p] to me and say, 'The LORD did not
6:30 appear to you'?"
2 Then the LORD said to him, "What is that in
4:2 your hand?"
[q]ver 17,20 "A staff,"[q] he replied.
3 The LORD said, "Throw it on the ground."
Moses threw it on the ground and it became a
snake, and he ran from it. 4 Then the LORD said to
him, "Reach out your hand and take it by the
tail." So Moses reached out and took hold of the
snake and it turned back into a staff in his hand.
4:5 5 "This," said the LORD, "is so that they may
[r]Ex 19:9 believe[r] that the LORD, the God of their fathers—
the God of Abraham, the God of Isaac and the God
of Jacob—has appeared to you."
6 Then the LORD said, "Put your hand inside your
4:6 cloak." So Moses put his hand into his cloak, and
[s]Nu 12:10; when he took it out, it was leprous,[b] like snow.[s]
2Ki 5:1,27 7 "Now put it back into your cloak," he said. So
Moses put his hand back into his cloak, and when

[a] *15* The Hebrew for *LORD* sounds like and may be derived from the Hebrew for *I AM* in verse 14. [b] *6* The Hebrew word was used for various diseases affecting the skin—not necessarily leprosy.

God Keeps His Promises

EX 3:21–22

God lets Moses know in detail that he will be able *to accomplish the task to which he is being called—delivering the* Hebrew nation out of Egypt. *When Moses was younger, his own people had rejected him* (Ex 2:14), *but now the Hebrew elders will listen to him* (Ex 3:18). *Egypt's pharaoh will be forced to comply with the demand to release Israel* (Ex 3:19–20). Furthermore, God *says his people will leave Egypt rich because of the silver, gold and clothing that the Egyptians will give to them.*

***It seems almost impossible to* think that the Egyptians, *who do not want to lose the work force* Israel represents, will send them *away laden with wealth; but it happens just as* God says it will (Ex 12:35–36). *Even more amazing, this promise fulfills a pledge* God made to Abraham in Genesis 15:12–14! *We need never fear.* God always keeps his promises (2Co 1:20).**

No Partial Obedience

EX 4:24–26

Exodus 4:24–26 is difficult to understand. What can we make of it? God demands full obedience from this man he has commissioned for leadership. In a parallel situation, when David moves the ark (2Sa 6:1–11), a life is lost because of partial obedience. Here in Exodus Moses almost dies because he has neglected God's command to circumcise one (or both) of his sons (Ge 17:10). Leaders are held to a strict standard of judgment (Jas 3:1).

What about Zipporah? Was she grieved by her husband's lack of obedience or was she jolted into action by the thought of her husband's death? We do not know, but she took up the knife to do Moses' job. "Surely you are a bridegroom of blood" may be a statement of anger or it may be a statement of faith by which she expresses some understanding of redemption—that life is kept safe only through the shedding of blood.

he took it out, it was restored,[t] like the rest of his
flesh.
8Then the LORD said, "If they do not believe you
or pay attention to the first miraculous sign, they
may believe the second. 9But if they do not believe
these two signs or listen to you, take some water
from the Nile and pour it on the dry ground. The
water you take from the river will become blood[u]
on the ground."
10Moses said to the LORD, "O Lord, I have never
been eloquent, neither in the past nor since you
have spoken to your servant. I am slow of speech
and tongue."[v]
11The LORD said to him, "Who gave man his
mouth? Who makes him deaf or mute? Who gives
him sight or makes him blind?[w] Is it not I, the
LORD? 12Now go; I will help you speak and will
teach you what to say."[x]
13But Moses said, "O Lord, please send someone else to do it."
14Then the LORD's anger burned against Moses
and he said, "What about your brother, Aaron the
Levite? I know he can speak well. He is already
on his way to meet[y] you, and his heart will be
glad when he sees you. 15You shall speak to him
and put words in his mouth;[z] I will help both of
you speak and will teach you what to do. 16He
will speak to the people for you, and it will be as
if he were your mouth[a] and as if you were God to
him. 17But take this staff[b] in your hand so you can
perform miraculous signs[c] with it."

Moses Returns to Egypt

18Then Moses went back to Jethro his father-in-
law and said to him, "Let me go back to my own
people in Egypt to see if any of them are still alive."
Jethro said, "Go, and I wish you well."
19Now the LORD had said to Moses in Midian,
"Go back to Egypt, for all the men who wanted to
kill[d] you are dead."[e] 20So Moses took his wife and
sons, put them on a donkey and started back to
Egypt. And he took the staff[f] of God in his hand.
21The LORD said to Moses, "When you return to
Egypt, see that you perform before Pharaoh all the
wonders[g] I have given you the power to do. But I
will harden his heart[h] so that he will not let the
people go. 22Then say to Pharaoh, 'This is what
the LORD says: Israel is my firstborn son,[i] 23and I
told you, "Let my son go,[j] so he may worship me."
But you refused to let him go; so I will kill your
firstborn son.' "[k]
24At a lodging place on the way, the LORD met
⌊Moses,⌋[a] and was about to kill[l] him. 25But Zipporah took a flint knife, cut off her son's foreskin[m]
and touched ⌊Moses'⌋ feet with it.[b] "Surely you are
a bridegroom of blood to me," she said. 26So the
LORD let him alone. (At that time she said "bridegroom of blood," referring to circumcision.)

4:7 [t]Nu 12:13-15; Dt 32:39; 2Ki 5:14; Mt 8:3
4:9 [u]Ex 7:17-21
4:10 [v]Ex 6:12; Jer 1:6
4:11 [w]Ps 94:9; Mt 11:5
4:12 [x]Isa 50:4; Jer 1:9; Mt 10:19-20; Mk 13:11; Lk 12:12; 21:14-15
4:14 [y]ver 27
4:15 [z]Nu 23:5,12,16
4:16 [a]Ex 7:1-2
4:17 [b]ver 2 [c]Ex 7:9-21
4:19 [d]Ex 2:15 [e]Ex 2:23
4:20 [f]Ex 17:9; Nu 20:8-9,11
4:21 [g]Ex 3:19,20 [h]Ex 7:3,13; 9:12,35; 14:4,8; Dt 2:30; Isa 63:17; Jn 12:40; Ro 9:18
4:22 [i]Isa 63:16; 64:8; Jer 31:9; Hos 11:1; Ro 9:4
4:23 [j]Ex 5:1; 7:16 [k]Ex 11:5; 12:12,29
4:24 [l]Nu 22:22
4:25 [m]Ge 17:14; Jos 5:2,3

[a] 24 Or ⌊*Moses' son*⌋; Hebrew *him* [b] 25 Or *and drew near* ⌊*Moses'*⌋ *feet*

4:27 27The LORD said to Aaron, "Go into the desert to
nEx 3:1 meet Moses." So he met Moses at the mountain[n]
over 14 of God and kissed[o] him. 28Then Moses told Aaron
4:28 everything the LORD had sent him to say,[p] and also
pver 8-9,16 about all the miraculous signs he had commanded him to perform.
4:29 29Moses and Aaron brought together all the el-
qEx 3:16 ders[q] of the Israelites, 30and Aaron told them
everything the LORD had said to Moses. He also
performed the signs before the people, 31and they
4:31 believed.[r] And when they heard that the LORD was
rver 8; Ex 3:18 concerned[s] about them and had seen their misery,
sEx 2:25 they bowed down and worshiped.

Bricks Without Straw

5 Afterward Moses and Aaron went to Pharaoh
and said, "This is what the LORD, the God of
Israel, says: 'Let my people go, so that they may
5:1 tEx 3:18 hold a festival[t] to me in the desert.' "
2Pharaoh said, "Who is the LORD,[u] that I should
5:2 obey him and let Israel go? I do not know the LORD
u2Ki 18:35; Job 21:15 and I will not let Israel go."[v]
vEx 3:19 3Then they said, "The God of the Hebrews has
met with us. Now let us take a three-day journey
5:3 into the desert to offer sacrifices to the LORD our
wEx 3:18 God, or he may strike us with plagues[w] or with
the sword."
4But the king of Egypt said, "Moses and Aaron,
5:4 why are you taking the people away from their
xEx 1:11 labor?[x] Get back to your work!" 5Then Pharaoh
said, "Look, the people of the land are now numer-
5:5 yEx 1:7,9 ous,[y] and you are stopping them from working."
6That same day Pharaoh gave this order to the
slave drivers and foremen in charge of the people:
7"You are no longer to supply the people with
straw for making bricks; let them go and gather
their own straw. 8But require them to make the
same number of bricks as before; don't reduce the
quota. They are lazy; that is why they are crying
out, 'Let us go and sacrifice to our God.' 9Make the
work harder for the men so that they keep working and pay no attention to lies."
10Then the slave drivers and the foremen went
out and said to the people, "This is what Pharaoh
says: 'I will not give you any more straw. 11Go and
get your own straw wherever you can find it, but
your work will not be reduced at all.' " 12So the
people scattered all over Egypt to gather stubble to
use for straw. 13The slave drivers kept pressing
them, saying, "Complete the work required of you
for each day, just as when you had straw." 14The
5:14 Israelite foremen appointed by Pharaoh's slave
zIsa 10:24 drivers were beaten[z] and were asked, "Why didn't
you meet your quota of bricks yesterday or today,
as before?"
15Then the Israelite foremen went and appealed
to Pharaoh: "Why have you treated your servants
this way? 16Your servants are given no straw, yet
we are told, 'Make bricks!' Your servants are being
beaten, but the fault is with your own people."
17Pharaoh said, "Lazy, that's what you are—

Making Bricks

EX 5:6-9

Many believe that Moses was born under the reign of the Egyptian pharaoh Thutmose I (1526-1512 B.C.). This king's daughter Hatshepsut may have been the princess who discovered Moses in the reeds of the Nile. When Moses returned to Egypt at the age of 80, Amunhotep II was likely the pharaoh. The empire was steadily expanding and many new buildings were being erected.

The pyramids and temples were made of granite, limestone and sandstone, but the Egyptians used bricks as standard materials for most other buildings. Brick making dates back to the time of the Babylonians (3500 B.C.). Egyptian brick was made of clay and sand mixed with water, then shaped by hand or poured into molds. Straw was added to make the bricks more durable. Most bricks were sun dried.

One site, which may or may not be tied to Hebrew slavery, shows three forms of brick in one building. The first layer contains brick with straw; the second layer, only stubble; and the third layer, no straw or stubble.

God, the "LORD"

EX 6:2

This is not the first time that God is called "LORD" (*Yahweh*) in the Scriptures (Ge 4:26). But now he connects this name with special aspects of his relationship with Israel—his covenant (Ex 6:4), his hearing the groans of the Israelites (Ex 6:5), his great deliverance of the nation (Ex 6:6), and his taking them as his special people (Ex 6:7). As God Almighty (Ge 17:1–2), he has promised to keep his covenant and to bless Israel, but the name "LORD" also speaks of God's faithfulness and intimate love for his people. Furthermore, the name Yahweh literally means "I AM WHO I AM" (Ex 3:14). Therefore, we know that the covenant-keeping Lord is also the eternal God, the One who always was, the One who will forever be and the One who is present with us in a way that no other being can be.

lazy![a] That is why you keep saying, 'Let us go and
sacrifice to the LORD.' [18]Now get to work. You will
not be given any straw, yet you must produce
your full quota of bricks."
[19]The Israelite foremen realized they were in
trouble when they were told, "You are not to reduce
the number of bricks required of you for each day."
[20]When they left Pharaoh, they found Moses and
Aaron waiting to meet them, [21]and they said, "May
the LORD look upon you and judge you! You have
made us a stench[b] to Pharaoh and his officials and
have put a sword in their hand to kill us."[c]

God Promises Deliverance

[22]Moses returned to the LORD and said, "O Lord,
why have you brought trouble upon this people?[d]
Is this why you sent me? [23]Ever since I went to
Pharaoh to speak in your name, he has brought
trouble upon this people, and you have not rescued[e] your people at all."

6 Then the LORD said to Moses, "Now you will
see what I will do to Pharaoh: Because of my
mighty hand[f] he will let them go;[g] because of my
mighty hand he will drive them out of his
country."[h]
[2]God also said to Moses, "I am the LORD. [3]I
appeared to Abraham, to Isaac and to Jacob as
God Almighty,[a][i] but by my name[j] the LORD[b][k] I did
not make myself known to them.[c] [4]I also established my covenant[l] with them to give them the
land of Canaan, where they lived as aliens.[m]
[5]Moreover, I have heard the groaning[n] of the Israelites, whom the Egyptians are enslaving, and I
have remembered my covenant.
[6]"Therefore, say to the Israelites: 'I am the LORD,
and I will bring you out from under the yoke of
the Egyptians. I will free you from being slaves to
them, and I will redeem[o] you with an outstretched
arm[p] and with mighty acts of judgment. [7]I will
take you as my own people, and I will be your
God.[q] Then you will know[r] that I am the LORD
your God, who brought you out from under the
yoke of the Egyptians. [8]And I will bring you to the
land[s] I swore with uplifted hand[t] to give to Abraham, to Isaac and to Jacob.[u] I will give it to you as
a possession. I am the LORD.' "
[9]Moses reported this to the Israelites, but they
did not listen to him because of their discouragement and cruel bondage.
[10]Then the LORD said to Moses, [11]"Go, tell Pharaoh king of Egypt to let the Israelites go out of his
country."
[12]But Moses said to the LORD, "If the Israelites
will not listen to me, why would Pharaoh listen
to me, since I speak with faltering lips[d]?"[v]

[a] 3 Hebrew *El-Shaddai* [b] 3 See note at Exodus 3:15.
[c] 3 Or *Almighty, and by my name the LORD did I not let myself be known to them?* [d] 12 Hebrew *I am uncircumcised of lips*; also in verse 30

5:17 [a]ver 8
5:21 [b]Ge 34:30 [c]Ex 14:11
5:22 [d]Nu 11:11
5:23 [e]Jer 4:10
6:1 [f]Ex 3:19 [g]Ex 3:20 [h]Ex 12:31, 33,39
6:3 [i]Ge 17:1 [j]Ps 68:4; 83:18; Isa 52:6 [k]Ex 3:14
6:4 [l]Ge 15:18 [m]Ge 28:4,13
6:5 [n]Ex 2:23
6:6 [o]Dt 7:8; 1Ch 17:21 [p]Dt 26:8
6:7 [q]Dt 4:20; 2Sa 7:24 [r]Ex 16:12; Isa 41:20
6:8 [s]Ge 15:18; 26:3 [t]Ge 14:22 [u]Ps 136:21-22
6:12 [v]ver 30; Ex 4:10; Jer 1:6

Family Record of Moses and Aaron

13 Now the LORD spoke to Moses and Aaron about the Israelites and Pharaoh king of Egypt, and he commanded them to bring the Israelites out of Egypt.

14 These were the heads of their families[a]:[w]

The sons of Reuben the firstborn son of Israel were Hanoch and Pallu, Hezron and Carmi. These were the clans of Reuben.

15 The sons of Simeon[x] were Jemuel, Jamin, Ohad, Jakin, Zohar and Shaul the son of a Canaanite woman. These were the clans of Simeon.

16 These were the names of the sons of Levi according to their records: Gershon,[y] Kohath and Merari.[z] Levi lived 137 years.

17 The sons of Gershon, by clans, were Libni and Shimei.[a]

18 The sons of Kohath were Amram, Izhar, Hebron and Uzziel.[b] Kohath lived 133 years.

19 The sons of Merari were Mahli and Mushi.[c]

These were the clans of Levi according to their records.

20 Amram married his father's sister Jochebed, who bore him Aaron and Moses.[d] Amram lived 137 years.

21 The sons of Izhar[e] were Korah, Nepheg and Zicri.

22 The sons of Uzziel were Mishael, Elzaphan[f] and Sithri.

23 Aaron married Elisheba, daughter of Amminadab[g] and sister of Nahshon, and she bore him Nadab and Abihu,[h] Eleazar[i] and Ithamar.[j]

24 The sons of Korah[k] were Assir, Elkanah and Abiasaph. These were the Korahite clans.

25 Eleazar son of Aaron married one of the daughters of Putiel, and she bore him Phinehas.[l]

These were the heads of the Levite families, clan by clan.

26 It was this same Aaron and Moses to whom the LORD said, "Bring the Israelites out of Egypt by their divisions."[m] 27 They were the ones who spoke to Pharaoh king of Egypt about bringing the Israelites out of Egypt. It was the same Moses and Aaron.

Aaron to Speak for Moses

28 Now when the LORD spoke to Moses in Egypt, 29 he said to him, "I am the LORD.[n] Tell Pharaoh king of Egypt everything I tell you."

30 But Moses said to the LORD, "Since I speak with faltering lips,[o] why would Pharaoh listen to me?"

6:14 [w]Ge 46:9
6:15 [x]Ge 46:10; 1Ch 4:24
6:16 [y]Ge 46:11 [z]Nu 3:17
6:17 [a]1Ch 6:17
6:18 [b]1Ch 6:2,18
6:19 [c]Nu 33:20-33; 1Ch 6:19; 23:21
6:20 [d]Ex 2:1-2; Nu 26:59
6:21 [e]1Ch 6:38
6:22 [f]Lev 10:4; Nu 3:30
6:23 [g]Ru 4:19,20 [h]Lev 10:1 [i]Nu 3:2,32 [j]Nu 26:60
6:24 [k]Nu 26:11
6:25 [l]Nu 25:7,11; Jos 24:33; Ps 106:30
6:26 [m]Ex 7:4; 12:17,41,51
6:29 [n]ver 11; Ex 7:2
6:30 [o]ver 12; Ex 4:10

[a] *14* The Hebrew for *families* here and in verse 25 refers to units larger than clans.

The only way to meet *affliction* is to pass through it solemnly, slowly, with humility and faith, *as the Israelites passed through the sea.* Then its very *waves of misery* will divide, and *become to us a wall,* on the right side and on the left, until the *gulf narrows before our eyes,* and we land safe on the opposite shore.

—Dinah Maria Mulock Craik (1826-1887)

7 Then the LORD said to Moses, "See, I have made
you like God[p] to Pharaoh, and your brother
Aaron will be your prophet. 2You are to say everything I command you, and your brother Aaron is
to tell Pharaoh to let the Israelites go out of his
country. 3But I will harden Pharaoh's heart,[q] and
though I multiply my miraculous signs and wonders in Egypt, 4he will not listen[r] to you. Then I
will lay my hand on Egypt and with mighty acts of
judgment[s] I will bring out my divisions, my people
the Israelites. 5And the Egyptians will know that I
am the LORD[t] when I stretch out my hand[u] against
Egypt and bring the Israelites out of it."
6Moses and Aaron did just as the LORD commanded[v] them. 7Moses was eighty years old[w] and
Aaron eighty-three when they spoke to Pharaoh.

Aaron's Staff Becomes a Snake

8The LORD said to Moses and Aaron, 9"When
Pharaoh says to you, 'Perform a miracle,[x]' then
say to Aaron, 'Take your staff and throw it down
before Pharaoh,' and it will become a snake."[y]
10So Moses and Aaron went to Pharaoh and did
just as the LORD commanded. Aaron threw his staff
down in front of Pharaoh and his officials, and it
became a snake. 11Pharaoh then summoned wise
men and sorcerers, and the Egyptian magicians[z]
also did the same things by their secret arts:[a]
12Each one threw down his staff and it became a
snake. But Aaron's staff swallowed up their staffs.
13Yet Pharaoh's heart[b] became hard and he would
not listen to them, just as the LORD had said.

The Plague of Blood

14Then the LORD said to Moses, "Pharaoh's heart
is unyielding;[c] he refuses to let the people go. 15Go
to Pharaoh in the morning as he goes out to the
water. Wait on the bank of the Nile to meet him,
and take in your hand the staff that was changed
into a snake. 16Then say to him, 'The LORD, the
God of the Hebrews, has sent me to say to you:
Let my people go, so that they may worship[d] me
in the desert. But until now you have not listened.
17This is what the LORD says: By this you will
know that I am the LORD:[e] With the staff that is in
my hand I will strike the water of the Nile, and it
will be changed into blood.[f] 18The fish in the Nile
will die, and the river will stink; the Egyptians
will not be able to drink its water.' "[g]
19The LORD said to Moses, "Tell Aaron, 'Take
your staff and stretch out your hand[h] over the
waters of Egypt—over the streams and canals, over
the ponds and all the reservoirs'—and they will
turn to blood. Blood will be everywhere in Egypt,
even in the wooden buckets and stone jars."
20Moses and Aaron did just as the LORD had
commanded. He raised his staff in the presence of
Pharaoh and his officials and struck the water of
the Nile,[i] and all the water was changed into
blood.[j] 21The fish in the Nile died, and the river

7:1 [p]Ex 4:16
7:3 [q]Ex 4:21; 11:9
7:4 [r]Ex 11:9 [s]Ex 3:20; 6:6
7:5 [t]ver 17; Ex 8:19,22 [u]Ex 3:20
7:6 [v]ver 2
7:7 [w]Dt 31:2; 34:7; Ac 7:23,30
7:9 [x]Isa 7:11; Jn 2:18 [y]Ex 4:2-5
7:11 [z]Ge 41:8; 2Ti 3:8 [a]ver 22; Ex 8:7,18
7:13 [b]Ex 4:21
7:14 [c]Ex 8:15,32; 10:1,20,27
7:16 [d]Ex 3:18; 5:1,3
7:17 [e]Ex 5:2 [f]Ex 4:9; Rev 11:6; 16:4
7:18 [g]ver 21,24
7:19 [h]Ex 8:5-6,16; 9:22; 10:12, 21; 14:21
7:20 [i]Ex 17:5 [j]Ps 78:44; 105:29

Hardened Hearts

EX 7:3

We see in God's words in Exodus 7:3 the interplay that exists between the free will of humans and the sovereignty of God. God twice predicts that he will harden Pharaoh's heart (Ex 4:21; 7:3). As the story plays itself out, however, we see six times when Pharaoh chooses to harden his own heart (Ex 7:13-14,22; 8:15,19,32; 9:7). Only after the sixth plague does the Bible say that God hardened Pharaoh's heart (Ex 9:12). We again read that Pharaoh hardened his own heart in Exodus 9:34. As the story continues, God does the hardening (Ex 10:1,20,27; 11:10; 14:4,8). The warning to us is clear: Repeated, stubborn disobedience charts a course of life that can become virtually irreversible, a path that God may also use as a means of active judgment in our lives.

smelled so bad that the Egyptians could not drink
its water. Blood was everywhere in Egypt.
22But the Egyptian magicians did the same
7:22 [k]ver 11 things by their secret arts,[k] and Pharaoh's heart
became hard; he would not listen to Moses and
Aaron, just as the LORD had said. 23Instead, he
turned and went into his palace, and did not take
even this to heart. 24And all the Egyptians dug
along the Nile to get drinking water, because they
could not drink the water of the river.

The Plague of Frogs

25Seven days passed after the LORD struck the Nile.
8 1Then the LORD said to Moses, "Go to Pharaoh
and say to him, 'This is what the LORD says:
8:1 [l]Ex 3:12,18; 4:23 Let my people go, so that they may worship[l] me.
2If you refuse to let them go, I will plague your
whole country with frogs. 3The Nile will teem
with frogs. They will come up into your palace
and your bedroom and onto your bed, into the
8:3 [m]Ex 10:6 houses of your officials and on your people,[m] and
into your ovens and kneading troughs. 4The frogs
will go up on you and your people and all your
officials.' "
5Then the LORD said to Moses, "Tell Aaron,
8:5 [n]Ex 7:19 'Stretch out your hand with your staff[n] over the
streams and canals and ponds, and make frogs
come up on the land of Egypt.' "
8:6 [o]Ps 78:45; 105:30 6So Aaron stretched out his hand over the
waters of Egypt, and the frogs[o] came up and covered the land. 7But the magicians did the same
8:7 [p]Ex 7:11 things by their secret arts;[p] they also made frogs
come up on the land of Egypt.
8:8 [q]ver 28; Ex 9:28; 10:17 8Pharaoh summoned Moses and Aaron and
said, "Pray[q] to the LORD to take the frogs away
from me and my people, and I will let your people
[r]ver 25 go to offer sacrifices[r] to the LORD."
9Moses said to Pharaoh, "I leave to you the hon-
or of setting the time for me to pray for you and
your officials and your people that you and your
houses may be rid of the frogs, except for those
that remain in the Nile."
10"Tomorrow," Pharaoh said.
Moses replied, "It will be as you say, so that you
8:10 [s]Ex 9:14; Dt 4:35; 33:26; 2Sa 7:22; 1Ch 17:20; Ps 86:8; Isa 46:9; Jer 10:6 may know there is no one like the LORD our God.[s]
11The frogs will leave you and your houses, your
officials and your people; they will remain only
in the Nile."
12After Moses and Aaron left Pharaoh, Moses
cried out to the LORD about the frogs he had
brought on Pharaoh. 13And the LORD did what
Moses asked. The frogs died in the houses, in the
courtyards and in the fields. 14They were piled
into heaps, and the land reeked of them. 15But
when Pharaoh saw that there was relief, he hard-
8:15 [t]Ex 7:14 ened his heart[t] and would not listen to Moses and
Aaron, just as the LORD had said.

The Plague of Gnats

16Then the LORD said to Moses, "Tell Aaron,

Masters of the Occult

EX 7:22

How did the Egyptian magicians imitate the first two plagues (Ex 7:22; 8:7)? *Although some believe that they took advantage of natural phenomena, perhaps a better explanation for these events is that the magicians used demonic powers to perform these supernatural acts. Egyptian idolatry, with its multiple gods and goddesses, opened the door to the demonic world, and its priests and magicians became masters of the occult. The power of demons can be manifested in supernatural events (Ac 16:16). However, this demonic power is limited. In the second plague, when Pharaoh can no longer tolerate frogs overrunning the land, he turns to Moses, not his magicians, to take them away (Ex 8:8). In the third plague, the magicians attempt to produce gnats from dust, but they completely fail. At this point (Ex 8:18–19), they recognize that Moses is empowered by a God greater than any of the gods of Egypt.*

Set Apart

EX 8:22-23

Beginning with the fourth plague, God begins to protect his people from the effects of the disasters overtaking Egypt. A *careful examination of the story reveals that God protects his people from the plagues in some cases* (Ex 9:6,25-26; 10:23; 11:7); *but in other cases, whether he does so is not clearly stated in the text* (Ex 9:8-12; 10:4-6). Even if the *Israelites were not protected from all of the plagues, they were clearly protected from the most destructive, severe ones.* God *declares his reason for this in* Exodus 8:22-23. This visible distinction *is not only a statement of God's presence and power on behalf of his people to deliver them but also a statement of judgment against the Egyptians.* Throughout Scripture, God calls his people to *be distinctive in lifestyle and promises to distinguish them with blessings and protection.* For other *clear statements of this principle and the impact it has on a watching world, see* Exodus 19:5-6; Deuteronomy 7:6; 10:15-22; Philippians 1:27-28; 1 Peter 2:9-12; 3:13-16.

'Stretch out your staff and strike the dust of the
ground,' and throughout the land of Egypt the dust
will become gnats." 17 They did this, and when Aaron stretched out his hand with the staff and struck
the dust of the ground, gnats[u] came upon men and
animals. All the dust throughout the land of Egypt
became gnats. 18 But when the magicians[v] tried to
produce gnats by their secret arts,[w] they could not.
And the gnats were on men and animals.
19 The magicians said to Pharaoh, "This is the
finger[x] of God." But Pharaoh's heart was hard and
he would not listen, just as the LORD had said.

The Plague of Flies

20 Then the LORD said to Moses, "Get up early in
the morning[y] and confront Pharaoh as he goes to
the water and say to him, 'This is what the LORD
says: Let my people go, so that they may worship[z]
me. 21 If you do not let my people go, I will send
swarms of flies on you and your officials, on your
people and into your houses. The houses of the
Egyptians will be full of flies, and even the ground
where they are.
22 " 'But on that day I will deal differently with
the land of Goshen, where my people live;[a] no
swarms of flies will be there, so that you will
know[b] that I, the LORD, am in this land. 23 I will
make a distinction[a] between my people and your
people. This miraculous sign will occur tomorrow.' "
24 And the LORD did this. Dense swarms of flies
poured into Pharaoh's palace and into the houses
of his officials, and throughout Egypt the land was
ruined by the flies.[c]
25 Then Pharaoh summoned[d] Moses and Aaron
and said, "Go, sacrifice to your God here in the
land."
26 But Moses said, "That would not be right. The
sacrifices we offer the LORD our God would be
detestable to the Egyptians.[e] And if we offer sacrifices that are detestable in their eyes, will they
not stone us? 27 We must take a three-day journey
into the desert to offer sacrifices[f] to the LORD our
God, as he commands us."
28 Pharaoh said, "I will let you go to offer sacrifices to the LORD your God in the desert, but you
must not go very far. Now pray[g] for me."
29 Moses answered, "As soon as I leave you, I
will pray to the LORD, and tomorrow the flies will
leave Pharaoh and his officials and his people.
Only be sure that Pharaoh does not act deceitfully[h] again by not letting the people go to offer sacrifices to the LORD."
30 Then Moses left Pharaoh and prayed to the
LORD,[i] 31 and the LORD did what Moses asked: The
flies left Pharaoh and his officials and his people;
not a fly remained. 32 But this time also Pharaoh
hardened his heart[j] and would not let the people go.

8:17 [u]Ps 105:31
8:18 [v]Ex 9:11; Da 5:8 [w]Ex 7:11
8:19 [x]Ex 7:5; 10:7; Ps 8:3; Lk 11:20
8:20 [y]Ex 7:15; 9:13 [z]ver 1; Ex 3:18
8:22 [a]Ex 9:4,6, 26; 10:23; 11:7 [b]Ex 7:5; 9:29
8:24 [c]Ps 78:45; 105:31
8:25 [d]ver 8; Ex 9:27
8:26 [e]Ge 43:32; 46:34
8:27 [f]Ex 3:18
8:28 [g]ver 8; Ex 9:28; 1Ki 13:6
8:29 [h]ver 15
8:30 [i]ver 12
8:32 [j]ver 8,15; Ex 4:21

[a] *23* Septuagint and Vulgate; Hebrew *will put a deliverance*

The Plague on Livestock

9 Then the LORD said to Moses, “Go to Pharaoh
and say to him, ‘This is what the LORD, the God
of the Hebrews, says: “Let my people go, so that
9:1 [k]Ex 8:1 they may worship[k] me.” [2]If you refuse to let them
go and continue to hold them back, [3]the hand[l] of
9:3 [l]Ex 7:4 the LORD will bring a terrible plague on your livestock in the field—on your horses and donkeys and
camels and on your cattle and sheep and goats.
9:4 [4]But the LORD will make a distinction between the
[m]ver 26; livestock of Israel and that of Egypt,[m] so that no
Ex 8:22 animal belonging to the Israelites will die.’ ”
[5]The LORD set a time and said, “Tomorrow the
LORD will do this in the land.” [6]And the next day
9:6 [n]ver 19-21; the LORD did it: All the livestock[n] of the Egyptians
Ex 11:5 [o]Ps 78:48-50 died,[o] but not one animal belonging to the Israelites died. [7]Pharaoh sent men to investigate and
found that not even one of the animals of the Isra-
9:7 elites had died. Yet his heart was unyielding and
[p]Ex 7:14; 8:32 he would not let the people go.[p]

The Plague of Boils

[8]Then the LORD said to Moses and Aaron, “Take
handfuls of soot from a furnace and have Moses
toss it into the air in the presence of Pharaoh. [9]It
will become fine dust over the whole land of
9:9 [q]Dt 28:27, Egypt, and festering boils[q] will break out on men
35; Rev 16:2 and animals throughout the land.”
[10]So they took soot from a furnace and stood
before Pharaoh. Moses tossed it into the air, and
9:11 festering boils broke out on men and animals.
[r]Ex 8:18 [11]The magicians[r] could not stand before Moses
because of the boils that were on them and on all
9:12 the Egyptians. [12]But the LORD hardened Pharaoh’s
[s]Ex 4:21 hearts[s] and he would not listen to Moses and Aaron, just as the LORD had said to Moses.

The Plague of Hail

[13]Then the LORD said to Moses, “Get up early in
the morning, confront Pharaoh and say to him,
9:13 ‘This is what the LORD, the God of the Hebrews,
[t]Ex 8:20 says: Let my people go, so that they may worship[t]
me, [14]or this time I will send the full force of my
9:14 plagues against you and against your officials and
[u]Ex 8:10 your people, so you may know[u] that there is no
[v]2Sa 7:22; 1Ch 17:20; one like[v] me in all the earth. [15]For by now I could
Ps 86:8; have stretched out my hand and struck you and
Isa 46:9; Jer 10:6 your people[w] with a plague that would have
wiped you off the earth. [16]But I have raised you
9:15 [w]Ex 3:20 up[a] for this very purpose,[x] that I might show you
my power[y] and that my name might be pro-
9:16 [x]Pr 16:4 claimed in all the earth. [17]You still set yourself
[y]Ro 9:17* against my people and will not let them go.
9:18 [18]Therefore, at this time tomorrow I will send the
[z]ver 23 worst hailstorm[z] that has ever fallen on Egypt,
[a]ver 24 from the day it was founded till now.[a] [19]Give an
order now to bring your livestock and everything
you have in the field to a place of shelter, because

[a] 16 Or *have spared you*

A Holy Demonstration

EX 9:13-16

These verses reveal that God’s desire is not so much to destroy Pharaoh as to demonstrate his power and majesty to, and through, him. He has chosen to spare him through the first six plagues, giving Pharaoh every opportunity to repent. But even though Pharaoh does not respond personally to this message, God still uses this pharaoh to make his own name known.

The same is true in the world today. God’s patience in waiting to judge is meant to bring us to repentance (2Pe 3:9) so that we might know him personally. He uses the rebellion and rejection of unbelieving people to display his glory (Ro 9:17-24). And through the words of Paul to the Philippians, God reminds us that everyone—whether humble and obedient or proud and rebellious—will one day bow on their knees before his son Jesus Christ (Php 2:9-10).

A Horrific Hailstorm

EX 9:20,24

The severity of this hailstorm surpassed all previously recorded storms (Ex 9:24). In our own time, hail has occasionally accumulated to more than a foot deep. Because this was a supernatural storm, the hail likely exceeded that depth. The Exodus account emphasizes the destructiveness of this storm, but it also shows the kindness of God. He wants the Egyptians to protect their livestock (Ex 9:19), and some of the officials believe and heed this warning. Can we assume that the Egyptians who fear "the word of the LORD" (Ex 9:20) are true believers? There is no way to know. Likewise, people today can act on the principles and wisdom of Scripture in terms of relationships, marriage or business but still not put their trust in Jesus Christ. The wisdom of God's Word makes life more manageable for all who heed it. But its ultimate purpose is much greater than that: to bring us to personal salvation.

the hail will fall on every man and animal that
has not been brought in and is still out in the
field, and they will die.' "

20 Those officials of Pharaoh who feared[b] the
word of the LORD hurried to bring their slaves and
their livestock inside. 21 But those who ignored the
word of the LORD left their slaves and livestock in
the field.

22 Then the LORD said to Moses, "Stretch out
your hand toward the sky so that hail will fall all
over Egypt—on men and animals and on everything growing in the fields of Egypt." 23 When
Moses stretched out his staff toward the sky, the
LORD sent thunder[c] and hail,[d] and lightning
flashed down to the ground. So the LORD rained
hail on the land of Egypt; 24 hail fell and lightning
flashed back and forth. It was the worst storm in
all the land of Egypt since it had become a nation.
25 Throughout Egypt hail struck everything in the
fields—both men and animals; it beat down
everything growing in the fields and stripped
every tree.[e] 26 The only place it did not hail was
the land of Goshen,[f] where the Israelites were.[g]

27 Then Pharaoh summoned Moses and Aaron.
"This time I have sinned,"[h] he said to them. "The
LORD is in the right,[i] and I and my people are in
the wrong. 28 Pray[j] to the LORD, for we have had
enough thunder and hail. I will let you go;[k] you
don't have to stay any longer."

29 Moses replied, "When I have gone out of the
city, I will spread out my hands[l] in prayer to the
LORD. The thunder will stop and there will be no
more hail, so you may know that the earth[m] is the
LORD's. 30 But I know that you and your officials
still do not fear the LORD God."

31 (The flax and barley[n] were destroyed, since
the barley had headed and the flax was in bloom.
32 The wheat and spelt, however, were not
destroyed, because they ripen later.)

33 Then Moses left Pharaoh and went out of the
city. He spread out his hands toward the LORD; the
thunder and hail stopped, and the rain no longer
poured down on the land. 34 When Pharaoh saw
that the rain and hail and thunder had stopped,
he sinned again: He and his officials hardened
their hearts. 35 So Pharaoh's heart[o] was hard and
he would not let the Israelites go, just as the LORD
had said through Moses.

The Plague of Locusts

10 Then the LORD said to Moses, "Go to Pharaoh, for I have hardened his heart[p] and the
hearts of his officials so that I may perform these
miraculous signs[q] of mine among them 2 that you
may tell your children[r] and grandchildren how I
dealt harshly with the Egyptians and how I performed my signs among them, and that you may
know that I am the LORD."

3 So Moses and Aaron went to Pharaoh and
said to him, "This is what the LORD, the God of
the Hebrews, says: 'How long will you refuse to

9:20 [b]Pr 13:13
9:23 [c]Ps 18:13 [d]Jos 10:11; Ps 78:47; 105:32; Isa 30:30; Eze 38:22; Rev 8:7; 16:21
9:25 [e]Ps 105:32-33
9:26 [f]ver 4 [g]Ex 8:22; 10:23; 11:7; 12:13
9:27 [h]Ex 10:16 [i]2Ch 12:6; Ps 129:4; La 1:18
9:28 [j]Ex 10:17 [k]Ex 8:8
9:29 [l]1Ki 8:22,38; Ps 143:6; Isa 1:15 [m]Ex 19:5; Ps 24:1; 1Co 10:26
9:31 [n]Ru 1:22; 2:23
9:35 [o]Ex 4:21
10:1 [p]Ex 4:21 [q]Ex 7:3
10:2 [r]Ex 12:26-27; 13:8,14; Dt 4:9; Ps 44:1; 78:4,5; Joel 1:3

10:3 humble[s] yourself before me? Let my people go,
[s]1Ki 21:29; so that they may worship me. 4If you refuse to
Jas 4:10; let them go, I will bring locusts[t] into your coun-
1Pe 5:6 10:4 try tomorrow. 5They will cover the face of the
[t]Rev 9:3 ground so that it cannot be seen. They will
10:5 devour what little you have left[u] after the hail,
[u]Ex 9:32; including every tree that is growing in your
Joel 1:4 fields. 6They will fill your houses and those of
all your officials and all the Egyptians—something neither your fathers nor your forefathers
have ever seen from the day they settled in this
land till now.' " Then Moses turned and left
Pharaoh.
10:7 7Pharaoh's officials said to him, "How long will
[v]Ex 23:33; this man be a snare[v] to us? Let the people go, so
Jos 23:13; 1Sa 18:21; that they may worship the LORD their God. Do you
Ecc 7:26 not yet realize that Egypt is ruined?"[w]
[w]Ex 8:19 8Then Moses and Aaron were brought back to
10:8 Pharaoh. "Go, worship[x] the LORD your God," he
[x]Ex 8:8 said. "But just who will be going?"
9Moses answered, "We will go with our young
and old, with our sons and daughters, and with
our flocks and herds, because we are to celebrate
a festival to the LORD."
10Pharaoh said, "The LORD be with you—if I let
you go, along with your women and children!
Clearly you are bent on evil.[a] 11No! Have only the
men go; and worship the LORD, since that's what
you have been asking for." Then Moses and Aaron were driven out of Pharaoh's presence.
10:12 12And the LORD said to Moses, "Stretch out your
[y]Ex 7:19 hand[y] over Egypt so that locusts will swarm over
the land and devour everything growing in the
fields, everything left by the hail."
13So Moses stretched out his staff over Egypt,
and the LORD made an east wind blow across the
land all that day and all that night. By morning
10:13 the wind had brought the locusts;[z] 14they invaded
[z]Ps 105:34 all Egypt and settled down in every area of the
10:14 country in great numbers. Never before had there
[a]Ps 78:46; Joel 2:1-11, been such a plague of locusts,[a] nor will there ever
25 be again. 15They covered all the ground until it
10:15 was black. They devoured[b] all that was left after
[b]ver 5; the hail—everything growing in the fields and the
Ps 105:34-35 fruit on the trees. Nothing green remained on tree
or plant in all the land of Egypt.
16Pharaoh quickly summoned Moses and Aaron
10:16 and said, "I have sinned[c] against the LORD your
[c]Ex 9:27 God and against you. 17Now forgive my sin once
10:17 more and pray[d] to the LORD your God to take this
[d]Ex 8:8 deadly plague away from me."
18Moses then left Pharaoh and prayed to the
10:18 LORD.[e] 19And the LORD changed the wind to a very
[e]Ex 8:30 strong west wind, which caught up the locusts
10:20 and carried them into the Red Sea.[b] Not a locust
[f]Ex 4:21; was left anywhere in Egypt. 20But the LORD hard-
11:10 ened Pharaoh's heart,[f] and he would not let the
Israelites go.

[a] 10 Or *Be careful, trouble is in store for you!* [b] 19 Hebrew *Yam Suph*; that is, Sea of Reeds

Pharaoh Resists

EX 10:9-11

Pharaoh refuses Moses' request to take the Hebrew women and children into the desert to worship along with the men. For one thing, from his perspective only men participate fully in worship. But more important to the king, he is fearful they will not return; and with the economic destruction the plagues have brought on Egypt, he does not want to further deplete his kingdom's wealth and lose the assets represented by this slave-people. They will play, he assumes, an essential role in rebuilding his devastated economy. Therefore he attempts to bargain with Moses and keep the men's families in Egypt. Moses stands firm against Pharaoh's scheme, and, in the process, he reveals to us a deeper spiritual principle as well. God desires to see entire families growing in true faith and calls families to stand firm together to nurture and protect the spiritual life of the home (Dt 6:4-9; Pr 4:1-4).

God's Power

EX 11:10

The plagues bring economic disaster to Egypt, but, more significant, God uses them to communicate that the gods the Egyptians trust are not truly gods (Ex 12:12). The bull god Apis, the goddess Isis and the ram god Khnum are associated with the power and blessing of the Nile River. The Nile is called the bloodstream of Osiris, the god of earth and vegetation. The first plague undermines the supposed authority of these deities, and each subsequent plague communicates a similar message. Heqt, the goddess of birth, has a frog's head. Ra, the sun god, is represented by the fly. Hathor is a goddess with a cow's head. Nut controls the sky, and Sekhmet is thought to protect against diseases and boils. The tenth plague, with its death of the firstborn, also has enormous spiritual implications. The Egyptians believe the pharaoh and his firstborn son are gods. Every god the Egyptians trust is being overpowered. Piece by piece God is dismantling the false beliefs and hopes of the most powerful nation on earth and showing his power as the true God through a nation of displaced slaves.

The Plague of Darkness

21Then the LORD said to Moses, "Stretch out your 10:21
hand toward the sky so that darkness[g] will spread [g]Dt 28:29
over Egypt—darkness that can be felt." 22So Moses
stretched out his hand toward the sky, and total 10:22
darkness[h] covered all Egypt for three days. 23No [h]Ps 105:28;
one could see anyone else or leave his place for Rev 16:10
three days. Yet all the Israelites had light in the 10:23
places where they lived.[i] [i]Ex 8:22
24Then Pharaoh summoned Moses and said,
"Go, worship the LORD. Even your women and
children[j] may go with you; only leave your flocks 10:24
and herds behind." [j]ver 8-10
25But Moses said, "You must allow us to have
sacrifices and burnt offerings to present to the
LORD our God. 26Our livestock too must go with
us; not a hoof is to be left behind. We have to use
some of them in worshiping the LORD our God,
and until we get there we will not know what we
are to use to worship the LORD."
27But the LORD hardened Pharaoh's heart,[k] and 10:27
he was not willing to let them go. 28Pharaoh said [k]ver 20;
to Moses, "Get out of my sight! Make sure you do Ex 4:21
not appear before me again! The day you see my
face you will die."
29"Just as you say," Moses replied, "I will never 10:29
appear[l] before you again." [l]Heb 11:27

The Plague on the Firstborn

11 Now the LORD had said to Moses, "I will
bring one more plague on Pharaoh and on
Egypt. After that, he will let you go from here, and
when he does, he will drive you out completely.
2Tell the people that men and women alike are to
ask their neighbors for articles of silver and 11:2
gold."[m] 3(The LORD made the Egyptians favorably [m]Ex 3:21,22
disposed toward the people, and Moses himself
was highly regarded[n] in Egypt by Pharaoh's offi- 11:3
cials and by the people.) [n]Dt 34:11
4So Moses said, "This is what the LORD says:
'About midnight[o] I will go throughout Egypt. 11:4
5Every firstborn[p] son in Egypt will die, from the [o]Ex 12:29
firstborn son of Pharaoh, who sits on the throne, 11:5
to the firstborn son of the slave girl, who is at her [p]Ex 4:23;
hand mill, and all the firstborn of the cattle as Ps 78:51
well. 6There will be loud wailing[q] throughout 11:6
Egypt—worse than there has ever been or ever [q]Ex 12:30
will be again. 7But among the Israelites not a dog
will bark at any man or animal.' Then you will 11:7
know that the LORD makes a distinction[r] between [r]Ex 8:22
Egypt and Israel. 8All these officials of yours will
come to me, bowing down before me and saying,
'Go,[s] you and all the people who follow you!' 11:8
After that I will leave." Then Moses, hot with [s]Ex 12:31-33
anger, left Pharaoh.
9The LORD had said to Moses, "Pharaoh will 11:9
refuse to listen[t] to you—so that my wonders may [t]Ex 7:4
be multiplied in Egypt." 10Moses and Aaron performed all these wonders before Pharaoh, but the

LORD hardened Pharaoh's heart,[u] and he would
not let the Israelites go out of his country.

The Passover

12 The LORD said to Moses and Aaron in Egypt,
2"This month is to be for you the first
month,[v] the first month of your year. 3Tell the
whole community of Israel that on the tenth day
of this month each man is to take a lamb[a] for his
family, one for each household. 4If any household
is too small for a whole lamb, they must share one
with their nearest neighbor, having taken into
account the number of people there are. You are to
determine the amount of lamb needed in accordance with what each person will eat. 5The animals you choose must be year-old males without
defect,[w] and you may take them from the sheep
or the goats. 6Take care of them until the fourteenth day of the month,[x] when all the people of
the community of Israel must slaughter them at
twilight.[y] 7Then they are to take some of the blood
and put it on the sides and tops of the doorframes
of the houses where they eat the lambs. 8That
same night[z] they are to eat the meat roasted[a] over
the fire, along with bitter herbs,[b] and bread made
without yeast.[c] 9Do not eat the meat raw or
cooked in water, but roast it over the fire—head,
legs and inner parts. 10Do not leave any of it till
morning;[d] if some is left till morning, you must
burn it. 11This is how you are to eat it: with your
cloak tucked into your belt, your sandals on your
feet and your staff in your hand. Eat it in haste;[e] it
is the LORD's Passover.[f]

12"On that same night I will pass through[g] Egypt
and strike down every firstborn—both men and
animals—and I will bring judgment on all the
gods[h] of Egypt. I am the LORD.[i] 13The blood will
be a sign for you on the houses where you are;
and when I see the blood, I will pass over you. No
destructive plague will touch you when I strike
Egypt.

14"This is a day you are to commemorate;[j] for
the generations to come you shall celebrate it as a
festival to the LORD—a lasting ordinance.[k] 15For
seven days you are to eat bread made without
yeast.[l] On the first day remove the yeast from your
houses, for whoever eats anything with yeast in it
from the first day through the seventh must be cut
off[m] from Israel. 16On the first day hold a sacred
assembly, and another one on the seventh day. Do
no work at all on these days, except to prepare
food for everyone to eat—that is all you may do.

17"Celebrate the Feast of Unleavened Bread,
because it was on this very day that I brought
your divisions out of Egypt.[n] Celebrate this day as
a lasting ordinance for the generations to come.
18In the first month[o] you are to eat bread made
without yeast, from the evening of the fourteenth
day until the evening of the twenty-first day. 19For

11:10 [u]Ex 4:21; 10:20,27
12:2 [v]Ex 13:4; Dt 16:1
12:5 [w]Lev 22:18-21; Heb 9:14
12:6 [x]Lev 23:5; Nu 9:1-3,5,11 [y]Ex 16:12; Dt 16:4,6
12:8 [z]Ex 34:25; Nu 9:12 [a]Dt 16:7 [b]Nu 9:11 [c]Dt 16:3-4; 1Co 5:8
12:10 [d]Ex 23:18; 34:25
12:11 [e]Dt 16:3 [f]ver 13,21,27,43; Dt 16:1
12:12 [g]Ex 11:4; Am 5:17 [h]Nu 33:4 [i]Ex 6:2
12:14 [j]Ex 13:9 [k]ver 17,24; Ex 13:5,10; 2Ki 23:21
12:15 [l]Ex 13:6-7; 23:15; 34:18; Lev 23:6; Dt 16:3 [m]Ge 17:14; Nu 9:13
12:17 [n]ver 41; Ex 13:3
12:18 [o]ver 2; Lev 23:5-8; Nu 28:16-25

[a] 3 The Hebrew word can mean *lamb* or *kid;* also in verse 4.

The First Passover

EX 12:2–3,8–11

The first Passover is a meal that the Israelites prepare and eat in obedience to God's instructions and in faith that he will protect them from "the destroyer" (Ex 12:23). A powerful visual aid and community event, it will serve the nation for generations by proclaiming that only through a blood sacrifice can they be protected from death. In every way, the Passover points ahead to Jesus Christ. (See what John the Baptist said in John 1:29.)

Because the meal is celebrated in households and not in a central place of worship, women are intimately involved in its preparation and celebration. As they work in their own homes, God gives them the opportunity to participate firsthand in all that the meal symbolizes. As the meal is observed year after year (Ex 12:24–27), mothers and fathers have an opportunity to remind their children of the wonderful deliverance God gave the nation of Israel at the exodus.

seven days no yeast is to be found in your houses.
And whoever eats anything with yeast in it must
be cut off from the community of Israel, whether
he is an alien or native-born. 20Eat nothing made
with yeast. Wherever you live, you must eat
unleavened bread."
21Then Moses summoned all the elders of Israel and said to them, "Go at once and select the
animals for your families and slaughter the
Passover[p] lamb. 22Take a bunch of hyssop, dip it
into the blood in the basin and put some of the
blood[q] on the top and on both sides of the doorframe. Not one of you shall go out the door of his
house until morning. 23When the LORD goes
through the land to strike down the Egyptians, he
will see the blood[r] on the top and sides of the
doorframe and will pass over[s] that doorway, and
he will not permit the destroyer[t] to enter your
houses and strike you down.
24"Obey these instructions as a lasting ordinance
for you and your descendants. 25When you enter
the land that the LORD will give you as he promised, observe this ceremony. 26And when your children[u] ask you, 'What does this ceremony mean to
you?' 27then tell them, 'It is the Passover[v] sacrifice
to the LORD, who passed over the houses of the
Israelites in Egypt and spared our homes when he
struck down the Egyptians.' " Then the people
bowed down and worshiped.[w] 28The Israelites did
just what the LORD commanded Moses and Aaron.
29At midnight[x] the LORD struck down all the
firstborn[y] in Egypt, from the firstborn of Pharaoh,
who sat on the throne, to the firstborn of the prisoner, who was in the dungeon, and the firstborn
of all the livestock[z] as well. 30Pharaoh and all his
officials and all the Egyptians got up during the
night, and there was loud wailing[a] in Egypt, for
there was not a house without someone dead.

The Exodus

31During the night Pharaoh summoned Moses
and Aaron and said, "Up! Leave my people, you
and the Israelites! Go, worship[b] the LORD as you
have requested. 32Take your flocks and herds,[c] as
you have said, and go. And also bless me."
33The Egyptians urged the people to hurry and
leave[d] the country. "For otherwise," they said, "we
will all die!" 34So the people took their dough
before the yeast was added, and carried it on their
shoulders in kneading troughs wrapped in clothing. 35The Israelites did as Moses instructed and
asked the Egyptians for articles of silver and gold[e]
and for clothing. 36The LORD had made the Egyptians favorably disposed toward the people, and
they gave them what they asked for; so they plundered[f] the Egyptians.
37The Israelites journeyed from Rameses to Succoth.[g] There were about six hundred thousand
men[h] on foot, besides women and children.
38Many other people[i] went up with them, as well
as large droves of livestock, both flocks and herds.

12:21 [p]ver 11; Mk 14:12-16
12:22 [q]ver 7; Heb 11:28
12:23 [r]Rev 7:3 [s]ver 13 [t]1Co 10:10; Heb 11:28
12:26 [u]Ex 10:2; 13:8,14-15; Jos 4:6
12:27 [v]ver 11 [w]Ex 4:31
12:29 [x]Ex 11:4 [y]Ex 4:23; Ps 78:51 [z]Ex 9:6
12:30 [a]Ex 11:6
12:31 [b]Ex 8:8
12:32 [c]Ex 10:9,26
12:33 [d]Ps 105:38
12:35 [e]Ex 3:22
12:36 [f]Ex 3:22
12:37 [g]Nu 33:3-5 [h]Ex 38:26; Nu 1:46; 11:13,21
12:38 [i]Nu 11:4

Growth

EX 12:37-38

Four hundred thirty years in Egypt have turned Jacob's family of 70 people into an immense multitude. If each of the 600,000 men represents a family group of just 4, then the total number can easily be more than two million. In addition, many other non-Jewish people (primarily Egyptians) decide to go along (Ex 12:38). While some of these became true believers when they saw God's power displayed, others are merely eager to escape plague-devastated Egypt. These people, however, eventually become a source of trouble (Nu 11:4).

Imagine the chaos, noise and confusion of the great multitude as they hurry out of Egypt with all their worldly possessions, including the invaluable livestock. We can only assume that Moses had planned some sort of organizational strategy for the exodus. A relay communication system is in place through 70 recognized elders (Ex 12:21; 24:1), and the people are arranged into divisions for the journey into the desert (Ex 12:41, 51). Even so, the sight, the dust, the confusion and the reality of such a movement must have been overwhelming.

39With the dough they had brought from Egypt,
they baked cakes of unleavened bread. The dough
was without yeast because they had been driven
out[j] of Egypt and did not have time to prepare
food for themselves.
40Now the length of time the Israelite people
lived in Egypt[a] was 430 years.[k] 41At the end of the
430 years, to the very day, all the LORD's divisions[l]
left Egypt.[m] 42Because the LORD kept vigil that
night to bring them out of Egypt, on this night all
the Israelites are to keep vigil to honor the LORD
for the generations to come.[n]

Passover Restrictions

43The LORD said to Moses and Aaron, "These are
the regulations for the Passover:[o]
"No foreigner[p] is to eat of it. 44Any slave you
have bought may eat of it after you have circumcised[q] him, 45but a temporary resident and a hired
worker[r] may not eat of it.
46"It must be eaten inside one house; take none
of the meat outside the house. Do not break any of
the bones.[s] 47The whole community of Israel must
celebrate it.
48"An alien living among you who wants to celebrate the LORD's Passover must have all the males
in his household circumcised; then he may take
part like one born in the land.[t] No uncircumcised
male may eat of it. 49The same law applies to the
native-born and to the alien[u] living among you."
50All the Israelites did just what the LORD had
commanded Moses and Aaron. 51And on that very
day the LORD brought the Israelites out of Egypt
by their divisions.[v]

Consecration of the Firstborn

13 The LORD said to Moses, 2"Consecrate to me
every firstborn male.[w] The first offspring of
every womb among the Israelites belongs to me,
whether man or animal."
3Then Moses said to the people, "Commemorate
this day, the day you came out of Egypt, out of the
land of slavery, because the LORD brought you out
of it with a mighty hand.[x] Eat nothing containing
yeast.[y] 4Today, in the month of Abib,[z] you are
leaving. 5When the LORD brings you into the land
of the Canaanites, Hittites, Amorites, Hivites and
Jebusites[a]—the land he swore to your forefathers
to give you, a land flowing with milk and honey—you are to observe this ceremony[b] in this
month: 6For seven days eat bread made without
yeast and on the seventh day hold a festival[c] to
the LORD. 7Eat unleavened bread during those sev-
en days; nothing with yeast in it is to be seen
among you, nor shall any yeast be seen anywhere
within your borders. 8On that day tell your son,[d]
'I do this because of what the LORD did for me

[a] *40* Masoretic Text; Samaritan Pentateuch and Septuagint *Egypt and Canaan*

12:39 [j]ver 31-33; Ex 6:1; 11:1
12:40 [k]Ge 15:13; Ac 7:6; Gal 3:17
12:41 [l]ver 17; Ex 6:26 [m]Ex 3:10
12:42 [n]Ex 13:10; Dt 16:1,6
12:43 [o]ver 11 [p]ver 48; Nu 9:14
12:44 [q]Ge 17:12-13
12:45 [r]Lev 22:10
12:46 [s]Nu 9:12; Jn 19:36*
12:48 [t]Nu 9:14
12:49 [u]Nu 15:15-16,29; Gal 3:28
12:51 [v]ver 41; Ex 6:26
13:2 [w]ver 12,13, 15; Ex 22:29; Nu 3:13; Dt 15:19; Lk 2:23*
13:3 [x]Ex 3:20; 6:1 [y]Ex 12:19
13:4 [z]Ex 12:2
13:5 [a]Ex 3:8 [b]Ex 12:25-26
13:6 [c]Ex 12:15-20
13:8 [d]ver 14; Ex 10:2; Ps 78:5-6

Unleavened Bread

EX 12:39

The Israelites leave Egypt so quickly that they have no yeast with which to make their bread. The bread they eat is a flat, unrisen variety. Subsequent Passover celebrations begin with six days in which only unleavened bread may be eaten. During that time, the Jews must make sure that no yeast is even present in their homes (Ex 12:17–20). Why such a restriction? Yeast in the Scripture is often used as a symbol for sin (1Co 5:8), and it is a fitting picture. Only a small amount of yeast is needed to change the nature of a large amount of flour and water. It invades, penetrates and grows within the dough until every particle is affected. Similarly, what seems to be only a small sin can have widespread impact in our lives.

The Pillar

EX 13:20-22

The words in these verses reveal God's tender love for Israel as he guides them out of Egypt. Not only do they have Moses and Aaron to lead them, but they also have a miraculous manifestation of God himself. This pillar of cloud by day and pillar of fire by night (Nu 9:15-16) guides the Israelites—when and where to stop and camp, when and where to move (see Nu 9:17-23; Dt 1:32-33; Ne 9:19)—and protects them (Ex 14:19-20). The pillar is a visual reminder for the Israelites that God is positively present with them (Ex 33:9-10; Nu 14:14).

Even greater than this cloud, Jesus is the visible fulfillment of God's commitment to be near to us. His name is Immanuel, which means "God with us" (Mt 1:23). Before he left this earth, Jesus declared that something even better would be available for us: the Holy Spirit to not only be near us but also to live within *us (Jn 14:15-20; 1Co 6:19).*

when I came out of Egypt.' 9This observance will
be for you like a sign on your hand and a
reminder on your forehead[e] that the law of the
LORD is to be on your lips. For the LORD brought
you out of Egypt with his mighty hand. 10You
must keep this ordinance[f] at the appointed time
year after year.

11"After the LORD brings you into the land of the
Canaanites and gives it to you, as he promised on
oath to you and your forefathers, 12you are to give
over to the LORD the first offspring of every womb.
All the firstborn males of your livestock belong to
the LORD.[g] 13Redeem with a lamb every firstborn
donkey, but if you do not redeem it, break its
neck.[h] Redeem every firstborn among your sons.[i]

14"In days to come, when your son[j] asks you,
'What does this mean?' say to him, 'With a
mighty hand the LORD brought us out of Egypt,
out of the land of slavery.[k] 15When Pharaoh stubbornly refused to let us go, the LORD killed every
firstborn in Egypt, both man and animal. This is
why I sacrifice to the LORD the first male offspring
of every womb and redeem each of my firstborn
sons.'[l] 16And it will be like a sign on your hand
and a symbol on your forehead[m] that the LORD
brought us out of Egypt with his mighty hand."

Crossing the Sea

17When Pharaoh let the people go, God did not
lead them on the road through the Philistine
country, though that was shorter. For God said, "If
they face war, they might change their minds and
return to Egypt."[n] 18So God led[o] the people around
by the desert road toward the Red Sea.[a] The Israelites went up out of Egypt armed for battle.[p]

19Moses took the bones of Joseph[q] with him
because Joseph had made the sons of Israel swear
an oath. He had said, "God will surely come to
your aid, and then you must carry my bones up
with you from this place."[b][r]

20After leaving Succoth they camped at Etham
on the edge of the desert.[s] 21By day the LORD went
ahead of them in a pillar of cloud[t] to guide them
on their way and by night in a pillar of fire to give
them light, so that they could travel by day or
night. 22Neither the pillar of cloud by day nor the
pillar of fire by night left its place in front of the
people.

14 Then the LORD said to Moses, 2"Tell the Israelites to turn back and encamp near Pi
Hahiroth, between Migdol[u] and the sea. They are
to encamp by the sea, directly opposite Baal
Zephon. 3Pharaoh will think, 'The Israelites are
wandering around the land in confusion, hemmed
in by the desert.' 4And I will harden Pharaoh's
heart,[v] and he will pursue them. But I will gain
glory[w] for myself through Pharaoh and all his

13:9 [e]ver 16; Dt 6:8; 11:18
13:10 [f]Ex 12:24-25
13:12 [g]Lev 27:26; Lk 2:23*
13:13 [h]Ex 34:20 [i]Nu 18:15
13:14 [j]Ex 10:2; 12:26-27; Dt 6:20 [k]ver 3,9
13:15 [l]Ex 12:29
13:16 [m]ver 9
13:17 [n]Ex 14:11; Nu 14:1-4; Dt 17:16
13:18 [o]Ps 136:16 [p]Jos 1:14
13:19 [q]Jos 24:32; Ac 7:16 [r]Ge 50:24-25
13:20 [s]Nu 33:6
13:21 [t]Ex 14:19, 24; 33:9-10; Nu 9:16; Dt 1:33; Ne 9:12,19; Ps 78:14; 99:7; 105:39; Isa 4:5; 1Co 10:1
14:2 [u]Nu 33:7; Jer 44:1
14:4 [v]Ex 4:21 [w]Ro 9:17,22-23

[a] *18* Hebrew *Yam Suph*; that is, Sea of Reeds [b] *19* See Gen. 50:25.

army, and the Egyptians will know that I am the
LORD."[x] So the Israelites did this.
5 When the king of Egypt was told that the people had fled, Pharaoh and his officials changed
their minds about them and said, "What have we
done? We have let the Israelites go and have lost
their services!" 6 So he had his chariot made ready
and took his army with him. 7 He took six hundred of the best chariots, along with all the other
chariots of Egypt, with officers over all of them.
8 The LORD hardened the heart[y] of Pharaoh king of
Egypt, so that he pursued the Israelites, who were
marching out boldly.[z] 9 The Egyptians—all Pharaoh's horses and chariots, horsemen[a] and
troops—pursued the Israelites and overtook[a] them
as they camped by the sea near Pi Hahiroth, opposite Baal Zephon.
10 As Pharaoh approached, the Israelites looked
up, and there were the Egyptians, marching after
them. They were terrified and cried[b] out to the
LORD. 11 They said to Moses, "Was it because there
were no graves in Egypt that you brought us to
the desert to die?[c] What have you done to us by
bringing us out of Egypt? 12 Didn't we say to you in
Egypt, 'Leave us alone; let us serve the Egyptians'? It would have been better for us to serve
the Egyptians than to die in the desert!"
13 Moses answered the people, "Do not be
afraid.[d] Stand firm and you will see[e] the deliverance the LORD will bring you today. The Egyptians
you see today you will never see[f] again. 14 The LORD
will fight[g] for you; you need only to be still."[h]
15 Then the LORD said to Moses, "Why are you
crying out to me? Tell the Israelites to move on.
16 Raise your staff[i] and stretch out your hand over
the sea to divide the water[j] so that the Israelites
can go through the sea on dry ground. 17 I will
harden the hearts of the Egyptians so that they
will go in after them.[k] And I will gain glory
through Pharaoh and all his army, through his
chariots and his horsemen. 18 The Egyptians will
know that I am the LORD when I gain glory
through Pharaoh, his chariots and his horsemen."
19 Then the angel of God, who had been traveling in front of Israel's army, withdrew and went
behind them. The pillar of cloud[l] also moved from
in front and stood behind them, 20 coming between
the armies of Egypt and Israel. Throughout the
night the cloud brought darkness to the one side
and light to the other side; so neither went near
the other all night long.
21 Then Moses stretched out his hand over the
sea, and all that night the LORD drove the sea back
with a strong east wind[m] and turned it into dry
land. The waters were divided,[n] 22 and the Israelites went through the sea on dry ground,[o] with a
wall of water on their right and on their left.
23 The Egyptians pursued them, and all Pharaoh's
horses and chariots and horsemen followed them

14:4 [x]Ex 7:5
14:8 [y]ver 4; Ex 11:10 [z]Nu 33:3; Ac 13:17
14:9 [a]Ex 15:9
14:10 [b]Jos 24:7; Ne 9:9; Ps 34:17
14:11 [c]Ps 106:7-8
14:13 [d]Ge 15:1 [e]2Ch 20:17; Isa 41:10,13-14 [f]ver 30
14:14 [g]ver 25; Ex 15:3; Dt 1:30; 3:22; 2Ch 20:29 [h]Ps 37:7; 46:10; Isa 30:15
14:16 [i]Ex 4:17; Nu 20:8-9,11 [j]Isa 10:26
14:17 [k]ver 4
14:19 [l]Ex 13:21
14:21 [m]Ex 15:8 [n]Ps 74:13; 114:5; Isa 63:12
14:22 [o]Ex 15:19; Ne 9:11; Ps 66:6; Heb 11:29

[a] 9 Or *charioteers*; also in verses 17, 18, 23, 26 and 28

Moving Out in Faith

EX 14:13-15

In *a* place of fear and confusion, God's words are strong: Don't be afraid! Stand firm! Be still! Stop crying out! Move on! To believe those words, trapped between the Red Sea and the approaching Egyptian army, stretches even Moses' faith. But the Israelites have little choice—except perhaps to collapse in fear and panic.

God's words to Israel, when they are caught between the rock of Pharaoh's angry army and the hard place of churning water, can help to relieve our fears and control our panic when we find ourselves in a stressful situation. We have the same choice as the Israelites—God's promises or our fears. God hears our terrified and desperate cries, just as he heard those of the Israelites. And he can deliver us—just as surely as he delivered them—if we pray, listen to him, follow his guidance and trust that he will open a way for our deliverance (Php 4:6-7).

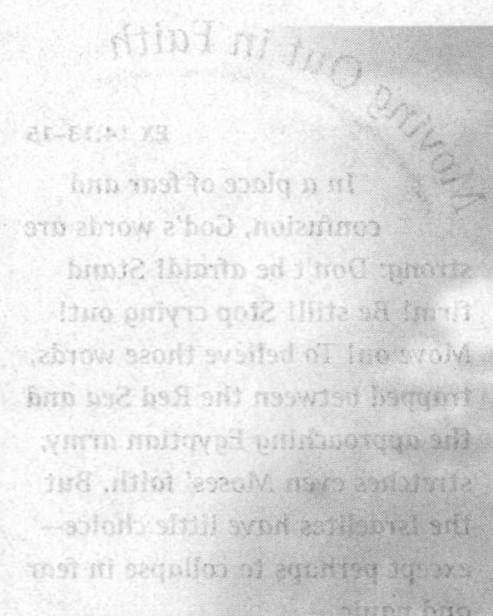

W**hatever may have happened in your past is over and should be done with. It's history. *You can pack your guilt and shame away in a box, use duct tape around all the edges to seal it tightly, and put it in the trash where it belongs. It doesn't need to haunt you any longer. Why?* Because Jesus cares about what happened in your past. And he cares even more about what you're doing today to recover from it. He *wants you to bring it to him, so he can fulfill his promise to you.***

—Thelma Wells

into the sea. 24During the last watch of the night
the LORD looked down from the pillar of fire and
cloud[p] at the Egyptian army and threw it into confusion. 25He made the wheels of their chariots
come off[a] so that they had difficulty driving. And
the Egyptians said, "Let's get away from the Israelites! The LORD is fighting[q] for them against Egypt."
26Then the LORD said to Moses, "Stretch out your
hand over the sea so that the waters may flow back
over the Egyptians and their chariots and horsemen." 27Moses stretched out his hand over the sea,
and at daybreak the sea went back to its place.[r]
The Egyptians were fleeing toward[b] it, and the
LORD swept them into the sea.[s] 28The water flowed
back and covered the chariots and horsemen—the
entire army of Pharaoh that had followed the Israelites into the sea. Not one of them survived.
29But the Israelites went through the sea on dry
ground,[t] with a wall of water on their right and
on their left. 30That day the LORD saved[u] Israel
from the hands of the Egyptians, and Israel saw
the Egyptians lying dead on the shore. 31And
when the Israelites saw the great power the LORD
displayed against the Egyptians, the people feared
the LORD and put their trust[v] in him and in Moses
his servant.

The Song of Moses and Miriam

15 Then Moses and the Israelites sang this
song[w] to the LORD:

"I will sing[x] to the LORD,
for he is highly exalted.
The horse and its rider
he has hurled into the sea.
2The LORD is my strength[y] and my song;
he has become my salvation.[z]
He is my God,[a] and I will praise him,
my father's God, and I will exalt[b] him.
3The LORD is a warrior;[c]
the LORD is his name.[d]
4Pharaoh's chariots and his army[e]
he has hurled into the sea.
The best of Pharaoh's officers
are drowned in the Red Sea.[c]
5The deep waters have covered them;
they sank to the depths like a stone.[f]

6"Your right hand,[g] O LORD,
was majestic in power.
Your right hand, O LORD,
shattered the enemy.
7In the greatness of your majesty
you threw down those who opposed
you.
You unleashed your burning anger;[h]
it consumed them like stubble.
8By the blast of your nostrils[i]

14:24 [p]Ex 13:21
14:25 [q]ver 14
14:27 [r]Jos 4:18 [s]Ex 15:1,21; Ps 78:53; 106:11
14:29 [t]ver 22
14:30 [u]Ps 106:8, 10, 21
14:31 [v]Ps 106:12; Jn 2:11
15:1 [w]Rev 15:3 [x]Ps 106:12
15:2 [y]Ps 59:17 [z]Ps 18:2,46; Isa 12:2; Hab 3:18 [a]Ge 28:21 [b]Ex 3:6,15-16; Isa 25:1
15:3 [c]Ex 14:14; Ps 24:8; Rev 19:11 [d]Ex 6:2-3, 7-8; Ps 83:18
15:4 [e]Ex 14:6-7
15:5 [f]ver 10; Ne 9:11
15:6 [g]Ps 118:15
15:7 [h]Ps 78:49-50
15:8 [i]Ex 14:21

[a] *25* Or *He jammed the wheels of their chariots* (see Samaritan Pentateuch, Septuagint and Syriac) [b] *27* Or *from*
[c] *4* Hebrew *Yam Suph*; that is, Sea of Reeds; also in verse 22

15:8 [j]Ps 78:13 [k]Ex 14:22

the waters piled up.[j]
The surging waters stood firm like a
wall;[k]
the deep waters congealed in the
heart of the sea.

15:9 [l]Ex 14:5-9 [m]Jdg 5:30; Isa 53:12

9 "The enemy boasted,
'I will pursue,[l] I will overtake them.
I will divide the spoils;[m]
I will gorge myself on them.
I will draw my sword
and my hand will destroy them.'
10 But you blew with your breath,
and the sea covered them.
They sank like lead
in the mighty waters.[n]

15:10 [n]ver 5; Ex 14:27-28

15:11 [o]Ex 8:10; Dt 3:24; Ps 77:13 [p]Isa 6:3; Rev 4:8 [q]Ps 8:1

11 "Who among the gods is like you,[o]
O LORD?
Who is like you—
majestic in holiness,[p]
awesome in glory,[q]
working wonders?
12 You stretched out your right hand
and the earth swallowed them.

15:13 [r]Ne 9:12; Ps 77:20 [s]Ps 78:54

13 "In your unfailing love you will lead[r]
the people you have redeemed.
In your strength you will guide them
to your holy dwelling.[s]

15:14 [t]Dt 2:25

14 The nations will hear and tremble;[t]
anguish will grip the people of
Philistia.

15:15 [u]Ge 36:15 [v]Nu 22:3 [w]Jos 5:1

15 The chiefs[u] of Edom will be terrified,
the leaders of Moab will be seized
with trembling,[v]
the people[a] of Canaan will melt[w] away;

15:16 [x]Ex 23:27; Jos 2:9 [y]1Sa 25:37 [z]Ps 74:2

16 terror[x] and dread will fall upon them.
By the power of your arm
they will be as still as a stone[y]—
until your people pass by, O LORD,
until the people you bought[b][z] pass by.

15:17 [a]Ps 44:2 [b]Ps 78:54,68

17 You will bring them in and plant[a] them
on the mountain[b] of your
inheritance—
the place, O LORD, you made for your
dwelling,
the sanctuary, O Lord, your hands
established.
18 The LORD will reign
for ever and ever."

15:19 [c]Ex 14:28 [d]Ex 14:22

15:20 [e]Nu 26:59 [f]Jdg 4:4 [g]Jdg 11:34; 1Sa 18:6; Ps 30:11; 150:4

19 When Pharaoh's horses, chariots and horsemen[c] went into the sea,[c] the LORD brought the
waters of the sea back over them, but the Israelites walked through the sea on dry ground.[d]
20 Then Miriam[e] the prophetess,[f] Aaron's sister,
took a tambourine in her hand, and all the
women followed her, with tambourines and dancing.[g] 21 Miriam sang to them:

Let's Dance!

EX 15:20

Cries of fear quickly turn to cries of joy when the Israelites realize they never need to fear Pharaoh and his armies again. What a relief! What a miracle! No wonder they break out in dancing!

Miriam, Moses' sister, leads the women of Israel in exuberant worship after their extraordinary deliverance. We know from 1 Samuel 18:6, 2 Samuel 6:14-15 and Psalms 149:3 and 150:4 that God's people celebrate and worship him with musical instruments, dancing and singing.

Miriam is the first woman in the Bible called a prophetess. What sort of ministry did she, a woman, have in early Israelite culture? First, Micah 6:4 speaks of the leadership role she shared with Moses and Aaron in bringing the Israelites out of Egypt. Second, from Numbers 12:1, 2, 6 we understand that God spoke to Miriam in visions and dreams. Finally, as a prophetess, she led God's people in worship and praise. *(See character sketch for Miriam on page 401.)*

[a] *15* Or *rulers* [b] *16* Or *created* [c] *19* Or *charioteers*

Our Patient God

EX 15:24

Only a short trip from a show-stopping miracle, and the Israelites are already grumbling. Their faith is shaken to its foundations because they have no water. Again and again we see this pattern of fear, grumbling and unbelief in the lives of God's people in the desert (Ex 16:2–3; 32:1–14). Israel's refusal to believe God in the face of difficulties and challenges eventually sends them wandering in the desert for 40 years (Nu 14:1–34). We wonder how God could have endured the whiney Israelites with such patience!

Yet as we look at our own hearts, we see the same tendency to quickly forget God's blessings and promises. Like Israel, we test God with our unbelief. Psalm 95:7–11 urges us to not harden our hearts when we hear God's word, like the Israelites did at Meribah and Massah (Ex 17:7); and Hebrews 3:7–19 confronts us even more passionately with this important warning.

"Sing to the LORD,
for he is highly exalted.
The horse and its rider
he has hurled into the sea."[h]

The Waters of Marah and Elim

22Then Moses led Israel from the Red Sea and
they went into the Desert of Shur. For three days
they traveled in the desert without finding water.
23When they came to Marah, they could not drink
its water because it was bitter. (That is why the
place is called Marah.[a][i]) 24So the people grumbled[j]
against Moses, saying, "What are we to drink?"
25Then Moses cried out[k] to the LORD, and the
LORD showed him a piece of wood. He threw it
into the water, and the water became sweet.
There the LORD made a decree and a law for
them, and there he tested[l] them. 26He said, "If you
listen carefully to the voice of the LORD your God
and do what is right in his eyes, if you pay attention to his commands and keep all his decrees,[m] I
will not bring on you any of the diseases[n] I
brought on the Egyptians, for I am the LORD, who
heals[o] you."
27Then they came to Elim, where there were
twelve springs and seventy palm trees, and they
camped[p] there near the water.

Manna and Quail

16 The whole Israelite community set out from
Elim and came to the Desert of Sin,[q] which
is between Elim and Sinai, on the fifteenth day of
the second month after they had come out of
Egypt. 2In the desert the whole community grumbled[r] against Moses and Aaron. 3The Israelites
said to them, "If only we had died by the LORD's
hand in Egypt![s] There we sat around pots of meat
and ate all the food[t] we wanted, but you have
brought us out into this desert to starve this entire
assembly to death."
4Then the LORD said to Moses, "I will rain down
bread from heaven[u] for you. The people are to go
out each day and gather enough for that day. In
this way I will test them and see whether they will
follow my instructions. 5On the sixth day they are
to prepare what they bring in, and that is to be
twice[v] as much as they gather on the other days."
6So Moses and Aaron said to all the Israelites,
"In the evening you will know that it was the
LORD who brought you out of Egypt,[w] 7and in the
morning you will see the glory[x] of the LORD,
because he has heard your grumbling[y] against
him. Who are we, that you should grumble
against us?"[z] 8Moses also said, "You will know
that it was the LORD when he gives you meat to
eat in the evening and all the bread you want in
the morning, because he has heard your grumbling against him. Who are we? You are not grumbling against us, but against the LORD."[a]

15:21 [h]ver 1; Ex 14:27
15:23 [i]Nu 33:8
15:24 [j]Ex 14:12; 16:2
15:25 [k]Ex 14:10 [l]Jdg 3:4
15:26 [m]Dt 7:12 [n]Dt 28:27, 58-60 [o]Ex 23:25-26
15:27 [p]Nu 33:9
16:1 [q]Nu 33:11,12
16:2 [r]Ex 14:11; 15:24; 1Co 10:10
16:3 [s]Ex 17:3 [t]Nu 11:4,34
16:4 [u]Dt 8:3; Jn 6:31*
16:5 [v]ver 22
16:6 [w]Ex 6:6
16:7 [x]ver 10; Isa 35:2; 40:5 [y]ver 12; Nu 14:2,27, 28 [z]Nu 16:11
16:8 [a]1Sa 8:7; Ro 13:2

[a] 23 *Marah* means *bitter.*

9Then Moses told Aaron, "Say to the entire Israelite community, 'Come before the LORD, for he
has heard your grumbling.' "
10While Aaron was speaking to the whole Isra-
16:10 [b]ver 7; elite community, they looked toward the desert,
Nu 16:19 and there was the glory[b] of the LORD appearing in
[c]Ex 13:21; the cloud.[c]
1Ki 8:10 11The LORD said to Moses, 12"I have heard the
16:12 grumbling[d] of the Israelites. Tell them, 'At twilight
[d]ver 7 you will eat meat, and in the morning you will be
filled with bread. Then you will know that I am
the LORD your God.' "
16:13 13That evening quail[e] came and covered the
[e]Nu 11:31; Ps 78:27-28; camp, and in the morning there was a layer of
105:40 dew[f] around the camp. 14When the dew was gone,
[f]Nu 11:9 thin flakes like frost[g] on the ground appeared on
16:14 the desert floor. 15When the Israelites saw it, they
[g]ver 31; Nu 11:7-9; said to each other, "What is it?" For they did not
Ps 105:40 know what it was.
Moses said to them, "It is the bread[h] the LORD
16:15 [h]ver 4; has given you to eat. 16This is what the LORD has
Jn 6:31 commanded: 'Each one is to gather as much as he
needs. Take an omer[a][i] for each person you have
16:16 [i]ver 32,36 in your tent.' "
17The Israelites did as they were told; some
gathered much, some little. 18And when they
measured it by the omer, he who gathered much
16:18 did not have too much, and he who gathered lit-
[j]2Co 8:15* tle did not have too little.[j] Each one gathered as
much as he needed.
16:19 19Then Moses said to them, "No one is to keep
[k]ver 23; any of it until morning."[k]
Ex 12:10; 23:18 20However, some of them paid no attention to
Moses; they kept part of it until morning, but it
was full of maggots and began to smell. So Moses
was angry with them.
21Each morning everyone gathered as much as
he needed, and when the sun grew hot, it melted
away. 22On the sixth day, they gathered twice[l] as
16:22 [l]ver 5 much—two omers[b] for each person—and the
[m]Ex 34:31 leaders of the community[m] came and reported this
to Moses. 23He said to them, "This is what the
16:23 LORD commanded: 'Tomorrow is to be a day of
[n]Ge 2:3; rest, a holy Sabbath[n] to the LORD. So bake what
Ex 20:8; 23:12; you want to bake and boil what you want to boil.
Lev 23:3 Save whatever is left and keep it until morning.' "
24So they saved it until morning, as Moses commanded, and it did not stink or get maggots in it.
25"Eat it today," Moses said, "because today is a
Sabbath to the LORD. You will not find any of it on
16:26 the ground today. 26Six days you are to gather it,
[o]Ex 20:9-10 but on the seventh day, the Sabbath,[o] there will
not be any."
27Nevertheless, some of the people went out on
16:28 [p]2Ki 17:14; the seventh day to gather it, but they found none.
Ps 78:10; 28Then the LORD said to Moses, "How long will
106:13 you[c] refuse to keep my commands[p] and my

[a] *16* That is, probably about 2 quarts (about 2 liters); also in verses 18, 32, 33 and 36 [b] *22* That is, probably about 4 quarts (about 4.5 liters) [c] *28* The Hebrew is plural.

Manna

EX 16:31

***Manna* derives directly from a Hebrew word meaning "What is it?" (see NIV footnote on Ex 16:31; see also Ex 16:15). We do not know exactly what it was. We know it was white, tasted like wafers made with honey, and could be baked or boiled. Numbers 11:7–8 adds that it was waxy, like resin, had the flavor of something cooked in olive oil, and had to be ground or crushed before cooking. No matter how interesting it was at first, a steady diet of this one substance quickly became tiresome to the Israelites. But remember—God's plan was not a 40-year desert trek but a short trip across Sinai into the promised land (Ex 16:35; Nu 14:1–34).**

Manna Preserves

EX 16:33-34

When the manna first appears, God commands Moses to save a day's provision of manna in a jar and place it before the Testimony, the tablets on which the Ten Commandments were inscribed (Ex 34:28-29). God chooses to miraculously preserve that manna so it will be a reminder to the people of his faithfulness. All other saved manna spoiled within a few hours (Ex 16:20), except the manna kept for the Sabbath, which stayed fresh for two days (Ex 16:23-24).

Later when the ark is built (Ex 25:10-22), the tablets of the law are placed in the ark (Ex 25:21; Ex 34:28-29—"the Testimony") alongside the jar of manna and Aaron's rod (Nu 17:10). All three serve as perpetual reminders of God's faithfulness in giving his people three essential gifts: his commandments to give them life and understanding, his daily provision to sustain them, and his leaders to guide them.

instructions? [29]Bear in mind that the LORD has giv-
en you the Sabbath; that is why on the sixth day
he gives you bread for two days. Everyone is to
stay where he is on the seventh day; no one is to
go out." [30]So the people rested on the seventh day.
[31]The people of Israel called the bread manna.[a][q] **16:31** [q]Nu 11:7-9
It was white like coriander seed and tasted like
wafers made with honey. [32]Moses said, "This is
what the LORD has commanded: 'Take an omer of
manna and keep it for the generations to come, so
they can see the bread I gave you to eat in the
desert when I brought you out of Egypt.'"
[33]So Moses said to Aaron, "Take a jar and put **16:33** [r]Heb 9:4
an omer of manna[r] in it. Then place it before the
LORD to be kept for the generations to come."
[34]As the LORD commanded Moses, Aaron put **16:34** [s]Ex 25:16,
the manna in front of the Testimony,[s] that it might 21,22; 40:20;
be kept. [35]The Israelites ate manna[t] forty years,[u] Nu 17:4,10
until they came to a land that was settled; they ate **16:35** [t]Jn 6:31,49
manna until they reached the border of Canaan.[v] [u]Ne 9:21
[36](An omer is one tenth of an ephah.) [v]Jos 5:12

Water From the Rock

17 The whole Israelite community set out from **17:1** [w]Ex 16:1
the Desert of Sin,[w] traveling from place to [x]Nu 33:14
place as the LORD commanded. They camped at
Rephidim, but there was no water[x] for the people
to drink. [2]So they quarreled with Moses and said, **17:2** [y]Nu 20:2
"Give us water[y] to drink." [z]Dt 6:16;
Moses replied, "Why do you quarrel with me? Ps 78:18,41;
Why do you put the LORD to the test?"[z] 1Co 10:9
[3]But the people were thirsty for water there, and **17:3** [a]Ex 15:24;
they grumbled[a] against Moses. They said, "Why 16:2-3
did you bring us up out of Egypt to make us and
our children and livestock die of thirst?"
[4]Then Moses cried out to the LORD, "What am I
to do with these people? They are almost ready to **17:4** [b]Nu 14:10;
stone[b] me." 1Sa 30:6
[5]The LORD answered Moses, "Walk on ahead of
the people. Take with you some of the elders of
Israel and take in your hand the staff with which **17:5** [c]Ex 7:20
you struck the Nile,[c] and go. [6]I will stand there
before you by the rock at Horeb. Strike the rock,
and water[d] will come out of it for the people to **17:6** [d]Nu 20:11;
drink." So Moses did this in the sight of the elders Ps 114:8;
of Israel. [7]And he called the place Massah[b] and 1Co 10:4
Meribah[c][e] because the Israelites quarreled and **17:7** [e]Nu 20:13,
because they tested the LORD saying, "Is the LORD 24; Ps 81:7
among us or not?"

The Amalekites Defeated

[8]The Amalekites[f] came and attacked the Israel- **17:8** [f]Ge 36:12;
ites at Rephidim. [9]Moses said to Joshua, "Choose Dt 25:17-19
some of our men and go out to fight the Ama-
lekites. Tomorrow I will stand on top of the hill **17:9** [g]Ex 4:17
with the staff[g] of God in my hands."
[10]So Joshua fought the Amalekites as Moses had **17:10** [h]Ex 24:14
ordered, and Moses, Aaron and Hur[h] went to the

[a] *31 Manna* means *What is it?* (see verse 15). [b] *7 Massah* means *testing.* [c] *7 Meribah* means *quarreling.*

17:11 top of the hill. 11 As long as Moses held up his
[i]Jas 5:16 hands, the Israelites were winning,[i] but whenever he lowered his hands, the Amalekites were
winning. 12 When Moses' hands grew tired, they
took a stone and put it under him and he sat on it.
Aaron and Hur held his hands up—one on one
side, one on the other—so that his hands
remained steady till sunset. 13 So Joshua overcame
the Amalekite army with the sword.

17:14 14 Then the LORD said to Moses, "Write[j] this on a
[j]Ex 24:4; 34:27; scroll as something to be remembered and make
Nu 33:2 sure that Joshua hears it, because I will com-
[k]1Sa 15:3; 30:17-18 pletely blot out the memory of Amalek[k] from
under heaven."

15 Moses built an altar and called it The LORD is
my Banner. 16 He said, "For hands were lifted up
to the throne of the LORD. The[a] LORD will be at war
against the Amalekites from generation to
generation."

Jethro Visits Moses

18:1 **18** Now Jethro, the priest of Midian[l] and
[l]Ex 2:16; 3:1 father-in-law of Moses, heard of everything
God had done for Moses and for his people Israel,
and how the LORD had brought Israel out of Egypt.
18:2 2 After Moses had sent away his wife Zipporah,[m]
[m]Ex 2:21; 4:25 his father-in-law Jethro received her 3 and her two
sons.[n] One son was named Gershom,[b] for Moses
18:3 [n]Ex 4:20; said, "I have become an alien in a foreign land";[o]
Ac 7:29 4 and the other was named Eliezer,[c][p] for he said,
[o]Ex 2:22 "My father's God was my helper; he saved me
18:4 from the sword of Pharaoh."
[p]1Ch 23:15 5 Jethro, Moses' father-in-law, together with
18:5 Moses' sons and wife, came to him in the desert,
[q]Ex 3:1 where he was camped near the mountain[q] of God.
6 Jethro had sent word to him, "I, your father-in-
law Jethro, am coming to you with your wife and
her two sons."

7 So Moses went out to meet his father-in-law
18:7 [r]Ge 43:28 and bowed down[r] and kissed[s] him. They greeted
[s]Ge 29:13 each other and then went into the tent. 8 Moses
told his father-in-law about everything the LORD
had done to Pharaoh and the Egyptians for Israel's
18:8 sake and about all the hardships they had met
[t]Ex 15:6,16; along the way and how the LORD had saved[t] them.
Ps 81:7 9 Jethro was delighted to hear about all the good
things the LORD had done for Israel in rescuing
them from the hand of the Egyptians. 10 He said,
18:10 "Praise be to the LORD,[u] who rescued you from the
[u]Ge 14:20; Ps 68:19-20 hand of the Egyptians and of Pharaoh, and who
rescued the people from the hand of the Egyp-
tians. 11 Now I know that the LORD is greater than
18:11 [v]Ex 12:12; all other gods,[v] for he did this to those who had
15:11; 2Ch 2:5 treated Israel arrogantly."[w] 12 Then Jethro, Moses'
[w]Lk 1:51 father-in-law, brought a burnt offering and other
sacrifices to God, and Aaron came with all the el-

[a] 16 Or *"Because a hand was against the throne of the LORD, the* [b] 3 *Gershom* sounds like the Hebrew for *an alien there.* [c] 4 *Eliezer* means *my God is helper.*

Wiped From Memory

EX 17:14

God's promise that he will wipe out the memory of the Amalekites means that he will destroy their significance as a people, not that he will eliminate the memory of their existence. The same Hebrew word for *memory* is translated as "renown" or "fame" in Hosea 12:5 and Hosea 14:7. The Amalekites are a nomadic people, descendants of Esau's grandson Amalek (Ge 36:12). They attack Israel, and a fierce battle develops. Exodus 17:10–13 gives a fascinating commentary on how that battle was won. The Amalekites continue to be a hostile and bothersome enemy of the Israelites until they are dealt two final blows, first by David (1Sa 30) and then by King Hezekiah's men (1Ch 4:41–43). Thus God's promise fully comes to pass. Like many of the challenges of our lives, the enemy is not destroyed in a single battle but through a series of encounters over a long period of time.

On Eagles' Wings

EX 19:4

After three months in the desert, God is ready to give his people his law. As he begins, he wants them to clearly understand that their relationship with him is rooted in his love and care. He uses a surprising image to describe their relationship. He says he has carried them on "eagles' wings." A mother eagle flies beneath her babies with her wings outstretched so she can rescue them if they begin to falter—a powerful image of our God, who tenderly, constantly cares for and supports his people.

God continues by saying, "I . . . brought you to myself." He frees his people and protects them in order to bring them into the center of his heart as his "treasured possession" (Ex 19:5). His only request? That his people love and obey him.

ders of Israel to eat bread with Moses' father-in-
law in the presence[x] of God.
13 The next day Moses took his seat to serve as
judge for the people, and they stood around him
from morning till evening. 14 When his father-in-
law saw all that Moses was doing for the people,
he said, "What is this you are doing for the people?
Why do you alone sit as judge, while all these people stand around you from morning till evening?"
15 Moses answered him, "Because the people
come to me to seek God's will.[y] 16 Whenever they
have a dispute, it is brought to me, and I decide
between the parties and inform them of God's
decrees and laws."[z]
17 Moses' father-in-law replied, "What you are
doing is not good. 18 You and these people who
come to you will only wear yourselves out. The
work is too heavy for you; you cannot handle it
alone.[a] 19 Listen now to me and I will give you
some advice, and may God be with you.[b] You
must be the people's representative before God
and bring their disputes[c] to him. 20 Teach them the
decrees and laws,[d] and show them the way to live[e]
and the duties they are to perform.[f] 21 But select
capable men[g] from all the people—men who fear
God, trustworthy men who hate dishonest gain[h]—
and appoint them as officials[i] over thousands,
hundreds, fifties and tens. 22 Have them serve as
judges for the people at all times, but have them
bring every difficult case[j] to you; the simple cases
they can decide themselves. That will make your
load lighter, because they will share[k] it with you.
23 If you do this and God so commands, you will
be able to stand the strain, and all these people
will go home satisfied."
24 Moses listened to his father-in-law and did
everything he said. 25 He chose capable men from
all Israel and made them leaders of the people,
officials over thousands, hundreds, fifties and
tens.[l] 26 They served as judges for the people at all
times. The difficult cases they brought to Moses,
but the simple ones they decided themselves.[m]
27 Then Moses sent his father-in-law on his way,
and Jethro returned to his own country.[n]

At Mount Sinai

19 In the third month after the Israelites left
Egypt—on the very day—they came to the
Desert of Sinai. 2 After they set out from Rephidim,[o] they entered the Desert of Sinai, and Israel
camped there in the desert in front of the
mountain.[p]
3 Then Moses went up to God, and the LORD
called[q] to him from the mountain and said, "This
is what you are to say to the house of Jacob and
what you are to tell the people of Israel: 4 'You
yourselves have seen what I did to Egypt,[r] and
how I carried you on eagles' wings[s] and brought
you to myself. 5 Now if you obey me fully[t] and
keep my covenant,[u] then out of all nations you
will be my treasured possession.[v] Although the

18:12 [x]Dt 12:7
18:15 [y]Nu 9:6,8; Dt 17:8-13
18:16 [z]Lev 24:12
18:18 [a]Nu 11:11, 14,17
18:19 [b]Ex 3:12 [c]Nu 27:5
18:20 [d]Dt 5:1 [e]Ps 143:8 [f]Dt 1:18
18:21 [g]Ac 6:3 [h]Dt 16:19; Ps 15:5; Eze 18:8 [i]Dt 1:13,15; 2Ch 19:5-10
18:22 [j]Dt 1:17-18 [k]Nu 11:17
18:25 [l]Dt 1:13-15
18:26 [m]ver 22
18:27 [n]Nu 10:29-30
19:2 [o]Ex 17:1 [p]Ex 3:1
19:3 [q]Ex 3:4; Ac 7:38
19:4 [r]Dt 29:2 [s]Isa 63:9
19:5 [t]Ex 15:26 [u]Dt 5:2 [v]Dt 14:2; Ps 135:4

whole earth[w] is mine, **6**you[a] will be for me a kingdom of priests[x] and a holy nation.'[y] These are the
words you are to speak to the Israelites."
7So Moses went back and summoned the elders
of the people and set before them all the words
the LORD had commanded him to speak. **8**The people all responded together, "We will do everything
the LORD has said."[z] So Moses brought their
answer back to the LORD.
9The LORD said to Moses, "I am going to come to
you in a dense cloud,[a] so that the people will hear
me speaking[b] with you and will always put their
trust in you." Then Moses told the LORD what the
people had said.
10And the LORD said to Moses, "Go to the people and consecrate[c] them today and tomorrow.
Have them wash their clothes[d] **11**and be ready by
the third day,[e] because on that day the LORD will
come down on Mount Sinai in the sight of all the
people. **12**Put limits for the people around the
mountain and tell them, 'Be careful that you do
not go up the mountain or touch the foot of it.
Whoever touches the mountain shall surely be
put to death. **13**He shall surely be stoned[f] or shot
with arrows; not a hand is to be laid on him.
Whether man or animal, he shall not be permitted
to live.' Only when the ram's horn sounds a long
blast may they go up to the mountain."
14After Moses had gone down the mountain to
the people, he consecrated them, and they washed
their clothes. **15**Then he said to the people, "Prepare yourselves for the third day. Abstain from
sexual relations."
16On the morning of the third day there was
thunder and lightning, with a thick cloud over the
mountain, and a very loud trumpet blast.[g] Everyone in the camp trembled.[h] **17**Then Moses led the
people out of the camp to meet with God, and
they stood at the foot of the mountain. **18**Mount
Sinai was covered with smoke,[i] because the LORD
descended on it in fire.[j] The smoke billowed up
from it like smoke from a furnace,[k] the whole
mountain[b] trembled[l] violently, **19**and the sound of
the trumpet grew louder and louder. Then Moses
spoke and the voice[m] of God answered[n] him.[c]
20The LORD descended to the top of Mount Sinai
and called Moses to the top of the mountain. So
Moses went up **21**and the LORD said to him, "Go
down and warn the people so they do not force
their way through to see[o] the LORD and many of
them perish. **22**Even the priests, who approach[p]
the LORD, must consecrate themselves, or the LORD
will break out against them."[q]
23Moses said to the LORD, "The people cannot
come up Mount Sinai, because you yourself

19:5 [w]Ex 9:29; Dt 10:14
19:6 [x]1Pe 2:5 [y]Dt 7:6; 26:19; Isa 62:12
19:8 [z]Ex 24:3,7; Dt 5:27
19:9 [a]ver 16; Ex 24:15-16 [b]Dt 4:12,36
19:10 [c]Lev 11:44; Heb 10:22 [d]Ge 35:2
19:11 [e]ver 16
19:13 [f]Heb 12:20*
19:16 [g]Heb 12:18-19; Rev 4:1 [h]Heb 12:21
19:18 [i]Ps 104:32 [j]Ex 3:2; 24:17; Dt 4:11; 2Ch 7:1; Ps 18:8; Heb 12:18 [k]Ge 19:28 [l]Jdg 5:5; Ps 68:8; Jer 4:24
19:19 [m]Ne 9:13 [n]Ps 81:7
19:21 [o]Ex 3:5; 1Sa 6:19
19:22 [p]Lev 10:3 [q]2Sa 6:7

[a] 5,6 Or *possession, for the whole earth is mine.* [6]*You*
[b] *18* Most Hebrew manuscripts; a few Hebrew manuscripts and Septuagint *all the people*
[c] *19* Or *and God answered him with thunder*

A Sacred Relationship

EX 19:14–15

God is bringing Israel into a covenant with himself (Ex 19:5–6). In order to reinforce the significance and holiness of this relationship, God includes a number of specific instructions for his people's preparation. ***Washing their clothes is a visible sign of cleansing. Abstaining from sexual relationships is not an assertion that marital sex is sinful but is a call to focus solely on the Lord.*** **In 1 Corinthians 7:5, Paul encour-** ***ages abstinence if a married couple agrees to set aside a time for concentrated prayer.***

The Israelites' preparation for ***this covenant ceremony parallels a bride's preparation for her wedding day. Because this day is unique and wonderful, a bride beautifies herself as she does for no other day. God's covenant relationship with his people is like a marriage—loyal, loving and holy—and he wants us to make personal choices appropriate to the sacredness and beauty of that relationship*** **(Isa 54:5–6).**

Timeless Standards

EX 20:2–17

The Ten Commandments set God's standard for our relationships with him and with others. They are the spiritual and moral centerpiece of the entire law—a law that includes religious ceremony as well as civil functions.

Are Christians obligated to keep the law today? The civil law, while containing many timeless principles for society, applies specifically to the nation of Israel. The New Testament declares clearly that Jesus Christ fulfilled every ceremonial requirement the law set forth by his sinless life and perfect sacrifice (Mt 5:17–18; Eph 2:15–16). When our faith is in Christ, we will not be judged by the law (Ro 6:14; 8:1–4; Php 3:7–9).

Still, the Ten Commandments express God's unchanging standards for moral living, and, rather than discarding them, Jesus actually drives these issues to the heart in Matthew 5:21–28. We are called not only to a personal relationship with God through Christ but also to an ethical, practical holiness that mirrors his character (1Pe 1:14–16).

warned us, 'Put limits[r] around the mountain and
set it apart as holy.' "
24 The LORD replied, "Go down and bring Aaron[s]
up with you. But the priests and the people must
not force their way through to come up to the
LORD, or he will break out against them."
25 So Moses went down to the people and told
them.

The Ten Commandments

20 And God spoke all these words:

2 "I am the LORD your God, who brought
you out of Egypt, out of the land of
slavery.[t]
3 "You shall have no other gods before[a] me.[u]
4 "You shall not make for yourself an idol[v] in
the form of anything in heaven above or
on the earth beneath or in the waters
below. 5 You shall not bow down to them
or worship[w] them; for I, the LORD your
God, am a jealous God,[x] punishing the
children for the sin of the fathers to the
third and fourth generation[y] of those
who hate me, 6 but showing love to a
thousand[z] ⌞generations⌟ of those who
love me and keep my commandments.
7 "You shall not misuse the name of the LORD
your God, for the LORD will not hold anyone guiltless who misuses his name.[a]
8 "Remember the Sabbath[b] day by keeping it
holy. 9 Six days you shall labor and do all
your work,[c] 10 but the seventh day is a
Sabbath to the LORD your God. On it you
shall not do any work, neither you, nor
your son or daughter, nor your manservant or maidservant, nor your animals,
nor the alien within your gates. 11 For in
six days the LORD made the heavens and
the earth, the sea, and all that is in them,
but he rested[d] on the seventh day. Therefore the LORD blessed the Sabbath day
and made it holy.
12 "Honor your father and your mother,[e] so that
you may live long in the land the LORD
your God is giving you.
13 "You shall not murder.[f]
14 "You shall not commit adultery.[g]
15 "You shall not steal.[h]
16 "You shall not give false testimony against
your neighbor.[i]
17 "You shall not covet[j] your neighbor's house.
You shall not covet your neighbor's wife,
or his manservant or maidservant, his ox
or donkey, or anything that belongs to
your neighbor."

18 When the people saw the thunder and lightning and heard the trumpet[k] and saw the moun-

19:23 [r]ver 12
19:24 [s]Ex 24:1,9
20:2 [t]Ex 13:3
20:3 [u]Dt 6:14; Jer 35:15
20:4 [v]Lev 26:1; Dt 4:15-19, 23; 27:15
20:5 [w]Isa 44:15, 17,19 [x]Ex 34:14; Dt 4:24 [y]Nu 14:18; Jer 32:18
20:6 [z]Dt 7:9
20:7 [a]Lev 19:12; Mt 5:33
20:8 [b]Ex 31:13-16; Lev 26:2
20:9 [c]Ex 34:21; Lk 13:14
20:11 [d]Ge 2:2
20:12 [e]Mt 15:4*; Mk 7:10*; Eph 6:2
20:13 [f]Mt 5:21*; Ro 13:9*
20:14 [g]Mt 19:18*
20:15 [h]Lev 19:11, 13; Mt 19:18*
20:16 [i]Ex 23:1,7; Mt 19:18*
20:17 [j]Ro 7:7*; 13:9*; Eph 5:3
20:18 [k]Ex 19:16-19; Heb 12:18-19

[a] 3 Or *besides*

Meeting a Fearsome God

Thunder and lightning, a thick cloud, smoke, loud trumpeting and then the voice of God. The Israelites experience all this when God descends to the top of Mount Sinai (Ex 19:16-19). They tremble "with fear" (Ex 20:18). Imagine the crying and the chaos as mothers call for their children and as families huddle together. They cower in God's fearsome presence, expecting death.

Have you experienced the immensity of God's power, majesty and holiness? Few people have—and few want to. It's much more pleasant to think about the beautiful, peaceful, loving face of God than his mightiness, holiness and power. Does God want us to be afraid of him?

What distinction does Moses make between being afraid of God and fearing God (Ex 20:20)?

If fearing God is not the same as being afraid of God, what does it mean to "fear God" (Heb 12:18-29)?

What are the benefits of fearing God (Ps 25:14; 31:19; 34:9; Pr 14:26-27)?

What are the consequences of not fearing God (Jer 5:21-25)? The Israelites put their trust in other gods, in human strength, in power and in wealth. Have you put your trust in something or someone other than God?

To fear God is to acknowledge his holiness and power, to respect and honor him and to stand in awe of him. Those who rebel against God should be afraid of him. Their rebellion incurs his anger (Ps 90:7-11). But if you are his child, God does not want you to be afraid of him.

Enjoying God THROUGH the Word

Read Exodus 3:1-6 (page 92). Moses' first encounter with God terrifies him. However, as their relationship becomes more intimate, God speaks to Moses "face to face, as a man speaks with his friend" (Ex 33:11). Later Moses boldly asks God, "Show me your glory" (Ex 33:18). God then comes down in the cloud and stands there with Moses, proclaiming that he is "the LORD, the compassionate and gracious God, slow to anger, abounding in love and faithfulness, maintaining love to thousands, and forgiving wickedness" (Ex 34:5-7). As Moses comes to know God more intimately, he is less afraid and more fearful—that is, awed by God's holiness.

Are you afraid of God? Or do you fear him? God desires an intimate relationship with you. If you want to see his face, you can be certain that one day your desire will be realized (Rev 22:4).

Enjoying God THROUGH Experience

The Israelites prepare themselves for meeting God by consecrating themselves and washing their clothes (Ex 19:10). Purity is a necessity in the presence of a holy God. You are made pure through Jesus' blood (Heb 13:11-12; 1Jn 1:7). He is your righteousness (1Co 1:30).

Use the Scriptures (such as Psalm 99:1-5) to express your adoration to God. Write your own psalm of praise, or sing a song to God in order to release your feelings of love for him. As you draw near to God, he will draw near to you (Jas 4:8). The time you spend with him is time like no other because he is like no other (Jer 10:6-7). If you are afraid, ask God to show himself to you as your loving and compassionate friend. The Holy Spirit will be your helper as you yield to God, learn to trust him and begin to enjoy his presence.

Go to page 222 for your next weekly study.

Slavery

EX 21:2–6

As difficult as the words of Exodus 21:2–6 are to our ears, God is here providing a way for a person to pay off indebtedness or avoid living in poverty. Upon release, these indentured servants/slaves are to be treated liberally (Dt 15:12–15).

In the ancient world, some men from a lower economic class might have sold themselves or even their daughters to wealthier families, hoping to thereby secure a higher standard of living. The stipulations recorded here shielded these individuals from abuse and ensured they were provided for.

Although God gives these regulations to protect people within an imperfect world, we can in no way conclude that God endorses slavery. Paul's call to his friend Philemon to accept his runaway slave as a dear brother in the Lord is a picture of what God truly desires (Phm 8–21).

tain in smoke, they trembled with fear. They
stayed at a distance 19 and said to Moses, "Speak 20:19
to us yourself and we will listen. But do not have [l]Dt 5:5,23-
God speak to us or we will die."[l] 27; Gal 3:19
20 Moses said to the people, "Do not be afraid. 20:20
God has come to test you, so that the fear[m] of God [m]Dt 4:10;
will be with you to keep you from sinning."[n] Isa 8:13
21 The people remained at a distance, while Moses [n]Pr 16:6
approached the thick darkness[o] where God was. 20:21 [o]Dt 5:22

Idols and Altars

22 Then the LORD said to Moses, "Tell the Israelites this: 'You have seen for yourselves that I have
spoken to you from heaven:[p] 23 Do not make any 20:22
gods to be alongside me;[q] do not make for your- [p]Ne 9:13
selves gods of silver or gods of gold.[r] 20:23
24 " 'Make an altar of earth for me and sacrifice [q]ver 3
on it your burnt offerings and fellowship offer- [r]Ex 32:4,8,
ings,[a] your sheep and goats and your cattle. Wher- 31
ever I cause my name[s] to be honored, I will come 20:24
to you and bless[t] you. 25 If you make an altar of [s]Dt 12:5;
stones for me, do not build it with dressed stones, 16:6,11; 2Ch 6:6
for you will defile it if you use a tool[u] on it. 26 And [t]Ge 12:2
do not go up to my altar on steps, lest your naked- 20:25
ness be exposed on it.' [u]Dt 27:5-6

21 "These are the laws[v] you are to set before 21:1
them: [v]Dt 4:14

Hebrew Servants

2 "If you buy a Hebrew servant, he is to serve you
for six years. But in the seventh year, he shall go
free,[w] without paying anything. 3 If he comes alone, 21:2
he is to go free alone; but if he has a wife when he [w]Jer 34:8,14
comes, she is to go with him. 4 If his master gives
him a wife and she bears him sons or daughters,
the woman and her children shall belong to her
master, and only the man shall go free.
5 "But if the servant declares, 'I love my master
and my wife and children and do not want to go 21:5
free,'[x] 6 then his master must take him before the [x]Dt 15:16
judges.[b][y] He shall take him to the door or the 21:6
doorpost and pierce his ear with an awl. Then he [y]Ex 22:8-9
will be his servant for life.[z] [z]Ne 5:5
7 "If a man sells his daughter as a servant, she is
not to go free as menservants do. 8 If she does not
please the master who has selected her for himself,[c] he must let her be redeemed. He has no right
to sell her to foreigners, because he has broken
faith with her. 9 If he selects her for his son, he
must grant her the rights of a daughter. 10 If he marries another woman, he must not deprive the first
one of her food, clothing and marital rights.[a] 11 If 21:10
he does not provide her with these three things, [a]1Co 7:3-5
she is to go free, without any payment of money.

Personal Injuries

12 "Anyone who strikes a man and kills him

[a] 24 Traditionally *peace offerings* [b] 6 Or *before God*
[c] 8 Or *master so that he does not choose her*

shall surely be put to death.[b] 13 However, if he does
not do it intentionally, but God lets it happen, he
is to flee to a place[c] I will designate. 14 But if a man
schemes and kills another man deliberately,[d] take
him away from my altar and put him to death.[e]
15 "Anyone who attacks[a] his father or his mother must be put to death.
16 "Anyone who kidnaps another and either
sells[f] him or still has him when he is caught must
be put to death.[g]
17 "Anyone who curses his father or mother
must be put to death.[h]
18 "If men quarrel and one hits the other with a
stone or with his fist[b] and he does not die but is
confined to bed, 19 the one who struck the blow
will not be held responsible if the other gets up
and walks around outside with his staff; however,
he must pay the injured man for the loss of his
time and see that he is completely healed.
20 "If a man beats his male or female slave with
a rod and the slave dies as a direct result, he must
be punished, 21 but he is not to be punished if the
slave gets up after a day or two, since the slave is
his property.[i]
22 "If men who are fighting hit a pregnant
woman and she gives birth prematurely[c] but there
is no serious injury, the offender must be fined
whatever the woman's husband demands[j] and the
court allows. 23 But if there is serious injury, you
are to take life for life,[k] 24 eye for eye, tooth for
tooth,[l] hand for hand, foot for foot, 25 burn for
burn, wound for wound, bruise for bruise.
26 "If a man hits a manservant or maidservant in
the eye and destroys it, he must let the servant go
free to compensate for the eye. 27 And if he knocks
out the tooth of a manservant or maidservant, he
must let the servant go free to compensate for the
tooth.
28 "If a bull gores a man or a woman to death,
the bull must be stoned to death,[m] and its meat
must not be eaten. But the owner of the bull will
not be held responsible. 29 If, however, the bull has
had the habit of goring and the owner has been
warned but has not kept it penned up and it kills
a man or woman, the bull must be stoned and the
owner also must be put to death. 30 However, if
payment is demanded of him, he may redeem his
life by paying whatever is demanded.[n] 31 This law
also applies if the bull gores a son or daughter. 32 If
the bull gores a male or female slave, the owner
must pay thirty shekels[d][o] of silver to the master
of the slave, and the bull must be stoned.
33 "If a man uncovers a pit or digs one and fails
to cover it and an ox or a donkey falls into it, 34 the
owner of the pit must pay for the loss; he must
pay its owner, and the dead animal will be his.
35 "If a man's bull injures the bull of another and

21:12 [b]Ge 9:6; Mt 26:52
21:13 [c]Nu 35:10-34; Dt 19:2-13; Jos 20:9; 1Sa 24:4,10,18
21:14 [d]Heb 10:26 [e]Dt 19:11-12; 1Ki 2:28-34
21:16 [f]Ge 37:28 [g]Ex 22:4; Dt 24:7
21:17 [h]Lev 20:9-10; Mt 15:4*; Mk 7:10*
21:21 [i]Lev 25:44-46
21:22 [j]ver 30; Dt 22:18-19
21:23 [k]Lev 24:19; Dt 19:21
21:24 [l]Mt 5:38*
21:28 [m]ver 32; Ge 9:5
21:30 [n]ver 22; Nu 35:31
21:32 [o]Zec 11:12-13; Mt 26:15; 27:3,9

[a] 15 Or *kills* [b] 18 Or *with a tool* [c] 22 Or *she has a miscarriage* [d] 32 That is, about 12 ounces (about 0.3 kilogram)

Vengeance

EX 21:12-36

Before the Israelites have traveled very far, God gives laws to regulate cases of violence and retribution. God's desire to protect life, the home and parental authority are made clear in the four crimes that demand the death penalty (Ex 21:12-17). God then lists crimes and accidents that demand payment for damages or injury. In every case, the law of retaliation strictly limits the consequence for wrongdoing. The punishment cannot exceed the crime. These restrictions provided a safeguard in the ancient world, where many crimes carried the death penalty and vengeance often extended as far as killing the entire family of a criminal.

It is human nature to wish to inflict more pain than we suffer, and this series of laws was intended to control this inclination to violence. Eventually, Jesus called his followers to an even higher level of love and forgiveness (Mt 5:38-42).

Laws of Restitution

EX 22:1–15

Specific regulations concerning property, animals, grazing rights, goods kept by a neighbor, and use of another's possessions reveal God's desire for his people to have a deep respect for personal property, just as they were to have a deep respect for the life and safety of others.

Unlike the restrictions in Exodus 21:12–36 that limit penalties for personal injury to "an eye for an eye," this group of laws often demands double payment as restitution. Although the laws are complex and specific to various situations, essentially they are an elaboration of the eighth commandment, "You shall not steal" (Ex 20:15). Carefully examining these laws makes it clear that God cares about the property of others but also about the potential for cruelty, greed and malice in the hearts of his people.

it dies, they are to sell the live one and divide both
the money and the dead animal equally. 36However,
if it was known that the bull had the habit of
goring, yet the owner did not keep it penned up,
the owner must pay, animal for animal, and the
dead animal will be his.

Protection of Property

22 "If a man steals an ox or a sheep and
slaughters it or sells it, he must pay back[p]
five head of cattle for the ox and four sheep for
the sheep.
2"If a thief is caught breaking in[q] and is struck
so that he dies, the defender is not guilty of bloodshed;[r] 3but if it happens[a] after sunrise, he is guilty
of bloodshed.
"A thief must certainly make restitution, but if
he has nothing, he must be sold[s] to pay for his
theft.
4"If the stolen animal is found alive in his possession—whether ox or donkey or sheep—he
must pay back double.[t]
5"If a man grazes his livestock in a field or vineyard and lets them stray and they graze in another man's field, he must make restitution from the
best of his own field or vineyard.
6"If a fire breaks out and spreads into thornbushes so that it burns shocks of grain or standing
grain or the whole field, the one who started the
fire must make restitution.
7"If a man gives his neighbor silver or goods for
safekeeping and they are stolen from the neighbor's house, the thief, if he is caught, must pay
back double.[u] 8But if the thief is not found, the
owner of the house must appear before the
judges[b][v] to determine whether he has laid his
hands on the other man's property. 9In all cases
of illegal possession of an ox, a donkey, a sheep, a
garment, or any other lost property about which
somebody says, 'This is mine,' both parties are to
bring their cases before the judges.[w] The one
whom the judges declare[c] guilty must pay back
double to his neighbor.
10"If a man gives a donkey, an ox, a sheep or
any other animal to his neighbor for safekeeping
and it dies or is injured or is taken away while no
one is looking, 11the issue between them will be
settled by the taking of an oath[x] before the LORD
that the neighbor did not lay hands on the other
person's property. The owner is to accept this, and
no restitution is required. 12But if the animal was
stolen from the neighbor, he must make restitution to the owner. 13If it was torn to pieces by a
wild animal, he shall bring in the remains as evidence and he will not be required to pay for the
torn animal.[y]
14"If a man borrows an animal from his neighbor and it is injured or dies while the owner is not

22:1 [p]2Sa 12:6; Pr 6:31; Lk 19:8
22:2 [q]Mt 6:19-20; 24:43 [r]Nu 35:27
22:3 [s]Ex 21:2; Mt 18:25
22:4 [t]Ge 43:12
22:7 [u]ver 4
22:8 [v]Ex 21:6; Dt 17:8-9; 19:17
22:9 [w]ver 28; Dt 25:1
22:11 [x]Heb 6:16
22:13 [y]Ge 31:39

[a] 3 Or *if he strikes him* [b] 8 Or *before God*; also in verse 9
[c] 9 Or *whom God declares*

present, he must make restitution. 15But if the
owner is with the animal, the borrower will not
have to pay. If the animal was hired, the money
paid for the hire covers the loss.

Social Responsibility

16"If a man seduces a virgin[z] who is not pledged
to be married and sleeps with her, he must pay
the bride-price, and she shall be his wife. 17If her
father absolutely refuses to give her to him, he
must still pay the bride-price for virgins.
18"Do not allow a sorceress[a] to live.
19"Anyone who has sexual relations with an
animal[b] must be put to death.
20"Whoever sacrifices to any god other than the
LORD must be destroyed.[a][c]
21"Do not mistreat an alien[d] or oppress him, for
you were aliens[e] in Egypt.
22"Do not take advantage of a widow or an
orphan.[f] 23If you do and they cry out[g] to me, I will
certainly hear their cry.[h] 24My anger will be
aroused, and I will kill you with the sword; your
wives will become widows and your children
fatherless.[i]
25"If you lend money to one of my people
among you who is needy, do not be like a moneylender; charge him no interest.[b][j] 26If you take
your neighbor's cloak as a pledge,[k] return it to
him by sunset, 27because his cloak is the only covering he has for his body. What else will he sleep
in? When he cries out to me, I will hear, for I am
compassionate.[l]
28"Do not blaspheme God[c][m] or curse the ruler
of your people.[n]
29"Do not hold back offerings[o] from your granaries or your vats.[d]
"You must give me the firstborn of your sons.[p]
30Do the same with your cattle and your sheep.[q]
Let them stay with their mothers for seven days,
but give them to me on the eighth day.[r]
31"You are to be my holy people.[s] So do not eat
the meat of an animal torn by wild beasts;[t] throw
it to the dogs.

Laws of Justice and Mercy

23 "Do not spread false reports.[u] Do not help a
wicked man by being a malicious witness.[v]
2"Do not follow the crowd in doing wrong.
When you give testimony in a lawsuit, do not pervert justice[w] by siding with the crowd, 3and do not
show favoritism to a poor man in his lawsuit.
4"If you come across your enemy's ox or donkey wandering off, be sure to take it back to him.[x]
5If you see the donkey[y] of someone who hates you
fallen down under its load, do not leave it there;
be sure you help him with it.

22:16 [z]Dt 22:28
22:18 [a]Lev 20:27; Dt 18:11; 1Sa 28:3
22:19 [b]Lev 18:23; Dt 27:21
22:20 [c]Dt 17:2-5
22:21 [d]Lev 19:33 [e]Dt 10:19
22:22 [f]Dt 24:6,10, 12,17
22:23 [g]Lk 18:7 [h]Dt 15:9; Ps 18:6
22:24 [i]Ps 69:24; 109:9
22:25 [j]Lev 25:35-37; Dt 23:20; Ps 15:5
22:26 [k]Dt 24:6
22:27 [l]Ex 34:6
22:28 [m]Lev 24:11, 16 [n]Ecc 10:20; Ac 23:5*
22:29 [o]Ex 23:15, 16,19 [p]Ex 13:2
22:30 [q]Ex 13:12; Dt 15:19 [r]Lev 22:27
22:31 [s]Lev 19:2 [t]Eze 4:14
23:1 [u]Ex 20:16; Ps 101:5 [v]Ps 35:11; Ac 6:11
23:2 [w]Dt 16:19
23:4 [x]Dt 22:1-3
23:5 [y]Dt 22:4

[a] 20 The Hebrew term refers to the irrevocable giving over of things or persons to the LORD, often by totally destroying them.
[b] 25 Or *excessive interest* [c] 28 Or *Do not revile the judges*
[d] 29 The meaning of the Hebrew for this phrase is uncertain.

Widows, Orphans and Aliens

EX 22:22–24

The ancient world had no safe place for orphans, widows or aliens. If a family or community refused to care for its own needy members, no one else was obligated to do so.

In this passage God sets a radically different standard. He calls his people to remember their own suffering in Egypt (Ex 22:21; 23:9) and to give to others the same mercy they have received. Grain is to be left in the fields for orphans, widows and aliens (Lev 19:9–10; Dt 24:19–22). Families are to include them on festival days (Dt 16:11–14). Produce from the nation's tithe is given for their support (Dt 14:28–29). God calls us to no less than he called the nation of Israel: to be a compassionate, giving people; and to remember that we ourselves were in need of God's mercy and should, therefore, extend that same mercy to the helpless and needy around us.

Sabbath Keeping

EX 23:10–13

Christians generally find themselves in agreement over what each of the Ten Commandments means for us today, except the fourth: "Remember the Sabbath day by keeping it holy" (Ex 20:8). The Sabbath is a reminder that God rested when he finished creation. He did not require physical rest, but he wished to demonstrate that what he had done was complete.

What do these things mean for us today? Jesus said that the Jews' intricate rules for keeping the Sabbath missed God's point. The Sabbath was meant to bless his people, not stifle them (Mk 2:27–28). That truth is as authentic today as it was in New Testament times.

Hebrews 4:9–10 teaches there is a spiritual Sabbath available to us, a "Sabbath-rest." We find spiritual rest as we grow in our understanding that we are saved by grace and not by works. God is our re-Creator, accomplishing our salvation and completing our transformation into spiritual maturity (Php 1:6), just as he completed physical creation.

6"Do not deny justice[z] to your poor people in
their lawsuits. 7Have nothing to do with a false
charge[a] and do not put an innocent or honest person to death, for I will not acquit the guilty.
8"Do not accept a bribe,[b] for a bribe blinds those
who see and twists the words of the righteous.
9"Do not oppress an alien;[c] you yourselves
know how it feels to be aliens, because you were
aliens in Egypt.

Sabbath Laws

10"For six years you are to sow your fields and
harvest the crops, 11but during the seventh year
let the land lie unplowed and unused. Then the
poor among your people may get food from it, and
the wild animals may eat what they leave. Do the
same with your vineyard and your olive grove.
12"Six days do your work,[d] but on the seventh
day do not work, so that your ox and your donkey
may rest and the slave born in your household,
and the alien as well, may be refreshed.
13"Be careful[e] to do everything I have said to
you. Do not invoke the names of other gods; do
not let them be heard on your lips.

The Three Annual Festivals

14"Three times[f] a year you are to celebrate a festival to me.
15"Celebrate the Feast of Unleavened Bread;[g] for
seven days eat bread made without yeast, as I
commanded you. Do this at the appointed time in
the month of Abib, for in that month you came
out of Egypt.
"No one is to appear before me empty-handed.[h]
16"Celebrate the Feast of Harvest with the firstfruits[i] of the crops you sow in your field.
"Celebrate the Feast of Ingathering at the end of
the year, when you gather in your crops from the
field.[j]
17"Three times[k] a year all the men are to appear
before the Sovereign LORD.
18"Do not offer the blood of a sacrifice to me
along with anything containing yeast.[l]
"The fat of my festival offerings must not be
kept until morning.[m]
19"Bring the best of the firstfruits[n] of your soil to
the house of the LORD your God.
"Do not cook a young goat in its mother's milk.[o]

God's Angel to Prepare the Way

20"See, I am sending an angel[p] ahead of you to
guard you along the way and to bring you to the
place I have prepared.[q] 21Pay attention to him and
listen[r] to what he says. Do not rebel against him;
he will not forgive your rebellion,[s] since my Name
is in him. 22If you listen carefully to what he says
and do all that I say, I will be an enemy[t] to your
enemies and will oppose those who oppose you.
23My angel will go ahead of you and bring you
into the land of the Amorites, Hittites, Perizzites,

23:6 [z]ver 2
23:7 [a]Eph 4:25
23:8 [b]Dt 10:17; 16:19; Pr 15:27
23:9 [c]Ex 22:21
23:12 [d]Ex 20:9
23:13 [e]1Ti 4:16
23:14 [f]Ex 34:23,24
23:15 [g]Ex 12:17 [h]Ex 34:20
23:16 [i]Ex 34:22 [j]Dt 16:13
23:17 [k]Dt 16:16
23:18 [l]Ex 34:25 [m]Dt 16:4
23:19 [n]Ex 22:29; Dt 26:2,10 [o]Dt 14:21
23:20 [p]Ex 14:19; 32:34 [q]Ex 15:17
23:21 [r]Nu 14:11; Dt 18:19 [s]Ps 78:8,40, 56
23:22 [t]Ge 12:3; Dt 30:7

Canaanites, Hivites and Jebusites,[u] and I will wipe
them out. [24]Do not bow down before their gods or
worship[v] them or follow their practices.[w] You
must demolish[x] them and break their sacred
stones to pieces. [25]Worship the LORD your God,[y]
and his blessing[z] will be on your food and water.
I will take away sickness[a] from among you, [26]and
none will miscarry or be barren[b] in your land. I
will give you a full life span.[c]

[27]"I will send my terror[d] ahead of you and throw
into confusion[e] every nation you encounter. I will
make all your enemies turn their backs and run.
[28]I will send the hornet[f] ahead of you to drive the
Hivites, Canaanites and Hittites out of your way.
[29]But I will not drive them out in a single year,
because the land would become desolate and the
wild animals[g] too numerous for you. [30]Little by little I will drive them out before you, until you have
increased enough to take possession of the land.

[31]"I will establish your borders from the Red
Sea[a] to the Sea of the Philistines,[b] and from the
desert to the River.[c][h] I will hand over to you the
people who live in the land and you will drive
them out[i] before you. [32]Do not make a covenant[j]
with them or with their gods. [33]Do not let them
live in your land, or they will cause you to sin
against me, because the worship of their gods will
certainly be a snare[k] to you."

The Covenant Confirmed

24 Then he said to Moses, "Come up to the
LORD, you and Aaron, Nadab and Abihu,[l]
and seventy of the elders[m] of Israel. You are to
worship at a distance, [2]but Moses alone is to
approach the LORD; the others must not come
near. And the people may not come up with him."

[3]When Moses went and told the people all the
LORD's words and laws, they responded with one
voice, "Everything the LORD has said we will do."[n]
[4]Moses then wrote[o] down everything the LORD had
said.

He got up early the next morning and built an
altar at the foot of the mountain and set up twelve
stone pillars[p] representing the twelve tribes of
Israel. [5]Then he sent young Israelite men, and
they offered burnt offerings and sacrificed young
bulls as fellowship offerings[d] to the LORD. [6]Moses
took half of the blood[q] and put it in bowls, and
the other half he sprinkled on the altar. [7]Then he
took the Book of the Covenant[r] and read it to the
people. They responded, "We will do everything
the LORD has said; we will obey."

[8]Moses then took the blood, sprinkled it on the
people and said, "This is the blood of the covenant[s] that the LORD has made with you in accordance with all these words."

[9]Moses and Aaron, Nadab and Abihu, and the

23:23 [u]ver 20; Jos 24:8,11
23:24 [v]Ex 20:5 [w]Dt 12:30-31 [x]Ex 34:13; Nu 33:52
23:25 [y]Dt 6:13; Mt 4:10 [z]Dt 7:12-15; 28:1-14 [a]Ex 15:26
23:26 [b]Dt 7:14; Mal 3:11 [c]Job 5:26
23:27 [d]Ex 15:14; Dt 2:25 [e]Dt 7:23
23:28 [f]Dt 7:20; Jos 24:12
23:29 [g]Dt 7:22
23:31 [h]Ge 15:18 [i]Jos 21:44; 24:12,18
23:32 [j]Ex 34:12; Dt 7:2
23:33 [k]Dt 7:16; Ps 106:36
24:1 [l]Ex 6:23; Lev 10:1-2 [m]Nu 11:16
24:3 [n]Ex 19:8; Dt 5:27
24:4 [o]Dt 31:9 [p]Ge 28:18
24:6 [q]Heb 9:18
24:7 [r]Heb 9:19
24:8 [s]Heb 9:20*; 1Pe 1:2

Thy will is the treasure I seek,
For thou art as faithful as strong;
There let me, obedient and meek,
Repose myself all the day long.
My spirit and faculties fail;
Oh, finish what love has begun!
Destroy what is sinful and frail,
And dwell in the soul thou hast won!
Dear theme of my wonder and praise,
I cry, who is worthy as thou?
I can only be silent and gaze!
'Tis all that is left to me now.

—*Madame Guyon* (1647–1717)

[a] *31* Hebrew *Yam Suph*; that is, Sea of Reeds [b] *31* That is, the Mediterranean [c] *31* That is, the Euphrates
[d] *5* Traditionally *peace offerings*

The Glory of God

EX 24:15–18

Words are never adequate to describe God's glory. The word glory itself means "heavy." God's very nature is so weighted with the beauty of holiness, the majesty of his greatness and the splendor of his love that it is almost unbearable to be near him. He is altogether wonderful and altogether powerful, too awesome, too other, to be treated lightly or indifferently.

God wants his people to know the tenderness of his love (Ex 19:4–6), but he also wants them to realize he is to be feared and obeyed. Here in Exodus 24:17 the glory of God is said to be "like" a consuming fire, a beautiful and accurate description. We love fire's light, warmth, blessing and benefits, but it is powerful and dangerous if treated without respect.

seventy elders[t] of Israel went up 10 and saw[u] the God of Israel. Under his feet was something like a pavement made of sapphire,[a][v] clear as the sky[w] itself. 11 But God did not raise his hand against these leaders of the Israelites; they saw[x] God, and they ate and drank.

12 The LORD said to Moses, "Come up to me on the mountain and stay here, and I will give you the tablets of stone,[y] with the law and commands I have written for their instruction."

13 Then Moses set out with Joshua[z] his aide, and Moses went up on the mountain[a] of God. 14 He said to the elders, "Wait here for us until we come back to you. Aaron and Hur are with you, and anyone involved in a dispute can go to them."

15 When Moses went up on the mountain, the cloud[b] covered it, 16 and the glory[c] of the LORD settled on Mount Sinai. For six days the cloud covered the mountain, and on the seventh day the LORD called to Moses from within the cloud.[d] 17 To the Israelites the glory of the LORD looked like a consuming fire[e] on top of the mountain. 18 Then Moses entered the cloud as he went on up the mountain. And he stayed on the mountain forty[f] days and forty nights.[g]

Offerings for the Tabernacle

25 The LORD said to Moses, 2 "Tell the Israelites to bring me an offering. You are to receive the offering for me from each man whose heart prompts[h] him to give. 3 These are the offerings you are to receive from them: gold, silver and bronze; 4 blue, purple and scarlet yarn and fine linen; goat hair; 5 ram skins dyed red and hides of sea cows[b]; acacia wood; 6 olive oil[i] for the light; spices for the anointing oil and for the fragrant incense; 7 and onyx stones and other gems to be mounted on the ephod[j] and breastpiece.[k]

8 "Then have them make a sanctuary[l] for me, and I will dwell[m] among them. 9 Make this tabernacle and all its furnishings exactly like the pattern[n] I will show you.

The Ark

10 "Have them make a chest[o] of acacia wood—two and a half cubits long, a cubit and a half wide, and a cubit and a half high.[c] 11 Overlay it with pure gold, both inside and out, and make a gold molding around it. 12 Cast four gold rings for it and fasten them to its four feet, with two rings on one side and two rings on the other. 13 Then make poles of acacia wood and overlay them with gold. 14 Insert the poles into the rings on the sides of the chest to carry it. 15 The poles are to remain in the rings of this ark; they are not to be removed.[p] 16 Then put in the ark the Testimony,[q] which I will give you.

24:9 [t]ver 1
24:10 [u]Mt 17:2; Jn 1:18; 6:46 [v]Eze 1:26 [w]Rev 4:3
24:11 [x]Ge 32:30; Ex 19:21
24:12 [y]Ex 32:15-16
24:13 [z]Ex 17:9 [a]Ex 3:1
24:15 [b]Ex 19:9
24:16 [c]Ex 16:10 [d]Ps 99:7
24:17 [e]Ex 3:2; Dt 4:36; Heb 12:18, 29
24:18 [f]Dt 9:9 [g]Ex 34:28
25:2 [h]Ex 35:21; 1Ch 29:5,7, 9; Ezr 2:68; 2Co 8:11-12; 9:7
25:6 [i]Ex 27:20; 30:22-32
25:7 [j]Ex 28:4,6-14 [k]Ex 28:15-30
25:8 [l]Ex 36:1-5; Heb 9:1-2 [m]Ex 29:45; 1Ki 6:13; 2Co 6:16; Rev 21:3
25:9 [n]ver 40; Ac 7:44; Heb 8:5
25:10 [o]Dt 10:1-5; Heb 9:4
25:15 [p]1Ki 8:8
25:16 [q]Dt 31:26; Heb 9:4

[a] *10* Or *lapis lazuli* [b] *5* That is, dugongs [c] *10* That is, about 3 3/4 feet (about 1.1 meters) long and 2 1/4 feet (about 0.7 meter) wide and high

25:17 [r]Ro 3:25
25:20 [s]1Ki 8:7; 1Ch 28:18; Heb 9:5
25:21 [t]Ex 26:34 [u]ver 16
25:22 [v]Nu 7:89; 1Sa 4:4; 2Sa 6:2; 2Ki 19:15; Ps 80:1; Isa 37:16 [w]Ex 29:42-43
25:23 [x]Heb 9:2
25:29 [y]Nu 4:7
25:30 [z]Lev 24:5-9
25:31 [a]1Ki 7:49; Zec 4:2; Heb 9:2; Rev 1:12
25:37 [b]Ex 27:21; Lev 24:3-4; Nu 8:2

17"Make an atonement cover[a][r] of pure gold—
two and a half cubits long and a cubit and a half
wide.[b] 18And make two cherubim out of hammered gold at the ends of the cover. 19Make one
cherub on one end and the second cherub on the
other; make the cherubim of one piece with the
cover, at the two ends. 20The cherubim are to have
their wings spread upward, overshadowing[s] the
cover with them. The cherubim are to face each
other, looking toward the cover. 21Place the cover
on top of the ark[t] and put in the ark the Testimony,[u] which I will give you. 22There, above the cover between the two cherubim[v] that are over the
ark of the Testimony, I will meet[w] with you and
give you all my commands for the Israelites.

The Table

23"Make a table[x] of acacia wood—two cubits
long, a cubit wide and a cubit and a half high.[c]
24Overlay it with pure gold and make a gold molding around it. 25Also make around it a rim a handbreadth[d] wide and put a gold molding on the rim.
26Make four gold rings for the table and fasten
them to the four corners, where the four legs are.
27The rings are to be close to the rim to hold the
poles used in carrying the table. 28Make the poles
of acacia wood, overlay them with gold and carry
the table with them. 29And make its plates and
dishes of pure gold, as well as its pitchers and
bowls for the pouring out of offerings.[y] 30Put the
bread of the Presence[z] on this table to be before
me at all times.

The Lampstand

31"Make a lampstand[a] of pure gold and hammer
it out, base and shaft; its flowerlike cups, buds
and blossoms shall be of one piece with it. 32Six
branches are to extend from the sides of the lampstand—three on one side and three on the other.
33Three cups shaped like almond flowers with
buds and blossoms are to be on one branch, three
on the next branch, and the same for all six
branches extending from the lampstand. 34And on
the lampstand there are to be four cups shaped
like almond flowers with buds and blossoms.
35One bud shall be under the first pair of branches
extending from the lampstand, a second bud
under the second pair, and a third bud under the
third pair—six branches in all. 36The buds and
branches shall all be of one piece with the lampstand, hammered out of pure gold.
37"Then make its seven lamps[b] and set them up
on it so that they light the space in front of it. 38Its
wick trimmers and trays are to be of pure gold.
39A talent[e] of pure gold is to be used for the lamp-

[a] *17* Traditionally *a mercy seat* [b] *17* That is, about 3 3/4 feet (about 1.1 meters) long and 2 1/4 feet (about 0.7 meter) wide [c] *23* That is, about 3 feet (about 0.9 meter) long and 1 1/2 feet (about 0.5 meter) wide and 2 1/4 feet (about 0.7 meter) high [d] *25* That is, about 3 inches (about 8 centimeters) [e] *39* That is, about 75 pounds (about 34 kilograms)

All That Gold!

EX 25

God intends his house to be a place of exquisite beauty. These former slaves have many valuable items in their possession (gold, silver, bronze, fine linen material, animal skins, spices, gemstones). Where did all this come from? The most likely answer: from Egypt. The Israelite slaves "plundered" Egypt, taking with them many valuable Egyptian articles (Ge 15:13-14; Ex 12:35-36).

When Moses calls the people to give for the tabernacle's construction, their eager generosity proves so great that Moses has to tell them to stop bringing gifts (Ex 36:2-7)! What they contribute staggers our minds. Over 2,000 pounds of gold alone went into the construction (Ex 38:24; see NIV footnote).

Why does God want all this golden beauty? It is more than a lesson in the value of worship. As the place where God meets with his people, the tabernacle pictures Christ. John 1:14 says, literally, "The Word became flesh and made his dwelling [or *tabernacled*] among us."

An Educated Leader

EX 25:40

During Moses' early years, Egypt is at a high point as an international power, with a written history and a highly developed culture of artisans. Acts 7:22 says, "Moses was educated in all the wisdom of the Egyptians." He is capable of negotiating in Pharaoh's court, organizing an exodus of two million people, and recording what God says (Ex 17:14, 24:4, 34:28). His education gives him the expertise to direct the building of the tabernacle to precisely match the pattern God has given. Moses' full obedience is critical because the tabernacle is a picture of a true holy place in heaven (Heb 8:5; 9:24). As Moses ensures that the artisans under him follow God's pattern exactly, the tabernacle unfolds to become a visual picture of the story of salvation that Christ would one day bring. See Hebrews 7:1—10:22 for a full discussion of the meaning of the priesthood and the tabernacle.

stand and all these accessories. 40See that you make them according to the pattern[c] shown you on the mountain.

The Tabernacle

26 "Make the tabernacle with ten curtains of finely twisted linen and blue, purple and scarlet yarn, with cherubim worked into them by a skilled craftsman. 2All the curtains are to be the same size—twenty-eight cubits long and four cubits wide.[a] 3Join five of the curtains together, and do the same with the other five. 4Make loops of blue material along the edge of the end curtain in one set, and do the same with the end curtain in the other set. 5Make fifty loops on one curtain and fifty loops on the end curtain of the other set, with the loops opposite each other. 6Then make fifty gold clasps and use them to fasten the curtains together so that the tabernacle is a unit.

7"Make curtains of goat hair for the tent over the tabernacle—eleven altogether. 8All eleven curtains are to be the same size—thirty cubits long and four cubits wide.[b] 9Join five of the curtains together into one set and the other six into another set. Fold the sixth curtain double at the front of the tent. 10Make fifty loops along the edge of the end curtain in one set and also along the edge of the end curtain in the other set. 11Then make fifty bronze clasps and put them in the loops to fasten the tent together as a unit. 12As for the additional length of the tent curtains, the half curtain that is left over is to hang down at the rear of the tabernacle. 13The tent curtains will be a cubit[c] longer on both sides; what is left will hang over the sides of the tabernacle so as to cover it. 14Make for the tent a covering of ram skins dyed red, and over that a covering of hides of sea cows.[d][d]

15"Make upright frames of acacia wood for the tabernacle. 16Each frame is to be ten cubits long and a cubit and a half wide,[e] 17with two projections set parallel to each other. Make all the frames of the tabernacle in this way. 18Make twenty frames for the south side of the tabernacle 19and make forty silver bases to go under them—two bases for each frame, one under each projection. 20For the other side, the north side of the tabernacle, make twenty frames 21and forty silver bases—two under each frame. 22Make six frames for the far end, that is, the west end of the tabernacle, 23and make two frames for the corners at the far end. 24At these two corners they must be double from the bottom all the way to the top, and fitted into a single ring; both shall be like that. 25So there will be eight frames and sixteen silver bases—two under each frame.

25:40 [c]Ex 26:30; Nu 8:4; Ac 7:44; Heb 8:5*

26:14 [d]Ex 36:19; Nu 4:25

[a] *2* That is, about 42 feet (about 12.5 meters) long and 6 feet (about 1.8 meters) wide [b] *8* That is, about 45 feet (about 13.5 meters) long and 6 feet (about 1.8 meters) wide [c] *13* That is, about 1 1/2 feet (about 0.5 meter) [d] *14* That is, dugongs [e] *16* That is, about 15 feet (about 4.5 meters) long and 2 1/4 feet (about 0.7 meter) wide

26“Also make crossbars of acacia wood: five for
the frames on one side of the tabernacle, 27five for
those on the other side, and five for the frames on
the west, at the far end of the tabernacle. 28The
center crossbar is to extend from end to end at the
middle of the frames. 29Overlay the frames with
gold and make gold rings to hold the crossbars.
Also overlay the crossbars with gold.
30“Set up the tabernacle according to the plan[e]
shown you on the mountain.
31“Make a curtain[f] of blue, purple and scarlet
yarn and finely twisted linen, with cherubim[g]
worked into it by a skilled craftsman. 32Hang it
with gold hooks on four posts of acacia wood
overlaid with gold and standing on four silver
bases. 33Hang the curtain from the clasps and
place the ark of the Testimony behind the curtain.[h] The curtain will separate the Holy Place
from the Most Holy Place.[i] 34Put the atonement
cover[j] on the ark of the Testimony in the Most
Holy Place. 35Place the table[k] outside the curtain
on the north side of the tabernacle and put the
lampstand[l] opposite it on the south side.
36“For the entrance to the tent make a curtain
of blue, purple and scarlet yarn and finely twisted
linen—the work of an embroiderer. 37Make gold
hooks for this curtain and five posts of acacia
wood overlaid with gold. And cast five bronze
bases for them.

26:30 [e]Ex 25:9,40; Ac 7:44; Heb 8:5
26:31 [f]2Ch 3:14; Mt 27:51; Heb 9:3 [g]Ex 36:35
26:33 [h]Ex 40:3,21; Lev 16:2 [i]Heb 9:2-3
26:34 [j]Ex 25:21; 40:20; Heb 9:5
26:35 [k]Heb 9:2 [l]Ex 40:22,24

The Altar of Burnt Offering

27 “Build an altar[m] of acacia wood, three
cubits[a] high; it is to be square, five cubits
long and five cubits wide.[b] 2Make a horn[n] at each
of the four corners, so that the horns and the altar
are of one piece, and overlay the altar with
bronze. 3Make all its utensils of bronze—its pots
to remove the ashes, and its shovels, sprinkling
bowls, meat forks and firepans. 4Make a grating
for it, a bronze network, and make a bronze ring
at each of the four corners of the network. 5Put it
under the ledge of the altar so that it is halfway
up the altar. 6Make poles of acacia wood for the
altar and overlay them with bronze. 7The poles
are to be inserted into the rings so they will be on
two sides of the altar when it is carried. 8Make the
altar hollow, out of boards. It is to be made just
as you were shown[o] on the mountain.

27:1 [m]Eze 43:13
27:2 [n]Ps 118:27
27:8 [o]Ex 25:9,40

The Courtyard

9“Make a courtyard for the tabernacle. The south
side shall be a hundred cubits[c] long and is to have
curtains of finely twisted linen, 10with twenty posts
and twenty bronze bases and with silver hooks
and bands on the posts. 11The north side shall also
be a hundred cubits long and is to have curtains,

[a] *1* That is, about 4 1/2 feet (about 1.3 meters) [b] *1* That is, about 7 1/2 feet (about 2.3 meters) long and wide [c] *9* That is, about 150 feet (about 46 meters); also in verse 11

A Special Curtain

EXODUS 26:31–37

As slaves in Egypt, the Israelites learn to make exquisite cloth. They make this cloth by twisting together many fine strands of linen and then weaving them into fabric. This method produces a soft, heavy, extremely strong cloth. Once it is embroidered, this colorful curtain will enclose the Most Holy Place, which is where the ark, the symbol of God’s presence, will sit (Ex 25:22). The high priest can enter the Most Holy Place only once a year. There he makes atonement before God for the nation’s sins (Lev 16:2–3, 29–30).

In startling and graphic language, Matthew 27:51 records that as Jesus dies, this curtain is torn in two from top to bottom. Christ’s death provides total cleansing. There is no longer any need for separation from our holy God. We can now freely approach God because of Christ’s perfect sacrifice (Heb 10:19–22).

The Gold Lampstand

EXODUS 27:20-21

Exodus 25:31-40 gives the details for crafting the large, ornate, gold lampstand with seven lights (stems and bowls for holding olive oil) that God commands must be continually lit. This lampstand provides light for the priests to perform their duties. But more than that, the light from the lampstand symbolizes the presence of God. Since he has promised never to leave (Dt 31:6), he commands that this light should never be extinguished. Ultimately, the lampstand points to Christ, the light of the world (Jn 8:12).

During their years in the desert, the oil for these seven lights must have come either from the goods the Israelites took with them from Egypt or from trading with other nomadic groups. Once the Israelites settle in the promised land and begin cultivating olive groves, olive oil becomes a staple in both life and worship.

with twenty posts and twenty bronze bases and with silver hooks and bands on the posts.

12 "The west end of the courtyard shall be fifty cubits[a] wide and have curtains, with ten posts and ten bases. 13 On the east end, toward the sunrise, the courtyard shall also be fifty cubits wide. 14 Curtains fifteen cubits[b] long are to be on one side of the entrance, with three posts and three bases, 15 and curtains fifteen cubits long are to be on the other side, with three posts and three bases.

16 "For the entrance to the courtyard, provide a curtain twenty cubits[c] long, of blue, purple and scarlet yarn and finely twisted linen—the work of an embroiderer—with four posts and four bases. 17 All the posts around the courtyard are to have silver bands and hooks, and bronze bases. 18 The courtyard shall be a hundred cubits long and fifty cubits wide,[d] with curtains of finely twisted linen five cubits[e] high, and with bronze bases. 19 All the other articles used in the service of the tabernacle, whatever their function, including all the tent pegs for it and those for the courtyard, are to be of bronze.

Oil for the Lampstand

20 "Command the Israelites to bring you clear oil of pressed olives for the light so that the lamps may be kept burning. 21 In the Tent of Meeting,[p] outside the curtain that is in front of the Testimony,[q] Aaron and his sons are to keep the lamps[r] burning before the LORD from evening till morning. This is to be a lasting ordinance[s] among the Israelites for the generations to come.

The Priestly Garments

28 "Have Aaron[t] your brother brought to you from among the Israelites, along with his sons Nadab and Abihu, Eleazar and Ithamar, so they may serve me as priests.[u] 2 Make sacred garments[v] for your brother Aaron, to give him dignity and honor. 3 Tell all the skilled men[w] to whom I have given wisdom[x] in such matters that they are to make garments for Aaron, for his consecration, so he may serve me as priest. 4 These are the garments they are to make: a breastpiece,[y] an ephod, a robe,[z] a woven tunic,[a] a turban and a sash. They are to make these sacred garments for your brother Aaron and his sons, so they may serve me as priests. 5 Have them use gold, and blue, purple and scarlet yarn, and fine linen.

The Ephod

6 "Make the ephod of gold, and of blue, purple and scarlet yarn, and of finely twisted linen—the work of a skilled craftsman. 7 It is to have two

27:21 [p]Ex 28:43 [q]Ex 26:31,33 [r]Ex 25:37; 30:8; 1Sa 3:3; 2Ch 13:11 [s]Ex 29:9; Lev 3:17; 16:34; Nu 18:23; 19:21

28:1 [t]Heb 5:4 [u]Nu 18:1-7; Heb 5:1

28:2 [v]Ex 29:5,29; 31:10; 39:1; Lev 8:7-9,30

28:3 [w]Ex 31:6; 36:1 [x]Ex 31:3

28:4 [y]ver 15-30 [z]ver 31-35 [a]ver 39

[a] *12* That is, about 75 feet (about 23 meters); also in verse 13
[b] *14* That is, about 22 1/2 feet (about 6.9 meters); also in verse 15
[c] *16* That is, about 30 feet (about 9 meters)
[d] *18* That is, about 150 feet (about 46 meters) long and 75 feet (about 23 meters) wide
[e] *18* That is, about 7 1/2 feet (about 2.3 meters)

shoulder pieces attached to two of its corners, so
it can be fastened. 8Its skillfully woven waistband
is to be like it—of one piece with the ephod and
made with gold, and with blue, purple and scarlet
yarn, and with finely twisted linen.
9"Take two onyx stones and engrave on them
the names of the sons of Israel 10in the order of
their birth—six names on one stone and the
remaining six on the other. 11Engrave the names of
the sons of Israel on the two stones the way a gem
cutter engraves a seal. Then mount the stones in
gold filigree settings 12and fasten them on the
shoulder pieces of the ephod as memorial stones
for the sons of Israel. Aaron is to bear the names
on his shoulders as a memorial before the LORD.
13Make gold filigree settings 14and two braided
chains of pure gold, like a rope, and attach the
chains to the settings.

The Breastpiece

15"Fashion a breastpiece for making decisions—
the work of a skilled craftsman. Make it like the
ephod: of gold, and of blue, purple and scarlet
yarn, and of finely twisted linen. 16It is to be
square—a span[a] long and a span wide—and folded double. 17Then mount four rows of precious
stones on it. In the first row there shall be a ruby,
a topaz and a beryl; 18in the second row a
turquoise, a sapphire[b] and an emerald; 19in the
third row a jacinth, an agate and an amethyst; 20in
the fourth row a chrysolite, an onyx and a jasper.[c]
Mount them in gold filigree settings. 21There are to
be twelve stones, one for each of the names of the
sons of Israel, each engraved like a seal with the
name of one of the twelve tribes.
22"For the breastpiece make braided chains of
pure gold, like a rope. 23Make two gold rings for it
and fasten them to two corners of the breastpiece.
24Fasten the two gold chains to the rings at the
corners of the breastpiece, 25and the other ends of
the chains to the two settings, attaching them to
the shoulder pieces of the ephod at the front.
26Make two gold rings and attach them to the other two corners of the breastpiece on the inside
edge next to the ephod. 27Make two more gold
rings and attach them to the bottom of the shoulder pieces on the front of the ephod, close to the
seam just above the waistband of the ephod. 28The
rings of the breastpiece are to be tied to the rings
of the ephod with blue cord, connecting it to the
waistband, so that the breastpiece will not swing
28:29 out from the ephod.
[b]ver 12 29"Whenever Aaron enters the Holy Place,[b] he
28:30 will bear the names of the sons of Israel over his
[c]Lev 8:8; heart on the breastpiece of decision as a continu-
Nu 27:21; ing memorial before the LORD. 30Also put the Urim
Dt 33:8; Ezr 2:63; and the Thummim[c] in the breastpiece, so they
Ne 7:65

[a] *16* That is, about 9 inches (about 22 centimeters) [b] *18* Or *lapis lazuli* [c] *20* The precise identification of some of these precious stones is uncertain.

The Breastpiece

EX 28:15-30

The breastpiece of the high priest's garment pictures God's heart for his people and his commitment to give them wisdom. Twelve precious stones are placed on the breastpiece and engraved with the names of the Hebrew tribes—[ruby (Reuben), topaz (Simeon), beryl (Levi), turquoise (Judah), sapphire (Issachar), emerald (Zebulun), jacinth (Dan), agate (Naphtali), amethyst (Gad), chrysolite (Asher), onyx (Joseph), jasper (Benjamin)]. The symbolism is clear: God knows his people by name (Isa 43:1); he carries their burdens; he holds them close to his heart (Ex 19:4).

The Urim and the Thummim placed inside the breastpiece are puzzling. Literally these two words mean "curses" and "perfections." The priests use these two items to seek answers and direction from God (Nu 27:21; 1Sa 30:7-8; Ezr 2:63). However, their exact nature, and how they functioned, is unknown.

may be over Aaron's heart whenever he enters the
presence of the LORD. Thus Aaron will always bear
the means of making decisions for the Israelites
over his heart before the LORD.

Other Priestly Garments

31"Make the robe of the ephod entirely of blue
cloth, 32with an opening for the head in its center.
There shall be a woven edge like a collar[a] around
this opening, so that it will not tear. 33Make pomegranates of blue, purple and scarlet yarn around
the hem of the robe, with gold bells between
them. 34The gold bells and the pomegranates are
to alternate around the hem of the robe. 35Aaron
must wear it when he ministers. The sound of the
bells will be heard when he enters the Holy Place
before the LORD and when he comes out, so that
he will not die.

36"Make a plate of pure gold and engrave on it as
on a seal: HOLY TO THE LORD.[d] 37Fasten a blue cord to
it to attach it to the turban; it is to be on the front
of the turban. 38It will be on Aaron's forehead, and
he will bear the guilt[e] involved in the sacred gifts
the Israelites consecrate, whatever their gifts may
be. It will be on Aaron's forehead continually so
that they will be acceptable to the LORD.

39"Weave the tunic of fine linen and make the
turban of fine linen. The sash is to be the work of
an embroiderer. 40Make tunics, sashes and headbands for Aaron's sons,[f] to give them dignity and
honor. 41After you put these clothes on your brother Aaron and his sons, anoint[g] and ordain them.
Consecrate them so they may serve me as priests.[h]

42"Make linen undergarments[i] as a covering for
the body, reaching from the waist to the thigh.
43Aaron and his sons must wear them whenever
they enter the Tent of Meeting[j] or approach the
altar to minister in the Holy Place, so that they
will not incur guilt and die.[k]

"This is to be a lasting ordinance[l] for Aaron and
his descendants.

Consecration of the Priests

29 "This is what you are to do to consecrate
them, so they may serve me as priests: Take
a young bull and two rams without defect. 2And
from fine wheat flour, without yeast, make bread,
and cakes mixed with oil, and wafers spread with
oil.[m] 3Put them in a basket and present them in
it—along with the bull and the two rams. 4Then
bring Aaron and his sons to the entrance to the
Tent of Meeting and wash them with water.[n] 5Take
the garments[o] and dress Aaron with the tunic, the
robe of the ephod, the ephod itself and the breastpiece. Fasten the ephod on him by its skillfully
woven waistband.[p] 6Put the turban on his head
and attach the sacred diadem[q] to the turban. 7Take
the anointing oil[r] and anoint him by pouring it on
his head. 8Bring his sons and dress them in tunics

The more they abandon themselves, the more they find [God].

—Catherine of Siena (1347-1380)

28:36 [d]Zec 14:20
28:38 [e]Lev 10:17; 22:9,16; Nu 18:1; Heb 9:28; 1Pe 2:24
28:40 [f]ver 4; Ex 39:41
28:41 [g]Ex 29:7; Lev 10:7 [h]Ex 29:7-9; 30:30; 40:15; Lev 8:1-36; Heb 7:28
28:42 [i]Lev 6:10; 16:4,23; Eze 44:18
28:43 [j]Ex 27:21 [k]Ex 20:26 [l]Lev 17:7
29:2 [m]Lev 2:1,4; 6:19-23
29:4 [n]Ex 40:12; Heb 10:22
29:5 [o]Ex 28:2; Lev 8:7 [p]Ex 28:8
29:6 [q]Lev 8:9
29:7 [r]Ex 30:25, 30,31; Lev 8:12; 21:10; Nu 35:25; Ps 133:2

[a] *32* The meaning of the Hebrew for this word is uncertain.

29:9 9and put headbands on them. Then tie sashes on
sEx 28:40 Aaron and his sons.[a][s] The priesthood is theirs by
tEx 40:15; a lasting ordinance.[t] In this way you shall ordain
Nu 3:10; Aaron and his sons.
18:7; 25:13; 10"Bring the bull to the front of the Tent of Meet-
Dt 18:5 ing, and Aaron and his sons shall lay their hands
on its head. 11Slaughter it in the LORD's presence at
the entrance to the Tent of Meeting. 12Take some
29:12 of the bull's blood and put it on the horns[u] of the
uEx 27:2 altar with your finger, and pour out the rest of it at
29:13 the base of the altar. 13Then take all the fat[v] around
vLev 3:3,5,9 the inner parts, the covering of the liver, and both
kidneys with the fat on them, and burn them on
29:14 the altar. 14But burn the bull's flesh and its hide
wLev 4:11- and its offal outside the camp.[w] It is a sin offering.
12,21; 15"Take one of the rams, and Aaron and his sons
Heb 13:11 shall lay their hands on its head. 16Slaughter it
and take the blood and sprinkle it against the altar
on all sides. 17Cut the ram into pieces and wash
the inner parts and the legs, putting them with the
head and the other pieces. 18Then burn the entire
ram on the altar. It is a burnt offering to the LORD,
29:18 a pleasing aroma,[x] an offering made to the LORD
xGe 8:21 by fire.
29:19 19"Take the other ram,[y] and Aaron and his sons
yver 3 shall lay their hands on its head. 20Slaughter it,
take some of its blood and put it on the lobes of
the right ears of Aaron and his sons, on the
thumbs of their right hands, and on the big toes of
their right feet. Then sprinkle blood against the
29:21 zHeb 9:22 altar on all sides. 21And take some of the blood[z]
aEx 30:25,31 on the altar and some of the anointing oil[a] and
bver 1 sprinkle it on Aaron and his garments and on his
sons and their garments. Then he and his sons
and their garments will be consecrated.[b]
22"Take from this ram the fat, the fat tail, the fat
around the inner parts, the covering of the liver,
both kidneys with the fat on them, and the right
thigh. (This is the ram for the ordination.) 23From
the basket of bread made without yeast, which is
before the LORD, take a loaf, and a cake made with
oil, and a wafer. 24Put all these in the hands of
29:24 Aaron and his sons and wave them before the
cLev 7:30 LORD as a wave offering.[c] 25Then take them from
their hands and burn them on the altar along with
the burnt offering for a pleasing aroma to the
LORD, an offering made to the LORD by fire. 26After
you take the breast of the ram for Aaron's ordina-
29:26 tion, wave it before the LORD as a wave offering,
dLev 7:31-34 and it will be your share.[d]
29:27 eLev 7:31,34; 27"Consecrate those parts of the ordination ram
Dt 18:3 that belong to Aaron and his sons:[e] the breast that
was waved and the thigh that was presented.
28This is always to be the regular share from the
Israelites for Aaron and his sons. It is the contri-
29:28 bution the Israelites are to make to the LORD from
fLev 10:15 their fellowship offerings.[b][f]
29"Aaron's sacred garments will belong to his

[a] 9 Hebrew; Septuagint *on them* [b] 28 Traditionally *peace offerings*

Anointing Body Parts

EX 29:19-20

As Aaron and his sons are set apart for their priestly life and duties, a ram is killed and some of its blood is put on the lobes of their right ears, the thumbs of their right hands, and the big toes of their right feet. Odd ceremony, don't you think? What did it mean?

Placing blood on these three body parts may have been God's reminder to his priests that they should constantly guard every part of their lives. They must submit to God's will in what they listen to and how eagerly they devote themselves to his word (the ear lobe). They must guard their actions and choices (the thumb), and they must carefully watch their walk through life (the big toe). In many cultures of the world, the right side of the body is favored, so to anoint body parts with blood on the right side is to say that the very best of a person's life has been consecrated for service to God.

Pressed Olives

EX 29:38–41

Olives were an essential part of the ancient Middle Eastern diet. Olive oil was used for cooking, for anointing and as a medicine. Olive oil was produced by a strenuous and tedious process of pressing olives in a mill, moved either by an animal or by human power. Each olive produced only a few drops of oil, so there was great effort involved in producing only a single pint of oil.

God's requirement that every morning and evening sacrifice include a quarter of a hin (about one quart) of olive oil called for true commitment from his people. They were being asked to daily give back to him something essential to their well-being and something that represented significant labor on their part.

descendants so that they can be anointed and ordained in them.[g] 30The son[h] who succeeds him as priest and comes to the Tent of Meeting to minister in the Holy Place is to wear them seven days.

31"Take the ram for the ordination and cook the meat in a sacred place. 32At the entrance to the Tent of Meeting, Aaron and his sons are to eat the meat of the ram and the bread[i] that is in the basket. 33They are to eat these offerings by which atonement was made for their ordination and consecration. But no one else may eat[j] them, because they are sacred. 34And if any of the meat of the ordination ram or any bread is left over till morning,[k] burn it up. It must not be eaten, because it is sacred.

35"Do for Aaron and his sons everything I have commanded you, taking seven days to ordain them. 36Sacrifice a bull each day[l] as a sin offering to make atonement. Purify the altar by making atonement for it, and anoint it to consecrate[m] it. 37For seven days make atonement for the altar and consecrate it. Then the altar will be most holy, and whatever touches it will be holy.[n]

38"This is what you are to offer on the altar regularly each day:[o] two lambs a year old. 39Offer one in the morning and the other at twilight.[p] 40With the first lamb offer a tenth of an ephah[a] of fine flour mixed with a quarter of a hin[b] of oil from pressed olives, and a quarter of a hin of wine as a drink offering. 41Sacrifice the other lamb at twilight with the same grain offering and its drink offering as in the morning—a pleasing aroma, an offering made to the LORD by fire.

42"For the generations to come[q] this burnt offering is to be made regularly at the entrance to the Tent of Meeting before the LORD. There I will meet you and speak to you;[r] 43there also I will meet with the Israelites, and the place will be consecrated by my glory.[s]

44"So I will consecrate the Tent of Meeting and the altar and will consecrate Aaron and his sons to serve me as priests.[t] 45Then I will dwell[u] among the Israelites and be their God.[v] 46They will know that I am the LORD their God, who brought them out of Egypt so that I might dwell among them. I am the LORD their God.[w]

The Altar of Incense

30 "Make an altar[x] of acacia wood for burning incense.[y] 2It is to be square, a cubit long and a cubit wide, and two cubits high[c]—its horns[z] of one piece with it. 3Overlay the top and all the sides and the horns with pure gold, and make a gold molding around it. 4Make two gold rings for the altar below the molding—two on opposite sides—to hold the poles used to carry it. 5Make

29:29 [g]Nu 20:26, 28
29:30 [h]Nu 20:28
29:32 [i]Mt 12:4
29:33 [j]Lev 10:14; 22:10,13
29:34 [k]Ex 12:10
29:36 [l]Heb 10:11 [m]Ex 40:10
29:37 [n]Ex 30:28-29; 40:10; Mt 23:19
29:38 [o]Nu 28:3-8; 1Ch 16:40; Da 12:11
29:39 [p]Eze 46:13-15
29:42 [q]Ex 30:8 [r]Ex 25:22
29:43 [s]1Ki 8:11
29:44 [t]Lev 21:15
29:45 [u]Ex 25:8; Lev 26:12; Zec 2:10; Jn 14:17 [v]2Co 6:16; Rev 21:3
29:46 [w]Ex 20:2
30:1 [x]Ex 37:25 [y]Rev 8:3
30:2 [z]Ex 27:2

[a] *40* That is, probably about 2 quarts (about 2 liters)
[b] *40* That is, probably about 1 quart (about 1 liter)
[c] *2* That is, about 1 1/2 feet (about 0.5 meter) long and wide and about 3 feet (about 0.9 meter) high

Lot's Wife

Excess Baggage

If the most sinful act of your life were frozen in stone, what would you be doing? Where would you be? Few of us consider a backward glance as justification for freezing a person as a pillar of salt. Does the example of Lot's wife mean that God is just waiting for us to make one wrong move so he can zap us? No. There is more going on here than a look back over the shoulder.

Lot and his wife had enjoyed following along with Abraham, Lot's uncle. God had blessed Abraham with great riches, which Lot's family shared. But, unlike Abraham, Lot's family had not connected with the God who gave the blessing.

Perhaps in the beginning Lot's family was able to avoid the wicked mind-set pervading Sodom. But daily exposure to Sodom's culture began to erode their sense of right and wrong. They seemed to have had no strong sense of faith in God or knowledge of him by which to judge what was going on around them. Tolerance of the gross sins of their neighbors seemed a small price to pay for their overall sense of well-being. That they were affected by the prevailing moral culture is suggested by Lot's offering his two daughters to the men who surrounded his house (Ge 19:6–8) and by the incestuous activities of Lot's daughters after they'd fled Sodom (Ge 19:30–38).

Abraham's prayer on behalf of the city was the only thing that stood between Lot's family and utter destruction. And though angels escorted them, they argued. One of God's demands was nonnegotiable, however. The break from sin must be complete. No looking back, no baggage from the wicked past—all of their wealth was left behind.

But it appears that Lot's wife regretted leaving Sodom and all its comforts. Her backward glance suggests that even in the very presence of God she longed for the life and the things that led to destruction. She didn't believe, and she disobeyed the angel's command. God remained true to his word.

Lot and his family flirted with temptation and lost everything. We too are swayed by our culture in ways we don't even realize. It's not enough to be a good person, to associate with other good people and to share in their blessings, as Lot's family shared Abraham's prosperity. In the face of God's judgment, only Jesus stands between us and eternal destruction. Only Jesus can cover all the refuse of our lives and proclaim us righteous.

Lot's Wife
Genesis 19:1–29
Luke 17:29–33

Candid SNAPSHOT Then the LORD rained down burning sulfur on Sodom and Gomorrah . . . But Lot's wife looked back, and she became a pillar of salt (Genesis 19:24,26).

Rebekah

Giving God a Hand

It was a moment that touched her deepest being. As her hands pressed against her belly that bounced with life, Rebekah whispered to God, "What will my child be like?" She had been waiting for this for twenty years, and her pregnancy was a great wonder of self-discovery and communion with her Maker. God answered Rebekah's question with startling clarity.

Twins! Not only did the Lord reveal the number, but also the character of the children within her and the essence of his plan for their lives. This was a remarkable gift to Rebekah from the Lord. The problem lay in what she did with the information, for Rebekah tried to take her children's futures out of God's hands and into her own. She shouldn't have; God could have handled the job.

As her sons, Esau and Jacob, grew older, their own choices revealed their inclinations. Esau had so little regard for his spiritual birthright that he sold it to Jacob for a bowl of soup! Jacob showed his crafty nature by duping his father—with Rebekah's urging and help.

Rebekah probably believed that her actions furthered God's cause. She certainly did not intentionally foster the family division and strife that lasted for generations. But in truth, Rebekah could never have fashioned the perfect plan to bring about God's will. No human can. It isn't our job. The Lord has said, "As the heavens are higher than the earth, so are my ways higher than your ways and my thoughts than your thoughts" (Isa 55:9).

Perhaps most sadly of all, Rebekah's need to elevate Jacob prevented her from encouraging and nurturing Esau. Largely by her own activities, she missed out on the greatest joy a mother can have—watching her sons grow into men of integrity, set on pleasing God. As a matter of fact, when she sent Jacob away to Haran, she lost him for good. From the text it appears that she died before he returned some twenty years later (Ge 35:27–29).

If God gives us insight into the lives of our children or other loved ones, it is for his glory. We love him all the more as we recognize his hand in their lives, and we can cooperate with what he is doing. Knowing that he is in control gives us hope in setbacks or reversals. We can pray in the faith that God's plan will not be thwarted. We have no right to manipulate and connive, as Rebekah did, to accomplish what we think is God's will in our children's lives.

Rebekah
(ensnarer)

Genesis 24; 25:20–28; 26:7–28:5; 49:31
Romans 9:6–16

Candid SNAPSHOT *Now, my son, listen carefully and do what I tell you: Go out to the flock and bring me two choice young goats, so I can prepare some tasty food for your father, just the way he likes it. Then take it to your father to eat, so that he may give you his blessing before he dies (Genesis 27:8–10).*

the poles of acacia wood and overlay them with
gold. 6Put the altar in front of the curtain that is
before the ark of the Testimony—before the atone-
30:6 [a]Ex 25:22; 26:34 — ment cover[a] that is over the Testimony—where I
will meet with you.
30:7 [b]ver 34-35; Ex 27:21; 1Sa 2:28 — 7"Aaron must burn fragrant incense[b] on the altar
every morning when he tends the lamps. 8He must
burn incense again when he lights the lamps at
twilight so incense will burn regularly before the
LORD for the generations to come. 9Do not offer on
30:9 [c]Lev 10:1 — this altar any other incense[c] or any burnt offering
or grain offering, and do not pour a drink offering
30:10 [d]Lev 16:18-19,30 — on it. 10Once a year Aaron shall make atonement[d]
on its horns. This annual atonement must be made
with the blood of the atoning sin offering for the
generations to come. It is most holy to the LORD."

Atonement Money

11Then the LORD said to Moses, 12"When you
30:12 [e]Ex 38:25; Nu 1:2,49; 2Sa 24:1 [f]Nu 31:50; Mt 20:28 [g]2Sa 24:13 — take a census[e] of the Israelites to count them, each
one must pay the LORD a ransom[f] for his life at the
time he is counted. Then no plague[g] will come on
them when you number them. 13Each one who
crosses over to those already counted is to give a
30:13 [h]Nu 3:47; Mt 17:24 — half shekel,[a] according to the sanctuary shekel,[h]
which weighs twenty gerahs. This half shekel is
an offering to the LORD. 14All who cross over, those
twenty years old or more, are to give an offering
30:15 [i]Pr 22:2; Eph 6:9 — to the LORD. 15The rich are not to give more than a
half shekel and the poor are not to give less[i] when
you make the offering to the LORD to atone for your
lives. 16Receive the atonement money from the
Israelites and use it for the service of the Tent of
30:16 [j]Ex 38:25-28 — Meeting.[j] It will be a memorial for the Israelites
before the LORD, making atonement for your lives."

Basin for Washing

30:18 [k]Ex 38:8; 40:7,30 — 17Then the LORD said to Moses, 18"Make a bronze
basin,[k] with its bronze stand, for washing. Place it
between the Tent of Meeting and the altar, and put
30:19 [l]Ex 40:31-32; Isa 52:11 [m]Ps 26:6 — water in it. 19Aaron and his sons are to wash their
hands and feet[l] with water[m] from it. 20Whenever
they enter the Tent of Meeting, they shall wash
with water so that they will not die. Also, when
they approach the altar to minister by presenting
an offering made to the LORD by fire, 21they shall
wash their hands and feet so that they will not die.
30:21 [n]Ex 27:21; 28:43 — This is to be a lasting ordinance[n] for Aaron and his
descendants for the generations to come."

Anointing Oil

22Then the LORD said to Moses, 23"Take the fol-
30:23 [o]Ge 37:25 — lowing fine spices: 500 shekels[b] of liquid myrrh,[o]
half as much (that is, 250 shekels) of fragrant cin-
30:24 [p]Ps 45:8 — namon, 250 shekels of fragrant cane, 24500
shekels of cassia[p]—all according to the sanctuary
shekel—and a hin[c] of olive oil. 25Make these into

[a] *13* That is, about 1/5 ounce (about 6 grams); also in verse 15
[b] *23* That is, about 12 1/2 pounds (about 6 kilograms)
[c] *24* That is, probably about 4 quarts (about 4 liters)

Recipe for Anointing Oil

EX 30:22-33

God gives very specific instructions for making the oil that will be used to anoint the tabernacle, its furnishings and the priests. The Israelites are to use precious and rare items in this oil. The fine spices may have been part of the spoil that the Israelites took with them from Egypt. One-half of a shekel represented about one-fifth of an ounce, so in our measurements the recipe for the anointing oil included 12½ pounds of myrrh, 6¼ pounds of cinnamon (from the bark of the cinnamon tree), 6¼ pounds of fragrant cane, 12½ pounds of cassia (from the dried flowers of the cinnamon tree), and about 4 quarts of olive oil. Because the oil was used exclusively for specific spiritual purposes, it was probably mixed by the Levites from offerings made by the people.

Recipe for Incense

EX 30:34–38

The recipe God gives for the special incense in these verses is to be used only for sacred purposes, similar to the anointing oil in the previous verses. This special incense is never to be used merely as a perfume for enjoyment—note the severe penalty exacted for personal use (Ex 30:38).

Four ingredients in equal amounts make up the incense. Gum resin, a rare and valuable substance, was taken from hardened drops of myrrh. The identity of onycha is uncertain, though it may have come from clam or mollusk shells. Galbanum is a plant found in Syria and Persia having a bitter, aromatic smell. Frankincense is a fragrant resin taken from a tree found in Asia.

The burning of incense and its fragrance in the tabernacle symbolized the people's prayers going up to God. In 2 Corinthians Paul describes the presence of Christians in the world as the "aroma of Christ" (2Co 2:15), spreading "everywhere the fragrance of the knowledge of him" (2Co 2:14).

a sacred anointing oil, a fragrant blend, the work
of a perfumer.[q] It will be the sacred anointing oil.[r]
26 Then use it to anoint[s] the Tent of Meeting, the
ark of the Testimony, 27 the table and all its articles, the lampstand and its accessories, the altar
of incense, 28 the altar of burnt offering and all its
utensils, and the basin with its stand. 29 You shall
consecrate them so they will be most holy, and
whatever touches them will be holy.[t]
30 "Anoint Aaron and his sons and consecrate[u]
them so they may serve me as priests. 31 Say to the
Israelites, 'This is to be my sacred anointing oil
for the generations to come. 32 Do not pour it on
men's bodies and do not make any oil with the
same formula. It is sacred, and you are to consider it sacred.[v] 33 Whoever makes perfume like it and
whoever puts it on anyone other than a priest
must be cut off[w] from his people.' "

Incense

34 Then the LORD said to Moses, "Take fragrant
spices—gum resin, onycha and galbanum—and
pure frankincense, all in equal amounts, 35 and
make a fragrant blend of incense, the work of a
perfumer.[x] It is to be salted and pure and sacred.
36 Grind some of it to powder and place it in front
of the Testimony in the Tent of Meeting, where I
will meet with you. It shall be most holy[y] to you.
37 Do not make any incense with this formula for
yourselves; consider it holy[z] to the LORD. 38 Whoever makes any like it to enjoy its fragrance must
be cut off[a] from his people."

Bezalel and Oholiab

31 Then the LORD said to Moses, 2 "See, I have
chosen Bezalel[b] son of Uri, the son of Hur,
of the tribe of Judah, 3 and I have filled him with
the Spirit of God, with skill, ability and knowledge in all kinds of crafts[c]— 4 to make artistic
designs for work in gold, silver and bronze, 5 to
cut and set stones, to work in wood, and to
engage in all kinds of craftsmanship. 6 Moreover, I
have appointed Oholiab son of Ahisamach, of the
tribe of Dan, to help him. Also I have given skill to
all the craftsmen to make everything I have commanded you: 7 the Tent of Meeting,[d] the ark of the
Testimony[e] with the atonement cover[f] on it, and
all the other furnishings of the tent— 8 the table[g]
and its articles, the pure gold lampstand[h] and all
its accessories, the altar of incense, 9 the altar of
burnt offering and all its utensils, the basin with
its stand— 10 and also the woven garments[i], both
the sacred garments for Aaron the priest and the
garments for his sons when they serve as priests,
11 and the anointing oil[j] and fragrant incense for
the Holy Place. They are to make them just as I
commanded you."

The Sabbath

12 Then the LORD said to Moses, 13 "Say to the

30:25 [q]Ex 37:29 [r]Ex 40:9
30:26 [s]Ex 40:9; Lev 8:10; Nu 7:1
30:29 [t]Ex 29:37
30:30 [u]Ex 29:7; Lev 8:2,12, 30
30:32 [v]ver 25,37
30:33 [w]ver 38; Ge 17:14
30:35 [x]ver 25
30:36 [y]ver 32; Ex 29:37; Lev 2:3
30:37 [z]ver 32
30:38 [a]ver 33
31:2 [b]Ex 36:1,2; 1Ch 2:20
31:3 [c]1Ki 7:14
31:7 [d]Ex 36:8-38 [e]Ex 37:1-5 [f]Ex 37:6
31:8 [g]Ex 37:10-16 [h]Ex 37:17-24
31:10 [i]Ex 28:2; 39:1,41
31:11 [j]Ex 30:22-32

31:13 Israelites, ‘You must observe my Sabbaths.[k] This
[k]Ex 20:8; Lev 19:3,30 will be a sign[l] between me and you for the gener-
[l]Eze 20:12, 20 ations to come, so you may know that I am the
[m]Lev 11:44 LORD, who makes you holy.[a][m]
14“ ‘Observe the Sabbath, because it is holy to
31:14 you. Anyone who desecrates it must be put to
[n]Nu 15:32-36 death;[n] whoever does any work on that day must
be cut off from his people. 15For six days, work[o] is
31:15 to be done, but the seventh day is a Sabbath of
[o]Ex 20:8-11 rest,[p] holy to the LORD. Whoever does any work
[p]Ge 2:3; Ex 16:23 on the Sabbath day must be put to death. 16The
Israelites are to observe the Sabbath, celebrating it
31:17 for the generations to come as a lasting covenant.
[q]ver 13 17It will be a sign[q] between me and the Israelites
[r]Ge 2:2-3 forever, for in six days the LORD made the heavens
and the earth, and on the seventh day he
abstained from work and rested.[r]’ ”
31:18 18When the LORD finished speaking to Moses on
[s]Ex 24:12 Mount Sinai, he gave him the two tablets of the
[t]Ex 32:15-16; 34:1,28; Testimony, the tablets of stone[s] inscribed by the
Dt 4:13; 5:22 finger of God.[t]

The Golden Calf

32 When the people saw that Moses was so
32:1 [u]Ex 24:18; long in coming down from the mountain,[u]
Dt 9:9-12 they gathered around Aaron and said, “Come,
[v]Ac 7:40* make us gods[b] who will go before us. As for this
fellow Moses who brought us up out of Egypt, we
don't know what has happened to him.”[v]
2Aaron answered them, “Take off the gold ear-
32:2 [w]Ex 35:22 rings[w] that your wives, your sons and your
daughters are wearing, and bring them to me.”
3So all the people took off their earrings and
brought them to Aaron. 4He took what they handed him and made it into an idol cast in the shape
32:4 [x]Dt 9:16; of a calf,[x] fashioning it with a tool. Then they
Ne 9:18; said, “These are your gods,[c] O Israel, who brought
Ps 106:19; Ac 7:41 you up out of Egypt.”
5When Aaron saw this, he built an altar in front
32:5 [y]Lev 23:2, of the calf and announced, “Tomorrow there will
37; 2Ki 10:20 be a festival[y] to the LORD.” 6So the next day the
people rose early and sacrificed burnt offerings
32:6 [z]Nu 25:2; and presented fellowship offerings.[d][z] Afterward
Ac 7:41 they sat down to eat and drink and got up to
[a]ver 17-19; 1Co 10:7* indulge in revelry.[a]
7Then the LORD said to Moses, “Go down,
32:7 [b]ver 4,11 because your people, whom you brought up out
[c]Ge 6:11-12; of Egypt,[b] have become corrupt.[c] 8They have been
Dt 9:12 quick to turn away from what I commanded them
32:8 and have made themselves an idol[d] cast in the
[d]Ex 20:4 [e]Ex 22:20 shape of a calf. They have bowed down to it and
[f]1Ki 12:28 sacrificed[e] to it and have said, ‘These are your
gods, O Israel, who brought you up out of Egypt.’[f]
32:9 9“I have seen these people,” the LORD said to
[g]Ex 33:3,5; Moses, “and they are a stiff-necked[g] people. 10Now
34:9; Isa 48:4; Ac 7:51 leave me alone so that my anger may burn against

[a] 13 Or *who sanctifies you*; or *who sets you apart as holy*
[b] 1 Or *a god*; also in verses 23 and 31 [c] 4 Or *This is your god*; also in verse 8 [d] 6 Traditionally *peace offerings*

The Finger of God

EX 31:18

The phrase “the finger of God” is a picturesque description of God's power. Pharaoh's magicians recognize the creation of gnats from dust as “the finger of God” (Ex 8:19). Psalm 8:3 declares that the heavens are the finger work of God. Jesus speaks in Luke 11:20 of demons being driven out by the finger of God. God wrote his commandments for his people with his own finger. Whether taken figuratively or literally, the picture is of a God who is powerfully and intimately involved in the lives of his people.

Disaster Averted

EX 32:11-14

God is a holy God. The magnitude of Israel's rebellion against his holiness requires punishment. Though it may seem harsh to us today, God's plan to destroy Israel and begin a new nation through Moses was a just response to their defiance. In an amazing act, Moses steps in as a mediator between God and the people to avert this judgment. He appeals to God's name and glory. Moses does not want the Egyptians to have reason to criticize God because of his treatment of his people. Moses reminds God of the promises he made to Abraham. And he reminds God that he is a God who keeps his promises.

Moses' impassioned plea does not fall on deaf ears. God relents. He punishes, but he does not destroy. In his effort to avert the judgment of God, Moses is a picture of Jesus, the only true mediator between God and human beings, the one who has turned the judgment of God from us, who deserve it, to himself (1Ti 2:5).

them and that I may destroy them. Then I will
make you into a great nation."[h]
11But Moses sought the favor[i] of the LORD his
God. "O LORD," he said, "why should your anger
burn against your people, whom you brought out
of Egypt with great power and a mighty hand?[j]
12Why should the Egyptians say, 'It was with evil
intent that he brought them out, to kill them in
the mountains and to wipe them off the face of
the earth'?[k] Turn from your fierce anger; relent
and do not bring disaster on your people.
13Remember[l] your servants Abraham, Isaac and
Israel, to whom you swore by your own self:[m] 'I
will make your descendants as numerous as the
stars[n] in the sky and I will give your descendants
all this land[o] I promised them, and it will be their
inheritance forever.' " 14Then the LORD relented[p]
and did not bring on his people the disaster he
had threatened.
15Moses turned and went down the mountain
with the two tablets of the Testimony[q] in his
hands.[r] They were inscribed on both sides, front
and back. 16The tablets were the work of God; the
writing was the writing of God, engraved on the
tablets.[s]
17When Joshua heard the noise of the people
shouting, he said to Moses, "There is the sound of
war in the camp."
18Moses replied:

"It is not the sound of victory,
it is not the sound of defeat;
it is the sound of singing that I hear."

19When Moses approached the camp and saw
the calf[t] and the dancing, his anger burned and
he threw the tablets out of his hands, breaking
them to pieces[u] at the foot of the mountain. 20And
he took the calf they had made and burned it in
the fire; then he ground it to powder, scattered it
on the water[v] and made the Israelites drink it.
21He said to Aaron, "What did these people do
to you, that you led them into such great sin?"
22"Do not be angry, my lord," Aaron answered.
"You know how prone these people are to evil.[w]
23They said to me, 'Make us gods who will go
before us. As for this fellow Moses who brought
us up out of Egypt, we don't know what has happened to him.'[x] 24So I told them, 'Whoever has
any gold jewelry, take it off.' Then they gave me
the gold, and I threw it into the fire, and out came
this calf!"[y]
25Moses saw that the people were running wild
and that Aaron had let them get out of control and
so become a laughingstock to their enemies. 26So
he stood at the entrance to the camp and said,
"Whoever is for the LORD, come to me." And all
the Levites rallied to him.
27Then he said to them, "This is what the LORD,
the God of Israel, says: 'Each man strap a sword to
his side. Go back and forth through the camp
from one end to the other, each killing his broth-

32:10 [h]Nu 14:12; Dt 9:14
32:11 [i]Dt 9:18 [j]Dt 9:26
32:12 [k]Nu 14:13-16; Dt 9:28
32:13 [l]Ex 2:24 [m]Ge 22:16; Heb 6:13 [n]Ge 15:5; 26:4 [o]Ge 12:7
32:14 [p]2Sa 24:16; Ps 106:45
32:15 [q]Ex 31:18 [r]Dt 9:15
32:16 [s]Ex 31:18
32:19 [t]Dt 9:16 [u]Dt 9:17
32:20 [v]Dt 9:21
32:22 [w]Dt 9:24
32:23 [x]ver 1
32:24 [y]ver 4

32:27 er and friend and neighbor.' "[z] 28The Levites did
[z]Nu 25:3,5; as Moses commanded, and that day about three
Dt 33:9 thousand of the people died. 29Then Moses said,
"You have been set apart to the LORD today, for
you were against your own sons and brothers,
and he has blessed you this day."
32:30 30The next day Moses said to the people, "You
[a]1Sa 12:20 have committed a great sin.[a] But now I will go up
[b]Lev 1:4; to the LORD; perhaps I can make atonement[b] for
Nu 25:13 your sin."
31So Moses went back to the LORD and said,
32:31 "Oh, what a great sin these people have commit-
[c]Dt 9:18 [d]Ex 20:23 ted![c] They have made themselves gods of gold.[d]
32:32 32But now, please forgive their sin—but if not,
[e]Ro 9:3 then blot me[e] out of the book[f] you have written."
[f]Ps 69:28; 33The LORD replied to Moses, "Whoever has
Da 12:1; Php 4:3; sinned against me I will blot out[g] of my book.
Rev 3:5; 21:27 34Now go, lead the people to the place[h] I spoke of,
and my angel[i] will go before you. However, when
32:33 the time comes for me to punish,[j] I will punish
[g]Dt 29:20; Ps 9:5 them for their sin."
35And the LORD struck the people with a plague
32:34 because of what they did with the calf[k] Aaron had
[h]Ex 3:17 [i]Ex 23:20 made.
[j]Dt 32:35; 33 Then the LORD said to Moses, "Leave this
Ps 99:8; place, you and the people you brought up
Ro 2:5-6 out of Egypt, and go up to the land I promised on
32:35 oath to Abraham, Isaac and Jacob, saying, 'I will
[k]ver 4 give it to your descendants.'[l] 2I will send an angel[m]
33:1 before you and drive out the Canaanites, Amorites,
[l]Ge 12:7 Hittites, Perizzites, Hivites and Jebusites.[n] 3Go up to
the land flowing with milk and honey.[o] But I will
33:2 not go with you, because you are a stiff-necked[p]
[m]Ex 32:34 [n]Ex 23:27-31; Jos 24:11 people and I might destroy[q] you on the way."
4When the people heard these distressing words,
33:3 they began to mourn[r] and no one put on any orna-
[o]Ex 3:8 ments. 5For the LORD had said to Moses, "Tell the
[p]Ex 32:9 Israelites, 'You are a stiff-necked people. If I were
[q]Ex 32:10 to go with you even for a moment, I might destroy
33:4 you. Now take off your ornaments and I will
[r]Nu 14:39 decide what to do with you.' " 6So the Israelites
stripped off their ornaments at Mount Horeb.

The Tent of Meeting

7Now Moses used to take a tent and pitch it outside the camp some distance away, calling it the
33:7 "tent of meeting."[s] Anyone inquiring of the LORD
[s]Ex 29:42-43 would go to the tent of meeting outside the camp.
8And whenever Moses went out to the tent, all the
33:8 people rose and stood at the entrances to their
[t]Nu 16:27 tents,[t] watching Moses until he entered the tent.
33:9 9As Moses went into the tent, the pillar of cloud[u]
[u]Ex 13:21 would come down and stay at the entrance, while
[v]Ex 31:18; the LORD spoke[v] with Moses. 10Whenever the peo-
Ps 99:7 ple saw the pillar of cloud standing at the
entrance to the tent, they all stood and worshiped,
33:11 each at the entrance to his tent. 11The LORD would
[w]Nu 12:8; speak to Moses face to face,[w] as a man speaks
Dt 34:10 with his friend. Then Moses would return to the
camp, but his young aide Joshua son of Nun did
not leave the tent.

True Love

EX 32:32

Here is true and amazing love in action. If it will save the Israelites, Moses is willing to be blotted out of God's book. He is willing to have his name removed from the list of people whom God claims as his own (Ps 69:28; Da 12:1; Mal 3:16; Rev 3:5; 20:12,15). But the Lord immediately rejects Moses' generous offer, stating that the person who sins is held responsible for his or her own sin (Ex 32:33).

The apostle Paul loves as powerfully as Moses did. In Romans 9:3 he says he is willing to be cursed, to be separated from Christ, if it will bring about the salvation of his fellow Israelites. Such sacrificial love is ultimately a picture of Jesus himself, who willingly became "a curse," willingly took the punishment we rightfully deserve—that we might be saved (Gal 3:13).

God's Presence

EX 33:15

In Exodus 32 Moses intervenes on behalf of the people so that God will not destroy them. But now in Exodus 33, God is contemplating a judgment that is just as devastating. God threatens to leave the Israelites to journey alone, sending in his place an angel to go before them (Ex 33:2–5). Moses knows the absolute blessing of friendship with God (Ex 33:11), so he begs God to stay near to him and to the people (Ex 33:12–16). He recognizes that unless God is personally present, Israel is no different from other nations. In that vulnerable condition, they would easily be destroyed. He also knows that unless God's presence is actively with them, they will not experience God's favor. God graciously gives Moses more than he asks. He will go with them, and he will give them *rest* (Ex 33:14), a tranquillity and confidence in the future that only God's presence can impart.

Moses and the Glory of the LORD

12Moses said to the LORD, "You have been telling
me, 'Lead these people,'[x] but you have not let me
know whom you will send with me. You have
said, 'I know you by name[y] and you have found
favor with me.' 13If you are pleased with me, teach
me your ways[z] so I may know you and continue
to find favor with you. Remember that this nation
is your people."[a]
14The LORD replied, "My Presence[b] will go with
you, and I will give you rest."[c]
15Then Moses said to him, "If your Presence
does not go with us, do not send us up from here.
16How will anyone know that you are pleased with
me and with your people unless you go with us?[d]
What else will distinguish me and your people
from all the other people on the face of the earth?"[e]
17And the LORD said to Moses, "I will do the
very thing you have asked, because I am pleased
with you and I know you by name."
18Then Moses said, "Now show me your glory."
19And the LORD said, "I will cause all my goodness to pass in front of you, and I will proclaim
my name, the LORD, in your presence. I will have
mercy on whom I will have mercy, and I will have
compassion on whom I will have compassion.[f]
20But," he said, "you cannot see my face, for no
one may see[g] me and live."
21Then the LORD said, "There is a place near me
where you may stand on a rock. 22When my glory passes by, I will put you in a cleft in the rock
and cover you with my hand[h] until I have passed
by. 23Then I will remove my hand and you will
see my back; but my face must not be seen."

The New Stone Tablets

34 The LORD said to Moses, "Chisel out two
stone tablets like the first ones, and I will
write on them the words that were on the first
tablets,[i] which you broke.[j] 2Be ready in the morning, and then come up on Mount Sinai.[k] Present
yourself to me there on top of the mountain. 3No
one is to come with you or be seen anywhere on
the mountain;[l] not even the flocks and herds may
graze in front of the mountain."
4So Moses chiseled out two stone tablets like
the first ones and went up Mount Sinai early in
the morning, as the LORD had commanded him;
and he carried the two stone tablets in his hands.
5Then the LORD came down in the cloud and stood
there with him and proclaimed his name, the
LORD.[m] 6And he passed in front of Moses, proclaiming, "The LORD, the LORD, the compassionate[n] and gracious God, slow to anger,[o] abounding
in love[p] and faithfulness,[q] 7maintaining love to
thousands,[r] and forgiving wickedness, rebellion
and sin.[s] Yet he does not leave the guilty unpunished;[t] he punishes the children and their children
for the sin of the fathers to the third and fourth
generation."

33:12 [x]Ex 3:10 [y]ver 17; Jn 10:14-15; 2Ti 2:19
33:13 [z]Ps 25:4; 86:11; 119:33 [a]Ex 34:9; Dt 9:26,29
33:14 [b]Isa 63:9 [c]Jos 21:44; 22:4
33:16 [d]Nu 14:14 [e]Ex 34:10
33:19 [f]Ro 9:15*
33:20 [g]Ge 32:30; Isa 6:5
33:22 [h]Ps 91:4
34:1 [i]Dt 10:2,4 [j]Ex 32:19
34:2 [k]Ex 19:11
34:3 [l]Ex 19:12-13, 21
34:5 [m]Ex 33:19
34:6 [n]Ps 86:15 [o]Nu 14:18; Ro 2:4 [p]Ne 9:17; Ps 103:8; Joel 2:13 [q]Ps 108:4
34:7 [r]Ex 20:6 [s]Ps 103:3; 130:4,8; Da 9:9; 1Jn 1:9 [t]Job 10:14; Na 1:3

8Moses bowed to the ground at once and worshiped. 9"O Lord, if I have found favor in your
eyes," he said, "then let the Lord go with us.[u]
Although this is a stiff-necked people, forgive our
wickedness and our sin, and take us as your
inheritance."[v]
10Then the LORD said: "I am making a covenant[w]
with you. Before all your people I will do wonders
never before done in any nation in all the world.[x]
The people you live among will see how awesome
is the work that I, the LORD, will do for you.
11Obey what I command you today. I will drive out
before you the Amorites, Canaanites, Hittites, Perizzites, Hivites and Jebusites.[y] 12Be careful not to
make a treaty with those who live in the land
where you are going, or they will be a snare[z]
among you. 13Break down their altars, smash their
sacred stones and cut down their Asherah poles.[a][a]
14Do not worship any other god,[b] for the LORD,
whose name is Jealous, is a jealous God.[c]
15"Be careful not to make a treaty with those
who live in the land; for when they prostitute[d]
themselves to their gods and sacrifice to them,
they will invite you and you will eat their sacrifices.[e] 16And when you choose some of their
daughters as wives[f] for your sons and those
daughters prostitute themselves to their gods,[g]
they will lead your sons to do the same.
17"Do not make cast idols.[h]
18"Celebrate the Feast of Unleavened Bread.[i] For
seven days eat bread made without yeast,[j] as I
commanded you. Do this at the appointed time in
the month of Abib,[k] for in that month you came
out of Egypt.
19"The first offspring[l] of every womb belongs to
me, including all the firstborn males of your livestock, whether from herd or flock. 20Redeem the
firstborn donkey with a lamb, but if you do not
redeem it, break its neck.[m] Redeem all your firstborn sons.
"No one is to appear before me empty-handed.[n]
21"Six days you shall labor, but on the seventh
day you shall rest;[o] even during the plowing season and harvest you must rest.
22"Celebrate the Feast of Weeks with the firstfruits of the wheat harvest, and the Feast of Ingathering[p] at the turn of the year.[b] 23Three times[q] a year
all your men are to appear before the Sovereign
LORD, the God of Israel. 24I will drive out nations[r]
before you and enlarge your territory, and no one
will covet your land when you go up three times
each year to appear before the LORD your God.
25"Do not offer the blood of a sacrifice to me
along with anything containing yeast,[s] and do not
let any of the sacrifice from the Passover Feast
remain until morning.[t]
26"Bring the best of the firstfruits of your soil to
the house of the LORD your God.

[a] *13* That is, symbols of the goddess Asherah [b] *22* That is, in the fall

34:9 [u]Ex 33:15 [v]Ps 33:12
34:10 [w]Dt 5:2-3 [x]Ex 33:16; Dt 4:32
34:11 [y]Ex 33:2
34:12 [z]Ex 23:32-33
34:13 [a]Ex 23:24; Dt 12:3; 2Ki 18:4
34:14 [b]Ex 20:3 [c]Ex 20:5; Dt 4:24
34:15 [d]Jdg 2:17 [e]Nu 25:2; 1Co 8:4
34:16 [f]Dt 7:3 [g]1Ki 11:4
34:17 [h]Ex 32:8
34:18 [i]Ex 12:17 [j]Ex 12:15 [k]Ex 12:2
34:19 [l]Ex 13:2
34:20 [m]Ex 13:13, 15 [n]Ex 23:15; Dt 16:16
34:21 [o]Ex 20:9; Lk 13:14
34:22 [p]Ex 23:16
34:23 [q]Ex 23:14
34:24 [r]Ex 23:28; 33:2; Ps 78:55
34:25 [s]Ex 23:18 [t]Ex 12:8,10

Our Jealous God

EX 34:14

In Exodus 34:14 God calls his people to absolute allegiance to himself. He is a jealous God, tolerating no rivals, unwilling to take any place except first in our lives. How can jealousy be part of a holy God's character when human jealousy is so sinful and destructive? As we examine God's character, we begin to understand his demand. In Exodus 34:6–7 God reveals his loyal love and his holiness. In Exodus 34:10–11 he promises to act powerfully on behalf of his people, to bless them as they could never bless themselves. To ask for their full love and devotion in return springs out of God's desire for only the best for his people. *(See character sketch for Skilled Women on page 402.)*

A Radiant Face

EX 34:29-35

Moses' conversations with God transform his countenance so radically that his face shines with the glory of God. Why then does he wear a veil and hide that glory from the people of Israel?

In 2 Corinthians 3:7-18, Paul gives his interpretation. Paul saw the fading of the glory on Moses' face as evidence that the old covenant was temporary and would be replaced by a much more glorious—and unfading—new covenant. Only in Jesus Christ is the veil removed so that as believers we can see and experience the Holy Spirit's "glorious" ministry (2Co 3:10) in us.

"Do not cook a young goat in its mother's
milk."[u]
27 Then the LORD said to Moses, "Write[v] down
these words, for in accordance with these words I
have made a covenant with you and with Israel."
28 Moses was there with the LORD forty days and
forty nights[w] without eating bread or drinking
water. And he wrote on the tablets[x] the words of
the covenant—the Ten Commandments.[y]

The Radiant Face of Moses

29 When Moses came down from Mount Sinai
with the two tablets of the Testimony in his
hands,[z] he was not aware that his face was radiant[a] because he had spoken with the LORD. 30 When
Aaron and all the Israelites saw Moses, his face
was radiant, and they were afraid to come near
him. 31 But Moses called to them; so Aaron and all
the leaders of the community came back to him,
and he spoke to them. 32 Afterward all the Israelites came near him, and he gave them all the commands[b] the LORD had given him on Mount Sinai.
33 When Moses finished speaking to them, he
put a veil[c] over his face. 34 But whenever he
entered the LORD's presence to speak with him,
he removed the veil until he came out. And when
he came out and told the Israelites what he had
been commanded, 35 they saw that his face was
radiant. Then Moses would put the veil back over
his face until he went in to speak with the LORD.

Sabbath Regulations

35 Moses assembled the whole Israelite community and said to them, "These are the
things the LORD has commanded[d] you to do: 2 For
six days, work is to be done, but the seventh day
shall be your holy day, a Sabbath[e] of rest to the
LORD. Whoever does any work on it must be put
to death. 3 Do not light a fire in any of your
dwellings on the Sabbath day.[f]"

Materials for the Tabernacle

4 Moses said to the whole Israelite community,
"This is what the LORD has commanded: 5 From
what you have, take an offering for the LORD.
Everyone who is willing is to bring to the LORD an
offering of gold, silver and bronze; 6 blue, purple
and scarlet yarn and fine linen; goat hair; 7 ram
skins dyed red and hides of sea cows[a]; acacia
wood; 8 olive oil for the light; spices for the anointing oil and for the fragrant incense; 9 and onyx
stones and other gems to be mounted on the
ephod and breastpiece.
10 "All who are skilled among you are to come
and make everything the LORD has commanded:[g]
11 the tabernacle[h] with its tent and its covering,
clasps, frames, crossbars, posts and bases; 12 the
ark[i] with its poles and the atonement cover and
the curtain that shields it; 13 the table[j] with its poles

34:26 [u]Ex 23:19
34:27 [v]Ex 17:14; 24:4
34:28 [w]Ge 7:4; Ex 24:18; Mt 4:2 [x]ver 1; Ex 31:18 [y]Dt 4:13; 10:4
34:29 [z]Ex 32:15 [a]Ps 34:5; Mt 17:2; 2Co 3:7,13
34:32 [b]Ex 24:3
34:33 [c]2Co 3:13
35:1 [d]Ex 34:32
35:2 [e]Ex; 20:9-10; 34:21; Lev 23:3
35:3 [f]Ex 16:23
35:10 [g]Ex 31:6
35:11 [h]Ex 26:1-37
35:12 [i]Ex 25:10-22
35:13 [j]Ex 25:23-30; Lev 24:5-6

[a] 7 That is, dugongs; also in verse 23

and all its articles and the bread of the Presence;
35:14 [k]Ex 25:31 14the lampstand[k] that is for light with its accessories, lamps and oil for the light; 15the altar[l] of
35:15 [l]Ex 30:1-6 incense with its poles, the anointing oil[m] and the
[m]Ex 30:25 fragrant incense;[n] the curtain for the doorway at
[n]Ex 30:34-38 the entrance to the tabernacle; 16the altar[o] of burnt
35:16 offering with its bronze grating, its poles and all
[o]Ex 27:1-8 its utensils; the bronze basin with its stand; 17the
35:17 curtains of the courtyard with its posts and bases,
[p]Ex 27:9 and the curtain for the entrance to the courtyard;[p]
18the tent pegs for the tabernacle and for the courtyard, and their ropes; 19the woven garments worn
for ministering in the sanctuary—both the sacred
35:19 [q]Ex 28:2; garments[q] for Aaron the priest and the garments
31:10; 39:1 for his sons when they serve as priests."
20Then the whole Israelite community withdrew from Moses' presence, 21and everyone who
was willing and whose heart moved him came
and brought an offering to the LORD for the work
on the Tent of Meeting, for all its service, and for
the sacred garments. 22All who were willing, men
and women alike, came and brought gold jewelry
of all kinds: brooches, earrings, rings and ornaments. They all presented their gold as a wave
35:23 offering to the LORD. 23Everyone who had blue,
[r]1Ch 29:8 purple or scarlet yarn[r] or fine linen, or goat hair,
ram skins dyed red or hides of sea cows brought
them. 24Those presenting an offering of silver or
bronze brought it as an offering to the LORD, and
35:25 everyone who had acacia wood for any part of the
[s]Ex 28:3 work brought it. 25Every skilled woman[s] spun
with her hands and brought what she had spun—
blue, purple or scarlet yarn or fine linen. 26And all
the women who were willing and had the skill
35:27 [t]1Ch 29:6; spun the goat hair. 27The leaders[t] brought onyx
Ezr 2:68 stones and other gems to be mounted on the
ephod and breastpiece. 28They also brought spices
35:28 [u]Ex 25:6 and olive oil for the light and for the anointing oil
and for the fragrant incense.[u] 29All the Israelite
35:29 [v]ver 21; men and women who were willing[v] brought to
1Ch 29:9 the LORD freewill offerings[w] for all the work the
[w]ver 4-9; LORD through Moses had commanded them to do.
Ex 25:1-7; 36:3; 2Ki 12:4

Bezalel and Oholiab

30Then Moses said to the Israelites, "See, the
LORD has chosen Bezalel son of Uri, the son of Hur,
of the tribe of Judah, 31and he has filled him with
35:31 the Spirit of God, with skill, ability and knowledge
[x]ver 35; in all kinds of crafts[x]— 32to make artistic designs
2Ch 2:7,14 for work in gold, silver and bronze, 33to cut and
set stones, to work in wood and to engage in all
35:34 [y]Ex 31:6 kinds of artistic craftsmanship. 34And he has given
[z]2Ch 2:14 both him and Oholiab[y] son of Ahisamach, of the
tribe of Dan, the ability to teach[z] others. 35He has
35:35 [a]ver 31; filled them with skill to do all kinds of work[a] as
Ex 31:3,6; craftsmen, designers, embroiderers in blue, purple
1Ki 7:14 and scarlet yarn and fine linen, and weavers—all
36:1 36 of them master craftsmen and designers. 1So
[b]Ex 28:3 Bezalel, Oholiab and every skilled person[b]
to whom the LORD has given skill and ability to
know how to carry out all the work of construct-

The Artistry of God

EX 35:25-26,30-35

As we read the story of the construction of the tabernacle, we are impressed both by the richness of the materials used and by the tremendous artistic ability that was needed to accomplish the work according to the pattern God had given. God loves beauty. His creation shouts it; the tabernacle was to mirror it. Exodus 35:31,34 reveal the source of this ability to not only create but also to teach others to create: the Spirit of God.

As women, the creative abilities we have been given—that we take the time to develop and that we teach to others—are all opportunities for the Spirit of God to express his artistry through us. God intends for all expressions of art to draw us into deeper fellowship with him. He is the ultimate creator of beauty, and being in his image means we are to create beauty as well—to his glory (Col 3:23; 1Co 10:31). (See character sketch for Skilled Women on page 402.)

Giving Cheerfully

EX 36:5-7

Considering their history of disbelief and disobedience, what now motivates the Israelites to give so freely and abundantly to the building of the tabernacle? Several possibilities make sense. First, they may recognize, in ways we sometimes fail to, that the wealth they have is truly God's. He had provided it as part of their miraculous escape from Egypt, so they realize it is not something they have earned themselves. Second, having seen God's provision in these first months in the desert, they can be sure that no matter what they give away, God will meet their needs. Third, they know the deep rebellion of their own hearts. They know they deserved to die after the golden-calf incident. Only because of God's mercy were they not destroyed; so their generosity may be a response of gratitude to God. In many ways their abundant giving mirrors principles of generosity Paul expresses in 2 Corinthians 8–9.

ing the sanctuary[c] are to do the work just as the
LORD has commanded."
2 Then Moses summoned Bezalel[d] and Oholiab[e]
and every skilled person to whom the LORD had
given ability and who was willing[f] to come and
do the work. 3 They received from Moses all the
offerings[g] the Israelites had brought to carry out
the work of constructing the sanctuary. And the
people continued to bring freewill offerings morning after morning. 4 So all the skilled craftsmen
who were doing all the work on the sanctuary left
their work 5 and said to Moses, "The people are
bringing more than enough[h] for doing the work
the LORD commanded to be done."
6 Then Moses gave an order and they sent this
word throughout the camp: "No man or woman
is to make anything else as an offering for the
sanctuary." And so the people were restrained
from bringing more, 7 because what they already
had was more[i] than enough to do all the work.

The Tabernacle

8 All the skilled men among the workmen made
the tabernacle with ten curtains of finely twisted
linen and blue, purple and scarlet yarn, with cherubim worked into them by a skilled craftsman.
9 All the curtains were the same size—twenty-
eight cubits long and four cubits wide.[a] 10 They
joined five of the curtains together and did the
same with the other five. 11 Then they made loops
of blue material along the edge of the end curtain
in one set, and the same was done with the end
curtain in the other set. 12 They also made fifty
loops on one curtain and fifty loops on the end
curtain of the other set, with the loops opposite
each other. 13 Then they made fifty gold clasps and
used them to fasten the two sets of curtains
together so that the tabernacle was a unit.[j]
14 They made curtains of goat hair for the tent
over the tabernacle—eleven altogether. 15 All
eleven curtains were the same size—thirty cubits
long and four cubits wide.[b] 16 They joined five of
the curtains into one set and the other six into
another set. 17 Then they made fifty loops along
the edge of the end curtain in one set and also
along the edge of the end curtain in the other set.
18 They made fifty bronze clasps to fasten the tent
together as a unit.[k] 19 Then they made for the tent
a covering of ram skins dyed red, and over that a
covering of hides of sea cows.[c]
20 They made upright frames of acacia wood for
the tabernacle. 21 Each frame was ten cubits long
and a cubit and a half wide,[d] 22 with two projections set parallel to each other. They made all the
frames of the tabernacle in this way. 23 They made
twenty frames for the south side of the tabernacle

36:1 [c]Ex 25:8
36:2 [d]Ex 31:2 [e]Ex 31:6 [f]Ex 25:2; 35:21,26; 1Ch 29:5
36:3 [g]Ex 35:29
36:5 [h]2Ch 24:14; 31:10; 2Co 8:2-3
36:7 [i]1Ki 7:47
36:13 [j]ver 18
36:18 [k]ver 13

[a] *9* That is, about 42 feet (about 12.5 meters) long and 6 feet (about 1.8 meters) wide [b] *15* That is, about 45 feet (about 13.5 meters) long and 6 feet (about 1.8 meters) wide [c] *19* That is, dugongs [d] *21* That is, about 15 feet (about 4.5 meters) long and 2 1/4 feet (about 0.7 meter) wide

[24]and made forty silver bases to go under them—two bases for each frame, one under each projection. [25]For the other side, the north side of the tabernacle, they made twenty frames [26]and forty silver bases—two under each frame. [27]They made six frames for the far end, that is, the west end of the tabernacle, [28]and two frames were made for the corners of the tabernacle at the far end. [29]At these two corners the frames were double from the bottom all the way to the top and fitted into a single ring; both were made alike. [30]So there were eight frames and sixteen silver bases—two under each frame.

[31]They also made crossbars of acacia wood: five for the frames on one side of the tabernacle, [32]five for those on the other side, and five for the frames on the west, at the far end of the tabernacle. [33]They made the center crossbar so that it extended from end to end at the middle of the frames. [34]They overlaid the frames with gold and made gold rings to hold the crossbars. They also overlaid the crossbars with gold.

[35]They made the curtain[l] of blue, purple and scarlet yarn and finely twisted linen, with cherubim worked into it by a skilled craftsman. [36]They made four posts of acacia wood for it and overlaid them with gold. They made gold hooks for them and cast their four silver bases. [37]For the entrance to the tent they made a curtain of blue, purple and scarlet yarn and finely twisted linen—the work of an embroiderer;[m] [38]and they made five posts with hooks for them. They overlaid the tops of the posts and their bands with gold and made their five bases of bronze.

The Ark

37 Bezalel[n] made the ark[o] of acacia wood—two and a half cubits long, a cubit and a half wide, and a cubit and a half high.[a] [2]He overlaid it with pure gold,[p] both inside and out, and made a gold molding around it. [3]He cast four gold rings for it and fastened them to its four feet, with two rings on one side and two rings on the other. [4]Then he made poles of acacia wood and overlaid them with gold. [5]And he inserted the poles into the rings on the sides of the ark to carry it.

[6]He made the atonement cover[q] of pure gold—two and a half cubits long and a cubit and a half wide.[b] [7]Then he made two cherubim[r] out of hammered gold at the ends of the cover. [8]He made one cherub on one end and the second cherub on the other; at the two ends he made them of one piece with the cover. [9]The cherubim had their wings spread upward, overshadowing[s] the cover with them. The cherubim faced each other, looking toward the cover.[t]

36:35 [l]Ex 39:38; Mt 27:51; Lk 23:45; Heb 9:3
36:37 [m]Ex 27:16
37:1 [n]Ex 31:2 [o]Ex 30:6; 39:35; Dt 10:3
37:2 [p]ver 11,26
37:6 [q]Ex 26:34; 31:7; Heb 9:5
37:7 [r]Eze 41:18
37:9 [s]Heb 9:5 [t]Dt 10:3

[a] *1* That is, about 3 3/4 feet (about 1.1 meters) long and 2 1/4 feet (about 0.7 meter) wide and high [b] *6* That is, about 3 3/4 feet (about 1.1 meters) long and 2 1/4 feet (about 0.7 meter) wide

The Ark

EX 37:1-9

The chief craftsman Bezalel makes the ark, the piece of furniture at the very center of the Israelites' worship. Based on a cubit of 18 inches, the ark is 3¾ feet long and 2¼ feet wide and high. The wood for its construction comes from the acacia tree, common to the Sinai peninsula. It is overlaid, both inside and out, with pure gold.

Two cherubim—winged angelic creatures—face each other on the lid of the ark. This lid is known as the "atonement cover," the place where God dwells. It is upon this lid that the high priest once a year sprinkles the blood of a sacrifice to make atonement for (that is, to cover) the sins of the people (Lev 16).

The Gold Lampstand

EX 37:17–24

In several ways the ornate gold lampstand that is part of the tabernacle furnishings is a precursor to the familiar Jewish menorah. The word *menorah* is the Hebrew word for "lampstand." The lampstand is made of pure gold, with seven flower-shaped cups for holding oil and wicks.

The Table

10 They[a] made the table[u] of acacia wood—two 37:10
cubits long, a cubit wide, and a cubit and a half [u]Heb 9:2
high.[b] 11 Then they overlaid it with pure gold[v] and 37:11
made a gold molding around it. 12 They also made [v]ver 2
around it a rim a handbreadth[c] wide and put a gold
molding on the rim. 13 They cast four gold rings for
the table and fastened them to the four corners,
where the four legs were. 14 The rings[w] were put 37:14
close to the rim to hold the poles used in carrying [w]ver 27
the table. 15 The poles for carrying the table were
made of acacia wood and were overlaid with gold.
16 And they made from pure gold the articles for the
table—its plates and dishes and bowls and its pitchers for the pouring out of drink offerings.

The Lampstand

17 They made the lampstand[x] of pure gold and 37:17
hammered it out, base and shaft; its flowerlike [x]Heb 9:2;
cups, buds and blossoms were of one piece with Rev 1:12
it. 18 Six branches extended from the sides of the
lampstand—three on one side and three on the
other. 19 Three cups shaped like almond flowers
with buds and blossoms were on one branch,
three on the next branch and the same for all six
branches extending from the lampstand. 20 And on
the lampstand were four cups shaped like almond
flowers with buds and blossoms. 21 One bud was
under the first pair of branches extending from
the lampstand, a second bud under the second
pair, and a third bud under the third pair—six
branches in all. 22 The buds and the branches were
all of one piece with the lampstand, hammered 37:22
out of pure gold.[y] [y]ver 17;
Nu 8:4

23 They made its seven lamps,[z] as well as its
wick trimmers and trays, of pure gold. 24 They 37:23
made the lampstand and all its accessories from [z]Ex 40:4,25
one talent[d] of pure gold.

The Altar of Incense

25 They made the altar of incense[a] out of acacia 37:25
wood. It was square, a cubit long and a cubit wide, [a]Ex 30:34-36; Lk 1:11;
and two cubits high[e]—its horns[b] of one piece with Heb 9:4;
it. 26 They overlaid the top and all the sides and the Rev 8:3
horns with pure gold, and made a gold molding [b]Ex 27:2;
around it. 27 They made two gold rings[c] below the Rev 9:13
molding—two on opposite sides—to hold the poles 37:27
used to carry it. 28 They made the poles of acacia [c]ver 14
wood and overlaid them with gold.[d] 37:28
[d]Ex 25:13

29 They also made the sacred anointing oil[e] and 37:29
the pure, fragrant incense[f]—the work of a [e]Ex 31:11
perfumer. [f]Ex 30:1,25; 39:38

[a] *10* Or *He*; also in verses 11–29 [b] *10* That is, about 3 feet (about 0.9 meter) long, 1 1/2 feet (about 0.5 meter) wide, and 2 1/4 feet (about 0.7 meter) high [c] *12* That is, about 3 inches (about 8 centimeters) [d] *24* That is, about 75 pounds (about 34 kilograms) [e] *25* That is, about 1 1/2 feet (about 0.5 meter) long and wide, and about 3 feet (about 0.9 meter) high

The Altar of Burnt Offering

38 They[a] built the altar of burnt offering of
acacia wood, three cubits[b] high; it was
square, five cubits long and five cubits wide.[c]
2They made a horn at each of the four corners, so
that the horns and the altar were of one piece, and
38:2 they overlaid the altar with bronze.[g] 3They made
[g]2Ch 1:5 all its utensils[h] of bronze—its pots, shovels, sprin-
38:3 kling bowls, meat forks and firepans. 4They made
[h]Ex 31:9 a grating for the altar, a bronze network, to be
under its ledge, halfway up the altar. 5They cast
bronze rings to hold the poles for the four corners
of the bronze grating. 6They made the poles of
acacia wood and overlaid them with bronze.
7They inserted the poles into the rings so they
would be on the sides of the altar for carrying it.
They made it hollow, out of boards.

Basin for Washing

38:8
[i]Ex 30:18; 40:7
[j]Dt 23:17; 1Sa 2:22; 1Ki 14:24

8They made the bronze basin[i] and its bronze
stand from the mirrors of the women[j] who served
at the entrance to the Tent of Meeting.

The Courtyard

9Next they made the courtyard. The south side
was a hundred cubits[d] long and had curtains of
finely twisted linen, 10with twenty posts and
twenty bronze bases, and with silver hooks and
bands on the posts. 11The north side was also a
hundred cubits long and had twenty posts and
twenty bronze bases, with silver hooks and bands
on the posts.
12The west end was fifty cubits[e] wide and had
curtains, with ten posts and ten bases, with silver
hooks and bands on the posts. 13The east end,
toward the sunrise, was also fifty cubits wide.
14Curtains fifteen cubits[f] long were on one side of
the entrance, with three posts and three bases,
15and curtains fifteen cubits long were on the other side of the entrance to the courtyard, with three
posts and three bases. 16All the curtains around
the courtyard were of finely twisted linen. 17The
bases for the posts were bronze. The hooks and
bands on the posts were silver, and their tops were
overlaid with silver; so all the posts of the courtyard had silver bands.
18The curtain for the entrance to the courtyard
was of blue, purple and scarlet yarn and finely
twisted linen—the work of an embroiderer. It was
twenty cubits[g] long and, like the curtains of the
courtyard, five cubits[h] high, 19with four posts and
four bronze bases. Their hooks and bands were
silver, and their tops were overlaid with silver.

[a] *1* Or *He*; also in verses 2–9 [b] *1* That is, about 4 1/2 feet (about 1.3 meters) [c] *1* That is, about 7 1/2 feet (about 2.3 meters) long and wide [d] *9* That is, about 150 feet (about 46 meters) [e] *12* That is, about 75 feet (about 23 meters) [f] *14* That is, about 22 1/2 feet (about 6.9 meters) [g] *18* That is, about 30 feet (about 9 meters) [h] *18* That is, about 7 1/2 feet (about 2.3 meters)

Bronze Mirrors

EX 38:8

A mirror in ancient times was a prized possession. Made from highly polished bronze, these mirrors were probably part of the treasure the Israelite women took from Egypt. The bronze basin, where the priests washed their hands, was made from the bronze mirrors of the women who "served at the entrance to the Tent of Meeting." Who were these women? Perhaps they led the women worshipers as Miriam did (Ex 15:20–21), or perhaps they were responsible for some of the physical labor involved in the care of the tabernacle. We know they were not temple prostitutes. The cultic religions of the Mediterranean area involved temple prostitution, but God had clearly and forcefully forbidden this practice (Dt 23:17–18).

At the Age of Twenty

EX 38:26

The count of 603,550 men corresponds to the number of men of military age who left in the exodus (Ex 12:37; Nu 1:45–46). Evidently 20 years is seen as the age when a young man is ready for the responsibilities of war and the responsibilities of supporting the worship that will take place at the tabernacle. Exodus 30:11–16 explains that whenever a census is taken, every adult male, excluding the Levites (Nu 1:47–49), is to give an offering. This offering will support the ministry of the tabernacle. God says the offering represents ransom money for their lives, and he promises to protect them from plagues when they give it (Ex 30:12).

20All the tent pegs[k] of the tabernacle and of the
surrounding courtyard were bronze.

The Materials Used

21These are the amounts of the materials used
for the tabernacle, the tabernacle of the Testimony,[l] which were recorded at Moses' command by
the Levites under the direction of Ithamar[m] son of
Aaron, the priest. 22(Bezalel[n] son of Uri, the son of
Hur, of the tribe of Judah, made everything the
LORD commanded Moses; 23with him was Oholiab[o] son of Ahisamach, of the tribe of Dan—a
craftsman and designer, and an embroiderer in
blue, purple and scarlet yarn and fine linen.)
24The total amount of the gold from the wave
offering used for all the work on the sanctuary[p]
was 29 talents and 730 shekels,[a] according to the
sanctuary shekel.[q]

25The silver obtained from those of the community who were counted in the census[r] was 100 talents and 1,775 shekels,[b] according to the sanctuary shekel— 26one beka per person,[s] that is, half a
shekel,[c] according to the sanctuary shekel,[t] from
everyone who had crossed over to those counted,
twenty years old or more,[u] a total of 603,550
men.[v] 27The 100 talents[d] of silver were used to cast
the bases[w] for the sanctuary and for the curtain—
100 bases from the 100 talents, one talent for each
base. 28They used the 1,775 shekels[e] to make the
hooks for the posts, to overlay the tops of the
posts, and to make their bands.

29The bronze from the wave offering was 70 talents and 2,400 shekels.[f] 30They used it to make
the bases for the entrance to the Tent of Meeting,
the bronze altar with its bronze grating and all its
utensils, 31the bases for the surrounding courtyard
and those for its entrance and all the tent pegs for
the tabernacle and those for the surrounding
courtyard.

The Priestly Garments

39 From the blue, purple and scarlet yarn[x] they
made woven garments for ministering in
the sanctuary.[y] They also made sacred garments[z]
for Aaron, as the LORD commanded Moses.

The Ephod

2They[g] made the ephod of gold, and of blue,
purple and scarlet yarn, and of finely twisted
linen. 3They hammered out thin sheets of gold
and cut strands to be worked into the blue, purple
and scarlet yarn and fine linen—the work of a
skilled craftsman. 4They made shoulder pieces for

38:20 [k]Ex 35:18
38:21 [l]Nu 1:50,53; 8:24; 9:15; 10:11; 17:7; 1Ch 23:32; 2Ch 24:6; Ac 7:44; Rev 15:5 [m]Nu 4:28,33
38:22 [n]Ex 31:2
38:23 [o]Ex 31:6
38:24 [p]Ex 30:16 [q]Ex 30:13; Lev 27:25; Nu 3:47; 18:16
38:25 [r]Ex 30:12
38:26 [s]Ex 30:12 [t]Ex 30:13 [u]Ex 30:14 [v]Ex 12:37; Nu 1:46
38:27 [w]Ex 26:19
39:1 [x]Ex 35:23 [y]Ex 35:19 [z]ver 41; Ex 28:2

[a] *24* The weight of the gold was a little over one ton (about 1 metric ton). [b] *25* The weight of the silver was a little over 3 3/4 tons (about 3.4 metric tons). [c] *26* That is, about 1/5 ounce (about 5.5 grams) [d] *27* That is, about 3 3/4 tons (about 3.4 metric tons) [e] *28* That is, about 45 pounds (about 20 kilograms) [f] *29* The weight of the bronze was about 2 1/2 tons (about 2.4 metric tons). [g] *2* Or *He*; also in verses 7, 8 and 22

the ephod, which were attached to two of its corners, so it could be fastened. 5 Its skillfully woven
waistband was like it—of one piece with the
ephod and made with gold, and with blue, purple
and scarlet yarn, and with finely twisted linen, as
the LORD commanded Moses.
6 They mounted the onyx stones in gold filigree
settings and engraved them like a seal with the
names of the sons of Israel. 7 Then they fastened
them on the shoulder pieces of the ephod as
39:7 [a]Lev 24:7; Jos 4:7 memorial[a] stones for the sons of Israel, as the
LORD commanded Moses.

The Breastpiece

39:8 [b]Lev 8:8 8 They fashioned the breastpiece[b]—the work of a
skilled craftsman. They made it like the ephod: of
gold, and of blue, purple and scarlet yarn, and of
finely twisted linen. 9 It was square—a span[a] long
and a span wide—and folded double. 10 Then they
mounted four rows of precious stones on it. In the
first row there was a ruby, a topaz and a beryl; 11 in
the second row a turquoise, a sapphire[b] and an
emerald; 12 in the third row a jacinth, an agate and
an amethyst; 13 in the fourth row a chrysolite, an
onyx and a jasper.[c] They were mounted in gold
filigree settings. 14 There were twelve stones, one
for each of the names of the sons of Israel, each
39:14 [c]Rev 21:12 engraved like a seal with the name of one of the
twelve tribes.[c]
15 For the breastpiece they made braided chains
of pure gold, like a rope. 16 They made two gold
filigree settings and two gold rings, and fastened
the rings to two of the corners of the breastpiece.
17 They fastened the two gold chains to the rings at
the corners of the breastpiece, 18 and the other
ends of the chains to the two settings, attaching
them to the shoulder pieces of the ephod at the
front. 19 They made two gold rings and attached
them to the other two corners of the breastpiece
on the inside edge next to the ephod. 20 Then they
made two more gold rings and attached them to
the bottom of the shoulder pieces on the front of
the ephod, close to the seam just above the waistband of the ephod. 21 They tied the rings of the
breastpiece to the rings of the ephod with blue
cord, connecting it to the waistband so that the
breastpiece would not swing out from the
ephod—as the LORD commanded Moses.

Other Priestly Garments

22 They made the robe of the ephod entirely of
blue cloth—the work of a weaver— 23 with an
opening in the center of the robe like the opening
of a collar,[d] and a band around this opening, so
that it would not tear. 24 They made pomegranates
of blue, purple and scarlet yarn and finely twisted

[a] 9 That is, about 9 inches (about 22 centimeters) [b] *11* Or *lapis lazuli* [c] *13* The precise identification of some of these precious stones is uncertain. [d] *23* The meaning of the Hebrew for this word is uncertain.

"Life is hard and then you die." Does that sound discouraging? Actually, it's the strongest message of encouragement I know, because we have not even begun to taste the glory, love, grace, and joy that God intends for us!

—Barbara Johnson

A Blessing

EX 39:43

When the work for the tabernacle is finished, the Israelites are at a high point spiritually. In chapter 39 alone, the text records ten times that the Israelites did everything "as the LORD had commanded Moses." Seeing this full obedience, an obedience that is costly in gifts and in labor, Moses blesses the people.

***Blessing* can point toward God or toward humans. When we bless God, we come before him in praise and adoration. (In Hebrew, the same word for "bless" is also used for the word "kneel.") When we bless others, we are asking God's favor and goodness to be with them.**

linen around the hem of the robe. 25And they
made bells of pure gold and attached them around
the hem between the pomegranates. 26The bells
and pomegranates alternated around the hem of
the robe to be worn for ministering, as the LORD
commanded Moses.
27For Aaron and his sons, they made tunics of
fine linen[d]—the work of a weaver—28and the turban[e] of fine linen, the linen headbands and the
undergarments of finely twisted linen. 29The sash
was of finely twisted linen and blue, purple and
scarlet yarn—the work of an embroiderer—as the
LORD commanded Moses.
30They made the plate, the sacred diadem, out
of pure gold and engraved on it, like an inscription on a seal: HOLY TO THE LORD. 31Then they fastened a blue cord to it to attach it to the turban, as
the LORD commanded Moses.

Moses Inspects the Tabernacle

32So all the work on the tabernacle, the Tent of
Meeting, was completed. The Israelites did everything just as the LORD commanded Moses.[f] 33Then
they brought the tabernacle to Moses: the tent and
all its furnishings, its clasps, frames, crossbars,
posts and bases; 34the covering of ram skins dyed
red, the covering of hides of sea cows[a] and the
shielding curtain; 35the ark of the Testimony[g] with
its poles and the atonement cover; 36the table with
all its articles and the bread of the Presence; 37the
pure gold lampstand[h] with its row of lamps and
all its accessories, and the oil for the light; 38the
gold altar,[i] the anointing oil, the fragrant incense,
and the curtain[j] for the entrance to the tent; 39the
bronze altar with its bronze grating, its poles and
all its utensils; the basin with its stand; 40the curtains of the courtyard with its posts and bases,
and the curtain for the entrance to the courtyard;[k]
the ropes and tent pegs for the courtyard; all the
furnishings for the tabernacle, the Tent of Meeting; 41and the woven garments worn for ministering in the sanctuary, both the sacred garments for
Aaron the priest and the garments for his sons
when serving as priests.
42The Israelites had done all the work just as the
LORD had commanded Moses.[l] 43Moses inspected
the work and saw that they had done it just as the
LORD had commanded. So Moses blessed[m] them.

Setting Up the Tabernacle

40 Then the LORD said to Moses: 2"Set up the
tabernacle, the Tent of Meeting,[n] on the first
day of the first month.[o] 3Place the ark[p] of the Testimony in it and shield the ark with the curtain.
4Bring in the table and set out what belongs on
it.[q] Then bring in the lampstand[r] and set up its
lamps. 5Place the gold altar[s] of incense in front of
the ark of the Testimony and put the curtain at the
entrance to the tabernacle.

39:27 [d]Lev 6:10
39:28 [e]Ex 28:4
39:32 [f]ver 42-43; Ex 25:9
39:35 [g]Ex 30:6
39:37 [h]Ex 25:31
39:38 [i]Ex 30:1-10 [j]Ex 36:35
39:40 [k]Ex 27:9-19
39:42 [l]Ex 25:9
39:43 [m]Lev 9:22, 23; Nu 6:23-27; 2Sa 6:18; 1Ki 8:14,55; 2Ch 30:27
40:2 [n]Nu 1:1 [o]ver 17; Ex 12:2
40:3 [p]ver 21; Nu 4:5; Ex 26:33
40:4 [q]Ex 25:30 [r]ver 22-25; Ex 26:35
40:5 [s]ver 26; Ex 30:1

[a] *34* That is, dugongs

6 “Place the altar of burnt offering in front of the entrance to the tabernacle, the Tent of Meeting; 7 place the basin[t] between the Tent of Meeting and the altar and put water in it. 8 Set up the courtyard around it and put the curtain at the entrance to the courtyard.

9 “Take the anointing oil and anoint[u] the tabernacle and everything in it; consecrate it and all its furnishings, and it will be holy. 10 Then anoint the altar of burnt offering and all its utensils; consecrate[v] the altar, and it will be most holy. 11 Anoint the basin and its stand and consecrate them.

12 “Bring Aaron and his sons to the entrance to the Tent of Meeting and wash them with water.[w] 13 Then dress Aaron in the sacred garments,[x] anoint him and consecrate[y] him so he may serve me as priest. 14 Bring his sons and dress them in tunics. 15 Anoint them just as you anointed their father, so they may serve me as priests. Their anointing will be to a priesthood that will continue for all generations to come.[z]” 16 Moses did everything just as the LORD commanded him.

17 So the tabernacle[a] was set up on the first day of the first month[b] in the second year. 18 When Moses set up the tabernacle, he put the bases in place, erected the frames, inserted the crossbars and set up the posts. 19 Then he spread the tent over the tabernacle and put the covering over the tent, as the LORD commanded him.

20 He took the Testimony[c] and placed it in the ark, attached the poles to the ark and put the atonement cover over it. 21 Then he brought the ark into the tabernacle and hung the shielding curtain[d] and shielded the ark of the Testimony, as the LORD commanded him.

22 Moses placed the table[e] in the Tent of Meeting on the north side of the tabernacle outside the curtain 23 and set out the bread[f] on it before the LORD, as the LORD commanded him.

24 He placed the lampstand[g] in the Tent of Meeting opposite the table on the south side of the tabernacle 25 and set up the lamps[h] before the LORD, as the LORD commanded him.

26 Moses placed the gold altar[i] in the Tent of Meeting in front of the curtain 27 and burned fragrant incense on it, as the LORD commanded[j] him. 28 Then he put up the curtain[k] at the entrance to the tabernacle.

29 He set the altar of burnt offering near the entrance to the tabernacle, the Tent of Meeting, and offered on it burnt offerings and grain offerings,[l] as the LORD commanded him.

30 He placed the basin[m] between the Tent of Meeting and the altar and put water in it for washing, 31 and Moses and Aaron and his sons used it to wash their hands and feet. 32 They washed whenever they entered the Tent of Meeting or approached the altar,[n] as the LORD commanded Moses.

33 Then Moses set up the courtyard[o] around the tabernacle and altar and put up the curtain[p] at the

40:7 [t]ver 30; Ex 30:18
40:9 [u]Ex 30:26; Lev 8:10
40:10 [v]Ex 29:36
40:12 [w]Lev 8:1-13
40:13 [x]Ex 28:41 [y]Lev 8:12
40:15 [z]Ex 29:9; Nu 25:13
40:17 [a]Nu 7:1 [b]ver 2
40:20 [c]Ex 16:34; 25:16; Dt 10:5; 1Ki 8:9; Heb 9:4
40:21 [d]Ex 26:33
40:22 [e]Ex 26:35
40:23 [f]ver 4
40:24 [g]Ex 26:35
40:25 [h]ver 4; Ex 25:37
40:26 [i]ver 5; Ex 30:6
40:27 [j]Ex 30:7
40:28 [k]Ex 26:36
40:29 [l]ver 6; Ex 29:38-42
40:30 [m]ver 7
40:32 [n]Ex 30:20
40:33 [o]Ex 27:9 [p]ver 8

Living our lives with certain things unresolved is what faith is all about. I believe that many things happen that we simply can’t explain. When we look back after many years, we still have little understanding of what went on. But we have the knowledge and assurance that Jesus was there with us through every moment, walking by our side, guiding our footsteps. We never needed to fear the questions, because Jesus was answer enough.

—Sheila Walsh

entrance to the courtyard. And so Moses finished
the work.

The Glory of the LORD

[34]Then the cloud[q] covered the Tent of Meeting,
and the glory of the LORD filled the tabernacle.
[35]Moses could not enter the Tent of Meeting
because the cloud had settled upon it, and the glory of the LORD filled the tabernacle.[r]
[36]In all the travels of the Israelites, whenever
the cloud lifted from above the tabernacle, they
would set out;[s] [37]but if the cloud did not lift, they
did not set out—until the day it lifted. [38]So the
cloud[t] of the LORD was over the tabernacle by day,
and fire was in the cloud by night, in the sight of
all the house of Israel during all their travels.

40:34 [q]Nu 9:15-23; 1Ki 8:12
40:35 [r]1Ki 8:11; 2Ch 5:13-14
40:36 [s]Nu 9:17-23; 10:13; Ne 9:19
40:38 [t]Ex 13:21; Nu 9:15; 1Co 10:1

Don't take yourself too seriously. It just makes life all the harder. It'll all come out in the wash anyway, because God's glory eventually will eclipse everything that goes wrong on this earth.

—Luci Swindoll

Leviticus

A holy law defined by a holy God.

Ultimately, the book of Leviticus is a book about relationships: God's relationship with his people and their relationships with each other. The laws and guidelines in Leviticus provide a formula for a holy lifestyle based on God's principles. The laws cover every aspect of daily life, from worship on holy days to proper eating habits, from clothing to cleansing, from sexual activity to rewards for obedience and punishments for disobedience.

Leviticus devotes several chapters to the Israelite system of sacrifices (Lev 1-7). These offerings were designed to remind the Israelites of their need for God's love and forgiveness, while illustrating the essential characteristics of God's nature. The intimately detailed rules for daily living found throughout Leviticus provide the regulations necessary to maintain order in Israelite society. In Leviticus we learn about God's concerns for a proper diet (Lev 11), his interest in the proper care of diseased skin (Lev 13–14), our natural bodily functions and God's provisions for cleansing (Lev 15). The detailed lists of sexual regulations and guidelines for moral behavior found in Leviticus 18–19 reveal not so much a God who is "picky" as a God who is intimately concerned with every aspect of life. The goal of Leviticus is to produce a people who are holy before a holy God.

Quick Study

Author
Generally thought to be Moses.

Date Written
Probably written during the 1400s B.C., at the time of Israel's wandering in the desert.

Setting
Mount Sinai.

Key Passage
Leviticus 11:45 "I am the LORD who brought you up out of Egypt to be your God; therefore be holy, because I am holy."

Outline

Instructions for offerings.
Lev 1-7

Aaron and his sons.
Lev 8-10

Rules for clean living.
Lev 11-15

The Day of Atonement.
Lev 16

Eating blood is forbidden.
Lev 17

Sexual laws.
Lev 18

Various laws.
Lev 19

Punishments for sin.
Lev 20

Rules for priests.
Lev 21-22

Instructions for feasts and special days.
Lev 23-25

Rewards for obedience.
Lev 26:1-13

Punishments for disobedience.
Lev 26:14-46

Laws of redemption.
Lev 27

The Women of Leviticus

Priests' daughters *Tough punishment for defilement.* Lev 21:9

Shelomith *Mother of a blasphemer.* Lev 24:10-13

The Burnt Offering

1 The LORD called to Moses[a] and spoke to him
from the Tent of Meeting.[b] He said, 2"Speak to
the Israelites and say to them: 'When any of you
brings an offering to the LORD, bring as your offering an animal from either the herd or the flock.[c]
3" 'If the offering is a burnt offering from the
herd, he is to offer a male without defect.[d] He
must present it at the entrance to the Tent[e] of
Meeting so that it[a] will be acceptable to the LORD.
4He is to lay his hand on the head[f] of the burnt
offering, and it will be accepted on his behalf to
make atonement[g] for him. 5He is to slaughter[h] the
young bull before the LORD, and then Aaron's sons
the priests shall bring the blood and sprinkle it
against the altar on all sides[i] at the entrance to the
Tent of Meeting. 6He is to skin[j] the burnt offering
and cut it into pieces. 7The sons of Aaron the
priest are to put fire on the altar and arrange
wood[k] on the fire. 8Then Aaron's sons the priests
shall arrange the pieces, including the head and
the fat,[l] on the burning wood that is on the altar.
9He is to wash the inner parts and the legs with
water, and the priest is to burn all of it on the
altar.[m] It is a burnt offering, an offering made by
fire, an aroma pleasing to the LORD.[n]
10" 'If the offering is a burnt offering from the
flock, from either the sheep or the goats,[o] he is to
offer a male without defect. 11He is to slaughter it
at the north side of the altar before the LORD, and
Aaron's sons the priests shall sprinkle its blood
against the altar on all sides.[p] 12He is to cut it into
pieces, and the priest shall arrange them, including the head and the fat, on the burning wood
that is on the altar. 13He is to wash the inner parts
and the legs with water, and the priest is to bring
all of it and burn it on the altar. It is a burnt offering, an offering made by fire, an aroma pleasing to
the LORD.
14" 'If the offering to the LORD is a burnt offering
of birds, he is to offer a dove or a young pigeon.[q]
15The priest shall bring it to the altar, wring off the
head and burn it on the altar; its blood shall be
drained out on the side of the altar.[r] 16He is to
remove the crop with its contents[b] and throw it to
the east side of the altar, where the ashes[s] are.
17He shall tear it open by the wings, not severing
it completely,[t] and then the priest shall burn it on
the wood[u] that is on the fire on the altar. It is a
burnt offering, an offering made by fire, an aroma pleasing to the LORD.

The Grain Offering

2 " 'When someone brings a grain offering[v] to
the LORD, his offering is to be of fine flour. He
is to pour oil[w] on it, put incense on it 2and take it
to Aaron's sons the priests. The priest shall take a
handful of the fine flour[x] and oil, together with all

1:1 [a]Ex 19:3; 25:22 [b]Nu 7:89
1:2 [c]Lev 22:18-19
1:3 [d]Ex 12:5; Dt 15:21; Heb 9:14; 1Pe 1:19 [e]Lev 17:9
1:4 [f]Ex 29:10,15; Lev 3:2 [g]2Ch 29:23-24
1:5 [h]Lev 3:2,8 [i]Heb 12:24; 1Pe 1:2
1:6 [j]Lev 7:8
1:7 [k]Lev 6:12
1:8 [l]ver 12
1:9 [m]Ex 29:18 [n]ver 13; Ge 8:21; Nu 15:8-10; Eph 5:2
1:10 [o]ver 3; Ex 12:5
1:11 [p]ver 5
1:14 [q]Ge 15:9; Lev 5:7; Lk 2:24
1:15 [r]Lev 5:9
1:16 [s]Lev 6:10
1:17 [t]Ge 15:10 [u]Lev 5:8
2:1 [v]Lev 6:14-18 [w]Nu 15:4
2:2 [x]Lev 5:11

[a] *3* Or *he* [b] *16* Or *crop and the feathers*; the meaning of the Hebrew for this word is uncertain.

To Atone for Sin

LEV 1:9

Because God is holy and people are sinful, it is impossible for any human to have a relationship with God without atonement for their sins first being made. Levitical law requires regular sacrifices throughout the calendar year, as well as public fasts and feasts, to atone for the sins of the people. Due to people's sinful nature, daily, individual sacrifices are also required.

In order to make payment for sins and to demonstrate devotion to God, the sinner offers up one animal for sacrifice. The type of animal required—a bull, goat or sheep, or young pigeon or dove—is determined on a "sliding scale" basis, contingent on the donor's wealth or standing in the community. The monetary value of the animal does not gain the donor more or less forgiveness; only its lack of blemish and the heart repentance of the sinner matter to God.

Grain and Fellowship Offerings

LEV 2:1—3:17

While the burnt offering atones for sin, the grain offering is an act of worship made in recognition of God's favor and blessing. The grain itself represents the finest of people's labors. This offering is never made on its own. Rather, it accompanies a burnt offering, fellowship offering or sin offering (Lev 9:3–4). The added salt likely represents friendship and permanence and the faithfulness of God's love for his people.

The fellowship offering, or peace offering, is the only sacrifice in which the worshiper actively participates. The priest, as part of God's provision for him, eats a portion of this offering (Lev 7:28–34), and the worshiper eats the remainder. The offering must be eaten within a two-day period (Lev 7:15–18), therefore, the worshiper often invites friends, neighbors, relatives or the poor to share the meal. In this way, the people could fellowship—in a sense, have a meal—with God.

the incense,[y] and burn this as a memorial portion[z]
on the altar, an offering made by fire, an aroma
pleasing to the LORD. 3The rest of the grain offering
belongs to Aaron and his sons;[a] it is a most holy
part of the offerings made to the LORD by fire.
4“ ‘If you bring a grain offering baked in an
oven, it is to consist of fine flour: cakes made
without yeast and mixed with oil, or[a] wafers
made without yeast and spread with oil.[b] 5If your
grain offering is prepared on a griddle, it is to be
made of fine flour mixed with oil, and without
yeast. 6Crumble it and pour oil on it; it is a grain
offering. 7If your grain offering is cooked in a
pan,[c] it is to be made of fine flour and oil. 8Bring
the grain offering made of these things to the
LORD; present it to the priest, who shall take it to
the altar. 9He shall take out the memorial portion[d]
from the grain offering and burn it on the altar as
an offering made by fire, an aroma pleasing to the
LORD.[e] 10The rest of the grain offering belongs to
Aaron and his sons;[f] it is a most holy part of the
offerings made to the LORD by fire.
11“ ‘Every grain offering you bring to the LORD
must be made without yeast,[g] for you are not to
burn any yeast or honey in an offering made to
the LORD by fire. 12You may bring them to the LORD
as an offering of the firstfruits,[h] but they are not to
be offered on the altar as a pleasing aroma. 13Sea-
son all your grain offerings with salt. Do not leave
the salt of the covenant[i] of your God out of your
grain offerings; add salt to all your offerings.
14“ ‘If you bring a grain offering of firstfruits[j] to
the LORD, offer crushed heads of new grain roasted in the fire. 15Put oil and incense on it; it is a
grain offering. 16The priest shall burn the memorial portion[k] of the crushed grain and the oil,
together with all the incense, as an offering made
to the LORD by fire.

The Fellowship Offering

3 “ ‘If someone’s offering is a fellowship offering,[b][l] and he offers an animal from the herd,
whether male or female, he is to present before
the LORD an animal without defect.[m] 2He is to lay
his hand on the head[n] of his offering and slaughter it[o] at the entrance to the Tent of Meeting. Then
Aaron’s sons the priests shall sprinkle the blood
against the altar on all sides. 3From the fellowship
offering he is to bring a sacrifice made to the LORD
by fire: all the fat[p] that covers the inner parts or is
connected to them, 4both kidneys with the fat on
them near the loins, and the covering of the liver,
which he will remove with the kidneys. 5Then
Aaron’s sons[q] are to burn it on the altar on top of
the burnt offering[r] that is on the burning wood,
as an offering made by fire, an aroma pleasing to
the LORD.
6“ ‘If he offers an animal from the flock as a fel-

2:2 [y]Lev 6:15; Isa 66:3 [z]ver 9,16; Lev 5:12; 6:15; 24:7; Ac 10:4
2:3 [a]ver 10; Lev 6:16; 10:12,13
2:4 [b]Ex 29:2
2:7 [c]Lev 7:9
2:9 [d]ver 2 [e]Ex 29:18; Lev 6:15
2:10 [f]ver 3
2:11 [g]Ex 23:18; 34:25; Lev 6:16
2:12 [h]Lev 7:13; 23:10
2:13 [i]Nu 18:19; Eze 43:24
2:14 [j]Lev 23:10
2:16 [k]ver 2
3:1 [l]Lev 7:11-34 [m]Lev 1:3; 22:21
3:2 [n]Ex 29:10,15 [o]Lev 1:5
3:3 [p]Ex 29:13
3:5 [q]Lev 7:29-34 [r]Ex 29:13, 38-42

[a] *4* Or *and* [b] *1* Traditionally *peace offering;* also in verses 3, 6 and 9

lowship offering[s] to the LORD, he is to offer a male or female without defect. 7If he offers a lamb, he is to present it before the LORD.[t] 8He is to lay his hand on the head of his offering and slaughter it[u] in front of the Tent of Meeting. Then Aaron's sons shall sprinkle its blood against the altar on all sides. 9From the fellowship offering he is to bring a sacrifice made to the LORD by fire: its fat, the entire fat tail cut off close to the backbone, all the fat that covers the inner parts or is connected to them, 10both kidneys with the fat on them near the loins, and the covering of the liver, which he will remove with the kidneys. 11The priest shall burn them on the altar[v] as food,[w] an offering made to the LORD by fire.

12" 'If his offering is a goat, he is to present it before the LORD. 13He is to lay his hand on its head and slaughter it in front of the Tent of Meeting. Then Aaron's sons shall sprinkle[x] its blood against the altar on all sides. 14From what he offers he is to make this offering to the LORD by fire: all the fat that covers the inner parts or is connected to them, 15both kidneys with the fat on them near the loins, and the covering of the liver, which he will remove with the kidneys. 16The priest shall burn them on the altar as food, an offering made by fire, a pleasing aroma. All the fat is the LORD's.[y]

17" 'This is a lasting ordinance for the generations to come,[z] wherever you live: You must not eat any fat or any blood.[a]' "

The Sin Offering

4 The LORD said to Moses, 2"Say to the Israelites: 'When anyone sins unintentionally[b] and does what is forbidden in any of the LORD's commands—

3" 'If the anointed priest sins, bringing guilt on the people, he must bring to the LORD a young bull[c] without defect as a sin offering[d] for the sin he has committed. 4He is to present the bull at the entrance to the Tent of Meeting before the LORD.[e] He is to lay his hand on its head and slaughter it before the LORD. 5Then the anointed priest shall take some of the bull's blood[f] and carry it into the Tent of Meeting. 6He is to dip his finger into the blood and sprinkle some of it seven times before the LORD, in front of the curtain of the sanctuary. 7The priest shall then put some of the blood on the horns of the altar of fragrant incense that is before the LORD in the Tent of Meeting. The rest of the bull's blood he shall pour out at the base of the altar[g] of burnt offering[h] at the entrance to the Tent of Meeting. 8He shall remove all the fat[i] from the bull of the sin offering—the fat that covers the inner parts or is connected to them, 9both kidneys with the fat on them near the loins, and the covering of the liver, which he will remove with the kidneys[j]— 10just as the fat is removed from the ox[a]

3:6 [s]ver 1
3:7 [t]Lev 17:8-9
3:8 [u]ver 2; Lev 1:5
3:11 [v]ver 5 [w]ver 16; Lev 21:6,17
3:13 [x]Ex 24:6
3:16 [y]1Sa 2:16
3:17 [z]Lev 6:18; 17:7 [a]Ge 9:4; Lev 7:25-26; 17:10-16; Dt 12:16; Ac 15:20
4:2 [b]Lev 5:15-18; Ps 19:12; Heb 9:7
4:3 [c]ver 14; Ps 66:15 [d]Lev 9:2-22; Heb 9:13-14
4:4 [e]Lev 1:3
4:5 [f]Lev 16:14
4:7 [g]ver 34; Lev 8:15 [h]ver 18,30; Lev 5:9; 9:9; 16:18
4:8 [i]Lev 3:3-5
4:9 [j]Lev 3:4

[a] *10* The Hebrew word can include both male and female.

The Sin Offering

LEV 4:1–5:13

Even when sins are committed unintentionally, the Israelites are held accountable. A sacrifice of blood is required to pay for their sin. In a sin offering, the sinner's guilt is transferred to the animal to be sacrificed through the laying on of hands. After the animal is slaughtered, some of the blood of the sacrifice—a substitute for the sinner's own blood and life—is spread on the horns of the altar of incense. Smoke from the incense drifts heavenward as an offering to God.

Several different animals could be given as a sin offering, depending on the ranking of the individual or group; the greater the position, the greater the responsibility. For the sins of a high priest or the entire community, a bull must be sacrificed; for a leader, a male goat; for a common citizen, a female goat or lamb; for the poor, two doves or two pigeons; and for the very poor, and offering of fine flour.

sacrificed as a fellowship offering.[a] Then the
priest shall burn them on the altar of burnt offering. 11But the hide of the bull and all its flesh, as
well as the head and legs, the inner parts and
offal[k]— 12that is, all the rest of the bull—he must
take outside the camp[l] to a place ceremonially
clean,[m] where the ashes are thrown, and burn it
in a wood fire on the ash heap.

13" 'If the whole Israelite community sins unintentionally[n] and does what is forbidden in any of
the LORD's commands, even though the community is unaware of the matter, they are guilty.
14When they become aware of the sin they committed, the assembly must bring a young bull[o] as
a sin offering[p] and present it before the Tent of
Meeting. 15The elders of the community are to lay
their hands on the bull's head[q] before the LORD,
and the bull shall be slaughtered before the LORD.
16Then the anointed priest is to take some of the
bull's blood[r] into the Tent of Meeting. 17He shall
dip his finger into the blood and sprinkle it before
the LORD[s] seven times in front of the curtain. 18He
is to put some of the blood on the horns of the
altar that is before the LORD[t] in the Tent of Meeting. The rest of the blood he shall pour out at the
base of the altar of burnt offering at the entrance
to the Tent of Meeting. 19He shall remove all the
fat[u] from it and burn it on the altar, 20and do with
this bull just as he did with the bull for the sin
offering. In this way the priest will make atonement[v] for them, and they will be forgiven.[w]
21Then he shall take the bull outside the camp and
burn it as he burned the first bull. This is the sin
offering for the community.[x]

22" 'When a leader[y] sins unintentionally[z] and
does what is forbidden in any of the commands
of the LORD his God, he is guilty. 23When he is
made aware of the sin he committed, he must
bring as his offering a male goat without defect.
24He is to lay his hand on the goat's head and
slaughter it at the place where the burnt offering
is slaughtered before the LORD. It is a sin offering.
25Then the priest shall take some of the blood of
the sin offering with his finger and put it on the
horns of the altar of burnt offering and pour out
the rest of the blood at the base of the altar.[a] 26He
shall burn all the fat on the altar as he burned the
fat of the fellowship offering. In this way the
priest will make atonement for the man's sin, and
he will be forgiven.[b]

27" 'If a member of the community sins unintentionally[c] and does what is forbidden in any of
the LORD's commands, he is guilty. 28When he is
made aware of the sin he committed, he must
bring as his offering[d] for the sin he committed a
female goat[e] without defect. 29He is to lay his hand
on the head[f] of the sin offering[g] and slaughter it at

4:11 [k]Ex 29:14; Lev 9:11; Nu 19:5
4:12 [l]Heb 13:11 [m]Lev 6:11
4:13 [n]ver 2; Lev 5:2-4,17; Nu 15:24-26
4:14 [o]ver 3 [p]ver 23,28
4:15 [q]Lev 1:4; 8:14,22; Nu 8:10
4:16 [r]ver 5
4:17 [s]ver 6
4:18 [t]ver 7
4:19 [u]ver 8
4:20 [v]Heb 10:10-12 [w]Nu 15:25
4:21 [x]Lev 16:5,15
4:22 [y]Nu 31:13 [z]ver 2
4:25 [a]ver 7,18,30,34; Lev 9:9
4:26 [b]Lev 5:10
4:27 [c]ver 2; Nu 15:27
4:28 [d]ver 23 [e]ver 3
4:29 [f]ver 4,24 [g]Lev 1:4

"All I wish for, all I long for is to be a holy woman. Thank *you, Father, that you have released* the power for me to do so, and *that everything in this life that* comes my way—the instruments *that bring joy or sorrow—is held* by your divine hands, carving the *very nature, the very heart of* Jesus in me."
—Kathy Troccoli

[a] *10* Traditionally *peace offering*; also in verses 26, 31 and 35

the place of the burnt offering. 30 Then the priest is
4:30 to take some of the blood with his finger and put
hver 7 it on the horns of the altar of burnt offering[h] and
pour out the rest of the blood at the base of the
altar. 31 He shall remove all the fat, just as the fat is
removed from the fellowship offering, and the
4:31 priest shall burn it on the altar as an aroma pleas-
iGe 8:21 ing to the LORD.[i] In this way the priest will make
atonement for him, and he will be forgiven.
32 " 'If he brings a lamb as his sin offering, he is
4:32 to bring a female without defect.[j] 33 He is to lay his
jver 28 hand on its head and slaughter it for a sin offering
at the place where the burnt offering is slaugh-
4:33 tered.[k] 34 Then the priest shall take some of the
kver 29 blood of the sin offering with his finger and put it
4:34 on the horns of the altar of burnt offering and pour
lver 7 out the rest of the blood at the base of the altar.[l]
35 He shall remove all the fat, just as the fat is
4:35 removed from the lamb of the fellowship offering,
mver 26,31 and the priest shall burn it on the altar[m] on top of
the offerings made to the LORD by fire. In this way
the priest will make atonement for him for the sin
he has committed, and he will be forgiven.

5:1 **5** " 'If a person sins because he does not speak
nPr 29:24 up when he hears a public charge to testify[n]
over 17 regarding something he has seen or learned
about, he will be held responsible.[o]
2 " 'Or if a person touches anything ceremonially unclean—whether the carcasses of unclean
5:2 wild animals or of unclean livestock or of unclean
pLev 11:11, 24-40; Dt 14:8 creatures that move along the ground[p]—even
though he is unaware of it, he has become
unclean and is guilty.
5:3 3 " 'Or if he touches human uncleanness[q]—any-
qNu 19:11-16 thing that would make him unclean—even
though he is unaware of it, when he learns of it he
5:4 will be guilty.
rNu 30:6,8 4 " 'Or if a person thoughtlessly takes an oath[r]
to do anything, whether good or evil—in any matter one might carelessly swear about—even
though he is unaware of it, in any case when he
learns of it he will be guilty.
5:5 5 " 'When anyone is guilty in any of these ways,
sLev 16:21; 26:40; Nu 5:7; Pr 28:13 he must confess[s] in what way he has sinned 6 and,
as a penalty for the sin he has committed, he must
bring to the LORD a female lamb or goat from the
5:6 flock as a sin offering;[t] and the priest shall make
tLev 4:28 atonement for him for his sin.
7 " 'If he cannot afford[u] a lamb, he is to bring
5:7 two doves or two young pigeons to the LORD as a
uLev 12:8; 14:21 penalty for his sin—one for a sin offering and the
other for a burnt offering. 8 He is to bring them to
5:8 the priest, who shall first offer the one for the sin
vLev 1:15 offering. He is to wring its head from its neck,[v]
wLev 1:17 not severing it completely,[w] 9 and is to sprinkle
some of the blood of the sin offering against the
5:9 side of the altar; the rest of the blood must be
xLev 4:7,18 drained out at the base of the altar.[x] It is a sin
5:10 offering. 10 The priest shall then offer the other as
yLev 1:14-17 a burnt offering in the prescribed way[y] and make

Rules for Healthy Living

LEV 5:2-3

Only in recent history has it been proven that some illnesses are caused by the spread of disease-producing microorganisms. Yet even before the development of the germ theory, God's laws helped to safeguard his people against the spread of disease. By avoiding the things that make them ceremonially unclean, such as the carcasses of wild animals, the Israelites not only remain clean before God but experience God's protection—one of the many benefits of adhering to his rules for healthy living.

The Guilt Offering

LEV 5:14—6:7

When an Israelite commits a sin in regard to property, a guilt offering is required and restitution must be made. The only acceptable sacrifice in such cases is a ram. Additionally, the sinner is obligated to fully repay the one who was sinned against, with an additional 20 percent given as compensation. Examples of sins requiring a guilt offering might be: failure to return lost or borrowed property, cheating a neighbor or mishandling "holy things" (Lev 5:15), that is, sacrifices or any other thing connected with offerings to God. A guilt offering not only restored relationship between the sinner and God, but also between the sinner and the rest of the community.

atonement for him for the sin he has committed, 5:10
and he will be forgiven.[z] [z]Lev 4:26
11“ ‘If, however, he cannot afford two doves or
two young pigeons, he is to bring as an offering 5:11
for his sin a tenth of an ephah[a] of fine flour[a] for a [a]Lev 2:1
sin offering. He must not put oil or incense on it,
because it is a sin offering. 12He is to bring it to
the priest, who shall take a handful of it as a
memorial portion and burn it on the altar on top
of the offerings made to the LORD by fire. It is a sin
offering. 13In this way the priest will make atone- 5:13
ment[b] for him for any of these sins he has com- [b]Lev 4:26
mitted, and he will be forgiven. The rest of the [c]Lev 2:3
offering will belong to the priest,[c] as in the case of
the grain offering.’ ”

The Guilt Offering

14The LORD said to Moses: 15“When a person
commits a violation and sins unintentionally in
regard to any of the LORD’s holy things, he is to 5:15
bring to the LORD as a penalty[d] a ram[e] from the [d]Lev 22:14
flock, one without defect and of the proper value [e]Nu 5:8
in silver, according to the sanctuary shekel.[b][f] It is a [f]Ex 30:13
guilt offering. 16He must make restitution[g] for what 5:16
he has failed to do in regard to the holy things, add [g]Lev 6:4
a fifth of the value[h] to that and give it all to the [h]Lev 22:14; Nu 5:7
priest, who will make atonement for him with the
ram as a guilt offering, and he will be forgiven.
17“If a person sins and does what is forbidden in
any of the LORD’s commands, even though he does
not know it,[i] he is guilty and will be held respon- 5:17
sible. 18He is to bring to the priest as a guilt offer- [i]ver 15;
ing a ram from the flock, one without defect and Lev 4:2
of the proper value. In this way the priest will
make atonement for him for the wrong he has
committed unintentionally, and he will be forgiv- 5:18
en.[j] 19It is a guilt offering; he has been guilty of[c] [j]ver 15
wrongdoing against the LORD.”

6 The LORD said to Moses: 2“If anyone sins and 6:2
is unfaithful to the LORD[k] by deceiving his [k]Nu 5:6;
neighbor[l] about something entrusted to him or Ac 5:4; Col 3:9
left in his care[m] or stolen, or if he cheats him, 3or [l]Pr 24:28
if he finds lost property and lies about it,[n] or if he [m]Ex 22:7
swears falsely, or if he commits any such sin that 6:3
people may do— 4when he thus sins and becomes [n]Dt 22:1-3
guilty, he must return[o] what he has stolen or tak- 6:4
en by extortion, or what was entrusted to him, or [o]Lk 19:8
the lost property he found, 5or whatever it was he 6:5
swore falsely about. He must make restitution[p] in [p]Nu 5:7
full, add a fifth of the value to it and give it all to [q]Lev 5:15
the owner on the day he presents his guilt offer- 6:6
ing.[q] 6And as a penalty he must bring to the [r]Lev 5:15
priest, that is, to the LORD, his guilt offering,[r] a 6:7
ram from the flock, one without defect and of the [s]Lev 4:26
proper value. 7In this way the priest will make
atonement[s] for him before the LORD, and he will

[a] *11* That is, probably about 2 quarts (about 2 liters)
[b] *15* That is, about 2/5 ounce (about 11.5 grams)
[c] *19* Or *has made full expiation for his*

be forgiven for any of these things he did that made him guilty.”

The Burnt Offering

8The LORD said to Moses: 9“Give Aaron and his sons this command: ‘These are the regulations for the burnt offering: The burnt offering is to remain on the altar hearth throughout the night, till morning, and the fire must be kept burning on the altar. 10The priest shall then put on his linen clothes, with linen undergarments next to his body,[t] and shall remove the ashes of the burnt offering that the fire has consumed on the altar and place them beside the altar. 11Then he is to take off these clothes and put on others, and carry the ashes outside the camp to a place that is ceremonially clean.[u] 12The fire on the altar must be kept burning; it must not go out. Every morning the priest is to add firewood and arrange the burnt offering on the fire and burn the fat of the fellowship offerings[a] on it. 13The fire must be kept burning on the altar continuously; it must not go out.

The Grain Offering

14“ ‘These are the regulations for the grain offering:[v] Aaron’s sons are to bring it before the LORD, in front of the altar. 15The priest is to take a handful of fine flour and oil, together with all the incense on the grain offering,[w] and burn the memorial portion[x] on the altar as an aroma pleasing to the LORD. 16Aaron and his sons[y] shall eat the rest[z] of it, but it is to be eaten without yeast[a] in a holy place;[b] they are to eat it in the courtyard of the Tent of Meeting. 17It must not be baked with yeast; I have given it as their share of the offerings made to me by fire. Like the sin offering and the guilt offering, it is most holy.[c] 18Any male descendant of Aaron may eat it.[d] It is his regular share of the offerings made to the LORD by fire for the generations to come. Whatever touches them will become holy.[b][e]’ ”

19The LORD also said to Moses, 20“This is the offering Aaron and his sons are to bring to the LORD on the day he[c] is anointed: a tenth of an ephah[d][f] of fine flour as a regular grain offering,[g] half of it in the morning and half in the evening. 21Prepare it with oil on a griddle;[h] bring it well-mixed and present the grain offering broken[e] in pieces as an aroma pleasing to the LORD. 22The son who is to succeed him as anointed priest shall prepare it. It is the LORD’s regular share and is to be burned completely. 23Every grain offering of a priest shall be burned completely; it must not be eaten.”

The Sin Offering

24The LORD said to Moses, 25“Say to Aaron and

6:10 [t]Ex 28:39-42, 43; 39:28
6:11 [u]Lev 4:12
6:14 [v]Lev 2:1; 15:4
6:15 [w]Lev 2:9 [x]Lev 2:2
6:16 [y]Lev 2:3 [z]Eze 44:29 [a]Lev 2:11 [b]Lev 10:13
6:17 [c]ver 29; Ex 40:10; Nu 18:9,10
6:18 [d]ver 29; Nu 18:9-10 [e]ver 27
6:20 [f]Ex 16:36 [g]Ex 29:2
6:21 [h]Lev 2:5

[a] *12* Traditionally *peace offerings* [b] *18* Or *Whoever touches them must be holy*; similarly in verse 27 [c] *20* Or *each*
[d] *20* That is, probably about 2 quarts (about 2 liters)
[e] *21* The meaning of the Hebrew for this word is uncertain.

Linen Clothes

LEV 6:10

A cloth woven from fibers of the flax plant, linen was a fine, breathable fabric that was particularly desirable during Biblical times. Due to its high cost, linen was considered a luxury item and was generally worn only by the wealthy and by the priests, who wore it only inside the tabernacle. When Christ returns to earth, the armies of heaven will accompany him, riding white horses and dressed in “fine linen, white and clean” (Rev 19:14).

Clay Pots

LEV 6:28

Because clay pots are made of a porous material, juices from the meat of the sin offering are absorbed during the cooking process. A part of the sacrifice then remains within the pot even after the offering has been completed. If a bronze pot is used, none of the sacrifice is absorbed into it. It can simply be washed and then reused. However, since the clay pot can never be fully separated from the meat of the sacrifice, it must be broken and not used again. This process keeps the sacred, a sacrifice or offering, from coming into contact with the ordinary or profane if the pot is used again.

his sons: 'These are the regulations for the sin offering: The sin offering is to be slaughtered before the LORD[i] in the place[j] the burnt offering is slaughtered; it is most holy. 26 The priest who offers it shall eat it; it is to be eaten in a holy place,[k] in the courtyard[l] of the Tent of Meeting. 27 Whatever touches any of the flesh will become holy,[m] and if any of the blood is spattered on a garment, you must wash it in a holy place. 28 The clay pot[n] the meat is cooked in must be broken; but if it is cooked in a bronze pot, the pot is to be scoured and rinsed with water. 29 Any male in a priest's family may eat it;[o] it is most holy.[p] 30 But any sin offering whose blood is brought into the Tent of Meeting to make atonement in the Holy Place[q] must not be eaten; it must be burned.[r]

The Guilt Offering

7 " 'These are the regulations for the guilt offering,[s] which is most holy: 2 The guilt offering is to be slaughtered in the place where the burnt offering is slaughtered, and its blood is to be sprinkled against the altar on all sides. 3 All its fat[t] shall be offered: the fat tail and the fat that covers the inner parts, 4 both kidneys with the fat on them near the loins, and the covering of the liver, which is to be removed with the kidneys. 5 The priest shall burn them on the altar as an offering made to the LORD by fire. It is a guilt offering. 6 Any male in a priest's family may eat it,[u] but it must be eaten in a holy place; it is most holy.[v]

7 " 'The same law applies to both the sin offering and the guilt offering: They belong to the priest[w] who makes atonement with them. 8 The priest who offers a burnt offering for anyone may keep its hide for himself. 9 Every grain offering baked in an oven or cooked in a pan or on a griddle[x] belongs to the priest who offers it, 10 and every grain offering, whether mixed with oil or dry, belongs equally to all the sons of Aaron.

The Fellowship Offering

11 " 'These are the regulations for the fellowship offering[a] a person may present to the LORD:

12 " 'If he offers it as an expression of thankfulness, then along with this thank offering[y] he is to offer cakes of bread made without yeast and mixed with oil, wafers[z] made without yeast and spread with oil, and cakes of fine flour well-kneaded and mixed with oil. 13 Along with his fellowship offering of thanksgiving he is to present an offering with cakes of bread made with yeast.[a] 14 He is to bring one of each kind as an offering, a contribution to the LORD; it belongs to the priest who sprinkles the blood of the fellowship offerings. 15 The meat of his fellowship offering of thanksgiving must be eaten on the day it is offered; he must leave none of it till morning.[b]

16 " 'If, however, his offering is the result of a

6:25 [i]Lev 1:3 [j]Lev 1:5,11
6:26 [k]ver 16 [l]Lev 10:17-18
6:27 [m]Ex 29:37
6:28 [n]Lev 11:33; 15:12
6:29 [o]ver 18 [p]ver 17
6:30 [q]Lev 4:18 [r]Lev 4:12
7:1 [s]Lev 5:14-6:7
7:3 [t]Ex 29:13; Lev 3:4,9
7:6 [u]Lev 6:18; Nu 18:9-10 [v]Lev 2:3
7:7 [w]Lev 6:17, 26; 1Co 9:13
7:9 [x]Lev 2:5
7:12 [y]ver 13,15 [z]Lev 2:4; Nu 6:15
7:13 [a]Lev 23:17; Am 4:5
7:15 [b]Lev 22:30

[a] *11* Traditionally *peace offering*; also in verses 13–37

vow or is a freewill offering, the sacrifice shall be
eaten on the day he offers it, but anything left over
7:16 may be eaten on the next day.[c] 17Any meat of the
cLev 19:5-8 sacrifice left over till the third day must be burned
up. 18If any meat of the fellowship offering is eat-
7:18 dLev 19:7 en on the third day, it will not be accepted.[d] It will
eNu 18:27 not be credited[e] to the one who offered it, for it is
impure; the person who eats any of it will be held
responsible.

19" 'Meat that touches anything ceremonially
unclean must not be eaten; it must be burned up.
As for other meat, anyone ceremonially clean may
eat it. 20But if anyone who is unclean eats any meat
7:20 of the fellowship offering belonging to the LORD,
fLev 22:3-7 that person must be cut off from his people.[f] 21If
7:21 anyone touches something unclean[g]—whether
gLev 5:2; 11:24,28 human uncleanness or an unclean animal or any
unclean, detestable thing—and then eats any of the
meat of the fellowship offering belonging to the
LORD, that person must be cut off from his people.' "

Eating Fat and Blood Forbidden

22The LORD said to Moses, 23"Say to the Israelites: 'Do not eat any of the fat of cattle, sheep or
7:23 hLev 3:17; 17:13-14 goats.[h] 24The fat of an animal found dead or torn
by wild animals[i] may be used for any other pur-
pose, but you must not eat it. 25Anyone who eats
7:24 iEx 22:31 the fat of an animal from which an offering by fire
may be[a] made to the LORD must be cut off from
7:26 his people. 26And wherever you live, you must not
jGe 9:4 eat the blood[j] of any bird or animal. 27If anyone
7:27 eats blood,[k] that person must be cut off from his
kLev 17:10-24; Ac 15:20, 29 people.' "

The Priests' Share

28The LORD said to Moses, 29"Say to the Israelites: 'Anyone who brings a fellowship offering to
the LORD is to bring part of it as his sacrifice to the
LORD. 30With his own hands he is to bring the
offering made to the LORD by fire; he is to bring
the fat, together with the breast, and wave the
7:30 lEx 29:24; breast before the LORD as a wave offering.[l] 31The
Nu 6:20 priest shall burn the fat on the altar, but the breast
7:31 belongs to Aaron and his sons.[m] 32You are to give
mver 34 the right thigh of your fellowship offerings to the
7:32 priest as a contribution.[n] 33The son of Aaron who
nver 34; offers the blood and the fat of the fellowship offer-
Lev 9:21; ing shall have the right thigh as his share. 34From
Nu 6:20 the fellowship offerings of the Israelites, I have
7:34 taken the breast that is waved and the thigh[o] that
oLev 10:15 pEx 29:27; is presented and have given them to Aaron the
Nu 18:18-19 priest and his sons[p] as their regular share from the
Israelites.' "

35This is the portion of the offerings made to the
LORD by fire that were allotted to Aaron and his
7:36 sons on the day they were presented to serve the
qEx 40:13, LORD as priests. 36On the day they were anointed,[q]
15; Lev 8:12, 30 the LORD commanded that the Israelites give this

a 25 Or *fire is*

Eating Fat and Blood

LEV 7:22-27

The injunctions given in these verses—to refrain from eating fat and blood—are given primarily for spiritual, rather than physical, reasons. These animals are offerings to the Lord and their fat and blood is dedicated to him.

The Israelites are, however, commanded never to eat blood, though eating blood was common in other cultures of the day (Lev 17). The Israelites obviously did not have access to the medical studies we have at our disposal today. They were not privy to current information about disease and the link to diet. Yet where their knowledge falls short, God's wisdom steps in, providing guidelines that protect the health and welfare of his people. Though the commands for eating have their basis in the spiritual, they also have implications for the physical lives of the Israelites. For more on the sacred connection between blood and life, see the note on Leviticus 17:11.

The Priesthood of Aaron

LEV 8:5-10

Aaron and his sons are consecrated here for the priesthood, representing the entire Israelite nation before God. Aaron is from the tribe of Levi. The Levites as a whole are set apart for the care of the tabernacle and the furnishing of the tabernacle. However, only the descendants of Aaron are called to be priests.

God chooses Aaron for the priesthood, though he is far from perfect. He had not only made a golden idol for the Israelites to worship (Ex 32), he also rebelled against Moses' special position (Nu 12). The truth of the matter is, there is no perfect person available to act as a priestly mediator between God and his people. Leviticus 8 outlines the process of purification that Aaron goes through before he is able to begin his priestly duties. The only perfect priest is, of course, Jesus Christ, our mediator, our atonement, our perfect Savior.

to them as their regular share for the generations
to come.

37These, then, are the regulations for the burnt
offering,[r] the grain offering,[s] the sin offering, the
guilt offering, the ordination offering[t] and the fellowship offering, 38which the LORD gave Moses on
Mount Sinai on the day he commanded the Israelites to bring their offerings to the LORD,[u] in the
Desert of Sinai.

The Ordination of Aaron and His Sons

8 The LORD said to Moses, 2"Bring Aaron and his
sons, their garments, the anointing oil,[v] the
bull for the sin offering, the two rams and the basket containing bread made without yeast,[w] 3and
gather the entire assembly[x] at the entrance to the
Tent of Meeting." 4Moses did as the LORD commanded him, and the assembly gathered at the
entrance to the Tent of Meeting.

5Moses said to the assembly, "This is what the
LORD has commanded to be done." 6Then Moses
brought Aaron and his sons forward and washed
them with water.[y] 7He put the tunic on Aaron, tied
the sash around him, clothed him with the robe
and put the ephod on him. He also tied the ephod
to him by its skillfully woven waistband; so it was
fastened on him.[z] 8He placed the breastpiece on
him and put the Urim and Thummim[a] in the
breastpiece. 9Then he placed the turban on Aaron's
head and set the gold plate, the sacred diadem,[b] on
the front of it, as the LORD commanded Moses.

10Then Moses took the anointing oil[c] and
anointed[d] the tabernacle and everything in it, and
so consecrated them. 11He sprinkled some of the
oil on the altar seven times, anointing the altar
and all its utensils and the basin with its stand, to
consecrate them.[e] 12He poured some of the anointing oil on Aaron's head and anointed[f] him to consecrate him.[g] 13Then he brought Aaron's sons forward, put tunics on them, tied sashes around
them and put headbands on them, as the LORD
commanded Moses.

14He then presented the bull[h] for the sin offering,[i] and Aaron and his sons laid their hands on
its head. 15Moses slaughtered the bull and took
some of the blood, and with his finger he put it
on all the horns of the altar[j] to purify the altar.[k]
He poured out the rest of the blood at the base of
the altar. So he consecrated it to make atonement
for it.[l] 16Moses also took all the fat around the
inner parts, the covering of the liver, and both kidneys and their fat, and burned it on the altar. 17But
the bull with its hide and its flesh and its offal[m] he
burned up outside the camp,[n] as the LORD commanded Moses.

18He then presented the ram[o] for the burnt offering, and Aaron and his sons laid their hands on its
head. 19Then Moses slaughtered the ram and
sprinkled the blood against the altar on all sides.
20He cut the ram into pieces and burned the head,

7:37 [r]Lev 6:9 [s]Lev 6:14 [t]ver 1,11
7:38 [u]Lev 1:2
8:2 [v]Ex 30:23-25,30 [w]Ex 29:2-3
8:3 [x]Nu 8:9
8:6 [y]Ex 29:4; 30:19; Ps 26:6; Ac 22:16; 1Co 6:11; Eph 5:26
8:7 [z]Ex 28:4
8:8 [a]Ex 28:30
8:9 [b]Ex 28:36
8:10 [c]ver 2 [d]Ex 30:26
8:11 [e]Ex 30:29
8:12 [f]Lev 21:10,12 [g]Ex 30:30
8:14 [h]Lev 4:3 [i]Ps 66:15; Eze 43:19
8:15 [j]Lev 4:7 [k]Heb 9:22 [l]Eze 43:20
8:17 [m]Lev 4:11 [n]Lev 4:12
8:18 [o]ver 2

the pieces and the fat. [21]He washed the inner parts
and the legs with water and burned the whole
ram on the altar as a burnt offering, a pleasing
aroma, an offering made to the LORD by fire, as the
LORD commanded Moses.
8:22 [22]He then presented the other ram, the ram for
[p]ver 2 the ordination,[p] and Aaron and his sons laid their
hands on its head. [23]Moses slaughtered the ram
and took some of its blood and put it on the lobe
of Aaron's right ear, on the thumb of his right
hand and on the big toe of his right foot. [24]Moses
also brought Aaron's sons forward and put some
of the blood on the lobes of their right ears, on the
thumbs of their right hands and on the big toes of
their right feet. Then he sprinkled blood against
8:24 the altar on all sides.[q] [25]He took the fat, the fat tail,
[q]Heb 9:18-22 all the fat around the inner parts, the covering of
the liver, both kidneys and their fat and the right
thigh. [26]Then from the basket of bread made without
yeast, which was before the LORD, he took a
cake of bread, and one made with oil, and a
wafer; he put these on the fat portions and on the
right thigh. [27]He put all these in the hands of Aaron
and his sons and waved them before the LORD
as a wave offering. [28]Then Moses took them from
their hands and burned them on the altar on top
of the burnt offering as an ordination offering, a
pleasing aroma, an offering made to the LORD by
8:29 fire. [29]He also took the breast—Moses' share of the
[r]Lev 7:31-34 ordination ram[r]—and waved it before the LORD as
a wave offering, as the LORD commanded Moses.
[30]Then Moses took some of the anointing oil
and some of the blood from the altar and sprin-
8:30 kled them on Aaron and his garments[s] and on his
[s]Ex 28:2 [t]Nu 3:3 sons and their garments. So he consecrated[t] Aaron and his garments and his sons and their
garments.
[31]Moses then said to Aaron and his sons, "Cook
the meat at the entrance to the Tent of Meeting and
eat it there with the bread from the basket of ordination
offerings, as I commanded, saying,[a] 'Aaron
and his sons are to eat it.' [32]Then burn up the rest of
the meat and the bread. [33]Do not leave the entrance
to the Tent of Meeting for seven days, until the days
of your ordination are completed, for your ordination
8:34 tion will last seven days. [34]What has been done
[u]Heb 7:16 today was commanded by the LORD[u] to make atonement for you. [35]You must stay at the entrance to the
8:35 Tent of Meeting day and night for seven days and
[v]Nu 3:7; do what the LORD requires,[v] so you will not die; for
9:19; that is what I have been commanded." [36]So Aaron
Dt 11:1; 1Ki 2:3; and his sons did everything the LORD commanded
Eze 48:11 through Moses.

The Priests Begin Their Ministry

9:1 **9** On the eighth day[w] Moses summoned Aaron
[w]Eze 43:27 and his sons and the elders of Israel. [2]He said
to Aaron, "Take a bull calf for your sin offering and
a ram for your burnt offering, both without defect,

[a] 31 Or *I was commanded:*

Were there no God, we would be in this glorious world with grateful hearts: and no one to thank.

—Christina Georgina Rossetti (1830-1894)

and present them before the LORD. 3 Then say to the
Israelites: 'Take a male goat for a sin offering, a
calf and a lamb—both a year old and without
defect—for a burnt offering, 4 and an ox[a] and a ram 9:4
for a fellowship offering[b] to sacrifice before the [x]Ex 29:43
LORD, together with a grain offering mixed with
oil. For today the LORD will appear to you.[x]' "
5 They took the things Moses commanded to the
front of the Tent of Meeting, and the entire assembly came near and stood before the LORD. 6 Then
Moses said, "This is what the LORD has com- 9:6
manded you to do, so that the glory of the LORD[y] [y]ver 23;
may appear to you." Ex 24:16
7 Moses said to Aaron, "Come to the altar and
sacrifice your sin offering and your burnt offering
and make atonement for yourself and the people;
sacrifice the offering that is for the people and
make atonement for them, as the LORD has com- 9:7
manded.[z]" [z]Heb 5:1,3; 7:27
8 So Aaron came to the altar and slaughtered the
calf as a sin offering[a] for himself. 9 His sons brought 9:8
the blood to him,[b] and he dipped his finger into the [a]Lev 4:1-12
blood and put it on the horns of the altar; the rest 9:9
of the blood he poured out at the base of the altar.[c] [b]ver 12,18 [c]Lev 4:7
10 On the altar he burned the fat, the kidneys and
the covering of the liver from the sin offering, as 9:11
the LORD commanded Moses; 11 the flesh and the [d]Lev 4:11
hide[d] he burned up outside the camp.[e] [e]Lev 4:12; 8:17
12 Then he slaughtered the burnt offering. His
sons handed him the blood, and he sprinkled it
against the altar on all sides. 13 They handed him
the burnt offering piece by piece, including the
head, and he burned them on the altar.[f] 14 He 9:13
washed the inner parts and the legs and burned [f]Lev 1:8
them on top of the burnt offering on the altar.
15 Aaron then brought the offering that was for 9:15
the people.[g] He took the goat for the people's sin [g]Lev 4:27-31
offering and slaughtered it and offered it for a sin
offering as he did with the first one.
16 He brought the burnt offering and offered it in
the prescribed way.[h] 17 He also brought the grain 9:16
offering, took a handful of it and burned it on the [h]Lev 1:1-13
altar in addition to the morning's burnt offering.[i] 9:17
18 He slaughtered the ox and the ram as the fel- [i]Lev 2:1-2; 3:5
lowship offering for the people.[j] His sons handed
him the blood, and he sprinkled it against the 9:18
altar on all sides. 19 But the fat portions of the ox [j]Lev 3:1-11
and the ram—the fat tail, the layer of fat, the kidneys and the covering of the liver— 20 these they
laid on the breasts, and then Aaron burned the fat
on the altar. 21 Aaron waved the breasts and the 9:21
right thigh before the LORD as a wave offering,[k] as [k]Ex 29:24, 26; Lev 7:30-34
Moses commanded.
22 Then Aaron lifted his hands toward the people
and blessed them.[l] And having sacrificed the sin 9:22
offering, the burnt offering and the fellowship [l]Nu 6:23; Dt 21:5;
offering, he stepped down. Lk 24:50

When we reach the end of our strength, wisdom, and personal resources, we enter into the beginning of his glorious provisions. And that's a wondrous place to be.

—Patsy Clairmont

[a] *4* The Hebrew word can include both male and female; also in verses 18 and 19. [b] *4* Traditionally *peace offering*; also in verses 18 and 22

23 Moses and Aaron then went into the Tent of
Meeting. When they came out, they blessed the
people; and the glory of the LORD[m] appeared to all
the people. 24 Fire[n] came out from the presence of
the LORD and consumed the burnt offering and the
fat portions on the altar. And when all the people
saw it, they shouted for joy and fell facedown.[o]

The Death of Nadab and Abihu

10 Aaron's sons Nadab and Abihu[p] took their
censers, put fire in them[q] and added
incense; and they offered unauthorized fire before
the LORD, contrary to his command.[r] 2 So fire came
out from the presence of the LORD and consumed
them,[s] and they died before the LORD. 3 Moses then
said to Aaron, "This is what the LORD spoke of
when he said:

> " 'Among those who approach me[t]
> I will show myself holy;[u]
> in the sight of all the people
> I will be honored.[v]' "

Aaron remained silent.
4 Moses summoned Mishael and Elzaphan,[w]
sons of Aaron's uncle Uzziel,[x] and said to them,
"Come here; carry your cousins outside the
camp,[y] away from the front of the sanctuary." 5 So
they came and carried them, still in their tunics,[z]
outside the camp, as Moses ordered.
6 Then Moses said to Aaron and his sons Eleazar
and Ithamar, "Do not let your hair become
unkempt,[a][a] and do not tear your clothes, or you
will die and the LORD will be angry with the whole
community.[b] But your relatives, all the house of
Israel, may mourn for those the LORD has destroyed
by fire. 7 Do not leave the entrance to the Tent of
Meeting or you will die, because the LORD's anointing oil[c] is on you." So they did as Moses said.
8 Then the LORD said to Aaron, 9 "You and your
sons are not to drink wine[d] or other fermented
drink[e] whenever you go into the Tent of Meeting,
or you will die. This is a lasting ordinance for the
generations to come. 10 You must distinguish
between the holy and the common, between the
unclean and the clean,[f] 11 and you must teach[g] the
Israelites all the decrees the LORD has given them
through Moses.[h]"
12 Moses said to Aaron and his remaining sons,
Eleazar and Ithamar, "Take the grain offering left
over from the offerings made to the LORD by fire
and eat it prepared without yeast beside the altar,[i]
for it is most holy. 13 Eat it in a holy place, because
it is your share and your sons' share of the offerings made to the LORD by fire; for so I have been
commanded. 14 But you and your sons and your
daughters may eat the breast that was waved and
the thigh that was presented. Eat them in a ceremonially clean place;[j] they have been given to you
and your children as your share of the Israelites'

[a] 6 Or *Do not uncover your heads*

9:23 [m]ver 6
9:24 [n]Jdg 6:21; 2Ch 7:1 [o]1Ki 18:39
10:1 [p]Ex 24:1; Nu 3:2-4; 26:61 [q]Lev 16:12 [r]Ex 30:9
10:2 [s]Nu 3:4; 16:35; 26:61
10:3 [t]Ex 19:22 [u]Ex 30:29; Lev 21:6; Eze 28:22 [v]Isa 49:3
10:4 [w]Ex 6:22 [x]Ex 6:18 [y]Ac 5:6,9,10
10:5 [z]Lev 8:13
10:6 [a]Lev 21:10 [b]Nu 1:53; 16:22; Jos 7:1; 22:18; 2Sa 24:1
10:7 [c]Ex 28:41; Lev 21:12
10:9 [d]Hos 4:11 [e]Pr 20:1; Isa 28:7; Eze 44:21; Lk 1:15; Eph 5:18; 1Ti 3:3; Tit 1:7
10:10 [f]Lev 11:47; 20:25; Eze 22:26
10:11 [g]Mal 2:7 [h]Dt 24:8
10:12 [i]Lev 6:14-18; 21:22
10:14 [j]Ex 29:24, 26-27; Lev 7:31,34; Nu 18:11

Aaron's Sons Sin

LEV 10:1–7

What exactly this "unauthorized fire" was remains uncertain. The fire in Aaron's sons' censers may have come from someplace other than the altar, they may have offered the incense at the wrong time, or they may have used improper utensils to perform their task. In any case, they have taken matters into their own hands—acting presumptuously and disobeying God's specific commands.

Divine retribution is immediate, and those who sin by fire are quickly consumed by fire. Aaron is stunned into silence (Lev 10:3). Because of his position as high priest, Aaron is not allowed the traditional expressions of grief (Lev 10:6; 21:10–12). Instead, Aaron and his remaining sons suffer deeply but quietly.

Some scholars speculate that Nadab and Abihu had been drinking before the incident with the fire and that the wine had clouded their judgment. This would explain the immediate directive from God that the priests not consume any fermented drink before entering the Tent of Meeting (Lev 10:8–11).

Clean and Unclean Foods

LEV 11

As we scan the lists of allowed and disallowed foods, some of the designations seem reasonable; others appear arbitrary. It would be ridiculous to attempt to second-guess God; however, the text itself may provide some clues to God's reasoning. After giving a long list of instructions about clean and unclean foods, the Lord himself states: "Consecrate yourselves and be holy, because I am holy. Do not make yourselves unclean" (Lev 11:44). Each of the prohibited animals is unclean for one reason or another—perhaps due to societal custom, physical repulsion, superstition or a connection to heathen deities. Whatever the reasoning, the purpose is clear: By avoiding these unclean foods, God's people set themselves apart and keep themselves pure and holy for him.

fellowship offerings.[a] 15The thigh[k] that was presented and the breast that was waved must be brought with the fat portions of the offerings made by fire, to be waved before the LORD as a wave offering. This will be the regular share for you and your children, as the LORD has commanded."

16When Moses inquired about the goat of the sin offering[l] and found that it had been burned up, he was angry with Eleazar and Ithamar, Aaron's remaining sons, and asked, 17"Why didn't you eat the sin offering[m] in the sanctuary area? It is most holy; it was given to you to take away the guilt of the community by making atonement for them before the LORD. 18Since its blood was not taken into the Holy Place,[n] you should have eaten the goat in the sanctuary area, as I commanded."

19Aaron replied to Moses, "Today they sacrificed their sin offering and their burnt offering[o] before the LORD, but such things as this have happened to me. Would the LORD have been pleased if I had eaten the sin offering today?" 20When Moses heard this, he was satisfied.

Clean and Unclean Food

11 The LORD said to Moses and Aaron, 2"Say to the Israelites: 'Of all the animals that live on land, these are the ones you may eat:[p] 3You may eat any animal that has a split hoof completely divided and that chews the cud.

4" 'There are some that only chew the cud or only have a split hoof, but you must not eat them. The camel, though it chews the cud, does not have a split hoof; it is ceremonially unclean for you. 5The coney,[b] though it chews the cud, does not have a split hoof; it is unclean for you. 6The rabbit, though it chews the cud, does not have a split hoof; it is unclean for you. 7And the pig,[q] though it has a split hoof completely divided, does not chew the cud; it is unclean for you. 8You must not eat their meat or touch their carcasses; they are unclean for you.[r]

9" 'Of all the creatures living in the water of the seas and the streams, you may eat any that have fins and scales. 10But all creatures in the seas or streams that do not have fins and scales—whether among all the swarming things or among all the other living creatures in the water—you are to detest.[s] 11And since you are to detest them, you must not eat their meat and you must detest their carcasses. 12Anything living in the water that does not have fins and scales is to be detestable to you.

13" 'These are the birds you are to detest and not eat because they are detestable: the eagle, the vulture, the black vulture, 14the red kite, any kind of black kite, 15any kind of raven, 16the horned owl, the screech owl, the gull, any kind of hawk, 17the little owl, the cormorant, the great owl, 18the

10:15 [k]Lev 7:34
10:16 [l]Lev 9:3
10:17 [m]Lev 6:24-30
10:18 [n]Lev 6:26,30
10:19 [o]Lev 9:12
11:2 [p]Ac 10:12-14
11:7 [q]Isa 65:4; 66:3,17
11:8 [r]Isa 52:11; Heb 9:10
11:10 [s]Lev 7:18

[a] *14* Traditionally *peace offerings* [b] *5* That is, the hyrax or rock badger

white owl, the desert owl, the osprey, [19]the stork,
any kind of heron, the hoopoe and the bat.[a]
[20]" 'All flying insects that walk on all fours are
11:20 [t]Ac 10:14 to be detestable to you.[t] [21]There are, however,
some winged creatures that walk on all fours that
you may eat: those that have jointed legs for hop-
11:22 ping on the ground. [22]Of these you may eat any
[u]Mt 3:4; kind of locust,[u] katydid, cricket or grasshopper.
Mk 1:6 [23]But all other winged creatures that have four
legs you are to detest.
[24]" 'You will make yourselves unclean by these;
whoever touches their carcasses will be unclean
11:25 till evening. [25]Whoever picks up one of their car-
[v]Lev 14:8, casses must wash his clothes,[v] and he will be
47; 15:5 unclean till evening.[w]
[w]ver 40; [26]" 'Every animal that has a split hoof not com-
Nu 31:24 pletely divided or that does not chew the cud is
unclean for you; whoever touches ⌊the carcass of⌋
any of them will be unclean. [27]Of all the animals
that walk on all fours, those that walk on their
paws are unclean for you; whoever touches their
carcasses will be unclean till evening. [28]Anyone
who picks up their carcasses must wash his
clothes, and he will be unclean till evening. They
are unclean for you.
[29]" 'Of the animals that move about on the
ground, these are unclean for you: the weasel, the
11:29 rat,[x] any kind of great lizard, [30]the gecko, the mon-
[x]Isa 66:17 itor lizard, the wall lizard, the skink and the
chameleon. [31]Of all those that move along the
ground, these are unclean for you. Whoever
touches them when they are dead will be unclean
till evening. [32]When one of them dies and falls on
something, that article, whatever its use, will be
unclean, whether it is made of wood, cloth, hide
11:32 [y]Lev 15:12 or sackcloth.[y] Put it in water; it will be unclean
till evening, and then it will be clean. [33]If one of
them falls into a clay pot, everything in it will be
11:33 [z]Lev 6:28; unclean, and you must break the pot.[z] [34]Any food
15:12 that could be eaten but has water on it from such
a pot is unclean, and any liquid that could be
drunk from it is unclean. [35]Anything that one of
their carcasses falls on becomes unclean; an oven
or cooking pot must be broken up. They are
unclean, and you are to regard them as unclean.
[36]A spring, however, or a cistern for collecting
water remains clean, but anyone who touches one
of these carcasses is unclean. [37]If a carcass falls on
any seeds that are to be planted, they remain
clean. [38]But if water has been put on the seed and
a carcass falls on it, it is unclean for you.
[39]" 'If an animal that you are allowed to eat
dies, anyone who touches the carcass will be
unclean till evening. [40]Anyone who eats some of
the carcass must wash his clothes, and he will be
11:40 [a]Lev 17:15; unclean till evening.[a] Anyone who picks up the
22:8; carcass must wash his clothes, and he will be
Eze 44:31 unclean till evening.

[a] *19* The precise identification of some of the birds, insects and animals in this chapter is uncertain.

There is so much beauty around us, if we will only take the time to notice it. You can make a conscious effort to . . . develop an appreciation for the beautiful things in life. Your days will seem a lot less harried, I promise you. Beauty has a way of totally capturing our senses, making us forget the fact that the car stalled on the way to work this morning, that the kids spilled chocolate milk on the carpet, that the workload keeps piling up. For a few brief shining moments, nothing else seems to matter. And the wonderful thing about beauty is that we can store it in our minds to be played over and over again.

—Luci Swindoll

Giving Birth

LEV 12

When a woman gives birth to a child, it is the bleeding involved, not the birth or the child itself, that causes her to be unclean. God's prescribed manner for dealing with a new mother's condition is both gentle and thoughtful. If a woman gives birth to a son, she remains in seclusion for one week, unclean for a total of 40 days; if she bears a daughter, she is secluded for two weeks, unclean (and therefore exempt from public religious observances) for a total of 80 days. Like God's other laws, such boundaries are to the mother's benefit.

The difference in duration may reflect popular cultural views of the time. Possibly, the people believed that a woman bled longer after bearing a daughter. Ancient society certainly placed a higher value on males than on females. But God did—and does—not. Throughout Scripture we see evidence of God's love for women and the tremendous worth we have to him.

41 " 'Every creature that moves about on the ground is detestable; it is not to be eaten. 42 You are not to eat any creature that moves about on the ground, whether it moves on its belly or walks on all fours or on many feet; it is detestable. 43 Do not defile yourselves by any of these creatures.[b] Do not make yourselves unclean by means of them or be made unclean by them. 44 I am the LORD your God;[c] consecrate yourselves[d] and be holy,[e] because I am holy.[f] Do not make yourselves unclean by any creature that moves about on the ground. 45 I am the LORD who brought you up out of Egypt[g] to be your God;[h] therefore be holy, because I am holy.[i]

46 " 'These are the regulations concerning animals, birds, every living thing that moves in the water and every creature that moves about on the ground. 47 You must distinguish between the unclean and the clean, between living creatures that may be eaten and those that may not be eaten.[j] ' "

Purification After Childbirth

12 The LORD said to Moses, 2 "Say to the Israelites: 'A woman who becomes pregnant and gives birth to a son will be ceremonially unclean for seven days, just as she is unclean during her monthly period.[k] 3 On the eighth day the boy is to be circumcised.[l] 4 Then the woman must wait thirty-three days to be purified from her bleeding. She must not touch anything sacred or go to the sanctuary until the days of her purification are over. 5 If she gives birth to a daughter, for two weeks the woman will be unclean, as during her period. Then she must wait sixty-six days to be purified from her bleeding.

6 " 'When the days of her purification for a son or daughter are over,[m] she is to bring to the priest at the entrance to the Tent of Meeting a year-old lamb[n] for a burnt offering and a young pigeon or a dove for a sin offering.[o] 7 He shall offer them before the LORD to make atonement for her, and then she will be ceremonially clean from her flow of blood.

" 'These are the regulations for the woman who gives birth to a boy or a girl. 8 If she cannot afford a lamb, she is to bring two doves or two young pigeons,[p] one for a burnt offering and the other for a sin offering.[q] In this way the priest will make atonement for her, and she will be clean.[r] ' "

Regulations About Infectious Skin Diseases

13 The LORD said to Moses and Aaron, 2 "When anyone has a swelling[s] or a rash or a bright spot[t] on his skin that may become an infectious skin disease,[a][u] he must be brought to Aaron the priest[v] or to one of his sons[b] who is a priest. 3 The priest is to examine the sore on his skin, and if

11:43 [b]Lev 20:25
11:44 [c]Ex 6:2,7; Isa 43:3; 51:15 [d]Lev 20:7 [e]Ex 19:6 [f]Lev 19:2; Ps 99:3; Eph 1:4; 1Th 4:7; 1Pe 1:15,16*
11:45 [g]Lev 25:38, 55; Ex 6:7; 20:2 [h]Ge 17:7 [i]Ex 19:6; 1Pe 1:16*
11:47 [j]Lev 10:10
12:2 [k]Lev 15:19; 18:19
12:3 [l]Ge 17:12; Lk 1:59; 2:21
12:6 [m]Lk 2:22 [n]Ex 29:38; Lev 23:12; Nu 6:12,14; 7:15 [o]Lev 5:7
12:8 [p]Ge 15:9; Lev 14:22 [q]Lev 5:7; Lk 2:22-24* [r]Lev 4:26
13:2 [s]ver 10,19, 28,43 [t]ver 4,38,39; Lev 14:56 [u]ver 3,9,15; Ex 4:6; Lev 14:3,32; Nu 5:2; Dt 24:8 [v]Dt 24:8

[a] *2* Traditionally *leprosy*; the Hebrew word was used for various diseases affecting the skin—not necessarily leprosy; also elsewhere in this chapter. [b] *2* Or *descendants*

the hair in the sore has turned white and the sore
appears to be more than skin deep,[a] it is an infec-
13:3 tious skin disease. When the priest examines him,
[w]ver 8,11, he shall pronounce him ceremonially unclean.[w]
20,30; Lev 21:1; 4If the spot[x] on his skin is white but does not
Nu 9:6 appear to be more than skin deep and the hair in
13:4 it has not turned white, the priest is to put the
[x]ver 2 infected person in isolation for seven days.[y] 5On
[y]ver 5,21,26, the seventh day[z] the priest is to examine him,[a]
33,46; Lev 14:38; and if he sees that the sore is unchanged and has
Nu 12:14,15; not spread in the skin, he is to keep him in isola-
Dt 24:9 tion another seven days. 6On the seventh day the
13:5 priest is to examine him again, and if the sore has
[z]Lev 14:9 faded and has not spread in the skin, the priest
[a]ver 27,32, 34,51 shall pronounce him clean;[b] it is only a rash. The
man must wash his clothes,[c] and he will be
13:6 [b]ver 13,17, clean.[d] 7But if the rash does spread in his skin
23,28,34; after he has shown himself to the priest to be pro-
Mt 8:3; Lk 5:12-14 nounced clean, he must appear before the priest
[c]Lev 11:25 again.[e] 8The priest is to examine him, and if the
[d]Lev 11:25; 14:8,9,20, rash has spread in the skin, he shall pronounce
48; 15:8; him unclean; it is an infectious disease.
Nu 8:7 9"When anyone has an infectious skin disease,
he must be brought to the priest. 10The priest is to
13:7 [e]Lk 5:14 examine him, and if there is a white swelling in
the skin that has turned the hair white and if
there is raw flesh in the swelling, 11it is a chronic
13:11 skin disease[f] and the priest shall pronounce him
[f]Ex 4:6; Lev 14:8; unclean. He is not to put him in isolation, because
Nu 12:10; Mt 8:2 he is already unclean.
12"If the disease breaks out all over his skin and,
so far as the priest can see, it covers all the skin of
the infected person from head to foot, 13the priest is
to examine him, and if the disease has covered his
whole body, he shall pronounce that person clean.
Since it has all turned white, he is clean. 14But
whenever raw flesh appears on him, he will be
unclean. 15When the priest sees the raw flesh, he
13:15 shall pronounce him unclean. The raw flesh is
[g]ver 2 unclean; he has an infectious disease.[g] 16Should the
raw flesh change and turn white, he must go to the
priest. 17The priest is to examine him, and if the
sores have turned white, the priest shall pronounce
13:17 [h]ver 6 the infected person clean;[h] then he will be clean.
18"When someone has a boil[i] on his skin and it
13:18 [i]Ex 9:9 heals, 19and in the place where the boil was, a
white swelling or reddish-white[j] spot[k] appears, he
13:19 must present himself to the priest. 20The priest is to
[j]ver 24,42; examine it, and if it appears to be more than skin
Lev 14:37 [k]ver 2 deep and the hair in it has turned white, the priest
shall pronounce him unclean. It is an infectious
13:20 [l]ver 2 skin disease[l] that has broken out where the boil
was. 21But if, when the priest examines it, there is
no white hair in it and it is not more than skin
deep and has faded, then the priest is to put him in
isolation for seven days. 22If it is spreading in the
skin, the priest shall pronounce him unclean; it is
infectious. 23But if the spot is unchanged and has

[a] 3 Or *be lower than the rest of the skin*; also elsewhere in this chapter

Priests As Doctors

LEV 13:8

While the priests do not try to cure disease, they do identify it and isolate those who suffer from certain diseases. The "skin diseases" in this chapter refer to a variety of ailments, from simple dermatitis to skin cancers and leprosy. Since these diseases are outwardly obvious, they quickly identify a person as unclean, not "whole," and therefore not able to come into God's presence. These distinctions provide a clear visual lesson for the Israelites not only on their uncleanness but also on the holiness of their God and the necessity of spiritual cleanliness when coming before him.

Skin Diseases

LEV 13

Many of the skin diseases in this chapter could be evidence of some variety of communicable disease: measles, scarlet fever, small pox, and the like, although some may also have been simple forms of dermatitis or eczema. The isolation of the diseased person prevents the spread of deadly diseases and protects the community. Though the edict in Leviticus 13:46 seems harsh—the diseased person must live alone, outside the camp—the protection it affords the rest of the people cannot be discounted.

The Levitical priests are vigilant in their watch for signs of leprosy. Although we know today that leprosy is one of the least infectious of the contagious diseases, the fact remains that leprosy is transmissible, and the people in the nation of Israel greatly feared it.

not spread, it is only a scar from the boil, and the
priest shall pronounce him clean.[m]
24“When someone has a burn on his skin and a
reddish-white or white spot appears in the raw
flesh of the burn, 25the priest is to examine the
spot, and if the hair in it has turned white, and it
appears to be more than skin deep, it is an infectious disease that has broken out in the burn. The
priest shall pronounce him unclean; it is an infectious skin disease.[n] 26But if the priest examines it
and there is no white hair in the spot and if it is
not more than skin deep and has faded, then the
priest is to put him in isolation for seven days.[o]
27On the seventh day the priest is to examine
him,[p] and if it is spreading in the skin, the priest
shall pronounce him unclean; it is an infectious
skin disease. 28If, however, the spot is unchanged
and has not spread in the skin but has faded, it is
a swelling from the burn, and the priest shall pronounce him clean; it is only a scar from the burn.[q]
29“If a man or woman has a sore on the head[r] or
on the chin, 30the priest is to examine the sore,
and if it appears to be more than skin deep and
the hair in it is yellow and thin, the priest shall
pronounce that person unclean; it is an itch, an
infectious disease of the head or chin. 31But if,
when the priest examines this kind of sore, it does
not seem to be more than skin deep and there is
no black hair in it, then the priest is to put the
infected person in isolation for seven days.[s] 32On
the seventh day the priest is to examine the sore,[t]
and if the itch has not spread and there is no yellow hair in it and it does not appear to be more
than skin deep, 33he must be shaved except for the
diseased area, and the priest is to keep him in isolation another seven days. 34On the seventh day
the priest is to examine the itch,[u] and if it has not
spread in the skin and appears to be no more than
skin deep, the priest shall pronounce him clean.
He must wash his clothes, and he will be clean.[v]
35But if the itch does spread in the skin after he is
pronounced clean, 36the priest is to examine him,
and if the itch has spread in the skin, the priest
does not need to look for yellow hair; the person
is unclean.[w] 37If, however, in his judgment it is
unchanged and black hair has grown in it, the
itch is healed. He is clean, and the priest shall
pronounce him clean.
38“When a man or woman has white spots on
the skin, 39the priest is to examine them, and if
the spots are dull white, it is a harmless rash that
has broken out on the skin; that person is clean.
40“When a man has lost his hair and is bald,[x]
he is clean. 41If he has lost his hair from the front
of his scalp and has a bald forehead, he is clean.
42But if he has a reddish-white sore on his bald
head or forehead, it is an infectious disease breaking out on his head or forehead. 43The priest is to
examine him, and if the swollen sore on his head
or forehead is reddish-white like an infectious
skin disease, 44the man is diseased and is unclean.

13:23 [m]ver 6
13:25 [n]ver 11
13:26 [o]ver 4
13:27 [p]ver 5
13:28 [q]ver 2
13:29 [r]ver 43,44
13:31 [s]ver 4
13:32 [t]ver 5
13:34 [u]ver 5 [v]Lev 11:25
13:36 [w]ver 30
13:40 [x]Lev 21:5; 2Ki 2:23; Isa 3:24; 15:2; 22:12; Eze 27:31; 29:18; Am 8:10; Mic 1:16

The priest shall pronounce him unclean because
of the sore on his head.
[45]"The person with such an infectious disease
must wear torn clothes,[y] let his hair be unkempt,[a]
cover the lower part of his face[z] and cry out,
'Unclean! Unclean!'[a] [46]As long as he has the infection he remains unclean. He must live alone; he
must live outside the camp.[b]

Regulations About Mildew

[47]"If any clothing is contaminated with mildew—any woolen or linen clothing, [48]any woven
or knitted material of linen or wool, any leather or
anything made of leather— [49]and if the contamination in the clothing, or leather, or woven or
knitted material, or any leather article, is greenish or reddish, it is a spreading mildew and must
be shown to the priest.[c] [50]The priest is to examine
the mildew[d] and isolate the affected article for sev-
en days. [51]On the seventh day he is to examine it,[e]
and if the mildew has spread in the clothing, or
the woven or knitted material, or the leather,
whatever its use, it is a destructive mildew; the
article is unclean.[f] [52]He must burn up the clothing, or the woven or knitted material of wool or
linen, or any leather article that has the contamination in it, because the mildew is destructive; the
article must be burned up.[g]
[53]"But if, when the priest examines it, the mildew has not spread in the clothing, or the woven
or knitted material, or the leather article, [54]he
shall order that the contaminated article be
washed. Then he is to isolate it for another seven
days. [55]After the affected article has been washed,
the priest is to examine it, and if the mildew has
not changed its appearance, even though it has
not spread, it is unclean. Burn it with fire,
whether the mildew has affected one side or the
other. [56]If, when the priest examines it, the mildew has faded after the article has been washed,
he is to tear the contaminated part out of the
clothing, or the leather, or the woven or knitted
material. [57]But if it reappears in the clothing, or
in the woven or knitted material, or in the leather
article, it is spreading, and whatever has the mildew must be burned with fire. [58]The clothing, or
the woven or knitted material, or any leather article that has been washed and is rid of the mildew,
must be washed again, and it will be clean."
[59]These are the regulations concerning contamination by mildew in woolen or linen clothing,
woven or knitted material, or any leather article,
for pronouncing them clean or unclean.

Cleansing From Infectious Skin Diseases

14 The LORD said to Moses, [2]"These are the regulations for the diseased person at the time
of his ceremonial cleansing, when he is brought
to the priest:[h] [3]The priest is to go outside the camp

13:45 [y]Lev 10:6 [z]Eze 24:17, 22; Mic 3:7 [a]Lev 5:2; La 4:15; Lk 17:12
13:46 [b]Nu 5:1-4; 12:14; 2Ki 7:3; 15:5; Lk 17:12
13:49 [c]Mk 1:44
13:50 [d]Eze 44:23
13:51 [e]ver 5 [f]Lev 14:44
13:52 [g]ver 55,57
14:2 [h]Mt 8:2-4; Mk 1:40-44; Lk 5:12-14; 17:14

[a]45 Or *clothes, uncover his head*

Mildew

LEV 13:47-59

In today's society, a woman can handle the problem of mildew with one hand tied behind her back. At her disposal are a full arsenal of cleaning products—industrial-strength bathroom cleansers and sprays guaranteed to zap out spots and germs. Coming from this background, we may struggle to understand why so much time and attention is given to Biblical rules concerning mildew.

Remember, however, the Israelites are God's chosen people, and their efforts are directed at drawing close to him. Because God is holy, nothing can exist in his presence that is unhealthy or unwhole. The mildew in question is persistent and destructive. If it is not brought under control, it will damage the article on which it is found. If God is to dwell with his people, their place of dwelling must be clean. The regulations regarding mildew accomplish this cleanliness.

Two Birds

LEV 14:5-7

The two clean birds used in this sacrifice are representative of the unclean person. The slaughtered bird symbolizes the unclean person as he or she once was and might have remained: dead to the world, separated from the Lord and his people. The bird that was freed beautifully illustrates the revival of life to the former outcast, newly cleansed and restored to the community of God.

The significance of the other elements (hyssop, cedar wood and scarlet yarn) is uncertain. We do know that hyssop was used to sprinkle blood on the door frames in Egypt (Ex 12:22) and that it was a sign of spiritual cleansing from sin (Ps 51:7). The color scarlet was frequently used in the tabernacle and was known as a sign of prosperity.

and examine him.[i] If the person has been healed
of his infectious skin disease,[a] 4the priest shall
order that two live clean birds and some cedar
wood, scarlet yarn and hyssop be brought for the
one to be cleansed.[j] 5Then the priest shall order
that one of the birds be killed over fresh water in
a clay pot. 6He is then to take the live bird and dip
it, together with the cedar wood, the scarlet yarn
and the hyssop, into the blood of the bird that was
killed over the fresh water.[k] 7Seven times he shall
sprinkle[l] the one to be cleansed of the infectious
disease and pronounce him clean. Then he is to
release the live bird in the open fields.
8"The person to be cleansed must wash his
clothes,[m] shave off all his hair and bathe with
water;[n] then he will be ceremonially clean.[o] After
this he may come into the camp,[p] but he must
stay outside his tent for seven days. 9On the seventh day he must shave off all his hair; he must
shave his head, his beard, his eyebrows and the
rest of his hair. He must wash his clothes and
bathe himself with water, and he will be clean.
10"On the eighth day[q] he must bring two male
lambs and one ewe lamb a year old, each without
defect, along with three-tenths of an ephah[b] of
fine flour mixed with oil for a grain offering,[r] and
one log[c] of oil.[s] 11The priest who pronounces him
clean shall present both the one to be cleansed
and his offerings before the LORD at the entrance
to the Tent of Meeting.
12"Then the priest is to take one of the male
lambs and offer it as a guilt offering,[t] along with
the log of oil; he shall wave them before the LORD
as a wave offering.[u] 13He is to slaughter the lamb
in the holy place[v] where the sin offering and the
burnt offering are slaughtered. Like the sin offering, the guilt offering belongs to the priest;[w] it is
most holy. 14The priest is to take some of the
blood of the guilt offering and put it on the lobe of
the right ear of the one to be cleansed, on the
thumb of his right hand and on the big toe of his
right foot.[x] 15The priest shall then take some of the
log of oil, pour it in the palm of his own left hand,
16dip his right forefinger into the oil in his palm,
and with his finger sprinkle some of it before the
LORD seven times. 17The priest is to put some of
the oil remaining in his palm on the lobe of the
right ear of the one to be cleansed, on the thumb
of his right hand and on the big toe of his right
foot, on top of the blood of the guilt offering.
18The rest of the oil in his palm the priest shall put
on the head of the one to be cleansed and make
atonement for him before the LORD.
19"Then the priest is to sacrifice the sin offering
and make atonement for the one to be cleansed
from his uncleanness. After that, the priest shall

14:3 [i]Lev 13:46
14:4 [j]ver 6,49,51, 52; Nu 19:6; Ps 51:7
14:6 [k]ver 4
14:7 [l]2Ki 5:10,14; Isa 52:15; Eze 36:25
14:8 [m]Lev 11:25; 13:6 [n]ver 9 [o]ver 20 [p]Nu 5:2,3; 12:14,15; 2Ch 26:21
14:10 [q]Mt 8:4; Mk 1:44; Lk 5:14 [r]Lev 2:1 [s]ver 12,15, 21,24
14:12 [t]Lev 5:18; 6:6-7 [u]Ex 29:24
14:13 [v]Ex 29:11 [w]Lev 6:24-30; 7:7
14:14 [x]Ex 29:20; Lev 8:23

[a] *3* Traditionally *leprosy;* the Hebrew word was used for various diseases affecting the skin—not necessarily leprosy; also elsewhere in this chapter. [b] *10* That is, probably about 6 quarts (about 6.5 liters) [c] *10* That is, probably about 2/3 pint (about 0.3 liter); also in verses 12, 15, 21 and 24

slaughter the burnt offering 20 and offer it on the
14:20 altar, together with the grain offering, and make
[y]ver 8 atonement for him, and he will be clean.[y]
14:21 21 "If, however, he is poor[z] and cannot afford
[z]Lev 5:7; these,[a] he must take one male lamb as a guilt
12:8 offering to be waved to make atonement for him,
[a]ver 22,32 together with a tenth of an ephah[a] of fine flour
mixed with oil for a grain offering, a log of oil,
14:22 22 and two doves or two young pigeons,[b] which he
[b]Lev 5:7 can afford, one for a sin offering and the other for
a burnt offering.
23 "On the eighth day he must bring them for his
cleansing to the priest at the entrance to the Tent
14:23 of Meeting, before the LORD.[c] 24 The priest is to take
[c]ver 10,11 the lamb for the guilt offering,[d] together with the
14:24 log of oil,[e] and wave them before the LORD as a
[d]Nu 6:14 [e]ver 10 wave offering.[f] 25 He shall slaughter the lamb for
[f]ver 12 the guilt offering and take some of its blood and
14:25 put it on the lobe of the right ear of the one to be
[g]ver 14; cleansed, on the thumb of his right hand and on
Ex 29:20 the big toe of his right foot.[g] 26 The priest is to pour
14:26 some of the oil into the palm of his own left
[h]ver 15 hand,[h] 27 and with his right forefinger sprinkle
some of the oil from his palm seven times before
the LORD. 28 Some of the oil in his palm he is to put
on the same places he put the blood of the guilt
offering—on the lobe of the right ear of the one to
be cleansed, on the thumb of his right hand and
on the big toe of his right foot. 29 The rest of the
oil in his palm the priest shall put on the head of
the one to be cleansed, to make atonement for
14:29 [i]ver 18 him before the LORD.[i] 30 Then he shall sacrifice the
14:30 doves or the young pigeons, which the person can
[j]Lev 5:7 afford,[j] 31 one[b] as a sin offering and the other as a
burnt offering,[k] together with the grain offering.
14:31 [k]ver 22; In this way the priest will make atonement before
Lev 5:7; the LORD on behalf of the one to be cleansed.[l]"
15:15,30 [l]ver 18,19 32 These are the regulations for anyone who has
an infectious skin disease[m] and who cannot afford
14:32 [m]Lev 13:2 the regular offerings[n] for his cleansing.
[n]ver 21

Cleansing From Mildew

33 The LORD said to Moses and Aaron, 34 "When
14:34 [o]Ge 12:5; you enter the land of Canaan,[o] which I am giving
Ex 6:4; Nu 13:2 you as your possession,[p] and I put a spreading
[p]Ge 17:8; mildew in a house in that land, 35 the owner of the
48:4; Nu 27:12; house must go and tell the priest, 'I have seen
32:22; something that looks like mildew in my house.'
Dt 3:27; 7:1; 36 The priest is to order the house to be emptied
32:49 before he goes in to examine the mildew, so that
nothing in the house will be pronounced unclean.
After this the priest is to go in and inspect the
14:37 house. 37 He is to examine the mildew on the
[q]Lev 13:19 walls, and if it has greenish or reddish[q] depres-
sions that appear to be deeper than the surface of
14:38 the wall, 38 the priest shall go out the doorway of
[r]Lev 13:4 the house and close it up for seven days.[r] 39 On the

[a] *21* That is, probably about 2 quarts (about 2 liters)
[b] *31* Septuagint and Syriac; Hebrew *31 such as the person can afford, one*

Sorrow is divine. Sorrow is reigning on all the thrones of the universe, and the crown of all crowns has been one of thorns. There have been many books that treat of the sympathy of sorrow, but only one that bids us glory in tribulation, and count it all joy when we fall into divers afflictions, that so we may be associated with that great fellowship of suffering of which the incarnate Son of God is the head, and through which he is carrying a redemptive conflict to a glorious victory over evil. If we suffer with him, we shall also reign with him.

—Harriet Beecher Stowe (1811-1896)

Bodily Discharges

LEV 15

The discharge referred to in Leviticus 15:2 is not seminal in nature; the description given is consistent with a form of gonorrhea that causes excessive secretion of mucous. Other possibilities are diarrhea or urethral discharge from an infection. In any case, the secretions are surely caused by disease or illness. The instructions given by God emphasize the importance of good hygiene in interacting with the infected individual.

Secretions caused by disease are not the only bodily fluids that make a person symbolically unclean. Any secretion from the body causes the individual to be defiled; the manner of dealing with the matter varies, however, depending on the cause of the discharge (Lev 15:1–33).

seventh day[s] the priest shall return to inspect the 14:39
house. If the mildew has spread on the walls, 40he [s]Lev 13:5
is to order that the contaminated stones be torn
out and thrown into an unclean place outside the 14:40
town.[t] 41He must have all the inside walls of the [t]ver 45
house scraped and the material that is scraped off
dumped into an unclean place outside the town.
42Then they are to take other stones to replace
these and take new clay and plaster the house.
43"If the mildew reappears in the house after the
stones have been torn out and the house scraped
and plastered, 44the priest is to go and examine it
and, if the mildew has spread in the house, it is a 14:44
destructive mildew; the house is unclean.[u] 45It must [u]Lev 13:51
be torn down—its stones, timbers and all the plas-
ter—and taken out of the town to an unclean place.
46"Anyone who goes into the house while it is 14:46
closed up will be unclean till evening.[v] 47Anyone [v]Lev 11:24
who sleeps or eats in the house must wash his
clothes.[w] 14:47
48"But if the priest comes to examine it and the [w]Lev 11:25
mildew has not spread after the house has been 14:48
plastered, he shall pronounce the house clean,[x]
because the mildew is gone. 49To purify the house [x]Lev 13:6
he is to take two birds and some cedar wood, scar-
let yarn and hyssop.[y] 50He shall kill one of the 14:49 [y]ver 4;
birds over fresh water in a clay pot.[z] 51Then he is 1Ki 4:33;
to take the cedar wood, the hyssop,[a] the scarlet ver 4
yarn and the live bird, dip them into the blood of
the dead bird and the fresh water, and sprinkle the 14:50
house seven times.[b] 52He shall purify the house [z]ver 5
with the bird's blood, the fresh water, the live 14:51 [a]ver 6;
bird, the cedar wood, the hyssop and the scarlet Ps 51:7
yarn. 53Then he is to release the live bird in the [b]ver 4,7
open fields[c] outside the town. In this way he will 14:53
make atonement for the house, and it will be [c]ver 7
clean.[d]" [d]ver 20
54These are the regulations for any infectious 14:54
skin disease,[e] for an itch, 55for mildew[f] in clothing [e]Lev 13:2,30
or in a house, 56and for a swelling, a rash or a 14:55
bright spot,[g] 57to determine when something is [f]Lev 13:47-
clean or unclean. 52
These are the regulations for infectious skin dis- 14:56
eases and mildew.[h] [g]Lev 13:2 14:57 [h]Lev 10:10

Discharges Causing Uncleanness

15 The LORD said to Moses and Aaron, 2"Speak
to the Israelites and say to them: 'When any 15:2
man has a bodily discharge,[i] the discharge is [i]ver 16,32;
unclean. 3Whether it continues flowing from his Lev 22:4;
body or is blocked, it will make him unclean. This Nu 5:2;
is how his discharge will bring about unclean- 2Sa 3:29;
ness: Mt 9:20
4" 'Any bed the man with a discharge lies on
will be unclean, and anything he sits on will be
unclean. 5Anyone who touches his bed must 15:5
wash his clothes[j] and bathe with water,[k] and he [j]Lev 11:25
will be unclean till evening.[l] 6Whoever sits on [k]Lev 14:8
anything that the man with a discharge sat on [l]Lev 11:24
must wash his clothes and bathe with water, and
he will be unclean till evening.

15:7 ᵐver 19; Lev 22:5 7“ ‘Whoever touches the man[m] who has a dis-
ⁿver 16; Lev 22:4 charge[n] must wash his clothes and bathe with
water, and he will be unclean till evening.
8“ ‘If the man with the discharge spits[o] on
15:8 °Nu 12:14 someone who is clean, that person must wash his
clothes and bathe with water, and he will be
unclean till evening.
9“ ‘Everything the man sits on when riding will
be unclean, 10and whoever touches any of the
things that were under him will be unclean till
15:10 evening; whoever picks up those things[p] must
ᵖNu 19:10 wash his clothes and bathe with water, and he
will be unclean till evening.
11“ ‘Anyone the man with a discharge touches
without rinsing his hands with water must wash
his clothes and bathe with water, and he will be
15:12 unclean till evening.
ᵠLev 6:28 12“ ‘A clay pot[q] that the man touches must be
ʳLev 11:32 broken, and any wooden article[r] is to be rinsed
with water.
13“ ‘When a man is cleansed from his discharge,
15:13 ˢLev 8:33 he is to count off seven days[s] for his ceremonial
ᵗver 5 cleansing; he must wash his clothes and bathe
himself with fresh water, and he will be clean.[t]
15:14 14On the eighth day he must take two doves or two
ᵘLev 14:22 young pigeons[u] and come before the LORD to the
entrance to the Tent of Meeting and give them to
15:15 the priest. 15The priest is to sacrifice them, the one
ᵛLev 5:7 for a sin offering[v] and the other for a burnt offer-
ʷLev 14:31 ˣLev 14:18, ing.[w] In this way he will make atonement before
19 the LORD for the man because of his discharge.[x]
15:16 16“ ‘When a man has an emission of semen,[y] he
ʸver 2; must bathe his whole body with water, and he
Lev 22:4; Dt 23:10 will be unclean till evening.[z] 17Any clothing or
ᶻver 5; leather that has semen on it must be washed with
Dt 23:11 water, and it will be unclean till evening. 18When
15:18 a man lies with a woman and there is an emission
ᵃ1Sa 21:4 of semen,[a] both must bathe with water, and they
will be unclean till evening.
15:19 19“ ‘When a woman has her regular flow of
ᵇver 24; blood, the impurity of her monthly period[b] will
Lev 12:2 last seven days, and anyone who touches her will
be unclean till evening.
20“ ‘Anything she lies on during her period will
be unclean, and anything she sits on will be
unclean. 21Whoever touches her bed must wash
15:21 his clothes and bathe with water, and he will be
ᶜver 27 unclean till evening.[c] 22Whoever touches anything
she sits on must wash his clothes and bathe with
water, and he will be unclean till evening.
23Whether it is the bed or anything she was sitting on, when anyone touches it, he will be
unclean till evening.
15:24 ᵈver 19; 24“ ‘If a man lies with her and her monthly
Lev 12:2; flow[d] touches him, he will be unclean for seven
18:19; 20:18; Eze 18:6 days; any bed he lies on will be unclean.
25“ ‘When a woman has a discharge of blood for
15:25 many days at a time other than her monthly peri-
ᵉMt 9:20; Mk 5:25; od[e] or has a discharge that continues beyond her
Lk 8:43 period, she will be unclean as long as she has the
discharge, just as in the days of her period. 26Any

Menstruation

LEV 15:19-24

The restrictions for a menstruating woman appear severe. But upon closer inspection, we see that requirements of a woman experiencing a natural flow of blood are not unrealistic. It is true that during her period a woman is set apart from the community. God also commands that no one touch her body, bed or any chairs she might have sat upon. An obvious reason for these rules is good hygiene. Presumably, anything that comes in direct contact with the woman's genital area has the potential to be contaminated.

Yet, notably, there is no mention of anything else that the woman might touch. All that she contacts with clean hands is apparently not defiled. While in seclusion from the greater population, she lives in the comfort of her own home, in the company of her own family. There, she is able to go about her normal, daily business: cooking, cleaning and interacting with those she loves.

Most Holy Place

LEV 16:2

No one can enter the presence of God in the Most Holy Place except the high priest. And even Aaron and his successors as high priests may not go in whenever they please. Only once a year, on the Day of Atonement, may the high priest step behind the sacred veil in the tabernacle, and then only in the manner that God prescribes. The high priest must bathe and put on special priestly clothing. He must also offer a sacrifice for his own sin before he can enter God's presence (Heb 5:1–3). Christ, our high priest and the perfect Lamb of God, has no need to offer a sacrifice for his own sin. Instead, as the sinless one, he offers himself as a sacrifice for our sins so that we can enter God's presence (Heb 7:26–28).

bed she lies on while her discharge continues will
be unclean, as is her bed during her monthly period, and anything she sits on will be unclean, as
during her period. 27Whoever touches them will
be unclean; he must wash his clothes and bathe
with water, and he will be unclean till evening.
28" 'When she is cleansed from her discharge,
she must count off seven days, and after that she
will be ceremonially clean. 29On the eighth day
she must take two doves or two young pigeons[f]
and bring them to the priest at the entrance to the
Tent of Meeting. 30The priest is to sacrifice one for
a sin offering and the other for a burnt offering. In
this way he will make atonement for her before
the LORD for the uncleanness of her discharge.[g]
31" 'You must keep the Israelites separate from
things that make them unclean, so they will not
die in their uncleanness for defiling my dwelling
place,[a][h] which is among them.' "
32These are the regulations for a man with a discharge, for anyone made unclean by an emission
of semen,[i] 33for a woman in her monthly period,
for a man or a woman with a discharge, and for a
man who lies with a woman who is ceremonially
unclean.[j]

The Day of Atonement

16 The LORD spoke to Moses after the death of
the two sons of Aaron who died when they
approached the LORD.[k] 2The LORD said to Moses:
"Tell your brother Aaron not to come whenever
he chooses[l] into the Most Holy Place[m] behind the
curtain in front of the atonement cover on the ark,
or else he will die, because I appear[n] in the cloud[o]
over the atonement cover.
3"This is how Aaron is to enter the sanctuary
area:[p] with a young bull for a sin offering and a
ram for a burnt offering. 4He is to put on the
sacred linen tunic, with linen undergarments next
to his body; he is to tie the linen sash around him
and put on the linen turban.[q] These are sacred
garments;[r] so he must bathe himself with water[s]
before he puts them on. 5From the Israelite community[t] he is to take two male goats[u] for a sin
offering and a ram for a burnt offering.
6"Aaron is to offer the bull for his own sin offering to make atonement for himself and his household.[v] 7Then he is to take the two goats and present them before the LORD at the entrance to the
Tent of Meeting. 8He is to cast lots for the two
goats—one lot for the LORD and the other for the
scapegoat.[b] 9Aaron shall bring the goat whose lot
falls to the LORD and sacrifice it for a sin offering.
10But the goat chosen by lot as the scapegoat shall
be presented alive before the LORD to be used for
making atonement[w] by sending it into the desert
as a scapegoat.
11"Aaron shall bring the bull for his own sin

15:29 [f]Lev 14:22
15:30 [g]Lev 5:10; 14:20,31; 18:19; 2Sa 11:4; Mk 5:25; Lk 8:43
15:31 [h]Lev 20:3; Nu 5:3; 19:13,20; 2Sa 15:25; 2Ki 21:7; Ps 33:14; 74:7; 76:2; Eze 5:11; 23:38
15:32 [i]ver 2
15:33 [j]ver 19,24, 25
16:1 [k]Lev 10:1
16:2 [l]Ex 30:10; Heb 9:7 [m]Heb 9:25; 10:19 [n]Ex 25:22 [o]Ex 40:34
16:3 [p]Heb 9:24, 25
16:4 [q]Ex 28:39 [r]Ex 28:42 [s]ver 24; Heb 10:22
16:5 [t]Lev 4:13-21 [u]2Ch 29:23
16:6 [v]Lev 9:7; Heb 5:3; 7:27; 9:7,12
16:10 [w]Isa 53:4-10; Ro 3:25; 1Jn 2:2

[a] *31* Or *my tabernacle* [b] *8* That is, the goat of removal; Hebrew *azazel*; also in verses 10 and 26

offering to make atonement for himself and his
household,[x] and he is to slaughter the bull for his
own sin offering. 12 He is to take a censer full of
burning coals[y] from the altar before the LORD and
two handfuls of finely ground fragrant incense[z]
and take them behind the curtain. 13 He is to put
the incense on the fire before the LORD, and the
smoke of the incense will conceal the atonement
cover above the Testimony, so that he will not die.[a]
14 He is to take some of the bull's blood[b] and with
his finger sprinkle it on the front of the atonement
cover; then he shall sprinkle some of it with his
finger seven times before the atonement cover.[c]
15 "He shall then slaughter the goat for the sin
offering for the people[d] and take its blood behind
the curtain[e] and do with it as he did with the
bull's blood: He shall sprinkle it on the atonement
cover and in front of it. 16 In this way he will make
atonement[f] for the Most Holy Place because of the
uncleanness and rebellion of the Israelites, whatever their sins have been. He is to do the same for
the Tent of Meeting, which is among them in the
midst of their uncleanness. 17 No one is to be in
the Tent of Meeting from the time Aaron goes in to
make atonement in the Most Holy Place until he
comes out, having made atonement for himself,
his household and the whole community of Israel.
18 "Then he shall come out to the altar[g] that is
before the LORD and make atonement for it. He
shall take some of the bull's blood and some of the
goat's blood and put it on all the horns of the altar.[h]
19 He shall sprinkle some of the blood on it with his
finger seven times to cleanse it and to consecrate it
from the uncleanness of the Israelites.[i]
20 "When Aaron has finished making atonement
for the Most Holy Place, the Tent of Meeting and
the altar, he shall bring forward the live goat. 21 He
is to lay both hands on the head of the live goat
and confess[j] over it all the wickedness and rebellion of the Israelites—all their sins—and put them
on the goat's head. He shall send the goat away
into the desert in the care of a man appointed for
the task. 22 The goat will carry on itself all their
sins[k] to a solitary place; and the man shall release
it in the desert.
23 "Then Aaron is to go into the Tent of Meeting
and take off the linen garments he put on before
he entered the Most Holy Place, and he is to leave
them there.[l] 24 He shall bathe himself with water
in a holy place and put on his regular garments.[m]
Then he shall come out and sacrifice the burnt
offering for himself and the burnt offering for the
people, to make atonement for himself and for the
people. 25 He shall also burn the fat of the sin offering on the altar.
26 "The man who releases the goat as a scapegoat must wash his clothes[n] and bathe himself
with water; afterward he may come into the
camp. 27 The bull and the goat for the sin offerings,
whose blood was brought into the Most Holy
Place to make atonement, must be taken outside

16:11 [x]Heb 7:27; 9:7
16:12 [y]Lev 10:1 [z]Ex 30:34-38
16:13 [a]Ex 28:43; Lev 22:9
16:14 [b]Lev 4:5; Heb 9:7,13, 25 [c]Lev 4:6
16:15 [d]Heb 9:7,12 [e]Heb 9:3
16:16 [f]Ex 29:36
16:18 [g]Lev 4:7 [h]Lev 4:25
16:19 [i]Eze 43:20
16:21 [j]Lev 5:5
16:22 [k]Isa 53:12
16:23 [l]Eze 42:14; 44:19
16:24 [m]ver 3-5
16:26 [n]Lev 11:25

Day of Atonement

LEV 16

Occurring on the tenth day of the seventh month (September/October of the Hebrew calendar), the Day of Atonement serves as a public reminder of the sin that separates the Israelites from God and of their need for atonement. On this day, the people fast and the high priest makes sacrificial atonement for their sins.

Two goats are involved in the ritual of the Day of Atonement. The first goat is sacrificed and its blood sprinkled on the atonement cover, or mercy seat, of the ark in the Most Holy Place, symbolizing the death that covers sin. The second goat is sent off into the desert, symbolizing the removal of sin from the people.

Christ's death on the cross is the final and consummate Day of Atonement. His death covers our sins once and for all (Heb 10:11–14). No other sacrifice is required. No scapegoats. No Most Holy Place. No high priest. Christ's supreme sacrifice atones for it all.

Blood and Life

LEV 17:11

Throughout the Bible blood is associated with life. This is an important concept to grasp when reading Leviticus, for much of the text deals with the sacrificial offering of blood. Because of sin, every person is separated from God (Ro 3:23). The price that must be paid for sin is one's life (Ro 6:23). Yet God desires us to be reconciled to him and throughout history has consistently provided the means for that reconciliation to take place. From the days of Moses to the death and resurrection of Jesus Christ, the sacrificial system outlined in the Old Testament is the vehicle used to bring about that restored relationship (Heb 9:22).

Christ's death closes that chapter of history, however. The perfect Lamb of God completes the reconciliation required for relationship with God (Jn 1:29). The old ways are gone. A new way is instituted. No longer is continual sacrifice needed. Christ's sacrifice once and for all paid for our sin and opened the curtain into the very presence of God (Heb 10:19–22).

the camp;[o] their hides, flesh and offal are to be
burned up. 28The man who burns them must
wash his clothes and bathe himself with water;
afterward he may come into the camp.
29"This is to be a lasting ordinance for you: On
the tenth day of the seventh month you must deny
yourselves[a][p] and not do any work—whether
native-born or an alien living among you—
30because on this day atonement will be made for
you, to cleanse you. Then, before the LORD, you
will be clean from all your sins.[q] 31It is a sabbath of
rest, and you must deny yourselves;[r] it is a lasting
ordinance. 32The priest who is anointed and
ordained to succeed his father as high priest is to
make atonement. He is to put on the sacred linen
garments[s] 33and make atonement for the Most Holy
Place, for the Tent of Meeting and the altar, and for
the priests and all the people of the community.[t]
34"This is to be a lasting ordinance for you:
Atonement is to be made once a year[u] for all the
sins of the Israelites."

And it was done, as the LORD commanded
Moses.

Eating Blood Forbidden

17 The LORD said to Moses, 2"Speak to Aaron
and his sons and to all the Israelites and say
to them: 'This is what the LORD has commanded:
3Any Israelite who sacrifices an ox,[b] a lamb or a
goat in the camp or outside of it 4instead of bringing it to the entrance to the Tent of Meeting to
present it as an offering to the LORD in front of the
tabernacle of the LORD[v]—that man shall be considered guilty of bloodshed; he has shed blood
and must be cut off from his people.[w] 5This is so
the Israelites will bring to the LORD the sacrifices
they are now making in the open fields. They
must bring them to the priest, that is, to the LORD,
at the entrance to the Tent of Meeting and sacrifice
them as fellowship offerings.[c] 6The priest is to
sprinkle the blood against the altar of the LORD[x]
at the entrance to the Tent of Meeting and burn
the fat as an aroma pleasing to the LORD.[y] 7They
must no longer offer any of their sacrifices to the
goat idols[d][z] to whom they prostitute themselves.[a]
This is to be a lasting ordinance for them and for
the generations to come.'
8"Say to them: 'Any Israelite or any alien living
among them who offers a burnt offering or sacrifice 9and does not bring it to the entrance to the
Tent of Meeting[b] to sacrifice it to the LORD—that
man must be cut off from his people.
10" 'Any Israelite or any alien living among
them who eats any blood—I will set my face
against that person who eats blood[c] and will cut
him off from his people. 11For the life of a creature
is in the blood,[d] and I have given it to you to make

16:27 [o]Lev 4:12,21; Heb 13:11
16:29 [p]Lev 23:27, 32; Nu 29:7; Isa 58:3
16:30 [q]Jer 33:8; Eph 5:26
16:31 [r]Isa 58:3,5
16:32 [s]ver 4; Nu 20:26,28
16:33 [t]ver 11,16-18
16:34 [u]Heb 9:7,25
17:4 [v]Dt 12:5-21 [w]Ge 17:14
17:6 [x]Lev 3:2 [y]Nu 18:17
17:7 [z]Ex 22:20; 2Ch 11:15 [a]Ex 32:8; 34:15; Dt 32:17; 1Co 10:20
17:9 [b]ver 4
17:10 [c]Ge 9:4; Lev 3:17; Dt 12:16,23; 1Sa 14:33
17:11 [d]ver 14; Ge 9:4

[a] 29 Or *must fast;* also in verse 31 [b] 3 The Hebrew word can include both male and female. [c] 5 Traditionally *peace offerings* [d] 7 Or *demons*

atonement for yourselves on the altar; it is the
17:11 [e]Heb 9:22 blood that makes atonement for one's life.[e]
12Therefore I say to the Israelites, "None of you
may eat blood, nor may an alien living among
you eat blood."
13" 'Any Israelite or any alien living among you
17:13 who hunts any animal or bird that may be eaten
[f]Lev 7:26; must drain out the blood and cover it with earth,[f]
Dt 12:16 14because the life of every creature is its blood.
That is why I have said to the Israelites, "You must
not eat the blood of any creature, because the life
17:14 of every creature is its blood; anyone who eats it
[g]ver 11; must be cut off."[g]
Ge 9:4 15" 'Anyone, whether native-born or alien, who
17:15 eats anything found dead or torn by wild animals[h]
[h]Ex 22:31; must wash his clothes and bathe with water, and
Dt 14:21 he will be ceremonially unclean till evening; then
he will be clean. 16But if he does not wash his
clothes and bathe himself, he will be held
responsible.' "

Unlawful Sexual Relations

18 The LORD said to Moses, 2"Speak to the Israelites and say to them: 'I am the LORD your
18:2 God.[i] 3You must not do as they do in Egypt, where
[i]Ex 6:7; you used to live, and you must not do as they do
Lev 11:44; in the land of Canaan, where I am bringing you.
Eze 20:5 Do not follow their practices.[j] 4You must obey my
18:3 laws and be careful to follow my decrees. I am the
[j]ver 24-30; Ex 23:24; LORD your God.[k] 5Keep my decrees and laws, for
Lev 20:23 the man who obeys them will live by them.[l] I am
18:4 the LORD.
[k]ver 2 6" 'No one is to approach any close relative to
18:5 have sexual relations. I am the LORD.
[l]Eze 20:11; 7" 'Do not dishonor your father[m] by having sex-
Ro 10:5*; ual relations with your mother.[n] She is your moth-
Gal 3:12* er; do not have relations with her.
18:7 [m]Lev 20:11 8" 'Do not have sexual relations with your
[n]Eze 22:10 father's wife;[o] that would dishonor your father.[p]
18:8 9" 'Do not have sexual relations with your sis-
[o]1Co 5:1 ter,[q] either your father's daughter or your moth-
[p]Lev 20:11 er's daughter, whether she was born in the same
18:9 home or elsewhere.
[q]Lev 20:17 10" 'Do not have sexual relations with your
son's daughter or your daughter's daughter; that
would dishonor you.
11" 'Do not have sexual relations with the
daughter of your father's wife, born to your
father; she is your sister.
18:12 12" 'Do not have sexual relations with your
[r]Lev 20:19 father's sister;[r] she is your father's close relative.
13" 'Do not have sexual relations with your
mother's sister, because she is your mother's close
relative.
14" 'Do not dishonor your father's brother by
approaching his wife to have sexual relations; she
18:14 [s]Lev 20:20 is your aunt.[s]
15" 'Do not have sexual relations with your
18:15 daughter-in-law.[t] She is your son's wife; do not
[t]Lev 20:12 have relations with her.

Clear-Cut Guidelines

LEV 18

When a mother tells her son or daughter not to do something, the child's response is often a whiny, "Whyyyyy?" Not knowing the reason for a specific rule is not a legitimate excuse for the one who has disobeyed it. But many parents find that, in explaining certain rules and expectations, they help their children internalize the principles behind the commands.

In Leviticus 18 God does more than just lay down the law. He spells out specifics, leaving no room for loopholes or misinterpretations. He explains why certain behaviors are unacceptable. For example, a man who has sexual relations with his granddaughter brings dishonor on himself (Lev 18:10). However, God's primary reason is much simpler and is given clearly in the introduction to chapter 18, as well as in verses 4, 5, 6, 21, and 30: "I am the LORD." No greater reason exists for obedience.

Results of Sexual Sin

LEV 18:24-28

The laundry list of sexual sins that God gives Moses sounds more like the plotline for a bad soap opera than the ways of a functioning society. But the Canaanites, inhabitants of the land God had promised to the Israelites, had committed every one.

God speaks to Moses about the matter to prepare his people for a completely different sort of lifestyle. In giving his people these specific sexual laws, God provides tangible boundaries for them. He also equips the leaders to combat ungodly behavior, so that they might help the Israelites avoid the same perverse mistakes, and the same fate, as their predecessors.

16“ ‘Do not have sexual relations with your
brother’s wife;[u] that would dishonor your brother.
17“ ‘Do not have sexual relations with both a
woman and her daughter.[v] Do not have sexual
relations with either her son’s daughter or her
daughter’s daughter; they are her close relatives.
That is wickedness.
18“ ‘Do not take your wife’s sister as a rival wife
and have sexual relations with her while your
wife is living.
19“ ‘Do not approach a woman to have sexual
relations during the uncleanness of her monthly
period.[w]
20“ ‘Do not have sexual relations with your
neighbor’s wife[x] and defile yourself with her.
21“ ‘Do not give any of your children[y] to be sacrificed[a] to Molech,[z] for you must not profane the
name of your God.[a] I am the LORD.
22“ ‘Do not lie with a man as one lies with a
woman;[b] that is detestable.
23“ ‘Do not have sexual relations with an animal and defile yourself with it. A woman must
not present herself to an animal to have sexual
relations with it; that is a perversion.[c]
24“ ‘Do not defile yourselves in any of these
ways, because this is how the nations that I am
going to drive out before you[d] became defiled.[e]
25Even the land was defiled; so I punished it for
its sin,[f] and the land vomited out its inhabitants.[g]
26But you must keep my decrees and my laws. The
native-born and the aliens living among you must
not do any of these detestable things, 27for all
these things were done by the people who lived
in the land before you, and the land became
defiled. 28And if you defile the land, it will vomit
you out as it vomited out the nations that were
before you.
29“ ‘Everyone who does any of these detestable
things—such persons must be cut off from their
people. 30Keep my requirements[h] and do not follow any of the detestable customs that were practiced before you came and do not defile yourselves
with them. I am the LORD your God.[i] ’ ”

Various Laws

19 The LORD said to Moses, 2“Speak to the
entire assembly of Israel and say to them:
‘Be holy because I, the LORD your God, am holy.[j]
3“ ‘Each of you must respect his mother and
father,[k] and you must observe my Sabbaths. I am
the LORD your God.[l]
4“ ‘Do not turn to idols or make gods of cast
metal for yourselves.[m] I am the LORD your God.
5“ ‘When you sacrifice a fellowship offering[b] to
the LORD, sacrifice it in such a way that it will be
accepted on your behalf. 6It shall be eaten on the
day you sacrifice it or on the next day; anything
left over until the third day must be burned up.

18:16 [u]Lev 20:21
18:17 [v]Lev 20:14
18:19 [w]Lev 15:24; 20:18
18:20 [x]Ex 20:14; Lev 20:10; Mt 5:27,28; 1Co 6:9; Heb 13:4
18:21 [y]Dt 12:31 [z]Lev 20:2-5 [a]Lev 19:12; 21:6; Eze 36:20
18:22 [b]Lev 20:13; Dt 23:18; Ro 1:27
18:23 [c]Ex 22:19; Lev 20:15; Dt 27:21
18:24 [d]ver 3,27,30 [e]Dt 18:12
18:25 [f]Lev 20:23; Dt 9:5; 18:12 [g]ver 28; Lev 20:22
18:30 [h]Dt 11:1 [i]ver 2
19:2 [j]1Pe 1:16*; Lev 11:44
19:3 [k]Ex 20:12 [l]Lev 11:44
19:4 [m]Ex 20:4,23; 34:17; Lev 26:1; Ps 96:5; 115:4-7

[a] 21 Or *to be passed through* ⌞*the fire*⌟ [b] 5 Traditionally *peace offering*

7If any of it is eaten on the third day, it is impure
and will not be accepted. 8Whoever eats it will be
held responsible because he has desecrated what
is holy to the LORD; that person must be cut off
from his people.
9" 'When you reap the harvest of your land, do
not reap to the very edges of your field or gather
the gleanings of your harvest.[n] 10Do not go over
your vineyard a second time or pick up the grapes
that have fallen. Leave them for the poor and the
alien. I am the LORD your God.
11" 'Do not steal.[o]
" 'Do not lie.[p]
" 'Do not deceive one another.
12" 'Do not swear falsely by my name[q] and so
profane the name of your God. I am the LORD.
13" 'Do not defraud your neighbor or rob him.[r]
" 'Do not hold back the wages of a hired man
overnight.[s]
14" 'Do not curse the deaf or put a stumbling
block in front of the blind,[t] but fear your God. I
am the LORD.
15" 'Do not pervert justice;[u] do not show partiality[v] to the poor or favoritism to the great, but
judge your neighbor fairly.
16" 'Do not go about spreading slander[w] among
your people.
" 'Do not do anything that endangers your
neighbor's life.[x] I am the LORD.
17" 'Do not hate your brother in your heart.[y]
Rebuke your neighbor frankly[z] so you will not
share in his guilt.
18" 'Do not seek revenge[a] or bear a grudge[b]
against one of your people, but love your neighbor
as yourself.[c] I am the LORD.
19" 'Keep my decrees.
" 'Do not mate different kinds of animals.
" 'Do not plant your field with two kinds of
seed.[d]
" 'Do not wear clothing woven of two kinds of
material.[e]
20" 'If a man sleeps with a woman who is a
slave girl promised to another man but who has
not been ransomed or given her freedom, there
must be due punishment. Yet they are not to be
put to death, because she had not been freed.
21The man, however, must bring a ram to the
entrance to the Tent of Meeting for a guilt offering to the LORD.[f] 22With the ram of the guilt offering the priest is to make atonement for him before
the LORD for the sin he has committed, and his sin
will be forgiven.
23" 'When you enter the land and plant any
kind of fruit tree, regard its fruit as forbidden.[a] For
three years you are to consider it forbidden[a]; it
must not be eaten. 24In the fourth year all its fruit
will be holy,[g] an offering of praise to the LORD.
25But in the fifth year you may eat its fruit. In this

19:9 [n]Lev 23:10, 22; Dt 24:19-22
19:11 [o]Ex 20:15 [p]Eph 4:25
19:12 [q]Ex 20:7; Mt 5:33
19:13 [r]Ex 22:15, 25-27 [s]Dt 24:15; Jas 5:4
19:14 [t]Dt 27:18
19:15 [u]Ex 23:2,6 [v]Dt 1:17
19:16 [w]Ps 15:3; Eze 22:9 [x]Ex 23:7
19:17 [y]1Jn 2:9; 3:15 [z]Mt 18:15; Lk 17:3
19:18 [a]Ro 12:19 [b]Ps 103:9 [c]Mt 5:43*; 19:16*; 22:39*; Mk 12:31*; Lk 10:27*; Jn 13:34; Ro 13:9*; Gal 5:14*; Jas 2:8*
19:19 [d]Dt 22:9 [e]Dt 22:11
19:21 [f]Lev 5:15
19:24 [g]Pr 3:9

[a] 23 Hebrew *uncircumcised*

Be Compassionate

LEV 19

Many of the rules God imparts through Moses compel the Israelites to deal compassionately with the disabled and the disadvantaged. A great number of the concepts presented here were not common to the cultures of the day and therefore were a new way of thinking for God's people. As a result of these injunctions, destitute people and foreigners are able to glean food from partially harvested fields, the poor who live hand-to-mouth are paid daily, the deaf and blind are not tormented by those with hearing and sight, and men who sleep with betrothed slave girls are held accountable for their actions. Israel's God is not merely a God who imposes arbitrary rules for them to follow. He is a God who cares about the helpless and wants his people to care also.

Hairstyles and Tattoos

LEV 19:27–28

Because God is holy, nothing that is profane—not even something as seemingly trivial as a hairstyle—can be allowed in his presence. In the land surrounding the Israelites, pagan worshipers cut their hair in a particular manner, put tattoos on their bodies, or disfigured themselves in an effort to please their false gods. Adopting such behavior would have brought the people of Israel and their God great dishonor. To protect them against this, God presents strict laws regarding hairstyles—styles that are still worn by Orthodox Jews today.

way your harvest will be increased. I am the LORD
your God.
26" 'Do not eat any meat with the blood still
in it.[h]
" 'Do not practice divination or sorcery.[i]
27" 'Do not cut the hair at the sides of your head
or clip off the edges of your beard.[j]
28" 'Do not cut your bodies for the dead or put
tattoo marks on yourselves. I am the LORD.
29" 'Do not degrade your daughter by making
her a prostitute,[k] or the land will turn to prostitution and be filled with wickedness.
30" 'Observe my Sabbaths and have reverence
for my sanctuary. I am the LORD.[l]
31" 'Do not turn to mediums or seek out spiritists,[m] for you will be defiled by them. I am the
LORD your God.
32" 'Rise in the presence of the aged, show
respect for the elderly[n] and revere your God. I am
the LORD.
33" 'When an alien lives with you in your land,
do not mistreat him. 34The alien living with you
must be treated as one of your native-born.[o] Love
him as yourself, for you were aliens in Egypt.[p] I
am the LORD your God.
35" 'Do not use dishonest standards when measuring length, weight or quantity. 36Use honest
scales and honest weights, an honest ephah[a] and
an honest hin.[b][q] I am the LORD your God, who
brought you out of Egypt.
37" 'Keep all my decrees and all my laws and
follow them. I am the LORD.' "

Punishments for Sin

20 The LORD said to Moses, 2"Say to the Israelites: 'Any Israelite or any alien living in
Israel who gives[c] any of his children to Molech
must be put to death. The people of the community are to stone him. 3I will set my face against
that man and I will cut him off from his people;
for by giving his children to Molech, he has
defiled my sanctuary[r] and profaned my holy
name.[s] 4If the people of the community close their
eyes when that man gives one of his children to
Molech and they fail to put him to death,[t] 5I will
set my face against that man and his family and
will cut off from their people both him and all
who follow him in prostituting themselves to
Molech.
6" 'I will set my face against the person who
turns to mediums and spiritists to prostitute himself by following them, and I will cut him off from
his people.[u]
7" 'Consecrate yourselves and be holy,[v] because
I am the LORD your God. 8Keep my decrees and
follow them. I am the LORD, who makes you
holy.[d][w]

19:26 [h]Lev 17:10 [i]Dt 18:10
19:27 [j]Lev 21:5
19:29 [k]Dt 23:18
19:30 [l]Lev 26:2
19:31 [m]Lev 20:6; Isa 8:19
19:32 [n]1Ti 5:1
19:34 [o]Ex 12:48 [p]Dt 10:19
19:36 [q]Dt 25:13-15
20:3 [r]Lev 15:31 [s]Lev 18:21
20:4 [t]Dt 17:2-5
20:6 [u]Lev 19:31
20:7 [v]Eph 1:4; 1Pe 1:16*
20:8 [w]Ex 31:13

[a] *36* An ephah was a dry measure. [b] *36* A hin was a liquid measure. [c] *2* Or *sacrifices*; also in verses 3 and 4 [d] *8* Or *who sanctifies you*; or *who sets you apart as holy*

9 “ ‘If anyone curses his father or mother,[x] he must be put to death.[y] He has cursed his father or his mother, and his blood will be on his own head.[z]

10 “ ‘If a man commits adultery with another man’s wife[a]—with the wife of his neighbor—both the adulterer and the adulteress must be put to death.

11 “ ‘If a man sleeps with his father’s wife, he has dishonored his father.[b] Both the man and the woman must be put to death; their blood will be on their own heads.

12 “ ‘If a man sleeps with his daughter-in-law,[c] both of them must be put to death. What they have done is a perversion; their blood will be on their own heads.

13 “ ‘If a man lies with a man as one lies with a woman, both of them have done what is detestable.[d] They must be put to death; their blood will be on their own heads.

14 “ ‘If a man marries both a woman and her mother,[e] it is wicked. Both he and they must be burned in the fire, so that no wickedness will be among you.[f]

15 “ ‘If a man has sexual relations with an animal,[g] he must be put to death, and you must kill the animal.

16 “ ‘If a woman approaches an animal to have sexual relations with it, kill both the woman and the animal. They must be put to death; their blood will be on their own heads.

17 “ ‘If a man marries his sister[h], the daughter of either his father or his mother, and they have sexual relations, it is a disgrace. They must be cut off before the eyes of their people. He has dishonored his sister and will be held responsible.

18 “ ‘If a man lies with a woman during her monthly period[i] and has sexual relations with her, he has exposed the source of her flow, and she has also uncovered it. Both of them must be cut off from their people.

19 “ ‘Do not have sexual relations with the sister of either your mother or your father,[j] for that would dishonor a close relative; both of you would be held responsible.

20 “ ‘If a man sleeps with his aunt,[k] he has dishonored his uncle. They will be held responsible; they will die childless.

21 “ ‘If a man marries his brother’s wife,[l] it is an act of impurity; he has dishonored his brother. They will be childless.

22 “ ‘Keep all my decrees and laws and follow them, so that the land[m] where I am bringing you to live may not vomit you out. 23 You must not live according to the customs of the nations[n] I am going to drive out before you.[o] Because they did all these things, I abhorred them. 24 But I said to you, “You will possess their land; I will give it to you as an inheritance, a land flowing with milk and honey.”[p] I am the LORD your God, who has set you apart from the nations.[q]

20:9 [x]Dt 27:16 [y]Ex 21:17; Mt 15:4*; Mk 7:10* [z]ver 11; 2Sa 1:16
20:10 [a]Ex 20:14; Dt 5:18; 22:22
20:11 [b]Lev 18:7; Dt 27:23
20:12 [c]Lev 18:15
20:13 [d]Lev 18:22
20:14 [e]Lev 18:17 [f]Dt 27:23
20:15 [g]Lev 18:23
20:17 [h]Lev 18:9
20:18 [i]Lev 15:24; 18:19
20:19 [j]Lev 18:12-13
20:20 [k]Lev 18:14
20:21 [l]Lev 18:16
20:22 [m]Lev 18:25-28
20:23 [n]Lev 18:3 [o]Lev 18:24, 27,30
20:24 [p]Ex 3:8; 13:5; 33:3 [q]Ex 33:16

Sex During Menstruation

LEV 20:18

Because the flow of any bodily fluid or secretion makes a person unclean, to engage in the sacred act of intercourse while a woman is menstruating is, according to Israelite religious law, to willingly defile one’s body. The consequence of such an act is severe, possibly because to sin in this manner is a direct and willful disobedience of God’s laws. This sin appears on a list of sexual sins of which the Israelites’ neighbors are guilty. Having sexual relations during a woman’s menstrual period may be acceptable in other communities, but God’s people are to be distinct in all ways, set apart and holy.

Although believers today are no longer bound to the ceremonial laws of the Old Testament (Ga 3:25), the call to a life of holiness remains (1Pe 1:14-16).

A Treasured Possession

LEV 20:26

The people of Israel belong to the Lord God. *They are not just his responsibility, they are his "treasured possession" (Ex 19:5). Because God is holy, they too are to be holy and pure. While the people from the surrounding nations cavort and carouse, worshiping idols and spurning the God who created them, God calls the Israelites apart, to uphold the knowledge and worship of the Lord. God has blessed them far more than other nations. With that great blessing comes great responsibility.*

It's a hard course to navigate when trying to determine which of these laws still apply to our world today and which are cultural and intended only for the Israelites. Perhaps the best approach is to determine the spirit of the law and begin to apply that to daily life. God's call to Israel to be a special people, distinct from those around them in their attitudes and behaviors, is no less than our call today to be a distinct—often countercultural—and holy people.

25“ ‘You must therefore make a distinction
between clean and unclean animals and between
unclean and clean birds.[r] Do not defile yourselves
by any animal or bird or anything that moves
along the ground—those which I have set apart
as unclean for you. 26You are to be holy to me[a]
because I, the LORD, am holy,[s] and I have set you
apart from the nations to be my own.
27“ ‘A man or woman who is a medium or spiritist among you must be put to death.[t] You are to
stone them; their blood will be on their own
heads.’ ”

Rules for Priests

21 The LORD said to Moses, “Speak to the
priests, the sons of Aaron, and say to them:
‘A priest must not make himself ceremonially
unclean for any of his people who die,[u] 2except
for a close relative, such as his mother or father,
his son or daughter, his brother, 3or an unmarried sister who is dependent on him since she has
no husband—for her he may make himself
unclean. 4He must not make himself unclean for
people related to him by marriage,[b] and so defile
himself.
5“ ‘Priests must not shave their heads or shave
off the edges of their beards[v] or cut their bodies.[w]
6They must be holy to their God and must not profane the name of their God.[x] Because they present
the offerings made to the LORD by fire,[y] the food of
their God, they are to be holy.
7“ ‘They must not marry women defiled by
prostitution or divorced from their husbands,[z]
because priests are holy to their God.[a] 8Regard
them as holy,[b] because they offer up the food of
your God. Consider them holy, because I the LORD
am holy—I who make you holy.[c]
9“ ‘If a priest's daughter defiles herself by
becoming a prostitute, she disgraces her father;
she must be burned in the fire.[c]
10“ ‘The high priest, the one among his brothers who has had the anointing oil poured on his
head and who has been ordained to wear the
priestly garments,[d] must not let his hair become
unkempt[d] or tear his clothes.[e] 11He must not enter
a place where there is a dead body.[f] He must not
make himself unclean,[g] even for his father or
mother, 12nor leave the sanctuary of his God or
desecrate it, because he has been dedicated by the
anointing oil[h] of his God. I am the LORD.
13“ ‘The woman he marries must be a virgin.[i]
14He must not marry a widow, a divorced woman,
or a woman defiled by prostitution, but only a virgin from his own people, 15so he will not defile
his offspring among his people. I am the LORD,
who makes him holy.[e]’ ”

20:25 [r]Lev 11:1-47; Dt 14:3-21
20:26 [s]Lev 19:2
20:27 [t]Lev 19:31
21:1 [u]Eze 44:25
21:5 [v]Eze 44:20 [w]Lev 19:28; Dt 14:1
21:6 [x]Lev 18:21 [y]Lev 3:11
21:7 [z]ver 13,14 [a]Eze 44:22
21:8 [b]ver 6
21:9 [c]Ge 38:24; Lev 19:29
21:10 [d]Lev 16:32 [e]Lev 10:6
21:11 [f]Nu 19:11, 13,14 [g]Lev 19:28
21:12 [h]Ex 29:6-7; Lev 10:7
21:13 [i]Eze 44:22

[a] 26 Or *be my holy ones* [b] 4 Or *unclean as a leader among his people* [c] 8 Or *who sanctify you*; or *who set you apart as holy* [d] 10 Or *not uncover his head* [e] 15 Or *who sanctifies him*; or *who sets him apart as holy*

16The LORD said to Moses, 17"Say to Aaron: 'For
the generations to come none of your descendants
who has a defect may come near to offer the food
21:17 of his God.[j] 18No man who has any defect[k] may
jver 6 come near: no man who is blind or lame, disfig-
21:18 ured or deformed; 19no man with a crippled foot
kLev 22:19- or hand, 20or who is hunchbacked or dwarfed, or
25 who has any eye defect, or who has festering or
21:20 running sores or damaged testicles.[l] 21No descen-
lDt 23:1; Isa 56:3 dant of Aaron the priest who has any defect is to
come near to present the offerings made to the
LORD by fire. He has a defect; he must not come
near to offer the food of his God. 22He may eat the
21:22 most holy food of his God,[m] as well as the holy
m1Co 9:13 food; 23yet because of his defect, he must not go
near the curtain or approach the altar, and so desecrate my sanctuary. I am the LORD, who makes
them holy.[a]' "
24So Moses told this to Aaron and his sons and
to all the Israelites.

22 The LORD said to Moses, 2"Tell Aaron and
his sons to treat with respect the sacred
offerings the Israelites consecrate to me, so they
will not profane my holy name. I am the LORD.
3"Say to them: 'For the generations to come, if
any of your descendants is ceremonially unclean
and yet comes near the sacred offerings that the
22:3 Israelites consecrate to the LORD, that person must
nLev 7:20, be cut off from my presence.[n] I am the LORD.
21; Nu 19:13 4" 'If a descendant of Aaron has an infectious
22:4 skin disease[b] or a bodily discharge,[o] he may not
oLev 14:1-32; eat the sacred offerings until he is cleansed. He
15:2-15 pLev 11:24- will also be unclean if he touches something
28,39 defiled by a corpse[p] or by anyone who has an
22:5 emission of semen, 5or if he touches any crawling
qLev 11:24- thing[q] that makes him unclean, or any person[r]
28,43 rLev 15:7 who makes him unclean, whatever the uncleanness may be. 6The one who touches any such
thing will be unclean till evening. He must not eat
any of the sacred offerings unless he has bathed
himself with water. 7When the sun goes down, he
22:7 will be clean, and after that he may eat the sacred
sNu 18:11 offerings, for they are his food.[s] 8He must not eat
22:8 anything found dead[t] or torn by wild animals,[u]
tLev 11:39 and so become unclean[v] through it. I am the LORD.
uEx 22:31; 9" 'The priests are to keep my requirements so
Lev 17:15 that they do not become guilty and die[w] for treat-
vLev 11:40 ing them with contempt. I am the LORD, who
22:9 makes them holy.[c]
wver 16; 10" 'No one outside a priest's family may eat the
Ex 28:43 sacred offering, nor may the guest of a priest or
his hired worker eat it. 11But if a priest buys a
22:11 slave with money, or if a slave is born in his
xGe 17:13; household, that slave may eat his food.[x] 12If a
Ex 12:44 priest's daughter marries anyone other than a
priest, she may not eat any of the sacred contri-

[a] 23 Or *who sanctifies them*; or *who sets them apart as holy*
[b] 4 Traditionally *leprosy*; the Hebrew word was used for various diseases affecting the skin—not necessarily leprosy.
[c] 9 Or *who sanctifies them*; or *who sets them apart as holy*; also in verse 16

A Perfect Priesthood

LEV 21:16-23

God himself is holy and perfect. Along with the sacrificial animals which had to be unblemished, the priests who serve before God, as a picture of the future perfect priest—that is, Jesus—must also be perfect, without any "defect" (Lev 21:17). No callousness or discrimination on God's part produced this rule, only his desire that his people should see before them, in his holy sanctuary, a picture of the perfect holiness he requires. These lame and blind and impaired individuals are still able to eat of the holy foods, and are, therefore, provided for; but they are not allowed to serve within the sanctuary.

Our perfect priest, Jesus Christ, has now produced for us the clearest, most beautiful picture of the holiness of God. All his people are part of a new "royal priesthood" (1Pe 2:9). Every defect, every sin, every imperfection is covered by Jesus' blood and grace. All who belong to him are acceptable, able to come before him in worship and in service.

butions. 13But if a priest's daughter becomes a
widow or is divorced, yet has no children, and she
returns to live in her father's house as in her
youth, she may eat of her father's food. No unauthorized person, however, may eat any of it.
14"'If anyone eats a sacred offering by mistake,
he must make restitution to the priest for the
offering and add a fifth of the value[y] to it. 15The 22:14 [y]Lev 5:15
priests must not desecrate the sacred offerings the 22:15
Israelites present to the LORD[z] 16by allowing them [z]Nu 18:32
to eat the sacred offerings and so bring upon them
guilt requiring payment.[a] I am the LORD, who 22:16
makes them holy.' " [a]ver 9

Unacceptable Sacrifices

17The LORD said to Moses, 18"Speak to Aaron
and his sons and to all the Israelites and say to
them: 'If any of you—either an Israelite or an
alien living in Israel—presents a gift[b] for a burnt 22:18
offering to the LORD, either to fulfill a vow or as a [b]Lev 1:2
freewill offering, 19you must present a male with-
out defect[c] from the cattle, sheep or goats in order 22:19 [c]Lev 1:3
that it may be accepted on your behalf. 20Do not
bring anything with a defect,[d] because it will not 22:20
be accepted on your behalf. 21When anyone brings [d]Dt 15:21; 17:1;
from the herd or flock a fellowship offering[ae] to Mal 1:8,14;
the LORD to fulfill a special vow or as a freewill Heb 9:14;
offering, it must be without defect or blemish to 1Pe 1:19
be acceptable. 22Do not offer to the LORD the blind, 22:21
the injured or the maimed, or anything with warts [e]Lev 3:6; Nu 15:3,8
or festering or running sores. Do not place any of
these on the altar as an offering made to the LORD
by fire. 23You may, however, present as a freewill
offering an ox[b] or a sheep that is deformed or
stunted, but it will not be accepted in fulfillment
of a vow. 24You must not offer to the LORD an animal whose testicles are bruised, crushed, torn or
cut.[f] You must not do this in your own land, 25and 22:24
you must not accept such animals from the hand [f]Lev 21:20
of a foreigner and offer them as the food of your
God.[g] They will not be accepted on your behalf, 22:25 [g]Lev 21:6
because they are deformed and have defects.' "
26The LORD said to Moses, 27"When a calf, a
lamb or a goat is born, it is to remain with its 22:27
mother for seven days.[h] From the eighth day on, it [h]Ex 22:30
will be acceptable as an offering made to the LORD
by fire. 28Do not slaughter a cow or a sheep and its 22:28 [i]Dt 22:6,7
young on the same day.[i]
29"When you sacrifice a thank offering[j] to the 22:29
LORD, sacrifice it in such a way that it will be [j]Lev 7:12; Ps 107:22
accepted on your behalf. 30It must be eaten that
same day; leave none of it till morning.[k] I am the 22:30 [k]Lev 7:15
LORD.
31"Keep[l] my commands and follow them. I am 22:31 [l]Dt 4:2,40;
the LORD. 32Do not profane my holy name.[m] I must Ps 105:45
be acknowledged as holy by the Israelites.[n] I am
the LORD, who makes[c] you holy[d] 33and who 22:32 [m]Lev 18:21 [n]Lev 10:3

[a] 21 Traditionally *peace offering* [b] 23 The Hebrew word can include both male and female. [c] 32 Or *made* [d] 32 Or *who sanctifies you*; or *who sets you apart as holy*

I believe that each person has a spiritual obligation before God to learn how to live well, to live fully, as opposed to knowing only how to live comfortably.

—Luci Swindoll

brought you out of Egypt to be your God.[o] I am
the LORD."

23 The LORD said to Moses, 2"Speak to the Israelites and say to them: 'These are my
appointed feasts,[p] the appointed feasts of the
LORD, which you are to proclaim as sacred
assemblies.[q]

The Sabbath

3" 'There are six days when you may work,[r] but
the seventh day is a Sabbath of rest,[s] a day of
sacred assembly. You are not to do any work;
wherever you live, it is a Sabbath to the LORD.

The Passover and Unleavened Bread

4" 'These are the LORD's appointed feasts, the
sacred assemblies you are to proclaim at their
appointed times: 5The LORD's Passover begins at
twilight on the fourteenth day of the first month.[t]
6On the fifteenth day of that month the LORD's
Feast of Unleavened Bread begins; for seven days
you must eat bread made without yeast. 7On the
first day hold a sacred assembly[u] and do no regular work. 8For seven days present an offering
made to the LORD by fire. And on the seventh day
hold a sacred assembly and do no regular work.' "

Firstfruits

9The LORD said to Moses, 10"Speak to the Israelites and say to them: 'When you enter the land I
am going to give you and you reap its harvest,
bring to the priest a sheaf[v] of the first grain you harvest. 11He is to wave the sheaf before the LORD[w] so
it will be accepted on your behalf; the priest is to
wave it on the day after the Sabbath. 12On the day
you wave the sheaf, you must sacrifice as a burnt
offering to the LORD a lamb a year old without
defect, 13together with its grain offering[x] of two-
tenths of an ephah[a] of fine flour mixed with oil—an
offering made to the LORD by fire, a pleasing aroma—and its drink offering of a quarter of a hin[b] of
wine. 14You must not eat any bread, or roasted or
new grain, until the very day you bring this offering to your God.[y] This is to be a lasting ordinance
for the generations to come,[z] wherever you live.

Feast of Weeks

15" 'From the day after the Sabbath, the day you
brought the sheaf of the wave offering, count off
seven full weeks. 16Count off fifty days up to the
day after the seventh Sabbath,[a] and then present
an offering of new grain to the LORD. 17From wherever you live, bring two loaves made of two-tenths
of an ephah of fine flour, baked with yeast, as a
wave offering of firstfruits[b] to the LORD. 18Present
with this bread seven male lambs, each a year old
and without defect, one young bull and two rams.

[a] *13* That is, probably about 4 quarts (about 4.5 liters); also in verse 17 [b] *13* That is, probably about 1 quart (about 1 liter)

22:33 [o]Lev 11:45
23:2 [p]ver 4,37, 44; Nu 29:39 [q]ver 21,27
23:3 [r]Ex 20:9 [s]Ex 20:10; 31:13-17; Lev 19:3; Dt 5:13; Heb 4:9,10
23:5 [t]Ex 12:18-19; Nu 28:16-17; Dt 16:1-8
23:7 [u]ver 3,8
23:10 [v]Ex 23:16, 19; 34:26
23:11 [w]Ex 29:24
23:13 [x]Lev 2:14-16; 6:20
23:14 [y]Ex 34:26 [z]Nu 15:21
23:16 [a]Nu 28:26; Ac 2:1
23:17 [b]Ex 34:22; Lev 2:12

Passover Celebrations

LEV 23:4-8

The great Jewish Feast of the Passover serves as a commemoration of the Israelites' flight from Egypt. Passover begins on the 14th day of the first month of the Hebrew calendar (our March/April) with a ceremonial dinner. At this meal, the story of the exodus is read and symbolic foods are eaten in remembrance of the Israelites' captivity and journey. Throughout the seven days of Passover, only unleavened bread (bread without yeast) is eaten. This reflects the haste with which the Israelites left Egypt, with no time to add yeast to their bread.

The Feast of the Passover is one of the three feasts that all ceremonially clean Hebrew men, normally accompanied by their families, are required to attend. The other two are the Feast of Weeks (Lev 23:15-22) and the Feast of Tabernacles (Lev 23:33-43).

They will be a burnt offering to the LORD, together with their grain offerings and drink offerings—
an offering made by fire, an aroma pleasing to the
LORD. 19Then sacrifice one male goat for a sin
offering and two lambs, each a year old, for a fellowship offering.[a] 20The priest is to wave the two
lambs before the LORD as a wave offering, together with the bread of the firstfruits. They are a
sacred offering to the LORD for the priest. 21On that
same day you are to proclaim a sacred assembly[c]
and do no regular work.[d] This is to be a lasting
ordinance for the generations to come, wherever
you live.

22" 'When you reap the harvest[e] of your land,
do not reap to the very edges of your field or gather the gleanings of your harvest.[f] Leave them for
the poor and the alien. I am the LORD your God.' "

Feast of Trumpets

23The LORD said to Moses, 24"Say to the Israelites: 'On the first day of the seventh month you
are to have a day of rest, a sacred assembly commemorated with trumpet blasts.[g] 25Do no regular
work,[h] but present an offering made to the LORD
by fire.' "

Day of Atonement

26The LORD said to Moses, 27"The tenth day of
this seventh month[i] is the Day of Atonement.[j]
Hold a sacred assembly[k] and deny yourselves,[b]
and present an offering made to the LORD by fire.
28Do no work on that day, because it is the Day of
Atonement, when atonement is made for you
before the LORD your God. 29Anyone who does not
deny himself on that day must be cut off from his
people.[l] 30I will destroy from among his people[m]
anyone who does any work on that day. 31You
shall do no work at all. This is to be a lasting ordinance for the generations to come, wherever you
live. 32It is a sabbath of rest for you, and you must
deny yourselves. From the evening of the ninth
day of the month until the following evening you
are to observe your sabbath."

Feast of Tabernacles

33The LORD said to Moses, 34"Say to the Israelites: 'On the fifteenth day of the seventh month
the LORD's Feast of Tabernacles[n] begins, and it
lasts for seven days. 35The first day is a sacred
assembly; do no regular work. 36For seven days
present offerings made to the LORD by fire, and on
the eighth day hold a sacred assembly[o] and present an offering made to the LORD by fire. It is the
closing assembly; do no regular work.

37(" 'These are the LORD's appointed feasts,
which you are to proclaim as sacred assemblies
for bringing offerings made to the LORD by fire—
the burnt offerings and grain offerings, sacrifices

23:21 [c]ver 2 [d]ver 3
23:22 [e]Lev 19:9 [f]Lev 19:10; Dt 24:19-21; Ru 2:15
23:24 [g]Lev 25:9; Nu 10:9, 10; 29:1
23:25 [h]ver 21
23:27 [i]Lev 16:29 [j]Ex 30:10 [k]Nu 29:7
23:29 [l]Ge 17:14; Nu 5:2
23:30 [m]Lev 20:3
23:34 [n]Ex 23:16; Dt 16:13; Ezr 3:4; Ne 8:14; Zec 14:16; Jn 7:2
23:36 [o]2Ch 7:9; Ne 8:18; Jn 7:37

My soul is like a *mirror in which the glory of God is reflected, but sin, however insignificant, covers the mirror with smoke.*

—Teresa of Avila (1515-1582)

[a] *19* Traditionally *peace offering* [b] *27* Or *and fast*; also in verses 29 and 32

23:37 [p]ver 2,4 and drink offerings[p] required for each day. [38]These
offerings are in addition to those for the LORD's
23:38 Sabbaths[q] and[a] in addition to your gifts and what-
[q]Eze 45:17 ever you have vowed and all the freewill offerings
you give to the LORD.)
[39]" 'So beginning with the fifteenth day of the
seventh month, after you have gathered the crops
of the land, celebrate the festival to the LORD for
23:39 [r]Ex 23:16; seven days;[r] the first day is a day of rest, and the
Dt 16:13 eighth day also is a day of rest. [40]On the first day
you are to take choice fruit from the trees, and
23:40 [s]Ne 8:14-17 palm fronds, leafy branches and poplars,[s] and
rejoice before the LORD your God for seven days.
[41]Celebrate this as a festival to the LORD for seven
days each year. This is to be a lasting ordinance
for the generations to come; celebrate it in the
23:42 [t]Ne 8:14-16 seventh month. [42]Live in booths[t] for seven days:
All native-born Israelites are to live in booths [43]so
23:43 [u]Dt 31:13; your descendants will know[u] that I had the Isra-
Ps 78:5 elites live in booths when I brought them out of
Egypt. I am the LORD your God.' "
[44]So Moses announced to the Israelites the
appointed feasts of the LORD.

Oil and Bread Set Before the LORD

24 The LORD said to Moses, [2]"Command the
Israelites to bring you clear oil of pressed
olives for the light so that the lamps may be kept
burning continually. [3]Outside the curtain of the
Testimony in the Tent of Meeting, Aaron is to tend
the lamps before the LORD from evening till morning, continually. This is to be a lasting ordinance
for the generations to come. [4]The lamps on the
24:4 [v]Ex 25:31; pure gold lampstand[v] before the LORD must be
31:8 tended continually.
24:5 [5]"Take fine flour and bake twelve loaves of
[w]Ex 25:30 bread,[w] using two-tenths of an ephah[b] for each
24:6 loaf. [6]Set them in two rows, six in each row, on
[x]Ex 25:23- the table of pure gold[x] before the LORD. [7]Along
30; 1Ki 7:48 each row put some pure incense as a memorial
24:7 portion[y] to represent the bread and to be an offer-
[y]Lev 2:2 ing made to the LORD by fire. [8]This bread is to be
24:8 set out before the LORD regularly,[z] Sabbath after
[z]Nu 4:7; Sabbath,[a] on behalf of the Israelites, as a lasting
1Ch 9:32; covenant. [9]It belongs to Aaron and his sons,[b] who
2Ch 2:4 [a]Mt 12:5 are to eat it in a holy place, because it is a most
holy part of their regular share of the offerings
24:9 [b]Lev 8:31; Mt 12:4; Mk 2:26; Lk 6:4 made to the LORD by fire."

A Blasphemer Stoned

[10]Now the son of an Israelite mother and an
Egyptian father went out among the Israelites,
and a fight broke out in the camp between him
and an Israelite. [11]The son of the Israelite woman
24:11 [c]Ex 3:15 blasphemed the Name[c] with a curse; so they
brought him to Moses. (His mother's name was
Shelomith, the daughter of Dibri the Danite.)

a 38 Or *These feasts are in addition to the LORD's Sabbaths, and these offerings are* *b* 5 That is, probably about 4 quarts (about 4.5 liters)

Blasphemy

LEV 24:10-16,23

To blaspheme is not simply to spout off in anger; it is to challenge the honor and authority of God. Laws against blasphemy are designed to protect the sacred. Anyone who devalues sacred places or improperly uses the sacred name of God is guilty of this offense. Left unchallenged, the sin of blasphemy has the potential to chip away at the foundation of Israelite society, which is built on a faith in, and a reverence for, the Lord their God. Severe punishment for one who commits blasphemy, though it may appear unnecessarily harsh to us, is not only well deserved, it is necessary for the protection of God's people.

Eye for Eye

LEV 24:17-22

The laws of retaliation provide reasonable limitations to the punishments that can be exacted for certain crimes. These rules ensure that serious crimes will reap serious penalties. They also provide realistic restrictions that will, for example, prevent an aggrieved individual from demanding the death penalty for an enemy who has broken his arm in a fight.

Religious and civil law are one and the same thing in Israelite society. When Jesus revokes the eye-for-an-eye principle (Mt 5:38–42), he is not revoking civil laws of retribution but a tendency of the people to exact extreme forms of personal revenge instead of responding in love. We must never forget Jesus Christ's command to forgive, which transcends the exacting measure of the law.

12They put him in custody until the will of the
LORD should be made clear to them.[d]
13Then the LORD said to Moses: 14"Take the blasphemer outside the camp. All those who heard
him are to lay their hands on his head, and the
entire assembly is to stone him.[e] 15Say to the Israelites: 'If anyone curses his God,[f] he will be held
responsible; 16anyone who blasphemes the name
of the LORD must be put to death.[g] The entire
assembly must stone him. Whether an alien or
native-born, when he blasphemes the Name, he
must be put to death.
17" 'If anyone takes the life of a human being,
he must be put to death.[h] 18Anyone who takes the
life of someone's animal must make restitution[i]—
life for life. 19If anyone injures his neighbor, whatever he has done must be done to him: 20fracture
for fracture, eye for eye, tooth for tooth.[j] As he has
injured the other, so he is to be injured. 21Whoev-
er kills an animal must make restitution, but whoever kills a man must be put to death.[k] 22You are
to have the same law for the alien[l] and the native-
born.[m] I am the LORD your God.' "
23Then Moses spoke to the Israelites, and they
took the blasphemer outside the camp and stoned
him. The Israelites did as the LORD commanded
Moses.

The Sabbath Year

25 The LORD said to Moses on Mount Sinai,
2"Speak to the Israelites and say to them:
'When you enter the land I am going to give you,
the land itself must observe a sabbath to the LORD.
3For six years sow your fields, and for six years
prune your vineyards and gather their crops.[n] 4But
in the seventh year the land is to have a sabbath of
rest, a sabbath to the LORD. Do not sow your fields
or prune your vineyards. 5Do not reap what grows
of itself or harvest the grapes of your untended
vines. The land is to have a year of rest. 6Whatev-
er the land yields during the sabbath year[o] will be
food for you—for yourself, your manservant and
maidservant, and the hired worker and temporary
resident who live among you, 7as well as for your
livestock and the wild animals in your land.
Whatever the land produces may be eaten.

The Year of Jubilee

8" 'Count off seven sabbaths of years—seven
times seven years—so that the seven sabbaths of
years amount to a period of forty-nine years.
9Then have the trumpet[p] sounded everywhere on
the tenth day of the seventh month; on the Day of
Atonement sound the trumpet throughout your
land. 10Consecrate the fiftieth year and proclaim
liberty[q] throughout the land to all its inhabitants.
It shall be a jubilee[r] for you; each one of you is to
return to his family property and each to his own
clan. 11The fiftieth year shall be a jubilee for you;
do not sow and do not reap what grows of itself or

24:12 [d]Ex 18:16; Nu 15:34
24:14 [e]Lev 20:27; Dt 13:9; 17:5,7; 21:21
24:15 [f]Ex 22:28
24:16 [g]1Ki 21:10, 13; Mt 26:66
24:17 [h]Ge 9:6; Ex 21:12; Nu 35:30-31; Dt 27:24
24:18 [i]ver 21
24:20 [j]Ex 21:24; Mt 5:38*
24:21 [k]ver 17
24:22 [l]Ex 12:49 [m]Nu 9:14; 15:16
25:3 [n]Ex 23:10
25:6 [o]ver 20
25:9 [p]Lev 23:24
25:10 [q]Isa 61:1; Jer 34:8,15, 17; Lk 4:19 [r]Nu 36:4

harvest the untended vines. 12For it is a jubilee
and is to be holy for you; eat only what is taken
directly from the fields.
13" 'In this Year of Jubilee[s] everyone is to return
to his own property.
14" 'If you sell land to one of your countrymen
or buy any from him, do not take advantage of
each other.[t] 15You are to buy from your countryman on the basis of the number of years[u] since
the Jubilee. And he is to sell to you on the basis of
the number of years left for harvesting crops.
16When the years are many, you are to increase
the price, and when the years are few, you are to
decrease the price,[v] because what he is really selling you is the number of crops. 17Do not take
advantage of each other,[w] but fear your God.[x] I am
the LORD your God.[y]
18" 'Follow my decrees and be careful to obey
my laws, and you will live safely in the land.[z]
19Then the land will yield its fruit,[a] and you will
eat your fill and live there in safety. 20You may
ask, "What will we eat in the seventh year[b] if we
do not plant or harvest our crops?" 21I will send
you such a blessing[c] in the sixth year that the land
will yield enough for three years. 22While you
plant during the eighth year, you will eat from the
old crop and will continue to eat from it until the
harvest of the ninth year comes in.[d]
23" 'The land must not be sold permanently,
because the land is mine[e] and you are but aliens[f]
and my tenants. 24Throughout the country that
you hold as a possession, you must provide for
the redemption of the land.
25" 'If one of your countrymen becomes poor
and sells some of his property, his nearest relative[g] is to come and redeem[h] what his countryman has sold. 26If, however, a man has no one to
redeem it for him but he himself prospers and
acquires sufficient means to redeem it, 27he is to
determine the value for the years since he sold it
and refund the balance to the man to whom he
sold it; he can then go back to his own property.
28But if he does not acquire the means to repay
him, what he sold will remain in the possession of
the buyer until the Year of Jubilee. It will be
returned in the Jubilee, and he can then go back
to his property.[i]
29" 'If a man sells a house in a walled city, he
retains the right of redemption a full year after its
sale. During that time he may redeem it. 30If it is
not redeemed before a full year has passed, the
house in the walled city shall belong permanently to the buyer and his descendants. It is not to be
returned in the Jubilee. 31But houses in villages
without walls around them are to be considered
as open country. They can be redeemed, and they
are to be returned in the Jubilee.
32" 'The Levites always have the right to redeem
their houses in the Levitical towns,[j] which they
possess. 33So the property of the Levites is
redeemable—that is, a house sold in any town

25:13 [s]ver 10
25:14 [t]Lev 19:13; 1Sa 12:3,4
25:15 [u]Lev 27:18, 23
25:16 [v]ver 27,51, 52
25:17 [w]Pr 22:22; Jer 7:5,6; 1Th 4:6 [x]Lev 19:14 [y]Lev 19:32
25:18 [z]Lev 26:4,5; Dt 12:10; Ps 4:8; Jer 23:6
25:19 [a]Lev 26:4
25:20 [b]ver 4
25:21 [c]Dt 28:8,12; Hag 2:19; Mal 3:10
25:22 [d]Lev 26:10
25:23 [e]Ex 19:5 [f]Ge 23:4; 1Ch 29:15; Ps 39:12; Heb 11:13; 1Pe 2:11
25:25 [g]Ru 2:20; Jer 32:7 [h]Lev 27:13, 19,31; Ru 4:4
25:28 [i]ver 10
25:32 [j]Nu 35:1-8; Jos 21:2

Year of Jubilee

LEV 25:8–55

What a wonderful concept! A Year of Jubilee! *Slaves are freed, debts are cancelled, fields lie fallow, and everyone returns to their home property. God ordains that in Israel every 50th year be a Year of Jubilee. These rules are designed to keep the people from taking advantage of one another and to keep the rich from accumulating more while the poor get less and less.*

There is evidence, however, that the Israelites did not celebrate the Jubilee in its entirety. The writer of Chronicles says that the land will finally get its "sabbath rests" (2Ch 36:21) during the exile, implying that the Hebrews had not been following at least this particular aspect of the Year of Jubilee. The prophet Jeremiah chastises Judah for not freeing Hebrew slaves in accordance with the laws of Jubilee and cites this as a reason for the coming destruction and exile (Jer 34:8–22).

Redeemed

LEV 25:47–55

To be redeemed is to be freed through the payment of a required price. In the Old Testament, redemption occurs when an individual who has sold himself or herself into indentured service is freed through monetary payment to the owner. The price to be paid is determined by the number of years until Jubilee—more years equals a larger payment, fewer years equals a smaller payment. During the Year of Jubilee, regardless of any debt still owed, the slave goes free.

In the New Testament, redemption refers to the salvation of humankind. Believers have been redeemed through the payment of Jesus' shed blood on the cross (Ro 3:22–25).

they hold—and is to be returned in the Jubilee,
because the houses in the towns of the Levites are
their property among the Israelites. 34 But the pastureland belonging to their towns must not be
sold; it is their permanent possession.[k]
35 " 'If one of your countrymen becomes poor[l]
and is unable to support himself among you, help
him[m] as you would an alien or a temporary resident, so he can continue to live among you. 36 Do
not take interest[n] of any kind[a] from him, but fear
your God, so that your countryman may continue
to live among you. 37 You must not lend him money at interest or sell him food at a profit. 38 I am the
LORD your God, who brought you out of Egypt to
give you the land of Canaan and to be your God.[o]
39 " 'If one of your countrymen becomes poor
among you and sells himself to you, do not make
him work as a slave.[p] 40 He is to be treated as a
hired worker or a temporary resident among you;
he is to work for you until the Year of Jubilee.
41 Then he and his children are to be released, and
he will go back to his own clan and to the property[q] of his forefathers. 42 Because the Israelites are
my servants, whom I brought out of Egypt, they
must not be sold as slaves. 43 Do not rule over
them ruthlessly,[r] but fear your God.
44 " 'Your male and female slaves are to come
from the nations around you; from them you may
buy slaves. 45 You may also buy some of the temporary residents living among you and members
of their clans born in your country, and they will
become your property. 46 You can will them to
your children as inherited property and can make
them slaves for life, but you must not rule over
your fellow Israelites ruthlessly.
47 " 'If an alien or a temporary resident among
you becomes rich and one of your countrymen
becomes poor and sells himself to the alien living
among you or to a member of the alien's clan,
48 he retains the right of redemption after he has
sold himself. One of his relatives[s] may redeem
him: 49 An uncle or a cousin or any blood relative
in his clan may redeem him. Or if he prospers,[t] he
may redeem himself. 50 He and his buyer are to
count the time from the year he sold himself up to
the Year of Jubilee. The price for his release is to
be based on the rate paid to a hired man[u] for that
number of years. 51 If many years remain, he must
pay for his redemption a larger share of the price
paid for him. 52 If only a few years remain until the
Year of Jubilee, he is to compute that and pay for
his redemption accordingly. 53 He is to be treated
as a man hired from year to year; you must see to
it that his owner does not rule over him
ruthlessly.
54 " 'Even if he is not redeemed in any of these
ways, he and his children are to be released in the
Year of Jubilee, 55 for the Israelites belong to me as

25:34 [k]Nu 35:2-5
25:35 [l]Dt 24:14,15 [m]Dt 15:8; Ps 37:21,26; Lk 6:35
25:36 [n]Ex 22:25; Dt 23:19-20
25:38 [o]Ge 17:7; Lev 11:45
25:39 [p]Ex 21:2; Dt 15:12; 1Ki 9:22
25:41 [q]ver 28
25:43 [r]Ex 1:13; Eze 34:4; Col 4:1
25:48 [s]Ne 5:5
25:49 [t]ver 26
25:50 [u]Job 7:1; Isa 16:14; 21:16

[a] 36 Or *take excessive interest*; similarly in verse 37

servants. They are my servants, whom I brought
out of Egypt. I am the LORD your God.

Reward for Obedience

26 “ ‘Do not make idols[v] or set up an image or
a sacred stone[w] for yourselves, and do not
place a carved stone[x] in your land to bow down
before it. I am the LORD your God.
2“ ‘Observe my Sabbaths and have reverence for
my sanctuary.[y] I am the LORD.
3“ ‘If you follow my decrees and are careful to
obey[z] my commands, 4I will send you rain[a] in its
season, and the ground will yield its crops and the
trees of the field their fruit.[b] 5Your threshing will
continue until grape harvest and the grape harvest
will continue until planting, and you will eat all
the food you want[c] and live in safety in your land.[d]
6“ ‘I will grant peace in the land,[e] and you will lie
down[f] and no one will make you afraid.[g] I will
remove savage beasts[h] from the land, and the sword
will not pass through your country. 7You will pursue your enemies, and they will fall by the sword
before you. 8Five of you will chase a hundred, and
a hundred of you will chase ten thousand, and your
enemies will fall by the sword before you.[i]
9“ ‘I will look on you with favor and make you
fruitful and increase your numbers,[j] and I will
keep my covenant[k] with you. 10You will still be
eating last year’s harvest when you will have to
move it out to make room for the new.[l] 11I will put
my dwelling place[a][m] among you, and I will not
abhor you. 12I will walk[n] among you and be your
God, and you will be my people.[o] 13I am the LORD
your God, who brought you out of Egypt so that
you would no longer be slaves to the Egyptians; I
broke the bars of your yoke[p] and enabled you to
walk with heads held high.

Punishment for Disobedience

14“ ‘But if you will not listen to me and carry
out all these commands,[q] 15and if you reject my
decrees and abhor my laws and fail to carry out
all my commands and so violate my covenant,
16then I will do this to you: I will bring upon you
sudden terror, wasting diseases and fever[r] that
will destroy your sight and drain away your life.[s]
You will plant seed in vain, because your enemies
will eat it.[t] 17I will set my face[u] against you so that
you will be defeated by your enemies; those who
hate you will rule over you,[v] and you will flee
even when no one is pursuing you.[w]
18“ ‘If after all this you will not listen to me, I will
punish you for your sins seven times over.[x] 19I will
break down your stubborn pride[y] and make the
sky above you like iron and the ground beneath
you like bronze.[z] 20Your strength will be spent in
vain,[a] because your soil will not yield its crops, nor
will the trees of the land yield their fruit.[b]
21“ ‘If you remain hostile toward me and refuse

[a] 11 Or *my tabernacle*

26:1 [v]Ex 20:4; Lev 19:4; Dt 5:8 [w]Ex 23:24 [x]Nu 33:52
26:2 [y]Lev 19:30
26:3 [z]Dt 7:12; 11:13,22; 28:1,9
26:4 [a]Dt 11:14 [b]Ps 67:6
26:5 [c]Dt 11:15; Joel 2:19,26; Am 9:13 [d]Lev 25:18
26:6 [e]Ps 29:11; 85:8; 147:14 [f]Ps 4:8 [g]Zep 3:13 [h]ver 22
26:8 [i]Dt 32:30; Jos 23:10
26:9 [j]Ge 17:6; Ne 9:23 [k]Ge 17:7
26:10 [l]Lev 25:22
26:11 [m]Ex 25:8; Ps 76:2; Eze 37:27
26:12 [n]Ge 3:8 [o]2Co 6:16*
26:13 [p]Eze 34:27
26:14 [q]Dt 28:15-68; Mal 2:2
26:16 [r]Dt 28:22,35 [s]1Sa 2:33 [t]Job 31:8
26:17 [u]Lev 17:10 [v]Ps 106:41 [w]ver 36,37; Dt 28:7,25; Ps 53:5
26:18 [x]ver 21
26:19 [y]Isa 25:11 [z]Dt 28:23
26:20 [a]Ps 127:1; Isa 17:11 [b]Dt 11:17

Rewards and Punishments

LEV 26

God promises the people of Israel immediate, tangible rewards for their compliance with the law, affirming his pleasure in their obedience. However, the opposite is also true. God is offended by disobedience, and he manifests his displeasure by bringing terror, disease, hunger and defeat on those who disregard his laws.

In the New Testament, God’s attitudes toward obedience and disobedience are the same, but he apparently takes a different approach to meting out rewards and punishments. Neither blessings nor trials should be taken as signs of his pleasure or displeasure, for “he causes his sun to rise on the evil and the good, and sends rain on the righteous and the unrighteous” alike (Mt 5:45). Instead, God emphasizes the eternal, heavenly rewards that await the faithful (Mt 5:12; Lk 6:23).

to listen to me, I will multiply your afflictions sev-
en times over,[c] as your sins deserve. 22 I will send
wild animals[d] against you, and they will rob you
of your children, destroy your cattle and make you
so few in number that your roads will be deserted.
23 " 'If in spite of these things you do not accept
my correction[e] but continue to be hostile toward
me, 24 I myself will be hostile toward you and will
afflict you for your sins seven times over. 25 And I
will bring the sword upon you to avenge the
breaking of the covenant. When you withdraw
into your cities, I will send a plague[f] among you,
and you will be given into enemy hands. 26 When
I cut off your supply of bread,[g] ten women will be
able to bake your bread in one oven, and they will
dole out the bread by weight. You will eat, but you
will not be satisfied.
27 " 'If in spite of this you still do not listen to
me but continue to be hostile toward me, 28 then in
my anger I will be hostile toward you, and I
myself will punish you for your sins seven times
over. 29 You will eat the flesh of your sons and the
flesh of your daughters.[h] 30 I will destroy your high
places,[i] cut down your incense altars[j] and pile
your dead bodies on the lifeless forms of your
idols,[k] and I will abhor you. 31 I will turn your cities into ruins and lay waste your sanctuaries,[l] and
I will take no delight in the pleasing aroma of
your offerings. 32 I will lay waste the land,[m] so that
your enemies who live there will be appalled. 33 I
will scatter you among the nations[n] and will draw
out my sword and pursue you. Your land will be
laid waste, and your cities will lie in ruins. 34 Then
the land will enjoy its sabbath years all the time
that it lies desolate and you are in the country of
your enemies;[o] then the land will rest and enjoy
its sabbaths. 35 All the time that it lies desolate, the
land will have the rest it did not have during the
sabbaths you lived in it.
36 " 'As for those of you who are left, I will make
their hearts so fearful in the lands of their enemies
that the sound of a windblown leaf will put them
to flight.[p] They will run as though fleeing from
the sword, and they will fall, even though no one
is pursuing them. 37 They will stumble over one
another as though fleeing from the sword, even
though no one is pursuing them. So you will not
be able to stand before your enemies.[q] 38 You will
perish among the nations; the land of your enemies will devour you.[r] 39 Those of you who are left
will waste away in the lands of their enemies
because of their sins; also because of their fathers'
sins they will waste away.[s]
40 " 'But if they will confess their sins and the sins
of their fathers[t]—their treachery against me and
their hostility toward me, 41 which made me hostile
toward them so that I sent them into the land of
their enemies—then when their uncircumcised
hearts[u] are humbled and they pay for their sin, 42 I
will remember my covenant with Jacob[v] and my
covenant with Isaac[w] and my covenant with Abra-

26:21 [c]ver 18
26:22 [d]Dt 32:24
26:23 [e]Jer 2:30; 5:3
26:25 [f]Nu 14:12; Eze 5:17
26:26 [g]Ps 105:16; Isa 3:1; Mic 6:14
26:29 [h]Dt 28:53
26:30 [i]2Ch 34:3; Eze 6:3 [j]Eze 6:6 [k]Eze 6:13
26:31 [l]Ps 74:3-7
26:32 [m]Jer 9:11
26:33 [n]Dt 4:27; Eze 12:15; 20:23; Zec 7:14
26:34 [o]ver 43; 2Ch 36:21
26:36 [p]Eze 21:7
26:37 [q]Jos 7:12
26:38 [r]Dt 4:26
26:39 [s]Eze 4:17
26:40 [t]Jer 3:12-15; Lk 15:18; 1Jn 1:9
26:41 [u]Eze 44:7,9; Ac 7:51
26:42 [v]Ge 22:15-18; 28:15 [w]Ge 26:5

This world is not conclusion;
A sequel stands beyond,
Invisible, as music,
But positive, as sound.
It beckons and it baffles;
Philosophies don't know,
And through a riddle, at the last,
Sagacity must go.
To guess it puzzles scholars;
To gain it, men have shown
Contempt of generations,
And crucifixion known.

—Emily Dickinson (1830-1886)

Not Getting What You Want Most

Jacob thought he had a deal. Seven years working for Laban would make Rachel his wife. Other young men had to rely on their parents to arrange suitable marriages, but Jacob got to choose for himself—or so he thought.

Even if the deal was not straightforward, God honored it. Leah was Jacob's wife. But Leah got cheated at least as much as Jacob did. Jacob wanted what he wanted. He didn't rest until he got it. Jacob wanted Rachel, so he never gave Leah a chance to win his heart. But—to his credit—neither did he cast her aside.

The text says that "when the LORD saw that Leah was not loved, he opened her womb"—he gave her children in some way of compensation. Leah longed for Jacob's love. She hoped that having sons would turn his heart toward her. At least, they probably caused him to spend more time with her. Leah was blessed with fruitfulness, and she rejoiced and thanked God for each child. And although Jacob favored Rachel, God ordained that the priestly and the Messianic lines came through Leah's sons Levi and Judah. It is curious to note that Rachel, who had captured the devotion that Leah so desired, was as jealous of Leah as Leah was of her! Neither woman had all that she wanted.

Perhaps Jacob eventually recognized Leah's worth, her strong relationship with God and the respect due her as his wife, because just before he died in Egypt, he instructed his sons: "Bury me with my fathers in the cave in the field of Ephron the Hittite . . . There Abraham and his wife Sarah were buried, there Isaac and his wife Rebekah were buried, and there I buried Leah" (Ge 49:29-31).

Many of us don't get the one thing we want most in our personal lives. Some of us dream of a husband's love and don't have it, some desire children and don't have them. One of the greatest challenges in life is to accept the compensations God gives and, through Christ, live in faith and without envy, even when we don't get what we desire most deeply.

Leah
(possibly *wild cow*, or *gazelle*)

Genesis 29—30; 49:31

Ruth 4:11

Candid SNAPSHOT Then Leah said, "God has presented me with a precious gift. This time my husband will treat me with honor, because I have borne him six sons" (Genesis 30:19-20).

Rachel

A Bitter Reality

Rachel could hardly believe it! The good-looking stranger who was at the well when she arrived to water the sheep was her cousin! All her life she had heard the story of how her father's sister had gone away with a servant she'd met at this very spot, to marry a wealthy relative she'd never met. And now this stranger arrived, their son. Could he be the one God had for her? She went to sleep that night and dreamt about marrying the rich young stranger and having a dozen handsome sons.

But Rachel hit the wall of reality years later when she realized that Leah had children and she did not. Rachel fixed on one goal: to have children, no matter what it took. So began the obsession and the destructive rivalry with her sister that deprived them both of satisfaction and contentment.

Rachel's relationship with the Lord appears tenuous at best. She stole her father's idols when she left home, apparently still affected by gods (false as they were) she could see and touch. She bargained with Leah for some mandrake—a plant superstitiously believed by some to aid conception. And rather than crying out to God for the children she so desired, she blamed Jacob for not delivering (Ge 30:1-2)!

We must not be too hard on Rachel. After all, in her time a woman's chief duty, purpose, and worth were defined by childbearing. Still, we see in her a woman who is never able to rise above her own self-interest to find the joy of loving others. Instead, her need to be affirmed consumed her. The Lord was speaking to Rachel through her barrenness. It isn't clear if she eventually turned wholeheartedly to God, but the text does say, "God remembered Rachel; he listened to her and opened her womb" (Ge 30:22). Perhaps for those six or seven years after Joseph's birth and before she died in childbirth with Benjamin, Rachel was fulfilled.

When we don't get what we deeply desire, it's easy to look only at what we don't have and ignore the good things we do have. Only Jesus Christ can help us rise above our needs and desires to find joy and purpose in loving others.

Rachel
(ewe or lamb)

Genesis 29–31; 33:1-2, 7; 35:16-26; 48:7

Ruth 4:11

Jeremiah 31:15

Matthew 2:18

Candid SNAPSHOT When Rachel saw that she was not bearing Jacob any children, she became jealous of her sister. So she said to Jacob, "Give me children, or I'll die!" (Genesis 30:1).

ham, and I will remember the land. 43 For the land
will be deserted by them and will enjoy its sabbaths while it lies desolate without them. They will
pay for their sins because they rejected my laws
and abhorred my decrees. 44 Yet in spite of this,
26:44 when they are in the land of their enemies, I will
[x]Ro 11:2 not reject them or abhor[x] them so as to destroy
[y]Dt 4:31; Jer 30:11 them completely,[y] breaking my covenant[z] with
[z]Jer 33:26 them. I am the LORD their God. 45 But for their sake
26:45 I will remember[a] the covenant with their ancestors
[a]Ge 17:7 whom I brought out of Egypt[b] in the sight of the
[b]Ex 6:8; Lev 25:38 nations to be their God. I am the LORD.' "
46 These are the decrees, the laws and the regu-
26:46 lations that the LORD established on Mount Sinai
[c]Lev 7:38; 27:34 between himself and the Israelites through Moses.[c]

Redeeming What Is the LORD's

27 The LORD said to Moses, 2 "Speak to the Israelites and say to them: 'If anyone makes a
27:2 special vow[d] to dedicate persons to the LORD by
[d]Nu 6:2 giving equivalent values, 3 set the value of a male
27:3 between the ages of twenty and sixty at fifty
[e]Ex 30:13; Nu 3:47; 18:16 shekels[a] of silver, according to the sanctuary
shekel[b];[e] 4 and if it is a female, set her value at thirty shekels.[c] 5 If it is a person between the ages of
five and twenty, set the value of a male at twenty
shekels[d] and of a female at ten shekels.[e] 6 If it is a
person between one month and five years, set the
27:6 value of a male at five shekels[f][f] of silver and that
[f]Nu 18:16 of a female at three shekels[g] of silver. 7 If it is a person sixty years old or more, set the value of a male
at fifteen shekels[h] and of a female at ten shekels.
27:8 8 If anyone making the vow is too poor to pay[g] the
[g]Lev 5:11 specified amount, he is to present the person to
[h]ver 12,14 the priest, who will set the value[h] for him according to what the man making the vow can afford.
9 " 'If what he vowed is an animal that is acceptable as an offering to the LORD, such an animal giv-
en to the LORD becomes holy. 10 He must not
exchange it or substitute a good one for a bad one,
27:10 or a bad one for a good one;[i] if he should substi-
[i]ver 33 tute one animal for another, both it and the substitute become holy. 11 If what he vowed is a ceremonially unclean animal—one that is not acceptable
as an offering to the LORD—the animal must be presented to the priest, 12 who will judge its quality as
good or bad. Whatever value the priest then sets,
27:13 that is what it will be. 13 If the owner wishes to
[j]ver 15,19; Lev 25:25 redeem[j] the animal, he must add a fifth to its value.
14 " 'If a man dedicates his house as something
holy to the LORD, the priest will judge its quality
as good or bad. Whatever value the priest then
sets, so it will remain. 15 If the man who dedicates

[a] 3 That is, about 1 1/4 pounds (about 0.6 kilogram); also in verse 16 [b] 3 That is, about 2/5 ounce (about 11.5 grams); also in verse 25 [c] 4 That is, about 12 ounces (about 0.3 kilogram) [d] 5 That is, about 8 ounces (about 0.2 kilogram) [e] 5 That is, about 4 ounces (about 110 grams); also in verse 7 [f] 6 That is, about 2 ounces (about 55 grams) [g] 6 That is, about 1 1/4 ounces (about 35 grams) [h] 7 That is, about 6 ounces (about 170 grams)

Not an Indication of Value

LEV 27:3

In Western culture, women have long fought to dispel the view that men are in some way more valuable than women. For this reason, some women respond negatively to this passage. Yet, a careful review of the facts reveals that the monetary amounts cited are not an indication of value but are, rather, related to the capacity of work women and men were expected to give at the temple.

In Israel's earlier days, people who were dedicated to the Lord remained in the service of the priests. At the time this was written, these dedications were covered instead by a monetary payment. That payment compensated the priests for the labor they would have received. For this reason, the amount paid for a man in his prime was greater than that paid for a woman of equal age; the amount for the elderly was less than that paid for the young. These amounts were a matter of practicality and had nothing to do with the intrinsic value of human beings of either gender.

Devoted

LEV 27:28

To "dedicate" something to the Lord is a voluntary act and can, therefore, later be redeemed. "Devoting" a possession to the Lord, however, is a much more serious matter. Any item that is devoted to God can be used only for his service. It cannot be redeemed by a payment of money. It belongs totally and wholly to God.

When, as believers, we use the word devoted to describe our commitment to Jesus Christ, we should not do so lightly. With our devotion comes a total and wholehearted surrender to God, a willingness to be used for his purposes and a desire to deny self and serve only him (Mt 16:24; Gal 2:20).

his house redeems it,[k] he must add a fifth to its
value, and the house will again become his.
16“ ‘If a man dedicates to the LORD part of his
family land, its value is to be set according to the
amount of seed required for it—fifty shekels of silver to a homer[a] of barley seed. 17If he dedicates his
field during the Year of Jubilee, the value that has
been set remains. 18But if he dedicates his field
after the Jubilee, the priest will determine the value according to the number of years that remain[l]
until the next Year of Jubilee, and its set value will
be reduced. 19If the man who dedicates the field
wishes to redeem it, he must add a fifth to its value, and the field will again become his. 20If, however, he does not redeem the field, or if he has sold
it to someone else, it can never be redeemed.
21When the field is released in the Jubilee,[m] it will
become holy, like a field devoted to the LORD;[n] it
will become the property of the priests.[b]
22“ ‘If a man dedicates to the LORD a field he has
bought, which is not part of his family land, 23the
priest will determine its value up to the Year of
Jubilee, and the man must pay its value on that
day as something holy to the LORD. 24In the Year of
Jubilee the field will revert to the person from
whom he bought it,[o] the one whose land it was.
25Every value is to be set according to the sanctuary shekel,[p] twenty gerahs[q] to the shekel.
26“ ‘No one, however, may dedicate the firstborn
of an animal, since the firstborn already belongs
to the LORD;[r] whether an ox[c] or a sheep, it is the
LORD's. 27If it is one of the unclean animals,[s] he
may buy it back at its set value, adding a fifth of
the value to it. If he does not redeem it, it is to be
sold at its set value.
28“ ‘But nothing that a man owns and devotes[d][t]
to the LORD—whether man or animal or family
land—may be sold or redeemed; everything so
devoted is most holy to the LORD.
29“ ‘No person devoted to destruction[e] may be
ransomed; he must be put to death.
30“ ‘A tithe[u] of everything from the land,
whether grain from the soil or fruit from the trees,
belongs to the LORD; it is holy to the LORD. 31If a
man redeems any of his tithe, he must add a fifth
of the value to it. 32The entire tithe of the herd and
flock—every tenth animal that passes under the
shepherd's rod[v]—will be holy to the LORD. 33He
must not pick out the good from the bad or make
any substitution.[w] If he does make a substitution,
both the animal and its substitute become holy
and cannot be redeemed.’ ”

34These are the commands the LORD gave Moses
on Mount Sinai for the Israelites.[x]

27:15 [k]ver 13,20
27:18 [l]Lev 25:15
27:21 [m]Lev 25:10 [n]ver 28; Nu 18:14; Eze 44:29
27:24 [o]Lev 25:28
27:25 [p]Ex 30:13; Nu 18:16 [q]Nu 3:47; Eze 45:12
27:26 [r]Ex 13:2,12
27:27 [s]ver 11
27:28 [t]Nu 18:14; Jos 6:17-19
27:30 [u]Ge 28:22; 2Ch 31:6; Mal 3:8
27:32 [v]Jer 33:13; Eze 20:37
27:33 [w]ver 10
27:34 [x]Lev 26:46; Dt 4:5

[a] *16* That is, probably about 6 bushels (about 220 liters)
[b] *21* Or *priest* [c] *26* The Hebrew word can include both male and female. [d] *28* The Hebrew term refers to the irrevocable giving over of things or persons to the LORD. [e] *29* The Hebrew term refers to the irrevocable giving over of things or persons to the LORD, often by totally destroying them.

Numbers

Wanderings of a faithless generation.

The historical account of Numbers demonstrates God's great mercy and forgiveness for his people despite their repeated rebellion, disobedience and complaining. Time and again the Israelites choose to disobey God rather than to submit to his will. Their lack of faith brings about the death of an entire generation and 40 years of wandering in the Sinai desert.

The book of Numbers introduces some interesting women as it recounts the struggles and growth of the fledgling nation of Israel. Miriam, Moses' sister, joins forces with their brother, Aaron, in a short-lived revolt against Moses' leadership. God's judgment on their insurrection is visible and instantaneous, as Miriam is stricken with leprosy. Yet God also demonstrates his mercy when he forgives their sin, heals Miriam and restores the sister and brother to the community (Nu 12). Zelophehad's daughters take center stage when the Israelites receive their land allocations. In a patriarchal society these brave women discover that they are not second-class citizens in God's economy (Nu 27). Numbers also reminds us that God holds women, as well as men, accountable when it comes to sexual immorality and unfaithfulness in marriage (Nu 5).

Forty years of wandering in the desert provide ample opportunity for God's people to learn to trust him in every circumstance. The Israelites' example in Numbers assures us that God's purposes will not be thwarted. With our eyes focused on God's promises and on his eternal faithfulness, we can face our futures with courage. What God says, he will do.

Quick Study

Author
Generally thought to be Moses.

Date Written
Probably written during the 1400s B.C., at the time of Israel's wandering in the desert.

Setting
Most of Numbers takes place in the desert area between Egypt and Canaan.

Key Passage
Numbers 14:18 "The LORD is slow to anger, abounding in love and forgiving sin and rebellion."

Outline

The first census. Nu 1
Setting up camp. Nu 2
Numbering special groups. Nu 3-4
Camp regulations. Nu 5-6
Dedicating the tabernacle. Nu 7:1—10:10
Leaving Sinai. Nu 10:11-36
The Israelites grumble. Nu 11
Miriam and Aaron rebel. Nu 12
Exploring Canaan. Nu 13:1-25
Conflicting reports. Nu 13:26-33
Rebellion. Nu 14
Offerings. Nu 15:1-31
A stoning. Nu 15:32-36
Tassels on garments. Nu 15:37-41
Rebellion and plague. Nu 16
Aaron's budding staff. Nu 17
Duties of the priests. Nu 18-19
The sin of Moses. Nu 20:1-13
Edom denies Israel passage. Nu 20:14-31
Aaron's death. Nu 20:22-29
Meeting various nations. Nu 21:1—21:35
Balak and Balaam. Nu 22-24
Seduction by Moabite women. Nu 25
The second census. Nu 26
The request of Zelophehad's daughters. Nu 27:1-11
Joshua to succeed Moses. Nu 27:12-23
More regulations. Nu 28-30
Vengeance on the Midianites. Nu 31
The Transjordan tribes. Nu 32
The journey continues. Nu 33
Information on Canaan. Nu 34-35
Inheritance of Zelophehad's daughters. Nu 36

The Women of Numbers

Moses' Cushite wife	*Verbally attacked by her husband's family.* Nu 12:1
Miriam	*Paid a stiff penalty for rebellion.* Nu 12:1-15; 20:1; 26:59 (page 401)
Cozbi	*Killed for her part in Israel's seduction into idolatry and immorality.* Nu 25:6-18
Mahlah, Noah, Hoglah, Milcah, Tirzah	*Zelophehad's daughters.* Nu 26:33; 27:1-11; 36:1-12

Denotes a sketch written about this character

The Census

1 The LORD spoke to Moses in the Tent of Meeting[a] in the Desert of Sinai[b] on the first day of
the second month[c] of the second year after the
Israelites came out of Egypt. He said: 2“Take a census[d] of the whole Israelite community by their
clans and families, listing every man by name,
one by one. 3You and Aaron are to number by
their divisions all the men in Israel twenty years
old or more[e] who are able to serve in the army.
4One man from each tribe, each the head of his
family,[f] is to help you.[g] 5These are the names of
the men who are to assist you:

from Reuben,[h] Elizur son of Shedeur;
6from Simeon, Shelumiel son of Zurishaddai;
7from Judah,[i] Nahshon son of Amminadab;[j]
8from Issachar,[k] Nethanel son of Zuar;
9from Zebulun,[l] Eliab son of Helon;
10from the sons of Joseph:
from Ephraim,[m] Elishama son of Ammihud;
from Manasseh, Gamaliel son of Pedahzur;
11from Benjamin, Abidan son of Gideoni;
12from Dan,[n] Ahiezer son of Ammishaddai;
13from Asher,[o] Pagiel son of Ocran;
14from Gad, Eliasaph son of Deuel;[p]
15from Naphtali,[q] Ahira son of Enan.”

16These were the men appointed from the community, the leaders[r] of their ancestral tribes. They
were the heads of the clans of Israel.[s]
17Moses and Aaron took these men whose
names had been given, 18and they called the
whole community together on the first day of the
second month.[t] The people indicated their ancestry[u] by their clans and families, and the men
twenty years old or more were listed by name, one
by one, 19as the LORD commanded Moses. And so
he counted them in the Desert of Sinai:

20From the descendants of Reuben[v] the firstborn
son of Israel:
All the men twenty years old or more who
were able to serve in the army were listed
by name, one by one, according to the
records of their clans and families. 21The
number from the tribe of Reuben was
46,500.

22From the descendants of Simeon:[w]
All the men twenty years old or more who
were able to serve in the army were counted and listed by name, one by one, according to the records of their clans and families. 23The number from the tribe of
Simeon was 59,300.

24From the descendants of Gad:[x]
All the men twenty years old or more who
were able to serve in the army were listed
by name, according to the records of their

1:1 [a]Ex 40:2 [b]Ex 19:1 [c]Ex 40:17
1:2 [d]Ex 30:11-16; Nu 26:2
1:3 [e]Ex 30:14
1:4 [f]ver 16 [g]Ex 18:21; Dt 1:15
1:5 [h]Ge 29:32; Dt 33:6; Rev 7:5
1:7 [i]Ge 29:35; Ps 78:68 [j]Ru 4:20; 1Ch 2:10; Lk 3:32
1:8 [k]Ge 30:18
1:9 [l]ver 30
1:10 [m]ver 32
1:12 [n]ver 38
1:13 [o]ver 40
1:14 [p]Nu 2:14
1:15 [q]ver 42
1:16 [r]Ex 18:25 [s]ver 4; Ex 18:21; Nu 7:2
1:18 [t]ver 1 [u]Ezr 2:59; Heb 7:3
1:20 [v]Nu 26:5-11; Rev 7:5
1:22 [w]Nu 26:12-14; Rev 7:7
1:24 [x]Ge 30:11; Nu 26:15-18; Rev 7:5

A Fitting Name

NU 1

The opening chapters show clearly why Numbers is a fitting name for the fourth book of the Bible. From an accounting of Israel's army to a census of the Levitical work force, scores of names and numbers are meticulously recorded within these pages.

Such a detailed accounting is not only valuable to the people of Israel, it is necessary to their survival. God orders this census through Moses just days before the beginning of the Israelites' journey into the promised land. The initial census brings organization and a sense of discipline to this group of former slaves just when they need it most. Now soldiers instead of slaves, the census serves as a military draft list and prepares the Israelites to face the enemies and hardships that lay ahead.

clans and families. 25The number from the
tribe of Gad was 45,650.

26From the descendants of Judah:[y]
All the men twenty years old or more who
were able to serve in the army were listed
by name, according to the records of their
clans and families. 27The number from the
tribe of Judah was 74,600.

28From the descendants of Issachar:[z]
All the men twenty years old or more who
were able to serve in the army were listed
by name, according to the records of their
clans and families. 29The number from the
tribe of Issachar was 54,400.

30From the descendants of Zebulun:[a]
All the men twenty years old or more who
were able to serve in the army were listed
by name, according to the records of their
clans and families. 31The number from the
tribe of Zebulun was 57,400.

32From the sons of Joseph:
From the descendants of Ephraim:[b]
All the men twenty years old or more who
were able to serve in the army were listed
by name, according to the records of their
clans and families. 33The number from the
tribe of Ephraim was 40,500.

34From the descendants of Manasseh:[c]
All the men twenty years old or more who
were able to serve in the army were listed
by name, according to the records of their
clans and families. 35The number from the
tribe of Manasseh was 32,200.

36From the descendants of Benjamin:[d]
All the men twenty years old or more who
were able to serve in the army were listed
by name, according to the records of their
clans and families. 37The number from the
tribe of Benjamin was 35,400.

38From the descendants of Dan:[e]
All the men twenty years old or more who
were able to serve in the army were listed
by name, according to the records of their
clans and families. 39The number from the
tribe of Dan was 62,700.

40From the descendants of Asher:[f]
All the men twenty years old or more who
were able to serve in the army were listed
by name, according to the records of their
clans and families. 41The number from the
tribe of Asher was 41,500.

42From the descendants of Naphtali:[g]
All the men twenty years old or more who
were able to serve in the army were listed
by name, according to the records of their
clans and families. 43The number from the
tribe of Naphtali was 53,400.

1:26 [y]Ge 29:35; Nu 26:19-22; Mt 1:2; Rev 7:5
1:28 [z]Nu 26:23-25; Rev 7:7
1:30 [a]Nu 26:26-27; Rev 7:8
1:32 [b]Nu 26:35-37
1:34 [c]Nu 26:28-34; Rev 7:6
1:36 [d]Nu 26:38-41; 2Ch 17:17; Rev 7:8
1:38 [e]Ge 30:6; Nu 26:42-43
1:40 [f]Nu 26:44-47; Rev 7:6
1:42 [g]Nu 26:48-50; Rev 7:6

You must not break away from holy prayer for any reason except obedience or charity. For often during the time scheduled for prayer, the devil comes with all sorts of struggles and annoyances—even more than when you are not at prayer. He does this to make you weary of holy prayer. Often he will say, "This sort of prayer is worthless to you. You should not think about or pay attention to anything except vocal prayer." He makes it seem this way so that you will become weary and confused, and abandon the exercise of prayer. But prayer is a weapon with which you can defend yourself against every enemy. If you hold it with love's hand and the arm of free choice, this weapon, with the light of most holy faith, will be your defense.

—Catherine of Siena (1347-1380)

44 These were the men counted by Moses and
Aaron[h] and the twelve leaders of Israel, each one
representing his family. 45 All the Israelites twenty
years old or more who were able to serve in Israel's army were counted according to their families. 46 The total number was 603,550.[i]
47 The families of the tribe of Levi,[j] however,
were not counted[k] along with the others. 48 The
LORD had said to Moses: 49 "You must not count
the tribe of Levi or include them in the census of
the other Israelites. 50 Instead, appoint the Levites
to be in charge of the tabernacle of the Testimony[l]—over all its furnishings and everything
belonging to it. They are to carry the tabernacle
and all its furnishings; they are to take care of it
and encamp around it. 51 Whenever the tabernacle
is to move, the Levites are to take it down, and
whenever the tabernacle is to be set up, the
Levites shall do it.[m] Anyone else who goes near it
shall be put to death. 52 The Israelites are to set up
their tents by divisions, each man in his own
camp under his own standard.[n] 53 The Levites,
however, are to set up their tents around the tabernacle of the Testimony so that wrath will not
fall[o] on the Israelite community. The Levites are
to be responsible for the care of the tabernacle of
the Testimony.[p]"
54 The Israelites did all this just as the LORD commanded Moses.

The Arrangement of the Tribal Camps

2 The LORD said to Moses and Aaron: 2 "The Israelites are to camp around the Tent of Meeting
some distance from it, each man under his standard[q] with the banners of his family."

3 On the east, toward the sunrise, the divisions of the camp of Judah are to encamp
under their standard. The leader of the people of Judah is Nahshon son of Amminadab.[r]
4 His division numbers 74,600.
5 The tribe of Issachar will camp next to
them. The leader of the people of Issachar is
Nethanel son of Zuar.[s] 6 His division numbers
54,400.
7 The tribe of Zebulun will be next. The
leader of the people of Zebulun is Eliab son of
Helon.[t] 8 His division numbers 57,400.
9 All the men assigned to the camp of
Judah, according to their divisions, number
186,400. They will set out first.[u]

10 On the south will be the divisions of the
camp of Reuben under their standard. The
leader of the people of Reuben is Elizur son
of Shedeur.[v] 11 His division numbers 46,500.
12 The tribe of Simeon will camp next to
them. The leader of the people of Simeon is
Shelumiel son of Zurishaddai.[w] 13 His division
numbers 59,300.
14 The tribe of Gad will be next. The leader

1:44 [h]Nu 26:64
1:46 [i]Ex 12:37; 38:26; Nu 2:32; 26:51
1:47 [j]Nu 2:33; 26:57 [k]Nu 4:3,49
1:50 [l]Ex 38:21; Ac 7:44
1:51 [m]Nu 3:38; 4:1-33
1:52 [n]Nu 2:2; Ps 20:5
1:53 [o]Lev 10:6; Nu 16:46; 18:5 [p]Nu 18:2-4
2:2 [q]Nu 1:52; Ps 74:4; Isa 31:9
2:3 [r]Nu 10:14; Ru 4:20; 1Ch 2:10
2:5 [s]Nu 1:8
2:7 [t]Nu 1:9
2:9 [u]Nu 10:14
2:10 [v]Nu 1:5
2:12 [w]Nu 1:6

Tabernacle of Testimony

NU 1:50

The phrase "tabernacle of the Testimony" appears just 6 times throughout Scripture (Ex 38:21; Nu 1:50,53; 10:11; Ac 7:44; Rev 15:5). The "tabernacle," the worship center of the Israelites, houses the "Testimony," the Ten Commandments or the Law. God commands that the Testimony, written on stone tablets, be placed in the "ark of the Testimony." This sacred chest—also known as the ark of God, the ark of the Lord and the ark of the covenant—is kept in the innermost room of the tabernacle, the Most Holy Place.

Camping Arrangements

NU 2

These details regarding the march and camping order of the Israelites may seem immaterial at first glance. Yet a closer look reveals important insights into God's character. Through his commands to Moses and Aaron, we learn that our God is an orderly God, one who values organization over chaos. At the same time, we see God symbolically positioning himself in the middle of his people. The Israelites camp around the Tent of Meeting. God himself lives in the midst of his chosen people—demonstrating his desire to be at the very center of human existence.

God's desire is the same today as it was during Moses' lifetime: to be at the center of our existence. Where is God in your world today? At the center? Or relegated only to the fringes? Be honest with yourself and with God. Ask him to help you live your life with him at its center.

of the people of Gad is Eliasaph son of Deuel.[a][x] 15His division numbers 45,650. 2:14
16All the men assigned to the camp of Reu- [x]Nu 1:14
ben,[y] according to their divisions, number 2:16
151,450. They will set out second. [y]Nu 10:18

17Then the Tent of Meeting and the camp 2:17
of the Levites[z] will set out in the middle of [z]Nu 1:53;
the camps. They will set out in the same 10:21
order as they encamp, each in his own place
under his standard.

18On the west will be the divisions of the 2:18
camp of Ephraim[a] under their standard. The [a]Ge 48:20;
leader of the people of Ephraim is Elishama Jer 31:18-20
son of Ammihud.[b] 19His division numbers [b]Nu 1:10
40,500.
20The tribe of Manasseh will be next to
them. The leader of the people of Manasseh
is Gamaliel son of Pedahzur.[c] 21His division 2:20
numbers 32,200. [c]Nu 1:10
22The tribe of Benjamin will be next. The
leader of the people of Benjamin is Abidan
son of Gideoni.[d] 23His division numbers 2:22
35,400. [d]Nu 1:11;
24All the men assigned to the camp of Ps 68:27
Ephraim,[e] according to their divisions, num- 2:24
ber 108,100. They will set out third.[f] [e]Nu 10:22
[f]Ps 80:2

25On the north will be the divisions of the
camp of Dan, under their standard. The
leader of the people of Dan is Ahiezer son of 2:25
Ammishaddai.[g] 26His division numbers [g]Nu 1:12
62,700.
27The tribe of Asher will camp next to
them. The leader of the people of Asher is 2:27
Pagiel son of Ocran.[h] 28His division numbers [h]Nu 1:13
41,500.
29The tribe of Naphtali will be next. The
leader of the people of Naphtali is Ahira son 2:29
of Enan.[i] 30His division numbers 53,400. [i]Nu 1:15
31All the men assigned to the camp of Dan 2:31
number 157,600. They will set out last,[j] [j]Nu 10:25
under their standards.

32These are the Israelites, counted according to their families. All those in the camps, 2:32
by their divisions, number 603,550.[k] 33The [k]Ex 38:26;
Levites, however, were not counted[l] along Nu 1:46
with the other Israelites, as the LORD com- 2:33
manded Moses. [l]Nu 1:47;
26:57-62

34So the Israelites did everything the LORD commanded Moses; that is the way they encamped
under their standards, and that is the way they set
out, each with his clan and family.

[a] *14* Many manuscripts of the Masoretic Text, Samaritan Pentateuch and Vulgate (see also Num. 1:14); most manuscripts of the Masoretic Text *Reuel*

The Levites

3 This is the account of the family of Aaron and
3:1 [m]Ex 6:27 Moses[m] at the time the LORD talked with
Moses on Mount Sinai.
2 The names of the sons of Aaron were Nadab the
3:2 [n]Ex 6:23; firstborn and Abihu, Eleazar and Ithamar.[n] 3 Those
Nu 26:60 were the names of Aaron's sons, the anointed
priests,[o] who were ordained to serve as priests.
3:3 [o]Ex 28:41 4 Nadab and Abihu, however, fell dead before the
3:4 LORD[p] when they made an offering with unautho-
[p]Lev 10:2 rized fire before him in the Desert of Sinai.[q] They
[q]Lev 10:1 had no sons; so only Eleazar and Ithamar served
[r]1Ch 24:1 as priests during the lifetime of their father Aaron.[r]
3:6 5 The LORD said to Moses, 6 "Bring the tribe of
[s]Dt 10:8; Levi[s] and present them to Aaron the priest to assist
31:9; 1Ch 15:2 him.[t] 7 They are to perform duties for him and for
[t]Nu 8:6-22; the whole community at the Tent of Meeting by
18:1-7; 2Ch 29:11 doing the work[u] of the tabernacle. 8 They are to
take care of all the furnishings of the Tent of Meet-
3:7 [u]Lev 8:35; ing, fulfilling the obligations of the Israelites by
Nu 1:50 doing the work of the tabernacle. 9 Give the Levites
3:9 to Aaron and his sons;[v] they are the Israelites who
[v]Nu 8:19; are to be given wholly to him.[a] 10 Appoint Aaron
18:6 and his sons to serve as priests;[w] anyone else who
3:10 approaches the sanctuary must be put to death."[x]
[w]Ex 29:9 11 The LORD also said to Moses, 12 "I have taken
[x]Nu 1:51 the Levites[y] from among the Israelites in place of
3:12 the first male offspring[z] of every Israelite woman.
[y]Mal 2:4 The Levites are mine,[a] 13 for all the firstborn are
[z]ver 41; Nu 8:16,18 mine.[b] When I struck down all the firstborn in
[a]Ex 13:2 Egypt, I set apart for myself every firstborn in Israel, whether man or animal. They are to be mine.
3:13 [b]Ex 13:12 I am the LORD."
3:15 14 The LORD said to Moses in the Desert of Sinai,
[c]ver 39 15 "Count[c] the Levites by their families and clans.
[d]Nu 26:62 Count every male a month old or more."[d] 16 So
Moses counted them, as he was commanded by
the word of the LORD.
3:17 [e]Ge 46:11 17 These were the names of the sons of Levi:[e]
[f]Ex 6:16 Gershon, Kohath and Merari.[f]
18 These were the names of the Gershonite
clans:
3:18 [g]Ex 6:17 Libni and Shimei.[g]
19 The Kohathite clans:
3:19 [h]Ex 6:18 Amram, Izhar, Hebron and Uzziel.[h]
20 The Merarite clans:[i]
3:20 [i]Ge 46:11 Mahli and Mushi.[j]
[j]Ex 6:19 These were the Levite clans, according to their
families.

21 To Gershon belonged the clans of the Libnites
3:21 [k]Ex 6:17 and Shimeites;[k] these were the Gershonite clans.
22 The number of all the males a month old or
more who were counted was 7,500. 23 The Gershonite clans were to camp on the west, behind
the tabernacle. 24 The leader of the families of the
Gershonites was Eliasaph son of Lael. 25 At the

[a] 9 Most manuscripts of the Masoretic Text; some manuscripts of the Masoretic Text, Samaritan Pentateuch and Septuagint (see also Num. 8:16) *to me*

How Many Tribes?

NU 3

The confederacy of Israel is traditionally comprised of twelve tribes, named after the sons of Jacob who founded them. In Genesis 35:23–26, the following sons are identified: Reuben, Simeon, Levi, Judah, Dan, Naphtali, Gad, Asher, Issachar, Zebulun, Joseph and Benjamin. This is *one accounting* of the twelve tribes of Israel.

Years later, when the Israelites settle in the promised land and the tribe of Levi receives no "inheritance among the rest" (Jos 14:4), the number twelve is maintained by counting both Ephraim and Manasseh, Joseph's sons whom Jacob adopted (Ge 48:5).

In Revelation 7 yet another accounting of the tribes is offered: Judah, Reuben, Gad, Asher, Naphtali, Manasseh, Simeon, Levi, Issachar, Zebulun, Joseph and Benjamin. Note the inclusion here of the tribe of Levi as well as exclusion of the original tribe of Dan (Joseph and Manasseh keep the count at twelve). Dan may have been excluded because they did not support the other tribes (Jdg 5:17), because of traditional belief that the antichrist will come from Dan (Ge 49:17; Jer 8:16–17) or because of the idolatry practiced by the tribe (Jdg 18:30).

When we empty ourselves of all that is creature and rid ourselves of it for the love of God, that same Lord will fill our souls with himself.

—Teresa of Avila (1515-1582)

Tent of Meeting the Gershonites were responsible
for the care of the tabernacle[l] and tent, its coverings,[m] the curtain at the entrance[n] to the Tent of
Meeting, 26 the curtains of the courtyard[o], the curtain at the entrance to the courtyard surrounding
the tabernacle and altar, and the ropes[p]—and
everything related to their use.

27 To Kohath belonged the clans of the Amramites, Izharites, Hebronites and Uzzielites;[q]
these were the Kohathite clans. 28 The number of
all the males a month old or more was 8,600.[a] The
Kohathites were responsible for the care of the
sanctuary. 29 The Kohathite clans were to camp on
the south side[r] of the tabernacle. 30 The leader of
the families of the Kohathite clans was Elizaphan
son of Uzziel. 31 They were responsible for the care
of the ark,[s] the table,[t] the lampstand,[u] the altars,[v]
the articles of the sanctuary used in ministering,
the curtain,[w] and everything related to their use.[x]
32 The chief leader of the Levites was Eleazar son of
Aaron, the priest. He was appointed over those
who were responsible for the care of the sanctuary.

33 To Merari belonged the clans of the Mahlites
and the Mushites;[y] these were the Merarite clans.
34 The number of all the males a month old or
more who were counted was 6,200. 35 The leader
of the families of the Merarite clans was Zuriel
son of Abihail; they were to camp on the north
side of the tabernacle.[z] 36 The Merarites were
appointed[a] to take care of the frames of the tabernacle, its crossbars, posts, bases, all its equipment,
and everything related to their use, 37 as well as
the posts of the surrounding courtyard with their
bases, tent pegs and ropes.

38 Moses and Aaron and his sons were to camp
to the east[b] of the tabernacle, toward the sunrise,
in front of the Tent of Meeting.[c] They were responsible for the care of the sanctuary[d] on behalf of
the Israelites. Anyone else who approached the
sanctuary was to be put to death.[e]

39 The total number of Levites counted at the
LORD's command by Moses and Aaron according
to their clans, including every male a month old
or more, was 22,000.[f]

40 The LORD said to Moses, "Count all the firstborn Israelite males who are a month old or more[g]
and make a list of their names. 41 Take the Levites
for me in place of all the firstborn of the Israelites,[h] and the livestock of the Levites in place of all
the firstborn of the livestock of the Israelites. I am
the LORD."

42 So Moses counted all the firstborn of the Israelites, as the LORD commanded him. 43 The total

a 28 Hebrew; some Septuagint manuscripts *8,300*

3:25 [l]Ex 25:9 [m]Ex 26:14 [n]Ex 26:36; Nu 4:25
3:26 [o]Ex 27:9 [p]Ex 35:18
3:27 [q]1Ch 26:23
3:29 [r]Nu 1:53
3:31 [s]Ex 25:10-22 [t]Ex 25:23 [u]Ex 25:31 [v]Ex 27:1; 30:1 [w]Ex 26:33 [x]Nu 4:15
3:33 [y]Ex 6:19
3:35 [z]Nu 1:53; 2:25
3:36 [a]Nu 4:32
3:38 [b]Nu 2:3 [c]Nu 1:53 [d]ver 7; Nu 18:5 [e]ver 10; Nu 1:51
3:39 [f]Nu 26:62
3:40 [g]ver 15
3:41 [h]ver 12

number of firstborn males a month old or more, listed by name, was 22,273.[i]

44The LORD also said to Moses, 45"Take the Levites in place of all the firstborn of Israel, and the livestock of the Levites in place of their livestock. The Levites are to be mine. I am the LORD. 46To redeem[j] the 273 firstborn Israelites who exceed the number of the Levites, 47collect five shekels[a][k] for each one, according to the sanctuary shekel,[l] which weighs twenty gerahs.[m] 48Give the money for the redemption of the additional Israelites to Aaron and his sons."

49So Moses collected the redemption money from those who exceeded the number redeemed by the Levites. 50From the firstborn of the Israelites he collected silver weighing 1,365 shekels,[b][n] according to the sanctuary shekel. 51Moses gave the redemption money to Aaron and his sons, as he was commanded by the word of the LORD.

The Kohathites

4 The LORD said to Moses and Aaron: 2"Take a census[o] of the Kohathite branch of the Levites by their clans and families. 3Count all the men from thirty to fifty years of age[p] who come to serve in the work in the Tent of Meeting.

4"This is the work of the Kohathites in the Tent of Meeting: the care of the most holy things.[q] 5When the camp is to move, Aaron and his sons are to go in and take down the shielding curtain[r] and cover the ark of the Testimony with it.[s] 6Then they are to cover this with hides of sea cows,[c] spread a cloth of solid blue over that and put the poles[t] in place.

7"Over the table of the Presence[u] they are to spread a blue cloth and put on it the plates, dishes and bowls, and the jars for drink offerings; the bread that is continually there[v] is to remain on it. 8Over these they are to spread a scarlet cloth, cover that with hides of sea cows and put its poles in place.

9"They are to take a blue cloth and cover the lampstand that is for light, together with its lamps, its wick trimmers and trays,[w] and all its jars for the oil used to supply it. 10Then they are to wrap it and all its accessories in a covering of hides of sea cows and put it on a carrying frame.

11"Over the gold altar[x] they are to spread a blue cloth and cover that with hides of sea cows and put its poles in place.

12"They are to take all the articles used for ministering in the sanctuary, wrap them in a blue cloth, cover that with hides of sea cows and put them on a carrying frame.

13"They are to remove the ashes from the bronze altar[y] and spread a purple cloth over it. 14Then they are to place on it all the utensils used

3:43 [i]ver 39
3:46 [j]Ex 13:13; Nu 18:15
3:47 [k]Lev 27:6 [l]Ex 30:13 [m]Lev 27:25
3:50 [n]ver 46-48
4:2 [o]Ex 30:12
4:3 [p]ver 23; Nu 8:25; 1Ch 23:3,24, 27; Ezr 3:8
4:4 [q]ver 19
4:5 [r]Ex 26:31,33 [s]Ex 25:10,16
4:6 [t]Ex 25:13-15; 1Ki 8:7; 2Ch 5:8
4:7 [u]Ex 25:23, 29; Lev 24:6 [v]Ex 25:30
4:9 [w]Ex 25:31, 37,38
4:11 [x]Ex 30:1
4:13 [y]Ex 27:1-8

[a] *47* That is, about 2 ounces (about 55 grams) [b] *50* That is, about 35 pounds (about 15.5 kilograms) [c] *6* That is, dugongs; also in verses 8, 10, 11, 12, 14 and 25

Beautiful Colors

NU 4:1-13

Blue (Nu 4:6,7,9,11,12), scarlet (Nu 4:8) and purple (Nu 4:13)—*the significance of these colors is uncertain. The dyed cloths are perhaps used to identify the sacred items they cover. It is also likely that the colors themselves carry some meaning. The color blue is often used in tabernacle tapestries; both blue and purple are considered royal hues and are worn by the wealthy. Scarlet also is used in the tabernacle and is seen as a sign of prosperity.*

The Israelites are skilled at both weaving and dyeing. Their dyes are commonly drawn from vegetable and animal sources. Both blue and purple come from different species of shellfish as well as the rind of the pomegranate; scarlet, from insects such as weevils. The quality of dyes varies greatly, and the recipes for dyes are closely guarded secrets.

Sea Cows

NU 4:14

A large, plant-eating aquatic mammal, the sea cow—or dugong—is found commonly in tropical waters such as the Red Sea, which borders Egypt. From the top of its round head to the tip of its tail fin, the seal-like sea cow can grow up to 15 feet in length and weigh as much as 1,500 pounds. In the desert, hides from these marine animals are rare and valuable, making them especially appropriate for use in the tabernacle.

for ministering at the altar, including the firepans,
meat forks,[z] shovels and sprinkling bowls.[a] Over
it they are to spread a covering of hides of sea
cows and put its poles[b] in place.
15"After Aaron and his sons have finished covering the holy furnishings and all the holy articles, and when the camp is ready to move, the
Kohathites are to come to do the carrying.[c] But
they must not touch the holy things or they will
die.[d] The Kohathites are to carry those things that
are in the Tent of Meeting.
16"Eleazar[e] son of Aaron, the priest, is to have
charge of the oil for the light,[f] the fragrant
incense, the regular grain offering[g] and the
anointing oil. He is to be in charge of the entire
tabernacle and everything in it, including its holy
furnishings and articles."
17The LORD said to Moses and Aaron, 18"See that
the Kohathite tribal clans are not cut off from the
Levites. 19So that they may live and not die when
they come near the most holy things,[h] do this for
them: Aaron and his sons are to go into the sanctuary and assign to each man his work and what
he is to carry. 20But the Kohathites must not go in
to look[i] at the holy things, even for a moment, or
they will die."

The Gershonites

21The LORD said to Moses, 22"Take a census also
of the Gershonites by their families and clans.
23Count all the men from thirty to fifty years of
age[j] who come to serve in the work at the Tent of
Meeting.
24"This is the service of the Gershonite clans as
they work and carry burdens: 25They are to carry
the curtains of the tabernacle,[k] the Tent of Meeting,[l] its covering[m] and the outer covering of hides
of sea cows, the curtains for the entrance to the
Tent of Meeting, 26the curtains of the courtyard
surrounding the tabernacle and altar, the curtain
for the entrance, the ropes and all the equipment
used in its service. The Gershonites are to do all
that needs to be done with these things. 27All their
service, whether carrying or doing other work, is
to be done under the direction of Aaron and his
sons. You shall assign to them as their responsibility all they are to carry. 28This is the service of
the Gershonite clans[n] at the Tent of Meeting. Their
duties are to be under the direction of Ithamar son
of Aaron, the priest.

The Merarites

29"Count the Merarites by their clans and families.[o] 30Count all the men from thirty to fifty years
of age who come to serve in the work at the Tent
of Meeting. 31This is their duty as they perform
service at the Tent of Meeting: to carry the frames
of the tabernacle, its crossbars, posts and bases,[p]
32as well as the posts of the surrounding courtyard
with their bases, tent pegs, ropes, all their equip-

4:14 [z]2Ch 4:16 [a]Jer 52:18 [b]Ex 27:6
4:15 [c]Nu 7:9 [d]Nu 1:51; 2Sa 6:6,7
4:16 [e]Lev 10:6 [f]Ex 25:6 [g]Ex 29:41; Lev 6:14-23
4:19 [h]ver 15
4:20 [i]Ex 19:21; 1Sa 6:19
4:23 [j]ver 3; 1Ch 23:3,24, 27
4:25 [k]Ex 27:10-18; Nu 3:26 [l]Nu 3:25 [m]Ex 26:14
4:28 [n]Nu 7:7
4:29 [o]Ge 46:11
4:31 [p]Nu 3:36

ment and everything related to their use. Assign to
each man the specific things he is to carry. [33]This
is the service of the Merarite clans as they work at
the Tent of Meeting under the direction of Ithamar
son of Aaron, the priest."

The Numbering of the Levite Clans

[34]Moses, Aaron and the leaders of the commu-
4:34 nity counted the Kohathites[q] by their clans and
[q]ver 2 families. [35]All the men from thirty to fifty years of
age who came to serve in the work in the Tent of
Meeting, [36]counted by clans, were 2,750. [37]This
4:37 was the total of all those in the Kohathite clans[r]
[r]Nu 3:27 who served in the Tent of Meeting. Moses and
Aaron counted them according to the LORD's command through Moses.
4:38 [s]Ge 46:11 [38]The Gershonites[s] were counted by their clans
and families. [39]All the men from thirty to fifty
years of age who came to serve in the work at the
Tent of Meeting, [40]counted by their clans and families, were 2,630. [41]This was the total of those in
the Gershonite clans who served at the Tent of
Meeting. Moses and Aaron counted them according to the LORD's command.
[42]The Merarites were counted by their clans and
families. [43]All the men from thirty to fifty years of
age who came to serve in the work at the Tent of
Meeting, [44]counted by their clans, were 3,200.
4:45 [t]ver 29 [45]This was the total of those in the Merarite clans.[t]
Moses and Aaron counted them according to the
LORD's command through Moses.
[46]So Moses, Aaron and the leaders of Israel
counted all the Levites by their clans and families.
4:47 [u]ver 3 [47]All the men from thirty to fifty years of age[u] who
came to do the work of serving and carrying the
4:48 [v]Nu 3:39 Tent of Meeting [48]numbered 8,580.[v] [49]At the
LORD's command through Moses, each was
assigned his work and told what to carry.
4:49 [w]Nu 1:47 Thus they were counted,[w] as the LORD commanded Moses.

The Purity of the Camp

5 The LORD said to Moses, [2]"Command the Israelites to send away from the camp anyone
5:2 who has an infectious skin disease[a][x] or a dis-
[x]Lev 13:46 charge[y] of any kind, or who is ceremonially
[y]Lev 15:2; Mt 9:20 unclean[z] because of a dead body. [3]Send away
[z]Lev 13:3; male and female alike; send them outside the
Nu 9:6-10 camp so they will not defile their camp, where I
5:3 dwell among them.[a]" [4]The Israelites did this; they
[a]Lev 26:12; Nu 35:34; sent them outside the camp. They did just as the
2Co 6:16 LORD had instructed Moses.

Restitution for Wrongs

[5]The LORD said to Moses, [6]"Say to the Israelites:
5:6 'When a man or woman wrongs another in any
[b]Lev 6:2 way[b] and so is unfaithful[b] to the LORD, that per-

[a] 2 Traditionally *leprosy*; the Hebrew word was used for various diseases affecting the skin—not necessarily leprosy.
[b] 6 Or *woman commits any wrong common to mankind*

Numbering the Levites

NU 4:34–48

The census taken of the Levites is completely separate from, and conducted for a totally different purpose than, that of the other tribes. The accounting of the people described in Numbers 1 serves, in part, as a military draft, from which the priestly tribe of Levi is exempted. The count taken of the Levites in Numbers 4 is for the purpose of priestly service. The first census counts all males over 20 years of age (Nu 1:3) who are fit for military service. The count of the Levites includes all men ages 30 to 50 (Nu 4:43) who are fit for service in the tabernacle.

Test for Unfaithfulness

NU 5:11-31

To today's reader, it seems unfair that an innocent woman might be subjected to the test for an unfaithful wife. But this test, in fact, provides physical protection for women accused of adultery in Old Testament times. Without it, a jealous husband might be inclined to take matters into his own hands—possibly beating or even killing his wife. The test described by God provides a structured system for dealing with the unfortunate situation of suspected adultery.

An equivalent test for husbands does not exist, most likely because there is no need for their physical protection in this male-dominated society. Once the sin of adultery is discovered, however, the man and woman who have committed it are subject to the same punishment—death (Lev 20:10).

son is guilty[c] [7]and must confess[d] the sin he has 5:6
committed. He must make full restitution[e] for his [c]Lev 5:14-6:7
wrong, add one fifth to it and give it all to the per- 5:7
son he has wronged. [8]But if that person has no [d]Lev 5:5; 26:40;
close relative to whom restitution can be made for Jos 7:19;
the wrong, the restitution belongs to the LORD and Lk 19:8
must be given to the priest, along with the ram [e]Lev 6:5
with which atonement is made for him.[f] [9]All the 5:8
sacred contributions the Israelites bring to a priest [f]Lev 6:6,7;
will belong to him.[g] [10]Each man's sacred gifts are 7:7
his own, but what he gives to the priest will 5:9
belong to the priest.[h]' " [g]Lev 6:17; 7:6-14

The Test for an Unfaithful Wife 5:10

[11]Then the LORD said to Moses, [12]"Speak to the [h]Lev 10:13
Israelites and say to them: 'If a man's wife goes
astray[i] and is unfaithful to him [13]by sleeping with 5:12 [i]Ex 20:14
another man,[j] and this is hidden from her husband
and her impurity is undetected (since there is no 5:13
witness against her and she has not been caught in [j]Lev 18:20; 20:10
the act), [14]and if feelings of jealousy[k] come over
her husband and he suspects his wife and she is 5:14
impure—or if he is jealous and suspects her even [k]Pr 6:34;
though she is not impure— [15]then he is to take his SS 8:6
wife to the priest. He must also take an offering of
a tenth of an ephah[a][l] of barley flour[m] on her 5:15 [l]Ex 16:36
behalf. He must not pour oil on it or put incense [m]Lev 6:20
on it, because it is a grain offering for jealousy, a [n]Eze 29:16
reminder[n] offering to draw attention to guilt.
[16]" 'The priest shall bring her and have her
stand before the LORD. [17]Then he shall take some
holy water in a clay jar and put some dust from
the tabernacle floor into the water. [18]After the
priest has had the woman stand before the LORD,
he shall loosen her hair[o] and place in her hands 5:18
the reminder offering, the grain offering for jeal- [o]Lev 10:6;
ousy, while he himself holds the bitter water that 1Co 11:6
brings a curse. [19]Then the priest shall put the
woman under oath and say to her, "If no other
man has slept with you and you have not gone
astray[p] and become impure while married to your 5:19
husband, may this bitter water that brings a curse [p]ver 12,29
not harm you. [20]But if you have gone astray[q] 5:20 [q]ver 12
while married to your husband and you have
defiled yourself by sleeping with a man other than
your husband"— [21]here the priest is to put the 5:21
woman under this curse of the oath[r]—"may the [r]Jos 6:26;
LORD cause your people to curse and denounce 1Sa 14:24;
you when he causes your thigh to waste away and Ne 10:29
your abdomen to swell.[b] [22]May this water[s] that 5:22
brings a curse[t] enter your body so that your [s]Ps 109:18 [t]ver 18
abdomen swells and your thigh wastes away.[c]" [u]Dt 27:15
" 'Then the woman is to say, "Amen. So be it.[u]"
[23]" 'The priest is to write these curses on a 5:23
scroll[v] and then wash them off into the bitter [v]Jer 45:1
water. [24]He shall have the woman drink the bitter

[a] *15* That is, probably about 2 quarts (about 2 liters)
[b] *21* Or *causes you to have a miscarrying womb and barrenness*
[c] *22* Or *body and cause you to be barren and have a miscarrying womb*

water that brings a curse, and this water will enter
her and cause bitter suffering. 25 The priest is to
take from her hands the grain offering for jealousy, wave it before the LORD[w] and bring it to the
altar. 26 The priest is then to take a handful of the
grain offering as a memorial offering and burn it
on the altar; after that, he is to have the woman
drink the water. 27 If she has defiled herself and
been unfaithful to her husband, then when she is
made to drink the water that brings a curse, it will
go into her and cause bitter suffering; her
abdomen will swell and her thigh waste away,[a]
and she will become accursed[x] among her people.
28 If, however, the woman has not defiled herself
and is free from impurity, she will be cleared of
guilt and will be able to have children.
29 " 'This, then, is the law of jealousy when a
woman goes astray[y] and defiles herself while married to her husband, 30 or when feelings of jealousy
come over a man because he suspects his wife.
The priest is to have her stand before the LORD and
is to apply this entire law to her. 31 The husband
will be innocent of any wrongdoing, but the
woman will bear the consequences[z] of her sin.' "

The Nazirite

6 The LORD said to Moses, 2 "Speak to the Israelites and say to them: 'If a man or woman
wants to make a special vow[a], a vow of separation to the LORD as a Nazirite,[b] 3 he must abstain
from wine[c] and other fermented drink and must
not drink vinegar[d] made from wine or from other
fermented drink. He must not drink grape juice
or eat grapes or raisins. 4 As long as he is a Nazirite, he must not eat anything that comes from the
grapevine, not even the seeds or skins.
5 " 'During the entire period of his vow of separation no razor[e] may be used on his head.[f] He
must be holy until the period of his separation to
the LORD is over; he must let the hair of his head
grow long. 6 Throughout the period of his separation to the LORD he must not go near a dead body.[g]
7 Even if his own father or mother or brother or
sister dies, he must not make himself ceremonially unclean[h] on account of them, because the
symbol of his separation to God is on his head.
8 Throughout the period of his separation he is
consecrated to the LORD.
9 " 'If someone dies suddenly in his presence,
thus defiling the hair he has dedicated,[i] he must
shave his head on the day of his cleansing[j]—the
seventh day. 10 Then on the eighth day he must
bring two doves or two young pigeons[k] to the
priest at the entrance to the Tent of Meeting. 11 The
priest is to offer one as a sin offering and the other as a burnt offering[l] to make atonement[m] for
him because he sinned by being in the presence of
the dead body. That same day he is to consecrate

5:25 [w]Lev 8:27
5:27 [x]Isa 43:28; 65:15; Jer 26:6; 29:18; 42:18; 44:12,22; Zec 8:13
5:29 [y]ver 19
5:31 [z]Lev 5:1; 20:17
6:2 [a]Ge 28:20; Ac 21:23 [b]Jdg 13:5; 16:17; Am 2:11,12
6:3 [c]Lk 1:15 [d]Ru 2:14; Ps 69:21; Pr 10:26
6:5 [e]Ps 52:2; 57:4; 59:7; Isa 7:20; Eze 5:1 [f]1Sa 1:11
6:6 [g]Lev 21:1-3; Nu 19:11-22
6:7 [h]Nu 9:6
6:9 [i]ver 18 [j]Lev 14:9
6:10 [k]Lev 5:7; 14:22
6:11 [l]Ge 8:20 [m]Ex 29:36

[a] 27 Or *suffering; she will have barrenness and a miscarrying womb*

The Nazirite Vow

NU 6:1-21

While only those Israelites from the tribe of Levi can become priests, any person—man or woman—can become a Nazirite. Taken from the Hebrew verb *nazar*, which means "to separate," the name Nazirite is given to those who specially devote themselves to God for a specific period of time, a time during which strict rules in regard to diet, appearance and associations must be observed. Throughout this period, the Nazirite abstains from consuming any product of the grape vine, probably to prevent him or her from being ruled by anything other than God's Spirit (Eph 5:18). Nazirites are further restricted from cutting their hair and shaving (the length of the Nazirite's hair provides an outward sign, particularly for a male, of the length of the vow) and from going near dead bodies.

The length of time for this consecration is not defined in Scripture, but tradition holds that it lasted from 30 days to a lifetime—as in the cases of Samson, Samuel and John the Baptist, whose parents made the vows for them before their births.

The Blessing

NU 6:24–26

The Aaronic benediction—given to the Israelites at God's command—is still commonly used today and is a tradition at Jewish weddings. Poetic and powerful, this priestly prayer is used to call forth God's favor on his people by claiming for them the blessings associated with his name and his character.

As women today, we can petition God for these same gifts. Take five minutes to memorize Numbers 6:24–26. Make a mental list of some ways and places you could use this prayer. Practice two or three possibilities this week. Try placing a hand on your children's heads and blessing them before they go off to school. Integrate this appeal into your quiet time as you pray for your friends, church and community. Hold hands with your husband and recite it together. At the end of the week, choose one application that you can use in your life on a regular basis.

his head. 12 He must dedicate himself to the LORD
for the period of his separation and must bring a
year-old male lamb as a guilt offering. The previous days do not count, because he became defiled
during his separation.
13 " 'Now this is the law for the Nazirite when
the period of his separation is over.[n] He is to be
brought to the entrance to the Tent of Meeting.
14 There he is to present his offerings to the LORD:
a year-old male lamb without defect for a burnt
offering, a year-old ewe lamb without defect for a
sin offering,[o] a ram without defect for a fellowship offering,[a] 15 together with their grain offerings
and drink offerings,[p] and a basket of bread made
without yeast—cakes made of fine flour mixed
with oil, and wafers spread with oil.[q]
16 " 'The priest is to present them before the
LORD and make the sin offering and the burnt
offering. 17 He is to present the basket of unleavened bread and is to sacrifice the ram as a fellowship offering to the LORD, together with its grain
offering and drink offering.
18 " 'Then at the entrance to the Tent of Meeting,
the Nazirite must shave off the hair that he dedicated.[r] He is to take the hair and put it in the fire
that is under the sacrifice of the fellowship offering.
19 " 'After the Nazirite has shaved off the hair of
his dedication, the priest is to place in his hands a
boiled shoulder of the ram, and a cake and a
wafer from the basket, both made without yeast.
20 The priest shall then wave them before the LORD
as a wave offering; they are holy and belong to
the priest, together with the breast that was waved
and the thigh that was presented. After that, the
Nazirite may drink wine.[s]
21 " 'This is the law of the Nazirite who vows his
offering to the LORD in accordance with his separation, in addition to whatever else he can afford.
He must fulfill the vow he has made, according to
the law of the Nazirite.' "

The Priestly Blessing

22 The LORD said to Moses, 23 "Tell Aaron and his
sons, 'This is how you are to bless[t] the Israelites.
Say to them:

24 " ' "The LORD bless you[u]
and keep you;[v]
25 the LORD make his face shine upon you[w]
and be gracious to you;[x]
26 the LORD turn his face[y] toward you
and give you peace.[z]" '

27 "So they will put my name[a] on the Israelites,
and I will bless them."

Offerings at the Dedication of the Tabernacle

7 When Moses finished setting up the tabernacle,[b] he anointed it and consecrated it and all
its furnishings.[c] He also anointed and consecrated

6:13 [n]Ac 21:26
6:14 [o]Lev 14:10; Nu 15:27
6:15 [p]Nu 15:1-7 [q]Ex 29:2; Lev 2:4
6:18 [r]ver 9; Ac 21:24
6:20 [s]Ecc 9:7
6:23 [t]Dt 21:5; 1Ch 23:13
6:24 [u]Dt 28:3-6; Ps 28:9 [v]1Sa 2:9; Ps 17:8
6:25 [w]Job 29:24; Ps 31:16; 80:3; 119:135 [x]Ge 43:29; Ps 25:16; 86:16
6:26 [y]Ps 4:6; 44:3 [z]Ps 29:11; 37:11,37; Jn 14:27
6:27 [a]Dt 28:10; 2Sa 7:23; 2Ch 7:14; Ne 9:10; Jer 25:29
7:1 [b]Ex 40:17 [c]Ex 40:9

[a] 14 Traditionally *peace offering;* also in verses 17 and 18

the altar and all its utensils.[d] 2 Then the leaders of
Israel,[e] the heads of families who were the tribal
leaders in charge of those who were counted,
made offerings. 3 They brought as their gifts before
the LORD six covered carts and twelve oxen—an
ox from each leader and a cart from every two.
These they presented before the tabernacle.

4 The LORD said to Moses, 5 "Accept these from
them, that they may be used in the work at the
Tent of Meeting. Give them to the Levites as each
man's work requires."

6 So Moses took the carts and oxen and gave
them to the Levites. 7 He gave two carts and four
oxen to the Gershonites,[f] as their work required,
8 and he gave four carts and eight oxen to the Merarites,[g] as their work required. They were all
under the direction of Ithamar son of Aaron, the
priest. 9 But Moses did not give any to the Kohathites, because they were to carry on their shoulders[h] the holy things, for which they were
responsible.

10 When the altar was anointed,[i] the leaders
brought their offerings for its dedication[j] and presented them before the altar. 11 For the LORD had
said to Moses, "Each day one leader is to bring his
offering for the dedication of the altar."

12 The one who brought his offering on the first
day was Nahshon son of Amminadab of the tribe
of Judah.

13 His offering was one silver plate weighing a
hundred and thirty shekels,[a] and one silver
sprinkling bowl weighing seventy shekels,[b]
both according to the sanctuary shekel,[k] each
filled with fine flour mixed with oil as a grain
offering;[l] 14 one gold dish weighing ten
shekels,[c] filled with incense;[m] 15 one young
bull,[n] one ram and one male lamb a year old,
for a burnt offering;[o] 16 one male goat for a sin
offering;[p] 17 and two oxen, five rams, five male
goats and five male lambs a year old, to be
sacrificed as a fellowship offering.[d][q] This was
the offering of Nahshon son of Amminadab.[r]

18 On the second day Nethanel son of Zuar,[s] the
leader of Issachar, brought his offering.

19 The offering he brought was one silver plate
weighing a hundred and thirty shekels, and
one silver sprinkling bowl weighing seventy
shekels, both according to the sanctuary
shekel, each filled with fine flour mixed with
oil as a grain offering; 20 one gold dish[t] weighing ten shekels, filled with incense; 21 one
young bull, one ram and one male lamb a
year old, for a burnt offering; 22 one male goat
for a sin offering; 23 and two oxen, five rams,

7:1 [d]ver 84,88; Ex 40:10
7:2 [e]Nu 1:5-16
7:7 [f]Nu 4:24-26, 28
7:8 [g]Nu 4:31-33
7:9 [h]Nu 4:15
7:10 [i]ver 1 [j]2Ch 7:9
7:13 [k]Ex 30:13; Nu 3:47 [l]Lev 2:1
7:14 [m]Ex 30:34
7:15 [n]Ex 24:5; 29:3; Nu 28:11 [o]Lev 1:3
7:16 [p]Lev 4:3,23
7:17 [q]Lev 3:1 [r]Nu 1:7
7:18 [s]Nu 1:8
7:20 [t]ver 14

[a] *13* That is, about 3 1/4 pounds (about 1.5 kilograms); also elsewhere in this chapter [b] *13* That is, about 1 3/4 pounds (about 0.8 kilogram); also elsewhere in this chapter
[c] *14* That is, about 4 ounces (about 110 grams); also elsewhere in this chapter [d] *17* Traditionally *peace offering*; also elsewhere in this chapter

Importance of Ceremony

NU 7

Empty rituals, practiced without heart, have little or no meaning. Yet, when used properly, ritual can play a key role in the development of our spiritual lives. Numbers 7 emphasizes the importance of ceremony through its detailed description of the leaders' repetitive offerings. Though Moses could have saved time, effort and paper by describing just once the offering given by all twelve leaders, he lets the entire account unfold, one piece at a time—demonstrating the importance of sacred tradition.

What rituals or traditions in your life allow you to more fully experience the sacred? Is it morning coffee in the breakfast nook with God? Regular quiet times? The lighting of candles as you read or pray? A special song of worship sung each day? What small, simple rituals can you add to your life that will feed your spirit and soul?

five male goats and five male lambs a year
old, to be sacrificed as a fellowship offering.
This was the offering of Nethanel son of Zuar.

24 On the third day, Eliab son of Helon,[u] the leader 7:24
of the people of Zebulun, brought his offering. [u]Nu 1:9
25 His offering was one silver plate weighing a
hundred and thirty shekels, and one silver
sprinkling bowl weighing seventy shekels,
both according to the sanctuary shekel, each
filled with fine flour mixed with oil as a grain
offering; 26 one gold dish weighing ten
shekels, filled with incense; 27 one young bull,
one ram and one male lamb a year old, for a
burnt offering; 28 one male goat for a sin offering; 29 and two oxen, five rams, five male
goats and five male lambs a year old, to be
sacrificed as a fellowship offering. This was
the offering of Eliab son of Helon.

30 On the fourth day Elizur son of Shedeur,[v] the 7:30
leader of the people of Reuben, brought his [v]Nu 1:5
offering.
31 His offering was one silver plate weighing
a hundred and thirty shekels, and one silver
sprinkling bowl weighing seventy shekels,
both according to the sanctuary shekel, each
filled with fine flour mixed with oil as a grain
offering; 32 one gold dish weighing ten
shekels, filled with incense; 33 one young bull,
one ram and one male lamb a year old, for a
burnt offering; 34 one male goat for a sin offering; 35 and two oxen, five rams, five male
goats and five male lambs a year old, to be
sacrificed as a fellowship offering. This was
the offering of Elizur son of Shedeur.

36 On the fifth day Shelumiel son of Zurishaddai,[w] 7:36
the leader of the people of Simeon, brought his [w]Nu 1:6
offering.
37 His offering was one silver plate weighing a
hundred and thirty shekels, and one silver
sprinkling bowl weighing seventy shekels,
both according to the sanctuary shekel, each
filled with fine flour mixed with oil as a grain
offering; 38 one gold dish weighing ten
shekels, filled with incense; 39 one young bull,
one ram and one male lamb a year old, for a
burnt offering; 40 one male goat for a sin offering; 41 and two oxen, five rams, five male
goats and five male lambs a year old, to be
sacrificed as a fellowship offering. This was
the offering of Shelumiel son of Zurishaddai.

42 On the sixth day Eliasaph son of Deuel,[x] the 7:42
leader of the people of Gad, brought his offering. [x]Nu 1:14
43 His offering was one silver plate weighing a
hundred and thirty shekels, and one silver
sprinkling bowl weighing seventy shekels,
both according to the sanctuary shekel, each
filled with fine flour mixed with oil as a grain
offering; 44 one gold dish weighing ten
shekels, filled with incense; 45 one young bull,

Source of love, and
light of day,
Tear me from myself away;
Every view and thought of mine
Cast into the mould of thine;
Teach, O teach this faithless heart
A consistent constant part.

—Madame Guyon (1647–1717)

one ram and one male lamb a year old, for a
burnt offering; 46one male goat for a sin offering; 47and two oxen, five rams, five male
goats and five male lambs a year old, to be
sacrificed as a fellowship offering. This was
the offering of Eliasaph son of Deuel.

7:48 48On the seventh day Elishama son of Ammihud,[y]
yNu 1:10 the leader of the people of Ephraim, brought his
offering.

49His offering was one silver plate weighing a
hundred and thirty shekels, and one silver
sprinkling bowl weighing seventy shekels,
both according to the sanctuary shekel, each
filled with fine flour mixed with oil as a grain
offering; 50one gold dish weighing ten
shekels, filled with incense; 51one young bull,
one ram and one male lamb a year old, for a
burnt offering; 52one male goat for a sin offering; 53and two oxen, five rams, five male
goats and five male lambs a year old, to be
7:53 sacrificed as a fellowship offering. This was
zNu 1:10 the offering of Elishama son of Ammihud.[z]

7:54 54On the eighth day Gamaliel son of Pedahzur,[a]
aNu 1:10; 2:20 the leader of the people of Manasseh, brought his
offering.

55His offering was one silver plate weighing a
hundred and thirty shekels, and one silver
sprinkling bowl weighing seventy shekels,
both according to the sanctuary shekel, each
filled with fine flour mixed with oil as a grain
offering; 56one gold dish weighing ten
shekels, filled with incense; 57one young bull,
one ram and one male lamb a year old, for a
burnt offering; 58one male goat for a sin offering; 59and two oxen, five rams, five male
goats and five male lambs a year old, to be
sacrificed as a fellowship offering. This was
the offering of Gamaliel son of Pedahzur.

7:60 60On the ninth day Abidan son of Gideoni,[b] the
bNu 1:11 leader of the people of Benjamin, brought his
offering.

61His offering was one silver plate weighing
a hundred and thirty shekels, and one silver
sprinkling bowl weighing seventy shekels,
both according to the sanctuary shekel, each
filled with fine flour mixed with oil as a grain
offering; 62one gold dish weighing ten
shekels, filled with incense; 63one young bull,
one ram and one male lamb a year old, for a
burnt offering; 64one male goat for a sin offering; 65and two oxen, five rams, five male
goats and five male lambs a year old, to be
sacrificed as a fellowship offering. This was
the offering of Abidan son of Gideoni.

7:66 66On the tenth day Ahiezer son of Ammishaddai,[c]
cNu 1:12; 2:25 the leader of the people of Dan, brought his
offering.

67His offering was one silver plate weighing a
hundred and thirty shekels, and one silver

No coward soul is mine,
No trembler in the world's storm-troubled sphere:
I see Heaven's glories shine,
And faith shines equal, arming me from fear.

—Emily Brontë (1818–1848)

The Shekel

NU 7:84–86

Prior to the existence of coins, people in Old Testament times generally exchanged precious metals, measured into specific weights (shekel means "weight"). The shekel was a part of the Mesopotamian weight system used by both the Canaanites and Israelites. At about half an ounce, the silver sanctuary shekel weighed the same amount as the common shekel.

For 12 successive days, a leader from a different tribe presents one silver plate, one silver bowl, and one gold dish to God. The pomp and ceremony of their presentation day by day moves beyond the actual weight or value of their gift. The leaders present to the Lord the hearts of the people along with the gifts. The Lord's pleasure in these gifts is indicated by his audible voice speaking to Moses from between the cherubim (Nu 7:89) after the gifts are received. God's pleasure in gifts that are given with heart—not out of obligation or ritual but out of love for him—is evident throughout Scripture (Ps 51:16–17; 2Co 9:7).

sprinkling bowl weighing seventy shekels,
both according to the sanctuary shekel, each
filled with fine flour mixed with oil as a grain
offering; [68]one gold dish weighing ten
shekels, filled with incense; [69]one young bull,
one ram and one male lamb a year old, for a
burnt offering; [70]one male goat for a sin offering; [71]and two oxen, five rams, five male
goats and five male lambs a year old, to be
sacrificed as a fellowship offering. This was
the offering of Ahiezer son of Ammishaddai.

[72]On the eleventh day Pagiel son of Ocran,[d] the 7:72
leader of the people of Asher, brought his offering. [d]Nu 1:13

[73]His offering was one silver plate weighing a
hundred and thirty shekels, and one silver
sprinkling bowl weighing seventy shekels,
both according to the sanctuary shekel, each
filled with fine flour mixed with oil as a grain
offering; [74]one gold dish weighing ten
shekels, filled with incense; [75]one young bull,
one ram and one male lamb a year old, for a
burnt offering; [76]one male goat for a sin offering; [77]and two oxen, five rams, five male
goats and five male lambs a year old, to be
sacrificed as a fellowship offering. This was
the offering of Pagiel son of Ocran.

[78]On the twelfth day Ahira son of Enan,[e] the 7:78
leader of the people of Naphtali, brought his [e]Nu 1:15;
offering. 2:29

[79]His offering was one silver plate weighing a
hundred and thirty shekels, and one silver
sprinkling bowl weighing seventy shekels,
both according to the sanctuary shekel, each
filled with fine flour mixed with oil as a grain
offering; [80]one gold dish weighing ten
shekels, filled with incense; [81]one young bull,
one ram and one male lamb a year old, for a
burnt offering; [82]one male goat for a sin offering; [83]and two oxen, five rams, five male
goats and five male lambs a year old, to be
sacrificed as a fellowship offering. This was
the offering of Ahira son of Enan.

[84]These were the offerings of the Israelite leaders for the dedication of the altar when it was
anointed:[f] twelve silver plates, twelve silver sprin- 7:84
kling bowls[g] and twelve gold dishes.[h] [85]Each sil- [f]ver 1,10 [g]Nu 4:14
ver plate weighed a hundred and thirty shekels, [h]ver 14
and each sprinkling bowl seventy shekels. Altogether, the silver dishes weighed two thousand
four hundred shekels,[a] according to the sanctuary
shekel. [86]The twelve gold dishes filled with
incense weighed ten shekels each, according to
the sanctuary shekel. Altogether, the gold dishes
weighed a hundred and twenty shekels.[b] [87]The
total number of animals for the burnt offering
came to twelve young bulls, twelve rams and
twelve male lambs a year old, together with their

[a] *85* That is, about 60 pounds (about 28 kilograms)
[b] *86* That is, about 3 pounds (about 1.4 kilograms)

grain offering. Twelve male goats were used for
the sin offering. 88The total number of animals for
the sacrifice of the fellowship offering came to
twenty-four oxen, sixty rams, sixty male goats and
sixty male lambs a year old. These were the offer-
7:88 ings for the dedication of the altar after it was
[i]ver 1,10 anointed.[i]
7:89 89When Moses entered the Tent of Meeting to
[j]Ex 25:21,22; speak with the LORD,[j] he heard the voice speaking
33:9,11 to him from between the two cherubim above the
[k]Ps 80:1; 99:1 atonement cover[k] on the ark of the Testimony.
And he spoke with him.

Setting Up the Lamps

8 The LORD said to Moses, 2"Speak to Aaron and
say to him, 'When you set up the seven lamps,
8:2 they are to light the area in front of the lamp-
[l]Ex 25:37; Lev 24:2,4 stand.[l]' "
3Aaron did so; he set up the lamps so that they
faced forward on the lampstand, just as the LORD
8:4 commanded Moses. 4This is how the lampstand
[m]Ex 25:18, was made: It was made of hammered gold[m]—
36; 25:18 [n]Ex 25:9 from its base to its blossoms. The lampstand was
made exactly like the pattern[n] the LORD had
shown Moses.

The Setting Apart of the Levites

5The LORD said to Moses: 6"Take the Levites
from among the other Israelites and make them
8:6 ceremonially clean.[o] 7To purify them, do this:
[o]Lev 22:2; Sprinkle the water of cleansing[p] on them; then
Isa 1:16; 52:11 have them shave their whole bodies[q] and wash
their clothes,[r] and so purify themselves. 8Have
8:7 [p]Nu 19:9,17 them take a young bull with its grain offering of
[q]Lev 14:9; Dt 21:12 fine flour mixed with oil;[s] then you are to take a
[r]Lev 14:8 second young bull for a sin offering. 9Bring the
8:8 Levites to the front of the Tent of Meeting[t] and
[s]Lev 2:1; assemble the whole Israelite community.[u] 10You
Nu 15:8-10 are to bring the Levites before the LORD, and the
8:9 Israelites are to lay their hands on them.[v] 11Aaron
[t]Ex 40:12 is to present the Levites before the LORD as a wave
[u]Lev 8:3 offering[w] from the Israelites, so that they may be
8:10 ready to do the work of the LORD.
[v]Ac 6:6 12"After the Levites lay their hands on the heads
8:11 of the bulls,[x] use the one for a sin offering to the
[w]Lev 7:30 LORD and the other for a burnt offering, to make
8:12 atonement[y] for the Levites. 13Have the Levites
[x]Ex 29:10 stand in front of Aaron and his sons and then
[y]Ex 29:36 present them as a wave offering to the LORD. 14In
8:14 this way you are to set the Levites apart from the
[z]Nu 3:12 other Israelites, and the Levites will be mine.[z]
8:15 15"After you have purified the Levites and pre-
[a]Ex 29:24 sented them as a wave offering,[a] they are to come
to do their work at the Tent of Meeting. 16They are
the Israelites who are to be given wholly to me. I
have taken them as my own in place of the first-
8:16 born, the first male offspring[b] from every Israel-
[b]Nu 3:12 ite woman. 17Every firstborn male in Israel,
8:17 whether man or animal,[c] is mine. When I struck
[c]Ex 4:23 down all the firstborn in Egypt, I set them apart

God's Presence

NU 7:89

This verse records the culmination of the story, a resounding end to 12 days of ceremony. Standing within the sanctuary, but outside the veil that separates the Most Holy Place from the Holy Place, Moses hears the audible voice of God speaking from between the cherubim. Some ancient scholars believe that this manifestation of God's voice was an incarnation of the Son of God: the Word who would one day take human form and come to live among his people. Such a belief seems reasonable, for Jesus is indeed identified as the one through whom God chooses to make himself fully known to his people (Jn 1:14; Heb 1:1–3).

The Voice of God

Imagine actually hearing the voice of God! Moses seems to accept this as a normal occurrence. And, in fact, it is normal for Moses. The words "the LORD said to Moses" appear 138 times in the Old Testament, the words "the LORD said," 290 times. God wasn't silent then, and he's not silent today. Even though he might not speak audibly, God still has much to say to us.

Has the Lord ever spoken to you (see Jn 14:26; 1Jn 2:27)? What are some ways the Holy Spirit might communicate with you? And how do you know if the voice is God's?

The Bible is the chief way the Spirit speaks and is the test for all the other voices that claim to be God's. It is "living and active" (Heb 4:12). It tells us who God is and who we are. What particular insight has it given you lately about God or about yourself?

The Holy Spirit sometimes spoke directly to Paul; however, other times he used people to guide Paul (Ac 21:10–11). Has God ever seemed to use someone to guide you? Describe what happened. As you look back, do you think the guidance passes the test of agreement with the Scriptures? Why or why not?

The Spirit sometimes speaks through visions and dreams. Peter learned an important lesson through a vision (Ac 10:9–20). Have you ever had a dream or a vision that you felt was from God? What was the dream or vision like? What did it reveal to you? As you look back, do you think the dream or vision passes the test of agreeing with the Scriptures? Why or why not?

The Holy Spirit sometimes uses circumstances to communicate with people. God used Esther's circumstances to save his people. When have you felt that God used your circumstances to speak to you? Looking back, do you think your interpretation of the circumstances agrees with Scripture's teachings? Why or why not?

The Spirit can put thoughts in people's minds. He put the plans for the temple into David's mind (1Ch 28:12,19). Have you ever had plans, ideas or mental impressions that you felt were from God? Describe them. As you look back on them, do you think your ideas were in keeping with Scripture? Why or why not?

God is a person. He wants to have a relationship with you. A good relationship requires communication. In other words, he may be speaking, but are you listening? And if you're listening, are you testing the voice to see if it's God's?

Enjoying God THROUGH the Word

Read Jeremiah 32:6–9 (page 1288). Jeremiah receives word from God telling him to buy a field. He doesn't act immediately. Perhaps he isn't sure the message is from God. Only when his cousin comes to him and says, "Buy my field," is Jeremiah certain the message comes from God.

What should you do if you think you hear God speaking, but you're not sure? Try to test a mental impression to see if it is from the Lord (1Jn 4:1–3). A word from God will always (1) agree with the Bible. He will not contradict himself. A word from God will also (2) be consistent with Christ's character. If you are a believer in Christ, you have the Holy Spirit in you and you should (3) sense agreement with a message that's truly from God. Ask yourself: Am I fixing my spiritual eyes on Jesus, or have my own wishes tainted the impression? Am I obeying Scripture, or am I being deceived?

Enjoying God THROUGH Experience

During your prayer time, listen for the Lord to speak to your heart, perhaps through a Bible verse, a song, a mental impression or a reaction of some kind. You may sense a response in yourself of faith, awe, peace, praise or healing. The Spirit speaks to the core of your being, filling that deep place in you—that place no one else can reach.

Go to page 294 for your next weekly study.

8:17 for myself.[d] 18And I have taken the Levites in place
[d]Ex 13:2; of all the firstborn sons in Israel.[e] 19Of all the Isra-
Lk 2:23 elites, I have given the Levites as gifts to Aaron
8:18 and his sons[f] to do the work at the Tent of Meet-
[e]Nu 3:12 ing on behalf of the Israelites[g] and to make atone-
8:19 ment for them[h] so that no plague will strike the
[f]Nu 3:9 Israelites when they go near the sanctuary."
[g]Nu 1:53 20Moses, Aaron and the whole Israelite com-
[h]Nu 16:46 munity did with the Levites just as the LORD commanded Moses. 21The Levites purified themselves
8:21 and washed their clothes.[i] Then Aaron presented
[i]ver 7 them as a wave offering before the LORD and made
[j]ver 12 atonement for them to purify them.[j] 22After that,
the Levites came to do their work at the Tent of
Meeting under the supervision of Aaron and his
sons. They did with the Levites just as the LORD
commanded Moses.
23The LORD said to Moses, 24"This applies to the
8:24 Levites: Men twenty-five years old or more[k] shall
[k]1Ch 23:3 come to take part in the work at the Tent of Meet-
[l]Ex 38:21; ing,[l] 25but at the age of fifty, they must retire from
Nu 4:3 their regular service and work no longer. 26They
may assist their brothers in performing their
duties at the Tent of Meeting, but they themselves
must not do the work. This, then, is how you are
to assign the responsibilities of the Levites."

The Passover

9:1 9 The LORD spoke to Moses in the Desert of Sinai
[m]Ex 40:2 in the first month[m] of the second year after
[n]Nu 1:1 they came out of Egypt.[n] He said, 2"Have the Israelites celebrate the Passover at the appointed time.
3Celebrate it at the appointed time, at twilight on
the fourteenth day of this month, in accordance
9:3 with all its rules and regulations.[o]"
[o]Ex 12:2-11, 43-49; 4So Moses told the Israelites to celebrate the
Lev 23:5-8; Passover, 5and they did so in the Desert of Sinai
Dt 16:1-8 at twilight on the fourteenth day of the first
9:5 month.[p] The Israelites did everything just as the
[p]Ex 12:1-13; LORD commanded Moses.
Jos 5:10 6But some of them could not celebrate the
Passover on that day because they were ceremo-
9:6 nially unclean[q] on account of a dead body. So they
[q]Lev 5:3 [r]Ex 18:15; came to Moses and Aaron[r] that same day 7and
Nu 27:2 said to Moses, "We have become unclean because
of a dead body, but why should we be kept from
presenting the LORD's offering with the other Israelites at the appointed time?"
8Moses answered them, "Wait until I find out
9:8 what the LORD commands concerning you."[s]
[s]Ex 18:15; 9Then the LORD said to Moses, 10"Tell the Israel-
Nu 27:5,21; ites: 'When any of you or your descendants are
Ps 85:8 9:10 unclean because of a dead body or are away on a
[t]2Ch 30:2 journey, they may still celebrate[t] the LORD's
Passover. 11They are to celebrate it on the four-
9:11 teenth day of the second month at twilight. They
[u]Ex 12:8 are to eat the lamb, together with unleavened
bread and bitter herbs.[u] 12They must not leave any
9:12 [v]Ex 12:10,43 of it till morning[v] or break any of its bones.[w]
[w]Ex 12:46; When they celebrate the Passover, they must fol-
Jn 19:36* low all the regulations. 13But if a man who is cer-

Seeking Direction

NU 9:6–10

When the people come to Moses with their problem, he does not rule immediately. Instead, he asks them to wait while he seeks direction from God.

His actions provide a useful example for us today. Far too often, we respond impulsively to the situations around us. It is tempting for us to think that, because we are walking with God, we will make right choices. Yet Moses—who walks and talks with God as with a friend (Ex 33:11)—knows the importance of seeking the Lord's counsel. Operating out of his own wisdom, Moses might have ordered the unclean Israelites not to participate in the Passover; instead, he receives direction from God that allows the Israelites in question to join in the celebration.

What decisions have you made entirely on your own recently? What were the results? Ask God to remind you to bring future problems to him—and to teach you to patiently wait for his counsel.

God's Presence

NU 9:15

The pillar that directs the Israelites in their journey through the desert appears to them as a cloud by day and fire by night. This miraculous pillar of fire and cloud provides them with illumination for their travels as well as with visual evidence of God's presence and will for his people (Ex 13:21–22).

After the tabernacle is built, God's presence is also manifested in a cloud. This cloud is not in the form of a pillar, yet it does have several similarities to the column that previously guided them. During the day, the cloud appears over the tabernacle; at night, the same cloud is present, but to the people it looks like fire.

Often, we as modern-day believers long for a similar physical manifestation of God's presence to lead us. Although he may give us a sign indicating his direction, we have no guarantee that he will do so. At such times, it's important to remember that we have advantages that the Israelites did not: knowledge of the good news of Jesus Christ and the indwelling of God's Spirit, who faithfully guides us.

emonially clean and not on a journey fails to celebrate the Passover, that person must be cut off from his people[x] because he did not present the LORD's offering at the appointed time. That man will bear the consequences of his sin.

14" 'An alien[y] living among you who wants to celebrate the LORD's Passover must do so in accordance with its rules and regulations. You must have the same regulations for the alien and the native-born.' "

The Cloud Above the Tabernacle

15 On the day the tabernacle, the Tent of the Testimony, was set up, the cloud[z] covered it. From evening till morning the cloud above the tabernacle looked like fire.[a] 16 That is how it continued to be; the cloud covered it, and at night it looked like fire. 17 Whenever the cloud lifted from above the Tent, the Israelites set out; wherever the cloud settled, the Israelites encamped.[b] 18 At the LORD's command the Israelites set out, and at his command they encamped. As long as the cloud stayed over the tabernacle, they remained in camp. 19 When the cloud remained over the tabernacle a long time, the Israelites obeyed the LORD's order and did not set out. 20 Sometimes the cloud was over the tabernacle only a few days; at the LORD's command they would encamp, and then at his command they would set out. 21 Sometimes the cloud stayed only from evening till morning, and when it lifted in the morning, they set out. Whether by day or by night, whenever the cloud lifted, they set out. 22 Whether the cloud stayed over the tabernacle for two days or a month or a year, the Israelites would remain in camp and not set out; but when it lifted, they would set out. 23 At the LORD's command they encamped, and at the LORD's command they set out. They obeyed the LORD's order, in accordance with his command through Moses.

The Silver Trumpets

10 The LORD said to Moses: 2"Make two trumpets[c] of hammered silver, and use them for calling the community[d] together and for having the camps set out. 3 When both are sounded, the whole community is to assemble before you at the entrance to the Tent of Meeting. 4 If only one is sounded, the leaders[e]—the heads of the clans of Israel—are to assemble before you. 5 When a trumpet blast is sounded, the tribes camping on the east are to set out.[f] 6 At the sounding of a second blast, the camps on the south are to set out.[g] The blast will be the signal for setting out. 7 To gather the assembly, blow the trumpets,[h] but not with the same signal.[i]

8"The sons of Aaron, the priests, are to blow the trumpets. This is to be a lasting ordinance for you and the generations to come.[j] 9 When you go into battle in your own land against an enemy who is

9:13 [x]Ge 17:14; Ex 12:15
9:14 [y]Ex 12:48,49
9:15 [z]Ex 40:34 [a]Ex 13:21
9:17 [b]Ex 40:36-38; Nu 10:11, 12; 1Co 10:1
10:2 [c]Ne 12:35; Ps 47:5 [d]Jer 4:5,19; 6:1; Hos 5:8; Joel 2:1,15; Am 3:6
10:4 [e]Ex 18:21; Nu 1:16; 7:2
10:5 [f]ver 14
10:6 [g]ver 18
10:7 [h]Eze 33:3; Joel 2:1 [i]1Co 14:8
10:8 [j]Nu 31:6

10:9 oppressing you,[k] sound a blast on the trumpets.
[k]Jdg 2:18; 6:9; Then you will be remembered[l] by the LORD your
1Sa 10:18; God and rescued from your enemies.[m] 10Also at
Ps 106:42 [l]Ge 8:1 your times of rejoicing—your appointed feasts
[m]Ps 106:4 and New Moon festivals[n]—you are to sound the
10:10 trumpets[o] over your burnt offerings and fellow-
[n]Ps 81:3 ship offerings,[a] and they will be a memorial for
[o]Lev 23:24 you before your God. I am the LORD your God."

The Israelites Leave Sinai

11On the twentieth day of the second month of
10:11 [p]Ex 40:17 the second year,[p] the cloud lifted[q] from above the
[q]Nu 9:17 tabernacle of the Testimony. 12Then the Israelites
set out from the Desert of Sinai and traveled from
place to place until the cloud came to rest in the
10:13 Desert of Paran. 13They set out, this first time, at
[r]Dt 1:6 the LORD's command through Moses.[r]
14The divisions of the camp of Judah went first,
10:14 [s]Nu 2:3-9 under their standard.[s] Nahshon son of Ammin-
[t]Nu 1:7 adab[t] was in command. 15Nethanel son of Zuar
was over the division of the tribe of Issachar, 16and
Eliab son of Helon was over the division of the
tribe of Zebulun. 17Then the tabernacle was taken
down, and the Gershonites and Merarites, who
10:17 carried it, set out.[u]
[u]Nu 4:21-32 18The divisions of the camp of Reuben went
10:18 [v]Nu 2:10-16 next, under their standard.[v] Elizur son of Shedeur
was in command. 19Shelumiel son of Zurishaddai
was over the division of the tribe of Simeon, 20and
Eliasaph son of Deuel was over the division of the
tribe of Gad. 21Then the Kohathites set out, carry-
10:21 [w]Nu 4:20 ing the holy things.[w] The tabernacle was to be set
[x]ver 17 up before they arrived.[x]
22The divisions of the camp of Ephraim[y] went
10:22 [y]Nu 2:24 next, under their standard. Elishama son of
Ammihud was in command. 23Gamaliel son of
Pedahzur was over the division of the tribe of
Manasseh, 24and Abidan son of Gideoni was over
the division of the tribe of Benjamin.
10:25 25Finally, as the rear guard[z] for all the units, the
[z]Nu 2:31; Jos 6:9 divisions of the camp of Dan set out, under their
standard. Ahiezer son of Ammishaddai was in
command. 26Pagiel son of Ocran was over the division of the tribe of Asher, 27and Ahira son of Enan
was over the division of the tribe of Naphtali.
28This was the order of march for the Israelite divisions as they set out.
10:29 29Now Moses said to Hobab[a] son of Reuel[b] the
[a]Jdg 4:11 [b]Ex 2:18 Midianite, Moses' father-in-law,[c] "We are setting
[c]Ex 3:1 out for the place about which the LORD said, 'I will
[d]Ge 12:7 give it to you.'[d] Come with us and we will treat
you well, for the LORD has promised good things
to Israel."
10:30 [e]Mt 21:29 30He answered, "No, I will not go;[e] I am going
back to my own land and my own people."
31But Moses said, "Please do not leave us. You
know where we should camp in the desert, and
10:31 [f]Job 29:15 you can be our eyes.[f] 32If you come with us, we

[a] 10 Traditionally *peace offerings*

Silver Trumpets

NU 10:10

There are two types of trumpets described in the Old Testament: one is made of a ram's horn; the other, of silver. Long and thin, these silver trumpets—very different from today's trumpet styles—are tubular in shape with flared ends. The Lord ordered that these two trumpets be made of "hammered silver" (Nu 10:2) and be used to call the people into an orderly marching sequence. They are also sounded as a means of calling God to give them victory in battle (Nu 10:9) and as a call to times of feasting and celebration.

A Steady Diet

NU 11:4–5,7

After the variety of foods the people had consumed in Egypt—many of them well seasoned—a daily dose of manna seems extraordinarily dull and tasteless. The non-Israelites in the group ("the rabble") are particularly put out by this repetitive meal. Despite its blandness, manna is a sorely needed provision of food in the desert and is clearly God given. This "bread from heaven" (Ex 16:4), which appears miraculously on the ground each morning, can be boiled, baked, fried or ground into cakes.

There are many possible explanations for the phenomenon of manna. Some suggest that manna was a product of the secretion of two kinds of insects on a tamarisk shrub. The regularly changing pattern of the manna's appearance (double portions every sixth day, nothing on the seventh day), however, defies explanation and testifies to the divine nature of its provision, given by a loving God who cares for the welfare of his people (see the note on Exodus 16:31, page 113).

will share with you[g] whatever good things the **10:32** [g]Dt 10:18
LORD gives us.[h]" [h]Ps 22:27-31; 67:5-7
[33]So they set out[i] from the mountain of the LORD
and traveled for three days. The ark of the cov- **10:33**
enant of the LORD[j] went before them during those [i]ver 12;
three days to find them a place to rest. [34]The cloud Dt 1:33
of the LORD was over them by day when they set [j]Jos 3:3
out from the camp.[k] **10:34**
[35]Whenever the ark set out, Moses said, [k]Nu 9:15-23

"Rise up, O LORD! **10:35**
May your enemies be scattered;[l] [l]Ps 68:1
may your foes flee before you.[m]" [m]Dt 7:10; 32:41;
[36]Whenever it came to rest, he said, Ps 68:2; Isa 17:12-14

"Return,[n] O LORD, **10:36** [n]Isa 63:17
to the countless thousands of Israel.[o]" [o]Dt 1:10

Fire From the LORD

11 Now the people complained about their
hardships in the hearing of the LORD, and
when he heard them his anger was aroused. Then
fire from the LORD burned among them[p] and con- **11:1** [p]Lev 10:2
sumed some of the outskirts of the camp. [2]When
the people cried out to Moses, he prayed to the
LORD[q] and the fire died down. [3]So that place was **11:2** [q]Nu 21:7
called Taberah,[a][r] because fire from the LORD had **11:3**
burned among them. [r]Dt 9:22

Quail From the LORD

[4]The rabble with them began to crave other
food,[s] and again the Israelites started wailing[t] and **11:4** [s]Ex 12:38
said, "If only we had meat to eat! [5]We remember [t]Ps 78:18;
the fish we ate in Egypt at no cost—also the 1Co 10:6
cucumbers, melons, leeks, onions and garlic.[u]
[6]But now we have lost our appetite; we never see **11:5** [u]Ex 16:3
anything but this manna!"
[7]The manna was like coriander seed[v] and **11:7** [v]Ex 16:31
looked like resin.[w] [8]The people went around gath- [w]Ge 2:12
ering it, and then ground it in a handmill or
crushed it in a mortar. They cooked it in a pot or
made it into cakes. And it tasted like something
made with olive oil. [9]When the dew[x] settled on **11:9** [x]Ex 16:13
the camp at night, the manna also came down.
[10]Moses heard the people of every family wailing, each at the entrance to his tent. The LORD
became exceedingly angry, and Moses was troubled. [11]He asked the LORD, "Why have you
brought this trouble on your servant? What have **11:11** [y]Ex 5:22
I done to displease you that you put the burden of
all these people on me?[y] [12]Did I conceive all these **11:12**
people? Did I give them birth? Why do you tell me [z]Isa 40:11; 49:23
to carry them in my arms, as a nurse carries an [a]Ex 13:5
infant,[z] to the land you promised on oath to their
forefathers?[a] [13]Where can I get meat for all these **11:13**
people?[b] They keep wailing to me, 'Give us meat [b]Jn 6:5-9
to eat!' [14]I cannot carry all these people by myself; **11:14** [c]Ex 18:18
the burden is too heavy for me.[c] [15]If this is how
you are going to treat me, put me to death[d] right **11:15** [d]Ex 32:32

[a] 3 *Taberah* means *burning.*

now[e]—if I have found favor in your eyes—and do not let me face my own ruin."

16The LORD said to Moses: "Bring me seventy of Israel's elders who are known to you as leaders and officials among the people. Have them come to the Tent of Meeting, that they may stand there with you. 17I will come down and speak with you there, and I will take of the Spirit that is on you and put the Spirit on them.[f] They will help you carry the burden of the people so that you will not have to carry it alone.[g]

18"Tell the people: 'Consecrate yourselves[h] in preparation for tomorrow, when you will eat meat. The LORD heard you when you wailed,[i] "If only we had meat to eat! We were better off in Egypt!"[j] Now the LORD will give you meat, and you will eat it. 19You will not eat it for just one day, or two days, or five, ten or twenty days, 20but for a whole month—until it comes out of your nostrils and you loathe it[k]—because you have rejected the LORD,[l] who is among you, and have wailed before him, saying, "Why did we ever leave Egypt?" ' "

21But Moses said, "Here I am among six hundred thousand men[m] on foot, and you say, 'I will give them meat to eat for a whole month!' 22Would they have enough if flocks and herds were slaughtered for them? Would they have enough if all the fish in the sea were caught for them?"[n]

23The LORD answered Moses, "Is the LORD's arm too short?[o] You will now see whether or not what I say will come true for you.[p]"

24So Moses went out and told the people what the LORD had said. He brought together seventy of their elders and had them stand around the Tent. 25Then the LORD came down in the cloud[q] and spoke with him,[r] and he took of the Spirit[s] that was on him and put the Spirit on the seventy elders.[t] When the Spirit rested on them, they prophesied,[u] but they did not do so again.[*a*]

26However, two men, whose names were Eldad and Medad, had remained in the camp. They were listed among the elders, but did not go out to the Tent. Yet the Spirit also rested on them, and they prophesied in the camp. 27A young man ran and told Moses, "Eldad and Medad are prophesying in the camp."

28Joshua son of Nun, who had been Moses' aide[v] since youth, spoke up and said, "Moses, my lord, stop them!"[w]

29But Moses replied, "Are you jealous for my sake? I wish that all the LORD's people were prophets[x] and that the LORD would put his Spirit on them!" 30Then Moses and the elders of Israel returned to the camp.

31Now a wind went out from the LORD and drove quail[y] in from the sea. It brought them[*b*] down all around the camp to about three feet[*c*] above the

11:15 [e]1Ki 19:4; Jnh 4:3
11:17 [f]ver 25,29; 1Sa 10:6; 2Ki 2:9,15; Joel 2:28 [g]Ex 18:18
11:18 [h]Ex 19:10 [i]Ex 16:7 [j]ver 5; Ac 7:39
11:20 [k]Ps 78:29; 106:14,15 [l]Jos 24:27; 1Sa 10:19
11:21 [m]Ex 12:37
11:22 [n]Mt 15:33
11:23 [o]Isa 50:2; 59:1 [p]Nu 23:19; Eze 12:25; 24:14
11:25 [q]Nu 12:5 [r]ver 17 [s]1Sa 10:6 [t]Ac 2:17 [u]1Sa 10:10
11:28 [v]Ex 33:11; Jos 1:1 [w]Mk 9:38-40
11:29 [x]1Co 14:5
11:31 [y]Ex 16:13; Ps 78:26-28

a 25 Or *prophesied and continued to do so* *b* 31 Or *They flew*
c 31 Hebrew *two cubits* (about 1 meter)

Help for the Task

NU 11:16-17

The job Moses has been given is not an easy one. Already much of the difficult work—leading the people out of Egypt—has been completed. But the road ahead is long, and Moses is struggling under the burden he alone carries. Exhausted and frustrated, he cries out, dramatically asking God to end his suffering (Nu 11:14-15).

When we try to handle things solo, we're certain to burn out. Moses' father-in-law knows this (Ex 18:13-24). So does God. In response to Moses' venting, the Lord compassionately instructs him to recruit others to share the burden. God blesses these other leaders with an outpouring of his Spirit to equip them for their work (Nu 11:24-25).

What overwhelming responsibilities are you currently shouldering alone—difficult relationships, job, home duties, community responsibilities, parenting tasks, personal life? Make a list of people—at home, at work, at church—on whom you can call to share your burdens.

ground, as far as a day's walk in any direction. 32All that day and night and all the next day the people went out and gathered quail. No one gathered less than ten homers.[a] Then they spread them out all around the camp. 33But while the meat was still between their teeth[z] and before it could be consumed, the anger of the LORD burned against the people, and he struck them with a severe plague.[a] 34Therefore the place was named Kibroth Hattaavah,[b][b] because there they buried the people who had craved other food.

35From Kibroth Hattaavah the people traveled to Hazeroth[c] and stayed there.

Miriam and Aaron Oppose Moses

12 Miriam and Aaron began to talk against Moses because of his Cushite wife,[d] for he had married a Cushite. 2"Has the LORD spoken only through Moses?" they asked. "Hasn't he also spoken through us?"[e] And the LORD heard this.[f]

3(Now Moses was a very humble man,[g] more humble than anyone else on the face of the earth.)

4At once the LORD said to Moses, Aaron and Miriam, "Come out to the Tent of Meeting, all three of you." So the three of them came out. 5Then the LORD came down in a pillar of cloud;[h] he stood at the entrance to the Tent and summoned Aaron and Miriam. When both of them stepped forward, 6he said, "Listen to my words:

"When a prophet of the LORD is among you,
I reveal myself to him in visions,[i]
I speak to him in dreams.[j]
7But this is not true of my servant Moses;[k]
he is faithful in all my house.[l]
8With him I speak face to face,
clearly and not in riddles;[m]
he sees the form of the LORD.[n]
Why then were you not afraid
to speak against my servant Moses?"

9The anger of the LORD burned against them, and he left them.[o]

10When the cloud lifted from above the Tent, there stood Miriam—leprous,[c] like snow.[p] Aaron turned toward her and saw that she had leprosy;[q] 11and he said to Moses, "Please, my lord, do not hold against us the sin we have so foolishly committed.[r] 12Do not let her be like a stillborn infant coming from its mother's womb with its flesh half eaten away."

13So Moses cried out to the LORD, "O God, please heal her![s]"

14The LORD replied to Moses, "If her father had spit in her face,[t] would she not have been in dis-

11:33 [z]Ps 78:30 [a]Ps 106:15
11:34 [b]Dt 9:22
11:35 [c]Nu 33:17
12:1 [d]Ex 2:21
12:2 [e]Nu 16:3 [f]Nu 11:1
12:3 [g]Mt 11:29
12:5 [h]Nu 11:25
12:6 [i]Ge 15:1; 46:2 [j]Ge 31:10; 1Ki 3:5; Heb 1:1
12:7 [k]Jos 1:1-2; Ps 105:26 [l]Heb 3:2,5
12:8 [m]Dt 34:10 [n]Ex 20:4; Ps 17:15
12:9 [o]Ge 17:22
12:10 [p]Ex 4:6; Dt 24:9 [q]2Ki 5:1,27
12:11 [r]2Sa 19:19; 24:10
12:13 [s]Isa 30:26; Jer 17:14
12:14 [t]Dt 25:9; Job 17:6; 30:9-10; Isa 50:6

[a] *32* That is, probably about 60 bushels (about 2.2 kiloliters)
[b] *34* *Kibroth Hattaavah* means *graves of craving.*
[c] *10* The Hebrew word was used for various diseases affecting the skin—not necessarily leprosy.

Face to Face

NU 12:6–8

A prophet unlike any other, Moses shares a deep relationship with God. The statement that God speaks "face to face" (Nu 12:8) with him appears to be metaphoric. Though Moses cannot view the face of God and live (Ex 33:20), he is intimately acquainted with God, and God speaks to him as to a friend (Ex 33:11). Moses is certainly not the only prophet God uses; the Old Testament is filled with the accounts of people to whom God speaks through visions, dreams and other revelations. But the Lord's relationship with Moses and the manner in which he speaks to him—at times audibly (Nu 7:89)—are truly unique.

Moses' face-to-face relationship with God is unique for his time. Today, however, through the redemptive work of Jesus Christ, all believers can experience this close relationship with God. Jesus' death and resurrection have removed the barriers of sin, and a vital, fresh, face-to-face relationship with the Father can be ours.

grace for seven days? Confine her outside the
12:14 [u]Lev 13:46; Nu 5:2-3 camp[u] for seven days; after that she can be
brought back." 15 So Miriam was confined outside
the camp for seven days, and the people did not
move on till she was brought back.
12:16 [v]Nu 11:35 16 After that, the people left Hazeroth[v] and
encamped in the Desert of Paran.

Exploring Canaan

13 The LORD said to Moses, 2 "Send some men
13:2 [w]Dt 1:22 to explore[w] the land of Canaan, which I am
giving to the Israelites. From each ancestral tribe
send one of its leaders."
3 So at the LORD's command Moses sent them
out from the Desert of Paran. All of them were
leaders of the Israelites. 4 These are their names:

from the tribe of Reuben, Shammua son of Zaccur;
5 from the tribe of Simeon, Shaphat son of Hori;
13:6 [x]ver 30; Nu 14:6,24; 34:19; Jdg 1:12-15 6 from the tribe of Judah, Caleb son of Jephunneh;[x]
7 from the tribe of Issachar, Igal son of Joseph;
8 from the tribe of Ephraim, Hoshea son of Nun;
9 from the tribe of Benjamin, Palti son of Raphu;
10 from the tribe of Zebulun, Gaddiel son of Sodi;
11 from the tribe of Manasseh (a tribe of Joseph), Gaddi son of Susi;
12 from the tribe of Dan, Ammiel son of Gemalli;
13 from the tribe of Asher, Sethur son of Michael;
14 from the tribe of Naphtali, Nahbi son of Vophsi;
15 from the tribe of Gad, Geuel son of Maki.

16 These are the names of the men Moses sent to
13:16 [y]ver 8 explore the land. (Moses gave Hoshea son of Nun[y]
[z]Dt 32:44 the name Joshua.)[z]
17 When Moses sent them to explore Canaan, he
13:17 [a]Ge 12:9 said, "Go up through the Negev[a] and on into the
[b]Jdg 1:9 hill country.[b] 18 See what the land is like and
whether the people who live there are strong or
weak, few or many. 19 What kind of land do they
live in? Is it good or bad? What kind of towns do
they live in? Are they unwalled or fortified? 20 How
13:20 [c]Dt 1:25 is the soil? Is it fertile or poor? Are there trees on
it or not? Do your best to bring back some of the
13:21 [d]Nu 20:1; fruit of the land.[c]" (It was the season for the first
27:14; 33:36; ripe grapes.)
Jos 15:1 21 So they went up and explored the land from
[e]Jos 19:28 the Desert of Zin[d] as far as Rehob,[e] toward Lebo[a]
[f]Jos 13:5 Hamath.[f] 22 They went up through the Negev and
13:22 [g]Jos 15:14 came to Hebron, where Ahiman, Sheshai and Tal-
[h]Jos 15:13 mai,[g] the descendants of Anak,[h] lived. (Hebron
[i]Ps 78:12,43; had been built seven years before Zoan in Egypt.)[i]
Isa 19:11,13

[a] 21 Or *toward the entrance to*

Why Only Miriam?

NU 12:10-15

Though both Miriam and Aaron rebel against Moses, only Miriam is struck with leprosy. Why is Aaron spared? Perhaps Miriam is the first one to gripe, or perhaps her grumbling is worse than Aaron's. Or possibly Aaron is spared because of his position as high priest, so the worship of the Israelites will not be disrupted. Certainly, though Aaron is spared the disease, he suffers as he watches his sister bear the punishment for a sin both of them committed.

In any case, the objections regarding Moses' Cushite wife are apparently a cover for Miriam and Aaron's true complaint: "Has the LORD spoken only through Moses? . . . Hasn't he also spoken through us?" (Nu 12:2). God quickly and dramatically demonstrates that he will not tolerate jealousy among his servants.

Perspective on Challenges

NU 13:26–33

In their report about the land of Canaan, most of the Israelite spies emphasize the overwhelming size of its inhabitants. Though God has promised them they will inherit the land, they do not believe that its people can be conquered. Only Caleb and Joshua remain convinced that God can, and will, make Canaan their new home (Nu 14:6–8). Their statements minimize, rather than emphasize, the danger (Nu 14:9).

The Israelites' attitudes negatively impact their ability to move forward. When they see the size of the people of Canaan, fear grips them. They obsess about the size of the problem instead of focusing on the greatness of God's power.

What tough challenge do you face today? Write down a list of words related to your situation (for example, fear, love, forgiveness). Using a concordance, look up several verses on the subject. Write out one related Bible promise or insight that you can memorize and claim this week and focus on God's power rather than the problem at hand.

23When they reached the Valley of Eshcol,[a] they
cut off a branch bearing a single cluster of grapes.
Two of them carried it on a pole between them,
along with some pomegranates and figs. 24That
place was called the Valley of Eshcol because of
the cluster of grapes the Israelites cut off there.
25At the end of forty days they returned from
exploring the land.

Report on the Exploration

26They came back to Moses and Aaron and the
whole Israelite community at Kadesh in the
Desert of Paran. There they reported to them[j] and
to the whole assembly and showed them the fruit
of the land. 27They gave Moses this account: "We
went into the land to which you sent us, and it
does flow with milk and honey![k] Here is its fruit.[l]
28But the people who live there are powerful, and
the cities are fortified and very large.[m] We even
saw descendants of Anak there. 29The Amalekites
live in the Negev; the Hittites, Jebusites and Amorites live in the hill country; and the Canaanites
live near the sea and along the Jordan."
30Then Caleb silenced the people before Moses
and said, "We should go up and take possession of
the land, for we can certainly do it."
31But the men who had gone up with him said,
"We can't attack those people; they are stronger
than we are."[n] 32And they spread among the Israelites a bad report[o] about the land they had
explored. They said, "The land we explored
devours[p] those living in it. All the people we saw
there are of great size.[q] 33We saw the Nephilim[r]
there (the descendants of Anak[s] come from the
Nephilim). We seemed like grasshoppers in our
own eyes, and we looked the same to them."

The People Rebel

14 That night all the people of the community
raised their voices and wept aloud. 2All the
Israelites grumbled against Moses and Aaron, and
the whole assembly said to them, "If only we had
died in Egypt! Or in this desert![t] 3Why is the LORD
bringing us to this land only to let us fall by the
sword? Our wives and children will be taken as
plunder. Wouldn't it be better for us to go back to
Egypt?" 4And they said to each other, "We should
choose a leader and go back to Egypt.[u]"
5Then Moses and Aaron fell facedown[v] in front
of the whole Israelite assembly gathered there.
6Joshua son of Nun and Caleb son of Jephunneh,
who were among those who had explored the
land, tore their clothes 7and said to the entire Israelite assembly, "The land we passed through and
explored is exceedingly good.[w] 8If the LORD is
pleased with us,[x] he will lead us into that land, a
land flowing with milk and honey,[y] and will give
it to us. 9Only do not rebel[z] against the LORD. And
do not be afraid of the people of the land,[a] because

13:26 [j]Nu 32:8
13:27 [k]Ex 3:8 [l]Dt 1:25
13:28 [m]Dt 1:28; 9:1,2
13:31 [n]Dt 1:28; 9:1; Jos 14:8
13:32 [o]Nu 14:36, 37 [p]Eze 36:13, 14 [q]Am 2:9
13:33 [r]Ge 6:4 [s]Dt 1:28
14:2 [t]Nu 11:1
14:4 [u]Ne 9:17
14:5 [v]Nu 16:4,22, 45
14:7 [w]Nu 13:27; Dt 1:25
14:8 [x]Dt 10:15 [y]Nu 13:27
14:9 [z]Dt 1:26; 9:7,23,24 [a]Dt 1:21; 7:18; 20:1

[a] 23 *Eshcol* means *cluster*; also in verse 24.

we will swallow them up. Their protection is gone, but the LORD is with us. Do not be afraid of them."

10 But the whole assembly talked about stoning[b] them. Then the glory of the LORD[c] appeared at the Tent of Meeting to all the Israelites. 11 The LORD said to Moses, "How long will these people treat me with contempt? How long will they refuse to believe in me,[d] in spite of all the miraculous signs I have performed among them? 12 I will strike them down with a plague and destroy them, but I will make you into a nation[e] greater and stronger than they."

13 Moses said to the LORD, "Then the Egyptians will hear about it! By your power you brought these people up from among them.[f] 14 And they will tell the inhabitants of this land about it. They have already heard[g] that you, O LORD, are with these people and that you, O LORD, have been seen face to face, that your cloud stays over them, and that you go before them in a pillar of cloud by day and a pillar of fire by night.[h] 15 If you put these people to death all at one time, the nations who have heard this report about you will say, 16 'The LORD was not able to bring these people into the land he promised them on oath; so he slaughtered them in the desert.'[i]

17 "Now may the Lord's strength be displayed, just as you have declared: 18 'The LORD is slow to anger, abounding in love and forgiving sin and rebellion.[j] Yet he does not leave the guilty unpunished; he punishes the children for the sin of the fathers to the third and fourth generation.'[k] 19 In accordance with your great love, forgive[l] the sin of these people,[m] just as you have pardoned them from the time they left Egypt until now."[n]

20 The LORD replied, "I have forgiven them,[o] as you asked. 21 Nevertheless, as surely as I live[p] and as surely as the glory of the LORD fills the whole earth,[q] 22 not one of the men who saw my glory and the miraculous signs I performed in Egypt and in the desert but who disobeyed me and tested me ten times[r]— 23 not one of them will ever see the land I promised on oath[s] to their forefathers. No one who has treated me with contempt will ever see it.[t] 24 But because my servant Caleb has a different spirit and follows me wholeheartedly,[u] I will bring him into the land he went to, and his descendants will inherit it.[v] 25 Since the Amalekites and Canaanites are living in the valleys, turn[w] back tomorrow and set out toward the desert along the route to the Red Sea.[a]"

26 The LORD said to Moses and Aaron: 27 "How long will this wicked community grumble against me? I have heard the complaints of these grumbling Israelites.[x] 28 So tell them, 'As surely as I live,[y] declares the LORD, I will do to you the very things I heard you say: 29 In this desert your bodies will fall[z]—every one of you twenty years old or more[a] who was counted in the census and who has grumbled against me. 30 Not one of you will

14:10 [b]Ex 17:4 [c]Lev 9:23
14:11 [d]Ps 78:22; 106:24
14:12 [e]Ex 32:10
14:13 [f]Ex 32:11-14; Ps 106:23
14:14 [g]Ex 15:14 [h]Ex 13:21
14:16 [i]Jos 7:7
14:18 [j]Ex 34:6; Ps 145:8; Jnh 4:2 [k]Ex 20:5
14:19 [l]Ex 34:9 [m]Ps 106:45 [n]Ps 78:38
14:20 [o]Ps 106:23; Mic 7:18-20
14:21 [p]Dt 32:40; Isa 49:18 [q]Ps 72:19; Isa 6:3; Hab 2:14
14:22 [r]Ex 14:11; 32:1; 1Co 10:5
14:23 [s]Nu 32:11 [t]Heb 3:18
14:24 [u]ver 6-9; Jos 14:8,14 [v]Nu 32:12
14:25 [w]Dt 1:40
14:27 [x]Ex 16:12
14:28 [y]ver 21
14:29 [z]Nu 26:65 [a]Nu 1:45

[a] 25 Hebrew *Yam Suph*; that is, Sea of Reeds

Moses Intercedes

NU 14:13-19

In his intercession for the Israelites, Moses cites the very nature of God—his forgiveness, love and slowness to anger—as he pleads with God not to destroy them. He uses God's own words to reason with him (Ex 34:6-7). Yet even Moses recognizes that God's forgiveness will not erase the consequences of sin (Nu 14:18). God confirms this in his response. He honors Moses' request to spare the lives of the Israelites, but at the same time he specifies consequences for their rebellious behavior.

It is tempting to ask God to save us from our own sins. But, although he will forgive us if we repent, he loves us too much to let us live consequence-free lives. Just as parents discipline their children so they can reach their full potential, so God allows life's lessons to help us become all that we may be in him.

Forty Days = Forty Years

NU 14:34

The Israelites' sentence of wandering 40 years in the desert is not randomly chosen by God; each year of their nomadic existence corresponds to a day that they explored the land. This 40-year lesson is experienced not only in the lives of the people but also in their deaths. For their act of rebellion, all those 20 years and older (those who would have been old enough and able to conquer the land) will die in the desert. For 40 years the Israelites will not only live and wander in the desert; they will also watch as, one by one, they die for their sin. Thankfully, a compassionate God does not, however, totally write them off or destroy them. A young force of Israelites will eventually reach the gateway to the promised land and will then trust God for power to conquer.

enter the land I swore with uplifted hand to make
your home, except Caleb son of Jephunneh and
Joshua son of Nun. 31 As for your children that you
said would be taken as plunder, I will bring them
in to enjoy the land you have rejected.[b] 32 But
you—your bodies will fall[c] in this desert. 33 Your
children will be shepherds here for forty years,
suffering for your unfaithfulness, until the last of
your bodies lies in the desert. 34 For forty years—
one year for each of the forty days you explored
the land[d]—you will suffer for your sins and know
what it is like to have me against you.' 35 I, the
LORD, have spoken, and I will surely do these
things[e] to this whole wicked community, which
has banded together against me. They will meet
their end in this desert; here they will die."
36 So the men Moses had sent[f] to explore the land,
who returned and made the whole community
grumble against him by spreading a bad report[g]
about it— 37 these men responsible for spreading
the bad report[h] about the land were struck down
and died of a plague[i] before the LORD. 38 Of the men
who went to explore the land, only Joshua son of
Nun and Caleb son of Jephunneh survived.[j]
39 When Moses reported this to all the Israelites,
they mourned[k] bitterly. 40 Early the next morning
they went up toward the high hill country. "We
have sinned[l]," they said. "We will go up to the
place the LORD promised."
41 But Moses said, "Why are you disobeying the
LORD's command? This will not succeed![m] 42 Do not
go up, because the LORD is not with you. You will
be defeated by your enemies,[n] 43 for the Amalekites
and Canaanites will face you there. Because you
have turned away from the LORD, he will not be
with you and you will fall by the sword."
44 Nevertheless, in their presumption they went
up[o] toward the high hill country, though neither
Moses nor the ark of the LORD's covenant moved
from the camp.[p] 45 Then the Amalekites and
Canaanites who lived in that hill country came
down and attacked them and beat them down all
the way to Hormah.[q]

Supplementary Offerings

15 The LORD said to Moses, 2 "Speak to the Israelites and say to them: 'After you enter the
land I am giving you[r] as a home 3 and you present
to the LORD offerings made by fire, from the herd
or the flock,[s] as an aroma pleasing to the LORD[t]—
whether burnt offerings[u] or sacrifices, for special
vows or freewill offerings[v] or festival offerings[w]—
4 then the one who brings his offering shall present to the LORD a grain offering[x] of a tenth of an
ephah[a] of fine flour mixed with a quarter of a hin[b]
of oil. 5 With each lamb for the burnt offering or
the sacrifice, prepare a quarter of a hin of wine[y] as
a drink offering.

[a] *4* That is, probably about 2 quarts (about 2 liters) [b] *4* That is, probably about 1 quart (about 1 liter); also in verse 5

14:31 [b]Ps 106:24
14:32 [c]1Co 10:5
14:34 [d]Nu 13:25
14:35 [e]Nu 23:19
14:36 [f]Nu 13:4-16 [g]Nu 13:32
14:37 [h]1Co 10:10 [i]Nu 16:49
14:38 [j]Jos 14:6
14:39 [k]Ex 33:4
14:40 [l]Dt 1:41
14:41 [m]2Ch 24:20
14:42 [n]Dt 1:42
14:44 [o]Dt 1:43 [p]Nu 31:6
14:45 [q]Nu 21:3; Dt 1:44; Jdg 1:17
15:2 [r]Lev 23:10
15:3 [s]Lev 1:2 [t]ver 24; Ge 8:21; Ex 29:18 [u]Nu 28:19, 27 [v]Lev 22:18, 21; Ezr 1:4 [w]Lev 23:1-44
15:4 [x]Lev 2:1; 6:14
15:5 [y]Nu 28:7,14

15:6 [6]" 'With a ram[z] prepare a grain offering[a] of two-
[z]Lev 5:15 tenths of an ephah[a] of fine flour mixed with a
[a]Nu 28:12 [b]Eze 46:14 third of a hin[b] of oil,[b] [7]and a third of a hin of wine
as a drink offering. Offer it as an aroma pleasing
to the LORD.
[8]" 'When you prepare a young bull as a burnt
15:8 offering or sacrifice, for a special vow or a fellow-
[c]Lev 1:3; 3:1 ship offering[cc] to the LORD, [9]bring with the bull a
grain offering of three-tenths of an ephah[dd] of fine
15:9 [d]Lev 14:10 flour mixed with half a hin[e] of oil. [10]Also bring
half a hin of wine as a drink offering. It will be
an offering made by fire, an aroma pleasing to the
LORD. [11]Each bull or ram, each lamb or young
goat, is to be prepared in this manner. [12]Do this
for each one, for as many as you prepare.
15:13 [13]" 'Everyone who is native-born[e] must do these
[e]Lev 16:29 things in this way when he brings an offering
made by fire as an aroma pleasing to the LORD.
[14]For the generations to come, whenever an alien
or anyone else living among you presents an
offering made by fire as an aroma pleasing to the
LORD, he must do exactly as you do. [15]The community is to have the same rules for you and for
the alien living among you; this is a lasting ordi-
15:15 [f]ver 29; nance for the generations to come.[f] You and the
Nu 9:14 alien shall be the same before the LORD: [16]The
15:16 same laws and regulations will apply both to you
[g]Nu 9:14 and to the alien living among you.[g]' "
[17]The LORD said to Moses, [18]"Speak to the Israelites and say to them: 'When you enter the land
to which I am taking you [19]and you eat the food of
15:19 [h]Jos 5:11,12 the land,[h] present a portion as an offering to the
LORD. [20]Present a cake from the first of your
15:20 ground meal[i] and present it as an offering from
[i]Ex 34:26; Lev 23:14; the threshing floor.[j] [21]Throughout the generations
Dt 26:2,10 to come you are to give this offering to the LORD
[j]Lev 2:14 from the first of your ground meal.[k]
15:21 [k]Ro 11:16

Offerings for Unintentional Sins

15:22 [22]" 'Now if you unintentionally fail to keep any
[l]Lev 4:2 of these commands the LORD gave Moses[l]— [23]any
of the LORD's commands to you through him, from
the day the LORD gave them and continuing
through the generations to come— [24]and if this is
15:24 done unintentionally without the community
[m]Lev 5:15 being aware of it,[m] then the whole community is
[n]Lev 4:14 [o]Lev 4:3 to offer a young bull for a burnt offering[n] as an
aroma pleasing to the LORD, along with its pre-
scribed grain offering and drink offering, and a
male goat for a sin offering.[o] [25]The priest is to
make atonement for the whole Israelite commu-
15:25 nity, and they will be forgiven,[p] for it was not
[p]Lev 4:20; Ro 3:25; intentional and they have brought to the LORD for
Heb 2:17 their wrong an offering made by fire and a sin
offering. [26]The whole Israelite community and the
aliens living among them will be forgiven,

[a] 6 That is, probably about 4 quarts (about 4.5 liters)
[b] 6 That is, probably about 1 1/4 quarts (about 1.2 liters); also in verse 7 [c] 8 Traditionally *peace offering* [d] 9 That is, probably about 6 quarts (about 6.5 liters) [e] 9 That is, probably about 2 quarts (about 2 liters); also in verse 10

Enjoying fellowship is *one of life's sweetest blessings and joys. What would we do without people and the many shadings of companionship and camaraderie? We need friends in our lives, friends with whom we not only discuss "deep" issues and confide our secrets, fears or sorrows, but with whom we can laugh, play and even cry. The best times in life are made a thousand times better when shared with a dear friend.*

—Luci Swindoll

Sin Is Sin

NU 15:22-41

All sin is sin and requires atonement. Yet Scripture also distinguishes between two kinds of sin, prescribing different methods for dealing with each. In Numbers 15, God calls for unintentional sin—sin that is committed accidentally—to be handled gently and mercifully, with the motive of the sinner ever in mind. At the same time, God orders that intentional sin—especially sin that is committed in deliberate defiance of him—must receive swift, strict and severe consequences.

In order to help keep the Israelites from sinning in either manner, God commands them to wear blue tassels on their clothing. Like a string tied around a finger, these tassels serve as daily reminders not to sin. Today, we have something far better than such a physical reminder: the Holy Spirit, who lives within our hearts and who, moment-by-moment, reminds us of God's commands and pricks our consciences when necessary, encouraging us to be obedient.

because all the people were involved in the unintentional wrong.[q]
27“ ‘But if just one person sins unintentionally,[r]
he must bring a year-old female goat for a sin
offering. 28The priest is to make atonement before
the LORD for the one who erred by sinning unintentionally, and when atonement has been made
for him, he will be forgiven.[s] 29One and the same
law applies to everyone who sins unintentionally,
whether he is a native-born Israelite or an alien.
30“ ‘But anyone who sins defiantly,[t] whether
native-born or alien,[u] blasphemes the LORD, and
that person must be cut off from his people.
31Because he has despised the LORD's word and
broken his commands,[v] that person must surely
be cut off; his guilt remains on him.[w]’ ”

The Sabbath-Breaker Put to Death

32While the Israelites were in the desert, a man
was found gathering wood on the Sabbath day.[x]
33Those who found him gathering wood brought
him to Moses and Aaron and the whole assembly, 34and they kept him in custody, because it
was not clear what should be done to him.[y]
35Then the LORD said to Moses, “The man must
die.[z] The whole assembly must stone him outside
the camp.[a]” 36So the assembly took him outside
the camp and stoned him to death, as the LORD
commanded Moses.

Tassels on Garments

37The LORD said to Moses, 38“Speak to the Israelites and say to them: ‘Throughout the generations
to come you are to make tassels on the corners of
your garments,[b] with a blue cord on each tassel.
39You will have these tassels to look at and so you
will remember[c] all the commands of the LORD, that
you may obey them and not prostitute yourselves
by going after the lusts of your own hearts and
eyes. 40Then you will remember to obey all my
commands and will be consecrated to your God.[d]
41I am the LORD your God, who brought you out of
Egypt to be your God. I am the LORD your God.’ ”

Korah, Dathan and Abiram

16 Korah[e] son of Izhar, the son of Kohath, the
son of Levi, and certain Reubenites—
Dathan and Abiram, sons of Eliab,[f] and On son of
Peleth—became insolent[a] 2and rose up against
Moses. With them were 250 Israelite men, well-
known community leaders who had been
appointed members of the council.[g] 3They came
as a group to oppose Moses and Aaron[h] and said
to them, “You have gone too far! The whole community is holy,[i] every one of them, and the LORD
is with them.[j] Why then do you set yourselves
above the LORD's assembly?”[k]
4When Moses heard this, he fell facedown.[l]
5Then he said to Korah and all his followers: “In

15:26 [q]ver 24
15:27 [r]Lev 4:27
15:28 [s]Lev 4:35
15:30 [t]Nu 14:40-44; Dt 1:43; 17:13; Ps 19:13 [u]ver 14
15:31 [v]2Sa 12:9; Ps 119:126; Pr 13:13 [w]Lev 5:1; Eze 18:20
15:32 [x]Ex 31:14, 15; 35:2,3
15:34 [y]Nu 9:8
15:35 [z]Ex 31:14, 15; Dt 21:21 [a]Lev 20:2; 24:14; Ac 7:58
15:38 [b]Dt 22:12; Mt 23:5
15:39 [c]Dt 4:23; 6:12; Ps 73:27
15:40 [d]Lev 11:44; Ro 12:1; Col 1:22; 1Pe 1:15
16:1 [e]Jude 1:11 [f]Nu 26:8; Dt 11:6
16:2 [g]Nu 1:16; 26:9
16:3 [h]ver 7; Ps 106:16 [i]Ex 19:6 [j]Nu 14:14 [k]Nu 12:2
16:4 [l]Nu 14:5

[a] 1 Or *Peleth—took men*

the morning the LORD will show who belongs to
16:5 him and who is holy,[m] and he will have that person come near him. The man he chooses[n] he will
cause to come near him. 6You, Korah, and all your
followers are to do this: Take censers 7and tomorrow put fire and incense in them before the LORD.
The man the LORD chooses will be the one who is
holy. You Levites have gone too far!"
8Moses also said to Korah, "Now listen, you
Levites! 9Isn't it enough for you that the God of
Israel has separated you from the rest of the Israelite community and brought you near himself to
do the work at the LORD's tabernacle and to stand
16:9 before the community and minister to them?[o] 10He
has brought you and all your fellow Levites near
himself, but now you are trying to get the priest-
16:10 hood too.[p] 11It is against the LORD that you and all
your followers have banded together. Who is Aaron that you should grumble[q] against him?[r]"
16:11 12Then Moses summoned Dathan and Abiram,
the sons of Eliab. But they said, "We will not
come! 13Isn't it enough that you have brought us
up out of a land flowing with milk and honey to
16:13 kill us in the desert?[s] And now you also want to
lord it over us?[t] 14Moreover, you haven't brought
us into a land flowing with milk and honey[u] or
16:14 given us an inheritance of fields and vineyards.[v]
Will you gouge out the eyes of[a] these men?[w] No,
we will not come!"
15Then Moses became very angry and said to
the LORD, "Do not accept their offering. I have not
16:15 taken so much as a donkey[x] from them, nor have
I wronged any of them."
16Moses said to Korah, "You and all your followers are to appear before the LORD tomorrow—you
16:16 and they and Aaron.[y] 17Each man is to take his
censer and put incense in it—250 censers in all—
and present it before the LORD. You and Aaron are
to present your censers also." 18So each man took
his censer, put fire and incense in it, and stood with
Moses and Aaron at the entrance to the Tent of
16:19 Meeting. 19When Korah had gathered all his followers in opposition to them[z] at the entrance to the
Tent of Meeting, the glory of the LORD[a] appeared to
the entire assembly. 20The LORD said to Moses and
Aaron, 21"Separate yourselves from this assembly
16:21 so I can put an end to them at once."[b]
22But Moses and Aaron fell facedown[c] and cried
16:22 out, "O God, God of the spirits of all mankind,[d]
will you be angry with the entire assembly when
only one man sins?"[e]
23Then the LORD said to Moses, 24"Say to the
assembly, 'Move away from the tents of Korah,
Dathan and Abiram.' "
25Moses got up and went to Dathan and Abiram, and the elders of Israel followed him. 26He
16:26 warned the assembly, "Move back from the tents
of these wicked men![f] Do not touch anything
belonging to them, or you will be swept away[g]

16:5 [m]Lev 10:3; 2Ti 2:19* [n]Nu 17:5; Ps 65:4
16:9 [o]Nu 3:6; Dt 10:8
16:10 [p]Nu 3:10; 18:7
16:11 [q]1Co 10:10 [r]Ex 16:7
16:13 [s]Nu 14:2 [t]Ac 7:27,35
16:14 [u]Lev 20:24 [v]Ex 22:5; 23:11; Nu 20:5 [w]Jdg 16:21; 1Sa 11:2
16:15 [x]1Sa 12:3
16:16 [y]ver 6
16:19 [z]ver 42 [a]Ex 16:7; Nu 14:10; 20:6
16:21 [b]Ex 32:10
16:22 [c]Nu 14:5 [d]Nu 27:16; Job 12:10; Heb 12:9 [e]Ge 18:23
16:26 [f]Isa 52:11 [g]Ge 19:15

[a] 14 Or *you make slaves of*; or *you deceive*

The Glory of the Lord

NU 16:19

The "glory of the LORD appeared to the entire assembly." Surely that must have been a frightening sight, and surely these people must remember the other times when the glory of the Lord had appeared to them. They know that an appearance of God's glory is not always a sign of his pleasure with them. When the Israelites grumbled against God because they missed the food of Egypt, the glory of the Lord appeared to them (Ex 16:7–10). Later, when they rebelled and tried to stone Caleb and Joshua, it appeared again (Nu 14:1–25). At that time, God threatened to destroy the people but relented after Moses interceded on their behalf.

After the uprising of Korah, Dathan and Abiram, the glory of the Lord appears once more, and again Moses must step in and plead for God's mercy (Nu 16:22). Fortunately for the Israelites, God's anger is appeased, and those outside of the seditious group are spared.

because of all their sins." 27 So they moved away from the tents of Korah, Dathan and Abiram. Dathan and Abiram had come out and were standing with their wives, children and little ones at the entrances to their tents.

28 Then Moses said, "This is how you will know that the LORD has sent me[h] to do all these things and that it was not my idea: 29 If these men die a natural death and experience only what usually happens to men, then the LORD has not sent me.[i] 30 But if the LORD brings about something totally new, and the earth opens its mouth and swallows them, with everything that belongs to them, and they go down alive into the grave,[a][j] then you will know that these men have treated the LORD with contempt."

31 As soon as he finished saying all this, the ground under them split apart[k] 32 and the earth opened its mouth and swallowed them,[l] with their households and all Korah's men and all their possessions. 33 They went down alive into the grave, with everything they owned; the earth closed over them, and they perished and were gone from the community. 34 At their cries, all the Israelites around them fled, shouting, "The earth is going to swallow us too!"

35 And fire came out from the LORD[m] and consumed[n] the 250 men who were offering the incense.

36 The LORD said to Moses, 37 "Tell Eleazar son of Aaron, the priest, to take the censers out of the smoldering remains and scatter the coals some distance away, for the censers are holy— 38 the censers of the men who sinned at the cost of their lives.[o] Hammer the censers into sheets to overlay the altar, for they were presented before the LORD and have become holy. Let them be a sign[p] to the Israelites."

39 So Eleazar the priest collected the bronze censers brought by those who had been burned up, and he had them hammered out to overlay the altar, 40 as the LORD directed him through Moses. This was to remind the Israelites that no one except a descendant of Aaron should come to burn incense[q] before the LORD,[r] or he would become like Korah and his followers.[s]

41 The next day the whole Israelite community grumbled against Moses and Aaron. "You have killed the LORD's people," they said.

42 But when the assembly gathered in opposition[t] to Moses and Aaron and turned toward the Tent of Meeting, suddenly the cloud covered it and the glory of the LORD appeared. 43 Then Moses and Aaron went to the front of the Tent of Meeting, 44 and the LORD said to Moses, 45 "Get away from this assembly so I can put an end to them at once." And they fell facedown.

46 Then Moses said to Aaron, "Take your censer and put incense in it, along with fire from the altar, and hurry to the assembly[u] to make atone-

16:28 [h]Ex 3:12; Jn 5:36; 6:38
16:29 [i]Ecc 3:19
16:30 [j]ver 33; Ps 55:15
16:31 [k]Mic 1:3-4
16:32 [l]Nu 26:11; Dt 11:6; Ps 106:17
16:35 [m]Nu 11:1-3; 26:10 [n]Lev 10:2
16:38 [o]Pr 20:2 [p]Nu 26:10; Eze 14:8; 2Pe 2:6
16:40 [q]Ex 30:7-10; Nu 1:51 [r]2Ch 26:18 [s]Nu 3:10
16:42 [t]ver 19; Nu 20:6
16:46 [u]Lev 10:6

[a] *30* Hebrew *Sheol*; also in verse 33

Korah's Sons

NU 16:31-33

A second census of the Israelites reveals that Korah's line is not totally extinguished in this catastrophe (Nu 26:11). Later in Israelite history, 11 psalms bear the name of his descendants (Ps 42-49, 84-85, 87-88; see the note on Ps 88, page 951). It appears that Korah's sons do not support their father's position and thus are not killed. The other followers of Korah, as well as Dathan and Abiram, however, are destroyed. Since Dathan and Abiram are Reubenites, this destruction may account for the decreased numbers in that tribe recorded in the second census (compare Nu 1:21 and 26:7-11).

More than 14,700 Israelites die because of this rebellion (Nu 16:49), the consequence of arousing God's righteous anger. We, too, suffer when we disobediently turn from God's perfect ways. Confess to God your tendency toward rebellion, and ask him to turn your heart toward him and his ways (Isa 55:7).

16:46 [v]Nu 18:5; 25:13; Dt 9:22 [w]Nu 8:19; Ps 106:29 ment[v] for them. Wrath has come out from the
LORD; the plague[w] has started." 47So Aaron did as
Moses said, and ran into the midst of the assembly. The plague had already started among the
people,[x] but Aaron offered the incense and made
16:47 [x]Nu 25:6-8 atonement for them. 48He stood between the living and the dead, and the plague stopped.[y] 49But
16:48 [y]Nu 25:8; Ps 106:30 14,700 people died from the plague, in addition to
those who had died because of Korah.[z] 50Then
Aaron returned to Moses at the entrance to the
16:49 [z]ver 32 Tent of Meeting, for the plague had stopped.

The Budding of Aaron's Staff

17 The LORD said to Moses, 2"Speak to the Israelites and get twelve staffs from them, one
from the leader of each of their ancestral tribes.
Write the name of each man on his staff. 3On the
17:3 [a]Nu 1:3 staff of Levi write Aaron's name,[a] for there must
be one staff for the head of each ancestral tribe.
4Place them in the Tent of Meeting in front of the
17:4 [b]ver 7 [c]Ex 25:22 Testimony,[b] where I meet with you.[c] 5The staff
belonging to the man I choose[d] will sprout, and I
17:5 [d]Nu 16:5 will rid myself of this constant grumbling against
you by the Israelites."
6So Moses spoke to the Israelites, and their leaders gave him twelve staffs, one for the leader of
each of their ancestral tribes, and Aaron's staff
17:7 [e]Ex 38:21; Ac 7:44 was among them. 7Moses placed the staffs before
the LORD in the Tent of the Testimony.[e]
8The next day Moses entered the Tent of the Testimony and saw that Aaron's staff, which represented the house of Levi, had not only sprouted
17:8 [f]Eze 17:24; Heb 9:4 but had budded, blossomed and produced
almonds.[f] 9Then Moses brought out all the staffs
from the LORD's presence to all the Israelites. They
looked at them, and each man took his own staff.
10The LORD said to Moses, "Put back Aaron's
staff in front of the Testimony, to be kept as a sign
17:10 [g]Dt 9:24 to the rebellious.[g] This will put an end to their
grumbling against me, so that they will not die."
11Moses did just as the LORD commanded him.
12The Israelites said to Moses, "We will die! We
17:12 [h]Isa 6:5 are lost, we are all lost![h] 13Anyone who even
comes near the tabernacle of the LORD will die.[i]
17:13 [i]Nu 1:51 Are we all going to die?"

Duties of Priests and Levites

18 The LORD said to Aaron, "You, your sons
and your father's family are to bear the
18:1 [j]Ex 28:38 responsibility for offenses against the sanctuary,[j]
and you and your sons alone are to bear the
responsibility for offenses against the priesthood.
2Bring your fellow Levites from your ancestral
tribe to join you and assist you when you and
18:2 [k]Nu 3:10 your sons minister[k] before the Tent of the Testimony. 3They are to be responsible to you and are
18:3 [l]Nu 1:51 [m]ver 7; Nu 4:15 to perform all the duties of the Tent,[l] but they
must not go near the furnishings of the sanctuary
or the altar, or both they and you will die.[m] 4They
are to join you and be responsible for the care of

A Budding Staff

NU 17

In Old Testament times, a leader's authority was represented by his staff or rod (Ex 4:20; Isa 14:5). The Hebrew word *metteh* is sometimes translated "tribe," other times, "rod." Thus, in selecting one rod, God demonstrates not only his ultimate authority but also his selection of one man (Aaron) and one tribe (the tribe of Levi) to lead Israel's worship.

While God's most recent signs to Israel have been destructive in nature due to the need to squelch rebellion, the sprouting of Aaron's rod is affirming and life-giving. Not only does God meet the criteria of the test by making the staff bud, but he also goes beyond all human expectation, causing it to blossom and bear fruit.

The Israelites respond to this miracle with fear (Nu 17:12). While the plague and the wholesale destruction of several families didn't convince them (perhaps they thought these judgments came from Moses or Aaron rather than God himself), this latest sign from the Lord does. He is holy, and he is to be obeyed. They finally recognize, at least momentarily, the seriousness of their rebellion.

Only Men Allowed

NU 18:10

These grain, sin and guilt offerings are "most holy" (Nu 18:9), special offerings to God. Levitical law requires that these remain within the courtyard of the Tent of Meeting (Lev 6:16–18,26; 7:6–7). Only males are allowed to enter this space; therefore, women are not allowed to eat these portions. The priests' wives and children do, however, receive and enjoy the wave offerings (Nu 18:11), as well as the best oils, wines, grains and fruits (Nu 18:12–13).

the Tent of Meeting—all the work at the Tent—
and no one else may come near where you are.
5"You are to be responsible for the care of the
sanctuary and the altar,[n] so that wrath will not fall
on the Israelites again. 6I myself have selected
your fellow Levites from among the Israelites as
a gift to you,[o] dedicated to the LORD to do the work
at the Tent of Meeting. 7But only you and your
sons may serve as priests in connection with
everything at the altar and inside the curtain.[p] I
am giving you the service of the priesthood as a
gift.[q] Anyone else who comes near the sanctuary
must be put to death.[r]"

Offerings for Priests and Levites

8Then the LORD said to Aaron, "I myself have
put you in charge of the offerings presented to me;
all the holy offerings the Israelites give me I give
to you and your sons as your portion and regular
share.[s] 9You are to have the part of the most holy
offerings that is kept from the fire. From all the
gifts they bring me as most holy offerings,
whether grain[t] or sin[u] or guilt offerings,[v] that part
belongs to you and your sons. 10Eat it as something most holy; every male shall eat it.[w] You
must regard it as holy.

11"This also is yours: whatever is set aside from
the gifts of all the wave offerings[x] of the Israelites.
I give this to you and your sons and daughters as
your regular share. Everyone in your household
who is ceremonially clean[y] may eat it.

12"I give you all the finest olive oil and all the
finest new wine and grain they give the LORD as
the firstfruits of their harvest.[z] 13All the land's
firstfruits that they bring to the LORD will be
yours.[a] Everyone in your household who is ceremonially clean may eat it.

14"Everything in Israel that is devoted[a] to the
LORD[b] is yours. 15The first offspring of every
womb, both man and animal, that is offered to the
LORD is yours.[c] But you must redeem[d] every firstborn son and every firstborn male of unclean animals.[e] 16When they are a month old, you must
redeem them at the redemption price set at five
shekels[b][f] of silver, according to the sanctuary
shekel,[g] which weighs twenty gerahs.

17"But you must not redeem the firstborn of an
ox, a sheep or a goat; they are holy.[h] Sprinkle their
blood[i] on the altar and burn their fat as an offering made by fire, an aroma pleasing to the LORD.
18Their meat is to be yours, just as the breast of
the wave offering[j] and the right thigh are yours.
19Whatever is set aside from the holy offerings the
Israelites present to the LORD I give to you and
your sons and daughters as your regular share. It
is an everlasting covenant of salt[k] before the LORD
for both you and your offspring."

18:5 [n]Nu 16:46
18:6 [o]Nu 3:9
18:7 [p]Heb 9:3,6 [q]ver 20; Ex 29:9 [r]Nu 3:10
18:8 [s]Lev 6:16; 7:6,31-34,36
18:9 [t]Lev 2:1 [u]Lev 6:25 [v]Lev 5:15; 7:7
18:10 [w]Lev 6:16
18:11 [x]Ex 29:26 [y]Lev 22:1-16
18:12 [z]Ex 23:19; Ne 10:35
18:13 [a]Ex 22:29; 23:19
18:14 [b]Lev 27:28
18:15 [c]Ex 13:2 [d]Nu 3:46 [e]Ex 13:13
18:16 [f]Lev 27:6 [g]Ex 30:13
18:17 [h]Dt 15:19 [i]Lev 3:2
18:18 [j]Lev 7:30
18:19 [k]Lev 2:13; 2Ch 13:5

a 14 The Hebrew term refers to the irrevocable giving over of things or persons to the LORD. *b 16* That is, about 2 ounces (about 55 grams)

20 The LORD said to Aaron, "You will have no
18:20 inheritance in their land, nor will you have any
[l]Dt 12:12 share among them;[l] I am your share and your
[m]Dt 10:9; inheritance[m] among the Israelites.
14:27; 18:1-2; 21 "I give to the Levites all the tithes[n] in Israel as
Jos 13:33; their inheritance[o] in return for the work they do
Eze 44:28 while serving at the Tent of Meeting. 22 From now
18:21 on the Israelites must not go near the Tent of
[n]Dt 14:22; Meeting, or they will bear the consequences of
Mal 3:8 [o]Lev 27:30- their sin and will die.[p] 23 It is the Levites who are
33; Heb 7:5 to do the work at the Tent of Meeting and bear the
responsibility for offenses against it. This is a last-
18:22 [p]Lev 22:9; ing ordinance for the generations to come. They
Nu 1:51 will receive no inheritance[q] among the Israelites.
18:23 24 Instead, I give to the Levites as their inheritance
[q]ver 20 the tithes that the Israelites present as an offering
to the LORD. That is why I said concerning them:
'They will have no inheritance among the Israelites.' "
25 The LORD said to Moses, 26 "Speak to the Levites
and say to them: 'When you receive from the Isra-
18:26 elites the tithe I give you[r] as your inheritance, you
[r]ver 21 [s]Ne 10:38 must present a tenth of that tithe as the LORD's
offering.[s] 27 Your offering will be reckoned to you
as grain from the threshing floor or juice from the
winepress. 28 In this way you also will present an
18:28 offering to the LORD from all the tithes[t] you receive
[t]Mal 3:8 from the Israelites. From these tithes you must give
the LORD's portion to Aaron the priest. 29 You must
present as the LORD's portion the best and holiest
part of everything given to you.'
30 "Say to the Levites: 'When you present the
18:30 best part, it will be reckoned to you as the product
[u]ver 27 of the threshing floor or the winepress.[u] 31 You and
your households may eat the rest of it anywhere,
for it is your wages for your work at the Tent of
18:32 Meeting. 32 By presenting the best part[v] of it you
[v]Lev 22:15 will not be guilty in this matter; then you will not
[w]Lev 19:8 defile the holy offerings[w] of the Israelites, and you
will not die.' "

19:2 [x]Ge 15:9;

The Water of Cleansing

Heb 9:13 **19** The LORD said to Moses and Aaron: 2 "This is
[y]Lev 22:19-25 a requirement of the law that the LORD has
[z]Dt 21:3; commanded: Tell the Israelites to bring you a red
1Sa 6:7 heifer[x] without defect or blemish[y] and that has
19:3 never been under a yoke.[z] 3 Give it to Eleazar[a] the
[a]Nu 3:4 priest; it is to be taken outside the camp[b] and
[b]Lev 4:12, 21; slaughtered in his presence. 4 Then Eleazar the
Heb 13:11 priest is to take some of its blood on his finger and
19:4 sprinkle[c] it seven times toward the front of the
[c]Lev 4:17 Tent of Meeting. 5 While he watches, the heifer is
19:5 to be burned—its hide, flesh, blood and offal.[d]
[d]Ex 29:14 6 The priest is to take some cedar wood, hyssop[e]
19:6 and scarlet wool[f] and throw them onto the burn-
[e]ver 18; ing heifer. 7 After that, the priest must wash his
Ps 51:7 clothes and bathe himself with water.[g] He may
[f]Lev 14:4 then come into the camp, but he will be ceremo-
19:7 nially unclean till evening. 8 The man who burns
[g]Lev 11:25; it must also wash his clothes and bathe with
16:26,28; 22:6 water, and he too will be unclean till evening.

The Levites' Inheritance

NU 18:20

God promises that, while the other tribes of Israel will inherit land, he himself will be the inheritance of the Levites. If the Levites were allowed to own property, it would be necessary for them to care for it—time that would take them away from their priestly duties. God instead orders that they receive a percentage of the tithes and offerings. In this way, the Levites are not only set apart for God, they are completely dependent on him for their provision (Neh 13:10–12).

As Christians, we too are heirs of God (Ac 20:32; Col 3:24); our inheritance is forgiveness of sins and a place among the redeemed. What is important to you? Take five minutes to reflect on what you have—here and now, and what's waiting for you in heaven.

Three and Seven

NU 19:12

Cleansing from the uncleanness of touching a dead body requires sprinkling water on the unclean person on the third and seventh days. The water used for this cleansing had to be the "water of cleansing" described in Numbers 19:1-10. Water is mixed with the ashes produced from burning a red heifer (a cow that has never had a calf). The color red signifies the blood required to purify from sin.

The unclean person had to be sprinkled with this water on the third and seventh days. The numbers three and seven appear often in Scripture, their presence generally signifying fullness or completion. God created the world in six days and rested on the seventh (Ge 1:1—2:3). The seventh day of the week is to be a day of rest, a holy day (Ex 20:10). The triune God is made up of three persons: Father, Son and Spirit (Mt 28:19).

9"A man who is clean shall gather up the ashes
of the heifer[h] and put them in a ceremonially clean
place outside the camp. They shall be kept by the
Israelite community for use in the water of cleansing;[i] it is for purification from sin. 10The man who
gathers up the ashes of the heifer must also wash
his clothes, and he too will be unclean till evening.
This will be a lasting ordinance both for the Israelites and for the aliens living among them.
11"Whoever touches the dead body[j] of anyone
will be unclean for seven days.[k] 12He must purify
himself with the water on the third day and on
the seventh day;[l] then he will be clean. But if he
does not purify himself on the third and seventh
days, he will not be clean. 13Whoever touches the
dead body[m] of anyone and fails to purify himself
defiles the LORD's tabernacle.[n] That person must
be cut off from Israel.[o] Because the water of
cleansing has not been sprinkled on him, he is
unclean;[p] his uncleanness remains on him.
14"This is the law that applies when a person
dies in a tent: Anyone who enters the tent and
anyone who is in it will be unclean for seven
days, 15and every open container without a lid fastened on it will be unclean.
16"Anyone out in the open who touches someone who has been killed with a sword or someone who has died a natural death,[q] or anyone
who touches a human bone or a grave,[r] will be
unclean for seven days.
17"For the unclean person, put some ashes[s] from
the burned purification offering into a jar and pour
fresh water over them. 18Then a man who is ceremonially clean is to take some hyssop,[t] dip it in
the water and sprinkle the tent and all the furnishings and the people who were there. He must
also sprinkle anyone who has touched a human
bone or a grave or someone who has been killed or
someone who has died a natural death. 19The man
who is clean is to sprinkle the unclean person on
the third and seventh days, and on the seventh day
he is to purify him.[u] The person being cleansed
must wash his clothes and bathe with water, and
that evening he will be clean. 20But if a person who
is unclean does not purify himself, he must be cut
off from the community, because he has defiled
the sanctuary of the LORD. The water of cleansing
has not been sprinkled on him, and he is unclean.
21This is a lasting ordinance for them.

"The man who sprinkles the water of cleansing
must also wash his clothes, and anyone who
touches the water of cleansing will be unclean till
evening. 22Anything that an unclean[v] person
touches becomes unclean, and anyone who
touches it becomes unclean till evening."

Water From the Rock

20 In the first month the whole Israelite community arrived at the Desert of Zin,[w] and
they stayed at Kadesh.[x] There Miriam[y] died and
was buried.

19:9 [h]Heb 9:13 [i]ver 13; Nu 8:7
19:11 [j]Lev 21:1; Nu 5:2 [k]Nu 31:19
19:12 [l]ver 19; Nu 31:19
19:13 [m]Lev 20:3 [n]Lev 15:31; 2Ch 36:14 [o]Lev 7:20; 22:3 [p]Hag 2:13
19:16 [q]Nu 31:19 [r]Mt 23:27
19:17 [s]ver 9
19:18 [t]ver 6
19:19 [u]Eze 36:25; Heb 10:22
19:22 [v]Lev 5:2; Hag 2:13,14
20:1 [w]Nu 13:21 [x]Nu 33:36 [y]Ex 15:20

20:2 2Now there was no water for the community,[z]
[z]Ex 17:1 [a]Nu 16:19 and the people gathered in opposition[a] to Moses
and Aaron. 3They quarreled[b] with Moses and said,
20:3 [b]Ex 17:2 "If only we had died when our brothers fell dead
[c]Nu 14:2; before the LORD![c] 4Why did you bring the LORD's
16:31-35 community into this desert, that we and our live-
20:4 stock should die here?[d] 5Why did you bring us up
[d]Ex 14:11; out of Egypt to this terrible place? It has no grain
17:3; Nu 14:3; or figs, grapevines or pomegranates.[e] And there is
16:13 no water to drink!"

6Moses and Aaron went from the assembly to
20:5 [e]Nu 16:14 the entrance to the Tent of Meeting and fell facedown,[f] and the glory of the LORD[g] appeared to
20:6 [f]Nu 14:5 them. 7The LORD said to Moses, 8"Take the staff,[h]
[g]Nu 16:19 and you and your brother Aaron gather the
20:8 assembly together. Speak to that rock before their
[h]Ex 4:17,20 eyes and it will pour out its water.[i] You will bring
[i]Ex 17:6; Isa 43:20 water out of the rock for the community so they
and their livestock can drink."

9So Moses took the staff from the LORD's pres-
20:9 [j]Nu 17:10 ence,[j] just as he commanded him. 10He and Aaron
gathered the assembly together in front of the
rock and Moses said to them, "Listen, you rebels,
20:10 [k]Ps 106:32, must we bring you water out of this rock?"[k]
33 11Then Moses raised his arm and struck the rock
20:11 twice with his staff. Water[l] gushed out, and the
[l]Ex 17:6; community and their livestock drank.

Dt 8:15; 12But the LORD said to Moses and Aaron,
Ps 78:16; Isa 48:2; "Because you did not trust in me enough to hon-
1Co 10:4 or me as holy[m] in the sight of the Israelites, you
20:12 will not bring this community into the land I give
[m]Nu 27:14 them."[n]

[n]ver 24; Dt 1:37; 3:27 13These were the waters of Meribah,[a][o] where
the Israelites quarreled[p] with the LORD and where
20:13 [o]Ex 17:7 he showed himself holy among them.

[p]Dt 33:8; Ps 95:8; 106:32

Edom Denies Israel Passage

14Moses sent messengers from Kadesh[q] to the
20:14 [q]Jdg 11:16- king of Edom,[r] saying:

17 [r]Dt 2:4 "This is what your brother Israel says: You
[s]Jos 2:11; 9:9 know[s] about all the hardships that have come
upon us. 15Our forefathers went down into
20:15 [t]Ge 46:6 Egypt,[t] and we lived there many years.[u] The
[u]Ge 15:13; Ex 12:40 Egyptians mistreated[v] us and our fathers,
[v]Ex 1:11; 16but when we cried out to the LORD, he heard
Dt 26:6 our cry[w] and sent an angel[x] and brought us
out of Egypt.

20:16 [w]Ex 2:23; "Now we are here at Kadesh, a town on the
3:7 edge of your territory. 17Please let us pass
[x]Ex 14:19 through your country. We will not go through
any field or vineyard, or drink water from
any well. We will travel along the king's
highway and not turn to the right or to the
left until we have passed through your
20:17 [y]Nu 21:22 territory."[y]

18But Edom answered:

"You may not pass through here; if you try,

[a] 13 *Meribah* means *quarreling.*

Complete Obedience

NU 20:1-12

Because God is a holy God, he will not allow any sin to go unpunished—even that of his chosen leaders. At the Tent of Meeting, the Lord clearly tells Moses to speak to the rock, promising that water for the people will come forth. Instead, Moses strikes the rock—possibly with Aaron's support, since we know that both sin and both are punished (Nu 20:12,24).

The exact nature of the men's rebellion remains uncertain. We do know that they disobey God's orders, exhibit a lack of faith, and dishonor the holiness of the Lord. Possibly they begin to see themselves as Israel's providers, trusting in their own strength and claiming God's glory for themselves (Nu 20:10). Certainly, Moses, in his anger, speaks rashly (Ps 106:32-33).

Does their punishment seem harsh? Perhaps, as some scholars suggest, there was more to the sin than meets the eye or is recorded in Scripture. In any case, we can trust that God, in his infinite and superior wisdom, disciplined the two fairly.

The End

NU 20:22–29

Together, Aaron, Moses and Eleazar bravely make the journey to the top of Mount Hor, fully knowing that when they reach their destination, Aaron's earthly life will end. Following God's command, Aaron submits himself to the ministrations of his brother, Moses, who carefully removes Aaron's priestly garments and passes them on to his son, Eleazar. According to God's command, these clothes are to be passed down to Aaron's successor, who will wear them in his role as high priest (Ex 29:29–30). They are a sign of the God-given authority and the holy consecration of the one who wears them (Ex 39). As Aaron releases his claim on the robes, he releases his claim to the priesthood as well.

On Mount Hor Aaron is "gathered to his people" (Nu 20:24), a common Biblical phrase for death. The words describe one who dies righteously and at an old age.

we will march out and attack you with the
sword."

19 The Israelites replied:

"We will go along the main road, and if we
or our livestock[z] drink any of your water, we 20:19
will pay for it.[a] We only want to pass through [z]Ex 12:38
on foot—nothing else." [a]Dt 2:6,28

20 Again they answered:

"You may not pass through."

Then Edom came out against them with a large
and powerful army. 21 Since Edom refused to let
them go through their territory, Israel turned 20:21
away from them.[b] [b]Dt 2:8; Jdg 11:18

The Death of Aaron

22 The whole Israelite community set out from
Kadesh and came to Mount Hor.[c] 23 At Mount Hor, 20:22
near the border of Edom,[d] the LORD said to Moses [c]Nu 33:37
and Aaron, 24 "Aaron will be gathered to his peo- 20:23
ple.[e] He will not enter the land I give the Israelites, [d]Nu 33:37
because both of you rebelled against my com- 20:24
mand[f] at the waters of Meribah. 25 Get Aaron and [e]Ge 25:8
his son Eleazar and take them up Mount Hor.[g] [f]ver 10
26 Remove Aaron's garments and put them on his 20:25
son Eleazar, for Aaron will be gathered to his peo- [g]Nu 33:38
ple;[h] he will die there." 20:26
27 Moses did as the LORD commanded: They [h]ver 24
went up Mount Hor in the sight of the whole community. 28 Moses removed Aaron's garments and
put them on his son Eleazar.[i] And Aaron died 20:28
there[j] on top of the mountain. Then Moses and [i]Ex 29:29
Eleazar came down from the mountain, 29 and [j]Nu 33:38; Dt 10:6;
when the whole community learned that Aaron 32:50
had died, the entire house of Israel mourned for 20:29
him[k] thirty days. [k]Dt 34:8

Arad Destroyed

21 When the Canaanite king of Arad,[l] who 21:1
lived in the Negev,[m] heard that Israel was [l]Nu 33:40; Jos 12:14
coming along the road to Atharim, he attacked the [m]Jdg 1:9,16
Israelites and captured some of them. 2 Then Israel made this vow to the LORD: "If you will deliver
these people into our hands, we will totally
destroy[a] their cities." 3 The LORD listened to Israel's plea and gave the Canaanites over to them.
They completely destroyed them and their towns;
so the place was named Hormah.[b]

The Bronze Snake

4 They traveled from Mount Hor[n] along the route 21:4 [n]Nu 20:22
to the Red Sea,[c] to go around Edom. But the peo- [o]Dt 2:8;
ple grew impatient on the way;[o] 5 they spoke Jdg 11:18
against God[p] and against Moses, and said, "Why 21:5
have you brought us up out of Egypt to die in the [p]Ps 78:19

[a] 2 The Hebrew term refers to the irrevocable giving over of things or persons to the LORD, often by totally destroying them; also in verse 3. [b] 3 *Hormah* means *destruction*.
[c] 4 Hebrew *Yam Suph*; that is, Sea of Reeds

21:5 desert?[q] There is no bread! There is no water! And
[q]Nu 14:2,3 [r]Nu 11:6 we detest this miserable food!"[r]
[6]Then the LORD sent venomous snakes[s] among
21:6 [s]Dt 8:15; them; they bit the people and many Israelites died.[t]
Jer 8:17 [7]The people came to Moses[u] and said, "We sinned
[t]1Co 10:9 when we spoke against the LORD and against you.
21:7 Pray that the LORD[v] will take the snakes away from
[u]Ps 78:34; us." So Moses prayed[w] for the people.
Hos 5:15 [v]Ex 8:8; [8]The LORD said to Moses, "Make a snake and put
Ac 8:24 it up on a pole;[x] anyone who is bitten can look at it
[w]Nu 11:2 and live." [9]So Moses made a bronze snake[y] and put
21:8 it up on a pole. Then when anyone was bitten by a
[x]Jn 3:14 snake and looked at the bronze snake, he lived.[z]

21:9 [y]2Ki 18:4

The Journey to Moab

[z]Jn 3:14-15 [10]The Israelites moved on and camped at
21:10 Oboth.[a] [11]Then they set out from Oboth and
[a]Nu 33:43 camped in Iye Abarim, in the desert that faces
21:11 Moab[b] toward the sunrise. [12]From there they
[b]Nu 33:44 moved on and camped in the Zered Valley.[c] [13]They
21:12 set out from there and camped alongside the
[c]Dt 2:13,14 Arnon[d], which is in the desert extending into
Amorite territory. The Arnon is the border of
21:13 [d]Nu 22:36; Moab, between Moab and the Amorites. [14]That is
Jdg 11:13,18 why the Book of the Wars of the LORD says:

"... Waheb in Suphah[a] and the ravines,
the Arnon [15]and[b] the slopes of the
ravines
21:15 that lead to the site of Ar[e]
[e]ver 28; Dt 2:9,18 and lie along the border of Moab."

21:16 [16]From there they continued on to Beer,[f] the well
[f]Jdg 9:21 where the LORD said to Moses, "Gather the people
together and I will give them water."
21:17 [g]Ex 15:1 [17]Then Israel sang this song:[g]

"Spring up, O well!
Sing about it,
[18]about the well that the princes dug,
that the nobles of the people sank—
the nobles with scepters and staffs."

Then they went from the desert to Mattanah,
[19]from Mattanah to Nahaliel, from Nahaliel to
Bamoth, [20]and from Bamoth to the valley in Moab
where the top of Pisgah overlooks the wasteland.

Defeat of Sihon and Og

21:21 [21]Israel sent messengers to say to Sihon[h] king
[h]Dt 1:4; 2:26-27; of the Amorites:

Jdg 11:19-21 [22]"Let us pass through your country. We
will not turn aside into any field or vineyard,
or drink water from any well. We will travel
along the king's highway until we have
21:22 [i]Nu 20:17 passed through your territory.[i]"

21:23 [23]But Sihon would not let Israel pass through
[j]Nu 20:21 his territory.[j] He mustered his entire army and

[a] *14* The meaning of the Hebrew for this phrase is uncertain.
[b] *14,15* Or *"I have been given from Suphah and the ravines / of the Arnon [15]to*

An Unusual Antidote

NU 21:4-9

When Moses prays for a rescue from poisonous snakes, God provides an unusual remedy: a bronze snake that the people may look on in faith to receive healing. The snake itself has no power to cure. It only serves as an object of focus for the Israelites, a reminder of the punishment God decrees and of the remedy he provides.

Not surprisingly, the Israelites take God's good gift and turn it into an idol for worship. We do not know at what point this sinful adoration begins. But many years later, during the reign of King Hezekiah of Judah, that very symbol remains the recipient of their misguided homage (2Ki 18:4). Righteous King Hezekiah destroys it.

Modern-day believers are equally guilty of elevating God's gifts above God himself. Think for a moment. Is there a "bronze snake" in your life that needs to be demoted—or possibly even destroyed?

Chemosh

NU 21:29

Chemosh was the national god of the Moabites and possibly the Ammonites. He was little known other than through Biblical references until the discovery of the Moabite Stone in 1868. Inscriptions on the stone reveal Chemosh as a savage war god. Like Molech, another of the pagan gods worshiped by the Canaanites, worship of Chemosh required human sacrifice, including perhaps children (2Ki 3:27). Solomon built a temple for Chemosh when his foreign wives led him away from God (1Ki 11:7). Josiah destroyed this temple about 300 years later (2Ki 23:13).

marched out into the desert against Israel. When
he reached Jahaz,[k] he fought with Israel. 24Israel,
however, put him to the sword[l] and took over his
land from the Arnon to the Jabbok, but only as
far as the Ammonites,[m] because their border was
fortified. 25Israel captured all the cities of the Amorites[n] and occupied them, including Heshbon and
all its surrounding settlements. 26Heshbon was the
city of Sihon[o] king of the Amorites, who had
fought against the former king of Moab and had
taken from him all his land as far as the Arnon.
27That is why the poets say:

> "Come to Heshbon and let it be rebuilt;
> let Sihon's city be restored.
>
> 28"Fire went out from Heshbon,
> a blaze from the city of Sihon.[p]
> It consumed Ar[q] of Moab,
> the citizens of Arnon's heights.[r]
> 29Woe to you, O Moab![s]
> You are destroyed, O people of
> Chemosh![t]
> He has given up his sons as fugitives[u]
> and his daughters as captives[v]
> to Sihon king of the Amorites.
>
> 30"But we have overthrown them;
> Heshbon is destroyed all the way to
> Dibon.[w]
> We have demolished them as far as
> Nophah,
> which extends to Medeba."

31So Israel settled in the land of the Amorites.
32After Moses had sent spies to Jazer,[x] the Israelites captured its surrounding settlements and
drove out the Amorites who were there. 33Then
they turned and went up along the road toward
Bashan[y],[z] and Og king of Bashan and his whole
army marched out to meet them in battle at
Edrei.[a]
34The LORD said to Moses, "Do not be afraid of
him, for I have handed him over to you, with his
whole army and his land. Do to him what you did
to Sihon king of the Amorites, who reigned in
Heshbon.[b]"
35So they struck him down, together with his
sons and his whole army, leaving them no survivors. And they took possession of his land.

Balak Summons Balaam

22 Then the Israelites traveled to the plains of
Moab and camped along the Jordan across
from Jericho.[a][c]
2Now Balak son of Zippor[d] saw all that Israel
had done to the Amorites, 3and Moab was terrified because there were so many people. Indeed,
Moab was filled with dread[e] because of the
Israelites.

21:23 [k]Dt 2:32; Jdg 11:20
21:24 [l]Dt 2:33; Ps 135:10-11; Am 2:9 [m]Dt 2:37
21:25 [n]Nu 13:29; Jdg 10:11; Am 2:10
21:26 [o]Dt 29:7; Ps 135:11
21:28 [p]Jer 48:45 [q]ver 15 [r]Nu 22:41; Isa 15:2
21:29 [s]Isa 25:10; Jer 48:46 [t]Jdg 11:24; 1Ki 11:7,33; 2Ki 23:13; Jer 48:7,46 [u]Isa 15:5 [v]Isa 16:2
21:30 [w]Nu 32:3; Isa 15:2; Jer 48:18,22
21:32 [x]Nu 32:1,3, 35; Jer 48:32
21:33 [y]Dt 3:3 [z]Dt 3:4 [a]Dt 1:4; 3:1, 10; Jos 13:12,31
21:34 [b]Dt 3:2
22:1 [c]Nu 33:48
22:2 [d]Jdg 11:25
22:3 [e]Ex 15:15

[a] *1* Hebrew *Jordan of Jericho*; possibly an ancient name for the Jordan River

4 The Moabites said to the elders of Midian, "This horde is going to lick up everything around us, as an ox licks up the grass of the field."

So Balak son of Zippor, who was king of Moab at that time, 5 sent messengers to summon Balaam son of Beor,[f] who was at Pethor, near the River,[a] in his native land. Balak said:

> "A people has come out of Egypt; they cover the face of the land and have settled next to me. 6 Now come and put a curse[g] on these people, because they are too powerful for me. Perhaps then I will be able to defeat them and drive them out of the country. For I know that those you bless are blessed, and those you curse are cursed."

7 The elders of Moab and Midian left, taking with them the fee for divination.[h] When they came to Balaam, they told him what Balak had said.

8 "Spend the night here," Balaam said to them, "and I will bring you back the answer the LORD gives me.[i]" So the Moabite princes stayed with him.

9 God came to Balaam[j] and asked,[k] "Who are these men with you?"

10 Balaam said to God, "Balak son of Zippor, king of Moab, sent me this message: 11 'A people that has come out of Egypt covers the face of the land. Now come and put a curse on them for me. Perhaps then I will be able to fight them and drive them away.' "

12 But God said to Balaam, "Do not go with them. You must not put a curse on those people, because they are blessed.[l]"

13 The next morning Balaam got up and said to Balak's princes, "Go back to your own country, for the LORD has refused to let me go with you."

14 So the Moabite princes returned to Balak and said, "Balaam refused to come with us."

15 Then Balak sent other princes, more numerous and more distinguished than the first. 16 They came to Balaam and said:

> "This is what Balak son of Zippor says: Do not let anything keep you from coming to me, 17 because I will reward you handsomely[m] and do whatever you say. Come and put a curse[n] on these people for me."

18 But Balaam answered them, "Even if Balak gave me his palace filled with silver and gold, I could not do anything great or small to go beyond the command of the LORD my God.[o] 19 Now stay here tonight as the others did, and I will find out what else the LORD will tell me.[p]"

20 That night God came to Balaam[q] and said, "Since these men have come to summon you, go with them, but do only what I tell you."[r]

22:5 [f]Dt 23:4; Jos 13:22; 24:9; Ne 13:2; Mic 6:5; 2Pe 2:15
22:6 [g]ver 12,17; Nu 23:7,11, 13
22:7 [h]Nu 23:23; 24:1
22:8 [i]ver 19
22:9 [j]Ge 20:3 [k]ver 20
22:12 [l]Ge 12:2; 22:17; Nu 23:20
22:17 [m]ver 37; Nu 24:11 [n]ver 6
22:18 [o]ver 38; Nu 23:12,26; 24:13; 1Ki 22:14; 2Ch 18:13; Jer 42:4
22:19 [p]ver 8
22:20 [q]Ge 20:3 [r]ver 35,38; Nu 23:5,12, 16,26; 24:13; 2Ch 18:13

[a] 5 That is, the Euphrates

Balaam

NU 22:5

King Balak believes military might cannot save his kingdom from the Israelite onslaught. He turns instead to witchcraft and summons Balaam, a magician and soothsayer with a widespread reputation for success (Nu 22:6). Though Balaam claims loyalty to the Lord (Nu 22:18), he more likely worships numerous pagan gods and conveniently includes the one true God among them.

Balaam obeys when God tells him not to go with the king's emissaries (Nu 22:13). However, when they return a second time with the same request, God gives his permission (Nu 22:20). But now that Balaam is on his way, God is "very angry" (Nu 22:22). It appears as though Balaam outwardly obeys God's commands (Nu 22:20–21), yet has evil intentions. God, who sees the heart, knows the truth and takes extreme measures to get Balaam's attention.

A Talking Donkey

NU 22:21-39

God could have gotten Balaam's attention in any number of ways, but it is difficult to imagine a more effective method than the one he chooses. As a highly sought after fortuneteller, Balaam is considered great in the eyes of men. He is a seer who claims special communication and power from the gods. Presumably, he would have been honored to receive a message from an angel of the Lord. Balaam does in fact receive such a message, but rather than coming in a manner Balaam would probably think was his due, the message comes through the mouth of a lowly beast of burden. The wise and mighty seer receives the truth from a donkey. No doubt, this experience is simultaneously humbling, eye opening and highly memorable.

Balaam's Donkey

21 Balaam got up in the morning, saddled his donkey and went with the princes of Moab. 22 But God
was very angry[s] when he went, and the angel of
the LORD[t] stood in the road to oppose him. Balaam
was riding on his donkey, and his two servants
were with him. 23 When the donkey saw the angel
of the LORD standing in the road with a drawn
sword[u] in his hand, she turned off the road into a
field. Balaam beat her[v] to get her back on the road.
24 Then the angel of the LORD stood in a narrow
path between two vineyards, with walls on both
sides. 25 When the donkey saw the angel of the
LORD, she pressed close to the wall, crushing
Balaam's foot against it. So he beat her again.
26 Then the angel of the LORD moved on ahead
and stood in a narrow place where there was no
room to turn, either to the right or to the left.
27 When the donkey saw the angel of the LORD, she
lay down under Balaam, and he was angry[w] and
beat her with his staff. 28 Then the LORD opened
the donkey's mouth,[x] and she said to Balaam,
"What have I done to you to make you beat me
these three times?[y]"
29 Balaam answered the donkey, "You have
made a fool of me! If I had a sword in my hand, I
would kill you right now.[z]"
30 The donkey said to Balaam, "Am I not your
own donkey, which you have always ridden, to this
day? Have I been in the habit of doing this to you?"
"No," he said.
31 Then the LORD opened Balaam's eyes,[a] and he
saw the angel of the LORD standing in the road
with his sword drawn. So he bowed low and fell
facedown.
32 The angel of the LORD asked him, "Why have
you beaten your donkey these three times? I have
come here to oppose you because your path is a
reckless one before me.[a] 33 The donkey saw me
and turned away from me these three times. If she
had not turned away, I would certainly have killed
you by now,[b] but I would have spared her."
34 Balaam said to the angel of the LORD, "I have
sinned.[c] I did not realize you were standing in the
road to oppose me. Now if you are displeased, I
will go back."
35 The angel of the LORD said to Balaam, "Go
with the men, but speak only what I tell you." So
Balaam went with the princes of Balak.
36 When Balak heard that Balaam was coming,
he went out to meet him at the Moabite town on
the Arnon[d] border, at the edge of his territory.
37 Balak said to Balaam, "Did I not send you an
urgent summons? Why didn't you come to me?
Am I really not able to reward you?"
38 "Well, I have come to you now," Balaam
replied. "But can I say just anything? I must speak
only what God puts in my mouth."[e]
39 Then Balaam went with Balak to Kiriath

22:22 [s]Ex 4:14 [t]Ge 16:7; Ex 23:20; Jdg 13:3,6, 13
22:23 [u]Jos 5:13 [v]ver 25,27
22:27 [w]Nu 11:1; Jas 1:19
22:28 [x]2Pe 2:16 [y]ver 32
22:29 [z]Dt 25:4; Pr 12:10; 27:23-27; Mt 15:19
22:31 [a]Ge 21:19
22:33 [b]ver 29
22:34 [c]Ge 39:9; Nu 14:40; 1Sa 15:24, 30; 2Sa 12:13; 24:10; Job 33:27; Ps 51:4
22:36 [d]Nu 21:13
22:38 [e]Nu 23:5,16, 26

[a] *32* The meaning of the Hebrew for this clause is uncertain.

22:40 [f]Nu 23:1,14, 29; Eze 45:23 Huzoth. 40 Balak sacrificed cattle and sheep,[f] and
gave some to Balaam and the princes who were
with him. 41 The next morning Balak took Balaam
22:41 [g]Nu 21:28 up to Bamoth Baal,[g] and from there he saw part of
[h]Nu 23:13 the people.[h]

Balaam's First Oracle

23:1 [i]Nu 22:40 **23** Balaam said, "Build me seven altars here,
and prepare seven bulls and seven rams[i] for
me." 2 Balak did as Balaam said, and the two of
23:2 [j]ver 14,30 them offered a bull and a ram on each altar.[j]
3 Then Balaam said to Balak, "Stay here beside
your offering while I go aside. Perhaps the LORD
23:3 [k]ver 15 will come to meet with me.[k] Whatever he reveals
to me I will tell you." Then he went off to a barren
height.
23:4 [l]ver 16 4 God met with him,[l] and Balaam said, "I have
prepared seven altars, and on each altar I have
offered a bull and a ram."
23:5 [m]Dt 18:18; 5 The LORD put a message in Balaam's mouth[m]
Jer 1:9 and said, "Go back to Balak and give him this
[n]Nu 22:20 message."[n]
6 So he went back to him and found him stand-
23:6 ing beside his offering, with all the princes of
[o]ver 17 Moab.[o] 7 Then Balaam[p] uttered his oracle:[q]

23:7 [p]Nu 22:5 "Balak brought me from Aram,
[q]ver 18; the king of Moab from the eastern
Nu 24:3,21 mountains.
[r]Nu 22:6; 'Come,' he said, 'curse Jacob for me;
Dt 23:4 come, denounce Israel.'[r]
8 How can I curse
23:8 [s]Nu 22:12 those whom God has not cursed?[s]
How can I denounce
those whom the LORD has not
denounced?
9 From the rocky peaks I see them,
from the heights I view them.
I see a people who live apart
and do not consider themselves one of
23:9 [t]Ex 33:16; the nations.[t]
Dt 32:8; 33:28 10 Who can count the dust of Jacob[u]
or number the fourth part of Israel?
23:10 [u]Ge 13:16 Let me die the death of the righteous,[v]
[v]Ps 116:15; Isa 57:1 and may my end be like theirs![w]"
[w]Ps 37:37 11 Balak said to Balaam, "What have you done
23:11 to me? I brought you to curse my enemies, but
[x]Nu 24:10; you have done nothing but bless them!"[x]
Ne 13:2 12 He answered, "Must I not speak what the
23:12 LORD puts in my mouth?"[y]
[y]Nu 22:20, 38

Balaam's Second Oracle

13 Then Balak said to him, "Come with me to
another place where you can see them; you will
see only a part but not all of them. And from
there, curse them for me." 14 So he took him to the
field of Zophim on the top of Pisgah, and there he
23:14 built seven altars and offered a bull and a ram on
[z]ver 2 each altar.[z]

An Oracle

NU 23-24

The word *oracle* is used 46 times in the Old Testament. It most often refers to a *message from God given through an intermediary. God gives his messages to his prophets (for example,* Isa 23:1; Jer 23:33-38), *and they pass the messages on to the people. Often the word oracle is used to denote an upsetting or difficult message.*

The Greeks considered an *oracle to be both a prophetic speech made by a pagan god via a human, as well as the human being who delivered it. Such prophecies were often made while the human oracle was under a sort of trance.*

Does God Change His Mind?

NU 23:19

God is not a fickle God, nor is his a changing nature. He is, however, a compassionate and caring Lord, willing to be influenced by the attitudes, actions and petitions of his people. His desire is to relate to the people he created, and relationships are a dynamic phenomenon—they involve give-and-take, growth and development. At no time does God change who he is; however, he does at times alter his responses to his people.

15Balaam said to Balak, "Stay here beside your
offering while I meet with him over there."
16The LORD met with Balaam and put a message
in his mouth[a] and said, "Go back to Balak and
give him this message."
17So he went to him and found him standing
beside his offering, with the princes of Moab.
Balak asked him, "What did the LORD say?"
18Then he uttered his oracle:

"Arise, Balak, and listen;
hear me, son of Zippor.
19God is not a man,[b] that he should lie,
nor a son of man, that he should
change his mind.[c]
Does he speak and then not act?
Does he promise and not fulfill?
20I have received a command to bless;
he has blessed,[d] and I cannot change
it.[e]

21"No misfortune is seen in Jacob,[f]
no misery observed in Israel.[a][g]
The LORD their God is with them;[h]
the shout of the King[i] is among them.
22God brought them out of Egypt;[j]
they have the strength of a wild ox.[k]
23There is no sorcery against Jacob,
no divination[l] against Israel.
It will now be said of Jacob
and of Israel, 'See what God has
done!'
24The people rise like a lioness;[m]
they rouse themselves like a lion[n]
that does not rest till he devours his
prey
and drinks the blood of his victims."

25Then Balak said to Balaam, "Neither curse
them at all nor bless them at all!"
26Balaam answered, "Did I not tell you I must
do whatever the LORD says?"

Balaam's Third Oracle

27Then Balak said to Balaam, "Come, let me
take you to another place.[o] Perhaps it will please
God to let you curse them for me from there."
28And Balak took Balaam to the top of Peor,[p] overlooking the wasteland.
29Balaam said, "Build me seven altars here, and
prepare seven bulls and seven rams for me."
30Balak did as Balaam had said, and offered a bull
and a ram on each altar.

24 Now when Balaam saw that it pleased the
LORD to bless Israel, he did not resort to sorcery[q] as at other times, but turned his face toward
the desert.[r] 2When Balaam looked out and saw
Israel encamped tribe by tribe, the Spirit of God
came upon him[s] 3and he uttered his oracle:

23:16 [a]Nu 22:38
23:19 [b]Isa 55:9; Hos 11:9 [c]1Sa 15:29; Mal 3:6; Tit 1:2; Jas 1:17
23:20 [d]Ge 22:17; Nu 22:12 [e]Isa 43:13
23:21 [f]Ps 32:2,5; Ro 4:7-8 [g]Isa 40:2; Jer 50:20 [h]Ex 29:45, 46; Ps 145:18 [i]Dt 33:5; Ps 89:15-18
23:22 [j]Nu 24:8 [k]Dt 33:17; Job 39:9
23:23 [l]Nu 24:1; Jos 13:22
23:24 [m]Na 2:11 [n]Ge 49:9
23:27 [o]ver 13
23:28 [p]Ps 106:28
24:1 [q]Nu 23:23 [r]Nu 23:28
24:2 [s]Nu 11:25, 26; 1Sa 10:10; 19:20; 2Ch 15:1

[a] 21 Or *He has not looked on Jacob's offenses / or on the wrongs found in Israel.*

"The oracle of Balaam son of Beor,
the oracle of one whose eye sees
clearly,
4 the oracle of one who hears the words
of God,[t]
who sees a vision from the
Almighty,[a][u]
who falls prostrate, and whose eyes
are opened:
5 "How beautiful are your tents, O Jacob,
your dwelling places, O Israel!

6 "Like valleys they spread out,
like gardens beside a river,
like aloes[v] planted by the LORD,
like cedars beside the waters.[w]
7 Water will flow from their buckets;
their seed will have abundant water.

"Their king will be greater than Agag;[x]
their kingdom will be exalted.[y]

8 "God brought them out of Egypt;
they have the strength of a wild ox.
They devour hostile nations
and break their bones in pieces;[z]
with their arrows they pierce them.[a]
9 Like a lion they crouch and lie down,
like a lioness[b]—who dares to rouse
them?

"May those who bless you be blessed
and those who curse you be cursed!"[c]

10 Then Balak's anger burned against Balaam.
He struck his hands together[d] and said to him, "I
summoned you to curse my enemies, but you
have blessed them[e] these three times.[f] 11 Now leave
at once and go home! I said I would reward you
handsomely,[g] but the LORD has kept you from
being rewarded."
12 Balaam answered Balak, "Did I not tell the
messengers you sent me,[h] 13 'Even if Balak gave
me his palace filled with silver and gold, I could
not do anything of my own accord, good or bad,
to go beyond the command of the LORD[i]—and I
must say only what the LORD says'?[j] 14 Now I am
going back to my people, but come, let me warn
you of what this people will do to your people in
days to come."[k]

Balaam's Fourth Oracle

15 Then he uttered his oracle:

"The oracle of Balaam son of Beor,
the oracle of one whose eye sees
clearly,
16 the oracle of one who hears the words
of God,
who has knowledge from the Most
High,

[a] 4 Hebrew *Shaddai*; also in verse 16

24:4 [t]Nu 22:20 [u]Ge 15:1
24:6 [v]Ps 45:8 [w]Ps 1:3; 104:16
24:7 [x]2Sa 15:8 [y]2Sa 5:12; 1Ch 14:2; Ps 145:11-13
24:8 [z]Ps 2:9; Jer 50:17 [a]Ps 45:5
24:9 [b]Ge 49:9; Nu 23:24 [c]Ge 12:3
24:10 [d]Eze 21:14 [e]Nu 23:11 [f]Ne 13:2
24:11 [g]Nu 22:17
24:12 [h]Nu 22:18
24:13 [i]Nu 22:18 [j]Nu 22:20
24:14 [k]Ge 49:1; Nu 31:8,16; Da 2:28; Mic 6:5

The more they abandon themselves, the more they find [God].

—Catherine of Siena (1347-1380)

Women of Moab and Midian

NU 25:1–3,6

Apparently at the suggestion of Balaam (Nu 31:16; Rev 2:14), Midianite women seduce Israelite men. The women's interest in the men is not idle; their seduction of the Israelites is likely a part of a plan to woo them away from the Lord and to their own pagan gods. To accomplish this, the foreign women invite the men to participate in their fertility festival, which includes not only worship of the pagan god Baal but also having sex with temple prostitutes—sins expressly forbidden by God (Ex 20:3–5). Knowing that the Israelites are susceptible to these sins, God warns them against making any kind of alliance with those living in the land where they were going (Ex 34:15–16); yet they do not listen, and 24,000 die (Nu 25:9) because of their disobedience.

who sees a vision from the Almighty,
who falls prostrate, and whose eyes
are opened:
17 "I see him, but not now;
I behold him, but not near.[l]
A star will come out of Jacob;[m]
a scepter will rise out of Israel.[n]
He will crush the foreheads of Moab,[o]
the skulls[a] of[b] all the sons of Sheth.[c]
18 Edom[p] will be conquered;
Seir, his enemy, will be conquered,
but Israel will grow strong.
19 A ruler will come out of Jacob[q]
and destroy the survivors of the city."

Balaam's Final Oracles

20 Then Balaam saw Amalek[r] and uttered his
oracle:

"Amalek was first among the nations,
but he will come to ruin at last."

21 Then he saw the Kenites[s] and uttered his
oracle:

"Your dwelling place is secure,
your nest is set in a rock;
22 yet you Kenites will be destroyed
when Asshur[t] takes you captive."

23 Then he uttered his oracle:

"Ah, who can live when God does this?[d]
24 Ships will come from the shores of
Kittim;[u]
they will subdue Asshur and Eber,[v]
but they too will come to ruin.[w]"

25 Then Balaam[x] got up and returned home and
Balak went his own way.

Moab Seduces Israel

25 While Israel was staying in Shittim,[y] the
men began to indulge in sexual immorality[z] with Moabite women,[a] 2 who invited them to
the sacrifices[b] to their gods.[c] The people ate and
bowed down before these gods. 3 So Israel joined
in worshiping the Baal of Peor.[d] And the LORD's
anger burned against them.
4 The LORD said to Moses, "Take all the leaders of
these people, kill them and expose them in broad
daylight before the LORD,[e] so that the LORD's fierce
anger[f] may turn away from Israel."
5 So Moses said to Israel's judges, "Each of you
must put to death[g] those of your men who have
joined in worshiping the Baal of Peor."
6 Then an Israelite man brought to his family a
Midianite woman right before the eyes of Moses

24:17 [l]Rev 1:7 [m]Mt 2:2 [n]Ge 49:10 [o]Nu 21:29; Isa 15:1-16:14
24:18 [p]Am 9:12
24:19 [q]Ge 49:10; Mic 5:2
24:20 [r]Ex 17:14
24:21 [s]Ge 15:19
24:22 [t]Ge 10:22
24:24 [u]Ge 10:4 [v]Ge 10:21 [w]ver 20
24:25 [x]Nu 31:8
25:1 [y]Jos 2:1; Mic 6:5 [z]1Co 10:8; Rev 2:14 [a]Nu 31:16
25:2 [b]Ex 34:15 [c]Ex 20:5; Dt 32:38; 1Co 10:20
25:3 [d]Ps 106:28; Hos 9:10
25:4 [e]Dt 4:3 [f]Dt 13:17
25:5 [g]Ex 32:27

[a] *17* Samaritan Pentateuch (see also Jer. 48:45); the meaning of the word in the Masoretic Text is uncertain. [b] *17* Or possibly *Moab, / batter* [c] *17* Or *all the noisy boasters*
[d] *23* Masoretic Text; with a different word division of the Hebrew *A people will gather from the north.*

and the whole assembly of Israel while they were
weeping at the entrance to the Tent of Meeting.
7When Phinehas son of Eleazar, the son of Aaron,
the priest, saw this, he left the assembly, took a
spear in his hand 8and followed the Israelite into
the tent. He drove the spear through both of
them—through the Israelite and into the woman's
body. Then the plague against the Israelites was
25:8 [h]Nu 16:46-48; Ps 106:30 stopped;[h] 9but those who died in the plague[i] numbered 24,000.[j]
10The LORD said to Moses, 11"Phinehas son of
25:9 [i]Nu 14:37; 1Co 10:8 [j]Nu 31:16 Eleazar, the son of Aaron, the priest, has turned
my anger away from the Israelites;[k] for he was as
zealous as I am for my honor[l] among them, so
that in my zeal I did not put an end to them.
25:11 [k]Ps 106:30 [l]Ex 20:5; Dt 32:16,21; Ps 78:58 12Therefore tell him I am making my covenant of
peace[m] with him. 13He and his descendants will
have a covenant of a lasting priesthood,[n] because
he was zealous for the honor of his God and made
25:12 [m]Isa 54:10; Eze 34:25; Mal 2:4,5 atonement[o] for the Israelites."
14The name of the Israelite who was killed with
the Midianite woman was Zimri son of Salu, the
leader of a Simeonite family. 15And the name of
25:13 [n]Ex 29:9 [o]Nu 16:46 the Midianite woman who was put to death was
Cozbi[p] daughter of Zur, a tribal chief of a Midian-
ite family.[q]
25:15 [p]ver 18 [q]Nu 31:8; Jos 13:21 16The LORD said to Moses, 17"Treat the Midianites[r] as enemies and kill them, 18because they
treated you as enemies when they deceived you in
25:17 [r]Nu 31:1-3 the affair of Peor[s] and their sister Cozbi, the daughter of a Midianite leader, the woman who was
25:18 [s]Nu 31:16 killed when the plague came as a result of Peor."

The Second Census

26 After the plague the LORD said to Moses and
Eleazar son of Aaron, the priest, 2"Take a
26:2 [t]Ex 30:11-16; 38:25-26; Nu 1:2 [u]Nu 1:3 census[t] of the whole Israelite community by families—all those twenty years old or more who are
able to serve in the army[u] of Israel." 3So on the
plains of Moab[v] by the Jordan across from Jeri-
26:3 [v]Nu 33:48 [w]Nu 22:1 cho,[a][w] Moses and Eleazar the priest spoke with
them and said, 4"Take a census of the men twenty
years old or more, as the LORD commanded Moses."

These were the Israelites who came out of
Egypt:

5The descendants of Reuben, the firstborn son of
Israel, were:
26:5 [x]Ge 46:9 [y]1Ch 5:3 through Hanoch,[x] the Hanochite clan;
through Pallu,[y] the Palluite clan;
6through Hezron, the Hezronite clan;
through Carmi, the Carmite clan.
7These were the clans of Reuben; those numbered
were 43,730.
8The son of Pallu was Eliab, 9and the sons of
26:9 [z]Nu 16:1 [a]Nu 1:16 Eliab[z] were Nemuel, Dathan and Abiram. The
same Dathan and Abiram were the community[a]
officials who rebelled against Moses and Aaron

[a] 3 Hebrew *Jordan of Jericho;* possibly an ancient name for the Jordan River; also in verse 63

A Perpetual Priesthood

NU 25:12-13

This covenant of a "lasting priesthood" (Nu 25:13) assures that the descendants of Phinehas will continue to serve as the high priests of Israel throughout the existence of the tabernacle and temple, as long as human, priestly intervention is required.

Centuries later, we still need a mediator to petition our case before God. Yet, unlike the Old Testament priesthood, Jesus himself now serves as our high priest (Heb 2:17; 4:15). Though the ancient priests had to offer continuous blood sacrifices for the people's sins, Jesus atones for our sins once and for all, through the shedding of his own blood (1Pe 3:18). The priests who descended from Phinehas were from the tribe of Aaron; Jesus' priesthood, described as being "in the order of the Melchizedek" (Heb 5:10), is vastly superior and supersedes every priesthood of the past (see the note on Heb 7:11-26, page 1998).

Another Census

NU 26:7-10

The second census records a reduction in numbers in the tribe of Reuben and refers to Dathan and Abiram, the two Reubenites who joined the Levite Korah in challenging Moses' authority (Nu 16:1–3). Had Dathan and Abiram not rebelled, they and their families would presumably have been spared, as were the sons of Korah (Nu 26:11; see also the note on Nu 16:31-33, page 236). Consequently, the tribe of Reuben would have grown larger and stronger. More than just an accounting of the people, this second census serves as a clear reminder of the consequences of sinful rebellion.

and were among Korah's followers when they
rebelled against the LORD.[b] 10 The earth opened its
mouth and swallowed them along with Korah,
whose followers died when the fire devoured the
250 men. And they served as a warning sign.[c]
11 The line of Korah,[d] however, did not die out.[e]

12 The descendants of Simeon by their clans were:
through Nemuel, the Nemuelite clan;
through Jamin,[f] the Jaminite clan;
through Jakin, the Jakinite clan;
13 through Zerah,[g] the Zerahite clan;
through Shaul, the Shaulite clan.
14 These were the clans of Simeon; there were
22,200 men.[h]

15 The descendants of Gad by their clans were:
through Zephon,[i] the Zephonite clan;
through Haggi, the Haggite clan;
through Shuni, the Shunite clan;
16 through Ozni, the Oznite clan;
through Eri, the Erite clan;
17 through Arodi,[a] the Arodite clan;
through Areli, the Arelite clan.
18 These were the clans of Gad;[j] those numbered
were 40,500.

19 Er and Onan were sons of Judah, but they died[k]
in Canaan.
20 The descendants of Judah by their clans were:
through Shelah,[l] the Shelanite clan;
through Perez, the Perezite clan;
through Zerah, the Zerahite clan.[m]
21 The descendants of Perez were:
through Hezron,[n] the Hezronite clan;
through Hamul, the Hamulite clan.
22 These were the clans of Judah;[o] those numbered
were 76,500.

23 The descendants of Issachar by their clans were:
through Tola,[p] the Tolaite clan;
through Puah, the Puite[b] clan;
24 through Jashub,[q] the Jashubite clan;
through Shimron, the Shimronite clan.
25 These were the clans of Issachar;[r] those numbered were 64,300.

26 The descendants of Zebulun by their clans were:
through Sered, the Seredite clan;
through Elon, the Elonite clan;
through Jahleel, the Jahleelite clan.
27 These were the clans of Zebulun;[s] those numbered were 60,500.

28 The descendants of Joseph by their clans
through Manasseh and Ephraim were:

29 The descendants of Manasseh:
through Makir,[t] the Makirite clan (Makir was
the father of Gilead[u]);

[a] *17* Samaritan Pentateuch and Syriac (see also Gen. 46:16); Masoretic Text *Arod* [b] *23* Samaritan Pentateuch, Septuagint, Vulgate and Syriac (see also 1 Chron. 7:1); Masoretic Text *through Puvah, the Punite*

26:9 [b]Nu 16:2
26:10 [c]Nu 16:35, 38
26:11 [d]Ex 6:24 [e]Nu 16:33; Dt 24:16
26:12 [f]1Ch 4:24
26:13 [g]Ge 46:10
26:14 [h]Nu 1:23
26:15 [i]Ge 46:16
26:18 [j]Nu 1:25; Jos 13:24-28
26:19 [k]Ge 38:2-10; 46:12
26:20 [l]1Ch 2:3 [m]Jos 7:17
26:21 [n]Ru 4:19; 1Ch 2:9
26:22 [o]Nu 1:27
26:23 [p]Ge 46:13; 1Ch 7:1
26:24 [q]Ge 46:13
26:25 [r]Nu 1:29
26:27 [s]Nu 1:31
26:29 [t]Jos 17:1 [u]Jdg 11:1

through Gilead, the Gileadite clan.
26:30 [v]Jos 17:2; Jdg 6:11 30 These were the descendants of Gilead:
through Iezer,[v] the Iezerite clan;
through Helek, the Helekite clan;
31 through Asriel, the Asrielite clan;
through Shechem, the Shechemite clan;
32 through Shemida, the Shemidaite clan;
through Hepher, the Hepherite clan.
26:33 [w]Nu 27:1 [x]Nu 36:11 33 (Zelophehad[w] son of Hepher had no sons;
he had only daughters, whose names were
Mahlah, Noah, Hoglah, Milcah and
Tirzah.)[x]
34 These were the clans of Manasseh; those num-
26:34 [y]Nu 1:35 bered were 52,700.[y]

35 These were the descendants of Ephraim by their
clans:
through Shuthelah, the Shuthelahite clan;
through Beker, the Bekerite clan;
through Tahan, the Tahanite clan.
36 These were the descendants of Shuthelah:
through Eran, the Eranite clan.
26:37 [z]Nu 1:33 37 These were the clans of Ephraim;[z] those numbered were 32,500.

These were the descendants of Joseph by their
clans.

26:38 [a]Ge 46:21; 1Ch 7:6 38 The descendants of Benjamin[a] by their clans
were:
through Bela, the Belaite clan;
through Ashbel, the Ashbelite clan;
through Ahiram, the Ahiramite clan;
39 through Shupham,[a] the Shuphamite clan;
through Hupham, the Huphamite clan.
26:40 [b]Ge 46:21; 1Ch 8:3 40 The descendants of Bela through Ard[b] and
Naaman were:
through Ard,[b] the Ardite clan;
through Naaman, the Naamite clan.
26:41 [c]Nu 1:37 41 These were the clans of Benjamin;[c] those numbered were 45,600.

42 These were the descendants of Dan by their
clans:
26:42 [d]Ge 46:23 through Shuham,[d] the Shuhamite clan.
These were the clans of Dan: 43 All of them were
Shuhamite clans; and those numbered were
64,400.

44 The descendants of Asher by their clans were:
through Imnah, the Imnite clan;
through Ishvi, the Ishvite clan;
through Beriah, the Beriite clan;
45 and through the descendants of Beriah:
through Heber, the Heberite clan;
through Malkiel, the Malkielite clan.
46 (Asher had a daughter named Serah.)

[a] *39* A few manuscripts of the Masoretic Text, Samaritan Pentateuch, Vulgate and Syriac (see also Septuagint); most manuscripts of the Masoretic Text *Shephupham*
[b] *40* Samaritan Pentateuch and Vulgate (see also Septuagint); Masoretic Text does not have *through Ard.*

Daughters in the Census

NU 26:33,46

Because ancient Israelite society was patriarchal and because Biblical accounts often reflected the values of the days in which they were written, the names of females rarely appear in Scriptural genealogies. The use of a census for military purposes also limited the inclusion of women in official accounts. This very scarcity causes us to sit up and take notice when such references do occur.

The mention of Asher's daughter Serah (Nu 26:46) is as mysterious as it is remarkable. No explanation is given for its inclusion, though some speculate that Serah may have been Jacob's only granddaughter, just as Dinah was his only daughter.

The listing of Zelophehad's daughters (Nu 26:33) is probably given as background for their story, recorded in Numbers 27:1–11 and Numbers 36. To approach Moses and Aaron about their father's inheritance took great courage and conviction; these five sisters are some of the most valiant female role models found in Scripture.

Comparing Census Totals

NU 26:51

In 40 years of desert wandering, the Israelite population has decreased very little. Despite the hardships the people have faced and the massive loss of life that has resulted from their own disobedience (Nu 16:31–35,49; 25:6–9), the number of males available for military service has remained nearly constant since the flight from Egypt, evidence of God's continued faithfulness to his chosen people.

Comparison of the First and Second Censuses

Tribe	First Census	Second Census
Reuben	46,500	43,730
Simeon	59,300	22,200
Gad	45,650	40,500
Judah	74,600	76,500
Issachar	54,400	64,300
Zebulun	57,400	60,500
Ephraim	40,500	32,500
Manasseh	32,200	52,700
Benjamin	35,400	45,600
Dan	62,700	64,400
Asher	41,500	53,400
Naphtali	53,400	45,400
TOTAL	603,550	601,730

The tribe of Simeon is the only tribe to experience significant loss. Possibly the recent plague, where 24,000 die because of the sin of Zimri, a Simeonite, is the cause (Nu 25:6–9,14).

47These were the clans of Asher;[e] those numbered
were 53,400.

48The descendants of Naphtali[f] by their clans
were:
through Jahzeel, the Jahzeelite clan;
through Guni, the Gunite clan;
49through Jezer, the Jezerite clan;
through Shillem, the Shillemite clan.
50These were the clans of Naphtali;[g] those numbered were 45,400.

51The total number of the men of Israel was
601,730.[h]

52The LORD said to Moses, 53"The land is to be
allotted to them as an inheritance based on the
number of names.[i] 54To a larger group give a larger inheritance, and to a smaller group a smaller
one; each is to receive its inheritance according to
the number[j] of those listed. 55Be sure that the land
is distributed by lot.[k] What each group inherits
will be according to the names for its ancestral
tribe. 56Each inheritance is to be distributed by lot
among the larger and smaller groups."

57These were the Levites[l] who were counted by
their clans:
through Gershon, the Gershonite clan;
through Kohath, the Kohathite clan;
through Merari, the Merarite clan.
58These also were Levite clans:
the Libnite clan,
the Hebronite clan,
the Mahlite clan,
the Mushite clan,
the Korahite clan.
(Kohath was the forefather of Amram;[m] 59the
name of Amram's wife was Jochebed,[n] a
descendant of Levi, who was born to the
Levites[a] in Egypt. To Amram she bore Aaron,
Moses[o] and their sister Miriam. 60Aaron was
the father of Nadab and Abihu, Eleazar and
Ithamar.[p] 61But Nadab and Abihu[q] died when
they made an offering before the LORD with
unauthorized fire.)[r]

62All the male Levites a month old or more numbered 23,000.[s] They were not counted[t] along with
the other Israelites because they received no
inheritance[u] among them.[v]

63These are the ones counted by Moses and Eleazar the priest when they counted the Israelites
on the plains of Moab[w] by the Jordan across from
Jericho. 64Not one of them was among those
counted[x] by Moses and Aaron the priest when
they counted the Israelites in the Desert of Sinai.
65For the LORD had told those Israelites they would
surely die in the desert,[y] and not one of them was

26:47 [e]Nu 1:41
26:48 [f]Ge 46:24; 1Ch 7:13
26:50 [g]Nu 1:43
26:51 [h]Ex 12:37; 38:26; Nu 1:46; 11:21
26:53 [i]Jos 11:23; 14:1; Eze 45:8
26:54 [j]Nu 33:54
26:55 [k]Nu 34:14
26:57 [l]Ge 46:11; Ex 6:16-19
26:58 [m]Ex 6:20
26:59 [n]Ex 2:1 [o]Ex 6:20
26:60 [p]Nu 3:2
26:61 [q]Lev 10:1-2 [r]Nu 3:4
26:62 [s]Nu 3:39 [t]Nu 1:47 [u]Nu 18:23 [v]Nu 2:33; Dt 10:9
26:63 [w]ver 3
26:64 [x]Nu 14:29; Dt 2:14-15; Heb 3:17
26:65 [y]Nu 14:28; 1Co 10:5

[a] 59 Or *Jochebed, a daughter of Levi, who was born to Levi*

left except Caleb son of Jephunneh and Joshua
son of Nun.[z]

Zelophehad's Daughters

27 The daughters of Zelophehad[a] son of
Hepher,[b] the son of Gilead, the son of
Makir,[c] the son of Manasseh, belonged to the clans
of Manasseh son of Joseph. The names of the
daughters were Mahlah, Noah, Hoglah, Milcah
and Tirzah. They approached 2the entrance to the
Tent of Meeting and stood before Moses, Eleazar
the priest, the leaders and the whole assembly, and
said, 3"Our father died in the desert.[d] He was not
among Korah's followers, who banded together
against the LORD,[e] but he died for his own sin and
left no sons.[f] 4Why should our father's name disappear from his clan because he had no son? Give
us property among our father's relatives."
5So Moses brought their case[g] before the LORD[h]
6and the LORD said to him, 7"What Zelophehad's
daughters are saying is right. You must certainly
give them property as an inheritance[i] among their
father's relatives and turn their father's inheritance over to them.[j]
8"Say to the Israelites, 'If a man dies and leaves
no son, turn his inheritance over to his daughter.
9If he has no daughter, give his inheritance to his
brothers. 10If he has no brothers, give his inheritance to his father's brothers. 11If his father had no
brothers, give his inheritance to the nearest relative in his clan, that he may possess it. This is to
be a legal requirement[k] for the Israelites, as the
LORD commanded Moses.' "

Joshua to Succeed Moses

12Then the LORD said to Moses, "Go up this
mountain in the Abarim range[l] and see the land[m]
I have given the Israelites. 13After you have seen
it, you too will be gathered to your people,[n] as
your brother Aaron[o] was, 14for when the community rebelled at the waters in the Desert of Zin,
both of you disobeyed my command to honor me
as holy[p] before their eyes." (These were the
waters of Meribah[q] Kadesh, in the Desert of Zin.)
15Moses said to the LORD, 16"May the LORD, the
God of the spirits of all mankind,[r] appoint a man
over this community 17to go out and come in
before them, one who will lead them out and
bring them in, so the LORD's people will not be
like sheep without a shepherd."[s]
18So the LORD said to Moses, "Take Joshua son
of Nun, a man in whom is the spirit,[a][t] and lay
your hand on him.[u] 19Have him stand before Eleazar the priest and the entire assembly and commission him[v] in their presence.[w] 20Give him some
of your authority so the whole Israelite community will obey him.[x] 21He is to stand before Eleazar
the priest, who will obtain decisions for him by
inquiring[y] of the Urim[z] before the LORD. At his

26:65 [z]Jos 14:6-10
27:1 [a]Nu 26:33 [b]Jos 17:2,3 [c]Nu 36:1
27:3 [d]Nu 26:65 [e]Nu 16:2 [f]Nu 26:33
27:5 [g]Ex 18:19 [h]Nu 9:8
27:7 [i]Job 42:15 [j]Jos 17:4
27:11 [k]Nu 35:29
27:12 [l]Nu 33:47; Jer 22:20 [m]Dt 3:23-27; 32:48-52
27:13 [n]Nu 31:2 [o]Nu 20:28
27:14 [p]Nu 20:12 [q]Ex 17:7; Dt 32:51; Ps 106:32
27:16 [r]Nu 16:22
27:17 [s]Dt 31:2; 1Ki 22:17; Eze 34:5; Zec 10:2; Mt 9:36; Mk 6:34
27:18 [t]Ge 41:38; Nu 11:25-29 [u]ver 23; Dt 34:9
27:19 [v]Dt 3:28; 31:14,23 [w]Dt 31:7
27:20 [x]Jos 1:16,17
27:21 [y]Jos 9:14 [z]Ex 28:30

[a] 18 Or *Spirit*

Moses' Successor

NU 27:15-18

In selecting a new ruler for Israel, Moses wisely defers to "the God of the spirits of all mankind" (Nu 27:16). God himself created humans, and he can clearly read the spirit of every one. No candidate can fool him by appearances, and he is far more able than Moses to choose a worthy successor. This same spirit is present in Joshua, Moses' appointed successor. His spirit—or God's Spirit within him—is in alignment with his outward actions and gives him the wisdom and righteous characteristics required of the leader of God's people.

While our actions speak volumes about the state of our hearts, that's only half the battle, for even good actions can be performed with sinful motives. Search your heart today to see if there is any way in which you are trying to "pull the wool" over God's eyes—or anyone else's. Consider what you must do—starting today—to bring your inner and outer lives into alignment.

command he and the entire community of the
Israelites will go out, and at his command they
will come in."
22Moses did as the LORD commanded him. He
took Joshua and had him stand before Eleazar the
priest and the whole assembly. 23Then he laid his
hands on him and commissioned him, as the LORD
instructed through Moses.

Daily Offerings

28 The LORD said to Moses, 2"Give this command to the Israelites and say to them: 'See
that you present to me at the appointed time the
food[a] for my offerings made by fire, as an aroma
pleasing to me.' 3Say to them: 'This is the offering
made by fire that you are to present to the LORD:
two lambs a year old without defect, as a regular
burnt offering each day.[b] 4Prepare one lamb in the
morning and the other at twilight, 5together with
a grain offering of a tenth of an ephah[a] of fine
flour mixed with a quarter of a hin[b] of oil[c] from
pressed olives. 6This is the regular burnt offering
instituted at Mount Sinai[d] as a pleasing aroma, an
offering made to the LORD by fire. 7The accompanying drink offering[e] is to be a quarter of a hin of
fermented drink with each lamb. Pour out the
drink offering to the LORD at the sanctuary.[f] 8Pre-
pare the second lamb at twilight, along with the
same kind of grain offering and drink offering that
you prepare in the morning. This is an offering
made by fire, an aroma pleasing to the LORD.[g]

Sabbath Offerings

9" 'On the Sabbath[h] day, make an offering of
two lambs a year old without defect, together with
its drink offering and a grain offering of two-
tenths of an ephah[c][i] of fine flour mixed with oil.
10This is the burnt offering for every Sabbath, in
addition to the regular burnt offering[j] and its
drink offering.

Monthly Offerings

11" 'On the first of every month,[k] present to the
LORD a burnt offering of two young bulls, one ram
and seven male lambs a year old, all without
defect.[l] 12With each bull there is to be a grain
offering[m] of three-tenths of an ephah[d][n] of fine
flour mixed with oil; with the ram, a grain offering of two-tenths of an ephah of fine flour mixed
with oil; 13and with each lamb, a grain offering[o] of
a tenth of an ephah of fine flour mixed with oil.
This is for a burnt offering, a pleasing aroma, an
offering made to the LORD by fire. 14With each bull
there is to be a drink offering[p] of half a hin[e] of

28:2 [a]Lev 3:11
28:3 [b]Ex 29:38
28:5 [c]Lev 2:1; Nu 15:4
28:6 [d]Ex 19:3
28:7 [e]Ex 29:41 [f]Lev 3:7
28:8 [g]Lev 1:9
28:9 [h]Ex 20:10 [i]Lev 23:13
28:10 [j]ver 3
28:11 [k]Nu 10:10 [l]Lev 1:3
28:12 [m]Nu 15:6 [n]Nu 15:9
28:13 [o]Lev 6:14
28:14 [p]Nu 15:7

[a] *5* That is, probably about 2 quarts (about 2 liters); also in verses 13, 21 and 29 [b] *5* That is, probably about 1 quart (about 1 liter); also in verses 7 and 14 [c] *9* That is, probably about 4 quarts (about 4.5 liters); also in verses 12, 20 and 28 [d] *12* That is, probably about 6 quarts (about 6.5 liters); also in verses 20 and 28 [e] *14* That is, probably about 2 quarts (about 2 liters)

The Lord does not look so much at the magnitude of anything we do as at the love with which we do it.

—Teresa of Avila (1515-1582)

wine; with the ram, a third of a hin[a]; and with
28:14 each lamb, a quarter of a hin. This is the month-
qEzr 3:5 ly burnt offering to be made at each new moon[q]
28:15 during the year. 15Besides the regular burnt offer-
rver 3,23,24 ing[r] with its drink offering, one male goat is to be
sLev 4:3 presented to the LORD as a sin offering.[s]

The Passover

28:16 16“ ‘On the fourteenth day of the first month the
tEx 12:6,18; LORD’s Passover[t] is to be held. 17On the fifteenth
Lev 23:5; day of this month there is to be a festival; for sev-
Dt 16:1 en days[u] eat bread made without yeast.[v] 18On the
28:17 first day hold a sacred assembly and do no regular
uEx 12:19 vEx 23:15; work.[w] 19Present to the LORD an offering made by
34:18; fire, a burnt offering of two young bulls, one ram
Lev 23:6; and seven male lambs a year old, all without
Dt 16:3-8 defect. 20With each bull prepare a grain offering
28:18 of three-tenths of an ephah[x] of fine flour mixed
wEx 12:16; Lev 23:7 with oil; with the ram, two-tenths; 21and with
each of the seven lambs, one-tenth. 22Include one
28:20 male goat as a sin offering[y] to make atonement
xLev 14:10 for you.[z] 23Prepare these in addition to the regular
28:22 morning burnt offering. 24In this way prepare the
yRo 8:3 food for the offering made by fire every day for
zNu 15:28 seven days as an aroma pleasing to the LORD; it is
to be prepared in addition to the regular burnt
offering and its drink offering. 25On the seventh
day hold a sacred assembly and do no regular
work.

Feast of Weeks

28:26 26“ ‘On the day of firstfruits,[a] when you present
aEx 34:22 to the LORD an offering of new grain during the
bEx 23:16 cver 18; Feast of Weeks,[b] hold a sacred assembly and do
Dt 16:10 no regular work.[c] 27Present a burnt offering of two
young bulls, one ram and seven male lambs a
year old as an aroma pleasing to the LORD. 28With
each bull there is to be a grain offering of three-
tenths of an ephah of fine flour mixed with oil;
with the ram, two-tenths; 29and with each of the
28:29 seven lambs, one-tenth.[d] 30Include one male goat
dver 13 to make atonement for you. 31Prepare these
together with their drink offerings, in addition to
28:31 the regular burnt offering[e] and its grain offering.
ever 3,19 Be sure the animals are without defect.

Feast of Trumpets

29 “ ‘On the first day of the seventh month
29:1 hold a sacred assembly and do no regular
fLev 23:24 work.[f] It is a day for you to sound the trumpets.
29:2 2As an aroma pleasing to the LORD,[g] prepare a
gNu 28:2 burnt offering of one young bull, one ram and
hNu 28:3 seven male lambs a year old, all without defect.[h]
3With the bull prepare a grain offering of three-
tenths of an ephah[b] of fine flour mixed with oil;
with the ram, two-tenths[c]; 4and with each of the

I clearly recognize that all good is in God alone, and that in me, without divine grace, there is nothing but deficiency . . . The one sole thing in myself in which I glory, is that I see in myself nothing in which I can glory.

—Catherine of Genoa (1447–1510)

[a] *14* That is, probably about 1 1/4 quarts (about 1.2 liters)
[b] *3* That is, probably about 6 quarts (about 6.5 liters); also in verses 9 and 14 [c] *3* That is, probably about 4 quarts (about 4.5 liters); also in verses 9 and 14

There is a certain work to be accomplished. We are to be delivered from the power of sin . . . We are to be transformed by the renewing of our minds . . . Besetting sins are to be conquered. Evil habits are to be overcome. Wrong dispositions and feelings are to be rooted out, and holy tempers and emotions are to be begotten. A positive transformation is to take place. So at least the Bible teaches. Now somebody must do this. Either we must do it for ourselves, or another must do it for us. We have most of us tried to do it for ourselves at first, and have grievously failed; then we discover from the Scriptures and from our own experience that it is a work we are utterly unable to do for ourselves, but that the Lord Jesus Christ has come on purpose to do it, and that He will do it for all who put themselves wholly into His hand, and trust Him to do it. Now under these circumstances, what is the part of the believer, and what is the part of the Lord? Plainly the believer can do nothing but trust; while the Lord, in whom he trusts, actually does the work.

—Hannah Whitall Smith (1832-1911)

seven lambs, one-tenth.[a] 5 Include one male goat[i]
as a sin offering to make atonement for you.
6 These are in addition to the monthly[j] and daily
burnt offerings[k] with their grain offerings and
drink offerings as specified. They are offerings
made to the LORD by fire—a pleasing aroma.

Day of Atonement

7 " 'On the tenth day of this seventh month hold
a sacred assembly. You must deny yourselves[b][l]
and do no work.[m] 8 Present as an aroma pleasing
to the LORD a burnt offering of one young bull,
one ram and seven male lambs a year old, all
without defect. 9 With the bull prepare a grain
offering[n] of three-tenths of an ephah of fine flour
mixed with oil; with the ram, two-tenths; 10 and
with each of the seven lambs, one-tenth.[o]
11 Include one male goat as a sin offering, in addition to the sin offering for atonement and the regular burnt offering[p] with its grain offering, and
their drink offerings.

Feast of Tabernacles

12 " 'On the fifteenth day of the seventh[q] month,[r]
hold a sacred assembly and do no regular work.
Celebrate a festival to the LORD for seven days.
13 Present an offering made by fire as an aroma
pleasing to the LORD, a burnt offering of thirteen
young bulls, two rams and fourteen male lambs a
year old, all without defect. 14 With each of the thirteen bulls prepare a grain offering[s] of three-tenths
of an ephah of fine flour mixed with oil; with each
of the two rams, two-tenths; 15 and with each of the
fourteen lambs, one-tenth. 16 Include one male goat
as a sin offering, in addition to the regular burnt
offering with its grain offering and drink offering.[t]
17 " 'On the second day[u] prepare twelve young
bulls, two rams and fourteen male lambs a year
old, all without defect.[v] 18 With the bulls, rams and
lambs, prepare their grain offerings[w] and drink
offerings[x] according to the number specified.[y]
19 Include one male goat as a sin offering,[z] in addition to the regular burnt offering with its grain
offering, and their drink offerings.
20 " 'On the third day prepare eleven bulls, two
rams and fourteen male lambs a year old, all without defect.[a] 21 With the bulls, rams and lambs, prepare their grain offerings and drink offerings
according to the number specified.[b] 22 Include one
male goat as a sin offering, in addition to the regular burnt offering with its grain offering and
drink offering.
23 " 'On the fourth day prepare ten bulls, two
rams and fourteen male lambs a year old, all without defect. 24 With the bulls, rams and lambs, prepare their grain offerings and drink offerings
according to the number specified. 25 Include one
male goat as a sin offering, in addition to the reg-

29:5 [i]Nu 28:15
29:6 [j]Nu 28:11 [k]Nu 28:3
29:7 [l]Ac 27:9 [m]Ex 31:15; Lev 16:29; 23:26-32
29:9 [n]ver 3,18
29:10 [o]Nu 28:13
29:11 [p]Lev 16:3; Nu 28:3
29:12 [q]1Ki 8:2 [r]Lev 23:24
29:14 [s]ver 3
29:16 [t]ver 6
29:17 [u]Lev 23:36 [v]Nu 28:3
29:18 [w]ver 9 [x]Nu 28:7 [y]Nu 15:4-12
29:19 [z]Nu 28:15
29:20 [a]ver 17
29:21 [b]ver 18

[a] 4 That is, probably about 2 quarts (about 2 liters); also in verses 10 and 15 [b] 7 Or *must fast*

ular burnt offering with its grain offering and
drink offering.
26“ ‘On the fifth day prepare nine bulls, two rams
and fourteen male lambs a year old, all without
defect. 27With the bulls, rams and lambs, prepare
their grain offerings and drink offerings according
to the number specified. 28Include one male goat
as a sin offering, in addition to the regular burnt
offering with its grain offering and drink offering.
29“ ‘On the sixth day prepare eight bulls, two
rams and fourteen male lambs a year old, all without defect. 30With the bulls, rams and lambs, prepare their grain offerings and drink offerings
according to the number specified. 31Include one
male goat as a sin offering, in addition to the regular burnt offering with its grain offering and
drink offering.
32“ ‘On the seventh day prepare seven bulls, two
rams and fourteen male lambs a year old, all without defect. 33With the bulls, rams and lambs, prepare their grain offerings and drink offerings
according to the number specified. 34Include one
male goat as a sin offering, in addition to the regular burnt offering with its grain offering and
29:35 drink offering.
[c]Lev 23:36 35“ ‘On the eighth day hold an assembly[c] and
do no regular work. 36Present an offering made by
29:36 fire as an aroma pleasing to the LORD,[d] a burnt
[d]Lev 1:9 [e]ver 2 offering of one bull, one ram and seven male
lambs a year old,[e] all without defect. 37With the
bull, the ram and the lambs, prepare their grain
offerings and drink offerings according to the
number specified. 38Include one male goat as a sin
offering, in addition to the regular burnt offering
29:39 with its grain offering and drink offering.
[f]Nu 6:2 39“ ‘In addition to what you vow[f] and your
[g]Lev 23:2 freewill offerings, prepare these for the LORD at
[h]Lev 1:3; 1Ch 23:31; your appointed feasts:[g] your burnt offerings,[h]
2Ch 31:3 grain offerings, drink offerings and fellowship
offerings.[a]’ ”
40Moses told the Israelites all that the LORD commanded him.

Vows

30 Moses said to the heads of the tribes of Isra-
30:1 [i]Nu 1:4 el:[i] “This is what the LORD commands:
2When a man makes a vow to the LORD or takes
an oath to obligate himself by a pledge, he must
30:2 not break his word but must do everything he
[j]Dt 23:21-23; said.[j]
Jdg 11:35; 3“When a young woman still living in her
Job 22:27; father's house makes a vow to the LORD or obli-
Ps 22:25; 50:14; gates herself by a pledge 4and her father hears
116:14; about her vow or pledge but says nothing to her,
Pr 20:25; then all her vows and every pledge by which she
Ecc 5:4,5; Jnh 1:16 obligated herself will stand.[k] 5But if her father for-
30:4 bids her when he hears about it, none of her vows
[k]ver 7 or the pledges by which she obligated herself will

[a] 39 Traditionally *peace offerings*

Women's Vows

NU 30

It seems peculiar to the contemporary female mind that a father is allowed to interfere in his daughter's religious experience or a husband in his wife's. But this law regarding women's vows—the only regulation of its kind—is made for the protection of women, as were so many of God's other laws (see the note on Nu 5:11-31, page 214).

The primary regulation regarding vows—taken by men and women alike—is that they be fulfilled. *Women at that time were under the authority of the men in their lives. God knows that their responsibilities to their families and to their husbands may at times conflict with their vows and obligations to God. He therefore here provides a clause that will release women from their vows, eliminating the source of contention—and possible abuse—between women and those who had authority over them.*

More on Women's Vows

NU 30:9

In situations where women are not subject to the authority of a father or husband, they are required to honor their vows, just as men are. These include general vows, made for any purpose, and specific religious vows, such as those taken by the Nazirites (see the note on Nu 6:1–21, page 215).

There are no parallel laws for men in Scripture because there is no need for them. Since men are in authority and are not at risk for abuse in Israelite society, nothing prevents them from honoring their pledges before God. They, along with independent women such as divorcees and widows, are required to fulfill every vow and oath they make.

stand; the LORD will release her because her father has forbidden her.

6"If she marries after she makes a vow[l] or after her lips utter a rash promise by which she obligates herself 7and her husband hears about it but says nothing to her, then her vows or the pledges by which she obligated herself will stand. 8But if her husband[m] forbids her when he hears about it, he nullifies the vow that obligates her or the rash promise by which she obligates herself, and the LORD will release her.

9"Any vow or obligation taken by a widow or divorced woman will be binding on her.

10"If a woman living with her husband makes a vow or obligates herself by a pledge under oath 11and her husband hears about it but says nothing to her and does not forbid her, then all her vows or the pledges by which she obligated herself will stand. 12But if her husband nullifies them when he hears about them, then none of the vows or pledges that came from her lips will stand.[n] Her husband has nullified them, and the LORD will release her. 13Her husband may confirm or nullify any vow she makes or any sworn pledge to deny herself. 14But if her husband says nothing to her about it from day to day, then he confirms all her vows or the pledges binding on her. He confirms them by saying nothing to her when he hears about them. 15If, however, he nullifies them some time after he hears about them, then he is responsible for her guilt."

16These are the regulations the LORD gave Moses concerning relationships between a man and his wife, and between a father and his young daughter still living in his house.

Vengeance on the Midianites

31 The LORD said to Moses, 2"Take vengeance on the Midianites[o] for the Israelites. After that, you will be gathered to your people.[p]"

3So Moses said to the people, "Arm some of your men to go to war against the Midianites and to carry out the LORD's vengeance[q] on them. 4Send into battle a thousand men from each of the tribes of Israel." 5So twelve thousand men armed for battle, a thousand from each tribe, were supplied from the clans of Israel. 6Moses sent them into battle, a thousand from each tribe, along with Phinehas son of Eleazar, the priest, who took with him articles from the sanctuary[r] and the trumpets[s] for signaling.

7They fought against Midian, as the LORD commanded Moses, and killed every man.[t] 8Among their victims were Evi, Rekem, Zur, Hur and Reba[u]—the five kings of Midian.[v] They also killed Balaam son of Beor with the sword.[w] 9The Israelites captured the Midianite women and children and took all the Midianite herds, flocks and goods as plunder. 10They burned all the towns where the Midianites had settled, as well as all their camps.[x] 11They took all the plunder and spoils, including the people and animals,[y] 12and brought the cap-

30:6 [l]Lev 5:4
30:8 [m]Ge 3:16
30:12 [n]Eph 5:22; Col 3:18
31:2 [o]Ge 25:2 [p]Nu 20:26; 27:13
31:3 [q]Jdg 11:36; 1Sa 24:12; 2Sa 4:8; 22:48; Ps 94:1; 149:7
31:6 [r]Nu 14:44 [s]Nu 10:9
31:7 [t]Dt 20:13; Jdg 21:11; 1Ki 11:15,16
31:8 [u]Jos 13:21 [v]Nu 25:15 [w]Jos 13:22
31:10 [x]Ge 25:16; 1Ch 6:54; Ps 69:25; Eze 25:4
31:11 [y]Dt 20:14

tives, spoils and plunder to Moses and Eleazar the
31:12 [z]Nu 27:2 priest and the Israelite assembly[z] at their camp on
the plains of Moab, by the Jordan across from
Jericho.[a]
13 Moses, Eleazar the priest and all the leaders
of the community went to meet them outside the
camp. 14 Moses was angry with the officers of the
31:14 [a]ver 48; Ex 18:21; Dt 1:15 army[a]—the commanders of thousands and commanders of hundreds—who returned from the
battle.
15 "Have you allowed all the women to live?" he
asked them. 16 "They were the ones who followed
31:16 [b]2Pe 2:15; Rev 2:14 [c]Nu 25:1-9 Balaam's advice[b] and were the means of turning
the Israelites away from the LORD in what happened
at Peor,[c] so that a plague struck the LORD's people.
17 Now kill all the boys. And kill every woman who
31:17 [d]Dt 7:2; 20:16-18; Jdg 21:11 has slept with a man,[d] 18 but save for yourselves
every girl who has never slept with a man.
19 "All of you who have killed anyone or touched
anyone who was killed[e] must stay outside the
31:19 [e]Nu 19:16 [f]Nu 19:12 camp seven days. On the third and seventh days
you must purify yourselves[f] and your captives.
31:20 [g]Nu 19:19 20 Purify every garment[g] as well as everything
made of leather, goat hair or wood."
21 Then Eleazar the priest said to the soldiers who
had gone into battle, "This is the requirement of the
law that the LORD gave Moses: 22 Gold, silver,
31:22 [h]Jos 6:19; 22:8 bronze, iron,[h] tin, lead 23 and anything else that can
withstand fire must be put through the fire,[i] and
31:23 [i]1Co 3:13 [j]Nu 19:9,17 then it will be clean. But it must also be purified
with the water of cleansing.[j] And whatever cannot
withstand fire must be put through that water. 24 On
31:24 [k]Lev 11:25 the seventh day wash your clothes and you will be
clean.[k] Then you may come into the camp."

Dividing the Spoils

25 The LORD said to Moses, 26 "You and Eleazar
the priest and the family heads of the community
31:26 [l]Nu 1:19 are to count all the people[l] and animals that were
captured. 27 Divide[m] the spoils between the sol-
31:27 [m]Jos 22:8; 1Sa 30:24 diers who took part in the battle and the rest of
the community. 28 From the soldiers who fought in
the battle, set apart as tribute for the LORD[n] one
31:28 [n]Nu 18:21 out of every five hundred, whether persons, cattle,
donkeys, sheep or goats. 29 Take this tribute from
their half share and give it to Eleazar the priest as
the LORD's part. 30 From the Israelites' half, select
one out of every fifty, whether persons, cattle,
donkeys, sheep, goats or other animals. Give them
31:30 [o]Nu 3:7; 18:3 to the Levites, who are responsible for the care of
the LORD's tabernacle.[o]" 31 So Moses and Eleazar
the priest did as the LORD commanded Moses.
32 The plunder remaining from the spoils that
the soldiers took was 675,000 sheep, 33 72,000 cattle, 34 61,000 donkeys 35 and 32,000 women who
had never slept with a man.
36 The half share of those who fought in the battle was:

[a] *12* Hebrew *Jordan of Jericho*; possibly an ancient name for the Jordan River

Vengeance on the Midianites

NU 31:15-19

The Midianite women are just as much to blame for the attack on God's people as are the Midianite men, for they played an active role in seducing the Israelites into idolatry (see the note on Nu 25:1-3,6, page 250). Yet the Israelite soldiers are reluctant to put them to death. God's response makes it clear that both men and women will be held accountable for their actions. Every Midianite who poses a threat to Israel is killed: all boys—the Midianites' future army—and all sexually active women.

Presumably, these sexually active women participated in Midianite fertility festivals and worship of the pagan god Baal. They include those who earlier seduced the Israelite men. Also they likely would have remained loyal to their own tribe and religion in the future. Virgin women, however, could not have been part of the seduction and could more easily be assimilated into Israelite culture, following the directives given in Deuteronomy 21:10-14.

An excerpt from Lady Jane Grey's address to the crowd that gathered to watch her execution for refusing to renounce the Protestant faith and for treason. She was only 17 years old at the time of her death.

Before God and the face of you, good Christian people, this day I pray you all, to bear me witness that I die a true Christian woman, and that I look to be saved by none other means, but only by the mercy of God, in the merits of the blood of his only son, Jesus Christ. And I confess, when I did know the word of God, I neglected the same, loved myself and the world, and thereto the plague or punishment is happily and worthily happened unto me for my sins. And yet, I thank God of His goodness that he hath thus given me a time and respite to repent. And now good people, while I am alive, I pray you to assist me with your prayers.

—Lady Jane Grey (1537-1554)

337,500 sheep, 37 of which the tribute for the LORD[p] was 675;
38 36,000 cattle, of which the tribute for the LORD was 72;
39 30,500 donkeys, of which the tribute for the LORD was 61;
40 16,000 people, of which the tribute for the LORD was 32.

41 Moses gave the tribute to Eleazar the priest as the LORD's part,[q] as the LORD commanded Moses.

42 The half belonging to the Israelites, which Moses set apart from that of the fighting men— 43 the community's half—was 337,500 sheep, 44 36,000 cattle, 45 30,500 donkeys 46 and 16,000 people. 47 From the Israelites' half, Moses selected one out of every fifty persons and animals, as the LORD commanded him, and gave them to the Levites, who were responsible for the care of the LORD's tabernacle.

48 Then the officers who were over the units of the army—the commanders of thousands and commanders of hundreds—went to Moses 49 and said to him, "Your servants have counted the soldiers under our command, and not one is missing.[r] 50 So we have brought as an offering to the LORD the gold articles each of us acquired—armlets, bracelets, signet rings, earrings and necklaces—to make atonement for ourselves[s] before the LORD."

51 Moses and Eleazar the priest accepted from them the gold—all the crafted articles. 52 All the gold from the commanders of thousands and commanders of hundreds that Moses and Eleazar presented as a gift to the LORD weighed 16,750 shekels.[a] 53 Each soldier had taken plunder[t] for himself. 54 Moses and Eleazar the priest accepted the gold from the commanders of thousands and commanders of hundreds and brought it into the Tent of Meeting as a memorial[u] for the Israelites before the LORD.

The Transjordan Tribes

32 The Reubenites and Gadites, who had very large herds and flocks, saw that the lands of Jazer[v] and Gilead were suitable for livestock.[w] 2 So they came to Moses and Eleazar the priest and to the leaders of the community, and said, 3 "Ataroth,[x] Dibon, Jazer, Nimrah,[y] Heshbon, Elealeh,[z] Sebam, Nebo and Beon[a]— 4 the land the LORD subdued[b] before the people of Israel—are suitable for livestock,[c] and your servants have livestock. 5 If we have found favor in your eyes," they said, "let this land be given to your servants as our possession. Do not make us cross the Jordan."

6 Moses said to the Gadites and Reubenites, "Shall your countrymen go to war while you sit here? 7 Why do you discourage the Israelites from going over into the land the LORD has given them?[d] 8 This is what your fathers did when I sent

31:37 [p]ver 38-41
31:41 [q]Nu 5:9; 18:8
31:49 [r]Jer 23:4
31:50 [s]Ex 30:16
31:53 [t]Dt 20:14
31:54 [u]Ex 28:12
32:1 [v]Nu 21:32 [w]Ex 12:38
32:3 [x]ver 34 [y]ver 36 [z]ver 37; Isa 15:4; 16:9; Jer 48:34 [a]ver 38; Jos 13:17; Eze 25:9
32:4 [b]Nu 21:34 [c]Ex 12:38
32:7 [d]Nu 13:27-14:4

[a] 52 That is, about 420 pounds (about 190 kilograms)

32:8 them from Kadesh Barnea to look over the land.[e]
eNu 13:3,26; [9]After they went up to the Valley of Eshcol[f] and
Dt 1:19-25 viewed the land, they discouraged the Israelites
32:9 from entering the land the LORD had given them.
fNu 13:23; [10]The LORD's anger was aroused[g] that day and he
Dt 1:24 swore this oath: [11]'Because they have not followed
32:10 me wholeheartedly, not one of the men twenty
gNu 11:1 years old or more[h] who came up out of Egypt will
32:11 see the land I promised on oath[i] to Abraham,
hEx 30:14 iNu 14:23 Isaac and Jacob[j]— [12]not one except Caleb son of
jNu 14:28-30 Jephunneh the Kenizzite and Joshua son of Nun,
for they followed the LORD wholeheartedly.'[k] [13]The
32:12 kNu 14:24, LORD's anger burned against Israel[l] and he made
30; Dt 1:36; them wander in the desert forty years, until the
Ps 63:8 whole generation of those who had done evil in
32:13 his sight was gone.[m]
lEx 4:14 [14]"And here you are, a brood of sinners, stand-
mNu 14:28- ing in the place of your fathers and making the
35; 26:64,65 LORD even more angry with Israel.[n] [15]If you turn
32:14 away from following him, he will again leave all
nver 10; Dt 1:34; this people in the desert, and you will be the
Ps 78:59 cause of their destruction.[o]"
32:15 [16]Then they came up to him and said, "We
oDt 30:17- would like to build pens here for our livestock[p] and
18; 2Ch 7:20 cities for our women and children. [17]But we are
32:16 ready to arm ourselves and go ahead of the Israel-
pEx 12:38; ites[q] until we have brought them to their place.[r]
Dt 3:19 Meanwhile our women and children will live in
32:17 fortified cities, for protection from the inhabitants
qJos 4:12,13 of the land. [18]We will not return to our homes until
rNu 22:4; every Israelite has received his inheritance.[s] [19]We
Dt 3:20 will not receive any inheritance with them on the
32:18 other side of the Jordan, because our inheritance
sJos 22:1-4 has come to us on the east side of the Jordan."[t]
32:19 [20]Then Moses said to them, "If you will do
tJos 12:1 this—if you will arm yourselves before the LORD
32:20 for battle,[u] [21]and if all of you will go armed over
uDt 3:18 the Jordan before the LORD until he has driven his
32:22 enemies out before him— [22]then when the land is
vJos 22:4 subdued before the LORD, you may return[v] and be
wDt 3:18-20 free from your obligation to the LORD and to Israel. And this land will be your possession before
the LORD.[w]
[23]"But if you fail to do this, you will be sinning
against the LORD; and you may be sure that your
32:23 sin will find you out.[x] [24]Build cities for your
xGe 4:7; 44:16; women and children, and pens for your flocks,[y]
Isa 59:12 but do what you have promised.[z]"
32:24 [25]The Gadites and Reubenites said to Moses,
yver 1,16 "We your servants will do as our lord commands.
zNu 30:2 [26]Our children and wives, our flocks and herds
32:26 will remain here in the cities of Gilead.[a] [27]But your
aJos 1:14 servants, every man armed for battle, will cross
over to fight before the LORD, just as our lord says."
32:28 [28]Then Moses gave orders about them[b] to Elea-
bDt 3:18-20; zar the priest and Joshua son of Nun and to the
Jos 1:13 family heads of the Israelite tribes. [29]He said to
them, "If the Gadites and Reubenites, every man
armed for battle, cross over the Jordan with you
before the LORD, then when the land is subdued
before you, give them the land of Gilead as their

Angry Moses

NU 32:1-15

Moses has good reason to be angry. A lack of support from Reuben and Gad will be emotionally discouraging and deeply damaging to the rest of the population as they enter the promised land. Moses reminds these tribes of God's anger 40 years earlier at the Israelites' unwillingness to enter the promised land. He suggests that further unwillingness could bring additional judgment. Their reluctance to claim the promised land—which Moses knows he will never be allowed to enter—most likely leaves him feeling both incensed and incredulous. They eventually strike an agreement, ensuring that the tribes east of the Jordan do not neglect defending their brothers and sisters simply because their immediate needs are met (Nu 32:17).

Though God promises that he has a plan for our future (Jer 29:11), we too often ask him for more immediate pleasures, such as the job, fiancé, or home we desire. As you continue in your study of God's Word, jot down his promises about your future. Read them every time you feel dissatisfied with your present situation.

The East Side of the Jordan

NU 32:33

The Reubenites and Gadites wish to settle on the east side of the Jordan river, as it is well suited to meet the needs of their people (Nu 32:1–4). After Moses reaches an agreement with them (Nu 32:20–27), half of the tribe of Manasseh decide they want to remain east of Jordan, too. Manasseh is the only group to settle on both sides of the Jordan, and it—along with the tribes of Gad and Reuben—is allowed to do so only after lending military support to the other tribes.

possession. 30But if they do not cross over with you armed, they must accept their possession with you in Canaan."

31The Gadites and Reubenites answered, "Your servants will do what the LORD has said.[c] 32We will cross over before the LORD into Canaan armed, but the property we inherit will be on this side of the Jordan."

33Then Moses gave to the Gadites,[d] the Reubenites and the half-tribe of Manasseh son of Joseph the kingdom of Sihon king of the Amorites[e] and the kingdom of Og king of Bashan—the whole land with its cities and the territory around them.[f]

34The Gadites built up Dibon, Ataroth, Aroer,[g] 35Atroth Shophan, Jazer,[h] Jogbehah, 36Beth Nimrah[i] and Beth Haran as fortified cities, and built pens for their flocks. 37And the Reubenites rebuilt Heshbon, Elealeh and Kiriathaim, 38as well as Nebo[j] and Baal Meon (these names were changed) and Sibmah. They gave names to the cities they rebuilt.

39The descendants of Makir[k] son of Manasseh went to Gilead, captured it and drove out the Amorites who were there. 40So Moses gave Gilead to the Makirites,[l] the descendants of Manasseh, and they settled there. 41Jair, a descendant of Manasseh, captured their settlements and called them Havvoth Jair.[a][m] 42And Nobah captured Kenath and its surrounding settlements and called it Nobah after himself.[n]

Stages in Israel's Journey

33 Here are the stages in the journey of the Israelites when they came out of Egypt[o] by divisions under the leadership of Moses and Aaron.[p] 2At the LORD's command Moses recorded the stages in their journey. This is their journey by stages:

3The Israelites set out from Rameses on the fifteenth day of the first month, the day after the Passover.[q] They marched out boldly[r] in full view of all the Egyptians, 4who were burying all their firstborn, whom the LORD had struck down among them; for the LORD had brought judgment on their gods.[s]

5The Israelites left Rameses and camped at Succoth.[t]

6They left Succoth and camped at Etham, on the edge of the desert.[u]

7They left Etham, turned back to Pi Hahiroth, to the east of Baal Zephon,[v] and camped near Migdol.[w]

8They left Pi Hahiroth[b] and passed through the sea[x] into the desert, and when they had traveled for three days in the Desert of Etham, they camped at Marah.[y]

9They left Marah and went to Elim, where

32:31 [c]ver 29
32:33 [d]Jos 13:24-28; 1Sa 13:7 [e]Dt 2:26 [f]Nu 21:24; Jos 12:6
32:34 [g]Dt 2:36; Jdg 11:26
32:35 [h]ver 3
32:36 [i]ver 3
32:38 [j]ver 3; Isa 15:2; Jer 48:1,22
32:39 [k]Ge 50:23
32:40 [l]Dt 3:15; Jos 17:1
32:41 [m]Dt 3:14; Jos 13:30; Jdg 10:4; 1Ch 2:23
32:42 [n]2Sa 18:18; Ps 49:11
33:1 [o]Mic 6:4 [p]Ps 77:20
33:3 [q]Ex 13:4 [r]Ex 14:8
33:4 [s]Ex 12:12
33:5 [t]Ex 12:37
33:6 [u]Ex 13:20
33:7 [v]Ex 14:9 [w]Ex 14:2
33:8 [x]Ex 14:22 [y]Ex 15:23

[a] *41* Or *them the settlements of Jair* [b] *8* Many manuscripts of the Masoretic Text, Samaritan Pentateuch and Vulgate; most manuscripts of the Masoretic Text *left from before Hahiroth*

33:9 there were twelve springs and seventy palm
[z]Ex 15:27 trees, and they camped[z] there.
10 They left Elim and camped by the Red
Sea.[a]
11 They left the Red Sea and camped in the
33:11 Desert of Sin.[a]
[a]Ex 16:1 12 They left the Desert of Sin and camped at
Dophkah.
13 They left Dophkah and camped at Alush.
14 They left Alush and camped at Rephidim,
where there was no water for the people to
33:15 drink.
[b]Ex 17:1 15 They left Rephidim[b] and camped in the
[c]Ex 19:1 Desert of Sinai.[c]
16 They left the Desert of Sinai and camped
33:16 at Kibroth Hattaavah.[d]
[d]Nu 11:34 17 They left Kibroth Hattaavah and camped
33:17 at Hazeroth.[e]
[e]Nu 11:35 18 They left Hazeroth and camped at
Rithmah.
19 They left Rithmah and camped at Rimmon Perez.
20 They left Rimmon Perez and camped at
33:20 Libnah.[f]
[f]Jos 10:29 21 They left Libnah and camped at Rissah.
22 They left Rissah and camped at
Kehelathah.
23 They left Kehelathah and camped at
Mount Shepher.
24 They left Mount Shepher and camped at
Haradah.
25 They left Haradah and camped at
Makheloth.
26 They left Makheloth and camped at
Tahath.
27 They left Tahath and camped at Terah.
28 They left Terah and camped at Mithcah.
29 They left Mithcah and camped at
Hashmonah.
30 They left Hashmonah and camped at
33:30 Moseroth.[g]
[g]Dt 10:6 31 They left Moseroth and camped at Bene
Jaakan.
32 They left Bene Jaakan and camped at Hor
Haggidgad.
33 They left Hor Haggidgad and camped at
33:33 Jotbathah.[h]
[h]Dt 10:7 34 They left Jotbathah and camped at
Abronah.
33:35 35 They left Abronah and camped at Ezion
[i]Dt 2:8; Geber.[i]
1Ki 9:26; 22:48 36 They left Ezion Geber and camped at
33:36 Kadesh, in the Desert of Zin.[j]
[j]Nu 20:1 37 They left Kadesh and camped at Mount
33:37 Hor,[k] on the border of Edom.[l] 38 At the LORD's
[k]Nu 20:22 command Aaron the priest went up Mount
[l]Nu 20:16; 21:4 Hor, where he died[m] on the first day of the
33:38 fifth month of the fortieth year after the Isra-
[m]Dt 10:6 elites came out of Egypt.[n] 39 Aaron was a hun-
[n]Nu 20:25-28

[a] *10* Hebrew *Yam Suph*; that is, Sea of Reeds; also in verse 11

A Nomadic Itinerary

NU 33

Moses has carefully recorded the details of the Israelites' journey, but it is not until Numbers 33 that we see a full itinerary: Ramses to Succoth. Succoth to Etham. And so on, and so on, and so on . . .

This itinerary provides an inspiring record of God's provision for, and deliverance of, his people. However, even to the most practiced packer and mover, more than 40 address changes in 40 years sounds like a lot of uprooting. This must have been particularly difficult for the women, the "nesters" of the nation.

Many of us wish that God would just let us settle into a job, a marriage, a home or some other aspect of life. We feel like we are constantly in transition. How might our current desert experiences be preparing us for the "promised land" of our future? Do any present circumstances serve as reminders of the consequences of past actions? How could our current situation be used to bring glory to God?

A Warning

NU 33:50-56

These verses carry a warning about the consequences for those who allow themselves to be pulled away from God into evil lifestyles. God's instructions here are clear: Every inhabitant, every carved image, every cast idol and every high place of worship must be destroyed. Any remnant left will be a temptation and a trouble to the Israelites, described graphically as "barbs in [their] eyes and thorns in [their] sides" (Nu 33:55).

How do we as a people still practice idolatry today? Most of us do not have the power to banish those who attempt to drag us down. But we are *responsible for how we respond to ungodly influence and counsel. If we ask, God's Spirit will protect us and give us wisdom and strength to escape temptation (1Co 10:13). Also, there are people in our lives who can hold us accountable in our areas of temptation.*

dred and twenty-three years old when he
died on Mount Hor.
40 The Canaanite king of Arad,[o] who lived
in the Negev of Canaan, heard that the Israelites were coming.
41 They left Mount Hor and camped at Zalmonah.
42 They left Zalmonah and camped at
Punon.
43 They left Punon and camped at Oboth.[p]
44 They left Oboth and camped at Iye Abarim, on the border of Moab.[q]
45 They left Iyim[a] and camped at Dibon Gad.
46 They left Dibon Gad and camped at
Almon Diblathaim.
47 They left Almon Diblathaim and camped
in the mountains of Abarim,[r] near Nebo.
48 They left the mountains of Abarim and
camped on the plains of Moab by the Jordan
across from Jericho.[b][s] 49 There on the plains
of Moab they camped along the Jordan from
Beth Jeshimoth to Abel Shittim.[t]
50 On the plains of Moab by the Jordan across
from Jericho the LORD said to Moses, 51 "Speak to
the Israelites and say to them: 'When you cross
the Jordan into Canaan,[u] 52 drive out all the inhabitants of the land before you. Destroy all their
carved images and their cast idols, and demolish
all their high places.[v] 53 Take possession of the
land and settle in it, for I have given you the land
to possess.[w] 54 Distribute the land by lot, according to your clans.[x] To a larger group give a larger
inheritance, and to a smaller group a smaller one.
Whatever falls to them by lot will be theirs. Distribute it according to your ancestral tribes.
55 " 'But if you do not drive out the inhabitants
of the land, those you allow to remain will
become barbs in your eyes and thorns[y] in your
sides. They will give you trouble in the land
where you will live. 56 And then I will do to you
what I plan to do to them.' "

Boundaries of Canaan

34 The LORD said to Moses, 2 "Command the
Israelites and say to them: 'When you
enter Canaan, the land that will be allotted to
you as an inheritance[z] will have these boundaries:[a]
3 " 'Your southern side will include some of the
Desert of Zin[b] along the border of Edom. On the
east, your southern boundary will start from the
end of the Salt Sea,[c][c] 4 cross south of Scorpion[d]
Pass,[d] continue on to Zin and go south of Kadesh
Barnea.[e] Then it will go to Hazar Addar and over

33:40 [o]Nu 21:1
33:43 [p]Nu 21:10
33:44 [q]Nu 21:11
33:47 [r]Nu 27:12
33:48 [s]Nu 22:1
33:49 [t]Nu 25:1
33:51 [u]Jos 3:17
33:52 [v]Ex 23:24; 34:13; Lev 26:1; Dt 7:2,5; 12:3; Jos 11:12; Ps 106:34-36
33:53 [w]Dt 11:31; Jos 21:43
33:54 [x]Nu 26:54
33:55 [y]Jos 23:13; Jdg 2:3; Ps 106:36
34:2 [z]Ge 17:8; Dt 1:7-8; Ps 78:54-55 [a]Eze 47:15
34:3 [b]Jos 15:1-3 [c]Ge 14:3
34:4 [d]Jos 15:3 [e]Nu 32:8

[a] *45* That is, Iye Abarim [b] *48* Hebrew *Jordan of Jericho*; possibly an ancient name for the Jordan River; also in verse 50 [c] *3* That is, the Dead Sea; also in verse 12 [d] *4* Hebrew *Akrabbim*

Tamar

In Jesus' Family Line

She sat at the side of the road with a come-hither look. Though dressed like a prostitute, Tamar was confident in her cause. She had been *wronged.*

Judah and his brothers had sold Joseph to a passing caravan and had told Jacob, their father, that Joseph had been killed by a wild animal. Perhaps Judah couldn't bear to see his father's grief day in and day out. He left home, married and raised three sons. Judah's eldest son, Er, married Tamar. Er died, and Tamar was married to his brother, as was the custom, but he also died. Shelah, the last brother, was still too young to marry. So Judah sent Tamar to her father's home to wait, while Judah dragged his feet. His older sons had displeased God and the Lord put each to death at an early age. But Judah blamed Tamar. He had only one son left, and he was not going to chance losing him too. So he put off the marriage between Shelah and Tamar.

Years passed. Shelah grew up. Judah's wife died. Soon Tamar would be past childbearing age and would have no prospects of marriage to another man. She believed that if she were to have a child and the place and respect due her, she would have to take things into her own hands. She carefully laid her trap, making sure she would be safe from retribution. She had thought of everything, and her plan worked better than she dared dream. She was pregnant—by Judah—and he was none the wiser. She now only had to wait for vindication.

Tamar chose deceit, incest and cunning to achieve her ends. She committed a grave sin. Yet when Judah discovered the whole story, he claimed she was more righteous than he. She—a Canaanite—had been living more righteously than he, a son of the promise. God used Tamar to wake up Judah. Judah returned to his father and brothers to take up his God-given responsibilities to his family. And he never slept with Tamar again.

Tamar had twin sons named Perez and Zerah. Through Perez, Tamar became an ancestor of the Messiah. Though her ruse was reprehensible, through Tamar God shows us something about himself. When Jesus came to earth, he became wholly human, including having sinful ancestors. The blood that flowed from his side on the cross included Canaanite genes—and was shed for people of every race. He did not place himself above us but became one of us. And his choice was out of his grace, not our merit.

Tamar
(palm)
Genesis 38
Ruth 4:12
1 Chronicles 2:4
Matthew 1:3

Candid SNAPSHOT She took off her widow's clothes, covered herself with a veil to disguise herself, and then sat down at the entrance to Enaim, which is on the road to Timnah. For she saw that, though Shelah had now grown up, she had not been given to him as his wife (Genesis 38:14).

Shiphrah and Puah

Obedience With a Price Tag

No one in ancient Egypt would trifle with the pharaoh. In fact, Egyptians believed he was a god. His word was law, and he owned everything. Yet the foreigners who lived among them were a threat to this all-powerful pharaoh. He was afraid the Hebrews would grow too powerful and turn against the Egyptians (Ex 1:9-10). So Pharaoh ordered the Hebrew midwives, Shiphrah and Puah, to carry out his decree: Kill the Hebrew boys as soon as they're born. But the midwives didn't obey.

Think about it. These women were not the intellectual elite. They simply helped women have their babies under stark conditions. They cut the cord, bathed and rubbed the baby with salt, then swaddled it (Eze 16:4). In the rare event of twins, the midwife also marked the first twin born (Ge 38:28). Their duties were not mysterious or deeply spiritual. Yet, these lowly slave women refused to follow the orders of mighty Pharaoh.

Where did they find the courage to disobey? Pharaoh had squared off with God. Shiphrah and Puah knew where the real power lay. Obeying Pharaoh meant disobeying God. And they loved the Lord more than they loved their own lives. They didn't argue with Pharaoh or try to shout him down. That would have been foolhardy. In the intimate moments of a newborn boy's first breath, they simply let him live.

It was not long before Pharaoh recognized there had been no reduction in the number of Hebrew boys born—the moment of truth for Puah and Shiphrah. They told him, "Hebrew women are not like Egyptian women; they are vigorous and give birth before the midwives arrive" (Ex 1:19). Whether Pharaoh believed them or not, he let them go. Their story really didn't matter. It was their trust in God that saved their lives.

Scripture goes on to say that the Lord was kind to the midwives, giving them honored places in history as well as families of their own. Life propagated life, and that which they held precious was returned to them in good measure. Puah and Shiphrah didn't risk their lives for a reward. They did it because it was the right thing to do. But God saw and was pleased, and he blessed them.

Scripture exhorts us to obey those who are over us: "Everyone must submit himself to the governing authorities, for there is no authority except that which God has established" (Ro 13:1). Nevertheless, there may be a time when we have to choose either to obey an authority or to obey God. It is not a choice to make lightly. The choice may even carry a high cost. But if God is the author of the decision, he will be with us, no matter what the outcome.

Shiphrah and Puah
(prolific **and** ***joy of parent)***
Exodus 1:15-22

Candid SNAPSHOT The midwives, however, feared God and did not do what the king of Egypt had told them to do; they let the boys live (Exodus 1:17).

34:5 to Azmon, 5 where it will turn, join the Wadi of
[f]Ge 15:18; Egypt[f] and end at the Sea.[a]
Jos 15:4 6 " 'Your western boundary will be the coast of
the Great Sea. This will be your boundary on the
west.
34:7 7 " 'For your northern boundary,[g] run a line
[g]Eze 47:15-17 from the Great Sea to Mount Hor 8 and from Mount
Hor to Lebo[b] Hamath.[h] Then the boundary will go
34:8 [h]Nu 13:21; to Zedad, 9 continue to Ziphron and end at Hazar
Jos 13:5 Enan. This will be your boundary on the north.
10 " 'For your eastern boundary, run a line from
Hazar Enan to Shepham. 11 The boundary will go
34:11 [i]2Ki 23:33; down from Shepham to Riblah[i] on the east side of
Jer 39:5 Ain and continue along the slopes east of the Sea
[j]Dt 3:17; of Kinnereth.[c][j] 12 Then the boundary will go down
Jos 11:2; 13:27 along the Jordan and end at the Salt Sea.
" 'This will be your land, with its boundaries
on every side.' "
13 Moses commanded the Israelites: "Assign this
34:13 [k]Jos 14:1-5 land by lot as an inheritance.[k] The LORD has
ordered that it be given to the nine and a half
tribes, 14 because the families of the tribe of Reuben, the tribe of Gad and the half-tribe of Manas-
34:14 [l]Nu 32:33; seh have received their inheritance.[l] 15 These two
Jos 14:3 and a half tribes have received their inheritance
on the east side of the Jordan of Jericho,[d] toward
the sunrise."
16 The LORD said to Moses, 17 "These are the
names of the men who are to assign the land for
you as an inheritance: Eleazar the priest and Josh-
34:17 [m]Jos 14:1 ua[m] son of Nun. 18 And appoint one leader from
34:18 each tribe to help[n] assign the land. 19 These are
[n]Nu 1:4,16 their names:

34:19 Caleb[o] son of Jephunneh,
[o]Nu 26:65 [p]Ge 29:35; from the tribe of Judah;[p]
Dt 33:7 20 Shemuel son of Ammihud,
from the tribe of Simeon;[q]
34:20 [q]Ge 49:5 21 Elidad son of Kislon,
from the tribe of Benjamin;[r]
34:21 [r]Ge 49:27; 22 Bukki son of Jogli,
Ps 68:27 the leader from the tribe of Dan;
23 Hanniel son of Ephod,
the leader from the tribe of Manasseh son
of Joseph;
24 Kemuel son of Shiphtan,
the leader from the tribe of Ephraim son of
Joseph;
25 Elizaphan son of Parnach,
the leader from the tribe of Zebulun;
26 Paltiel son of Azzan,
the leader from the tribe of Issachar;
34:27 27 Ahihud son of Shelomi,
[s]Nu 1:40 the leader from the tribe of Asher;[s]
28 Pedahel son of Ammihud,
the leader from the tribe of Naphtali."
29 These are the men the LORD commanded to

[a] 5 That is, the Mediterranean; also in verses 6 and 7 [b] 8 Or *to the entrance to* [c] 11 That is, Galilee [d] 15 *Jordan of Jericho* was possibly an ancient name for the Jordan River.

Canaan's Bo

The geograp ***that God proclaims*** ***el are, at the point in history when he announces them to Moses, only an ideal. Not until many years later, during the lifetimes of Kings David and Solomon, will these boundaries be more or less realized (see Map 4: Land of the Twelve Tribes at the back of this Bible).***

Cities of Refuge

NU 35:6–29

As a nomadic nation, Israel has long relied on customary tribal law for the protection of the community. Such law calls for retaliation or revenge by a family member—an "avenger of blood" (Nu 35:19)—for any individual who has been killed. Now that Israel is sinking in roots, however, it is necessary to live under civil law. Unfortunately, there is a real possibility that those accused of manslaughter will themselves be killed before they have an opportunity to stand trial.

In response to this problem, God establishes the cities of refuge. These cities provide a temporary sanctuary for those who have killed accidently (see the note on Jos 20:7–9 on page 363). Lawbreakers stay in a city of refuge until the time comes for them to be judged. If they are then convicted of murder, they are put to death by a blood avenger. If it is found that they have killed accidentally, they can seek sanctuary in a city of refuge, where they must remain until the death of the high priest (see Map 4: Land of the Twelve Tribes at the back of this Bible).

assign the inheritance to the Israelites in the land
of Canaan.

Towns for the Levites

35 On the plains of Moab by the Jordan across
from Jericho,[a] the LORD said to Moses,
2“Command the Israelites to give the Levites
towns to live in[t] from the inheritance the Israelites
will possess. And give them pasturelands around
the towns. 3Then they will have towns to live in
and pasturelands for their cattle, flocks and all
their other livestock.
4“The pasturelands around the towns that you
give the Levites will extend out fifteen hundred
feet[b] from the town wall. 5Outside the town, measure three thousand feet[c] on the east side, three
thousand on the south side, three thousand on the
west and three thousand on the north, with the
town in the center. They will have this area as
pastureland for the towns.

Cities of Refuge

6“Six of the towns you give the Levites will be
cities of refuge, to which a person who has killed
someone may flee.[u] In addition, give them forty-
two other towns. 7In all you must give the Levites
forty-eight towns, together with their pasturelands. 8The towns you give the Levites from the
land the Israelites possess are to be given in proportion to the inheritance of each tribe: Take
many towns from a tribe that has many, but few
from one that has few.”[v]
9Then the LORD said to Moses: 10“Speak to the
Israelites and say to them: ‘When you cross the
Jordan into Canaan,[w] 11select some towns to be
your cities of refuge, to which a person who has
killed someone[x] accidentally[y] may flee. 12They
will be places of refuge from the avenger,[z] so that
a person accused of murder may not die before he
stands trial before the assembly. 13These six towns
you give will be your cities of refuge. 14Give three
on this side of the Jordan and three in Canaan as
cities of refuge. 15These six towns will be a place
of refuge for Israelites, aliens and any other people
living among them, so that anyone who has killed
another accidentally can flee there.
16“ ‘If a man strikes someone with an iron
object so that he dies, he is a murderer; the murderer shall be put to death.[a] 17Or if anyone has a
stone in his hand that could kill, and he strikes
someone so that he dies, he is a murderer; the
murderer shall be put to death. 18Or if anyone has
a wooden object in his hand that could kill, and
he hits someone so that he dies, he is a murderer;
the murderer shall be put to death. 19The avenger
of blood shall put the murderer to death; when he
meets him, he shall put him to death.[b] 20If anyone

35:2 [t]Lev 25:32-34; Jos 14:3, 4
35:6 [u]Jos 20:7-9; 21:3,13
35:8 [v]Nu 26:54; 33:54; Jos 21:1-42
35:10 [w]Jos 20:2
35:11 [x]ver 22-25 [y]Ex 21:13; Dt 19:1-13
35:12 [z]Dt 19:6; Jos 20:3
35:16 [a]Ex 21:12; Lev 24:17
35:19 [b]ver 21

[a] *1* Hebrew *Jordan of Jericho;* possibly an ancient name for the Jordan River [b] *4* Hebrew *a thousand cubits* (about 450 meters) [c] *5* Hebrew *two thousand cubits* (about 900 meters)

with malice aforethought shoves another or
35:20 [c]Ge 4:8; Ex 21:14; Dt 19:11; 2Sa 3:27; 20:10
throws something at him intentionally[c] so that he
dies 21or if in hostility he hits him with his fist so
that he dies, that person shall be put to death; he
is a murderer. The avenger of blood shall put the
murderer to death when he meets him.
22" 'But if without hostility someone suddenly
shoves another or throws something at him unin-
35:22 [d]ver 11; Ex 21:13
tentionally[d] 23or, without seeing him, drops a stone
on him that could kill him, and he dies, then since
he was not his enemy and he did not intend to
35:24 [e]ver 12; Jos 20:6
harm him, 24the assembly[e] must judge between
him and the avenger of blood according to these
regulations. 25The assembly must protect the one
accused of murder from the avenger of blood and
send him back to the city of refuge to which he
fled. He must stay there until the death of the high
35:25 [f]Ex 29:7
priest, who was anointed with the holy oil.[f]
26" 'But if the accused ever goes outside the limits of the city of refuge to which he has fled 27and
the avenger of blood finds him outside the city,
the avenger of blood may kill the accused without being guilty of murder. 28The accused must
stay in his city of refuge until the death of the high
priest; only after the death of the high priest may
he return to his own property.
35:29 [g]Nu 27:11
29" 'These are to be legal requirements[g] for you
throughout the generations to come, wherever
you live.
30" 'Anyone who kills a person is to be put to
death as a murderer only on the testimony of witnesses. But no one is to be put to death on the tes-
35:30 [h]ver 16; Dt 17:6; 19:15; Mt 18:16; Jn 7:51; 2Co 13:1; Heb 10:28
timony of only one witness.[h]
31" 'Do not accept a ransom for the life of a murderer, who deserves to die. He must surely be put
to death.
32" 'Do not accept a ransom for anyone who has
fled to a city of refuge and so allow him to go back
and live on his own land before the death of the
high priest.
33" 'Do not pollute the land where you are.
35:33 [i]Ge 9:6; Ps 106:38; Mic 4:11
Bloodshed pollutes the land,[i] and atonement cannot be made for the land on which blood has been
shed, except by the blood of the one who shed it.
35:34 [j]Lev 18:24, 25 [k]Ex 29:45
34Do not defile the land[j] where you live and where
I dwell,[k] for I, the LORD, dwell among the Israelites.' "

Inheritance of Zelophehad's Daughters

36:1 [l]Nu 26:29 [m]Nu 27:2
36 The family heads of the clan of Gilead[l] son
of Makir, the son of Manasseh, who were
from the clans of the descendants of Joseph, came
and spoke before Moses and the leaders,[m] the
heads of the Israelite families. 2They said, "When
the LORD commanded my lord to give the land as
an inheritance to the Israelites by lot, he ordered
you to give the inheritance of our brother
36:2 [n]Nu 26:33; 27:1,7
Zelophehad[n] to his daughters. 3Now suppose they
marry men from other Israelite tribes; then their
inheritance will be taken from our ancestral
inheritance and added to that of the tribe they

Avenger of Blood

NU 35:19–34

The avenger of blood is the closest male blood relative of any individual who has been killed. His responsibility is to avenge the death of his relative by finding, and putting to death, the victim's killer. This can, and often did, bring further retaliation from the family of the accused, and sometimes the initiation of bloody feuds.

Zelophehad's Daughters

NU 36:1-13

Just as Zelophehad's daughters want to keep their father's property within the family (Nu 27:1-11), so also the family heads wish to keep Zelophehad's land within the tribe. In his earlier ruling, God ensured that the unmarried women would receive their father's inheritance. Here, he protects the interests of their tribe, ruling that all female heirs must marry within their own tribal clan. This ruling does not appear to have been a hardship for the sisters. The women have great freedom in selecting their husbands. Only one restriction applies: "They may marry anyone they please as long as they marry within the tribal clan of their father" (Nu 36:6).

marry into. And so part of the inheritance allotted to us will be taken away. 4When the Year of **36:4**
Jubilee[o] for the Israelites comes, their inheritance [o]Lev 25:10
will be added to that of the tribe into which they
marry, and their property will be taken from the
tribal inheritance of our forefathers."
5Then at the LORD's command Moses gave this
order to the Israelites: "What the tribe of the
descendants of Joseph is saying is right. 6This is
what the LORD commands for Zelophehad's
daughters: They may marry anyone they please
as long as they marry within the tribal clan of **36:7**
their father. 7No inheritance[p] in Israel is to pass [p]1Ki 21:3
from tribe to tribe, for every Israelite shall keep
the tribal land inherited from his forefathers.
8Every daughter who inherits land in any Israelite
tribe must marry someone in her father's tribal **36:8**
clan,[q] so that every Israelite will possess the inher- [q]1Ch 23:22
itance of his fathers. 9No inheritance may pass
from tribe to tribe, for each Israelite tribe is to
keep the land it inherits."
10So Zelophehad's daughters did as the LORD
commanded Moses. 11Zelophehad's daughters—
Mahlah, Tirzah, Hoglah, Milcah and Noah[r]—mar- **36:11**
ried their cousins on their father's side. 12They [r]Nu 26:33;
married within the clans of the descendants of 27:1
Manasseh son of Joseph, and their inheritance
remained in their father's clan and tribe.
13These are the commands and regulations the **36:13**
LORD gave through Moses[s] to the Israelites on the [s]Lev 26:46;
plains of Moab by the Jordan across from Jeri- 27:34
cho.[a][t] [t]Nu 22:1

[a] *13* Hebrew *Jordan of Jericho*; possibly an ancient name for the Jordan River

Deuteronomy

Obedience brings blessing; disobedience brings punishment.

Deuteronomy restates the covenant of love between God and his people issued earlier in Exodus. As he prepares to die and relinquish leadership to Joshua, Moses delivers three sermons. Each sermon reminds this new generation of Israelites of the journey from Egypt, through the desert, to Canaan. In his final words, Moses renews the Israelites' covenant with God by reminding them of what God has done in the past, specifying how God wants them to live in the present, and announcing what God promises for their future.

Woven throughout the historic events of Deuteronomy are opportunities to look at life's choices from God's perspective. We are cautioned to keep our focus on God and to not allow idolatry to take hold in our lives (Dt 4). We are reminded to love God in everything we do, say or think and to pass this information along to our children (Dt 6). We learn that even the little things in our lives matter to God, and we are urged to avoid practices that, though acceptable in our society, may be detestable in God's eyes (Dt 18).

Moses ends Deuteronomy with a song and a blessing (Dt 32-33). These final words urge the Israelites—and us—to learn from the past and to prepare for the future by choosing to walk in covenant faith with God.

Quick Study

Author
Generally thought to be Moses.

Date Written
Probably written during the 1400s B.C., at the time of Israel's wandering in the desert.

Setting
Near the Jordan River, across from the promised land.

Key Passage
Deuteronomy 6:5-7
"These commandments that I give you today are to be upon your hearts. Impress them on your children. Talk about them when you sit at home and when you walk along the road, when you lie down and when you get up."

Outline

Moses' first speech.
Dt 1:1–4:40

Cities of refuge.
Dt 4:41-43

God's law.
Dt 4:44–6:25

Driving out the nations.
Dt 7

Remembering the Lord.
Dt 8:1–9:6

Recalling the golden calf.
Dt 9:7-29

Loving and obeying God.
Dt 10-11

Regulations for worship.
Dt 12-13

Clean and unclean food.
Dt 14

Canceling debts.
Dt 15

Passover and other regulations.
Dt 16-18

Cities of refuge.
Dt 19

More rules and regulations.
Dt 20-25

Giving God what is his.
Dt 26

Curses from Mount Ebal.
Dt 27

Blessings and punishments.
Dt 28

God's promises.
Dt 29-30

Moses' successor.
Dt 31:1-29

Moses' song and impending death.
Dt 31:30–32:52

Moses' blessing.
Dt 33

Moses' death.
Dt 34

The Women of Deuteronomy

Captive women	*Proper treatment by their captors outlined.* Dt 21:10-14
⚘ **Miriam**	*Leprosy and healing.* Dt 24:9 (page 401)
Widows	*A call to benevolence.* Dt 24:17-21

⚘ *Denotes a sketch written about this character*

The Command to Leave Horeb

1 These are the words Moses spoke to all Israel
in the desert east of the Jordan—that is, in the
Arabah—opposite Suph, between Paran and
Tophel, Laban, Hazeroth and Dizahab. 2(It takes
eleven days to go from Horeb[a] to Kadesh Barnea[b]
by the Mount Seir road.)
3In the fortieth year,[c] on the first day of the
eleventh month, Moses proclaimed[d] to the Israelites all that the LORD had commanded him concerning them. 4This was after he had defeated
Sihon[e] king of the Amorites, who reigned in Heshbon,[f] and at Edrei had defeated Og[g] king of
Bashan, who reigned in Ashtaroth.
5East of the Jordan in the territory of Moab,
Moses began to expound this law, saying:
6The LORD our God said to us[h] at Horeb,[i] "You
have stayed long enough at this mountain. 7Break
camp and advance into the hill country of the
Amorites; go to all the neighboring peoples in the
Arabah, in the mountains, in the western
foothills, in the Negev[j] and along the coast, to the
land of the Canaanites and to Lebanon,[k] as far as
the great river, the Euphrates. 8See, I have given
you this land. Go in and take possession of the
land that the LORD swore[l] he would give to your
fathers—to Abraham, Isaac and Jacob—and to
their descendants after them."

The Appointment of Leaders

9At that time I said to you, "You are too heavy a
burden for me to carry alone.[m] 10The LORD your
God has increased your numbers so that today
you are as many[n] as the stars in the sky.[o] 11May
the LORD, the God of your fathers, increase you a
thousand times and bless you as he has promised![p] 12But how can I bear your problems and
your burdens and your disputes all by myself?
13Choose some wise, understanding and respected
men[q] from each of your tribes, and I will set them
over you."
14You answered me, "What you propose to do is
good."
15So I took[r] the leading men of your tribes, wise
and respected men, and appointed them to have
authority over you—as commanders of thousands, of hundreds, of fifties and of tens and as
tribal officials. 16And I charged your judges at that
time: Hear the disputes between your brothers
and judge fairly,[s] whether the case is between
brother Israelites or between one of them and an
alien.[t] 17Do not show partiality[u] in judging; hear
both small and great alike. Do not be afraid of any
man,[v] for judgment belongs to God. Bring me any
case too hard for you, and I will hear it.[w] 18And at
that time I told you everything you were to do.

Spies Sent Out

19Then, as the LORD our God commanded us, we
set out from Horeb and went toward the hill coun-

1:2 [a]Ex 3:1 [b]Nu 13:26; Dt 9:23
1:3 [c]Nu 33:38 [d]Dt 4:1-2
1:4 [e]Nu 21:21-26 [f]Nu 21:25 [g]Nu 21:33-35; Jos 13:12
1:6 [h]Nu 10:13 [i]Ex 3:1
1:7 [j]Jos 10:40 [k]Dt 11:24
1:8 [l]Ge 12:7; 15:18; 17:7-8; 26:4; 28:13
1:9 [m]Ex 18:18
1:10 [n]Ge 15:5 [o]Dt 10:22; 28:62
1:11 [p]Ge 22:17; Ex 32:13
1:13 [q]Ex 18:21
1:15 [r]Ex 18:25
1:16 [s]Dt 16:18; Jn 7:24 [t]Lev 24:22
1:17 [u]Lev 19:15; Dt 16:19; Pr 24:23; Jas 2:1 [v]2Ch 19:6 [w]Ex 18:26

On the Edge of Promise

DT 1:10

As the book of Deuteronomy opens, the Israelites *stand at the entrance to the promised land.* They have been here before. *Forty years earlier their ancestors surveyed Canaan and did not believe that they could possess the land.* With slumped shoulders and shattered faith, they *turned away from Canaan to wander in the desert.*

Will it be different this time? **Moses brilliantly begins by *reminding them of an ancient promise*—one made by God to Abraham—that their people would *one day multiply and become "as numerous as the stars in the sky"* (Ge 22:17). As they look into one *another's faces,* they are reminded *of a promise that has survived* death, disease, plagues, sibling *rivalry, manipulative relatives, decaying civilizations,* tyrannical superpowers, disobedience, idola*try and 40 years of wandering* and marking time. Possessing the promises of God begins with the *unshakable certainty* that God will *never* forget what he has promised.**

Lifeline to God's Promise

DT 1:39

Moses reminds the people that their ancestors' failed faith 40 years before had devastating results: All those who were 20 years old or older at that time are now dead. God disqualified those who would have been physically able to conquer their new land and who should have been spiritually mature.

Knowing "good from bad" is a Hebrew way of saying that they understood and lived by God's laws. Moses reminds the people, at the brink of the promised land, that possessing the promise of God is linked to knowing—heart and soul—God's Word. In fact, the Hebrew title for Deuteronomy is translated "These are the words." Moses encourages his troops by reminding them that God has given him the words that are the lifeline to the promised land. They must have hung on every word!

try of the Amorites through all that vast and
dreadful desert[x] that you have seen, and so we
reached Kadesh Barnea.[y] 20Then I said to you,
"You have reached the hill country of the Amorites, which the LORD our God is giving us. 21See,
the LORD your God has given you the land. Go up
and take possession of it as the LORD, the God of
your fathers, told you. Do not be afraid;[z] do not
be discouraged."
22Then all of you came to me and said, "Let us
send men ahead to spy out the land for us and
bring back a report about the route we are to take
and the towns we will come to."
23The idea seemed good to me; so I selected[a]
twelve of you, one man from each tribe. 24They
left and went up into the hill country, and came to
the Valley of Eshcol[b] and explored it. 25Taking
with them some of the fruit of the land, they
brought it down to us and reported,[c] "It is a good
land that the LORD our God is giving us."

Rebellion Against the LORD

26But you were unwilling to go up;[d] you
rebelled against the command of the LORD your
God. 27You grumbled[e] in your tents and said, "The
LORD hates us; so he brought us out of Egypt to
deliver us into the hands of the Amorites to
destroy us. 28Where can we go? Our brothers have
made us lose heart. They say, 'The people are
stronger and taller[f] than we are; the cities are
large, with walls up to the sky. We even saw the
Anakites[g] there.' "
29Then I said to you, "Do not be terrified; do not
be afraid of them. 30The LORD your God, who is
going before you, will fight[h] for you, as he did for
you in Egypt, before your very eyes, 31and in the
desert. There you saw how the LORD your God carried[i] you, as a father carries his son, all the way
you went until you reached this place."
32In spite of this, you did not trust[j] in the LORD
your God, 33who went ahead of you on your journey, in fire by night and in a cloud by day,[k] to
search[l] out places for you to camp and to show
you the way you should go.
34When the LORD heard what you said, he was
angry and solemnly swore:[m] 35"Not a man of this
evil generation shall see the good land[n] I swore to
give your forefathers, 36except Caleb son of
Jephunneh. He will see it, and I will give him and
his descendants the land he set his feet on,
because he followed the LORD wholeheartedly.[o]"
37Because of you the LORD became angry[p] with
me also and said, "You shall not enter[q] it, either.
38But your assistant, Joshua[r] son of Nun, will
enter it. Encourage[s] him, because he will lead[t]
Israel to inherit it. 39And the little ones that you
said would be taken captive,[u] your children who
do not yet know[v] good from bad—they will enter
the land. I will give it to them and they will take
possession of it. 40But as for you, turn around and

1:19 [x]Dt 8:15; Jer 2:2,6 [y]ver 2; Nu 13:26
1:21 [z]Jos 1:6,9,18
1:23 [a]Nu 13:1-3
1:24 [b]Nu 13:21-25
1:25 [c]Nu 13:27
1:26 [d]Nu 14:1-4
1:27 [e]Dt 9:28; Ps 106:25
1:28 [f]Nu 13:32 [g]Nu 13:33; Dt 9:1-3
1:30 [h]Ex 14:14; Dt 3:22; Ne 4:20
1:31 [i]Dt 32:10-12; Isa 46:3-4; 63:9; Hos 11:3; Ac 13:18
1:32 [j]Ps 106:24; Jude 1:5
1:33 [k]Ex 13:21; Ps 78:14 [l]Nu 10:33
1:34 [m]Nu 14:23, 28-30
1:35 [n]Ps 95:11
1:36 [o]Nu 14:24; Jos 14:9
1:37 [p]Dt 3:26; 4:21 [q]Nu 20:12
1:38 [r]Nu 14:30 [s]Dt 31:7 [t]Dt 3:28
1:39 [u]Nu 14:3 [v]Isa 7:15-16

set out toward the desert along the route to the
1:40 [w]Nu 14:25 Red Sea.[a][w]"
41 Then you replied, "We have sinned against the
LORD. We will go up and fight, as the LORD our
God commanded us." So every one of you put on
his weapons, thinking it easy to go up into the hill
country.
42 But the LORD said to me, "Tell them, 'Do not go
1:42 up and fight, because I will not be with you. You
[x]Nu 14:41-43 will be defeated by your enemies.' "[x]
43 So I told you, but you would not listen. You
rebelled against the LORD's command and in your
arrogance you marched up into the hill country.
1:44 44 The Amorites who lived in those hills came out
[y]Ps 118:12 against you; they chased you like a swarm of bees[y]
and beat you down from Seir all the way to Hor-
mah. 45 You came back and wept before the LORD,
but he paid no attention to your weeping and
1:46 turned a deaf ear to you. 46 And so you stayed in
[z]Nu 20:1; Jdg 11:17 Kadesh[z] many days—all the time you spent there.

Wanderings in the Desert

2 Then we turned back and set out toward the
2:1 desert along the route to the Red Sea,[a][a] as the
[a]Nu 21:4 LORD had directed me. For a long time we made
our way around the hill country of Seir.
2 Then the LORD said to me, 3 "You have made
your way around this hill country long enough;
2:4 now turn north. 4 Give the people these orders:[b]
[b]Nu 20:14-21 'You are about to pass through the territory of your
brothers the descendants of Esau, who live in Seir.
They will be afraid of you, but be very careful. 5 Do
not provoke them to war, for I will not give you
any of their land, not even enough to put your foot
on. I have given Esau the hill country of Seir as his
2:5 own.[c] 6 You are to pay them in silver for the food
[c]Ge 36:8; Jos 24:4 you eat and the water you drink.' "
7 The LORD your God has blessed you in all the
2:7 work of your hands. He has watched[d] over your
[d]Dt 8:2-4 journey through this vast desert. These forty years
the LORD your God has been with you, and you
have not lacked anything.
8 So we went on past our brothers the descendants of Esau, who live in Seir. We turned from
the Arabah road, which comes up from Elath and
2:8 Ezion Geber,[e] and traveled along the desert road of
[e]1Ki 9:26 [f]Jdg 11:18 Moab.[f]
9 Then the LORD said to me, "Do not harass the
2:9 Moabites or provoke them to war, for I will not
[g]Nu 21:15 give you any part of their land. I have given Ar[g] to
[h]Ge 19:36-38 the descendants of Lot[h] as a possession."
10 (The Emites[i] used to live there—a people
2:10 strong and numerous, and as tall as the Anakites.[j]
[i]Ge 14:5 [j]Nu 13:22,33 11 Like the Anakites, they too were considered
Rephaites, but the Moabites called them Emites.
12 Horites used to live in Seir, but the descendants
of Esau drove them out. They destroyed the
Horites from before them and settled in their

[a] *40,1* Hebrew *Yam Suph*; that is, Sea of Reeds

An Important Travelogue

DT 2:5

Moses reminds the Israelites of where they have been. He reviews the geography of their 40-year walk bordering the territories of the Edomites, Moabites and Ammonites. This travelogue is important because it illustrates that they initially reach an entrance to Canaan only 11 days after leaving Mount Sinai (Dt 1:2), but because of faltering faith they wander for 40 years in lands outside the promise (see Map 3: Exodus and Conquest of Canaan at the back of this Bible).

Note how often throughout this book Moses reminds and instructs the people not to "forget." He has learned, in a desert of wandering, how faith is strengthened. When we remember where we've been and learn from our mistakes and failures, we are ready to move ahead with humility and wisdom as companions to our faith.

place, just as Israel did[k] in the land the LORD gave them as their possession.)

13 And the LORD said, "Now get up and cross the Zered Valley." So we crossed the valley.

14 Thirty-eight years passed from the time we left Kadesh Barnea[l] until we crossed the Zered Valley. By then, that entire generation[m] of fighting men had perished from the camp, as the LORD had sworn to them.[n] 15 The LORD's hand was against them until he had completely eliminated[o] them from the camp.

16 Now when the last of these fighting men among the people had died, 17 the LORD said to me, 18 "Today you are to pass by the region of Moab at Ar. 19 When you come to the Ammonites,[p] do not harass them or provoke them to war, for I will not give you possession of any land belonging to the Ammonites. I have given it as a possession to the descendants of Lot.[q]"

20 (That too was considered a land of the Rephaites, who used to live there; but the Ammonites called them Zamzummites. 21 They were a people strong and numerous, and as tall as the Anakites.[r] The LORD destroyed them from before the Ammonites, who drove them out and settled in their place. 22 The LORD had done the same for the descendants of Esau, who lived in Seir,[s] when he destroyed the Horites from before them. They drove them out and have lived in their place to this day. 23 And as for the Avvites[t] who lived in villages as far as Gaza, the Caphtorites[u] coming out from Caphtor[a][v] destroyed them and settled in their place.)

Defeat of Sihon King of Heshbon

24 "Set out now and cross the Arnon Gorge.[w] See, I have given into your hand Sihon the Amorite, king of Heshbon, and his country. Begin to take possession of it and engage him in battle. 25 This very day I will begin to put the terror[x] and fear[y] of you on all the nations under heaven. They will hear reports of you and will tremble[z] and be in anguish because of you."

26 From the desert of Kedemoth I sent messengers to Sihon king of Heshbon offering peace and saying, 27 "Let us pass through your country. We will stay on the main road; we will not turn aside to the right or to the left.[a] 28 Sell us food to eat and water to drink for their price in silver. Only let us pass through on foot[b]— 29 as the descendants of Esau, who live in Seir, and the Moabites, who live in Ar, did for us—until we cross the Jordan into the land the LORD our God is giving us." 30 But Sihon king of Heshbon refused to let us pass through. For the LORD[c] your God had made his spirit stubborn[d] and his heart obstinate in order to give him into your hands, as he has now done.

31 The LORD said to me, "See, I have begun to

2:12 [k]ver 22
2:14 [l]Nu 13:26 [m]Nu 14:29-35 [n]Dt 1:34-35
2:15 [o]Ps 106:26
2:19 [p]Ge 19:38 [q]ver 9
2:21 [r]ver 10
2:22 [s]Ge 36:8
2:23 [t]Jos 13:3 [u]Ge 10:14 [v]Am 9:7
2:24 [w]Nu 21:13-14; Jdg 11:13,18
2:25 [x]Dt 11:25 [y]Jos 2:9,11 [z]Ex 15:14-16
2:27 [a]Nu 21:21-22
2:28 [b]Nu 20:19
2:30 [c]Jos 11:20 [d]Ex 4:21; Nu 21:23; Ro 9:18

We know that whatever God sends into our lives has first passed through his filter. NOTHING comes into the life of a Christian that God doesn't know about. Believing that, we can relax and know that God will be with us during the trials ahead.

—Barbara Johnson

[a] *23* That is, Crete

deliver Sihon and his country over to you. Now
2:31 [e]Dt 1:8 begin to conquer and possess his land."[e]
32 When Sihon and all his army came out to
2:32 [f]Nu 21:23 meet us in battle[f] at Jahaz, 33 the LORD our God
delivered him over to us and we struck him
2:33 [g]Dt 29:7 down,[g] together with his sons and his whole
army. 34 At that time we took all his towns and
2:34 [h]Dt 3:6; 7:2 completely destroyed[a][h] them—men, women and
children. We left no survivors. 35 But the livestock
and the plunder from the towns we had captured
2:36 we carried off for ourselves. 36 From Aroer[i] on the
[i]Dt 3:12; rim of the Arnon Gorge, and from the town in the
4:48; Jos 13:9 gorge, even as far as Gilead, not one town was too
[j]Ps 44:3 strong for us. The LORD our God gave[j] us all of
them. 37 But in accordance with the command of
2:37 [k]ver 18-19 the LORD our God,[k] you did not encroach on any
[l]Nu 21:24 of the land of the Ammonites,[l] neither the land
[m]Ge 32:22; Dt 3:16 along the course of the Jabbok[m] nor that around
the towns in the hills.

Defeat of Og King of Bashan

3 Next we turned and went up along the road
toward Bashan, and Og king of Bashan with
his whole army marched out to meet us in battle
3:1 [n]Nu 21:33 at Edrei.[n] 2 The LORD said to me, "Do not be afraid[o]
of him, for I have handed him over to you with
3:2 [o]Nu 21:34 his whole army and his land. Do to him what you
did to Sihon king of the Amorites, who reigned in
Heshbon."
3 So the LORD our God also gave into our hands
Og king of Bashan and all his army. We struck
3:3 [p]Nu 21:35 them down, leaving no survivors.[p] 4 At that time
we took all his cities. There was not one of the
sixty cities that we did not take from them—the
3:4 [q]1Ki 4:13 whole region of Argob, Og's kingdom in Bashan.[q] 5 All these cities were fortified with high
walls and with gates and bars, and there were
also a great many unwalled villages. 6 We completely destroyed[a] them, as we had done with
3:6 [r]Dt 2:24,34 Sihon king of Heshbon, destroying[a][r] every city—
men, women and children. 7 But all the livestock
and the plunder from their cities we carried off
for ourselves.
8 So at that time we took from these two kings of
the Amorites the territory east of the Jordan, from
the Arnon Gorge as far as Mount Hermon. 9 (Her-
3:9 [s]Dt 4:48; mon is called Sirion[s] by the Sidonians; the Amo-
Ps 29:6 rites call it Senir.)[t] 10 We took all the towns on the
[t]1Ch 5:23 plateau, and all Gilead, and all Bashan as far as
3:10 Salecah[u] and Edrei, towns of Og's kingdom in
[u]Jos 13:11 Bashan. 11 (Only Og king of Bashan was left of the
3:11 remnant of the Rephaites.[v] His bed[b] was made of
[v]Ge 14:5 iron and was more than thirteen feet long and six
[w]2Sa 12:26; Jer 49:2 feet wide.[c] It is still in Rabbah[w] of the Ammonites.)

[a] *34,6* The Hebrew term refers to the irrevocable giving over of things or persons to the LORD, often by totally destroying them. [b] *11* Or *sarcophagus* [c] *11* Hebrew *nine cubits long and four cubits wide* (about 4 meters long and 1.8 meters wide)

Devotion and Destruction

DT 2:34; 3:3

Moses reminds the Israelites of their victories over two Amorite kings. Twice he describes conquests in which there are no enemy survivors, underscoring the principle of herem. The Hebrew word herem means "a devoted thing" and is applied to the wartime practice of complete annihilation. What is the link between devotion and destruction? God commands this destruction in order to preserve his people. He knows if these enemies survive, they will turn the Israelites away from their devotion to God and toward false religions (Dt 20:18). This destruction is also God's means of judging the Amorites for their sin and rebellion against him (Ge 15:16).

Possessing the promises of God requires that we look within and identify what is turning our hearts from God and that we be willing to "demolish arguments and every pretension that sets itself up against the knowledge of God, and we take captive every thought to make it obedient to Christ" (2Co 10:5).

Rest in Obedience

DT 3:18-20

Moses' first sermon is almost over. So far, he has reviewed Israelite history and reminded them of their failures and victories. He is getting ready to charge the Israelites to go forward, to fight valiantly, and to conquer and possess Canaan. He wisely takes a moment to encourage them with a promise of the peace and rest that is to come. Moses knows that possessing the promised land will end their homeless wandering and bring the Israelites peace and stability. Obedience to God's Word, even in the midst of conflict and struggle, allows our hearts to rest and find shelter in God's leadership. The battle may surround us, but there is peace in the promise: "My Presence will go with you, and I will give you rest" (Ex 33:14).

Division of the Land

12 Of the land that we took over at that time, I
gave the Reubenites and the Gadites the territory
north of Aroer[x] by the Arnon Gorge, including
half the hill country of Gilead, together with its
towns. 13 The rest of Gilead and also all of Bashan,
the kingdom of Og, I gave to the half-tribe of
Manasseh. (The whole region of Argob in Bashan
used to be known as a land of the Rephaites.
14 Jair,[y] a descendant of Manasseh, took the whole
region of Argob as far as the border of the Geshurites and the Maacathites; it was named after him,
so that to this day Bashan is called Havvoth Jair.[a])
15 And I gave Gilead to Makir.[z] 16 But to the Reubenites and the Gadites I gave the territory extending from Gilead down to the Arnon Gorge (the
middle of the gorge being the border) and out to
the Jabbok River,[a] which is the border of the
Ammonites. 17 Its western border was the Jordan
in the Arabah, from Kinnereth[b] to the Sea of the
Arabah (the Salt Sea[b c]), below the slopes of
Pisgah.

18 I commanded you at that time: "The LORD
your God has given you this land to take possession of it. But all your able-bodied men, armed for
battle, must cross over ahead of your brother Israelites.[d] 19 However, your wives, your children and
your livestock (I know you have much livestock)
may stay in the towns I have given you, 20 until the
LORD gives rest to your brothers as he has to you,
and they too have taken over the land that the
LORD your God is giving them, across the Jordan.
After that, each of you may go back to the possession I have given you."

Moses Forbidden to Cross the Jordan

21 At that time I commanded Joshua: "You have
seen with your own eyes all that the LORD your
God has done to these two kings. The LORD will
do the same to all the kingdoms over there where
you are going. 22 Do not be afraid[e] of them; the
LORD your God himself will fight[f] for you."

23 At that time I pleaded with the LORD: 24 "O Sovereign LORD, you have begun to show to your servant your greatness[g] and your strong hand. For
what god[h] is there in heaven or on earth who can
do the deeds and mighty works[i] you do?[j] 25 Let me
go over and see the good land[k] beyond the Jordan—that fine hill country and Lebanon."

26 But because of you the LORD was angry[l] with
me and would not listen to me. "That is enough,"
the LORD said. "Do not speak to me anymore
about this matter. 27 Go up to the top of Pisgah and
look west and north and south and east. Look at
the land with your own eyes, since you are not
going to cross this Jordan.[m] 28 But commission[n]
Joshua, and encourage and strengthen him, for he
will lead this people across[o] and will cause them

3:12 [x]Nu 32:32-38; Dt 2:36; Jos 13:8-13
3:14 [y]Nu 32:41; 1Ch 2:22
3:15 [z]Nu 32:39-40
3:16 [a]Nu 21:24
3:17 [b]Nu 34:11; Jos 13:27 [c]Ge 14:3; Jos 12:3
3:18 [d]Nu 32:17
3:22 [e]Dt 1:29 [f]Ex 14:14; Dt 20:4
3:24 [g]Dt 11:2 [h]Ex 15:11; Ps 86:8 [i]Ps 71:16,19 [j]2Sa 7:22
3:25 [k]Dt 4:22
3:26 [l]Dt 1:37; 31:2
3:27 [m]Nu 27:12
3:28 [n]Nu 27:18-23 [o]Dt 31:3,23

[a] *14* Or *called the settlements of Jair* [b] *17* That is, the Dead Sea

to inherit the land that you will see." 29So we stayed in the valley near Beth Peor.[p]

Obedience Commanded

4 Hear now, O Israel, the decrees and laws I am about to teach you. Follow them so that you may live[q] and may go in and take possession of the land that the LORD, the God of your fathers, is giving you. 2Do not add[r] to what I command you and do not subtract from it, but keep the commands of the LORD your God that I give you.

3You saw with your own eyes what the LORD did at Baal Peor.[s] The LORD your God destroyed from among you everyone who followed the Baal of Peor, 4but all of you who held fast to the LORD your God are still alive today.

5See, I have taught you decrees and laws as the LORD my God commanded me, so that you may follow them in the land you are entering to take possession of it. 6Observe them carefully, for this will show your wisdom[t] and understanding to the nations, who will hear about all these decrees and say, "Surely this great nation is a wise and understanding people."[u] 7What other nation is so great[v] as to have their gods near[w] them the way the LORD our God is near us whenever we pray to him? 8And what other nation is so great as to have such righteous decrees and laws as this body of laws I am setting before you today?

9Only be careful,[x] and watch yourselves closely so that you do not forget the things your eyes have seen or let them slip from your heart as long as you live. Teach[y] them to your children[z] and to their children after them. 10Remember the day you stood before the LORD your God at Horeb,[a] when he said to me, "Assemble the people before me to hear my words so that they may learn to revere me as long as they live in the land and may teach them to their children." 11You came near and stood at the foot of the mountain while it blazed with fire[b] to the very heavens, with black clouds and deep darkness. 12Then the LORD spoke[c] to you out of the fire. You heard the sound of words but saw no form; there was only a voice. 13He declared to you his covenant,[d] the Ten Commandments,[e] which he commanded you to follow and then wrote them on two stone tablets. 14And the LORD directed me at that time to teach you the decrees and laws you are to follow in the land that you are crossing the Jordan to possess.

Idolatry Forbidden

15You saw no form[f] of any kind the day the LORD spoke to you at Horeb out of the fire. Therefore watch yourselves very carefully,[g] 16so that you do not become corrupt and make for yourselves an idol,[h] an image of any shape, whether formed like a man or a woman, 17or like any animal on earth or any bird that flies in the air, 18or like any creature that moves along the ground or any fish in

3:29 [p]Dt 4:46; 34:6
4:1 [q]Dt 5:33; 8:1; 16:20; 30:15-20; Eze 20:11; Ro 10:5
4:2 [r]Dt 12:32; Jos 1:7; Rev 22:18-19
4:3 [s]Nu 25:1-9; Ps 106:28
4:6 [t]Dt 30:19-20; Ps 19:7; Pr 1:7 [u]Job 28:28
4:7 [v]2Sa 7:23 [w]Ps 46:1; Isa 55:6
4:9 [x]Pr 4:23 [y]Ge 18:19; Eph 6:4 [z]Ps 78:5-6
4:10 [a]Ex 19:9,16
4:11 [b]Ex 19:18; Heb 12:18-19
4:12 [c]Ex 20:22; Dt 5:4,22
4:13 [d]Dt 9:9,11 [e]Ex 24:12; 31:18; 34:28
4:15 [f]Isa 40:18 [g]Jos 23:11
4:16 [h]Ex 20:4-5; 32:7; Dt 5:8; Ro 1:23

Knowing God

DT 4:12

In Deuteronomy 1-3, Moses reminds the people who *they are*. In Deuteronomy 4 he tells them who *God* is. He begins by underscoring the very real fact that their God is not like the gods of gold, silver, wood and stone that can be found in every neighboring nation. How then is their God made known? Moses recalls how God revealed himself to them through his voice, *a voice* they all clearly heard (Dt 4:12). Once *again* Moses highlights the theme of Deuteronomy—the importance of God's *Word* (see the note on Dt 1:39).

Where do we get our concept of God? A view of God based on his Word inevitably results in a meaningful life of work and worship.

the waters below. 19 And when you look up to the
sky and see the sun,[i] the moon and the stars—all
the heavenly array[j]—do not be enticed into bowing down to them and worshiping things the LORD
your God has apportioned to all the nations under
heaven. 20 But as for you, the LORD took you and
brought you out of the iron-smelting furnace,[k] out
of Egypt, to be the people of his inheritance,[l] as
you now are.
21 The LORD was angry with me[m] because of you,
and he solemnly swore that I would not cross the
Jordan and enter the good land the LORD your God
is giving you as your inheritance. 22 I will die in
this land; I will not cross the Jordan; but you are
about to cross over and take possession of that
good land.[n] 23 Be careful not to forget the covenant[o] of the LORD your God that he made with
you; do not make for yourselves an idol[p] in the
form of anything the LORD your God has forbidden. 24 For the LORD your God is a consuming fire,[q]
a jealous God.
25 After you have had children and grandchildren and have lived in the land a long time—if
you then become corrupt and make any kind of
idol, doing evil[r] in the eyes of the LORD your God
and provoking him to anger, 26 I call heaven and
earth as witnesses against you[s] this day that you
will quickly perish from the land that you are
crossing the Jordan to possess. You will not live
there long but will certainly be destroyed. 27 The
LORD will scatter[t] you among the peoples, and
only a few of you will survive among the nations
to which the LORD will drive you. 28 There you will
worship man-made gods[u] of wood and stone,
which cannot see or hear or eat or smell.[v] 29 But if
from there you seek[w] the LORD your God, you will
find him if you look for him with all your heart[x]
and with all your soul.[y] 30 When you are in distress and all these things have happened to you,
then in later days[z] you will return to the LORD
your God and obey him. 31 For the LORD your God
is a merciful[a] God; he will not abandon or destroy
you or forget the covenant with your forefathers,
which he confirmed to them by oath.

The LORD Is God

32 Ask[b] now about the former days, long before
your time, from the day God created man on the
earth;[c] ask from one end of the heavens to the other.[d] Has anything so great as this ever happened,
or has anything like it ever been heard of? 33 Has
any other people heard the voice of God[a] speaking
out of fire, as you have, and lived?[e] 34 Has any god
ever tried to take for himself one nation out of
another nation,[f] by testings, by miraculous signs[g]
and wonders,[h] by war, by a mighty hand and an
outstretched arm,[i] or by great and awesome
deeds,[j] like all the things the LORD your God did
for you in Egypt before your very eyes?

[a] 33 Or *of a god*

4:19 [i]Dt 17:3; Job 31:26 [j]2Ki 17:16; 21:3; Ro 1:25
4:20 [k]1Ki 8:51; Jer 11:4 [l]Ex 19:5; Dt 9:29
4:21 [m]Nu 20:12; Dt 1:37
4:22 [n]Dt 3:25
4:23 [o]ver 9,16 [p]Ex 20:4
4:24 [q]Ex 24:17; Dt 9:3; Heb 12:29
4:25 [r]2Ki 17:2,17
4:26 [s]Dt 30:18-19; Isa 1:2; Mic 6:2
4:27 [t]Lev 26:33; Dt 28:36,64; Ne 1:8
4:28 [u]Dt 28:36, 64; 1Sa 26:19; Jer 16:13 [v]Ps 115:4-8; 135:15-18
4:29 [w]2Ch 15:4; Isa 55:6 [x]Jer 29:13 [y]Dt 30:1-3, 10
4:30 [z]Dt 31:29; Jer 23:20; Hos 3:5
4:31 [a]2Ch 30:9; Ne 9:31; Ps 116:5; Jnh 4:2
4:32 [b]Dt 32:7; Job 8:8 [c]Ge 1:27 [d]Mt 24:31
4:33 [e]Ex 20:22; Dt 5:24-26
4:34 [f]Ex 6:6 [g]Ex 7:3 [h]Dt 7:19; 26:8 [i]Ex 13:3 [j]Dt 34:12

Sometimes I [God] *allow the world to show them what it is, so that, feeling its diverse and various passions, they may know how little stability it has, and may come to lift their desire beyond it, and seek their native country, which is the Eternal Life. And so I draw them by these, and by many other ways, for the eye cannot see, nor the tongue relate, nor the heart think, how many are the roads and ways which I use, through love alone, to lead them back to grace, so that My truth may be fulfilled in them.*

—Catherine of Siena (1347-1380)

35You were shown these things so that you
might know that the LORD is God; besides him
there is no other.[k] 36From heaven he made you
hear his voice[l] to discipline you. On earth he
showed you his great fire, and you heard his
words from out of the fire. 37Because he loved[m]
your forefathers and chose their descendants after
them, he brought you out of Egypt by his Presence and his great strength,[n] 38to drive out before
you nations greater and stronger than you and to
bring you into their land to give it to you for your
inheritance,[o] as it is today.

39Acknowledge and take to heart this day that
the LORD is God in heaven above and on the earth
below. There is no other.[p] 40Keep[q] his decrees and
commands, which I am giving you today, so that
it may go well[r] with you and your children after
you and that you may live long[s] in the land the
LORD your God gives you for all time.

Cities of Refuge

41Then Moses set aside three cities east of the
Jordan, 42to which anyone who had killed a person could flee if he had unintentionally killed his
neighbor without malice aforethought. He could
flee into one of these cities and save his life. 43The
cities were these: Bezer in the desert plateau, for
the Reubenites; Ramoth in Gilead, for the Gadites;
and Golan in Bashan, for the Manassites.

Introduction to the Law

44This is the law Moses set before the Israelites.
45These are the stipulations, decrees and laws
Moses gave them when they came out of Egypt
46and were in the valley near Beth Peor east of the
Jordan, in the land of Sihon[t] king of the Amorites,
who reigned in Heshbon and was defeated by
Moses and the Israelites as they came out of
Egypt. 47They took possession of his land and the
land of Og king of Bashan, the two Amorite kings
east of the Jordan. 48This land extended from Aro-
er[u] on the rim of the Arnon Gorge to Mount
Siyon[a][v] (that is, Hermon), 49and included all the
Arabah east of the Jordan, as far as the Sea of the
Arabah,[b] below the slopes of Pisgah.

The Ten Commandments

5 Moses summoned all Israel and said:
Hear, O Israel, the decrees and laws I declare
in your hearing today. Learn them and be sure to
follow them. 2The LORD our God made a covenant[w] with us at Horeb. 3It was not with our
fathers that the LORD made this covenant, but with
us, with all of us who are alive here today.[x] 4The
LORD spoke[y] to you face to face out of the fire on
the mountain. 5(At that time I stood between[z] the
LORD and you to declare to you the word of the

4:35 [k]Dt 32:39; 1Sa 2:2; Isa 45:5,18
4:36 [l]Ex 19:9,19
4:37 [m]Dt 10:15 [n]Ex 13:3,9, 14
4:38 [o]Dt 7:1; 9:5
4:39 [p]ver 35; Jos 2:11
4:40 [q]Lev 22:31; Dt 5:33 [r]Dt 5:16 [s]Dt 6:3,18; Eph 6:2-3
4:46 [t]Nu 21:26; Dt 3:29
4:48 [u]Dt 2:36 [v]Dt 3:9
5:2 [w]Ex 19:5
5:3 [x]Heb 8:9
5:4 [y]Dt 4:12,33, 36
5:5 [z]Gal 3:19

[a] 48 Hebrew; Syriac (see also Deut. 3:9) *Sirion* [b] 49 That is, the Dead Sea

The Law of Love

DT 4:37-40

Throughout the book of Deuteronomy, Moses declares the law of love: "Because he loved your forefathers and chose their descendants after them, he brought you out of Egypt by his Presence and his great strength . . . Acknowledge and take to heart this day that the LORD is God in heaven above and on the earth below. There is no other" (Dt 4:37,39). How can God's love be taken "to heart" in the midst of disappointments, challenges, desert wanderings or seasons when God's voice is dim? Moses repeatedly reminds the Israelites of God's unshakable love. As difficult as it is at times for the Israelites, the reality is still there: God loves them . . . and there is no other. They may be attracted to other gods; they may follow other gods. But no other god loves them, and, Moses reminds them, even commands them, to remember: There actually is no other god!

LORD, because you were afraid[a] of the fire and did
not go up the mountain.) And he said:

6 "I am the LORD your God, who brought
you out of Egypt, out of the land of
slavery.
7 "You shall have no other gods before[a] me.
8 "You shall not make for yourself an idol in
the form of anything in heaven above or
on the earth beneath or in the waters
below. 9 You shall not bow down to them
or worship them; for I, the LORD your
God, am a jealous God, punishing the
children for the sin of the fathers to the
third and fourth generation of those who
hate me,[b] 10 but showing love to a thousand ⌊generations⌋ of those who love me
and keep my commandments.[c]
11 "You shall not misuse the name of the LORD
your God, for the LORD will not hold anyone guiltless who misuses his name.[d]
12 "Observe the Sabbath day by keeping it holy,[e]
as the LORD your God has commanded
you. 13 Six days you shall labor and do all
your work, 14 but the seventh day[f] is a
Sabbath to the LORD your God. On it you
shall not do any work, neither you, nor
your son or daughter, nor your manservant or maidservant, nor your ox, your
donkey or any of your animals, nor the
alien within your gates, so that your
manservant and maidservant may rest,
as you do. 15 Remember that you were
slaves in Egypt and that the LORD your
God brought you out of there with a
mighty hand and an outstretched arm.[g]
Therefore the LORD your God has commanded you to observe the Sabbath day.
16 "Honor your father and your mother,[h] as the
LORD your God has commanded you, so
that you may live long[i] and that it may
go well with you in the land the LORD
your God is giving you.
17 "You shall not murder.[j]
18 "You shall not commit adultery.[k]
19 "You shall not steal.
20 "You shall not give false testimony against
your neighbor.
21 "You shall not covet your neighbor's wife.
You shall not set your desire on your
neighbor's house or land, his manservant or maidservant, his ox or donkey,
or anything that belongs to your neighbor."[l]

22 These are the commandments the LORD proclaimed in a loud voice to your whole assembly
there on the mountain from out of the fire, the
cloud and the deep darkness; and he added noth-

[a] 7 Or *besides*

5:5 [a]Ex 20:18,21
5:9 [b]Ex 34:7
5:10 [c]Jer 32:18
5:11 [d]Lev 19:12; Mt 5:33-37
5:12 [e]Ex 20:8
5:14 [f]Ge 2:2; Heb 4:4
5:15 [g]Dt 4:34
5:16 [h]Ex 20:12; Lev 19:3; Dt 27:16; Eph 6:2-3*; Col 3:20 [i]Dt 4:40
5:17 [j]Mt 5:21-22*
5:18 [k]Mt 5:27-30; Lk 18:20*; Jas 2:11*
5:21 [l]Ro 7:7*; 13:9*

**I love my God, but with
no love of mine
For I have none to give;
I love thee, Lord, but all that
love is thine,
For by thy life I live.
I am as nothing, and rejoice
to be
Emptied and lost and
swallowed up in Thee.**

—*Madame Guyon* (1647–1717)

ing more. Then he wrote them on two stone tablets[m] and gave them to me.

23 When you heard the voice out of the darkness, while the mountain was ablaze with fire, all the leading men of your tribes and your elders came to me. 24 And you said, "The LORD our God has shown us his glory and his majesty, and we have heard his voice from the fire. Today we have seen that a man can live even if God speaks with him.[n] 25 But now, why should we die? This great fire will consume us, and we will die if we hear the voice of the LORD our God any longer.[o] 26 For what mortal man has ever heard the voice of the living God speaking out of fire, as we have, and survived?[p] 27 Go near and listen to all that the LORD our God says. Then tell us whatever the LORD our God tells you. We will listen and obey."

28 The LORD heard you when you spoke to me and the LORD said to me, "I have heard what this people said to you. Everything they said was good.[q] 29 Oh, that their hearts would be inclined to fear me[r] and keep all my commands[s] always, so that it might go well with them and their children forever![t]

30 "Go, tell them to return to their tents. 31 But you stay here[u] with me so that I may give you all the commands, decrees and laws you are to teach them to follow in the land I am giving them to possess."

32 So be careful to do what the LORD your God has commanded you; do not turn aside to the right or to the left.[v] 33 Walk in all the way that the LORD your God has commanded you,[w] so that you may live and prosper and prolong your days[x] in the land that you will possess.

Love the LORD Your God

6 These are the commands, decrees and laws the LORD your God directed me to teach you to observe in the land that you are crossing the Jordan to possess, 2 so that you, your children and their children after them may fear[y] the LORD your God as long as you live by keeping all his decrees and commands that I give you, and so that you may enjoy long life. 3 Hear, O Israel, and be careful to obey so that it may go well with you and that you may increase greatly[z] in a land flowing with milk and honey,[a] just as the LORD, the God of your fathers, promised you.

4 Hear, O Israel: The LORD our God, the LORD is one.[a][b] 5 Love[c] the LORD your God with all your heart and with all your soul and with all your strength.[d] 6 These commandments that I give you today are to be upon your hearts.[e] 7 Impress them on your children. Talk about them when you sit at home and when you walk along the road, when you lie down and when you get up.[f] 8 Tie them as symbols on your hands and bind them on your foreheads.[g] 9 Write them on the doorframes of your houses and on your gates.[h]

[a] 4 Or *The LORD our God is one LORD*; or *The LORD is our God, the LORD is one*; or *The LORD is our God, the LORD alone*

5:22 [m]Ex 24:12; 31:18; Dt 4:13
5:24 [n]Ex 19:19
5:25 [o]Dt 18:16
5:26 [p]Dt 4:33
5:28 [q]Dt 18:17
5:29 [r]Ps 81:8,13 [s]Dt 11:1; Isa 48:18 [t]Dt 4:1,40
5:31 [u]Ex 24:12
5:32 [v]Dt 17:11,20; 28:14; Jos 1:7; 23:6; Pr 4:27
5:33 [w]Jer 7:23 [x]Dt 4:40
6:2 [y]Ex 20:20; Dt 10:12-13
6:3 [z]Dt 5:33 [a]Ex 3:8
6:4 [b]Mk 12:29*; 1Co 8:4
6:5 [c]Mt 22:37*; Mk 12:30*; Lk 10:27* [d]Dt 10:12
6:6 [e]Dt 11:18
6:7 [f]Dt 4:9; 11:19; Eph 6:4
6:8 [g]Ex 13:9,16; Dt 11:18
6:9 [h]Dt 11:20

Sticky Notes to Live By

DT 6:8–9

Moses recites the cornerstone of Deuteronomy in the commandment Jesus reiterates as the most important in all of Scripture: Love God with all your heart, soul and strength (Dt 6:5; Mt 22:37–38). Moses then gives the Israelites some exceptional instructions: Write this commandment on your hands and foreheads, post it on your front door and all your interior doors, and talk about it at breakfast, at work and when you are getting ready for bed.

We share two commonalities of heart with the Israelites: (1) we want to love God, and (2) we get sidetracked all too easily. Try posting some notes on the refrigerator, dashboard or bathroom mirror as a reminder of the primary requirement for really living!

Take Care to Obey

DT 6:25

Moses continues speaking to an increasingly enthusiastic crowd. They are beginning to believe that the promised land is within their reach! Imagine the effect when he pauses and speaks with fierce intensity: "Be careful. Obedience is the key to sustaining a relationship with God that is right-living and strength-giving." Moses has already reminded them of the terrible, 40-year consequence they suffered for being careless about obedience. As women, very little frustrates or discourages us more in relationships than passivity. God is no different. He longs to see an outward expression of our internal commitment to him. The life of love is marked by activity, and obedience prompts us to live passionate, not passive, lives.

10When the LORD your God brings you into the
land he swore to your fathers, to Abraham, Isaac
and Jacob, to give you—a land with large, flourishing cities you did not build,[i] 11houses filled **6:10**
with all kinds of good things you did not provide, [i]Jos 24:13
wells you did not dig, and vineyards and olive
groves you did not plant—then when you eat and **6:11**
are satisfied,[j] 12be careful that you do not forget [j]Dt 8:10
the LORD, who brought you out of Egypt, out of
the land of slavery.
13Fear the LORD[k] your God, serve him only[l] and **6:13**
take your oaths in his name. 14Do not follow other [k]Dt 10:20 [l]Mt 4:10*;
gods, the gods of the peoples around you; 15for the Lk 4:8*
LORD your God[m], who is among you, is a jealous **6:15**
God and his anger will burn against you, and he [m]Dt 4:24
will destroy you from the face of the land. 16Do not **6:16**
test the LORD your God[n] as you did at Massah. 17Be [n]Ex 17:7;
sure to keep the commands of the LORD your God Mt 4:7*;
and the stipulations and decrees he has given you.[o] Lk 4:12*
18Do what is right and good in the LORD's sight, so **6:17**
that it may go well[p] with you and you may go in [o]Dt 11:22;
and take over the good land that the LORD prom- Ps 119:4
ised on oath to your forefathers, 19thrusting out all **6:18**
your enemies before you, as the LORD said. [p]Dt 4:40
20In the future, when your son asks you,[q] "What **6:20**
is the meaning of the stipulations, decrees and [q]Ex 13:14
laws the LORD our God has commanded you?" 21tell
him: "We were slaves of Pharaoh in Egypt, but the
LORD brought us out of Egypt with a mighty hand.
22Before our eyes the LORD sent miraculous signs
and wonders—great and terrible—upon Egypt and
Pharaoh and his whole household. 23But he
brought us out from there to bring us in and give
us the land that he promised on oath to our forefathers. 24The LORD commanded us to obey all
these decrees and to fear the LORD our God,[r] so that **6:24**
we might always prosper and be kept alive, as is [r]Dt 10:12;
the case today.[s] 25And if we are careful to obey all Jer 32:39 [s]Ps 41:2
this law before the LORD our God, as he has com- **6:25**
manded us, that will be our righteousness.[t]" [t]Dt 24:13;

Driving Out the Nations Ro 10:3,5

7 When the LORD your God brings you into the
land you are entering to possess and drives out
before you many nations[u]—the Hittites, Girga- **7:1**
shites, Amorites, Canaanites, Perizzites, Hivites [u]Dt 31:3;
and Jebusites, seven nations larger and stronger Ac 13:19
than you— 2and when the LORD your God has
delivered them over to you and you have defeated
them, then you must destroy them totally.[a] Make **7:2** [v]Ex 23:32
no treaty[v] with them, and show them no mercy.[w] [w]Dt 13:8
3Do not intermarry with them.[x] Do not give your
daughters to their sons or take their daughters for **7:3**
your sons, 4for they will turn your sons away from [x]Ex 34:15-
following me to serve other gods, and the LORD's 16; Ezr 9:2
anger will burn against you and will quickly **7:4**
destroy[y] you. 5This is what you are to do to them: [y]Dt 6:15

[a] *2* The Hebrew term refers to the irrevocable giving over of things or persons to the LORD, often by totally destroying them; also in verse 26.

Break down their altars, smash their sacred stones,
7:5 cut down their Asherah poles[a] and burn their idols
[z]Ex 23:24; in the fire.[z] 6For you are a people holy[a] to the LORD
Dt 12:2-3 your God.[b] The LORD your God has chosen[c] you
7:6 out of all the peoples on the face of the earth to be
[a]Ex 19:5-6; his people, his treasured possession.
1Pe 2:9 7The LORD did not set his affection on you and
[b]Ps 50:5; Jer 2:3 choose you because you were more numerous
[c]Dt 14:2 than other peoples, for you were the fewest of all
7:7 peoples.[d] 8But it was because the LORD loved[e] you
[d]Dt 10:22 and kept the oath he swore[f] to your forefathers
7:8 that he brought you out with a mighty hand and
[e]Dt 10:15 redeemed you from the land of slavery,[g] from the
[f]Ex 32:13 power of Pharaoh king of Egypt. 9Know therefore
[g]Ex 13:14 that the LORD your God is God;[h] he is the faithful
7:9 God,[i] keeping his covenant of love[j] to a thousand
[h]Dt 4:35 generations of those who love him and keep his
[i]1Co 1:9; 2Ti 2:13 commands. 10But

[j]Ne 1:5; Da 9:4

> those who hate him he will repay to
> their face by destruction;
> he will not be slow to repay to their
> face those who hate him.

11Therefore, take care to follow the commands,
decrees and laws I give you today.
12If you pay attention to these laws and are careful to follow them, then the LORD your God will
keep his covenant of love with you, as he swore to
7:12 your forefathers.[k] 13He will love you and bless
[k]Lev 26:3-13; Dt 28:1-14; you[l] and increase your numbers. He will bless the
Ps 105:8-9 fruit of your womb, the crops of your land—your
grain, new wine and oil—the calves of your herds
7:13 and the lambs of your flocks in the land that he
[l]Jn 14:21 swore to your forefathers to give you.[m] 14You will
[m]Dt 28:4 be blessed more than any other people; none of
7:14 your men or women will be childless, nor any of
[n]Ex 23:26 your livestock without young.[n] 15The LORD will
7:15 keep you free from every disease.[o] He will not
[o]Ex 15:26 inflict on you the horrible diseases you knew in
Egypt, but he will inflict them on all who hate
you. 16You must destroy all the peoples the LORD
7:16 your God gives over to you. Do not look on them
[p]ver 2; with pity[p] and do not serve their gods, for that
Ex 23:33 will be a snare[q] to you.
[q]Jdg 8:27 17You may say to yourselves, "These nations are
stronger than we are. How can we drive them
7:17 out?[r]" 18But do not be afraid[s] of them; remember
[r]Nu 33:53 well what the LORD your God did to Pharaoh and
7:18 to all Egypt.[t] 19You saw with your own eyes the
[s]Dt 31:6 great trials, the miraculous signs and wonders, the
[t]Ps 105:5 mighty hand and outstretched arm, with which
7:19 the LORD your God brought you out. The LORD
[u]Dt 4:34 your God will do the same to all the peoples you
7:20 now fear.[u] 20Moreover, the LORD your God will
[v]Ex 23:28; send the hornet[v] among them until even the sur-
Jos 24:12 vivors who hide from you have perished. 21Do not
7:21 be terrified by them, for the LORD your God, who
[w]Jos 3:10 is among you,[w] is a great and awesome God.[x]
[x]Dt 10:17; Ne 9:32

[a] 5 That is, symbols of the goddess Asherah; here and elsewhere in Deuteronomy

The Heart of the Matter

DT 7:6

Moses reminds the Israelites that underscoring every command, no matter how hard it may sound, is a reality more radical than any they could possibly imagine: The Lord God has chosen them to be his. When God's instructions seem challenging or unfair, Moses encourages these wanderers that there is One who longs for them and loves them with a passionate intensity. His commands are intended to protect that treasured relationship.

The story of the Israelites foreshadows our own story of how God chose us, sent his Son to die for us, lives to love and sustain us, and is preparing a place for us.

Meditations in the Meantime

DT 8:7-9

Do you think the children get restless while Moses is preaching these rather lengthy sermons? Do any of the women's minds wander to sorting the possessions they will bring with them into Canaan? Perhaps a few mothers are calculating the hazards of the journey ahead and anticipating how best to prepare their families. Moses periodically jolts the Israelites to attention with reminders of where they are going (Dt 6:3,10–11; 7:13–15; 8:7–9; 11:8–12). This land is abundant, fruitful, verdant. If they follow their God faithfully while living there, they will be happy and fulfilled. They will lack nothing.

These people certainly were not any less human than we are. Sometimes the daily details of life—sick children, overdrawn bank accounts and mounting piles of laundry—distract, discourage and trick us into believing that life is overwhelming or not very meaningful. Where are we headed? Can you picture it? Hope in the future is an important meditation while we live in the meantime.

22 The LORD your God will drive out those nations
before you, little by little.[y] You will not be allowed
to eliminate them all at once, or the wild animals
will multiply around you. 23 But the LORD your God
will deliver them over to you, throwing them into
great confusion until they are destroyed. 24 He will
give their kings into your hand, and you will wipe
out their names from under heaven. No one will
be able to stand up against you;[z] you will destroy
them. 25 The images of their gods you are to burn[a]
in the fire. Do not covet[b] the silver and gold on
them, and do not take it for yourselves, or you
will be ensnared[c] by it, for it is detestable[d] to the
LORD your God. 26 Do not bring a detestable thing
into your house or you, like it, will be set apart
for destruction.[e] Utterly abhor and detest it, for it
is set apart for destruction.

Do Not Forget the LORD

8 Be careful to follow every command I am giving you today, so that you may live[f] and
increase and may enter and possess the land that
the LORD promised on oath to your forefathers.
2 Remember how the LORD your God led[g] you all
the way in the desert these forty years, to humble
you and to test you in order to know what was in
your heart, whether or not you would keep his
commands. 3 He humbled you, causing you to
hunger and then feeding you with manna,[h] which
neither you nor your fathers had known, to teach
you that man does not live on bread alone but on
every word that comes from the mouth of the
LORD.[i] 4 Your clothes did not wear out and your
feet did not swell during these forty years.[j] 5 Know
then in your heart that as a man disciplines his
son, so the LORD your God disciplines you.[k]
6 Observe the commands of the LORD your God,
walking in his ways and revering him.[l] 7 For the
LORD your God is bringing you into a good land—
a land with streams and pools of water, with
springs flowing in the valleys and hills;[m] 8 a land
with wheat and barley, vines and fig trees, pomegranates, olive oil and honey; 9 a land where bread
will not be scarce and you will lack nothing; a
land where the rocks are iron and you can dig
copper out of the hills.
10 When you have eaten and are satisfied,[n] praise
the LORD your God for the good land he has given
you. 11 Be careful that you do not forget the LORD
your God, failing to observe his commands, his
laws and his decrees that I am giving you this day.
12 Otherwise, when you eat and are satisfied, when
you build fine houses and settle down,[o] 13 and when
your herds and flocks grow large and your silver
and gold increase and all you have is multiplied,
14 then your heart will become proud and you will
forget[p] the LORD your God, who brought you out of
Egypt, out of the land of slavery. 15 He led you
through the vast and dreadful desert,[q] that thirsty
and waterless land, with its venomous snakes[r] and
scorpions. He brought you water out of hard rock.[s]

7:22 [y]Ex 23:28-30
7:24 [z]Jos 23:9
7:25 [a]Ex 32:20; 1Ch 14:12 [b]Jos 7:21 [c]Jdg 8:27 [d]Dt 17:1
7:26 [e]Lev 27:28-29
8:1 [f]Dt 4:1
8:2 [g]Am 2:10
8:3 [h]Ex 16:12, 14,35 [i]Ex 16:2-3; Mt 4:4*; Lk 4:4*
8:4 [j]Dt 29:5; Ne 9:21
8:5 [k]2Sa 7:14; Pr 3:11-12; Heb 12:5-11; Rev 3:19
8:6 [l]Dt 5:33
8:7 [m]Dt 11:9-12
8:10 [n]Dt 6:10-12
8:12 [o]Hos 13:6
8:14 [p]Ps 106:21
8:15 [q]Jer 2:6 [r]Nu 21:6 [s]Nu 20:11; Ps 78:15; 114:8

16 He gave you manna to eat in the desert, some-
8:16 [t]Ex 16:15 thing your fathers had never known,[t] to humble
and to test you so that in the end it might go well
8:17 [u]Dt 9:4,7,24 with you. 17 You may say to yourself,[u] "My power
and the strength of my hands have produced this
wealth for me." 18 But remember the LORD your God,
for it is he who gives you the ability to produce
8:18 [v]Pr 10:22; wealth,[v] and so confirms his covenant, which he
Hos 2:8 swore to your forefathers, as it is today.
19 If you ever forget the LORD your God and follow other gods and worship and bow down to
them, I testify against you today that you will
8:19 [w]Dt 4:26; surely be destroyed.[w] 20 Like the nations the LORD
30:18 destroyed before you, so you will be destroyed for
not obeying the LORD your God.

Not Because of Israel's Righteousness

9 Hear, O Israel. You are now about to cross the
Jordan to go in and dispossess nations greater
9:1 [x]Dt 4:38; and stronger than you,[x] with large cities that have
11:23,31 walls up to the sky.[y] 2 The people are strong and
[y]Dt 1:28 tall—Anakites! You know about them and have
9:2 heard it said: "Who can stand up against the Ana-
[z]Nu 13:22, kites?"[z] 3 But be assured today that the LORD your
28,32-33 God is the one who goes across ahead of you[a] like
9:3 a devouring fire.[b] He will destroy them; he will
[a]Dt 31:3; subdue them before you. And you will drive them
Jos 3:11 [b]Dt 4:24; out and annihilate them quickly,[c] as the LORD has
Heb 12:29 promised you.
[c]Ex 23:31; Dt 7:23-24 4 After the LORD your God has driven them out
before you, do not say to yourself,[d] "The LORD has
9:4 [d]Dt 8:17 brought me here to take possession of this land
[e]Lev 18:21, because of my righteousness." No, it is on account
24-30; of the wickedness of these nations[e] that the LORD is
Dt 18:9-14 going to drive them out before you. 5 It is not
9:5 [f]Tit 3:5 because of your righteousness or your integrity[f]
[g]Ge 12:7; that you are going in to take possession of their
13:15; 15:7; land; but on account of the wickedness of these
17:8; 26:4 nations, the LORD your God will drive them out
before you, to accomplish what he swore[g] to your
fathers, to Abraham, Isaac and Jacob. 6 Understand,
then, that it is not because of your righteousness
9:6 that the LORD your God is giving you this good
[h]ver 13; land to possess, for you are a stiff-necked people.[h]
Ex 32:9; Dt 31:27

The Golden Calf

7 Remember this and never forget how you provoked the LORD your God to anger in the desert.
From the day you left Egypt until you arrived
here, you have been rebellious against the LORD.
8 At Horeb you aroused the LORD's wrath so that
9:8 he was angry enough to destroy you.[i] 9 When I
[i]Ex 32:7-10; went up on the mountain to receive the tablets of
Ps 106:19 stone, the tablets of the covenant that the LORD
9:9 had made with you, I stayed on the mountain
[j]Ex 24:12, forty days and forty nights; I ate no bread and
15,18; 34:28 drank no water.[j] 10 The LORD gave me two stone
9:10 tablets inscribed by the finger of God.[k] On them
[k]Ex 31:18; Dt 4:13 were all the commandments the LORD proclaimed

The Gift of Failure

DT 9:6

Moses reminds the Israelites that they are a "stiff-necked," stubborn and rebellious group of people. In fact, he charges that they have been "rebellious against the LORD" ever since he has known them" (Dt 9:24). He repeatedly reviews their dismal failures. Why? The book of Deuteronomy, although categorized as one of the law books, is a book about grace. Moses rehearses their failures with an admonition to remember and live differently in the grace of a second chance. They are unworthy of God's gift, but, out of grace, he gives it.

Failure has the potential to teach us that we must pay attention, that we need God, and that we must encourage one another to stay the course. We may stumble, but we certainly won't fall, because the Lord has us by the hand (Ps 37:23-24).

to you on the mountain out of the fire, on the day
of the assembly.
11 At the end of the forty days and forty nights,
the LORD gave me the two stone tablets, the tablets
of the covenant. 12 Then the LORD told me, "Go
down from here at once, because your people
whom you brought out of Egypt have become corrupt.[l] They have turned away quickly[m] from what
I commanded them and have made a cast idol for
themselves."
13 And the LORD said to me, "I have seen this
people[n], and they are a stiff-necked people indeed!
14 Let me alone,[o] so that I may destroy them and
blot out[p] their name from under heaven. And I
will make you into a nation stronger and more
numerous than they."
15 So I turned and went down from the mountain while it was ablaze with fire. And the two
tablets of the covenant were in my hands.[a][q]
16 When I looked, I saw that you had sinned
against the LORD your God; you had made for
yourselves an idol cast in the shape of a calf.[r] You
had turned aside quickly from the way that the
LORD had commanded you. 17 So I took the two
tablets and threw them out of my hands, breaking them to pieces before your eyes.
18 Then once again I fell[s] prostrate before the
LORD for forty days and forty nights; I ate no bread
and drank no water, because of all the sin you had
committed, doing what was evil in the LORD's
sight and so provoking him to anger. 19 I feared the
anger and wrath of the LORD, for he was angry
enough with you to destroy you.[t] But again the
LORD listened to me.[u] 20 And the LORD was angry
enough with Aaron to destroy him, but at that
time I prayed for Aaron too. 21 Also I took that sinful thing of yours, the calf you had made, and
burned it in the fire. Then I crushed it and ground
it to powder as fine as dust and threw the dust
into a stream that flowed down the mountain.[v]
22 You also made the LORD angry at Taberah,[w] at
Massah[x] and at Kibroth Hattaavah.[y]
23 And when the LORD sent you out from Kadesh
Barnea, he said, "Go up and take possession of the
land I have given you." But you rebelled against
the command of the LORD your God. You did not
trust[z] him or obey him. 24 You have been rebellious
against the LORD ever since I have known you.[a]
25 I lay prostrate before the LORD those forty days
and forty nights because the LORD had said he
would destroy you.[b] 26 I prayed to the LORD and said,
"O Sovereign LORD, do not destroy your people,
your own inheritance that you redeemed by your
great power and brought out of Egypt with a
mighty hand.[c] 27 Remember your servants Abraham, Isaac and Jacob. Overlook the stubbornness
of this people, their wickedness and their sin.
28 Otherwise, the country from which you brought

9:12 [l]Ex 32:7-8; Dt 31:29 [m]Jdg 2:17
9:13 [n]ver 6; Ex 32:9; Dt 10:16
9:14 [o]Ex 32:10 [p]Nu 14:12; Dt 29:20
9:15 [q]Ex 19:18; 32:15
9:16 [r]Ex 32:19
9:18 [s]Ex 34:28
9:19 [t]Ex 32:10-11, 14 [u]Dt 10:10
9:21 [v]Ex 32:20
9:22 [w]Nu 11:3 [x]Ex 17:7 [y]Nu 11:34
9:23 [z]Ps 106:24
9:24 [a]ver 7; Dt 31:27
9:25 [b]ver 18
9:26 [c]Ex 32:11

Nobody can deny but religion is a comfort to the distressed, a cordial to the sick, and sometimes a restraint on the wicked; therefore, whoever would laugh or argue it out of the world, without giving some equivalent for it, ought to be treated as a common enemy.

—Mary Wortley Montagu (1689–1762)

[a] *15* Or *And I had the two tablets of the covenant with me, one in each hand*

us will say, 'Because the LORD was not able to take
them into the land he had promised them, and
because he hated them, he brought them out to put
them to death in the desert.'[d] 29 But they are your
people, your inheritance[e] that you brought out by
your great power and your outstretched arm.[f]"

Tablets Like the First Ones

10 At that time the LORD said to me, "Chisel out
two stone tablets[g] like the first ones and
come up to me on the mountain. Also make a
wooden chest.[a] 2 I will write on the tablets the
words that were on the first tablets, which you
broke. Then you are to put them in the chest."[h]
3 So I made the ark out of acacia wood[i] and chiseled[j] out two stone tablets like the first ones, and I
went up on the mountain with the two tablets in
my hands. 4 The LORD wrote on these tablets what
he had written before, the Ten Commandments he
had proclaimed[k] to you on the mountain, out of the
fire, on the day of the assembly. And the LORD gave
them to me. 5 Then I came back down the mountain[l] and put the tablets in the ark[m] I had made, as
the LORD commanded me, and they are there now.[n]
6 (The Israelites traveled from the wells of the
Jaakanites to Moserah.[o] There Aaron died and
was buried, and Eleazar his son succeeded him as
priest.[p] 7 From there they traveled to Gudgodah
and on to Jotbathah, a land with streams of
water.[q] 8 At that time the LORD set apart the tribe of
Levi[r] to carry the ark of the covenant of the LORD,
to stand before the LORD to minister[s] and to pronounce blessings[t] in his name, as they still do
today. 9 That is why the Levites have no share or
inheritance among their brothers; the LORD is their
inheritance,[u] as the LORD your God told them.)
10 Now I had stayed on the mountain forty days
and nights, as I did the first time, and the LORD listened to me at this time also. It was not his will to
destroy you.[v] 11 "Go," the LORD said to me, "and
lead the people on their way, so that they may
enter and possess the land that I swore to their
fathers to give them."

Fear the LORD

12 And now, O Israel, what does the LORD your
God ask of you[w] but to fear the LORD your God, to
walk in all his ways, to love him,[x] to serve the
LORD your God with all your heart[y] and with all
your soul, 13 and to observe the LORD's commands
and decrees that I am giving you today for your
own good?
14 To the LORD your God belong the heavens, even
the highest heavens,[z] the earth and everything in
it.[a] 15 Yet the LORD set his affection on your forefathers and loved[b] them, and he chose you, their
descendants, above all the nations, as it is today.
16 Circumcise[c] your hearts, therefore, and do not be
stiff-necked[d] any longer. 17 For the LORD your God is

9:28 [d]Ex 32:12; Nu 14:16
9:29 [e]Dt 4:20; 1Ki 8:51 [f]Dt 4:34; Ne 1:10
10:1 [g]Ex 25:10; 34:1-2
10:2 [h]Ex 25:16, 21; Dt 4:13
10:3 [i]Ex 25:5,10; 37:1-9 [j]Ex 34:4
10:4 [k]Ex 20:1
10:5 [l]Ex 34:29 [m]Ex 40:20 [n]1Ki 8:9
10:6 [o]Nu 33:30-31,38 [p]Nu 20:25-28
10:7 [q]Nu 33:32-34
10:8 [r]Nu 3:6 [s]Dt 18:5 [t]Dt 21:5
10:9 [u]Nu 18:20; Dt 18:1-2; Eze 44:28
10:10 [v]Ex 33:17; 34:28; Dt 9:18-19, 25
10:12 [w]Mic 6:8 [x]Dt 5:33; 6:13; Mt 22:37 [y]Dt 6:5
10:14 [z]1Ki 8:27 [a]Ex 19:5
10:15 [b]Dt 4:37
10:16 [c]Jer 4:4 [d]Dt 9:6

[a] *1* That is, an ark

Energy of the Heart

DT 10:12–13

Once again Moses emphasizes that the whole law is summed up in loving God wholeheartedly. Moses repeatedly cautions the Israelites about where they spend the passion or energy of their hearts. The Israelites have already demonstrated how quickly their passion for God can be twisted and turned into a passion for a mere golden calf. Their hearts are still divided—not given wholly to God. When we give ourselves, heart and soul, wholly to God, there is no "heart" left for twisting or turning—all our being is tuned, passionately, to love for God.

Heart Surgery

DT 10:16

Moses uses vivid imagery to instruct the Israelites on how to care for their hearts. He suggests that they "circumcise" their hearts, and they know what he means: to cut away all things that might restrict, interfere or diminish their spiritual lives. Often those who suffer debilitating physical heart disease do not detect it until the damage is irreparable. When heart pains send them to the emergency room, they are shocked and frightened to learn that only part of their heart is functioning. Spiritually, we too may walk around with a heart that is diseased and deadened—living far below the level at which God designed us to function—without even realizing it. Look inward and see if anything can be cut away to strengthen your heart for God.

God of gods[e] and Lord of lords, the great God,
mighty and awesome, who shows no partiality[f]
and accepts no bribes. 18He defends the cause of
the fatherless and the widow,[g] and loves the alien,
giving him food and clothing. 19And you are to
love those who are aliens, for you yourselves were
aliens in Egypt.[h] 20Fear the LORD your God and
serve him.[i] Hold fast[j] to him and take your oaths
in his name.[k] 21He is your praise;[l] he is your God,
who performed for you those great and awesome
wonders[m] you saw with your own eyes. 22Your
forefathers who went down into Egypt were seventy in all,[n] and now the LORD your God has made
you as numerous as the stars in the sky.[o]

Love and Obey the LORD

11 Love[p] the LORD your God and keep his
requirements, his decrees, his laws and his
commands always.[q] 2Remember today that your
children were not the ones who saw and experienced the discipline of the LORD your God:[r] his
majesty, his mighty hand, his outstretched arm;
3the signs he performed and the things he did in
the heart of Egypt, both to Pharaoh king of Egypt
and to his whole country; 4what he did to the Egyptian army, to its horses and chariots, how he overwhelmed them with the waters of the Red Sea[a][s] as
they were pursuing you, and how the LORD brought
lasting ruin on them. 5It was not your children who
saw what he did for you in the desert until you
arrived at this place, 6and what he did[t] to Dathan
and Abiram, sons of Eliab the Reubenite, when the
earth opened its mouth right in the middle of all
Israel and swallowed them up with their households, their tents and every living thing that
belonged to them. 7But it was your own eyes that
saw all these great things the LORD has done.

8Observe therefore all the commands I am giving you today, so that you may have the strength
to go in and take over the land that you are crossing the Jordan to possess,[u] 9and so that you may
live long[v] in the land that the LORD swore[w] to your
forefathers to give to them and their descendants,
a land flowing with milk and honey.[x] 10The land
you are entering to take over is not like the land of
Egypt, from which you have come, where you
planted your seed and irrigated it by foot as in a
vegetable garden. 11But the land you are crossing
the Jordan to take possession of is a land of mountains and valleys that drinks rain from heaven.[y]
12It is a land the LORD your God cares for; the eyes[z]
of the LORD your God are continually on it from
the beginning of the year to its end.

13So if you faithfully obey[a] the commands I am
giving you today—to love[b] the LORD your God and
to serve him with all your heart and with all your
soul— 14then I will send rain[c] on your land in its
season, both autumn and spring rains,[d] so that
you may gather in your grain, new wine and oil.

10:17 [e]Jos 22:22; Da 2:47 [f]Ac 10:34; Ro 2:11; Eph 6:9
10:18 [g]Ps 68:5
10:19 [h]Lev 19:34
10:20 [i]Mt 4:10 [j]Dt 11:22 [k]Ps 63:11
10:21 [l]Ex 15:2; Jer 17:14 [m]Ps 106:21-22
10:22 [n]Ge 46:26-27 [o]Ge 15:5; Dt 1:10
11:1 [p]Dt 10:12 [q]Zec 3:7
11:2 [r]Dt 5:24; 8:5
11:4 [s]Ex 14:27
11:6 [t]Nu 16:1-35
11:8 [u]Jos 1:7
11:9 [v]Dt 4:40; Pr 10:27 [w]Dt 9:5 [x]Ex 3:8
11:11 [y]Dt 8:7
11:12 [z]1Ki 9:3
11:13 [a]Dt 6:17 [b]Dt 10:12
11:14 [c]Lev 26:4; Dt 28:12 [d]Joel 2:23; Jas 5:7

[a] 4 Hebrew *Yam Suph*; that is, Sea of Reeds

15I will provide grass[e] in the fields for your cattle,
and you will eat and be satisfied.[f]
16Be careful, or you will be enticed to turn away
and worship other gods and bow down to them.[g]
17Then the LORD's anger[h] will burn against you, and
he will shut[i] the heavens so that it will not rain and
the ground will yield no produce, and you will
soon perish[j] from the good land the LORD is giving
you. 18Fix these words of mine in your hearts and
minds; tie them as symbols on your hands and
bind them on your foreheads.[k] 19Teach them to
your children,[l] talking about them when you sit at
home and when you walk along the road, when
you lie down and when you get up.[m] 20Write them
on the doorframes of your houses and on your
gates,[n] 21so that your days and the days of your children may be many[o] in the land that the LORD swore
to give your forefathers, as many as the days that
the heavens are above the earth.[p]
22If you carefully observe[q] all these commands I
am giving you to follow—to love the LORD your
God, to walk in all his ways and to hold fast[r] to
him— 23then the LORD will drive out all these
nations before you, and you will dispossess nations
larger and stronger than you.[s] 24Every place where
you set your foot will be yours:[t] Your territory will
extend from the desert to Lebanon, and from the
Euphrates River to the western sea.[a] 25No man will
be able to stand against you. The LORD your God, as
he promised you, will put the terror and fear of you
on the whole land, wherever you go.[u]
26See, I am setting before you today a blessing
and a curse[v]— 27the blessing[w] if you obey the
commands of the LORD your God that I am giving
you today; 28the curse if you disobey[x] the commands of the LORD your God and turn from the
way that I command you today by following other gods, which you have not known. 29When the
LORD your God has brought you into the land you
are entering to possess, you are to proclaim on
Mount Gerizim the blessings, and on Mount Ebal
the curses.[y] 30As you know, these mountains are
across the Jordan, west of the road,[b] toward the
setting sun, near the great trees of Moreh,[z] in the
territory of those Canaanites living in the Arabah
in the vicinity of Gilgal.[a] 31You are about to cross
the Jordan to enter and take possession[b] of the
land the LORD your God is giving you. When you
have taken it over and are living there, 32be sure
that you obey all the decrees and laws I am setting before you today.

The One Place of Worship

12 These are the decrees and laws you must be
careful to follow in the land that the LORD,
the God of your fathers, has given you to possess—as long as you live in the land.[c] 2Destroy
completely all the places on the high mountains
and on the hills and under every spreading tree[d]

11:15 [e]Ps 104:14 [f]Dt 6:11
11:16 [g]Dt 8:19; 29:18; Job 31:9,27
11:17 [h]Dt 6:15 [i]1Ki 8:35; 2Ch 6:26 [j]Dt 4:26
11:18 [k]Dt 6:6-8
11:19 [l]Dt 6:7 [m]Dt 4:9-10
11:20 [n]Dt 6:9
11:21 [o]Pr 3:2; 4:10 [p]Ps 72:5
11:22 [q]Dt 6:17 [r]Dt 10:20
11:23 [s]Dt 4:38; 9:1
11:24 [t]Ge 15:18; Ex 23:31; Jos 1:3; 14:9
11:25 [u]Ex 23:27; Dt 7:24
11:26 [v]Dt 30:1,15,19
11:27 [w]Dt 28:1-14
11:28 [x]Dt 28:15
11:29 [y]Dt 27:12-13; Jos 8:33
11:30 [z]Ge 12:6 [a]Jos 4:19
11:31 [b]Dt 9:1; Jos 1:11
12:1 [c]Dt 4:9-10; 1Ki 8:40
12:2 [d]2Ki 16:4; 17:10

Search the Scriptures

DT 12:1

In Deuteronomy 12-26 Moses gives specific instructions for the Israelites to live in obedience to God and to successfully inhabit Canaan. Some of these commandments seem strange and irrelevant to us, such as, "Make tassels on the four corners of the cloak you wear" (Dt 22:12). These peculiar laws and Moses' encouragement that blessing will follow obeying these laws raise two questions: (1) Does God intend for *us* to follow these commands? and (2) Is success guaranteed to those who obey? Answer these questions for yourself as you read these chapters looking for: (1) themes or principles throughout the instructions that are unchangeable regardless of time or culture; and (2) God's definition of "success."

[a] *24* That is, the Mediterranean [b] *30* Or *Jordan, westward*

Week 4

God's Dwelling Place

God has given precise details to Moses regarding offerings, sacrifices and tithes. Yet at this point in Israel's history, God has not told the Israelites where they will worship him. He says he himself will choose the place where his Name will dwell (Dt 12:5,11; 16:2,6,11; 26:2).

What is the symbol of God's presence (Lev 16:2; Nu 7:89)?

What place does God choose as his sanctuary so that he can dwell with his people (Ex 25:8–9)? What place does God choose as a more permanent dwelling for his Name (2Ch 6:2; 7:11–12)? How did God dwell among the disciples (Jn 1:14)?

Where does God dwell now (1Co 3:16–17)? Aren't you amazed? God chooses where he will dwell, and he has chosen to live in you!

What does Jesus say regarding the place true worshipers will worship (Jn 4:21–23)? How will God be worshiped by true worshipers (Jn 4:24)?

Enjoying God THROUGH the Word

Read Exodus 25:17–22 and Exodus 26:31–34 (pages 127 and 129). These passages describe the ark, the curtain separating the Holy Place from the Most Holy Place and the Most Holy Place itself, where God meets with Moses. Notice the dimensions of the court: 150 feet; the Holy Place: 30 feet; and the Most Holy Place: 15 feet. Each location gets successively smaller. The court has to be large because many worshipers gather there. The Holy Place is smaller because only priests can enter. And the Most Holy Place is smallest—only the high priest can enter. Each location brings the worshiper closer to the actual presence of God.

The curtain separating the Holy Place from the Most Holy Place shields the ark (the symbol of God's presence) from view. This shield not only keeps the priests from seeing God's glory, but also prevents God's glory from being in the presence of sin, which would mean certain death for those in the tabernacle. At Christ's death, this curtain was wondrously torn in two from top to bottom (Mt 27:51). All believers today, not just the high priest, have access to the Most Holy Place because of the shed blood of Jesus (Heb 10:19–20). Christ's blood covers sin and allows believers full access to and intimacy with Almighty God.

Does your busyness in the work of the outer court keep you from worship? Do you long to worship your Lord in the Holy Place? Are you yearning for the intimacy of the Most Holy Place?

Enjoying God THROUGH Experience

God has cleared the way for you to enter his presence. Ask the Holy Spirit to move in you with such intensity that you will no longer be content to remain in either the outer court or the Holy Place but will be satisfied only with the full intimacy of the Most Holy Place.

Picture Jesus standing between the Holy Place and the Most Holy Place with his arms outstretched, his hands holding the edges of the torn curtain. If you desire to go beyond the curtain, you must walk into his arms. When you do, his arms will enfold you, drawing the edges of the curtain around you, closing you off from everything but his presence. Nothing else will matter. You will be complete in him, enjoying his presence and love.

Go to page 337 for your next weekly study.

where the nations you are dispossessing worship
their gods. 3Break down their altars, smash[e] their
sacred stones and burn their Asherah poles in the
fire; cut down the idols of their gods and wipe out
their names from those places.
4You must not worship the LORD your God in
their way. 5But you are to seek the place the LORD
your God will choose from among all your tribes
to put his Name there for his dwelling.[f] To that
place you must go; 6there bring your burnt offerings and sacrifices, your tithes[g] and special gifts,
what you have vowed to give and your freewill
offerings, and the firstborn of your herds and
flocks. 7There, in the presence of the LORD your
God, you and your families shall eat and shall
rejoice[h] in everything you have put your hand to,
because the LORD your God has blessed you.
8You are not to do as we do here today, everyone as he sees fit, 9since you have not yet reached
the resting place and the inheritance the LORD
your God is giving you. 10But you will cross the
Jordan and settle in the land the LORD your God
is giving[i] you as an inheritance, and he will give
you rest from all your enemies around you so that
you will live in safety. 11Then to the place the LORD
your God will choose as a dwelling for his
Name[j]—there you are to bring everything I command you: your burnt offerings and sacrifices,
your tithes and special gifts, and all the choice
possessions you have vowed to the LORD. 12And
there rejoice[k] before the LORD your God, you, your
sons and daughters, your menservants and maidservants, and the Levites from your towns, who
have no allotment or inheritance[l] of their own.
13Be careful not to sacrifice your burnt offerings
anywhere you please. 14Offer them only at the
place the LORD will choose[m] in one of your tribes,
and there observe everything I command you.
15Nevertheless, you may slaughter your animals
in any of your towns and eat as much of the meat
as you want, as if it were gazelle or deer,[n] according to the blessing the LORD your God gives you.
Both the ceremonially unclean and the clean may
eat it. 16But you must not eat the blood;[o] pour it
out on the ground like water.[p] 17You must not eat
in your own towns the tithe of your grain and
new wine and oil, or the firstborn of your herds
and flocks, or whatever you have vowed to give,
or your freewill offerings or special gifts.
18Instead, you are to eat[q] them in the presence of
the LORD your God at the place the LORD your God
will choose[r]—you, your sons and daughters, your
menservants and maidservants, and the Levites
from your towns—and you are to rejoice[s] before
the LORD your God in everything you put your
hand to. 19Be careful not to neglect the Levites[t] as
long as you live in your land.
20When the LORD your God has enlarged your
territory[u] as he promised[v] you, and you crave
meat and say, "I would like some meat," then you
may eat as much of it as you want. 21If the place

12:3 [e]Nu 33:52; Dt 7:5; Jdg 2:2
12:5 [f]ver 11,13; 2Ch 7:12,16
12:6 [g]Dt 14:22-23
12:7 [h]ver 12,18; Lev 23:40; Dt 14:26
12:10 [i]Dt 11:31
12:11 [j]ver 5; Dt 15:20; 16:2
12:12 [k]ver 7 [l]Dt 10:9; 14:29
12:14 [m]ver 11
12:15 [n]ver 20-23; Dt 14:5; 15:22
12:16 [o]Ge 9:4; Lev 7:26; 17:10-12 [p]Dt 15:23
12:18 [q]Dt 14:23 [r]ver 5 [s]ver 7,12
12:19 [t]Dt 14:27
12:20 [u]Dt 19:8 [v]Ge 15:18; Dt 11:24

A Land Full of Idols

DT 12:3

One theme in the instructions of Moses is to avoid idolatry at all costs. This is a big task for the Israelites because their land is "full of idols" (Isa 2:8). God hates idolatry because it replaces him as the pivotal point of the universe and their lives. It results in defeat, emptiness and danger for the idol worshiper.

Idolatry is present whenever we bend our hearts toward any person, behavior or idea other than God. How much better to choose with the psalmist: "I will praise you, O LORD, with all my heart; before the 'gods' I will sing your praise. I will bow down toward your holy temple and will praise your name for your love and your faithfulness, for you have exalted above all things your name and your word" (Ps 138:1-2).

Sacrificing Children

DT 12:31

One of the unthinkable practices of some of Israel's neighboring cultures is burning their children as sacrifices to idols in hopes of improving their quality of life. Why does God have to warn his *own* people about sacrificing *their* children? Unbelievable! Unthinkable! But, unfortunately, not impossible (Jer 19:5). God knows his people seldom jump into idolatry with both feet. Most often they slowly, subtly and gradually wade into idolatry as they make choices about where they will spend their passion.

Are we guilty of the unthinkable? Do we sacrifice our children to pleasure, work or even ministry in hopes of an improved quality of life? This might be a good place to jot down some prayerful thoughts about God's picture of a "successful" family.

where the LORD your God chooses to put his Name
is too far away from you, you may slaughter animals from the herds and flocks the LORD has giv-
en you, as I have commanded you, and in your
own towns you may eat as much of them as you
want. 22Eat them as you would gazelle or deer.[w]
Both the ceremonially unclean and the clean may
eat. 23But be sure you do not eat the blood,[x]
because the blood is the life, and you must not eat
the life with the meat. 24You must not eat the
blood; pour it out on the ground like water. 25Do
not eat it, so that it may go well[y] with you and
your children after you, because you will be doing
what is right[z] in the eyes of the LORD.
26But take your consecrated things and whatever you have vowed to give,[a] and go to the place
the LORD will choose. 27Present your burnt offerings[b] on the altar of the LORD your God, both the
meat and the blood. The blood of your sacrifices
must be poured beside the altar of the LORD your
God, but you may eat the meat. 28Be careful to
obey all these regulations I am giving you, so that
it may always go well[c] with you and your children
after you, because you will be doing what is good
and right in the eyes of the LORD your God.
29The LORD your God will cut off[d] before you the
nations you are about to invade and dispossess.
But when you have driven them out and settled
in their land, 30and after they have been destroyed
before you, be careful not to be ensnared by
inquiring about their gods, saying, "How do these
nations serve their gods? We will do the same."
31You must not worship the LORD your God in their
way, because in worshiping their gods, they do all
kinds of detestable things the LORD hates.[e] They
even burn their sons[f] and daughters in the fire as
sacrifices to their gods.
32See that you do all I command you; do not
add[g] to it or take away from it.

Worshiping Other Gods

13 If a prophet,[h] or one who foretells by
dreams, appears among you and announces
to you a miraculous sign or wonder, 2and if the
sign or wonder of which he has spoken takes
place, and he says, "Let us follow other gods"[i]
(gods you have not known) "and let us worship
them," 3you must not listen to the words of that
prophet or dreamer. The LORD your God is testing[j]
you to find out whether you love him with all
your heart and with all your soul. 4It is the LORD
your God you must follow,[k] and him you must
revere. Keep his commands and obey him; serve
him and hold fast[l] to him. 5That prophet or
dreamer must be put to death, because he
preached rebellion against the LORD your God,
who brought you out of Egypt and redeemed you
from the land of slavery; he has tried to turn you
from the way the LORD your God commanded you
to follow. You must purge the evil[m] from among
you.

12:22 [w]ver 15
12:23 [x]ver 16; Ge 9:4; Lev 17:11,14
12:25 [y]Dt 4:40; Isa 3:10 [z]Ex 15:26; Dt 13:18; 1Ki 11:38
12:26 [a]ver 17; Nu 5:9-10
12:27 [b]Lev 1:5,9, 13
12:28 [c]ver 25; Dt 4:40
12:29 [d]Jos 23:4
12:31 [e]Dt 9:5 [f]Dt 18:10; Jer 32:35
12:32 [g]Dt 4:2; Jos 1:7; Rev 22:18-19
13:1 [h]Mt 24:24; Mk 13:22; 2Th 2:9
13:2 [i]ver 6,13
13:3 [j]Dt 8:2,16
13:4 [k]2Ki 23:3; 2Ch 34:31 [l]Dt 10:20
13:5 [m]Dt 17:7,12; 1Co 5:13

6If your very own brother, or your son or
13:6 daughter, or the wife you love, or your closest
[n]Dt 17:2-7; friend secretly entices[n] you, saying, "Let us go and
29:18 worship other gods" (gods that neither you nor
your fathers have known, 7gods of the peoples
13:8 around you, whether near or far, from one end of
[o]Pr 1:10 the land to the other), 8do not yield[o] to him or listen to him. Show him no pity. Do not spare him or
13:9 shield him. 9You must certainly put him to death.[p]
[p]Dt 17:5,7 Your hand must be the first in putting him to
death, and then the hands of all the people.
10Stone him to death, because he tried to turn you
away from the LORD your God, who brought you
13:11 out of Egypt, out of the land of slavery. 11Then all
[q]Dt 19:20 Israel will hear and be afraid,[q] and no one among
you will do such an evil thing again.
12If you hear it said about one of the towns the
13:13 LORD your God is giving you to live in 13that
[r]ver 2,6; wicked men[r] have arisen among you and have led
1Jn 2:19 the people of their town astray, saying, "Let us go
and worship other gods" (gods you have not
known), 14then you must inquire, probe and
investigate it thoroughly. And if it is true and it
has been proved that this detestable thing has
been done among you, 15you must certainly put
to the sword all who live in that town. Destroy it
completely,[a] both its people and its livestock.
16Gather all the plunder of the town into the middle of the public square and completely burn the
town and all its plunder as a whole burnt offer-
13:16 ing to the LORD your God.[s] It is to remain a ruin[t]
[s]Jos 6:24 [t]Jos 8:28; forever, never to be rebuilt. 17None of those con-
Jer 49:2 demned things[a] shall be found in your hands, so
13:17 that the LORD will turn from his fierce anger;[u] he
[u]Nu 25:4 will show you mercy, have compassion[v] on you,
[v]Dt 30:3 [w]Dt 7:13 and increase your numbers,[w] as he promised[x] on
[x]Ge 22:17; oath to your forefathers, 18because you obey the
26:4,24; LORD your God, keeping all his commands that I
28:14 am giving you today and doing what is right[y] in
13:18 [y]Dt 12:25,28 his eyes.

Clean and Unclean Food

14:1 **14** You are the children[z] of the LORD your God.
[z]Lev 19:28; 21:5; Do not cut yourselves or shave the front of
Jer 16:6; your heads for the dead, 2for you are a people holy
41:5; to the LORD your God.[a] Out of all the peoples on
Ro 8:14; 9:8; Gal 3:26 the face of the earth, the LORD has chosen you to
14:2 be his treasured possession.[b]
[a]Lev 20:26 3Do not eat any detestable thing.[c] 4These are the
[b]Dt 7:6; animals you may eat:[d] the ox, the sheep, the goat,
26:18-19 5the deer, the gazelle, the roe deer, the wild goat,
14:3 the ibex, the antelope and the mountain sheep.[b]
[c]Eze 4:14 6You may eat any animal that has a split hoof
14:4 divided in two and that chews the cud. 7However,
[d]Lev 11:2-45; of those that chew the cud or that have a split
Ac 10:14 hoof completely divided you may not eat the

[a] *15,17* The Hebrew term refers to the irrevocable giving over of things or persons to the LORD, often by totally destroying them. [b] *5* The precise identification of some of the birds and animals in this chapter is uncertain.

Tough Words

DT 13:6-10

If the Israelites ever wonder if God means what he says about worshiping other Gods, these words dispel any doubts. Moses tells them: If anyone "entices" (the word has the sense of allure, of fascination) you to worship other gods, don't show pity and don't protect that person. Whoever it is must be put to death—even if it's your mom or your husband or one of your children.

God tells his people he is a jealous God (Ex 34:14). He will allow devotion to no one except himself. And why shouldn't he? After all, as Moses asserts several times, those other gods are false and powerless. But this jealous God is the only God, the one who holds the power of life and death and healing in his hands (Dt 32:39).

camel, the rabbit or the coney.[a] Although they chew the cud, they do not have a split hoof; they are ceremonially unclean for you. 8The pig is also unclean; although it has a split hoof, it does not chew the cud. You are not to eat their meat or touch their carcasses.[e]

9Of all the creatures living in the water, you may eat any that has fins and scales. 10But anything that does not have fins and scales you may not eat; for you it is unclean.

11You may eat any clean bird. 12But these you may not eat: the eagle, the vulture, the black vulture, 13the red kite, the black kite, any kind of falcon, 14any kind of raven, 15the horned owl, the screech owl, the gull, any kind of hawk, 16the little owl, the great owl, the white owl, 17the desert owl, the osprey, the cormorant, 18the stork, any kind of heron, the hoopoe and the bat.

19All flying insects that swarm are unclean to you; do not eat them. 20But any winged creature that is clean you may eat.

21Do not eat anything you find already dead.[f] You may give it to an alien living in any of your towns, and he may eat it, or you may sell it to a foreigner. But you are a people holy to the LORD your God.[g]

Do not cook a young goat in its mother's milk.[h]

Tithes

22Be sure to set aside a tenth[i] of all that your fields produce each year. 23Eat the tithe of your grain, new wine and oil, and the firstborn of your herds and flocks in the presence of the LORD your God at the place he will choose as a dwelling for his Name,[j] so that you may learn[k] to revere the LORD your God always. 24But if that place is too distant and you have been blessed by the LORD your God and cannot carry your tithe (because the place where the LORD will choose to put his Name is so far away), 25then exchange your tithe for silver, and take the silver with you and go to the place the LORD your God will choose. 26Use the silver to buy whatever you like: cattle, sheep, wine or other fermented drink, or anything you wish. Then you and your household shall eat there in the presence of the LORD your God and rejoice.[l] 27And do not neglect the Levites[m] living in your towns, for they have no allotment or inheritance of their own.[n]

28At the end of every three years, bring all the tithes of that year's produce and store it in your towns,[o] 29so that the Levites (who have no allotment[p] or inheritance of their own) and the aliens,[q] the fatherless and the widows who live in your towns may come and eat and be satisfied, and so that the LORD your God may bless[r] you in all the work of your hands.

The Year for Canceling Debts

15 At the end of every seven years you must cancel debts.[s] 2This is how it is to be done:

[a] 7 That is, the hyrax or rock badger

14:8 [e]Lev 11:26-27
14:21 [f]Lev 17:15; 22:8 [g]ver 2 [h]Ex 23:19; 34:26
14:22 [i]Lev 27:30; Dt 12:6,17; Ne 10:37
14:23 [j]Dt 12:5 [k]Dt 4:10
14:26 [l]Dt 12:7-8
14:27 [m]Dt 12:19 [n]Nu 18:20
14:28 [o]Dt 26:12
14:29 [p]ver 27 [q]Dt 26:12 [r]Dt 15:10; Mal 3:10
15:1 [s]Dt 31:10

Sunshine let it be, or frost,
Storm or calm, as Thou shalt choose;
Though Thine every gift were lost,
Thee Thyself we cannot lose.

—Mary Elizabeth Coleridge (1861-1907)

Every creditor shall cancel the loan he has made
to his fellow Israelite. He shall not require payment from his fellow Israelite or brother, because
the LORD's time for canceling debts has been proclaimed. 3You may require payment from a for-
15:3 tDt 23:20 eigner,[t] but you must cancel any debt your brother owes you. 4However, there should be no poor
among you, for in the land the LORD your God is
15:4 giving you to possess as your inheritance, he will
uDt 28:8 richly bless[u] you, 5if only you fully obey the LORD
15:5 your God and are careful to follow[v] all these com-
vDt 28:1 mands I am giving you today. 6For the LORD your
God will bless you as he has promised, and you
will lend to many nations but will borrow from
none. You will rule over many nations but none
15:6 wDt 28:12-13,44 will rule over you.[w]
7If there is a poor man among your brothers in
any of the towns of the land that the LORD your
15:7 God is giving you, do not be hardhearted or tight-
x1Jn 3:17 fisted[x] toward your poor brother. 8Rather be
15:8 openhanded[y] and freely lend him whatever he
yMt 5:42; Lk 6:34 needs. 9Be careful not to harbor this wicked
thought: "The seventh year, the year for canceling
15:9 debts,[z] is near," so that you do not show ill will[a]
zver 1 toward your needy brother and give him nothing.
aMt 20:15 He may then appeal to the LORD against you, and
bDt 24:15 you will be found guilty of sin.[b] 10Give generous-
15:10 ly to him and do so without a grudging heart;[c]
c2Co 9:5 dDt 14:29; 24:19 then because of this the LORD your God will bless[d]
you in all your work and in everything you put
your hand to. 11There will always be poor people
in the land. Therefore I command you to be open-
15:11 handed toward your brothers and toward the poor
eMt 26:11; Mk 14:7; Jn 12:8 and needy in your land.[e]

Freeing Servants

12If a fellow Hebrew, a man or a woman, sells
15:12 himself to you and serves you six years, in the
fEx 21:2; Lev 25:39; Jer 34:14 seventh year you must let him go free.[f] 13And
when you release him, do not send him away
empty-handed. 14Supply him liberally from your
flock, your threshing floor and your winepress.
Give to him as the LORD your God has blessed you.
15:15 gDt 5:15 15Remember that you were slaves[g] in Egypt and
hDt 16:12 the LORD your God redeemed you.[h] That is why I
give you this command today.
16But if your servant says to you, "I do not want
to leave you," because he loves you and your family and is well off with you, 17then take an awl
and push it through his ear lobe into the door, and
he will become your servant for life. Do the same
for your maidservant.
18Do not consider it a hardship to set your servant free, because his service to you these six
years has been worth twice as much as that of a
hired hand. And the LORD your God will bless you
in everything you do.

The Firstborn Animals

19Set apart for the LORD your God every firstborn

A Living Sacrifice

DT 15:16-17

Moses reminds the Israelites of Hebrew law and reveals a wonderful picture of wholehearted service to God. Hebrews enslaved by Hebrews are to be released after six years (Dt 15:12). A slave, however, might choose a lifetime of service. This commitment is marked by piercing the ear of the slave in a ceremony at the door of the master's house. A lifelong commitment to service ensures the security of the slave, gives stability and security to his or her family, and testifies to a consecrated relationship between the slave and the master. The commitment is voluntary. The apostle Paul exhorts us to make a similar commitment: "Offer your bodies as living sacrifices, holy and pleasing to God—this is your spiritual act of worship" (Ro 12:1).

Festivals for Families

DT 16:1-17

The Israelites had a lot of feasts, ceremonies and festivals—rituals. Why? Although very different from our times and lives, they struggled, too, with balancing family, work, rest and worship. The many rituals of the Hebrew people link them together through shared tradition. These rituals powerfully affect families, giving them a respite from the ordinary, everyday tasks that make up their world, reminding them of who they are as a people, what they believe and how they want to live. These festivals strengthen the fabric of their society at every level: family, neighborhood, town, religious, civic.

What rituals do you already have as a family or civic or religious community? How can you build on and strengthen those rituals? What new rituals might benefit your family? Your community? Your church?

male[i] of your herds and flocks. Do not put the firstborn of your oxen to work, and do not shear the firstborn of your sheep. 20 Each year you and your family are to eat them in the presence of the LORD your God at the place he will choose.[j] 21 If an animal has a defect, is lame or blind, or has any serious flaw, you must not sacrifice it to the LORD your God.[k] 22 You are to eat it in your own towns. Both the ceremonially unclean and the clean may eat it, as if it were gazelle or deer.[l] 23 But you must not eat the blood; pour it out on the ground like water.[m]

Passover

16 Observe the month of Abib[n] and celebrate the Passover of the LORD your God, because in the month of Abib he brought you out of Egypt by night. 2 Sacrifice as the Passover to the LORD your God an animal from your flock or herd at the place the LORD will choose as a dwelling for his Name.[o] 3 Do not eat it with bread made with yeast, but for seven days eat unleavened bread, the bread of affliction,[p] because you left Egypt in haste[q]—so that all the days of your life you may remember the time of your departure from Egypt.[r] 4 Let no yeast be found in your possession in all your land for seven days. Do not let any of the meat you sacrifice on the evening of the first day remain until morning.[s]

5 You must not sacrifice the Passover in any town the LORD your God gives you 6 except in the place he will choose as a dwelling for his Name. There you must sacrifice the Passover in the evening, when the sun goes down, on the anniversary[a][t] of your departure from Egypt. 7 Roast[u] it and eat it at the place the LORD your God will choose. Then in the morning return to your tents. 8 For six days eat unleavened bread and on the seventh day hold an assembly[v] to the LORD your God and do no work.

Feast of Weeks

9 Count off seven weeks[w] from the time you begin to put the sickle to the standing grain.[x] 10 Then celebrate the Feast of Weeks to the LORD your God by giving a freewill offering in proportion to the blessings the LORD your God has given you. 11 And rejoice[y] before the LORD your God at the place he will choose as a dwelling for his Name—you, your sons and daughters, your menservants and maidservants, the Levites[z] in your towns, and the aliens, the fatherless and the widows living among you. 12 Remember that you were slaves in Egypt,[a] and follow carefully these decrees.

Feast of Tabernacles

13 Celebrate the Feast of Tabernacles for seven days after you have gathered the produce of your threshing floor[b] and your winepress.[c] 14 Be joyful[d] at your Feast—you, your sons and daughters, your

15:19 [i]Ex 13:2
15:20 [j]Dt 12:5-7, 17,18; 14:23
15:21 [k]Lev 22:19-25
15:22 [l]Dt 12:15,22
15:23 [m]Dt 12:16
16:1 [n]Ex 12:2; 13:4
16:2 [o]Dt 12:5,26
16:3 [p]Ex 12:8,39; 34:18 [q]Ex 12:11, 15,19 [r]Ex 13:3,6-7
16:4 [s]Ex 12:10; 34:25
16:6 [t]Ex 12:6; Dt 12:5
16:7 [u]Ex 12:8; 2Ch 35:13
16:8 [v]Ex 12:16; 13:6; Lev 23:8
16:9 [w]Ex 34:22; Lev 23:15 [x]Ex 23:16; Nu 28:26
16:11 [y]Dt 12:7 [z]Dt 12:12
16:12 [a]Dt 15:15
16:13 [b]Lev 23:34 [c]Ex 23:16
16:14 [d]ver 11

[a] 6 Or *down, at the time of day*

menservants and maidservants, and the Levites,
the aliens, the fatherless and the widows who live
in your towns. 15For seven days celebrate the Feast
to the LORD your God at the place the LORD will
choose. For the LORD your God will bless you in
16:15 [e]Lev 23:39 all your harvest and in all the work of your hands,
and your joy[e] will be complete.
16Three times a year all your men must appear
before the LORD your God at the place he will
16:16 [f]Ex 23:14,16 [g]Ex 34:20 choose: at the Feast of Unleavened Bread, the
Feast of Weeks and the Feast of Tabernacles.[f] No
man should appear before the LORD empty-handed:[g] 17Each of you must bring a gift in proportion
to the way the LORD your God has blessed you.

Judges

16:18 [h]Dt 1:16 18Appoint judges[h] and officials for each of your
tribes in every town the LORD your God is giving
16:19 [i]Ex 23:2,8 [j]Lev 19:15; Dt 1:17 [k]Ecc 7:7 you, and they shall judge the people fairly. 19Do not
pervert justice[i] or show partiality.[j] Do not accept a
bribe,[k] for a bribe blinds the eyes of the wise and
twists the words of the righteous. 20Follow justice
and justice alone, so that you may live and possess
the land the LORD your God is giving you.

Worshiping Other Gods

16:21 [l]Dt 7:5 [m]Ex 34:13; 2Ki 17:16; 21:3; 2Ch 33:3 21Do not set up any wooden Asherah pole[a][l]
beside the altar you build to the LORD your God,[m]
22and do not erect a sacred stone,[n] for these the
LORD your God hates.
16:22 [n]Lev 26:1 17 Do not sacrifice to the LORD your God an ox
or a sheep that has any defect[o] or flaw in it,
for that would be detestable to him.[p]
17:1 [o]Mal 1:8,13 [p]Dt 15:21 2If a man or woman living among you in one
of the towns the LORD gives you is found doing
17:2 [q]Dt 13:6-11 evil in the eyes of the LORD your God in violation
of his covenant,[q] 3and contrary to my command[r]
17:3 [r]Jer 7:22-23 [s]Job 31:26 has worshiped other gods, bowing down to them
or to the sun[s] or the moon or the stars of the sky,
4and this has been brought to your attention, then
17:4 [t]Dt 13:12-14 you must investigate it thoroughly. If it is true and
it has been proved that this detestable thing has
been done in Israel,[t] 5take the man or woman
who has done this evil deed to your city gate and
17:5 [u]Lev 24:14 stone that person to death.[u] 6On the testimony of
two or three witnesses a man shall be put to
17:6 [v]Nu 35:30; Dt 19:15; Jos 7:25; Mt 18:16; Jn 8:17; 2Co 13:1; 1Ti 5:19; Heb 10:28 death, but no one shall be put to death on the testimony of only one witness.[v] 7The hands of the
witnesses must be the first in putting him to
death, and then the hands of all the people. You
must purge the evil[w] from among you.

Law Courts

17:7 [w]Dt 13:5,9 8If cases come before your courts that are too difficult for you to judge—whether bloodshed, law-
17:8 [x]2Ch 19:10 [y]Dt 12:5; Hag 2:11 suits or assaults[x]—take them to the place the LORD
your God will choose.[y] 9Go to the priests, who are
Levites, and to the judge who is in office at that
time. Inquire of them and they will give you the

[a] 21 Or *Do not plant any tree dedicated to Asherah*

Celebrate!

DT 16:15

The Israelites give us a pattern for celebrating with three distinguishing characteristics: (1) commemoration; (2) invocation; and (3) thanksgiving. The festivals of the Israelites commemorate God's goodness to them in the far or recent past. The festivals also call the people back to God, with worship, prayer and fellowship as a part of almost every feast day. And thanksgiving! How can they not be thankful when they worship God and recall his goodness? Moses then reminds the Israelites of the foremost activity: to rejoice. The festivals are a time of immense joy as the Israelites remember past struggles and God's faithfulness and provision. They break out in sheer fun and laughter together.

Bring the party hats, recall stories, give thanks, and joy will overflow in our living rooms too! What can we celebrate? Birthdays and anniversaries, certainly. But how about getting braces, learning the multiplication tables, attending the first day of middle school? Choosing events and experiences to commemorate honors and strengthens family life.

Choosing a King

DT 17:16–18

Moses anticipates that the Israelites will want an earthly king, like all the other nations, and gives instructions for choosing a king wisely. Why would God give guidelines for doing something he doesn't want done? Because he knows everything—even human weakness—that we are always looking for something or someone to rescue us. The wonder of God's insight is that it is joined with his compassion. As often as the Israelites look to horses and chariots to deliver them, God continues to answer them when they finally call on him (Ps 20). Kings, horses, chariots. Success, government, prosperity. Salvation never comes from around us, but only from above, from our Rescuer-Redeemer-Savior.

verdict.[z] 10You must act according to the decisions
they give you at the place the LORD will choose. Be
careful to do everything they direct you to do. 11Act
according to the law they teach you and the decisions they give you. Do not turn aside from what
they tell you, to the right or to the left.[a] 12The man
who shows contempt[b] for the judge or for the
priest who stands ministering there to the LORD
your God must be put to death. You must purge
the evil from Israel. 13All the people will hear and
be afraid, and will not be contemptuous again.[c]

The King

14When you enter the land the LORD your God is
giving you and have taken possession of it and settled in it, and you say, "Let us set a king over us
like all the nations around us,"[d] 15be sure to
appoint over you the king the LORD your God
chooses. He must be from among your own brothers.[e] Do not place a foreigner over you, one who is
not a brother Israelite. 16The king, moreover, must
not acquire great numbers of horses for himself[f] or
make the people return to Egypt[g] to get more of
them,[h] for the LORD has told you, "You are not to
go back that way again."[i] 17He must not take many
wives,[j] or his heart will be led astray. He must not
accumulate large amounts of silver and gold.
18When he takes the throne of his kingdom, he
is to write[k] for himself on a scroll a copy of this
law, taken from that of the priests, who are
Levites. 19It is to be with him, and he is to read it
all the days of his life[l] so that he may learn to
revere the LORD his God and follow carefully all
the words of this law and these decrees 20and not
consider himself better than his brothers and turn
from the law[m] to the right or to the left.[n] Then he
and his descendants will reign a long time over
his kingdom in Israel.

Offerings for Priests and Levites

18 The priests, who are Levites—indeed the
whole tribe of Levi—are to have no allotment or inheritance with Israel. They shall live on
the offerings made to the LORD by fire, for that is
their inheritance.[o] 2They shall have no inheritance
among their brothers; the LORD is their inheritance, as he promised them.
3This is the share due the priests from the people who sacrifice a bull or a sheep: the shoulder,
the jowls and the inner parts.[p] 4You are to give
them the firstfruits of your grain, new wine and
oil, and the first wool from the shearing of your
sheep,[q] 5for the LORD your God has chosen them[r]
and their descendants out of all your tribes to
stand and minister[s] in the LORD's name always.
6If a Levite moves from one of your towns anywhere in Israel where he is living, and comes in
all earnestness to the place the LORD will choose,[t]
7he may minister in the name of the LORD his God
like all his fellow Levites who serve there in the

17:9 [z]Dt 19:17; Eze 44:24
17:11 [a]Dt 25:1
17:12 [b]Nu 15:30
17:13 [c]Dt 13:11; 19:20
17:14 [d]Dt 11:31; 1Sa 8:5,19-20
17:15 [e]Jer 30:21
17:16 [f]1Ki 4:26; 10:26 [g]Isa 31:1; Hos 11:5 [h]1Ki 10:28; Eze 17:15 [i]Ex 13:17
17:17 [j]1Ki 11:3
17:18 [k]Dt 31:22,24
17:19 [l]Jos 1:8
17:20 [m]1Ki 15:5 [n]Dt 5:32
18:1 [o]Dt 10:9; 1Co 9:13
18:3 [p]Lev 7:28-34
18:4 [q]Ex 22:29; Nu 18:12
18:5 [r]Ex 28:1 [s]Dt 10:8
18:6 [t]Nu 35:2-3

presence of the LORD. 8 He is to share equally in
18:8 their benefits, even though he has received mon-
[u]2Ch 31:4; Ne 12:44,47 ey from the sale of family possessions.[u]

Detestable Practices

9 When you enter the land the LORD your God is
18:9 [v]Dt 12:29-31 giving you, do not learn to imitate[v] the detestable
ways of the nations there. 10 Let no one be found
18:10 [w]Dt 12:31 among you who sacrifices his son or daughter in[a]
[x]Lev 19:31 the fire, who practices divination[w] or sorcery,
interprets omens, engages in witchcraft,[x] 11 or casts
spells, or who is a medium or spiritist or who consults the dead. 12 Anyone who does these things is
detestable to the LORD, and because of these
detestable practices the LORD your God will drive
18:12 out those nations before you.[y] 13 You must be
[y]Lev 18:24; Dt 9:4 blameless before the LORD your God.

The Prophet

14 The nations you will dispossess listen to those
who practice sorcery or divination. But as for you,
the LORD your God has not permitted you to do so.
15 The LORD your God will raise up for you a proph-
18:15 [z]Jn 1:21; et like me from among your own brothers.[z] You
Ac 3:22*; 7:37* must listen to him. 16 For this is what you asked of
the LORD your God at Horeb on the day of the
assembly when you said, "Let us not hear the
18:16 voice of the LORD our God nor see this great fire
[a]Ex 20:19; anymore, or we will die."[a]
Dt 5:23-27 17 The LORD said to me: "What they say is good.
18 I will raise up for them a prophet like you from
18:18 [b]Isa 51:16; among their brothers; I will put my words[b] in his
Jn 17:8 mouth, and he will tell them everything I com-
[c]Jn 4:25-26; mand him.[c] 19 If anyone does not listen to my
8:28; 12:49-50 words that the prophet speaks in my name, I
myself will call him to account.[d] 20 But a prophet
18:19 [d]Ac 3:23* who presumes to speak in my name anything I
have not commanded him to say, or a prophet
18:20 [e]Jer 14:14 who speaks in the name of other gods,[e] must be
[f]Dt 13:1-5 put to death."[f]

21 You may say to yourselves, "How can we
know when a message has not been spoken by
the LORD?" 22 If what a prophet proclaims in the
18:22 name of the LORD does not take place or come
[g]Jer 28:9 true, that is a message the LORD has not spoken.[g]
[h]ver 20 That prophet has spoken presumptuously.[h] Do not
be afraid of him.

Cities of Refuge

19 When the LORD your God has destroyed the
nations whose land he is giving you, and
when you have driven them out and settled in
19:1 their towns and houses,[i] 2 then set aside for your-
[i]Dt 12:29 selves three cities centrally located in the land the
LORD your God is giving you to possess. 3 Build
roads to them and divide into three parts the land
the LORD your God is giving you as an inheritance,
so that anyone who kills a man may flee there.
4 This is the rule concerning the man who kills

[a] 10 *Or who makes his son or daughter pass through*

Trading God's Glory

DT 18:9-13

The Israelites are about to take up residence in Canaan, and Moses warns that the Canaanites are spiritual people. He delineates the pagan rites the Canaanites use to worship their many gods and to communicate with the departed. Notice the clear judgments and strong warnings Moses gives when referring to these practices. He knows that participation in these rites will mar the Israelites' relationship with God.

***Spirituality abounds today, as well, in every conceivable form. Consulting a horoscope or investigating Eastern religious practices may seem innocent. But when viewed through the lens of Deuteronomy, it becomes detestable at worst and a waste of time at best. The apostle Paul describes the tragic pursuit of spirituality apart from the true and living God as "exchang[ing] the glory of the immortal God for images made to look like mortal man and birds and animals and reptiles"* (Ro 1:23).**

Good Neighbors

DT 19:14–19

Moses begins his treatise on the laws of Israel in the same way Jesus Christ begins his instructions in the New Testament: Love the Lord your God (Dt 6:5). Love your neighbor as you love yourself (Mt 22:37–40). Loving God and loving others is inextricably linked. In this passage Moses explains the laws of love regarding taking another's property or reputation. Boundary stones permanently mark a person's property. Moving the stones is equivalent to stealing the land. Individual reputation is guarded just as zealously. In fact, those who bring false charges are to suffer the same punishment they had hoped would be given to the one accused. These ancient laws are good reminders that respecting someone's reputation is as important as respecting their property.

another and flees there to save his life—one who
kills his neighbor unintentionally, without malice
aforethought. 5For instance, a man may go into
the forest with his neighbor to cut wood, and as
he swings his ax to fell a tree, the head may fly
off and hit his neighbor and kill him. That man
may flee to one of these cities and save his life.
6Otherwise, the avenger of blood[j] might pursue
him in a rage, overtake him if the distance is too
great, and kill him even though he is not deserving of death, since he did it to his neighbor without malice aforethought. 7This is why I command
you to set aside for yourselves three cities.
8If the LORD your God enlarges your territory, as
he promised on oath to your forefathers, and gives
you the whole land he promised them, 9because
you carefully follow all these laws I command you
today—to love the LORD your God and to walk
always in his ways[k]—then you are to set aside
three more cities. 10Do this so that innocent blood
will not be shed in your land, which the LORD
your God is giving you as your inheritance, and
so that you will not be guilty of bloodshed.[l]
11But if a man hates his neighbor and lies in
wait for him, assaults and kills him,[m] and then
flees to one of these cities, 12the elders of his town
shall send for him, bring him back from the city,
and hand him over to the avenger of blood to die.
13Show him no pity.[n] You must purge from Israel
the guilt of shedding innocent blood,[o] so that it
may go well with you.
14Do not move your neighbor's boundary stone
set up by your predecessors in the inheritance you
receive in the land the LORD your God is giving
you to possess.[p]

Witnesses

15One witness is not enough to convict a man
accused of any crime or offense he may have committed. A matter must be established by the testimony of two or three witnesses.[q]
16If a malicious witness[r] takes the stand to
accuse a man of a crime, 17the two men involved
in the dispute must stand in the presence of the
LORD before the priests and the judges[s] who are in
office at the time. 18The judges must make a thorough investigation, and if the witness proves to
be a liar, giving false testimony against his brother, 19then do to him as he intended to do to his
brother.[t] You must purge the evil from among you.
20The rest of the people will hear of this and be
afraid,[u] and never again will such an evil thing be
done among you. 21Show no pity:[v] life for life, eye
for eye, tooth for tooth, hand for hand, foot for
foot.[w]

Going to War

20 When you go to war against your enemies
and see horses and chariots and an army
greater than yours,[x] do not be afraid[y] of them,[z]

19:6 [j]Nu 35:12
19:9 [k]Jos 20:7-8
19:10 [l]Nu 35:33; Dt 21:1-9
19:11 [m]Nu 35:16
19:13 [n]Dt 7:2 [o]1Ki 2:31
19:14 [p]Dt 27:17; Pr 22:28; Hos 5:10
19:15 [q]Nu 35:30; Dt 17:6; Mt 18:16*; Jn 8:17; 2Co 13:1*; 1Ti 5:19; Heb 10:28
19:16 [r]Ex 23:1; Ps 27:12
19:17 [s]Dt 17:9
19:19 [t]Pr 19:5,9
19:20 [u]Dt 17:13; 21:21
19:21 [v]ver 13 [w]Ex 21:24; Lev 24:20; Mt 5:38*
20:1 [x]Ps 20:7; Isa 31:1 [y]Dt 31:6,8 [z]2Ch 32:7-8

because the LORD your God, who brought you up
out of Egypt, will be with you. 2When you are
about to go into battle, the priest shall come forward and address the army. 3He shall say: "Hear,
O Israel, today you are going into battle against
20:3 [a]Jos 23:10 your enemies. Do not be fainthearted[a] or afraid;
do not be terrified or give way to panic before
them. 4For the LORD your God is the one who goes
20:4 [b]Dt 1:30; 3:22; Jos 23:10 with you to fight[b] for you against your enemies to
give you victory."
5The officers shall say to the army: "Has any-
20:5 [c]Ne 12:27 one built a new house and not dedicated[c] it? Let
him go home, or he may die in battle and some-
one else may dedicate it. 6Has anyone planted a
vineyard and not begun to enjoy it? Let him go
home, or he may die in battle and someone else
enjoy it. 7Has anyone become pledged to a woman
and not married her? Let him go home, or he may
20:7 [d]Dt 24:5 die in battle and someone else marry her.[d]" 8Then
the officers shall add, "Is any man afraid or fainthearted? Let him go home so that his brothers will
20:8 [e]Jdg 7:3 not become disheartened too."[e] 9When the officers have finished speaking to the army, they shall
appoint commanders over it.
10When you march up to attack a city, make its
20:10 [f]Lk 14:31-32 people an offer of peace.[f] 11If they accept and open
their gates, all the people in it shall be subject to
20:11 [g]1Ki 9:21 forced labor[g] and shall work for you. 12If they
refuse to make peace and they engage you in bat-
tle, lay siege to that city. 13When the LORD your
God delivers it into your hand, put to the sword
20:13 [h]Nu 31:7 all the men in it.[h] 14As for the women, the chil-
20:14 [i]Jos 8:2; 22:8 dren, the livestock[i] and everything else in the city,
you may take these as plunder for yourselves. And
you may use the plunder the LORD your God gives
you from your enemies. 15This is how you are to
treat all the cities that are at a distance from you
and do not belong to the nations nearby.
16However, in the cities of the nations the LORD
your God is giving you as an inheritance, do not
20:16 [j]Ex 23:31-33; Nu 21:2-3; Dt 7:2; Jos 11:14 leave alive anything that breathes.[j] 17Completely
destroy[a] them—the Hittites, Amorites, Canaanites,
Perizzites, Hivites and Jebusites—as the LORD
your God has commanded you. 18Otherwise, they
20:18 [k]Ex 34:16; Dt 7:4; 12:30-31 will teach you to follow all the detestable things
they do in worshiping their gods,[k] and you will
[l]Ex 23:33 sin[l] against the LORD your God.
19When you lay siege to a city for a long time,
fighting against it to capture it, do not destroy its
trees by putting an ax to them, because you can
eat their fruit. Do not cut them down. Are the
trees of the field people, that you should besiege
them?[b] 20However, you may cut down trees that
you know are not fruit trees and use them to build
siege works until the city at war with you falls.

[a] *17* The Hebrew term refers to the irrevocable giving over of things or persons to the LORD, often by totally destroying them.
[b] *19* Or *down to use in the siege, for the fruit trees are for the benefit of man.*

God Is in the Details

DT 20:19-20

In these verses Moses reminds the conquering Israelites to spare the fruit trees because they provide sustenance. Historically, conquering nations often completely destroyed the areas they conquered, cutting down all trees and produce, burning cities to the ground, and spreading salt over it all. The conquered areas became unproductive for generations.

That is not God's way. The nations being conquered by the Israelites are suffering for their rebellion against God. However, God thinks of everything! Though the nation has rebelled, the produce of that nation is important for the Israelites and should be preserved. Read Psalm 139 and make a list of all of life's "details" that the psalmist records as important to God.

Atonement for an Unsolved Murder

21 If a man is found slain, lying in a field in
the land the LORD your God is giving you to
possess, and it is not known who killed him,
2your elders and judges shall go out and measure
the distance from the body to the neighboring
towns. 3Then the elders of the town nearest the
body shall take a heifer that has never been
worked and has never worn a yoke 4and lead her
down to a valley that has not been plowed or
planted and where there is a flowing stream.
There in the valley they are to break the heifer's
neck. 5The priests, the sons of Levi, shall step forward, for the LORD your God has chosen them to
minister and to pronounce blessings[m] in the name
of the LORD and to decide all cases of dispute and
assault.[n] 6Then all the elders of the town nearest
the body shall wash their hands[o] over the heifer
whose neck was broken in the valley, 7and they
shall declare: "Our hands did not shed this blood,
nor did our eyes see it done. 8Accept this atonement for your people Israel, whom you have
redeemed, O LORD, and do not hold your people
guilty of the blood of an innocent man." And the
bloodshed will be atoned for.[p] 9So you will purge[q]
from yourselves the guilt of shedding innocent
blood, since you have done what is right in the
eyes of the LORD.

21:5 [m]1Ch 23:13 [n]Dt 17:8-11
21:6 [o]Mt 27:24
21:8 [p]Nu 35:33-34
21:9 [q]Dt 19:13

Marrying a Captive Woman

10When you go to war against your enemies and
the LORD your God delivers them into your hands[r]
and you take captives, 11if you notice among the
captives a beautiful woman and are attracted to
her, you may take her as your wife. 12Bring her
into your home and have her shave her head,[s]
trim her nails 13and put aside the clothes she was
wearing when captured. After she has lived in
your house and mourned her father and mother
for a full month,[t] then you may go to her and be
her husband and she shall be your wife. 14If you
are not pleased with her, let her go wherever she
wishes. You must not sell her or treat her as a
slave, since you have dishonored her.[u]

21:10 [r]Jos 21:44
21:12 [s]Lev 14:9; Nu 6:9
21:13 [t]Ps 45:10
21:14 [u]Ge 34:2

The Right of the Firstborn

15If a man has two wives, and he loves one but
not the other, and both bear him sons but the firstborn is the son of the wife he does not love,[v]
16when he wills his property to his sons, he must
not give the rights of the firstborn to the son of
the wife he loves in preference to his actual firstborn, the son of the wife he does not love.[w] 17He
must acknowledge the son of his unloved wife as
the firstborn by giving him a double share of all
he has. That son is the first sign of his father's
strength.[x] The right of the firstborn belongs to
him.[y]

21:15 [v]Ge 29:33
21:16 [w]1Ch 26:10
21:17 [x]Ge 49:3 [y]Ge 25:31

I thought that Jesus said, "Come unto me all who are weary and burdened, and I will give you more to *do* than anyone else!" But Jesus didn't say that. He promised me rest. But I couldn't find it. My constant struggle to be "godly" left me tired, empty, lonely on the inside, and ready to give up.

. . . [So,] I gave up. I surrendered . . . I stopped being in charge of my spiritual goodness, because I didn't have any spiritual goodness. I had worked for God and yet withheld my heart from him. I'd sought to please him . . . and missed that he was pleased with me. I tried to do so many things *for* God that I missed being *with* God . . . I discovered that the Christian life is not about trying harder. It is not about keeping it all together. It is about trusting in the One who can keep it all together.

—Nicole Johnson

A Rebellious Son

18 If a man has a stubborn and rebellious son who does not obey his father and mother[z] and will not listen to them when they discipline him, 19 his father and mother shall take hold of him and bring him to the elders at the gate of his town. 20 They shall say to the elders, "This son of ours is stubborn and rebellious. He will not obey us. He is a profligate and a drunkard." 21 Then all the men of his town shall stone him to death. You must purge the evil[a] from among you. All Israel will hear of it and be afraid.[b]

Various Laws

22 If a man guilty of a capital offense[c] is put to death and his body is hung on a tree, 23 you must not leave his body on the tree overnight.[d] Be sure to bury him that same day, because anyone who is hung on a tree is under God's curse.[e] You must not desecrate[f] the land the LORD your God is giving you as an inheritance.

22 If you see your brother's ox or sheep straying, do not ignore it but be sure to take it back to him.[g] 2 If the brother does not live near you or if you do not know who he is, take it home with you and keep it until he comes looking for it. Then give it back to him. 3 Do the same if you find your brother's donkey or his cloak or anything he loses. Do not ignore it.

4 If you see your brother's donkey[h] or his ox fallen on the road, do not ignore it. Help him get it to its feet.

5 A woman must not wear men's clothing, nor a man wear women's clothing, for the LORD your God detests anyone who does this.

6 If you come across a bird's nest beside the road, either in a tree or on the ground, and the mother is sitting on the young or on the eggs, do not take the mother with the young.[i] 7 You may take the young, but be sure to let the mother go, so that it may go well with you and you may have a long life.[j]

8 When you build a new house, make a parapet around your roof so that you may not bring the guilt of bloodshed on your house if someone falls from the roof.

9 Do not plant two kinds of seed in your vineyard;[k] if you do, not only the crops you plant but also the fruit of the vineyard will be defiled.[a]

10 Do not plow with an ox and a donkey yoked together.[l]

11 Do not wear clothes of wool and linen woven together.[m]

12 Make tassels on the four corners of the cloak you wear.[n]

Marriage Violations

13 If a man takes a wife and, after lying with

21:18 [z]Pr 1:8; Isa 30:1; Eph 6:1-3
21:21 [a]Dt 19:19; 1Co 5:13* [b]Dt 13:11
21:22 [c]Dt 22:26; Mk 14:64; Ac 23:29
21:23 [d]Jos 8:29; 10:27; Jn 19:31 [e]Gal 3:13* [f]Lev 18:25; Nu 35:34
22:1 [g]Ex 23:4-5
22:4 [h]Ex 23:5
22:6 [i]Lev 22:28
22:7 [j]Dt 4:40
22:9 [k]Lev 19:19
22:10 [l]2Co 6:14
22:11 [m]Lev 19:19
22:12 [n]Nu 15:37-41; Mt 23:5

[a] 9 Or *be forfeited to the sanctuary*

Various Laws

DT 22:5

These "various laws" cover a variety of issues, from social and cultural to humanitarian. Each one has its reason for existence, although we may not always understand the issue behind the law. Often the purpose is simply to help the Israelites become a people distinct from the cultures around them. That is perhaps why God commands that dissimilar things not be mixed (clothing, Dt 22:5; other articles, Dt 22:9–11). The purpose of some of the laws is humanitarian, such as helping up a fallen donkey or ox (Dt 22:4), leaving a hen to have another brood (Dt 22:6–7) and building a railing on a roof to prevent an accidental death (Dt 22:8). Some of the laws promote honesty in dealing with acquaintances as well as strangers (Dt 22:1–3). God's purpose is to produce a people who belong exclusively to him and whose actions reveal their loyalty and love.

A Top Priority

DT 22:13–30

Moses reminds the Israelites of the laws in place to protect family life. Note that these laws address the relationship between husband and wife. From the beginning, God decrees that the bond between husband and wife is the primary building block of the family and should be honored, guarded and lovingly attended to above all other human relationships (Ge 2:23–24). These Hebrew laws are good reminders to us to pay attention to our marriages.

her[o], dislikes her [14]and slanders her and gives her a bad name, saying, "I married this woman, but when I approached her, I did not find proof of her virginity," [15]then the girl's father and mother shall bring proof that she was a virgin to the town elders at the gate. [16]The girl's father will say to the elders, "I gave my daughter in marriage to this man, but he dislikes her. [17]Now he has slandered her and said, 'I did not find your daughter to be a virgin.' But here is the proof of my daughter's virginity." Then her parents shall display the cloth before the elders of the town, [18]and the elders[p] shall take the man and punish him. [19]They shall fine him a hundred shekels of silver[a] and give them to the girl's father, because this man has given an Israelite virgin a bad name. She shall continue to be his wife; he must not divorce her as long as he lives.

[20]If, however, the charge is true and no proof of the girl's virginity can be found, [21]she shall be brought to the door of her father's house and there the men of her town shall stone her to death. She has done a disgraceful thing[q] in Israel by being promiscuous while still in her father's house. You must purge the evil from among you.

[22]If a man is found sleeping with another man's wife, both the man who slept with her and the woman must die.[r] You must purge the evil from Israel.

[23]If a man happens to meet in a town a virgin pledged to be married and he sleeps with her, [24]you shall take both of them to the gate of that town and stone them to death—the girl because she was in a town and did not scream for help, and the man because he violated another man's wife. You must purge the evil from among you.[s]

[25]But if out in the country a man happens to meet a girl pledged to be married and rapes her, only the man who has done this shall die. [26]Do nothing to the girl; she has committed no sin deserving death. This case is like that of someone who attacks and murders his neighbor, [27]for the man found the girl out in the country, and though the betrothed girl screamed, there was no one to rescue her.

[28]If a man happens to meet a virgin who is not pledged to be married and rapes her and they are discovered,[t] [29]he shall pay the girl's father fifty shekels of silver.[b] He must marry the girl, for he has violated her. He can never divorce her as long as he lives.

[30]A man is not to marry his father's wife; he must not dishonor his father's bed.[u]

22:13 [o]Dt 24:1
22:18 [p]Ex 18:21
22:21 [q]Ge 34:7; Dt 13:5; 23:17-18; Jdg 20:6; 2Sa 13:12
22:22 [r]Lev 20:10; Jn 8:5
22:24 [s]ver 21-22; 1Co 5:13*
22:28 [t]Ex 22:16
22:30 [u]Lev 18:8; 20:11; 18:8; Dt 27:20; 1Co 5:1

Exclusion From the Assembly

23 No one who has been emasculated by crushing or cutting may enter the assembly of the LORD.

[a] *19* That is, about 2 1/2 pounds (about 1 kilogram)
[b] *29* That is, about 1 1/4 pounds (about 0.6 kilogram)

2 No one born of a forbidden marriage[a] nor any
of his descendants may enter the assembly of the
LORD, even down to the tenth generation.
3 No Ammonite or Moabite or any of his descendants may enter the assembly of the LORD, even
23:3 down to the tenth generation.[v] 4 For they did not
[v]Ne 13:2 come to meet you with bread and water on your
23:4 way when you came out of Egypt, and they hired
[w]Nu 22:5-6; 23:7; Balaam[w] son of Beor from Pethor in Aram Naha-
2Pe 2:15 raim[b] to pronounce a curse on you. 5 However, the
LORD your God would not listen to Balaam but
23:5 turned the curse[x] into a blessing for you, because
[x]Pr 26:2 the LORD your God loves you. 6 Do not seek a treaty
23:6 of friendship with them as long as you live.[y]
[y]Ezr 9:12 7 Do not abhor an Edomite, for he is your broth-
23:7 er.[z] Do not abhor an Egyptian, because you lived
[z]Ge 25:26; Ob 1:10,12 as an alien in his country.[a] 8 The third generation
[a]Ex 22:21; 23:9; of children born to them may enter the assembly
Lev 19:34; Dt 10:19 of the LORD.

Uncleanness in the Camp

9 When you are encamped against your enemies, keep away from everything impure. 10 If one
of your men is unclean because of a nocturnal
emission, he is to go outside the camp and stay
23:10 there.[b] 11 But as evening approaches he is to wash
[b]Lev 15:16 himself, and at sunset he may return to the camp.
12 Designate a place outside the camp where you
can go to relieve yourself. 13 As part of your equipment have something to dig with, and when you
relieve yourself, dig a hole and cover up your
23:14 excrement. 14 For the LORD your God moves[c] about
[c]Lev 26:12 [d]Ex 3:5 in your camp to protect you and to deliver your
enemies to you. Your camp must be holy,[d] so that
he will not see among you anything indecent and
turn away from you.

Miscellaneous Laws

15 If a slave has taken refuge with you, do not
23:15 [e]1Sa 30:15 hand him over to his master.[e] 16 Let him live
23:16 among you wherever he likes and in whatever
[f]Ex 22:21 town he chooses. Do not oppress[f] him.
17 No Israelite man[g] or woman is to become a
23:17 [g]Ge 19:25; shrine prostitute.[h] 18 You must not bring the earn-
2Ki 23:7 ings of a female prostitute or of a male prostitute[c]
[h]Lev 19:29; Dt 22:21 into the house of the LORD your God to pay any
vow, because the LORD your God detests them both.
19 Do not charge your brother interest, whether
23:19 on money or food or anything else that may earn
[i]Ex 22:25; interest.[i] 20 You may charge a foreigner interest,
Lev 25:35-37 but not a brother Israelite, so that the LORD your
23:20 God may bless[j] you in everything you put your
[j]Dt 15:10; 28:12 hand to in the land you are entering to possess.
21 If you make a vow to the LORD your God, do not
be slow to pay it, for the LORD your God will certainly demand it of you and you will be guilty of
23:21 [k]Nu 30:1-2; sin.[k] 22 But if you refrain from making a vow, you
Ecc 5:4-5; Mt 5:33 will not be guilty. 23 Whatever your lips utter you

[a] 2 Or *one of illegitimate birth* [b] 4 That is, Northwest Mesopotamia [c] 18 Hebrew *of a dog*

Preventive Medicine

DT 23:12–13

Again God shows his concern for protecting the whole person. Following these laws of personal hygiene will keep the Israelites from experiencing many of the health problems and plagues prevalent in other cultures of that time. Between the lines of these laws is the tender concern of a loving Father. We long to believe that God cares about the details of our lives. These detailed, sometimes strange, laws testify that he notices us, knows us, thinks about us and plans for us. No concern is too small to escape the light of his love.

A High and Holy Calling

DT 24:5

What a great idea! God's idea. For one year, a new husband is to stay home and bring happiness to his wife. The Hebrew word for happiness can also be translated "bliss." These laws indicate that God holds high the goal of marital bliss. Our modern lifestyle does not accommodate such a law, but following the spirit of the law means that we will see marriage as sacred. We choose to honor it, guard it, nurture it. A marriage lived out under the awareness that it is sacred looks different. It calls us to more*—more than a mundane, ordinary or "sitcom" marriage. To see marriage as sacred means we have a calling—a vocation—to pray, risk, create, struggle, sacrifice . . . and to hug, listen, caress and laugh a lot. It is some of the most important work in the kingdom!*

must be sure to do, because you made your vow
freely to the LORD your God with your own mouth.
24If you enter your neighbor's vineyard, you may
eat all the grapes you want, but do not put any in
your basket. 25If you enter your neighbor's grain-
field, you may pick kernels with your hands, but
you must not put a sickle to his standing grain.[l]

24 If a man marries a woman who becomes
displeasing to him[m] because he finds something indecent about her, and he writes her a certificate of divorce,[n] gives it to her and sends her
from his house, 2and if after she leaves his house
she becomes the wife of another man, 3and her
second husband dislikes her and writes her a certificate of divorce, gives it to her and sends her
from his house, or if he dies, 4then her first husband, who divorced her, is not allowed to marry
her again after she has been defiled. That would
be detestable in the eyes of the LORD. Do not bring
sin upon the land the LORD[o] your God is giving
you as an inheritance.
5If a man has recently married, he must not be
sent to war or have any other duty laid on him.
For one year he is to be free to stay at home and
bring happiness to the wife he has married.[p]
6Do not take a pair of millstones—not even the
upper one—as security for a debt, because that
would be taking a man's livelihood as security.
7If a man is caught kidnapping one of his brother Israelites and treats him as a slave or sells him,
the kidnapper must die.[q] You must purge the evil
from among you.
8In cases of leprous[a] diseases be very careful to
do exactly as the priests, who are Levites, instruct
you. You must follow carefully what I have commanded them.[r] 9Remember what the LORD your
God did to Miriam along the way after you came
out of Egypt.[s]
10When you make a loan of any kind to your
neighbor, do not go into his house to get what he
is offering as a pledge. 11Stay outside and let the
man to whom you are making the loan bring the
pledge out to you. 12If the man is poor, do not go
to sleep with his pledge in your possession.
13Return his cloak to him by sunset[t] so that he
may sleep in it. Then he will thank you, and it
will be regarded as a righteous act in the sight of
the LORD your God.[u]
14Do not take advantage of a hired man who is
poor and needy, whether he is a brother Israelite
or an alien living in one of your towns.[v] 15Pay him
his wages each day before sunset, because he is
poor[w] and is counting on it.[x] Otherwise he may
cry to the LORD against you, and you will be guilty
of sin.[y]
16Fathers shall not be put to death for their children, nor children put to death for their fathers;
each is to die for his own sin.[z]

23:25 [l]Mt 12:1; Mk 2:23; Lk 6:1
24:1 [m]Dt 22:13 [n]Mt 5:31*; 19:7-9; Mk 10:4-5
24:4 [o]Jer 3:1
24:5 [p]Dt 20:7
24:7 [q]Ex 21:16
24:8 [r]Lev 13:1-46; 14:2
24:9 [s]Nu 12:10
24:13 [t]Ex 22:26 [u]Dt 6:25; Da 4:27
24:14 [v]Lev 25:35-43; Dt 15:12-18
24:15 [w]Jer 22:13 [x]Lev 19:13 [y]Dt 15:9; Jas 5:4
24:16 [z]2Ki 14:6; 2Ch 25:4; Jer 31:29-30; Eze 18:20

[a] *8* The Hebrew word was used for various diseases affecting the skin—not necessarily leprosy.

17Do not deprive the alien or the fatherless of
24:17 [a]Dt 1:17; justice,[a] or take the cloak of the widow as a
10:17-18; pledge. 18Remember that you were slaves in Egypt
16:19 and the LORD your God redeemed you from there.
That is why I command you to do this.
19When you are harvesting in your field and
24:19 [b]Lev 19:9; you overlook a sheaf, do not go back to get it.[b]
23:22 Leave it for the alien, the fatherless and the wid-
[c]Pr 19:17 ow, so that the LORD your God may bless[c] you in
all the work of your hands. 20When you beat the
olives from your trees, do not go over the
24:20 [d]Lev 19:10 branches a second time.[d] Leave what remains for
the alien, the fatherless and the widow. 21When
you harvest the grapes in your vineyard, do not
go over the vines again. Leave what remains for
the alien, the fatherless and the widow. 22Remem-
24:22 ber that you were slaves in Egypt. That is why I
[e]ver 18 command you to do this.[e]

25 When men have a dispute, they are to take
25:1 it to court and the judges will decide the
[f]Dt 19:17 case,[f] acquitting the innocent and condemning the
[g]Dt 1:16-17 guilty.[g] 2If the guilty man deserves to be beaten,[h]
25:2 the judge shall make him lie down and have him
[h]Lk 12:47-48 flogged in his presence with the number of lashes
25:3 his crime deserves, 3but he must not give him
[i]2Co 11:24 more than forty lashes.[i] If he is flogged more than
[j]Job 18:3 that, your brother will be degraded in your eyes.[j]
25:4 4Do not muzzle an ox while it is treading out
[k]Pr 12:10; the grain.[k]
1Co 9:9*; 1Ti 5:18* 5If brothers are living together and one of them
25:5 dies without a son, his widow must not marry
[l]Mt 22:24; outside the family. Her husband's brother shall
Mk 12:19; take her and marry her and fulfill the duty of a
Lk 20:28 brother-in-law to her.[l] 6The first son she bears
25:6 shall carry on the name of the dead brother so
[m]Ge 38:9; Ru 4:5,10 that his name will not be blotted out from Israel.[m]
7However, if a man does not want to marry his
brother's wife, she shall go to the elders at the
town gate and say, "My husband's brother refuses
25:7 to carry on his brother's name in Israel. He will
[n]Ru 4:1-2, 5-6 not fulfill the duty of a brother-in-law to me."[n]
8Then the elders of his town shall summon him
and talk to him. If he persists in saying, "I do not
want to marry her," 9his brother's widow shall go
25:9 up to him in the presence of the elders, take off
[o]Ru 4:7-8, 11 one of his sandals,[o] spit in his face and say, "This
is what is done to the man who will not build up
his brother's family line." 10That man's line shall
be known in Israel as The Family of the Unsan-
daled.
11If two men are fighting and the wife of one of
them comes to rescue her husband from his
assailant, and she reaches out and seizes him by
25:12 his private parts, 12you shall cut off her hand.
[p]Dt 19:13 Show her no pity.[p]
25:13 13Do not have two differing weights in your
[q]Lev 19:35-37; Pr 11:1; bag—one heavy, one light.[q] 14Do not have two dif-
Eze 45:10; fering measures in your house—one large, one
Mic 6:11 small. 15You must have accurate and honest
25:15 weights and measures, so that you may live long[r]
[r]Ex 20:12 in the land the LORD your God is giving you. 16For

Life in Community

DT 25:13-16

Moses follows the commandments regarding family life with solemn instructions about community life. He warns the people not to mistreat the poor, not to steal, and not to withhold what rightfully belongs to another. For example, by using a heavier weight for buying than for selling, a merchant can easily defraud others. Moses repeatedly reminds the Israelites of their freedom from slavery, at least in part to encourage them to treat others fairly. Families and communities are at their best when they care for one another. God's code of conduct yields a meaningful and satisfying life based on commitment, justice, truthfulness and community.

O World, I cannot hold
thee close enough!
Thy winds, thy wide grey skies!
Thy mists, that roll and rise!
Thy woods, this autumn day, that ache and sag
And all but cry with colour! That gaunt crag
To crush! To lift the lean of that black bluff!
World, World, I cannot get thee close enough!

Long have I known a glory in it all,
But never knew I this;
Here such a passion is
As stretcheth me apart—Lord, I do fear
Thou'st made the world too beautiful this year;
My soul is all but out of me—let fall
No burning leaf; prithee, let no bird call.

—*Edna St. Vincent Millay (1892–1950)*

the LORD your God detests anyone who does these
things, anyone who deals dishonestly.[s]
17 Remember what the Amalekites[t] did to you
along the way when you came out of Egypt.
18 When you were weary and worn out, they met
you on your journey and cut off all who were lag-
ging behind; they had no fear of God.[u] 19 When the
LORD your God gives you rest from all the enemies
around you in the land he is giving you to possess
as an inheritance, you shall blot out the memory
of Amalek[v] from under heaven. Do not forget!

Firstfruits and Tithes

26 When you have entered the land the LORD
your God is giving you as an inheritance
and have taken possession of it and settled in it,
2 take some of the firstfruits[w] of all that you produce from the soil of the land the LORD your God
is giving you and put them in a basket. Then go to
the place the LORD your God will choose as a
dwelling for his Name[x] 3 and say to the priest in
office at the time, "I declare today to the LORD your
God that I have come to the land the LORD swore
to our forefathers to give us." 4 The priest shall
take the basket from your hands and set it down
in front of the altar of the LORD your God. 5 Then
you shall declare before the LORD your God: "My
father was a wandering Aramean,[y] and he went
down into Egypt with a few people[z] and lived
there and became a great nation, powerful and
numerous. 6 But the Egyptians mistreated us and
made us suffer,[a] putting us to hard labor. 7 Then
we cried out to the LORD, the God of our fathers,
and the LORD heard our voice[b] and saw[c] our misery, toil and oppression. 8 So the LORD brought us
out of Egypt with a mighty hand and an outstretched arm, with great terror and with miraculous signs and wonders.[d] 9 He brought us to this
place and gave us this land, a land flowing with
milk and honey;[e] 10 and now I bring the firstfruits
of the soil that you, O LORD, have given me." Place
the basket before the LORD your God and bow
down before him. 11 And you and the Levites[f] and
the aliens among you shall rejoice[g] in all the good
things the LORD your God has given to you and
your household.
12 When you have finished setting aside a tenth[h]
of all your produce in the third year, the year of
the tithe,[i] you shall give it to the Levite, the alien,
the fatherless and the widow, so that they may eat
in your towns and be satisfied. 13 Then say to the
LORD your God: "I have removed from my house
the sacred portion and have given it to the Levite,
the alien, the fatherless and the widow, according
to all you commanded. I have not turned aside
from your commands nor have I forgotten any of
them.[j] 14 I have not eaten any of the sacred portion
while I was in mourning, nor have I removed any
of it while I was unclean,[k] nor have I offered any
of it to the dead. I have obeyed the LORD my God;
I have done everything you commanded me.

25:16 [s]Pr 11:1
25:17 [t]Ex 17:8
25:18 [u]Ps 36:1; Ro 3:18
25:19 [v]1Sa 15:2-3
26:2 [w]Ex 22:29; 23:16,19; Nu 18:13; Pr 3:9 [x]Dt 12:5
26:5 [y]Hos 12:12 [z]Ge 43:1-2; 45:7,11; 46:27; Dt 10:22
26:6 [a]Ex 1:11,14
26:7 [b]Ex 2:23-25 [c]Ex 3:9
26:8 [d]Dt 4:34
26:9 [e]Ex 3:8
26:11 [f]Dt 12:7 [g]Dt 16:11
26:12 [h]Lev 27:30 [i]Nu 18:24; Dt 14:28-29; Heb 7:5,9
26:13 [j]Ps 119:141, 153,176
26:14 [k]Lev 7:20; Hos 9:4

26:15 [l]Isa 63:15; 15 Look down from heaven,[l] your holy dwelling
Zec 2:13 place, and bless your people Israel and the land
you have given us as you promised on oath to our
forefathers, a land flowing with milk and honey."

Follow the LORD's Commands

16 The LORD your God commands you this day to
follow these decrees and laws; carefully observe
26:16 [m]Dt 4:29 them with all your heart and with all your soul.[m]
17 You have declared this day that the LORD is your
God and that you will walk in his ways, that you
will keep his decrees, commands and laws, and
that you will obey him. 18 And the LORD has
26:18 declared this day that you are his people, his trea-
[n]Ex 6:7; sured possession[n] as he promised, and that you
19:5; Dt 7:6; are to keep all his commands. 19 He has declared
14:2; 28:9 that he will set you in praise, fame and honor
26:19 high above all the nations[o] he has made and that
[o]Dt 4:7-8; 28:1,13,44 you will be a people holy[p] to the LORD your God,
[p]Ex 19:6; as he promised.
Dt 7:6;
1Pe 2:9

The Altar on Mount Ebal

27 Moses and the elders of Israel commanded
the people: "Keep all these commands that
I give you today. 2 When you have crossed the Jordan into the land the LORD your God is giving you,
set up some large stones and coat them with plas-
27:2 [q]Jos 8:31 ter.[q] 3 Write on them all the words of this law
when you have crossed over to enter the land the
27:3 LORD your God is giving you, a land flowing with
[r]Dt 26:9 milk and honey,[r] just as the LORD, the God of your
fathers, promised you. 4 And when you have
crossed the Jordan, set up these stones on Mount
27:4 [s]Dt 11:29 Ebal,[s] as I command you today, and coat them
with plaster. 5 Build there an altar[t] to the LORD your
27:5 God, an altar of stones. Do not use any iron tool[u]
[t]Jos 8:31 [u]Ex 20:25 upon them. 6 Build the altar of the LORD your God
with fieldstones and offer burnt offerings on it to
the LORD your God. 7 Sacrifice fellowship offerings[a]
there, eating them and rejoicing in the presence
of the LORD your God. 8 And you shall write very
clearly all the words of this law on these stones
you have set up."

Curses From Mount Ebal

9 Then Moses and the priests, who are Levites,
said to all Israel, "Be silent, O Israel, and listen!
You have now become the people of the LORD your
27:9 [v]Dt 26:18 God.[v] 10 Obey the LORD your God and follow his
commands and decrees that I give you today."
11 On the same day Moses commanded the
people:
12 When you have crossed the Jordan, these
27:12 [w]Dt 11:29 tribes shall stand on Mount Gerizim[w] to bless the
[x]Jos 8:35 people: Simeon, Levi, Judah, Issachar, Joseph and
Benjamin.[x] 13 And these tribes shall stand on
Mount Ebal to pronounce curses: Reuben, Gad,
Asher, Zebulun, Dan and Naphtali.

[a] 7 Traditionally *peace offerings*

Preparing for Worship

DT 27:5

Moses gives instructions for the renewal of the covenant under Joshua's leadership, including directions for constructing an altar at the foot of Mount Ebal. The Israelites are to use uncut stones that have not been ornamented with iron tools. Their place of worship is to be distinct from heathen altars, which are cut by iron tools and decorated with elaborate and sometimes erotic designs of idols.

It should not surprise us that God wants the Israelites to guard their place of worship. Worship is to see God as worthy. God himself meets us and is present with us. Worship fills our hearts and minds with wonder of him. Worship requires something from us—a time set apart, a surrendered heart, a single-minded focus. As we read about the Israelites' work to prepare for worship, now may be a good time for us to evaluate our dedication and preparation for worship.

Living Faith

DT 27:14

The Israelites can tell, no doubt, that Moses is nearing the end of his instructions. *Perhaps he stands up straighter, pauses for emphasis or spends a few minutes making eye contact with the crowd.* He begins a series of statements that are intended to guide the Israelites in living well within the promised land. Moses, together with the priests, reminds the people that in confessing their allegiance to these commands, they are testifying openly that they are God's people.

The theme of Deuteronomy is *no less relevant today: We display* our allegiance to God and his *Word when we live and love well.* Pay attention today. In the minutes and hours, chores and choices, and words and actions of your day, would anyone guess to whom you belong?

[14]The Levites shall recite to all the people of
Israel in a loud voice:

[15]"Cursed is the man who carves an image or casts an idol[y]—a thing detestable to the LORD, the work of the craftsman's hands—and sets it up in secret."

Then all the people shall say, "Amen!"

[16]"Cursed is the man who dishonors his father or his mother."[z]

Then all the people shall say, "Amen!"

[17]"Cursed is the man who moves his neighbor's boundary stone."[a]

Then all the people shall say, "Amen!"

[18]"Cursed is the man who leads the blind astray on the road."[b]

Then all the people shall say, "Amen!"

[19]"Cursed is the man who withholds justice from the alien,[c] the fatherless or the widow."[d]

Then all the people shall say, "Amen!"

[20]"Cursed is the man who sleeps with his father's wife, for he dishonors his father's bed."[e]

Then all the people shall say, "Amen!"

[21]"Cursed is the man who has sexual relations with any animal."[f]

Then all the people shall say, "Amen!"

[22]"Cursed is the man who sleeps with his sister, the daughter of his father or the daughter of his mother."[g]

Then all the people shall say, "Amen!"

[23]"Cursed is the man who sleeps with his mother-in-law."[h]

Then all the people shall say, "Amen!"

[24]"Cursed is the man who kills[i] his neighbor secretly."

Then all the people shall say, "Amen!"

[25]"Cursed is the man who accepts a bribe to kill an innocent person."[j]

Then all the people shall say, "Amen!"

[26]"Cursed is the man who does not uphold the words of this law by carrying them out."[k]

Then all the people shall say, "Amen!"

Blessings for Obedience

28 If you fully obey the LORD your God and
carefully follow all his commands[l] I give
you today, the LORD your God will set you high
above all the nations on earth.[m] [2]All these blessings will come upon you[n] and accompany you if
you obey the LORD your God:

[3]You will be blessed[o] in the city and blessed in the country.[p]

[4]The fruit of your womb will be blessed, and the crops of your land and the young of your livestock—the calves of your herds and the lambs of your flocks.[q]

[5]Your basket and your kneading trough will be blessed.

27:15 [y]Ex 20:4; 34:17; Lev 19:4; 26:1; Dt 4:16,23; 5:8; Isa 44:9
27:16 [z]Ex 20:12; 21:17; Lev 19:3; 20:9
27:17 [a]Dt 19:14; Pr 22:28
27:18 [b]Lev 19:14
27:19 [c]Ex 22:21; Dt 24:19 [d]Dt 10:18
27:20 [e]Lev 18:7; Dt 22:30
27:21 [f]Lev 18:23
27:22 [g]Lev 18:9; 20:17
27:23 [h]Lev 20:14
27:24 [i]Lev 24:17; Nu 35:31
27:25 [j]Ex 23:7-8; Dt 10:17; Eze 22:12
27:26 [k]Jer 11:3; Gal 3:10*
28:1 [l]Ex 15:26; Lev 26:3; Dt 7:12-26 [m]Dt 26:19
28:2 [n]Zec 1:6
28:3 [o]Ps 128:1,4 [p]Ge 39:5
28:4 [q]Ge 49:25; Pr 10:22

6You will be blessed when you come in and
28:6 [r]Ps 121:8 blessed when you go out.[r]

7The LORD will grant that the enemies who rise
up against you will be defeated before you. They
28:7 will come at you from one direction but flee from
[s]Lev 26:8,17 you in seven.[s]
8The LORD will send a blessing on your barns and
on everything you put your hand to. The LORD your
God will bless you in the land he is giving you.
28:9 9The LORD will establish you as his holy people,[t]
[t]Ex 19:6; Dt 7:6 as he promised you on oath, if you keep the commands of the LORD your God and walk in his ways.
10Then all the peoples on earth will see that you
28:10 are called by the name[u] of the LORD, and they will
[u]2Ch 7:14 fear you. 11The LORD will grant you abundant prosperity—in the fruit of your womb, the young of
28:11 your livestock and the crops of your ground—in
[v]Dt 30:9; the land he swore to your forefathers to give you.[v]
Pr 10:22 12The LORD will open the heavens, the storehouse
28:12 of his bounty, to send rain[w] on your land in season
[w]Lev 26:4 and to bless all the work of your hands. You will
[x]Dt 15:3,6 lend to many nations but will borrow from none.[x]
13The LORD will make you the head, not the tail. If
you pay attention to the commands of the LORD
your God that I give you this day and carefully follow them, you will always be at the top, never at
the bottom. 14Do not turn aside from any of the
commands I give you today, to the right or to the
28:14 [y]Dt 5:32 left,[y] following other gods and serving them.

Curses for Disobedience

28:15 15However, if you do not obey[z] the LORD your
[z]Lev 26:14 [a]Jos 23:15; God and do not carefully follow all his commands
Da 9:11; Mal 2:2 and decrees I am giving you today, all these curses
will come upon you and overtake you:[a]

16You will be cursed in the city and cursed
in the country.
17Your basket and your kneading trough
will be cursed.
18The fruit of your womb will be cursed,
and the crops of your land, and the calves of
your herds and the lambs of your flocks.
19You will be cursed when you come in and
cursed when you go out.

28:20 [b]Mal 2:2 20The LORD will send on you curses,[b] confusion
[c]Isa 51:20; 66:15 and rebuke[c] in everything you put your hand to,
until you are destroyed and come to sudden ruin[d]
[d]Dt 4:26 because of the evil you have done in forsaking
him.[a] 21The LORD will plague you with diseases
28:21 until he has destroyed you from the land you are
[e]Lev 26:25; Jer 24:10 entering to possess.[e] 22The LORD will strike you
with wasting disease, with fever and inflammation, with scorching heat and drought,[f] with
28:22 [f]Lev 26:16 blight and mildew, which will plague you until
[g]Am 4:9 you perish.[g] 23The sky over your head will be
28:23 bronze, the ground beneath you iron.[h] 24The LORD
[h]Lev 26:19 will turn the rain of your country into dust and

[a]20 Hebrew *me*

Beatitudes for Daily Living

DT 28:1–14

Do you look for God in everything? Moses informs the Israelites that maintaining a right relationship with God will affect their whole pattern of living. He attaches a relationship with the Most Holy One to the consequences of living in a very real world, and he promises that wholehearted devotion to God will infuse the Israelites' daily lives with power for living well.

As women, these "beatitudes" stir something within us, because they are connected with the most intimate parts of our lives: children, home, friendships. We long to be righteous women who serve God with all our hearts, but we are undone by piles of laundry, fussy children and snoring husbands. Consider writing a prayer or meditation for doing the laundry, rocking your baby or dusting the living room, inviting God into all the moments of your life.

Heads or Tails?

DT 28:43–44

Moses warns the Israelites that a breakdown in their relationship with God will result in the disintegration of the blessings of obedience. Aliens in the land of promise will prosper and oversee the Israelites. This warning is a good reminder that freedom is not the absence of restraint, but it is found in choosing whom we will serve. In choosing to disobey God and his Word, the Israelites return to bondage. In choosing to serve God, they become free for the blessings of God to reign in their lives. Moses uses a "heads or tails" metaphor familiar to the Hebrews (Dt 28:13,44; Isa 9:14; 19:15).

Throughout Scripture God reminds us that to be first is to submit to God's authority; to increase is to agree to decrease the control and rule of our lives; and to be free, really free, is to lose our lives in surrender to the One who sets captives free (Mt 10:39; 20:16; Jn 3:30).

powder; it will come down from the skies until
you are destroyed.
25 The LORD will cause you to be defeated before
your enemies. You will come at them from one
direction but flee from them in seven,[i] and you
will become a thing of horror to all the kingdoms
on earth.[j] 26 Your carcasses will be food for all the
birds of the air and the beasts of the earth, and
there will be no one to frighten them away.[k] 27 The
LORD will afflict you with the boils of Egypt[l] and
with tumors, festering sores and the itch, from
which you cannot be cured. 28 The LORD will afflict
you with madness, blindness and confusion of
mind. 29 At midday you will grope[m] about like a
blind man in the dark. You will be unsuccessful in
everything you do; day after day you will be
oppressed and robbed, with no one to rescue you.
30 You will be pledged to be married to a
woman, but another will take her and ravish her.[n]
You will build a house, but you will not live in it.[o]
You will plant a vineyard, but you will not even
begin to enjoy its fruit.[p] 31 Your ox will be slaughtered before your eyes, but you will eat none of it.
Your donkey will be forcibly taken from you and
will not be returned. Your sheep will be given to
your enemies, and no one will rescue them.
32 Your sons and daughters will be given to another nation,[q] and you will wear out your eyes
watching for them day after day, powerless to lift
a hand. 33 A people that you do not know will eat
what your land and labor produce, and you will
have nothing but cruel oppression all your days.[r]
34 The sights you see will drive you mad. 35 The
LORD will afflict your knees and legs with painful
boils[s] that cannot be cured, spreading from the
soles of your feet to the top of your head.
36 The LORD will drive you and the king[t] you set
over you to a nation unknown to you or your
fathers.[u] There you will worship other gods, gods
of wood and stone.[v] 37 You will become a thing of
horror and an object of scorn and ridicule to all
the nations where the LORD will drive you.[w]
38 You will sow much seed in the field but you
will harvest little,[x] because locusts will devour[y] it.
39 You will plant vineyards and cultivate them but
you will not drink the wine or gather the grapes,
because worms will eat them.[z] 40 You will have
olive trees throughout your country but you will
not use the oil, because the olives will drop off.[a]
41 You will have sons and daughters but you will
not keep them, because they will go into captivity.[b] 42 Swarms of locusts will take over all your
trees and the crops of your land.
43 The alien who lives among you will rise above
you higher and higher, but you will sink lower
and lower.[c] 44 He will lend to you, but you will not
lend to him.[d] He will be the head, but you will be
the tail.[e]
45 All these curses will come upon you. They
will pursue you and overtake you until you are
destroyed,[f] because you did not obey the LORD

28:25 [i]Isa 30:17 [j]Jer 15:4; 24:9; Eze 23:46
28:26 [k]Jer 7:33; 16:4; 34:20
28:27 [l]ver 60-61; 1Sa 5:6
28:29 [m]Job 5:14; Isa 59:10
28:30 [n]Job 31:10; Jer 8:10 [o]Am 5:11 [p]Jer 12:13
28:32 [q]ver 41
28:33 [r]Jer 5:15-17
28:35 [s]ver 27
28:36 [t]2Ki 17:4,6; 24:12,14; 25:7,11 [u]Jer 16:13 [v]Dt 4:28
28:37 [w]Jer 24:9
28:38 [x]Mic 6:15; Hag 1:6,9 [y]Joel 1:4
28:39 [z]Isa 5:10; 17:10-11
28:40 [a]Mic 6:15
28:41 [b]ver 32
28:43 [c]ver 13
28:44 [d]ver 12 [e]ver 13
28:45 [f]ver 15

your God and observe the commands and decrees
he gave you. [46]They will be a sign and a wonder
to you and your descendants forever.[g] [47]Because
you did not serve[h] the LORD your God joyfully and
gladly[i] in the time of prosperity, [48]therefore in
hunger and thirst, in nakedness and dire poverty,
you will serve the enemies the LORD sends against
you. He will put an iron yoke[j] on your neck until
he has destroyed you.
[49]The LORD will bring a nation against you from
far away, from the ends of the earth,[k] like an
eagle[l] swooping down, a nation whose language
you will not understand, [50]a fierce-looking nation
without respect for the old[m] or pity for the young.
[51]They will devour the young of your livestock
and the crops of your land until you are destroyed.
They will leave you no grain, new wine or oil, nor
any calves of your herds or lambs of your flocks
until you are ruined.[n] [52]They will lay siege to all
the cities throughout your land until the high fortified walls in which you trust fall down. They
will besiege all the cities throughout the land the
LORD your God is giving you.[o]
[53]Because of the suffering that your enemy will
inflict on you during the siege, you will eat the
fruit of the womb, the flesh of the sons and
daughters the LORD your God has given you.[p]
[54]Even the most gentle and sensitive man among
you will have no compassion on his own brother
or the wife he loves or his surviving children,
[55]and he will not give to one of them any of the
flesh of his children that he is eating. It will be all
he has left because of the suffering your enemy
will inflict on you during the siege of all your cities. [56]The most gentle and sensitive[q] woman
among you—so sensitive and gentle that she
would not venture to touch the ground with the
sole of her foot—will begrudge the husband she
loves and her own son or daughter [57]the afterbirth
from her womb and the children she bears. For
she intends to eat them secretly during the siege
and in the distress that your enemy will inflict on
you in your cities.
[58]If you do not carefully follow all the words of
this law, which are written in this book, and do
not revere[r] this glorious and awesome name[s]—the
LORD your God— [59]the LORD will send fearful
plagues on you and your descendants, harsh and
prolonged disasters, and severe and lingering illnesses. [60]He will bring upon you all the diseases
of Egypt[t] that you dreaded, and they will cling to
you. [61]The LORD will also bring on you every kind
of sickness and disaster not recorded in this Book
of the Law, until you are destroyed.[u] [62]You who
were as numerous as the stars in the sky[v] will be
left but few in number, because you did not obey
the LORD your God. [63]Just as it pleased[w] the LORD
to make you prosper and increase in number, so it
will please[x] him to ruin and destroy you. You will
be uprooted[y] from the land you are entering to
possess.

28:46 [g]Isa 8:18; Eze 14:8
28:47 [h]Dt 32:15 [i]Ne 9:35
28:48 [j]Jer 28:13-14
28:49 [k]Jer 5:15; 6:22 [l]La 4:19; Hos 8:1
28:50 [m]Isa 47:6
28:51 [n]ver 33
28:52 [o]Jer 10:18; Zep 1:14-16, 17
28:53 [p]Lev 26:29; 2Ki 6:28-29; Jer 19:9; La 2:20; 4:10
28:56 [q]ver 54
28:58 [r]Mal 1:14 [s]Ex 6:3
28:60 [t]ver 27
28:61 [u]Dt 4:25-26
28:62 [v]Dt 4:27; 10:22; Ne 9:23
28:63 [w]Jer 32:41 [x]Pr 1:26 [y]Jer 12:14; 45:4

Womanhood

DT 28:56-57

Moses continues to warn of the disastrous results of disobedience. He doesn't hold back. The women he describes in this passage are as far from their God-given design as conceivably possible—to the horrifying extreme of devouring their own children. Moses' warning finds fulfillment later in Israel's history (2Ki 6:24-29).

We lose the essence of who we are made to be when we wander from God and his Word. When we don't understand God's design for us as women, we may shrink to fill the small and superficial pictures prescribed by advertising and media executives. Where do you look to discover who you are? Begin a comprehensive study of the subject of women in the Bible. Write down everything that resonates with you, and pray for intimate application to your own life.

Memory and Miracle

DT 29:5

Moses reminds the Israelites of the miraculous provisions of God for everyday desert living, including clothes and sandals that did not wear out. *Why did they need to be reminded of these supernatural blessings? A mere three days after the Israelites had escaped from Egypt through the parted Red Sea, they had pleaded, "Just let us go back to what we know"* (Nu 14:2-3).

God gives the Israelites 40 *years of struggle in order to weave together miracle and memory into a tapestry of faith-filled living. We may think that dramatic miracles would bolster our faith and that we would never forget them, but we are not that different from the Hebrew wanderers. Look for God's blessings everywhere—in joyful circumstances, in painful memories, in the humdrum of everyday life. Write them down; etch them on your soul to strengthen you for the journey ahead.*

64Then the LORD will scatter[z] you among all
nations,[a] from one end of the earth to the other.
There you will worship other gods—gods of wood
and stone, which neither you nor your fathers
have known. 65Among those nations you will find
no repose, no resting place for the sole of your
foot. There the LORD will give you an anxious
mind, eyes weary with longing, and a despairing
heart.[b] 66You will live in constant suspense, filled
with dread both night and day, never sure of your
life. 67In the morning you will say, "If only it were
evening!" and in the evening, "If only it were
morning!"—because of the terror that will fill
your hearts and the sights that your eyes will see.[c]
68The LORD will send you back in ships to Egypt
on a journey I said you should never make again.
There you will offer yourselves for sale to your
enemies as male and female slaves, but no one
will buy you.

Renewal of the Covenant

29 These are the terms of the covenant the
LORD commanded Moses to make with the
Israelites in Moab, in addition to the covenant he
had made with them at Horeb.[d]

2Moses summoned all the Israelites and said to
them:

Your eyes have seen all that the LORD did in
Egypt to Pharaoh, to all his officials and to all his
land.[e] 3With your own eyes you saw those great
trials, those miraculous signs and great wonders.[f]
4But to this day the LORD has not given you a mind
that understands or eyes that see or ears that
hear.[g] 5During the forty years that I led you
through the desert, your clothes did not wear out,
nor did the sandals on your feet.[h] 6You ate no
bread and drank no wine or other fermented
drink. I did this so that you might know that I am
the LORD your God.[i]

7When you reached this place, Sihon[j] king of
Heshbon and Og king of Bashan came out to fight
against us, but we defeated them.[k] 8We took their
land and gave it as an inheritance to the Reubenites, the Gadites and the half-tribe of Manasseh.[l]

9Carefully follow[m] the terms of this covenant,
so that you may prosper in everything you do.[n]
10All of you are standing today in the presence of
the LORD your God—your leaders and chief men,
your elders and officials, and all the other men of
Israel, 11together with your children and your
wives, and the aliens living in your camps who
chop your wood and carry your water.[o] 12You are
standing here in order to enter into a covenant
with the LORD your God, a covenant the LORD is
making with you this day and sealing with an
oath, 13to confirm you this day as his people,[p] that
he may be your God[q] as he promised you and as
he swore to your fathers, Abraham, Isaac and
Jacob. 14I am making this covenant,[r] with its oath,
not only with you 15who are standing here with

28:64 [z]Lev 26:33; Dt 4:27 [a]Ne 1:8
28:65 [b]Lev 26:16, 36
28:67 [c]ver 34; Job 7:4
29:1 [d]Dt 5:2-3
29:2 [e]Ex 19:4
29:3 [f]Dt 4:34; 7:19
29:4 [g]Isa 6:10; Ac 28:26-27; Ro 11:8*; Eph 4:18
29:5 [h]Dt 8:4
29:6 [i]Dt 8:3
29:7 [j]Dt 2:32; 3:1 [k]Nu 21:21-24,33-35
29:8 [l]Nu 32:33; Dt 3:12-13
29:9 [m]Dt 4:6; Jos 1:7 [n]1Ki 2:3
29:11 [o]Jos 9:21,23, 27
29:13 [p]Dt 28:9 [q]Ge 17:7; Ex 6:7
29:14 [r]Jer 31:31

us today in the presence of the LORD our God but also with those who are not here today.[s]

16 You yourselves know how we lived in Egypt and how we passed through the countries on the way here. 17 You saw among them their detestable images and idols of wood and stone, of silver and gold.[t] 18 Make sure there is no man or woman, clan or tribe among you today whose heart turns away from the LORD our God to go and worship the gods of those nations; make sure there is no root among you that produces such bitter poison.[u]

19 When such a person hears the words of this oath, he invokes a blessing on himself and therefore thinks, "I will be safe, even though I persist in going my own way." This will bring disaster on the watered land as well as the dry.[a] 20 The LORD will never be willing to forgive him; his wrath and zeal[v] will burn[w] against that man. All the curses written in this book will fall upon him, and the LORD will blot[x] out his name from under heaven. 21 The LORD will single him out from all the tribes of Israel for disaster, according to all the curses of the covenant written in this Book of the Law.

22 Your children who follow you in later generations and foreigners who come from distant lands will see the calamities that have fallen on the land and the diseases with which the LORD has afflicted it.[y] 23 The whole land will be a burning waste[z] of salt[a] and sulfur—nothing planted, nothing sprouting, no vegetation growing on it. It will be like the destruction of Sodom and Gomorrah,[b] Admah and Zeboiim, which the LORD overthrew in fierce anger. 24 All the nations will ask: "Why has the LORD done this to this land?[c] Why this fierce, burning anger?"

25 And the answer will be: "It is because this people abandoned the covenant of the LORD, the God of their fathers, the covenant he made with them when he brought them out of Egypt. 26 They went off and worshiped other gods and bowed down to them, gods they did not know, gods he had not given them. 27 Therefore the LORD's anger burned against this land, so that he brought on it all the curses written in this book.[d] 28 In furious anger and in great wrath the LORD uprooted[e] them from their land and thrust them into another land, as it is now."

29 The secret things belong to the LORD our God, but the things revealed belong to us and to our children forever, that we may follow all the words of this law.

Prosperity After Turning to the LORD

30 When all these blessings and curses[f] I have set before you come upon you and you take them to heart wherever the LORD your God disperses you among the nations,[g] 2 and when you and your children return[h] to the LORD your God and obey him with all your heart and with all

29:15 [s]Ac 2:39
29:17 [t]Dt 28:36
29:18 [u]Dt 11:16; Heb 12:15
29:20 [v]Eze 23:25 [w]Ps 74:1; 79:5 [x]Ex 32:33; Dt 9:14
29:22 [y]Jer 19:8
29:23 [z]Isa 34:9 [a]Jer 17:6 [b]Ge 19:24, 25; Zep 2:9
29:24 [c]1Ki 9:8; Jer 22:8-9
29:27 [d]Da 9:11,13, 14
29:28 [e]1Ki 14:15; 2Ch 7:20; Ps 52:5; Pr 2:22
30:1 [f]ver 15,19; Dt 11:26 [g]Lev 26:40-45; Dt 28:64; 29:28; 1Ki 8:47
30:2 [h]Dt 4:30; Ne 1:9

Hope for the Future

DT 29:14-15

In renewing the covenant between God and his people, Moses proclaims that the promises are not only for those people who are present with him on this very day, but they are also for all God's people yet to come. He encourages them with the wonderful promise of God's enduring love and concern for them, now and for the generations to come (Ac 2:39).

*This aspect of God's character—*enduring love*—brings special comfort to parents. Nothing stirs longing within mothers like their children. We long for them to be happy, successful and good. When our children struggle due to their unique make-up or their bad choices, we hurt and wonder what will become of them. We can take comfort from God's character—his love not only endures through foolish wandering, but it reaches into the future with compassion and concern. There is One who longs for and loves our children more than we do, and he promises: "I know the plans I have for you . . . to give you hope and a future" (Jer 29:11).*

[a] 19 Or *way, in order to add drunkenness to thirst."*

Choose Life!

DT 30:19-20

Moses defines life—not merely living, but living well, living abundantly. Love God, listen to his Word and hold fast to him. Moses repeatedly reminds the Israelites that the only choice that will guard them, guide them, and guarantee living well is the choice to love God with all their heart, soul and mind—to turn their hearts toward him in struggle and victory, in daily life and dramatic adventure, in times of faith and moments of doubt.

Can we make the choice for life when that choice is hard, when doing so requires every ounce of faith we can eke out? The story of Deuteronomy becomes our story when we believe that each moment in which we love God, listen to his Word, and cling to him for dear life *we are really living*! ***May our hearts echo together in prayerful determination: "We do not want to live any other way."***

your soul according to everything I command you
today, 3then the LORD your God will restore your
fortunes[a][i] and have compassion on you and gather[j] you again from all the nations where he scattered you.[k] 4Even if you have been banished to the
most distant land under the heavens, from there
the LORD your God will gather you and bring you
back.[l] 5He will bring[m] you to the land that
belonged to your fathers, and you will take possession of it. He will make you more prosperous
and numerous than your fathers. 6The LORD your
God will circumcise your hearts and the hearts of
your descendants,[n] so that you may love him with
all your heart and with all your soul, and live.
7The LORD your God will put all these curses on
your enemies who hate and persecute you.[o] 8You
will again obey the LORD and follow all his commands I am giving you today. 9Then the LORD
your God will make you most prosperous in all
the work of your hands and in the fruit of your
womb, the young of your livestock and the crops
of your land.[p] The LORD will again delight in you
and make you prosperous, just as he delighted in
your fathers, 10if you obey the LORD your God and
keep his commands and decrees that are written
in this Book of the Law and turn to the LORD your
God with all your heart and with all your soul.[q]

The Offer of Life or Death

11Now what I am commanding you today is not
too difficult for you or beyond your reach.[r] 12It is
not up in heaven, so that you have to ask, "Who
will ascend into heaven to get it and proclaim it to
us so we may obey it?"[s] 13Nor is it beyond the sea,
so that you have to ask, "Who will cross the sea to
get it and proclaim it to us so we may obey it?"
14No, the word is very near you; it is in your
mouth and in your heart so you may obey it.

15See, I set before you today life and prosperity,
death and destruction.[t] 16For I command you
today to love the LORD your God, to walk in his
ways, and to keep his commands, decrees and
laws; then you will live and increase, and the
LORD your God will bless you in the land you are
entering to possess.

17But if your heart turns away and you are not
obedient, and if you are drawn away to bow down
to other gods and worship them, 18I declare to you
this day that you will certainly be destroyed.[u] You
will not live long in the land you are crossing the
Jordan to enter and possess.

19This day I call heaven and earth as witnesses
against you[v] that I have set before you life and
death, blessings and curses.[w] Now choose life, so
that you and your children may live 20and that
you may love[x] the LORD your God, listen to his
voice, and hold fast to him. For the LORD is your
life,[y] and he will give you many years in the land

30:3 [i]Ps 126:4 [j]Ps 147:2; Jer 32:37; Eze 34:13 [k]Jer 29:14
30:4 [l]Ne 1:8-9; Isa 43:6
30:5 [m]Jer 29:14
30:6 [n]Dt 10:16; Jer 32:39
30:7 [o]Dt 7:15
30:9 [p]Dt 28:11; Jer 31:28; 32:41
30:10 [q]Dt 4:29
30:11 [r]Isa 45:19,23
30:12 [s]Ro 10:6*
30:15 [t]Dt 11:26
30:18 [u]Dt 8:19
30:19 [v]Dt 4:26 [w]ver 1
30:20 [x]Dt 6:5; 10:20 [y]Ps 27:1; Jn 11:25

[a] 3 Or *will bring you back from captivity*

he swore to give to your fathers, Abraham, Isaac and Jacob.

Joshua to Succeed Moses

31 Then Moses went out and spoke these words to all Israel: 2"I am now a hundred and twenty years old[z] and I am no longer able to lead you.[a] The LORD has said to me, 'You shall not cross the Jordan.'[b] 3The LORD your God himself will cross[c] over ahead of you.[d] He will destroy these nations before you, and you will take possession of their land. Joshua also will cross[e] over ahead of you, as the LORD said. 4And the LORD will do to them what he did to Sihon and Og, the kings of the Amorites, whom he destroyed along with their land. 5The LORD will deliver[f] them to you, and you must do to them all that I have commanded you. 6Be strong and courageous.[g] Do not be afraid or terrified[h] because of them, for the LORD your God goes with you;[i] he will never leave you[j] nor forsake[k] you."

7Then Moses summoned Joshua and said[l] to him in the presence of all Israel, "Be strong and courageous, for you must go with this people into the land that the LORD swore to their forefathers to give them, and you must divide it among them as their inheritance. 8The LORD himself goes before you and will be with you;[m] he will never leave you nor forsake you. Do not be afraid; do not be discouraged."

The Reading of the Law

9So Moses wrote down this law and gave it to the priests, the sons of Levi, who carried[n] the ark of the covenant of the LORD, and to all the elders of Israel. 10Then Moses commanded them: "At the end of every seven years, in the year for canceling debts,[o] during the Feast of Tabernacles,[p] 11when all Israel comes to appear[q] before the LORD your God at the place he will choose, you shall read this law[r] before them in their hearing. 12Assemble the people—men, women and children, and the aliens living in your towns—so they can listen and learn[s] to fear the LORD your God and follow carefully all the words of this law. 13Their children,[t] who do not know this law, must hear it and learn to fear the LORD your God as long as you live in the land you are crossing the Jordan to possess."

Israel's Rebellion Predicted

14The LORD said to Moses, "Now the day of your death[u] is near. Call Joshua and present yourselves at the Tent of Meeting, where I will commission him." So Moses and Joshua came and presented themselves at the Tent of Meeting.

15Then the LORD appeared at the Tent in a pillar of cloud, and the cloud stood over the entrance to the Tent.[v] 16And the LORD said to Moses: "You are going to rest with your fathers, and these people

31:2 [z]Dt 34:7 [a]Nu 27:17; 1Ki 3:7 [b]Dt 3:23,26
31:3 [c]Nu 27:18 [d]Dt 9:3 [e]Dt 3:28
31:5 [f]Dt 7:2
31:6 [g]Jos 10:25; 1Ch 22:13 [h]Dt 7:18 [i]Dt 1:29; 20:4 [j]Jos 1:5 [k]Heb 13:5*
31:7 [l]Dt 1:38; 3:28
31:8 [m]Ex 13:21; 33:14
31:9 [n]ver 25; Nu 4:15; Jos 3:3
31:10 [o]Dt 15:1 [p]Lev 23:34
31:11 [q]Dt 16:16 [r]Jos 8:34-35; 2Ki 23:2
31:12 [s]Dt 4:10
31:13 [t]Dt 11:2; Ps 78:6-7
31:14 [u]Nu 27:13; Dt 32:49-50
31:15 [v]Ex 33:9

The Source of Our Faith

DT 31:10-11

The priests are responsible for reading the law publicly to the people every seven years. Moses ends his remarks to the Israelites as he began them, with a reminder that possessing the promises of God is inextricably linked to reading, hearing, meditating on and obeying God's Word. Moses knows that in the days ahead the people will face great obstacles and mundane daily tasks that will test their faith and stretch it to its very limits. He reminds the Israelites of their source of wisdom, power and life itself—the Word of God. The book of Deuteronomy clearly and pointedly reveals the source of faith for people of God of all ages: "Faith comes from hearing the message, and the message is heard through the word of Christ" (Ro 10:17).

The Law's Purpose

DT 31:26

Moses instructs the Israelites to keep a copy of God's laws with the ark because he knows they will forget and falter and need to be challenged, rebuked and reminded of the words of God. If you read ahead in the story (Judges, 1 and 2 Kings), you'll discover that indeed the Israelites break God's laws, worship false gods and are conquered by other nations. It's a bit discouraging. And a bit familiar. If there's one thing we've all experienced, it's that "when I want to do good, evil is right there with me" (Ro 7:21). Deuteronomy teaches us that the law is "holy, righteous and good" (Ro 7:12), but we can't keep it. We need help. "Who will rescue [us] . . . ? Thanks be to God—through Jesus Christ our Lord" (Ro 7:24-25). The book of Deuteronomy points us straight to Jesus.

will soon prostitute[w] themselves to the foreign
gods of the land they are entering. They will forsake[x] me and break the covenant I made with
them. 17 On that day I will become angry[y] with
them and forsake[z] them; I will hide[a] my face from
them, and they will be destroyed. Many disasters
and difficulties will come upon them, and on that
day they will ask, 'Have not these disasters come
upon us because our God is not with us?'[b] 18 And
I will certainly hide my face on that day because
of all their wickedness in turning to other gods.
19 "Now write down for yourselves this song and
teach it to the Israelites and have them sing it, so
that it may be a witness for me against them.
20 When I have brought them into the land flowing
with milk and honey, the land I promised on oath
to their forefathers,[c] and when they eat their fill
and thrive, they will turn to other gods[d] and worship them, rejecting me and breaking my covenant.[e] 21 And when many disasters and difficulties come upon them,[f] this song will testify
against them, because it will not be forgotten by
their descendants. I know what they are disposed
to do,[g] even before I bring them into the land I
promised them on oath." 22 So Moses wrote[h] down
this song that day and taught it to the Israelites.
23 The LORD gave this command[i] to Joshua son of
Nun: "Be strong and courageous,[j] for you will
bring the Israelites into the land I promised them
on oath, and I myself will be with you."
24 After Moses finished writing in a book the
words of this law from beginning to end, 25 he gave
this command to the Levites who carried the ark
of the covenant of the LORD: 26 "Take this Book of
the Law and place it beside the ark of the covenant of the LORD your God. There it will remain
as a witness against you.[k] 27 For I know how rebellious and stiff-necked[l] you are. If you have been
rebellious against the LORD while I am still alive
and with you, how much more will you rebel
after I die! 28 Assemble before me all the elders of
your tribes and all your officials, so that I can
speak these words in their hearing and call heav-
en and earth to testify against them.[m] 29 For I know
that after my death you are sure to become utterly corrupt[n] and to turn from the way I have commanded you. In days to come, disaster[o] will fall
upon you because you will do evil in the sight of
the LORD and provoke him to anger by what your
hands have made."

The Song of Moses

30 And Moses recited the words of this song from
beginning to end in the hearing of the whole
assembly of Israel:

32 Listen, O heavens,[p] and I will speak;
hear, O earth, the words of my mouth.
2 Let my teaching fall like rain
and my words descend like dew,[q]
like showers[r] on new grass,

31:16 [w]Jdg 2:12 [x]Jdg 10:6,13
31:17 [y]Jdg 2:14,20 [z]Jdg 6:13; 2Ch 15:2 [a]Dt 32:20; Isa 1:15; 8:17 [b]Nu 14:42
31:20 [c]Dt 6:10-12 [d]Dt 32:15-17 [e]ver 16
31:21 [f]ver 17 [g]Hos 5:3
31:22 [h]ver 19
31:23 [i]ver 7 [j]Jos 1:6
31:26 [k]ver 19
31:27 [l]Ex 32:9; Dt 9:6,24
31:28 [m]Dt 4:26; 30:19; 32:1
31:29 [n]Dt 32:5; Jdg 2:19 [o]Dt 28:15
32:1 [p]Isa 1:2
32:2 [q]Isa 55:11 [r]Ps 72:6

like abundant rain on tender plants.
3 I will proclaim the name of the LORD.[s]
Oh, praise the greatness[t] of our God!
4 He is the Rock,[u] his works are perfect,[v]
and all his ways are just.
A faithful God[w] who does no wrong,
upright and just is he.
5 They have acted corruptly toward him;
to their shame they are no longer his
children,
but a warped and crooked
generation.[a][x]
6 Is this the way you repay[y] the LORD,
O foolish and unwise people?[z]
Is he not your Father,[a] your Creator,[b]
who made you and formed you?[b]
7 Remember the days of old;
consider the generations long past.
Ask your father and he will tell you,
your elders, and they will explain to
you.[c]
8 When the Most High gave the nations
their inheritance,
when he divided all mankind,[d]
he set up boundaries for the peoples
according to the number of the sons
of Israel.[c]
9 For the LORD's portion[e] is his people,
Jacob his allotted inheritance.[f]
10 In a desert[g] land he found him,
in a barren and howling waste.
He shielded him and cared for him;
he guarded him as the apple of his
eye,[h]
11 like an eagle that stirs up its nest
and hovers over its young,[i]
that spreads its wings to catch them
and carries them on its pinions.
12 The LORD alone led him;
no foreign god was with him.[j]
13 He made him ride on the heights[k] of the
land
and fed him with the fruit of the
fields.
He nourished him with honey from the
rock,
and with oil[l] from the flinty crag,
14 with curds and milk from herd and
flock
and with fattened lambs and goats,
with choice rams of Bashan
and the finest kernels of wheat.[m]
You drank the foaming blood of the
grape.[n]

32:3 [s]Ex 33:19 [t]Dt 3:24
32:4 [u]ver 15,18, 30 [v]2Sa 22:31 [w]Dt 7:9
32:5 [x]Dt 31:29
32:6 [y]Ps 116:12 [z]Ps 74:2 [a]Dt 1:31; Isa 63:16 [b]ver 15
32:7 [c]Ex 13:14
32:8 [d]Ge 11:8; Ac 17:26
32:9 [e]Jer 10:16 [f]1Ki 8:51,53
32:10 [g]Jer 2:6 [h]Ps 17:8; Zec 2:8
32:11 [i]Ex 19:4
32:12 [j]ver 39
32:13 [k]Isa 58:14 [l]Job 29:6
32:14 [m]Ps 81:16; 147:14 [n]Ge 49:11

[a] 5 Or *Corrupt are they and not his children, / a generation warped and twisted to their shame* [b] 6 Or *Father, who bought you* [c] 8 Masoretic Text; Dead Sea Scrolls (see also Septuagint) *sons of God*

The Song of Moses

DT 32:1-43

One of the most repeated words in the book of Deuteronomy is *remember*. Moses knows all too well the reality of human forgetfulness. He wisely gives this song to the Hebrews, knowing that, in recalling their deliverance, they are more likely to live as free people. Since few Israelites can read or write, history has to be passed down in oral forms. A song, with its rhythm and literary patterns, helps the people remember more easily than straight narrative might.

Construct your own song of deliverance. You might never sing it publicly, but remembering God's work in your life will strengthen you to live like someone who has been set free. Remember past blessings, personal forgiveness, evidence of God's presence in the world, and moments of intimate connection with God. Remember, "It is for freedom that Christ has set us free" (Gal 5:1). Sing a song of freedom!

God used common folks for the most sacred, esteemed assignment in human history: The birth of his only begotten Son. Jesus' birth was a consummate example of the extraordinary swaddled in the ordinary. And God, in his outrageous love, continues to use ordinary people—you and me—to ring in his kingdom today . . . God chooses and uses people who are willing to be used by him. Whether what we have seems great or small, God makes it much when we let him have his way in us. He took the loaves and fish from an ordinary little boy and multiplied it to feed over five thousand people. That's what he wants to do with us. God himself set the example of how to love by living and dying in service to the unlovely. His humble birth into human form—all for the love of humankind—was outrageous! God's very ordinariness is a stunning insult to the proud, a tender delight to the grateful. Every day we are also called to live extraordinary lives in ordinary ways.

—Thelma Wells

15 Jeshurun[a] grew fat[o] and kicked;
filled with food, he became heavy and sleek.
He abandoned[p] the God who made him
and rejected the Rock[q] his Savior.
16 They made him jealous[r] with their foreign gods
and angered[s] him with their detestable idols.
17 They sacrificed to demons, which are not God—
gods they had not known,[t]
gods that recently appeared,[u]
gods your fathers did not fear.
18 You deserted the Rock, who fathered you;
you forgot[v] the God who gave you birth.

19 The LORD saw this and rejected them[w]
because he was angered by his sons and daughters.[x]
20 "I will hide my face[y] from them," he said,
"and see what their end will be;
for they are a perverse generation,[z]
children who are unfaithful.
21 They made me jealous[a] by what is no god
and angered me with their worthless idols.[b]
I will make them envious by those who are not a people;
I will make them angry by a nation that has no understanding.[c]
22 For a fire has been kindled by my wrath,
one that burns to the realm of death[b] below.[d]
It will devour the earth and its harvests
and set afire the foundations of the mountains.

23 "I will heap calamities[e] upon them
and spend my arrows[f] against them.
24 I will send wasting famine against them,
consuming pestilence[g] and deadly plague;[h]
I will send against them the fangs of wild beasts,[i]
the venom of vipers[j] that glide in the dust.
25 In the street the sword will make them childless;
in their homes terror will reign.[k]
Young men and young women will perish,
infants and gray-haired men.[l]
26 I said I would scatter[m] them

32:15 [o]Dt 31:20 [p]ver 6; Isa 1:4,28 [q]ver 4
32:16 [r]1Co 10:22 [s]Ps 78:58
32:17 [t]Dt 28:64 [u]Jdg 5:8
32:18 [v]Isa 17:10
32:19 [w]Jer 44:21-23 [x]Ps 106:40
32:20 [y]Dt 31:17,29 [z]ver 5
32:21 [a]1Co 10:22 [b]1Ki 16:13, 26 [c]Ro 10:19*
32:22 [d]Ps 18:7-8; Jer 15:14; La 4:11
32:23 [e]Dt 29:21 [f]Ps 7:13; Eze 5:16
32:24 [g]Dt 28:22 [h]Ps 91:6 [i]Lev 26:22 [j]Am 5:18-19
32:25 [k]Eze 7:15 [l]2Ch 36:17; La 2:21
32:26 [m]Dt 4:27

[a] 15 *Jeshurun* means *the upright one*, that is, Israel.
[b] 22 Hebrew *to Sheol*

and blot out their memory from
32:26 [n]Ps 34:16 — mankind,[n]
27 but I dreaded the taunt of the enemy,
lest the adversary misunderstand
and say, 'Our hand has triumphed;
32:27 [o]Isa 10:13 — the LORD has not done all this.' "[o]

28 They are a nation without sense,
there is no discernment in them.
29 If only they were wise and would
32:29 [p]Dt 5:29; Ps 81:13 — understand this[p]
and discern what their end will be!
30 How could one man chase a thousand,
32:30 [q]Lev 26:8 [r]Ps 44:12 — or two put ten thousand to flight,[q]
unless their Rock had sold them,
unless the LORD had given them up?[r]
31 For their rock is not like our Rock,
as even our enemies concede.
32 Their vine comes from the vine of
Sodom
and from the fields of Gomorrah.
Their grapes are filled with poison,
and their clusters with bitterness.
33 Their wine is the venom of serpents,
32:33 [s]Ps 58:4 — the deadly poison of cobras.[s]

32:34 [t]Jer 2:22; Hos 13:12 — 34 "Have I not kept this in reserve
and sealed it in my vaults?[t]
35 It is mine to avenge; I will repay.[u]
32:35 [u]Ro 12:19*; Heb 10:30* [v]Jer 23:12 [w]Eze 7:8-9 — In due time their foot will slip;[v]
their day of disaster is near
and their doom rushes upon them.[w]"
36 The LORD will judge his people
32:36 [x]Dt 30:1-3; Ps 135:14; Joel 2:14 — and have compassion on his servants[x]
when he sees their strength is gone
and no one is left, slave or free.
37 He will say: "Now where are their gods,
32:37 [y]Jdg 10:14; Jer 2:28 — the rock they took refuge in,[y]
38 the gods who ate the fat of their
sacrifices
and drank the wine of their drink
offerings?
Let them rise up to help you!
Let them give you shelter!

32:39 [z]Isa 41:4 [a]Isa 45:5 [b]1Sa 2:6; Ps 68:20 [c]Hos 6:1 [d]Ps 50:22 — 39 "See now that I myself am He![z]
There is no god besides me.[a]
I put to death and I bring to life,[b]
I have wounded and I will heal,[c]
and no one can deliver out of my
hand.[d]
40 I lift my hand to heaven and declare:
As surely as I live forever,
32:41 [e]Isa 34:6; 66:16; Eze 21:9-10 [f]Jer 50:29 — 41 when I sharpen my flashing sword[e]
and my hand grasps it in judgment,
I will take vengeance on my adversaries
and repay those who hate me.[f]
42 I will make my arrows drunk with
32:42 [g]ver 23 [h]Jer 46:10,14 — blood,[g]
while my sword devours flesh:[h]
the blood of the slain and the captives,
the heads of the enemy leaders."

A Lesson in Grammar

DT 32:31

Moses uses a favorite Hebrew metaphor to remind the Israelites of a truth about God. He refers to God as "our Rock" and to pagan gods as "their rock." The Hebrew grammatical distinction reminds us that God is worthy of honor, that our relationship with him is to be set apart from all other relationships. Moses recalls how their Rock has come to their defense time and again and that even Israel's enemies can't help but concede that Israel's Rock is greater than their rock.

Just as Moses calls God a "Rock" in his song, so David also refers to God as a "Rock" in his psalms: "From the ends of the earth I call to you, I call as my heart grows faint; lead me to the rock that is higher than I" (Ps 61:2). We also call God our Rock, the one who will be our source of stability and comfort in a world of change and unrest.

43 Rejoice,[i] O nations, with his people,[a,b]
for he will avenge the blood of his
servants;[j]
he will take vengeance on his enemies
and make atonement for his land and
people.[k]

44 Moses came with Joshua[c][l] son of Nun and
spoke all the words of this song in the hearing of
the people. 45 When Moses finished reciting all
these words to all Israel, 46 he said to them, "Take
to heart all the words I have solemnly declared to
you this day,[m] so that you may command your
children to obey carefully all the words of this
law. 47 They are not just idle words for you—they
are your life.[n] By them you will live long in the
land you are crossing the Jordan to possess."

Moses to Die on Mount Nebo

48 On that same day the LORD told Moses, 49 "Go
up into the Abarim[o] Range to Mount Nebo in
Moab, across from Jericho, and view Canaan, the
land I am giving the Israelites as their own possession. 50 There on the mountain that you have
climbed you will die[p] and be gathered to your
people, just as your brother Aaron died on Mount
Hor and was gathered to his people. 51 This is
because both of you broke faith with me in the
presence of the Israelites at the waters of Meribah
Kadesh in the Desert of Zin[q] and because you did
not uphold my holiness among the Israelites.[r]
52 Therefore, you will see the land only from a distance;[s] you will not enter[t] the land I am giving to
the people of Israel."

Moses Blesses the Tribes

33 This is the blessing that Moses the man of
God[u] pronounced on the Israelites before
his death. 2 He said:

"The LORD came from Sinai[v]
and dawned over them from Seir;[w]
he shone forth from Mount Paran.[x]
He came with[d] myriads of holy ones[y]
from the south, from his mountain
slopes.[e]
3 Surely it is you who love[z] the people;
all the holy ones are in your hand.[a]
At your feet they all bow down,[b]
and from you receive instruction,
4 the law that Moses gave us,[c]
the possession of the assembly of
Jacob.[d]
5 He was king over Jeshurun[f]
when the leaders of the people
assembled,

[a] 43 Or *Make his people rejoice, O nations* [b] 43 Masoretic Text; Dead Sea Scrolls (see also Septuagint) *people, / and let all the angels worship him /* [c] 44 Hebrew *Hoshea,* a variant of *Joshua* [d] 2 Or *from* [e] 2 The meaning of the Hebrew for this phrase is uncertain. [f] 5 *Jeshurun* means *the upright one,* that is, Israel; also in verse 26.

32:43 [i]Ro 15:10* [j]2Ki 9:7 [k]Ps 65:3; 85:1; Rev 19:2
32:44 [l]Nu 13:8,16
32:46 [m]Eze 40:4
32:47 [n]Dt 30:20
32:49 [o]Nu 27:12
32:50 [p]Ge 25:8
32:51 [q]Nu 20:11-13 [r]Nu 27:14
32:52 [s]Dt 34:1-3 [t]Dt 1:37
33:1 [u]Jos 14:6
33:2 [v]Ex 19:18; Ps 68:8 [w]Jdg 5:4 [x]Hab 3:3 [y]Da 7:10; Ac 7:53; Rev 5:11
33:3 [z]Hos 11:1 [a]Dt 14:2 [b]Lk 10:39
33:4 [c]Jn 1:17 [d]Ps 119:111

Tonic for the Soul

DT 32:47

***Where do we find life?* We know we are relying on a false god when the inevitable difficulties, disappointments and struggles of living cause us to despair and consider quitting.** Moses reminds the Israelites that the Word of God is not idle—or impotent—but is tonic for the soul, uplifting to the spirit and empowering for the daily exercise of faith. Promises of strength for really living come at us from all sides. When we are saturated with media magic and faster-than-the-speed-of-light technology, we need to be reminded as often as the Israelites that true life is found only as we immerse ourselves in God's Word.

along with the tribes of Israel.
6 "Let Reuben live and not die,
nor[a] his men be few."

33:7 [e]Ge 49:10

7 And this he said about Judah:[e]

"Hear, O LORD, the cry of Judah;
bring him to his people.
With his own hands he defends his cause.
Oh, be his help against his foes!"

8 About Levi he said:

33:8 [f]Ex 28:30 [g]Ex 17:7

"Your Thummim and Urim[f] belong
to the man you favored.
You tested him at Massah;
you contended with him at the waters of Meribah.[g]

33:9 [h]Ex 32:26-29 [i]Mal 2:5

9 He said of his father and mother,[h]
'I have no regard for them.'
He did not recognize his brothers
or acknowledge his own children,
but he watched over your word
and guarded your covenant.[i]

33:10 [j]Lev 10:11; Dt 31:9-13 [k]Ps 51:19

10 He teaches your precepts to Jacob
and your law to Israel.[j]
He offers incense before you
and whole burnt offerings on your altar.[k]

33:11 [l]2Sa 24:23

11 Bless all his skills, O LORD,
and be pleased with the work of his hands.[l]
Smite the loins of those who rise up against him;
strike his foes till they rise no more."

12 About Benjamin he said:

33:12 [m]Dt 12:10 [n]Ex 28:12

"Let the beloved of the LORD rest secure in him,[m]
for he shields him all day long,
and the one the LORD loves rests between his shoulders.[n]"

33:13 [o]Ge 49:25 [p]Ge 27:28

13 About Joseph[o] he said:

"May the LORD bless his land
with the precious dew from heaven above
and with the deep waters that lie below;[p]
14 with the best the sun brings forth
and the finest the moon can yield;

33:15 [q]Hab 3:6

15 with the choicest gifts of the ancient mountains[q]
and the fruitfulness of the everlasting hills;
16 with the best gifts of the earth and its fullness
and the favor of him who dwelt in the burning bush.[r]

33:16 [r]Ex 3:2

[a] 6 Or *but let*

Family Ties

DT 33:9

As women, we may find this passage a bit unsettling. Forget our families? Is that what Moses is commending these Levites for? Not quite. Moses is actually praising the Levites for their commitment to God's Word above all else, including family ties. Does this mean they ignored their families, concentrating all their efforts instead on their God-given ministry tasks? Not at all. But their commitments are to maintain a strong connection first to God, then to family.

Sometimes, when our children wander far from home or our marriage is disappointing, we are tempted to do the opposite of the Levites and forget God. Whether in good or bad times, our hearts need to be turned first to God's Word, because it alone is a "lamp to [our] feet and a light for [our] path" (Ps 119:105). In a divine paradox, we find that a wholehearted commitment to God's Word—putting him first—enlarges our hearts and provides greater vigor to love our families.

Let all these rest on the head of Joseph,
on the brow of the prince among[a] his brothers.
17 In majesty he is like a firstborn bull;
his horns are the horns of a wild ox.[s]
With them he will gore[t] the nations,
even those at the ends of the earth.
Such are the ten thousands of Ephraim;
such are the thousands of Manasseh."

18 About Zebulun[u] he said:

"Rejoice, Zebulun, in your going out,
and you, Issachar, in your tents.
19 They will summon peoples to the mountain[v]
and there offer sacrifices of righteousness;[w]
they will feast on the abundance of the seas,[x]
on the treasures hidden in the sand."

20 About Gad[y] he said:

"Blessed is he who enlarges Gad's domain!
Gad lives there like a lion,
tearing at arm or head.
21 He chose the best land for himself;[z]
the leader's portion was kept for him.
When the heads of the people assembled,
he carried out the LORD's righteous will,[a]
and his judgments concerning Israel."

22 About Dan[b] he said:

"Dan is a lion's cub,
springing out of Bashan."

23 About Naphtali he said:

"Naphtali is abounding with the favor of the LORD
and is full of his blessing;
he will inherit southward to the lake."

24 About Asher[c] he said:

"Most blessed of sons is Asher;
let him be favored by his brothers,
and let him bathe his feet in oil.[d]
25 The bolts of your gates will be iron and bronze,
and your strength will equal your days.[e]
26 "There is no one like the God of Jeshurun,[f]
who rides on the heavens to help you[g]
and on the clouds in his majesty.

[a] 16 Or *of the one separated from*

33:17 [s]Nu 23:22 [t]1Ki 22:11; Ps 44:5
33:18 [u]Ge 49:13-15
33:19 [v]Ex 15:17; Isa 2:3 [w]Ps 4:5 [x]Isa 60:5, 11
33:20 [y]Ge 49:19
33:21 [z]Nu 32:1-5, 31-32 [a]Jos 4:12; 22:1-3
33:22 [b]Ge 49:16
33:24 [c]Ge 49:21 [d]Ge 49:20; Job 29:6
33:25 [e]Dt 4:40; 32:47
33:26 [f]Ex 15:11 [g]Ps 104:3

We only live once, and if we do it well enough, once is enough.

—Nicole Johnson

Jochebed

The Power of a Mother's Love

The pains of labor took her breath away, making her want to cry out. But Jochebed knew she must be silent. These were evil times, and Pharaoh was killing male babies. So Jochebed bit her lip and held back the scream as she pushed the child to his first breath. It was a boy! What joy! And what terror.

Mother love—in its powerful bonding force—enveloped her as she cradled her son Moses in her arms. Her time with him would be brief. Jochebed must give him up to save his life. God would make a way.

Jochebed and her husband, Amram, had a plan. Keep the baby hidden for now. Savor every moment. The baby was vigorous, with a lusty cry. Surely someone soon would hear from the street and come to seize him. So his parents decided that when he became too difficult to hide, they would give him back to God—in a basket.

Perhaps Jochebed knew that Pharaoh's daughter came to bathe at a certain spot in the river. It is also possible, however, that it was completely by "chance" that one so great found the child. Either way, it took tremendous faith for Jochebed to place her three-month-old baby so precariously on a river that could easily sweep him away on its current and that was home to hundreds of hungry crocodiles.

Imagine Jochebed's joy when she was hired to nurse her own baby for Pharaoh's daughter. Now she could treasure her child without fear. In the time she had—probably about three years—Jochebed knit Moses securely to his family. The rest she would have to trust to prayer, the powerful force that pours out of a mother's heart. It would be enough.

Only the deepest kind of love could surrender a child—even for the child's own good. Jochebed's deep love and her faith in God allowed Moses not only to live but to receive the best advantages: education, diplomacy in Pharaoh's court, language, literature. Egypt trained Moses for his destiny as the leader of Israel and author of the Pentateuch (the first five books of the Bible). But Jochebed's influence established his connection to the Hebrew people and, most importantly, to the God of Israel.

We worry about the influence of the world on the next generation. Its potential impact daunts us. But we can take comfort from the example of Jochebed. Her opportunity to shape her children was fleeting, but her legacy to and through her children lasted a lifetime—and far beyond. The time with our children is short, but our power to influence, great.

Jochebed
(Yahweh is glory)

Exodus 2:1-10; 6:20
Numbers 26:59
Hebrews 11:23

Candid SNAPSHOT Pharaoh's daughter said to her, "Take this baby and nurse him for me, and I will pay you." So the woman took the baby and nursed him. When the child grew older, she took him to Pharaoh's daughter and he became her son (Exodus 2:9-10).

Pharaoh's Daughter

Instrument of God

She sighed as she walked to the river for her bath. Life was so predictable, so boring. As Pharaoh's daughter she had every material advantage anyone could want, but she lacked purpose. But this day turned out like no other. The events of this day gave her a vision to last many years.

In a basket among the reeds, she found a baby. The boy was Hebrew, there could be no doubt. He was crying, and she felt sorry for him. She knew she could not let him be sacrificed to her father's insecurities. This baby was a gift from the gods. He would grow up to be great. She knew it. In fact, she would see to it.

A Hebrew woman to nurse the child? Excellent. She was probably the baby's mother, but no matter. Who could better nurture him in these critical early years than his own mother?

So began God's plan to raise up Moses as a leader to take his people to the promised land. Even though she was an idolater, Pharaoh's daughter was the perfect person in the perfect place to mold Moses into the man God wanted him to be.

She raised Moses as her own son. She provided every opportunity at her disposal for his education and grooming as a leader. Through the years, she probably also allowed him some contact with his birth family, for when God came to him in the desert, Moses clearly knew his brother Aaron's character and gifts.

Was her heart broken when Moses killed an Egyptian and fled for his life? Probably. She certainly had other plans for him. And perhaps she didn't live to see her adopted son return from the desert as God's appointed leader, gifted and strong enough to face one of the most powerful men on earth—the new pharaoh (who may have been her own brother). Moses had given her life purpose and direction. It is even possible—although not recorded—that she met the God of Israel along the way.

God's plans are far beyond our comprehension. He can use anyone he chooses to raise up a leader of his people, whether it is a single mother or a young couple from Pakistan or an impoverished Chinese mother and father or an unbelieving Egyptian princess. Even when things seemed most grim for his people, God was still at work, even using his people's enemies to bring about their deliverance. This should give us hope when our circumstances are most dire. God is still at work on our behalf, to accomplish his purposes in our lives.

Pharaoh's Daughter
Exodus 2:5–10
Acts 7:21
Hebrews 11:24

Candid SNAPSHOT She opened [the basket] and saw the baby. He was crying, and she felt sorry for him. "This is one of the Hebrew babies," she said (Exodus 2:6).

33:27 [h]Ps 90:1 27 The eternal God is your refuge,[h]
[i]Jos 24:18 and underneath are the everlasting
[j]Dt 7:2 arms.
He will drive out your enemy before
you,[i]
saying, 'Destroy him!'[j]
33:28 28 So Israel will live in safety alone;[k]
[k]Nu 23:9; Jer 23:6 Jacob's spring is secure
[l]Ge 27:28 in a land of grain and new wine,
where the heavens drop dew.[l]
33:29 29 Blessed are you, O Israel![m]
[m]Ps 144:15 [n]Ps 18:44 Who is like you,[n]
[o]2Sa 7:23 a people saved by the LORD?[o]
[p]Ps 115:9-11 He is your shield and helper[p]
[q]Dt 32:13 and your glorious sword.
Your enemies will cower before you,
and you will trample down their high
places.[a][q]"

The Death of Moses

34:1 **34** Then Moses climbed Mount Nebo from the
[r]Dt 32:49 [s]Dt 32:52 plains of Moab to the top of Pisgah, across
from Jericho.[r] There the LORD showed[s] him the
34:2 whole land—from Gilead to Dan, 2 all of Naphtali,
[t]Dt 11:24 the territory of Ephraim and Manasseh, all the
34:3 land of Judah as far as the western sea,[b][t] 3 the Neg-
[u]Jdg 1:16; 3:13; ev and the whole region from the Valley of Jeri-
2Ch 28:15 cho, the City of Palms,[u] as far as Zoar. 4 Then the
LORD said to him, "This is the land I promised on
34:4 [v]Ge 28:13 oath[v] to Abraham, Isaac and Jacob when I said, 'I
[w]Ge 12:7 will give it[w] to your descendants.' I have let you
[x]Dt 3:27 see it with your eyes, but you will not cross[x] over
34:5 into it."
[y]Nu 12:7 5 And Moses the servant of the LORD[y] died[z] there
[z]Dt 32:50; Jos 1:1-2 in Moab, as the LORD had said. 6 He buried him[c] in
Moab, in the valley opposite Beth Peor,[a] but to this
34:6 day no one knows where his grave is.[b] 7 Moses
[a]Dt 3:29 was a hundred and twenty years old[c] when he
[b]Jude 1:9 died, yet his eyes were not weak[d] nor his strength
34:7 gone. 8 The Israelites grieved for Moses in the
[c]Dt 31:2 [d]Ge 27:1 plains of Moab thirty days, until the time of weeping and mourning[e] was over.
34:8 9 Now Joshua son of Nun was filled with the
[e]Ge 50:3,10; spirit[d] of wisdom[f] because Moses had laid his
2Sa 11:27 hands on him.[g] So the Israelites listened to him
34:9 and did what the LORD had commanded Moses.
[f]Ge 41:38; 10 Since then, no prophet has risen in Israel like
Isa 11:2; Da 6:3 [g]Nu 27:18, Moses,[h] whom the LORD knew face to face,[i] 11 who
23 did all those miraculous signs and wonders[j] the
34:10 LORD sent him to do in Egypt—to Pharaoh and to
[h]Dt 18:15,18 all his officials[k] and to his whole land. 12 For no
[i]Ex 33:11; one has ever shown the mighty power or per-
Nu 12:6,8; Dt 5:4 formed the awesome deeds that Moses did in the
34:11 [j]Dt 4:34 [k]Dt 7:19 sight of all Israel.

When the Arrows Fly

DT 33:29

Moses ends his words to the Israelites with a metaphor comparing God to a shield and a sword. But unlike the shield held only in front or the sword wielded against a single attacker, God is able to surround his people and gloriously go both before them and behind them. Moses asks the people to join him in lifting their eyes to the One who has chosen them, surrounds them, has plans for them, and promises to deliver them. When they face obstacles, they need to remember that God is their sword and shield. He goes before and behind them on the battlefield. When the arrows start to fly, they can look beyond themselves to the One who is their Promise. "But you are a shield around me, O LORD; you bestow glory on me and lift up my head. To the LORD I cry aloud, and he answers me from his holy hill (Ps 3:3-4).

[a] *29* Or *will tread upon their bodies* [b] *2* That is, the Mediterranean [c] *6* Or *He was buried* [d] *9* Or *Spirit*

Joshua

Victory comes through faith in God.

Quick Study

Author
Joshua probably wrote the book in its earliest form with Eleazar, son of Aaron, adding the conclusion. Later editing may have been done, possibly by Samuel.

Date Written
The original manuscript was probably written sometime in the 1300s B.C., with additions and edits at later dates, possibly during the early monarchy of Israel.

Setting
The land of Canaan.

Key Passage
Joshua 24:15 "Choose for yourselves this day whom you will serve, whether the gods your forefathers served beyond the River, or the gods of the Amorites, in whose land you are living. But as for me and my household, we will serve the LORD."

The faithfulness of God is apparent throughout the narrative of Joshua. As the Israelites begin to put down roots in their new homeland, they shift from a nomadic band of wanderers to a settled community whose existence is totally dependent on God. Although the Israelites are faced with temptations and obstacles, Joshua's strong leadership brings them to success as they rely on and obey God.

In the opening chapter of Joshua, we're reminded of God's presence and power as he inspires Joshua to face seemingly insurmountable obstacles with courage. We watch as Rahab, the prostitute with resourcefulness and bravery, assists Israel in its triumph over Jericho (Jos 2). This unlikely member of the family of God reinforces another lesson from the book of Joshua—that faithfulness to God brings rewards (Jos 14). We smile as Acsah charms her father, Caleb, into giving her and her husband not only a field but also springs to water the field (Jos 15:13–19). We are amazed at the miracle of the sun standing still (Jos 10) and marvel as the Canaanites' land is transformed into the Israelites' land when each tribe is allotted towns, cities and fields (Jos 13–22).

In the final chapters of the book, Joshua gathers the people together for his farewell speeches. Knowing their inclination toward disobedience and idolatry, he challenges them to choose whom they will serve (Jos 23–24), an exhortation that's as fitting for us today as it was for the Israelites thousands of years ago.

Outline

Encouragement for Joshua.
Jos 1

Rahab and the spies.
Jos 2

Crossing the Jordan.
Jos 3–4

Circumcision at Gilgal.
Jos 5:1–12

Conquering Jericho.
Jos 5:13–6:27

Achan's sin.
Jos 7

Ai destroyed.
Jos 8:1–29

The covenant renewed at Mount Ebal.
Jos 8:30–35

The Gibeonite deception.
Jos 9

The triumphant Israelites.
Jos 10–12

Dividing the land.
Jos 13–19

Cities of refuge.
Jos 20

Levite towns.
Jos 21

Return of the eastern tribes.
Jos 22

Joshua's farewell challenges.
Jos 23:1–24:27

Joshua's death.
Jos 24:28–33

The Women of Joshua

☙ **Rahab** — *A most unlikely ally.* Jos 2; 6:17–25; Mt 1:5; Heb 11:31; Jas 2:25 (page 469)

Acsah — *She knew what she wanted—and got it.* Jos 15:16–19

☙ Denotes a sketch written about this character

True Success

JOS 1:8

"If you are faithful to God, you will get rich." Is that the message God is giving to Joshua, the people of Israel and believers through all history? The answer is yes and no.

Prosperity and success come in many forms. Our Savior did not have a place to lay his head (Mt 8:20). The Lord of glory was born in a stable and worked as a common carpenter. He never made the top ten list for wealthiest people of his day. Yet Jesus was both prosperous and successful. The apostle Paul traded position and power in the religious establishment of his day for beatings, sleepless nights and the utter joy of planting churches. Successful? Prosperous? Absolutely!

God's promise to his people is that if they follow him and walk in faithfulness, he will bless them. This blessing can take many shapes. Sometimes it will mean monetary provision. Many Biblical characters experienced this. Yet it is a bigger picture than just dollars and cents. Just ask Jesus and Paul.

The LORD Commands Joshua

1 After the death of Moses the servant of the
LORD,[a] the LORD said to Joshua[b] son of Nun, 1:1
Moses' aide: 2"Moses my servant is dead. Now [a]Nu 12:7; Dt 34:5
then, you and all these people, get ready to cross [b]Ex 24:13;
the Jordan River[c] into the land I am about to give Dt 1:38
to them—to the Israelites. 3I will give you every 1:2
place where you set your foot,[d] as I promised [c]ver 11
Moses. 4Your territory will extend from the desert 1:3
to Lebanon, and from the great river, the Euphra- [d]Dt 11:24
tes[e]—all the Hittite country—to the Great Sea[a] on 1:4
the west.[f] 5No one will be able to stand up against [e]Ge 15:18
you[g] all the days of your life. As I was with[h] [f]Nu 34:2-12
Moses, so I will be with you; I will never leave
you nor forsake[i] you. 1:5
6"Be strong and courageous, because you will [g]Dt 7:24
lead these people to inherit the land I swore to [h]Jos 3:7; 6:27
their forefathers[j] to give them. 7Be strong and very [i]Dt 31:6-8
courageous. Be careful to obey all the law my ser- 1:6
vant Moses gave you; do not turn from it to the [j]Dt 31:23
right or to the left,[k] that you may be successful 1:7
wherever you go.[l] 8Do not let this Book of the Law [k]Dt 5:32;
depart from your mouth; meditate on it day and 28:14
night, so that you may be careful to do everything [l]Jos 11:15
written in it. Then you will be prosperous and
successful.[m] 9Have I not commanded you? Be 1:8
strong and courageous. Do not be terrified;[n] do [m]Dt 29:9; Ps 1:1-3
not be discouraged, for the LORD your God will be
with you wherever you go."[o] 1:9
10So Joshua ordered the officers of the people: [n]Ps 27:1
11"Go through the camp and tell the people, 'Get [o]ver 7;
your supplies ready. Three days from now you Dt 31:7-8; Jer 1:8
will cross the Jordan here to go in and take possession[p] of the land the LORD your God is giving 1:11
you for your own.' " [p]Joel 3:2
12But to the Reubenites, the Gadites and the half-
tribe of Manasseh,[q] Joshua said, 13"Remember the 1:12
command that Moses the servant of the LORD gave [q]Nu 32:20-22
you: 'The LORD your God is giving you rest[r] and
has granted you this land.' 14Your wives, your chil- 1:13
dren and your livestock may stay in the land that [r]Dt 3:18-20
Moses gave you east of the Jordan, but all your
fighting men, fully armed, must cross over ahead
of your brothers. You are to help your brothers
15until the LORD gives them rest, as he has done for
you, and until they too have taken possession of
the land that the LORD your God is giving them.
After that, you may go back and occupy your own
land, which Moses the servant of the LORD gave
you east of the Jordan toward the sunrise."[s] 1:15
16Then they answered Joshua, "Whatever you [s]Jos 22:1-4
have commanded us we will do, and wherever
you send us we will go. 17Just as we fully obeyed
Moses, so we will obey you.[t] Only may the LORD 1:17
your God be with you as he was with Moses. [t]ver 5,9
18Whoever rebels against your word and does not
obey your words, whatever you may command
them, will be put to death. Only be strong and
courageous!"

[a] *4* That is, the Mediterranean

Rahab and the Spies

2:1 **2** Then Joshua son of Nun secretly sent two
uJas 2:25 spies[u] from Shittim.[v] "Go, look over the land,"
vNu 25:1; he said, "especially Jericho." So they went and
Jos 3:1 entered the house of a prostitute[a] named Rahab[w]
wHeb 11:31 and stayed there.
2 The king of Jericho was told, "Look! Some of
the Israelites have come here tonight to spy out
the land." 3 So the king of Jericho sent this message to Rahab: "Bring out the men who came to
you and entered your house, because they have
come to spy out the whole land."
2:4 4 But the woman had taken the two men and
x2Sa 17:19- hidden them.[x] She said, "Yes, the men came to
20 me, but I did not know where they had come
from. 5 At dusk, when it was time to close the city
gate, the men left. I don't know which way they
went. Go after them quickly. You may catch up
with them." 6 (But she had taken them up to the
2:6 roof and hidden them under the stalks of flax[y] she
yJas 2:25 had laid out on the roof.)[z] 7 So the men set out in
zEx 1:17,19; pursuit of the spies on the road that leads to the
2Sa 17:19 fords of the Jordan, and as soon as the pursuers
had gone out, the gate was shut.
8 Before the spies lay down for the night, she
went up on the roof 9 and said to them, "I know
that the LORD has given this land to you and that
2:9 a great fear[a] of you has fallen on us, so that all
aGe 35:5; Ex 23:27; who live in this country are melting in fear
Dt 2:25 because of you. 10 We have heard how the LORD
2:10 dried up[b] the water of the Red Sea[b] for you when
bEx 14:21 cNu 23:22 you came out of Egypt,[c] and what you did to
dNu 21:21, Sihon and Og,[d] the two kings of the Amorites east
24,34-35 of the Jordan, whom you completely destroyed.[c]
2:11 11 When we heard of it, our hearts melted and
eEx 15:14; everyone's courage failed because of you,[e] for the
Jos 5:1; 7:5; Ps 22:14; LORD your God is God in heaven above and on the
Isa 13:7 earth[f] below. 12 Now then, please swear to me by
fDt 4:39 the LORD that you will show kindness to my fam-
2:12 ily, because I have shown kindness to you. Give
gver 18 me a sure sign[g] 13 that you will spare the lives of
my father and mother, my brothers and sisters,
and all who belong to them, and that you will
save us from death."
14 "Our lives for your lives!" the men assured
her. "If you don't tell what we are doing, we will
2:14 treat you kindly and faithfully[h] when the LORD
hJdg 1:24; Mt 5:7 gives us the land."
2:15 15 So she let them down by a rope through the
iAc 9:25 window,[i] for the house she lived in was part of
the city wall. 16 Now she had said to them, "Go to
the hills so the pursuers will not find you. Hide
2:16 jJas 2:25 yourselves there three days[j] until they return, and
kHeb 11:31 then go on your way."[k]
2:17 17 The men said to her, "This oath[l] you made us
lGe 24:8 swear will not be binding on us 18 unless, when

[a] *1* Or possibly *an innkeeper* [b] *10* Hebrew *Yam Suph*; that is, Sea of Reeds [c] *10* The Hebrew term refers to the irrevocable giving over of things or persons to the LORD, often by totally destroying them.

Israel Is Different

JOS 2:8-11

When the nation of Israel begins to march toward a city, their enemies tremble in their sandals! They may be fearless and seasoned warriors, but their hearts melt with fear. Why? What is so different about Israel?

The answer is simple. God is leading this nation. As Israel marches forward, the seas part, cities fall and miracles are performed. The people of the land realize that God is with these people. In a time when each people group believes in its own territorial god who rules the nation, they are confronted by a people whose God is the "God in heaven above and on the earth below" (Jos 2:11). They might be able to stand up against a foreign army, but who can stand against the power of almighty God?

A Scarlet Cord

JOS 2:21

Some have called it the "scarlet thread" that weaves its way through all of Scripture. The place of blood in the salvation story begins long before this Jericho event. In Moses' day the sacrificial system required the blood of animals to cover the cost of sin. At the Passover, the blood of a spotless lamb marks the door of each home, and the angel of death passes over it.

When Rahab ties the scarlet cord in the window of her house, there is a guarantee that all those within will be "passed over." They will be spared the judgment that is to fall on their city. The image reminds us of the first Passover, yet it also points to a future day. One day all those who have been marked by the blood of the spotless Lamb of God, Jesus Christ, will be spared judgment and taken into the presence of God. Those who do not bear this mark will be outside of God's covering and will be lost. (See character sketch for Rahab on page 469.)

we enter the land, you have tied this scarlet cord
in the window through which you let us down,
and unless you have brought your father and
mother, your brothers and all your family[m] into
your house. 19If anyone goes outside your house
into the street, his blood will be on his own head;[n]
we will not be responsible. As for anyone who is
in the house with you, his blood will be on our
head[o] if a hand is laid on him. 20But if you tell
what we are doing, we will be released from the
oath you made us swear."

21"Agreed," she replied. "Let it be as you say."
So she sent them away and they departed. And
she tied the scarlet cord in the window.

22When they left, they went into the hills and
stayed there three days, until the pursuers had
searched all along the road and returned without
finding them. 23Then the two men started back.
They went down out of the hills, forded the river
and came to Joshua son of Nun and told him
everything that had happened to them. 24They
said to Joshua, "The LORD has surely given the
whole land into our hands;[p] all the people are
melting in fear because of us."

Crossing the Jordan

3 Early in the morning Joshua and all the Israelites set out from Shittim[q] and went to the
Jordan, where they camped before crossing over.
2After three days the officers went throughout the
camp,[r] 3giving orders to the people: "When you
see the ark of the covenant[s] of the LORD your God,
and the priests,[t] who are Levites, carrying it, you
are to move out from your positions and follow it.
4Then you will know which way to go, since you
have never been this way before. But keep a distance of about a thousand yards[a] between you and
the ark; do not go near it."

5Joshua told the people, "Consecrate yourselves,[u] for tomorrow the LORD will do amazing
things among you."

6Joshua said to the priests, "Take up the ark of
the covenant and pass on ahead of the people." So
they took it up and went ahead of them.

7And the LORD said to Joshua, "Today I will
begin to exalt you[v] in the eyes of all Israel, so they
may know that I am with you as I was with
Moses.[w] 8Tell the priests[x] who carry the ark of the
covenant: 'When you reach the edge of the Jordan's waters, go and stand in the river.' "

9Joshua said to the Israelites, "Come here and
listen to the words of the LORD your God. 10This is
how you will know that the living God[y] is among
you and that he will certainly drive out before you
the Canaanites, Hittites, Hivites, Perizzites, Girgashites, Amorites and Jebusites.[z] 11See, the ark of
the covenant of the Lord of all the earth[a] will go
into the Jordan ahead of you. 12Now then, choose
twelve men[b] from the tribes of Israel, one from

2:18 [m]ver 12; Jos 6:23
2:19 [n]Eze 33:4 [o]Mt 27:25
2:24 [p]ver 9; Jos 6:2
3:1 [q]Jos 2:1
3:2 [r]Jos 1:11
3:3 [s]Nu 10:33 [t]Dt 31:9
3:5 [u]Ex 19:10, 14; Lev 20:7; Jos 7:13; 1Sa 16:5; Joel 2:16
3:7 [v]Jos 4:14; 1Ch 29:25 [w]Jos 1:5
3:8 [x]ver 3
3:10 [y]Dt 5:26; 1Sa 17:26, 36; 2Ki 19:4, 16; Hos 1:10; Mt 16:16; 1Th 1:9 [z]Ex 33:2; Dt 7:1
3:11 [a]ver 13; Job 41:11; Zec 6:5
3:12 [b]Jos 4:2,4

[a]4 Hebrew *about two thousand cubits* (about 900 meters)

Week 5

Uncharted Waters

Moses has died, and Joshua stands with the people of Israel at the edge of the Jordan River. Normally only about a hundred feet wide, the river is at flood stage—much wider and treacherous to cross. How will Joshua get all the Israelites, including the women and children, across? And where will he lead them then?

God has a plan. He himself will lead them. The waters of the Jordan part, but only when the priests walk forward by faith, and their feet touch the water's edge (Jos 3:15-16).

Have you ever sensed God leading you into uncharted waters, to a place you've never been before? How can you discover God's will?

- What is a prerequisite for knowing God's will (1Co 2:14-16)? How can you be sure that you meet this requirement (1Jn 5:11,20)?
- What is the first thing you must do when you seek God's will (Jas 1:5)?
- What are some of the blessings you receive when you follow God's will (Ps 37:4-6; Isa 30:21; Mt 12:50)?
- You have three primary resources for knowing God's will: the Bible (Ps 119:105; 2Ti 3:14-17), the Holy Spirit (Jn 14:26; 1Jn 2:20, 27) and the "mind of Christ" (1Co 2:15-16). How are you utilizing these means of guidance?

God has promised that he will instruct you (Ps 32:8). He has plans for you (Jer 29:11), but you must choose to follow (Jn 7:17).

Enjoying God THROUGH the Word

Read 1 Chronicles 13:1-10 (page 650). Notice that David confers with his officers and commanders, with the priests and Levites and with the people about bringing the ark to Jerusalem. Although he is concerned about God's will (1Ch 13:2), he doesn't stop to actually determine what God's will is. Big mistake! David uses a cart to move the ark instead of moving it the way God had instructed (Ex 25:12-15). When the cart tips, Uzzah supports it—and dies. David's mistake incites God's holy anger (1Ch 15:11-15).

The daily business of life may lead to a false sense of security. You're busy, you're doing good things, so you think you're following God's will. But if you haven't actually consulted him, you can miss doing God's will (Heb 10:36). Those who follow God's will discover the truth of his promise: "I will lead the blind by ways they have not known, along unfamiliar paths I will guide them; I will turn the darkness into light before them and make the rough places smooth" (Isa 42:16; see 58:11).

Enjoying God THROUGH Experience

When you pray, ask God to reveal his will to you. Expect an answer, but don't be surprised if you must wait. Remember: Sin and disobedience can hinder your prayers (Dt 1:42-45; 1Pe 3:12). Physical or emotional exhaustion can prevent you from hearing the Lord's direction (1Ki 19:3-9). Allowing your own desires, rather than the Holy Spirit, to control your life will blind you to God's will (Ro 8:5-8). If you have not obeyed the Spirit's leading, you can choose to do so today. If you are a believer in Jesus, God has sent his Holy Spirit to guide you (Ps 73:23-24; Jn 16:13). You may, however, have to put your feet into the water first, as the priests did at the edge of the Jordan (Jos 3:15-16). That means you must begin to obey God's clear commands before you will see the path opened in front of you.

Go to page 445 for your next weekly study.

A Step of Faith

JOS 3:14–17

As the Israelites move forward, they hit another roadblock: the Jordan River. At certain times of the year the Jordan River meanders slowly southward until it reaches the stagnant and salty waters of the Dead Sea. During these times it is not difficult to wade across it. The Israelites, however, reach the Jordan at flood season, when the snows are melting, the spring rains are falling, and the water is rushing past at 10 to 12 feet deep.

It is easy to step into the shallow and slow-moving Jordan River. But God calls the people of Israel to take their step of faith into the Jordan at the peak of the flood season! They obey, and immediately the river stops flowing.

"Step out in faith." "Take a leap of faith." "Move forward and watch what God will do!" Great advice to give, but hard to take. We can all use a clear reminder of our need to trust God and walk confidently forward as he leads.

each tribe. 13And as soon as the priests who carry
the ark of the LORD—the Lord of all the earth[c]—set
foot in the Jordan, its waters flowing downstream[d]
will be cut off and stand up in a heap.[e]"
14So when the people broke camp to cross the
Jordan, the priests carrying the ark of the covenant[f] went ahead[g] of them. 15Now the Jordan is
at flood stage[h] all during harvest. Yet as soon as
the priests who carried the ark reached the Jordan and their feet touched the water's edge, 16the
water from upstream stopped flowing.[i] It piled up
in a heap a great distance away, at a town called
Adam in the vicinity of Zarethan,[j] while the water
flowing down[k] to the Sea of the Arabah[l] (the Salt
Sea[a][m]) was completely cut off. So the people
crossed over opposite Jericho. 17The priests who
carried the ark of the covenant of the LORD stood
firm on dry ground in the middle of the Jordan,
while all Israel passed by until the whole nation
had completed the crossing on dry ground.[n]

4 When the whole nation had finished crossing
the Jordan,[o] the LORD said to Joshua, 2"Choose
twelve men[p] from among the people, one from
each tribe, 3and tell them to take up twelve
stones[q] from the middle of the Jordan from right
where the priests stood and to carry them over
with you and put them down at the place where
you stay tonight.[r]"
4So Joshua called together the twelve men he
had appointed from the Israelites, one from each
tribe, 5and said to them, "Go over before the ark of
the LORD your God into the middle of the Jordan.
Each of you is to take up a stone on his shoulder,
according to the number of the tribes of the Israelites, 6to serve as a sign among you. In the future,
when your children ask you, 'What do these
stones mean?'[s] 7tell them that the flow of the Jordan was cut off[t] before the ark of the covenant of
the LORD. When it crossed the Jordan, the waters
of the Jordan were cut off. These stones are to be
a memorial[u] to the people of Israel forever."
8So the Israelites did as Joshua commanded
them. They took twelve stones from the middle of
the Jordan, according to the number of the tribes
of the Israelites, as the LORD had told Joshua;[v] and
they carried them over with them to their camp,
where they put them down. 9Joshua set up the
twelve stones[w] that had been[b] in the middle of the
Jordan at the spot where the priests who carried
the ark of the covenant had stood. And they are
there to this day.
10Now the priests who carried the ark remained
standing in the middle of the Jordan until everything the LORD had commanded Joshua was done
by the people, just as Moses had directed Joshua.
The people hurried over, 11and as soon as all of
them had crossed, the ark of the LORD and the
priests came to the other side while the people

3:13 [c]ver 11 [d]ver 16 [e]Ex 15:8; Ps 78:13
3:14 [f]Ps 132:8 [g]Ac 7:44-45
3:15 [h]Jos 4:18; 1Ch 12:15
3:16 [i]Ps 66:6; 74:15 [j]1Ki 4:12; 7:46 [k]ver 13 [l]Dt 1:1 [m]Ge 14:3
3:17 [n]Ex 14:22,29
4:1 [o]Dt 27:2
4:2 [p]Jos 3:12
4:3 [q]ver 20 [r]ver 19
4:6 [s]ver 21; Ex 12:26; 13:14
4:7 [t]Jos 3:13 [u]Ex 12:14
4:8 [v]ver 20
4:9 [w]Ge 28:18; Jos 24:26; 1Sa 7:12

[a] *16* That is, the Dead Sea [b] *9* Or *Joshua also set up twelve stones*

watched. 12The men of Reuben, Gad and the half-
4:12 tribe of Manasseh crossed over, armed, in front of
xNu 32:27 the Israelites,[x] as Moses had directed them. 13About
forty thousand armed for battle crossed over before
the LORD to the plains of Jericho for war.
4:14 14That day the LORD exalted[y] Joshua in the sight
yJos 3:7 of all Israel; and they revered him all the days of
his life, just as they had revered Moses.
15Then the LORD said to Joshua, 16"Command
4:16 zEx 25:22 the priests carrying the ark of the Testimony[z] to
come up out of the Jordan."
17So Joshua commanded the priests, "Come up
out of the Jordan."
18And the priests came up out of the river carrying the ark of the covenant of the LORD. No
sooner had they set their feet on the dry ground
4:18 than the waters of the Jordan returned to their
aJos 3:15 place and ran at flood stage[a] as before.
4:19 19On the tenth day of the first month the people
bJos 5:9 went up from the Jordan and camped at Gilgal[b]
4:20 on the eastern border of Jericho. 20And Joshua set
cver 3,8 up at Gilgal the twelve stones[c] they had taken out
of the Jordan. 21He said to the Israelites, "In the
future when your descendants ask their fathers,
4:21 dver 6 'What do these stones mean?'[d] 22tell them, 'Israel
crossed the Jordan on dry ground.'[e] 23For the LORD
4:22 eJos 3:17 your God dried up the Jordan before you until you
had crossed over. The LORD your God did to the
Jordan just what he had done to the Red Sea[a]
when he dried it up before us until we had
4:23 crossed over.[f] 24He did this so that all the peoples
fEx 14:21 of the earth might know[g] that the hand of the
4:24 LORD is powerful[h] and so that you might always
g1Ki 8:42-43; 2Ki 19:19; fear the LORD your God.[i]"
Ps 106:8; Jer 10:7

Circumcision at Gilgal

hEx 15:16; 1Ch 29:12; 5 Now when all the Amorite kings west of the
Ps 89:13 Jordan and all the Canaanite kings along the
iEx 14:31 coast[j] heard how the LORD had dried up the Jordan
5:1 before the Israelites until we had crossed over,
jNu 13:29 kJos 2:9-11 their hearts melted[k] and they no longer had the
courage to face the Israelites.
2At that time the LORD said to Joshua, "Make
5:2 flint knives[l] and circumcise the Israelites again."
lEx 4:25 3So Joshua made flint knives and circumcised the
5:4 Israelites at Gibeath Haaraloth.[b]
mDt 2:14 4Now this is why he did so: All those who came
out of Egypt—all the men of military age—died in
the desert on the way after leaving Egypt.[m] 5All the
people that came out had been circumcised, but
all the people born in the desert during the journey
from Egypt had not. 6The Israelites had moved
5:6 about in the desert forty years[n] until all the men
nDt 2:7 who were of military age when they left Egypt had
oNu 14:23, 29-35; died, since they had not obeyed the LORD. For the
Dt 2:14 LORD had sworn to them that they would not see
the land that he had solemnly promised their
fathers to give us,[o] a land flowing with milk and

[a] 23 Hebrew *Yam Suph*; that is, Sea of Reeds [b] 3 *Gibeath Haaraloth* means *hill of foreskins.*

Memorial Stones

JOS 4:6-7,20-24

When God does a mighty work, the Israelites leave a memorial in the very place where God acted on their behalf. Often they set up a pile of stones as a reminder. The Israelites cross the Jordan on dry land, a great miracle of God. They enter the land without so much as a wet sandal. And then God says, "Don't ever forget this moment! Pile up 12 stones as a perpetual reminder of this day." Every time a family passes that spot, they tell the story again! "Grandpa, tell us again what God did when we entered the land." "Mom, tell the story one more time."

What a powerful example for us today! We can become a generation that builds and establishes memorials that point us and our children back to those moments when God moved in powerful ways. We need to tell the stories again and again so that we never forget God's deeds on our behalf.

honey.[p] 7So he raised up their sons in their place,
and these were the ones Joshua circumcised. They
were still uncircumcised because they had not
been circumcised on the way. 8And after the whole
nation had been circumcised, they remained
where they were in camp until they were healed.[q]
9Then the LORD said to Joshua, "Today I have
rolled away the reproach of Egypt from you." So
the place has been called Gilgal[a] to this day.
10On the evening of the fourteenth day of the
month,[r] while camped at Gilgal on the plains of
Jericho, the Israelites celebrated the Passover.
11The day after the Passover, that very day, they
ate some of the produce of the land:[s] unleavened
bread and roasted grain.[t] 12The manna stopped the
day after[b] they ate this food from the land; there
was no longer any manna for the Israelites, but
that year they ate of the produce of Canaan.[u]

The Fall of Jericho

13Now when Joshua was near Jericho, he
looked up and saw a man[v] standing in front of
him with a drawn sword[w] in his hand. Joshua
went up to him and asked, "Are you for us or for
our enemies?"
14"Neither," he replied, "but as commander of
the army of the LORD I have now come." Then
Joshua fell facedown[x] to the ground in reverence,
and asked him, "What message does my Lord[c]
have for his servant?"
15The commander of the LORD's army replied,
"Take off your sandals, for the place where you
are standing is holy."[y] And Joshua did so.

6 Now Jericho[z] was tightly shut up because of the
Israelites. No one went out and no one came in.
2Then the LORD said to Joshua, "See, I have delivered[a] Jericho into your hands, along with its king
and its fighting men. 3March around the city once
with all the armed men. Do this for six days. 4Have
seven priests carry trumpets of rams' horns in front
of the ark. On the seventh day, march around the
city seven times, with the priests blowing the
trumpets.[b] 5When you hear them sound a long
blast[c] on the trumpets, have all the people give a
loud shout;[d] then the wall of the city will collapse
and the people will go up, every man straight in."
6So Joshua son of Nun called the priests and
said to them, "Take up the ark of the covenant
of the LORD and have seven priests carry trumpets
in front of it." 7And he ordered the people, "Advance[e]! March around the city, with the armed
guard going ahead of the ark of the LORD."
8When Joshua had spoken to the people, the
seven priests carrying the seven trumpets before
the LORD went forward, blowing their trumpets,
and the ark of the LORD's covenant followed them.
9The armed guard marched ahead of the priests
who blew the trumpets, and the rear guard[f] fol-

Give plenty of what is
given to you,
And listen to pity's call;
Don't think the little you give
is great
And the much you get is
small.

—*Phoebe Cary (1824–1871)*

[a] 9 *Gilgal* sounds like the Hebrew for *roll.* [b] 12 Or *the day* [c] 14 Or *lord*

5:6 [p]Ex 3:8
5:8 [q]Ge 34:25
5:10 [r]Ex 12:6
5:11 [s]Nu 15:19 [t]Lev 23:14
5:12 [u]Ex 16:35
5:13 [v]Ge 18:2; 32:24 [w]Nu 22:23
5:14 [x]Ge 17:3
5:15 [y]Ex 3:5; Ac 7:33
6:1 [z]Jos 24:11
6:2 [a]Dt 7:24; Jos 2:9,24; 8:1
6:4 [b]Lev 25:9; Nu 10:8
6:5 [c]Ex 19:13 [d]ver 20; 1Sa 4:5; Ps 42:4; Isa 42:13
6:7 [e]Ex 14:15
6:9 [f]ver 13; Isa 52:12

lowed the ark. All this time the trumpets were
sounding. 10 But Joshua had commanded the people, "Do not give a war cry, do not raise your
6:10 voices, do not say a word until the day I tell you to
[g]ver 20 shout. Then shout![g]" 11 So he had the ark of the
LORD carried around the city, circling it once. Then
the people returned to camp and spent the night
there.
12 Joshua got up early the next morning and the
priests took up the ark of the LORD. 13 The seven
priests carrying the seven trumpets went forward,
marching before the ark of the LORD and blowing
the trumpets. The armed men went ahead of them
and the rear guard followed the ark of the LORD,
while the trumpets kept sounding. 14 So on the second day they marched around the city once and
returned to the camp. They did this for six days.
15 On the seventh day, they got up at daybreak
and marched around the city seven times in the
same manner, except that on that day they circled
6:15 the city seven times.[h] 16 The seventh time around,
[h]1Ki 18:44 when the priests sounded the trumpet blast, Joshua commanded the people, "Shout! For the LORD
has given you the city! 17 The city and all that is
6:17 in it are to be devoted[a][i] to the LORD. Only Rahab
[i]Lev 27:28; Dt 20:17 the prostitute[b] and all who are with her in her
[j]Jos 2:4 house shall be spared, because she hid[j] the spies
6:18 we sent. 18 But keep away from the devoted
[k]Jos 7:1 things,[k] so that you will not bring about your own
[l]Jos 7:12 [m]Jos 7:25,26 destruction by taking any of them. Otherwise you
will make the camp of Israel liable to destruction[l]
6:19 and bring trouble[m] on it. 19 All the silver and gold
[n]ver 24; and the articles of bronze and iron[n] are sacred to
Nu 31:22 the LORD and must go into his treasury."
6:20 20 When the trumpets sounded,[o] the people
[o]Jdg 6:34; Jer 4:21; shouted, and at the sound of the trumpet, when
Am 2:2 the people gave a loud shout,[p] the wall collapsed;
[p]ver 5 so every man charged straight in, and they took
[q]Heb 11:30 the city.[q] 21 They devoted the city to the LORD and
6:21 [r]Dt 20:16 destroyed[r] with the sword every living thing in
it—men and women, young and old, cattle, sheep
and donkeys.
22 Joshua said to the two men who had spied out
the land, "Go into the prostitute's house and bring
6:22 her out and all who belong to her, in accordance
[s]Jos 2:14; with your oath to her.[s]" 23 So the young men who
Heb 11:31 had done the spying went in and brought out
Rahab, her father and mother and brothers and all
6:23 who belonged to her.[t] They brought out her entire
[t]Jos 2:13 family and put them in a place outside the camp
of Israel.
24 Then they burned the whole city and every-
6:24 thing in it, but they put the silver and gold and
[u]ver 19 the articles of bronze and iron[u] into the treasury
6:25 of the LORD's house. 25 But Joshua spared Rahab
[v]Heb 11:31 the prostitute,[v] with her family and all who

[a] *17* The Hebrew term refers to the irrevocable giving over of things or persons to the LORD, often by totally destroying them; also in verses 18 and 21. [b] *17* Or possibly *innkeeper*; also in verses 22 and 25

Tumbling Down

JOS 6:20

Set on a hill and probably thirty feet high, Jericho's wall is a monstrous structure. To the approaching army of Israel, it looks like an impenetrable fortress. To the people of Jericho, it is absolute assurance that no army can ever invade the security of their city . . . or so they think.

Archaeological evidence of Joshua's conquest of Jericho is scant, likely due to the fact that it was so thoroughly destroyed at this time and then was subject to five centuries of erosion. Joshua's curse on the man who would rebuild Jericho (Jos 6:26)—in violation of the city's destruction remaining an ongoing testimony of God's judgment on the Canaanites and provision of Israel—was fulfilled in the days of King Ahab (1Ki 16:34). The story of Joshua and the city of Jericho is a reminder of the utter holiness of God, the supreme power of God and the reality that no obstacle is too big to stand in the way when God is at work.

One Man's Sin

JOS 7

"What she doesn't know won't hurt her!" Sometimes we try to pretend that we can sin and no one else will be affected. The sin of Achan wakes us up to the stark reality that no one sins in a vacuum. Like a rock thrown into the middle of a still pond, the ripple effect of our sins touches everyone and everything around us.

Achan thinks he can save some of the plunder that is devoted to God. Just a few of the best things: clothing, silver and gold. He can gather them with no one watching and bury them under his tent. And he gets away with it . . . he thinks. But God is watching. Achan's rebellion costs him his life, and the ripple effect of his sin reaches his family and everything he owns. The picture is crystal clear: There are no secret sins.

belonged to her, because she hid the men Joshua had sent as spies to Jericho[w]—and she lives among the Israelites to this day.

26 At that time Joshua pronounced this solemn oath: "Cursed before the LORD is the man who undertakes to rebuild this city, Jericho:

"At the cost of his firstborn son
 will he lay its foundations;
at the cost of his youngest
 will he set up its gates."[x]

27 So the LORD was with Joshua,[y] and his fame spread[z] throughout the land.

Achan's Sin

7 But the Israelites acted unfaithfully in regard to the devoted things[a];[a] Achan son of Carmi, the son of Zimri,[b] the son of Zerah,[b] of the tribe of Judah, took some of them. So the LORD's anger burned against Israel.

2 Now Joshua sent men from Jericho to Ai, which is near Beth Aven[c] to the east of Bethel, and told them, "Go up and spy out the region." So the men went up and spied out Ai.

3 When they returned to Joshua, they said, "Not all the people will have to go up against Ai. Send two or three thousand men to take it and do not weary all the people, for only a few men are there." 4 So about three thousand men went up; but they were routed by the men of Ai,[d] 5 who killed about thirty-six of them. They chased the Israelites from the city gate as far as the stone quarries[c] and struck them down on the slopes. At this the hearts of the people melted[e] and became like water.

6 Then Joshua tore his clothes[f] and fell facedown to the ground before the ark of the LORD, remaining there till evening. The elders of Israel did the same, and sprinkled dust[g] on their heads. 7 And Joshua said, "Ah, Sovereign LORD, why did you ever bring this people across the Jordan to deliver us into the hands of the Amorites to destroy us?[h] If only we had been content to stay on the other side of the Jordan! 8 O Lord, what can I say, now that Israel has been routed by its enemies? 9 The Canaanites and the other people of the country will hear about this and they will surround us and wipe out our name from the earth.[i] What then will you do for your own great name?"

10 The LORD said to Joshua, "Stand up! What are you doing down on your face? 11 Israel has sinned; they have violated my covenant,[j] which I commanded them to keep. They have taken some of the devoted things; they have stolen, they have lied,[k] they have put them with their own possessions. 12 That is why the Israelites cannot stand against their enemies;[l] they turn their backs and

6:25 [w] Jos 2:6
6:26 [x] 1Ki 16:34
6:27 [y] Ge 39:2; Jos 1:5 [z] Jos 9:1
7:1 [a] Jos 6:18 [b] Jos 22:20
7:2 [c] Jos 18:12; 1Sa 13:5; 14:23
7:4 [d] Lev 26:17; Dt 28:25
7:5 [e] Lev 26:36; Jos 2:9,11; Eze 21:7; Na 2:10
7:6 [f] Ge 37:29 [g] 1Sa 4:12; 2Sa 13:19; Ne 9:1; Job 2:12; La 2:10; Rev 18:19
7:7 [h] Ex 5:22
7:9 [i] Ex 32:12; Dt 9:28
7:11 [j] Jos 6:17-19 [k] Ac 5:1-2
7:12 [l] Nu 14:45; Jdg 2:14

[a] *1* The Hebrew term refers to the irrevocable giving over of things or persons to the LORD, often by totally destroying them; also in verses 11, 12, 13 and 15. [b] *1* See Septuagint and 1 Chron. 2:6; Hebrew *Zabdi*; also in verses 17 and 18.
[c] *5* Or *as far as Shebarim*

run because they have been made liable to
7:12 [m]Jos 6:18 destruction.[m] I will not be with you anymore
unless you destroy whatever among you is devot-
ed to destruction.
13 "Go, consecrate the people. Tell them, 'Conse-
7:13 [n]Jos 3:5; 6:18 crate yourselves[n] in preparation for tomorrow; for
this is what the LORD, the God of Israel, says: That
which is devoted is among you, O Israel. You cannot stand against your enemies until you remove it.
14 " 'In the morning, present yourselves tribe by
7:14 [o]Pr 16:33 tribe. The tribe that the LORD takes[o] shall come forward clan by clan; the clan that the LORD takes shall
come forward family by family; and the family that
the LORD takes shall come forward man by man.
15 He who is caught with the devoted things shall
be destroyed by fire, along with all that belongs to
7:15 [p]1Sa 14:39 [q]ver 11 [r]Ge 34:7 him.[p] He has violated the covenant[q] of the LORD
and has done a disgraceful thing in Israel!' "[r]
16 Early the next morning Joshua had Israel
come forward by tribes, and Judah was taken.
17 The clans of Judah came forward, and he took
7:17 [s]Nu 26:20 the Zerahites.[s] He had the clan of the Zerahites
come forward by families, and Zimri was taken.
18 Joshua had his family come forward man by
man, and Achan son of Carmi, the son of Zimri,
the son of Zerah, of the tribe of Judah, was taken.
19 Then Joshua said to Achan, "My son, give glo-
7:19 [t]1Sa 6:5; Jer 13:16; Jn 9:24* [u]1Sa 14:43 ry[t] to the LORD,[a] the God of Israel, and give him
the praise.[b] Tell[u] me what you have done; do not
hide it from me."
20 Achan replied, "It is true! I have sinned against
the LORD, the God of Israel. This is what I have
done: 21 When I saw in the plunder a beautiful robe
7:21 [v]Dt 7:25; Eph 5:5; 1Ti 6:10 from Babylonia,[c] two hundred shekels[d] of silver
and a wedge of gold weighing fifty shekels,[e] I cov-
eted[v] them and took them. They are hidden in the
ground inside my tent, with the silver underneath."
22 So Joshua sent messengers, and they ran to
the tent, and there it was, hidden in his tent, with
the silver underneath. 23 They took the things from
the tent, brought them to Joshua and all the Israelites and spread them out before the LORD.
24 Then Joshua, together with all Israel, took
Achan son of Zerah, the silver, the robe, the gold
wedge, his sons and daughters, his cattle, donkeys
7:24 [w]ver 26; Jos 15:7 and sheep, his tent and all that he had, to the Valley of Achor.[w] 25 Joshua said, "Why have you
brought this trouble[x] on us? The LORD will bring
7:25 [x]Jos 6:18 [y]Dt 17:5 trouble on you today."
Then all Israel stoned him,[y] and after they had
stoned the rest, they burned them. 26 Over Achan
7:26 [z]Nu 25:4; Dt 13:17 [a]ver 24; Isa 65:10; Hos 2:15 they heaped up a large pile of rocks, which
remains to this day. Then the LORD turned from
his fierce anger.[z] Therefore that place has been
called the Valley of Achor[f a] ever since.

[a] *19* A solemn charge to tell the truth [b] *19* Or *and confess to him* [c] *21* Hebrew *Shinar* [d] *21* That is, about 5 pounds (about 2.3 kilograms) [e] *21* That is, about 1 1/4 pounds (about 0.6 kilogram) [f] *26* *Achor* means *trouble.*

Swift and Final Judgment

JOS 7:19–25

There are some passages in the Bible that are difficult to understand. They fly in the face of the way we think things should be. This is one such passage. Achan's punishment is so immediate, so severe, so final. We agree that Achan is wrong. But isn't the death penalty a bit much?

Although severe judgment is not normative, there are times in the Bible when swift and final judgment falls. Most often, these events occur when a new work of God is at a decisive starting point. The people must understand the holiness of God and the essential call to obedience. At the beginning of the sacrificial system, two of Aaron's sons are judged (Lev 10:1–3). Later, a defiant Sabbath-breaker is stoned (Nu 15:32–36). Even in the New Testament, Ananias and Sapphira pay dearly for their lies (Acts 5:1–11). All of these are tough passages. If nothing else, they stand as powerful reminders that we serve a holy God.

> **I would rather walk with God in the dark than go alone in the light.**
>
> *—Mary Gardiner Brainard (1860)*

Ai Destroyed

8 Then the LORD said to Joshua, "Do not be afraid;[b] do not be discouraged.[c] Take the whole army[d] with you, and go up and attack Ai. For I have delivered[e] into your hands the king of Ai, his people, his city and his land. 2You shall do to Ai and its king as you did to Jericho and its king, except that you may carry off their plunder and livestock for yourselves.[f] Set an ambush behind the city."

3So Joshua and the whole army moved out to attack Ai. He chose thirty thousand of his best fighting men and sent them out at night 4with these orders: "Listen carefully. You are to set an ambush behind the city. Don't go very far from it. All of you be on the alert. 5I and all those with me will advance on the city, and when the men come out against us, as they did before, we will flee from them. 6They will pursue us until we have lured them away from the city, for they will say, 'They are running away from us as they did before.' So when we flee from them, 7you are to rise up from ambush and take the city. The LORD your God will give it into your hand.[g] 8When you have taken the city, set it on fire.[h] Do what the LORD has commanded.[i] See to it; you have my orders."

9Then Joshua sent them off, and they went to the place of ambush[j] and lay in wait between Bethel and Ai, to the west of Ai—but Joshua spent that night with the people.

10Early the next morning[k] Joshua mustered his men, and he and the leaders of Israel[l] marched before them to Ai. 11The entire force that was with him marched up and approached the city and arrived in front of it. They set up camp north of Ai, with the valley between them and the city. 12Joshua had taken about five thousand men and set them in ambush between Bethel and Ai, to the west of the city. 13They had the soldiers take up their positions—all those in the camp to the north of the city and the ambush to the west of it. That night Joshua went into the valley.

14When the king of Ai saw this, he and all the men of the city hurried out early in the morning to meet Israel in battle at a certain place overlooking the Arabah.[m] But he did not know[n] that an ambush had been set against him behind the city. 15Joshua and all Israel let themselves be driven back[o] before them, and they fled toward the desert.[p] 16All the men of Ai were called to pursue them, and they pursued Joshua and were lured away[q] from the city. 17Not a man remained in Ai or Bethel who did not go after Israel. They left the city open and went in pursuit of Israel.

18Then the LORD said to Joshua, "Hold out toward Ai the javelin[r] that is in your hand,[s] for into your hand I will deliver the city." So Joshua held out his javelin[t] toward Ai. 19As soon as he did this, the men in the ambush rose quickly[u] from their

8:1 [b]Dt 31:6 [c]Dt 1:21; 7:18; Jos 1:9 [d]Jos 10:7 [e]Jos 6:2
8:2 [f]ver 27; Dt 20:14
8:7 [g]Jdg 7:7; 1Sa 23:4
8:8 [h]Jdg 20:29-38 [i]ver 19
8:9 [j]2Ch 13:13
8:10 [k]Ge 22:3 [l]Jos 7:6
8:14 [m]Dt 1:1 [n]Jdg 20:34
8:15 [o]Jdg 20:36 [p]Jos 15:61; 16:1; 18:12
8:16 [q]Jdg 20:31
8:18 [r]Job 41:26; Ps 35:3 [s]Ex 4:2; 14:16; 17:9-12 [t]ver 26
8:19 [u]Jdg 20:33

position and rushed forward. They entered the city
and captured it and quickly set it on fire.[v]
20The men of Ai looked back and saw the
smoke of the city rising against the sky,[w] but they
had no chance to escape in any direction, for the
Israelites who had been fleeing toward the desert
had turned back against their pursuers. 21For
when Joshua and all Israel saw that the ambush
had taken the city and that smoke was going up
from the city, they turned around and attacked the
men of Ai. 22The men of the ambush also came
out of the city against them, so that they were
caught in the middle, with Israelites on both sides.
Israel cut them down, leaving them neither survivors nor fugitives.[x] 23But they took the king of
Ai alive[y] and brought him to Joshua.
24When Israel had finished killing all the men
of Ai in the fields and in the desert where they had
chased them, and when every one of them had
been put to the sword, all the Israelites returned
to Ai and killed those who were in it. 25Twelve
thousand men and women fell that day—all the
people of Ai.[z] 26For Joshua did not draw back the
hand that held out his javelin until he had
destroyed[a][a] all who lived in Ai.[b] 27But Israel did
carry off for themselves the livestock and plunder
of this city, as the LORD had instructed Joshua.[c]
28So Joshua burned[d] Ai[e] and made it a permanent heap of ruins,[f] a desolate place to this day.[g]
29He hung the king of Ai on a tree and left him
there until evening. At sunset,[h] Joshua ordered
them to take his body from the tree and throw it
down at the entrance of the city gate. And they
raised a large pile of rocks[i] over it, which remains
to this day.

The Covenant Renewed at Mount Ebal

30Then Joshua built on Mount Ebal[j] an altar[k] to
the LORD, the God of Israel, 31as Moses the servant
of the LORD had commanded the Israelites. He
built it according to what is written in the Book of
the Law of Moses—an altar of uncut stones, on
which no iron tool[l] had been used. On it they
offered to the LORD burnt offerings and sacrificed
fellowship offerings.[b][m] 32There, in the presence of
the Israelites, Joshua copied on stones the law of
Moses, which he had written.[n] 33All Israel, aliens
and citizens[o] alike, with their elders, officials and
judges, were standing on both sides of the ark of
the covenant of the LORD, facing those who carried it—the priests, who were Levites.[p] Half of the
people stood in front of Mount Gerizim and half of
them in front of Mount Ebal,[q] as Moses the servant of the LORD had formerly commanded when
he gave instructions to bless the people of Israel.
34Afterward, Joshua read all the words of the
law—the blessings and the curses—just as it is

8:19 [v]ver 8
8:20 [w]Jdg 20:40
8:22 [x]Dt 7:2; Jos 10:1
8:23 [y]1Sa 15:8
8:25 [z]Dt 20:16-18
8:26 [a]Nu 21:2 [b]Ex 17:12
8:27 [c]ver 2
8:28 [d]Nu 31:10 [e]Jos 7:2; Jer 49:3 [f]Dt 13:16; Jos 10:1 [g]Ge 35:20
8:29 [h]Dt 21:23; Jn 19:31 [i]2Sa 18:17
8:30 [j]Dt 11:29 [k]Ex 20:24
8:31 [l]Ex 20:25 [m]Dt 27:6-7
8:32 [n]Dt 27:8
8:33 [o]Lev 16:29 [p]Dt 31:12 [q]Dt 11:29; 27:11-14

[a] *26* The Hebrew term refers to the irrevocable giving over of things or persons to the LORD, often by totally destroying them.
[b] *31* Traditionally *peace offerings*

Joshua's Leadership

JOS 8:30-35

Moses, the man who speaks with God "face to face, as a man speaks with his friend" (Ex. 33:11), is gone. Moses, who led the people of Israel from bondage to freedom, is no longer there to guide them. The people of God are facing the age-old problem of moving from the old leadership to a new administration. Joshua is called by God to lead the people. Will he honor Moses' legacy? Will he continue forward in a way that honors God? Anyone who wonders if Joshua will deviate from the direction set by God does not have to wonder for long. Joshua fulfills the detailed instructions Moses gave the Israelites for their entrance into the promised land (Dt 27:1-13): He builds an altar for worship according to the instructions God had given through Moses and offers the prescribed sacrifices; he copies on stones the Law of Moses; and then before the people he reads the words of the law—emphasizing both blessings and curses (Ex 20:25). With these acts Joshua honors Moses' direction and God's authority as he leads the people into the future.

Sobering Words

JOS 9:14

Here are some sobering words: "[They] did not inquire of the LORD" (Jos 9:14).

The people of Gibeon devise an elaborate strategy. They know the Israelites are on the move. They have heard the stories of waters parting, walls falling and nations being driven out. They know their day is coming. So, they plan their own preemptive strike. Not a military strike, but a ploy. The plan of the Gibeonites will never work if the people of Israel simply inquire of the Lord. But they don't. They fail to seek God's face, and they take the bait of the Gibeonites—hook, line and sinker!

What a great reminder for us to lean on God's wisdom and not our own: "Trust in the LORD with all your heart and lean not on your own understanding" (Pr 3:5). God calls us to live in the wise balance of using the minds he has given us, while also seeking his wisdom in all things. May it never be said of us: "They did not inquire of the LORD."

written in the Book of the Law.[r] 35There was not a
word of all that Moses had commanded that Joshua did not read to the whole assembly of Israel,
including the women and children, and the aliens
who lived among them.[s]

The Gibeonite Deception

9 Now when all the kings west of the Jordan
heard about these things—those in the hill
country, in the western foothills, and along the
entire coast of the Great Sea[a][t] as far as Lebanon
(the kings of the Hittites, Amorites, Canaanites,
Perizzites, Hivites and Jebusites)[u]— 2they came
together to make war against Joshua and Israel.
3However, when the people of Gibeon[v] heard
what Joshua had done to Jericho and Ai, 4they
resorted to a ruse: They went as a delegation
whose donkeys were loaded[b] with worn-out sacks
and old wineskins, cracked and mended. 5The
men put worn and patched sandals on their feet
and wore old clothes. All the bread of their food
supply was dry and moldy. 6Then they went to
Joshua in the camp at Gilgal[w] and said to him and
the men of Israel, "We have come from a distant
country; make a treaty with us."
7The men of Israel said to the Hivites,[x] "But perhaps you live near us. How then can we make a
treaty[y] with you?"
8"We are your servants,[z]" they said to Joshua.
But Joshua asked, "Who are you and where do
you come from?"
9They answered: "Your servants have come
from a very distant country[a] because of the fame
of the LORD your God. For we have heard reports[b]
of him: all that he did in Egypt, 10and all that he
did to the two kings of the Amorites east of the
Jordan—Sihon king of Heshbon, and Og king of
Bashan,[c] who reigned in Ashtaroth.[d] 11And our
elders and all those living in our country said to
us, 'Take provisions for your journey; go and meet
them and say to them, "We are your servants;
make a treaty with us." ' 12This bread of ours was
warm when we packed it at home on the day we
left to come to you. But now see how dry and
moldy it is. 13And these wineskins that we filled
were new, but see how cracked they are. And our
clothes and sandals are worn out by the very long
journey."
14The men of Israel sampled their provisions
but did not inquire[e] of the LORD. 15Then Joshua
made a treaty of peace[f] with them to let them live,
and the leaders of the assembly ratified it by oath.
16Three days after they made the treaty with the
Gibeonites, the Israelites heard that they were
neighbors, living near them. 17So the Israelites set
out and on the third day came to their cities: Gib-

8:34 [r]Dt 28:61; 31:11; Jos 1:8
8:35 [s]Ex 12:38; Dt 31:12
9:1 [t]Nu 34:6 [u]Ex 3:17; Jos 3:10
9:3 [v]ver 17; Jos 10:2; 2Sa 2:12; 2Ch 1:3; Isa 28:21
9:6 [w]Jos 5:10
9:7 [x]ver 1; Jos 11:19 [y]Ex 23:32; Dt 7:2
9:8 [z]Dt 20:11; 2Ki 10:5
9:9 [a]Dt 20:15 [b]ver 24; Jos 2:9
9:10 [c]Nu 21:33 [d]Nu 21:24, 35
9:14 [e]Nu 27:21
9:15 [f]Ex 23:32; Jos 11:19; 2Sa 21:2

[a] *1* That is, the Mediterranean [b] *4* Most Hebrew manuscripts; some Hebrew manuscripts, Vulgate and Syriac (see also Septuagint) *They prepared provisions and loaded their donkeys*

9:17 eon, Kephirah, Beeroth[g] and Kiriath Jearim.[h] 18But
gJos 18:25 the Israelites did not attack them, because the
h1Sa 7:1-2 leaders of the assembly had sworn an oath[i] to
9:18 them by the LORD, the God of Israel.
iPs 15:4 The whole assembly grumbled[j] against the
jEx 15:24 leaders, 19but all the leaders answered, "We have
given them our oath by the LORD, the God of Israel, and we cannot touch them now. 20This is what
we will do to them: We will let them live, so that
wrath will not fall on us for breaking the oath we
9:21 swore to them." 21They continued, "Let them live,[k]
kver 15 but let them be woodcutters and water carriers[l]
lDt 29:11 for the entire community." So the leaders' promise
to them was kept.
22Then Joshua summoned the Gibeonites and
said, "Why did you deceive us by saying, 'We live
9:22 mver 6 a long way[m] from you,' while actually you live
nver 16 near[n] us? 23You are now under a curse:[o] You will
9:23 never cease to serve as woodcutters and water car-
oGe 9:25 riers for the house of my God."
9:24 24They answered Joshua, "Your servants were
pver 9 clearly told[p] how the LORD your God had commanded his servant Moses to give you the whole
land and to wipe out all its inhabitants from
before you. So we feared for our lives because of
9:25 you, and that is why we did this. 25We are now in
qGe 16:6 your hands.[q] Do to us whatever seems good and
right to you."
26So Joshua saved them from the Israelites, and
they did not kill them. 27That day he made the
Gibeonites woodcutters and water carriers for the
community and for the altar of the LORD at the
9:27 place the LORD would choose.[r] And that is what
rDt 12:5 they are to this day.

The Sun Stands Still

10:1 sJdg 1:7 **10** Now Adoni-Zedek king of Jerusalem[s] heard
tJos 8:1 that Joshua had taken Ai[t] and totally
uDt 20:16; destroyed[a][u] it, doing to Ai and its king as he had
Jos 8:22 done to Jericho and its king, and that the people
vJos 9:15 of Gibeon had made a treaty of peace[v] with Israel
and were living near them. 2He and his people
were very much alarmed at this, because Gibeon
was an important city, like one of the royal cities;
it was larger than Ai, and all its men were good
10:3 fighters. 3So Adoni-Zedek king of Jerusalem
wGe 13:18 appealed to Hoham king of Hebron,[w] Piram king
x2Ch 11:9; of Jarmuth, Japhia king of Lachish[x] and Debir
25:27; Ne 11:30; king of Eglon. 4"Come up and help me attack Gib-
Isa 36:2; eon," he said, "because it has made peace[y] with
37:8; Jer 34:7; Joshua and the Israelites."
Mic 1:13 5Then the five kings of the Amorites[z]—the
10:4 kings of Jerusalem, Hebron, Jarmuth, Lachish and
yJos 9:15 Eglon—joined forces. They moved up with all
their troops and took up positions against Gibeon
10:5 zNu 13:29 and attacked it.
6The Gibeonites then sent word to Joshua in the

[a] *1* The Hebrew term refers to the irrevocable giving over of things or persons to the LORD, often by totally destroying them; also in verses 28, 35, 37, 39 and 40.

Curses

JOS 9:23,26-27

In the book of Genesis, Noah predicts Canaan will someday become the servant of Shem (Ge 9:25-26). This curse in Joshua 9 may be part of the fulfillment of Noah's ancient prophecy. The Gibeonites, people of Canaan, are placed in a position of servitude to the people of Israel.

Tabernacle worship requires an ongoing need for water and firewood for the continual offering of sacrifices. The menial task of bringing the water and wood to the tabernacle becomes the responsibility of the Gibeonites. In a strange and roundabout way, these people become servants of the Lord, providing some of what is needed for the sacrificial work of the priests. One simple piece of evidence reveals the significance of their participation in the worship of Israel: When Solomon becomes king, the altar of God and the tabernacle are located at Gibeon, the region inhabited by the Gibeonites.

The Book of Jashar

JOS 10:13

The Book of Jashar is a collection of Hebrew poetic literature that records the military exploits of the nation of Israel. This group of writings tells the stories of Israel's national heroes and some of the high points of their history. This literary source is never acknowledged as Scripture, but was in existence when some historical books of the Bible were being written. No copies of the Book of Jashar exist today, so what we know about it is secondhand through quotes like the one here in Joshua and in 2 Samuel 1:18.

We certainly can't explain the scientific implications of the sun and moon standing still, but we know we serve a God who is above and beyond the rules of the physical universe. The God who spoke all things into existence, the One who sustains the universe, the One who raised Christ from the dead, would have no trouble accomplishing this miracle with a single word.

camp at Gilgal: "Do not abandon your servants.
Come up to us quickly and save us! Help us,
because all the Amorite kings from the hill country
have joined forces against us."
7 So Joshua marched up from Gilgal with his
entire army,[a] including all the best fighting men.
8 The LORD said to Joshua, "Do not be afraid[b] of
them; I have given them into your hand. Not one
of them will be able to withstand you."
9 After an all-night march from Gilgal, Joshua
took them by surprise. 10 The LORD threw them
into confusion before Israel,[c] who defeated them
in a great victory at Gibeon. Israel pursued them
along the road going up to Beth Horon[d] and cut
them down all the way to Azekah[e] and Makkedah.
11 As they fled before Israel on the road down
from Beth Horon to Azekah, the LORD hurled large
hailstones[f] down on them from the sky, and more
of them died from the hailstones than were killed
by the swords of the Israelites.
12 On the day the LORD gave the Amorites[g] over
to Israel, Joshua said to the LORD in the presence
of Israel:

"O sun, stand still over Gibeon,
O moon, over the Valley of Aijalon.[h]"
13 So the sun stood still,[i]
and the moon stopped,
till the nation avenged itself on[a] its
enemies,
as it is written in the Book of Jashar.[j]

The sun stopped[k] in the middle of the sky and
delayed going down about a full day. 14 There has
never been a day like it before or since, a day
when the LORD listened to a man. Surely the LORD
was fighting[l] for Israel!
15 Then Joshua returned with all Israel to the
camp at Gilgal.[m]

Five Amorite Kings Killed

16 Now the five kings had fled and hidden in the
cave at Makkedah. 17 When Joshua was told that
the five kings had been found hiding in the cave
at Makkedah, 18 he said, "Roll large rocks up to the
mouth of the cave, and post some men there to
guard it. 19 But don't stop! Pursue your enemies,
attack them from the rear and don't let them
reach their cities, for the LORD your God has given
them into your hand."
20 So Joshua and the Israelites destroyed them
completely[n]—almost to a man—but the few who
were left reached their fortified cities. 21 The whole
army then returned safely to Joshua in the camp
at Makkedah, and no one uttered a word against
the Israelites.
22 Joshua said, "Open the mouth of the cave and
bring those five kings out to me." 23 So they
brought the five kings out of the cave—the kings
of Jerusalem, Hebron, Jarmuth, Lachish and

10:7 [a]Jos 8:1
10:8 [b]Dt 3:2; Jos 1:9
10:10 [c]Dt 7:23 [d]Jos 16:3,5 [e]Jos 15:35
10:11 [f]Ps 18:12; Isa 28:2,17
10:12 [g]Am 2:9 [h]Jdg 1:35; 12:12
10:13 [i]Hab 3:11 [j]2Sa 1:18 [k]Isa 38:8
10:14 [l]ver 42; Ex 14:14; Dt 1:30; Ps 106:43; 136:24
10:15 [m]ver 43
10:20 [n]Dt 20:16

[a] 13 Or *nation triumphed over*

Eglon. 24When they had brought these kings to
Joshua, he summoned all the men of Israel and
said to the army commanders who had come with
10:24 him, "Come here and put your feet[o] on the necks
[o]Mal 4:3 of these kings." So they came forward and placed
[p]Ps 110:1 their feet[p] on their necks.
10:25 25Joshua said to them, "Do not be afraid; do not
[q]Dt 31:6 be discouraged. Be strong and courageous.[q] This
is what the LORD will do to all the enemies you are
going to fight." 26Then Joshua struck and killed
the kings and hung them on five trees, and they
were left hanging on the trees until evening.
10:27 [r]Dt 21:23; 27At sunset[r] Joshua gave the order and they
Jos 8:9,29 took them down from the trees and threw them
into the cave where they had been hiding. At the
mouth of the cave they placed large rocks, which
are there to this day.
28That day Joshua took Makkedah. He put the
10:28 city and its king to the sword and totally de-
[s]Dt 20:16 stroyed everyone in it. He left no survivors.[s] And
[t]Jos 6:21 he did to the king of Makkedah as he had done to
the king of Jericho.[t]

Southern Cities Conquered

29Then Joshua and all Israel with him moved
on from Makkedah to Libnah and attacked it.
30The LORD also gave that city and its king into
Israel's hand. The city and everyone in it Joshua
put to the sword. He left no survivors there. And
he did to its king as he had done to the king of
Jericho.
31Then Joshua and all Israel with him moved on
from Libnah to Lachish; he took up positions
against it and attacked it. 32The LORD handed
Lachish over to Israel, and Joshua took it on the
second day. The city and everyone in it he put to
10:33 the sword, just as he had done to Libnah. 33Mean-
[u]Jos 16:3,10; while, Horam king of Gezer[u] had come up to help
Jdg 1:29; Lachish, but Joshua defeated him and his army—
1Ki 9:15 until no survivors were left.
34Then Joshua and all Israel with him moved
on from Lachish to Eglon; they took up positions
against it and attacked it. 35They captured it that
same day and put it to the sword and totally
destroyed everyone in it, just as they had done to
Lachish.
10:36 36Then Joshua and all Israel with him went up
[v]Jos 14:13; from Eglon to Hebron[v] and attacked it. 37They
15:13; took the city and put it to the sword, together with
Jdg 1:10 its king, its villages and everyone in it. They left
no survivors. Just as at Eglon, they totally
destroyed it and everyone in it.
38Then Joshua and all Israel with him turned
10:38 around and attacked Debir.[w] 39They took the city,
[w]Jos 15:15; its king and its villages, and put them to the
Jdg 1:11 sword. Everyone in it they totally destroyed. They
left no survivors. They did to Debir and its king
as they had done to Libnah and its king and to
Hebron.
10:40 40So Joshua subdued the whole region, includ-
[x]Ge 12:9; ing the hill country, the Negev,[x] the western
Jos 12:8

On Their Necks

JOS 10:24

In the ancient world, when a powerful enemy was defeated, the victorious people publicly humiliated the leaders of the fallen nation. This practice assured the citizens of the victorious nation that these kings and leaders would no longer be a threat.

When the Israelites win a mighty victory over the five kings of the Amorites, Joshua and his people follow this ancient practice. They place their feet on the necks of their captives, a visible sign of victory for Israel and humiliation for the Amorites. The Amorite kings are then executed and their bodies publicly hung, a clear warning to all who challenge Israel. Joshua calls the people to abandon fear and discouragement and to be strong and courageous.

This whole scene might seem brutal to us today. But the Israelites were involved in a holy conquest, taking the land God promised them. Every square mile of territory came into their possession only by courage and hard-fought battles.

Hamstringing Horses

JOS 11:6

Joshua is an effective and powerful military commander. He understands both the power of God for victory and good military strategy. Why, then, does he cripple the captive horses and burn all the chariots? These are the armored vehicles of the day, powerful weapons for future battles. Yet Joshua destroys them. What kind of military strategy is this?

This is not an issue of cruelty to animals, nor a sign that he has made a poor military decision. Joshua is simply following the orders of his senior commander, the Lord of hosts. So the question becomes: Why would God call Joshua to this drastic action? The answer is found in one of David's psalms: "Some trust in chariots and some in horses, but we trust in the name of the Lord our God" (Ps 20:7). The core issue is trust. Will Joshua and his army place their trust in advanced military weapons or in the might of their God? The answer rings clear. Their trust is in God.

foothills and the mountain slopes,[y] together with
all their kings.[z] He left no survivors. He totally
destroyed all who breathed, just as the LORD, the
God of Israel, had commanded.[a] 41Joshua subdued
them from Kadesh Barnea[b] to Gaza[c] and from the
whole region of Goshen[d] to Gibeon. 42All these
kings and their lands Joshua conquered in one
campaign, because the LORD, the God of Israel,
fought[e] for Israel.
43Then Joshua returned with all Israel to the
camp at Gilgal.[f]

Northern Kings Defeated

11 When Jabin[g] king of Hazor[h] heard of this, he
sent word to Jobab king of Madon, to the
kings of Shimron[i] and Acshaph, 2and to the northern kings who were in the mountains, in the Arabah[j] south of Kinnereth,[k] in the western foothills
and in Naphoth Dor[a][l] on the west; 3to the Canaanites in the east and west; to the Amorites, Hittites,
Perizzites and Jebusites in the hill country; and to
the Hivites[m] below Hermon in the region of Mizpah.[n] 4They came out with all their troops and a
large number of horses and chariots—a huge army,
as numerous as the sand on the seashore.[o] 5All
these kings joined forces[p] and made camp together
at the Waters of Merom, to fight against Israel.
6The LORD said to Joshua, "Do not be afraid of
them, because by this time tomorrow I will hand
all of them over[q] to Israel, slain. You are to ham-
string[r] their horses and burn their chariots."
7So Joshua and his whole army came against
them suddenly at the Waters of Merom and
attacked them, 8and the LORD gave them into the
hand of Israel. They defeated them and pursued
them all the way to Greater Sidon, to Misrephoth
Maim,[s] and to the Valley of Mizpah on the east,
until no survivors were left. 9Joshua did to them
as the LORD had directed: He hamstrung their
horses and burned their chariots.
10At that time Joshua turned back and captured
Hazor and put its king to the sword. (Hazor had
been the head of all these kingdoms.) 11Everyone
in it they put to the sword. They totally destroyed[b]
them, not sparing anything that breathed,[t] and he
burned up Hazor itself.
12Joshua took all these royal cities and their
kings and put them to the sword. He totally
destroyed them, as Moses the servant of the LORD
had commanded.[u] 13Yet Israel did not burn any of
the cities built on their mounds—except Hazor,
which Joshua burned. 14The Israelites carried off
for themselves all the plunder and livestock of
these cities, but all the people they put to the
sword until they completely destroyed them, not
sparing anyone that breathed.[v] 15As the LORD
commanded his servant Moses, so Moses com-

10:40 [y]Dt 1:7 [z]Dt 7:24 [a]Dt 20:16-17
10:41 [b]Ge 14:7 [c]Ge 10:19 [d]Jos 11:16; 15:51
10:42 [e]ver 14
10:43 [f]ver 15; Jos 5:9
11:1 [g]Jdg 4:2,7, 23 [h]ver 10; 1Sa 12:9 [i]Jos 19:15
11:2 [j]Jos 12:3 [k]Nu 34:11 [l]Jos 17:11; Jdg 1:27; 1Ki 4:11
11:3 [m]Dt 7:1; Jdg 3:3,5; 1Ki 9:20 [n]Ge 31:49; Jos 15:38; 18:26
11:4 [o]Jdg 7:12; 1Sa 13:5
11:5 [p]Jdg 5:19
11:6 [q]Jos 10:8 [r]2Sa 8:4
11:8 [s]Jos 13:6
11:11 [t]Dt 20:16-17
11:12 [u]Nu 33:50-52; Dt 7:2
11:14 [v]Nu 31:11-12

[a] 2 Or *in the heights of Dor* [b] 11 The Hebrew term refers to the irrevocable giving over of things or persons to the LORD, often by totally destroying them; also in verses 12, 20 and 21.

manded Joshua, and Joshua did it; he left noth-
11:15 ing undone of all that the LORD commanded
[w]Ex 34:11; Moses.[w]
Jos 1:7 16So Joshua took this entire land: the hill country, all the Negev, the whole region of Goshen, the
11:16 western foothills,[x] the Arabah and the mountains
[x]Jos 10:41 of Israel with their foothills, 17from Mount Halak,
which rises toward Seir, to Baal Gad in the Valley of
11:17 [y]Jos 12:7 Lebanon[y] below Mount Hermon. He captured all
[z]Dt 7:24 their kings and struck them down, putting them to
death.[z] 18Joshua waged war against all these kings
for a long time. 19Except for the Hivites living in
11:19 [a]Jos 9:3 Gibeon,[a] not one city made a treaty of peace with
the Israelites, who took them all in battle. 20For it
11:20 [b]Ex 14:17; was the LORD himself who hardened their hearts[b] to
Ro 9:18 wage war against Israel, so that he might destroy
[c]Dt 7:16; them totally, exterminating them without mercy, as
Jdg 14:4 the LORD had commanded Moses.[c]
21At that time Joshua went and destroyed the
11:21 [d]Nu 13:22, Anakites[d] from the hill country: from Hebron, De-
33; Dt 9:2 bir and Anab, from all the hill country of Judah,
and from all the hill country of Israel. Joshua
totally destroyed them and their towns. 22No Anakites were left in Israelite territory; only in Gaza,
11:22 [e]1Sa 17:4; Gath[e] and Ashdod[f] did any survive. 23So Joshua
1Ki 2:39; took the entire land,[g] just as the LORD had direct-
1Ch 8:13 [f]1Sa 5:1; ed Moses, and he gave it as an inheritance[h] to
Isa 20:1 Israel according to their tribal divisions.[i]
Then the land had rest from war.[j]

11:23 [g]Jos 21:43-45 [h]Dt 1:38;

List of Defeated Kings

12:9-10; **12** These are the kings of the land whom the
25:19 [i]Nu 26:53 Israelites had defeated and whose territory
[j]Jos 14:15 they took over east of the Jordan, from the Arnon
12:1 [k]Dt 3:8 Gorge to Mount Hermon,[k] including all the eastern side of the Arabah:

2Sihon king of the Amorites,
who reigned in Heshbon. He ruled from Aroer on the rim of the Arnon Gorge—from the
middle of the gorge—to the Jabbok River,
which is the border of the Ammonites. This
12:2 [l]Dt 2:36 included half of Gilead.[l] 3He also ruled over
the eastern Arabah from the Sea of Kinne-
12:3 [m]Jos 11:2 reth[a][m] to the Sea of the Arabah (the Salt
[n]Jos 13:20 Sea[b]), to Beth Jeshimoth,[n] and then southward below the slopes of Pisgah.

12:4 [o]Nu 21:21, 4And the territory of Og king of Bashan,[o]
33; Dt 3:11 one of the last of the Rephaites, who reigned
[p]Dt 1:4 in Ashtaroth[p] and Edrei. 5He ruled over
12:5 [q]Dt 3:10 Mount Hermon, Salecah,[q] all of Bashan to the
[r]1Sa 27:8 border of the people of Geshur[r] and Maacah,[s]
[s]Dt 3:14 and half of Gilead to the border of Sihon king
of Heshbon.

6Moses, the servant of the LORD, and the Israelites conquered them. And Moses the servant of
the LORD gave their land to the Reubenites, the

Real People

JOS 11:15

The Bible does not portray candy-coated saints who never struggle or sin. From King David's adultery to the apostle Paul's pre-Christian persecution of the church, the Bible paints a picture of real people learning to follow a real God. No makeovers. Just real people—warts, blemishes and all.

Knowing this, we quickly realize how incredible is Joshua's character and tenacious obedience to God. We have no evidence of skeletons in Joshua's closet. He shows a consistent commitment to walk in the ways of the Lord. This does not mean he is sinless or never stumbles. It simply means that he lives an exemplary life of faithfulness. What a pleasure it is when we meet those people who have learned to live a yielded and surrendered life. We need to thank God for people of exceptional faith who inspire us and call us to a life of higher commitment.

[a] 3 That is, Galilee [b] 3 That is, the Dead Sea

Defeated Kings

JOS 12

When God calls Joshua and the people of Israel to enter the promised land, he tells them this will be their home, "their inheritance forever" (Ex 32:13). Perhaps we picture this land as open territory with no people, lots of produce, homes divinely built and fortified cities with gates wide open. Nothing could be further from the truth.

The land is rich and fertile, but many people inhabit it. If Israel is going to occupy the land, they are going to have to fight for it! Joshua 12 chronicles the cities and kings who are defeated by Joshua and the people of Israel—one king or ruler for each city. At this time in history, a king is the ruler of a city or group of people. God gives a record of the kings that are defeated and the cities that are conquered . . . an everlasting reminder that God keeps his promises.

Gadites and the half-tribe of Manasseh to be their
possession.[t]
7These are the kings of the land that Joshua and
the Israelites conquered on the west side of the
Jordan, from Baal Gad in the Valley of Lebanon[u]
to Mount Halak, which rises toward Seir (their
lands Joshua gave as an inheritance to the tribes
of Israel according to their tribal divisions— 8the
hill country, the western foothills, the Arabah, the
mountain slopes, the desert and the Negev[v]—the
lands of the Hittites, Amorites, Canaanites, Perizzites, Hivites and Jebusites):

9 the king of Jericho[w] one
the king of Ai[x] (near Bethel) one
10 the king of Jerusalem[y] one
the king of Hebron one
11 the king of Jarmuth one
the king of Lachish one
12 the king of Eglon one
the king of Gezer[z] one
13 the king of Debir one
the king of Geder one
14 the king of Hormah one
the king of Arad[a] one
15 the king of Libnah one
the king of Adullam one
16 the king of Makkedah one
the king of Bethel[b] one
17 the king of Tappuah one
the king of Hepher[c] one
18 the king of Aphek[d] one
the king of Lasharon one
19 the king of Madon one
the king of Hazor one
20 the king of Shimron Meron one
the king of Acshaph[e] one
21 the king of Taanach one
the king of Megiddo one
22 the king of Kedesh[f] one
the king of Jokneam in Carmel[g] one
23 the king of Dor (in Naphoth Dor[a][h]) one
the king of Goyim in Gilgal one
24 the king of Tirzah one
thirty-one kings in all.[i]

Land Still to Be Taken

13 When Joshua was old and well advanced in
years,[j] the LORD said to him, "You are very
old, and there are still very large areas of land to
be taken over.

2"This is the land that remains: all the regions
of the Philistines and Geshurites: 3from the
Shihor River[k] on the east of Egypt to the territory of Ekron[l] on the north, all of it counted
as Canaanite (the territory of the five Philistine rulers[m] in Gaza, Ashdod, Ashkelon, Gath
and Ekron—that of the Avvites);[n] 4from the
south, all the land of the Canaanites, from

12:6 [t]Nu 32:29, 33; Jos 13:8
12:7 [u]Jos 11:17
12:8 [v]Jos 11:16
12:9 [w]Jos 6:2 [x]Jos 8:29
12:10 [y]Jos 10:23
12:12 [z]Jos 10:33
12:14 [a]Nu 21:1
12:16 [b]Jos 7:2
12:17 [c]1Ki 4:10
12:18 [d]Jos 13:4
12:20 [e]Jos 11:1
12:22 [f]Jos 19:37; 20:7; 21:32 [g]1Sa 15:12
12:23 [h]Jos 11:2
12:24 [i]Ps 135:11; Dt 7:24
13:1 [j]Ge 24:1; Jos 14:10
13:3 [k]Jer 2:18 [l]Jdg 1:18 [m]Jdg 3:3 [n]Dt 2:23

[a] 23 Or *in the heights of Dor*

Arah of the Sidonians as far as Aphek,[o] the
region of the Amorites,[p] 5 the area of the Gebal-
ites[a];[q] and all Lebanon[r] to the east, from Baal
Gad below Mount Hermon to Lebo[b] Hamath.

6 "As for all the inhabitants of the mountain
regions from Lebanon to Misrephoth Maim,[s] that
is, all the Sidonians, I myself will drive them out
before the Israelites. Be sure to allocate this land
to Israel for an inheritance, as I have instructed
you,[t] 7 and divide it as an inheritance[u] among the
nine tribes and half of the tribe of Manasseh."

Division of the Land East of the Jordan

8 The other half of Manasseh,[c] the Reubenites and
the Gadites had received the inheritance that
Moses had given them east of the Jordan, as he,
the servant of the LORD, had assigned[v] it to them.

9 It extended from Aroer[w] on the rim of the
Arnon Gorge, and from the town in the middle of the gorge, and included the whole plateau[x] of Medeba as far as Dibon,[y] 10 and all the
towns of Sihon king of the Amorites, who
ruled in Heshbon, out to the border of the
Ammonites.[z] 11 It also included Gilead, the territory of the people of Geshur and Maacah,
all of Mount Hermon and all Bashan as far as
Salecah[a]— 12 that is, the whole kingdom of Og
in Bashan,[b] who had reigned in Ashtaroth[c]
and Edrei and had survived as one of the last
of the Rephaites.[d] Moses had defeated them
and taken over their land. 13 But the Israelites
did not drive out the people of Geshur[e] and
Maacah,[f] so they continue to live among the
Israelites to this day.

14 But to the tribe of Levi he gave no inheritance,
since the offerings made by fire to the LORD, the
God of Israel, are their inheritance, as he promised them.[g]

15 This is what Moses had given to the tribe of Reuben, clan by clan:

16 The territory from Aroer[h] on the rim of the
Arnon Gorge, and from the town in the middle of the gorge, and the whole plateau past
Medeba[i] 17 to Heshbon and all its towns on
the plateau, including Dibon,[j] Bamoth Baal,
Beth Baal Meon,[k] 18 Jahaz,[l] Kedemoth, Mephaath,[m] 19 Kiriathaim,[n] Sibmah, Zereth Shahar
on the hill in the valley, 20 Beth Peor,[o] the
slopes of Pisgah, and Beth Jeshimoth 21—all
the towns on the plateau and the entire realm
of Sihon king of the Amorites, who ruled at
Heshbon. Moses had defeated him and the
Midianite chiefs,[p] Evi, Rekem, Zur, Hur and
Reba[q]—princes allied with Sihon—who lived
in that country. 22 In addition to those slain in
battle, the Israelites had put to the sword

13:4 [o] Jos 12:18; 19:30 [p] Am 2:10
13:5 [q] 1Ki 5:18; Ps 83:7; Eze 27:9 [r] Jos 12:7
13:6 [s] Jos 11:8 [t] Nu 33:54
13:7 [u] Jos 11:23; Ps 78:55
13:8 [v] Jos 12:6
13:9 [w] ver 16; Jdg 11:26 [x] Jer 48:8,21 [y] Nu 21:30
13:10 [z] Nu 21:24
13:11 [a] Jos 12:5
13:12 [b] Dt 3:11 [c] Jos 12:4 [d] Ge 14:5
13:13 [e] Jos 12:5 [f] Dt 3:14
13:14 [g] ver 33; Dt 18:1-2
13:16 [h] ver 9; Jos 12:2 [i] Nu 21:30
13:17 [j] Nu 32:3 [k] 1Ch 5:8
13:18 [l] Nu 21:23 [m] Jer 48:21
13:19 [n] Nu 32:37
13:20 [o] Dt 3:29
13:21 [p] Nu 25:15 [q] Nu 31:8

[a] *5* That is, the area of Byblos [b] *5* Or *to the entrance to*
[c] *8* Hebrew *With it* (that is, with the other half of Manasseh)

Father, I feel like I'm truly beginning to learn that without you everything is nothing, and with you, nothing is everything.

—Kathy Troccoli

Drawing Lots

JOS 14:2

When we think of the concept of drawing lots, we perhaps picture children pulling pieces of paper out of a hat to see who gets chosen for a certain event. There is a great deal more going on here. The division of the land among the people of Israel relates directly to their inheritance. This land will be the possession of each tribe for all time! Important decisions are being made.

With this in mind, God calls the people to draw lots to see which portion of the land will belong to each tribe (see Map 4: Land of the Twelve Tribes at the back of this Bible). There are at least two important things to note when we think of this seemingly random way of allocating the land. First, drawing lots takes away the possibility of various tribes fighting over which tribe gets what portion. Second, it puts God in charge of the process. There is no room for political or human manipulation.

Balaam son of Beor,[r] who practiced divination. 23 The boundary of the Reubenites was the bank of the Jordan. These towns and their villages were the inheritance of the Reubenites, clan by clan.

24 This is what Moses had given to the tribe of Gad, clan by clan:

25 The territory of Jazer,[s] all the towns of Gilead and half the Ammonite country as far as Aroer, near Rabbah; 26 and from Heshbon[t] to Ramath Mizpah and Betonim, and from Mahanaim to the territory of Debir;[u] 27 and in the valley, Beth Haram, Beth Nimrah, Succoth[v] and Zaphon with the rest of the realm of Sihon king of Heshbon (the east side of the Jordan, the territory up to the end of the Sea of Kinnereth[a][w]). 28 These towns and their villages were the inheritance of the Gadites,[x] clan by clan.

29 This is what Moses had given to the half-tribe of Manasseh, that is, to half the family of the descendants of Manasseh, clan by clan:

30 The territory extending from Mahanaim[y] and including all of Bashan, the entire realm of Og king of Bashan—all the settlements of Jair[z] in Bashan, sixty towns, 31 half of Gilead, and Ashtaroth and Edrei (the royal cities of Og in Bashan). This was for the descendants of Makir[a] son of Manasseh—for half of the sons of Makir, clan by clan.

32 This is the inheritance Moses had given when he was in the plains of Moab across the Jordan east of Jericho. 33 But to the tribe of Levi, Moses had given no inheritance; the LORD, the God of Israel, is their inheritance,[b] as he promised them.[c]

Division of the Land West of the Jordan

14 Now these are the areas the Israelites received as an inheritance in the land of Canaan, which Eleazar the priest, Joshua son of Nun and the heads of the tribal clans of Israel allotted to them.[d] 2 Their inheritances were assigned by lot[e] to the nine-and-a-half tribes, as the LORD had commanded through Moses. 3 Moses had granted the two-and-a-half tribes their inheritance east of the Jordan[f] but had not granted the Levites an inheritance among the rest,[g] 4 for the sons of Joseph had become two tribes—Manasseh and Ephraim.[h] The Levites received no share of the land but only towns to live in, with pasturelands for their flocks and herds. 5 So the Israelites divided the land, just as the LORD had commanded Moses.[i]

Hebron Given to Caleb

6 Now the men of Judah approached Joshua at Gilgal, and Caleb son of Jephunneh[j] the Kenizzite said to him, "You know what the LORD said to

13:22 [r]Nu 22:5; 31:8
13:25 [s]Nu 21:32; Jos 21:39
13:26 [t]Nu 21:25; Jer 49:3 [u]Jos 10:3
13:27 [v]Ge 33:17 [w]Nu 34:11
13:28 [x]Nu 32:33
13:30 [y]Ge 32:2 [z]Nu 32:41
13:31 [a]Ge 50:23
13:33 [b]Nu 18:20 [c]ver 14; Jos 18:7
14:1 [d]Nu 34:17-18
14:2 [e]Nu 26:55
14:3 [f]Nu 32:33 [g]Jos 13:14
14:4 [h]Ge 41:52; 48:5
14:5 [i]Nu 34:13; 35:2; Jos 21:2
14:6 [j]Nu 13:6; 14:30

[a] *27* That is, Galilee

14:6 [k]Nu 13:26 Moses the man of God at Kadesh Barnea[k] about
you and me. 7 I was forty years old when Moses
14:7 [l]Nu 13:17 [m]Nu 13:30; 14:6-9 the servant of the LORD sent me from Kadesh Barnea to explore the land.[l] And I brought him back
a report according to my convictions,[m] 8 but my
brothers who went up with me made the hearts
14:8 [n]Nu 13:31 [o]Nu 14:24 of the people melt with fear.[n] I, however, followed
the LORD my God wholeheartedly.[o] 9 So on that day
Moses swore to me, 'The land on which your feet
have walked will be your inheritance and that of
14:9 [p]Nu 14:24; Dt 1:36 your children[p] forever, because you have followed
the LORD my God wholeheartedly.'[a]
14:10 [q]Nu 14:30 10 "Now then, just as the LORD promised,[q] he has
kept me alive for forty-five years since the time he
said this to Moses, while Israel moved about in the
desert. So here I am today, eighty-five years old!
14:11 [r]Dt 34:7 11 I am still as strong[r] today as the day Moses sent
me out; I'm just as vigorous to go out to battle now
as I was then. 12 Now give me this hill country that
the LORD promised me that day. You yourself heard
14:12 [s]Nu 13:33 [t]Nu 13:28 then that the Anakites[s] were there and their cities
were large and fortified,[t] but, the LORD helping me,
I will drive them out just as he said."
14:13 [u]Jos 22:6,7 [v]Jos 10:36 [w]Jdg 1:20; 1Ch 6:56 13 Then Joshua blessed[u] Caleb son of Jephunneh
and gave him Hebron[v] as his inheritance.[w] 14 So
Hebron has belonged to Caleb son of Jephunneh
the Kenizzite ever since, because he followed the
LORD, the God of Israel, wholeheartedly. 15 (Hebron
14:15 [x]Ge 23:2 [y]Jos 15:13 [z]Jos 11:23 used to be called Kiriath Arba[x] after Arba,[y] who
was the greatest man among the Anakites.)
Then the land had rest[z] from war.

Allotment for Judah

15 The allotment for the tribe of Judah, clan
by clan, extended down to the territory of
15:1 [a]Nu 34:3 [b]Nu 33:36 Edom,[a] to the Desert of Zin[b] in the extreme south.
2 Their southern boundary started from the
bay at the southern end of the Salt Sea,[b]
15:3 [c]Nu 34:4 3 crossed south of Scorpion[c] Pass,[c] continued
on to Zin and went over to the south of
Kadesh Barnea. Then it ran past Hezron up
to Addar and curved around to Karka. 4 It
15:4 [d]Nu 34:5 [e]Ge 15:18 then passed along to Azmon[d] and joined the
Wadi of Egypt,[e] ending at the sea. This is
their[d] southern boundary.
15:5 [f]Nu 34:10 [g]Jos 18:15-19 5 The eastern boundary[f] is the Salt Sea as
far as the mouth of the Jordan.
The northern boundary[g] started from the
bay of the sea at the mouth of the Jordan,
15:6 [h]Jos 18:19, 21 [i]Jos 18:17 6 went up to Beth Hoglah[h] and continued
north of Beth Arabah to the Stone of Bohan[i]
son of Reuben. 7 The boundary then went up
to Debir from the Valley of Achor[j] and turned
15:7 [j]Jos 7:24 [k]2Sa 17:17; 1Ki 1:9 north to Gilgal, which faces the Pass of
Adummim south of the gorge. It continued
along to the waters of En Shemesh and came
out at En Rogel.[k] 8 Then it ran up the Valley of
Ben Hinnom along the southern slope of the

[a] 9 Deut. 1:36 [b] 2 That is, the Dead Sea; also in verse 5
[c] 3 Hebrew *Akrabbim* [d] 4 Hebrew *your*

Caleb

JOS 14:10-14

If you live to see your 85th birthday, what do you think people will say about you? What a blessing it would be to have people say of you what the Israelites say of Caleb: "He followed the LORD, the God of Israel, wholeheartedly" (Jos 14:14). Although Caleb is in his 80s, he is still as physically fit as he had been 45 years before. This might seem impressive, but there is something even more noteworthy. Caleb is still as spiritually fit and healthy as he was all those years before.

What a blessing it would be to reach 85 and be physically strong. What a greater testimony to reach this age and say we have spent a lifetime following God wholeheartedly!

An Arranged Marriage

JOS 15:16-19

Arranged marriages seem like a completely foreign concept to those who come from the Western world. Yet this practice was very common in Old Testament days and is still in practice in some parts of the world. This passage might make it appear that Caleb is offering his daughter as a prize to the one who wins a certain battle and conquers a specific city. Yet there is more to the story. Caleb knows that only a mighty warrior and brave man can accomplish such a feat. Only a leader who can rally troops and inspire courage can take this city—just the kind of person Caleb wants his daughter to marry. It so happens that the one who rises to this task is indeed courageous and a strong leader. His name is Othniel, and he is such a powerful leader that he becomes the first judge of Israel (Jdg 3:9).

Jebusite[l] city (that is, Jerusalem). From there
it climbed to the top of the hill west of the
Hinnom Valley at the northern end of the Valley of Rephaim. 9From the hilltop the boundary headed toward the spring of the waters of
Nephtoah,[m] came out at the towns of Mount
Ephron and went down toward Baalah[n] (that
is, Kiriath Jearim). 10Then it curved westward
from Baalah to Mount Seir, ran along the
northern slope of Mount Jearim (that is, Kes-
alon), continued down to Beth Shemesh and
crossed to Timnah.[o] 11It went to the northern
slope of Ekron, turned toward Shikkeron,
passed along to Mount Baalah and reached
Jabneel.[p] The boundary ended at the sea.
12The western boundary is the coastline of
the Great Sea.[a][q]
These are the boundaries around the people of
Judah by their clans.

13In accordance with the LORD's command to
him, Joshua gave to Caleb son of Jephunneh a
portion in Judah—Kiriath Arba, that is, Hebron.
(Arba was the forefather of Anak.)[r] 14From
Hebron Caleb drove out the three Anakites[s]—Sheshai, Ahiman and Talmai[t]—descendants of Anak.[u]
15From there he marched against the people living in Debir (formerly called Kiriath Sepher).
16And Caleb said, "I will give my daughter Acsah[v]
in marriage to the man who attacks and captures
Kiriath Sepher." 17Othniel[w] son of Kenaz, Caleb's
brother, took it; so Caleb gave his daughter Acsah
to him in marriage.
18One day when she came to Othniel, she urged
him[b] to ask her father for a field. When she got
off her donkey, Caleb asked her, "What can I do
for you?"
19She replied, "Do me a special favor. Since you
have given me land in the Negev, give me also
springs of water." So Caleb gave her the upper and
lower springs.

20This is the inheritance of the tribe of Judah,
clan by clan:
21The southernmost towns of the tribe of Judah in
the Negev toward the boundary of Edom were:
Kabzeel, Eder,[x] Jagur, 22Kinah, Dimonah,
Adadah, 23Kedesh, Hazor, Ithnan, 24Ziph,[y]
Telem, Bealoth, 25Hazor Hadattah, Kerioth
Hezron (that is, Hazor), 26Amam, Shema,
Moladah,[z] 27Hazar Gaddah, Heshmon, Beth
Pelet, 28Hazar Shual, Beersheba,[a] Biziothiah,
29Baalah,[b] Iim, Ezem, 30Eltolad,[c] Kesil, Hormah, 31Ziklag,[d] Madmannah, Sansannah,
32Lebaoth, Shilhim, Ain and Rimmon[e]—a
total of twenty-nine towns and their villages.

15:8 [l]ver 63; Jos 18:16, 28; Jdg 1:21; 19:10
15:9 [m]Jos 18:15 [n]1Ch 13:6
15:10 [o]Ge 38:12; Jdg 14:1
15:11 [p]Jos 19:33
15:12 [q]Nu 34:6
15:13 [r]Jos 14:13-15
15:14 [s]Nu 13:33 [t]Nu 13:22 [u]Jdg 1:10,20
15:16 [v]Jdg 1:12
15:17 [w]Jdg 3:9,11
15:21 [x]Ge 35:21
15:24 [y]1Sa 23:14
15:26 [z]1Ch 4:28
15:28 [a]Ge 21:31
15:29 [b]ver 9
15:30 [c]Jos 19:4
15:31 [d]1Sa 27:6
15:32 [e]Jdg 20:45

[a] *12* That is, the Mediterranean; also in verse 47
[b] *18* Hebrew and some Septuagint manuscripts; other Septuagint manuscripts (see also note at Judges 1:14) *Othniel, he urged her*

33 In the western foothills:
Eshtaol,[f] Zorah, Ashnah, 34 Zanoah,[g] En
Gannim, Tappuah, Enam, 35 Jarmuth,[h] Adullam,[i] Socoh, Azekah, 36 Shaaraim, Adithaim
and Gederah[j] (or Gederothaim)[a]—fourteen
towns and their villages.
37 Zenan, Hadashah, Migdal Gad, 38 Dilean,
Mizpah, Joktheel,[k] 39 Lachish,[l] Bozkath,[m]
Eglon, 40 Cabbon, Lahmas, Kitlish, 41 Gederoth,
Beth Dagon, Naamah and Makkedah[n]—sixteen towns and their villages.
42 Libnah, Ether, Ashan,[o] 43 Iphtah, Ashnah,
Nezib, 44 Keilah, Aczib[p] and Mareshah[q]—nine
towns and their villages.
45 Ekron, with its surrounding settlements
and villages; 46 west of Ekron, all that were in
the vicinity of Ashdod, together with their
villages; 47 Ashdod,[r] its surrounding settlements and villages; and Gaza, its settlements
and villages, as far as the Wadi of Egypt[s] and
the coastline of the Great Sea.[t]

48 In the hill country:
Shamir, Jattir,[u] Socoh, 49 Dannah, Kiriath
Sannah (that is, Debir[v]), 50 Anab, Eshtemoh,[w]
Anim, 51 Goshen,[x] Holon and Giloh—eleven
towns and their villages.
52 Arab, Dumah,[y] Eshan, 53 Janim, Beth Tappuah, Aphekah, 54 Humtah, Kiriath Arba (that
is, Hebron) and Zior—nine towns and their
villages.
55 Maon, Carmel,[z] Ziph, Juttah, 56 Jezreel,[a]
Jokdeam, Zanoah, 57 Kain, Gibeah[b] and Timnah—ten towns and their villages.
58 Halhul, Beth Zur,[c] Gedor, 59 Maarath, Beth
Anoth and Eltekon—six towns and their
villages.
60 Kiriath Baal (that is, Kiriath Jearim[d]) and
Rabbah[e]—two towns and their villages.

61 In the desert:
Beth Arabah, Middin, Secacah, 62 Nibshan,
the City of Salt and En Gedi[f]—six towns and
their villages.
63 Judah could not[g] dislodge the Jebusites[h], who
were living in Jerusalem; to this day the Jebusites
live there with the people of Judah.

Allotment for Ephraim and Manasseh

16 The allotment for Joseph began at the
Jordan of Jericho,[b] east of the waters of
Jericho, and went up from there through the
desert[i] into the hill country of Bethel. 2 It went
on from Bethel (that is, Luz[j]),[c] crossed over to
the territory of the Arkites in Ataroth,
3 descended westward to the territory of the
Japhletites as far as the region of Lower Beth
Horon[k] and on to Gezer,[l] ending at the sea.

15:33 [f] Jdg 13:25; 16:31
15:34 [g] 1Ch 4:18; Ne 3:13
15:35 [h] Jos 10:3 [i] 1Sa 22:1
15:36 [j] 1Ch 12:4
15:38 [k] 2Ki 14:7
15:39 [l] Jos 10:3; 2Ki 14:19 [m] 2Ki 22:1
15:41 [n] Jos 10:10
15:42 [o] 1Sa 30:30
15:44 [p] Jdg 1:31 [q] Mic 1:15
15:47 [r] Jos 11:22 [s] ver 4 [t] Nu 34:6
15:48 [u] 1Sa 30:27
15:49 [v] Jos 10:3
15:50 [w] Jos 21:14
15:51 [x] Jos 10:41; 11:16
15:52 [y] Ge 25:14
15:55 [z] Jos 12:22
15:56 [a] Jos 17:16
15:57 [b] Jos 18:28; Jdg 19:12
15:58 [c] 1Ch 2:45
15:60 [d] Jos 18:14 [e] Dt 3:11
15:62 [f] 1Sa 23:29
15:63 [g] Jdg 1:21 [h] 2Sa 5:6
16:1 [i] Jos 8:15; 18:12
16:2 [j] Jos 18:13
16:3 [k] 2Ch 8:5 [l] Jos 10:33; 1Ki 9:15

[a] *36* Or *Gederah and Gederothaim* [b] *1* *Jordan of Jericho* was possibly an ancient name for the Jordan River.
[c] *2* Septuagint; Hebrew *Bethel to Luz*

The Land of the Jebusites

JOS 15:63

The land of the Jebusites is part of the territory given by God to the tribe of Benjamin. The book of Judges records the people of Judah conquering this portion of the land (Jdg 1:8). Yet we read here that the Jebusites are still living in the city of Jerusalem when Joshua is written. Evidently Judah drove out their enemy only to have them return and inhabit the land again. Their failure to trust God's promise to help them drive the Jebusites out eventually leads to the fulfillment of the prophecies given in Deuteronomy 7:1–6.

What a powerful reminder that accomplishing the will of God is a partnership of the Lord's divine power and our action in obedience to his leading. Fulfilling the will of God does not always happen overnight. Sometimes it takes years or even generations. Our call is to be faithful and keep moving forward.

Zelophehad's Daughters

JOS 17:3–4

In a time when the land is under the control of the men in the community, a request like the one in this passage is extraordinary. The five daughters of Zelophehad come to Joshua and Eleazar the priest and request a portion of the land as their inheritance. Their request is based on God's command to Moses (Nu 27:1–7). Joshua grants their request.

Five strong women step forward in a time when women are found behind the scenes. And a generous God grants their request. Zelophehad's daughters give women of all times and cultures hope—hope that though they may seem insignificant in the eyes of the world, they are under the watchful, caring eye of their Father God.

4 So Manasseh and Ephraim, the descendants of Joseph, received their inheritance.[m]

5 This was the territory of Ephraim, clan by clan:

The boundary of their inheritance went from Ataroth Addar[n] in the east to Upper Beth Horon 6 and continued to the sea. From Micmethath[o] on the north it curved eastward to Taanath Shiloh, passing by it to Janoah on the east. 7 Then it went down from Janoah to Ataroth[p] and Naarah, touched Jericho and came out at the Jordan. 8 From Tappuah the border went west to the Kanah Ravine[q] and ended at the sea. This was the inheritance of the tribe of the Ephraimites, clan by clan. 9 It also included all the towns and their villages that were set aside for the Ephraimites within the inheritance of the Manassites.

10 They did not dislodge the Canaanites living in Gezer; to this day the Canaanites live among the people of Ephraim but are required to do forced labor.[r]

17 This was the allotment for the tribe of Manasseh as Joseph's firstborn,[s] that is, for Makir,[t] Manasseh's firstborn. Makir was the ancestor of the Gileadites, who had received Gilead and Bashan because the Makirites were great soldiers. 2 So this allotment was for the rest of the people of Manasseh—the clans of Abiezer,[u] Helek, Asriel, Shechem, Hepher and Shemida. These are the other male descendants of Manasseh son of Joseph by their clans.

3 Now Zelophehad son of Hepher,[v] the son of Gilead, the son of Makir, the son of Manasseh, had no sons but only daughters,[w] whose names were Mahlah, Noah, Hoglah, Milcah and Tirzah. 4 They went to Eleazar the priest, Joshua son of Nun, and the leaders and said, "The LORD commanded Moses to give us an inheritance among our brothers." So Joshua gave them an inheritance along with the brothers of their father, according to the LORD's command.[x] 5 Manasseh's share consisted of ten tracts of land besides Gilead and Bashan east of the Jordan, 6 because the daughters of the tribe of Manasseh received an inheritance among the sons. The land of Gilead belonged to the rest of the descendants of Manasseh.

7 The territory of Manasseh extended from Asher to Micmethath[y] east of Shechem.[z] The boundary ran southward from there to include the people living at En Tappuah. 8 (Manasseh had the land of Tappuah, but Tappuah[a] itself, on the boundary of Manasseh, belonged to the Ephraimites.) 9 Then the boundary continued south to the Kanah Ravine.[b] There were towns belonging to Ephraim lying among the towns of Manasseh, but the boundary of Manasseh was the northern side of the ravine and ended at the sea. 10 On the south the land belonged to Ephraim, on the north to Manasseh. The territory of

16:4 [m]Jos 17:14
16:5 [n]Jos 18:13
16:6 [o]Jos 17:7
16:7 [p]1Ch 7:28
16:8 [q]Jos 17:9
16:10 [r]Jos 17:13; Jdg 1:28-29; 1Ki 9:16
17:1 [s]Ge 41:51 [t]Ge 50:23
17:2 [u]Nu 26:30; 1Ch 7:18
17:3 [v]Nu 27:1 [w]Nu 26:33
17:4 [x]Nu 27:5-7
17:7 [y]Jos 16:6 [z]Ge 12:6; Jos 21:21
17:8 [a]Jos 16:8
17:9 [b]Jos 16:8

Manasseh reached the sea and bordered Ash-
17:10 [c]Ge 30:18 er on the north and Issachar[c] on the east.
11Within Issachar and Asher, Manasseh
17:11 [d]1Sa 31:10; also had Beth Shan,[d] Ibleam and the people
1Ki 4:12; of Dor,[e] Endor,[f] Taanach and Megiddo,[g]
1Ch 7:29 [e]Jos 11:2 together with their surrounding settlements
[f]1Sa 28:7; (the third in the list is Naphoth[a]).
Ps 83:10 12Yet the Manassites were not able[h] to occupy these
[g]1Ki 9:15 towns, for the Canaanites were determined to live
17:12 in that region. 13However, when the Israelites grew
[h]Jdg 1:27 stronger, they subjected the Canaanites to forced
17:13 labor but did not drive them out completely.[i]
[i]Jos 16:10 14The people of Joseph said to Joshua, "Why
have you given us only one allotment and one
portion for an inheritance? We are a numerous
17:14 [j]Nu 26:28-37 people and the LORD has blessed us abundantly."[j]
15"If you are so numerous," Joshua answered,
"and if the hill country of Ephraim is too small for
you, go up into the forest and clear land for yourselves there in the land of the Perizzites and
17:15 [k]Ge 14:5 Rephaites.[k]"
16The people of Joseph replied, "The hill coun-
17:16 try is not enough for us, and all the Canaanites
[l]Jdg 1:19; who live in the plain have iron chariots,[l] both
4:3,13 those in Beth Shan and its settlements and those
in the Valley of Jezreel."
17But Joshua said to the house of Joseph—to
Ephraim and Manasseh—"You are numerous and
very powerful. You will have not only one allotment 18but the forested hill country as well. Clear
it, and its farthest limits will be yours; though the
17:18 Canaanites have iron chariots[m] and though they
[m]ver 16 are strong, you can drive them out."

Division of the Rest of the Land

18 The whole assembly of the Israelites gath-
18:1 ered at Shiloh[n] and set up the Tent of Meet-
[n]Jos 19:51; ing[o] there. The country was brought under their
21:2; control, 2but there were still seven Israelite tribes
Jdg 18:31; 21:12,19; who had not yet received their inheritance.
1Sa 1:3; 4:3; 3So Joshua said to the Israelites: "How long will
Jer 7:12; 26:6 you wait before you begin to take possession of
[o]Ex 27:21 the land that the LORD, the God of your fathers,
has given you? 4Appoint three men from each
tribe. I will send them out to make a survey of the
land and to write a description of it, according to
18:4 [p]Mic 2:5 the inheritance of each.[p] Then they will return to
me. 5You are to divide the land into seven parts.
Judah is to remain in its territory on the south[q]
and the house of Joseph in its territory on the
18:5 north.[r] 6After you have written descriptions of the
[q]Jos 15:1 seven parts of the land, bring them here to me and
[r]Jos 16:1-4 18:6 I will cast lots[s] for you in the presence of the LORD
[s]Jos 14:2 our God. 7The Levites, however, do not get a por-
18:7 tion among you, because the priestly service of
[t]Jos 13:33 the LORD is their inheritance.[t] And Gad, Reuben
and the half-tribe of Manasseh have already
received their inheritance on the east side of the

[a] *11* That is, Naphoth Dor

The Ecology of Israel

JOS 17:18

Travelers to Israel today see a desert that is blossoming. Through irrigation and careful planting and watering, modern-day Israel is a place of amazing agricultural production. Countless trees have been planted. Where there is water and an effort to grow produce, the desert is a garden. However, where there is no water and no effort to plant, the land lies barren.

In the days of Joshua, fertile hillsides are covered with dense brush and forests. So many trees cover the land that the tribes of Ephraim and Manasseh have to clear them out to inhabit the area. Over time the forested area is stripped bare and the fields are over-grazed. Until the 1940s little effort was made to remedy the damage to the land. However, since the reestablishment of Israel as a nation, the land has begun to blossom again.

Shiloh

JOS 18:8

For the first time, a specific location becomes the place of worship for the nation of Israel. Now that they are settled in the land, Shiloh, a town in the territory of Ephraim, becomes the central place of worship where the Tent of Meeting is set up.

When people think of Israelite worship, many think of Jerusalem. However, for many years Shiloh is the primary gathering place for God's people. When they gather here, they are "in the presence of the LORD" (Jos 18:8; 19:51). Through the time of the judges and several of the kings, Shiloh is the place of worship. Unfortunately, Shiloh is not always the primary location for worship, since the Israelites at times ignore it in favor of local high places (see note on 1Ki 14:23, page 553). The priest Eli ministers before the Lord in Shiloh, and Samuel grows up and begins his prophetic ministry here.

Jordan. Moses the servant of the LORD gave it to
them.[u]"
8 As the men started on their way to map out the
land, Joshua instructed them, "Go and make a survey of the land and write a description of it. Then
return to me, and I will cast lots for you here at Shiloh[v] in the presence of the LORD." 9 So the men left
and went through the land. They wrote its description on a scroll, town by town, in seven parts, and
returned to Joshua in the camp at Shiloh. 10 Joshua
then cast lots[w] for them in Shiloh in the presence[x]
of the LORD, and there he distributed the land to the
Israelites according to their tribal divisions.[y]

Allotment for Benjamin

11 The lot came up for the tribe of Benjamin, clan
by clan. Their allotted territory lay between the
tribes of Judah and Joseph:

12 On the north side their boundary began
at the Jordan, passed the northern slope of
Jericho and headed west into the hill country, coming out at the desert[z] of Beth Aven.[a]
13 From there it crossed to the south slope of
Luz[b] (that is, Bethel[c]) and went down to Ataroth Addar[d] on the hill south of Lower Beth
Horon.

14 From the hill facing Beth Horon[e] on the
south the boundary turned south along the
western side and came out at Kiriath Baal
(that is, Kiriath Jearim), a town of the people
of Judah. This was the western side.

15 The southern side began at the outskirts
of Kiriath Jearim on the west, and the
boundary came out at the spring of the
waters of Nephtoah.[f] 16 The boundary went
down to the foot of the hill facing the Valley
of Ben Hinnom, north of the Valley of Rephaim. It continued down the Hinnom Valley[g]
along the southern slope of the Jebusite city
and so to En Rogel.[h] 17 It then curved north,
went to En Shemesh, continued to Geliloth,
which faces the Pass of Adummim, and ran
down to the Stone of Bohan[i] son of Reuben.
18 It continued to the northern slope of Beth
Arabah[a][j] and on down into the Arabah. 19 It
then went to the northern slope of Beth Hoglah and came out at the northern bay of the
Salt Sea,[b][k] at the mouth of the Jordan in the
south. This was the southern boundary.

20 The Jordan formed the boundary on the
eastern side.

These were the boundaries that marked out the
inheritance of the clans of Benjamin on all sides.[l]

21 The tribe of Benjamin, clan by clan, had the following cities:

Jericho, Beth Hoglah, Emek Keziz, 22 Beth
Arabah, Zemaraim, Bethel,[m] 23 Avvim, Parah,

18:7 [u] Jos 13:8
18:8 [v] ver 1
18:10 [w] Nu 34:13 [x] ver 1; Jer 7:12 [y] Nu 33:54; Jos 19:51
18:12 [z] Jos 16:1 [a] Jos 7:2
18:13 [b] Ge 28:19 [c] Jdg 1:23 [d] Jos 16:5
18:14 [e] Jos 10:10
18:15 [f] Jos 15:9
18:16 [g] Jos 15:8; 2Ki 23:10 [h] Jos 15:7
18:17 [i] Jos 15:6
18:18 [j] Jos 15:6
18:19 [k] Ge 14:3
18:20 [l] Jos 21:4,17; 1Sa 9:1
18:22 [m] Jos 16:1

[a] *18* Septuagint; Hebrew *slope facing the Arabah* [b] *19* That is, the Dead Sea

18:24 Ophrah, 24Kephar Ammoni, Ophni and
[n]Isa 10:29 Geba[n]—twelve towns and their villages.
18:25 25Gibeon,[o] Ramah,[p] Beeroth,[q] 26Mizpah,[r]
[o]Jos 9:3 Kephirah, Mozah, 27Rekem, Irpeel, Taralah,
[p]Jdg 4:5 [q]Jos 9:17 28Zelah,[s] Haeleph, the Jebusite city[t] (that is,
18:26 Jerusalem[u]), Gibeah[v] and Kiriath—fourteen
[r]Jos 11:3 towns and their villages.
This was the inheritance of Benjamin for its clans.

18:28 [s]2Sa 21:14

Allotment for Simeon

[t]Jos 15:8 [u]Jos 10:1 **19** The second lot came out for the tribe of
[v]Jos 15:57 Simeon, clan by clan. Their inheritance lay
19:1 [w]ver 9; within the territory of Judah.[w] 2It included:
Ge 49:7 Beersheba[x] (or Sheba),[a] Moladah, 3Hazar
Shual, Balah, Ezem, 4Eltolad, Bethul, Hor-
19:2 [x]Ge 21:14; mah, 5Ziklag, Beth Marcaboth, Hazar Susah,
1Ki 19:3 6Beth Lebaoth and Sharuhen—thirteen towns
and their villages;
19:7 [y]Jos 15:42 7Ain, Rimmon, Ether and Ashan[y]—four
towns and their villages— 8and all the villages around these towns as far as Baalath
19:8 [z]Jos 10:40 Beer (Ramah in the Negev).[z]
This was the inheritance of the tribe of the Simeonites, clan by clan. 9The inheritance of the Sim-
19:9 [a]Ge 49:7 eonites was taken from the share of Judah,[a]
[b]Eze 48:24 because Judah's portion was more than they
needed. So the Simeonites received their inheritance within the territory of Judah.[b]

Allotment for Zebulun

19:10 [c]Jos 21:7,34 10The third lot came up for Zebulun,[c] clan by clan:
The boundary of their inheritance went as
far as Sarid. 11Going west it ran to Maralah,
touched Dabbesheth, and extended to the
19:11 [d]Jos 12:22 ravine near Jokneam.[d] 12It turned east from
Sarid toward the sunrise to the territory of
Kisloth Tabor and went on to Daberath and
up to Japhia. 13Then it continued eastward to
Gath Hepher and Eth Kazin; it came out at
19:13 [e]Jos 15:32 Rimmon[e] and turned toward Neah. 14There
the boundary went around on the north to
Hannathon and ended at the Valley of Iphtah
El. 15Included were Kattath, Nahalal, Shim-
19:15 [f]Ge 35:19 ron, Idalah and Bethlehem.[f] There were
twelve towns and their villages.
19:16 [g]ver 10; 16These towns and their villages were the inheri-
Jos 21:7 tance of Zebulun,[g] clan by clan.[h]
[h]Eze 48:26

Allotment for Issachar

19:17 17The fourth lot came out for Issachar,[i] clan by
[i]Ge 30:18 clan. 18Their territory included:
19:18 Jezreel,[j] Kesulloth, Shunem,[k] 19Hapharaim,
[j]Jos 15:56 Shion, Anaharath, 20Rabbith, Kishion, Ebez,
[k]1Sa 28:4; 21Remeth, En Gannim, En Haddah and Beth
2Ki 4:8 Pazzez. 22The boundary touched Tabor,[l] Sha-
19:22 [l]Jdg 4:6,12; hazumah and Beth Shemesh,[m] and ended at
Ps 89:12 the Jordan. There were sixteen towns and
[m]Jos 15:10 their villages.

[a] 2 Or *Beersheba, Sheba*; 1 Chron. 4:28 does not have *Sheba*.

Simeon's Inheritance

JOS 19:1,9

This passage addresses the issue of fairness in the distribution of land for the tribes of Israel. God gives the people the land, but he also calls them to fight for it. This promised and holy land is inhabited with people who are not ready to pack their things and leave. The land is won mile by mile and city by city through a campaign of military battles.

Simeon's inheritance falls entirely within the boundaries of Judah. What is going on here? Doesn't God give each tribe a portion of the land? Yes, each tribe has its own allotment. Yet Judah goes in and takes their land with a fury! Their invasion spreads beyond the area designated for them and into Simeon's territory. Judah ends up with more land than they need. Simeon teams up with Judah and takes a part of that land so that both tribes have their inheritance and both tribes have enough land (see Map 4: Land of the Twelve Tribes at the back of this Bible).

[23]These towns and their villages were the inheritance of the tribe of Issachar,[n] clan by clan.[o]

Allotment for Asher

[24]The fifth lot came out for the tribe of Asher,[p]
clan by clan. [25]Their territory included:
Helkath, Hali, Beten, Acshaph, [26]Allam-
melech, Amad and Mishal. On the west the
boundary touched Carmel[q] and Shihor Lib-
nath. [27]It then turned east toward Beth
Dagon, touched Zebulun[r] and the Valley of
Iphtah El, and went north to Beth Emek and
Neiel, passing Cabul[s] on the left. [28]It went to
Abdon,[a] Rehob,[t] Hammon[u] and Kanah, as far
as Greater Sidon.[v] [29]The boundary then
turned back toward Ramah[w] and went to the
fortified city of Tyre,[x] turned toward Hosah
and came out at the sea in the region of
Aczib,[y] [30]Ummah, Aphek and Rehob. There
were twenty-two towns and their villages.
[31]These towns and their villages were the inheritance of the tribe of Asher,[z] clan by clan.

Allotment for Naphtali

[32]The sixth lot came out for Naphtali, clan by clan:
[33]Their boundary went from Heleph and
the large tree in Zaanannim, passing Adami
Nekeb and Jabneel to Lakkum and ending at
the Jordan. [34]The boundary ran west through
Aznoth Tabor and came out at Hukkok. It
touched Zebulun on the south, Asher on the
west and the Jordan[b] on the east. [35]The fortified cities were Ziddim, Zer, Hammath, Rak-
kath, Kinnereth,[a] [36]Adamah, Ramah,[b] Hazor,[c]
[37]Kedesh, Edrei,[d] En Hazor, [38]Iron, Migdal El,
Horem, Beth Anath and Beth Shemesh. There
were nineteen towns and their villages.
[39]These towns and their villages were the inheritance of the tribe of Naphtali, clan by clan.[e]

Allotment for Dan

[40]The seventh lot came out for the tribe of Dan,
clan by clan. [41]The territory of their inheritance
included:
Zorah, Eshtaol, Ir Shemesh, [42]Shaalabbin,
Aijalon,[f] Ithlah, [43]Elon, Timnah,[g] Ekron,
[44]Eltekeh, Gibbethon, Baalath, [45]Jehud, Bene
Berak, Gath Rimmon,[h] [46]Me Jarkon and Rak-
kon, with the area facing Joppa.[i]
[47](But the Danites had difficulty taking possession of their territory,[j] so they went up and
attacked Leshem[k], took it, put it to the sword and
occupied it. They settled in Leshem and named it
Dan after their forefather.)[l]
[48]These towns and their villages were the inheritance of the tribe of Dan,[m] clan by clan.

I smiled to think God's greatness
Flowed around our incompleteness—
Round our restlessness, His rest.
—Elizabeth Barrett Browning (1806-1861)

19:23 [n]Jos 17:10 [o]Ge 49:15; Eze 48:25
19:24 [p]Jos 17:7
19:26 [q]Jos 12:22
19:27 [r]ver 10 [s]1Ki 9:13
19:28 [t]Jdg 1:31 [u]1Ch 6:76 [v]Ge 10:19; Jos 11:8
19:29 [w]Jos 18:25 [x]2Sa 5:11; 24:7; Isa 23:1; Jer 25:22; Eze 26:2 [y]Jdg 1:31
19:31 [z]Ge 30:13; Eze 48:2
19:35 [a]Jos 11:2
19:36 [b]Jos 18:25 [c]Jos 11:1
19:37 [d]Nu 21:33
19:39 [e]Dt 33:23; Eze 48:3
19:42 [f]Jdg 1:35
19:43 [g]Ge 38:12
19:45 [h]Jos 21:24; 1Ch 6:69
19:46 [i]2Ch 2:16; Jnh 1:3
19:47 [j]Jdg 18:1 [k]Jdg 18:7,14 [l]Jdg 18:27, 29
19:48 [m]Ge 30:6

[a] *28* Some Hebrew manuscripts (see also Joshua 21:30); most Hebrew manuscripts *Ebron* [b] *34* Septuagint; Hebrew *west, and Judah, the Jordan,*

Allotment for Joshua

49 When they had finished dividing the land into
its allotted portions, the Israelites gave Joshua son
of Nun an inheritance among them, 50 as the LORD
had commanded. They gave him the town he
19:50 [n]Jos 24:30 asked for—Timnath Serah[a][n] in the hill country of
Ephraim. And he built up the town and settled
there.
51 These are the territories that Eleazar the priest,
Joshua son of Nun and the heads of the tribal clans
of Israel assigned by lot at Shiloh in the presence of
19:51 [o]Jos 14:1; the LORD at the entrance to the Tent of Meeting.
18:10; Ac 13:19 And so they finished dividing the land.[o]

Cities of Refuge

20 Then the LORD said to Joshua: 2 "Tell the
Israelites to designate the cities of refuge, as
I instructed you through Moses, 3 so that anyone
who kills a person accidentally and unintention-
20:3 [p]Lev 4:2 ally[p] may flee there and find protection from the
[q]Nu 35:12 avenger of blood.[q]
20:4 4 "When he flees to one of these cities, he is to
[r]Ru 4:1; stand in the entrance of the city gate[r] and state his
Jer 38:7 case before the elders[s] of that city. Then they are
[s]Jos 7:6 to admit him into their city and give him a place
to live with them. 5 If the avenger of blood pursues
him, they must not surrender the one accused,
because he killed his neighbor unintentionally
and without malice aforethought. 6 He is to stay in
20:6 that city until he has stood trial before the assem-
[t]Nu 35:12 bly[t] and until the death of the high priest who is
serving at that time. Then he may go back to his
20:7 own home in the town from which he fled."
[u]Jos 21:32; 7 So they set apart Kedesh[u] in Galilee in the hill
1Ch 6:76 [v]Ge 12:6 country of Naphtali, Shechem[v] in the hill country
[w]Jos 10:36; of Ephraim, and Kiriath Arba (that is, Hebron[w]) in
21:11 the hill country of Judah.[x] 8 On the east side of the
[x]Lk 1:39 Jordan of Jericho[b] they designated Bezer[y] in the
20:8 desert on the plateau in the tribe of Reuben,
[y]Jos 21:36; Ramoth in Gilead[z] in the tribe of Gad, and Golan
1Ch 6:78 [z]Jos 12:2 in Bashan in the tribe of Manasseh. 9 Any of the
Israelites or any alien living among them who
killed someone accidentally could flee to these des-
20:9 ignated cities and not be killed by the avenger of
[a]Ex 21:13; Nu 35:15 blood prior to standing trial before the assembly.[a]

Towns for the Levites

21 Now the family heads of the Levites
approached Eleazar the priest, Joshua son
of Nun, and the heads of the other tribal families
21:1 [b]Jos 14:1 of Israel[b] 2 at Shiloh[c] in Canaan and said to them,
"The LORD commanded through Moses that you
21:2 [c]Jos 18:1 give us towns to live in, with pasturelands for our
[d]Nu 35:2-3 livestock."[d] 3 So, as the LORD had commanded, the
Israelites gave the Levites the following towns and
pasturelands out of their own inheritance:
4 The first lot came out for the Kohathites, clan

[a] *50* Also known as *Timnath Heres* (see Judges 2:9)
[b] *8* *Jordan of Jericho* was possibly an ancient name for the Jordan River.

Cities of Refuge

JOS 20:7-9

It is a day of "an eye for an eye" and "blood for blood" revenge. Justice at this time in history is swift and harsh. During this time there are really two conflicting systems of justice. There is ancient tribal law and a developing sense of civil law (see the note on Nu 35:6-29, page 270).

When people commit a murder, manslaughter or even kill someone accidentally, they can be hunted down and killed. However, if they escape to one of the six cities of refuge, they are assured protection and a trial. These six cities of refuge are carefully selected by location. There are three on each side of the Jordan, one in the south, one in the north, and one in the middle of the land (see Map 4: Land of the Twelve Tribes at the back of this Bible). This makes the cities accessible to anyone in need, one more way God extends protection and care for his people.

Levite Inheritance

JOS 21

Although the Levites do not receive large areas of land as do the other tribes of Israel (see the note on Nu 18:20, page 239), they are allotted specific cities. The cities of refuge listed here are among those assigned to the Levites. This should not surprise us. In these cities an accused murderer can find sanctuary and a fair trial when an avenger is pursuing him or her.

Who better to live in these cities of refuge than the Levites? The Levites are the ministers of the day. They teach the people of God, offer the sacrifices and stand before the Lord on behalf of the nation. The call of God on the Levites to inhabit these cities is just another reminder of God's intentional love for his people and his commitment to give them more than just the land of Canaan. God is helping them build a nation.

by clan. The Levites who were descendants of
Aaron the priest were allotted thirteen towns from
the tribes of Judah, Simeon and Benjamin.[e] 5The
rest of Kohath's descendants were allotted ten
towns from the clans of the tribes of Ephraim,
Dan and half of Manasseh.[f]

6The descendants of Gershon were allotted thirteen towns from the clans of the tribes of Issachar,[g] Asher, Naphtali and the half-tribe of Manasseh in Bashan.

7The descendants of Merari,[h] clan by clan,
received twelve towns from the tribes of Reuben,
Gad and Zebulun.[i]

8So the Israelites allotted to the Levites these
towns and their pasturelands, as the LORD had
commanded through Moses.

9From the tribes of Judah and Simeon they allotted the following towns by name 10(these towns
were assigned to the descendants of Aaron who
were from the Kohathite clans of the Levites,
because the first lot fell to them):

11They gave them Kiriath Arba (that is,
Hebron[j]), with its surrounding pastureland,
in the hill country of Judah. (Arba was the
forefather of Anak.) 12But the fields and villages around the city they had given to Caleb
son of Jephunneh as his possession.

13So to the descendants of Aaron the priest
they gave Hebron (a city of refuge for one
accused of murder), Libnah,[k] 14Jattir,[l] Eshtemoa,[m] 15Holon,[n] Debir, 16Ain, Juttah[o] and
Beth Shemesh,[p] together with their pasturelands—nine towns from these two tribes.

17And from the tribe of Benjamin they gave
them Gibeon, Geba,[q] 18Anathoth and Almon,
together with their pasturelands—four
towns.

19All the towns for the priests, the descendants of
Aaron, were thirteen, together with their
pasturelands.

20The rest of the Kohathite clans of the Levites
were allotted towns from the tribe of Ephraim:

21In the hill country of Ephraim they were
given Shechem[r] (a city of refuge for one
accused of murder) and Gezer, 22Kibzaim and
Beth Horon,[s] together with their pasturelands—four towns.[t]

23Also from the tribe of Dan they received
Eltekeh, Gibbethon, 24Aijalon and Gath Rimmon,[u] together with their pasturelands—four
towns.

25From half the tribe of Manasseh they
received Taanach and Gath Rimmon, together with their pasturelands—two towns.

26All these ten towns and their pasturelands were
given to the rest of the Kohathite clans.

27The Levite clans of the Gershonites were given:
from the half-tribe of Manasseh,
Golan in Bashan[v] (a city of refuge for one

21:4 [e]ver 19
21:5 [f]ver 26
21:6 [g]Ge 30:18
21:7 [h]Ex 6:16 [i]Jos 19:10
21:11 [j]Jos 15:13; 1Ch 6:55
21:13 [k]Jos 15:42; 1Ch 6:57
21:14 [l]Jos 15:48 [m]Jos 15:50
21:15 [n]Jos 15:51
21:16 [o]Jos 15:55 [p]Jos 15:10
21:17 [q]Jos 18:24
21:21 [r]Jos 17:7; 20:7
21:22 [s]Jos 10:10 [t]1Sa 1:1
21:24 [u]Jos 19:45
21:27 [v]Jos 12:5

21:27 accused of murder[w]) and Be Eshtarah, togeth-
[w]Nu 35:6 er with their pasturelands—two towns;
21:28 28 from the tribe of Issachar,[x]
[x]Ge 30:18 Kishion, Daberath, 29 Jarmuth and En Gannim, together with their pasturelands—four
towns;
21:30 30 from the tribe of Asher,[y]
[y]Jos 17:7 Mishal, Abdon, 31 Helkath and Rehob, together with their pasturelands—four towns;
21:32 32 from the tribe of Naphtali,
[z]Jos 12:22 Kedesh[z] in Galilee (a city of refuge for one
[a]Nu 35:6; accused of murder[a]), Hammoth Dor and Kar-
Jos 20:7 tan, together with their pasturelands—three
towns.
21:33 33 All the towns of the Gershonite[b] clans were thir-
[b]ver 6 teen, together with their pasturelands.
34 The Merarite clans (the rest of the Levites) were
21:34 given:
[c]Jos 19:10; from the tribe of Zebulun,[c]
1Ch 6:77 Jokneam, Kartah, 35 Dimnah and Nahalal,
together with their pasturelands—four
towns;
36 from the tribe of Reuben,
21:36 Bezer,[d] Jahaz, 37 Kedemoth and Mephaath,
[d]Jos 20:8 together with their pasturelands—four
towns;
38 from the tribe of Gad,
21:38 Ramoth[e] in Gilead (a city of refuge for one
[e]Dt 4:43 accused of murder), Mahanaim,[f] 39 Heshbon
[f]Ge 32:2 and Jazer, together with their pasturelands—
four towns in all.
40 All the towns allotted to the Merarite clans, who
were the rest of the Levites, were twelve.
41 The towns of the Levites in the territory held
21:41 by the Israelites were forty-eight in all, together
[g]Nu 35:7 with their pasturelands.[g] 42 Each of these towns
had pasturelands surrounding it; this was true for
all these towns.
43 So the LORD gave Israel all the land he had
21:43 sworn to give their forefathers,[h] and they took
[h]Dt 34:4 possession[i] of it and settled there.[j] 44 The LORD gave
[i]Dt 11:31 them rest[k] on every side, just as he had sworn to
[j]Dt 17:14 their forefathers. Not one of their enemies[l] with-
21:44 stood them; the LORD handed all their enemies[m]
[k]Ex 33:14; over to them.[n] 45 Not one of all the LORD's good
Jos 1:13 promises[o] to the house of Israel failed; every one
[l]Dt 6:19 was fulfilled.
[m]Ex 23:31
[n]Dt 7:24;
21:10

21:45
[o]Jos 23:14;
Ne 9:8

Eastern Tribes Return Home

22 Then Joshua summoned the Reubenites,
the Gadites and the half-tribe of Manasseh
22:2 2 and said to them, "You have done all that Moses
[p]Nu 32:25 the servant of the LORD commanded,[p] and you
have obeyed me in everything I commanded. 3 For
a long time now—to this very day—you have not
deserted your brothers but have carried out the
mission the LORD your God gave you. 4 Now that
22:4 the LORD your God has given your brothers rest as
[q]Nu 32:22; he promised, return to your homes[q] in the land
Dt 3:20 that Moses the servant of the LORD gave you on

God's Faithfulness

JOS 21:45

Many people in our day and age are no longer surprised when someone breaks a promise. As a matter of fact, what astounds them is when someone actually keeps his or her word. From business deals gone bad to divorces to confidences broken, faithfulness and promise-keeping have fallen on hard times.

Then we read these words: "Not one of all the LORD's good promises to the house of Israel failed; every one was fulfilled" (Jos 21:45). What an excellent thought to lock away in our hearts and minds. In a day and age when we can grow a little cynical and untrusting, we can be certain of one thing . . . God never breaks a promise! Great is his faithfulness! If the Lord was faithful to his people in Joshua's day, you can know with confidence that he will be just as faithful today.

Misunderstanding

JOS 22:10-20

Misunderstandings can erupt over little things and big things. When this happens, the best course of action is to openly communicate, a lesson learned in an immense way by the people of Israel.

The tribes of Reuben, Gad and the half-tribe of Manasseh build an altar near the Jordan. All the other people of Israel hear of this and are outraged. They assume this is a new place of worship and that the tribes on the east side of the Jordan will no longer come to Shiloh for worship. They are angry . . . angry enough to go to war! Until they talk.

The leaders from each side of the Jordan express their concern and intentions. By the end of the conversation, the tribes on the west side of the Jordan celebrate this memorial of their unity. It is not a rival altar. It is a visual reminder that the tribes of Israel ought to always stand together. What is meant for peace almost leads to war, until the people communicate!

the other side of the Jordan.[r] 5But be very careful
to keep the commandment[s] and the law that
Moses the servant of the LORD gave you: to love
the LORD your God, to walk in all his ways, to
obey his commands,[t] to hold fast to him and to
serve him with all your heart and all your soul.[u]"

6Then Joshua blessed[v] them and sent them
away, and they went to their homes. 7(To the half-
tribe of Manasseh Moses had given land in
Bashan,[w] and to the other half of the tribe Joshua
gave land on the west side[x] of the Jordan with
their brothers.) When Joshua sent them home, he
blessed them, 8saying, "Return to your homes
with your great wealth—with large herds of livestock,[y] with silver, gold, bronze and iron, and a
great quantity of clothing—and divide[z] with your
brothers the plunder[a] from your enemies."

9So the Reubenites, the Gadites and the half-
tribe of Manasseh left the Israelites at Shiloh in
Canaan to return to Gilead,[b] their own land,
which they had acquired in accordance with the
command of the LORD through Moses.

10When they came to Geliloth near the Jordan
in the land of Canaan, the Reubenites, the Gadites
and the half-tribe of Manasseh built an imposing
altar there by the Jordan. 11And when the Israelites heard that they had built the altar on the border of Canaan at Geliloth near the Jordan on the
Israelite side, 12the whole assembly of Israel gathered at Shiloh[c] to go to war against them.

13So the Israelites sent Phinehas[d] son of Eleazar,[e] the priest, to the land of Gilead—to Reuben,
Gad and the half-tribe of Manasseh. 14With him
they sent ten of the chief men, one for each of the
tribes of Israel, each the head of a family division
among the Israelite clans.[f]

15When they went to Gilead—to Reuben, Gad
and the half-tribe of Manasseh—they said to
them: 16"The whole assembly of the LORD says:
'How could you break faith[g] with the God of Israel like this? How could you turn away from the
LORD and build yourselves an altar in rebellion[h]
against him now? 17Was not the sin of Peor[i]
enough for us? Up to this very day we have not
cleansed ourselves from that sin, even though a
plague fell on the community of the LORD! 18And
are you now turning away from the LORD?

" 'If you rebel against the LORD today, tomorrow
he will be angry with the whole community[j] of
Israel. 19If the land you possess is defiled, come
over to the LORD's land, where the LORD's tabernacle stands, and share the land with us. But do
not rebel against the LORD or against us by building an altar for yourselves, other than the altar of
the LORD our God. 20When Achan son of Zerah acted unfaithfully regarding the devoted things,[a][k] did
not wrath[l] come upon the whole community of

22:4 [r]Nu 32:18; Jos 1:13-15
22:5 [s]Isa 43:22 [t]Dt 5:29 [u]Dt 6:6,17
22:6 [v]Ex 39:43
22:7 [w]Nu 32:33; Jos 12:5 [x]Jos 17:2,5
22:8 [y]Dt 20:14 [z]Nu 31:27 [a]Ge 49:27; 1Sa 30:16; Isa 9:3
22:9 [b]Nu 32:26, 29
22:12 [c]Jos 18:1
22:13 [d]Nu 25:7 [e]Nu 3:32; Jos 24:33
22:14 [f]Nu 1:4
22:16 [g]Dt 13:14 [h]Dt 12:13-14
22:17 [i]Nu 25:1-9
22:18 [j]Lev 10:6; Nu 16:22
22:20 [k]Jos 7:1 [l]Ps 7:11

[a] *20* The Hebrew term refers to the irrevocable giving over of things or persons to the LORD, often by totally destroying them.

22:20 [m]Jos 7:5
Israel? He was not the only one who died for his
sin.' "[m]
21Then Reuben, Gad and the half-tribe of
Manasseh replied to the heads of the clans of Israel: 22"The Mighty One, God, the LORD! The Mighty
22:22 [n]Dt 10:17 [o]Ps 50:1 [p]1Ki 8:39; Job 10:7; Ps 44:21; Jer 17:10
One, God,[n] the LORD![o] He knows![p] And let Israel
know! If this has been in rebellion or disobedience to the LORD, do not spare us this day. 23If we
have built our own altar to turn away from the
LORD and to offer burnt offerings and grain offer-
22:23 [q]Jer 41:5 [r]Dt 12:11; 18:19; 1Sa 20:16
ings,[q] or to sacrifice fellowship offerings[a] on it,
may the LORD himself call us to account.[r]
24"No! We did it for fear that some day your
descendants might say to ours, 'What do you have
to do with the LORD, the God of Israel? 25The LORD
has made the Jordan a boundary between us and
you—you Reubenites and Gadites! You have no
share in the LORD.' So your descendants might
cause ours to stop fearing the LORD.
26"That is why we said, 'Let us get ready and
build an altar—but not for burnt offerings or sac-
22:27 [s]Ge 21:30; Jos 24:27 [t]Dt 12:6
rifices.' 27On the contrary, it is to be a witness[s]
between us and you and the generations that follow, that we will worship the LORD at his sanctuary with our burnt offerings, sacrifices and fellowship offerings.[t] Then in the future your
descendants will not be able to say to ours, 'You
have no share in the LORD.'
28"And we said, 'If they ever say this to us, or to
our descendants, we will answer: Look at the
replica of the LORD's altar, which our fathers built,
not for burnt offerings and sacrifices, but as a witness between us and you.'
22:29 [u]Jos 24:16 [v]Dt 12:13-14
29"Far be it from us to rebel[u] against the LORD
and turn away from him today by building an
altar for burnt offerings, grain offerings and sacrifices, other than the altar of the LORD our God
that stands before his tabernacle.[v]"
30When Phinehas the priest and the leaders of
the community—the heads of the clans of the Israelites—heard what Reuben, Gad and Manasseh
had to say, they were pleased. 31And Phinehas son
of Eleazar, the priest, said to Reuben, Gad and
Manasseh, "Today we know that the LORD is with
22:31 [w]Lev 26:11-12; 2Ch 15:2
us,[w] because you have not acted unfaithfully
toward the LORD in this matter. Now you have rescued the Israelites from the LORD's hand."
32Then Phinehas son of Eleazar, the priest, and
the leaders returned to Canaan from their meeting with the Reubenites and Gadites in Gilead and
22:33 [x]1Ch 29:20; Da 2:19; Lk 2:28
reported to the Israelites. 33They were glad to hear
the report and praised God.[x] And they talked no
more about going to war against them to devastate the country where the Reubenites and the
Gadites lived.
22:34 [y]Ge 21:30
34And the Reubenites and the Gadites gave the
altar this name: A Witness[y] Between Us that the
LORD is God.

[a] 23 Traditionally *peace offerings*; also in verse 27

What we don't have shapes us more than what we have. We are like Swiss cheese, and the holes in us are actually supposed to be there. The holes are the things that make us who we are. The holes are the places God has reserved in us for himself! The longings identify our real hunger. A hunger that drives us to him to be satisfied. ***If . . . big if . . . we listen.***

. . . There are [holes] in my life that I cannot get filled outside of God. I can do some temporary filling, but not the kind my soul craves. The longing to be filled, the longing to be known, and the longing for heaven all draw me to him with an intense pull that began the day he made me.

—Nicole Johnson

A Biblical Euphemism

JOS 23:14

A euphemism is a nice way of saying something not quite so nice. When women go to the "powder room," we know exactly what they mean. When someone has the "gift of gab," we know that the conversation won't be ending right away.

One such Biblical euphemism is the phrase that someone is "about to go the way of all the earth" (Jos 23:14; 1Ki 2:2). This is a nice way of saying that someone is about to die; the end is near. For Joshua in this passage and David in 1 Kings, it is the time to give final words of exhortation and blessing to those they love and those who will lead the people after them. They are preparing to die, to go the way all things eventually go, "the way of all the earth."

Joshua's Farewell to the Leaders

23 After a long time had passed and the LORD
had given Israel rest[z] from all their enemies
around them, Joshua, by then old and well
advanced in years,[a] 2summoned all Israel—their
elders,[b] leaders, judges and officials[c]—and said to
them: "I am old and well advanced in years. 3You
yourselves have seen everything the LORD your
God has done to all these nations for your sake; it
was the LORD your God who fought for you.[d]
4Remember how I have allotted[e] as an inheritance
for your tribes all the land of the nations that
remain—the nations I conquered—between the
Jordan and the Great Sea[a][f] in the west. 5The LORD
your God himself will drive them out of your way.
He will push them out before you, and you will
take possession of their land, as the LORD your
God promised you.[g]

6"Be very strong; be careful to obey all that is
written in the Book of the Law of Moses, without
turning aside to the right or to the left.[h] 7Do not
associate with these nations that remain among
you; do not invoke the names of their gods or
swear[i] by them. You must not serve them or bow
down[j] to them. 8But you are to hold fast to the
LORD[k] your God, as you have until now.

9"The LORD has driven out before you great and
powerful nations;[l] to this day no one has been
able to withstand you.[m] 10One of you routs a thousand,[n] because the LORD your God fights for you,[o]
just as he promised. 11So be very careful to love
the LORD[p] your God.

12"But if you turn away and ally yourselves with
the survivors of these nations that remain among
you and if you intermarry with them[q] and associate with them,[r] 13then you may be sure that the
LORD your God will no longer drive out these
nations before you. Instead, they will become
snares[s] and traps for you, whips on your backs
and thorns in your eyes,[t] until you perish from
this good land, which the LORD your God has giv-
en you.

14"Now I am about to go the way of all the
earth.[u] You know with all your heart and soul that
not one of all the good promises the LORD your
God gave you has failed. Every promise has been
fulfilled; not one has failed.[v] 15But just as every
good promise of the LORD your God has come true,
so the LORD will bring on you all the evil he has
threatened, until he has destroyed you from this
good land he has given you.[w] 16If you violate the
covenant of the LORD your God, which he commanded you, and go and serve other gods and
bow down to them, the LORD's anger will burn
against you, and you will quickly perish from the
good land he has given you.[x]"

23:1 [z]Dt 12:9; Jos 21:44 [a]Jos 13:1
23:2 [b]Jos 7:6 [c]Jos 24:1
23:3 [d]Ex 14:14
23:4 [e]Jos 19:51 [f]Nu 34:6
23:5 [g]Ex 23:30; Nu 33:53
23:6 [h]Dt 5:32; Jos 1:7
23:7 [i]Ex 23:13; Ps 16:4; Jer 5:7 [j]Ex 20:5
23:8 [k]Dt 10:20
23:9 [l]Dt 11:23 [m]Dt 7:24
23:10 [n]Lev 26:8 [o]Ex 14:14; Dt 3:22
23:11 [p]Jos 22:5
23:12 [q]Dt 7:3 [r]Ex 34:16; Ps 106:34-35
23:13 [s]Ex 23:33 [t]Nu 33:55
23:14 [u]1Ki 2:2 [v]Jos 21:45
23:15 [w]Lev 26:17; Dt 28:15
23:16 [x]Dt 4:25-26

[a] *4* That is, the Mediterranean

The Covenant Renewed at Shechem

24 Then Joshua assembled all the tribes of
24:1 Israel at Shechem. He summoned the el-
[y]Jos 23:2 ders, leaders, judges and officials of Israel,[y] and
they presented themselves before God.
2 Joshua said to all the people, "This is what the
LORD, the God of Israel, says: 'Long ago your forefathers, including Terah the father of Abraham
24:2 and Nahor, lived beyond the River[a] and worshiped
[z]Ge 11:32 other gods.[z] 3 But I took your father Abraham from
24:3 the land beyond the River and led him throughout
[a]Ge 12:1 Canaan[a] and gave him many descendants.[b] I gave
[b]Ge 15:5 him Isaac,[c] 4 and to Isaac I gave Jacob and Esau.[d]
[c]Ge 21:3 I assigned the hill country of Seir[e] to Esau, but
24:4 Jacob and his sons went down to Egypt.[f]
[d]Ge 25:26 5 " 'Then I sent Moses and Aaron,[g] and I afflicted
[e]Dt 2:5 [f]Ge 46:5-6 the Egyptians by what I did there, and I brought you
out. 6 When I brought your fathers out of Egypt, you
24:5 came to the sea, and the Egyptians pursued them
[g]Ex 3:10 with chariots and horsemen[b][h] as far as the Red Sea.[c]
24:6 7 But they cried to the LORD for help, and he put
[h]Ex 14:9 darkness[i] between you and the Egyptians; he
24:7 brought the sea over them and covered them.[j] You
[i]Ex 14:20 [j]Ex 14:28 saw with your own eyes what I did to the Egyp-
[k]Dt 1:46 tians. Then you lived in the desert for a long time.[k]
8 " 'I brought you to the land of the Amorites
who lived east of the Jordan. They fought against
you, but I gave them into your hands. I destroyed
24:8 them from before you, and you took possession of
[l]Nu 21:31 their land.[l] 9 When Balak son of Zippor,[m] the king
24:9 of Moab, prepared to fight against Israel, he sent
[m]Nu 22:2 for Balaam son of Beor to put a curse on you.[n]
[n]Nu 22:6 10 But I would not listen to Balaam, so he blessed
24:10 you[o] again and again, and I delivered you out of
[o]Nu 23:11; his hand.
Dt 23:5 11 " 'Then you crossed the Jordan[p] and came to
24:11 Jericho.[q] The citizens of Jericho fought against
[p]Jos 3:16-17 you, as did also the Amorites, Perizzites, Canaan-
[q]Jos 6:1 [r]Ex 23:23; ites, Hittites, Girgashites, Hivites and Jebusites,
Dt 7:1 but I gave them into your hands.[r] 12 I sent the hor-
24:12 net[s] ahead of you, which drove them out before
[s]Ex 23:28; you—also the two Amorite kings. You did not do
Dt 7:20; it with your own sword and bow. 13 So I gave you
Ps 44:3,6-7 a land on which you did not toil and cities you
did not build; and you live in them and eat from
24:13 vineyards and olive groves that you did not plant.'[t]
[t]Dt 6:10-11 14 "Now fear the LORD and serve him with all
24:14 faithfulness.[u] Throw away the gods[v] your forefa-
[u]Dt 10:12; thers worshiped beyond the River and in Egypt,[w]
18:13; 1Sa 12:24; and serve the LORD. 15 But if serving the LORD
2Co 1:12 seems undesirable to you, then choose for your-
[v]ver 23 [w]Eze 23:3 selves this day whom you will serve, whether the
gods your forefathers served beyond the River, or
24:15 [x]Jdg 6:10; the gods of the Amorites,[x] in whose land you are
Ru 1:15 living. But as for me and my household, we will
[y]Ru 1:16; 1Ki 18:21 serve the LORD."[y]
16 Then the people answered, "Far be it from us
to forsake the LORD to serve other gods! 17 It was

[a] 2 That is, the Euphrates; also in verses 3, 14 and 15 [b] 6 Or *charioteers* [c] 6 Hebrew *Yam Suph*; that is, Sea of Reeds

My Household

JOS 24:15

In our culture today we define a household in very narrow terms. When a census is taken, or when a church counts households, often there is one household for every living unit. Each house, apartment or mobile home counts as one household. This was not the case in Joshua's day. A household included the extended family, and a family was seen as a very broad group of relatives, adopted family members and even servants. Often these people lived in one tent, a series of connected tents or in a permanent structure that could easily be added to as more family members came in. There are still many places in Israel today where homes are built with additional rooms for family members who may join them in the future. When Joshua says, "as for me and my household" he means more than just his immediate family. He is speaking of his entire extended household.

the LORD our God himself who brought us and our
fathers up out of Egypt, from that land of slavery,
and performed those great signs before our eyes.
He protected us on our entire journey and among
all the nations through which we traveled. 18 And
the LORD drove out before us all the nations,
including the Amorites, who lived in the land. We
too will serve the LORD, because he is our God."

19 Joshua said to the people, "You are not able to
serve the LORD. He is a holy God;[z] he is a jealous
God.[a] He will not forgive your rebellion[b] and your
sins. 20 If you forsake the LORD[c] and serve foreign
gods, he will turn[d] and bring disaster on you and
make an end of you,[e] after he has been good to you."

21 But the people said to Joshua, "No! We will
serve the LORD."

22 Then Joshua said, "You are witnesses against
yourselves that you have chosen[f] to serve the
LORD."

"Yes, we are witnesses," they replied.

23 "Now then," said Joshua, "throw away the
foreign gods[g] that are among you and yield your
hearts[h] to the LORD, the God of Israel."

24 And the people said to Joshua, "We will serve
the LORD our God and obey him."[i]

25 On that day Joshua made a covenant[j] for the
people, and there at Shechem he drew up for them
decrees and laws.[k] 26 And Joshua recorded these
things in the Book of the Law of God.[l] Then he
took a large stone[m] and set it up there under the
oak near the holy place of the LORD.

27 "See!" he said to all the people. "This stone
will be a witness[n] against us. It has heard all the
words the LORD has said to us. It will be a witness
against you if you are untrue to your God."

Buried in the Promised Land

28 Then Joshua sent the people away, each to his
own inheritance.

29 After these things, Joshua son of Nun, the servant of the LORD, died at the age of a hundred and
ten.[o] 30 And they buried him in the land of his
inheritance, at Timnath Serah[a][p] in the hill country
of Ephraim, north of Mount Gaash.

31 Israel served the LORD throughout the lifetime
of Joshua and of the elders[q] who outlived him and
who had experienced everything the LORD had
done for Israel.

32 And Joseph's bones, which the Israelites had
brought up from Egypt,[r] were buried at Shechem
in the tract of land[s] that Jacob bought for a hundred pieces of silver[b] from the sons of Hamor, the
father of Shechem. This became the inheritance
of Joseph's descendants.

33 And Eleazar son of Aaron[t] died and was
buried at Gibeah, which had been allotted to his
son Phinehas[u] in the hill country of Ephraim.

[a] *30* Also known as *Timnath Heres* (see Judges 2:9)
[b] *32* Hebrew *hundred kesitahs*; a kesitah was a unit of money of unknown weight and value.

24:19 [z]Lev 19:2; 20:26 [a]Ex 20:5 [b]Ex 23:21
24:20 [c]1Ch 28:9,20 [d]Ac 7:42 [e]Jos 23:15
24:22 [f]Ps 119:30, 173
24:23 [g]ver 14 [h]1Ki 8:58; Ps 119:36; 141:4
24:24 [i]Ex 19:8; 24:3,7; Dt 5:27
24:25 [j]Ex 24:8 [k]Ex 15:25
24:26 [l]Dt 31:24 [m]Ge 28:18
24:27 [n]Jos 22:27
24:29 [o]Jdg 2:8
24:30 [p]Jos 19:50
24:31 [q]Jdg 2:7
24:32 [r]Ge 50:25; Ex 13:19 [s]Ge 33:19; Jn 4:5; Ac 7:16
24:33 [t]Jos 22:13 [u]Ex 6:25

The Oak at Shechem

JOS 24:26

To the modern mind, location may not seem terribly important, but to the people of Israel, each location is filled with significance and history. When a specific place is mentioned, their minds are filled with a flood of stories of great men and women of God and mighty acts of God. Jesus' brief interaction with the woman at the well (Jn 4) highlights how important location is to John, the author, and to his readers:

This is near the plot of land given to Joseph by Jacob.

Jacob's well is there.

Jerusalem is the central place of worship.

References to places and people are woven into the fabric of Israelite history. When we read of Joshua under the great oak at Shechem, we realize that every Jew will quickly remember Abraham in this same location (Gen 12:6), receiving the promise of God, building an altar and worshiping the Lord. Continuity of place and the work of God all go together in the Israelite mind and Israelite history.

The cycle of sin and salvation.

Judges records Israel's history immediately after the death of Joshua. Now established in the promised land, the Israelites waver in their obedience to God and begin to follow the sinful practices of neighboring nations. The resulting cycle of oppression and deliverance clearly reveals the tragic consequences of incomplete commitment to God.

Throughout Israel's cycle of sin and redemption, God provides deliverers who help to restore peace and spiritual vitality. Deborah serves as a godly example with her servant's heart, ability to delegate, authoritative leadership and willingness to follow God at any cost (Jdg 4–5). Jael (Jdg 4:17–22) and the woman of Thebez (Jdg 9:50–57) are lesser-known women, but they are still used by God in extraordinary ways to further his plan. The story of Jephthah and his daughter stands as a grievous reminder of the consequences of careless promises (Jdg 11:30–40). Samson's mother reveals the blessings that are available to those who comply with God's will (Jdg 13), whereas Micah's mother exposes the misery that accompanies superstition and unfaithfulness (Jdg 17–18). When Samson takes credit for successes that come from God's hand, he becomes vulnerable, and Delilah's seduction leads to his downfall (Jdg 16).

The nation of Israel suffers political and social misery for repeatedly ignoring God's direct commands. However, not only God's judgment but also his never-ending love and forgiveness shine through the chapters of Judges.

Quick Study

Author
Traditionally thought to be Samuel; however, actual authorship is uncertain.

Date Written
The book was likely written during the early monarchy, probably around 1000 B.C. It covers a time period of 330 years.

Setting
The land of Canaan.

Key Passage
Judges 21:25 "In those days Israel had no king; everyone did as he saw fit."

Outline

Incomplete conquest of Canaan.
Jdg 1:1–3:6

Judge Othniel.
Jdg 3:7–11

Judge Ehud.
Jdg 3:12–30

Judge Shamgar.
Jdg 3:31

Judge Deborah.
Jdg 4:1–5:31

Judge Gideon.
Jdg 6:6–8

The wickedness of Abimelech.
Jdg 9

Judge Tola.
Jdg 10:1–2

Judge Jair.
Jdg 10:3–5

Judge Jephthah.
Jdg 10:6–12:7

Judges Ibzan, Elon, Abdon.
Jdg 12:8–15

Judge Samson.
Jdg 13–16

The Israelites battle with each other.
Jdg 17–21

The Women of Judges

⚘ **Deborah**	*She went where no man dared to go alone.* Jdg 4–5 (page 470)
⚘ **Jael**	*A barbaric but faithful act.* Jdg 4:17–22; 5:24–27 (page 535)
Sisera's mother	*Waiting in vain for her son.* Jdg 5:28–30
The woman of Thebez	*A millstone provided a weapon.* Jdg 9:50–57
Jephthah's daughter	*A virgin doomed.* Jdg 11:30–40
⚘ **Samson's mother**	*A faithful mother with a foolish son.* Jdg 13; 14:1–7 (page 536)
⚘ **Delilah**	*Beauty used for evil.* Jdg 16:4–22 (page 603)
Micah's mother	*Twisted thinking.* Jdg 17:1–6
Levite's concubine	*The recipient of men's brutality.* Jdg 19
400 virgins	*At the mercy of the Benjamites.* Jdg 21

⚘ Denotes a sketch written about this character

Israel Fights the Remaining Canaanites

1:1 1 After the death[a] of Joshua, the Israelites asked
[a]Jos 24:29 [b]Nu 27:21 the LORD, "Who will be the first[b] to go up and
[c]ver 27; Jdg 3:1-6 fight for us against the Canaanites?[c]"
2 The LORD answered, "Judah[d] is to go; I have
1:2 given the land into their hands.[e]"
[d]Ge 49:8 [e]ver 4; 3 Then the men of Judah said to the Simeonites
Jdg 3:28 their brothers, "Come up with us into the territory allotted to us, to fight against the Canaanites.
1:3 We in turn will go with you into yours." So the
[f]ver 17 Simeonites[f] went with them.
4 When Judah attacked, the LORD gave the
1:4 [g]Ge 13:7; Canaanites and Perizzites[g] into their hands and
Jos 3:10 they struck down ten thousand men at Bezek.[h] 5 It
[h]1Sa 11:8 was there that they found Adoni-Bezek and fought
against him, putting to rout the Canaanites and Perizzites. 6 Adoni-Bezek fled, but they chased him and
caught him, and cut off his thumbs and big toes.
7 Then Adoni-Bezek said, "Seventy kings with
their thumbs and big toes cut off have picked up
scraps under my table. Now God has paid me
1:7 [i]Lev 24:19 back[i] for what I did to them." They brought him
to Jerusalem, and he died there.
1:8 [j]ver 21; 8 The men of Judah attacked Jerusalem[j] also and
Jos 15:63 took it. They put the city to the sword and set it on
fire.
9 After that, the men of Judah went down to
fight against the Canaanites living in the hill
1:9 [k]Nu 13:17 country,[k] the Negev[l] and the western foothills.
[l]Nu 21:1 10 They advanced against the Canaanites living in
1:10 Hebron[m] (formerly called Kiriath Arba[n]) and
[m]Ge 13:18 defeated Sheshai, Ahiman and Talmai.[o]
[n]Ge 35:27 11 From there they advanced against the people
[o]Jos 15:14 living in Debir[p] (formerly called Kiriath Sepher).
1:11 12 And Caleb said, "I will give my daughter Acsah
[p]Jos 15:15 in marriage to the man who attacks and captures
Kiriath Sepher." 13 Othniel son of Kenaz, Caleb's
younger brother, took it; so Caleb gave his daughter Acsah to him in marriage.
14 One day when she came to Othniel, she urged
him[a] to ask her father for a field. When she got
off her donkey, Caleb asked her, "What can I do
for you?"
15 She replied, "Do me a special favor. Since you
have given me land in the Negev, give me also
springs of water." Then Caleb gave her the upper
1:16 and lower springs.
[q]Nu 10:29 16 The descendants of Moses' father-in-law,[q] the
[r]Ge 15:19; Jdg 4:11 Kenite,[r] went up from the City of Palms[b][s] with the
[s]Dt 34:3; men of Judah to live among the people of the
Jdg 3:13 Desert of Judah in the Negev near Arad.[t]
[t]Nu 21:1 17 Then the men of Judah went with the Sime-
1:17 onites[u] their brothers and attacked the Canaanites
[u]ver 3 [v]Nu 21:3 living in Zephath, and they totally destroyed[c] the
city. Therefore it was called Hormah.[d][v] 18 The men

[a] 14 Hebrew; Septuagint and Vulgate *Othniel, he urged her*
[b] 16 That is, Jericho [c] 17 The Hebrew term refers to the irrevocable giving over of things or persons to the LORD, often by totally destroying them. [d] 17 *Hormah* means *destruction.*

Mutilated Soldiers

JDG 1:6

No thumbs. No big toes.

Such mutilation makes the conquered people unable to fight ever again. A soldier with no thumbs cannot swing a weapon, and a soldier with no big toes just simply cannot run. As well as making the soldier unfit to fight, the practice may have at least some background in defiling defeated peoples. Compare this verse with Exodus 29:20, where Aaron and his sons were consecrated as priests when some of the blood of the sacrifice was placed on their right ear lobes, their right thumbs and their right big toes.

As gruesome as it sounds, mutilation of conquered soldiers and their leaders was not uncommon in the ancient world, when hand-to-hand combat was the primary means of battle. King Adoni-Bezek takes his punishment in stride and mentions the number of defeated kings he has rendered helpless in the same way, humiliating them further by making them eat the scraps under his table.

Drive Them Out

JDG 1:27-36

Before ever entering the land of Canaan, God promised the Israelites that he would drive the Canaanites out of the land and give it* wholly *to them* (Ex 34:11,24; Dt 4:38; Jos 3:10). *These early verses in Judges, however, give a disturbing report. Stopping short of complete conquest, the Israelites allow to remain the very nations God had promised to completely drive out. Oh, the Israelites force them into slave labor, but they continue to live in the land and continue to interact and influence the Israelites.

Going their own willful way, perhaps thinking that what God requires is just too hard, the Israelites stop short of complete obedience. And they pay the price. The wars and disturbances recorded in Judges begin, fulfilling God's warning that, unless they drive them out completely, these nations will become "barbs in [their] eyes and thorns in [their] sides"* (Nu 33:55). *Never is anything less than* complete *obedience* true *obedience.

of Judah also took[a] Gaza,[w] Ashkelon and Ekron—each city with its territory.

[19]The LORD was with[x] the men of Judah. They took possession of the hill country, but they were unable to drive the people from the plains, because they had iron chariots.[y] [20]As Moses had promised, Hebron[z] was given to Caleb, who drove from it the three sons of Anak.[a] [21]The Benjamites, however, failed[b] to dislodge the Jebusites, who were living in Jerusalem;[c] to this day the Jebusites live there with the Benjamites.

[22]Now the house of Joseph attacked Bethel, and the LORD was with them. [23]When they sent men to spy out Bethel (formerly called Luz),[d] [24]the spies saw a man coming out of the city and they said to him, "Show us how to get into the city and we will see that you are treated well.[e]" [25]So he showed them, and they put the city to the sword but spared[f] the man and his whole family. [26]He then went to the land of the Hittites, where he built a city and called it Luz, which is its name to this day.

[27]But Manasseh did not drive out the people of Beth Shan or Taanach or Dor or Ibleam[g] or Megiddo and their surrounding settlements, for the Canaanites[h] were determined to live in that land. [28]When Israel became strong, they pressed the Canaanites into forced labor but never drove them out completely. [29]Nor did Ephraim drive out the Canaanites living in Gezer,[i] but the Canaanites continued to live there among them.[j] [30]Neither did Zebulun drive out the Canaanites living in Kitron or Nahalol, who remained among them; but they did subject them to forced labor. [31]Nor did Asher drive out those living in Acco or Sidon or Ahlab or Aczib[k] or Helbah or Aphek or Rehob, [32]and because of this the people of Asher lived among the Canaanite inhabitants of the land. [33]Neither did Naphtali drive out those living in Beth Shemesh or Beth Anath[l]; but the Naphtalites too lived among the Canaanite inhabitants of the land, and those living in Beth Shemesh and Beth Anath became forced laborers for them. [34]The Amorites[m] confined the Danites to the hill country, not allowing them to come down into the plain. [35]And the Amorites were determined also to hold out in Mount Heres, Aijalon[n] and Shaalbim, but when the power of the house of Joseph increased, they too were pressed into forced labor. [36]The boundary of the Amorites was from Scorpion[b] Pass[o] to Sela and beyond.

The Angel of the LORD at Bokim

2 The angel of the LORD[p] went up from Gilgal to Bokim[q] and said, "I brought you up out of Egypt[r] and led you into the land that I swore to give to your forefathers.[s] I said, 'I will never break my covenant with you,[t] [2]and you shall not make a covenant with the people of this land,[u] but you

1:18 [w]Jos 11:22
1:19 [x]ver 2 [y]Jos 17:16
1:20 [z]Jos 14:9; 15:13-14 [a]ver 10; Jos 14:13
1:21 [b]Jos 15:63 [c]ver 8
1:23 [d]Ge 28:19
1:24 [e]Jos 2:12,14
1:25 [f]Jos 6:25
1:27 [g]Jos 17:11 [h]ver 1
1:29 [i]1Ki 9:16 [j]Jos 16:10
1:31 [k]Jdg 10:6
1:33 [l]Jos 19:38
1:34 [m]Ex 3:17
1:35 [n]Jos 19:42
1:36 [o]Jos 15:3
2:1 [p]Jdg 6:11 [q]ver 5 [r]Ex 20:2 [s]Ge 17:8 [t]Lev 26:42-44; Dt 7:9
2:2 [u]Ex 23:32; 34:12; Dt 7:2

[a] *18* Hebrew; Septuagint *Judah did not take* [b] *36* Hebrew *Akrabbim*

2:2 shall break down their altars.[v] Yet you have dis-
[v]Ex 34:13 obeyed me. Why have you done this? 3 Now there-
2:3 fore I tell you that I will not drive them out before
[w]Jos 23:13 [x]Nu 33:55 you;[w] they will be ⌊thorns⌋[x] in your sides and their
[y]Dt 7:16; gods will be a snare[y] to you."
Jdg 3:6; 4 When the angel of the LORD had spoken these
Ps 106:36 things to all the Israelites, the people wept aloud,
5 and they called that place Bokim.[a] There they
offered sacrifices to the LORD.

Disobedience and Defeat

6 After Joshua had dismissed the Israelites, they
went to take possession of the land, each to his
own inheritance. 7 The people served the LORD
throughout the lifetime of Joshua and of the elders who outlived him and who had seen all the
great things the LORD had done for Israel.
8 Joshua son of Nun, the servant of the LORD,
died at the age of a hundred and ten. 9 And they
buried him in the land of his inheritance, at Tim-
2:9 nath Heres[b][z] in the hill country of Ephraim, north
[z]Jos 19:50 of Mount Gaash.
2:10 [a]Ex 5:2; 10 After that whole generation had been gathered
1Sa 2:12; to their fathers, another generation grew up, who
1Ch 28:9; knew neither the LORD nor what he had done for
Gal 4:8 Israel.[a] 11 Then the Israelites did evil in the eyes of
2:11 the LORD[b] and served the Baals.[c] 12 They forsook
[b]Jdg 3:12; the LORD, the God of their fathers, who had
4:1; 6:1; 10:6 [c]Jdg 3:7; brought them out of Egypt. They followed and
8:33 worshiped various gods[d] of the peoples around
2:12 them.[e] They provoked the LORD to anger 13 because
[d]Ps 106:36 they forsook him and served Baal and the Ash-
[e]Dt 31:16; toreths.[f] 14 In his anger[g] against Israel the LORD
Jdg 10:6 handed them over[h] to raiders who plundered
2:13 them. He sold them[i] to their enemies all around,
[f]Jdg 10:6 whom they were no longer able to resist.[j] 15 When-
2:14 ever Israel went out to fight, the hand of the LORD
[g]Dt 31:17 was against them to defeat them, just as he had
[h]Ps 106:41 [i]Dt 32:30; sworn to them. They were in great distress.
Jdg 3:8 16 Then the LORD raised up judges,[c][k] who saved[l]
[j]Dt 28:25 them out of the hands of these raiders. 17 Yet they
2:16 would not listen to their judges but prostituted[m]
[k]Ac 13:20 themselves to other gods and worshiped them.
[l]Ps 106:43 Unlike their fathers, they quickly turned from the
2:17 way in which their fathers had walked, the way of
[m]Ex 34:15 obedience to the LORD's commands.[n] 18 Whenever
[n]ver 7 the LORD raised up a judge for them, he was with
the judge and saved them out of the hands of their
2:18 enemies as long as the judge lived; for the LORD
[o]Dt 32:36; had compassion[o] on them as they groaned[p] under
Jos 1:5 [p]Ps 106:44 those who oppressed and afflicted them. 19 But
when the judge died, the people returned to ways
2:19 [q]Jdg 3:12 even more corrupt[q] than those of their fathers, fol-
[r]Jdg 4:1; lowing other gods and serving and worshiping
8:33 them.[r] They refused to give up their evil practices
2:20 and stubborn ways.
[s]ver 14; Jos 23:16 20 Therefore the LORD was very angry[s] with Isra-

[a] *5 Bokim* means *weepers.* [b] *9* Also known as *Timnath Serah* (see Joshua 19:50 and 24:30) [c] *16* Or *leaders;* similarly in verses 17–19

Teach Your Children

JDG 2:10

Amazing! One generation sees the power of the Lord—food in the desert, Jericho's walls falling down, nation after nation conquered, a new land possessed—and the *very next* generation knows "neither the LORD nor what he had done for Israel."

What happened? It's so simple, it's scary: *They didn't teach their children.* Those little ones grew up with parents who had experienced firsthand the amazing power of God, and they weren't even told about him. They reach adulthood knowing nothing of the Lord and what he has done.

There's a lesson here, a rather obvious one. Children won't learn about the Lord by osmosis. They have to be *taught.* And God puts the responsibility for that teaching squarely on the adults who have influence in their lives. His words to the Israelites ring as true today as they did then: "These commandments that I give you today are to be upon your hearts. Impress them on your children" (Dt 6:6–7).

Forgetting God

JDG 3:7

The Israelites "forgot" God. Attracted by the gods of the people they failed to drive out of Canaan, they abandon the true God and serve the "Baals and the Asherahs." It is bad enough that they forget the One who miraculously delivered them from slavery and provided them with a homeland. But then, adding insult to injury, they begin to serve these phantom gods.

Ancient Baal worshipers believed that their god was responsible for the fertility of the land, animals and people. Baal worship, therefore, involved human sexual fertility rites that supposedly induced the god to act. The worship of Asherah involved similar lascivious activities.

Throughout their history, the Israelites are tempted to abandon the worship of the true God for these false gods. Each time, God calls them back and offers forgiveness and love (Ne 9:29–31). This true God, who can't be seen or touched like some idol, but whose mercy and grace can be experienced by his people, offers grace to anyone who, instead of forgetting him, remembers.

el and said, "Because this nation has violated the
covenant that I laid down for their forefathers and
has not listened to me, 21I will no longer drive out[t]
before them any of the nations Joshua left when
he died. 22I will use them to test[u] Israel and see
whether they will keep the way of the LORD and
walk in it as their forefathers did." 23The LORD had
allowed those nations to remain; he did not drive
them out at once by giving them into the hands
of Joshua.

3 These are the nations the LORD left to test[v] all
those Israelites who had not experienced any
of the wars in Canaan 2(he did this only to teach
warfare to the descendants of the Israelites who
had not had previous battle experience): 3the five[w]
rulers of the Philistines, all the Canaanites, the
Sidonians, and the Hivites living in the Lebanon
mountains from Mount Baal Hermon to Lebo[a]
Hamath. 4They were left to test[x] the Israelites to
see whether they would obey the LORD's commands, which he had given their forefathers
through Moses.
5The Israelites lived[y] among the Canaanites,
Hittites, Amorites, Perizzites, Hivites and
Jebusites. 6They took their daughters in marriage
and gave their own daughters to their sons, and
served their gods.[z]

Othniel

7The Israelites did evil in the eyes of the LORD;
they forgot the LORD[a] their God and served the
Baals and the Asherahs.[b] 8The anger of the LORD
burned against Israel so that he sold[c] them into
the hands of Cushan-Rishathaim king of Aram
Naharaim,[b] to whom the Israelites were subject
for eight years. 9But when they cried out[d] to the
LORD, he raised up for them a deliverer, Othniel[e]
son of Kenaz, Caleb's younger brother, who saved
them. 10The Spirit of the LORD came upon him,[f] so
that he became Israel's judge[c] and went to war.
The LORD gave Cushan-Rishathaim king of Aram
into the hands of Othniel, who overpowered him.
11So the land had peace for forty years, until Othniel son of Kenaz died.

Ehud

12Once again the Israelites did evil in the eyes
of the LORD,[g] and because they did this evil the
LORD gave Eglon king of Moab[h] power over Israel.
13Getting the Ammonites and Amalekites to join
him, Eglon came and attacked Israel, and they
took possession of the City of Palms.[d][i] 14The Israelites were subject to Eglon king of Moab for
eighteen years.
15Again the Israelites cried out to the LORD, and
he gave them a deliverer[j]—Ehud, a left-handed
man, the son of Gera the Benjamite. The Israelites
sent him with tribute to Eglon king of Moab. 16Now

2:21 [t]Jos 23:13
2:22 [u]Dt 8:2,16; Jdg 3:1,14
3:1 [v]Jdg 2:21-22
3:3 [w]Jos 13:3
3:4 [x]Dt 8:2; Jdg 2:22
3:5 [y]Ps 106:35
3:6 [z]Ex 34:16; Dt 7:3-4
3:7 [a]Dt 4:9 [b]Ex 34:13; Jdg 2:11,13
3:8 [c]Jdg 2:14
3:9 [d]ver 15; Jdg 6:6,7; 10:10; Ps 106:44 [e]Jdg 1:13
3:10 [f]Nu 11:25, 29; 24:2; Jdg 6:34; 11:29; 13:25; 14:6,19; 1Sa 11:6
3:12 [g]Jdg 2:11,14 [h]1Sa 12:9
3:13 [i]Jdg 1:16
3:15 [j]ver 9; Ps 78:34; 107:13

[a] *3* Or *to the entrance to* [b] *8* That is, Northwest Mesopotamia [c] *10* Or *leader* [d] *13* That is, Jericho

Ehud had made a double-edged sword about a foot
and a half[a] long, which he strapped to his right
thigh under his clothing. 17He presented the tribute to Eglon king of Moab, who was a very fat
3:17 kver 12 man.[k] 18After Ehud had presented the tribute, he
sent on their way the men who had carried it. 19At
the idols[b] near Gilgal he himself turned back and
said, "I have a secret message for you, O king."
The king said, "Quiet!" And all his attendants
left him.
20Ehud then approached him while he was sitting alone in the upper room of his summer
palace[c] and said, "I have a message from God for
you." As the king rose from his seat, 21Ehud
reached with his left hand, drew the sword from
his right thigh and plunged it into the king's belly. 22Even the handle sank in after the blade,
which came out his back. Ehud did not pull the
sword out, and the fat closed in over it. 23Then
Ehud went out to the porch[d]; he shut the doors of
the upper room behind him and locked them.
24After he had gone, the servants came and
found the doors of the upper room locked. They
3:24 l1Sa 24:3 said, "He must be relieving himself[l] in the inner
room of the house." 25They waited to the point of
3:25 m2Ki 2:17; embarrassment,[m] but when he did not open the
8:11 doors of the room, they took a key and unlocked
them. There they saw their lord fallen to the floor,
dead.
26While they waited, Ehud got away. He passed
by the idols and escaped to Seirah. 27When he
3:27 nJdg 6:34; arrived there, he blew a trumpet[n] in the hill coun-
1Sa 13:3 try of Ephraim, and the Israelites went down with
him from the hills, with him leading them.
28"Follow me," he ordered, "for the LORD has
3:28 oJdg 7:9,15 given Moab, your enemy, into your hands.[o]" So
pJos 2:7; they followed him down and, taking possession
Jdg 7:24; of the fords of the Jordan[p] that led to Moab, they
12:5 allowed no one to cross over. 29At that time they
struck down about ten thousand Moabites, all vigorous and strong; not a man escaped. 30That day
Moab was made subject to Israel, and the land
3:30 qver 11 had peace[q] for eighty years.

Shamgar

3:31 rJdg 5:6 31After Ehud came Shamgar son of Anath,[r] who
sJos 23:10 struck down six hundred[s] Philistines with an
oxgoad. He too saved Israel.

Deborah

4 After Ehud died, the Israelites once again did
4:1 tJdg 2:19 evil[t] in the eyes of the LORD. 2So the LORD sold
4:2 them into the hands of Jabin, a king of Canaan,
uJos 11:1 who reigned in Hazor.[u] The commander of his
vver 13,16; army was Sisera,[v] who lived in Harosheth Hag-
1Sa 12:9; goyim. 3Because he had nine hundred iron chari-
Ps 83:9

You will find humility in the knowledge of yourself when you see that even your own existence comes not from yourself but from me [God], for I loved you before you came into being. And in my unspeakable love for you I willed to create you anew in grace.

—Catherine of Siena (1347–1380)

[a] *16* Hebrew *a cubit* (about 0.5 meter) [b] *19* Or *the stone quarries*; also in verse 26 [c] *20* The meaning of the Hebrew for this phrase is uncertain. [d] *23* The meaning of the Hebrew for this word is uncertain.

Warrior Woman

JDG 4:1-10

Deborah is a woman among men—brave, intelligent, trustworthy, sure of God's word and confident of God's presence. Deborah rules Israel under a palm tree that bears her name. The Israelites bring all their disputes to her. But more than an arbitrator, Deborah is a conduit of God's will for the people. And God's will is that they go into battle. She summons Barak. He refuses to go unless she goes along. So she goes.

Deborah steps outside of that day's common cultural position for women. She judges while most women are at home weaving. She prophesies when her peers are cooking meals. And she goes into battle while other women stay home with the children.

The key issue here, however, is not what Deborah does but whom she follows. Deborah willingly does whatever God asks of her. She would have been just as willing to stay at home with the kids. But God calls her into battle. Deborah doesn't quibble or quake. She obeys (see the character sketch for Deborah on page 470).

ots[w] and had cruelly oppressed[x] the Israelites for 4:3
twenty years, they cried to the LORD for help. [w]Jdg 1:19
4Deborah, a prophetess, the wife of Lappidoth, [x]Ps 106:42
was leading[a] Israel at that time. 5She held court
under the Palm of Deborah between Ramah and
Bethel[y] in the hill country of Ephraim, and the 4:5
Israelites came to her to have their disputes decid- [y]Ge 35:8
ed. 6She sent for Barak son of Abinoam[z] from 4:6
Kedesh in Naphtali and said to him, "The LORD, [z]Heb 11:32
the God of Israel, commands you: 'Go, take with
you ten thousand men of Naphtali and Zebulun
and lead the way to Mount Tabor. 7I will lure Sisera, the commander of Jabin's army, with his
chariots and his troops to the Kishon River[a] and 4:7
give him into your hands.' " [a]Ps 83:9
8Barak said to her, "If you go with me, I will go;
but if you don't go with me, I won't go."
9"Very well," Deborah said, "I will go with you.
But because of the way you are going about this,[b] 4:9
the honor will not be yours, for the LORD will [b]ver 21;
hand Sisera over to a woman." So Deborah went Jdg 2:14
with Barak to Kedesh,[b] 10where he summoned[c] 4:10 [c]ver 14;
Zebulun and Naphtali. Ten thousand men fol- Jdg 5:15,18
lowed him, and Deborah also went with him.
11Now Heber the Kenite had left the other 4:11
Kenites,[d] the descendants of Hobab,[e] Moses' [d]Jdg 1:16
brother-in-law,[c] and pitched his tent by the great [e]Nu 10:29
tree in Zaanannim[f] near Kedesh. [f]Jos 19:33
12When they told Sisera that Barak son of Abinoam had gone up to Mount Tabor, 13Sisera gath-
ered together his nine hundred iron chariots[g] and 4:13 [g]ver 3
all the men with him, from Harosheth Haggoyim
to the Kishon River.
14Then Deborah said to Barak, "Go! This is the
day the LORD has given Sisera into your hands.
Has not the LORD gone ahead[h] of you?" So Barak 4:14 [h]Dt 9:3;
went down Mount Tabor, followed by ten thou- 2Sa 5:24;
sand men. 15At Barak's advance, the LORD routed[i] Ps 68:7
Sisera and all his chariots and army by the sword,
and Sisera abandoned his chariot and fled on foot. 4:15
16But Barak pursued the chariots and army as far [i]Jos 10:10;
as Harosheth Haggoyim. All the troops of Sisera Ps 83:9-10
fell by the sword; not a man was left.[j] 4:16 [j]Ps 83:9
17Sisera, however, fled on foot to the tent of Jael,
the wife of Heber the Kenite, because there were
friendly relations between Jabin king of Hazor
and the clan of Heber the Kenite.
18Jael went out to meet Sisera and said to him,
"Come, my lord, come right in. Don't be afraid."
So he entered her tent, and she put a covering
over him.
19"I'm thirsty," he said. "Please give me some
water." She opened a skin of milk,[k] gave him a 4:19 [k]Jdg 5:25
drink, and covered him up.
20"Stand in the doorway of the tent," he told
her. "If someone comes by and asks you, 'Is anyone here?' say 'No.' "
21But Jael, Heber's wife, picked up a tent peg

[a] 4 Traditionally *judging* [b] 9 Or *But on the expedition you are undertaking* [c] 11 Or *father-in-law*

and a hammer and went quietly to him while he
lay fast asleep, exhausted. She drove the peg
through his temple into the ground, and he
4:21 [l]Jdg 5:26 died.[l]
[22]Barak came by in pursuit of Sisera, and Jael
went out to meet him. "Come," she said, "I will
show you the man you're looking for." So he went
in with her, and there lay Sisera with the tent peg
through his temple—dead.
4:23 [m]Ne 9:24; Ps 18:47 [23]On that day God subdued[m] Jabin, the Canaanite king, before the Israelites. [24]And the hand of
the Israelites grew stronger and stronger against
Jabin, the Canaanite king, until they destroyed
him.

The Song of Deborah

5:1 [n]Ex 15:1 **5** On that day Deborah and Barak son of Abinoam sang this song:[n]

[2]"When the princes in Israel take the
lead,
5:2 [o]2Ch 17:16; Ps 110:3 [p]ver 9 when the people willingly offer[o]
themselves—
praise the LORD![p]

[3]"Hear this, you kings! Listen, you
rulers!
5:3 [q]Ps 27:6 I will sing to[a] the LORD, I will sing;
I will make music to[b] the LORD, the
God of Israel.[q]

5:4 [r]Dt 33:2 [s]Ps 68:8 [4]"O LORD, when you went out from Seir,[r]
when you marched from the land of
Edom,
the earth shook, the heavens poured,
the clouds poured down water.[s]
5:5 [t]Ex 19:18; Ps 68:8; 97:5; Isa 64:3 [5]The mountains quaked[t] before the LORD,
the One of Sinai,
before the LORD, the God of Israel.

5:6 [u]Jdg 3:31 [v]Jdg 4:17 [w]Isa 33:8 [6]"In the days of Shamgar son of Anath,[u]
in the days of Jael,[v] the roads[w] were
abandoned;
travelers took to winding paths.
[7]Village life[c] in Israel ceased,
ceased until I,[d] Deborah, arose,
arose a mother in Israel.
5:8 [x]Dt 32:17 [8]When they chose new gods,[x]
war came to the city gates,
and not a shield or spear was seen
among forty thousand in Israel.
[9]My heart is with Israel's princes,
5:9 [y]ver 2 with the willing volunteers[y] among
the people.
Praise the LORD!

5:10 [z]Jdg 10:4; 12:14 [10]"You who ride on white donkeys,[z]
sitting on your saddle blankets,
and you who walk along the road,

[a]3 Or *of* [b]3 Or / *with song I will praise* [c]7 Or *Warriors*
[d]7 Or *you*

Jael Brings Victory

JDG 4:21

It's hard to imagine any woman committing such a brutal act. Inviting General Sisera into her tent (an improper act for a married woman), Jael tenderly covers the tired warrior, offers him milk to drink and watches over him as he sleeps. Then, when he is most vulnerable, she takes a tent peg and hammer—domestic tools with which she is familiar since she puts up the tent each time the family moves—and drives the peg through Sisera's temple. He dies instantly.

Is God a part of such a barbarous act? Is Deborah right in singing Jael's praises (Jdg 5:24–27)? The times of the judges were violent times. While that doesn't justify Jael's actions, it may help to understand them. Sisera's people have been brutally oppressing the Israelites for years. Now God's judgment comes down through the act of a woman. Was the act God's will? Perhaps not. But it did fulfill God's purpose by ending the oppression of Israel at the hands of the Canaanites. (See character sketch for Jael on page 535.)

Mary Artemesia Lathbury, daughter of a Methodist minister and author of Women's Christian Temperance materials, wrote this song on the shore of Lake Chautauqua in New York.

Day Is Dying in the West

Day is dying in the west;
Heaven is touching earth with rest;
Wait and worship while the night
Sets the evening lamps alight
Through all the sky.

Holy, holy, holy, Lord God of Hosts!
Heaven and earth are full of Thee!
Heaven and earth are praising Thee,
O Lord most high!

Lord of life, beneath the dome
Of the universe, Thy home,
Gather us who seek Thy face
To the fold of Thy embrace,
For Thou art nigh.

When forever from our sight
Pass the stars, the day, the night,
Lord of angels, on our eyes
Let eternal morning rise
And shadows end.

—Mary Artemesia Lathbury (1841-1913)

consider [11]the voice of the singers[a] at the
watering places.
They recite the righteous acts[a] of the
LORD,
the righteous acts of his warriors[b] in
Israel.

"Then the people of the LORD
went down to the city gates.[b]
12 'Wake up,[c] wake up, Deborah!
Wake up, wake up, break out in song!
Arise, O Barak!
Take captive your captives,[d] O son of
Abinoam.'

13 "Then the men who were left
came down to the nobles;
the people of the LORD
came to me with the mighty.
14 Some came from Ephraim, whose roots
were in Amalek;[e]
Benjamin was with the people who
followed you.
From Makir captains came down,
from Zebulun those who bear a
commander's staff.
15 The princes of Issachar were with
Deborah;[f]
yes, Issachar was with Barak,
rushing after him into the valley.
In the districts of Reuben
there was much searching of heart.
16 Why did you stay among the campfires[c]
to hear the whistling for the flocks?[g]
In the districts of Reuben
there was much searching of heart.
17 Gilead stayed beyond the Jordan.
And Dan, why did he linger by the
ships?
Asher remained on the coast[h]
and stayed in his coves.
18 The people of Zebulun risked their very
lives;
so did Naphtali on the heights of the
field.[i]

19 "Kings came[j], they fought;
the kings of Canaan fought
at Taanach by the waters of Megiddo,[k]
but they carried off no silver, no
plunder.[l]
20 From the heavens[m] the stars fought,
from their courses they fought against
Sisera.
21 The river Kishon[n] swept them away,
the age-old river, the river Kishon.
March on, my soul; be strong!
22 Then thundered the horses' hoofs—
galloping, galloping go his mighty
steeds.

5:11 [a]1Sa 12:7; Mic 6:5 [b]ver 8
5:12 [c]Ps 57:8 [d]Ps 68:18; Eph 4:8
5:14 [e]Jdg 3:13
5:15 [f]Jdg 4:10
5:16 [g]Nu 32:1
5:17 [h]Jos 19:29
5:18 [i]Jdg 4:6, 10
5:19 [j]Jos 11:5; Jdg 4:13 [k]Jdg 1:27 [l]ver 30
5:20 [m]Jos 10:11
5:21 [n]Jdg 4:7

[a] *11* Or *archers*; the meaning of the Hebrew for this word is uncertain. [b] *11* Or *villagers* [c] *16* Or *saddlebags*

23 'Curse Meroz,' said the angel of the
LORD.
'Curse its people bitterly,
because they did not come to help the
LORD,
to help the LORD against the mighty.'

5:24 [o]Jdg 4:17 24 "Most blessed of women be Jael,[o]
the wife of Heber the Kenite,
most blessed of tent-dwelling women.
25 He asked for water, and she gave him
5:25 milk;[p]
[p]Jdg 4:19 in a bowl fit for nobles she brought
him curdled milk.
26 Her hand reached for the tent peg,
her right hand for the workman's
hammer.
5:26 She struck Sisera, she crushed his head,
[q]Jdg 4:21 she shattered and pierced his temple.[q]
27 At her feet he sank,
he fell; there he lay.
At her feet he sank, he fell;
where he sank, there he fell—dead.

28 "Through the window peered Sisera's
mother;
5:28 behind the lattice she cried out,[r]
[r]Pr 7:6 'Why is his chariot so long in coming?
Why is the clatter of his chariots
delayed?'
29 The wisest of her ladies answer her;
indeed, she keeps saying to herself,
30 'Are they not finding and dividing the
5:30 spoils:[s]
[s]Ex 15:9; 1Sa 30:24 a girl or two for each man,
colorful garments as plunder for
Sisera,
colorful garments embroidered,
highly embroidered garments for my
neck—
all this as plunder?'

31 "So may all your enemies perish,
O LORD!
5:31 But may they who love you be like
[t]2Sa 23:4; the sun[t]
Ps 19:4; 89:36 when it rises in its strength."
[u]Jdg 3:11

Then the land had peace[u] forty years.

Gideon

6:1
[v]Jdg 2:11 6 Again the Israelites did evil in the eyes of the
[w]Nu 25:15-18; 31:1-3 LORD,[v] and for seven years he gave them into
the hands of the Midianites.[w] 2 Because the power
6:2 of Midian was so oppressive,[x] the Israelites pre-
[x]1Sa 13:6; pared shelters for themselves in mountain clefts,
Isa 8:21 [y]Heb 11:38 caves and strongholds.[y] 3 Whenever the Israelites
planted their crops, the Midianites, Amalekites[z]
6:3 and other eastern peoples invaded the country.
[z]Jdg 3:13 4 They camped on the land and ruined the crops[a]
6:4 all the way to Gaza and did not spare a living
[a]Lev 26:16; Dt 28:30,51 thing for Israel, neither sheep nor cattle nor don-

Contrasts

JDG 5:24-31

Deborah's song ends with two contrasts. The first compares the joyful victory of one mother with the anguished defeat of another. Deborah, "a mother in Israel" (Jdg 5:7), sings an exuberant song of victory over the enemies of Israel and God. The battle looks like it should go to Israel's enemy, with its stronger force of 900 chariots. But appearances don't always add up in God's economy. Israel wins the battle, thanks in part to Jael's initiative. Deborah's joy is contrasted with the anguish of Sisera's mother as she waits for the return of her son.

The second contrast compares what will happen to those who are God's enemies with what will happen to those who love him. The first will be destroyed while the second will rise in power. The victory may not be immediate. It may look like the odds are against us. But the winner is always the one who is on God's side.

Threshing in a Winepress

JDG 6:11

It's absurd. Why ever would Gideon thresh wheat in a winepress? A winepress is for pressing grapes.

Traditionally, wheat is threshed on a threshing floor, and often threshing floors are located on hilltops, where the breezes can carry away the chaff, leaving only the fresh grain. But threshing on a hilltop would have made Gideon a "sitting duck" for any passing Midianite looking for food or revenge. Instead Gideon threshes his grain in a winepress. A winepress is a large vat, often hewn out of solid stone, where grapes are pressed for their juices. It's not an ideal place for threshing grain. But it's an apt one, considering the recent activities of the Midianites.

Read the first six verses of Judges 6 for a shattering description of the suffering the Midianites cause the Israelites. Gideon, doing what he could to survive, threshes grain in a winepress, while God plans a rescue with Gideon as his champion.

keys. 5They came up with their livestock and their
tents like swarms of locusts.[b] It was impossible to
count the men and their camels;[c] they invaded the
land to ravage it. 6Midian so impoverished the
Israelites that they cried out[d] to the LORD for help.
7When the Israelites cried to the LORD because
of Midian, 8he sent them a prophet, who said,
"This is what the LORD, the God of Israel, says: I
brought you up out of Egypt,[e] out of the land of
slavery. 9I snatched you from the power of Egypt
and from the hand of all your oppressors. I drove
them from before you and gave you their land.[f] 10I
said to you, 'I am the LORD your God; do not worship[g] the gods of the Amorites,[h] in whose land
you live.' But you have not listened to me."
11The angel of the LORD[i] came and sat down
under the oak in Ophrah that belonged to Joash
the Abiezrite,[j] where his son Gideon[k] was threshing wheat in a winepress to keep it from the Midianites. 12When the angel of the LORD appeared to
Gideon, he said, "The LORD is with you,[l] mighty
warrior."
13"But sir," Gideon replied, "if the LORD is with
us, why has all this happened to us? Where are
all his wonders that our fathers told[m] us about
when they said, 'Did not the LORD bring us up out
of Egypt?' But now the LORD has abandoned[n] us
and put us into the hand of Midian."
14The LORD turned to him and said, "Go in the
strength you have[o] and save Israel out of Midian's
hand. Am I not sending you?"
15"But Lord,[a]" Gideon asked, "how can I save
Israel? My clan is the weakest in Manasseh, and I
am the least in my family.[p]"
16The LORD answered, "I will be with you[q], and
you will strike down all the Midianites together."
17Gideon replied, "If now I have found favor in
your eyes, give me a sign[r] that it is really you talking to me. 18Please do not go away until I come
back and bring my offering and set it before you."
And the LORD said, "I will wait until you
return."
19Gideon went in, prepared a young goat, and
from an ephah[b] of flour he made bread without
yeast. Putting the meat in a basket and its broth in
a pot, he brought them out and offered them to
him under the oak.[s]
20The angel of God said to him, "Take the meat
and the unleavened bread, place them on this
rock,[t] and pour out the broth." And Gideon did
so. 21With the tip of the staff that was in his hand,
the angel of the LORD touched the meat and the
unleavened bread.[u] Fire flared from the rock, consuming the meat and the bread. And the angel of
the LORD disappeared. 22When Gideon realized[v]
that it was the angel of the LORD, he exclaimed,
"Ah, Sovereign LORD! I have seen the angel of the
LORD face to face!"[w]

6:5 [b]Jdg 7:12 [c]Jdg 8:10
6:6 [d]Jdg 3:9
6:8 [e]Jdg 2:1
6:9 [f]Ps 44:2
6:10 [g]2Ki 17:35 [h]Jer 10:2
6:11 [i]Ge 16:7 [j]Jos 17:2 [k]Heb 11:32
6:12 [l]Jos 1:5; Jdg 13:3; Lk 1:11,28
6:13 [m]Ps 44:1 [n]2Ch 15:2
6:14 [o]Heb 11:34
6:15 [p]Ex 3:11; 1Sa 9:21
6:16 [q]Ex 3:12; Jos 1:5
6:17 [r]ver 36-37; Ge 24:14; Isa 38:7-8
6:19 [s]Ge 18:7-8
6:20 [t]Jdg 13:19
6:21 [u]Lev 9:24
6:22 [v]Jdg 13:16, 21 [w]Ge 32:30; Ex 33:20; Jdg 13:22

[a] *15* Or *sir* [b] *19* That is, probably about 3/5 bushel (about 22 liters)

23But the LORD said to him, "Peace! Do not be
6:23 [x]Da 10:19 afraid.[x] You are not going to die."
24So Gideon built an altar to the LORD there and
6:24 [y]Ge 22:14 called[y] it The LORD is Peace. To this day it stands in
[z]Jdg 8:32 Ophrah[z] of the Abiezrites.
25That same night the LORD said to him, "Take
the second bull from your father's herd, the one
6:25 [a]Ex 34:13; seven years old.[a] Tear down your father's altar to
Dt 7:5 Baal and cut down the Asherah pole[b][a] beside it.
26Then build a proper kind of[c] altar to the LORD
your God on the top of this height. Using the
wood of the Asherah pole that you cut down, offer
the second[d] bull as a burnt offering."
27So Gideon took ten of his servants and did as
the LORD told him. But because he was afraid of
his family and the men of the town, he did it at
night rather than in the daytime.
28In the morning when the men of the town got
6:28 [b]1Ki 16:32 up, there was Baal's altar,[b] demolished, with the
Asherah pole beside it cut down and the second
bull sacrificed on the newly built altar!
29They asked each other, "Who did this?"
When they carefully investigated, they were
told, "Gideon son of Joash did it."
30The men of the town demanded of Joash,
"Bring out your son. He must die, because he has
broken down Baal's altar and cut down the Asherah pole beside it."
31But Joash replied to the hostile crowd around
him, "Are you going to plead Baal's cause? Are
you trying to save him? Whoever fights for him
shall be put to death by morning! If Baal really is
a god, he can defend himself when someone
breaks down his altar." 32So that day they called
6:32 [c]Jdg 7:1; Gideon "Jerub-Baal,[e][c]" saying, "Let Baal contend
8:29,35; with him," because he broke down Baal's altar.
1Sa 12:11 33Now all the Midianites, Amalekites and other
eastern peoples[d] joined forces and crossed over
6:33 [d]ver 3 the Jordan and camped in the Valley of Jezreel.[e]
[e]Jos 17:16 34Then the Spirit of the LORD came upon[f] Gideon,
6:34 [f]Jdg 3:10; and he blew a trumpet,[g] summoning the Abiez-
1Ch 12:18; rites to follow him. 35He sent messengers through-
2Ch 24:20 out Manasseh, calling them to arms, and also into
[g]Jdg 3:27 Asher, Zebulun and Naphtali,[h] so that they too
6:35 went up to meet them.
[h]Jdg 4:6 36Gideon said to God, "If you will save[i] Israel by
6:36 my hand as you have promised— 37look, I will
[i]ver 14 place a wool fleece on the threshing floor.[j] If there
is dew only on the fleece and all the ground is dry,
6:37 [j]Ex 4:3-7 then I will know[k] that you will save Israel by my
[k]Ge 24:14 hand, as you said." 38And that is what happened.
Gideon rose early the next day; he squeezed the
fleece and wrung out the dew—a bowlful of
water.
39Then Gideon said to God, "Do not be angry
6:39 [l]Ge 18:32 with me. Let me make just one more request.[l]

[a] *25* Or *Take a full-grown, mature bull from your father's herd*
[b] *25* That is, a symbol of the goddess Asherah; here and elsewhere in Judges
[c] *26* Or *build with layers of stone an*
[d] *26* Or *full-grown;* also in verse 28
[e] *32* *Jerub-Baal* means *let Baal contend.*

The Source of True Courage

JDG 6:34

When God calls Gideon to lead the Israelites against their oppressors, Gideon comes up with every excuse imaginable. "I'm the weakest. I'm the smallest" (Jdg 6:15). "I'm not sure you're really speaking to me" (Jdg 6:17). "I need a sign" (Jdg 6:36-40).

Yet this same Gideon is the "mighty warrior" (Jdg 6:12) that we know as the one God used to defeat the mighty Midianites. Where does this ordinary man gain the courage to accomplish this extraordinary task? The key is found in Judges 6:34: "Then the Spirit of the LORD came upon Gideon." The language used here literally means that the Spirit "clothed himself with Gideon." The mighty Spirit of God takes on new clothing, that of the man Gideon, and accomplishes astounding things through him—things the mere human being could never have done on his own. If God can use a Gideon, don't you think he can use us? We just need to be like Gideon—not strong or brave or powerful, simply *willing*.

Ready for Battle

JDG 7:1–8

Gideon's army of 32,000 men faces an enemy of enormous proportions and strength (Jdg 7:12). Gideon bravely moves forward—until God stops him—and tells him he has way too many soldiers. Gideon obeys God and tells all those who are scared about the coming battle to go home. A "mere" 22,000 leave. What? Still too many? Another 9,700 are weeded out through a riverbank test.

Now Gideon is left with a paltry 300 soldiers to fight an enemy as numerous as locusts. Foolhardy. Suicidal. But divine. God wants to be sure the Israelites get the lesson and get it crystal clear. A mere 300 men can never conquer so huge an enemy. The Israelites' victory has nothing to do with their strength or number and everything to do with God's power and love . . . the same power and love that is at work today conquering enemies too big and too powerful for us to fight alone.

Allow me one more test with the fleece. This time
make the fleece dry and the ground covered with
dew." 40That night God did so. Only the fleece was
dry; all the ground was covered with dew.

Gideon Defeats the Midianites

7 Early in the morning, Jerub-Baal[m] (that is, **7:1**
Gideon) and all his men camped at the spring [m]Jdg 6:32
of Harod. The camp of Midian was north of them [n]Ge 12:6
in the valley near the hill of Moreh.[n] 2The LORD
said to Gideon, "You have too many men for me to
deliver Midian into their hands. In order that Israel may not boast against me that her own
strength[o] has saved her, 3announce now to the **7:2**
people, 'Anyone who trembles with fear may turn [o]Dt 8:17;
back and leave Mount Gilead.[p]' " So twenty-two 2Co 4:7
thousand men left, while ten thousand remained. **7:3**
4But the LORD said to Gideon, "There are still too [p]Dt 20:8
many[q] men. Take them down to the water, and I **7:4**
will sift them for you there. If I say, 'This one shall [q]1Sa 14:6
go with you,' he shall go; but if I say, 'This one
shall not go with you,' he shall not go."
5So Gideon took the men down to the water.
There the LORD told him, "Separate those who lap
the water with their tongues like a dog from those
who kneel down to drink." 6Three hundred men
lapped with their hands to their mouths. All the
rest got down on their knees to drink.
7The LORD said to Gideon, "With the three hundred men that lapped I will save you and give the
Midianites into your hands. Let all the other men
go, each to his own place."[r] 8So Gideon sent the **7:7**
rest of the Israelites to their tents but kept the [r]1Sa 14:6
three hundred, who took over the provisions and
trumpets of the others.
Now the camp of Midian lay below him in the
valley. 9During that night the LORD said to Gideon, "Get up, go down against the camp, because I **7:9**
am going to give it into your hands.[s] 10If you are [s]Jos 2:24;
afraid to attack, go down to the camp with your 10:8; 11:6
servant Purah 11and listen to what they are saying. Afterward, you will be encouraged to attack
the camp." So he and Purah his servant went
down to the outposts of the camp. 12The Midian-
ites, the Amalekites[t] and all the other eastern peo- **7:12**
ples had settled in the valley, thick as locusts.[u] [t]Jdg 8:10 [u]Jdg 6:5
Their camels[v] could no more be counted than the [v]Jer 49:29
sand on the seashore.[w] [w]Jos 11:4
13Gideon arrived just as a man was telling a
friend his dream. "I had a dream," he was saying.
"A round loaf of barley bread came tumbling into
the Midianite camp. It struck the tent with such
force that the tent overturned and collapsed."
14His friend responded, "This can be nothing
other than the sword of Gideon son of Joash, the
Israelite. God has given the Midianites and the
whole camp into his hands."
15When Gideon heard the dream and its inter- **7:15**
pretation, he worshiped God.[x] He returned to the [x]1Sa 15:31
camp of Israel and called out, "Get up! The LORD
has given the Midianite camp into your hands."

16Dividing the three hundred men[y] into three com-
7:16 [y]Ge 14:15 panies,[z] he placed trumpets and empty jars in the
[z]2Sa 18:2 hands of all of them, with torches inside.
17"Watch me," he told them. "Follow my lead.
When I get to the edge of the camp, do exactly as
I do. 18When I and all who are with me blow our
7:18 [a]Jdg 3:27 trumpets,[a] then from all around the camp blow
yours and shout, 'For the LORD and for Gideon.' "
19Gideon and the hundred men with him
reached the edge of the camp at the beginning of
the middle watch, just after they had changed the
guard. They blew their trumpets and broke the
jars that were in their hands. 20The three companies blew the trumpets and smashed the jars.
Grasping the torches in their left hands and hold-
7:20 ing in their right hands the trumpets they were to
[b]ver 14 blow, they shouted, "A sword[b] for the LORD and
for Gideon!" 21While each man held his position
around the camp, all the Midianites ran, crying
7:21 out as they fled.[c]
[c]2Ki 7:7 22When the three hundred trumpets sounded,[d]
7:22 the LORD caused the men throughout the camp to
[d]Jos 6:20 turn on each other[e] with their swords. The army
[e]1Sa 14:20; 2Ch 20:23 fled to Beth Shittah toward Zererah as far as the
[f]1Ki 4:12; 19:16 border of Abel Meholah[f] near Tabbath. 23Israelites
from Naphtali, Asher and all Manasseh were
7:23 called out,[g] and they pursued the Midianites.
[g]Jdg 6:35 24Gideon sent messengers throughout the hill
country of Ephraim, saying, "Come down against
7:24 the Midianites and seize the waters of the Jordan[h]
[h]Jdg 3:28 ahead of them as far as Beth Barah."
So all the men of Ephraim were called out and
they took the waters of the Jordan as far as Beth
Barah. 25They also captured two of the Midianite
7:25 leaders, Oreb and Zeeb[i]. They killed Oreb at the
[i]Jdg 8:3; Ps 83:11 rock of Oreb,[j] and Zeeb at the winepress of Zeeb.
[j]Isa 10:26 They pursued the Midianites and brought the
[k]Jdg 8:4 heads of Oreb and Zeeb to Gideon, who was by
the Jordan.[k]

Zebah and Zalmunna

8 Now the Ephraimites asked Gideon, "Why
have you treated us like this? Why didn't you
8:1 call us when you went to fight Midian?"[l] And they
[l]Jdg 12:1 [m]2Sa 19:41 criticized him sharply.[m]
2But he answered them, "What have I accomplished compared to you? Aren't the gleanings of
Ephraim's grapes better than the full grape har-
8:3 vest of Abiezer? 3God gave Oreb and Zeeb,[n] the
[n]Jdg 7:25; Pr 15:1 Midianite leaders, into your hands. What was I
able to do compared to you?" At this, their resentment against him subsided.
4Gideon and his three hundred men, exhausted
8:4 yet keeping up the pursuit, came to the Jordan[o]
[o]Jdg 7:25 and crossed it. 5He said to the men of Succoth,[p]
8:5 "Give my troops some bread; they are worn out,
[p]Ge 33:17 and I am still pursuing Zebah and Zalmunna,[q] the
[q]Ps 83:11 kings of Midian."
6But the officials of Succoth said, "Do you
already have the hands of Zebah and Zalmunna

Shout to the Lord

JDG 7:20

Three hundred soldiers with torches covered by jars in their left hands and trumpets in their right hands. Where are the swords and shields? What hands did they use to hold their weapons?

At the designated moment, the soldiers hold their positions, simultaneously blow on their trumpets and break their jars so the torches flare; then they roar, "A sword for the LORD and for Gideon!" Their terrified enemies turn on each other with their own swords, and 120,000 swordsmen are killed that day (Jdg 8:10).

There can be no doubt whatsoever who is the victor in this battle. It is not the brave little band of Israelite soldiers who aren't even holding weapons. It is not General Gideon. The Victor is the Lord.

in your possession? Why should we give bread[r] to
your troops?"[s]
7 Then Gideon replied, "Just for that, when the
LORD has given Zebah and Zalmunna[t] into my
hand, I will tear your flesh with desert thorns and
briers."
8 From there he went up to Peniel[a][u] and made
the same request of them, but they answered as
the men of Succoth had. 9 So he said to the men of
Peniel, "When I return in triumph, I will tear
down this tower."[v]
10 Now Zebah and Zalmunna were in Karkor with
a force of about fifteen thousand men, all that were
left of the armies of the eastern peoples; a hundred
and twenty thousand swordsmen had fallen.[w]
11 Gideon went up by the route of the nomads east
of Nobah[x] and Jogbehah[y] and fell upon the unsuspecting army. 12 Zebah and Zalmunna, the two
kings of Midian, fled, but he pursued them and
captured them, routing their entire army.
13 Gideon son of Joash then returned from the
battle by the Pass of Heres. 14 He caught a young
man of Succoth and questioned him, and the
young man wrote down for him the names of the
seventy-seven officials of Succoth, the elders of
the town. 15 Then Gideon came and said to the
men of Succoth, "Here are Zebah and Zalmunna,
about whom you taunted me by saying, 'Do you
already have the hands of Zebah and Zalmunna
in your possession? Why should we give bread to
your exhausted men?[z]' " 16 He took the elders of
the town and taught the men of Succoth a lesson[a]
by punishing them with desert thorns and briers.
17 He also pulled down the tower of Peniel and
killed the men of the town.[b]
18 Then he asked Zebah and Zalmunna, "What
kind of men did you kill at Tabor?[c]"
"Men like you," they answered, "each one with
the bearing of a prince."
19 Gideon replied, "Those were my brothers, the
sons of my own mother. As surely as the LORD
lives, if you had spared their lives, I would not kill
you." 20 Turning to Jether, his oldest son, he said,
"Kill them!" But Jether did not draw his sword,
because he was only a boy and was afraid.
21 Zebah and Zalmunna said, "Come, do it yourself. 'As is the man, so is his strength.' " So Gideon stepped forward and killed them, and took the
ornaments[d] off their camels' necks.

Gideon's Ephod

22 The Israelites said to Gideon, "Rule over us—
you, your son and your grandson—because you
have saved us out of the hand of Midian."
23 But Gideon told them, "I will not rule over
you, nor will my son rule over you. The LORD will
rule[e] over you." 24 And he said, "I do have one
request, that each of you give me an earring from

[a] 8 Hebrew *Penuel,* a variant of *Peniel;* also in verses 9 and 17

8:6 [r] 1Sa 25:11 [s] ver 15
8:7 [t] Jdg 7:15
8:8 [u] Ge 32:30; 1Ki 12:25
8:9 [v] ver 17
8:10 [w] Jdg 6:5; 7:12; Isa 9:4
8:11 [x] Nu 32:42 [y] Nu 32:35
8:15 [z] ver 6
8:16 [a] ver 7
8:17 [b] ver 9
8:18 [c] Jos 19:22; Jdg 4:6
8:21 [d] ver 26; Ps 83:11
8:23 [e] Ex 16:8; 1Sa 8:7; 10:19; 12:12

My Mother's Sons

JDG 8:19

Notice how Gideon identifies these dead men as his brothers: "[They are] my brothers, the *sons of my own mother*" (emphasis added). These are the days of multiple wives for one husband, so these specific brothers need to be distinguished from other brothers who have the same father but a different mother.

When God instituted marriage in the Garden of Eden, his plan was for one man to marry one woman (Ge 2:24). However, early on even the patriarchs had more than one wife, seemingly without disapproval from God. Gideon's father has several wives, and Gideon himself has "many wives" (Jdg 8:30).

The teachings of Jesus (Mt 19:4–6; Mk 10:11–12) underscore the benefits and beauty of the marriage of one man to one woman for life. Paul urges Timothy and Titus to choose leaders who have only "one wife" (1Ti 3:2,12; Tit 1:6), supporting God's first and best choice for marriage.

your share of the plunder." (It was the custom of
8:24 [f]Ge 25:13 the Ishmaelites[f] to wear gold earrings.)
[25]They answered, "We'll be glad to give them."
So they spread out a garment, and each man
threw a ring from his plunder onto it. [26]The
weight of the gold rings he asked for came to seventeen hundred shekels,[a] not counting the ornaments, the pendants and the purple garments
worn by the kings of Midian or the chains that
were on their camels' necks. [27]Gideon made the
8:27 [g]Jdg 17:5; gold into an ephod,[g] which he placed in Ophrah,
18:14 his town. All Israel prostituted themselves by wor-
[h]Dt 7:16; shiping it there, and it became a snare[h] to Gideon
Ps 106:39 and his family.

Gideon's Death

[28]Thus Midian was subdued before the Israelites and did not raise its head again. During Gid-
8:28 [i]Jdg 5:31 eon's lifetime, the land enjoyed peace[i] forty years.
[29]Jerub-Baal[j] son of Joash went back home to
8:29 [j]Jdg 7:1 live. [30]He had seventy sons[k] of his own, for he had
many wives. [31]His concubine, who lived in She-
8:30 [k]Jdg 9:2,5, chem, also bore him a son, whom he named
18,24 Abimelech.[l] [32]Gideon son of Joash died at a good
old age[m] and was buried in the tomb of his father
8:31 [l]Jdg 9:1 Joash in Ophrah of the Abiezrites.
[33]No sooner had Gideon died than the Israelites
8:32 [m]Ge 25:8 again prostituted themselves to the Baals.[n] They
set up Baal-Berith[o] as their god[p] and [34]did not
8:33 remember[q] the LORD their God, who had rescued
[n]Jdg 2:11,13, 19 them from the hands of all their enemies on every
[o]Jdg 9:4 side. [35]They also failed to show kindness to the
[p]Jdg 9:27,46 family of Jerub-Baal (that is, Gideon) for all the
8:34 [q]Jdg 3:7; Dt 4:9; good things he had done for them.[r]

Abimelech

Ps 78:11,42 **9** Abimelech[s] son of Jerub-Baal went to his
8:35 mother's brothers in Shechem and said to them
[r]Jdg 9:16 and to all his mother's clan, [2]"Ask all the citizens
9:1 of Shechem, 'Which is better for you: to have all
[s]Jdg 8:31 seventy of Jerub-Baal's sons rule over you, or just
9:2 one man?' Remember, I am your flesh and blood.[t]"
[t]Ge 29:14; [3]When the brothers repeated all this to the citi-
Jdg 8:30 zens of Shechem, they were inclined to follow
Abimelech, for they said, "He is our brother."
9:4 [4]They gave him seventy shekels[b] of silver from the
[u]Jdg 8:33 [v]Jdg 11:3; temple of Baal-Berith,[u] and Abimelech used it to
2Ch 13:7 hire reckless adventurers,[v] who became his followers. [5]He went to his father's home in Ophrah
9:5 [w]ver 2; and on one stone murdered his seventy brothers,[w]
Jdg 8:30 the sons of Jerub-Baal. But Jotham, the youngest
[x]2Ki 11:2 son of Jerub-Baal, escaped by hiding.[x] [6]Then all
the citizens of Shechem and Beth Millo gathered
beside the great tree at the pillar in Shechem to
crown Abimelech king.
[7]When Jotham was told about this, he climbed
9:7 [y]Dt 11:29; up on the top of Mount Gerizim[y] and shouted to
27:12; Jn 4:20 them, "Listen to me, citizens of Shechem, so that

[a] 26 That is, about 43 pounds (about 19.5 kilograms)
[b] 4 That is, about 1 3/4 pounds (about 0.8 kilogram)

Gideon's Ephod

JDG 8:22–27

After the Midianite war, the people give a share of their plunder to Gideon: one gold earring each. Gideon takes the gold and forms it into an ephod, an article of clothing connected with worshiping God (Ex 28:6). Unfortunately, Gideon's ephod has no such high purpose. Soon after he makes it, the Israelites begin to worship it. So quickly they forget their miraculous deliverance from the Midianites, so quickly they turn from God to go their own way—a story repeated time after time throughout Judges and throughout the history of the church as well. God forgives, God delivers. We're thankful and close to him for a time, but then we soon forget and go our own way—a cycle that God will continue to work to break.

God may listen to you. 8One day the trees went
out to anoint a king for themselves. They said to
the olive tree, 'Be our king.'
9"But the olive tree answered, 'Should I give up
my oil, by which both gods and men are honored,
to hold sway over the trees?'
10"Next, the trees said to the fig tree, 'Come and
be our king.'
11"But the fig tree replied, 'Should I give up my
fruit, so good and sweet, to hold sway over the
trees?'
12"Then the trees said to the vine, 'Come and be
our king.'
13"But the vine answered, 'Should I give up my
wine,[z] which cheers both gods and men, to hold 9:13
sway over the trees?' [z]Ecc 2:3
14"Finally all the trees said to the thornbush,
'Come and be our king.'
15"The thornbush said to the trees, 'If you really
want to anoint me king over you, come and take 9:15
refuge in my shade;[a] but if not, then let fire come [a]Isa 30:2 [b]ver 20
out[b] of the thornbush and consume the cedars of [c]Isa 2:13
Lebanon!'[c]
16"Now if you have acted honorably and in good
faith when you made Abimelech king, and if you
have been fair to Jerub-Baal and his family, and if
you have treated him as he deserves— 17and to
think that my father fought for you, risked his life
to rescue you from the hand of Midian 18(but
today you have revolted against my father's fami- 9:18
ly, murdered his seventy sons[d] on a single stone, [d]ver 5-6;
and made Abimelech, the son of his slave girl, Jdg 8:30
king over the citizens of Shechem because he is
your brother)— 19if then you have acted honorably and in good faith toward Jerub-Baal and his
family today, may Abimelech be your joy, and
may you be his, too! 20But if you have not, let fire 9:20
come out[e] from Abimelech and consume you, cit- [e]ver 15
izens of Shechem and Beth Millo, and let fire
come out from you, citizens of Shechem and Beth
Millo, and consume Abimelech!"
21Then Jotham fled, escaping to Beer, and he
lived there because he was afraid of his brother
Abimelech.
22After Abimelech had governed Israel three 9:23
years, 23God sent an evil spirit[f] between Abim- [f]1Sa 16:14,
elech and the citizens of Shechem, who acted 23; 18:10;
treacherously against Abimelech. 24God did this 1Ki 22:22;
in order that the crime against Jerub-Baal's sev- Isa 19:14;
enty sons, the shedding[g] of their blood, might be 33:1 9:24
avenged[h] on their brother Abimelech and on the [g]Nu 35:33;
citizens of Shechem, who had helped him[i] murder 1Ki 2:32 [h]ver 56-57
his brothers. 25In opposition to him these citizens [i]Dt 27:25
of Shechem set men on the hilltops to ambush
and rob everyone who passed by, and this was
reported to Abimelech.
26Now Gaal son of Ebed moved with his brothers into Shechem, and its citizens put their confidence in him. 27After they had gone out into the
fields and gathered the grapes and trodden[j] them, 9:27 [j]Am 9:13
they held a festival in the temple of their god.[k] [k]Jdg 8:33

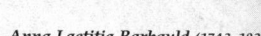

Life! we have been long together,
Through pleasant and through cloudy weather;
'Tis hard to part when friends are dear;
Perhaps 'twill cost a sigh, a tear—
Then steal away, give little warning,
Choose thine own time;
Say not Good-night, but in some brighter clime
Bid me Good-morning!

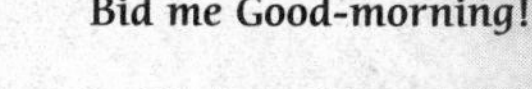

—Anna Laetitia Barbauld (1743-1825)

While they were eating and drinking, they cursed
9:28 [l]1Sa 25:10; Abimelech. 28 Then Gaal son of Ebed said, "Who[l]
1Ki 12:16 is Abimelech, and who is Shechem, that we
[m]Ge 34:2,6 should be subject to him? Isn't he Jerub-Baal's
son, and isn't Zebul his deputy? Serve the men of
Hamor,[m] Shechem's father! Why should we serve
Abimelech? 29 If only this people were under my
9:29 command![n] Then I would get rid of him. I would
[n]2Sa 15:4 say to Abimelech, 'Call out your whole army!' "[a]
30 When Zebul the governor of the city heard
what Gaal son of Ebed said, he was very angry.
31 Under cover he sent messengers to Abimelech,
saying, "Gaal son of Ebed and his brothers have
come to Shechem and are stirring up the city
against you. 32 Now then, during the night you and
9:32 your men should come and lie in wait[o] in the
[o]Jos 8:2 fields. 33 In the morning at sunrise, advance
against the city. When Gaal and his men come out
9:33 against you, do whatever your hand finds to do.[p]"
[p]1Sa 10:7 34 So Abimelech and all his troops set out by
night and took up concealed positions near Shechem in four companies. 35 Now Gaal son of Ebed
had gone out and was standing at the entrance to
9:35 the city gate just as Abimelech and his soldiers
[q]Ps 32:7; came out from their hiding place.[q]
Jer 49:10 36 When Gaal saw them, he said to Zebul,
"Look, people are coming down from the tops of
the mountains!"

Zebul replied, "You mistake the shadows of the
mountains for men."

37 But Gaal spoke up again: "Look, people are
coming down from the center of the land, and a
company is coming from the direction of the
soothsayers' tree."

38 Then Zebul said to him, "Where is your big
talk now, you who said, 'Who is Abimelech that
we should be subject to him?' Aren't these the
9:38 men you ridiculed?[r] Go out and fight them!"
[r]ver 28-29 39 So Gaal led out[b] the citizens of Shechem and
fought Abimelech. 40 Abimelech chased him, and
many fell wounded in the flight—all the way to
the entrance to the gate. 41 Abimelech stayed in
Arumah, and Zebul drove Gaal and his brothers
out of Shechem.

42 The next day the people of Shechem went out
to the fields, and this was reported to Abimelech.
43 So he took his men, divided them into three
9:43 companies[s] and set an ambush in the fields.
[s]Jdg 7:16 When he saw the people coming out of the city,
he rose to attack them. 44 Abimelech and the companies with him rushed forward to a position at
the entrance to the city gate. Then two companies
rushed upon those in the fields and struck them
down. 45 All that day Abimelech pressed his attack
against the city until he had captured it and killed
9:45 its people. Then he destroyed the city[t] and scat-
[t]ver 20; 2Ki 3:25 tered salt[u] over it.
[u]Dt 29:23

[a] 29 Septuagint; Hebrew *him." Then he said to Abimelech, "Call out your whole army!"* [b] 39 Or *Gaal went out in the sight of*

When Christ went to Calvary, I am so *glad* he had absolutely no prejudices or biases; . . . he died for us all. If God were prejudiced, I might have been relegated to the you-can't-make-it-to-heaven group. I was poor and fat once, and I'll be black all my life. Praise God, none of that matters. The *only* things that matter are my love for God and my faith in his Son, Jesus Christ.

—Thelma Wells

A Woman's Tool

JDG 9:50–57

For the second time in judges, a woman kills the aggressor in a conflict. Just as Jael killed Sisera using a familiar tool (Jdg 4:21), so this woman of Thebez uses a domestic tool to kill Abimelech when he attacks her town. In the tower where she and her neighbors take refuge, this woman doesn't crouch in fear, but she stands near the edge, dropping her millstone on Abimelech's head at the opportune moment.

This woman takes her millstone, an indispensable domestic tool, with her when she runs from her home to the tower, probably thinking ahead to the need to continue to provide bread for her family. Her act is one of optimism in a time of horror. Her uncommon use of her common domestic tool provides the deliverance she and her neighbors seek and is God's means of bringing judgment on Abimelech for his wickedness.

46 On hearing this, the citizens in the tower of
Shechem went into the stronghold of the temple[v] **9:46**
of El-Berith. 47 When Abimelech heard that they [v]Jdg 8:33
had assembled there, 48 he and all his men went up
Mount Zalmon.[w] He took an ax and cut off some **9:48**
branches, which he lifted to his shoulders. He [w]Ps 68:14
ordered the men with him, "Quick! Do what you
have seen me do!" 49 So all the men cut branches
and followed Abimelech. They piled them against
the stronghold and set it on fire over the people
inside. So all the people in the tower of Shechem,
about a thousand men and women, also died.
50 Next Abimelech went to Thebez[x] and besieged **9:50**
it and captured it. 51 Inside the city, however, was a [x]2Sa 11:21
strong tower, to which all the men and women—
all the people of the city—fled. They locked themselves in and climbed up on the tower roof.
52 Abimelech went to the tower and stormed it. But
as he approached the entrance to the tower to set
it on fire, 53 a woman dropped an upper millstone
on his head and cracked his skull.[y] **9:53**
54 Hurriedly he called to his armor-bearer, [y]2Sa 11:21
"Draw your sword and kill me,[z] so that they can't **9:54**
say, 'A woman killed him.'" So his servant ran [z]1Sa 31:4;
him through, and he died. 55 When the Israelites 2Sa 1:9
saw that Abimelech was dead, they went home.
56 Thus God repaid the wickedness that Abimelech had done to his father by murdering his seventy brothers. 57 God also made the men of She- **9:57**
chem pay for all their wickedness.[a] The curse of [a]ver 20
Jotham son of Jerub-Baal came on them.

Tola

10 After the time of Abimelech a man of Issa-
char,[b] Tola son of Puah,[c] the son of Dodo, **10:1** [b]Ge 30:18
rose to save[d] Israel. He lived in Shamir, in the hill [c]Ge 46:13
country of Ephraim. 2 He led[a] Israel twenty-three [d]Jdg 2:16; 6:14
years; then he died, and was buried in Shamir.

Jair

3 He was followed by Jair of Gilead, who led
Israel twenty-two years. 4 He had thirty sons, who
rode thirty donkeys. They controlled thirty towns
in Gilead, which to this day are called Havvoth **10:4**
Jair.[b][e] 5 When Jair died, he was buried in Kamon. [e]Nu 32:41

Jephthah

6 Again the Israelites did evil in the eyes of the
Lord.[f] They served the Baals and the Ashtoreths,[g] **10:6** [f]Jdg 2:11
and the gods of Aram, the gods of Sidon, the gods [g]Jdg 2:13
of Moab, the gods of the Ammonites and the gods [h]Jdg 2:12
of the Philistines.[h] And because the Israelites for- [i]Dt 32:15
sook the Lord[i] and no longer served him, 7 he
became angry[j] with them. He sold them[k] into the **10:7** [j]Dt 31:17
hands of the Philistines and the Ammonites, 8 who [k]Dt 32:30;
that year shattered and crushed them. For eigh- Jdg 2:14;
teen years they oppressed all the Israelites on the 1Sa 12:9
east side of the Jordan in Gilead, the land of the

[a] 2 Traditionally *judged*; also in verse 3 [b] 4 Or *called the settlements of Jair*

Amorites. 9The Ammonites also crossed the Jordan to fight against Judah, Benjamin and the
house of Ephraim; and Israel was in great distress.
10Then the Israelites cried out to the LORD, "We
have sinned against you, forsaking our God and
10:10 [l]1Sa 12:10 serving the Baals."[l]
11The LORD replied, "When the Egyptians,[m] the
10:11 [m]Ex 14:30 [n]Nu 21:21; Jdg 3:13 [o]Jdg 3:31 Amorites, the Ammonites,[n] the Philistines,[o] 12the
Sidonians, the Amalekites and the Maonites[a]
oppressed you[p] and you cried to me for help, did
I not save you from their hands? 13But you have
10:12 [p]Ps 106:42 forsaken me and served other gods, so I will no
longer save you. 14Go and cry out to the gods you
10:14 [q]Dt 32:37 have chosen. Let them save you when you are in
trouble![q]"
15But the Israelites said to the LORD, "We have
10:15 [r]1Sa 3:18; 2Sa 15:26 sinned. Do with us whatever you think best,[r] but
please rescue us now." 16Then they got rid of the
10:16 [s]Jos 24:23; Jer 18:8 [t]Isa 63:9 [u]Dt 32:36; Ps 106:44-45 foreign gods among them and served the LORD.[s]
And he could bear Israel's misery[t] no longer.[u]
17When the Ammonites were called to arms and
camped in Gilead, the Israelites assembled and
camped at Mizpah.[v] 18The leaders of the people of
10:17 [v]Ge 31:49; Jdg 11:29 Gilead said to each other, "Whoever will launch
the attack against the Ammonites will be the
head[w] of all those living in Gilead."
10:18 [w]Jdg 11:8,9 11 Jephthah[x] the Gileadite was a mighty warrior.[y] His father was Gilead; his mother was
11:1 [x]Heb 11:32 [y]Jdg 6:12 a prostitute. 2Gilead's wife also bore him sons, and
when they were grown up, they drove Jephthah
away. "You are not going to get any inheritance in
our family," they said, "because you are the son of
11:3 [z]2Sa 10:6,8 [a]Jdg 9:4 another woman." 3So Jephthah fled from his
brothers and settled in the land of Tob,[z] where a
group of adventurers[a] gathered around him and
followed him.
11:4 [b]Jdg 10:9 4Some time later, when the Ammonites[b] made
war on Israel, 5the elders of Gilead went to get
Jephthah from the land of Tob. 6"Come," they
said, "be our commander, so we can fight the
Ammonites."
7Jephthah said to them, "Didn't you hate me
11:7 [c]Ge 26:27 and drive me from my father's house?[c] Why do
you come to me now, when you're in trouble?"
8The elders of Gilead said to him, "Nevertheless,
we are turning to you now; come with us to fight
11:8 [d]Jdg 10:18 the Ammonites, and you will be our head[d] over
all who live in Gilead."
9Jephthah answered, "Suppose you take me
back to fight the Ammonites and the LORD gives
them to me—will I really be your head?"
10The elders of Gilead replied, "The LORD is our
11:10 [e]Ge 31:50; Jer 42:5 witness;[e] we will certainly do as you say." 11So
Jephthah went with the elders of Gilead, and the
people made him head and commander over
11:11 [f]Jos 11:3; Jdg 10:17; 20:1; 1Sa 10:17 them. And he repeated all his words before the
LORD in Mizpah.[f]
12Then Jephthah sent messengers to the Ammon-

[a] *12* Hebrew; some Septuagint manuscripts *Midianites*

Worshiping False Gods

JDG 10:6

This one verse gives a distressingly long list of the false gods that the Israelites worship. These false gods claim control over the fertility of the land in this agricultural economy. The Israelites depend on successful crops for survival. Why risk the anger of neighboring "fertility" gods? So they combine worship of false gods with worship of the one true God, thinking they then have themselves "covered." These local gods aren't seen to be omniscient and can even be manipulated, something the Israelites could not even begin to do with their God, who declares, "My thoughts are not your thoughts, neither are your ways my ways" (Isa 55:8).

Their attraction to these powerless false gods may seem foolish and offensive to us today. However, today's false gods are no less attractive or fascinating, though they may be less obvious. Money, pleasure, success—anything that comes between us and our relationship with God—are false gods, idols just as surely as the "Baals and the Ashtoreths."

ite king with the question: "What do you have
against us that you have attacked our country?"
13 The king of the Ammonites answered Jephthah's messengers, "When Israel came up out of
Egypt, they took away my land from the Arnon to
the Jabbok,[g] all the way to the Jordan. Now give
it back peaceably."
14 Jephthah sent back messengers to the
Ammonite king, 15 saying:

"This is what Jephthah says: Israel did not
take the land of Moab[h] or the land of the
Ammonites.[i] 16 But when they came up out of
Egypt, Israel went through the desert to the
Red Sea[a][j] and on to Kadesh.[k] 17 Then Israel
sent messengers[l] to the king of Edom, saying,
'Give us permission to go through your country,'[m] but the king of Edom would not listen.
They sent also to the king of Moab, and he
refused.[n] So Israel stayed at Kadesh.
18 "Next they traveled through the desert,
skirted the lands of Edom[o] and Moab, passed
along the eastern side[p] of the country of
Moab, and camped on the other side of the
Arnon.[q] They did not enter the territory of
Moab, for the Arnon was its border.
19 "Then Israel sent messengers to Sihon
king of the Amorites, who ruled in Heshbon,
and said to him, 'Let us pass through your
country to our own place.'[r] 20 Sihon, however,
did not trust Israel[b] to pass through his territory. He mustered all his men and encamped
at Jahaz and fought with Israel.[s]
21 "Then the LORD, the God of Israel, gave
Sihon and all his men into Israel's hands, and
they defeated them. Israel took over all the
land of the Amorites who lived in that country, 22 capturing all of it from the Arnon to the
Jabbok and from the desert to the Jordan.[t]
23 "Now since the LORD, the God of Israel, has
driven the Amorites out before his people Israel, what right have you to take it over? 24 Will
you not take what your god Chemosh[u] gives
you? Likewise, whatever the LORD our God has
given us, we will possess. 25 Are you better
than Balak son of Zippor,[v] king of Moab? Did
he ever quarrel with Israel or fight with
them?[w] 26 For three hundred years Israel occupied[x] Heshbon, Aroer, the surrounding settlements and all the towns along the Arnon.
Why didn't you retake them during that time?
27 I have not wronged you, but you are doing
me wrong by waging war against me. Let the
LORD, the Judge,[c][y] decide[z] the dispute this day
between the Israelites and the Ammonites."

28 The king of Ammon, however, paid no attention
to the message Jephthah sent him.

11:13 [g]Ge 32:22; Nu 21:24
11:15 [h]Dt 2:9 [i]Dt 2:19
11:16 [j]Nu 14:25; Dt 1:40 [k]Nu 20:1
11:17 [l]Nu 20:14 [m]Nu 20:18, 21 [n]Jos 24:9
11:18 [o]Nu 21:4 [p]Dt 2:8 [q]Nu 21:13
11:19 [r]Nu 21:21-22; Dt 2:26-27
11:20 [s]Nu 21:23; Dt 2:32
11:22 [t]Dt 2:36
11:24 [u]Nu 21:29; Jos 3:10; 1Ki 11:7
11:25 [v]Nu 22:2 [w]Jos 24:9
11:26 [x]Nu 21:25
11:27 [y]Ge 18:25 [z]Ge 16:5; 31:53; 1Sa 24:12, 15

Jesus, who said, "If you have seen me you have seen the Father," experienced every feeling, every nuance of emotion, every temptation on this earth that you and I do. If this truth is a reality to us, we can't help but be humbled by his graciousness in continually working to conform us to his image. What an awesome privilege that in our rebellious state he loves us and welcomes us always as part of the family—not because of what we do, but because of what he did on the cross.

—Marilyn Meberg

[a] *16* Hebrew *Yam Suph*; that is, Sea of Reeds [b] *20* Or *however, would not make an agreement for Israel* [c] *27* Or *Ruler*

11:29 29 Then the Spirit[a] of the LORD came upon Jeph-
aNu 11:25; thah. He crossed Gilead and Manasseh, passed
Jdg 3:10; through Mizpah of Gilead, and from there he
6:34; 14:6, advanced against the Ammonites. 30 And Jephthah
19; 15:14; made a vow[b] to the LORD: "If you give the
1Sa 11:6; Ammonites into my hands, 31 whatever comes out
16:13; Isa 11:2 of the door of my house to meet me when I return
11:30 bGe 28:20 in triumph from the Ammonites will be the
LORD's, and I will sacrifice it as a burnt offering."
32 Then Jephthah went over to fight the
Ammonites, and the LORD gave them into his
11:33 hands. 33 He devastated twenty towns from Aroer
cEze 27:17 to the vicinity of Minnith,[c] as far as Abel Kera-
mim. Thus Israel subdued Ammon.
34 When Jephthah returned to his home in Mizpah, who should come out to meet him but his
11:34 daughter, dancing to the sound of tambourines![d]
dEx 15:20; Jer 31:4 She was an only child. Except for her he had neither son nor daughter. 35 When he saw her, he tore
his clothes and cried, "Oh! My daughter! You have
made me miserable and wretched, because I have
11:35 made a vow to the LORD that I cannot break.[e]"
eNu 30:2; Ecc 5:2,4,5 36 "My father," she replied, "you have given your
word to the LORD. Do to me just as you promised,[f]
11:36 now that the LORD has avenged you of your ene-
fLk 1:38 g2Sa 18:19 mies,[g] the Ammonites. 37 But grant me this one
request," she said. "Give me two months to roam
the hills and weep with my friends, because I will
never marry."
38 "You may go," he said. And he let her go for
two months. She and the girls went into the hills
and wept because she would never marry. 39 After
the two months, she returned to her father and he
did to her as he had vowed. And she was a virgin.
From this comes the Israelite custom 40 that each
year the young women of Israel go out for four
days to commemorate the daughter of Jephthah
the Gileadite.

Jephthah and Ephraim

12 The men of Ephraim called out their forces,
crossed over to Zaphon and said to Jephthah, "Why did you go to fight the Ammonites
12:1 without calling us to go with you?[h] We're going
hJdg 8:1 to burn down your house over your head."
2 Jephthah answered, "I and my people were
engaged in a great struggle with the Ammonites,
and although I called, you didn't save me out of
their hands. 3 When I saw that you wouldn't help,
12:3 I took my life in my hands[i] and crossed over to
i1Sa 19:5; 28:21; fight the Ammonites, and the LORD gave me the
Job 13:14 victory over them. Now why have you come up
today to fight me?"
4 Jephthah then called together the men of Gilead and fought against Ephraim. The Gileadites
struck them down because the Ephraimites had
said, "You Gileadites are renegades from Ephraim
12:5 and Manasseh." 5 The Gileadites captured the fords
jJos 22:11; of the Jordan[j] leading to Ephraim, and whenever
Jdg 3:28 a survivor of Ephraim said, "Let me cross over,"
the men of Gilead asked him, "Are you an

Keeping Vows

JDG 11:30

Foolish Jephthah. God has already sent his Spirit on him. No vow is necessary for God to reveal his power and use Jephthah to gain victory over the Ammonites. But Jephthah jumps ahead and makes a bargain with God, a foolish one that has devastating consequences.

What actually happens in this story isn't totally clear. Perhaps Jephthah doesn't physically sacrifice his daughter, but condemns her to a life of servitude and virginity. However, the stark wording of verse 39—"he did to her as he had vowed"—makes this seem unlikely. It appears that in order to keep his vow, something every Israelite takes very seriously, Jephthah sacrifices his only daughter, his only child. Was it more important to fulfill his vow than to save his daughter? Was fulfilling a vow more important than obeying God, who had forbidden human sacrifice?

This leader, chosen by God, chose to bargain with God rather than simply trust him. He got his victory, but at great price.

His Claim to Fame

JDG 12:13–15

Scripture tells us very little about the judge Abdon, who rules Israel for eight years, other than that he has an amazing 40 sons and 30 grandsons, all of whom are noted because they ride on 70 donkeys. While the reputation of donkeys today leaves something to be desired, in the time of the judges, those of power and influence rode on donkeys. That Abdon's sons and grandsons ride on donkeys marks them as prestigious and probably wealthy men, definitely worth noticing. A horse seems to us to be a more suitable animal for riding. However, horses are not in common use until after the time of Solomon, who imports them from Egypt.

When Jesus enters Jerusalem, he does not choose to ride a horse as a sign of power or authority. He instead chooses a donkey and distinguishes himself as one worthy of notice because of his humility and grace.

Ephraimite?" If he replied, "No," 6 they said, "All
right, say 'Shibboleth.' " If he said, "Sibboleth,"
because he could not pronounce the word correctly, they seized him and killed him at the fords
of the Jordan. Forty-two thousand Ephraimites
were killed at that time.
7 Jephthah led[a] Israel six years. Then Jephthah
the Gileadite died, and was buried in a town in
Gilead.

Ibzan, Elon and Abdon

8 After him, Ibzan of Bethlehem led Israel. 9 He
had thirty sons and thirty daughters. He gave his
daughters away in marriage to those outside his
clan, and for his sons he brought in thirty young
women as wives from outside his clan. Ibzan led
Israel seven years. 10 Then Ibzan died, and was
buried in Bethlehem.
11 After him, Elon the Zebulunite led Israel ten
years. 12 Then Elon died, and was buried in Aijalon
in the land of Zebulun.
13 After him, Abdon son of Hillel, from Pirathon,
led Israel. 14 He had forty sons and thirty grandsons,[k] who rode on seventy donkeys.[l] He led Israel eight years. 15 Then Abdon son of Hillel died,
and was buried at Pirathon in Ephraim, in the hill
country of the Amalekites.[m]

The Birth of Samson

13 Again the Israelites did evil in the eyes of
the LORD, so the LORD delivered them into
the hands of the Philistines[n] for forty years.
2 A certain man of Zorah,[o] named Manoah, from
the clan of the Danites, had a wife who was sterile
and remained childless. 3 The angel of the LORD[p]
appeared to her[q] and said, "You are sterile and
childless, but you are going to conceive and have
a son.[r] 4 Now see to it that you drink no wine or
other fermented drink and that you do not eat anything unclean,[s] 5 because you will conceive and
give birth to a son. No razor[t] may be used on his
head, because the boy is to be a Nazirite,[u] set apart
to God from birth, and he will begin[v] the deliverance of Israel from the hands of the Philistines."
6 Then the woman went to her husband and told
him, "A man of God[w] came to me. He looked like
an angel of God,[x] very awesome. I didn't ask him
where he came from, and he didn't tell me his
name. 7 But he said to me, 'You will conceive and
give birth to a son. Now then, drink no wine or
other fermented drink and do not eat anything
unclean, because the boy will be a Nazirite of God
from birth until the day of his death.' "
8 Then Manoah prayed to the LORD: "O Lord, I
beg you, let the man of God you sent to us come
again to teach us how to bring up the boy who is
to be born."
9 God heard Manoah, and the angel of God came
again to the woman while she was out in the field;

12:14 [k]Jdg 10:4 [l]Jdg 5:10
12:15 [m]Jdg 5:14
13:1 [n]Jdg 2:11; 1Sa 12:9
13:2 [o]Jos 15:33; 19:41
13:3 [p]ver 6, 8; Jdg 6:12 [q]ver 10 [r]Lk 1:13
13:4 [s]ver 14; Nu 6:2-4; Lk 1:15
13:5 [t]Nu 6:5; 1Sa 1:11 [u]Nu 6:2, 13 [v]1Sa 7:13
13:6 [w]ver 8; 1Sa 2:27; 9:6 [x]ver 17-18; Mt 28:3

[a] 7 Traditionally *judged;* also in verses 8–14

but her husband Manoah was not with her. 10 The
woman hurried to tell her husband, "He's here!
The man who appeared to me the other day!"
11 Manoah got up and followed his wife. When
he came to the man, he said, "Are you the one
who talked to my wife?"
"I am," he said.
12 So Manoah asked him, "When your words are
fulfilled, what is to be the rule for the boy's life
and work?"
13 The angel of the LORD answered, "Your wife
must do all that I have told her. 14 She must not eat
anything that comes from the grapevine, nor
drink any wine or other fermented drink[y] nor eat
anything unclean.[z] She must do everything I have
commanded her."
15 Manoah said to the angel of the LORD, "We
would like you to stay until we prepare a young
goat[a] for you."
16 The angel of the LORD replied, "Even though
you detain me, I will not eat any of your food. But
if you prepare a burnt offering,[b] offer it to the
LORD." (Manoah did not realize that it was the
angel of the LORD.)
17 Then Manoah inquired of the angel of the
LORD, "What is your name,[c] so that we may hon-
or you when your word comes true?"
18 He replied, "Why do you ask my name?[d] It is
beyond understanding.[a]" 19 Then Manoah took a
young goat, together with the grain offering, and
sacrificed it on a rock[e] to the LORD. And the LORD
did an amazing thing while Manoah and his wife
watched: 20 As the flame[f] blazed up from the altar
toward heaven, the angel of the LORD ascended in
the flame. Seeing this, Manoah and his wife fell
with their faces to the ground.[g] 21 When the angel
of the LORD did not show himself again to Manoah and his wife, Manoah realized[h] that it was the
angel of the LORD.
22 "We are doomed[i] to die!" he said to his wife.
"We have seen[j] God!"
23 But his wife answered, "If the LORD had meant
to kill us, he would not have accepted a burnt
offering and grain offering from our hands, nor
shown us all these things or now told us this."[k]
24 The woman gave birth to a boy and named
him Samson.[l] He grew[m] and the LORD blessed
him,[n] 25 and the Spirit of the LORD began to stir[o]
him while he was in Mahaneh Dan,[p] between
Zorah and Eshtaol.

Samson's Marriage

14 Samson went down to Timnah[q] and saw
there a young Philistine woman. 2 When he
returned, he said to his father and mother, "I have
seen a Philistine woman in Timnah; now get her
for me as my wife."[r]
3 His father and mother replied, "Isn't there an
acceptable woman among your relatives or

13:14 [y]Nu 6:4 [z]ver 4
13:15 [a]ver 3; Jdg 6:19
13:16 [b]Jdg 6:20
13:17 [c]Ge 32:29
13:18 [d]Isa 9:6
13:19 [e]Jdg 6:20
13:20 [f]Lev 9:24 [g]1Ch 21:16; Eze 1:28; Mt 17:6
13:21 [h]ver 16; Jdg 6:22
13:22 [i]Dt 5:26 [j]Ge 32:30; Jdg 6:22
13:23 [k]Ps 25:14
13:24 [l]Heb 11:32 [m]1Sa 3:19 [n]Lk 1:80
13:25 [o]Jdg 3:10 [p]Jdg 18:12
14:1 [q]Ge 38:12
14:2 [r]Ge 21:21; 34:4

[a] 18 Or *is wonderful*

Practical Mrs. Manoah

JDG 13:23

An angel appears first to Manoah's wife and then to her and her husband together. When they offer a burnt offering in the angel's presence, the angel ascends "in the flame" (Jdg 13:20). Quite naturally, they are terrified. Manoah cries out, "We're going to die!" But what is the response of Manoah's wife? With a "come on now" attitude, she tells her husband that if the angel was going to kill them, he would already have done so. Instead the angel tells them they will have a son.

This isn't, of course, the only case in history when a husband and wife temper each other's personality. Perhaps it's one of the nicer functions of becoming "one" (Ge 2:24). Our excitability is tempered by his practicality. His temper is lightened by our patience. Our less-than-pleasant character traits are moderated by our spouse. We soften each other's rough edges. Together we are more whole than we ever would be alone (see the character sketch for Samson's mother on page 536).

Marrying an Outsider

JDG 14:1-4

Samson's parents react with shock when he asks them to get a wife for him from their Philistine neighbors. They think he should marry one of the local Israelite girls, but Samson will have none of it.

God has commanded the Israelites not to intermarry with the nations that surround them (Dt 7:3-4). He knows that within marriage the influences of these pagan cultures will dilute the worship of the true God. So why does Judges 14:4 include this "aside": "His parents did not know that this was from the LORD"? Did God actually want Samson to break God's own commandments? Of course not. But the Lord uses Samson's weakness to bring about his own good purpose: the punishment of the Philistines, who are oppressing the Israelites at this time. Samson's early story is just one more manifestation of an amazing God who is willing to use all of us—our good intentions and our courageous acts as well as our disobedience and waywardness—to accomplish his good purposes.

among all our people?[s] Must you go to the uncircumcised[t] Philistines to get a wife?[u]"
But Samson said to his father, "Get her for me.
She's the right one for me." 4(His parents did not
know that this was from the LORD, who was seeking an occasion to confront the Philistines;[v] for at
that time they were ruling over Israel.)[w] 5Samson
went down to Timnah together with his father
and mother. As they approached the vineyards of
Timnah, suddenly a young lion came roaring
toward him. 6The Spirit of the LORD came upon
him in power[x] so that he tore the lion apart with
his bare hands as he might have torn a young
goat. But he told neither his father nor his mother what he had done. 7Then he went down and
talked with the woman, and he liked her.
8Some time later, when he went back to marry
her, he turned aside to look at the lion's carcass. In
it was a swarm of bees and some honey, 9which he
scooped out with his hands and ate as he went
along. When he rejoined his parents, he gave them
some, and they too ate it. But he did not tell them
that he had taken the honey from the lion's carcass.
10Now his father went down to see the woman.
And Samson made a feast there, as was customary
for bridegrooms. 11When he appeared, he was giv-
en thirty companions.
12"Let me tell you a riddle,[y]" Samson said to
them. "If you can give me the answer within the
seven days of the feast,[z] I will give you thirty linen
garments and thirty sets of clothes.[a] 13If you can't
tell me the answer, you must give me thirty linen
garments and thirty sets of clothes."
"Tell us your riddle," they said. "Let's hear it."
14He replied,

> "Out of the eater, something to eat;
> out of the strong, something sweet."

For three days they could not give the answer.
15On the fourth[a] day, they said to Samson's
wife, "Coax[b] your husband into explaining the
riddle for us, or we will burn you and your
father's household to death.[c] Did you invite us
here to rob us?"
16Then Samson's wife threw herself on him,
sobbing, "You hate me! You don't really love me.[d]
You've given my people a riddle, but you haven't
told me the answer."
"I haven't even explained it to my father or
mother," he replied, "so why should I explain it
to you?" 17She cried the whole seven days[e] of the
feast. So on the seventh day he finally told her,
because she continued to press him. She in turn
explained the riddle to her people.
18Before sunset on the seventh day the men of
the town said to him,

> "What is sweeter than honey?
> What is stronger than a lion?"[f]

14:3 [s]Ge 24:4 [t]Dt 7:3 [u]Ex 34:16
14:4 [v]Jos 11:20 [w]Jdg 13:1
14:6 [x]Jdg 3:10; 13:25
14:12 [y]1Ki 10:1; Eze 17:2 [z]Ge 29:27 [a]Ge 45:22; 2Ki 5:5
14:15 [b]Jdg 16:5; Ecc 7:26 [c]Jdg 15:6
14:16 [d]Jdg 16:15
14:17 [e]Est 1:5
14:18 [f]ver 14

[a] *15* Some Septuagint manuscripts and Syriac; Hebrew *seventh*

Samson said to them,

"If you had not plowed with my heifer,
you would not have solved my
riddle."

19Then the Spirit of the LORD came upon him in power.[g] He went down to Ashkelon, struck down thirty of their men, stripped them of their belongings and gave their clothes to those who had explained the riddle. Burning with anger,[h] he went up to his father's house. 20And Samson's wife was given to the friend[i] who had attended him at his wedding.

Samson's Vengeance on the Philistines

15 Later on, at the time of wheat harvest, Samson took a young goat[j] and went to visit his wife. He said, "I'm going to my wife's room." But her father would not let him go in.

2"I was so sure you thoroughly hated her," he said, "that I gave her to your friend.[k] Isn't her younger sister more attractive? Take her instead."

3Samson said to them, "This time I have a right to get even with the Philistines; I will really harm them." 4So he went out and caught three hundred foxes and tied them tail to tail in pairs. He then fastened a torch to every pair of tails, 5lit the torches and let the foxes loose in the standing grain of the Philistines. He burned up the shocks and standing grain, together with the vineyards and olive groves.

6When the Philistines asked, "Who did this?" they were told, "Samson, the Timnite's son-in-law, because his wife was given to his friend."

So the Philistines went up and burned her and her father to death.[l] 7Samson said to them, "Since you've acted like this, I won't stop until I get my revenge on you." 8He attacked them viciously and slaughtered many of them. Then he went down and stayed in a cave in the rock of Etam.

9The Philistines went up and camped in Judah, spreading out near Lehi.[m] 10The men of Judah asked, "Why have you come to fight us?"

"We have come to take Samson prisoner," they answered, "to do to him as he did to us."

11Then three thousand men from Judah went down to the cave in the rock of Etam and said to Samson, "Don't you realize that the Philistines are rulers over us?[n] What have you done to us?"

He answered, "I merely did to them what they did to me."

12They said to him, "We've come to tie you up and hand you over to the Philistines."

Samson said, "Swear to me that you won't kill me yourselves."

13"Agreed," they answered. "We will only tie you up and hand you over to them. We will not kill you." So they bound him with two new ropes and led him up from the rock. 14As he approached Lehi, the Philistines came toward him shouting. The Spirit of the LORD came upon him in power.[o] The ropes on his arms became like charred flax,

14:19 [g]Nu 11:25; Jdg 3:10; 6:34; 11:29; 13:25; 15:14; 1Sa 11:6; 16:13; 1Ki 18:46; 2Ch 24:20; Isa 11:2 [h]1Sa 11:6
14:20 [i]Jdg 15:2,6; Jn 3:29
15:1 [j]Ge 38:17
15:2 [k]Jdg 14:20
15:6 [l]Jdg 14:15
15:9 [m]ver 14,17, 19
15:11 [n]Jdg 13:1; 14:4; Ps 106:40-42
15:14 [o]Jdg 3:10; 14:19; 1Sa 11:6

Not So Sweet

JDG 14:12-20

Riddles. We still enjoy them today. They spring up at dinners, at parties and on e-mail. Samson's riddle is beyond his opponents' ability to figure out. So they resort to deception. Instead of acting fairly to figure out the riddle, they seek out Samson's new wife, his "heifer." They "plow" with her; they threaten her and her family. She buckles and pesters Samson, using deceit herself ("If you loved me, you'd tell me!" [Jdg 14:16]) until he gives in and tells her the solution to his riddle (see the character sketch for Delilah on page 603).

Samson responds to the deception of his opponents and his new wife with "burning" anger (Jdg 14:19). He kills 30 of their own countrymen in order to get the sets of clothing he now owes, and in so doing, he brings about God's continued judgment against the Philistines. It seems to be a rather contorted way for God to punish the Philistines. However, God's purposes will be fulfilled, in spite of Samson's foolishness . . . or ours.

The Number Seven

JDG 16:7

Samson tells Delilah that he should be tied up with "seven fresh thongs." (See character sketch for Delilah on page 603.) He also wears his long, uncut hair in seven braids (Jdg 16:13). Is there some significance for the use of seven?

The earth was created in seven days (Ge 2:2); seven of each clean animal accompany Noah into the ark (Ge 7:2–3); Jacob worked seven years for Laban in order to gain Rachel as his wife (Ge 29:18); Egypt suffered seven years of famine (Ge 41:54); the Israelites marched around Jericho seven days and seven times on the seventh day (Jos 6:4); and Jesus says we are to forgive each other not a mere seven times but seventy times seven (Mt 18:21–22, see NIV footnote). These are only a few examples of the hundreds of times the number seven appears in Scripture. For ancient people, the number seven signified completeness (see the note at Rev 15–16, page 2075). A "perfect" number, it gives a sense of finality or fullness to whatever is being counted.

and the bindings dropped from his hands. [15]Find-
ing a fresh jawbone of a donkey, he grabbed it and
struck down a thousand men.[p]
[16]Then Samson said,

"With a donkey's jawbone
I have made donkeys of them.[a]
With a donkey's jawbone
I have killed a thousand men."

[17]When he finished speaking, he threw away the
jawbone; and the place was called Ramath Lehi.[b]
[18]Because he was very thirsty, he cried out to
the LORD,[q] "You have given your servant this great
victory. Must I now die of thirst and fall into the
hands of the uncircumcised?" [19]Then God opened
up the hollow place in Lehi, and water came out
of it. When Samson drank, his strength returned
and he revived.[r] So the spring was called En Hakkore,[c] and it is still there in Lehi.
[20]Samson led[d] Israel for twenty years[s] in the
days of the Philistines.

Samson and Delilah

16 One day Samson went to Gaza, where he
saw a prostitute. He went in to spend the
night with her. [2]The people of Gaza were told,
"Samson is here!" So they surrounded the place
and lay in wait for him all night at the city gate.[t]
They made no move during the night, saying, "At
dawn we'll kill him."
[3]But Samson lay there only until the middle of
the night. Then he got up and took hold of the
doors of the city gate, together with the two posts,
and tore them loose, bar and all. He lifted them to
his shoulders and carried them to the top of the
hill that faces Hebron.[u]
[4]Some time later, he fell in love[v] with a woman
in the Valley of Sorek whose name was Delilah.
[5]The rulers of the Philistines[w] went to her and
said, "See if you can lure[x] him into showing you
the secret of his great strength and how we can
overpower him so we may tie him up and subdue
him. Each one of us will give you eleven hundred
shekels[e] of silver."[y]
[6]So Delilah said to Samson, "Tell me the secret
of your great strength and how you can be tied up
and subdued."
[7]Samson answered her, "If anyone ties me with
seven fresh thongs[f] that have not been dried, I'll
become as weak as any other man."
[8]Then the rulers of the Philistines brought her
seven fresh thongs that had not been dried, and
she tied him with them. [9]With men hidden in the
room,[z] she called to him, "Samson, the Philistines
are upon you!" But he snapped the thongs as easily as a piece of string snaps when it comes close

[a] 16 Or *made a heap or two*; the Hebrew for *donkey* sounds like the Hebrew for *heap.* [b] 17 *Ramath Lehi* means *jawbone hill.* [c] 19 *En Hakkore* means *caller's spring.* [d] 20 Traditionally *judged* [e] 5 That is, about 28 pounds (about 13 kilograms) [f] 7 Or *bowstrings*; also in verses 8 and 9

15:15 [p]Lev 26:8; Jos 23:10; Jdg 3:31
15:18 [q]Jdg 16:28
15:19 [r]Ge 45:27; Isa 40:29
15:20 [s]Jdg 13:1; 16:31; Heb 11:32
16:2 [t]1Sa 23:26; Ps 118:10-12; Ac 9:24
16:3 [u]Jos 10:36
16:4 [v]Ge 24:67
16:5 [w]Jos 13:3 [x]Ex 10:7; Jdg 14:15 [y]ver 18
16:9 [z]ver 12

to a flame. So the secret of his strength was not
discovered.
[10]Then Delilah said to Samson, "You have made
16:10 [a]ver 13 a fool of me;[a] you lied to me. Come now, tell me
how you can be tied."
16:11 [11]He said, "If anyone ties me securely with new
[b]Jdg 15:13 ropes[b] that have never been used, I'll become as
weak as any other man."
[12]So Delilah took new ropes and tied him with
them. Then, with men hidden in the room, she
called to him, "Samson, the Philistines are upon
you!" But he snapped the ropes off his arms as if
they were threads.
[13]Delilah then said to Samson, "Until now, you
have been making a fool of me and lying to me.
Tell me how you can be tied."
He replied, "If you weave the seven braids of
my head into the fabric ⌞on the loom⌟ and tighten
it with the pin, I'll become as weak as any other
man." So while he was sleeping, Delilah took the
seven braids of his head, wove them into the fabric [14]and[a] tightened it with the pin.
16:14 Again she called to him, "Samson, the Philis-
[c]ver 9,20 tines are upon you!"[c] He awoke from his sleep and
pulled up the pin and the loom, with the fabric.
[15]Then she said to him, "How can you say, 'I
16:15 love you,'[d] when you won't confide in me? This is
[d]Jdg 14:16 [e]Nu 24:10 the third time[e] you have made a fool of me and
[f]ver 5 haven't told me the secret of your great strength.[f]"
[16]With such nagging she prodded him day after
day until he was tired to death.
16:17 [17]So he told her everything.[g] "No razor has ever
[g]Mic 7:5 [h]Nu 6:2,5; been used on my head," he said, "because I have
Jdg 13:5 been a Nazirite[h] set apart to God since birth. If my
head were shaved, my strength would leave me,
and I would become as weak as any other man."
[18]When Delilah saw that he had told her everything, she sent word to the rulers of the Philis-
16:18 tines[i], "Come back once more; he has told me
[i]Jos 13:3; everything." So the rulers of the Philistines
1Sa 5:8 returned with the silver in their hands. [19]Having
put him to sleep on her lap, she called a man to
shave off the seven braids of his hair, and so
16:19 began to subdue him.[b] And his strength left him.[j]
[j]Pr 7:26-27 [20]Then she called, "Samson, the Philistines are
upon you!"
He awoke from his sleep and thought, "I'll go
16:20 out as before and shake myself free." But he did
[k]Nu 14:42; not know that the LORD had left him.[k]
Jos 7:12; 1Sa 16:14; [21]Then the Philistines[l] seized him, gouged out
18:12; 28:15 his eyes[m] and took him down to Gaza. Binding
16:21 him with bronze shackles, they set him to grind-
[l]Jer 47:1 [m]Nu 16:14 ing[n] in the prison. [22]But the hair on his head
[n]Job 31:10; Isa 47:2 began to grow again after it had been shaved.

[a] *13,14* Some Septuagint manuscripts; Hebrew *"I can⌟ if you weave the seven braids of my head into the fabric ⌞on the loom⌟." [14]So she* [b] *19* Hebrew; some Septuagint manuscripts *and he began to weaken*

God Left

JDG 16:20

Sad words here describe the truth of what happens when Delilah's cohorts shave Samson's long hair: "He did not know that the LORD had left him." When Samson allows his hair to be cut, he thereby renounces his Nazirite vow (Nu 6:5), which is the basis for God's special presence in his life.

"But the hair on his head began to grow again after it had been shaved" (Jdg 16:22). With these words, we know God has not abandoned Samson forever, nor has his love for him been fully expended. Samson by now realizes his foolish ways and asks God to be with him "just once more" (Jdg 16:28). God responds in power.

We may look with contempt on Samson, but perhaps we're not too different. We have at times gone our own way, deliberately turning from God's plan. But, like Samson, God does not abandon us, nor is his love for us ever exhausted.

Two Pillars

JDG 16:26

The structure of some ancient temples depended on the support of large wooden pillars mounted on stone bases. The central pillars of Dagon's temple support a large, flat roof where several thousand Dagon worshipers gather to celebrate Samson's capture. They watch with glee as he is humiliated and forced to perform for them.

But while they celebrate, God is planning their punishment. Samson asks his captors to place him near the supporting pillars of the temple, seemingly so that he can lean on them. With one last request of God and one last burst of supernatural power, Samson pushes the wooden pillars off their stone foundations and brings the entire structure down. Samson's final act is one of unselfish willingness to be used by God one last time. This flawed hero of Israel fulfills his destiny and gains his place in Hebrews' "hall of fame" of the faithful (Heb 11:32–34).

The Death of Samson

23 Now the rulers of the Philistines assembled to offer a great sacrifice to Dagon[o] their god and to celebrate, saying, "Our god has delivered Samson, our enemy, into our hands."

24 When the people saw him, they praised their god,[p] saying,

> "Our god has delivered our enemy
> into our hands,[q]
> the one who laid waste our land
> and multiplied our slain."

25 While they were in high spirits,[r] they shouted, "Bring out Samson to entertain us." So they called Samson out of the prison, and he performed for them.

When they stood him among the pillars, 26 Samson said to the servant who held his hand, "Put me where I can feel the pillars that support the temple, so that I may lean against them." 27 Now the temple was crowded with men and women; all the rulers of the Philistines were there, and on the roof[s] were about three thousand men and women watching Samson perform. 28 Then Samson prayed to the LORD,[t] "O Sovereign LORD, remember me. O God, please strengthen me just once more, and let me with one blow get revenge[u] on the Philistines for my two eyes." 29 Then Samson reached toward the two central pillars on which the temple stood. Bracing himself against them, his right hand on the one and his left hand on the other, 30 Samson said, "Let me die with the Philistines!" Then he pushed with all his might, and down came the temple on the rulers and all the people in it. Thus he killed many more when he died than while he lived.

31 Then his brothers and his father's whole family went down to get him. They brought him back and buried him between Zorah and Eshtaol in the tomb of Manoah[v] his father. He had led[a][w] Israel twenty years.[x]

Micah's Idols

17 Now a man named Micah[y] from the hill country of Ephraim 2 said to his mother, "The eleven hundred shekels[b] of silver that were taken from you and about which I heard you utter a curse—I have that silver with me; I took it."

Then his mother said, "The LORD bless you,[z] my son!"

3 When he returned the eleven hundred shekels of silver to his mother, she said, "I solemnly consecrate my silver to the LORD for my son to make a carved image and a cast idol.[a] I will give it back to you."

4 So he returned the silver to his mother, and she took two hundred shekels[c] of silver and gave them

16:23 [o]1Sa 5:2; 1Ch 10:10
16:24 [p]Da 5:4 [q]1Sa 31:9; 1Ch 10:9
16:25 [r]Jdg 9:27; Ru 3:7; Est 1:10
16:27 [s]Dt 22:8; Jos 2:8
16:28 [t]Jdg 15:18 [u]Jer 15:15
16:31 [v]Jdg 13:2 [w]Ru 1:1; 1Sa 4:18 [x]Jdg 15:20
17:1 [y]Jdg 18:2,13
17:2 [z]Ru 2:20; 1Sa 15:13; 2Sa 2:5
17:3 [a]Ex 20:4,23; 34:17; Lev 19:4

[a] *31* Traditionally *judged* [b] *2* That is, about 28 pounds (about 13 kilograms) [c] *4* That is, about 5 pounds (about 2.3 kilograms)

Miriam

In Her Brother's Shadow

Miriam held her breath as she watched from the bank of the river. What would happen when Pharaoh's daughter saw her brother? Surely the circumstances and his features would give him away—he was a Hebrew. Would the woman call for someone to come and exterminate him? No. Rather, the highborn Egyptian woman looked on the child with compassion and tenderly drew him from the water. Miriam, with exceptional courage for one so young, approached the pharaoh's daughter to ask if she needed help.

God favored all three of Jochebed and Amram's children with extraordinary gifts. Years later, Moses, Aaron and Miriam formed the leadership team that led the Israelites across the desert. Miriam was clearly a leader (Mic 6:4) in a time when leadership roles were reserved for men. Her ability to inspire and galvanize others into action was unparalleled.

But there came a time when Miriam and Aaron challenged Moses' leadership. Why? The text suggests there had been a falling out among them over Moses' Cushite wife. Perhaps they grew tired of taking a backseat to Moses. Through the years, Miriam had seen Moses make a lot of mistakes, and she perhaps thought she could do it better. And maybe she could have, but that wasn't the point. Moses was God's *choice.*

Miriam and Aaron questioned the wisdom of God when they confronted Moses. They implied that God didn't know what he was doing when he made Moses the leader. And for that they were corrected and judged. Miriam became leprous in an instant. The punishment of Miriam brought everything back into proper perspective. God's election can't be contested. Our lives are his to spend as he chooses.

The people waited out her quarantine before they moved on. Miriam had made a mistake, but her value to the nation remained indisputable. Others emulated her courage and strength long after her death, and the story of her dance at the parting of the sea became a treasured collective memory.

It can be difficult for a gifted woman to stand back and let others be in charge, especially when it is someone she knows as well as a brother. But it is vital to understand God's unique call on each *life. There is a place, a time and a purpose given to each of us. We will thrive and be most content in the niche God appoints.*

Miriam
(possibly *beloved, bitter,* or *rebellion*)

Exodus 2:1-10; 15:20-21

Numbers 12:1-15; 20:1

Deuteronomy 24:9

Micah 6:4

Candid SNAPSHOT When Pharaoh's horses, chariots and horsemen went into the sea, the LORD brought the waters of the sea back over them, but the Israelites walked through the sea on dry ground. Then Miriam the prophetess, Aaron's sister, took a tambourine in her hand, and all the women followed her, with tambourines and dancing (Exodus 15:20).

Skilled Women

Give With a Willing Heart

Moses invited the people of Israel: Surrender your jewels, your gold, your silver as an offering to the Lord. They didn't *have* to do it. It was voluntary. The Lord did not demand; he invited their gifts. How different was Yahweh from the pagan gods who, without mouths, gobbled up their resources.

The people's hearts burned with shame when they remembered how quickly they had abandoned the one true God (Ex 32). But now they had the chance to redeem themselves for their reprehensible act of false worship. This time it was a project worth investing in—a dwelling suitable for the God who speaks, the God who provides, the merciful God of the second chance.

They had given the jewels that were easy to part with for the golden calf. The ones they still had were those they treasured. But what better gift? Not the blemished lamb but the unblemished—only the best for the Lord!

God appointed two gifted men to assemble the tabernacle and its furnishings of wood and precious metals. But women played a vital role as well. They had the skills to weave the waterproof curtains of goat hair for the outer tent and to fashion the ornate tapestries of rare blue, purple and scarlet yarns or fine linen to fit the interior. The women spun the thread and wove the cloth entirely by hand, digging out their precious threads of royal hue, which they hoarded for their most festal garments.

The momentum grew as they began to experience the joy of giving back to the Lord, of being a part of his work. An air of excitement and cooperation replaced idleness and grumbling. Their designs and workmanship reached new heights of creativity. More and more riches came out of their stores, as each morning the people brought contributions for the work. Moses finally had to tell them to stop. They had enough—more than they needed—to finish the work (Ex 36:3-7).

Skilled Women
Exodus 35:20-29

Something remarkable happens when we offer our gifts to the Lord. They multiply in our hands. Doing some task for the first time in our lives, we recognize ways that he has prepared us in the past. We find a deeper level of companionship with others of like mind. Our skills are sharpened and refined as we find ourselves able to do things we never thought we could do, enjoying things we never thought we would enjoy. And we thought *we* were the ones doing the giving!

Candid SNAPSHOT *Every skilled woman spun with her hands and brought what she had spun—blue, purple or scarlet yarn or fine linen. And all the women who were willing and had the skill spun the goat hair (Exodus 35:25-26).*

to a silversmith, who made them into the image
17:4 [b]Ex 32:4; and the idol.[b] And they were put in Micah's house.
Isa 17:8 5 Now this man Micah had a shrine,[c] and he
made an ephod[d] and some idols[e] and installed[f]
17:5 [c]Isa 44:13; one of his sons as his priest.[g] 6 In those days Isra-
Eze 8:10 el had no king;[h] everyone did as he saw fit.[i]
[d]Jdg 8:27 7 A young Levite from Bethlehem in Judah,[j]
[e]Ge 31:19; Jdg 18:14 who had been living within the clan of Judah,
[f]Nu 16:10 [g]Ex 29:9; 8 left that town in search of some other place to
Jdg 18:24 stay. On his way[a] he came to Micah's house in the
hill country of Ephraim.
17:6 [h]Jdg 18:1; 9 Micah asked him, "Where are you from?"
19:1; 21:25 "I'm a Levite from Bethlehem in Judah," he
[i]Dt 12:8 said, "and I'm looking for a place to stay."
17:7 [j]Jdg 19:1; 10 Then Micah said to him, "Live with me and be
Ru 1:1-2; my father and priest,[k] and I'll give you ten shekels[b]
Mic 5:2; of silver a year, your clothes and your food." 11 So
Mt 2:1 the Levite agreed to live with him, and the young
17:10 man was to him like one of his sons. 12 Then Micah
[k]Jdg 18:19 installed[l] the Levite, and the young man became
his priest and lived in his house. 13 And Micah said,
17:12 [l]Nu 16:10 "Now I know that the LORD will be good to me,
since this Levite has become my priest."

Danites Settle in Laish

18:1 [m]Jdg 17:6; 19:1 **18** In those days Israel had no king.[m]
And in those days the tribe of the Danites
[n]Jos 19:47 was seeking a place of their own where they
might settle, because they had not yet come into
an inheritance among the tribes of Israel.[n] 2 So the
18:2 [o]Jdg 13:25 Danites[o] sent five warriors from Zorah and Eshta-
[p]Jos 2:1 ol to spy out the land and explore it. These men
[q]Jdg 17:1 represented all their clans. They told them, "Go,
explore the land."[p]
The men entered the hill country of Ephraim
and came to the house of Micah,[q] where they
spent the night. 3 When they were near Micah's
house, they recognized the voice of the young
Levite; so they turned in there and asked him,
"Who brought you here? What are you doing in
this place? Why are you here?"
4 He told them what Micah had done for him,
18:4 [r]Jdg 17:12 and said, "He has hired me and I am his priest.[r]"
5 Then they said to him, "Please inquire of God[s]
18:5 [s]1Ki 22:5 to learn whether our journey will be successful."
6 The priest answered them, "Go in peace[t]. Your
18:6 [t]1Ki 22:6 journey has the LORD's approval."
7 So the five men left and came to Laish,[u] where
18:7 [u]Jos 19:47 they saw that the people were living in safety, like
[v]ver 28 the Sidonians, unsuspecting and secure. And since
their land lacked nothing, they were prosperous.[c]
Also, they lived a long way from the Sidonians[v]
and had no relationship with anyone else.[d]
8 When they returned to Zorah and Eshtaol,
their brothers asked them, "How did you find
things?"

[a] 8 Or *To carry on his profession* [b] *10* That is, about 4 ounces (about 110 grams) [c] *7* The meaning of the Hebrew for this clause is uncertain. [d] *7* Hebrew; some Septuagint manuscripts *with the Arameans*

As He Saw Fit

JDG 17:6

This dark chapter in Judges is illustrated by these words: "Everyone did as he saw fit" (Jdg 17:6; 21:25). God's people choose to simply live however each sees fit to live. There is no moral compass that applies to all, no commandment important enough for all to obey, no direction of God attractive enough for all to embrace. Each simply goes his or her own way, following his or her own whims and desires.

Instead of worshiping the true God as God has commanded, Micah establishes not only his own household idols but also his own place of worship with his own Levite priest. Perhaps he thinks that having a Levite priest will in some way legitimize his idol worship. But Micah's thinking is defective. Never does one legitimate piece purify illegitimate worship. Keeping ourselves and our worship pure before God is a high priority, not simply because it's our desire (something we see "fit" to do) but because it's God's command.

Children in Front

JDG 18:21

The Danites head out after stealing Micah's idols. They know Micah and his men will follow and that a battle might develop. To protect themselves, they put the children, presumably with their mothers, out in front of the 600 soldiers (Jdg 18:16). Does that appear cruel and cowardly? Perhaps so. However, it's not the first time women and children are used as a shield. Jacob employs a similar tactic when meeting Esau and fearing a battle (Ge 33:2–3).

These two incidents are contrary to the Bible as a whole, which reveals a loving attitude toward children. Children are worthy to be taught the love and laws of God (Dt 6:7; Ps 78:5–6) and can participate in worship (Ps 8:2). Children are a source of happiness for their mothers (Ps 113:9) and a blessing and gift from God (Ps 115:14; 127:3; Pr 17:6). Jesus blesses and loves little children (Mt 19:13) and sets an example for us in treating them not only with love but also with respect.

9 They answered, "Come on, let's attack them!
We have seen that the land is very good. Aren't
you going to do something? Don't hesitate to go
there and take it over.[w] 10 When you get there, you
will find an unsuspecting people and a spacious
land that God has put into your hands, a land that
lacks nothing[x] whatever.[y]"
11 Then six hundred men[z] from the clan of the
Danites,[a] armed for battle, set out from Zorah and
Eshtaol. 12 On their way they set up camp near Kiriath
Jearim in Judah. This is why the place west
of Kiriath Jearim is called Mahaneh Dan[a][b] to this
day. 13 From there they went on to the hill country
of Ephraim and came to Micah's house.
14 Then the five men who had spied out the land
of Laish said to their brothers, "Do you know that
one of these houses has an ephod, other household
gods, a carved image and a cast idol?[c] Now
you know what to do." 15 So they turned in there
and went to the house of the young Levite at
Micah's place and greeted him. 16 The six hundred
Danites,[d] armed for battle, stood at the entrance
to the gate. 17 The five men who had spied out the
land went inside and took the carved image, the
ephod, the other household gods[e] and the cast
idol while the priest and the six hundred armed
men stood at the entrance to the gate.
18 When these men went into Micah's house and
took[f] the carved image, the ephod, the other
household gods and the cast idol, the priest said to
them, "What are you doing?"
19 They answered him, "Be quiet![g] Don't say a
word. Come with us, and be our father and
priest.[h] Isn't it better that you serve a tribe and
clan in Israel as priest rather than just one man's
household?" 20 Then the priest was glad. He took
the ephod, the other household gods and the
carved image and went along with the people.
21 Putting their little children, their livestock and
their possessions in front of them, they turned
away and left.
22 When they had gone some distance from
Micah's house, the men who lived near Micah
were called together and overtook the Danites.
23 As they shouted after them, the Danites turned
and said to Micah, "What's the matter with you
that you called out your men to fight?"
24 He replied, "You took the gods I made, and my
priest, and went away. What else do I have? How
can you ask, 'What's the matter with you?' "
25 The Danites answered, "Don't argue with us,
or some hot-tempered men will attack you, and
you and your family will lose your lives." 26 So the
Danites went their way, and Micah, seeing that
they were too strong for him,[i] turned around and
went back home.
27 Then they took what Micah had made, and
his priest, and went on to Laish, against a peaceful
and unsuspecting people.[j] They attacked them

18:9 [w]Nu 13:30; 1Ki 22:3
18:10 [x]ver 7,27; Dt 8:9 [y]1Ch 4:40
18:11 [z]ver 16,17 [a]Jdg 13:2
18:12 [b]Jdg 13:25
18:14 [c]Ge 31:19; Jdg 17:5
18:16 [d]ver 11
18:17 [e]Ge 31:19; Mic 5:13
18:18 [f]Isa 46:2; Jer 43:11; Hos 10:5
18:19 [g]Job 21:5; 29:9; 40:4; Mic 7:16 [h]Jdg 17:10
18:26 [i]Ps 18:17; 35:10
18:27 [j]ver 7,10

[a] 12 *Mahaneh Dan* means *Dan's camp.*

18:27 [k]Ge 49:17; with the sword and burned down their city.[k]
Jos 19:47 28 There was no one to rescue them because they
lived a long way from Sidon[l] and had no relation-
18:28 [l]ver 7 ship with anyone else. The city was in a valley
[m]Nu 13:21; near Beth Rehob.[m]
2Sa 10:6 The Danites rebuilt the city and settled there.
18:29 29 They named it Dan[n] after their forefather Dan,
[n]Ge 14:14 who was born to Israel—though the city used to
[o]Jos 19:47; be called Laish.[o] 30 There the Danites set up for
1Ki 15:20 themselves the idols, and Jonathan son of Ger-
18:30 shom,[p] the son of Moses,[a] and his sons were
[p]Ex 2:22; priests for the tribe of Dan until the time of the
Jdg 17:3,5 captivity of the land. 31 They continued to use the
18:31 idols Micah had made, all the time the house of
[q]Jdg 19:18 [r]Jos 18:1; God[q] was in Shiloh.[r]
Jer 7:14

A Levite and His Concubine

19 In those days Israel had no king.
19:1 Now a Levite who lived in a remote area in
[s]Jdg 18:1 the hill country of Ephraim[s] took a concubine
[t]Ru 1:1 from Bethlehem in Judah.[t] 2 But she was unfaithful to him. She left him and went back to her
father's house in Bethlehem, Judah. After she had
been there four months, 3 her husband went to her
to persuade her to return. He had with him his
servant and two donkeys. She took him into her
father's house, and when her father saw him, he
gladly welcomed him. 4 His father-in-law, the girl's
father, prevailed upon him to stay; so he remained
19:4 with him three days, eating and drinking,[u] and
[u]Ex 32:6 sleeping there.

5 On the fourth day they got up early and he prepared to leave, but the girl's father said to his son-
19:5 [v]ver 8; in-law, "Refresh yourself[v] with something to eat;
Ge 18:5 then you can go." 6 So the two of them sat down to
19:6 eat and drink together. Afterward the girl's father
[w]ver 9,22; Jdg 16:25 said, "Please stay tonight and enjoy yourself.[w]"
7 And when the man got up to go, his father-in-law
persuaded him, so he stayed there that night. 8 On
the morning of the fifth day, when he rose to go,
the girl's father said, "Refresh yourself. Wait till
afternoon!" So the two of them ate together.

9 Then when the man, with his concubine and
his servant, got up to leave, his father-in-law, the
girl's father, said, "Now look, it's almost evening.
Spend the night here; the day is nearly over. Stay
and enjoy yourself. Early tomorrow morning you
can get up and be on your way home." 10 But,
unwilling to stay another night, the man left and
19:10 went toward Jebus[x] (that is, Jerusalem), with his
[x]Ge 10:16; two saddled donkeys and his concubine.
Jos 15:8; 1Ch 11:4-5 11 When they were near Jebus and the day was
almost gone, the servant said to his master,
19:11 "Come, let's stop at this city of the Jebusites[y] and
[y]Jos 3:10 spend the night."

12 His master replied, "No. We won't go into an
alien city, whose people are not Israelites. We will
go on to Gibeah." 13 He added, "Come, let's try to

[a] *30* An ancient Hebrew scribal tradition, some Septuagint manuscripts and Vulgate; Masoretic Text *Manasseh*

Concubines

JDG 19:1

During Old Testament times a concubine was a legitimate wife of her husband, not merely his mistress; however, she held a position below that of the primary wife. She had no claim to any inheritance, and her children, though considered legitimate, also had no inheritance rights. The only right a concubine held was the right to live with her husband, and even that was tenuous since her husband could lawfully send her and her children away with only a small gift.

A number of Old Testament men had concubines: Nahor, Abraham's brother (Ge 22:24), Jacob (Ge 35:22), Gideon (Jdg 8:31), the Levite mentioned in this passage, King Saul (2Sa 3:7), King David (2Sa 5:13), and King Solomon, who had an amazing 300 hundred (1Ki 11:3). Even godly men in ancient times practiced polygamy, though monogamy is definitely God's divine intention for marriage (Ge 2:23–24).

Hospitality

JDG 19:15

In the ancient Middle East, hospitality was not considered merely a custom but was seen as a highly regarded virtue and a sacred obligation. In a time when there were no motels or hotels, travelers stopped for the night in the town square and waited for an invitation from a local resident. To leave a traveler alone in the dark in the town square was a violation of all that hospitality demanded. Therefore, that this Levite and his concubine were left to wait for an invitation is an indication of the corruption of the local culture, the depths of which this story quickly reveals.

reach Gibeah or Ramah[z] and spend the night in
one of those places." 14So they went on, and the
sun set as they neared Gibeah in Benjamin.[a]
15There they stopped to spend the night. They
went and sat in the city square,[b] but no one took
them into his home for the night.
16That evening[c] an old man from the hill country of Ephraim,[d] who was living in Gibeah (the
men of the place were Benjamites), came in from
his work in the fields. 17When he looked and saw
the traveler in the city square, the old man asked,
"Where are you going? Where did you come
from?"[e]
18He answered, "We are on our way from Bethlehem in Judah to a remote area in the hill country of Ephraim where I live. I have been to Bethlehem in Judah and now I am going to the house
of the LORD.[f] No one has taken me into his house.
19We have both straw and fodder[g] for our donkeys
and bread and wine[h] for ourselves your servants—me, your maidservant, and the young man
with us. We don't need anything."
20"You are welcome at my house," the old man
said. "Let me supply whatever you need. Only
don't spend the night in the square." 21So he took
him into his house and fed his donkeys. After they
had washed their feet, they had something to eat
and drink.[i]
22While they were enjoying themselves,[j] some of
the wicked men[k] of the city surrounded the house.
Pounding on the door, they shouted to the old man
who owned the house, "Bring out the man who
came to your house so we can have sex with him.[l]"
23The owner of the house went outside[m] and
said to them, "No, my friends, don't be so vile.
Since this man is my guest, don't do this disgraceful thing.[n] 24Look, here is my virgin daughter,[o] and his concubine. I will bring them out to
you now, and you can use them and do to them
whatever you wish. But to this man, don't do
such a disgraceful thing."
25But the men would not listen to him. So the
man took his concubine and sent her outside to
them, and they raped her and abused her[p]
throughout the night, and at dawn they let her go.
26At daybreak the woman went back to the house
where her master was staying, fell down at the
door and lay there until daylight.
27When her master got up in the morning and
opened the door of the house and stepped out to
continue on his way, there lay his concubine, fall-
en in the doorway of the house, with her hands
on the threshold. 28He said to her, "Get up; let's
go." But there was no answer. Then the man put
her on his donkey and set out for home.
29When he reached home, he took a knife[q] and
cut up his concubine, limb by limb, into twelve
parts and sent them into all the areas of Israel.[r]
30Everyone who saw it said, "Such a thing has
never been seen or done, not since the day the

19:13 [z]Jos 18:25
19:14 [a]1Sa 10:26; Isa 10:29
19:15 [b]Ge 19:2
19:16 [c]Ps 104:23 [d]ver 1
19:17 [e]Ge 29:4
19:18 [f]Jdg 18:31
19:19 [g]Ge 24:25 [h]Ge 14:18
19:21 [i]Ge 24:32-33; Lk 7:44
19:22 [j]Jdg 16:25 [k]Dt 13:13 [l]Ge 19:4-5; Jdg 20:5; Ro 1:26-27
19:23 [m]Ge 19:6 [n]Ge 34:7; Lev 19:29; Dt 22:21; Jdg 20:6; 2Sa 13:12; Ro 1:27
19:24 [o]Ge 19:8; Dt 21:14
19:25 [p]1Sa 31:4
19:29 [q]Ge 22:6 [r]Jdg 20:6; 1Sa 11:7

19:30 [s]Hos 9:9 Israelites came up out of Egypt.[s] Think about it!
[t]Jdg 20:7; Pr 13:10 Consider it! Tell us what to do![t]"

Israelites Fight the Benjamites

20:1 [u]Jdg 21:5 **20** Then all the Israelites[u] from Dan to Beershe-
[v]1Sa 3:20; ba[v] and from the land of Gilead came out as
2Sa 3:10; one man[w] and assembled[x] before the LORD in Miz-
1Ki 4:25 pah. 2 The leaders of all the people of the tribes of
[w]1Sa 11:7 Israel took their places in the assembly of the peo-
[x]1Sa 7:5 ple of God, four hundred thousand soldiers[y] armed
20:2 [y]Jdg 8:10 with swords. 3 (The Benjamites heard that the Israelites had gone up to Mizpah.) Then the Israelites
said, "Tell us how this awful thing happened."
4 So the Levite, the husband of the murdered
20:4 woman, said, "I and my concubine came to Gibe-
[z]Jos 15:57 ah[z] in Benjamin to spend the night.[a] 5 During the
[a]Jdg 19:15 night the men of Gibeah came after me and sur-
20:5 rounded the house, intending to kill me.[b] They
[b]Jdg 19:22 raped my concubine, and she died.[c] 6 I took my
[c]Jdg 19:25-26 concubine, cut her into pieces and sent one piece
20:6 to each region of Israel's inheritance,[d] because
[d]Jdg 19:29 they committed this lewd and disgraceful act[e] in
[e]Jos 7:15; Israel. 7 Now, all you Israelites, speak up and give
Jdg 19:23 your verdict.[f]"
20:7 8 All the people rose as one man, saying, "None
[f]Jdg 19:30 of us will go home. No, not one of us will return
20:9 to his house. 9 But now this is what we'll do to
[g]Lev 16:8 Gibeah: We'll go up against it as the lot directs.[g]
10 We'll take ten men out of every hundred from
all the tribes of Israel, and a hundred from a thousand, and a thousand from ten thousand, to get
provisions for the army. Then, when the army
arrives at Gibeah[a] in Benjamin, it can give them
what they deserve for all this vileness done in
20:11 Israel." 11 So all the men of Israel got together and
[h]ver 1 united as one man[h] against the city.
12 The tribes of Israel sent men throughout the
tribe of Benjamin, saying, "What about this awful
crime that was committed among you? 13 Now sur-
20:13 [i]Dt 13:13; render those wicked men[i] of Gibeah so that we
Jdg 19:22 may put them to death and purge the evil from
[j]Dt 17:12 Israel.[j]"
But the Benjamites would not listen to their fellow Israelites. 14 From their towns they came
together at Gibeah to fight against the Israelites.
15 At once the Benjamites mobilized twenty-six
thousand swordsmen from their towns, in addition to seven hundred chosen men from those living in Gibeah. 16 Among all these soldiers there
20:16 were seven hundred chosen men who were left-
[k]Jdg 3:15; handed,[k] each of whom could sling a stone at a
1Ch 12:2 hair and not miss.
17 Israel, apart from Benjamin, mustered four
hundred thousand swordsmen, all of them fighting men.
18 The Israelites went up to Bethel[b] and inquired

[a] *10* One Hebrew manuscript; most Hebrew manuscripts *Geba,* a variant of *Gibeah* [b] *18* Or *to the house of God*; also in verse 26

Moral Outrage

JDG 19:30

Finally a righteous reaction to the appalling events of this story! The Levite's concubine has been repeatedly raped until she dies while trying to return to him. He reacts with anger and proceeds to cut the woman into 12 pieces, sending one piece to each tribe of Israel. All the while the events of the story are taking place, the inhabitants of the area are going about their daily business, ignoring the injustice and horror of what is being done to the woman.

But now, at last, there is a reaction. The Israelites are shocked out of their moral lethargy. They spring to action, gathering together "as one man" (Jdg 20:1), seek the Lord's direction, and mete out the punishment.

Perhaps now the Israelites have learned and will follow God, worshiping only him and obeying his commands. Sadly, their obedience is as short-lived as before. After punishing the Benjamites, they return to their own towns and "everyone [again] did as he saw fit" (Jdg 21:25).

The Ark

JDG 20:27

This is the only time the ark of the covenant is mentioned in the book of Judges, probably an indication of the lack of reverence the people have for God. Instead of following his commands and seeking his will, they go their own way. Their way leads them into sin and chaos as a nation.

The Levite and his host put their own comfort and their own welfare above the safety of a woman (Jdg 19:20–26). The result is the death not only of the innocent woman but also of 25,100 Benjamite warriors.

Whenever a people follow their own course of action and ignore God's commands, chaos results. The innocent suffer, the helpless are ignored and a decent, orderly way of life is replaced with discord and even anarchy. God's laws are not in place merely to satisfy his whim or to make life difficult. They are beautifully designed to give life structure and wholeness.

of God.[l] They said, "Who of us shall go first to
fight[m] against the Benjamites?"
The LORD replied, "Judah shall go first."
19 The next morning the Israelites got up and
pitched camp near Gibeah. 20 The men of Israel
went out to fight the Benjamites and took up battle positions against them at Gibeah. 21 The Benjamites came out of Gibeah and cut down twenty-
two thousand Israelites[n] on the battlefield that
day. 22 But the men of Israel encouraged one
another and again took up their positions where
they had stationed themselves the first day. 23 The
Israelites went up and wept before the LORD until
evening,[o] and they inquired of the LORD. They
said, "Shall we go up again to battle[p] against the
Benjamites, our brothers?"
The LORD answered, "Go up against them."
24 Then the Israelites drew near to Benjamin the
second day. 25 This time, when the Benjamites
came out from Gibeah to oppose them, they cut
down another eighteen thousand Israelites,[q] all of
them armed with swords.
26 Then the Israelites, all the people, went up to
Bethel, and there they sat weeping before the
LORD.[r] They fasted that day until evening and presented burnt offerings and fellowship offerings[a]
to the LORD.[s] 27 And the Israelites inquired of the
LORD. (In those days the ark of the covenant of
God[t] was there, 28 with Phinehas son of Eleazar,[u]
the son of Aaron, ministering before it.)[v] They
asked, "Shall we go up again to battle with Benjamin our brother, or not?"
The LORD responded, "Go, for tomorrow I will
give them into your hands.[w]"
29 Then Israel set an ambush[x] around Gibeah.
30 They went up against the Benjamites on the
third day and took up positions against Gibeah as
they had done before. 31 The Benjamites came out
to meet them and were drawn away[y] from the city.
They began to inflict casualties on the Israelites
as before, so that about thirty men fell in the open
field and on the roads—the one leading to Bethel
and the other to Gibeah.
32 While the Benjamites were saying, "We are
defeating them as before,"[z] the Israelites were saying, "Let's retreat and draw them away from the
city to the roads."
33 All the men of Israel moved from their places
and took up positions at Baal Tamar, and the Israelite ambush charged out of its place[a] on the west[b]
of Gibeah.[c] 34 Then ten thousand of Israel's finest
men made a frontal attack on Gibeah. The fighting was so heavy that the Benjamites did not realize[b] how near disaster was.[c] 35 The LORD defeated
Benjamin[d] before Israel, and on that day the Israelites struck down 25,100 Benjamites, all armed

20:18 [l]ver 26-27; Nu 27:21 [m]ver 23,28
20:21 [n]ver 25
20:23 [o]Jos 7:6 [p]ver 18
20:25 [q]ver 21
20:26 [r]ver 23 [s]Jdg 21:4
20:27 [t]Jos 18:1
20:28 [u]Jos 24:33 [v]Dt 18:5 [w]Jdg 7:9
20:29 [x]Jos 8:2,4
20:31 [y]Jos 8:16
20:32 [z]ver 39
20:33 [a]Jos 8:19
20:34 [b]Jos 8:14 [c]Isa 47:11
20:35 [d]1Sa 9:21

[a] *26* Traditionally *peace offerings* [b] *33* Some Septuagint manuscripts and Vulgate; the meaning of the Hebrew for this word is uncertain. [c] *33* Hebrew *Geba,* a variant of *Gibeah*

with swords. 36Then the Benjamites saw that they
20:36 were beaten.
eJos 8:15 Now the men of Israel had given way[e] before
Benjamin, because they relied on the ambush
they had set near Gibeah. 37The men who had
been in ambush made a sudden dash into Gibe-
20:37 ah, spread out and put the whole city to the
fJos 8:19 sword.[f] 38The men of Israel had arranged with the
20:38 ambush that they should send up a great cloud of
gJos 8:20 smoke[g] from the city, 39and then the men of Israel would turn in the battle.
The Benjamites had begun to inflict casualties
on the men of Israel (about thirty), and they said,
20:39 "We are defeating them as in the first battle."[h]
hver 32 40But when the column of smoke began to rise
from the city, the Benjamites turned and saw the
20:40 smoke of the whole city going up into the sky.[i]
iJos 8:20 41Then the men of Israel turned on them, and the
men of Benjamin were terrified, because they realized that disaster had come upon them. 42So they
fled before the Israelites in the direction of the
desert, but they could not escape the battle. And
the men of Israel who came out of the towns cut
them down there. 43They surrounded the Benjamites, chased them and easily[a] overran them in
the vicinity of Gibeah on the east. 44Eighteen thou-
20:44 sand Benjamites fell, all of them valiant fighters.[j]
jPs 76:5 45As they turned and fled toward the desert to the
20:45 rock of Rimmon,[k] the Israelites cut down five
kJos 15:32; thousand men along the roads. They kept pressing
Jdg 21:13 after the Benjamites as far as Gidom and struck
down two thousand more.
46On that day twenty-five thousand Benjamite
swordsmen fell, all of them valiant fighters. 47But
six hundred men turned and fled into the desert to
the rock of Rimmon, where they stayed four
months. 48The men of Israel went back to Benjamin and put all the towns to the sword, including
20:48 the animals and everything else they found. All
lJdg 21:23 the towns they came across they set on fire.[l]

Wives for the Benjamites

21:1
mJos 9:18 **21** The men of Israel had taken an oath[m] at
nJdg 20:1 Mizpah:[n] "Not one of us will give[o] his
over 7,18 daughter in marriage to a Benjamite."
2The people went to Bethel,[b] where they sat
before God until evening, raising their voices and
weeping bitterly. 3"O LORD, the God of Israel," they
cried, "why has this happened to Israel? Why
should one tribe be missing from Israel today?"
4Early the next day the people built an altar and
21:4 presented burnt offerings and fellowship offer-
pJdg 20:26; ings.[c][p]
2Sa 24:25 5Then the Israelites asked, "Who from all the
21:5 tribes of Israel[q] has failed to assemble before the
qJdg 5:23; LORD?" For they had taken a solemn oath that any-
20:1 one who failed to assemble before the LORD at
Mizpah should certainly be put to death.

[a] *43* The meaning of the Hebrew for this word is uncertain.
[b] *2* Or *to the house of God*   [c] *4* Traditionally *peace offerings*

Glorious, Almighty,
First, and without end!
When wilt thou melt the
mountains and descend?
When wilt thou shoot abroad
thy conquering rays,
And teach these atoms, thou
hast made, thy praise?

—*Madame Guyon* (1647-1717)

Compounded Calamity

JDG 21:1–25

The Israelites compound the calamity as they try to extricate themselves from the web their actions and vows have created. They go beyond God's design of punishment for the Benjamites and almost annihilate the entire tribe, leaving only 600 men alive (Jdg 20:47). They had also taken an oath not to give any of their daughters to these Benjamite men in marriage (Jdg 21:1), adding to their previous oath to kill any Israelite who didn't come to help them in their punishment of the Benjamites (Jdg. 21:5). Now they grieve the results. The tribe of Benjamin may cease to exist. Their actions to remedy the situation perfectly illustrate what we already know: another wrong doesn't correct a previous wrong. It only compounds the problem.

The root of the Israelites' problem is simply and sadly summed up again in the last verse of the book: "Everyone did as he saw fit." The standards and commands of God are ignored, and the bedlam of these last chapters is the result.

6Now the Israelites grieved for their brothers,
the Benjamites. "Today one tribe is cut off from
Israel," they said. 7"How can we provide wives for
those who are left, since we have taken an oath[r] 21:7
by the LORD not to give them any of our daughters [r]ver 1
in marriage?" 8Then they asked, "Which one of
the tribes of Israel failed to assemble before the
LORD at Mizpah?" They discovered that no one
from Jabesh Gilead[s] had come to the camp for the 21:8
assembly. 9For when they counted the people, [s]1Sa 11:1;
they found that none of the people of Jabesh Gil- 31:11
ead were there.

10So the assembly sent twelve thousand fighting
men with instructions to go to Jabesh Gilead and
put to the sword those living there, including the
women and children. 11"This is what you are to
do," they said. "Kill every male and every woman 21:11
who is not a virgin.[t]" 12They found among the [t]Nu 31:17-18
people living in Jabesh Gilead four hundred young
women who had never slept with a man, and they 21:12
took them to the camp at Shiloh[u] in Canaan. [u]Jos 18:1

13Then the whole assembly sent an offer of 21:13
peace[v] to the Benjamites at the rock of Rimmon.[w] [v]Dt 20:10
14So the Benjamites returned at that time and were [w]Jdg 20:47
given the women of Jabesh Gilead who had been
spared. But there were not enough for all of them.

15The people grieved for Benjamin,[x] because the 21:15
LORD had made a gap in the tribes of Israel. 16And [x]ver 6
the elders of the assembly said, "With the women
of Benjamin destroyed, how shall we provide
wives for the men who are left? 17The Benjamite
survivors must have heirs," they said, "so that a
tribe of Israel will not be wiped out. 18We can't
give them our daughters as wives, since we Israelites have taken this oath: 'Cursed be anyone who 21:18
gives[y] a wife to a Benjamite.' 19But look, there is [y]ver 1
the annual festival of the LORD in Shiloh,[z] to the
north of Bethel, and east of the road that goes from 21:19
Bethel to Shechem, and to the south of Lebonah." [z]Jos 18:1; Jdg 18:31; 1Sa 1:3

20So they instructed the Benjamites, saying, "Go
and hide in the vineyards 21and watch. When the
girls of Shiloh come out to join in the dancing,[a] 21:21
then rush from the vineyards and each of you [a]Ex 15:20;
seize a wife from the girls of Shiloh and go to the Jdg 11:34
land of Benjamin. 22When their fathers or brothers
complain to us, we will say to them, 'Do us a
kindness by helping them, because we did not get
wives for them during the war, and you are inno- 21:22
cent, since you did not give[b] your daughters to [b]ver 1,18
them.' "

23So that is what the Benjamites did. While the
girls were dancing, each man caught one and carried her off to be his wife. Then they returned to
their inheritance and rebuilt the towns and settled 21:23
in them.[c] [c]Jdg 20:48

24At that time the Israelites left that place and
went home to their tribes and clans, each to his
own inheritance. 21:25

25In those days Israel had no king; everyone did [d]Dt 12:8; Jdg 17:6;
as he saw fit.[d] 18:1; 19:1

Ruth

Sacrifice is a hallmark of genuine love.

The book of Ruth is a surprising love story that illustrates the kindness, grace and loyalty that can flourish in times of crisis. Set against the backdrop of the depressing era of Israel's judges, this brief narrative recounts the struggles of three widows and the choices they make to survive in hard economic times. A widowed daughter-in-law's love and devotion toward her widowed mother-in-law shapes the destiny of future generations.

Naomi epitomizes a woman who recognizes God's control in her life despite devastating hardship (Ru 1). Daughter-in-law Orpah makes choices that cause her to quickly fade into Biblical obscurity (Ru 1). Daughter-in-law Ruth, on the other hand, recognizes that she holds a permanent place in Naomi's family. No crisis or obstacle can sever her promise of faithfulness nor her willingness to submit to Naomi's guidance (Ru 1). Though Ruth and Naomi face uncertainty and unforeseeable dangers from those who could take advantage of them, their commitment to each other and to God's care brings them great peace and unexpected blessings (Ru 2–3). Ultimately both widows find joy—Ruth in remarriage and motherhood and Naomi in her role as grandmother (Ru 4).

The book of Ruth is a poignant reminder to us of God's unceasing faithfulness. Whether we come from religious families or from disreputable backgrounds, when we seek God and surrender to his plan we can find the same peace and purpose discovered by Ruth and Naomi so many years ago.

Quick Study

Author
Unknown.

Date Written
Most likely during the monarchy, around 1000 B.C.

Setting
Moab and Bethlehem.

Key Passage
Ruth 1:16 "Don't urge me to leave you or to turn back from you. Where you go I will go, and where you stay I will stay. Your people will be my people and your God my God."

Outline

Naomi in Moab.
Ru 1:1-5

Orpah chooses to stay in Moab.
Ru 1:6-14

Ruth accompanies Naomi to Bethlehem.
Ru 1:15-22

Gleaning in Boaz's fields.
Ru 2

At the threshing floor.
Ru 3

The marriage of Ruth and Boaz.
Ru 4:1-12

A son for Ruth and Boaz.
Ru 4:13-16

Ruth's part in the genealogy of David.
Ru 4:17-22

The Women of Ruth

Naomi	*Bitterness turned to blessing.* Ru 1-4 (page 604)
Orpah	*Destiny unknown.* Ru 1 (page 669)
Ruth	*Future secure.* Ru 1-4 (page 670)
Rachel	*Mother of the house of Israel.* Ru 4:11 (page 200)
Leah	*Mother of the house of Israel.* Ru 4:11 (page 199)
Tamar	*God brought good from bad in her life too.* Ru 4:12 (page 267)

Denotes a sketch written about this character

Naomi and Ruth

1 In the days when the judges ruled,[a][a] there was a famine in the land,[b] and a man from Bethlehem in Judah, together with his wife and two sons, went to live for a while in the country of Moab.[c] 2The man's name was Elimelech, his wife's name Naomi, and the names of his two sons were Mahlon and Kilion. They were Ephrathites from Bethlehem,[d] Judah. And they went to Moab and lived there.

3Now Elimelech, Naomi's husband, died, and she was left with her two sons. 4They married Moabite women, one named Orpah and the other Ruth.[e] After they had lived there about ten years, 5both Mahlon and Kilion also died, and Naomi was left without her two sons and her husband.

6When she heard in Moab that the LORD had come to the aid of his people[f] by providing food[g] for them, Naomi and her daughters-in-law prepared to return home from there. 7With her two daughters-in-law she left the place where she had been living and set out on the road that would take them back to the land of Judah.

8Then Naomi said to her two daughters-in-law, "Go back, each of you, to your mother's home. May the LORD show kindness[h] to you, as you have shown to your dead[i] and to me. 9May the LORD grant that each of you will find rest[j] in the home of another husband."

Then she kissed them and they wept aloud 10and said to her, "We will go back with you to your people."

11But Naomi said, "Return home, my daughters. Why would you come with me? Am I going to have any more sons, who could become your husbands?[k] 12Return home, my daughters; I am too old to have another husband. Even if I thought there was still hope for me—even if I had a husband tonight and then gave birth to sons— 13would you wait until they grew up? Would you remain unmarried for them? No, my daughters. It is more bitter for me than for you, because the LORD's hand has gone out against me![l]"

14At this they wept again. Then Orpah kissed her mother-in-law[m] good-by, but Ruth clung to her.[n]

15"Look," said Naomi, "your sister-in-law is going back to her people and her gods.[o] Go back with her."

16But Ruth replied, "Don't urge me to leave you[p] or to turn back from you. Where you go I will go, and where you stay I will stay. Your people will be my people and your God my God.[q] 17Where you die I will die, and there I will be buried. May the LORD deal with me, be it ever so severely,[r] if anything but death separates you and me." 18When Naomi realized that Ruth was determined to go with her, she stopped urging her.[s]

19So the two women went on until they came to Bethlehem. When they arrived in Bethlehem, the

1:1 [a]Jdg 2:16-18 [b]Ge 12:10; Ps 105:16 [c]Jdg 3:30
1:2 [d]Ge 35:19
1:4 [e]Mt 1:5
1:6 [f]Ex 4:31; Jer 29:10; Zep 2:7 [g]Ps 132:15; Mt 6:11
1:8 [h]Ru 2:20; 2Ti 1:16 [i]ver 5
1:9 [j]Ru 3:1
1:11 [k]Ge 38:11; Dt 25:5
1:13 [l]Jdg 2:15; Job 4:5; 19:21; Ps 32:4
1:14 [m]Ru 2:11 [n]Pr 17:17; 18:24
1:15 [o]Jos 24:14; Jdg 11:24
1:16 [p]2Ki 2:2 [q]Ru 2:11,12
1:17 [r]1Sa 3:17; 25:22; 2Sa 19:13; 2Ki 6:31
1:18 [s]Ac 21:14

[a] *1* Traditionally *judged*

A Radical Commitment

RU 1:16–17

Ruth's story begins with loss and disappointment in relationships and then takes a radical turn with a renewed commitment to relationships. Ruth's statement of devotion in these verses seems even more radical when you consider the object of her commitment. Naomi is not the most winsome friend at the time. It is after Naomi's harsh words (Ru 1:13,15) that Ruth makes her incredible declaration. Doesn't Ruth see the bitter woman in front of her? The whole story of the book hinges on the fact that Ruth does not. Read on in the story. Ruth's exceptional commitment to Naomi will wondrously impact not only the two of them but also generations to come (see the character sketches for Orpah and Ruth on pages 669 and 670).

A Radical Response

RUTH 2:2–7

Naomi's response to Ruth's commitment is a bit disappointing. Can you imagine how Naomi's "non-introduction" of Ruth to the women in her hometown might have hurt Ruth (Ru 1:19–22)? (See the character sketch for Naomi on page 604.) Aren't you curious to know what Ruth's first recorded words to Naomi were after this dismal introduction? Don't you think it's about time for Ruth to confront Naomi and point out her cruelty, bitterness and lack of faith? Instead, Ruth volunteers to help (Ru 2:2)! She offers to give of herself—not because Naomi is particularly lovely or deserving at the moment, but on the strength of her commitment to Naomi. Ruth surveys the state of their relationship and asks, "What can I do?" Her commitment keeps her from focusing on changing Naomi and sets her on a course that will transform a woman from Moab into the great-grandmother of Israel's most famous king . . . and part of the lineage of Christ, the King of kings!

whole town was stirred[t] because of them, and the
women exclaimed, "Can this be Naomi?"
[20]"Don't call me Naomi,[a]" she told them. "Call
me Mara,[b] because the Almighty[c][u] has made my
life very bitter.[v] [21]I went away full, but the LORD
has brought me back empty.[w] Why call me Naomi? The LORD has afflicted[d] me; the Almighty has
brought misfortune upon me."
[22]So Naomi returned from Moab accompanied
by Ruth the Moabitess, her daughter-in-law, arriving in Bethlehem as the barley harvest[x] was
beginning.[y]

Ruth Meets Boaz

2 Now Naomi had a relative[z] on her husband's
side, from the clan of Elimelech,[a] a man of
standing, whose name was Boaz.[b]
[2]And Ruth the Moabitess said to Naomi, "Let
me go to the fields and pick up the leftover grain[c]
behind anyone in whose eyes I find favor."
Naomi said to her, "Go ahead, my daughter."
[3]So she went out and began to glean in the fields
behind the harvesters. As it turned out, she found
herself working in a field belonging to Boaz, who
was from the clan of Elimelech.
[4]Just then Boaz arrived from Bethlehem and
greeted the harvesters, "The LORD be with you![d]"
"The LORD bless you![e]" they called back.
[5]Boaz asked the foreman of his harvesters,
"Whose young woman is that?"
[6]The foreman replied, "She is the Moabitess[f]
who came back from Moab with Naomi. [7]She
said, 'Please let me glean and gather among the
sheaves behind the harvesters.' She went into the
field and has worked steadily from morning till
now, except for a short rest in the shelter."
[8]So Boaz said to Ruth, "My daughter, listen to
me. Don't go and glean in another field and don't
go away from here. Stay here with my servant
girls. [9]Watch the field where the men are harvesting, and follow along after the girls. I have told
the men not to touch you. And whenever you are
thirsty, go and get a drink from the water jars the
men have filled."
[10]At this, she bowed down with her face to the
ground.[g] She exclaimed, "Why have I found such
favor in your eyes that you notice me[h]—a
foreigner?[i]"
[11]Boaz replied, "I've been told all about what
you have done for your mother-in-law[j] since the
death of your husband—how you left your father
and mother and your homeland and came to live
with a people you did not know before.[k] [12]May the
LORD repay you for what you have done. May you
be richly rewarded by the LORD,[l] the God of Israel,
under whose wings[m] you have come to take
refuge.[n]"

1:19 [t]Mt 21:10
1:20 [u]Ex 6:3 [v]ver 13; Job 6:4
1:21 [w]Job 1:21
1:22 [x]Ex 9:31; Ru 2:23 [y]2Sa 21:9
2:1 [z]Ru 3:2,12 [a]Ru 1:2 [b]Ru 4:21
2:2 [c]ver 7; Lev 19:9; 23:22; Dt 24:19
2:4 [d]Jdg 6:12; Lk 1:28; 2Th 3:16 [e]Ps 129:7-8
2:6 [f]Ru 1:22
2:10 [g]1Sa 25:23 [h]Ps 41:1 [i]Dt 15:3
2:11 [j]Ru 1:14 [k]Ru 1:16-17
2:12 [l]1Sa 24:19 [m]Ps 17:8; 36:7; 57:1; 61:4; 63:7; 91:4 [n]Ru 1:16

[a] *20* *Naomi* means *pleasant*; also in verse 21. [b] *20* *Mara* means *bitter.* [c] *20* Hebrew *Shaddai*; also in verse 21
[d] *21* Or *has testified against*

[13]“May I continue to find favor in your eyes, my
lord,” she said. “You have given me comfort and
have spoken kindly to your servant—though I do
not have the standing of one of your servant girls.”
[14]At mealtime Boaz said to her, “Come over
here. Have some bread and dip it in the wine
vinegar.”
When she sat down with the harvesters, he
2:14 offered her some roasted grain. She ate all she
[o]ver 18 wanted and had some left over.[o] [15]As she got up to
glean, Boaz gave orders to his men, “Even if she
gathers among the sheaves, don’t embarrass her.
[16]Rather, pull out some stalks for her from the
bundles and leave them for her to pick up, and
don’t rebuke her.”
[17]So Ruth gleaned in the field until evening
Then she threshed the barley she had gath
and it amounted to about an ephah.[a] [18]Sh
it back to town, and her mother-in
much she had gathered. Ruth
2:18 [p]ver 14 and gave her what she ha
eaten enough.
[19]Her mother-in-law a
glean today? Where di
2:19 [q]ver 10; man who took
Ps 41:1 Then Ruth
one at who
name of th
she said.
[20]“The
daugh
ki

2:2
[r]Ru

A Radical Redeemer

RUTH 2:13–3:4

Ruth and Naomi’s losses result in the worst possible life situation for them—the loss their rightful inherit lehem. There is on loss can be rest required. a kins

uncover his feet and lie down. He will tell you
what to do."
[5]"I will do whatever you say,"[x] Ruth answered.
[6]So she went down to the threshing floor and did
everything her mother-in-law told her to do.
[7]When Boaz had finished eating and drinking
and was in good spirits,[y] he went over to lie down
at the far end of the grain pile. Ruth approached
quietly, uncovered his feet and lay down. [8]In the
middle of the night something startled the man,
and he turned and discovered a woman lying at
his feet.
[9]"Who are you?" he asked.
"I am your servant Ruth," she said. "Spread the
corner of your garment[z] over me, since you are a
kinsman-redeemer.[a]"
[10]"The LORD bless you, my daughter," he replied.
indness is greater than that which you
lier: You have not run after the younger
or poor. [11]And now, my daugh-
ll do for you all you ask. All
ow that you are a woman
ough it is true that I am
sman-redeemer[c] nearer
t, and in the morn-
let him redeem.
he LORD lives[f]
ng, but got
ed; and he
came to

3:5 [x]Eph 6:1; Col 3:20
3:7 [y]Jdg 19:6,9, 22; 2Sa 13:28; 1Ki 21:7; Est 1:10
3:9 [z]Eze 16:8 [a]ver 12; Ru 2:20
3:11 [b]Pr 12:4; 31:10
3:12 [c]ver 9 [d]Ru 4:1
3:13 [e]Dt 25:5; Ru 4:5; Mt 22:24 [f]Jdg 8:19; Jer 4:2
3:14 [g]Ro 14:16; Co 8:21

gest that you buy it in the presence of these seated
here and in the presence of the elders of my people. If you will redeem it, do so. But if you[a] will
not, tell me, so I will know. For no one has the
right to do it except you,[k] and I am next in line."
"I will redeem it," he said.
[5]Then Boaz said, "On the day you buy the land
from Naomi and from Ruth the Moabitess, you
acquire[b] the dead man's widow, in order to maintain the name of the dead with his property."[l]
[6]At this, the kinsman-redeemer said, "Then I
cannot redeem[m] it because I might endanger my
own estate. You redeem it yourself. I cannot do it."
[7](Now in earlier times in Israel, for the redemption and transfer of property to become final, one
party took off his sandal and gave it to the other.
This was the method of legalizing transactions i
Israel.)[n]
[8]So the kinsman-redeemer said to Bo
yourself." And he removed his san
[9]Then Boaz announced to
people, "Today you are
bought from Naomi all th
Kilion and Mahlon. [10]I
the Moabitess, Mahl
order to maintai
property, so th
among his
Today you a
[11]Then th
"We are
woma
R

4:4 [k]Lev 25:25; Jer 32:7-8
4:5 [l]Ge 38:8; Dt 25:5-6; Ru 3:13; Mt 22:24
4:6 [m]Lev 25:25; Ru 3:13
4:7 [n]Dt 25:7-9
4:10 [o]Dt 25:6
4:11 [p]Dt 25:9 [q]Ps 127:3; 128:3 [r]Ge 35:16

A Radical Ending

RUTH 4:22

No words in the book of Ruth speak more elo- ...ently about redemption than ...ords. Ruth, a foreigner ...comes the great- ...avid, Israel's ...God longs to

Ram the father of Amminadab,[y]
20 Amminadab the father of Nahshon,
Nahshon the father of Salmon,[a]
21 Salmon the father of Boaz,[z]
Boaz the father of Obed,
22 Obed the father of Jesse,
and Jesse the father of David.

4:19 [y]Ex 6:23

4:21 [z]Ru 2:1

1 Samuel

A change in leadership.

The book of 1 Samuel continues the history of Israel as it connects the end of the era of the judges under Samuel with the reign of Israel's first king, Saul. The nation of Israel faces disconcerting transitions as it rejects God's theocratic rule and clamors for a monarchy like that of its neighbors. Though grieved by Israel's choice, God grants the people's request and installs Saul as king. Ultimately Saul falls prey to the sin of pride, and Samuel anoints Saul's successor, David.

Godly women play important roles in the unfolding drama of 1 Samuel. We feel the anguish of Hannah's barrenness and share her ultimate joy when God grants her desire for a child (1Sa 1:1–2:26). We revel in the blush of first love as Michal reveals her feelings for David and sympathize as she incurs her father's wrath when she attempts to protect David (1Sa 18:20-29; 19:9-17). We applaud Abigail's intelligence and resourcefulness as she dares to do what's right despite her husband's evil intentions (1Sa 25).

Some characters in 1 Samuel exhibit weaknesses that serve as vivid lessons. Eli's poor parenting results in children who lack moral strength (1Sa 3:1-18). Saul's preoccupation with success at any cost brings about his ultimate removal from leadership (1Sa 15). And Jesse's lack of discernment blinds him to God's perspective in choosing a new leader (1Sa 16:1-13). Throughout 1 Samuel one truth rings loudly and clearly: God doesn't necessarily opt to use those with tremendous talents or leadership skills. He uses those who are *willing* to be used and who value obedience above all else.

Quick Study

Author
Unknown.

Date Written
Sometime after the division of Israel into the northern and southern kingdoms, around 930 B.C.

Setting
Israel.

Key Passage
1 Samuel 16:7 "The LORD does not look at the things man looks at. Man looks at the outward appearance, but the LORD looks at the heart."

Outline

Hannah prays for a son.
1Sa 1:1–20

Hannah returns Samuel to God.
1Sa 1:21–28

Hannah's prayer.
1Sa 2:1–11

The house of Eli.
1Sa 2:12–36

The call of Samuel.
1Sa 3

Misuse of the ark.
1Sa 4–7

Israel's first king.
1Sa 8–11

Samuel's farewell speech.
1Sa 12

King Saul rebels.
1Sa 12–15

Samuel anoints David.
1Sa 16

David and Goliath.
1Sa 17

Saul's jealousy and David's exploits.
1Sa 18–24

Abigail's bravery.
1Sa 25

More exploits of David.
1Sa 26–27

Saul and a witch.
1Sa 28

Still more exploits of David.
1Sa 29–30

Saul's death.
1Sa 31

The Women of 1 Samuel

⚘ **Hannah**	*Grief turned to a song.* 1Sa 1–2 (page 739)
Peninnah	*The annoying "other" woman.* 1Sa 1:1–8
Elkanah's daughters	*Daughters of Peninnah and Hannah.* 1Sa 1:4; 2:21
Ichabod's mother	*Prophetic dying words.* 1Sa 4:19–22
Merab	*Saul's older daughter.* 1Sa 14:49;18:17–19
Ahinoam	*Saul's wife.* 1Sa 14:50
⚘ **Michal**	*A pawn in her father's hands.* 1Sa 14:49; 18:20–30; 19:11–17; 25:44 (page 740)
⚘ **Abigail**	*A gutsy woman.* 1Sa 25; 27:3; 30:5 (page 805)
Abigail's five maids	*Followed their mistress.* 1Sa 25:42
Ahinoam	*One of David's wives.* 1 Sa 25:43; 27:3; 30:5
⚘ **Witch (or medium) of Endor**	*An evil and dangerous practice.* 1Sa 28 (page 806)

⚘ Denotes a sketch written about this character

The Birth of Samuel

1 There was a certain man from Ramathaim, a
1:1 [a]Jos 17:17-18 [b]1Ch 6:27,34 Zuphite[a] from the hill country[a] of Ephraim,
whose name was Elkanah[b] son of Jeroham, the
son of Elihu, the son of Tohu, the son of Zuph, an
1:2 [c]Dt 21:15-17; Lk 2:36 Ephraimite. 2He had two wives;[c] one was called
Hannah and the other Peninnah. Peninnah had
children, but Hannah had none.
1:3 [d]ver 21; Ex 23:14; 34:23; Lk 2:41 [e]Dt 12:5-7 [f]Jos 18:1 3Year after year[d] this man went up from his town
to worship[e] and sacrifice to the LORD Almighty at
Shiloh,[f] where Hophni and Phinehas, the two sons
of Eli, were priests of the LORD. 4Whenever the day
came for Elkanah to sacrifice,[g] he would give portions of the meat to his wife Peninnah and to all
1:4 [g]Dt 12:17-18 her sons and daughters. 5But to Hannah he gave a
double portion because he loved her, and the LORD
1:5 [h]Ge 16:1; 30:2 had closed her womb.[h] 6And because the LORD had
closed her womb, her rival kept provoking her in
order to irritate her.[i] 7This went on year after year.
1:6 [i]Job 24:21 Whenever Hannah went up to the house of the
LORD, her rival provoked her till she wept and
would not eat. 8Elkanah her husband would say to
her, "Hannah, why are you weeping? Why don't
you eat? Why are you downhearted? Don't I mean
1:8 [j]Ru 4:15 more to you than ten sons?[j]"
9Once when they had finished eating and drinking in Shiloh, Hannah stood up. Now Eli the
1:9 [k]1Sa 3:3 priest was sitting on a chair by the doorpost of the
LORD's temple.[b k] 10In bitterness of soul[l] Hannah
1:10 [l]Job 7:11 wept much and prayed to the LORD. 11And she
made a vow, saying, "O LORD Almighty, if you will
1:11 [m]Ge 8:1; 28:20; 29:32 [n]Nu 6:1-21; Jdg 13:5 only look upon your servant's misery and remember[m] me, and not forget your servant but give her
a son, then I will give him to the LORD for all the
days of his life, and no razor[n] will ever be used on
his head."
12As she kept on praying to the LORD, Eli
observed her mouth. 13Hannah was praying in her
heart, and her lips were moving but her voice was
not heard. Eli thought she was drunk 14and said to
her, "How long will you keep on getting drunk?
Get rid of your wine."
15"Not so, my lord," Hannah replied, "I am a
1:15 [o]Ps 42:4; 62:8; La 2:19 woman who is deeply troubled. I have not been
drinking wine or beer; I was pouring[o] out my soul
to the LORD. 16Do not take your servant for a
wicked woman; I have been praying here out of
my great anguish and grief."
1:17 [p]Jdg 18:6; 1Sa 25:35; 2Ki 5:19; Mk 5:34 [q]Ps 20:3-5 17Eli answered, "Go in peace,[p] and may the God
of Israel grant you what you have asked of him.[q]"
18She said, "May your servant find favor in your
eyes.[r]" Then she went her way and ate something,
and her face was no longer downcast.[s]
1:18 [r]Ru 2:13 [s]Ecc 9:7; Ro 15:13 19Early the next morning they arose and worshiped before the LORD and then went back to
their home at Ramah. Elkanah lay with Hannah
1:19 [t]Ge 4:1; 30:22 his wife, and the LORD remembered[t] her. 20So in
the course of time Hannah conceived and gave

[a] *1* Or *from Ramathaim Zuphim* [b] *9* That is, tabernacle

A Closed Womb

1SA 1:1-2

In Hebrew society, one of the greatest tragedies that could befall a woman was to be barren. The Hebrews knew that children are a blessing from God (Ps 127:3-5). The reverse of this, they assumed, was that a lack of children was a curse. So was God actually cursing Hannah by causing her infertility? Scripture does state that God had "closed" Hannah's womb (1Sa 1:5), but there is no indication that it was the result of a curse.

In today's culture, we would probably say God *allowed* but did not *cause* Hannah's infertility. Other Old Testament women who are described as barren include Sarah, Rebekah and Rachel. Each of these women received a child (or children) after seeking God. God may not answer every childless woman as he did Hannah or these other women, yet even then, we can trust in God's healing—healing for the brokenhearted (Ps 147:3). (See character sketch for Hannah on page 739.)

Dedicating Children

1SA 1:24–28

In Bible times, a person at times made a vow to the Lord when they asked something specific of him. Then, when the request was granted, the vow or dedication had to be fulfilled. A person might dedicate himself or herself, or a slave or a child, to the tabernacle or temple for service (see the note on Lev 27:3, page 201).

It must be heart wrenching for Hannah to give up her only child when he is but a toddler. However, her goal is not her own happiness or comfort—her goal is to fulfill the promise she made to the Lord (1Sa 1:11). She is a remarkable model for us of someone who is willing to completely fulfill her vow, no matter how difficult. Our children are just as precious to us today, and Hannah's commitment and devotion are worthy of our attention.

birth to a son. She named[u] him Samuel,[a] saying,
"Because I asked the LORD for him."

Hannah Dedicates Samuel

21 When the man Elkanah went up with all his
family to offer the annual[v] sacrifice to the LORD
and to fulfill his vow,[w] 22 Hannah did not go. She
said to her husband, "After the boy is weaned, I
will take him and present[x] him before the LORD,
and he will live there always."

23 "Do what seems best to you," Elkanah her
husband told her. "Stay here until you have
weaned him; only may the LORD make good[y] his[b]
word." So the woman stayed at home and nursed
her son until she had weaned him.

24 After he was weaned, she took the boy with
her, young as he was, along with a three-year-old
bull,[c][z] an ephah[d] of flour and a skin of wine, and
brought him to the house of the LORD at Shiloh.
25 When they had slaughtered the bull, they
brought the boy to Eli, 26 and she said to him, "As
surely as you live, my lord, I am the woman who
stood here beside you praying to the LORD. 27 I
prayed[a] for this child, and the LORD has granted
me what I asked of him. 28 So now I give him to
the LORD. For his whole life[b] he will be given over
to the LORD." And he worshiped the LORD there.

Hannah's Prayer

2 Then Hannah prayed and said:[c]

"My heart rejoices[d] in the LORD;
in the LORD my horn[e][e] is lifted high.
My mouth boasts over my enemies,
for I delight in your deliverance.

2 "There is no one holy[f][f] like the LORD;
there is no one besides you;
there is no Rock[g] like our God.

3 "Do not keep talking so proudly
or let your mouth speak such
arrogance,[h]
for the LORD is a God who knows,
and by him deeds[i] are weighed.[j]
4 "The bows of the warriors are broken,[k]
but those who stumbled are armed
with strength.
5 Those who were full hire themselves out
for food,
but those who were hungry hunger
no more.
She who was barren[l] has borne seven
children,

1:20 [u]Ge 41:51-52; Ex 2:10, 22; Mt 1:21
1:21 [v]ver 3 [w]Dt 12:11
1:22 [x]ver 11,28; Lk 2:22
1:23 [y]ver 17; Nu 30:7
1:24 [z]Nu 15:8-10; Dt 12:5; Jos 18:1
1:27 [a]ver 11-13; Ps 66:19-20
1:28 [b]ver 11,22; Ge 24:26,52
2:1 [c]Lk 1:46-55 [d]Ps 9:14; 13:5 [e]Ps 89:17, 24; 92:10; Isa 12:2-3
2:2 [f]Ex 15:11; Lev 19:2 [g]Dt 32:30-31; 2Sa 22:2,32
2:3 [h]Pr 8:13 [i]1Sa 16:7; 1Ki 8:39 [j]Pr 16:2; 24:11-12
2:4 [k]Ps 37:15
2:5 [l]Ps 113:9; Jer 15:9

[a] 20 *Samuel* sounds like the Hebrew for *heard of God.*
[b] 23 Masoretic Text; Dead Sea Scrolls, Septuagint and Syriac *your* [c] 24 Dead Sea Scrolls, Septuagint and Syriac; Masoretic Text *with three bulls* [d] 24 That is, probably about 3/5 bushel (about 22 liters) [e] 1 *Horn* here symbolizes strength; also in verse 10. [f] 2 Or *no Holy One*

but she who has had many sons pines
away.
[6]"The LORD brings death and makes
alive;[m]
he brings down to the grave[a] and
raises up.[n]
[7]The LORD sends poverty and wealth;[o]
he humbles and he exalts.[p]
[8]He raises[q] the poor from the dust
and lifts the needy from the ash heap;
he seats them with princes
and has them inherit a throne of
honor.[r]
"For the foundations[s] of the earth are
the LORD's;
upon them he has set the world.
[9]He will guard the feet[t] of his saints,
but the wicked will be silenced in
darkness.[u]
"It is not by strength[v] that one prevails;
10 those who oppose the LORD will be
shattered.[w]
He will thunder[x] against them from
heaven;
the LORD will judge[y] the ends of the
earth.
"He will give strength[z] to his king
and exalt the horn[a] of his anointed."

[11]Then Elkanah went home to Ramah, but the
boy ministered[b] before the LORD under Eli the
priest.

Eli's Wicked Sons

[12]Eli's sons were wicked men; they had no
regard[c] for the LORD. [13]Now it was the practice of
the priests with the people that whenever anyone
offered a sacrifice and while the meat[d] was being
boiled, the servant of the priest would come with
a three-pronged fork in his hand. [14]He would
plunge it into the pan or kettle or caldron or pot,
and the priest would take for himself whatever
the fork brought up. This is how they treated all
the Israelites who came to Shiloh. [15]But even
before the fat was burned, the servant of the priest
would come and say to the man who was sacrificing, "Give the priest some meat to roast; he
won't accept boiled meat from you, but only raw."
[16]If the man said to him, "Let the fat be burned
up first, and then take whatever you want," the
servant would then answer, "No, hand it over
now; if you don't, I'll take it by force."
[17]This sin of the young men was very great in
the LORD's sight, for they[b] were treating the LORD's
offering with contempt.[e]
[18]But Samuel was ministering[f] before the
LORD—a boy wearing a linen ephod.[g] [19]Each year

2:6 [m]Dt 32:39 [n]Isa 26:19
2:7 [o]Dt 8:18 [p]Job 5:11; Ps 75:7
2:8 [q]Ps 113:7-8 [r]Job 36:7 [s]Job 38:4
2:9 [t]Ps 91:12 [u]Mt 8:12 [v]Ps 33:16-17
2:10 [w]Ps 2:9 [x]Ps 18:13 [y]Ps 96:13 [z]Ps 21:1 [a]Ps 89:24
2:11 [b]ver 18; 1Sa 3:1
2:12 [c]Jer 2:8; 9:6
2:13 [d]Lev 7:29-34
2:17 [e]Mal 2:7-9
2:18 [f]ver 11; 1Sa 3:1 [g]ver 28

a6 Hebrew *Sheol* *b17* Or *men*

Eli's Wicked Sons

1SA 2:12-17

Eli is both a priest and a judge. He leads Israel for 40 years (1Sa 4:18). But his reputation is marred. Eli is a passive father, and his sons, Hophni and Phinehas, steal from the sacrifices offered to God and sleep with the women who help at the Tent of Meeting (1Sa 2:22). This troubles the Lord so much that he promises both sons will die on the same day (1Sa 2:34). Even more than that, he vows that there will not be an old man in Eli's family line (1Sa 2:31).

God's judgment of Eli's sons is carried out through the Philistines when Hophni and Phinehas carry the ark of the covenant into battle. Both sons are killed and the ark is captured (1Sa 4:11). God's final judgment is fulfilled in 1 Samuel 22:18-19 when Saul's warriors kill Eli's descendants—priests, men and women, children and infants—in the city of Nob.

Her Faithfulness Rewarded

1SA 2:19

Can you picture Hannah stitching a new garment for little Samuel each year, wondering how big he has grown since she last saw him? Imagine her excitement as she travels with her husband to the tabernacle for the annual sacrifice. But that happens only once a year. Many other days her empty arms must have ached to hold her son. Yet God rewards Hannah's faithfulness. He gives her three more sons and two daughters! God also takes care of Samuel. The young boy "grew up in the presence of the LORD" (1Sa 2:21). God answers Hannah's prayers in ways she never could have dreamed—Samuel experiences God the Father's loving and caring embrace when his mother's arms can't reach him.

his mother made him a little robe and took it to
him when she went up with her husband to offer
the annual[h] sacrifice. 20Eli would bless Elkanah
and his wife, saying, "May the LORD give you children by this woman to take the place of the one
she prayed[i] for and gave to the LORD." Then they
would go home. 21And the LORD was gracious to
Hannah;[j] she conceived and gave birth to three
sons and two daughters. Meanwhile, the boy Samuel grew[k] up in the presence of the LORD.

22Now Eli, who was very old, heard about
everything his sons were doing to all Israel and
how they slept with the women[l] who served at the
entrance to the Tent of Meeting. 23So he said to
them, "Why do you do such things? I hear from
all the people about these wicked deeds of yours.
24No, my sons; it is not a good report that I hear
spreading among the LORD's people. 25If a man
sins against another man, God[a] may mediate for
him; but if a man sins against the LORD, who will[m]
intercede[n] for him?" His sons, however, did not
listen to their father's rebuke, for it was the LORD's
will to put them to death.

26And the boy Samuel continued to grow[o] in
stature and in favor with the LORD and with men.

Prophecy Against the House of Eli

27Now a man of God[p] came to Eli and said to
him, "This is what the LORD says: 'Did I not clearly reveal myself to your father's house when they
were in Egypt under Pharaoh? 28I chose[q] your
father out of all the tribes of Israel to be my priest,
to go up to my altar, to burn incense, and to wear
an ephod[r] in my presence. I also gave your
father's house all the offerings made with fire by
the Israelites. 29Why do you[b] scorn my sacrifice
and offering[s] that I prescribed for my dwelling?[t]
Why do you honor your sons more than me by
fattening yourselves on the choice parts of every
offering made by my people Israel?'

30"Therefore the LORD, the God of Israel, declares:
'I promised that your house and your father's
house would minister before me forever.[u]' But now
the LORD declares: 'Far be it from me! Those who
honor me I will honor,[v] but those who despise[w] me
will be disdained. 31The time is coming when I will
cut short your strength and the strength of your
father's house, so that there will not be an old man
in your family line[x] 32and you will see distress in
my dwelling. Although good will be done to Israel,
in your family line there will never be an old man.[y]
33Every one of you that I do not cut off from my
altar will be spared only to blind your eyes with
tears and to grieve your heart, and all your descendants will die in the prime of life.

34" 'And what happens to your two sons, Hophni and Phinehas, will be a sign to you—they will
both die[z] on the same day.[a] 35I will raise up for
myself a faithful priest,[b] who will do according to

2:19 [h]1Sa 1:3
2:20 [i]1Sa 1:11,27-28; Lk 2:34
2:21 [j]Ge 21:1 [k]ver 26; Jdg 13:24; 1Sa 3:19; Lk 2:40
2:22 [l]Ex 38:8
2:25 [m]Nu 15:30; Jos 11:20 [n]Dt 1:17; 1Sa 3:14; Heb 10:26
2:26 [o]ver 21; Lk 2:52
2:27 [p]Ex 4:14-16; 1Ki 13:1
2:28 [q]Ex 28:1 [r]Lev 8:7-8
2:29 [s]ver 12-17 [t]Dt 12:5; Mt 10:37
2:30 [u]Ex 29:9 [v]Ps 50:23; 91:15 [w]Mal 2:9
2:31 [x]1Sa 4:11-18; 22:16-20
2:32 [y]1Ki 2:26-27; Zec 8:4
2:34 [z]1Sa 4:11 [a]1Ki 13:3
2:35 [b]1Sa 12:3; 1Ki 2:35

[a] *25* Or *the judges* [b] *29* The Hebrew is plural.

what is in my heart and mind. I will firmly establish his house, and he will minister before my anointed[c] one always. 36Then everyone left in your family line will come and bow down before him for a piece of silver and a crust of bread and plead, "Appoint me to some priestly office so I can have food to eat.[d]" ' "

The LORD Calls Samuel

3 The boy Samuel ministered[e] before the LORD under Eli. In those days the word of the LORD was rare;[f] there were not many visions.[g]

2One night Eli, whose eyes[h] were becoming so weak that he could barely see, was lying down in his usual place. 3The lamp[i] of God had not yet gone out, and Samuel was lying down in the temple[a] of the LORD, where the ark of God was. 4Then the LORD called Samuel.

Samuel answered, "Here I am.[j]" 5And he ran to Eli and said, "Here I am; you called me."

But Eli said, "I did not call; go back and lie down." So he went and lay down.

6Again the LORD called, "Samuel!" And Samuel got up and went to Eli and said, "Here I am; you called me."

"My son," Eli said, "I did not call; go back and lie down."

7Now Samuel did not yet know the LORD: The word of the LORD had not yet been revealed[k] to him.

8The LORD called Samuel a third time, and Samuel got up and went to Eli and said, "Here I am; you called me."

Then Eli realized that the LORD was calling the boy. 9So Eli told Samuel, "Go and lie down, and if he calls you, say, 'Speak, LORD, for your servant is listening.' " So Samuel went and lay down in his place.

10The LORD came and stood there, calling as at the other times, "Samuel! Samuel!"

Then Samuel said, "Speak, for your servant is listening."

11And the LORD said to Samuel: "See, I am about to do something in Israel that will make the ears of everyone who hears of it tingle.[l] 12At that time I will carry out against Eli everything[m] I spoke against his family—from beginning to end. 13For I told him that I would judge his family forever because of the sin he knew about; his sons made themselves contemptible,[b] and he failed to restrain[n] them. 14Therefore, I swore to the house of Eli, 'The guilt of Eli's house will never be atoned[o] for by sacrifice or offering.' "

15Samuel lay down until morning and then opened the doors of the house of the LORD. He was afraid to tell Eli the vision, 16but Eli called him and said, "Samuel, my son."

Samuel answered, "Here I am."

[a] *3* That is, tabernacle [b] *13* Masoretic Text; an ancient Hebrew scribal tradition and Septuagint *sons blasphemed God*

2:35 [c]1Sa 16:13; 2Sa 7:11,27; 1Ki 11:38
2:36 [d]1Ki 2:27
3:1 [e]1Sa 2:11 [f]Ps 74:9 [g]Am 8:11
3:2 [h]1Sa 4:15
3:3 [i]Lev 24:1-4
3:4 [j]Isa 6:8
3:7 [k]Ac 19:12
3:11 [l]2Ki 21:12; Jer 19:3
3:12 [m]1Sa 2:27-36
3:13 [n]1Sa 2:12, 17,22,29-31
3:14 [o]Lev 15:30-31; 1Sa 2:25; Isa 22:14

Knowing God's Voice

1SA 3:10

As a young boy, Samuel hears the voice of God calling him. This is significant because during these days the word of the Lord is "rare" (1Sa 3:1). After Samuel runs to Eli three times, Eli helps Samuel understand God is speaking.

In our own lives, although we cannot always easily discern God's will, we can listen and follow him when:

1. ***We seek to do what God desires, not what we desire* (Mt 6:33)**
2. ***We know God's Word and realize anything contrary to it cannot be his will* (Ps 119:11)**
3. ***We live each day not in and of ourselves, but in Jesus Christ* (Jn 15:5)**
4. ***We depend on the Lord's strength, not our own, to complete the task he asks of us* (2Co 12:9)**

Trustworthy Words

1SA 3:19

As Samuel grows, he discovers that God is faithful to keep his promises. God speaks, Samuel listens and Scripture says, "He let none of his words fall to the ground." This construction probably has a double meaning here. Through experience, Samuel knows God's words are true—not one of God's words to him falls to the ground or fails. Samuel's words to others are reliable as well; people find they can trust what he says (1Sa 9:6).

17“What was it he said to you?” Eli asked. “Do
not hide it from me. May God deal with you, be it
ever so severely,[p] if you hide from me anything he
told you.” 18So Samuel told him everything, hiding nothing from him. Then Eli said, “He is the
LORD; let him do what is good in his eyes.”[q]
19The LORD was with[r] Samuel as he grew[s] up,
and he let none[t] of his words fall to the ground.
20And all Israel from Dan to Beersheba[u] recognized
that Samuel was attested as a prophet of the LORD.
21The LORD continued to appear at Shiloh, and there
he revealed[v] himself to Samuel through his word.
4 And Samuel's word came to all Israel.

The Philistines Capture the Ark

Now the Israelites went out to fight against the
Philistines. The Israelites camped at Ebenezer,[w]
and the Philistines at Aphek.[x] 2The Philistines
deployed their forces to meet Israel, and as the
battle spread, Israel was defeated by the Philistines, who killed about four thousand of them on
the battlefield. 3When the soldiers returned to
camp, the elders of Israel asked, “Why[y] did the
LORD bring defeat upon us today before the Philistines? Let us bring the ark[z] of the LORD's covenant from Shiloh, so that it[a] may go with us and
save us from the hand of our enemies.”
4So the people sent men to Shiloh, and they
brought back the ark of the covenant of the LORD
Almighty, who is enthroned between the cherubim.[a] And Eli's two sons, Hophni and Phinehas,
were there with the ark of the covenant of God.
5When the ark of the LORD's covenant came into
the camp, all Israel raised such a great shout[b] that
the ground shook. 6Hearing the uproar, the Philistines asked, “What's all this shouting in the
Hebrew camp?”
When they learned that the ark of the LORD had
come into the camp, 7the Philistines were afraid.[c]
“A god has come into the camp,” they said. “We're
in trouble! Nothing like this has happened before.
8Woe to us! Who will deliver us from the hand of
these mighty gods? They are the gods who struck
the Egyptians with all kinds of plagues in the
desert. 9Be strong, Philistines! Be men, or you will
be subject to the Hebrews, as they[d] have been to
you. Be men, and fight!”
10So the Philistines fought, and the Israelites
were defeated[e] and every man fled to his tent. The
slaughter was very great; Israel lost thirty thousand foot soldiers. 11The ark of God was captured,
and Eli's two sons, Hophni and Phinehas, died.[f]

Death of Eli

12That same day a Benjamite ran from the battle
line and went to Shiloh, his clothes torn and dust[g]
on his head. 13When he arrived, there was Eli[h] sitting on his chair by the side of the road, watch-

[a] 3 Or *he*

3:17 [p]Ru 1:17; 2Sa 3:35
3:18 [q]Job 2:10; Isa 39:8
3:19 [r]Ge 21:22; 39:2 [s]1Sa 2:21 [t]1Sa 9:6
3:20 [u]Jdg 20:1
3:21 [v]ver 10
4:1 [w]1Sa 7:12 [x]Jos 12:18; 1Sa 29:1
4:3 [y]Jos 7:7 [z]Nu 10:35; Jos 6:7
4:4 [a]Ex 25:22; 2Sa 6:2
4:5 [b]Jos 6:5, 10
4:7 [c]Ex 15:14
4:9 [d]Jdg 13:1; 1Co 16:13
4:10 [e]ver 2; Dt 28:25; 2Sa 18:17; 2Ki 14:12
4:11 [f]1Sa 2:34; Ps 78:61, 64
4:12 [g]Jos 7:6; 2Sa 1:2; 15:32; Ne 9:1; Job 2:12
4:13 [h]ver 18; 1Sa 1:9

ing, because his heart feared for the ark of God.
When the man entered the town and told what
had happened, the whole town sent up a cry.
14Eli heard the outcry and asked, "What is the
meaning of this uproar?"
The man hurried over to Eli, 15who was ninety-
4:15 [i]1Sa 3:2 eight years old and whose eyes[i] were set so that
he could not see. 16He told Eli, "I have just come
from the battle line; I fled from it this very day."
Eli asked, "What happened, my son?"
17The man who brought the news replied, "Israel fled before the Philistines, and the army has
suffered heavy losses. Also your two sons, Hophni and Phinehas, are dead, and the ark of God has
been captured."
18When he mentioned the ark of God, Eli fell
backward off his chair by the side of the gate. His
neck was broken and he died, for he was an old
4:18 [j]ver 13 man and heavy. He had led[a][j] Israel forty years.
19His daughter-in-law, the wife of Phinehas,
was pregnant and near the time of delivery. When
she heard the news that the ark of God had been
captured and that her father-in-law and her husband were dead, she went into labor and gave
birth, but was overcome by her labor pains. 20As
she was dying, the women attending her said,
"Don't despair; you have given birth to a son." But
she did not respond or pay any attention.
4:21 [k]Ge 35:18 21She named the boy Ichabod,[b][k] saying, "The
[l]Ps 26:8; Jer 2:11 glory[l] has departed from Israel"—because of the
capture of the ark of God and the deaths of her
father-in-law and her husband. 22She said, "The
glory has departed from Israel, for the ark of God
has been captured."

The Ark in Ashdod and Ekron

5 After the Philistines had captured the ark of
5:1 [m]1Sa 4:1; 7:12 [n]Jos 13:3 God, they took it from Ebenezer[m] to Ashdod.[n]
2Then they carried the ark into Dagon's temple and
set it beside Dagon.[o] 3When the people of Ashdod
5:2 [o]Jdg 16:23 rose early the next day, there was Dagon, fallen[p] on
his face on the ground before the ark of the LORD!
5:3 [p]Isa 19:1; 46:7 They took Dagon and put him back in his place.
4But the following morning when they rose, there
was Dagon, fallen on his face on the ground before
5:4 [q]Eze 6:6; Mic 1:7 the ark of the LORD! His head and hands had been
broken[q] off and were lying on the threshold; only
his body remained. 5That is why to this day neither
the priests of Dagon nor any others who enter
5:5 [r]Zep 1:9 Dagon's temple at Ashdod step on the threshold.[r]
6The LORD's hand[s] was heavy upon the people
5:6 [s]ver 7; Ex 9:3; Ps 32:4; Ac 13:11 [t]ver 11; Ps 78:66 [u]Dt 28:27; 1Sa 6:5 of Ashdod and its vicinity; he brought devastation[t]
upon them and afflicted them with tumors.[c][u]
7When the men of Ashdod saw what was happening, they said, "The ark of the god of Israel
must not stay here with us, because his hand is
heavy upon us and upon Dagon our god." 8So

[a] 18 Traditionally *judged* [b] 21 *Ichabod* means *no glory.*
[c] 6 Hebrew; Septuagint and Vulgate *tumors. And rats appeared in their land, and death and destruction were throughout the city*

Not a Good Luck Charm

1SA 4:21–22

The ark of the covenant is the Israelites' most important sacred object. They believe that the ark is God's throne, the place that represents God's presence among them (see the note on Ex 37:1–9, page 147). But as years pass, the people become less interested in God and more interested in using the ark as a good luck charm. They begin to trust in the "power" of the ark itself rather than in the Power behind it. After the ark is taken away, the people are devastated. They feel that with the ark gone, God's glory and presence have also departed.

While few of us today place our faith in physical objects, we, too, can feel abandoned by God when a surge of tough situations washes over our lives. Like the Israelites, those moments challenge us to grow our roots deeper into the steady soil of God's unchanging character.

O eternal God, light surpassing all other light because all light comes forth from you! O fire surpassing every fire because you alone are the fire that burns without consuming! You consume whatever sin and selfishness you find in the soul. Yet your consuming does not distress the soul but fattens her with insatiable love, for though you satisfy her she is never sated but longs for you constantly. The more she possesses you the more she seeks you, and the more she seeks and desires you the more she finds and enjoys you.

—Catherine of Siena (1347–1380)

they called together all the rulers of the Philistines
and asked them, "What shall we do with the ark
of the god of Israel?"
They answered, "Have the ark of the god of 5:8
Israel moved to Gath.[v]" So they moved the ark of [v]ver 11
the God of Israel.
[9]But after they had moved it, the LORD's hand
was against that city, throwing it into a great pan- 5:9
ic.[w] He afflicted the people of the city, both young [w]ver 6,11;
and old, with an outbreak of tumors.[a] [10]So they Dt 2:15;
sent the ark of God to Ekron. 1Sa 7:13;
As the ark of God was entering Ekron, the peo- Ps 78:66
ple of Ekron cried out, "They have brought the ark
of the god of Israel around to us to kill us and our 5:11
people." [11]So they called together all the rulers[x] of [x]ver 6,8-9
the Philistines and said, "Send the ark of the god
of Israel away; let it go back to its own place, or it[b]
will kill us and our people." For death had filled
the city with panic; God's hand was very heavy
upon it. [12]Those who did not die were afflicted
with tumors, and the outcry of the city went up
to heaven.

The Ark Returned to Israel

6 When the ark of the LORD had been in Philistine territory seven months, [2]the Philistines
called for the priests and the diviners[y] and said, 6:2
"What shall we do with the ark of the LORD? Tell [y]Ge 41:8; Ex 7:11;
us how we should send it back to its place." Isa 2:6
[3]They answered, "If you return the ark of the 6:3
god of Israel, do not send it away empty,[z] but by [z]Ex 23:15;
all means send a guilt offering[a] to him. Then you Dt 16:16 [a]Lev 5:15
will be healed, and you will know why his hand[b] [b]ver 9
has not been lifted from you."
[4]The Philistines asked, "What guilt offering
should we send to him?"
They replied, "Five gold tumors and five gold 6:4
rats, according to the number[c] of the Philistine [c]ver 17-18;
rulers, because the same plague has struck both Jos 13:3;
you and your rulers. [5]Make models of the tumors[d] Jdg 3:3
and of the rats that are destroying the country, and 6:5
pay honor[e] to Israel's god. Perhaps he will lift his [d]1Sa 5:6-11
hand from you and your gods and your land. [e]Jos 7:19;
[6]Why do you harden[f] your hearts as the Egyptians Isa 42:12;
and Pharaoh did? When he[c] treated them harshly, Jn 9:24; Rev 14:7
did they[g] not send the Israelites out so they could
go on their way? 6:6
[7]"Now then, get a new cart[h] ready, with two [f]Ex 7:13; 8:15; 9:34;
cows that have calved and have never been 14:17
yoked.[i] Hitch the cows to the cart, but take their [g]Ex 12:31,33
calves away and pen them up. [8]Take the ark of the 6:7
LORD and put it on the cart, and in a chest beside [h]2Sa 6:3
it put the gold objects you are sending back to [i]Nu 19:2
him as a guilt offering. Send it on its way, [9]but
keep watching it. If it goes up to its own territory,
toward Beth Shemesh,[j] then the LORD has brought 6:9
this great disaster on us. But if it does not, then [j]ver 3; Jos 15:10; 21:16

[a] 9 Or *with tumors in the groin* (see Septuagint) [b] 11 Or *he*
[c] 6 That is, God

we will know that it was not his hand that struck
us and that it happened to us by chance."
[10]So they did this. They took two such cows and
hitched them to the cart and penned up their
calves. [11]They placed the ark of the LORD on the
cart and along with it the chest containing the
gold rats and the models of the tumors. [12]Then the
cows went straight up toward Beth Shemesh,
keeping on the road and lowing all the way; they
did not turn to the right or to the left. The rulers
of the Philistines followed them as far as the border of Beth Shemesh.
[13]Now the people of Beth Shemesh were harvesting their wheat in the valley, and when they
looked up and saw the ark, they rejoiced at the
sight. [14]The cart came to the field of Joshua of
Beth Shemesh, and there it stopped beside a large
rock. The people chopped up the wood of the cart
6:14 [k]2Sa 24:22; and sacrificed the cows as a burnt offering[k] to the
1Ki 19:21 LORD. [15]The Levites[l] took down the ark of the
LORD, together with the chest containing the gold
6:15 [l]Jos 3:3 objects, and placed them on the large rock. On
that day the people of Beth Shemesh offered burnt
offerings and made sacrifices to the LORD. [16]The
five rulers of the Philistines saw all this and then
returned that same day to Ekron.
[17]These are the gold tumors the Philistines sent
6:17 [m]ver 4 as a guilt offering to the LORD—one each[m] for Ashdod, Gaza, Ashkelon, Gath and Ekron. [18]And the
number of the gold rats was according to the
number of Philistine towns belonging to the five
rulers—the fortified towns with their country villages. The large rock, on which[a] they set the ark
of the LORD, is a witness to this day in the field of
Joshua of Beth Shemesh.
6:19 [19]But God struck down[n] some of the men of
[n]2Sa 6:7 [o]Ex 19:21; Beth Shemesh, putting seventy[b] of them to death
Nu 4:5,15, 20 because they had looked[o] into the ark of the LORD.
The people mourned because of the heavy blow
the LORD had dealt them, [20]and the men of Beth
6:20 [p]2Sa 6:9; Shemesh asked, "Who can stand[p] in the presence
Mal 3:2; of the LORD, this holy[q] God? To whom will the ark
Rev 6:17 [q]Lev 11:45 go up from here?"
[21]Then they sent messengers to the people of
6:21 Kiriath Jearim,[r] saying, "The Philistines have
[r]Jos 9:17; 15:9,60; returned the ark of the LORD. Come down and take
1Ch 13:5-6 **7** it up to your place." [1]So the men of Kiriath Jearim came and took up the ark of the LORD. They
7:1 took it to Abinadab's[s] house on the hill and conse-
[s]2Sa 6:3 crated Eleazar his son to guard the ark of the LORD.

Samuel Subdues the Philistines at Mizpah

[2]It was a long time, twenty years in all, that the
ark remained at Kiriath Jearim, and all the people
of Israel mourned and sought after the LORD. [3]And
Samuel said to the whole house of Israel, "If you

[a] *18* A few Hebrew manuscripts (see also Septuagint); most Hebrew manuscripts *villages as far as Greater Abel, where*
[b] *19* A few Hebrew manuscripts; most Hebrew manuscripts and Septuagint *50,070*

God's Secret Things

1SA 6:19–7:1

For many years the ark has been housed behind a veil, seen only by the high priest once a year. Now here it is, in front of common people! Yet, instead of treating the ark with the honor it deserves, these people gratify their curiosity, prying into the holy things of God. God has told his people not to touch, or even look on, the ark (Nu 4:15, 20). The people of Beth Shemesh disregard these commands, and 70 men perish. This may seem like a stiff penalty, but the ark represents the manifestation of God's holiness and presence among his people. By protecting the ark, God is protecting his honor and holiness.

Poured Out

1SA 7:6

The people are sorry. They "mourned and sought after the LORD" (1Sa 7:2). It may seem strange to us, but in Biblical times, custom encouraged vivid expressions of grief. In this passage, the people's mourning leads to acts of fasting, confession and the pouring out of water. These first two acts are somewhat familiar to us, but why pour out water? To the Israelites it symbolizes the pouring out of their hearts before God. It is a sign that they have come to the end of their own resources. Our displays of repentance may not be as animated, but when we, too, are willing to pour out everything to God—with no hope of collecting it back—God is faithful to answer (1Sa 7:9). And he usually answers in a greater way then we could ever imagine, as he did with the Israelites (1Sa 7:10–11).

are returning[t] to the LORD with all your hearts,
then rid[u] yourselves of the foreign gods and the
Ashtoreths[v] and commit[w] yourselves to the LORD
and serve him only,[x] and he will deliver you out
of the hand of the Philistines." 4So the Israelites
put away their Baals and Ashtoreths, and served
the LORD only.
5Then Samuel said, "Assemble all Israel at Mizpah[y] and I will intercede with the LORD for you."
6When they had assembled at Mizpah, they drew
water and poured[z] it out before the LORD. On that
day they fasted and there they confessed, "We
have sinned against the LORD." And Samuel was
leader[a a] of Israel at Mizpah.
7When the Philistines heard that Israel had
assembled at Mizpah, the rulers of the Philistines
came up to attack them. And when the Israelites
heard of it, they were afraid[b] because of the Philistines. 8They said to Samuel, "Do not stop crying[c] out to the LORD our God for us, that he may
rescue us from the hand of the Philistines." 9Then
Samuel[d] took a suckling lamb and offered it up as
a whole burnt offering to the LORD. He cried out to
the LORD on Israel's behalf, and the LORD
answered him.[e]
10While Samuel was sacrificing the burnt offering, the Philistines drew near to engage Israel in
battle. But that day the LORD thundered[f] with loud
thunder against the Philistines and threw them
into such a panic[g] that they were routed before the
Israelites. 11The men of Israel rushed out of Mizpah and pursued the Philistines, slaughtering
them along the way to a point below Beth Car.
12Then Samuel took a stone[h] and set it up
between Mizpah and Shen. He named it Ebenezer,[b] saying, "Thus far has the LORD helped us."
13So the Philistines were subdued[i] and did not
invade Israelite territory again.
Throughout Samuel's lifetime, the hand of the
LORD was against the Philistines. 14The towns
from Ekron to Gath that the Philistines had captured from Israel were restored to her, and Israel
delivered the neighboring territory from the power of the Philistines. And there was peace between
Israel and the Amorites.
15Samuel[j] continued as judge over Israel all the
days of his life. 16From year to year he went on a
circuit from Bethel to Gilgal to Mizpah, judging
Israel in all those places. 17But he always went
back to Ramah,[k] where his home was, and there
he also judged Israel. And he built an altar[l] there
to the LORD.

Israel Asks for a King

8 When Samuel grew old, he appointed[m] his
sons as judges for Israel. 2The name of his
firstborn was Joel and the name of his second was
Abijah, and they served at Beersheba.[n] 3But his
sons did not walk in his ways. They turned aside

7:3 [t]Dt 30:10; Isa 55:7; Hos 6:1 [u]Ge 35:2; Jos 24:14 [v]Jdg 2:12-13; 1Sa 31:10 [w]Joel 2:12 [x]Dt 6:13; Mt 4:10; Lk 4:8
7:5 [y]Jdg 20:1
7:6 [z]Ps 62:8; La 2:19 [a]Jdg 10:10; Ne 9:1; Ps 106:6
7:7 [b]1Sa 17:11
7:8 [c]1Sa 12:19, 23; Isa 37:4; Jer 15:1
7:9 [d]Ps 99:6 [e]Jer 15:1
7:10 [f]1Sa 2:10; 2Sa 22:14-15 [g]Jos 10:10
7:12 [h]Ge 35:14; Jos 4:9
7:13 [i]Jdg 13:1,5; 1Sa 13:5
7:15 [j]ver 6; 1Sa 12:11
7:17 [k]1Sa 1:19; 8:4 [l]Jdg 21:4
8:1 [m]Dt 16:18-19
8:2 [n]Ge 22:19; 1Ki 19:3; Am 5:4-5

[a] 6 Traditionally *judge* [b] 12 *Ebenezer* means *stone of help.*

after dishonest gain and accepted bribes[o] and perverted justice.
4So all the elders of Israel gathered together and
came to Samuel at Ramah.[p] 5They said to him,
"You are old, and your sons do not walk in your
ways; now appoint a king[q] to lead[a] us, such as all
the other nations have."
6But when they said, "Give us a king to lead
us," this displeased[r] Samuel; so he prayed to the
LORD. 7And the LORD told him: "Listen to all that
the people are saying to you; it is not you they
have rejected, but they have rejected me as their
king.[s] 8As they have done from the day I brought
them up out of Egypt until this day, forsaking me
and serving other gods, so they are doing to you.
9Now listen to them; but warn them solemnly and
let them know[t] what the king who will reign over
them will do."
10Samuel told all the words of the LORD to the
people who were asking him for a king. 11He said,
"This is what the king who will reign over you
will do: He will take[u] your sons and make them
serve with his chariots and horses, and they will
run in front of his chariots.[v] 12Some he will assign
to be commanders[w] of thousands and commanders of fifties, and others to plow his ground and
reap his harvest, and still others to make weapons
of war and equipment for his chariots. 13He will
take your daughters to be perfumers and cooks
and bakers. 14He will take the best of your[x] fields
and vineyards[y] and olive groves and give them to
his attendants. 15He will take a tenth of your grain
and of your vintage and give it to his officials and
attendants. 16Your menservants and maidservants
and the best of your cattle[b] and donkeys he will
take for his own use. 17He will take a tenth of your
flocks, and you yourselves will become his slaves.
18When that day comes, you will cry out for relief
from the king you have chosen, and the LORD will
not answer[z] you in that day."
19But the people refused[a] to listen to Samuel.
"No!" they said. "We want a king over us. 20Then
we will be like all the other nations,[b] with a king
to lead us and to go out before us and fight our
battles."
21When Samuel heard all that the people said,
he repeated[c] it before the LORD. 22The LORD answered, "Listen[d] to them and give them a king."
Then Samuel said to the men of Israel, "Everyone go back to his town."

Samuel Anoints Saul

9 There was a Benjamite, a man of standing,
whose name was Kish[e] son of Abiel, the son of
Zeror, the son of Becorath, the son of Aphiah of
Benjamin. 2He had a son named Saul, an impressive young man without equal[f] among the Israelites—a head taller[g] than any of the others.

8:3 [o]Ex 23:8; Dt 16:19; Ps 15:5
8:4 [p]1Sa 7:17
8:5 [q]Dt 17:14-20
8:6 [r]1Sa 15:11
8:7 [s]Ex 16:8; 1Sa 10:19
8:9 [t]ver 11-18; 1Sa 10:25
8:11 [u]1Sa 10:25; 14:52 [v]Dt 17:16; 2Sa 15:1
8:12 [w]1Sa 22:7
8:14 [x]Eze 46:18 [y]1Ki 21:7,15
8:18 [z]Pr 1:28; Isa 1:15; Mic 3:4
8:19 [a]Isa 66:4; Jer 44:16
8:20 [b]ver 5
8:21 [c]Jdg 11:11
8:22 [d]ver 7
9:1 [e]1Sa 14:51; 1Ch 8:33; 9:39
9:2 [f]1Sa 10:24 [g]1Sa 10:23

[a] 5 Traditionally *judge*; also in verses 6 and 20
[b] 16 Septuagint; Hebrew *young men*

Behold, Our King

1SA 8:10-18

The old saying goes, "Be careful what you ask for; you just might get it." The people ask for a king, and they get one—but not before being warned exactly what a king will require of them. Samuel tries to dissuade them (1Sa 8:10-11). He knows that once the kind of king they are asking for gains power, he might not rely on the Lord or take responsibility for his own actions. And why should he? He is the king! Still the people want to be like the pagan nations around them. Instead of being special, *they wanted to be* similar. *So the Israelites enslave themselves to a king, who will exact heavy taxes and require the services of their children—a king who might be unresponsive to God—instead of devoting themselves to the King, who cares intimately for them.*

Hebrew Gift-Giving

1SA 9:8

This is one of the few places in the Bible where a fraction of a shekel is mentioned. Here it is one-quarter of a shekel. These pieces are probably fragments of gold or silver bars rather than shaped coins. Saul and his servant need assistance, and they don't want to go before the man of God empty-handed. They have no food or gifts to offer, but at least they can offer some token of respect, even if it is very small. Their gift is not a required payment for services but rather a way to show respect. It is common practice to give gifts to men of God in exchange for their help (1Ki 13:7; 14:3; 2Ki 5:5). *It seems the amount of the gift did not matter so much as simply having something to give.*

[3]Now the donkeys belonging to Saul's father
Kish were lost, and Kish said to his son Saul, "Take
one of the servants with you and go and look for
the donkeys." [4]So he passed through the hill[h]
country of Ephraim and through the area around
Shalisha,[i] but they did not find them. They went
on into the district of Shaalim, but the donkeys
were not there. Then he passed through the territory of Benjamin, but they did not find them.
[5]When they reached the district of Zuph,[j] Saul
said to the servant who was with him, "Come,
let's go back, or my father will stop thinking
about the donkeys and start worrying[k] about us."
[6]But the servant replied, "Look, in this town
there is a man of God;[l] he is highly respected, and
everything[m] he says comes true. Let's go there
now. Perhaps he will tell us what way to take."
[7]Saul said to his servant, "If we go, what can
we give the man? The food in our sacks is gone.
We have no gift[n] to take to the man of God. What
do we have?"
[8]The servant answered him again. "Look," he
said, "I have a quarter of a shekel[a] of silver. I will
give it to the man of God so that he will tell us
what way to take." [9](Formerly in Israel, if a man
went to inquire of God, he would say, "Come, let
us go to the seer," because the prophet of today
used to be called a seer.)[o]
[10]"Good," Saul said to his servant. "Come, let's
go." So they set out for the town where the man of
God was.
[11]As they were going up the hill to the town,
they met some girls coming out to draw[p] water,
and they asked them, "Is the seer here?"
[12]"He is," they answered. "He's ahead of you.
Hurry now; he has just come to our town today,
for the people have a sacrifice[q] at the high place.[r]
[13]As soon as you enter the town, you will find him
before he goes up to the high place to eat. The
people will not begin eating until he comes,
because he must bless the sacrifice; afterward,
those who are invited will eat. Go up now; you
should find him about this time."
[14]They went up to the town, and as they were
entering it, there was Samuel, coming toward
them on his way up to the high place.
[15]Now the day before Saul came, the LORD had
revealed this to Samuel: [16]"About this time tomorrow I will send you a man from the land of Benjamin. Anoint[s] him leader over my people Israel;
he will deliver[t] my people from the hand of the
Philistines. I have looked upon my people, for
their cry has reached me."
[17]When Samuel caught sight of Saul, the LORD
said to him, "This[u] is the man I spoke to you
about; he will govern my people."
[18]Saul approached Samuel in the gateway and
asked, "Would you please tell me where the seer's
house is?"

9:4 [h]Jos 24:33 [i]2Ki 4:42
9:5 [j]1Sa 1:1 [k]1Sa 10:2
9:6 [l]Dt 33:1; 1Ki 13:1 [m]1Sa 3:19
9:7 [n]1Ki 14:3; 2Ki 5:5,15; 8:8
9:9 [o]2Sa 24:11; 2Ki 17:13; 1Ch 9:22; 26:28; 29:29; Isa 30:10; Am 7:12
9:11 [p]Ge 24:11,13
9:12 [q]Nu 28:11-15; 1Sa 7:17 [r]Ge 31:54; 1Sa 10:5; 1Ki 3:2
9:16 [s]1Sa 10:1 [t]Ex 3:7-9
9:17 [u]1Sa 16:12

[a] *8* That is, about 1/10 ounce (about 3 grams)

19"I am the seer," Samuel replied. "Go up ahead
of me to the high place, for today you are to eat
with me, and in the morning I will let you go and
9:20 will tell you all that is in your heart. 20As for the
[v]ver 3 donkeys[v] you lost three days ago, do not worry
[w]1Sa 8:5; about them; they have been found. And to whom
12:13 is all the desire[w] of Israel turned, if not to you and
all your father's family?"
9:21 21Saul answered, "But am I not a Benjamite,
[x]1Sa 15:17 from the smallest tribe[x] of Israel, and is not my
[y]Jdg 20:35, clan the least of all the clans of the tribe of Benja-
46 min?[y] Why do you say such a thing to me?"
22Then Samuel brought Saul and his servant
into the hall and seated them at the head of those
who were invited—about thirty in number. 23Sam-
uel said to the cook, "Bring the piece of meat I
gave you, the one I told you to lay aside."
9:24 24So the cook took up the leg[z] with what was
[z]Lev 7:32-34; on it and set it in front of Saul. Samuel said, "Here
Nu 18:18 is what has been kept for you. Eat, because it was
set aside for you for this occasion, from the time I
said, 'I have invited guests.' " And Saul dined with
Samuel that day.
25After they came down from the high place to
9:25 the town, Samuel talked with Saul on the roof[a] of
[a]Dt 22:8; Ac 10:9 his house. 26They rose about daybreak and Samuel called to Saul on the roof, "Get ready, and I will
send you on your way." When Saul got ready, he
and Samuel went outside together. 27As they were
going down to the edge of the town, Samuel said
to Saul, "Tell the servant to go on ahead of us"—
and the servant did so—"but you stay here awhile,
so that I may give you a message from God."
10:1 [b]1Sa 16:13; **10** Then Samuel took a flask[b] of oil and poured
2Ki 9:1,3,6 it on Saul's head and kissed him, saying,
[c]Ps 2:12 [d]Dt 32:9; "Has not the LORD anointed[c] you leader over his
Ps 78:62,71 inheritance?[a d] 2When you leave me today, you
10:2 will meet two men near Rachel's tomb,[e] at Zelzah
[e]Ge 35:20 on the border of Benjamin. They will say to you,
[f]1Sa 9:4 'The donkeys[f] you set out to look for have been
[g]1Sa 9:5 found. And now your father has stopped thinking
about them and is worried[g] about you. He is asking, "What shall I do about my son?" '
3"Then you will go on from there until you
reach the great tree of Tabor. Three men going up
10:3 [h]Ge 28:22; to God at Bethel[h] will meet you there. One will be
35:7-8 carrying three young goats, another three loaves
of bread, and another a skin of wine. 4They will
greet you and offer you two loaves of bread,
10:5 which you will accept from them.
[i]1Sa 13:3 [j]1Sa 9:12 5"After that you will go to Gibeah of God, where
[k]2Ki 3:15 there is a Philistine outpost.[i] As you approach the
[l]1Sa 19:20; 1Co 14:1 town, you will meet a procession of prophets coming down from the high place[j] with lyres, tam-
10:6 [m]ver 10; bourines, flutes and harps[k] being played before
Nu 11:25; 1Sa 19:23-24 them, and they will be prophesying.[l] 6The Spirit[m]

[a] *1* Hebrew; Septuagint and Vulgate *over his people Israel? You will reign over the LORD's people and save them from the power of their enemies round about. And this will be a sign to you that the LORD has anointed you leader over his inheritance:*

Who Am I?

1SA 9:21

In one sentence Samuel prophetically identifies the future king (1Sa 9:20). Saul must have tried to hide his amusement. He asks, "Don't you know where I come from? Why would you say such a thing?" Sure, this young man is impressive in stature, but aside from that, he is an ordinary man, doing ordinary work. He is from the smallest of the tribes and clans, and at this moment is tired and filthy after searching for lost donkeys! Yet despite Saul's doubts, God knows him and has a plan for him.

Do you ever say the same thing? "Don't you know where I come from, God? Don't you know what I am? Who am I to do your work?" Remember Saul and remember Jeremiah 29:11: "'For I know the plans I have for you,' declares the LORD, 'plans to prosper you and not to harm you, plans to give you hope and a future.'"

God Is With You

1SA 10:7

Samuel tells Saul, "Do whatever your hand finds to do, for God is with you." Whatever does that mean? Can we take it literally? The answer lies in the second part of the statement: ". . . for God is with you." Moses spoke these same words to Israel as the people prepared to enter the promised land (Dt 20:1). An angel spoke these words to Gideon as he fretted about facing the Midianites (Jdg 6:12). Now Samuel speaks these words to Saul.

When God is with us, powerful things happen. When God is with us and we are attuned to him, we *can* do whatever our "hand finds to do," because it will be God working through us, directing us, fulfilling his purposes through us.

of the LORD will come upon you in power, and you
will prophesy with them; and you will be changed
into a different person. 7Once these signs are fulfilled, do whatever[n] your hand finds to do, for God
is with[o] you.
8"Go down ahead of me to Gilgal.[p] I will surely
come down to you to sacrifice burnt offerings and
fellowship offerings,[a] but you must wait seven
days until I come to you and tell you what you are
to do."

Saul Made King

9As Saul turned to leave Samuel, God changed[q]
Saul's heart, and all these signs were fulfilled that
day. 10When they arrived at Gibeah, a procession
of prophets met him; the Spirit of God came upon
him in power, and he joined in their prophesying.[r]
11When all those who had formerly known him
saw him prophesying with the prophets, they asked
each other, "What is this[s] that has happened to the
son of Kish? Is Saul also among the prophets?"[t]
12A man who lived there answered, "And who is
their father?" So it became a saying: "Is Saul also
among the prophets?" 13After Saul stopped prophesying, he went to the high place.
14Now Saul's uncle[u] asked him and his servant,
"Where have you been?"

"Looking for the donkeys," he said. "But when
we saw they were not to be found, we went to
Samuel."
15Saul's uncle said, "Tell me what Samuel said
to you."
16Saul replied, "He assured us that the donkeys[v]
had been found." But he did not tell his uncle
what Samuel had said about the kingship.
17Samuel summoned the people of Israel to the
LORD at Mizpah[w] 18and said to them, "This is what
the LORD, the God of Israel, says: 'I brought Israel
up out of Egypt, and I delivered you from the
power of Egypt and all the kingdoms that
oppressed[x] you.' 19But you have now rejected your
God, who saves you out of all your calamities and
distresses. And you have said, 'No, set a king[y]
over us.' So now present[z] yourselves before the
LORD by your tribes and clans."
20When Samuel brought all the tribes of Israel
near, the tribe of Benjamin was chosen. 21Then he
brought forward the tribe of Benjamin, clan by
clan, and Matri's clan was chosen. Finally Saul
son of Kish was chosen. But when they looked for
him, he was not to be found. 22So they inquired[a]
further of the LORD, "Has the man come here yet?"

And the LORD said, "Yes, he has hidden himself
among the baggage."
23They ran and brought him out, and as he
stood among the people he was a head taller[b] than
any of the others. 24Samuel said to all the people,
"Do you see the man the LORD has chosen?[c] There
is no one like him among all the people."

10:7 [n]Ecc 9:10 [o]Jos 1:5; Jdg 6:12; Heb 13:5
10:8 [p]1Sa 11:14-15
10:9 [q]ver 6
10:10 [r]ver 5-6; 1Sa 19:20
10:11 [s]Mt 13:54; Jn 7:15 [t]1Sa 19:24
10:14 [u]1Sa 14:50
10:16 [v]1Sa 9:20
10:17 [w]Jdg 20:1; 1Sa 7:5
10:18 [x]Jdg 6:8-9
10:19 [y]1Sa 8:5-7; 12:12 [z]Jos 7:14; 24:1
10:22 [a]1Sa 23:2,4, 9-11
10:23 [b]1Sa 9:2
10:24 [c]Dt 17:15; 2Sa 21:6

[a] 8 Traditionally *peace offerings*

10:24 [d]1Ki 1:25, 34,39 Then the people shouted, "Long live[d] the king!"
[25]Samuel explained to the people the regula-
tions[e] of the kingship. He wrote them down on a
10:25 [e]Dt 17:14-20; 1Sa 8:11-18 scroll and deposited it before the LORD. Then Samuel dismissed the people, each to his own home.
[26]Saul also went to his home in Gibeah,[f] accom-
10:26 [f]1Sa 11:4 panied by valiant men whose hearts God had
10:27 [g]Dt 13:13 [h]1Ki 10:25; 2Ch 17:5 touched. [27]But some troublemakers[g] said, "How
can this fellow save us?" They despised him and
brought him no gifts.[h] But Saul kept silent.

Saul Rescues the City of Jabesh

11:1 [i]1Sa 12:12 [j]Jdg 21:8 [k]1Ki 20:34; Eze 17:13 11 Nahash[i] the Ammonite went up and
besieged Jabesh Gilead.[j] And all the men of
Jabesh said to him, "Make a treaty[k] with us, and
we will be subject to you."
[2]But Nahash the Ammonite replied, "I will
make a treaty with you only on the condition that
11:2 [l]Nu 16:14 [m]1Sa 17:26 I gouge[l] out the right eye of every one of you and
so bring disgrace[m] on all Israel."
[3]The elders of Jabesh said to him, "Give us sev-
en days so we can send messengers throughout
Israel; if no one comes to rescue us, we will surrender to you."
11:4 [n]1Sa 10:5, 26; 15:34 [o]Jdg 2:4; 1Sa 30:4 [4]When the messengers came to Gibeah[n] of Saul
and reported these terms to the people, they all
wept[o] aloud. [5]Just then Saul was returning from
the fields, behind his oxen, and he asked, "What
is wrong with the people? Why are they weeping?" Then they repeated to him what the men of
Jabesh had said.
11:6 [p]Jdg 3:10; 6:34; 13:25; 14:6; 1Sa 10:10; 16:13 [6]When Saul heard their words, the Spirit[p] of
God came upon him in power, and he burned
with anger. [7]He took a pair of oxen, cut them into
pieces, and sent the pieces by messengers
throughout Israel,[q] proclaiming, "This is what
11:7 [q]Jdg 19:29 [r]Jdg 21:5 will be done to the oxen of anyone[r] who does not
follow Saul and Samuel." Then the terror of the
LORD fell on the people, and they turned out as
11:8 [s]Jdg 20:2 [t]Jdg 1:4 one man. [8]When Saul mustered[s] them at Bezek,[t]
the men of Israel numbered three hundred thou-
sand and the men of Judah thirty thousand.
[9]They told the messengers who had come, "Say
to the men of Jabesh Gilead, 'By the time the sun is
hot tomorrow, you will be delivered.' " When the
messengers went and reported this to the men of
11:10 [u]ver 3 Jabesh, they were elated. [10]They said to the
Ammonites, "Tomorrow we will surrender[u] to you,
and you can do to us whatever seems good to you."
11:11 [v]Jdg 7:16 [11]The next day Saul separated his men into
three divisions;[v] during the last watch of the night
they broke into the camp of the Ammonites and
slaughtered them until the heat of the day. Those
who survived were scattered, so that no two of
them were left together.

Saul Confirmed as King

11:12 [w]1Sa 10:27; Lk 19:27 [12]The people then said to Samuel, "Who[w] was it
that asked, 'Shall Saul reign over us?' Bring these
men to us and we will put them to death."

Filled for Service

1SA 11:6

Saul is a reluctant leader. He questions Samuel's prophecy (1Sa 9:21); he doesn't tell his uncle about the kingship (1Sa 10:16); and he hides when the people want to acknowledge him as their king (1Sa 10:21–22). Yet the Spirit of God transforms him. First Samuel 11:6 literally reads, "the Spirit of God energized *Saul" (emphasis added). In the Old Testament, the presence or absence of the Spirit had nothing to do with salvation. Rather, the Holy Spirit often came on an individual in order to give that person power for a particular task (Jdg 3:10; 6:34). For Saul, the Spirit comes with a righteous anger and gives him the power to be a dynamic leader. But in the same way that the Spirit is given, it is also removed when Saul acts arrogantly and independently of the Lord (1Sa 16:14).*

In the Name of Progress

1SA 12:1–5

Samuel has been in service to Israel for many years. He stoops slightly after years of carrying the weight of government on his shoulders. He's seen many things. He's experienced God in many ways. Now it's time for him to step down. A handsome, strong king replaces an old, gray prophet. With this, a new civil government replaces a divine administration. The people rejoice, but Samuel's heart is broken. Like a magnificent oak cut down, this ancient strength is dismissed in the name of progress. The prophet, who spoke for God on many occasions, now reveals his own heart. "What have I done against you? What have I done to deserve this?" he asks. The people confirm his innocence, yet their desires do not waver. At this moment, a king who will require everything (1Sa 8:11) replaces a prophet who asked for nothing.

13 But Saul said, "No one shall be put to death
today,[x] for this day the LORD has rescued[y] Israel."
14 Then Samuel said to the people, "Come, let us
go to Gilgal[z] and there reaffirm the kingship.[a]" 15 So
all the people went to Gilgal[b] and confirmed Saul
as king in the presence of the LORD. There they sacrificed fellowship offerings[a] before the LORD, and
Saul and all the Israelites held a great celebration.

Samuel's Farewell Speech

12 Samuel said to all Israel, "I have listened[c]
to everything you said to me and have set a
king[d] over you. 2 Now you have a king as your
leader.[e] As for me, I am old and gray, and my sons
are here with you. I have been your leader from
my youth until this day. 3 Here I stand. Testify
against me in the presence of the LORD and his
anointed.[f] Whose ox have I taken? Whose donkey[g] have I taken? Whom have I cheated? Whom
have I oppressed? From whose hand have I
accepted a bribe[h] to make me shut my eyes? If I
have done[i] any of these, I will make it right."
4 "You have not cheated or oppressed us," they
replied. "You have not taken anything from anyone's hand."
5 Samuel said to them, "The LORD is witness
against you, and also his anointed is witness this
day, that you have not found anything[j] in my
hand.[k]"
"He is witness," they said.
6 Then Samuel said to the people, "It is the LORD
who appointed Moses and Aaron and brought[l]
your forefathers up out of Egypt. 7 Now then, stand
here, because I am going to confront[m] you with evidence before the LORD as to all the righteous acts
performed by the LORD for you and your fathers.
8 "After Jacob entered Egypt, they cried[n] to the
LORD for help, and the LORD sent[o] Moses and Aaron, who brought your forefathers out of Egypt and
settled them in this place.
9 "But they forgot[p] the LORD their God; so he sold
them into the hand of Sisera,[q] the commander of
the army of Hazor, and into the hands of the Philistines[r] and the king of Moab,[s] who fought
against them. 10 They cried out to the LORD and
said, 'We have sinned; we have forsaken[t] the LORD
and served the Baals and the Ashtoreths.[u] But
now deliver us from the hands of our enemies,
and we will serve you.' 11 Then the LORD sent
Jerub-Baal,[b][v] Barak,[c][w] Jephthah[x] and Samuel,[d]
and he delivered you from the hands of your enemies on every side, so that you lived securely.
12 "But when you saw that Nahash[y] king[z] of the
Ammonites was moving against you, you said to
me, 'No, we want a king to rule[a] over us'—even
though the LORD your God was your king. 13 Now
here is the king[b] you have chosen, the one you

11:13 [x]2Sa 19:22 [y]Ex 14:13; 1Sa 19:5
11:14 [z]1Sa 10:8 [a]1Sa 10:25
11:15 [b]1Sa 10:8,17
12:1 [c]1Sa 8:7 [d]1Sa 10:24; 11:15
12:2 [e]1Sa 8:5
12:3 [f]1Sa 10:1; 24:6; 2Sa 1:14 [g]Nu 16:15 [h]Dt 16:19 [i]Ac 20:33
12:5 [j]Ac 23:9; 24:20 [k]Ex 22:4
12:6 [l]Ex 6:26; Mic 6:4
12:7 [m]Isa 1:18; Mic 6:1-5
12:8 [n]Ex 2:23 [o]Ex 3:10; 4:16
12:9 [p]Jdg 3:7 [q]Jdg 4:2 [r]Jdg 10:7; 13:1 [s]Jdg 3:12
12:10 [t]Jdg 10:10,15 [u]Jdg 2:13
12:11 [v]Jdg 6:14,32 [w]Jdg 4:6 [x]Jdg 11:1
12:12 [y]1Sa 11:1 [z]1Sa 8:5 [a]Jdg 8:23; 1Sa 8:6,19
12:13 [b]1Sa 8:5; Hos 13:11

[a] *15* Traditionally *peace offerings* [b] *11* Also called *Gideon*
[c] *11* Some Septuagint manuscripts and Syriac; Hebrew *Bedan*
[d] *11* Hebrew; some Septuagint manuscripts and Syriac *Samson*

asked[c] for; see, the LORD has set a king over you. 14 If you fear[d] the LORD and serve and obey him and do not rebel against his commands, and if both you and the king who reigns over you follow the LORD your God—good! 15 But if you do not obey the LORD, and if you rebel against[e] his commands, his hand will be against you, as it was against your fathers.

16 "Now then, stand still and see[f] this great thing the LORD is about to do before your eyes! 17 Is it not wheat harvest[g] now? I will call[h] upon the LORD to send thunder and rain.[i] And you will realize what an evil[j] thing you did in the eyes of the LORD when you asked for a king."

18 Then Samuel called upon the LORD, and that same day the LORD sent thunder and rain. So all the people stood in awe[k] of the LORD and of Samuel.

19 The people all said to Samuel, "Pray[l] to the LORD your God for your servants so that we will not die, for we have added to all our other sins the evil of asking for a king."

20 "Do not be afraid," Samuel replied. "You have done all this evil; yet do not turn away from the LORD, but serve the LORD with all your heart. 21 Do not turn away after useless[m] idols.[n] They can do you no good, nor can they rescue you, because they are useless. 22 For the sake[o] of his great name[p] the LORD will not reject[q] his people, because the LORD was pleased to make[r] you his own. 23 As for me, far be it from me that I should sin against the LORD by failing to pray[s] for you. And I will teach[t] you the way that is good and right. 24 But be sure to fear[u] the LORD and serve him faithfully with all your heart; consider[v] what great[w] things he has done for you. 25 Yet if you persist[x] in doing evil, both you and your king will be swept[y] away."

Samuel Rebukes Saul

13 Saul was ⌞thirty⌟[a] years old when he became king, and he reigned over Israel ⌞forty-⌟[b] two years.

2 Saul[c] chose three thousand men from Israel; two thousand were with him at Micmash and in the hill country of Bethel, and a thousand were with Jonathan at Gibeah[z] in Benjamin. The rest of the men he sent back to their homes.

3 Jonathan attacked the Philistine outpost[a] at Geba, and the Philistines heard about it. Then Saul had the trumpet blown throughout the land and said, "Let the Hebrews hear!" 4 So all Israel heard the news: "Saul has attacked the Philistine outpost, and now Israel has become a stench[b] to the Philistines." And the people were summoned to join Saul at Gilgal.

5 The Philistines assembled to fight Israel, with

[a] *1* A few late manuscripts of the Septuagint; Hebrew does not have *thirty.* [b] *1* See the round number in Acts 13:21; Hebrew does not have *forty-.* [c] *1,2* Or *and when he had reigned over Israel two years, ²he*

12:13 [c]1Sa 10:24
12:14 [d]Jos 24:14
12:15 [e]ver 9; Jos 24:20; Isa 1:20
12:16 [f]Ex 14:13
12:17 [g]1Sa 7:9-10 [h]Jas 5:18 [i]Pr 26:1 [j]1Sa 8:6-7
12:18 [k]Ex 14:31
12:19 [l]ver 23; Ex 9:28; Jas 5:18; 1Jn 5:16
12:21 [m]Isa 41:24, 29; Jer 16:19; Hab 2:18 [n]Dt 11:16
12:22 [o]Ps 106:8 [p]Jos 7:9 [q]1Ki 6:13 [r]Dt 7:7; 1Pe 2:9
12:23 [s]Ro 1:9-10; Col 1:9; 2Ti 1:3 [t]1Ki 8:36; Ps 34:11; Pr 4:11
12:24 [u]Ecc 12:13 [v]Isa 5:12 [w]Dt 10:21
12:25 [x]1Sa 31:1-5 [y]Jos 24:20
13:2 [z]1Sa 10:26
13:3 [a]1Sa 10:5
13:4 [b]Ge 34:30

Stand Still and See!

1SA 12:16

"What does it take to get your attention?" Samuel seems to be asking. Enough with the loving reprimands. Israel needs a reminder that it has rejected God's as their king (1Sa 12:12). "Stand still and see this great thing the LORD is about to do before your eyes!" Samuel says. He then asks for thunder and rain. The Lord provides both so forcefully that the people think they're about to die (1Sa 12:19). Many today would call a storm like that a "freak of nature," revealing how easily we cast off God's mastery as "random chance." Samuel wants the people to be aware. By asking them to "stand still and see," he urges them to actively look for a display of God's power.

Power Behind the Iron

1SA 13:19

"Not a blacksmith could be found in the whole land of Israel." This isn't for lack of know-how, since the first smith, Tubal-Cain, is mentioned way back in Genesis. He worked with bronze and iron (Ge 4:22). It isn't for lack of resources either, since Israel is a "a land where the rocks are iron" (Dt 8:9). The lack of blacksmiths is due to the Philistines' control. They close the blacksmith shops and exile the smiths into their own country. They prohibit, by severe penalties, any Israelite from practicing the trade. Not only does this keep the Israelites from making weapons (1Sa 13:22), but it also allows the Philistines to grow rich off payment for blacksmith work that needs to be done (1Sa 13:20-21). Yet this did not always assure victory (1Sa 14:13-14). The Philistines forget one thing—which nation has God on its side.

three thousand[a] chariots, six thousand charioteers, and soldiers as numerous as the sand[c] on
the seashore. They went up and camped at Micmash, east of Beth Aven. 6 When the men of Israel saw that their situation was critical and that
their army was hard pressed, they hid in caves
and thickets, among the rocks, and in pits and cisterns.[d] 7 Some Hebrews even crossed the Jordan to
the land of Gad[e] and Gilead.
Saul remained at Gilgal, and all the troops with
him were quaking with fear. 8 He waited seven[f]
days, the time set by Samuel; but Samuel did not
come to Gilgal, and Saul's men began to scatter. 9 So
he said, "Bring me the burnt offering and the fellowship offerings.[b]" And Saul offered[g] up the burnt
offering. 10 Just as he finished making the offering,
Samuel[h] arrived, and Saul went out to greet him.
11 "What have you done?" asked Samuel.
Saul replied, "When I saw that the men were
scattering, and that you did not come at the set
time, and that the Philistines were assembling at
Micmash,[i] 12 I thought, 'Now the Philistines will
come down against me at Gilgal, and I have not
sought the LORD's favor.[j]' So I felt compelled to
offer the burnt offering."
13 "You acted foolishly,[k]" Samuel said. "You have
not kept[l] the command the LORD your God gave
you; if you had, he would have established your
kingdom over Israel for all time. 14 But now your
kingdom[m] will not endure; the LORD has sought
out a man after his own heart[n] and appointed[o]
him leader of his people, because you have not
kept the LORD's command."
15 Then Samuel left Gilgal[c] and went up to Gibeah[p] in Benjamin, and Saul counted the men who
were with him. They numbered about six hundred.

Israel Without Weapons

16 Saul and his son Jonathan and the men with
them were staying in Gibeah[d] in Benjamin, while
the Philistines camped at Micmash. 17 Raiding[q]
parties went out from the Philistine camp in three
detachments. One turned toward Ophrah[r] in the
vicinity of Shual, 18 another toward Beth Horon,[s]
and the third toward the borderland overlooking
the Valley of Zeboim[t] facing the desert.
19 Not a blacksmith[u] could be found in the
whole land of Israel, because the Philistines had
said, "Otherwise the Hebrews will make swords
or spears!" 20 So all Israel went down to the Philistines to have their plowshares, mattocks, axes and
sickles[e] sharpened. 21 The price was two thirds of a
shekel[f] for sharpening plowshares and mattocks,

13:5 [c] Jos 11:4
13:6 [d] Jdg 6:2
13:7 [e] Nu 32:33
13:8 [f] 1Sa 10:8
13:9 [g] 2Sa 24:25; 1Ki 3:4
13:10 [h] 1Sa 15:13
13:11 [i] ver 2,5,16, 23
13:12 [j] Jer 26:19
13:13 [k] 2Ch 16:9 [l] 1Sa 15:23, 24
13:14 [m] 1Sa 15:28 [n] Ac 7:46; 13:22 [o] 2Sa 6:21
13:15 [p] 1Sa 14:2
13:17 [q] 1Sa 14:15 [r] Jos 18:23
13:18 [s] Jos 18:13-14 [t] Ne 11:34
13:19 [u] 2Ki 24:14; Jer 24:1

[a] *5* Some Septuagint manuscripts and Syriac; Hebrew *thirty thousand* [b] *9* Traditionally *peace offerings* [c] *15* Hebrew; Septuagint *Gilgal and went his way; the rest of the people went after Saul to meet the army, and they went out of Gilgal* [d] *16* Two Hebrew manuscripts; most Hebrew manuscripts *Geba,* a variant of *Gibeah* [e] *20* Septuagint; Hebrew *plowshares* [f] *21* Hebrew *pim*; that is, about 1/4 ounce (about 8 grams)

and a third of a shekel[a] for sharpening forks and
axes and for repointing goads.
22So on the day of the battle not a soldier with
13:22 v1Ch 9:39 Saul and Jonathan[v] had a sword or spear[w] in his
wJdg 5:8 hand; only Saul and his son Jonathan had them.

Jonathan Attacks the Philistines

23Now a detachment of Philistines had gone out
13:23 **14** to the pass[x] at Micmash. 1One day Jonathan
x1Sa 14:4 son of Saul said to the young man bearing
his armor, "Come, let's go over to the Philistine
outpost on the other side." But he did not tell his
father.
2Saul was staying on the outskirts of Gibeah[y]
14:2 y1Sa 13:15 under a pomegranate tree in Migron.[z] With him
zIsa 10:28 were about six hundred men, 3among whom was
Ahijah, who was wearing an ephod. He was a son
14:3 a1Sa 4:21 of Ichabod's[a] brother Ahitub[b] son of Phinehas, the
b1Sa 22:11, 20 son of Eli,[c] the LORD's priest in Shiloh. No one was
c1Sa 2:28 aware that Jonathan had left.
4On each side of the pass[d] that Jonathan intend-
14:4 ed to cross to reach the Philistine outpost was a
d1Sa 13:23 cliff; one was called Bozez, and the other Seneh.
5One cliff stood to the north toward Micmash, the
other to the south toward Geba.
6Jonathan said to his young armor-bearer,
"Come, let's go over to the outpost of those uncir-
14:6 e1Sa 17:26, cumcised[e] fellows. Perhaps the LORD will act in
36; Jer 9:26 fHeb 11:34 our behalf. Nothing[f] can hinder the LORD from
gJdg 7:4 saving, whether by many[g] or by few.[h]"
h1Sa 17:46-47 7"Do all that you have in mind," his armor-bearer said. "Go ahead; I am with you heart and soul."
8Jonathan said, "Come, then; we will cross over
toward the men and let them see us. 9If they say to
us, 'Wait there until we come to you,' we will stay
where we are and not go up to them. 10But if they
say, 'Come up to us,' we will climb up, because
14:10 iGe 24:14; that will be our sign[i] that the LORD has given them
Jdg 6:36-37 into our hands."
11So both of them showed themselves to the
Philistine outpost. "Look!" said the Philistines.
"The Hebrews are crawling out of the holes they
14:11 j1Sa 13:6 were hiding[j] in." 12The men of the outpost shouted to Jonathan and his armor-bearer, "Come up to
14:12 k1Sa 17:43-44 us and we'll teach you a lesson.[k]"
So Jonathan said to his armor-bearer, "Climb up
l2Sa 5:24 after me; the LORD has given them into the hand[l]
of Israel."
13Jonathan climbed up, using his hands and
feet, with his armor-bearer right behind him. The
Philistines fell before Jonathan, and his armor-
bearer followed and killed behind him. 14In that
first attack Jonathan and his armor-bearer killed
some twenty men in an area of about half an acre.[b]

Israel Routs the Philistines

14:15 mGe 35:5; 2Ki 7:5-7 15Then panic[m] struck the whole army—those in

[a] *21* That is, about 1/8 ounce (about 4 grams) [b] *14* Hebrew *half a yoke*; a "yoke" was the land plowed by a yoke of oxen in one day.

Points of Reference

1SA 14:2

In the Old Testament, trees are often used as points of reference. (People who live in rural areas where road signs are few and far between have a good understanding of this!) In 1 Samuel 14:2, Saul and his men stay under a pomegranate tree. Deborah, the judge, held court under a palm tree (Jdg 4:5). And Rebekah's nurse is buried under an oak tree (Ge 35:8). Trees are also used as landmarks, to tell distance (Ge 12:6), to mark boundaries (Jos 19:33), and as gathering places (Jdg 9:6). Also, trees are a symbol of prosperity. During Solomon's lifetime every person in Judah and Israel lives in safety "under his own vine and fig tree" (1Ki 4:25). Since trees are so valued, it is no wonder that King David calls a man who delights in the Lord "a tree planted by streams of water, which yields its fruit in season and whose leaf does not wither" (Ps 1:3).

the camp and field, and those in the outposts and
raiding[n] parties—and the ground shook. It was a
panic sent by God.[a]
16Saul's lookouts[o] at Gibeah in Benjamin saw
the army melting away in all directions. 17Then
Saul said to the men who were with him, "Muster
the forces and see who has left us." When they
did, it was Jonathan and his armor-bearer who
were not there.
18Saul said to Ahijah, "Bring[p] the ark of God."
(At that time it was with the Israelites.)[b] 19While
Saul was talking to the priest, the tumult in the
Philistine camp increased more and more. So Saul
said to the priest,[q] "Withdraw your hand."
20Then Saul and all his men assembled and
went to the battle. They found the Philistines in
total confusion, striking[r] each other with their
swords. 21Those Hebrews who had previously
been with the Philistines and had gone up with
them to their camp went[s] over to the Israelites
who were with Saul and Jonathan. 22When all the
Israelites who had hidden[t] in the hill country of
Ephraim heard that the Philistines were on the
run, they joined the battle in hot pursuit. 23So the
LORD rescued[u] Israel that day, and the battle
moved on beyond Beth Aven.[v]

Jonathan Eats Honey

24Now the men of Israel were in distress that
day, because Saul had bound the people under an
oath,[w] saying, "Cursed be any man who eats food
before evening comes, before I have avenged
myself on my enemies!" So none of the troops
tasted food.
25The entire army[c] entered the woods, and there
was honey on the ground. 26When they went into
the woods, they saw the honey oozing out, yet no
one put his hand to his mouth, because they
feared the oath. 27But Jonathan had not heard that
his father had bound the people with the oath, so
he reached out the end of the staff that was in his
hand and dipped it into the honeycomb.[x] He
raised his hand to his mouth, and his eyes brightened.[d] 28Then one of the soldiers told him, "Your
father bound the army under a strict oath, saying,
'Cursed be any man who eats food today!' That is
why the men are faint."
29Jonathan said, "My father has made trouble[y]
for the country. See how my eyes brightened[e]
when I tasted a little of this honey. 30How much
better it would have been if the men had eaten
today some of the plunder they took from their
enemies. Would not the slaughter of the Philistines have been even greater?"
31That day, after the Israelites had struck down
the Philistines from Micmash to Aijalon,[z] they

14:15 [n]1Sa 13:17
14:16 [o]2Sa 18:24
14:18 [p]1Sa 30:7
14:19 [q]Nu 27:21
14:20 [r]Jdg 7:22; 2Ch 20:23
14:21 [s]1Sa 29:4
14:22 [t]1Sa 13:6
14:23 [u]Ex 14:30; Ps 44:6-7 [v]1Sa 13:5
14:24 [w]Jos 6:26
14:27 [x]ver 43; 1Sa 30:12
14:29 [y]Jos 7:25; 1Ki 18:18
14:31 [z]Jos 10:12

[a] 15 Or *a terrible panic* [b] 18 Hebrew; Septuagint *"Bring the ephod." (At that time he wore the ephod before the Israelites.)* [c] 25 Or *Now all the people of the land* [d] 27 Or *his strength was renewed* [e] 29 Or *my strength was renewed*

When [my sister] Vanessa began talking about the love of Christ, God moved me. At that point her words ceased to be words, and I felt an earthquake in my soul. I didn't open my heart; I slowly cracked the door to peep out, and God tore the door off the hinges. His love entered my life like *a raging river*, and I was lost *in a new way*, in the intensity and passion of *the greatest love* I had ever known.

—Nicole Johnson

14:32 [a]1Sa 15:19 [b]Ge 9:4; Lev 3:17; 7:26; 17:10-14; 19:26; Dt 12:16,23-24 were exhausted. 32They pounced on the plunder[a]
and, taking sheep, cattle and calves, they
butchered them on the ground and ate them,
together with the blood.[b] 33Then someone said to
Saul, "Look, the men are sinning against the LORD
by eating meat that has blood in it."

"You have broken faith," he said. "Roll a large
stone over here at once." 34Then he said, "Go out
among the men and tell them, 'Each of you bring
me your cattle and sheep, and slaughter them
here and eat them. Do not sin against the LORD by
eating meat with blood still in it.' "

So everyone brought his ox that night and
14:35 [c]1Sa 7:17 slaughtered it there. 35Then Saul built an altar[c] to
the LORD; it was the first time he had done this.

36Saul said, "Let us go down after the Philistines
by night and plunder them till dawn, and let us
not leave one of them alive."

"Do whatever seems best to you," they replied.

But the priest said, "Let us inquire of God here."

37So Saul asked God, "Shall I go down after the
Philistines? Will you give them into Israel's
14:37 [d]1Sa 10:22; 28:6,15 hand?" But God did not answer[d] him that day.

38Saul therefore said, "Come here, all you who
are leaders of the army, and let us find out what
14:38 [e]Jos 7:11; 1Sa 10:19 sin has been committed[e] today. 39As surely as the
LORD who rescues Israel lives,[f] even if it lies with
14:39 [f]2Sa 12:5 my son Jonathan, he must die." But not one of the
men said a word.

40Saul then said to all the Israelites, "You stand
over there; I and Jonathan my son will stand over
here."

"Do what seems best to you," the men replied.

14:41 [g]Ac 1:24 [h]Pr 16:33 41Then Saul prayed to the LORD, the God of
Israel, "Give[g] me the right[h] answer."[a] And Jonathan and Saul were taken by lot, and the men
were cleared. 42Saul said, "Cast the lot between
me and Jonathan my son." And Jonathan was
taken.

14:43 [i]Jos 7:19 [j]ver 27 43Then Saul said to Jonathan, "Tell me what you
have done."[i]

So Jonathan told him, "I merely tasted a little
honey[j] with the end of my staff. And now must I
die?"

14:44 [k]Ru 1:17 [l]ver 39 44Saul said, "May God deal with me, be it ever
so severely,[k] if you do not die, Jonathan.[l]"

45But the men said to Saul, "Should Jonathan
die—he who has brought about this great deliverance in Israel? Never! As surely as the LORD lives,
14:45 [m]1Ki 1:52; Lk 21:18; Ac 27:34 [n]2Sa 14:11 not a hair[m] of his head will fall to the ground, for
he did this today with God's help." So the men
rescued[n] Jonathan, and he was not put to death.

46Then Saul stopped pursuing the Philistines,
and they withdrew to their own land.

47After Saul had assumed rule over Israel, he
fought against their enemies on every side: Moab,

[a] 41 Hebrew; Septuagint *"Why have you not answered your servant today? If the fault is in me or my son Jonathan, respond with Urim, but if the men of Israel are at fault, respond with Thummim."*

Standing for Integrity

1SA 14:24–45

The Israelites are at war. Eager for victory, Saul vows, "Cursed be any man who eats food before evening comes!" (1Sa 14:24). Jonathan, not hearing, eats wild honey (1Sa 14:27). Later, when Saul discovers that the Lord is displeased with the people, he makes another foolish vow: Whoever has caused the Lord's displeasure will be killed (1Sa 14:38–39). It turns out the offender is the king's own son, Jonathan—yet the men rescue him from death.

Now the question that begs an answer—who is right? Saul, Jonathan or the men? Jonathan has unintentionally become entangled in his father's rashness. And though Saul shows much zeal, he shows little discretion. Not to be humiliated, he is willing to kill his own son. But the men discern the truth. They stand by the man of integrity. Saul is a rash king—Jonathan, a war hero. Saul they disobey—Jonathan they save.

Involuntary Service

1SA 14:52

The prophet Samuel had warned Israel when they cried out for a king, "He will take your sons and make them serve with his chariots and horses" (1Sa 8:11). The people would not listen, and now Samuel's prophecy is fulfilled. Fathers, sons and brothers are dragged away in service to their king.

And so it often is with the things we desire most: wealth, success, prosperity, a desire to "keep up" with those around us. Often the things we ask for are the very things that enslave us, as they recruit our time, our energy, our service and even our hearts.

the Ammonites,[o] Edom, the kings[a] of Zobah,[p] and
the Philistines. Wherever he turned, he inflicted
punishment on them.[b] 48He fought valiantly and
defeated the Amalekites,[q] delivering Israel from
the hands of those who had plundered them.

Saul's Family

49Saul's sons were Jonathan, Ishvi and Malki-
Shua.[r] The name of his older daughter was Merab,
and that of the younger was Michal.[s] 50His wife's
name was Ahinoam daughter of Ahimaaz. The
name of the commander of Saul's army was
Abner son of Ner, and Ner was Saul's uncle.
51Saul's father Kish[t] and Abner's father Ner were
sons of Abiel.
52All the days of Saul there was bitter war with
the Philistines, and whenever Saul saw a mighty
or brave man, he took[u] him into his service.

The LORD Rejects Saul as King

15 Samuel said to Saul, "I am the one the LORD
sent to anoint[v] you king over his people
Israel; so listen now to the message from the LORD.
2This is what the LORD Almighty says: 'I will punish the Amalekites[w] for what they did to Israel
when they waylaid them as they came up from
Egypt. 3Now go, attack the Amalekites and totally[x] destroy[c] everything that belongs to them. Do
not spare them; put to death men and women,
children and infants, cattle and sheep, camels and
donkeys.' "
4So Saul summoned the men and mustered
them at Telaim—two hundred thousand foot soldiers and ten thousand men from Judah. 5Saul
went to the city of Amalek and set an ambush in
the ravine. 6Then he said to the Kenites,[y] "Go
away, leave the Amalekites so that I do not
destroy you along with them; for you showed
kindness to all the Israelites when they came up
out of Egypt." So the Kenites moved away from
the Amalekites.
7Then Saul attacked the Amalekites[z] all the way
from Havilah to Shur,[a] to the east of Egypt. 8He
took Agag king of the Amalekites alive,[b] and all
his people he totally destroyed with the sword.
9But Saul and the army spared[c] Agag and the best
of the sheep and cattle, the fat calves[d] and lambs—
everything that was good. These they were unwilling to destroy completely, but everything that was
despised and weak they totally destroyed.
10Then the word of the LORD came to Samuel:
11"I am grieved[d] that I have made Saul king,
because he has turned[e] away from me and has not
carried out my instructions."[f] Samuel was troubled,[g] and he cried out to the LORD all that night.

14:47 [o]1Sa 11:1-13 [p]ver 52; 2Sa 10:6
14:48 [q]1Sa 15:2,7
14:49 [r]1Sa 31:2; 1Ch 8:33 [s]1Sa 18:17-20
14:51 [t]1Sa 9:1
14:52 [u]1Sa 8:11
15:1 [v]1Sa 9:16
15:2 [w]Ex 17:8-14; Nu 24:20; Dt 25:17-19
15:3 [x]Nu 24:20; Dt 20:16-18; Jos 6:17; 1Sa 22:19
15:6 [y]Ex 18:10, 19; Nu 10:29-32; 24:22; Jdg 1:16; 4:1
15:7 [z]1Sa 14:48 [a]Ge 16:7; 25:17-18; Ex 15:22
15:8 [b]1Sa 30:1
15:9 [c]ver 3,15
15:11 [d]Ge 6:6; 2Sa 24:16 [e]Jos 22:16 [f]1Sa 13:13; 1Ki 9:6-7 [g]ver 35

[a] 47 Masoretic Text; Dead Sea Scrolls and Septuagint *king*
[b] 47 Hebrew; Septuagint *he was victorious* [c] 3 The Hebrew term refers to the irrevocable giving over of things or persons to the LORD, often by totally destroying them; also in verses 8, 9, 15, 18, 20 and 21. [d] 9 Or *the grown bulls*; the meaning of the Hebrew for this phrase is uncertain.

[12]Early in the morning Samuel got up and went
15:12 to meet Saul, but he was told, "Saul has gone to
[h]Jos 15:55 Carmel.[h] There he has set up a monument in his
own honor and has turned and gone on down to
Gilgal."
[13]When Samuel reached him, Saul said, "The
LORD bless you! I have carried out the LORD's
instructions."
[14]But Samuel said, "What then is this bleating
of sheep in my ears? What is this lowing of cattle
that I hear?"
[15]Saul answered, "The soldiers brought them
from the Amalekites; they spared the best of the
sheep and cattle to sacrifice to the LORD your God,
but we totally destroyed the rest."
[16]"Stop!" Samuel said to Saul. "Let me tell you
what the LORD said to me last night."
"Tell me," Saul replied.
15:17 [17]Samuel said, "Although you were once small[i]
[i]1Sa 9:21 in your own eyes, did you not become the head
of the tribes of Israel? The LORD anointed you king
over Israel. [18]And he sent you on a mission, saying, 'Go and completely destroy those wicked
people, the Amalekites; make war on them until
you have wiped them out.' [19]Why did you not
obey the LORD? Why did you pounce on the plun-
15:19 [j]1Sa 14:32 der[j] and do evil in the eyes of the LORD?"
[20]"But I did obey[k] the LORD," Saul said. "I went
15:20 [k]ver 13 on the mission the LORD assigned me. I completely destroyed the Amalekites and brought back
Agag their king. [21]The soldiers took sheep and cattle from the plunder, the best of what was devoted to God, in order to sacrifice them to the LORD
your God at Gilgal."
[22]But Samuel replied:

"Does the LORD delight in burnt
offerings and sacrifices
15:22 [l]Ps 40:6-8; 51:16; Isa 1:11-15; Jer 7:22; Hos 6:6; Mic 6:6-8; Mt 12:7; Mk 12:33; Heb 10:6-9 as much as in obeying the voice of the
LORD?
To obey is better than sacrifice,
and to heed is better than the fat of
rams.
[23]For rebellion is like the sin of
divination,[m]
and arrogance like the evil of idolatry.
15:23 [m]Dt 18:10 Because you have rejected[n] the word of
[n]1Sa 13:13 the LORD,
he has rejected you as king."

15:24 [o]2Sa 12:13 [24]Then Saul said to Samuel, "I have sinned.[o] I
[p]Pr 29:25; Isa 51:12-13 violated the LORD's command and your instructions. I was afraid[p] of the people and so I gave in to
15:25 them. [25]Now I beg you, forgive[q] my sin and come
[q]Ex 10:17 back with me, so that I may worship the LORD."
15:26 [26]But Samuel said to him, "I will not go back
[r]1Sa 13:14 with you. You have rejected[r] the word of the LORD,
and the LORD has rejected you as king over Israel!"
15:27 [s]1Ki 11:11,31 [27]As Samuel turned to leave, Saul caught hold
of the hem of his robe, and it tore.[s] [28]Samuel said
15:28 [t]1Sa 28:17; 1Ki 11:31 to him, "The LORD has torn[t] the kingdom of Israel
from you today and has given it to one of your

Obedience or Sacrifice

1SA 15:22

"To obey is better than sacrifice." The essence of this passage is worded in various ways throughout Scripture: "For I desire mercy, not sacrifice, and acknowledgment of God rather than burnt offerings" (Hos 6:6), or "To love him with all your heart . . . is more important than all burnt offerings and sacrifices" (Mk 12:33). If God states his desire so clearly, why did the Israelites—and why do we—have such difficulty following it?

God makes it clear that what he wants from us is our hearts. We can "play" at religious activity. We can go through the "appropriate" religious motions, offering sacrifices, singing the right songs, bringing burnt offerings, attending the right services. But none of it means anything unless our hearts are tuned to God, offering him more than our gestures, offering him our obedience and love.

Think about how this applies in your own life. Is there an area where you are offering sacrifice instead of obedience to the Lord?

God's Regrets

1SA 15:35

The word grieve *in this passage literally means God "was sorry." This is not the only passage where God tells of his regret. Genesis 6:6 says, "The* LORD *was grieved that he had made man on the earth, and his heart was filled with pain." Yet, in both these cases, it is people who have changed, not God. Saul's own actions and decisions transform him from a humble man into an arrogant and rebellious king. Since God is all knowing, he obviously knows Saul's heart. And he gives Saul a chance to prove himself worthy of the role of king of God's people. But Saul ignores God and goes his own way,* grieving *the very God who had placed him in his exalted position.*

neighbors—to one better than you. 29He who is
the Glory of Israel does not lie[u] or change[v] his 15:29
mind; for he is not a man, that he should change u1Ch 29:11;
his mind." Tit 1:2 vNu 23:19;
30Saul replied, "I have sinned. But please hon- Eze 24:14
or[w] me before the elders of my people and before 15:30
Israel; come back with me, so that I may worship wIsa 29:13; Jn 5:44;
the LORD your God." 31So Samuel went back with 12:43
Saul, and Saul worshiped the LORD.
32Then Samuel said, "Bring me Agag king of the
Amalekites."
Agag came to him confidently,[a] thinking, "Surely the bitterness of death is past."
33But Samuel said,

"As your sword has made women
childless,
so will your mother be childless
among women."[x] 15:33

xGe 9:6; Jdg 1:7

And Samuel put Agag to death before the LORD at
Gilgal.
34Then Samuel left for Ramah,[y] but Saul went up 15:34 y1Sa 7:17
to his home in Gibeah[z] of Saul. 35Until the day Sam- z1Sa 11:4
uel[a] died, he did not go to see Saul again, though 15:35
Samuel mourned[b] for him. And the LORD was a1Sa 19:24
grieved that he had made Saul king over Israel. b1Sa 16:1

Samuel Anoints David

16 The LORD said to Samuel, "How long will you 16:1
mourn[c] for Saul, since I have rejected[d] him c1Sa 15:35
as king over Israel? Fill your horn with oil[e] and be d1Sa 15:23
on your way; I am sending you to Jesse[f] of Bethle- e2Ki 9:1
hem. I have chosen[g] one of his sons to be king." fRu 4:17; 1Sa 9:16
2But Samuel said, "How can I go? Saul will hear gPs 78:70;
about it and kill me." Ac 13:22
The LORD said, "Take a heifer with you and say,
'I have come to sacrifice to the LORD.' 3Invite Jesse to the sacrifice, and I will show[h] you what to 16:3 hEx 4:15
do. You are to anoint[i] for me the one I indicate." iDt 17:15;
4Samuel did what the LORD said. When he 1Sa 9:16
arrived at Bethlehem,[j] the elders of the town 16:4
trembled when they met him. They asked, "Do jGe 48:7; Lk 2:4
you come in peace?[k]" k1Ki 2:13;
5Samuel replied, "Yes, in peace; I have come to 2Ki 9:17
sacrifice to the LORD. Consecrate[l] yourselves and 16:5
come to the sacrifice with me." Then he conse- lEx 19:10,22
crated Jesse and his sons and invited them to the
sacrifice.
6When they arrived, Samuel saw Eliab[m] and 16:6
thought, "Surely the LORD's anointed stands here m1Sa 17:13
before the LORD."
7But the LORD said to Samuel, "Do not consider
his appearance or his height, for I have rejected
him. The LORD does not look at the things man 16:7
looks at. Man looks at the outward appearance,[n] nPs 147:10
but the LORD looks at the heart."[o] o1Ki 8:39; 1Ch 28:9;
8Then Jesse called Abinadab[p] and had him pass Isa 55:8
in front of Samuel. But Samuel said, "The LORD 16:8
has not chosen this one either." 9Jesse then had p1Sa 17:13

[a] 32 Or *him trembling, yet*

Week 6

Broken Relationships

One of the saddest chapters in the Bible, 1 Samuel 15 tells of disobedience, greed, lies, denial and shifting blame. The outcome: broken relationships with people and with God. How does Saul go from being God's chosen king to being rejected by God? Well, it certainly didn't happen overnight, and rejecting Saul wasn't a snap decision on God's part. Here is a portrait of a man who is more like us than we care to admit.

What command does God give to Saul in 1 Samuel 15:3? To "totally destroy" seems abhorrent to us today. But God used total destruction to punish nations for their sin and to preserve Israel from vile influences. How does Saul disobey this command (1Sa 15:8–9)?

How does offering to God (through death) the "despised and weak" animals (1Sa 15:9) show disrespect for God (Mal 1:7–12)? How does keeping the best animals for themselves show greed (1Sa 15:9,19)? What are some ways you have saved the best for yourself?

How does Saul reveal his pride (1Sa 15:12)?

Saul takes the credit for what is done right, and he blames others for what is done wrong (1Sa 15:15,24). Do you ever play the shifting blame game? How does this interfere with your relationship to God?

What is Saul's punishment (1Sa 15:23, 26)? How does this go beyond the punishment he had previously received for disobedience (1Sa 13:14)? What does this reveal about God (Joel 2:13)?

What does Saul's unconscious use of the pronoun "your" (1Sa 15:15,21,30) say about his relationship with God? How does he try to keep up outward appearances of having a relationship with God (1Sa 15:30)? Have you ever done this? When? Why?

How does Saul reveal that his repentance is not heartfelt but simply an attempt to escape judgment (1Sa 15:24–25)? When have you made excuses for your sin when God required true repentance? How does this prevent reconciliation with God?

Enjoying God THROUGH the Word

Read 2 Samuel 12:1–14 (page 491). If you are unfamiliar with the story of David and Bathsheba, you may also want to read 2 Samuel 11.

David committed adultery with Bathsheba and then had Bathsheba's husband, Uriah, killed to cover up what he had done. Nathan the prophet confronts David with his sin. Although David's confession is the same as Saul's—"I have sinned" (1Sa 15:24; 2Sa 12:13)—David's attitude is totally different. He responds with true repentance and is immediately forgiven (2Sa 12:13).

True repentance is more than a simple "You're right; I'm sorry." True repentance is a heartfelt recognition of guilt, accompanied by a desire for restoration and a turning away from sin. God forgives David's sin and David devotes himself to the Lord all the rest of his life. He is remembered as one who "had done what was right in the eyes of the LORD and had not failed to keep any of the LORD's commands all the days of his life—except in the case of Uriah the Hittite" (1Ki 15:5).

Enjoying God THROUGH Experience

Are you alienated from God because of sin and disobedience? Return to him. He will not turn away from a broken and contrite heart (Ps 51:17). Your broken relationship can be restored only if your heart is broken in repentance. Bring the pieces of your heart and your life to Jesus, the only One who can mend them.

Go to page 484 for your next weekly study.

Music Therapy

1SA 16:23

Studying the benefits of music has become popular in recent years. Classical music has been said to help students study better and even help plants grow stronger! David's music therapy settles Saul's soul. Music has a natural tendency to calm the mind when it is disturbed or melancholy. David's harp playing is so soothing that even after Saul grows to loathe David, Saul cannot do without his service. The therapeutic quality of music also calms Elisha's spirit and opens his heart to God's message (2Ki 3:14-15). When was the last time you allowed music to soothe you? Take time today to listen to relaxing strains of music or to make a joyful noise by creating your own melody for one of David's psalms.

Shammah pass by, but Samuel said, "Nor has the
LORD chosen this one." 10 Jesse had seven of his
sons pass before Samuel, but Samuel said to him,
"The LORD has not chosen these." 11 So he asked
Jesse, "Are these all[q] the sons you have?"

"There is still the youngest," Jesse answered,
"but he is tending the sheep."

Samuel said, "Send for him; we will not sit
down[a] until he arrives."

12 So he[r] sent and had him brought in. He was
ruddy, with a fine appearance and handsome[s]
features.

Then the LORD said, "Rise and anoint him; he is
the one."

13 So Samuel took the horn of oil and anointed
him in the presence of his brothers, and from that
day on the Spirit of the LORD[t] came upon David in
power.[u] Samuel then went to Ramah.

David in Saul's Service

14 Now the Spirit of the LORD had departed[v] from
Saul, and an evil[b] spirit[w] from the LORD tormented
him.

15 Saul's attendants said to him, "See, an evil
spirit from God is tormenting you. 16 Let our lord
command his servants here to search for someone
who can play the harp.[x] He will play when the
evil spirit from God comes upon you, and you will
feel better."

17 So Saul said to his attendants, "Find someone
who plays well and bring him to me."

18 One of the servants answered, "I have seen a
son of Jesse of Bethlehem who knows how to play
the harp. He is a brave man and a warrior. He
speaks well and is a fine-looking man. And the
LORD is with[y] him."

19 Then Saul sent messengers to Jesse and said,
"Send me your son David, who is with the sheep."
20 So Jesse took a donkey loaded with bread,[z] a
skin of wine and a young goat and sent them with
his son David to Saul.

21 David came to Saul and entered his service.[a]
Saul liked him very much, and David became one
of his armor-bearers. 22 Then Saul sent word to Jesse, saying, "Allow David to remain in my service,
for I am pleased with him."

23 Whenever the spirit from God came upon
Saul, David would take his harp and play. Then
relief would come to Saul; he would feel better,
and the evil spirit[b] would leave him.

David and Goliath

17 Now the Philistines gathered their forces for
war and assembled[c] at Socoh in Judah.
They pitched camp at Ephes Dammim, between
Socoh[d] and Azekah. 2 Saul and the Israelites
assembled and camped in the Valley of Elah[e] and
drew up their battle line to meet the Philistines.

16:11 [q] 1Sa 17:12
16:12 [r] 1Sa 9:17 [s] Ge 39:6; 1Sa 17:42
16:13 [t] Nu 27:18; Jdg 11:29 [u] 1Sa 10:1,6, 9-10; 11:6
16:14 [v] Jdg 16:20 [w] Jdg 9:23; 1Sa 18:10
16:16 [x] ver 23; 1Sa 18:10; 19:9; 2Ki 3:15
16:18 [y] 1Sa 3:19; 17:32-37
16:20 [z] 1Sa 10:27; Pr 18:16
16:21 [a] Ge 41:46; Pr 22:29
16:23 [b] ver 14-16
17:1 [c] 1Sa 13:5 [d] Jos 15:35; 2Ch 28:18
17:2 [e] 1Sa 21:9

[a] *11* Some Septuagint manuscripts; Hebrew *not gather around*
[b] *14* Or *injurious*; also in verses 15, 16 and 23

3The Philistines occupied one hill and the Israelites another, with the valley between them.
4A champion named Goliath,[f] who was from
Gath, came out of the Philistine camp. He was over
nine feet[a] tall. 5He had a bronze helmet on his head
and wore a coat of scale armor of bronze weighing
five thousand shekels[b]; 6on his legs he wore bronze
greaves, and a bronze javelin[g] was slung on his
back. 7His spear shaft was like a weaver's rod,[h] and
its iron point weighed six hundred shekels.[c] His
shield bearer[i] went ahead of him.
8Goliath stood and shouted to the ranks of Israel,
"Why do you come out and line up for battle? Am I
not a Philistine, and are you not the servants of
Saul? Choose[j] a man and have him come down to
me. 9If he is able to fight and kill me, we will
become your subjects; but if I overcome him and
kill him, you will become our subjects and serve
us." 10Then the Philistine said, "This day I defy[k] the
ranks of Israel! Give me a man and let us fight each
other." 11On hearing the Philistine's words, Saul
and all the Israelites were dismayed and terrified.
12Now David was the son of an Ephrathite
named Jesse,[l] who was from Bethlehem[m] in
Judah. Jesse had eight[n] sons, and in Saul's time
he was old and well advanced in years. 13Jesse's
three oldest sons had followed Saul to the war:
The firstborn was Eliab;[o] the second, Abinadab;
and the third, Shammah.[p] 14David was the
youngest. The three oldest followed Saul, 15but
David went back and forth from Saul to tend his
father's sheep[q] at Bethlehem.
16For forty days the Philistine came forward
every morning and evening and took his stand.
17Now Jesse said to his son David, "Take this
ephah[d] of roasted grain[r] and these ten loaves of
bread for your brothers and hurry to their camp.
18Take along these ten cheeses to the commander
of their unit.[e] See how your brothers[s] are and
bring back some assurance[f] from them. 19They are
with Saul and all the men of Israel in the Valley of
Elah, fighting against the Philistines."
20Early in the morning David left the flock with
a shepherd, loaded up and set out, as Jesse had
directed. He reached the camp as the army was
going out to its battle positions, shouting the war
cry. 21Israel and the Philistines were drawing up
their lines facing each other. 22David left his things
with the keeper of supplies, ran to the battle lines
and greeted his brothers. 23As he was talking with
them, Goliath, the Philistine champion from Gath,
stepped out from his lines and shouted his usual[t]
defiance, and David heard it. 24When the Israelites
saw the man, they all ran from him in great fear.
25Now the Israelites had been saying, "Do you
see how this man keeps coming out? He comes

17:4 [f]Jos 11:21-22; 2Sa 21:19
17:6 [g]ver 45
17:7 [h]2Sa 21:19 [i]ver 41
17:8 [j]1Sa 8:17
17:10 [k]ver 26,45; 2Sa 21:21
17:12 [l]Ru 4:17; 1Ch 2:13-15 [m]Ge 35:19 [n]1Sa 16:11
17:13 [o]1Sa 16:6 [p]1Sa 16:9
17:15 [q]1Sa 16:19
17:17 [r]1Sa 25:18
17:18 [s]Ge 37:14
17:23 [t]ver 8-10

[a] 4 Hebrew *was six cubits and a span* (about 3 meters)
[b] 5 That is, about 125 pounds (about 57 kilograms) [c] 7 That is, about 15 pounds (about 7 kilograms) [d] 17 That is, probably about 3/5 bushel (about 22 liters) [e] 18 Hebrew *thousand* [f] 18 Or *some token*; or *some pledge of spoils*

Daily Faithfulness

1SA 17:3-25

David must have considered Samuel's anointing a distant dream. David is anointed, he goes to serve the king, but then he returns home to care for his father's sheep. Yet in the mundane, as he serves his father at a thankless job, David is unknowingly being prepared for the challenges to come. In obeying Jesse (1Sa 17:17), David learns to obey his heavenly Father. On quiet hillsides while guarding sheep, Israel's God becomes living and real in David's life. Through daily troubles David's faith grows, and he discovers his God-given strengths (1Sa 17:34-37). How could he possibly have known that by becoming skilled with a sling to save his father's sheep, he would someday save God's lost sheep—Israel? David has no idea how his faithfulness in daily living plays into God's bigger plan . . . and neither do we.

Nobody can deny but religion is a comfort to the distressed, a cordial to the sick, and sometimes a restraint on the wicked; therefore, whoever would laugh or argue it out of the world, without giving some equivalent for it, ought to be treated as a common enemy.

—Mary Wortley Montagu (1689-1762)

out to defy Israel. The king will give great wealth
to the man who kills him. He will also give him
his daughter[u] in marriage and will exempt his
father's family from taxes in Israel."
26David asked the men standing near him,
"What will be done for the man who kills this
Philistine and removes this disgrace[v] from Israel?
Who is this uncircumcised[w] Philistine that he
should defy[x] the armies of the living[y] God?"
27They repeated to him what they had been saying and told him, "This is what will be done for
the man who kills him."
28When Eliab, David's oldest brother, heard him
speaking with the men, he burned with anger[z] at
him and asked, "Why have you come down here?
And with whom did you leave those few sheep in
the desert? I know how conceited you are and
how wicked your heart is; you came down only
to watch the battle."
29"Now what have I done?" said David. "Can't I
even speak?" 30He then turned away to someone
else and brought up the same matter, and the men
answered him as before. 31What David said was
overheard and reported to Saul, and Saul sent for
him.
32David said to Saul, "Let no one lose heart[a] on
account of this Philistine; your servant will go and
fight him."
33Saul replied,[b] "You are not able to go out
against this Philistine and fight him; you are only
a boy, and he has been a fighting man from his
youth."
34But David said to Saul, "Your servant has been
keeping his father's sheep. When a lion[c] or a bear
came and carried off a sheep from the flock, 35I
went after it, struck it and rescued the sheep from
its mouth. When it turned on me, I seized it by its
hair, struck it and killed it. 36Your servant has
killed both the lion and the bear; this uncircumcised Philistine will be like one of them, because
he has defied the armies of the living God. 37The
LORD who delivered[d] me from the paw of the lion[e]
and the paw of the bear will deliver me from the
hand of this Philistine."
Saul said to David, "Go, and the LORD be with[f]
you."
38Then Saul dressed David in his own tunic. He
put a coat of armor on him and a bronze helmet
on his head. 39David fastened on his sword over
the tunic and tried walking around, because he
was not used to them.
"I cannot go in these," he said to Saul, "because
I am not used to them." So he took them off.
40Then he took his staff in his hand, chose five
smooth stones from the stream, put them in the
pouch of his shepherd's bag and, with his sling in
his hand, approached the Philistine.
41Meanwhile, the Philistine, with his shield
bearer in front of him, kept coming closer to
David. 42He looked David over and saw that he
was only a boy, ruddy and handsome,[g] and he

17:25 [u]Jos 15:16; 1Sa 18:17
17:26 [v]1Sa 11:2 [w]1Sa 14:6 [x]ver 10 [y]Dt 5:26
17:28 [z]Ge 37:4,8, 11; Pr 18:19; Mt 10:36
17:32 [a]Dt 20:3; 1Sa 16:18
17:33 [b]Nu 13:31
17:34 [c]Jer 49:19; Am 3:12
17:37 [d]2Co 1:10 [e]2Ti 4:17 [f]1Sa 20:13; 1Ch 22:11,16
17:42 [g]1Sa 16:12

despised[h] him. 43 He said to David, "Am I a dog,[i]
that you come at me with sticks?" And the Philistine cursed David by his gods. 44 "Come here," he
said, "and I'll give your flesh to the birds of the
air and the beasts of the field![j]"
45 David said to the Philistine, "You come against
me with sword and spear and javelin, but I come
against you in the name[k] of the LORD Almighty,
the God of the armies of Israel, whom you have
defied.[l] 46 This day the LORD will hand you over to
me, and I'll strike you down and cut off your
head. Today I will give the carcasses[m] of the Philistine army to the birds of the air and the beasts
of the earth, and the whole world[n] will know that
there is a God in Israel.[o] 47 All those gathered here
will know that it is not by sword[p] or spear that
the LORD saves;[q] for the battle[r] is the LORD's, and
he will give all of you into our hands."
48 As the Philistine moved closer to attack him,
David ran quickly toward the battle line to meet
him. 49 Reaching into his bag and taking out a
stone, he slung it and struck the Philistine on the
forehead. The stone sank into his forehead, and
he fell facedown on the ground.
50 So David triumphed over the Philistine with a
sling[s] and a stone; without a sword in his hand
he struck down the Philistine and killed him.
51 David ran and stood over him. He took hold of
the Philistine's sword and drew it from the scabbard. After he killed him, he cut[t] off his head with
the sword.[u]
When the Philistines saw that their hero was
dead, they turned and ran. 52 Then the men of Israel and Judah surged forward with a shout and
pursued the Philistines to the entrance of Gath[a]
and to the gates of Ekron.[v] Their dead were
strewn along the Shaaraim[w] road to Gath and
Ekron. 53 When the Israelites returned from chasing the Philistines, they plundered their camp.
54 David took the Philistine's head and brought it
to Jerusalem, and he put the Philistine's weapons
in his own tent.
55 As Saul watched David[x] going out to meet the
Philistine, he said to Abner, commander of the
army, "Abner, whose son is that young man?"
Abner replied, "As surely as you live, O king, I
don't know."
56 The king said, "Find out whose son this
young man is."
57 As soon as David returned from killing the
Philistine, Abner took him and brought him
before Saul, with David still holding the Philistine's head.
58 "Whose son are you, young man?" Saul asked
him.
David said, "I am the son of your servant Jesse[y]
of Bethlehem."

17:42 [h]Ps 123:3-4; Pr 16:18
17:43 [i]1Sa 24:14; 2Sa 3:8; 9:8; 2Ki 8:13
17:44 [j]1Ki 20:10-11
17:45 [k]2Sa 22:33, 35; 2Ch 32:8; Ps 124:8; Heb 11:32-34 [l]ver 10
17:46 [m]Dt 28:26 [n]Jos 4:24; 1Ki 8:43; Isa 52:10 [o]1Ki 18:36; 2Ki 19:19; Isa 37:20
17:47 [p]Hos 1:7; Zec 4:6 [q]1Sa 14:6; 2Ch 14:11 [r]2Ch 20:15; Ps 44:6-7
17:50 [s]2Sa 23:21
17:51 [t]Heb 11:34 [u]1Sa 21:9
17:52 [v]Jos 15:11 [w]Jos 15:36
17:55 [x]1Sa 16:21
17:58 [y]ver 12

The Name of the LORD

1SA 17:45

David stands against Goliath with "the name of the LORD" as his defense. David's confidence is understandable when we look into the meaning behind these words. By calling on God's "name," David is making an appeal to God's honor, authority, character and presence. He is recalling God's mighty works and putting the outcome of the battle in God's hands. David does not base his confidence on his own expertise or on something he has done. He places his confidence solely in God's power. The same use of the word name *is found in Psalm 25:11: "For the sake of your name, O LORD, forgive my iniquity, though it is great." The psalmist asks for forgiveness, not based on himself or his own works, but based on God's name and his works.*

Many of us have obstacles looming in the distance. We can approach them with the same confidence as David: When we pray in the Lord's name, remember what God has done and confidently place the results in his hands.

[a] 52 Some Septuagint manuscripts; Hebrew *a valley*

An Evil Spirit From God

1SA 18:10

We may rub our eyes in confusion as we read this verse. What is an evil spirit from God? And why would God send one to Saul? Here, evil is defined as "distressful" or "injurious" (see NIV footnote.) Saul acts out this distress by "prophesying," most likely in a display of frantic pacing and ranting. But does God actually send this evil spirit to Saul? We can debate whether God sends the evil spirit or allows it to enter Saul. However, the writer of 1 Samuel, in characteristic Old Testament style, simply states that the evil spirit is "from God," recognizing God's control over everything. This evil spirit may find a place within Saul simply because he has ignored God, creating a spiritual void within himself that allows room for an evil spirit to enter. Or Saul's increasing awareness that his sin has caused God's blessing to leave him may have caused his extreme torment, characterized by an evil spirit. The truth of the passage is comforting, even in its distressful circumstances: Evil spirits are under God's control and do not function within this world except under his divine authority.

Saul's Jealousy of David

18 After David had finished talking with Saul,
Jonathan became one in spirit with David,
and he loved[z] him as himself.[a] 2From that day
Saul kept David with him and did not let him
return to his father's house. 3And Jonathan made
a covenant[b] with David because he loved him as
himself. 4Jonathan took off the robe[c] he was wearing and gave it to David, along with his tunic, and
even his sword, his bow and his belt.
5Whatever Saul sent him to do, David did it so
successfully[a] that Saul gave him a high rank in
the army. This pleased all the people, and Saul's
officers as well.
6When the men were returning home after
David had killed the Philistine, the women came
out from all the towns of Israel to meet King Saul
with singing and dancing,[d] with joyful songs and
with tambourines[e] and lutes. 7As they danced,
they sang:[f]

"Saul has slain his thousands,
and David his tens[g] of thousands."

8Saul was very angry; this refrain galled him.
"They have credited David with tens of thousands," he thought, "but me with only thousands.
What more can he get but the kingdom?[h]" 9And
from that time on Saul kept a jealous eye on David.
10The next day an evil[b] spirit[i] from God came
forcefully upon Saul. He was prophesying in his
house, while David was playing the harp, as he
usually[j] did. Saul had a spear in his hand 11and he
hurled it, saying to himself,[k] "I'll pin David to the
wall." But David eluded[l] him twice.
12Saul was afraid[m] of David, because the LORD[n]
was with[o] David but had left Saul. 13So he sent
David away from him and gave him command
over a thousand men, and David led[p] the troops in
their campaigns.[q] 14In everything he did he had
great success,[c][r] because the LORD was with[s] him.
15When Saul saw how successful[d] he was, he was
afraid of him. 16But all Israel and Judah loved
David, because he led them in their campaigns.[t]
17Saul said to David, "Here is my older daughter[u] Merab. I will give her to you in marriage; only
serve me bravely and fight the battles[v] of the
LORD." For Saul said to himself,[w] "I will not raise
a hand against him. Let the Philistines do that!"
18But David said to Saul, "Who am I,[x] and what
is my family or my father's clan in Israel, that I
should become the king's son-in-law?[y]" 19So[e]
when the time came for Merab,[z] Saul's daughter,
to be given to David, she was given in marriage to
Adriel of Meholah.[a]
20Now Saul's daughter Michal[b] was in love with
David, and when they told Saul about it, he was
pleased. 21"I will give her to him," he thought, "so
that she may be a snare[c] to him and so that the

18:1 [z]2Sa 1:26 [a]Ge 44:30
18:3 [b]1Sa 20:8, 16,17,42
18:4 [c]Ge 41:42
18:6 [d]Ex 15:20 [e]Jdg 11:34; Ps 68:25
18:7 [f]Ex 15:21 [g]1Sa 21:11; 29:5
18:8 [h]1Sa 15:8
18:10 [i]1Sa 16:14 [j]1Sa 19:7
18:11 [k]1Sa 20:7,33 [l]1Sa 19:10
18:12 [m]ver 15,29 [n]1Sa 16:13 [o]1Sa 28:15
18:13 [p]ver 16; Nu 27:17 [q]2Sa 5:2
18:14 [r]Ge 39:3 [s]Ge 39:2,23; Jos 6:27; 1Sa 16:18
18:16 [t]ver 5
18:17 [u]1Sa 17:25 [v]Nu 21:14; 1Sa 25:28 [w]ver 25
18:18 [x]1Sa 9:21; 2Sa 7:18 [y]ver 23
18:19 [z]2Sa 21:8 [a]Jdg 7:22
18:20 [b]ver 28
18:21 [c]ver 17,26

[a] 5 Or *wisely* [b] 10 Or *injurious* [c] 14 Or *he was very wise*
[d] 15 Or *wise* [e] 19 Or *However,*

hand of the Philistines may be against him." So
Saul said to David, "Now you have a second
opportunity to become my son-in-law."
22 Then Saul ordered his attendants: "Speak to
David privately and say, 'Look, the king is pleased
with you, and his attendants all like you; now
become his son-in-law.' "
23 They repeated these words to David. But
David said, "Do you think it is a small matter to
become the king's son-in-law? I'm only a poor
man and little known."
24 When Saul's servants told him what David
had said, 25 Saul replied, "Say to David, 'The king

18:25 [d]Ge 34:12; Ex 22:17; 1Sa 14:24 [e]ver 17

wants no other price[d] for the bride than a hundred Philistine foreskins, to take revenge on his
enemies.' " Saul's plan[e] was to have David fall by
the hands of the Philistines.
26 When the attendants told David these things,
he was pleased to become the king's son-in-law.
So before the allotted time elapsed, 27 David and
his men went out and killed two hundred Philistines. He brought their foreskins and presented
the full number to the king so that he might

18:27 [f]ver 13; 2Sa 3:14

become the king's son-in-law. Then Saul gave him
his daughter Michal[f] in marriage.
28 When Saul realized that the LORD was with
David and that his daughter Michal loved David,
29 Saul became still more afraid of him, and he
remained his enemy the rest of his days.
30 The Philistine commanders continued to go
out to battle, and as often as they did, David met

18:30 [g]ver 5; 2Sa 11:1

with more success[a][g] than the rest of Saul's officers, and his name became well known.

Saul Tries to Kill David

19:1 [h]1Sa 18:1 [i]1Sa 18:9

19 Saul told his son Jonathan[h] and all the
attendants to kill[i] David. But Jonathan was
very fond of David 2 and warned him, "My father
Saul is looking for a chance to kill you. Be on your
guard tomorrow morning; go into hiding and stay
there. 3 I will go out and stand with my father in

19:3 [j]1Sa 20:12

the field where you are. I'll speak[j] to him about
you and will tell you what I find out."

19:4 [k]1Sa 20:32; Pr 31:8,9; Jer 18:20 [l]Ge 42:22; Pr 17:13

4 Jonathan spoke[k] well of David to Saul his
father and said to him, "Let not the king do
wrong[l] to his servant David; he has not wronged
you, and what he has done has benefited you
greatly. 5 He took his life in his hands when he
killed the Philistine. The LORD won a great victo-

19:5 [m]1Sa 11:13; 17:49-50; 1Ch 11:14 [n]Dt 19:10-13; 1Sa 20:32; Mt 27:4

ry[m] for all Israel, and you saw it and were glad.
Why then would you do wrong to an innocent[n]
man like David by killing him for no reason?"
6 Saul listened to Jonathan and took this oath:
"As surely as the LORD lives, David will not be put
to death."
7 So Jonathan called David and told him the

19:7 [o]1Sa 16:21; 18:2,13

whole conversation. He brought him to Saul, and
David was with Saul as before.[o]
8 Once more war broke out, and David went out

[a] 30 Or *David acted more wisely*

Saul's Scheme, David's Success

1SA 18:22-30

Saul has a plan. He asks a huge—and grotesque—bride price for his daughter's hand in marriage: 100 Philistine foreskins. The foreskins mean nothing to Saul. In actuality, he wants David to die while trying to acquire them. If David sees behind the ploy, it doesn't seem to faze or disturb him. David is "pleased to become the king's son-in-law" (1Sa 18:26). In his own eyes, he has no money or fame (1Sa 18:23), nothing that would make him worthy to marry a princess. But he is a mighty warrior, and he can earn the right to be a part of the royal family. Saul's plan fails. David doesn't die but returns with 200 foreskins, becoming an even greater hero (1Sa 18:30). Once again, divinely orchestrated events prove that what people contrive in order to harm, God uses to accomplish his ultimate purposes (Ge 50:20).

and fought the Philistines. He struck them with
such force that they fled before him.
9But an evil[a] spirit[p] from the LORD came upon
Saul as he was sitting in his house with his spear
in his hand. While David was playing the harp,
10Saul tried to pin him to the wall with his spear,
but David eluded[q] him as Saul drove the spear into
the wall. That night David made good his escape.
11Saul sent men to David's house to watch[r] it
and to kill him in the morning. But Michal,
David's wife, warned him, "If you don't run for
your life tonight, tomorrow you'll be killed." 12So
Michal let David down through a window,[s] and
he fled and escaped. 13Then Michal took an idol[b]
and laid it on the bed, covering it with a garment
and putting some goats' hair at the head.
14When Saul sent the men to capture David,
Michal said,[t] "He is ill."
15Then Saul sent the men back to see David and
told them, "Bring him up to me in his bed so that
I may kill him." 16But when the men entered,
there was the idol in the bed, and at the head was
some goats' hair.
17Saul said to Michal, "Why did you deceive me
like this and send my enemy away so that he
escaped?"
Michal told him, "He said to me, 'Let me get
away. Why should I kill you?' "
18When David had fled and made his escape, he
went to Samuel at Ramah[u] and told him all that
Saul had done to him. Then he and Samuel went
to Naioth and stayed there. 19Word came to Saul:
"David is in Naioth at Ramah"; 20so he sent men
to capture him. But when they saw a group of
prophets[v] prophesying, with Samuel standing
there as their leader, the Spirit of God came upon[w]
Saul's men and they also prophesied.[x] 21Saul was
told about it, and he sent more men, and they
prophesied too. Saul sent men a third time, and
they also prophesied. 22Finally, he himself left for
Ramah and went to the great cistern at Secu. And
he asked, "Where are Samuel and David?"
"Over in Naioth at Ramah," they said.
23So Saul went to Naioth at Ramah. But the
Spirit of God came even upon him, and he walked
along prophesying[y] until he came to Naioth. 24He
stripped[z] off his robes and also prophesied in
Samuel's presence. He lay that way all that day
and night. This is why people say, "Is Saul also
among the prophets?"[a]

David and Jonathan

20 Then David fled from Naioth at Ramah and
went to Jonathan and asked, "What have I
done? What is my crime? How have I wronged[b]
your father, that he is trying to take my life?"
2"Never!" Jonathan replied. "You are not going
to die! Look, my father doesn't do anything, great

19:9 [p]1Sa 16:14; 18:10-11
19:10 [q]1Sa 18:11
19:11 [r]Ps 59 Title
19:12 [s]Jos 2:15; Ac 9:25
19:14 [t]Jos 2:4
19:18 [u]1Sa 7:17
19:20 [v]ver 11,14; Jn 7:32,45 [w]Nu 11:25 [x]1Sa 10:5; Joel 2:28
19:23 [y]1Sa 10:13
19:24 [z]2Sa 6:20; Isa 20:2; Mic 1:8 [a]1Sa 10:11
20:1 [b]1Sa 24:9

I see not a step before me
as I tread on another year;
But I've left the Past in God's
keeping—
The Future His mercy shall
clear;
And what looks dark in the dis-
tance may brighten as I
draw near.

—Mary Gardiner Brainard (1860)

[a] 9 Or *injurious* [b] 13 Hebrew *teraphim*; also in verse 16

or small, without confiding in me. Why would he
20:3 hide this from me? It's not so!"
[c]Dt 6:13 3But David took an oath[c] and said, "Your father
knows very well that I have found favor in your
eyes, and he has said to himself, 'Jonathan must
not know this or he will be grieved.' Yet as surely
as the LORD lives and as you live, there is only a
step between me and death."
4Jonathan said to David, "Whatever you want
me to do, I'll do for you."
20:5 5So David said, "Look, tomorrow is the New
[d]Nu 10:10; Moon festival,[d] and I am supposed to dine with
28:11 the king; but let me go and hide[e] in the field until
[e]1Sa 19:2 the evening of the day after tomorrow. 6If your
20:6 father misses me at all, tell him, 'David earnestly
[f]1Sa 17:58 asked my permission to hurry to Bethlehem,[f] his
[g]Dt 12:5 hometown, because an annual[g] sacrifice is being
made there for his whole clan.' 7If he says, 'Very
well,' then your servant is safe. But if he loses his
20:7 [h]1Sa 25:17 temper,[h] you can be sure that he is determined to
harm me. 8As for you, show kindness to your ser-
20:8 [i]1Sa 18:3; vant, for you have brought him into a covenant[i]
23:18 with you before the LORD. If I am guilty, then kill[j]
[j]2Sa 14:32 me yourself! Why hand me over to your father?"
9"Never!" Jonathan said. "If I had the least
inkling that my father was determined to harm
you, wouldn't I tell you?"
10David asked, "Who will tell me if your father
answers you harshly?"
11"Come," Jonathan said, "let's go out into the
field." So they went there together.
12Then Jonathan said to David: "By the LORD,
the God of Israel, I will surely sound out my father
by this time the day after tomorrow! If he is favorably disposed toward you, will I not send you
word and let you know? 13But if my father is
inclined to harm you, may the LORD deal with me,
20:13 [k]Ru 1:17; be it ever so severely,[k] if I do not let you know and
1Sa 3:17 send you away safely. May the LORD be with[l] you
[l]Jos 1:5; 1Sa 17:37; as he has been with my father. 14But show me
18:12; unfailing kindness like that of the LORD as long as
1Ch 22:11,16 I live, so that I may not be killed, 15and do not ever
20:15 cut off your kindness from my family[m]—not even
[m]2Sa 9:7 when the LORD has cut off every one of David's
20:16 enemies from the face of the earth."
[n]1Sa 25:22 16So Jonathan made a covenant[n] with the house
of David, saying, "May the LORD call David's ene-
20:17 mies to account." 17And Jonathan had David reaf-
[o]1Sa 18:3 firm his oath[o] out of love for him, because he
loved him as he loved himself.
18Then Jonathan said to David: "Tomorrow is
20:18 the New Moon festival. You will be missed,
[p]ver 5,25 because your seat will be empty.[p] 19The day after
20:19 tomorrow, toward evening, go to the place where
[q]1Sa 19:2 you hid[q] when this trouble began, and wait by the
stone Ezel. 20I will shoot three arrows to the side
of it, as though I were shooting at a target. 21Then
I will send a boy and say, 'Go, find the arrows.' If
I say to him, 'Look, the arrows are on this side of
you; bring them here,' then come, because, as
surely as the LORD lives, you are safe; there is no

Discouragement

1SA 20:3

"There is only a step between me and death."

The prospect of death at the hand of King Saul overwhelms David with grief and sorrow. Focusing on his problems instead of his call and anointing, David becomes discouraged and convinced that King Saul will do him harm. But God has other plans in mind. If David will turn his focus on God instead of on his problems, he will find peace.

When trouble comes, when things don't go our way, it's easy to follow the same path of discouragement that David journeyed. Just as God anointed David and had a throne awaiting him, he has called us as his children and anointed us as heirs to his kingdom (Ro 8:17). Our present may be discouraging and look hopeless, but our future is assured!

Uncommon Friendship

1SA 20:16-42

Probably the most famous—and most unlikely—friendship in the Bible is the one between Jonathan and David. First Samuel 20:17 says that Jonathan loved David "as he loved himself." David is a lowly shepherd. Jonathan is heir to the throne of Israel. More than that, David has been anointed as the next king of Israel—he stands in the way of Jonathan becoming king (1Sa 16:1,12; 20:31). But instead of seeking his rightful place, Jonathan humbly confirms David's kingship (1Sa 23:17). David likewise shows respect for Jonathan by bowing before him as a servant (1Sa 20:41). Their love for each other is seen most clearly in their parting—the two young men separate with great affection and tears, promising a covenant of friendship not only between themselves but also between their descendants. The application to our own lives is obvious: We, too, have many opportunities to serve, respect and love our friends.

danger. 22 But if I say to the boy, 'Look, the arrows are beyond[r] you,' then you must go, because the LORD has sent you away. 23 And about the matter you and I discussed—remember, the LORD is witness[s] between you and me forever."

24 So David hid in the field, and when the New Moon festival came, the king sat down to eat. 25 He sat in his customary place by the wall, opposite Jonathan,[a] and Abner sat next to Saul, but David's place was empty.[t] 26 Saul said nothing that day, for he thought, "Something must have happened to David to make him ceremonially unclean—surely he is unclean.[u]" 27 But the next day, the second day of the month, David's place was empty again. Then Saul said to his son Jonathan, "Why hasn't the son of Jesse come to the meal, either yesterday or today?"

28 Jonathan answered, "David earnestly asked me for permission[v] to go to Bethlehem. 29 He said, 'Let me go, because our family is observing a sacrifice in the town and my brother has ordered me to be there. If I have found favor in your eyes, let me get away to see my brothers.' That is why he has not come to the king's table."

30 Saul's anger flared up at Jonathan and he said to him, "You son of a perverse and rebellious woman! Don't I know that you have sided with the son of Jesse to your own shame and to the shame of the mother who bore you? 31 As long as the son of Jesse lives on this earth, neither you nor your kingdom will be established. Now send and bring him to me, for he must die!"

32 "Why[w] should he be put to death? What[x] has he done?" Jonathan asked his father. 33 But Saul hurled his spear at him to kill him. Then Jonathan knew that his father intended[y] to kill David.

34 Jonathan got up from the table in fierce anger; on that second day of the month he did not eat, because he was grieved at his father's shameful treatment of David.

35 In the morning Jonathan went out to the field for his meeting with David. He had a small boy with him, 36 and he said to the boy, "Run and find the arrows I shoot." As the boy ran, he shot an arrow beyond him. 37 When the boy came to the place where Jonathan's arrow had fallen, Jonathan called out after him, "Isn't the arrow beyond[z] you?" 38 Then he shouted, "Hurry! Go quickly! Don't stop!" The boy picked up the arrow and returned to his master. 39 (The boy knew nothing of all this; only Jonathan and David knew.) 40 Then Jonathan gave his weapons to the boy and said, "Go, carry them back to town."

41 After the boy had gone, David got up from the south side ⌊of the stone⌋ and bowed down before Jonathan three times, with his face to the ground. Then they kissed each other and wept together—but David wept the most.

42 Jonathan said to David, "Go in peace,[a] for we

20:22 [r]ver 37
20:23 [s]ver 14-15; Ge 31:50
20:25 [t]ver 18
20:26 [u]Lev 7:20-21; 15:5; 1Sa 16:5
20:28 [v]ver 6
20:32 [w]1Sa 19:4; Mt 27:23 [x]Ge 31:36; Lk 23:22
20:33 [y]ver 7; 1Sa 18:11,17
20:37 [z]ver 22
20:42 [a]ver 22; 1Sa 1:17

[a] 25 Septuagint; Hebrew *wall. Jonathan arose*

20:42 have sworn friendship[b] with each other in the
[b]2Sa 1:26; name of the LORD, saying, 'The LORD is witness
Pr 18:24 between you and me, and between your descendants and my descendants forever.' " Then David
left, and Jonathan went back to the town.

David at Nob

21:1 **21** David went to Nob,[c] to Ahimelech the
[c]1Sa 14:3; 22:9,19; priest. Ahimelech trembled[d] when he met
Ne 11:32; Isa 10:32 him, and asked, "Why are you alone? Why is no
[d]1Sa 16:4 one with you?"
[2]David answered Ahimelech the priest, "The
king charged me with a certain matter and said to
me, 'No one is to know anything about your mission and your instructions.' As for my men, I have
told them to meet me at a certain place. [3]Now
then, what do you have on hand? Give me five
loaves of bread, or whatever you can find."
21:4 [4]But the priest answered David, "I don't have
[e]Lev 24:8-9 any ordinary bread[e] on hand; however, there is
[f]Ex 25:30; Mt 12:4 some consecrated[f] bread here—provided the men
[g]Ex 19:15 have kept[g] themselves from women."
21:5 [5]David replied, "Indeed women have been kept
[h]1Th 4:4 from us, as usual whenever[a] I set out. The men's
things[b] are holy[h] even on missions that are not
holy. How much more so today!" [6]So the priest
21:6 gave him the consecrated bread,[i] since there was
[i]Lev 24:8-9; Mt 12:3-4; no bread there except the bread of the Presence
Mk 2:25-28; Lk 6:1-5 that had been removed from before the LORD and
replaced by hot bread on the day it was taken
away.
21:7 [7]Now one of Saul's servants was there that day,
[j]1Sa 22:9,22 detained before the LORD; he was Doeg[j] the Edom-
[k]1Sa 14:47; Ps 52 Title ite,[k] Saul's head shepherd.
[8]David asked Ahimelech, "Don't you have a
spear or a sword here? I haven't brought my
sword or any other weapon, because the king's
business was urgent."
21:9 [9]The priest replied, "The sword[l] of Goliath the
[l]1Sa 17:51 Philistine, whom you killed in the Valley of Elah,[m]
[m]1Sa 17:2 is here; it is wrapped in a cloth behind the ephod.
If you want it, take it; there is no sword here but
that one."
David said, "There is none like it; give it to me."

David at Gath

21:10 [10]That day David fled from Saul and went[n] to
[n]1Sa 27:2 Achish king of Gath. [11]But the servants of Achish
said to him, "Isn't this David, the king of the land?
Isn't he the one they sing about in their dances:

" 'Saul has slain his thousands,
21:11 and David his tens of thousands'?"[o]
[o]1Sa 18:7; 29:5; Ps 56 Title

[12]David took these words to heart and was very
much afraid of Achish king of Gath. [13]So he pre-
21:13 tended to be insane[p] in their presence; and while
[p]Ps 34 Title he was in their hands he acted like a madman,
making marks on the doors of the gate and letting
saliva run down his beard.

[a] 5 Or *from us in the past few days since* [b] 5 Or *bodies*

Consecrated Bread

1SA 21:4

The consecrated bread that Ahimelech the priest offers is described in Leviticus 24:5-9. Twelve loaves of bread are baked and, each Sabbath, are placed on the table of pure gold. The bread is a gift that represents the people's gratitude to God for his provision. When the bread is removed, only priests may eat it. Since this is the only bread available, Ahimelech offers it to David, but only if David's men have "kept themselves from women." According to Levitical law, a man who has had an emission of semen after sexual contact with a woman must bathe with water and is considered unclean until evening (Lev 15:16). In order to eat this holy bread, the men must be ceremonially clean. After David's confirmation, Ahimelech considers the men clean, and he gives David the consecrated bread. It is interesting to note that Jesus recalls this incident in order to teach the Pharisees that doing good takes precedence over ritualistic adherence to ceremonial law (Lk 6:1-5).

David's Motley Crew

1SA 22:2

David's band of renegades is a motley crew—there's not a trained warrior or rich man in the bunch. Running from King Saul, David is considered an outlaw, and those who are drawn to him are those who are "in distress or in debt or discontented." Yet David readily accepts any who will enlist in his service and follow his leadership. Like Jesus centuries later, David is a magnet for lost and hurting souls.

[14]Achish said to his servants, "Look at the man!
He is insane! Why bring him to me? [15]Am I so
short of madmen that you have to bring this fellow here to carry on like this in front of me? Must
this man come into my house?"

David at Adullam and Mizpah

22 David left Gath and escaped to the cave[q] of
Adullam. When his brothers and his
father's household heard about it, they went
down to him there. [2]All those who were in distress or in debt or discontented gathered[r] around
him, and he became their leader. About four hundred men were with him.

22:1 q2Sa 23:13; Ps 57 Title; 142 Title
22:2 r1Sa 23:13; 25:13; 2Sa 15:20

[3]From there David went to Mizpah in Moab and
said to the king of Moab, "Would you let my
father and mother come and stay with you until I
learn what God will do for me?" [4]So he left them
with the king of Moab, and they stayed with him
as long as David was in the stronghold.
[5]But the prophet Gad[s] said to David, "Do not
stay in the stronghold. Go into the land of Judah."
So David left and went to the forest of Hereth.

22:5 s2Sa 24:11; 1Ch 21:9; 29:29; 2Ch 29:25

Saul Kills the Priests of Nob

[6]Now Saul heard that David and his men had
been discovered. And Saul, spear in hand, was
seated[t] under the tamarisk[u] tree on the hill at Gibeah, with all his officials standing around him.
[7]Saul said to them, "Listen, men of Benjamin!
Will the son of Jesse give all of you fields and
vineyards? Will he make all of you commanders[v]
of thousands and commanders of hundreds? [8]Is
that why you have all conspired against me? No
one tells me when my son makes a covenant[w]
with the son of Jesse. None of you is concerned[x]
about me or tells me that my son has incited my
servant to lie in wait for me, as he does today."
[9]But Doeg[y] the Edomite, who was standing with
Saul's officials, said, "I saw the son of Jesse come to
Ahimelech son of Ahitub at Nob.[z] [10]Ahimelech
inquired[a] of the LORD for him; he also gave him provisions[b] and the sword of Goliath the Philistine."

22:6 tJdg 4:5 uGe 21:33
22:7 v1Sa 8:14
22:8 w1Sa 18:3; 20:16 x1Sa 23:21
22:9 y1Sa 21:7; Ps 52 Title z1Sa 21:1
22:10 aNu 27:21; 1Sa 10:22 b1Sa 21:6

[11]Then the king sent for the priest Ahimelech
son of Ahitub and his father's whole family, who
were the priests at Nob, and they all came to the
king. [12]Saul said, "Listen now, son of Ahitub."
"Yes, my lord," he answered.
[13]Saul said to him, "Why have you conspired[c]
against me, you and the son of Jesse, giving him
bread and a sword and inquiring of God for him,
so that he has rebelled against me and lies in wait
for me, as he does today?"
[14]Ahimelech answered the king, "Who[d] of all
your servants is as loyal as David, the king's son-
in-law, captain of your bodyguard and highly
respected in your household? [15]Was that day the
first time I inquired of God for him? Of course not!
Let not the king accuse your servant or any of his

22:13 cver 8
22:14 d1Sa 19:4

father's family, for your servant knows nothing at
all about this whole affair."
16But the king said, "You will surely die, Ahimelech, you and your father's whole family."
17Then the king ordered the guards at his side:
"Turn and kill the priests of the LORD, because
they too have sided with David. They knew he
was fleeing, yet they did not tell me."
22:17 But the king's officials were not willing[e] to raise
[e]Ex 1:17 a hand to strike the priests of the LORD.
18The king then ordered Doeg, "You turn and
strike down the priests." So Doeg the Edomite
turned and struck them down. That day he killed
22:18 eighty-five men who wore the linen ephod.[f] 19He
[f]1Sa 2:18,31 also put to the sword[g] Nob, the town of the
22:19 priests, with its men and women, its children and
[g]1Sa 15:3 infants, and its cattle, donkeys and sheep.
22:20 20But Abiathar,[h] a son of Ahimelech son of Ahi-
[h]1Sa 23:6,9; 30:7; tub, escaped and fled to join David.[i] 21He told
1Ki 2:22,26, David that Saul had killed the priests of the LORD.
27 22Then David said to Abiathar: "That day, when
[i]1Sa 2:32 Doeg[j] the Edomite was there, I knew he would be
22:22 sure to tell Saul. I am responsible for the death of
[j]1Sa 21:7 your father's whole family. 23Stay with me; don't
22:23 be afraid; the man who is seeking your life[k] is
[k]1Ki 2:26 seeking mine also. You will be safe with me."

David Saves Keilah

23 When David was told, "Look, the Philis-
23:1 tines are fighting against Keilah[l] and are
[l]Jos 15:44 looting the threshing floors," 2he inquired[m] of the
23:2 LORD, saying, "Shall I go and attack these Philis-
[m]ver 4,12; 1Sa 30:8; tines?"
2Sa 5:19,23 The LORD answered him, "Go, attack the Philistines and save Keilah."
3But David's men said to him, "Here in Judah
we are afraid. How much more, then, if we go to
Keilah against the Philistine forces!"
4Once again David inquired of the LORD, and the
23:4 LORD answered him, "Go down to Keilah, for I am
[n]Jos 8:7; going to give the Philistines into your hand.[n]" 5So
Jdg 7:7 David and his men went to Keilah, fought the Philistines and carried off their livestock. He inflicted
23:6 heavy losses on the Philistines and saved the peo-
[o]1Sa 22:20 ple of Keilah. 6(Now Abiathar[o] son of Ahimelech
had brought the ephod down with him when he
fled to David at Keilah.)

Saul Pursues David

7Saul was told that David had gone to Keilah,
and he said, "God has handed him over to me, for
David has imprisoned himself by entering a town
with gates and bars." 8And Saul called up all his
forces for battle, to go down to Keilah to besiege
David and his men.
23:9 9When David learned that Saul was plotting
[p]ver 6; against him, he said to Abiathar[p] the priest, "Bring
1Sa 22:20; the ephod." 10David said, "O LORD, God of Israel,
30:7 your servant has heard definitely that Saul plans
to come to Keilah and destroy the town on account

David's Hard Lesson

1SA 22:17–22

Saul's anger is growing, spreading, consuming him. No longer content with destroying David, Saul insists on killing anyone assisting this enemy of the king—even God's anointed priests. Yet the king's guards refuse to comply. They know that by striking out at the priests, they are striking out at God himself. Saul's zeal is not quenched, and he commands Doeg, an Edomite, to do the dirty work. In the end, only one priest escapes with his life—and another distressed soul joins David's band. Not surprisingly, David takes responsibility for the massacre. After all, Saul wants David, not the priests. And David neglected to take precautions to prevent Doeg from telling Saul about David's encounter with Ahimelech the priest (1Sa 22:9–10). Through this incident David learns a hard lesson: Sometimes those hurt most by hostilities are the innocent.

A Third Covenant

1SA 23:16

Saul is in hot pursuit of David. He can't seem to catch up with him; yet Saul's son Jonathan finds a way. Jonathan offers comfort. He encourages David to look to God. He reminds David of his rightful place as future king. He offers hope. He confirms God's plan, and the friends make a covenant for the third time (1Sa 23:17–18). This third covenant goes beyond the earlier covenants between the two men (1Sa 18:3; 20:16–17). This new agreement places Jonathan in a position as second-in-command to David, offering the benefit of rallying together the followers of both David and of Saul.

of me. 11Will the citizens of Keilah surrender me
to him? Will Saul come down, as your servant has
heard? O LORD, God of Israel, tell your servant."
And the LORD said, "He will."
12Again David asked, "Will the citizens of Kei- **23:12**
lah surrender[q] me and my men to Saul?" [q]ver 20
And the LORD said, "They will." **23:13**
13So David and his men,[r] about six hundred in [r]1Sa 22:2;
number, left Keilah and kept moving from place 25:13
to place. When Saul was told that David had
escaped from Keilah, he did not go there.
14David stayed in the desert strongholds and in **23:14**
the hills of the Desert of Ziph.[s] Day after day Saul [s]Jos 15:24,
searched[t] for him, but God did not[u] give David 55
into his hands. [t]Ps 54:3-4
[u]Ps 32:7
15While David was at Horesh in the Desert of
Ziph, he learned that Saul had come out to take
his life. 16And Saul's son Jonathan went to David
at Horesh and helped him find strength[v] in God. **23:16**
17"Don't be afraid," he said. "My father Saul will [v]1Sa 30:6
not lay a hand on you. You will be king[w] over **23:17**
Israel, and I will be second to you. Even my father [w]1Sa 20:31;
Saul knows this." 18The two of them made a cov- 24:20
enant[x] before the LORD. Then Jonathan went **23:18**
home, but David remained at Horesh. [x]1Sa 18:3;
19The Ziphites[y] went up to Saul at Gibeah and 20:16,42;
said, "Is not David hiding among us[z] in the 2Sa 9:1; 21:7
strongholds at Horesh, on the hill of Hakilah,[a] **23:19**
south of Jeshimon? 20Now, O king, come down [y]1Sa 26:1
whenever it pleases you to do so, and we will be [z]Ps 54 Title
responsible for handing[b] him over to the king." [a]1Sa 26:3
21Saul replied, "The LORD bless you for your **23:20**
concern[c] for me. 22Go and make further prepara- [b]ver 12
tion. Find out where David usually goes and who **23:21**
has seen him there. They tell me he is very crafty. [c]1Sa 22:8
23Find out about all the hiding places he uses and
come back to me with definite information.[a] Then
I will go with you; if he is in the area, I will track
him down among all the clans of Judah."
24So they set out and went to Ziph ahead of
Saul. Now David and his men were in the Desert
of Maon,[d] in the Arabah south of Jeshimon. 25Saul **23:24**
and his men began the search, and when David [d]Jos 15:55;
was told about it, he went down to the rock and 1Sa 25:2
stayed in the Desert of Maon. When Saul heard
this, he went into the Desert of Maon in pursuit of
David.
26Saul[e] was going along one side of the moun- **23:26**
tain, and David and his men were on the other [e]Ps 17:9
side, hurrying to get away from Saul. As Saul and
his forces were closing in on David and his men to
capture them, 27a messenger came to Saul, saying,
"Come quickly! The Philistines are raiding the
land." 28Then Saul broke off his pursuit of David
and went to meet the Philistines. That is why they
call this place Sela Hammahlekoth.[b] 29And David
went up from there and lived in the strongholds of **23:29**
En Gedi.[f] [f]2Ch 20:2

[a] 23 Or *me at Nacon* [b] 28 *Sela Hammahlekoth* means *rock of parting.*

David Spares Saul's Life

24 After Saul returned from pursuing the Philistines, he was told, "David is in the Desert
of En Gedi.[g]" 2So Saul took three thousand chosen
men from all Israel and set out to look[h] for David
and his men near the Crags of the Wild Goats.
3He came to the sheep pens along the way; a
cave[i] was there, and Saul went in to relieve[j] himself. David and his men were far back in the cave.
4The men said, "This is the day the LORD spoke[k] of
when he said[a] to you, 'I will give your enemy into
your hands for you to deal with as you wish.' "[l]
Then David crept up unnoticed and cut off a corner of Saul's robe.
5Afterward, David was conscience-stricken[m] for
having cut off a corner of his robe. 6He said to his
men, "The LORD forbid that I should do such a
thing to my master, the LORD's anointed,[n] or lift
my hand against him; for he is the anointed of the
LORD." 7With these words David rebuked his men
and did not allow them to attack Saul. And Saul
left the cave and went his way.
8Then David went out of the cave and called out
to Saul, "My lord the king!" When Saul looked
behind him, David bowed down and prostrated
himself with his face to the ground.[o] 9He said to
Saul, "Why do you listen when men say, 'David is
bent on harming you'? 10This day you have seen
with your own eyes how the LORD delivered you
into my hands in the cave. Some urged me to kill
you, but I spared you; I said, 'I will not lift my
hand against my master, because he is the LORD's
anointed.' 11See, my father, look at this piece of
your robe in my hand! I cut off the corner of your
robe but did not kill you. Now understand and
recognize that I am not guilty[p] of wrongdoing or
rebellion. I have not wronged you, but you are
hunting[q] me down to take my life. 12May the LORD
judge[r] between you and me. And may the LORD
avenge[s] the wrongs you have done to me, but my
hand will not touch you. 13As the old saying goes,
'From evildoers come evil deeds,[t]' so my hand
will not touch you.
14"Against whom has the king of Israel come
out? Whom are you pursuing? A dead dog?[u] A
flea?[v] 15May the LORD be our judge[w] and decide
between us. May he consider my cause and
uphold[x] it; may he vindicate[y] me by delivering[z]
me from your hand."
16When David finished saying this, Saul asked,
"Is that your voice,[a] David my son?" And he wept
aloud. 17"You are more righteous than I,"[b] he said.
"You have treated me well,[c] but I have treated you
badly. 18You have just now told me of the good
you did to me; the LORD delivered[d] me into your
hands, but you did not kill me. 19When a man
finds his enemy, does he let him get away
unharmed? May the LORD reward you well for the
way you treated me today. 20I know that you will

24:1 [g]1Sa 23:28-29
24:2 [h]1Sa 26:2
24:3 [i]Ps 57 Title; 142 Title [j]Jdg 3:24
24:4 [k]1Sa 25:28-30 [l]1Sa 23:17; 26:8
24:5 [m]2Sa 24:10
24:6 [n]1Sa 26:11
24:8 [o]1Sa 25:23-24
24:11 [p]Ps 7:3 [q]1Sa 23:14, 23; 1Sa 26:20
24:12 [r]Ge 16:5; 31:53; Job 5:8 [s]Jdg 11:27; 1Sa 26:10
24:13 [t]Mt 7:20
24:14 [u]1Sa 17:43; 2Sa 9:8 [v]1Sa 26:20
24:15 [w]ver 12 [x]Ps 35:1,23; Mic 7:9 [y]Ps 43:1 [z]Ps 119:134, 154
24:16 [a]1Sa 26:17
24:17 [b]Ge 38:26; 1Sa 26:21 [c]Mt 5:44
24:18 [d]1Sa 26:23

[a] 4 Or *"Today the LORD is saying*

A God-Centered Person

1SA 24

David faces real enemies. Killing is not new to him. Tens of thousands have been slain under his command. But when his adversary Saul is helpless before him, David is conscience stricken merely because he cuts off a corner of the king's robe. David knows the symbolic nature of what he has done. To hold the corner of someone's robe showed loyalty, while cutting off the corner revealed rebellion.

This passage serves as a vivid comparison between a self-centered person and a God-centered person. While one strives for power, the other takes a place of humility. While one seeks to destroy, the other desires to uplift those whom God sees as worthy. While one strives to kill without regret, the other feels remorse over the smallest act of disrespect. Read this passage again, taking note of David's example of considering others for God's sake. Then, consider practical ways to follow this in daily living.

Sheepshearing Festivities

1SA 25:7-8

In Old Testament days the Israelites celebrated feasts and festivals on a community scale. Even the poor, the widows and the orphans were invited. So when David seeks help from Nabal, he makes a point of reminding Nabal that it is sheep-shearing time—a "festive time" (1Sa 25:8). As the flock owner, part of the purpose of Nabal's celebration is to share his bounty with those who attend. And David feels his men have earned the right to join the feast by protecting Nabal's flocks. If David had approached Nabal at any other time, Nabal could have claimed he had nothing to spare. But during a holiday, when supplies are plentiful, Nabal is without excuse.

Just like Nabal, we also are without excuse when we refuse to give out of our abundance. God has given us much. In return he only asks that we open our hearts and hands to others.

surely be king[e] and that the kingdom[f] of Israel will be established in your hands. 21 Now swear[g] to me by the LORD that you will not cut off my descendants or wipe out my name from my father's family.[h]"

22 So David gave his oath to Saul. Then Saul returned home, but David and his men went up to the stronghold.[i]

David, Nabal and Abigail

25 Now Samuel died,[j] and all Israel assembled and mourned[k] for him; and they buried him at his home in Ramah.[l]

Then David moved down into the Desert of Maon.[a] 2 A certain man in Maon,[m] who had property there at Carmel, was very wealthy. He had a thousand goats and three thousand sheep, which he was shearing in Carmel. 3 His name was Nabal and his wife's name was Abigail.[n] She was an intelligent and beautiful woman, but her husband, a Calebite,[o] was surly and mean in his dealings.

4 While David was in the desert, he heard that Nabal was shearing sheep. 5 So he sent ten young men and said to them, "Go up to Nabal at Carmel and greet him in my name. 6 Say to him: 'Long life to you! Good health[p] to you and your household! And good health to all that is yours![q]

7 " 'Now I hear that it is sheep-shearing time. When your shepherds were with us, we did not mistreat[r] them, and the whole time they were at Carmel nothing of theirs was missing. 8 Ask your own servants and they will tell you. Therefore be favorable toward my young men, since we come at a festive time. Please give your servants and your son David whatever[s] you can find for them.' "

9 When David's men arrived, they gave Nabal this message in David's name. Then they waited.

10 Nabal answered David's servants, "Who[t] is this David? Who is this son of Jesse? Many servants are breaking away from their masters these days. 11 Why should I take my bread[u] and water, and the meat I have slaughtered for my shearers, and give it to men coming from who knows where?"

12 David's men turned around and went back. When they arrived, they reported every word. 13 David said to his men, "Put on your swords!" So they put on their swords, and David put on his. About four hundred men went[v] up with David, while two hundred stayed with the supplies.[w]

14 One of the servants told Nabal's wife Abigail: "David sent messengers from the desert to give our master his greetings,[x] but he hurled insults at them. 15 Yet these men were very good to us. They did not mistreat[y] us, and the whole time we were out in the fields near them nothing was missing.[z] 16 Night and day they were a wall[a] around us all the time we were herding our sheep near them. 17 Now think it over and see what you can do, because disaster is hanging over our master and

24:20 [e]1Sa 23:17 [f]1Sa 13:14
24:21 [g]Ge 21:23; 2Sa 21:1-9 [h]1Sa 20:14-15
24:22 [i]1Sa 23:29
25:1 [j]1Sa 28:3 [k]Nu 20:29; Dt 34:8 [l]Ge 21:21; 2Ch 33:20
25:2 [m]Jos 15:55; 1Sa 23:24
25:3 [n]Pr 31:10 [o]Jos 15:13
25:6 [p]Ps 122:7; Lk 10:5 [q]1Ch 12:18
25:7 [r]ver 15
25:8 [s]Ne 8:10
25:10 [t]Jdg 9:28
25:11 [u]Jdg 8:6
25:13 [v]1Sa 23:13 [w]1Sa 30:24
25:14 [x]1Sa 13:10
25:15 [y]ver 7 [z]ver 21
25:16 [a]Ex 14:22; Job 1:10

[a] *1* Some Septuagint manuscripts; Hebrew *Paran*

25:17 his whole household. He is such a wicked[b] man
b1Sa 20:7 that no one can talk to him."
[18]Abigail lost no time. She took two hundred
loaves of bread, two skins of wine, five dressed
sheep, five seahs[a] of roasted grain, a hundred
25:18 cakes of raisins[c] and two hundred cakes of pressed
c1Ch 12:40 d2Sa 16:1 figs, and loaded them on donkeys.[d] [19]Then she told
her servants, "Go on ahead;[e] I'll follow you." But
25:19 she did not tell her husband Nabal.
eGe 32:20 [20]As she came riding her donkey into a mountain ravine, there were David and his men
descending toward her, and she met them. [21]David
had just said, "It's been useless—all my watching
25:21 over this fellow's property in the desert so that
fPs 109:5 nothing of his was missing. He has paid[f] me back
evil for good. [22]May God deal with David,[b] be it
25:22 g1Sa 3:17; ever so severely,[g] if by morning I leave alive one
20:13 male[h] of all who belong to him!"
h1Ki 14:10; [23]When Abigail saw David, she quickly got off
21:21; 2Ki 9:8 her donkey and bowed down before David with
her face to the ground.[i] [24]She fell at his feet and
25:23 i1Sa 20:41 said: "My lord, let the blame be on me alone.
Please let your servant speak to you; hear what
your servant has to say. [25]May my lord pay no
attention to that wicked man Nabal. He is just like
25:25 jPr 14:16 his name—his name is Fool,[j] and folly goes with
him. But as for me, your servant, I did not see the
men my master sent.
[26]"Now since the LORD has kept you, my mas-
25:26 ter, from bloodshed[k] and from avenging[l] yourself
kver 33 lHeb 10:30 with your own hands, as surely as the LORD lives
m2Sa 18:32 and as you live, may your enemies and all who
intend to harm my master be like Nabal.[m] [27]And
25:27 nGe 33:11; let this gift,[n] which your servant has brought to
1Sa 30:26 my master, be given to the men who follow you.
25:28 [28]Please forgive[o] your servant's offense, for the
over 24 LORD will certainly make a lasting[p] dynasty for my
p2Sa 7:11,26 q1Sa 18:17 master, because he fights the LORD's battles.[q] Let
r1Sa 24:11 no wrongdoing[r] be found in you as long as you
live. [29]Even though someone is pursuing you to
take your life, the life of my master will be bound
securely in the bundle of the living by the LORD
25:29 your God. But the lives of your enemies he will
sJer 10:18 hurl[s] away as from the pocket of a sling. [30]When
the LORD has done for my master every good thing
25:30 he promised concerning him and has appointed
t1Sa 13:14 him leader[t] over Israel, [31]my master will not have
on his conscience the staggering burden of need-
less bloodshed or of having avenged himself. And
when the LORD has brought my master success,
25:31 uGe 40:14 remember[u] your servant."
[32]David said to Abigail, "Praise[v] be to the LORD,
25:32 vGe 24:27; the God of Israel, who has sent you today to meet
Ex 18:10; me. [33]May you be blessed for your good judgment
Lk 1:68 and for keeping me from bloodshed[w] this day and
25:33 from avenging myself with my own hands. [34]Oth-
wver 26 erwise, as surely as the LORD, the God of Israel,

[a] *18* That is, probably about a bushel (about 37 liters)
[b] *22* Some Septuagint manuscripts; Hebrew *with David's enemies*

Real Security

1SA 25:29

Abigail literally throws herself at David's feet. She ***sees this as her only chance to save her husband and the others in her household.*** **She offers David** ***a generous gift of food and drink, and then she asks forgiveness for her husband's harshness.*** **Abigail** ***makes it clear that she is aware of what her husband is . . . and who*** **David is, "for the LORD will cer-** ***tainly make a lasting dynasty for my master, because he fights the*** **LORD's battles" (1Sa 25:28). She** ***ends by prophesying that God will*** **keep David "bound securely in the bundle of the living." In essence** ***she is saying,*** **"David, you will not be killed, but God will secure your** ***place among the living in the same way we hold close all that is pre- cious to us"*** **(see the character sketch for Abigail on page 805).**

Multiple Wives

1SA 25:39,42–44

Although God intends for *one man and one woman* to be united in marriage (Ge 2:24), polygamy—the practice of taking multiple wives—is common in early Biblical times, especially among royalty. In the space of three verses, David marries two women. In his mind, and as a symbol to those around him, David proves his rank and importance. Both marriages are politically important because they align David with important clans and regions. But his marriages do not stop here: "David took more concubines and wives in Jerusalem, and more sons and daughters were born to him" (2Sa 5:13). While God seems to tolerate this practice in Old Testament times (see the note on 1Ch 14:3, page 651), he makes his ideal clear to the early church: *one man, one women, one flesh* (1Ti 3:2,12).

lives, who has kept me from harming you, if you had not come quickly to meet me, not one male belonging to Nabal would have been left alive by daybreak."

35 Then David accepted from her hand what she had brought him and said, "Go home in peace. I have heard your words and granted[x] your request."

36 When Abigail went to Nabal, he was in the house holding a banquet like that of a king. He was in high[y] spirits and very drunk.[z] So she told[a] him nothing until daybreak. 37 Then in the morning, when Nabal was sober, his wife told him all these things, and his heart failed him and he became like a stone. 38 About ten days later, the LORD struck[b] Nabal and he died.

39 When David heard that Nabal was dead, he said, "Praise be to the LORD, who has upheld my cause against Nabal for treating me with contempt. He has kept his servant from doing wrong and has brought Nabal's wrongdoing down on his own head."

Then David sent word to Abigail, asking her to become his wife. 40 His servants went to Carmel and said to Abigail, "David has sent us to you to take you to become his wife."

41 She bowed down with her face to the ground and said, "Here is your maidservant, ready to serve you and wash the feet of my master's servants." 42 Abigail[c] quickly got on a donkey and, attended by her five maids, went with David's messengers and became his wife. 43 David had also married Ahinoam[d] of Jezreel, and they both were his wives.[e] 44 But Saul had given his daughter Michal, David's wife, to Paltiel[a][f] son of Laish, who was from Gallim.[g]

David Again Spares Saul's Life

26 The Ziphites[h] went to Saul at Gibeah and said, "Is not David hiding[i] on the hill of Hakilah, which faces Jeshimon?"

2 So Saul went down to the Desert of Ziph, with his three thousand chosen men of Israel, to search[j] there for David. 3 Saul made his camp beside the road on the hill of Hakilah facing Jeshimon, but David stayed in the desert. When he saw that Saul had followed him there, 4 he sent out scouts and learned that Saul had definitely arrived.[b]

5 Then David set out and went to the place where Saul had camped. He saw where Saul and Abner[k] son of Ner, the commander of the army, had lain down. Saul was lying inside the camp, with the army encamped around him.

6 David then asked Ahimelech the Hittite and Abishai son of Zeruiah,[l] Joab's brother, "Who will go down into the camp with me to Saul?"

"I'll go with you," said Abishai.

7 So David and Abishai went to the army by night, and there was Saul, lying asleep inside the

25:35 [x]Ge 19:21; 1Sa 20:42; 2Ki 5:19
25:36 [y]2Sa 13:23 [z]Pr 20:1; Isa 5:11,22; Hos 4:11 [a]ver 19
25:38 [b]1Sa 26:10; 2Sa 6:7
25:42 [c]Ge 24:61-67
25:43 [d]Jos 15:56 [e]1Sa 27:3; 30:5
25:44 [f]2Sa 3:15 [g]Isa 10:30
26:1 [h]1Sa 23:19 [i]Ps 54 Title
26:2 [j]1Sa 13:2; 24:2
26:5 [k]1Sa 14:50; 17:55
26:6 [l]Jdg 7:10-11; 1Ch 2:16

[a] 44 Hebrew *Palti*, a variant of *Paltiel* [b] 4 Or *had come to Nacon*

camp with his spear stuck in the ground near his
head. Abner and the soldiers were lying around
him.
8Abishai said to David, "Today God has delivered your enemy into your hands. Now let me pin
him to the ground with one thrust of my spear; I
won't strike him twice."
9But David said to Abishai, "Don't destroy him!
26:9 Who can lay a hand on the LORD's anointed[m] and
[m]2Sa 1:14 be guiltless?[n] 10As surely as the LORD lives," he
[n]1Sa 24:5 said, "the LORD himself will strike[o] him; either his
26:10 time[p] will come and he will die,[q] or he will go into
[o]1Sa 25:38; Ro 12:19 battle and perish. 11But the LORD forbid that I
[p]Ge 47:29; should lay a hand on the LORD's anointed. Now
Dt 31:14; Ps 37:13 get the spear and water jug that are near his head,
[q]1Sa 31:6; 2Sa 1:1 and let's go."
12So David took the spear and water jug near
Saul's head, and they left. No one saw or knew
about it, nor did anyone wake up. They were all
26:12 sleeping, because the LORD had put them into a
[r]Ge 2:21; 15:12 deep sleep.[r]
13Then David crossed over to the other side and
stood on top of the hill some distance away; there
was a wide space between them. 14He called out
to the army and to Abner son of Ner, "Aren't you
going to answer me, Abner?"
Abner replied, "Who are you who calls to the
king?"
15David said, "You're a man, aren't you? And
who is like you in Israel? Why didn't you guard
your lord the king? Someone came to destroy your
lord the king. 16What you have done is not good.
As surely as the LORD lives, you and your men
deserve to die, because you did not guard your
master, the LORD's anointed. Look around you.
Where are the king's spear and water jug that
were near his head?"
26:17 17Saul recognized David's voice and said, "Is
[s]1Sa 24:16 that your voice,[s] David my son?"
David replied, "Yes it is, my lord the king."
18And he added, "Why is my lord pursuing his ser-
26:18 vant? What have I done, and what wrong[t] am I
[t]1Sa 24:9,11-14 guilty of? 19Now let my lord the king listen to his
servant's words. If the LORD has incited you against
26:19 me, then may he accept an offering.[u] If, however,
[u]2Sa 16:11 [v]2Sa 14:16 men have done it, may they be cursed before the
LORD! They have now driven me from my share in
the LORD's inheritance[v] and have said, 'Go, serve
other gods.' 20Now do not let my blood fall to the
26:20 ground far from the presence of the LORD. The king
[w]1Sa 24:14 of Israel has come out to look for a flea[w]—as one
hunts a partridge in the mountains."
26:21 21Then Saul said, "I have sinned.[x] Come back,
[x]Ex 9:27; 1Sa 15:24 David my son. Because you considered my life pre-
[y]1Sa 24:17 cious[y] today, I will not try to harm you again. Surely I have acted like a fool and have erred greatly."
22"Here is the king's spear," David answered.
26:23 "Let one of your young men come over and get it.
[z]Ps 62:12 23The LORD rewards[z] every man for his righteous-
[a]Ps 7:8; 18:20,24 ness[a] and faithfulness. The LORD delivered you
into my hands today, but I would not lay a hand

God's Perfect Timing

1SA 26:9-11

In today's society we feel the sooner we reach the top and grasp our rightful place, the better. David, on the other hand, finds contentment in his position as God's servant, whether that means fulfilling the occupation of a shepherd, a warrior or a king. **David not only refuses to kill Saul when the opportunity presents itself, but David also refuses to allow others to do so. Instead, he puts Saul's end in God's hand (1Sa 26:10). To David, God's perfect timing matters more than his own desire to reign. David's *example is one we can follow as we replace our own longing for success with a yearning for God's* plans and God's paths.**

Humble or Brutal?

1SA 27:5,9

David's life among the Philistines may seem confusing. He behaves humbly—or so it seems (1Sa 27:5). Yet this "humility" allows him to live apart from the king's watchful eye. And while David's brutality seems inexcusable to us, the destruction of peoples and cities is a continuation of the conquest of Canaan begun by Joshua. David may live among his enemies, but if we take a closer look, we see that he is not under their submission. While Achish trusts David and believes that David has cut himself off from Israel (1Sa 27:12), David actually uses his protected life in the land of the Philistines to defeat Israel's enemies for the benefit of God's people.

on the LORD's anointed. 24As surely as I valued
your life today, so may the LORD value my life and
deliver[b] me from all trouble."
25Then Saul said to David, "May you be blessed,
my son David; you will do great things and surely triumph."

So David went on his way, and Saul returned home.

David Among the Philistines

27 But David thought to himself, "One of these days I will be destroyed by the hand of Saul. The best thing I can do is to escape to the land of the Philistines. Then Saul will give up searching for me anywhere in Israel, and I will slip out of his hand."
2So David and the six hundred men[c] with him
left and went[d] over to Achish[e] son of Maoch king
of Gath. 3David and his men settled in Gath with
Achish. Each man had his family with him, and
David had his two wives:[f] Ahinoam of Jezreel and
Abigail of Carmel, the widow of Nabal. 4When
Saul was told that David had fled to Gath, he no
longer searched for him.
5Then David said to Achish, "If I have found
favor in your eyes, let a place be assigned to me in one of the country towns, that I may live there. Why should your servant live in the royal city with you?"
6So on that day Achish gave him Ziklag,[g] and it
has belonged to the kings of Judah ever since.
7David lived[h] in Philistine territory a year and four
months.
8Now David and his men went up and raided
the Geshurites,[i] the Girzites and the Amalekites.[j]
(From ancient times these peoples had lived in the
land extending to Shur[k] and Egypt.) 9Whenever
David attacked an area, he did not leave a man or woman alive,[l] but took sheep and cattle, donkeys and camels, and clothes. Then he returned to Achish.
10When Achish asked, "Where did you go raid-
ing today?" David would say, "Against the Negev
of Judah" or "Against the Negev of Jerahmeel[m]"
or "Against the Negev of the Kenites.[n]" 11He did
not leave a man or woman alive to be brought to Gath, for he thought, "They might inform on us and say, 'This is what David did.' " And such was his practice as long as he lived in Philistine territory. 12Achish trusted David and said to himself,
"He has become so odious to his people, the Israelites, that he will be my servant forever."

Saul and the Witch of Endor

28 In those days the Philistines gathered[o] their forces to fight against Israel. Achish said to David, "You must understand that you and your men will accompany me in the army."
2David said, "Then you will see for yourself
what your servant can do."

26:24 [b]Ps 54:7
27:2 [c]1Sa 25:13 [d]1Sa 21:10 [e]1Ki 2:39
27:3 [f]1Sa 25:43; 30:3
27:6 [g]Jos 15:31; 19:5; Ne 11:28
27:7 [h]1Sa 29:3
27:8 [i]Jos 13:2,13 [j]Ex 17:8; 1Sa 15:7-8 [k]Ex 15:22
27:9 [l]1Sa 15:3
27:10 [m]1Sa 30:29; 1Ch 2:9,25 [n]Jdg 1:16
28:1 [o]1Sa 29:1

Achish replied, "Very well, I will make you my
bodyguard for life."
3 Now Samuel was dead,[p] and all Israel had
mourned for him and buried him in his own town
of Ramah.[q] Saul had expelled the mediums and
spiritists[r] from the land.
4 The Philistines assembled and came and set up
camp at Shunem,[s] while Saul gathered all the Israelites and set up camp at Gilboa.[t] 5 When Saul saw
the Philistine army, he was afraid; terror filled his
heart. 6 He inquired[u] of the LORD, but the LORD did
not answer him by dreams[v] or Urim[w] or prophets.
7 Saul then said to his attendants, "Find me a
woman who is a medium,[x] so I may go and
inquire of her."
"There is one in Endor,[y]" they said.
8 So Saul disguised[z] himself, putting on other
clothes, and at night he and two men went to the
woman. "Consult[a] a spirit for me," he said, "and
bring up for me the one I name."
9 But the woman said to him, "Surely you know
what Saul has done. He has cut off[b] the mediums
and spiritists from the land. Why have you set a
trap for my life to bring about my death?"
10 Saul swore to her by the LORD, "As surely as
the LORD lives, you will not be punished for this."
11 Then the woman asked, "Whom shall I bring
up for you?"
"Bring up Samuel," he said.
12 When the woman saw Samuel, she cried out
at the top of her voice and said to Saul, "Why
have you deceived me? You are Saul!"
13 The king said to her, "Don't be afraid. What
do you see?"
The woman said, "I see a spirit[a] coming up out
of the ground."
14 "What does he look like?" he asked.
"An old man wearing a robe[c] is coming up," she
said.
Then Saul knew it was Samuel, and he bowed
down and prostrated himself with his face to the
ground.
15 Samuel said to Saul, "Why have you disturbed
me by bringing me up?"
"I am in great distress," Saul said. "The Philistines are fighting against me, and God has turned[d]
away from me. He no longer answers me, either
by prophets or by dreams. So I have called on you
to tell me what to do."
16 Samuel said, "Why do you consult me, now
that the LORD has turned away from you and
become your enemy? 17 The LORD has done what
he predicted through me. The LORD has torn[e] the
kingdom out of your hands and given it to one of
your neighbors—to David. 18 Because you did not
obey[f] the LORD or carry out his fierce wrath[g]
against the Amalekites, the LORD has done this to
you today. 19 The LORD will hand over both Israel
and you to the Philistines, and tomorrow you and

28:3 [p]1Sa 25:1 [q]1Sa 7:17 [r]Ex 22:18; Lev 19:31; 20:27; Dt 18:10-11; 1Sa 15:23
28:4 [s]Jos 19:18; 2Ki 4:8 [t]1Sa 31:1,3
28:6 [u]1Sa 14:37; 1Ch 10:13-14; Pr 1:28 [v]Nu 12:6 [w]Ex 28:30; Nu 27:21
28:7 [x]Ac 16:16 [y]Jos 17:11
28:8 [z]2Ch 18:29; 35:22 [a]Dt 18:10-11; 1Ch 10:13; Isa 8:19
28:9 [b]ver 3
28:14 [c]1Sa 15:27; 24:8
28:15 [d]ver 6; 1Sa 18:12
28:17 [e]1Sa 15:28
28:18 [f]1Sa 15:20 [g]1Ki 20:42

[a] *13* Or *see spirits*; or *see gods*

The Spirit World

1SA 28:12

While we can't determine what exactly happens in this passage—whether the spirit truly is Samuel (1Sa 28:14) or a demon playing the role of Samuel—we can note a few things. First, this passage confirms that a spirit world does exist. Second, the spirit confirms the message Samuel spoke in his life—the kingdom will be taken from Saul and given to David (1Sa 28:17). Third, the spirit predicts the death of Saul and his sons (1Sa 28:19). This comes to pass just as this spirit says (1Sa 31:6). Saul discovers the truth, but only by seeking it in the darkness. Rather than continually seeking God's direction and believing what Samuel had spoken from God, Saul chooses to find his answers from a dark source. Too late to rectify his wrongly placed loyalties, Saul pays the ultimate price. *(See character sketch for the Witch of Endor on page 806.)*

Sheol

1SA 28:16–20

In Old Testament times, the Hebrew people considered death as the time of entrance to Sheol. Sheol was thought to be a dwelling place inside the earth where the dead endured a shadowy existence, cut off from life but still reachable by God (Ps 139:8). The righteous and the unrighteous alike were thought to go there. Whether Saul believes the spirit is speaking of Sheol when it says, "Tomorrow you and your sons will be with me" (1Sa 28:19), is uncertain. What is certain is that Saul knows his spirit will be separated from his body; he and his sons will soon join the dead. Saul also recognizes this as being from the hand of the Lord who "brings death and makes alive; he brings down to the grave and raises up" (1Sa 2:6).

your sons[h] will be with me. The LORD will also
hand over the army of Israel to the Philistines."
20Immediately Saul fell full length on the
ground, filled with fear because of Samuel's
words. His strength was gone, for he had eaten
nothing all that day and night.
21When the woman came to Saul and saw that
he was greatly shaken, she said, "Look, your
maidservant has obeyed you. I took my life[i] in my
hands and did what you told me to do. 22Now
please listen to your servant and let me give you
some food so you may eat and have the strength
to go on your way."
23He refused[j] and said, "I will not eat."
But his men joined the woman in urging him,
and he listened to them. He got up from the
ground and sat on the couch.
24The woman had a fattened calf at the house,
which she butchered at once. She took some flour,
kneaded it and baked bread without yeast. 25Then
she set it before Saul and his men, and they ate.
That same night they got up and left.

Achish Sends David Back to Ziklag

29 The Philistines gathered[k] all their forces at
Aphek,[l] and Israel camped by the spring in
Jezreel.[m] 2As the Philistine rulers marched with
their units of hundreds and thousands, David and
his men were marching at the rear[n] with Achish.
3The commanders of the Philistines asked, "What
about these Hebrews?"
Achish replied, "Is this not David, who was an
officer of Saul king of Israel? He has already been
with me for over a year,[o] and from the day he left
Saul until now, I have found no fault in him."
4But the Philistine commanders were angry
with him and said, "Send[p] the man back, that he
may return to the place you assigned him. He
must not go with us into battle, or he will turn[q]
against us during the fighting. How better could
he regain his master's favor than by taking the
heads of our own men? 5Isn't this the David they
sang about in their dances:

" 'Saul has slain his thousands,
and David his tens of thousands'?"[r]

6So Achish called David and said to him, "As
surely as the LORD lives, you have been reliable,
and I would be pleased to have you serve with me
in the army. From the day[s] you came to me until
now, I have found no fault in you, but the rulers[t]
don't approve of you. 7Turn back and go in peace;
do nothing to displease the Philistine rulers."
8"But what have I done?" asked David. "What
have you found against your servant from the day
I came to you until now? Why can't I go and fight
against the enemies of my lord the king?"
9Achish answered, "I know that you have been
as pleasing in my eyes as an angel[u] of God; nevertheless, the Philistine commanders[v] have said,
'He must not go up with us into battle.' 10Now get

28:19 [h]1Sa 31:2
28:21 [i]Jdg 12:3; 1Sa 19:5; Job 13:14
28:23 [j]2Ki 5:13
29:1 [k]1Sa 28:1 [l]Jos 12:18; 1Sa 4:1 [m]2Ki 9:30
29:2 [n]1Sa 28:2
29:3 [o]1Sa 27:7; Da 6:5
29:4 [p]1Ch 12:19 [q]1Sa 14:21
29:5 [r]1Sa 18:7; 21:11
29:6 [s]1Sa 27:8-12 [t]ver 3
29:9 [u]2Sa 14:17, 20; 19:27 [v]ver 4

up early, along with your master's servants who
29:10 [w]1Ch 12:19 have come with you, and leave[w] in the morning
as soon as it is light."
11So David and his men got up early in the
morning to go back to the land of the Philistines,
and the Philistines went up to Jezreel.

David Destroys the Amalekites

30:1 **30** David and his men reached Ziklag[x] on the
[x]1Sa 29:4,11 third day. Now the Amalekites[y] had raided
[y]1Sa 15:7; 27:8 the Negev and Ziklag. They had attacked Ziklag
and burned it, 2and had taken captive the women
and all who were in it, both young and old. They
killed none of them, but carried them off as they
went on their way.
3When David and his men came to Ziklag, they
found it destroyed by fire and their wives and sons
and daughters taken captive. 4So David and his
men wept aloud until they had no strength left to
30:5 [z]1Sa 25:43; weep. 5David's two wives[z] had been captured—
2Sa 2:2 Ahinoam of Jezreel and Abigail, the widow of
30:6 Nabal of Carmel. 6David was greatly distressed
[a]Ex 17:4; because the men were talking of stoning[a] him;
Jn 8:59 each one was bitter in spirit because of his sons
[b]Ps 27:14; 56:3-4,11; and daughters. But David found strength[b] in the
Ro 4:20 LORD his God.
7Then David said to Abiathar[c] the priest, the
30:7 [c]1Sa 22:20 son of Ahimelech, "Bring me the ephod.[d]" Abia-
[d]1Sa 23:9 thar brought it to him, 8and David inquired[e] of the
30:8 LORD, "Shall I pursue this raiding party? Will I
[e]1Sa 23:2 overtake them?"
[f]ver 18 "Pursue them," he answered. "You will certainly overtake them and succeed[f] in the rescue."
30:9 9David and the six hundred men[g] with him
[g]1Sa 27:2 came to the Besor Ravine, where some stayed
behind, 10for two hundred men were too exhaust-
30:10 [h]ver 9,21 ed[h] to cross the ravine. But David and four hundred men continued the pursuit.
11They found an Egyptian in a field and brought
him to David. They gave him water to drink and
food to eat— 12part of a cake of pressed figs and
30:12 two cakes of raisins. He ate and was revived,[i] for
[i]Jdg 15:19 he had not eaten any food or drunk any water for
three days and three nights.
13David asked him, "To whom do you belong,
and where do you come from?"
He said, "I am an Egyptian, the slave of an
Amalekite. My master abandoned me when I
became ill three days ago. 14We raided the Negev
30:14 of the Kerethites[j] and the territory belonging to
[j]2Sa 8:18; Judah and the Negev of Caleb.[k] And we burned[l]
1Ki 1:38,44; Ziklag."
Eze 25:16; 15David asked him, "Can you lead me down to
Zep 2:5 [k]ver 16; this raiding party?"
Jos 14:13; He answered, "Swear to me before God that you
15:13 will not kill me or hand me over to my master,
[l]ver 1 and I will take you down to them."
16He led David down, and there they were, scat-
30:16 tered over the countryside, eating, drinking and
[m]Lk 12:19 reveling[m] because of the great amount of plunder[n]
[n]ver 14 they had taken from the land of the Philistines

The Ephod

1SA 30:7-8

In early Israelite history, the priests used the Urim and Thummim to determine God's will. They are stored in a breastpiece that is part of the ephod, which is a sacred priestly garment. Carefully phrased questions are posed.

Since the Urim and Thummim are part of the ephod, it is also called "the breastpiece of decision" (Ex 28:29) or judgment. In fact, in Exodus 28:15, God tells Moses to "fashion a breastpiece for making decisions" (see the note on Ex 28:30, page 131). How exactly the Urim and Thummim worked, or what exactly they were, remains a mystery. However, we do know that God used them to tell his people his will.

God apparently approves of David's use of this method since David receives correct answers (1Sa 23:9-11; 30:7-8). Saul also seeks God in this manner, but the Bible says he receives no answer from the Lord "by dreams or Urim or prophets" (1Sa 28:6).

and from Judah. 17 David fought[o] them from dusk until the evening of the next day, and none of them got away, except four hundred young men who rode off on camels and fled.[p] 18 David recovered[q] everything the Amalekites had taken, including his two wives. 19 Nothing was missing: young or old, boy or girl, plunder or anything else they had taken. David brought everything back. 20 He took all the flocks and herds, and his men drove them ahead of the other livestock, saying, "This is David's plunder."

21 Then David came to the two hundred men who had been too exhausted[r] to follow him and who were left behind at the Besor Ravine. They came out to meet David and the people with him. As David and his men approached, he greeted them. 22 But all the evil men and troublemakers among David's followers said, "Because they did not go out with us, we will not share with them the plunder we recovered. However, each man may take his wife and children and go."

23 David replied, "No, my brothers, you must not do that with what the LORD has given us. He has protected us and handed over to us the forces that came against us. 24 Who will listen to what you say? The share of the man who stayed with the supplies is to be the same as that of him who went down to the battle. All will share alike.[s]" 25 David made this a statute and ordinance for Israel from that day to this.

26 When David arrived in Ziklag, he sent some of the plunder to the elders of Judah, who were his friends, saying, "Here is a present for you from the plunder of the LORD's enemies."

27 He sent it to those who were in Bethel,[t] Ramoth[u] Negev and Jattir;[v] 28 to those in Aroer,[w] Siphmoth, Eshtemoa[x] 29 and Racal; to those in the towns of the Jerahmeelites[y] and the Kenites;[z] 30 to those in Hormah,[a] Bor Ashan,[b] Athach 31 and Hebron;[c] and to those in all the other places where David and his men had roamed.

Saul Takes His Life

31 Now the Philistines fought against Israel; the Israelites fled before them, and many fell slain on Mount Gilboa.[d] 2 The Philistines pressed hard after Saul and his sons, and they killed his sons Jonathan, Abinadab and Malki-Shua. 3 The fighting grew fierce around Saul, and when the archers overtook him, they wounded[e] him critically.

4 Saul said to his armor-bearer, "Draw your sword and run me through,[f] or these uncircumcised[g] fellows will come and run me through and abuse me."

But his armor-bearer was terrified and would not do it; so Saul took his own sword and fell on it. 5 When the armor-bearer saw that Saul was dead, he too fell on his sword and died with him. 6 So Saul and his three sons and his armor-bearer and all his men died together that same day.

30:17 [o]1Sa 11:11 [p]1Sa 15:3
30:18 [q]Ge 14:16
30:21 [r]ver 10
30:24 [s]Nu 31:27; Jos 22:8
30:27 [t]Jos 7:2 [u]Jos 19:8 [v]Jos 15:48
30:28 [w]Jos 13:16 [x]Jos 15:50
30:29 [y]1Sa 27:10 [z]Jdg 1:16; 1Sa 15:6
30:30 [a]Nu 14:45; Jdg 1:17 [b]Jos 15:42
30:31 [c]Jos 14:13; 2Sa 2:1,4
31:1 [d]1Sa 28:4; 1Ch 10:1-12
31:3 [e]2Sa 1:6
31:4 [f]Jdg 9:54; 2Sa 1:6,10 [g]1Sa 14:6

The soul on earth is an immortal guest,
Compelled to starve at an unreal feast;
A pilgrim panting for the rest to come;
An exile, anxious for his native home.

—Hannah More (1745–1833)

Rahab

A New Future for a Woman With a Past

It wasn't unusual for strange men to appear at her door. She was, after all, a prostitute. The Israelite spies came to Rahab looking for a place to hide, and they put their lives in her hands.

Who could have failed to hear about the Israelites? They had been in the desert for 40 years and now were heading straight toward Jericho. But Rahab told the spies she had heard of the *God* of Israel and the deeds *he* had done on behalf of his people. It was as if she was just waiting for evidence of him in her own life. When she saw her chance, she did not hesitate. She joined the cause of this God whom she believed to be greater than the gods worshiped by her people: "for the LORD your God is God in heaven above and on the earth below" (Jos 2:11).

What if these men betrayed her? What if their God failed her? There could be no turning back. Risking her own death, she was obedient to the conviction of truth within her—no debate, no consultation, no wavering.

Within minutes of her decision, Rahab revealed her extraordinary heart. Rahab interceded for her family's safety as well as her own. Her family heeded her, for when the walls of Jericho came down, her relatives were with her.

Over the ensuing years, Rahab surely needed to learn a new way of relating to men. Perhaps her restoration required the greatest faith of all—everyday choices, without drama or spotlight, to be chaste, to forgive, to trust again. Scripture reveals that she continued to hold on to the God who gave her a new beginning. Matthew 1:5 lists Rahab among the forebears of Jesus. But she is not called "the prostitute," for the stigma of her past is overshadowed by the honor given her by God. And by choosing her—a Gentile sinner—God confirms that he is the Savior of all peoples, for all time and in all circumstances.

Is there hope for a woman with a past, someone who has made bad decisions and given herself to a life of sin? Our enemy wants us to believe that nothing good can come from such wreckage. But Rahab's life demonstrates the benefits of believing *God* instead. When Rahab chose him, he gave her a completely new life. And he set no limits on her potential as his child. None.

Rahab
(broad)
Joshua 2; 6:17–25
Matthew 1:5
Hebrews 11:31
James 2:25

Candid SNAPSHOT But Joshua spared Rahab the prostitute, with her family and all who belonged to her, because she hid the men Joshua had sent as spies to Jericho—and she lives among the Israelites to this day (Joshua 6:25).

Deborah

Leading Woman

The long line of people waiting their turn snaked across the desert. People came to Deborah for answers and justice because of her great wisdom. She spent most of her time meeting their needs, judging under a tree known throughout Israel as "the Palm of Deborah" (Jdg 4:5).

Mosaic Law did not prohibit women from taking responsibilities ordinarily reserved for men. Deborah was one of the wisest people in Israel, so she became the judge. She called herself "a mother in Israel" (Jdg 5:7)—a mother to comfort, to encourage, to challenge, to train, to give birth to faith. Deborah was also a prophetess, and God spoke to her in her role as the leader of his people. God told her that Barak was to lead the troops into battle, and he, God, would deliver the enemy into their hands.

For 20 years the Israelites had suffered under Canaanite oppression. The Canaanites' cruel commander, Sisera, seemed invincible. "The roads were abandoned; travelers took to winding paths. Village life in Israel ceased" (Jdg 5:6–7). The Israelites cried to the Lord for help. And he was about to deliver them! Deborah did not doubt the outcome—God had spoken. The Israelites had merely to obey.

When Deborah gave Barak the good news, he stipulated that Deborah go with him. Perhaps he did not believe Deborah, did not believe God or did not believe in himself. But Barak would not get the glory for winning the battle. Instead, it would go to a woman. And it happened just as Deborah said—a woman, Jael, killed the mighty Sisera.

Some have said that in times when men are spiritually weak God uses women instead. It is probably more accurate to say the deeds and faith of women are simply more apparent in those times. For the Lord gives gifts and callings to *all* of his people. The time of the judges is a prime example. Here we see Deborah, Jael, Samson's mother, Naomi and Ruth, among others, all extolled as heroes of the faith—in a time when men wrote about the deeds of men.

There is much to do before the Lord's return. He will not spurn *any* worker of good heart—and his gifts do not carry a gender label. If we soberly assess our talents and seek confirmation from others who know us well, we can move in confidence to the fullness of our ability, spreading God's Good News. We too are in a war. We already know the outcome—God has spoken. And we need merely to obey.

Deborah
(bee)
Judges 4–5

Candid SNAPSHOT Then Deborah said to Barak, "Go! This is the day the LORD has given Sisera into your hands. Has not the LORD gone ahead of you?" So Barak went down Mount Tabor, followed by ten thousand men (Judges 4:14).

7 When the Israelites along the valley and those
across the Jordan saw that the Israelite army had
fled and that Saul and his sons had died, they
abandoned their towns and fled. And the Philistines came and occupied them.
8 The next day, when the Philistines came to
strip the dead, they found Saul and his three sons
fallen on Mount Gilboa. 9 They cut off his head
and stripped off his armor, and they sent messengers throughout the land of the Philistines to proclaim the news[h] in the temple of their idols and
among their people.[i] 10 They put his armor in the
temple of the Ashtoreths[j] and fastened his body
to the wall of Beth Shan.[k]
11 When the people of Jabesh Gilead[l] heard of
what the Philistines had done to Saul, 12 all their
valiant men journeyed through the night to Beth
Shan. They took down the bodies of Saul and his
sons from the wall of Beth Shan and went to
Jabesh, where they burned[m] them. 13 Then they
took their bones[n] and buried them under a tamarisk[o] tree at Jabesh, and they fasted[p] seven days.[q]

31:9 [h]2Sa 1:20 [i]Jdg 16:24
31:10 [j]Jdg 2:12-13; 1Sa 7:3 [k]Jos 17:11; 2Sa 21:12
31:11 [l]1Sa 11:1
31:12 [m]2Sa 2:4-7; 2Ch 16:14; Am 6:10
31:13 [n]2Sa 21:12-14 [o]1Sa 22:6 [p]2Sa 1:12 [q]Ge 50:10

Gift of a Decent Burial

1SA 31:7-13

The men of Jabesh Gilead are horrified to hear what has happened to the bodies of Saul and his sons. Saul's armor is put in the temple of the Philistines' goddess (1Sa 31:10), and Saul's head is hung in the temple of the god Dagon (1Ch 10:10). The Philistines fasten Saul's body and the bodies of his sons to the wall of a village (1Sa 31:10). The Israelites retrieve the bodies, burn them and then bury the bones. The burning is possibly meant to prevent any further abuse of the bodies or perhaps to prevent contamination or illness from their decomposition. Or it could be that they burned spices to perfume the bodies, a common practice for royalty (2Ch 16:14). Either way, this act is most likely completed in honor since the people of Jabesh Gilead owed Saul their very lives (1Sa 11). The burning and burying is their last act of service to their king.

2 Samuel

A nation and its leader.

The book of 2 Samuel records the events in the life of one of the brightest lights of the Biblical narrative—King David. Continuing Israel's history from the death of Saul to the end of David's 40-year reign, this book chronicles David's highest achievements as well as his lowest failures. An able administrator, David brings the nation of Israel to political, economic and military supremacy. His godly example strengthens his people's commitment to the Lord, and yet his failure to control his passions and his family transforms this kingdom from peace to dissension.

This uncensored story of David's triumphs and troubles gives us a glimpse of life in the royal palace at Jerusalem. We encounter the resentment of David's wife, Michal, who has become a political pawn instead of a beloved spouse (2Sa 6:20-23). We trace the slippery slide of adultery and cover-up as Bathsheba becomes an unwitting partner to David's passions and suffers the death of her child as a result (2Sa 11:1–12:25). We experience revulsion and horror at the rape of Tamar by her half-brother (2Sa 13). We applaud the wise analogy of the woman of Tekoa who confronts the king with his weakness (2Sa 14:1-22). And we mourn with Rizpah as she stands vigil over her unburied family (2Sa 21).

With its candid examination of the life of David, the book of 2 Samuel stands as a graphic reminder that there are devastating consequences to sin. Only confession and repentance can heal the wounds, and only faithful obedience to God can keep us on the right track.

Quick Study

Author
Unknown.

Date Written
Sometime after the division of Israel into the northern and southern kingdoms, around 930 B.C.

Setting
Israel.

Key Passage
2 Samuel 7:22-24 "How great you are, O Sovereign LORD! There is no one like you, and there is no God but you, as we have heard with our own ears . . . You have established your people Israel as your very own forever, and you, O LORD, have become their God."

Outline

King David of Judah.
2Sa 1–4

King David of Israel.
2Sa 5:1–5

David's victories.
2Sa 5:6–10:19

David and Bathsheba.
2Sa 11–12

Tamar and Amnon.
2Sa 13:1–22

Absalom's rebellion and death.
2Sa 13:23–18:18

David mourns Absalom.
2Sa 18:19–19:8

David returns to Jerusalem.
2Sa 19:9–43

The woman of Tekoa.
2Sa 20

Gibeonites and Philistines.
2Sa 21

David's song.
2Sa 22

David's last words.
2Sa 23:1–7

David's mighty men.
2Sa 23:8–39

David's census of fighting men.
2Sa 24:1–17

David builds an altar.
2Sa 24:18–25

The Women of 2 Samuel

Ahinoam	*David's first wife.* 2Sa 3:2
Abigail	*Married David after her husband Nabal died.* 2Sa 3:3
Maacah, Haggith, Abital, Eglah	*David's other wives.* 2Sa 3:3–5
Rizpah	*Bravely honored her dead sons.* 2Sa 3:7; 21:8–14 (page 874)
Mephibosheth's nurse	*Protector of Jonathan's son.* 2Sa 4:4 (page 873)
Bathsheba	*David's lover.* 2Sa 11–12 (page 939)
Tamar	*Raped by her own half-brother.* 2Sa 13 (page 940)
Woman of Tekoa	*A skillful actress.* 2Sa 14:1–22
Tamar	*Absalom's beautiful daughter.* 2Sa 14:27
	David's ten concubines. 2Sa 17:3
Servant girl	*An informant for David.* 2Sa 17:17
Wife of a man in Bahurim	*Used a well to protect David's men.* 2Sa 17:18–20
Wise woman of Abel Beth Maacah	*A wise but gruesome act.* 2Sa 20:14–22 (page 1009)

Denotes a sketch written about this character

David Mourns Saul

2SA 1:1–19

The Amalekite runs to David's camp with the news of Saul's death and expects David to be relieved and joyful. After all, Saul has harassed David for years, even demanding David's death. And with Saul gone, David's kingship is assured. Why wouldn't he be grateful for the news? But instead of being elated, David mourns and fasts (2Sa 1:12), not only for the humiliating blow to Israel but also for the loss of Saul and Jonathan. David's lamentations are sincere. He respected Saul as the Lord's anointed king, if for nothing else. Here again, David proves his unselfish love and concern for his people and his God rather than for what might benefit him personally.

David Hears of Saul's Death

1 After the death[a] of Saul, David returned from defeating[b] the Amalekites and stayed in Ziklag two days. 2On the third day a man[c] arrived from Saul's camp, with his clothes torn and with dust on his head.[d] When he came to David, he fell to the ground to pay him honor.

3"Where have you come from?" David asked him.

He answered, "I have escaped from the Israelite camp."

4"What happened?" David asked. "Tell me."

He said, "The men fled from the battle. Many of them fell and died. And Saul and his son Jonathan are dead."

5Then David said to the young man who brought him the report, "How do you know that Saul and his son Jonathan are dead?"

6"I happened to be on Mount Gilboa,[e]" the young man said, "and there was Saul, leaning on his spear, with the chariots and riders almost upon him. 7When he turned around and saw me, he called out to me, and I said, 'What can I do?'

8"He asked me, 'Who are you?'

" 'An Amalekite,[f]' I answered.

9"Then he said to me, 'Stand over me and kill me! I am in the throes of death, but I'm still alive.'

10"So I stood over him and killed him, because I knew that after he had fallen he could not survive. And I took the crown[g] that was on his head and the band on his arm and have brought them here to my lord."

11Then David and all the men with him took hold of their clothes and tore[h] them. 12They mourned and wept and fasted till evening for Saul and his son Jonathan, and for the army of the LORD and the house of Israel, because they had fallen by the sword.

13David said to the young man who brought him the report, "Where are you from?"

"I am the son of an alien, an Amalekite,[i]" he answered.

14David asked him, "Why were you not afraid to lift your hand to destroy the LORD's anointed?[j]"

15Then David called one of his men and said, "Go, strike him down!"[k] So he struck him down, and he died.[l] 16For David had said to him, "Your blood be on your own head.[m] Your own mouth testified against you when you said, 'I killed the LORD's anointed.' "

David's Lament for Saul and Jonathan

17David took up this lament[n] concerning Saul and his son Jonathan, 18and ordered that the men of Judah be taught this lament of the bow (it is written in the Book of Jashar):[o]

19"Your glory, O Israel, lies slain on your
heights.
How the mighty have fallen![p]

1:1 [a]1Sa 31:6 [b]1Sa 30:17
1:2 [c]2Sa 4:10 [d]1Sa 4:12
1:6 [e]1Sa 28:4; 31:2-4
1:8 [f]1Sa 15:2; 30:13,17
1:10 [g]Jdg 9:54; 2Ki 11:12
1:11 [h]Ge 37:29; 2Sa 3:31; 13:31
1:13 [i]ver 8
1:14 [j]1Sa 24:6; 26:9
1:15 [k]2Sa 4:12 [l]2Sa 4:10
1:16 [m]Lev 20:9; 2Sa 3:28-29; 1Ki 2:32; Mt 27:24-25; Ac 18:6
1:17 [n]2Ch 35:25
1:18 [o]Jos 10:13; 1Sa 31:3
1:19 [p]ver 27

1:20 [q]Mic 1:10 [r]1Sa 31:8 [s]Ex 15:20; 1Sa 18:6

20 "Tell it not in Gath,[q]
proclaim it not in the streets of
Ashkelon,
lest the daughters of the Philistines[r] be
glad,
lest the daughters of the
uncircumcised rejoice.[s]

1:21 [t]ver 6; 1Sa 31:1 [u]Eze 31:15 [v]Isa 21:5

21 "O mountains of Gilboa,[t]
may you have neither dew nor rain,
nor fields that yield offerings[u] ⌊of
grain⌋.
For there the shield of the mighty was
defiled,
the shield of Saul—no longer rubbed
with oil.[v]

1:22 [w]Isa 34:3,7 [x]Dt 32:42; 1Sa 18:4

22 From the blood[w] of the slain,
from the flesh of the mighty,
the bow[x] of Jonathan did not turn back,
the sword of Saul did not return
unsatisfied.
23 "Saul and Jonathan—
in life they were loved and gracious,
and in death they were not parted.

1:23 [y]Dt 28:49; Jer 4:13 [z]Jdg 14:18

They were swifter than eagles,[y]
they were stronger than lions.[z]

24 "O daughters of Israel,
weep for Saul,
who clothed you in scarlet and finery,
who adorned your garments with
ornaments of gold.
25 "How the mighty have fallen in battle!
Jonathan lies slain on your heights.

1:26 [a]1Sa 20:42 [b]1Sa 18:1

26 I grieve for you, Jonathan my brother;[a]
you were very dear to me.
Your love for me was wonderful,[b]
more wonderful than that of women.

1:27 [c]ver 19,25; 1Sa 2:4

27 "How the mighty have fallen!
The weapons of war have perished!"[c]

David Anointed King Over Judah

2:1 [d]1Sa 23:2,11-12 [e]Ge 13:18; 1Sa 30:31

2 In the course of time, David inquired[d] of the
LORD. "Shall I go up to one of the towns of
Judah?" he asked.
The LORD said, "Go up."
David asked, "Where shall I go?"
"To Hebron,"[e] the LORD answered.

2:2 [f]1Sa 25:43; 30:5 [g]1Sa 25:42

2 So David went up there with his two wives,[f]
Ahinoam of Jezreel and Abigail,[g] the widow of

2:3 [h]1Sa 27:2; 30:9

Nabal of Carmel. 3 David also took the men who
were with him,[h] each with his family, and they
settled in Hebron and its towns. 4 Then the men of

2:4 [i]1Sa 30:31 [j]1Sa 2:35; 2Sa 5:3-5 [k]1Sa 31:11-13

Judah came to Hebron[i] and there they anointed[j]
David king over the house of Judah.
When David was told that it was the men of
Jabesh Gilead[k] who had buried Saul, 5 he sent
messengers to the men of Jabesh Gilead to say to

2:5 [l]1Sa 23:21

them, "The LORD bless[l] you for showing this kindness to Saul your master by burying him. 6 May

Laments

2SA 1:19–27

The word *lament* means "to wail." Biblical custom called for loud and intense grieving when someone died. Along with wailing, common forms of mourning included tearing one's clothes (2Sa 1:11); wearing a form of clothing made from coarse cloth or goat hair, called sackcloth (2Sa 3:31); fasting (Ps 35:13); and placing ashes on one's head (2Sa 13:19). David also expresses his grief by putting his lament into the poem recorded in these verses. The Hebrews sometimes hired professional mourners to assist in their wailing (Jer 9:17). While mourning has its place, and grief is a natural response to a sad situation, God puts limitations on its expression: "You are the children of the LORD your God. Do not cut yourselves or shave the front of your heads for the dead, for you are a people holy to the LORD your God" (Dt 14:1–2). This same message is confirmed in the New Testament when believers are reminded that they do not need to "grieve like the rest of men, who have no hope" (1Th 4:13).

David's Progression As King

2SA 2:1–7; 5:1–5

David begins his reign over the tribe of Judah at 30 *years of age*. But he must wait *another seven years and six months* before he reigns over all Israel (2Sa 5:5). Instead of following the lineage of Saul, Judah chooses to be ruled by the king God has anointed. David's anointing in Hebron (2Sa 2:4) is the second of three anointings. He is first privately anointed by Samuel as the *future* king (1Sa 16:13). Then he is publicly anointed king of one tribe, Judah (2Sa 2:4.) Finally, years later, David is anointed king over all of Israel (2Sa 5:3). Although many years pass before God's promise is fulfilled completely, David chooses to trust rather than take matters into his own hands. He knows who has put him in this position and who will orchestrate events to bring it to fulfillment.

the LORD now show you kindness and faithfulness,[m] and I too will show you the same favor because you have done this. [7]Now then, be strong and brave, for Saul your master is dead, and the house of Judah has anointed me king over them."

War Between the Houses of David and Saul

[8]Meanwhile, Abner[n] son of Ner, the commander of Saul's army, had taken Ish-Bosheth son of Saul and brought him over to Mahanaim.[o] [9]He made him king over Gilead,[p] Ashuri[a][q] and Jezreel, and also over Ephraim, Benjamin and all Israel.[r]

[10]Ish-Bosheth son of Saul was forty years old when he became king over Israel, and he reigned two years. The house of Judah, however, followed David. [11]The length of time David was king in Hebron over the house of Judah was seven years and six months.[s]

[12]Abner son of Ner, together with the men of Ish-Bosheth son of Saul, left Mahanaim and went to Gibeon.[t] [13]Joab[u] son of Zeruiah and David's men went out and met them at the pool of Gibeon. One group sat down on one side of the pool and one group on the other side.

[14]Then Abner said to Joab, "Let's have some of the young men get up and fight hand to hand in front of us."

"All right, let them do it," Joab said.

[15]So they stood up and were counted off—twelve men for Benjamin and Ish-Bosheth son of Saul, and twelve for David. [16]Then each man grabbed his opponent by the head and thrust his dagger into his opponent's side, and they fell down together. So that place in Gibeon was called Helkath Hazzurim.[b]

[17]The battle that day was very fierce, and Abner and the men of Israel were defeated[v] by David's men.

[18]The three sons of Zeruiah[w] were there: Joab,[x] Abishai[y] and Asahel.[z] Now Asahel was as fleet-footed as a wild gazelle.[a] [19]He chased Abner, turning neither to the right nor to the left as he pursued him. [20]Abner looked behind him and asked, "Is that you, Asahel?"

"It is," he answered.

[21]Then Abner said to him, "Turn aside to the right or to the left; take on one of the young men and strip him of his weapons." But Asahel would not stop chasing him.

[22]Again Abner warned Asahel, "Stop chasing me! Why should I strike you down? How could I look your brother Joab in the face?"[b]

[23]But Asahel refused to give up the pursuit; so Abner thrust the butt of his spear into Asahel's stomach,[c] and the spear came out through his back. He fell there and died on the spot. And every man stopped when he came to the place where Asahel had fallen and died.[d]

2:6 [m]Ex 34:6; 1Ti 1:16
2:8 [n]1Sa 14:50 [o]Ge 32:2
2:9 [p]Nu 32:26 [q]Jdg 1:32 [r]1Ch 12:29
2:11 [s]2Sa 5:5
2:12 [t]Jos 18:25
2:13 [u]2Sa 8:16; 1Ch 2:16; 11:6
2:17 [v]2Sa 3:1
2:18 [w]2Sa 3:39 [x]2Sa 3:30 [y]1Sa 26:6 [z]1Ch 2:16 [a]1Ch 12:8
2:22 [b]2Sa 3:27
2:23 [c]2Sa 3:27; 4:6 [d]2Sa 20:12

[a] 9 Or *Ashur* [b] 16 *Helkath Hazzurim* means *field of daggers* or *field of hostilities.*

24 But Joab and Abishai pursued Abner, and as
the sun was setting, they came to the hill of
Ammah, near Giah on the way to the wasteland of
Gibeon. 25 Then the men of Benjamin rallied
behind Abner. They formed themselves into a
group and took their stand on top of a hill.
2:26 26 Abner called out to Joab, "Must the sword
[e]Dt 32:42; devour[e] forever? Don't you realize that this will
Jer 46:10,14 end in bitterness? How long before you order your
men to stop pursuing their brothers?"
27 Joab answered, "As surely as God lives, if you
had not spoken, the men would have continued
the pursuit of their brothers until morning.[a]"
2:28 [f]2Sa 18:16 28 So Joab[f] blew the trumpet,[g] and all the men
[g]Jdg 3:27 came to a halt; they no longer pursued Israel, nor
did they fight anymore.
29 All that night Abner and his men marched
through the Arabah. They crossed the Jordan,
continued through the whole Bithron[b] and came
2:29 [h]ver 8 to Mahanaim.[h]
30 Then Joab returned from pursuing Abner and
assembled all his men. Besides Asahel, nineteen
of David's men were found missing. 31 But David's
men had killed three hundred and sixty Ben-
2:32 jamites who were with Abner. 32 They took Asahel
[i]Ge 49:29 and buried him in his father's tomb[i] at Bethlehem. Then Joab and his men marched all night
and arrived at Hebron by daybreak.
3 The war between the house of Saul and the
3:1 [j]1Ki 14:30 house of David lasted a long time.[j] David grew
[k]2Sa 5:10 stronger and stronger,[k] while the house of Saul
[l]2Sa 2:17 grew weaker and weaker.[l]
2 Sons were born to David in Hebron:
His firstborn was Amnon the son of Ahin-
3:2 [m]1Sa 25:43; 1Ch 3:1-3 oam[m] of Jezreel;
3 his second, Kileab the son of Abigail[n] the
widow of Nabal of Carmel;
3:3 [n]1Sa 25:42 the third, Absalom[o] the son of Maacah
[o]2Sa 13:1,28 daughter of Talmai king of Geshur;[p]
[p]1Sa 27:8; 2Sa 13:37; 14:32; 15:8 4 the fourth, Adonijah[q] the son of Haggith;
the fifth, Shephatiah the son of Abital;
3:4 [q]1Ki 1:5,11 5 and the sixth, Ithream the son of David's
wife Eglah.
These were born to David in Hebron.

Abner Goes Over to David

6 During the war between the house of Saul and
the house of David, Abner had been strengthening
his own position in the house of Saul. 7 Now Saul
3:7 [r]2Sa 16:21-22 had had a concubine[r] named Rizpah[s] daughter of
Aiah. And Ish-Bosheth said to Abner, "Why did
[s]2Sa 21:8-11 you sleep with my father's concubine?"
8 Abner was very angry because of what Ish-
Bosheth said and he answered, "Am I a dog's
3:8 [t]1Sa 24:14; head[t]—on Judah's side? This very day I am loyal
2Sa 9:8; 16:9 to the house of your father Saul and to his family

[a] 27 Or *spoken this morning, the men would not have taken up the pursuit of their brothers*; or *spoken, the men would have given up the pursuit of their brothers by morning* [b] 29 Or *morning*; or *ravine*; the meaning of the Hebrew for this word is uncertain.

The King's Concubine

2SA 3:6–7

Concubines were female slaves or mistresses, legal members of a household, but without the benefits of a primary wife. The man of the household could lawfully have sexual intercourse with her. The law protected a concubine by not allowing her to be sold if she was no longer of interest to the man (Ex 21:7–11; see also the note on Jdg 19:1, page 405). Later in Israelite history, the practice of keeping concubines became a privilege of kings only—and they took full advantage of the situation. Solomon had 700 wives and 300 concubines (1Ki 11:3). To sleep with a king's concubine was to threaten the king's power—which happened when Absalom slept with David's concubines (see the note on 2Sa 16:22, page 500). In this passage Ish-Bosheth considers Abner's actions treason since, as successor to the throne, only Ish-Bosheth has a right to Saul's concubines.

David Asks for Michal

2SA 3:13–14

Three possibilities could explain why David asks for the return of Michal. First, at one time David showed his devotion to Michal by paying a high bride-price for her. She was still his wife when, out of anger, Saul gave her to Paltiel. Now that Saul is dead, David has the chance to reclaim her. Second, as the king's son-in-law again, David can claim to be a legitimate heir to the throne. And third, David may still love Michal. We know that at one time Michal loved David (1Sa 18:20) and even saved him from her father's threats (1Sa 19:11–13). Apparently during their time apart, however, Michal's affections have cooled (2Sa 6:16).

Like many women over the centuries, Michal is a victim of circumstances and of the men in her life. She cannot control her circumstances; however, she can control her response to them. She chooses bitterness and hatred both toward the men who have made her a pawn (see note on 1Ch 15:29, page 653) and toward her God . . . and she pays a high price (2Sa 6:23). (See a character sketch for Michal on page 740.)

and friends. I haven't handed you over to David. Yet now you accuse me of an offense involving this woman! 9 May God deal with Abner, be it ever so severely, if I do not do for David what the LORD promised[u] him on oath 10 and transfer the kingdom from the house of Saul and establish David's throne over Israel and Judah from Dan to Beersheba."[v] 11 Ish-Bosheth did not dare to say another word to Abner, because he was afraid of him.

12 Then Abner sent messengers on his behalf to say to David, "Whose land is it? Make an agreement with me, and I will help you bring all Israel over to you."

13 "Good," said David. "I will make an agreement with you. But I demand one thing of you: Do not come into my presence unless you bring Michal daughter of Saul when you come to see me."[w] 14 Then David sent messengers to Ish-Bosheth son of Saul, demanding, "Give me my wife Michal,[x] whom I betrothed to myself for the price of a hundred Philistine foreskins."

15 So Ish-Bosheth gave orders and had her taken away from her husband[y] Paltiel[z] son of Laish. 16 Her husband, however, went with her, weeping behind her all the way to Bahurim.[a] Then Abner said to him, "Go back home!" So he went back.

17 Abner conferred with the elders[b] of Israel and said, "For some time you have wanted to make David your king. 18 Now do it! For the LORD promised David, 'By my servant David I will rescue my people Israel from the hand of the Philistines[c] and from the hand of all their enemies.[d]' "

19 Abner also spoke to the Benjamites in person. Then he went to Hebron to tell David everything that Israel and the whole house of Benjamin[e] wanted to do. 20 When Abner, who had twenty men with him, came to David at Hebron, David prepared a feast for him and his men. 21 Then Abner said to David, "Let me go at once and assemble all Israel for my lord the king, so that they may make a compact[f] with you, and that you may rule over all that your heart desires."[g] So David sent Abner away, and he went in peace.

Joab Murders Abner

22 Just then David's men and Joab returned from a raid and brought with them a great deal of plunder. But Abner was no longer with David in Hebron, because David had sent him away, and he had gone in peace. 23 When Joab and all the soldiers with him arrived, he was told that Abner son of Ner had come to the king and that the king had sent him away and that he had gone in peace.

24 So Joab went to the king and said, "What have you done? Look, Abner came to you. Why did you let him go? Now he is gone! 25 You know Abner son of Ner; he came to deceive you and observe your movements and find out everything you are doing."

26 Joab then left David and sent messengers after Abner, and they brought him back from the well of Sirah. But David did not know it. 27 Now when

3:9 [u] 1Sa 15:28; 1Ki 19:2
3:10 [v] Jdg 20:1; 1Sa 3:20
3:13 [w] Ge 43:5; 1Sa 18:20
3:14 [x] 1Sa 18:27
3:15 [y] Dt 24:1-4 [z] 1Sa 25:44
3:16 [a] 2Sa 16:5; 19:16
3:17 [b] Jdg 11:11
3:18 [c] 1Sa 9:16 [d] 1Sa 15:28; 2Sa 8:6
3:19 [e] 1Sa 10:20-21; 1Ch 12:2, 16,29
3:21 [f] ver 10,12 [g] 1Ki 11:37

3:27 [h]2Sa 2:8 [i]2Sa 2:22; 20:9-10; 1Ki 2:5 Abner[h] returned to Hebron, Joab took him aside
into the gateway, as though to speak with him
privately. And there, to avenge the blood of his
brother Asahel, Joab stabbed him in the stomach,
and he died.[i]
28 Later, when David heard about this, he said, "I
3:28 [j]ver 37; Dt 21:9 and my kingdom are forever innocent[j] before the
LORD concerning the blood of Abner son of Ner.
29 May his blood[k] fall upon the head of Joab and
3:29 [k]Lev 20:9 [l]1Ki 2:31-33 [m]Lev 15:2 upon all his father's house![l] May Joab's house
never be without someone who has a running
sore[m] or leprosy[a] or who leans on a crutch or who
falls by the sword or who lacks food."
30 (Joab and his brother Abishai murdered
Abner because he had killed their brother Asahel
in the battle at Gibeon.)
3:31 [n]2Sa 1:2,11; Ps 30:11; Isa 20:2 [o]Ge 37:34 31 Then David said to Joab and all the people
with him, "Tear your clothes and put on sackcloth[n]
and walk in mourning[o] in front of Abner." King
David himself walked behind the bier. 32 They
buried Abner in Hebron, and the king wept[p] aloud
3:32 [p]Nu 14:1; Pr 24:17 at Abner's tomb. All the people wept also.
33 The king sang this lament[q] for Abner:

3:33 [q]2Sa 1:17 "Should Abner have died as the lawless
die?
34 Your hands were not bound,
your feet were not fettered.
You fell as one falls before wicked men."

And all the people wept over him again.
35 Then they all came and urged David to eat
something while it was still day; but David took
an oath, saying, "May God deal with me, be it ever
3:35 [r]Ru 1:17; 1Sa 3:17 [s]1Sa 31:13; 2Sa 1:12; 12:17; Jer 16:7 so severely,[r] if I taste bread[s] or anything else
before the sun sets!"
36 All the people took note and were pleased;
indeed, everything the king did pleased them. 37 So
on that day all the people and all Israel knew that
3:37 [t]ver 28 the king had no part[t] in the murder of Abner son
of Ner.
3:38 [u]2Sa 1:19 38 Then the king said to his men, "Do you not
realize that a prince and a great man has fallen[u] in
Israel this day? 39 And today, though I am the
3:39 [v]2Sa 2:18 [w]2Sa 19:5-7 [x]1Ki 2:5-6, 33-34; Ps 41:10; 101:8 anointed king, I am weak, and these sons of Zeruiah[v] are too strong for me.[w] May the LORD repay[x]
the evildoer according to his evil deeds!"

Ish-Bosheth Murdered

4:1 [y]2Sa 3:27; Ezr 4:4 4 When Ish-Bosheth son of Saul heard that
Abner[y] had died in Hebron, he lost courage,
and all Israel became alarmed. 2 Now Saul's son
4:2 [z]Jos 9:17; 18:25 had two men who were leaders of raiding bands.
One was named Baanah and the other Recab; they
were sons of Rimmon the Beerothite from the
4:3 [a]Ne 11:33 tribe of Benjamin—Beeroth[z] is considered part of
Benjamin, 3 because the people of Beeroth fled to
4:4 [b]1Sa 18:1 Gittaim[a] and have lived there as aliens to this day.
4 (Jonathan[b] son of Saul had a son who was

[a] 29 The Hebrew word was used for various diseases affecting the skin—not necessarily leprosy.

David Mourns Abner

2SA 3:38-39

Abner, King Saul's cousin, obtains for Saul's successor, Ish-Bosheth, the allegiance of all the tribes but Judah. But when Ish-Bosheth insinuates that Abner is aiming for the crown himself by taking Saul's concubine, Abner switches his allegiance to David and offers all the tribes of Israel to him. Then Joab, David's general, kills Abner.

David knows that Abner's death will look like the execution of an opponent. To prove that he had no involvement in Abner's death, David reprimands Joab and mourns Abner. As David washes his hands of the guilt of Abner's blood, he heaps curses on Joab and his family (2Sa 3:29). The respect David pays to Abner pleases the people, proving his noble character to them once again. So, too, when we look to God rather than to human effort to deal with our "enemies," and when we honor those who have opposed us, our good character will be recognized and respected.

Mephibosheth

2SA 4:4

Mephibosheth is Jonathan's son and Saul's grandson. He is only five years old when his grandfather and father are killed. Since a new king often kills anyone with a claim to the throne, Mephibosheth's nurse flees with the boy, but he is injured as they run and becomes crippled. Mephibosheth is mentioned again when David seeks a way to honor his friend Jonathan (2Sa 9:3-7). When David learns that Jonathan's son is alive, he gives Mephibosheth everything that had once belonged to Saul's family, including the honor of sitting at the king's table. David's care is an example of faithfully keeping our promises made to one another (1Sa 20:12-15,42) and a picture of the beauty of long-lasting friendships. (See character sketch for Mephibosheth's nurse on page 873.)

lame in both feet. He was five years old when the
news[c] about Saul and Jonathan came from Jezreel. His nurse picked him up and fled, but as she
hurried to leave, he fell and became crippled.[d] His
name was Mephibosheth.)[e]
5Now Recab and Baanah, the sons of Rimmon
the Beerothite, set out for the house of Ish-Bosheth,[f]
and they arrived there in the heat of the day while
he was taking his noonday rest. 6They went into
the inner part of the house as if to get some wheat,
and they stabbed[g] him in the stomach. Then Recab
and his brother Baanah slipped away.
7They had gone into the house while he was
lying on the bed in his bedroom. After they
stabbed and killed him, they cut off his head. Taking it with them, they traveled all night by way of
the Arabah. 8They brought the head of Ish-
Bosheth to David at Hebron and said to the king,
"Here is the head of Ish-Bosheth son of Saul,[h]
your enemy, who tried to take your life. This day
the LORD has avenged my lord the king against
Saul and his offspring."
9David answered Recab and his brother Baanah,
the sons of Rimmon the Beerothite, "As surely as
the LORD lives, who has delivered[i] me out of all
trouble, 10when a man told me, 'Saul is dead,' and
thought he was bringing good news, I seized him
and put him to death in Ziklag.[j] That was the
reward I gave him for his news! 11How much
more—when wicked men have killed an innocent
man in his own house and on his own bed—
should I not now demand his blood[k] from your
hand and rid the earth of you!"
12So David gave an order to his men, and they
killed them.[l] They cut off their hands and feet and
hung the bodies by the pool in Hebron. But they
took the head of Ish-Bosheth and buried it in
Abner's tomb at Hebron.

David Becomes King Over Israel

5 All the tribes of Israel[m] came to David at
Hebron and said, "We are your own flesh and
blood.[n] 2In the past, while Saul was king over us,
you were the one who led Israel on their military
campaigns.[o] And the LORD said to you, 'You will
shepherd[p] my people Israel, and you will become
their ruler.[q]' "
3When all the elders of Israel had come to King
David at Hebron, the king made a compact[r] with
them at Hebron before the LORD, and they anointed[s] David king over Israel.
4David was thirty years old[t] when he became
king, and he reigned[u] forty[v] years. 5In Hebron he
reigned over Judah seven years and six months,[w]
and in Jerusalem he reigned over all Israel and
Judah thirty-three years.

David Conquers Jerusalem

6The king and his men marched to Jerusalem[x]
to attack the Jebusites,[y] who lived there. The Jeb-

4:4 [c]1Sa 31:1-4 [d]Lev 21:18 [e]2Sa 9:3,6; 1Ch 8:34; 9:40
4:5 [f]2Sa 2:8
4:6 [g]2Sa 2:23
4:8 [h]1Sa 24:4; 25:29
4:9 [i]Ge 48:16; 1Ki 1:29
4:10 [j]2Sa 1:2-16
4:11 [k]Ge 9:5; Ps 9:12
4:12 [l]2Sa 1:15
5:1 [m]2Sa 19:43 [n]1Ch 11:1
5:2 [o]1Sa 18:5, 13,16 [p]1Sa 16:1; 2Sa 7:7 [q]1Sa 25:30
5:3 [r]2Sa 3:21 [s]2Sa 2:4
5:4 [t]Lk 3:23 [u]1Ki 2:11; 1Ch 3:4 [v]1Ch 26:31; 29:27
5:5 [w]2Sa 2:11; 1Ch 3:4
5:6 [x]Jdg 1:8 [y]Jos 15:8

usites said to David, "You will not get in here;
even the blind and the lame can ward you off."
They thought, "David cannot get in here." 7Nev-
ertheless, David captured the fortress of Zion, the
5:7 [z]2Sa 6:12, 16; 1Ki 2:10 City of David.[z]
8On that day, David said, "Anyone who conquers the Jebusites will have to use the water
shaft[a] to reach those 'lame and blind' who are
David's enemies.[b]" That is why they say, "The
'blind and lame' will not enter the palace."
9David then took up residence in the fortress
5:9 [a]ver 7; 1Ki 9:15,24 and called it the City of David. He built up the area
around it, from the supporting terraces[ca] inward.
10And he became more and more powerful,[b]
5:10 [b]2Sa 3:1 because the LORD God Almighty was with him.
11Now Hiram[c] king of Tyre sent messengers to
5:11 [c]1Ki 5:1,18; 1Ch 14:1 David, along with cedar logs and carpenters and
stonemasons, and they built a palace for David.
12And David knew that the LORD had established
him as king over Israel and had exalted his kingdom for the sake of his people Israel.
13After he left Hebron, David took more concu-
5:13 [d]Dt 17:17; 1Ch 3:9 bines and wives[d] in Jerusalem, and more sons and
daughters were born to him. 14These are the
5:14 [e]1Ch 3:5 names of the children born to him there:[e] Shammua, Shobab, Nathan, Solomon, 15Ibhar, Elishua,
Nepheg, Japhia, 16Elishama, Eliada and Eliphelet.

David Defeats the Philistines

17When the Philistines heard that David had
been anointed king over Israel, they went up in
5:17 [f]2Sa 23:14; 1Ch 11:16 full force to search for him, but David heard about
it and went down to the stronghold.[f] 18Now the
Philistines had come and spread out in the Valley
5:18 [g]Jos 15:8; 17:15; 18:16 of Rephaim;[g] 19so David inquired[h] of the LORD,
"Shall I go and attack the Philistines? Will you
hand them over to me?"
5:19 [h]1Sa 23:2; 2Sa 2:1 The LORD answered him, "Go, for I will surely
hand the Philistines over to you."
20So David went to Baal Perazim, and there he
defeated them. He said, "As waters break out, the
LORD has broken out against my enemies before
5:20 [i]Isa 28:21 me." So that place was called Baal Perazim.[di]
21The Philistines abandoned their idols there, and
5:21 [j]Dt 7:5; 1Ch 14:12; Isa 46:2 David and his men carried them off.[j]
22Once more the Philistines came up and spread
out in the Valley of Rephaim; 23so David inquired
of the LORD, and he answered, "Do not go straight
up, but circle around behind them and attack
5:24 [k]2Ki 7:6 [l]Jdg 4:14 them in front of the balsam trees. 24As soon as you
hear the sound[k] of marching in the tops of the bal-
sam trees, move quickly, because that will mean
the LORD has gone out in front[l] of you to strike the
Philistine army." 25So David did as the LORD com-
5:25 [m]Isa 28:21 [n]1Ch 14:16 manded him, and he struck down the Philistines
all the way from Gibeon[em] to Gezer.[n]

[a] *8* Or *use scaling hooks* [b] *8* Or *are hated by David* [c] *9* Or *the Millo* [d] *20* *Baal Perazim* means *the lord who breaks out.* [e] *25* Septuagint (see also 1 Chron. 14:16); Hebrew *Geba*

God Goes Before

2SA 5:24

When the Israelites go into a battle that is sanctioned by God, he leads them, or, as this verse states, he goes "out in front" of them. Many times the Lord uses supernatural means to bring victory to his people. In 2 Kings 7:5–6, the Arameans hear "the sound of chariots and horses and a great army." Is there such an army? No! But the Lord produces the sound of it, and the Arameans run in fright and confusion. In 1 Samuel 14:15, God makes the ground shake, causing the enemy army to panic. God opens the eyes of Elisha's servant so that he can see the supernatural "horses and chariots of fire" (2Ki 6:17) sent to protect Elisha. God manifests his power in a miraculous way in the battle recorded in this verse also. The troops hear "the sound of marching in the tops of the balsam trees." They hear the sound of God's armies, a heavenly host, marching out to aid his people in battle.

Uzzah's Death

2SA 6:6–8

Poor Uzzah. He is, after all, only trying to protect the ark of God. And for that he must die? Why? Very simply, because Uzzah disregards God's holiness: "The LORD's anger burned against Uzzah because of his irreverent act" (2Sa 6:7). By pulling it on a cart with a team of oxen, those involved here do not follow the Lord's very specific instructions for carrying the ark (1Ch 15:15). Only the Kohathites, a special branch of the tribe of Levi, are allowed to carry the ark, and even they may not touch it or they will die (Nu 4:15). While all of the men, including David, are irreverent, God shows his mercy by only striking the one man who directly violates God's specific instructions—good intentions notwithstanding.

The Ark Brought to Jerusalem

6 David again brought together out of Israel chosen men, thirty thousand in all. 2He and all his
men set out from Baalah[o] of Judah[a] to bring up
from there the ark[p] of God, which is called by the
Name,[b][q] the name of the LORD Almighty, who is
enthroned[r] between the cherubim[s] that are on the
ark. 3They set the ark of God on a new cart[t] and
brought it from the house of Abinadab, which was
on the hill. Uzzah and Ahio, sons of Abinadab,
were guiding the new cart 4with the ark of God on
it,[c] and Ahio was walking in front of it. 5David and
the whole house of Israel were celebrating with all
their might before the LORD, with songs[d] and with
harps, lyres, tambourines, sistrums and cymbals.[u]
6When they came to the threshing floor of
Nacon, Uzzah reached out and took hold of[v] the
ark of God, because the oxen stumbled. 7The
LORD's anger burned against Uzzah because of his
irreverent act;[w] therefore God struck him down[x]
and he died there beside the ark of God.
8Then David was angry because the LORD's
wrath[y] had broken out against Uzzah, and to this
day that place is called Perez Uzzah.[e][z]
9David was afraid of the LORD that day and said,
"How[a] can the ark of the LORD ever come to me?"
10He was not willing to take the ark of the LORD to
be with him in the City of David. Instead, he took
it aside to the house of Obed-Edom[b] the Gittite.
11The ark of the LORD remained in the house of
Obed-Edom the Gittite for three months, and the
LORD blessed him and his entire household.[c]
12Now King David[d] was told, "The LORD has
blessed the household of Obed-Edom and everything he has, because of the ark of God." So David
went down and brought up the ark of God from
the house of Obed-Edom to the City of David with
rejoicing. 13When those who were carrying the
ark of the LORD had taken six steps, he sacrificed[e]
a bull and a fattened calf. 14David, wearing a linen
ephod,[f] danced[g] before the LORD with all his
might, 15while he and the entire house of Israel
brought up the ark of the LORD with shouts and
the sound of trumpets.[h]
16As the ark of the LORD was entering the City of
David,[i] Michal daughter of Saul watched from a
window. And when she saw King David leaping
and dancing before the LORD, she despised him in
her heart.
17They brought the ark of the LORD and set it in
its place inside the tent that David had pitched for
it,[j] and David sacrificed burnt offerings[k] and fel-

6:2 [o]Jos 15:9 [p]1Sa 4:4; 7:1 [q]Lev 24:16; Isa 63:14 [r]Ps 99:1 [s]Ex 25:22; 1Ch 13:5-6
6:3 [t]Nu 7:4-9; 1Sa 6:7
6:5 [u]1Sa 18:6-7; Ezr 3:10; Ps 150:5
6:6 [v]Nu 4:15,19-20; 1Ch 13:9
6:7 [w]1Ch 15:13-15 [x]Ex 19:22; 1Sa 6:19
6:8 [y]Ps 7:11 [z]Ge 38:29
6:9 [a]Ps 119:120
6:10 [b]1Ch 13:13; 26:4-5
6:11 [c]Ge 30:27; 39:5
6:12 [d]1Ki 8:1; 1Ch 15:25
6:13 [e]1Ki 8:5,62
6:14 [f]Ex 19:6; 1Sa 2:18 [g]Ex 15:20
6:15 [h]Ps 47:5; 98:6
6:16 [i]2Sa 5:7
6:17 [j]1Ch 15:1; 2Ch 1:4 [k]Lev 1:1-17; 1Ki 8:62-64

[a] *2* That is, Kiriath Jearim; Hebrew *Baale Judah,* a variant of *Baalah of Judah* [b] *2* Hebrew; Septuagint and Vulgate do not have *the Name.* [c] *3,4* Dead Sea Scrolls and some Septuagint manuscripts; Masoretic Text *cart* [4]*and they brought it with the ark of God from the house of Abinadab, which was on the hill* [d] *5* See Dead Sea Scrolls, Septuagint and 1 Chronicles 13:8; Masoretic Text *celebrating before the LORD with all kinds of instruments made of pine.* [e] *8* *Perez Uzzah* means *outbreak against Uzzah.*

lowship offerings[a] before the LORD. 18After he had
6:18 [l]1Ki 8:22 finished sacrificing[l] the burnt offerings and fellowship offerings, he blessed the people in the
name of the LORD Almighty. 19Then he gave a loaf
6:19 [m]Hos 3:1 of bread, a cake of dates and a cake of raisins[m] to
[n]Ne 8:10 each person in the whole crowd of Israelites, both
men and women.[n] And all the people went to
their homes.
20When David returned home to bless his
household, Michal daughter of Saul came out to
meet him and said, "How the king of Israel has
6:20 [o]ver 14,16 distinguished himself today, disrobing[o] in the
sight of the slave girls of his servants as any vul-
gar fellow would!"
21David said to Michal, "It was before the LORD,
who chose me rather than your father or anyone
6:21 [p]1Sa 13:14; from his house when he appointed[p] me ruler over
15:28 the LORD's people Israel—I will celebrate before
the LORD. 22I will become even more undignified
than this, and I will be humiliated in my own
eyes. But by these slave girls you spoke of, I will
be held in honor."
23And Michal daughter of Saul had no children
to the day of her death.

God's Promise to David

7:1 **7** After the king was settled in his palace[q] and
[q]1Ch 17:1 the LORD had given him rest from all his enemies around him, 2he said to Nathan the prophet,
7:2 "Here I am, living in a palace[r] of cedar, while the
[r]2Sa 5:11 [s]Ex 26:1; ark of God remains in a tent."[s]
Ac 7:45-46 3Nathan replied to the king, "Whatever you
have in mind, go ahead and do it, for the LORD is
with you."
4That night the word of the LORD came to
Nathan, saying:

5"Go and tell my servant David, 'This is
7:5 what the LORD says: Are you[t] the one to build
[t]1Ki 8:19; 1Ch 22:8 me a house to dwell in?[u] 6I have not dwelt in
[u]1Ki 5:3-5 a house from the day I brought the Israelites
7:6 up out of Egypt to this day. I have been mov-
[v]Ex 40:18,34 ing from place to place with a tent[v] as my
[w]1Ki 8:16 dwelling.[w] 7Wherever I have moved with all
7:7 the Israelites,[x] did I ever say to any of their
[x]Dt 23:14 rulers whom I commanded to shepherd[y] my
[y]2Sa 5:2 people Israel, "Why have you not built me a
[z]Lev 26:11-12 house of cedar?[z]" '
8"Now then, tell my servant David, 'This is
what the LORD Almighty says: I took you from
7:8 the pasture and from following the flock[a] to
[a]1Sa 16:11 [b]2Sa 6:21 be ruler[b] over my people Israel.[c] 9I have been
[c]Ps 78:70-72; with you wherever you have gone,[d] and I
2Co 6:18* have cut off all your enemies from before
7:9 you.[e] Now I will make your name great, like
[d]2Sa 5:10 the names of the greatest men of the earth.
[e]Ps 18:37-42 10And I will provide a place for my people
7:10 Israel and will plant[f] them so that they can
[f]Ex 15:17; Isa 5:1-7 have a home of their own and no longer be

God Sees the Heart

2SA 6:21–23

After being passed between two men according to their whims and those of her father, Michal is a bitter and ungracious woman (see note on 2Sa 3:13–14, page 478). When she sees David disrobe and dance in the streets, she is disgusted. More than that, she despises him (2Sa 6:16). David wears only an ephod (a thigh-length, sleeveless garment that is worn by priests and is associated with worship), and dances with abandon (2Sa 6:14). Michal feels that David's behavior dishonors him and his throne (2Sa 6:20). She doesn't speak out of concern for David or for her nation's best interests, but rather out of contempt for David (see character sketch for Michal on page 740). Unperturbed, David claims he'd go even further, be even more "undignified," even be "humiliated" (2Sa 6:22) in order to truly worship his God. As David clearly exhibits, our hearts are what God cares about, not our traditions or cultural expectations. Worship from the heart honors God, regardless of how it may appear to others.

[a] *17* Traditionally *peace offerings;* also in verse 18

Extravagant Worship

For Christians, worship expresses reverence, awe and praise to God. Because true worship is personal, it has unlimited styles of expression and can stir up strong emotions. What is your worship style? Is it quiet and dignified or extravagant and spontaneous?

David abandons himself to God and worships him in ways some people feel are undignified and irreverent. David removes his royal robes (2Sa 6:20) and dances "before the LORD with all his might" (2Sa 6:14). He is not concerned with how others view him. His dance of praise is joyously unrestrained. But David's wife Michal watches and despises him "in her heart" (2Sa 6:16).

Why is Michal so angry with David? Whose honor is at stake (2Sa 6:20-22)? Whose honor and reputation are you concerned with when you worship?

How does David respond to Michal's criticism (2Sa 6:21-22)? How should you respond if someone criticizes your worship?

What does Jesus say about the extravagant worship of his followers when the Pharisees criticize them (Lk 19:37-40)? What should you do when your worship brings pressure from critics?

What type of worship does God abhor (Mk 7:6-8)? What type of worship pleases God (Jn 4:23-24)? How would you describe your worship?

God's honor is the issue here—not your own honor or the honor of those around you. At times, your praise or worship of God may even be offensive or embarrassing to others. But what people think of you or of your mode of worship is irrelevant. David's response to Michal revealed his true focus—God. Don't let fear of others rob you of the wonder that comes from joyful abandonment to God (Pr 29:25).

Enjoying God THROUGH the Word

Read Luke 7:36-50 (pages 1698-1699). This "sinful" woman endures ridicule when she comes into the house of a Pharisee and approaches Jesus. Her tears wet his feet; she wipes his feet with her hair and kisses them. Then she pours her perfume over them. What a beautiful act of worship! But those around her respond with indignation and offense. Her expression of worship is completely misunderstood by everyone except Jesus.

Imagine you are this woman. Are you embarrassed? Or are you focusing so intently on Jesus that you neither notice nor care about the reactions of others? Worship is a time of intimacy between you and your Lord. Don't let a desire for the approval of others prevent you from offering loving abandonment to God (Jn 12:42-43).

Enjoying God THROUGH Experience

Worship *style* is not the real issue here; heart attitude is. True worship is a spirit-to-spirit encounter with God. Do you lift your hands in praise? Do you bow with your face to the floor? Do you dance? Whisper? Clap? Shout? Think about your most comfortable style of worship. Now take a deep breath spiritually and try something new. If you tend to have a quiet and reflective worship style, put on praise music, in the privacy of your home, and dance before the Lord. If you usually sing and shout to the Lord in praise, slow down, to experience the peace of contemplative worship. Offering a "sacrifice of praise" (Heb 13:15) to the Lord requires that you sacrifice your own ideas and those of others in order to hold God's honor as supreme. Whatever your style, whatever your circumstance, whatever your condition—praise him!

Go to page 560 for your next weekly study.

7:10 [g]Ps 89:22-23 [h]Isa 60:18 disturbed. Wicked[g] people will not oppress
them anymore,[h] as they did at the beginning
11 and have done ever since the time I
7:11 [i]Jdg 2:16; 1Sa 12:9-11 [j]ver 1 [k]1Sa 25:28 [l]ver 27 appointed leaders[a][i] over my people Israel. I
will also give you rest from all your enemies.[j]
"'The LORD declares to you that the LORD
himself will establish[k] a house[l] for you:
12 When your days are over and you rest[m]
7:12 [m]1Ki 2:1 [n]Ps 132:11-12 with your fathers, I will raise up your offspring to succeed you, who will come from
your own body,[n] and I will establish his kingdom. 13 He is the one who will build a house
7:13 [o]1Ki 5:5; 8:19,29 [p]Isa 9:7 for my Name,[o] and I will establish the throne
of his kingdom forever.[p] 14 I will be his father,
and he will be my son.[q] When he does
7:14 [q]Ps 89:26; Heb 1:5* [r]Ps 89:30-33 wrong, I will punish him with the rod[r] of
men, with floggings inflicted by men. 15 But
my love will never be taken away from him,
as I took it away from Saul,[s] whom I removed
7:15 [s]1Sa 15:23, 28 from before you. 16 Your house and your kingdom will endure forever before me[b]; your
7:16 [t]Ps 89:36-37 [u]ver 13 throne[t] will be established forever.[u]' "

17 Nathan reported to David all the words of this
entire revelation.

David's Prayer

18 Then King David went in and sat before the
LORD, and he said:

7:18 [v]Ex 3:11; 1Sa 18:18 "Who am I,[v] O Sovereign LORD, and what is
my family, that you have brought me this far?
19 And as if this were not enough in your
sight, O Sovereign LORD, you have also spoken about the future of the house of your ser-
7:19 [w]Isa 55:8-9 vant. Is this your usual way of dealing with
man,[w] O Sovereign LORD?

7:20 [x]Jn 21:17 [y]1Sa 16:7 20 "What more can David say to you? For
you know[x] your servant,[y] O Sovereign LORD.
21 For the sake of your word and according to
your will, you have done this great thing and
made it known to your servant.

7:22 [z]Ps 48:1; 86:10; Jer 10:6 [a]Dt 3:24 [b]Ex 15:11 [c]Ex 10:2; Ps 44:1 22 "How great[z] you are,[a] O Sovereign LORD!
There is no one like you, and there is no God[b]
but you, as we have heard with our own
ears.[c] 23 And who is like your people Israel[d]—
the one nation on earth that God went out to
redeem as a people for himself, and to make
7:23 [d]Dt 4:32-38 [e]Dt 10:21 [f]Dt 9:26; 15:15 a name for himself, and to perform great and
awesome wonders[e] by driving out nations
and their gods from before your people,
whom you redeemed[f] from Egypt?[c] 24 You
have established your people Israel as your
7:24 [g]Dt 26:18 [h]Ex 6:6-7; Ps 48:14 very own[g] forever, and you, O LORD, have
become their God.[h]

25 "And now, LORD God, keep forever the
promise you have made concerning your ser-

[a] *11* Traditionally *judges* [b] *16* Some Hebrew manuscripts and Septuagint; most Hebrew manuscripts *you* [c] *23* See Septuagint and 1 Chron. 17:21; Hebrew *wonders for your land and before your people, whom you redeemed from Egypt, from the nations and their gods.*

God's Promised Rest

2SA 7:11

God promises David "rest from all [his] enemies." *This is fulfilled for a time during* David's reign (2Sa 7:1); *yet God's promise doesn't end there. It continues after David's death and is fulfilled completely through Jesus Christ's reign as King of kings. A descendent of David, Jesus is the fulfillment of God's promises to David of a king forever on the throne* (2Sa 7:13) *and of rest from his enemies* (2Sa 7:11). *Read* Luke 1:31–33, *underlining the passage and noting its connection to this wonderful promise.*

vant and his house. Do as you promised, 26so
that your name will be great forever. Then
men will say, 'The LORD Almighty is God over
Israel!' And the house of your servant David
will be established before you.
27"O LORD Almighty, God of Israel, you
have revealed this to your servant, saying, 'I
will build a house for you.' So your servant
has found courage to offer you this prayer.
28O Sovereign LORD, you are God! Your words 7:28
are trustworthy,[i] and you have promised [i]Ex 34:6;
these good things to your servant. 29Now be Jn 17:17
pleased to bless the house of your servant,
that it may continue forever in your sight; for
you, O Sovereign LORD, have spoken, and 7:29
with your blessing[j] the house of your servant [j]Nu 6:23-27
will be blessed forever."

David's Victories

8 In the course of time, David defeated the Philistines and subdued them, and he took
Metheg Ammah from the control of the Philistines.
2David also defeated the Moabites.[k] He made 8:2
them lie down on the ground and measured them [k]Ge 19:37;
off with a length of cord. Every two lengths of Nu 24:17
them were put to death, and the third length was
allowed to live. So the Moabites became subject
to David and brought tribute.
3Moreover, David fought Hadadezer[l] son of 8:3
Rehob, king of Zobah,[m] when he went to restore [l]2Sa 10:16,
his control along the Euphrates River. 4David cap- 19
tured a thousand of his chariots, seven thousand [m]1Sa 14:47
charioteers[a] and twenty thousand foot soldiers. He
hamstrung[n] all but a hundred of the chariot horses. 8:4
5When the Arameans of Damascus[o] came to [n]Jos 11:9
help Hadadezer king of Zobah, David struck 8:5
down twenty-two thousand of them. 6He put gar- [o]1Ki 11:24
risons in the Aramean kingdom of Damascus, and
the Arameans became subject to him and brought
tribute. The LORD gave David victory wherever he 8:6
went.[p] [p]ver 14;
7David took the gold shields[q] that belonged to 2Sa 3:18; 7:9
the officers of Hadadezer and brought them to Je- 8:7
rusalem. 8From Tebah[b] and Berothai,[r] towns that [q]1Ki 10:16
belonged to Hadadezer, King David took a great 8:8
quantity of bronze. [r]Eze 47:16
9When Tou[c] king of Hamath[s] heard that David 8:9
had defeated the entire army of Hadadezer, 10he [s]1Ki 8:65;
sent his son Joram[d] to King David to greet him and 2Ch 8:4
congratulate him on his victory in battle over
Hadadezer, who had been at war with Tou. Joram
brought with him articles of silver and gold and
bronze.
11King David dedicated[t] these articles to the 8:11
LORD, as he had done with the silver and gold [t]1Ki 7:51; 1Ch 26:26

I think our best plan is to ***place ourselves in the Lord's presence, meditate upon his mercy and grace and upon our own lowliness, and leave him to give us what he wills, whether it be water or aridity. He knows best what is good for us, and in this way we shall walk in tranquillity and the devil will have less opportunity to fool us.***

—*Teresa of Avila* (1515-1582)

[a] *4* Septuagint (see also Dead Sea Scrolls and 1 Chron. 18:4); Masoretic Text *captured seventeen hundred of his charioteers*
[b] *8* See some Septuagint manuscripts (see also 1 Chron. 18:8); Hebrew *Betah.*
[c] *9* Hebrew *Toi,* a variant of *Tou;* also in verse 10
[d] *10* A variant of *Hadoram*

from all the nations he had subdued: 12Edom[a] and
8:12 [u]ver 2 Moab,[u] the Ammonites[v] and the Philistines,[w] and
[v]2Sa 10:14 Amalek.[x] He also dedicated the plunder taken
[w]2Sa 5:25 [x]1Sa 27:8 from Hadadezer son of Rehob, king of Zobah.
8:13 13And David became famous[y] after he returned
[y]2Sa 7:9 from striking down eighteen thousand Edomites[b]
[z]2Ki 14:7; in the Valley of Salt.[z]
1Ch 18:12 14He put garrisons throughout Edom, and all
8:14 the Edomites[a] became subject to David.[b] The LORD
[a]Nu 24:17-18 gave David victory wherever he went.[c]

[b]Ge 27:29, 37-40 [c]ver 6

David's Officials

8:16 15David reigned over all Israel, doing what was
[d]2Sa 19:13; just and right for all his people. 16Joab[d] son of Zer-
1Ch 11:6 uiah was over the army; Jehoshaphat[e] son of Ahi-
[e]2Sa 20:24; lud was recorder; 17Zadok[f] son of Ahitub and
1Ki 4:3 Ahimelech son of Abiathar were priests; Seraiah
was secretary;[g] 18Benaiah[h] son of Jehoiada was
8:17 over the Kerethites[i] and Pelethites; and David's
[f]2Sa 15:24, 29; sons were royal advisers.[c]

1Ch 16:39; 24:3

David and Mephibosheth

[g]1Ki 4:3; 2Ki 12:10 9 David asked, "Is there anyone still left of the
8:18 house of Saul to whom I can show kindness
[h]2Sa 20:23; for Jonathan's sake?"[j]
1Ki 1:8,38; 2Now there was a servant of Saul's household
1Ch 18:17 [i]1Sa 30:14 named Ziba.[k] They called him to appear before
David, and the king said to him, "Are you Ziba?"
9:1 "Your servant," he replied.
[j]1Sa 20:14-17,42 3The king asked, "Is there no one still left of the
house of Saul to whom I can show God's kindness?"
9:2 [k]2Sa 16:1-4; Ziba answered the king, "There is still a son of
19:17,26,29 Jonathan;[l] he is crippled[m] in both feet."
4"Where is he?" the king asked.
9:3 [l]1Sa 20:14 Ziba answered, "He is at the house of Makir[n]
[m]2Sa 4:4 son of Ammiel in Lo Debar."
9:4 5So King David had him brought from Lo Debar,
[n]2Sa 17:27-29 from the house of Makir son of Ammiel.
6When Mephibosheth son of Jonathan, the son
9:6 of Saul, came to David, he bowed down to pay
[o]2Sa 16:4; 19:24-30 him honor.[o]
David said, "Mephibosheth!"
"Your servant," he replied.
7"Don't be afraid," David said to him, "for I will
surely show you kindness for the sake of your
father Jonathan. I will restore to you all the land
9:7 that belonged to your grandfather Saul, and you
[p]ver 1,3; will always eat at my table.[p]"
2Sa 12:8; 8Mephibosheth bowed down and said, "What is
19:28; 1Ki 2:7; your servant, that you should notice a dead dog[q]
2Ki 25:29 like me?"
9:8 9Then the king summoned Ziba, Saul's servant,
[q]2Sa 16:9 and said to him, "I have given your master's
grandson everything that belonged to Saul and his
family. 10You and your sons and your servants are
to farm the land for him and bring in the crops, so

[a] 12 Some Hebrew manuscripts, Septuagint and Syriac (see also 1 Chron. 18:11); most Hebrew manuscripts *Aram*
[b] 13 A few Hebrew manuscripts, Septuagint and Syriac (see also 1 Chron. 18:12); most Hebrew manuscripts *Aram* (that is, Arameans) [c] 18 Or *were priests*

Treatment of the Lame

2SA 9:3

In David's day, neither the sick nor the crippled nor the lame could serve in the temple (Lev 21:17-21). The lame were at the mercy of those who took care of them and carried them from place to place (Mt 15:30; Ac 3:2). Since they often had no way to support themselves, they resorted to begging (Ac 3:2).

Mephibosheth most likely has lived in obscurity out of his fear of David, but his deformity may also have driven him into seclusion—for the grandson of great King Saul calls himself a "dead dog" (2Sa 9:8). Mephibosheth displays again this same self-deprecating spirit in 2 Samuel 19:26-28. Like David, who rescues Mephibosheth, God is a rescuer of the lame (Zep 3:19). And he calls us to be the same. We are to follow David's example by helping those who cannot help themselves and those who have nothing to offer us in return (Lk 14:13-14).

Gross Indignities

2SA 10:4

When the Ammonite king dies, David sends a delegation to express his sympathy to Hanun, the new Ammonite king. Suspecting the delegation of ulterior motives, Hanun seizes the men of the delegation. He then proceeds to humiliate them in the most insulting manner he can think of: He cuts off half of each man's beard (probably the right or left half), and he cuts off each man's robe at the buttocks. Public nakedness is considered shameful, so exposing the men's buttocks is embarrassing for them. Also, men's beards are their personal badge of dignity and a sign of freedom since slaves are usually shaved. When David hears of the humiliation of his men, he graciously allows them to stay in Jericho until their beards have grown back. The Ammonites realize their error, gather an army for the onslaught they know David will undertake and suffer a tremendous defeat in the battles that ensue.

that your master's grandson[r] may be provided for.
And Mephibosheth, grandson of your master, will
always eat at my table." (Now Ziba had fifteen
sons and twenty servants.)
11Then Ziba said to the king, "Your servant will
do whatever my lord the king commands his servant to do." So Mephibosheth ate at David's[a] table
like one of the king's sons.[s]
12Mephibosheth had a young son named Mica,
and all the members of Ziba's household were servants of Mephibosheth.[t] 13And Mephibosheth
lived in Jerusalem, because he always ate at the
king's table, and he was crippled in both feet.

David Defeats the Ammonites

10 In the course of time, the king of the
Ammonites died, and his son Hanun succeeded him as king. 2David thought, "I will show
kindness to Hanun son of Nahash,[u] just as his
father showed kindness to me." So David sent a
delegation to express his sympathy to Hanun concerning his father.
When David's men came to the land of the
Ammonites, 3the Ammonite nobles said to Hanun
their lord, "Do you think David is honoring your
father by sending men to you to express sympathy? Hasn't David sent them to you to explore the
city and spy it out and overthrow it?" 4So Hanun
seized David's men, shaved off half of each man's
beard,[v] cut off their garments in the middle at the
buttocks,[w] and sent them away.
5When David was told about this, he sent messengers to meet the men, for they were greatly
humiliated. The king said, "Stay at Jericho till
your beards have grown, and then come back."
6When the Ammonites realized that they had
become a stench[x] in David's nostrils, they hired
twenty thousand Aramean[y] foot soldiers from
Beth Rehob[z] and Zobah, as well as the king of
Maacah[a] with a thousand men, and also twelve
thousand men from Tob.
7On hearing this, David sent Joab out with the
entire army of fighting men. 8The Ammonites
came out and drew up in battle formation at the
entrance to their city gate, while the Arameans of
Zobah and Rehob and the men of Tob and Maacah were by themselves in the open country.
9Joab saw that there were battle lines in front
of him and behind him; so he selected some of the
best troops in Israel and deployed them against
the Arameans. 10He put the rest of the men under
the command of Abishai his brother and deployed
them against the Ammonites. 11Joab said, "If the
Arameans are too strong for me, then you are to
come to my rescue; but if the Ammonites are too
strong for you, then I will come to rescue you.
12Be strong[b] and let us fight bravely for our people
and the cities of our God. The LORD will do what
is good in his sight."[c]

[a] *11* Septuagint; Hebrew *my*

9:10 [r]ver 7,11,13; 2Sa 19:28
9:11 [s]Job 36:7; Ps 113:8
9:12 [t]1Ch 8:34
10:2 [u]1Sa 11:1
10:4 [v]Lev 19:27; Isa 15:2; Jer 48:37 [w]Isa 20:4
10:6 [x]Ge 34:30 [y]2Sa 8:5 [z]Jdg 18:28 [a]Dt 3:14
10:12 [b]Dt 31:6; 1Co 16:13; Eph 6:10 [c]Jdg 10:15; 1Sa 3:18; Ne 4:14

13Then Joab and the troops with him advanced
to fight the Arameans, and they fled before him.
14When the Ammonites saw that the Arameans
were fleeing, they fled before Abishai and went
inside the city. So Joab returned from fighting the
Ammonites and came to Jerusalem.
15After the Arameans saw that they had been
routed by Israel, they regrouped. 16Hadadezer had
Arameans brought from beyond the River[a]; they
went to Helam, with Shobach the commander of
Hadadezer's army leading them.
17When David was told of this, he gathered all
Israel, crossed the Jordan and went to Helam. The
Arameans formed their battle lines to meet David
and fought against him. 18But they fled before
Israel, and David killed seven hundred of their
charioteers and forty thousand of their foot soldiers.[b] He also struck down Shobach the commander of their army, and he died there. 19When
all the kings who were vassals of Hadadezer saw
that they had been defeated by Israel, they made
10:19 [d]2Sa 8:6 peace with the Israelites and became subject[d] to
[e]1Ki 11:25; 2Ki 5:1 them.
So the Arameans[e] were afraid to help the
Ammonites anymore.

David and Bathsheba

11:1 [f]1Ki 20:22, 26 [g]2Sa 2:18 [h]1Ch 20:1 [i]2Sa 12:26-28
11 In the spring,[f] at the time when kings go off
to war, David sent Joab[g] out with the king's
men and the whole Israelite army.[h] They
destroyed the Ammonites and besieged Rabbah.[i]
But David remained in Jerusalem.
11:2 [j]Dt 22:8; Jos 2:8 [k]Mt 5:28
2One evening David got up from his bed and
walked around on the roof[j] of the palace. From
the roof he saw[k] a woman bathing. The woman
was very beautiful, 3and David sent someone to
find out about her. The man said, "Isn't this
11:3 [l]1Ch 3:5 [m]2Sa 23:34 [n]2Sa 23:39
Bathsheba,[l] the daughter of Eliam[m] and the wife
of Uriah[n] the Hittite?" 4Then David sent messengers to get her.[o] She came to him, and he slept[p]
11:4 [o]Lev 20:10; Ps 51 Title; Jas 1:14-15 [p]Dt 22:22 [q]Lev 15:25-30; 18:19
with her. (She had purified herself from her
uncleanness.)[q] Then[c] she went back home. 5The
woman conceived and sent word to David, saying, "I am pregnant."
6So David sent this word to Joab: "Send me Uriah[r] the Hittite." And Joab sent him to David.
11:6 [r]1Ch 11:41
7When Uriah came to him, David asked him how
Joab was, how the soldiers were and how the war
was going. 8Then David said to Uriah, "Go down
11:8 [s]Ge 18:4; 43:24; Lk 7:44
to your house and wash your feet."[s] So Uriah left
the palace, and a gift from the king was sent after
him. 9But Uriah slept at the entrance to the palace
with all his master's servants and did not go down
to his house.
10When David was told, "Uriah did not go

[a] *16* That is, the Euphrates [b] *18* Some Septuagint manuscripts (see also 1 Chron. 19:18); Hebrew *horsemen*
[c] *4* Or *with her. When she purified herself from her uncleanness,*

Royal Rape?

2SA 11:2-5

Does Bathsheba bear any responsibility in her sexual encounter with David? Or is this episode an instance of royal rape? First, the Bible does not mention whether Bathsheba offers any resistance. Nor does it give any indication that her bathing is inappropriate (see the character sketch for Bathsheba on page 939). Instead of turning away and respecting her privacy, David continues to look. His lust for Bathsheba is not stifled when he hears she is married. And although it is common for kings of that day to take whomever they wish for their harem, taking a married woman is against Israelite law. Later, when Nathan rebukes David for this sin, he does not reprove Bathsheba (2Sa 12:1–13). David takes full responsibility. While the events in this story are troubling, it provides us with a beautiful assurance that should we commit great sin, we can repent to a great God. Read Psalm 51, David's prayer of repentance. Underline David's pleas and consider how David's image of God affects his petitions.

The Spark of Sin

2SA 11:6–27

It starts simply—as most sin does. David looks at a beautiful woman, he wants her; and before he knows it, he has not only committed adultery but also murder. We can note three things about sin as we read this story:

1. Sin is a flame that quickly grows and spreads.

2. Sin engulfs others. In this case, not only David, but Uriah, Bathsheba and an innocent baby pay the price for David's offense (2Sa 12:18).

3. Any sin against a human being is a sin against God. David realizes this truth and expresses it in Psalm 51:4: "Against you, you only, have I sinned and done what is evil in your sight."

Sadly, David discovers the progression of sin too late. The more he tries to cover it up, the more harm he causes. In your Bible, number the progressive steps of David's sin, and then remember them the next time the smallest offense sparks in your heart. (See character sketch for Bathsheba on page 939.)

home," he asked him, "Haven't you just come
from a distance? Why didn't you go home?"
11 Uriah said to David, "The ark[t] and Israel and
Judah are staying in tents, and my master Joab
and my lord's men are camped in the open fields.
How could I go to my house to eat and drink and
lie with my wife? As surely as you live, I will not
do such a thing!"
12 Then David said to him, "Stay here one more
day, and tomorrow I will send you back." So Uriah remained in Jerusalem that day and the next.
13 At David's invitation, he ate and drank with
him, and David made him drunk. But in the
evening Uriah went out to sleep on his mat among
his master's servants; he did not go home.
14 In the morning David wrote a letter[u] to Joab
and sent it with Uriah. 15 In it he wrote, "Put Uriah in the front line where the fighting is fiercest.
Then withdraw from him so he will be struck
down[v] and die.[w]"
16 So while Joab had the city under siege, he put
Uriah at a place where he knew the strongest
defenders were. 17 When the men of the city came
out and fought against Joab, some of the men in
David's army fell; moreover, Uriah the Hittite
died.
18 Joab sent David a full account of the battle.
19 He instructed the messenger: "When you have
finished giving the king this account of the battle,
20 the king's anger may flare up, and he may ask
you, 'Why did you get so close to the city to fight?
Didn't you know they would shoot arrows from
the wall? 21 Who killed Abimelech[x] son of Jerub-
Besheth[a]? Didn't a woman throw an upper millstone on him from the wall,[y] so that he died in
Thebez? Why did you get so close to the wall?' If
he asks you this, then say to him, 'Also, your servant Uriah the Hittite is dead.' "
22 The messenger set out, and when he arrived
he told David everything Joab had sent him to say.
23 The messenger said to David, "The men overpowered us and came out against us in the open,
but we drove them back to the entrance to the city
gate. 24 Then the archers shot arrows at your servants from the wall, and some of the king's men
died. Moreover, your servant Uriah the Hittite is
dead."
25 David told the messenger, "Say this to Joab:
'Don't let this upset you; the sword devours one
as well as another. Press the attack against the city
and destroy it.' Say this to encourage Joab."
26 When Uriah's wife heard that her husband
was dead, she mourned for him. 27 After the time
of mourning was over, David had her brought to
his house, and she became his wife and bore him
a son. But the thing David had done displeased[z]
the LORD.

11:11 [t]2Sa 7:2
11:14 [u]1Ki 21:8
11:15 [v]2Sa 12:9 [w]2Sa 12:12
11:21 [x]Jdg 8:31 [y]Jdg 9:50-54
11:27 [z]2Sa 12:9; Ps 51:4-5

[a] 21 Also known as *Jerub-Baal* (that is, Gideon)

Nathan Rebukes David

12 The LORD sent Nathan[a] to David.[b] When he
came to him,[c] he said, "There were two
men in a certain town, one rich and the other
poor. 2The rich man had a very large number of
sheep and cattle, 3but the poor man had nothing
except one little ewe lamb he had bought. He
raised it, and it grew up with him and his children. It shared his food, drank from his cup and
even slept in his arms. It was like a daughter to
him.
4"Now a traveler came to the rich man, but the
rich man refrained from taking one of his own
sheep or cattle to prepare a meal for the traveler
who had come to him. Instead, he took the ewe
lamb that belonged to the poor man and prepared
it for the one who had come to him."
5David[d] burned with anger against the man and
said to Nathan, "As surely as the LORD lives, the
man who did this deserves to die! 6He must pay
for that lamb four times over,[e] because he did
such a thing and had no pity."
7Then Nathan said to David, "You are the man!
This is what the LORD, the God of Israel, says: 'I
anointed[f] you[g] king over Israel, and I delivered
you from the hand of Saul. 8I gave your master's
house to you,[h] and your master's wives into your
arms. I gave you the house of Israel and Judah.
And if all this had been too little, I would have
given you even more. 9Why did you despise[i] the
word of the LORD by doing what is evil in his eyes?
You struck down[j] Uriah the Hittite with the sword
and took his wife to be your own. You killed him
with the sword of the Ammonites. 10Now, therefore, the sword[k] will never depart from your
house, because you despised me and took the wife
of Uriah the Hittite to be your own.'
11"This is what the LORD says: 'Out of your own
household I am going to bring calamity upon
you.[l] Before your very eyes I will take your wives
and give them to one who is close to you, and he
will lie with your wives in broad daylight. 12You
did it in secret,[m] but I will do this thing in broad
daylight[n] before all Israel.' "
13Then David said to Nathan, "I have sinned[o]
against the LORD."
Nathan replied, "The LORD has taken away[p]
your sin.[q] You are not going to die.[r] 14But because
by doing this you have made the enemies of the
LORD show utter contempt,[a][s] the son born to you
will die."
15After Nathan had gone home, the LORD struck[t]
the child that Uriah's wife had borne to David,
and he became ill. 16David pleaded with God for
the child. He fasted and went into his house and
spent the nights lying[u] on the ground. 17The elders of his household stood beside him to get him

12:1 [a]2Sa 7:2; 1Ki 20:35-41 [b]Ps 51 Title [c]2Sa 14:4
12:5 [d]1Ki 20:40
12:6 [e]Ex 22:1; Lk 19:8
12:7 [f]1Sa 16:13 [g]1Ki 20:42
12:8 [h]2Sa 9:7
12:9 [i]Nu 15:31; 1Sa 15:19 [j]2Sa 11:15
12:10 [k]2Sa 13:28; 18:14-15; 1Ki 2:25
12:11 [l]Dt 28:30; 2Sa 16:21-22
12:12 [m]2Sa 11:4-15 [n]2Sa 16:22
12:13 [o]Ge 13:13; Nu 22:34; 1Sa 15:24; 2Sa 24:10 [p]Ps 32:1-5; 51:1,9; 103:12; Zec 3:4,9 [q]Pr 28:13; Mic 7:18-19 [r]Lev 20:10; 24:17
12:14 [s]Isa 52:5; Ro 2:24
12:15 [t]1Sa 25:38
12:16 [u]2Sa 13:31; Ps 5:7

[a] 14 Masoretic Text; an ancient Hebrew scribal tradition *this you have shown utter contempt for the LORD*

David's Secret

2SA 12:11-12

David thinks he has a secret. Yet how will he keep it when all of heaven knows? The prophet Nathan confronts David and proclaims the Lord's judgment. The tables turn, and God promises that David will now experience the same pain he has caused others. The judgment that Nathan describes is fulfilled in 2 Samuel 16:22. Someone close to David—his own son—sleeps with David's concubines. David's sin is done in secret and is diligently concealed. But the punishment is fulfilled on the roof of the palace "in the sight of all Israel" (2Sa 16:22). Solomon, who is later born to David and Bathsheba, writes, "For God will bring every deed into judgment, including every hidden thing, whether it is good or evil" (Ecc 12:14). Perhaps Solomon's words come from seeing this truth play out in his own father's household.

Two Names

2SA 12:24–25

A second child is born to David and Bathsheba. The names given to this child indicate that both God and his parents love him. The past is redeemed, and this new child is a reason for rejoicing. David and Bathsheba name their baby Solomon, which is a form of the Hebrew word shalom, *meaning "peace." God calls the child Jedidiah, which means, "loved by the* Lord.*" Both names are fulfilled as the child grows. Solomon/Jedidiah becomes the peaceful builder of the temple and the first king of Israel to trade commercial goods profitably with other nations. God loves Solomon and blesses him by making him the wisest, richest and most honored king of his day and perhaps of all time (1Ki 3:10–14).*

up from the ground, but he refused, and he would
not eat any food with them.[v]
18 On the seventh day the child died. David's servants were afraid to tell him that the child was
dead, for they thought, "While the child was still
living, we spoke to David but he would not listen
to us. How can we tell him the child is dead? He
may do something desperate."
19 David noticed that his servants were whispering among themselves and he realized the child
was dead. "Is the child dead?" he asked.
"Yes," they replied, "he is dead."
20 Then David got up from the ground. After he
had washed,[w] put on lotions and changed his
clothes,[x] he went into the house of the Lord and
worshiped. Then he went to his own house, and
at his request they served him food, and he ate.
21 His servants asked him, "Why are you acting
this way? While the child was alive, you fasted
and wept,[y] but now that the child is dead, you get
up and eat!"
22 He answered, "While the child was still alive,
I fasted and wept. I thought, 'Who knows?[z] The
Lord may be gracious to me and let the child
live.'[a] 23 But now that he is dead, why should I fast?
Can I bring him back again? I will go to him,[b] but
he will not return to me."[c]
24 Then David comforted his wife Bathsheba,[d]
and he went to her and lay with her. She gave
birth to a son, and they named him Solomon.[e]
The Lord loved him; 25 and because the Lord loved
him, he sent word through Nathan the prophet to
name him Jedidiah.[a][f]
26 Meanwhile Joab fought against Rabbah[g] of the
Ammonites and captured the royal citadel. 27 Joab
then sent messengers to David, saying, "I have
fought against Rabbah and taken its water supply.
28 Now muster the rest of the troops and besiege
the city and capture it. Otherwise I will take the
city, and it will be named after me."
29 So David mustered the entire army and went to
Rabbah, and attacked and captured it. 30 He took the
crown[h] from the head of their king[b]—its weight
was a talent[c] of gold, and it was set with precious
stones—and it was placed on David's head. He
took a great quantity of plunder from the city 31 and
brought out the people who were there, consigning them to labor with saws and with iron picks
and axes, and he made them work at brickmaking.[d] He did this to all the Ammonite[i] towns. Then
David and his entire army returned to Jerusalem.

Amnon and Tamar

13 In the course of time, Amnon[j] son of David
fell in love with Tamar,[k] the beautiful sister
of Absalom[l] son of David.

12:17 [v]2Sa 3:35
12:20 [w]Mt 6:17 [x]Job 1:20
12:21 [y]Jdg 20:26
12:22 [z]Jnh 3:9 [a]Isa 38:1-5
12:23 [b]Ge 37:35 [c]1Sa 31:13; 2Sa 13:39; Job 7:10; 10:21
12:24 [d]1Ki 1:11 [e]1Ki 1:10; 1Ch 22:9; 28:5; Mt 1:6
12:25 [f]Ne 13:26
12:26 [g]Dt 3:11; 1Ch 20:1-3
12:30 [h]1Ch 20:2; Est 8:15; Ps 21:3; 132:18
12:31 [i]1Sa 14:47
13:1 [j]2Sa 3:2 [k]2Sa 14:27; 1Ch 3:9 [l]2Sa 3:3

[a] *25 Jedidiah* means *loved by the Lord.* [b] *30* Or *of Milcom* (that is, Molech) [c] *30* That is, about 75 pounds (about 34 kilograms) [d] *31* The meaning of the Hebrew for this clause is uncertain.

2 Amnon became frustrated to the point of illness on account of his sister Tamar, for she was a
virgin, and it seemed impossible for him to do
anything to her.
3 Now Amnon had a friend named Jonadab son
13:3 [m]1Sa 16:9 of Shimeah,[m] David's brother. Jonadab was a very
shrewd man. 4 He asked Amnon, "Why do you,
the king's son, look so haggard morning after
morning? Won't you tell me?"
Amnon said to him, "I'm in love with Tamar,
my brother Absalom's sister."
5 "Go to bed and pretend to be ill," Jonadab said.
"When your father comes to see you, say to him,
'I would like my sister Tamar to come and give
me something to eat. Let her prepare the food in
my sight so I may watch her and then eat it from
her hand.' "
6 So Amnon lay down and pretended to be ill.
When the king came to see him, Amnon said to
him, "I would like my sister Tamar to come and
make some special bread in my sight, so I may eat
from her hand."
7 David sent word to Tamar at the palace: "Go to
the house of your brother Amnon and prepare
some food for him." 8 So Tamar went to the house
of her brother Amnon, who was lying down. She
took some dough, kneaded it, made the bread in
his sight and baked it. 9 Then she took the pan and
13:9 served him the bread, but he refused to eat.
[n]Ge 45:1 "Send everyone out of here,"[n] Amnon said. So
everyone left him. 10 Then Amnon said to Tamar,
"Bring the food here into my bedroom so I may
eat from your hand." And Tamar took the bread
she had prepared and brought it to her brother
Amnon in his bedroom. 11 But when she took it to
13:11 [o]Ge 39:12 him to eat, he grabbed[o] her and said, "Come to
[p]Ge 38:16 bed with me, my sister."[p]
12 "Don't, my brother!" she said to him. "Don't
force me. Such a thing should not be done in Isra-
13:12 [q]Lev 20:17; Jdg 20:6 el![q] Don't do this wicked thing.[r] 13 What about
[r]Ge 34:7; Jdg 19:23 me?[s] Where could I get rid of my disgrace? And
what about you? You would be like one of the
wicked fools in Israel. Please speak to the king;
13:13 [s]Ge 20:12; he will not keep me from being married to you."
Lev 18:9; 14 But he refused to listen to her, and since he was
Dt 22:21,23-24 stronger than she, he raped her.[t]
15 Then Amnon hated her with intense hatred.
13:14 [t]Ge 34:2; In fact, he hated her more than he had loved her.
Dt 22:25; Amnon said to her, "Get up and get out!"
Eze 22:11 16 "No!" she said to him. "Sending me away
would be a greater wrong than what you have
already done to me."
13:18 But he refused to listen to her. 17 He called his
[u]Ge 37:23; Jdg 5:30 personal servant and said, "Get this woman out of
here and bolt the door after her." 18 So his servant
13:19 put her out and bolted the door after her. She was
[v]Jos 7:6; wearing a richly ornamented[a] robe,[u] for this was
1Sa 4:12; 2Sa 1:2; the kind of garment the virgin daughters of the
Est 4:1; Da 9:3 king wore. 19 Tamar put ashes[v] on her head and

[a] 18 The meaning of the Hebrew for this phrase is uncertain.

The Horror of Rape

2SA 13:1-18

Amnon believes he is in love with his half-sister. Actually, however, lust runs through his veins. He devises a plan to get Tamar alone. And he rapes her. The word for rape *here literally means "to seize," "bind," "restrain," and "ravish." The Mosaic Law concerning the rape of a young girl who is not pledged to be married is recorded in* Deuteronomy 22:28-29: *"If a man happens to meet a virgin who is not pledged to be married and rapes her . . . he must marry the girl, for he has violated her." Tamar begs Amnon to marry her rather than to humiliate her by sending her away. By Israelite custom, if he will not marry her, she will be forced to remain unmarried for the rest of her life. He sends Tamar away, victimizing her not just once, but twice* *(see character sketch for Tamar on page 940)*.

Tamar's Advocate?

2SA 13:19–22

Tamar mourns, and yet no one comes forward as her advocate—not even her father, King David, who alone has the power to discipline Amnon. Perhaps because of his own scandalous behavior with Bathsheba, David feels he has no right to rebuke his son. Or, perhaps, as the ancient Greek translation of the Old Testament (the Septuagint) states: David "would not hurt Amnon because he was his eldest son and he loved him." David's inertia not only hurts Tamar but also causes a seed of hatred to grow in Absalom's heart. If David will not avenge Tamar, Absalom will.

Absalom is kind enough to take Tamar into his home, but he adds this insensitive advice: "Don't take this to heart" (2Sa 13:20)! As if she can forget her physical and emotional violation! But if he counsels his sister to forget, Absalom himself does not. Biding his time, two years later he kills Amnon (2Sa 13:29).

tore the ornamented[a] robe she was wearing. She
put her hand on her head and went away, weeping aloud as she went.
20 Her brother Absalom said to her, "Has that
Amnon, your brother, been with you? Be quiet
now, my sister; he is your brother. Don't take this
thing to heart." And Tamar lived in her brother
Absalom's house, a desolate woman.
21 When King David heard all this, he was furious.[w] 22 Absalom never said a word to Amnon,
either good or bad;[x] he hated[y] Amnon because he
had disgraced his sister Tamar.

Absalom Kills Amnon

23 Two years later, when Absalom's sheepshear-
ers[z] were at Baal Hazor near the border of Ephraim, he invited all the king's sons to come there.
24 Absalom went to the king and said, "Your servant has had shearers come. Will the king and his
officials please join me?"
25 "No, my son," the king replied. "All of us
should not go; we would only be a burden to
you." Although Absalom urged him, he still
refused to go, but gave him his blessing.
26 Then Absalom said, "If not, please let my
brother Amnon come with us."
The king asked him, "Why should he go with
you?" 27 But Absalom urged him, so he sent with
him Amnon and the rest of the king's sons.
28 Absalom[a] ordered his men, "Listen! When
Amnon is in high[b] spirits from drinking wine and
I say to you, 'Strike Amnon down,' then kill him.
Don't be afraid. Have not I given you this order?
Be strong and brave.[c]" 29 So Absalom's men did to
Amnon what Absalom had ordered. Then all the
king's sons got up, mounted their mules and fled.
30 While they were on their way, the report came
to David: "Absalom has struck down all the king's
sons; not one of them is left." 31 The king stood up,
tore[d] his clothes and lay down on the ground; and
all his servants stood by with their clothes torn.
32 But Jonadab son of Shimeah, David's brother,
said, "My lord should not think that they killed all
the princes; only Amnon is dead. This has been
Absalom's expressed intention ever since the day
Amnon raped his sister Tamar. 33 My lord the king
should not be concerned about the report that all
the king's sons are dead. Only Amnon is dead."
34 Meanwhile, Absalom had fled.
Now the man standing watch looked up and
saw many people on the road west of him, coming
down the side of the hill. The watchman went and
told the king, "I see men in the direction of Horonaim, on the side of the hill."[b]
35 Jonadab said to the king, "See, the king's sons
are here; it has happened just as your servant said."
36 As he finished speaking, the king's sons came

13:21 [w]Ge 34:7
13:22 [x]Ge 31:24 [y]Lev 19:17-18; 1Jn 2:9-11
13:23 [z]1Sa 25:7
13:28 [a]2Sa 3:3 [b]Jdg 19:6,9, 22; Ru 3:7; 1Sa 25:36 [c]2Sa 12:10
13:31 [d]Nu 14:6; 2Sa 1:11; 12:16

[a] *19* The meaning of the Hebrew for this word is uncertain.
[b] *34* Septuagint; Hebrew does not have this sentence.

in, wailing loudly. The king, too, and all his ser-
13:37 vants wept very bitterly.
[e]ver 34; 37 Absalom fled and went to Talmai[e] son of
2Sa 3:3; Ammihud, the king of Geshur. But King David
14:23,32 mourned for his son every day.
38 After Absalom fled and went to Geshur, he
13:39 stayed there three years. 39 And the spirit of the
[f]2Sa 14:13 king[a] longed to go to Absalom,[f] for he was con-
[g]2Sa 12:19-23 soled[g] concerning Amnon's death.

Absalom Returns to Jerusalem

14:1 [h]2Sa 2:18 **14** Joab[h] son of Zeruiah knew that the king's
14:2 heart longed for Absalom. 2 So Joab sent
[i]2Ch 11:6; Ne 3:5; someone to Tekoa[i] and had a wise woman[j]
Jer 6:1; brought from there. He said to her, "Pretend you
Am 1:1 are in mourning. Dress in mourning clothes, and
[j]2Sa 20:16 don't use any cosmetic lotions.[k] Act like a woman
[k]Ru 3:3; 2Sa 12:20; who has spent many days grieving for the dead.
Isa 1:6 3 Then go to the king and speak these words to
14:3 him." And Joab[l] put the words in her mouth.
[l]ver 19 4 When the woman from Tekoa went[b] to the
king, she fell with her face to the ground to pay
him honor, and she said, "Help me, O king!"
5 The king asked her, "What is troubling you?"
She said, "I am indeed a widow; my husband
is dead. 6 I your servant had two sons. They got
into a fight with each other in the field, and no
one was there to separate them. One struck the
other and killed him. 7 Now the whole clan has
risen up against your servant; they say, 'Hand
14:7 over the one who struck his brother down, so that
[m]Nu 35:19 we may put him to death[m] for the life of his broth-
[n]Mt 21:38 er whom he killed; then we will get rid of the
[o]Dt 19:10-13 heir[n] as well.' They would put out the only burning coal I have left,[o] leaving my husband neither
name nor descendant on the face of the earth."
14:8 8 The king said to the woman, "Go home,[p] and I
[p]1Sa 25:35 will issue an order in your behalf."
14:9 9 But the woman from Tekoa said to him, "My
[q]1Sa 25:24 lord the king, let the blame[q] rest on me and on
[r]Mt 27:25 my father's family,[r] and let the king and his
[s]1Sa 25:28; 1Ki 2:33 throne be without guilt.[s]"
10 The king replied, "If anyone says anything to
you, bring him to me, and he will not bother you
again."
11 She said, "Then let the king invoke the LORD
14:11 [t]Nu 35:12,21 his God to prevent the avenger[t] of blood from
[u]Mt 10:30 adding to the destruction, so that my son will not
[v]1Sa 14:45 be destroyed."
"As surely as the LORD lives," he said, "not one
hair[u] of your son's head will fall to the ground.[v]"
12 Then the woman said, "Let your servant speak
a word to my lord the king."
"Speak," he replied.
13 The woman said, "Why then have you
devised a thing like this against the people of God?

[a] *39* Dead Sea Scrolls and some Septuagint manuscripts; Masoretic Text *But* ⸤*the spirit of*⸥ *David the king* [b] *4* Many Hebrew manuscripts, Septuagint, Vulgate and Syriac; most Hebrew manuscripts *spoke*

Friend, when we become *disappointed, angry, frustrated* and *desperate, Satan can have a* field day in our minds. He can load our minds with so much junk that we can't hear God or won't *pay attention to the Holy Spirit* when he's trying to talk to us. It doesn't matter how much we study the Bible, how long we pray, how *constantly we praise God, Satan* and his demons are waiting for *one tiny port of entry into our* minds to deceive us. Satan's job is to confuse and frustrate us to the point of retaliation, rebellion, dis*obedience and distrust in God. He* is always out to disturb our peace *of mind while we're waiting for* the manifestation of God's prom*ises to us.*

—Thelma Wells

Absalom's Beauty

2SA 14:25-26

In the middle of these passages about rape, murder, revenge and rebellion, we find this description of Absalom's beauty. It is probably placed here to set the stage for Absalom's use of his good looks and charm to take over his father's throne (2Sa 15:1-6). The source of Absalom's beauty, his thick hair, is perhaps what causes his head to become entangled in a tree branch, contributing to his death (2Sa 18:9).

It is human nature to follow beautiful people. The Israelites turn to Absalom because of his charm and beauty, and today we do the same. In choosing whom we will appoint as our leaders and whom we will follow, we would be wise to remember that "the LORD does not look at the things man looks at. Man looks at the outward appearance, but the LORD looks at the heart" (1Sa 16:7).

When the king says this, does he not convict himself,[w] for the king has not brought back his banished son?[x] 14 Like water[y] spilled on the ground,
which cannot be recovered, so we must die.[z] But
God does not take away life; instead, he devises
ways so that a banished person[a] may not remain
estranged from him.
15 "And now I have come to say this to my lord
the king because the people have made me afraid.
Your servant thought, 'I will speak to the king;
perhaps he will do what his servant asks. 16 Perhaps the king will agree to deliver his servant from
the hand of the man who is trying to cut off both
me and my son from the inheritance[b] God gave us.'
17 "And now your servant says, 'May the word
of my lord the king bring me rest, for my lord the
king is like an angel[c] of God in discerning[d] good
and evil. May the LORD your God be with you.' "
18 Then the king said to the woman, "Do not
keep from me the answer to what I am going to
ask you."
"Let my lord the king speak," the woman said.
19 The king asked, "Isn't the hand of Joab[e] with
you in all this?"
The woman answered, "As surely as you live,
my lord the king, no one can turn to the right or
to the left from anything my lord the king says.
Yes, it was your servant Joab who instructed me
to do this and who put all these words into the
mouth of your servant. 20 Your servant Joab did
this to change the present situation. My lord has
wisdom[f] like that of an angel of God—he knows
everything that happens in the land.[g]"
21 The king said to Joab, "Very well, I will do it.
Go, bring back the young man Absalom."
22 Joab fell with his face to the ground to pay
him honor, and he blessed the king.[h] Joab said,
"Today your servant knows that he has found
favor in your eyes, my lord the king, because the
king has granted his servant's request."
23 Then Joab went to Geshur and brought Absalom back to Jerusalem. 24 But the king said, "He
must go to his own house; he must not see my
face." So Absalom went to his own house and did
not see the face of the king.
25 In all Israel there was not a man so highly
praised for his handsome appearance as Absalom.
From the top of his head to the sole of his foot
there was no blemish in him. 26 Whenever he cut
the hair of his head[i]—he used to cut his hair from
time to time when it became too heavy for him—
he would weigh it, and its weight was two hundred shekels[a] by the royal standard.
27 Three sons[j] and a daughter were born to
Absalom. The daughter's name was Tamar,[k] and
she became a beautiful woman.
28 Absalom lived two years in Jerusalem without seeing the king's face. 29 Then Absalom sent
for Joab in order to send him to the king, but Joab

14:13 [w]2Sa 12:7; 1Ki 20:40 [x]2Sa 13:38-39
14:14 [y]Job 14:11; Ps 58:7; Isa 19:5 [z]Job 10:8; 17:13; 30:23; Ps 22:15; Heb 9:27 [a]Nu 35:15, 25-28; Job 34:15
14:16 [b]Ex 34:9; 1Sa 26:19
14:17 [c]ver 20; 1Sa 29:9; 2Sa 19:27 [d]1Ki 3:9; Da 2:21
14:19 [e]ver 3
14:20 [f]1Ki 3:12,28; Isa 28:6 [g]ver 17; 2Sa 18:13; 19:27
14:22 [h]Ge 47:7
14:26 [i]2Sa 18:9; Eze 44:20
14:27 [j]2Sa 18:18 [k]2Sa 13:1

[a] *26* That is, about 5 pounds (about 2.3 kilograms)

refused to come to him. So he sent a second time,
but he refused to come. 30 Then he said to his servants, “Look, Joab’s field is next to mine, and he
14:30 has barley[l] there. Go and set it on fire.” So Absa-
[l]Ex 9:31 lom’s servants set the field on fire.
31 Then Joab did go to Absalom’s house and he
14:31 said to him, “Why have your servants set my field
[m]Jdg 15:5 on fire?[m]”
32 Absalom said to Joab, “Look, I sent word to
you and said, ‘Come here so I can send you to the
14:32 king to ask, “Why have I come from Geshur?[n] It
[n]2Sa 3:3 would be better for me if I were still there!” ’ Now
[o]1Sa 20:8 then, I want to see the king’s face, and if I am
guilty of anything, let him put me to death.”[o]
33 So Joab went to the king and told him this.
Then the king summoned Absalom, and he came
14:33 in and bowed down with his face to the ground
[p]Ge 33:4; Lk 15:20 before the king. And the king kissed[p] Absalom.

Absalom’s Conspiracy

15:1 **15** In the course of time,[q] Absalom provided
[q]2Sa 12:11 [r]1Sa 8:11; 1Ki 1:5 himself with a chariot[r] and horses and with
fifty men to run ahead of him. 2 He would get up
15:2 early and stand by the side of the road leading to
[s]Ge 23:10; 2Sa 19:8 the city gate.[s] Whenever anyone came with a
complaint to be placed before the king for a deci-
sion, Absalom would call out to him, “What town
are you from?” He would answer, “Your servant is
from one of the tribes of Israel.” 3 Then Absalom
would say to him, “Look, your claims are valid
15:3 and proper, but there is no representative of the
[t]Pr 12:2 king to hear you.”[t] 4 And Absalom would add, “If
15:4 only I were appointed judge in the land![u] Then
[u]Jdg 9:29 everyone who has a complaint or case could come
to me and I would see that he gets justice.”
5 Also, whenever anyone approached him to
bow down before him, Absalom would reach out
his hand, take hold of him and kiss him. 6 Absalom behaved in this way toward all the Israelites
15:6 who came to the king asking for justice, and so
[v]Ro 16:18 he stole the hearts[v] of the men of Israel.
7 At the end of four[a] years, Absalom said to the
king, “Let me go to Hebron and fulfill a vow I
made to the LORD. 8 While your servant was living
15:8 at Geshur[w] in Aram, I made this vow:[x] ‘If the LORD
[w]2Sa 3:3; 13:37-38 takes me back to Jerusalem, I will worship the
[x]Ge 28:20 LORD in Hebron.[b]’ ”
9 The king said to him, “Go in peace.” So he
went to Hebron.
10 Then Absalom sent secret messengers
15:10 throughout the tribes of Israel to say, “As soon as
[y]1Ki 1:34, 39; 2Ki 9:13 you hear the sound of the trumpets,[y] then say,
‘Absalom is king in Hebron.’ ” 11 Two hundred men
from Jerusalem had accompanied Absalom. They
had been invited as guests and went quite inno-
cently, knowing nothing about the matter. 12 While
Absalom was offering sacrifices, he also sent for

[a] 7 Some Septuagint manuscripts, Syriac and Josephus; Hebrew *forty* [b] 8 Some Septuagint manuscripts; Hebrew does not have *in Hebron.*

Absalom’s Scheme

2SA 15:1-12

Absalom devises a clever, fourfold plan to take over his father’s throne:

1. He flatters the people by pronouncing favorable verdicts concerning their cases.

2. He makes the people discontented by accusing the king of laxness in trying cases. (We have no extraneous evidence to judge the merit of Absalom’s accusation.)

3. He suggests an easy remedy by becoming king (“judge” [2Sa 15:4]).

4. Finally by crossing the invisible line separating royalty from the commoner and kissing his constituents, he endeared himself to the people.

Absalom carries out his plan like a professional politician. He finds fault with the man in power, and he praises himself and his abilities. Absalom pulls off this trickery because of his high rank, his handsome appearance and his courtesy to even the lowliest persons. In so doing, he steals the hearts of the Israelites. Yet through it all, David, an indulgent father, does not take Absalom’s actions seriously.

"King" Absalom

2SA 15:19

David again flees, fearing for his life—only this time the pursuer is his son Absalom, not King Saul. David hears that Absalom has been proclaimed king at Hebron (2Sa 15:10)—the city where David himself was first proclaimed king (2Sa 2:4). David also is told, "The hearts of the men of Israel are with Absalom" (2Sa 15:13). It appears that Absalom's revolt has been successful, and David accepts Absalom's position by calling him "King Absalom" (2Sa 15:19). But Ittai, David's advisor, does not embrace such a defeat. He says to David, "Wherever my lord the king may be, whether it means life or death, there will your servant be" (2Sa 15:21). Underline Ittai's response in your Bible; then, consider how his words must have encouraged David during this difficult time.

Ahithophel[z] the Gilonite, David's counselor,[a] to
come from Giloh,[b] his hometown. And so the conspiracy gained strength, and Absalom's following
kept on increasing.[c]

David Flees

13 A messenger came and told David, "The
hearts of the men of Israel are with Absalom."
14 Then David said to all his officials who were
with him in Jerusalem, "Come! We must flee,[d] or
none of us will escape from Absalom.[e] We must
leave immediately, or he will move quickly to
overtake us and bring ruin upon us and put the
city to the sword."
15 The king's officials answered him, "Your servants are ready to do whatever our lord the king
chooses."
16 The king set out, with his entire household
following him; but he left ten concubines[f] to take
care of the palace. 17 So the king set out, with all
the people following him, and they halted at a
place some distance away. 18 All his men marched
past him, along with all the Kerethites[g] and
Pelethites; and all the six hundred Gittites who
had accompanied him from Gath marched before
the king.
19 The king said to Ittai[h] the Gittite, "Why should
you come along with us? Go back and stay with
King Absalom. You are a foreigner,[i] an exile from
your homeland. 20 You came only yesterday. And
today shall I make you wander[j] about with us,
when I do not know where I am going? Go back,
and take your countrymen. May kindness and
faithfulness[k] be with you."
21 But Ittai replied to the king, "As surely as the
LORD lives, and as my lord the king lives, wherever my lord the king may be, whether it means life
or death, there will your servant be."[l]
22 David said to Ittai, "Go ahead, march on." So
Ittai the Gittite marched on with all his men and
the families that were with him.
23 The whole countryside wept aloud as all the
people passed by. The king also crossed the Kidron Valley,[m] and all the people moved on toward
the desert.
24 Zadok[n] was there, too, and all the Levites who
were with him were carrying the ark[o] of the covenant of God. They set down the ark of God, and
Abiathar[p] offered sacrifices[a] until all the people
had finished leaving the city.
25 Then the king said to Zadok, "Take the ark of
God back into the city. If I find favor in the LORD's
eyes, he will bring me back and let me see it and
his dwelling place[q] again. 26 But if he says, 'I am
not pleased with you,' then I am ready; let him do
to me whatever seems good to him.[r]"
27 The king also said to Zadok the priest, "Aren't
you a seer?[s] Go back to the city in peace, with
your son Ahimaaz and Jonathan[t] son of Abiathar.

[a] 24 Or *Abiathar went up*

15:12 [z] ver 31,34; 2Sa 16:15, 23; 1Ch 27:33 [a] Job 19:14; Ps 41:9; 55:13; Jer 9:4 [b] Jos 15:51 [c] Ps 3:1

15:14 [d] 2Sa 12:11; 1Ki 2:26; Ps 132:1; Ps 3 Title [e] 2Sa 19:9

15:16 [f] 2Sa 16:21-22; 20:3

15:18 [g] 1Sa 30:14; 2Sa 8:18; 20:7,23; 1Ki 1:38,44; 1Ch 18:17

15:19 [h] 2Sa 18:2 [i] Ge 31:15

15:20 [j] 1Sa 23:13 [k] 2Sa 2:6

15:21 [l] Ru 1:16-17; Pr 17:17

15:23 [m] 2Ch 29:16

15:24 [n] 2Sa 8:17 [o] Nu 4:15 [p] 1Sa 22:20

15:25 [q] Ex 15:13; Ps 43:3; Jer 25:30

15:26 [r] 1Sa 3:18; 2Sa 22:20; 1Ki 10:9

15:27 [s] 1Sa 9:9 [t] 2Sa 17:17

You and Abiathar take your two sons with you. 28I will wait at the fords[u] in the desert until word comes from you to inform me." 29So Zadok and Abiathar took the ark of God back to Jerusalem and stayed there.

30But David continued up the Mount of Olives, weeping[v] as he went; his head[w] was covered and he was barefoot. All the people with him covered their heads too and were weeping as they went up. 31Now David had been told, "Ahithophel[x] is among the conspirators with Absalom." So David prayed, "O LORD, turn Ahithophel's counsel into foolishness."

32When David arrived at the summit, where people used to worship God, Hushai the Arkite[y] was there to meet him, his robe torn and dust[z] on his head. 33David said to him, "If you go with me, you will be a burden[a] to me. 34But if you return to the city and say to Absalom, 'I will be your servant, O king; I was your father's servant in the past, but now I will be your servant,'[b] then you can help me by frustrating Ahithophel's advice. 35Won't the priests Zadok and Abiathar be there with you? Tell them anything you hear in the king's palace.[c] 36Their two sons, Ahimaaz son of Zadok and Jonathan[d] son of Abiathar, are there with them. Send them to me with anything you hear."

37So David's friend Hushai[e] arrived at Jerusalem as Absalom[f] was entering the city.

David and Ziba

16 When David had gone a short distance beyond the summit, there was Ziba,[g] the steward of Mephibosheth, waiting to meet him. He had a string of donkeys saddled and loaded with two hundred loaves of bread, a hundred cakes of raisins, a hundred cakes of figs and a skin of wine.[h]

2The king asked Ziba, "Why have you brought these?"

Ziba answered, "The donkeys are for the king's household to ride on, the bread and fruit are for the men to eat, and the wine is to refresh[i] those who become exhausted in the desert."

3The king then asked, "Where is your master's grandson?"[j]

Ziba said to him, "He is staying in Jerusalem, because he thinks, 'Today the house of Israel will give me back my grandfather's kingdom.' "

4Then the king said to Ziba, "All that belonged to Mephibosheth is now yours."

"I humbly bow," Ziba said. "May I find favor in your eyes, my lord the king."

Shimei Curses David

5As King David approached Bahurim,[k] a man from the same clan as Saul's family came out from there. His name was Shimei[l] son of Gera, and he cursed[m] as he came out. 6He pelted David and all the king's officials with stones, though

15:28 [u]2Sa 17:16
15:30 [v]2Sa 19:4; Ps 126:6 [w]Est 6:12; Isa 20:2-4
15:31 [x]ver 12; 2Sa 16:23; 17:14,23
15:32 [y]Jos 16:2 [z]2Sa 1:2
15:33 [a]2Sa 19:35
15:34 [b]2Sa 16:19
15:35 [c]2Sa 17:15-16
15:36 [d]ver 27; 2Sa 17:17
15:37 [e]2Sa 16:16-17; 1Ch 27:33 [f]2Sa 16:15
16:1 [g]2Sa 9:1-13 [h]1Sa 25:18
16:2 [i]2Sa 17:27-29
16:3 [j]2Sa 9:9-10; 19:26-27
16:5 [k]2Sa 3:16 [l]2Sa 19:16-23; 1Ki 2:8-9,36,44 [m]Ex 22:28

Hopeful Weeping

2SA 15:30-36

David weeps as he travels to the Mount of Olives. His *bare feet and covered head are signs of the depth of his grief. Yet even in his despair, he has hope.* Instead of complete surrender, David sends his faithful servant Hushai to spy on Absalom. How is *it possible for David to remain hopeful during such a discouraging time?* Because David looks upward instead of outward (Ps 3). He focuses on God, not on circumstances or people. David knows *that if it is God's desire, he will be returned to his rightful position, and he prays to that end.* Then he *takes prayerful action, thereby placing his kingship in the hands* of the King of kings.

Absalom Replaces David

2SA 16:22

In the sight of Israel, Absalom pitches a tent on the roof of the palace and has sex with his father's concubines. His action serves two purposes:

1. Taking over the king's harem indicates to the people that Absalom is now king of Israel.

2. The action also indicates an irreversible break between father and son. When he takes that first concubine, the possibility for peace between father and son is obliterated.

Absalom's actions fulfill Nathan's prophecy in 2 Samuel 12:11–12 (see the note on page 491). Absalom violates God's law, which declares, "Do not have sexual relations with your father's wife; that would dishonor your father" (Lev 18:8).

all the troops and the special guard were on
David's right and left. 7As he cursed, Shimei
said, "Get out, get out, you man of blood, you
scoundrel! 8The LORD has repaid you for all the
blood you shed in the household of Saul, in
whose place you have reigned.[n] The LORD has
handed the kingdom over to your son Absalom.
You have come to ruin because you are a man of
blood!"

9Then Abishai[o] son of Zeruiah said to the king,
"Why should this dead dog curse my lord the
king? Let me go over and cut off his head."[p]

10But the king said, "What do you and I have in
common, you sons of Zeruiah?[q] If he is cursing
because the LORD said to him, 'Curse David,' who
can ask, 'Why do you do this?' "[r]

11David then said to Abishai and all his officials,
"My son,[s] who is of my own flesh, is trying to
take my life. How much more, then, this Benjamite! Leave him alone; let him curse, for the
LORD has told him to.[t] 12It may be that the LORD
will see my distress[u] and repay me with good[v] for
the cursing I am receiving today.[w]"

13So David and his men continued along the
road while Shimei was going along the hillside
opposite him, cursing as he went and throwing
stones at him and showering him with dirt. 14The
king and all the people with him arrived at their
destination exhausted.[x] And there he refreshed
himself.

The Advice of Ahithophel and Hushai

15Meanwhile, Absalom[y] and all the men of Israel came to Jerusalem, and Ahithophel[z] was with
him. 16Then Hushai[a] the Arkite, David's friend,
went to Absalom and said to him, "Long live the
king! Long live the king!"

17Absalom asked Hushai, "Is this the love you
show your friend? Why didn't you go with your
friend?"[b]

18Hushai said to Absalom, "No, the one chosen
by the LORD, by these people, and by all the men
of Israel—his I will be, and I will remain with
him. 19Furthermore, whom should I serve? Should
I not serve the son? Just as I served your father, so
I will serve you."[c]

20Absalom said to Ahithophel, "Give us your
advice. What should we do?"

21Ahithophel answered, "Lie with your father's
concubines whom he left to take care of the
palace. Then all Israel will hear that you have
made yourself a stench in your father's nostrils,
and the hands of everyone with you will be
strengthened." 22So they pitched a tent for Absalom on the roof, and he lay with his father's concubines in the sight of all Israel.[d]

23Now in those days the advice[e] Ahithophel
gave was like that of one who inquires of God.
That was how both David[f] and Absalom regarded
all of Ahithophel's advice.

16:8 [n]2Sa 21:9
16:9 [o]2Sa 9:8 [p]Ex 22:28; Lk 9:54
16:10 [q]2Sa 19:22 [r]Ro 9:20
16:11 [s]2Sa 12:11 [t]Ge 45:5
16:12 [u]Ps 4:1; 25:18 [v]Dt 23:5; Ro 8:28 [w]Ps 109:28
16:14 [x]2Sa 17:2
16:15 [y]2Sa 15:37 [z]2Sa 15:12
16:16 [a]2Sa 15:37
16:17 [b]2Sa 19:25
16:19 [c]2Sa 15:34
16:22 [d]2Sa 12:11-12; 15:16
16:23 [e]2Sa 17:14, 23 [f]2Sa 15:12

17 Ahithophel said to Absalom, "I would[a]
choose twelve thousand men and set out
17:2 tonight in pursuit of David. 2I would[b] attack him
[g]2Sa 16:14 while he is weary and weak.[g] I would[b] strike him
[h]1Ki 22:31; with terror, and then all the people with him will
Zec 13:7 flee. I would[b] strike down only the king[h] 3and
bring all the people back to you. The death of the
man you seek will mean the return of all; all the
people will be unharmed." 4This plan seemed
good to Absalom and to all the elders of Israel.
17:5 5But Absalom said, "Summon also Hushai[i] the
[i]2Sa 15:32 Arkite, so we can hear what he has to say." 6When
Hushai came to him, Absalom said, "Ahithophel
has given this advice. Should we do what he says?
If not, give us your opinion."
7Hushai replied to Absalom, "The advice
Ahithophel has given is not good this time. 8You
know your father and his men; they are fighters,
17:8 and as fierce as a wild bear robbed of her cubs.[j]
[j]Hos 13:8 [k]1Sa 16:18 Besides, your father is an experienced fighter;[k] he
17:9 will not spend the night with the troops. 9Even
[l]Jer 41:9 now, he is hidden in a cave or some other place.[l]
If he should attack your troops first,[c] whoever
hears about it will say, 'There has been a slaughter among the troops who follow Absalom.' 10Then
17:10 even the bravest soldier, whose heart is like the
[m]1Ch 12:8 heart of a lion,[m] will melt[n] with fear, for all Israel
[n]Jos 2:9,11; knows that your father is a fighter and that those
Eze 21:15 with him are brave.[o]
[o]2Sa 23:8; 1Ch 11:11 11"So I advise you: Let all Israel, from Dan to
17:11 Beersheba[p]—as numerous as the sand[q] on the
[p]Jdg 20:1 seashore—be gathered to you, with you yourself
[q]Ge 12:2; 22:17; leading them into battle. 12Then we will attack
Jos 11:4 him wherever he may be found, and we will fall
on him as dew settles on the ground. Neither he
nor any of his men will be left alive. 13If he with-
17:13 draws into a city, then all Israel will bring ropes to
[r]Mic 1:6 that city, and we will drag it down to the valley[r]
until not even a piece of it can be found."
14Absalom and all the men of Israel said, "The
17:14 advice[s] of Hushai the Arkite is better than that of
[s]2Sa 16:23 [t]2Sa 15:12 Ahithophel."[t] For the LORD had determined to
[u]2Sa 15:34; Ne 4:15 frustrate[u] the good advice of Ahithophel in order
[v]Ps 9:16 to bring disaster[v] on Absalom.[w]
[w]2Ch 10:8 15Hushai told Zadok and Abiathar, the priests,
"Ahithophel has advised Absalom and the elders
of Israel to do such and such, but I have advised
them to do so and so. 16Now send a message
17:16 immediately and tell David, 'Do not spend the
[x]2Sa 15:28 night at the fords in the desert;[x] cross over with-
[y]2Sa 15:35 out fail, or the king and all the people with him
will be swallowed up.[y]'"
17:17 17Jonathan[z] and Ahimaaz were staying at En
[z]2Sa 15:27, 36 Rogel.[a] A servant girl was to go and inform them,
[a]Jos 15:7; 18:16 and they were to go and tell King David, for they
could not risk being seen entering the city. 18But a
young man saw them and told Absalom. So the
two of them left quickly and went to the house of

[a] 1 Or *Let me* [b] 2 Or *will* [c] 9 Or *When some of the men fall at the first attack*

Good Advice?

2SA 16:15–17:23

Absalom seeks the advice of two men, Ahithophel and Hushai. Ahithophel is helping the prince overtake his father's throne. Hushai, on the other hand, is David's spy. At first Ahithophel's advice sounds good—and most likely David and his men would have been overtaken had it been followed. But Hushai, caring about David and not Absalom, baits the prince by flattering his pride and ambition (2Sa 17:11-12). He compares Absalom's mighty army to the dew on the ground, winning Absalom's favor. Several years later another king, Rehoboam, also seeks counsel (1Ki 12:6-11), but instead of listening to wise elders, he follows his friends' recommendations—to the demise of his kingdom.

From whom can we get good advice? How can we know if the advice is wise or unwise? It is difficult at times to distinguish between the two. However, one lesson can be learned from Absalom and Rehoboam. Flattery isn't a component of good advice. Carefully weigh all that advisors recommend, viewing with skepticism any advice that is laced with empty flattery.

Suicide

Good Advice?

2SA 17:23

Although the word *suicide* is not used in the Bible, *there are several instances when* men take their own lives. Saul *takes his life out of fear of torture by his enemies* (1Sa 31:4). Zimri, *king of Israel, dies in a palace fire he sets himself because he, too, is afraid of his enemies* (1Ki 16:18). In the New Testament, Judas *betrays Jesus, then goes out and hangs himself when he is over-whelmed with grief and shame* (Mt 27:5).

Ahithophel hangs himself *either because he is angry that* Absalom didn't follow his advice *or because he thinks Absalom's* plan will fail. Ahithophel knows *that if Absalom fails, he'll be found guilty of treason and exe-cuted. No matter what the circum-stances, suicide is detestable to the* Hebrews *because of the high value they place on human life. God val-ues our lives also, and he is in control of our days . . . and our* deaths (Job 1:21).

a man in Bahurim.[b] He had a well in his courtyard, and they climbed down into it. 19His wife
took a covering and spread it out over the opening
of the well and scattered grain over it. No one
knew anything about it.[c]
20When Absalom's men came to the woman[d] at
the house, they asked, "Where are Ahimaaz and
Jonathan?"
The woman answered them, "They crossed
over the brook."[a] The men searched but found no
one, so they returned to Jerusalem.
21After the men had gone, the two climbed out
of the well and went to inform King David. They
said to him, "Set out and cross the river at once;
Ahithophel has advised such and such against
you." 22So David and all the people with him set
out and crossed the Jordan. By daybreak, no one
was left who had not crossed the Jordan.
23When Ahithophel saw that his advice[e] had
not been followed, he saddled his donkey and set
out for his house in his hometown. He put his
house in order[f] and then hanged himself. So he
died and was buried in his father's tomb.
24David went to Mahanaim,[g] and Absalom
crossed the Jordan with all the men of Israel.
25Absalom had appointed Amasa[h] over the army
in place of Joab. Amasa was the son of a man
named Jether,[b][i] an Israelite[c] who had married Abigail,[d] the daughter of Nahash and sister of Zeruiah the mother of Joab. 26The Israelites and Absalom camped in the land of Gilead.
27When David came to Mahanaim, Shobi son of
Nahash[j] from Rabbah[k] of the Ammonites, and
Makir[l] son of Ammiel from Lo Debar, and Barzillai[m] the Gileadite[n] from Rogelim 28brought bedding and bowls and articles of pottery. They also
brought wheat and barley, flour and roasted grain,
beans and lentils,[e] 29honey and curds, sheep, and
cheese from cows' milk for David and his people
to eat.[o] For they said, "The people have become
hungry and tired and thirsty in the desert.[p]"

Absalom's Death

18 David mustered the men who were with
him and appointed over them commanders
of thousands and commanders of hundreds.
2David sent the troops out[q]—a third under the
command of Joab, a third under Joab's brother
Abishai[r] son of Zeruiah, and a third under Ittai[s]
the Gittite. The king told the troops, "I myself will
surely march out with you."
3But the men said, "You must not go out; if we
are forced to flee, they won't care about us. Even
if half of us die, they won't care; but you are

17:18 [b]2Sa 3:16; 16:5
17:19 [c]Jos 2:6
17:20 [d]Ex 1:19; Jos 2:3-5; 1Sa 19:12-17
17:23 [e]2Sa 15:12; 16:23 [f]2Ki 20:1; Mt 27:5
17:24 [g]Ge 32:2; 2Sa 2:8
17:25 [h]2Sa 19:13; 20:4,9-12; 1Ki 2:5,32; 1Ch 12:18 [i]1Ch 2:13-17
17:27 [j]1Sa 11:1 [k]Dt 3:11; 2Sa 10:1-2; 12:26,29 [l]2Sa 9:4 [m]2Sa 19:31-39; 1Ki 2:7 [n]2Sa 19:31; Ezr 2:61
17:29 [o]1Ch 12:40 [p]2Sa 16:2; Ro 12:13
18:2 [q]Jdg 7:16; 1Sa 11:11 [r]1Sa 26:6 [s]2Sa 15:19

[a] 20 Or *"They passed by the sheep pen toward the water."*
[b] 25 Hebrew *Ithra,* a variant of *Jether* [c] 25 Hebrew and some Septuagint manuscripts; other Septuagint manuscripts (see also 1 Chron. 2:17) *Ishmaelite* or *Jezreelite*
[d] 25 Hebrew *Abigal,* a variant of *Abigail* [e] 28 Most Septuagint manuscripts and Syriac; Hebrew *lentils, and roasted grain*

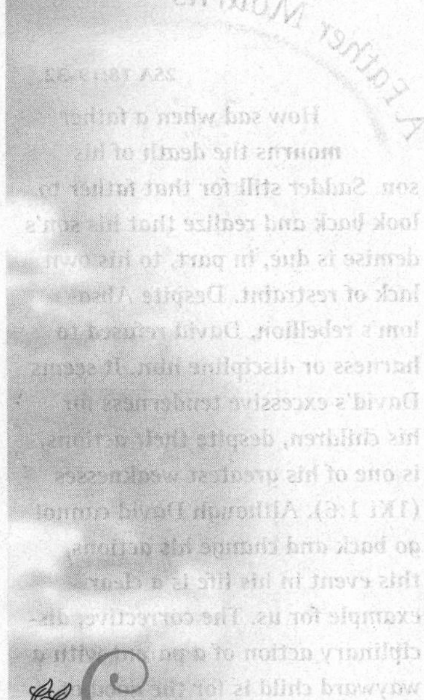

18:3 worth ten[t] thousand of us.[a] It would be better now
[t]1Sa 18:7 for you to give us support from the city."[u]
[u]2Sa 21:17 4The king answered, "I will do whatever seems
best to you."

So the king stood beside the gate while all the
men marched out in units of hundreds and of
thousands. 5The king commanded Joab, Abishai
and Ittai, "Be gentle with the young man Absalom
for my sake." And all the troops heard the king
giving orders concerning Absalom to each of the
commanders.

18:6 6The army marched into the field to fight Israel,
[v]Jos 17:18 and the battle took place in the forest[v] of Ephraim.
7There the army of Israel was defeated by David's
men, and the casualties that day were great—
twenty thousand men. 8The battle spread out over
the whole countryside, and the forest claimed
more lives that day than the sword.

9Now Absalom happened to meet David's men.
He was riding his mule, and as the mule went
18:9 under the thick branches of a large oak, Absa-
[w]2Sa 14:26 lom's head[w] got caught in the tree. He was left
hanging in midair, while the mule he was riding
kept on going.

10When one of the men saw this, he told Joab, "I
just saw Absalom hanging in an oak tree."

11Joab said to the man who had told him this,
"What! You saw him? Why didn't you strike[x] him
18:11 to the ground right there? Then I would have had
[x]2Sa 3:39 to give you ten shekels[b] of silver and a warrior's
[y]1Sa 18:4 belt.[y]"

12But the man replied, "Even if a thousand
shekels[c] were weighed out into my hands, I would
not lift my hand against the king's son. In our
hearing the king commanded you and Abishai
18:13 and Ittai, 'Protect the young man Absalom for my
[z]2Sa 14:19- sake.[d]' 13And if I had put my life in jeopardy[e]—
20 and nothing is hidden from the king[z]—you would
have kept your distance from me."

18:14 14Joab[a] said, "I'm not going to wait like this for
[a]2Sa 2:18; you." So he took three javelins in his hand and
14:30 plunged them into Absalom's heart while Absalom was still alive in the oak tree. 15And ten of
Joab's armor-bearers surrounded Absalom, struck
18:15 him and killed him.[b]
[b]2Sa 12:10 16Then Joab[c] sounded the trumpet, and the
18:16 troops stopped pursuing Israel, for Joab halted
[c]2Sa 2:28; them. 17They took Absalom, threw him into a big
20:22 pit in the forest and piled up[d] a large heap of
18:17 rocks[e] over him. Meanwhile, all the Israelites fled
[d]Jos 7:26 to their homes.
[e]Jos 8:29 18During his lifetime Absalom had taken a pillar
18:18 and erected it in the King's Valley[f] as a monu-
[f]Ge 14:17

[a] *3* Two Hebrew manuscripts, some Septuagint manuscripts and Vulgate; most Hebrew manuscripts *care; for now there are ten thousand like us* [b] *11* That is, about 4 ounces (about 115 grams) [c] *12* That is, about 25 pounds (about 11 kilograms) [d] *12* A few Hebrew manuscripts, Septuagint, Vulgate and Syriac; most Hebrew manuscripts may be translated *Absalom, whoever you may be.* [e] *13* Or *Otherwise, if I had acted treacherously toward him*

God's mill grinds slowly but exceedingly fine. His refining fire is hot, and nothing can come into your life except through the filter of God's love.

—Barbara Johnson

A Father Mourns

2SA 18:19–32

How sad when a father mourns the death of his son. Sadder still for that father to look back and realize that his son's demise is due, in part, to his own lack of restraint. Despite Absalom's rebellion, David refused to harness or discipline him. It seems David's excessive tenderness for his children, despite their actions, is one of his greatest weaknesses (1Ki 1:6). Although David cannot go back and change his actions, this event in his life is a clear example for us. The corrective, disciplinary action of a parent with a wayward child is for the good of the child (Pr 13:24; Heb 12:6–11). David refuses to discipline or punish, but God's judgment is unavoidable. Consequently, Absalom dies, and David mourns.

ment[g] to himself, for he thought, "I have no son[h]
to carry on the memory of my name." He named
the pillar after himself, and it is called Absalom's
Monument to this day.

David Mourns

19 Now Ahimaaz[i] son of Zadok said, "Let me run
and take the news to the king that the LORD has
delivered him from the hand of his enemies.[j]"
20 "You are not the one to take the news today,"
Joab told him. "You may take the news another
time, but you must not do so today, because the
king's son is dead."
21 Then Joab said to a Cushite, "Go, tell the king
what you have seen." The Cushite bowed down
before Joab and ran off.
22 Ahimaaz son of Zadok again said to Joab,
"Come what may, please let me run behind the
Cushite."

But Joab replied, "My son, why do you want to
go? You don't have any news that will bring you a
reward."
23 He said, "Come what may, I want to run."

So Joab said, "Run!" Then Ahimaaz ran by way
of the plain[a] and outran the Cushite.
24 While David was sitting between the inner
and outer gates, the watchman[k] went up to the
roof of the gateway by the wall. As he looked out,
he saw a man running alone. 25 The watchman
called out to the king and reported it.

The king said, "If he is alone, he must have
good news." And the man came closer and closer.
26 Then the watchman saw another man running, and he called down to the gatekeeper,
"Look, another man running alone!"

The king said, "He must be bringing good
news,[l] too."
27 The watchman said, "It seems to me that the
first one runs like[m] Ahimaaz son of Zadok."

"He's a good man," the king said. "He comes
with good news."
28 Then Ahimaaz called out to the king, "All is
well!" He bowed down before the king with his
face to the ground and said, "Praise be to the LORD
your God! He has delivered up the men who lifted their hands against my lord the king."
29 The king asked, "Is the young man Absalom
safe?"

Ahimaaz answered, "I saw great confusion just
as Joab was about to send the king's servant and
me, your servant, but I don't know what it was."
30 The king said, "Stand aside and wait here." So
he stepped aside and stood there.
31 Then the Cushite arrived and said, "My lord
the king, hear the good news! The LORD has delivered you today from all who rose up against you."
32 The king asked the Cushite, "Is the young
man Absalom safe?"

The Cushite replied, "May the enemies of my

18:18 [g]Ge 50:5; Nu 32:42; 1Sa 15:12 [h]2Sa 14:27
18:19 [i]2Sa 15:36 [j]ver 31; Jdg 11:36
18:24 [k]1Sa 14:16; 2Sa 19:8; 2Ki 9:17; Jer 51:12
18:26 [l]1Ki 1:42; Isa 52:7; 61:1
18:27 [m]2Ki 9:20

[a] *23* That is, the plain of the Jordan

lord the king and all who rise up to harm you be
18:32 [n]Jdg 5:31; like that young man."[n]
1Sa 25:26 33The king was shaken. He went up to the room
over the gateway and wept. As he went, he said:
18:33 "O my son Absalom! My son, my son Absalom! If
[o]Ex 32:32 only I had died[o] instead of you—O Absalom, my
[p]Ge 43:14; 2Sa 19:4; son, my son!"[p]
Ro 9:3 **19** Joab was told, "The king is weeping and
mourning for Absalom." 2And for the whole
army the victory that day was turned into mourning, because on that day the troops heard it said,
"The king is grieving for his son." 3The men stole
into the city that day as men steal in who are
ashamed when they flee from battle. 4The king
covered his face and cried aloud, "O my son Absalom! O Absalom, my son, my son!"
5Then Joab went into the house to the king and
said, "Today you have humiliated all your men,
who have just saved your life and the lives of your
sons and daughters and the lives of your wives
and concubines. 6You love those who hate you
and hate those who love you. You have made it
clear today that the commanders and their men
mean nothing to you. I see that you would be
pleased if Absalom were alive today and all of us
were dead. 7Now go out and encourage your men.
I swear by the LORD that if you don't go out, not a
man will be left with you by nightfall. This will be
worse for you than all the calamities that have
19:7 [q]Pr 14:28 come upon you from your youth till now."[q]
8So the king got up and took his seat in the
19:8 gateway. When the men were told, "The king is
[r]2Sa 15:2 sitting in the gateway,[r]" they all came before him.

David Returns to Jerusalem

Meanwhile, the Israelites had fled to their
homes. 9Throughout the tribes of Israel, the people were all arguing with each other, saying, "The
king delivered us from the hand of our enemies;
19:9 he is the one who rescued us from the hand of the
[s]2Sa 8:1-14 Philistines.[s] But now he has fled the country
[t]2Sa 15:14 because of Absalom;[t] 10and Absalom, whom we
anointed to rule over us, has died in battle. So
why do you say nothing about bringing the king
19:11 back?"
[u]2Sa 15:24 11King David sent this message to Zadok[u] and
Abiathar, the priests: "Ask the elders of Judah,
'Why should you be the last to bring the king
back to his palace, since what is being said
throughout Israel has reached the king at his
quarters? 12You are my brothers, my own flesh
and blood. So why should you be the last to bring
19:13 back the king?' 13And say to Amasa,[v] 'Are you not
[v]2Sa 17:25 my own flesh and blood?[w] May God deal with me,
[w]Ge 29:14 be it ever so severely,[x] if from now on you are not
[x]Ru 1:17; 1Ki 19:2; the commander of my army in place of Joab.[y]' "
8:16 14He won over the hearts of all the men of
[y]2Sa 2:13 Judah as though they were one man. They sent
word to the king, "Return, you and all your men."
15Then the king returned and went as far as the
Jordan.

A Father Cries

2SA 18:33

The political victory David has achieved cannot compare to the personal loss he has sustained. David's cry is the heart cry of any parent when a child is lost. Like any parent, David loves even when his child is unlovely and unloving. His agony reaches across the centuries to another time and another passage: "For God so loved the world that he gave his one and only Son, that whoever believes in him shall not perish but have eternal life" (Jn 3:16). What David wishes to fulfill—exchanging his life for another—God fulfills when he sends his Son, Jesus.

Now the men of Judah had come to Gilgal[z] to go out and meet the king and bring him across the Jordan. [16]Shimei[a] son of Gera, the Benjamite from Bahurim, hurried down with the men of Judah to meet King David. [17]With him were a thousand Benjamites, along with Ziba,[b] the steward of Saul's household,[c] and his fifteen sons and twenty servants. They rushed to the Jordan, where the king was. [18]They crossed at the ford to take the king's household over and to do whatever he wished.

When Shimei son of Gera crossed the Jordan, he fell prostrate before the king [19]and said to him, "May my lord not hold me guilty. Do not remember how your servant did wrong on the day my lord the king left Jerusalem.[d] May the king put it out of his mind. [20]For I your servant know that I have sinned, but today I have come here as the first of the whole house of Joseph to come down and meet my lord the king."

[21]Then Abishai[e] son of Zeruiah said, "Shouldn't Shimei be put to death for this? He cursed[f] the LORD's anointed."[g]

[22]David replied, "What do you and I have in common, you sons of Zeruiah?[h] This day you have become my adversaries! Should anyone be put to death in Israel today?[i] Do I not know that today I am king over Israel?" [23]So the king said to Shimei, "You shall not die." And the king promised him on oath.[j]

[24]Mephibosheth,[k] Saul's grandson, also went down to meet the king. He had not taken care of his feet or trimmed his mustache or washed his clothes from the day the king left until the day he returned safely. [25]When he came from Jerusalem to meet the king, the king asked him, "Why didn't you go with me,[l] Mephibosheth?"

[26]He said, "My lord the king, since I your servant am lame,[m] I said, 'I will have my donkey saddled and will ride on it, so I can go with the king.' But Ziba[n] my servant betrayed me. [27]And he has slandered your servant to my lord the king. My lord the king is like an angel[o] of God; so do whatever pleases you. [28]All my grandfather's descendants deserved nothing but death[p] from my lord the king, but you gave your servant a place among those who eat at your table.[q] So what right do I have to make any more appeals to the king?"

[29]The king said to him, "Why say more? I order you and Ziba to divide the fields."

[30]Mephibosheth said to the king, "Let him take everything, now that my lord the king has arrived home safely."

[31]Barzillai[r] the Gileadite also came down from Rogelim to cross the Jordan with the king and to send him on his way from there. [32]Now Barzillai was a very old man, eighty years of age. He had provided for the king during his stay in Mahanaim, for he was a very wealthy[s] man. [33]The king said to Barzillai, "Cross over with me and stay with me in Jerusalem, and I will provide for you."

[34]But Barzillai answered the king, "How many

19:15 [z]Jos 5:9; 1Sa 11:15
19:16 [a]2Sa 16:5-13; 1Ki 2:8
19:17 [b]2Sa 9:2; 16:1-2 [c]Ge 43:16
19:19 [d]1Sa 22:15; 2Sa 16:6-8
19:21 [e]1Sa 26:6 [f]Ex 22:28 [g]1Sa 12:3; 26:9; 2Sa 16:7-8
19:22 [h]2Sa 2:18; 16:10 [i]1Sa 11:13
19:23 [j]1Ki 2:8,42
19:24 [k]2Sa 4:4; 9:6-10
19:25 [l]2Sa 16:17
19:26 [m]Lev 21:18 [n]2Sa 9:2
19:27 [o]1Sa 29:9; 2Sa 14:17,20
19:28 [p]2Sa 16:8; 21:6-9 [q]2Sa 9:7,13
19:31 [r]2Sa 17:27-29; 1Ki 2:7
19:32 [s]1Sa 25:2; 2Sa 17:27

Those of us who have accepted Jesus Christ as our Savior are a part of the greatest family ever created. We belong to the family (household) of God. God is our Father; we are his children. He accepts us, protects us, directs us, comforts us, disciplines us, loves us and cares for us better than any human being could ever hope to do.

—Thelma Wells

more years will I live, that I should go up to Jerusalem with the king? 35I am now eighty[t] years old.
Can I tell the difference between what is good and
what is not? Can your servant taste what he eats
and drinks? Can I still hear the voices of men and
women singers?[u] Why should your servant be an
added[v] burden to my lord the king? 36Your servant
will cross over the Jordan with the king for a short
distance, but why should the king reward me in
this way? 37Let your servant return, that I may die
in my own town near the tomb of my father[w] and
mother. But here is your servant Kimham.[x] Let
him cross over with my lord the king. Do for him
whatever pleases you."

38The king said, "Kimham shall cross over with
me, and I will do for him whatever pleases you.
And anything you desire from me I will do for
you."

39So all the people crossed the Jordan, and then
the king crossed over. The king kissed Barzillai
and gave him his blessing,[y] and Barzillai returned
to his home.

40When the king crossed over to Gilgal, Kimham crossed with him. All the troops of Judah
and half the troops of Israel had taken the king
over.

41Soon all the men of Israel were coming to the
king and saying to him, "Why did our brothers,
the men of Judah, steal the king away and bring
him and his household across the Jordan, together with all his men?"[z]

42All the men of Judah answered the men of
Israel, "We did this because the king is closely
related to us. Why are you angry about it? Have
we eaten any of the king's provisions? Have we
taken anything for ourselves?"

43Then the men of Israel[a] answered the men of
Judah, "We have ten shares in the king; and
besides, we have a greater claim on David than
you have. So why do you treat us with contempt?
Were we not the first to speak of bringing back
our king?"

But the men of Judah responded even more
harshly than the men of Israel.

Sheba Rebels Against David

20 Now a troublemaker named Sheba son of
Bicri, a Benjamite, happened to be there. He
sounded the trumpet and shouted,

> "We have no share[b] in David,[c]
> no part in Jesse's son![d]
> Every man to his tent, O Israel!"

2So all the men of Israel deserted David to follow Sheba son of Bicri. But the men of Judah
stayed by their king all the way from the Jordan to
Jerusalem.

3When David returned to his palace in Jerusalem, he took the ten concubines[e] he had left to
take care of the palace and put them in a house
under guard. He provided for them, but did not

19:35 [t]Ps 90:10 [u]2Ch 35:25; Ezr 2:65; Ecc 2:8; 12:1; Isa 5:11-12 [v]2Sa 15:33
19:37 [w]Ge 49:29; 1Ki 2:7 [x]ver 40; Jer 41:17
19:39 [y]Ge 31:55; Ge 47:7
19:41 [z]Jdg 8:1; 12:1
19:43 [a]2Sa 5:1
20:1 [b]Ge 31:14 [c]Ge 29:14; 1Ki 12:16 [d]1Sa 22:7-8; 2Ch 10:16
20:3 [e]2Sa 15:16; 16:21-22

Barzillai's Request

2SA 19:34–37

When David and his people are running from Absalom, they land in the town of Mahanaim (2Sa 17:27–29). They have few supplies with them, and Barzillai comes to their aid, generously providing bedding and dishes and food. Now that Absalom's rebellion is squelched, David wishes to reward the old man. Instead of accepting David's favor for himself, however, Barzillai asks that the rewards be given to Kimham, possibly one of his sons. David honors Barzillai's request, and later, when the time comes for David to die, he reminds Solomon to do the same (1Ki 2:7). Because of his kindness and love toward his king, Barzillai's heirs are honored for years to come. Like Barzillai, we too can seek favor from our King for those we love. We can pray that God will honor our faithfulness to him by doing for our family members "whatever pleases" him (2Sa 19:37).

Kiss of Death

2SA 20:9

It's a fascinating picture. Joab takes hold of Amasa's beard with his right hand to kiss him. In Biblical times, this was a typical greeting between two friends and is still customary in parts of the East today. Notice that Joab uses his right hand. The right hand is considered more honorable than the left hand, but it also is an indication of peace, since it is the weapon hand and must be empty in order to grab a beard. If Joab means to harm Amasa, he is more likely to use his right hand to wield a weapon than to reach out to hold Amasa's beard. Joab's actions toward David's army commander are a compliment, and Amasa, no doubt, prepares to return the honor. Yet what Amasa takes as a sign of friendship, Joab intends for death. In a similar incident, Judas uses a kiss, a sign friendship, to betray Jesus (Lk 22:47–48).

lie with them. They were kept in confinement till
the day of their death, living as widows.
4Then the king said to Amasa,[f] "Summon the
men of Judah to come to me within three days,
and be here yourself." 5But when Amasa went to
summon Judah, he took longer than the time the
king had set for him.
6David said to Abishai,[g] "Now Sheba son of Bicri will do us more harm than Absalom did. Take
your master's men and pursue him, or he will
find fortified cities and escape from us." 7So Joab's
men and the Kerethites[h] and Pelethites and all the
mighty warriors went out under the command of
Abishai. They marched out from Jerusalem to
pursue Sheba son of Bicri.
8While they were at the great rock in Gibeon,[i]
Amasa came to meet them. Joab[j] was wearing his
military tunic, and strapped over it at his waist
was a belt with a dagger in its sheath. As he
stepped forward, it dropped out of its sheath.
9Joab said to Amasa, "How are you, my brother?" Then Joab took Amasa by the beard with his
right hand to kiss him. 10Amasa was not on his
guard against the dagger[k] in Joab's[l] hand, and
Joab plunged it into his belly, and his intestines
spilled out on the ground. Without being stabbed
again, Amasa died. Then Joab and his brother
Abishai pursued Sheba son of Bicri.
11One of Joab's men stood beside Amasa and
said, "Whoever favors Joab, and whoever is for
David, let him follow Joab!" 12Amasa lay wallowing in his blood in the middle of the road, and the
man saw that all the troops came to a halt[m] there.
When he realized that everyone who came up to
Amasa stopped, he dragged him from the road into
a field and threw a garment over him. 13After Amasa had been removed from the road, all the men
went on with Joab to pursue Sheba son of Bicri.
14Sheba passed through all the tribes of Israel to
Abel Beth Maacah[a] and through the entire region
of the Berites,[n] who gathered together and followed him. 15All the troops with Joab came and
besieged Sheba in Abel Beth Maacah.[o] They built
a siege ramp[p] up to the city, and it stood against
the outer fortifications. While they were battering
the wall to bring it down, 16a wise woman[q] called
from the city, "Listen! Listen! Tell Joab to come
here so I can speak to him." 17He went toward her,
and she asked, "Are you Joab?"

"I am," he answered.

She said, "Listen to what your servant has to say."

"I'm listening," he said.

18She continued, "Long ago they used to say, 'Get
your answer at Abel,' and that settled it. 19We are
the peaceful[r] and faithful in Israel. You are trying to
destroy a city that is a mother in Israel. Why do you
want to swallow up the LORD's inheritance?"[s]
20"Far be it from me!" Joab replied, "Far be it

20:4 [f]2Sa 17:25; 19:13
20:6 [g]2Sa 21:17
20:7 [h]1Sa 30:14; 2Sa 8:18; 15:18; 1Ki 1:38
20:8 [i]Jos 9:3 [j]2Sa 2:18
20:10 [k]Jdg 3:21; 2Sa 2:23; 3:27 [l]1Ki 2:5
20:12 [m]2Sa 2:23
20:14 [n]Nu 21:16
20:15 [o]1Ki 15:20; 2Ki 15:29 [p]2Ki 19:32; Isa 37:33; Jer 6:6; 32:24
20:16 [q]2Sa 14:2
20:19 [r]Dt 2:26 [s]1Sa 26:19; 2Sa 21:3

[a] 14 Or *Abel, even Beth Maacah*; also in verse 15

from me to swallow up or destroy! 21 That is not
the case. A man named Sheba son of Bicri, from
the hill country of Ephraim, has lifted up his hand
against the king, against David. Hand over this
one man, and I'll withdraw from the city."
The woman said to Joab, "His head[t] will be
thrown to you from the wall."
22 Then the woman went to all the people with
her wise advice,[u] and they cut off the head of Sheba son of Bicri and threw it to Joab. So he sounded the trumpet, and his men dispersed from the
city, each returning to his home. And Joab went
back to the king in Jerusalem.
23 Joab[v] was over Israel's entire army; Benaiah
son of Jehoiada was over the Kerethites and
Pelethites; 24 Adoniram[a][w] was in charge of forced
labor; Jehoshaphat[x] son of Ahilud was recorder;
25 Sheva was secretary; Zadok[y] and Abiathar were
priests; 26 and Ira the Jairite was David's priest.

The Gibeonites Avenged

21 During the reign of David, there was a
famine[z] for three successive years; so David
sought[a] the face of the LORD. The LORD said, "It is
on account of Saul and his blood-stained house; it
is because he put the Gibeonites to death."
2 The king summoned the Gibeonites[b] and
spoke to them. (Now the Gibeonites were not a
part of Israel but were survivors of the Amorites;
the Israelites had sworn to ⌊spare⌋ them, but Saul
in his zeal for Israel and Judah had tried to annihilate them.) 3 David asked the Gibeonites, "What
shall I do for you? How shall I make amends so
that you will bless the LORD's inheritance?"[c]
4 The Gibeonites answered him, "We have no
right to demand silver or gold from Saul or his
family, nor do we have the right to put anyone in
Israel to death."[d]
"What do you want me to do for you?" David
asked.
5 They answered the king, "As for the man who
destroyed us and plotted against us so that we
have been decimated and have no place anywhere
in Israel, 6 let seven of his male descendants be
given to us to be killed and exposed[e] before the
LORD at Gibeah of Saul—the LORD's chosen[f] one."
So the king said, "I will give them to you."
7 The king spared Mephibosheth[g] son of Jonathan, the son of Saul, because of the oath[h] before
the LORD between David and Jonathan son of
Saul. 8 But the king took Armoni and Mephibosheth, the two sons of Aiah's daughter Rizpah,[i]
whom she had borne to Saul, together with the
five sons of Saul's daughter Merab,[b] whom she
had borne to Adriel son of Barzillai the Meho-
lathite.[j] 9 He handed them over to the Gibeonites,

20:21 [t]2Sa 4:8
20:22 [u]Ecc 9:13
20:23 [v]2Sa 2:28; 8:16-18; 24:2
20:24 [w]1Ki 4:6; 5:14; 12:18; 2Ch 10:18 [x]2Sa 8:16; 1Ki 4:3
20:25 [y]1Sa 2:35; 2Sa 8:17
21:1 [z]Ge 12:10; Dt 32:24 [a]Ex 32:11
21:2 [b]Jos 9:15
21:3 [c]1Sa 26:19; 2Sa 20:19
21:4 [d]Nu 35:33-34
21:6 [e]Nu 25:4 [f]1Sa 10:24
21:7 [g]2Sa 4:4 [h]1Sa 18:3; 20:8,15; 2Sa 9:7
21:8 [i]2Sa 3:7 [j]1Sa 18:19

[a] *24* Some Septuagint manuscripts (see also 1 Kings 4:6 and 5:14); Hebrew *Adoram* [b] *8* Two Hebrew manuscripts, some Septuagint manuscripts and Syriac (see also 1 Samuel 18:19); most Hebrew and Septuagint manuscripts *Michal*

Wise Woman

2SA 20:22

A woman calls out to Joab, halting his attack on her city. She quickly promises to toss Sheba's head over the wall to Joab. When the act is completed, the attack on the city is halted. One woman's wisdom saves a city (see the character sketch for this woman on page 1009). This is not the only time Joab enlists the help of a woman. During some times of difficulty with Absalom, Joab used another wise woman to bring a message to King David (2Sa 14:2). Both incidents indicate that wise women are respected in Israel. These women probably follow the example of Deborah the judge (Jdg 4). Such accounts are sprinkled throughout Scripture and impress on us that God, the commander of all things, also respects women of wisdom and wishes to use them on behalf of his people.

A Mother's Love

2SA 21:10

Rizpah's sons are executed in the spring. The rains usually come in October. That means Rizpah's devoted watch may have lasted up to six months! According to Deuteronomy 21:22–23, executed individuals are to be buried before evening. But the law is set aside in this case. In the East, vultures flock instantly to a carcass (Mt 24:28). Keeping them away is no easy task. Yet Rizpah keeps watch by day, exposing herself to the fierce summer heat. And she keeps watch by night as wild animals roam. No doubt her heart is even more pained than her flesh as she watches her beloved sons' bodies waste away. In this brief passage, we find strong mother's love and maternal tenderness in greater measure than most books hold in all their pages (see the character sketch for Rizpah on page 874).

who killed and exposed them on a hill before the
LORD. All seven of them fell together; they were
put to death[k] during the first days of the harvest,
just as the barley harvest was beginning.[l]
10 Rizpah daughter of Aiah took sackcloth and
spread it out for herself on a rock. From the beginning of the harvest till the rain poured down from
the heavens on the bodies, she did not let the
birds of the air touch them by day or the wild animals by night.[m] 11 When David was told what
Aiah's daughter Rizpah, Saul's concubine, had
done, 12 he went and took the bones of Saul[n] and
his son Jonathan from the citizens of Jabesh Gilead. (They had taken them secretly from the public square at Beth Shan,[o] where the Philistines had
hung[p] them after they struck Saul down on Gilboa.) 13 David brought the bones of Saul and his
son Jonathan from there, and the bones of those
who had been killed and exposed were gathered up.
14 They buried the bones of Saul and his son
Jonathan in the tomb of Saul's father Kish, at
Zela[q] in Benjamin, and did everything the king
commanded. After that,[r] God answered prayer[s] in
behalf of the land.

Wars Against the Philistines

15 Once again there was a battle between the
Philistines[t] and Israel. David went down with his
men to fight against the Philistines, and he
became exhausted. 16 And Ishbi-Benob, one of the
descendants of Rapha, whose bronze spearhead
weighed three hundred shekels[a] and who was
armed with a new ⌊sword⌋, said he would kill
David. 17 But Abishai[u] son of Zeruiah came to
David's rescue; he struck the Philistine down and
killed him. Then David's men swore to him, saying, "Never again will you go out with us to battle, so that the lamp[v] of Israel will not be extinguished.[w]"
18 In the course of time, there was another battle
with the Philistines, at Gob. At that time Sibbecai[x]
the Hushathite killed Saph, one of the descendants of Rapha.
19 In another battle with the Philistines at Gob,
Elhanan son of Jaare-Oregim[b] the Bethlehemite
killed Goliath[c] the Gittite, who had a spear with a
shaft like a weaver's rod.[y]
20 In still another battle, which took place at
Gath, there was a huge man with six fingers on
each hand and six toes on each foot—twenty-four
in all. He also was descended from Rapha. 21 When
he taunted Israel, Jonathan son of Shimeah,[z]
David's brother, killed him.
22 These four were descendants of Rapha in
Gath, and they fell at the hands of David and his
men.

21:9 [k]2Sa 16:8 [l]Ru 1:22
21:10 [m]ver 8; Dt 21:23; 1Sa 17:44
21:12 [n]1Sa 31:11-13 [o]Jos 17:11 [p]1Sa 31:10
21:14 [q]Jos 18:28 [r]Jos 7:26 [s]2Sa 24:25
21:15 [t]2Sa 5:25
21:17 [u]2Sa 20:6 [v]1Ki 11:36 [w]2Sa 18:3
21:18 [x]1Ch 11:29; 20:4; 27:11
21:19 [y]1Sa 17:7
21:21 [z]1Sa 16:9

[a] *16* That is, about 7 1/2 pounds (about 3.5 kilograms)
[b] *19* Or *son of Jair the weaver* [c] *19* Hebrew and Septuagint; 1 Chron. 20:5 *son of Jair killed Lahmi the brother of Goliath*

David's Song of Praise

22 David sang[a] to the LORD the words of this
song when the LORD delivered him from the
hand of all his enemies and from the hand of Saul.
2 He said:

"The LORD is my rock,[b] my fortress[c] and
my deliverer;[d]
3 my God is my rock, in whom I take
refuge,[e]
my shield[f] and the horn[ag] of my
salvation.
He is my stronghold,[h] my refuge and my
savior—
from violent men you save me.
4 I call to the LORD, who is worthy[i] of
praise,
and I am saved from my enemies.
5 "The waves[j] of death swirled about me;
the torrents of destruction
overwhelmed me.
6 The cords of the grave[bk] coiled around
me;
the snares of death confronted me.
7 In my distress[l] I called[m] to the LORD;
I called out to my God.
From his temple he heard my voice;
my cry came to his ears.
8 "The earth[n] trembled and quaked,[o]
the foundations[p] of the heavens[c]
shook;
they trembled because he was angry.
9 Smoke rose from his nostrils;
consuming fire[q] came from his
mouth,
burning coals blazed out of it.
10 He parted the heavens and came down;
dark clouds[r] were under his feet.
11 He mounted the cherubim and flew;
he soared[d] on the wings of the wind.[s]
12 He made darkness his canopy around
him—
the dark[e] rain clouds of the sky.
13 Out of the brightness of his presence
bolts of lightning[t] blazed forth.
14 The LORD thundered[u] from heaven;
the voice of the Most High resounded.
15 He shot arrows[v] and scattered ⌊the
enemies⌋,
bolts of lightning and routed them.
16 The valleys of the sea were exposed
and the foundations of the earth laid
bare
at the rebuke[w] of the LORD,
at the blast of breath from his nostrils.

22:1 [a]Ex 15:1; Jdg 5:1; Ps 18:2-50
22:2 [b]Dt 32:4; Ps 71:3 [c]Ps 31:3; 91:2 [d]Ps 144:2
22:3 [e]Dt 32:37; Jer 16:19 [f]Ge 15:1 [g]Lk 1:69 [h]Ps 9:9
22:4 [i]Ps 48:1; 96:4
22:5 [j]Ps 69:14-15; 93:4; Jnh 2:3
22:6 [k]Ps 116:3
22:7 [l]Ps 120:1 [m]Ps 34:6,15; 116:4
22:8 [n]Jdg 5:4; Ps 97:4 [o]Ps 77:18 [p]Job 26:11
22:9 [q]Ps 97:3; Heb 12:29
22:10 [r]1Ki 8:12; Na 1:3
22:11 [s]Ps 104:3
22:13 [t]ver 9
22:14 [u]1Sa 2:10
22:15 [v]Dt 32:23
22:16 [w]Na 1:4

[a] *3 Horn* here symbolizes strength. [b] *6* Hebrew *Sheol*
[c] *8* Hebrew; Vulgate and Syriac (see also Psalm 18:7) *mountains* [d] *11* Many Hebrew manuscripts (see also Psalm 18:10); most Hebrew manuscripts *appeared* [e] *12* Septuagint and Vulgate (see also Psalm 18:11); Hebrew *massed*

None other Lamb,
none other Name,
None other hope in heav'n or
earth or sea,
None other hiding place from guilt
and shame,
None beside Thee!

My faith burns low, my hope
burns low;
Only my heart's desire cries out
in me
By the deep thunder of its want
and woe,
Cries out to Thee.

Lord, Thou art Life, though I be
dead;
Love's fire Thou art, however cold
I be:
Nor heav'n have I, nor place to lay
my head,
Nor home, but Thee.

—Christina Georgina Rossetti (1830-1894)

David the Poet

2SA 22

David's days are ending. In this book of history, we have seen him as a shepherd, musician, soldier and great leader. However, the record of his life would not be complete without meeting David, the poet. The words of this song are also found in Psalm 18. David writes this poem after he has escaped Saul and become king, after he has triumphed over foreign nations but before his sin with Bathsheba. The psalm gives thanks for the Lord's deliverance and mighty help. It forms an overview of a life spent trusting in God. Read 2 Samuel 22:2–4 aloud, underlining any parts that also apply to your life. Then take time to thank God for the way he has helped and delivered you.

17 "He reached down from on high[x] and took hold of me;
he drew[y] me out of deep waters.
18 He rescued me from my powerful enemy,
from my foes, who were too strong for me.
19 They confronted me in the day of my disaster,
but the LORD was my support.[z]
20 He brought me out into a spacious[a] place;
he rescued[b] me because he delighted[c] in me.[d]

21 "The LORD has dealt with me according to my righteousness;[e]
according to the cleanness of my hands[f] he has rewarded me.
22 For I have kept[g] the ways of the LORD;
I have not done evil by turning from my God.
23 All his laws are before me;[h]
I have not turned[i] away from his decrees.
24 I have been blameless[j] before him
and have kept myself from sin.
25 The LORD has rewarded me according to my righteousness,[k]
according to my cleanness[a] in his sight.

26 "To the faithful you show yourself faithful,
to the blameless you show yourself blameless,
27 to the pure[l] you show yourself pure,
but to the crooked you show yourself shrewd.[m]
28 You save the humble,[n]
but your eyes are on the haughty to bring them low.[o]
29 You are my lamp,[p] O LORD;
the LORD turns my darkness into light.
30 With your help I can advance against a troop[b];
with my God I can scale a wall.

31 "As for God, his way is perfect;[q]
the word of the LORD is flawless.[r]
He is a shield
for all who take refuge in him.
32 For who is God besides the LORD?
And who is the Rock[s] except our God?
33 It is God who arms me with strength[c]
and makes my way perfect.
34 He makes my feet like the feet of a deer;[t]

22:17 [x]Ps 144:7 [y]Ex 2:10
22:19 [z]Ps 23:4
22:20 [a]Ps 31:8 [b]Ps 118:5 [c]Ps 22:8 [d]2Sa 15:26
22:21 [e]1Sa 26:23 [f]Ps 24:4
22:22 [g]Ge 18:19; Ps 128:1; Pr 8:32
22:23 [h]Dt 6:4-9; Ps 119:30-32 [i]Ps 119:102
22:24 [j]Ge 6:9; Eph 1:4
22:25 [k]ver 21
22:27 [l]Mt 5:8 [m]Lev 26:23-24
22:28 [n]Ex 3:8; Ps 72:12-13 [o]Isa 2:12,17; 5:15
22:29 [p]Ps 27:1
22:31 [q]Dt 32:4; Mt 5:48 [r]Ps 12:6; 119:140; Pr 30:5-6
22:32 [s]1Sa 2:2
22:34 [t]Hab 3:19

[a] *25* Hebrew; Septuagint and Vulgate (see also Psalm 18:24) *to the cleanness of my hands* [b] *30* Or *can run through a barricade* [c] *33* Dead Sea Scrolls, some Septuagint manuscripts, Vulgate and Syriac (see also Psalm 18:32); Masoretic Text *who is my strong refuge*

he enables me to stand on the
heights.[u]
35 He trains my hands[v] for battle;
my arms can bend a bow of bronze.
36 You give me your shield[w] of victory;
you stoop down to make me great.
37 You broaden the path[x] beneath me,
so that my ankles do not turn.

38 "I pursued my enemies and crushed
them;
I did not turn back till they were
destroyed.
39 I crushed[y] them completely, and they
could not rise;
they fell beneath my feet.
40 You armed me with strength for battle;
you made my adversaries bow at my
feet.[z]
41 You made my enemies turn their backs[a]
in flight,
and I destroyed my foes.
42 They cried for help,[b] but there was no
one to save them—[c]
to the LORD, but he did not answer.
43 I beat them as fine as the dust of the
earth;
I pounded and trampled[d] them like
mud[e] in the streets.

44 "You have delivered[f] me from the
attacks of my people;
you have preserved[g] me as the head of
nations.
People[h] I did not know are subject to
me,
45 and foreigners come cringing[i] to me;
as soon as they hear me, they obey
me.
46 They all lose heart;
they come trembling[a][j] from their
strongholds.

47 "The LORD lives! Praise be to my Rock!
Exalted be God, the Rock, my Savior![k]
48 He is the God who avenges me,[l]
who puts the nations under me,
49 who sets me free from my enemies.[m]
You exalted me above my foes;
from violent men you rescued me.
50 Therefore I will praise you, O LORD,
among the nations;
I will sing praises to your name.[n]
51 He gives his king great victories;[o]
he shows unfailing kindness to his
anointed,[p]
to David[q] and his descendants
forever."[r]

22:34 [u]Dt 32:13
22:35 [v]Ps 144:1
22:36 [w]Eph 6:16
22:37 [x]Pr 4:11
22:39 [y]Mal 4:3
22:40 [z]Ps 44:5
22:41 [a]Ex 23:27
22:42 [b]Isa 1:15 [c]Ps 50:22
22:43 [d]Mic 7:10 [e]Isa 10:6; Mic 7:10
22:44 [f]2Sa 3:1 [g]Dt 28:13 [h]2Sa 8:1-14; Isa 55:3-5
22:45 [i]Ps 66:3; 81:15
22:46 [j]Mic 7:17
22:47 [k]Ps 89:26
22:48 [l]Ps 94:1; 144:2; 1Sa 25:39
22:49 [m]Ps 140:1,4
22:50 [n]Ro 15:9*
22:51 [o]Ps 144:9-10 [p]Ps 89:20 [q]2Sa 7:13 [r]Ps 89:24,29

[a] *46* Some Septuagint manuscripts and Vulgate (see also Psalm 18:45); Masoretic Text *they arm themselves.*

Overcoming Enemies

2SA 22:35-43

David is, first and foremost, a warrior. Even his poetry portrays violent images. David's enemies are strong, mighty, flesh-and-blood warriors—quite different from the enemies we face today. Nevertheless our enemies are just as real and just as dangerous. "For our struggle is not against flesh and blood, but against the rulers, against the authorities, against the powers of this dark world and against the spiritual forces of evil in the heavenly realms" (Eph 6:12). Consider these spiritual enemies. How do they mount forces against us? How are they similar to the enemies David faced? How are they different? Read 2 Samuel 22:35-37 as a prayer of strength for spiritual battles. Underline the ways God prepares us for battle. Now, mark this passage and come back to it when spiritual enemies mount up and threaten to overwhelm you.

The Last Words of David

23 These are the last words of David:

"The oracle of David son of Jesse,
the oracle of the man exalted[s] by the Most High,
the man anointed[t] by the God of Jacob,
Israel's singer of songs[a]:

2 "The Spirit[u] of the LORD spoke through me;
his word was on my tongue.
3 The God of Israel spoke,
the Rock[v] of Israel said to me:
'When one rules over men in righteousness,[w]
when he rules in the fear of God,[x]
4 he is like the light of morning at sunrise[y]
on a cloudless morning,
like the brightness after rain
that brings the grass from the earth.'

5 "Is not my house right with God?
Has he not made with me an everlasting covenant,[z]
arranged and secured in every part?
Will he not bring to fruition my salvation
and grant me my every desire?
6 But evil men are all to be cast aside like thorns,[a]
which are not gathered with the hand.
7 Whoever touches thorns
uses a tool of iron or the shaft of a spear;
they are burned up where they lie."

David's Mighty Men

8 These are the names of David's mighty men:
Josheb-Basshebeth,[b] a Tahkemonite,[c] was chief
of the Three; he raised his spear against eight
hundred men, whom he killed[d] in one encounter.
9 Next to him was Eleazar son of Dodai[b] the
Ahohite.[c] As one of the three mighty men, he was
with David when they taunted the Philistines
gathered ⌞at Pas Dammim⌟[e] for battle. Then the
men of Israel retreated, 10 but he stood his ground
and struck down the Philistines till his hand grew
tired and froze to the sword. The LORD brought
about a great victory that day. The troops returned
to Eleazar, but only to strip the dead.
11 Next to him was Shammah son of Agee the

23:1 [s]2Sa 7:8-9; Ps 78:70-71; 89:27 [t]1Sa 16:12-13; Ps 89:20
23:2 [u]Mt 22:43; 2Pe 1:21
23:3 [v]Dt 32:4; 2Sa 22:2,32 [w]Ps 72:3 [x]2Ch 19:7,9; Isa 11:1-5
23:4 [y]Jdg 5:31; Ps 89:36
23:5 [z]Ps 89:29; Isa 55:3
23:6 [a]Mt 13:40-41
23:9 [b]1Ch 27:4 [c]1Ch 8:4

Then this soul, as it were, like one intoxicated, could not contain herself, but standing before the face of God, exclaimed, "How great is the Eternal Mercy with which You cover the sins of Your creatures!"

—*Catherine of Siena (1347-1380)*

[a] *1* Or *Israel's beloved singer* [b] *8* Hebrew; some Septuagint manuscripts suggest *Ish-Bosheth,* that is, *Esh-Baal* (see also 1 Chron. 11:11 *Jashobeam*). [c] *8* Probably a variant of *Hacmonite* (see 1 Chron. 11:11) [d] *8* Some Septuagint manuscripts (see also 1 Chron. 11:11); Hebrew and other Septuagint manuscripts *Three; it was Adino the Eznite who killed eight hundred men* [e] *9* See 1 Chron. 11:13; Hebrew *gathered there.*

Hararite. When the Philistines banded together at a place where there was a field full of lentils, Israel's troops fled from them. 12 But Shammah took his stand in the middle of the field. He defended it and struck the Philistines down, and the LORD brought about a great victory.

13 During harvest time, three of the thirty chief men came down to David at the cave of Adullam,[d] while a band of Philistines was encamped in the Valley of Rephaim.[e] 14 At that time David was in the stronghold,[f] and the Philistine garrison was at Bethlehem.[g] 15 David longed for water and said, "Oh, that someone would get me a drink of water from the well near the gate of Bethlehem!" 16 So the three mighty men broke through the Philistine lines, drew water from the well near the gate of Bethlehem and carried it back to David. But he refused to drink it; instead, he poured[h] it out before the LORD. 17 "Far be it from me, O LORD, to do this!" he said. "Is it not the blood[i] of men who went at the risk of their lives?" And David would not drink it.

Such were the exploits of the three mighty men.

18 Abishai[j] the brother of Joab son of Zeruiah was chief of the Three.[a] He raised his spear against three hundred men, whom he killed, and so he became as famous as the Three. 19 Was he not held in greater honor than the Three? He became their commander, even though he was not included among them.

20 Benaiah[k] son of Jehoiada was a valiant fighter from Kabzeel,[l] who performed great exploits. He struck down two of Moab's best men. He also went down into a pit on a snowy day and killed a lion. 21 And he struck down a huge Egyptian. Although the Egyptian had a spear in his hand, Benaiah went against him with a club. He snatched the spear from the Egyptian's hand and killed him with his own spear. 22 Such were the exploits of Benaiah son of Jehoiada; he too was as famous as the three mighty men. 23 He was held in greater honor than any of the Thirty, but he was not included among the Three. And David put him in charge of his bodyguard.

24 Among the Thirty were:

Asahel[m] the brother of Joab,
Elhanan son of Dodo from Bethlehem,
25 Shammah the Harodite,[n]
Elika the Harodite,
26 Helez[o] the Paltite,
Ira son of Ikkesh from Tekoa,
27 Abiezer from Anathoth,[p]
Mebunnai[b] the Hushathite,
28 Zalmon the Ahohite,
Maharai[q] the Netophathite,[r]
29 Heled[c] son of Baanah the Netophathite,

23:13 [d]1Sa 22:1 [e]2Sa 5:18
23:14 [f]1Sa 22:4-5 [g]Ru 1:19
23:16 [h]Ge 35:14
23:17 [i]Lev 17:10-12
23:18 [j]2Sa 10:10, 14; 1Ch 11:20
23:20 [k]2Sa 8:18; 20:23 [l]Jos 15:21
23:24 [m]2Sa 2:18
23:25 [n]Jdg 7:1; 1Ch 11:27
23:26 [o]1Ch 27:10
23:27 [p]Jos 21:18
23:28 [q]1Ch 27:13 [r]2Ki 25:23; Ne 7:26

[a] *18* Most Hebrew manuscripts (see also 1 Chron. 11:20); two Hebrew manuscripts and Syriac *Thirty* [b] *27* Hebrew; some Septuagint manuscripts (see also 1 Chron. 11:29) *Sibbecai* [c] *29* Some Hebrew manuscripts and Vulgate (see also 1 Chron. 11:30); most Hebrew manuscripts *Heleb*

Life-Risking Loyalty

2SA 23:13-17

Three men risk their lives to fetch water for David. Instead of drinking it, however, David pours it out. Scholars offer four explanations for his action:

1. This story also is recounted in 1 Chronicles 11:18-19 in which David says, "Should I drink the blood of these men who went at the risk of their lives?" David proclaims by his action that a little refreshment is not worth his men's blood—lest they attempt such a stunt again.

2. David pours out the water as a drink offering to the Lord.

3. David sees the devotion his men have toward him, and he realizes that such life-risking loyalty belongs only to the Lord, so he pours out their gift before the Lord.

4. Despite how it appears to us, David's actions show his tender regard for his soldiers. By pouring out the water, he communicates regret for a foolish request that causes three men to risk their lives.

Inciting a Census

2SA 24:1

This is a puzzling passage. Second Samuel 24:1 says that God "incited," which literally means "seduced," David to count his fighting men. The parallel account in 1 Chronicles 21:1 says, "Satan . . . incited David to take a census." Since God permits all temptation, and evil tempts us only as God's allows (Job 1:12), these two passages may not be as different as they seem. God himself isn't the author of temptation, but he is in control of even this part of our lives, allowing Satan to tempt us only under his watchful eye.

The second point of confusion: What is wrong with taking a census and counting the fighting men? When David counts his soldiers, he will perhaps turn his focus from God and begin to boast about the strength of his men. God wants David to count on and boast in God's strength alone (see note on 1Ch 27:23–24, page 673).

Ithai son of Ribai from Gibeah[s] in Benjamin,
30 Benaiah the Pirathonite,[t]
Hiddai[a] from the ravines of Gaash,[u]
31 Abi-Albon the Arbathite,
Azmaveth the Barhumite,[v]
32 Eliahba the Shaalbonite,
the sons of Jashen,
Jonathan 33 son of[b] Shammah the Hararite,
Ahiam son of Sharar[c] the Hararite,
34 Eliphelet son of Ahasbai the Maacathite,
Eliam[w] son of Ahithophel[x] the Gilonite,
35 Hezro the Carmelite,[y]
Paarai the Arbite,
36 Igal son of Nathan from Zobah,[z]
the son of Hagri,[d]
37 Zelek the Ammonite,
Naharai the Beerothite, the armor-bearer of Joab son of Zeruiah,
38 Ira the Ithrite,[a]
Gareb the Ithrite
39 and Uriah[b] the Hittite.

There were thirty-seven in all.

David Counts the Fighting Men

24 Again[c] the anger of the LORD burned against
Israel, and he incited David against them,
saying, "Go and take a census of[d] Israel and
Judah."
2 So the king said to Joab[e] and the army commanders[e] with him, "Go throughout the tribes of
Israel from Dan to Beersheba[f] and enroll the fighting men, so that I may know how many there are."
3 But Joab replied to the king, "May the LORD your
God multiply the troops a hundred times over,[g] and
may the eyes of my lord the king see it. But why
does my lord the king want to do such a thing?"
4 The king's word, however, overruled Joab and
the army commanders; so they left the presence
of the king to enroll the fighting men of Israel.
5 After crossing the Jordan, they camped near
Aroer,[h] south of the town in the gorge, and then
went through Gad and on to Jazer.[i] 6 They went to
Gilead and the region of Tahtim Hodshi, and on
to Dan Jaan and around toward Sidon.[j] 7 Then
they went toward the fortress of Tyre[k] and all the
towns of the Hivites and Canaanites. Finally, they
went on to Beersheba[l] in the Negev[m] of Judah.
8 After they had gone through the entire land,
they came back to Jerusalem at the end of nine
months and twenty days.
9 Joab reported the number of the fighting men
to the king: In Israel there were eight hundred

23:29 [s]Jos 15:57
23:30 [t]Jdg 12:13 [u]Jos 24:30
23:31 [v]2Sa 3:16
23:34 [w]2Sa 11:3 [x]2Sa 15:12
23:35 [y]Jos 12:22
23:36 [z]1Sa 14:47
23:38 [a]2Sa 20:26; 1Ch 2:53
23:39 [b]2Sa 11:3
24:1 [c]Jos 9:15 [d]1Ch 27:23
24:2 [e]2Sa 20:23 [f]Jdg 20:1; 2Sa 3:10
24:3 [g]Dt 1:11
24:5 [h]Dt 2:36; Jos 13:9 [i]Nu 21:32
24:6 [j]Ge 10:19; Jos 19:28; Jdg 1:31
24:7 [k]Jos 19:29 [l]Ge 21:22-33 [m]Dt 1:7; Jos 11:3

[a] *30* Hebrew; some Septuagint manuscripts (see also 1 Chron. 11:32) *Hurai* [b] *33* Some Septuagint manuscripts (see also 1 Chron. 11:34); Hebrew does not have *son of.* [c] *33* Hebrew; some Septuagint manuscripts (see also 1 Chron. 11:35) *Sacar* [d] *36* Some Septuagint manuscripts (see also 1 Chron. 11:38); Hebrew *Haggadi* [e] *2* Septuagint (see also verse 4 and 1 Chron. 21:2); Hebrew *Joab the army commander*

thousand able-bodied men who could handle a
24:9 [n]Nu 1:44-46; sword, and in Judah five hundred thousand.[n]
1Ch 21:5 [10]David was conscience-stricken[o] after he had
counted the fighting men, and he said to the LORD,
24:10 [o]1Sa 24:5 "I have sinned[p] greatly in what I have done. Now,
[p]2Sa 12:13 O LORD, I beg you, take away the guilt of your ser-
[q]Nu 12:11; 1Sa 13:13 vant. I have done a very foolish thing.[q]"
[11]Before David got up the next morning, the word
24:11 [r]1Sa 22:5 of the LORD had come to Gad[r] the prophet, David's
[s]1Sa 9:9; seer:[s] [12]"Go and tell David, 'This is what the LORD
1Ch 29:29 says: I am giving you three options. Choose one of
them for me to carry out against you.' "
[13]So Gad went to David and said to him, "Shall
24:13 [t]Dt 28:38-42, there come upon you three[a] years of famine[t] in
48; your land? Or three months of fleeing from your
Eze 14:21 enemies while they pursue you? Or three days of
[u]Lev 26:25 plague[u] in your land? Now then, think it over and
decide how I should answer the one who sent me."
[14]David said to Gad, "I am in deep distress. Let us
24:14 [v]Ne 9:28; fall into the hands of the LORD, for his mercy[v] is
Ps 51:1; great; but do not let me fall into the hands of men."
103:8,13; [15]So the LORD sent a plague on Israel from that
130:4 morning until the end of the time designated, and
seventy thousand of the people from Dan to Beer-
24:15 [w]1Ch 27:24 sheba died.[w] [16]When the angel stretched out his
hand to destroy Jerusalem, the LORD was grieved[x]
24:16 [x]Ge 6:6; because of the calamity and said to the angel who
1Sa 15:11 was afflicting the people, "Enough! Withdraw
[y]Ex 12:23; your hand." The angel of the LORD[y] was then at
Ac 12:23 the threshing floor of Araunah the Jebusite.
[17]When David saw the angel who was striking
down the people, he said to the LORD, "I am the
24:17 one who has sinned and done wrong. These are
[z]Ps 74:1 but sheep.[z] What have they done? Let your hand
[a]Jnh 1:12 fall upon me and my family."[a]

David Builds an Altar

[18]On that day Gad went to David and said to
him, "Go up and build an altar to the LORD on the
threshing floor of Araunah the Jebusite." [19]So
David went up, as the LORD had commanded
through Gad. [20]When Araunah looked and saw
the king and his men coming toward him, he
went out and bowed down before the king with
his face to the ground.
[21]Araunah said, "Why has my lord the king
come to his servant?"
"To buy your threshing floor," David answered,
"so I can build an altar to the LORD, that the
24:21 plague on the people may be stopped."[b]
[b]Nu 16:44-50 [22]Araunah said to David, "Let my lord the king
24:22 take whatever pleases him and offer it up. Here are
[c]1Sa 6:14; oxen[c] for the burnt offering, and here are threshing
1Ki 19:21 sledges and ox yokes for the wood. [23]O king, Arau-
24:23 nah gives[d] all this to the king." Araunah also said
[d]Eze 20:40-41 to him, "May the LORD your God accept you."
[24]But the king replied to Araunah, "No, I insist
on paying you for it. I will not sacrifice to the

[a] *13* Septuagint (see also 1 Chron. 21:12); Hebrew *seven*

The Plague

2SA 24:13–15

David is given three options as a punishment for taking a census: three years of famine, three months of fleeing from his enemies or three days of plague. Each of these is chosen to humble David and to diminish his confidence in human power and resources. Of the three, David chooses the plague that comes directly from God. David realizes that human vengeance knows no limits, while our wise and gracious Lord is capable of exhibiting mercy to repentant sinners if he so chooses. Still, it doesn't seem fair. Why do 70,000 have to die? Even David is upset by the consequences of his sin on innocent people. Yet we must remember that the Lord is already angry **before** ***David takes a census (2Sa 24:1). For this reason, some see this plague not so much as punishment for David's personal sin as it is punishment of a nation of people for their sin.***

Costly Sacrifices

2SA 24:24

Araunah is honored to be in his king's presence (2Sa 24:20). When David states his intent to buy Araunah's threshing floor and build an altar, Araunah offers to give David not only the site, but also his oxen for the sacrifice and his sledges and yokes for wood. But David refuses his offer. David knows that a sacrifice must cost him something, otherwise it could not truly be considered a "sacrifice."

This realization should be planted deeply in our hearts, too. We want to sacrificially offer God our best, not just what costs us little or nothing and not simply cheap and easy worship. Underline 2 Samuel 24:24. What do we have that we can offer to God? Our time? Our energy? Our finances? What do we have that would be costly to offer? Give God one thing—one thing that costs much.

LORD my God burnt offerings that cost me nothing."[e]
So David bought the threshing floor and the
oxen and paid fifty shekels[a] of silver for them.
25 David built an altar[f] to the LORD there and sacrificed burnt offerings and fellowship offerings.[b]
Then the LORD answered prayer[g] in behalf of the
land, and the plague on Israel was stopped.

24:24 [e]Mal 1:13-14

24:25 [f]1Sa 7:17 [g]2Sa 21:14

[a] 24 That is, about 1 1/4 pounds (about 0.6 kilogram)
[b] 25 Traditionally *peace offerings*

1 Kings

From wisest to vilest.

Quick Study

Author
Unknown.

Date Written
Probably written during Israel's Babylonian exile, around 550 B.C.

Setting
Israel and Judah.

Key Passage
1 Kings 2:2–3 "Be strong, show yourself a man, and observe what the LORD your God requires: Walk in his ways, and keep his decrees and commands, his laws and requirements, as written in the Law of Moses, so that you may prosper in all you do and wherever you go."

The book of 1 Kings records the final years of the united nation of Israel and its subsequent breakup into two separate kingdoms—Israel and Judah. The opening chapters describe Solomon's divinely given wisdom and the golden years of his reign. But the dangers of success ultimately cause Solomon to take his eyes off God and focus instead on power, influence, wealth and foreign idols. Because of his disobedience, civil war breaks out, the kingdom is torn in two and the two kingdoms slip deeper into wickedness.

Within this account of Israel's decline, we meet those who stand firm in their commitment to God, as well as those who actively campaign against him. We feel the heartache of a mother who is willing to give away her child to preserve his life (1Ki 3:16–28). We applaud the respect accorded to the queen of Sheba as she questions Solomon (1Ki 10). We sorrowfully observe the negative impact brought about by Solomon's devotion to things other than God himself (1Ki 11). We are humbled by the trusting belief of the widow of Zarephath (1Ki 17:7–24) but horrified by the manipulative wickedness of Jezebel (1Ki 18–21).

The chapters of 1 Kings illustrate a clear correlation between a leader's personal morality and the course of those who follow that leader. Success in a leadership role requires taking God's commands and promises seriously. Disobedience to God's commands will bring devastating consequences that may affect several generations, but obedience to God's way will bring far-reaching blessings.

Outline

Solomon's early kingship and wisdom.
1Ki 1-4

Solomon's building projects.
1Ki 5:1—8:21

The temple dedication.
1Ki 8:22-66

The Lord appears to Solomon.
1Ki 9:1-9

Solomon's other activities.
1Ki 9:10-28

The queen of Sheba visits Solomon.
1Ki 10:1-13

Solomon's splendor.
1Ki 10:14-29

Solomon's wives.
1Ki 11:1-13

Solomon's troubles.
1Ki 11:14-43

King Rehoboam.
1Ki 12-14

Kings of Israel and Judah.
1Ki 15-16

Elijah the prophet.
1Ki 17-19

The reign of wicked King Ahab's reign.
1Ki 20:1—22:40

Jehoshaphat and Ahaziah.
1Ki 22:41-53

The Women of 1 Kings

Bathsheba	*Assured her son's succession to the throne.* 2Sa 11; 12:24; 1Ki 1-2; 2Ch 35; Ps 51:1 (page 939)
Haggith	*Mother of usurper Adonijah.* 1Ki 1:5,11; 2:13
Abishag	*Young comforter for an old king.* 2Sa 3:4; 1Ki 1:1-4,15; 2:13-25; 2Ch 3:2
Two prostitute mothers	*One honest, one a liar.* 1Ki 3 (page 1010)
Taphath	*Solomon's daughter.* 1Ki 4:11
Basemath	*Solomon's daughter.* 1Ki 4:15
Huram's mother	*Hebrew mother of a skilled bronze worker.* 1Ki 7:13-45
Queen of Sheba	*Awed by Solomon's wealth and wisdom.* 1Ki 10: 1-13; 2Ch 9:1-12; Mt 12:42 (page 1075)
Solomon's wives and concubines	*Solomon's downfall.* 1Ki 11:1-13
Tahpenes	*Pharaoh's queen.* 1Ki 11:19-20
Hadad's wife	*Sister of Queen Tahpenes.* 1Ki 11:19-20
Zeruah	*Mother of rebel Jeroboam.* 1Ki 11:26
Jeroboam's wife	*Only bad news for her.* 1Ki 14:1-18
Naamah	*Ammonite mother of Rehoboam.* 1Ki 14:21,31; 2Ch 12:13
Maacah	*Mother of Abijah, grandmother of Asa.* 1Ki 15:1-2,13; 1Ch 11:20-22
Jezebel	*Infamous for her wickedness.* 1Ki 16:29-31; 18:1—19:2; 21:5-25; 2Ki 9:6-37 (page 1076)
Widow of Zarephath	*Sharing resulted in survival.* 1Ki 17:8-24; Lk 4:26 (page 1143)
Azubah	*King Jehoshaphat's mother.* 1Ki 22:42; 2Ch 20:31

Denotes a sketch written about this character

Adonijah Sets Himself Up as King

1 When King David was old and well advanced
in years, he could not keep warm even when
they put covers over him. 2So his servants said to
him, "Let us look for a young virgin to attend the
king and take care of him. She can lie beside him
so that our lord the king may keep warm."
3Then they searched throughout Israel for a
1:3 beautiful girl and found Abishag, a Shunammite,[a]
[a]Jos 19:18 and brought her to the king. 4The girl was very
beautiful; she took care of the king and waited on
him, but the king had no intimate relations with
her.
1:5 [b]2Sa 3:4 5Now Adonijah,[b] whose mother was Haggith,
[c]2Sa 15:1 put himself forward and said, "I will be king." So
he got chariots[c] and horses[a] ready, with fifty men
to run ahead of him. 6(His father had never inter-
1:6 fered[d] with him by asking, "Why do you behave
[d]2Sa 3:3-4 as you do?" He was also very handsome and was
born next after Absalom.)
1:7 [e]1Ki 2:22,28; 7Adonijah conferred with Joab[e] son of Zeruiah
1Ch 11:6 and with Abiathar[f] the priest, and they gave him
[f]1Sa 22:20; their support. 8But Zadok[g] the priest, Benaiah[h] son
2Sa 20:25 of Jehoiada, Nathan[i] the prophet, Shimei[j] and Rei[b]
1:8 and David's special guard[k] did not join Adonijah.
[g]2Sa 20:25 9Adonijah then sacrificed sheep, cattle and fat-
[h]2Sa 8:18 [i]2Sa 12:1 tened calves at the Stone of Zoheleth near En
[j]1Ki 4:18 [k]2Sa 23:8 Rogel.[l] He invited all his brothers, the king's sons,
and all the men of Judah who were royal officials,
1:9 10but he did not invite Nathan the prophet or Bena-
[l]2Sa 17:17 iah or the special guard or his brother Solomon.[m]
1:10 11Then Nathan asked Bathsheba,[n] Solomon's
[m]2Sa 12:24 mother, "Have you not heard that Adonijah,[o] the
1:11 son of Haggith, has become king without our lord
[n]2Sa 12:24 David's knowing it? 12Now then, let me advise[p]
[o]2Sa 3:4 you how you can save your own life and the life of
1:12 your son Solomon. 13Go in to King David and say
[p]Pr 15:22 to him, 'My lord the king, did you not swear[q] to
1:13 me your servant: "Surely Solomon your son shall
[q]ver 30; be king after me, and he will sit on my throne"?
1Ch 22:9-13 Why then has Adonijah become king?' 14While
you are still there talking to the king, I will come
in and confirm what you have said."
1:15 15So Bathsheba went to see the aged king in his
[r]ver 1 room, where Abishag[r] the Shunammite was
attending him. 16Bathsheba bowed low and knelt
before the king.
"What is it you want?" the king asked.
1:17 17She said to him, "My lord, you yourself swore[s]
[s]ver 13,30 to me your servant by the LORD your God: 'Solomon your son shall be king after me, and he will
sit on my throne.' 18But now Adonijah has become
1:19 king, and you, my lord the king, do not know
[t]ver 9 about it. 19He has sacrificed[t] great numbers of cattle, fattened calves, and sheep, and has invited all
the king's sons, Abiathar the priest and Joab the
commander of the army, but he has not invited
Solomon your servant. 20My lord the king, the
eyes of all Israel are on you, to learn from you

[a] 5 Or *charioteers* [b] 8 Or *and his friends*

More Nurse Than Wife

1KI 1:3–4

Youthful and lovely, Abishag is given to David in an attempt to restore his vigor—for in his old age, the king has become weak and chilled. At the time of David's reign, a ruler's virility was taken as a sign of the strength and vitality of his people. David's servants hope that Abishag's charms will revitalize the king, but their plan fails. Abishag ends up being more of a nurse than a lover to David.

Although the relationship between Abishag and David is never consummated, she is considered to be a part of his harem, even one of his wives. This is significant, for a claim to a king's wives and harem signals a claim to the throne. After David's death, Adonijah attempts to take the throne by requesting Abishag as his bride. Solomon sees through his ploy, knowing Adonijah has more in mind than a new wife, and takes quick and decisive action to protect his throne (1Ki 2:13–25).

"I have nothing to glory in but my infirmities and my unworthiness, since, in that everlasting marriage-union thou hast made with me, I brought with me nothing but weakness, sin and misery. How I rejoice to owe all to thee, and that thou favorest my heart with a sight of the treasures and boundless riches of thy grace and love! Thou hast dealt by me, as if a magnificent king should marry a poor slave, forget her slavery, give her all the ornaments which may render her pleasing in his eyes, and freely pardon her all the faults and ill qualities which her ignorance and bad education had given her . . . . My poverty is become my riches, and in the extremity of my weakness I have found my strength."

—Madame Guyon (1647-1717)

who will sit on the throne of my lord the king after him. 21 Otherwise, as soon as my lord the king is laid to rest[u] with his fathers, I and my son Solomon will be treated as criminals."

22 While she was still speaking with the king, Nathan the prophet arrived. 23 And they told the king, "Nathan the prophet is here." So he went before the king and bowed with his face to the ground.

24 Nathan said, "Have you, my lord the king, declared that Adonijah shall be king after you, and that he will sit on your throne? 25 Today he has gone down and sacrificed great numbers of cattle, fattened calves, and sheep. He has invited all the king's sons, the commanders of the army and Abiathar the priest. Right now they are eating and drinking with him and saying, 'Long live King Adonijah!' 26 But me your servant, and Zadok the priest, and Benaiah son of Jehoiada, and your servant Solomon he did not invite.[v] 27 Is this something my lord the king has done without letting his servants know who should sit on the throne of my lord the king after him?"

David Makes Solomon King

28 Then King David said, "Call in Bathsheba." So she came into the king's presence and stood before him.

29 The king then took an oath: "As surely as the LORD lives, who has delivered me out of every trouble,[w] 30 I will surely carry out today what I swore[x] to you by the LORD, the God of Israel: Solomon your son shall be king after me, and he will sit on my throne in my place."

31 Then Bathsheba bowed low with her face to the ground and, kneeling before the king, said, "May my lord King David live forever!"

32 King David said, "Call in Zadok the priest, Nathan the prophet and Benaiah son of Jehoiada." When they came before the king, 33 he said to them: "Take your lord's servants with you and set Solomon my son on my own mule[y] and take him down to Gihon.[z] 34 There have Zadok the priest and Nathan the prophet anoint[a] him king over Israel. Blow the trumpet[b] and shout, 'Long live King Solomon!' 35 Then you are to go up with him, and he is to come and sit on my throne and reign in my place. I have appointed him ruler over Israel and Judah."

36 Benaiah son of Jehoiada answered the king, "Amen! May the LORD, the God of my lord the king, so declare it. 37 As the LORD was with my lord the king, so may he be with[c] Solomon to make his throne even greater[d] than the throne of my lord King David!"

38 So Zadok[e] the priest, Nathan the prophet, Benaiah son of Jehoiada, the Kerethites[f] and the Pelethites went down and put Solomon on King David's mule and escorted him to Gihon.[g] 39 Zadok the priest took the horn of oil[h] from the sacred tent and anointed Solomon. Then they sounded

1:21 [u]Dt 31:16; 1Ki 2:10
1:26 [v]ver 8,10
1:29 [w]2Sa 4:9
1:30 [x]ver 13,17
1:33 [y]2Sa 20:6-7 [z]2Ch 32:30; 33:14
1:34 [a]1Sa 10:1; 16:3,12; 1Ki 19:16; 2Ki 9:3,13 [b]ver 25; 2Sa 5:3; 15:10
1:37 [c]Jos 1:5,17; 1Sa 20:13 [d]ver 47
1:38 [e]ver 8 [f]2Sa 8:18 [g]ver 33
1:39 [h]Ex 30:23-32; Ps 89:20

1:39 the trumpet and all the people shouted,[i] "Long
[i]ver 34; live King Solomon!" 40And all the people went up
1Sa 10:24 after him, playing flutes and rejoicing greatly, so
that the ground shook with the sound.
41Adonijah and all the guests who were with
him heard it as they were finishing their feast. On
hearing the sound of the trumpet, Joab asked,
"What's the meaning of all the noise in the city?"
1:42 42Even as he was speaking, Jonathan[j] son of
[j]2Sa 15:27, 36 Abiathar the priest arrived. Adonijah said, "Come
[k]2Sa 18:26 in. A worthy man like you must be bringing good
news."[k]
43"Not at all!" Jonathan answered. "Our lord
King David has made Solomon king. 44The king
has sent with him Zadok the priest, Nathan the
prophet, Benaiah son of Jehoiada, the Kerethites
and the Pelethites, and they have put him on the
king's mule, 45and Zadok the priest and Nathan
the prophet have anointed him king at Gihon.
1:45 From there they have gone up cheering, and the
[l]ver 40 city resounds[l] with it. That's the noise you hear.
46Moreover, Solomon has taken his seat on the
royal throne. 47Also, the royal officials have come
to congratulate our lord King David, saying, 'May
1:47 your God make Solomon's name more famous
[m]ver 37; than yours and his throne greater[m] than yours!'
Ge 47:31 And the king bowed in worship on his bed 48and
said, 'Praise be to the LORD, the God of Israel, who
1:48 has allowed my eyes to see a successor[n] on my
[n]2Sa 7:12; 1Ki 3:6 throne today.' "
49At this, all Adonijah's guests rose in alarm and
1:50 dispersed. 50But Adonijah, in fear of Solomon,
[o]1Ki 2:28 went and took hold of the horns[o] of the altar.
51Then Solomon was told, "Adonijah is afraid of
King Solomon and is clinging to the horns of the
altar. He says, 'Let King Solomon swear to me
today that he will not put his servant to death
with the sword.' "
1:52 52Solomon replied, "If he shows himself to be a
[p]1Sa 14:45; worthy man, not a hair[p] of his head will fall to the
2Sa 14:11 ground; but if evil is found in him, he will die."
53Then King Solomon sent men, and they brought
him down from the altar. And Adonijah came and
bowed down to King Solomon, and Solomon said,
2:1 "Go to your home."
[q]Ge 47:29; Dt 31:14

David's Charge to Solomon

2:2 **2** When the time drew near for David to die,[q] he
[r]Jos 23:14 gave a charge to Solomon his son.
[s]Dt 31:7,23; Jos 1:6 2"I am about to go the way of all the earth,"[r] he
said. "So be strong,[s] show yourself a man, 3and
2:3 observe[t] what the LORD your God requires: Walk
[t]Dt 17:14-20; Jos 1:7 in his ways, and keep his decrees and commands,
[u]1Ch 22:13 his laws and requirements, as written in the Law
of Moses, so that you may prosper[u] in all you do
2:4 and wherever you go, 4and that the LORD may
[v]2Sa 7:13, 25; 1Ki 8:25 keep his promise[v] to me: 'If your descendants
[w]2Ki 20:3; watch how they live, and if they walk faithfully[w]
Ps 132:12 before me with all their heart and soul, you will
2:5 never fail to have a man on the throne of Israel.'
[x]2Sa 2:18; 18:5,12,14 5"Now you yourself know what Joab[x] son of

The Horns of the Altar

1Ki 1:50

Both the altar at the temple and the altar at the tabernacle were designed with four horns or vertical projections, one at each of the four corners (Ex 27:2). Fugitives who sought asylum clung to these horns while waiting to learn of their fate. Refuge at the altar was only temporary, however; if a person was judged guilty of murder, he was removed and executed (Ex 21:13–14). Both Adonijah and Joab seek refuge at the horns of the altar—but with different results (1Ki 1:49–53; 2:28–34).

Joab's Future

1KI 2:5–6

For political reasons, Joab intentionally murders two men: Abner and his own cousin, Amasa (2Sa 3:22–27; 20:9–10). The penalty required for these crimes is Joab's life (Ex 21:13–14). King David knows this but is apparently reluctant to carry out the sentence himself. David's reluctance may stem from the fact that Joab had faithfully served for many years as David's military commander, even standing by him at the time of Absalom's attempted coup. Family ties may also be behind his lack of action. Joab is David's nephew, the son of his sister Zeruiah. Yet despite his feelings for Joab, David knows that he must be punished and leaves the task to Solomon. Though Joab could have gone down in history as a man known for his valor and honor, he instead leaves a legacy of dishonor and violence, receiving a well-deserved punishment at the hands of David's son (1Ki 2:31).

Zeruiah did to me—what he did to the two com- 2:5
manders of Israel's armies, Abner[y] son of Ner and [y]2Sa 3:27
Amasa[z] son of Jether. He killed them, shedding [z]2Sa 20:10
their blood in peacetime as if in battle, and with
that blood stained the belt around his waist and
the sandals on his feet. 6 Deal with him according
to your wisdom,[a] but do not let his gray head go 2:6
down to the grave[a] in peace. [a]ver 9
7 "But show kindness to the sons of Barzillai[b] of 2:7 [b]2Sa 17:27;
Gilead and let them be among those who eat at 19:31-39
your table.[c] They stood by me when I fled from [c]2Sa 9:7
your brother Absalom.
8 "And remember, you have with you Shimei[d] 2:8 [d]2Sa 16:5-13
son of Gera, the Benjamite from Bahurim, who [e]2Sa 19:18-
called down bitter curses on me the day I went to 23
Mahanaim. When he came down to meet me at
the Jordan, I swore[e] to him by the LORD: 'I will not
put you to death by the sword.' 9 But now, do not
consider him innocent. You are a man of wisdom;[f] 2:9
you will know what to do to him. Bring his gray [f]ver 6
head down to the grave in blood."
10 Then David rested with his fathers and was 2:10
buried[g] in the City of David.[h] 11 He had reigned[i] [g]Ac 2:29;
forty years over Israel—seven years in Hebron and 13:36
thirty-three in Jerusalem. 12 So Solomon sat on the [h]2Sa 5:7
throne[j] of his father David, and his rule was firm- 2:11
ly established.[k] [i]2Sa 5:4,5

Solomon's Throne Established 2:12 [j]1Ch 29:23

13 Now Adonijah, the son of Haggith, went to [k]2Ch 1:1
Bathsheba, Solomon's mother. Bathsheba asked 2:13
him, "Do you come peacefully?"[l] [l]1Sa 16:4
He answered, "Yes, peacefully." 14 Then he
added, "I have something to say to you."
"You may say it," she replied.
15 "As you know," he said, "the kingdom was
mine. All Israel looked to me as their king. But
things changed, and the kingdom has gone to my
brother; for it has come to him from the LORD.
16 Now I have one request to make of you. Do not
refuse me."
"You may make it," she said.
17 So he continued, "Please ask King Solomon— 2:17
he will not refuse you—to give me Abishag[m] the [m]1Ki 1:3
Shunammite as my wife."
18 "Very well," Bathsheba replied, "I will speak
to the king for you."
19 When Bathsheba went to King Solomon to
speak to him for Adonijah, the king stood up to
meet her, bowed down to her and sat down on his
throne. He had a throne brought for the king's
mother,[n] and she sat down at his right hand.[o] 2:19 [n]1Ki 15:13
20 "I have one small request to make of you," she [o]Ps 45:9
said. "Do not refuse me."
The king replied, "Make it, my mother; I will
not refuse you."
21 So she said, "Let Abishag[p] the Shunammite be 2:21
given in marriage to your brother Adonijah." [p]1Ki 1:3
22 King Solomon answered his mother, "Why do

[a] 6 Hebrew *Sheol*; also in verse 9

2:22 you request Abishag[q] the Shunammite for Adoni-
[q]2Sa 12:8; 1Ki 1:3 jah? You might as well request the kingdom for
[r]1Ch 3:2 him—after all, he is my older brother[r]—yes, for
him and for Abiathar the priest and Joab son of
Zeruiah!"
[23]Then King Solomon swore by the LORD: "May
2:23 [s]Ru 1:17 God deal with me, be it ever so severely,[s] if Adonijah does not pay with his life for this request!
[24]And now, as surely as the LORD lives—he who
has established me securely on the throne of my
2:24 father David and has founded a dynasty for me as
[t]2Sa 7:11; he promised[t]—Adonijah shall be put to death
1Ch 22:10 today!" [25]So King Solomon gave orders to Bena-
2:25 iah[u] son of Jehoiada, and he struck down Adoni-
[u]2Sa 8:18 jah and he died.
[26]To Abiathar[v] the priest the king said, "Go back
2:26 [v]1Sa 22:20 to your fields in Anathoth.[w] You deserve to die,
[w]Jos 21:18 but I will not put you to death now, because you
[x]2Sa 15:24 carried the ark[x] of the Sovereign LORD before my
[y]1Sa 23:6 father David and shared all my father's hardships."[y] [27]So Solomon removed Abiathar from the
2:27 priesthood of the LORD, fulfilling[z] the word the
[z]1Sa 2:27-36 LORD had spoken at Shiloh about the house of Eli.
[28]When the news reached Joab, who had con-
spired with Adonijah though not with Absalom,
he fled to the tent of the LORD and took hold of the
2:28 horns[a] of the altar. [29]King Solomon was told that
[a]1Ki 1:7,50 Joab had fled to the tent of the LORD and was
2:29 beside the altar. Then Solomon ordered Benaiah[b]
[b]ver 25 son of Jehoiada, "Go, strike him down!"
[30]So Benaiah entered the tent of the LORD and
2:30 said to Joab, "The king says, 'Come out![c]'"
[c]Ex 21:14 But he answered, "No, I will die here."
Benaiah reported to the king, "This is how Joab
answered me."
[31]Then the king commanded Benaiah, "Do as
he says. Strike him down and bury him, and so
clear me and my father's house of the guilt of the
2:31 innocent blood[d] that Joab shed. [32]The LORD will
[d]Nu 35:33; Dt 19:13; repay[e] him for the blood he shed,[f] because with-
21:8-9 out the knowledge of my father David he attacked
2:32 two men and killed them with the sword. Both of
[e]Jdg 9:57; them—Abner son of Ner, commander of Israel's
Ps 7:16 [f]Jdg 9:24 army, and Amasa[g] son of Jether, commander of
[g]2Sa 3:27; Judah's army—were better[h] men and more
20:10 upright than he. [33]May the guilt of their blood rest
[h]2Ch 21:13 on the head of Joab and his descendants forever.
But on David and his descendants, his house and
his throne, may there be the LORD's peace forever."
[34]So Benaiah son of Jehoiada went up and
struck down Joab and killed him, and he was
2:35 [i]1Ki 4:4 buried on his own land[a] in the desert. [35]The king
[j]ver 27; put Benaiah[i] son of Jehoiada over the army in
1Ch 29:22 Joab's position and replaced Abiathar with Zadok[j]
the priest.
2:36 [36]Then the king sent for Shimei[k] and said to him,
[k]ver 8; "Build yourself a house in Jerusalem and live there,
2Sa 16:5 but do not go anywhere else. [37]The day you leave

[a] 34 Or *buried in his tomb*

Joab's Death

1KI 2:28-34

A man who grasps the horns of the altar is safe—but not indefinitely. Once he is judged guilty of murder, he is removed from the altar and put to death. Joab hopes that if he refuses to leave the holy place, his life will be spared. Indeed, Benaiah is reluctant to follow his orders, understandably hesitant to execute someone in the sacred tent of God. But after receiving assurance from Solomon that God has authorized the punishment, Benaiah enters the tent and executes Joab.

Shimei's Future

1KI 2:36–46

A descendant of Saul, Shimei deeply resents the fact that David has seized the throne from his family. When David is running from Absalom, Shimei meets him outside Bahurim and curses him bitterly (2Sa 16:5–14). These curses have a profound affect on the king, for he believes that God is allowing them as a part of the punishment for his sins against Uriah the Hittite (2Sa 11). After Absalom's death, Shimei repents of his actions, and David allows him to live (2Sa 19:18–23). Before his death, however, David charges Solomon to "bring his gray head down to the grave in blood" (1Ki 2:9). Solomon meets with Shimei and agrees to spare his life—but only under certain conditions. When Shimei ignores those conditions, Solomon orders his execution.

and cross the Kidron Valley,[l] you can be sure you
will die; your blood will be on your own head."[m]
38 Shimei answered the king, "What you say is
good. Your servant will do as my lord the king has
said." And Shimei stayed in Jerusalem for a long
time.
39 But three years later, two of Shimei's slaves ran
off to Achish[n] son of Maacah, king of Gath, and
Shimei was told, "Your slaves are in Gath." 40 At
this, he saddled his donkey and went to Achish at
Gath in search of his slaves. So Shimei went away
and brought the slaves back from Gath.
41 When Solomon was told that Shimei had gone
from Jerusalem to Gath and had returned, 42 the
king summoned Shimei and said to him, "Did I
not make you swear by the LORD and warn you,
'On the day you leave to go anywhere else, you
can be sure you will die'? At that time you said to
me, 'What you say is good. I will obey.' 43 Why
then did you not keep your oath to the LORD and
obey the command I gave you?"
44 The king also said to Shimei, "You know in
your heart all the wrong[o] you did to my father
David. Now the LORD will repay you for your
wrongdoing. 45 But King Solomon will be blessed,
and David's throne will remain secure[p] before the
LORD forever."
46 Then the king gave the order to Benaiah son
of Jehoiada, and he went out and struck Shimei
down and killed him.
The kingdom was now firmly established[q] in
Solomon's hands.

Solomon Asks for Wisdom

3 Solomon made an alliance with Pharaoh king
of Egypt and married[r] his daughter.[s] He
brought her to the City of David[t] until he finished
building his palace[u] and the temple of the LORD,
and the wall around Jerusalem. 2 The people, however, were still sacrificing at the high places,[v]
because a temple had not yet been built for the
Name of the LORD. 3 Solomon showed his love[w] for
the LORD by walking according to the statutes[x] of
his father David, except that he offered sacrifices
and burned incense on the high places.
4 The king went to Gibeon[y] to offer sacrifices, for
that was the most important high place, and Solomon offered a thousand burnt offerings on that
altar. 5 At Gibeon the LORD appeared[z] to Solomon
during the night in a dream,[a] and God said, "Ask
for whatever you want me to give you."
6 Solomon answered, "You have shown great
kindness to your servant, my father David,
because he was faithful[b] to you and righteous and
upright in heart. You have continued this great
kindness to him and have given him a son[c] to sit
on his throne this very day.
7 "Now, O LORD my God, you have made your
servant king in place of my father David. But I am
only a little child[d] and do not know how to carry
out my duties. 8 Your servant is here among the

2:37 [l]2Sa 15:23 [m]Lev 20:9; Jos 2:19; 2Sa 1:16
2:39 [n]1Sa 27:2
2:44 [o]1Sa 25:39; 2Sa 16:5-13; Eze 17:19
2:45 [p]2Sa 7:13; Pr 25:5
2:46 [q]ver 12; 2Ch 1:1
3:1 [r]1Ki 7:8 [s]1Ki 9:24 [t]2Sa 5:7 [u]1Ki 7:1; 9:15,19
3:2 [v]Lev 17:3-5; Dt 12:2,4-5; 1Ki 22:43
3:3 [w]Dt 6:5; Ps 31:23; 1Co 8:3 [x]1Ki 2:3; 9:4; 11:4,6,38
3:4 [y]1Ch 16:39
3:5 [z]1Ki 9:2 [a]Nu 12:6; Mt 1:20
3:6 [b]1Ki 2:4; 9:4 [c]1Ki 1:48
3:7 [d]Nu 27:17; 1Ch 29:1

people you have chosen,[e] a great people, too
numerous to count or number.[f] 9So give your servant a discerning[g] heart to govern your people
and to distinguish[h] between right and wrong. For
who is able[i] to govern this great people of yours?"
10The Lord was pleased that Solomon had asked
for this. 11So God said to him, "Since you have
asked[j] for this and not for long life or wealth for
yourself, nor have asked for the death of your enemies but for discernment in administering justice,
12I will do what you have asked.[k] I will give you a
wise[l] and discerning heart, so that there will never have been anyone like you, nor will there ever
be. 13Moreover, I will give you what you have not[m]
asked for—both riches and honor[n]—so that in
your lifetime you will have no equal[o] among
kings. 14And if you walk[p] in my ways and obey
my statutes and commands as David your father
did, I will give you a long life."[q] 15Then Solomon
awoke[r]—and he realized it had been a dream.
He returned to Jerusalem, stood before the ark
of the Lord's covenant and sacrificed burnt offerings[s] and fellowship offerings.[a][t] Then he gave a
feast[u] for all his court.

A Wise Ruling

16Now two prostitutes came to the king and
stood before him. 17One of them said, "My lord,
this woman and I live in the same house. I had a
baby while she was there with me. 18The third day
after my child was born, this woman also had a
baby. We were alone; there was no one in the
house but the two of us.
19"During the night this woman's son died
because she lay on him. 20So she got up in the
middle of the night and took my son from my side
while I your servant was asleep. She put him by
her breast and put her dead son by my breast.
21The next morning, I got up to nurse my son—
and he was dead! But when I looked at him closely in the morning light, I saw that it wasn't the
son I had borne."
22The other woman said, "No! The living one is
my son; the dead one is yours."
But the first one insisted, "No! The dead one is
yours; the living one is mine." And so they argued
before the king.
23The king said, "This one says, 'My son is alive
and your son is dead,' while that one says, 'No!
Your son is dead and mine is alive.' "
24Then the king said, "Bring me a sword." So
they brought a sword for the king. 25He then gave
an order: "Cut the living child in two and give half
to one and half to the other."
26The woman whose son was alive was filled
with compassion[v] for her son and said to the king,
"Please, my lord, give her the living baby! Don't
kill him!"

3:8 [e]Dt 7:6 [f]Ge 15:5
3:9 [g]2Sa 14:17; Jas 1:5 [h]Pr 2:3-9; Heb 5:14 [i]Ps 72:1-2
3:11 [j]Jas 4:3
3:12 [k]1Jn 5:14-15 [l]1Ki 4:29,30, 31; 5:12; 10:23; Ecc 1:16
3:13 [m]Mt 6:33; Eph 3:20 [n]1Ki 4:21-24; Pr 3:1-2,16 [o]1Ki 10:23
3:14 [p]ver 6; Pr 3:1-2,16 [q]Ps 61:6; 91:16
3:15 [r]Ge 41:7 [s]1Ki 8:65 [t]Mk 6:21 [u]Est 1:3,9; Da 5:1
3:26 [v]Ge 43:30; Isa 49:15; Jer 31:20; Hos 11:8

Solomon's Wisdom

1KI 3:4-15

At Gibeon, the Lord appears to Solomon in a dream, promising to grant whatever he desires. While he could ask for fame or riches, Solomon instead asks for wisdom, demonstrating a keen awareness of his youth (he is about 20 years old when he becomes king) and his lack of experience in ruling a nation. Solomon's request pleases the Lord, and he promises to give the young king the wisdom he desires—plus much more. Though Solomon becomes the most prosperous ruler of his time, it is for his wisdom, not his wealth, that he is best known. The story of Solomon's ruling in the case of the two quarreling mothers is perhaps the most famous example of his wisdom in action (1Ki 3:16-27; see the character sketch for these women on page 1010).

[a] *15* Traditionally *peace offerings*

Solomon's Household

1KI 4:6-7

***As the official in charge of the palace, Ahishar is most likely responsible for both the administration of the king's residence and the stewardship of his land. This is a position of great importance with many complex duties. Just feeding the members of Solomon's household is a massive undertaking, for the king, his servants, the court officials and all their families consume an astonishing amount of food each day* (1Ki 4:22-23). *The exact number of people in Solomon's household is unknown, but Solomon's wives and concubines alone would have numbered more than one thousand* (1Ki 11:3).**

But the other said, "Neither I nor you shall have
him. Cut him in two!"
[27]Then the king gave his ruling: "Give the living
baby to the first woman. Do not kill him; she is
his mother."
[28]When all Israel heard the verdict the king had
given, they held the king in awe, because they
saw that he had wisdom[w] from God to administer
justice.

Solomon's Officials and Governors

4 So King Solomon ruled over all Israel. [2]And
these were his chief officials:

Azariah[x] son of Zadok—the priest;
[3]Elihoreph and Ahijah, sons of Shisha—secretaries;
Jehoshaphat[y] son of Ahilud—recorder;
[4]Benaiah[z] son of Jehoiada—commander in chief;
Zadok[a] and Abiathar—priests;
[5]Azariah son of Nathan—in charge of the district officers;
Zabud son of Nathan—a priest and personal adviser to the king;
[6]Ahishar—in charge of the palace;
Adoniram son of Abda—in charge of forced labor.

[7]Solomon also had twelve district governors
over all Israel, who supplied provisions for the
king and the royal household. Each one had to
provide supplies for one month in the year. [8]These
are their names:

Ben-Hur—in the hill country[b] of Ephraim;
[9]Ben-Deker—in Makaz, Shaalbim,[c] Beth Shemesh[d] and Elon Bethhanan;
[10]Ben-Hesed—in Arubboth (Socoh[e] and all the land of Hepher[f] were his);
[11]Ben-Abinadab—in Naphoth Dor[a][g] (he was married to Taphath daughter of Solomon);
[12]Baana son of Ahilud—in Taanach and Megiddo, and in all of Beth Shan[h] next to Zarethan[i] below Jezreel, from Beth Shan to Abel Meholah[j] across to Jokmeam;[k]
[13]Ben-Geber—in Ramoth Gilead (the settlements of Jair[l] son of Manasseh in Gilead were his, as well as the district of Argob in Bashan and its sixty large walled cities[m] with bronze gate bars);
[14]Ahinadab son of Iddo—in Mahanaim;[n]
[15]Ahimaaz[o]—in Naphtali (he had married Basemath daughter of Solomon);
[16]Baana son of Hushai[p]—in Asher and in Aloth;
[17]Jehoshaphat son of Paruah—in Issachar;
[18]Shimei[q] son of Ela—in Benjamin;
[19]Geber son of Uri—in Gilead (the country of Sihon king of the Amorites and the country

3:28 [w]ver 9,11-12; Col 2:3
4:2 [x]1Ch 6:10
4:3 [y]2Sa 8:16
4:4 [z]1Ki 2:35 [a]1Ki 2:27
4:8 [b]Jos 24:33
4:9 [c]Jdg 1:35 [d]Jos 21:16
4:10 [e]Jos 15:35 [f]Jos 12:17
4:11 [g]Jos 11:2
4:12 [h]Jos 17:11; Jdg 5:19 [i]Jos 3:16 [j]1Ki 19:16 [k]1Ch 6:68
4:13 [l]Nu 32:41 [m]Dt 3:4
4:14 [n]Jos 13:26
4:15 [o]2Sa 15:27
4:16 [p]2Sa 15:32
4:18 [q]1Ki 1:8

[a] *11* Or *in the heights of Dor*

4:19 [r]Dt 3:8-10 of Og[r] king of Bashan). He was the only
governor over the district.

Solomon's Daily Provisions

20The people of Judah and Israel were as
4:20 [s]Ge 22:17; 32:12; 1Ki 3:8 numerous as the sand[s] on the seashore; they ate,
they drank and they were happy. 21And Solomon
ruled[t] over all the kingdoms from the River[a][u] to
4:21 [t]2Ch 9:26; Ps 72:11 [u]Jos 1:4; Ps 72:8 [v]Ge 15:18 [w]Ps 68:29 the land of the Philistines, as far as the border of
Egypt.[v] These countries brought tribute[w] and were
Solomon's subjects all his life.
22Solomon's daily provisions were thirty cors[b]
of fine flour and sixty cors[c] of meal, 23ten head of
stall-fed cattle, twenty of pasture-fed cattle and a
hundred sheep and goats, as well as deer,
gazelles, roebucks and choice fowl. 24For he ruled
4:24 [x]Ps 72:11 [y]1Ch 22:9 over all the kingdoms west of the River, from
Tiphsah[x] to Gaza, and had peace[y] on all sides.
25During Solomon's lifetime Judah and Israel,
4:25 [z]Jdg 20:1 [a]Jer 23:6 [b]Mic 4:4; Zec 3:10 from Dan to Beersheba,[z] lived in safety,[a] each man
under his own vine and fig tree.[b]
26Solomon had four[d] thousand stalls for chariot
horses,[c] and twelve thousand horses.[e]
4:26 [c]1Ki 10:26; 2Ch 1:14 27The district officers,[d] each in his month, supplied provisions for King Solomon and all who
came to the king's table. They saw to it that noth-
4:27 [d]ver 7 ing was lacking. 28They also brought to the proper place their quotas of barley and straw for the
chariot horses and the other horses.

Solomon's Wisdom

4:29 [e]1Ki 3:12 29God gave Solomon wisdom[e] and very great
insight, and a breadth of understanding as measureless as the sand on the seashore. 30Solomon's
wisdom was greater than the wisdom of all the
4:30 [f]Ge 25:6 [g]Ac 7:22 men of the East,[f] and greater than all the wisdom
of Egypt.[g] 31He was wiser[h] than any other man,
including Ethan the Ezrahite—wiser than Heman,
4:31 [h]1Ki 3:12; 1Ch 2:6; 6:33; 15:19; Ps 89 Title Calcol and Darda, the sons of Mahol. And his fame
spread to all the surrounding nations. 32He spoke
three thousand proverbs[i] and his songs[j] numbered
a thousand and five. 33He described plant life, from
4:32 [i]Pr 1:1; Ecc 12:9 [j]SS 1:1 the cedar of Lebanon to the hyssop that grows out
of walls. He also taught about animals and birds,
reptiles and fish. 34Men of all nations came to lis-
4:34 [k]1Ki 10:1; 2Ch 9:23 ten to Solomon's wisdom, sent by all the kings[k] of
the world, who had heard of his wisdom.

Preparations for Building the Temple

5:1 [l]ver 10,18; 2Sa 5:11; 1Ch 14:1 **5** When Hiram[l] king of Tyre heard that Solomon
had been anointed king to succeed his father
David, he sent his envoys to Solomon, because he
had always been on friendly terms with David.
2Solomon sent back this message to Hiram:
5:3 [m]1Ch 22:8; 28:3 3"You know that because of the wars[m]

[a] *21* That is, the Euphrates; also in verse 24 [b] *22* That is, probably about 185 bushels (about 6.6 kiloliters) [c] *22* That is, probably about 375 bushels (about 13.2 kiloliters)
[d] *26* Some Septuagint manuscripts (see also 2 Chron. 9:25); Hebrew *forty* [e] *26* Or *charioteers*

Peace and Prosperity

1KI 4:20,25

Under Solomon's rule, the nation of Israel experiences peace unlike any they have known before. The author of 1 and 2 Kings emphasizes the prosperity of the times using images of flourishing vines and fig trees, symbols of fertility and wealth. If each man has his own vine and fig tree and the leisure to sit under it, that can only mean that the people are experiencing a time of both peace and abundance.

God repeatedly promised that if his people obey him he would grant them rest from their enemies (Lev 26:36; Dt 28:17); during Solomon's lifetime, this promise is fulfilled (1Ki 8:56). In this period of harmony with Israel's neighbors, Solomon at last can devote the nation's resources to constructing a temple to God (1Ki 5:4–5).

A Massive Effort

1KI 5:13–18

Years before, the prophet Samuel predicted the burdensome demands a king would one day make on the people (1Sa 8:11–18). These verses record the fulfillment of Samuel's prophecy. Though the conscripted workers from Israel are not actually slaves (1Ki 9:22), they are in a sense "drafted" into the work force and have no choice as to whether they will, or will not, serve.

When ancient architectural accomplishments are viewed from a 21st century perspective, the question is often asked: "How did they do it without modern equipment?" This passage of Scripture provides at least part of the answer: a massive labor force. In the building of Solomon's temple, 30,000 laborers, 70,000 carriers and 80,000 stonecutters are required to complete the monumental project.

waged against my father David from all sides,
he could not build a temple for the Name of
the LORD his God until the LORD put his enemies under his feet. 4But now the LORD my **5:4**
God has given me rest[n] on every side, and [n]1Ki 4:24;
there is no adversary or disaster. 5I intend, 1Ch 22:9
therefore, to build a temple[o] for the Name of **5:5**
the LORD my God, as the LORD told my father [o]1Ch 17:12
David, when he said, 'Your son whom I will [p]2Sa 7:13;
put on the throne in your place will build the 1Ch 22:10
temple for my Name.'[p]
6"So give orders that cedars of Lebanon be
cut for me. My men will work with yours, and
I will pay you for your men whatever wages
you set. You know that we have no one so
skilled in felling timber as the Sidonians."

7When Hiram heard Solomon's message, he
was greatly pleased and said, "Praise be to the
LORD today, for he has given David a wise son to
rule over this great nation."
8So Hiram sent word to Solomon:

"I have received the message you sent me
and will do all you want in providing the cedar
and pine logs. 9My men will haul them down **5:9**
from Lebanon to the sea[q], and I will float them [q]Ezr 3:7
in rafts by sea to the place you specify. There I [r]Eze 27:17;
will separate them and you can take them Ac 12:20
away. And you are to grant my wish by providing food[r] for my royal household."

10In this way Hiram kept Solomon supplied
with all the cedar and pine logs he wanted, 11and
Solomon gave Hiram twenty thousand cors[a] of
wheat as food for his household, in addition to
twenty thousand baths[b,c] of pressed olive oil. Solomon continued to do this for Hiram year after
year. 12The LORD gave Solomon wisdom,[s] just as **5:12**
he had promised him. There were peaceful rela- [s]1Ki 3:12
tions between Hiram and Solomon, and the two [t]Am 1:9
of them made a treaty.[t]
13King Solomon conscripted laborers[u] from all **5:13**
Israel—thirty thousand men. 14He sent them off [u]1Ki 9:15
to Lebanon in shifts of ten thousand a month, so
that they spent one month in Lebanon and two
months at home. Adoniram[v] was in charge of the **5:14**
forced labor. 15Solomon had seventy thousand car- [v]1Ki 4:6;
riers and eighty thousand stonecutters in the hills, 2Ch 10:18
16as well as thirty-three hundred[d] foremen[w] who **5:16**
supervised the project and directed the workmen. [w]1Ki 9:23
17At the king's command they removed from the **5:17**
quarry[x] large blocks of quality stone[y] to provide a [x]1Ki 6:7
foundation of dressed stone for the temple. 18The [y]1Ch 22:2
craftsmen of Solomon and Hiram and the men of
Gebal[e z] cut and prepared the timber and stone for **5:18**
the building of the temple. [z]Jos 13:5

[a] *11* That is, probably about 125,000 bushels (about 4,400 kiloliters) [b] *11* Septuagint (see also 2 Chron. 2:10); Hebrew *twenty cors* [c] *11* That is, about 115,000 gallons (about 440 kiloliters) [d] *16* Hebrew; some Septuagint manuscripts (see also 2 Chron. 2:2, 18) *thirty-six hundred* [e] *18* That is, Byblos

Solomon Builds the Temple

6:1 6 In the four hundred and eightieth[a] year after
[a]Ac 7:47 the Israelites had come out of Egypt, in the
fourth year of Solomon's reign over Israel, in the
month of Ziv, the second month, he began to
build the temple of the LORD.[a]
6:2 [2]The temple[b] that King Solomon built for the
[b]Eze 41:1 LORD was sixty cubits long, twenty wide and thirty high.[b] [3]The portico at the front of the main
hall of the temple extended the width of the temple, that is twenty cubits,[c] and projected ten
6:4 cubits[d] from the front of the temple. [4]He made
[c]Eze 40:16; narrow clerestory windows[c] in the temple.
41:16 [5]Against the walls of the main hall and inner
6:5 sanctuary he built a structure around the build-
[d]ver 16,19- ing, in which there were side rooms.[d] [6]The low-
21; est floor was five cubits[e] wide, the middle floor
Eze 41:5-6 six cubits[f] and the third floor seven.[g] He made
offset ledges around the outside of the temple so
that nothing would be inserted into the temple
6:7 walls.
[e]Ex 20:25 [7]In building the temple, only blocks dressed[e] at
[f]Dt 27:5 the quarry were used, and no hammer, chisel or
any other iron tool[f] was heard at the temple site
while it was being built.
[8]The entrance to the lowest[h] floor was on the
south side of the temple; a stairway led up to the
middle level and from there to the third. [9]So he
6:9 built the temple and completed it, roofing it with
[g]ver 14,38 beams and cedar[g] planks. [10]And he built the side
rooms all along the temple. The height of each
was five cubits, and they were attached to the
temple by beams of cedar.
[11]The word of the LORD came to Solomon: [12]"As
6:12 for this temple you are building, if you follow my
[h]2Sa 7:12- decrees, carry out my regulations and keep all my
16; 1Ki 2:4; commands and obey them, I will fulfill through
9:5 you the promise[h] I gave to David your father.
6:13 [13]And I will live among the Israelites and will not
[i]Ex 25:8; abandon[i] my people Israel."
Lev 26:11; [14]So Solomon built the temple and completed[j]
Dt 31:6; it. [15]He lined its interior walls with cedar boards,
Heb 13:5
6:14 paneling them from the floor of the temple to the
[j]ver 9,38 ceiling,[k] and covered the floor of the temple with
6:15 planks of pine. [16]He partitioned off twenty cubits[c]
[k]1Ki 7:7 at the rear of the temple with cedar boards from
floor to ceiling to form within the temple an inner
6:16 sanctuary, the Most Holy Place.[l] [17]The main hall
[l]Ex 26:33; in front of this room was forty cubits[i] long. [18]The
Lev 16:2; inside of the temple was cedar,[m] carved with
1Ki 8:6
6:18 gourds and open flowers. Everything was cedar;
[m]1Ki 7:24; no stone was to be seen.
Ps 74:6

[a] *1* Hebrew; Septuagint *four hundred and fortieth* [b] *2* That is, about 90 feet (about 27 meters) long and 30 feet (about 9 meters) wide and 45 feet (about 13.5 meters) high
[c] *3,16* That is, about 30 feet (about 9 meters) [d] *3* That is, about 15 feet (about 4.5 meters) [e] *6* That is, about 7 1/2 feet (about 2.3 meters); also in verses 10 and 24 [f] *6* That is, about 9 feet (about 2.7 meters) [g] *6* That is, about 10 1/2 feet (about 3.1 meters) [h] *8* Septuagint; Hebrew *middle*
[i] *17* That is, about 60 feet (about 18 meters)

No Hammers or Chisels

1KI 6:7

Though the sound of tools is not heard at the construction site, the use of equipment is not banned at the quarry where the stones are actually prepared for building. The limited use of tools had a spiritual explanation. Moses commanded no cut stone to be used in building altars to God. Using iron tools to dress and ornament stones for sacred altars and buildings was a practice connected with pagan worship and was therefore forbidden (Ex 20:25; see the note on Dt 27:5, page 299). The practice of using tools off-site may have also been practical in nature. Using stones that had been previously fit together at the quarry may have made the on-site construction go much more quickly and smoothly.

A Comparison

1KI 6:38–7:1

While the construction of the temple takes 7 years, Solomon invests almost twice as much time—a full 13 years—in the building of his own palace. The contrast between the two schedules is striking and perhaps points to the beginning of a shift in priorities. As Solomon's power and wealth grow, so does his distance from the Lord.

How we respond to times of prosperity tells much about our spiritual health. Good times can find us drifting away from the Lord, focusing instead on wealth or power or our own abilities. Struggles, however, can make us more dependent on him. As we read of the shift in Solomon's priorities, we can also assess our own and make sure they are in proper order.

19 He prepared the inner sanctuary[n] within the temple to set the ark of the covenant[o] of the LORD there. 20 The inner sanctuary[p] was twenty cubits long, twenty wide and twenty high.[a] He overlaid the inside with pure gold, and he also overlaid the altar of cedar. 21 Solomon covered the inside of the temple with pure gold, and he extended gold chains across the front of the inner sanctuary, which was overlaid with gold. 22 So he overlaid the whole interior with gold. He also overlaid with gold the altar that belonged to the inner sanctuary.

23 In the inner sanctuary he made a pair of cherubim[q] of olive wood, each ten cubits[b] high. 24 One wing of the first cherub was five cubits long, and the other wing five cubits—ten cubits from wing tip to wing tip. 25 The second cherub also measured ten cubits, for the two cherubim were identical in size and shape. 26 The height of each cherub was ten cubits. 27 He placed the cherubim[r] inside the innermost room of the temple, with their wings spread out. The wing of one cherub touched one wall, while the wing of the other touched the other wall, and their wings touched each other in the middle of the room. 28 He overlaid the cherubim with gold.

29 On the walls all around the temple, in both the inner and outer rooms, he carved cherubim,[s] palm trees and open flowers. 30 He also covered the floors of both the inner and outer rooms of the temple with gold.

31 For the entrance of the inner sanctuary he made doors of olive wood with five-sided jambs. 32 And on the two olive wood doors he carved cherubim, palm trees and open flowers, and overlaid the cherubim and palm trees with beaten gold. 33 In the same way he made four-sided jambs of olive wood for the entrance to the main hall. 34 He also made two pine doors, each having two leaves that turned in sockets. 35 He carved cherubim, palm trees and open flowers on them and overlaid them with gold hammered evenly over the carvings.

36 And he built the inner courtyard of three courses[t] of dressed stone and one course of trimmed cedar beams.

37 The foundation of the temple of the LORD was laid in the fourth year, in the month of Ziv. 38 In the eleventh year in the month of Bul, the eighth month, the temple was finished in all its details according to its specifications.[u] He had spent seven years building it.

Solomon Builds His Palace

7 It took Solomon thirteen years, however, to complete the construction of his palace.[v] 2 He built the Palace[w] of the Forest of Lebanon[x] a hundred cubits long, fifty wide and thirty high,[c] with

6:19 [n]1Ki 8:6 [o]1Sa 3:3
6:20 [p]Eze 41:3-4
6:23 [q]Ex 37:1-9
6:27 [r]Ex 25:20; 37:9; 1Ki 8:7; 2Ch 5:8
6:29 [s]ver 32,35
6:36 [t]1Ki 7:12; Ezr 6:4
6:38 [u]Heb 8:5
7:1 [v]1Ki 9:10; 2Ch 8:1
7:2 [w]2Sa 7:2 [x]1Ki 10:17; 2Ch 9:16

[a] *20* That is, about 30 feet (about 9 meters) long, wide and high [b] *23* That is, about 15 feet (about 4.5 meters)
[c] *2* That is, about 150 feet (about 46 meters) long, 75 feet (about 23 meters) wide and 45 feet (about 13.5 meters) high

four rows of cedar columns supporting trimmed
cedar beams. 3It was roofed with cedar above the
beams that rested on the columns—forty-five
beams, fifteen to a row. 4Its windows were placed
high in sets of three, facing each other. 5All the
doorways had rectangular frames; they were in
the front part in sets of three, facing each other.[a]
6He made a colonnade fifty cubits long and thirty wide.[b] In front of it was a portico, and in front
of that were pillars and an overhanging roof.
7He built the throne hall, the Hall of Justice,
where he was to judge,[y] and he covered it with
cedar from floor to ceiling.[c][z] 8And the palace in
which he was to live, set farther back, was similar
in design. Solomon also made a palace like this hall
for Pharaoh's daughter, whom he had married.[a]
9All these structures, from the outside to the
great courtyard and from foundation to eaves,
were made of blocks of high-grade stone cut to
size and trimmed with a saw on their inner and
outer faces. 10The foundations were laid with large
stones of good quality, some measuring ten
cubits[d] and some eight.[e] 11Above were high-grade
stones, cut to size, and cedar beams. 12The great
courtyard was surrounded by a wall of three
courses[b] of dressed stone and one course of
trimmed cedar beams, as was the inner courtyard
of the temple of the LORD with its portico.

The Temple's Furnishings

13King Solomon sent to Tyre and brought
Huram,[f][c] 14whose mother was a widow from the
tribe of Naphtali and whose father was a man of
Tyre and a craftsman in bronze. Huram was highly skilled[d] and experienced in all kinds of bronze
work. He came to King Solomon and did all[e] the
work assigned to him.
15He cast two bronze pillars,[f] each eighteen
cubits high and twelve cubits around,[g] by line.
16He also made two capitals[g] of cast bronze to set
on the tops of the pillars; each capital was five
cubits[h] high. 17A network of interwoven chains
festooned the capitals on top of the pillars, seven
for each capital. 18He made pomegranates in two
rows[i] encircling each network to decorate the capitals on top of the pillars.[j] He did the same for
each capital. 19The capitals on top of the pillars in
the portico were in the shape of lilies, four cubits[k]

7:7 [y]Ps 122:5; Pr 20:8 [z]1Ki 6:15
7:8 [a]1Ki 3:1; 2Ch 8:11
7:12 [b]1Ki 6:36
7:13 [c]2Ch 2:13
7:14 [d]Ex 31:2-5; 35:31; 36:1; 2Ch 2:14 [e]2Ch 4:11,16
7:15 [f]2Ki 25:17; 2Ch 3:15; 4:12; 52:17, 21
7:16 [g]2Ki 25:17

Separate Living Quarters

1KI 7:8

Solomon forms an alliance with Egypt by marrying Pharaoh's daughter, but he builds special living quarters for her and will not allow her to live anywhere the ark of the Lord has been (2Ch 8:11). Sadly, despite such initial integrity, Solomon eventually allows his foreign wives to persuade him to worship their pagan gods. This attraction to his wives and their gods ultimately proves to be his downfall (see the note on 1Ki 11:1–6, page 545).

Like Solomon, we too are known to fall back on our promises to God. Most of us have areas where we long to "get back on track" with the Lord. God doesn't desire our feelings of shame. He desires our repentance and a renewed commitment to him. He also promises that if we stumble again (and again), he will welcome us back with open arms.

[a] *5* The meaning of the Hebrew for this verse is uncertain.
[b] *6* That is, about 75 feet (about 23 meters) long and 45 feet (about 13.5 meters) wide [c] *7* Vulgate and Syriac; Hebrew *floor* [d] *10* That is, about 15 feet (about 4.5 meters)
[e] *10* That is, about 12 feet (about 3.6 meters) [f] *13* Hebrew *Hiram,* a variant of *Huram;* also in verses 40 and 45
[g] *15* That is, about 27 feet (about 8.1 meters) high and 18 feet (about 5.4 meters) around [h] *16* That is, about 7 1/2 feet (about 2.3 meters); also in verse 23 [i] *18* Two Hebrew manuscripts and Septuagint; most Hebrew manuscripts *made the pillars, and there were two rows* [j] *18* Many Hebrew manuscripts and Syriac; most Hebrew manuscripts *pomegranates* [k] *19* That is, about 6 feet (about 1.8 meters); also in verse 38

The Sea

1KI 7:23-26

An immense reservoir of water, the temple Sea is used by the priests in the ritual washing before they offer sacrifices (2Ch 4:6), just as the bronze basin was used in the tabernacle (Ex 30:17-21). The basin is so massive (a cubit is the equivalent of 18 inches in length, making the Sea a full 15 feet from rim to rim), it can hold approximately 11,500 gallons of water, about the size of a small, modern swimming pool.

high. 20On the capitals of both pillars, above the
bowl-shaped part next to the network, were the 7:20
two hundred pomegranates[h] in rows all around. h2Ch 3:16;
21He erected the pillars at the portico of the tem- 4:13;
ple. The pillar to the south he named Jakin[a] and Jer 52:23
the one to the north Boaz.[b][i] 22The capitals on top 7:21
were in the shape of lilies. And so the work on the i1Ki 6:3; 2Ch 3:17
pillars was completed.
23He made the Sea[j] of cast metal, circular in 7:23
shape, measuring ten cubits[c] from rim to rim and j2Ki 25:13; 1Ch 18:8;
five cubits high. It took a line of thirty cubits[d] to Jer 52:17
measure around it. 24Below the rim, gourds encircled it—ten to a cubit. The gourds were cast in
two rows in one piece with the Sea.
25The Sea stood on twelve bulls,[k] three facing 7:25
north, three facing west, three facing south and k2Ch 4:4-5; Jer 52:20
three facing east. The Sea rested on top of them,
and their hindquarters were toward the center. 26It
was a handbreadth[e] in thickness, and its rim was
like the rim of a cup, like a lily blossom. It held
two thousand baths.[f]
27He also made ten movable stands[l] of bronze; 7:27
each was four cubits long, four wide and three lver 38; 2Ch 4:14
high.[g] 28This is how the stands were made: They
had side panels attached to uprights. 29On the
panels between the uprights were lions, bulls and
cherubim—and on the uprights as well. Above
and below the lions and bulls were wreaths of
hammered work. 30Each stand[m] had four bronze 7:30
wheels with bronze axles, and each had a basin m2Ki 16:17
resting on four supports, cast with wreaths on
each side. 31On the inside of the stand there was
an opening that had a circular frame one cubit[h]
deep. This opening was round, and with its base-
work it measured a cubit and a half.[i] Around its
opening there was engraving. The panels of the
stands were square, not round. 32The four wheels
were under the panels, and the axles of the
wheels were attached to the stand. The diameter
of each wheel was a cubit and a half. 33The
wheels were made like chariot wheels; the axles,
rims, spokes and hubs were all of cast metal.
34Each stand had four handles, one on each corner, projecting from the stand. 35At the top of the
stand there was a circular band half a cubit[j] deep.
The supports and panels were attached to the top
of the stand. 36He engraved cherubim, lions and
palm trees on the surfaces of the supports and on
the panels, in every available space, with wreaths
all around. 37This is the way he made the ten

[a] *21* Jakin probably means *he establishes.* [b] *21* Boaz probably means *in him is strength.* [c] *23* That is, about 15 feet (about 4.5 meters) [d] *23* That is, about 45 feet (about 13.5 meters) [e] *26* That is, about 3 inches (about 8 centimeters) [f] *26* That is, probably about 11,500 gallons (about 44 kiloliters); the Septuagint does not have this sentence. [g] *27* That is, about 6 feet (about 1.8 meters) long and wide and about 4 1/2 feet (about 1.3 meters) high [h] *31* That is, about 1 1/2 feet (about 0.5 meter) [i] *31* That is, about 2 1/4 feet (about 0.7 meter); also in verse 32 [j] *35* That is, about 3/4 foot (about 0.2 meter)

Strength for the Battle

Sisera was a cruel man who had preyed on the Israelites for 20 years. But this time something had gone wrong. Sisera needed a place to hide. He needed Jael's help.

Jael knew if Sisera were to escape, he would continue his reign of terror and bloodshed. He was an evil man—and he was in her tent. Jael knew what she must do. She just had to figure out how to do it. She took her cues from Sisera himself.

Sisera thought he was safe with Jael, a member of a family friendly with his people. He began to relax. He reclined in her tent and let her cover him to hide him. He was thirsty and asked for water. But she gave him milk to make him sleepy and to buy her time.

Sisera fell asleep. The Lord disarmed Sisera and gave Jael the courage and strength to do what she knew she must. Having no weapons, she used what she had at hand: a simple tent peg and a hammer.

Jael was a Gentile woman. We don't know what kind of relationship Jael had with God or with the Israelites. She had not gone looking for trouble—it had come to her. She easily could have said that this wasn't her battle. But she didn't.

No one could have expected Jael to be the one to bring down the mighty warrior. When the opportunity presented itself, however, she gathered up her courage and her strength and made certain Sisera would never survive the blow. Undoubtedly when the deed was done, she shuddered in horror at the scene before her. Anyone would.

Just as Jael probably wasn't prepared to take on the task of putting an end to Sisera's bloodshed, many women today face situations for which they are not prepared. Whether the situation is a frustrating daily task or a difficult struggle, they face it alone. They are single, widowed or married to a man who is uninvolved, whether by choice or necessity. In the absence of a husband, a woman must find the strength and courage to fend off the world and the enemy at the door without the aid a husband might provide. A Christian woman does not need to panic or feel abandoned. She *can* do what must be done. The Lord is there, providing wisdom, courage and the strength to win the battle.

Jael
(wild goat)

Judges 4:17–22; 5:6,24–27

Candid SNAPSHOT But Jael, Heber's wife, picked up a tent peg and a hammer and went quietly to him while he lay fast asleep, exhausted. She drove the peg through his temple into the ground, and he died (Judges 4:21).

Samson's Mother

A Secondhand Faith

She was a simple woman living a simple life. Then one day an angel appeared to her—an *angel*—in an age of spiritual darkness, a time when "everyone did as he saw fit" (Jdg 17:6).

Samson's mother had been barren. Now she was to have a son, the angel said, "set apart to God from birth," who "will begin the deliverance of Israel from the hands of the Philistines" (Jdg 13:5). Wonderful news! But how does one raise such a child? Her husband, Manoah, asked the question, and the angel was quick to answer: "Your wife must do all that I have told her. She must not eat anything that comes from the grapevine, nor drink any wine or other fermented drink nor eat anything unclean. She must do everything I have commanded her" (Jdg 13:12–14). Clearly, obedience was the first step, but Samson's parents were walking in unfamiliar territory, without a living model.

The responsibility for raising Samson fell largely to his mother. How she must have grieved when the early promise of Samson's life derailed, for as a teenager he rebelled. Fornication and lust eventually led to his death at an early age. Along the way, he recklessly broke many of God's laws and hid his transgressions from his parents. Clearly, Samson was out of control. What had happened?

The problem seems to rest more with what had *not* happened. Samson's mother had succeeded in instilling outward appearances of holiness—Samson never drank wine or cut his hair—but he did not surrender his will to the Lord. Samson lacked the relationship with God that his call deserved.

Samson's mother lived in a time of spiritual and moral darkness, a time even worse than our own. Godly mentors were in short supply, and she did her best to please God. But Samson was responsible for his own choices, and his mother had to make peace with her own limitations.

God accomplished his will through Samson despite Samson's obvious weaknesses. Samson ruled Israel as a judge for 20 years. In the end, he connected with God. Praying for strength from *the Lord*, "he killed many more [Philistines] when he died than while he lived" (Jdg 16:30). This one act of faith was Samson's legacy. God was true to the prophecy given about Samson before his birth.

God has a plan for every child. We parents cannot know the end at the beginning. Yet even through our mistakes and our children's poor choices, God is faithful. We must partner with him to raise our children with genuine faith of their own.

Samson's Mother
Judges 13; 14:1-7

Candid SNAPSHOT [The angel] said to me, "You will conceive and give birth to a son. Now then, drink no wine or other fermented drink and do not eat anything unclean, because the boy will be a Nazirite of God from birth until the day of his death" (Judges 13:7).

stands. They were all cast in the same molds and
7:38 were identical in size and shape.
[n]Ex 30:18; 38He then made ten bronze basins,[n] each hold-
2Ch 4:6 ing forty baths[a] and measuring four cubits across,
one basin to go on each of the ten stands. 39He
placed five of the stands on the south side of the
temple and five on the north. He placed the Sea
on the south side, at the southeast corner of the
temple. 40He also made the basins and shovels and
sprinkling bowls.

So Huram finished all the work he had undertaken for King Solomon in the temple of the LORD:

41 the two pillars;
the two bowl-shaped capitals on top of the pillars;
the two sets of network decorating the two bowl-shaped capitals on top of the pillars;
42 the four hundred pomegranates for the two sets of network (two rows of pomegranates
7:42 for each network, decorating the bowl-
[o]ver 20 shaped capitals[o] on top of the pillars);
43 the ten stands with their ten basins;
44 the Sea and the twelve bulls under it;
7:45 [p]Ex 27:3 45 the pots, shovels and sprinkling bowls.[p]

All these objects that Huram made for King Solomon for the temple of the LORD were of burnished bronze. 46The king had them cast in clay
7:46 [q]2Ch 4:17 molds in the plain[q] of the Jordan between Suc-
[r]Ge 33:17; coth[r] and Zarethan.[s] 47Solomon left all these
Jos 13:27 things unweighed,[t] because there were so many;
[s]Jos 3:16 the weight of the bronze was not determined.
7:47 48Solomon also made all the furnishings that
[t]1Ch 22:3 were in the LORD's temple:

7:48 the golden altar;
[u]Ex 37:10 the golden table[u] on which was the bread of
[v]Ex 25:30 the Presence;[v]
7:49 49 the lampstands[w] of pure gold (five on the
[w]Ex 25:31-38 right and five on the left, in front of the inner sanctuary);
the gold floral work and lamps and tongs;
7:50 50 the pure gold basins, wick trimmers, sprin-
[x]2Ki 25:13 kling bowls, dishes and censers;[x]
and the gold sockets for the doors of the innermost room, the Most Holy Place, and also for the doors of the main hall of the temple.

51When all the work King Solomon had done for
the temple of the LORD was finished, he brought in
7:51 the things his father David had dedicated[y]—the sil-
[y]2Sa 8:11 ver and gold and the furnishings—and he placed
them in the treasuries of the LORD's temple.

The Ark Brought to the Temple

8 Then King Solomon summoned into his pres-
8:1 ence at Jerusalem the elders of Israel, all the
[z]Nu 7:2 heads of the tribes and the chiefs[z] of the Israelite
[a]2Sa 6:17 families, to bring up the ark[a] of the LORD's covenant

[a] *38* That is, about 230 gallons (about 880 liters)

As a daughter of the King, remember this: No matter how little money is in your purse, you're already rich anyway. You may be broke, but you'll never be poor.

—Luci Swindoll

Ark of the Covenant

1KI 8:1,8

Years before, trusting in the powers of the ark of the covenant rather than in the Lord their God, the Israelites had carried the ark into battle against the Philistines (1Sa 4:1–11). The Philistines captured it, but they later returned it when it brought them only tragedy (1Sa 5–6). The ark then stayed at Kiriath Jearim in Abinadab's house (1Sa 7:1) until David attempted to bring it to Jerusalem. Because they carried the ark improperly and didn't give it the reverence it was due, Uzzah died that day, and David instead placed the ark in the home of Obed-Edom (2Sa 6:1–10). Obed-Edom's family enjoyed exceptional blessing for the three months that the ark resided in their home (2Sa 6:11). Later, David prepared a tent for the ark in Jerusalem (1Ch 15:1), bringing it there by following the carefully laid orders for moving it (Ex 37:5; Dt 10:8). It remained there until the building of Solomon's temple.

from Zion, the City of David.[b] 2All the men of Israel came together to King Solomon at the time of the
festival[c] in the month of Ethanim, the seventh
month.[d]
3When all the elders of Israel had arrived, the
priests[e] took up the ark, 4and they brought up
the ark of the LORD and the Tent of Meeting[f] and all
the sacred furnishings in it. The priests and Levites
carried them up, 5and King Solomon and the entire
assembly of Israel that had gathered about him
were before the ark, sacrificing[g] so many sheep and
cattle that they could not be recorded or counted.
6The priests then brought the ark of the LORD's
covenant[h] to its place in the inner sanctuary of the
temple, the Most Holy Place, and put it beneath the
wings of the cherubim.[i] 7The cherubim spread
their wings over the place of the ark and overshadowed the ark and its carrying poles. 8These poles
were so long that their ends could be seen from the
Holy Place in front of the inner sanctuary, but not
from outside the Holy Place; and they are still there
today.[j] 9There was nothing in the ark except the
two stone tablets[k] that Moses had placed in it at
Horeb, where the LORD made a covenant with the
Israelites after they came out of Egypt.
10When the priests withdrew from the Holy
Place, the cloud[l] filled the temple of the LORD.
11And the priests could not perform their service
because of the cloud, for the glory of the LORD
filled his temple.
12Then Solomon said, "The LORD has said that
he would dwell in a dark cloud;[m] 13I have indeed
built a magnificent temple for you, a place for you
to dwell[n] forever."
14While the whole assembly of Israel was standing there, the king turned around and blessed[o]
them. 15Then he said:

"Praise be to the LORD,[p] the God of Israel,
who with his own hand has fulfilled what he
promised with his own mouth to my father
David. For he said, 16'Since the day I brought
my people Israel out of Egypt, I have not chosen a city in any tribe of Israel to have a temple built for my Name[q] to be there, but I have
chosen[r] David[s] to rule my people Israel.'
17"My father David had it in his heart to
build a temple[t] for the Name of the LORD, the
God of Israel. 18But the LORD said to my father
David, 'Because it was in your heart to build
a temple for my Name, you did well to have
this in your heart. 19Nevertheless, you[u] are
not the one to build the temple, but your son,
who is your own flesh and blood—he is the
one who will build the temple for my Name.'[v]
20"The LORD has kept the promise he made:
I have succeeded David my father and now I
sit on the throne of Israel, just as the LORD
promised, and I have built[w] the temple for the
Name of the LORD, the God of Israel. 21I have
provided a place there for the ark, in which is

8:1 [b]2Sa 5:7
8:2 [c]2Ch 7:8 [d]Lev 23:34
8:3 [e]Nu 7:9; Jos 3:3
8:4 [f]1Ki 3:4; 2Ch 1:3
8:5 [g]2Sa 6:13
8:6 [h]2Sa 6:17 [i]1Ki 6:19,27
8:8 [j]Ex 25:13-15
8:9 [k]Ex 24:7-8; 25:21; 40:20; Dt 10:2-5; Heb 9:4
8:10 [l]Ex 40:34-35; 2Ch 7:1-2
8:12 [m]Ps 18:11; 97:2
8:13 [n]Ex 15:17; 2Sa 7:13; Ps 132:13
8:14 [o]2Sa 6:18
8:15 [p]2Sa 7:12-13; 1Ch 29:10, 20; Ne 9:5; Lk 1:68
8:16 [q]Dt 12:5 [r]1Sa 16:1 [s]2Sa 7:4-6,8
8:17 [t]2Sa 7:2; 1Ch 17:1
8:19 [u]2Sa 7:5 [v]2Sa 7:13; 1Ki 5:3,5
8:20 [w]1Ch 28:6

the covenant of the LORD that he made with
our fathers when he brought them out of
Egypt."

Solomon's Prayer of Dedication

22Then Solomon stood before the altar of the
8:22 LORD in front of the whole assembly of Israel,
[x]Ex 9:29; Ezr 9:5 spread out his hands[x] toward heaven 23and said:

8:23 "O LORD, God of Israel, there is no God like[y]
[y]1Sa 2:2; you in heaven above or on earth below—you
2Sa 7:22 who keep your covenant of love[z] with your
[z]Dt 7:9,12; servants who continue wholeheartedly in
Ne 1:5; 9:32; Da 9:4 your way. 24You have kept your promise to
your servant David my father; with your
mouth you have promised and with your
hand you have fulfilled it—as it is today.
25"Now LORD, God of Israel, keep for your
8:25 [a]1Ki 2:4 servant David my father the promises[a] you
made to him when you said, 'You shall nev-
er fail to have a man to sit before me on the
throne of Israel, if only your sons are careful
in all they do to walk before me as you have
8:26 done.' 26And now, O God of Israel, let your
[b]2Sa 7:25 word that you promised[b] your servant David
my father come true.
8:27 27"But will God really dwell[c] on earth? The
[c]Ac 7:48 heavens, even the highest heaven, cannot
[d]2Ch 2:6; Ps 139:7-16; contain[d] you. How much less this temple I
Isa 66:1; Jer 23:24 have built! 28Yet give attention to your servant's prayer and his plea for mercy, O LORD
my God. Hear the cry and the prayer that your
servant is praying in your presence this day.
8:29 [e]2Ch 7:15; 29May your eyes be open[e] toward[f] this temple
Ne 1:6 [f]Da 6:10 night and day, this place of which you said,
[g]Dt 12:11 'My Name[g] shall be there,' so that you will
hear the prayer your servant prays toward this
place. 30Hear the supplication of your servant
and of your people Israel when they pray
toward this place. Hear from heaven, your
8:30 [h]Ps 85:2 dwelling place, and when you hear, forgive.[h]
31"When a man wrongs his neighbor and
is required to take an oath and he comes and
8:31 [i]Ex 22:11 swears the oath[i] before your altar in this temple, 32then hear from heaven and act. Judge
between your servants, condemning the
guilty and bringing down on his own head
what he has done. Declare the innocent not
8:32 [j]Dt 25:1 guilty, and so establish his innocence.[j]
8:33 33"When your people Israel have been
[k]Lev 26:17; Dt 28:25 defeated[k] by an enemy because they have
[l]Lev 26:39 sinned[l] against you, and when they turn back
to you and confess your name, praying and
making supplication to you in this temple,
34then hear from heaven and forgive the sin
of your people Israel and bring them back to
the land you gave to their fathers.
8:35 35"When the heavens are shut up and there
[m]Lev 26:19; Dt 28:24 is no rain[m] because your people have sinned
against you, and when they pray toward this
place and confess your name and turn from

An Enigma

1KI 8:22

To the contemporary reader of 1 Kings, Solomon is an enigma. On the one hand, he marries an Egyptian wife who worships pagan gods (1Ki 7:8). On the other hand, he offers praises to the Lord and prayers of dedication before the people of Israel when the temple is dedicated.

We cannot see into Solomon's heart to discover where his true loyalties are, anymore than others can see into our hearts. We may be just as much an enigma to others as Solomon is to us. We, too, can appear simultaneously devoted to the world and to the Lord. Let's prayerfully ask God to help us line up our hearts and lives so that others can clearly see that our loyalties lie only with the God and Savior we follow.

God's Desire

1KI 8:41–43

It is God's desire that the whole world might come to know him through his chosen people. His blessing is never intended for Israel alone, for he states that all the people of the earth (not just some of them) will be blessed through Abraham's descendants (Ge 12:3). In praying for foreigners, Solomon is acting in alignment with God's will and purpose.

Who are the "foreigners" in our lives? The homeless man we pass on our way to work in the morning? Our blatantly atheistic aunt? Our best friend from college who sees our religious fervor as "nutty"? How might God be calling us to bless them? How can we pray for them? How often and how passionately do we ask God to make himself known to each one?

their sin because you have afflicted them,
36 then hear from heaven and forgive the sin of
your servants, your people Israel. Teach[n] them
the right way[o] to live, and send rain on the
land you gave your people for an inheritance.
37 "When famine[p] or plague comes to the
land, or blight[q] or mildew, locusts or grasshoppers, or when an enemy besieges them in any
of their cities, whatever disaster or disease
may come, 38 and when a prayer or plea is
made by any of your people Israel—each one
aware of the afflictions of his own heart, and
spreading out his hands toward this temple—
39 then hear from heaven, your dwelling place.
Forgive and act; deal with each man according to all he does, since you know[r] his heart
(for you alone know the hearts of all men),
40 so that they will fear[s] you all the time they
live in the land you gave our fathers.
41 "As for the foreigner who does not belong
to your people Israel but has come from a distant land because of your name— 42 for men
will hear of your great name and your mighty
hand[t] and your outstretched arm—when he
comes and prays toward this temple, 43 then
hear from heaven, your dwelling place, and
do whatever the foreigner asks of you, so that
all the peoples of the earth may know[u] your
name and fear[v] you, as do your own people
Israel, and may know that this house I have
built bears your Name.
44 "When your people go to war against
their enemies, wherever you send them, and
when they pray to the LORD toward the city
you have chosen and the temple I have built
for your Name, 45 then hear from heaven their
prayer and their plea, and uphold their cause.
46 "When they sin against you—for there is
no one who does not sin[w]—and you become
angry with them and give them over to the
enemy, who takes them captive[x] to his own
land, far away or near; 47 and if they have a
change of heart in the land where they are
held captive, and repent and plead[y] with you
in the land of their conquerors and say, 'We
have sinned, we have done wrong, we have
acted wickedly';[z] 48 and if they turn back to
you with all their heart[a] and soul in the land
of their enemies who took them captive, and
pray[b] to you toward the land you gave their
fathers, toward the city you have chosen and
the temple[c] I have built for your Name; 49 then
from heaven, your dwelling place, hear their
prayer and their plea, and uphold their cause.
50 And forgive your people, who have sinned
against you; forgive all the offenses they have
committed against you, and cause their conquerors to show them mercy;[d] 51 for they are
your people and your inheritance,[e] whom
you brought out of Egypt, out of that iron-
smelting furnace.[f]

8:36 [n]1Sa 12:23; Ps 25:4; 94:12 [o]Ps 5:8; 27:11; Jer 6:16
8:37 [p]Lev 26:26 [q]Dt 28:22
8:39 [r]1Sa 16:7; 1Ch 28:9; Ps 11:4; Jer 17:10; Jn 2:24; Ac 1:24
8:40 [s]Ps 130:4
8:42 [t]Dt 3:24
8:43 [u]1Sa 17:46; 2Ki 19:19 [v]Ps 102:15
8:46 [w]Pr 20:9; Ecc 7:20; Ro 3:9; 1Jn 1:8-10 [x]Lev 26:33-39; Dt 28:64
8:47 [y]Lev 26:40; Ne 1:6 [z]Ps 106:6; Da 9:5
8:48 [a]Dt 4:29; Jer 29:12-14 [b]Da 6:10 [c]Jnh 2:4
8:50 [d]2Ch 30:9; Ps 106:46
8:51 [e]Dt 4:20; 9:29; Ne 1:10 [f]Jer 11:4

52“May your eyes be open to your servant’s plea and to the plea of your people Israel, and may you listen to them whenever they cry out to you. 53For you singled them out from all the nations of the world to be your own inheritance,[g] just as you declared through your servant Moses when you, O Sovereign LORD, brought our fathers out of Egypt.”

54When Solomon had finished all these prayers and supplications to the LORD, he rose from before the altar of the LORD, where he had been kneeling with his hands spread out toward heaven. 55He stood and blessed[h] the whole assembly of Israel in a loud voice, saying:

56“Praise be to the LORD, who has given rest[i] to his people Israel just as he promised. Not one word has failed of all the good promises[j] he gave through his servant Moses. 57May the LORD our God be with us as he was with our fathers; may he never leave us nor forsake[k] us. 58May he turn our hearts[l] to him, to walk in all his ways and to keep the commands, decrees and regulations he gave our fathers. 59And may these words of mine, which I have prayed before the LORD, be near to the LORD our God day and night, that he may uphold the cause of his servant and the cause of his people Israel according to each day’s need, 60so that all the peoples[m] of the earth may know that the LORD is God and that there is no other.[n] 61But your hearts must be fully committed[o] to the LORD our God, to live by his decrees and obey his commands, as at this time.”

The Dedication of the Temple

62Then the king and all Israel with him offered sacrifices before the LORD. 63Solomon offered a sacrifice of fellowship offerings[a] to the LORD: twenty-two thousand cattle and a hundred and twenty thousand sheep and goats. So the king and all the Israelites dedicated the temple of the LORD.

64On that same day the king consecrated the middle part of the courtyard in front of the temple of the LORD, and there he offered burnt offerings, grain offerings and the fat of the fellowship offerings, because the bronze altar[p] before the LORD was too small to hold the burnt offerings, the grain offerings and the fat of the fellowship offerings.

65So Solomon observed the festival[q] at that time, and all Israel with him—a vast assembly, people from Lebo[b] Hamath[r] to the Wadi of Egypt.[s] They celebrated it before the LORD our God for seven days and seven days more, fourteen days in all. 66On the following day he sent the people away. They blessed the king and then went home, joyful and glad in heart for all the good things the LORD had done for his servant David and his people Israel.

8:53 [g]Ex 19:5; Dt 9:26-29
8:55 [h]ver 14; 2Sa 6:18
8:56 [i]Dt 12:10 [j]Jos 21:45; 23:15
8:57 [k]Dt 31:6; Jos 1:5; Heb 13:5
8:58 [l]Ps 119:36
8:60 [m]Jos 4:24; 1Sa 17:46 [n]Dt 4:35; 1Ki 18:39; Jer 10:10-12
8:61 [o]1Ki 11:4; 15:3,14; 2Ki 20:3
8:64 [p]2Ch 4:1
8:65 [q]ver 2; Lev 23:34 [r]Nu 34:8; Jos 13:5; Jdg 3:3; 2Ki 14:25 [s]Ge 15:18

[a] 63 Traditionally *peace offerings;* also in verse 64 [b] 65 Or *from the entrance to*

God’s Will and Ours

1KI 8:58

God has given people a choice to serve him or reject him (Jos 24:15). Yet it is impossible to make the right choice if God does not first extend his grace. Since the fall of the human race in the garden, humans have been held captive by sin. Our sinful nature makes it impossible for us to come to God in our own wisdom, righteousness and strength—for we have none. Solomon’s prayer is that God will grant the people divine wisdom, righteousness and strength, so that they might see past Satan’s lies to the truth of God and enter into relationship with him.

The LORD Appears to Solomon

9 When Solomon had finished[t] building the 9:1
temple of the LORD and the royal palace, and [t]1Ki 7:1;
had achieved all he had desired to do, 2the LORD 2Ch 8:6
appeared[u] to him a second time, as he had 9:2
appeared to him at Gibeon. 3The LORD said to him: [u]1Ki 3:5

"I have heard[v] the prayer and plea you 9:3 [v]2Ki 20:5;
have made before me; I have consecrated this Ps 10:17 [w]Dt 11:12;
temple, which you have built, by putting my 1Ki 8:29
Name there forever. My eyes[w] and my heart
will always be there.

4"As for you, if you walk before me in 9:4
integrity of heart[x] and uprightness, as David[y] [x]Ge 17:1
your father did, and do all I command and [y]1Ki 15:5
observe my decrees and laws, 5I will estab- 9:5
lish[z] your royal throne over Israel forever, as [z]1Ch 22:10
I promised David your father when I said, [a]2Sa 7:15;
'You shall never fail[a] to have a man on the 1Ki 2:4
throne of Israel.' 9:6

6"But if you[a] or your sons turn away[b] from [b]2Sa 7:14
me and do not observe the commands and
decrees I have given you[a] and go off to serve
other gods and worship them, 7then I will cut 9:7
off Israel from the land[c] I have given them [c]2Ki 17:23;
and will reject this temple I have consecrated 25:21 [d]Jer 7:14
for my Name.[d] Israel will then become a [e]Ps 44:14
byword[e] and an object of ridicule[f] among all [f]Dt 28:37
peoples. 8And though this temple is now
imposing, all who pass by will be appalled
and will scoff and say, 'Why has the LORD
done such a thing to this land and to this 9:8
temple?'[g] 9People will answer, 'Because they [g]Dt 29:24;
have forsaken the LORD their God, who Jer 22:8-9
brought their fathers out of Egypt, and have
embraced other gods, worshiping and serving them—that is why the LORD brought all
this disaster on them.'"

Solomon's Other Activities

10At the end of twenty years, during which Solomon built these two buildings—the temple of the
LORD and the royal palace— 11King Solomon gave
twenty towns in Galilee to Hiram king of Tyre,
because Hiram had supplied him with all the cedar
and pine and gold[h] he wanted. 12But when Hiram 9:11
went from Tyre to see the towns that Solomon had [h]2Ch 8:2
given him, he was not pleased with them. 13"What
kind of towns are these you have given me, my
brother?" he asked. And he called them the Land 9:13
of Cabul,[b][i] a name they have to this day. 14Now [i]Jos 19:27
Hiram had sent to the king 120 talents[c] of gold.

15Here is the account of the forced labor King 9:15
Solomon conscripted[j] to build the LORD's temple, [j]Jos 16:10;
his own palace, the supporting terraces,[d][k] the wall 1Ki 5:13 [k]ver 24;
of Jerusalem, and Hazor,[l] Megiddo and Gezer.[m] 2Sa 5:9
16(Pharaoh king of Egypt had attacked and cap- [l]Jos 19:36 [m]Jos 17:11

[a] *6* The Hebrew is plural. [b] *13* *Cabul* sounds like the Hebrew for *good-for-nothing.* [c] *14* That is, about 4 1/2 tons (about 4 metric tons) [d] *15* Or *the Millo*; also in verse 24

"There is no God," the
foolish saith,
But none, "There is no sor-
row":
And nature oft the cry of faith
In bitter need will borrow.
Eyes, which the preacher could
not school,
By wayside *graves are raised;*
And lips say, "God be pitiful,"
Who ne'er said, "God be
praised.

—Elizabeth Barrett Browning (1806–1861)

tured Gezer. He had set it on fire. He killed its Canaanite inhabitants and then gave it as a wedding gift to his daughter, Solomon's wife. [17]And Solomon rebuilt Gezer.) He built up Lower Beth Horon,[n] [18]Baalath,[o] and Tadmor[a] in the desert, within his land, [19]as well as all his store cities[p] and the towns for his chariots[q] and for his horses[b]—whatever he desired to build in Jerusalem, in Lebanon and throughout all the territory he ruled.

[20]All the people left from the Amorites, Hittites, Perizzites, Hivites and Jebusites (these peoples were not Israelites), [21]that is, their descendants[r] remaining in the land, whom the Israelites could not exterminate[c][s]—these Solomon conscripted for his slave labor force,[t] as it is to this day. [22]But Solomon did not make slaves[u] of any of the Israelites; they were his fighting men, his government officials, his officers, his captains, and the commanders of his chariots and charioteers. [23]They were also the chief officials[v] in charge of Solomon's projects—550 officials supervising the men who did the work.

[24]After Pharaoh's daughter[w] had come up from the City of David to the palace Solomon had built for her, he constructed the supporting terraces.[x]

[25]Three[y] times a year Solomon sacrificed burnt offerings and fellowship offerings[d] on the altar he had built for the LORD, burning incense before the LORD along with them, and so fulfilled the temple obligations.

[26]King Solomon also built ships[z] at Ezion Geber,[a] which is near Elath in Edom, on the shore of the Red Sea.[e] [27]And Hiram sent his men—sailors[b] who knew the sea—to serve in the fleet with Solomon's men. [28]They sailed to Ophir[c] and brought back 420 talents[f] of gold, which they delivered to King Solomon.

The Queen of Sheba Visits Solomon

10 When the queen of Sheba[d] heard about the fame of Solomon and his relation to the name of the LORD, she came to test him with hard questions.[e] [2]Arriving at Jerusalem with a very great caravan—with camels carrying spices, large quantities of gold, and precious stones—she came to Solomon and talked with him about all that she had on her mind. [3]Solomon answered all her questions; nothing was too hard for the king to explain to her. [4]When the queen of Sheba saw all the wisdom of Solomon and the palace he had built, [5]the food on his table,[f] the seating of his officials, the attending servants in their robes, his cupbearers, and the burnt offerings he made at[g] the temple of the LORD, she was overwhelmed.

9:17 [n]Jos 16:3; 2Ch 8:5
9:18 [o]Jos 19:44
9:19 [p]ver 1 [q]1Ki 4:26
9:21 [r]Ge 9:25-26 [s]Jos 15:63; 17:12; Jdg 1:21,27, 29 [t]Ezr 2:55,58
9:22 [u]Lev 25:39
9:23 [v]1Ki 5:16
9:24 [w]1Ki 3:1; 7:8 [x]2Sa 5:9; 1Ki 11:27; 2Ch 32:5
9:25 [y]Ex 23:14; 2Ch 8:12-13, 16
9:26 [z]1Ki 22:48 [a]Nu 33:35; Dt 2:8
9:27 [b]1Ki 10:11; Eze 27:8
9:28 [c]1Ch 29:4
10:1 [d]Ge 10:7,28; Mt 12:42; Lk 11:31 [e]Jdg 14:12
10:5 [f]1Ch 26:16

[a] *18* The Hebrew may also be read *Tamar.* [b] *19* Or *charioteers* [c] *21* The Hebrew term refers to the irrevocable giving over of things or persons to the LORD, often by totally destroying them. [d] *25* Traditionally *peace offerings* [e] *26* Hebrew *Yam Suph*; that is, Sea of Reeds [f] *28* That is, about 16 tons (about 14.5 metric tons) [g] *5* Or *the ascent by which he went up to*

The Queen of Sheba

1KI 10:1–2

The journey from Sheba, a great trading nation in southwest Arabia, to Jerusalem is long and arduous. Jesus himself later notes that "she [the queen of Sheba] came from the ends of the earth to listen to Solomon's wisdom" (Mt 12:42). The queen has several reasons for her trip. Her curiosity is certainly a factor, for rumors of Solomon's great wealth and wisdom have spread throughout Arabia. Possibly she also wants to enter a trade agreement with Israel, for her ships and caravans and Solomon's both do commerce throughout the known world of the day.

Though the queen is impressed with the Lord of Israel (1Ki 10:9), there is no evidence that she comes to know him as her own, personal God. She probably simply accepts him as she would any other god: legitimate, geographical (that is, with power over his own area and nation, but not over others), and equal to other gods she knows and worships. *(See character sketch for the Queen of Sheba on page 1075.)*

666

1KI 10:14

There does not appear to be any significance to the number 666 as it is used here, except as a measure of Solomon's impressive yearly income. This many talents of gold—666—weighs approximately 25 tons (or 23 metric tons). The value of this much gold on today's market would probably be in the billion-dollar range. On top of this astronomical figure, Solomon collects additional funds from merchants, traders, Arabian kings and governors.

6She said to the king, "The report I heard in my
own country about your achievements and your
wisdom is true. 7But I did not believe these things
until I came and saw with my own eyes. Indeed, 10:7
not even half was told me; in wisdom and wealth[g] [g]1Ch 29:25
you have far exceeded the report I heard. 8How
happy your men must be! How happy your offi- 10:8
cials, who continually stand before you and hear[h] [h]Pr 8:34
your wisdom! 9Praise[i] be to the LORD your God, 10:9
who has delighted in you and placed you on the [i]1Ki 5:7
throne of Israel. Because of the LORD's eternal love [j]2Sa 8:15;
for Israel, he has made you king, to maintain jus- Ps 33:5; 72:2
tice[j] and righteousness."
10And she gave the king 120 talents[a] of gold,[k] 10:10
large quantities of spices, and precious stones. [k]ver 2
Never again were so many spices brought in as
those the queen of Sheba gave to King Solomon. 10:11
11(Hiram's ships brought gold from Ophir;[l] and [l]Ge 10:29;
from there they brought great cargoes of almug- 1Ki 9:27-28
wood[b] and precious stones. 12The king used the
almugwood to make supports for the temple of
the LORD and for the royal palace, and to make
harps and lyres for the musicians. So much
almugwood has never been imported or seen
since that day.)
13King Solomon gave the queen of Sheba all she
desired and asked for, besides what he had given
her out of his royal bounty. Then she left and
returned with her retinue to her own country.

Solomon's Splendor

14The weight of the gold[m] that Solomon 10:14
received yearly was 666 talents,[c] 15not including [m]1Ki 9:28
the revenues from merchants and traders and
from all the Arabian kings and the governors of
the land.
16King Solomon made two hundred large 10:16
shields[n] of hammered gold; six hundred bekas[d] of [n]1Ki 14:26-
gold went into each shield. 17He also made three 28
hundred small shields of hammered gold, with
three minas[e] of gold in each shield. The king put 10:17
them in the Palace of the Forest of Lebanon.[o] [o]1Ki 7:2
18Then the king made a great throne inlaid with
ivory and overlaid with fine gold. 19The throne had
six steps, and its back had a rounded top. On both
sides of the seat were armrests, with a lion standing beside each of them. 20Twelve lions stood on
the six steps, one at either end of each step. Nothing like it had ever been made for any other kingdom. 21All King Solomon's goblets were gold, and
all the household articles in the Palace of the Forest of Lebanon were pure gold. Nothing was made
of silver, because silver was considered of little
value in Solomon's days. 22The king had a fleet of 10:22
trading ships[f][p] at sea along with the ships of [p]1Ki 9:26

[a] *10* That is, about 4 1/2 tons (about 4 metric tons)
[b] *11* Probably a variant of *algumwood*; also in verse 12
[c] *14* That is, about 25 tons (about 23 metric tons) [d] *16* That is, about 7 1/2 pounds (about 3.5 kilograms) [e] *17* That is, about 3 3/4 pounds (about 1.7 kilograms) [f] *22* Hebrew of *ships of Tarshish*

Hiram. Once every three years it returned, carrying
10:23 gold, silver and ivory, and apes and baboons.
q1Ki 3:13 23King Solomon was greater in riches[q] and wis-
r1Ki 4:30 dom[r] than all the other kings of the earth. 24The
whole world sought audience with Solomon to
10:24 hear the wisdom[s] God had put in his heart. 25Year
s1Ki 3:9,12, 28 after year, everyone who came brought a gift—
articles of silver and gold, robes, weapons and
spices, and horses and mules.
10:26 26Solomon accumulated chariots and horses;[t] he
tDt 17:16; had fourteen hundred chariots and twelve thou-
1Ki 4:26; 9:19; sand horses,[a] which he kept in the chariot cities
2Ch 1:14; and also with him in Jerusalem. 27The king made
9:25 silver as common[u] in Jerusalem as stones, and
10:27 cedar as plentiful as sycamore-fig trees in the
uDt 17:17 foothills. 28Solomon's horses were imported from
10:29 Egypt[b] and from Kue[c]—the royal merchants pur-
v2Ki 7:6-7 chased them from Kue. 29They imported a chariot
from Egypt for six hundred shekels[d] of silver, and
a horse for a hundred and fifty.[e] They also exported them to all the kings of the Hittites[v] and of the
Arameans.

Solomon's Wives

11 King Solomon, however, loved many for-
11:1 eign women[w] besides Pharaoh's daughter—
wDt 17:17; Ne 13:26 Moabites, Ammonites, Edomites, Sidonians and
Hittites. 2They were from nations about which the
11:2 LORD had told the Israelites, "You must not inter-
xEx 34:16; marry[x] with them, because they will surely turn
Dt 7:3-4 your hearts after their gods." Nevertheless, Solomon held fast to them in love. 3He had seven
hundred wives of royal birth and three hundred
concubines, and his wives led him astray. 4As Sol-
11:4 omon grew old, his wives turned his heart after
y1Ki 8:61; other gods, and his heart was not fully devoted[y] to
9:4 the LORD his God, as the heart of David his father
11:5 had been. 5He followed Ashtoreth[z] the goddess of
zver 33; the Sidonians, and Molech[f][a] the detestable god of
Jdg 2:13; 2Ki 23:13 the Ammonites. 6So Solomon did evil in the eyes
aver 7 of the LORD; he did not follow the LORD completely, as David his father had done.
11:7 7On a hill east[b] of Jerusalem, Solomon built a
b2Ki 23:13 high place for Chemosh[c] the detestable god of
cNu 21:29; Jdg 11:24 Moab, and for Molech[d] the detestable god of the
dLev 20:2-5; Ac 7:43 Ammonites. 8He did the same for all his foreign
wives, who burned incense and offered sacrifices
to their gods.
9The LORD became angry with Solomon because
11:9 his heart had turned away from the LORD, the God
ever 2-3; of Israel, who had appeared[e] to him twice.
1Ki 3:5; 9:2 10Although he had forbidden Solomon to follow
11:10 other gods,[f] Solomon did not keep the LORD's com-
f1Ki 9:6 mand.[g] 11So the LORD said to Solomon, "Since this
g1Ki 6:12 is your attitude and you have not kept my covenant and my decrees, which I commanded you,

[a] 26 Or *charioteers* [b] 28 Or possibly *Muzur*, a region in Cilicia; also in verse 29 [c] 28 Probably *Cilicia* [d] 29 That is, about 15 pounds (about 7 kilograms) [e] 29 That is, about 3 3/4 pounds (about 1.7 kilograms) [f] 5 Hebrew *Milcom*; also in verse 33

Solomon's Foreign Wives

1KI 11:1-6

In addition to granting Solomon the wisdom he asked for, God promised—and delivered—abundant wealth and fame (1Ki 3:10–14). Yet despite all that he receives from the Lord, Solomon insists on taking many wives (many, *many* wives—1Ki 11:3), a practice forbidden by God (Dt 17:17). Even worse, many of Solomon's wives are foreigners, married to form political alliances. They worship pagan gods. The Lord knew what the result of such unions would be and had commanded that the Israelites not intermarry with foreigners (Ex 34:16). Solomon, however, apparently believes he is above the law. Just as Joshua predicted (Jos 23:12–13), close association with these pagan worshipers leads to disaster.

Though he is known worldwide for his wisdom, Solomon fails to take his own good advice. Perhaps he is blinded by love. Perhaps in matters of worship he finds it easier to stray than to stay. In any case, his foolish behavior leads to the loss of the Lord's favor.

One Tribe

1KI 11:9–13

The Lord reveals to Solomon that his lack of commitment to the one true God will cost his son the kingdom. Only one full tribe of Israel will remain under the authority of his son, Rehoboam. The entire tribe of Judah stays faithful to Rehoboam after Solomon's death, as does most of the tribe of Benjamin. The remaining northern tribes follow Jeroboam, one of Solomon's overseers, fulfilling God's decree that he would give Solomon's kingdom to one of his "subordinates" (1Ki 11:11).

How sad to watch Solomon—someone with so much promise, so much of God's heart available to him—be lured away. His story is a clear call to us today to be sure that nothing, and no one, comes between us and our worship and obedience.

I will most certainly tear[h] the kingdom away from you and give it to one of your subordinates. 12Nevertheless, for the sake of David your father, I will not do it during your lifetime. I will tear it out of the hand of your son. 13Yet I will not tear the whole kingdom from him, but will give him one tribe[i] for the sake[j] of David my servant and for the sake of Jerusalem, which I have chosen."[k]

Solomon's Adversaries

14Then the LORD raised up against Solomon an adversary, Hadad the Edomite, from the royal line of Edom. 15Earlier when David was fighting with Edom, Joab the commander of the army, who had gone up to bury the dead, had struck down all the men in Edom.[l] 16Joab and all the Israelites stayed there for six months, until they had destroyed all the men in Edom. 17But Hadad, still only a boy, fled to Egypt with some Edomite officials who had served his father. 18They set out from Midian and went to Paran.[m] Then taking men from Paran with them, they went to Egypt, to Pharaoh king of Egypt, who gave Hadad a house and land and provided him with food.

19Pharaoh was so pleased with Hadad that he gave him a sister of his own wife, Queen Tahpenes, in marriage. 20The sister of Tahpenes bore him a son named Genubath, whom Tahpenes brought up in the royal palace. There Genubath lived with Pharaoh's own children.

21While he was in Egypt, Hadad heard that David rested with his fathers and that Joab the commander of the army was also dead. Then Hadad said to Pharaoh, "Let me go, that I may return to my own country."

22"What have you lacked here that you want to go back to your own country?" Pharaoh asked.

"Nothing," Hadad replied, "but do let me go!"

23And God raised up against Solomon another adversary,[n] Rezon son of Eliada, who had fled from his master, Hadadezer[o] king of Zobah. 24He gathered men around him and became the leader of a band of rebels when David destroyed the forces[a] ⌞of Zobah⌟; the rebels went to Damascus,[p] where they settled and took control. 25Rezon was Israel's adversary as long as Solomon lived, adding to the trouble caused by Hadad. So Rezon ruled in Aram[q] and was hostile toward Israel.

Jeroboam Rebels Against Solomon

26Also, Jeroboam son of Nebat rebelled[r] against the king. He was one of Solomon's officials, an Ephraimite from Zeredah, and his mother was a widow named Zeruah.

27Here is the account of how he rebelled against the king: Solomon had built the supporting terraces[b][s] and had filled in the gap in the wall of the city of David his father. 28Now Jeroboam was a man of standing,[t] and when Solomon saw how well[u] the

11:11 [h]ver 31; 1Ki 12:15-16; 2Ki 17:21
11:13 [i]1Ki 12:20 [j]2Sa 7:15 [k]Dt 12:11
11:15 [l]Dt 20:13; 2Sa 8:14; 1Ch 18:12
11:18 [m]Nu 10:12
11:23 [n]ver 14 [o]2Sa 8:3
11:24 [p]2Sa 8:5; 10:8,18
11:25 [q]2Sa 10:19
11:26 [r]2Sa 20:21; 1Ki 12:2; 2Ch 13:6
11:27 [s]1Ki 9:24
11:28 [t]Ru 2:1 [u]Pr 22:29

[a] 24 Hebrew *destroyed them* [b] 27 Or *the Millo*

young man did his work, he put him in charge of
the whole labor force of the house of Joseph.
[29]About that time Jeroboam was going out of Je-
11:29 [v]1Ki 12:15; rusalem, and Ahijah[v] the prophet of Shiloh met
14:2; him on the way, wearing a new cloak. The two of
2Ch 9:29 them were alone out in the country, [30]and Ahijah
11:30 took hold of the new cloak he was wearing and
[w]1Sa 15:27 tore[w] it into twelve pieces. [31]Then he said to Jeroboam, "Take ten pieces for yourself, for this is
what the LORD, the God of Israel, says: 'See, I am
11:31 [x]ver 11 going to tear[x] the kingdom out of Solomon's hand
and give you ten tribes. [32]But for the sake of my
servant David and the city of Jerusalem, which I
have chosen out of all the tribes of Israel, he will
11:33 [y]ver 5-7 have one tribe. [33]I will do this because they have[a]
[z]1Ki 3:3 forsaken me and worshiped[y] Ashtoreth the goddess of the Sidonians, Chemosh the god of the
Moabites, and Molech the god of the Ammonites,
and have not walked in my ways, nor done what
is right in my eyes, nor kept my statutes[z] and laws
as David, Solomon's father, did.
[34]" 'But I will not take the whole kingdom out
of Solomon's hand; I have made him ruler all the
days of his life for the sake of David my servant,
whom I chose and who observed my commands
and statutes. [35]I will take the kingdom from his
11:36 son's hands and give you ten tribes. [36]I will give
[a]ver 13; one tribe[a] to his son so that David my servant may
1Ki 12:17 [b]1Ki 15:4; always have a lamp[b] before me in Jerusalem, the
2Ki 8:19 city where I chose to put my Name. [37]However, as
11:37 for you, I will take you, and you will rule over all
[c]2Sa 3:21 that your heart desires;[c] you will be king over
Israel. [38]If you do whatever I command you and
11:38 walk in my ways and do what is right in my eyes
[d]Dt 17:19 by keeping my statutes[d] and commands, as David
[e]Jos 1:5; my servant did, I will be with you. I will build you
2Sa 7:11,27 a dynasty[e] as enduring as the one I built for David
and will give Israel to you. [39]I will humble David's
descendants because of this, but not forever.' "
[40]Solomon tried to kill Jeroboam, but Jeroboam
11:40 [f]2Ch 12:2 fled to Egypt, to Shishak[f] the king, and stayed
there until Solomon's death.

Solomon's Death

[41]As for the other events of Solomon's reign—all
he did and the wisdom he displayed—are they not
written in the book of the annals of Solomon?
[42]Solomon reigned in Jerusalem over all Israel
forty years. [43]Then he rested with his fathers and
11:43 was buried in the city of David his father. And
[g]1Ki 14:21; Mt 1:7 Rehoboam[g] his son succeeded him as king.

Israel Rebels Against Rehoboam

12 Rehoboam went to Shechem, for all the
Israelites had gone there to make him king.
12:2 [2]When Jeroboam son of Nebat heard this (he was
[h]1Ki 11:40 still in Egypt, where he had fled[h] from King Solomon), he returned from[b] Egypt. [3]So they sent for

[a] 33 Hebrew; Septuagint, Vulgate and Syriac *because he has*
[b] 2 Or *he remained in*

Ten Tribes

1KI 11:35,38–39

The Lord promises to give Jeroboam ten tribes (1Ki 11:35) and to allow Solomon's son Rehoboam to keep only one (1Ki 11:36). That leaves a twelfth tribe unaccounted for. This may have been the tribe of Levi, since the Levites live interspersed throughout the land and have no specific allotment of land that might be claimed by Jeroboam. Or it may have been the tribe of Simeon, which has essentially been absorbed into Judah's territory. A third possibility is that the twelfth tribe is Benjamin, since some of the Benjamites serve Israel and some remain faithful to Judah—making it difficult for them to be claimed by either party.

Through Ahijah (1Ki 11:29), God assures Jeroboam that he will give him ten tribes to rule over, a dynasty comparable to David's. Yet all this will be his only if he obeys the Lord's commands, walks in the Lord's ways and does what is right in the Lord's eyes. As is usual in Israelite history, blessing is tied to obedience.

Spoiled Rich Kids

1KI 12:1-11

Though Rehoboam is 41 years old when he becomes king, it seems that he is still associating with his childhood friends, for it is their counsel he seeks—and follows—in regard to the Israelites' pleas. The elders who served his father, Solomon, give him sound advice, yet Rehoboam turns instead to men who are far younger and less experienced to guide him.

As part of the royal inner circle, these "young men" (1Ki 12:8) know little—and apparently care even less—about the heavy burden carried by the people. Spoiled and rich, they demonstrate no concept of what real life is like and no mercy to those less fortunate than themselves.

We can be like Rehoboam and his young friends—or not—when we face those who earn less than we do, those whose plight causes them to to depend on governmental aid, or even those whose own foolishness has caused their predicament. We can respond as Rehoboam and his young counselors did, with little mercy and kindness, or we can respond with a godly heart of compassion (Dt 15:7; Pr 19:7).

Jeroboam, and he and the whole assembly of Israel went to Rehoboam and said to him: 4"Your
father put a heavy yoke[i] on us, but now lighten
the harsh labor and the heavy yoke he put on us,
and we will serve you."
5Rehoboam answered, "Go away for three days
and then come back to me." So the people went
away.
6Then King Rehoboam consulted the elders[j]
who had served his father Solomon during his
lifetime. "How would you advise me to answer
these people?" he asked.
7They replied, "If today you will be a servant to
these people and serve them and give them a favorable answer,[k] they will always be your servants."
8But Rehoboam rejected the advice the elders
gave him and consulted the young men who had
grown up with him and were serving him. 9He
asked them, "What is your advice? How should
we answer these people who say to me, 'Lighten
the yoke your father put on us'?"
10The young men who had grown up with him
replied, "Tell these people who have said to you,
'Your father put a heavy yoke on us, but make our
yoke lighter'—tell them, 'My little finger is thicker than my father's waist. 11My father laid on you
a heavy yoke; I will make it even heavier. My
father scourged you with whips; I will scourge
you with scorpions.' "
12Three days later Jeroboam and all the people
returned to Rehoboam, as the king had said,
"Come back to me in three days." 13The king
answered the people harshly. Rejecting the advice
given him by the elders, 14he followed the advice
of the young men and said, "My father made your
yoke heavy; I will make it even heavier. My father
scourged[l] you with whips; I will scourge you with
scorpions." 15So the king did not listen to the people, for this turn of events was from the LORD,[m] to
fulfill the word the LORD had spoken to Jeroboam
son of Nebat through Ahijah[n] the Shilonite.
16When all Israel saw that the king refused to
listen to them, they answered the king:

> "What share do we have in David,
> what part in Jesse's son?
> To your tents, O Israel![o]
> Look after your own house, O David!"

So the Israelites went home. 17But as for the Israelites who were living in the towns of Judah,[p]
Rehoboam still ruled over them.
18King Rehoboam sent out Adoniram,[a][q] who
was in charge of forced labor, but all Israel stoned
him to death. King Rehoboam, however, managed
to get into his chariot and escape to Jerusalem.
19So Israel has been in rebellion against the house
of David[r] to this day.
20When all the Israelites heard that Jeroboam

12:4 [i]1Sa 8:11-18; 1Ki 4:20-28
12:6 [j]1Ki 4:2
12:7 [k]Pr 15:1
12:14 [l]Ex 1:14; 5:5-9,16-18
12:15 [m]ver 24; Dt 2:30; Jdg 14:4; 2Ch 22:7; 25:20 [n]1Ki 11:29
12:16 [o]2Sa 20:1
12:17 [p]1Ki 11:13, 36
12:18 [q]2Sa 20:24; 1Ki 4:6; 5:14
12:19 [r]2Ki 17:21

[a] *18* Some Septuagint manuscripts and Syriac (see also 1 Kings 4:6 and 5:14); Hebrew *Adoram*

had returned, they sent and called him to the
assembly and made him king over all Israel. Only
the tribe of Judah remained loyal to the house of
12:20 [s]1Ki 11:13, 32 David.[s]
21When Rehoboam arrived in Jerusalem, he
mustered the whole house of Judah and the tribe
12:21 [t]2Ch 11:1 of Benjamin—a hundred and eighty thousand
fighting men—to make war[t] against the house of
Israel and to regain the kingdom for Rehoboam
son of Solomon.
12:22 [u]2Ch 12:5-7 22But this word of God came to Shemaiah[u] the
man of God: 23"Say to Rehoboam son of Solomon
king of Judah, to the whole house of Judah and
Benjamin, and to the rest of the people, 24'This is
what the LORD says: Do not go up to fight against
your brothers, the Israelites. Go home, every one
of you, for this is my doing.' " So they obeyed the
word of the LORD and went home again, as the
LORD had ordered.

Golden Calves at Bethel and Dan

12:25 [v]Jdg 9:45 [w]Jdg 8:8,17 25Then Jeroboam fortified Shechem[v] in the hill
country of Ephraim and lived there. From there
he went out and built up Peniel.[a][w]
26Jeroboam thought to himself, "The kingdom
will now likely revert to the house of David. 27If
12:27 [x]Dt 12:5-6 these people go up to offer sacrifices at the temple
of the LORD in Jerusalem,[x] they will again give their
allegiance to their lord, Rehoboam king of Judah.
They will kill me and return to King Rehoboam."
12:28 [y]Ex 32:4; 2Ki 10:29; 17:16 [z]Ex 32:8 28After seeking advice, the king made two gold-
en calves.[y] He said to the people, "It is too much
for you to go up to Jerusalem. Here are your gods,
O Israel, who brought you up out of Egypt."[z]
12:29 [a]Ge 28:19 [b]Jdg 18:27-31 29One he set up in Bethel,[a] and the other in Dan.[b]
30And this thing became a sin;[c] the people went
even as far as Dan to worship the one there.
31Jeroboam built shrines[d] on high places and
12:30 [c]1Ki 13:34; 2Ki 17:21 appointed priests[e] from all sorts of people, even
though they were not Levites. 32He instituted a fes-
tival on the fifteenth day of the eighth[f] month, like
12:31 [d]1Ki 13:32 [e]Nu 3:10; 1Ki 13:33; 2Ki 17:32; 2Ch 11:14-15; 13:9 the festival held in Judah, and offered sacrifices
on the altar. This he did in Bethel, sacrificing to
the calves he had made. And at Bethel he also
installed priests at the high places he had made.
33On the fifteenth day of the eighth month, a
12:32 [f]Lev 23:33-34; Nu 29:12 month of his own choosing, he offered sacrifices
on the altar he had built at Bethel.[g] So he institut-
ed the festival for the Israelites and went up to the
12:33 [g]Nu 15:39; 1Ki 13:1; Am 7:13 altar to make offerings.

The Man of God From Judah

13:1 [h]2Ki 23:17 [i]1Ki 12:32-33 **13** By the word of the LORD a man of God[h]
came from Judah to Bethel,[i] as Jeroboam
was standing by the altar to make an offering. 2He
cried out against the altar by the word of the LORD:
13:2 [j]2Ki 23:15-16,20 "O altar, altar! This is what the LORD says: 'A son
named Josiah[j] will be born to the house of David.
On you he will sacrifice the priests of the high

[a] 25 Hebrew *Penuel*, a variant of *Peniel*

A Message From God

1KI 12:24

With the entire house of Judah and a portion of Benjamin armed and ready, Rehoboam fully intends to go to battle against Israel. Yet with one word from Shemaiah, he is willing to scrap all his plans. In this sense, at least, the king demonstrates some wisdom. Rehoboam is not alone in his esteem of prophetic words. Without the revelation of written Scripture to guide them, the Israelites and their leaders only have the Lord's prophets to reveal to them God's will. When such messages come, they are not taken lightly, for the words of the prophets are words from the Lord himself. Only the messages of those prophets who are not from God—whose past prophecies did not come true or led the people away from the one true God—can be safely ignored (Dt 13:1-3; 18:21,22).

What softens my response to what in my human understanding could seem autocratic of God is to remember the nature of God. The nature of God is love. For a rich reminder of this attribute of his, just look up all the verses on his love for you in a Bible concordance. It will soften your resistance and inspire a reciprocal love for him. His love is simply too great and too all-encompassing to step around.

Based on that love platform is the realization that I am not incidental in the grand scheme of things. In Ephesians 1:4, the apostle Paul tells us, "For he chose us in him before the creation of the world" . . . I am not an afterthought. All God's love-inspired preplanning for each of us is not haphazard or impersonal. His timing may throw me or his sovereign plan may grieve me, but I am always sheltered in his sovereign hand. Can I rest in that . . . can I quit resisting that? Not always, but that's my humanness interfering with my acceptance of his divineness.

—Marilyn Meberg

places who now make offerings here, and human
bones will be burned on you.' " 3That same day
the man of God gave a sign:[k] "This is the sign the
LORD has declared: The altar will be split apart and
the ashes on it will be poured out."
4When King Jeroboam heard what the man of
God cried out against the altar at Bethel, he
stretched out his hand from the altar and said,
"Seize him!" But the hand he stretched out toward
the man shriveled up, so that he could not pull it
back. 5Also, the altar was split apart and its ashes
poured out according to the sign given by the man
of God by the word of the LORD.
6Then the king said to the man of God, "Intercede[l] with the LORD your God and pray for me that
my hand may be restored." So the man of God
interceded with the LORD, and the king's hand was
restored and became as it was before.
7The king said to the man of God, "Come home
with me and have something to eat, and I will
give you a gift."[m]
8But the man of God answered the king, "Even
if you were to give me half your possessions,[n] I
would not go with you, nor would I eat bread[o] or
drink water here. 9For I was commanded by the
word of the LORD: 'You must not eat bread or
drink water or return by the way you came.' " 10So
he took another road and did not return by the
way he had come to Bethel.
11Now there was a certain old prophet living in
Bethel, whose sons came and told him all that the
man of God had done there that day. They also
told their father what he had said to the king.
12Their father asked them, "Which way did he
go?" And his sons showed him which road the
man of God from Judah had taken. 13So he said to
his sons, "Saddle the donkey for me." And when
they had saddled the donkey for him, he mounted it 14and rode after the man of God. He found
him sitting under an oak tree and asked, "Are you
the man of God who came from Judah?"
"I am," he replied.
15So the prophet said to him, "Come home with
me and eat."
16The man of God said, "I cannot turn back and
go with you, nor can I eat bread[p] or drink water
with you in this place. 17I have been told by the
word of the LORD: 'You must not eat bread or drink
water there or return by the way you came.' "
18The old prophet answered, "I too am a prophet, as you are. And an angel said to me by the word
of the LORD: 'Bring him back with you to your
house so that he may eat bread and drink water.' "
(But he was lying[q] to him.) 19So the man of God
returned with him and ate and drank in his house.
20While they were sitting at the table, the word
of the LORD came to the old prophet who had
brought him back. 21He cried out to the man of
God who had come from Judah, "This is what the
LORD says: 'You have defied[r] the word of the LORD
and have not kept the command the LORD your

13:3 [k]Jdg 6:17; Isa 7:14; Jn 2:11; 1Co 1:22

13:6 [l]Ex 8:8; 9:28; 10:17; Lk 6:27-28; Ac 8:24; Jas 5:16

13:7 [m]1Sa 9:7; 2Ki 5:15

13:8 [n]Nu 22:18; 24:13 [o]ver 16

13:16 [p]ver 8

13:18 [q]Dt 13:3

13:21 [r]ver 26

God gave you. 22 You came back and ate bread and
drank water in the place where he told you not to
eat or drink. Therefore your body will not be
buried in the tomb of your fathers.' "
23 When the man of God had finished eating and
drinking, the prophet who had brought him back
13:24 saddled his donkey for him. 24 As he went on his
[s]1Ki 20:36 way, a lion[s] met him on the road and killed him,
and his body was thrown down on the road, with
both the donkey and the lion standing beside it.
25 Some people who passed by saw the body
thrown down there, with the lion standing beside
the body, and they went and reported it in the city
where the old prophet lived.
26 When the prophet who had brought him back
from his journey heard of it, he said, "It is the
man of God who defied the word of the LORD. The
LORD has given him over to the lion, which has
mauled him and killed him, as the word of the
LORD had warned him."
27 The prophet said to his sons, "Saddle the donkey for me," and they did so. 28 Then he went out
and found the body thrown down on the road, with
the donkey and the lion standing beside it. The lion
had neither eaten the body nor mauled the donkey.
29 So the prophet picked up the body of the man of
God, laid it on the donkey, and brought it back to
his own city to mourn for him and bury him.
30 Then he laid the body in his own tomb, and they
13:30 mourned over him and said, "Oh, my brother!"[t]
[t]Jer 22:18 31 After burying him, he said to his sons, "When
I die, bury me in the grave where the man of God
13:31 is buried; lay my bones[u] beside his bones. 32 For
[u]2Ki 23:18 the message he declared by the word of the LORD
13:32 against the altar in Bethel and against all the
[v]ver 2; shrines on the high places[v] in the towns of
Lev 26:30 Samaria[w] will certainly come true."[x]
[w]1Ki 16:24, 28 33 Even after this, Jeroboam did not change his
[x]2Ki 23:16 evil ways, but once more appointed priests for the
13:33 high places from all sorts[y] of people. Anyone who
[y]1Ki 12:31; wanted to become a priest he consecrated for the
2Ch 11:15; high places. 34 This was the sin[z] of the house of
13:9 Jeroboam that led to its downfall and to its
13:34 destruction[a] from the face of the earth.
[z]1Ki 12:30
[a]1Ki 14:10

Ahijah's Prophecy Against Jeroboam

14 At that time Abijah son of Jeroboam
became ill, 2 and Jeroboam said to his wife,
"Go, disguise yourself, so you won't be recog-
14:2 nized as the wife of Jeroboam. Then go to Shiloh.
[b]1Sa 28:8; Ahijah[b] the prophet is there—the one who told
2Sa 14:2; 1Ki 11:29 me I would be king over this people. 3 Take ten
loaves of bread[c] with you, some cakes and a jar
14:3 of honey, and go to him. He will tell you what will
[c]1Sa 9:7 happen to the boy." 4 So Jeroboam's wife did what
he said and went to Ahijah's house in Shiloh.
Now Ahijah could not see; his sight was gone
because of his age. 5 But the LORD had told Ahijah,
"Jeroboam's wife is coming to ask you about her
son, for he is ill, and you are to give her such and

Jeroboam's Sin

1KI 13:33–34

When God revealed to Jeroboam that he would make him king of Israel, he explained clearly that Solomon's idol worship was the cause of the change in leadership (1Ki 11:33). Jeroboam was warned that he must behave differently—he must obey God's commands and walk uprightly—if he is to remain in God's favor.

Yet after he becomes king, Jeroboam supports, and even goes so far as to initiate, idol worship among his people. Even after being warned by the prophet from Judah, Jeroboam continues to appoint priests at the pagan high places "from all sorts of people" (1Ki 13:33), a clear violation of God's command that only Levites serve in the priesthood.

In the historical narrative of 2 Kings, the chorus becomes: "He did evil in the eyes of the LORD and did not turn away from any of the sins of Jeroboam son of Nebat, which he had caused Israel to commit" (2Ki 13:11; see also 2Ki 10:29,31; 13:6; 14:24; 15:9, etc.). Instead of a legacy of justice and blessing, Jeroboam's legacy, recalled over and over again, is one of deliberate waywardness (see the note on 2Ki 15:9, page 599).

Bad News

1KI 14:12-18

Jeroboam wants to know what the prophet Ahijah can tell him about his son's illness, but he is reluctant to go to see the prophet himself. Perhaps an awareness of his own guilt makes him embarrassed to face the prophet. Perhaps he thinks the prophecy will be impacted negatively if Ahijah knows whose family it concerns. In either case, he sends his wife to do his dirty work, telling her to disguise herself.

She obeys. But their trick is to no avail. Ahijah knows who she is and who her husband is. She receives from the prophet what is undoubtedly the most devastating news a mother can hear: Her son will die.

Note, however, that his death is a matter of honor, for this son "is the only one in the house of Jeroboam in whom the LORD . . . has found anything good" (1Ki 14:13). He will, therefore, be honored with a decent burial and a period of mourning by the people, something no one else in Jeroboam's family receives (1Ki 15:28–30).

such an answer. When she arrives, she will pretend to be someone else."
6So when Ahijah heard the sound of her footsteps at the door, he said, "Come in, wife of Jeroboam. Why this pretense? I have been sent to you
with bad news. 7Go, tell Jeroboam that this is
what the LORD, the God of Israel, says: 'I raised
you up from among the people and made you a
leader[d] over my people Israel. 8I tore[e] the kingdom
away from the house of David and gave it to you,
but you have not been like my servant David, who
kept my commands and followed me with all his
heart, doing only what was right[f] in my eyes. 9You
have done more evil than all who lived before
you. You have made for yourself other gods, idols[g]
made of metal; you have provoked me to anger
and thrust me behind your back.[h]
10" 'Because of this, I am going to bring disaster
on the house of Jeroboam. I will cut off from Jeroboam every last male in Israel—slave or free.[i] I
will burn up the house of Jeroboam as one burns
dung, until it is all gone.[j] 11Dogs[k] will eat those
belonging to Jeroboam who die in the city, and
the birds of the air will feed on those who die in
the country. The LORD has spoken!'
12"As for you, go back home. When you set foot
in your city, the boy will die. 13All Israel will
mourn for him and bury him. He is the only one
belonging to Jeroboam who will be buried,
because he is the only one in the house of Jeroboam in whom the LORD, the God of Israel, has
found anything good.[l]
14"The LORD will raise up for himself a king over
Israel who will cut off the family of Jeroboam.
This is the day! What? Yes, even now.[a] 15And the
LORD will strike Israel, so that it will be like a reed
swaying in the water. He will uproot[m] Israel from
this good land that he gave to their forefathers and
scatter them beyond the River,[b] because they provoked[n] the LORD to anger by making Asherah[o]
poles.[c] 16And he will give Israel up because of the
sins[p] Jeroboam has committed and has caused
Israel to commit."
17Then Jeroboam's wife got up and left and went
to Tirzah.[q] As soon as she stepped over the threshold of the house, the boy died. 18They buried him,
and all Israel mourned for him, as the LORD had
said through his servant the prophet Ahijah.
19The other events of Jeroboam's reign, his wars
and how he ruled, are written in the book of the
annals of the kings of Israel. 20He reigned for
twenty-two years and then rested with his fathers.
And Nadab his son succeeded him as king.

Rehoboam King of Judah

21Rehoboam son of Solomon was king in Judah.
He was forty-one years old when he became king,

14:7 [d]2Sa 12:7-8; 1Ki 16:2
14:8 [e]1Ki 11:31, 33,38 [f]1Ki 15:5
14:9 [g]Ex 34:17; 1Ki 12:28; 2Ch 11:15 [h]Ne 9:26; Ps 50:17; Eze 23:35
14:10 [i]Dt 32:36; 1Ki 21:21; 2Ki 9:8-9; 14:26 [j]1Ki 15:29
14:11 [k]1Ki 16:4; 21:24
14:13 [l]2Ch 12:12; 19:3
14:15 [m]Dt 29:28; 2Ki 15:29; 17:6; Ps 52:5 [n]Jos 23:15-16 [o]Ex 34:13; Dt 12:3
14:16 [p]1Ki 12:30; 13:34; 15:30, 34; 16:2
14:17 [q]ver 12; 1Ki 15:33; 16:6-9

[a] *14* The meaning of the Hebrew for this sentence is uncertain.
[b] *15* That is, the Euphrates [c] *15* That is, symbols of the goddess Asherah; here and elsewhere in 1 Kings

and he reigned seventeen years in Jerusalem, the
city the LORD had chosen out of all the tribes of
Israel in which to put his Name. His mother's
name was Naamah; she was an Ammonite.[r]
22 Judah[s] did evil in the eyes of the LORD. By the
sins they committed they stirred up his jealous
anger[t] more than their fathers had done. 23 They
also set up for themselves high places, sacred
stones[u] and Asherah poles on every high hill and
under every spreading tree.[v] 24 There were even
male shrine prostitutes[w] in the land; the people
engaged in all the detestable practices of the
nations the LORD had driven out before the Israelites.
25 In the fifth year of King Rehoboam, Shishak
king of Egypt attacked[x] Jerusalem. 26 He carried off
the treasures of the temple[y] of the LORD and the
treasures of the royal palace. He took everything,
including all the gold shields[z] Solomon had made.
27 So King Rehoboam made bronze shields to
replace them and assigned these to the commanders of the guard on duty at the entrance to the royal palace. 28 Whenever the king went to the LORD's
temple, the guards bore the shields, and afterward
they returned them to the guardroom.
29 As for the other events of Rehoboam's reign,
and all he did, are they not written in the book of
the annals of the kings of Judah? 30 There was continual warfare[a] between Rehoboam and Jeroboam. 31 And Rehoboam rested with his fathers and
was buried with them in the City of David. His
mother's name was Naamah; she was an Ammonite.[b] And Abijah[a] his son succeeded him as king.

Abijah King of Judah

15 In the eighteenth year of the reign of Jeroboam son of Nebat, Abijah[b] became king of
Judah, 2 and he reigned in Jerusalem three years.
His mother's name was Maacah[c] daughter of
Abishalom.[c]
3 He committed all the sins his father had done
before him; his heart was not fully devoted[d] to the
LORD his God, as the heart of David his forefather
had been. 4 Nevertheless, for David's sake the LORD
his God gave him a lamp[e] in Jerusalem by raising
up a son to succeed him and by making Jerusalem strong. 5 For David had done what was right
in the eyes of the LORD and had not failed to keep[f]
any of the LORD's commands all the days of his
life—except in the case of Uriah[g] the Hittite.
6 There was war[h] between Rehoboam[d] and Jeroboam throughout ⌞Abijah's⌟ lifetime. 7 As for the
other events of Abijah's reign, and all he did, are
they not written in the book of the annals of the

14:21 [r]ver 31; 1Ki 11:1; 2Ch 12:13
14:22 [s]2Ch 12:1 [t]Dt 32:21; Ps 78:58; 1Co 10:22
14:23 [u]Dt 16:22; 2Ki 17:9-10; Eze 16:24-25 [v]Dt 12:2; Isa 57:5
14:24 [w]Dt 23:17; 1Ki 15:12; 2Ki 23:7
14:25 [x]1Ki 11:40; 2Ch 12:2
14:26 [y]1Ki 15:15, 18 [z]1Ki 10:17
14:30 [a]1Ki 12:21; 15:6
14:31 [b]ver 21; 2Ch 12:16
15:2 [c]2Ch 11:20; 13:2
15:3 [d]1Ki 11:4; Ps 119:80
15:4 [e]2Sa 21:17; 1Ki 11:36; 2Ch 21:7
15:5 [f]1Ki 9:4; 14:8 [g]2Sa 11:2-27; 12:9
15:6 [h]1Ki 14:30

[a] *31* Some Hebrew manuscripts and Septuagint (see also 2 Chron. 12:16); most Hebrew manuscripts *Abijam*
[b] *1* Some Hebrew manuscripts and Septuagint (see also 2 Chron. 12:16); most Hebrew manuscripts *Abijam*; also in verses 7 and 8 [c] *2* A variant of *Absalom*; also in verse 10
[d] *6* Most Hebrew manuscripts; some Hebrew manuscripts and Syriac *Abijam* (that is, Abijah)

High Places

1KI 14:23

Places that are high in elevation have long been perceived as being above the ordinary. Even today, key moments in life are referred to as "mountain-top experiences." In ancient times, worshipers often went to the top of a hill or mountain to separate themselves from their daily routines and draw closer to their pagan gods, many of whom they believed lived in the sky. Places of worship, which came to be known as "high places," were eventually established on many of the hills and mounts of Israel. Worship at such locations was expressly forbidden to the people of God (Lev 26:30; Nu 33:52).

Constant War

1KI 15:16–17

Since the division of Israel, war between Judah and the northern tribes has been the norm. The two parties are not always engaged in active combat; however, the hostility between them is long-standing and chronic, having begun during the reigns of Rehoboam and Jeroboam (1Ki 15:6). The animosity continues throughout the reigns of King Baasha of Israel and King Abijah of Judah.

When Asa comes to power in Judah, he initiates numerous religious reforms, committing himself to the worship of the one true God. However, he, too, battles against Baasha, who has now fortified Ramah, a city of Benjamin on the border between Judah and Israel. Baasha's move has a double intent: to block the trade route to Jerusalem and to block the road to keep people of the northern kingdom from traveling to Jerusalem to worship.

kings of Judah? There was war between Abijah
and Jeroboam. 8And Abijah rested with his fathers
and was buried in the City of David. And Asa his
son succeeded him as king.

Asa King of Judah

9In the twentieth year of Jeroboam king of Israel, Asa became king of Judah, 10and he reigned in
Jerusalem forty-one years. His grandmother's
name was Maacah[i] daughter of Abishalom.
11Asa did what was right in the eyes of the LORD,
as his father David had done. 12He expelled the
male shrine prostitutes[j] from the land and got rid of
all the idols his fathers had made. 13He even
deposed his grandmother Maacah from her position as queen mother, because she had made a
repulsive Asherah pole. Asa cut the pole down[k] and
burned it in the Kidron Valley. 14Although he did
not remove the high places, Asa's heart was fully
committed[l] to the LORD all his life. 15He brought
into the temple of the LORD the silver and gold and
the articles that he and his father had dedicated.[m]
16There was war[n] between Asa and Baasha king
of Israel throughout their reigns. 17Baasha king of
Israel went up against Judah and fortified Ramah[o]
to prevent anyone from leaving or entering the
territory of Asa king of Judah.
18Asa then took all the silver and gold that was
left in the treasuries of the LORD's temple[p] and of
his own palace. He entrusted it to his officials and
sent[q] them to Ben-Hadad[r] son of Tabrimmon, the
son of Hezion, the king of Aram, who was ruling in
Damascus. 19"Let there be a treaty between me and
you," he said, "as there was between my father and
your father. See, I am sending you a gift of silver
and gold. Now break your treaty with Baasha king
of Israel so he will withdraw from me."
20Ben-Hadad agreed with King Asa and sent the
commanders of his forces against the towns of Israel. He conquered[s] Ijon, Dan, Abel Beth Maacah and
all Kinnereth in addition to Naphtali. 21When Baasha heard this, he stopped building Ramah and
withdrew to Tirzah. 22Then King Asa issued an
order to all Judah—no one was exempt—and they
carried away from Ramah the stones and timber
Baasha had been using there. With them King Asa
built up Geba[t] in Benjamin, and also Mizpah.
23As for all the other events of Asa's reign, all
his achievements, all he did and the cities he
built, are they not written in the book of the
annals of the kings of Judah? In his old age, however, his feet became diseased. 24Then Asa rested
with his fathers and was buried with them in the
city of his father David. And Jehoshaphat[u] his son
succeeded him as king.

Nadab King of Israel

25Nadab son of Jeroboam became king of Israel
in the second year of Asa king of Judah, and he
reigned over Israel two years. 26He did evil in the

15:10 [i]ver 2
15:12 [j]1Ki 14:24; 22:46
15:13 [k]Ex 32:20
15:14 [l]ver 3; 1Ki 8:61; 22:43
15:15 [m]1Ki 7:51
15:16 [n]ver 32
15:17 [o]Jos 18:25; 1Ki 12:27
15:18 [p]ver 15; 1Ki 14:26 [q]2Ki 12:18 [r]1Ki 11:23-24
15:20 [s]Jdg 18:29; 2Sa 20:14; 2Ki 15:29
15:22 [t]Jos 18:24; 21:17
15:24 [u]Mt 1:8

eyes of the LORD, walking in the ways of his
father[v] and in his sin, which he had caused Israel
to commit.
27Baasha son of Ahijah of the house of Issachar
plotted against him, and he struck him down[w] at
Gibbethon,[x] a Philistine town, while Nadab and
all Israel were besieging it. 28Baasha killed Nadab
in the third year of Asa king of Judah and succeeded him as king.
29As soon as he began to reign, he killed Jeroboam's whole family.[y] He did not leave Jeroboam
anyone that breathed, but destroyed them all,
according to the word of the LORD given through
his servant Ahijah the Shilonite— 30because of the
sins[z] Jeroboam had committed and had caused
Israel to commit, and because he provoked the
LORD, the God of Israel, to anger.
31As for the other events of Nadab's reign, and
all he did, are they not written in the book of the
annals of the kings of Israel? 32There was war[a]
between Asa and Baasha king of Israel throughout their reigns.

Baasha King of Israel

33In the third year of Asa king of Judah, Baasha
son of Ahijah became king of all Israel in Tirzah,
and he reigned twenty-four years. 34He did evil[b]
in the eyes of the LORD, walking in the ways of Jeroboam and in his sin, which he had caused Israel to commit.

16 Then the word of the LORD came to Jehu[c]
son of Hanani[d] against Baasha: 2"I lifted
you up from the dust[e] and made you leader[f] of my
people Israel, but you walked in the ways of Jeroboam and caused[g] my people Israel to sin and to
provoke me to anger by their sins. 3So I am about
to consume Baasha and his house,[h] and I will
make your house like that of Jeroboam son of
Nebat. 4Dogs[i] will eat those belonging to Baasha
who die in the city, and the birds of the air will
feed on those who die in the country."
5As for the other events of Baasha's reign, what
he did and his achievements, are they not written
in the book of the annals[j] of the kings of Israel?
6Baasha rested with his fathers and was buried in
Tirzah.[k] And Elah his son succeeded him as king.
7Moreover, the word of the LORD came[l] through
the prophet Jehu[m] son of Hanani to Baasha and
his house, because of all the evil he had done in
the eyes of the LORD, provoking him to anger by
the things he did, and becoming like the house of
Jeroboam—and also because he destroyed it.

Elah King of Israel

8In the twenty-sixth year of Asa king of Judah,
Elah son of Baasha became king of Israel, and he
reigned in Tirzah two years.
9Zimri, one of his officials, who had command
of half his chariots, plotted against him. Elah was
in Tirzah at the time, getting drunk[n] in the home

15:26 [v]1Ki 12:30; 14:16
15:27 [w]1Ki 14:14 [x]Jos 19:44; 21:23
15:29 [y]1Ki 14:10, 14
15:30 [z]1Ki 14:9,16
15:32 [a]ver 16
15:34 [b]ver 26; 1Ki 12:28-29; 13:33; 14:16
16:1 [c]ver 7; 2Ch 19:2; 20:34 [d]2Ch 16:7
16:2 [e]1Sa 2:8 [f]1Ki 14:7-9 [g]1Ki 15:34
16:3 [h]ver 11; 1Ki 14:10; 15:29; 21:22
16:4 [i]1Ki 14:11
16:5 [j]1Ki 14:19; 15:31
16:6 [k]1Ki 14:17; 15:33
16:7 [l]1Ki 15:27, 29 [m]ver 1
16:9 [n]2Ki 9:30-33

Having friends adds such sweetness to life . . . We all want to be close to someone who is tender toward us. Understanding. Loving. Kind. When we receive those qualities from others, it generally makes us more that way ourselves.

—Luci Swindoll

of Arza, the man in charge[o] of the palace at Tirzah. 10 Zimri came in, struck him down and killed him in the twenty-seventh year of Asa king of Judah. Then he succeeded him as king.

11 As soon as he began to reign and was seated on the throne, he killed off Baasha's whole family.[p] He did not spare a single male, whether relative or friend. 12 So Zimri destroyed the whole family of Baasha, in accordance with the word of the LORD spoken against Baasha through the prophet Jehu— 13 because of all the sins Baasha and his son Elah had committed and had caused Israel to commit, so that they provoked the LORD, the God of Israel, to anger by their worthless idols.[q]

14 As for the other events of Elah's reign, and all he did, are they not written in the book of the annals of the kings of Israel?

Zimri King of Israel

15 In the twenty-seventh year of Asa king of Judah, Zimri reigned in Tirzah seven days. The army was encamped near Gibbethon,[r] a Philistine town. 16 When the Israelites in the camp heard that Zimri had plotted against the king and murdered him, they proclaimed Omri, the commander of the army, king over Israel that very day there in the camp. 17 Then Omri and all the Israelites with him withdrew from Gibbethon and laid siege to Tirzah. 18 When Zimri saw that the city was taken, he went into the citadel of the royal palace and set the palace on fire around him. So he died, 19 because of the sins he had committed, doing evil in the eyes of the LORD and walking in the ways of Jeroboam and in the sin he had committed and had caused Israel to commit.

20 As for the other events of Zimri's reign, and the rebellion he carried out, are they not written in the book of the annals of the kings of Israel?

Omri King of Israel

21 Then the people of Israel were split into two factions; half supported Tibni son of Ginath for king, and the other half supported Omri. 22 But Omri's followers proved stronger than those of Tibni son of Ginath. So Tibni died and Omri became king.

23 In the thirty-first year of Asa king of Judah, Omri became king of Israel, and he reigned twelve years, six of them in Tirzah.[s] 24 He bought the hill of Samaria from Shemer for two talents[a] of silver and built a city on the hill, calling it Samaria,[t] after Shemer, the name of the former owner of the hill.

25 But Omri did evil[u] in the eyes of the LORD and sinned more than all those before him. 26 He walked in all the ways of Jeroboam son of Nebat and in his sin, which he had caused[v] Israel to commit, so that they provoked the LORD, the God of Israel, to anger by their worthless idols.[w]

27 As for the other events of Omri's reign, what

[a] *24* That is, about 150 pounds (about 70 kilograms)

16:9 [o]1Ki 18:3
16:11 [p]ver 3
16:13 [q]Dt 32:21; 1Sa 12:21; Isa 41:29
16:15 [r]Jos 19:44; 1Ki 15:27
16:23 [s]1Ki 15:21
16:24 [t]1Ki 13:32; Jn 4:4
16:25 [u]Dt 4:25; Mic 6:16
16:26 [v]ver 19 [w]Dt 32:21

The Annals

1KI 16:14,20

The author of 1 and 2 Kings used a number of sources in compiling his historical account, including "the book of the annals of the kings of Israel" (1Ki 16:14,20), "the book of the annals of Solomon" (1Ki 11:41), and "the book of the annals of the kings of Judah" (1Ki 14:29). These books may have been official court records from the royal archives in Jerusalem and Samaria, although it is uncertain whether such documents would have included details about conspiracies such as those cited in 1 Kings 16:20 and 2 Kings 15:15. It appears as though these annals were accessible to anyone interested in an in-depth study of a king's reign, which probably would not have been the case if they were a part of the official royal archives. Another possibility is that these records were a compilation of materials gathered by a series of prophets throughout the kingdom period (1Ch 29:29; 2Ch 9:29). These writings no longer exist.

he did and the things he achieved, are they not
written in the book of the annals of the kings of
Israel? [28]Omri rested with his fathers and was
buried in Samaria. And Ahab his son succeeded
him as king.

Ahab Becomes King of Israel

[29]In the thirty-eighth year of Asa king of Judah,
Ahab son of Omri became king of Israel, and he
reigned in Samaria over Israel twenty-two years.
16:30 [x]ver 25; 1Ki 14:9 [30]Ahab son of Omri did more[x] evil in the eyes of
the LORD than any of those before him. [31]He not
only considered it trivial to commit the sins of Jer-
16:31 [y]Dt 7:3; 1Ki 11:2 [z]Jdg 18:7; 2Ki 9:34 oboam son of Nebat, but he also married[y] Jezebel
daughter[z] of Ethbaal king of the Sidonians, and
began to serve Baal[a] and worship him. [32]He set up
[a]2Ki 10:18; 17:16 an altar for Baal in the temple[b] of Baal that he built
in Samaria. [33]Ahab also made an Asherah pole[c] and
16:32 [b]2Ki 10:21, 27; 11:18 did more[d] to provoke the LORD, the God of Israel,
to anger than did all the kings of Israel before him.
16:33 [c]2Ki 13:6 [d]ver 29,30; 1Ki 14:9; 21:25 [34]In Ahab's time, Hiel of Bethel rebuilt Jericho.
He laid its foundations at the cost of his firstborn
son Abiram, and he set up its gates at the cost of
his youngest son Segub, in accordance with the
word of the LORD spoken by Joshua son of Nun.[e]
16:34 [e]Jos 6:26

Elijah Fed by Ravens

17:1 [f]Mal 4:5; Jas 5:17 [g]Jdg 12:4 [h]Dt 10:8; 1Ki 18:1; 2Ki 3:14; Lk 4:25 17 Now Elijah[f] the Tishbite, from Tishbe[a] in
Gilead,[g] said to Ahab, "As the LORD, the God
of Israel, lives, whom I serve, there will be neither
dew nor rain[h] in the next few years except at my
word."
[2]Then the word of the LORD came to Elijah:
[3]"Leave here, turn eastward and hide in the Kerith
Ravine, east of the Jordan. [4]You will drink from
17:4 [i]Ge 8:7 the brook, and I have ordered the ravens[i] to feed
you there."
[5]So he did what the LORD had told him. He went
to the Kerith Ravine, east of the Jordan, and
stayed there. [6]The ravens brought him bread and
17:6 [j]Ex 16:8 meat in the morning[j] and bread and meat in the
evening, and he drank from the brook.

The Widow at Zarephath

[7]Some time later the brook dried up because
there had been no rain in the land. [8]Then the
word of the LORD came to him: [9]"Go at once to
17:9 [k]Ob 1:20 [l]Lk 4:26 Zarephath[k] of Sidon and stay there. I have commanded a widow[l] in that place to supply you with
food." [10]So he went to Zarephath. When he came
to the town gate, a widow was there gathering
sticks. He called to her and asked, "Would you
bring me a little water in a jar so I may have a
17:10 [m]Ge 24:17; Jn 4:7 drink?"[m] [11]As she was going to get it, he called,
"And bring me, please, a piece of bread."
[12]"As surely as the LORD your God lives," she
17:12 [n]ver 1; 2Ki 4:2 replied, "I don't have any bread—only a handful of
flour in a jar and a little oil[n] in a jug. I am gather-

[a] 1 Or *Tishbite, of the settlers*

Rebuilding Jericho

1KI 16:34

Israelites continued to live in Jericho after its destruction (Jos 18:21); however, the city remained unwalled and unfortified. During Ahab's time, a man named Hiel rebuilds the walls of Jericho. He goes against God's desire that Jericho remain a ruin as a reminder to Israel that their land has been provided by the might of the Lord God, not by their own military strength or superior battle planning. Joshua, who led the people on the successive trips around Jericho, vowed that anyone who sought to rebuild Jericho's walls would do so at the cost of his own children's lives (Jos 6:26). Hiel's actions lead to the deaths of his oldest and youngest sons, clearly a fulfillment of Joshua's curse.

Extraordinary Sustenance

1KI 17:14

A widow and her son reach the absolute end of their resources, never imagining the miracle God has planned. The same God who caused the drought is perfectly able to give sustenance to this woman and her son and, through them, to his prophet. The provision of food for Elijah via the ravens is extraordinary enough (1Ki 17:1–6); the supernatural abundance of the flour jar and oil jug seem still more miraculous—and mysterious. When our own resources appear to be tapped out, we, too, can trust that our God is greater than our natural circumstances (see character sketch for this woman on page 1143).

ing a few sticks to take home and make a meal for
myself and my son, that we may eat it—and die."
13 Elijah said to her, "Don't be afraid. Go home
and do as you have said. But first make a small
cake of bread for me from what you have and
bring it to me, and then make something for yourself and your son. 14 For this is what the LORD, the
God of Israel, says: 'The jar of flour will not be
used up and the jug of oil will not run dry until
the day the LORD gives rain on the land.' "
15 She went away and did as Elijah had told her.
So there was food every day for Elijah and for the
woman and her family. 16 For the jar of flour was
not used up and the jug of oil did not run dry, in
keeping with the word of the LORD spoken by
Elijah.
17 Some time later the son of the woman who
owned the house became ill. He grew worse and
worse, and finally stopped breathing. 18 She said
to Elijah, "What do you have against me, man of
God? Did you come to remind me of my sin[o] and
kill my son?"
19 "Give me your son," Elijah replied. He took
him from her arms, carried him to the upper room
where he was staying, and laid him on his bed.
20 Then he cried out to the LORD, "O LORD my God,
have you brought tragedy also upon this widow I
am staying with, by causing her son to die?"
21 Then he stretched[p] himself out on the boy three
times and cried to the LORD, "O LORD my God, let
this boy's life return to him!"
22 The LORD heard Elijah's cry, and the boy's life
returned to him, and he lived. 23 Elijah picked up
the child and carried him down from the room
into the house. He gave him to his mother and
said, "Look, your son is alive!"
24 Then the woman said to Elijah, "Now I know[q]
that you are a man of God and that the word of
the LORD from your mouth is the truth."[r]

17:18 [o]2Ki 3:13; Lk 5:8

17:21 [p]2Ki 4:34; Ac 20:10

17:24 [q]Jn 3:2; 16:30 [r]Ps 119:43; Jn 17:17

Elijah and Obadiah

18 After a long time, in the third[s] year, the word
of the LORD came to Elijah: "Go and present
yourself to Ahab, and I will send rain[t] on the
land." 2 So Elijah went to present himself to Ahab.
Now the famine was severe in Samaria, 3 and
Ahab had summoned Obadiah, who was in
charge[u] of his palace. (Obadiah was a devout
believer[v] in the LORD. 4 While Jezebel[w] was killing
off the LORD's prophets, Obadiah had taken a hundred prophets and hidden[x] them in two caves,
fifty in each, and had supplied them with food
and water.) 5 Ahab had said to Obadiah, "Go
through the land to all the springs and valleys.
Maybe we can find some grass to keep the horses
and mules alive so we will not have to kill any of
our animals." 6 So they divided the land they were
to cover, Ahab going in one direction and Obadiah in another.
7 As Obadiah was walking along, Elijah met him.

18:1 [s]1Ki 17:1; Lk 4:25; Jas 5:17 [t]Dt 28:12

18:3 [u]1Ki 16:9 [v]Ne 7:2

18:4 [w]2Ki 9:7 [x]ver 13; Isa 16:3

18:7 Obadiah recognized[y] him, bowed down to the
[y]2Ki 1:8 ground, and said, "Is it really you, my lord Elijah?"
8"Yes," he replied. "Go tell your master, 'Elijah
is here.' "
9"What have I done wrong," asked Obadiah,
"that you are handing your servant over to Ahab
to be put to death? 10As surely as the LORD your
God lives, there is not a nation or kingdom where
18:10 [z]1Ki 17:3 my master has not sent someone to look[z] for you.
And whenever a nation or kingdom claimed you
were not there, he made them swear they could
not find you. 11But now you tell me to go to my
master and say, 'Elijah is here.' 12I don't know
18:12 [a]2Ki 2:16; where the Spirit[a] of the LORD may carry you when
Eze 3:14; I leave you. If I go and tell Ahab and he doesn't
Ac 8:39 find you, he will kill me. Yet I your servant have
worshiped the LORD since my youth. 13Haven't
you heard, my lord, what I did while Jezebel was
killing the prophets of the LORD? I hid a hundred
of the LORD's prophets in two caves, fifty in each,
and supplied them with food and water. 14And
now you tell me to go to my master and say, 'Elijah is here.' He will kill me!"
15Elijah said, "As the LORD Almighty lives,
18:15 whom I serve, I will surely present[b] myself to
[b]1Ki 17:1 Ahab today."

Elijah on Mount Carmel

16So Obadiah went to meet Ahab and told him,
and Ahab went to meet Elijah. 17When he saw Eli-
18:17 [c]Jos 7:25; jah, he said to him, "Is that you, you troubler[c] of
1Ki 21:20; Israel?"
Ac 16:20 18"I have not made trouble for Israel," Elijah
18:18 replied. "But you[d] and your father's family have.
[d]1Ki 16:31, You have abandoned[e] the LORD's commands and
33; 21:25 [e]2Ch 15:2 have followed the Baals. 19Now summon the people from all over Israel to meet me on Mount Car-
18:19 [f]Jos 19:26 mel.[f] And bring the four hundred and fifty prophets of Baal and the four hundred prophets of
Asherah, who eat at Jezebel's table."
20So Ahab sent word throughout all Israel and
assembled the prophets on Mount Carmel. 21Elijah
went before the people and said, "How long will
18:21 you waver[g] between two opinions? If the LORD is
[g]Jos 24:15; 2Ki 17:41; God, follow him; but if Baal is God, follow him."
Mt 6:24 But the people said nothing.
22Then Elijah said to them, "I am the only one of
18:22 [h]1Ki 19:10 the LORD's prophets left,[h] but Baal has four hundred
[i]ver 19 and fifty prophets.[i] 23Get two bulls for us. Let them
choose one for themselves, and let them cut it into
pieces and put it on the wood but not set fire to it.
I will prepare the other bull and put it on the wood
but not set fire to it. 24Then you call on the name of
your god, and I will call on the name of the LORD.
18:24 [j]ver 38; The god who answers by fire[j]—he is God."
1Ch 21:26 Then all the people said, "What you say is
good."
25Elijah said to the prophets of Baal, "Choose
one of the bulls and prepare it first, since there are
so many of you. Call on the name of your god, but

Troubler of Israel

1KI 18:21

The people of Israel believe that they can simultaneously worship two gods—the *pagan god Baal and the one true God—and receive blessings from* both. Elijah, the Lord's prophet, makes it clear that nothing could be further from the truth. Long before, *when he gave the Ten Com*mandments at Mount Sinai, the Lord himself announced that he, *a* jealous God, would not tolerate the worship of other gods (Ex 20:3–4). Yet the people will not choose him over their idols, and their two-faced behavior is loathsome to him.

Like the Israelites, believers *today often attempt to serve both* the gods of this world and the Lord. Many things can steal our worship from God: money, control, possessions, people. Whatever takes up most of our thoughts and energy may be an object of worship. *We have a choice to make,* one that the Israelites failed to *make so long ago on Mount Car*mel. *May our legacy be very dif*ferent from theirs: "But the people said nothing" (1Ki 18:21).

Week 8

Embracing Grace and Faith

Imagine the sight: Elijah and King Ahab, with 850 prophets of Baal and Asherah, standing on the high ridge of Mount Carmel overlooking the Mediterranean Sea. In that place Elijah confronts the people: "How long will you waver between two opinions? If the LORD is God, follow him; but if Baal is God, follow him" (1Ki 18:21). If this were a movie, the background music would swell with drama—what will they decide?

"But the people said nothing" (1Ki 18:21).

What? They say *nothing?* Do they think, "We're God's chosen people, what's Elijah's point?" Elijah says they need to choose. That day they choose by not choosing. Even today you can choose to follow other gods by not choosing to follow God.

Is faith simply an intellectual assent to truth (Lk 10:21; Jas 2:19; 1Jn 2:4)? Intellectually accepting that Christ is the Savior is a necessary step toward faith (Ro 10:17), but it is not—by itself—saving faith. Even calling Jesus "Lord" does not necessarily make you a Christian (Mt 7:21-23).

Is knowing your Bible proof that you're a Christian (Jn 5:37-40)? The Pharisees could quote a Scripture text for any occasion. But they were Jesus' enemies.

What is saving faith (Heb 11:1)? Peter affirms that Jesus is the Christ (Mt. 16:16), not simply as a product of his intellect or emotions, but because God himself reveals it to him (Mt 16:17). Something happens spiritually within Peter. God's Spirit enlightens him, and he embraces the truth and declares Jesus as Christ with true faith.

Is faith received through diligent effort (Eph 2:8-9)? Faith is a gift of God just as salvation is a gift of grace. It cannot be earned or conjured up. You won't have faith by saying, "I have faith; I have faith." Faith is a sovereign gift from God as he reveals Christ to us in his word (Ro 10:17).

Enjoying God THROUGH the Word

Read Matthew 7:21-23 (page 1591). These people know Jesus Christ's teaching and have even been out on the "mission field," casting out demons and performing miracles. What causes Jesus to reject them?

Jesus says that only those who do the will of God will enter the kingdom of heaven. Evidently these people resist God's will. Their absence of a relationship with God reveals the true condition of their "faith": "Then I will tell them plainly, 'I never *knew* you' " (Mt 7:23, emphasis added). They make an intellectual assent, but their hearts are not touched or changed.

What makes your faith more than mere intellectual assent or family tradition? True faith is experienced—not just affirmed (1Sa 3:7). It is your heart's "Aha!" when you discover the hope and power found only in a relationship with Jesus Christ. That faith drives all you do. That faith compels you to do God's will.

Enjoying God THROUGH Experience

If you have not accepted the gift of faith that the Holy Spirit offers, receive his grace and allow him to bring a new revelation to your heart of who Jesus is. If you have embraced the truth of Jesus, if, by faith, you know him in a way you cannot prove but will never deny, you can stand with the hosts of heaven and shout, "Worthy is the Lamb!" (Rev 5:12). Spend some time in prayer simply praising God—in your own unique way—for the gifts of grace, faith and, most of all, Jesus.

Go to page 581 for your next weekly study.

do not light the fire." 26 So they took the bull given them and prepared it.

Then they called on the name of Baal from morning till noon. "O Baal, answer us!" they shouted. But there was no response;[k] no one answered. And they danced around the altar they had made.

27 At noon Elijah began to taunt them. "Shout louder!" he said. "Surely he is a god! Perhaps he is deep in thought, or busy, or traveling. Maybe he is sleeping and must be awakened."[l] 28 So they shouted louder and slashed[m] themselves with swords and spears, as was their custom, until their blood flowed. 29 Midday passed, and they continued their frantic prophesying until the time for the evening sacrifice.[n] But there was no response, no one answered, no one paid attention.[o]

30 Then Elijah said to all the people, "Come here to me." They came to him, and he repaired the altar[p] of the LORD, which was in ruins. 31 Elijah took twelve stones, one for each of the tribes descended from Jacob, to whom the word of the LORD had come, saying, "Your name shall be Israel."[q] 32 With the stones he built an altar in the name[r] of the LORD, and he dug a trench around it large enough to hold two seahs[a] of seed. 33 He arranged[s] the wood, cut the bull into pieces and laid it on the wood. Then he said to them, "Fill four large jars with water and pour it on the offering and on the wood."

34 "Do it again," he said, and they did it again.

"Do it a third time," he ordered, and they did it the third time. 35 The water ran down around the altar and even filled the trench.

36 At the time of sacrifice, the prophet Elijah stepped forward and prayed: "O LORD, God of Abraham,[t] Isaac and Israel, let it be known[u] today that you are God in Israel and that I am your servant and have done all these things at your command.[v] 37 Answer me, O LORD, answer me, so these people will know that you, O LORD, are God, and that you are turning their hearts back again."

38 Then the fire[w] of the LORD fell and burned up the sacrifice, the wood, the stones and the soil, and also licked up the water in the trench.

39 When all the people saw this, they fell prostrate and cried, "The LORD—he is God! The LORD—he is God!"[x]

40 Then Elijah commanded them, "Seize the prophets of Baal. Don't let anyone get away!" They seized them, and Elijah had them brought down to the Kishon Valley[y] and slaughtered[z] there.

41 And Elijah said to Ahab, "Go, eat and drink, for there is the sound of a heavy rain." 42 So Ahab went off to eat and drink, but Elijah climbed to the top of Carmel, bent down to the ground and put his face between his knees.[a]

43 "Go and look toward the sea," he told his servant. And he went up and looked.

"There is nothing there," he said.

18:26 [k]Ps 115:4-5; Jer 10:5; 1Co 8:4; 12:2
18:27 [l]Hab 2:19
18:28 [m]Lev 19:28; Dt 14:1
18:29 [n]Ex 29:41 [o]ver 26
18:30 [p]1Ki 19:10
18:31 [q]Ge 32:28; 35:10; 2Ki 17:34
18:32 [r]Col 3:17
18:33 [s]Ge 22:9; Lev 1:6-8
18:36 [t]Ex 3:6; Mt 22:32 [u]1Ki 8:43; 2Ki 19:19 [v]Nu 16:28
18:38 [w]Lev 9:24; Jdg 6:21; 1Ch 21:26; 2Ch 7:1; Job 1:16
18:39 [x]ver 24
18:40 [y]Jdg 4:7 [z]Dt 13:5; 18:20; 2Ki 10:24-25
18:42 [a]ver 19-20; Jas 5:18

[a] 32 That is, probably about 13 quarts (about 15 liters)

Simple Faith

1KI 18:36-37

No trickery. No desperate pleas. No artifice or fraud. Elijah uses simple but dramatic methods to prove to the Israelites who is the true God. First, in a time of drought, he pours jug after jug of water on the sacrifice. He wants to make certain the fire that burns the sacrifice can only be divinely sent—no ordinary fire can burn this wet offering. Then he offers a simple prayer. No desperate cutting, no bloody Canaanite rituals. Elijah prays in absolute faith that God will answer.

We can put ourselves on that mountain, either saying nothing (1Ki 18:21) or praying Elijah's prayer of faith in God. The choice is that simple. And that difficult.

Ups and Downs

1KI 19:3-5

On the heels of an incredible victory, Elijah immediately sinks into a profound depression. Jezebel's threats would certainly have thrown a damper on any positive feelings he might have had. But even without her interference, the melancholy prophet may still have suffered a "let down" after being used by God in such a mighty way.

God doesn't leave the prophet alone in his melancholy, however. He sends an angel to minister to him—not mentally or emotionally, but physically. The angel twice prepares nourishing food and drink and allows the worn-out prophet healing sleep. When Elijah's physical resources are restored, he's ready to move on.

It is the same in our own lives. Often after times of great joy or success or happiness, our spirits slump and—in contrast to earlier experiences of euphoria—we feel as if God is no longer present. Yet even when negative emotions rock our world, God's faithfulness remains unshakable.

Seven times Elijah said, "Go back."
44 The seventh time the servant reported, "A
cloud[b] as small as a man's hand is rising from the
sea."
So Elijah said, "Go and tell Ahab, 'Hitch up
your chariot and go down before the rain stops
you.' "
45 Meanwhile, the sky grew black with clouds,
the wind rose, a heavy rain came on and Ahab
rode off to Jezreel. 46 The power[c] of the LORD came
upon Elijah and, tucking his cloak into his belt,[d]
he ran ahead of Ahab all the way to Jezreel.

Elijah Flees to Horeb

19 Now Ahab told Jezebel everything Elijah
had done and how he had killed[e] all the
prophets with the sword. 2 So Jezebel sent a messenger to Elijah to say, "May the gods deal with
me, be it ever so severely,[f] if by this time tomorrow I do not make your life like that of one of
them."
3 Elijah was afraid[a] and ran[g] for his life. When
he came to Beersheba in Judah, he left his servant
there, 4 while he himself went a day's journey into
the desert. He came to a broom tree, sat down
under it and prayed that he might die. "I have had
enough, LORD," he said. "Take my life;[h] I am no
better than my ancestors." 5 Then he lay down
under the tree and fell asleep.[i]
All at once an angel touched him and said, "Get
up and eat." 6 He looked around, and there by his
head was a cake of bread baked over hot coals,
and a jar of water. He ate and drank and then lay
down again.
7 The angel of the LORD came back a second time
and touched him and said, "Get up and eat, for
the journey is too much for you." 8 So he got up
and ate and drank. Strengthened by that food, he
traveled forty[j] days and forty nights until he
reached Horeb,[k] the mountain of God. 9 There he
went into a cave[l] and spent the night.

The LORD Appears to Elijah

And the word of the LORD came to him: "What
are you doing here, Elijah?"
10 He replied, "I have been very zealous[m] for the
LORD God Almighty. The Israelites have rejected
your covenant, broken down your altars, and put
your prophets to death with the sword. I am the
only one left,[n] and now they are trying to kill me
too."
11 The LORD said, "Go out and stand on the
mountain[o] in the presence of the LORD, for the
LORD is about to pass by."
Then a great and powerful wind[p] tore the
mountains apart and shattered the rocks before
the LORD, but the LORD was not in the wind. After
the wind there was an earthquake, but the LORD
was not in the earthquake. 12 After the earthquake

18:44 [b]Lk 12:54
18:46 [c]2Ki 3:15 [d]2Ki 4:29; 9:1
19:1 [e]1Ki 18:40
19:2 [f]1Ki 20:10; 2Ki 6:31; Ru 1:17
19:3 [g]Ge 31:21
19:4 [h]Nu 11:15; Jer 20:18; Jnh 4:8
19:5 [i]Ge 28:11
19:8 [j]Ex 24:18; 34:28; Dt 9:9-11,18; Mt 4:2 [k]Ex 3:1
19:9 [l]Ex 33:22
19:10 [m]Nu 25:13 [n]1Ki 18:4, 22; Ro 11:3*
19:11 [o]Ex 24:12 [p]Eze 1:4; 37:7

[a] 3 Or *Elijah saw*

came a fire, but the LORD was not in the fire. And
19:12 [q]Job 4:16; Zec 4:6 after the fire came a gentle whisper.[q] [13]When Elijah heard it, he pulled his cloak over his face[r] and
19:13 [r]ver 9; Ex 3:6 went out and stood at the mouth of the cave.
Then a voice said to him, "What are you doing
here, Elijah?"
[14]He replied, "I have been very zealous for the
LORD God Almighty. The Israelites have rejected
your covenant, broken down your altars, and put
your prophets to death with the sword. I am the
19:14 [s]ver 10 only one left,[s] and now they are trying to kill me
too."
[15]The LORD said to him, "Go back the way you
19:15 [t]2Ki 8:7-15 came, and go to the Desert of Damascus. When
you get there, anoint Hazael[t] king over Aram.
19:16 [u]2Ki 9:1-3,6 [v]ver 21; 2Ki 2:9,15 [16]Also, anoint[u] Jehu son of Nimshi king over Israel, and anoint Elisha[v] son of Shaphat from Abel
Meholah to succeed you as prophet. [17]Jehu will
put to death any who escape the sword of Haza-
19:17 [w]2Ki 8:12, 29; 9:14; 13:3,7,22 el,[w] and Elisha will put to death any who escape
the sword of Jehu. [18]Yet I reserve[x] seven thousand
in Israel—all whose knees have not bowed down
19:18 [x]Ro 11:4* [y]Hos 13:2 to Baal and all whose mouths have not kissed[y]
him."

The Call of Elisha

[19]So Elijah went from there and found Elisha
son of Shaphat. He was plowing with twelve yoke
19:19 [z]2Ki 2:8,14 of oxen, and he himself was driving the twelfth
pair. Elijah went up to him and threw his cloak[z]
around him. [20]Elisha then left his oxen and ran
after Elijah. "Let me kiss my father and mother
19:20 [a]Mt 8:21-22; Lk 9:61 good-by,"[a] he said, "and then I will come with
you."
"Go back," Elijah replied. "What have I done to
you?"
[21]So Elisha left him and went back. He took his
19:21 [b]2Sa 24:22 [c]ver 16 yoke of oxen[b] and slaughtered them. He burned
the plowing equipment to cook the meat and gave
it to the people, and they ate. Then he set out to
follow Elijah and became his attendant.[c]

Ben-Hadad Attacks Samaria

20:1 [d]1Ki 15:18; 22:31; 2Ki 6:24 **20** Now Ben-Hadad[d] king of Aram mustered
his entire army. Accompanied by thirty-two
kings with their horses and chariots, he went up
and besieged Samaria and attacked it. [2]He sent
messengers into the city to Ahab king of Israel,
saying, "This is what Ben-Hadad says: [3]'Your silver and gold are mine, and the best of your wives
and children are mine.' "
[4]The king of Israel answered, "Just as you say,
my lord the king. I and all I have are yours."
[5]The messengers came again and said, "This is
what Ben-Hadad says: 'I sent to demand your silver and gold, your wives and your children. [6]But
about this time tomorrow I am going to send my
officials to search your palace and the houses of
your officials. They will seize everything you value and carry it away.' "

A Gentle Whisper

1KI 19:12

Elijah is physically rejuvenated but still feeling the effects of the events 40 days before. God is now ready to teach him an important lesson. He will "pass by" Elijah (Does Elijah have any idea how special he is?), giving Elijah a glimpse of his holiness.

The wind, the lightening and the earthquake increase Elijah's awareness of his own weaknesses. But God is present in none of these things. Instead, he manifests himself in a "gentle whisper," revealing to Elijah that strength and power are not always found in the dramatic or sensational, but at times in gentleness and calm. Elijah immediately recognizes God in the quiet murmur, responding with awe and reverence.

7The king of Israel summoned all the elders of
the land and said to them, "See how this man is 20:7
looking for trouble![e] When he sent for my wives [e]2Ki 5:7
and my children, my silver and my gold, I did not
refuse him."
8The elders and the people all answered, "Don't
listen to him or agree to his demands."
9So he replied to Ben-Hadad's messengers, "Tell
my lord the king, 'Your servant will do all you
demanded the first time, but this demand I cannot meet.' " They left and took the answer back to
Ben-Hadad.
10Then Ben-Hadad sent another message to
Ahab: "May the gods deal with me, be it ever so 20:10
severely, if enough dust[f] remains in Samaria to [f]2Sa 22:43;
give each of my men a handful." 1Ki 19:2
11The king of Israel answered, "Tell him: 'One
who puts on his armor should not boast[g] like one 20:11 [g]Pr 27:1;
who takes it off.' " Jer 9:23
12Ben-Hadad heard this message while he and 20:12
the kings were drinking[h] in their tents,[a] and he [h]ver 16;
ordered his men: "Prepare to attack." So they pre- 1Ki 16:9
pared to attack the city.

Ahab Defeats Ben-Hadad

13Meanwhile a prophet came to Ahab king of
Israel and announced, "This is what the LORD
says: 'Do you see this vast army? I will give it into
your hand today, and then you will know[i] that I 20:13
am the LORD.' " [i]ver 28; Ex 6:7
14"But who will do this?" asked Ahab.
The prophet replied, "This is what the LORD
says: 'The young officers of the provincial commanders will do it.' "
"And who will start[j] the battle?" he asked. 20:14
The prophet answered, "You will." [j]Jdg 1:1
15So Ahab summoned the young officers of the
provincial commanders, 232 men. Then he
assembled the rest of the Israelites, 7,000 in all.
16They set out at noon while Ben-Hadad and the
32 kings allied with him were in their tents get- 20:16
ting drunk.[k] 17The young officers of the provincial [k]ver 12;
commanders went out first. 1Ki 16:9
Now Ben-Hadad had dispatched scouts, who
reported, "Men are advancing from Samaria."
18He said, "If they have come out for peace, take
them alive; if they have come out for war, take
them alive."
19The young officers of the provincial commanders marched out of the city with the army
behind them 20and each one struck down his
opponent. At that, the Arameans fled, with the
Israelites in pursuit. But Ben-Hadad king of Aram
escaped on horseback with some of his horsemen.
21The king of Israel advanced and overpowered
the horses and chariots and inflicted heavy losses
on the Arameans.
22Afterward, the prophet[l] came to the king of 20:22
Israel and said, "Strengthen your position and see [l]ver 13

[a] 12 Or *in Succoth*; also in verse 16

Build a little fence of trust
Around today;
Fill the space with loving work,
And therein stay;
Look not through the sheltering bars
Upon to-morrow;
God will help thee bear what comes
Of joy or sorrow.

—Mary Frances Butts (1836–1902)

20:22 what must be done, because next spring[m] the king
[m]ver 26; 2Sa 11:1 of Aram will attack you again."
23Meanwhile, the officials of the king of Aram
20:23 [n]1Ki 14:23; advised him, "Their gods are gods[n] of the hills.
Ro 1:21-23 That is why they were too strong for us. But if we
fight them on the plains, surely we will be
stronger than they. 24Do this: Remove all the kings
from their commands and replace them with other officers. 25You must also raise an army like the
one you lost—horse for horse and chariot for
chariot—so we can fight Israel on the plains. Then
surely we will be stronger than they." He agreed
with them and acted accordingly.
20:26 [o]ver 22 26The next spring[o] Ben-Hadad mustered the
[p]2Ki 13:17 Arameans and went up to Aphek[p] to fight against
Israel. 27When the Israelites were also mustered
and given provisions, they marched out to meet
them. The Israelites camped opposite them like
20:27 two small flocks of goats, while the Arameans
[q]Jdg 6:6; 1Sa 13:6 covered the countryside.[q]
28The man of God came up and told the king of
Israel, "This is what the LORD says: 'Because the
Arameans think the LORD is a god of the hills and
20:28 [r]ver 23 not a god[r] of the valleys, I will deliver this vast
[s]ver 13 army into your hands, and you will know[s] that I
am the LORD.' "
29For seven days they camped opposite each
other, and on the seventh day the battle was
joined. The Israelites inflicted a hundred thousand
casualties on the Aramean foot soldiers in one
day. 30The rest of them escaped to the city of
20:30 [t]ver 26 Aphek,[t] where the wall collapsed on twenty-sev-
[u]1Ki 22:25; en thousand of them. And Ben-Hadad fled to the
2Ch 18:24 city and hid[u] in an inner room.
31His officials said to him, "Look, we have heard
that the kings of the house of Israel are merciful.
20:31 [v]Ge 37:34 Let us go to the king of Israel with sackcloth[v]
around our waists and ropes around our heads.
Perhaps he will spare your life."
32Wearing sackcloth around their waists and
ropes around their heads, they went to the king
of Israel and said, "Your servant Ben-Hadad says:
'Please let me live.' "
The king answered, "Is he still alive? He is my
brother."
33The men took this as a good sign and were
quick to pick up his word. "Yes, your brother Ben-
Hadad!" they said.
"Go and get him," the king said. When Ben-
Hadad came out, Ahab had him come up into his
chariot.
20:34 34"I will return the cities[w] my father took from
[w]1Ki 15:20 [x]Jer 49:23-27 your father," Ben-Hadad offered. "You may set up
[y]Ex 23:32 your own market areas in Damascus,[x] as my
father did in Samaria."
⌞Ahab said,⌟ "On the basis of a treaty[y] I will set
you free." So he made a treaty with him, and let
him go.

A Prophet Condemns Ahab

35By the word of the LORD one of the sons of the

Hill Gods

1KI 20:23

The Aramean soldiers are a force to be reckoned with on flat land. Their chariots and horses give them the battle edge whenever they fight on the plains. But the Israelites are much more skilled at fighting in the hills and successfully rout the Aramean soldiers. The Israelites, the Arameans reason, must have a hill god who aids them in their battles. They plan, therefore, to fight on the plains the next time, thereby gaining the advantage. But they don't take into account the true God who is behind Israel's victories, the God of the hills and the valleys. He enables the Israelite army to again defeat the Arameans.

Steward of the Land

1KI 21:3

Naboth's refusal to make a deal with Ahab is not an act of stubborn self-will but of loyalty to God's laws. Naboth knows that his family's land has merely been loaned to him. All the land of Israel, including this vineyard of Naboth, actually belongs to the Lord. Naboth sees himself, not as an owner, but as a steward of God's property. To sell it permanently to Ahab would have been a direct violation of the law (Lev 25:23). So Naboth refuses.

prophets said to his companion, "Strike me with
your weapon," but the man refused.[z] **20:35** [z]1Ki 13:21;
36So the prophet said, "Because you have not 2Ki 2:3-7
obeyed the LORD, as soon as you leave me a lion[a] **20:36**
will kill you." And after the man went away, a [a]1Ki 13:24
lion found him and killed him.
37The prophet found another man and said,
"Strike me, please." So the man struck him and
wounded him. 38Then the prophet went and stood
by the road waiting for the king. He disguised
himself with his headband down over his eyes.
39As the king passed by, the prophet called out to
him, "Your servant went into the thick of the battle, and someone came to me with a captive and
said, 'Guard this man. If he is missing, it will be **20:39**
your life for his life,[b] or you must pay a talent[a] of [b]2Ki 10:24
silver.' 40While your servant was busy here and
there, the man disappeared."
"That is your sentence," the king of Israel said.
"You have pronounced it yourself."
41Then the prophet quickly removed the headband from his eyes, and the king of Israel recognized him as one of the prophets. 42He said to the
king, "This is what the LORD says: 'You have set **20:42**
free a man I had determined should die.[bc] There- [c]Jer 48:10
fore it is your life for his life,[d] your people for his [d]ver 39;
people.' " 43Sullen and angry,[e] the king of Israel Jos 2:14;
went to his palace in Samaria. 1Ki 22:31-37

20:43 [e]1Ki 21:4

Naboth's Vineyard

21 Some time later there was an incident **21:1**
involving a vineyard belonging to Naboth[f] [f]2Ki 9:21
the Jezreelite. The vineyard was in Jezreel,[g] close [g]1Ki 18:45-
to the palace of Ahab king of Samaria. 2Ahab said 46
to Naboth, "Let me have your vineyard to use for
a vegetable garden, since it is close to my palace.
In exchange I will give you a better vineyard or, if
you prefer, I will pay you whatever it is worth."
3But Naboth replied, "The LORD forbid that I **21:3**
should give you the inheritance[h] of my fathers." [h]Lev 25:23;
4So Ahab went home, sullen and angry[i] because Nu 36:7;
Naboth the Jezreelite had said, "I will not give you Eze 46:18
the inheritance of my fathers." He lay on his bed **21:4**
sulking and refused to eat. [i]1Ki 20:43
5His wife Jezebel came in and asked him, "Why
are you so sullen? Why won't you eat?"
6He answered her, "Because I said to Naboth the
Jezreelite, 'Sell me your vineyard; or if you prefer,
I will give you another vineyard in its place.' But
he said, 'I will not give you my vineyard.' "
7Jezebel his wife said, "Is this how you act as
king over Israel? Get up and eat! Cheer up. I'll get **21:7**
you the vineyard[j] of Naboth the Jezreelite." [j]1Sa 8:14
8So she wrote letters in Ahab's name, placed his **21:8**
seal[k] on them, and sent them to the elders and [k]Ge 38:18;
nobles who lived in Naboth's city with him. 9In Est 3:12; 8:8,
those letters she wrote: 10

[a] *39* That is, about 75 pounds (about 34 kilograms)
[b] *42* The Hebrew term refers to the irrevocable giving over of things or persons to the LORD, often by totally destroying them.

"Proclaim a day of fasting and seat Naboth
in a prominent place among the people. 10But
seat two scoundrels[l] opposite him and have
them testify that he has cursed[m] both God
and the king. Then take him out and stone
him to death."

11So the elders and nobles who lived in Naboth's
city did as Jezebel directed in the letters she had
written to them. 12They proclaimed a fast[n] and
seated Naboth in a prominent place among the people. 13Then two scoundrels came and sat opposite
him and brought charges against Naboth before the
people, saying, "Naboth has cursed both God and
the king." So they took him outside the city and
stoned him to death.[o] 14Then they sent word to Jezebel: "Naboth has been stoned and is dead."

15As soon as Jezebel heard that Naboth had
been stoned to death, she said to Ahab, "Get up
and take possession of the vineyard[p] of Naboth
the Jezreelite that he refused to sell you. He is no
longer alive, but dead." 16When Ahab heard that
Naboth was dead, he got up and went down to
take possession of Naboth's vineyard.

17Then the word of the LORD came to Elijah the
Tishbite: 18"Go down to meet Ahab king of Israel,
who rules in Samaria. He is now in Naboth's vineyard, where he has gone to take possession of it.
19Say to him, 'This is what the LORD says: Have you
not murdered a man and seized his property?'
Then say to him, 'This is what the LORD says: In
the place where dogs licked up Naboth's blood,[q]
dogs[r] will lick up your blood—yes, yours!' "

20Ahab said to Elijah, "So you have found me,
my enemy!"[s]

"I have found you," he answered, "because you
have sold[t] yourself to do evil in the eyes of the LORD.
21'I am going to bring disaster on you. I will consume your descendants and cut off from Ahab every
last male[u] in Israel—slave or free. 22I will make your
house[v] like that of Jeroboam son of Nebat and that
of Baasha son of Ahijah, because you have provoked me to anger and have caused Israel to sin.'[w]

23"And also concerning Jezebel the LORD says:
'Dogs[x] will devour Jezebel by the wall of[a] Jezreel.'

24"Dogs[y] will eat those belonging to Ahab who
die in the city, and the birds of the air will feed on
those who die in the country."

25(There was never[z] a man like Ahab, who sold
himself to do evil in the eyes of the LORD, urged on
by Jezebel his wife. 26He behaved in the vilest
manner by going after idols, like the Amorites[a]
the LORD drove out before Israel.)

27When Ahab heard these words, he tore his
clothes, put on sackcloth[b] and fasted. He lay in
sackcloth and went around meekly.

28Then the word of the LORD came to Elijah the
Tishbite: 29"Have you noticed how Ahab has humbled himself before me? Because he has humbled

21:10 [l]Ac 6:11 [m]Ex 22:28; Lev 24:15-16
21:12 [n]Isa 58:4
21:13 [o]2Ki 9:26
21:15 [p]1Sa 8:14
21:19 [q]2Ki 9:26; Ps 9:12; Isa 14:20 [r]1Ki 22:38
21:20 [s]1Ki 18:17 [t]ver 25; 2Ki 17:17; Ro 7:14
21:21 [u]1Ki 14:10; 2Ki 9:8
21:22 [v]1Ki 15:29; 16:3 [w]1Ki 12:30
21:23 [x]2Ki 9:10,34-36
21:24 [y]1Ki 14:11; 16:4
21:25 [z]ver 20; 1Ki 16:33
21:26 [a]Ge 15:16; Lev 18:25-30; 2Ki 21:11
21:27 [b]Ge 37:34; 2Sa 3:31; 2Ki 6:30

[a] *23* Most Hebrew manuscripts; a few Hebrew manuscripts, Vulgate and Syriac (see also 2 Kings 9:26) *the plot of ground at*

Good Versus Evil

1KI 21:25

Traditionally known as the most evil of all the kings **of Israel and Judah (1Ki 16:30–33),** ***Ahab wields the power of wickedness in various ways. At times his depravity is obvious, as in the establishment of Baal worship*** **(1Ki 16:31–32)** ***and in his pursuit of Elijah*** **(1Ki 18:10).** ***At other times Ahab's evil ways are manifested more subtly, as in his attempt to gain Naboth's land*** **(1Ki 21:1–16).** ***Both subtle as well as obvious crimes are used by those in power to manipulate the weak and vulnerable. But those who practice evil are infinitely weaker than the God of goodness. Like Ahab, they will eventually pay the ultimate price for their choices.***

himself, I will not bring this disaster in his day, but
I will bring it on his house in the days of his son."[c]

Micaiah Prophesies Against Ahab

22 For three years there was no war between
Aram and Israel. 2But in the third year
Jehoshaphat king of Judah went down to see the
king of Israel. 3The king of Israel had said to his
officials, "Don't you know that Ramoth Gilead[d]
belongs to us and yet we are doing nothing to
retake it from the king of Aram?"

4So he asked Jehoshaphat, "Will you go with
me to fight[e] against Ramoth Gilead?"

Jehoshaphat replied to the king of Israel, "I am
as you are, my people as your people, my horses as
your horses." 5But Jehoshaphat also said to the
king of Israel, "First seek the counsel[f] of the LORD."

6So the king of Israel brought together the
prophets—about four hundred men—and asked
them, "Shall I go to war against Ramoth Gilead, or
shall I refrain?"

"Go,"[g] they answered, "for the Lord will give it
into the king's hand."

7But Jehoshaphat asked, "Is there not a prophet[h] of the LORD here whom we can inquire of?"

8The king of Israel answered Jehoshaphat,
"There is still one man through whom we can
inquire of the LORD, but I hate[i] him because he
never prophesies anything good[j] about me, but
always bad. He is Micaiah son of Imlah."

"The king should not say that," Jehoshaphat
replied.

9So the king of Israel called one of his officials
and said, "Bring Micaiah son of Imlah at once."

10Dressed in their royal robes, the king of Israel
and Jehoshaphat king of Judah were sitting on
their thrones at the threshing floor[k] by the entrance
of the gate of Samaria, with all the prophets prophesying before them. 11Now Zedekiah son of Kenaanah had made iron horns[l] and he declared, "This is
what the LORD says: 'With these you will gore the
Arameans until they are destroyed.' "

12All the other prophets were prophesying the
same thing. "Attack Ramoth Gilead and be victorious," they said, "for the LORD will give it into the
king's hand."

13The messenger who had gone to summon
Micaiah said to him, "Look, as one man the other
prophets are predicting success for the king. Let
your word agree with theirs, and speak favorably."

14But Micaiah said, "As surely as the LORD lives,
I can tell him only what the LORD tells me."[m]

15When he arrived, the king asked him, "Micaiah, shall we go to war against Ramoth Gilead, or
shall I refrain?"

"Attack and be victorious," he answered, "for
the LORD will give it into the king's hand."

16The king said to him, "How many times must
I make you swear to tell me nothing but the truth
in the name of the LORD?"

21:29 [c]2Ki 9:26
22:3 [d]Dt 4:43; Jos 21:38
22:4 [e]2Ki 3:7
22:5 [f]Ex 33:7; 2Ki 3:11
22:6 [g]1Ki 18:19
22:7 [h]2Ki 3:11
22:8 [i]Am 5:10 [j]Isa 5:20
22:10 [k]ver 6
22:11 [l]Dt 33:17; Zec 1:18-21
22:14 [m]Nu 22:18; 24:13; 1Ki 18:10,15

Prophets

1KI 22:7

Jehoshaphat clearly does not trust the prophets of the land, possibly because they serve under the evil King Ahab. Perhaps he also has contacts in the north who tell him which prophets can and cannot be trusted. Or perhaps God has given Jehoshaphat the ability to discern which prophets truly represent the Lord God. Ahab does not want to recommend Micaiah, a proven prophet, because Micaiah's prophecies about him are always negative (1Ki 22:8).

Perhaps at times we are more like Ahab than we like to admit. We pray for insight and revelation from the Lord—then reject a message that displeases us. God reveals truth to us, particularly through his Word, but many times it isn't exactly what we are waiting to hear. For example, God never promises that Christians won't suffer. In fact, he says the exact opposite (Php 1:29; 2Ti 3:12). We don't like hearing that or experiencing it! But God does promise that all things work for the good of those who love him (Ro 8:28).

22:17 17 Then Micaiah answered, "I saw all Israel scat-
[n]ver 34-36; tered on the hills like sheep without a shepherd,[n]
Nu 27:17; and the LORD said, 'These people have no master.
Mt 9:36 Let each one go home in peace.' "
18 The king of Israel said to Jehoshaphat, "Didn't
I tell you that he never prophesies anything good
about me, but only bad?"
19 Micaiah continued, "Therefore hear the word
22:19 of the LORD: I saw the LORD sitting on his throne[o]
[o]Isa 6:1; with all the host[p] of heaven standing around him
Eze 1:26; on his right and on his left. 20 And the LORD said,
Da 7:9 'Who will entice Ahab into attacking Ramoth Gil-
[p]Job 1:6; 2:1; ead and going to his death there?'
Ps 103:20-21; "One suggested this, and another that. 21 Finally,
Mt 18:10; a spirit came forward, stood before the LORD and
Heb 1:7,14 said, 'I will entice him.'
22 " 'By what means?' the LORD asked.
22:22 " 'I will go out and be a lying[q] spirit in the
[q]Jdg 9:23; mouths of all his prophets,' he said.
1Sa 16:14; " 'You will succeed in enticing him,' said the
18:10; 19:9; LORD. 'Go and do it.'
Eze 14:9; 23 "So now the LORD has put a lying spirit in the
2Th 2:11 mouths of all these prophets[r] of yours. The LORD
22:23 has decreed disaster for you."
[r]Eze 14:9 24 Then Zedekiah[s] son of Kenaanah went up and
22:24 slapped[t] Micaiah in the face. "Which way did the
[s]ver 11 spirit from[a] the LORD go when he went from me to
[t]Ac 23:2 speak to you?" he asked.
25 Micaiah replied, "You will find out on the day
22:25 you go to hide[u] in an inner room."
[u]1Ki 20:30 26 The king of Israel then ordered, "Take Micaiah
and send him back to Amon the ruler of the city
and to Joash the king's son 27 and say, 'This is
22:27 what the king says: Put this fellow in prison[v] and
[v]2Ch 16:10 give him nothing but bread and water until I
return safely.' "
28 Micaiah declared, "If you ever return safely,
22:28 the LORD has not spoken[w] through me." Then he
[w]Dt 18:22 added, "Mark my words, all you people!"

Ahab Killed at Ramoth Gilead

29 So the king of Israel and Jehoshaphat king of
Judah went up to Ramoth Gilead. 30 The king of Israel said to Jehoshaphat, "I will enter the battle in dis-
22:30 guise,[x] but you wear your royal robes." So the king
[x]2Ch 35:32 of Israel disguised himself and went into battle.
31 Now the king of Aram had ordered his thirty-
two chariot commanders, "Do not fight with any-
22:31 one, small or great, except the king[y] of Israel."
[y]2Sa 17:2 32 When the chariot commanders saw Jehoshaphat, they thought, "Surely this is the king of Israel." So they turned to attack him, but when
Jehoshaphat cried out, 33 the chariot commanders
saw that he was not the king of Israel and stopped
pursuing him.
22:34 34 But someone drew his bow[z] at random and hit
[z]2Ch 35:23 the king of Israel between the sections of his armor.
The king told his chariot driver, "Wheel around
and get me out of the fighting. I've been wound-

[a] 24 Or *Spirit of*

At Random?

1KI 22:34

The author of 1 and 2 Kings suggests that a soldier draws a bow at random and wounds King Ahab. Yet nothing is truly "random," for our sovereign God is always in control. This supposedly "random" act leads to Ahab's death, which one of God's prophets had foretold: "In the place where dogs licked up Naboth's blood, dogs will lick up your blood—yes, yours!" (1Ki 21:19).

The "random" acts that occur in our lives today also fall under the authority of the Lord. We "accidentally" find ourselves in situations that impact our families, our homes, our health, our careers . . . even our worship. Let's not think of any part of life as "random," but ask God today to orchestrate every detail of our circumstances to bring glory to him as well as to experience his blessings on our lives.

Ahab's Legacy

1KI 22:39

At the end of his life, King Ahab leaves a legacy of a beautiful palace and fortified cities. But sadly, the treasures that matter most—a love and reverence for his God and Creator—are nowhere to be found.

No matter how much wealth we acquire, in the end it is all just "stuff." While there is nothing wrong with building a lovely home or prospering in various ways, material wealth has no eternal value. Jesus warns, "Do not store up for yourselves treasures on earth . . . But store up for yourselves treasures in heaven . . . For where your treasure is, there your heart will be also" (Mt 6:19–21). It's never too late to add to the balance in our heavenly treasure accounts.

ed." 35All day long the battle raged, and the king
was propped up in his chariot facing the Arameans. The blood from his wound ran onto the floor
of the chariot, and that evening he died. 36As the
sun was setting, a cry spread through the army:
"Every man to his town; everyone to his land!"[a]
37So the king died and was brought to Samaria,
and they buried him there. 38They washed the
chariot at a pool in Samaria (where the prostitutes
bathed),[a] and the dogs[b] licked up his blood, as the
word of the LORD had declared.
39As for the other events of Ahab's reign,
including all he did, the palace he built and inlaid
with ivory,[c] and the cities he fortified, are they not
written in the book of the annals of the kings of
Israel? 40Ahab rested with his fathers. And Ahaziah his son succeeded him as king.

Jehoshaphat King of Judah

41Jehoshaphat son of Asa became king of Judah
in the fourth year of Ahab king of Israel. 42Jehosh-
aphat was thirty-five years old when he became
king, and he reigned in Jerusalem twenty-five
years. His mother's name was Azubah daughter
of Shilhi. 43In everything he walked in the ways
of his father Asa[d] and did not stray from them; he
did what was right in the eyes of the LORD. The
high places,[e] however, were not removed, and the
people continued to offer sacrifices and burn
incense there. 44Jehoshaphat was also at peace
with the king of Israel.
45As for the other events of Jehoshaphat's reign,
the things he achieved and his military exploits,
are they not written in the book of the annals of
the kings of Judah? 46He rid the land of the rest of
the male shrine prostitutes[f] who remained there
even after the reign of his father Asa. 47There was
then no king[g] in Edom; a deputy ruled.
48Now Jehoshaphat built a fleet of trading
ships[b][h] to go to Ophir for gold, but they never set
sail—they were wrecked at Ezion Geber. 49At that
time Ahaziah son of Ahab said to Jehoshaphat,
"Let my men sail with your men," but Jehoshaphat refused.
50Then Jehoshaphat rested with his fathers and
was buried with them in the city of David his
father. And Jehoram his son succeeded him.

Ahaziah King of Israel

51Ahaziah son of Ahab became king of Israel in
Samaria in the seventeenth year of Jehoshaphat
king of Judah, and he reigned over Israel two
years. 52He did evil[i] in the eyes of the LORD,
because he walked in the ways of his father and
mother and in the ways of Jeroboam son of Nebat,
who caused Israel to sin. 53He served and worshiped Baal[j] and provoked the LORD, the God of
Israel, to anger, just as his father[k] had done.

22:36 [a]2Ki 14:12
22:38 [b]1Ki 21:19
22:39 [c]2Ch 9:17; Am 3:15
22:43 [d]2Ch 17:3 [e]1Ki 3:2; 15:14; 2Ki 12:3
22:46 [f]Dt 23:17; 1Ki 14:24; 15:12
22:47 [g]2Sa 8:14; 2Ki 3:9; 8:20
22:48 [h]1Ki 9:26; 10:22
22:52 [i]1Ki 15:26; 21:25
22:53 [j]Jdg 2:11 [k]1Ki 16:30-32

[a] 38 Or *Samaria and cleaned the weapons* [b] 48 Hebrew *of ships of Tarshish*

2 Kings

The peril of refusing to obey God's prophets.

The book of 2 Kings details the steady downfall of the kingdoms of Israel and Judah. Beginning with the ministries of two prophets, Elijah and Elisha, it traces the reigns of the kings of both nations, highlighting the price that each kingdom pays for failing to heed the message of God's prophets. Because of sin and spiritual blindness, Israel is exiled to Assyria. Judah's failure to learn from Israel's example leads it down a similar path to exile in Babylon.

In 2 Kings the rebellion of the majority is contrasted with the faithfulness of a minority. We rejoice as a prophet's widow finds provision when she follows God's direction and closes her door to outside distractions (2Ki 4:1–7). We're delighted when a Shunammite woman bears a long-awaited child, and we grieve with her as the child's death tests her faith (2Ki 4:8–37). We revel in the bravery of a young slave girl who remembers the lessons of childhood and makes a recommendation to her sick master (2Ki 5:1–19). We're horrified at the brutal death of wicked Jezebel (2Ki 9:30–37) but gladdened when Jehosheba is able to save young Joash from certain death (2Ki 11:1–12).

As the fabric of morality slowly unravels in both Israel and Judah, the lines of right and wrong become blurred. The majority of their leaders show little regard for godly lifestyles. They become easy marks for idolatry, trusting that their status as God's chosen will insulate them from destruction—if they care about God at all. As the people of 2 Kings learn, the negative effects of persistent sin intensify over time. Compromising God's standards will result in moral and physical collapse. Obedience is the only sure path to blessing.

Quick Study

Author
Unknown.

Date Written
Probably written during Israel's Babylonian exile, around 550 B.C.

Setting
Israel and Judah.

Key Passage
2 Kings 13:23 "But the LORD was gracious to them and had compassion and showed concern for them because of his covenant with Abraham, Isaac and Jacob. To this day he has been unwilling to destroy them or banish them from his presence."

Outline

Elijah's ministry.
2Ki 1:1–2:18

Elisha's ministry.
2Ki 2:19–3:27

Two women in need.
2Ki 4:1–37

Feeding hungry people.
2Ki 4:38–48

Naaman's leprosy.
2Ki 5

More on Elisha's ministry.
2Ki 6:1–8:15

Two kings of Judah.
2Ki 8:16–29

Reign of Jehu; death of Ahab's family.
2Ki 9–10

The rescue and reign of Joash.
2Ki 11–12

Kings of Judah and Israel.
2Ki 13–16

Israel exiled to Assyria.
2Ki 17

Good king Hezekiah.
2Ki 18–20

The last kings of Judah.
2Ki 21–24

The fall of Jerusalem.
2Ki 25

The Women of 2 Kings

❦ **Widow with jars of oil**	*Rewarded for her faithful act.* 2Ki 4:1–7 (page 1144)
❦ **Shunammite woman**	*Experienced great joy and great sorrow.* 2Ki 4:8–37; 8:1–6 (page 1211)
❦ **Servant girl of Naaman's wife**	*A brave young woman.* 2Ki 5:–19; Lk 4:27 (page 1212)
Mothers who ate their sons	*Horrific acts of desperation.* 2Ki 6:26–30
❦ **Athaliah**	*Ambition run wild.* 2Ki 8:26; 11; 2Ch 22; 23:12–21 (page 1277)
❦ **Jehosheba**	*A brave act to save a prince.* 2Ki 11:2–3; 2Ch 22:11 (page 1278)
Zibiah	*Mother of King Joash.* 2Ki 12:1; 2Ch 24:1
Shimeath, Shomer	*Mothers of assassins.* 2Ki 12:21 (see also 2Ch 24:26)
Jehoaddin	*Mother of Amaziah.* 2Ki 14:2; 2Ch 25:1
Jecoliah	*Mother of Azariah.* 2Ki 15:2; 2Ch 26:3
Jerusha	*Mother of Jotham.* 2Ki 15:33; 2Ch 27:1
Abijah	*Mother of Hezekiah.* 2Ki 18:2; 2Ch 29:1
Hephzibah	*Mother of Manasseh.* 2Ki 21:1
Meshullemeth	*Mother of Amon.* 2Ki 21:19
Jedidah	*Mother of child-king Josiah.* 2Ki 22:1–2
Huldah	*Prophetess with bad news for Josiah.* 2Ki 22:14–20; 2Ch 34:22
Hamutal	*Mother of kings Jehoahaz and Zedekiah.* 2Ki 23:31; 24:18; Jer 52:1
Zebidah	*Mother of Jehoiakim.* 2Ki 23:36
Nehushta	*Mother of Jehoiachin.* 2Ki 24:8

❦ Denotes a sketch written about this character

The LORD's Judgment on Ahaziah

1 After Ahab's death, Moab[a] rebelled against Israel. 2Now Ahaziah had fallen through the lattice of his upper room in Samaria and injured himself. So he sent messengers,[b] saying to them, "Go and consult Baal-Zebub,[c] the god of Ekron,[d] to see if I will recover[e] from this injury."

3But the angel[f] of the LORD said to Elijah[g] the Tishbite, "Go up and meet the messengers of the king of Samaria and ask them, 'Is it because there is no God in Israel[h] that you are going off to consult Baal-Zebub, the god of Ekron?' 4Therefore this is what the LORD says: 'You will not leave[i] the bed you are lying on. You will certainly die!' " So Elijah went.

5When the messengers returned to the king, he asked them, "Why have you come back?"

6"A man came to meet us," they replied. "And he said to us, 'Go back to the king who sent you and tell him, "This is what the LORD says: Is it because there is no God in Israel that you are sending men to consult Baal-Zebub, the god of Ekron? Therefore you will not leave the bed you are lying on. You will certainly die!" ' "

7The king asked them, "What kind of man was it who came to meet you and told you this?"

8They replied, "He was a man with a garment of hair[j] and with a leather belt around his waist."

The king said, "That was Elijah the Tishbite."

9Then he sent[k] to Elijah a captain[l] with his company of fifty men. The captain went up to Elijah, who was sitting on the top of a hill, and said to him, "Man of God, the king says, 'Come down!' "

10Elijah answered the captain, "If I am a man of God, may fire come down from heaven and consume you and your fifty men!" Then fire[m] fell from heaven and consumed the captain and his men.

11At this the king sent to Elijah another captain with his fifty men. The captain said to him, "Man of God, this is what the king says, 'Come down at once!' "

12"If I am a man of God," Elijah replied, "may fire come down from heaven and consume you and your fifty men!" Then the fire of God fell from heaven and consumed him and his fifty men.

13So the king sent a third captain with his fifty men. This third captain went up and fell on his knees before Elijah. "Man of God," he begged, "please have respect for my life[n] and the lives of these fifty men, your servants! 14See, fire has fallen from heaven and consumed the first two captains and all their men. But now have respect for my life!"

15The angel[o] of the LORD said to Elijah, "Go down with him; do not be afraid[p] of him." So Elijah got up and went down with him to the king.

16He told the king, "This is what the LORD says: Is it because there is no God in Israel for you to consult that you have sent messengers[q] to consult Baal-Zebub, the god of Ekron? Because you have done

1:1 [a]Ge 19:37; 2Sa 8:2; 2Ki 3:5
1:2 [b]ver 16 [c]Mk 3:22 [d]1Sa 6:2; Isa 2:6; 14:29; Mt 10:25 [e]Jdg 18:5; 2Ki 8:7-10
1:3 [f]ver 15; Ge 16:7 [g]1Ki 17:1 [h]1Sa 28:8
1:4 [i]ver 6,16; Ps 41:8
1:8 [j]1Ki 18:7; Zec 13:4; Mt 3:4; Mk 1:6
1:9 [k]2Ki 6:14 [l]Ex 18:25; Isa 3:3
1:10 [m]1Ki 18:38; Lk 9:54; Rev 11:5; 13:13
1:13 [n]1Sa 26:21; Ps 72:14
1:15 [o]ver 3 [p]Isa 51:12; 57:11; Jer 1:17; Eze 2:6
1:16 [q]ver 2

[God's] mercy is incomparably greater than all the sins anyone could commit.

—Catherine of Siena (1347-1380)

A Whirlwind of a Prophet

2KI 2:1–11

Though a fiery chariot descends from heaven, Elijah is apparently not caught up in it. Rather, he goes up to heaven in the whirlwind itself. One of the most beautiful and poetic passages in Scripture, this account describes a fitting exit for a prophet who was himself a kind of whirlwind in life, calling down fire from heaven (1Ki 18:36–38), parting river waters (2Ki 2:8) and suddenly appearing and disappearing (1Ki 18:9–12,16).

this, you will never leave[r] the bed you are lying on.
You will certainly die!" 17So he died,[s] according to
the word of the LORD that Elijah had spoken.
Because Ahaziah had no son, Joram[a][t] succeeded him as king in the second year of Jehoram son
of Jehoshaphat king of Judah. 18As for all the other events of Ahaziah's reign, and what he did, are
they not written in the book of the annals of the
kings of Israel?

Elijah Taken Up to Heaven

2 When the LORD was about to take[u] Elijah up
to heaven in a whirlwind,[v] Elijah and Elisha[w]
were on their way from Gilgal.[x] 2Elijah said to Elisha, "Stay here;[y] the LORD has sent me to Bethel."
But Elisha said, "As surely as the LORD lives and
as you live, I will not leave you."[z] So they went
down to Bethel.
3The company[a] of the prophets at Bethel came
out to Elisha and asked, "Do you know that the
LORD is going to take your master from you today?"
"Yes, I know," Elisha replied, "but do not speak
of it."
4Then Elijah said to him, "Stay here, Elisha; the
LORD has sent me to Jericho.[b]"
And he replied, "As surely as the LORD lives and
as you live, I will not leave you." So they went to
Jericho.
5The company[c] of the prophets at Jericho went
up to Elisha and asked him, "Do you know that the
LORD is going to take your master from you today?"
"Yes, I know," he replied, "but do not speak
of it."
6Then Elijah said to him, "Stay here;[d] the LORD
has sent me to the Jordan."[e]
And he replied, "As surely as the LORD lives and
as you live, I will not leave you."[f] So the two of
them walked on.
7Fifty men of the company of the prophets went
and stood at a distance, facing the place where Elijah and Elisha had stopped at the Jordan. 8Elijah
took his cloak,[g] rolled it up and struck[h] the water
with it. The water divided[i] to the right and to the
left, and the two of them crossed over on dry[j]
ground.
9When they had crossed, Elijah said to Elisha,
"Tell me, what can I do for you before I am taken
from you?"
"Let me inherit a double[k] portion of your spirit,"[l] Elisha replied.
10"You have asked a difficult thing," Elijah said,
"yet if you see me when I am taken from you, it
will be yours—otherwise not."
11As they were walking along and talking
together, suddenly a chariot of fire[m] and horses of
fire appeared and separated the two of them, and
Elijah went up to heaven[n] in a whirlwind.[o] 12Elisha saw this and cried out, "My father! My father!
The chariots[p] and horsemen of Israel!" And Eli-

[a] 17 Hebrew *Jehoram,* a variant of *Joram*

1:16 [r]ver 4
1:17 [s]2Ki 8:15; Jer 20:6; 28:17 [t]2Ki 3:1; 8:16
2:1 [u]Ge 5:24; Heb 11:5 [v]ver 11; 1Ki 19:11; Isa 5:28; 66:15; Jer 4:13; Na 1:3 [w]1Ki 19:16, 21 [x]Dt 11:30; 2Ki 4:38
2:2 [y]ver 6 [z]Ru 1:16; 1Sa 1:26; 2Ki 4:30
2:3 [a]1Sa 10:5; 2Ki 4:1,38
2:4 [b]Jos 3:16; 6:26
2:5 [c]ver 3
2:6 [d]ver 2 [e]Jos 3:15 [f]Ru 1:16
2:8 [g]1Ki 19:19 [h]ver 14 [i]Ex 14:21 [j]Ex 14:22,29
2:9 [k]Dt 21:17 [l]Nu 11:17
2:11 [m]2Ki 6:17; Ps 68:17; 104:3,4; Isa 66:15; Hab 3:8; Zec 6:1 [n]Ge 5:24 [o]ver 1
2:12 [p]2Ki 6:17; 13:14

2:12 sha saw him no more. Then he took hold of his
[q]Ge 37:29 own clothes and tore[q] them apart.
13He picked up the cloak that had fallen from
2:14 Elijah and went back and stood on the bank of the
[r]1Ki 19:19 Jordan. 14Then he took the cloak[r] that had fallen
[s]ver 8 from him and struck[s] the water with it. "Where
now is the LORD, the God of Elijah?" he asked.
When he struck the water, it divided to the right
2:15 and to the left, and he crossed over.
[t]ver 7; 15The company[t] of the prophets from Jericho,
1Sa 10:5 who were watching, said, "The spirit[u] of Elijah is
[u]Nu 11:17 resting on Elisha." And they went to meet him
and bowed to the ground before him. 16"Look,"
they said, "we your servants have fifty able men.
Let them go and look for your master. Perhaps the
2:16 [v]1Ki 18:12 Spirit[v] of the LORD has picked him up[w] and set
[w]Ac 8:39 him down on some mountain or in some valley."
2:17 "No," Elisha replied, "do not send them."
[x]2Ki 8:11 17But they persisted until he was too ashamed[x]
to refuse. So he said, "Send them." And they sent
fifty men, who searched for three days but did not
find him. 18When they returned to Elisha, who
was staying in Jericho, he said to them, "Didn't I
tell you not to go?"

Healing of the Water

19The men of the city said to Elisha, "Look, our
lord, this town is well situated, as you can see, but
the water is bad and the land is unproductive."
20"Bring me a new bowl," he said, "and put salt
in it." So they brought it to him.
2:21 21Then he went out to the spring and threw[y] the
[y]Ex 15:25; salt into it, saying, "This is what the LORD says: 'I
2Ki 4:41; 6:6 have healed this water. Never again will it cause
2:22 death or make the land unproductive.' " 22And the
[z]Ex 15:25 water has remained wholesome[z] to this day,
according to the word Elisha had spoken.

2:23
Elisha Is Jeered

[a]Ex 22:28; 23From there Elisha went up to Bethel. As he
2Ch 36:16; Job 19:18; was walking along the road, some youths came
Ps 31:18 out of the town and jeered[a] at him. "Go on up,
2:24 you baldhead!" they said. "Go on up, you bald-
[b]Ge 4:11; head!" 24He turned around, looked at them and
Ne 13:25-27 called down a curse[b] on them in the name[c] of the
[c]Dt 18:19 2:25 LORD. Then two bears came out of the woods and
[d]1Ki 18:20; mauled forty-two of the youths. 25And he went on
2Ki 4:25 to Mount Carmel[d] and from there returned to
3:1 Samaria.
[e]2Ki 1:17

Moab Revolts

3:2
[f]1Ki 15:26 3 Joram[a][e] son of Ahab became king of Israel in
[g]1Ki 16:30-32 Samaria in the eighteenth year of Jehoshaphat
[h]Ex 23:24; king of Judah, and he reigned twelve years. 2He
2Ki 10:18, did evil[f] in the eyes of the LORD, but not as his
26-28 father[g] and mother had done. He got rid of the
3:3 sacred stone[h] of Baal that his father had made.
[i]1Ki 12:28-32; 14:9,16 3Nevertheless he clung to the sins[i] of Jeroboam

[a] *1* Hebrew *Jehoram,* a variant of *Joram;* also in verse 6

Clear Consequences

2KI 2:23–24

It may seem as though Elisha's response is a bit excessive. But it is, in fact, appropriate in light of what is occurring around him. The youths he encounters are likely in their late teens, and there are a good number them. Many of us today feel wary when we encounter just one or two angry-looking teenagers. These young men—there are at least 42 of them—don't just look antagonistic, they go out of their way to pick a fight.

Despite their taunts, it seems unlikely that Elisha is spurred to action because he is personally offended. More likely, he is disturbed by their rejection of prophetic authority and of the God he represents. He responds by calling on the Lord, and God deals with the youths in the manner he sees fit—sending a clear message about the consequences that await those who blaspheme the Lord.

The Sheep of Moab

2KI 3:4-5

The sheep owned by the king of Moab are probably of a small and not particularly impressive-looking breed, yet they can be counted on to yield great amounts of quality wool. The number of sheep Mesha reportedly owes to the king of Israel is extraordinarily high for an annual tribute. This may have been due to the vast amounts of pastureland he controls. The amount also could be a poetic, rather than a literal, figure—representing the complete submission required of Mesha by the king of Israel. Or it may possibly refer to a penalty assessed against Moab for its rebellion after the death of Ahab.

son of Nebat, which he had caused Israel to commit; he did not turn away from them.
4 Now Mesha king of Moab[j] raised sheep, and
he had to supply the king of Israel with a hundred
thousand lambs[k] and with the wool of a hundred
thousand rams. 5 But after Ahab died, the king of
Moab rebelled[l] against the king of Israel. 6 So at
that time King Joram set out from Samaria and
mobilized all Israel. 7 He also sent this message to
Jehoshaphat king of Judah: "The king of Moab
has rebelled against me. Will you go with me to
fight[m] against Moab?"
"I will go with you," he replied. "I am as you
are, my people as your people, my horses as your
horses."
8 "By what route shall we attack?" he asked.
"Through the Desert of Edom," he answered.
9 So the king of Israel set out with the king of
Judah and the king of Edom.[n] After a roundabout
march of seven days, the army had no more water
for themselves or for the animals with them.
10 "What!" exclaimed the king of Israel. "Has the
LORD called us three kings together only to hand
us over to Moab?"
11 But Jehoshaphat asked, "Is there no prophet
of the LORD here, that we may inquire[o] of the LORD
through him?"
An officer of the king of Israel answered, "Elisha[p] son of Shaphat is here. He used to pour water
on the hands of Elijah.[a][q]"
12 Jehoshaphat said, "The word[r] of the LORD is
with him." So the king of Israel and Jehoshaphat
and the king of Edom went down to him.
13 Elisha said to the king of Israel, "What do we
have to do with each other? Go to the prophets of
your father and the prophets of your mother."
"No," the king of Israel answered, "because it
was the LORD who called us three kings together
to hand us over to Moab."
14 Elisha said, "As surely as the LORD Almighty
lives, whom I serve, if I did not have respect for
the presence of Jehoshaphat king of Judah, I
would not look at you or even notice you. 15 But
now bring me a harpist."[s]
While the harpist was playing, the hand[t] of the
LORD came upon Elisha 16 and he said, "This is
what the LORD says: Make this valley full of
ditches. 17 For this is what the LORD says: You will
see neither wind nor rain, yet this valley will be
filled with water,[u] and you, your cattle and your
other animals will drink. 18 This is an easy[v] thing
in the eyes of the LORD; he will also hand Moab
over to you. 19 You will overthrow every fortified
city and every major town. You will cut down
every good tree, stop up all the springs, and ruin
every good field with stones."
20 The next morning, about the time[w] for offering the sacrifice, there it was—water flowing from

3:4 [j]Ge 19:37; 2Ki 1:1 [k]Ezr 7:17; Isa 16:1
3:5 [l]2Ki 1:1
3:7 [m]1Ki 22:4
3:9 [n]1Ki 22:47
3:11 [o]Ge 25:22; 1Ki 22:7 [p]Ge 20:7 [q]1Ki 19:16
3:12 [r]Nu 11:17
3:15 [s]1Sa 16:23 [t]Jer 15:17; Eze 1:3
3:17 [u]Ps 107:35; Isa 32:2; 35:6; 41:18
3:18 [v]Ge 18:14; 2Ki 20:10; Isa 49:6; Jer 32:17,27; Mk 10:27
3:20 [w]Ex 29:39-40

[a] *11* That is, he was Elijah's personal servant.

3:20 the direction of Edom! And the land was filled
[x]Ex 17:6 with water.[x]
21 Now all the Moabites had heard that the kings
had come to fight against them; so every man,
young and old, who could bear arms was called up
and stationed on the border. 22 When they got up
early in the morning, the sun was shining on the
water. To the Moabites across the way, the water
looked red—like blood. 23 "That's blood!" they said.
"Those kings must have fought and slaughtered
each other. Now to the plunder, Moab!"
24 But when the Moabites came to the camp of
Israel, the Israelites rose up and fought them until
they fled. And the Israelites invaded the land and
slaughtered the Moabites. 25 They destroyed the
towns, and each man threw a stone on every good
field until it was covered. They stopped up all the
3:25 springs and cut down every good tree. Only Kir
[y]ver 19; Hareseth[y] was left with its stones in place, but
Isa 15:1; men armed with slings surrounded it and
16:7; attacked it as well.
Jer 48:31,36 26 When the king of Moab saw that the battle
had gone against him, he took with him seven
hundred swordsmen to break through to the king
of Edom, but they failed. 27 Then he took his first-
3:27 [z]Dt 12:31; born[z] son, who was to succeed him as king, and
2Ki 16:3; offered him as a sacrifice on the city wall. The
21:6; 2Ch 28:3; fury against Israel was great; they withdrew and
Ps 106:38; returned to their own land.
Jer 19:4-5; Am 2:1; Mic 6:7

The Widow's Oil

4:1 [a]1Sa 10:5; **4** The wife of a man from the company[a] of the
2Ki 2:3 prophets cried out to Elisha, "Your servant my
[b]Ex 22:26; husband is dead, and you know that he revered
Lev 25:39- the LORD. But now his creditor[b] is coming to take
43; Ne 5:3-5; my two boys as his slaves."
Job 22:6; 2 Elisha replied to her, "How can I help you? Tell
24:9 me, what do you have in your house?"
4:2 "Your servant has nothing there at all," she
[c]1Ki 17:12 said, "except a little oil."[c]
3 Elisha said, "Go around and ask all your neighbors for empty jars. Don't ask for just a few. 4 Then
go inside and shut the door behind you and your
sons. Pour oil into all the jars, and as each is
filled, put it to one side."
5 She left him and afterward shut the door
behind her and her sons. They brought the jars to
her and she kept pouring. 6 When all the jars were
full, she said to her son, "Bring me another one."
But he replied, "There is not a jar left." Then
the oil stopped flowing.
4:7 7 She went and told the man of God,[d] and he
[d]1Ki 12:22 said, "Go, sell the oil and pay your debts. You and
your sons can live on what is left."

The Shunammite's Son Restored to Life

4:8 8 One day Elisha went to Shunem.[e] And a well-
[e]Jos 19:18 to-do woman was there, who urged him to stay for
a meal. So whenever he came by, he stopped there
to eat. 9 She said to her husband, "I know that this

Complete Destruction

2KI 3:25

The destruction of the land of the Moabites is not *indiscriminate, nor is it done without reason. Standard practices of warfare at the time called for soldiers to destroy their enemy's agricultural potential. The extreme action taken here is due primarily to the idolatry and wickedness of the Moabites and the threat for idolatry that they represent to the people of Israel.*

The soldiers could have done *nothing, however, if Elisha had not been present to call on the Lord. Because of God's actions, the Moabites see pools of water in the desert that they take to be blood, giving them a false sense of confidence. The likely source of this water was rainfall over neighboring Edom. The reflection of the rising sun on the water caused it to appear red like blood.*

Hospitality

2KI 4:10

Scripture teaches that each person has a spiritual gift that he or she is to use to bless others (Ro 12:4–8). The Shunammite woman has the gift of hospitality, and she uses *it. Not only does she graciously bring Elisha into her home, but she also prepares a special room for him. All of this is done with no thought to what she will receive; the woman is simply delighted to give.*

In our busy lives, it is difficult to make room for activities that don't seem to give us some return on our efforts. Yet we are definitely called to use the gifts God has given us to touch the lives of others. We can discover a variety of gifts if we study Romans 12 and *1 Corinthians 12. Then we can follow the example of the Shunammite woman and use our gift to God's glory (see the character sketch for this woman on page 1211).*

man who often comes our way is a holy man of
God. [10]Let's make a small room on the roof and put
in it a bed and a table, a chair and a lamp for him.
Then he can stay[f] there whenever he comes to us."
[11]One day when Elisha came, he went up to his
room and lay down there. [12]He said to his servant
Gehazi, "Call the Shunammite."[g] So he called her,
and she stood before him. [13]Elisha said to him,
"Tell her, 'You have gone to all this trouble for us.
Now what can be done for you? Can we speak on
your behalf to the king or the commander of the
army?' "

She replied, "I have a home among my own
people."

[14]"What can be done for her?" Elisha asked.

Gehazi said, "Well, she has no son and her husband is old."

[15]Then Elisha said, "Call her." So he called her,
and she stood in the doorway. [16]"About this time[h]
next year," Elisha said, "you will hold a son in
your arms."

"No, my lord," she objected. "Don't mislead
your servant, O man of God!"

[17]But the woman became pregnant, and the
next year about that same time she gave birth to a
son, just as Elisha had told her.

[18]The child grew, and one day he went out to
his father, who was with the reapers.[i] [19]"My head!
My head!" he said to his father.

His father told a servant, "Carry him to his
mother." [20]After the servant had lifted him up and
carried him to his mother, the boy sat on her lap
until noon, and then he died. [21]She went up and
laid him on the bed[j] of the man of God, then shut
the door and went out.

[22]She called her husband and said, "Please send
me one of the servants and a donkey so I can go to
the man of God quickly and return."

[23]"Why go to him today?" he asked. "It's not the
New Moon[k] or the Sabbath."

"It's all right," she said.

[24]She saddled the donkey and said to her servant, "Lead on; don't slow down for me unless I
tell you." [25]So she set out and came to the man of
God at Mount Carmel.[l]

When he saw her in the distance, the man of
God said to his servant Gehazi, "Look! There's the
Shunammite! [26]Run to meet her and ask her, 'Are
you all right? Is your husband all right? Is your
child all right?' "

"Everything is all right," she said.

[27]When she reached the man of God at the
mountain, she took hold of his feet. Gehazi came
over to push her away, but the man of God said,
"Leave her alone! She is in bitter distress,[m] but the
LORD has hidden it from me and has not told me
why."

[28]"Did I ask you for a son, my lord?" she said.
"Didn't I tell you, 'Don't raise my hopes'?"

[29]Elisha said to Gehazi, "Tuck your cloak into
your belt,[n] take my staff[o] in your hand and run. If

4:10 [f]Mt 10:41; Ro 12:13
4:12 [g]2Ki 8:1
4:16 [h]Ge 18:10
4:18 [i]Ru 2:3
4:21 [j]ver 32
4:23 [k]Nu 10:10; 1Ch 23:31; Ps 81:3
4:25 [l]1Ki 18:20; 2Ki 2:25
4:27 [m]1Sa 1:15
4:29 [n]1Ki 18:46; 2Ki 2:8,14; 9:1 [o]Ex 4:2; 7:19; 14:16

you meet anyone, do not greet him, and if anyone
greets you, do not answer. Lay my staff on the
boy's face."
[30]But the child's mother said, "As surely as the
LORD lives and as you live, I will not leave you."
So he got up and followed her.
[31]Gehazi went on ahead and laid the staff on the
boy's face, but there was no sound or response.
So Gehazi went back to meet Elisha and told him,
"The boy has not awakened."
[32]When Elisha reached the house, there was the
4:32 [p]ver 21 boy lying dead on his couch.[p] [33]He went in, shut
the door on the two of them and prayed[q] to the
4:33 [q]1Ki 17:20; LORD. [34]Then he got on the bed and lay upon the
Mt 6:6 boy, mouth to mouth, eyes to eyes, hands to
4:34 hands. As he stretched[r] himself out upon him, the
[r]1Ki 17:21; boy's body grew warm. [35]Elisha turned away and
Ac 20:10 walked back and forth in the room and then got
4:35 on the bed and stretched out upon him once
[s]Jos 6:15 more. The boy sneezed seven times[s] and opened
[t]2Ki 8:5 his eyes.[t]
[36]Elisha summoned Gehazi and said, "Call the
4:36 Shunammite." And he did. When she came, he
[u]Heb 11:35 said, "Take your son."[u] [37]She came in, fell at his
feet and bowed to the ground. Then she took her
son and went out.

Death in the Pot

4:38 [v]2Ki 2:1 [38]Elisha returned to Gilgal[v] and there was a
[w]Lev 26:26; famine[w] in that region. While the company of the
2Ki 8:1 prophets was meeting with him, he said to his servant, "Put on the large pot and cook some stew
for these men."
[39]One of them went out into the fields to gather
herbs and found a wild vine. He gathered some of
its gourds and filled the fold of his cloak. When he
returned, he cut them up into the pot of stew,
though no one knew what they were. [40]The stew
was poured out for the men, but as they began to
eat it, they cried out, "O man of God, there is
death in the pot!" And they could not eat it.
[41]Elisha said, "Get some flour." He put it into
the pot and said, "Serve it to the people to eat."
4:41 [x]Ex 15:25; 2Ki 2:21 And there was nothing harmful in the pot.[x]

Feeding of a Hundred

4:42 [y]1Sa 9:4 [42]A man came from Baal Shalishah,[y] bringing
[z]Mt 14:17; 15:36 the man of God twenty loaves[z] of barley bread[a]
[a]1Sa 9:7 baked from the first ripe grain, along with some
heads of new grain. "Give it to the people to eat,"
Elisha said.
[43]"How can I set this before a hundred men?"
his servant asked.
But Elisha answered, "Give it to the people to
4:43 [b]Lk 9:13 eat.[b] For this is what the LORD says: 'They will eat
[c]Mt 14:20; and have some left over.[c]' " [44]Then he set it before
Jn 6:12 them, and they ate and had some left over, according to the word of the LORD.

Death in the Pot

2KI 4:38–44

Elisha's visit to Gilgal comes at a time of famine. Not long after his arrival, a group of prophets meets to share a meal. When one of the men returns from gathering herbs for the stew, a poisonous ingredient is accidentally added to the meal. Once the men begin to eat, the bitter taste of the stew reveals the mistake. Using the powers given to him by God, Elisha quickly renders the food safe.

In a second food-related miracle, Elisha orders that 20 barley loaves be used to feed 100 hungry men until satisfied—with food to spare. This episode shares many similarities with Jesus' feeding of the 5,000 (Mt 14:20), although it occurs on a much smaller scale.

A Servant Girl's Faith

2KI 5:1-15

Very little is known about the girl who serves Naaman's wife. We know that she is an Israelite; we know that she is a captive—and we know that her faith in God is strong. Although she is far from home, she shows no sign of bitterness. Her desire is for her master's healing, and she doesn't hesitate to tell of her conviction that the prophet of God can heal him.

She could have thought she was too young, too weak, too inexperienced or too trapped in her own difficult circumstances to have any real impact on the situation. We all feel that way at times. But as this young servant girl reveals, we don't have to be mature, experienced or untouched by heartache to be used by God. We simply need to be faithful (see the character sketch for this girl on page 1212).

Naaman Healed of Leprosy

5 Now Naaman was commander of the army of 5:1
the king of Aram.[d] He was a great man in the [d]Ge 10:22;
sight of his master and highly regarded, because 2Sa 10:19
through him the LORD had given victory to Aram. [e]Ex 4:6;
He was a valiant soldier, but he had leprosy.[a][e] Nu 12:10; Lk 4:27
[2]Now bands[f] from Aram had gone out and had
taken captive a young girl from Israel, and she 5:2
served Naaman's wife. [3]She said to her mistress, [f]2Ki 6:23; 13:20; 24:2
"If only my master would see the prophet[g] who is 5:3
in Samaria! He would cure him of his leprosy." [g]Ge 20:7
[4]Naaman went to his master and told him what
the girl from Israel had said. [5]"By all means, go,"
the king of Aram replied. "I will send a letter to
the king of Israel." So Naaman left, taking with 5:5
him ten talents[b] of silver, six thousand shekels[c] of [h]ver 22;
gold and ten sets of clothing.[h] [6]The letter that he Ge 24:53;
took to the king of Israel read: "With this letter I Jdg 14:12;
am sending my servant Naaman to you so that 1Sa 9:7
you may cure him of his leprosy." 5:7
[7]As soon as the king of Israel read the letter,[i] he [i]2Ki 19:14
tore his robes and said, "Am I God?[j] Can I kill and [j]Ge 30:2
bring back to life?[k] Why does this fellow send [k]Dt 32:39; 1Sa 2:6
someone to me to be cured of his leprosy? See [l]1Ki 20:7
how he is trying to pick a quarrel[l] with me!"
[8]When Elisha the man of God heard that the
king of Israel had torn his robes, he sent him this
message: "Why have you torn your robes? Have
the man come to me and he will know that there
is a prophet[m] in Israel." [9]So Naaman went with 5:8
his horses and chariots and stopped at the door of [m]1Ki 22:7
Elisha's house. [10]Elisha sent a messenger to say to 5:10
him, "Go, wash[n] yourself seven times[o] in the Jor- [n]Jn 9:7
dan, and your flesh will be restored and you will [o]Ge 33:3;
be cleansed." Lev 14:7
[11]But Naaman went away angry and said, "I
thought that he would surely come out to me and
stand and call on the name of the LORD his God, 5:11
wave his hand[p] over the spot and cure me of my [p]Ex 7:19
leprosy. [12]Are not Abana and Pharpar, the rivers 5:12
of Damascus, better than any of the waters[q] of [q]Isa 8:6
Israel? Couldn't I wash in them and be cleansed?" [r]Pr 14:17,29;
So he turned and went off in a rage.[r] 19:11; 29:11
[13]Naaman's servants went to him and said, "My 5:13
father,[s] if the prophet had told you to do some [s]2Ki 6:21;
great thing, would you not have done it? How 13:14
much more, then, when he tells you, 'Wash and 5:14
be cleansed'!" [14]So he went down and dipped [t]Ge 33:3; Lev 14:7;
himself in the Jordan seven times,[t] as the man of Jos 6:15
God had told him, and his flesh was restored[u] and [u]Ex 4:7
became clean like that of a young boy.[v] [v]Job 33:25; Lk 4:27
[15]Then Naaman and all his attendants went 5:15
back to the man of God[w]. He stood before him and [w]Jos 2:11
said, "Now I know[x] that there is no God in all the [x]Jos 4:24;
world except in Israel. Please accept now a gift[y] 1Sa 17:46; Da 2:47
from your servant." [y]1Sa 9:7; 25:27

[a] *1* The Hebrew word was used for various diseases affecting the skin—not necessarily leprosy; also in verses 3, 6, 7, 11 and 27. [b] *5* That is, about 750 pounds (about 340 kilograms)
[c] *5* That is, about 150 pounds (about 70 kilograms)

Not What You Expect

Naaman, the bigwig, the commander of Aram's armies, has the respect of his men; he has courage; he has political clout; he has leprosy. Naaman goes to the king and tells him about a prophet in Israel who might be able to cure him. The king says, "Go."

When Naaman arrives at Elisha's house, Elisha doesn't even come out to meet him (not quite what Naaman expects). Instead, Elisha sends a messenger to tell Naaman to wash seven times in the Jordan River.

What does Naaman do (2Ki 5:11)? What circumstances might cause you to assume that your standing as God's child entitles you to a special hearing or healing?

What does Naaman say (2Ki 5:12)? Does his answer surprise you? Sound arrogant, even? What sort of circumstances might cause you to answer in much the same way? Perhaps, for example, when God asks something of you that seems too hard or unexpected or doesn't fit in with your tradition or theology?

What changes Naaman's mind (2Ki 5:13)? What will godly friends do for you in a time of testing?

What is the result of Naaman's obedience (2Ki 5:14)? When you don't understand God and his ways, it's easy to think your way is best. What results can you expect if you obey God even when what he requires seems outside your expectations or comfort zone?

After his healing, Naaman goes back to Elisha and, standing before all his attendants, makes a public statement of belief in the one true God (2Ki 5:15). What impact do you think this has on his attendants?

God is not confined to human ideas or opinions (Isa 55:8). If you keep him in the box that you have designed for him, he will show he is bigger than your box. If you refuse to accept his bigness, you will miss out on all the great things he wants you to discover and experience.

Enjoying God THROUGH the Word

Read John 9:1-7 (page 1761). Jesus already has a reputation for being a miracle worker. He heals the sick, usually with a touch or a word. But Jesus does the unexpected to this blind man. He spits on the ground, makes mud pie and puts it on the man's eyes. Then he tells the man to go to the Pool of Siloam and wash away the mud. Suppose the man had said, "Ugh! That's disgusting! I'm not going to embarrass myself by walking through town with this mud made with spittle on my face!" Do you think he would have been healed anyway? Sometimes God comes in unexpected ways. Sometimes God does things that seem totally unlike the way you think he should act. Have you ever tried to squeeze God into your human standards? Are you amazed that you would ever try? How have you limited God's handiwork and healing by a rigid set of standards and expectations?

Enjoying God THROUGH Experience

In prayer, ask the Holy Spirit to awaken fresh faith in you to look for the unexpected and to believe what seems unbelievable. "Call to me and I will answer you and tell you great and unsearchable things you do not know" (Jer 33:3). "Can you fathom the mysteries of God? Can you probe the limits of the Almighty? They are higher than the heavens—what can you do? They are deeper than the depths of the grave—what can you know? Their measure is longer than the earth and wider than the sea" (Job 11:7-9). Enjoying God can be a wonderful adventure of the unexpected. Come along!

Go to page 678 for your next weekly study.

Gehazi's Costly Mistake

2KI 5:20-27

For some time, Gehazi has been a faithful servant to Elisha. Gehazi accompanied Elisha when he went to the aid of the Shunammite woman (2Ki 4:29-37). Elisha's faith in his servant was so strong, in fact, that he entrusted Gehazi with his staff and gave him instructions regarding the boy's possible healing.

In the face of Naaman's wealth, however, Gehazi loses sight of what matters most. So great is his desire for wealth that he is willing to lie and betray his master in order to gain it. The poetic justice of his punishment cannot be missed: The Israelite who dishonors his God is struck with leprosy, while the pagan who honors God is miraculously healed of it.

16 The prophet answered, "As surely as the LORD
lives, whom I serve, I will not accept a thing."
And even though Naaman urged him, he refused.[z]
17 "If you will not," said Naaman, "please let me,
your servant, be given as much earth[a] as a pair of
mules can carry, for your servant will never again
make burnt offerings and sacrifices to any other
god but the LORD. 18 But may the LORD forgive your
servant for this one thing: When my master enters
the temple of Rimmon to bow down and he is
leaning[b] on my arm and I bow there also—when
I bow down in the temple of Rimmon, may the
LORD forgive your servant for this."
19 "Go in peace,"[c] Elisha said.
After Naaman had traveled some distance,
20 Gehazi, the servant of Elisha the man of God,
said to himself, "My master was too easy on Naaman, this Aramean, by not accepting from him
what he brought. As surely as the LORD[d] lives, I
will run after him and get something from him."
21 So Gehazi hurried after Naaman. When Naaman saw him running toward him, he got down
from the chariot to meet him. "Is everything all
right?" he asked.
22 "Everything is all right," Gehazi answered.
"My master sent me to say, 'Two young men from
the company of the prophets have just come to me
from the hill country of Ephraim. Please give
them a talent[a] of silver and two sets of clothing.' "[e]
23 "By all means, take two talents," said Naaman. He urged Gehazi to accept them, and then
tied up the two talents of silver in two bags, with
two sets of clothing. He gave them to two of his
servants, and they carried them ahead of Gehazi.
24 When Gehazi came to the hill, he took the
things from the servants and put them away in the
house. He sent the men away and they left. 25 Then
he went in and stood before his master Elisha.
"Where have you been, Gehazi?" Elisha asked.
"Your servant didn't go anywhere," Gehazi answered.
26 But Elisha said to him, "Was not my spirit
with you when the man got down from his chariot to meet you? Is this the time[f] to take money,
or to accept clothes, olive groves, vineyards,
flocks, herds, or menservants and maidservants?[g]
27 Naaman's leprosy[h] will cling to you and to your
descendants forever." Then Gehazi[i] went from Elisha's presence and he was leprous, as white as
snow.[j]

An Axhead Floats

6 The company[k] of the prophets said to Elisha,
"Look, the place where we meet with you is
too small for us. 2 Let us go to the Jordan, where
each of us can get a pole; and let us build a place
there for us to live."
And he said, "Go."

5:16 [z]ver 20,26; Ge 14:23; Da 5:17
5:17 [a]Ex 20:24
5:18 [b]2Ki 7:2
5:19 [c]1Sa 1:17; Ac 15:33
5:20 [d]Ex 20:7
5:22 [e]ver 5; Ge 45:22
5:26 [f]ver 16 [g]Jer 45:5
5:27 [h]Nu 12:10; 2Ki 15:5 [i]Col 3:5 [j]Ex 4:6
6:1 [k]1Sa 10:5; 2Ki 4:38

[a] *22* That is, about 75 pounds (about 34 kilograms)

[3]Then one of them said, "Won't you please
come with your servants?"
"I will," Elisha replied. [4]And he went with
them.
They went to the Jordan and began to cut down
trees. [5]As one of them was cutting down a tree,
the iron axhead fell into the water. "Oh, my lord,"
he cried out, "it was borrowed!"
[6]The man of God asked, "Where did it fall?"
When he showed him the place, Elisha cut a stick
6:6
and threw[l] it there, and made the iron float. [7]"Lift
[l]Ex 15:25;
it out," he said. Then the man reached out his
2Ki 2:21
hand and took it.

Elisha Traps Blinded Arameans

[8]Now the king of Aram was at war with Israel.
After conferring with his officers, he said, "I will
set up my camp in such and such a place."
6:9
[9]The man of God sent word to the king[m] of Isra-
[m]ver 12
el: "Beware of passing that place, because the Arameans are going down there." [10]So the king of
6:10
Israel checked on the place indicated by the man
[n]Jer 11:18
of God. Time and again Elisha warned[n] the king,
so that he was on his guard in such places.
[11]This enraged the king of Aram. He summoned
his officers and demanded of them, "Will you not
tell me which of us is on the side of the king of
Israel?"
6:12
[12]"None of us, my lord the king[o]," said one of
[o]ver 9
his officers, "but Elisha, the prophet who is in
Israel, tells the king of Israel the very words you
speak in your bedroom."
[13]"Go, find out where he is," the king ordered,
"so I can send men and capture him." The report
6:13
[p]Ge 37:17
came back: "He is in Dothan."[p] [14]Then he sent[q]
horses and chariots and a strong force there. They
6:14
went by night and surrounded the city.
[q]2Ki 1:9
[15]When the servant of the man of God got up
and went out early the next morning, an army
with horses and chariots had surrounded the city.
"Oh, my lord, what shall we do?" the servant
asked.
6:16
[16]"Don't be afraid,"[r] the prophet answered.
[r]Ge 15:1
[s]2Ch 32:7;
"Those who are with us are more[s] than those who
Ps 55:18;
are with them."
Ro 8:31;
1Jn 4:4
[17]And Elisha prayed, "O LORD, open his eyes so
he may see." Then the LORD opened the servant's
6:17
eyes, and he looked and saw the hills full of
[t]2Ki 2:11,12;
horses and chariots[t] of fire all around Elisha.
Ps 68:17;
Zec 6:1-7
[18]As the enemy came down toward him, Elisha
prayed to the LORD, "Strike these people with
6:18
blindness."[u] So he struck them with blindness, as
[u]Ge 19:11;
Ac 13:11
Elisha had asked.
[19]Elisha told them, "This is not the road and this
is not the city. Follow me, and I will lead you to
the man you are looking for." And he led them to
Samaria.
[20]After they entered the city, Elisha said, "LORD,
open the eyes of these men so they can see." Then
the LORD opened their eyes and they looked, and
there they were, inside Samaria.

Borrowing

2KI 6:1-7

In Old Testament times, the poor borrowed items they could not afford to own themselves. The commandments of God dictate that the Israelites should freely lend to their poor neighbors whatever they need (Dt 15:7-11). The fact that the ax is borrowed probably indicates that the prophets are too impoverished to own their own. They are also too poor to purchase a replacement if the axhead is lost. While the sinking of an axhead may not appear to us to be an earth-shattering event, its loss causes the company of prophets no small amount of worry. In God's eyes, the problem is deserving of a miracle.

In our own lives, we often feel hesitant to bring God our "axhead" problems. Yet there is no reason to hold back. For God cares about the tiniest details of our lives, and he wants us to bring even the smallest practical concerns to him.

Extreme Behavior

2KI 6:28–29

The woman's actions—cooking and eating her own son—are despicable. But perhaps she is not in her right mind when she performs them. At this point, the country has experienced famine for so long that the entire city is on the verge of starvation. History has shown that extremes of hunger can lead people to engage in extreme behaviors—even the cannibalism described here.

21 When the king of Israel saw them, he asked Elisha, "Shall I kill them, my father?[v] Shall I kill them?"

22 "Do not kill them," he answered. "Would you kill men you have captured[w] with your own sword or bow? Set food and water before them so that they may eat and drink and then go back to their master." 23 So he prepared a great feast for them, and after they had finished eating and drinking, he sent them away, and they returned to their master. So the bands[x] from Aram stopped raiding Israel's territory.

Famine in Besieged Samaria

24 Some time later, Ben-Hadad[y] king of Aram mobilized his entire army and marched up and laid siege[z] to Samaria. 25 There was a great famine[a] in the city; the siege lasted so long that a donkey's head sold for eighty shekels[a] of silver, and a quarter of a cab[b] of seed pods[c][b] for five shekels.[d]

26 As the king of Israel was passing by on the wall, a woman cried to him, "Help me, my lord the king!"

27 The king replied, "If the LORD does not help you, where can I get help for you? From the threshing floor? From the winepress?" 28 Then he asked her, "What's the matter?"

She answered, "This woman said to me, 'Give up your son so we may eat him today, and tomorrow we'll eat my son.' 29 So we cooked my son and ate[c] him. The next day I said to her, 'Give up your son so we may eat him,' but she had hidden him."

30 When the king heard the woman's words, he tore[d] his robes. As he went along the wall, the people looked, and there, underneath, he had sackcloth[e] on his body. 31 He said, "May God deal with me, be it ever so severely, if the head of Elisha son of Shaphat remains on his shoulders today!"

32 Now Elisha was sitting in his house, and the elders[f] were sitting with him. The king sent a messenger ahead, but before he arrived, Elisha said to the elders, "Don't you see how this murderer[g] is sending someone to cut off my head?[h] Look, when the messenger comes, shut the door and hold it shut against him. Is not the sound of his master's footsteps behind him?"

33 While he was still talking to them, the messenger came down to him. And ⌊the king⌋ said, "This disaster is from the LORD. Why should I wait[i] for the LORD any longer?"

7 Elisha said, "Hear the word of the LORD. This is what the LORD says: About this time tomorrow, a seah[e] of flour will sell for a shekel[f] and two

6:21 [v]2Ki 5:13
6:22 [w]Dt 20:11; 2Ch 28:8-15; Ro 12:20
6:23 [x]2Ki 5:2
6:24 [y]1Ki 15:18; 20:1; 2Ki 8:7 [z]Dt 28:52
6:25 [a]Lev 26:26; Ru 1:1 [b]Isa 36:12
6:29 [c]Lev 26:29; Dt 28:53-55
6:30 [d]2Ki 18:37; Isa 22:15 [e]Ge 37:34; 1Ki 21:27
6:32 [f]Eze 8:1; 14:1; 20:1 [g]1Ki 18:4 [h]ver 31
6:33 [i]Lev 24:11; Job 2:9; 14:14; Isa 40:31

[a] *25* That is, about 2 pounds (about 1 kilogram) [b] *25* That is, probably about 1/2 pint (about 0.3 liter) [c] *25* Or *of doves' dung* [d] *25* That is, about 2 ounces (about 55 grams) [e] *1* That is, probably about 7 quarts (about 7.3 liters); also in verses 16 and 18 [f] *1* That is, about 2/5 ounce (about 11 grams); also in verses 16 and 18

7:1 seahs[a] of barley for a shekel[j] at the gate of
[j]ver 16 Samaria."
[2]The officer on whose arm the king was lean-
7:2 [k]2Ki 5:18 ing[k] said to the man of God, "Look, even if the
[l]ver 19; LORD should open the floodgates[l] of the heavens,
Ge 7:11; Ps 78:23; could this happen?"
Mal 3:10 "You will see it with your own eyes," answered
[m]ver 17 Elisha, "but you will not eat[m] any of it!"

The Siege Lifted

7:3 [3]Now there were four men with leprosy[b][n] at the
[n]Lev 13:45-46; Nu 5:1-4 entrance of the city gate. They said to each other,
"Why stay here until we die? [4]If we say, 'We'll go
into the city'—the famine is there, and we will die.
And if we stay here, we will die. So let's go over to
the camp of the Arameans and surrender. If they
spare us, we live; if they kill us, then we die."
[5]At dusk they got up and went to the camp of
the Arameans. When they reached the edge of the
7:6 camp, not a man was there, [6]for the Lord had
[o]Ex 14:24; caused the Arameans to hear the sound[o] of chari-
2Sa 5:24; ots and horses and a great army, so that they said
Eze 1:24 [p]2Sa 10:6; to one another, "Look, the king of Israel has hired[p]
Jer 46:21 the Hittite[q] and Egyptian kings to attack us!" [7]So
[q]Nu 13:29 they got up and fled[r] in the dusk and abandoned
7:7 their tents and their horses and donkeys. They left
[r]Jdg 7:21; the camp as it was and ran for their lives.
Ps 48:4-6; [8]The men who had leprosy[s] reached the edge of
Pr 28:1; Isa 30:17 the camp and entered one of the tents. They ate
7:8 and drank, and carried away silver, gold and
[s]Isa 33:23; clothes, and went off and hid them. They returned
35:6 and entered another tent and took some things
from it and hid them also.
[9]Then they said to each other, "We're not doing
right. This is a day of good news and we are keeping it to ourselves. If we wait until daylight, punishment will overtake us. Let's go at once and
report this to the royal palace."
[10]So they went and called out to the city gatekeepers and told them, "We went into the Aramean camp and not a man was there—not a sound of
anyone—only tethered horses and donkeys, and
the tents left just as they were." [11]The gatekeepers
shouted the news, and it was reported within the
palace.
[12]The king got up in the night and said to his
officers, "I will tell you what the Arameans have
done to us. They know we are starving; so they
7:12 have left the camp to hide[t] in the countryside,
[t]Jos 8:4; thinking, 'They will surely come out, and then we
2Ki 6:25-29 will take them alive and get into the city.' "
[13]One of his officers answered, "Have some men
take five of the horses that are left in the city.
Their plight will be like that of all the Israelites
left here—yes, they will only be like all these Isra-

[a] *1* That is, probably about 13 quarts (about 15 liters); also in verses 16 and 18 [b] *3* The Hebrew word is used for various diseases affecting the skin—not necessarily leprosy; also in verse 8.

The Life of a Leper

2KI 7:1-11

The life of a leper in Old Testament times was nothing but grim. Lepers were required to live outside the city, separate from those who were healthy. Those stricken with the disease lived in isolation (see the note on Lev 13, page 173), with little hope for the future.

After famine strikes the land, things go from bad to worse for the lepers living outside Samaria. Whereas their families might have once passed them bits of food, now there is no nourishment to be found even within the city. Under such conditions, four lepers fatalistically decide to turn themselves over to the enemy—these four lepers, diseased, hungry, isolated and without much hope, are God's messengers of hope and healing to a besieged city. Their actions prove to have amazing results, for when they enter the Aramean camp, they find it empty of people, but full of plunder.

The Town of Shunem

2KI 8:1–6

A border town belonging to the tribe of Issachar (Jos 19:17–18), Shunem was located approximately three miles north of Jezreel. The Philistines camped at Shunem before Saul's last battle (1Sa 28:4). Shunem was the town of the unnamed Shunammite woman whose son was raised from the dead by Elisha (2Ki 4:8–36), as well as of Abishag, the young virgin who served King David in his old age (1Ki 1:3).

The story here of what happens to the Shunammite woman provides a beautiful example of the far-reaching impact of godly deeds. Though it would be unworthy of us to do good for others solely for the purpose of personal gain, it is at the same time encouraging—and empowering—to note that there is spiritual truth to the concept that blessing leads to blessing.

elites who are doomed. So let us send them to find
out what happened."
14So they selected two chariots with their
horses, and the king sent them after the Aramean
army. He commanded the drivers, "Go and find
out what has happened." 15They followed them as
far as the Jordan, and they found the whole road
strewn with the clothing and equipment the Arameans had thrown away in their headlong flight.
So the messengers returned and reported to the
king. 16Then the people went out and plundered[u]
the camp of the Arameans. So a seah of flour sold
for a shekel, and two seahs of barley sold for a
shekel,[v] as the LORD had said.
17Now the king had put the officer on whose
arm he leaned in charge of the gate, and the people trampled him in the gateway, and he died,[w]
just as the man of God had foretold when the king
came down to his house. 18It happened as the man
of God had said to the king: "About this time
tomorrow, a seah of flour will sell for a shekel and
two seahs of barley for a shekel at the gate of
Samaria."
19The officer had said to the man of God, "Look,
even if the LORD should open the floodgates[x] of the
heavens, could this happen?" The man of God had
replied, "You will see it with your own eyes, but
you will not eat any of it!" 20And that is exactly
what happened to him, for the people trampled
him in the gateway, and he died.

The Shunammite's Land Restored

8 Now Elisha had said to the woman[y] whose
son he had restored to life, "Go away with
your family and stay for a while wherever you
can, because the LORD has decreed a famine[z] in
the land that will last seven years."[a] 2The woman
proceeded to do as the man of God said. She and
her family went away and stayed in the land of
the Philistines seven years.
3At the end of the seven years she came back
from the land of the Philistines and went to the
king to beg for her house and land. 4The king was
talking to Gehazi, the servant of the man of God,
and had said, "Tell me about all the great things
Elisha has done." 5Just as Gehazi was telling the
king how Elisha had restored[b] the dead to life, the
woman whose son Elisha had brought back to life
came to beg the king for her house and land.
Gehazi said, "This is the woman, my lord the
king, and this is her son whom Elisha restored to
life." 6The king asked the woman about it, and
she told him.
Then he assigned an official to her case and
said to him, "Give back everything that belonged
to her, including all the income from her land
from the day she left the country until now."

Hazael Murders Ben-Hadad

7Elisha went to Damascus,[c] and Ben-Hadad[d]

7:16 [u]Isa 33:4,23 [v]ver 1
7:17 [w]ver 2; 2Ki 6:32
7:19 [x]ver 2
8:1 [y]2Ki 4:8-37 [z]Lev 26:26; Dt 28:22; Ru 1:1 [a]Ge 12:10; Ps 105:16; Hag 1:11
8:5 [b]2Ki 4:35
8:7 [c]2Sa 8:5; 1Ki 11:24 [d]2Ki 6:24

king of Aram was ill. When the king was told, "The man of God has come all the way up here," 8 he said to Hazael,[e] "Take a gift[f] with you and go to meet the man of God. Consult[g] the LORD through him; ask him, 'Will I recover from this illness?' "

9 Hazael went to meet Elisha, taking with him as a gift forty camel-loads of all the finest wares of Damascus. He went in and stood before him, and said, "Your son Ben-Hadad king of Aram has sent me to ask, 'Will I recover from this illness?' "

10 Elisha answered, "Go and say to him, 'You will certainly recover';[h] but[a] the LORD has revealed to me that he will in fact die." 11 He stared at him with a fixed gaze until Hazael felt ashamed.[i] Then the man of God began to weep.[j]

12 "Why is my lord weeping?" asked Hazael.

"Because I know the harm[k] you will do to the Israelites," he answered. "You will set fire to their fortified places, kill their young men with the sword, dash[l] their little children[m] to the ground, and rip open[n] their pregnant women."

13 Hazael said, "How could your servant, a mere dog,[o] accomplish such a feat?"

"The LORD has shown me that you will become king[p] of Aram," answered Elisha.

14 Then Hazael left Elisha and returned to his master. When Ben-Hadad asked, "What did Elisha say to you?" Hazael replied, "He told me that you would certainly recover." 15 But the next day he took a thick cloth, soaked it in water and spread it over the king's face, so that he died.[q] Then Hazael succeeded him as king.

Jehoram King of Judah

16 In the fifth year of Joram[r] son of Ahab king of Israel, when Jehoshaphat was king of Judah, Jehoram[s] son of Jehoshaphat began his reign as king of Judah. 17 He was thirty-two years old when he became king, and he reigned in Jerusalem eight years. 18 He walked in the ways of the kings of Israel, as the house of Ahab had done, for he married a daughter[t] of Ahab. He did evil in the eyes of the LORD. 19 Nevertheless, for the sake of his servant David, the LORD was not willing to destroy[u] Judah. He had promised to maintain a lamp[v] for David and his descendants forever.

20 In the time of Jehoram, Edom rebelled against Judah and set up its own king.[w] 21 So Jehoram[b] went to Zair with all his chariots. The Edomites surrounded him and his chariot commanders, but he rose up and broke through by night; his army, however, fled back home. 22 To this day Edom has been in rebellion[x] against Judah. Libnah[y] revolted at the same time.

23 As for the other events of Jehoram's reign, and all he did, are they not written in the book of the annals of the kings of Judah? 24 Jehoram rested

[a] *10* The Hebrew may also be read *Go and say, 'You will certainly not recover,' for.* [b] *21* Hebrew *Joram,* a variant of *Jehoram;* also in verses 23 and 24

8:8 [e] 1Ki 19:15 [f] Ge 32:20; 1Sa 9:7; 2Ki 1:2 [g] Jdg 18:5
8:10 [h] Isa 38:1
8:11 [i] Jdg 3:25 [j] Lk 19:41
8:12 [k] 1Ki 19:17; 2Ki 10:32; 12:17; 13:3, 7 [l] Ps 137:9; Isa 13:16; Hos 13:16; Na 3:10; Lk 19:44 [m] Ge 34:29 [n] 2Ki 15:16; Am 1:13
8:13 [o] 1Sa 17:43; 2Sa 3:8 [p] 1Ki 19:15
8:15 [q] 2Ki 1:17
8:16 [r] 2Ki 1:17; 3:1 [s] 2Ch 21:1-4
8:18 [t] ver 26; 2Ki 11:1
8:19 [u] Ge 6:13 [v] 2Sa 21:17; 7:13; 1Ki 11:36; Rev 21:23
8:20 [w] 1Ki 22:47
8:22 [x] Ge 27:40 [y] Nu 33:20; Jos 21:13; 2Ki 19:8

Elisha and Aram

2KI 8:7-15

Elisha's meeting with Hazael, an official under King Ben-Hadad, is not his first interaction with a leader from Aram (2Ki 5:1-19; 6:8-23). Though Elisha is accustomed to dealing with the Arameans, he is overwhelmed by the prophecy that God reveals to him in Hazael's presence. God tells Elisha that Hazael will not only become king of Aram but also that he will terrorize the Israelites. This news distresses the prophet, yet he does not argue or plead with God. Elisha understands that God has sovereign control over his people. No circumstance or event will happen to them that God does not ordain, control or allow.

Unlike Elisha's quiet acceptance of God's will, many of us rail against God in response to our difficulties. We can't understand why he allows certain things to occur in our lives. Elisha's response can teach us—and all believers—about dealing with difficult circumstances. God sees the forest when often all we can see are the trees. "Now we see but a poor reflection as in a mirror; then we shall see face to face" (1Co 13:12).

Influential but Wicked

2KI 8:25-29

In ancient times, women were generally considered subordinate to men. But there is no denying that at times they wielded great influence. Athaliah—daughter of Israel's King Ahab and possibly Queen Jezebel, wife to Judah's King Jehoram, and mother of Judah's King Ahaziah—has great influence over both her husband and son. Both men despise the Lord, an attitude that the godless Athaliah most certainly promotes and applauds.

Ahaziah reigns only one year in Jerusalem, and Athaliah seizes the opportunity to extend her influence. Rather than stand by as another son or grandson takes the throne, the full measure of this woman's wickedness is revealed when she massacres "the whole royal family" (2Ki 11:1) and takes the throne for herself. (See character sketch for Athaliah on page 1277.)

with his fathers and was buried with them in the
City of David. And Ahaziah his son succeeded
him as king.

Ahaziah King of Judah

25 In the twelfth[z] year of Joram son of Ahab king
of Israel, Ahaziah son of Jehoram king of Judah
began to reign. 26 Ahaziah was twenty-two years
old when he became king, and he reigned in Jerusalem one year. His mother's name was Athaliah,[a]
a granddaughter of Omri[b] king of Israel. 27 He
walked in the ways of the house of Ahab[c] and did
evil[d] in the eyes of the LORD, as the house of Ahab
had done, for he was related by marriage to
Ahab's family.

28 Ahaziah went with Joram son of Ahab to war
against Hazael king of Aram at Ramoth Gilead.[e]
The Arameans wounded Joram; 29 so King Joram
returned to Jezreel[f] to recover from the wounds
the Arameans had inflicted on him at Ramoth[a] in
his battle with Hazael[g] king of Aram.

Then Ahaziah son of Jehoram king of Judah
went down to Jezreel to see Joram son of Ahab,
because he had been wounded.

Jehu Anointed King of Israel

9 The prophet Elisha summoned a man from the
company[h] of the prophets and said to him,
"Tuck your cloak into your belt,[i] take this flask of
oil[j] with you and go to Ramoth Gilead.[k] 2 When
you get there, look for Jehu son of Jehoshaphat,
the son of Nimshi. Go to him, get him away from
his companions and take him into an inner room.
3 Then take the flask and pour the oil[l] on his head
and declare, 'This is what the LORD says: I anoint
you king over Israel.' Then open the door and run;
don't delay!"

4 So the young man, the prophet, went to
Ramoth Gilead. 5 When he arrived, he found the
army officers sitting together. "I have a message
for you, commander," he said.

"For which of us?" asked Jehu.

"For you, commander," he replied.

6 Jehu got up and went into the house. Then the
prophet poured the oil[m] on Jehu's head and
declared, "This is what the LORD, the God of Israel, says: 'I anoint you king over the LORD's people
Israel. 7 You are to destroy the house of Ahab your
master, and I will avenge[n] the blood of my servants[o] the prophets and the blood of all the LORD's
servants shed by Jezebel.[p] 8 The whole house[q] of
Ahab will perish. I will cut off from Ahab every
last male[r] in Israel—slave or free. 9 I will make the
house of Ahab like the house of Jeroboam[s] son of
Nebat and like the house of Baasha[t] son of Ahijah. 10 As for Jezebel, dogs[u] will devour her on the
plot of ground at Jezreel, and no one will bury
her.' " Then he opened the door and ran.

11 When Jehu went out to his fellow officers, one

[a] 29 Hebrew *Ramah*, a variant of *Ramoth*

8:25 [z]2Ki 9:29
8:26 [a]ver 18 [b]1Ki 16:23
8:27 [c]1Ki 16:30 [d]1Ki 15:26
8:28 [e]Dt 4:43; 1Ki 22:3,29
8:29 [f]2Ki 9:15 [g]1Ki 19:15, 17
9:1 [h]1Sa 10:5 [i]2Ki 4:29 [j]1Sa 10:1 [k]2Ki 8:28
9:3 [l]1Ki 19:16
9:6 [m]1Ki 19:16; 2Ch 22:7
9:7 [n]Ge 4:24; Rev 6:10 [o]Dt 32:43 [p]1Ki 18:4; 21:15
9:8 [q]2Ki 10:17 [r]Dt 32:36; 1Sa 25:22; 1Ki 21:21; 2Ki 14:26
9:9 [s]1Ki 14:10; 15:29; 16:3, 11 [t]1Ki 16:3
9:10 [u]ver 35-36; 1Ki 21:23

9:11 of them asked him, “Is everything all right? Why
[v]Jer 29:26; did this madman[v] come to you?”
Jn 10:20; “You know the man and the sort of things he
Ac 26:24 says,” Jehu replied.
12“That’s not true!” they said. “Tell us.”
Jehu said, “Here is what he told me: ‘This is
what the LORD says: I anoint you king over
Israel.’ ”
9:13 13They hurried and took their cloaks and
[w]Mt 21:8; spread[w] them under him on the bare steps. Then
Lk 19:36 they blew the trumpet[x] and shouted, “Jehu is
[x]2Sa 15:10; 1Ki 1:34,39 king!”

Jehu Kills Joram and Ahaziah

14So Jehu son of Jehoshaphat, the son of Nim-
9:14 shi, conspired against Joram. (Now Joram and all
[y]Dt 4:43; Israel had been defending Ramoth Gilead[y] against
2Ki 8:28 Hazael king of Aram, 15but King Joram[a] had
9:15 returned to Jezreel to recover[z] from the wounds
[z]2Ki 8:29 the Arameans had inflicted on him in the battle
with Hazael king of Aram.) Jehu said, “If this is
the way you feel, don’t let anyone slip out of the
city to go and tell the news in Jezreel.” 16Then he
got into his chariot and rode to Jezreel, because
9:16 [a]2Ch 22:7 Joram was resting there and Ahaziah[a] king of
Judah had gone down to see him.
9:17 [b]Isa 21:6 17When the lookout[b] standing on the tower in
[c]1Sa 16:4 Jezreel saw Jehu’s troops approaching, he called
out, “I see some troops coming.”
“Get a horseman,” Joram ordered. “Send him to
meet them and ask, ‘Do you come in peace?[c]’ ”
18The horseman rode off to meet Jehu and said,
“This is what the king says: ‘Do you come in
peace?’ ”
“What do you have to do with peace?” Jehu
replied. “Fall in behind me.”
The lookout reported, “The messenger has
reached them, but he isn’t coming back.”
19So the king sent out a second horseman.
When he came to them he said, “This is what the
king says: ‘Do you come in peace?’ ”
Jehu replied, “What do you have to do with
peace? Fall in behind me.”
20The lookout reported, “He has reached them,
9:20 but he isn’t coming back either. The driving is
[d]2Sa 18:27 like[d] that of Jehu son of Nimshi—he drives like a
madman.”
21“Hitch up my chariot,” Joram ordered. And
when it was hitched up, Joram king of Israel and
Ahaziah king of Judah rode out, each in his own
9:21 chariot, to meet Jehu. They met him at the plot of
[e]ver 26; ground that had belonged to Naboth[e] the Jezree-
1Ki 21:1-7, lite. 22When Joram saw Jehu he asked, “Have you
15-19 9:22 come in peace, Jehu?”
[f]1Ki 16:30- “How can there be peace,” Jehu replied, “as
33; 18:19; long as all the idolatry and witchcraft of your
2Ch 21:13; mother Jezebel[f] abound?”
Rev 2:20

[a] *15* Hebrew *Jehoram,* a variant of *Joram;* also in verses 17 and 21–24

I find that my joy is enlarged by understanding that, *as a child of God, even my pain* has purpose. That realization doesn’t eliminate my pain, but it makes it more manageable.

—Patsy Clairmont

Prophecy Fulfilled

2KI 9:24-37

Years before, the Lord had told the prophet Elijah that he would bring disaster on the house of Ahab in the days of the king's son because of Ahab's extreme wickedness (1Ki 21:19-29). With the deaths of Joram, Ahab's son, and Ahaziah, Ahab's grandson, the prophecy begins to see fulfillment. The rest of the gory end of Ahab's family is described in 2 Kings 10:1-17 (see note on next page). Elijah had also predicted that dogs would devour Jezebel by the wall of Jezreel (1Ki 21:23). (See character sketch for Jezebel on page 1076.) This prophecy also is fulfilled (2Ki 9:30-37), and justice for Naboth is accomplished.

23 Joram turned about and fled, calling out to
Ahaziah, "Treachery,[g] Ahaziah!"
24 Then Jehu drew his bow[h] and shot Joram
between the shoulders. The arrow pierced his
heart and he slumped down in his chariot. 25 Jehu
said to Bidkar, his chariot officer, "Pick him up
and throw him on the field that belonged to
Naboth the Jezreelite. Remember how you and I
were riding together in chariots behind Ahab his
father when the LORD made this prophecy[i] about
him: 26 'Yesterday I saw the blood of Naboth[j] and
the blood of his sons, declares the LORD, and I will
surely make you pay for it on this plot of ground,
declares the LORD.'[a] Now then, pick him up and
throw him on that plot, in accordance with the
word of the LORD."[k]
27 When Ahaziah king of Judah saw what had
happened, he fled up the road to Beth Haggan.[b]
Jehu chased him, shouting, "Kill him too!" They
wounded him in his chariot on the way up to Gur
near Ibleam,[l] but he escaped to Megiddo[m] and died
there. 28 His servants took him by chariot[n] to Jerusalem and buried him with his fathers in his tomb in
the City of David. 29 (In the eleventh[o] year of Joram
son of Ahab, Ahaziah had become king of Judah.)

Jezebel Killed

30 Then Jehu went to Jezreel. When Jezebel
heard about it, she painted[p] her eyes, arranged her
hair and looked out of a window. 31 As Jehu
entered the gate, she asked, "Have you come in
peace, Zimri,[q] you murderer of your master?"[c]
32 He looked up at the window and called out,
"Who is on my side? Who?" Two or three eunuchs
looked down at him. 33 "Throw her down!" Jehu
said. So they threw her down, and some of her
blood spattered the wall and the horses as they
trampled her underfoot.[r]
34 Jehu went in and ate and drank. "Take care of
that cursed woman," he said, "and bury her, for
she was a king's daughter."[s] 35 But when they went
out to bury her, they found nothing except her
skull, her feet and her hands. 36 They went back
and told Jehu, who said, "This is the word of the
LORD that he spoke through his servant Elijah the
Tishbite: On the plot of ground at Jezreel dogs[t] will
devour Jezebel's flesh.[d][u] 37 Jezebel's body will be
like refuse[v] on the ground in the plot at Jezreel, so
that no one will be able to say, 'This is Jezebel.' "

Ahab's Family Killed

10 Now there were in Samaria[w] seventy sons[x]
of the house of Ahab. So Jehu wrote letters
and sent them to Samaria: to the officials of Jezreel,[e][y] to the elders and to the guardians[z] of Ahab's
children. He said, 2 "As soon as this letter reaches

[a] *26* See 1 Kings 21:19. [b] *27* Or *fled by way of the garden house* [c] *31* Or *"Did Zimri have peace, who murdered his master?"* [d] *36* See 1 Kings 21:23. [e] *1* Hebrew; some Septuagint manuscripts and Vulgate *of the city*

9:23 [g] 2Ki 11:14
9:24 [h] 1Ki 22:34
9:25 [i] 1Ki 21:19-22,24-29
9:26 [j] 1Ki 21:19 [k] 1Ki 21:29
9:27 [l] Jdg 1:27 [m] 2Ki 23:29
9:28 [n] 2Ki 14:20; 23:30
9:29 [o] 2Ki 8:25
9:30 [p] Jer 4:30; Eze 23:40
9:31 [q] 1Ki 16:9-10
9:33 [r] Ps 7:5
9:34 [s] 1Ki 16:31; 21:25
9:36 [t] Ps 68:23; Jer 15:3 [u] 1Ki 21:23
9:37 [v] Ps 83:10; Isa 5:25; Jer 8:2; 9:22; 16:4; 25:33; Zep 1:17
10:1 [w] 1Ki 13:32 [x] Jdg 8:30 [y] 1Ki 21:1 [z] ver 5

you, since your master's sons are with you and
you have chariots and horses, a fortified city and
weapons, 3choose the best and most worthy of
your master's sons and set him on his father's
throne. Then fight for your master's house."
4But they were terrified and said, "If two kings
could not resist him, how can we?"
5So the palace administrator, the city governor,
10:5 the elders and the guardians sent this message to
[a]Jos 9:8; Jehu: "We are your servants[a] and we will do any-
1Ki 20:4,32 thing you say. We will not appoint anyone as
king; you do whatever you think best."
6Then Jehu wrote them a second letter, saying,
"If you are on my side and will obey me, take the
heads of your master's sons and come to me in
Jezreel by this time tomorrow."
Now the royal princes, seventy of them, were
with the leading men of the city, who were rear-
10:7 ing them. 7When the letter arrived, these men
[b]1Ki 21:21 took the princes and slaughtered all seventy[b] of
[c]2Sa 4:8 them. They put their heads[c] in baskets and sent
them to Jehu in Jezreel. 8When the messenger
arrived, he told Jehu, "They have brought the
heads of the princes."
Then Jehu ordered, "Put them in two piles at
the entrance of the city gate until morning."
9The next morning Jehu went out. He stood
before all the people and said, "You are innocent. It
was I who conspired against my master and killed
him, but who killed all these? 10Know then, that
not a word the LORD has spoken against the house
10:10 of Ahab will fail. The LORD has done what he prom-
[d]2Ki 9:7-10 ised[d] through his servant Elijah."[e] 11So Jehu[f] killed
[e]1Ki 21:29 10:11 everyone in Jezreel who remained of the house of
[f]Hos 1:4 Ahab, as well as all his chief men, his close friends
[g]ver 14; and his priests, leaving him no survivor.[g]
Job 18:19 12Jehu then set out and went toward Samaria.
At Beth Eked of the Shepherds, 13he met some relatives of Ahaziah king of Judah and asked, "Who
are you?"
10:13 They said, "We are relatives of Ahaziah,[h] and
[h]2Ki 8:24, we have come down to greet the families of the
29; 2Ch 22:8 king and of the queen mother.[i]"
[i]1Ki 2:19 14"Take them alive!" he ordered. So they took
them alive and slaughtered them by the well of
Beth Eked—forty-two men. He left no survivor.
15After he left there, he came upon Jehonadab[j]
10:15 son of Recab,[k] who was on his way to meet him.
[j]Jer 35:6,14-19 Jehu greeted him and said, "Are you in accord
[k]1Ch 2:55; with me, as I am with you?"
Jer 35:2 "I am," Jehonadab answered.
[l]Ezr 10:19; "If so," said Jehu, "give me your hand."[l] So he
Eze 17:18 did, and Jehu helped him up into the chariot.
10:16 16Jehu said, "Come with me and see my zeal[m] for
[m]Nu 25:13; the LORD." Then he had him ride along in his
1Ki 19:10 chariot.
17When Jehu came to Samaria, he killed all
10:17 who were left there of Ahab's family;[n] he
[n]2Ki 9:8 destroyed them, according to the word of the LORD
spoken to Elijah.

A Bloody Massacre

2KI 10:1-17

The account of the massacre of Ahab's family is extraordinarily difficult to read. In fact, it is hard to imagine a more bloody, horrifying scene. Yet the atrocities committed by the house of Ahab are also great; his descendants cannot be allowed to retain power. Each of the 70 princes has a legitimate claim to the throne. Jehu cannot afford to leave a single one alive.

In addition to eliminating the competition, Jehu's atrocities clearly establish his authority before the people. They also leave an unforgettable impression of his ruthlessness in the minds of any who might dare oppose him.

But all of those political purposes aside, the death of the dynasty of Ahab is God's just judgment for Ahab's sin and his family's sin. God waits for the repentance of his people and even stayed his judgment of Ahab when Ahab showed a repentant spirit (1Ki 21:27-29). But the price for sin must finally be paid.

Wholehearted Service

2KI 10:18-31

Again, Jehu exacts bloody justice on evil—in this case, on the ministers of Baal. Using deception, he gathers all the priests of Baal together in one place and has them killed. What a gory and disturbing sequel to the massacre of Ahab's family, but justifiable; according to the Law of Moses, the penalty for idolatry is death (Dt 17:2-7).

Jehu is God's instrument of judgment on the dynasty of Israelite king Ahab (2Ki 9:6-7). He is commended for his obedience, but the commendation is qualified. Jehu is obedient only to a point. He destroys Baal worship in Israel, but he allows worship of the golden calves at Bethel and Dan to continue (2Ki 10:29). A politically expedient move on Jehu's part, he recognizes the importance of the golden calves and their worship locations in uniting the northern tribes (see the note on 2Ki 15:9 on page 599). It would appear that Jehu's obedience in fulfilling God's judgment stems as much from his political aspirations as his true zeal for the Lord.

Ministers of Baal Killed

18 Then Jehu brought all the people together and said to them, "Ahab served[o] Baal a little; Jehu will serve him much. 19 Now summon[p] all the prophets of Baal, all his ministers and all his priests. See that no one is missing, because I am going to hold a great sacrifice for Baal. Anyone who fails to come will no longer live." But Jehu was acting deceptively in order to destroy the ministers of Baal.

20 Jehu said, "Call an assembly[q] in honor of Baal." So they proclaimed it. 21 Then he sent word throughout Israel, and all the ministers of Baal came; not one stayed away. They crowded into the temple of Baal until it was full from one end to the other. 22 And Jehu said to the keeper of the wardrobe, "Bring robes for all the ministers of Baal." So he brought out robes for them.

23 Then Jehu and Jehonadab son of Recab went into the temple of Baal. Jehu said to the ministers of Baal, "Look around and see that no servants of the LORD are here with you—only ministers of Baal." 24 So they went in to make sacrifices and burnt offerings. Now Jehu had posted eighty men outside with this warning: "If one of you lets any of the men I am placing in your hands escape, it will be your life for his life."[r]

25 As soon as Jehu had finished making the burnt offering, he ordered the guards and officers: "Go in and kill[s] them; let no one escape."[t] So they cut them down with the sword. The guards and officers threw the bodies out and then entered the inner shrine of the temple of Baal. 26 They brought the sacred stone[u] out of the temple of Baal and burned it. 27 They demolished the sacred stone of Baal and tore down the temple[v] of Baal, and people have used it for a latrine to this day.

28 So Jehu[w] destroyed Baal worship in Israel. 29 However, he did not turn away from the sins[x] of Jeroboam son of Nebat, which he had caused Israel to commit—the worship of the golden calves[y] at Bethel[z] and Dan.

30 The LORD said to Jehu, "Because you have done well in accomplishing what is right in my eyes and have done to the house of Ahab all I had in mind to do, your descendants will sit on the throne of Israel to the fourth generation."[a] 31 Yet Jehu was not careful[b] to keep the law of the LORD, the God of Israel, with all his heart. He did not turn away from the sins[c] of Jeroboam, which he had caused Israel to commit.

32 In those days the LORD began to reduce[d] the size of Israel. Hazael[e] overpowered the Israelites throughout their territory 33 east of the Jordan in all the land of Gilead (the region of Gad, Reuben and Manasseh), from Aroer[f] by the Arnon Gorge through Gilead to Bashan.

34 As for the other events of Jehu's reign, all he did, and all his achievements, are they not written in the book of the annals[g] of the kings of Israel?

10:18 [o]Jdg 2:11; 1Ki 16:31-32
10:19 [p]1Ki 18:19; 22:6
10:20 [q]Ex 32:5; Joel 1:14
10:24 [r]1Ki 20:39
10:25 [s]Ex 22:20; 2Ki 11:18 [t]1Ki 18:40
10:26 [u]1Ki 14:23
10:27 [v]1Ki 16:32
10:28 [w]1Ki 19:17
10:29 [x]1Ki 12:30 [y]1Ki 12:28-29 [z]1Ki 12:32
10:30 [a]ver 35; 2Ki 15:12
10:31 [b]Pr 4:23 [c]1Ki 12:30
10:32 [d]2Ki 13:25 [e]1Ki 19:17; 2Ki 8:12
10:33 [f]Nu 32:34; Dt 2:36; Jdg 11:26; Isa 17:2
10:34 [g]1Ki 15:31

35 Jehu rested with his fathers and was buried in
Samaria. And Jehoahaz his son succeeded him as
king. 36 The time that Jehu reigned over Israel in
Samaria was twenty-eight years.

Athaliah and Joash

11 When Athaliah[h] the mother of Ahaziah saw
that her son was dead, she proceeded to
destroy the whole royal family. 2 But Jehosheba,
the daughter of King Jehoram[a] and sister of Ahaziah, took Joash[i] son of Ahaziah and stole him
away from among the royal princes, who were
about to be murdered. She put him and his nurse
in a bedroom to hide him from Athaliah; so he
was not killed.[j] 3 He remained hidden with his
nurse at the temple of the LORD for six years while
Athaliah ruled the land.

4 In the seventh year Jehoiada sent for the commanders of units of a hundred, the Carites[k] and
the guards and had them brought to him at the
temple of the LORD. He made a covenant with
them and put them under oath at the temple of
the LORD. Then he showed them the king's son.
5 He commanded them, saying, "This is what you
are to do: You who are in the three companies that
are going on duty on the Sabbath[l]—a third of you
guarding the royal palace,[m] 6 a third at the Sur
Gate, and a third at the gate behind the guard,
who take turns guarding the temple— 7 and you
who are in the other two companies that normally go off Sabbath duty are all to guard the temple
for the king. 8 Station yourselves around the king,
each man with his weapon in his hand. Anyone
who approaches your ranks[b] must be put to death.
Stay close to the king wherever he goes."

9 The commanders of units of a hundred did just
as Jehoiada the priest ordered. Each one took his
men—those who were going on duty on the Sabbath and those who were going off duty—and
came to Jehoiada the priest. 10 Then he gave the
commanders the spears and shields[n] that had
belonged to King David and that were in the temple of the LORD. 11 The guards, each with his
weapon in his hand, stationed themselves around
the king—near the altar and the temple, from the
south side to the north side of the temple.

12 Jehoiada brought out the king's son and put
the crown on him; he presented him with a copy
of the covenant[o] and proclaimed him king. They
anointed[p] him, and the people clapped their
hands[q] and shouted, "Long live the king!"[r]

13 When Athaliah heard the noise made by the
guards and the people, she went to the people at
the temple of the LORD. 14 She looked and there was
the king, standing by the pillar,[s] as the custom
was. The officers and the trumpeters were beside
the king, and all the people of the land were rejoic-

11:1 h2Ki 8:18
11:2 iver 21; 2Ki 12:1 jJdg 9:5
11:4 kver 19
11:5 l1Ch 9:25 m1Ki 14:27
11:10 n2Sa 8:7; 1Ch 18:7
11:12 oEx 25:16; 2Ki 23:3 p1Sa 9:16; 1Ki 1:39 qPs 47:1; 98:8; Isa 55:12 r1Sa 10:24
11:14 s1Ki 7:15; 2Ki 23:3; 2Ch 34:31

[a] 2 Hebrew *Joram,* a variant of *Jehoram* [b] 8 Or *approaches the precincts*

A Covenant for a King

2KI 11:12

This "copy of the covenant" may have been the Ten Commandments, the entire book of Deuteronomy or perhaps information about the king's responsibilities in regard to God's covenant with his people. The Law of Moses decreed that at a king's inauguration, he was to be given his own copy of the law (Dt 17:18–20). Some scholars believe that the king himself was required to copy the law out by hand; others think he was simply presented with a personal copy. In either case, he was to make a serious study of it. By meditating daily on the law, the king learned reverence for the Lord, gained knowledge that would help him follow the law throughout his reign, and learned the value of humility. God promised that if a king obeyed these commandments, he and his family would enjoy a prolonged reign over Israel.

Repairing the Temple

2KI 12:4–5

In recent years, the temple had suffered greatly. During the reign of Rehoboam, Shishak, king of Egypt, stole the temple's riches (1Ki 14:25–26). Later, temple treasures were used by Asa, king of Judah, to buy the support of a pagan king (1Ki 15:18). Presumably, the temple building itself had also suffered neglect during this period.

ing and blowing trumpets.[t] Then Athaliah tore[u]
her robes and called out, "Treason! Treason!"[v]
15 Jehoiada the priest ordered the commanders
of units of a hundred, who were in charge of the
troops: "Bring her out between the ranks[a] and put
to the sword anyone who follows her." For the
priest had said, "She must not be put to death in
the temple[w] of the LORD." 16 So they seized her as
she reached the place where the horses enter[x] the
palace grounds, and there she was put to death.[y]
17 Jehoiada then made a covenant[z] between the
LORD and the king and people that they would be
the LORD's people. He also made a covenant
between the king and the people.[a] 18 All the people
of the land went to the temple[b] of Baal and tore it
down. They smashed[c] the altars and idols to
pieces and killed Mattan the priest[d] of Baal in
front of the altars.
Then Jehoiada the priest posted guards at the
temple of the LORD. 19 He took with him the commanders
of hundreds, the Carites,[e] the guards and
all the people of the land, and together they
brought the king down from the temple of the LORD
and went into the palace, entering by way of the
gate of the guards. The king then took his place on
the royal throne, 20 and all the people of the land
rejoiced.[f] And the city was quiet, because Athaliah
had been slain with the sword at the palace.
21 Joash[b] was seven years old when he began to
reign.

Joash Repairs the Temple

12 In the seventh year of Jehu, Joash[c][g] became
king, and he reigned in Jerusalem forty
years. His mother's name was Zibiah; she was
from Beersheba. 2 Joash did what was right in the
eyes of the LORD all the years Jehoiada the priest
instructed him. 3 The high places,[h] however, were
not removed; the people continued to offer sacrifices
and burn incense there.
4 Joash said to the priests, "Collect[i] all the money
that is brought as sacred offerings[j] to the temple
of the LORD—the money collected in the census,[k]
the money received from personal vows and
the money brought voluntarily[l] to the temple. 5 Let
every priest receive the money from one of the
treasurers, and let it be used to repair whatever
damage is found in the temple."
6 But by the twenty-third year of King Joash the
priests still had not repaired the temple. 7 Therefore
King Joash summoned Jehoiada the priest
and the other priests and asked them, "Why aren't
you repairing the damage done to the temple?
Take no more money from your treasurers, but
hand it over for repairing the temple." 8 The priests
agreed that they would not collect any more mon-

11:14 [t]1Ki 1:39 [u]Ge 37:29 [v]2Ki 9:23
11:15 [w]1Ki 2:30
11:16 [x]Ne 3:28; Jer 31:40 [y]Ge 4:14
11:17 [z]Ex 24:8; 2Sa 5:3; 2Ch 15:12; 23:3; 29:10; 34:31; Ezr 10:3 [a]2Ki 23:3; Jer 34:8
11:18 [b]1Ki 16:32 [c]Dt 12:3 [d]1Ki 18:40; 2Ki 10:25; 23:20
11:19 [e]ver 4
11:20 [f]Pr 11:10; 28:12; 29:2
12:1 [g]2Ki 11:2
12:3 [h]1Ki 3:3; 2Ki 14:4; 15:35; 18:4
12:4 [i]2Ki 22:4 [j]Ex 35:5 [k]Ex 30:12 [l]Ex 35:29; 1Ch 29:3-9

[a] *15* Or *out from the precincts* [b] *21* Hebrew *Jehoash,* a variant of *Joash* [c] *1* Hebrew *Jehoash,* a variant of *Joash;* also in verses 2, 4, 6, 7 and 18

ey from the people and that they would not repair
the temple themselves.
9 Jehoiada the priest took a chest and bored a
hole in its lid. He placed it beside the altar, on the
12:9 right side as one enters the temple of the LORD.
[m]Jer 35:4 The priests who guarded the entrance[m] put into
[n]2Ch 24:8; Mk 12:41; the chest all the money[n] that was brought to the
Lk 21:1 temple of the LORD. 10 Whenever they saw that
there was a large amount of money in the chest,
12:10 [o]2Sa 8:17 the royal secretary[o] and the high priest came,
counted the money that had been brought into the
temple of the LORD and put it into bags. 11 When
the amount had been determined, they gave the
money to the men appointed to supervise the
work on the temple. With it they paid those who
worked on the temple of the LORD—the carpenters
12:12 and builders, 12 the masons and stonecutters.[p]
[p]2Ki 22:5-6 They purchased timber and dressed stone for the
repair of the temple of the LORD, and met all the
other expenses of restoring the temple.
13 The money brought into the temple was not
spent for making silver basins, wick trimmers,
sprinkling bowls, trumpets or any other articles
12:13 of gold[q] or silver for the temple of the LORD; 14 it
[q]1Ki 7:48-51; 2Ch 24:14 was paid to the workmen, who used it to repair
the temple. 15 They did not require an accounting
from those to whom they gave the money to pay
the workers, because they acted with complete
12:15 honesty.[r] 16 The money from the guilt offerings[s]
[r]2Ki 22:7; 1Co 4:2 and sin offerings[t] was not brought into the temple
of the LORD; it belonged[u] to the priests.
12:16 17 About this time Hazael[v] king of Aram went up
[s]Lev 5:14-19; Nu 18:9 and attacked Gath and captured it. Then he turned
[t]Lev 4:1-35 to attack Jerusalem. 18 But Joash king of Judah
[u]Lev 7:7 took all the sacred objects dedicated by his
12:17 fathers—Jehoshaphat, Jehoram and Ahaziah, the
[v]2Ki 8:12 kings of Judah—and the gifts he himself had dedicated and all the gold found in the treasuries of
the temple of the LORD and of the royal palace, and
12:18 [w]1Ki 15:18; he sent[w] them to Hazael king of Aram, who then
2Ch 21:16-17 [x]1Ki 15:21 withdrew[x] from Jerusalem.
19 As for the other events of the reign of Joash,
12:20 and all he did, are they not written in the book of
[y]2Ki 14:5 the annals of the kings of Judah? 20 His officials[y]
[z]2Ch 24:25 [a]Jdg 9:6 conspired against him and assassinated[z] him at
Beth Millo,[a] on the road down to Silla. 21 The officials who murdered him were Jozabad son of
Shimeath and Jehozabad son of Shomer. He died
and was buried with his fathers in the City of
David. And Amaziah his son succeeded him as
king.

Jehoahaz King of Israel

13 In the twenty-third year of Joash son of
Ahaziah king of Judah, Jehoahaz son of
Jehu became king of Israel in Samaria, and he
13:2 reigned seventeen years. 2 He did evil[b] in the eyes
[b]1Ki 12:26-33 of the LORD by following the sins of Jeroboam son
of Nebat, which he had caused Israel to commit,
13:3 and he did not turn away from them. 3 So the
[c]Dt 31:17; Jdg 2:14 LORD's anger[c] burned against Israel, and for a long

Results of Joash's Wickedness

2KI 12:17-18

When Queen Athaliah killed all the royal family except Joash, the child was hidden at the temple for six years (2Ki 11:1-3). (See character sketch for Jehosheba on page 1278.) When the time came for Joash to be crowned king, the priest Jehoiada seized power for him and served as his mentor and advisor. Joash, in turn, enjoyed God's favor as long as he followed the godly direction of the priest. However, after Jehoiada's death, Joash fell under the influence of the idolatrous officials of Judah (2Ch 24:17-22). When Jehoiada's son, Zechariah, confronted the king about his disobedience to God, Joash had him killed. Zechariah's dying words called for God to bring justice for the king's actions.

Now the army of Aram has attacked Jerusalem. God allows this invasion because of Judah's disobedience and the murder of Zechariah. Without God on his side, Joash can do little against Hazael, so he turns to the temple's treasures as a means to pay off his enemy.

time he kept them under the power[d] of Hazael king of Aram and Ben-Hadad[e] his son. 4 Then Jehoahaz sought[f] the LORD's favor, and the LORD listened to him, for he saw[g] how severely the king of Aram was oppressing[h] Israel. 5 The LORD provided a deliverer[i] for Israel, and they escaped from the power of Aram. So the Israelites lived in their own homes as they had before. 6 But they did not turn away from the sins[j] of the house of Jeroboam, which he had caused Israel to commit; they continued in them. Also, the Asherah pole[a][k] remained standing in Samaria.

7 Nothing had been left[l] of the army of Jehoahaz except fifty horsemen, ten chariots and ten thousand foot soldiers, for the king of Aram had destroyed the rest and made them like the dust[m] at threshing time.

8 As for the other events of the reign of Jehoahaz, all he did and his achievements, are they not written in the book of the annals of the kings of Israel? 9 Jehoahaz rested with his fathers and was buried in Samaria. And Jehoash[b] his son succeeded him as king.

Jehoash King of Israel

10 In the thirty-seventh year of Joash king of Judah, Jehoash son of Jehoahaz became king of Israel in Samaria, and he reigned sixteen years. 11 He did evil in the eyes of the LORD and did not turn away from any of the sins of Jeroboam son of Nebat, which he had caused Israel to commit; he continued in them.

12 As for the other events of the reign of Jehoash, all he did and his achievements, including his war against Amaziah[n] king of Judah, are they not written in the book of the annals[o] of the kings of Israel? 13 Jehoash rested with his fathers, and Jeroboam[p] succeeded him on the throne. Jehoash was buried in Samaria with the kings of Israel.

14 Now Elisha was suffering from the illness from which he died. Jehoash king of Israel went down to see him and wept over him. "My father! My father!" he cried. "The chariots[q] and horsemen of Israel!"

15 Elisha said, "Get a bow and some arrows,"[r] and he did so. 16 "Take the bow in your hands," he said to the king of Israel. When he had taken it, Elisha put his hands on the king's hands.

17 "Open the east window," he said, and he opened it. "Shoot!"[s] Elisha said, and he shot. "The LORD's arrow of victory, the arrow of victory over Aram!" Elisha declared. "You will completely destroy the Arameans at Aphek."[t]

18 Then he said, "Take the arrows," and the king took them. Elisha told him, "Strike the ground." He struck it three times and stopped. 19 The man of God was angry with him and said, "You should have

13:3 [d]1Ki 8:12; 12:17; 19:17 [e]ver 24
13:4 [f]Dt 4:29; Ps 78:34 [g]Ex 3:7; Dt 26:7 [h]2Ki 14:26
13:5 [i]ver 25; 2Ki 14:25,27
13:6 [j]1Ki 12:30 [k]1Ki 16:33
13:7 [l]2Ki 10:32-33 [m]2Sa 22:43
13:12 [n]2Ki 14:15 [o]1Ki 15:31
13:13 [p]2Ki 14:23; Hos 1:1
13:14 [q]2Ki 2:12
13:15 [r]1Sa 20:20
13:17 [s]Jos 8:18 [t]1Ki 20:26

Allow me to know the depth of you, to incorporate that into my whole being. I desire to be a temple for you, Lord, for you to live through me, a walking piece of love, so others may touch you, taste of you, experience Jesus on this earth. Live your life over again in me.

—*Kathy Troccoli*

[a] 6 That is, a symbol of the goddess Asherah; here and elsewhere in 2 Kings [b] 9 Hebrew *Joash*, a variant of *Jehoash*; also in verses 12–14 and 25

struck the ground five or six times; then you would have defeated Aram and completely destroyed it. But now you will defeat it only three times."[u]

20 Elisha died and was buried.

Now Moabite raiders[v] used to enter the country every spring. 21 Once while some Israelites were burying a man, suddenly they saw a band of raiders; so they threw the man's body into Elisha's tomb. When the body touched Elisha's bones, the man came to life[w] and stood up on his feet.

22 Hazael king of Aram oppressed[x] Israel throughout the reign of Jehoahaz. 23 But the LORD was gracious to them and had compassion and showed concern for them because of his covenant[y] with Abraham, Isaac and Jacob. To this day he has been unwilling to destroy[z] them or banish them from his presence.[a]

24 Hazael king of Aram died, and Ben-Hadad[b] his son succeeded him as king. 25 Then Jehoash son of Jehoahaz recaptured from Ben-Hadad son of Hazael the towns he had taken in battle from his father Jehoahaz. Three times[c] Jehoash defeated him, and so he recovered[d] the Israelite towns.

Amaziah King of Judah

14 In the second year of Jehoash[a] son of Jehoahaz king of Israel, Amaziah son of Joash king of Judah began to reign. 2 He was twenty-five years old when he became king, and he reigned in Jerusalem twenty-nine years. His mother's name was Jehoaddin; she was from Jerusalem. 3 He did what was right in the eyes of the LORD, but not as his father David had done. In everything he followed the example of his father Joash. 4 The high places,[e] however, were not removed; the people continued to offer sacrifices and burn incense there.

5 After the kingdom was firmly in his grasp, he executed[f] the officials[g] who had murdered his father the king. 6 Yet he did not put the sons of the assassins to death, in accordance with what is written in the Book of the Law[h] of Moses where the LORD commanded: "Fathers shall not be put to death for their children, nor children put to death for their fathers; each is to die for his own sins."[b][i]

7 He was the one who defeated ten thousand Edomites in the Valley of Salt[j] and captured Sela[k] in battle, calling it Joktheel, the name it has to this day.

8 Then Amaziah sent messengers to Jehoash son of Jehoahaz, the son of Jehu, king of Israel, with the challenge: "Come, meet me face to face."

9 But Jehoash king of Israel replied to Amaziah king of Judah: "A thistle[l] in Lebanon sent a message to a cedar in Lebanon, 'Give your daughter to my son in marriage.' Then a wild beast in Lebanon came along and trampled the thistle underfoot. 10 You have indeed defeated Edom and now

13:19 [u]ver 25
13:20 [v]2Ki 3:7; 24:2
13:21 [w]Mt 27:52
13:22 [x]1Ki 19:17; 2Ki 8:12
13:23 [y]Ge 13:16-17; Ex 2:24 [z]Dt 29:20 [a]Ex 33:15; 2Ki 14:27; 17:18; 24:3, 20
13:24 [b]ver 3
13:25 [c]ver 18,19 [d]2Ki 10:32
14:4 [e]2Ki 12:3; 16:4
14:5 [f]2Ki 21:24 [g]2Ki 12:20
14:6 [h]Dt 28:61 [i]Nu 26:11; Job 21:20; Jer 31:30; 44:3; Eze 18:4,20
14:7 [j]2Sa 8:13; 2Ch 25:11 [k]Jdg 1:36
14:9 [l]Jdg 9:8-15

[a] *1* Hebrew *Joash,* a variant of *Jehoash*; also in verses 13, 23 and 27 [b] *6* Deut. 24:16

Elisha's God Still Lives

2KI 13:20-21

Despite appearances, Elisha's bones do not actually raise this man from the dead. Only God has the power to defeat death, though he has at times allowed his servants to restore life on his behalf (2Ki 4:8-37). The bones in Elisha's tomb are dry and lifeless. Yet this miracle provides a tangible and astonishing sign that the God Elisha served is still living and working among his people.

Jonah 2KI 14:25

In the Biblical book that bears his name, Jonah appears as a reluctant prophet who runs from God's will. In these verses he is identified, with no negative disclaimers, as an effective servant of the Lord—one who prophesies about the increase in Israel's territory that occurs under Jeroboam II's rule. Though little is known about Jonah, this verse sheds a bit of light on his life, identifying his home as Gath Hepher, an Israelite town in Zebulun, about two or three miles from Nazareth.

you are arrogant.[m] Glory in your victory, but stay
at home! Why ask for trouble and cause your own
downfall and that of Judah also?”
11 Amaziah, however, would not listen, so Jehoash king of Israel attacked. He and Amaziah king
of Judah faced each other at Beth Shemesh[n] in
Judah. 12 Judah was routed by Israel, and every
man fled to his home.[o] 13 Jehoash king of Israel
captured Amaziah king of Judah, the son of
Joash, the son of Ahaziah, at Beth Shemesh. Then
Jehoash went to Jerusalem and broke down the
wall[p] of Jerusalem from the Ephraim Gate[q] to the
Corner Gate[r]—a section about six hundred feet
long.[a] 14 He took all the gold and silver and all the
articles found in the temple of the LORD and in the
treasuries of the royal palace. He also took hostages and returned to Samaria.
15 As for the other events of the reign of Jehoash, what he did and his achievements, including
his war[s] against Amaziah king of Judah, are they
not written in the book of the annals of the kings
of Israel? 16 Jehoash rested with his fathers and
was buried in Samaria with the kings of Israel.
And Jeroboam his son succeeded him as king.
17 Amaziah son of Joash king of Judah lived for
fifteen years after the death of Jehoash son of
Jehoahaz king of Israel. 18 As for the other events
of Amaziah's reign, are they not written in the
book of the annals of the kings of Judah?
19 They conspired[t] against him in Jerusalem, and
he fled to Lachish,[u] but they sent men after him to
Lachish and killed him there. 20 He was brought
back by horse[v] and was buried in Jerusalem with
his fathers, in the City of David.
21 Then all the people of Judah took Azariah,[b][w]
who was sixteen years old, and made him king in
place of his father Amaziah. 22 He was the one
who rebuilt Elath[x] and restored it to Judah after
Amaziah rested with his fathers.

Jeroboam II King of Israel

23 In the fifteenth year of Amaziah son of Joash
king of Judah, Jeroboam[y] son of Jehoash king of
Israel became king in Samaria, and he reigned
forty-one years. 24 He did evil in the eyes of the
LORD and did not turn away from any of the sins
of Jeroboam son of Nebat, which he had caused
Israel to commit.[z] 25 He was the one who restored
the boundaries of Israel from Lebo[c] Hamath[a] to
the Sea of the Arabah,[d][b] in accordance with the
word of the LORD, the God of Israel, spoken
through his servant Jonah[c] son of Amittai, the
prophet from Gath Hepher.
26 The LORD had seen how bitterly everyone in
Israel, whether slave or free,[d] was suffering;[e] there
was no one to help them.[f] 27 And since the LORD
had not said he would blot out[g] the name of Isra-

[a] *13* Hebrew *four hundred cubits* (about 180 meters)
[b] *21* Also called *Uzziah* [c] *25* Or *from the entrance to*
[d] *25* That is, the Dead Sea

14:10 [m]Dt 8:14; 2Ch 26:16; 32:25
14:11 [n]Jos 15:10
14:12 [o]2Sa 18:17
14:13 [p]1Ki 3:1; 2Ch 33:14; 36:19; Jer 39:2 [q]Ne 8:16; 12:39 [r]2Ch 25:23; Jer 31:38; Zec 14:10
14:15 [s]2Ki 13:12
14:19 [t]2Ki 12:20 [u]Jos 10:3; 2Ki 18:14,17
14:20 [v]2Ki 9:28
14:21 [w]2Ki 15:1; 2Ch 26:23
14:22 [x]1Ki 9:26; 2Ki 16:6
14:23 [y]2Ki 13:13
14:24 [z]1Ki 15:30
14:25 [a]Nu 13:21; 1Ki 8:65 [b]Dt 3:17 [c]Jnh 1:1; Mt 12:39
14:26 [d]Dt 32:36 [e]2Ki 13:4 [f]Ps 18:41; 22:11; 72:12; 107:12; Isa 63:5; La 1:7
14:27 [g]2Ki 13:23

14:27 [h]Jdg 6:14 el from under heaven, he saved[h] them by the
hand of Jeroboam son of Jehoash.
28 As for the other events of Jeroboam's reign,
all he did, and his military achievements, includ-
14:28 ing how he recovered for Israel both Damascus[i]
[i]2Sa 8:5; and Hamath,[j] which had belonged to Yaudi,[a] are
1Ki 11:24 they not written in the book of the annals[k] of the
[j]2Ch 8:3 [k]1Ki 15:31 kings of Israel? 29 Jeroboam rested with his fathers,
the kings of Israel. And Zechariah his son suc-
ceeded him as king.

Azariah King of Judah

15:1 **15** In the twenty-seventh year of Jeroboam
[l]ver 32; king of Israel, Azariah[l] son of Amaziah
2Ki 14:21 king of Judah began to reign. 2 He was sixteen
years old when he became king, and he reigned in
Jerusalem fifty-two years. His mother's name was
Jecoliah; she was from Jerusalem. 3 He did what
was right in the eyes of the LORD, just as his father
Amaziah had done. 4 The high places, however,
were not removed; the people continued to offer
sacrifices and burn incense there.
15:5 5 The LORD afflicted[m] the king with leprosy[b] until
[m]Ge 12:17 the day he died, and he lived in a separate
[n]Lev 13:46 [o]2Ch 27:1 house.[cn] Jotham[o] the king's son had charge of the
[p]Ge 41:40 palace[p] and governed the people of the land.
6 As for the other events of Azariah's reign, and
15:7 all he did, are they not written in the book of the
[q]Isa 6:1; annals of the kings of Judah? 7 Azariah rested[q]
14:28 with his fathers and was buried near them in the
[r]ver 5 City of David. And Jotham[r] his son succeeded him
as king.

Zechariah King of Israel

8 In the thirty-eighth year of Azariah king of
Judah, Zechariah son of Jeroboam became king
of Israel in Samaria, and he reigned six months.
15:9 [s]1Ki 15:26 9 He did evil[s] in the eyes of the LORD, as his fathers
had done. He did not turn away from the sins of
Jeroboam son of Nebat, which he had caused Israel to commit.
10 Shallum son of Jabesh conspired against
Zechariah. He attacked him in front of the peo-
15:10 [t]2Ki 12:20 ple,[d] assassinated[t] him and succeeded him as
king. 11 The other events of Zechariah's reign are
15:11 [u]1Ki 15:31 written in the book of the annals[u] of the kings of
Israel. 12 So the word of the LORD spoken to Jehu
15:12 was fulfilled:[v] "Your descendants will sit on the
[v]2Ki 10:30 throne of Israel to the fourth generation."[e]

Shallum King of Israel

13 Shallum son of Jabesh became king in the
15:13 [w]ver 1,8 thirty-ninth year of Uzziah king of Judah, and he
15:14 reigned in Samaria[w] one month. 14 Then Menahem
[x]1Ki 14:17 son of Gadi went from Tirzah[x] up to Samaria. He

[a] *28* Or *Judah* [b] *5* The Hebrew word was used for various diseases affecting the skin—not necessarily leprosy.
[c] *5* Or *in a house where he was relieved of responsibility*
[d] *10* Hebrew; some Septuagint manuscripts *in Ibleam*
[e] *12* 2 Kings 10:30

The Sins of Jeroboam

2KI 15:9

After the death of Solomon, a delegation of leaders led by Jeroboam approached Solomon's son, Rehoboam, and urged him to lighten the yoke of service on the people. When Rehoboam threatened instead to make the servitude worse, the ten northern tribes of Israel revolted and made Jeroboam their king. Fearing that the tribes might one day reunite if the people continued to travel to Jerusalem for religious festivals and feasts, Jeroboam initiated and promoted local idol worship. He appointed as priests men who did not serve the one true God and who were not from the tribe of Levi (1Ki 13:33).

Jeroboam's sins brought God's wrath on his entire family (1Ki 13:34). Subsequent generations continued to serve idols (1Ki 16:31–32; 2Ki 15:9) before the line was eventually destroyed (1Ki 15:29–30). The repeated references to Jeroboam's sins emphasize the far-reaching implications of his actions and remind us of the harsh consequences for those who worship anyone or anything but God (see the note on 1Ki 13:33–34, page 551).

Brutal Practices of War

2KI 15:16

Brutalizing pregnant women and killing children are among the most horrifying practices of war. When Elisha learned that Hazael and the Arameans would torment the people of Israel in this manner, he wept bitterly (2Ki 8:10–12). The atrocities committed by Menahem in the Israelite town of Tiphsah are as great as those of Hazael, king of Aram. By killing unborn children, ancient warriors sought to prevent the survival of those who might one day grow up to fight against them. Yet the emotional impact of this extreme violence does far more than the loss of any future army to debilitate those who have lost their beloved wives and children.

**attacked Shallum son of Jabesh in Samaria, assas-
sinated[y] him and succeeded him as king.
15 The other events of Shallum's reign, and the
conspiracy he led, are written in the book of the
annals[z] of the kings of Israel.
16 At that time Menahem, starting out from Tirzah, attacked Tiphsah[a] and everyone in the city
and its vicinity, because they refused to open[b]
their gates. He sacked Tiphsah and ripped open
all the pregnant women.**

Menahem King of Israel

**17 In the thirty-ninth year of Azariah king of
Judah, Menahem son of Gadi became king of Israel, and he reigned in Samaria ten years. 18 He did
evil in the eyes of the LORD. During his entire reign
he did not turn away from the sins of Jeroboam son
of Nebat, which he had caused Israel to commit.
19 Then Pul[a][c] king of Assyria invaded the land,
and Menahem gave him a thousand talents[b] of silver to gain his support and strengthen his own
hold on the kingdom. 20 Menahem exacted this
money from Israel. Every wealthy man had to
contribute fifty shekels[c] of silver to be given to the
king of Assyria. So the king of Assyria withdrew[d]
and stayed in the land no longer.
21 As for the other events of Menahem's reign,
and all he did, are they not written in the book of
the annals of the kings of Israel? 22 Menahem rested with his fathers. And Pekahiah his son succeeded him as king.**

Pekahiah King of Israel

**23 In the fiftieth year of Azariah king of Judah,
Pekahiah son of Menahem became king of Israel
in Samaria, and he reigned two years. 24 Pekahiah
did evil in the eyes of the LORD. He did not turn
away from the sins of Jeroboam son of Nebat,
which he had caused Israel to commit. 25 One of
his chief officers, Pekah[e] son of Remaliah, conspired against him. Taking fifty men of Gilead
with him, he assassinated[f] Pekahiah, along with
Argob and Arieh, in the citadel of the royal palace
at Samaria. So Pekah killed Pekahiah and succeeded him as king.
26 The other events of Pekahiah's reign, and all
he did, are written in the book of the annals of the
kings of Israel.**

Pekah King of Israel

**27 In the fifty-second year of Azariah king of
Judah, Pekah[g] son of Remaliah[h] became king of
Israel in Samaria, and he reigned twenty years.
28 He did evil in the eyes of the LORD. He did not
turn away from the sins of Jeroboam son of Nebat,
which he had caused Israel to commit.
29 In the time of Pekah king of Israel, Tiglath-**

15:14 [y]2Ki 12:20
15:15 [z]1Ki 15:31
15:16 [a]1Ki 4:24 [b]2Ki 8:12; Hos 13:16
15:19 [c]1Ch 5:6,26
15:20 [d]2Ki 12:18
15:25 [e]2Ch 28:6; Isa 7:1 [f]2Ki 12:20
15:27 [g]2Ch 28:6; Isa 7:1 [h]Isa 7:4

[a] *19* Also called *Tiglath-Pileser* [b] *19* That is, about 37 tons (about 34 metric tons) [c] *20* That is, about 1 1/4 pounds (about 0.6 kilogram)

Pileser[i] king of Assyria came and took Ijon,[j] Abel
Beth Maacah, Janoah, Kedesh and Hazor. He took
Gilead and Galilee, including all the land of Naphtali,[k] and deported[l] the people to Assyria. 30Then
Hoshea[m] son of Elah conspired against Pekah son
of Remaliah. He attacked and assassinated[n] him,
and then succeeded him as king in the twentieth
year of Jotham son of Uzziah.
31As for the other events of Pekah's reign, and
all he did, are they not written in the book of the
annals of the kings of Israel?

Jotham King of Judah

32In the second year of Pekah son of Remaliah
king of Israel, Jotham[o] son of Uzziah king of
Judah began to reign. 33He was twenty-five years
old when he became king, and he reigned in Jerusalem sixteen years. His mother's name was Jerusha daughter of Zadok. 34He did what was right[p]
in the eyes of the LORD, just as his father Uzziah
had done. 35The high places,[q] however, were not
removed; the people continued to offer sacrifices
and burn incense there. Jotham rebuilt the Upper
Gate[r] of the temple of the LORD.
36As for the other events of Jotham's reign, and
what he did, are they not written in the book of
the annals of the kings of Judah? 37(In those days
the LORD began to send Rezin[s] king of Aram and
Pekah son of Remaliah against Judah.) 38Jotham
rested with his fathers and was buried with them
in the City of David, the city of his father. And
Ahaz his son succeeded him as king.

Ahaz King of Judah

16 In the seventeenth year of Pekah son of
Remaliah, Ahaz[t] son of Jotham king of
Judah began to reign. 2Ahaz was twenty years old
when he became king, and he reigned in Jerusalem sixteen years. Unlike David his father, he did
not do what was right[u] in the eyes of the LORD his
God. 3He walked in the ways of the kings of Israel and even sacrificed his son[v] in[a] the fire, following the detestable[w] ways of the nations the LORD
had driven out before the Israelites. 4He offered
sacrifices and burned incense at the high places,
on the hilltops and under every spreading tree.[x]
5Then Rezin[y] king of Aram and Pekah son of
Remaliah king of Israel marched up to fight
against Jerusalem and besieged Ahaz, but they
could not overpower him. 6At that time, Rezin[z]
king of Aram recovered Elath[a] for Aram by driving out the men of Judah. Edomites then moved
into Elath and have lived there to this day.
7Ahaz sent messengers to say to Tiglath-Pileser[b]
king of Assyria, "I am your servant and vassal.
Come up and save[c] me out of the hand of the king
of Aram and of the king of Israel, who are attacking me." 8And Ahaz took the silver and gold found
in the temple of the LORD and in the treasuries of

15:29 [i] 2Ki 16:7; 17:6; 1Ch 5:26; 2Ch 28:20; Jer 50:17 [j] 1Ki 15:20 [k] 2Ki 16:9; 17:24; 2Ch 16:4; Isa 9:1 [l] 2Ki 24:14-16; 1Ch 5:22; Isa 14:6,17; 36:17; 45:13
15:30 [m] 2Ki 17:1 [n] 2Ki 12:20
15:32 [o] 1Ch 5:17
15:34 [p] ver 3; 1Ki 14:8; 2Ch 26:4-5
15:35 [q] 2Ki 12:3 [r] 2Ch 23:20
15:37 [s] 2Ki 16:5; Isa 7:1
16:1 [t] Isa 1:1; 14:28
16:2 [u] 1Ki 14:8
16:3 [v] Lev 18:21; 2Ki 21:6 [w] Lev 18:3; Dt 9:4; 12:31
16:4 [x] Dt 12:2; Eze 6:13
16:5 [y] 2Ki 15:37; Isa 7:1,4
16:6 [z] Isa 9:12 [a] 2Ki 14:22; 2Ch 26:2
16:7 [b] 2Ki 15:29 [c] Isa 2:6; Jer 2:18; Eze 16:28; Hos 10:6

[a] 3 Or *even made his son pass through*

Human Sacrifice

2KI 16:3

God's people have long demonstrated their willingness to participate in the pagan practices of their neighbors. Human sacrifice was one such rite. At the time of Ahaz's rule, the pagans believed that the sacrifice of one's firstborn son—far more than a simple animal sacrifice—would buy the favor of the gods. Ahaz's desire for success, particularly during a time of political turmoil, is greater than any feelings of warmth he might feel toward his child.

While human sacrifice would probably never occur to us, we, too, can be guilty of putting personal desires and goals above the well-being of our children. The grace of Jesus Christ and the leading of God's Spirit can guide us and reveal to us any wrong priorities. If these are present, we can repent and trust God for his guidance in restoring things to their proper order.

The Sabbath Canopy

2KI 16:18

The Sabbath canopy is mentioned only in this one place in the Bible. The phrase may describe a canopied seat of some kind or an awning, cover or screen made of metal. Biblical scholars have suggested that it may have been a place where the king attended Sabbath services, a special entry used by the priests or a location where teaching took place.

the royal palace and sent it as a gift[d] to the king of
Assyria. 9The king of Assyria complied by attacking Damascus[e] and capturing it. He deported its
inhabitants to Kir[f] and put Rezin to death.
10Then King Ahaz went to Damascus to meet
Tiglath-Pileser king of Assyria. He saw an altar in
Damascus and sent to Uriah[g] the priest a sketch of
the altar, with detailed plans for its construction.
11So Uriah the priest built an altar in accordance
with all the plans that King Ahaz had sent from
Damascus and finished it before King Ahaz
returned. 12When the king came back from
Damascus and saw the altar, he approached it and
presented offerings[a][h] on it. 13He offered up his
burnt offering[i] and grain offering, poured out his
drink offering, and sprinkled the blood of his fellowship offerings[b][j] on the altar. 14The bronze
altar[k] that stood before the LORD he brought from
the front of the temple—from between the new
altar and the temple of the LORD—and put it on
the north side of the new altar.
15King Ahaz then gave these orders to Uriah the
priest: "On the large new altar, offer the morning[l]
burnt offering and the evening grain offering, the
king's burnt offering and his grain offering, and
the burnt offering of all the people of the land,
and their grain offering and their drink offering.
Sprinkle on the altar all the blood of the burnt
offerings and sacrifices. But I will use the bronze
altar for seeking guidance."[m] 16And Uriah the
priest did just as King Ahaz had ordered.
17King Ahaz took away the side panels and
removed the basins from the movable stands. He
removed the Sea from the bronze bulls that supported it and set it on a stone base.[n] 18He took
away the Sabbath canopy[c] that had been built at
the temple and removed the royal entryway outside the temple of the LORD, in deference to the
king of Assyria.[o]
19As for the other events of the reign of Ahaz,
and what he did, are they not written in the book
of the annals of the kings of Judah? 20Ahaz rested
with his fathers and was buried with them in the
City of David. And Hezekiah his son succeeded
him as king.

Hoshea Last King of Israel

17 In the twelfth year of Ahaz king of Judah,
Hoshea[p] son of Elah became king of Israel
in Samaria, and he reigned nine years. 2He did
evil in the eyes of the LORD, but not like the kings
of Israel who preceded him.
3Shalmaneser[q] king of Assyria came up to
attack Hoshea, who had been Shalmaneser's vassal and had paid him tribute. 4But the king of
Assyria discovered that Hoshea was a traitor, for
he had sent envoys to So[d] king of Egypt, and he

16:8 [d]2Ki 12:18
16:9 [e]2Ki 15:29 [f]Isa 22:6; Am 1:5; 9:7
16:10 [g]Isa 8:2
16:12 [h]2Ch 26:16
16:13 [i]Lev 6:8-13 [j]Lev 7:11-21
16:14 [k]2Ch 4:1
16:15 [l]Ex 29:38-41 [m]1Sa 9:9
16:17 [n]1Ki 7:27
16:18 [o]Eze 16:28
17:1 [p]2Ki 15:30
17:3 [q]2Ki 18:9-12; Hos 10:14

[a] 12 Or *and went up* [b] 13 Traditionally *peace offerings*
[c] 18 Or *the dais of his throne* (see Septuagint) [d] 4 Or *to Sais, to the*; So is possibly an abbreviation for *Osorkon*.

Delilah

An Army of One

Samson thought she was on *his* side. The Philistine rulers thought she was on *their* side. But Delilah was only on *Delilah's* side. If she could disarm Samson, she would make a lot of money.

The Philistines did not consider Samson a wise leader to be feared. They understood his weakness—Samson acted more like a Philistine than a Philistine! It would only take a little cunning, and he would fall into their hands by his own doing. Yes, Delilah was just the ticket.

She must have been remarkably beautiful. Samson immediately fell under her spell. She was shrewd—like a spider she patiently spun her web until he had no way to escape. She did not tip her hand before she was completely satisfied that Samson's secret was her own.

She was a great actress. While he should have been wary of her motives, he treated her like a child to be humored, which only whetted her appetite for victory. She manipulated by whining, wheedling and nagging. Her persistence finally wore Samson down. She manipulated him with accusations that he didn't love her, and these must have struck a nerve. Samson's Philistine wife—who had suffered a tragic death (Jdg 15:6)—had used the same technique to pry his secrets from him (Jdg 14:15-17). Whether he thought he could trust Delilah or he simply could not imagine life without her, Samson told her everything. Waiting until he was asleep, Delilah had his hair cut so his strength would leave him, and then she handed him over to his enemies.

But she had never contended with a God who uses even his people's weaknesses. Without her knowledge or consent, Delilah also was used by God. Her actions imprisoned Samson behind enemy lines and within striking distance of the Philistine government and its ruling class. When the Philistines mocked Samson and boasted that their god Dagon had delivered Samson into their hands, God's wrath brought their temple down on their own heads—through Samson (Jdg 16:23-30).

Delilah used her beauty and intelligence to further her own ends. It is possible even for Christians to be tempted to manipulate those who love us to get what we want. Desire for money, fame and material things can motivate us to walk down roads that we would otherwise never consider.

Delilah
(dainty one)
Judges 16:4-22

Candid SNAPSHOT Having put him to sleep on her lap, she called a man to shave off the seven braids of his hair, and so began to subdue him. And his strength left him (Judges 16:19).

Naomi

Not Forsaken

Naomi stood on the road to Judah feeling overwhelmed with a sense of responsibility and pain for her daughters-in-law—and for herself. The downward spiral doesn't give you much to hang on to on the way down. Naomi had been sliding for years, and now she had hit the bottom. The daughters-in-law, Ruth and Orpah, cried with Naomi. She was like a mother to them and had introduced them to the God of Israel. But it was difficult to see that in Naomi now, with defeat and hopelessness pulling at her features.

Naomi's trials had begun when her husband, Elimelech, abandoned his inheritance in the promised land during a famine to try to provide for his family in Moab. There Naomi's sons, Mahlon and Kilion, married Moabite wives. Though Naomi came to love both Ruth and Orpah, she had struggled with her sons' choices. The Law expressly prohibited pagan wives. Then came the deaths in rapid succession: Elimelech, Mahlon and Kilion.

Naomi's faith was at its lowest ebb. Could she ever lift her head again in the presence of her friends? But God knew Naomi's heart. For all her despair, Naomi was a godly woman full of love for others. The Lord was patient with her. He had an exquisite and elaborate plan that required Naomi's participation—a plan to mentor Ruth and bring together a man and a woman of exceptional virtue.

Ruth went to Judah with Naomi and met Naomi's kinsman Boaz. Naomi knew the hand of God when she saw it. Of course! Boaz! Her hope swelled as she prayed for Ruth's future, as well as for her own deliverance. Boaz would do the right thing. He had both the character and the resources to do whatever God asked of him. Naomi had foreseen the Lord's redemption. Boaz reclaimed the plot of land belonging to Elimelech and married Ruth as the kinsman-redeemer, according to Israelite law. Ruth and Boaz counted their first child, Obed, as Naomi's, to continue the families of Elimelech, Mahlon and Kilion. Obed was the grandfather of David and an ancestor of Christ Jesus (1Ch 2:12-15; Mt 1:5-6).

There are times in life when we have no faith. In times of great grief—when life seems like ashes in our mouths—the Lord sees our hearts. He understands our pain and fear for the future. He even knows how it feels when it seems God has abandoned us. But he will never forget or forsake us. He has a plan. In Naomi's case, it came as close to a fairytale ending as we will find.

Naomi
(pleasantness)

Ruth 1-4

Candid SNAPSHOT "Praise be to the LORD, who this day has not left you without a kinsman-redeemer. May he become famous throughout Israel! He will renew your life and sustain you in your old age. For your daughter-in-law, who loves you and who is better to you than seven sons, has given him birth" (Ruth 4:14-15).

no longer paid tribute to the king of Assyria, as
he had done year by year. Therefore Shalmaneser
seized him and put him in prison. 5The king of
Assyria invaded the entire land, marched against
Samaria and laid siege[r] to it for three years. 6In
the ninth year of Hoshea, the king of Assyria captured Samaria[s] and deported[t] the Israelites to
Assyria. He settled them in Halah, in Gozan[u] on
the Habor River and in the towns of the Medes.

Israel Exiled Because of Sin

7All this took place because the Israelites had
sinned[v] against the LORD their God, who had
brought them up out of Egypt[w] from under the
power of Pharaoh king of Egypt. They worshiped
other gods 8and followed the practices of the
nations[x] the LORD had driven out before them, as
well as the practices that the kings of Israel had
introduced. 9The Israelites secretly did things
against the LORD their God that were not right.
From watchtower to fortified city[y] they built themselves high places in all their towns. 10They set up
sacred stones and Asherah poles[z] on every high
hill and under every spreading tree.[a] 11At every
high place they burned incense, as the nations
whom the LORD had driven out before them had
done. They did wicked things that provoked the
LORD to anger. 12They worshiped idols,[b] though
the LORD had said, "You shall not do this."[a] 13The
LORD warned Israel and Judah through all his
prophets and seers:[c] "Turn from your evil ways.[d]
Observe my commands and decrees, in accordance with the entire Law that I commanded your
fathers to obey and that I delivered to you through
my servants the prophets."

14But they would not listen and were as stiff-
necked[e] as their fathers, who did not trust in the
LORD their God. 15They rejected his decrees and
the covenant[f] he had made with their fathers and
the warnings he had given them. They followed
worthless idols[g] and themselves became worthless. They imitated the nations[h] around them
although the LORD had ordered them, "Do not do
as they do," and they did the things the LORD had
forbidden them to do.

16They forsook all the commands of the LORD
their God and made for themselves two idols cast
in the shape of calves,[i] and an Asherah[j] pole. They
bowed down to all the starry hosts,[k] and they
worshiped Baal.[l] 17They sacrificed[m] their sons and
daughters in[b] the fire. They practiced divination
and sorcery[n] and sold[o] themselves to do evil in the
eyes of the LORD, provoking him to anger.

18So the LORD was very angry with Israel and
removed them from his presence. Only the tribe of
Judah was left, 19and even Judah did not keep the
commands of the LORD their God. They followed
the practices Israel had introduced.[p] 20Therefore

17:5 [r]Hos 13:16
17:6 [s]Hos 13:16 [t]Dt 28:36,64; 2Ki 18:10-11 [u]1Ch 5:26
17:7 [v]Jos 23:16; Jdg 6:10 [w]Ex 14:15-31
17:8 [x]Lev 18:3; Dt 18:9; 2Ki 16:3
17:9 [y]2Ki 18:8
17:10 [z]Ex 34:13; Mic 5:14 [a]1Ki 14:23
17:12 [b]Ex 20:4
17:13 [c]1Sa 9:9 [d]Jer 18:11; 25:5; 35:15
17:14 [e]Ex 32:9; Dt 31:27; Ac 7:51
17:15 [f]Dt 29:25 [g]Dt 32:21; Ro 1:21-23 [h]Dt 12:30-31
17:16 [i]1Ki 12:28 [j]1Ki 14:15, 23 [k]2Ki 21:3 [l]1Ki 16:31
17:17 [m]Dt 18:10-12; 2Ki 16:3 [n]Lev 19:26 [o]1Ki 21:20
17:19 [p]1Ki 14:22-23; 2Ki 16:3

[a] 12 Exodus 20:4,5 [b] 17 Or *They made their sons and daughters pass through*

Secret Sins

2KI 17:9

The Israelites foolishly believe that they are sinning in secret. Though they know well the commands of God and continue to worship him, they also choose to simultaneously worship false idols "behind his back." The Psalms testify that it is the arrogant and the wicked who believe that their deeds go unseen by God (Ps 90:7-8; 94:7), and the long list of sinful acts performed by the Israelites confirms this belief (2Ki 17:7-17).

The people are deceived, however, if they believe that God does not see what they are doing. God was—and is—aware of the thoughts and occurrences in every life, down to the tiniest detail (Ps 139). No matter where we go, God is with us. This is both a warning and a comfort; God knows every sin we commit, yet he is also intimately aware of our every need.

Resettling Samaria

2KI 17:22–24

After God sends the Israelites into exile for their wickedness, the king of Assyria resettles Samaria with people from other conquered parts of his empire. The reason for this action is simple: As the Assyrian empire expands, it becomes more and more difficult for the king to manage all the different people groups under his rule. Specific populations can be controlled, however, by moving them to a place where they are unfamiliar with the land and culture. This relocation causes widespread panic and misery, weakens national and cultural identities, and decreases the likelihood that the people will rebel against their Assyrian captors. The inhabitants of Israel are resettled in the eastern regions of Assyria, and captives from other regions are brought in to resettle Israel's cities and towns.

the LORD rejected all the people of Israel; he afflicted them and gave them into the hands of plunderers,[q] until he thrust them from his presence.
21 When he tore[r] Israel away from the house of
David, they made Jeroboam son of Nebat their
king.[s] Jeroboam enticed Israel away from following the LORD and caused them to commit a great
sin. 22 The Israelites persisted in all the sins of Jeroboam and did not turn away from them 23 until the
LORD removed them from his presence, as he had
warned through all his servants the prophets. So
the people of Israel were taken from their homeland into exile in Assyria, and they are still there.

Samaria Resettled

24 The king of Assyria[t] brought people from Babylon, Cuthah, Avva, Hamath and Sepharvaim[u]
and settled them in the towns of Samaria to
replace the Israelites. They took over Samaria and
lived in its towns. 25 When they first lived there,
they did not worship the LORD; so he sent lions[v]
among them and they killed some of the people.
26 It was reported to the king of Assyria: "The people you deported and resettled in the towns of
Samaria do not know what the god of that country requires. He has sent lions among them,
which are killing them off, because the people do
not know what he requires."
27 Then the king of Assyria gave this order: "Have
one of the priests you took captive from Samaria
go back to live there and teach the people what the
god of the land requires." 28 So one of the priests
who had been exiled from Samaria came to live in
Bethel and taught them how to worship the LORD.
29 Nevertheless, each national group made its
own gods in the several towns[w] where they settled, and set them up in the shrines[x] the people of
Samaria had made at the high places.[y] 30 The men
from Babylon made Succoth Benoth, the men
from Cuthah made Nergal, and the men from
Hamath made Ashima; 31 the Avvites made Nibhaz
and Tartak, and the Sepharvites burned their children in the fire as sacrifices to Adrammelech[z] and
Anammelech, the gods of Sepharvaim.[a] 32 They
worshiped the LORD, but they also appointed all
sorts[b] of their own people to officiate for them as
priests in the shrines at the high places. 33 They
worshiped the LORD, but they also served their
own gods in accordance with the customs of the
nations from which they had been brought.
34 To this day they persist in their former practices. They neither worship the LORD nor adhere
to the decrees and ordinances, the laws and commands that the LORD gave the descendants of
Jacob, whom he named Israel.[c] 35 When the LORD
made a covenant with the Israelites, he commanded them: "Do not worship[d] any other gods
or bow down to them, serve them or sacrifice to
them. 36 But the LORD, who brought you up out of
Egypt with mighty power and outstretched arm,[e]
is the one you must worship. To him you shall

17:20 [q]2Ki 15:29
17:21 [r]1Ki 11:11 [s]1Ki 12:20
17:24 [t]Ezr 4:2,10 [u]2Ki 18:34
17:25 [v]Ge 37:20
17:29 [w]Jer 2:28 [x]1Ki 12:31 [y]Mic 4:5
17:31 [z]2Ki 19:37 [a]ver 24
17:32 [b]1Ki 12:31
17:34 [c]Ge 32:28; 35:10; 1Ki 18:31
17:35 [d]Ex 20:5; Jdg 6:10
17:36 [e]Ex 3:20; 6:6; Ps 136:12

bow down and to him offer sacrifices. 37 You must
always be careful[f] to keep the decrees and ordinances, the laws and commands he wrote for you.
Do not worship other gods. 38 Do not forget[g] the
covenant I have made with you, and do not worship other gods. 39 Rather, worship the LORD your
God; it is he who will deliver you from the hand
of all your enemies."
40 They would not listen, however, but persisted
in their former practices. 41 Even while these people were worshiping the LORD,[h] they were serving
their idols. To this day their children and grandchildren continue to do as their fathers did.

Hezekiah King of Judah

18 In the third year of Hoshea son of Elah king
of Israel, Hezekiah[i] son of Ahaz king of
Judah began to reign. 2 He was twenty-five years
old when he became king, and he reigned in Jerusalem twenty-nine years.[j] His mother's name was
Abijah[a] daughter of Zechariah. 3 He did what was
right in the eyes of the LORD, just as his father
David[k] had done. 4 He removed[l] the high places,
smashed the sacred stones[m] and cut down the
Asherah poles. He broke into pieces the bronze
snake[n] Moses had made, for up to that time the
Israelites had been burning incense to it. (It was
called[b] Nehushtan.[c])
5 Hezekiah trusted[o] in the LORD, the God of Israel. There was no one like him among all the kings
of Judah, either before him or after him. 6 He held
fast[p] to the LORD and did not cease to follow him;
he kept the commands the LORD had given Moses.
7 And the LORD was with him; he was successful[q]
in whatever he undertook. He rebelled[r] against
the king of Assyria and did not serve him. 8 From
watchtower to fortified city,[s] he defeated the Philistines, as far as Gaza and its territory.
9 In King Hezekiah's fourth year,[t] which was the
seventh year of Hoshea son of Elah king of Israel,
Shalmaneser king of Assyria marched against
Samaria and laid siege to it. 10 At the end of three
years the Assyrians took it. So Samaria was captured in Hezekiah's sixth year, which was the
ninth year of Hoshea king of Israel. 11 The king[u] of
Assyria deported Israel to Assyria and settled
them in Halah, in Gozan on the Habor River and
in towns of the Medes. 12 This happened because
they had not obeyed the LORD their God, but had
violated his covenant[v]—all that Moses the servant
of the LORD commanded.[w] They neither listened
to the commands[x] nor carried them out.
13 In the fourteenth year of King Hezekiah's reign,
Sennacherib king of Assyria attacked all the fortified cities of Judah[y] and captured them. 14 So Hezekiah king of Judah sent this message to the king of
Assyria at Lachish: "I have done wrong.[z] Withdraw

17:37 [f]Dt 5:32
17:38 [g]Dt 4:23; 6:12
17:41 [h]ver 32-33; 1Ki 18:21; Mt 6:24
18:1 [i]Isa 1:1; 2Ch 28:27
18:2 [j]Isa 38:5
18:3 [k]Isa 38:5
18:4 [l]2Ch 31:1 [m]Ex 23:24 [n]Nu 21:9
18:5 [o]2Ki 19:10; 23:25
18:6 [p]Dt 10:20; Jos 23:8
18:7 [q]Ge 39:3; 1Sa 18:14 [r]2Ki 16:7
18:8 [s]2Ki 17:9; Isa 14:29
18:9 [t]Isa 1:1
18:11 [u]Isa 37:12
18:12 [v]2Ki 17:15 [w]Da 9:6,10 [x]1Ki 9:6
18:13 [y]2Ch 32:1; Isa 1:7; Mic 1:9
18:14 [z]Isa 24:5

[a] 2 Hebrew *Abi,* a variant of *Abijah* [b] 4 Or *He called it*
[c] 4 *Nehushtan* sounds like the Hebrew for *bronze* and *snake* and *unclean thing.*

The Meaning of "Father"

2KI 18:3

In ancient times, the term *father's house* referred to a person's extended family; similarly, the word *father* could refer to any male ancestor. The phrase *father David* appears more than 40 times in Scripture. David is called the "father" of Hezekiah here, as well as of Ahaz in 2 Kings 16:2. Both men are descendants of King David: Ahaz, nine generations away from David, and Hezekiah, ten (Mt 1:6–10). Yet the two men—one the father, one the son; one righteous, one ungodly—are in many ways extreme opposites.

Temple and Palace Treasures

2KI 18:15

Again and again kings of Judah used the temple treasures to pacify an enemy. Shishak, king of Egypt, carried away the riches from the temple during Rehoboam's reign in exchange for peace (1Ki 14:26). King Asa built an alliance with the king of Aram by presenting him with similar treasures (1Ki 15:18). Not long after King Joash had the temple refurbished, he himself stripped it, presenting its contents to the invading king of Aram (2Ki 12:18). Later, Ahaz purchased the loyalty of the king of Assyria with gold and silver taken from the temple (2Ki 16:8). Not only did the kings of Judah pay tribute to other kings to gain peace or protection, but also the kings of other nations at times paid tribute to Judah (2Ch 17:11; 26:8). As the fortunes of wars and campaigns dwindled or increased, so did the fortunes of the kings and the temple treasures.

from me, and I will pay whatever you demand of
me." The king of Assyria exacted from Hezekiah
king of Judah three hundred talents[a] of silver and **18:15**
thirty talents[b] of gold. 15So Hezekiah gave[a] him all [a]1Ki 15:18;
the silver that was found in the temple of the LORD 2Ki 16:8
and in the treasuries of the royal palace.
16At this time Hezekiah king of Judah stripped
off the gold with which he had covered the doors
and doorposts of the temple of the LORD, and gave
it to the king of Assyria.

Sennacherib Threatens Jerusalem

17The king of Assyria sent his supreme com-
mander,[b] his chief officer and his field command- **18:17**
er with a large army, from Lachish to King Heze- [b]Isa 20:1
kiah at Jerusalem. They came up to Jerusalem and [c]2Ki 20:20; 2Ch 32:4,30; Isa 7:3
stopped at the aqueduct of the Upper Pool,[c] on the
road to the Washerman's Field. 18They called for
the king; and Eliakim[d] son of Hilkiah the palace **18:18**
administrator, Shebna[e] the secretary, and Joah son [d]2Ki 19:2; Isa 22:20
of Asaph the recorder went out to them. [e]Isa 22:15
19The field commander said to them, "Tell
Hezekiah:

" 'This is what the great king, the king of
Assyria, says: On what are you basing this
confidence of yours? 20You say you have strategy and military strength—but you speak only
empty words. On whom are you depending,
that you rebel against me? 21Look now, you are
depending on Egypt,[f] that splintered reed of a **18:21**
staff,[g] which pierces a man's hand and [f]Isa 20:5; Eze 29:6
wounds him if he leans on it! Such is Pharaoh [g]Isa 30:5,7
king of Egypt to all who depend on him. 22And
if you say to me, "We are depending on the
LORD our God"—isn't he the one whose high
places and altars Hezekiah removed, saying to
Judah and Jerusalem, "You must worship
before this altar in Jerusalem"?

23" 'Come now, make a bargain with my
master, the king of Assyria: I will give you
two thousand horses—if you can put riders on
them! 24How can you repulse one officer[h] of **18:24** [h]Isa 10:8
the least of my master's officials, even though
you are depending on Egypt for chariots and
horsemen[c]? 25Furthermore, have I come to
attack and destroy this place without word
from the LORD?[i] The LORD himself told me to **18:25** [i]2Ki 19:6,22
march against this country and destroy it.' "

26Then Eliakim son of Hilkiah, and Shebna and
Joah said to the field commander, "Please speak to
your servants in Aramaic,[j] since we understand **18:26** [j]Ezr 4:7
it. Don't speak to us in Hebrew in the hearing of
the people on the wall."
27But the commander replied, "Was it only to
your master and you that my master sent me to
say these things, and not to the men sitting on the

[a] *14* That is, about 11 tons (about 10 metric tons) [b] *14* That is, about 1 ton (about 1 metric ton) [c] *24* Or *charioteers*

wall—who, like you, will have to eat their own
filth and drink their own urine?"
28 Then the commander stood and called out in
Hebrew: "Hear the word of the great king, the
king of Assyria! 29 This is what the king says: Do
not let Hezekiah deceive[k] you. He cannot deliver
you from my hand. 30 Do not let Hezekiah persuade you to trust in the LORD when he says, 'The
LORD will surely deliver us; this city will not be
given into the hand of the king of Assyria.'
31 "Do not listen to Hezekiah. This is what the
king of Assyria says: Make peace with me and
come out to me. Then every one of you will eat
from his own vine and fig tree[l] and drink water
from his own cistern,[m] 32 until I come and take you
to a land like your own, a land of grain and new
wine, a land of bread and vineyards, a land of
olive trees and honey. Choose life[n] and not death!
"Do not listen to Hezekiah, for he is misleading
you when he says, 'The LORD will deliver us.'
33 Has the god[o] of any nation ever delivered his
land from the hand of the king of Assyria?
34 Where are the gods of Hamath[p] and Arpad?[q]
Where are the gods of Sepharvaim, Hena and
Ivvah? Have they rescued Samaria from my hand?
35 Who of all the gods of these countries has been
able to save his land from me? How then can the
LORD deliver Jerusalem from my hand?"[r]
36 But the people remained silent and said nothing in reply, because the king had commanded,
"Do not answer him."
37 Then Eliakim son of Hilkiah the palace
administrator, Shebna the secretary and Joah son
of Asaph the recorder went to Hezekiah, with
their clothes torn,[s] and told him what the field
commander had said.

Jerusalem's Deliverance Foretold

19 When King Hezekiah heard this, he tore[t] his
clothes and put on sackcloth and went into
the temple of the LORD. 2 He sent Eliakim the palace
administrator, Shebna the secretary and the leading priests, all wearing sackcloth, to the prophet
Isaiah[u] son of Amoz. 3 They told him, "This is what
Hezekiah says: This day is a day of distress and
rebuke and disgrace, as when children come to the
point of birth and there is no strength to deliver
them. 4 It may be that the LORD your God will hear
all the words of the field commander, whom his
master, the king of Assyria, has sent to ridicule[v]
the living God, and that he will rebuke[w] him for
the words the LORD your God has heard. Therefore
pray for the remnant that still survives."
5 When King Hezekiah's officials came to Isaiah,
6 Isaiah said to them, "Tell your master, 'This is
what the LORD says: Do not be afraid of what you
have heard—those words with which the under-
lings of the king of Assyria have blasphemed[x] me.
7 Listen! I am going to put such a spirit in him that
when he hears a certain report, he will return to

18:29 [k]2Ki 19:10
18:31 [l]Nu 13:23; 1Ki 4:25 [m]Jer 14:3; La 4:4
18:32 [n]Dt 8:7-9; 30:19
18:33 [o]2Ki 19:12; Isa 10:10-11
18:34 [p]2Ki 17:24; 19:13 [q]Isa 10:9
18:35 [r]Ps 2:1-2
18:37 [s]2Ki 6:30
19:1 [t]Ge 37:34; 1Ki 21:27; 2Ch 32:20-22
19:2 [u]Isa 1:1
19:4 [v]2Ki 18:35 [w]2Sa 16:12
19:6 [x]2Ki 18:25

When I prayerfully remember my shortcomings, I'm not informing the Lord of anything he doesn't already know. But when I enumerate my failings, I take responsibility before him, and he then releases me from dirty shame, grimy guilt, and scummy sin.

—Patsy Clairmont

his own country, and there I will have him cut
down with the sword.[y]' "
8When the field commander heard that the king
of Assyria had left Lachish,[z] he withdrew and
found the king fighting against Libnah.
9Now Sennacherib received a report that Tirha-
kah, the Cushite[a] king ⌞of Egypt⌟, was marching
out to fight against him. So he again sent messengers to Hezekiah with this word: 10"Say to Hezekiah king of Judah: Do not let the god you depend[a]
on deceive[b] you when he says, 'Jerusalem will not
be handed over to the king of Assyria.' 11Surely you
have heard what the kings of Assyria have done to
all the countries, destroying them completely. And
will you be delivered? 12Did the gods of the nations
that were destroyed by my forefathers deliver[c]
them: the gods of Gozan,[d] Haran,[e] Rezeph and the
people of Eden who were in Tel Assar? 13Where is
the king of Hamath, the king of Arpad, the king of
the city of Sepharvaim, or of Hena or Ivvah?"[f]

Hezekiah's Prayer

14Hezekiah received the letter from the messengers and read it. Then he went up to the temple of
the LORD and spread it out before the LORD. 15And
Hezekiah prayed to the LORD: "O LORD, God of
Israel, enthroned between the cherubim,[g] you
alone are God over all the kingdoms of the earth.
You have made heaven and earth. 16Give ear,[h]
O LORD, and hear;[i] open your eyes,[j] O LORD, and
see; listen to the words Sennacherib has sent to
insult the living God.
17"It is true, O LORD, that the Assyrian kings
have laid waste these nations and their lands.
18They have thrown their gods into the fire and
destroyed them, for they were not gods[k] but only
wood and stone, fashioned by men's hands.[l]
19Now, O LORD our God, deliver us from his hand,
so that all kingdoms[m] on earth may know[n] that
you alone, O LORD, are God."

Isaiah Prophesies Sennacherib's Fall

20Then Isaiah son of Amoz sent a message to
Hezekiah: "This is what the LORD, the God of Israel, says: I have heard[o] your prayer concerning
Sennacherib king of Assyria. 21This is the word
that the LORD has spoken against him:

" 'The Virgin Daughter[p] of Zion
despises you and mocks[q] you.
The Daughter of Jerusalem
tosses her head[r] as you flee.
22Who is it you have insulted and
blasphemed?
Against whom have you raised your
voice
and lifted your eyes in pride?
Against the Holy One[s] of Israel!
23By your messengers

[a]9 That is, from the upper Nile region

19:7 [y]ver 37
19:8 [z]2Ki 18:14
19:10 [a]2Ki 18:5 [b]2Ki 18:29
19:12 [c]2Ki 18:33 [d]2Ki 17:6 [e]Ge 11:31
19:13 [f]2Ki 18:34
19:15 [g]Ex 25:22
19:16 [h]Ps 31:2 [i]1Ki 8:29 [j]ver 4; 2Ch 6:40
19:18 [k]Isa 44:9-11; Jer 10:3-10 [l]Ps 115:4; Ac 17:29
19:19 [m]1Ki 8:43 [n]Ps 83:18
19:20 [o]2Ki 20:5
19:21 [p]Jer 14:17; La 2:13 [q]Ps 22:7-8 [r]Job 16:4; Ps 109:25
19:22 [s]Ps 71:22; Isa 5:24

In God is my being, my me, my strength, my beatitude, my good and my delight.

—Catherine of Genoa (1447-1510)

you have heaped insults on the Lord.
19:23 [t]Isa 10:18 [u]Ps 20:7
And you have said,[t]
"With my many chariots[u]
I have ascended the heights of the mountains,
the utmost heights of Lebanon.
I have cut down its tallest cedars,
the choicest of its pines.
I have reached its remotest parts,
the finest of its forests.
24 I have dug wells in foreign lands
and drunk the water there.
With the soles of my feet
I have dried up all the streams of Egypt."

19:25 [v]Isa 40:21,28 [w]Isa 10:5; 45:7 [x]Mic 1:6
25 " 'Have you not heard?[v]
Long ago I ordained it.
In days of old I planned[w] it;
now I have brought it to pass,
that you have turned fortified cities
into piles of stone.[x]
26 Their people, drained of power,
19:26 [y]Ps 6:10 [z]Isa 4:2 [a]Ps 129:6
are dismayed[y] and put to shame.
They are like plants in the field,
like tender green shoots,[z]
like grass sprouting on the roof,
scorched[a] before it grows up.

19:27 [b]Ps 139:1-4
27 " 'But I know[b] where you stay
and when you come and go
and how you rage against me.
28 Because you rage against me
and your insolence has reached my ears,
19:28 [c]Eze 19:9; 29:4 [d]Isa 30:28 [e]ver 33
I will put my hook[c] in your nose
and my bit[d] in your mouth,
and I will make you return[e]
by the way you came.'

19:29 [f]2Ki 20:8-9; Lk 2:12 [g]Lev 25:5 [h]Ps 107:37
29 "This will be the sign[f] for you, O Hezekiah:
"This year you will eat what grows by itself,[g]
and the second year what springs from that.
But in the third year sow and reap,
plant vineyards[h] and eat their fruit.
30 Once more a remnant of the house of Judah
19:30 [i]2Ch 32:22-23
will take root[i] below and bear fruit above.
31 For out of Jerusalem will come a remnant,
and out of Mount Zion a band of survivors.
19:31 [j]Isa 9:7
The zeal[j] of the LORD Almighty will accomplish this.

32 "Therefore this is what the LORD says concerning the king of Assyria:

"He will not enter this city

A Return to Normal

2KI 19:29

Isaiah's prophecy tells King Hezekiah that there will be no harvest, in the traditional sense, until the third year. The first year, the people of Judah will eat only the fruit of those plants that have grown naturally; the next, they will be fed by the crops that come from those plants' seeds. In the third year, normal planting and harvesting will resume—a sign of life returning to a welcome normalcy.

Isaiah makes this prophecy while Sennacherib besieges Jerusalem. He's already conquered every other Judean city. Why would Jerusalem escape? Because of the prayers of their godly king, Hezekiah (2Ki 19:20). God is punishing Judah because of their sins; however, he stops short of total destruction because of their faithful king. A staggering number of Sennacherib's soldiers die in one night, and Sennacherib returns to Nineveh without conquering Jerusalem (2Ki 19:35-36).

A Sign From God

2KI 20:10-11

Confused by the two conflicting messages about his death (2Ki 20:1,6), Hezekiah doesn't know whether he will truly recover. Seeking reassurance, he asks for a sign. Isaiah obliges, prophesying that the Lord will alter the shadow on the sundial by ten steps.

How God accomplishes this miracle is uncertain. Perhaps he used atmospheric conditions, clouds that refract the light of the sun. Perhaps he even, as many have long suggested, reversed the earth's rotation—after all, the one who created the universe can make his creation behave any way he chooses! No matter how he accomplished this supernatural resetting of the "clock," God fulfilled his promise through an impressive display of his power over the natural world.

or shoot an arrow here.
He will not come before it with shield
or build a siege ramp against it.
33 By the way that he came he will return;[k] **19:33** [k]ver 28
he will not enter this city,
declares the LORD.
34 I will defend[l] this city and save it, **19:34** [l]2Ki 20:6 [m]1Ki 11:12-13
for my sake and for the sake of
David[m] my servant."

35 That night the angel of the LORD[n] went out **19:35** [n]Ex 12:23 [o]Job 24:24
and put to death a hundred and eighty-five thou-
sand men in the Assyrian camp. When the people got up the next morning—there were all the
dead bodies![o] 36 So Sennacherib king of Assyria
broke camp and withdrew. He returned to Nineveh[p] and stayed there. **19:36** [p]Ge 10:11; Jnh 1:2
37 One day, while he was worshiping in the temple of his god Nisroch, his sons Adrammelech and
Sharezer cut him down with the sword,[q] and they **19:37** [q]ver 7 [r]Ge 8:4 [s]Ezr 4:2
escaped to the land of Ararat.[r] And Esarhaddon[s]
his son succeeded him as king.

Hezekiah's Illness

20 In those days Hezekiah became ill and was
at the point of death. The prophet Isaiah
son of Amoz went to him and said, "This is what
the LORD says: Put your house in order, because
you are going to die; you will not recover."
2 Hezekiah turned his face to the wall and
prayed to the LORD, 3 "Remember,[t] O LORD, how I **20:3** [t]Ne 13:22 [u]2Ki 18:3-6
have walked before you faithfully[u] and with
wholehearted devotion and have done what is
good in your eyes." And Hezekiah wept bitterly.
4 Before Isaiah had left the middle court, the
word of the LORD came to him: 5 "Go back and tell
Hezekiah, the leader of my people, 'This is what
the LORD, the God of your father David, says: I
have heard[v] your prayer and seen your tears;[w] I **20:5** [v]1Sa 9:16; 1Ki 9:3; 2Ki 19:20 [w]Ps 39:12; 56:8
will heal you. On the third day from now you will
go up to the temple of the LORD. 6 I will add fifteen
years to your life. And I will deliver you and this
city from the hand of the king of Assyria. I will
defend[x] this city for my sake and for the sake of **20:6** [x]2Ki 19:34
my servant David.' "
7 Then Isaiah said, "Prepare a poultice of figs." **20:7** [y]Isa 38:21
They did so and applied it to the boil,[y] and he
recovered.
8 Hezekiah had asked Isaiah, "What will be the
sign that the LORD will heal me and that I will go
up to the temple of the LORD on the third day from
now?" **20:9** [z]Dt 13:2; Jer 44:29
9 Isaiah answered, "This is the LORD's sign[z] to
you that the LORD will do what he has promised:
Shall the shadow go forward ten steps, or shall it
go back ten steps?"
10 "It is a simple matter for the shadow to go forward ten steps," said Hezekiah. "Rather, have it
go back ten steps."
11 Then the prophet Isaiah called upon the LORD,

and the LORD made the shadow go back[a] the ten steps it had gone down on the stairway of Ahaz.

Envoys From Babylon

12At that time Merodach-Baladan son of Baladan king of Babylon sent Hezekiah letters and a gift, because he had heard of Hezekiah's illness. 13Hezekiah received the messengers and showed them all that was in his storehouses—the silver, the gold, the spices and the fine oil—his armory and everything found among his treasures. There was nothing in his palace or in all his kingdom that Hezekiah did not show them.

14Then Isaiah the prophet went to King Hezekiah and asked, "What did those men say, and where did they come from?"

"From a distant land," Hezekiah replied. "They came from Babylon."

15The prophet asked, "What did they see in your palace?"

"They saw everything in my palace," Hezekiah said. "There is nothing among my treasures that I did not show them."

16Then Isaiah said to Hezekiah, "Hear the word of the LORD: 17The time will surely come when everything in your palace, and all that your fathers have stored up until this day, will be carried off to Babylon.[b] Nothing will be left, says the LORD. 18And some of your descendants,[c] your own flesh and blood, that will be born to you, will be taken away, and they will become eunuchs in the palace of the king of Babylon."

19"The word of the LORD you have spoken is good," Hezekiah replied. For he thought, "Will there not be peace and security in my lifetime?"

20As for the other events of Hezekiah's reign, all his achievements and how he made the pool[d] and the tunnel by which he brought water into the city, are they not written in the book of the annals of the kings of Judah? 21Hezekiah rested with his fathers. And Manasseh his son succeeded him as king.

Manasseh King of Judah

21 Manasseh was twelve years old when he became king, and he reigned in Jerusalem fifty-five years. His mother's name was Hephzibah.[e] 2He did evil[f] in the eyes of the LORD, following the detestable practices[g] of the nations the LORD had driven out before the Israelites. 3He rebuilt the high places[h] his father Hezekiah had destroyed; he also erected altars to Baal[i] and made an Asherah pole, as Ahab king of Israel had done. He bowed down to all the starry hosts[j] and worshiped them. 4He built altars[k] in the temple of the LORD, of which the LORD had said, "In Jerusalem I will put my Name."[l] 5In both courts[m] of the temple of the LORD, he built altars to all the starry hosts. 6He sacrificed his own son[n] in[a] the fire,

20:11 [a]Jos 10:13
20:17 [b]2Ki 24:13; 25:13; 2Ch 36:10; Jer 27:22; 52:17-23
20:18 [c]2Ki 24:15; 2Ch 33:11; Da 1:3
20:20 [d]Ne 3:16
21:1 [e]Isa 62:4
21:2 [f]Jer 15:4 [g]2Ki 16:3
21:3 [h]2Ki 18:4 [i]Jdg 6:28; 1Ki 16:32 [j]Dt 17:3; 2Ki 17:16
21:4 [k]Jer 32:34 [l]2Sa 7:13; 1Ki 8:29
21:5 [m]1Ki 7:12; 2Ki 23:12
21:6 [n]Lev 18:21; Dt 18:10; 2Ki 16:3; 17:17

[a] 6 Or *He made his own son pass through*

The Siloam Tunnel

2KI 20:20

Hezekiah builds the Siloam tunnel in a far-sighted effort to supply water to the city of Jerusalem when it is under threat of invasion by Assyria. Approximately 6 feet high, 2 feet wide, and 1800 feet long, the tunnel taps into the Gihon spring outside Jerusalem, guaranteeing a water supply for the city. The water is carried through the tunnel, under the city walls and into the Pool of Siloam inside Jerusalem's walls, where the people can access it. In building the tunnel, two teams of men channel through solid rock. One crew works from the direction of the city and the other from the spring, until the two meet in the middle. This feat of engineering, which is marked by a commemorative inscription at the entrance to the tunnel, is a great success and supplies the city with plenty of water for its people.

> **O**ur part is the trusting, it is His to accomplish the results. And when we do our part, He never fails to do His, for no one ever trusted in the Lord and was confounded. Do not be afraid, then, that if you trust, or tell others to trust, the matter will end there. Trust is only the beginning and the continual foundation; when we trust, the Lord works, and His work is the important part of the whole matter.
>
> *—Hannah Whitall Smith (1832-1911)*

practiced sorcery and divination, and consulted
mediums and spiritists.[o] He did much evil in the
eyes of the LORD, provoking him to anger.
7He took the carved Asherah pole[p] he had made
and put it in the temple, of which the LORD had
said to David and to his son Solomon, "In this
temple and in Jerusalem, which I have chosen out
of all the tribes of Israel, I will put my Name[q] forever. 8I will not again[r] make the feet of the Israelites wander from the land I gave their forefathers,
if only they will be careful to do everything I commanded them and will keep the whole Law that
my servant Moses[s] gave them." 9But the people
did not listen. Manasseh led them astray, so that
they did more evil[t] than the nations[u] the LORD had
destroyed before the Israelites.
10The LORD said through his servants the prophets: 11"Manasseh king of Judah has committed
these detestable sins. He has done more evil[v] than
the Amorites[w] who preceded him and has led
Judah into sin with his idols. 12Therefore this is
what the LORD, the God of Israel, says: I am going
to bring such disaster[x] on Jerusalem and Judah
that the ears of everyone who hears of it will tingle.[y] 13I will stretch out over Jerusalem the measuring line used against Samaria and the plumb
line[z] used against the house of Ahab. I will wipe[a]
out Jerusalem as one wipes a dish, wiping it and
turning it upside down. 14I will forsake[b] the remnant[c] of my inheritance and hand them over to
their enemies. They will be looted and plundered
by all their foes, 15because they have done evil[d] in
my eyes and have provoked[e] me to anger from the
day their forefathers came out of Egypt until this
day."
16Moreover, Manasseh also shed so much innocent blood[f] that he filled Jerusalem from end to
end—besides the sin that he had caused Judah to
commit, so that they did evil in the eyes of the
LORD.
17As for the other events of Manasseh's reign,
and all he did, including the sin he committed,
are they not written in the book of the annals of
the kings of Judah? 18Manasseh rested with his
fathers and was buried in his palace garden,[g] the
garden of Uzza. And Amon his son succeeded
him as king.

Amon King of Judah

19Amon was twenty-two years old when he
became king, and he reigned in Jerusalem two
years. His mother's name was Meshullemeth
daughter of Haruz; she was from Jotbah. 20He did
evil[h] in the eyes of the LORD, as his father Manasseh had done. 21He walked in all the ways of his
father; he worshiped the idols his father had worshiped, and bowed down to them. 22He forsook
the LORD, the God of his fathers, and did not walk[i]
in the way of the LORD.
23Amon's officials conspired against him and
assassinated[j] the king in his palace. 24Then the

21:6 [o]Lev 19:31
21:7 [p]Dt 16:21; 2Ki 23:4 [q]2Sa 7:13; 1Ki 8:29; 9:3; 2Ki 23:27; Jer 32:34
21:8 [r]2Sa 7:10 [s]2Ki 18:12
21:9 [t]Pr 29:12 [u]Dt 9:4
21:11 [v]2Ki 24:3-4 [w]Ge 15:16; 1Ki 21:26
21:12 [x]2Ki 23:26; 24:3; Jer 15:4 [y]1Sa 3:11; Jer 19:3
21:13 [z]Isa 34:11; La 2:8; Am 7:7-9 [a]2Ki 23:27
21:14 [b]Ps 78:58-60 [c]2Ki 19:4; Mic 2:12
21:15 [d]Ex 32:22 [e]Jer 25:7
21:16 [f]2Ki 24:4
21:18 [g]ver 26
21:20 [h]ver 2-6
21:22 [i]1Ki 11:33
21:23 [j]2Ki 12:20; 2Ch 33:24-25

21:24 people of the land killed[k] all who had plotted
[k]2Ki 14:5 against King Amon, and they made Josiah his son
king in his place.
25As for the other events of Amon's reign, and
what he did, are they not written in the book of
the annals of the kings of Judah? 26He was buried
21:26 in his grave in the garden[l] of Uzza. And Josiah his
[l]ver 18 son succeeded him as king.

The Book of the Law Found

22 Josiah was eight years old when he became
king, and he reigned in Jerusalem thirty-
one years. His mother's name was Jedidah daugh-
22:1 ter of Adaiah; she was from Bozkath.[m] 2He did
[m]Jos 15:39 what was right[n] in the eyes of the LORD and
22:2 walked in all the ways of his father David, not
[n]Dt 17:19 [o]Dt 5:32 turning aside to the right[o] or to the left.
3In the eighteenth year of his reign, King Josiah
22:3 sent the secretary, Shaphan[p] son of Azaliah, the
[p]2Ch 34:20; Jer 39:14 son of Meshullam, to the temple of the LORD. He
said: 4"Go up to Hilkiah the high priest and have
him get ready the money that has been brought
into the temple of the LORD, which the doorkeep-
22:4 ers have collected[q] from the people. 5Have them
[q]2Ki 12:4-5 entrust it to the men appointed to supervise the
work on the temple. And have these men pay the
22:5 workers who repair[r] the temple of the LORD— 6the
[r]2Ki 12:5,11-14 carpenters, the builders and the masons. Also
have them purchase timber and dressed stone to
22:6 repair the temple.[s] 7But they need not account for
[s]2Ki 12:11-12 the money entrusted to them, because they are
22:7 acting faithfully."[t]
[t]2Ki 12:15 8Hilkiah the high priest said to Shaphan the sec-
22:8 retary, "I have found the Book of the Law[u] in the
[u]Dt 31:24 temple of the LORD." He gave it to Shaphan, who
read it. 9Then Shaphan the secretary went to the
king and reported to him: "Your officials have
paid out the money that was in the temple of the
LORD and have entrusted it to the workers and
supervisors at the temple." 10Then Shaphan the
secretary informed the king, "Hilkiah the priest
has given me a book." And Shaphan read from it
22:10 [v]Jer 36:21 in the presence of the king.[v]
11When the king heard the words of the Book of
22:12 the Law, he tore his robes. 12He gave these orders
[w]2Ki 25:22; to Hilkiah the priest, Ahikam[w] son of Shaphan,
Jer 26:24 Acbor son of Micaiah, Shaphan the secretary and
Asaiah the king's attendant: 13"Go and inquire of
the LORD for me and for the people and for all
Judah about what is written in this book that has
22:13 been found. Great is the LORD's anger[x] that burns
[x]Dt 29:24-28; 31:17 against us because our fathers have not obeyed the
words of this book; they have not acted in accor-
dance with all that is written there concerning us."
14Hilkiah the priest, Ahikam, Acbor, Shaphan
and Asaiah went to speak to the prophetess Huldah, who was the wife of Shallum son of Tikvah,
the son of Harhas, keeper of the wardrobe. She
lived in Jerusalem, in the Second District.
15She said to them, "This is what the LORD, the
God of Israel, says: Tell the man who sent you to

Rediscovering God's Law

2KI 22:8

The Book of the Law—or the Book of the Covenant—*is the name of the laws God gave* to Moses at Mount Sinai. Some *scholars believe that Hilkiah's statement refers to a copy of the entire Pentateuch,* Genesis through *Deuteronomy; others suggest that he found all or part of the book of* Deuteronomy.

Under the 55-year reign of *Josiah's grandfather, evil king* Manasseh, *the people of Judah worshiped idols rather than the* true God. *Not many people remember God's laws; fewer still* obey them. Under these condi*tions, the law was essentially* lost—forgotten by all but the old*est, most faithful priests.* Presum*ably, these old documents come to* Hilkiah's *attention while the tem*ple repairs *are in process.*

Restoration

2KI 23:4–8

Stunned and humbled by Hilkiah's discovery, King Josiah zealously attempts to restore Judah's relationship with the God of Israel. He immediately begins the process of ridding Jerusalem and Judah of pagan idols and shrines. The temple itself is cleansed by burning all of the pagan articles, including the Asherah pole, and destroying the pagan altars and living quarters occupied by male prostitutes.

The reform does not stop there, however. While earlier kings had made half-hearted efforts to please the Lord, Josiah is the first to destroy the high places—sites generally dedicated to the worship of pagan gods.

The litany of destruction of pagan sites in 2 Kings 23 is as much an indictment of the people for the depth of their wickedness as it is an honor to the king who takes God's laws to heart. Josiah's efforts are not merely for show; they are born of a deep passion for the Lord. Perhaps more than any other figure in the Bible, Josiah demonstrates how God desires us to respond to his law: with all of our heart, soul and strength (2Ki 23:25).

me, 16'This is what the LORD says: I am going to bring disaster[y] on this place and its people, according to everything written in the book[z] the king of Judah has read. 17Because they have forsaken[a] me and burned incense to other gods and provoked me to anger by all the idols their hands have made,[a] my anger will burn against this place and will not be quenched.' 18Tell the king of Judah, who sent you to inquire[b] of the LORD, 'This is what the LORD, the God of Israel, says concerning the words you heard: 19Because your heart was responsive and you humbled[c] yourself before the LORD when you heard what I have spoken against this place and its people, that they would become accursed[d] and laid waste,[e] and because you tore your robes and wept in my presence, I have heard you, declares the LORD. 20Therefore I will gather you to your fathers, and you will be buried in peace.[f] Your eyes will not see all the disaster I am going to bring on this place.'"

So they took her answer back to the king.

Josiah Renews the Covenant

23 Then the king called together all the elders of Judah and Jerusalem. 2He went up to the temple of the LORD with the men of Judah, the people of Jerusalem, the priests and the prophets—all the people from the least to the greatest. He read[g] in their hearing all the words of the Book of the Covenant, which had been found in the temple of the LORD. 3The king stood by the pillar and renewed the covenant[h] in the presence of the LORD—to follow[i] the LORD and keep his commands, regulations and decrees with all his heart and all his soul, thus confirming the words of the covenant written in this book. Then all the people pledged themselves to the covenant.

4The king ordered Hilkiah the high priest, the priests next in rank and the doorkeepers[j] to remove[k] from the temple of the LORD all the articles made for Baal and Asherah and all the starry hosts. He burned them outside Jerusalem in the fields of the Kidron Valley and took the ashes to Bethel. 5He did away with the pagan priests appointed by the kings of Judah to burn incense on the high places of the towns of Judah and on those around Jerusalem—those who burned incense to Baal, to the sun and moon, to the constellations and to all the starry hosts.[l] 6He took the Asherah pole from the temple of the LORD to the Kidron Valley outside Jerusalem and burned it there. He ground it to powder and scattered the dust over the graves of the common people.[m] 7He also tore down the quarters of the male shrine prostitutes,[n] which were in the temple of the LORD and where women did weaving for Asherah.

8Josiah brought all the priests from the towns of Judah and desecrated the high places, from Geba[o] to Beersheba, where the priests had burned

22:16 [y]Dt 31:29; Jos 23:15 [z]Dt 29:27; Da 9:11
22:17 [a]Dt 29:25-27
22:18 [b]2Ch 34:26; Jer 21:2
22:19 [c]Ex 10:3; 1Ki 21:29; Ps 51:17; Isa 57:15; Mic 6:8 [d]Jer 26:6 [e]Lev 26:31
22:20 [f]Isa 57:1
23:2 [g]Dt 31:11; 2Ki 22:8
23:3 [h]2Ki 11:14, 17 [i]Dt 13:4
23:4 [j]2Ki 25:18 [k]2Ki 21:7
23:5 [l]2Ki 21:3; Jer 8:2
23:6 [m]Jer 26:23
23:7 [n]1Ki 14:24; 15:12; Eze 16:16
23:8 [o]1Ki 15:22

[a] 17 Or *by everything they have done*

incense. He broke down the shrines[a] at the
gates—at the entrance to the Gate of Joshua, the
city governor, which is on the left of the city gate.
23:9 9 Although the priests of the high places did not
[p]Eze 44:10-14 serve[p] at the altar of the LORD in Jerusalem, they
ate unleavened bread with their fellow priests.
23:10 10 He desecrated Topheth,[q] which was in the Val-
[q]Isa 30:33; ley of Ben Hinnom,[r] so no one could use it to sac-
Jer 7:31,32; 19:6 rifice his son[s] or daughter in[b] the fire to Molech.
[r]Jos 15:8 11 He removed from the entrance to the temple of
[s]Lev 18:21; Dt 18:10 the LORD the horses that the kings of Judah had
dedicated to the sun. They were in the court near
23:11 the room of an official named Nathan-Melech. Josi-
[t]Dt 4:19 ah then burned the chariots dedicated to the sun.[t]
12 He pulled down the altars the kings of Judah
23:12 had erected on the roof[u] near the upper room of
[u]Jer 19:13; Zep 1:5 Ahaz, and the altars Manasseh had built in the
[v]2Ki 21:5 two courts[v] of the temple of the LORD. He removed
them from there, smashed them to pieces and
threw the rubble into the Kidron Valley. 13 The
king also desecrated the high places that were east
of Jerusalem on the south of the Hill of Corrup-
23:13 tion—the ones Solomon[w] king of Israel had built
[w]1Ki 11:7 for Ashtoreth the vile goddess of the Sidonians,
for Chemosh the vile god of Moab, and for
23:14 Molech[c] the detestable god of the people of
[x]Ex 23:24; Ammon. 14 Josiah smashed[x] the sacred stones and
Dt 7:5,25 cut down the Asherah poles and covered the sites
23:15 with human bones.
[y]1Ki 13:1-3 15 Even the altar[y] at Bethel, the high place made
[z]1Ki 12:33 by Jeroboam[z] son of Nebat, who had caused Israel to sin—even that altar and high place he demolished. He burned the high place and ground it to
23:16 powder, and burned the Asherah pole also. 16 Then
[a]1Ki 13:2 Josiah[a] looked around, and when he saw the
tombs that were there on the hillside, he had the
bones removed from them and burned on the altar
to defile it, in accordance with the word of the
LORD proclaimed by the man of God who foretold
these things.
17 The king asked, "What is that tombstone I
see?"
The men of the city said, "It marks the tomb of
the man of God who came from Judah and pronounced against the altar of Bethel the very things
you have done to it."
18 "Leave it alone," he said. "Don't let anyone
23:18 disturb his bones[b]." So they spared his bones and
[b]1Ki 13:31 those of the prophet who had come from Samaria.
19 Just as he had done at Bethel, Josiah removed
and defiled all the shrines at the high places that
23:20 the kings of Israel had built in the towns of
[c]Ex 22:20; 2Ki 10:25; Samaria that had provoked the LORD to anger.
11:18 20 Josiah slaughtered[c] all the priests of those high
[d]1Ki 13:2 places on the altars and burned human bones[d] on
23:21 them. Then he went back to Jerusalem.
[e]Ex 12:11; 21 The king gave this order to all the people: "Cel-
Nu 9:2; Dt 16:1-8 ebrate the Passover[e] to the LORD your God, as it is

[a] 8 Or *high places* [b] 10 Or *to make his son or daughter pass through* [c] 13 Hebrew *Milcom*

Burning Human Bones

2KI 23:14

To desecrate the high places east of Jerusalem and in the towns of Samaria, Josiah probably uses bones from nearby tombs, as he does at Bethel (2Ki 23:16). The remains of those whom Josiah knows to be righteous—the man of God who came from Judah and the unnamed prophet from Samaria—are spared (2Ki 23:17–18). In burning human bones on the altars, Josiah effectively defiles the sites, making them unfit for pagan worship in the future.

Only for a Season

2KI 23:26

The leaders and the people of Judah apparently obey their king's commands regarding pagan worship—but only for a season. After King Josiah is killed in battle (2Ki 23:29), his descendants return to the evil ways of their ancestors (2Ki 23:32, 37; 24:9). Josiah's repentance and humility cause him to find favor in the sight of the Lord, yet his godliness does not save the people from the consequences of their disobedience (2Ki 22:19–20).

written in this Book of the Covenant." 22 Not since the days of the judges who led Israel, nor throughout the days of the kings of Israel and the kings of Judah, had any such Passover been observed. 23 But in the eighteenth year of King Josiah, this Passover was celebrated to the LORD in Jerusalem.

24 Furthermore, Josiah got rid of the mediums and spiritists,[f] the household gods,[g] the idols and all the other detestable things seen in Judah and Jerusalem. This he did to fulfill the requirements of the law written in the book that Hilkiah the priest had discovered in the temple of the LORD. 25 Neither before nor after Josiah was there a king like him who turned[h] to the LORD as he did—with all his heart and with all his soul and with all his strength, in accordance with all the Law of Moses.

26 Nevertheless, the LORD did not turn away from the heat of his fierce anger, which burned against Judah because of all that Manasseh[i] had done to provoke him to anger. 27 So the LORD said, "I will remove[j] Judah also from my presence[k] as I removed Israel, and I will reject Jerusalem, the city I chose, and this temple, about which I said, 'There shall my Name be.'[a]"

28 As for the other events of Josiah's reign, and all he did, are they not written in the book of the annals of the kings of Judah?

29 While Josiah was king, Pharaoh Neco[l] king of Egypt went up to the Euphrates River to help the king of Assyria. King Josiah marched out to meet him in battle, but Neco faced him and killed him at Megiddo.[m] 30 Josiah's servants brought his body in a chariot[n] from Megiddo to Jerusalem and buried him in his own tomb. And the people of the land took Jehoahaz son of Josiah and anointed him and made him king in place of his father.

Jehoahaz King of Judah

31 Jehoahaz[o] was twenty-three years old when he became king, and he reigned in Jerusalem three months. His mother's name was Hamutal[p] daughter of Jeremiah; she was from Libnah. 32 He did evil in the eyes of the LORD, just as his fathers had done. 33 Pharaoh Neco put him in chains at Riblah[q] in the land of Hamath[b][r] so that he might not reign in Jerusalem, and he imposed on Judah a levy of a hundred talents[c] of silver and a talent[d] of gold. 34 Pharaoh Neco made Eliakim[s] son of Josiah king in place of his father Josiah and changed Eliakim's name to Jehoiakim. But he took Jehoahaz and carried him off to Egypt, and there he died.[t] 35 Jehoiakim paid Pharaoh Neco the silver and gold he demanded. In order to do so, he taxed the land and exacted the silver and gold from the people of the land according to their assessments.[u]

23:24 [f]Lev 19:31; Dt 18:11; 2Ki 21:6 [g]Ge 31:19
23:25 [h]2Ki 18:5
23:26 [i]2Ki 21:12; Jer 15:4
23:27 [j]2Ki 21:13 [k]2Ki 18:11
23:29 [l]Jer 46:2 [m]Zec 12:11
23:30 [n]2Ki 9:28
23:31 [o]1Ch 3:15; Jer 22:11 [p]2Ki 24:18
23:33 [q]2Ki 25:6 [r]1Ki 8:65
23:34 [s]1Ch 3:15; 2Ch 36:5-8 [t]Jer 22:12; Eze 19:3-4
23:35 [u]ver 33

[a] *27* 1 Kings 8:29 [b] *33* Hebrew; Septuagint (see also 2 Chron. 36:3) *Neco at Riblah in Hamath removed him*
[c] *33* That is, about 3 3/4 tons (about 3.4 metric tons)
[d] *33* That is, about 75 pounds (about 34 kilograms)

Jehoiakim King of Judah

23:36 [36]Jehoiakim[v] was twenty-five years old when he
[v]Jer 26:1 became king, and he reigned in Jerusalem eleven
years. His mother's name was Zebidah daughter of
Pedaiah; she was from Rumah. [37]And he did evil in
the eyes of the LORD, just as his fathers had done.

24 During Jehoiakim's reign, Nebuchadnez-
24:1 zar[w] king of Babylon invaded the land, and
[w]Jer 25:1,9; Da 1:1 Jehoiakim became his vassal for three years. But
then he changed his mind and rebelled against
24:2 Nebuchadnezzar. [2]The LORD sent Babylonian,[a]
[x]Jer 35:11 Aramean,[x] Moabite and Ammonite raiders against
[y]Jer 25:9 him. He sent them to destroy[y] Judah, in accordance with the word of the LORD proclaimed by
his servants the prophets. [3]Surely these things
happened to Judah according to the LORD's com-
24:3 mand,[z] in order to remove them from his presence
[z]2Ki 18:25 [a]2Ki 21:12; because of the sins of Manasseh[a] and all he had
23:26 done, [4]including the shedding of innocent blood.[b]
24:4 For he had filled Jerusalem with innocent blood,
[b]2Ki 21:16 and the LORD was not willing to forgive.
[5]As for the other events of Jehoiakim's reign,
and all he did, are they not written in the book of
the annals of the kings of Judah? [6]Jehoiakim rest-
24:6 [c]Jer 22:19 ed[c] with his fathers. And Jehoiachin his son succeeded him as king.
24:7 [7]The king of Egypt[d] did not march out from his
[d]Ge 15:18 [e]Jer 37:5-7; own country again, because the king of Babylon[e]
46:2 had taken all his territory, from the Wadi of Egypt
to the Euphrates River.

Jehoiachin King of Judah

24:8 [f]1Ch 3:16 [8]Jehoiachin[f] was eighteen years old when he
became king, and he reigned in Jerusalem three
months. His mother's name was Nehushta daughter of Elnathan; she was from Jerusalem. [9]He did
evil in the eyes of the LORD, just as his father had
done.
24:10 [g]Da 1:1 [10]At that time the officers of Nebuchadnezzar[g]
king of Babylon advanced on Jerusalem and laid
siege to it, [11]and Nebuchadnezzar himself came
up to the city while his officers were besieging it.
[12]Jehoiachin king of Judah, his mother, his atten-
24:12 [h]2Ki 25:27; dants, his nobles and his officials all surrendered[h]
Jer 22:24-30; to him.
24:1; 25:1; In the eighth year of the reign of the king of
29:2; 52:28 Babylon, he took Jehoiachin prisoner. [13]As the
24:13 [i]2Ki 20:17 LORD had declared,[i] Nebuchadnezzar removed all
[j]2Ki 25:15; the treasures[j] from the temple of the LORD and
Isa 39:6 from the royal palace, and took away all the gold
[k]2Ki 25:14; articles[k] that Solomon[l] king of Israel had made for
Jer 20:5 [l]1Ki 7:51 the temple of the LORD. [14]He carried into exile[m] all
24:14 Jerusalem: all the officers and fighting men, and
[m]Jer 24:1; 52:28 all the craftsmen and artisans—a total of ten thou-
[n]2Ki 25:12; sand. Only the poorest[n] people of the land were
Jer 40:7; left.
52:16 [15]Nebuchadnezzar took Jehoiachin captive to
Babylon. He also took from Jerusalem to Babylon

[a] 2 Or *Chaldean*

God's Mercy and Justice

2KI 24:3–4

God is always willing to forgive those who turn from disobedient ways and back to him. *Sadly, the people of Jerusalem consistently do the opposite.* Though God listens, hoping to hear them speak of their sincere love and repentance, it does not occur (Jer 8:5–6).

God desires to forgive us as *well. He is always waiting, listening—eager to embrace us as we turn from our sin.* But never forget: He requires true repentance of *believers today, just as in Old Testament times.* We glibly toss up a quick, "God, please forgive me!" only to find ourselves committing *the same offense the next day (or hour or minute).* We long to see *our lives more accurately reflect the values of our hearts.* If we ask, *and if we meditate on him and his Word, the Lord will reveal the sins that need to be confessed and will give the power to live changed lives.*

Deportation

2KI 24:13–16

Following King Jehoiachin's surrender, Nebuchadnezzar strips the temple of its riches and deports the wealthiest and most prominent of Jerusalem's citizens—including leaders, soldiers, craftsmen and artisans—those with usable skills and trades. All are taken to Babylon to serve as slaves; only the very poor remain.

More than a decade later, a second mass deportation takes place. After seizing Judah's new king, Zedekiah, Nebuchadnezzar destroys Jerusalem, burning the temple and other major buildings and breaking down the walls. Those left after the first deportation are now taken to Babylon, leaving only the poorest of the poor to work the land as best they can (2Ki 25:1–12).

the king's mother,[o] his wives, his officials and the
leading men[p] of the land. 16The king of Babylon
also deported to Babylon the entire force of seven
thousand fighting men, strong and fit for war, and
a thousand craftsmen and artisans.[q] 17He made
Mattaniah, Jehoiachin's uncle, king in his place
and changed his name to Zedekiah.[r]

Zedekiah King of Judah

18Zedekiah[s] was twenty-one years old when he
became king, and he reigned in Jerusalem eleven
years. His mother's name was Hamutal[t] daughter
of Jeremiah; she was from Libnah. 19He did evil
in the eyes of the LORD, just as Jehoiakim had
done. 20It was because of the LORD's anger that all
this happened to Jerusalem and Judah, and in the
end he thrust[u] them from his presence.

The Fall of Jerusalem

Now Zedekiah rebelled against the king of
Babylon.

25 So in the ninth year of Zedekiah's reign, on
the tenth day of the tenth month, Nebuchadnezzar[v] king of Babylon marched against Jerusalem with his whole army. He encamped outside the city and built siege works[w] all around it.
2The city was kept under siege until the eleventh
year of King Zedekiah. 3By the ninth day of the
⌞fourth⌟[a] month the famine[x] in the city had
become so severe that there was no food for the
people to eat. 4Then the city wall was broken
through,[y] and the whole army fled at night
through the gate between the two walls near the
king's garden, though the Babylonians[b] were surrounding[z] the city. They fled toward the Arabah,[c]
5but the Babylonian[d] army pursued the king and
overtook him in the plains of Jericho. All his soldiers were separated from him and scattered,[a]
6and he was captured.[b] He was taken to the king
of Babylon at Riblah,[c] where sentence was pronounced on him. 7They killed the sons of Zedekiah before his eyes. Then they put out his eyes,
bound him with bronze shackles and took him to
Babylon.[d]

8On the seventh day of the fifth month, in the
nineteenth year of Nebuchadnezzar king of Babylon, Nebuzaradan commander of the imperial
guard, an official of the king of Babylon, came to
Jerusalem. 9He set fire[e] to the temple of the LORD,
the royal palace and all the houses of Jerusalem.
Every important building he burned down.[f] 10The
whole Babylonian army, under the commander of
the imperial guard, broke down the walls[g] around
Jerusalem. 11Nebuzaradan the commander of the
guard carried into exile[h] the people who remained
in the city, along with the rest of the populace and
those who had gone over to the king of Babylon.[i]

24:15 [o]Jer 22:24-28 [p]Est 2:6; Eze 17:12-14
24:16 [q]Jer 52:28
24:17 [r]1Ch 3:15; 2Ch 36:11; Jer 37:1
24:18 [s]Jer 52:1 [t]2Ki 23:31
24:20 [u]Dt 4:26; 29:27
25:1 [v]Jer 34:1-7 [w]Eze 24:2
25:3 [x]Jer 14:18; La 4:9
25:4 [y]Eze 33:21 [z]Jer 4:17
25:5 [a]Eze 12:14
25:6 [b]Jer 34:21-22 [c]2Ki 23:33
25:7 [d]Jer 21:7; 32:4-5; Eze 12:11
25:9 [e]Isa 60:7 [f]Ps 74:3-8; Jer 2:15; Am 2:5; Mic 3:12
25:10 [g]Ne 1:3
25:11 [h]2Ki 24:14 [i]2Ki 24:1

[a] *3* See Jer. 52:6. [b] *4* Or *Chaldeans*; also in verses 13, 25 and 26 [c] *4* Or *the Jordan Valley* [d] *5* Or *Chaldean*; also in verses 10 and 24

12But the commander left behind some of the poorest people[j] of the land to work the vineyards and fields.

13The Babylonians broke up the bronze pillars, the movable stands and the bronze Sea that were at the temple of the LORD and they carried the bronze to Babylon. 14They also took away the pots, shovels, wick trimmers, dishes and all the bronze articles[k] used in the temple service. 15The commander of the imperial guard took away the censers and sprinkling bowls—all that were made of pure gold or silver.

16The bronze from the two pillars, the Sea and the movable stands, which Solomon had made for the temple of the LORD, was more than could be weighed. 17Each pillar[l] was twenty-seven feet[a] high. The bronze capital on top of one pillar was four and a half feet[b] high and was decorated with a network and pomegranates of bronze all around. The other pillar, with its network, was similar.

18The commander of the guard took as prisoners Seraiah[m] the chief priest, Zephaniah[n] the priest next in rank and the three doorkeepers. 19Of those still in the city, he took the officer in charge of the fighting men and five royal advisers. He also took the secretary who was chief officer in charge of conscripting the people of the land and sixty of his men who were found in the city. 20Nebuzaradan the commander took them all and brought them to the king of Babylon at Riblah. 21There at Riblah, in the land of Hamath, the king had them executed.

So Judah went into captivity, away from her land.[o]

22Nebuchadnezzar king of Babylon appointed Gedaliah[p] son of Ahikam, the son of Shaphan, to be over the people he had left behind in Judah. 23When all the army officers and their men heard that the king of Babylon had appointed Gedaliah as governor, they came to Gedaliah at Mizpah—Ishmael son of Nethaniah, Johanan son of Kareah, Seraiah son of Tanhumeth the Netophathite, Jaazaniah the son of the Maacathite, and their men. 24Gedaliah took an oath to reassure them and their men. "Do not be afraid of the Babylonian officials," he said. "Settle down in the land and serve the king of Babylon, and it will go well with you."

25In the seventh month, however, Ishmael son of Nethaniah, the son of Elishama, who was of royal blood, came with ten men and assassinated Gedaliah and also the men of Judah and the Babylonians who were with him at Mizpah. 26At this, all the people from the least to the greatest, together with the army officers, fled to Egypt[q] for fear of the Babylonians.

25:12 [j]2Ki 24:14
25:14 [k]Ex 27:3; 1Ki 7:47-50
25:17 [l]1Ki 7:15-22
25:18 [m]1Ch 6:14; Ezr 7:1; Ne 11:11 [n]Jer 21:1; 29:25
25:21 [o]Ge 12:7; Dt 28:64; Jos 23:13; 2Ki 23:27
25:22 [p]Jer 39:14; 40:5,7
25:26 [q]Isa 30:2; Jer 43:7

[a] *17* Hebrew *eighteen cubits* (about 8.1 meters)
[b] *17* Hebrew *three cubits* (about 1.3 meters)

More Looting

2KI 25:13-15

Once again the Babylonians plunder the temple, this time taking mostly items made of bronze: pillars, stands, pots, dishes and the remarkable cast bronze basin known as the Sea (see the note at 1Ki 7:23-26, page 534). Note the interesting description of the pillars and the amount of bronze taken (2Ki 25:16-17). Very little gold and silver remain in the city for them to take, the majority having been stolen by Nebuchadnezzar during his first looting of Jerusalem (2Ki 24:13).

Captivity for a King

2KI 25:28-30

After the assassination of Gedaliah by Ishmael, the people of Judah are thrown into even greater chaos. Fearing retribution by Babylon, they seek refuge in Egypt (2Ki 25:26; Jer 41:17).

Meanwhile, Jehoiachin, the exiled king of Judah, remains in prison until the crowning of a new Babylonian king. At 55 years old, with only a three-month reign behind him—and that when he was only 18 (2Ki 24:8)—Jehoiachin is apparently no longer considered a threat. Along with several other captive kings, he is set free. For the rest of his days, Jehoiachin enjoys a position of prominence in the royal court, where he eats his meals comfortably with the king.

Jehoiachin Released

27In the thirty-seventh year of the exile of
Jehoiachin king of Judah, in the year Evil-Mero-
dach[a] became king of Babylon, he released
Jehoiachin[r] from prison on the twenty-seventh
day of the twelfth month. 28He spoke kindly to
him and gave him a seat of honor[s] higher than
those of the other kings who were with him in
Babylon. 29So Jehoiachin put aside his prison
clothes and for the rest of his life ate regularly at
the king's table.[t] 30Day by day the king gave
Jehoiachin a regular allowance as long as he
lived.[u]

25:27 [r]2Ki 24:12; Jer 52:31-34
25:28 [s]Ezr 5:5; Ne 2:1; Da 2:48
25:29 [t]2Sa 9:7
25:30 [u]Est 2:9; Jer 28:4

[a] *27* Also called *Amel-Marduk*

1 Chronicles

A godly king makes a nation strong.

The books of 1 and 2 Chronicles were originally one large volume. Later divided by the translators of the Septuagint (the Greek Old Testament) into separate books, the two volumes portray the history of Israel before the time of the exile. The book of 1 Chronicles helps the returning Jewish exiles rediscover their godly heritage as they rebuild their homeland. Emphasizing the need for obedience to God's commands, 1 Chronicles highlights the importance of true worship, the positive aspects of David's reign and the continuation of his family line.

While the opening chapters of 1 Chronicles seem like an endless list of nondescript names, they are actually much more than that. The lengthy genealogy asserts God's love for individuals. He knows each by name and never forgets even one. In addition, when we look more closely we see that the genealogies unveil familiar women. We meet Keturah, the joy of Abraham's life after Sarah's death (1Ch 1:32–33). We recognize Abigail and Acsah, women whose resourcefulness brings blessing to their families (1Ch 2:16–17; 49). We find Tamar and Bathsheba, women who suffer the consequences of sexual sin (1Ch 3:5–9). And we find Miriam, who learns the importance of following God's leaders (1Ch 6:3).

Studying the positive aspects of David's reign helps us to understand the importance of doing things God's way. Rather than forcing his way onto the throne, David waits for God's timing and unifies the nation (1Ch 10–12). Instead of bemoaning his inability to build the temple, David energetically assembles the materials for its construction (1Ch 22). David's choice to follow God's plan and God's timing instead of his own brings blessing to Israel.

Quick Study

Author
Jewish tradition puts Ezra as the author, although this is not certain.

Date Written
Around 450 B.C.

Setting
Israel.

Key Passage
1 Chronicles 16:13–15
**"O descendants of Israel his servant,
O sons of Jacob, his chosen ones.
He is the LORD our God;
his judgments are in all the earth.
He remembers his covenant forever,
the word he commanded, for a thousand generations."**

Outline

Genealogies.
1Ch 1-9

King Saul.
1Ch 10

King David begins his reign.
1Ch 11-12

The return of the ark.
1Ch 13:1–16:6

David communicates with God.
1Ch 16:7–17:27

David's victories.
1Ch 18-20

David's census.
1Ch 21

Temple preparation.
1Ch 22-26

Armies and officers.
1Ch 27

Temple plans and gifts.
1Ch 28:1–29:9

The end of David's life.
1Ch 29:10-30

The Women of 1 Chronicles

Keturah	*Abraham's concubine.* 1Ch 1:32-33
Timna	*Lotan's sister.* 1Ch 1:39
Matred, Mehetabel	*Mother and daughter.* 1Ch 1:50
Tamar	*Judah's daughter-in-law and mother of two of his sons.* 1Ch 2:4 (page 940)
Abigail, Zeruiah	*David's sisters.* 1Ch 2:16
Azubah, Jerioth, Ephrathah, Azubah, Ephrath	*Caleb's wives.* 1Ch 2:18-19,50; 4:4
Abijah	*Hezron's wife.* 1Ch 2:24
Atarah	*Jerahmeel's second wife.* 1Ch 2:26
Abihail	*Abishur's wife.* 1Ch 2:29
Ahlai	*Married to her father's Egyptian servant.* 1Ch 2:31,34
Ephah, Maacah	*Caleb's concubines.* 1Ch 2:46,48
Acsah	*Caleb's daughter.* 1Ch 2:49
Ahinoam, Abigail, Maacah, Haggith, Abital, Eglah, Bathsheba	*David's wives.* 1Ch 3:1-4,5
Tamar	*David's daughter.* 1Ch 3:9
Shelomith	*Zerubbabel's daughter.* 1Ch 3:19
Hazzelelponi	*Etam's daughter.* 1Ch 4:3
Helah, Naarah	*Ashhur's wives.* 1Ch 4:5-7
Jabez's mother	*Mother of an honorable man.* 1Ch 4:9-10
Bithiah	*Daughter of Pharaoh and wife of Mered.* 1Ch 4:18
Shimei's daughters	*Six in all.* 1Ch 4:27
Bilhah	*Mother of the tribe of Naphtali.* 1Ch 7:13
Maacah	*Makir's wife.* 1Ch 7:16
Hammoleketh	*Gilead's sister.* 1Ch 7:18
Sheerah	*Female builder of cities.* 1Ch 7:24
Serah	*Asher's daughter.* 1Ch 7:30
Shua	*Heber's daughter.* 1Ch 7:32
Hushim, Baara	*Divorced wives.* 1Ch 8:8,11
Hodesh	*Shaharaim's wife.* 1Ch 8:9
Maacah	*Jeiel's wife.* 1Ch 8:29; 9:35
Michal	*David's wife, who came to despise her husband.* 1Ch 15:29 (page 740)
Heman's daughters	*A fulfillment of God's promise.* 1Ch 25:5

Denotes a sketch written about this character

Historical Records From Adam to Abraham

To Noah's Sons

1:1 [a]Ge 5:1-32; Lk 3:36-38
1:2 [b]Ge 5:9 [c]Ge 5:12 [d]Ge 5:15
1:3 [e]Ge 5:18; Jude 1:14 [f]Ge 5:21 [g]Ge 5:25 [h]Ge 5:29
1:4 [i]Ge 6:10; 10:1 [j]Ge 5:32

1 Adam,[a] Seth, Enosh, 2Kenan,[b] Mahalalel,[c]
Jared,[d] 3Enoch,[e] Methuselah,[f] Lamech,[g]
Noah.[h]

4The sons of Noah:[a][i]
Shem, Ham and Japheth.[j]

The Japhethites

5The sons[b] of Japheth:
Gomer, Magog, Madai, Javan, Tubal, Meshech and Tiras.
6The sons of Gomer:
Ashkenaz, Riphath[c] and Togarmah.
7The sons of Javan:
Elishah, Tarshish, the Kittim and the Rodanim.

The Hamites

8The sons of Ham:
Cush, Mizraim,[d] Put and Canaan.
9The sons of Cush:
Seba, Havilah, Sabta, Raamah and Sabteca.
The sons of Raamah:
Sheba and Dedan.
10Cush was the father[e] of
Nimrod, who grew to be a mighty warrior on earth.
11Mizraim was the father of
the Ludites, Anamites, Lehabites, Naphtuhites,
12Pathrusites, Casluhites (from whom the Philistines came) and Caphtorites.
13Canaan was the father of
Sidon his firstborn,[f] and of the Hittites,
14Jebusites, Amorites, Girgashites,
15Hivites, Arkites, Sinites, 16Arvadites,
Zemarites and Hamathites.

The Semites

17The sons of Shem:
Elam, Asshur, Arphaxad, Lud and Aram.
The sons of Aram:[g]
Uz, Hul, Gether and Meshech.
18Arphaxad was the father of Shelah,
and Shelah the father of Eber.
19Two sons were born to Eber:
One was named Peleg,[h] because in his time

[a] *4* Septuagint; Hebrew does not have this line [b] *5 Sons* may mean *descendants* or *successors* or *nations*; also in verses 6–10, 17 and 20. [c] *6* Many Hebrew manuscripts and Vulgate (see also Septuagint and Gen. 10:3); most Hebrew manuscripts *Diphath* [d] *8* That is, Egypt; also in verse 11 [e] *10 Father* may mean *ancestor* or *predecessor* or *founder*; also in verses 11, 13, 18 and 20. [f] *13* Or *of the Sidonians, the foremost* [g] *17* One Hebrew manuscript and some Septuagint manuscripts (see also Gen. 10:23); most Hebrew manuscripts do not have this line. [h] *19* *Peleg* means *division.*

Not Just a List of Names

1CH 1–9

The long list of names in 1 Chronicles may not be the Bible's most inspirational reading, but these nine chapters offer the reader vital information. We need to "think Hebrew" to understand their value. The genealogies help establish inheritance rights for Jewish exiles moving back to Judah. The lists assist the leaders in recruiting workers and assigning tasks. For example, since God said that all who perform priestly duties must come from Aaron's clan within the Levite tribe, it is essential to verify each person's lineage. In addition, these extensive genealogical tables help the people reconnect with their ancestors and reestablish their faith in God. They need assurance he will be with them as they rebuild their ruined nation.

The genealogies affirm God's covenant with Abraham (Ge 12:2–3) and his pledge to David (2Sa 7:12–16.) This covenant promise is also ours today as Abraham's descendants by faith in God's Son Jesus Christ (Gal 3:8–9).

Accepting others as they are is a perfect picture of seeing theory lived out in practicality. We may say we accept others, but until we actually do it, it is only theory. No one can actually change anyone else, so why do we try so hard? Present to them the gospel? Yes! Attempt to introduce them to Christ? Fine. Suggest a better way of life or standard of living? They'll probably appreciate it. But change them? No . . .

I am learning that if we want our associates to change, two things must occur: We must leave their alteration to the work of God—to his Spirit and timing; and we must accept them (preferably love them) as they are. Acceptance has an important side effect, too, related to honesty or openness. If I know I am going to be accepted by another person, no matter what I say or do—if I know that I will not be judged for my behavior or comments—then I am more apt to be transparent with them. In fact, I will be open only to the degree that I know I'm going to be accepted. The less judgmental we are, the more easily other people will open their hearts to us.

—Luci Swindoll

the earth was divided; his brother was
named Joktan.
20 Joktan was the father of
Almodad, Sheleph, Hazarmaveth, Jerah,
21 Hadoram, Uzal, Diklah, 22 Obal,[a] Abimael,
Sheba, 23 Ophir, Havilah and Jobab. All
these were sons of Joktan.

24 Shem,[k] Arphaxad,[b] Shelah,
25 Eber, Peleg, Reu,
26 Serug, Nahor, Terah
27 and Abram (that is, Abraham).

1:24 [k]Ge 10:21-25; Lk 3:34-36

The Family of Abraham

28 The sons of Abraham:
Isaac and Ishmael.

Descendants of Hagar

29 These were their descendants:
Nebaioth the firstborn of Ishmael, Kedar,
Adbeel, Mibsam, 30 Mishma, Dumah, Massa, Hadad, Tema, 31 Jetur, Naphish and Kedemah. These were the sons of Ishmael.

Descendants of Keturah

32 The sons born to Keturah, Abraham's concu-
bine:[l]
Zimran, Jokshan, Medan, Midian, Ishbak
and Shuah.
The sons of Jokshan:
Sheba and Dedan.[m]
33 The sons of Midian:
Ephah, Epher, Hanoch, Abida and Eldaah.
All these were descendants of Keturah.

1:32 [l]Ge 22:24 [m]Ge 10:7

Descendants of Sarah

34 Abraham[n] was the father of Isaac.[o]
The sons of Isaac:
Esau and Israel.[p]

1:34 [n]Lk 3:34 [o]Ge 21:2-3; Mt 1:2; Ac 7:8 [p]Ge 17:5; 25:25-26

Esau's Sons

35 The sons of Esau:[q]
Eliphaz, Reuel,[r] Jeush, Jalam and Korah.
36 The sons of Eliphaz:
Teman, Omar, Zepho,[c] Gatam and Kenaz;
by Timna: Amalek.[d][s]
37 The sons of Reuel:[t]
Nahath, Zerah, Shammah and Mizzah.

1:35 [q]Ge 36:19 [r]Ge 36:4
1:36 [s]Ex 17:14
1:37 [t]Ge 36:17

The People of Seir in Edom

38 The sons of Seir:
Lotan, Shobal, Zibeon, Anah, Dishon, Ezer
and Dishan.

[a] *22* Some Hebrew manuscripts and Syriac (see also Gen. 10:28); most Hebrew manuscripts *Ebal* [b] *24* Hebrew; some Septuagint manuscripts *Arphaxad, Cainan* (see also note at Gen. 11:10) [c] *36* Many Hebrew manuscripts, some Septuagint manuscripts and Syriac (see also Gen. 36:11); most Hebrew manuscripts *Zephi* [d] *36* Some Septuagint manuscripts (see also Gen. 36:12); Hebrew *Gatam, Kenaz, Timna and Amalek*

[39]The sons of Lotan:
Hori and Homam. Timna was Lotan's sister.
[40]The sons of Shobal:
1:40 [u]Ge 36:2
Alvan,[a] Manahath, Ebal, Shepho and Onam.
The sons of Zibeon:
Aiah and Anah.[u]
[41]The son of Anah:
Dishon.
The sons of Dishon:
Hemdan,[b] Eshban, Ithran and Keran.
[42]The sons of Ezer:
Bilhan, Zaavan and Akan.[c]
The sons of Dishan[d]:
Uz and Aran.

The Rulers of Edom

[43]These were the kings who reigned in Edom before any Israelite king reigned[e]:
Bela son of Beor, whose city was named Dinhabah.
[44]When Bela died, Jobab son of Zerah from Bozrah succeeded him as king.
[45]When Jobab died, Husham from the land of
1:45 [v]Ge 36:11
the Temanites[v] succeeded him as king.
[46]When Husham died, Hadad son of Bedad, who defeated Midian in the country of Moab, succeeded him as king. His city was named Avith.
[47]When Hadad died, Samlah from Masrekah succeeded him as king.
[48]When Samlah died, Shaul from Rehoboth on the river[f] succeeded him as king.
[49]When Shaul died, Baal-Hanan son of Acbor succeeded him as king.
[50]When Baal-Hanan died, Hadad succeeded him as king. His city was named Pau,[g] and his wife's name was Mehetabel daughter of Matred, the daughter of Me-Zahab.
[51]Hadad also died.
The chiefs of Edom were:
Timna, Alvah, Jetheth, [52]Oholibamah, Elah, Pinon, [53]Kenaz, Teman, Mibzar, [54]Magdiel and Iram. These were the chiefs of Edom.

Israel's Sons

2 These were the sons of Israel:
Reuben, Simeon, Levi, Judah, Issachar,

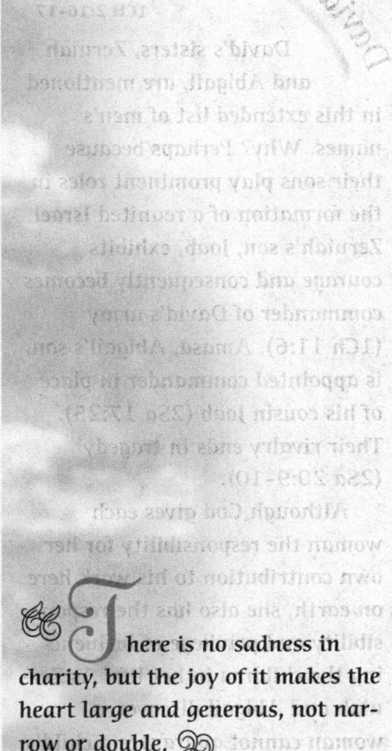

There is no sadness in charity, but the joy of it makes the heart large and generous, not narrow or double.

—Catherine of Siena (1347–1380)

[a] *40* Many Hebrew manuscripts and some Septuagint manuscripts (see also Gen. 36:23); most Hebrew manuscripts *Alian* [b] *41* Many Hebrew manuscripts and some Septuagint manuscripts (see also Gen. 36:26); most Hebrew manuscripts *Hamran* [c] *42* Many Hebrew and Septuagint manuscripts (see also Gen. 36:27); most Hebrew manuscripts *Zaavan, Jaakan* [d] *42* Hebrew *Dishon,* a variant of *Dishan* [e] *43* Or *before an Israelite king reigned over them* [f] *48* Possibly the Euphrates [g] *50* Many Hebrew manuscripts, some Septuagint manuscripts, Vulgate and Syriac (see also Gen. 36:39); most Hebrew manuscripts *Pai*

David's Sisters

1CH 2:16-17

David's sisters, Zeruiah and Abigail, are mentioned in this extended list of men's names. Why? Perhaps because their sons play prominent roles in the formation of a reunited Israel. Zeruiah's son, Joab, exhibits courage and consequently becomes commander of David's army (1Ch 11:6). Amasa, Abigail's son, is appointed commander in place of his cousin Joab (2Sa 17:25). Their rivalry ends in tragedy (2Sa 20:9-10).

Although God gives each woman the responsibility for her own contribution to his work here on earth, she also has the responsibility and privilege of influencing the children in her life. As Zeruiah and Abigail discover, a woman cannot guarantee a child's future decisions. However, she can *live her life with faith and consistency, providing a godly example for them to follow.*

Zebulun, [2]Dan, Joseph, Benjamin, Naphtali, Gad and Asher.

Judah

To Hezron's Sons

[3]The sons of Judah:[w]
Er, Onan and Shelah.[x] These three were
born to him by a Canaanite woman, the
daughter of Shua.[y] Er, Judah's firstborn,
was wicked in the LORD's sight; so the LORD
put him to death.[z] [4]Tamar,[a] Judah's daughter-in-law,[b] bore him Perez[c] and Zerah.
Judah had five sons in all.

[5]The sons of Perez:[d]
Hezron[e] and Hamul.
[6]The sons of Zerah:
Zimri, Ethan, Heman, Calcol and Darda[a]—five in all.
[7]The son of Carmi:
Achar,[b f] who brought trouble on Israel by violating the ban on taking devoted things.[c g]
[8]The son of Ethan:
Azariah.
[9]The sons born to Hezron[h] were:
Jerahmeel, Ram and Caleb.[d]

From Ram Son of Hezron

[10]Ram[i] was the father of
Amminadab[j], and Amminadab the father of
Nahshon,[k] the leader of the people of Judah.
[11]Nahshon was the father of Salmon,[e] Salmon the father of Boaz, [12]Boaz[l] the father of
Obed and Obed the father of Jesse.[m]
[13]Jesse[n] was the father of
Eliab[o] his firstborn; the second son was
Abinadab, the third Shimea, [14]the fourth
Nethanel, the fifth Raddai, [15]the sixth
Ozem and the seventh David. [16]Their sisters were Zeruiah[p] and Abigail. Zeruiah's[q]
three sons were Abishai, Joab[r] and Asahel.
[17]Abigail was the mother of Amasa,[s] whose
father was Jether the Ishmaelite.

Caleb Son of Hezron

[18]Caleb son of Hezron had children by his wife
Azubah (and by Jerioth). These were her
sons: Jesher, Shobab and Ardon. [19]When
Azubah died, Caleb[t] married Ephrath, who
bore him Hur. [20]Hur was the father of Uri,
and Uri the father of Bezalel.[u]
[21]Later, Hezron lay with the daughter of Makir

2:3 [w]Ge 29:35; 38:2-10 [x]Ge 38:5 [y]Ge 38:2 [z]Nu 26:19
2:4 [a]Ge 38:11-30 [b]Ge 11:31 [c]Ge 38:29
2:5 [d]Ge 46:12 [e]Nu 26:21
2:7 [f]Jos 7:1 [g]Jos 6:18
2:9 [h]Nu 26:21
2:10 [i]Lk 3:32-33 [j]Ex 6:23 [k]Nu 1:7
2:12 [l]Ru 2:1 [m]Ru 4:17
2:13 [n]Ru 4:17 [o]1Sa 16:6
2:16 [p]1Sa 26:6 [q]2Sa 2:18 [r]2Sa 2:13
2:17 [s]2Sa 17:25
2:19 [t]ver 42,50
2:20 [u]Ex 31:2

[a] *6* Many Hebrew manuscripts, some Septuagint manuscripts and Syriac (see also 1 Kings 4:31); most Hebrew manuscripts *Dara* [b] *7* *Achar* means *trouble*; *Achar* is called *Achan* in Joshua. [c] *7* The Hebrew term refers to the irrevocable giving over of things or persons to the LORD, often by totally destroying them. [d] *9* Hebrew *Kelubai*, a variant of *Caleb* [e] *11* Septuagint (see also Ruth 4:21); Hebrew *Salma*

the father of Gilead[v] (he had married her
2:21 when he was sixty years old), and she bore
[v]Nu 27:1 him Segub. 22 Segub was the father of Jair,
2:23 who controlled twenty-three towns in Gil-
[w]Nu 32:41; Dt 3:14; Jos 13:30 ead. 23 (But Geshur and Aram captured
Havvoth Jair,[a][w] as well as Kenath[x] with its
[x]Nu 32:42 surrounding settlements—sixty towns.) All
these were descendants of Makir the father
of Gilead.

24 After Hezron died in Caleb Ephrathah, Abi-
2:24 jah the wife of Hezron bore him Ashhur[y]
[y]1Ch 4:5 the father[b] of Tekoa.

Jerahmeel Son of Hezron

25 The sons of Jerahmeel the firstborn of Hezron:
Ram his firstborn, Bunah, Oren, Ozem
and[c] Ahijah. 26 Jerahmeel had another wife,
whose name was Atarah; she was the
mother of Onam.

27 The sons of Ram the firstborn of Jerahmeel:
Maaz, Jamin and Eker.

28 The sons of Onam:
Shammai and Jada.

The sons of Shammai:
Nadab and Abishur.

29 Abishur's wife was named Abihail, who bore
him Ahban and Molid.

30 The sons of Nadab:
Seled and Appaim. Seled died without
children.

31 The son of Appaim:
Ishi, who was the father of Sheshan.
Sheshan was the father of Ahlai.

32 The sons of Jada, Shammai's brother:
Jether and Jonathan. Jether died without
children.

33 The sons of Jonathan:
Peleth and Zaza.

These were the descendants of Jerahmeel.

34 Sheshan had no sons—only daughters.
He had an Egyptian servant named Jarha.
35 Sheshan gave his daughter in marriage to
his servant Jarha, and she bore him Attai.

36 Attai was the father of Nathan,
2:36 Nathan the father of Zabad,[z]
[z]1Ch 11:41 37 Zabad the father of Ephlal,
Ephlal the father of Obed,
38 Obed the father of Jehu,
Jehu the father of Azariah,
39 Azariah the father of Helez,
Helez the father of Eleasah,
40 Eleasah the father of Sismai,
Sismai the father of Shallum,
41 Shallum the father of Jekamiah,
and Jekamiah the father of Elishama.

[a] *23* Or *captured the settlements of Jair* [b] *24* *Father* may mean *civic leader* or *military leader*; also in verses 42, 45, 49–52 and possibly elsewhere. [c] *25* Or *Oren and Ozem, by*

Inheritance

1CH 2:34–35

Since the property an Israelite family owns in the promised land is believed to be a gift from God, it is vital that the property remains in the family. Upon the father's death, the property is divided among all the sons with a double portion going to the oldest who then cares for his mother and unmarried sisters. However, when a husband and his wife have no sons, God gives permission for the land to be given to his daughters (Nu 27:1–8.) Another option for keeping the inheritance within the family is for the father to adopt one of his servants. Abraham thought about doing this with his servant Eliezer (Ge 15:2–3). It seems that Sheshan wants a double assurance that his property will remain within his family. Therefore, he marries his daughter to his servant.

The development of a laugh attitude begins internally. It begins with a foundation that is God-inspired and God-constructed. That foundation gives us security as we stand confidently on the strength of his incomparable love for us. Faith in that solid foundation then leads to personal rest and divine security. Without this internal peace, the laughter inspired by all the zany antics we can think of will ultimately die in the wind, leaving a hollow void waiting to be filled with the next antic or joke.

I guess if I were to reduce all of these words about developing a laugh lifestyle into one sure first step, it would be: Become personally acquainted with the Author and giver of joy. His name is Jesus.

—*Marilyn Meberg*

The Clans of Caleb

42 The sons of Caleb[a] the brother of Jerahmeel:
Mesha his firstborn, who was the father of
Ziph, and his son Mareshah,[a] who was the
father of Hebron.
43 The sons of Hebron:
Korah, Tappuah, Rekem and Shema. 44 Shema was the father of Raham, and Raham
the father of Jorkeam. Rekem was the
father of Shammai. 45 The son of Shammai
was Maon[b], and Maon was the father of
Beth Zur.[c]
46 Caleb's concubine Ephah was the mother of
Haran, Moza and Gazez. Haran was the
father of Gazez.
47 The sons of Jahdai:
Regem, Jotham, Geshan, Pelet, Ephah and
Shaaph.
48 Caleb's concubine Maacah was the mother of
Sheber and Tirhanah. 49 She also gave birth
to Shaaph the father of Madmannah[d] and
to Sheva the father of Macbenah and Gib-
ea. Caleb's daughter was Acsah.[e] 50 These
were the descendants of Caleb.

The sons of Hur[f] the firstborn of Ephrathah:
Shobal the father of Kiriath Jearim,[g] 51 Sal-
ma the father of Bethlehem, and Hareph
the father of Beth Gader.
52 The descendants of Shobal the father of Kiriath Jearim were:
Haroeh, half the Manahathites, 53 and the
clans of Kiriath Jearim: the Ithrites,[h]
Puthites, Shumathites and Mishraites.
From these descended the Zorathites and
Eshtaolites.
54 The descendants of Salma:
Bethlehem, the Netophathites,[i] Atroth Beth
Joab, half the Manahathites, the Zorites,
55 and the clans of scribes[b] who lived at
Jabez: the Tirathites, Shimeathites and
Sucathites. These are the Kenites[j] who
came from Hammath,[k] the father of the
house of Recab.[c][l]

The Sons of David

3 These were the sons of David[m] born to him in
Hebron:
The firstborn was Amnon the son of Ahinoam of Jezreel;[n]
the second, Daniel the son of Abigail[o] of
Carmel;
2 the third, Absalom the son of Maacah
daughter of Talmai king of Geshur;
the fourth, Adonijah[p] the son of Haggith;
3 the fifth, Shephatiah the son of Abital;
and the sixth, Ithream, by his wife Eglah.
4 These six were born to David in Hebron,[q]

2:42 [a]ver 19
2:45 [b]Jos 15:55 [c]Jos 15:58
2:49 [d]Jos 15:31 [e]Jos 15:16
2:50 [f]1Ch 4:4 [g]ver 19
2:53 [h]2Sa 23:38
2:54 [i]Ezr 2:22; Ne 7:26; 12:28
2:55 [j]Ge 15:19; Jdg 1:16; Jdg 4:11 [k]Jos 19:35 [l]2Ki 10:15, 23; Jer 35:2-19
3:1 [m]1Ch 14:3; 28:5 [n]Jos 15:56 [o]1Sa 25:42
3:2 [p]1Ki 2:22
3:4 [q]2Sa 5:4; 1Ch 29:27

[a] 42 The meaning of the Hebrew for this phrase is uncertain.
[b] 55 Or *of the Sopherites* [c] 55 Or *father of Beth Recab*

where he reigned seven years and six
months.[r]
David reigned in Jerusalem thirty-three years,
5 and these were the children born to him there:
Shammua,[a] Shobab, Nathan and Solomon.
These four were by Bathsheba[b][s] daughter
of Ammiel. 6 There were also Ibhar, Elishua,[c] Eliphelet, 7 Nogah, Nepheg, Japhia,
8 Elishama, Eliada and Eliphelet—nine in
all. 9 All these were the sons of David,
besides his sons by his concubines. And
Tamar[t] was their sister.[u]

The Kings of Judah

10 Solomon's son was Rehoboam,[v]
Abijah his son,
Asa his son,
Jehoshaphat[w] his son,
11 Jehoram[d][x] his son,
Ahaziah[y] his son,
Joash[z] his son,
12 Amaziah[a] his son,
Azariah his son,
Jotham[b] his son,
13 Ahaz[c] his son,
Hezekiah[d] his son,
Manasseh[e] his son,
14 Amon[f] his son,
Josiah[g] his son.
15 The sons of Josiah:
Johanan the firstborn,
Jehoiakim[h] the second son,
Zedekiah[i] the third,
Shallum[j] the fourth.
16 The successors of Jehoiakim:
Jehoiachin[e][k] his son,
and Zedekiah.[l]

The Royal Line After the Exile

17 The descendants of Jehoiachin the captive:
Shealtiel[m] his son, 18 Malkiram, Pedaiah,
Shenazzar,[n] Jekamiah, Hoshama and
Nedabiah.[o]
19 The sons of Pedaiah:
Zerubbabel[p] and Shimei.
The sons of Zerubbabel:
Meshullam and Hananiah.
Shelomith was their sister.
20 There were also five others:
Hashubah, Ohel, Berekiah, Hasadiah and
Jushab-Hesed.
21 The descendants of Hananiah:
Pelatiah and Jeshaiah, and the sons of

3:4 [r]2Sa 2:11; 5:5
3:5 [s]2Sa 11:3; 12:24
3:9 [t]2Sa 13:1 [u]1Ch 14:4
3:10 [v]1Ki 11:43; 14:21-31; 2Ch 12:16 [w]2Ch 17:1-21:3
3:11 [x]2Ki 8:16-24; 2Ch 21:1 [y]2Ch 22:1-10 [z]2Ki 11:1-12:21
3:12 [a]2Ki 14:1-22; 2Ch 25:1-28 [b]Isa 1:1; Hos 1:1; Mic 1:1
3:13 [c]2Ki 16:1-20; 2Ch 28:1; Isa 7:1 [d]2Ki 18:1-20:21; 2Ch 29:1; Jer 26:19 [e]2Ch 33:1
3:14 [f]2Ki 21:19-26; 2Ch 33:21; Zep 1:1 [g]2Ch 34:1; Jer 1:2; 3:6; 25:3
3:15 [h]2Ki 23:34 [i]Jer 37:1 [j]2Ki 23:31
3:16 [k]2Ki 24:6,8; Mt 1:11 [l]2Ki 24:18
3:17 [m]Ezr 3:2
3:18 [n]Ezr 1:8; 5:14 [o]Jer 22:30
3:19 [p]Ezr 2:2; 3:2; 5:2; Ne 7:7; 12:1; Hag 1:1; 2:2; Zec 4:6

[a] *5* Hebrew *Shimea,* a variant of *Shammua* [b] *5* One Hebrew manuscript and Vulgate (see also Septuagint and 2 Samuel 11:3); most Hebrew manuscripts *Bathshua* [c] *6* Two Hebrew manuscripts (see also 2 Samuel 5:15 and 1 Chron. 14:5); most Hebrew manuscripts *Elishama* [d] *11* Hebrew *Joram,* a variant of *Jehoram* [e] *16* Hebrew *Jeconiah,* a variant of *Jehoiachin;* also in verse 17

King David's Sons

1CH 3:5

In the first few verses of 1 Chronicles 3, Solomon is listed with the rest of King David's sons. He is not David's firstborn son, but he succeeds David on the throne of Israel. This is God's plan.

Although David longs to build a temple for the Lord, God has other plans. God tells David that his son Solomon will accomplish this massive construction project (1Ch 28:6). At the same time, God promises David that his kingdom will last forever (2Sa 7:8–17).

Since David's reign ends, as does the reign of every human king, God's promise of an eternal kingdom must refer to the future rule of the Messiah. David understood this truth and so did the Hebrew people. Today God's true followers acknowledge that the Son of David came into the world as Jesus Christ, the Messiah, our forever king (Isa 9:7; Lk 1:29–33).

A Message From Jabez

1CH 4:9–10

Nestled in the middle of this family tree is an anecdote that presents a profound message about one man's choices. While it is fairly common to include brief historical comments in genealogical records, these parenthetical remarks include more than the usual facts or figures.

As a result of an extremely painful childbirth, the mother in 1 Chronicles 4:9 names her son Jabez, which means "sorrow" and "pain." Since names are significant to the Hebrew people, Jabez has a strike against him from the day he enters the world.

Yet Jabez wants more than the sad heritage his family offers. So he makes a wise decision. He goes to God. "I want your blessing," Jabez prays. "Nourish and grow me beyond my present situation. Direct me with your powerful hand and help me to rise above my painful, depressing past." And God did!

Rephaiah, of Arnan, of Obadiah and of Shecaniah.

22 The descendants of Shecaniah:
Shemaiah and his sons:
Hattush,[q] Igal, Bariah, Neariah and Shaphat—six in all.

23 The sons of Neariah:
Elioenai, Hizkiah and Azrikam—three in all.

24 The sons of Elioenai:
Hodaviah, Eliashib, Pelaiah, Akkub, Johanan, Delaiah and Anani—seven in all.

Other Clans of Judah

4 The descendants of Judah:[r]
Perez, Hezron,[s] Carmi, Hur and Shobal.

2 Reaiah son of Shobal was the father of Jahath, and Jahath the father of Ahumai and Lahad. These were the clans of the Zorathites.

3 These were the sons[a] of Etam:
Jezreel, Ishma and Idbash. Their sister was named Hazzelelponi. 4 Penuel was the father of Gedor, and Ezer the father of Hushah.
These were the descendants of Hur,[t] the firstborn of Ephrathah and father[b] of Bethlehem.[u]

5 Ashhur[v] the father of Tekoa had two wives, Helah and Naarah.

6 Naarah bore him Ahuzzam, Hepher, Temeni and Haahashtari. These were the descendants of Naarah.

7 The sons of Helah:
Zereth, Zohar, Ethnan, 8 and Koz, who was the father of Anub and Hazzobebah and of the clans of Aharhel son of Harum.

9 Jabez was more honorable than his brothers.
His mother had named him Jabez,[c] saying, "I gave
birth to him in pain." 10 Jabez cried out to the God
of Israel, "Oh, that you would bless me and
enlarge my territory! Let your hand be with me,
and keep me from harm so that I will be free from
pain." And God granted his request.

11 Kelub, Shuhah's brother, was the father of Mehir, who was the father of Eshton. 12 Eshton was the father of Beth Rapha, Paseah and Tehinnah the father of Ir Nahash.[d] These were the men of Recah.

13 The sons of Kenaz:
Othniel[w] and Seraiah.
The sons of Othniel:
Hathath and Meonothai.[e] 14 Meonothai was the father of Ophrah.

3:22 [q]Ezr 8:2-3
4:1 [r]Ge 29:35; 46:12; 1Ch 2:3 [s]Nu 26:21
4:4 [t]1Ch 2:50 [u]Ru 1:19
4:5 [v]1Ch 2:24
4:13 [w]Jos 15:17

[a] 3 Some Septuagint manuscripts (see also Vulgate); Hebrew *father* [b] 4 *Father* may mean *civic leader* or *military leader*; also in verses 12, 14, 17, 18 and possibly elsewhere.
[c] 9 *Jabez* sounds like the Hebrew for *pain.* [d] 12 Or *of the city of Nahash* [e] 13 Some Septuagint manuscripts and Vulgate; Hebrew does not have *and Meonothai.*

Seraiah was the father of Joab,
the father of Ge Harashim.[a] It was called
this because its people were craftsmen.
15 The sons of Caleb son of Jephunneh:
Iru, Elah and Naam.
The son of Elah:
Kenaz.
16 The sons of Jehallelel:
Ziph, Ziphah, Tiria and Asarel.
17 The sons of Ezrah:
4:17 Jether, Mered, Epher and Jalon. One of
[x]Ex 15:20 Mered's wives gave birth to Miriam,[x]
Shammai and Ishbah the father of Eshtemoa. 18 (His Judean wife gave birth to Jered
the father of Gedor, Heber the father of
4:18 [y]Jos 15:34 Soco, and Jekuthiel the father of Zanoah.[y])
These were the children of Pharaoh's
daughter Bithiah, whom Mered had
married.
19 The sons of Hodiah's wife, the sister of
4:19 Naham:
[z]Jos 15:44 the father of Keilah[z] the Garmite, and Esh-
[a]Dt 3:14 temoa the Maacathite.[a]
20 The sons of Shimon:
Amnon, Rinnah, Ben-Hanan and Tilon.
The descendants of Ishi:
4:21 Zoheth and Ben-Zoheth.
[b]Ge 38:5 21 The sons of Shelah[b] son of Judah:
Er the father of Lecah, Laadah the father of
Mareshah and the clans of the linen workers at Beth Ashbea, 22 Jokim, the men of
Cozeba, and Joash and Saraph, who ruled
in Moab and Jashubi Lehem. (These
records are from ancient times.) 23 They
were the potters who lived at Netaim and
Gederah; they stayed there and worked for
the king.

Simeon

4:24 [c]Ge 29:33 24 The descendants of Simeon:[c]
[d]Nu 26:12 Nemuel, Jamin, Jarib,[d] Zerah and Shaul;
25 Shallum was Shaul's son, Mibsam his son
and Mishma his son.
26 The descendants of Mishma:
Hammuel his son, Zaccur his son and
4:28 Shimei his son.
[e]Ge 21:14 27 Shimei had sixteen sons and six daughters,
[f]Jos 15:26 but his brothers did not have many children; so
4:29 their entire clan did not become as numerous as
[g]Jos 15:29 the people of Judah. 28 They lived in Beersheba,[e]
4:30 Moladah,[f] Hazar Shual, 29 Bilhah, Ezem,[g] Tolad,
[h]Nu 14:45 30 Bethuel, Hormah,[h] Ziklag, 31 Beth Marcaboth,
4:31 Hazar Susim, Beth Biri and Shaaraim.[i] These were
[i]Jos 15:36 their towns until the reign of David. 32 Their sur-
4:32 rounding villages were Etam, Ain,[j] Rimmon,
[j]Nu 34:11 Token and Ashan[k]—five towns— 33 and all the vil-
[k]Jos 15:42 lages around these towns as far as Baalath.[b] These

[a] *14 Ge Harashim* means *valley of craftsmen.* [b] *33* Some Septuagint manuscripts (see also Joshua 19:8); Hebrew *Baal*

I will never say anything about myself, either good or bad, lest I should come to esteem myself of some importance; and when I have sometimes heard myself spoken of by others, especially if I were praised, I have said inwardly: "If you knew what I am within, you would not speak thus." And then, turning to myself, I say: "When thou hearest thyself named, or listenest to words which perhaps may seem to praise thee, know that they are not spoken of what is thine; for the only virtue and glory thou hast belong to God.

—*Catherine of Genoa (1447-1510)*

Simeon's Clan

1CH 4:39–43

Simeon's clan prospers until their current acreage is no longer adequate. They search and find a peaceful area with lush pastureland, a prime example of the "milk and honey" image God had promised to them (Dt 26:15). They decide this spot will make a good home for their growing families and herds. But the enemies of God live in this quiet locale. Acting on an earlier mandate from God (Dt 20:17–18), the Simeonites move these people off the land and completely destroy them in the process.

These devastating attacks may be troubling to us. We view God as compassionate and merciful. However, there is evidence that these people not only ignore and deliberately oppose God and his ways but also try to influence the Israelites to turn against God. Like any caring parent, God makes hard rules in order to protect his children.

were their settlements. And they kept a genealogical record.

34 Meshobab, Jamlech, Joshah son of Amaziah, 35 Joel, Jehu son of Joshibiah, the son of
Seraiah, the son of Asiel, 36 also Elioenai, Jaa-
kobah, Jeshohaiah, Asaiah, Adiel, Jesimiel,
Benaiah, 37 and Ziza son of Shiphi, the son of
Allon, the son of Jedaiah, the son of Shimri,
the son of Shemaiah.

38 The men listed above by name were leaders
of their clans. Their families increased greatly,
39 and they went to the outskirts of Gedor[l] to the
east of the valley in search of pasture for their
flocks. 40 They found rich, good pasture, and the
land was spacious, peaceful and quiet.[m] Some
Hamites had lived there formerly.

41 The men whose names were listed came in
the days of Hezekiah king of Judah. They
attacked the Hamites in their dwellings and also
the Meunites[n] who were there and completely
destroyed[a] them, as is evident to this day. Then
they settled in their place, because there was pasture for their flocks. 42 And five hundred of these
Simeonites, led by Pelatiah, Neariah, Rephaiah
and Uzziel, the sons of Ishi, invaded the hill country of Seir.[o] 43 They killed the remaining Amalekites[p] who had escaped, and they have lived
there to this day.

Reuben

5 The sons of Reuben[q] the firstborn of Israel (he
was the firstborn, but when he defiled his
father's marriage bed,[r] his rights as firstborn were
given to the sons of Joseph[s] son of Israel;[t] so he
could not be listed in the genealogical record in
accordance with his birthright,[u] 2 and though
Judah[v] was the strongest of his brothers and a
ruler[w] came from him, the rights of the firstborn[x]
belonged to Joseph)— 3 the sons of Reuben[y] the
firstborn of Israel:

Hanoch, Pallu,[z] Hezron and Carmi.

4 The descendants of Joel:

Shemaiah his son, Gog his son,
Shimei his son, 5 Micah his son,
Reaiah his son, Baal his son,
6 and Beerah his son, whom Tiglath-Pileser[b][a]
king of Assyria took into exile. Beerah was
a leader of the Reubenites.

7 Their relatives by clans,[b] listed according to
their genealogical records:

Jeiel the chief, Zechariah, 8 and Bela son of
Azaz, the son of Shema, the son of Joel.
They settled in the area from Aroer[c] to Nebo
and Baal Meon. 9 To the east they occupied
the land up to the edge of the desert that

4:39 [l]Jos 15:58
4:40 [m]Jdg 18:7-10
4:41 [n]2Ch 20:1; 26:7
4:42 [o]Ge 14:6
4:43 [p]1Sa 15:8; 30:17; 2Sa 8:12; Est 3:1; 9:16
5:1 [q]Ge 29:32 [r]Ge 35:22; 49:4 [s]Ge 48:16, 22; 49:26 [t]Ge 48:5 [u]1Ch 26:10
5:2 [v]Ge 49:10,12 [w]1Sa 9:16; 12:12; 2Sa 6:21; 1Ch 11:2; 2Ch 7:18; Ps 60:7; Mic 5:2; Mt 2:6 [x]Ge 25:31
5:3 [y]Ge 29:32; 46:9; Ex 6:14; Nu 26:5-11 [z]Nu 26:5
5:6 [a]ver 26; 2Ki 15:19; 16:10; 2Ch 28:20
5:7 [b]ver 17
5:8 [c]Nu 32:34

[a] *41* The Hebrew term refers to the irrevocable giving over of things or persons to the LORD, often by totally destroying them.
[b] *6* Hebrew *Tilgath-Pilneser,* a variant of *Tiglath-Pileser*; also in verse 26

extends to the Euphrates River, because
their livestock had increased in Gilead.[d]

5:9 [d]Nu 32:26; Jos 22:9

10 During Saul's reign they waged war
against the Hagrites[e], who were defeated at
their hands; they occupied the dwellings of
the Hagrites throughout the entire region east
of Gilead.

5:10 [e]ver 18-21

Gad

5:11 [f]Jos 13:24-28 [g]Dt 3:10; Jos 13:11

11 The Gadites[f] lived next to them in Bashan, as
far as Salecah:[g]
12 Joel was the chief, Shapham the second,
then Janai and Shaphat, in Bashan.
13 Their relatives, by families, were:
Michael, Meshullam, Sheba, Jorai, Jacan,
Zia and Eber—seven in all.
14 These were the sons of Abihail son of Huri,
the son of Jaroah, the son of Gilead, the
son of Michael, the son of Jeshishai, the
son of Jahdo, the son of Buz.
15 Ahi son of Abdiel, the son of Guni, was
head of their family.
16 The Gadites lived in Gilead, in Bashan and its
outlying villages, and on all the pasturelands of Sharon as far as they extended.

5:17 [h]2Ki 15:32 [i]2Ki 14:16, 28

17 All these were entered in the genealogical
records during the reigns of Jotham[h] king of
Judah and Jeroboam[i] king of Israel.

5:18 [j]Nu 1:3

18 The Reubenites, the Gadites and the half-tribe
of Manasseh had 44,760 men ready for military
service[j]—able-bodied men who could handle
shield and sword, who could use a bow, and who
were trained for battle. 19 They waged war against
the Hagrites, Jetur,[k] Naphish and Nodab. 20 They
were helped[l] in fighting them, and God handed the
Hagrites and all their allies over to them, because
they cried[m] out to him during the battle. He
answered their prayers, because they trusted[n] in
him. 21 They seized the livestock of the Hagrites—
fifty thousand camels, two hundred fifty thousand
sheep and two thousand donkeys. They also took
one hundred thousand people captive, 22 and many
others fell slain, because the battle[o] was God's.
And they occupied the land until the exile.[p]

5:19 [k]ver 10; Ge 25:15; 1Ch 1:31

5:20 [l]Ps 37:40 [m]1Ki 8:44; 2Ch 13:14; 14:11; Ps 20:7-9; 22:5 [n]Ps 26:1; Da 6:23

5:22 [o]2Ch 32:8 [p]2Ki 15:29; 17:6

The Half-Tribe of Manasseh

23 The people of the half-tribe of Manasseh were
numerous; they settled in the land from Bashan
to Baal Hermon, that is, to Senir (Mount Hermon).[q]

5:23 [q]Dt 3:8,9; SS 4:8

24 These were the heads of their families: Epher,
Ishi, Eliel, Azriel, Jeremiah, Hodaviah and Jahdi-
el. They were brave warriors, famous men, and
heads of their families. 25 But they were unfaithful[r] to the God of their fathers and prostituted[s]
themselves to the gods of the peoples of the land,
whom God had destroyed before them. 26 So the
God of Israel stirred up the spirit of Pul[t] king of
Assyria (that is, Tiglath-Pileser[u] king of Assyria),
who took the Reubenites, the Gadites and the

5:25 [r]Dt 32:15-18; 2Ki 17:7; 1Ch 9:1; 2Ch 26:16 [s]Ex 34:15

5:26 [t]2Ki 15:19 [u]2Ki 15:29

**Thy will is the treasure
I seek,
For thou art as faithful as strong;
There let me, obedient and meek,
Repose myself all the day long.
My spirit and faculties fail;
Oh, finish what love has begun!
Destroy what is sinful and frail,
And dwell in the soul thou hast
won!
Dear theme of my wonder and
praise,
I cry, who is worthy as thou?
I can only be silent and gaze!
'Tis all that is left to me now.**

—Madame Guyon (1647-1717)

The Tribe of Levi

1CH 6

God "set apart" (Nu 3:12–13; 8:14) the Levite tribe to lead the Israelites in their worship. They perform various tasks in the tabernacle (Nu 4) and then in the temple. All the men of the tribe of Levi are dedicated to God for this purpose. However, only the Levites who are descendants of Aaron are designated as priests who may offer sacrifices on behalf of the people (Ex 28:1; 1Ch 6:49). Only a priest, a descendant of Aaron, may come into the Most Holy Place and atone for the people's sins.

After their 70-year captivity, the people realize they need to authenticate the Levites' lineage. The genealogies in chapter 6 achieve this purpose and ease the exiles' concern that they are faithfully following God's commands regarding worship.

The Jewish exiles *look forward* to the day when the Messiah will usher in the kingdom of God, canceling the need for a Levite priest's repeated sacrifice and wiping away forever the people's sins. With grateful hearts, we *look back* to the kingdom of God Jesus ushered in and his sacrificial death on the cross.

half-tribe of Manasseh into exile. He took them to Halah,[v] Habor, Hara and the river of Gozan, where they are to this day.

Levi

6 The sons of Levi:[w]
Gershon, Kohath and Merari.
2 The sons of Kohath:
Amram, Izhar, Hebron and Uzziel.
3 The children of Amram:
Aaron, Moses and Miriam.
The sons of Aaron:
Nadab, Abihu,[x] Eleazar and Ithamar.
4 Eleazar was the father of Phinehas,
Phinehas the father of Abishua,
5 Abishua the father of Bukki,
Bukki the father of Uzzi,
6 Uzzi the father of Zerahiah,
Zerahiah the father of Meraioth,
7 Meraioth the father of Amariah,
Amariah the father of Ahitub,
8 Ahitub the father of Zadok,[y]
Zadok the father of Ahimaaz,
9 Ahimaaz the father of Azariah,
Azariah the father of Johanan,
10 Johanan the father of Azariah[z] (it was he who served as priest in the temple Solomon built in Jerusalem),
11 Azariah the father of Amariah,
Amariah the father of Ahitub,
12 Ahitub the father of Zadok,
Zadok the father of Shallum,
13 Shallum the father of Hilkiah,[a]
Hilkiah the father of Azariah,
14 Azariah the father of Seraiah,[b]
and Seraiah the father of Jehozadak.
15 Jehozadak[c] was deported when the LORD sent Judah and Jerusalem into exile by the hand of Nebuchadnezzar.
16 The sons of Levi:[d]
Gershon,[a] Kohath and Merari.[e]
17 These are the names of the sons of Gershon:
Libni and Shimei.
18 The sons of Kohath:
Amram, Izhar, Hebron and Uzziel.
19 The sons of Merari:[f]
Mahli and Mushi.
These are the clans of the Levites listed according to their fathers:
20 Of Gershon:
Libni his son, Jehath his son,
Zimmah his son, 21 Joah his son,
Iddo his son, Zerah his son
and Jeatherai his son.
22 The descendants of Kohath:
Amminadab his son, Korah[g] his son,
Assir his son, 23 Elkanah his son,
Ebiasaph his son, Assir his son,

[a] *16* Hebrew *Gershom,* a variant of *Gershon;* also in verses 17, 20, 43, 62 and 71

5:26 [v] 2Ki 17:6; 18:11
6:1 [w] Ge 46:11; Ex 6:16; Nu 26:57; 1Ch 23:6
6:3 [x] Lev 10:1
6:8 [y] 2Sa 8:17; 15:27; Ezr 7:2
6:10 [z] 1Ki 4:2; 6:1; 2Ch 3:1; 26:17-18
6:13 [a] 2Ki 22:1-20; 2Ch 34:9; 35:8
6:14 [b] 2Ki 25:18; Ezr 2:2; Ne 11:11
6:15 [c] 2Ki 25:18; Ne 12:1; Hag 1:1,14; 2:2,4; Zec 6:11
6:16 [d] Ge 29:34; Ex 6:16; Nu 3:17-20 [e] Nu 26:57
6:19 [f] Ge 46:11; 1Ch 23:21; 24:26
6:22 [g] Ex 6:24

6:24
h1Ch 15:5

24 Tahath his son, Uriel[h] his son,
Uzziah his son and Shaul his son.
25 The descendants of Elkanah:
Amasai, Ahimoth,
26 Elkanah his son,[a] Zophai his son,
Nahath his son, 27 Eliab his son,
Jeroham his son, Elkanah[i] his son
and Samuel[j] his son.[b]
28 The sons of Samuel:
Joel[c][k] the firstborn
and Abijah the second son.
29 The descendants of Merari:
Mahli, Libni his son,
Shimei his son, Uzzah his son,
30 Shimea his son, Haggiah his son
and Asaiah his son.

6:27
i1Sa 1:1
j1Sa 1:20

6:28
kver 33;
1Sa 8:2

The Temple Musicians

31 These are the men[l] David put in charge of the
music[m] in the house of the LORD after the ark
came to rest there. 32 They ministered with music
before the tabernacle, the Tent of Meeting, until
Solomon built the temple of the LORD in
Jerusalem. They performed their duties according
to the regulations laid down for them.
33 Here are the men who served, together with
their sons:
From the Kohathites:
Heman,[n] the musician,
the son of Joel,[o] the son of Samuel,
34 the son of Elkanah,[p] the son of Jeroham,
the son of Eliel, the son of Toah,
35 the son of Zuph, the son of Elkanah,
the son of Mahath, the son of Amasai,
36 the son of Elkanah, the son of Joel,
the son of Azariah, the son of Zephaniah,
37 the son of Tahath, the son of Assir,
the son of Ebiasaph, the son of Korah,[q]
38 the son of Izhar,[r] the son of Kohath,
the son of Levi, the son of Israel;
39 and Heman's associate Asaph,[s] who served
at his right hand:
Asaph son of Berekiah, the son of Shimea,[t]
40 the son of Michael, the son of Baaseiah,[d]
the son of Malkijah, 41 the son of Ethni,
the son of Zerah, the son of Adaiah,
42 the son of Ethan, the son of Zimmah,
the son of Shimei, 43 the son of Jahath,
the son of Gershon, the son of Levi;
44 and from their associates, the Merarites, at
his left hand:
Ethan son of Kishi, the son of Abdi,

6:31
l1Ch 25:1;
2Ch 29:25-26; Ne 12:45
m1Ch 9:33;
15:19;
Ezr 3:10;
Ps 68:25

6:33
n1Ki 4:31;
1Ch 15:17;
25:1
over 28

6:34
p1Sa 1:1

6:37
qEx 6:24

6:38
rEx 6:21

6:39
s1Ch 25:1,9;
2Ch 29:13;
Ne 11:17
t1Ch 15:17

[a] *26* Some Hebrew manuscripts, Septuagint and Syriac; most Hebrew manuscripts *Ahimoth* [26]*and Elkanah. The sons of Elkanah:* [b] *27* Some Septuagint manuscripts (see also 1 Samuel 1:19,20 and 1 Chron. 6:33,34); Hebrew does not have *and Samuel his son.* [c] *28* Some Septuagint manuscripts and Syriac (see also 1 Samuel 8:2 and 1 Chron. 6:33); Hebrew does not have *Joel.* [d] *40* Most Hebrew manuscripts; some Hebrew manuscripts, one Septuagint manuscript and Syriac *Maaseiah*

Temple Musicians

1CH 6:31-32

David appoints music ministers from the tribe of Levi, charging them with using music to worship God (1Ch 15:16). Many of these musicians write their own praise lyrics and set them to music. Some of these songs are recorded in the the book of Psalms. Compare the titles of Psalms 39, 42, 44–50 and 73–88 with this list of temple musicians.

One of the temple musicians, Asaph became well known for his compositions (1Ch 15:17,19; 16:5,7). Many believe that Asaph taught music and perhaps formed a musical guild. Like other Levitical musicians, he probably held a prophetic ministry position as well (1Ch 25:1). Asaph, or perhaps his son or a music student, wrote 12 psalms. One of Asaph's psalms includes this heart cry of ancient and contemporary worshipers: "My flesh and my heart may fail, but God is the strength of my heart and my portion forever" (Ps 73:26).

the son of Malluch, [45]the son of Hashabiah,
the son of Amaziah, the son of Hilkiah,
[46]the son of Amzi, the son of Bani,
the son of Shemer, [47]the son of Mahli,
the son of Mushi, the son of Merari,
the son of Levi.

[48]Their fellow Levites[u] were assigned to all the other duties of the tabernacle, the house of God. [49]But Aaron and his descendants were the ones who presented offerings on the altar[v] of burnt offering and on the altar of incense[w] in connection with all that was done in the Most Holy Place, making atonement for Israel, in accordance with all that Moses the servant of God had commanded.

[50]These were the descendants of Aaron:
Eleazar his son, Phinehas his son,
Abishua his son, [51]Bukki his son,
Uzzi his son, Zerahiah his son,
[52]Meraioth his son, Amariah his son,
Ahitub his son, [53]Zadok[x] his son
and Ahimaaz his son.

[54]These were the locations of their settlements[y] allotted as their territory (they were assigned to the descendants of Aaron who were from the Kohathite clan, because the first lot was for them):

[55]They were given Hebron in Judah with its surrounding pasturelands. [56]But the fields and villages around the city were given to Caleb son of Jephunneh.[z]

[57]So the descendants of Aaron were given Hebron (a city of refuge), and Libnah,[a][a] Jattir,[b] Eshtemoa, [58]Hilen, Debir,[c] [59]Ashan,[d] Juttah[b] and Beth Shemesh, together with their pasturelands. [60]And from the tribe of Benjamin they were given Gibeon,[c] Geba, Alemeth and Anathoth,[e] together with their pasturelands.

These towns, which were distributed among the Kohathite clans, were thirteen in all.

[61]The rest of Kohath's descendants were allotted ten towns from the clans of half the tribe of Manasseh.

[62]The descendants of Gershon, clan by clan, were allotted thirteen towns from the tribes of Issachar, Asher and Naphtali, and from the part of the tribe of Manasseh that is in Bashan.

[63]The descendants of Merari, clan by clan, were allotted twelve towns from the tribes of Reuben, Gad and Zebulun.

[64]So the Israelites gave the Levites these towns[f] and their pasturelands. [65]From the tribes of Judah, Simeon and Benjamin they allotted the previously named towns.

[66]Some of the Kohathite clans were given as their territory towns from the tribe of Ephraim.

6:48 [u]1Ch 23:32
6:49 [v]Ex 27:1-8 [w]Ex 30:1-7, 10; 2Ch 26:18
6:53 [x]2Sa 8:17
6:54 [y]Nu 31:10
6:56 [z]Jos 14:13; 15:13
6:57 [a]Nu 33:20 [b]Jos 15:48
6:58 [c]Jos 10:3
6:59 [d]Jos 15:42
6:60 [e]Jer 1:1
6:64 [f]Nu 35:1-8; Jos 21:3,41-42

[a] *57* See Joshua 21:13; Hebrew *given the cities of refuge: Hebron, Libnah.* [b] *59* Syriac (see also Septuagint and Joshua 21:16); Hebrew does not have *Juttah.* [c] *60* See Joshua 21:17; Hebrew does not have *Gibeon.*

What a liberating concept: that our hate—our *anger*—needs to be prayed. Burying it will not make it go away. Suppressing it contaminates our souls. If we fail to take it to God, it will leak out *and destroy the* world.

—Sheila Walsh

67 In the hill country of Ephraim they were
given Shechem (a city of refuge), and Gezer,[a][g]
68 Jokmeam,[h] Beth Horon,[i] 69 Aijalon[j] and Gath
Rimmon,[k] together with their pasturelands.
70 And from half the tribe of Manasseh the
Israelites gave Aner and Bileam, together
with their pasturelands, to the rest of the
Kohathite clans.

71 The Gershonites[l] received the following:
From the clan of the half-tribe of Manasseh
they received Golan in Bashan[m] and also
Ashtaroth, together with their pasturelands;
72 from the tribe of Issachar
they received Kedesh, Daberath,[n] 73 Ramoth
and Anem, together with their pasturelands;
74 from the tribe of Asher
they received Mashal, Abdon,[o] 75 Hukok[p]
and Rehob,[q] together with their pasturelands;
76 and from the tribe of Naphtali
they received Kedesh in Galilee, Hammon[r]
and Kiriathaim,[s] together with their pasturelands.

77 The Merarites (the rest of the Levites)
received the following:
From the tribe of Zebulun
they received Jokneam, Kartah,[b] Rimmono
and Tabor, together with their pasturelands;
78 from the tribe of Reuben across the Jordan
east of Jericho
they received Bezer[t] in the desert, Jahzah,
79 Kedemoth[u] and Mephaath, together with
their pasturelands;
80 and from the tribe of Gad
they received Ramoth in Gilead,[v] Mahanaim,[w] 81 Heshbon and Jazer,[x] together with
their pasturelands.[y]

Issachar

7 The sons of Issachar:[z]
Tola, Puah,[a] Jashub and Shimron—four in
all.
2 The sons of Tola:
Uzzi, Rephaiah, Jeriel, Jahmai, Ibsam and
Samuel—heads of their families. During
the reign of David, the descendants of Tola
listed as fighting men in their genealogy
numbered 22,600.
3 The son of Uzzi:
Izrahiah.
The sons of Izrahiah:
Michael, Obadiah, Joel and Isshiah. All five
of them were chiefs. 4 According to their

6:67 [g] Jos 10:33
6:68 [h] 1Ki 4:12; [i] Jos 10:10
6:69 [j] Jos 10:12; [k] Jos 19:45
6:71 [l] 1Ch 23:7; [m] Jos 20:8
6:72 [n] Jos 19:12
6:74 [o] Jos 19:28
6:75 [p] Jos 19:34; [q] Nu 13:21
6:76 [r] Jos 19:28; [s] Nu 32:37
6:78 [t] Jos 20:8
6:79 [u] Dt 2:26
6:80 [v] Jos 20:8; [w] Ge 32:2
6:81 [x] Nu 21:32; [y] 2Ch 11:14
7:1 [z] Ge 30:18; Nu 26:23; [a] Ge 46:13

[a] 67 See Joshua 21:21; Hebrew *given the cities of refuge: Shechem, Gezer.* [b] 77 See Septuagint and Joshua 21:34; Hebrew does not have *Jokneam, Kartah.*

With Pasturelands

1CH 6:64-80

When God calls the tribe of Levi to meet his people's religious and spiritual needs, he asks the other tribes to provide for the Levites' physical needs (Jos 21:1–3). The Levites own no land, so they are given cities (and the adjoining pasturelands for their crops and herds) within the other tribes' districts. The people's tithes and offerings help support the Levites.

This living arrangement fulfills Jacob's prediction that the Levites will be scattered in Israel (Ge 49:5,7), and it guarantees that every tribe will be taught God's Word. The Levites perform the duties of the tabernacle (and later, the temple), but their specific responsibilities change over the years. They carry the ark of the covenant, assist the priests, manage the temple's inventory and finances, serve as music leaders and teach God's law to the people. Like today's pastors and church workers, the Levites depended on the love, generosity and prayers of God's people.

No Sons

1CH 7:15

"Zelophehad . . . had only daughters." This unimpressive phrase in Manasseh's family tree represents a story with an encouraging word for contemporary women. Zelophehad wanders between Egypt and the promised land with Moses and more than a million other Israelites. He has five daughters and no sons. He dies during the desert journey and leaves the five sisters without a father to protect and provide for them. They want to preserve their father's name and guarantee their future.

Consequently, these five women go before Moses and the community council to request that their father's inheritance rights be transferred to them. Moses takes their case before the Lord. The Lord says, "They are right." Previously only sons could inherit family property. Because of these women, God issues an exception to the rule (Nu 27:7-11). These wise and courageous sisters understand God's law and Hebrew tradition. Yet they take a risk and stand up for what they believe is right. Their brave action changes their world and the world of generations of women to come (see the note on Jos 17:3-4, page 358).

family genealogy, they had 36,000 men
ready for battle, for they had many wives
and children.
5 The relatives who were fighting men belonging to all the clans of Issachar, as listed in
their genealogy, were 87,000 in all.

Benjamin

6 Three sons of Benjamin:[b] 7:6 [b]Ge 46:21; Nu 26:38; 1Ch 8:1-40
Bela, Beker and Jediael.
7 The sons of Bela:
Ezbon, Uzzi, Uzziel, Jerimoth and Iri,
heads of families—five in all. Their
genealogical record listed 22,034 fighting
men.
8 The sons of Beker:
Zemirah, Joash, Eliezer, Elioenai, Omri,
Jeremoth, Abijah, Anathoth and Alemeth.
All these were the sons of Beker. 9 Their
genealogical record listed the heads of families and 20,200 fighting men.
10 The son of Jediael:
Bilhan.
The sons of Bilhan:
Jeush, Benjamin, Ehud, Kenaanah, Zethan,
Tarshish and Ahishahar. 11 All these sons of
Jediael were heads of families. There were
17,200 fighting men ready to go out to war.
12 The Shuppites and Huppites were the descendants of Ir, and the Hushites the descendants of Aher.

Naphtali

13 The sons of Naphtali:[c] 7:13 [c]Ge 30:8; 46:24
Jahziel, Guni, Jezer and Shillem[a]—the
descendants of Bilhah.

Manasseh

14 The descendants of Manasseh:[d] 7:14 [d]Ge 41:51; Jos 17:1; 1Ch 5:23 [e]Nu 26:30
Asriel was his descendant through his Ara-
mean concubine. She gave birth to Makir the
father of Gilead.[e] 15 Makir took a wife from
among the Huppites and Shuppites. His sister's name was Maacah.
Another descendant was named Zelophe-
had,[f] who had only daughters. 7:15 [f]Nu 26:33; 36:1-12
16 Makir's wife Maacah gave birth to a son
and named him Peresh. His brother was
named Sheresh, and his sons were Ulam and
Rakem.
17 The son of Ulam:
Bedan.
These were the sons of Gilead[g] son of Makir, 7:17 [g]Nu 26:30; 1Sa 12:11
the son of Manasseh. 18 His sister Ham-
moleketh gave birth to Ishhod, Abiezer[h]
and Mahlah. 7:18 [h]Jos 17:2
19 The sons of Shemida were:
Ahian, Shechem, Likhi and Aniam.

[a] *13* Some Hebrew and Septuagint manuscripts (see also Gen. 46:24 and Num. 26:49); most Hebrew manuscripts *Shallum*

Ephraim

7:20 20 The descendants of Ephraim:[i]
[i]Ge 41:52; Shuthelah, Bered his son,
Nu 1:33; Tahath his son, Eleadah his son,
26:35 Tahath his son, 21 Zabad his son
and Shuthelah his son.
Ezer and Elead were killed by the native-
born men of Gath, when they went down to
seize their livestock. 22 Their father Ephraim
mourned for them many days, and his relatives came to comfort him. 23 Then he lay
with his wife again, and she became pregnant and gave birth to a son. He named him
Beriah,[a] because there had been misfortune
7:24 in his family. 24 His daughter was Sheerah,
[j]Jos 10:10; who built Lower and Upper Beth Horon[j] as
16:3,5 well as Uzzen Sheerah.
25 Rephah was his son, Resheph his son,[b]
Telah his son, Tahan his son,
26 Ladan his son, Ammihud his son,
Elishama his son, 27 Nun his son
and Joshua his son.
28 Their lands and settlements included Bethel
7:28 and its surrounding villages, Naaran to the east,
[k]Jos 10:33; Gezer[k] and its villages to the west, and Shechem
16:7 and its villages all the way to Ayyah and its vil-
7:29 lages. 29 Along the borders of Manasseh were Beth
[l]Jos 17:11 Shan,[l] Taanach, Megiddo and Dor,[m] together with
[m]Jos 11:2 their villages. The descendants of Joseph son of
Israel lived in these towns.

Asher

7:30
[n]Ge 46:17; 30 The sons of Asher:[n]
Nu 1:40; Imnah, Ishvah, Ishvi and Beriah. Their sis-
26:44 ter was Serah.
31 The sons of Beriah:
Heber and Malkiel, who was the father of
Birzaith.
32 Heber was the father of Japhlet, Shomer and
Hotham and of their sister Shua.
33 The sons of Japhlet:
Pasach, Bimhal and Ashvath.
These were Japhlet's sons.
34 The sons of Shomer:
Ahi, Rohgah,[c] Hubbah and Aram.
35 The sons of his brother Helem:
Zophah, Imna, Shelesh and Amal.
36 The sons of Zophah:
Suah, Harnepher, Shual, Beri, Imrah,
37 Bezer, Hod, Shamma, Shilshah, Ithran[d]
and Beera.
38 The sons of Jether:
Jephunneh, Pispah and Ara.
39 The sons of Ulla:
Arah, Hanniel and Rizia.
40 All these were descendants of Asher—heads

[a] 23 *Beriah* sounds like the Hebrew for *misfortune.*
[b] 25 Some Septuagint manuscripts; Hebrew does not have *his son.* [c] 34 Or *of his brother Shomer: Rohgah* [d] 37 Possibly a variant of *Jether*

She Builds Towns

1CH 7:24

Sheerah. *Every woman should remember her name, but few probably do. Sheerah is listed in this genealogy with this interesting historical note: She builds cities.*

A lone woman in an extended list of men, Ms. Sheerah is noted not for the usual activities of a woman, but for an activity that is usually the domain of men. She must have been a strong and able worker and leader, for she built not just one or two cities, but three. Uzzen is mentioned only here, but Upper and Lower Beth Horon are referred to several times in the Old Testament (Jos 10:10–11; 16:3,5; 18:13–14; 1Sa 13:18; 2Ch 8:5). These two cities form an important pass between Jerusalem and Joppa (near the modern city of Tel Aviv; see Map 3: Exodus and Conquest of Canaan at the back of this Bible).

Sheerah does not allow the traditional thinking that only men can successfully organize and manage large projects to keep her from fulfilling her potential and making her mark on the world. Her example is an inspiration to women of all ages to use their God-given abilities to fulfill not just cultural expectations but God's divine purposes.

Divorce

1CH 8:8

Old Testament law allowed a man to divorce his wife if she became "displeasing to him because he found something indecent about her" (Dt 24:1). It seems too easy, doesn't it? But this law of Moses was enacted to *protect* women, since husbands were in the practice of abandoning their wives without explanation. A husband had time to think about his decision as he prepared a "certificate of divorce" and gave it to his wife.

Jesus says divorce is allowed because those involved have hard hearts (Mt 19:8). The rabbis tried to drag Jesus into their continuing debate about the definition of "something indecent," but he refuses to join the argument (Mt 19:3–6). He quotes God's original intent for marriage: A man and woman are to leave their parents and come together as one (Ge 2:24). The fall of Adam and Eve has blighted the beauty of the relationship, but God's exquisite design for marriage can still be fulfilled, and couples can still enjoy a mutually joyful and permanent relationship.

of families, choice men, brave warriors and outstanding leaders. The number of men ready for battle, as listed in their genealogy, was 26,000.

The Genealogy of Saul the Benjamite

8 Benjamin[o] was the father of Bela his firstborn,
Ashbel the second son, Aharah the third,
2 Nohah the fourth and Rapha the fifth.
3 The sons of Bela were:
Addar,[p] Gera, Abihud,[a] 4 Abishua, Naaman,
Ahoah,[q] 5 Gera, Shephuphan and Huram.
6 These were the descendants of Ehud,[r] who
were heads of families of those living in
Geba and were deported to Manahath:
7 Naaman, Ahijah, and Gera, who deported
them and who was the father of Uzza and
Ahihud.
8 Sons were born to Shaharaim in Moab after he
had divorced his wives Hushim and Baara.
9 By his wife Hodesh he had Jobab, Zibia,
Mesha, Malcam, 10 Jeuz, Sakia and Mirmah.
These were his sons, heads of families. 11 By
Hushim he had Abitub and Elpaal.
12 The sons of Elpaal:
Eber, Misham, Shemed (who built Ono[s]
and Lod with its surrounding villages),
13 and Beriah and Shema, who were heads
of families of those living in Aijalon[t] and
who drove out the inhabitants of Gath.[u]
14 Ahio, Shashak, Jeremoth, 15 Zebadiah, Arad,
Eder, 16 Michael, Ishpah and Joha were the
sons of Beriah.
17 Zebadiah, Meshullam, Hizki, Heber, 18 Ishmerai, Izliah and Jobab were the sons of
Elpaal.
19 Jakim, Zicri, Zabdi, 20 Elienai, Zillethai, Eliel,
21 Adaiah, Beraiah and Shimrath were the
sons of Shimei.
22 Ishpan, Eber, Eliel, 23 Abdon, Zicri, Hanan,
24 Hananiah, Elam, Anthothijah, 25 Iphdeiah
and Penuel were the sons of Shashak.
26 Shamsherai, Shehariah, Athaliah, 27 Jaareshiah, Elijah and Zicri were the sons of
Jeroham.
28 All these were heads of families, chiefs as listed in their genealogy, and they lived in Jerusalem.
29 Jeiel[b] the father[c] of Gibeon lived in Gibeon.[v]
His wife's name was Maacah, 30 and his
firstborn son was Abdon, followed by Zur,
Kish, Baal, Ner,[d] Nadab, 31 Gedor, Ahio,
Zeker 32 and Mikloth, who was the father of
Shimeah. They too lived near their relatives in Jerusalem.
33 Ner[w] was the father of Kish,[x] Kish the father

8:1 [o]Ge 46:21; 1Ch 7:6
8:3 [p]Ge 46:21
8:4 [q]2Sa 23:9
8:6 [r]Jdg 3:12-30; 1Ch 2:52
8:12 [s]Ezr 2:33; Ne 6:2; 7:37; 11:35
8:13 [t]Jos 10:12 [u]Jos 11:22
8:29 [v]Jos 9:3
8:33 [w]1Sa 28:19 [x]1Sa 9:1

[a] 3 Or *Gera the father of Ehud* [b] 29 Some Septuagint manuscripts (see also 1 Chron. 9:35); Hebrew does not have *Jeiel.* [c] 29 *Father* may mean *civic leader* or *military leader.* [d] 30 Some Septuagint manuscripts (see also 1 Chron. 9:36); Hebrew does not have *Ner.*

8:33 [y]1Sa 14:49 [z]2Sa 2:8 of Saul[y], and Saul the father of Jonathan,
Malki-Shua, Abinadab and Esh-Baal.[a][z]
34 The son of Jonathan:[a]
8:34 [a]2Sa 9:12 [b]2Sa 4:4 Merib-Baal,[b][b] who was the father of Micah.
35 The sons of Micah:
Pithon, Melech, Tarea and Ahaz.
36 Ahaz was the father of Jehoaddah, Jehoaddah was the father of Alemeth, Azmaveth and Zimri, and Zimri was the father of Moza.
37 Moza was the father of Binea; Raphah was his son, Eleasah his son and Azel his son.
38 Azel had six sons, and these were their names:
Azrikam, Bokeru, Ishmael, Sheariah, Obadiah and Hanan. All these were the sons of Azel.
39 The sons of his brother Eshek:
Ulam his firstborn, Jeush the second son and Eliphelet the third.
40 The sons of Ulam were brave warriors who could handle the bow. They had many sons and grandsons—150 in all.
8:40 [c]Nu 26:38 All these were the descendants of Benjamin.[c]

9 All Israel was listed in the genealogies recorded in the book of the kings of Israel.

The People in Jerusalem

The people of Judah were taken captive to Babylon because of their unfaithfulness.[d]
9:1 [d]1Ch 5:25
2 Now the first to resettle on their own property in their own towns[e] were some Israelites, priests, Levites and temple servants.[f]
9:2 [e]Jos 9:27; Ezr 2:70 [f]Ezr 2:43,58; 8:20; Ne 7:60

3 Those from Judah, from Benjamin, and from Ephraim and Manasseh who lived in Jerusalem were:
4 Uthai son of Ammihud, the son of Omri, the son of Imri, the son of Bani, a descendant of Perez son of Judah.[g]
9:4 [g]Ge 38:29; 46:12
5 Of the Shilonites:
Asaiah the firstborn and his sons.
6 Of the Zerahites:
Jeuel.
The people from Judah numbered 690.
7 Of the Benjamites:
Sallu son of Meshullam, the son of Hodaviah, the son of Hassenuah;
8 Ibneiah son of Jeroham; Elah son of Uzzi, the son of Micri; and Meshullam son of Shephatiah, the son of Reuel, the son of Ibnijah.
9 The people from Benjamin, as listed in their genealogy, numbered 956. All these men were heads of their families.
10 Of the priests:
Jedaiah; Jehoiarib; Jakin;
11 Azariah son of Hilkiah, the son of Meshullam, the son of Zadok, the son of Meraioth,

[a] 33 Also known as *Ish-Bosheth* [b] 34 Also known as *Mephibosheth*

***S**leep at last has fled*
these eyes,
Nor do I regret his flight,
More alert my spirits rise,
And my heart is free and light.

Nature silent all around,
Not a single witness near;
God as soon as sought is found;
And the flame of love burns clear.

Interruption, all day long,
Checks the current of my joys;
Creatures press me with a throng,
And perplex me with their noise.

Undisturbed I muse all night,
On the first Eternal Fair;
Nothing there obstructs delight,
Love is renovated there.

Life, with its perpetual stir,
Proves a foe to love and me;
Fresh entanglements occur—
Comes the night, and sets me free.

Hush the world, that I may wake
To the taste of pure delights;
Oh the pleasures I partake—
God, the partner of my
nights!

—Madame Guyon (1647-1717)

The Gatekeepers

1CH 9:22-27

According to 2 Kings 12:9, gatekeepers are "priests who [guard] the entrance" of the temple. They come from the tribe of Levi and have distinct duties, which include collecting the worshipers' monetary offerings and guarding the storerooms and "treasuries" (1Ch 9:26). Their primary job is to protect around the clock the doorways to the house of the Lord, guarding the temple from anyone or anything that might damage or defile it.

There are some who may think that the position of gatekeeper is humble and insignificant, perhaps based on the words of Psalm 84:10. However, there is actually no low or menial task when work is being done for God. Whether doorkeeper or high priest, janitor or pastor, church school teacher or usher—no task is unimportant when it is done for the Lord. Go to Psalm 84 and write in the margin what task others might consider insignificant that you would be willing to do for God's glory.

the son of Ahitub, the official in charge of
the house of God;
12 Adaiah son of Jeroham, the son of Pashhur,[h] the son of Malkijah; and Maasai son
of Adiel, the son of Jahzerah, the son of
Meshullam, the son of Meshillemith, the
son of Immer.
13 The priests, who were heads of families,
numbered 1,760. They were able men,
responsible for ministering in the house of
God.
14 Of the Levites:
Shemaiah son of Hasshub, the son of Azrikam, the son of Hashabiah, a Merarite;
15 Bakbakkar, Heresh, Galal and Mattaniah[i]
son of Mica, the son of Zicri, the son of
Asaph; 16 Obadiah son of Shemaiah, the son
of Galal, the son of Jeduthun; and Berekiah
son of Asa, the son of Elkanah, who lived
in the villages of the Netophathites.[j]
17 The gatekeepers:[k]
Shallum, Akkub, Talmon, Ahiman and
their brothers, Shallum their chief 18 being
stationed at the King's Gate[l] on the east, up
to the present time. These were the gatekeepers belonging to the camp of the
Levites. 19 Shallum[m] son of Kore, the son of
Ebiasaph, the son of Korah, and his fellow
gatekeepers from his family (the Korahites)
were responsible for guarding the thresholds of the Tent[a] just as their fathers had
been responsible for guarding the entrance
to the dwelling of the LORD. 20 In earlier
times Phinehas[n] son of Eleazar was in
charge of the gatekeepers, and the LORD
was with him. 21 Zechariah[o] son of Meshelemiah was the gatekeeper at the entrance
to the Tent of Meeting.
22 Altogether, those chosen to be gatekeepers[p] at
the thresholds numbered 212. They were registered by genealogy in their villages. The gatekeepers had been assigned to their positions of
trust by David and Samuel the seer.[q] 23 They and
their descendants were in charge of guarding the
gates of the house of the LORD—the house called
the Tent. 24 The gatekeepers were on the four sides:
east, west, north and south. 25 Their brothers in
their villages had to come from time to time and
share their duties for seven-day[r] periods. 26 But the
four principal gatekeepers, who were Levites,
were entrusted with the responsibility for the
rooms and treasuries[s] in the house of God. 27 They
would spend the night stationed around the house
of God,[t] because they had to guard it; and they
had charge of the key[u] for opening it each
morning.
28 Some of them were in charge of the articles
used in the temple service; they counted them
when they were brought in and when they were

9:12 [h]Ezr 2:38; 10:22; Ne 10:3; Jer 21:1; 38:1
9:15 [i]2Ch 20:14; Ne 11:22
9:16 [j]Ne 12:28
9:17 [k]ver 22; 1Ch 26:1; 2Ch 8:14; 31:14; Ezr 2:42; Ne 7:45
9:18 [l]1Ch 26:14; Eze 43:1; 46:1
9:19 [m]Jer 35:4
9:20 [n]Nu 25:7-13
9:21 [o]1Ch 26:2,14
9:22 [p]ver 17; 1Ch 26:1-2; 2Ch 31:15, 18 [q]1Sa 9:9
9:25 [r]2Ki 11:5; 2Ch 23:8
9:26 [s]1Ch 26:22
9:27 [t]Nu 3:38; 1Ch 23:30-32 [u]Isa 22:22

[a] *19* That is, the temple; also in verses 21 and 23

taken out. [29]Others were assigned to take care of
9:29 the furnishings and all the other articles of the
[v]Nu 3:28; sanctuary,[v] as well as the flour and wine, and the
1Ch 23:29 oil, incense and spices. [30]But some[w] of the priests
9:30 took care of mixing the spices. [31]A Levite named
[w]Ex 30:23-25 Mattithiah, the firstborn son of Shallum the
Korahite, was entrusted with the responsibility for
baking the offering bread. [32]Some of their Kohath-
9:32 ite brothers were in charge of preparing for every
[x]Lev 24:5-8; Sabbath the bread set out on the table.[x]
1Ch 23:29; [33]Those who were musicians,[y] heads of Levite
2Ch 13:11 families, stayed in the rooms of the temple and
9:33 were exempt from other duties because they were
[y]1Ch 6:31; responsible for the work day and night.[z]
25:1-31 [34]All these were heads of Levite families, chiefs
[z]Ps 134:1 as listed in their genealogy, and they lived in
Jerusalem.

The Genealogy of Saul

9:35 [35]Jeiel[a] the father[a] of Gibeon lived in Gibeon.
[a]1Ch 8:29 His wife's name was Maacah, [36]and his
firstborn son was Abdon, followed by Zur,
Kish, Baal, Ner, Nadab, [37]Gedor, Ahio,
Zechariah and Mikloth. [38]Mikloth was the
father of Shimeam. They too lived near
their relatives in Jerusalem.
9:39 [39]Ner[b] was the father of Kish,[c] Kish the father
[b]1Ch 8:33 of Saul, and Saul the father of Jonathan,[d]
[c]1Sa 9:1 Malki-Shua, Abinadab and Esh-Baal.[be]
[d]1Sa 13:22 [40]The son of Jonathan:
[e]2Sa 2:8 Merib-Baal,[cf] who was the father of Micah.
9:40 [41]The sons of Micah:
[f]2Sa 4:4 Pithon, Melech, Tahrea and Ahaz.[d]
[42]Ahaz was the father of Jadah, Jadah[e] was
the father of Alemeth, Azmaveth and Zimri, and Zimri was the father of Moza.
[43]Moza was the father of Binea; Rephaiah
was his son, Eleasah his son and Azel his
son.
[44]Azel had six sons, and these were their
names:
Azrikam, Bokeru, Ishmael, Sheariah, Obadiah and Hanan. These were the sons of
Azel.

Saul Takes His Life

10 Now the Philistines fought against Israel; the
Israelites fled before them, and many fell
slain on Mount Gilboa. [2]The Philistines pressed
hard after Saul and his sons, and they killed his
sons Jonathan, Abinadab and Malki-Shua. [3]The
fighting grew fierce around Saul, and when the
archers overtook him, they wounded him.
[4]Saul said to his armor-bearer, "Draw your

[a] *35* *Father* may mean *civic leader* or *military leader.*
[b] *39* Also known as *Ish-Bosheth* [c] *40* Also known as *Mephibosheth* [d] *41* Vulgate and Syriac (see also Septuagint and 1 Chron. 8:35); Hebrew does not have *and Ahaz.*
[e] *42* Some Hebrew manuscripts and Septuagint (see also 1 Chron. 8:36); most Hebrew manuscripts *Jarah, Jarah*

Kings and Chronicles

1CH 10

With chapter 10 the writer of 1 Chronicles *leaves the genealogies behind and turns to the history of the southern kingdom of Judah. In 1 and 2 Kings, we read about historical events that occur over a 400-year period, including the histories of both the northern and southern kingdoms. First Chronicles focuses on the southern kingdom, emphasizing especially the godly reign of David. With this goal in mind, the writer omits some less-than-inspirational circumstances (sins and failures) in David's life that the book of Kings includes.*

First Chronicles is written to *encourage the recently released Jewish captives, who question whether God's covenant is still relevant to them. Chronicles gives the exiles reason to believe God will be with them as he was with King David. The genealogies assure them that each individual has a part in their nation's godly heritage.*

Though they made sinful *choices in the past, God still offers them his love and forgiveness. This truth empowers them to move ahead, and that is precisely the writer's objective.*

Conquering Jerusalem

1CH 11:4–5

David, the newly crowned king of "all Israel" (1Ch 11:1), goes to the city of Jebus to stake his claim. The Jebusites who live there boast that David and his men will never overpower their fortress. Nevertheless, the Israelite soldiers conquer Jerusalem, which soon becomes known as the "City of David."

Centuries before, near this same location, Melchizedek, the king of "Salem," blessed Abraham (Ge 14:18–20). Abraham obeyed the command to offer Isaac as a sacrifice in this same area (Ge 22:2). Here, years after David's death, Solomon builds the temple atop the threshing floor David purchased as an altar (2Sa 24:18). Today the Muslim mosque, the Dome of the Rock, stands on this site.

God chooses Jerusalem as the place for his people to worship him (Dt 12:13–14; 1Ki 14:21), and David, "a man after [God's] own heart" (Ac 13:22), establishes the city as the royal and religious capital of Israel. In Psalm 122:6 David challenges God's people to "pray for the peace of Jerusalem." It is a challenge as appropriate for us today as it was for the Israelites in David's time.

sword and run me through, or these uncircumcised fellows will come and abuse me."
But his armor-bearer was terrified and would
not do it; so Saul took his own sword and fell on it.
5When the armor-bearer saw that Saul was dead,
he too fell on his sword and died. 6So Saul and his
three sons died, and all his house died together.
7When all the Israelites in the valley saw that
the army had fled and that Saul and his sons had
died, they abandoned their towns and fled. And
the Philistines came and occupied them.
8The next day, when the Philistines came to
strip the dead, they found Saul and his sons fall-
en on Mount Gilboa. 9They stripped him and
took his head and his armor, and sent messengers throughout the land of the Philistines to proclaim the news among their idols and their people. 10They put his armor in the temple of their
gods and hung up his head in the temple of
Dagon.[g]
11When all the inhabitants of Jabesh Gilead[h]
heard of everything the Philistines had done to
Saul, 12all their valiant men went and took the
bodies of Saul and his sons and brought them to
Jabesh. Then they buried their bones under the
great tree in Jabesh, and they fasted seven days.
13Saul died[i] because he was unfaithful[j] to the
LORD; he did not keep[k] the word of the LORD and
even consulted a medium[l] for guidance, 14and did
not inquire of the LORD. So the LORD put him to
death and turned[m] the kingdom[n] over to David
son of Jesse.

David Becomes King Over Israel

11 All Israel[o] came together to David at
Hebron[p] and said, "We are your own flesh
and blood. 2In the past, even while Saul was king,
you were the one who led Israel on their military
campaigns.[q] And the LORD your God said to you,
'You will shepherd[r] my people Israel, and you will
become their ruler.[s]' "
3When all the elders of Israel had come to King
David at Hebron, he made a compact with them at
Hebron before the LORD, and they anointed[t] David
king over Israel, as the LORD had promised
through Samuel.

David Conquers Jerusalem

4David and all the Israelites marched to Jerusalem (that is, Jebus). The Jebusites[u] who lived
there 5said to David, "You will not get in here."
Nevertheless, David captured the fortress of Zion,
the City of David.
6David had said, "Whoever leads the attack on
the Jebusites will become commander-in-chief."
Joab[v] son of Zeruiah went up first, and so he
received the command.
7David then took up residence in the fortress,
and so it was called the City of David. 8He built
up the city around it, from the supporting

10:10 [g]Jdg 16:23
10:11 [h]Jdg 21:8
10:13 [i]2Sa 1:1 [j]1Sa 15:23; 1Ch 5:25 [k]1Sa 13:13 [l]Lev 19:31; 20:6; Dt 18:9-14; 1Sa 28:7
10:14 [m]1Ch 12:23 [n]1Sa 13:14; 15:28
11:1 [o]1Ch 9:1 [p]Ge 13:18; 23:19
11:2 [q]1Sa 18:5,16 [r]Ps 78:71; Mt 2:6 [s]1Ch 5:2
11:3 [t]1Sa 16:1-13
11:4 [u]Ge 10:16; 15:18-21; Jos 3:10; 15:8; Jdg 1:21; 19:10
11:6 [v]2Sa 2:13; 8:16

11:8 terraces[a][w] to the surrounding wall, while Joab
w2Sa 5:9; restored the rest of the city. 9And David became
2Ch 32:5 more and more powerful,[x] because the LORD Al-
11:9 x2Sa 3:1; mighty was with him.
Est 9:4

David's Mighty Men

11:10 10These were the chiefs of David's mighty
yver 1 zver 3; men—they, together with all Israel,[y] gave his
1Ch 12:23 kingship strong support to extend it over the
whole land, as the LORD had promised[z]— 11this is
11:11 the list of David's mighty men:[a]
a2Sa 17:10 Jashobeam,[b] a Hacmonite, was chief of the officers[c]; he raised his spear against three hundred
men, whom he killed in one encounter.
12Next to him was Eleazar son of Dodai the
Ahohite, one of the three mighty men. 13He was
with David at Pas Dammim when the Philistines
gathered there for battle. At a place where there
was a field full of barley, the troops fled from the
Philistines. 14But they took their stand in the middle of the field. They defended it and struck the
Philistines down, and the LORD brought about a
11:14 great victory.[b]
bEx 14:30; 15Three of the thirty chiefs came down to David
1Sa 11:13 to the rock at the cave of Adullam, while a band of
11:15 c1Ch 14:9; Philistines was encamped in the Valley[c] of Reph-
Isa 17:5 aim. 16At that time David was in the stronghold,[d]
11:16 and the Philistine garrison was at Bethlehem.
d2Sa 5:17 17David longed for water and said, "Oh, that someone would get me a drink of water from the well
near the gate of Bethlehem!" 18So the Three broke
through the Philistine lines, drew water from the
well near the gate of Bethlehem and carried it
11:18 back to David. But he refused to drink it; instead,
eDt 12:16 he poured[e] it out before the LORD. 19"God forbid
that I should do this!" he said. "Should I drink the
blood of these men who went at the risk of their
lives?" Because they risked their lives to bring it
back, David would not drink it.
11:20 Such were the exploits of the three mighty men.
f1Sa 26:6 20Abishai[f] the brother of Joab was chief of the
Three. He raised his spear against three hundred
men, whom he killed, and so he became as
famous as the Three. 21He was doubly honored
above the Three and became their commander,
even though he was not included among them.
22Benaiah son of Jehoiada was a valiant fighter
11:22 gJos 15:21 from Kabzeel,[g] who performed great exploits. He
h1Sa 17:36 struck down two of Moab's best men. He also
went down into a pit on a snowy day and killed a
lion.[h] 23And he struck down an Egyptian who was
seven and a half feet[d] tall. Although the Egyptian
11:23 had a spear like a weaver's rod[i] in his hand, Bena-
i1Sa 17:7 iah went against him with a club. He snatched the
spear from the Egyptian's hand and killed him
with his own spear. 24Such were the exploits of
Benaiah son of Jehoiada; he too was as famous as

[a] *8* Or *the Millo* [b] *11* Possibly a variant of *Jashob-Baal*
[c] *11* Or *Thirty*; some Septuagint manuscripts *Three* (see also 2 Samuel 23:8) [d] *23* Hebrew *five cubits* (about 2.3 meters)

David's Power

1CH 11:9

Why does David become a strong and powerful leader? Because the Lord Almighty is with him (1Ch 11:9). How is David *able to inspire loyalty and encourage faith?* Because the Lord is with him (1Ch 12:18). Why is David *able to guide the people in worshiping and serving the one true God?* Because the Lord God is with him (1Ch 17:18–19). David starts *out as a shepherd boy and ends up as king of all Israel,* because God Almighty is with him.

David knows God motivates, *energizes, enables and strengthens* him. The longing of David's soul is *to be in God's presence every day* of his life (Ps 27:4). David writes *and sings about God's righteousness, love, forgiveness and mercy.* He never forgets that it is only *through God's grace* that he enjoys success. What is true for David is, *we know,* true also for us. Only *through God's power* can we find true success in this life.

David's Mighty Men

1CH 11:10–47

The writer of 1 Chronicles wants to encourage the newly released Jewish people that God is able to reestablish Israel and make it a strong nation again. He accomplishes this purpose by listing all the "mighty men" who join David's great army.

Many of these men come from the tribes of Judah, which is not surprising since David comes from Judah. What is more unusual is that men from former King Saul's tribe join David's forces. But most remarkable is the number of foreigners who join David's ranks: men from the Ammonites, the Hittites, the Moabites and a variety of other nations.

The returning Jews gain confidence in God as they learn about King David's military support. And they begin to realize that they can receive God's blessing, as David had, if they will only follow David's example of godliness.

the three mighty men. 25He was held in greater
honor than any of the Thirty, but he was not
included among the Three. And David put him in
charge of his bodyguard.

26The mighty men were:
Asahel[j] the brother of Joab, **11:26** [j]2Sa 2:18
Elhanan son of Dodo from Bethlehem,
27Shammoth[k] the Harorite, **11:27** [k]1Ch 27:8
Helez the Pelonite,
28Ira son of Ikkesh from Tekoa,
Abiezer[l] from Anathoth, **11:28** [l]1Ch 27:12
29Sibbecai[m] the Hushathite,
Ilai the Ahohite, **11:29** [m]2Sa 21:18
30Maharai the Netophathite,
Heled son of Baanah the Netophathite,
31Ithai son of Ribai from Gibeah in Benjamin,
Benaiah[n] the Pirathonite,[o] **11:31** [n]1Ch 27:14 [o]Jdg 12:13
32Hurai from the ravines of Gaash,
Abiel the Arbathite,
33Azmaveth the Baharumite,
Eliahba the Shaalbonite,
34the sons of Hashem the Gizonite,
Jonathan son of Shagee the Hararite,
35Ahiam son of Sacar the Hararite,
Eliphal son of Ur,
36Hepher the Mekerathite,
Ahijah the Pelonite,
37Hezro the Carmelite,
Naarai son of Ezbai,
38Joel the brother of Nathan,
Mibhar son of Hagri,
39Zelek the Ammonite,
Naharai the Berothite, the armor-bearer of Joab son of Zeruiah,
40Ira the Ithrite,
Gareb the Ithrite,
41Uriah[p] the Hittite, **11:41** [p]2Sa 11:6
Zabad[q] son of Ahlai, [q]1Ch 2:36
42Adina son of Shiza the Reubenite, who was chief of the Reubenites, and the thirty with him,
43Hanan son of Maacah,
Joshaphat the Mithnite,
44Uzzia the Ashterathite,[r] **11:44** [r]Dt 1:4
Shama and Jeiel the sons of Hotham the Aroerite,
45Jediael son of Shimri,
his brother Joha the Tizite,
46Eliel the Mahavite,
Jeribai and Joshaviah the sons of Elnaam,
Ithmah the Moabite,
47Eliel, Obed and Jaasiel the Mezobaite.

Warriors Join David

12 These were the men who came to David at
Ziklag,[s] while he was banished from the **12:1** [s]Jos 15:31;
presence of Saul son of Kish (they were among 1Sa 27:2-6
the warriors who helped him in battle; 2they were
armed with bows and were able to shoot arrows

12:2 or to sling stones right-handed or left-handed;[t]
[t]Jdg 3:15; 20:16 they were kinsmen of Saul[u] from the tribe of
[u]2Sa 3:19 Benjamin):
3 Ahiezer their chief and Joash the sons of She-
maah the Gibeathite; Jeziel and Pelet the sons
of Azmaveth; Beracah, Jehu the Anathothite,
4 and Ishmaiah the Gibeonite, a mighty man
among the Thirty, who was a leader of the
Thirty; Jeremiah, Jahaziel, Johanan, Jozabad
12:4 the Gederathite,[v] 5 Eluzai, Jerimoth, Bealiah,
[v]Jos 15:36 Shemariah and Shephatiah the Haruphite;
6 Elkanah, Isshiah, Azarel, Joezer and
Jashobeam the Korahites; 7 and Joelah and
12:7 [w]Jos 15:58 Zebadiah the sons of Jeroham from Gedor.[w]
12:8 8 Some Gadites[x] defected to David at his strong-
[x]Ge 30:11 hold in the desert. They were brave warriors,
[y]2Sa 17:10 [z]2Sa 2:18 ready for battle and able to handle the shield and
spear. Their faces were the faces of lions,[y] and
they were as swift as gazelles[z] in the mountains.
9 Ezer was the chief,
Obadiah the second in command, Eliab the
third,
10 Mishmannah the fourth, Jeremiah the fifth,
11 Attai the sixth, Eliel the seventh,
12 Johanan the eighth, Elzabad the ninth,
13 Jeremiah the tenth and Macbannai the
eleventh.
14 These Gadites were army commanders; the
12:14 least was a match for a hundred,[a] and the greatest
[a]Lev 26:8 [b]Dt 32:30 for a thousand.[b] 15 It was they who crossed the
Jordan in the first month when it was overflowing
12:15 [c]Jos 3:15 all its banks,[c] and they put to flight everyone living in the valleys, to the east and to the west.
12:16 [d]2Sa 3:19 16 Other Benjamites[d] and some men from Judah
also came to David in his stronghold. 17 David
went out to meet them and said to them, "If you
have come to me in peace, to help me, I am ready
to have you unite with me. But if you have come
to betray me to my enemies when my hands are
free from violence, may the God of our fathers see
it and judge you."
12:18 18 Then the Spirit[e] came upon Amasai,[f] chief of
[e]Jdg 3:10; 6:34; 1Ch 28:12; 2Ch 15:1; 20:14; 24:20 the Thirty, and he said:

"We are yours, O David!
[f]2Sa 17:25 We are with you, O son of Jesse!
[g]1Sa 25:5-6 Success,[g] success to you,
and success to those who help you,
for your God will help you."

So David received them and made them leaders
of his raiding bands.
19 Some of the men of Manasseh defected to
David when he went with the Philistines to fight
against Saul. (He and his men did not help the Philistines because, after consultation, their rulers sent
him away. They said, "It will cost us our heads if he
12:19 [h]1Sa 29:2-11 deserts to his master Saul.")[h] 20 When David went
to Ziklag,[i] these were the men of Manasseh who
12:20 [i]1Sa 27:6 defected to him: Adnah, Jozabad, Jediael, Michael, Jozabad, Elihu and Zillethai, leaders of units of

Common Sense and Caution

1CH 12:16–18

Even before David becomes king of reunited Israel, skilled military men from many different backgrounds join his ranks. Some defect from other armies. On one occasion, David sees a group of warriors approaching him. He does not know their purpose. Instead of attacking the men without cause, he first asks them for an explanation. Do they come in peace or to betray him?

God's Spirit influences the men, and they bless David with an incredible affirmation: "We are yours, David. May peace come to you and all those who join you, for we know that God is the power behind your success." Consequently, David acquires additional experienced soldiers for his army.

David does not jump to a premature conclusion when he faces an unfamiliar and potentially explosive situation. He trusts God for protection, exercises his common sense and asks questions. His three-step approach has much to recommend to us as we also face potentially explosive situations.

An Army of God

1CH 12:22–23

Military men from all around join together at Hebron to support David as the new king. These soldiers volunteer to serve, coming "armed for battle" (1Ch 12:23). Scripture refers to David's troops as a "great army, like the army of God" (1Ch 12:22). Why? Perhaps the answer is found in verse 23: "Men . . . came to David at Hebron to turn Saul's kingdom over to him as the Lord had said" (emphasis added). The Lord God is the one who chooses David the shepherd boy to become David the king. God himself calls together this massive gathering of skilled soldiers, an "army of God."

King David and his mighty army of loyal, joyous and "armed for battle" volunteers remind us of Jesus the coming King and his immense army of devoted and "ready to serve" followers. Believers from every tribe and nation join together to make up the vast and devoted army of God (Rev 5:9).

a thousand in Manasseh. 21 They helped David
against raiding bands, for all of them were brave
warriors, and they were commanders in his army.
22 Day after day men came to help David, until he
had a great army, like the army of God.[a]

Others Join David at Hebron

23 These are the numbers of the men armed for
battle who came to David at Hebron[j] to turn[k]
Saul's kingdom over to him, as the LORD had said:[l]
24 men of Judah, carrying shield and spear—
6,800 armed for battle;
25 men of Simeon, warriors ready for battle—
7,100;
26 men of Levi—4,600, 27 including Jehoiada,
leader of the family of Aaron, with 3,700
men, 28 and Zadok,[m] a brave young warrior,
with 22 officers from his family;
29 men of Benjamin,[n] Saul's kinsmen—3,000,
most[o] of whom had remained loyal to
Saul's house until then;
30 men of Ephraim, brave warriors, famous in
their own clans—20,800;
31 men of half the tribe of Manasseh, designated
by name to come and make David
king—18,000;
32 men of Issachar, who understood the times
and knew what Israel should do[p]—200
chiefs, with all their relatives under their
command;
33 men of Zebulun, experienced soldiers prepared
for battle with every type of weapon,
to help David with undivided loyalty—
50,000;
34 men of Naphtali—1,000 officers, together
with 37,000 men carrying shields and
spears;
35 men of Dan, ready for battle—28,600;
36 men of Asher, experienced soldiers prepared
for battle—40,000;
37 and from east of the Jordan, men of Reuben,
Gad and the half-tribe of Manasseh, armed
with every type of weapon—120,000.
38 All these were fighting men who volunteered
to serve in the ranks. They came to Hebron fully
determined to make David king over all Israel.[q]
All the rest of the Israelites were also of one mind
to make David king. 39 The men spent three days
there with David, eating and drinking,[r] for their
families had supplied provisions for them. 40 Also,
their neighbors from as far away as Issachar, Zebulun
and Naphtali came bringing food on donkeys,
camels, mules and oxen. There were plentiful
supplies[s] of flour, fig cakes, raisin[t] cakes, wine,
oil, cattle and sheep, for there was joy[u] in Israel.

Bringing Back the Ark

13 David conferred with each of his officers,
the commanders of thousands and com-

12:23 [j]2Sa 2:3-4 [k]1Ch 10:14 [l]1Sa 16:1; 1Ch 11:10
12:28 [m]2Sa 8:17; 1Ch 6:8; 15:11; 16:39; 27:17
12:29 [n]2Sa 3:19 [o]2Sa 2:8-9
12:32 [p]Est 1:13
12:38 [q]2Sa 5:1-3; 1Ch 9:1
12:39 [r]2Sa 3:20; Isa 25:6-8
12:40 [s]2Sa 16:1; 17:29 [t]1Sa 25:18 [u]1Ch 29:22

[a] 22 Or *a great and mighty army*

manders of hundreds. 2He then said to the whole
assembly of Israel, "If it seems good to you and if
it is the will of the LORD our God, let us send word
far and wide to the rest of our brothers throughout
the territories of Israel, and also to the priests and
Levites who are with them in their towns and pas-
13:3 turelands, to come and join us. 3Let us bring the
[v]1Sa 7:1-2 ark of our God back to us,[v] for we did not inquire[w]
[w]2Ch 1:5 of[a] it[b] during the reign of Saul." 4The whole
assembly agreed to do this, because it seemed
right to all the people.
13:5 [x]1Ch 11:1; 5So David assembled all the Israelites,[x] from the
15:3 [y]Jos 13:3 Shihor River[y] in Egypt to Lebo[c] Hamath,[z] to bring
[z]Nu 13:21 the ark of God from Kiriath Jearim.[a] 6David and all
[a]1Sa 6:21; the Israelites with him went to Baalah[b] of Judah
7:2 (Kiriath Jearim) to bring up from there the ark of
13:6 God the LORD, who is enthroned between the cher-
[b]Jos 15:9; 2Sa 6:2 ubim[c]—the ark that is called by the Name.
[c]Ex 25:22; 7They moved the ark of God from Abinadab's[d]
2Ki 19:15 house on a new cart, with Uzzah and Ahio guiding
13:7 it. 8David and all the Israelites were celebrating with
[d]Nu 4:15; all their might before God, with songs and with
1Sa 7:1 harps, lyres, tambourines, cymbals and trumpets.[e]
13:8 9When they came to the threshing floor of
[e]2Sa 6:5; Kidon, Uzzah reached out his hand to steady the
1Ch 15:16, 19,24; ark, because the oxen stumbled. 10The LORD's
2Ch 5:12; anger[f] burned against Uzzah, and he struck him
Ps 92:3 down[g] because he had put his hand on the ark.
13:10 So he died there before God.
[f]1Ch 15:13, 15 11Then David was angry because the LORD's
[g]Lev 10:2 wrath had broken out against Uzzah, and to this
day that place is called Perez Uzzah.[d][h]
13:11 [h]1Ch 15:13; 12David was afraid of God that day and asked,
Ps 7:11 "How can I ever bring the ark of God to me?" 13He
did not take the ark to be with him in the City of
David. Instead, he took it aside to the house of
13:13 [i]1Ch 15:18, Obed-Edom[i] the Gittite. 14The ark of God re-
24; 16:38; mained with the family of Obed-Edom in his
26:4-5,15 house for three months, and the LORD blessed his
13:14 [j]2Sa 6:11; household[j] and everything he had.
1Ch 26:4-5

David's House and Family

14:1 [k]2Ch 2:3; **14** Now Hiram king of Tyre sent messengers to
Ezr 3:7 David, along with cedar logs,[k] stonemasons
and carpenters to build a palace for him. 2And
David knew that the LORD had established him as
king over Israel and that his kingdom had been
14:2 [l]Nu 24:7; highly exalted[l] for the sake of his people Israel.
Dt 26:19 3In Jerusalem David took more wives and
14:3 [m]1Ch 3:1 became the father of more sons[m] and daughters.
4These are the names of the children born to him
14:4 [n]1Ch 3:9 there:[n] Shammua, Shobab, Nathan, Solomon,
5Ibhar, Elishua, Elpelet, 6Nogah, Nepheg, Japhia,
7Elishama, Beeliada[e] and Eliphelet.

David Defeats the Philistines

8When the Philistines heard that David had been

[a] 3 Or *we neglected* [b] 3 Or *him* [c] 5 Or *to the entrance to*
[d] 11 *Perez Uzzah* means *outbreak against Uzzah.*
[e] 7 A variant of *Eliada*

Many Wives

1CH 14:3

God's original plan for marriage is one spouse for a lifetime (Ge 2:24; Mt 19:6), yet David, "a man after [God's] own heart" (Ac 13:22), had many wives. Why did David follow God's directives for most decisions but ignore God's design for a king's marriage (Dt 17:17)? How can Scripture teach that God values monogamy over polygamy and then list David's many children by numerous different women as a blessing (1Ch 3:1–9)?

Old Testament society put great value on having many children. Perhaps this is why God allowed David's behavior. We cannot be certain. What we do know from Old Testament stories of polygamy (or extramarital) arrangements is that they invariably produced heartache and persistent problems. This was true for Abraham, Jacob, David and his son Solomon. Their mistakes are good examples for us of what not *to do (see the note on 1Sa 25:39,43–44, page 462).*

anointed king over all Israel,[o] they went up in full
force to search for him, but David heard about it
and went out to meet them. 9Now the Philistines
had come and raided the Valley[p] of Rephaim; 10so
David inquired of God: "Shall I go and attack the
Philistines? Will you hand them over to me?"
The LORD answered him, "Go, I will hand them
over to you."
11So David and his men went up to Baal Perazim,[q] and there he defeated them. He said, "As
waters break out, God has broken out against my
enemies by my hand." So that place was called
Baal Perazim.[a] 12The Philistines had abandoned
their gods there, and David gave orders to burn[r]
them in the fire.[s]
13Once more the Philistines raided the valley;[t]
14so David inquired of God again, and God
answered him, "Do not go straight up, but circle
around them and attack them in front of the balsam trees. 15As soon as you hear the sound of
marching in the tops of the balsam trees, move
out to battle, because that will mean God has gone
out in front of you to strike the Philistine army."
16So David did as God commanded him, and they
struck down the Philistine army, all the way from
Gibeon[u] to Gezer.[v]
17So David's fame[w] spread throughout every
land, and the LORD made all the nations fear[x] him.

The Ark Brought to Jerusalem

15 After David had constructed buildings for
himself in the City of David, he prepared[y] a
place for the ark of God and pitched[z] a tent for it.
2Then David said, "No one but the Levites[a] may
carry[b] the ark of God, because the LORD chose
them to carry the ark of the LORD and to minister[c]
before him forever."
3David assembled all Israel[d] in Jerusalem to
bring up the ark of the LORD to the place he had
prepared for it. 4He called together the descendants of Aaron and the Levites:
5From the descendants of Kohath,
Uriel the leader and 120 relatives;
6from the descendants of Merari,
Asaiah the leader and 220 relatives;
7from the descendants of Gershon,[b]
Joel the leader and 130 relatives;
8from the descendants of Elizaphan,[e]
Shemaiah the leader and 200 relatives;
9from the descendants of Hebron,[f]
Eliel the leader and 80 relatives;
10from the descendants of Uzziel,
Amminadab the leader and 112 relatives.
11Then David summoned Zadok[g] and Abiathar[h]
the priests, and Uriel, Asaiah, Joel, Shemaiah, Eliel and Amminadab the Levites. 12He said to them,
"You are the heads of the Levitical families; you
and your fellow Levites are to consecrate[i] your-

14:8 [o]1Ch 11:1
14:9 [p]ver 13; Jos 15:8; 1Ch 11:15
14:11 [q]Isa 28:21
14:12 [r]Ex 32:20 [s]Jos 7:15
14:13 [t]ver 9
14:16 [u]Jos 9:3 [v]Jos 10:33
14:17 [w]Jos 6:27; 2Ch 26:8 [x]Ex 15:14-16; Dt 2:25
15:1 [y]Ps 132:1-18 [z]1Ch 16:1; 17:1
15:2 [a]Nu 4:15; Dt 10:8; 2Ch 5:5 [b]Dt 31:9 [c]1Ch 23:13
15:3 [d]1Ki 8:1; 1Ch 13:5
15:8 [e]Ex 6:22
15:9 [f]Ex 6:18
15:11 [g]1Ch 12:28 [h]1Sa 22:20
15:12 [i]Ex 19:14-15; Lev 11:44; 2Ch 35:6

[a] 11 *Baal Perazim* means *the lord who breaks out.*
[b] 7 Hebrew *Gershom,* a variant of *Gershon*

***M**ost Christians are like a man who was toiling along the road, bending under a heavy burden, when a wagon overtook him, and the driver kindly offered to help him on his journey. He joyfully accepted the offer, but when seated, continued to bend beneath his burden, which he still kept on his shoulders. "Why do you not lay down your burden?" asked the kind-hearted driver. "Oh!" replied the man, "I feel that it is almost too much to ask you to carry me, and I could not think of letting you carry my burden too." And so Christians, who have given themselves into the care and keeping of the Lord Jesus, still continue to bend beneath the weight of their burden, and often go weary and heavy-laden throughout the whole length of their journey.*

—Hannah Whitall Smith (1832-1911)

selves and bring up the ark of the LORD, the God of
15:13 Israel, to the place I have prepared for it. 13 It was
[j]1Ki 8:4 because you, the Levites,[j] did not bring it up the
[k]2Sa 6:3; first time that the LORD our God broke out in anger
1Ch 13:7-10 against us.[k] We did not inquire of him about how
to do it in the prescribed way." 14 So the priests and
Levites consecrated themselves in order to bring
up the ark of the LORD, the God of Israel. 15 And
15:15 the Levites carried the ark of God with the poles
[l]Ex 25:14; on their shoulders, as Moses had commanded[l] in
Nu 4:5,15 accordance with the word of the LORD.
15:16 16 David told the leaders of the Levites to appoint
[m]Ps 68:25 their brothers as singers[m] to sing joyful songs,
[n]1Ch 13:8; 25:1; accompanied by musical instruments: lyres, harps
Ne 12:27,36 and cymbals.[n]
15:17 17 So the Levites appointed Heman[o] son of Joel;
[o]1Ch 6:33 from his brothers, Asaph[p] son of Berekiah; and from
[p]1Ch 6:39 their brothers the Merarites,[q] Ethan son of Kusha-
[q]1Ch 6:44 iah; 18 and with them their brothers next in rank:
15:18 Zechariah,[a] Jaaziel, Shemiramoth, Jehiel, Unni, Eli-
[r]1Ch 26:4-5 ab, Benaiah, Maaseiah, Mattithiah, Eliphelehu,
Mikneiah, Obed-Edom[r] and Jeiel,[b] the gatekeepers.
15:19 19 The musicians Heman,[s] Asaph and Ethan
[s]1Ch 25:6 were to sound the bronze cymbals; 20 Zechariah,
Aziel, Shemiramoth, Jehiel, Unni, Eliab, Maaseiah and Benaiah were to play the lyres according
to *alamoth*,[c] 21 and Mattithiah, Eliphelehu, Mikneiah, Obed-Edom, Jeiel and Azaziah were to play
the harps, directing according to *sheminith*.[c]
22 Kenaniah the head Levite was in charge of the
singing; that was his responsibility because he
was skillful at it.
23 Berekiah and Elkanah were to be doorkeepers
for the ark. 24 Shebaniah, Joshaphat, Nethanel,
15:24 Amasai, Zechariah, Benaiah and Eliezer the
[t]ver 28; priests were to blow trumpets[t] before the ark of
1Ch 16:6; God. Obed-Edom and Jehiah were also to be door-
2Ch 7:6 keepers for the ark.
25 So David and the elders of Israel and the commanders of units of a thousand went to bring up
15:25 the ark[u] of the covenant of the LORD from the
[u]1Ch 13:13; house of Obed-Edom, with rejoicing. 26 Because
2Ch 1:4 God had helped the Levites who were carrying the
15:26 ark of the covenant of the LORD, seven bulls and
[v]Nu 23:1-4, seven rams[v] were sacrificed. 27 Now David was
29 clothed in a robe of fine linen, as were all the
Levites who were carrying the ark, and as were
the singers, and Kenaniah, who was in charge of
the singing of the choirs. David also wore a linen
ephod. 28 So all Israel brought up the ark of the
15:28 covenant of the LORD with shouts, with the sound-
[w]1Ch 13:8 ing of rams' horns[w] and trumpets, and of cymbals,
and the playing of lyres and harps.
29 As the ark of the covenant of the LORD was
entering the City of David, Michal daughter of
Saul watched from a window. And when she saw

[a] *18* Three Hebrew manuscripts and most Septuagint manuscripts (see also verse 20 and 1 Chron. 16:5); most Hebrew manuscripts *Zechariah son and* or *Zechariah, Ben and*
[b] *18* Hebrew; Septuagint (see also verse 21) *Jeiel and Azaziah*
[c] *20,21* Probably a musical term

David's Wife Michal

1CH 15:29

When the ark of the covenant, which represents God's presence with his people, is back in its rightful place, the people of Israel shout, sing and dance. King David takes an active, exuberant part in the celebration. David's wife Michal chooses not to join the praise festival. From the sidelines she watches her husband-king sway with the music, and she cannot suppress her bitterness (2Sa 6:16).

What causes Michal's venomous response? The blame can be laid at the feet of the two men who should be most caring of Michal but who, instead, use her for their own purposes: her father, King Saul, and her husband, King David (see the note on 2Sa 3:13–14, page 478). Undoubtedly, her anger is justified. However, Michal allows her anger to deteriorate into smoldering resentment and hatred that ignites in a bitter torrent of accusations (2Sa 6:20). Consequently, she finds no joy in the Lord's presence, and she concludes her life lonely and alone (see the note on 2Sa 6:21–23, page 483; also see character sketch for Michal on page 740).

King David dancing and celebrating, she despised
him in her heart.

16 They brought the ark of God and set it inside
the tent that David had pitched[x] for it, and — 16:1 x1Ch 15:1
they presented burnt offerings and fellowship offerings[a] before God. 2 After David had finished sacrificing the burnt offerings and fellowship offerings, — 16:2
he blessed[y] the people in the name of the LORD. — yEx 39:43
3 Then he gave a loaf of bread, a cake of dates and
a cake of raisins to each Israelite man and woman.

4 He appointed some of the Levites to minister[z] — 16:4
before the ark of the LORD, to make petition, to — z1Ch 15:2
give thanks, and to praise the LORD, the God of
Israel: 5 Asaph was the chief, Zechariah second,
then Jeiel, Shemiramoth, Jehiel, Mattithiah, Eliab, Benaiah, Obed-Edom and Jeiel. They were to
play the lyres and harps, Asaph was to sound the
cymbals, 6 and Benaiah and Jahaziel the priests
were to blow the trumpets regularly before the ark
of the covenant of God.

David's Psalm of Thanks

7 That day David first committed to Asaph and — 16:7
his associates this psalm[a] of thanks to the LORD: — a2Sa 23:1

8 Give thanks[b] to the LORD, call on his name; — 16:8 bver 34;
make known among the nations[c] — Ps 136:1
what he has done. — c2Ki 19:19
9 Sing to him, sing praise[d] to him;
tell of all his wonderful acts. — 16:9
10 Glory in his holy name; — dEx 15:1
let the hearts of those who seek the
LORD rejoice.
11 Look to the LORD and his strength;
seek[e] his face always. — 16:11
12 Remember[f] the wonders he has done, — e1Ch 28:9;
his miracles,[g] and the judgments he — 2Ch 7:14; Ps 24:6;
pronounced, — 119:2,58
13 O descendants of Israel his servant, — 16:12
O sons of Jacob, his chosen ones. — fPs 77:11 gPs 78:43

14 He is the LORD our God; — 16:14
his judgments[h] are in all the earth. — hIsa 26:9
15 He remembers[b] his covenant forever,
the word he commanded, for a
thousand generations, — 16:16 iGe 12:7;
16 the covenant[i] he made with Abraham, — 15:18; 17:2;
the oath he swore to Isaac. — 22:16-18;
17 He confirmed it to Jacob[j] as a decree, — 26:3; 28:13; 35:11
to Israel as an everlasting covenant:
18 "To you I will give the land of Canaan[k] — 16:17 jGe 35:9-12
as the portion you will inherit."

19 When they were but few in number,[l] — 16:18 kGe 13:14-17
few indeed, and strangers in it,
20 they[c] wandered from nation to nation, — 16:19 lGe 34:30; Dt 7:7

[a] *1* Traditionally *peace offerings*; also in verse 2 [b] *15* Some Septuagint manuscripts (see also Psalm 105:8); Hebrew *Remember* [c] *18–20* One Hebrew manuscript, Septuagint and Vulgate (see also Psalm 105:12); most Hebrew manuscripts *inherit, / [19]though you are but few in number, / few indeed, and strangers in it." / [20]They*

Calm on the bosom of
thy God,
Fair spirit, rest thee now!
E'en while with ours thy footsteps
trod,
His seal was on thy brow.

Dust, to its narrow house
beneath!
Soul, to its place on high!
They that have seen thy look in
death
No more may fear to die. 

—*Felicia Dorothea Hemans (1793-1835)*

from one kingdom to another.
21 He allowed no man to oppress them;
for their sake he rebuked kings:[m]
22 "Do not touch my anointed ones;
do my prophets[n] no harm."
23 Sing to the LORD, all the earth;
proclaim his salvation day after day.
24 Declare his glory among the nations,
his marvelous deeds among all
peoples.
25 For great is the LORD and most worthy of
praise;[o]
he is to be feared[p] above all gods.[q]
26 For all the gods of the nations are idols,
but the LORD made the heavens.[r]
27 Splendor and majesty are before him;
strength and joy in his dwelling place.
28 Ascribe to the LORD, O families of
nations,
ascribe to the LORD glory and
strength,[s]
29 ascribe to the LORD the glory due his
name.
Bring an offering and come before him;
worship the LORD in the splendor of
his[a] holiness.[t]
30 Tremble[u] before him, all the earth!
The world is firmly established; it
cannot be moved.
31 Let the heavens rejoice, let the earth be
glad;[v]
let them say among the nations, "The
LORD reigns![w]"
32 Let the sea resound, and all that is in it;[x]
let the fields be jubilant, and
everything in them!
33 Then the trees[y] of the forest will sing,
they will sing for joy before the LORD,
for he comes to judge[z] the earth.
34 Give thanks[a] to the LORD, for he is
good;[b]
his love endures forever.[c]
35 Cry out, "Save us, O God our Savior;[d]
gather us and deliver us from the
nations,
that we may give thanks to your holy
name,
that we may glory in your praise."
36 Praise be to the LORD, the God of Israel,[e]
from everlasting to everlasting.

Then all the people said "Amen" and "Praise the
LORD."

37 David left Asaph and his associates before the
ark of the covenant of the LORD to minister there
regularly, according to each day's requirements.[f]
38 He also left Obed-Edom[g] and his sixty-eight

16:21 [m]Ge 12:17; 20:3; Ex 7:15-18
16:22 [n]Ge 20:7
16:25 [o]Ps 48:1 [p]Ps 76:7; 89:7 [q]Dt 32:39
16:26 [r]Lev 19:4; Ps 102:25
16:28 [s]Ps 29:1-2
16:29 [t]Ps 29:1-2
16:30 [u]Ps 114:7
16:31 [v]Isa 44:23; 49:13 [w]Ps 93:1
16:32 [x]Ps 98:7
16:33 [y]Isa 55:12 [z]Ps 96:10; 98:9
16:34 [a]ver 8 [b]Na 1:7 [c]2Ch 5:13; 7:3; Ezr 3:11; Ps 136:1-26; Jer 33:11
16:35 [d]Mic 7:7
16:36 [e]Dt 27:15; 1Ki 8:15; Ps 72:18-19
16:37 [f]2Ch 8:14
16:38 [g]1Ch 13:13

[a] 29 Or *LORD with the splendor of*

Nature Sings to God

1CH 16:32-33

Nature passionately declares the creativity and power of the God of creation. Just by being, just by displaying God's handiwork, nature "sings" God's praise. The language in these verses is figurative. The ocean, fields and forest do not have the ability to voice, or the intellect to compose, a message of thanksgiving or joy. Only we, as God's human creation, have the capability to form words of glory and honor to the Master Creator.

Still, there are times when we cannot adequately express how deeply we appreciate God's goodness and love. So we join with nature and attempt to paint a poetic word picture of God's majesty and grace. David did this eloquently, perhaps because he knew both God and his creation intimately.

Read Psalm 19:1-4 or Psalm 93:3-4 and circle the words that remind you of David's prayer of thanksgiving in 1 Chronicles 16. Picture in your mind the heavens rejoicing, the seas resounding and the trees singing. Can you hear it? Will you join in their praise?

Updated Directions

1CH 17:1–4

A prophet is called to listen for God's instructions and then deliver that message to a specific audience. The prophet Nathan's special audience includes King David and those who work in his royal court.

David shares his heart's desire with Nathan: He wants to build a house for the Lord. Nathan tells David to proceed with his plans. He bases his response on what he knows about God's will thus far. David is God's appointed king. However, during the night, God gives Nathan updated directions. Nathan listens and immediately tells David that God has a different plan.

Nathan is not necessarily out of God's will when he tells David to go ahead with his plans to build the temple. He makes his decision according to what God has revealed to him in the past. Then he remains sensitive and open to God's clarification for the present and the future.

associates to minister with them. Obed-Edom son
of Jeduthun, and also Hosah,[h] were gatekeepers. **16:38** [h]1Ch 26:10
39 David left Zadok[i] the priest and his fellow **16:39** [i]2Sa 8:17;
priests before the tabernacle of the LORD at the 1Ch 15:11
high place in Gibeon[j] 40 to present burnt offerings [j]1Ki 3:4;
to the LORD on the altar of burnt offering regular- 2Ch 1:3
ly, morning and evening, in accordance with
everything written in the Law[k] of the LORD, which **16:40** [k]Ex 29:38;
he had given Israel. 41 With them were Heman[l] Nu 28:1-8
and Jeduthun and the rest of those chosen and
designated by name to give thanks to the LORD, **16:41** [l]1Ch 6:33;
"for his love endures forever." 42 Heman and Jedu- 25:1-6;
thun were responsible for the sounding of the 2Ch 5:13
trumpets and cymbals and for the playing of the **16:42**
other instruments for sacred song.[m] The sons of [m]2Ch 7:6
Jeduthun were stationed at the gate.
43 Then all the people left, each for his own
home, and David returned home to bless his
family.

God's Promise to David

17 After David was settled in his palace, he
said to Nathan the prophet, "Here I am, liv-
ing in a palace of cedar, while the ark of the cov- **17:1**
enant of the LORD is under a tent.[n]" [n]1Ch 15:1
2 Nathan replied to David, "Whatever you have **17:2**
in mind,[o] do it, for God is with you." [o]2Ch 6:7
3 That night the word of God came to Nathan,
saying:

4 "Go and tell my servant David, 'This is
what the LORD says: You[p] are not the one to **17:4**
build me a house to dwell in. 5 I have not [p]1Ch 28:3
dwelt in a house from the day I brought Israel up out of Egypt to this day. I have moved
from one tent site to another, from one
dwelling place to another. 6 Wherever I have
moved with all the Israelites, did I ever say to
any of their leaders[a] whom I commanded to
shepherd my people, "Why have you not
built me a house of cedar?" '
7 "Now then, tell my servant David, 'This is
what the LORD Almighty says: I took you from
the pasture and from following the flock, to
be ruler[q] over my people Israel. 8 I have been **17:7** [q]2Sa 6:21
with you wherever you have gone, and I have
cut off all your enemies from before you.
Now I will make your name like the names of
the greatest men of the earth. 9 And I will provide a place for my people Israel and will
plant them so that they can have a home of
their own and no longer be disturbed.
Wicked people will not oppress them any-
more, as they did at the beginning 10 and have **17:10**
done ever since the time I appointed leaders[r] [r]Jdg 2:16
over my people Israel. I will also subdue all
your enemies.
" 'I declare to you that the LORD will build
a house for you: 11 When your days are over

[a] 6 Traditionally *judges*; also in verse 10

and you go to be with your fathers, I will
raise up your offspring to succeed you, one
of your own sons, and I will establish his
17:12 [s]1Ki 5:5 kingdom. [12]He is the one who will build[s] a
[t]2Ch 7:18 house for me, and I will establish his throne
17:13 forever.[t] [13]I will be his father,[u] and he will be
[u]2Co 6:18 my son.[v] I will never take my love away from
[v]Lk 1:32; Heb 1:5* him, as I took it away from your predecessor.
17:14 [14]I will set him over my house and my king-
[w]1Ki 2:12; dom forever; his throne[w] will be established
1Ch 28:5 [x]Ps 132:11; forever.[x]' "

Jer 33:17 [15]Nathan reported to David all the words of this
entire revelation.

David's Prayer

[16]Then King David went in and sat before the
LORD, and he said:

"Who am I, O LORD God, and what is my
family, that you have brought me this far?
[17]And as if this were not enough in your
sight, O God, you have spoken about the
future of the house of your servant. You have
looked on me as though I were the most
exalted of men, O LORD God.

[18]"What more can David say to you for
17:19 honoring your servant? For you know your
[y]2Sa 7:16-17; servant, [19]O LORD. For the sake[y] of your ser-
2Ki 20:6; Isa 9:7; vant and according to your will, you have
37:35; 55:3 [z]2Sa 7:25 done this great thing and made known all
these great promises.[z]

17:20 [20]"There is no one like you, O LORD, and
[a]Ex 8:10; 9:14; 15:11; there is no God but you,[a] as we have heard
Isa 44:6; with our own ears. [21]And who is like your
46:9 people Israel—the one nation on earth whose
17:21 God went out to redeem[b] a people for him-
[b]Ex 6:6 self, and to make a name for yourself, and to
perform great and awesome wonders by driving out nations from before your people,
17:22 whom you redeemed from Egypt? [22]You made
[c]Ex 19:5-6 your people Israel your very own forever,[c]
17:23 and you, O LORD, have become their God.
[d]1Ki 8:25 [23]"And now, LORD, let the promise[d] you have
made concerning your servant and his house
be established forever. Do as you promised,
[24]so that it will be established and that your
name will be great forever. Then men will say,
'The LORD Almighty, the God over Israel, is
Israel's God!' And the house of your servant
David will be established before you.

[25]"You, my God, have revealed to your servant that you will build a house for him. So
your servant has found courage to pray to
you. [26]O LORD, you are God! You have promised these good things to your servant. [27]Now
you have been pleased to bless the house of
17:27 your servant, that it may continue forever in
[e]Ps 16:11; 21:6 your sight;[e] for you, O LORD, have blessed it,
and it will be blessed forever."

Humble David

1CH 17:16

Nathan's prophetic words to David include a change in direction. David is not to build a temple for the Lord. That privilege will go to David's son. Any disappointment that David might feel is quickly dispelled by the promise the Lord graciously includes: David's house and throne will last forever (1Ch 17:10–14).

Such a promise could produce pride, perhaps a bit of haughtiness, maybe even arrogance. But how does David respond? "Who am I, O LORD God, and what is my family, that you have brought me this far?" In this moment, the awesome reality of God's "forever" plan dawns on David. He is more than the king of reunited Israel; he is an instrument of God's grace-filled purpose for all people for all time. From David's lineage will come the Messiah, the eternal King, the Savior of the world. David sees himself as God sees him: deeply fallen, profoundly human, sinful and prone to wander, but redeemed by God's grace, loved and raised to a privileged position of usefulness.

David's Victories

18 In the course of time, David defeated the
Philistines and subdued them, and he took
Gath and its surrounding villages from the control of the Philistines.
2 David also defeated the Moabites,[f] and they
became subject to him and brought tribute.
3 Moreover, David fought Hadadezer king of
Zobah,[g] as far as Hamath, when he went to establish his control along the Euphrates River.[h] 4 David
captured a thousand of his chariots, seven thousand charioteers and twenty thousand foot soldiers. He hamstrung[i] all but a hundred of the
chariot horses.
5 When the Arameans of Damascus[j] came to help
Hadadezer king of Zobah, David struck down
twenty-two thousand of them. 6 He put garrisons in
the Aramean kingdom of Damascus, and the Arameans became subject to him and brought tribute.
The LORD gave David victory everywhere he went.
7 David took the gold shields carried by the officers of Hadadezer and brought them to Jerusalem.
8 From Tebah[a] and Cun, towns that belonged to
Hadadezer, David took a great quantity of bronze,
which Solomon used to make the bronze Sea,[k] the
pillars and various bronze articles.
9 When Tou king of Hamath heard that David
had defeated the entire army of Hadadezer king
of Zobah, 10 he sent his son Hadoram to King
David to greet him and congratulate him on his
victory in battle over Hadadezer, who had been at
war with Tou. Hadoram brought all kinds of articles of gold and silver and bronze.
11 King David dedicated these articles to the
LORD, as he had done with the silver and gold he
had taken from all these nations: Edom[l] and
Moab, the Ammonites and the Philistines, and
Amalek.[m]
12 Abishai son of Zeruiah struck down eighteen
thousand Edomites[n] in the Valley of Salt. 13 He put
garrisons in Edom, and all the Edomites became
subject to David. The LORD gave David victory
everywhere he went.

David's Officials

14 David reigned[o] over all Israel,[p] doing what
was just and right for all his people. 15 Joab[q] son of
Zeruiah was over the army; Jehoshaphat son of
Ahilud was recorder; 16 Zadok[r] son of Ahitub and
Ahimelech[b][s] son of Abiathar were priests; Shav-
sha was secretary; 17 Benaiah son of Jehoiada was
over the Kerethites and Pelethites;[t] and David's
sons were chief officials at the king's side.

The Battle Against the Ammonites

19 In the course of time, Nahash king of the
Ammonites[u] died, and his son succeeded

[a] 8 Hebrew *Tibhath,* a variant of *Tebah* [b] 16 Some Hebrew manuscripts, Vulgate and Syriac (see also 2 Samuel 8:17); most Hebrew manuscripts *Abimelech*

18:2 [f]Nu 21:29
18:3 [g]1Ch 19:6 [h]Ge 2:14
18:4 [i]Ge 49:6
18:5 [j]2Ki 16:9; 1Ch 19:6
18:8 [k]1Ki 7:23; 2Ch 4:12,15-16
18:11 [l]Nu 24:18 [m]Nu 24:20
18:12 [n]1Ki 11:15
18:14 [o]1Ch 29:26 [p]1Ch 11:1
18:15 [q]2Sa 5:6-8; 1Ch 11:6
18:16 [r]2Sa 8:17; 1Ch 6:8 [s]1Ch 24:6
18:17 [t]1Sa 30:14; 2Sa 8:18; 15:18
19:1 [u]Ge 19:38; Jdg 10:17-11:33; 2Ch 20:1-2; Zep 2:8-11

I know that strength *arising from obedience has a way of simplifying things which seem impossible.*

—*Teresa of Avila (1515-1582)*

him as king. 2David thought, "I will show kindness to Hanun son of Nahash, because his father
showed kindness to me." So David sent a delegation to express his sympathy to Hanun concerning his father.
When David's men came to Hanun in the land
of the Ammonites to express sympathy to him,
3the Ammonite nobles said to Hanun, "Do you
think David is honoring your father by sending
men to you to express sympathy? Haven't his men
19:3 come to you to explore and spy out[v] the country
[v]Nu 21:32 and overthrow it?" 4So Hanun seized David's men,
shaved them, cut off their garments in the middle
at the buttocks, and sent them away.
5When someone came and told David about the
men, he sent messengers to meet them, for they
were greatly humiliated. The king said, "Stay at
Jericho till your beards have grown, and then
come back."
6When the Ammonites realized that they had
19:6 become a stench[w] in David's nostrils, Hanun and
[w]Ge 34:30 [x]1Ch 18:3, 5,9 the Ammonites sent a thousand talents[a] of silver
to hire chariots and charioteers from Aram Naha-
raim,[b] Aram Maacah and Zobah.[x] 7They hired
thirty-two thousand chariots and charioteers, as
19:7 well as the king of Maacah with his troops, who
[y]Nu 21:30; Jos 13:9,16 came and camped near Medeba,[y] while the
Ammonites were mustered from their towns and
moved out for battle.
8On hearing this, David sent Joab out with the
entire army of fighting men. 9The Ammonites
came out and drew up in battle formation at the
entrance to their city, while the kings who had
come were by themselves in the open country.
10Joab saw that there were battle lines in front
of him and behind him; so he selected some of the
best troops in Israel and deployed them against the
Arameans. 11He put the rest of the men under the
19:11 command of Abishai[z] his brother, and they were
[z]1Sa 26:6 deployed against the Ammonites. 12Joab said, "If
the Arameans are too strong for me, then you are
to rescue me; but if the Ammonites are too strong
for you, then I will rescue you. 13Be strong and let
us fight bravely for our people and the cities of our
God. The LORD will do what is good in his sight."
14Then Joab and the troops with him advanced
to fight the Arameans, and they fled before him.
15When the Ammonites saw that the Arameans
were fleeing, they too fled before his brother
Abishai and went inside the city. So Joab went
back to Jerusalem.
16After the Arameans saw that they had been
routed by Israel, they sent messengers and had
Arameans brought from beyond the River,[c] with
Shophach the commander of Hadadezer's army
leading them.
17When David was told of this, he gathered all
19:17 Israel[a] and crossed the Jordan; he advanced
[a]1Ch 9:1

[a] *6* That is, about 37 tons (about 34 metric tons) [b] *6* That is, Northwest Mesopotamia [c] *16* That is, the Euphrates

Compassionate David

1CH 19:1-5

In addition to David's other admirable character traits, he is a compassionate and understanding supervisor. When David hears that his men have been humiliated and insulted while on an assignment for him (see the note on 2Sa 10:4, page 488), he wants to ease their embarrassment. To protect his ambassadors from additional public shame, he sends word for them to remain in a remote area until their beards and dignity return.

No wonder the people adore him. David is a capable leader who chooses to treat others with respect. His wise actions inspire loyalty and cultivate a safe atmosphere in which to work and serve.

David Prepares the Way

1CH 20

When the Israelites, under the direction of Moses, first scouted out the territory referred to as the promised land, they noticed a group of people so strong and tall that all but a few were afraid to proceed (Dt 1:28). These giant idol worshipers were known as Anakites or Rephaites (see the note on Nu 13:26–33, page 230). Their history is not entirely clear, but they were associated with the Philistines, the Israelites' primary enemy.

While David is still a shepherd boy, he kills Goliath, a Philistine giant. David's military men kill giants also (2Sa 21:15–22). Through the years the Israelites face the Philistines many times. With the description of the Philistine defeat in 1 Chronicles 20, the writer of Chronicles accomplishes his goal: to help the reader understand how King David prepares the way for his son Solomon to have a peaceful reign (1Ch 22:8–9). There are no wars during Solomon's rule, allowing him to build God's house as a "man of peace and rest" (1Ch 22:9).

against them and formed his battle lines opposite them. David formed his lines to meet the Arameans in battle, and they fought against him. 18But they fled before Israel, and David killed seven thousand of their charioteers and forty thousand of their foot soldiers. He also killed Shophach the commander of their army.

19When the vassals of Hadadezer saw that they had been defeated by Israel, they made peace with David and became subject to him.

So the Arameans were not willing to help the Ammonites anymore.

The Capture of Rabbah

20 In the spring, at the time when kings go off to war, Joab led out the armed forces. He laid waste the land of the Ammonites and went to Rabbah[b] and besieged it, but David remained in Jerusalem. Joab attacked Rabbah and left it in ruins.[c] 2David took the crown from the head of their king[a]—its weight was found to be a talent[b] of gold, and it was set with precious stones—and it was placed on David's head. He took a great quantity of plunder from the city 3and brought out the people who were there, consigning them to labor with saws and with iron picks and axes.[d] David did this to all the Ammonite towns. Then David and his entire army returned to Jerusalem.

20:1 [b]Dt 3:11; 2Sa 12:26 [c]Am 1:13-15
20:3 [d]Dt 29:11

War With the Philistines

4In the course of time, war broke out with the Philistines, at Gezer.[e] At that time Sibbecai the Hushathite killed Sippai, one of the descendants of the Rephaites,[f] and the Philistines were subjugated.

5In another battle with the Philistines, Elhanan son of Jair killed Lahmi the brother of Goliath the Gittite, who had a spear with a shaft like a weaver's rod.[g]

6In still another battle, which took place at Gath, there was a huge man with six fingers on each hand and six toes on each foot—twenty-four in all. He also was descended from Rapha. 7When he taunted Israel, Jonathan son of Shimea, David's brother, killed him.

8These were descendants of Rapha in Gath, and they fell at the hands of David and his men.

20:4 [e]Jos 10:33 [f]Ge 14:5
20:5 [g]1Sa 17:7

David Numbers the Fighting Men

21 Satan[h] rose up against Israel and incited David to take a census[i] of Israel. 2So David said to Joab and the commanders of the troops, "Go and count[j] the Israelites from Beersheba to Dan. Then report back to me so that I may know how many there are."

3But Joab replied, "May the LORD multiply his troops a hundred times over.[k] My lord the king, are they not all my lord's subjects? Why does my

21:1 [h]2Ch 18:21; Ps 109:6 [i]2Ch 14:8; 25:5
21:2 [j]1Ch 27:23-24
21:3 [k]Dt 1:11

[a] 2 Or *of Milcom,* that is, Molech [b] 2 That is, about 75 pounds (about 34 kilograms)

lord want to do this? Why should he bring guilt
on Israel?"
4The king's word, however, overruled Joab; so
Joab left and went throughout Israel and then
came back to Jerusalem. 5Joab reported the num-
21:5 [l]1Ch 9:1 ber of the fighting men to David: In all Israel[l]
there were one million one hundred thousand
men who could handle a sword, including four
hundred and seventy thousand in Judah.
6But Joab did not include Levi and Benjamin in
the numbering, because the king's command was
repulsive to him. 7This command was also evil in
the sight of God; so he punished Israel.
8Then David said to God, "I have sinned greatly
by doing this. Now, I beg you, take away the guilt
of your servant. I have done a very foolish thing."
21:9 [m]1Sa 22:5 9The LORD said to Gad,[m] David's seer,[n] 10"Go and
[n]1Sa 9:9 tell David, 'This is what the LORD says: I am giving
you three options. Choose one of them for me to
carry out against you.' "
11So Gad went to David and said to him, "This is
what the LORD says: 'Take your choice: 12three years
21:12 [o]Dt 32:24 of famine,[o] three months of being swept away[a]
[p]Eze 30:25 before your enemies, with their swords overtaking
[q]Ge 19:13 you, or three days of the sword[p] of the LORD[q]—days
of plague in the land, with the angel of the LORD
ravaging every part of Israel.' Now then, decide
how I should answer the one who sent me."
21:13 13David said to Gad, "I am in deep distress. Let
[r]Ps 6:4; me fall into the hands of the LORD, for his mercy[r]
86:15; is very great; but do not let me fall into the hands
130:4,7 of men."
21:14 14So the LORD sent a plague on Israel, and seven-
[s]1Ch 27:24 ty thousand men of Israel fell dead.[s] 15And God sent
an angel[t] to destroy Jerusalem.[u] But as the angel
21:15 [t]Ge 32:1 was doing so, the LORD saw it and was grieved[v]
[u]Ps 125:2 because of the calamity and said to the angel who
[v]Ge 6:6; Ex 32:14 was destroying[w] the people, "Enough! Withdraw
[w]Ge 19:13 your hand." The angel of the LORD was then standing at the threshing floor of Araunah[b] the Jebusite.
16David looked up and saw the angel of the
LORD standing between heaven and earth, with a
drawn sword in his hand extended over Jerusalem. Then David and the elders, clothed in sackcloth, fell facedown.[x]
21:16 [x]Nu 14:5; 17David said to God, "Was it not I who ordered
Jos 7:6 the fighting men to be counted? I am the one who
has sinned and done wrong. These are but sheep.[y]
21:17 [y]2Sa 7:8; What have they done? O LORD my God, let your
Ps 74:1 hand fall upon me and my family,[z] but do not let
[z]Jnh 1:12 this plague remain on your people."
18Then the angel of the LORD ordered Gad to tell
David to go up and build an altar to the LORD on
21:18 the threshing floor[a] of Araunah the Jebusite. 19So
[a]2Ch 3:1 David went up in obedience to the word that Gad
had spoken in the name of the LORD.
21:20 [b]Jdg 6:11 20While Araunah was threshing wheat,[b] he

[a] *12* Hebrew; Septuagint and Vulgate (see also 2 Samuel 24:13) *of fleeing* [b] *15* Hebrew *Ornan,* a variant of *Araunah;* also in verses 18–28

Angel Messengers

1CH 21:15-20

Throughout the history of the Bible, angels function as God's messengers or agents. They come to earth for different purposes, depending on the circumstances. They might make an announcement: Moses (Ex 3:2-6), Mary (Lk 1:26-38); protect someone from pain or harm: Hagar (Ge 21:17-18), Isaac (Ge 22:11-12), Elijah (1Ki 19:1-8), Daniel (Da 6:22); or deliver punishment: on Jerusalem (1Ch 21:15), on the Assyrian army (2Ch 32:21).

This chapter of Chronicles records a sad page in the history of the Israelites and their godly king. God sends an angel to punish his own people. Both David and the people have sinned, and a just God cannot ignore it. Punishment is the inevitable consequence. However, when God sees the angel raise his sword to destroy Jerusalem, he is "grieved because of the calamity" (1Ch 21:15) and stops the angel he had sent. Though this story is difficult to read, it gives us a glimpse of both the just and merciful character of our God.

Painter, student of French, and teacher of literature, logic, history and botany, Lucy Larcom was also a prolific writer, at one time declaring she would only write hymns if she could get her publishers to accept them.

Draw Thou My Soul, O Christ

Draw Thou my soul, O Christ,
closer to Thine;
Breathe into every wish Thy will
divine;
Raised my low self above, won by
Thy deathless love,
Ever, O Christ, through mine let
Thy life shine.

Lead forth my soul, O Christ, one
with Thine own,
Joyful to follow Thee through paths
unknown;
In Thee my strength renew; give me
Thy work to do;
Through me Thy truth be shown,
Thy love made known.

Not for myself alone may my prayer
be;
Lift Thou Thy world, O Christ,
closer to Thee;
Cleanse it from guilt and wrong;
teach it salvation's song
Till earth, as heaven, fulfills God's
holy will.

—*Lucy Larcom (1824–1893)*

turned and saw the angel; his four sons who were
with him hid themselves. 21Then David approached, and when Araunah looked and saw
him, he left the threshing floor and bowed down
before David with his face to the ground.
22David said to him, "Let me have the site of
your threshing floor so I can build an altar to the
LORD, that the plague on the people may be
stopped. Sell it to me at the full price."
23Araunah said to David, "Take it! Let my lord
the king do whatever pleases him. Look, I will
give the oxen for the burnt offerings, the threshing
sledges for the wood, and the wheat for the grain
offering. I will give all this."
24But King David replied to Araunah, "No, I
insist on paying the full price. I will not take for
the LORD what is yours, or sacrifice a burnt offering that costs me nothing."
25So David paid Araunah six hundred shekels[a]
of gold for the site. 26David built an altar to the
LORD there and sacrificed burnt offerings and fellowship offerings.[b] He called on the LORD, and the
LORD answered him with fire[c] from heaven on the
altar of burnt offering.
27Then the LORD spoke to the angel, and he put
his sword back into its sheath. 28At that time,
when David saw that the LORD had answered him
on the threshing floor of Araunah the Jebusite, he
offered sacrifices there. 29The tabernacle of the
LORD, which Moses had made in the desert, and
the altar of burnt offering were at that time on the
high place at Gibeon.[d] 30But David could not go
before it to inquire of God, because he was afraid
of the sword of the angel of the LORD.

22 Then David said, "The house of the LORD
God[e] is to be here, and also the altar of
burnt offering for Israel."

Preparations for the Temple

2So David gave orders to assemble the aliens[f] living in Israel, and from among them he appointed
stonecutters[g] to prepare dressed stone for building
the house of God. 3He provided a large amount of
iron to make nails for the doors of the gateways
and for the fittings, and more bronze than could
be weighed.[h] 4He also provided more cedar logs[i]
than could be counted, for the Sidonians and Tyr-
ians had brought large numbers of them to David.
5David said, "My son Solomon is young[j] and
inexperienced, and the house to be built for the
LORD should be of great magnificence and fame
and splendor in the sight of all the nations. Therefore I will make preparations for it." So David
made extensive preparations before his death.
6Then he called for his son Solomon and
charged him to build[k] a house for the LORD, the
God of Israel. 7David said to Solomon: "My son, I
had it in my heart[l] to build[m] a house for the Name[n]

21:26 [c]Lev 9:24; Jdg 6:21
21:29 [d]1Ki 3:4; 1Ch 16:39
22:1 [e]Ge 28:17; 1Ch 21:18-29; 2Ch 3:1
22:2 [f]1Ki 9:21; Isa 56:6 [g]1Ki 5:17-18
22:3 [h]ver 14; 1Ki 7:47; 1Ch 29:2-5
22:4 [i]1Ki 5:6
22:5 [j]1Ki 3:7; 1Ch 29:1
22:6 [k]Ac 7:47
22:7 [l]1Ch 17:2 [m]2Sa 7:2; 1Ki 8:17 [n]Dt 12:5,11

[a] 25 That is, about 15 pounds (about 7 kilograms)
[b] 26 Traditionally *peace offerings*

of the LORD my God. 8 But this word of the LORD
came to me: 'You have shed much blood and have
fought many wars.[o] You are not to build a house
for my Name,[p] because you have shed much blood
on the earth in my sight. 9 But you will have a son
who will be a man of peace[q] and rest, and I will
give him rest from all his enemies on every side.
His name will be Solomon,[a r] and I will grant Israel peace and quiet[s] during his reign. 10 He is the one
who will build a house for my Name.[t] He will be
my son,[u] and I will be his father. And I will establish the throne of his kingdom over Israel forever.'[v]

11 "Now, my son, the LORD be with[w] you, and
may you have success and build the house of the
LORD your God, as he said you would. 12 May the
LORD give you discretion and understanding[x]
when he puts you in command over Israel, so that
you may keep the law of the LORD your God.
13 Then you will have success if you are careful to
observe the decrees and laws[y] that the LORD gave
Moses for Israel. Be strong and courageous.[z] Do
not be afraid or discouraged.

14 "I have taken great pains to provide for the
temple of the LORD a hundred thousand talents[b] of
gold, a million talents[c] of silver, quantities of
bronze and iron too great to be weighed, and
wood and stone. And you may add to them.[a] 15 You
have many workmen: stonecutters, masons and
carpenters, as well as men skilled in every kind
of work 16 in gold and silver, bronze and iron—
craftsmen[b] beyond number. Now begin the work,
and the LORD be with you."

17 Then David ordered[c] all the leaders of Israel
to help his son Solomon. 18 He said to them, "Is
not the LORD your God with you? And has he not
granted you rest[d] on every side?[e] For he has handed the inhabitants of the land over to me, and the
land is subject to the LORD and to his people.
19 Now devote your heart and soul to seeking the
LORD your God.[f] Begin to build the sanctuary of
the LORD God, so that you may bring the ark of
the covenant of the LORD and the sacred articles
belonging to God into the temple that will be built
for the Name of the LORD."

The Levites

23 When David was old and full of years, he
made his son Solomon[g] king over Israel.[h]

2 He also gathered together all the leaders of Israel, as well as the priests and Levites. 3 The Levites
thirty years old or more[i] were counted, and the
total number of men was thirty-eight thousand.[j]
4 David said, "Of these, twenty-four thousand are
to supervise[k] the work of the temple of the LORD
and six thousand are to be officials and judges.[l]
5 Four thousand are to be gatekeepers and four

22:8 [o]1Ki 5:3 [p]1Ch 28:3
22:9 [q]1Ki 5:4 [r]2Sa 12:24 [s]1Ki 4:20
22:10 [t]1Ch 17:12 [u]2Sa 7:13 [v]2Sa 7:14; 2Ch 6:15
22:11 [w]ver 16
22:12 [x]1Ki 3:9-12; 2Ch 1:10
22:13 [y]1Ch 28:7 [z]Dt 31:6; Jos 1:6-9; 1Ch 28:20
22:14 [a]ver 3; 1Ch 29:2-5, 19
22:16 [b]ver 11; 2Ch 2:7
22:17 [c]1Ch 28:1-6
22:18 [d]ver 9; 1Ch 23:25 [e]2Sa 7:1
22:19 [f]ver 7; 1Ki 8:6; 1Ch 28:9; 2Ch 5:7; 7:14
23:1 [g]1Ki 1:33-39; 1Ch 28:5 [h]1Ki 1:30; 1Ch 29:28
23:3 [i]ver 24; Nu 8:24 [j]Nu 4:3-49
23:4 [k]Ezr 3:8 [l]1Ch 26:29; 2Ch 19:8

[a] 9 *Solomon* sounds like and may be derived from the Hebrew for *peace.* [b] 14 That is, about 3,750 tons (about 3,450 metric tons) [c] 14 That is, about 37,500 tons (about 34,500 metric tons)

Solomon-Jedidiah

1CH 22:9

Through the prophet Nathan, God tells David and Bathsheba to give their newborn son the name Jedidiah, which means "loved by the LORD" (see the note on 2Sa 12:24–25, page 492). The baby's parents have already named him Solomon, meaning "peace." Despite David and Bathsheba's adultery and the death of their first child, God shows his love to their son Solomon from the time he is born.

Later, Solomon lives out the peaceful meaning of his name. God says David's son will build the temple, for he will be a "man of peace and rest" (1Ch 22:9). The peace the Israelites experience during Solomon's reign is more than the absence of military action. The Hebrew word for peace includes a tranquility of mind and heart based on knowing that all is right between God and his people. This extraordinary time of peace foreshadows the permanent peace God offers through Jesus, the Son of David, the Prince of Peace.

thousand are to praise the LORD with the musical instruments[m] I have provided for that purpose."[n]
6 David divided[o] the Levites into groups corresponding to the sons of Levi: Gershon, Kohath and Merari.

Gershonites

7 Belonging to the Gershonites:
Ladan and Shimei.
8 The sons of Ladan:
Jehiel the first, Zetham and Joel—three in all.
9 The sons of Shimei:
Shelomoth, Haziel and Haran—three in all.
These were the heads of the families of Ladan.
10 And the sons of Shimei:
Jahath, Ziza,[a] Jeush and Beriah.
These were the sons of Shimei—four in all.
11 Jahath was the first and Ziza the second, but Jeush and Beriah did not have many sons; so they were counted as one family with one assignment.

Kohathites

12 The sons of Kohath:[p]
Amram, Izhar, Hebron and Uzziel—four in all.
13 The sons of Amram:[q]
Aaron and Moses.
Aaron was set apart,[r] he and his descendants forever, to consecrate the most holy things, to offer sacrifices before the LORD, to minister before him and to pronounce blessings[s] in his name forever.
14 The sons of Moses the man[t] of God were counted as part of the tribe of Levi.
15 The sons of Moses:
Gershom and Eliezer.[u]
16 The descendants of Gershom:[v]
Shubael was the first.
17 The descendants of Eliezer:
Rehabiah was the first.
Eliezer had no other sons, but the sons of Rehabiah were very numerous.
18 The sons of Izhar:
Shelomith was the first.
19 The sons of Hebron:[w]
Jeriah the first, Amariah the second, Jahaziel the third and Jekameam the fourth.
20 The sons of Uzziel:
Micah the first and Isshiah the second.

Merarites

21 The sons of Merari:[x]
Mahli and Mushi.
The sons of Mahli:
Eleazar and Kish.

23:5 [m]1Ch 15:16 [n]Ne 12:45
23:6 [o]2Ch 8:14; 29:25
23:12 [p]Ex 6:18
23:13 [q]Ex 6:20; 28:1 [r]Ex 30:7-10; Dt 21:5 [s]Nu 6:23
23:14 [t]Dt 33:1
23:15 [u]Ex 18:4
23:16 [v]1Ch 26:24-28
23:19 [w]1Ch 24:23
23:21 [x]1Ch 24:26

[a] *10* One Hebrew manuscript, Septuagint and Vulgate (see also verse 11); most Hebrew manuscripts *Zina*

Praise God from whom all blessings flow.
Praise him who sendeth joy and woe.
The Lord who takes,—the Lord who gives,—
O praise him all that dies and lives.
—Dinah Maria Mulock Craik (1826-1887)

22 Eleazar died without having sons: he had
only daughters. Their cousins, the sons of
Kish, married them.
23 The sons of Mushi:
Mahli, Eder and Jerimoth—three in all.

24 These were the descendants of Levi by their
families—the heads of families as they were registered under their names and counted individually, that is, the workers twenty years old or more[y]
who served in the temple of the LORD. 25 For David
had said, "Since the LORD, the God of Israel, has
granted rest[z] to his people and has come to dwell
in Jerusalem forever, 26 the Levites no longer need
to carry the tabernacle or any of the articles used
in its service."[a] 27 According to the last instructions
of David, the Levites were counted from those
twenty years old or more.

28 The duty of the Levites was to help Aaron's
descendants in the service of the temple of the
LORD: to be in charge of the courtyards, the side
rooms, the purification[b] of all sacred things and
the performance of other duties at the house of
God. 29 They were in charge of the bread set out on
the table,[c] the flour for the grain offerings,[d] the
unleavened wafers, the baking and the mixing,
and all measurements of quantity and size.[e] 30 They
were also to stand every morning to thank and
praise the LORD. They were to do the same in the
evening[f] 31 and whenever burnt offerings were presented to the LORD on Sabbaths and at New Moon[g]
festivals and at appointed feasts.[h] They were to
serve before the LORD regularly in the proper number and in the way prescribed for them.

32 And so the Levites[i] carried out their respon-
sibilities for the Tent of Meeting,[j] for the Holy
Place and, under their brothers the descendants of
Aaron, for the service of the temple of the LORD.[k]

The Divisions of Priests

24 These were the divisions[l] of the sons of
Aaron:[m]
The sons of Aaron were Nadab, Abihu, Eleazar
and Ithamar.[n] 2 But Nadab and Abihu died before
their father did,[o] and they had no sons; so Eleazar
and Ithamar served as the priests. 3 With the help
of Zadok[p] a descendant of Eleazar and Ahimelech
a descendant of Ithamar, David separated them
into divisions for their appointed order of ministering. 4 A larger number of leaders were found
among Eleazar's descendants than among Ithamar's, and they were divided accordingly: sixteen
heads of families from Eleazar's descendants and
eight heads of families from Ithamar's descendants. 5 They divided them impartially by drawing
lots,[q] for there were officials of the sanctuary and
officials of God among the descendants of both
Eleazar and Ithamar.

6 The scribe Shemaiah son of Nethanel, a Levite,
recorded their names in the presence of the king
and of the officials: Zadok the priest, Ahimelech[r]

23:24 [y]Nu 4:3; 10:17,21
23:25 [z]1Ch 22:9
23:26 [a]Nu 4:5,15; 7:9; Dt 10:8
23:28 [b]2Ch 29:15; Ne 13:9; Mal 3:3
23:29 [c]Ex 25:30 [d]Lev 2:4-7; 6:20-23 [e]Lev 19:35-36; 1Ch 9:29,32
23:30 [f]1Ch 9:33; Ps 134:1
23:31 [g]2Ki 4:23 [h]Lev 23:4; Nu 28:9-29:39; Isa 1:13-14; Col 2:16
23:32 [i]Nu 1:53; 1Ch 6:48 [j]Nu 3:6-8,38 [k]2Ch 23:18; 31:2; Eze 44:14
24:1 [l]1Ch 23:6; 28:13; 2Ch 5:11; 8:14; 23:8; 31:2; 35:4,5; Ezr 6:18 [m]Nu 3:2-4 [n]Ex 6:23
24:2 [o]Lev 10:1-2; Nu 3:4
24:3 [p]2Sa 8:17
24:5 [q]ver 31; 1Ch 25:8
24:6 [r]1Ch 18:16

Drawing Lots

1CH 24:5

The Hebrew people often make decisions by "drawing lots." They believe God directs the results, as he does all of life (Pr 16:33). We are not certain what lots looked like or how decisions were determined. However, the Bible records the use of this practice on many important occasions: when the promised land was divided into territories (see the note on Jos 14:2, page 354), when Saul was chosen as king (1Sa 10:20–24), and when the tasks of the priests are assigned (1Ch 24:5).

David's goal is to divide the tasks of the "officials of the sanctuary and the officials of God" in an impartial way. Although this decision-making method seems haphazard to us, it is God's will for his people under the old covenant. The last recorded use of lots is found in Acts 1:26; there lots were used to choose a disciple to replace Judas Iscariot. One verse later the Holy Spirit comes to dwell within believers, and the Bible never records the use of lots again. Today we have the privilege of communicating directly with God through his Spirit's work in our minds and spirits.

son of Abiathar and the heads of families of the
priests and of the Levites—one family being taken
from Eleazar and then one from Ithamar.

7 The first lot fell to Jehoiarib,
the second to Jedaiah,[s]
8 the third to Harim,[t]
the fourth to Seorim,
9 the fifth to Malkijah,
the sixth to Mijamin,
10 the seventh to Hakkoz,
the eighth to Abijah,[u]
11 the ninth to Jeshua,
the tenth to Shecaniah,
12 the eleventh to Eliashib,
the twelfth to Jakim,
13 the thirteenth to Huppah,
the fourteenth to Jeshebeab,
14 the fifteenth to Bilgah,
the sixteenth to Immer,[v]
15 the seventeenth to Hezir,[w]
the eighteenth to Happizzez,
16 the nineteenth to Pethahiah,
the twentieth to Jehezkel,
17 the twenty-first to Jakin,
the twenty-second to Gamul,
18 the twenty-third to Delaiah
and the twenty-fourth to Maaziah.

19 This was their appointed order of ministering
when they entered the temple of the LORD, according to the regulations prescribed for them by their
forefather Aaron, as the LORD, the God of Israel,
had commanded him.

The Rest of the Levites

20 As for the rest of the descendants of Levi:[x]
from the sons of Amram: Shubael;
from the sons of Shubael: Jehdeiah.
21 As for Rehabiah,[y] from his sons:
Isshiah was the first.
22 From the Izharites: Shelomoth;
from the sons of Shelomoth: Jahath.
23 The sons of Hebron:[z] Jeriah the first,[a] Amariah the second, Jahaziel the third and Jekameam the fourth.
24 The son of Uzziel: Micah;
from the sons of Micah: Shamir.
25 The brother of Micah: Isshiah;
from the sons of Isshiah: Zechariah.
26 The sons of Merari:[a] Mahli and Mushi.
The son of Jaaziah: Beno.
27 The sons of Merari:
from Jaaziah: Beno, Shoham, Zaccur and
Ibri.
28 From Mahli: Eleazar, who had no sons.
29 From Kish: the son of Kish:
Jerahmeel.

[a] *23* Two Hebrew manuscripts and some Septuagint manuscripts (see also 1 Chron. 23:19); most Hebrew manuscripts *The sons of Jeriah:*

24:7 [s] Ezr 2:36; Ne 12:6
24:8 [t] Ezr 2:39; Ne 10:5
24:10 [u] Ne 12:4,17; Lk 1:5
24:14 [v] Jer 20:1
24:15 [w] Ne 10:20
24:20 [x] 1Ch 23:6
24:21 [y] 1Ch 23:17
24:23 [z] 1Ch 23:19
24:26 [a] 1Ch 6:19; 23:21

Aspirations after the holy [are] the only aspirations in which the soul can be assured it will never meet with disappointment.

—Maria McIntosh (1805–1878)

30 And the sons of Mushi: Mahli, Eder and Jerimoth.

These were the Levites, according to their families. 31 They also cast lots,[b] just as their brothers the descendants of Aaron did, in the presence of King David and of Zadok, Ahimelech, and the heads of families of the priests and of the Levites. The families of the oldest brother were treated the same as those of the youngest.

24:31 [b]ver 5

The Singers

25 David, together with the commanders of the army, set apart some of the sons of Asaph,[c] Heman[d] and Jeduthun[e] for the ministry of prophesying,[f] accompanied by harps, lyres and cymbals.[g] Here is the list of the men[h] who performed this service:[i]

2 From the sons of Asaph:

Zaccur, Joseph, Nethaniah and Asarelah. The sons of Asaph were under the supervision of Asaph, who prophesied under the king's supervision.

3 As for Jeduthun, from his sons:[j]

Gedaliah, Zeri, Jeshaiah, Shimei,[a] Hashabiah and Mattithiah, six in all, under the supervision of their father Jeduthun, who prophesied, using the harp[k] in thanking and praising the LORD.

4 As for Heman, from his sons:

Bukkiah, Mattaniah, Uzziel, Shubael and Jerimoth; Hananiah, Hanani, Eliathah, Giddalti and Romamti-Ezer; Joshbekashah, Mallothi, Hothir and Mahazioth. 5 All these were sons of Heman the king's seer. They were given him through the promises of God to exalt him.[b] God gave Heman fourteen sons and three daughters.

25:1 [c]1Ch 6:39 [d]1Ch 6:33 [e]1Ch 16:41, 42; Ne 11:17 [f]1Sa 10:5; 2Ki 3:15 [g]1Ch 15:16 [h]1Ch 6:31 [i]2Ch 5:12; 8:14; 34:12; 35:15; Ezr 3:10

25:3 [j]1Ch 16:41-42 [k]Ge 4:21; Ps 33:2

6 All these men were under the supervision of their fathers[l] for the music of the temple of the LORD, with cymbals, lyres and harps, for the ministry at the house of God. Asaph, Jeduthun and Heman[m] were under the supervision of the king.[n] 7 Along with their relatives—all of them trained and skilled in music for the LORD—they numbered 288. 8 Young and old alike, teacher as well as student, cast lots[o] for their duties.

25:6 [l]1Ch 15:16 [m]1Ch 15:19 [n]2Ch 23:18; 29:25

25:8 [o]1Ch 26:13

25:9 [p]1Ch 6:39

9 The first lot, which was for Asaph,[p]
fell to Joseph,
his sons and relatives,[c] 12[d]
the second to Gedaliah,
he and his relatives and sons, 12
10 the third to Zaccur,
his sons and relatives, 12

[a] 3 One Hebrew manuscript and some Septuagint manuscripts (see also verse 17); most Hebrew manuscripts do not have *Shimei.* [b] 5 Hebrew *exalt the horn* [c] 9 See Septuagint; Hebrew does not have *his sons and relatives.* [d] 9 See the total in verse 7; Hebrew does not have *twelve.*

David the Musician

1CH 25:1

David was a musician long before he became king. He used his God-given musical gifts in various ways: as a harpist (1Sa 16:18), as a singer and songwriter (Ps 101:1) and as a music administrator (1Ch 6:31). It is not surprising, therefore, that David values music as a method of worship in the house of the Lord. He appoints singers and musicians to minister at the worship services. These worship leaders use voice and dance as well as instruments, including the trumpet, harp, lyre, tambourine, flute, strings and cymbals (Ps 150).

Through the years, music has played an important role in the life of God's church. Martin Luther said, "[Music] is no invention of ours; it is the gift of God." What a privilege to worship God, using the gift of music he has given to us!

He sendeth sun, he sendeth shower,
Alike they're needful to the flower;
And joys and tears alike are sent
To give the soul fit nourishment.
As comes to me of cloud or sun,
Father! Thy will, not mine, be done.

—*Sarah Fuller Flower Adams (1805–1848)*

11 the fourth to Izri,[a]
his sons and relatives, 12
12 the fifth to Nethaniah,
his sons and relatives, 12
13 the sixth to Bukkiah,
his sons and relatives, 12
14 the seventh to Jesarelah,[b]
his sons and relatives, 12
15 the eighth to Jeshaiah,
his sons and relatives, 12
16 the ninth to Mattaniah,
his sons and relatives, 12
17 the tenth to Shimei,
his sons and relatives, 12
18 the eleventh to Azarel,[c]
his sons and relatives, 12
19 the twelfth to Hashabiah,
his sons and relatives, 12
20 the thirteenth to Shubael,
his sons and relatives, 12
21 the fourteenth to Mattithiah,
his sons and relatives, 12
22 the fifteenth to Jerimoth,
his sons and relatives, 12
23 the sixteenth to Hananiah,
his sons and relatives, 12
24 the seventeenth to Joshbekashah,
his sons and relatives, 12
25 the eighteenth to Hanani,
his sons and relatives, 12
26 the nineteenth to Mallothi,
his sons and relatives, 12
27 the twentieth to Eliathah,
his sons and relatives, 12
28 the twenty-first to Hothir,
his sons and relatives, 12
29 the twenty-second to Giddalti,
his sons and relatives, 12
30 the twenty-third to Mahazioth,
his sons and relatives, 12
31 the twenty-fourth to Romamti-Ezer, 25:31 [q]1Ch 9:33
his sons and relatives, 12[q]

The Gatekeepers

26 The divisions of the gatekeepers:[r] 26:1 [r]1Ch 9:17
From the Korahites: Meshelemiah son of
Kore, one of the sons of Asaph.
2 Meshelemiah had sons: 26:2
Zechariah[s] the firstborn, [s]1Ch 9:21
Jediael the second,
Zebadiah the third,
Jathniel the fourth,
3 Elam the fifth,
Jehohanan the sixth
and Eliehoenai the seventh.
4 Obed-Edom also had sons:
Shemaiah the firstborn,

[a] *11* A variant of *Zeri* [b] *14* A variant of *Asarelah*
[c] *18* A variant of *Uzziel*

Orpah

Playing It Safe

Her eyes filled with tears as she battled indecision. Orpah loved Naomi and Ruth. They were family to her. In fact, if all the Israelites proved to be as wise and kind as Naomi, Bethlehem would be a wonderful place to live. But with their husbands dead and no men to care for them, the three women would have no means of support. Naomi had even lost her plot of land in Israel when she moved to Moab. In Orpah's mind, Bethlehem promised only more problems.

She decided. Naomi was right; she would go back to her mother. It was the practical thing to do. She would not need to learn new ways, relate to foreign people, or learn to worship a new God. Yes, Orpah would return. That way, she would not be a burden to Naomi.

Orpah took what appeared to be the path of least resistance. She could imagine a future in her own land, the possibility of remarriage to a man of her own people. At the very least, she would be provided for and safe with her family. She returned to the familiar rather than stepping out into the unknown.

Though Orpah perhaps didn't see herself as a risk taker, in truth, she took a risk either way. Going forward meant risking her life with God; going back meant risking her life without him. Trusting her own perception and understanding gave her a feeling of more control, but she forfeited the blessings and adventure of being a daughter of the living God.

We do not know if Orpah ever learned what happened to Ruth and Naomi in Bethlehem or if she ever regretted her decision. We only know that as she stood on the road to Judah, she chose the lesser part, to her loss.

Following God presents many challenges. Admittedly, much in our lives is beyond our control. But isn't that where our greatest security lies? Relinquishing control to the God who is the master planner? Every morning we have a chance to choose again the path we will take that day. Choose God's path. Live the adventure only he can bring. Only then are we *absolutely* safe—forever.

Orpah
(neck, that is, stubbornness)
Ruth 1:1–15

Candid SNAPSHOT At this they wept again. Then Orpah kissed her mother-in-law good-by (Ruth 1:14).

Ruth

Rejecting Rejection

The Moabite Ruth was as welcome in Bethlehem as a roach raiding the pantry. Her ancestor Moab had been born out of an act of incest between Lot and his elder daughter (Ge 19:30–38). Moab's descendants had hired Balaam to curse Israel while Israel camped in Moab during the journey from Egypt to the promised land (Nu 22–24). Though Balaam could only bless and not curse, the Israelites were seduced into worshiping the gods of the Moabites, and 24,000 Israelites died in the plague that was their judgment (Nu 25:1–9). And after the Israelites settled in Canaan, Moab attacked and oppressed them. So Israelite hatred for Moabites ran deep.

Naomi, Ruth's mother-in-law, had tried to dissuade Ruth from following her, convinced that Ruth had a more promising future in Moab. But Ruth could never turn away from the love she'd found. She was not going to let go of Naomi or of Naomi's God.

Ruth was not naïve. She likely had faced the indignation of her own people when she married Mahlon, an Israelite. She was aware of the initial resentment against her in Bethlehem. But she refused to accept rejection. Instead, she placed herself in the Lord's hands as she went out to glean in the fields of any "in whose eyes I find favor" (Ru 2:2). By "chance" she chose the fields of Boaz, a relative of Naomi's late husband, by Israelite law a kinsman-redeemer and one Israelite with a heart big enough to overlook her Moabite heritage.

When Ruth decided to give her life to the God of Israel, she also decided to trust his people. And God blessed her. He placed her with trustworthy people, like Naomi and Boaz, who had her best interests at heart—and who feared God.

Ruth might have lived out her life as a victim of harsh circumstances. Instead, she focused on providing for herself and for Naomi—winning her neighbors' good opinions in the process. Even when she went to lie at Boaz's feet, as a request for marriage, she showed her willingness to follow the divine law rather than her own preferences, for Naomi's sake (Ru 3:10). Her care for Naomi culminated in her final recorded act: She counted her first son, Obed, as Naomi's, to perpetuate the family name of Elimelech, Mahlon and Kilion.

Ruth
(female companion)
Ruth 1–4
Matthew 1:5

What can we find in Ruth's character to emulate? Everything. We too can refuse to accept the rejection that the world uses to keep us from following hard after God. We have a Kinsman-Redeemer far greater than Boaz. The Lord Jesus Christ will advise, protect and provide for us for the rest of our lives. Count on it.

Candid SNAPSHOT But Ruth replied, "Don't urge me to leave you or to turn back from you. Where you go I will go, and where you stay I will stay. Your people will be my people and your God my God" (Ruth 1:16).

Jehozabad the second,
Joah the third,
Sacar the fourth,
Nethanel the fifth,
5 Ammiel the sixth,
Issachar the seventh
26:5 and Peullethai the eighth.
t2Sa 6:10; 1Ch 13:13; 16:38 (For God had blessed Obed-Edom.[t])
6 His son Shemaiah also had sons, who were
leaders in their father's family because
they were very capable men. 7 The sons of
Shemaiah: Othni, Rephael, Obed and Elzabad; his relatives Elihu and Semakiah were
also able men. 8 All these were descendants
of Obed-Edom; they and their sons and
their relatives were capable men with the
strength to do the work—descendants of
Obed-Edom, 62 in all.
9 Meshelemiah had sons and relatives, who
were able men—18 in all.
10 Hosah the Merarite had sons: Shimri the first
(although he was not the firstborn, his
26:10 father had appointed him the first),[u] 11 Hil-
uDt 21:16; 1Ch 5:1 kiah the second, Tabaliah the third and
Zechariah the fourth. The sons and rela-
tives of Hosah were 13 in all.
12 These divisions of the gatekeepers, through
26:12 v1Ch 9:22 their chief men, had duties for ministering[v] in the
temple of the LORD, just as their relatives had.
26:13 wIch 24:5, 31; 25:8 13 Lots[w] were cast for each gate, according to their
families, young and old alike.
26:14 14 The lot for the East Gate[x] fell to Shelemiah.[a]
x1Ch 9:18 Then lots were cast for his son Zechariah,[y] a wise
y1Ch 9:21 counselor, and the lot for the North Gate fell to
26:15 him. 15 The lot for the South Gate fell to Obed-
z1Ch 13:13; 2Ch 25:24 Edom,[z] and the lot for the storehouse fell to his
sons. 16 The lots for the West Gate and the
Shalleketh Gate on the upper road fell to Shuppim
and Hosah.
Guard was alongside of guard: 17 There were six
Levites a day on the east, four a day on the north,
four a day on the south and two at a time at the
storehouse. 18 As for the court to the west, there
were four at the road and two at the court itself.
19 These were the divisions of the gatekeepers
26:19 a2Ch 35:15; Ne 7:1; Eze 44:11 who were descendants of Korah and Merari.[a]

The Treasurers and Other Officials

26:20 20 Their fellow Levites[b] were[b] in charge of the
b2Ch 24:5 treasuries of the house of God and the treasuries
c1Ch 28:12 for the dedicated things.[c]
21 The descendants of Ladan, who were Gershonites through Ladan and who were heads of
26:21 families belonging to Ladan the Gershonite,[d] were
d1Ch 23:7; 29:8 Jehieli, 22 the sons of Jehieli, Zetham and his
brother Joel. They were in charge of the treasur-
26:22 e1Ch 9:26 ies[e] of the temple of the LORD.

[a] *14* A variant of *Meshelemiah* [b] *20* Septuagint; Hebrew *As for the Levites, Ahijah was*

The Firstborn

1CH 26:10

After the Israelites left Egypt, God told Moses that parents must dedicate their firstborn sons to the Lord in memory of the death of Egypt's firstborn sons and the safekeeping of Israel's firstborn sons (Ex 13:11–16). A firstborn son enjoyed unique privileges and responsibilities, inherited a double portion of his father's estate and became the family's leader after his father died.

We are not told why Hosah appoints the firstborn inheritance rights to Shimri, a younger son. However, we know that a firstborn could sell his inheritance rights, as Esau did (Ge 25:29–34), or could be forced to forfeit his rights because of wrongdoing, as in the case of Reuben (Ge 35:22; 1Ch 5:1).

Jesus Christ came as the firstborn son of Mary (Lk 2:7), the firstborn son of God (Heb 1:6), the firstborn son over creation (Col 1:15) and the firstborn from among the dead (Col 1:18). As children redeemed by Christ's death and resurrection, we now have privileged status as firstborn children of God, the glorious "church of the firstborn" (Heb 12:23).

A Theocracy

1CH 26:26–28

The Israel of the Old Testament is a theocracy—God rules through his chosen leaders. Secular and spiritual things are intertwined, and there is no separation of church and state.

When Israel goes to war and wins, the soldiers bring back anything of value and add it to the nation's temple treasuries. The Levites manage these "treasuries for the dedicated things" (1Ch 26:20). The valuable items are dedicated to God, and the people expect this precious property to be used only for God's purposes.

God protects the Israelites and repeatedly gives them victory over their enemies. All that they acquire is the result of God's provision and mercy, and they count it a privilege to honor God with their abundance.

23 From the Amramites, the Izharites, the
Hebronites and the Uzzielites:[f] 26:23 [f]Nu 3:27

24 Shubael,[g] a descendant of Gershom son of 26:24 [g]1Ch 23:16
Moses, was the officer in charge of the trea-
suries. 25 His relatives through Eliezer:
Rehabiah his son, Jeshaiah his son, Joram
his son, Zicri his son and Shelomith[h] his 26:25 [h]1Ch 23:18
son. 26 Shelomith and his relatives were in
charge of all the treasuries for the things
dedicated[i] by King David, by the heads of 26:26 [i]2Sa 8:11
families who were the commanders of
thousands and commanders of hundreds,
and by the other army commanders.
27 Some of the plunder taken in battle they
dedicated for the repair of the temple of the
LORD. 28 And everything dedicated by Sam-
uel the seer[j] and by Saul son of Kish, 26:28 [j]1Sa 9:9
Abner son of Ner and Joab son of Zeruiah,
and all the other dedicated things were in
the care of Shelomith and his relatives.

29 From the Izharites: Kenaniah and his sons
were assigned duties away from the tem-
ple, as officials and judges[k] over Israel. 26:29 [k]Dt 17:8-13; 1Ch 23:4; Ne 11:16

30 From the Hebronites: Hashabiah[l] and his relatives—seventeen hundred able men—were
responsible in Israel west of the Jordan for 26:30 [l]1Ch 27:17
all the work of the LORD and for the king's
service. 31 As for the Hebronites,[m] Jeriah was 26:31 [m]1Ch 23:19
their chief according to the genealogical [n]2Sa 5:4
records of their families. In the fortieth[n] year
of David's reign a search was made in the
records, and capable men among the
Hebronites were found at Jazer in Gilead.
32 Jeriah had twenty-seven hundred relatives,
who were able men and heads of families,
and King David put them in charge of the
Reubenites, the Gadites and the half-tribe of
Manasseh for every matter pertaining to
God and for the affairs of the king.

Army Divisions

27 This is the list of the Israelites—heads of
families, commanders of thousands and
commanders of hundreds, and their officers, who
served the king in all that concerned the army
divisions that were on duty month by month
throughout the year. Each division consisted of
24,000 men.

2 In charge of the first division, for the first 27:2 [o]2Sa 23:8; 1Ch 11:11
month, was Jashobeam[o] son of Zabdiel.
There were 24,000 men in his division. 3 He
was a descendant of Perez and chief of all the
army officers for the first month.

4 In charge of the division for the second month
was Dodai[p] the Ahohite; Mikloth was the 27:4 [p]2Sa 23:9
leader of his division. There were 24,000 men
in his division.

5 The third army commander, for the third 27:5
month, was Benaiah[q] son of Jehoiada the [q]2Sa 23:20

priest. He was chief and there were 24,000
men in his division. 6 This was the Benaiah
who was a mighty man among the Thirty
and was over the Thirty. His son Ammizabad
was in charge of his division.
7 The fourth, for the fourth month, was Asahel[r]
the brother of Joab; his son Zebadiah was his
successor. There were 24,000 men in his
division.
8 The fifth, for the fifth month, was the commander Shamhuth[s] the Izrahite. There were
24,000 men in his division.
9 The sixth, for the sixth month, was Ira[t] the son
of Ikkesh the Tekoite. There were 24,000 men
in his division.
10 The seventh, for the seventh month, was Helez[u]
the Pelonite, an Ephraimite. There were
24,000 men in his division.
11 The eighth, for the eighth month, was Sibbecai[v]
the Hushathite, a Zerahite. There were 24,000
men in his division.
12 The ninth, for the ninth month, was Abiezer[w]
the Anathothite, a Benjamite. There were
24,000 men in his division.
13 The tenth, for the tenth month, was Maharai[x]
the Netophathite, a Zerahite. There were
24,000 men in his division.
14 The eleventh, for the eleventh month, was
Benaiah[y] the Pirathonite, an Ephraimite.
There were 24,000 men in his division.
15 The twelfth, for the twelfth month, was Heldai[z]
the Netophathite, from the family of Othniel.[a] There were 24,000 men in his division.

Officers of the Tribes

16 The officers over the tribes of Israel:

over the Reubenites: Eliezer son of Zicri;
over the Simeonites: Shephatiah son of Maacah;
17 over Levi: Hashabiah[b] son of Kemuel;
over Aaron: Zadok;[c]
18 over Judah: Elihu, a brother of David;
over Issachar: Omri son of Michael;
19 over Zebulun: Ishmaiah son of Obadiah;
over Naphtali: Jerimoth son of Azriel;
20 over the Ephraimites: Hoshea son of Azaziah;
over half the tribe of Manasseh: Joel son of Pedaiah;
21 over the half-tribe of Manasseh in Gilead: Iddo son of Zechariah;
over Benjamin: Jaasiel son of Abner;
22 over Dan: Azarel son of Jeroham.

These were the officers over the tribes of Israel.

23 David did not take the number of the men
twenty years old or less,[d] because the LORD had
promised to make Israel as numerous as the stars[e]
in the sky. 24 Joab son of Zeruiah began to count
the men but did not finish. Wrath came on Israel
on account of this numbering,[f] and the number

27:7 [r]2Sa 2:18; 1Ch 11:26
27:8 [s]1Ch 11:27
27:9 [t]2Sa 23:26; 1Ch 11:28
27:10 [u]2Sa 23:26; 1Ch 11:27
27:11 [v]2Sa 21:18
27:12 [w]2Sa 23:27; 1Ch 11:28
27:13 [x]2Sa 23:28; 1Ch 11:30
27:14 [y]1Ch 11:31
27:15 [z]2Sa 23:29 [a]Jos 15:17
27:17 [b]1Ch 26:30 [c]2Sa 8:17; 1Ch 12:28
27:23 [d]1Ch 21:2-5 [e]Ge 15:5
27:24 [f]2Sa 24:15; 1Ch 21:7

Counting the Men

1CH 27:23–24

It is difficult to understand David's stubborn determination to count his troops and God's vehement response. Previously, God had commanded census taking (Nu 1:1–3). So why is it now considered a sinful thing? These verses help dispel the confusion.

David numbers only the fighting men (those 21 years old and older). He does not take a total census but insists on counting only his soldiers, which indicates that perhaps David's victories have caused him to trust in his army's strength rather than in the power of God. Afterward, David realizes his sinful thinking and repents. One of his compositions reveals his genuine belief: "Some trust in chariots and some in horses, but we trust in the name of the LORD our God" (Ps 20:7).

We may not have men to count or horses and chariots to depend on, but, like David, we all have times when we trust in ourselves rather than in God's power. David's actions and his repentant response can be a valuable lesson to all of us.

God's Footstool

1CH 28:2

When the tomb of Egypt's Tutankhamen (King Tut) was unearthed, archaeologists discovered among his many treasures a footstool carved with pictures of his enemies. Since ancient times, the footstool has represented power or dominion. In Isaiah 66:1 and Matthew 5:34–35, the earth is described as God's footstool. In Psalm 110:1 and several New Testament verses, the Messiah's enemies become his footstool (see the note on Ps 99:5, page 962).

David explains to Solomon and the people that his heart's desire has been to build a special house for the ark of the covenant, which he calls "the footstool of our God" (1Ch 28:2). David is perhaps referring to the mercy seat of the ark, the slab of pure gold that covers the ark.

Regardless of interpretation, the message of this image remains the same: God is the sovereign authority, worthy to be praised and honored. We are his creation, his children, his subjects, and we willingly worship at his footstool (Ps 99:5).

was not entered in the book[a] of the annals of King
David.

The King's Overseers

25 Azmaveth son of Adiel was in charge of the
royal storehouses.
Jonathan son of Uzziah was in charge of the
storehouses in the outlying districts, in the towns,
the villages and the watchtowers.
26 Ezri son of Kelub was in charge of the field
workers who farmed the land.
27 Shimei the Ramathite was in charge of the
vineyards.
Zabdi the Shiphmite was in charge of the produce of the vineyards for the wine vats.
28 Baal-Hanan the Gederite was in charge of the **27:28**
olive and sycamore-fig[g] trees in the western [g]1Ki 10:27;
foothills. 2Ch 1:15
Joash was in charge of the supplies of olive oil.
29 Shitrai the Sharonite was in charge of the
herds grazing in Sharon.
Shaphat son of Adlai was in charge of the herds
in the valleys.
30 Obil the Ishmaelite was in charge of the
camels.
Jehdeiah the Meronothite was in charge of the
donkeys.
31 Jaziz the Hagrite[h] was in charge of the flocks. **27:31** [h]1Ch 5:10
All these were the officials in charge of King
David's property.

32 Jonathan, David's uncle, was a counselor, a
man of insight and a scribe. Jehiel son of Hacmo-
ni took care of the king's sons.
33 Ahithophel[i] was the king's counselor. **27:33** [i]2Sa 15:12
Hushai[j] the Arkite was the king's friend. [j]2Sa 15:37
34 Ahithophel was succeeded by Jehoiada son of
Benaiah and by Abiathar.[k] **27:34** [k]1Ki 1:7
Joab[l] was the commander of the royal army. [l]1Ch 11:6

David's Plans for the Temple

28 David summoned all the officials[m] of Israel **28:1** [m]1Ch 11:10;
to assemble at Jerusalem: the officers over 27:1-31
the tribes, the commanders of the divisions in the
service of the king, the commanders of thousands
and commanders of hundreds, and the officials in
charge of all the property and livestock belonging
to the king and his sons, together with the palace
officials, the mighty men and all the brave
warriors.
2 King David rose to his feet and said: "Listen to **28:2** [n]1Ch 17:2
me, my brothers and my people. I had it in my [o]Ps 99:5;
heart[n] to build a house as a place of rest for the 132:7
ark of the covenant of the LORD, for the footstool[o] **28:3**
of our God, and I made plans to build it. 3 But God [p]2Sa 7:5
said to me,[p] 'You are not to build a house for my [q]1Ch 22:8
Name,[q] because you are a warrior and have shed [r]1Ki 5:3; 1Ch 17:4
blood.'[r] **28:4**
4 "Yet the LORD, the God of Israel, chose me[s] from [s]1Ch 17:23, 27; 2Ch 6:6

[a] *24* Septuagint; Hebrew *number*

28:4 [t]1Sa 16:1-13 my whole family[t] to be king over Israel forever. He
[u]Ge 49:10; chose Judah[u] as leader, and from the house of
1Ch 5:2 Judah he chose my family, and from my father's
sons he was pleased to make me king over all Israel. 5Of all my sons—and the LORD has given me
28:5 many[v]—he has chosen my son Solomon[w] to sit on
[v]1Ch 3:1 [w]1Ch 22:9; the throne of the kingdom of the LORD over Israel.
23:1 6He said to me: 'Solomon your son is the one who
will build my house and my courts, for I have cho-
28:6 [x]2Sa 7:13; sen him to be my son,[x] and I will be his father. 7I
1Ch 22:9-10 will establish his kingdom forever if he is
28:7 unswerving in carrying out my commands and
[y]1Ch 22:13 laws,[y] as is being done at this time.'
8"So now I charge you in the sight of all Israel
and of the assembly of the LORD, and in the hearing of our God: Be careful to follow all the com-
28:8 [z]Dt 6:1 mands[z] of the LORD your God, that you may pos-
[a]Dt 4:1 sess this good land and pass it on as an
inheritance to your descendants forever.[a]
9"And you, my son Solomon, acknowledge the
God of your father, and serve him with whole-
28:9 [b]1Ch 29:19 hearted devotion[b] and with a willing mind, for the
[c]1Sa 16:7; LORD searches every heart[c] and understands every
Ps 7:9 motive behind the thoughts. If you seek him,[d] he
[d]Ps 40:16; Jer 29:13 will be found by you; but if you forsake[e] him, he
[e]Jos 24:20; 2Ch 15:2 will reject[f] you forever. 10Consider now, for the
[f]Ps 44:23 LORD has chosen you to build a temple as a sanctuary. Be strong and do the work."
28:11 11Then David gave his son Solomon the plans[g]
[g]Ex 25:9 for the portico of the temple, its buildings, its storerooms, its upper parts, its inner rooms and the
place of atonement. 12He gave him the plans of all
28:12 [h]1Ch 12:18 that the Spirit[h] had put in his mind for the courts
[i]1Ch 26:20 of the temple of the LORD and all the surrounding
rooms, for the treasuries of the temple of God and
for the treasuries for the dedicated things.[i] 13He
28:13 gave him instructions for the divisions[j] of the
[j]1Ch 24:1 priests and Levites, and for all the work of serving
in the temple of the LORD, as well as for all the articles to be used in its service. 14He designated the
weight of gold for all the gold articles to be used in
various kinds of service, and the weight of silver
for all the silver articles to be used in various kinds
of service: 15the weight of gold for the gold lamp-
28:15 [k]Ex 25:31 stands[k] and their lamps, with the weight for each
lampstand and its lamps; and the weight of silver
for each silver lampstand and its lamps, according
to the use of each lampstand; 16the weight of gold
28:16 [l]Ex 25:23 for each table[l] for consecrated bread; the weight of
silver for the silver tables; 17the weight of pure gold
28:17 for the forks, sprinkling bowls[m] and pitchers; the
[m]Ex 27:3 weight of gold for each gold dish; the weight of sil-
28:18 ver for each silver dish; 18and the weight of the
[n]Ex 30:1-10 refined gold for the altar of incense.[n] He also gave
[o]Ex 25:18-22 [p]Ex 25:20 him the plan for the chariot,[o] that is, the cherubim
of gold that spread their wings and shelter[p] the ark
of the covenant of the LORD.
19"All this," David said, "I have in writing from
28:19 the hand of the LORD upon me, and he gave me
[q]1Ki 6:38 [r]Ex 25:9 understanding in all the details[q] of the plan.[r]"
20David also said to Solomon his son, "Be strong

God's Plans

1CH 28:11-12,19

David has a dream: to build a magnificent house for his Lord. Since his objective is to honor God, David believes he can go forward with his plans. But David and the prophet Nathan discover that God has a different idea: David's son Solomon will see the dream to fruition (see the note on 1Ch 17:1-4, page 656).

David accepts this change of plans. He does not want his vision, *however noble, to mean more to him than God himself. David tells Solomon and the people that God's own hand wrote the plans he is sharing with them (1Ch 28:19). Perhaps God actually "inscribed" his directives as he "inscribed" the commandments for Moses (Ex 31:18). Or perhaps the Spirit simply inspired David's mind with a plan for the temple. Either way, God does not leave the temple details to human imagination alone. God's Spirit controls the process, and the results honor him.*

Be Strong and Courageous

1CH 28:20-21

King David is probably weak and old by this time, but he *stands up* (1Ch 28:2) to deliver this important message to his young son Solomon and the Israelite people. The aging king gives the incoming ruler specific instructions about the temple building project and then assures him that the plans are from God.

"I know you have an enormous task ahead of you," says David. "Don't be intimidated by the magnitude of this job. I know, without a doubt, that my God, who is your God also, will be with you through every phase of the project. Work hard. Walk straight through your fear with your head up. God will not fail you. He will never walk away. He has promised, and he will not retract his pledge. Trust him when you are tired. Trust him when there is opposition. Trust him when something threatens to go wrong. He will see the project through to completion. He is in control."

and courageous,[s] and do the work. Do not be
afraid or discouraged, for the LORD God, my God, is
with you. He will not fail you or forsake[t] you until
all the work for the service of the temple of the
LORD is finished.[u] 21The divisions of the priests and
Levites are ready for all the work on the temple of
God, and every willing man skilled[v] in any craft
will help you in all the work. The officials and all
the people will obey your every command."

Gifts for Building the Temple

29 Then King David said to the whole assembly: "My son Solomon, the one whom God
has chosen, is young and inexperienced.[w] The task
is great, because this palatial structure is not for
man but for the LORD God. 2With all my resources
I have provided for the temple of my God—gold[x]
for the gold work, silver for the silver, bronze for
the bronze, iron for the iron and wood for the
wood, as well as onyx for the settings, turquoise,[a][y]
stones of various colors, and all kinds of fine stone
and marble—all of these in large quantities.[z]
3Besides, in my devotion to the temple of my God
I now give my personal treasures of gold and silver
for the temple of my God, over and above everything I have provided[a] for this holy temple: 4three
thousand talents[b] of gold (gold of Ophir)[b] and sev-
en thousand talents[c] of refined silver,[c] for the over-
laying of the walls of the buildings, 5for the gold
work and the silver work, and for all the work to
be done by the craftsmen. Now, who is willing to
consecrate himself today to the LORD?"

6Then the leaders of families, the officers of the
tribes of Israel, the commanders of thousands and
commanders of hundreds, and the officials[d] in
charge of the king's work gave willingly.[e] 7They[f]
gave toward the work on the temple of God five
thousand talents[d] and ten thousand darics[e] of gold,
ten thousand talents[f] of silver, eighteen thousand
talents[g] of bronze and a hundred thousand talents[h]
of iron. 8Any who had precious stones[g] gave them
to the treasury of the temple of the LORD in the custody of Jehiel the Gershonite.[h] 9The people rejoiced
at the willing response of their leaders, for they
had given freely and wholeheartedly[i] to the LORD.
David the king also rejoiced greatly.

David's Prayer

10David praised the LORD in the presence of the
whole assembly, saying,

"Praise be to you, O LORD,
God of our father Israel,
from everlasting to everlasting.

28:20 [s]Dt 31:6; 1Ch 22:13; 2Ch 19:11; Hag 2:4 [t]Dt 4:31; Jos 24:20 [u]1Ki 6:14; 2Ch 7:11
28:21 [v]Ex 35:25-36:5
29:1 [w]1Ki 3:7; 1Ch 22:5; 2Ch 13:7
29:2 [x]ver 7,14, 16; Ezr 1:4; 6:5; Hag 2:8 [y]Isa 54:11 [z]1Ch 22:2-5
29:3 [a]2Ch 24:10; 31:3; 35:8
29:4 [b]Ge 10:29 [c]1Ch 22:14
29:6 [d]1Ch 27:1; 28:1 [e]ver 9; Ex 25:1-8; 35:20-29; 36:2; 2Ch 24:10; Ezr 7:15
29:7 [f]Ex 25:2; Ne 7:70-71
29:8 [g]Ex 35:27 [h]1Ch 26:21
29:9 [i]1Ki 8:61; 2Co 9:7

[a] *2* The meaning of the Hebrew for this word is uncertain. [b] *4* That is, about 110 tons (about 100 metric tons) [c] *4* That is, about 260 tons (about 240 metric tons) [d] *7* That is, about 190 tons (about 170 metric tons) [e] *7* That is, about 185 pounds (about 84 kilograms) [f] *7* That is, about 375 tons (about 345 metric tons) [g] *7* That is, about 675 tons (about 610 metric tons) [h] *7* That is, about 3,750 tons (about 3,450 metric tons)

29:11 [j]Ps 24:8; 59:17; 62:11 [k]Ps 89:11 [l]Rev 5:12-13

11 Yours, O LORD, is the greatness and the
power[j]
and the glory and the majesty and the
splendor,
for everything in heaven and earth is
yours.[k]
Yours, O LORD, is the kingdom;
you are exalted as head over all.[l]

29:12 [m]2Ch 1:12 [n]2Ch 20:6; Ro 11:36

12 Wealth and honor[m] come from you;
you are the ruler[n] of all things.
In your hands are strength and power
to exalt and give strength to all.
13 Now, our God, we give you thanks,
and praise your glorious name.

14 "But who am I, and who are my people, that
we should be able to give as generously as this?
Everything comes from you, and we have given
you only what comes from your hand. 15 We are

29:15 [o]Ps 39:12; Heb 11:13 [p]Job 14:2

aliens and strangers[o] in your sight, as were all our
forefathers. Our days on earth are like a shadow,[p]
without hope. 16 O LORD our God, as for all this
abundance that we have provided for building
you a temple for your Holy Name, it comes from
your hand, and all of it belongs to you. 17 I know,

29:17 [q]Ps 139:23; Pr 15:11; 17:3; Jer 11:20; 17:10 [r]1Ch 28:9; Ps 15:1-5

my God, that you test the heart[q] and are pleased
with integrity. All these things have I given willingly and with honest intent. And now I have
seen with joy how willingly your people who are
here have given to you.[r] 18 O LORD, God of our
fathers Abraham, Isaac and Israel, keep this desire
in the hearts of your people forever, and keep their
hearts loyal to you. 19 And give my son Solomon

29:19 [s]1Ch 28:9 [t]Ps 72:1 [u]1Ch 22:14

the wholehearted devotion[s] to keep your commands, requirements and decrees[t] and to do
everything to build the palatial structure for
which I have provided."[u]

20 Then David said to the whole assembly,
"Praise the LORD your God." So they all praised the
LORD, the God of their fathers; they bowed low
and fell prostrate before the LORD and the king.

Solomon Acknowledged as King

21 The next day they made sacrifices to the LORD

29:21 [v]1Ki 8:62

and presented burnt offerings to him:[v] a thousand
bulls, a thousand rams and a thousand male
lambs, together with their drink offerings, and
other sacrifices in abundance for all Israel. 22 They

29:22 [w]1Ch 23:1 [x]1Ki 1:33-39

ate and drank with great joy[w] in the presence of
the LORD that day.

Then they acknowledged Solomon son of David
as king a second time, anointing him before the
LORD to be ruler and Zadok[x] to be priest. 23 So

29:23 [y]1Ki 2:12

Solomon sat on the throne[y] of the LORD as king in
place of his father David. He prospered and all
Israel obeyed him. 24 All the officers and mighty
men, as well as all of King David's sons, pledged
their submission to King Solomon.

29:25 [z]2Ch 1:1,12 [a]1Ki 3:13; Ecc 2:9

25 The LORD highly exalted Solomon in the sight
of all Israel and bestowed on him royal splendor[z]
such as no king over Israel ever had before.[a]

Godly Qualities

1CH 29:17

By this time in his life, David recognizes the attitudes and behavior that please his Lord. In his prayer he mentions some of these godly character qualities: integrity, honesty, generosity, joyfulness and teachability. Through the years David has become more familiar with the way God examines and grows us.

When God "tests" a heart, it is not to shame or manipulate, but to liberate and empower. God wants to coach us into becoming the generous, teachable, honest and joyful people he designed us to be. He is delighted when we live intentionally, choosing to cultivate a willing and happy attitude and behavior that demonstrates integrity and truthfulness.

Friends, family or associates may not take the time to understand us—our vision, passion, spiritual desires or motives. But God examines our hearts, and he knows the real you and the real me. And even more remarkable, he loves us.

Week 10

Praise to the King!

King David's life is drawing to a close. He has received the plans for the temple from the Spirit of God (1Ch 28:12) and has provided materials for building it (1Ch 29:2–3). Now he asks the leaders of Israel to step forward with their own gifts of consecration—total dedication— to God. David is moved by the generosity of Israel's leaders to offer this beautiful prayer of praise. David proclaims God's worthiness to receive all that they have—everything in heaven and earth—because all belongs to God.

Have you begun to discover the worthiness of God? Has your heart ever simply overflowed with praise? Genuine praise includes both your heart and your mind; it wells up from within until your spirit bursts with exclamations of God's greatness and worth.

What truths about God (for example, God is eternal, 1Ch 29:10) are found in David's prayer of praise? *Praise acknowledges God's greatness.*

What produces praise (Lk 10:21; Jas 5:13)? *Praise flows naturally out of your joy and gratitude to God for all he is and all he does.*

What benefits do you receive when you praise God (2Ch 5:13–14; Ps 16:11; 63:4–5)? *Praise brings God close and satisfies the soul.*

Why is it important to praise God when you're in the middle of a spiritual battle (2Ch 20:1–23; Ps 8:2; 18:3; 144:1–2)?

What are some ways to praise God (1Ch 29:20; Ezr 3:11; Ps 69:30; 150)?

Who should praise God (Ps 66:1–4; 103:20–21; 145:21)?

A heart full of love for God cannot keep quiet. But, whether in anguish or in praise, the heart needs to express its passion (Ps 39:2–3). God is worthy of all praise. Jesus said that if his disciples kept quiet, "the stones [would] cry out" (Lk 19:40).

Enjoying God THROUGH the Word

Read Psalm 103:1–5 (page 965). If you have a difficult time getting into the spirit of praise, you may have simply forgotten what God has done for you. God has forgiven your sins, healed your diseases, redeemed your life from the pit, crowned you with love and compassion, satisfied your desires with good things and renewed your life. Don't just pass over these items as mere words. These are the great and mighty deeds God has done for *you!* Praise pleases God (Ps 69:30–31) and brings you into his presence. Praise him!

Enjoying God THROUGH Experience

Find a Scripture of praise (such as 2 Samuel 22; Job 26; Psalm 148). Use it as a prayer of praise to God. Don't just read the words—allow the majesty and wonder of who God is and of what he has done to permeate your heart. Continue praying in your own words, giving glory and honor to God. Sing a song—one you know or one that the Holy Spirit puts in your heart for this occasion. If you are willing to step out of your comfort zone, you may wish to dance or bow with your face to the floor, showing God your adoration through the posture of your body.

Abandon yourself to giving God the praise due him. He alone, he *alone,* is worthy (Rev 5:12).

Go to page 726 for your next weekly study.

The Death of David

29:26 26 David son of Jesse was king[b] over all Israel.
b1Ch 18:14 27 He ruled over Israel forty years—seven in
29:27 Hebron and thirty-three in Jerusalem.[c] 28 He died[d]
c2Sa 5:4-5; at a good old age, having enjoyed long life, wealth
1Ki 2:11; and honor. His son Solomon succeeded him as
1Ch 3:4 king.[e]
29:28 29 As for the events of King David's reign, from
dGe 15:15; Ac 13:36 beginning to end, they are written in the records
e1Ch 23:1 of Samuel the seer,[f] the records of Nathan[g] the
29:29 prophet and the records of Gad[h] the seer, 30 togeth-
f1Sa 9:9 er with the details of his reign and power, and the
g2Sa 7:2 circumstances that surrounded him and Israel and
h1Sa 22:5 the kingdoms of all the other lands.

Flawed but Respected

1CH 29:28

David lived a full and satisfying life. He was a shepherd, a singer, a soldier, a songwriter, a friend, a father, a husband and a man of God. As king of all Israel, he commanded armies to victory and managed well the nation's political and religious matters. Other countries' leaders respected him. The people under his rule honored him. Through the years David's wealth increased, and he willingly gave it back to the Lord (1Ch 29:17).

Yet, during his lifetime David made some major mistakes. His sinful choices brought others pain and even death. David was a faulty human being, like every other person who has ever walked the face of the earth. But the beautiful thing about David is that, in spite of his imperfection, his heart was right, and God is pleased (Ac 13:22). From the lineage of this faithful earthly king comes "the Son of the Most High . . . His kingdom will never end" (Lk 1:32–33).

2 Chronicles

A nation that honors God will be successful.

The book of 2 Chronicles emphasizes for the returning Jewish exiles the blessings of following God. This continuation of the history of Israel from King Solomon to the exile gives little coverage to her wicked kings, while describing in great detail the lives of those kings who sought to do things God's way. With such a focus, 2 Chronicles warns the people against disobedience to God and reminds them that the nation that honors God will experience success.

We can find faithful followers of God in this lengthy account of a nation's downward slide into corruption, idolatry and compromise. Solomon's wise start ends in foolish disobedience (2Ch 1–9). Yet the Queen of Sheba praises God because of his rich blessing on Solomon's kingdom (2Ch 9:1-12). Queen Athaliah's idolatry holds the nation under the influence of Baal (2Ch 22:10—23:21). Yet Jehosheba places her life on the line for six years to hide from this wicked queen the rightful heir to the throne (2Ch 22:10-12). Years of idolatrous practices harden the people to God's ways, but the prophetess Huldah bravely speaks God's words of commendation and warning (2Ch 34:22-28).

While the influence for good is present in Israel, the choice to disobey God ultimately wins out. After years of political turmoil, beloved Jerusalem falls, the temple is destroyed and the people find themselves in exile. But 2 Chronicles doesn't end on that discouraging note. The last words of the book are a reminder of Jeremiah's prophecy of restoration and a decree from King Cyrus of Persia that any of the exiles who wish to return to Jerusalem may do so (2Ch 36:23).

Quick Study

Author
Jewish tradition puts Ezra as the author, although this is not certain.

Date Written
Around 450 B.C.

Setting
Israel and Judah (after the kingdom is divided).

Key Passage
2 Chronicles 7:14 "If my people, who are called by my name, will humble themselves and pray and seek my face and turn from their wicked ways, then will I hear from heaven and will forgive their sin and will heal their land."

Outline

Solomon's request.
2Ch 1

Building the temple.
2Ch 2:1–6:11

Dedicating the temple.
2Ch 6:12–7:10

The Lord appears to Solomon.
2Ch7:11-22

Solomon's accomplishments.
2Ch 8

The queen of Sheba visits Solomon.
2Ch 9:1-12

Solomon's splendor.
2Ch 9:13-28

Solomon's death.
2Ch 9:29-31

The kingdom divided.
2Ch 10-12

King Abijah.
2Ch 13:1–14:1

King Asa.
2Ch 14:2–16:14

Kings Jehoshaphat and Ahab.
2Ch 17:1–21:3

King Jehoram.
2Ch 21:4-20

Kings Ahaziah and Joash.
2Ch 22-24

King Amaziah.
2Ch 25

King Uzziah.
2Ch 26

King Jotham and Ahaz.
2Ch 27-28

King Hezekiah.
2Ch 29-32

Kings Manasseh and Amon.
2Ch 33

King Josiah.
2Ch 34:1–36:1

Kings Jehoahaz and Jehoiakim.
2Ch 36:2-8

Kings Jehoiachin and Zedekiah.
2Ch 36:9-14

Jerusalem falls.
2Ch 36:15-23

The Women of 2 Chronicles

	Huram's mother	*Originally from Dan.* 2Ch 2:13-14
⚘	**Queen of Sheba**	*Amazed by Solomon.* 2Ch 9:1-12 (page 1075)
	Abihail	*Jesse's granddaughter.* 2Ch 11:18
	Mahalath	*Rehoboam's wife.* 2Ch 11:18
	Maacah	*Rehoboam's best-loved wife.* 2Ch 11:20-22; 13:2; 15:16
	Naamah	*Rehoboam's mother.* 2Ch 12:13
	Azubah	*Jehoshaphat's mother.* 2Ch 20:31
⚘	**Athaliah**	*Killed her own sons and grandsons.* 2Ch 22:10-12; 23:12-21; 24:7 (page 1277)
⚘	**Jehosheba**	*Saved the prince.* 2Ch 22:11-12 (page 1278)
	Zibiah	*Mother of young king Joash.* 2Ch 24:1
	Shimeath, Shimrith	*Mothers of Joash's assassins.* 2Ch 24:26
	Jehoaddin	*Amaziah's mother.* 2Ch 25:1
	Jecoliah	*Uzziah's mother.* 2Ch 26:3
	Jerusha	*Jotham's mother.* 2Ch 27:1
	Abijah	*Hezekiah's mother.* 2Ch 29:1
	Huldah	*Brave prophetess.* 2Ch 34:22-28

⚘ Denotes a sketch written about this character

Solomon Asks for Wisdom

1 Solomon son of David established[a] himself
firmly over his kingdom, for the LORD his God
was with[b] him and made him exceedingly great.[c]
2Then Solomon spoke to all Israel[d]—to the commanders of thousands and commanders of hundreds, to the judges and to all the leaders in Israel,
the heads of families— 3and Solomon and the
whole assembly went to the high place at Gibeon,
for God's Tent of Meeting[e] was there, which Moses[f]
the LORD's servant had made in the desert. 4Now
David had brought up the ark[g] of God from Kiriath
Jearim to the place he had prepared for it, because
he had pitched a tent[h] for it in Jerusalem. 5But the
bronze altar[i] that Bezalel[j] son of Uri, the son of
Hur, had made was in Gibeon in front of the tabernacle of the LORD; so Solomon and the assembly
inquired[k] of him there. 6Solomon went up to the
bronze altar before the LORD in the Tent of Meeting
and offered a thousand burnt offerings on it.
7That night God appeared[l] to Solomon and said
to him, "Ask for whatever you want me to give
you."
8Solomon answered God, "You have shown great
kindness to David my father and have made me[m]
king in his place. 9Now, LORD God, let your promise[n] to my father David be confirmed, for you have
made me king over a people who are as numerous
as the dust of the earth.[o] 10Give me wisdom and
knowledge, that I may lead[p] this people, for who is
able to govern this great people of yours?"
11God said to Solomon, "Since this is your
heart's desire and you have not asked for wealth,[q]
riches or honor, nor for the death of your enemies,
and since you have not asked for a long life but
for wisdom and knowledge to govern my people
over whom I have made you king, 12therefore wisdom and knowledge will be given you. And I will
also give you wealth, riches and honor,[r] such as
no king who was before you ever had and none
after you will have.[s]"
13Then Solomon went to Jerusalem from the
high place at Gibeon, from before the Tent of
Meeting. And he reigned over Israel.
14Solomon accumulated chariots[t] and horses; he
had fourteen hundred chariots and twelve thousand horses,[a] which he kept in the chariot cities
and also with him in Jerusalem. 15The king made
silver and gold[u] as common in Jerusalem as
stones, and cedar as plentiful as sycamore-fig trees
in the foothills. 16Solomon's horses were imported
from Egypt[b] and from Kue[c]—the royal merchants
purchased them from Kue. 17They imported a
chariot[v] from Egypt for six hundred shekels[d] of
silver, and a horse for a hundred and fifty.[e] They

1:1 [a]1Ki 2:12,26; 2Ch 12:1 [b]Ge 21:22; 39:2; Nu 14:43 [c]1Ch 29:25
1:2 [d]1Ch 9:1; 28:1
1:3 [e]Ex 36:8 [f]Ex 40:18
1:4 [g]2Sa 6:2; 1Ch 15:25 [h]2Sa 6:17; 1Ch 15:1
1:5 [i]Ex 38:2 [j]Ex 31:2 [k]1Ch 13:3
1:7 [l]2Ch 7:12
1:8 [m]1Ch 23:1; 28:5
1:9 [n]2Sa 7:25; 1Ki 8:25 [o]Ge 12:2
1:10 [p]Nu 27:17; 2Sa 5:2; Pr 8:15-16
1:11 [q]Dt 17:17
1:12 [r]1Ch 29:12 [s]1Ch 29:25; 2Ch 9:22; Ne 13:26
1:14 [t]1Sa 8:11; 1Ki 4:26; 9:19
1:15 [u]1Ki 9:28; Isa 60:5
1:17 [v]SS 1:9

Saint Augustine says that our souls will never find their rest until they find it in God. *He* is the treasure. Our longings will point the way to him every single time. Each longing in my life that I have discovered, or that has discovered me, drives me to confront a truth that I might not have confronted otherwise: I need God. I am thirsty for God. Desperately thirsty. In every area of my life. I was made by him and for him, and apart from him, I will not be satisfied.

—Nicole Johnson

[a] 14 Or *charioteers* [b] 16 Or possibly *Muzur,* a region in Cilicia; also in verse 17 [c] 16 Probably Cilicia [d] 17 That is, about 15 pounds (about 7 kilograms) [e] 17 That is, about 3 3/4 pounds (about 1.7 kilograms)

also exported them to all the kings of the Hittites
and of the Arameans.

Preparations for Building the Temple

2:1 [w]Dt 12:5 **2** Solomon gave orders to build a temple[w] for the
[x]Ecc 2:4 Name of the LORD and a royal palace for himself.[x] 2He conscripted seventy thousand men as carriers and eighty thousand as stonecutters in the
2:2 hills and thirty-six hundred as foremen over them.[y]
[y]ver 18; 2Ch 10:4 3Solomon sent this message to Hiram[a][z] king of
2:3 Tyre:

[z]2Sa 5:11 "Send me cedar logs[a] as you did for my
[a]1Ch 14:1 father David when you sent him cedar to
build a palace to live in. 4Now I am about to
2:4 [b]ver 1; build a temple[b] for the Name of the LORD my
Dt 12:5 God and to dedicate it to him for burning fra-
[c]Ex 30:7 grant incense[c] before him, for setting out the
[d]Ex 25:30 consecrated bread[d] regularly, and for making
[e]Ex 29:42; 2Ch 13:11 burnt offerings[e] every morning and evening
[f]Nu 28:9-10 and on Sabbaths[f] and New Moons and at the
appointed feasts of the LORD our God. This is
a lasting ordinance for Israel.
5"The temple I am going to build will be
2:5 [g]1Ch 22:5; great,[g] because our God is greater than all
Ps 135:5 other gods.[h] 6But who is able to build a tem-
[h]1Ch 16:25 ple for him, since the heavens, even the high-
2:6 est heavens, cannot contain him?[i] Who then
[i]1Ki 8:27; am I[j] to build a temple for him, except as a
2Ch 6:18; Jer 23:24 place to burn sacrifices before him?
[j]Ex 3:11 7"Send me, therefore, a man skilled to
work in gold and silver, bronze and iron, and
in purple, crimson and blue yarn, and experienced in the art of engraving, to work in
2:7 Judah and Jerusalem with my skilled crafts-
[k]ver 13-14; men,[k] whom my father David provided.
Ex 35:31; 8"Send me also cedar, pine and algum[b] logs
1Ch 22:16 from Lebanon, for I know that your men are
skilled in cutting timber there. My men will
work with yours 9to provide me with plenty
of lumber, because the temple I build must
be large and magnificent. 10I will give your
servants, the woodsmen who cut the timber,
twenty thousand cors[c] of ground wheat,
twenty thousand cors of barley, twenty thou-
2:10 sand baths[d] of wine and twenty thousand
[l]Ezr 3:7 baths of olive oil.[l]"

11Hiram king of Tyre replied by letter to Solomon:

2:11 [m]1Ki 10:9; "Because the LORD loves[m] his people, he
2Ch 9:8 has made you their king."

12And Hiram added:

2:12 [n]Ne 9:6; "Praise be to the LORD, the God of Israel,
Ps 8:3; 33:6; 102:25 who made heaven and earth![n] He has given

[a] *3* Hebrew *Huram*, a variant of *Hiram*; also in verses 11 and 12 [b] *8* Probably a variant of *almug*; possibly juniper
[c] *10* That is, probably about 125,000 bushels (about 4,400 kiloliters) [d] *10* That is, probably about 115,000 gallons (about 440 kiloliters)

Too Big

2CH 2:5-6

Solomon sends a message to Hiram, the king of Tyre, informing him of his plan to build a magnificent temple for God. This new temple will take the place of the traveling tabernacle or tent where the people have worshiped since their desert journey days with Moses. The tabernacle has sheltered the ark of the covenant, the symbol of God's presence with his people (Ex 25:22). Now the temple will be the center of Israelite worship, for this will be God's house (1Ch 17:12).

But Solomon, with his God-given wisdom (2Ch 1:11–12), sees beyond this symbol, and he includes his insights in his letter to Hiram. Solomon understands the omnipresent character and sovereignty of the Lord and consequently knows God cannot be contained in a building. He recognizes that God's willingness to create a symbol of his presence here on earth is a unique and inspiring illustration of his grace and love for finite human beings.

Superior Lumber

2CH 2:16

Solomon diplomatically pursues the political relationship David started with King Hiram of Tyre (1Ki 5:11) and in so doing offers us a worthy example of wise interaction with others who may not agree with our political or spiritual ideology.

From Hiram, Solomon requests the services of a skilled craftsman and orders logs of "cedar, pine and algum" to use in building the temple (1Ch 2:8). The fragrant cedars of Lebanon are resistant to rot and superior to the lumbers available in Israel. Pine trees (perhaps cypress) provide pliable woods required in the construction. The rare algum wood (possibly from red sandalwoods) is used as paneling and for musical instruments.

Hiram makes Tyre, a city along the Great Sea (now called the Mediterranean Sea), a major seaport and himself a respected world trader. He floats the logs from Tyre down the seacoast 90 miles to Joppa and then Solomon's men transport them over the 35-mile pass to Jerusalem.

King David a wise son, endowed with intelligence and discernment, who will build a
temple for the LORD and a palace for himself.
13"I am sending you Huram-Abi,[o] a man of
great skill, 14whose mother was from Dan[p]
and whose father was from Tyre. He is
trained[q] to work in gold and silver, bronze
and iron, stone and wood, and with purple
and blue[r] and crimson yarn and fine linen.
He is experienced in all kinds of engraving
and can execute any design given to him. He
will work with your craftsmen and with
those of my lord, David your father.
15"Now let my lord send his servants the
wheat and barley and the olive oil[s] and wine
he promised, 16and we will cut all the logs
from Lebanon that you need and will float
them in rafts by sea down to Joppa.[t] You can
then take them up to Jerusalem."

17Solomon took a census of all the aliens[u] who
were in Israel, after the census[v] his father David
had taken; and they were found to be 153,600.
18He assigned[w] 70,000 of them to be carriers and
80,000 to be stonecutters in the hills, with 3,600
foremen over them to keep the people working.

Solomon Builds the Temple

3 Then Solomon began to build[x] the temple of
the LORD[y] in Jerusalem on Mount Moriah,
where the LORD had appeared to his father David.
It was on the threshing floor of Araunah[a][z] the Jebusite, the place provided by David. 2He began
building on the second day of the second month
in the fourth year of his reign.[a]
3The foundation Solomon laid for building the
temple of God was sixty cubits long and twenty
cubits wide[b][b] (using the cubit of the old standard).
4The portico at the front of the temple was twenty cubits[c] long across the width of the building
and twenty cubits[d] high.
He overlaid the inside with pure gold. 5He paneled the main hall with pine and covered it with
fine gold and decorated it with palm tree[c] and
chain designs. 6He adorned the temple with precious stones. And the gold he used was gold of
Parvaim. 7He overlaid the ceiling beams, doorframes, walls and doors of the temple with gold,
and he carved cherubim[d] on the walls.
8He built the Most Holy Place,[e] its length corresponding to the width of the temple—twenty
cubits long and twenty cubits wide. He overlaid
the inside with six hundred talents[e] of fine gold.

2:13 [o]1Ki 7:13
2:14 [p]Ex 31:6 [q]Ex 35:31 [r]Ex 35:35
2:15 [s]ver 10; Ezr 3:7
2:16 [t]Jos 19:46; Jnh 1:3
2:17 [u]1Ch 22:2 [v]2Sa 24:2
2:18 [w]ver 2; 1Ch 22:2; 2Ch 8:8
3:1 [x]Ac 7:47 [y]Ge 28:17 [z]2Sa 24:18; 1Ch 21:18
3:2 [a]Ezr 5:11
3:3 [b]Eze 41:2
3:5 [c]Eze 40:16
3:7 [d]Ge 3:24; 1Ki 6:29-35; Eze 41:18
3:8 [e]Ex 26:33

[a] *1* Hebrew *Ornan,* a variant of *Araunah* [b] *3* That is, about 90 feet (about 27 meters) long and 30 feet (about 9 meters) wide [c] *4* That is, about 30 feet (about 9 meters); also in verses 8, 11 and 13 [d] *4* Some Septuagint and Syriac manuscripts; Hebrew *and a hundred and twenty* [e] *8* That is, about 23 tons (about 21 metric tons)

3:9 9The gold nails[f] weighed fifty shekels.[a] He also
[f]Ex 26:32 overlaid the upper parts with gold.
3:10 10In the Most Holy Place he made a pair[g] of
[g]Ex 25:18 sculptured cherubim and overlaid them with gold.
11The total wingspan of the cherubim was twenty
cubits. One wing of the first cherub was five cubits[b]
long and touched the temple wall, while its other
wing, also five cubits long, touched the wing of the
other cherub. 12Similarly one wing of the second
cherub was five cubits long and touched the other
temple wall, and its other wing, also five cubits
long, touched the wing of the first cherub. 13The
wings of these cherubim[h] extended twenty cubits.
3:13 They stood on their feet, facing the main hall.[c]
[h]Ex 25:18 14He made the curtain[i] of blue, purple and crim-
3:14 son yarn and fine linen, with cherubim[j] worked
[i]Ex 26:31,33; Heb 9:3 into it.
[j]Ge 3:24 15In the front of the temple he made two pil-
3:15 lars,[k] which ⌞together⌟ were thirty-five cubits[d]
[k]1Ki 7:15; long, each with a capital[l] on top measuring five
Rev 3:12 cubits. 16He made interwoven chains[e][m] and put
[l]1Ki 7:22 them on top of the pillars. He also made a hun-
3:16 dred pomegranates[n] and attached them to the
[m]1Ki 7:17 chains. 17He erected the pillars in the front of the
[n]1Ki 7:20 temple, one to the south and one to the north. The
one to the south he named Jakin[f] and the one to
the north Boaz.[g]

The Temple's Furnishings

4:1 4 He made a bronze altar[o] twenty cubits long,
[o]Ex 20:24; 27:1-2; 40:6; twenty cubits wide and ten cubits high.[h] 2He
1Ki 8:64; made the Sea[p] of cast metal, circular in shape,
2Ki 16:14 measuring ten cubits from rim to rim and five
4:2 cubits[i] high. It took a line of thirty cubits[j] to mea-
[p]Rev 4:6; sure around it. 3Below the rim, figures of bulls
15:2 encircled it—ten to a cubit.[k] The bulls were cast in
two rows in one piece with the Sea.
4The Sea stood on twelve bulls, three facing
north, three facing west, three facing south and
4:4 three facing east.[q] The Sea rested on top of them,
[q]Nu 2:3-25; and their hindquarters were toward the center. 5It
Eze 48:30-34; was a handbreadth[l] in thickness, and its rim was
Rev 21:13 like the rim of a cup, like a lily blossom. It held
4:6 three thousand baths.[m]
[r]Ex 30:18 6He then made ten basins[r] for washing and
[s]Ne 13:5,9; placed five on the south side and five on the
Eze 40:38 north. In them the things to be used for the burnt
offerings[s] were rinsed, but the Sea was to be used
by the priests for washing.

[a] 9 That is, about 1 1/4 pounds (about 0.6 kilogram)
[b] 11 That is, about 7 1/2 feet (about 2.3 meters); also in verse 15
[c] 13 Or *facing inward*
[d] 15 That is, about 52 feet (about 16 meters)
[e] 16 Or possibly *made chains in the inner sanctuary*; the meaning of the Hebrew for this phrase is uncertain.
[f] 17 *Jakin* probably means *he establishes.*
[g] 17 *Boaz* probably means *in him is strength.*
[h] 1 That is, about 30 feet (about 9 meters) long and wide, and about 15 feet (about 4.5 meters) high
[i] 2 That is, about 7 1/2 feet (about 2.3 meters)
[j] 2 That is, about 45 feet (about 13.5 meters)
[k] 3 That is, about 1 1/2 feet (about 0.5 meter)
[l] 5 That is, about 3 inches (about 8 centimeters)
[m] 5 That is, about 17,500 gallons (about 66 kiloliters)

Jakin and Boaz

2CH 3:17

Solomon orders two large, ornate pillars to be erected in front of the temple. These pillars are made of bronze and measure approximately 27 feet high and 18 feet around (1Ki 7:15 and its footnote). Some scholars believe these pillars were freestanding, but others suggest they may have supported a roof that formed a covered portico. The fact that Solomon designates names for these pillars seems to indicate that they had symbolic significance for the Jewish people. One pillar is named Jakin, which probably means "he establishes." The other pillar is called Boaz, which possibly means "in him is strength."

Throughout Scripture, pillars represent real or symbolic strength or support (Jdg 16:26; Gal. 2:9). In the last book of the Bible, John writes a message from Jesus Christ to the church in Philadelphia, promising that believers who remain loyal and strong despite difficulties on earth will be called pillars in the temple of God in the city where Jesus reigns as king forever (Rev 3:12).

Take My Silver and My Gold

2CH 5:1

King David prepares the architectural plans and provides resources for the temple construction project that his son, Solomon, will supervise (1Ch 28:11; 29:2). In addition, he donates his spersonal fortune of silver and gold (1Ch 29:3). Some estimate the gold alone would be worth an astounding seven billion dollars by today's standards. After completing the temple construction, Solomon places David's silver and gold donations into the temple treasury.

David's generous gift reminds us of the words of an old hymn of the church: "Take my silver and my gold, not a mite would I withhold. Take my love, my God, I pour at Thy feet its treasure store." Like David, the writer of this hymn, Frances Ridley Havergal, knew the true joy of giving from a grateful and willing heart (see more on this hymn on page 2020).

7 He made ten gold lampstands[t] according to the specifications[u] for them and placed them in the temple, five on the south side and five on the north. 8 He made ten tables[v] and placed them in the temple, five on the south side and five on the north. He also made a hundred gold sprinkling bowls.[w]

9 He made the courtyard[x] of the priests, and the large court and the doors for the court, and overlaid the doors with bronze. 10 He placed the Sea on the south side, at the southeast corner.

11 He also made the pots and shovels and sprinkling bowls.

So Huram finished[y] the work he had undertaken for King Solomon in the temple of God:

12 the two pillars;
the two bowl-shaped capitals on top of the pillars;
the two sets of network decorating the two bowl-shaped capitals on top of the pillars;
13 the four hundred pomegranates for the two sets of network (two rows of pomegranates for each network, decorating the bowl-shaped capitals on top of the pillars);
14 the stands[z] with their basins;
15 the Sea and the twelve bulls under it;
16 the pots, shovels, meat forks and all related articles.

All the objects that Huram-Abi[a] made for King Solomon for the temple of the LORD were of polished bronze. 17 The king had them cast in clay molds in the plain of the Jordan between Succoth[b] and Zarethan.[a] 18 All these things that Solomon made amounted to so much that the weight of the bronze[c] was not determined.

19 Solomon also made all the furnishings that were in God's temple:

the golden altar;
the tables[d] on which was the bread of the Presence;
20 the lampstands[e] of pure gold with their lamps, to burn in front of the inner sanctuary as prescribed;
21 the gold floral work and lamps and tongs (they were solid gold);
22 the pure gold wick trimmers, sprinkling bowls, dishes[f] and censers;[g] and the gold doors of the temple: the inner doors to the Most Holy Place and the doors of the main hall.

5 When all the work Solomon had done for the temple of the LORD was finished,[h] he brought in the things his father David had dedicated[i]—the silver and gold and all the furnishings—and he placed them in the treasuries of God's temple.

4:7 [t]Ex 25:31 [u]Ex 25:40
4:8 [v]Ex 25:23 [w]Nu 4:14
4:9 [x]1Ki 6:36; 2Ki 21:5; 2Ch 33:5
4:11 [y]1Ki 7:14
4:14 [z]1Ki 7:27-30
4:16 [a]1Ki 7:13
4:17 [b]Ge 33:17
4:18 [c]1Ki 7:23
4:19 [d]Ex 25:23,30
4:20 [e]Ex 25:31
4:22 [f]Nu 7:14 [g]Lev 10:1
5:1 [h]1Ki 6:14 [i]2Sa 8:11

[a] 17 Hebrew *Zeredatha,* a variant of *Zarethan*

The Ark Brought to the Temple

2 Then Solomon summoned to Jerusalem the
elders of Israel, all the heads of the tribes and the
chiefs of the Israelite families, to bring up the ark[j]
of the LORD's covenant from Zion, the City of
David. 3 And all the men of Israel[k] came together
to the king at the time of the festival in the seventh month.

4 When all the elders of Israel had arrived, the
Levites took up the ark, 5 and they brought up the
ark and the Tent of Meeting and all the sacred furnishings in it. The priests, who were Levites,[l] carried them up; 6 and King Solomon and the entire
assembly of Israel that had gathered about him
were before the ark, sacrificing so many sheep and
cattle that they could not be recorded or counted.

7 The priests then brought the ark[m] of the LORD's
covenant to its place in the inner sanctuary of the
temple, the Most Holy Place, and put it beneath
the wings of the cherubim. 8 The cherubim[n] spread
their wings over the place of the ark and covered
the ark and its carrying poles. 9 These poles were
so long that their ends, extending from the ark,
could be seen from in front of the inner sanctuary,
but not from outside the Holy Place; and they are
still there today. 10 There was nothing in the ark
except[o] the two tablets[p] that Moses had placed in it
at Horeb, where the LORD made a covenant with
the Israelites after they came out of Egypt.

11 The priests then withdrew from the Holy
Place. All the priests who were there had consecrated themselves, regardless of their divisions.[q]
12 All the Levites who were musicians[r]—Asaph,
Heman, Jeduthun and their sons and relatives—
stood on the east side of the altar, dressed in fine
linen and playing cymbals, harps and lyres. They
were accompanied by 120 priests sounding trumpets.[s] 13 The trumpeters and singers joined in unison, as with one voice, to give praise and thanks
to the LORD. Accompanied by trumpets, cymbals
and other instruments, they raised their voices in
praise to the LORD and sang:

> "He is good;
> his love endures forever."[t]

Then the temple of the LORD was filled with a
cloud, 14 and the priests could not perform[u] their
service because of the cloud,[v] for the glory[w] of the
LORD filled the temple of God.

6 Then Solomon said, "The LORD has said that
he would dwell in a dark cloud;[x] 2 I have built
a magnificent temple for you, a place for you to
dwell forever.[y]"

3 While the whole assembly of Israel was standing there, the king turned around and blessed
them. 4 Then he said:

> "Praise be to the LORD, the God of Israel,
> who with his hands has fulfilled what he
> promised with his mouth to my father David.
> For he said, 5 'Since the day I brought my peo-

5:2 [j]Nu 3:31; 2Sa 6:12; 1Ch 15:25
5:3 [k]1Ch 9:1; 2Ch 7:8-10
5:5 [l]Nu 3:31; 1Ch 15:2
5:7 [m]Rev 11:19
5:8 [n]Ge 3:24
5:10 [o]Heb 9:4 [p]Ex 16:34; Dt 10:2
5:11 [q]1Ch 24:1
5:12 [r]1Ki 10:12; 1Ch 25:1; Ps 68:25 [s]1Ch 13:8; 15:24
5:13 [t]1Ch 16:34, 41; 2Ch 7:3; 20:21; Ezr 3:11; Ps 100:5; 136:1; Jer 33:11
5:14 [u]Ex 40:35; Rev 15:8 [v]Ex 19:16 [w]Ex 29:43; 2Ch 7:2
6:1 [x]Ex 19:9; 1Ki 8:12-50
6:2 [y]Ezr 6:12; 7:15; Ps 135:21

God's Glory

2CH 5:13–6:3

As 120 priests play trumpets and a choir praises God to the accompaniment of cymbals and other instruments, the glory of the Lord fills the newly completed temple. God's majesty is beyond comprehension. He is too holy to be viewed by the human eye, but he gives the Israelites a visual expression of his glory.

The glory cloud, representing God's presence, protected and led the people on their flight out of Egypt (Ex 13:21). God descended in the cloud to speak to the Israelites during times of crisis (Nu 12:5). At the dedication of the tabernacle, the cloud covered the tent and God's glory filled it (Ex 40:34-35). And at the temple dedication, God's glory cloud fills the temple as a sign to Israel that God is real and active in their lives.

Centuries later, God's glory comes to earth through his Son, Jesus. Turn to Hebrews 1:3, and underline these splendid words: "The Son is the radiance of God's glory and the exact representation of his being."

Kneeling to Pray

2CH 6:13

In a beautiful act of reverence and submission, the king kneels before the King. "The whole assembly of Israel" watches as King Solomon kneels to pray during the temple dedication ceremony. The writer of this account uses a Hebrew word for kneel that indicates a close connection between bowing the knee and receiving a blessing.

A person may kneel when making a request of someone who is able to grant the favor (or blessing). For example, a young man kneels before the woman he loves to ask her to become his wife. A willing servant bends his knee before a master, seeking approval and blessing. Prisoners are forced to kneel before their captors, but appreciative subjects bow in willing surrender.

With this definition in mind, we understand why kneeling is a meaningful prayer position. Certainly, we can talk to our Lord whether we kneel, stand, sit or lie down, but kneeling reveals the attitude of our hearts. One day all people—believers and unbelievers alike—will kneel before Jesus Christ, the eternal King (Php 2:10).

ple out of Egypt, I have not chosen a city in
any tribe of Israel to have a temple built for
my Name to be there, nor have I chosen anyone to be the leader over my people Israel.
6But now I have chosen Jerusalem[z] for my
Name[a] to be there, and I have chosen David[b]
to rule my people Israel.'
7"My father David had it in his heart[c] to
build a temple for the Name of the LORD, the
God of Israel. 8But the LORD said to my father
David, 'Because it was in your heart to build
a temple for my Name, you did well to have
this in your heart. 9Nevertheless, you are not
the one to build the temple, but your son,
who is your own flesh and blood—he is the
one who will build the temple for my Name.'
10"The LORD has kept the promise he made.
I have succeeded David my father and now I
sit on the throne of Israel, just as the LORD
promised, and I have built the temple for the
Name of the LORD, the God of Israel. 11There I
have placed the ark, in which is the covenant[d] of the LORD that he made with the people of Israel."

Solomon's Prayer of Dedication

12Then Solomon stood before the altar of the
LORD in front of the whole assembly of Israel and
spread out his hands. 13Now he had made a
bronze platform,[e] five cubits[a] long, five cubits
wide and three cubits[b] high, and had placed it in
the center of the outer court. He stood on the platform and then knelt down[f] before the whole
assembly of Israel and spread out his hands
toward heaven. 14He said:
"O LORD, God of Israel, there is no God like
you[g] in heaven or on earth—you who keep
your covenant of love[h] with your servants
who continue wholeheartedly in your way.
15You have kept your promise to your servant
David my father; with your mouth you have
promised[i] and with your hand you have fulfilled it—as it is today.
16"Now LORD, God of Israel, keep for your
servant David my father the promises you
made to him when you said, 'You shall never fail[j] to have a man to sit before me on the
throne of Israel, if only your sons are careful
in all they do to walk before me according to
my law,[k] as you have done.' 17And now,
O LORD, God of Israel, let your word that you
promised your servant David come true.
18"But will God really dwell[l] on earth with
men? The heavens,[m] even the highest heavens,
cannot contain you. How much less this temple I have built! 19Yet give attention to your
servant's prayer and his plea for mercy, O LORD
my God. Hear the cry and the prayer that your

6:6 [z]Dt 12:5; Isa 14:1 [a]Ex 20:24; 2Ch 12:13 [b]1Ch 28:4
6:7 [c]1Sa 10:7; 1Ch 17:2; 28:2; Ac 7:46
6:11 [d]Dt 10:2; 2Ch 5:10; Ps 25:10; 50:5
6:13 [e]Ne 8:4 [f]Ps 95:6
6:14 [g]Ex 8:10; 15:11 [h]Dt 7:9
6:15 [i]1Ch 22:10
6:16 [j]2Sa 7:13,15; 1Ki 2:4; 2Ch 7:18; 23:3 [k]Ps 132:12
6:18 [l]Rev 21:3 [m]2Ch 2:6; Ps 11:4; Isa 40:22; 66:1; Ac 7:49

[a] *13* That is, about 7 1/2 feet (about 2.3 meters) [b] *13* That is, about 4 1/2 feet (about 1.3 meters)

servant is praying in your presence. 20 May
your eyes[n] be open toward this temple day and
night, this place of which you said you would
put your Name[o] there. May you hear[p] the
prayer your servant prays toward this place.
21 Hear the supplications of your servant and of
your people Israel when they pray toward this
place. Hear from heaven, your dwelling place;
and when you hear, forgive.[q]
22 "When a man wrongs his neighbor and
is required to take an oath[r] and he comes and
swears the oath before your altar in this temple, 23 then hear from heaven and act. Judge
between your servants, repaying[s] the guilty
by bringing down on his own head what he
has done. Declare the innocent not guilty and
so establish his innocence.
24 "When your people Israel have been
defeated[t] by an enemy because they have
sinned against you and when they turn back
and confess your name, praying and making
supplication before you in this temple, 25 then
hear from heaven and forgive the sin of your
people Israel and bring them back to the land
you gave to them and their fathers.
26 "When the heavens are shut up and there
is no rain[u] because your people have sinned
against you, and when they pray toward this
place and confess your name and turn from
their sin because you have afflicted them,
27 then hear from heaven and forgive[v] the sin of
your servants, your people Israel. Teach them
the right way to live, and send rain on the land
you gave your people for an inheritance.
28 "When famine[w] or plague comes to the
land, or blight or mildew, locusts or grasshoppers, or when enemies besiege them in
any of their cities, whatever disaster or disease may come, 29 and when a prayer or plea
is made by any of your people Israel—each
one aware of his afflictions and pains, and
spreading out his hands toward this temple—
30 then hear from heaven, your dwelling
place. Forgive,[x] and deal with each man
according to all he does, since you know his
heart (for you alone know the hearts of
men),[y] 31 so that they will fear you[z] and walk
in your ways all the time they live in the land
you gave our fathers.
32 "As for the foreigner who does not belong
to your people Israel but has come[a] from a
distant land because of your great name and
your mighty hand[b] and your outstretched
arm—when he comes and prays toward this
temple, 33 then hear from heaven, your
dwelling place, and do whatever the foreigner[c] asks of you, so that all the peoples of the
earth may know your name and fear you, as
do your own people Israel, and may know
that this house I have built bears your Name.
34 "When your people go to war against

6:20 [n]Ex 3:16; Ps 34:15 [o]Dt 12:11 [p]2Ch 7:14; 30:20
6:21 [q]Ps 51:1; Isa 33:24; 40:2; 43:25; 44:22; 55:7; Mic 7:18
6:22 [r]Ex 22:11
6:23 [s]Isa 3:11; 65:6; Mt 16:27
6:24 [t]Lev 26:17
6:26 [u]Lev 26:19; Dt 11:17; 28:24; 2Sa 1:21; 1Ki 17:1
6:27 [v]ver 30,39; 2Ch 7:14
6:28 [w]2Ch 20:9
6:30 [x]ver 27 [y]1Sa 16:7; 1Ch 28:9; Ps 7:9; 44:21; Pr 16:2; 17:3
6:31 [z]Ps 103:11, 13; Pr 8:13
6:32 [a]2Ch 9:6; Jn 12:20; Ac 8:27 [b]Ex 3:19,20
6:33 [c]2Ch 7:14

Our All-Knowing God

2CH 6:30

God is omniscient; he has complete and unlimited knowledge, awareness and understanding. *The wise King Solomon grasps this truth and incorporates it into his eloquent prayer at the temple dedication service. God knows all things—past, present and future. Nothing gets by him. He knows what every individual thinks and feels (Ps 7:9). To the unbeliever, this is disturbing news; to the believer, it is a comforting reality (Ps. 44:20–21; 139:23–24).*

Even King Solomon, the most discerning man ever (1Ki 3:12), could not read the heart of another person. God can look inside, however, and see the motives behind our behavior (Pr 16:2). Others may doubt our sincerity, our passion and our purpose, but God, who looks beyond what others see, knows our genuine heart's desire (1Sa 16:7). Solomon understands God's attributes and prays that all Israel will learn to respect, love and follow their all-knowing God (2Ch 6:31).

Pray Toward Jerusalem

2CH 6:38

One phrase in Solomon's dedicatory prayer indicates that the people are to pray facing in the direction of the temple. The Israelite people take these words literally. While in captivity in Babylon, Daniel prays toward Jerusalem (Da 6:10). Today Jews visit the temple Wailing Wall (the only remnant of the temple left standing) and pray facing it. The temple and the ark it is constructed to hold provide the Israelites with symbols of God's presence among them (Ex 25:21–22; 2Ch 7:16). When they pray toward the temple, it helps them focus on the one true God.

their enemies,[d] wherever you send them, and when they pray[e] to you toward this city you have chosen and the temple I have built for your Name, [35]then hear from heaven their prayer and their plea, and uphold their cause.

[36]"When they sin against you—for there is no one who does not sin[f]—and you become angry with them and give them over to the enemy, who takes them captive[g] to a land far away or near; [37]and if they have a change of heart[h] in the land where they are held captive, and repent and plead with you in the land of their captivity and say, 'We have sinned, we have done wrong and acted wickedly'; [38]and if they turn back to you with all their heart and soul in the land of their captivity where they were taken, and pray toward the land you gave their fathers, toward the city you have chosen and toward the temple I have built for your Name; [39]then from heaven, your dwelling place, hear their prayer and their pleas, and uphold their cause. And forgive your people, who have sinned against you.

[40]"Now, my God, may your eyes be open and your ears attentive[i] to the prayers offered in this place.

[41] "Now arise,[j] O LORD God, and come to
your resting place,[k]
you and the ark of your might.
May your priests,[l] O LORD God, be
clothed with salvation,
may your saints rejoice in your
goodness.[m]
[42] O LORD God, do not reject your
anointed one.
Remember the great love[n] promised
to David your servant."

The Dedication of the Temple

7 When Solomon finished praying, fire[o] came down from heaven and consumed the burnt offering and the sacrifices, and the glory of the LORD filled[p] the temple.[q] [2]The priests could not enter[r] the temple of the LORD because the glory[s] of the LORD filled it. [3]When all the Israelites saw the fire coming down and the glory of the LORD above the temple, they knelt on the pavement with their faces to the ground, and they worshiped and gave thanks to the LORD, saying,

"He is good;
his love endures forever."[t]

[4]Then the king and all the people offered sacrifices before the LORD. [5]And King Solomon offered a sacrifice of twenty-two thousand head of cattle and a hundred and twenty thousand sheep and goats. So the king and all the people dedicated the temple of God. [6]The priests took their positions, as did the Levites[u] with the LORD's musical instru-

6:34 [d]Dt 28:7 [e]1Ch 5:20
6:36 [f]Job 15:14; Ps 143:2; Ecc 7:20; Jer 17:9; Jas 3:1; 1Jn 1:8-10 [g]Lev 26:44
6:37 [h]2Ch 7:14; 33:12,19,23; Jer 29:13
6:40 [i]2Ch 7:15; Ne 1:6,11; Ps 17:1,6
6:41 [j]Isa 33:10 [k]1Ch 28:2 [l]Ps 132:16 [m]Ps 116:12
6:42 [n]Ps 89:24, 28; Isa 55:3
7:1 [o]Lev 9:24; 1Ki 18:38 [p]Ex 16:10 [q]Ps 26:8
7:2 [r]1Ki 8:11 [s]Ex 29:43; 40:35; 2Ch 5:14
7:3 [t]1Ch 16:34; 2Ch 5:13; 20:21
7:6 [u]1Ch 15:16

7:6 ments,[v] which King David had made for praising
[v]2Ch 5:12 the LORD and which were used when he gave
thanks, saying, "His love endures forever." Opposite the Levites, the priests blew their trumpets,
and all the Israelites were standing.
7Solomon consecrated the middle part of the
courtyard in front of the temple of the LORD, and
there he offered burnt offerings and the fat of the
fellowship offerings,[a] because the bronze altar he
had made could not hold the burnt offerings, the
grain offerings and the fat portions.
7:8 [w]2Ch 30:26 8So Solomon observed the festival[w] at that time
[x]Ge 15:18 for seven days, and all Israel with him—a vast
assembly, people from Lebo[b] Hamath to the Wadi
of Egypt.[x] 9On the eighth day they held an assembly, for they had celebrated the dedication of the
7:9 altar for seven days and the festival[y] for seven
[y]Lev 23:36 days more. 10On the twenty-third day of the seventh month he sent the people to their homes,
joyful and glad in heart for the good things the
LORD had done for David and Solomon and for his
people Israel.

The LORD Appears to Solomon

11When Solomon had finished the temple of the
LORD and the royal palace, and had succeeded in
carrying out all he had in mind to do in the temple of the LORD and in his own palace, 12the LORD
appeared to him at night and said:

7:12 [z]Dt 12:5 "I have heard your prayer and have chosen
7:13 this place for myself[z] as a temple for sacri-
[a]2Ch 6:26-28; Am 4:7 fices.
13"When I shut up the heavens so that
7:14 there is no rain,[a] or command locusts to
[b]Lev 26:41; devour the land or send a plague among my
2Ch 6:37; people, 14if my people, who are called by my
Jas 4:10 [c]1Ch 16:11 name, will humble[b] themselves and pray and
[d]Isa 55:7; seek my face[c] and turn[d] from their wicked
Zec 1:4 [e]2Ch 6:27 ways, then will I hear from heaven and will
[f]2Ch 30:20; forgive[e] their sin and will heal[f] their land.
Isa 30:26; 15Now my eyes will be open and my ears
57:18 attentive to the prayers offered in this place.[g]
7:15 16I have chosen[h] and consecrated this temple
[g]2Ch 6:40 so that my Name may be there forever. My
7:16 eyes and my heart will always be there.
[h]ver 12; 17"As for you, if you walk before me[i] as
2Ch 6:6 David your father did, and do all I command,
7:17 and observe my decrees and laws, 18I will
[i]1Ki 9:4 establish your royal throne, as I covenanted
7:18 with David your father when I said, 'You shall
[j]2Ch 6:16 never fail to have a man[j] to rule over Israel.'[k]
[k]2Sa 7:13; 19"But if you[c] turn away[l] and forsake[m] the
2Ch 13:5 decrees and commands I have given you[c] and
7:19 go off to serve other gods and worship them,
[l]Dt 28:15 [m]Lev 26:14, 20then I will uproot[n] Israel from my land,[o]
33 which I have given them, and will reject this
7:20 temple I have consecrated for my Name. I
[n]Dt 29:28 [o]1Ki 14:15 will make it a byword and an object of

[a] 7 Traditionally *peace offerings* [b] 8 *Or from the entrance to*
[c] 19 The Hebrew is plural.

True Repentance

2CH 7:14

Solomon spends 7 years building the temple and 13 years constructing his royal palace (1Ki 6:38; 7:1). After finishing both projects, the Lord comes to Solomon a second time during the night (2Ch 1:7; 7:12). Although God's nocturnal meeting with Solomon is recorded in both 1 Kings and 2 Chronicles, the Chronicles account has an additional message from the Lord.

God says, "If my people will bend their knees and hearts (after disobeying me) and take time to talk with me about it and stop the behavior creating distance between us, then I will listen attentively to their prayers and will pardon their habitual sin and repair their lives—both corporate and individual" (2Ch 7:14, author's paraphrase). God gives Solomon and the Israelites a "recipe" for renewal and blessing. The ingredients include humility, prayer, commitment and repentance.

The "recipe" is still valid today. If you wish to see renewal and blessing in your personal life or in the life of your church, the same ingredients must be used.

ridicule[p] among all peoples. 21 And though 7:20
this temple is now so imposing, all who pass [p]Dt 28:37
by will be appalled and say,[q] 'Why has the 7:21
LORD done such a thing to this land and to [q]Dt 29:24
this temple?' 22 People will answer, 'Because
they have forsaken the LORD, the God of their
fathers, who brought them out of Egypt, and
have embraced other gods, worshiping and
serving them—that is why he brought all this
disaster on them.' "

Solomon's Other Activities

8 At the end of twenty years, during which Solomon built the temple of the LORD and his own
palace, 2 Solomon rebuilt the villages that Hiram[a]
had given him, and settled Israelites in them. 3 Solomon then went to Hamath Zobah and captured
it. 4 He also built up Tadmor in the desert and all
the store cities he had built in Hamath. 5 He rebuilt 8:5
Upper Beth Horon[r] and Lower Beth Horon as for- [r]1Ch 7:24;
tified cities, with walls and with gates and bars, 2Ch 14:7
6 as well as Baalath and all his store cities, and all
the cities for his chariots and for his horses[b]—
whatever he desired to build in Jerusalem, in Lebanon and throughout all the territory he ruled.
7 All the people left from the Hittites, Amorites,
Perizzites, Hivites and Jebusites[s] (these peoples 8:7
were not Israelites), 8 that is, their descendants [s]Ge 10:16
remaining in the land, whom the Israelites had 8:8
not destroyed—these Solomon conscripted[t] for his [t]1Ki 4:6; 9:21
slave labor force, as it is to this day. 9 But Solomon
did not make slaves of the Israelites for his work;
they were his fighting men, commanders of his
captains, and commanders of his chariots and
charioteers. 10 They were also King Solomon's
chief officials—two hundred and fifty officials
supervising the men.
11 Solomon brought Pharaoh's daughter[u] up 8:11
from the City of David to the palace he had built [u]1Ki 3:1; 7:8
for her, for he said, "My wife must not live in the
palace of David king of Israel, because the places
the ark of the LORD has entered are holy."
12 On the altar[v] of the LORD that he had built in 8:12
front of the portico, Solomon sacrificed burnt [v]1Ki 8:64;
offerings to the LORD, 13 according to the daily 2Ch 4:1; 15:8
requirement[w] for offerings commanded by Moses 8:13
for Sabbaths,[x] New Moons and the three[y] annual [w]Ex 29:38;
feasts—the Feast of Unleavened Bread, the Feast Nu 28:3 [x]Nu 28:9
of Weeks[z] and the Feast of Tabernacles. 14 In keep- [y]Ex 23:14;
ing with the ordinance of his father David, he Dt 16:16
appointed the divisions[a] of the priests for their [z]Ex 23:16
duties, and the Levites[b] to lead the praise and to 8:14
assist the priests according to each day's require- [a]1Ch 24:1 [b]1Ch 25:1
ment. He also appointed the gatekeepers[c] by divi- [c]1Ch 9:17;
sions for the various gates, because this was what 26:1
David the man of God[d] had ordered.[e] 15 They did [d]Ne 12:24,36 [e]1Ch 23:6;
not deviate from the king's commands to the Ne 12:45

[a] 2 Hebrew *Huram,* a variant of *Hiram;* also in verse 18
[b] 6 Or *charioteers*

Earth's crammed with heaven,
And every common bush afire with God,
And only he who *sees* takes off his shoes,
The rest sit round and pluck blackberries.

—Elizabeth Barrett Browning (1806-1861)

priests or to the Levites in any matter, including
that of the treasuries.
16All Solomon's work was carried out, from the
day the foundation of the temple of the LORD was
laid until its completion. So the temple of the LORD
was finished.
17Then Solomon went to Ezion Geber and Elath
on the coast of Edom. 18And Hiram sent him ships
commanded by his own officers, men who knew
the sea. These, with Solomon's men, sailed to
8:18 Ophir and brought back four hundred and fifty
[f]2Ch 9:9 talents[a] of gold,[f] which they delivered to King
Solomon.

The Queen of Sheba Visits Solomon

9:1 9 When the queen of Sheba[g] heard of Solomon's
[g]Ge 10:7; Eze 23:42; fame, she came to Jerusalem to test him with
Mt 12:42; Lk 11:31 hard questions. Arriving with a very great caravan—with camels carrying spices, large quanti-
ties of gold, and precious stones—she came to Solomon and talked with him about all she had on
her mind. 2Solomon answered all her questions;
nothing was too hard for him to explain to her.
9:3 3When the queen of Sheba saw the wisdom of Sol-
[h]1Ki 5:12 omon,[h] as well as the palace he had built, 4the
food on his table, the seating of his officials, the
attending servants in their robes, the cupbearers
in their robes and the burnt offerings he made at[b]
the temple of the LORD, she was overwhelmed.
5She said to the king, "The report I heard in my
own country about your achievements and your
wisdom is true. 6But I did not believe what they
9:6 said until I came[i] and saw with my own eyes.
[i]2Ch 6:32 Indeed, not even half the greatness of your wisdom was told me; you have far exceeded the
report I heard. 7How happy your men must be!
How happy your officials, who continually stand
before you and hear your wisdom! 8Praise be to
9:8 the LORD your God, who has delighted in you and
[j]1Ki 2:12; placed you on his throne[j] as king to rule for the
1Ch 17:14; 28:5; 29:23; LORD your God. Because of the love of your God
2Ch 13:8 for Israel and his desire to uphold them forever,
[k]2Ch 2:11 he has made you king[k] over them, to maintain
justice and righteousness."
9:9 9Then she gave the king 120 talents[c] of gold,[l]
[l]2Ch 8:18 large quantities of spices, and precious stones.
There had never been such spices as those the
queen of Sheba gave to King Solomon.
10(The men of Hiram and the men of Solomon
9:10 brought gold from Ophir;[m] they also brought
[m]2Ch 8:18 algumwood[d] and precious stones. 11The king used
the algumwood to make steps for the temple of
the LORD and for the royal palace, and to make
harps and lyres for the musicians. Nothing like
them had ever been seen in Judah.)
12King Solomon gave the queen of Sheba all she
desired and asked for; he gave her more than she

[a] *18* That is, about 17 tons (about 16 metric tons) [b] *4* Or *the ascent by which he went up to* [c] *9* That is, about 4 1/2 tons (about 4 metric tons) [d] *10* Probably a variant of *almugwood*

There are briers besetting
every path,
Which call for patient care;
There is a cross in every lot,
And an earnest need for
prayer;
But a lowly heart that leans on
Thee
Is happy anywhere.

—Alice Cary (1820-1871)

had brought to him. Then she left and returned
with her retinue to her own country.

Solomon's Splendor

13The weight of the gold that Solomon received
yearly was 666 talents,[a] 14not including the revenues brought in by merchants and traders. Also
all the kings of Arabia[n] and the governors of the 9:14 [n]2Ch 17:11;
land brought gold and silver to Solomon. Isa 21:13;
15King Solomon made two hundred large Jer 25:24;
shields of hammered gold; six hundred bekas[b] of Eze 27:21; 30:5
hammered gold went into each shield. 16He also 9:16
made three hundred small shields[o] of hammered [o]2Ch 12:9
gold, with three hundred bekas[c] of gold in each [p]1Ki 7:2
shield. The king put them in the Palace of the Forest of Lebanon.[p]
17Then the king made a great throne inlaid with 9:17
ivory[q] and overlaid with pure gold. 18The throne [q]1Ki 22:39
had six steps, and a footstool of gold was attached
to it. On both sides of the seat were armrests, with
a lion standing beside each of them. 19Twelve lions
stood on the six steps, one at either end of each
step. Nothing like it had ever been made for any
other kingdom. 20All King Solomon's goblets were
gold, and all the household articles in the Palace of
the Forest of Lebanon were pure gold. Nothing was
made of silver, because silver was considered of
little value in Solomon's day. 21The king had a fleet
of trading ships[d] manned by Hiram's[e] men. Once
every three years it returned, carrying gold, silver
and ivory, and apes and baboons.
22King Solomon was greater in riches and wis- 9:22
dom than all the other kings of the earth.[r] 23All [r]1Ki 3:13;
the kings[s] of the earth sought audience with Sol- 2Ch 1:12
omon to hear the wisdom God had put in his 9:23
heart. 24Year after year, everyone who came [s]1Ki 4:34
brought a gift[t]—articles of silver and gold, and 9:24
robes, weapons and spices, and horses and mules. [t]2Ch 32:23;
25Solomon had four thousand stalls for horses Ps 45:12;
and chariots,[u] and twelve thousand horses,[f] which 68:29; 72:10;
he kept in the chariot cities and also with him in Isa 18:7
Jerusalem. 26He ruled[v] over all the kings from the 9:25
River[g][w] to the land of the Philistines, as far as the [u]1Sa 8:11;
border of Egypt.[x] 27The king made silver as com- 1Ki 4:26
mon in Jerusalem as stones, and cedar as plentiful 9:26
as sycamore-fig trees in the foothills. 28Solomon's [v]1Ki 4:21
horses were imported from Egypt[h] and from all [w]Ps 72:8-9
other countries. [x]Ge 15:18-21

Solomon's Death

29As for the other events of Solomon's reign,
from beginning to end, are they not written in 9:29
the records of Nathan[y] the prophet, in the proph- [y]2Sa 7:2;
ecy of Ahijah[z] the Shilonite and in the visions of 1Ch 29:29 [z]1Ki 11:29
Iddo the seer concerning Jeroboam[a] son of [a]2Ch 10:2

[a] *13* That is, about 25 tons (about 23 metric tons) [b] *15* That is, about 7 1/2 pounds (about 3.5 kilograms) [c] *16* That is, about 3 3/4 pounds (about 1.7 kilograms) [d] *21* Hebrew *of ships that could go to Tarshish* [e] *21* Hebrew *Huram,* a variant of *Hiram* [f] *25* Or *charioteers* [g] *26* That is, the Euphrates [h] *28* Or possibly *Muzur,* a region in Cilicia

Apes and Baboons

2CH 9:21

Solomon, an accomplished botanist and zoologist, enjoys gathering extensive information about plants, birds, insects, animals and fish (1Ki 4:33). He brings exotic animals and other goods to Israel on trading boats that may have resembled the large, well-constructed ships of Tarshish (a famous seaport at the southern tip of Spain nearly 2,000 miles away).

Solomon's ability to retain knowledge, instruct others, negotiate with foreign dignitaries, supervise building projects and successfully manage Israel comes to him as a gift of God (1Ki 3:10-13). In addition to his studies of plant and animal life, Solomon writes 3,000 proverbs and 1,005 songs (1Ki 4:32-33). Kings from all over the world send their advisors to study under Solomon (1Ki 4:34), and the famed queen of Sheba makes a journey of thousands of miles to see if what she has heard about him is true (1Ki 10:1). Solomon's wisdom is recorded in two psalms (Ps 72; 127), the books of Proverbs, Song of Songs and probably also Ecclesiastes.

Nebat? 30 Solomon reigned in Jerusalem over all
9:31 Israel forty years. 31 Then he rested with his
[b]1Ki 2:10 fathers and was buried in the city of David[b] his
father. And Rehoboam his son succeeded him as
king.

Israel Rebels Against Rehoboam

10 Rehoboam went to Shechem, for all the Israelites had gone there to make him king.
10:2 [c]2Ch 9:29 2 When Jeroboam[c] son of Nebat heard this (he was
[d]1Ki 11:40 in Egypt, where he had fled[d] from King Solomon),
10:3 he returned from Egypt. 3 So they sent for Jerobo-
[e]1Ch 9:1 am, and he and all Israel[e] went to Rehoboam and
10:4 said to him: 4 "Your father put a heavy yoke on us,[f]
[f]2Ch 2:2 but now lighten the harsh labor and the heavy
yoke he put on us, and we will serve you."
5 Rehoboam answered, "Come back to me in
three days." So the people went away.
10:6 6 Then King Rehoboam consulted the elders[g]
[g]Job 8:8-9; 12:12; 15:10; who had served his father Solomon during his
32:7 lifetime. "How would you advise me to answer
these people?" he asked.
7 They replied, "If you will be kind to these peo-
10:7 ple and please them and give them a favorable
[h]Pr 15:1 answer,[h] they will always be your servants."
10:8 8 But Rehoboam rejected[i] the advice the elders[j]
[i]2Sa 17:14 gave him and consulted the young men who had
[j]Pr 13:20 grown up with him and were serving him. 9 He
asked them, "What is your advice? How should
we answer these people who say to me, 'Lighten
the yoke your father put on us'?"
10 The young men who had grown up with him
replied, "Tell the people who have said to you,
'Your father put a heavy yoke on us, but make our
yoke lighter'—tell them, 'My little finger is thicker than my father's waist. 11 My father laid on you
a heavy yoke; I will make it even heavier. My
father scourged you with whips; I will scourge
you with scorpions.' "
12 Three days later Jeroboam and all the people
returned to Rehoboam, as the king had said,
"Come back to me in three days." 13 The king
answered them harshly. Rejecting the advice of
the elders, 14 he followed the advice of the young
men and said, "My father made your yoke heavy;
I will make it even heavier. My father scourged
you with whips; I will scourge you with scorpions." 15 So the king did not listen to the people, for
10:15 this turn of events was from God,[k] to fulfill the
[k]2Ch 11:4; 25:16-20 word the LORD had spoken to Jeroboam son of
[l]1Ki 11:29 Nebat through Ahijah the Shilonite.[l]
10:16 16 When all Israel[m] saw that the king refused to
[m]1Ch 9:1 listen to them, they answered the king:

[n]ver 19; 2Sa 20:1 "What share do we have in David,[n]
what part in Jesse's son?
To your tents, O Israel!
Look after your own house, O David!"

So all the Israelites went home. 17 But as for the
Israelites who were living in the towns of Judah,
Rehoboam still ruled over them.

Rehoboam's Advisors

2CH 10:8

As the spokesman for the common people, Jeroboam asks newly crowned Rehoboam to modify the harsh tax and labor system Solomon had initiated. Rehoboam's elder advisors counsel him to lighten the load of these overworked people and win their cooperation. However, Rehoboam snubs this sensible idea and consults advisors closer to his own age. These younger advisors may have been Rehoboam's brothers or the sons of other nobility, who have had as sheltered and opulent a background as his own. Obviously they do not understand the plight of the common person.

When Rehoboam denies Jeroboam's request, the people revolt and make Jeroboam their king. This initiates the split between the north and south (see the note on 1Ki 11:35,38–39, page 547). Rehoboam listens to poor advice and makes a bad decision with long-term consequences—unlike his grandfather, King David, who was cautiously understanding in his dealings with other people (see the note on 1Ch 12:16–18, page 649).

Often our tendency is to seek advice from people who will feed our egos or tell us what we want to hear. True humility—and for that matter, wisdom—obliges us to be teachable and willing to heed advice from those whom we don't necessarily agree (Prov 15:22).

Jeroboam and Rehoboam

2CH 11:13-17

Jeroboam worries his people will revert to following Rehoboam if they travel to worship in the temple at Jerusalem. Instead of trusting God's message to him through the prophet of Shiloh (1Ki 11:29-31,38), he acts foolishly by setting up idols and false worship centers, appointing counterfeit priests and introducing a new way to worship God.

Many (including the priests and Levites) abandon Jeroboam and travel to Jerusalem to worship the true God. They support King Rehoboam for three years. Why only three years? Probably because after Rehoboam experiences success, he abandons God and his ways (2Ch 12:1), and God sends the king of Egypt to attack Jerusalem and capture the surrounding cities (1Ch 12:2,4). When Rehoboam and his leaders turn back to God, destruction is averted (1Ch 12:6,12). However, Rehoboam appears only to follow God when he needs him and abandons him when everything is going well (2Ch 12:14).

18King Rehoboam sent out Adoniram,[a][o] who
was in charge of forced labor, but the Israelites
stoned him to death. King Rehoboam, however,
managed to get into his chariot and escape to Jerusalem. 19So Israel has been in rebellion against
the house of David to this day.

11 When Rehoboam arrived in Jerusalem,[p] he
mustered the house of Judah and Benjamin—a hundred and eighty thousand fighting
men—to make war against Israel and to regain the
kingdom for Rehoboam.
2But this word of the LORD came to Shemaiah[q]
the man of God: 3"Say to Rehoboam son of Solomon king of Judah and to all the Israelites in
Judah and Benjamin, 4'This is what the LORD says:
Do not go up to fight against your brothers.[r] Go
home, every one of you, for this is my doing.'" So
they obeyed the words of the LORD and turned
back from marching against Jeroboam.

Rehoboam Fortifies Judah

5Rehoboam lived in Jerusalem and built up
towns for defense in Judah: 6Bethlehem, Etam,
Tekoa, 7Beth Zur, Soco, Adullam, 8Gath, Mareshah, Ziph, 9Adoraim, Lachish, Azekah, 10Zorah,
Aijalon and Hebron. These were fortified cities in
Judah and Benjamin. 11He strengthened their
defenses and put commanders in them, with supplies of food, olive oil and wine. 12He put shields
and spears in all the cities, and made them very
strong. So Judah and Benjamin were his.
13The priests and Levites from all their districts
throughout Israel sided with him. 14The Levites[s]
even abandoned their pasturelands and property,[t]
and came to Judah and Jerusalem because Jeroboam and his sons had rejected them as priests of the
LORD. 15And he appointed[u] his own priests[v] for the
high places and for the goat[w] and calf[x] idols he had
made. 16Those from every tribe of Israel[y] who set
their hearts on seeking the LORD, the God of Israel,
followed the Levites to Jerusalem to offer sacrifices
to the LORD, the God of their fathers. 17They
strengthened[z] the kingdom of Judah and supported Rehoboam son of Solomon three years, walking
in the ways of David and Solomon during this time.

Rehoboam's Family

18Rehoboam married Mahalath, who was the
daughter of David's son Jerimoth and of Abihail,
the daughter of Jesse's son Eliab. 19She bore him
sons: Jeush, Shemariah and Zaham. 20Then he
married Maacah[a] daughter of Absalom, who bore
him Abijah,[b] Attai, Ziza and Shelomith. 21Reho-
boam loved Maacah daughter of Absalom more
than any of his other wives and concubines. In
all, he had eighteen wives[c] and sixty concubines,
twenty-eight sons and sixty daughters.
22Rehoboam appointed Abijah[d] son of Maacah
to be the chief prince among his brothers, in order

10:18 [o]1Ki 5:14
11:1 [p]1Ki 12:21
11:2 [q]2Ch 12:5-7, 15
11:4 [r]2Ch 28:8-11
11:14 [s]Nu 35:2-5 [t]2Ch 13:9
11:15 [u]1Ki 13:33 [v]1Ki 12:31 [w]Lev 17:7 [x]1Ki 12:28; 2Ch 13:8
11:16 [y]2Ch 15:9
11:17 [z]2Ch 12:1
11:20 [a]1Ki 15:2 [b]2Ch 13:2
11:21 [c]Dt 17:17
11:22 [d]Dt 21:15-17

[a] *18* Hebrew *Hadoram,* a variant of *Adoniram*

to make him king. 23He acted wisely, dispersing
some of his sons throughout the districts of Judah
and Benjamin, and to all the fortified cities. He
gave them abundant provisions and took many
wives for them.

Shishak Attacks Jerusalem

12 After Rehoboam's position as king was
12:1 [e]ver 13 established[e] and he had become strong,[f] he
[f]2Ch 11:17 and all Israel[a] with him abandoned the law of the
LORD. 2Because they had been unfaithful[g] to the
12:2 [g]1Ki 14:22-24 LORD, Shishak[h] king of Egypt attacked Jerusalem
in the fifth year of King Rehoboam. 3With twelve
[h]1Ki 11:40 hundred chariots and sixty thousand horsemen
12:3 and the innumerable troops of Libyans, Sukkites
[i]2Ch 16:8; Na 3:9 and Cushites[b][i] that came with him from Egypt,
4he captured the fortified cities[j] of Judah and
12:4 came as far as Jerusalem.
[j]2Ch 11:10 5Then the prophet Shemaiah[k] came to Rehobo-
12:5 am and to the leaders of Judah who had assem-
[k]2Ch 11:2 bled in Jerusalem for fear of Shishak, and he said
[l]Dt 28:15; 2Ch 15:2 to them, "This is what the LORD says, 'You have
abandoned me; therefore, I now abandon[l] you to
Shishak.' "
6The leaders of Israel and the king humbled
12:6 themselves and said, "The LORD is just."[m]
[m]Ex 9:27; Da 9:14 7When the LORD saw that they humbled themselves, this word of the LORD came to Shemaiah:
"Since they have humbled themselves, I will not
destroy them but will soon give them deliver-
12:7 ance.[n] My wrath will not be poured out on Jerusa-
[n]1Ki 21:29; lem through Shishak. 8They will, however,
Ps 78:38 become subject[o] to him, so that they may learn
12:8 [o]Dt 28:48 the difference between serving me and serving the
kings of other lands."
9When Shishak king of Egypt attacked Jerusalem, he carried off the treasures of the temple of
the LORD and the treasures of the royal palace. He
12:9 [p]2Ch 9:16 took everything, including the gold shields[p] Solomon had made. 10So King Rehoboam made bronze
shields to replace them and assigned these to the
commanders of the guard on duty at the entrance
to the royal palace. 11Whenever the king went to
the LORD's temple, the guards went with him,
bearing the shields, and afterward they returned
them to the guardroom.
12Because Rehoboam humbled himself, the
LORD's anger turned from him, and he was not
12:12 [q]1Ki 14:13; totally destroyed. Indeed, there was some good[q]
2Ch 19:3 in Judah.
13King Rehoboam established himself firmly in
Jerusalem and continued as king. He was forty-one
years old when he became king, and he reigned
seventeen years in Jerusalem, the city the LORD had
chosen out of all the tribes of Israel in which to put
12:13 [r]Dt 12:5; his Name.[r] His mother's name was Naamah; she
2Ch 6:6 was an Ammonite. 14He did evil because he had not
set his heart on seeking the LORD.

[a] *1* That is, Judah, as frequently in 2 Chronicles [b] *3* That is, people from the upper Nile region

The Consequences

2CH 12:2-6

Through Moses, God told the Israelites what blessings they could expect if they followed his ways. Likewise, Moses informed them of the negative consequences they would experience if they abandoned their loving God. These explicit directives (known as Israel's covenant) are recorded in Deuteronomy 27-30. Moses told them that what God was asking was not unreasonable—or "too difficult" (Dt 30:11). They only needed to love the Lord and obey his directives, and their lives would be blessed (Dt 30:11, 15-16). But Rehoboam and "all Israel" abandon God and suffer the negative consequences (2Ch 12:1-2).

God provides redemption for the Israelites' sins through the sacrificial system (Lev 16:21-24). Sinful human beings can have a relationship with the perfect Lord. The Israelites live under the old covenant, yet achieve fellowship with God through obedience. All this God arranges as a prelude to the new covenant that we now enjoy in Christ Jesus, his Son (1Jn 4:10).

Covenant of Salt

2CH 13:5

King Abijah of Judah delivers a speech to the northern king, emphasizing God's alliance with the southern kingdom (David and his descendants) "by a covenant of salt" (2Ch 13:5). What does he mean? What exactly is a "covenant of salt"?

God instructs the Israelites to salt their offerings (Lev 2:13) and to add salt to their holy incense (Ex 30:34–35). Since salt is an important preservative, perhaps God wants it added to the sacrifices as an illustration that his covenant with Israel is permanent and, like salt, will not decay (Nu 18:19).

When King Abijah mentions the "covenant of salt," he is probably referring to God's "permanent" promise to David: His throne will be established forever (2Sa 7:16). Jesus comes from David's lineage and by his death and resurrection now rules believers' hearts. This enduring covenant between God and his people will only be completely fulfilled when Jesus returns to reign over all things (Rev 11:15).

15As for the events of Rehoboam's reign, from
beginning to end, are they not written in the
records of Shemaiah[s] the prophet and of Iddo the
seer that deal with genealogies? There was continual warfare between Rehoboam and Jeroboam.
16Rehoboam rested with his fathers and was
buried in the City of David. And Abijah[t] his son
succeeded him as king.

Abijah King of Judah

13 In the eighteenth year of the reign of Jeroboam, Abijah became king of Judah, 2and he
reigned in Jerusalem three years. His mother's
name was Maacah,[a] a daughter[b] of Uriel of Gibeah.
There was war between Abijah[u] and Jeroboam.[v] 3Abijah went into battle with a force of four
hundred thousand able fighting men, and Jeroboam drew up a battle line against him with eight
hundred thousand able troops.
4Abijah stood on Mount Zemaraim,[w] in the hill
country of Ephraim, and said, "Jeroboam and all
Israel,[x] listen to me! 5Don't you know that the
LORD, the God of Israel, has given the kingship of
Israel to David and his descendants forever[y] by a
covenant of salt?[z] 6Yet Jeroboam son of Nebat, an
official of Solomon son of David, rebelled[a] against
his master. 7Some worthless scoundrels[b] gathered
around him and opposed Rehoboam son of Solomon when he was young and indecisive and not
strong enough to resist them.
8"And now you plan to resist the kingdom of the
LORD, which is in the hands of David's descendants. You are indeed a vast army and have with
you the golden calves[c] that Jeroboam made to be
your gods. 9But didn't you drive out the priests of
the LORD,[d] the sons of Aaron, and the Levites, and
make priests of your own as the peoples of other
lands do? Whoever comes to consecrate himself
with a young bull[e] and seven rams may become a
priest of what are not gods.[f]
10"As for us, the LORD is our God, and we have
not forsaken him. The priests who serve the LORD
are sons of Aaron, and the Levites assist them.
11Every morning and evening[g] they present burnt
offerings and fragrant incense to the LORD. They
set out the bread on the ceremonially clean table[h]
and light the lamps on the gold lampstand every
evening. We are observing the requirements of the
LORD our God. But you have forsaken him. 12God
is with us; he is our leader. His priests with their
trumpets will sound the battle cry against you.[i]
Men of Israel, do not fight against the LORD,[j] the
God of your fathers, for you will not succeed."
13Now Jeroboam had sent troops around to the
rear, so that while he was in front of Judah the
ambush[k] was behind them. 14Judah turned and
saw that they were being attacked at both front

12:15 [s]2Ch 9:29; 11:2
12:16 [t]2Ch 11:20
13:2 [u]2Ch 11:20 [v]1Ki 15:6
13:4 [w]Jos 18:22 [x]1Ch 11:1
13:5 [y]2Sa 7:13 [z]Lev 2:13; Nu 18:19
13:6 [a]1Ki 11:26
13:7 [b]Jdg 9:4
13:8 [c]1Ki 12:28; 2Ch 11:15
13:9 [d]2Ch 11:14-15 [e]Ex 29:35-36 [f]Jer 2:11
13:11 [g]Ex 29:39; 2Ch 2:4 [h]Lev 24:5-9
13:12 [i]Nu 10:8-9 [j]Ac 5:39
13:13 [k]Jos 8:9

[a] *2* Most Septuagint manuscripts and Syriac (see also 2 Chron. 11:20 and 1 Kings 15:2); Hebrew *Micaiah* [b] *2* Or *granddaughter*

13:14 and rear. Then they cried out[l] to the LORD. The
[l]2Ch 14:11 priests blew their trumpets 15and the men of
Judah raised the battle cry. At the sound of their
13:15 [m]2Ch 14:12 battle cry, God routed Jeroboam and all Israel[m]
before Abijah and Judah. 16The Israelites fled
13:16 [n]2Ch 16:8 before Judah, and God delivered[n] them into their
hands. 17Abijah and his men inflicted heavy losses
on them, so that there were five hundred thousand casualties among Israel's able men. 18The
men of Israel were subdued on that occasion, and
the men of Judah were victorious because they
13:18 [o]1Ch 5:20; relied[o] on the LORD, the God of their fathers.
2Ch 14:11; 19Abijah pursued Jeroboam and took from him
Ps 22:5 the towns of Bethel, Jeshanah and Ephron, with
their surrounding villages. 20Jeroboam did not
regain power during the time of Abijah. And the
LORD struck him down and he died.
21But Abijah grew in strength. He married fourteen wives and had twenty-two sons and sixteen
daughters.
22The other events of Abijah's reign, what he
did and what he said, are written in the annotations of the prophet Iddo.

14 And Abijah rested with his fathers and was
buried in the City of David. Asa his son succeeded him as king, and in his days the country
was at peace for ten years.

Asa King of Judah

2Asa did what was good and right in the eyes of
the LORD his God. 3He removed the foreign altars
and the high places, smashed the sacred stones
14:3 [p]Ex 34:13; and cut down the Asherah poles.[a][p] 4He command-
Dt 7:5; ed Judah to seek the LORD, the God of their fathers,
1Ki 15:12-14 and to obey his laws and commands. 5He removed
14:5 [q]2Ch 34:4,7 the high places and incense altars[q] in every town
in Judah, and the kingdom was at peace under
him. 6He built up the fortified cities of Judah, since
the land was at peace. No one was at war with him
14:6 [r]1Ch 22:9; during those years, for the LORD gave him rest.[r]
2Ch 15:15 7"Let us build up these towns," he said to
Judah, "and put walls around them, with towers,
gates and bars. The land is still ours, because we
have sought the LORD our God; we sought him and
he has given us rest on every side." So they built
and prospered.
8Asa had an army of three hundred thousand
men from Judah, equipped with large shields and
with spears, and two hundred and eighty thousand from Benjamin, armed with small shields
and with bows. All these were brave fighting men.
9Zerah the Cushite[s] marched out against them
14:9 [s]2Ch 12:3; with a vast army[b] and three hundred chariots, and
16:8 came as far as Mareshah.[t] 10Asa went out to meet
[t]2Ch 11:8 him, and they took up battle positions in the Valley of Zephathah near Mareshah.

[a]3 That is, symbols of the goddess Asherah; here and elsewhere in 2 Chronicles [b]9 Hebrew *with an army of a thousand thousands* or *with an army of thousands upon thousands*

A Time of Peace

2CH 14:1-7

Since Asa abolishes idols and encourages spiritual reform, God blesses his reign with ten years of peace. Believing it would be wise during peaceful times to prepare for future possible trouble, Asa instructs the people to "build up these towns . . . and put walls around them, with towers, gates and bars" (2Ch 14:7).

Walls of stone, up to 20–30 feet thick, protect Israel's larger towns against invasion. Since gates are the most vulnerable part of the wall, they are usually flanked by towers (tall silo-like structures erected so the town's inhabitants can watch for approaching enemies). Iron and bronze bars strengthen the heavy wooden gates, which are usually closed at night and, of course, when the town is under attack.

During this time of peace, the Israelites wisely prepare themselves and their towns for potential trouble. We, too, can prepare ourselves and our families for future adversity by praying, planning and making God our strong tower of protection (Ps 61:3).

Be Strong

2CH 15:1–8

The prophet Azariah comes to encourage King Asa. Azariah first recalls when Israel endured a frightening era of war and turmoil (2Ch 15:5–6), probably during the time of the judges. Even traveling from town to town was a dangerous experience. Azariah reminds Asa that during that time, when the people sought God, he delivered them. He then encourages Asa to continue the good work he has begun.

Asa listens to the prophet's reassuring words. With God-given boldness, he confronts the adamant idol worshipers and destroys their gods (1Ki 15:12–13). Asa faces intimidating circumstances. Perhaps he recalls what his ancestor, King David, wrote: "When I am afraid, I will trust in [God]" (Ps 56:3). Both Asa and David acknowledge that Almighty God is the believer's source of courage. Underline the phrase "the LORD is with you" (2Ch 15:2) and then draw an arrow to the word "courage" (2Ch 15:8) to remind you of the source of courage.

11 Then Asa called[u] to the LORD his God and said,
"LORD, there is no one like you to help the powerless against the mighty. Help us, O LORD our God,
for we rely[v] on you, and in your name[w] we have
come against this vast army. O LORD, you are our
God; do not let man prevail[x] against you."
12 The LORD struck down[y] the Cushites before
Asa and Judah. The Cushites fled, 13 and Asa and
his army pursued them as far as Gerar.[z] Such a
great number of Cushites fell that they could not
recover; they were crushed before the LORD and
his forces. The men of Judah carried off a large
amount of plunder. 14 They destroyed all the villages around Gerar, for the terror[a] of the LORD had
fallen upon them. They plundered all these villages, since there was much booty there. 15 They
also attacked the camps of the herdsmen and carried off droves of sheep and goats and camels.
Then they returned to Jerusalem.

Asa's Reform

15 The Spirit of God came upon[b] Azariah son
of Oded. 2 He went out to meet Asa and said
to him, "Listen to me, Asa and all Judah and Benjamin. The LORD is with you[c] when you are with
him.[d] If you seek[e] him, he will be found by you,
but if you forsake him, he will forsake you.[f] 3 For
a long time Israel was without the true God, without a priest to teach[g] and without the law.[h] 4 But in
their distress they turned to the LORD, the God of
Israel, and sought him,[i] and he was found by
them. 5 In those days it was not safe to travel
about,[j] for all the inhabitants of the lands were in
great turmoil. 6 One nation was being crushed by
another and one city by another,[k] because God
was troubling them with every kind of distress.
7 But as for you, be strong[l] and do not give up, for
your work will be rewarded."[m]
8 When Asa heard these words and the prophecy of Azariah son of[a] Oded the prophet, he took
courage. He removed the detestable idols from the
whole land of Judah and Benjamin and from the
towns he had captured[n] in the hills of Ephraim.
He repaired the altar[o] of the LORD that was in front
of the portico of the LORD's temple.
9 Then he assembled all Judah and Benjamin
and the people from Ephraim, Manasseh and Simeon who had settled among them, for large numbers[p] had come over to him from Israel when they
saw that the LORD his God was with him.
10 They assembled at Jerusalem in the third
month of the fifteenth year of Asa's reign. 11 At that
time they sacrificed to the LORD seven hundred
head of cattle and seven thousand sheep and goats
from the plunder[q] they had brought back. 12 They
entered into a covenant[r] to seek the LORD,[s] the God
of their fathers, with all their heart and soul. 13 All
who would not seek the LORD, the God of Israel,

14:11 [u]2Ch 13:14 [v]2Ch 13:18 [w]1Sa 17:45 [x]1Sa 14:6; Ps 9:19
14:12 [y]2Ch 13:15
14:13 [z]Ge 10:19
14:14 [a]Ge 35:5; 2Ch 17:10
15:1 [b]Nu 11:25, 26; 24:2; 2Ch 20:14; 24:20
15:2 [c]ver 4,15; 2Ch 20:17 [d]Jas 4:8 [e]Jer 29:13 [f]1Ch 28:9; 2Ch 24:20
15:3 [g]Lev 10:11 [h]2Ch 17:9; La 2:9
15:4 [i]Dt 4:29
15:5 [j]Jdg 5:6
15:6 [k]Mt 24:7
15:7 [l]Jos 1:7,9 [m]Ps 58:11
15:8 [n]2Ch 13:19 [o]2Ch 8:12
15:9 [p]2Ch 11:16-17
15:11 [q]2Ch 14:13
15:12 [r]2Ki 11:17; 2Ch 23:16; 34:31 [s]1Ch 16:11

[a] *8* Vulgate and Syriac (see also Septuagint and verse 1); Hebrew does not have *Azariah son of*.

15:13 were to be put to death,[t] whether small or great,
[t]Ex 22:20; man or woman. [14]They took an oath to the LORD
Dt 13:9-16 with loud acclamation, with shouting and with
trumpets and horns. [15]All Judah rejoiced about the
15:15 oath because they had sworn it wholeheartedly.
[u]Dt 4:29 They sought God[u] eagerly, and he was found by
[v]1Ch 22:9; 2Ch 14:7 them. So the LORD gave them rest[v] on every side.
[16]King Asa also deposed his grandmother Maa-
15:16 cah from her position as queen mother, because
[w]Ex 34:13; she had made a repulsive Asherah pole.[w] Asa cut
2Ch 14:2-5 the pole down, broke it up and burned it in the
Kidron Valley. [17]Although he did not remove the
high places from Israel, Asa's heart was fully committed ⌊to the LORD⌋ all his life. [18]He brought into
the temple of God the silver and gold and the articles that he and his father had dedicated.
[19]There was no more war until the thirty-fifth
year of Asa's reign.

Asa's Last Years

16:1 **16** In the thirty-sixth year of Asa's reign Baa-
[x]Jer 41:9 sha[x] king of Israel went up against Judah
and fortified Ramah to prevent anyone from leaving or entering the territory of Asa king of Judah.
[2]Asa then took the silver and gold out of the
treasuries of the LORD's temple and of his own
palace and sent it to Ben-Hadad king of Aram,
who was ruling in Damascus. [3]"Let there be a
16:3 treaty[y] between me and you," he said, "as there
[y]2Ch 20:35 was between my father and your father. See, I am
sending you silver and gold. Now break your
treaty with Baasha king of Israel so he will withdraw from me."
[4]Ben-Hadad agreed with King Asa and sent the
commanders of his forces against the towns of
Israel. They conquered Ijon, Dan, Abel Maim[a] and
all the store cities of Naphtali. [5]When Baasha
heard this, he stopped building Ramah and abandoned his work. [6]Then King Asa brought all the
men of Judah, and they carried away from Ramah
the stones and timber Baasha had been using.
With them he built up Geba and Mizpah.
16:7 [7]At that time Hanani[z] the seer came to Asa king
[z]1Ki 16:1 of Judah and said to him: "Because you relied on
the king of Aram and not on the LORD your God,
the army of the king of Aram has escaped from
16:8 your hand. [8]Were not the Cushites[b][a] and Libyans
[a]2Ch 12:3; 14:9 a mighty army with great numbers of chariots and
[b]2Ch 13:16 horsemen[c]? Yet when you relied on the LORD, he
16:9 delivered[b] them into your hand. [9]For the eyes[c] of
[c]Pr 15:3; the LORD range throughout the earth to strengthen
Jer 16:17; Zec 4:10 those whose hearts are fully committed to him.
[d]1Sa 13:13 You have done a foolish[d] thing, and from now on
you will be at war."
[10]Asa was angry with the seer because of this;
he was so enraged that he put him in prison. At
the same time Asa brutally oppressed some of the
people.

[a]4 Also known as *Abel Beth Maacah* [b]8 That is, people from the upper Nile region [c]8 Or *charioteers*

Faith Above Family

2CH 15:16

King Asa's grandmother, Maacah, worships idols and erects a "repulsive" Asherah pole. Asherah poles are affiliated with the worship of Baal's goddess-companion, Asherah. Asa removes all the authority and power Maacah holds as queen mother. He knows she is not a good influence on the people. Perhaps this highly uncomfortable situation is one reason Asa needs courage (2Ch 15:8). No doubt, Asa finds it difficult to put his faith above his family, but it is the right decision.

Jesus addresses this family-versus-faith dilemma when he says, "Anyone who loves his father or mother more than me is not worthy of me" (Mt 10:37). Jesus does not mean we should hate our family members or treat them poorly. He simply wants us to put our relationship with the triune God above all other relationships.

Help From the Lord

2CH 16:12

Asa is classified as a "good" king, yet toward the end of his life he turns his back on God. Instead of asking for God's help when Judah's relations with Israel begin to sour, he seeks a foreign king's help and pays him with money from the temple treasury to resolve the problem (2Ch 16:2–5). Then he incarcerates a prophet and oppresses his people (2Ch 16:10). Later, when he contracts a serious foot disease, he refuses to go to God for help, but instead seeks only the advice of physicians. Asa appears to willfully choose not *to seek help from God.*

Like his ancestor King David, Asa makes sinful choices (2Sa 12:7–13). Each king has the opportunity and privilege to repent. David does. We have no record, however, of Asa's repentance. He dies after a 41-year reign and is buried with honors.

11The events of Asa's reign, from beginning to
end, are written in the book of the kings of Judah
and Israel. 12In the thirty-ninth year of his reign
Asa was afflicted with a disease in his feet.
Though his disease was severe, even in his illness
he did not seek help from the LORD,[e] but only from
the physicians. 13Then in the forty-first year of his
reign Asa died and rested with his fathers. 14They
buried him in the tomb that he had cut out for
himself in the City of David. They laid him on a
bier covered with spices and various blended perfumes,[f] and they made a huge fire[g] in his honor.

Jehoshaphat King of Judah

17 Jehoshaphat his son succeeded him as king
and strengthened himself against Israel. 2He
stationed troops in all the fortified cities of Judah
and put garrisons in Judah and in the towns of
Ephraim that his father Asa had captured.[h]
3The LORD was with Jehoshaphat because in his
early years he walked in the ways his father David[i]
had followed. He did not consult the Baals 4but
sought[j] the God of his father and followed his commands rather than the practices of Israel. 5The LORD
established the kingdom under his control; and all
Judah brought gifts[k] to Jehoshaphat, so that he had
great wealth and honor.[l] 6His heart was devoted[m] to
the ways of the LORD; furthermore, he removed the
high places[n] and the Asherah poles[o] from Judah.[p]
7In the third year of his reign he sent his officials Ben-Hail, Obadiah, Zechariah, Nethanel and
Micaiah to teach[q] in the towns of Judah. 8With
them were certain Levites[r]—Shemaiah, Nethaniah, Zebadiah, Asahel, Shemiramoth, Jehonathan,
Adonijah, Tobijah and Tob-Adonijah—and the
priests Elishama and Jehoram. 9They taught
throughout Judah, taking with them the Book of
the Law[s] of the LORD; they went around to all the
towns of Judah and taught the people.
10The fear[t] of the LORD fell on all the kingdoms
of the lands surrounding Judah, so that they did
not make war with Jehoshaphat. 11Some Philistines brought Jehoshaphat gifts and silver as tribute, and the Arabs[u] brought him flocks:[v] seven
thousand seven hundred rams and seven thousand seven hundred goats.
12Jehoshaphat became more and more powerful; he built forts and store cities in Judah 13and
had large supplies in the towns of Judah. He also
kept experienced fighting men in Jerusalem.
14Their enrollment[w] by families was as follows:

From Judah, commanders of units of 1,000:
Adnah the commander, with 300,000 fighting men;
15next, Jehohanan the commander, with 280,000;
16next, Amasiah son of Zicri, who volunteered[x] himself for the service of the LORD, with 200,000.

17From Benjamin:[y]

16:12 [e]Jer 17:5-6
16:14 [f]Ge 50:2; Jn 19:39-40 [g]2Ch 21:19; Jer 34:5
17:2 [h]2Ch 15:8
17:3 [i]1Ki 22:43
17:4 [j]1Ki 12:28; 2Ch 22:9
17:5 [k]1Sa 10:27 [l]2Ch 18:1
17:6 [m]1Ki 8:61; 2Ch 15:17 [n]1Ki 15:14; 2Ch 19:3; 20:33 [o]Ex 34:13 [p]2Ch 21:12
17:7 [q]Lev 10:11; Dt 6:4-9; 2Ch 15:3; 35:3
17:8 [r]2Ch 19:8; Ne 8:7-8
17:9 [s]Dt 6:4-9; 28:61
17:10 [t]Ge 35:5; Dt 2:25; 2Ch 14:14
17:11 [u]2Ch 9:14; 26:8 [v]2Ch 21:16
17:14 [w]2Sa 24:2
17:16 [x]Jdg 5:9; 1Ch 29:9
17:17 [y]Nu 1:36

Eliada, a valiant soldier, with 200,000 men
armed with bows and shields;
18 next, Jehozabad, with 180,000 men armed
for battle.

17:19
[z]2Ch 11:10
[a]2Ch 25:5

19 These were the men who served the king,
besides those he stationed in the fortified cities[z]
throughout Judah.[a]

Micaiah Prophesies Against Ahab

18:1
[b]2Ch 17:5
[c]2Ch 19:1-3;
22:3
[d]2Ch 21:6

18 Now Jehoshaphat had great wealth and
honor,[b] and he allied[c] himself with Ahab[d]
by marriage. 2 Some years later he went down to
visit Ahab in Samaria. Ahab slaughtered many
sheep and cattle for him and the people with him
and urged him to attack Ramoth Gilead. 3 Ahab
king of Israel asked Jehoshaphat king of Judah,
"Will you go with me against Ramoth Gilead?"

Jehoshaphat replied, "I am as you are, and my
people as your people; we will join you in the
war." 4 But Jehoshaphat also said to the king of
Israel, "First seek the counsel of the LORD."

5 So the king of Israel brought together the
prophets—four hundred men—and asked them,
"Shall we go to war against Ramoth Gilead, or
shall I refrain?"

"Go," they answered, "for God will give it into
the king's hand."

6 But Jehoshaphat asked, "Is there not a prophet of the LORD here whom we can inquire of?"

7 The king of Israel answered Jehoshaphat,
"There is still one man through whom we can
inquire of the LORD, but I hate him because he
never prophesies anything good about me, but
always bad. He is Micaiah son of Imlah."

"The king should not say that," Jehoshaphat
replied.

8 So the king of Israel called one of his officials
and said, "Bring Micaiah son of Imlah at once."

9 Dressed in their royal robes, the king of Israel
and Jehoshaphat king of Judah were sitting on
their thrones at the threshing floor by the entrance
to the gate of Samaria, with all the prophets
prophesying before them. 10 Now Zedekiah son of
Kenaanah had made iron horns, and he declared,
"This is what the LORD says: 'With these you will
gore the Arameans until they are destroyed.' "

18:11
[e]2Ch 22:5

11 All the other prophets were prophesying the
same thing. "Attack Ramoth Gilead[e] and be victorious," they said, "for the LORD will give it into the
king's hand."

12 The messenger who had gone to summon
Micaiah said to him, "Look, as one man the other
prophets are predicting success for the king. Let
your word agree with theirs, and speak favorably."

18:13
[f]Nu 22:18,
20,35

13 But Micaiah said, "As surely as the LORD lives,
I can tell him only what my God says."[f]

14 When he arrived, the king asked him, "Micaiah, shall we go to war against Ramoth Gilead, or
shall I refrain?"

King Jehoshaphat

2CH 18:9

King Jehoshaphat aims to live a godly life (2Ch 17:3, 6). He develops a plan for teaching the Israelites (2Ch 17:9; 19:4) and clears out the idols (2Ch 17:6). He wins the respect of Israelites *and* foreigners.

Yet Jehoshaphat joins forces with corrupt King Ahab and marries his son to Ahab's idol-worshiping daughter (2Ch 18:1). The two kings agree to go to war against Ramoth Gilead (see Map 7: Prophets in Israel and Judah at the back of this Bible). Together they sit in all their royal regalia at the threshing floor (the widest open spot) of Samaria's city gate (a place for public business.) Stretched out before them are 400 of Ahab's "yes-men" (prophets), shouting assurances that God wants this war. It is quite a scene! Although King Jehoshaphat remains committed to God, his poor decision to align with wicked King Ahab produces long-term negative consequences for his family and the kingdom of Judah (2Ch 21:4-6).

We, too, can easily forget that the decisions we make may have long-ranging effects on others. Choosing *not* to confront the sin results in a child whose heart is far from God. Working long hours to afford a few of life's luxuries may mean forfeiting a closer family years later. The often-used adage "No man (or woman!) is an island" is true—our actions *do* affect others.

Ignoring the Prophet

2CH 18:12-34

Egotistical King Ahab makes up his mind to attack Ramoth Gilead. He does not care what God thinks. He calls on Micaiah to prophesy only because King Jehoshaphat of Judah asks him to obtain the advice of a true prophet of God. Ahab's 400 "yes-men" encourage the proposed war, but bold Micaiah says God is against it.

Then why does the godly King Jehoshaphat agree to join Ahab in this war? Maybe Jehoshaphat succumbs to the pressure of those who advise war. Perhaps he feels obligated because his son is married to Ahab's daughter. Maybe he knows it is a mistake and is just too timid or embarrassed to back out. Whatever the reason, Jehoshaphat puts himself and his soldiers in danger. God in his mercy spares Jehoshaphat as he cries out (2Ch 18:31). Evidently, Jehoshaphat realizes his error because later, when faced with another war, he fasts and prays and follows the directions he's given (2Ch 20).

"Attack and be victorious," he answered, "for
they will be given into your hand."
15 The king said to him, "How many times must
I make you swear to tell me nothing but the truth
in the name of the LORD?"
16 Then Micaiah answered, "I saw all Israel[g]
scattered on the hills like sheep without a shepherd,[h] and the LORD said, 'These people have no
master. Let each one go home in peace.' "
17 The king of Israel said to Jehoshaphat, "Didn't
I tell you that he never prophesies anything good
about me, but only bad?"
18 Micaiah continued, "Therefore hear the word
of the LORD: I saw the LORD sitting on his throne[i]
with all the host of heaven standing on his right
and on his left. 19 And the LORD said, 'Who will
entice Ahab king of Israel into attacking Ramoth
Gilead and going to his death there?'
"One suggested this, and another that. 20 Finally,
a spirit came forward, stood before the LORD and
said, 'I will entice him.'
" 'By what means?' the LORD asked.
21 " 'I will go and be a lying spirit[j] in the mouths
of all his prophets,' he said.
" 'You will succeed in enticing him,' said the
LORD. 'Go and do it.'
22 "So now the LORD has put a lying spirit in the
mouths of these prophets of yours.[k] The LORD has
decreed disaster for you."
23 Then Zedekiah son of Kenaanah went up and
slapped[l] Micaiah in the face. "Which way did the
spirit from[a] the LORD go when he went from me to
speak to you?" he asked.
24 Micaiah replied, "You will find out on the day
you go to hide in an inner room."
25 The king of Israel then ordered, "Take Micaiah
and send him back to Amon the ruler of the city
and to Joash the king's son, 26 and say, 'This is
what the king says: Put this fellow in prison[m] and
give him nothing but bread and water until I
return safely.' "
27 Micaiah declared, "If you ever return safely,
the LORD has not spoken through me." Then he
added, "Mark my words, all you people!"

Ahab Killed at Ramoth Gilead

28 So the king of Israel and Jehoshaphat king of
Judah went up to Ramoth Gilead. 29 The king of
Israel said to Jehoshaphat, "I will enter the battle
in disguise, but you wear your royal robes." So the
king of Israel disguised[n] himself and went into
battle.
30 Now the king of Aram had ordered his chariot commanders, "Do not fight with anyone, small
or great, except the king of Israel." 31 When the
chariot commanders saw Jehoshaphat, they
thought, "This is the king of Israel." So they
turned to attack him, but Jehoshaphat cried out,[o]
and the LORD helped him. God drew them away

18:16 [g]1Ch 9:1 [h]Nu 27:17; Eze 34:5-8
18:18 [i]Da 7:9
18:21 [j]1Ch 21:1; Job 1:6; Zec 3:1; Jn 8:44
18:22 [k]Job 12:16; Isa 19:14; Eze 14:9
18:23 [l]Jer 20:2; Mk 14:65; Ac 23:2
18:26 [m]2Ch 16:10; Heb 11:36
18:29 [n]1Sa 28:8
18:31 [o]2Ch 13:14

[a] 23 Or *Spirit of*

from him, 32for when the chariot commanders
saw that he was not the king of Israel, they
stopped pursuing him.
33But someone drew his bow at random and hit
the king of Israel between the sections of his
armor. The king told the chariot driver, "Wheel
around and get me out of the fighting. I've been
wounded." 34All day long the battle raged, and the
king of Israel propped himself up in his chariot
18:34 facing the Arameans until evening. Then at sunset
[p]2Ch 22:5 he died.[p]

19:2 **19** When Jehoshaphat king of Judah returned
safely to his palace in Jerusalem, 2Jehu[q] the
[q]1Ki 16:1 [r]2Ch 16:2-9 seer, the son of Hanani, went out to meet him and
[s]Ps 139:21-22 said to the king, "Should you help the wicked[r]
[t]2Ch 24:18; 32:25; and love[a] those who hate the LORD?[s] Because of
Ps 7:11 this, the wrath[t] of the LORD is upon you. 3There
is, however, some good[u] in you, for you have rid
19:3 the land of the Asherah poles[v] and have set your
[u]1Ki 14:13; 2Ch 12:12 heart on seeking God.[w]"

[v]2Ch 17:6 [w]2Ch 18:1; 20:35; 25:7; Ezr 7:10

Jehoshaphat Appoints Judges

4Jehoshaphat lived in Jerusalem, and he went
out again among the people from Beersheba to the
hill country of Ephraim and turned them back to
19:5 the LORD, the God of their fathers. 5He appointed
[x]Ge 47:6; judges[x] in the land, in each of the fortified cities of
Ex 18:26 Judah. 6He told them, "Consider carefully what
19:6 you do,[y] because you are not judging for man[z] but
[y]Lev 19:15 for the LORD, who is with you whenever you give
[z]Dt 1:17; a verdict. 7Now let the fear of the LORD be upon
16:18-20; 17:8-13 you. Judge carefully, for with the LORD our God
there is no injustice[a] or partiality[b] or bribery."
19:7 8In Jerusalem also, Jehoshaphat appointed
[a]Ge 18:25; Dt 32:4 some of the Levites, priests and heads of Israelite
[b]Dt 10:17; families to administer[c] the law of the LORD and to
Job 34:19; Ro 2:11; settle disputes. And they lived in Jerusalem. 9He
Col 3:25 gave them these orders: "You must serve faithful-
19:8 ly and wholeheartedly in the fear of the LORD. 10In
[c]2Ch 17:8-9 every case that comes before you from your fellow countrymen who live in the cities—whether
bloodshed or other concerns of the law, commands, decrees or ordinances—you are to warn
19:10 them not to sin against the LORD;[d] otherwise his
[d]Dt 17:8-13 wrath will come on you and your brothers. Do
this, and you will not sin.
11"Amariah the chief priest will be over you in
any matter concerning the LORD, and Zebadiah
son of Ishmael, the leader of the tribe of Judah,
will be over you in any matter concerning the
19:11 king, and the Levites will serve as officials before
[e]1Ch 28:20 you. Act with courage,[e] and may the LORD be with
those who do well."

Jehoshaphat Defeats Moab and Ammon

20:1 **20** After this, the Moabites and Ammonites
[f]1Ch 4:41 with some of the Meunites[b][f] came to make
war on Jehoshaphat.

[a] 2 Or *and make alliances with* [b] 1 Some Septuagint manuscripts; Hebrew *Ammonites*

Good King Jehoshaphat

2CH 19:4-11

After escaping from the dangerous battle against Syria, Jehoshaphat travels throughout his own kingdom challenging his people to recommit themselves to God. His name, Jehoshaphat, means "the LORD judges," and it is fitting for the king who reforms Judah's judicial system. Jehoshaphat implements an ingenious religious and judicial system that is a model years later for the Jewish exiles who return from Babylonian captivity to restore Jerusalem.

Perhaps this is one reason the writer of Chronicles dedicates so much space to Jehoshaphat's story. His writing goal is to inspire the returning exiles to trust their ancestors' God and to emulate the wise leadership of the godly kings. Since the northern kingdom had no *godly kings, the writer focuses on the devout kings of Judah. Asa, Jehoshaphat, Jotham, Hezekiah and Josiah join David and Solomon in doing what is "right in the eyes of the LORD" (2Ch 14:2; 20:32; 27:2; 29:2; 34:2), a commendable epitaph for anyone.*

A United People

2CH 20:13

As Moses and the Israelites headed toward the promised land, God instructed them not to aggravate the Edomites, Ammonites and the Moabites who lived east of the Jordan (Dt 2:2–6). They obeyed and avoided a confrontation at that time. However, during Jehoshaphat's reign the Moabites, Ammonites and Meunites march toward Judah with the intent to attack.

The worried king goes to God for help (2Ch 20:3). He calls all the people—men, women and children from every town—to come to the temple for prayer and fasting. This alarming situation affects everyone, and the king includes all in the solution. They stand united in prayer, admitting their powerlessness over this organized military action. God responds through one willing person, who steps forward and says, "Do not be afraid or discouraged . . . For the battle is not yours, but God's" (2Ch 20:15).

2Some men came and told Jehoshaphat, "A vast army is coming against you from Edom,[a] from the other side of the Sea.[b] It is already in Hazazon Tamar[g]" (that is, En Gedi). 3Alarmed, Jehoshaphat resolved to inquire of the LORD, and he proclaimed a fast[h] for all Judah. 4The people of Judah came together to seek help from the LORD; indeed, they came from every town in Judah to seek him.

5Then Jehoshaphat stood up in the assembly of Judah and Jerusalem at the temple of the LORD in the front of the new courtyard 6and said:

"O LORD, God of our fathers,[i] are you not the God who is in heaven?[j] You rule over all the kingdoms[k] of the nations. Power and might are in your hand, and no one can withstand you. 7O our God, did you not drive out the inhabitants of this land before your people Israel and give it forever to the descendants of Abraham your friend?[l] 8They have lived in it and have built in it a sanctuary[m] for your Name, saying, 9'If calamity comes upon us, whether the sword of judgment, or plague or famine,[n] we will stand in your presence before this temple that bears your Name and will cry out to you in our distress, and you will hear us and save us.'

10"But now here are men from Ammon, Moab and Mount Seir, whose territory you would not allow Israel to invade when they came from Egypt;[o] so they turned away from them and did not destroy them. 11See how they are repaying us by coming to drive us out of the possession[p] you gave us as an inheritance. 12O our God, will you not judge them?[q] For we have no power to face this vast army that is attacking us. We do not know what to do, but our eyes are upon you.[r]"

13All the men of Judah, with their wives and children and little ones, stood there before the LORD.

14Then the Spirit[s] of the LORD came upon Jahaziel son of Zechariah, the son of Benaiah, the son of Jeiel, the son of Mattaniah, a Levite and descendant of Asaph, as he stood in the assembly.

15He said: "Listen, King Jehoshaphat and all who live in Judah and Jerusalem! This is what the LORD says to you: 'Do not be afraid or discouraged[t] because of this vast army. For the battle[u] is not yours, but God's. 16Tomorrow march down against them. They will be climbing up by the Pass of Ziz, and you will find them at the end of the gorge in the Desert of Jeruel. 17You will not have to fight this battle. Take up your positions; stand firm and see[v] the deliverance the LORD will give you, O Judah and Jerusalem. Do not be afraid; do not be discouraged. Go out to face them tomorrow, and the LORD will be with you.' "

20:2 [g]Ge 14:7
20:3 [h]1Sa 7:6; 2Ch 19:3; Ezr 8:21; Jer 36:9; Jnh 3:5,7
20:6 [i]Mt 6:9 [j]Dt 4:39 [k]1Ch 29:11-12
20:7 [l]Isa 41:8; Jas 2:23
20:8 [m]2Ch 6:20
20:9 [n]2Ch 6:28
20:10 [o]Nu 20:14-21; Dt 2:4-6, 9,18-19
20:11 [p]Ps 83:1-12
20:12 [q]Jdg 11:27 [r]Ps 25:15; 121:1-2
20:14 [s]2Ch 15:1
20:15 [t]2Ch 32:7 [u]Ex 14:13-14; 1Sa 17:47
20:17 [v]Ex 14:13; 2Ch 15:2

[a] *2* One Hebrew manuscript; most Hebrew manuscripts, Septuagint and Vulgate *Aram* [b] *2* That is, the Dead Sea

20:18 18 Jehoshaphat bowed[w] with his face to the
[w]Ex 4:31 ground, and all the people of Judah and Jerusalem fell down in worship before the LORD. 19 Then
some Levites from the Kohathites and Korahites
stood up and praised the LORD, the God of Israel,
with a very loud voice.
20 Early in the morning they left for the Desert of
Tekoa. As they set out, Jehoshaphat stood and
20:20 said, "Listen to me, Judah and people of Jerusa-
[x]Isa 7:9 lem! Have faith[x] in the LORD your God and you
[y]Ge 39:3; will be upheld; have faith in his prophets and you
Pr 16:3 will be successful.[y]" 21 After consulting the people,
Jehoshaphat appointed men to sing to the LORD
20:21 and to praise him for the splendor of his[a] holi-
[z]1Ch 16:29; ness[z] as they went out at the head of the army,
Ps 29:2 saying:
[a]2Ch 5:13;

> "Give thanks to the LORD,
>
> Ps 136:1 for his love endures forever."[a]

20:22 22 As they began to sing and praise, the LORD set
[b]Jdg 7:22; ambushes[b] against the men of Ammon and Moab
2Ch 13:13 and Mount Seir who were invading Judah, and
20:23 they were defeated. 23 The men of Ammon[c] and
[c]Ge 19:38 Moab rose up against the men from Mount Seir[d]
[d]2Ch 21:8 to destroy and annihilate them. After they fin-
[e]Jdg 7:22; 1Sa 14:20; ished slaughtering the men from Seir, they helped
Eze 38:21 to destroy one another.[e]
24 When the men of Judah came to the place that
overlooks the desert and looked toward the vast
army, they saw only dead bodies lying on the
ground; no one had escaped. 25 So Jehoshaphat
and his men went to carry off their plunder, and
they found among them a great amount of equipment and clothing[b] and also articles of value—
more than they could take away. There was so
much plunder that it took three days to collect it.
26 On the fourth day they assembled in the Valley
of Beracah, where they praised the LORD. This is
why it is called the Valley of Beracah[c] to this day.
27 Then, led by Jehoshaphat, all the men of
Judah and Jerusalem returned joyfully to Jerusalem, for the LORD had given them cause to rejoice
over their enemies. 28 They entered Jerusalem and
went to the temple of the LORD with harps and
lutes and trumpets.
20:29 29 The fear[f] of God came upon all the kingdoms
[f]Ge 35:5; Dt 2:25; of the countries when they heard how the LORD
2Ch 14:14; had fought[g] against the enemies of Israel. 30 And
17:10 the kingdom of Jehoshaphat was at peace, for his
[g]Ex 14:14 God had given him rest[h] on every side.
20:30 [h]1Ch 22:9; 2Ch 14:6-7; 15:15

The End of Jehoshaphat's Reign

31 So Jehoshaphat reigned over Judah. He was
thirty-five years old when he became king of
Judah, and he reigned in Jerusalem twenty-five
years. His mother's name was Azubah daughter
of Shilhi. 32 He walked in the ways of his father

[a] 21 Or *him with the splendor of* [b] 25 Some Hebrew manuscripts and Vulgate; most Hebrew manuscripts *corpses* [c] 26 *Beracah* means *praise.*

The Lord God planted a garden
In the first white days of the world,
And He set there an angel warden
In a garment of light enfurled.

So near to the peace of Heaven,
That the hawk might nest with the wren,
For there in the cool of the even
God walked with the first of men.

And I dream that these garden-closes
With their shade and their sun-flecked sod
And their lilies and bowers of roses,
Were laid by the hand of God.

The kiss of the sun for pardon,
The song of the birds for mirth—
One is nearer God's heart in a garden
Than anywhere else on earth. 

—Dorothy Frances Gurney (1858-1932)

A Dangerous Alliance

2CH 21:6

Jehoshaphat jeopardized his family and his kingdom by aligning with wicked Ahab. This political alliance resulted in Jehoshaphat's eldest son, Jehoram, marrying the daughter of Ahab and Jezebel (2Ch 18:1).

As king, Jehoram rejects his father's godly lifestyle and adopts the beliefs of his idol-worshiping wife, Athaliah. He murders his brothers and institutes Baal worship. Eventually his wife, Athaliah, kills her own grandsons and becomes queen (2Ki 11:1-3). Athaliah never turns to God, and her life ends tragically (2Ki 11:16). (See character sketch for Athaliah on page 1277.)

Jehoshaphat's alliance with Ahab and Jehoram's marriage to Athaliah serve to clearly illustrate for us the dangers of associating with those who would turn us away from following God wholeheartedly. No less today than in their time, our close associations—those that involve our hearts—must be with those whose hearts are turned with ours toward serving God.

Asa and did not stray from them; he did what was **20:33**
right in the eyes of the LORD. 33The high places,[i] [i]2Ch 17:6;
however, were not removed, and the people still 19:3
had not set their hearts on the God of their fathers.
34The other events of Jehoshaphat's reign, from
beginning to end, are written in the annals of **20:34**
Jehu[j] son of Hanani, which are recorded in the [j]1Ki 16:1
book of the kings of Israel.
35Later, Jehoshaphat king of Judah made an **20:35**
alliance[k] with Ahaziah king of Israel, who was [k]2Ch 16:3
guilty of wickedness.[l] 36He agreed with him to [l]2Ch 19:1-3
construct a fleet of trading ships.[a] After these were
built at Ezion Geber, 37Eliezer son of Dodavahu of
Mareshah prophesied against Jehoshaphat, saying,
"Because you have made an alliance with
Ahaziah, the LORD will destroy what you have **20:37**
made." The ships[m] were wrecked and were not [m]1Ki 9:26;
able to set sail to trade.[b] 2Ch 9:21

21 Then Jehoshaphat rested with his fathers
and was buried with them in the City of **21:1**
David. And Jehoram[n] his son succeeded him as [n]1Ch 3:11
king. 2Jehoram's brothers, the sons of Jehoshaphat,
were Azariah, Jehiel, Zechariah, Azariahu,
Michael and Shephatiah. All these were sons of
Jehoshaphat king of Israel.[c] 3Their father had giv- **21:3**
en them many gifts[o] of silver and gold and arti- [o]2Ch 11:23
cles of value, as well as fortified cities[p] in Judah, [p]2Ch 11:10
but he had given the kingdom to Jehoram because
he was his firstborn son.

Jehoram King of Judah

4When Jehoram established[q] himself firmly **21:4** [q]1Ki 2:12
over his father's kingdom, he put all his brothers[r] [r]Jdg 9:5
to the sword along with some of the princes of
Israel. 5Jehoram was thirty-two years old when he
became king, and he reigned in Jerusalem eight
years. 6He walked in the ways of the kings of Isra-
el,[s] as the house of Ahab had done, for he mar- **21:6** [s]1Ki 12:28-
ried a daughter of Ahab.[t] He did evil in the eyes of 30
the LORD. 7Nevertheless, because of the covenant [t]2Ch 18:1;
the LORD had made with David,[u] the LORD was not 22:3
willing to destroy the house of David.[v] He had **21:7**
promised to maintain a lamp[w] for him and his [u]2Sa 7:13
descendants forever. [v]2Sa 7:15; 2Ch 23:3
8In the time of Jehoram, Edom[x] rebelled against [w]2Sa 21:17;
Judah and set up its own king. 9So Jehoram went 1Ki 11:36
there with his officers and all his chariots. The **21:8**
Edomites surrounded him and his chariot com- [x]2Ch 20:22-
manders, but he rose up and broke through by 23
night. 10To this day Edom has been in rebellion
against Judah.
Libnah[y] revolted at the same time, because **21:10** [y]Nu 33:20
Jehoram had forsaken the LORD, the God of his
fathers. 11He had also built high places on the hills
of Judah and had caused the people of Jerusalem
to prostitute themselves and had led Judah astray.

[a] 36 Hebrew *of ships that could go to Tarshish* [b] 37 Hebrew *sail for Tarshish* [c] 2 That is, Judah, as frequently in 2 Chronicles

21:12 [12]Jehoram received a letter from Elijah[z] the
[z]2Ki 1:16-17 [a]2Ch 17:3-6 prophet, which said:
[b]2Ch 14:2
“This is what the LORD, the God of your
father[a] David, says: ‘You have not walked in
the ways of your father Jehoshaphat or of
Asa[b] king of Judah. [13]But you have walked in
the ways of the kings of Israel, and you have
led Judah and the people of Jerusalem to
prostitute themselves, just as the house of
21:13 Ahab did.[c] You have also murdered your own
[c]ver 6,11; 1Ki 16:29-33 brothers, members of your father’s house,
[d]ver 4; 1Ki 2:32 men who were better[d] than you. [14]So now the
LORD is about to strike your people, your
sons, your wives and everything that is
yours, with a heavy blow. [15]You yourself will
21:15 be very ill with a lingering disease[e] of the
[e]ver 18-19; Nu 12:10 bowels, until the disease causes your bowels
to come out.’ ”

[16]The LORD aroused against Jehoram the hostil-
21:16 ity of the Philistines and of the Arabs[f] who lived
[f]2Ch 17:10-11; 22:1; 26:7 near the Cushites. [17]They attacked Judah, invaded it and carried off all the goods found in the
king’s palace, together with his sons and wives.
Not a son was left to him except Ahaziah,[a] the
21:17 youngest.[g]
[g]2Ki 12:18; 2Ch 22:1; 25:23; Joel 3:5 [18]After all this, the LORD afflicted Jehoram with
an incurable disease of the bowels. [19]In the course
of time, at the end of the second year, his bowels
came out because of the disease, and he died in
21:19 great pain. His people made no fire in his honor,[h]
[h]2Ch 16:14 as they had for his fathers.

[20]Jehoram was thirty-two years old when he
became king, and he reigned in Jerusalem eight
years. He passed away, to no one’s regret, and was
21:20 buried[i] in the City of David, but not in the tombs
[i]2Ch 24:25; 28:27; 33:20; Jer 22:18,28 of the kings.

Ahaziah King of Judah

22:1 **22** The people[j] of Jerusalem[k] made Ahaziah,
[j]2Ch 33:25; 36:1 Jehoram’s youngest son, king in his place,
[k]2Ch 23:20-21; 26:1 since the raiders,[l] who came with the Arabs into
[l]2Ch 21:16-17 the camp, had killed all the older sons. So Ahaziah son of Jehoram king of Judah began to reign.

[2]Ahaziah was twenty-two[b] years old when he
became king, and he reigned in Jerusalem one
year. His mother’s name was Athaliah, a granddaughter of Omri.

22:3 [3]He too walked[m] in the ways of the house of
[m]2Ch 18:1 [n]2Ch 21:6 Ahab,[n] for his mother encouraged him in doing
wrong. [4]He did evil in the eyes of the LORD, as the
house of Ahab had done, for after his father’s
death they became his advisers, to his undoing.
[5]He also followed their counsel when he went
22:5 with Joram[c] son of Ahab king of Israel to war
[o]2Ch 18:11, 34 against Hazael king of Aram at Ramoth Gilead.[o]

[a] *17* Hebrew *Jehoahaz,* a variant of *Ahaziah* [b] *2* Some Septuagint manuscripts and Syriac (see also 2 Kings 8:26); Hebrew *forty-two* [c] *5* Hebrew *Jehoram,* a variant of *Joram;* also in verses 6 and 7

Disease

2CH 21:15,18

Jehoram’s disease comes on him as a direct judgment from God for his idolatry. Though his father is the godly Jehoshaphat, Jehoram is influenced by his wife, the sinful daughter of Ahab and probably Jezebel. In a letter from the prophet Elijah, God lists the sins of Jehoram and then, in graphic language, describes the disease that will eventually kill him.

Exactly what disease strikes Jehoram is uncertain. It could have been related to dysentery, a common ailment at that time, or it could have been a cancerous attack on his intestinal system. Jehoram dies “in great pain” (2Ch 21:19). That in itself is sad enough. However, the epitaph that follows is a sadder still indictment of a man who refused to follow the God of his people: “He passed away, to no one’s regret” (2Ch 21:20).

Two Women—Two Choices

2CH 22:10-12

Athaliah dedicates her life to evil. Her dismal legacy is in the Bible for all to read. She is remembered as an evil influence on the lives of both her husband, Jehoram, and her son, Ahaziah (2Ch 21:6; 22:3).

Yet Ahaziah's sister, Jehosheba, leaves a completely different legacy. When Athaliah seizes the throne and kills all her grandchildren, Jehosheba hides her one-year-old nephew Joash (see the character sketch for Jehosheba on page 1278). She and her godly husband, Jehoiada the priest, nurture, teach and protect this young child, and he becomes king of Judah at the tender age of seven.

God promised that the Messiah would come through David's family line, but that line is almost annihilated by the sinful choices of one woman. However, by the wise decisions of another, God rescues David's line. There is never a doubt that God will find a way to carry out his covenant promise to his people. He just needs a willing person to accomplish his purpose, and Jehosheba is that woman.

The Arameans wounded Joram; 6so he returned to Jezreel to recover from the wounds they had inflicted on him at Ramoth[a] in his battle with Hazael[p] king of Aram.

Then Ahaziah[b] son of Jehoram king of Judah went down to Jezreel to see Joram son of Ahab because he had been wounded.

7Through Ahaziah's[q] visit to Joram, God brought about Ahaziah's downfall. When Ahaziah arrived, he went out with Joram to meet Jehu son of Nimshi, whom the LORD had anointed to destroy the house of Ahab. 8While Jehu was executing judgment on the house of Ahab,[r] he found the princes of Judah and the sons of Ahaziah's relatives, who had been attending Ahaziah, and he killed them. 9He then went in search of Ahaziah, and his men captured him while he was hiding[s] in Samaria. He was brought to Jehu and put to death. They buried him, for they said, "He was a son of Jehoshaphat, who sought[t] the LORD with all his heart." So there was no one in the house of Ahaziah powerful enough to retain the kingdom.

Athaliah and Joash

10When Athaliah the mother of Ahaziah saw that her son was dead, she proceeded to destroy the whole royal family of the house of Judah. 11But Jehosheba,[c] the daughter of King Jehoram, took Joash son of Ahaziah and stole him away from among the royal princes who were about to be murdered and put him and his nurse in a bedroom. Because Jehosheba,[c] the daughter of King Jehoram and wife of the priest Jehoiada, was Ahaziah's sister, she hid the child from Athaliah so she could not kill him. 12He remained hidden with them at the temple of God for six years while Athaliah ruled the land.

23 In the seventh year Jehoiada showed his strength. He made a covenant with the commanders of units of a hundred: Azariah son of Jeroham, Ishmael son of Jehohanan, Azariah son of Obed, Maaseiah son of Adaiah, and Elishaphat son of Zicri. 2They went throughout Judah and gathered the Levites[u] and the heads of Israelite families from all the towns. When they came to Jerusalem, 3the whole assembly made a covenant[v] with the king at the temple of God.

Jehoiada said to them, "The king's son shall reign, as the LORD promised concerning the descendants of David.[w] 4Now this is what you are to do: A third of you priests and Levites who are going on duty on the Sabbath are to keep watch at the doors, 5a third of you at the royal palace and a third at the Foundation Gate, and all the other men are to be in the courtyards of the temple of the LORD. 6No one is to enter the temple of the

22:6 [p]1Ki 19:15; 2Ki 8:13-15; 9:15
22:7 [q]2Ki 9:16; 2Ch 10:15
22:8 [r]2Ki 10:13
22:9 [s]Jdg 9:5 [t]2Ch 17:4
23:2 [u]Nu 35:2-5
23:3 [v]2Ki 11:17 [w]2Sa 7:12; 1Ki 2:4; 2Ch 6:16; 7:18; 21:7

[a] 6 Hebrew *Ramah,* a variant of *Ramoth* [b] 6 Some Hebrew manuscripts, Septuagint, Vulgate and Syriac (see also 2 Kings 8:29); most Hebrew manuscripts *Azariah* [c] 11 Hebrew *Jehoshabeath,* a variant of *Jehosheba*

LORD except the priests and Levites on duty; they
23:6 may enter because they are consecrated, but all
[x]1Ch 23:28- the other men are to guard[x] what the LORD has
29; Zec 3:7 assigned to them.[a] 7 The Levites are to station
themselves around the king, each man with his
weapons in his hand. Anyone who enters the
temple must be put to death. Stay close to the king
wherever he goes."
8 The Levites and all the men of Judah did just
23:8 [y]2Ki 11:9 as Jehoiada the priest ordered.[y] Each one took his
[z]1Ch 24:1 men—those who were going on duty on the Sabbath and those who were going off duty—for
Jehoiada the priest had not released any of the
divisions.[z] 9 Then he gave the commanders of
units of a hundred the spears and the large and
small shields that had belonged to King David and
that were in the temple of God. 10 He stationed all
the men, each with his weapon in his hand,
around the king—near the altar and the temple,
from the south side to the north side of the
temple.
11 Jehoiada and his sons brought out the king's
son and put the crown on him; they presented
23:11 [a]Ex 25:16; him with a copy[a] of the covenant and proclaimed
Dt 17:18; him king. They anointed him and shouted, "Long
1Sa 10:24 live the king!"
12 When Athaliah heard the noise of the people
running and cheering the king, she went to them
23:13 at the temple of the LORD. 13 She looked, and there
[b]1Ki 1:41 was the king,[b] standing by his pillar[c] at the
[c]1Ki 7:15 entrance. The officers and the trumpeters were
beside the king, and all the people of the land
were rejoicing and blowing trumpets, and singers
with musical instruments were leading the
praises. Then Athaliah tore her robes and shouted, "Treason! Treason!"
14 Jehoiada the priest sent out the commanders
of units of a hundred, who were in charge of the
troops, and said to them: "Bring her out between
the ranks[b] and put to the sword anyone who follows her." For the priest had said, "Do not put her
to death at the temple of the LORD." 15 So they
seized her as she reached the entrance of the
23:15 [d]Ne 3:28; Horse Gate[d] on the palace grounds, and there they
Jer 31:40 put her to death.
16 Jehoiada then made a covenant[e] that he and
23:16 [e]2Ch 29:10; the people and the king[c] would be the LORD's peo-
34:31; ple. 17 All the people went to the temple of Baal
Ne 9:38 and tore it down. They smashed the altars and
23:17 [f]Dt 13:6-9 idols and killed[f] Mattan the priest of Baal in front
of the altars.
18 Then Jehoiada placed the oversight of the tem-
23:18 ple of the LORD in the hands of the priests, who
[g]1Ch 23:28- were Levites,[g] to whom David had made assign-
32; 2Ch 5:5 ments in the temple,[h] to present the burnt offer-
[h]1Ch 23:6; ings of the LORD as written in the Law of Moses,
25:6 with rejoicing and singing, as David had ordered.

[a] 6 *Or to observe the LORD's command* ⌞*not to enter*⌟ [b] 14 *Or out from the precincts* [c] 16 *Or covenant between* ⌞*the LORD*⌟ *and the people and the king that they* (see 2 Kings 11:17)

Treason!

2CH 23:13

As the Levites, priests and soldiers guard the new young king, the people celebrate. *Athaliah hears the commotion and unsuspectingly walks over to the temple area. As soon as she realizes that her seven-year-old grandson (rightful heir to the throne) is alive and has been crowned king, she screams the first words that come into her evil mind: "Treason! Treason!"*

Perhaps she convinces herself that she has been genuinely wronged. Perhaps she thinks she can bluff her way back into power. She can continue to yell, "Treason!" for eternity, but the fact remains that she is the one who has committed treason, usurping God's chosen royal line. No amount of blaming, bluffing or bullying will help her now.

Repairing the Temple

2CH 24:5-6,10,13

Because of the past kings' neglect and the thievery and wickedness of Queen Athaliah and her family (2Ch 24:7), the temple needs refurbishing. King Joash determines to repair the damage and restore the temple to its former glory. He asks the priests and Levites to collect the annual dues from the cities around Judah. But the priests procrastinate. Perhaps they are just slow to begin or perhaps they worry that all the money collected will go to renovating the temple and they will not have enough to support their families.

Consequently, Joash meets with his aging mentor, Jehoiada the priest, and decides to implement a unique giving campaign. The king notifies the residents of Jerusalem and the surrounding cities to deposit their census tax in a special box at the temple gate. Under this new system everyone contributes "gladly" (2Ch 24:10) and then enjoys watching as their gifts and tax money bring positive changes to the temple.

19He also stationed doorkeepers[i] at the gates of the
LORD's temple so that no one who was in any way
unclean might enter.
20He took with him the commanders of hundreds, the nobles, the rulers of the people and all
the people of the land and brought the king down
from the temple of the LORD. They went into the
palace through the Upper Gate[j] and seated the
king on the royal throne, 21and all the people of
the land rejoiced. And the city was quiet, because
Athaliah had been slain with the sword.[k]

Joash Repairs the Temple

24 Joash was seven years old when he became
king, and he reigned in Jerusalem forty
years. His mother's name was Zibiah; she was
from Beersheba. 2Joash did what was right in the
eyes of the LORD[l] all the years of Jehoiada the
priest. 3Jehoiada chose two wives for him, and he
had sons and daughters.
4Some time later Joash decided to restore the
temple of the LORD. 5He called together the priests
and Levites and said to them, "Go to the towns of
Judah and collect the money[m] due annually from
all Israel,[n] to repair the temple of your God. Do it
now." But the Levites[o] did not act at once.
6Therefore the king summoned Jehoiada the
chief priest and said to him, "Why haven't you
required the Levites to bring in from Judah and
Jerusalem the tax imposed by Moses the servant
of the LORD and by the assembly of Israel for the
Tent of the Testimony?"[p]
7Now the sons of that wicked woman Athaliah
had broken into the temple of God and had used
even its sacred objects for the Baals.
8At the king's command, a chest was made and
placed outside, at the gate of the temple of the
LORD. 9A proclamation was then issued in Judah
and Jerusalem that they should bring to the LORD
the tax that Moses the servant of God had required
of Israel in the desert. 10All the officials and all the
people brought their contributions gladly,[q] dropping them into the chest until it was full. 11When-
ever the chest was brought in by the Levites to the
king's officials and they saw that there was a large
amount of money, the royal secretary and the officer of the chief priest would come and empty the
chest and carry it back to its place. They did this
regularly and collected a great amount of money.
12The king and Jehoiada gave it to the men who
carried out the work required for the temple of the
LORD. They hired[r] masons and carpenters to
restore the LORD's temple, and also workers in iron
and bronze to repair the temple.
13The men in charge of the work were diligent,
and the repairs progressed under them. They
rebuilt the temple of God according to its original
design and reinforced it. 14When they had finished, they brought the rest of the money to the
king and Jehoiada, and with it were made articles
for the LORD's temple: articles for the service and

23:19 [i]1Ch 9:22
23:20 [j]2Ki 15:35
23:21 [k]2Ch 22:1
24:2 [l]2Ch 25:2; 26:5
24:5 [m]Ex 30:16; Ne 10:32-33; Mt 17:24 [n]1Ch 11:1 [o]1Ch 26:20
24:6 [p]Ex 30:12-16; Nu 1:50
24:10 [q]Ex 25:2; 1Ch 29:3,6,9
24:12 [r]2Ch 34:11

for the burnt offerings, and also dishes and other
objects of gold and silver. As long as Jehoiada
lived, burnt offerings were presented continually
in the temple of the LORD.
15 Now Jehoiada was old and full of years, and
he died at the age of a hundred and thirty. 16 He
was buried with the kings in the City of David,
because of the good he had done in Israel for God
and his temple.

The Wickedness of Joash

17 After the death of Jehoiada, the officials of
Judah came and paid homage to the king, and he
listened to them. 18 They abandoned[s] the temple of
the LORD, the God of their fathers, and worshiped
Asherah poles and idols.[t] Because of their guilt,
God's anger[u] came upon Judah and Jerusalem.
19 Although the LORD sent prophets to the people
to bring them back to him, and though they testified against them, they would not listen.[v]
20 Then the Spirit[w] of God came upon Zechariah[x] son of Jehoiada the priest. He stood before the
people and said, "This is what God says: 'Why do
you disobey the LORD's commands? You will not
prosper.[y] Because you have forsaken the LORD, he
has forsaken[z] you.' "
21 But they plotted against him, and by order of
the king they stoned[a] him to death[b] in the courtyard of the LORD's temple.[c] 22 King Joash did not
remember the kindness Zechariah's father Jehoiada had shown him but killed his son, who said
as he lay dying, "May the LORD see this and call
you to account."[d]
23 At the turn of the year,[a] the army of Aram
marched against Joash; it invaded Judah and Jerusalem and killed all the leaders of the people.[e]
They sent all the plunder to their king in Damascus. 24 Although the Aramean army had come
with only a few men,[f] the LORD delivered into
their hands a much larger army.[g] Because Judah
had forsaken the LORD, the God of their fathers,
judgment was executed on Joash. 25 When the
Arameans withdrew, they left Joash severely
wounded. His officials conspired against him for
murdering the son of Jehoiada the priest, and
they killed him in his bed. So he died and was
buried[h] in the City of David, but not in the tombs
of the kings.
26 Those who conspired against him were
Zabad,[b] son of Shimeath an Ammonite woman,
and Jehozabad, son of Shimrith[c][i] a Moabite
woman.[j] 27 The account of his sons, the many
prophecies about him, and the record of the
restoration of the temple of God are written in the
annotations on the book of the kings. And Amaziah his son succeeded him as king.

24:18 [s]ver 4; Jos 24:20; 2Ch 7:19 [t]Ex 34:13; 1Ki 14:23; 2Ch 33:3; Jer 17:2 [u]Jos 22:20; 2Ch 19:2
24:19 [v]Nu 11:29; Jer 7:25; Zec 1:4
24:20 [w]Jdg 3:10; 1Ch 12:18; 2Ch 20:14 [x]Mt 23:35; Lk 11:51 [y]Nu 14:41 [z]Dt 31:17; 2Ch 15:2
24:21 [a]Jos 7:25; Ac 7:58-59 [b]Ne 9:26; Jer 26:21 [c]Jer 20:2; Mt 23:35
24:22 [d]Ge 9:5
24:23 [e]2Ki 12:17-18
24:24 [f]2Ch 14:9; 16:8; 20:2, 12 [g]Lev 26:23-25; Dt 28:25
24:25 [h]2Ch 21:20
24:26 [i]2Ki 12:21 [j]Ru 1:4

[a] *23* Probably in the spring [b] *26* A variant of *Jozabad*
[c] *26* A variant of *Shomer*

Buried With Kings

2CH 24:15-16

After Joash (later referred at as Jehoash), becomes king of Judah at the age of seven (2Ch 24:1), he relies on his spiritual mentor, Jehoiada the priest, to help him make wise decisions. Jehoiada influences the young king to restore the temple and reestablish the worship of the Lord (2Ch 24:14). God uses this dedicated priest to restore the line of David to the throne (2Ch 23:3).

Although Jehoiada is a priest (and not a king), he plays a significant role in influencing Judah for good. When he dies at the incredible age of 130, the people honor him by burying him with the kings. The writer of Chronicles always mentions where a king is buried as a way to help the reader ascertain the overall effect that king had on the nation. Jehoiada cooperates with God—and the way he lives his life changes the kingdom of Judah forever.

Amaziah King of Judah

25 Amaziah was twenty-five years old when he
became king, and he reigned in Jerusalem
twenty-nine years. His mother's name was
Jehoaddin[a]; she was from Jerusalem. 2He did what
was right in the eyes of the LORD, but not wholeheartedly.[k] 3After the kingdom was firmly in his
control, he executed the officials who had murdered his father the king. 4Yet he did not put their
sons to death, but acted in accordance with what
is written in the Law, in the Book of Moses,[l] where
the LORD commanded: "Fathers shall not be put to
death for their children, nor children put to death
for their fathers; each is to die for his own sins."[b][m]

5Amaziah called the people of Judah together
and assigned them according to their families to
commanders of thousands and commanders of
hundreds for all Judah and Benjamin. He then
mustered[n] those twenty years old[o] or more and
found that there were three hundred thousand
men ready for military service,[p] able to handle the
spear and shield. 6He also hired a hundred thousand fighting men from Israel for a hundred talents[c] of silver.

7But a man of God came to him and said, "O
king, these troops from Israel[q] must not march
with you, for the LORD is not with Israel—not with
any of the people of Ephraim. 8Even if you go and
fight courageously in battle, God will overthrow
you before the enemy, for God has the power to
help or to overthrow."[r]

9Amaziah asked the man of God, "But what
about the hundred talents I paid for these Israelite
troops?"

The man of God replied, "The LORD can give
you much more than that."[s]

10So Amaziah dismissed the troops who had
come to him from Ephraim and sent them home.
They were furious with Judah and left for home
in a great rage.[t]

11Amaziah then marshaled his strength and led
his army to the Valley of Salt, where he killed ten
thousand men of Seir. 12The army of Judah also
captured ten thousand men alive, took them to the
top of a cliff and threw them down so that all were
dashed to pieces.[u]

13Meanwhile the troops that Amaziah had sent
back and had not allowed to take part in the war
raided Judean towns from Samaria to Beth Horon.
They killed three thousand people and carried off
great quantities of plunder.

14When Amaziah returned from slaughtering the
Edomites, he brought back the gods of the people
of Seir. He set them up as his own gods,[v] bowed
down to them and burned sacrifices to them. 15The
anger of the LORD burned against Amaziah, and he
sent a prophet to him, who said, "Why do you con-

25:2 [k]ver 14; 1Ki 8:61; 2Ch 24:2
25:4 [l]Dt 28:61 [m]Nu 26:11; Dt 24:16
25:5 [n]2Sa 24:2 [o]Ex 30:14 [p]Nu 1:3; 1Ch 21:1; 2Ch 17:14-19
25:7 [q]2Ch 16:2-9; 19:1-3
25:8 [r]2Ch 14:11; 20:6
25:9 [s]Dt 8:18; Pr 10:22
25:10 [t]ver 13
25:12 [u]Ps 141:6; Ob 1:3
25:14 [v]Ex 20:3; 2Ch 28:23; Isa 44:15

He is my home. He is my family. He is my friend. Every situation, *every circumstance*—he proves himself true. *Never a want* without him knowing. *Never a* desire without him seeing. *Never a* need without him coming to meet it. He will. His way. He promises.

—Kathy Troccoli

[a] *1* Hebrew *Jehoaddan,* a variant of *Jehoaddin* [b] *4* Deut. 24:16 [c] *6* That is, about 3 3/4 tons (about 3.4 metric tons); also in verse 9

25:15 sult this people's gods, which could not save[w] their
ʷPs 96:5; Isa 36:20 own people from your hand?"
16While he was still speaking, the king said to
him, "Have we appointed you an adviser to the
king? Stop! Why be struck down?"
So the prophet stopped but said, "I know that
God has determined to destroy you, because you
have done this and have not listened to my
counsel."
17After Amaziah king of Judah consulted his
advisers, he sent this challenge to Jehoash[a] son of
Jehoahaz, the son of Jehu, king of Israel: "Come,
meet me face to face."
25:18 18But Jehoash king of Israel replied to Amaziah
ˣJdg 9:8-15 king of Judah: "A thistle[x] in Lebanon sent a message to a cedar in Lebanon, 'Give your daughter to
my son in marriage.' Then a wild beast in Lebanon came along and trampled the thistle underfoot. 19You say to yourself that you have defeated
Edom, and now you are arrogant and proud. But
stay at home! Why ask for trouble and cause your
own downfall and that of Judah also?"
20Amaziah, however, would not listen, for God
25:20 so worked that he might hand them over to
ʸ1Ki 12:15; ⌊Jehoash⌋, because they sought the gods of Edom.[y]
2Ch 10:15; 21So Jehoash king of Israel attacked. He and Ama-
22:7 ziah king of Judah faced each other at Beth Shemesh in Judah. 22Judah was routed by Israel, and
every man fled to his home. 23Jehoash king of
Israel captured Amaziah king of Judah, the son of
Joash, the son of Ahaziah,[b] at Beth Shemesh.
Then Jehoash brought him to Jerusalem and
25:23 broke down the wall of Jerusalem from the Ephra-
ᶻ2Ki 14:13; Ne 8:16; im Gate[z] to the Corner Gate[a]—a section about six
12:39 ᵃ2Ch 26:9; hundred feet[c] long. 24He took all the gold and sil-
Jer 31:38 ver and all the articles found in the temple of God
that had been in the care of Obed-Edom,[b] togeth-
25:24 er with the palace treasures and the hostages, and
ᵇ1Ch 26:15 returned to Samaria.
25Amaziah son of Joash king of Judah lived for
fifteen years after the death of Jehoash son of
Jehoahaz king of Israel. 26As for the other events
of Amaziah's reign, from beginning to end, are
they not written in the book of the kings of Judah
and Israel? 27From the time that Amaziah turned
25:27 away from following the LORD, they conspired
ᶜJos 10:3 against him in Jerusalem and he fled to Lachish[c],
but they sent men after him to Lachish and killed
him there. 28He was brought back by horse and
was buried with his fathers in the City of Judah.

Uzziah King of Judah

26:1 **26** Then all the people of Judah[d] took Uzziah,[d]
ᵈ2Ch 22:1 who was sixteen years old, and made him
king in place of his father Amaziah. 2He was the

[a] *17* Hebrew *Joash,* a variant of *Jehoash;* also in verses 18, 21, 23 and 25 [b] *23* Hebrew *Jehoahaz,* a variant of *Ahaziah*
[c] *23* Hebrew *four hundred cubits* (about 180 meters)
[d] *1* Also called *Azariah*

A Thistle and a Cedar

2CH 25:18

When King Amaziah of Judah provokes King Jehoash of Israel, saying, "Come, meet me face to face" (2Ch 25:17), Jehoash responds with a satirical allegory about the two nations. In effect Jehoash says, "My kingdom is a mighty cedar tree. Yours is a wimpy thistle plant. Don't try to take us on. You'll be crushed before you start. Stay home and stay alive."

Allegories—or word pictures—are used to make a point or teach a lesson subtly rather than directly. Allegorical statements and stories can be found in the Old Testament, and many of Jesus' parables are a form of allegory. Often Old Testament allegories contain a comparison, like the one Jehoash uses. Jesus knew the people of his day were accustomed to hearing stories, so he used parables to effectively communicate his message of God's love and reconciliation.

Creative Leadership

2CH 26:11–16

Uzziah, a capable and creative leader, succeeds at everything he does. He manages and equips his huge army to win every battle, gaining the respect of neighboring kingdoms. Uzziah ("Azariah" in 2Ki 15:1) builds up his cities and becomes well known for his agriculture talents (2Ch 26:10). During most of his 52-year reign, he follows God, and God helps him succeed—until "he became powerful" (2Ch 26:15).

Then Uzziah begins to think God's ideas are not good enough. He wants more. As if to say, "I, the powerful king, will show my passion for God," he walks into the "priest-only" area of the temple and burns incense on the altar. When confronted with his sin, he rages instead of repenting. Pride prevents him from admitting the truth. His response is ironic, since it was God who engineered his success (2Ch 26:5). The Chronicler ends with a sad commentary. Uzziah is not remembered as the gifted leader God used to strengthen Judah, but as the leper king.

one who rebuilt Elath and restored it to Judah
after Amaziah rested with his fathers.
3 Uzziah was sixteen years old when he became
king, and he reigned in Jerusalem fifty-two years.
His mother's name was Jecoliah; she was from Jerusalem. 4 He did what was right in the eyes of the
LORD, just as his father Amaziah had done. 5 He
sought God during the days of Zechariah, who
instructed him in the fear[a] of God.[e] As long as he
sought the LORD, God gave him success.[f]
6 He went to war against the Philistines[g] and
broke down the walls of Gath, Jabneh and Ashdod.[h] He then rebuilt towns near Ashdod and
elsewhere among the Philistines. 7 God helped him
against the Philistines and against the Arabs[i] who
lived in Gur Baal and against the Meunites.[j] 8 The
Ammonites[k] brought tribute to Uzziah, and his
fame spread as far as the border of Egypt, because
he had become very powerful.
9 Uzziah built towers in Jerusalem at the Corner
Gate,[l] at the Valley Gate[m] and at the angle of the
wall, and he fortified them. 10 He also built towers
in the desert and dug many cisterns, because he
had much livestock in the foothills and in the
plain. He had people working his fields and vineyards in the hills and in the fertile lands, for he
loved the soil.
11 Uzziah had a well-trained army, ready to go
out by divisions according to their numbers as
mustered by Jeiel the secretary and Maaseiah the
officer under the direction of Hananiah, one of the
royal officials. 12 The total number of family leaders over the fighting men was 2,600. 13 Under their
command was an army of 307,500 men trained
for war, a powerful force to support the king
against his enemies. 14 Uzziah provided shields,
spears, helmets, coats of armor, bows and slingstones for the entire army.[n] 15 In Jerusalem he
made machines designed by skillful men for use
on the towers and on the corner defenses to shoot
arrows and hurl large stones. His fame spread far
and wide, for he was greatly helped until he
became powerful.
16 But after Uzziah became powerful, his pride[o]
led to his downfall.[p] He was unfaithful[q] to the
LORD his God, and entered the temple of the LORD
to burn incense[r] on the altar of incense. 17 Azariah[s]
the priest with eighty other courageous priests of
the LORD followed him in. 18 They confronted him
and said, "It is not right for you, Uzziah, to burn
incense to the LORD. That is for the priests,[t] the
descendants[u] of Aaron,[v] who have been consecrated to burn incense.[w] Leave the sanctuary, for
you have been unfaithful; and you will not be
honored by the LORD God."
19 Uzziah, who had a censer in his hand ready to
burn incense, became angry. While he was raging
at the priests in their presence before the incense

26:5 [e] 2Ch 15:2; 24:2; Da 1:17 [f] 2Ch 27:6
26:6 [g] Isa 2:6; 11:14; 14:29; Jer 25:20 [h] Am 1:8; 3:9
26:7 [i] 2Ch 21:16 [j] 2Ch 20:1
26:8 [k] Ge 19:38; 2Ch 17:11
26:9 [l] 2Ki 14:13; 2Ch 25:23 [m] Ne 2:13; 3:13
26:14 [n] Jer 46:4
26:16 [o] 2Ki 14:10 [p] Dt 32:15; 2Ch 25:19 [q] 1Ch 5:25 [r] 2Ki 16:12
26:17 [s] 1Ki 4:2; 1Ch 6:10
26:18 [t] Nu 16:39 [u] Nu 18:1-7 [v] Ex 30:7 [w] 1Ch 6:49

[a] *5* Many Hebrew manuscripts, Septuagint and Syriac; other Hebrew manuscripts *vision*

26:19 altar in the LORD's temple, leprosy[a][x] broke out on
[x]Nu 12:10; his forehead. 20When Azariah the chief priest and
2Ki 5:25-27 all the other priests looked at him, they saw that
he had leprosy on his forehead, so they hurried
him out. Indeed, he himself was eager to leave,
because the LORD had afflicted him.
26:21 21King Uzziah had leprosy until the day he died.
[y]Ex 4:6; He lived in a separate house[b][y]—leprous, and
Lev 13:46; excluded from the temple of the LORD. Jotham his
14:8; Nu 5:2; son had charge of the palace and governed the
19:12 people of the land.
26:22 22The other events of Uzziah's reign, from begin-
[z]2Ki 15:1; ning to end, are recorded by the prophet Isaiah[z]
Isa 1:1; 6:1 son of Amoz. 23Uzziah[a] rested with his fathers and
26:23 was buried near them in a field for burial that
[a]Isa 1:1; 6:1 belonged to the kings, for people said, "He had lep-
[b]2Ki 14:21; rosy." And Jotham his son succeeded him as king.[b]
15:7; Am 1:1

Jotham King of Judah

27:1 **27** Jotham[c] was twenty-five years old when he
[c]2Ki 15:5,32; became king, and he reigned in Jerusalem
1Ch 3:12 sixteen years. His mother's name was Jerusha
daughter of Zadok. 2He did what was right in the
eyes of the LORD, just as his father Uzziah had
done, but unlike him he did not enter the temple
of the LORD. The people, however, continued their
corrupt practices. 3Jotham rebuilt the Upper Gate
27:3 of the temple of the LORD and did extensive work
[d]2Ch 33:14; on the wall at the hill of Ophel.[d] 4He built towns
Ne 3:26 in the Judean hills and forts and towers in the
wooded areas.
27:5 5Jotham made war on the king of the Ammon-
[e]Ge 19:38 ites[e] and conquered them. That year the Ammonites paid him a hundred talents[c] of silver, ten thousand cors[d] of wheat and ten thousand cors of
barley. The Ammonites brought him the same
27:6 amount also in the second and third years.
[f]2Ch 26:5 6Jotham grew powerful[f] because he walked
steadfastly before the LORD his God.
7The other events in Jotham's reign, including
all his wars and the other things he did, are written
in the book of the kings of Israel and Judah. 8He
was twenty-five years old when he became king,
and he reigned in Jerusalem sixteen years. 9Jotham
rested with his fathers and was buried in the City of
28:1 David. And Ahaz his son succeeded him as king.
[g]1Ch 3:13;
Isa 1:1

Ahaz King of Judah

28:2 **28** Ahaz[g] was twenty years old when he
[h]Ex 34:17; became king, and he reigned in Jerusalem
2Ch 22:3 sixteen years. Unlike David his father, he did not
28:3 do what was right in the eyes of the LORD. 2He
[i]Jos 15:8; walked in the ways of the kings of Israel and also
2Ki 23:10 made cast idols[h] for worshiping the Baals. 3He
[j]Lev 18:21; burned sacrifices in the Valley of Ben Hinnom[i]
2Ki 3:27; and sacrificed his sons[j] in the fire, following the
2Ch 33:6;
Eze 20:26

God will mend a broken heart, but he must have *all* the pieces. When you are hurting, really in despair . . . it is easy to show that your heart is broken. It lies in pieces all over your life . . . But God can heal your heart. God can rescue you from despair and give you something to rejoice about again. It won't happen overnight: There is some necessary mourning and recovery you have to go through first, but *it will happen.* All you have to do is be willing to give every piece of your broken heart to God . . . and he will begin the mending process. You will survive, times will get better and you will, with the grace of God, be able to help others with the gift of God's love.

—Barbara Johnson

[a] *19* The Hebrew word was used for various diseases affecting the skin—not necessarily leprosy; also in verses 20, 21 and 23.
[b] *21* Or *in a house where he was relieved of responsibilities*
[c] *5* That is, about 3 3/4 tons (about 3.4 metric tons) [d] *5* That is, probably about 62,000 bushels (about 2,200 kiloliters)

How Not to Live

2CH 28:1-14

Ahaz's life exemplifies what not to be and what not to do. He imitates the idolatrous ways of the surrounding pagan nations, becoming so corrupt that he throws his own sons into the sacrificial fire (2Ch 28:3-4).

The Lord will only tolerate such wickedness so long before acting. He gives Ahaz over to the forces of the king of Aram (Syria) and King Pekah of Israel. Ahaz's army suffers devastating losses with 120,000 killed in one day alone. The enemy takes 200,000 women and children as slaves, as well as large quantities of Judah's possessions.

Then an interesting thing happens. Oded the prophet admonishes the victorious army: "Although God let you win over Judah, you pushed it way too far. God is not pleased. Send the prisoners back" (2Ch 28:9-11, author's paraphrase).

Some courageous men support Oded's message and instigate a reversal. They give their captives new clothing, food and medicine and then escort them home. God wants his followers to exercise kindness and consideration even, or especially, when executing justice.

detestable[k] ways of the nations the LORD had driv-
en out before the Israelites. 4He offered sacrifices
and burned incense at the high places, on the hilltops and under every spreading tree.
5Therefore the LORD his God handed him over
to the king of Aram.[l] The Arameans defeated him
and took many of his people as prisoners and
brought them to Damascus.
He was also given into the hands of the king of
Israel, who inflicted heavy casualties on him. 6In
one day Pekah[m] son of Remaliah killed a hundred
and twenty thousand soldiers in Judah[n]—because
Judah had forsaken the LORD, the God of their
fathers. 7Zicri, an Ephraimite warrior, killed Maaseiah the king's son, Azrikam the officer in charge
of the palace, and Elkanah, second to the king.
8The Israelites took captive from their kinsmen[o]
two hundred thousand wives, sons and daughters.
They also took a great deal of plunder, which they
carried back to Samaria.[p]
9But a prophet of the LORD named Oded was
there, and he went out to meet the army when it
returned to Samaria. He said to them, "Because
the LORD, the God of your fathers, was angry[q] with
Judah, he gave them into your hand. But you
have slaughtered them in a rage that reaches to
heaven.[r] 10And now you intend to make the men
and women of Judah and Jerusalem your slaves.[s]
But aren't you also guilty of sins against the LORD
your God? 11Now listen to me! Send back your fellow countrymen you have taken as prisoners, for
the LORD's fierce anger rests on you.[t]"
12Then some of the leaders in Ephraim—Azariah son of Jehohanan, Berekiah son of Meshillemoth, Jehizkiah son of Shallum, and Amasa son
of Hadlai—confronted those who were arriving
from the war. 13"You must not bring those prisoners here," they said, "or we will be guilty before
the LORD. Do you intend to add to our sin and
guilt? For our guilt is already great, and his fierce
anger rests on Israel."
14So the soldiers gave up the prisoners and
plunder in the presence of the officials and all the
assembly. 15The men designated by name took the
prisoners, and from the plunder they clothed all
who were naked. They provided them with
clothes and sandals, food and drink,[u] and healing
balm. All those who were weak they put on donkeys. So they took them back to their fellow countrymen at Jericho, the City of Palms,[v] and
returned to Samaria.
16At that time King Ahaz sent to the king[a] of
Assyria[w] for help. 17The Edomites[x] had again come
and attacked Judah and carried away prisoners,[y]
18while the Philistines[z] had raided towns in the
foothills and in the Negev of Judah. They captured
and occupied Beth Shemesh, Aijalon[a] and Gederoth, as well as Soco, Timnah and Gimzo, with

28:3 [k]Dt 18:9; 2Ch 33:2
28:5 [l]Isa 7:1
28:6 [m]2Ki 15:25, 27 [n]ver 8; Isa 9:21; 11:13
28:8 [o]Dt 28:25-41; 2Ch 11:4 [p]2Ch 29:9
28:9 [q]2Ch 25:15; Isa 10:6; 47:6; Zec 1:15 [r]Ezr 9:6; Rev 18:5
28:10 [s]Lev 25:39-46
28:11 [t]2Ch 11:4; Jas 2:13
28:15 [u]2Ki 6:22; Pr 25:21-22 [v]Dt 34:3; Jdg 1:16
28:16 [w]2Ki 16:7
28:17 [x]Ps 137:7; Isa 34:5 [y]2Ch 29:9
28:18 [z]Eze 16:27, 57 [a]Jos 10:12

[a] *16* One Hebrew manuscript, Septuagint and Vulgate (see also 2 Kings 16:7); most Hebrew manuscripts *kings*

their surrounding villages. 19The LORD had humbled Judah because of Ahaz king of Israel,[a] for he
had promoted wickedness in Judah and had been
most unfaithful[b] to the LORD. 20Tiglath-Pileser[b][c]
king of Assyria came to him, but he gave him trouble instead of help.[d] 21Ahaz took some of the things
from the temple of the LORD and from the royal
palace and from the princes and presented them to
the king of Assyria, but that did not help him.
22In his time of trouble King Ahaz became even
more unfaithful[e] to the LORD. 23He offered sacrifices to the gods[f] of Damascus, who had defeated
him; for he thought, "Since the gods of the kings
of Aram have helped them, I will sacrifice to them
so they will help me."[g] But they were his downfall
and the downfall of all Israel.
24Ahaz gathered together the furnishings from
the temple of God[h] and took them away.[c] He shut
the doors[i] of the LORD's temple and set up altars[j] at
every street corner in Jerusalem. 25In every town
in Judah he built high places to burn sacrifices to
other gods and provoked the LORD, the God of his
fathers, to anger.
26The other events of his reign and all his ways,
from beginning to end, are written in the book of
the kings of Judah and Israel. 27Ahaz rested[k] with
his fathers and was buried[l] in the city of Jerusalem, but he was not placed in the tombs of the
kings of Israel. And Hezekiah his son succeeded
him as king.

Hezekiah Purifies the Temple

29 Hezekiah[m] was twenty-five years old when
he became king, and he reigned in Jerusalem twenty-nine years. His mother's name was
Abijah daughter of Zechariah. 2He did what was
right in the eyes of the LORD, just as his father
David[n] had done.
3In the first month of the first year of his reign,
he opened the doors of the temple of the LORD and
repaired[o] them. 4He brought in the priests and the
Levites, assembled them in the square on the east
side 5and said: "Listen to me, Levites! Consecrate[p]
yourselves now and consecrate the temple of the
LORD, the God of your fathers. Remove all defilement from the sanctuary. 6Our fathers[q] were
unfaithful;[r] they did evil in the eyes of the LORD
our God and forsook him. They turned their faces
away from the LORD's dwelling place and turned
their backs on him. 7They also shut the doors of
the portico and put out the lamps. They did not
burn incense or present any burnt offerings at the
sanctuary to the God of Israel. 8Therefore, the
anger of the LORD has fallen on Judah and Jerusalem; he has made them an object of dread and
horror[s] and scorn,[t] as you can see with your own
eyes. 9This is why our fathers have fallen by the

28:19 [b]2Ch 21:2
28:20 [c]2Ki 15:29; 1Ch 5:6 [d]2Ki 16:7
28:22 [e]Jer 5:3
28:23 [f]2Ch 25:14 [g]Jer 44:17-18
28:24 [h]2Ki 16:18 [i]2Ch 29:7 [j]2Ch 30:14
28:27 [k]Isa 14:28-32 [l]2Ch 21:20; 24:25
29:1 [m]1Ch 3:13
29:2 [n]2Ch 28:1; 34:2
29:3 [o]2Ch 28:24
29:5 [p]2Ch 35:6
29:6 [q]Ps 106:6-47; Jer 2:27 [r]1Ch 5:25; Eze 8:16
29:8 [s]Dt 28:25; 2Ch 24:18 [t]Jer 18:16; 19:8; 25:9, 18

[a] 19 That is, Judah, as frequently in 2 Chronicles
[b] 20 Hebrew *Tilgath-Pilneser,* a variant of *Tiglath-Pileser*
[c] 24 Or *and cut them up*

A Reprieve in Hezekiah

2CH 28:22—29:3

King Ahaz adopts the pagan mindset—"The conquering king's god must have true power, so I will worship him." When that god fails, he builds altars to another. Ahaz lives with no apparent spiritual focus. Evil rules his life, and he dies in disgrace, leaving Judah in a pathetic spiritual state.

Then Ahaz's son Hezekiah comes to the throne and *immediately* reverses the evil trend by opening the temple's doors and calling the people to God. Although his father, Ahaz, wanders purposelessly from one idol to another, Hezekiah makes an intentional decision to follow God (2Ch 29:10). He realizes that if he, as the political and spiritual leader, wishes to have a godly influence on the people of Judah, he must first make his own commitment to the Lord. Why not circle Hezekiah's words "now I intend" and then talk to God about your own spiritual intentions?

Hezekiah's Mentor

2CH 29:15-30

Corrupt King Ahaz is a poor role model for his son Hezekiah. Yet Hezekiah becomes a remarkable man of ethical and spiritual character. Who influenced him for good? How did Hezekiah learn to trust in God?

The Bible only suggests at the answer to these questions. Any king of God's chosen people learns about King David, his godly life and the important religious and political systems he initiated. Faithful priests, prophets (Isaiah and Micah are Hezekiah's contemporaries) or other devout men and women perhaps influence Hezekiah during his childhood. Or perhaps Hezekiah's mother, Abijah, gives him his godly spiritual heritage. She is the daughter of Zechariah (2Ch 29:1), who may have been the godly adviser to Hezekiah's great-grandfather, Uzziah (2Ch 26:5), or one of the Levites Hezekiah enlists to help restore the temple (2Ch 29:13.) Someone, somewhere along the way in his upbringing, influences Hezekiah for good, and that influence makes a profound impression on the nation.

sword and why our sons and daughters and our
wives are in captivity.[u] 10 Now I intend to make a 29:9 [u]2Ch 28:5-8, 17
covenant[v] with the LORD, the God of Israel, so that
his fierce anger will turn away from us. 11 My sons,
do not be negligent now, for the LORD has chosen 29:10 [v]2Ch 15:12; 23:16
you to stand before him and serve him,[w] to min-
ister[x] before him and to burn incense."
12 Then these Levites[y] set to work: 29:11 [w]Nu 3:6; 8:6, 14 [x]1Ch 15:2
from the Kohathites,
Mahath son of Amasai and Joel son of
Azariah; 29:12 [y]Nu 3:17-20 [z]2Ch 31:15
from the Merarites,
Kish son of Abdi and Azariah son of Jehallelel;
from the Gershonites,
Joah son of Zimmah and Eden[z] son of
Joah;
13 from the descendants of Elizaphan,
Shimri and Jeiel;
from the descendants of Asaph,[a] 29:13 [a]1Ch 6:39
Zechariah and Mattaniah;
14 from the descendants of Heman,
Jehiel and Shimei;
from the descendants of Jeduthun,
Shemaiah and Uzziel.
15 When they had assembled their brothers and 29:15 [b]ver 5; 1Ch 23:28; 2Ch 30:12
consecrated themselves, they went in to purify[b]
the temple of the LORD, as the king had ordered,
following the word of the LORD. 16 The priests went
into the sanctuary of the LORD to purify it. They
brought out to the courtyard of the LORD's temple
everything unclean that they found in the temple
of the LORD. The Levites took it and carried it out 29:16 [c]2Sa 15:23
to the Kidron Valley.[c] 17 They began the consecra-
tion on the first day of the first month, and by the
eighth day of the month they reached the portico
of the LORD. For eight more days they consecrated
the temple of the LORD itself, finishing on the sixteenth day of the first month.
18 Then they went in to King Hezekiah and
reported: "We have purified the entire temple of
the LORD, the altar of burnt offering with all its
utensils, and the table for setting out the consecrated bread, with all its articles. 19 We have prepared and consecrated all the articles[d] that King 29:19 [d]2Ch 28:24
Ahaz removed in his unfaithfulness while he was
king. They are now in front of the LORD's altar."
20 Early the next morning King Hezekiah gathered the city officials together and went up to the
temple of the LORD. 21 They brought seven bulls,
seven rams, seven male lambs and seven male 29:21 [e]Lev 4:13-14
goats as a sin offering[e] for the kingdom, for the
sanctuary and for Judah. The king commanded
the priests, the descendants of Aaron, to offer
these on the altar of the LORD. 22 So they slaughtered the bulls, and the priests took the blood and
sprinkled it on the altar; next they slaughtered the
rams and sprinkled their blood on the altar; then
they slaughtered the lambs and sprinkled their
blood[f] on the altar. 23 The goats for the sin offering 29:22 [f]Lev 4:18
were brought before the king and the assembly,

29:23 and they laid their hands[g] on them. [24]The priests
[g]Lev 4:15 then slaughtered the goats and presented their
29:24 blood on the altar for a sin offering to atone[h] for
[h]Ex 29:36; all Israel, because the king had ordered the burnt
Lev 4:26 offering and the sin offering for all Israel.
[25]He stationed the Levites in the temple of the
29:25 LORD with cymbals, harps and lyres in the way
[i]1Ch 25:6; prescribed by David[i] and Gad[j] the king's seer and
2Ch 8:14 Nathan the prophet; this was commanded by the
[j]1Sa 22:5; LORD through his prophets. [26]So the Levites stood
2Sa 24:11 ready with David's instruments,[k] and the priests
29:26 with their trumpets.[l]
[k]1Ch 15:16 [27]Hezekiah gave the order to sacrifice the burnt
[l]1Ch 15:24; 23:5; offering on the altar. As the offering began,
2Ch 5:12 singing to the LORD began also, accompanied by
29:27 trumpets and the instruments[m] of David king of
[m]2Ch 23:18 Israel. [28]The whole assembly bowed in worship,
while the singers sang and the trumpeters played.
All this continued until the sacrifice of the burnt
offering was completed.
[29]When the offerings were finished, the king
29:29 and everyone present with him knelt down and
[n]2Ch 20:18 worshiped.[n] [30]King Hezekiah and his officials
ordered the Levites to praise the LORD with the
words of David and of Asaph the seer. So they
sang praises with gladness and bowed their heads
and worshiped.
[31]Then Hezekiah said, "You have now dedicated
29:31 yourselves to the LORD. Come and bring sacrifices[o]
[o]Heb 13:15-16 and thank offerings to the temple of the LORD." So
[p]Ex 25:2; the assembly brought sacrifices and thank offer-
35:22 ings, and all whose hearts were willing[p] brought
burnt offerings.
[32]The number of burnt offerings the assembly
brought was seventy bulls, a hundred rams and
two hundred male lambs—all of them for burnt
offerings to the LORD. [33]The animals consecrated
as sacrifices amounted to six hundred bulls and
three thousand sheep and goats. [34]The priests,
29:34 however, were too few to skin all the burnt offer-
[q]2Ch 35:11 ings;[q] so their kinsmen the Levites helped them
[r]2Ch 30:3,15 until the task was finished and until other priests
had been consecrated,[r] for the Levites had been
more conscientious in consecrating themselves
than the priests had been. [35]There were burnt
29:35 offerings in abundance, together with the fat[s] of
[s]Ex 29:13; the fellowship offerings[a][t] and the drink offerings[u]
Lev 3:16
[t]Lev 7:11-21 that accompanied the burnt offerings.
[u]Nu 15:5-10 So the service of the temple of the LORD was
reestablished. [36]Hezekiah and all the people
rejoiced at what God had brought about for his
people, because it was done so quickly.

Hezekiah Celebrates the Passover

30 Hezekiah sent word to all Israel and Judah
and also wrote letters to Ephraim and
30:1 Manasseh,[v] inviting them to come to the temple of
[v]Ge 41:52 the LORD in Jerusalem and celebrate the Passover[w]
[w]Ex 12:11; Nu 28:16 to the LORD, the God of Israel. [2]The king and his

[a] 35 Traditionally *peace offerings*

Celebrating Passover

2CH 30:1-5

Hezekiah invites "all Israel" (2Ch 30:1) to come celebrate the Passover in Jerusalem. The timing is good for Hezekiah to unite the north and the south. The Assyrians (2Ki 17:1-6) control the north, and the influence of King Hoshea of Israel is vanquished. Some of the people of the northern tribes respond to Hezekiah's invitation, others do not (2Ch 30:10-12).

Both the temple and priesthood are in disarray because of the apostasy of Hezekiah's father. Hezekiah has much work to do before anyone can worship or sacrifice at the temple. He restores it as quickly as possible, yet all the preparations are not completed in time to have the Passover at the usual time on the "fourteenth day of the first month" (Lev 23:5). Hezekiah and his officials decide it is justifiable to celebrate the Passover in the second month due to an exception clause in Moses' law (Nu 9:10-11). Hezekiah chooses to follow God and his ways. He remains intentional about challenging and inspiring the people to follow.

officials and the whole assembly in Jerusalem decided to celebrate[x] the Passover in the second month. 3They had not been able to celebrate it at the regular time because not enough priests had consecrated[y] themselves and the people had not assembled in Jerusalem. 4The plan seemed right both to the king and to the whole assembly. 5They decided to send a proclamation throughout Israel, from Beersheba to Dan,[z] calling the people to come to Jerusalem and celebrate the Passover to the LORD, the God of Israel. It had not been celebrated in large numbers according to what was written.

6At the king's command, couriers went throughout Israel and Judah with letters from the king and from his officials, which read:

> "People of Israel, return to the LORD, the God of Abraham, Isaac and Israel, that he may return to you who are left, who have escaped from the hand of the kings of Assyria. 7Do not be like your fathers[a] and brothers, who were unfaithful to the LORD, the God of their fathers, so that he made them an object of horror,[b] as you see. 8Do not be stiff-necked,[c] as your fathers were; submit to the LORD. Come to the sanctuary, which he has consecrated forever. Serve the LORD your God, so that his fierce anger[d] will turn away from you. 9If you return[e] to the LORD, then your brothers and your children will be shown compassion[f] by their captors and will come back to this land, for the LORD your God is gracious and compassionate.[g] He will not turn his face from you if you return to him."

10The couriers went from town to town in Ephraim and Manasseh, as far as Zebulun, but the people scorned and ridiculed[h] them. 11Nevertheless, some men of Asher, Manasseh and Zebulun humbled themselves and went to Jerusalem.[i] 12Also in Judah the hand of God was on the people to give them unity[j] of mind to carry out what the king and his officials had ordered, following the word of the LORD.

13A very large crowd of people assembled in Jerusalem to celebrate the Feast of Unleavened Bread[k] in the second month. 14They removed the altars[l] in Jerusalem and cleared away the incense altars and threw them into the Kidron Valley.[m]

15They slaughtered the Passover lamb on the fourteenth day of the second month. The priests and the Levites were ashamed and consecrated[n] themselves and brought burnt offerings to the temple of the LORD. 16Then they took up their regular positions[o] as prescribed in the Law of Moses the man of God. The priests sprinkled the blood handed to them by the Levites. 17Since many in the crowd had not consecrated themselves, the Levites had to kill[p] the Passover lambs for all those who were not ceremonially clean and could not consecrate ⌊their lambs⌋ to the LORD. 18Although most of the many people who came

30:2 [x]Nu 9:10
30:3 [y]2Ch 29:34
30:5 [z]Jdg 20:1
30:7 [a]Ps 78:8,57; 106:6; Eze 20:18 [b]2Ch 29:8
30:8 [c]Ex 32:9 [d]Nu 25:4; 2Ch 29:10
30:9 [e]Dt 30:2-5; Isa 1:16; 55:7 [f]1Ki 8:50; Ps 106:46 [g]Ex 34:6-7; Dt 4:31; Mic 7:18
30:10 [h]2Ch 36:16
30:11 [i]ver 25
30:12 [j]Jer 32:39; Eze 11:19; Php 2:13
30:13 [k]Nu 28:16
30:14 [l]2Ch 28:24 [m]2Sa 15:23
30:15 [n]2Ch 29:34
30:16 [o]2Ch 35:10
30:17 [p]2Ch 29:34

Humor, in its many-splendored varieties, is a remarkable thing. Henri Bergson, the French philosopher, said, "Humor is a momentary anesthesia of the heart," and truly it is. A good laugh can aid in deadening the pain and difficulty that is frequently a part of our daily living. It can cross the barrier of language or culture. It can erase tension between friends. It can liven up a discussion or a school room, an office or a family. And it can certainly relieve boredom.

—Luci Swindoll

from Ephraim, Manasseh, Issachar and Zebulun
had not purified themselves,[q] yet they ate the
Passover, contrary to what was written. But Hezekiah prayed for them, saying, "May the LORD,
who is good, pardon everyone 19 who sets his heart
on seeking God—the LORD, the God of his
fathers—even if he is not clean according to the
rules of the sanctuary." 20 And the LORD heard[r]
Hezekiah and healed[s] the people.[t]

21 The Israelites who were present in Jerusalem
celebrated the Feast of Unleavened Bread[u] for sev-
en days with great rejoicing, while the Levites and
priests sang to the LORD every day, accompanied
by the LORD's instruments of praise.[a]

22 Hezekiah spoke encouragingly to all the
Levites, who showed good understanding of the
service of the LORD. For the seven days they ate
their assigned portion and offered fellowship offerings[b] and praised the LORD, the God of their fathers.

23 The whole assembly then agreed to celebrate[v]
the festival seven more days; so for another seven
days they celebrated joyfully. 24 Hezekiah king of
Judah provided[w] a thousand bulls and seven
thousand sheep and goats for the assembly, and
the officials provided them with a thousand bulls
and ten thousand sheep and goats. A great number of priests consecrated themselves. 25 The entire
assembly of Judah rejoiced, along with the priests
and Levites and all who had assembled from Israel[x], including the aliens who had come from Israel and those who lived in Judah. 26 There was
great joy in Jerusalem, for since the days of Solomon[y] son of David king of Israel there had been
nothing like this in Jerusalem. 27 The priests and
the Levites stood to bless[z] the people, and God
heard them, for their prayer reached heaven, his
holy dwelling place.

31 When all this had ended, the Israelites who
were there went out to the towns of Judah,
smashed the sacred stones and cut down[a] the
Asherah poles. They destroyed the high places
and the altars throughout Judah and Benjamin
and in Ephraim and Manasseh. After they had
destroyed all of them, the Israelites returned to
their own towns and to their own property.

Contributions for Worship

2 Hezekiah[b] assigned the priests and Levites to
divisions[c]—each of them according to their duties
as priests or Levites—to offer burnt offerings and
fellowship offerings,[b] to minister,[d] to give thanks
and to sing praises[e] at the gates of the LORD's
dwelling.[f] 3 The king contributed[g] from his own
possessions for the morning and evening burnt
offerings and for the burnt offerings on the Sabbaths, New Moons and appointed feasts as written
in the Law of the LORD.[h] 4 He ordered the people

30:18 [q]Ex 12:43-49; Nu 9:6-10
30:20 [r]2Ch 6:20 [s]2Ch 7:14; Mal 4:2 [t]Jas 5:16
30:21 [u]Ex 12:15, 17; 13:6
30:23 [v]1Ki 8:65; 2Ch 7:9
30:24 [w]1Ki 8:5; 2Ch 29:34; 35:7; Ezr 6:17; 8:35
30:25 [x]ver 11
30:26 [y]2Ch 7:8
30:27 [z]Ex 39:43; Nu 6:23; Dt 26:15; 2Ch 23:18; Ps 68:5
31:1 [a]2Ki 18:4; 2Ch 32:12; Isa 36:7
31:2 [b]2Ch 29:9 [c]1Ch 24:1 [d]1Ch 15:2 [e]Ps 7:17; 9:2; 47:6; 71:22 [f]1Ch 23:28-32
31:3 [g]1Ch 29:3; 2Ch 35:7; Eze 45:17 [h]Nu 28:1-29:40

Great Joy!

2CH 30:26–27

Hezekiah joins together "all Israel" (2Ch 30:1) for a true Passover celebration, the first since Solomon dedicated the new temple well over two centuries earlier. The priests rededicate their lives to God (2Ch 30:24), guide the people in fervent prayer (2Ch 30:27) and exuberantly sing and praise God every day (2Ch 30:21). Everyone is so filled with joy that they agree to extend the celebration another seven days (2Ch 30:23).

Then everyone comes down from the "mountaintop" experience to make a courageous difference in the surrounding communities. They destroy the pagan altars and high places (2Ch 31:1); then they go back to their homes to live for God, committed to positively influencing their world.

[a] 21 Or *priests praised the LORD every day with resounding instruments belonging to the LORD* [b] 22,2 Traditionally *peace offerings*

Heaps

2CH 31:6–10

God's plan is for his people to support the Levites by giving their annual tithes (Nu 18:24; 2Ch 31:4) so the Levites can be free to "devote themselves to the Law of the LORD" (31:4). When Hezekiah calls for this giving to begin again after years of neglect, the people respond enthusiastically—so much so that the gifts are piled in "heaps" (2Ch 31:6) in the temple area. The "heaps" are so large that Hezekiah notices them immediately and praises God for the people's generosity.

The writer of Chronicles composes the history of Judah's kings for the benefit of the newly released Babylonian captives. He wants to show them examples of what worked for God's people in the past, so they will know how to reestablish not only the temple worship in Jerusalem but also godly lifestyles in their towns. The returning exiles are reluctant to give their offerings (Mal 3:8–10). At times, the Levites are forced back into farming to support themselves (Ne 13:10). The story of how Hezekiah blesses the people for their generosity without criticizing them for their former neglect is exactly the encouragement the exiles need.

living in Jerusalem to give the portion[i] due the
priests and Levites so they could devote themselves to the Law of the LORD. 5As soon as the order
went out, the Israelites generously gave the firstfruits[j] of their grain, new wine,[k] oil and honey and
all that the fields produced. They brought a great
amount, a tithe of everything. 6The men of Israel
and Judah who lived in the towns of Judah also
brought a tithe[l] of their herds and flocks and a
tithe of the holy things dedicated to the LORD their
God, and they piled them in heaps.[m] 7They began
doing this in the third month and finished in the
seventh month.[n] 8When Hezekiah and his officials
came and saw the heaps, they praised the LORD
and blessed[o] his people Israel.

9Hezekiah asked the priests and Levites about
the heaps; 10and Azariah the chief priest, from the
family of Zadok,[p] answered, "Since the people
began to bring their contributions to the temple
of the LORD, we have had enough to eat and plenty to spare, because the LORD has blessed his people, and this great amount is left over."[q]

11Hezekiah gave orders to prepare storerooms in
the temple of the LORD, and this was done. 12Then
they faithfully brought in the contributions, tithes
and dedicated gifts. Conaniah,[r] a Levite, was in
charge of these things, and his brother Shimei was
next in rank. 13Jehiel, Azaziah, Nahath, Asahel,
Jerimoth, Jozabad,[s] Eliel, Ismakiah, Mahath and
Benaiah were supervisors under Conaniah and
Shimei his brother, by appointment of King Hezekiah and Azariah the official in charge of the
temple of God.

14Kore son of Imnah the Levite, keeper of the
East Gate, was in charge of the freewill offerings
given to God, distributing the contributions made
to the LORD and also the consecrated gifts. 15Eden,[t]
Miniamin, Jeshua, Shemaiah, Amariah and
Shecaniah assisted him faithfully in the towns[u] of
the priests, distributing to their fellow priests
according to their divisions, old and young alike.

16In addition, they distributed to the males three
years old or more whose names were in the
genealogical records[v]—all who would enter the
temple of the LORD to perform the daily duties of
their various tasks, according to their responsibilities and their divisions. 17And they distributed to
the priests enrolled by their families in the
genealogical records and likewise to the Levites
twenty years old or more, according to their
responsibilities and their divisions. 18They included all the little ones, the wives, and the sons and
daughters of the whole community listed in these
genealogical records. For they were faithful in
consecrating themselves.

19As for the priests, the descendants of Aaron,
who lived on the farm lands around their towns
or in any other towns,[w] men were designated by
name to distribute portions to every male among
them and to all who were recorded in the genealogies of the Levites.

31:4 [i]Nu 18:8; Dt 18:8; Ne 13:10; Mal 2:7

31:5 [j]Nu 18:12, 24; Ne 13:12; Eze 44:30 [k]Dt 12:17

31:6 [l]Lev 27:30; Ne 13:10-12 [m]Dt 14:28; Ru 3:7

31:7 [n]Ex 23:16

31:8 [o]Ps 144:13-15

31:10 [p]2Sa 8:17 [q]Ex 36:5; Eze 44:30; Mal 3:10-12

31:12 [r]2Ch 35:9

31:13 [s]2Ch 35:9

31:15 [t]2Ch 29:12 [u]Jos 21:9-19

31:16 [v]1Ch 23:3; Ezr 3:4

31:19 [w]ver 12-15; Lev 25:34; Nu 35:2-5

31:20 20 This is what Hezekiah did throughout Judah,
[x]2Ki 20:3; doing what was good and right and faithful[x] before
22:2 the LORD his God. 21 In everything that he undertook
in the service of God's temple and in obedience to
the law and the commands, he sought his God and
31:21 [y]Dt 29:9 worked wholeheartedly. And so he prospered.[y]

Sennacherib Threatens Jerusalem

32:1 **32** After all that Hezekiah had so faithfully
[z]2Ki 18:13- done, Sennacherib[z] king of Assyria came
19; Isa 36:1; and invaded Judah. He laid siege to the fortified
37:9,17,37 cities, thinking to conquer them for himself.
32:2 2 When Hezekiah saw that Sennacherib had come
[a]Isa 22:7; and that he intended to make war on Jerusalem,[a]
Jer 1:15 3 he consulted with his officials and military staff
about blocking off the water from the springs outside the city, and they helped him. 4 A large force
32:4 of men assembled, and they blocked all the
[b]2Ki 18:17; springs[b] and the stream that flowed through the
20:20; land. "Why should the kings[a] of Assyria come and
Isa 22:9,11; find plenty of water?" they said. 5 Then he worked
Na 3:14 hard repairing all the broken sections of the wall[c]
32:5 [c]2Ch 25:23; and building towers on it. He built another wall
Isa 22:10 outside that one and reinforced the supporting ter-
[d]1Ki 9:24; races[b][d] of the City of David. He also made large
1Ch 11:8 [e]Isa 22:8 numbers of weapons[e] and shields.

6 He appointed military officers over the people
and assembled them before him in the square at
the city gate and encouraged them with these
32:7 words: 7 "Be strong and courageous.[f] Do not be
[f]Dt 31:6; 1Ch 22:13 afraid or discouraged[g] because of the king of
[g]2Ch 20:15 Assyria and the vast army with him, for there is a
[h]Nu 14:9; 2Ki 6:16 greater power with us than with him.[h] 8 With him
is only the arm of flesh,[i] but with us[j] is the LORD
32:8 our God to help us and to fight our battles."[k] And
[i]Job 40:9; Isa 52:10; the people gained confidence from what Hezekiah
Jer 17:5; 32:21 the king of Judah said.

[j]Dt 3:22; 9 Later, when Sennacherib king of Assyria and
1Sa 17:45; all his forces were laying siege to Lachish,[l] he sent
2Ch 13:12 [k]1Ch 5:22; his officers to Jerusalem with this message for
2Ch 20:17; Hezekiah king of Judah and for all the people of
Ps 20:7; Isa 28:6 Judah who were there:

10 "This is what Sennacherib king of Assyr-
32:9 [l]Jos 10:3,31 ia says: On what are you basing your confidence,[m] that you remain in Jerusalem under
32:10 [m]Eze 29:16 siege? 11 When Hezekiah says, 'The LORD our
God will save us from the hand of the king of
32:11 [n]Isa 37:10 Assyria,' he is misleading[n] you, to let you die
of hunger and thirst. 12 Did not Hezekiah him-
self remove this god's high places and altars,
32:12 saying to Judah and Jerusalem, 'You must
[o]2Ch 31:1 worship before one altar[o] and burn sacrifices
on it'?

13 "Do you not know what I and my fathers
have done to all the peoples of the other
32:13 lands? Were the gods of those nations ever
[p]ver 15 able to deliver their land from my hand?[p]
14 Who of all the gods of these nations that my

Divine wisdom, intending to detain us some time on earth, has done well to cover with *a* veil the prospect of the life to come; for if our sight could clearly distinguish the opposite bank, who would remain on this tempestuous coast of time?

—Madame Anne-Louise-Germaine de Staël (1766-1817)

[a] 4 Hebrew; Septuagint and Syriac *king* [b] 5 Or *the Millo*

Week 11

Your Warrior King

You've honored the Lord, followed his ways to the best of your ability and stood up for what is right and godly. But now you're being attacked. Why is God allowing this to happen? You've been faithful to him, but now it seems he's turning his back on you. Are you going to have to fight this one alone? Well, take a look at someone who knows all about your situation: Hezekiah, king of Judah.

The nation of Israel is divided into two kingdoms, the northern kingdom, Israel, and the southern kingdom, Judah. The Assyrians are steadily expanding their territory. They attack Samaria, the capital of Israel. After the fall of Samaria, Judah experiences several years of relief from military pressures. Hezekiah uses those years to rebuild Judah and bring the people back to the Lord. He reconsecrates the temple (2Ch 29), reinstitutes the celebration of the Passover (2Ch 30) and takes steps to stop idolatry (2Ch 31:1). But in spite of all that he does, God allows Sennacherib, the king of Assyria, to invade Judah (2Ch 32:1). So what is a God-fearing king to do?

What words does Hezekiah have for the people (2Ch 32:7-8)? What words does the Lord have for you in your time of trouble (Dt 20:4)?

Does Hezekiah's trust in God deter Sennacherib (2Ch 32:14-15)? Will you lose hope if things don't get better immediately (Ps 33:17-22; Ps 62:5-8)?

What is Hezekiah's response to Sennacherib's threat (2Ch 32:20)? What will you do when faced with a battle (2Ch 20:21-22; Ps 32:6-7)?

How does God rescue Hezekiah and Jerusalem (2Ch 32:21-22)? How might God rescue you (Jer 15:20; Ps 27)?

How does God honor Hezekiah for his trust (2Ch 32:23)? How might God honor you (Ps 3:3)?

God is ready and able to fight for you. When you call to him, he will hear your voice. He is your warrior king, your fortress and your deliverer (Ps 18:1-2).

Enjoying God THROUGH the Word

Read 2 Samuel 22:7-20 (page 511). These incredibly beautiful images can give you strength and hope when you are in battle. No matter how powerful your enemy, God is greater (2Ch 32:7). No matter how many oppose you, there are more on your side than on the side of your enemy. God may send the mighty hosts of heaven to aid you (Mt 26:53-54). Often all we lack is the discernment to identify God's presence in our situation (2Ki 6:14-17). And you have his very Spirit within you, who is greater than all the enemies in this world (1Jn 4:4).

Your warrior king gives power and strength to his people and to you (Ps 68:32-35). He will triumph over his enemies, who are also *your* enemies (Isa 42:13). Your warrior king provides far greater security than any you can produce yourself (Pr 14:26).

Enjoying God THROUGH Experience

Use your prayer time to thank God that he is your warrior king. Read a Scripture (such as Psalm 24:7-10) that declares your praise and thanksgiving. Perhaps sing a song that describes God's power and praises him for it (such as "A Mighty Fortress Is Our God"). Allow the knowledge of his power to give you confidence, strength and hope. Your warrior king has declared, "Do not fear, for I am with you; do not be dismayed, for I am your God. I will strengthen you and help you; I will uphold you with my righteous right hand" (Isa 41:10).

Go to page 763 for your next weekly study.

fathers destroyed has been able to save his
people from me? How then can your god
deliver you from my hand? 15Now do not let
32:15 Hezekiah deceive[q] you and mislead you like
[q]Isa 37:10 this. Do not believe him, for no god of any
[r]Da 3:15 nation or kingdom has been able to deliver[r]
[s]Ex 5:2 his people from my hand or the hand of my
fathers.[s] How much less will your god deliver you from my hand!"

16Sennacherib's officers spoke further against
the LORD God and against his servant Hezekiah.
32:17 17The king also wrote letters[t] insulting[u] the LORD,
[t]Isa 37:14 the God of Israel, and saying this against him:
[u]Ps 74:22; "Just as the gods[v] of the peoples of the other lands
Isa 37:4,17 did not rescue their people from my hand, so the
[v]2Ki 19:12 god of Hezekiah will not rescue his people from
my hand." 18Then they called out in Hebrew to
the people of Jerusalem who were on the wall, to
terrify them and make them afraid in order to capture the city. 19They spoke about the God of Jeru-
32:19 salem as they did about the gods of the other peo-
[w]2Ki 19:18; ples of the world—the work of men's hands.[w]
Ps 115:4-8; 20King Hezekiah and the prophet Isaiah son of
Isa 2:8; 17:8 Amoz cried out in prayer to heaven about this.
32:21 21And the LORD sent an angel,[x] who annihilated
[x]Ge 19:13 all the fighting men and the leaders and officers in
[y]2Ki 19:7 the camp of the Assyrian king. So he withdrew to
his own land in disgrace. And when he went into
the temple of his god, some of his sons cut him
down with the sword.[y]

22So the LORD saved Hezekiah and the people of
Jerusalem from the hand of Sennacherib king of
Assyria and from the hand of all others. He took
32:23 care of them[a] on every side. 23Many brought offer-
[z]2Ch 9:24; ings to Jerusalem for the LORD and valuable gifts[z]
17:5; for Hezekiah king of Judah. From then on he was
Isa 45:14; highly regarded by all the nations.
Zec 14:16-17

Hezekiah's Pride, Success and Death

24In those days Hezekiah became ill and was at
the point of death. He prayed to the LORD, who
answered him and gave him a miraculous sign.
32:25 25But Hezekiah's heart was proud[a] and he did not
[a]2Ki 14:10; respond to the kindness shown him; therefore the
2Ch 26:16
[b]2Ch 19:2; LORD's wrath[b] was on him and on Judah and Jeru-
24:18 salem. 26Then Hezekiah repented[c] of the pride of
32:26 his heart, as did the people of Jerusalem; there-
[c]Jer 26:18-19 fore the LORD's wrath did not come upon them
[d]2Ch 34:27, during the days of Hezekiah.[d]
28; Isa 39:8

32:27 27Hezekiah had very great riches and honor,[e]
[e]1Ch 29:12 and he made treasuries for his silver and gold and
for his precious stones, spices, shields and all
kinds of valuables. 28He also made buildings to
store the harvest of grain, new wine and oil; and
he made stalls for various kinds of cattle, and
pens for the flocks. 29He built villages and
32:29 acquired great numbers of flocks and herds, for
[f]1Ch 29:12 God had given him very great riches.[f]

[a] 22 Hebrew; Septuagint and Vulgate *He gave them rest*

Taunting God

2CH 32:16-17

Sennacherib's egotistical taunts against the Israelites' God are based on a revoltingly warped belief system. Convinced that specific gods rule over different territories, he thinks the stronger gods will eventually crush the weaker gods. The Assyrian king believes he can expand his power base by adding his captives' gods to his idol collection. He assumes Hezekiah's "Lord" is merely one more god to conquer. It is the worst act of blasphemy to put the self-existing God into the same category as "the work of men's hands" (1Ch 32:19). No wonder Hezekiah tears his clothes and mourns (2Ki 19:1).

King Hezekiah and the prophet Isaiah take their heavy hearts to God (2Ch 32:20), and he assures them he has heard the blasphemous remarks of Sennacherib and his men. God sends an angel to destroy Sennacherib's soldiers, and the king goes back to Nineveh in "disgrace" (2Ch 32:21; see Map 8a: Assyrian Empire at the back of this Bible).

Manasseh

2CH 33:10–13

Hezekiah's son Manasseh fills most of his 55-year ***reign with evil activity—rebuilding the pagan shrines his father had destroyed, worshiping the stars, practicing witchcraft, consulting with psychics, sacrificing his own sons and leading the Israelites to forsake God and behave like the pagan nations around them.***

Both Biblical accounts of Manasseh's life record his evil deeds (2Ki 21:1–18; 2Ch 33:1–20). However, the writer of Kings dwells on Manasseh's sinful choices, ***picturing him as the major cause for Jerusalem's fall*** **(2Ki 21:10–15)** ***and does not mention the Chronicler's description of Manasseh's prison time in Babylon, his repentance and the restoration of his kingdom*** **(2Ch 33:10–13). Throughout 1 and 2 Chronicles, the writer seeks to show his readers** ***(the recently released Jewish exiles) the cause and effect of following or rejecting God. He wants them to understand that disobedience and sin always bring punishment, whereas repentance and trust in God renders blessing, restoration and peace.***

30 It was Hezekiah who blocked[g] the upper outlet of the Gihon[h] spring and channeled the water
down to the west side of the City of David. He succeeded in everything he undertook. 31 But when
envoys were sent by the rulers of Babylon[i] to ask
him about the miraculous sign[j] that had occurred
in the land, God left him to test[k] him and to know
everything that was in his heart.
32 The other events of Hezekiah's reign and his
acts of devotion are written in the vision of the
prophet Isaiah son of Amoz in the book of the
kings of Judah and Israel. 33 Hezekiah rested with
his fathers and was buried on the hill where the
tombs of David's descendants are. All Judah and
the people of Jerusalem honored him when he
died. And Manasseh his son succeeded him as
king.

Manasseh King of Judah

33 Manasseh[l] was twelve years old when he
became king, and he reigned in Jerusalem
fifty-five years. 2 He did evil in the eyes of the
LORD,[m] following the detestable[n] practices of the
nations the LORD had driven out before the Israelites. 3 He rebuilt the high places his father Hezekiah had demolished; he also erected altars to the
Baals and made Asherah poles.[o] He bowed down[p]
to all the starry hosts and worshiped them. 4 He
built altars in the temple of the LORD, of which the
LORD had said, "My Name[q] will remain in Jerusalem forever." 5 In both courts of the temple of the
LORD,[r] he built altars to all the starry hosts. 6 He
sacrificed his sons[s] in[a] the fire in the Valley of Ben
Hinnom, practiced sorcery, divination and witchcraft, and consulted mediums[t] and spiritists.[u] He
did much evil in the eyes of the LORD, provoking
him to anger.
7 He took the carved image he had made and put
it in God's temple,[v] of which God had said to
David and to his son Solomon, "In this temple and
in Jerusalem, which I have chosen out of all the
tribes of Israel, I will put my Name forever. 8 I will
not again make the feet of the Israelites leave the
land[w] I assigned to your forefathers, if only they
will be careful to do everything I commanded
them concerning all the laws, decrees and ordinances given through Moses." 9 But Manasseh led
Judah and the people of Jerusalem astray, so that
they did more evil than the nations the LORD had
destroyed before the Israelites.[x]
10 The LORD spoke to Manasseh and his people,
but they paid no attention. 11 So the LORD brought
against them the army commanders of the king of
Assyria, who took Manasseh prisoner,[y] put a hook
in his nose, bound him with bronze shackles[z] and
took him to Babylon. 12 In his distress he sought
the favor of the LORD his God and humbled[a] himself greatly before the God of his fathers. 13 And
when he prayed to him, the LORD was moved by

32:30 [g]2Ki 18:17 [h]1Ki 1:33
32:31 [i]Isa 39:1 [j]ver 24; Isa 38:7 [k]Ge 22:1; Dt 8:16
33:1 [l]1Ch 3:13
33:2 [m]Jer 15:4 [n]Dt 18:9; 2Ch 28:3
33:3 [o]Dt 16:21-22 [p]Dt 17:3; 2Ch 31:1
33:4 [q]2Ch 7:16
33:5 [r]2Ch 4:9
33:6 [s]Lev 18:21; Dt 18:10; 2Ch 28:3 [t]Lev 19:31 [u]1Sa 28:13
33:7 [v]2Ch 7:16
33:8 [w]2Sa 7:10
33:9 [x]Jer 15:4
33:11 [y]Dt 28:36 [z]Ps 149:8
33:12 [a]2Ch 6:37; 32:26; 1Pe 5:6

[a] 6 Or *He made his sons pass through*

his entreaty and listened to his plea; so he brought
him back to Jerusalem and to his kingdom. Then
Manasseh knew that the LORD is God.
33:14 14Afterward he rebuilt the outer wall of the City
b1Ki 1:33 of David, west of the Gihon[b] spring in the valley,
cNe 3:3; 12:39; as far as the entrance of the Fish Gate[c] and encir-
Zep 1:10 cling the hill of Ophel;[d] he also made it much
d2Ch 27:3; higher. He stationed military commanders in all
Ne 3:26 the fortified cities in Judah.
33:15 15He got rid of the foreign gods and removed[e] the
ever 3-7; 2Ki 23:12 image from the temple of the LORD, as well as all
the altars he had built on the temple hill and in Jerusalem; and he threw them out of the city. 16Then
33:16 he restored the altar of the LORD and sacrificed fel-
fLev 7:11-18 lowship offerings[a] and thank offerings[f] on it, and
told Judah to serve the LORD, the God of Israel.
17The people, however, continued to sacrifice at the
high places, but only to the LORD their God.
18The other events of Manasseh's reign, including his prayer to his God and the words the seers
spoke to him in the name of the LORD, the God of
Israel, are written in the annals of the kings of
Israel.[b] 19His prayer and how God was moved by
his entreaty, as well as all his sins and unfaithfulness, and the sites where he built high places and
set up Asherah poles and idols before he hum-
33:19 bled[g] himself—all are written in the records of the
g2Ch 6:37; h2Ki 21:17 seers.[c][h] 20Manasseh rested with his fathers and
33:20 was buried[i] in his palace. And Amon his son suc-
i2Ki 21:18; 2Ch 21:20 ceeded him as king.

Amon King of Judah

33:21 j1Ch 3:14 21Amon[j] was twenty-two years old when he
became king, and he reigned in Jerusalem two
years. 22He did evil in the eyes of the LORD, as his
father Manasseh had done. Amon worshiped and
offered sacrifices to all the idols Manasseh had
made. 23But unlike his father Manasseh, he did
33:23 kver 12; not humble[k] himself before the LORD; Amon
Ex 10:3; 2Ch 7:14; increased his guilt.
Ps 18:27; 147:6; 24Amon's officials conspired against him and
Pr 3:34 assassinated him in his palace. 25Then the people[l]
of the land killed all who had plotted against King
33:25 Amon, and they made Josiah his son king in his
l2Ch 22:1 place.

Josiah's Reforms

34:1 m1Ch 3:14 34 Josiah[m] was eight years old when he became
nZep 1:1 king,[n] and he reigned in Jerusalem thirty-
one years. 2He did what was right in the eyes of the
34:2 o2Ch 29:2 LORD and walked in the ways of his father David,[o]
not turning aside to the right or to the left.
3In the eighth year of his reign, while he was
34:3 p1Ki 13:2; still young, he began to seek the God[p] of his father
1Ch 16:11; David. In his twelfth year he began to purge
2Ch 15:2; Judah and Jerusalem of high places, Asherah
33:17,22 poles, carved idols and cast images. 4Under his

[a] *16* Traditionally *peace offerings* [b] *18* That is, Judah, as frequently in 2 Chronicles [c] *19* One Hebrew manuscript and Septuagint; most Hebrew manuscripts *of Hozai*

Good Kings, Bad Kings

2CH 33:18—34:2

Abraham's grandson Jacob (later called Israel) has 12 sons who become the ancestors of the 12 tribes of Israel. Through these tribes God plans to fulfill his covenant promise to Abraham (Ge 17:4). The 12 tribes exist as a united kingdom under 3 kings—Saul, David and Solomon.

When Solomon's son Rehoboam begins his reign, the northern tribes revolt and the divided kingdom begins (2Ch 10). The northern kingdom becomes known as Israel; the southern kingdom, as Judah. None of Israel's kings are "good," although several great prophets—Elijah, Elisha and Hosea—come from Israel.

Of the 20 kings of Judah, 5 are godly—Asa, Jehoshaphat, Jotham, Hezekiah and Josiah. Several make some good decisions: Uzziah (Azariah), Jehoash (Joash) and Manasseh; but the rest reject God and his ways. In this theocracy, each king is the Lord's representative. That is why it is such a spiritual tragedy for a king to ignore God and worship idols.

direction the altars of the Baals were torn down;
he cut to pieces the incense altars that were above
them, and smashed the Asherah poles,[q] the idols
and the images. These he broke to pieces and scattered over the graves of those who had sacrificed
to them.[r] 5He burned[s] the bones of the priests on
their altars, and so he purged Judah and Jerusalem. 6In the towns of Manasseh, Ephraim and
Simeon, as far as Naphtali, and in the ruins
around them, 7he tore down the altars and the
Asherah poles and crushed the idols to powder[t]
and cut to pieces all the incense altars throughout
Israel. Then he went back to Jerusalem.

8In the eighteenth year of Josiah's reign, to purify the land and the temple, he sent Shaphan son
of Azaliah and Maaseiah the ruler of the city, with
Joah son of Joahaz, the recorder, to repair the temple of the LORD his God.

9They went to Hilkiah[u] the high priest and gave
him the money that had been brought into the
temple of God, which the Levites who were the
doorkeepers had collected from the people of
Manasseh, Ephraim and the entire remnant of
Israel and from all the people of Judah and Benjamin and the inhabitants of Jerusalem. 10Then
they entrusted it to the men appointed to supervise the work on the LORD's temple. These men
paid the workers who repaired and restored the
temple. 11They also gave money[v] to the carpenters
and builders to purchase dressed stone, and timber for joists and beams for the buildings that the
kings of Judah had allowed to fall into ruin.[w]

12The men did the work faithfully.[x] Over them to
direct them were Jahath and Obadiah, Levites
descended from Merari, and Zechariah and
Meshullam, descended from Kohath. The Levites—
all who were skilled in playing musical instruments—[y] 13had charge of the laborers[z] and supervised all the workers from job to job. Some of the
Levites were secretaries, scribes and doorkeepers.

The Book of the Law Found

14While they were bringing out the money that
had been taken into the temple of the LORD, Hilkiah the priest found the Book of the Law of the
LORD that had been given through Moses. 15Hilki-
ah said to Shaphan the secretary, "I have found
the Book of the Law[a] in the temple of the LORD."
He gave it to Shaphan.

16Then Shaphan took the book to the king and
reported to him: "Your officials are doing everything that has been committed to them. 17They
have paid out the money that was in the temple of
the LORD and have entrusted it to the supervisors
and workers." 18Then Shaphan the secretary
informed the king, "Hilkiah the priest has given
me a book." And Shaphan read from it in the presence of the king.

19When the king heard the words of the Law,[b]
he tore[c] his robes. 20He gave these orders to Hilkiah, Ahikam son of Shaphan[d], Abdon son of

34:4 [q]Ex 34:13 [r]Ex 32:20; Lev 26:30; 2Ki 23:11; Mic 1:5
34:5 [s]1Ki 13:2
34:7 [t]Ex 32:20; 2Ch 31:1
34:9 [u]1Ch 6:13; 2Ch 35:8
34:11 [v]2Ch 24:12 [w]2Ch 33:4-7
34:12 [x]2Ki 12:15 [y]1Ch 25:1
34:13 [z]1Ch 23:4
34:15 [a]2Ki 22:8; Ezr 7:6; Ne 8:1
34:19 [b]Dt 28:3-68 [c]Jos 7:6; Isa 36:22; 37:1
34:20 [d]2Ki 22:3

People always like to be where the action is. Often we are inclined to wait until everything is copacetic before we reach out to anyone else. We don't feel our living quarters are nice enough, or finished enough, or furnished enough, or elaborate enough. But people don't come to check us out. They come to relax or have fun. And sometimes they come because they are hungry for fellowship. Don't wait until everything is perfect before you extend hospitality. That day will never come.

—Luci Swindoll

Micah,[a] Shaphan the secretary and Asaiah the
king's attendant: [21]"Go and inquire of the LORD for
me and for the remnant in Israel and Judah about
what is written in this book that has been found.
34:21 [e]2Ch 29:8; La 2:4; 4:11; Eze 36:18 Great is the LORD's anger that is poured out[e] on us
because our fathers have not kept the word of the
LORD; they have not acted in accordance with all
that is written in this book."
34:22 [f]Ex 15:20; Ne 6:14 [22]Hilkiah and those the king had sent with him[b]
went to speak to the prophetess[f] Huldah, who was
the wife of Shallum son of Tokhath,[c] the son of
Hasrah,[d] keeper of the wardrobe. She lived in Jerusalem, in the Second District.
[23]She said to them, "This is what the LORD, the
God of Israel, says: Tell the man who sent you to
34:24 [g]Pr 16:4; Isa 3:9; Jer 40:2; 42:10; 44:2, 11 [h]2Ch 36:14-20 [i]Dt 28:15-68 me, [24]'This is what the LORD says: I am going to
bring disaster[g] on this place and its people[h]—all
the curses[i] written in the book that has been read
in the presence of the king of Judah. [25]Because
they have forsaken me[j] and burned incense to
other gods and provoked me to anger by all that
their hands have made,[e] my anger will be poured
34:25 [j]2Ch 33:3-6; Jer 22:9 out on this place and will not be quenched.' [26]Tell
the king of Judah, who sent you to inquire of the
LORD, 'This is what the LORD, the God of Israel,
34:27 [k]2Ch 12:7; 32:26 [l]Ex 10:3; 2Ch 6:37 says concerning the words you heard: [27]Because
your heart was responsive[k] and you humbled[l]
yourself before God when you heard what he
spoke against this place and its people, and
because you humbled yourself before me and tore
your robes and wept in my presence, I have heard
you, declares the LORD. [28]Now I will gather you
34:28 [m]2Ch 35:20-25 [n]2Ch 32:26 to your fathers,[m] and you will be buried in peace.
Your eyes will not see all the disaster I am going
to bring on this place and on those who live
here.' "[n]
So they took her answer back to the king.
[29]Then the king called together all the elders of
Judah and Jerusalem. [30]He went up to the temple
34:30 [o]2Ki 23:2; Ne 8:1-3 of the LORD[o] with the men of Judah, the people of
Jerusalem, the priests and the Levites—all the
people from the least to the greatest. He read in
their hearing all the words of the Book of the Covenant, which had been found in the temple of the
34:31 [p]1Ki 7:15; 2Ki 11:14 [q]2Ki 11:17; 2Ch 23:16; 29:10 [r]Dt 13:4 LORD. [31]The king stood by his pillar[p] and renewed
the covenant[q] in the presence of the LORD—to follow[r] the LORD and keep his commands, regulations and decrees with all his heart and all his
soul, and to obey the words of the covenant written in this book.
[32]Then he had everyone in Jerusalem and Benjamin pledge themselves to it; the people of Jerusalem did this in accordance with the covenant of
God, the God of their fathers.
34:33 [s]ver 3-7; Dt 18:9 [33]Josiah removed all the detestable[s] idols from
all the territory belonging to the Israelites, and he

[a] 20 Also called *Acbor son of Micaiah* [b] 22 One Hebrew manuscript, Vulgate and Syriac; most Hebrew manuscripts do not have *had sent with him.* [c] 22 Also called *Tikvah* [d] 22 Also called *Harhas* [e] 25 Or *by everything they have done*

A Reprieve

2CH 34:28

When King Josiah compares God's written expectations in the Book of the Law (probably the book of Deuteronomy) with the disobedient actions of Judah's former kings, he tears his clothes in shock and grief (see the note on 2Ki 23:4-8, page 616). Worried that Judah will soon experience judgment for their sins, he sends his men to "inquire of the LORD" (2Ch 34:21). They consult with Huldah the prophetess, who does not sugarcoat her response to the king. She says punishment is certain, but God has heard Josiah's humble cries and will wait to send destruction until after his death.

Although Huldah probably prophesies on other occasions, evidenced by the fact that the men respect and accept her message and do not ask for Jeremiah or Zephaniah, the Bible only mentions her on this one occasion (2Ki 22:14; 2Ch 34:22). Huldah is a godly woman who is ready to be used by God—even if it means delivering sad news to her king.

Returning the Ark

2CH 35:3

The ark of the covenant is the symbol of God's holy presence with the Israelite people. At first, the ark (Hebrew for "chest" or "box") contains the stone tablets on which God wrote the Ten Commandments, a jar of manna and Aaron's staff (Heb 9:4). Levite priests carry the ark on their shoulders with poles, since no human is permitted to touch it.

When Solomon constructs the temple in Jerusalem, the priests place the ark in its permanent location inside the Most Holy Place. More than 300 years later, King Josiah asks the Levites to return the "sacred ark" to the temple. Scripture is not clear where the ark is at this time, but most Biblical scholars believe faithful priests may have moved the ark to a safe place during the desperately wicked reigns of Manasseh and Amon. Even during these times of corruption and depravity, a few remain faithful to God's will and wish to protect his holiness.

had all who were present in Israel serve the LORD
their God. As long as he lived, they did not fail to
follow the LORD, the God of their fathers.

Josiah Celebrates the Passover

35 Josiah celebrated the Passover[t] to the LORD
in Jerusalem, and the Passover lamb was
slaughtered on the fourteenth day of the first
month. 2 He appointed the priests to their duties
and encouraged them in the service of the LORD's
temple. 3 He said to the Levites, who instructed[u]
all Israel and who had been consecrated to the
LORD: "Put the sacred ark in the temple that Solomon son of David king of Israel built. It is not to
be carried about on your shoulders. Now serve the
LORD your God and his people Israel. 4 Prepare
yourselves by families in your divisions,[v] according to the directions written by David king of Israel and by his son Solomon.
5 "Stand in the holy place with a group of
Levites for each subdivision of the families of
your fellow countrymen, the lay people. 6 Slaughter the Passover lambs, consecrate yourselves[w]
and prepare ⌞the lambs⌟ for your fellow countrymen, doing what the LORD commanded through
Moses."
7 Josiah provided for all the lay people who were
there a total of thirty thousand sheep and goats
for the Passover offerings,[x] and also three thousand cattle—all from the king's own possessions.[y]
8 His officials also contributed[z] voluntarily to the
people and the priests and Levites. Hilkiah,[a]
Zechariah and Jehiel, the administrators of God's
temple, gave the priests twenty-six hundred
Passover offerings and three hundred cattle. 9 Also
Conaniah[b] along with Shemaiah and Nethanel,
his brothers, and Hashabiah, Jeiel and Jozabad,[c]
the leaders of the Levites, provided five thousand
Passover offerings and five hundred head of cattle
for the Levites.
10 The service was arranged and the priests stood
in their places with the Levites in their divisions[d]
as the king had ordered.[e] 11 The Passover lambs
were slaughtered,[f] and the priests sprinkled the
blood handed to them, while the Levites skinned
the animals. 12 They set aside the burnt offerings to
give them to the subdivisions of the families of the
people to offer to the LORD, as is written in the
Book of Moses. They did the same with the cattle.
13 They roasted the Passover animals over the fire
as prescribed,[g] and boiled the holy offerings in
pots, caldrons and pans and served them quickly
to all the people. 14 After this, they made preparations for themselves and for the priests, because
the priests, the descendants of Aaron, were sacrificing the burnt offerings and the fat portions[h]
until nightfall. So the Levites made preparations
for themselves and for the Aaronic priests.
15 The musicians,[i] the descendants of Asaph,
were in the places prescribed by David, Asaph,
Heman and Jeduthun the king's seer. The gate-

35:1 [t]Ex 12:1-30; Nu 9:3; 28:16
35:3 [u]Dt 33:10; 1Ch 23:26; 2Ch 5:7; 17:7
35:4 [v]ver 10; 1Ch 9:10-13; 24:1; 2Ch 8:14; Ezr 6:18
35:6 [w]Lev 11:44; 2Ch 29:5,15
35:7 [x]2Ch 30:24 [y]2Ch 31:3
35:8 [z]1Ch 29:3; 2Ch 29:31-36 [a]1Ch 6:13
35:9 [b]2Ch 31:12 [c]2Ch 31:13
35:10 [d]ver 4; Ezr 6:18 [e]2Ch 30:16
35:11 [f]2Ch 29:22, 34; 30:17
35:13 [g]Ex 12:2-11; Lev 6:25; 1Sa 2:13-15
35:14 [h]Ex 29:13
35:15 [i]1Ch 25:1; 26:12-19; 2Ch 29:30; Ne 12:46; Ps 68:25

keepers at each gate did not need to leave their
posts, because their fellow Levites made the
preparations for them.
[16]So at that time the entire service of the LORD
was carried out for the celebration of the Passover
and the offering of burnt offerings on the altar of
the LORD, as King Josiah had ordered. [17]The Israelites who were present celebrated the Passover at
that time and observed the Feast of Unleavened
Bread for seven days. [18]The Passover had not been
observed like this in Israel since the days of the
prophet Samuel; and none of the kings of Israel
had ever celebrated such a Passover as did Josiah,
with the priests, the Levites and all Judah and
Israel who were there with the people of Jerusalem. [19]This Passover was celebrated in the eighteenth year of Josiah's reign.

The Death of Josiah

[20]After all this, when Josiah had set the temple
35:20 in order, Neco king of Egypt went up to fight at
[j]Isa 10:9; Carchemish[j] on the Euphrates,[k] and Josiah
Jer 46:2 marched out to meet him in battle. [21]But Neco sent
[k]Ge 2:14 messengers to him, saying, "What quarrel is there
between you and me, O king of Judah? It is not
35:21 you I am attacking at this time, but the house with
[l]1Ki 13:18; which I am at war. God has told[l] me to hurry; so
2Ki 18:25 stop opposing God, who is with me, or he will
destroy you."
35:22 [22]Josiah, however, would not turn away from
[m]Jdg 5:19; him, but disguised[m] himself to engage him in bat-
1Sa 28:8; tle. He would not listen to what Neco had said at
2Ch 18:29 God's command but went to fight him on the
35:23 plain of Megiddo.
[n]1Ki 22:34 [23]Archers[n] shot King Josiah, and he told his officers, "Take me away; I am badly wounded." [24]So
they took him out of his chariot, put him in the
other chariot he had and brought him to Jerusalem, where he died. He was buried in the tombs
of his fathers, and all Judah and Jerusalem
mourned for him.
[25]Jeremiah composed laments for Josiah, and to
this day all the men and women singers com-
35:25 memorate Josiah in the laments.[o] These became
[o]Jer 22:10, a tradition in Israel and are written in the
15-16 Laments.
[26]The other events of Josiah's reign and his acts
of devotion, according to what is written in the Law
of the LORD— [27]all the events, from beginning to
end, are written in the book of the kings of Israel
36 and Judah. [1]And the people of the land took
Jehoahaz son of Josiah and made him king
in Jerusalem in place of his father.

Jehoahaz King of Judah

[2]Jehoahaz[a] was twenty-three years old when
he became king, and he reigned in Jerusalem
three months. [3]The king of Egypt dethroned him
in Jerusalem and imposed on Judah a levy of a

[a] 2 Hebrew *Joahaz,* a variant of *Jehoahaz;* also in verse 4

Laments

2CH 35:25

King Josiah's death shocks and saddens the people of Judah. Jeremiah the prophet shares their grief and writes a number of laments in Josiah's memory. Laments, mournful poems often set to music, offer the people an emotional outlet during times of deep sorrow.

Although Jeremiah writes these lamentations soon after Josiah's death, the Jewish people are still singing them 250 years later, when Chronicles is written. The laments mentioned in 2 Chronicles 35:25 are not the dirge poems found in the book of Lamentations. Jeremiah writes those to mourn the destruction of Jerusalem. Lamentations is, however, a good example of this literary form.

The people of Judah experienced a renewal of hope and joy as Josiah led them back to God. When he dies, they grieve not only for their king, but also for their lost hope. Their future is uncertain. Soon they will be chanting the laments of Jerusalem's fall.

The End of Judah

2CH 36:2-19

Josiah's son Jehoahaz rules only three dismal months before Egypt's king dethrones him and crowns his brother, Jehoiakim, as king. Jehoiakim arrogantly burns a written message God sends him through the prophet Jeremiah (Jer 36:32). When Jehoiakim dies, his son, Jehoiachin, reigns only three months and ten days before Nebuchadnezzar conquers Jerusalem and takes him captive. Nebuchadnezzar appoints Jehoiachin's uncle, Zedekiah, king over Judah. Zedekiah revolts against Babylon (2Ki 24:20), and Nebuchadnezzar responds by destroying Jerusalem and taking captive to Babylon everyone left alive after the bloodshed.

God gives the Israelites one opportunity after another to change (2Ch 36:15). They refused his mercy, however, going so far as to ridicule his messengers. Finally there is no "remedy," no just act except punishment. A holy God cannot be put off forever. Finally, judgment must be meted out to a people who refuse to repent and insist on going their own ways.

hundred talents[a] of silver and a talent[b] of gold. 4The king of Egypt made Eliakim, a brother of Jehoahaz, king over Judah and Jerusalem and changed Eliakim's name to Jehoiakim. But Neco[p] took Eliakim's brother Jehoahaz and carried him off to Egypt.

Jehoiakim King of Judah

5Jehoiakim[q] was twenty-five years old when he became king, and he reigned in Jerusalem eleven years. He did evil in the eyes of the LORD his God. 6Nebuchadnezzar[r] king of Babylon attacked him and bound him with bronze shackles to take him to Babylon.[s] 7Nebuchadnezzar also took to Babylon articles from the temple of the LORD and put them in his temple[c] there.[t]

8The other events of Jehoiakim's reign, the detestable things he did and all that was found against him, are written in the book of the kings of Israel and Judah. And Jehoiachin his son succeeded him as king.

Jehoiachin King of Judah

9Jehoiachin[u] was eighteen[d] years old when he became king, and he reigned in Jerusalem three months and ten days. He did evil in the eyes of the LORD. 10In the spring, King Nebuchadnezzar sent for him and brought him to Babylon,[v] together with articles of value from the temple of the LORD, and he made Jehoiachin's uncle,[e] Zedekiah, king over Judah and Jerusalem.

Zedekiah King of Judah

11Zedekiah[w] was twenty-one years old when he became king, and he reigned in Jerusalem eleven years. 12He did evil in the eyes of the LORD[x] his God and did not humble[y] himself before Jeremiah the prophet, who spoke the word of the LORD. 13He also rebelled against King Nebuchadnezzar, who had made him take an oath[z] in God's name. He became stiff-necked[a] and hardened his heart and would not turn to the LORD, the God of Israel. 14Furthermore, all the leaders of the priests and the people became more and more unfaithful,[b] following all the detestable practices of the nations and defiling the temple of the LORD, which he had consecrated in Jerusalem.

The Fall of Jerusalem

15The LORD, the God of their fathers, sent word to them through his messengers[c] again and again,[d] because he had pity on his people and on his dwelling place. 16But they mocked God's messengers, despised his words and scoffed[e] at his prophets until the wrath[f] of the LORD was aroused

36:4 [p]Jer 22:10-12
36:5 [q]Jer 22:18; 26:1; 35:1
36:6 [r]Jer 25:9; 27:6; Eze 29:18 [s]2Ch 33:11; Eze 19:9; Da 1:1
36:7 [t]2Ki 24:13; Ezr 1:7; Da 1:2
36:9 [u]Jer 22:24-28; 52:31
36:10 [v]ver 18; 2Ki 20:17; Ezr 1:7; Jer 22:25; 24:1; 29:1; 37:1; Eze 17:12
36:11 [w]2Ki 24:17; Jer 27:1; 28:1
36:12 [x]Jer 37:1-39:18 [y]Dt 8:3; 2Ch 7:14; 2Ch 33:23; Jer 21:3-7
36:13 [z]Eze 17:13 [a]2Ki 17:14; 2Ch 30:8
36:14 [b]1Ch 5:25
36:15 [c]Isa 5:4; 44:26; Jer 7:25; Hag 1:13; Zec 1:4; Mal 2:7; 3:1 [d]Jer 7:13,25; 25:3-4; 35:14,15; 44:4-6
36:16 [e]2Ki 2:23; Pr 1:25; Jer 5:13 [f]Ezr 5:12; Pr 1:30-31

[a] *3* That is, about 3 3/4 tons (about 3.4 metric tons) [b] *3* That is, about 75 pounds (about 34 kilograms) [c] *7* Or *palace* [d] *9* One Hebrew manuscript, some Septuagint manuscripts and Syriac (see also 2 Kings 24:8); most Hebrew manuscripts *eight* [e] *10* Hebrew *brother,* that is, relative (see 2 Kings 24:17)

against his people and there was no remedy.[g] 17 He
brought up against them the king of the Babylonians,[a] who killed their young men with the
sword in the sanctuary, and spared neither young
man[h] nor young woman, old man or aged. God
handed all of them over to Nebuchadnezzar.[i] 18 He
carried to Babylon all the articles[j] from the temple
of God, both large and small, and the treasures of
the LORD's temple and the treasures of the king
and his officials. 19 They set fire[k] to God's temple[l]
and broke down the wall[m] of Jerusalem; they
burned all the palaces and destroyed[n] everything
of value there.[o]

20 He carried into exile[p] to Babylon the remnant,
who escaped from the sword, and they became
servants[q] to him and his sons until the kingdom
of Persia came to power. 21 The land enjoyed its
sabbath rests;[r] all the time of its desolation it rested,[s] until the seventy years[t] were completed in fulfillment of the word of the LORD spoken by
Jeremiah.

22 In the first year of Cyrus[u] king of Persia, in
order to fulfill the word of the LORD spoken by Jeremiah, the LORD moved the heart of Cyrus king of
Persia to make a proclamation throughout his
realm and to put it in writing:

23 "This is what Cyrus king of Persia says:

" 'The LORD, the God of heaven, has given
me all the kingdoms of the earth and he has
appointed[v] me to build a temple for him at
Jerusalem in Judah. Anyone of his people
among you—may the LORD his God be with
him, and let him go up.' "

36:16 [g]2Ch 30:10; Pr 29:1; Zec 1:2
36:17 [h]Jer 6:11 [i]Ezr 5:12; Jer 32:28
36:18 [j]ver 7,10
36:19 [k]Jer 11:16; 17:27; 21:10, 14; 22:7; 32:29; 39:8; La 4:11; Eze 20:47; Am 2:5; Zec 11:1 [l]1Ki 9:8-9 [m]2Ki 14:13 [n]La 2:6 [o]Ps 79:1-3
36:20 [p]Lev 26:44; 2Ki 24:14; Ezr 2:1; Ne 7:6 [q]Jer 27:7
36:21 [r]Lev 25:4; 26:34 [s]1Ch 22:9 [t]Jer 1:1; 25:11; 27:22; 29:10; 40:1; Da 9:2; Zec 1:12; 7:5
36:22 [u]Isa 44:28; 45:1,13; Jer 25:12; 29:10; Da 1:21; 6:28; 10:1
36:23 [v]Jdg 4:10

A Sabbath Rest

2CH 36:21

God designs a sabbatical year for the benefit of the Israelites and the good of the land. Every seventh year the farmers are to "rest" the land and refrain from planting a new crop (Ex 23:10-11; Lev. 25:1-7). Just as God instructed Moses to set aside the seventh day as rest for the people and renewal before God, the seventh year is also to be set aside as a time of rest and renewal for the land.

The Israelites carelessly ignore this directive just as they disregard many of God's other laws. Looking back to Leviticus 26:33-35, the writer of Chronicles recalls God's warning that he will give the land a forced sabbath rest if the people do not obey him. But even in these words of judgment is a word of hope. God will not abandon his people forever. After 70 years, he will restore them and give them "hope and a future" (Jer 29:10-11). Thankfully, God's judgments are always tempered by his grace.

[a] 17 Or *Chaldeans*

Return to the promised land.

The book of Ezra sounds a clear reminder that God is in control of earthly events. The Jews have lived in Babylon as captives for 70 years. After the king finally allows the Israelites to return to the promised land, Ezra joins them to help restore true worship to the renewed nation. Ezra's commitment to teach the people God's Word brings a rebirth of hope, and the exiles experience spiritual revival.

Ezra's narrative opens with a list of the families who return to the promised land, tracing their lineage back into Israel's history (Ezr 2:1-63). This detailed list helps the exiles reestablish their roots by instilling a sense of community and by focusing on their need to work together to restore the land and the temple (Ezr 3). Though the people face adversity, their commitment to each other and to God's commands ultimately brings about religious revival, joyful celebration and a successful rebuilding program (Ezr 4-6). Ezra, who was both priest and scribe—"a teacher well versed in the Law of Moses" (Ezr 7:6)—arrives in Jerusalem, bringing many other exiles with him (Ezr 7-8). The remainder of the book contains Ezra's call for the people to return to total obedience to God's Word (Ezr 9-10).

Ezra's leadership provides a sure foundation for ordinary people who want their lives to count for God. Ezra not only listens to and learns from God's Word, but he also applies himself to sharing what he has learned (Ezr 7:10). Ezra's passion for God spills over into his daily life and helps bring revival to his nation.

Quick Study

Author
Possibly Ezra.

Date Written
About 440 B.C.

Setting
Judah.

Key Passage
Ezra 3:11-12 *"All the people gave a great shout of praise to the LORD, because the foundation of the house of the LORD was laid. But many of the older priests and Levites and family heads, who had seen the former temple, wept aloud when they saw the foundation of this temple being laid, while many others shouted for joy."*

Outline

Permission to return to Jerusalem.
Ezr 1

List of returning exiles.
Ezr 2

Rebuilding the altar and the temple.
Ezr 3

Rebuilding opposed.
Ezr 4–5

Decree of Darius.
Ezr 6:1–12

Completion and dedication of the temple.
Ezr 6:13–18

Passover celebrated.
Ezr 6:19–22

Return of Ezra and other Israelites.
Ezr 7–8

Intermarriage: discovery and confession.
Ezr 9–10

The Women of Ezra

Foreign women	*Disobedient Israelites married them.* Ezr 9:2; 10:2–4,18–19,44

The Captives Return

EZR 1:1–4

When Cyrus of Persia takes control of the Babylonian Empire, he changes the existing policy concerning the captives under his control. He gives specific written instructions that allow the Jewish exiles to return home to rebuild the temple at Jerusalem. Historical evidence indicates that Cyrus allowed other exiles to return to their homes and countries as well.

In making this strategic decision, Cyrus fulfills Jeremiah's prophecy that the captivity will last 70 years (Jer 25:11–12; 29:10). A century and a half earlier, another prophet, Isaiah, had predicted that God would "stir up" a leader named Cyrus to work on behalf of God and his people (Isa 41:2,25; 44:28; 45:1,13). We may think that Cyrus is an unlikely tool in God's hands, since he represents the pagan opposition. However, our sovereign God can and will use anyone or anything to accomplish his purposes. We need not panic when circumstances look impossible. Our God is in control. We can trust his word.

Cyrus Helps the Exiles to Return

1 In the first year of Cyrus king of Persia, in
order to fulfill the word of the LORD spoken by
Jeremiah,[a] the LORD moved the heart[b] of Cyrus
king of Persia to make a proclamation throughout
his realm and to put it in writing:

2"This is what Cyrus king of Persia says:
" 'The LORD, the God of heaven, has given
me all the kingdoms of the earth and he has
appointed[c] me to build[d] a temple for him at Jerusalem in Judah. 3Anyone of his people
among you—may his God be with him, and
let him go up to Jerusalem in Judah and build
the temple of the LORD, the God of Israel, the
God who is in Jerusalem. 4And the people of
any place where survivors[e] may now be living
are to provide him with silver and gold, with
goods and livestock, and with freewill offerings[f] for the temple of God in Jerusalem.' "[g]

5Then the family heads of Judah and Benjamin,[h] and the priests and Levites—everyone
whose heart God had moved[i]—prepared to go up
and build the house[j] of the LORD in Jerusalem. 6All
their neighbors assisted them with articles of silver and gold, with goods and livestock, and with
valuable gifts, in addition to all the freewill offerings. 7Moreover, King Cyrus brought out the articles belonging to the temple of the LORD, which
Nebuchadnezzar had carried away from Jerusalem and had placed in the temple of his god.[a][k]
8Cyrus king of Persia had them brought by Mithredath the treasurer, who counted them out to
Sheshbazzar[l] the prince of Judah.
9This was the inventory:

gold dishes	30
silver dishes	1,000
silver pans[b]	29
10 gold bowls	30
matching silver bowls	410
other articles	1,000

11In all, there were 5,400 articles of gold and of
silver. Sheshbazzar brought all these along when
the exiles came up from Babylon to Jerusalem.

The List of the Exiles Who Returned

2 Now these are the people of the province who
came up from the captivity of the exiles,[m]
whom Nebuchadnezzar king of Babylon[n] had tak-
en captive to Babylon (they returned to Jerusalem
and Judah, each to his own town,[o] 2in company
with Zerubbabel,[p] Jeshua,[q] Nehemiah, Seraiah,[r]
Reelaiah, Mordecai, Bilshan, Mispar, Bigvai,
Rehum and Baanah):

The list of the men of the people of Israel:

3 the descendants of Parosh[s]	2,172

1:1 [a]Jer 25:11-12; 29:10-14 [b]2Ch 36:22, 23
1:2 [c]Isa 44:28; 45:13 [d]Ezr 5:13
1:4 [e]Isa 10:20-22 [f]Nu 15:3; Ps 50:14; 54:6; 116:17 [g]Ezr 4:3; 5:13; 6:3,14
1:5 [h]Ezr 4:1; Ne 11:4 [i]ver 1; Ex 35:20-22; 2Ch 36:22; Hag 1:14; Php 2:13 [j]Ps 127:1
1:7 [k]2Ki 24:13; 2Ch 36:7,10; Ezr 5:14; 6:5
1:8 [l]Ezr 5:14
2:1 [m]2Ch 36:20; Ne 7:6 [n]2Ki 24:16; 25:12 [o]Ne 7:73
2:2 [p]1Ch 3:19 [q]Ezr 3:2 [r]Ne 10:2
2:3 [s]Ezr 8:3

[a] 7 Or *gods* [b] 9 The meaning of the Hebrew for this word is uncertain.

Hannah

A Mother At Last

Hannah was barren, and, to add insult to injury, Peninnah, her husband's other wife, ridiculed her endlessly.

In the house of the Lord, weeping in her grief because of her barrenness, Hannah prayed silently, mouthing the words. She prayed for a son, vowing to give him back to the Lord. Her behavior drew suspicion from Eli, the priest. He mistook her deep communication with God for drunkenness! Hannah explained herself, and Eli blessed her. Hannah felt comforted as she left the tabernacle.

Soon after, Hannah conceived and bore a son, Samuel. How Hannah must have treasured the short time she had with her child. Her joy was complete, her thanks and praise to God were lavish, and she kept her vow. "After he was weaned, she took the boy with her, young as he was . . . and brought him to the house of the LORD at Shiloh" (1Sa 1:24). There he was to stay—permanently.

Hannah knew how to handle the pain of Samuel's absence: She prayed. Every year when she went to the tabernacle at Shiloh, she took Samuel a new robe that she had sewn. Surely, every stitch in the garment represented a prayer for him. And because she'd kept her vow, Hannah was blessed with three more sons and two daughters.

Growing up in the tabernacle was far from the best environment for a young child. In fact, Samuel was surrounded by sin (1Sa 1:3; 2:12). Even so, he "continued to grow in stature and in favor with the LORD and with men" (1Sa 2:26). At the end of his long life as a prophet and judge, Samuel challenged the people to identify any instance of cheating, oppression or corruption on his part. They found none—and this in a time when "everyone did as he saw fit" (Jdg 21:25).

Prayer is effective and loaded with grace. When confronted with an overwhelming circumstance, we say, "All we can do is pray." It is enough. It is more than enough. It unlocks the presence and power of God himself.

Hannah
(gracious)

1 Samuel 1:1–2:21

Candid SNAPSHOT Hannah was praying in her heart, and her lips were moving but her voice was not heard (1 Samuel 1:13).

Michal

Royal Chattel

She was mere chattel—personal property sold to the highest bidder. Michal, daughter of a king! Her father, Saul, sold her first to David for a hundred Philistine foreskins, then Saul gave her to Paltiel, when the relationship between Saul and David disintegrated.

In the beginning Michal loved David. When David ran for his life, she surely expected to go to him as soon as it was safe. But Michal was under her father's control, and Saul was a powerful man. She was married to Paltiel. To her surprise, Paltiel was a good man who cherished her. Michal quite likely was content, and, as the years passed, David probably faded from her memory.

At first, David's rise to power following Saul's death had little impact on her life. But David ruled only part of the kingdom, and Michal was a political prize. David reclaimed her as his wife, making her a bargaining chip when Saul's general came over to David's side. Her husband Paltiel followed her in tears, begging for her release, but Abner, the general, brusquely sent him home. David had *paid* for her. Michal belonged to him, even though he had acquired other wives by this time.

Michal's anger crystallized into hatred for David. She saw him only through the lens of her own pain. She bitterly criticized him after he vigorously danced before the ark of the Lord. David responded quickly and bluntly to Michal's attack. His worship was before the God who had chosen him as king in place of her father Saul. He was not at all worried about Michal's estimation of him (2Sa 6:21-22). The last mention of Michal in Scripture is a sad statement assessing the rest of her life, the worst sort of curse for a woman of her time: she "had no children to the day of her death" (2Sa 6:23).

We want to think the best of David, the man after God's own heart. Perhaps if Michal had bared her heart to David instead of her bitterness, he might have relented and even allowed her to return to her life with Paltiel. But she didn't, and he didn't.

Many women respond with outrage when they are treated like property. Such mistreatment was never in God's heart or design. He can miraculously turn your suffering into something beautiful for him. And he can change your husband's heart toward you. In the meantime, do not suffer in silence. Take your grief to the God of all compassion. Take your outrage to a trusted friend or counselor. And if your husband's attitude leads to violence toward you or your children, take them and go to a safe place.

Michal
(Who is like God?)

1 Samuel 14:49; 18:20-28; 19:11-17; 25:44

2 Samuel 3:13-14; 6:16-23

1Chronicles 15:29

Candid SNAPSHOT As the ark of the LORD was entering the City of David, Michal daughter of Saul watched from a window. And when she saw King David leaping and dancing before the LORD, she despised him in her heart (2 Samuel 6:16).

4 of Shephatiah 372
5 of Arah 775
6 of Pahath-Moab (through the line
of Jeshua and Joab) 2,812
7 of Elam 1,254
8 of Zattu 945
9 of Zaccai 760
10 of Bani 642
11 of Bebai 623
12 of Azgad 1,222
13 of Adonikam[t] 666
14 of Bigvai 2,056
15 of Adin 454
16 of Ater (through Hezekiah) 98
17 of Bezai 323
18 of Jorah 112
19 of Hashum 223
20 of Gibbar 95

21 the men of Bethlehem[u] 123
22 of Netophah 56
23 of Anathoth 128
24 of Azmaveth 42
25 of Kiriath Jearim,[a] Kephirah and
Beeroth 743
26 of Ramah[v] and Geba 621
27 of Micmash 122
28 of Bethel and Ai[w] 223
29 of Nebo 52
30 of Magbish 156
31 of the other Elam 1,254
32 of Harim 320
33 of Lod, Hadid and Ono 725
34 of Jericho[x] 345
35 of Senaah 3,630

36 The priests:

the descendants of Jedaiah[y] (through
the family of Jeshua) 973
37 of Immer[z] 1,052
38 of Pashhur[a] 1,247
39 of Harim[b] 1,017

40 The Levites:[c]

the descendants of Jeshua[d] and
Kadmiel (through the line of
Hodaviah) 74

41 The singers:[e]

the descendants of Asaph 128

42 The gatekeepers[f] of the temple:

the descendants of
Shallum, Ater, Talmon,
Akkub, Hatita and Shobai 139

43 The temple servants:[g]

the descendants of
Ziha, Hasupha, Tabbaoth,
44 Keros, Siaha, Padon,

a 25 See Septuagint (see also Neh. 7:29); Hebrew *Kiriath Arim.*

2:13 [t]Ezr 8:13
2:21 [u]Mic 5:2
2:26 [v]Jos 18:25
2:28 [w]Ge 12:8
2:34 [x]1Ki 16:34; 2Ch 28:15
2:36 [y]1Ch 24:7
2:37 [z]1Ch 24:14
2:38 [a]1Ch 9:12
2:39 [b]1Ch 24:8
2:40 [c]Ge 29:34; Nu 3:9; Dt 18:6-7; 1Ch 16:4; Ezr 7:7; 8:15; Ne 12:24 [d]Ezr 3:9
2:41 [e]1Ch 15:16
2:42 [f]1Sa 3:15; 1Ch 9:17
2:43 [g]1Ch 9:2; Ne 11:21

It seems like an oxymoron to say we need to seek solitude to recover from isolation. But isolation is like desolation (*a desert*) to the soul, whereas solitude is like irrigation (*a garden*) to life. In isolation, I suffer rejection and barrenness. In solitude, I am restored by his acceptance and given the privilege of fruitfulness.

—Patsy Clairmont

Living in Captivity

EZR 2:64-69

After 70 years most Jewish exiles living in Babylon are leading comfortable lives. Though the deportation must have been painful and distressing, the generation now living recalls little or nothing of their homeland. Many of them are prosperous. They have grown up in Babylon, married and raised children there. It is the only home they know.

Consequently, when Cyrus grants them permission to leave, many decide to stay in Babylon. They are unwilling to forfeit their well-paying jobs and sheltered social lives for the hardships of the 900-mile trek back to a broken-down Judah (see Map 8b: Babylonian Empire at the back of this Bible).

Some sense God's prompting to return and reestablish Jerusalem, but the decision involves risk. They cannot predict what might happen. Those who stay behind retain their prosperous businesses and predictable schedules. Yet they miss the joyous fulfillment of joining God in his restorative work.

45 Lebanah, Hagabah, Akkub,
46 Hagab, Shalmai, Hanan,
47 Giddel, Gahar, Reaiah,
48 Rezin, Nekoda, Gazzam,
49 Uzza, Paseah, Besai,
50 Asnah, Meunim, Nephusim,
51 Bakbuk, Hakupha, Harhur,
52 Bazluth, Mehida, Harsha,
53 Barkos, Sisera, Temah,
54 Neziah and Hatipha

55 The descendants of the servants of Solomon:

the descendants of
Sotai, Hassophereth, Peruda,
56 Jaala, Darkon, Giddel,
57 Shephatiah, Hattil,
Pokereth-Hazzebaim and Ami

58 The temple servants[h] and the descendants of the servants of Solomon 392

59 The following came up from the towns of
Tel Melah, Tel Harsha, Kerub, Addon and
Immer, but they could not show that their
families were descended[i] from Israel:

60 The descendants of
Delaiah, Tobiah and Nekoda 652

61 And from among the priests:

The descendants of
Hobaiah, Hakkoz and Barzillai (a
man who had married a daughter of
Barzillai the Gileadite[j] and was called
by that name).

62 These searched for their family records,
but they could not find them and so were
excluded from the priesthood[k] as unclean.
63 The governor ordered them not to eat any of
the most sacred food[l] until there was a priest
ministering with the Urim and Thummim.[m]

64 The whole company numbered 42,360,
65 besides their 7,337 menservants and maidservants; and they also had 200 men and
women singers.[n] 66 They had 736 horses,[o] 245
mules, 67 435 camels and 6,720 donkeys.

68 When they arrived at the house of the LORD in
Jerusalem, some of the heads of the families[p] gave
freewill offerings toward the rebuilding of the
house of God on its site. 69 According to their ability they gave to the treasury for this work 61,000
drachmas[a] of gold, 5,000 minas[b] of silver and 100
priestly garments.

70 The priests, the Levites, the singers, the gatekeepers and the temple servants settled in their
own towns, along with some of the other people,
and the rest of the Israelites settled in their towns.[q]

2:58 [h] 1Ki 9:21; 1Ch 9:2
2:59 [i] Nu 1:18
2:61 [j] 2Sa 17:27
2:62 [k] Nu 3:10; 16:39-40
2:63 [l] Lev 2:3,10 [m] Ex 28:30; Nu 27:21
2:65 [n] 2Sa 19:35
2:66 [o] Isa 66:20
2:68 [p] Ex 25:2
2:70 [q] ver 1; 1Ch 9:2; Ne 11:3-4

[a] *69* That is, about 1,100 pounds (about 500 kilograms)
[b] *69* That is, about 3 tons (about 2.9 metric tons)

Rebuilding the Altar

3 When the seventh month came and the Israelites had settled in their towns,[r] the people
assembled[s] as one man in Jerusalem. 2Then Jeshua[t] son of Jozadak[u] and his fellow priests and
Zerubbabel son of Shealtiel[v] and his associates
began to build the altar of the God of Israel to sacrifice burnt offerings on it, in accordance with
what is written in the Law of Moses[w] the man of
God. 3Despite their fear[x] of the peoples around
them, they built the altar on its foundation and
sacrificed burnt offerings on it to the LORD, both
the morning and evening sacrifices.[y] 4Then in
accordance with what is written, they celebrated
the Feast of Tabernacles[z] with the required number
of burnt offerings prescribed for each day. 5After
that, they presented the regular burnt offerings,
the New Moon[a] sacrifices and the sacrifices for all
the appointed sacred feasts of the LORD,[b] as well as
those brought as freewill offerings to the LORD. 6On
the first day of the seventh month they began to
offer burnt offerings to the LORD, though the foundation of the LORD's temple had not yet been laid.

Rebuilding the Temple

7Then they gave money to the masons and carpenters, and gave food and drink and oil to the
people of Sidon and Tyre, so that they would bring
cedar logs[c] by sea from Lebanon[d] to Joppa, as
authorized by Cyrus[e] king of Persia.

8In the second month of the second year after
their arrival at the house of God in Jerusalem,
Zerubbabel[f] son of Shealtiel, Jeshua son of Jozadak and the rest of their brothers (the priests and
the Levites and all who had returned from the
captivity to Jerusalem) began the work, appointing Levites twenty[g] years of age and older to
supervise the building of the house of the LORD.
9Jeshua[h] and his sons and brothers and Kadmiel
and his sons (descendants of Hodaviah[a]) and the
sons of Henadad and their sons and brothers—all
Levites—joined together in supervising those
working on the house of God.

10When the builders laid[i] the foundation of the
temple of the LORD, the priests in their vestments
and with trumpets,[j] and the Levites (the sons of
Asaph) with cymbals, took their places to praise[k]
the LORD, as prescribed by David[l] king of Israel.[m]
11With praise and thanksgiving they sang to the
LORD:

> "He is good;
> his love to Israel endures forever."[n]

And all the people gave a great shout[o] of praise to
the LORD, because the foundation of the house of
the LORD was laid. 12But many of the older priests
and Levites and family heads, who had seen the
former temple,[p] wept aloud when they saw the

3:1 [r]Ne 7:73; 8:1 [s]Lev 23:24
3:2 [t]Ezr 2:2; Ne 12:1,8; Hag 2:2 [u]Hag 1:1; Zec 6:11 [v]1Ch 3:17 [w]Ex 20:24; Dt 12:5-6
3:3 [x]Ezr 4:4; Da 9:25 [y]Ex 29:39; Nu 28:1-8
3:4 [z]Ex 23:16; Nu 29:12-38; Ne 8:14-18; Zec 14:16-19
3:5 [a]Nu 28:3,11, 14; Col 2:16 [b]Lev 23:1-44; Nu 29:39
3:7 [c]1Ch 14:1 [d]Isa 35:2 [e]Ezr 1:2-4; 6:3
3:8 [f]Zec 4:9 [g]1Ch 23:24
3:9 [h]Ezr 2:40
3:10 [i]Ezr 5:16 [j]Nu 10:2; 1Ch 16:6 [k]1Ch 25:1 [l]1Ch 6:31 [m]Zec 6:12
3:11 [n]1Ch 16:34, 41; 2Ch 7:3; Ps 107:1; 118:1 [o]Ne 12:24
3:12 [p]Hag 2:3,9

[a] 9 Hebrew *Yehudah,* probably a variant of *Hodaviah*

The New Temple

EZR 3:12

The older leaders have a fascinating response as they watch the new temple foundation being laid. While others clap and shout for joy, they cry. The sounds of their mourning are as loud as the sounds of rejoicing! These older folks remember the grandeur of Jerusalem before the devastating destruction. It seems they fear that the new might not duplicate the magnificence of the old. And yet, surely they must be thankful for this opportunity to rebuild God's house.

Perhaps their tears are a mixture of sadness and joy—joy at being given a second chance and sadness at the lost years sin has caused. Their sadness is inevitable. They clearly understand that their spiritual rebelliousness and poor choices have damaged their relationship with God and each other. However, God offers them repeated opportunities to renew their commitment to him and his ways. They accept God's gracious "second chance," and their sorrow overflows into tears of joyful relief and hope.

Spontaneous Praise

EZR 3:13

It is springtime when the people of all ages, life experiences, temperaments and gifts begin the massive project of rebuilding the temple. When they finish laying the foundation, they stop their work, put down their tools and have a service of praise and worship. The older ones cry, recalling the past. Others cheer at the promise of a new beginning. Emotions run so high in this little Judean gathering that the sounds of their weeping and cheering are heard "far away."

God understands our individualized responses to circumstances and lovingly accepts all our genuine acts of worship. He invites us to come before him with our honest expressions of emotion, whatever they may be.

foundation of this temple being laid, while many
others shouted for joy. 13No one could distinguish
the sound of the shouts of joy[q] from the sound of
weeping, because the people made so much noise.
And the sound was heard far away.

Opposition to the Rebuilding

4 When the enemies of Judah and Benjamin
heard that the exiles were building a temple
for the LORD, the God of Israel, 2they came to
Zerubbabel and to the heads of the families and
said, "Let us help you build because, like you, we
seek your God and have been sacrificing to him
since the time of Esarhaddon[r] king of Assyria,
who brought us here."[s]
3But Zerubbabel, Jeshua and the rest of the heads
of the families of Israel answered, "You have no
part with us in building a temple to our God. We
alone will build it for the LORD, the God of Israel, as
King Cyrus, the king of Persia, commanded us."[t]
4Then the peoples around them set out to discourage
the people of Judah and make them
afraid to go on building.[a][u] 5They hired counselors
to work against them and frustrate their plans
during the entire reign of Cyrus king of Persia and
down to the reign of Darius king of Persia.

Later Opposition Under Xerxes and Artaxerxes

6At the beginning of the reign of Xerxes,[b][v] they
lodged an accusation against the people of Judah
and Jerusalem.[w]
7And in the days of Artaxerxes[x] king of Persia,
Bishlam, Mithredath, Tabeel and the rest of his
associates wrote a letter to Artaxerxes. The letter
was written in Aramaic script and in the Aramaic[y]
language.[c,d]
8Rehum the commanding officer and Shimshai
the secretary wrote a letter against Jerusalem to
Artaxerxes the king as follows:

> 9Rehum the commanding officer and Shimshai
> the secretary, together with the rest of
> their associates[z]—the judges and officials
> over the men from Tripolis, Persia,[e] Erech
> and Babylon, the Elamites of Susa, 10and the
> other people whom the great and honorable
> Ashurbanipal[f] deported and settled in the
> city of Samaria and elsewhere in Trans-Euphrates.[a]
>
> 11(This is a copy of the letter they sent him.)
>
> To King Artaxerxes,
>
> From your servants, the men of Trans-Euphrates:

3:13 [q]Job 8:21; Ps 27:6; Isa 16:9
4:2 [r]2Ki 17:24; 19:37 [s]2Ki 17:41
4:3 [t]Ezr 1:1-4; Ne 2:20
4:4 [u]Ezr 3:3
4:6 [v]Est 1:1; Da 9:1 [w]Est 3:13; 9:5
4:7 [x]Ezr 7:1; Ne 2:1 [y]2Ki 18:26; Isa 36:11; Da 2:4
4:9 [z]Ezr 5:6; 6:6, 13
4:10 [a]ver 17; Ne 4:2

[a] 4 Or *and troubled them as they built* [b] 6 Hebrew *Ahasuerus,* a variant of Xerxes' Persian name [c] 7 Or *written in Aramaic and translated* [d] 7 The text of Ezra 4:8—6:18 is in Aramaic. [e] 9 Or *officials, magistrates and governors over the men from* [f] 10 Aramaic *Osnappar,* a variant of Ashurbanipal

[12]The king should know that the Jews who
came up to us from you have gone to Jerusalem and are rebuilding that rebellious and
4:12 wicked city. They are restoring the walls and
[b]Ezr 5:3,9 repairing the foundations.[b]
[13]Furthermore, the king should know that
4:13 if this city is built and its walls are restored,
[c]Ezr 7:24; no more taxes, tribute or duty[c] will be paid,
Ne 5:4 and the royal revenues will suffer. [14]Now
since we are under obligation to the palace
and it is not proper for us to see the king dishonored, we are sending this message to
inform the king, [15]so that a search may be
4:15 [d]Ezr 5:17; made in the archives[d] of your predecessors.
6:1 In these records you will find that this city is
[e]Est 3:8 a rebellious city, troublesome to kings and
provinces, a place of rebellion from ancient
times. That is why this city was destroyed.[e]
[16]We inform the king that if this city is built
and its walls are restored, you will be left
with nothing in Trans-Euphrates.

[17]The king sent this reply:

To Rehum the commanding officer, Shimshai
the secretary and the rest of their associates
4:17 living in Samaria and elsewhere in Trans-
[f]ver 10 Euphrates:[f]
Greetings.

[18]The letter you sent us has been read and
4:19 translated in my presence. [19]I issued an order
[g]2Ki 18:7 and a search was made, and it was found that
4:20 this city has a long history of revolt[g] against
[h]Ge 15:18- kings and has been a place of rebellion and
21; Ex 23:31; sedition. [20]Jerusalem has had powerful kings
Jos 1:4; 1Ki 4:21; ruling over the whole of Trans-Euphrates,[h]
1Ch 18:3; and taxes, tribute and duty were paid to
Ps 72:8-11 them. [21]Now issue an order to these men to
4:22 stop work, so that this city will not be rebuilt
[i]Da 6:2 until I so order. [22]Be careful not to neglect this
4:23 matter. Why let this threat grow, to the detri-
[j]ver 9 ment of the royal interests?[i]

4:24 [23]As soon as the copy of the letter of King
[k]Ne 2:1-8; Da 9:25; Artaxerxes was read to Rehum and Shimshai the
Hag 1:1,15; secretary and their associates,[j] they went imme-
Zec 1:1 diately to the Jews in Jerusalem and compelled
5:1 them by force to stop.
[l]Ezr 6:14;
Hag 1:1,3,
12; 2:1,10,
20
[24]Thus the work on the house of God in Jerusa-
[m]Zec 1:1; 7:1 lem came to a standstill until the second year of
[n]Hag 1:14- the reign of Darius[k] king of Persia.
2:9; Zec 4:9-
10; 8:9

Tattenai's Letter to Darius

5:2 **5** Now Haggai[l] the prophet and Zechariah[m] the
[o]1Ch 3:19; prophet, a descendant of Iddo, prophesied[n] to
Hag 1:14; 2:21; the Jews in Judah and Jerusalem in the name of
Zec 4:6-10 the God of Israel, who was over them. [2]Then
[p]Ezr 2:2; 3:2 Zerubbabel[o] son of Shealtiel and Jeshua[p] son of
[q]ver 8; Hag 2:2-5 Jozadak set to work[q] to rebuild the house of God

Opposition Arises

EZR 4:24

The events of Ezra 4 seem confusing until we understand that the verses are not written in strict chronological order. The objective of this writer (most likely Ezra) is to inform us of the consistent opposition the people faced during the years they attempted to rebuild the temple.

The Jews' enemies utilize various techniques to sabotage the work. They pretend to follow God and offer to "help." Probably their real motive is to infiltrate the ranks and push their own agenda. When that does not work, they hire corrupt agents to harass the workers and spread false rumors. We then read how, years later (after the temple was rebuilt), the Jews' enemies would send an inflammatory letter filled with half-truths to the king. This tactic temporarily stops the work of rebuilding the walls of Jerusalem.

There will always be those who oppose the work of God. Over time this reality can cause God's people to doubt and wonder if he is in control. God understands, and he wants to replace our fears with faith in his ability to overcome any and all opposition.

The Eye of God

EZR 5:5

For 16 years the Jewish exiles have suffered opposition in their efforts to rebuild the temple. Finally they are forced to stop their work, and in the intervening years they lose their passion for rebuilding the temple, focusing instead on rebuilding their own homes and establishing businesses (Hag 1:1–5). They wonder why they aren't enjoying the success they had assumed would be a part of their return.

The prophets Haggai and Zechariah are quick to explain: It is because work on the temple has ceased (Hag 1:9; Zec 8:9). In spite of the opposition they face, the people obey God and his prophets and resume work on the temple (Ezr 5:1–2).

What inspires their renewed passion and commitment? The assurance that the "eye of their God" is watching over them (Ezr 5:5). When the people keep their focus on God, trusting him to guide and empower them, they find courage to face their difficulties and finish the work God has given them to do.

in Jerusalem. And the prophets of God were with
them, helping them.
3 At that time Tattenai,[r] governor of Trans-
Euphrates, and Shethar-Bozenai[s] and their associates went to them and asked, "Who authorized you
to rebuild this temple and restore this structure?"[t]
4 They also asked, "What are the names of the men
constructing this building?"[a] 5 But the eye of their
God[u] was watching over the elders of the Jews, and
they were not stopped until a report could go to
Darius and his written reply be received.
6 This is a copy of the letter that Tattenai, governor of Trans-Euphrates, and Shethar-Bozenai and
their associates, the officials of Trans-Euphrates,
sent to King Darius. 7 The report they sent him
read as follows:

To King Darius:
Cordial greetings.

8 The king should know that we went to the
district of Judah, to the temple of the great
God. The people are building it with large
stones and placing the timbers in the walls.
The work[v] is being carried on with diligence
and is making rapid progress under their
direction.
9 We questioned the elders and asked them,
"Who authorized you to rebuild this temple
and restore this structure?"[w] 10 We also asked
them their names, so that we could write
down the names of their leaders for your
information.
11 This is the answer they gave us:

"We are the servants of the God of heaven
and earth, and we are rebuilding the temple[x]
that was built many years ago, one that a great
king of Israel built and finished. 12 But because
our fathers angered[y] the God of heaven, he
handed them over to Nebuchadnezzar the
Chaldean, king of Babylon, who destroyed this
temple and deported the people to Babylon.[z]
13 "However, in the first year of Cyrus king
of Babylon, King Cyrus issued a decree[a] to
rebuild this house of God. 14 He even removed
from the temple[b] of Babylon the gold and silver articles of the house of God, which Nebuchadnezzar had taken from the temple in Jerusalem and brought to the temple[b] in Babylon.[b]

"Then King Cyrus gave them to a man
named Sheshbazzar,[c] whom he had appointed
governor, 15 and he told him, 'Take these articles and go and deposit them in the temple in
Jerusalem. And rebuild the house of God on
its site.' 16 So this Sheshbazzar came and laid
the foundations of the house of God[d] in Jerusalem. From that day to the present it has been
under construction but is not yet finished."

5:3 [r]Ezr 6:6 [s]Ezr 6:6 [t]ver 9; Ezr 1:3; 4:12
5:5 [u]2Ki 25:28; Ezr 7:6,9,28; 8:18,22,31; Ne 2:8,18; Ps 33:18; Isa 66:14
5:8 [v]ver 2
5:9 [w]Ezr 4:12
5:11 [x]1Ki 6:1; 2Ch 3:1-2
5:12 [y]2Ch 36:16 [z]Dt 21:10; 28:36; 2Ki 24:1; 25:8,9,11; Jer 1:3
5:13 [a]Ezr 1:1
5:14 [b]Ezr 1:7; 6:5; Da 5:2 [c]1Ch 3:18
5:16 [d]Ezr 3:10; 6:15

[a] 4 See Septuagint; Aramaic *4We told them the names of the men constructing this building.* [b] 14 *Or palace*

17 Now if it pleases the king, let a search be made in the royal archives[e] of Babylon to see if King Cyrus did in fact issue a decree to rebuild this house of God in Jerusalem. Then let the king send us his decision in this matter.

The Decree of Darius

6 King Darius then issued an order, and they searched in the archives[f] stored in the treasury at Babylon. 2 A scroll was found in the citadel of Ecbatana in the province of Media, and this was written on it:

Memorandum:

3 In the first year of King Cyrus, the king issued a decree concerning the temple of God in Jerusalem:

Let the temple be rebuilt as a place to present sacrifices, and let its foundations be laid.[g] It is to be ninety feet[a] high and ninety feet wide, 4 with three courses[h] of large stones and one of timbers. The costs are to be paid by the royal treasury.[i] 5 Also, the gold[j] and silver articles of the house of God, which Nebuchadnezzar took from the temple in Jerusalem and brought to Babylon, are to be returned to their places in the temple in Jerusalem; they are to be deposited in the house of God.[k]

6 Now then, Tattenai,[l] governor of Trans-Euphrates, and Shethar-Bozenai[m] and you, their fellow officials of that province, stay away from there. 7 Do not interfere with the work on this temple of God. Let the governor of the Jews and the Jewish elders rebuild this house of God on its site.

8 Moreover, I hereby decree what you are to do for these elders of the Jews in the construction of this house of God:

The expenses of these men are to be fully paid out of the royal treasury,[n] from the revenues[o] of Trans-Euphrates, so that the work will not stop. 9 Whatever is needed—young bulls, rams, male lambs for burnt offerings[p] to the God of heaven, and wheat, salt, wine and oil, as requested by the priests in Jerusalem—must be given them daily without fail, 10 so that they may offer sacrifices pleasing to the God of heaven and pray for the well-being of the king and his sons.[q]

11 Furthermore, I decree that if anyone changes this edict, a beam is to be pulled from his house and he is to be lifted up and impaled[r] on it. And for this crime his house is to be made a pile of rubble.[s] 12 May God, who has caused his Name to dwell there,[t] overthrow any king or people who lifts a hand to

[a] 3 Aramaic *sixty cubits* (about 27 meters)

5:17 [e] Ezr 4:15; 6:1,2
6:1 [f] Ezr 4:15; 5:17
6:3 [g] Ezr 3:10; Hag 2:3
6:4 [h] 1Ki 6:36 [i] ver 8; Ezr 7:20
6:5 [j] 1Ch 29:2 [k] Ezr 1:7; 5:14
6:6 [l] Ezr 5:3 [m] Ezr 5:3
6:8 [n] ver 4 [o] 1Sa 9:20
6:9 [p] Lev 1:3,10
6:10 [q] Ezr 7:23; 1Ti 2:1-2
6:11 [r] Dt 21:22-23; Est 2:23; 5:14; 9:14 [s] Ezr 7:26; Da 2:5; 3:29
6:12 [t] Ex 20:24; Dt 12:5; 1Ki 9:3; 2Ch 6:2

Hope for the Christian is much more than pie-in-the-sky wishful thinking. The dictionary defines hope as a verb of expectation—to "hope against hope," to actively and confidently expect fulfillment. Hope as a noun is defined as a confident expectation that a desire will be fulfilled. Hope as a virtue is described as the confidence with which a Christian looks for God's grace in this world and glory in the next . . . Did you get the common denominator? Hope is all about placing our confidence in what we can't yet see, about having high expectations that, in spite of all appearances to the contrary, our deepest longings will be fulfilled. And as Christians, that's exactly what we can count on.

—Thelma Wells

Celebrating Passover Again

EZR 6:19–22

When the people finish building the new temple in 516 B.C., they celebrate with a dedication service. Approximately one month later, they celebrate again by observing the Passover as a nation probably for the first time in over 100 years. They likely have not commemorated Passover in this way since the Book of the Law was discovered during the reign of godly King Josiah (2Ki 22:2,8; 23:21).

For seven days the people's joy is unrestrained. They praise God for changing the attitude of the ruler and for the completed temple. And they probably praise him simply because they are together again in their homeland. God has accomplished what once looked impossible: He has set them free from captivity and restored them to serve and celebrate again.

When God accomplishes what humans think is impossible, it is always a reason for joy. Healing from sickness, healing in a family or marriage, surviving a difficult or tragic event—God sees beyond the difficulties to the joy ahead and waits to take our hands to lead us into restoration.

change this decree or to destroy this temple
in Jerusalem.
I Darius[u] have decreed it. Let it be carried
out with diligence.

Completion and Dedication of the Temple

13 Then, because of the decree King Darius had
sent, Tattenai, governor of Trans-Euphrates, and
Shethar-Bozenai and their associates[v] carried it
out with diligence. 14 So the elders of the Jews continued to build and prosper under the preaching[w]
of Haggai the prophet and Zechariah, a descendant of Iddo. They finished building the temple
according to the command of the God of Israel
and the decrees of Cyrus,[x] Darius[y] and Artaxerxes,[z] kings of Persia. 15 The temple was completed
on the third day of the month Adar, in the sixth
year of the reign of King Darius.[a]
16 Then the people of Israel—the priests, the
Levites and the rest of the exiles—celebrated the
dedication[b] of the house of God with joy. 17 For the
dedication of this house of God they offered[c] a
hundred bulls, two hundred rams, four hundred
male lambs and, as a sin offering for all Israel,
twelve male goats, one for each of the tribes of
Israel. 18 And they installed the priests in their divisions[d] and the Levites in their groups[e] for the service of God at Jerusalem, according to what is
written in the Book of Moses.[f]

The Passover

19 On the fourteenth day of the first month, the
exiles celebrated the Passover.[g] 20 The priests and
Levites had purified themselves and were all ceremonially clean. The Levites slaughtered[h] the
Passover lamb for all the exiles, for their brothers
the priests and for themselves. 21 So the Israelites
who had returned from the exile ate it, together
with all who had separated themselves[i] from the
unclean practices[j] of their Gentile neighbors in
order to seek the LORD,[k] the God of Israel. 22 For
seven days they celebrated with joy the Feast of
Unleavened Bread,[l] because the LORD had filled
them with joy by changing the attitude[m] of the
king of Assyria, so that he assisted them in the
work on the house of God, the God of Israel.

Ezra Comes to Jerusalem

7 After these things, during the reign of Artaxerxes[n] king of Persia, Ezra son of Seraiah, the
son of Azariah, the son of Hilkiah,[o] 2 the son of
Shallum, the son of Zadok,[p] the son of Ahitub,[q]
3 the son of Amariah, the son of Azariah, the son of
Meraioth, 4 the son of Zerahiah, the son of Uzzi,
the son of Bukki, 5 the son of Abishua, the son of
Phinehas, the son of Eleazar, the son of Aaron the
chief priest— 6 this Ezra[r] came up from Babylon.
He was a teacher well versed in the Law of Moses,
which the LORD, the God of Israel, had given. The
king had granted him everything he asked, for the

6:12 [u]ver 14
6:13 [v]Ezr 4:9
6:14 [w]Ezr 5:1 [x]Ezr 1:1-4 [y]ver 12 [z]Ezr 7:1; Ne 2:1
6:15 [a]Zec 1:1; 4:9
6:16 [b]1Ki 8:63; 2Ch 7:5
6:17 [c]2Sa 6:13; 2Ch 29:21; 30:24; Ezr 8:35
6:18 [d]1Ch 23:6; 2Ch 35:4; Lk 1:5 [e]1Ch 24:1 [f]Nu 3:6-9; 8:9-11; 18:1-32
6:19 [g]Ex 12:11; Nu 28:16
6:20 [h]2Ch 30:15, 17; 35:11
6:21 [i]Ezr 9:1; Ne 9:2 [j]Dt 18:9; Ezr 9:11; Eze 36:25 [k]1Ch 22:19; Ps 14:2
6:22 [l]Ex 12:17 [m]Ezr 1:1
7:1 [n]Ezr 4:7; 6:14; Ne 2:1 [o]2Ki 22:4
7:2 [p]1Ki 1:8; 1Ch 6:8 [q]Ne 11:11
7:6 [r]Ne 12:36

7:6 hand of the LORD his God was on him.[s] 7Some of
[s]Ezr 5:5; the Israelites, including priests, Levites, singers,
Isa 41:20 gatekeepers and temple servants, also came up to
7:7 [t]Ezr 8:1 Jerusalem in the seventh year of King Artaxerxes.[t]
8Ezra arrived in Jerusalem in the fifth month of
the seventh year of the king. 9He had begun his
journey from Babylon on the first day of the first
month, and he arrived in Jerusalem on the first
7:9 day of the fifth month, for the gracious hand of
[u]ver 6 his God was on him.[u] 10For Ezra had devoted himself to the study and observance of the Law of the
7:10 [v]ver 25; LORD, and to teaching[v] its decrees and laws in
Dt 33:10; Israel.
Ne 8:1-8

King Artaxerxes' Letter to Ezra

11This is a copy of the letter King Artaxerxes had
given to Ezra the priest and teacher, a man
learned in matters concerning the commands and
decrees of the LORD for Israel:

7:12 [w]Eze 26:7; 12[a] Artaxerxes, king of kings,[w]
Da 2:37

To Ezra the priest, a teacher of the Law of the
God of heaven:

Greetings.

13Now I decree that any of the Israelites in
my kingdom, including priests and Levites,
who wish to go to Jerusalem with you, may
7:14 go. 14You are sent by the king and his seven
[x]Est 1:14 advisers[x] to inquire about Judah and Jerusalem with regard to the Law of your God,
which is in your hand. 15Moreover, you are
to take with you the silver and gold that the
7:15 king and his advisers have freely given[y] to
[y]1Ch 29:6 [z]1Ch 29:6,9; the God of Israel, whose dwelling[z] is in Jeru-
2Ch 6:2 salem, 16together with all the silver and gold[a]
7:16 [a]Ezr 8:25 you may obtain from the province of Bab-
[b]Zec 6:10 ylon, as well as the freewill offerings of the
people and priests for the temple of their God
in Jerusalem.[b] 17With this money be sure to
7:17 [c]2Ki 3:4 buy bulls, rams and male lambs,[c] together
[d]Nu 15:5-12 with their grain offerings and drink offer-
[e]Dt 12:5-11 ings,[d] and sacrifice[e] them on the altar of the
temple of your God in Jerusalem.

18You and your brother Jews may then do
whatever seems best with the rest of the silver and gold, in accordance with the will of
7:19 [f]Ezr 5:14; your God. 19Deliver[f] to the God of Jerusalem
Jer 27:22 all the articles entrusted to you for worship
in the temple of your God. 20And anything
else needed for the temple of your God that
you may have occasion to supply, you may
7:20 [g]Ezr 6:4 provide from the royal treasury.[g]

21Now I, King Artaxerxes, order all the
treasurers of Trans-Euphrates to provide with
diligence whatever Ezra the priest, a teacher
of the Law of the God of heaven, may ask of
you— 22up to a hundred talents[b] of silver, a

[a] *12* The text of Ezra 7:12–26 is in Aramaic. [b] *22* That is, about 3 3/4 tons (about 3.4 metric tons)

In a Holding Pattern

EZR 7:8

In approximately 458 B.C. Ezra leaves captivity in Babylon and travels to Jerusalem with the permission and support of King Artaxerxes of Persia. Evidently Ezra, under God's direction, approaches the king with a request to take a group of committed priests and temple workers to Jerusalem to serve in the new temple.

While in Babylon, Ezra is unable to perform his priestly duties in the traditional manner, since there is no temple there. Ezra probably feels frustrated that he cannot serve as he is called to do. Still, his limiting circumstances do not stop him from serving. He concentrates on what he can do: study God's law and encourage the other Israelites to trust God for the future.

Some of us are in life situations that prevent us from ministering as we planned. Like Ezra, we can focus on the ministry opportunities currently before us and then trust God for our future roles.

My favorite theological doctrine is that of "justification." It is the sovereign act of God whereby he declares the believing sinner righteous . . . In other words, when a person comes to God, just as she is . . . , God looks at her and because of what Jesus Christ did on the cross he proclaims her righteous. She does not have to clean up her act. She does not have to do penance. She does not have to be thin or good-looking or rich or famous or accomplished. All she has to do is believe God for the forgiveness of her sins . . . Salvation is a gift. He gives. You receive.

—Luci Swindoll

hundred cors[a] of wheat, a hundred baths[b] of
wine, a hundred baths[b] of olive oil, and salt
without limit. 23 Whatever the God of heaven
has prescribed, let it be done with diligence
for the temple of the God of heaven. Why
should there be wrath against the realm of
the king and of his sons?[h] 24 You are also to
know that you have no authority to impose
taxes, tribute or duty[i] on any of the priests,
Levites, singers, gatekeepers, temple servants
or other workers at this house of God.[j]

25 And you, Ezra, in accordance with the
wisdom of your God, which you possess,
appoint[k] magistrates and judges to administer justice to all the people of Trans-Euphrates—all who know the laws of your God. And
you are to teach[l] any who do not know them.
26 Whoever does not obey the law of your God
and the law of the king must surely be punished by death, banishment, confiscation of
property, or imprisonment.[m]

27 Praise be to the LORD, the God of our fathers,
who has put it into the king's heart[n] to bring hon-
or[o] to the house of the LORD in Jerusalem in this
way 28 and who has extended his good favor[p] to me
before the king and his advisers and all the king's
powerful officials. Because the hand of the LORD
my God was on me,[q] I took courage and gathered
leading men from Israel to go up with me.

List of the Family Heads Returning With Ezra

8 These are the family heads and those registered with them who came up with me from
Babylon during the reign of King Artaxerxes:[r]

2 of the descendants of Phinehas, Gershom;
of the descendants of Ithamar, Daniel;
of the descendants of David, Hattush 3 of the
descendants of Shecaniah;[s]

of the descendants of Parosh,[t] Zechariah, and
with him were registered 150 men;
4 of the descendants of Pahath-Moab,[u] Eliehoenai son of Zerahiah, and with him 200
men;
5 of the descendants of Zattu,[c] Shecaniah son
of Jahaziel, and with him 300 men;
6 of the descendants of Adin,[v] Ebed son of Jonathan, and with him 50 men;
7 of the descendants of Elam, Jeshaiah son of
Athaliah, and with him 70 men;
8 of the descendants of Shephatiah, Zebadiah
son of Michael, and with him 80 men;
9 of the descendants of Joab, Obadiah son of
Jehiel, and with him 218 men;

7:23 [h]Ezr 6:10
7:24 [i]Ezr 4:13 [j]Ezr 8:36
7:25 [k]Ex 18:21, 26; Dt 16:18 [l]ver 10; Lev 10:11
7:26 [m]Ezr 6:11
7:27 [n]Ezr 1:1; 6:22 [o]1Ch 29:12
7:28 [p]2Ki 25:28 [q]Ezr 5:5; 9:9
8:1 [r]Ezr 7:7
8:3 [s]1Ch 3:22 [t]Ezr 2:3
8:4 [u]Ezr 2:6
8:6 [v]Ezr 2:15; Ne 7:20; 10:16

[a] 22 That is, probably about 600 bushels (about 22 kiloliters)
[b] 22 That is, probably about 600 gallons (about 2.2 kiloliters)
[c] 5 Some Septuagint manuscripts (also 1 Esdras 8:32); Hebrew does not have *Zattu.*

10 of the descendants of Bani,[a] Shelomith son of
Josiphiah, and with him 160 men;
11 of the descendants of Bebai, Zechariah son of
Bebai, and with him 28 men;
12 of the descendants of Azgad, Johanan son of
8:13 Hakkatan, and with him 110 men;
[w]Ezr 2:13 13 of the descendants of Adonikam,[w] the last
ones, whose names were Eliphelet, Jeuel
and Shemaiah, and with them 60 men;
14 of the descendants of Bigvai, Uthai and Zaccur, and with them 70 men.

The Return to Jerusalem

8:15 15 I assembled them at the canal that flows
[x]ver 21,31 toward Ahava,[x] and we camped there three days.
[y]Ezr 2:40; When I checked among the people and the priests,
7:7 I found no Levites[y] there. 16 So I summoned Eliezer, Ariel, Shemaiah, Elnathan, Jarib, Elnathan,
Nathan, Zechariah and Meshullam, who were
leaders, and Joiarib and Elnathan, who were men
of learning, 17 and I sent them to Iddo, the leader in
8:17 Casiphia. I told them what to say to Iddo and his
[z]Ezr 2:43 kinsmen, the temple servants[z] in Casiphia, so that
they might bring attendants to us for the house of
our God. 18 Because the gracious hand of our God
8:18 was on us,[a] they brought us Sherebiah, a capable
[a]Ezr 5:5 man, from the descendants of Mahli son of Levi,
the son of Israel, and Sherebiah's sons and brothers, 18 men; 19 and Hashabiah, together with Jeshaiah from the descendants of Merari, and his broth-
8:20 ers and nephews, 20 men. 20 They also brought 220
[b]1Ch 9:2; of the temple servants[b]—a body that David and the
Ezr 2:43 officials had established to assist the Levites. All
8:21 were registered by name.
[c]ver 15; 21 There, by the Ahava Canal,[c] I proclaimed a
2Ch 20:3 fast, so that we might humble ourselves before
[d]Ps 5:8; 107:7 our God and ask him for a safe journey[d] for us
8:22 and our children, with all our possessions. 22 I was
[e]Ne 2:9; ashamed to ask the king for soldiers[e] and horse-
Ezr 7:6,9,28 men to protect us from enemies on the road,
[f]Ezr 5:5 because we had told the king, "The gracious hand
[g]Dt 31:17; 2Ch 15:2 of our God is on everyone[f] who looks to him, but
8:23 his great anger is against all who forsake him.[g]"
[h]2Ch 20:3; 23 So we fasted[h] and petitioned our God about this,
33:13 and he answered our prayer.
8:24 24 Then I set apart twelve of the leading priests,
[i]ver 18 together with Sherebiah,[i] Hashabiah and ten of
8:25 their brothers, 25 and I weighed out[j] to them the
[j]ver 33; offering of silver and gold and the articles that the
Ezr 7:15,16 king, his advisers, his officials and all Israel present
there had donated for the house of our God. 26 I
weighed out to them 650 talents[b] of silver, silver
articles weighing 100 talents,[c] 100 talents[c] of gold,
27 20 bowls of gold valued at 1,000 darics,[d] and two
fine articles of polished bronze, as precious as gold.
28 I said to them, "You as well as these articles

[a] *10* Some Septuagint manuscripts (also 1 Esdras 8:36); Hebrew does not have *Bani.* [b] *26* That is, about 25 tons (about 22 metric tons) [c] *26* That is, about 3 3/4 tons (about 3.4 metric tons) [d] *27* That is, about 19 pounds (about 8.5 kilograms)

The Hand of the Lord

EZR 8:10-28

In Ezra 7–8, variations of the faith-producing phrase "the hand of the LORD was upon us" occur six times. These words seem to summarize the life and teaching of Ezra, the dedicated priest who consistently urges God's people to stay committed to God's laws and ways.

Ezra relies on God for help when talking to people who might ordinarily intimidate him (Ezr 7:6), for courage in the face of fear (Ezr 7:28), for assistance in recruiting workers (Ezr 8:18), for assurance when he feels insecure (Ezr 8:22) and for protection in dangerous situations (Ezr 8:31).

To encourage your faith in God's trustworthiness, underline the phrase "Because the hand of the LORD my God was on me, I took courage" (Ezr 7:28), and then put your name above the word "me." God's protecting, encouraging and assisting hand is available to you just as it was to Ezra so many years ago.

The Action of Prayer

EZR 9

When Ezra learns that a number of Jewish men, including priests and Levites, had married non-Jews, something God had expressly forbidden (Dt 7:3–4), the news breaks his heart. He tears his clothing and then goes a step beyond that, pulling out hair from his head and beard. The pain in his heart must have surpassed the physical pain of such an action. By late afternoon Ezra picks himself up, falls before God and takes action—the action of prayer.

Ezra prays a gut-wrenching prayer, expressing his personal shame and the disgrace and guilt of this unfaithfulness—with Israel's leaders and officials leading the way. He acknowledges God's kindness and offer of restoration. God is far from offended by Ezra's extremely emotional response to sin. In fact, Ezra's passion causes a response of repentance in the people.

Like Ezra, when the pain in our heart is unbearable, we can go to God. When we feel the depth of our sin and need, God is waiting. If we fall on our knees before him, we can find acceptance and restoration.

are consecrated to the LORD.[k] The silver and gold
are a freewill offering to the LORD, the God of your
fathers. 29Guard them carefully until you weigh
them out in the chambers of the house of the LORD
in Jerusalem before the leading priests and the
Levites and the family heads of Israel." 30Then the
priests and Levites received the silver and gold
and sacred articles that had been weighed out to
be taken to the house of our God in Jerusalem.

31On the twelfth day of the first month we set
out from the Ahava Canal[l] to go to Jerusalem. The
hand of our God was on us, and he protected us
from enemies and bandits along the way. 32So we
arrived in Jerusalem, where we rested three days.[m]

33On the fourth day, in the house of our God,
we weighed out the silver and gold and the sacred
articles into the hands of Meremoth[n] son of Uriah,
the priest. Eleazar son of Phinehas was with him,
and so were the Levites Jozabad son of Jeshua and
Noadiah son of Binnui.[o] 34Everything was ac-
counted for by number and weight, and the entire
weight was recorded at that time.

35Then the exiles who had returned from captivity sacrificed burnt offerings to the God of Israel: twelve bulls for all Israel, ninety-six rams, seventy-seven male lambs and, as a sin offering,
twelve male goats.[p] All this was a burnt offering
to the LORD. 36They also delivered the king's
orders[q] to the royal satraps and to the governors of
Trans-Euphrates, who then gave assistance to the
people and to the house of God.[r]

Ezra's Prayer About Intermarriage

9 After these things had been done, the leaders
came to me and said, "The people of Israel,
including the priests and the Levites, have not
kept themselves separate[s] from the neighboring
peoples with their detestable practices, like those
of the Canaanites, Hittites, Perizzites, Jebusites,
Ammonites,[t] Moabites, Egyptians and Amorites.[u]
2They have taken some of their daughters[v] as
wives for themselves and their sons, and have
mingled the holy race[w] with the peoples around
them. And the leaders and officials have led the
way in this unfaithfulness."[x]

3When I heard this, I tore my tunic and cloak,
pulled hair from my head and beard and sat down
appalled. 4Then everyone who trembled[y] at the
words of the God of Israel gathered around me
because of this unfaithfulness of the exiles. And I
sat there appalled until the evening sacrifice.

5Then, at the evening sacrifice,[z] I rose from my
self-abasement, with my tunic and cloak torn, and
fell on my knees with my hands spread out to the
LORD my God 6and prayed:

"O my God, I am too ashamed and disgraced to lift up my face to you, my God,
because our sins are higher than our heads
and our guilt has reached to the heavens.[a]
7From the days of our forefathers[b] until now,

8:28 [k]Lev 21:6; 22:2-3
8:31 [l]ver 15
8:32 [m]Ge 40:13; Ne 2:11
8:33 [n]Ne 3:4,21 [o]Ne 3:24
8:35 [p]2Ch 29:21; Ezr 6:17
8:36 [q]Ezr 7:21-24 [r]Est 9:3
9:1 [s]Ezr 6:21; Ne 9:2 [t]Ge 19:38 [u]Ex 13:5
9:2 [v]Ex 34:16 [w]Ex 22:31 [x]Ezr 10:2
9:4 [y]Ezr 10:3
9:5 [z]Ex 29:41
9:6 [a]2Ch 28:9; Job 42:6; Ps 38:4; Rev 18:5
9:7 [b]2Ch 29:6

our guilt has been great. Because of our sins,
we and our kings and our priests have been
subjected to the sword[c] and captivity,[d] to pillage and humiliation[e] at the hand of foreign
kings, as it is today.
8“But now, for a brief moment, the LORD our
God has been gracious[f] in leaving us a remnant[g] and giving us a firm place[h] in his sanctuary, and so our God gives light to our eyes[i]
and a little relief in our bondage. 9Though we
are slaves,[j] our God has not deserted us in our
bondage. He has shown us kindness[k] in the
sight of the kings of Persia: He has granted us
new life to rebuild the house of our God and
repair its ruins,[l] and he has given us a wall of
protection in Judah and Jerusalem.
10“But now, O our God, what can we say
after this? For we have disregarded the commands[m] 11you gave through your servants the
prophets when you said: ‘The land you are
entering to possess is a land polluted[n] by the
corruption of its peoples. By their detestable
practices[o] they have filled it with their impurity from one end to the other. 12Therefore, do
not give your daughters in marriage to their
sons or take their daughters for your sons. Do
not seek a treaty of friendship with them[p] at
any time, that you may be strong and eat the
good things of the land and leave it to your
children as an everlasting inheritance.’
13“What has happened to us is a result of
our evil deeds and our great guilt, and yet, our
God, you have punished us less than our sins
have deserved[q] and have given us a remnant
like this. 14Shall we again break your commands and intermarry[r] with the peoples who
commit such detestable practices? Would you
not be angry enough with us to destroy us,[s]
leaving us no remnant[t] or survivor? 15O LORD,
God of Israel, you are righteous![u] We are left
this day as a remnant. Here we are before you
in our guilt, though because of it not one of us
can stand[v] in your presence.[w]”

The People’s Confession of Sin

10 While Ezra was praying and confessing,[x]
weeping and throwing himself down before
the house of God, a large crowd of Israelites—
men, women and children—gathered around him.
They too wept bitterly. 2Then Shecaniah son of
Jehiel, one of the descendants of Elam, said to
Ezra, “We have been unfaithful[y] to our God by
marrying foreign women from the peoples around
us. But in spite of this, there is still hope for Israel.[z] 3Now let us make a covenant[a] before our God
to send away[b] all these women and their children,
in accordance with the counsel of my lord and of
those who fear the commands of our God. Let it
be done according to the Law. 4Rise up; this matter is in your hands. We will support you, so take
courage and do it.”

9:7 [c]Eze 21:1-32 [d]Dt 28:64 [e]Dt 28:37
9:8 [f]Ps 25:16; Isa 33:2 [g]Ge 45:7 [h]Ecc 12:11; Isa 22:23 [i]Ps 13:3
9:9 [j]Ex 1:14; Ne 9:36 [k]Ezr 7:28 [l]Ps 69:35; Isa 43:1; Jer 32:44
9:10 [m]Dt 11:8; Isa 1:19-20
9:11 [n]Lev 18:25-28 [o]Dt 9:4
9:12 [p]Ex 34:15; Dt 7:3; 23:6
9:13 [q]Job 11:6; Ps 103:10
9:14 [r]Ne 13:27 [s]Dt 9:8 [t]Dt 9:14
9:15 [u]Ge 18:25; Ps 51:4; Jer 12:1; Da 9:7 [v]Ne 9:33; Ps 130:3; Mal 3:2 [w]1Ki 8:47
10:1 [x]2Ch 20:9; Da 9:20
10:2 [y]Ezr 9:2; Ne 13:27 [z]Dt 30:8-10
10:3 [a]2Ch 34:31 [b]Ex 34:16; Dt 7:2-3; Ezr 9:4

Remorse

EZR 10:1–6

The prophets often use visual illustrations to make a lasting impression on their audiences. This may have been Ezra’s intention as he continues to wail and throw himself down on the ground. However, Ezra’s grief over the people’s sin is so deep that this object lesson may have been a genuine display of remorse and not merely a dramatization. Either way, Ezra, a wise teacher, waits for his listeners to respond. Finally the Israelites admit they have sinned. “But there’s hope. We will do the right thing,” they say. Ezra promises they will do it together.

In Old Testament times, many did not or could not read the law for themselves. They relied on their priests for spiritual direction. They worked, learned and committed themselves to God as a whole society. Each individual’s spiritual life affected the entire community. Although Ezra did not actually commit the sin of intermarriage, he carried the burden of the people’s irresponsible behavior.

A Drastic Action

EZR 10:16–17

The people acknowledge that they have disregarded God's protective standard and broken his law by marrying women from the neighboring pagan countries (Dt 7:1–4). They also know they need to take drastic action to demonstrate their repentance. The foreign women and children must be sent away.

Does this action seem harsh? Yes, it does. It is *harsh. But extreme action has to be taken to protect the exilic community from the very sins that had originally caused their exile—abandonment of the ways of God. These marriages are not authentic according to God's explicit regulations.*

The people do not take the situation lightly. They spend three months investigating individual cases (Ezr 10:16–17). Perhaps exceptions are made for those women who have genuinely turned to God.

5So Ezra rose up and put the leading priests and
Levites and all Israel under oath[c] to do what had
been suggested. And they took the oath. 6Then
Ezra withdrew from before the house of God and
went to the room of Jehohanan son of Eliashib.
While he was there, he ate no food and drank no
water,[d] because he continued to mourn over the
unfaithfulness of the exiles.
7A proclamation was then issued throughout
Judah and Jerusalem for all the exiles to assemble
in Jerusalem. 8Anyone who failed to appear within three days would forfeit all his property, in
accordance with the decision of the officials and
elders, and would himself be expelled from the
assembly of the exiles.

9Within the three days, all the men of Judah
and Benjamin[e] had gathered in Jerusalem. And on
the twentieth day of the ninth month, all the people were sitting in the square before the house of
God, greatly distressed by the occasion and
because of the rain. 10Then Ezra the priest stood
up and said to them, "You have been unfaithful;
you have married foreign women, adding to Israel's guilt. 11Now make confession to the LORD, the
God of your fathers, and do his will. Separate
yourselves from the peoples around you and from
your foreign wives."[f]
12The whole assembly responded with a loud
voice:[g] "You are right! We must do as you say.
13But there are many people here and it is the
rainy season; so we cannot stand outside. Besides,
this matter cannot be taken care of in a day or
two, because we have sinned greatly in this thing.
14Let our officials act for the whole assembly.
Then let everyone in our towns who has married
a foreign woman come at a set time, along with
the elders and judges[h] of each town, until the
fierce anger[i] of our God in this matter is turned
away from us." 15Only Jonathan son of Asahel and
Jahzeiah son of Tikvah, supported by Meshullam
and Shabbethai[j] the Levite, opposed this.
16So the exiles did as was proposed. Ezra the
priest selected men who were family heads, one
from each family division, and all of them designated by name. On the first day of the tenth month
they sat down to investigate the cases, 17and by the
first day of the first month they finished dealing
with all the men who had married foreign women.

Those Guilty of Intermarriage

18Among the descendants of the priests, the following had married foreign women:[k]
From the descendants of Jeshua[l] son of Jozadak, and his brothers: Maaseiah, Eliezer,
Jarib and Gedaliah. 19(They all gave their
hands[m] in pledge to put away their wives,
and for their guilt they each presented a
ram from the flock as a guilt offering.)[n]
20From the descendants of Immer:[o]
Hanani and Zebadiah.

10:5 [c]Ne 5:12; 13:25
10:6 [d]Ex 34:28; Dt 9:18
10:9 [e]Ezr 1:5
10:11 [f]ver 3; Dt 24:1; Ne 9:2; Mal 2:10-16
10:12 [g]Jos 6:5
10:14 [h]Dt 16:18 [i]Nu 25:4; 2Ch 29:10; 30:8
10:15 [j]Ne 11:16
10:18 [k]Jdg 3:6 [l]Ezr 2:2
10:19 [m]2Ki 10:15 [n]Lev 5:15; 6:6
10:20 [o]1Ch 24:14

10:21 [p]1Ch 24:8
[21] From the descendants of Harim:[p]
Maaseiah, Elijah, Shemaiah, Jehiel and Uzziah.

10:22 [q]1Ch 9:12
[22] From the descendants of Pashhur:[q]
Elioenai, Maaseiah, Ishmael, Nethanel, Jozabad and Elasah.

10:23 [r]Ne 8:7; 9:4
[23] Among the Levites:[r]
Jozabad, Shimei, Kelaiah (that is, Kelita), Pethahiah, Judah and Eliezer.

[24] From the singers:
10:24 [s]Ne 3:1; 12:10; 13:7, 28
Eliashib.[s]
From the gatekeepers:
Shallum, Telem and Uri.

[25] And among the other Israelites:

10:25 [t]Ezr 2:3
From the descendants of Parosh:[t]
Ramiah, Izziah, Malkijah, Mijamin, Eleazar, Malkijah and Benaiah.

10:26 [u]ver 2
[26] From the descendants of Elam:[u]
Mattaniah, Zechariah, Jehiel, Abdi, Jeremoth and Elijah.

[27] From the descendants of Zattu:
Elioenai, Eliashib, Mattaniah, Jeremoth, Zabad and Aziza.

[28] From the descendants of Bebai:
Jehohanan, Hananiah, Zabbai and Athlai.

[29] From the descendants of Bani:
Meshullam, Malluch, Adaiah, Jashub, Sheal and Jeremoth.

[30] From the descendants of Pahath-Moab:
Adna, Kelal, Benaiah, Maaseiah, Mattaniah, Bezalel, Binnui and Manasseh.

[31] From the descendants of Harim:
Eliezer, Ishijah, Malkijah, Shemaiah, Shimeon, [32] Benjamin, Malluch and Shemariah.

[33] From the descendants of Hashum:
Mattenai, Mattattah, Zabad, Eliphelet, Jeremai, Manasseh and Shimei.

[34] From the descendants of Bani:
Maadai, Amram, Uel, [35] Benaiah, Bedeiah,
Keluhi, [36] Vaniah, Meremoth, Eliashib,
[37] Mattaniah, Mattenai and Jaasu.

[38] From the descendants of Binnui:[a]
Shimei, [39] Shelemiah, Nathan, Adaiah,
[40] Macnadebai, Shashai, Sharai, [41] Azarel,
Shelemiah, Shemariah, [42] Shallum, Amariah and Joseph.

[43] From the descendants of Nebo:
Jeiel, Mattithiah, Zabad, Zebina, Jaddai, Joel and Benaiah.

[44] All these had married foreign women, and some of them had children by these wives.[b]

[a] *37,38* See Septuagint (also 1 Esdras 9:34); Hebrew *Jaasu* [38] *and Bani and Binnui,* [b] *44* Or *and they sent them away with their children*

A Sad Chapter

EZR 10:18–44

A commission is formed to investigate the men who married pagan wives in violation of God's law. The commission's summary in Ezra 10:18–44 represents a sad chapter in the history of the Israelites.

This list is not included in the Bible, however, merely to shame or punish the wrongdoers. It serves as a record of legal proceedings, similar to a police report or public document in our day. The tragic reality is the same today as in Ezra's time. Unlawful acts have definite consequences. Yet there is hope. God lovingly waits for us to realize our need, confess our sin and change our behavior.

Nehemiah

Rebuilt walls and renewed faith.

The book of Nehemiah describes the rebuilding of the walls of Jerusalem, the renewal of the spiritual lives of the workers and the restoration of true worship in Israel. Nehemiah's role as cupbearer to the king places him in a favorable position to bring aid to the Jewish exiles who have returned to the promised land to rebuild Jerusalem. Through dependence on God and unswerving devotion to his task, Nehemiah reminds the exiles of their spiritual heritage and encourages them to successfully rebuild the city walls.

Strategies of godly leadership in Nehemiah's life surface throughout this historical account. Nehemiah's willingness to leave a secure position for an unknown future teaches a powerful lesson about trusting God's direction (Ne 1:1–2:10). The response of the people who help rebuild the walls despite opposition gives a glimpse of the power behind cheerful volunteering (Ne 2:11–4:23). Nehemiah's daily dependence on God, demonstrated by his frequent prayers throughout the book, reveals the unlimited strength available to go the distance despite troublesome situations. We rejoice when we read of the quick response of the people to the reading of the Law (Ne 8–10), and we celebrate Nehemiah's appeal to them to remember that their strength is in the joy of the Lord (Ne 8:10).

Nehemiah's example of godly leadership is as applicable today as it was when he was directing the rebuilding of Jerusalem's walls. Difficult assignments, accompanied by feelings of inadequacy, can only be accomplished by staying connected to God through prayer—every day and in every situation.

Quick Study

Author
Possibly Ezra.

Date Written
About 430 B.C.

Setting
Judah.

Key Passage
Nehemiah 8:10 "The joy of the LORD is your strength."

Outline

Nehemiah's prayer of concern.
Ne 1

Nehemiah returns to Jerusalem.
Ne 2

Workers begin rebuilding the walls.
Ne 3

Wall building is opposed.
Ne 4

Nehemiah helps the poor.
Ne 5

More opposition to wall building.
Ne 6:1–14

The wall is completed.
Ne 6:15–7:3

List of returning exiles.
Ne 7:4–73

Ezra reads the law.
Ne 8

The Israelites confess their sins.
Ne 9–10

New residents of Jerusalem.
Ne 11:1–12:26

The new wall is dedicated.
Ne 12:27–47

Nehemiah's final reforms.
Ne 13

The Women of Nehemiah

Artaxerxes' queen	*Sat beside her king.* Ne 2:6
Shallum's daughters	*Helped to rebuild Jerusalem's wall.* Ne 3:12
Noadiah	*Tried to intimidate Nehemiah.* Ne 6:14
Barzillai's daughter	*Her husband took her father's name.* Ne 7:63–64
Gentile women of mixed marriages	*Nehemiah beat their Jewish husbands.* Ne 13:23–27

Nehemiah

NE 1:1—2:3

Nehemiah, an Israelite born during the captivity, works for King Artaxerxes of Persia. When Nehemiah's brother comes from Judah to visit him at the palace, Nehemiah asks about the condition of Jerusalem and the situation of the Jewish people. After Nehemiah hears that Jerusalem's wall is "broken down" and that the people "are in great trouble and disgrace" (Ne 1:3), he weeps.

Nehemiah wants to do something to restore the people's dignity and repair the crushed wall. (A city without walls is open to attack and is considered insignificant.) For weeks he prays until God opens a door of opportunity. Nehemiah walks through his fear—as advocating for Jerusalem (as well as appearing sad in the king's presence) was in effect taking Nehemiah's life in his hands—to ask the king for permission to go rebuild the city.

God ignites a spark of revival in his servant Nehemiah. Nehemiah stokes the fire with prayer and a willing heart. Then God's power works through this caring and capable man to spread the revival fire over 500 miles to Jerusalem (see Map 8b: Babylonian Empire at the back of this Bible).

Nehemiah's Prayer

1 The words of Nehemiah son of Hacaliah:

In the month of Kislev[a] in the twentieth year, while I was in the citadel of Susa, 2Hanani,[b] one of my brothers, came from Judah with some other men, and I questioned them about the Jewish remnant[c] that survived the exile, and also about Jerusalem.

3They said to me, "Those who survived the exile and are back in the province are in great trouble and disgrace. The wall of Jerusalem is broken down, and its gates have been burned with fire.[d]"

4When I heard these things, I sat down and wept.[e] For some days I mourned and fasted[f] and prayed before the God of heaven. 5Then I said:

"O LORD, God of heaven, the great and awesome God,[g] who keeps his covenant of love[h] with those who love him and obey his commands, 6let your ear be attentive and your eyes open to hear[i] the prayer[j] your servant is praying before you day and night for your servants, the people of Israel. I confess the sins we Israelites, including myself and my father's house, have committed against you. 7We have acted very wickedly[k] toward you. We have not obeyed the commands, decrees and laws you gave your servant Moses.

8"Remember[l] the instruction you gave your servant Moses, saying, 'If you are unfaithful, I will scatter[m] you among the nations, 9but if you return to me and obey my commands, then even if your exiled people are at the farthest horizon, I will gather[n] them from there and bring them to the place I have chosen as a dwelling for my Name.'[o]

10"They are your servants and your people, whom you redeemed by your great strength and your mighty hand.[p] 11O Lord, let your ear be attentive[q] to the prayer of this your servant and to the prayer of your servants who delight in revering your name. Give your servant success today by granting him favor in the presence of this man."

I was cupbearer[r] to the king.

Artaxerxes Sends Nehemiah to Jerusalem

2 In the month of Nisan in the twentieth year of King Artaxerxes,[s] when wine was brought for him, I took the wine and gave it to the king. I had not been sad in his presence before; 2so the king asked me, "Why does your face look so sad when you are not ill? This can be nothing but sadness of heart."

I was very much afraid, 3but I said to the king, "May the king live forever![t] Why should my face not look sad when the city[u] where my fathers are buried lies in ruins, and its gates have been destroyed by fire?[v]"

1:1 [a]Ne 10:1; Zec 7:1
1:2 [b]Ne 7:2 [c]Jer 52:28
1:3 [d]2Ki 25:10; Ne 2:3,13,17
1:4 [e]Ps 137:1 [f]Ezr 9:4
1:5 [g]Dt 7:21; Ne 4:14 [h]Ex 20:6; Da 9:4
1:6 [i]1Ki 8:29 [j]Da 9:17
1:7 [k]Dt 28:14-15; Ps 106:6
1:8 [l]2Ki 20:3 [m]Lev 26:33
1:9 [n]Dt 30:4 [o]1Ki 8:48; Jer 29:14
1:10 [p]Ex 32:11; Dt 9:29
1:11 [q]ver 6 [r]Ge 40:1
2:1 [s]Ezr 7:1
2:3 [t]1Ki 1:31; Da 2:4; 5:10; 6:6,21 [u]Ps 137:6 [v]Ne 1:3

4 The king said to me, "What is it you want?"
Then I prayed to the God of heaven, 5 and I
answered the king, "If it pleases the king and if
your servant has found favor in his sight, let him
send me to the city in Judah where my fathers are
2:6 buried so that I can rebuild it."
[w]Ne 5:14; 6 Then the king[w], with the queen sitting beside
13:6 him, asked me, "How long will your journey take,
and when will you get back?" It pleased the king
to send me; so I set a time.
2:7 7 I also said to him, "If it pleases the king, may
[x]Ezr 8:36 I have letters to the governors of Trans-Euphrates,[x]
so that they will provide me safe-conduct until I
arrive in Judah? 8 And may I have a letter to
Asaph, keeper of the king's forest, so he will give
2:8 me timber to make beams for the gates of the
[y]Ne 7:2 citadel[y] by the temple and for the city wall and for
[z]ver 18; the residence I will occupy?" And because the
Ezr 5:5; 7:6 gracious hand of my God was upon me,[z] the king
granted my requests. 9 So I went to the governors
of Trans-Euphrates and gave them the king's letters. The king had also sent army officers and cav-
2:9 alry[a] with me.
[a]Ezr 8:22 10 When Sanballat[b] the Horonite and Tobiah[c] the
2:10 Ammonite official heard about this, they were
[b]ver 19; very much disturbed that someone had come to
Ne 4:1,7 promote the welfare of the Israelites.[d]
[c]Ne 4:3;
13:4-7
[d]Est 10:3

Nehemiah Inspects Jerusalem's Walls

2:11 11 I went to Jerusalem, and after staying there
[e]Ge 40:13 three days[e] 12 I set out during the night with a few
men. I had not told anyone what my God had put
in my heart to do for Jerusalem. There were no
2:13 mounts with me except the one I was riding on.
[f]2Ch 26:9 13 By night I went out through the Valley Gate[f]
[g]Ne 3:13 toward the Jackal[a] Well and the Dung Gate,[g]
[h]Ne 1:3 examining the walls[h] of Jerusalem, which had
been broken down, and its gates, which had been
2:14 destroyed by fire. 14 Then I moved on toward the
[i]Ne 3:15 Fountain Gate[i] and the King's Pool,[j] but there was
[j]2Ki 18:17 not enough room for my mount to get through;
15 so I went up the valley by night, examining the
wall. Finally, I turned back and reentered through
the Valley Gate. 16 The officials did not know
where I had gone or what I was doing, because as
yet I had said nothing to the Jews or the priests or
nobles or officials or any others who would be
doing the work.
17 Then I said to them, "You see the trouble we
are in: Jerusalem lies in ruins, and its gates have
2:17 been burned with fire.[k] Come, let us rebuild the
[k]Ne 1:3 wall[l] of Jerusalem, and we will no longer be in
[l]Ps 102:16; Isa 30:13; disgrace.[m]" 18 I also told them about the gracious
58:12 hand of my God upon me[n] and what the king had
[m]Eze 5:14 said to me.
2:18 They replied, "Let us start rebuilding." So they
[n]2Sa 2:7 began this good work.
2:19 19 But when Sanballat the Horonite, Tobiah the
[o]Ne 6:1,2,6 Ammonite official and Geshem[o] the Arab heard

[a] 13 Or *Serpent* or *Fig*

A Man of Prayer

NE 2:4–5

Nehemiah, a man of action, is also a man of prayer. The predicament of the Jewish people in Jerusalem breaks his heart and propels him to pray. His own comfortable position as trusted attendant to the king, in contrast to the sorry state of the people in Jerusalem, probably intensifies his sorrow.

Nehemiah praises God and asks for guidance in facing his boss with a request to go to Jerusalem. When God gives him the opportunity to act, Nehemiah is afraid (Ne 2:2). He shoots up a silent, "arrow" prayer for courage and plunges forward.

Prayer involves risk. We ask but don't know exactly how God will respond. We believe God will supply boldness and power, but we cannot guess his timing. So, like Nehemiah, we pray and trust that God is bigger than the risk we take. In order to remember Nehemiah and where he got his courage, draw an arrow from the phrase "very much afraid" to the words "Then I prayed" (Ne 2:2,4).

Women Wall Builders

NE 3:12

Although the reference in Nehemiah 3:12 to daughters working on the wall is an isolated case, it is very possible that other women were involved as well. Rebuilding Jerusalem's wall was an enormous community endeavor, and it was in everyone's best interest to complete the project as quickly as possible. So the women got involved.

As a wise leader, people motivator and team builder, Nehemiah gets many different people enthused about working on the wall project—men, women, sons, daughters, goldsmiths and perfume-makers (Ne 3:8). He allows people to work near their own homes, ensuring the wall will be built with excellence, commitment and speed (Ne 3:10). He keeps careful account of names, evidence that he values each worker's contribution. With detailed planning, careful team building and genuine appreciation, Nehemiah leads the people in this massive project. His example is one that men and women leaders will do well to imitate.

about it, they mocked and ridiculed us.[p] "What is
this you are doing?" they asked. "Are you rebelling
against the king?"
20 I answered them by saying, "The God of heav-
en will give us success. We his servants will start
rebuilding, but as for you, you have no share[q] in
Jerusalem or any claim or historic right to it."

Builders of the Wall

3 Eliashib[r] the high priest and his fellow priests
went to work and rebuilt[s] the Sheep Gate.[t]
They dedicated it and set its doors in place, building as far as the Tower of the Hundred, which
they dedicated, and as far as the Tower of Hananel.[u] 2 The men of Jericho[v] built the adjoining section, and Zaccur son of Imri built next to them.
3 The Fish Gate[w] was rebuilt by the sons of Has-
senaah. They laid its beams and put its doors and
bolts and bars in place. 4 Meremoth son of Uriah,
the son of Hakkoz, repaired the next section. Next
to him Meshullam son of Berekiah, the son of
Meshezabel, made repairs, and next to him Zadok
son of Baana also made repairs. 5 The next section
was repaired by the men of Tekoa,[x] but their
nobles would not put their shoulders to the work
under their supervisors.[a]

6 The Jeshanah[b] Gate[y] was repaired by Joiada
son of Paseah and Meshullam son of Besodeiah.
They laid its beams and put its doors and bolts
and bars in place. 7 Next to them, repairs were
made by men from Gibeon[z] and Mizpah—Melati-
ah of Gibeon and Jadon of Meronoth—places
under the authority of the governor of Trans-
Euphrates. 8 Uzziel son of Harhaiah, one of the
goldsmiths, repaired the next section; and Hananiah, one of the perfume-makers, made repairs
next to that. They restored[c] Jerusalem as far as the
Broad Wall.[a] 9 Rephaiah son of Hur, ruler of a half-
district of Jerusalem, repaired the next section.
10 Adjoining this, Jedaiah son of Harumaph made
repairs opposite his house, and Hattush son of
Hashabneiah made repairs next to him. 11 Malkijah son of Harim and Hasshub son of Pahath-
Moab repaired another section and the Tower of
the Ovens.[b] 12 Shallum son of Hallohesh, ruler of a
half-district of Jerusalem, repaired the next section with the help of his daughters.

13 The Valley Gate[c] was repaired by Hanun and
the residents of Zanoah.[d] They rebuilt it and put
its doors and bolts and bars in place. They also
repaired five hundred yards[d] of the wall as far as
the Dung Gate.[e]

14 The Dung Gate was repaired by Malkijah son
of Recab, ruler of the district of Beth Hakkerem.[f]

[a] 5 Or *their Lord* or *the governor* [b] 6 Or *Old* [c] 8 Or *They left out part of* [d] 13 Hebrew *a thousand cubits* (about 450 meters)

2:19 [p]Ps 44:13-16
2:20 [q]Ezr 4:3
3:1 [r]Ezr 10:24 [s]Isa 58:12 [t]ver 32; Ne 12:39 [u]Ne 12:39; Jer 31:38; Zec 14:10
3:2 [v]Ne 7:36
3:3 [w]2Ch 33:14; Ne 12:39
3:5 [x]2Sa 14:2
3:6 [y]Ne 12:39
3:7 [z]Jos 9:3; Ne 2:7
3:8 [a]Ne 12:38
3:11 [b]Ne 12:38
3:13 [c]2Ch 26:9 [d]Jos 15:34 [e]Ne 2:13
3:14 [f]Jer 6:1

He rebuilt it and put its doors and bolts and bars
in place.
[15]The Fountain Gate was repaired by Shallun
son of Col-Hozeh, ruler of the district of Mizpah.
He rebuilt it, roofing it over and putting its doors
and bolts and bars in place. He also repaired the
3:15 gIsa 8:6; wall of the Pool of Siloam,[a][g] by the King's Garden,
Jn 9:7 as far as the steps going down from the City of
3:16 David. [16]Beyond him, Nehemiah son of Azbuk,
hJos 15:58 ruler of a half-district of Beth Zur,[h] made repairs
iAc 2:29 up to a point opposite the tombs[b][i] of David, as far
as the artificial pool and the House of the Heroes.
[17]Next to him, the repairs were made by the
3:17 Levites under Rehum son of Bani. Beside him,
jJos 15:44 Hashabiah, ruler of half the district of Keilah,[j] carried out repairs for his district. [18]Next to him, the
repairs were made by their countrymen under
Binnui[c] son of Henadad, ruler of the other half-
district of Keilah. [19]Next to him, Ezer son of Jeshua, ruler of Mizpah, repaired another section,
from a point facing the ascent to the armory as far
as the angle. [20]Next to him, Baruch son of Zabbai
zealously repaired another section, from the angle
3:21 to the entrance of the house of Eliashib the high
kEzr 8:33 priest. [21]Next to him, Meremoth[k] son of Uriah, the
son of Hakkoz, repaired another section, from the
entrance of Eliashib's house to the end of it.
[22]The repairs next to him were made by the
priests from the surrounding region. [23]Beyond
them, Benjamin and Hasshub made repairs in
front of their house; and next to them, Azariah
son of Maaseiah, the son of Ananiah, made
3:24 repairs beside his house. [24]Next to him, Binnui[l]
lEzr 8:33 son of Henadad repaired another section, from
Azariah's house to the angle and the corner, [25]and
Palal son of Uzai worked opposite the angle and
3:25 the tower projecting from the upper palace near
mJer 32:2; the court of the guard.[m] Next to him, Pedaiah son
37:21; 39:14 nEzr 2:3 of Parosh[n] [26]and the temple servants[o] living on the
hill of Ophel[p] made repairs up to a point opposite
3:26 oNe 7:46; the Water Gate[q] toward the east and the projecting
11:21 tower. [27]Next to them, the men of Tekoa[r] repaired
p2Ch 33:14 another section, from the great projecting tower[s]
qNe 8:1,3, 16; 12:37 to the wall of Ophel.

3:27 [28]Above the Horse Gate,[t] the priests made
rver 5 sPs 48:12 repairs, each in front of his own house. [29]Next to
them, Zadok son of Immer made repairs opposite
3:28 his house. Next to him, Shemaiah son of Shecani-
t2Ki 11:16; ah, the guard at the East Gate, made repairs.
2Ch 23:15; Jer 31:40 [30]Next to him, Hananiah son of Shelemiah, and
Hanun, the sixth son of Zalaph, repaired another
section. Next to them, Meshullam son of Berekiah
made repairs opposite his living quarters. [31]Next
to him, Malkijah, one of the goldsmiths, made
repairs as far as the house of the temple servants

[a] *15* Hebrew *Shelah,* a variant of *Shiloah,* that is, Siloam
[b] *16* Hebrew; Septuagint, some Vulgate manuscripts and Syriac *tomb*
[c] *18* Two Hebrew manuscripts and Syriac (see also Septuagint and verse 24); most Hebrew manuscripts *Bavvai*

A Community Effort

NE 3:15-32

Although certain that God has called him to the task, Nehemiah knows he cannot build the wall of Jerusalem alone. He inspires others to join him in the massive undertaking. No doubt there are many competent leaders who are used to giving orders rather than taking them. Yet Nehemiah wins their cooperation, and the 52-day project becomes a splendid example of community effort.

Success is centered not on individuals being either independent or dependent, but on being interdependent. Interdependence means that each individual accepts responsibility for his or her own contribution to the inspired project at hand. This is how Nehemiah achieves his goal of rebuilding Jerusalem's wall and how we will reach the objectives God has given us for our churches and ministries.

Opposition

NE 4:1–2

In sending Nehemiah to Jerusalem, King Artaxerxes has made him the governor of Judah (Ne 5:14). Sanballat is the governor of Samaria, which borders Judah, and one of Nehemiah's most vehement opponents. As long as Jerusalem remains unprotected and the people unmotivated, Sanballat can exercise control over them. He does not appreciate a strong leader like Nehemiah coming into the area and usurping his power. He is afraid he will lose some of his influence. That fear erupts into an angry attempt to intimidate Nehemiah's workers to stop their work on the wall.

The people face opposition because they are trying to make positive changes in their circumstances and lives. Those who feel threatened by the transformation try to dissuade them. "Do you think God can use 'feeble Jews' like you?" they taunt (Ne 4:2). Nehemiah and the people refuse to accept this "false" shame and instead reaffirm their resolve to reconstruct both the wall and their honor. They do not allow Sanballat's opinion to mean more to them than God's.

and the merchants, opposite the Inspection Gate,
and as far as the room above the corner; 32 and
between the room above the corner and the Sheep
Gate[u] the goldsmiths and merchants made repairs.

Opposition to the Rebuilding

4 When Sanballat[v] heard that we were rebuilding the wall, he became angry and was greatly incensed. He ridiculed the Jews, 2 and in the
presence of his associates[w] and the army of
Samaria, he said, "What are those feeble Jews
doing? Will they restore their wall? Will they offer
sacrifices? Will they finish in a day? Can they
bring the stones back to life from those heaps of
rubble[x]—burned as they are?"
3 Tobiah[y] the Ammonite, who was at his side,
said, "What they are building—if even a fox
climbed up on it, he would break down their wall
of stones!"[z]
4 Hear us, O our God, for we are despised.[a] Turn
their insults back on their own heads. Give them
over as plunder in a land of captivity. 5 Do not cover up their guilt[b] or blot out their sins from your
sight,[c] for they have thrown insults in the face of[a]
the builders.
6 So we rebuilt the wall till all of it reached half its
height, for the people worked with all their heart.
7 But when Sanballat, Tobiah,[d] the Arabs, the
Ammonites and the men of Ashdod heard that the
repairs to Jerusalem's walls had gone ahead and
that the gaps were being closed, they were very
angry. 8 They all plotted together[e] to come and
fight against Jerusalem and stir up trouble against
it. 9 But we prayed to our God and posted a guard
day and night to meet this threat.
10 Meanwhile, the people in Judah said, "The
strength of the laborers[f] is giving out, and there is
so much rubble that we cannot rebuild the wall."
11 Also our enemies said, "Before they know it
or see us, we will be right there among them and
will kill them and put an end to the work."
12 Then the Jews who lived near them came and
told us ten times over, "Wherever you turn, they
will attack us."
13 Therefore I stationed some of the people
behind the lowest points of the wall at the exposed
places, posting them by families, with their
swords, spears and bows. 14 After I looked things
over, I stood up and said to the nobles, the officials
and the rest of the people, "Don't be afraid[g] of
them. Remember[h] the Lord, who is great and awesome,[i] and fight[j] for your brothers, your sons and
your daughters, your wives and your homes."
15 When our enemies heard that we were aware
of their plot and that God had frustrated it,[k] we all
returned to the wall, each to his own work.
16 From that day on, half of my men did the
work, while the other half were equipped with

3:32 [u]ver 1; Jn 5:2
4:1 [v]Ne 2:10
4:2 [w]Ezr 4:9-10 [x]Ps 79:1; Jer 26:18
4:3 [y]Ne 2:10 [z]Job 13:12; 15:3
4:4 [a]Ps 44:13; 79:12; 123:3-4; Jer 33:24
4:5 [b]Isa 2:9; La 1:22 [c]2Ki 14:27; Ps 51:1; 69:27-28; 109:14; Jer 18:23
4:7 [d]Ne 2:10
4:8 [e]Ps 2:2; 83:1-18
4:10 [f]1Ch 23:4
4:14 [g]Ge 28:15; Nu 14:9; Dt 1:29 [h]Ne 1:8 [i]Ne 1:5 [j]2Sa 10:12
4:15 [k]2Sa 17:14; Job 5:12

[a] 5 Or *have provoked you to anger before*

Week 12

Joy in Opposition

Satan will do anything to keep your faith in Jesus from growing. He wants you weak and susceptible to attack. As you grow and mature in Christ, the protective wall of faith guarding your heart grows taller, thicker and more impervious to attack.

Nehemiah found great opposition to building a wall. Let's learn from him.

What is the enemy's first response (Ne 4:1)? Satan will mock and harass you to keep you from growing in faith (Zec 3:1). When have you been ridiculed because of your faith?

What is the enemy's next assault (Ne 4:2–3)? Satan loves to tell you how weak and defenseless you are. But God has given you all you need to fight and overcome (2Sa 22:33–51). Who will fight for you (Ne 4:20; Jer 20:11)?

What is Nehemiah's response (Ne 4:4–6)? With God you can build a new wall or rebuild an old one. Who is your strength (Ps 118:14)?

What are the enemies of endurance (Ne 4:10–12)? Physical weariness ("strength . . . giving out"), emotional frustration ("there is so much rubble"), mental discouragement ("we cannot rebuild"), and fear from threats ("we will . . . kill them") cause discouragement. What is Nehemiah's response (Ne 4:13–23)?

Nehemiah's words provide a great plan of action when you're attacked. Protect your weak areas and pick up your weapons (Ne 4:13). Remember that your God is "great and awesome" (Ne 4:14). Be vigilant in your own work (Ne 4:15). Remember that those protecting the workers are as important as the workers themselves (Ne 4:16). Make sure your leaders are also armed for battle (Ne 4:16–17). And when (not if) the enemy attacks, stand together and be assured that God will fight for you (Ne 4:19–20).

Enjoying God THROUGH the Word

Read Ephesians 6:10–18 (page 1936). God has provided both offensive and defensive weapons for your use. You need the "full armor" (Eph 6:11,13), not just a piece of it:

- The Belt of Truth—your defense against the lies of the enemy. God's Word is a filter to differentiate between truth and lies (Eph 1:13).
- The Breastplate of Righteousness—your protection against the enemy's accusations. Jesus took your sin on himself, and you are now righteous in God's eyes (2Co 5:21).
- The Shoes of the Gospel of Peace—your defense against retreat. Your peace comes in knowing that you have all you need in Christ (1Jn 4:4).
- The Shield of Faith—your defense against doubt and guilt (1Co 16:13). Satan uses these to hinder your spiritual growth.
- The Helmet of Salvation—your defense against confusion and wrong thinking (Ro 12:2; 2Co 10:5). They rob you of your assurance of salvation.
- The Sword of the Spirit—the *rhema* ("spoken") word of God. When God says it and you speak it out, the Spirit cuts through the darkness like a sword (Heb 4:12).

Enjoying God THROUGH Experience

Put on—or "pray on"—God's armor every morning. Memorize Scripture. Pray the words of Scripture. Counter all lies with truth from Scripture. Pick up your sword and fight! God will protect you and bring you joy even in the battle because he is your strength and song (Ex 15:2).

Go to page 832 for your next weekly study.

Be Alert and Ready

NE 4:17

After the workers' lives are threatened (Ne 4:11), they begin to wonder if the restoration project will ever be completed. So Nehemiah and the people pray (Ne 4:9) and set into motion a new plan. They not only post guards in the most vulnerable areas, but the text also indicates that some workers carry a weapon in one hand and work with the other. Nehemiah and the workers stay on constant alert, day and night, not even stopping to change their clothes (Ne 4:23).

Their faith in a powerful God does not make them blind to the reality of their situation. The threats of their opposition are real. So they pray and act *simultaneously*. Prayer and alert action go hand in hand.

spears, shields, bows and armor. The officers posted themselves behind all the people of Judah
17 who were building the wall. Those who carried
materials did their work with one hand and held
a weapon[l] in the other, 18 and each of the builders 4:17 [l]Ps 149:6
wore his sword at his side as he worked. But the
man who sounded the trumpet[m] stayed with me. 4:18 [m]Nu 10:2
19 Then I said to the nobles, the officials and the
rest of the people, "The work is extensive and
spread out, and we are widely separated from
each other along the wall. 20 Wherever you hear
the sound of the trumpet,[n] join us there. Our God 4:20 [n]Eze 33:3
will fight[o] for us!" [o]Ex 14:14; Dt 1:30; 20:4; Jos 10:14
21 So we continued the work with half the men
holding spears, from the first light of dawn till the
stars came out. 22 At that time I also said to the
people, "Have every man and his helper stay
inside Jerusalem at night, so they can serve us as
guards by night and workmen by day." 23 Neither
I nor my brothers nor my men nor the guards
with me took off our clothes; each had his
weapon, even when he went for water.[a]

Nehemiah Helps the Poor

5 Now the men and their wives raised a great
outcry against their Jewish brothers. 2 Some
were saying, "We and our sons and daughters are
numerous; in order for us to eat and stay alive, we
must get grain."
3 Others were saying, "We are mortgaging our 5:3
fields,[p] our vineyards and our homes to get grain [p]Ps 109:11
during the famine."[q] [q]Ge 47:23
4 Still others were saying, "We have had to borrow money to pay the king's tax[r] on our fields and 5:4
vineyards. 5 Although we are of the same flesh and [r]Ezr 4:13
blood[s] as our countrymen and though our sons 5:5
are as good as theirs, yet we have to subject our [s]Ge 29:14
sons and daughters to slavery.[t] Some of our [t]Lev 25:39-43,47; 2Ki 4:1; Isa 50:1
daughters have already been enslaved, but we are
powerless, because our fields and our vineyards [u]Dt 15:7-11; 2Ki 4:1
belong to others."[u]
6 When I heard their outcry and these charges, I
was very angry. 7 I pondered them in my mind and
then accused the nobles and officials. I told them,
"You are exacting usury[v] from your own country- 5:7 [v]Ex 22:25-27;
men!" So I called together a large meeting to deal Lev 25:35-
with them 8 and said: "As far as possible, we have 37; Dt 23:19-
bought[w] back our Jewish brothers who were sold 20; 24:10-13
to the Gentiles. Now you are selling your brothers,
only for them to be sold back to us!" They kept 5:8 [w]Lev 25:47
quiet, because they could find nothing to say.[x] [x]Jer 34:8
9 So I continued, "What you are doing is not
right. Shouldn't you walk in the fear of our God to
avoid the reproach[y] of our Gentile enemies? 10 I 5:9 [y]Isa 52:5
and my brothers and my men are also lending the
people money and grain. But let the exacting of
usury stop![z] 11 Give back to them immediately 5:10 [z]Ex 22:25
their fields, vineyards, olive groves and houses,
and also the usury[a] you are charging them—the 5:11 [a]Isa 58:6

[a] *23* The meaning of the Hebrew for this clause is uncertain.

hundredth part of the money, grain, new wine
and oil.”
12“We will give it back,” they said. “And we will
not demand anything more from them. We will
do as you say.”
Then I summoned the priests and made the
5:12 bEzr 10:5 nobles and officials take an oath[b] to do what they
had promised. 13I also shook[c] out the folds of my
5:13 robe and said, “In this way may God shake out of
cMt 10:14; Ac 18:6 his house and possessions every man who does
dDt 27:15-26 not keep this promise. So may such a man be
shaken out and emptied!”
At this the whole assembly said, “Amen,”[d] and
praised the LORD. And the people did as they had
promised.
5:14 14Moreover, from the twentieth year of King
eNe 2:6; 13:6 Artaxerxes,[e] when I was appointed to be their
fGe 42:6; governor[f] in the land of Judah, until his thirty-sec-
Ezr 6:7; ond year—twelve years—neither I nor my broth-
Jer 40:7; Hag 1:1 ers ate the food allotted to the governor. 15But the
earlier governors—those preceding me—placed a
heavy burden on the people and took forty
shekels[a] of silver from them in addition to food
and wine. Their assistants also lorded it over the
5:15 gGe 20:11 people. But out of reverence for God[g] I did not act
like that. 16Instead,[h] I devoted myself to the work
5:16 on this wall. All my men were assembled there
h2Th 3:7-10 for the work; we[b] did not acquire any land.
17Furthermore, a hundred and fifty Jews and
officials ate at my table, as well as those who came
to us from the surrounding nations. 18Each day
5:18 i1Ki 4:23 one ox, six choice sheep and some poultry[i] were
prepared for me, and every ten days an abundant
supply of wine of all kinds. In spite of all this, I
never demanded the food allotted to the governor,
because the demands were heavy on these people.
5:19 19Remember[j] me with favor, O my God, for all I
jGe 8:1; 2Ki 20:3; have done for these people.

Ne 1:8; 13:14,22,31

Further Opposition to the Rebuilding

6:1 6 When word came to Sanballat, Tobiah,[k]
kNe 2:10 lNe 2:19 Geshem[l] the Arab and the rest of our enemies
that I had rebuilt the wall and not a gap was left in
it—though up to that time I had not set the doors
in the gates— 2Sanballat and Geshem sent me this
message: “Come, let us meet together in one of
6:2 m1Ch 8:12 the villages[c] on the plain of Ono.[m]”
But they were scheming to harm me; 3so I sent
messengers to them with this reply: “I am carrying on a great project and cannot go down. Why
should the work stop while I leave it and go down
to you?” 4Four times they sent me the same message, and each time I gave them the same answer.
6:5 5Then, the fifth time, Sanballat[n] sent his aide to
nNe 2:10 me with the same message, and in his hand was
an unsealed letter 6in which was written:

“It is reported among the nations—and

[a] *15* That is, about 1 pound (about 0.5 kilogram) [b] *16* Most Hebrew manuscripts; some Hebrew manuscripts, Septuagint, Vulgate and Syriac *I* [c] *2* Or *in Kephirim*

Hardships

NE 5

At the same time they are facing outside opposition, there is also dissatisfaction inside the Jewish community. Many suffer great economic hardships. They have large families and no money to buy food. Some are landowners but have had to mortgage all they own just to survive. Others have to borrow money to pay the exorbitant taxes. And then there are those who have only their children to use as collateral.

The people take their complaints to Nehemiah. He listens and then confronts the Jewish officials and nobles who are oppressing their needy neighbors. Nehemiah takes a stand against the mistreatment and neglect of the poor by reminding his Jewish brothers and sisters that God's standard calls for compassion and generosity (Dt 15:7–8). All God's people have the privilege and the responsibility to treat others, including the poor, with respect and kindness.

Only Fifty-Two Days

NE 6:15

On October 2, 445 B.C., the wall surrounding Jerusalem was completed. This wall had lain in ruin for nearly 150 years. Yet this entire reconstruction project took only 52 days, an amazing achievement. Some doubt that it could have been accomplished in such a short time span. Jewish historian Josephus mentions a much longer time spent in rebuilding; however, he is probably also including the time it took to beautify and further fortify the wall. Also, archaeologists suggest that Jerusalem during Nehemiah's leadership was a smaller city than before the exile.

The quick rebuilding of the wall has its effect on Israel's neighbors. While these neighbors threaten and try to frighten the Jews as they rebuilt, the completion of the wall frightens them. *And not just of the Jews themselves but of their God and his power.*

Geshem[a][o] says it is true—that you and the
Jews are plotting to revolt, and therefore you
are building the wall. Moreover, according to
these reports you are about to become their
king 7 and have even appointed prophets to
make this proclamation about you in Jerusalem: 'There is a king in Judah!' Now this
report will get back to the king; so come, let
us confer together."

8 I sent him this reply: "Nothing like what you
are saying is happening; you are just making it up
out of your head."

9 They were all trying to frighten us, thinking,
"Their hands will get too weak for the work, and
it will not be completed."

⌞But I prayed,⌟ "Now strengthen my hands."
10 One day I went to the house of Shemaiah son
of Delaiah, the son of Mehetabel, who was shut
in at his home. He said, "Let us meet in the house
of God, inside the temple[p], and let us close the
temple doors, because men are coming to kill
you—by night they are coming to kill you."
11 But I said, "Should a man like me run away?
Or should one like me go into the temple to save
his life? I will not go!" 12 I realized that God had
not sent him, but that he had prophesied against
me[q] because Tobiah and Sanballat[r] had hired him.
13 He had been hired to intimidate me so that I
would commit a sin by doing this, and then they
would give me a bad name to discredit me.[s]

14 Remember[t] Tobiah and Sanballat,[u] O my God,
because of what they have done; remember also
the prophetess[v] Noadiah and the rest of the prophets[w] who have been trying to intimidate me.

The Completion of the Wall

15 So the wall was completed on the twenty-fifth
of Elul, in fifty-two days. 16 When all our enemies
heard about this, all the surrounding nations were
afraid and lost their self-confidence, because they
realized that this work had been done with the
help of our God.
17 Also, in those days the nobles of Judah were
sending many letters to Tobiah, and replies from
Tobiah kept coming to them. 18 For many in Judah
were under oath to him, since he was son-in-law
to Shecaniah son of Arah, and his son Jehohanan
had married the daughter of Meshullam son of
Berekiah. 19 Moreover, they kept reporting to me
his good deeds and then telling him what I said.
And Tobiah sent letters to intimidate me.

7 After the wall had been rebuilt and I had set
the doors in place, the gatekeepers[x] and the
singers[y] and the Levites[z] were appointed. 2 I put in
charge of Jerusalem my brother Hanani,[a] along
with[b] Hananiah[b] the commander of the citadel,[c]
because he was a man of integrity and feared[d]

6:6 [o]Ne 2:19
6:10 [p]Nu 18:7
6:12 [q]Eze 13:22-23 [r]Ne 2:10
6:13 [s]Jer 20:10
6:14 [t]Ne 1:8 [u]Ne 2:10 [v]Ex 15:20; Eze 13:17-23; Ac 21:9; Rev 2:20 [w]Ne 13:29; Jer 23:9-40; Zec 13:2-3
7:1 [x]1Ch 9:27; 26:12-19; Ne 6:1,15 [y]Ps 68:25 [z]Ne 8:9
7:2 [a]Ne 1:2 [b]Ne 10:23 [c]Ne 2:8 [d]1Ki 18:3

[a] 6 Hebrew *Gashmu,* a variant of *Geshem* [b] 2 Or *Hanani, that is,*

God more than most men do. 3I said to them, "The
gates of Jerusalem are not to be opened until the
sun is hot. While the gatekeepers are still on duty,
have them shut the doors and bar them. Also
appoint residents of Jerusalem as guards, some at
their posts and some near their own houses."

The List of the Exiles Who Returned

4Now the city was large and spacious, but there
7:4 [e]Ne 11:1 were few people in it,[e] and the houses had not yet
been rebuilt. 5So my God put it into my heart to
assemble the nobles, the officials and the common
people for registration by families. I found the
genealogical record of those who had been the
first to return. This is what I found written there:

6These are the people of the province who
7:6 [f]2Ch 36:20; Ezr 2:1-70; Ne 1:2 came up from the captivity of the exiles[f]
whom Nebuchadnezzar king of Babylon had
taken captive (they returned to Jerusalem and
Judah, each to his own town, 7in company
7:7 [g]1Ch 3:19; Ezr 2:2 with Zerubbabel,[g] Jeshua, Nehemiah, Azariah, Raamiah, Nahamani, Mordecai, Bilshan,
Mispereth, Bigvai, Nehum and Baanah):

The list of the men of Israel:

8the descendants of Parosh 2,172
9of Shephatiah 372
10of Arah 652
11of Pahath-Moab (through the line of Jeshua and Joab) 2,818
12of Elam 1,254
13of Zattu 845
14of Zaccai 760
15of Binnui 648
16of Bebai 628
17of Azgad 2,322
18of Adonikam 667
19of Bigvai 2,067
7:20 [h]Ezr 8:6 20of Adin[h] 655
21of Ater (through Hezekiah) 98
22of Hashum 328
23of Bezai 324
24of Hariph 112
25of Gibeon 95

7:26 [i]2Sa 23:28; 1Ch 2:54 26the men of Bethlehem and Netophah[i] 188
27of Anathoth[j] 128
7:27 [j]Jos 21:18 28of Beth Azmaveth 42
29of Kiriath Jearim, Kephirah[k] and
7:29 [k]Jos 18:26 [l]Jos 18:25 Beeroth[l] 743
30of Ramah and Geba 621
31of Micmash 122
7:32 [m]Ge 12:8 32of Bethel and Ai[m] 123
33of the other Nebo 52
34of the other Elam 1,254
35of Harim 320
7:36 [n]Ne 3:2 36of Jericho[n] 345
37of Lod, Hadid and Ono[o] 721
7:37 [o]1Ch 8:12 38of Senaah 3,930

Jerusalem's Inhabitants

NE 7:4

Few people live inside the rebuilt walls of Jerusalem. When the Jewish people gain freedom from their Babylonian captors, many stay in their comfortable homes and jobs in Persia, some return and settle throughout Judah, but only a few settle in Jerusalem. Some probably feel uneasy about living in a small, unfortified city, and others prefer to settle in the towns of their ancestors.

The situation concerns Nehemiah, so this man of action and prayer talks to God and the Lord puts it into his "heart" (Ne 7:5) to call for a registration of the people. This allows Nehemiah to compare the existing population with records of the original returnees, helping to verify heritage and assign tasks. Some come willingly to settle in Jerusalem (Ne 11:2) while others are chosen by lot (Ne 11:1). Competent leaders and willing followers are needed to ensure that Jerusalem will grow and prosper (Ne 11:1).

[39]The priests:

the descendants of Jedaiah (through the family of Jeshua) 973
[40]of Immer 1,052
[41]of Pashhur 1,247
[42]of Harim 1,017

[43]The Levites:

the descendants of Jeshua (through Kadmiel through the line of Hodaviah) 74

[44]The singers:[p]

the descendants of Asaph 148

[45]The gatekeepers:[q]

the descendants of Shallum, Ater, Talmon, Akkub, Hatita and Shobai 138

[46]The temple servants:[r]

the descendants of
Ziha, Hasupha, Tabbaoth,
[47]Keros, Sia, Padon,
[48]Lebana, Hagaba, Shalmai,
[49]Hanan, Giddel, Gahar,
[50]Reaiah, Rezin, Nekoda,
[51]Gazzam, Uzza, Paseah,
[52]Besai, Meunim, Nephusim,
[53]Bakbuk, Hakupha, Harhur,
[54]Bazluth, Mehida, Harsha,
[55]Barkos, Sisera, Temah,
[56]Neziah and Hatipha

[57]The descendants of the servants of Solomon:

the descendants of
Sotai, Sophereth, Perida,
[58]Jaala, Darkon, Giddel,
[59]Shephatiah, Hattil, Pokereth-Hazzebaim and Amon

[60]The temple servants and the descendants of the servants of Solomon[s] 392

[61]The following came up from the towns of
Tel Melah, Tel Harsha, Kerub, Addon and
Immer, but they could not show that their
families were descended from Israel:

[62]the descendants of
Delaiah, Tobiah and Nekoda 642

[63]And from among the priests:

the descendants of
Hobaiah, Hakkoz and Barzillai (a man who had married a daughter of Barzillai the Gileadite and was called by that name).

[64]These searched for their family records,
but they could not find them and so were
excluded from the priesthood as unclean.
[65]The governor, therefore, ordered them not

7:44 [p]Ne 11:23
7:45 [q]1Ch 9:17
7:46 [r]Ne 3:26
7:60 [s]1Ch 9:2

You don't have to be happy to laugh. You become happy *because* you laugh.

—Barbara Johnson

to eat any of the most sacred food until there
7:65 should be a priest ministering with the Urim
[t]Ex 28:30; Ne 8:9 and Thummim.[t]

66The whole company numbered 42,360,
67besides their 7,337 menservants and maidservants; and they also had 245 men and
women singers. 68There were 736 horses, 245
mules,[a] 69435 camels and 6,720 donkeys.

70Some of the heads of the families contributed to the work. The governor gave to
the treasury 1,000 drachmas[b] of gold, 50
7:71 bowls and 530 garments for priests. 71Some
[u]1Ch 29:7 of the heads of the families[u] gave to the treasury for the work 20,000 drachmas[c] of gold
7:72 and 2,200 minas[d] of silver. 72The total given
[v]Ex 25:2 by the rest of the people was 20,000 drachmas of gold, 2,000 minas[e] of silver and 67
garments for priests.[v]
7:73 73The priests, the Levites, the gatekeepers,
[w]Ne 1:10; Ps 34:22; 103:21; 113:1; 135:1 the singers and the temple servants,[w] along
with certain of the people and the rest of the
[x]Ezr 3:1; Ne 11:1 Israelites, settled in their own towns.[x]
[y]Ezr 3:1

Ezra Reads the Law

When the seventh month came and the Israelites
8:1 had settled in their towns,[y] 1all the people
[z]Ne 3:26 8 assembled as one man in the square before the
[a]Dt 28:61; 2Ch 34:15; Ezr 7:6 Water Gate.[z] They told Ezra the scribe to bring out
the Book of the Law of Moses,[a] which the LORD had
commanded for Israel.
8:2 2So on the first day of the seventh month[b] Ezra
[b]Lev 23:23-25; Nu 29:1-6 the priest brought the Law[c] before the assembly,
[c]Dt 31:11 which was made up of men and women and all
who were able to understand. 3He read it aloud
from daybreak till noon as he faced the square
8:3 before the Water Gate[d] in the presence of the men,
[d]Ne 3:26 women and others who could understand. And all
the people listened attentively to the Book of the
Law.
4Ezra the scribe stood on a high wooden plat-
8:4 form[e] built for the occasion. Beside him on his
[e]2Ch 6:13 right stood Mattithiah, Shema, Anaiah, Uriah, Hilkiah and Maaseiah; and on his left were Pedaiah,
Mishael, Malkijah, Hashum, Hashbaddanah,
Zechariah and Meshullam.
5Ezra opened the book. All the people could see
8:5 him because he was standing[f] above them; and as
[f]Jdg 3:20 he opened it, the people all stood up. 6Ezra
8:6 praised the LORD, the great God; and all the people
[g]Ex 4:31; Ezr 9:5; 1Ti 2:8 lifted their hands[g] and responded, "Amen!
Amen!" Then they bowed down and worshiped
the LORD with their faces to the ground.
8:7 7The Levites[h]—Jeshua, Bani, Sherebiah, Jamin,
[h]Ezr 10:23 Akkub, Shabbethai, Hodiah, Maaseiah, Kelita, Aza-

[a] *68* Some Hebrew manuscripts (see also Ezra 2:66); most Hebrew manuscripts do not have this verse. [b] *70* That is, about 19 pounds (about 8.5 kilograms) [c] *71* That is, about 375 pounds (about 170 kilograms); also in verse 72
[d] *71* That is, about 1 1/3 tons (about 1.2 metric tons)
[e] *72* That is, about 1 1/4 tons (about 1.1 metric tons)

The People Respond

NE 8:5–8

The wall is complete, and the people realize they have participated in a wonderful, even miraculous, event. They respond by revealing their desire to know more of what God wants of them, asking Ezra to read God's Law. Although Ezra the scribe and priest had "devoted himself to the study and observance of the Law" (Ezr 7:10), he may not have read God's Law publicly before. Certainly, there is no record of "all the people" (Ne 8:3)—men, women and probably children—assembling to hear the Law read until this time.

As Ezra stands on a platform and opens the book, the people are so moved that they stand too. (Some communities of believers still stand when God's Word is read.) Ezra praises God, and the people respond by lifting their hands and shouting, "Amen!" Chosen Levites help Ezra explain the Law to the people. They need to hear and **understand** ***God's Word so it will penetrate their hearts and make a difference in the way they live, love and serve.***

The Joy of the Lord

NE 8:10

When the people hear God's Law, they experience deep sorrow at the way they have ignored and betrayed their sovereign and personal God. They sob at the thought of their sin. Their leaders don't pat them on the back and tell them how great it is to mourn their sin. Instead, they encourage the people to turn their mourning into celebration. Once they understand God's written message and accept his mercy, their joy overflows.

Jerusalem's wall is strong, restored. Now the people need to restore and strengthen their relationship with God. Nehemiah tells them that their delight in the Lord will be their inner fortification.

The people are no longer to focus on their inadequacies, mistakes or sins. As they repent and find their source of life and celebration in the Lord, their self-preoccupation diminishes. They come out of their sin-heavy "funk" and have a party! And they experience the truth of Nehemiah's words: "The joy of the LORD is your strength."

riah, Jozabad, Hanan and Pelaiah—instructed[i] the
people in the Law while the people were standing
there. 8 They read from the Book of the Law of God,
making it clear[a] and giving the meaning so that the
people could understand what was being read.
9 Then Nehemiah the governor, Ezra the priest
and scribe, and the Levites[j] who were instructing
the people said to them all, "This day is sacred to
the LORD your God. Do not mourn or weep."[k] For
all the people had been weeping as they listened
to the words of the Law.
10 Nehemiah said, "Go and enjoy choice food
and sweet drinks, and send some to those who
have nothing[l] prepared. This day is sacred to our
Lord. Do not grieve, for the joy[m] of the LORD is
your strength."
11 The Levites calmed all the people, saying, "Be
still, for this is a sacred day. Do not grieve."
12 Then all the people went away to eat and
drink, to send portions of food and to celebrate
with great joy,[n] because they now understood the
words that had been made known to them.
13 On the second day of the month, the heads of
all the families, along with the priests and the
Levites, gathered around Ezra the scribe to give
attention to the words of the Law. 14 They found
written in the Law, which the LORD had commanded through Moses, that the Israelites were to
live in booths during the feast of the seventh
month 15 and that they should proclaim this word
and spread it throughout their towns and in Jerusalem: "Go out into the hill country and bring
back branches from olive and wild olive trees, and
from myrtles, palms and shade trees, to make
booths"—as it is written.[b]
16 So the people went out and brought back
branches and built themselves booths on their
own roofs, in their courtyards, in the courts of the
house of God and in the square by the Water Gate
and the one by the Gate of Ephraim.[o] 17 The whole
company that had returned from exile built booths
and lived in them. From the days of Joshua son of
Nun until that day, the Israelites had not celebrated[p] it like this. And their joy was very great.
18 Day after day, from the first day to the last,
Ezra read[q] from the Book of the Law of God. They
celebrated the feast for seven days, and on the
eighth day, in accordance with the regulation,[r]
there was an assembly.

The Israelites Confess Their Sins

9 On the twenty-fourth day of the same month,
the Israelites gathered together, fasting and
wearing sackcloth and having dust on their
heads.[s] 2 Those of Israelite descent had separated
themselves from all foreigners.[t] They stood in
their places and confessed their sins and the
wickedness of their fathers.[u] 3 They stood where
they were and read from the Book of the Law of

8:7 [i]Lev 10:11; 2Ch 17:7
8:9 [j]Ne 7:1,65, 70 [k]Dt 12:7,12; 16:14-15
8:10 [l]1Sa 25:8; Lk 14:12-14 [m]Lev 23:40; Dt 12:18; 16:11,14-15
8:12 [n]Est 9:22
8:16 [o]2Ki 14:13; Ne 12:39
8:17 [p]2Ch 7:8; 8:13; 30:21
8:18 [q]Dt 31:11 [r]Lev 23:36, 40; Nu 29:35
9:1 [s]Jos 7:6; 1Sa 4:12
9:2 [t]Ne 13:3,30 [u]Ezr 10:11; Ps 106:6

[a] 8 Or *God, translating it* [b] 15 See Lev. 23:37–40.

the LORD their God for a quarter of the day, and
spent another quarter in confession and in worshiping the LORD their God. [4]Standing on the stairs
9:4 were the Levites[v]—Jeshua, Bani, Kadmiel, Sheba-
[v]Ezr 10:23 niah, Bunni, Sherebiah, Bani and Kenani—who
called with loud voices to the LORD their God.
[5]And the Levites—Jeshua, Kadmiel, Bani,
Hashabneiah, Sherebiah, Hodiah, Shebaniah and
Pethahiah—said: "Stand up and praise the LORD
9:5 [w]Ps 78:4 your God,[w] who is from everlasting to everlasting.[a]"

"Blessed be your glorious name, and may it
9:6 be exalted above all blessing and praise. [6]You
[x]Dt 6:4 alone are the LORD.[x] You made the heavens,[y]
[y]2Ki 19:15 even the highest heavens, and all their starry
[z]Ge 1:1; Isa 37:16 host, the earth[z] and all that is on it, the seas[a]
[a]Ps 95:5 and all that is in them.[b] You give life to every-
[b]Dt 10:14 thing, and the multitudes of heaven worship
you.
[7]"You are the LORD God, who chose Abram
9:7 [c]Ge 11:31 and brought him out of Ur of the Chaldeans[c]
[d]Ge 17:5 and named him Abraham.[d] [8]You found his
heart faithful to you, and you made a covenant
9:8 with him to give to his descendants the land of
[e]Ge 15:18-21 the Canaanites, Hittites, Amorites, Perizzites,
[f]Jos 21:45 [g]Ge 15:6; Jebusites and Girgashites.[e] You have kept your
Ezr 9:15 promise[f] because you are righteous.[g]
9:9 [9]"You saw the suffering of our forefathers
[h]Ex 3:7 in Egypt;[h] you heard their cry at the Red
[i]Ex 14:10-30 Sea.[b][i] [10]You sent miraculous signs[j] and won-
9:10 ders against Pharaoh, against all his officials
[j]Ex 10:1 and all the people of his land, for you knew
[k]Jer 32:20; Da 9:15 how arrogantly the Egyptians treated them.
You made a name[k] for yourself, which
9:11 remains to this day. [11]You divided the sea
[l]Ex 14:21; Ps 78:13 before them,[l] so that they passed through it
[m]Ex 15:4-5, on dry ground, but you hurled their pursuers
10; Heb 11:29 into the depths, like a stone into mighty
waters.[m] [12]By day you led[n] them with a pillar
9:12 [n]Ex 15:13 of cloud,[o] and by night with a pillar of fire to
[o]Ex 13:21 give them light on the way they were to take.
9:13 [13]"You came down on Mount Sinai;[p] you
[p]Ex 19:11 spoke[q] to them from heaven. You gave them
[q]Ex 19:19 regulations and laws that are just[r] and right,
[r]Ps 119:137 [s]Ex 20:1 and decrees and commands that are good.[s]
[14]You made known to them your holy Sab-
9:14 bath[t] and gave them commands, decrees and
[t]Ge 2:3; Ex 20:8-11 laws through your servant Moses. [15]In their
hunger you gave them bread from heaven[u]
9:15 [u]Ex 16:4; and in their thirst you brought them water
Jn 6:31 from the rock;[v] you told them to go in and
[v]Ex 17:6; Nu 20:7-13 take possession of the land you had sworn
[w]Dt 1:8,21 with uplifted hand to give them.[w]
[16]"But they, our forefathers, became arro-
9:16 gant and stiff-necked, and did not obey your
[x]Dt 1:26-33; 31:29 commands.[x] [17]They refused to listen and
failed to remember[y] the miracles you per-
9:17 [y]Ps 78:42 formed among them. They became stiff-

A Community Prayer

NE 9:5-15

After hearing God's Law read "day after day" for seven days (Ne 8:18), the Jewish people are prepared to solidify their commitment to God. They come before him and pray one of the most meaningful and expressive prayers recorded in the Bible. They honor and praise God by recalling and reciting his acts of goodness and faithfulness to them through the years. Even after exile and hardship, they have not forgotten God's works in their lives, and they now realize he has not forgotten them either.

Their God was and is actively at work in their lives and in their nation. Love, patience, forgiveness and grace are displayed in God's actions on their behalf (Ne 9:17). As you read through this passage, note all the verbs that indicate God's active participation in the lives of the Israelites. Then recall that this same God is still active today in his people's lives, including yours.

[a]5 Or *God for ever and ever* [b]9 Hebrew *Yam Suph*; that is, Sea of Reeds

A Lesson in History

NE 9:16-31

The recently rededicated Israelites recount their *nation's history as they talk with* God in prayer. They acknowledge *the rebellion and sin of their ancestors and the compassion, patience and mercy of God. They speak gratefully of God's second and third and fourth chances* (Ne 9:28). *By rehearsing the specific ways God has helped, sustained and restored their nation in the past, they gain courage to take risks of faith in the immediate future.*

As these people learned, it is a *faith-producing exercise to recall and record the events of one's history, while acknowledging God's presence and intervention in and through it.* God can combine our knowledge of *where we have been* with *who we are now* to help us discover *what to do next.* Perhaps *you would like to record some of the turning points from your past, times then God was right there with you as well as times when he seemed absent. Then, as you look where you've been, also record where you're going and jot down some goals for your future.*

necked and in their rebellion appointed a
leader in order to return to their slavery.[z] But
you are a forgiving God, gracious and compassionate, slow to anger[a] and abounding in
love.[b] Therefore you did not desert them,[c]
18even when they cast for themselves an
image of a calf[d] and said, 'This is your god,
who brought you up out of Egypt,' or when
they committed awful blasphemies.
19"Because of your great compassion you
did not abandon them in the desert. By day the
pillar of cloud did not cease to guide them on
their path, nor the pillar of fire by night to
shine on the way they were to take. 20You gave
your good Spirit[e] to instruct them. You did not
withhold your manna[f] from their mouths, and
you gave them water[g] for their thirst. 21For
forty years you sustained them in the desert;
they lacked nothing,[h] their clothes did not
wear out nor did their feet become swollen.[i]
22"You gave them kingdoms and nations,
allotting to them even the remotest frontiers.
They took over the country of Sihon[a][j] king of
Heshbon and the country of Og king of
Bashan.[k] 23You made their sons as numerous
as the stars in the sky, and you brought them
into the land that you told their fathers to enter
and possess. 24Their sons went in and took
possession of the land.[l] You subdued before
them the Canaanites, who lived in the land;
you handed the Canaanites over to them,
along with their kings and the peoples of the
land, to deal with them as they pleased. 25They
captured fortified cities and fertile land; they
took possession of houses filled with all kinds
of good things, wells already dug, vineyards,
olive groves and fruit trees in abundance. They
ate to the full and were well-nourished;[m] they
reveled in your great goodness.[n]
26"But they were disobedient and rebelled
against you; they put your law behind their
backs.[o] They killed your prophets,[p] who had
admonished them in order to turn them back
to you; they committed awful blasphemies.[q]
27So you handed them over to their enemies,[r]
who oppressed them. But when they were
oppressed they cried out to you. From heaven
you heard them, and in your great compassion[s] you gave them deliverers, who rescued
them from the hand of their enemies.
28"But as soon as they were at rest, they
again did what was evil in your sight. Then
you abandoned them to the hand of their
enemies so that they ruled over them. And
when they cried out to you again, you heard
from heaven, and in your compassion you
delivered them[t] time after time.
29"You warned them to return to your law,

9:17 [z]Nu 14:1-4 [a]Ex 34:6 [b]Nu 14:17-19 [c]Ps 78:11
9:18 [d]Ex 32:4
9:20 [e]Nu 11:17; Isa 63:11,14 [f]Ex 16:15 [g]Ex 17:6
9:21 [h]Dt 2:7 [i]Dt 8:4
9:22 [j]Nu 21:21 [k]Nu 21:33
9:24 [l]Jos 11:23
9:25 [m]Dt 6:10-12 [n]Nu 13:27; Dt 32:12-15
9:26 [o]1Ki 14:9 [p]Mt 21:35-36 [q]Jdg 2:12-13
9:27 [r]Jdg 2:14 [s]Ps 106:45
9:28 [t]Ps 106:43

[a] *22* One Hebrew manuscript and Septuagint; most Hebrew manuscripts *Sihon, that is, the country of the*

but they became arrogant[u] and disobeyed
your commands. They sinned against your
ordinances, by which a man will live if he
obeys them.[v] Stubbornly they turned their
backs on you, became stiff-necked and
refused to listen.[w] 30For many years you were
patient with them. By your Spirit you admonished them through your prophets.[x] Yet they
paid no attention, so you handed them over
to the neighboring peoples. 31But in your
great mercy you did not put an end[y] to them
or abandon them, for you are a gracious and
merciful God.

32"Now therefore, O our God, the great,
mighty[z] and awesome God, who keeps his
covenant of love,[a] do not let all this hardship
seem trifling in your eyes—the hardship that
has come upon us, upon our kings and leaders, upon our priests and prophets, upon our
fathers and all your people, from the days of
the kings of Assyria until today. 33In all that
has happened to us, you have been just;[b] you
have acted faithfully, while we did wrong.[c]
34Our kings,[d] our leaders, our priests and our
fathers[e] did not follow your law; they did not
pay attention to your commands or the warnings you gave them. 35Even while they were
in their kingdom, enjoying your great goodness[f] to them in the spacious and fertile land
you gave them, they did not serve you[g] or
turn from their evil ways.

36"But see, we are slaves[h] today, slaves in
the land you gave our forefathers so they
could eat its fruit and the other good things it
produces. 37Because of our sins, its abundant
harvest goes to the kings you have placed
over us. They rule over our bodies and our
cattle as they please. We are in great distress.[i]

The Agreement of the People

38"In view of all this, we are making a binding
agreement,[j] putting it in writing,[k] and our leaders, our Levites and our priests are affixing their
seals to it."

10 Those who sealed it were:

Nehemiah the governor, the son of Hacaliah.
Zedekiah, 2Seraiah,[l] Azariah, Jeremiah,
3Pashhur,[m] Amariah, Malkijah,
4Hattush, Shebaniah, Malluch,
5Harim,[n] Meremoth, Obadiah,
6Daniel, Ginnethon, Baruch,
7Meshullam, Abijah, Mijamin,
8Maaziah, Bilgai and Shemaiah.
These were the priests.

9The Levites:[o]

Jeshua son of Azaniah, Binnui of the sons of
Henadad, Kadmiel,
10and their associates: Shebaniah,

9:29 [u]Ps 5:5; Isa 2:11; Jer 43:2 [v]Dt 30:16 [w]Zec 7:11-12
9:30 [x]2Ki 17:13-18; 2Ch 36:16
9:31 [y]Isa 48:9; Jer 4:27
9:32 [z]Ps 24:8 [a]Dt 7:9
9:33 [b]Ge 18:25 [c]Jer 44:3; Da 9:7-8,14
9:34 [d]2Ki 23:11 [e]Jer 44:17
9:35 [f]Isa 63:7 [g]Dt 28:45-48
9:36 [h]Dt 28:48; Ezr 9:9
9:37 [i]Dt 28:33; La 5:5
9:38 [j]2Ch 23:16 [k]Isa 44:5
10:2 [l]Ezr 2:2
10:3 [m]1Ch 9:12
10:5 [n]1Ch 24:8
10:9 [o]Ne 12:1

Then and Now

NE 9:36–37

The people of Israel admit that their past kings and leaders failed to follow God's directives. Right when God is blessing them with spacious territories and abundant harvests, they are refusing to acknowledge his existence. They insist on doing what they want to do, when they want to do it, even when those actions directly oppose God's will.

The people know their current circumstances are the result of their ancestors' sinful choices. Though they now live in the land promised to Abraham and his descendants, they have no real authority. The Persian rulers take their profits and draft their sons into military service.

Even today, there is only tenuous peace in Israel. Enemies of the Jews still threaten them on every side. Jew and Gentile alike still look for peace but refuse to acknowledge the Prince of Peace, the only One who can bring harmony and restoration and the only One who can deliver us from our "great distress" (Ne 9:37).

An Oath and a Curse

NE 10:28–29

In Old Testament times, it was not unusual to bind a promise with an oath and a curse. The oath provided convincing evidence that a person would do what was promised. An added curse reinforced the oath, but it was not necessary. The curse invited injury or retribution if the person did not adhere to the commitment.

The Israelites actually ask for judgment, for rough treatment, if they do not keep their promise to obey the Law (Ne 10:29). Perhaps this is why Nehemiah is quite harsh with them when he discovers they have ignored their promises to God (Ne 13:25).

God gives the Israelites the privilege and the responsibility to choose how they will live—with integrity, keeping their vows, or with duplicity, reneging on their promises. They make the wrong choice. In the New Testament, Jesus encourages people not to take oaths. Instead, we should live honorably and let our word be our vow (Mt 5:33–37).

Hodiah, Kelita, Pelaiah, Hanan,
11 Mica, Rehob, Hashabiah,
12 Zaccur, Sherebiah, Shebaniah,
13 Hodiah, Bani and Beninu.

14 The leaders of the people:
Parosh, Pahath-Moab, Elam, Zattu, Bani,
15 Bunni, Azgad, Bebai,
16 Adonijah, Bigvai, Adin,[p]
17 Ater, Hezekiah, Azzur,
18 Hodiah, Hashum, Bezai,
19 Hariph, Anathoth, Nebai,
20 Magpiash, Meshullam, Hezir,[q]
21 Meshezabel, Zadok, Jaddua,
22 Pelatiah, Hanan, Anaiah,
23 Hoshea, Hananiah,[r] Hasshub,
24 Hallohesh, Pilha, Shobek,
25 Rehum, Hashabnah, Maaseiah,
26 Ahiah, Hanan, Anan,
27 Malluch, Harim and Baanah.

28 "The rest of the people—priests, Levites,
gatekeepers, singers, temple servants[s] and all
who separated themselves from the neighboring peoples[t] for the sake of the Law of
God, together with their wives and all their
sons and daughters who are able to understand— 29 all these now join their brothers the
nobles, and bind themselves with a curse and
an oath[u] to follow the Law of God given
through Moses the servant of God and to
obey carefully all the commands, regulations
and decrees of the LORD our Lord.
30 "We promise not to give our daughters in
marriage to the peoples around us or take
their daughters for our sons.[v]
31 "When the neighboring peoples bring
merchandise or grain to sell on the Sabbath,[w]
we will not buy from them on the Sabbath or
on any holy day. Every seventh year we will
forgo working the land[x] and will cancel all
debts.[y]
32 "We assume the responsibility for carrying out the commands to give a third of a
shekel[a] each year for the service of the house
of our God: 33 for the bread set out on the
table;[z] for the regular grain offerings and
burnt offerings; for the offerings on the Sabbaths, New Moon[a] festivals and appointed
feasts; for the holy offerings; for sin offerings
to make atonement for Israel; and for all the
duties of the house of our God.[b]
34 "We—the priests, the Levites and the people—have cast lots[c] to determine when each
of our families is to bring to the house of our
God at set times each year a contribution of
wood[d] to burn on the altar of the LORD our
God, as it is written in the Law.
35 "We also assume responsibility for bring-

10:16 [p]Ezr 8:6
10:20 [q]1Ch 24:15
10:23 [r]Ne 7:2
10:28 [s]Ps 135:1 [t]2Ch 6:26; Ne 9:2
10:29 [u]Nu 5:21; Ps 119:106
10:30 [v]Ex 34:16; Dt 7:3; Ne 13:23
10:31 [w]Ne 13:16, 18; Jer 17:27; Eze 23:38; Am 8:5 [x]Ex 23:11; Lev 25:1-7 [y]Dt 15:1
10:33 [z]Lev 24:6 [a]Nu 10:10; Ps 81:3; Isa 1:14 [b]2Ch 24:5
10:34 [c]Lev 16:8 [d]Ne 13:31

[a] 32 That is, about 1/8 ounce (about 4 grams)

ing to the house of the LORD each year the firstfruits[e] of our crops and of every fruit tree.[f]
36"As it is also written in the Law, we will bring the firstborn[g] of our sons and of our cattle, of our herds and of our flocks to the house of our God, to the priests ministering there.[h]
37"Moreover, we will bring to the storerooms of the house of our God, to the priests, the first of our ground meal, of our ⌊grain⌋ offerings, of the fruit of all our trees and of our new wine and oil.[i] And we will bring a tithe[j] of our crops to the Levites,[k] for it is the Levites who collect the tithes in all the towns where we work.[l] 38A priest descended from Aaron is to accompany the Levites when they receive the tithes, and the Levites are to bring a tenth of the tithes[m] up to the house of our God, to the storerooms of the treasury. 39The people of Israel, including the Levites, are to bring their contributions of grain, new wine and oil to the storerooms where the articles for the sanctuary are kept and where the ministering priests, the gatekeepers and the singers stay.

"We will not neglect the house of our God."[n]

The New Residents of Jerusalem

11 Now the leaders of the people settled in Jerusalem, and the rest of the people cast lots to bring one out of every ten to live in Jerusalem,[o] the holy city,[p] while the remaining nine were to stay in their own towns.[q] 2The people commended all the men who volunteered to live in Jerusalem.

3These are the provincial leaders who settled in Jerusalem (now some Israelites, priests, Levites, temple servants and descendants of Solomon's servants lived in the towns of Judah, each on his own property in the various towns,[r] 4while other people from both Judah and Benjamin[s] lived in Jerusalem):[t]

From the descendants of Judah:

> Athaiah son of Uzziah, the son of Zechariah, the son of Amariah, the son of Shephatiah, the son of Mahalalel, a descendant of Perez; 5and Maaseiah son of Baruch, the son of Col-Hozeh, the son of Hazaiah, the son of Adaiah, the son of Joiarib, the son of Zechariah, a descendant of Shelah. 6The descendants of Perez who lived in Jerusalem totaled 468 able men.

7From the descendants of Benjamin:

> Sallu son of Meshullam, the son of Joed, the son of Pedaiah, the son of Kolaiah, the son of Maaseiah, the son of Ithiel, the son of Jeshaiah, 8and his followers, Gabbai and Sallai—928 men. 9Joel son of Zicri was their chief officer, and Judah son of Hassenuah was over the Second District of the city.

10From the priests:

10:35 [e]Ex 22:29; 23:19; Nu 18:12 [f]Dt 26:1-11
10:36 [g]Ex 13:2; Nu 18:14-16 [h]Ne 13:31
10:37 [i]Lev 23:17; Nu 18:12 [j]Lev 27:30; Nu 18:21 [k]Dt 14:22-29 [l]Eze 44:30
10:38 [m]Nu 18:26
10:39 [n]Dt 12:6; Ne 13:11,12
11:1 [o]Ne 7:4 [p]ver 18; Isa 48:2; 52:1; 64:10; Zec 14:20-21 [q]Ne 7:73
11:3 [r]1Ch 9:2-3; Ezr 2:1
11:4 [s]Ezr 1:5 [t]Ezr 2:70

I can think of many "shadowy" moments in my life. And I know, if we could see the joy of the morning, we would make it through those dark nights. I think about how differently I would have handled my dark time if Christ had handed me my baby boy and said, "Sheila, this is your son. He won't be born for a few more years. Now look at him. He needs you to find courage to get up and get emotionally well." How much easier it would have been to hold that precious life, look into those eyes and find a reason to go on. But that didn't happen. Instead, Christ was there. And he asked me to get well and to believe, in faith, that he would make the crooked in my life straight . . . Whatever you're going through at the moment, remember this is not the end of your story. We are morning people, called to live by faith and not by sight, to lift our hearts to God in the darkness because we have the promise of the morning.

—Sheila Walsh

Regulating the Singers

NE 11:23

Music has always played an important role in Israel's daily life. They play instruments at family parties (Ge 31:27), dance with music to welcome home war heroes (1Sa 18:6), and crown their kings to the sound of music (1Ki 1:39–40). When King David outlines the Levites' various tasks and appoints some as temple singers, he places a high value on the temple's music ministry (see the note on 1Ch 6:31–32, page 637). He establishes musicians, singers and instrumentalists as a professional part of Israelite worship. The king of Persia encourages the temple singers by "regulat[ing] their daily activity," which probably means giving them a stipend for each day's work. Persia's king wants to maintain peace within his expanding kingdom, so he attempts to keep his subjects and their God or gods happy. As amazing as it sometimes seems, God can use anything or anyone, even a pagan king, to advance his work and provide for his children's spiritual, emotional and physical well-being.

Jedaiah; the son of Joiarib; Jakin; [11]Seraiah[u] son of Hilkiah, the son of Meshullam, the son of Zadok, the son of Meraioth, the son of Ahitub,[v] supervisor in the house of God, [12]and their associates, who carried on work for the temple—822 men; Adaiah son of Jeroham, the son of Pelaliah, the son of Amzi, the son of Zechariah, the son of Pashhur, the son of Malkijah, [13]and his associates, who were heads of families—242 men; Amashsai son of Azarel, the son of Ahzai, the son of Meshillemoth, the son of Immer, [14]and his[a] associates, who were able men—128. Their chief officer was Zabdiel son of Haggedolim.

[15]From the Levites:

Shemaiah son of Hasshub, the son of Azrikam, the son of Hashabiah, the son of Bunni; [16]Shabbethai[w] and Jozabad,[x] two of the heads of the Levites, who had charge of the outside work of the house of God; [17]Mattaniah[y] son of Mica, the son of Zabdi, the son of Asaph,[z] the director who led in thanksgiving and prayer; Bakbukiah, second among his associates; and Abda son of Shammua, the son of Galal, the son of Jeduthun.[a] [18]The Levites in the holy city[b] totaled 284.

[19]The gatekeepers:

Akkub, Talmon and their associates, who kept watch at the gates—172 men.

[20]The rest of the Israelites, with the priests and Levites, were in all the towns of Judah, each on his ancestral property.

[21]The temple servants[c] lived on the hill of Ophel, and Ziha and Gishpa were in charge of them.

[22]The chief officer of the Levites in Jerusalem was Uzzi son of Bani, the son of Hashabiah, the son of Mattaniah,[d] the son of Mica. Uzzi was one of Asaph's descendants, who were the singers responsible for the service of the house of God. [23]The singers[e] were under the king's orders, which regulated their daily activity.

[24]Pethahiah son of Meshezabel, one of the descendants of Zerah[f] son of Judah, was the king's agent in all affairs relating to the people.

[25]As for the villages with their fields, some of the people of Judah lived in Kiriath Arba[g] and its surrounding settlements, in Dibon[h] and its settlements, in Jekabzeel and its villages, [26]in Jeshua, in Moladah, in Beth Pelet,[i] [27]in Hazar Shual, in Beersheba[j] and its settlements, [28]in Ziklag,[k] in Meconah and its settlements, [29]in En Rimmon, in Zorah,[l] in Jarmuth,[m] [30]Zanoah, Adullam[n] and their villages, in Lachish[o] and its fields, and in Azekah[p] and its settlements. So they were living all the way from Beersheba[q] to the Valley of Hinnom.

11:11 [u]2Ki 25:18; Ezr 2:2 [v]Ezr 7:2
11:16 [w]Ezr 10:15 [x]Ezr 8:33
11:17 [y]1Ch 9:15; Ne 12:8 [z]2Ch 5:12 [a]1Ch 25:1
11:18 [b]Rev 21:2
11:21 [c]Ezr 2:43; Ne 3:26
11:22 [d]1Ch 9:15
11:23 [e]Ne 7:44
11:24 [f]Ge 38:30
11:25 [g]Ge 35:27; Jos 14:15 [h]Nu 21:30
11:26 [i]Jos 15:27
11:27 [j]Ge 21:14
11:28 [k]1Sa 27:6
11:29 [l]Jos 15:33 [m]Jos 10:3
11:30 [n]Jos 15:35 [o]Jos 10:3 [p]Jos 10:10 [q]Jos 15:28

[a] *14* Most Septuagint manuscripts; Hebrew *their*

[31]The descendants of the Benjamites from Geba[r]
lived in Micmash,[s] Aija, Bethel and its settlements, [32]in Anathoth,[t] Nob[u] and Ananiah, [33]in
Hazor,[v] Ramah and Gittaim,[w] [34]in Hadid, Zeboim[x]
and Neballat, [35]in Lod and Ono,[y] and in the Valley
of the Craftsmen.
[36]Some of the divisions of the Levites of Judah
settled in Benjamin.

Priests and Levites

12 These were the priests[z] and Levites who
returned with Zerubbabel[a] son of Shealtiel
and with Jeshua:[b]
Seraiah,[c] Jeremiah, Ezra,
[2]Amariah, Malluch, Hattush,
[3]Shecaniah, Rehum, Meremoth,
[4]Iddo,[d] Ginnethon,[a] Abijah,[e]
[5]Mijamin,[b] Moadiah, Bilgah,
[6]Shemaiah, Joiarib, Jedaiah,[f]
[7]Sallu, Amok, Hilkiah and Jedaiah.
These were the leaders of the priests and their
associates in the days of Jeshua.
[8]The Levites were Jeshua, Binnui, Kadmiel,
Sherebiah, Judah, and also Mattaniah,[g] who,
together with his associates, was in charge of the
songs of thanksgiving. [9]Bakbukiah and Unni, their
associates, stood opposite them in the services.
[10]Jeshua was the father of Joiakim, Joiakim the
father of Eliashib,[h] Eliashib the father of Joiada,
[11]Joiada the father of Jonathan, and Jonathan the
father of Jaddua.
[12]In the days of Joiakim, these were the heads
of the priestly families:
of Seraiah's family, Meraiah;
of Jeremiah's, Hananiah;
[13]of Ezra's, Meshullam;
of Amariah's, Jehohanan;
[14]of Malluch's, Jonathan;
of Shecaniah's,[c] Joseph;
[15]of Harim's, Adna;
of Meremoth's,[d] Helkai;
[16]of Iddo's,[i] Zechariah;
of Ginnethon's, Meshullam;
[17]of Abijah's, Zicri;
of Miniamin's and of Moadiah's, Piltai;
[18]of Bilgah's, Shammua;
of Shemaiah's, Jehonathan;
[19]of Joiarib's, Mattenai;
of Jedaiah's, Uzzi;
[20]of Sallu's, Kallai;
of Amok's, Eber;
[21]of Hilkiah's, Hashabiah;
of Jedaiah's, Nethanel.
[22]The family heads of the Levites in the days of
Eliashib, Joiada, Johanan and Jaddua, as well as

11:31 [r]Jos 21:17; Isa 10:29 [s]1Sa 13:2
11:32 [t]Jos 21:18; Isa 10:30 [u]1Sa 21:1
11:33 [v]Jos 11:1 [w]2Sa 4:3
11:34 [x]1Sa 13:18
11:35 [y]1Ch 8:12
12:1 [z]Ne 10:1-8 [a]1Ch 3:19 [b]Ezr 2:2 [c]Ezr 2:2
12:4 [d]Zec 1:1 [e]Lk 1:5
12:6 [f]1Ch 24:7
12:8 [g]Ne 11:17
12:10 [h]Ezr 10:24
12:16 [i]ver 4

[a] *4* Many Hebrew manuscripts and Vulgate (see also Neh. 12:16); most Hebrew manuscripts *Ginnethoi* [b] *5* A variant of *Miniamin* [c] *14* Very many Hebrew manuscripts, some Septuagint manuscripts and Syriac (see also Neh. 12:3); most Hebrew manuscripts *Shebaniah's* [d] *15* Some Septuagint manuscripts (see also Neh. 12:3); Hebrew *Meraioth's*

What a Job!

NE 12:8

Mattaniah, a relative of Asaph the psalm writer (Ne 11:17; see title of Ps 50), is "in charge of the songs of thanksgiving" (Ne 12:8). He has associates to help him with this "thank-full" job. What a job description they have: to write, compose and sing psalms and hymns of thanksgiving to God. (The book of Psalms is used as a hymnal or prayer book by the Israelite congregation, especially after the exile.) In addition, Mattaniah and his associates likely direct the choirs that perform for special celebrations (Ne 12:31, 38).

Some believe Psalm 147 was composed for the choir to sing at the dedication of the restored wall of Jerusalem. Read Psalm 147; then picture in your mind two great choirs marching along the newly constructed wall of Jerusalem, singing this psalm. What a sight! Can you see it? Can you hear it?

Antiphonal Praise

NE 12:24

King David introduces organized music, with professional musicians and singers from the Levite tribe, into the Israelites' worship services (1Ch 6:31). David's son Solomon follows through with his father's plans once the new temple is completed (2Ch 8:14). These temple musicians honor God with dignity, variety and creativity. One of the worship methods used by temple singers and worship leaders is antiphonal praise—songs or chants rendered responsively.

Psalm 118 may be one of the antiphonal praise songs used by the singers at the dedication of the wall. With the choir divided into two groups, one standing opposite the other, one side sings one line and the other side responds with: "His love endures forever."

those of the priests, were recorded in the reign of
Darius the Persian. 23 The family heads among the
descendants of Levi up to the time of Johanan son
of Eliashib were recorded in the book of the annals.
24 And the leaders of the Levites[j] were Hashabiah,
Sherebiah, Jeshua son of Kadmiel, and their associates, who stood opposite them to give praise and
thanksgiving, one section responding to the other,
as prescribed by David the man of God.

25 Mattaniah, Bakbukiah, Obadiah, Meshullam,
Talmon and Akkub were gatekeepers who guarded the storerooms at the gates. 26 They served in
the days of Joiakim son of Jeshua, the son of Jozadak, and in the days of Nehemiah the governor
and of Ezra the priest and scribe.

Dedication of the Wall of Jerusalem

27 At the dedication[k] of the wall of Jerusalem, the
Levites were sought out from where they lived and
were brought to Jerusalem to celebrate joyfully the
dedication with songs of thanksgiving and with the
music of cymbals,[l] harps and lyres.[m] 28 The singers
also were brought together from the region around
Jerusalem—from the villages of the Netophathites,[n]
29 from Beth Gilgal, and from the area of Geba and
Azmaveth, for the singers had built villages for
themselves around Jerusalem. 30 When the priests
and Levites had purified themselves ceremonially,
they purified the people,[o] the gates and the wall.
31 I had the leaders of Judah go up on top[a] of the
wall. I also assigned two large choirs to give
thanks. One was to proceed on top[b] of the wall to
the right, toward the Dung Gate.[p] 32 Hoshaiah and
half the leaders of Judah followed them, 33 along
with Azariah, Ezra, Meshullam, 34 Judah, Benjamin,[q] Shemaiah, Jeremiah, 35 as well as some
priests with trumpets,[r] and also Zechariah son of
Jonathan, the son of Shemaiah, the son of Mattaniah, the son of Micaiah, the son of Zaccur, the
son of Asaph, 36 and his associates—Shemaiah,
Azarel, Milalai, Gilalai, Maai, Nethanel, Judah
and Hanani—with musical instruments[s] ⌊prescribed by⌋ David the man of God.[t] Ezra[u] the
scribe led the procession. 37 At the Fountain Gate[v]
they continued directly up the steps of the City of
David on the ascent to the wall and passed above
the house of David to the Water Gate[w] on the east.

38 The second choir proceeded in the opposite
direction. I followed them on top[c] of the wall,
together with half the people—past the Tower of
the Ovens[x] to the Broad Wall,[y] 39 over the Gate of
Ephraim,[z] the Jeshanah[d] Gate,[a] the Fish Gate,[b] the
Tower of Hananel[c] and the Tower of the Hundred,[d]
as far as the Sheep Gate.[e] At the Gate of the Guard
they stopped.

40 The two choirs that gave thanks then took
their places in the house of God; so did I, together with half the officials, 41 as well as the priests—

12:24 [j]Ezr 2:40
12:27 [k]Dt 20:5 [l]2Sa 6:5 [m]1Ch 15:16, 28; 25:6; Ps 92:3
12:28 [n]1Ch 2:54; 9:16
12:30 [o]Ex 19:10; Job 1:5
12:31 [p]Ne 2:13
12:34 [q]Ezr 1:5
12:35 [r]Ezr 3:10
12:36 [s]1Ch 15:16 [t]2Ch 8:14 [u]Ezr 7:6
12:37 [v]Ne 2:14; 3:15 [w]Ne 3:26
12:38 [x]Ne 3:11 [y]Ne 3:8
12:39 [z]2Ki 14:13; Ne 8:16 [a]Ne 3:6 [b]2Ch 33:14; Ne 3:3 [c]Ne 3:1 [d]Ne 3:1 [e]Ne 3:1

[a] *31* Or *go alongside* [b] *31* Or *proceed alongside* [c] *38* Or *them alongside* [d] *39* Or *Old*

Eliakim, Maaseiah, Miniamin, Micaiah, Elioenai,
Zechariah and Hananiah with their trumpets—
42and also Maaseiah, Shemaiah, Eleazar, Uzzi,
Jehohanan, Malkijah, Elam and Ezer. The choirs
sang under the direction of Jezrahiah. 43And on
that day they offered great sacrifices, rejoicing
because God had given them great joy. The
women and children also rejoiced. The sound of
rejoicing in Jerusalem could be heard far away.
12:44 44At that time men were appointed to be in
[f]Ne 13:4,13 charge of the storerooms[f] for the contributions,
[g]Lev 27:30 firstfruits and tithes.[g] From the fields around the
[h]Dt 18:8 towns they were to bring into the storerooms the
portions required by the Law for the priests and
the Levites, for Judah was pleased with the ministering priests and Levites.[h] 45They performed the
service of their God and the service of purification,
12:45 as did also the singers and gatekeepers, according
[i]1Ch 25:1; 2Ch 8:14 to the commands of David[i] and his son Solomon.[j]
46For long ago, in the days of David and Asaph,[k]
[j]1Ch 6:31; 23:5 there had been directors for the singers and for the
songs of praise[l] and thanksgiving to God. 47So in
12:46 [k]2Ch 35:15 the days of Zerubbabel and of Nehemiah, all Isra-
[l]2Ch 29:27; el contributed the daily portions for the singers
Ps 137:4 and gatekeepers. They also set aside the portion
12:47 for the other Levites, and the Levites set aside the
[m]Nu 18:21; Dt 18:8 portion for the descendants of Aaron.[m]

Nehemiah's Final Reforms

13 On that day the Book of Moses was read
aloud in the hearing of the people and there
it was found written that no Ammonite or Moab-
13:1 ite should ever be admitted into the assembly of
[n]ver 23; God,[n] 2because they had not met the Israelites
Dt 23:3 with food and water but had hired Balaam[o] to call
13:2 a curse down on them.[p] (Our God, however,
[o]Nu 22:3-11 turned the curse into a blessing.)[q] 3When the peo-
[p]Nu 23:7; Dt 23:3 ple heard this law, they excluded from Israel all
[q]Nu 23:11; who were of foreign descent.[r]
Dt 23:4-5 4Before this, Eliashib the priest had been put in
13:3 charge of the storerooms[s] of the house of our God.
[r]ver 23; He was closely associated with Tobiah,[t] 5and he
Ne 9:2 had provided him with a large room formerly used
13:4 to store the grain offerings and incense and temple
[s]Ne 12:44 articles, and also the tithes[u] of grain, new wine and
[t]Ne 2:10 oil prescribed for the Levites, singers and gate-
13:5 keepers, as well as the contributions for the priests.
[u]Lev 27:30; 6But while all this was going on, I was not in
Nu 18:21 Jerusalem, for in the thirty-second year of Arta-
13:6 xerxes[v] king of Babylon I had returned to the
[v]Ne 2:6; 5:14 king. Some time later I asked his permission 7and
13:7 came back to Jerusalem. Here I learned about the
[w]Ezr 10:24 evil thing Eliashib[w] had done in providing Tobiah
13:8 a room in the courts of the house of God. 8I was
[x]Mt 21:12- greatly displeased and threw all Tobiah's house-
13; Jn 2:13-16 hold goods out of the room.[x] 9I gave orders to
purify the rooms,[y] and then I put back into them
13:9 the equipment of the house of God, with the grain
[y]1Ch 23:28; 2Ch 29:5 offerings and the incense.
13:10 10I also learned that the portions assigned to the
[z]Dt 12:19 Levites had not been given to them,[z] and that all

Do not cheat thy
Heart and tell her,
"Grief will pass away,
Hope for fairer times in future,
And forget to-day."
Tell her, if you will, that sorrow
Need not come in vain;
Tell her that the lesson taught her
Far outweighs the pain.

—Adelaide Ann Procter (1825–1864)

Keeping the Sabbath

NE 13:15-18

During Nehemiah's 12 years as Judah's governor (Ne 5:14), he encourages the Israelites to stay true to God. He then returns to Persia. "Some time later" (Ne 13:6-7) he travels back to Jerusalem to discover that the Israelites have reverted to their God-ignoring ways.

One Sabbath day, Nehemiah sees men making wine and hauling goods to Jerusalem to sell. They know better: They had listened to the reading of God's Law and had promised to obey its commands (Ne 10:29,31). It seems their greed drives them to work "overtime." God had established the Sabbath rest day as a specific time to focus on their covenant relationship with him (Ex 20:8-10). But the people again violate God's protective directives. Nehemiah quickly and resolutely sets them straight (Ne 13:19-22).

Today we live under the new covenant of grace, and every day is a day to concentrate on God. However, out of love for our Lord, we choose to set aside specific times to worship him with other believers (Heb 10:25).

the Levites and singers responsible for the service
had gone back to their own fields. 11 So I rebuked
the officials and asked them, "Why is the house of
God neglected?"[a] Then I called them together and
stationed them at their posts.
12 All Judah brought the tithes[b] of grain, new
wine and oil into the storerooms.[c] 13 I put Shelemiah the priest, Zadok the scribe, and a Levite
named Pedaiah in charge of the storerooms and
made Hanan son of Zaccur, the son of Mattaniah,
their assistant, because these men were considered trustworthy. They were made responsible for
distributing the supplies to their brothers.[d]

14 Remember[e] me for this, O my God, and do not
blot out what I have so faithfully done for the
house of my God and its services.

15 In those days I saw men in Judah treading
winepresses on the Sabbath and bringing in grain
and loading it on donkeys, together with wine,
grapes, figs and all other kinds of loads. And they
were bringing all this into Jerusalem on the Sabbath.[f] Therefore I warned them against selling food
on that day. 16 Men from Tyre who lived in Jerusalem were bringing in fish and all kinds of merchandise and selling them in Jerusalem on the Sabbath[g] to the people of Judah. 17 I rebuked the nobles
of Judah and said to them, "What is this wicked
thing you are doing—desecrating the Sabbath day?
18 Didn't your forefathers do the same things, so that
our God brought all this calamity upon us and
upon this city? Now you are stirring up more wrath
against Israel by desecrating the Sabbath."[h]
19 When evening shadows fell on the gates of Jerusalem before the Sabbath,[i] I ordered the doors to
be shut and not opened until the Sabbath was
over. I stationed some of my own men at the gates
so that no load could be brought in on the Sabbath
day. 20 Once or twice the merchants and sellers of
all kinds of goods spent the night outside Jerusalem. 21 But I warned them and said, "Why do you
spend the night by the wall? If you do this again, I
will lay hands on you." From that time on they no
longer came on the Sabbath. 22 Then I commanded
the Levites to purify themselves and go and guard
the gates in order to keep the Sabbath day holy.

Remember[j] me for this also, O my God, and
show mercy to me according to your great love.

23 Moreover, in those days I saw men of Judah
who had married[k] women from Ashdod, Ammon
and Moab.[l] 24 Half of their children spoke the language of Ashdod or the language of one of the
other peoples, and did not know how to speak the
language of Judah. 25 I rebuked them and called
curses down on them. I beat some of the men and
pulled out their hair. I made them take an oath[m]
in God's name and said: "You are not to give your
daughters in marriage to their sons, nor are you to
take their daughters in marriage for your sons or
for yourselves. 26 Was it not because of marriages

13:11 [a]Ne 10:37-39; Hag 1:1-9
13:12 [b]2Ch 31:6 [c]1Ki 7:51; Ne 10:37-39; Mal 3:10
13:13 [d]Ne 12:44; Ac 6:1-5
13:14 [e]Ge 8:1
13:15 [f]Ex 20:8-11; 34:21; Dt 5:12-15; Ne 10:31
13:16 [g]Ne 10:31
13:18 [h]Ne 10:31; Jer 17:21-23
13:19 [i]Lev 23:32
13:22 [j]Ge 8:1; Ne 12:30
13:23 [k]Ezr 9:1-2; Mal 2:11 [l]ver 1; Ne 10:30
13:25 [m]Ezr 10:5

like these that Solomon king of Israel sinned?
13:26 Among the many nations there was no king like
[n]1Ki 3:13; him.[n] He was loved by his God,[o] and God made
2Ch 1:12 him king over all Israel, but even he was led into
[o]2Sa 12:25 [p]1Ki 11:3 sin by foreign women.[p] 27 Must we hear now that
you too are doing all this terrible wickedness and
13:27 [q]Ezr 9:14; are being unfaithful to our God by marrying[q] for-
10:2 eign women?"
13:28 28 One of the sons of Joiada son of Eliashib[r] the
[r]Ezr 10:24 high priest was son-in-law to Sanballat[s] the Horo-
[s]Ne 2:10 nite. And I drove him away from me.

13:29 29 Remember[t] them, O my God, because they
[t]Ne 6:14 defiled the priestly office and the covenant of the
priesthood and of the Levites.

30 So I purified the priests and the Levites of
13:30 [u]Ne 10:30 everything foreign,[u] and assigned them duties,
each to his own task. 31 I also made provision for
13:31 [v]Ne 10:34 contributions of wood[v] at designated times, and
[w]ver 14,22; Ge 8:1 for the firstfruits.

Remember[w] me with favor, O my God.

Remember Me

NE 13:31

"Remember me with favor, O my God." Not just *a plea for God to keep track of his deeds, these words represent Nehemiah's life-long desire to serve God. Nehemiah is not asking God to remember him for his accomplishment of rebuilding Jerusalem's wall. Instead, he asks God to remember him for his passion for teaching the people to worship God (Ne 13:8–11), to honor God and his Law (Ne 13:15–22), and to remain pure and dedicated to God (Ne 13:26,30).*

Nehemiah is intentional about the way he lives. He longs to know God, which is evidenced by the time he spends in prayer. He chooses to please God, which is proven by the risks of faith he takes. He determines to serve God, which is confirmed by his willingness to leave a prestigious job. He desires to influence others for God, which is revealed by his commitment to inspiring spiritual revival.

God doesn't forget one of his children. Not you, not Nehemiah. He answers Nehemiah's prayer by including his story in the Bible. One generation after another reads his story and is inspired to be intentional about following God, just like Nehemiah.

The preservation of God's people.

God's name is never mentioned in this historical account of the events that lead to the establishment of the Jewish feast of Purim. Yet God's action behind the scenes is unmistakable as two faithful Jews risk their lives to save their people living in exile in Persia. Esther comes to the forefront when the Persian king chooses her to be his new queen. Courageously Esther heeds the advice of her cousin and foils the plot of a racist prince. Through God's providence the tables are turned and God's people are spared.

This profile of Esther's courage contains timeless lessons. We're amazed at Vashti's bold unwillingness to be exploited by her husband, even though he is king (Est 1). We thrill at the selfless actions of a caring relative who adopts Esther as his own child (Est 2:5-7). We enjoy reading of Esther's beauty regimen (Est 2:8-9). Her acceptance of Mordecai's advice splendidly models the importance of listening and learning from godly mentors (Est 4:12-17). And we marvel at Esther's brave willingness to put her life on the line and to use her influence with the king to help her people (Est 5:1–8:9).

Ultimately Queen Esther institutes the celebration of Purim to keep alive the memory of the preservation of the Jews (Est 9:17-32). Reasons to celebrate are abundant for us too when we recognize God's hand in the framework of the events that shape our lives. God took care of Esther; he will take care of us as well.

Quick Study

Author
Unknown.

Date Written
Sometime between 460 and 350 B.C.

Setting
Persia.

Key Passage
Esther 4:14 "Who knows but that you have come to royal position for such a time as this?"

Outline

Queen Vashti deposed.
Est 1

Esther becomes queen.
Est 2:1–18

Mordecai discovers a conspiracy.
Est 2:19–23

Haman devises a plot.
Est 3

Esther's brave actions.
Est 4–7

The king issues a new edict.
Est 8

The Jews are saved.
Est 9:1–17

Institution of the feast of Purim.
Est 9:19–32

Mordecai is honored.
Est 10

The Women of Esther

☙ **Vashti**	*Deposed as queen because of her defiance.* Est 1; 2:1 (page 1343)
☙ **Esther**	*The heroine of the story.* Est 2:7–9:32 (page 1344)
Zeresh	*Wiley Haman's wife.* Est 5:10,14; 6:13

☙ Denotes a sketch written about this character

Refusing to Obey

EST 1:1-17

Queen Vashti's refusal to obey a command from the king precipitates the story of Esther. The author gives us few hints to help us evaluate Vashti's decision. Some Bible students believe she violated the marriage covenant by her refusal. Others see her dilemma from a very different perspective. Perhaps the king's party was little more than a drunken brawl, and the king only wished to show her off as his ultimate prize. Perhaps she was to make her appearance wearing only her crown or she was to appear unveiled (a shameful thing in that culture). Regardless, Vashti knew if she was paraded before a group of drunken men, she would be seen only as an object of lust.

Acts 4:13-21 clearly reveals that there are situations in which divine and human purposes are in opposition to each other. In those instances we can choose God's way. However, that does not mean we will be protected from the consequences of our decision to act righteously in the face of evil. Vashti lost her position as queen when she refused to appear as she was commanded (see character sketch for Vashti on page 1343).

Queen Vashti Deposed

1 This is what happened during the time of Xerxes,[a][a] the Xerxes who ruled over 127
provinces[b] stretching from India to Cush[b]:[c] 2At
that time King Xerxes reigned from his royal
throne in the citadel of Susa,[d] 3and in the third
year of his reign he gave a banquet[e] for all his
nobles and officials. The military leaders of Persia and Media, the princes, and the nobles of the
provinces were present.
4For a full 180 days he displayed the vast wealth
of his kingdom and the splendor and glory of his
majesty. 5When these days were over, the king
gave a banquet, lasting seven days,[f] in the
enclosed garden[g] of the king's palace, for all the
people from the least to the greatest, who were in
the citadel of Susa. 6The garden had hangings of
white and blue linen, fastened with cords of white
linen and purple material to silver rings on marble pillars. There were couches[h] of gold and silver on a mosaic pavement of porphyry, marble,
mother-of-pearl and other costly stones. 7Wine
was served in goblets of gold, each one different
from the other, and the royal wine was abundant,
in keeping with the king's liberality.[i] 8By the
king's command each guest was allowed to drink
in his own way, for the king instructed all the
wine stewards to serve each man what he wished.
9Queen Vashti also gave a banquet[j] for the
women in the royal palace of King Xerxes.
10On the seventh day, when King Xerxes was in
high spirits[k] from wine,[l] he commanded the sev-
en eunuchs who served him—Mehuman, Biztha,
Harbona,[m] Bigtha, Abagtha, Zethar and Carcas—
11to bring[n] before him Queen Vashti, wearing her
royal crown, in order to display her beauty[o] to the
people and nobles, for she was lovely to look at.
12But when the attendants delivered the king's
command, Queen Vashti refused to come. Then
the king became furious and burned with anger.[p]
13Since it was customary for the king to consult
experts in matters of law and justice, he spoke
with the wise men who understood the times[q]
14and were closest to the king—Carshena, Shethar,
Admatha, Tarshish, Meres, Marsena and Memucan, the seven nobles[r] of Persia and Media who
had special access to the king and were highest in
the kingdom.
15"According to law, what must be done to
Queen Vashti?" he asked. "She has not obeyed the
command of King Xerxes that the eunuchs have
taken to her."
16Then Memucan replied in the presence of the
king and the nobles, "Queen Vashti has done
wrong, not only against the king but also against
all the nobles and the peoples of all the provinces
of King Xerxes. 17For the queen's conduct will
become known to all the women, and so they will

1:1 [a]Ezr 4:6; Da 9:1 [b]Est 9:30; Da 3:2; 6:1 [c]Est 8:9
1:2 [d]Ezr 4:9; Ne 1:1; Est 2:8
1:3 [e]1Ki 3:15; Est 2:18
1:5 [f]Jdg 14:17 [g]2Ki 21:18; Est 7:7-8
1:6 [h]Est 7:8; Eze 23:41; Am 3:12; 6:4
1:7 [i]Est 2:18; Da 5:2
1:9 [j]1Ki 3:15
1:10 [k]Jdg 16:25; Ru 3:7 [l]Ge 14:18; Est 3:15; 5:6; 7:2; Pr 31:4-7; Da 5:1-4 [m]Est 7:9
1:11 [n]SS 2:4 [o]Ps 45:11; Eze 16:14
1:12 [p]Ge 39:19; Est 2:21; 7:7; Pr 19:12
1:13 [q]1Ch 12:32; Jer 10:7; Da 2:12
1:14 [r]2Ki 25:19; Ezr 7:14

[a] *1* Hebrew *Ahasuerus,* a variant of Xerxes' Persian name; here and throughout Esther [b] *1* That is, the upper Nile region

despise their husbands and say, 'King Xerxes commanded Queen Vashti to be brought before him,
but she would not come.' 18This very day the Persian and Median women of the nobility who have
heard about the queen's conduct will respond to
all the king's nobles in the same way. There will
be no end of disrespect and discord.[s]
19"Therefore, if it pleases the king,[t] let him issue
a royal decree and let it be written in the laws of
Persia and Media, which cannot be repealed,[u] that
Vashti is never again to enter the presence of King
Xerxes. Also let the king give her royal position to
someone else who is better than she. 20Then when
the king's edict is proclaimed throughout all his
vast realm, all the women will respect their husbands, from the least to the greatest."
21The king and his nobles were pleased with
this advice, so the king did as Memucan proposed.
22He sent dispatches to all parts of the kingdom, to
each province in its own script and to each people
in its own language,[v] proclaiming in each people's
tongue that every man should be ruler over his
own household.

Esther Made Queen

2 Later when the anger of King Xerxes had subsided,[w] he remembered Vashti and what she
had done and what he had decreed about her.
2Then the king's personal attendants proposed,
"Let a search be made for beautiful young virgins
for the king. 3Let the king appoint commissioners
in every province of his realm to bring all these
beautiful girls into the harem at the citadel of
Susa. Let them be placed under the care of Hegai,
the king's eunuch, who is in charge of the
women; and let beauty treatments be given to
them. 4Then let the girl who pleases the king be
queen instead of Vashti." This advice appealed to
the king, and he followed it.
5Now there was in the citadel of Susa a Jew of
the tribe of Benjamin, named Mordecai son of
Jair, the son of Shimei, the son of Kish,[x] 6who had
been carried into exile from Jerusalem by Nebuchadnezzar king of Babylon, among those taken
captive with Jehoiachin[a][y] king of Judah.[z] 7Mor-
decai had a cousin named Hadassah, whom he
had brought up because she had neither father
nor mother. This girl, who was also known as
Esther,[a] was lovely[b] in form and features, and
Mordecai had taken her as his own daughter
when her father and mother died.
8When the king's order and edict had been proclaimed, many girls were brought to the citadel of
Susa[c] and put under the care of Hegai. Esther also
was taken to the king's palace and entrusted to
Hegai, who had charge of the harem. 9The girl
pleased him and won his favor.[d] Immediately he
provided her with her beauty treatments and special food.[e] He assigned to her seven maids select-

1:18 [s]Pr 19:13; 27:15
1:19 [t]Ecc 8:4 [u]Est 8:8; Da 6:8,12
1:22 [v]Ne 13:24; Est 8:9; Eph 5:22-24; 1Ti 2:12
2:1 [w]Est 1:19-20; 7:10
2:5 [x]1Sa 9:1; Est 3:2
2:6 [y]2Ki 24:6,15; 2Ch 36:10,20 [z]Da 1:1-5; 5:13
2:7 [a]Ge 41:45 [b]Ge 39:6
2:8 [c]ver 3,15; Ne 1:1; Est 1:2; Da 8:2
2:9 [d]Ge 39:21 [e]ver 3,12; Ge 37:3; 1Sa 9:22-24; 2Ki 25:30; Eze 16:9-13; Da 1:5

[a] 6 Hebrew *Jeconiah,* a variant of *Jehoiachin*

Adoption

EST 2:7

As part of the Jewish community in Persia, Mordecai and his cousin Esther have no status in society. Mordecai is from the tribe of Benjamin, and *his family is taken into captivity along with King Jehoiachin* (2Ki 24:8–17; Est 2:5–6). His *family may have ties to Israel's* nobility. *Although we are not sure about his ancestry, we know much* about his character. He exercises *compassion in raising an* orphaned cousin.

Although Hebrew law does not *regulate adoption, adoptions with*in extended families are an estab*lished Near Eastern custom. God* commands his people to be merci*ful to orphans and widows* (Ex 22:22–24). Abraham may *have adopted his servant Eliezer* (Ge 15:2–3), and Jacob adopted *two of his grandsons as sons* (Ge 48:5). Furthermore, God pic*tures his relationship with Israel as that of a father who adopts a* child (Ex 4:22; Jer 3:19).

Beauty Treatment

EST 2:12

Through Esther's conduct we see godly living in distressing circumstances. Esther has no choice but to enter the king's harem. She is subjected to at least a year of competition to become the king's next wife. Ancient literature describes women undergoing extensive beautification programs: ritual cleansings, plucking of eyebrows, removal of body hair, painting of hands and feet with henna, applying mixtures of pastes to lighten the skin and remove blemishes, painting the face with make-up and perfuming the body.

Surely the jealousies and infighting of a large group of women concentrating only on their looks and personal charm must have been wearying to Esther's spirit. Add to that the need for secrecy (Est 2:10), and Esther's position becomes even more difficult. Finally, as a Jew, Esther is forbidden to eat certain foods, to marry a foreigner or to have a sexual relationship with a man who is not her husband. Yet her circumstances force her into situations that are a violation of God's laws. Esther is caught up in political situations beyond her control—but all for good reason. (See character sketch for Esther on page 1344.)

ed from the king's palace and moved her and her
maids into the best place in the harem.
10Esther had not revealed her nationality and
family background, because Mordecai had forbidden her to do so.[f] 11Every day he walked back and
forth near the courtyard of the harem to find out
how Esther was and what was happening to her.
12Before a girl's turn came to go in to King Xerxes, she had to complete twelve months of beauty treatments prescribed for the women, six
months with oil of myrrh and six with perfumes[g]
and cosmetics. 13And this is how she would go to
the king: Anything she wanted was given her to
take with her from the harem to the king's palace.
14In the evening she would go there and in the
morning return to another part of the harem to
the care of Shaashgaz, the king's eunuch who was
in charge of the concubines.[h] She would not
return to the king unless he was pleased with her
and summoned her by name.[i]
15When the turn came for Esther (the girl Mordecai had adopted, the daughter of his uncle Abihail[j]) to go to the king,[k] she asked for nothing
other than what Hegai, the king's eunuch who
was in charge of the harem, suggested. And
Esther won the favor[l] of everyone who saw her.
16She was taken to King Xerxes in the royal residence in the tenth month, the month of Tebeth,
in the seventh year of his reign.
17Now the king was attracted to Esther more
than to any of the other women, and she won his
favor and approval more than any of the other virgins. So he set a royal crown on her head and
made her queen[m] instead of Vashti. 18And the king
gave a great banquet,[n] Esther's banquet, for all his
nobles and officials.[o] He proclaimed a holiday
throughout the provinces and distributed gifts
with royal liberality.[p]

Mordecai Uncovers a Conspiracy

19When the virgins were assembled a second
time, Mordecai was sitting at the king's gate.[q]
20But Esther had kept secret her family background and nationality just as Mordecai had told
her to do, for she continued to follow Mordecai's
instructions as she had done when he was bringing her up.[r]
21During the time Mordecai was sitting at the
king's gate, Bigthana[a] and Teresh, two of the
king's officers[s] who guarded the doorway, became
angry[t] and conspired to assassinate King Xerxes.
22But Mordecai found out about the plot and told
Queen Esther, who in turn reported it to the king,
giving credit to Mordecai. 23And when the report
was investigated and found to be true, the two
officials were hanged[u] on a gallows.[b] All this was
recorded in the book of the annals[v] in the presence of the king.

2:10 [f]ver 20
2:12 [g]Pr 27:9; SS 1:3; Isa 3:24
2:14 [h]1Ki 11:3; SS 6:8; Da 5:2 [i]Est 4:11
2:15 [j]Est 9:29 [k]Ps 45:14 [l]Ge 18:3; 30:27; Est 5:8
2:17 [m]Est 1:11; Eze 16:9-13
2:18 [n]1Ki 3:15; Est 1:3 [o]Ge 40:20 [p]Est 1:7
2:19 [q]ver 21; Est 3:2; 4:2; 5:13
2:20 [r]ver 10
2:21 [s]Ge 40:2; Est 6:2 [t]Est 1:12; 3:5; 5:9; 7:7
2:23 [u]Ge 40:19; Ps 7:14-16; Pr 26:27 [v]Est 6:1; 10:2

[a] 21 Hebrew *Bigthan,* a variant of *Bigthana* [b] 23 Or *were hung* (or *impaled*) *on poles*; similarly elsewhere in Esther

Haman's Plot to Destroy the Jews

3 After these events, King Xerxes honored
Haman son of Hammedatha, the Agagite,[w] elevating him and giving him a seat of honor higher
than that of all the other nobles. 2All the royal
officials at the king's gate knelt down and paid
honor to Haman, for the king had commanded
this concerning him. But Mordecai would not
kneel down or pay him honor.
3Then the royal officials at the king's gate asked
Mordecai, "Why do you disobey the king's command?"[x] 4Day after day they spoke to him but he
refused to comply.[y] Therefore they told Haman
about it to see whether Mordecai's behavior would
be tolerated, for he had told them he was a Jew.
5When Haman saw that Mordecai would not
kneel down or pay him honor, he was enraged.[z]
6Yet having learned who Mordecai's people were,
he scorned the idea of killing only Mordecai.
Instead Haman looked for a way[a] to destroy[b] all
Mordecai's people, the Jews,[c] throughout the
whole kingdom of Xerxes.
7In the twelfth year of King Xerxes, in the first
month, the month of Nisan, they cast the *pur*[d]
(that is, the lot[e]) in the presence of Haman to
select a day and month. And the lot fell on[a] the
twelfth month, the month of Adar.[f]
8Then Haman said to King Xerxes, "There is a
certain people dispersed and scattered among the
peoples in all the provinces of your kingdom
whose customs[g] are different from those of all other people and who do not obey[h] the king's laws; it
is not in the king's best interest to tolerate them.[i]
9If it pleases the king, let a decree be issued to
destroy them, and I will put ten thousand talents[b]
of silver into the royal treasury for the men who
carry out this business."[j]
10So the king took his signet ring[k] from his finger and gave it to Haman son of Hammedatha, the
Agagite, the enemy of the Jews. 11"Keep the money," the king said to Haman, "and do with the people as you please."
12Then on the thirteenth day of the first month
the royal secretaries were summoned. They wrote
out in the script of each province and in the language[l] of each people all Haman's orders to the
king's satraps, the governors of the various
provinces and the nobles of the various peoples.
These were written in the name of King Xerxes
himself and sealed[m] with his own ring. 13Dis-
patches were sent by couriers to all the king's
provinces with the order to destroy, kill and annihilate all the Jews[n]—young and old, women and
little children—on a single day, the thirteenth day
of the twelfth month, the month of Adar,[o] and to
plunder[p] their goods. 14A copy of the text of the
edict was to be issued as law in every province

3:1 [w]ver 10; Ex 17:8-16; Nu 24:7; Dt 25:17-19; 1Sa 14:48; Est 5:11
3:3 [x]Est 5:9; Da 3:12
3:4 [y]Ge 39:10
3:5 [z]Est 2:21; 5:9
3:6 [a]Pr 16:25 [b]Ps 74:8; 83:4 [c]Est 9:24
3:7 [d]Est 9:24,26 [e]Lev 16:8; 1Sa 10:21 [f]ver 13; Ezr 6:15; Est 9:19
3:8 [g]Ac 16:20-21 [h]Jer 29:7; Da 6:13 [i]Ezr 4:15
3:9 [j]Est 7:4
3:10 [k]Ge 41:42; Est 7:6; 8:2
3:12 [l]Ne 13:24 [m]Ge 38:18; 1Ki 21:8; Est 8:8-10
3:13 [n]1Sa 15:3; Ezr 4:6; Est 8:10-14 [o]ver 7 [p]Est 8:11; 9:10

[a] 7 Septuagint; Hebrew does not have *And the lot fell on.*
[b] 9 That is, about 375 tons (about 345 metric tons)

The Signet Ring

EST 3:9-10,13

Silver is the monetary standard of the Persian Empire, and Haman's offer represents a staggering sum: 375 tons of silver. That much silver represents more than 55 million dollars in today's economy. Haman may have been this rich; but more likely, he planned to seize the wealth from rich Jews as they were slaughtered.

The king's signet ring, mentioned in Esther 3:10, represents his authority throughout his empire. When used as a seal on a document (the design on the ring is pressed into soft clay or wax on papers from the king), that document is law. To allow another to use that ring means that the king has given full authority to that person.

For Such a Time As This

EST 4:14-16

Plans are in place to exterminate the Jewish people, and Mordecai begs Esther to intervene. At the same time he seems to understand that regardless of what Esther does, God will be faithful; he will not let his people be totally destroyed. Although this book never mentions God by name, Mordecai's statement in this passage points to a sovereign God who is at work in dreadful circumstances. Esther is in a place that requires great courage. She cannot hide her identity; she cannot count on the king's favor; and she cannot ignore an evil man at work in the kingdom. Esther's request that the Jews fast for three days is an admission that she needs more than courage to do her duty. Prayer usually accompanies fasting in the Old Testament (Ezr 8:21-23). Therefore, by her request, Esther acknowledges her need for others to pray for and with her.

and made known to the people of every nationality so they would be ready for that day.[q]
15 Spurred on by the king's command, the couriers went out, and the edict was issued in the
citadel of Susa.[r] The king and Haman sat down to
drink,[s] but the city of Susa was bewildered.[t]

Mordecai Persuades Esther to Help

4 When Mordecai learned of all that had been
done, he tore his clothes,[u] put on sackcloth and
ashes,[v] and went out into the city, wailing[w] loudly
and bitterly. 2 But he went only as far as the king's
gate,[x] because no one clothed in sackcloth was
allowed to enter it. 3 In every province to which the
edict and order of the king came, there was great
mourning among the Jews, with fasting, weeping
and wailing. Many lay in sackcloth and ashes.
4 When Esther's maids and eunuchs came and
told her about Mordecai, she was in great distress.
She sent clothes for him to put on instead of his
sackcloth, but he would not accept them. 5 Then
Esther summoned Hathach, one of the king's
eunuchs assigned to attend her, and ordered him
to find out what was troubling Mordecai and why.
6 So Hathach went out to Mordecai in the open
square of the city in front of the king's gate. 7 Mordecai told him everything that had happened to
him, including the exact amount of money
Haman had promised to pay into the royal treasury for the destruction of the Jews.[y] 8 He also
gave him a copy of the text of the edict for their
annihilation, which had been published in Susa,
to show to Esther and explain it to her, and he told
him to urge her to go into the king's presence to
beg for mercy and plead with him for her people.
9 Hathach went back and reported to Esther what
Mordecai had said. 10 Then she instructed him to
say to Mordecai, 11 "All the king's officials and the
people of the royal provinces know that for any
man or woman who approaches the king in the
inner court without being summoned[z] the king
has but one law:[a] that he be put to death. The only
exception to this is for the king to extend the gold
scepter[b] to him and spare his life. But thirty days
have passed since I was called to go to the king."
12 When Esther's words were reported to Mordecai, 13 he sent back this answer: "Do not think
that because you are in the king's house you
alone of all the Jews will escape. 14 For if you
remain silent[c] at this time, relief[d] and deliverance[e]
for the Jews will arise from another place, but you
and your father's family will perish. And who
knows but that you have come to royal position
for such a time as this?"[f]
15 Then Esther sent this reply to Mordecai: 16 "Go,
gather together all the Jews who are in Susa, and
fast[g] for me. Do not eat or drink for three days,
night or day. I and my maids will fast as you do.
When this is done, I will go to the king, even
though it is against the law. And if I perish, I
perish."[h]

3:14 [q]Est 8:8; 9:1
3:15 [r]Est 8:14 [s]Est 1:10 [t]Est 8:15
4:1 [u]Nu 14:6 [v]2Sa 13:19; Eze 27:30-31; Jnh 3:5-6 [w]Ex 11:6; Ps 30:11
4:2 [x]Est 2:19
4:7 [y]Est 3:9; 7:4
4:11 [z]Est 2:14 [a]Da 2:9 [b]Est 5:1,2; 8:4
4:14 [c]Ecc 3:7; Isa 62:1; Am 5:13 [d]Est 9:16,22 [e]Ge 45:7; Dt 28:29 [f]Ge 50:20
4:16 [g]2Ch 20:3; Est 9:31 [h]Ge 43:14

[17]So Mordecai went away and carried out all of
Esther's instructions.

Esther's Request to the King

5:1 [i]Est 4:16; Eze 16:13 [j]Est 6:4; Pr 21:1
5 On the third day Esther put on her royal robes[i]
and stood in the inner court of the palace, in
front of the king's[j] hall. The king was sitting on
his royal throne in the hall, facing the entrance.
[2]When he saw Queen Esther standing in the
court, he was pleased with her and held out to her
5:2 [k]Est 4:11; 8:4; Pr 21:1
the gold scepter that was in his hand. So Esther
approached and touched the tip of the scepter.[k]
[3]Then the king asked, "What is it, Queen
5:3 [l]Est 7:2; Da 5:16; Mk 6:23
Esther? What is your request? Even up to half the
kingdom,[l] it will be given you."
[4]"If it pleases the king," replied Esther, "let the
king, together with Haman, come today to a banquet I have prepared for him."
[5]"Bring Haman at once," the king said, "so that
we may do what Esther asks."
So the king and Haman went to the banquet
5:6 [m]Est 1:10 [n]Mk 6:23 [o]Est 7:2; 9:12
Esther had prepared. [6]As they were drinking
wine,[m] the king again asked Esther, "Now what is
your petition? It will be given you. And what is
your request? Even up to half the kingdom,[n] it
will be granted."[o]
[7]Esther replied, "My petition and my request is
5:8 [p]Est 2:15; 7:3; 8:5 [q]1Ki 3:15; Est 6:14
this: [8]If the king regards me with favor[p] and if it
pleases the king to grant my petition and fulfill
my request, let the king and Haman come tomorrow to the banquet[q] I will prepare for them. Then
I will answer the king's question."

Haman's Rage Against Mordecai

[9]Haman went out that day happy and in high
spirits. But when he saw Mordecai at the king's
5:9 [r]Est 2:21; Pr 14:17 [s]Est 3:3,5
gate and observed that he neither rose nor
showed fear in his presence, he was filled with
rage[r] against Mordecai.[s] [10]Nevertheless, Haman
restrained himself and went home.
5:10 [t]Est 6:13
Calling together his friends and Zeresh,[t] his
wife, [11]Haman boasted[u] to them about his vast
5:11 [u]Pr 13:16 [v]Est 9:7-10, 13
wealth, his many sons,[v] and all the ways the king
had honored him and how he had elevated him
above the other nobles and officials. [12]"And that's
5:12 [w]Job 22:29; Pr 16:18; 29:23
not all," Haman added. "I'm the only person[w]
Queen Esther invited to accompany the king to
the banquet she gave. And she has invited me
along with the king tomorrow. [13]But all this gives
5:13 [x]Est 2:19
me no satisfaction as long as I see that Jew Mordecai sitting at the king's gate.[x]"
[14]His wife Zeresh and all his friends said to him,
5:14 [y]Est 7:9 [z]Ezr 6:11; Est 6:4
"Have a gallows built, seventy-five feet[a] high,[y]
and ask the king in the morning to have Mordecai
hanged[z] on it. Then go with the king to the dinner
and be happy." This suggestion delighted Haman,
and he had the gallows built.

[a] 14 Hebrew *fifty cubits* (about 23 meters)

Coincidences

Delay

EST 5:7-8

There is no way to know for sure why Esther asks the king to a second banquet, rather than simply making her request. Does she lose courage at the last moment? Has this been part of her strategy all along? Does she sense during the first banquet that the time is not yet right to petition the king? The delay adds suspense to an already powerful story, but more than that, it draws us to examine how we conduct ourselves in difficult and frightening situations. Esther moves through the events of this story with a quiet dignity. We sense she is listening for God's wisdom in the midst of circumstances that do not have simple solutions.

A Series of "Coincidences"

EST 6:1

Humanly speaking, Esther 6 is a chapter of "coincidences." None of the events are unusual, but as they occur and converge, they reveal the sovereign and faithful hand of God as he cares for his people. The first event is the king's insomnia, providentially occurring the night before the second banquet. Since he cannot sleep, the king requests that someone read to him, either as a cure for insomnia or as a way to profitably use wakeful night hours. The portion read to the king relates Mordecai's exposure of an assassination plot against the king (Est 2:21–23). That Mordecai has not been rewarded earlier is a bureaucratic oversight; Persian kings are quick to honor subjects who exhibit this sort of loyalty. But God waits five years to bring this event to light at just the right time, one step along the way toward Haman's downfall.

Mordecai Honored

6 That night the king could not sleep;[a] so he
ordered the book of the chronicles,[b] the record
of his reign, to be brought in and read to him. 2It
was found recorded there that Mordecai had
exposed Bigthana and Teresh, two of the king's
officers who guarded the doorway, who had conspired to assassinate King Xerxes.
3"What honor and recognition has Mordecai
received for this?" the king asked.
"Nothing has been done for him,"[c] his attendants answered.
4The king said, "Who is in the court?" Now
Haman had just entered the outer court of the
palace to speak to the king about hanging Mordecai on the gallows he had erected for him.
5His attendants answered, "Haman is standing
in the court."
"Bring him in," the king ordered.
6When Haman entered, the king asked him,
"What should be done for the man the king
delights to honor?"
Now Haman thought to himself, "Who is there
that the king would rather honor than me?" 7So
he answered the king, "For the man the king
delights to honor, 8have them bring a royal robe[d]
the king has worn and a horse[e] the king has ridden, one with a royal crest placed on its head.
9Then let the robe and horse be entrusted to one
of the king's most noble princes. Let them robe
the man the king delights to honor, and lead him
on the horse through the city streets, proclaiming
before him, 'This is what is done for the man the
king delights to honor![f] ' "
10"Go at once," the king commanded Haman.
"Get the robe and the horse and do just as you
have suggested for Mordecai the Jew, who sits at
the king's gate. Do not neglect anything you have
recommended."
11So Haman got[g] the robe and the horse. He
robed Mordecai, and led him on horseback
through the city streets, proclaiming before him,
"This is what is done for the man the king
delights to honor!"
12Afterward Mordecai returned to the king's
gate. But Haman rushed home, with his head covered[h] in grief, 13and told Zeresh[i] his wife and all
his friends everything that had happened to him.
His advisers and his wife Zeresh said to him,
"Since Mordecai, before whom your downfall[j] has
started, is of Jewish origin, you cannot stand
against him—you will surely come to ruin!"
14While they were still talking with him, the
king's eunuchs arrived and hurried Haman away
to the banquet[k] Esther had prepared.

Haman Hanged

7 So the king and Haman went to dine[l] with
Queen Esther, 2and as they were drinking
wine[m] on that second day, the king again asked,

6:1 [a]Da 2:1; 6:18 [b]Est 2:23; 10:2
6:3 [c]Ecc 9:13-16
6:8 [d]Ge 41:42; Isa 52:1 [e]1Ki 1:33
6:9 [f]Ge 41:43
6:11 [g]Ge 41:42
6:12 [h]2Sa 15:30; Jer 14:3,4; Mic 3:7
6:13 [i]Est 5:10 [j]Ps 57:6; Pr 26:27; 28:18
6:14 [k]1Ki 3:15; Est 5:8
7:1 [l]Ge 40:20-22; Mt 22:1-14
7:2 [m]Est 1:10

"Queen Esther, what is your petition? It will be
7:2 given you. What is your request? Even up to half
[n]Est 5:3 the kingdom,[n] it will be granted.[o]"
[o]Est 9:12 3Then Queen Esther answered, "If I have found
7:3 favor[p] with you, O king, and if it pleases your
[p]Est 2:15 majesty, grant me my life—this is my petition.
And spare my people—this is my request. 4For I
and my people have been sold for destruction and
7:4 slaughter and annihilation.[q] If we had merely
[q]Est 3:9 been sold as male and female slaves, I would have
kept quiet, because no such distress would justify
disturbing the king.[a]"
5King Xerxes asked Queen Esther, "Who is he?
Where is the man who has dared to do such a
thing?"
6Esther said, "The adversary and enemy is this
vile Haman."
Then Haman was terrified before the king and
7:7 [r]Ge 34:7; queen. 7The king got up in a rage,[r] left his wine
Est 1:12; and went out into the palace garden.[s] But Haman,
Pr 19:12; 20:1-2 realizing that the king had already decided his
[s]2Ki 21:18 fate,[t] stayed behind to beg Queen Esther for his
[t]Est 6:13 life.
8Just as the king returned from the palace garden to the banquet hall, Haman was falling on the
7:8 [u]Est 1:6 couch[u] where Esther was reclining.[v]
[v]Ge 39:14 The king exclaimed, "Will he even molest the
[w]Ge 34:7 [x]Est 6:12 queen while she is with me in the house?"[w]
As soon as the word left the king's mouth, they
7:9 covered Haman's face.[x] 9Then Harbona,[y] one of
[y]Est 1:10 [z]Est 5:14 the eunuchs attending the king, said, "A gallows
[a]Ps 7:14-16; seventy-five feet[b] high[z] stands by Haman's house.
9:16; Pr 11:5-6; He had it made for Mordecai, who spoke up to
26:27; Mt 7:2 help the king."
The king said, "Hang him on it!"[a] 10So they
7:10 hanged Haman[b] on the gallows[c] he had prepared
[b]Pr 10:28 for Mordecai.[d] Then the king's fury subsided.[e]

[c]Est 9:25 [d]Da 6:24

The King's Edict in Behalf of the Jews

[e]Est 2:1 8 That same day King Xerxes gave Queen Esther
8:1 [f]Est 2:7; 7:6; the estate of Haman,[f] the enemy of the Jews.
Pr 22:22-23 And Mordecai came into the presence of the king,
for Esther had told how he was related to her.
8:2 2The king took off his signet ring,[g] which he had
[g]Ge 41:42; Est 3:10 reclaimed from Haman, and presented it to Mor-
[h]Pr 13:22; Da 2:48 decai. And Esther appointed him over Haman's
estate.[h]
3Esther again pleaded with the king, falling at
his feet and weeping. She begged him to put an
end to the evil plan of Haman the Agagite, which
he had devised against the Jews. 4Then the king
8:4 extended the gold scepter[i] to Esther and she arose
[i]Est 4:11; 5:2 and stood before him.
5"If it pleases the king," she said, "and if he
regards me with favor and thinks it the right thing
to do, and if he is pleased with me, let an order
be written overruling the dispatches that Haman

[a] 4 Or *quiet, but the compensation our adversary offers cannot be compared with the loss the king would suffer* [b] 9 Hebrew *fifty cubits* (about 23 meters)

Cover His Face

EST 7

Haman's desperate and untimely attempt to save his life only seals his fate. When the king leaves the banquet in a rage after hearing of Haman's plot against Esther's people, Haman stays behind to beg for mercy from Queen Esther. The king reappears at a providential moment, just as Haman is falling on Esther's couch. Assuming Haman is trying to molest his queen, the king now has double reason to execute him.

In the Greek and Roman worlds, the face of a person condemned to die was covered to indicate his sentence. Apparently this practice was also a Persian custom. The king's attendants, who are intimately aware of all the court intrigue, know of all the events that preceded this moment. They now feel free to reveal to the king the fact that Haman has erected gallows on which to hang Mordecai, the very person just honored by the king. If Xerxes has had any inclination to be lenient with Haman, this new piece of information seals Haman's fate. He is led out to be executed.

> It might be wise to remember that Satan is the enemy of our souls . . . It is his voice that whispers messages to discourage us, diminish us, and condemn us. It's his voice that suggests God could never forgive us, stick by us, or love us. It is his voice that tells us we aren't good enough, spiritual enough or worthy enough to receive salvation. And it is his voice that accuses us of inadequate faith and imperfect mental health. God calls him an "accuser" (Rev 12:10), and that very word is our cue to recognize when Satan is having a heyday in our souls. The Holy Spirit never accuses. Instead, he woos us, he wins us, and he loves us to behave better and to commit ourselves more deeply to him.
>
> *—Marilyn Meberg*

son of Hammedatha, the Agagite, devised and
wrote to destroy the Jews in all the king's
provinces. 6For how can I bear to see disaster fall
on my people? How can I bear to see the destruction of my family?"[j]
7King Xerxes replied to Queen Esther and to Mordecai the Jew, "Because Haman attacked the Jews,
I have given his estate to Esther, and they have
hanged him on the gallows. 8Now write another
decree[k] in the king's name in behalf of the Jews as
seems best to you, and seal it with the king's signet
ring[l]—for no document written in the king's name
and sealed with his ring can be revoked."[m]
9At once the royal secretaries were summoned—
on the twenty-third day of the third month, the
month of Sivan. They wrote out all Mordecai's
orders to the Jews, and to the satraps, governors
and nobles of the 127 provinces stretching from
India to Cush.[a][n] These orders were written in the
script of each province and the language of each
people and also to the Jews in their own script and
language.[o] 10Mordecai wrote in the name of King
Xerxes, sealed the dispatches with the king's signet
ring, and sent them by mounted couriers, who
rode fast horses especially bred for the king.
11The king's edict granted the Jews in every city
the right to assemble and protect themselves; to
destroy, kill and annihilate any armed force of any
nationality or province that might attack them
and their women and children; and to plunder[p]
the property of their enemies. 12The day appointed for the Jews to do this in all the provinces of
King Xerxes was the thirteenth day of the twelfth
month, the month of Adar.[q] 13A copy of the text of
the edict was to be issued as law in every province and made known to the people of every
nationality so that the Jews would be ready on
that day[r] to avenge themselves on their enemies.
14The couriers, riding the royal horses, raced
out, spurred on by the king's command. And the
edict was also issued in the citadel of Susa.
15Mordecai[s] left the king's presence wearing
royal garments of blue and white, a large crown of
gold and a purple robe of fine linen.[t] And the city
of Susa held a joyous celebration.[u] 16For the Jews
it was a time of happiness and joy,[v] gladness and
honor.[w] 17In every province and in every city,
wherever the edict of the king went, there was
joy[x] and gladness among the Jews, with feasting
and celebrating. And many people of other
nationalities became Jews because fear[y] of the
Jews had seized them.[z]

Triumph of the Jews

9 On the thirteenth day of the twelfth month,
the month of Adar,[a] the edict commanded by
the king was to be carried out. On this day the
enemies of the Jews had hoped to overpower
them, but now the tables were turned and the

8:6 [j]Est 7:4; 9:1
8:8 [k]Est 3:12-14 [l]Ge 41:42 [m]Est 1:19; Da 6:15
8:9 [n]Est 1:1 [o]Est 1:22
8:11 [p]Est 9:10,15, 16
8:12 [q]Est 3:13; 9:1
8:13 [r]Est 3:14
8:15 [s]Est 9:4 [t]Ge 41:42 [u]Est 3:15
8:16 [v]Ps 97:10-12 [w]Ps 112:4
8:17 [x]Est 9:19,27; Ps 35:27; Pr 11:10 [y]Ex 15:14, 16; Dt 11:25 [z]Est 9:3
9:1 [a]Est 8:12

[a] 9 That is, the upper Nile region

9:1 Jews got the upper hand[b] over those who hated
[b]Jer 29:4-7 [c]Est 3:12-14; them.[c] 2 The Jews assembled in their cities[d] in all
Pr 22:22-23 the provinces of King Xerxes to attack those seek-
ing their destruction. No one could stand against
9:2 [d]ver 15-18 them,[e] because the people of all the other nation-
[e]Est 8:11,17; Ps 71:13,24 alities were afraid of them. 3 And all the nobles of
the provinces, the satraps, the governors and the
9:3 king's administrators helped the Jews,[f] because
[f]Ezr 8:36 fear of Mordecai had seized them. 4 Mordecai was
9:4 prominent[g] in the palace; his reputation spread
[g]Ex 11:3 [h]2Sa 3:1; throughout the provinces, and he became more
1Ch 11:9 and more powerful.[h]
5 The Jews struck down all their enemies with
9:5 [i]Ezr 4:6 the sword, killing and destroying them,[i] and they
did what they pleased to those who hated them.
6 In the citadel of Susa, the Jews killed and
destroyed five hundred men. 7 They also killed
Parshandatha, Dalphon, Aspatha, 8 Poratha, Ada-
lia, Aridatha, 9 Parmashta, Arisai, Aridai and Vai-
9:10 [j]Est 5:11 zatha, 10 the ten sons[j] of Haman son of Hamme-
[k]Ge 14:23; datha, the enemy of the Jews. But they did not lay
1Sa 14:32; Est 3:13; their hands on the plunder.[k]
8:11 11 The number of those slain in the citadel of
Susa was reported to the king that same day. 12 The
king said to Queen Esther, "The Jews have killed
and destroyed five hundred men and the ten sons
of Haman in the citadel of Susa. What have they
done in the rest of the king's provinces? Now
what is your petition? It will be given you. What
9:12 [l]Est 5:6; 7:2 is your request? It will also be granted."[l]
13 "If it pleases the king," Esther answered, "give
the Jews in Susa permission to carry out this day's
9:13 [m]Est 5:11 edict tomorrow also, and let Haman's ten sons[m]
[n]Dt 21:22-23 be hanged[n] on gallows."
9:14 14 So the king commanded that this be done. An
[o]Ezr 6:11 edict was issued in Susa, and they hanged[o] the ten
sons of Haman. 15 The Jews in Susa came together
on the fourteenth day of the month of Adar, and
they put to death in Susa three hundred men, but
9:15 [p]Ge 14:23; they did not lay their hands on the plunder.[p]
Est 8:11 16 Meanwhile, the remainder of the Jews who
were in the king's provinces also assembled to
9:16 [q]Est 4:14 protect themselves and get relief[q] from their ene-
[r]Dt 25:19 [s]1Ch 4:43 mies.[r] They killed seventy-five thousand of them[s]
but did not lay their hands on the plunder. 17 This
happened on the thirteenth day of the month of
Adar, and on the fourteenth they rested and made
9:17 [t]1Ki 3:15 it a day of feasting[t] and joy.

Purim Celebrated

18 The Jews in Susa, however, had assembled on
the thirteenth and fourteenth, and then on the fifteenth they rested and made it a day of feasting
and joy.
19 That is why rural Jews—those living in vil-
9:19 [u]Est 3:7 lages—observe the fourteenth of the month of
[v]ver 22; Dt 16:11,14; Adar[u] as a day of joy and feasting, a day for giving
Ne 8:10,12; presents to each other.[v]
Est 2:9; 20 Mordecai recorded these events, and he sent
Rev 11:10 letters to all the Jews throughout the provinces of
King Xerxes, near and far, 21 to have them celebrate

No Plunder

EST 9:10,15-16

Unlike Haman, who saw the slaughter of the Jews as an opportunity to increase his wealth, the Jews' intentions are only to do away with their enemies in order to protect themselves and carry out God's judgment. In view of the fact that the king has given them permission to plunder their enemies (Est 8:11), the statement repeated in Esther 9:10, 15-16 is even more remarkable. By refusing to enrich themselves through their victory, they are following the example of Abraham in Genesis 14:22-24. In contrast, King Saul, the first king of Israel, did not conduct himself by the same high standard (1Sa 15:1-23). The end result for the Jews in Persia is that their victory becomes a day of feasting and joy, gift-giving and generosity to the poor (Est 9:19,22), not a day to delight in newly acquired wealth.

Purim

EST 9:22—10:3

Evidently Esther and Mordecai have no need to be seen as the heroes of this victory, but they have a great desire that their people not forget the deliverance God has given. Purim is not one of the feasts established by Mosaic Law, but it is still celebrated today by the Jewish people. A carnival-like atmosphere—with masquerades, amusing plays and gift-giving, along with reading the book of Esther aloud—marks the day as one of particular joy. The name chosen for this day, Purim, has special significance. As Esther 9:24 explains, the word is from the Persian word pur, *meaning "lot." Haman cast the* pur *to choose a day for the annihilation of the Jews (Est 3:7). In the midst of seemingly random events, in which God often appears absent, he is still sovereign. He works through circumstance and "happenstance" to faithfully protect his people.*

annually the fourteenth and fifteenth days of the
month of Adar 22 as the time when the Jews got
relief[w] from their enemies, and as the month
when their sorrow was turned into joy and their
mourning into a day of celebration.[x] He wrote
them to observe the days as days of feasting and
joy and giving presents of food[y] to one another
and gifts to the poor.
23 So the Jews agreed to continue the celebration
they had begun, doing what Mordecai had written to them. 24 For Haman son of Hammedatha,
the Agagite,[z] the enemy of all the Jews, had plotted against the Jews to destroy them and had cast
the *pur*[a] (that is, the lot[b]) for their ruin and
destruction. 25 But when the plot came to the
king's attention,[a] he issued written orders that the
evil scheme Haman had devised against the Jews
should come back onto his own head,[c] and that
he and his sons should be hanged[d] on the gallows.[e] 26 (Therefore these days were called Purim,
from the word *pur*.[f]) Because of everything written in this letter and because of what they had
seen and what had happened to them, 27 the Jews
took it upon themselves to establish the custom
that they and their descendants and all who join
them should without fail observe these two days
every year, in the way prescribed and at the time
appointed. 28 These days should be remembered
and observed in every generation by every family,
and in every province and in every city. And these
days of Purim should never cease to be celebrated
by the Jews, nor should the memory of them die
out among their descendants.
29 So Queen Esther, daughter of Abihail,[g] along
with Mordecai the Jew, wrote with full authority
to confirm this second letter concerning Purim.
30 And Mordecai sent letters to all the Jews in the
127 provinces[h] of the kingdom of Xerxes—words
of goodwill and assurance— 31 to establish these
days of Purim at their designated times, as Mordecai the Jew and Queen Esther had decreed for
them, and as they had established for themselves
and their descendants in regard to their times of
fasting[i] and lamentation.[j] 32 Esther's decree confirmed these regulations about Purim, and it was
written down in the records.

The Greatness of Mordecai

10 King Xerxes imposed tribute throughout the
empire, to its distant shores.[k] 2 And all his
acts of power and might, together with a full
account of the greatness of Mordecai[l] to which the
king had raised him,[m] are they not written in the
book of the annals[n] of the kings of Media and Persia? 3 Mordecai the Jew was second[o] in rank[p] to
King Xerxes,[q] preeminent among the Jews, and
held in high esteem by his many fellow Jews,
because he worked for the good of his people and
spoke up for the welfare of all the Jews.[r]

[a] 25 *Or when Esther came before the king*

9:22 [w]Est 4:14 [x]Ne 8:12; Ps 30:11-12 [y]2Ki 25:30
9:24 [z]Ex 17:8-16 [a]Est 3:7 [b]Lev 16:8
9:25 [c]Ps 7:16 [d]Dt 21:22-23 [e]Est 7:10
9:26 [f]ver 20; Est 3:7
9:29 [g]Est 2:15
9:30 [h]Est 1:1
9:31 [i]Est 4:16 [j]Est 4:1-3
10:1 [k]Ps 72:10; 97:1; Isa 24:15
10:2 [l]Est 8:15; 9:4 [m]Ge 41:44 [n]Est 2:23
10:3 [o]Da 5:7 [p]Ge 41:43 [q]Ge 41:40 [r]Ne 2:10; Jer 29:4-7; Da 6:3

Job

Even in suffering, God is sovereign.

The book of Job introduces us to a man named Job who is plagued by adversity. Job is a righteous, godly man, yet one catastrophe after another wreaks havoc on his life. After Satan spars with God, we are allowed to see pieces of the puzzle of Job's life that he himself cannot see. When Job's friends enter the picture, their words are based on incorrect assumptions. Instead of offering him the comfort he needs, they offer advice and try to find answers to his suffering. Job feels condemned instead of comforted.

In reading Job, we discern the identity of our true adversary and see how he manipulates events to snatch our focus away from God (Job 1:16–22). We reluctantly listen to Job's wife as she offers her advice, and we are awed by Job's righteous response (Job 2:9–10). We watch in dismay as Job's friends break their silence (Job 2:11–13), adding to his grief rather than alleviating it. We groan with Job under a burden of of suffering that is beyond understanding (Job 7). We marvel as Job learns to endure suffering by finding hope in the Lord (Job 19:23–27). And we cheer for Job's final restoration and reward for his faithfulness to God (Job 42:10–17).

Bad things *do* happen to good people. God *does* allow his children to undergo testing. But the book of Job reminds us that God is still in control. Even in the middle of the most horrific circumstances life throws our way, we can tie a mental knot in our faith and hang on to our trust in God. If we focus on his sovereignty and faithfulness, we can face any storm life has to offer and come through—scared and hurting perhaps—but victorious nonetheless.

Quick Study

Author
Unknown.

Date Written
The story of Job is presumed to be old, possibly dating back to the time of Abraham. It was most likely passed down in oral form until it was put into writing, probably sometime between Solomon's reign and the exile.

Setting
The land of Uz. It was likely a large area east of the Jordan River.

Key Passage
Job 2:10 " 'Shall we accept good from God, and not trouble?' In all this, Job did not sin in what he said."

Outline

Prologue.
Job 1:1-5

Job's first test.
Job 1:6-22

Job's second test.
Job 2:1-10

Job's friends grieve with him.
Job 2:11-13

Job speaks.
Job 3

Eliphaz speaks; Job replies.
Job 4-7

Bildad speaks; Job replies.
Job 8-10

Zophar speaks; Job replies.
Job 11-14

Eliphaz speaks; Job replies.
Job 15-17

Bildad speaks; Job replies.
Job 18-19

Zophar speaks; Job's replies.
Job 20-21

Eliphaz speaks; Job replies.
Job 22-24

Bildad speaks; Job replies.
Job 25-31

Elihu speaks.
Job 32-37

The Lord speaks.
Job 38-41

Job replies.
Job 42:1-6

Job is restored.
Job 42:7-17

The Women of Job

⚘ **Job's Wife**	*Not much help to Job.* Job 2:7-10; 19:17-19 (page 1411)
Jemimah, Keziah, Keren-Happuch	*Job's beautiful daughters.* Job 42:14-15

⚘ Denotes a sketch written about this character

Prologue

1:1 [a]Jer 25:20 [b]Eze 14:14, 20; Jas 5:11 [c]Ge 6:9; 17:1 [d]Ge 22:12; Ex 18:21 1 In the land of Uz[a] there lived a man whose
name was Job.[b] This man was blameless[c] and
upright; he feared God[d] and shunned evil. 2He had
seven sons and three daughters,[e] 3and he owned
seven thousand sheep, three thousand camels,
five hundred yoke of oxen and five hundred don-
1:2 [e]Job 42:13 keys, and had a large number of servants. He was
the greatest man[f] among all the people of the East.
1:3 [f]Job 29:25 4His sons used to take turns holding feasts in
their homes, and they would invite their three sisters to eat and drink with them. 5When a period of
feasting had run its course, Job would send and
1:5 [g]Ge 8:20; Job 42:8 [h]Job 8:4 [i]1Ki 21:10,13 have them purified. Early in the morning he
would sacrifice a burnt offering[g] for each of them,
thinking, "Perhaps my children have sinned[h] and
cursed God[i] in their hearts." This was Job's regular custom.

Job's First Test

1:6 [j]Job 38:7 [k]Job 2:1 6One day the angels[a][j] came to present themselves before the LORD, and Satan[b] also came with
them.[k] 7The LORD said to Satan, "Where have you
come from?"
Satan answered the LORD, "From roaming
1:7 [l]1Pe 5:8 through the earth and going back and forth in it."[l]
1:8 [m]Jos 1:7; Job 42:7-8 [n]ver 1 8Then the LORD said to Satan, "Have you considered my servant Job?[m] There is no one on earth
like him; he is blameless and upright, a man who
fears God and shuns evil."[n]
1:9 [o]1Ti 6:5 9"Does Job fear God for nothing?"[o] Satan replied.
10"Have you not put a hedge around him and his
1:10 [p]Ps 34:7 [q]ver 3; Job 29:6; 31:25; Ps 128:1-2 household and everything he has?[p] You have
blessed the work of his hands, so that his flocks
and herds are spread throughout the land.[q] 11But
stretch out your hand and strike everything he
has,[r] and he will surely curse you to your face."[s]
1:11 [r]Job 19:21 [s]Job 2:5 12The LORD said to Satan, "Very well, then,
everything he has is in your hands, but on the
man himself do not lay a finger."
Then Satan went out from the presence of the
LORD.
13One day when Job's sons and daughters were
feasting and drinking wine at the oldest brother's
house, 14a messenger came to Job and said, "The
1:15 [t]Ge 10:7; Job 6:19 oxen were plowing and the donkeys were grazing
nearby, 15and the Sabeans[t] attacked and carried
them off. They put the servants to the sword, and
I am the only one who has escaped to tell you!"
1:16 [u]Ge 19:24 [v]Lev 10:2; Nu 11:1-3 16While he was still speaking, another messenger
came and said, "The fire of God fell from the sky[u]
and burned up the sheep and the servants,[v] and I
am the only one who has escaped to tell you!"
1:17 [w]Ge 11:28,31 17While he was still speaking, another messenger came and said, "The Chaldeans[w] formed three
raiding parties and swept down on your camels
and carried them off. They put the servants to the

[a] 6 Hebrew *the sons of God* [b] 6 *Satan* means *accuser.*

In God's Holy Council

JOB 1:6-12

The "angels" referred to here are spiritual beings, literally "sons of God" in Hebrew, created by God to function as royal officials in his kingdom and to do his bidding. Strange then that Satan, an adversary of God, is allowed to enter this holy council. But some scholars suggest that Satan, "the accuser" (see NIV footnote on Job 1:6), appears here in his role of celestial spy, duty-bound to report to God and accuse humans on the basis of their behavior. Ultimately, however, all the officials in the King's court, including God's "fallen angel," are subject to his will and direction. See Psalm 89:5-8, which confirms that the Lord is "more awesome than all who surround him." Satan may have access to God and to God's servants, like Job, but the King of the ages will reign supreme (Rev 11:15-17; 12:10).

Job's Wife

JOB 2:9

Because Job's wife speaks only once in Scripture, we can only guess at all that is in her mind and heart when she urges Job to "cash in his chips." Although Job and his wife weren't Israelites, they may have had an innate appreciation of the Old Testament law which prescribed death for anyone who cursed God (Lev 24:15–16). Perhaps pessimistically assuming that Job had nothing to live for, she only wanted to hasten the day when he'd be put out of his misery.

Some commentators suggest that her role was that of temptress, that her sole function during Job's test of faith was to be Satan's instrument to derail her husband's faithfulness (see parallels in Adam and Eve's relationship in Ge 3:6). But this perspective overlooks the possibility that her own very human despair may simply have arisen from her own traumatic losses. After all, Job was not the only one to lose ten children and great wealth. Intense human suffering quickly reveals the condition of a person's faith. While Job's faith was strong enough to prevail, his wife's faith was undermined by these events (see character sketch for Job's wife on page 1411).

sword, and I am the only one who has escaped to
tell you!"
18 While he was still speaking, yet another messenger came and said, "Your sons and daughters
were feasting and drinking wine at the oldest
brother's house, 19 when suddenly a mighty wind[x]
swept in from the desert and struck the four corners of the house. It collapsed on them and they
are dead, and I am the only one who has escaped
to tell you!"
20 At this, Job got up and tore his robe[y] and
shaved his head. Then he fell to the ground in
worship[z] 21 and said:

"Naked I came from my mother's womb,
and naked I will depart.[a][a]
The LORD gave and the LORD has taken
away;[b]
may the name of the LORD be
praised."[c]

22 In all this, Job did not sin by charging God
with wrongdoing.[d]

Job's Second Test

2 On another day the angels[b] came to present
themselves before the LORD, and Satan also
came with them[e] to present himself before him.
2 And the LORD said to Satan, "Where have you
come from?"
Satan answered the LORD, "From roaming
through the earth and going back and forth in it."
3 Then the LORD said to Satan, "Have you considered my servant Job? There is no one on earth
like him; he is blameless and upright, a man who
fears God and shuns evil.[f] And he still maintains
his integrity,[g] though you incited me against him
to ruin him without any reason."[h]
4 "Skin for skin!" Satan replied. "A man will give
all he has for his own life. 5 But stretch out your
hand and strike his flesh and bones,[i] and he will
surely curse you to your face."[j]
6 The LORD said to Satan, "Very well, then, he is
in your hands; but you must spare his life."[k]
7 So Satan went out from the presence of the
LORD and afflicted Job with painful sores from the
soles of his feet to the top of his head.[l] 8 Then Job
took a piece of broken pottery and scraped himself
with it as he sat among the ashes.[m]
9 His wife said to him, "Are you still holding on
to your integrity? Curse God and die!"
10 He replied, "You are talking like a foolish[c]
woman. Shall we accept good from God, and not
trouble?"[n]
In all this, Job did not sin in what he said.[o]

Job's Three Friends

11 When Job's three friends, Eliphaz the Teman-

1:19 [x]Jer 4:11; 13:24
1:20 [y]Ge 37:29 [z]1Pe 5:6
1:21 [a]Ecc 5:15; 1Ti 6:7 [b]1Sa 2:7 [c]Job 2:10; Eph 5:20; 1Th 5:18
1:22 [d]Job 2:10
2:1 [e]Job 1:6
2:3 [f]Job 1:1,8 [g]Job 27:6 [h]Job 9:17
2:5 [i]Job 19:20 [j]Job 1:11
2:6 [k]Job 1:12
2:7 [l]Dt 28:35; Job 7:5
2:8 [m]Job 42:6; Jer 6:26; Eze 27:30; Mt 11:21
2:10 [n]Job 1:21 [o]Job 1:22; Ps 39:1; Jas 1:12; 5:11

[a] *21* Or *will return there* [b] *1* Hebrew *the sons of God*
[c] *10* The Hebrew word rendered *foolish* denotes moral deficiency.

ite,[p] Bildad the Shuhite[q] and Zophar the Naamathite, heard about all the troubles that had come
upon him, they set out from their homes and met
together by agreement to go and sympathize with
him and comfort him.[r] 12 When they saw him from
a distance, they could hardly recognize him; they
began to weep aloud, and they tore their robes
and sprinkled dust on their heads.[s] 13 Then they
sat on the ground with him for seven days and
seven nights.[t] No one said a word to him, because
they saw how great his suffering was.

Job Speaks

3 After this, Job opened his mouth and cursed
the day of his birth. 2 He said:

3 "May the day of my birth perish,
and the night it was said, 'A boy is born!'[u]
4 That day—may it turn to darkness;
may God above not care about it;
may no light shine upon it.
5 May darkness and deep shadow[a][v] claim it once more;
may a cloud settle over it;
may blackness overwhelm its light.
6 That night—may thick darkness[w] seize it;
may it not be included among the days of the year
nor be entered in any of the months.
7 May that night be barren;
may no shout of joy be heard in it.
8 May those who curse days[b] curse that day,
those who are ready to rouse Leviathan.[x]
9 May its morning stars become dark;
may it wait for daylight in vain
and not see the first rays of dawn,[y]
10 for it did not shut the doors of the womb on me
to hide trouble from my eyes.

11 "Why did I not perish at birth,
and die as I came from the womb?[z]
12 Why were there knees to receive me[a]
and breasts that I might be nursed?
13 For now I would be lying down[b] in peace;
I would be asleep and at rest[c]
14 with kings and counselors of the earth,[d]
who built for themselves places now lying in ruins,[e]
15 with rulers[f] who had gold,
who filled their houses with silver.[g]
16 Or why was I not hidden in the ground like a stillborn child,[h]
like an infant who never saw the light of day?

2:11 [p]Ge 36:11; Jer 49:7 [q]Ge 25:2 [r]Job 42:11; Ro 12:15
2:12 [s]Jos 7:6; Ne 9:1; La 2:10; Eze 27:30
2:13 [t]Ge 50:10; Eze 3:15
3:3 [u]Job 10:18-19; Jer 20:14-18
3:5 [v]Job 10:21, 22; Ps 23:4; Jer 2:6; 13:16
3:6 [w]Job 23:17
3:8 [x]Job 41:1,8, 10,25
3:9 [y]Job 41:18
3:11 [z]Job 10:18
3:12 [a]Ge 30:3; Isa 66:12
3:13 [b]Job 17:13 [c]Job 7:8-10, 21; 10:22; 14:10-12; 19:27; 21:13, 23
3:14 [d]Job 12:17 [e]Job 15:28
3:15 [f]Job 12:21 [g]Job 27:17
3:16 [h]Ps 58:8; Ecc 6:3

[a] 5 Or *and the shadow of death* [b] 8 Or *the sea*

Job's Friends

JOB 2:12

The first reaction of Job's friends to his calamities is sympathy. *In keeping with cultural norms, the men empathized with Job's grief by weeping loudly, ripping their clothes and sprinkling dust on their heads (see the note on 2Sa 1:19–27, page 475). In ancient culture, keeping a stiff upper lip was not expected during mourning. Even kings let their sobs be heard in public (2Sa 3:32). Tearing one's garments and covering one's head with dust were symbolic expressions of grief, disgrace and self-abasement (read about Tamar's dejection in 2Sa 13:10–19 and the prophet Ezra's anguish in Ezr 9:1–6). When we experience crisis and pain, we can take some cues from the people of old who were unashamed of their grief and threw themselves on God's mercy.*

Why?

JOB 3:23–26

Job's worst nightmares appear to have come true. He can hold in his anguish for only so long (a week to be exact). Finally he erupts in the natural human response to suffering: Why? Five times in this chapter he asks why. King David expresses his lament in the same way (Ps 22:1), as does Christ himself (Mt 27:46).

When we are suffering, Scripture makes it clear that pouring out our anguish, even our anger, is a natural and desirable response. In fact, if we keep everything inside, we only suffer more (Ps 32:3). The next time we are in physical or emotional pain, we can follow the examples of Job, of David, of Christ. We don't need to hide our feelings from the God who loves us and offers us refuge (Ps 38:8–9; 62:8).

17 There the wicked cease from turmoil,
and there the weary are at rest.[i]
18 Captives also enjoy their ease;
they no longer hear the slave driver's shout.[j]
19 The small and the great are there,
and the slave is freed from his master.

20 "Why is light given to those in misery,
and life to the bitter of soul,[k]
21 to those who long for death that does not come,[l]
who search for it more than for hidden treasure,[m]
22 who are filled with gladness
and rejoice when they reach the grave?
23 Why is life given to a man
whose way is hidden,
whom God has hedged in?[n]
24 For sighing comes to me instead of food;[o]
my groans pour out like water.[p]
25 What I feared has come upon me;
what I dreaded[q] has happened to me.
26 I have no peace, no quietness;
I have no rest,[r] but only turmoil."

Eliphaz

4 Then Eliphaz the Temanite replied:

2 "If someone ventures a word with you,
will you be impatient?
But who can keep from speaking?[s]
3 Think how you have instructed many,
how you have strengthened feeble hands.[t]
4 Your words have supported those who stumbled;
you have strengthened faltering knees.[u]
5 But now trouble comes to you, and you are discouraged;
it strikes[v] you, and you are dismayed.[w]
6 Should not your piety be your confidence[x]
and your blameless[y] ways your hope?

7 "Consider now: Who, being innocent, has ever perished?[z]
Where were the upright ever destroyed?[a]
8 As I have observed, those who plow evil[b]
and those who sow trouble reap it.[c]
9 At the breath of God[d] they are destroyed;
at the blast of his anger they perish.[e]
10 The lions may roar and growl,
yet the teeth of the great lions are broken.[f]
11 The lion perishes for lack of prey,[g]

3:17 [i]Job 17:16
3:18 [j]Job 39:7
3:20 [k]1Sa 1:10; Jer 20:18; Eze 27:30-31
3:21 [l]Rev 9:6 [m]Pr 2:4
3:23 [n]Job 19:6,8, 12; Ps 88:8; La 3:7
3:24 [o]Job 6:7; 33:20 [p]Ps 42:3,4
3:25 [q]Job 30:15
3:26 [r]Job 7:4,14
4:2 [s]Job 32:20
4:3 [t]Isa 35:3; Heb 12:12
4:4 [u]Isa 35:3; Heb 12:12
4:5 [v]Job 19:21 [w]Job 6:14
4:6 [x]Pr 3:26 [y]Job 1:1
4:7 [z]Job 36:7 [a]Job 8:20; Ps 37:25
4:8 [b]Job 15:35 [c]Pr 22:8; Hos 10:13; Gal 6:7-8
4:9 [d]Job 15:30; Isa 30:33; 2Th 2:8 [e]Job 40:13
4:10 [f]Job 5:15; Ps 58:6
4:11 [g]Job 27:14; Ps 34:10

and the cubs of the lioness are
scattered.

12 “A word was secretly brought to me,
my ears caught a whisper[h] of it.[i]
13 Amid disquieting dreams in the night,
when deep sleep falls on men,[j]
14 fear and trembling seized me
and made all my bones shake.[k]
15 A spirit glided past my face,
and the hair on my body stood on
end.
16 It stopped,
but I could not tell what it was.
A form stood before my eyes,
and I heard a hushed voice:
17 ‘Can a mortal be more righteous than
God?[l]
Can a man be more pure than his
Maker?[m]
18 If God places no trust in his servants,
if he charges his angels with error,[n]
19 how much more those who live in
houses of clay,[o]
whose foundations[p] are in the dust,[q]
who are crushed more readily than a
moth!
20 Between dawn and dusk they are
broken to pieces;
unnoticed, they perish forever.[r]
21 Are not the cords of their tent pulled
up,[s]
so that they die without wisdom?’[a][t]

5 “Call if you will, but who will answer you?
To which of the holy ones[u] will you turn?
2 Resentment kills a fool,
and envy slays the simple.[v]
3 I myself have seen a fool taking root,[w]
but suddenly his house was cursed.[x]
4 His children are far from safety,[y]
crushed in court[z] without a defender.
5 The hungry consume his harvest,[a]
taking it even from among thorns,
and the thirsty pant after his wealth.
6 For hardship does not spring from the
soil,
nor does trouble sprout from the
ground.
7 Yet man is born to trouble[b]
as surely as sparks fly upward.

8 “But if it were I, I would appeal to God;
I would lay my cause before him.[c]
9 He performs wonders that cannot be
fathomed,[d]
miracles that cannot be counted.
10 He bestows rain on the earth;
he sends water upon the countryside.[e]
11 The lowly he sets on high,[f]

4:12 [h]Job 26:14 [i]Job 33:14
4:13 [j]Job 33:15
4:14 [k]Jer 23:9; Hab 3:16
4:17 [l]Job 9:2 [m]Job 35:10
4:18 [n]Job 15:15
4:19 [o]Job 10:9 [p]Job 22:16 [q]Ge 2:7
4:20 [r]Job 14:2,20; 20:7; Ps 90:5-6
4:21 [s]Job 8:22 [t]Job 18:21; 36:12
5:1 [u]Job 15:15
5:2 [v]Pr 12:16
5:3 [w]Ps 37:35; Jer 12:2 [x]Job 24:18
5:4 [y]Job 4:11 [z]Am 5:12
5:5 [a]Job 18:8-10
5:7 [b]Job 14:1
5:8 [c]Ps 35:23; 50:15
5:9 [d]Job 42:3; Ps 40:5
5:10 [e]Job 36:28
5:11 [f]Ps 113:7-8

[a] *21* Some interpreters end the quotation after verse 17.

When Bad Things Happen

JOB 4:12-19

When bad things happen to good people, human nature seeks a logical explanation. Job’s friend Eliphaz is the first to offer his two cents. (Never mind that Job doesn’t ask for it.) Eliphaz bases his opinions and advice on a nightmare he had, which he assumes is a direct communiqué from the Almighty. In other words, he claims to speak for God when he counsels Job. How natural it is for Job’s well-meaning friends to try to “fix” Job’s problems and to view his situation through the lens of their own finite experiences. Eliphaz considers himself wise, but God puts him in his place later (Job 42:7). In the face of unexplainable suffering, we can humbly admit that we do not know all that is in God’s mind and simply comfort our friends rather than try to fix things for them.

The Cure

JOB 5:17–18

Because of Eliphaz's black-and-white, cause-and-effect logic, his conclusions *about the cure for Job's suffering are off base.* He wrongly assumes that Job has sinned and is being disciplined; thus, Job needs to *repent and seek God's mercy.* While Eliphaz's assumptions *about what God is up to in Job's life are wrong,* he does highlight *a wonderful truth about being God's child.* Because our Father loves us *as sons and daughters, he wisely and mercifully inflicts just the right "wounds" of discipline at just the right time for our unique situation* (Heb 12:5–11). The *painful consequences of our disobedience are gifts from a loving* God whose only desire is to draw us closer to his side, where joy awaits us (Ps 16:11).

and those who mourn are lifted to
safety.
[12]He thwarts the plans[g] of the crafty,
so that their hands achieve no
success.
[13]He catches the wise in their craftiness,[h]
and the schemes of the wily are swept
away.
[14]Darkness[i] comes upon them in the
daytime;
at noon they grope as in the night.[j]
[15]He saves the needy[k] from the sword in
their mouth;
he saves them from the clutches of the
powerful.[l]
[16]So the poor have hope,
and injustice shuts its mouth.[m]

[17]"Blessed is the man whom God
corrects;[n]
so do not despise the discipline[o] of the
Almighty.[a][p]
[18]For he wounds, but he also binds up;[q]
he injures, but his hands also heal.[r]
[19]From six calamities he will rescue you;
in seven no harm will befall you.[s]
[20]In famine[t] he will ransom you from
death,
and in battle from the stroke of the
sword.[u]
[21]You will be protected from the lash of
the tongue,[v]
and need not fear[w] when destruction
comes.
[22]You will laugh at destruction and
famine,
and need not fear the beasts of the
earth.[x]
[23]For you will have a covenant with the
stones[y] of the field,
and the wild animals will be at peace
with you.[z]
[24]You will know that your tent is secure;
you will take stock of your property
and find nothing missing.[a]
[25]You will know that your children will be
many,[b]
and your descendants like the grass of
the earth.[c]
[26]You will come to the grave in full vigor,[d]
like sheaves gathered in season.
[27]"We have examined this, and it is true.
So hear it and apply it to yourself."

Job

6

Then Job replied:
[2]"If only my anguish could be weighed

5:12 [g]Ne 4:15; Ps 33:10
5:13 [h]1Co 3:19*
5:14 [i]Job 12:25 [j]Dt 28:29
5:15 [k]Ps 35:10 [l]Job 4:10
5:16 [m]Ps 107:42
5:17 [n]Jas 1:12 [o]Ps 94:12; Pr 3:11 [p]Heb 12:5-11
5:18 [q]Isa 30:26 [r]1Sa 2:6
5:19 [s]Ps 34:19; 91:10
5:20 [t]Ps 33:19 [u]Ps 144:10
5:21 [v]Ps 31:20 [w]Ps 91:5
5:22 [x]Ps 91:13; Eze 34:25
5:23 [y]Ps 91:12 [z]Isa 11:6-9
5:24 [a]Job 8:6
5:25 [b]Ps 112:2 [c]Ps 72:16; Isa 44:3-4
5:26 [d]Ge 15:15

[a] *17* Hebrew *Shaddai*; here and throughout Job

and all my misery be placed on the
scales![e]
3 It would surely outweigh the sand[f] of
the seas—
no wonder my words have been
impetuous.[g]
4 The arrows[h] of the Almighty are in me,[i]
my spirit drinks[j] in their poison;
God's terrors[k] are marshaled against
me.[l]
5 Does a wild donkey bray when it has
grass,
or an ox bellow when it has fodder?
6 Is tasteless food eaten without salt,
or is there flavor in the white of an
egg[a]?
7 I refuse to touch it;
such food makes me ill.[m]

8 "Oh, that I might have my request,
that God would grant what I hope for,[n]
9 that God would be willing to crush me,
to let loose his hand and cut me off![o]
10 Then I would still have this
consolation—
my joy in unrelenting pain—
that I had not denied the words[p] of
the Holy One.[q]

11 "What strength do I have, that I should
still hope?
What prospects, that I should be
patient?[r]
12 Do I have the strength of stone?
Is my flesh bronze?
13 Do I have any power to help myself,[s]
now that success has been driven
from me?

14 "A despairing man[t] should have the
devotion[u] of his friends,
even though he forsakes the fear of
the Almighty.
15 But my brothers are as undependable as
intermittent streams,[v]
as the streams that overflow
16 when darkened by thawing ice
and swollen with melting snow,
17 but that cease to flow in the dry season,
and in the heat[w] vanish from their
channels.
18 Caravans turn aside from their routes;
they go up into the wasteland and
perish.
19 The caravans of Tema[x] look for water,
the traveling merchants of Sheba look
in hope.
20 They are distressed, because they had
been confident;

6:2 [e]Job 31:6
6:3 [f]Pr 27:3 [g]Job 23:2
6:4 [h]Ps 38:2 [i]Job 16:12, 13 [j]Job 21:20 [k]Job 30:15 [l]Ps 88:15-18
6:7 [m]Job 3:24
6:8 [n]Job 14:13
6:9 [o]Nu 11:15; 1Ki 19:4
6:10 [p]Job 22:22; 23:12 [q]Lev 19:2; Isa 57:15
6:11 [r]Job 21:4
6:13 [s]Job 26:2
6:14 [t]Job 4:5 [u]Job 15:4
6:15 [v]Ps 38:11; Jer 15:18
6:17 [w]Job 24:19
6:19 [x]Ge 25:15; Isa 21:14

[a] 6 The meaning of the Hebrew for this phrase is uncertain.

When Pain Is Relentless

JOB 6:8-10

Job's pain is relentless. Escape from this life seems like the best, or only, option. Yet he leaves his fate entirely up to his Creator. As much as he would like to be done with the agony his life has become, he doesn't consider ending it himself. While he suffers day after day, he doesn't even pretend to hope that things will get better, nor can he find reason for rejoicing in his trials. His only consolation is in believing that, in spite of everything, he has not brought dishonor to the God he loves. He has cursed the day he was born, even life itself, but he has not cursed God. Even while suffering, even while weakened by the pain of his circumstances, Job remains true. What an encouragement Job can be to us! When we suffer, we gain encouragement and strength as we endure anguish without denying our faith or taking our fate into our own hands.

Not Convinced

JOB 6:24–25

Job's friend Eliphaz has been eloquent and rational in his explanation of Job's suffering and his prescription for Job's restoration. Job, however, is unconvinced. He has communed intimately with God long enough to know where he stands. He doesn't categorically deny that he might have committed some sin; he is open to being shown the truth about himself. However, nothing within him resonates with his friend's assessment.

As women indwelled by God's Holy Spirit, we recognize that the whole truth about us is fully known by the One who loves us perfectly. While the insight and counsel of godly friends can be invaluable, we ultimately rely on the Spirit within us to convict us of sin and direct us toward righteousness. When we are uncertain about what is true, we can make the psalmist's prayer our own (Ps 25:4–5).

they arrive there, only to be
disappointed.[y]
21 Now you too have proved to be of no
help;
you see something dreadful and are
afraid.[z]
22 Have I ever said, 'Give something on my
behalf,
pay a ransom for me from your
wealth,
23 deliver me from the hand of the enemy,
ransom me from the clutches of the
ruthless'?

24 "Teach me, and I will be quiet;[a]
show me where I have been wrong.
25 How painful are honest words![b]
But what do your arguments prove?
26 Do you mean to correct what I say,
and treat the words of a despairing
man as wind?[c]
27 You would even cast lots[d] for the
fatherless
and barter away your friend.

28 "But now be so kind as to look at me.
Would I lie to your face?[e]
29 Relent, do not be unjust;
reconsider, for my integrity is at
stake.[a][f]
30 Is there any wickedness on my lips?[g]
Can my mouth not discern[h] malice?

7

"Does not man have hard service[i] on earth?[j]
Are not his days like those of a hired
man?[k]
2 Like a slave longing for the evening
shadows,
or a hired man waiting eagerly for his
wages,[l]
3 so I have been allotted months of
futility,
and nights of misery have been
assigned to me.[m]
4 When I lie down I think, 'How long
before I get up?'[n]
The night drags on, and I toss till
dawn.
5 My body is clothed with worms[o] and
scabs,
my skin is broken and festering.

6 "My days are swifter than a weaver's
shuttle,[p]
and they come to an end without
hope.[q]
7 Remember, O God, that my life is but a
breath;[r]
my eyes will never see happiness
again.[s]

6:20 [y]Jer 14:3
6:21 [z]Ps 38:11
6:24 [a]Ps 39:1
6:25 [b]Ecc 12:11
6:26 [c]Job 8:2; 15:3
6:27 [d]Joel 3:3; Na 3:10; 2Pe 2:3
6:28 [e]Job 27:4; 33:1,3; 36:3,4
6:29 [f]Job 23:7,10; 34:5,36; 42:6
6:30 [g]Job 27:4 [h]Job 12:11
7:1 [i]Job 14:14; Isa 40:2 [j]Job 5:7 [k]Job 14:6
7:2 [l]Lev 19:13
7:3 [m]Job 16:7; Ps 6:6
7:4 [n]Dt 28:67
7:5 [o]Job 17:14; Isa 14:11
7:6 [p]Job 9:25 [q]Job 13:15; 17:11,15
7:7 [r]Ps 78:39; Jas 4:14 [s]Job 9:25

[a] 29 Or *my righteousness still stands*

Abigail

A Wise Woman

Two hundred armed men marched toward her. They were dirty, smelly, hungry from weeks in the desert, and *angry*. Abigail—in an act of steely courage—knelt face down in the dirt and implored forgiveness. Nabal, her husband, was the cause of this terrifying threat of revenge against her entire household.

This certainly was not the first time that Abigail had to think fast to cover her husband's bad behavior. Nabal was a fool. Even his name meant "fool." But whatever he was, he was her husband. She asked David to put the blame on *her*. Her quick thinking to gather food for David's army reflected her intelligence; her assessment of David's character—and his relationship with the Lord—revealed profound wisdom.

Believing in his desire to please God, she wisely reached into David's soul to pull out his own better nature. Her trust was rewarded: The scales fell from his eyes. David realized that the Lord had used this beautiful woman to correct a knee-jerk reaction that he would have long regretted—a reaction that would have placed him outside God's will and favor. How sweet her assurance of success must have sounded to a man uncertain of his fate at Saul's hand. Surely, she brought him into God's presence and offered godly counsel.

When Nabal died a few days later by God's judgment, David quickly called Abigail to his side to become his wife. Without a backward glance, Abigail left her life of wealth to be with a man on the run.

It can be a challenge not to panic when faced with danger, to use mental resources and God-given insight to handle problems. In her life with Nabal, Abigail had learned to think quickly and to act decisively. She was capable and intelligent—and she earned David's admiration.

Whether in favorable circumstances or in harsh ones, the challenge is the same: to use our wisdom and abilities in the service of the will of God.

Abigail
(my father is joy)

1 Samuel 25; 27:3; 30:5

2 Samuel 3:3

1 Chronicles 3:1

Candid SNAPSHOT David said to Abigail, "Praise be to the LORD, the God of Israel, who has sent you today to meet me. May you be blessed for your good judgment and for keeping me from bloodshed (1 Samuel 25:32-33).

Witch of Endor

Smoke and Mirrors

Saul had failed as king. He had disobeyed God, and God was no longer available to him. Samuel was dead, and Saul had no one to turn to. He was terrified. Divination and witchcraft were expressly forbidden by the law as detestable to God (Dt 18:10–11; Lev 20:6). God didn't allow communication with the dead. Saul himself had expelled the mediums (witches) and spiritists from the land following Samuel's death. Yet, Saul himself now desperately turned to a medium because he could no longer hear God's voice.

When the witch saw Samuel and perceived that it was Saul who had come to her, she was alarmed. She knew she was in over her head. She had no scruples and made a good profit from the suffering of others. But this time, she was not in control. God used her illicit activity to clarify Saul's position beyond a shadow of a doubt. Saul was not comforted but rather was incapacitated by what he heard. Samuel declared that Saul and his sons would die the next day.

Regardless of the means by which the witch of Endor plied her trade in sorcery, what she did was *wrong*. She obviously knew God's commandments against the practice of witchcraft, or at the very least she knew that her king was enforcing those commandments (1Sa 28:9). But she knowingly disobeyed, plying her trade with apparent disregard for God's law and the king's.

Some even today carry on this woman's tradition. Don't be deceived, no matter how innocent it seems. They do not have their customers' happiness or well-being in mind. The Enemy never does. We have a human tendency to want to know the future. It began with Eve, in the Garden of Eden, wanting to be like God. We think that somehow we will be more prepared, more in control if we know what lies ahead. We won't be. Jesus said, "Do not worry about tomorrow, for tomorrow will worry about itself. Each day has enough trouble of its own" (Mt 6:34). Hearing and obeying God's voice for today is ample challenge. Our response to *him* shapes our tomorrows.

Witch of Endor

1 Samuel 28

Candid SNAPSHOT When the woman came to Saul and saw that he was greatly shaken, she said, "Look, your maidservant has obeyed you. I took my life in my hands and did what you told me to do" (1 Samuel 28:21).

8 The eye that now sees me will see me
no longer;
you will look for me, but I will be no
more.[t]
9 As a cloud vanishes and is gone,
so he who goes down to the grave[a][u]
does not return.[v]
10 He will never come to his house again;
his place[w] will know him no more.[x]

11 "Therefore I will not keep silent;[y]
I will speak out in the anguish of my
spirit,
I will complain in the bitterness of my
soul.[z]
12 Am I the sea, or the monster of the
deep,[a]
that you put me under guard?
13 When I think my bed will comfort me
and my couch will ease my
complaint,[b]
14 even then you frighten me with dreams
and terrify[c] me with visions,
15 so that I prefer strangling and death,[d]
rather than this body of mine.
16 I despise my life;[e] I would not live
forever.
Let me alone; my days have no
meaning.

17 "What is man that you make so much of
him,
that you give him so much attention,[f]
18 that you examine him every morning
and test him every moment?[g]
19 Will you never look away from me,
or let me alone even for an instant?[h]
20 If I have sinned, what have I done to
you,[i]
O watcher of men?
Why have you made me your target?[j]
Have I become a burden to you?[b]
21 Why do you not pardon my offenses
and forgive my sins?[k]
For I will soon lie down in the dust;[l]
you will search for me, but I will be
no more."

Bildad

8 Then Bildad the Shuhite replied:

2 "How long will you say such things?
Your words are a blustering wind.[m]
3 Does God pervert justice?[n]
Does the Almighty pervert what is
right?[o]
4 When your children sinned against him,

7:8 [t]Job 20:7,9, 21 **7:9** [u]Job 11:8 [v]2Sa 12:23; Job 30:15 **7:10** [w]Job 27:21, 23 [x]Job 8:18 **7:11** [y]Ps 40:9 [z]1Sa 1:10 **7:12** [a]Eze 32:2-3 **7:13** [b]Job 9:27 **7:14** [c]Job 9:34 **7:15** [d]1Ki 19:4 **7:16** [e]Job 9:21; 10:1 **7:17** [f]Ps 8:4; 144:3; Heb 2:6 **7:18** [g]Job 14:3 **7:19** [h]Job 9:18 **7:20** [i]Job 35:6 [j]Job 16:12 **7:21** [k]Job 10:14 [l]Job 10:9; Ps 104:29 **8:2** [m]Job 6:26 **8:3** [n]Dt 32:4; 2Ch 19:7; Ro 3:5 [o]Ge 18:25

[a] 9 Hebrew *Sheol* [b] 20 A few manuscripts of the Masoretic Text, an ancient Hebrew scribal tradition and Septuagint; most manuscripts of the Masoretic Text *I have become a burden to myself.*

Feeling Like a Target

JOB 7:17-20

While Job wants to keep his faith in God's goodness and love, his resolve is slipping. In Psalm 8:4 David asks almost the identical question Job asks: "What is man that you are mindful of him, the son of man that you care for him?" But David's question is expressed with wonder and praise, while Job's is uttered with frustration and bitterness. He's tired of feeling like God is using him for target practice. Jeremiah felt the same way (La 3:1-18).

When life is hard and there seems to be no end to suffering in sight, it's easy to feel like no one cares, possibly even God. If someone you care about is feeling despondent and disconnected from God, what encouragement can you offer (La 3:21-33; Ps 103:8-14)?

Bildad Speaks

JOB 8:8–10

Job's friend Bildad levels generally the same accusations at him that Eliphaz did: Job's apparent righteousness must be a ruse, and the only way out of his pain is to beg God's forgiveness for his sin. Unlike Eliphaz, however, Bildad supports his claim with the wisdom of "former generations" rather than with personal experience or divine inspiration. Operating under the assumption that history is destined to repeat itself if we don't learn from it, Bildad implies that if Job consults the wise traditions of those who lived before him, he'll be able to solve the puzzle of his predicament. Once again, a well-meaning friend assures Job that conclusive answers are available—this time in the annals of human wisdom. But God's wisdom is galaxies above human insight (Isa 55:8–9), and we demonstrate true wisdom when we look to him for our answers.

he gave them over to the penalty of
their sin.[p]
5 But if you will look to God
and plead[q] with the Almighty,
6 if you are pure and upright,
even now he will rouse himself on
your behalf[r]
and restore you to your rightful
place.[s]
7 Your beginnings will seem humble,
so prosperous[t] will your future be.

8 "Ask the former generations[u]
and find out what their fathers
learned,
9 for we were born only yesterday and
know nothing,[v]
and our days on earth are but a
shadow.[w]
10 Will they not instruct you and tell you?
Will they not bring forth words from
their understanding?
11 Can papyrus grow tall where there is no
marsh?
Can reeds thrive without water?
12 While still growing and uncut,
they wither more quickly than grass.[x]
13 Such is the destiny of all who forget
God;[y]
so perishes the hope of the
godless.[z]
14 What he trusts in is fragile[a];
what he relies on is a spider's web.[a]
15 He leans on his web,[b] but it gives way;
he clings to it, but it does not hold.[c]
16 He is like a well-watered plant in the
sunshine,
spreading its shoots[d] over the
garden;[e]
17 it entwines its roots around a pile of
rocks
and looks for a place among the
stones.
18 But when it is torn from its spot,
that place disowns it and says, 'I
never saw you.'[f]
19 Surely its life withers[g] away,
and[b] from the soil other plants grow.[h]

20 "Surely God does not reject a blameless[i]
man
or strengthen the hands of
evildoers.[j]
21 He will yet fill your mouth with
laughter[k]
and your lips with shouts of joy.[l]
22 Your enemies will be clothed in shame,[m]
and the tents of the wicked will be no
more."[n]

[a] 14 The meaning of the Hebrew for this word is uncertain.
[b] 19 Or *Surely all the joy it has / is that*

8:4 [p]Job 1:19
8:5 [q]Job 11:13
8:6 [r]Ps 7:6 [s]Job 5:24
8:7 [t]Job 42:12
8:8 [u]Dt 4:32; 32:7; Job 15:18
8:9 [v]Ge 47:9 [w]1Ch 29:15; Job 7:6
8:12 [x]Ps 129:6; Jer 17:6
8:13 [y]Ps 9:17 [z]Job 11:20; 13:16; 15:34; Pr 10:28
8:14 [a]Isa 59:5
8:15 [b]Job 27:18 [c]Ps 49:11
8:16 [d]Ps 80:11 [e]Ps 37:35; Jer 11:16
8:18 [f]Job 7:8; Ps 37:36
8:19 [g]Job 20:5 [h]Ecc 1:4
8:20 [i]Job 1:1 [j]Job 21:30
8:21 [k]Job 5:22 [l]Ps 126:2; 132:16
8:22 [m]Ps 35:26; 109:29; 132:18 [n]Job 18:6, 14,21

Job

9

Then Job replied:

2 “Indeed, I know that this is true.
But how can a mortal be righteous before God?[o]
3 Though one wished to dispute with him,
he could not answer him one time out of a thousand.[p]
4 His wisdom[q] is profound, his power is vast.[r]
Who has resisted him and come out unscathed?[s]
5 He moves mountains without their knowing it
and overturns them in his anger.[t]
6 He shakes the earth[u] from its place
and makes its pillars tremble.[v]
7 He speaks to the sun and it does not shine;
he seals off the light of the stars.[w]
8 He alone stretches out the heavens[x]
and treads on the waves of the sea.[y]
9 He is the Maker of the Bear and Orion,
the Pleiades and the constellations of the south.[z]
10 He performs wonders[a] that cannot be fathomed,
miracles that cannot be counted.[b]
11 When he passes me, I cannot see him;
when he goes by, I cannot perceive him.[c]
12 If he snatches away, who can stop him?[d]
Who can say to him, ‘What are you doing?’[e]
13 God does not restrain his anger;
even the cohorts of Rahab[f] cowered at his feet.

14 “How then can I dispute with him?
How can I find words to argue with him?
15 Though I were innocent, I could not answer him;[g]
I could only plead[h] with my Judge for mercy.
16 Even if I summoned him and he responded,
I do not believe he would give me a hearing.
17 He would crush me[i] with a storm[j]
and multiply[k] my wounds for no reason.[l]
18 He would not let me regain my breath
but would overwhelm me with misery.[m]
19 If it is a matter of strength, he is mighty!
And if it is a matter of justice, who will summon him[a]?

9:2 [o]Job 4:17; Ps 143:2; Ro 3:20
9:3 [p]Job 10:2; 40:2
9:4 [q]Job 11:6 [r]Job 36:5 [s]2Ch 13:12
9:5 [t]Mic 1:4
9:6 [u]Isa 2:21; Hag 2:6; Heb 12:26 [v]Job 26:11
9:7 [w]Isa 13:10; Eze 32:8
9:8 [x]Ge 1:6; Ps 104:2-3 [y]Job 38:16; Ps 77:19
9:9 [z]Ge 1:16; Job 38:31; Am 5:8
9:10 [a]Ps 71:15 [b]Job 5:9
9:11 [c]Job 23:8-9; 35:14
9:12 [d]Job 11:10 [e]Isa 45:9; Ro 9:20
9:13 [f]Job 26:12; Ps 89:10; Isa 30:7; 51:9
9:15 [g]Job 10:15 [h]Job 8:5
9:17 [i]Job 16:12 [j]Job 30:22 [k]Job 16:14 [l]Job 2:3
9:18 [m]Job 7:19; 27:2

The Truth

JOB 9:4–10

Job has barely begun to speak his mind here, but *even this early in the dialog Job hits on a truth that could have ended his complaining if only he’d truly embraced it. In magnifying the power and authority of the Creator, Job foreshadows the very response God ultimately gives him in Job 38.*

Make a list of the actions and *abilities Job ascribes to the Almighty in this passage. Then turn to God’s rhetorical speech in Job 38, and make a list of the claims he makes about himself. If Job had taken his own words to heart in chapter 9, how might they have helped him better cope with his situation?*

[a] *19* See Septuagint; Hebrew *me.*

A Mediator

JOB 9:32–35

It seems strange that so soon after testifying to God's supreme power and authority over the universe, Job is fantasizing about facing off with God in a court of law. Job entertains the idea of a righteous umpire who can level the playing field and referee the situation. In his cynical state, Job despairs of ever getting a fair hearing; he knows that as a mere mortal he can never really take on the Creator of the universe.

But as misguided as Job is, God has long foreseen and arranged to fulfill Job's desire for a mediator who will bridge the gap between himself and the Almighty. In Christ, God provides every human being with the only way into his holy presence (1Ti 2:5–6). Through faith in Christ the Mediator, we are both forgiven of sin and reconciled to God.

20 Even if I were innocent, my mouth
would condemn me;
if I were blameless, it would
pronounce me guilty.

21 "Although I am blameless,[n]
I have no concern for myself;
I despise my own life.[o]
22 It is all the same; that is why I say,
'He destroys both the blameless and
the wicked.'[p]
23 When a scourge[q] brings sudden death,
he mocks the despair of the innocent.[r]
24 When a land falls into the hands of the
wicked,[s]
he blindfolds its judges.[t]
If it is not he, then who is it?

25 "My days are swifter than a runner;[u]
they fly away without a glimpse of
joy.
26 They skim past like boats of papyrus,[v]
like eagles swooping down on their
prey.[w]
27 If I say, 'I will forget my complaint,[x]
I will change my expression, and
smile,'
28 I still dread[y] all my sufferings,
for I know you will not hold me
innocent.[z]
29 Since I am already found guilty,
why should I struggle in vain?[a]
30 Even if I washed myself with soap[a]
and my hands[b] with washing soda,[c]
31 you would plunge me into a slime pit
so that even my clothes would detest
me.

32 "He is not a man like me that I might
answer him,[d]
that we might confront each other in
court.[e]
33 If only there were someone to arbitrate
between us,[f]
to lay his hand upon us both,
34 someone to remove God's rod from me,[g]
so that his terror would frighten me
no more.
35 Then I would speak up without fear of
him,
but as it now stands with me, I
cannot.[h]

10

1 "I loathe my very life;[i]
therefore I will give free rein to my
complaint
and speak out in the bitterness of my
soul.[j]
2 I will say to God: Do not condemn me,
but tell me what charges[k] you have
against me.

9:21 [n]Job 1:1 [o]Job 7:16
9:22 [p]Job 10:8; Ecc 9:2,3; Eze 21:3
9:23 [q]Heb 11:36 [r]Job 24:1,12
9:24 [s]Job 10:3; 16:11 [t]Job 12:6
9:25 [u]Job 7:6
9:26 [v]Isa 18:2 [w]Hab 1:8
9:27 [x]Job 7:11
9:28 [y]Job 3:25; Ps 119:120 [z]Job 7:21
9:29 [a]Ps 37:33
9:30 [b]Job 31:7 [c]Jer 2:22
9:32 [d]Ro 9:20 [e]Ps 143:2; Ecc 6:10
9:33 [f]1Sa 2:25
9:34 [g]Job 13:21; Ps 39:10
9:35 [h]Job 13:21
10:1 [i]1Ki 19:4 [j]Job 7:11
10:2 [k]Job 9:29

[a] 30 Or *snow*

10:3 [l]Job 9:22 [m]Job 14:15; Ps 138:8; Isa 64:8 [n]Job 21:16; 22:18
10:4 [o]1Sa 16:7
10:5 [p]Ps 90:2,4; 2Pe 3:8
10:6 [q]Job 14:16
10:8 [r]Ps 119:73
10:9 [s]Isa 64:8 [t]Ge 2:7
10:11 [u]Ps 139:13, 15
10:12 [v]Job 33:4
10:13 [w]Job 23:13
10:14 [x]Job 7:21
10:15 [y]Job 9:13; Isa 3:11 [z]Job 9:15
10:16 [a]Isa 38:13; La 3:10 [b]Job 5:9
10:17 [c]Job 16:8 [d]Ru 1:21
10:18 [e]Job 3:11
10:20 [f]Job 14:1 [g]Job 7:19 [h]Job 7:16
10:21 [i]2Sa 12:23; Job 3:13; 16:22

3 Does it please you to oppress me,[l]
to spurn the work of your hands,[m]
while you smile on the schemes of the wicked?[n]
4 Do you have eyes of flesh?
Do you see as a mortal sees?[o]
5 Are your days like those of a mortal
or your years like those of a man,[p]
6 that you must search out my faults
and probe after my sin[q]—
7 though you know that I am not guilty
and that no one can rescue me from your hand?

8 "Your hands shaped[r] me and made me.
Will you now turn and destroy me?
9 Remember that you molded me like clay.[s]
Will you now turn me to dust again?[t]
10 Did you not pour me out like milk
and curdle me like cheese,
11 clothe me with skin and flesh
and knit me together[u] with bones and sinews?
12 You gave me life[v] and showed me kindness,
and in your providence watched over my spirit.

13 "But this is what you concealed in your heart,
and I know that this was in your mind:[w]
14 If I sinned, you would be watching me
and would not let my offense go unpunished.[x]
15 If I am guilty—woe to me![y]
Even if I am innocent, I cannot lift my head,[z]
for I am full of shame
and drowned in[a] my affliction.
16 If I hold my head high, you stalk me like a lion[a]
and again display your awesome power against me.[b]
17 You bring new witnesses against me[c]
and increase your anger toward me;[d]
your forces come against me wave upon wave.

18 "Why then did you bring me out of the womb?[e]
I wish I had died before any eye saw me.
19 If only I had never come into being,
or had been carried straight from the womb to the grave!
20 Are not my few days[f] almost over?[g]
Turn away from me[h] so I can have a moment's joy
21 before I go to the place of no return,[i]

[a] 15 Or *and aware of*

Now what will a poor creature like that do if [her deep troubles go] on for a very long time? If she prays . . . she is incapable of receiving any comfort, nor, even when her prayer is vocal, can she understand what she is saying; while mental prayer at such a time is certainly impossible—her faculties are not capable of it. Solitude is still worse for her, though it is also torture for her to be in anyone's company or to be spoken to; and so, despite all her efforts to conceal the fact, she becomes outwardly upset and despondent, to a very noticeable extent. Is it credible that she will be able to say what is the matter with her? The thing is inexpressible, for this distress and oppression are spiritual troubles and cannot be given a name. The best medicine—I do not say for removing the trouble, for I know of none for that, but for enabling the soul to endure it—is to occupy oneself with external affairs and works of charity and to hope in God's mercy, which never fails those who hope in Him. May He be blessed forever. Amen.

—Teresa of Avila (1515-1582)

Zophar Speaks

JOB 11:13–15

Like Eliphaz and Bildad, Zophar wrongly assumes that God is punishing Job for some hidden evil. Zophar's advice is even more simplistic than that of Job's other friends. "If you do this" Zophar claims, "then God will do that." In Zophar's view, if Job just does the right thing, then God is duty-bound to reward him with a "brighter than noonday" existence (Job 11:17).

God does not promise a carefree life, even to his most righteous servants. Nor does God always equate suffering with sin. In fact, in John 9:1–3, Jesus makes it clear that God sometimes allows hardship in order to display his glory in a person's life. Next time a well-meaning friend offers you a simplistic solution to a complex problem, take heart that even the sinless Christ suffered unto death, and he fully understands your situation.

to the land of gloom and deep
shadow,[a][j]
22 to the land of deepest night,
of deep shadow and disorder,
where even the light is like darkness."

Zophar

11 Then Zophar the Naamathite replied:

2 "Are all these words to go unanswered?[k]
Is this talker to be vindicated?
3 Will your idle talk reduce men to
silence?
Will no one rebuke you when you
mock?[l]
4 You say to God, 'My beliefs are flawless[m]
and I am pure[n] in your sight.'
5 Oh, how I wish that God would speak,
that he would open his lips against you
6 and disclose to you the secrets of
wisdom,[o]
for true wisdom has two sides.
Know this: God has even forgotten
some of your sin.[p]

7 "Can you fathom[q] the mysteries of God?
Can you probe the limits of the
Almighty?
8 They are higher than the heavens[r]—
what can you do?
They are deeper than the depths of
the grave[b]—what can you know?
9 Their measure is longer than the earth
and wider than the sea.

10 "If he comes along and confines you in
prison
and convenes a court, who can
oppose him?[s]
11 Surely he recognizes deceitful men;
and when he sees evil, does he not
take note?[t]
12 But a witless man can no more become
wise
than a wild donkey's colt can be born
a man.[c]

13 "Yet if you devote your heart[u] to him
and stretch out your hands to him,[v]
14 if you put away the sin that is in your
hand
and allow no evil[w] to dwell in your
tent,[x]
15 then you will lift up your face[y] without
shame;
you will stand firm and without fear.
16 You will surely forget your trouble,[z]
recalling it only as waters gone by.[a]
17 Life will be brighter than noonday,[b]

10:21 [j]Ps 23:4; 88:12
11:2 [k]Job 8:2
11:3 [l]Job 17:2; 21:3
11:4 [m]Job 6:10 [n]Job 10:7
11:6 [o]Job 9:4 [p]Ezr 9:13; Job 15:5
11:7 [q]Ecc 3:11; Ro 11:33
11:8 [r]Job 22:12
11:10 [s]Job 9:12; Rev 3:7
11:11 [t]Job 34:21-25; Ps 10:14
11:13 [u]1Sa 7:3; Ps 78:8 [v]Ps 88:9
11:14 [w]Ps 101:4 [x]Job 22:23
11:15 [y]Job 22:26; 1Jn 3:21
11:16 [z]Isa 65:16 [a]Job 22:11
11:17 [b]Job 22:28; Ps 37:6; Isa 58:8,10

[a] 21 Or *and the shadow of death;* also in verse 22 [b] 8 Hebrew *than Sheol* [c] 12 Or *wild donkey can be born tame*

and darkness will become like
morning.
18 You will be secure, because there is hope;
you will look about you and take your
rest[c] in safety.[d]
19 You will lie down, with no one to make
you afraid,[e]
and many will court your favor.[f]
20 But the eyes of the wicked will fail,[g]
and escape will elude them;[h]
their hope will become a dying gasp."[i]

Job

12

Then Job replied:

2 "Doubtless you are the people,
and wisdom will die with you![j]
3 But I have a mind as well as you;
I am not inferior to you.
Who does not know all these things?[k]

4 "I have become a laughingstock[l] to my
friends,
though I called upon God and he
answered[m]—
a mere laughingstock, though
righteous and blameless![n]
5 Men at ease have contempt for
misfortune
as the fate of those whose feet are
slipping.
6 The tents of marauders are
undisturbed,[o]
and those who provoke God are
secure[p]—
those who carry their god in their
hands.[a]

7 "But ask the animals, and they will
teach you,
or the birds of the air, and they will
tell you;
8 or speak to the earth, and it will teach
you,
or let the fish of the sea inform you.
9 Which of all these does not know
that the hand of the LORD has done
this?[q]
10 In his hand is the life of every creature
and the breath of all mankind.[r]
11 Does not the ear test words
as the tongue tastes food?[s]
12 Is not wisdom found among the aged?[t]
Does not long life bring
understanding?[u]

13 "To God belong wisdom[v] and power;[w]
counsel and understanding are his.[x]
14 What he tears down[y] cannot be rebuilt;[z]

11:18 [c]Ps 3:5 [d]Lev 26:6; Pr 3:24
11:19 [e]Lev 26:6 [f]Isa 45:14
11:20 [g]Dt 28:65; Job 17:5 [h]Job 27:22; 34:22 [i]Job 8:13
12:2 [j]Job 17:10
12:3 [k]Job 13:2
12:4 [l]Job 21:3 [m]Ps 91:15 [n]Job 6:29
12:6 [o]Job 22:18 [p]Job 9:24; 21:9
12:9 [q]Isa 41:20
12:10 [r]Job 27:3; 33:4; Ac 17:28
12:11 [s]Job 34:3
12:12 [t]Job 15:10 [u]Job 32:7,9
12:13 [v]Job 11:6 [w]Job 9:4 [x]Job 32:8; 38:36
12:14 [y]Job 19:10 [z]Job 37:7; Isa 25:2

[a] 6 Or *secure / in what God's hand brings them*

Job's Response

JOB 12:2–3

Job's friends have filled his ears with their "wisdom," but Job is tired of their condescending tone. After all, he points out, he could have given himself the same advice—if it was worth anything. Job knows his friends are off base, but it's hard to defend himself when they're lording it over him. He responds with biting sarcasm. If only his friends had approached him as their equal, as their beloved brother in the faith, then they might have had true wisdom and comfort to offer. When someone seems to be living under a cloud, it's easy to pass judgment and act as though we're superior just because the rain isn't falling on us. How much better to offer support, counsel, even admonishment to a fellow believer with humility and love rather than with arrogance (Ro 12:10; Eph 4:2).

Divine Wisdom

JOB 12:13–25

Job asserts again that his friends are out of their league in trying to analyze his misfortune or God's purposes. Only God is wise enough to know what's going on here. And because he is God, his ways are often incomprehensible and unpredictable. God cannot be put in a box, nor does he owe his people an explanation of why he creates and destroys as he sees fit.

To the person without faith in God's goodness, the Almighty's actions can appear capricious and even cruel. But to those who know "the whole story" of God's plan (which neither Job nor his friends were privy to), God's character and faithfulness are trustworthy. If you are feeling anxious about what God is up to in your life, spend some time meditating on Psalm 46. Write down the truths that reassure you that God is not only sovereign, but also good.

the man he imprisons cannot be
released.
15 If he holds back the waters,[a] there is
drought;[b]
if he lets them loose, they devastate
the land.[c]
16 To him belong strength and victory;
both deceived and deceiver are his.[d]
17 He leads counselors away stripped[e]
and makes fools of judges.[f]
18 He takes off the shackles[g] put on by
kings
and ties a loincloth[a] around their
waist.
19 He leads priests away stripped
and overthrows men long
established.[h]
20 He silences the lips of trusted advisers
and takes away the discernment of
elders.[i]
21 He pours contempt on nobles
and disarms the mighty.
22 He reveals the deep things of darkness[j]
and brings deep shadows[k] into the
light.[l]
23 He makes nations great, and destroys
them;[m]
he enlarges nations,[n] and disperses
them.
24 He deprives the leaders of the earth of
their reason;
he sends them wandering through a
trackless waste.[o]
25 They grope in darkness with no light;[p]
he makes them stagger like
drunkards.[q]

13 "My eyes have seen all this,
my ears have heard and understood it.
2 What you know, I also know;
I am not inferior to you.[r]
3 But I desire to speak to the Almighty
and to argue my case with God.[s]
4 You, however, smear me with lies;[t]
you are worthless physicians, all of
you!
5 If only you would be altogether silent!
For you, that would be wisdom.[u]
6 Hear now my argument;
listen to the plea of my lips.
7 Will you speak wickedly on God's
behalf?
Will you speak deceitfully for him?[v]
8 Will you show him partiality?[w]
Will you argue the case for God?
9 Would it turn out well if he examined
you?
Could you deceive him as you might
deceive men?[x]

12:15 [a]1Ki 8:35 [b]1Ki 17:1 [c]Ge 7:11
12:16 [d]Job 13:7,9
12:17 [e]Job 19:9 [f]Job 3:14
12:18 [g]Ps 116:16
12:19 [h]Job 24:12, 22; 34:20, 28; 35:9
12:20 [i]Job 32:9
12:22 [j]1Co 4:5 [k]Job 3:5 [l]Da 2:22
12:23 [m]Jer 25:9 [n]Ps 107:38; Isa 9:3; 26:15
12:24 [o]Ps 107:40
12:25 [p]Job 5:14 [q]Ps 107:27; Isa 24:20
13:2 [r]Job 12:3
13:3 [s]Job 23:3-4
13:4 [t]Ps 119:69; Jer 23:32
13:5 [u]Pr 17:28
13:7 [v]Job 36:4
13:8 [w]Lev 19:15
13:9 [x]Job 12:16; Gal 6:7

[a] 18 Or *shackles of kings / and ties a belt*

10 He would surely rebuke you
if you secretly showed partiality.
11 Would not his splendor[y] terrify you?
Would not the dread of him fall on
you?
12 Your maxims are proverbs of ashes;
your defenses are defenses of clay.

13 "Keep silent and let me speak;
then let come to me what may.
14 Why do I put myself in jeopardy
and take my life in my hands?
15 Though he slay me, yet will I hope[z] in
him;[a]
I will surely[a] defend my ways to his
face.[b]
16 Indeed, this will turn out for my
deliverance,[c]
for no godless man would dare come
before him!
17 Listen carefully to my words;[d]
let your ears take in what I say.
18 Now that I have prepared my case,[e]
I know I will be vindicated.
19 Can anyone bring charges against me?[f]
If so, I will be silent and die.[g]

20 "Only grant me these two things, O God,
and then I will not hide from you:
21 Withdraw your hand[h] far from me,
and stop frightening me with your
terrors.
22 Then summon me and I will answer,[i]
or let me speak, and you reply.[j]
23 How many wrongs and sins have I
committed?[k]
Show me my offense and my sin.
24 Why do you hide your face[l]
and consider me your enemy?[m]
25 Will you torment a windblown leaf?[n]
Will you chase after dry chaff?[o]
26 For you write down bitter things against
me
and make me inherit the sins of my
youth.[p]
27 You fasten my feet in shackles;[q]
you keep close watch on all my paths
by putting marks on the soles of my
feet.

28 "So man wastes away like something
rotten,
like a garment eaten by moths.[r]

14

"Man born of woman
is of few days and full of trouble.[s]
2 He springs up like a flower[t] and withers
away;[u]
like a fleeting shadow,[v] he does not
endure.
3 Do you fix your eye on such a one?[w]

13:11 [y]Job 31:23
13:15 [z]Job 7:6 [a]Ps 23:4; Pr 14:32 [b]Job 27:5
13:16 [c]Isa 12:1
13:17 [d]Job 21:2
13:18 [e]Job 23:4
13:19 [f]Job 40:4; Isa 50:8 [g]Job 10:8
13:21 [h]Ps 39:10
13:22 [i]Job 14:15 [j]Job 9:16
13:23 [k]1Sa 26:18
13:24 [l]Dt 32:20; Ps 13:1; Isa 8:17 [m]Job 19:11; La 2:5
13:25 [n]Lev 26:36 [o]Job 21:18; Isa 42:3
13:26 [p]Ps 25:7
13:27 [q]Job 33:11
13:28 [r]Isa 50:9; Jas 5:2
14:1 [s]Job 5:7; Ecc 2:23
14:2 [t]Jas 1:10 [u]Ps 90:5-6 [v]Job 8:9
14:3 [w]Ps 8:4; 144:3

[a] 15 Or *He will surely slay me; I have no hope — / yet I will*

Confidence in God

JOB 13:15–18

Although Job has been feeling baffled and betrayed by God, he now has a brief flash of confidence in God's righteousness. Surely the God he knows will be just in the end; surely the God who knows him won't judge him a hypocrite (Job 23:10; Pr 14:32). There is hope! Even if Job doesn't make it through his trials alive, his integrity will prevail because God's righteousness as a judge will prevail. God will ultimately clear him of all the charges his friends have leveled against him. Therefore, no matter what happens, Job will put his trust in God.

There is no such thing as premature death. Job 14:5 states, "Man's days are determined; you have decreed the number of his months and have set limits he cannot exceed."

And Psalm 139:16 says, "All the days ordained for me were written in your book before one of them came to be."

I find that realization comforting. In fact, it could be a cheer-up thought. To recognize God's sovereign determining of the number of days each of us is to have on earth relieves me of nagging questions like, "If I had just done this, eaten that, not eaten that, stayed home, not stayed home . . ."

This is not some kind of Christian fatalism in which we assume it doesn't matter if we take health and safety precautions. On the contrary, Scripture says our bodies are the temples of the Holy Spirit, and we must respect them as well as do our part in preserving them. But tension is released in me as I remember that the number of my days is in his hands and not mine . . . Based on Scripture, we do not die prematurely. We are ushered into God's presence at exactly the time God has chosen for us.

—*Marilyn Meberg*

Will you bring him[a] before you for
judgment?[x]
4 Who can bring what is pure[y] from the
impure?[z]
No one![a]
5 Man's days are determined;
you have decreed the number of his
months[b]
and have set limits he cannot exceed.
6 So look away from him and let him
alone,[c]
till he has put in his time like a hired
man.[d]

7 "At least there is hope for a tree:
If it is cut down, it will sprout again,
and its new shoots will not fail.
8 Its roots may grow old in the ground
and its stump die in the soil,
9 yet at the scent of water it will bud
and put forth shoots like a plant.
10 But man dies and is laid low;
he breathes his last and is no more.[e]
11 As water disappears from the sea
or a riverbed becomes parched and
dry,[f]
12 so man lies down and does not rise;
till the heavens are no more,[g] men
will not awake
or be roused from their sleep.[h]

13 "If only you would hide me in the
grave[b]
and conceal me till your anger has
passed![i]
If only you would set me a time
and then remember me!
14 If a man dies, will he live again?
All the days of my hard service
I will wait for my renewal[c] to come.
15 You will call and I will answer you;[j]
you will long for the creature your
hands have made.
16 Surely then you will count my steps[k]
but not keep track of my sin.[l]
17 My offenses will be sealed up in a bag;[m]
you will cover over my sin.[n]
18 "But as a mountain erodes and crumbles
and as a rock is moved from its place,
19 as water wears away stones
and torrents wash away the soil,
so you destroy man's hope.[o]
20 You overpower him once for all, and he
is gone;
you change his countenance and send
him away.
21 If his sons are honored, he does not
know it;

14:3 [x]Ps 143:2
14:4 [y]Ps 51:10 [z]Eph 2:1-3 [a]Jn 3:6; Ro 5:12
14:5 [b]Job 21:21
14:6 [c]Job 7:19 [d]Job 7:1,2; Ps 39:13
14:10 [e]Job 13:19
14:11 [f]Isa 19:5
14:12 [g]Rev 20:11; 21:1 [h]Ac 3:21
14:13 [i]Isa 26:20
14:15 [j]Job 13:22
14:16 [k]Ps 139:1-3; Pr 5:21; Jer 32:19 [l]Job 10:6
14:17 [m]Dt 32:34 [n]Hos 13:12
14:19 [o]Job 7:6

[a] *3* Septuagint, Vulgate and Syriac; Hebrew *me* [b] *13* Hebrew *Sheol* [c] *14* Or *release*

if they are brought low, he does not
see it.[p]
22 He feels but the pain of his own body
and mourns only for himself."

Eliphaz

15 Then Eliphaz the Temanite replied:

2 "Would a wise man answer with empty
notions
or fill his belly with the hot east
wind?[q]
3 Would he argue with useless words,
with speeches that have no value?
4 But you even undermine piety
and hinder devotion to God.
5 Your sin prompts your mouth;
you adopt the tongue of the crafty.[r]
6 Your own mouth condemns you, not
mine;
your own lips testify against you.[s]

7 "Are you the first man ever born?[t]
Were you brought forth before the
hills?[u]
8 Do you listen in on God's council?[v]
Do you limit wisdom to yourself?
9 What do you know that we do not
know?
What insights do you have that we do
not have?[w]
10 The gray-haired and the aged[x] are on
our side,
men even older than your father.
11 Are God's consolations[y] not enough for
you,
words[z] spoken gently to you?[a]
12 Why has your heart[b] carried you away,
and why do your eyes flash,
13 so that you vent your rage against God
and pour out such words from your
mouth?

14 "What is man, that he could be pure,
or one born of woman,[c] that he could
be righteous?[d]
15 If God places no trust in his holy ones,
if even the heavens are not pure in his
eyes,[e]
16 how much less man, who is vile and
corrupt,[f]
who drinks up evil like water![g]

17 "Listen to me and I will explain to you;
let me tell you what I have seen,
18 what wise men have declared,
hiding nothing received from their
fathers[h]
19 (to whom alone the land was given
when no alien passed among them):
20 All his days the wicked man suffers
torment,

14:21 [p]Ecc 9:5; Isa 63:16
15:2 [q]Job 6:26
15:5 [r]Job 5:13
15:6 [s]Lk 19:22
15:7 [t]Job 38:21 [u]Ps 90:2; Pr 8:25
15:8 [v]Ro 11:34; 1Co 2:11
15:9 [w]Job 13:2
15:10 [x]Job 32:6-7
15:11 [y]2Co 1:3-4 [z]Zec 1:13 [a]Job 36:16
15:12 [b]Job 11:13
15:14 [c]Job 14:4; 25:4 [d]Pr 20:9; Ecc 7:20
15:15 [e]Job 4:18; 25:5
15:16 [f]Ps 14:1 [g]Job 34:7; Pr 19:28
15:18 [h]Job 8:8

Human "Wisdom"

JOB 15:7-10

When we become convinced that we're right, that we're speaking for God, that there is only one way to look at a situation, we quickly become hard-hearted and self-righteous. Eliphaz is so sure of himself and the human "wisdom" of the ages that he is incapable of listening to what Job is really saying or to what God himself might want to reveal in Job's situation. When Job won't capitulate to his friends' viewpoint, Eliphaz only becomes more aggressive and mean-spirited. The fact that Eliphaz and the others, who are so sure they are right, turn out to be entirely wrong demonstrates that even the most righteous and educated should always place humility above conviction. The next time you find yourself feeling absolutely, positively, no-doubt-about-it sure you are right, practice closing your mouth and opening your mind and heart.

When you welcome God's companionship in the darkest hours of your life, when you keep on walking by faith on the darker parts of the path, you are gifted with moments of wonderful elation—as if you are joining with heaven in a celebration that is a tiny shadow of what it will be like when we get home. The closer we push into the heart of God, the more we are swept away by the joy that is his breath and life and gift to us all.

—Sheila Walsh

the ruthless through all the years
stored up for him.[i]
21 Terrifying sounds fill his ears;[j]
when all seems well, marauders
attack him.[k]
22 He despairs of escaping the darkness;
he is marked for the sword.[l]
23 He wanders about[m]—food for vultures[a];
he knows the day of darkness is at
hand.[n]
24 Distress and anguish fill him with
terror;
they overwhelm him, like a king
poised to attack,
25 because he shakes his fist at God
and vaunts himself against the
Almighty,[o]
26 defiantly charging against him
with a thick, strong shield.

27 "Though his face is covered with fat
and his waist bulges with flesh,[p]
28 he will inhabit ruined towns
and houses where no one lives,[q]
houses crumbling to rubble.[r]
29 He will no longer be rich and his wealth
will not endure,[s]
nor will his possessions spread over
the land.
30 He will not escape the darkness;[t]
a flame[u] will wither his shoots,
and the breath of God's mouth[v] will
carry him away.
31 Let him not deceive himself by trusting
what is worthless,[w]
for he will get nothing in return.
32 Before his time[x] he will be paid in full,[y]
and his branches will not flourish.[z]
33 He will be like a vine stripped of its
unripe grapes,[a]
like an olive tree shedding its
blossoms.
34 For the company of the godless will be
barren,
and fire will consume the tents of
those who love bribes.[b]
35 They conceive trouble and give birth to
evil;[c]
their womb fashions deceit."

Job

16 Then Job replied:

2 "I have heard many things like these;
miserable comforters are you all![d]
3 Will your long-winded speeches never
end?
What ails you that you keep on
arguing?[e]

15:20 [i]Job 24:1; 27:13-23
15:21 [j]Job 18:11; 20:25 [k]Job 27:20; 1Th 5:3
15:22 [l]Job 19:29; 27:14
15:23 [m]Ps 59:15; 109:10 [n]Job 18:12
15:25 [o]Job 36:9
15:27 [p]Ps 17:10
15:28 [q]Isa 5:9 [r]Job 3:14
15:29 [s]Job 27:16-17
15:30 [t]Job 5:14 [u]Job 22:20 [v]Job 4:9
15:31 [w]Isa 59:4
15:32 [x]Ecc 7:17 [y]Job 22:16; Ps 55:23 [z]Job 18:16
15:33 [a]Hab 3:17
15:34 [b]Job 8:22
15:35 [c]Ps 7:14; Isa 59:4; Hos 10:13
16:2 [d]Job 13:4
16:3 [e]Job 6:26

[a] 23 Or *about, looking for food*

4 I also could speak like you,
if you were in my place;
I could make fine speeches against you
and shake my head[f] at you.
5 But my mouth would encourage you;
comfort from my lips would bring you
relief.

6 "Yet if I speak, my pain is not relieved;
and if I refrain, it does not go away.
7 Surely, O God, you have worn me out;[g]
you have devastated my entire
household.
8 You have bound me—and it has become
a witness;
my gauntness[h] rises up and testifies
against me.[i]
9 God assails me and tears[j] me in his
anger
and gnashes his teeth at me;[k]
my opponent fastens on me his
piercing eyes.[l]
10 Men open their mouths[m] to jeer at me;
they strike my cheek[n] in scorn
and unite together against me.[o]
11 God has turned me over to evil men
and thrown me into the clutches of
the wicked.[p]
12 All was well with me, but he shattered
me;
he seized me by the neck and crushed
me.[q]
He has made me his target;[r]
13 his archers surround me.
Without pity, he pierces[s] my kidneys
and spills my gall on the ground.
14 Again and again[t] he bursts upon me;
he rushes at me like a warrior.[u]

15 "I have sewed sackcloth[v] over my skin
and buried my brow in the dust.
16 My face is red with weeping,
deep shadows ring my eyes;
17 yet my hands have been free of
violence[w]
and my prayer is pure.

18 "O earth, do not cover my blood;[x]
may my cry never be laid to rest![y]
19 Even now my witness[z] is in heaven;
my advocate is on high.
20 My intercessor is my friend[a]
as my eyes pour out[a] tears to God;
21 on behalf of a man he pleads[b] with God
as a man pleads for his friend.

22 "Only a few years will pass
before I go on the journey of no
return.[c]

17

1 My spirit is broken,
my days are cut short,

In Their Shoes

JOB 16:4–5

Now that Job has endured his friends' platitudes and criticisms, he's sure he would not behave the same way if he were in their shoes. He's confident he would offer only encouragement and solace, which is what he longs for himself.

Until we have suffered, until we have experienced the judgment and derision of others in the midst of our pain, we cannot know what it feels like. We cannot be sure we wouldn't treat a suffering friend with the same superficiality and ignorance. One of the greatest things we learn through suffering is how to empathize with others and how to comfort effectively as God comforts us (2Co 1:3–6). When our friends suffer, we can follow the advice of the writer of Hebrews to put ourselves in their shoes and love them tenaciously, with humility (Heb 13:3). Their suffering may one day be our own.

16:4 [f] Ps 22:7; 109:25; La 2:15; Zep 2:15; Mt 27:39
16:7 [g] Job 7:3
16:8 [h] Job 19:20 [i] Job 10:17
16:9 [j] Hos 6:1 [k] Ps 35:16; La 2:16; Ac 7:54 [l] Job 13:24
16:10 [m] Ps 22:13 [n] Isa 50:6; La 3:30; Mic 5:1; Ac 23:2 [o] Ps 35:15
16:11 [p] Job 1:15,17
16:12 [q] Job 9:17 [r] La 3:12
16:13 [s] Job 20:24
16:14 [t] Job 9:17 [u] Joel 2:7
16:15 [v] Ge 37:34
16:17 [w] Isa 59:6; Jnh 3:8
16:18 [x] Isa 26:21 [y] Ps 66:18-19
16:19 [z] Ge 31:50; Ro 1:9; 1Th 2:5
16:20 [a] La 2:19
16:21 [b] Ps 9:4
16:22 [c] Ecc 12:5

[a] 20 Or *My friends treat me with scorn*

Careful Comfort

JOB 17:10–12

Job claims his friends are too unwise, too glib. They try to help him with empty phrases, the proverbial, "Don't feel bad—everything will be okay" (contingent on Job's repentance). Job is facing the "darkness." Patting him on the shoulder and saying, "Light is near" (Job 17:12) is not only ineffective but also unwise. While it is gloriously true that a sovereign God works for our good in the midst of every circumstance (Ro 8:28), we cannot claim to know exactly how or when he will do so. Our primary comfort in those dark times is that he* is *in control and that he is concerned for our good.

the grave awaits me.[d]
2 Surely mockers[e] surround me;
my eyes must dwell on their hostility.

3 "Give me, O God, the pledge you demand.[f]
Who else will put up security[g] for me?[h]
4 You have closed their minds to understanding;
therefore you will not let them triumph.
5 If a man denounces his friends for reward,
the eyes of his children will fail.[i]

6 "God has made me a byword[j] to everyone,
a man in whose face people spit.
7 My eyes have grown dim with grief;[k]
my whole frame is but a shadow.
8 Upright men are appalled at this;
the innocent are aroused[l] against the ungodly.
9 Nevertheless, the righteous[m] will hold to their ways,
and those with clean hands[n] will grow stronger.

10 "But come on, all of you, try again!
I will not find a wise man among you.[o]
11 My days have passed, my plans are shattered,
and so are the desires of my heart.[p]
12 These men turn night into day;
in the face of darkness they say, 'Light is near.'
13 If the only home I hope for is the grave,[a][q]
if I spread out my bed in darkness,
14 if I say to corruption,[r] 'You are my father,'
and to the worm,[s] 'My mother' or 'My sister,'
15 where then is my hope?[t]
Who can see any hope for me?
16 Will it go down to the gates of death[a]?[u]
Will we descend together into the dust?"

Bildad

18 Then Bildad the Shuhite replied:

2 "When will you end these speeches?
Be sensible, and then we can talk.
3 Why are we regarded as cattle
and considered stupid in your sight?[v]
4 You who tear yourself[w] to pieces in your anger,

17:1 [d]Ps 88:3-4
17:2 [e]1Sa 1:6-7
17:3 [f]Ps 119:122 [g]Pr 6:1 [h]Isa 38:14
17:5 [i]Job 11:20
17:6 [j]Job 30:9
17:7 [k]Job 16:8
17:8 [l]Job 22:19
17:9 [m]Pr 4:18 [n]Job 22:30
17:10 [o]Job 12:2
17:11 [p]Job 7:6
17:13 [q]Job 3:13
17:14 [r]Job 13:28; 30:28,30; Ps 16:10 [s]Job 21:26
17:15 [t]Job 7:6
17:16 [u]Job 3:17-19; Jnh 2:6
18:3 [v]Ps 73:22
18:4 [w]Job 13:14

[a] 13,16 Hebrew *Sheol*

is the earth to be abandoned for your
sake?
Or must the rocks be moved from
their place?
5 "The lamp of the wicked is snuffed out;[x]
the flame of his fire stops burning.
6 The light in his tent becomes dark;
the lamp beside him goes out.
7 The vigor of his step is weakened;[y]
his own schemes[z] throw him down.[a]
8 His feet thrust him into a net[b]
and he wanders into its mesh.
9 A trap seizes him by the heel;
a snare holds him fast.
10 A noose is hidden for him on the
ground;
a trap lies in his path.
11 Terrors startle him on every side[c]
and dog[d] his every step.
12 Calamity is hungry[e] for him;
disaster is ready for him when he
falls.
13 It eats away parts of his skin;
death's firstborn devours his limbs.[f]
14 He is torn from the security of his tent[g]
and marched off to the king of terrors.
15 Fire resides[a] in his tent;
burning sulfur[h] is scattered over his
dwelling.
16 His roots dry up below[i]
and his branches wither above.[j]
17 The memory of him perishes from the
earth;
he has no name in the land.[k]
18 He is driven from light into darkness[l]
and is banished from the world.
19 He has no offspring[m] or descendants[n]
among his people,
no survivor where once he lived.[o]
20 Men of the west are appalled at his fate;[p]
men of the east are seized with
horror.
21 Surely such is the dwelling[q] of an evil
man;
such is the place of one who knows
not God."[r]

Job

19

Then Job replied:

2 "How long will you torment me
and crush me with words?
3 Ten times now you have reproached me;
shamelessly you attack me.
4 If it is true that I have gone astray,
my error[s] remains my concern alone.
5 If indeed you would exalt yourselves
above me[t]

18:5 [x]Job 21:17; Pr 13:9; 20:20; 24:20
18:7 [y]Pr 4:12 [z]Job 5:13 [a]Job 15:6
18:8 [b]Job 22:10; Ps 9:15; 35:7
18:11 [c]Job 15:21; Jer 6:25; 20:3 [d]Job 20:8
18:12 [e]Isa 8:21
18:13 [f]Zec 14:12
18:14 [g]Job 8:22
18:15 [h]Ps 11:6
18:16 [i]Isa 5:24; Hos 9:1-16; Am 2:9 [j]Job 15:30; Mal 4:1
18:17 [k]Ps 34:16; Pr 2:22; 10:7
18:18 [l]Job 5:14
18:19 [m]Jer 22:30 [n]Isa 14:22 [o]Job 27:14-15
18:20 [p]Ps 37:13; Jer 50:27,31
18:21 [q]Job 21:28 [r]Jer 9:3; 1Th 4:5
19:4 [s]Job 6:24
19:5 [t]Ps 35:26; 38:16; 55:12

God Alone Knows

JOB 19:4

Job claims his friends have overstepped their bounds. If he has done something wrong, it isn't up to them to convict him. The problem is between Job and God alone. Instead of trusting the living God to ultimately lead Job on the path of righteousness, they make it their mission to show him his wrongs and where he needs to change.

"Playing the Holy Spirit" in other people's lives is too often a popular pastime for Christians. We put minding another's conscience and behavior on our daily to-do list. In his letter to the Hebrews, the writer beautifully describes the way fellow believers are to draw near to God together, urge one another to live and love well, and cheer each other on (Heb 10:19–25). This positive approach to encouraging each other's righteousness and faithfulness is far superior to the critical approach Job's friends take. God alone fully knows our hearts, and he will judge rightly (Ps 96:13).

[a] 15 Or *Nothing he had remains*

Isolation

JOB 19:17–19

Job's words intimately reveal the intense shame and isolation he feels as he considers the state of his relationships. He's lost the respect of everyone, even "little boys." His most intimate friends hate him. His own wife can't stand to be near him (see character sketch for Job's wife on page 1411). He has been abandoned and betrayed by everyone he loves—and that on top of losing his ten precious children. His intense suffering and extreme loss and grief make it difficult for anyone to be around him.

It can be difficult, even frightening, to stay close to those who are truly hurting. The intensity of the emotion can be overwhelming; the unanswerable questions can be intimidating; the "negative" focus can be depressing. However, the truth is that as God's representatives in this world, we are called to "mourn with those who mourn" (Ro 12:15).

and use my humiliation against me,
6 then know that God has wronged me[u]
and drawn his net[v] around me.

7 "Though I cry, 'I've been wronged!' I get no response;[w]
though I call for help, there is no justice.[x]
8 He has blocked my way so I cannot pass;[y]
he has shrouded my paths in darkness.[z]
9 He has stripped[a] me of my honor
and removed the crown from my head.[b]
10 He tears me down[c] on every side till I am gone;
he uproots my hope[d] like a tree.[e]
11 His anger[f] burns against me;
he counts me among his enemies.[g]
12 His troops advance in force;[h]
they build a siege ramp[i] against me
and encamp around my tent.

13 "He has alienated my brothers[j] from me;
my acquaintances are completely estranged from me.[k]
14 My kinsmen have gone away;
my friends have forgotten me.
15 My guests and my maidservants count me a stranger;
they look upon me as an alien.
16 I summon my servant, but he does not answer,
though I beg him with my own mouth.
17 My breath is offensive to my wife;
I am loathsome to my own brothers.
18 Even the little boys[l] scorn me;
when I appear, they ridicule me.
19 All my intimate friends[m] detest me;[n]
those I love have turned against me.
20 I am nothing but skin and bones;[o]
I have escaped with only the skin of my teeth.[a]

21 "Have pity on me, my friends, have pity,
for the hand of God has struck me.
22 Why do you pursue[p] me as God does?
Will you never get enough of my flesh?[q]

23 "Oh, that my words were recorded,
that they were written on a scroll,[r]
24 that they were inscribed with an iron tool on[b] lead,
or engraved in rock forever!
25 I know that my Redeemer[c][s] lives,[t]
and that in the end he will stand upon the earth.[d]

19:6 [u]Job 27:2 [v]Job 18:8
19:7 [w]Job 30:20 [x]Job 9:24; Hab 1:2-4
19:8 [y]Job 3:23; La 3:7 [z]Job 30:26
19:9 [a]Job 12:17 [b]Ps 89:39, 44; La 5:16
19:10 [c]Job 12:14 [d]Job 7:6 [e]Job 24:20
19:11 [f]Job 16:9 [g]Job 13:24
19:12 [h]Job 16:13 [i]Job 30:12
19:13 [j]Ps 69:8 [k]Job 16:7; Ps 88:8
19:18 [l]2Ki 2:23
19:19 [m]Ps 55:12-13 [n]Ps 38:11
19:20 [o]Job 33:21; Ps 102:5
19:22 [p]Job 13:25; 16:11 [q]Ps 69:26
19:23 [r]Isa 30:8
19:25 [s]Ps 78:35; Pr 23:11; Isa 43:14; Jer 50:34 [t]Job 16:19

[a] *20* Or *only my gums* [b] *24* Or *and* [c] *25* Or *defender*
[d] *25* Or *upon my grave*

19:26 [u]Ps 17:15; Mt 5:8; 1Co 13:12; 1Jn 3:2
19:27 [v]Ps 73:26
19:29 [w]Job 15:22 [x]Job 22:4; Ps 1:5; 9:7

26 And after my skin has been destroyed,
yet[a] in[b] my flesh I will see God;[u]
27 I myself will see him
with my own eyes—I, and not another.
How my heart yearns[v] within me!

28 "If you say, 'How we will hound him,
since the root of the trouble lies in him,[c]'
29 you should fear the sword yourselves;
for wrath will bring punishment by the sword,[w]
and then you will know that there is judgment.[d]"[x]

Zophar

20 Then Zophar the Naamathite replied:

20:3 [y]Job 19:3
20:5 [z]Job 8:12; Ps 37:35-36; 73:19
20:6 [a]Isa 14:13-14; Ob 1:3-4
20:7 [b]Job 4:20 [c]Job 7:10; 8:18
20:8 [d]Ps 73:20 [e]Job 27:21-23 [f]Job 18:18 [g]Ps 90:5
20:9 [h]Job 7:8
20:10 [i]Job 5:4 [j]Job 27:16-17
20:11 [k]Job 13:26 [l]Job 21:26
20:13 [m]Nu 11:18-20

2 "My troubled thoughts prompt me to answer
because I am greatly disturbed.
3 I hear a rebuke[y] that dishonors me,
and my understanding inspires me to reply.

4 "Surely you know how it has been from of old,
ever since man[e] was placed on the earth,
5 that the mirth of the wicked is brief,
the joy of the godless lasts but a moment.[z]
6 Though his pride reaches to the heavens
and his head touches the clouds,[a]
7 he will perish forever,[b] like his own dung;
those who have seen him will say,
'Where is he?'[c]
8 Like a dream[d] he flies away,[e] no more to be found,
banished[f] like a vision of the night.[g]
9 The eye that saw him will not see him again;
his place will look on him no more.[h]
10 His children[i] must make amends to the poor;
his own hands must give back his wealth.[j]
11 The youthful vigor[k] that fills his bones
will lie with him in the dust.[l]

12 "Though evil is sweet in his mouth
and he hides it under his tongue,
13 though he cannot bear to let it go
and keeps it in his mouth,[m]

[a] 26 Or *And after I awake, / though this ˌbodyˌ has been destroyed, / then* [b] 26 Or */ apart from* [c] 28 Many Hebrew manuscripts, Septuagint and Vulgate; most Hebrew manuscripts *me* [d] 29 Or */ that you may come to know the Almighty* [e] 4 Or *Adam*

My Redeemer

JOB 19:25–27

As in his response to Zophar's first speech (Job 13), Job has a burst of renewed faith in the God he has long sought to know and serve. Throughout his life he has had faith that a Redeemer will come to vindicate the righteous, to raise the dead and to judge the earth. Although he sees no evidence of such good news in his current situation, he grasps onto faith in a God who promises to preserve his own (Ps 119:41–52).

Job's hope for the future is no longer in living through his ordeal, but in being united with a just and loving God. His confidence is not in anything the world or friends provide but only in God. He *knows* he will one day see him. He *longs* for that day to arrive!

Zophar Again

JOB 20

Zophar blasts Job again with the "proper theology": The righteous are rewarded; the wicked are punished. Zophar's lengthy and graphic description of a sinner's fate is his final attempt to get through to Job by scaring him into repentance. Job's friend is reciting the wisdom of the ages, an entrenched belief system that continues to prevail in our culture. We still tend to ask when we suffer, "What did I do to deserve this?" Our presumption is that life should be fair. But Job's story is just one of many in Scripture that proves we don't see the whole picture. Life isn't always "fair," and we simply won't ever have all the answers we seek. Therefore, our faith cannot rest on our theology, no matter how correct we think it is. Our comfort in our darkest hours can come only from the God who promises to never abandon us (Dt 31:6).

14 yet his food will turn sour in his
stomach;
it will become the venom of serpents
within him.
15 He will spit out the riches he swallowed;
God will make his stomach vomit
them up.
16 He will suck the poison[n] of serpents; **20:16** [n]Dt 32:32
the fangs of an adder will kill him.[o] [o]Dt 32:24
17 He will not enjoy the streams, **20:17**
the rivers flowing with honey[p] and [p]Dt 32:13
cream.[q] [q]Job 29:6
18 What he toiled for he must give back
uneaten;
he will not enjoy the profit from his
trading.
19 For he has oppressed the poor and left **20:19**
them destitute;[r] [r]Job 24:4,14;
he has seized houses he did not build. 35:9

20 "Surely he will have no respite from his **20:20**
craving;[s] [s]Ecc 5:12-14
he cannot save himself by his
treasure.
21 Nothing is left for him to devour; **20:21**
his prosperity will not endure.[t] [t]Job 15:29
22 In the midst of his plenty, distress will
overtake him;
the full force of misery will come
upon him.
23 When he has filled his belly,
God will vent his burning anger
against him
and rain down his blows upon him.[u] **20:23** [u]Ps 78:30-31
24 Though he flees[v] from an iron weapon,
a bronze-tipped arrow pierces him. **20:24**
25 He pulls it out of his back, [v]Isa 24:18;
the gleaming point out of his liver. Am 5:19
Terrors[w] will come over him;[x] **20:25** [w]Job 18:11
26 total darkness[y] lies in wait for his [x]Job 16:13
treasures.
A fire unfanned will consume him[z] **20:26** [y]Job 18:18
and devour what is left in his tent. [z]Ps 21:9
27 The heavens will expose his guilt; **20:27**
the earth will rise up against him.[a] [a]Dt 31:28
28 A flood will carry off his house,[b] **20:28**
rushing waters[a] on the day of God's [b]Dt 28:31
wrath.[c] [c]Job 21:17,
29 Such is the fate God allots the wicked, 20,30
the heritage appointed for them by **20:29**
God."[d] [d]Job 27:13

Job

21

Then Job replied:

2 "Listen carefully to my words;
let this be the consolation you give me.
3 Bear with me while I speak, **21:3**
and after I have spoken, mock on.[e] [e]Job 16:10

[a] 28 Or *The possessions in his house will be carried off, / washed away*

4 "Is my complaint directed to man?
Why should I not be impatient?[f]
5 Look at me and be astonished;
clap your hand over your mouth.[g]
6 When I think about this, I am terrified;
trembling seizes my body.
7 Why do the wicked live on,
growing old and increasing in power?[h]
8 They see their children established
around them,
their offspring before their eyes.[i]
9 Their homes are safe and free from fear;[j]
the rod of God is not upon them.
10 Their bulls never fail to breed;
their cows calve and do not miscarry.[k]
11 They send forth their children as a flock;
their little ones dance about.
12 They sing to the music of tambourine
and harp;
they make merry to the sound of the
flute.[l]
13 They spend their years in prosperity[m]
and go down to the grave[a] in peace.[b]
14 Yet they say to God, 'Leave us alone![n]
We have no desire to know your
ways.[o]
15 Who is the Almighty, that we should
serve him?
What would we gain by praying to
him?'[p]
16 But their prosperity is not in their own
hands,
so I stand aloof from the counsel of
the wicked.

17 "Yet how often is the lamp of the wicked
snuffed out?[q]
How often does calamity come upon
them,
the fate God allots in his anger?
18 How often are they like straw before the
wind,
like chaff[r] swept away by a gale?
19 ⌞It is said,⌟ 'God stores up a man's
punishment for his sons.'[s]
Let him repay the man himself, so
that he will know it!
20 Let his own eyes see his destruction;
let him drink[t] of the wrath of the
Almighty.[c][u]
21 For what does he care about the family
he leaves behind
when his allotted months[v] come to an
end?

22 "Can anyone teach knowledge to God,[w]
since he judges even the highest?[x]
23 One man dies in full vigor,

21:4 [f]Job 6:11
21:5 [g]Jdg 18:19; Job 29:9; 40:4
21:7 [h]Job 12:6; Ps 73:3; Jer 12:1; Hab 1:13
21:8 [i]Ps 17:14
21:9 [j]Ps 73:5
21:10 [k]Ex 23:26
21:12 [l]Ps 81:2
21:13 [m]Job 36:11
21:14 [n]Job 22:17 [o]Pr 1:29
21:15 [p]Ex 5:2; Job 34:9; Mal 3:14
21:17 [q]Job 18:5
21:18 [r]Job 13:25; Ps 1:4
21:19 [s]Ex 20:5; Jer 31:29; Eze 18:2
21:20 [t]Ps 75:8; Isa 51:17 [u]Jer 25:15; Rev 14:10
21:21 [v]Job 14:5
21:22 [w]Job 35:11; 36:22; Isa 40:13-14; Ro 11:34 [x]Ps 82:1

[a] *13* Hebrew *Sheol* [b] *13* Or *in an instant* [c] *17–20* Verses 17 and 18 may be taken as exclamations and 19 and 20 as declarations.

Julia Harriet Johnston lived all but the first six years of her life in Peoria, Illinois, and wrote more than 500 hymns, including this one expressing the marvelous grace given to sinners.

Marvelous Grace

Marvelous grace of our loving Lord,
Grace that exceeds our sin and our guilt!
Yonder on Calvary's mount outpoured,
There where the blood of the Lamb was spilled.

Sin and despair, like the sea waves cold,
Threaten the soul with infinite loss;
Grace that is greater, yes, grace untold,
Points to the refuge, the mighty cross.

Dark is the stain that we cannot hide.
What can we do to wash it away?
Look! There is flowing a crimson tide,
Brighter than snow you may be today.

Marvelous, infinite, matchless grace,
Freely bestowed on all who believe!
You that are longing to see His face,
Will you this moment His grace receive?

—Julia Harriet Johnston (1849–1919)

The Great Equalizer

JOB 21:22-26

Job argues logically that one quick look around contradicts everything his friends have said about divine retribution. He doesn't need to look far to see righteous people suffering and evil people prospering. And death awaits both the good and the wicked. God alone decides their fate. Vigorous people can drop dead; others breathe their last breath before ever enjoying themselves. Death is the great equalizer. The richest CEO and the poorest beggar, the meanest bully and the kindest friend will eventually return to the dust. What Job, in his depressed cynicism, forgets to mention is that the person who dies with faith in the Redeemer has a very different fate to look forward to than the one who renounces God. Believers are victorious over death and destined to live in joy for eternity (1Co 15:51-57; Rev 21:3-4).

completely secure and at ease,
24 his body[a] well nourished,
his bones rich with marrow.[y]
25 Another man dies in bitterness of soul,
never having enjoyed anything good.
26 Side by side they lie in the dust,
and worms cover them both.[z]

27 "I know full well what you are thinking,
the schemes by which you would
wrong me.
28 You say, 'Where now is the great man's[a]
house,
the tents where wicked men lived?'[b]
29 Have you never questioned those who
travel?
Have you paid no regard to their
accounts—
30 that the evil man is spared from the day
of calamity,[c]
that he is delivered from[b] the day of
wrath?[d]
31 Who denounces his conduct to his face?
Who repays him for what he has done?
32 He is carried to the grave,
and watch is kept over his tomb.
33 The soil in the valley is sweet to him;[e]
all men follow after him,
and a countless throng goes[c] before
him.[f]

34 "So how can you console me[g] with your
nonsense?
Nothing is left of your answers but
falsehood!"

Eliphaz

22 Then Eliphaz the Temanite replied:

2 "Can a man be of benefit to God?[h]
Can even a wise man benefit him?
3 What pleasure would it give the
Almighty if you were righteous?
What would he gain if your ways
were blameless?

4 "Is it for your piety that he rebukes you
and brings charges against you?[i]
5 Is not your wickedness great?
Are not your sins[j] endless?
6 You demanded security[k] from your
brothers for no reason;
you stripped men of their clothing,
leaving them naked.
7 You gave no water to the weary
and you withheld food from the
hungry,[l]
8 though you were a powerful man,
owning land—

21:24 [y]Pr 3:8
21:26 [z]Job 24:20; Ecc 9:2-3; Isa 14:11
21:28 [a]Job 1:3; 12:21; 31:37 [b]Job 8:22
21:30 [c]Pr 16:4 [d]Job 20:22, 28; 2Pe 2:9
21:33 [e]Job 3:22; 17:16; 24:24 [f]Job 3:19
21:34 [g]Job 16:2
22:2 [h]Lk 17:10
22:4 [i]Job 14:3; 19:29; Ps 143:2
22:5 [j]Job 11:6; 15:5
22:6 [k]Ex 22:26; Dt 24:6,17; Eze 18:12,16
22:7 [l]Job 31:17, 21,31

[a] *24* The meaning of the Hebrew for this word is uncertain.
[b] *30* Or *man is reserved for the day of calamity, / that he is brought forth to*
[c] *33* Or */ as a countless throng went*

an honored man,[m] living on it.
9 And you sent widows away empty-
handed[n]
and broke the strength of the
fatherless.
10 That is why snares are all around you,
why sudden peril terrifies you,
11 why it is so dark[o] you cannot see,
and why a flood of water covers you.[p]

12 "Is not God in the heights of heaven?[q]
And see how lofty are the highest
stars!
13 Yet you say, 'What does God know?[r]
Does he judge through such
darkness?[s]
14 Thick clouds[t] veil him, so he does not
see us
as he goes about in the vaulted
heavens.'
15 Will you keep to the old path
that evil men have trod?
16 They were carried off before their time,[u]
their foundations washed away by a
flood.[v]
17 They said to God, 'Leave us alone!
What can the Almighty do to us?'[w]
18 Yet it was he who filled their houses
with good things,[x]
so I stand aloof from the counsel of
the wicked.[y]

19 "The righteous see their ruin and
rejoice;[z]
the innocent mock[a] them, saying,
20 'Surely our foes are destroyed,
and fire[b] devours their wealth.'
21 "Submit to God and be at peace with
him;
in this way prosperity will come to
you.[c]
22 Accept instruction from his mouth
and lay up his words in your heart.
23 If you return[d] to the Almighty, you will
be restored:[e]
If you remove wickedness far from
your tent[f]
24 and assign your nuggets to the dust,
your gold of Ophir to the rocks in the
ravines,[g]
25 then the Almighty will be your gold,
the choicest silver for you.[h]
26 Surely then you will find delight in the
Almighty[i]
and will lift up your face to God.
27 You will pray to him,[j] and he will hear
you,
and you will fulfill your vows.
28 What you decide on will be done,
and light will shine on your ways.

22:8 [m]Isa 3:3; 9:15
22:9 [n]Job 24:3,21
22:11 [o]Job 5:14 [p]Ps 69:1-2; 124:4-5; La 3:54
22:12 [q]Job 11:8
22:13 [r]Ps 10:11; Isa 29:15 [s]Eze 8:12
22:14 [t]Job 26:9
22:16 [u]Job 15:32 [v]Job 14:19; Mt 7:26-27
22:17 [w]Job 21:15
22:18 [x]Job 12:6 [y]Job 21:16
22:19 [z]Ps 58:10; 107:42 [a]Ps 52:6
22:20 [b]Job 15:30
22:21 [c]Ps 34:8-10
22:23 [d]Job 8:5; Isa 31:6; Zec 1:3 [e]Isa 19:22; Ac 20:32 [f]Job 11:14
22:24 [g]Job 31:25
22:25 [h]Isa 33:6
22:26 [i]Job 27:10; Isa 58:14
22:27 [j]Job 33:26; 34:28; Isa 58:9

Good Advice, Poor Timing

JOB 22:21-27

Eliphaz offers some excellent advice, which is supported elsewhere in Scripture (2Ch 7:14). When sinners want to mend their relationships with the Almighty, the only way is through *humble repentance and fervent obedience.* Too bad Eliphaz's good theology is misapplied. He traces Job's suffering to his sin, but God declares Job blameless (Job 1:1). Again one of Job's friends displays his *ignorance about how God works.* Eliphaz's assumption is *that a good and obedient person will be rewarded in this life,* but such is not always the case. Jesus himself is the ultimate example of *a righteous man whose obedience led to his death* (Php 2:8).

Job's View of Himself

JOB 23:10–12

Considering how difficult it is to remain confident in the face of criticism, Job's view of himself is remarkable. Becoming defensive when someone judges us is natural, and Job has expressed a defensive tone in previous speeches. Here, however, he highlights his righteous track record with absolute confidence. His friends see him as extremely arrogant, but we know that Job speaks the truth about the way God sees him. While no one is truly sinless, the person justified and forgiven by a merciful God is graciously welcomed into his holy presence (Ro 3:10–12,22–26).

29 When men are brought low and you say,
'Lift them up!'
then he will save the downcast.[k]
30 He will deliver even one who is not innocent,
who will be delivered through the cleanness of your hands."[l]

Job

23

Then Job replied:

2 "Even today my complaint[m] is bitter;[n]
his hand[a] is heavy in spite of[b] my groaning.
3 If only I knew where to find him;
if only I could go to his dwelling!
4 I would state my case[o] before him
and fill my mouth with arguments.
5 I would find out what he would answer me,
and consider what he would say.
6 Would he oppose me with great power?[p]
No, he would not press charges against me.
7 There an upright man could present his case before him,[q]
and I would be delivered forever from my judge.

8 "But if I go to the east, he is not there;
if I go to the west, I do not find him.
9 When he is at work in the north, I do not see him;
when he turns to the south, I catch no glimpse of him.[r]
10 But he knows the way that I take;
when he has tested me,[s] I will come forth as gold.[t]
11 My feet have closely followed his steps;[u]
I have kept to his way without turning aside.[v]
12 I have not departed from the commands of his lips;[w]
I have treasured the words of his mouth more than my daily bread.[x]

13 "But he stands alone, and who can oppose him?
He does whatever he pleases.[y]
14 He carries out his decree against me,
and many such plans he still has in store.[z]
15 That is why I am terrified before him;
when I think of all this, I fear him.
16 God has made my heart faint;[a]
the Almighty[b] has terrified me.
17 Yet I am not silenced by the darkness,[c]

22:29 [k]Mt 23:12; 1Pe 5:5
22:30 [l]Job 42:7-8
23:2 [m]Job 7:11 [n]Job 6:3
23:4 [o]Job 13:18
23:6 [p]Job 9:4
23:7 [q]Job 13:3
23:9 [r]Job 9:11
23:10 [s]Ps 66:10; 139:1-3 [t]1Pe 1:7
23:11 [u]Ps 17:5 [v]Ps 44:18
23:12 [w]Job 6:10 [x]Jn 4:32,34
23:13 [y]Ps 115:3
23:14 [z]1Th 3:3
23:16 [a]Dt 20:3; Ps 22:14; Jer 51:46 [b]Job 27:2
23:17 [c]Job 19:8

[a] 2 Septuagint and Syriac; Hebrew / *the hand on me*
[b] 2 Or *heavy on me in*

by the thick darkness that covers my
face.

24

"Why does the Almighty not set times
for judgment?[d]
Why must those who know him look
in vain for such days?[e]
2 Men move boundary stones;[f]
they pasture flocks they have stolen.
3 They drive away the orphan's donkey
and take the widow's ox in pledge.[g]
4 They thrust the needy from the path
and force all the poor[h] of the land into
hiding.[i]
5 Like wild donkeys in the desert,
the poor go about their labor[j] of
foraging food;
the wasteland provides food for their
children.
6 They gather fodder in the fields
and glean in the vineyards of the
wicked.
7 Lacking clothes, they spend the night
naked;
they have nothing to cover themselves
in the cold.[k]
8 They are drenched by mountain rains
and hug[l] the rocks for lack of shelter.
9 The fatherless[m] child is snatched from
the breast;
the infant of the poor is seized for a
debt.
10 Lacking clothes, they go about naked;
they carry the sheaves, but still go
hungry.
11 They crush olives among the terraces[a];
they tread the winepresses, yet suffer
thirst.
12 The groans of the dying rise from the
city,
and the souls of the wounded cry out
for help.[n]
But God charges no one with
wrongdoing.[o]

13 "There are those who rebel against the
light,[p]
who do not know its ways
or stay in its paths.[q]
14 When daylight is gone, the murderer
rises up
and kills the poor and needy;
in the night he steals forth like a thief.[r]
15 The eye of the adulterer watches for
dusk;[s]
he thinks, 'No eye will see me,'[t]
and he keeps his face concealed.
16 In the dark, men break into houses,[u]
but by day they shut themselves in;

24:1 [d]Jer 46:10 [e]Ac 1:7
24:2 [f]Dt 19:14; 27:17; Pr 23:10
24:3 [g]Dt 24:6, 10, 12, 17; Job 22:6
24:4 [h]Job 29:12; 30:25; Ps 41:1 [i]Pr 28:28
24:5 [j]Ps 104:23
24:7 [k]Ex 22:27; Job 22:6
24:8 [l]La 4:5
24:9 [m]Dt 24:17
24:12 [n]Eze 26:15 [o]Job 9:23
24:13 [p]Jn 3:19-20 [q]Isa 5:20
24:14 [r]Ps 10:9
24:15 [s]Pr 7:8-9 [t]Ps 10:11
24:16 [u]Ex 22:2; Mt 6:19

[a] *11* Or *olives between the millstones*; the meaning of the Hebrew for this word is uncertain.

At Just the Right Time

JOB 24:1

Job's cry for a swift resolution to the injustice that he is suffering is a familiar one. Everyone wants God's timing to be their timing. It is so very hard to wait for him to act when everything within us is screaming for an end to the pain. But throughout the story of God, from Genesis to Revelation, God's timing is perfectly *perfect*. The apostle Peter reminds us that God operates on a whole different timetable than we do—for the best of reasons (2Pe 3:8-9).

Worm Theology

JOB 25:4–6

Bildad's last words cut to the chase: All human beings are maggots, worms. Not a pretty picture, but Bildad is right. No human being can be righteous on his or her own. But Bildad doesn't know the rest of the story. Jesus Christ came to pay the ultimate price for human unrighteousness by dying for a lost world. Because we are declared righteous through the shed blood of Jesus (Ro 3:21–25), we need never settle for being mere "worms" again! Christ did not die for worms, but for people he loves with abandon (Jn 3:16; Ro 5:8).

they want nothing to do with the
light.[v]
17 For all of them, deep darkness is their
morning[a];
they make friends with the terrors of
darkness.[b]

18 "Yet they are foam[w] on the surface of the
water;[x]
their portion of the land is cursed,
so that no one goes to the vineyards.
19 As heat and drought snatch away the
melted snow,[y]
so the grave[c][z] snatches away those
who have sinned.
20 The womb forgets them,
the worm feasts on them;
evil men are no longer remembered[a]
but are broken like a tree.[b]
21 They prey on the barren and childless
woman,
and to the widow show no kindness.[c]
22 But God drags away the mighty by his
power;
though they become established, they
have no assurance of life.[d]
23 He may let them rest in a feeling of
security,[e]
but his eyes are on their ways.[f]
24 For a little while they are exalted, and
then they are gone;[g]
they are brought low and gathered up
like all others;
they are cut off like heads of grain.[h]

25 "If this is not so, who can prove me
false
and reduce my words to nothing?"[i]

Bildad

25 Then Bildad the Shuhite replied:

2 "Dominion and awe belong to God;[j]
he establishes order in the heights of
heaven.
3 Can his forces be numbered?
Upon whom does his light not rise?[k]
4 How then can a man be righteous before
God?
How can one born of woman be
pure?[l]
5 If even the moon[m] is not bright
and the stars are not pure in his eyes,[n]
6 how much less man, who is but a
maggot—
a son of man,[o] who is only a worm!"[p]

24:16 [v]Jn 3:20
24:18 [w]Job 9:26 [x]Job 22:16
24:19 [y]Job 6:17 [z]Job 21:13
24:20 [a]Job 18:17; Pr 10:7 [b]Ps 31:12; Da 4:14
24:21 [c]Job 22:9
24:22 [d]Dt 28:66
24:23 [e]Job 12:6 [f]Job 11:11
24:24 [g]Job 14:21; Ps 37:10 [h]Isa 17:5
24:25 [i]Job 6:28; 27:4
25:2 [j]Job 9:4; Rev 1:6
25:3 [k]Jas 1:17
25:4 [l]Job 4:17; 14:4
25:5 [m]Job 31:26 [n]Job 15:15
25:6 [o]Job 7:17 [p]Ps 22:6

[a] 17 Or *them, their morning is like the shadow of death*
[b] 17 Or *of the shadow of death* [c] 19 Hebrew *Sheol*

Job

26

Then Job replied:

26:2 [q]Job 6:12 [r]Ps 71:9

2 "How you have helped the powerless![q]
How you have saved the arm that is feeble![r]
3 What advice you have offered to one without wisdom!
And what great insight you have displayed!
4 Who has helped you utter these words?
And whose spirit spoke from your mouth?

26:5 [s]Ps 88:10

5 "The dead are in deep anguish,[s]
those beneath the waters and all that live in them.

26:6 [t]Ps 139:8 [u]Job 41:11; Pr 15:11; Heb 4:13

6 Death[a][t] is naked before God;
Destruction[b] lies uncovered.[u]

26:7 [v]Job 9:8

7 He spreads out the northern ⌞skies⌟[v] over empty space;
he suspends the earth over nothing.

26:8 [w]Pr 30:4 [x]Job 37:11

8 He wraps up the waters[w] in his clouds,[x]
yet the clouds do not burst under their weight.

26:9 [y]Job 22:14; Ps 97:2

9 He covers the face of the full moon,
spreading his clouds[y] over it.

26:10 [z]Pr 8:27,29 [a]Job 38:8-11

10 He marks out the horizon on the face of the waters[z]
for a boundary between light and darkness.[a]
11 The pillars of the heavens quake,
aghast at his rebuke.

26:12 [b]Ex 14:21; Isa 51:15; Jer 31:35 [c]Job 12:13

12 By his power he churned up the sea;[b]
by his wisdom[c] he cut Rahab to pieces.

26:13 [d]Isa 27:1

13 By his breath the skies became fair;
his hand pierced the gliding serpent.[d]
14 And these are but the outer fringe of his works;
how faint the whisper we hear of him!

26:14 [e]Job 36:29

Who then can understand the thunder of his power?"[e]

27:1 [f]Job 29:1

27

And Job continued his discourse:[f]

27:2 [g]Job 34:5 [h]Job 9:18

2 "As surely as God lives, who has denied me justice,[g]
the Almighty, who has made me taste bitterness of soul,[h]

27:3 [i]Job 32:8; 33:4

3 as long as I have life within me,
the breath of God[i] in my nostrils,
4 my lips will not speak wickedness,
and my tongue will utter no deceit.[j]

27:4 [j]Job 6:28

5 I will never admit you are in the right;
till I die, I will not deny my integrity.[k]

27:5 [k]Job 2:9; 13:15

6 I will maintain my righteousness and never let go of it;

[a]6 Hebrew *Sheol* [b]6 Hebrew *Abaddon*

The Breath of God

JOB 27:2–5

The "breath of God" (Job 27:3) refers to the force that gives life itself, the Creator who literally breathes life into the first human being (Ge 2:7). With his breath, God both destroys and sustains (Job 4:9; 33:4). His enlivening breath is the only thing that keeps human hearts beating (Job 34:14–15). Job proclaims in no uncertain terms that as long as he is living, as long as "the breath of God" is in his "nostrils," he will not admit that his "friends" are right and that he deserves his pain.

Week 13

The Faint Whisper of God

Beautiful clouds, trees and flowers. Roaring thunderstorms. Millions of stars, each of which God calls by name (Isa 40:26) and gives particular splendor (1Co 15:41). Busy ants and peculiar insects. Giraffes. Platypuses! Peaceful snowfalls. Cascading waterfalls. Shadowed forests. All of these come from your incredible Creator.

Yet Job 26:14 says that what you see is a mere whisper of what your God truly is. He is indescribable and incomprehensible. Are there still times when you question him, his wisdom and his power? What questions are on your heart?

When in your life has it seemed to you that the wicked went unpunished (Job 24:1-4,22-24; 27:13-23)?

When did it seem that God was far away and unconcerned about your trials (Ps 6:3; 10:1)?

Job questions God and receives a lesson in humility. What contrasts does God make between his abilities and powers and Job's (Job 38:1-41)? When you become aware of who God truly is, what happens to your doubts about God or his ability to control your situation (Job 11:7-9)?

What is God's response to Job's questioning (Job 40:8-14)?

What does Job learn about questioning God (Job 42:1-6)?

God's treatment of Job may seem harsh; however, in the end, God commends Job (Job 42:7-9). Job learns much about himself and God through his trials. What have your trials taught you?

It's easy to forget just how exalted and how powerful God is. When you don't understand what God is doing in your life, it's easier to grab the phone and call a friend than to call on God. Job learns that friends sometimes point in the wrong direction. Their platitudes are not comforting, their instructions are not helpful and their attempts at spiritual wisdom are woefully simple and ignorant. When you're troubled, go to the One who has all the answers.

Enjoying God THROUGH the Word

Read Job 9 (pages 809-810). Job feels such despair that he despises his very life (Job 9:21). How can he even presume to confront God (Job 9:32-35)? If only he had someone to stand between him and God (Job 9:33). Have you ever felt like Job? Wishing for an arbitrator or mediator between you and God? Well, you have one (1Ti 2:5). Jesus understands you, sympathizes with your struggles and has gone to heaven on your behalf so that you can approach God's very throne with confidence (Heb 4:14-16). And you also have another helper. The Holy Spirit speaks to God on your behalf when you simply don't know how to express your need (Ro 8:26-27). God has provided for you. You can go to him—even with your doubt, fear or anger.

Enjoying God THROUGH Experience

Spiritually, you already are seated with Christ in the heavenly realms (Eph 2:6). You have been given the Holy Spirit as your helper and teacher. The Spirit will reveal the things of God to you (1Co 2:9-16) so that you can overcome the obstacles in your life.

Go outdoors to pray and praise. Look around; see the power and the glory of God. And remember, these things are but a whisper of him, very faint. Open your Bible and read Psalm 104:1-4 aloud. This is your God!

Go to page 893 for your next weekly study.

my conscience will not reproach me
as long as I live.[l]

7 "May my enemies be like the wicked,
my adversaries like the unjust!
8 For what hope has the godless[m] when
he is cut off,
when God takes away his life?[n]
9 Does God listen to his cry
when distress comes upon him?[o]
10 Will he find delight in the Almighty?[p]
Will he call upon God at all times?

11 "I will teach you about the power of
God;
the ways of the Almighty I will not
conceal.
12 You have all seen this yourselves.
Why then this meaningless talk?

13 "Here is the fate God allots to the
wicked,
the heritage a ruthless man receives
from the Almighty:[q]
14 However many his children, their fate is
the sword;[r]
his offspring will never have enough
to eat.[s]
15 The plague will bury those who survive
him,
and their widows will not weep for
them.[t]
16 Though he heaps up silver like dust
and clothes like piles of clay,[u]
17 what he lays up the righteous will
wear,[v]
and the innocent will divide his silver.
18 The house he builds is like a moth's
cocoon,[w]
like a hut[x] made by a watchman.
19 He lies down wealthy, but will do so no
more;[y]
when he opens his eyes, all is gone.
20 Terrors overtake him like a flood;[z]
a tempest snatches him away in the
night.[a]
21 The east wind carries him off, and he is
gone;
it sweeps him out of his place.[b]
22 It hurls itself against him without
mercy[c]
as he flees headlong from its power.[d]
23 It claps its hands in derision
and hisses him out of his place.[e]

28 "There is a mine for silver
and a place where gold is refined.
2 Iron is taken from the earth,
and copper is smelted from ore.[f]
3 Man puts an end to the darkness;[g]
he searches the farthest recesses
for ore in the blackest darkness.

27:6 [l]Job 2:3
27:8 [m]Job 8:13 [n]Job 11:20; Lk 12:20
27:9 [o]Job 35:12; Pr 1:28; Isa 1:15; Jer 14:12; Mic 3:4
27:10 [p]Job 22:26
27:13 [q]Job 15:20; 20:29
27:14 [r]Dt 28:41; Job 15:22; Hos 9:13 [s]Job 20:10
27:15 [t]Ps 78:64
27:16 [u]Zec 9:3
27:17 [v]Pr 28:8; Ecc 2:26
27:18 [w]Job 8:14 [x]Isa 1:8
27:19 [y]Job 7:8
27:20 [z]Job 15:21 [a]Job 20:8
27:21 [b]Job 7:10; 21:18
27:22 [c]Jer 13:14; Eze 5:11; 24:14 [d]Job 11:20
27:23 [e]Job 18:18
28:2 [f]Dt 8:9
28:3 [g]Ecc 1:13

There are some parts of our journey that are so dark and the terrain so bleak that it's hard to find the will to keep on walking. That is why we are called to walk by faith. We hold on to the promises of God not because they seem likely, for at times they don't, but because they come from God and it is not possible for him to lie. I pulled out an old diary the other day and read a verse that I wrote down when it was the last thing that I felt to be true about my life, "I am still confident of this: I will see the goodness of the LORD in the land of the living" (Psalm 27:13).

—Sheila Walsh

True Wisdom

JOB 28:12–24

We are all prone to believe that we are wise or that we can become so by some avenue apart from God. But Job reminds us that the invaluable spiritual commodity of wisdom cannot be found on earth, nor can it be purchased for any price. No matter how great our mastery of the physical world may become, God alone is great enough to understand all things and discern all mysteries. After all, God and wisdom have dwelled together since before the beginning of time (Pr 8:22–31). When we approach people or problems with the presumption of our own wisdom, we are likely to do damage, just as Job's friends have done. How much wiser we would be to be silent before our friends, and let the God who sees and knows all draw whatever conclusions need to be made.

4 Far from where people dwell he cuts a shaft,
in places forgotten by the foot of man;
far from men he dangles and sways.
5 The earth, from which food comes,[h]
is transformed below as by fire;
6 sapphires[a] come from its rocks,
and its dust contains nuggets of gold.
7 No bird of prey knows that hidden path,
no falcon's eye has seen it.
8 Proud beasts do not set foot on it,
and no lion prowls there.
9 Man's hand assaults the flinty rock
and lays bare the roots of the mountains.
10 He tunnels through the rock;
his eyes see all its treasures.
11 He searches[b] the sources of the rivers
and brings hidden things to light.

12 "But where can wisdom be found?[i]
Where does understanding dwell?
13 Man does not comprehend its worth;[j]
it cannot be found in the land of the living.
14 The deep says, 'It is not in me';
the sea says, 'It is not with me.'
15 It cannot be bought with the finest gold,
nor can its price be weighed in silver.[k]
16 It cannot be bought with the gold of Ophir,
with precious onyx or sapphires.
17 Neither gold nor crystal can compare with it,
nor can it be had for jewels of gold.[l]
18 Coral and jasper are not worthy of mention;
the price of wisdom is beyond rubies.[m]
19 The topaz of Cush cannot compare with it;
it cannot be bought with pure gold.[n]

20 "Where then does wisdom come from?
Where does understanding dwell?[o]
21 It is hidden from the eyes of every living thing,
concealed even from the birds of the air.
22 Destruction[c][p] and Death say,
'Only a rumor of it has reached our ears.'
23 God understands the way to it
and he alone knows where it dwells,[q]
24 for he views the ends of the earth[r]
and sees everything under the heavens.[s]
25 When he established the force of the wind

28:5 [h]Ps 104:14
28:12 [i]Ecc 7:24
28:13 [j]Pr 3:15; Mt 13:44-46
28:15 [k]Pr 3:13-14; 8:10-11; 16:16
28:17 [l]Pr 16:16
28:18 [m]Pr 3:15
28:19 [n]Pr 8:19
28:20 [o]ver 23,28
28:22 [p]Job 26:6
28:23 [q]Pr 8:22-31
28:24 [r]Ps 33:13-14 [s]Pr 15:3

[a] *6* Or *lapis lazuli;* also in verse 16 [b] *11* Septuagint, Aquila and Vulgate; Hebrew *He dams up* [c] *22* Hebrew *Abaddon*

and measured out the waters,[t]
26 when he made a decree for the rain
and a path for the thunderstorm,[u]
27 then he looked at wisdom and appraised it;
he confirmed it and tested it.
28 And he said to man,
'The fear of the Lord—that is wisdom,
and to shun evil is understanding.[v]' "

29

Job continued his discourse:[w]

2 "How I long for the months gone by,
for the days when God watched over me,[x]
3 when his lamp shone upon my head
and by his light I walked through darkness![y]
4 Oh, for the days when I was in my prime,
when God's intimate friendship
blessed my house,[z]
5 when the Almighty was still with me
and my children were around me,
6 when my path was drenched with cream[a]
and the rock[b] poured out for me
streams of olive oil.[c]

7 "When I went to the gate[d] of the city
and took my seat in the public square,
8 the young men saw me and stepped aside
and the old men rose to their feet;
9 the chief men refrained from speaking
and covered their mouths with their hands;[e]
10 the voices of the nobles were hushed,
and their tongues stuck to the roof of their mouths.[f]
11 Whoever heard me spoke well of me,
and those who saw me commended me,
12 because I rescued the poor[g] who cried for help,
and the fatherless[h] who had none to assist him.[i]
13 The man who was dying blessed me;[j]
I made the widow's[k] heart sing.
14 I put on righteousness[l] as my clothing;
justice was my robe and my turban.
15 I was eyes[m] to the blind
and feet to the lame.
16 I was a father to the needy;[n]
I took up the case of the stranger.
17 I broke the fangs of the wicked
and snatched the victims from their teeth.[o]

18 "I thought, 'I will die in my own house,
my days as numerous as the grains of sand.[p]

28:25 [t]Job 12:15; Ps 135:7
28:26 [u]Job 37:3,8, 11; 38:25,27
28:28 [v]Dt 4:6; Ps 111:10; Pr 1:7; 9:10
29:1 [w]Job 13:12; 27:1
29:2 [x]Jer 31:28
29:3 [y]Job 11:17
29:4 [z]Ps 25:14; Pr 3:32
29:6 [a]Job 20:17 [b]Ps 81:16 [c]Dt 32:13
29:7 [d]Job 31:21
29:9 [e]Job 21:5
29:10 [f]Ps 137:6
29:12 [g]Job 24:4 [h]Job 31:17, 21 [i]Ps 72:12; Pr 21:13
29:13 [j]Job 31:20 [k]Job 22:9
29:14 [l]Job 27:6; Ps 132:9; Isa 59:17; 61:10; Eph 6:14
29:15 [m]Nu 10:31
29:16 [n]Job 24:4; Pr 29:7
29:17 [o]Ps 3:7
29:18 [p]Ps 30:6

The Good Old Days

JOB 29:2–6

How natural it is to pine for the "good old days" when the present moment brings nothing but pain. Job's life before tragedy struck may not have been as perfect as he remembers it (we tend to see what we long for through rose-colored glasses), but his poignant recollections stir the sympathies of anyone who has also seen better days. Job's reference to "streams of olive oil" (Job 29:6) has special meaning for those listening to his lament at the time. Oil is considered a sign of God's favor and blessing (Jer 31:12), and pure olive oil in particular is associated with wealth, extravagance, honor, divine blessing and joy (Ex 30:22–25; Ps 92:10; 104:15; Isa 61:3; Eze 16:13). Job's current experience of life as "oil-less" is barren indeed.

The Fickleness of People

JOB 29:21–30:1

In the patriarchal society in which Job lived, being older than another person automatically merited the elder person authority and dignity. Unlike our society, in which the elderly are often marginalized and even looked down on, Job's culture esteemed its elders and looked to them for guidance.

For Job to literally be mocked by men younger than himself is the ultimate social disgrace. Job implies that insult is added to injury when he considers the caliber of the people who malign him: these upstarts' own fathers are no better than dogs. Dogs were considered vicious scavengers (Jer 15:3); therefore, to be compared to a dog was an appalling insult (1Sa 17:43). Job's experience of falling practically overnight from the pinnacle of social veneration to the desert floor of social scorn is a poignant reminder to all of us that we dare not place our security and self-worth into the hands of other people. Even our friends can be fickle; therefore, our trust can only rest secure in God (Ps 9:10).

19 My roots will reach to the water,[q]
and the dew will lie all night on my branches.
20 My glory will remain fresh in me,
the bow[r] ever new in my hand.'[s]

21 "Men listened to me expectantly,
waiting in silence for my counsel.
22 After I had spoken, they spoke no more;
my words fell gently on their ears.[t]
23 They waited for me as for showers
and drank in my words as the spring rain.
24 When I smiled at them, they scarcely believed it;
the light of my face was precious to them.[a]
25 I chose the way for them and sat as their chief;
I dwelt as a king[u] among his troops;
I was like one who comforts mourners.[v]

30

"But now they mock me,[w]
men younger than I,
whose fathers I would have disdained
to put with my sheep dogs.
2 Of what use was the strength of their hands to me,
since their vigor had gone from them?
3 Haggard from want and hunger,
they roamed[b] the parched land
in desolate wastelands at night.
4 In the brush they gathered salt herbs,
and their food[c] was the root of the broom tree.
5 They were banished from their fellow men,
shouted at as if they were thieves.
6 They were forced to live in the dry stream beds,
among the rocks and in holes in the ground.
7 They brayed among the bushes
and huddled in the undergrowth.
8 A base and nameless brood,
they were driven out of the land.

9 "And now their sons mock me[x] in song;[y]
I have become a byword[z] among them.
10 They detest me and keep their distance;
they do not hesitate to spit in my face.[a]
11 Now that God has unstrung my bow and afflicted me,[b]
they throw off restraint[c] in my presence.
12 On my right the tribe[d] attacks;

29:19 [q]Job 18:16; Jer 17:8
29:20 [r]Ps 18:34 [s]Ge 49:24
29:22 [t]Dt 32:2
29:25 [u]Job 1:3; 31:37 [v]Job 4:4
30:1 [w]Job 12:4
30:9 [x]Ps 69:11 [y]Job 12:4; La 3:14,63 [z]Job 17:6
30:10 [a]Nu 12:14; Dt 25:9; Isa 50:6; Mt 26:67
30:11 [b]Ru 1:21 [c]Ps 32:9

[a] *24* The meaning of the Hebrew for this clause is uncertain. [b] *3* Or *gnawed* [c] *4* Or *fuel* [d] *12* The meaning of the Hebrew for this word is uncertain.

they lay snares for my feet,[d]
they build their siege ramps against me.[e]
13 They break up my road;[f]
they succeed in destroying me—
without anyone's helping them.[a]
14 They advance as through a gaping breach;
amid the ruins they come rolling in.
15 Terrors overwhelm me;[g]
my dignity is driven away as by the wind,
my safety vanishes like a cloud.[h]

16 "And now my life ebbs away;[i]
days of suffering grip me.
17 Night pierces my bones;
my gnawing pains never rest.
18 In his great power ⌊God⌋ becomes like clothing to me[b];
he binds me like the neck of my garment.
19 He throws me into the mud,[j]
and I am reduced to dust and ashes.

20 "I cry out to you, O God, but you do not answer;[k]
I stand up, but you merely look at me.
21 You turn on me ruthlessly;[l]
with the might of your hand[m] you attack me.[n]
22 You snatch me up and drive me before the wind;[o]
you toss me about in the storm.[p]
23 I know you will bring me down to death,[q]
to the place appointed for all the living.[r]

24 "Surely no one lays a hand on a broken man
when he cries for help in his distress.[s]
25 Have I not wept for those in trouble?
Has not my soul grieved for the poor?[t]
26 Yet when I hoped for good, evil came;
when I looked for light, then came darkness.[u]
27 The churning inside me never stops;[v]
days of suffering confront me.
28 I go about blackened,[w] but not by the sun;
I stand up in the assembly and cry for help.[x]
29 I have become a brother of jackals,[y]
a companion of owls.[z]
30 My skin grows black and peels;[a]
my body burns with fever.[b]
31 My harp is tuned to mourning,[c]
and my flute to the sound of wailing.

30:12 [d]Ps 140:4-5 [e]Job 19:12
30:13 [f]Isa 3:12
30:15 [g]Job 31:23; Ps 55:4-5 [h]Job 3:25; Hos 13:3
30:16 [i]Job 3:24; Ps 22:14; 42:4
30:19 [j]Ps 69:2,14
30:20 [k]Job 19:7
30:21 [l]Job 19:6,22 [m]Job 16:9,14 [n]Job 10:3
30:22 [o]Job 27:21 [p]Job 9:17
30:23 [q]Job 9:22; 10:8 [r]Job 3:19
30:24 [s]Job 19:7
30:25 [t]Job 24:4; Ps 35:13-14; Ro 12:15
30:26 [u]Job 3:25-26; 19:8; Jer 8:15
30:27 [v]La 2:11
30:28 [w]Ps 38:6; 42:9; 43:2 [x]Job 19:7
30:29 [y]Ps 44:19 [z]Ps 102:6; Mic 1:8
30:30 [a]La 4:8 [b]Ps 102:3
30:31 [c]Isa 24:8

[a] 13 Or *me. / 'No one can help him,' ⌊they say⌋.* [b] 18 Hebrew; Septuagint *⌊God⌋ grasps my clothing*

When God Is Silent

JOB 30:20-22

Job is not alone in feeling like his prayers are slamming into an invisible ceiling. The psalmist expresses the same lament (Ps 22:1-2), as does Jeremiah (La 3:8,44). There is probably nothing worse than feeling like Almighty God, the only one who can save us, is indifferent to our plight. Nothing, perhaps, except watching his passivity turn to aggression. Job thinks God is not only turning a deaf ear to his cries, but also intentionally and maliciously making his life miserable. If only Job knew what we know: What he's accusing God of is actually the work of Satan. God is permitting the devil to have his way, but only temporarily. When we feel shut out of God's presence and battered by the storms of life, we can remember that the evil forces that hammer us will ultimately be crushed (Rev 20:10).

Proof of Innocence

JOB 31

Job has exhausted himself, passionately railing against life and God. Now he makes one last stab at proving his innocence, this time by a logical appeal to the judge who has established the laws with which Job has faithfully complied all his life. By methodically arguing that he has not committed any of the offenses that would warrant punishment, Job hopes to clear his name. How grateful we can be that under the new covenant we approach God, not as condemned defendants or clever attorneys, but as beloved children under grace (Heb 8:8–12).

31 "I made a covenant with my eyes
not to look lustfully at a girl.[d]
2 For what is man's lot from God above,
his heritage from the Almighty on high?[e]
3 Is it not ruin[f] for the wicked,
disaster for those who do wrong?[g]
4 Does he not see my ways[h]
and count my every step?[i]

5 "If I have walked in falsehood
or my foot has hurried after deceit[j]—
6 let God weigh me in honest scales[k]
and he will know that I am blameless—
7 if my steps have turned from the path,[l]
if my heart has been led by my eyes,
or if my hands[m] have been defiled,
8 then may others eat what I have sown,[n]
and may my crops be uprooted.[o]

9 "If my heart has been enticed[p] by a woman,
or if I have lurked at my neighbor's door,
10 then may my wife grind another man's grain,
and may other men sleep with her.[q]
11 For that would have been shameful,
a sin to be judged.[r]
12 It is a fire[s] that burns to Destruction[a];[t]
it would have uprooted my harvest.[u]

13 "If I have denied justice to my menservants and maidservants
when they had a grievance against me,[v]
14 what will I do when God confronts me?
What will I answer when called to account?
15 Did not he who made me in the womb make them?
Did not the same one form us both within our mothers?[w]

16 "If I have denied the desires of the poor[x]
or let the eyes of the widow[y] grow weary,
17 if I have kept my bread to myself,
not sharing it with the fatherless[z]—
18 but from my youth I reared him as would a father,
and from my birth I guided the widow—
19 if I have seen anyone perishing for lack of clothing,[a]
or a needy[b] man without a garment,
20 and his heart did not bless me
for warming him with the fleece from my sheep,

31:1 [d]Mt 5:28
31:2 [e]Job 20:29
31:3 [f]Job 21:30 [g]Job 34:22
31:4 [h]2Ch 16:9 [i]Pr 5:21
31:5 [j]Mic 2:11
31:6 [k]Job 6:2; 27:5-6
31:7 [l]Job 23:11 [m]Job 9:30
31:8 [n]Lev 26:16; Job 20:18 [o]Mic 6:15
31:9 [p]Job 24:15
31:10 [q]Dt 28:30; Jer 8:10
31:11 [r]Ge 38:24; Lev 20:10; Dt 22:22-24
31:12 [s]Job 15:30 [t]Job 26:6 [u]Job 20:28
31:13 [v]Dt 24:14-15
31:15 [w]Job 10:3
31:16 [x]Job 5:16; 20:19 [y]Job 22:9
31:17 [z]Job 22:7; 29:12
31:19 [a]Job 22:6 [b]Job 24:4

[a] 12 Hebrew *Abaddon*

31:21 [c]Job 22:9

21 if I have raised my hand against the
fatherless,[c]
knowing that I had influence in court,

31:22 [d]Job 38:15

22 then let my arm fall from the shoulder,
let it be broken off at the joint.[d]

31:23 [e]Job 13:11

23 For I dreaded destruction from God,
and for fear of his splendor[e] I could
not do such things.

31:24 [f]Job 22:25 [g]Mt 6:24; Mk 10:24

24 "If I have put my trust in gold[f]
or said to pure gold, 'You are my
security,'[g]

31:25 [h]Ps 62:10

25 if I have rejoiced over my great wealth,[h]
the fortune my hands had gained,

31:26 [i]Eze 8:16

26 if I have regarded the sun[i] in its
radiance
or the moon moving in splendor,
27 so that my heart was secretly enticed
and my hand offered them a kiss of
homage,

31:28 [j]Dt 17:2-7

28 then these also would be sins to be
judged,[j]
for I would have been unfaithful to
God on high.

31:29 [k]Ob 1:12 [l]Pr 17:5; 24:17-18

29 "If I have rejoiced at my enemy's
misfortune[k]
or gloated over the trouble that came
to him[l]—
30 I have not allowed my mouth to sin
by invoking a curse against his life—
31 if the men of my household have never
said,

31:31 [m]Job 22:7

'Who has not had his fill of Job's
meat?'[m]—
32 but no stranger had to spend the night
in the street,

31:32 [n]Ge 19:2-3; Ro 12:13

for my door was always open to the
traveler[n]—

31:33 [o]Pr 28:13 [p]Ge 3:8

33 if I have concealed[o] my sin as men do,[a]
by hiding[p] my guilt in my heart

31:34 [q]Ex 23:2

34 because I so feared the crowd[q]
and so dreaded the contempt of the
clans
that I kept silent and would not go
outside—

31:35 [r]Job 19:7; 30:28 [s]Job 27:7; 35:14

35 ("Oh, that I had someone to hear me![r]
I sign now my defense—let the
Almighty answer me;
let my accuser[s] put his indictment in
writing.
36 Surely I would wear it on my shoulder,
I would put it on like a crown.
37 I would give him an account of my
every step;

31:37 [t]Job 1:3; 29:25

like a prince[t] I would approach
him.)—

31:38 [u]Ge 4:10

38 "if my land cries out against me[u]
and all its furrows are wet with tears,

[a] 33 *Or as Adam did*

God is offering himself to you daily, and the rate of exchange is fixed: your sins for his forgiveness, your hurt for his balm of healing, your sorrow for his joy. Give him your pain. Give him the guilt you feel, the heartaches that come to us all. They are part of living, but if you focus on Jesus Christ, he alone can ease your heartache. Then he uses us to dry the tears of others.

—Barbara Johnson

The Words of Job End

JOB 31:40

When Job wraps up his final discourse, it is not with the hopeless resignation he expresses in some earlier chapters. He no longer appears to be waiting, or even wanting, to die. It is as if he remembers once again that God is just, even though his circumstances seem to prove otherwise, and his last hope is that the righteous appeal he's just presented will secure his redemption. While we know that not even the upright Job can win God's favor on human merit alone (Eph 2:8–9), Job's understanding of God's justice gives him boldness and a flicker of hope.

39 if I have devoured its yield without
payment[v]
or broken the spirit of its tenants,[w]
40 then let briers[x] come up instead of
wheat
and weeds instead of barley."

The words of Job are ended.

Elihu

32 So these three men stopped answering Job,
because he was righteous in his own eyes.[y]
2 But Elihu son of Barakel the Buzite,[z] of the family of Ram, became very angry with Job for justi-
fying himself rather than God.[a] 3 He was also
angry with the three friends, because they had
found no way to refute Job, and yet had condemned him.[a] 4 Now Elihu had waited before
speaking to Job because they were older than he.
5 But when he saw that the three men had nothing more to say, his anger was aroused.
6 So Elihu son of Barakel the Buzite said:

"I am young in years,
and you are old;[b]
that is why I was fearful,
not daring to tell you what I know.
7 I thought, 'Age should speak;
advanced years should teach wisdom.'
8 But it is the spirit[b] in a man,
the breath of the Almighty,[c] that gives
him understanding.[d]
9 It is not only the old[c] who are wise,[e]
not only the aged who understand
what is right.

10 "Therefore I say: Listen to me;
I too will tell you what I know.
11 I waited while you spoke,
I listened to your reasoning;
while you were searching for words,
12 I gave you my full attention.
But not one of you has proved Job
wrong;
none of you has answered his
arguments.
13 Do not say, 'We have found wisdom;[f]
let God refute him, not man.'
14 But Job has not marshaled his words
against me,
and I will not answer him with your
arguments.

15 "They are dismayed and have no more
to say;
words have failed them.
16 Must I wait, now that they are silent,
now that they stand there with no
reply?

31:39 [v]1Ki 21:19 [w]Lev 19:13; Jas 5:4
31:40 [x]Ge 3:18
32:1 [y]Job 10:7; 33:9
32:2 [z]Ge 22:21 [a]Job 27:5; 30:21
32:6 [b]Job 15:10
32:8 [c]Job 27:3; 33:4 [d]Pr 2:6
32:9 [e]1Co 1:26
32:13 [f]Jer 9:23

[a] 3 Masoretic Text; an ancient Hebrew scribal tradition *Job, and so had condemned God*   [b] 8 Or *Spirit*; also in verse 18
[c] 9 Or *many*; or *great*

17 I too will have my say;
I too will tell what I know.
18 For I am full of words,
and the spirit within me compels me;
19 inside I am like bottled-up wine,
like new wineskins ready to burst.
20 I must speak and find relief;
I must open my lips and reply.
21 I will show partiality[g] to no one,[h]
nor will I flatter any man;
22 for if I were skilled in flattery,
my Maker would soon take me away.

33

1 "But now, Job, listen to my words;
pay attention to everything I say.[i]
2 I am about to open my mouth;
my words are on the tip of my tongue.
3 My words come from an upright heart;
my lips sincerely speak what I know.[j]
4 The Spirit of God has made me;[k]
the breath of the Almighty[l] gives me life.
5 Answer me[m] then, if you can;
prepare[n] yourself and confront me.
6 I am just like you before God;
I too have been taken from clay.[o]
7 No fear of me should alarm you,
nor should my hand be heavy upon you.[p]

8 "But you have said in my hearing—
I heard the very words—
9 'I am pure[q] and without sin;[r]
I am clean and free from guilt.
10 Yet God has found fault with me;
he considers me his enemy.[s]
11 He fastens my feet in shackles;[t]
he keeps close watch on all my paths.'[u]

12 "But I tell you, in this you are not right,
for God is greater than man.[v]
13 Why do you complain to him[w]
that he answers none of man's words[a]?
14 For God does speak[x]—now one way,
now another—
though man may not perceive it.
15 In a dream,[y] in a vision of the night,
when deep sleep falls on men
as they slumber in their beds,
16 he may speak[z] in their ears
and terrify them with warnings,
17 to turn man from wrongdoing
and keep him from pride,
18 to preserve his soul from the pit,[b][a]
his life from perishing by the sword.[c][b]
19 Or a man may be chastened on a bed of pain

32:21 [g]Lev 19:15; Job 13:10 [h]Mt 22:16
33:1 [i]Job 13:6
33:3 [j]Job 6:28; 27:4; 36:4
33:4 [k]Ge 2:7; Job 10:3 [l]Job 27:3
33:5 [m]ver 32 [n]Job 13:18
33:6 [o]Job 4:19
33:7 [p]Job 9:34; 13:21; 2Co 2:4
33:9 [q]Job 10:7 [r]Job 13:23; 16:17
33:10 [s]Job 13:24
33:11 [t]Job 13:27 [u]Job 14:16
33:12 [v]Ecc 7:20
33:13 [w]Job 40:2; Isa 45:9
33:14 [x]Ps 62:11
33:15 [y]Job 4:13
33:16 [z]Job 36:10, 15
33:18 [a]ver 22,24, 28,30 [b]Job 15:22

[a] 13 Or *that he does not answer for any of his actions*
[b] 18 Or *preserve him from the grave*
[c] 18 Or *from crossing the River*

Elihu Speaks

JOB 32–33

Elihu has been listening from the wings to the various discourses of Job and his friends, apparently bursting to put in his two cents' worth but restrained from doing so by cultural mores. Not only was it considered disrespectful for young people to speak before their elders have had their say, but a young person's "wisdom" was often considered deficient. Elihu doesn't see it that way; in fact he, like the others, believes he speaks with divine inspiration (Job 32:8; 36:2–3). Elihu's lengthy speech does introduce important truths Job's other friends miss, especially the possibility of a gracious God using suffering to chasten and restore rather than to punish. But the young man's bombastic style and uninformed conclusions reveal that his wisdom is mostly in his own eyes.

with constant distress in his bones,[c]
20 so that his very being finds food[d]
repulsive
and his soul loathes the choicest
meal.[e]
21 His flesh wastes away to nothing,
and his bones, once hidden, now stick
out.[f]
22 His soul draws near to the pit,[a]
and his life to the messengers of
death.[b][g]

23 "Yet if there is an angel on his side
as a mediator, one out of a thousand,
to tell a man what is right for him,[h]
24 to be gracious to him and say,
'Spare him from going down to the
pit[c];[i]
I have found a ransom for him'—
25 then his flesh is renewed like a child's;
it is restored as in the days of his
youth.[j]
26 He prays to God and finds favor with
him,[k]
he sees God's face and shouts for joy;[l]
he is restored by God to his righteous
state.[m]
27 Then he comes to men and says,
'I sinned,[n] and perverted what was
right,[o]
but I did not get what I deserved.[p]
28 He redeemed my soul from going down
to the pit,[d]
and I will live to enjoy the light.'[q]
29 "God does all these things to a man[r]—
twice, even three times—
30 to turn back his soul from the pit,[e]
that the light of life[s] may shine on
him.
31 "Pay attention, Job, and listen to me;
be silent, and I will speak.
32 If you have anything to say, answer me;
speak up, for I want you to be
cleared.
33 But if not, then listen to me;
be silent, and I will teach you
wisdom.[t]"

34

Then Elihu said:

2 "Hear my words, you wise men;
listen to me, you men of learning.
3 For the ear tests words
as the tongue tastes food.[u]
4 Let us discern for ourselves what is
right;
let us learn together what is good.[v]

33:19 [c]Job 30:17
33:20 [d]Ps 107:18 [e]Job 3:24; 6:6
33:21 [f]Job 16:8; 19:20
33:22 [g]Ps 88:3
33:23 [h]Mic 6:8
33:24 [i]Isa 38:17
33:25 [j]2Ki 5:14
33:26 [k]Job 34:28 [l]Job 22:26 [m]Ps 50:15; 51:12
33:27 [n]2Sa 12:13 [o]Lk 15:21 [p]Ro 6:21
33:28 [q]Job 22:28
33:29 [r]1Co 12:6; Eph 1:11; Php 2:13
33:30 [s]Ps 56:13
33:33 [t]Ps 34:11
34:3 [u]Job 12:11
34:4 [v]1Th 5:21

[a] 22 Or *He draws near to the grave* [b] 22 Or *to the dead* [c] 24 Or *grave* [d] 28 Or *redeemed me from going down to the grave* [e] 30 Or *turn him back from the grave*

Suffering is seldom an item on our list of requests to the Lord. But when it crosses our path and we are able by his grace to keep on walking, our lives become messages of hope to the world and to the church.

—Sheila Walsh

[5]"Job says, 'I am innocent,[w]
but God denies me justice.[x]
[6]Although I am right,
I am considered a liar;
although I am guiltless,
his arrow inflicts an incurable
wound.'[y]
[7]What man is like Job,
who drinks scorn like water?[z]
[8]He keeps company with evildoers;
he associates with wicked men.[a]
[9]For he says, 'It profits a man nothing
when he tries to please God.'[b]

[10]"So listen to me, you men of
understanding.
Far be it from God to do evil,[c]
from the Almighty to do wrong.[d]
[11]He repays a man for what he has done;[e]
he brings upon him what his conduct
deserves.[f]
[12]It is unthinkable that God would do
wrong,
that the Almighty would pervert
justice.[g]
[13]Who appointed him over the earth?
Who put him in charge of the whole
world?[h]
[14]If it were his intention
and he withdrew his spirit[a] and
breath,[i]
[15]all mankind would perish together
and man would return to the dust.[j]

[16]"If you have understanding, hear this;
listen to what I say.
[17]Can he who hates justice govern?[k]
Will you condemn the just and
mighty One?[l]
[18]Is he not the One who says to kings,
'You are worthless,'
and to nobles, 'You are wicked,'[m]
[19]who shows no partiality[n] to princes
and does not favor the rich over the
poor,[o]
for they are all the work of his
hands?[p]
[20]They die in an instant, in the middle of
the night;[q]
the people are shaken and they pass
away;
the mighty are removed without
human hand.[r]

[21]"His eyes are on the ways of men;
he sees their every step.[s]
[22]There is no dark place,[t] no deep
shadow,[u]
where evildoers can hide.
[23]God has no need to examine men further,

34:5 [w]Job 33:9 [x]Job 27:2
34:6 [y]Job 6:4
34:7 [z]Job 15:16
34:8 [a]Job 22:15; Ps 50:18
34:9 [b]Job 21:15; 35:3
34:10 [c]Ge 18:25 [d]Dt 32:4; Job 8:3; Ro 9:14
34:11 [e]Ps 62:12; Mt 16:27; Ro 2:6; 2Co 5:10 [f]Jer 32:19; Eze 33:20
34:12 [g]Job 8:3
34:13 [h]Job 38:4,6
34:14 [i]Ps 104:29
34:15 [j]Ge 3:19; Job 9:22
34:17 [k]2Sa 23:3-4 [l]Job 40:8
34:18 [m]Ex 22:28
34:19 [n]Dt 10:17; Ac 10:34 [o]Lev 19:15 [p]Job 10:3
34:20 [q]Ex 12:29 [r]Job 12:19
34:21 [s]Job 31:4; Pr 15:3
34:22 [t]Ps 139:12 [u]Am 9:2-3

[a] 14 Or *Spirit*

The Author of Evil

JOB 34:10-15

Young Elihu makes a magnificent point here, one that both Abraham and Moses made (Ge 18:25; Dt 32:4). God is not the author of evil, although he allows the evil one to prowl the earth (1Pe 5:8). While Job, in his anguish and frustration, has accused God of acting unjustly (Job 24:12), Elihu wisely reminds him that God's scales balance perfectly and his mercy and goodwill sustain all.

When we see sin and suffering all around us, it's easy to blame God. After all, he is sovereign; is he not, then, responsible for evil? This mystery will never be solved to our satisfaction this side of heaven, but peace will come to our souls when we recall the words of Jesus: "In this world you will have trouble. But take heart! I have overcome the world" (Jn 16:33).

that they should come before him for
judgment.[v]
24 Without inquiry he shatters the mighty[w]
and sets up others in their place.[x]
25 Because he takes note of their deeds,
he overthrows them in the night and
they are crushed.
26 He punishes them for their wickedness
where everyone can see them,
27 because they turned from following him[y]
and had no regard for any of his ways.[z]
28 They caused the cry of the poor to come
before him,
so that he heard the cry of the needy.[a]
29 But if he remains silent, who can
condemn him?
If he hides his face, who can see him?
Yet he is over man and nation alike,
30 to keep a godless man from ruling,
from laying snares for the people.[b]

31 "Suppose a man says to God,
'I am guilty but will offend no more.
32 Teach me what I cannot see;[c]
if I have done wrong, I will not do so
again.'[d]
33 Should God then reward you on your
terms,
when you refuse to repent?[e]
You must decide, not I;
so tell me what you know.

34 "Men of understanding declare,
wise men who hear me say to me,
35 'Job speaks without knowledge;[f]
his words lack insight.'
36 Oh, that Job might be tested to the
utmost
for answering like a wicked man![g]
37 To his sin he adds rebellion;
scornfully he claps his hands[h] among
us
and multiplies his words against God."[i]

35 Then Elihu said:

2 "Do you think this is just?
You say, 'I will be cleared by God.[a]'
3 Yet you ask him, 'What profit is it to me,[b]
and what do I gain by not sinning?'[j]

4 "I would like to reply to you
and to your friends with you.
5 Look up at the heavens[k] and see;
gaze at the clouds so high above you.[l]
6 If you sin, how does that affect him?
If your sins are many, what does that
do to him?[m]
7 If you are righteous, what do you give to
him,[n]

34:23 [v]Job 11:11
34:24 [w]Job 12:19 [x]Da 2:21
34:27 [y]Ps 28:5; Isa 5:12 [z]1Sa 15:11
34:28 [a]Ex 22:23; Job 35:9; Jas 5:4
34:30 [b]Pr 29:2-12
34:32 [c]Job 35:11; Ps 25:4 [d]Job 33:27
34:33 [e]Job 41:11
34:35 [f]Job 35:16; 38:2
34:36 [g]Job 22:15
34:37 [h]Job 27:23 [i]Job 23:2
35:3 [j]Job 9:29-31; 34:9
35:5 [k]Ge 15:5 [l]Job 22:12
35:6 [m]Pr 8:36
35:7 [n]Ro 11:35

Our impatience to have God move now, to act in ways that make sense to us, will drive us to take control of our lives. God is moving in ways that we cannot see or understand. This means we are left with the question, "Do I trust him?" We can choose to bow the knee now and ask him to forgive us for trying to squeeze the answer we want out of heaven, or we will bow the knee later in remorse at our foolishness in thinking that we knew better than God.

We are all thirsty in different ways, deep down in our souls. It is a thirst as ancient as the hills. But it is a thirst that can be satisfied only in Christ.

—Sheila Walsh

[a] 2 Or *My righteousness is more than God's* [b] 3 Or *you*

or what does he receive[o] from your
hand?[p]
8 Your wickedness affects only a man like
yourself,
and your righteousness only the sons
of men.

9 "Men cry out[q] under a load of
oppression;
they plead for relief from the arm of
the powerful.[r]
10 But no one says, 'Where is God my
Maker,[s]
who gives songs in the night,[t]
11 who teaches[u] more to us than to[a] the
beasts of the earth
and makes us wiser than[b] the birds of
the air?'
12 He does not answer[v] when men cry out
because of the arrogance of the
wicked.
13 Indeed, God does not listen to their
empty plea;
the Almighty pays no attention to it.[w]
14 How much less, then, will he listen
when you say that you do not see
him,[x]
that your case[y] is before him
and you must wait for him,
15 and further, that his anger never
punishes
and he does not take the least notice
of wickedness.[c]
16 So Job opens his mouth with empty talk;
without knowledge he multiplies
words."[z]

36

Elihu continued:

2 "Bear with me a little longer and I will
show you
that there is more to be said in God's
behalf.
3 I get my knowledge from afar;
I will ascribe justice to my Maker.[a]
4 Be assured that my words are not false;[b]
one perfect in knowledge[c] is with you.

5 "God is mighty, but does not despise
men;[d]
he is mighty, and firm in his purpose.[e]
6 He does not keep the wicked alive[f]
but gives the afflicted their rights.[g]
7 He does not take his eyes off the
righteous;[h]
he enthrones them with kings[i]
and exalts them forever.
8 But if men are bound in chains,[j]
held fast by cords of affliction,

35:7 [o]Pr 9:12 [p]Job 22:2-3; Lk 17:10
35:9 [q]Ex 2:23 [r]Job 12:19
35:10 [s]Job 27:10; Isa 51:13 [t]Ps 42:8; 149:5; Ac 16:25
35:11 [u]Ps 94:12
35:12 [v]Pr 1:28
35:13 [w]Job 27:9; Pr 15:29; Isa 1:15; Jer 11:11
35:14 [x]Job 9:11 [y]Ps 37:6
35:16 [z]Job 34:35, 37
36:3 [a]Job 8:3; 37:23
36:4 [b]Job 33:3 [c]Job 37:5,16, 23
36:5 [d]Ps 22:24 [e]Job 12:13
36:6 [f]Job 8:22 [g]Job 5:15
36:7 [h]Ps 33:18 [i]Ps 113:8
36:8 [j]Ps 107:10,14

[a] 11 Or *teaches us by* [b] 11 Or *us wise by* [c] 15 Symmachus, Theodotion and Vulgate; the meaning of the Hebrew for this word is uncertain.

When you look at the response of Job's friends, it's amazing to see how little has actually changed over the years. They had no idea what Job was experiencing. The only thing they brought to their suffering friend was words, which they tossed his way to see if any would stick. Their impatience with him is obvious; he was disturbing the quiet of their waters, and they wanted life to be back to normal as soon as possible.

. . . When someone is in pain and at the beginning of the longest night of their lives, an endless barrage of words . . . is like thunder in the desert: a loud and comfortless noise.

. . . For Job, God pulled back the curtain for a moment and gave him a glimpse of who God is. All Job could say was, "My ears had heard you but now my eyes have seen you" (Job 42:5). This simple statement is one of the most profound in the entire canon of Scripture. It lays out the vast difference between head knowledge and heart knowledge . . . [God's words are] life to me, my bread and water and air.

—Sheila Walsh

By night when others soundly slept
And hath at once both ease and Rest,
My waking eyes were open kept
And so to lie I found it best.

I sought him whom my Soul did Love,
With tears I sought him earnestly.
He bow'd his ear down from Above.
In vain I did not seek or cry.

My hungry Soul he fill'd with Good;
He in his Bottle put my tears,
My smarting wounds washt in his blood,
And banisht thence my Doubts and fears.

What to my Saviour shall I give
Who freely hath done this for me?
I'll serve him here whilst I shall live
And Love him to Eternity. 

—*Anne Bradstreet (1612-1672)*

[9] he tells them what they have done—
that they have sinned arrogantly.[k] — **36:9** [k]Job 15:25
[10] He makes them listen[l] to correction — **36:10** [l]Job 33:16
and commands them to repent of their evil.[m] — [m]2Ki 17:13
[11] If they obey and serve him,[n] — **36:11** [n]Isa 1:19
they will spend the rest of their days in prosperity
and their years in contentment.
[12] But if they do not listen,
they will perish by the sword[a][o] — **36:12** [o]Job 15:22
and die without knowledge.[p] — [p]Job 4:21

[13] "The godless in heart[q] harbor resentment; — **36:13** [q]Ro 2:5
even when he fetters them, they do not cry for help.
[14] They die in their youth,
among male prostitutes of the shrines.[r] — **36:14** [r]Dt 23:17
[15] But those who suffer he delivers in their suffering;
he speaks to them in their affliction.
[16] "He is wooing[s] you from the jaws of distress — **36:16** [s]Hos 2:14 [t]Ps 23:5
to a spacious place free from restriction,
to the comfort of your table[t] laden with choice food.
[17] But now you are laden with the judgment due the wicked;
judgment and justice have taken hold of you.[u] — **36:17** [u]Job 22:11
[18] Be careful that no one entices you by riches;
do not let a large bribe turn you aside.[v] — **36:18** [v]Job 34:33
[19] Would your wealth
or even all your mighty efforts
sustain you so you would not be in distress?
[20] Do not long for the night,[w] — **36:20** [w]Job 34:20, 25
to drag people away from their homes.[b]
[21] Beware of turning to evil,[x] — **36:21** [x]Ps 66:18
which you seem to prefer to affliction.[y] — [y]Heb 11:25

[22] "God is exalted in his power. — **36:22** [z]Isa 40:13; 1Co 2:16
Who is a teacher like him?[z]
[23] Who has prescribed his ways for him,[a] — **36:23** [a]Job 34:13
or said to him, 'You have done wrong'?[b] — [b]Job 8:3
[24] Remember to extol his work,[c] — **36:24** [c]Ps 92:5; 138:5
which men have praised in song.[d] — [d]Ps 59:16; Rev 15:3
[25] All mankind has seen it;
men gaze on it from afar.
[26] How great is God—beyond our understanding![e] — **36:26** [e]1Co 13: 12

[a] 12 Or *will cross the River* [b] 20 The meaning of the Hebrew for verses 18–20 is uncertain.

36:26 [f]Job 10:5; Ps 90:2; 102:24; Heb 1:12
36:27 [g]Job 38:28; Ps 147:8
36:28 [h]Job 5:10
36:29 [i]Job 26:14; 37:16
36:31 [j]Job 37:13 [k]Ps 136:25; Ac 14:17
36:32 [l]Job 37:12, 15
37:2 [m]Ps 29:3-9
37:5 [n]Job 5:9
37:6 [o]Job 38:22 [p]Job 36:27
37:7 [q]Job 12:14
37:8 [r]Job 38:40; Ps 104:22
37:10 [s]Job 38:29-30; Ps 147:17
37:11 [t]Job 36:27, 29
37:12 [u]Ps 148:8
37:13 [v]1Sa 12:17 [w]Ex 9:18; 1Ki 18:45; Job 38:27

The number of his years is past
finding out.[f]
27 "He draws up the drops of water,
which distill as rain to the streams[a];[g]
28 the clouds pour down their moisture
and abundant showers fall on
mankind.[h]
29 Who can understand how he spreads
out the clouds,
how he thunders from his pavilion?[i]
30 See how he scatters his lightning about
him,
bathing the depths of the sea.
31 This is the way he governs[b] the nations[j]
and provides food in abundance.[k]
32 He fills his hands with lightning
and commands it to strike its mark.[l]
33 His thunder announces the coming storm;
even the cattle make known its
approach.[c]

37 "At this my heart pounds
and leaps from its place.
2 Listen! Listen to the roar of his voice,
to the rumbling that comes from his
mouth.[m]
3 He unleashes his lightning beneath the
whole heaven
and sends it to the ends of the earth.
4 After that comes the sound of his roar;
he thunders with his majestic voice.
When his voice resounds,
he holds nothing back.
5 God's voice thunders in marvelous ways;
he does great things beyond our
understanding.[n]
6 He says to the snow,[o] 'Fall on the earth,'
and to the rain shower, 'Be a mighty
downpour.'[p]
7 So that all men he has made may know
his work,
he stops every man from his labor.[d][q]
8 The animals take cover;
they remain in their dens.[r]
9 The tempest comes out from its chamber,
the cold from the driving winds.
10 The breath of God produces ice,
and the broad waters become frozen.[s]
11 He loads the clouds with moisture;
he scatters his lightning through them.[t]
12 At his direction they swirl around
over the face of the whole earth
to do whatever he commands them.[u]
13 He brings the clouds to punish men,[v]
or to water his earth[e] and show his
love.[w]

[a] 27 Or *distill from the mist as rain* [b] 31 Or *nourishes*
[c] 33 Or *announces his coming— / the One zealous against evil*
[d] 7 Or / *he fills all men with fear by his power* [e] 13 Or *to favor them*

Elihu's Picture of God

JOB 36:26—37:5

Elihu paints a majestic and true picture of God, highlighting the fact that the Almighty is far too great and mysterious for mere humanity to fully comprehend. This timely reminder is in stark contrast to previous statements by Job and his friends, which imply that God's ways should always make sense. The mystery, incomprehensibility and awesome majesty of God are truths that are woven throughout Scripture. Paul says that we will never fully understand God or his ways until we see him face to face (1Co 13:12).

So why pursue knowing the unknowable? Because, like Job, we're irresistibly drawn to him. And because through the God-man Jesus Christ, in whom all the fullness of God lives (Col 2:9), we can have a meaningful relationship with the Father who loves us. Cultivating our relationship with the Father while we're on earth prepares us to enjoy him forever (Ps 16:11).

Out of a Storm

JOB 38:1

Job's last plea is for the Almighty to respond to him (Job 31:35). Here he gets his wish, though not exactly as he'd envisioned it! When the Lord finally speaks, it is out of a raging storm, not an unusual accompaniment to God's appearances in the Old Testament (Ps 18:9–13; Eze 1:4). Apparently the fury, power and grandeur of a violent storm are seen as a fitting metaphor for an awesome God. Job's view of God has often been too small. He merely wants to argue his case before a righteous judge. But God is far more grand and multifaceted than Job imagines, as his forthcoming discourse will reveal.

14 "Listen to this, Job;
stop and consider God's wonders.
15 Do you know how God controls the clouds
and makes his lightning flash?
16 Do you know how the clouds hang poised,
those wonders of him who is perfect in knowledge?[x]
17 You who swelter in your clothes
when the land lies hushed under the south wind,
18 can you join him in spreading out the skies,[y]
hard as a mirror of cast bronze?

19 "Tell us what we should say to him;
we cannot draw up our case because of our darkness.
20 Should he be told that I want to speak?
Would any man ask to be swallowed up?
21 Now no one can look at the sun,
bright as it is in the skies
after the wind has swept them clean.
22 Out of the north he comes in golden splendor;
God comes in awesome majesty.
23 The Almighty is beyond our reach and exalted in power;[z]
in his justice[a] and great righteousness, he does not oppress.[b]
24 Therefore, men revere him,[c]
for does he not have regard for all the wise[d] in heart?[a]"

The LORD *Speaks*

38 Then the LORD answered Job out of the storm.[e] He said:

2 "Who is this that darkens my counsel
with words without knowledge?[f]
3 Brace yourself like a man;
I will question you,
and you shall answer me.[g]

4 "Where were you when I laid the earth's foundation?[h]
Tell me, if you understand.
5 Who marked off its dimensions?[i] Surely you know!
Who stretched a measuring line across it?
6 On what were its footings set,
or who laid its cornerstone[j]—
7 while the morning stars sang together
and all the angels[b] shouted for joy?

8 "Who shut up the sea behind doors[k]

37:16 [x]Job 36:4
37:18 [y]Job 9:8; Ps 104:2; Isa 44:24
37:23 [z]Job 9:4; 36:4; 1Ti 6:16 [a]Job 8:3 [b]Isa 63:9; Eze 18:23,32
37:24 [c]Mt 10:28 [d]Mt 11:25
38:1 [e]Job 40:6
38:2 [f]Job 35:16; 42:3; 1Ti 1:7
38:3 [g]Job 40:7
38:4 [h]Ps 104:5; Pr 8:29
38:5 [i]Pr 8:29; Isa 40:12
38:6 [j]Job 26:7
38:8 [k]Jer 5:22

[a] 24 Or *for he does not have regard for any who think they are wise.* [b] 7 Hebrew *the sons of God*

when it burst forth from the womb,[l]
[9] when I made the clouds its garment
and wrapped it in thick darkness,
[10] when I fixed limits for it[m]
and set its doors and bars in place,[n]
[11] when I said, 'This far you may come
and no farther;
here is where your proud waves halt'?[o]

[12] "Have you ever given orders to the
morning,
or shown the dawn its place,
[13] that it might take the earth by the edges
and shake the wicked[p] out of it?
[14] The earth takes shape like clay under a
seal;
its features stand out like those of a
garment.
[15] The wicked are denied their light,[q]
and their upraised arm is broken.[r]

[16] "Have you journeyed to the springs of
the sea
or walked in the recesses of the deep?[s]
[17] Have the gates of death[t] been shown to
you?
Have you seen the gates of the
shadow of death[a]?
[18] Have you comprehended the vast
expanses of the earth?[u]
Tell me, if you know all this.

[19] "What is the way to the abode of light?
And where does darkness reside?
[20] Can you take them to their places?
Do you know the paths[v] to their
dwellings?
[21] Surely you know, for you were already
born![w]
You have lived so many years!

[22] "Have you entered the storehouses of
the snow[x]
or seen the storehouses of the hail,
[23] which I reserve for times of trouble,[y]
for days of war and battle?[z]
[24] What is the way to the place where the
lightning is dispersed,
or the place where the east winds are
scattered over the earth?
[25] Who cuts a channel for the torrents of
rain,
and a path for the thunderstorm,[a]
[26] to water[b] a land where no man lives,
a desert with no one in it,
[27] to satisfy a desolate wasteland
and make it sprout with grass?[c]
[28] Does the rain have a father?[d]
Who fathers the drops of dew?
[29] From whose womb comes the ice?

38:8 [l] Ge 1:9-10
38:10 [m] Ps 33:7; 104:9 [n] Job 26:10
38:11 [o] Ps 89:9
38:13 [p] Ps 104:35
38:15 [q] Job 18:5 [r] Ps 10:15
38:16 [s] Ps 77:19
38:17 [t] Ps 9:13
38:18 [u] Job 28:24
38:20 [v] Job 26:10
38:21 [w] Job 15:7
38:22 [x] Job 37:6
38:23 [y] Isa 30:30; Eze 13:11 [z] Ex 9:18; Jos 10:11; Rev 16:21
38:25 [a] Job 28:26
38:26 [b] Job 36:27
38:27 [c] Ps 104:14; 107:35
38:28 [d] Ps 147:8; Jer 14:22

[a] 17 Or *gates of deep shadows*

Rhetorical Questions

JOB 38

The Lord immediately reveals his supreme wisdom by plying Job with rhetorical questions he can't possibly answer. Unlike Job's friends, who simply argue against Job point by point, God doesn't engage him in debate. God makes it clear that he does not consider Job his equal. God offers no answers, only more questions. One by one God catalogs his grand accomplishments, taking Job ever deeper into the mystery and majesty of his incomprehensible ways. When we are tempted, like Job, to challenge God to a verbal sparring match, we'd do well to remember that God will always win! His ways are so far above our own that our only sensible response is to fall down and worship.

God's Tender Care

JOB 39:1–4

Early in Job's trials he asks the agonizing question, "Why did I not perish at birth?" (Job 3:11). Now early in God's response he describes for Job how tenderly he oversees the process of birth and growth in *even lowly creatures like goats and deer.* How much more attentive he surely is to the same processes in his beloved children. When Job's life takes a terrible turn for the worse, he despises what he has become and begins to think that he's a mistake. But, as the saying goes, God doesn't make junk. He knits us together with great skill and care in our mother's womb (Ps 139:13–16). He establishes us as his own and ensures that we will flourish (Ps 92:12–13). God's tenderness and protection during physical birth assures us that our spiritual birth is *even more precious* to him (Tit 3:4–7).

Who gives birth to the frost from the
heavens[e]
30 when the waters become hard as stone,
when the surface of the deep is
frozen?[f]

31 "Can you bind the beautiful[a] Pleiades?
Can you loose the cords of Orion?[g]
32 Can you bring forth the constellations in
their seasons[b]
or lead out the Bear[c] with its cubs?
33 Do you know the laws[h] of the heavens?
Can you set up ⌞God's[d]⌟ dominion over
the earth?

34 "Can you raise your voice to the clouds
and cover yourself with a flood of
water?[i]
35 Do you send the lightning bolts on their
way?[j]
Do they report to you, 'Here we are'?
36 Who endowed the heart[e] with wisdom[k]
or gave understanding[l] to the mind[e]?
37 Who has the wisdom to count the
clouds?
Who can tip over the water jars of the
heavens
38 when the dust becomes hard
and the clods of earth stick together?

39 "Do you hunt the prey for the lioness
and satisfy the hunger of the lions[m]
40 when they crouch in their dens[n]
or lie in wait in a thicket?
41 Who provides food for the raven[o]
when its young cry out to God
and wander about for lack of food?[p]

39 "Do you know when the mountain
goats[q] give birth?
Do you watch when the doe bears her
fawn?
2 Do you count the months till they bear?
Do you know the time they give birth?
3 They crouch down and bring forth their
young;
their labor pains are ended.
4 Their young thrive and grow strong in
the wilds;
they leave and do not return.

5 "Who let the wild donkey[r] go free?
Who untied his ropes?
6 I gave him the wasteland[s] as his home,
the salt flats as his habitat.[t]
7 He laughs at the commotion in the
town;
he does not hear a driver's shout.[u]
8 He ranges the hills for his pasture

38:29 [e]Ps 147:16-17
38:30 [f]Job 37:10
38:31 [g]Job 9:9; Am 5:8
38:33 [h]Ps 148:6; Jer 31:36
38:34 [i]Job 22:11; 36:27-28
38:35 [j]Job 36:32; 37:3
38:36 [k]Job 9:4 [l]Job 32:8; Ps 51:6; Ecc 2:26
38:39 [m]Ps 104:21
38:40 [n]Job 37:8
38:41 [o]Lk 12:24 [p]Ps 147:9; Mt 6:26
39:1 [q]Dt 14:5
39:5 [r]Job 6:5; 11:12; 24:5
39:6 [s]Job 24:5; Ps 107:34; Jer 2:24 [t]Hos 8:9
39:7 [u]Job 3:18

[a] *31* Or *the twinkling;* or *the chains of the* [b] *32* Or *the morning star in its season* [c] *32* Or *out Leo* [d] *33* Or *his;* or *their* [e] *36* The meaning of the Hebrew for this word is uncertain.

and searches for any green thing.

9 "Will the wild ox[v] consent to serve you?
Will he stay by your manger at night?
10 Can you hold him to the furrow with a harness?
Will he till the valleys behind you?
11 Will you rely on him for his great strength?
Will you leave your heavy work to him?
12 Can you trust him to bring in your grain
and gather it to your threshing floor?

13 "The wings of the ostrich flap joyfully,
but they cannot compare with the pinions and feathers of the stork.
14 She lays her eggs on the ground
and lets them warm in the sand,
15 unmindful that a foot may crush them,
that some wild animal may trample them.
16 She treats her young harshly,[w] as if they were not hers;
she cares not that her labor was in vain,
17 for God did not endow her with wisdom
or give her a share of good sense.[x]
18 Yet when she spreads her feathers to run,
she laughs at horse and rider.

19 "Do you give the horse his strength
or clothe his neck with a flowing mane?
20 Do you make him leap like a locust,[y]
striking terror with his proud snorting?[z]
21 He paws fiercely, rejoicing in his strength,
and charges into the fray.[a]
22 He laughs at fear, afraid of nothing;
he does not shy away from the sword.
23 The quiver rattles against his side,
along with the flashing spear and lance.
24 In frenzied excitement he eats up the ground;
he cannot stand still when the trumpet sounds.[b]
25 At the blast of the trumpet[c] he snorts, 'Aha!'
He catches the scent of battle from afar,
the shout of commanders and the battle cry.[d]

26 "Does the hawk take flight by your wisdom
and spread his wings toward the south?
27 Does the eagle soar at your command
and build his nest on high?[e]

39:9 [v]Nu 23:22; Dt 33:17
39:16 [w]La 4:3
39:17 [x]Job 35:11
39:20 [y]Joel 2:4-5 [z]Jer 8:16
39:21 [a]Jer 8:6
39:24 [b]Jer 4:5,19; Eze 7:14; Am 3:6
39:25 [c]Jos 6:5 [d]Am 1:14; 2:2
39:27 [e]Jer 49:16; Ob 1:4

Amazing Animals

JOB 39:5-30

The Lord continues to humble Job by recounting the variety and peculiarities of the animals he has created. Job is reminded that even the seemingly foolish ostrich is a wondrous creation (Job 39:13–18). Who but God could conceive of endowing a small-brained bird with the speed of a stallion? Throughout Scripture God's animal menagerie is used to highlight his unfathomable creativity, supreme authority and tender care (Ps 50:9–12; 104:24; Pr 6:6–8). Jesus himself reminds us that even the most fragile birds are personally cared for by the Almighty; how much more faithfully will he tend to our needs (Mt 6:26)! When we are afraid, frustrated or ready to accuse God of not knowing what's best for us, we need only consider the work of his hands in nature. Surely a God who owns, rules and cares for all living things can be trusted to care for us (Ps 36:6).

God Questions Job

JOB 40:7

Earlier Job fantasized about presenting his case to the Almighty and calling God to account (Job 23:4–5). Job imagines that in a "fair" universe, God would answer Job's charges point by point. What a turn of events Job is in for! Instead of answering Job's questions, God does the very opposite: "I will question you, and you shall answer me" (Job 40:7, emphasis added). Of course, Job cannot answer the Lord's questions. Job is only a man; God is almighty! But God's gracious nature is beautifully displayed here, too, as he stoops to address a mere man. Job has complained that God excludes himself from the "duty" of confronting his accuser in court (Job 9:32), yet God willingly speaks to Job one-on-one when he could have remained righteously silent—or even destroyed Job and his friends with one sweep of his hand. Despite his rebuke of Job's presumptuous arrogance, God clearly honors Job's dignity as a human being by acknowledging, rather than dismissing, him.

28 He dwells on a cliff and stays there at night;
a rocky crag is his stronghold.
29 From there he seeks out his food;[f]
his eyes detect it from afar.
30 His young ones feast on blood,
and where the slain are, there is he."[g]

40

The LORD said to Job:[h]

2 "Will the one who contends with the Almighty correct him?
Let him who accuses God answer him!"

3 Then Job answered the LORD:

4 "I am unworthy[i]—how can I reply to you?
I put my hand over my mouth.[j]
5 I spoke once, but I have no answer[k]—
twice, but I will say no more."[l]

6 Then the LORD spoke to Job out of the storm:[m]

7 "Brace yourself like a man;
I will question you,
and you shall answer me.[n]
8 "Would you discredit my justice?[o]
Would you condemn me to justify yourself?
9 Do you have an arm like God's,[p]
and can your voice thunder like his?[q]
10 Then adorn yourself with glory and splendor,
and clothe yourself in honor and majesty.[r]
11 Unleash the fury of your wrath,[s]
look at every proud man and bring him low,[t]
12 look at every proud man and humble him,[u]
crush[v] the wicked where they stand.
13 Bury them all in the dust together;
shroud their faces in the grave.
14 Then I myself will admit to you
that your own right hand can save you.[w]
15 "Look at the behemoth,[a]
which I made along with you
and which feeds on grass like an ox.
16 What strength he has in his loins,
what power in the muscles of his belly!
17 His tail[b] sways like a cedar;
the sinews of his thighs are close-knit.
18 His bones are tubes of bronze,
his limbs like rods of iron.
19 He ranks first among the works of God,[x]

39:29 [f]Job 9:26
39:30 [g]Mt 24:28; Lk 17:37
40:1 [h]Job 10:2; 13:3; 23:4; 31:35; 33:13
40:4 [i]Job 42:6 [j]Job 29:9
40:5 [k]Job 9:3 [l]Job 9:15
40:6 [m]Job 38:1
40:7 [n]Job 38:3; 42:4
40:8 [o]Job 27:2; Ro 3:3
40:9 [p]2Ch 32:8 [q]Job 37:5; Ps 29:3-4
40:10 [r]Ps 93:1; 104:1
40:11 [s]Isa 42:25; Na 1:6 [t]Isa 2:11,12,17; Da 4:37
40:12 [u]1Sa 2:7 [v]Isa 13:11; 63:2-3,6
40:14 [w]Ps 20:6; 60:5; 108:6
40:19 [x]Job 41:33

[a] *15* Possibly the hippopotamus or the elephant
[b] *17* Possibly trunk

yet his Maker can approach him with
his sword.

40:20 [y]Ps 104:14 [z]Ps 104:26

20 The hills bring him their produce,[y]
and all the wild animals play[z] nearby.
21 Under the lotus plants he lies,
hidden among the reeds in the marsh.
22 The lotuses conceal him in their
shadow;

40:22 [a]Isa 44:4

the poplars by the stream[a] surround
him.
23 When the river rages, he is not alarmed;
he is secure, though the Jordan
should surge against his mouth.
24 Can anyone capture him by the eyes,[a]
or trap him and pierce his nose?[b]

40:24 [b]Job 41:2,7, 26

41 "Can you pull in the leviathan[bc] with a
fishhook
or tie down his tongue with a rope?

41:1 [c]Job 3:8; Ps 104:26; Isa 27:1

2 Can you put a cord through his nose
or pierce his jaw with a hook?[d]

41:2 [d]Isa 37:29

3 Will he keep begging you for mercy?
Will he speak to you with gentle
words?
4 Will he make an agreement with you
for you to take him as your slave for
life?[e]

41:4 [e]Ex 21:6

5 Can you make a pet of him like a bird
or put him on a leash for your girls?
6 Will traders barter for him?
Will they divide him up among the
merchants?
7 Can you fill his hide with harpoons
or his head with fishing spears?
8 If you lay a hand on him,
you will remember the struggle and
never do it again!
9 Any hope of subduing him is false;
the mere sight of him is
overpowering.
10 No one is fierce enough to rouse him.[f]
Who then is able to stand against
me?[g]

41:10 [f]Job 3:8 [g]Jer 50:44

11 Who has a claim against me that I must
pay?[h]
Everything under heaven belongs to
me.[i]

41:11 [h]Ro 11:35 [i]Ex 19:5; Dt 10:14; Ps 24:1; 50:12; 1Co 10:26

12 "I will not fail to speak of his limbs,
his strength and his graceful form.
13 Who can strip off his outer coat?
Who would approach him with a
bridle?
14 Who dares open the doors of his mouth,
ringed about with his fearsome teeth?
15 His back has[c] rows of shields
tightly sealed together;
16 each is so close to the next
that no air can pass between.

[a] 24 Or *by a water hole* [b] 1 Possibly the crocodile
[c] 15 Or *His pride is his*

Leviathan

JOB 41:1

The book of Job seems to use the word *leviathan* in two distinct ways. The legendary see monster Leviathan is referred to in Job 3:8, where Job expresses his desire that soothsayers could call up Leviathan to swallow the day of his birth. Ancient Canaanite myth depicted Leviathan as a chaos-stirring, many-headed sea dragon that was defeated at creation (Ps 74:14). In Isaiah 27:1, Leviathan is presented as the embodiment of evil—to be destroyed by the Lord.

Here in Job 41, as in Psalm 104:26, *leviathan* is used in a literal sense: as a large marine animal. As shown in the NIV footnote for Job 41:1, the leviathan in this passage is possibly the crocodile. Whether *Leviathan* or *leviathan*, no human being has power over this frightful creature. But the fact that the Lord has tamed him demonstrates yet again God's majesty and power.

Job Responds to God

JOB 42:1–6

Job has been brought to his knees, not by the exposure of some hidden past sin as his friends predicted, but by the wonder and majesty of his Creator and by his own smallness in the face of the infinite God. Now he knows to the core of his being, in a way he knew only in his head before, that God is eternally sovereign, powerful, just and gracious. God does not need to justify himself to anyone, for his ways are beyond human comprehension. In Romans 11, Paul's words could be considered a perfect summary of what Job has learned (Ro 11:33–36). As we follow Paul's thought into Romans 12:1–2, we quickly recognize that our only possible response to such a glorious God is to present ourselves to him as living sacrifices.

17 They are joined fast to one another;
they cling together and cannot be
parted.
18 His snorting throws out flashes of light;
his eyes are like the rays of dawn.[j]
19 Firebrands stream from his mouth;
sparks of fire shoot out.
20 Smoke pours from his nostrils
as from a boiling pot over a fire of
reeds.
21 His breath[k] sets coals ablaze,
and flames dart from his mouth.[l]
22 Strength resides in his neck;
dismay goes before him.
23 The folds of his flesh are tightly joined;
they are firm and immovable.
24 His chest is hard as rock,
hard as a lower millstone.
25 When he rises up, the mighty are
terrified;
they retreat before his thrashing.
26 The sword that reaches him has no
effect,
nor does the spear or the dart or the
javelin.
27 Iron he treats like straw
and bronze like rotten wood.
28 Arrows do not make him flee;
slingstones are like chaff to him.
29 A club seems to him but a piece of
straw;
he laughs at the rattling of the lance.
30 His undersides are jagged potsherds,
leaving a trail in the mud like a
threshing sledge.[m]
31 He makes the depths churn like a
boiling caldron
and stirs up the sea like a pot of
ointment.
32 Behind him he leaves a glistening wake;
one would think the deep had white
hair.
33 Nothing on earth is his equal[n]—
a creature without fear.
34 He looks down on all that are haughty;
he is king over all that are proud.[o]"

Job

42

Then Job replied to the LORD:

2 "I know that you can do all things;[p]
no plan of yours can be thwarted.[q]
3 ⌞You asked,⌟ 'Who is this that obscures
my counsel without knowledge?'[r]
Surely I spoke of things I did not
understand,
things too wonderful for me to know.[s]

4 ⌞"You said,⌟ 'Listen now, and I will
speak;
I will question you,

41:18 [j]Job 3:9
41:21 [k]Isa 40:7 [l]Ps 18:8
41:30 [m]Isa 41:15
41:33 [n]Job 40:19
41:34 [o]Job 28:8
42:2 [p]Ge 18:14; Mt 19:26 [q]2Ch 20:6
42:3 [r]Job 38:2 [s]Ps 40:5; 131:1; 139:6

and you shall answer me.'[t]
[5]My ears had heard of you[u]
but now my eyes have seen you.[v]
[6]Therefore I despise myself[w]
and repent in dust and ashes."[x]

Epilogue

[7]After the LORD had said these things to Job, he
said to Eliphaz the Temanite, "I am angry with
you and your two friends,[y] because you have not
spoken of me what is right, as my servant Job has.
[8]So now take seven bulls and seven rams[z] and go
to my servant Job and sacrifice a burnt offering[a]
for yourselves. My servant Job will pray for you,
and I will accept his prayer[b] and not deal with you
according to your folly.[c] You have not spoken of
me what is right, as my servant Job has." [9]So Eliphaz the Temanite, Bildad the Shuhite and Zophar
the Naamathite did what the LORD told them; and
the LORD accepted Job's prayer.
[10]After Job had prayed for his friends, the LORD
made him prosperous again[d] and gave him twice
as much as he had before.[e] [11]All his brothers and
sisters and everyone who had known him before[f]
came and ate with him in his house. They comforted and consoled him over all the trouble the
LORD had brought upon him, and each one gave
him a piece of silver[a] and a gold ring.
[12]The LORD blessed the latter part of Job's life
more than the first. He had fourteen thousand
sheep, six thousand camels, a thousand yoke of
oxen and a thousand donkeys. [13]And he also had
seven sons and three daughters. [14]The first daughter he named Jemimah, the second Keziah and the
third Keren-Happuch. [15]Nowhere in all the land
were there found women as beautiful as Job's
daughters, and their father granted them an inheritance along with their brothers.
[16]After this, Job lived a hundred and forty years;
he saw his children and their children to the
fourth generation. [17]And so he died, old and full
of years.[g]

42:4 [t]Job 38:3; 40:7
42:5 [u]Job 26:14; Ro 10:17 [v]Jdg 13:22; Isa 6:5; Eph 1:17-18
42:6 [w]Job 40:4 [x]Ezr 9:6
42:7 [y]Job 32:3
42:8 [z]Nu 23:1,29 [a]Job 1:5 [b]Ge 20:17; Jas 5:15-16; 1Jn 5:16 [c]Job 22:30
42:10 [d]Dt 30:3; Ps 14:7 [e]Job 1:3; Ps 85:1-3; 126:5-6
42:11 [f]Job 19:13
42:17 [g]Ge 15:15; 25:8

[a] *11* Hebrew *him a kesitah*; a kesitah was a unit of money of unknown weight and value.

A Gracious God

JOB 42:7-8

Job hasn't handled himself perfectly throughout his ordeal, so why does God commend him in the end? Perhaps to demonstrate that even when his children accuse God of failing them, he graciously listens beneath their frightened, angry words to their honest struggle. God delights in those who honor him with their honesty

God rebukes Job's friends for their lack of insight and for their self-righteousness, and he vindicates Job in the most amazing way possible: by restoring, in double measure, all he had lost. The lesson of the book of Job, learned as much from what his friends say as from Job's own life and words, is that relationship with God, not mere knowledge of God, should be our highest aspiration.

Psalms

Give praise to God.

Psalms is not a book of doctrine but rather a guide or hymnal for worship and prayer. Individuals or groups originally sang these songs to demonstrate God's love, holiness and intimate involvement in every aspect of life. The remarks that introduce the majority of psalms give information about the author and the purpose behind the psalm. David wrote more of these psalms than any other one writer. His entries furnish an intimate look at his relationship with God and the emotions behind many of the major events in his life.

In reading the psalms, we learn the benefit of following God's ways and see the downfall that results from disobedience (Ps 1–4; 119). We understand the nature of sin and forgiveness (Ps 6; 32; 38; 51). We find various reasons and circumstances in which to praise God (Ps 7–14; 32; 100; 150). We discover that God is our deliverer from distress and trouble (Ps 18; 27; 33; 46; 73; 113). We trust God as our protector (Ps 37; 41; 91; 116; 140) and our strength (Ps 21; 24; 28; 31; 59; 89; 147). And we take comfort in realizing that God can mend our broken hearts because he made us and cares for us (Ps 23; 34; 56; 139).

When words fail us, the book of Psalms can help us express our deepest emotions. Whether we face problems or peril, need God's protection or an encouraging promise or simply wish to praise God for who he is, the psalms give voice to the cries of our hearts as we pray and sing these words to the "LORD Most High" (Ps 47:2).

Quick Study

Author

No author is given for a number of the psalms; however, David is listed as the author in a great number of the titles preceding most psalms. Several superscriptions are ascribed to Asaph and to the sons of Korah.

Date Written

Because so many people contributed to the psalms, they were written in many different time periods. The individual pieces were gathered together into the book of Psalms by temple workers after the exile, probably in the third century B.C.

Setting

Again, since a variety of authors participated, a variety of locations is also likely.

Key Passage

Psalm 108:3–4 "I will praise you, O LORD, among the nations;
I will sing of you among the peoples.
For great is your love, higher than the heavens;
your faithfulness reaches to the skies."

Outline

Book I. Ps 1-41
Book II. Ps 42-72
Book III. Ps 73-89
Book IV. Ps 90-106
Book V. Ps 107-150

The Women of Psalms

Honored women, daughters of kings	*Part of a royal entourage.* Ps 45:9
The royal bride	*She dressed in gold.* Ps 45:9-14
Virgin companions	*Appropriate companions for the bride.* Ps 45:14-15
The barren woman	*God blessed her with children.* Ps 113:9
A maid and her mistress	*One was humbly dependent on the other.* Ps 123:2

Like a Tree

PS 1:3

The Psalms are packed with vivid word pictures and simple metaphors that make their messages immediately accessible and applicable. The person who loves and concentrates on God's words and ways is compared to a fruitful tree here—only one of several places in the Old Testament where God's people are compared to sturdy trees (Isa 44:2-4; Jer 17:7-8). In a description of the coming Messiah, Jesus Christ himself is depicted as a "splendid cedar" that will give shelter and shade to all who take refuge in him (Eze 17:22-24). The tree metaphor's richness is evident when we consider the elements of a healthy tree: the deep roots that feed and stabilize it, the branches that gracefully offer shade, the leaves that often possess healing properties, the fruit that nourishes. A blessed person is one who is deeply rooted in the soil of God's Word and who draws sustenance from his living water.

BOOK I

Psalms 1–41

Psalm 1

1 Blessed is the man
who does not walk[a] in the counsel of the wicked
or stand in the way of sinners
or sit[b] in the seat of mockers.
2 But his delight[c] is in the law of the LORD,[d]
and on his law he meditates[e] day and night.
3 He is like a tree[f] planted by streams of water,[g]
which yields its fruit[h] in season
and whose leaf does not wither.
Whatever he does prospers.[i]

4 Not so the wicked!
They are like chaff[j]
that the wind blows away.
5 Therefore the wicked will not stand[k] in the judgment,[l]
nor sinners in the assembly of the righteous.

6 For the LORD watches over[m] the way of the righteous,
but the way of the wicked will perish.[n]

Psalm 2

1 Why do the nations conspire[a]
and the peoples plot[o] in vain?
2 The kings[p] of the earth take their stand
and the rulers gather together
against the LORD
and against his Anointed[q] One.[b][r]
3 "Let us break their chains," they say,
"and throw off their fetters."[s]

4 The One enthroned in heaven laughs;[t]
the Lord scoffs at them.
5 Then he rebukes them in his anger
and terrifies them in his wrath,[u]
saying,
6 "I have installed my King[c]
on Zion, my holy hill."

7 I will proclaim the decree of the LORD:

He said to me, "You are my Son[d];
today I have become your Father.[e][v]
8 Ask of me,
and I will make the nations your inheritance,
the ends of the earth[w] your possession.
9 You will rule them with an iron scepter[f];[x]

1:1 [a]Pr 4:14 [b]Ps 26:4; Jer 15:17
1:2 [c]Ps 119:16, 35 [d]Ps 119:1 [e]Jos 1:8
1:3 [f]Ps 128:3 [g]Jer 17:8 [h]Eze 47:12 [i]Ge 39:3
1:4 [j]Job 21:18; Isa 17:13
1:5 [k]Ps 5:5 [l]Ps 9:7-8,16
1:6 [m]Ps 37:18; 2Ti 2:19 [n]Ps 9:6
2:1 [o]Ps 21:11
2:2 [p]Ps 48:4 [q]Jn 1:41 [r]Ps 74:18,23; Ac 4:25-26*
2:3 [s]Jer 5:5
2:4 [t]Ps 37:13; 59:8; Pr 1:26
2:5 [u]Ps 21:9; 78:49-50
2:7 [v]Ac 13:33*; Heb 1:5*
2:8 [w]Ps 22:27
2:9 [x]Rev 12:5

[a] *1* Hebrew; Septuagint *rage* [b] *2* Or *anointed one* [c] *6* Or *king* [d] *7* Or *son*; also in verse 12 [e] *7* Or *have begotten you* [f] *9* Or *will break them with a rod of iron*

2:9 [y]Ps 89:23 [z]Rev 2:27* you will dash them to pieces[y] like
pottery.[z]"

10 Therefore, you kings, be wise;
be warned, you rulers of the earth.
2:11 [a]Heb 12:28 [b]Ps 119:119-120 11 Serve the LORD with fear
and rejoice[a] with trembling.[b]
12 Kiss the Son,[c] lest he be angry
and you be destroyed in your way,
2:12 [c]Jn 5:23 [d]Rev 6:16 [e]Ps 34:8; Ro 9:33 for his wrath[d] can flare up in a moment.
Blessed are all who take refuge[e] in
him.

Psalm 3

3:1 [f]2Sa 15:14 A psalm of David. When he fled from his son Absalom.[f]

1 O LORD, how many are my foes!
How many rise up against me!
2 Many are saying of me,
3:2 [g]Ps 71:11 "God will not deliver him.[g]" *Selah*[a]

3:3 [h]Ge 15:1; Ps 28:7 [i]Ps 27:6 3 But you are a shield[h] around me,
O LORD;
you bestow glory on me and lift[b] up
my head.[i]
4 To the LORD I cry aloud,
and he answers me from his holy
3:4 [j]Ps 2:6 hill.[j] *Selah*
3:5 [k]Lev 26:6; Pr 3:24 5 I lie down and sleep;[k]
I wake again, because the LORD
sustains me.
3:6 [l]Ps 27:3 6 I will not fear[l] the tens of thousands
drawn up against me on every side.

3:7 [m]Ps 7:6 [n]Ps 6:4 [o]Job 16:10 [p]Ps 58:6 7 Arise,[m] O LORD!
Deliver me,[n] O my God!
Strike[o] all my enemies on the jaw;
break the teeth[p] of the wicked.

3:8 [q]Isa 43:3,11 8 From the LORD comes deliverance.[q]
May your blessing be on your people.
Selah

Psalm 4

For the director of music. With stringed instruments.
A psalm of David.

1 Answer me when I call to you,
O my righteous God.
Give me relief from my distress;
4:1 [r]Ps 25:16 [s]Ps 17:6 be merciful[r] to me and hear my
prayer.[s]

2 How long, O men, will you turn my
4:2 [t]Ps 31:6 glory into shame[c]?
How long will you love delusions and
seek false gods[d]?[t] *Selah*
4:3 [u]Ps 31:23 3 Know that the LORD has set apart the
godly[u] for himself;

a 2 A word of uncertain meaning, occurring frequently in the Psalms; possibly a musical term *b 3* Or *LORD, / my Glorious One, who lifts* *c 2* Or *you dishonor my Glorious One* *d 2* Or *seek lies*

I Lie Down and Sleep

PS 3:5

When we feel besieged by threats and worries, the restful relief of sleep can evade us. David, in flight for his life from his son Absalom, is fully aware of the dangers around him. Yet his spirit is at rest—so full of confidence in God's presence and protection that he can literally drift off to sleep even with his enemies in hot pursuit. In the midst of daily stress or life-altering distress, we can put our trust in the Lord alone, as the psalmist did (see also Ps 4:8). We do not need to be hyper-vigilant and self-reliant; rather, we can entrust our well-being to an ever-vigilant God, turning off our internal "antenna" and allowing the lullaby of his love to carry us into peaceful sleep. Only God has the power to shield our spirits and keep us eternally safe in his watchful care.

Internal Posture

PS 5:7

David shows us by example the proper internal posture for approaching the King of kings. Humility, reverence, submission and worship are natural responses when we're aware of who God is and who we are in relation to him. There is no place for arrogance in our lives when we are stunned by God's great mercy, mercy that welcomes sinners to his throne of grace (Heb 4:16). Whether we worship him in silence, with bowed head and folded hands, or in jubilance, with singing and dancing, our inner posture should be like David's: humbly reverent in the house of mercy.

the LORD will hear[v] when I call to him.

4 In your anger do not sin;[w]
when you are on your beds,[x]
search your hearts and be silent. *Selah*
5 Offer right sacrifices
and trust in the LORD.[y]

6 Many are asking, "Who can show us
any good?"
Let the light of your face shine upon
us,[z] O LORD.
7 You have filled my heart[a] with greater
joy[b]
than when their grain and new wine
abound.
8 I will lie down and sleep[c] in peace,
for you alone, O LORD,
make me dwell in safety.[d]

Psalm 5

For the director of music. For flutes. A psalm of David.

1 Give ear to my words, O LORD,
consider my sighing.
2 Listen to my cry for help,[e]
my King and my God,[f]
for to you I pray.
3 In the morning,[g] O LORD, you hear my
voice;
in the morning I lay my requests
before you
and wait in expectation.
4 You are not a God who takes pleasure in
evil;
with you the wicked[h] cannot dwell.
5 The arrogant[i] cannot stand[j] in your
presence;
you hate[k] all who do wrong.
6 You destroy those who tell lies;[l]
bloodthirsty and deceitful men
the LORD abhors.

7 But I, by your great mercy,
will come into your house;
in reverence will I bow down[m]
toward your holy temple.
8 Lead me, O LORD, in your righteousness[n]
because of my enemies—
make straight your way[o] before me.

9 Not a word from their mouth can be
trusted;
their heart is filled with destruction.
Their throat is an open grave;[p]
with their tongue they speak deceit.[q]
10 Declare them guilty, O God!
Let their intrigues be their downfall.
Banish them for their many sins,[r]
for they have rebelled[s] against you.

11 But let all who take refuge in you be
glad;

4:3 [v]Ps 6:8
4:4 [w]Eph 4:26* [x]Ps 77:6
4:5 [y]Dt 33:19; Ps 37:3
4:6 [z]Nu 6:25
4:7 [a]Ac 14:17 [b]Isa 9:3
4:8 [c]Ps 3:5 [d]Lev 25:18
5:2 [e]Ps 3:4 [f]Ps 84:3
5:3 [g]Ps 88:13
5:4 [h]Ps 11:5; 92:15
5:5 [i]Ps 73:3 [j]Ps 1:5 [k]Ps 11:5
5:6 [l]Ps 55:23; Rev 21:8
5:7 [m]Ps 138:2
5:8 [n]Ps 31:1 [o]Ps 27:11
5:9 [p]Lk 11:44 [q]Ro 3:13*
5:10 [r]Ps 9:16 [s]Ps 107:11

5:11 [t]Ps 2:12 [u]Ps 69:36 [v]Isa 65:13

let them ever sing for joy.[t]
Spread your protection over them,
that those who love your name[u] may rejoice in you.[v]
12 For surely, O LORD, you bless the righteous;

5:12 [w]Ps 32:7

you surround them[w] with your favor as with a shield.

Psalm 6

6:1 [x]Ps 38:1

For the director of music. With stringed instruments. According to *sheminith.*[a] A psalm of David.

1 O LORD, do not rebuke me in your anger[x]
or discipline me in your wrath.

6:2 [y]Hos 6:1 [z]Ps 22:14; 31:10

2 Be merciful to me, LORD, for I am faint;
O LORD, heal me,[y] for my bones are in agony.[z]

6:3 [a]Jn 12:27 [b]Ps 90:13

3 My soul is in anguish.[a]
How long,[b] O LORD, how long?

6:4 [c]Ps 17:13

4 Turn, O LORD, and deliver me;
save me because of your unfailing love.[c]

6:5 [d]Ps 30:9; 88:10-12; Ecc 9:10; Isa 38:18

5 No one remembers you when he is dead.
Who praises you from the grave[b]?[d]

6:6 [e]Ps 69:3 [f]Ps 42:3

6 I am worn out[e] from groaning;
all night long I flood my bed with weeping
and drench my couch with tears.[f]

6:7 [g]Ps 31:9

7 My eyes grow weak[g] with sorrow;
they fail because of all my foes.

6:8 [h]Ps 119:115 [i]Mt 7:23; Lk 13:27

8 Away from me,[h] all you who do evil,[i]
for the LORD has heard my weeping.

6:9 [j]Ps 116:1

9 The LORD has heard my cry for mercy;[j]
the LORD accepts my prayer.

6:10 [k]Ps 71:24; 73:19

10 All my enemies will be ashamed and dismayed;
they will turn back in sudden disgrace.[k]

Psalm 7

7:1 [l]Ps 31:15

A *shiggaion*[c] of David, which he sang to the LORD concerning Cush, a Benjamite.

1 O LORD my God, I take refuge in you;
save and deliver me from all who pursue me,[l]

7:2 [m]Isa 38:13 [n]Ps 50:22

2 or they will tear me like a lion[m]
and rip me to pieces with no one to rescue[n] me.

7:3 [o]1Sa 24:11; Isa 59:3

3 O LORD my God, if I have done this
and there is guilt on my hands[o]—
4 if I have done evil to him who is at peace with me

[a] Title: Probably a musical term [b] 5 Hebrew *Sheol* [c] Title: Probably a literary or musical term

Seeking God

PS 6:1-2

David's plea for mercy demonstrates his profound trust in the goodness and love of God. Even though he believes he is physically and emotionally tormented because of his own sin and God's resulting discipline, he does not try to hide from God and lick his wounds. Rather than withdrawing from the One who is bringing him agony, David seeks him out and, in childlike trust in a Father who loves even while he wounds, David begs for God to relent and restore him.

We can have the same confidence. Even when we suffer the consequences of our sin, our merciful God wants to reestablish us in his grace. So "come, let us return to the LORD. He has torn us to pieces but he will heal us; he has injured us but he will bind up our wounds" (Hos 6:1).

Declared Righteous

PS 7:8

Scripture clearly states that no human being is "good" or has cause to be self-righteous (Ro 3:10-12); only through faith in Jesus Christ, who shed his blood for our sin, are we declared righteous (Ro 3:20-26). David does not claim to be perfect, but he confidently asserts that, to the best of his knowledge, he is following God's will and does not deserve to be persecuted by his enemies. He acknowledges that he could have a blind spot (Ps 7:3-5), but he trusts that the perfect God who sees fully into every person's mind and heart will honor his sincere desire to be a man of integrity (Ps 7:9). Our God promises to reward those who earnestly seek him (Heb 11:6). When we pursue relationship with him, placing our ultimate faith in his character rather than in our own, we can be sure we will receive both justice and mercy.

or without cause have robbed my
foe—
5 then let my enemy pursue and overtake
me;
let him trample my life to the ground
and make me sleep in the dust. *Selah*

6 Arise,[p] O LORD, in your anger;
rise up against the rage of my
enemies.[q]
Awake,[r] my God; decree justice.
7 Let the assembled peoples gather
around you.
Rule over them from on high;
8 let the LORD judge the peoples.
Judge me, O LORD, according to my
righteousness,[s]
according to my integrity, O Most
High.
9 O righteous God,[t]
who searches minds and hearts,[u]
bring to an end the violence of the
wicked
and make the righteous secure.[v]

10 My shield[a] is God Most High,
who saves the upright in heart.[w]
11 God is a righteous judge,[x]
a God who expresses his wrath every
day.
12 If he does not relent,
he[b] will sharpen his sword;[y]
he will bend and string his bow.
13 He has prepared his deadly weapons;
he makes ready his flaming arrows.

14 He who is pregnant with evil
and conceives trouble gives birth[z] to
disillusionment.
15 He who digs a hole and scoops it out
falls into the pit he has made.[a]
16 The trouble he causes recoils on
himself;
his violence comes down on his own
head.

17 I will give thanks to the LORD because of
his righteousness[b]
and will sing praise[c] to the name of
the LORD Most High.

Psalm 8

For the director of music. According to *gittith*.[c]
A psalm of David.

1 O LORD, our Lord,
how majestic is your name in all the
earth!
You have set your glory
above the heavens.[d]

7:6 [p]Ps 94:2 [q]Ps 138:7 [r]Ps 44:23
7:8 [s]Ps 18:20; 96:13
7:9 [t]Jer 11:20 [u]1Ch 28:9; Ps 26:2; Rev 2:23 [v]Ps 37:23
7:10 [w]Ps 125:4
7:11 [x]Ps 50:6
7:12 [y]Dt 32:41
7:14 [z]Job 15:35; Isa 59:4; Jas 1:15
7:15 [a]Job 4:8
7:17 [b]Ps 71:15-16 [c]Ps 9:2
8:1 [d]Ps 57:5; 113:4; 148:13

[a] 10 Or *sovereign* [b] 12 Or *If a man does not repent, / God*
[c] Title: Probably a musical term

8:2 [e]Mt 21:16* [f]Ps 44:16; 1Co 1:27

2 From the lips of children and infants
you have ordained praise[a][e]
because of your enemies,
to silence the foe[f] and the avenger.

8:3 [g]Ps 89:11 [h]Ps 136:9

3 When I consider your heavens,[g]
the work of your fingers,
the moon and the stars,[h]
which you have set in place,
4 what is man that you are mindful of him,

8:4 [i]Job 7:17; Ps 144:3; Heb 2:6

the son of man that you care for him?[i]
5 You made him a little lower than the heavenly beings[b]

8:5 [j]Ps 21:5; 103:4

and crowned him with glory and honor.[j]

8:6 [k]Ge 1:28 [l]Heb 2:6-8* [m]1Co 15:25, 27*; Eph 1:22

6 You made him ruler[k] over the works of your hands;
you put everything under his feet:[l][m]
7 all flocks and herds,
and the beasts of the field,
8 the birds of the air,
and the fish of the sea,
all that swim the paths of the seas.

9 O LORD, our Lord,

8:9 [n]ver 1

how majestic is your name in all the earth![n]

Psalm 9[c]

For the director of music. To ⌞the tune of⌟ "The Death of the Son." A psalm of David.

9:1 [o]Ps 86:12 [p]Ps 26:7

1 I will praise you, O LORD, with all my heart;[o]
I will tell of all your wonders.[p]

9:2 [q]Ps 5:11 [r]Ps 92:1; 83:18

2 I will be glad and rejoice[q] in you;
I will sing praise to your name,[r]
O Most High.

3 My enemies turn back;
they stumble and perish before you.

9:4 [s]Ps 140:12 [t]1Pe 2:23

4 For you have upheld my right and my cause;[s]
you have sat on your throne, judging righteously.[t]
5 You have rebuked the nations and destroyed the wicked;

9:5 [u]Pr 10:7

you have blotted out their name[u] for ever and ever.
6 Endless ruin has overtaken the enemy,
you have uprooted their cities;

9:6 [v]Ps 34:16

even the memory of them[v] has perished.

7 The LORD reigns forever;

9:7 [w]Ps 89:14

he has established his throne[w] for judgment.

[a] 2 Or *strength* [b] 5 Or *than God* [c] Psalms 9 and 10 may have been originally a single acrostic poem, the stanzas of which begin with the successive letters of the Hebrew alphabet. In the Septuagint they constitute one psalm.

Children Praise Him

PS 8:2

The word *praise* here can also be translated "strength," but the implication is similar. It is God's nature to use human weakness to demonstrate his strength (Isa 40:29-31; 2Co 12:9-10) *and to elevate childlike faith over stuffy religion* (Mt 21:15-16). He does this in *order to turn proud human logic on its head and silence those who think they have life figured out and under control. When we* praise God in innocent trust and *rely on his strength in childlike weakness, we become showcases of his power and sovereignty in a world that ignores him.*

Mount Zion

PS 9:11

Mount Zion is the earthly place where God chooses to "reside" when David rules Jerusalem. David builds a citadel and a palace there and names it "the City of David" (2Sa 5:9). But it is significant to note that elsewhere David's city is referred to as the "city of God" (Ps 46:4; 87:3). David's son, Solomon, builds the temple there—a central place of worship that God promises to bless with his presence forever (2Ch 7:16). While God is not limited to a particular time or place, Biblical references to Zion and God's enthronement there are a figurative way of proclaiming his sovereign rule throughout eternity (Ps 9:7). God governs his kingdom from "the heavenly Jerusalem," where we will one day live with him forever in the presence of the angels (Heb 12:22–24).

8 He will judge the world in
righteousness;[x]
he will govern the peoples with
justice.
9 The LORD is a refuge for the oppressed,
a stronghold in times of trouble.[y]
10 Those who know your name[z] will trust
in you,
for you, LORD, have never forsaken[a]
those who seek you.

11 Sing praises to the LORD, enthroned in
Zion;[b]
proclaim among the nations[c] what he
has done.[d]
12 For he who avenges blood[e] remembers;
he does not ignore the cry of the
afflicted.

13 O LORD, see how my enemies[f] persecute
me!
Have mercy and lift me up from the
gates of death,
14 that I may declare your praises[g]
in the gates of the Daughter of Zion
and there rejoice in your salvation.[h]
15 The nations have fallen into the pit they
have dug;[i]
their feet are caught in the net they
have hidden.[j]
16 The LORD is known by his justice;
the wicked are ensnared by the work
of their hands. *Higgaion.*[a] *Selah*
17 The wicked return to the grave,[bk]
all the nations that forget God.[l]
18 But the needy will not always be
forgotten,
nor the hope[m] of the afflicted[n] ever
perish.

19 Arise, O LORD, let not man triumph;
let the nations be judged in your
presence.
20 Strike them with terror, O LORD;
let the nations know they are but
men.[o] *Selah*

Psalm 10[c]

1 Why, O LORD, do you stand far off?[p]
Why do you hide yourself[q] in times of
trouble?

2 In his arrogance the wicked man hunts
down the weak,
who are caught in the schemes he
devises.
3 He boasts[r] of the cravings of his heart;

9:8 [x]Ps 96:13
9:9 [y]Ps 32:7
9:10 [z]Ps 91:14 [a]Ps 37:28
9:11 [b]Ps 76:2 [c]Ps 107:22 [d]Ps 105:1
9:12 [e]Ge 9:5
9:13 [f]Ps 38:19
9:14 [g]Ps 106:2 [h]Ps 13:5; 51:12
9:15 [i]Ps 7:15-16 [j]Ps 35:8; 57:6
9:17 [k]Ps 49:14 [l]Job 8:13; Ps 50:22
9:18 [m]Ps 71:5; Pr 23:18 [n]Ps 12:5
9:20 [o]Ps 62:9; Isa 31:3
10:1 [p]Ps 22:1,11 [q]Ps 13:1
10:3 [r]Ps 94:4

[a] *16* Or *Meditation*; possibly a musical notation
[b] *17* Hebrew *Sheol* [c] Psalms 9 and 10 may have been originally a single acrostic poem, the stanzas of which begin with the successive letters of the Hebrew alphabet. In the Septuagint they constitute one psalm.

he blesses the greedy and reviles the
LORD.
4 In his pride the wicked does not seek
him;
in all his thoughts there is no room
for God.[s]
5 His ways are always prosperous;
he is haughty and your laws are far
from him;
he sneers at all his enemies.
6 He says to himself, "Nothing will shake
me;
I'll always be happy[t] and never have
trouble."
7 His mouth is full of curses[u] and lies and
threats;[v]
trouble and evil are under his
tongue.[w]
8 He lies in wait near the villages;
from ambush he murders the
innocent,[x]
watching in secret for his victims.
9 He lies in wait like a lion in cover;
he lies in wait to catch the helpless;[y]
he catches the helpless and drags
them off in his net.
10 His victims are crushed, they collapse;
they fall under his strength.
11 He says to himself, "God has forgotten;[z]
he covers his face and never sees."

12 Arise, LORD! Lift up your hand,[a] O God.
Do not forget the helpless.[b]
13 Why does the wicked man revile God?
Why does he say to himself,
"He won't call me to account"?
14 But you, O God, do see trouble[c] and grief;
you consider it to take it in hand.
The victim commits himself to you;[d]
you are the helper[e] of the fatherless.
15 Break the arm of the wicked and evil
man;[f]
call him to account for his wickedness
that would not be found out.

16 The LORD is King for ever and ever;[g]
the nations[h] will perish from his land.
17 You hear, O LORD, the desire of the
afflicted;[i]
you encourage them, and you listen to
their cry,
18 defending the fatherless[j] and the
oppressed,[k]
in order that man, who is of the earth,
may terrify no more.

Psalm 11

For the director of music. Of David.

1 In the LORD I take refuge.[l]
How then can you say to me:
"Flee like a bird to your mountain.

10:4 [s]Ps 14:1; 36:1
10:6 [t]Rev 18:7
10:7 [u]Ro 3:14* [v]Ps 73:8 [w]Ps 140:3
10:8 [x]Ps 94:6
10:9 [y]Ps 17:12; 59:3; 140:5
10:11 [z]Job 22:13
10:12 [a]Ps 17:7; Mic 5:9 [b]Ps 9:12
10:14 [c]Ps 22:11 [d]Ps 37:5 [e]Ps 68:5
10:15 [f]Ps 37:17
10:16 [g]Ps 29:10 [h]Dt 8:20
10:17 [i]1Ch 29:18; Ps 34:15
10:18 [j]Ps 82:3 [k]Ps 9:9
11:1 [l]Ps 56:11

God of the Victim

PS 10:14,17-18

In Matthew 25:31–46, ***Jesus paints a vivid portrait of how much the poor, needy, afflicted and oppressed are valued by a compassionate God—and how his children are to represent him on earth in the way they support and defend victimized and lonely people. Unfortunately, we do not always come through for those in need. But, as this psalm so superbly declares, God never overlooks them. In his eternal kingdom, the poor, the persecuted, the meek and the spiritually hungry are given special blessing (Mt 5:1–12). The first will be last, and the last will be first (Mt 20:16). Our heavenly Father has a very tender heart toward those who suffer and cry out to him. When they run to him for refuge, he promises to hear, encourage and defend them.***

Trustworthy Words

PS 12:2–6

David reveals in this psalm his knowledge of the notoriously difficult time human beings have keeping their tongues in check. Rather than letting God be the master of our words, we too often let loose with the lies and boasts that come naturally to us—and in the process, we hurt others and fail to be true friends. In contrast, God does not lie, never says something he doesn't mean, never fails to fulfill his promises (Nu 23:19). What a comfort it is to know that every word that comes from God is pure and completely trustworthy. Like precious silver refined to perfection, his promises have been "thoroughly tested" and will never let us down (Ps 119:140).

2 For look, the wicked bend their bows;
they set their arrows[m] against the strings
to shoot from the shadows
at the upright in heart.[n]
3 When the foundations[o] are being destroyed,
what can the righteous do[a]?"

4 The LORD is in his holy temple;[p]
the LORD is on his heavenly throne.[q]
He observes the sons of men;[r]
his eyes examine[s] them.
5 The LORD examines the righteous,[t]
but the wicked[b] and those who love violence
his soul hates.[u]
6 On the wicked he will rain
fiery coals and burning sulfur;[v]
a scorching wind[w] will be their lot.

7 For the LORD is righteous,[x]
he loves justice;[y]
upright men will see his face.[z]

11:2 [m]Ps 7:13 [n]Ps 64:3-4
11:3 [o]Ps 82:5
11:4 [p]Ps 18:6 [q]Ps 103:19 [r]Ps 33:13 [s]Ps 34:15-16
11:5 [t]Ge 22:1; Jas 1:12 [u]Ps 5:5
11:6 [v]Eze 38:22 [w]Jer 4:11-12
11:7 [x]Ps 7:9, 11; 45:7 [y]Ps 33:5 [z]Ps 17:15

Psalm 12

For the director of music. According to *sheminith.*[c] A psalm of David.

1 Help, LORD, for the godly are no more;[a]
the faithful have vanished from among men.
2 Everyone lies to his neighbor;
their flattering lips speak with deception.[b]

3 May the LORD cut off all flattering lips
and every boastful tongue[c]
4 that says, "We will triumph with our tongues;
we own our lips[d]—who is our master?"

5 "Because of the oppression of the weak
and the groaning of the needy,
I will now arise," says the LORD.
"I will protect them[d] from those who malign them."
6 And the words of the LORD are flawless,[e]
like silver refined in a furnace of clay,
purified seven times.

7 O LORD, you will keep us safe
and protect us from such people forever.[f]
8 The wicked freely strut[g] about
when what is vile is honored among men.

12:1 [a]Isa 57:1
12:2 [b]Ps 10:7; 41:6; 55:21; Ro 16:18
12:3 [c]Da 7:8; Rev 13:5
12:5 [d]Ps 10:18; 34:6
12:6 [e]2Sa 22:31; Ps 18:30; Pr 30:5
12:7 [f]Ps 37:28
12:8 [g]Ps 55:10-11

[a] 3 Or *what is the Righteous One doing* [b] 5 Or *The LORD, the Righteous One, examines the wicked, /* [c] Title: Probably a musical term [d] 4 Or */ our lips are our plowshares*

Psalm 13

For the director of music. A psalm of David.

13:1 [h]Job 13:24; Ps 44:24

1 How long, O LORD? Will you forget me
forever?
How long will you hide your face[h]
from me?

13:2 [i]Ps 42:4 [j]Ps 42:9

2 How long must I wrestle with my
thoughts[i]
and every day have sorrow in my
heart?
How long will my enemy triumph
over me?[j]

13:3 [k]Ps 5:1 [l]Ezr 9:8 [m]Jer 51:39

3 Look on me and answer,[k] O LORD my
God.
Give light to my eyes,[l] or I will sleep
in death;[m]

13:4 [n]Ps 25:2

4 my enemy will say, "I have overcome
him,[n]"
and my foes will rejoice when I fall.

13:5 [o]Ps 52:8 [p]Ps 9:14

5 But I trust in your unfailing love;[o]
my heart rejoices in your salvation.[p]

13:6 [q]Ps 116:7

6 I will sing[q] to the LORD,
for he has been good to me.

How Long?

PS 13:1–2

Like a child wailing in the night, David's plaintive cry, "How long, O LORD?" pierces the heart of anyone who knows what it feels like to suffer and wrestle with no end in sight. We all go through times in life when it seems like God is in hiding; we can't imagine what he's up to, and we feel abandoned and forgotten. This psalm of lament, like many others in the book, assures us that even godly people complain and feel desperate in the face of unrelenting pain. To cry out this way to God is not only perfectly acceptable to him, but such honesty is also the first step toward restoring our faith in a Maker who will truly never fail us (Ps 13:5–6).

Psalm 14

For the director of music. Of David.

14:1 [r]Ps 10:4

1 The fool[a] says in his heart,
"There is no God."[r]
They are corrupt, their deeds are vile;
there is no one who does good.

14:2 [s]Ps 33:13 [t]Ps 92:6

2 The LORD looks down from heaven[s]
on the sons of men
to see if there are any who understand,[t]
any who seek God.

14:3 [u]Ps 58:3 [v]Ps 143:2 [w]Ro 3:10-12*

3 All have turned aside,
they have together become corrupt;[u]
there is no one who does good,[v]
not even one.[w]

14:4 [x]Ps 82:5 [y]Ps 27:2 [z]Ps 79:6; Isa 64:7

4 Will evildoers never learn—[x]
those who devour my people[y] as men
eat bread
and who do not call on the LORD?[z]
5 There they are, overwhelmed with
dread,
for God is present in the company of
the righteous.

14:6 [a]Ps 9:9; 40:17

6 You evildoers frustrate the plans of the
poor,
but the LORD is their refuge.[a]

14:7 [b]Ps 53:6

7 Oh, that salvation for Israel would come
out of Zion!
When the LORD restores the fortunes[b]
of his people,
let Jacob rejoice and Israel be glad!

[a] *1* The Hebrew words rendered *fool* in Psalms denote one who is morally deficient.

God's Abundant Provision

PS 16:5–6

There is great beauty and joy in the metaphors used here for God's abundant and reliable provision. Most commentators agree that a "portion," drawing from the image of inheritance in the promised land, is one's lot in life; a "cup" is one's destiny. They are "assigned" by the Lord and are secure—they cannot be taken or changed—because God is in complete control of both. Knowing this can help us bear up confidently when our "portion" doesn't match our expectations as well as rejoice in gratitude when our "cup" overflows (Ps 23:5). God-ordained "boundary lines" determine our stake in a fertile heritage of God's favor. The great provider insures our inheritance of eternal life, bringing joy and delight to our soul. No matter what our earthly life presents us with, our ultimate and eternal "portion" is—unbelievably and gloriously—God himself (Ps 73:26).

Psalm 15

A psalm of David.

1 LORD, who may dwell in your
sanctuary?[c]
Who may live on your holy hill?[d]

2 He whose walk is blameless
and who does what is righteous,
who speaks the truth[e] from his heart
3 and has no slander[f] on his tongue,
who does his neighbor no wrong
and casts no slur on his fellowman,
4 who despises a vile man
but honors[g] those who fear the LORD,
who keeps his oath[h]
even when it hurts,
5 who lends his money without usury[i]
and does not accept a bribe[j] against
the innocent.

He who does these things
will never be shaken.[k]

Psalm 16

A *miktam*[a] of David.

1 Keep me safe,[l] O God,
for in you I take refuge.[m]

2 I said to the LORD, "You are my Lord;
apart from you I have no good thing."[n]
3 As for the saints who are in the land,[o]
they are the glorious ones in whom is
all my delight.[b]
4 The sorrows[p] of those will increase
who run after other gods.[q]
I will not pour out their libations of
blood
or take up their names[r] on my lips.

5 LORD, you have assigned me my portion[s]
and my cup;[t]
you have made my lot secure.
6 The boundary lines have fallen for me
in pleasant places;
surely I have a delightful inheritance.[u]
7 I will praise the LORD, who counsels me;[v]
even at night[w] my heart instructs me.
8 I have set the LORD always before me.
Because he is at my right hand,[x]
I will not be shaken.

9 Therefore my heart is glad[y] and my
tongue rejoices;
my body also will rest secure,[z]
10 because you will not abandon me to the
grave,[c]

15:1 [c]Ps 27:5-6 [d]Ps 24:3-5
15:2 [e]Ps 24:4; Zec 8:3,16; Eph 4:25
15:3 [f]Ex 23:1
15:4 [g]Ac 28:10 [h]Jdg 11:35
15:5 [i]Ex 22:25 [j]Ex 23:8; Dt 16:19 [k]2Pe 1:10
16:1 [l]Ps 17:8 [m]Ps 7:1
16:2 [n]Ps 73:25
16:3 [o]Ps 101:6
16:4 [p]Ps 32:10 [q]Ps 106:37-38 [r]Ex 23:13
16:5 [s]Ps 73:26 [t]Ps 23:5
16:6 [u]Ps 78:55; Jer 3:19
16:7 [v]Ps 73:24 [w]Ps 77:6
16:8 [x]Ps 73:23
16:9 [y]Ps 4:7; 30:11 [z]Ps 4:8

[a] Title: Probably a literary or musical term [b] 3 Or *As for the pagan priests who are in the land / and the nobles in whom all delight, I said:* [c] 10 Hebrew *Sheol*

16:10 nor will you let your Holy One[a] see
[a]Ac 13:35* decay.[a]
[11] You have made[b] known to me the path
16:11 of life;[b]
[b]Mt 7:14 you will fill me with joy in your
[c]Ac 2:25-28*
[d]Ps 36:7-8 presence,[c]
with eternal pleasures[d] at your right
hand.

Psalm 17

A prayer of David.

1 Hear, O LORD, my righteous plea;
17:1 listen to my cry.[e]
[e]Ps 61:1 Give ear to my prayer—
[f]Isa 29:13 it does not rise from deceitful lips.[f]
2 May my vindication come from you;
may your eyes see what is right.

3 Though you probe my heart and
17:3 examine me at night,
[g]Ps 26:2; though you test me,[g] you will find
66:10 nothing;[h]
[h]Job 23:10; I have resolved that my mouth will
Jer 50:20
[i]Ps 39:1 not sin.[i]
4 As for the deeds of men—
by the word of your lips
I have kept myself
from the ways of the violent.
5 My steps have held to your paths;[j]
17:5 my feet have not slipped.[k]
[j]Ps 44:18;
119:133
[k]Ps 18:36 6 I call on you, O God, for you will
answer me;[l]
17:6 give ear to me[m] and hear my prayer.[n]
[l]Ps 86:7
[m]Ps 116:2 7 Show the wonder of your great love,[o]
[n]Ps 88:2 you who save by your right hand[p]
17:7 those who take refuge in you from
[o]Ps 31:21 their foes.
[p]Ps 20:6 8 Keep me as the apple of your eye;[q]
17:8 hide me in the shadow of your wings
[q]Dt 32:10 9 from the wicked who assail me,
17:9 from my mortal enemies who
[r]Ps 31:20; surround me.[r]
109:3

10 They close up their callous hearts,[s]
17:10 and their mouths speak with
[s]Ps 73:7
[t]1Sa 2:3 arrogance.[t]
11 They have tracked me down, they now
17:11 surround me,[u]
[u]Ps 37:14;
88:17 with eyes alert, to throw me to the
17:12 ground.
[v]Ps 7:2; 10:9 12 They are like a lion[v] hungry for prey,
like a great lion crouching in cover.
17:13 13 Rise up, O LORD, confront them, bring
[w]Ps 7:12; them down;[w]
22:20; 73:18 rescue me from the wicked by your
sword.
14 O LORD, by your hand save me from
such men,

[a] 10 Or *your faithful one* [b] 11 Or *You will make*

***O**ur joy, our ability to laugh in the face of difficulties, has more to do with how we view God than how he views us. At times many of us fear that maybe God isn't all that interested in our daily lives. We've been taught the his-eye-is-on-the-sparrow-so-we-know-he-watches-us mentality, but we are far from convinced. Sometimes we see our lives running counter to our desires, wishes and prayers; we then assume God doesn't care. When these kinds of thoughts take over and undermine our faith, we have ceased to live in response to the abundance of God.*

The key word in this phrase is response. *Most of us have a good head-knowledge of God's abundance, but we often find ourselves unable to respond to that abundance. That inability to respond possibly comes from a growing fear that God is truly unaware of where we are and how we are. When this happens, we need bolstering, and there's no better source for faith-bolstering than God's living Word . . . I am not on a haphazard course of my own poor choosing. Psalm 16:11 assures me, "You have made known to me the path of life." I choose to believe God will indeed make life's path known to me, and that where I am on that path is no surprise to him.*

—Marilyn Meberg

The Strength of Our God

PS 18:2

The word pictures David uses here are vivid reminders of the kind of God we serve. He is rock solid in his faithfulness, unmoved by those who would do us harm. He is fortress-like in his unconquerable strength; we will always find safe refuge in him. He is impenetrable in his shield-like protection, powerful in his ability to save and utterly reliable as a stronghold in times of trouble. No wonder the psalmists come back to these images repeatedly in their praise of our mighty God (Ps 28:7; 37:39; 62:2,7; 91:2; 95:1; 144:2)!

from men of this world[x] whose
reward is in this life.[y]
You still the hunger of those you
cherish;
their sons have plenty,
and they store up wealth[y] for their
children.
15 And I—in righteousness I will see your
face;
when I awake, I will be satisfied with
seeing your likeness.[z]

Psalm 18

For the director of music. Of David the servant of the LORD. He sang to the LORD the words of this song when the LORD delivered him from the hand of all his enemies and from the hand of Saul. He said:

1 I love you, O LORD, my strength.
2 The LORD is my rock,[a] my fortress and
my deliverer;
my God is my rock, in whom I take
refuge.
He is my shield[b] and the horn[a] of my
salvation,[c] my stronghold.
3 I call to the LORD, who is worthy of
praise,[d]
and I am saved from my enemies.
4 The cords of death[e] entangled me;
the torrents[f] of destruction
overwhelmed me.
5 The cords of the grave[b] coiled around
me;
the snares of death[g] confronted me.
6 In my distress I called to the LORD;
I cried to my God for help.
From his temple he heard my voice;[h]
my cry came before him, into his ears.
7 The earth trembled and quaked,[i]
and the foundations of the mountains
shook;
they trembled because he was angry.[j]
8 Smoke rose from his nostrils;
consuming fire[k] came from his
mouth,
burning coals blazed out of it.
9 He parted the heavens and came down;[l]
dark clouds were under his feet.
10 He mounted the cherubim[m] and flew;
he soared on the wings of the wind.[n]
11 He made darkness his covering,[o] his
canopy around him—
the dark rain clouds of the sky.
12 Out of the brightness of his presence[p]
clouds advanced,
with hailstones and bolts of
lightning.[q]

17:14 [x]Lk 16:8 [y]Ps 73:3-7
17:15 [z]Nu 12:8; Ps 4:6-7; 16:11; 1Jn 3:2
18:2 [a]Ps 19:14 [b]Ps 59:11 [c]Ps 75:10
18:3 [d]Ps 48:1
18:4 [e]Ps 116:3 [f]Ps 124:4
18:5 [g]Ps 116:3
18:6 [h]Ps 34:15
18:7 [i]Jdg 5:4 [j]Ps 68:7-8
18:8 [k]Ps 50:3
18:9 [l]Ps 144:5
18:10 [m]Ps 80:1 [n]Ps 104:3
18:11 [o]Dt 4:11; Ps 97:2
18:12 [p]Ps 104:2 [q]Ps 97:3

[a] 2 *Horn* here symbolizes strength. [b] 5 Hebrew *Sheol*

13 The LORD thundered[r] from heaven;
the voice of the Most High
resounded.[a]
14 He shot his arrows and scattered ⌊the
enemies⌋,
great bolts of lightning and routed
them.[s]
15 The valleys of the sea were exposed
and the foundations of the earth laid
bare
at your rebuke,[t] O LORD,
at the blast of breath from your
nostrils.
16 He reached down from on high and took
hold of me;
he drew me out of deep waters.[u]
17 He rescued me from my powerful
enemy,
from my foes, who were too strong for
me.[v]
18 They confronted me in the day of my
disaster,
but the LORD was my support.[w]
19 He brought me out into a spacious
place;[x]
he rescued me because he delighted
in me.[y]

20 The LORD has dealt with me according to
my righteousness;
according to the cleanness of my
hands[z] he has rewarded me.
21 For I have kept the ways of the LORD;[a]
I have not done evil by turning[b] from
my God.
22 All his laws are before me;[c]
I have not turned away from his
decrees.
23 I have been blameless before him
and have kept myself from sin.
24 The LORD has rewarded me according to
my righteousness,[d]
according to the cleanness of my
hands in his sight.
25 To the faithful[e] you show yourself
faithful,
to the blameless you show yourself
blameless,
26 to the pure you show yourself pure,
but to the crooked you show yourself
shrewd.[f]
27 You save the humble
but bring low those whose eyes are
haughty.[g]
28 You, O LORD, keep my lamp burning;
my God turns my darkness into light.[h]

18:13 [r]Ps 29:3; 104:7
18:14 [s]Ps 144:6
18:15 [t]Ps 76:6; 106:9
18:16 [u]Ps 144:7
18:17 [v]Ps 35:10
18:18 [w]Ps 59:16
18:19 [x]Ps 31:8 [y]Ps 118:5
18:20 [z]Ps 24:4
18:21 [a]2Ch 34:33 [b]Ps 119:102
18:22 [c]Ps 119:30
18:24 [d]1Sa 26:23
18:25 [e]1Ki 8:32; Ps 62:12; Mt 5:7
18:26 [f]Pr 3:34
18:27 [g]Pr 6:17
18:28 [h]Job 18:6; 29:3

[a] *13* Some Hebrew manuscripts and Septuagint (see also 2 Samuel 22:14); most Hebrew manuscripts *resounded, / amid hailstones and bolts of lightning*

When emotions beat against our souls like wave after wave in the worst of a storm, there is nowhere to turn but to Christ. As I sit for a while and think about him, I hear the loneliest words in the world: "Jesus cried out in a loud voice, 'Eloi, Eloi, lama sabachthani?'—which means, 'My God, my God, why have you forsaken me?'" (Mt 27:46). On that brutal tree Christ embraced total isolation so that you and I never have to be alone. I am learning that that doesn't mean that life will be free of pain; it means that in the midst of the darkest night, he comes walking. Along the bleakest hospital corridors, he comes walking. When you think that the world has left you all alone, listen closely, he comes walking.

—Sheila Walsh

Broaden My Path

PS 18:36

Picture making your way along a high, narrow ledge, picking your way over rocks and snags as you try to escape a dangerous enemy who is quickly gaining on you. When the terrain of life becomes rocky, steep and narrow, the journey can be overwhelming. We are keenly aware of how easy it would be to turn an ankle, stumble and slip to our deaths. David's praise-filled proclamation of God's sustaining presence can be an affirmation of faith for us in daily life. Next time we find ourselves precariously perched on a dangerous precipice in a situation or relationship, we can say this verse aloud to the Lord. We can trust our Savior to broaden the path in front of us and keep our feet from slipping.

29 With your help[i] I can advance against a
troop[a];
with my God I can scale a wall.
30 As for God, his way is perfect;[j]
the word of the LORD is flawless.[k]
He is a shield
for all who take refuge[l] in him.
31 For who is God besides the LORD?[m]
And who is the Rock[n] except our God?
32 It is God who arms me with strength[o]
and makes my way perfect.
33 He makes my feet like the feet of a deer;[p]
he enables me to stand on the
heights.[q]
34 He trains my hands for battle;[r]
my arms can bend a bow of bronze.
35 You give me your shield of victory,
and your right hand sustains[s] me;
you stoop down to make me great.
36 You broaden the path beneath me,
so that my ankles do not turn.

37 I pursued my enemies[t] and overtook
them;
I did not turn back till they were
destroyed.
38 I crushed them so that they could not
rise;[u]
they fell beneath my feet.[v]
39 You armed me with strength for battle;
you made my adversaries bow at my
feet.
40 You made my enemies turn their backs[w]
in flight,
and I destroyed[x] my foes.
41 They cried for help, but there was no
one to save them[y]—
to the LORD, but he did not answer.[z]
42 I beat them as fine as dust borne on the
wind;
I poured them out like mud in the
streets.
43 You have delivered me from the attacks
of the people;
you have made me the head of
nations;[a]
people I did not know[b] are subject to
me.
44 As soon as they hear me, they obey me;
foreigners[c] cringe before me.
45 They all lose heart;
they come trembling from their
strongholds.[d]

46 The LORD lives! Praise be to my Rock!
Exalted be God my Savior![e]
47 He is the God who avenges me,
who subdues nations[f] under me,
48 who saves[g] me from my enemies.

18:29 [i]Heb 11:34
18:30 [j]Dt 32:4; Rev 15:3 [k]Ps 12:6 [l]Ps 17:7
18:31 [m]Dt 32:39; 86:8; Isa 45:5,6, 14,18,21 [n]Dt 32:31; 1Sa 2:2
18:32 [o]Isa 45:5
18:33 [p]Hab 3:19 [q]Dt 32:13
18:34 [r]Ps 144:1
18:35 [s]Ps 119:116
18:37 [t]Ps 37:20; 44:5
18:38 [u]Ps 36:12 [v]Ps 47:3
18:40 [w]Ps 21:12 [x]Ps 94:23
18:41 [y]Ps 50:22 [z]Job 27:9; Pr 1:28
18:43 [a]2Sa 8:1-14 [b]Isa 52:15; 55:5
18:44 [c]Ps 66:3
18:45 [d]Mic 7:17
18:46 [e]Ps 51:14
18:47 [f]Ps 47:3
18:48 [g]Ps 59:1

[a] 29 Or *can run through a barricade*

Mephibosheth's Nurse

Bridge Over Troubled Waters

Few of us will have our lives recorded in books or movies. Our stories will be etched in the lives of those whom God has given us to love. There are few words on paper about Mephibosheth's nurse, but the character of her charge discloses volumes.

It was a good life for an unattached woman of the times who loved children. The wealthy considered their nurse a valuable family member, and she often remained with them her whole life. It was a win-win arrangement, giving the nurse social status and personal security, the family a loyal servant devoted to the nurture of their children. Jonathan and his wife picked her carefully. They wanted the best. Little could anyone know at the time how critical their choice would be.

Mephibosheth was only five years old when everything in their lives fell apart. In one day, he lost his father and mother, his home, his friends, all his possessions and his health. As his nurse hurried to carry him out of danger in the power struggle for the throne, he fell and injured both feet. He was lame for the rest of his life.

Royalty cannot just blend in with the crowd. They are well-known public figures, subject to both the highs and lows of political favor. Stripped of all his possessions and personal history, Mephibosheth took on the lifestyle of a refugee, hiding from public view for years. He was a man who suffered much—physically, emotionally, materially and spiritually. He had every "right" to be bitter and demanding. Yet, when we meet him again many years later, we find a remarkably content and spiritually healthy person—thanks to his nurse.

Mephibosheth's nurse had provided continuity, safety and faith in turbulent times. He was a fortunate man, learning from her to embrace the simple joys of everyday life. He needed neither fame nor fortune for his happiness. His nurse had given him the tools to live the life God gave him with dignity and thankfulness. He was disabled, but he walked far taller than most men.

We have the power to do the same for those we love. Life is full of hardship and struggle, but it also offers joy. Love for God's simple gifts—a puppy's kiss, a walk in the woods, a balmy spring breeze on our face, a newborn's yawn—is an excellent heritage for our loved ones. It bonds them to the reality of a living God who loves us even in the midst of suffering.

Mephibosheth's Nurse

2 Samuel 4:4

Candid SNAPSHOT Jonathan son of Saul had a son who was lame in both feet. He was five years old when the news about Saul and Jonathan came from Jezreel. His nurse picked him up and fled, but as she hurried to leave, he fell and became crippled. His name was Mephibosheth (2 Samuel 4:4).

Rizpah

Love Beyond the Grave

Sleep would have to wait. Relaxing her vigil for even a moment would leave her sons prey to birds and other scavengers that would pick their bones. How could she endure the thought of her sons rotting on the ground? So Rizpah, Saul's concubine, watched, day and night. She protected, honored and mourned these men, born to such privilege and promise, now disgraced in death. She kept her watch until the rains came and washed their bones clean.

The house of Saul was no more. Saul and three of his sons had been killed fighting the Philistines. Now, seven more corpses—Rizpah's two sons and Saul's daughter's five sons—lay on a hillside in Gibeah. They'd been executed and exposed to the elements in restitution. Saul had broken the treaty established between Israel and Gibeah in Joshua's time and had attempted to annihilate the Gibeonites.

Rizpah had no part in war, no part in genocide. But her sons were dead, lying in a field without proper burial, and she would not be comforted. Her mourning was as intense as it was solitary. No family, no neighbors joined in her grief. There was only the wind and Rizpah—with her sackcloth, the rock she sat on, and the stench of the dead bodies rotting in the sun. No one else marked her sons' passing and helped her keep guard. The war between David and Saul was finally over, and the deaths of these seven atoned for Saul's savagery. But the mother only saw the familiar and beloved faces of her sons twisted and decaying in death.

As futile as her actions may have seemed to some, Rizpah's grief and her vigil touched David's heart. When he heard what she had done, he relented from his harsh position as the victor in war. In an act of deep respect, he collected the bones of Saul, Jonathan and the seven on the hillside and had them buried in the tomb of Saul's father.

The love of a godly mother does not end when her children make serious mistakes or fall victims to tragedy. Rizpah's love followed her sons to the grave. Hers was a mere shadowy reflection of God's love for us. He says through Isaiah: "Can a mother forget the baby at her breast and have no compassion on the child she has borne? Though she may forget, I will not forget you! See, I have engraved you on the palms of my hands" (Isa 49:15–16).

Rizpah
(hot stone)
2 Samuel 3:7; 21:8–14

Candid SNAPSHOT Rizpah daughter of Aiah took sackcloth and spread it out for herself on a rock. From the beginning of the harvest till the rain poured down from the heavens on the bodies, she did not let the birds of the air touch them by day or the wild animals by night (2 Samuel 21:10).

You exalted me above my foes;
from violent men you rescued me.
49 Therefore I will praise you among the nations, O LORD;
I will sing[h] praises to your name.[i]
50 He gives his king great victories;
he shows unfailing kindness to his anointed,
to David[j] and his descendants forever.[k]

Psalm 19

For the director of music. A psalm of David.

1 The heavens[l] declare[m] the glory of God;
the skies proclaim the work of his hands.
2 Day after day they pour forth speech;
night after night they display knowledge.[n]
3 There is no speech or language
where their voice is not heard.[a]
4 Their voice[b] goes out into all the earth,
their words to the ends of the world.[o]

In the heavens he has pitched a tent[p] for the sun,
5 which is like a bridegroom coming forth from his pavilion,
like a champion rejoicing to run his course.
6 It rises at one end of the heavens
and makes its circuit to the other;[q]
nothing is hidden from its heat.

7 The law of the LORD is perfect,
reviving the soul.[r]
The statutes of the LORD are trustworthy,[s]
making wise the simple.[t]
8 The precepts of the LORD are right,[u]
giving joy to the heart.
The commands of the LORD are radiant,
giving light to the eyes.
9 The fear of the LORD is pure,
enduring forever.
The ordinances of the LORD are sure
and altogether righteous.[v]
10 They are more precious than gold,[w]
than much pure gold;
they are sweeter than honey,
than honey from the comb.
11 By them is your servant warned;
in keeping them there is great reward.

12 Who can discern his errors?
Forgive my hidden faults.[x]
13 Keep your servant also from willful sins;
may they not rule over me.

18:49 [h]Ps 108:1 [i]Ro 15:9*
18:50 [j]Ps 144:10 [k]Ps 89:4
19:1 [l]Isa 40:22 [m]Ps 50:6; Ro 1:19
19:2 [n]Ps 74:16
19:4 [o]Ro 10:18* [p]Ps 104:2
19:6 [q]Ps 113:3; Ecc 1:5
19:7 [r]Ps 23:3 [s]Ps 93:5; 111:7 [t]Ps 119:98-100
19:8 [u]Ps 12:6; 119:128
19:9 [v]Ps 119:138, 142
19:10 [w]Pr 8:10
19:12 [x]Ps 51:2; 90:8; 139:6

[a] 3 Or *They have no speech, there are no words; / no sound is heard from them* [b] 4 Septuagint, Jerome and Syriac; Hebrew *line*

Frances Whitmarsh Wile wrote this beautiful expression of God's hand in the seasons at the request of a friend who was putting together a hymnal and wanted a song about winter.

All Beautiful the March of Days

All beautiful the march of days, as seasons come and go;
The Hand that shaped the rose hath wrought the crystal of the snow;
Hath sent the hoary frost of heaven, the flowing waters sealed,
And laid a silent loveliness on hill and wood and field.

O'er white expanses sparkling pure the radiant morns unfold;
The solemn splendors of the night burn brighter than the cold;
Life mounts in every throbbing vein, love deepens round the hearth,
And clearer sounds the angel hymn, "Good will to men on earth."

O Thou from Whose unfathomed law the year in beauty flows,
Thyself the vision passing by in crystal and in rose,
Day unto day doth utter speech, and night to night proclaim,
In ever changing words of light, the wonder of Thy Name.

—Frances Whitmarsh Wile (1878–1939)

Trust God

PS 20:7

David leads and engages in many military battles in his lifetime, but he is equally well acquainted with the moral battles common to us all. In any altercation with an enemy, be it physical or spiritual, David's confidence is not in himself or his resources, but in the power and authority of the Lord. When he is a mere boy, facing the giant Goliath, he proclaims that "the battle is the LORD's" (1Sa 17:47; see the note on 1Sa 17:45, page 449). He knows he is no match for the Philistine; he doesn't boast in his own strength or weaponry. Instead, he has absolute confidence in his victorious God. In that early face-off and during the battles throughout his life, David recalls his conviction that only God's strength and resources can be fully trusted. When we encounter spiritual battles in our own lives, we can use David's proclamations of faith to remind ourselves who rules the battleground. Satan may launch all his powers of darkness against us, but God will have the victory. Depend on it!

Then will I be blameless,
innocent of great transgression.

14 May the words of my mouth and the meditation of my heart
be pleasing[y] in your sight,
O LORD, my Rock[z] and my Redeemer.[a]

Psalm 20

For the director of music. A psalm of David.

1 May the LORD answer you when you are in distress;
may the name of the God of Jacob[b] protect you.[c]
2 May he send you help from the sanctuary[d]
and grant you support from Zion.
3 May he remember[e] all your sacrifices
and accept your burnt offerings.[f]
Selah
4 May he give you the desire of your heart[g]
and make all your plans succeed.
5 We will shout for joy when you are victorious
and will lift up our banners[h] in the name of our God.
May the LORD grant all your requests.[i]

6 Now I know that the LORD saves his anointed;[j]
he answers him from his holy heaven
with the saving power of his right hand.
7 Some trust in chariots and some in horses,[k]
but we trust in the name of the LORD our God.[l]
8 They are brought to their knees and fall,
but we rise up[m] and stand firm.[n]
9 O LORD, save the king!
Answer[a] us[o] when we call!

Psalm 21

For the director of music. A psalm of David.

1 O LORD, the king rejoices in your strength.
How great is his joy in the victories you give![p]
2 You have granted him the desire of his heart[q]
and have not withheld the request of his lips. *Selah*
3 You welcomed him with rich blessings
and placed a crown of pure gold[r] on his head.
4 He asked you for life, and you gave it to him—

19:14 [y]Ps 104:34 [z]Ps 18:2 [a]Isa 47:4
20:1 [b]Ps 46:7,11 [c]Ps 91:14
20:2 [d]Ps 3:4
20:3 [e]Ac 10:4 [f]Ps 51:19
20:4 [g]Ps 21:2; 145:16,19
20:5 [h]Ps 9:14; 60:4 [i]1Sa 1:17
20:6 [j]Ps 28:8; 41:11; Isa 58:9
20:7 [k]Ps 33:17; Isa 31:1 [l]2Ch 32:8
20:8 [m]Mic 7:8 [n]Ps 37:23
20:9 [o]Ps 3:7; 17:6
21:1 [p]Ps 59:16-17
21:2 [q]Ps 37:4
21:3 [r]2Sa 12:30

[a] 9 Or *save! / O King, answer*

21:4 [s]Ps 61:5-6; 91:16; 133:3

length of days, for ever and ever.[s]

21:5 [t]Ps 18:50

5 Through the victories[t] you gave, his
glory is great;
you have bestowed on him splendor
and majesty.

21:6 [u]Ps 43:4 [v]1Ch 17:27

6 Surely you have granted him eternal
blessings
and made him glad with the joy[u] of
your presence.[v]
7 For the king trusts in the LORD;
through the unfailing love of the Most
High
he will not be shaken.

21:8 [w]Isa 10:10

8 Your hand will lay hold[w] on all your
enemies;
your right hand will seize your foes.
9 At the time of your appearing
you will make them like a fiery
furnace.
In his wrath the LORD will swallow them
up,

21:9 [x]Ps 50:3; La 2:2; Mal 4:1

and his fire will consume them.[x]
10 You will destroy their descendants from
the earth,

21:10 [y]Dt 28:18; Ps 37:28

their posterity from mankind.[y]

21:11 [z]Ps 2:1 [a]Ps 10:2

11 Though they plot evil[z] against you
and devise wicked schemes,[a] they
cannot succeed;

21:12 [b]Ps 7:12-13; 18:40

12 for you will make them turn their backs[b]
when you aim at them with drawn
bow.

13 Be exalted, O LORD, in your strength;
we will sing and praise your might.

Psalm 22

For the director of music. To ⌊the tune of⌋ "The Doe of the Morning." A psalm of David.

22:1 [c]Mt 27:46*; Mk 15:34* [d]Ps 10:1

1 My God, my God, why have you
forsaken me?[c]
Why are you so far[d] from saving me,
so far from the words of my groaning?
2 O my God, I cry out by day, but you do
not answer,

22:2 [e]Ps 42:3

by night,[e] and am not silent.

22:3 [f]Ps 99:9 [g]Dt 10:21

3 Yet you are enthroned as the Holy One;[f]
you are the praise[g] of Israel.[a]
4 In you our fathers put their trust;
they trusted and you delivered them.
5 They cried to you and were saved;
in you they trusted and were not

22:5 [h]Isa 49:23

disappointed.[h]

22:6 [i]Job 25:6; Isa 41:14 [j]Ps 31:11 [k]Isa 49:7; 53:3

6 But I am a worm[i] and not a man,
scorned by men[j] and despised[k] by the
people.
7 All who see me mock me;

[a] 3 Or *Yet you are holy, / enthroned on the praises of Israel*

Dark Night of the Soul

PS 22:1

Part of the human condition is to encounter moments or seasons when God seems far, far away. We all experience the "dark night of the soul" at some point in our lives, and it is black indeed. How fortunate we are, however, to have a record of people who have felt exactly the same way, with the added benefit of knowing how their stories turn out. Many times David feels utterly dejected, forsaken by God and overwhelmed by life. But time after time God's mercy and faithfulness prevail; all of David's laments are eventually swallowed up in praise and thanksgiving. Our ultimate encouragement comes from Jesus Christ himself, whose last words on earth (other than the final, triumphant cry, "It is finished") are these same words of despair. In bearing our sin, he is crushed and momentarily separated from his Father. But his glorious destiny is sure, as is ours. Never again will anything or anyone have the power to separate us from God's love (Ro 8:31-39).

Our Maker Is With Us

PS 22:6–11

Like Job before him, David is scorned and mocked by those who watch him suffer. If the God he serves is so sovereign and powerful, where is this God now? When God doesn't seem to show up when David needs him most, does David conclude, as his faithless mockers do, that his trust has been in vain? Or does he choose instead to affirm the evidence of God's faithfulness to him over the long haul? David affirms here that God has always been in charge of his life—even before birth, even as a small child. His confidence is renewed: If anyone can help him now, it can only be God. Who but our Maker has been with us during every moment of our existence, preserving us and planning our lives, even before we knew anything about him (Ps 139:15–16)? Surely the God who has always been intimately present can be trusted to be faithful now and throughout eternity.

they hurl insults,[l] shaking their
heads:[m]
8 "He trusts in the LORD;
let the LORD rescue him.[n]
Let him deliver him,
since he delights[o] in him."

9 Yet you brought me out of the womb;[p]
you made me trust in you
even at my mother's breast.
10 From birth[q] I was cast upon you;
from my mother's womb you have
been my God.
11 Do not be far from me,
for trouble is near
and there is no one to help.[r]

12 Many bulls[s] surround me;
strong bulls of Bashan[t] encircle me.
13 Roaring lions[u] tearing their prey
open their mouths wide[v] against me.
14 I am poured out like water,
and all my bones are out of joint.[w]
My heart has turned to wax;
it has melted away[x] within me.
15 My strength is dried up like a potsherd,
and my tongue sticks to the roof of
my mouth;[y]
you lay me[a] in the dust[z] of death.
16 Dogs[a] have surrounded me;
a band of evil men has encircled me,
they have pierced[b][b] my hands and my
feet.
17 I can count all my bones;
people stare[c] and gloat over me.[d]
18 They divide my garments among them
and cast lots[e] for my clothing.

19 But you, O LORD, be not far off;
O my Strength, come quickly[f] to help
me.
20 Deliver my life from the sword,
my precious life[g] from the power of
the dogs.
21 Rescue me from the mouth of the lions;
save[c] me from the horns of the wild
oxen.

22 I will declare your name to my brothers;
in the congregation I will praise you.[h]
23 You who fear the LORD, praise him![i]
All you descendants of Jacob, honor
him!
Revere him,[j] all you descendants of
Israel!
24 For he has not despised or disdained
the suffering of the afflicted one;
he has not hidden his face[k] from him
but has listened to his cry for help.[l]

22:7 [l]Mt 27:39,44 [m]Mk 15:29
22:8 [n]Ps 91:14 [o]Mt 27:43
22:9 [p]Ps 71:6
22:10 [q]Isa 46:3
22:11 [r]Ps 72:12
22:12 [s]Ps 68:30 [t]Dt 32:14
22:13 [u]Ps 17:12 [v]Ps 35:21
22:14 [w]Ps 31:10 [x]Job 30:16; Da 5:6
22:15 [y]Ps 38:10; Jn 19:28 [z]Ps 104:29
22:16 [a]Ps 59:6 [b]Isa 53:5; Zec 12:10; Jn 19:34
22:17 [c]Lk 23:35 [d]Lk 23:27
22:18 [e]Mt 27:35*; Lk 23:34; Jn 19:24*
22:19 [f]Ps 70:5
22:20 [g]Ps 35:17
22:22 [h]Heb 2:12*
22:23 [i]Ps 86:12; 135:19 [j]Ps 33:8
22:24 [k]Ps 69:17 [l]Heb 5:7

[a] 15 Or / *I am laid* [b] 16 Some Hebrew manuscripts, Septuagint and Syriac; most Hebrew manuscripts / *like the lion,* [c] 21 Or / *you have heard*

22:25 [m]Ps 35:18 [n]Ecc 5:4

25 From you comes the theme of my praise
in the great assembly;[m]
before those who fear you[a] will I
fulfill my vows.[n]

22:26 [o]Ps 107:9 [p]Ps 40:16

26 The poor will eat[o] and be satisfied;
they who seek the LORD will praise
him—[p]
may your hearts live forever!

22:27 [q]Ps 2:8 [r]Ps 86:9

27 All the ends of the earth[q]
will remember and turn to the
LORD,
and all the families of the nations
will bow down before him,[r]

22:28 [s]Ps 47:7-8

28 for dominion belongs to the LORD[s]
and he rules over the nations.

22:29 [t]Ps 45:12 [u]Isa 26:19

29 All the rich[t] of the earth will feast and
worship;
all who go down to the dust[u] will
kneel before him—
those who cannot keep themselves
alive.

22:30 [v]Ps 102:28

30 Posterity[v] will serve him;
future generations will be told about
the Lord.

22:31 [w]Ps 78:6

31 They will proclaim his righteousness
to a people yet unborn[w]—
for he has done it.

Psalm 23

A psalm of David.

23:1 [x]Isa 40:11; Jn 10:11; 1Pe 2:25 [y]Php 4:19

1 The LORD is my shepherd,[x] I shall not be
in want.[y]
2 He makes me lie down in green
pastures,

23:2 [z]Eze 34:14; Rev 7:17

he leads me beside quiet waters,[z]
3 he restores my soul.[a]
He guides me in paths of
righteousness[b]
for his name's sake.

23:3 [a]Ps 19:7 [b]Ps 5:8; 85:13

4 Even though I walk
through the valley of the shadow of
death,[b][c]

23:4 [c]Job 10:21-22 [d]Ps 3:6; 27:1 [e]Isa 43:2

I will fear no evil,[d]
for you are with me;[e]
your rod and your staff,
they comfort me.

5 You prepare a table before me
in the presence of my enemies.

23:5 [f]Ps 92:10 [g]Ps 16:5

You anoint my head with oil;[f]
my cup[g] overflows.
6 Surely goodness and love will follow me
all the days of my life,
and I will dwell in the house of the LORD
forever.

[a]25 Hebrew *him* [b]4 Or *through the darkest valley*

Restoring the Soul

PS 23:2-3

The imagery in this snippet of the most known and beloved of all psalms could not be more soothing for women today. How often do we wish for nothing more than to "lie down," to enjoy peace and quiet, to rest and revive in the midst of our harried lives? If we think it is God who demands superhuman effort and impossible schedules, we are wrong. God wants us to move steadily forward on our journey through life (Ps 84:5-7), but rest and refreshment along the way are an integral part of his plan. He *makes* us lie down—in verdant, nourishing "pastures" of his presence. He does not leave us in the desert, but leads us directly to the banks of quiet pools of refreshment—if only we will follow. When we cooperate with the rejuvenating rhythms he has ordained for us each day, we will be physically, emotionally and spiritually restored so that we can renew our pilgrimage and follow him for eternity.

Psalm 24

Of David. A psalm.

1 The earth is the LORD's,[h] and everything in it,
the world, and all who live in it;[i]
2 for he founded it upon the seas
and established it upon the waters.

3 Who may ascend the hill[j] of the LORD?
Who may stand in his holy place?[k]
4 He who has clean hands[l] and a pure heart,[m]
who does not lift up his soul to an idol
or swear by what is false.[a]
5 He will receive blessing from the LORD
and vindication from God his Savior.
6 Such is the generation of those who seek him,
who seek your face,[n] O God of Jacob.[b]
Selah

7 Lift up your heads, O you gates;[o]
be lifted up, you ancient doors,
that the King of glory[p] may come in.
8 Who is this King of glory?
The LORD strong and mighty,
the LORD mighty in battle.[q]
9 Lift up your heads, O you gates;
lift them up, you ancient doors,
that the King of glory may come in.
10 Who is he, this King of glory?
The LORD Almighty—
he is the King of glory. *Selah*

Psalm 25[c]

Of David.

1 To you, O LORD, I lift up my soul;[r]
2 in you I trust,[s] O my God.
Do not let me be put to shame,
nor let my enemies triumph over me.
3 No one whose hope is in you
will ever be put to shame,[t]
but they will be put to shame
who are treacherous without excuse.

4 Show me your ways, O LORD,
teach me your paths;[u]
5 guide me in your truth and teach me,
for you are God my Savior,
and my hope is in you all day long.
6 Remember, O LORD, your great mercy and love,[v]
for they are from of old.
7 Remember not the sins of my youth[w]
and my rebellious ways;
according to your love[x] remember me,

24:1 [h]Ex 9:29; Job 41:11; Ps 89:11 [i]1Co 10:26*
24:3 [j]Ps 2:6 [k]Ps 15:1; 65:4
24:4 [l]Job 17:9 [m]Mt 5:8
24:6 [n]Ps 27:8
24:7 [o]Isa 26:2 [p]Ps 97:6; 1Co 2:8
24:8 [q]Ps 76:3-6
25:1 [r]Ps 86:4
25:2 [s]Ps 41:11
25:3 [t]Isa 49:23
25:4 [u]Ex 33:13
25:6 [v]Ps 103:17; Isa 63:7,15
25:7 [w]Job 13:26; Jer 3:25 [x]Ps 51:1

[In Psalm 23] David points out that he had to be led by the Lord to the still waters. I wonder if David had to be led because he was naturally drawn to the excitement of the rushing water? It certainly is that way with us. Left to our own *agendas*, we either run at breakneck speed right past the pasture, enamored with our frenzied pace, or sit in parched misery. The Shepherd, who understands our naiveté and our humanity . . . intervenes on our behalf to guide us with a strong hand onto a quiet path and into a calmer faith.

—Patsy Clairmont

[a] 4 Or *swear falsely* [b] 6 Two Hebrew manuscripts and Syriac (see also Septuagint); most Hebrew manuscripts *face, Jacob* [c] This psalm is an acrostic poem, the verses of which begin with the successive letters of the Hebrew alphabet.

for you are good, O LORD.
8 Good and upright[y] is the LORD;
therefore he instructs[z] sinners in his ways.
9 He guides[a] the humble in what is right
and teaches them[b] his way.
10 All the ways of the LORD are loving and faithful[c]
for those who keep the demands of his covenant.[d]
11 For the sake of your name,[e] O LORD,
forgive my iniquity, though it is great.
12 Who, then, is the man that fears the LORD?
He will instruct him in the way[f] chosen for him.
13 He will spend his days in prosperity,[g]
and his descendants will inherit the land.[h]
14 The LORD confides[i] in those who fear him;
he makes his covenant known[j] to them.
15 My eyes are ever on the LORD,[k]
for only he will release my feet from the snare.

16 Turn to me[l] and be gracious to me,
for I am lonely and afflicted.
17 The troubles of my heart have multiplied;
free me from my anguish.[m]
18 Look upon my affliction and my distress[n]
and take away all my sins.
19 See how my enemies[o] have increased
and how fiercely they hate me!
20 Guard my life[p] and rescue me;
let me not be put to shame,
for I take refuge in you.
21 May integrity[q] and uprightness protect me,
because my hope is in you.

22 Redeem Israel,[r] O God,
from all their troubles!

Psalm 26

Of David.

1 Vindicate me, O LORD,
for I have led a blameless life;[s]
I have trusted[t] in the LORD
without wavering.[u]
2 Test me,[v] O LORD, and try me,
examine my heart and my mind;[w]
3 for your love is ever before me,
and I walk continually[x] in your truth.
4 I do not sit[y] with deceitful men,
nor do I consort with hypocrites;
5 I abhor[z] the assembly of evildoers

25:8 [y]Ps 92:15 [z]Ps 32:8
25:9 [a]Ps 23:3 [b]Ps 27:11
25:10 [c]Ps 40:11 [d]Ps 103:18
25:11 [e]Ps 31:3; 79:9
25:12 [f]Ps 37:23
25:13 [g]Pr 19:23 [h]Ps 37:11
25:14 [i]Pr 3:32 [j]Jn 7:17
25:15 [k]Ps 141:8
25:16 [l]Ps 69:16
25:17 [m]Ps 107:6
25:18 [n]2Sa 16:12
25:19 [o]Ps 3:1
25:20 [p]Ps 86:2
25:21 [q]Ps 41:12
25:22 [r]Ps 130:8
26:1 [s]Ps 7:8; Pr 20:7 [t]Ps 28:7 [u]2Ki 20:3; Heb 10:23
26:2 [v]Ps 17:3 [w]Ps 7:9
26:3 [x]2Ki 20:3
26:4 [y]Ps 1:1
26:5 [z]Ps 31:6; 139:21

God's Name

PS 25:11

In Hebrew society, names carried rich meaning. In naming a person, place or thing, much thought was put into how to encapsulate attributes and characteristics in one label, a name. Thus, the Jews of David's day ascribed great importance to the "name" of God; they knew his name is a manifestation of his character, and he will do whatever is necessary to maintain the reputation associated with his name.

When David appeals for forgiveness, he isn't confident of it only because he knows God loves him. Rather, he knows that God has repeatedly promised to be faithful to his people, no matter how wayward they are at times, and that God's character is such that he cannot break a promise. God's reputation is at stake in the way he deals with his people. In Isaiah 48:9 God assures us that he will not cut us off in spite of our sin—not because we deserve his mercy, but for his own sake, that all creation will trust in his name and praise him.

One Thing I Ask

PS 27:4

Every day we are presented with myriad options for how we will spend our time and where we will put our focus. Our decisions reveal what we most value. As Jesus tells his friend Martha in Luke 10:41–42, there are so many things that demand our attention and energy, and certainly many are important. But "only one thing is needed"—a vital, constant fellowship with the Lord. David understands this, and it becomes his deepest desire. More than anything else he longs to be conscious of his Father's presence, to worship God's incomparable character, and to be guided moment to moment by his perfect wisdom. Such goals will always be the "one thing" that gives our lives meaning. Memorize David's heartfelt words and make them your prayer to the Lord today.

and refuse to sit with the wicked.
6 I wash my hands in innocence,[a]
and go about your altar, O LORD,
7 proclaiming aloud your praise
and telling of all your wonderful deeds.[b]
8 I love[c] the house where you live, O LORD,
the place where your glory dwells.
9 Do not take away my soul along with sinners,
my life with bloodthirsty men,[d]
10 in whose hands are wicked schemes,
whose right hands are full of bribes.[e]
11 But I lead a blameless life;
redeem me[f] and be merciful to me.
12 My feet stand on level ground;[g]
in the great assembly[h] I will praise the LORD.

Psalm 27

Of David.

1 The LORD is my light[i] and my salvation[j]—
whom shall I fear?
The LORD is the stronghold of my life—
of whom shall I be afraid?[k]
2 When evil men advance against me
to devour my flesh,[a]
when my enemies and my foes attack me,
they will stumble and fall.[l]
3 Though an army besiege me,
my heart will not fear;[m]
though war break out against me,
even then will I be confident.[n]
4 One thing[o] I ask of the LORD,
this is what I seek:
that I may dwell in the house of the LORD
all the days of my life,[p]
to gaze upon the beauty of the LORD
and to seek him in his temple.
5 For in the day of trouble
he will keep me safe in his dwelling;
he will hide me[q] in the shelter of his tabernacle
and set me high upon a rock.[r]
6 Then my head will be exalted[s]
above the enemies who surround me;
at his tabernacle will I sacrifice[t] with shouts of joy;
I will sing and make music to the LORD.
7 Hear my voice when I call, O LORD;
be merciful to me and answer me.[u]
8 My heart says of you, "Seek his[b] face!"

26:6 [a]Ps 73:13
26:7 [b]Ps 9:1
26:8 [c]Ps 27:4
26:9 [d]Ps 28:3
26:10 [e]1Sa 8:3
26:11 [f]Ps 69:18
26:12 [g]Ps 27:11; 40:2 [h]Ps 22:22
27:1 [i]Isa 60:19 [j]Ex 15:2 [k]Ps 118:6
27:2 [l]Ps 9:3; 14:4
27:3 [m]Ps 3:6 [n]Job 4:6
27:4 [o]Ps 90:17 [p]Ps 23:6; 26:8
27:5 [q]Ps 17:8; 31:20 [r]Ps 40:2
27:6 [s]Ps 3:3 [t]Ps 107:22
27:7 [u]Ps 13:3

[a] 2 Or *to slander me* [b] 8 Or *To you, O my heart, he has said, "Seek my*

Your face, LORD, I will seek.
27:9 [v]Ps 69:17 9 Do not hide your face[v] from me,
do not turn your servant away in anger;
you have been my helper.
Do not reject me or forsake me,
O God my Savior.
10 Though my father and mother forsake me,
the LORD will receive me.
11 Teach me your way, O LORD;
27:11 [w]Ps 5:8; 25:4; 86:11 lead me in a straight path[w]
because of my oppressors.
12 Do not turn me over to the desire of my foes,
27:12 [x]Mt 26:60; Ac 9:1 for false witnesses[x] rise up against me,
breathing out violence.

27:13 [y]Ps 31:19 [z]Jer 11:19; Eze 26:20 13 I am still confident of this:
I will see the goodness of the LORD[y]
in the land of the living.[z]
14 Wait[a] for the LORD;
27:14 [a]Ps 40:1 be strong and take heart
and wait for the LORD.

Psalm 28

Of David.

1 To you I call, O LORD my Rock;
28:1 [b]Ps 83:1 [c]Ps 88:4 do not turn a deaf ear to me.
For if you remain silent,[b]
I will be like those who have gone down to the pit.[c]
28:2 [d]Ps 138:2; 140:6 [e]Ps 5:7 2 Hear my cry for mercy[d]
as I call to you for help,
as I lift up my hands
toward your Most Holy Place.[e]

3 Do not drag me away with the wicked,
with those who do evil,
28:3 [f]Ps 12:2; Ps 26:9; Jer 9:8 who speak cordially with their neighbors
but harbor malice in their hearts.[f]
4 Repay them for their deeds
and for their evil work;
repay them for what their hands have
28:4 [g]2Ti 4:14; Rev 22:12 [h]Rev 18:6 done[g]
and bring back upon them what they deserve.[h]
5 Since they show no regard for the works of the LORD
28:5 [i]Isa 5:12 and what his hands have done,[i]
he will tear them down
and never build them up again.

6 Praise be to the LORD,
28:7 [j]Ps 18:1 [k]Ps 13:5 [l]Ps 40:3; 69:30 for he has heard my cry for mercy.
7 The LORD is my strength[j] and my shield;
my heart trusts[k] in him, and I am helped.
My heart leaps for joy
and I will give thanks to him in song.[l]
8 The LORD is the strength of his people,

Waiting

PS 27:13–14

When David is not talking directly to God in his psalms, he is usually talking to himself—speaking out affirmations of his faith so that his heart and soul can embrace the truths he's hidden away in his mind. When our circumstances appear bleak, when God answers our prayers with "wait," we can follow David's example. He knows from his own past experience that God will bring about his own perfect will in his own perfect time; reminding himself of this when times are tough gives him confidence and joy. When we are feeling uncertain or impatient about God's activity in our lives or in the life of someone we love, we can repeat David's affirmation and gain strength. If we meditate on the words of this psalm, we can give thanks to God. When we place our hope in him, we will never be disappointed.

I wonder if sometimes we gather for worship but leave too soon. We are encouraged by the volume of praise; it lifts our spirits, allowing us to lay aside our burdens for a while. But if we would wait, there is more. It is God's response to the worship of his children. An "unutterable beatitude" of blessing . . . We love to tell God how much we adore him, how he has changed our lives. We revel in the tidal waves of song, but then "time's up" and we move on. If we would just wait on God, let the silence fall, we could be gifted with the response of a loving Father to his children. In that holy moment we could receive a beatitude, a blessing that no human words could begin to frame.

—Sheila Walsh

a fortress of salvation for his anointed
one.[m]
9 Save your people and bless your
inheritance;[n]
be their shepherd[o] and carry them[p]
forever.

Psalm 29

A psalm of David.

1 Ascribe to the LORD,[q] O mighty ones,
ascribe to the LORD glory[r] and
strength.
2 Ascribe to the LORD the glory due his
name;
worship the LORD in the splendor of
his[a] holiness.[s]

3 The voice[t] of the LORD is over the waters;
the God of glory thunders,[u]
the LORD thunders over the mighty
waters.
4 The voice of the LORD is powerful;[v]
the voice of the LORD is majestic.
5 The voice of the LORD breaks the cedars;
the LORD breaks in pieces the cedars
of Lebanon.[w]
6 He makes Lebanon skip[x] like a calf,
Sirion[b][y] like a young wild ox.
7 The voice of the LORD strikes
with flashes of lightning.
8 The voice of the LORD shakes the desert;
the LORD shakes the Desert of
Kadesh.[z]
9 The voice of the LORD twists the oaks[c]
and strips the forests bare.
And in his temple all cry, "Glory!"[a]

10 The LORD sits[d] enthroned over the flood;[b]
the LORD is enthroned as King forever.[c]
11 The LORD gives strength to his people;[d]
the LORD blesses his people with
peace.[e]

Psalm 30

A psalm. A song. For the dedication of the temple.[e]
Of David.

1 I will exalt you, O LORD,
for you lifted me out of the depths
and did not let my enemies gloat over
me.[f]
2 O LORD my God, I called to you for help[g]
and you healed me.[h]
3 O LORD, you brought me up from the
grave[f];
you spared me from going down into
the pit.[i]

28:8 [m]Ps 20:6
28:9 [n]Dt 9:29; Ezr 1:4 [o]Isa 40:11 [p]Dt 1:31; 32:11
29:1 [q]1Ch 16:28 [r]Ps 96:7-9
29:2 [s]2Ch 20:21
29:3 [t]Job 37:5 [u]Ps 18:13
29:4 [v]Ps 68:33
29:5 [w]Jdg 9:15
29:6 [x]Ps 114:4 [y]Dt 3:9
29:8 [z]Nu 13:26
29:9 [a]Ps 26:8
29:10 [b]Ge 6:17 [c]Ps 10:16
29:11 [d]Ps 28:8 [e]Ps 37:11
30:1 [f]Ps 25:2; 28:9
30:2 [g]Ps 88:13 [h]Ps 6:2
30:3 [i]Ps 28:1; 86:13

[a] 2 Or *LORD with the splendor of* [b] 6 That is, Mount Hermon [c] 9 Or *LORD makes the deer give birth* [d] 10 Or *sat* [e] Title: Or *palace* [f] 3 Hebrew *Sheol*

30:4 [j]Ps 149:1 [k]Ps 97:12

4 Sing to the LORD, you saints[j] of his;
praise his holy name.[k]

30:5 [l]Ps 103:9 [m]2Co 4:17

5 For his anger[l] lasts only a moment,
but his favor lasts a lifetime;
weeping may remain for a night,
but rejoicing comes in the morning.[m]

6 When I felt secure, I said,
"I will never be shaken."
7 O LORD, when you favored me,
you made my mountain[a] stand firm;

30:7 [n]Dt 31:17; Ps 104:29

but when you hid your face,[n]
I was dismayed.

8 To you, O LORD, I called;
to the Lord I cried for mercy:

30:9 [o]Ps 6:5

9 "What gain is there in my destruction,[b]
in my going down into the pit?
Will the dust praise you?
Will it proclaim your faithfulness?[o]
10 Hear, O LORD, and be merciful to me;
O LORD, be my help."

11 You turned my wailing into dancing;
you removed my sackcloth and

30:11 [p]Ps 4:7; Jer 31:4,13

clothed me with joy,[p]
12 that my heart may sing to you and not
be silent.
O LORD my God, I will give you

30:12 [q]Ps 16:9 [r]Ps 44:8

thanks[q] forever.[r]

Psalm 31

For the director of music. A psalm of David.

1 In you, O LORD, I have taken refuge;
let me never be put to shame;
deliver me in your righteousness.
2 Turn your ear to me,
come quickly to my rescue;

31:2 [s]Ps 18:2

be my rock of refuge,[s]
a strong fortress to save me.

31:3 [t]Ps 18:2 [u]Ps 23:3

3 Since you are my rock and my fortress,[t]
for the sake of your name[u] lead and
guide me.

31:4 [v]Ps 25:15

4 Free me from the trap that is set for me,
for you are my refuge.[v]

31:5 [w]Lk 23:46; Ac 7:59

5 Into your hands I commit my spirit;[w]
redeem me, O LORD, the God of truth.

31:6 [x]Jnh 2:8

6 I hate those who cling to worthless idols;
I trust in the LORD.[x]

31:7 [y]Ps 90:14 [z]Ps 10:14; Jn 10:27

7 I will be glad and rejoice in your love,
for you saw my affliction[y]
and knew the anguish[z] of my soul.

31:8 [a]Dt 32:30

8 You have not handed me over[a] to the
enemy
but have set my feet in a spacious
place.

31:9 [b]Ps 6:7

9 Be merciful to me, O LORD, for I am in
distress;
my eyes grow weak with sorrow,[b]

[a] 7 Or *hill country* [b] 9 Or *there if I am silenced*

He Never Stops Loving

PS 30:5

Not many of us in this fallen world will experience a human relationship that remains steadfast and loving from the moment we are born to the moment we die. Friends come and go; not all parents love unconditionally; children sometimes break our hearts; even many spouses don't stick around for better and *for worse. What a profound comfort it is to know that our Creator, the lover of our souls, will never stop loving us.*

David knows that truth personally and experientially and expresses it in this song. God will be angry when we sin, and he will discipline us for our good, but he will never hold a grudge against us. His essential nature is gracious, not wrathful. Therefore, we can rejoice that no matter what the state of our circumstances or relationships, we are utterly secure in God's everlasting, unfailing love (Ps 36:7–8).

Into His Hands

PS 31:15

David experiences a great deal of distress in his life, including running from his enemies and being betrayed by his friends. With so many earthly forces against him, it is understandable if he feels like he is at the mercy of those who have it in for him. But David doesn't give that kind of power to anyone. At times he laments his fate bitterly, but he always returns to the truth he believes to the core of his being: God is in charge of his life, and God can be trusted. How often do we turn over a concern to God, only to take it back into our own hands? Like David, may we never hold on for long but commit our circumstances, our concerns and our very souls to God's care. Moment by moment David's words, like Christ's, can be our own: "Into your hands I commit my spirit" (Ps 31:5; Lk 23:46).

my soul and my body with grief.
10 My life is consumed by anguish
and my years by groaning;[c]
my strength fails because of my affliction,[a]
and my bones grow weak.[d]
11 Because of all my enemies,
I am the utter contempt of my neighbors;[e]
I am a dread to my friends—
those who see me on the street flee from me.
12 I am forgotten by them as though I were dead;[f]
I have become like broken pottery.
13 For I hear the slander of many;
there is terror on every side;[g]
they conspire against me
and plot to take my life.[h]

14 But I trust[i] in you, O LORD;
I say, "You are my God."
15 My times[j] are in your hands;
deliver me from my enemies
and from those who pursue me.
16 Let your face shine[k] on your servant;
save me in your unfailing love.
17 Let me not be put to shame,[l] O LORD,
for I have cried out to you;
but let the wicked be put to shame
and lie silent[m] in the grave.[b]
18 Let their lying lips[n] be silenced,
for with pride and contempt
they speak arrogantly[o] against the righteous.

19 How great is your goodness,[p]
which you have stored up for those who fear you,
which you bestow in the sight of men[q]
on those who take refuge in you.
20 In the shelter of your presence you hide[r] them
from the intrigues of men;[s]
in your dwelling you keep them safe
from accusing tongues.

21 Praise be to the LORD,
for he showed his wonderful love[t] to me
when I was in a besieged city.[u]
22 In my alarm[v] I said,
"I am cut off from your sight!"
Yet you heard my cry[w] for mercy
when I called to you for help.

23 Love the LORD, all his saints![x]
The LORD preserves the faithful,[y]
but the proud he pays back[z] in full.
24 Be strong and take heart,[a]
all you who hope in the LORD.

31:10 [c]Ps 13:2 [d]Ps 38:3; 39:11
31:11 [e]Job 19:13; Ps 38:11; 64:8; Isa 53:4
31:12 [f]Ps 88:4
31:13 [g]Jer 20:3,10; La 2:22 [h]Mt 27:1
31:14 [i]Ps 140:6
31:15 [j]Job 24:1; Ps 143:9
31:16 [k]Nu 6:25; Ps 4:6
31:17 [l]Ps 25:2-3 [m]Ps 115:17
31:18 [n]Ps 120:2 [o]Ps 94:4
31:19 [p]Ro 11:22 [q]Isa 64:4
31:20 [r]Ps 27:5 [s]Job 5:21
31:21 [t]Ps 17:7 [u]1Sa 23:7
31:22 [v]Ps 116:11 [w]La 3:54
31:23 [x]Ps 34:9 [y]Ps 145:20 [z]Ps 94:2
31:24 [a]Ps 27:14

[a] 10 Or *guilt* [b] 17 Hebrew *Sheol*

Psalm 32

Of David. A *maskil*.[a]

1 Blessed is he
32:1 [b]Ps 85:2 whose transgressions are forgiven,
whose sins are covered.[b]
2 Blessed is the man
32:2 [c]Ro 4:7-8*; 2Co 5:19 [d]Jn 1:47 whose sin the LORD does not count
against him[c]
and in whose spirit is no deceit.[d]

3 When I kept silent,
32:3 [e]Ps 31:10 my bones wasted away[e]
through my groaning all day long.
4 For day and night
32:4 [f]Job 33:7 your hand was heavy[f] upon me;
my strength was sapped
as in the heat of summer. *Selah*
5 Then I acknowledged my sin to you
and did not cover up my iniquity.
32:5 [g]Pr 28:13 [h]Ps 103:12 [i]Lev 26:40 I said, "I will confess[g]
my transgressions[h] to the LORD"—
and you forgave
the guilt of my sin.[i] *Selah*

6 Therefore let everyone who is godly
32:6 [j]Ps 69:13; Isa 55:6 [k]Isa 43:2 pray to you
while you may be found;[j]
surely when the mighty waters rise,
they will not reach him.[k]
7 You are my hiding place;
32:7 [l]Ps 9:9 [m]Ex 15:1 you will protect me from trouble[l]
and surround me with songs of
deliverance.[m] *Selah*

32:8 [n]Ps 25:8 [o]Ps 33:18 8 I will instruct[n] you and teach you in the
way you should go;
I will counsel you and watch over[o]
you.
9 Do not be like the horse or the mule,
which have no understanding
32:9 [p]Pr 26:3 but must be controlled by bit and bridle[p]
or they will not come to you.
32:10 [q]Ro 2:9 [r]Pr 16:20 10 Many are the woes of the wicked,[q]
but the LORD's unfailing love
surrounds the man who trusts[r] in
him.

32:11 [s]Ps 64:10 11 Rejoice in the LORD[s] and be glad, you
righteous;
sing, all you who are upright in heart!

Psalm 33

33:1 [t]Ps 147:1 [u]Ps 32:11 1 Sing joyfully to the LORD, you righteous;
it is fitting[t] for the upright[u] to praise
him.
2 Praise the LORD with the harp;
33:2 [v]Ps 92:3 make music to him on the ten-
stringed lyre.[v]
33:3 [w]Ps 96:1 3 Sing to him a new song;[w]

[a] Title: Probably a literary or musical term

A New Song

PS 33:3

Our God is a master at creating something from nothing—beauty from ashes, brand new from old. He loves new beginnings, and he promises that one day he will make everything new (Isa 65:17; Rev 21:5). As beings in his image, we too can create new realities, fresh starts, unique melodies. As a tribute to your God who makes all things new, create something new to honor him. Make up a song to sing or play. Write him an original psalm of praise. Create a simple work of art just for him—a drawing, a painting or a garden. And then thank him for his greatest new invention of all time: the new covenant that offers salvation to needy human souls (Heb 9:11-15).

A Mere Command

PS 33:6

In a poetic summary of the creation account in Genesis, the psalmist pays tribute to the power and sovereignty of God. All it takes for the whole grand creation to burst into existence is a mere command from the Almighty. With one word, one breath, he can bring forth anything in his awesome imagination. And what we can see and comprehend, Job reminds us, is "but the outer fringe of his works" (Job 26:14). What we can actually see and hear is but a whisper of the divine. "Who then can understand the thunder of his power?" (Job 26:14). If the Almighty God can speak the whole cosmos into existence with a breath, then surely he is creative and powerful enough to be the Lord of everything that concerns us.

play skillfully, and shout for joy.

4 For the word of the LORD is right[x] and true;
he is faithful in all he does.
5 The LORD loves righteousness and justice;[y]
the earth is full of his unfailing love.[z]

6 By the word[a] of the LORD were the heavens made,
their starry host by the breath of his mouth.
7 He gathers the waters of the sea into jars[a];
he puts the deep into storehouses.
8 Let all the earth fear the LORD;
let all the people of the world revere him.[b]
9 For he spoke, and it came to be;
he commanded,[c] and it stood firm.
10 The LORD foils the plans of the nations;[d]
he thwarts the purposes of the peoples.
11 But the plans of the LORD stand firm forever,
the purposes[e] of his heart through all generations.

12 Blessed is the nation whose God is the LORD,[f]
the people he chose[g] for his inheritance.
13 From heaven the LORD looks down
and sees all mankind;[h]
14 from his dwelling place[i] he watches
all who live on earth—
15 he who forms[j] the hearts of all,
who considers everything they do.[k]
16 No king is saved by the size of his army;[l]
no warrior escapes by his great strength.
17 A horse[m] is a vain hope for deliverance;
despite all its great strength it cannot save.
18 But the eyes[n] of the LORD are on those who fear him,
on those whose hope is in his unfailing love,[o]
19 to deliver them from death
and keep them alive in famine.[p]

20 We wait[q] in hope for the LORD;
he is our help and our shield.
21 In him our hearts rejoice,[r]
for we trust in his holy name.
22 May your unfailing love rest upon us, O LORD,
even as we put our hope in you.

33:4 [x]Ps 19:8
33:5 [y]Ps 11:7 [z]Ps 119:64
33:6 [a]Heb 11:3
33:8 [b]Ps 67:7; 96:9
33:9 [c]Ge 1:3; Ps 148:5
33:10 [d]Isa 8:10
33:11 [e]Job 23:13
33:12 [f]Ps 144:15 [g]Ex 19:5; Dt 7:6
33:13 [h]Job 28:24; Ps 11:4
33:14 [i]1Ki 8:39
33:15 [j]Job 10:8 [k]Jer 32:19
33:16 [l]Ps 44:6
33:17 [m]Ps 20:7; Pr 21:31
33:18 [n]Job 36:7; Ps 34:15 [o]Ps 147:11
33:19 [p]Job 5:20
33:20 [q]Ps 130:6
33:21 [r]Zec 10:7; Jn 16:22

[a] 7 Or *sea as into a heap*

Psalm 34[a]

Of David. When he pretended to be insane before Abimelech, who drove him away, and he left.

1 I will extol the LORD at all times;[s]
his praise will always be on my lips.
2 My soul will boast[t] in the LORD;
let the afflicted hear and rejoice.[u]
3 Glorify the LORD with me;
let us exalt[v] his name together.

4 I sought the LORD,[w] and he answered me;
he delivered me from all my fears.
5 Those who look to him are radiant;[x]
their faces are never covered with shame.[y]
6 This poor man called, and the LORD heard him;
he saved him out of all his troubles.
7 The angel of the LORD[z] encamps around those who fear him,
and he delivers them.

8 Taste and see that the LORD is good;[a]
blessed is the man who takes refuge[b] in him.
9 Fear the LORD, you his saints,
for those who fear him lack nothing.[c]
10 The lions may grow weak and hungry,
but those who seek the LORD lack no good thing.[d]

11 Come, my children, listen to me;
I will teach you[e] the fear of the LORD.
12 Whoever of you loves life[f]
and desires to see many good days,
13 keep your tongue from evil
and your lips from speaking lies.[g]
14 Turn from evil and do good;[h]
seek peace[i] and pursue it.

15 The eyes of the LORD[j] are on the righteous[k]
and his ears are attentive to their cry;
16 the face of the LORD is against[l] those who do evil,[m]
to cut off the memory[n] of them from the earth.
17 The righteous cry out, and the LORD hears[o] them;
he delivers them from all their troubles.
18 The LORD is close[p] to the brokenhearted[q]
and saves those who are crushed in spirit.

19 A righteous man may have many troubles,[r]
but the LORD delivers him from them all;[s]

34:1 [s]Ps 71:6; Eph 5:20
34:2 [t]Jer 9:24; 1Co 1:31 [u]Ps 119:74
34:3 [v]Lk 1:46
34:4 [w]Mt 7:7
34:5 [x]Ps 36:9 [y]Ps 25:3
34:7 [z]2Ki 6:17; Da 6:22
34:8 [a]1Pe 2:3 [b]Ps 2:12
34:9 [c]Ps 23:1
34:10 [d]Ps 84:11
34:11 [e]Ps 32:8
34:12 [f]1Pe 3:10
34:13 [g]1Pe 2:22
34:14 [h]Ps 37:27 [i]Heb 12:14
34:15 [j]Ps 33:18 [k]Job 36:7
34:16 [l]Lev 17:10; Jer 44:11 [m]1Pe 3:10-12* [n]Pr 10:7
34:17 [o]Ps 145:19
34:18 [p]Ps 145:18 [q]Isa 57:15
34:19 [r]ver 17 [s]ver 4,6; Pr 24:16

[a] This psalm is an acrostic poem, the verses of which begin with the successive letters of the Hebrew alphabet.

No Shame

PS 34:5

"Shame on you!" How many times have we had those sentiments aimed our way or said those belittling words to ourselves? Sometimes we behave badly and we need to make amends, but often the shame we feel is illegitimate and toxic. We want goodness from someone and he or she lets us down—and we feel ashamed. Someone doesn't like us—and we feel ashamed. In relationship with God, there is never shame. Christ has dealt once and for all with our guilt, and now we can interact with our Father without shame. In fact, when we look to him and depend on him, our lives will reflect the brilliance of his love because all "those who look to him are radiant" (Ps 34:5).

The Language of War

PS 35:1-3

The language of war may be somewhat foreign, even distasteful, to most women. *We may prefer to reflect on the gentler attributes and activities of God rather than on the battles and violence of Israel's history. But understanding God our warrior gives a much needed and glorious dimension to our experience of him. A righteous warrior defends the defenseless, stands firm for justice, even gives his or her life in the pursuit of peace. We all engage in personal battles; our world is literally a battleground between the forces of good and evil. What encouragement and confidence we can have when we realize we have a God who fights* for *us. He defends our cause and preserves our life (Ps 119:154); "there is no one like [him] to help the powerless against the mighty" (2Ch 14:11). We do no rely on our own strength or power or ability; we trust only in his might and his certain victory on our behalf (1Sa 17:47).*

20 he protects all his bones,
not one of them will be broken.[t] — **34:20** [t]Jn 19:36*
21 Evil will slay the wicked;[u]
the foes of the righteous will be condemned. — **34:21** [u]Ps 94:23
22 The LORD redeems[v] his servants;
no one will be condemned who takes refuge in him. — **34:22** [v]1Ki 1:29; Ps 71:23

Psalm 35

Of David.

1 Contend, O LORD, with those who contend with me;
fight[w] against those who fight against me. — **35:1** [w]Ps 43:1
2 Take up shield and buckler;
arise[x] and come to my aid. — **35:2** [x]Ps 62:2
3 Brandish spear and javelin[a]
against those who pursue me.
Say to my soul,
"I am your salvation."

4 May those who seek my life
be disgraced[y] and put to shame; — **35:4** [y]Ps 70:2
may those who plot my ruin
be turned back in dismay.
5 May they be like chaff[z] before the wind, — **35:5** [z]Job 21:18; Ps 1:4; Isa 29:5
with the angel of the LORD driving them away;
6 may their path be dark and slippery,
with the angel of the LORD pursuing them.
7 Since they hid their net for me without cause
and without cause dug a pit for me,
8 may ruin overtake them by surprise—[a] — **35:8** [a]1Th 5:3
may the net they hid entangle them, — [b]Ps 9:15
may they fall into the pit,[b] to their ruin.
9 Then my soul will rejoice[c] in the LORD — **35:9** [c]Lk 1:47
and delight in his salvation.[d] — [d]Isa 61:10
10 My whole being will exclaim,
"Who is like you,[e] O LORD? — **35:10** [e]Ex 15:11
You rescue the poor from those too strong[f] for them, — [f]Ps 18:17 [g]Ps 37:14
the poor and needy[g] from those who rob them."

11 Ruthless witnesses[h] come forward; — **35:11** [h]Ps 27:12
they question me on things I know nothing about.
12 They repay me evil for good[i] — **35:12** [i]Jn 10:32
and leave my soul forlorn.
13 Yet when they were ill, I put on sackcloth
and humbled myself with fasting.[j] — **35:13** [j]Job 30:25; Ps 69:10
When my prayers returned to me unanswered,
14 I went about mourning
as though for my friend or brother.

[a] 3 Or *and block the way*

I bowed my head in grief
as though weeping for my mother.
15 But when I stumbled, they gathered in glee;
attackers gathered against me when I was unaware.

35:15 [k]Job 30:1,8

They slandered[k] me without ceasing.
16 Like the ungodly they maliciously mocked[a];

35:16 [l]Job 16:9; La 2:16

they gnashed their teeth[l] at me.
17 O Lord, how long[m] will you look on?

35:17 [m]Hab 1:13 [n]Ps 22:20

Rescue my life from their ravages,
my precious life[n] from these lions.
18 I will give you thanks in the great assembly;[o]

35:18 [o]Ps 22:25 [p]Ps 22:22

among throngs of people I will praise you.[p]

19 Let not those gloat over me
who are my enemies without cause;
let not those who hate me without reason[q]

35:19 [q]Ps 38:19; 69:4; Jn 15:25* [r]Ps 13:4; Pr 6:13

maliciously wink the eye.[r]
20 They do not speak peaceably,
but devise false accusations
against those who live quietly in the land.
21 They gape[s] at me and say, "Aha! Aha![t]

35:21 [s]Ps 22:13 [t]Ps 40:15

With our own eyes we have seen it."

22 O LORD, you have seen[u] this; be not silent.

35:22 [u]Ex 3:7 [v]Ps 10:1; 28:1

Do not be far[v] from me, O Lord.
23 Awake,[w] and rise to my defense!

35:23 [w]Ps 44:23

Contend for me, my God and Lord.
24 Vindicate me in your righteousness,
O LORD my God;
do not let them gloat over me.
25 Do not let them think, "Aha, just what we wanted!"
or say, "We have swallowed him up."[x]

35:25 [x]La 2:16

26 May all who gloat over my distress
be put to shame[y] and confusion;

35:26 [y]Ps 40:14; 109:29 [z]Ps 38:16

may all who exalt themselves over me[z]
be clothed with shame and disgrace.
27 May those who delight in my vindication[a]

35:27 [a]Ps 9:4 [b]Ps 32:11 [c]Ps 40:16; 147:11

shout for joy[b] and gladness;
may they always say, "The LORD be exalted,
who delights[c] in the well-being of his servant."
28 My tongue will speak of your righteousness[d]

35:28 [d]Ps 51:14

and of your praises all day long.

[a] *16* Septuagint; Hebrew may mean *ungodly circle of mockers.*

Vengeance Is God's

PS 35:19-26

Being falsely accused or held up to public ridicule is an experience no one takes lightly. Even worse is to feel that someone is out to get us, almost "lying in wait" for us to make a wrong move so he or she can lord it over us. David experiences this dreadful reality. But he does not try to defend himself, stand up to his adversaries or clear his name. Rather, he turns the whole situation over to the Lord, trusting that God's righteousness will prevail and his enemies will eventually be put to shame. As believers we are charged to trust in God's vindication rather than exact vengeance on our own (Ro 12:19).

The Comforts of Home

PS 36:7–9

Refuge, abundance, delight, refreshment and light. All the comforts of home! In this psalm, David describes in fervent terms God's estate, David's spiritual "home." As God's children, we find there everything we could possibly need—and more. We never have to settle for crumbs from the King's table; we're welcome to feast *on his abundant provision. We need no money, no status, no resources of our own in order to fill up on the "richest of fare" (Isa 55:1–2). Jesus himself is the fountain of living water, and those who quench their spiritual thirst with him will never thirst again and never die (Jn 4:7–14).*

Psalm 36

For the director of music. Of David the servant of the LORD.

1 An oracle is within my heart
concerning the sinfulness of the wicked:[a]
There is no fear of God
before his eyes.[e]
2 For in his own eyes he flatters himself
too much to detect or hate his sin.
3 The words of his mouth[f] are wicked and deceitful;
he has ceased to be wise[g] and to do good.[h]
4 Even on his bed he plots evil;[i]
he commits himself to a sinful course[j]
and does not reject what is wrong.[k]

5 Your love, O LORD, reaches to the heavens,
your faithfulness to the skies.
6 Your righteousness is like the mighty mountains,
your justice like the great deep.[l]
O LORD, you preserve both man and beast.
7 How priceless is your unfailing love!
Both high and low among men
find[b] refuge in the shadow of your wings.[m]
8 They feast on the abundance of your house;[n]
you give them drink from your river[o] of delights.
9 For with you is the fountain of life;[p]
in your light[q] we see light.
10 Continue your love to those who know you,
your righteousness to the upright in heart.
11 May the foot of the proud not come against me,
nor the hand of the wicked drive me away.
12 See how the evildoers lie fallen—
thrown down, not able to rise![r]

Psalm 37[c]

Of David.

1 Do not fret because of evil men
or be envious[s] of those who do wrong;[t]
2 for like the grass they will soon wither,
like green plants they will soon die away.[u]

36:1 [e]Ro 3:18*
36:3 [f]Ps 10:7 [g]Ps 94:8 [h]Jer 4:22
36:4 [i]Pr 4:16; Mic 2:1 [j]Isa 65:2 [k]Ps 52:3; Ro 12:9
36:6 [l]Job 11:8; Ps 77:19; Ro 11:33
36:7 [m]Ru 2:12; Ps 17:8
36:8 [n]Ps 65:4 [o]Job 20:17; Rev 22:1
36:9 [p]Jer 2:13 [q]1Pe 2:9
36:12 [r]Ps 140:10
37:1 [s]Pr 23:17-18 [t]Ps 73:3
37:2 [u]Ps 90:6

[a] 1 Or *heart: / Sin proceeds from the wicked.* [b] 7 Or *love, O God! / Men find*; or *love! / Both heavenly beings and men / find* [c] This psalm is an acrostic poem, the stanzas of which begin with the successive letters of the Hebrew alphabet.

Week 14

God's River of Delights

Rivers fascinate us. Each has its own special qualities: the speed of the current, the color of the water, the pattern of the ripples formed by the water curling around a rock or a log. Some rivers project a sense of excitement and power by their fast-moving currents; others peacefully and calmly meander along their way.

Exodus 4:9, Daniel 7:10 and Revelation 22:1 mention unusual rivers (of blood, of fire and of life). But what is the "river of delights" of Psalm 36:5-9? Look for clues about what is flowing in this river of delights: love (Ps 36:5), preservation (Ps 36:6), refuge (Ps 36:7), abundance (Ps 36:8) and life (Ps 36:9). God's love is boundless, reaching to the heavens (Ps 36:5); it is priceless and unfailing (Ps 36:7). God is offering you a drink—a taste of all that he desires to lavish on you.

You can drink from God's river of delights as you answer the following questions:

- What are your general and specific blessings as a child of God (Ac 14:17; Eph 1:3-14)?
- What emotional needs do you have that God can fill (Jn 14:27; 1Pe 1:8)?
- How great is God's love for you (Ro 5:8; 8:38-39)? What is your response to this sort of love?
- Will God's love for you ever diminish (Ps 136:1-26; Isa 54:10)? How does that make you feel?
- Name one way you've experienced God's blessing in the past week. In the past year.
- Try to visualize what your life would be like if God didn't love and care for you. Be specific. What would be the same? What would be different?

God's river of delights is flowing out to you. God wants to satisfy your needs and your desires. Is something holding you back from receiving what he gives—past or present sin, a bad relationship that has soured you, a lackluster relationship with Jesus? Perhaps you've experienced God's river of delights but have wandered away. Come back and drink deeply of all God has for you.

Enjoying God THROUGH the Word

Read Ezekiel 47:1-12 (pages 1425-1426). Notice that Ezekiel enters the water where it is ankle-deep. As he is led farther into the water, it becomes knee-deep, then waist-deep, then deep enough to swim in—"a river that no one could cross" (Eze 47:5). When God invites you into his presence, you enter slowly; you experience his glory, but it does not overwhelm you. As your trust in God and desire for more of him increase, he leads you deeper into his glory until you are surrounded by his presence. Imagine that you are Ezekiel, being led into ever-deepening water. Are you afraid? Full of anticipation? Hesitant? Remember God's promise: "When you pass through the waters, I will be with you" (Isa 43:2).

Enjoying God THROUGH Experience

Write down and reflect on one or two of the Scripture verses from this study that seem to speak personally to you. Carry them with you for a few days so that they become familiar and appreciated. As you pray this week, meditate on God's love for you. As you quiet yourself in awareness of his presence, give the Holy Spirit freedom to speak to your heart. Step into his river of delights, even if only up to your ankles. When you delight in God, your deepest desires are met in him. When you delight in God, he delights in you (Ps 147:11).

Go to page 901 for your next weekly study.

Delighting in God

PS 37:4

David expresses in this psalm a deep truth that he's discovered: If he finds his life's delight in the Lord, all his desires are fulfilled. To delight in someone is to find joy in their presence, to welcome their unique qualities and to express pleasure in their company. When we make the Lord the object of our delight, spending time in his presence and reveling in his character, our deepest heart's desires gradually align themselves with his own. We discover that what we want is what he wants—and how delighted he is to honor our heart's desire by keeping us in the center of his will! As we believe in him and grow to love him more day by day, we will be "filled with an inexpressible and glorious joy," for we will be enjoying the ultimate prize of our faith, the ultimate desire of our hearts: the eternal salvation of our souls (1Pe 1:8-9).

3 Trust in the LORD and do good;
dwell in the land[v] and enjoy safe pasture.[w]
4 Delight[x] yourself in the LORD
and he will give you the desires of your heart.

5 Commit your way to the LORD;
trust in him[y] and he will do this:
6 He will make your righteousness[z] shine like the dawn,[a]
the justice of your cause like the noonday sun.

7 Be still[b] before the LORD and wait patiently[c] for him;
do not fret when men succeed in their ways,
when they carry out their wicked schemes.

8 Refrain from anger[d] and turn from wrath;
do not fret—it leads only to evil.
9 For evil men will be cut off,
but those who hope in the LORD will inherit the land.[e]
10 A little while, and the wicked will be no more;[f]
though you look for them, they will not be found.
11 But the meek will inherit the land[g]
and enjoy great peace.

12 The wicked plot against the righteous
and gnash their teeth[h] at them;
13 but the Lord laughs at the wicked,
for he knows their day is coming.[i]
14 The wicked draw the sword
and bend the bow[j]
to bring down the poor and needy,[k]
to slay those whose ways are upright.
15 But their swords will pierce their own hearts,[l]
and their bows will be broken.

16 Better the little that the righteous have
than the wealth[m] of many wicked;
17 for the power of the wicked will be broken,[n]
but the LORD upholds the righteous.

18 The days of the blameless are known to the LORD,[o]
and their inheritance will endure forever.
19 In times of disaster they will not wither;
in days of famine they will enjoy plenty.
20 But the wicked will perish:
The LORD's enemies will be like the beauty of the fields,
they will vanish—vanish like smoke.[p]

37:3 [v]Dt 30:20 [w]Isa 40:11; Jn 10:9
37:4 [x]Isa 58:14
37:5 [y]Ps 4:5; Ps 55:22; Pr 16:3; 1Pe 5:7
37:6 [z]Mic 7:9 [a]Job 11:17
37:7 [b]Ps 62:5; La 3:26 [c]Ps 40:1
37:8 [d]Eph 4:31; Col 3:8
37:9 [e]Isa 57:13; 60:21
37:10 [f]Job 7:10; 24:24
37:11 [g]Mt 5:5
37:12 [h]Ps 35:16
37:13 [i]1Sa 26:10; Ps 2:4
37:14 [j]Ps 11:2 [k]Ps 35:10
37:15 [l]Ps 9:16
37:16 [m]Pr 15:16
37:17 [n]Job 38:15; Ps 10:15
37:18 [o]Ps 1:6
37:20 [p]Ps 102:3

[21] The wicked borrow and do not repay,
but the righteous give generously;[q]
[22] those the LORD blesses will inherit the land,
but those he curses[r] will be cut off.

[23] If the LORD delights[s] in a man's way,
he makes his steps firm;[t]
[24] though he stumble, he will not fall,[u]
for the LORD upholds[v] him with his hand.

[25] I was young and now I am old,
yet I have never seen the righteous forsaken[w]
or their children begging bread.
[26] They are always generous and lend freely;
their children will be blessed.[x]

[27] Turn from evil and do good;[y]
then you will dwell in the land forever.
[28] For the LORD loves the just
and will not forsake his faithful ones.
They will be protected forever,
but the offspring of the wicked will be cut off;[z]
[29] the righteous will inherit the land[a]
and dwell in it forever.

[30] The mouth of the righteous man utters wisdom,
and his tongue speaks what is just.
[31] The law of his God is in his heart;[b]
his feet do not slip.[c]

[32] The wicked lie in wait[d] for the righteous,
seeking their very lives;
[33] but the LORD will not leave them in their power
or let them be condemned when brought to trial.[e]

[34] Wait for the LORD[f]
and keep his way.
He will exalt you to inherit the land;
when the wicked are cut off, you will see[g] it.

[35] I have seen a wicked and ruthless man
flourishing[h] like a green tree in its native soil,
[36] but he soon passed away and was no more;
though I looked for him, he could not be found.[i]

[37] Consider the blameless, observe the upright;
there is a future[a] for the man of peace.[j]

37:21 [q]Ps 112:5
37:22 [r]Job 5:3; Pr 3:33
37:23 [s]Ps 147:11 [t]1Sa 2:9
37:24 [u]Pr 24:16 [v]Ps 145:14; 147:6
37:25 [w]Heb 13:5
37:26 [x]Ps 147:13
37:27 [y]Ps 34:14
37:28 [z]Ps 21:10; Isa 14:20
37:29 [a]ver 9; Pr 2:21
37:31 [b]Dt 6:6; Ps 40:8; Isa 51:7 [c]ver 23
37:32 [d]Ps 10:8
37:33 [e]Ps 109:31; 2Pe 2:9
37:34 [f]Ps 27:14 [g]Ps 52:6
37:35 [h]Job 5:3
37:36 [i]Job 20:5
37:37 [j]Isa 57:1-2

[a] 37 Or *there will be posterity*

In my opinion, there are no coincidences. When we make Jesus Christ the Lord of our lives, the Lord orders everything that happens to us. Psalm 37:23-24 says that when the Lord approves of a person's path, he makes that person's steps firm; even if the person stumbles, he won't fall because the Lord upholds him.

—Thelma Wells

Divine Chastisement

PS 38:3-4

God has been known to punish sinful people with physical illness (see what happens to King Uzziah in 2Ch 26:16-20). We don't know if David's illness is a result of divine chastisement, but David clearly thinks it is. His estrangement from God causes him enormous suffering, "too heavy to bear" (Ps 38:4). In spite of his physical and mental anguish, however, David does not withdraw from the Lord and hide in a corner. Rather, he keeps his side of the communication going, pouring out his heart to God and trusting him in spite of his circumstances. The final words of this penitential psalm reveal David's faith: "Be not far from me, O my God . . . help me, O Lord my Savior" (Ps 38:21-22, emphasis added). Even though David feels rebuked and pierced by God, he still knows that he belongs to the Lord and can depend on him.

38 But all sinners will be destroyed;
the future[a] of the wicked will be cut off.[k]
39 The salvation[l] of the righteous comes from the LORD;
he is their stronghold in time of trouble.[m]
40 The LORD helps[n] them and delivers[o] them;
he delivers them from the wicked and saves them,
because they take refuge in him.

Psalm 38

A psalm of David. A petition.

1 O LORD, do not rebuke me in your anger
or discipline me in your wrath.[p]
2 For your arrows[q] have pierced me,
and your hand has come down upon me.
3 Because of your wrath there is no health in my body;
my bones[r] have no soundness
because of my sin.
4 My guilt has overwhelmed me
like a burden too heavy to bear.[s]

5 My wounds fester and are loathsome
because of my sinful folly.[t]
6 I am bowed down and brought very low;
all day long I go about mourning.[u]
7 My back is filled with searing pain;[v]
there is no health in my body.
8 I am feeble and utterly crushed;
I groan[w] in anguish of heart.

9 All my longings lie open before you, O Lord;
my sighing[x] is not hidden from you.
10 My heart pounds, my strength fails[y] me;
even the light has gone from my eyes.[z]
11 My friends and companions avoid me
because of my wounds;[a]
my neighbors stay far away.
12 Those who seek my life set their traps,[b]
those who would harm me talk of my ruin;[c]
all day long they plot deception.[d]

13 I am like a deaf man, who cannot hear,
like a mute, who cannot open his mouth;
14 I have become like a man who does not hear,
whose mouth can offer no reply.

37:38 [k]Ps 1:4
37:39 [l]Ps 3:8 [m]Ps 9:9
37:40 [n]1Ch 5:20 [o]Isa 31:5
38:1 [p]Ps 6:1
38:2 [q]Job 6:4; Ps 32:4
38:3 [r]Ps 6:2; Isa 1:6
38:4 [s]Ezr 9:6
38:5 [t]Ps 69:5
38:6 [u]Job 30:28; Ps 35:14; 42:9
38:7 [v]Ps 102:3
38:8 [w]Ps 22:1
38:9 [x]Job 3:24; Ps 6:6; 10:17
38:10 [y]Ps 31:10 [z]Ps 6:7
38:11 [a]Ps 31:11
38:12 [b]Ps 140:5 [c]Ps 35:4; 54:3 [d]Ps 35:20

[a] 38 Or *posterity*

38:15 [e]Ps 39:7 [f]Ps 17:6

15 I wait[e] for you, O LORD;
you will answer,[f] O Lord my God.

38:16 [g]Ps 35:26 [h]Ps 13:4

16 For I said, "Do not let them gloat[g]
or exalt themselves over me when my
foot slips."[h]

17 For I am about to fall,
and my pain is ever with me.

38:18 [i]Ps 32:5

18 I confess my iniquity;[i]
I am troubled by my sin.

38:19 [j]Ps 18:17 [k]Ps 35:19

19 Many are those who are my vigorous
enemies;[j]
those who hate me without reason[k]
are numerous.

38:20 [l]Ps 35:12; 1Jn 3:12

20 Those who repay my good with evil[l]
slander me when I pursue what is
good.

38:21 [m]Ps 35:22

21 O LORD, do not forsake me;
be not far[m] from me, O my God.

38:22 [n]Ps 40:13 [o]Ps 27:1

22 Come quickly to help me,[n]
O Lord my Savior.[o]

Psalm 39

For the director of music. For Jeduthun. A psalm of David.

39:1 [p]1Ki 2:4 [q]Job 2:10; Jas 3:2

1 I said, "I will watch my ways[p]
and keep my tongue from sin;[q]
I will put a muzzle on my mouth
as long as the wicked are in my
presence."

39:2 [r]Ps 38:13

2 But when I was silent[r] and still,
not even saying anything good,
my anguish increased.

3 My heart grew hot within me,
and as I meditated, the fire burned;
then I spoke with my tongue:

39:4 [s]Ps 90:12 [t]Ps 103:14

4 "Show me, O LORD, my life's end
and the number of my days;[s]
let me know how fleeting is my life.[t]

39:5 [u]Ps 89:45 [v]Ps 62:9

5 You have made my days[u] a mere
handbreadth;
the span of my years is as nothing
before you.
Each man's life is but a breath.[v] *Selah*

39:6 [w]1Pe 1:24 [x]Ps 127:2 [y]Lk 12:20

6 Man is a mere phantom[w] as he goes to
and fro:
He bustles about, but only in vain;[x]
he heaps up wealth, not knowing
who will get it.[y]

39:7 [z]Ps 38:15

7 "But now, Lord, what do I look for?
My hope is in you.[z]

39:8 [a]Ps 51:9 [b]Ps 44:13

8 Save me[a] from all my transgressions;[b]
do not make me the scorn of fools.

39:9 [c]Job 2:10

9 I was silent; I would not open my
mouth,[c]
for you are the one who has done
this.

10 Remove your scourge from me;

Muzzle My Mouth

PS 39:1

David is fearful of what he might say. He's been disciplined by God (Ps 39:10–11) and doesn't want to say anything in front of the unbelieving that might dishonor God. So he keeps silent.

Many of us were told when we were young, "If you can't say something nice, don't say anything at all." This familiar parental directive may actually be a Biblical principle! Jesus tells his followers that they are the light of the world and that when their redeemed character shines brightly, unbelievers will recognize God in them and give him praise (Mt 5:14–16). This is the power of Christian witness. But the opposite can also be true: We tarnish God's name by speaking foolishly or cruelly. "Reckless words pierce like a sword," Solomon warns (Pr 12:18). How crucial it is that we guard our tongues when we're in the company of those who don't know the Lord. They will judge our God by our behavior!

I am overcome by the blow of your
hand.[d]
[11] You rebuke[e] and discipline men for their
sin;
you consume their wealth like a
moth[f]—
each man is but a breath. *Selah*

[12] "Hear my prayer, O LORD,
listen to my cry for help;
be not deaf to my weeping.
For I dwell with you as an alien,[g]
a stranger,[h] as all my fathers were.
[13] Look away from me, that I may rejoice
again
before I depart and am no more."[i]

Psalm 40

For the director of music. Of David. A psalm.

[1] I waited patiently[j] for the LORD;
he turned to me and heard my cry.[k]
[2] He lifted me out of the slimy pit,
out of the mud and mire;[l]
he set my feet on a rock[m]
and gave me a firm place to stand.
[3] He put a new song[n] in my mouth,
a hymn of praise to our God.
Many will see and fear
and put their trust in the LORD.

[4] Blessed is the man[o]
who makes the LORD his trust,[p]
who does not look to the proud,
to those who turn aside to false
gods.[a]
[5] Many, O LORD my God,
are the wonders[q] you have done.
The things you planned for us
no one can recount[r] to you;
were I to speak and tell of them,
they would be too many to declare.
[6] Sacrifice and offering you did not
desire,[s]
but my ears you have pierced[b,c];
burnt offerings[t] and sin offerings
you did not require.
[7] Then I said, "Here I am, I have come—
it is written about me in the scroll.[d]
[8] I desire to do your will,[u] O my God;
your law is within my heart."[v]

[9] I proclaim righteousness in the great
assembly;[w]
I do not seal my lips,
as you know,[x] O LORD.
[10] I do not hide your righteousness in my
heart;

[a] 4 Or *to falsehood* [b] 6 Hebrew; Septuagint *but a body you have prepared for me* (see also Symmachus and Theodotion) [c] 6 Or *opened* [d] 7 Or *come / with the scroll written for me*

39:10 [d] Job 9:34; Ps 32:4
39:11 [e] 2Pe 2:16 [f] Job 13:28
39:12 [g] 1Pe 2:11 [h] Heb 11:13
39:13 [i] Job 10:21; 14:10
40:1 [j] Ps 27:14 [k] Ps 34:15
40:2 [l] Ps 69:14 [m] Ps 27:5
40:3 [n] Ps 33:3
40:4 [o] Ps 34:8 [p] Ps 84:12
40:5 [q] Ps 136:4 [r] Ps 139:18; Isa 55:8
40:6 [s] 1Sa 15:22; Am 5:22 [t] Isa 1:11
40:8 [u] Jn 4:34 [v] Ps 37:31
40:9 [w] Ps 22:25 [x] Jos 22:22; Ps 119:13

Pierced Ears

PS 40:6

In Hebrew culture an indentured servant was required to work faithfully for his master for six years. In the seventh year, he was allowed to go free; but if he had a good master whom he had grown to love, then he could choose to stay in his master's household. In that case, the servant's ear was pierced, marking him as belonging to his master for life (Ex 21:2–6; see the note on Dt 15:17, page 299).

David's use of this image reveals his heart attitude toward his God (Ps 40:8). Not only has he voluntarily chosen to serve the Lord for life, but the ears that are pierced as a mark of ownership are also wide open to his master's direction. When we belong to the Lord, our delight is to be taught by him and to do his will (Isa 50:4–5).

I speak of your faithfulness[y] and
salvation.
I do not conceal your love and your
truth
40:10 [y]Ps 89:1 [z]Ac 20:20 from the great assembly.[z]
11 Do not withhold your mercy from me,
O LORD;
40:11 [a]Pr 20:28 [b]Ps 43:3 may your love[a] and your truth[b]
always protect me.
40:12 [c]Ps 116:3 [d]Ps 38:4 [e]Ps 69:4 [f]Ps 73:26 12 For troubles[c] without number surround
me;
my sins have overtaken me, and I
cannot see.[d]
They are more than the hairs of my
head,[e]
and my heart fails[f] within me.
13 Be pleased, O LORD, to save me;
40:13 [g]Ps 70:1 O LORD, come quickly to help me.[g]
14 May all who seek to take my life
be put to shame and confusion;
40:14 [h]Ps 35:4 may all who desire my ruin[h]
be turned back in disgrace.
15 May those who say to me, "Aha! Aha!"
be appalled at their own shame.
16 But may all who seek you
rejoice and be glad in you;
may those who love your salvation
always say,
40:16 [i]Ps 35:27 "The LORD be exalted!"[i]

17 Yet I am poor and needy;
may the Lord think of me.
40:17 [j]Ps 70:5 You are my help and my deliverer;
O my God, do not delay.[j]

Psalm 41

For the director of music. A psalm of David.

41:1 [k]Ps 82:3-4; Pr 14:21 1 Blessed is he who has regard for the
weak;[k]
the LORD delivers him in times of
trouble.
2 The LORD will protect him and preserve
his life;
41:2 [l]Ps 37:22 [m]Ps 27:12 he will bless him in the land[l]
and not surrender him to the desire of
his foes.[m]
3 The LORD will sustain him on his
sickbed
and restore him from his bed of
illness.
41:4 [n]Ps 6:2 [o]Ps 51:4 4 I said, "O LORD, have mercy[n] on me;
heal me, for I have sinned[o] against
you."
5 My enemies say of me in malice,
41:5 [p]Ps 38:12 "When will he die and his name
perish?[p]"
41:6 [q]Ps 12:2 [r]Pr 26:24 6 Whenever one comes to see me,
he speaks falsely,[q] while his heart
gathers slander;[r]

Betrayed by Friends

PS 41:5-9

Most of us at one time or another have felt like everyone is against us—like there is no one we can trust. It's a terrible feeling to sense that the people around us are two-faced, talking behind our backs, wishing the worst for us. The ultimate hurt is to be betrayed by someone we consider a true friend. In describing this painful experience in his life, David foreshadows what Jesus Christ will endure: slander and malice from enemies, betrayal by close friends (Jn 13:18–38). Like David, Jesus is deeply troubled and hurt by this, yet the Lord's gracious forgiveness extends even to those who betray him unto death (Lk 23:33–34).

Thirsting for God

PS 42:1-5

This psalm was probably written by an exiled Levite who was recalling his former religious fervor, leading the people in worship at the temple. He was now not only exiled from the temple, but also from his home and nation and the presence of God there.

When the dry winds of life sap our spiritual lives, when we feel oppressed, lost, far from God's presence, we can use the psalmist's words as our prayer. Our souls thirst for God. The psalmist reminds us that we need not remain lost in the dark, nor must we find our way home by our own resources. We can pray that our loving Father will "send forth" the divine light and truth we need to guide us (Ps 43:3). The Lord is *our light; we do not need to be afraid (Ps 27:1). And all the truth and wisdom we need is within us through the indwelling of the Holy Spirit (1Jn 2:27). How comforting it is to know that no matter how lost and dejected we may feel at times, God's faithfulness ensures that we* will *find our way back into the fullness of his presence. We* will *yet praise him (Ps 42:5)!*

then he goes out and spreads it abroad.

7 All my enemies whisper together[s]
against me;
they imagine the worst for me, saying,
8 "A vile disease has beset him;
he will never get up from the place
where he lies."
9 Even my close friend,[t] whom I trusted,
he who shared my bread,
has lifted up his heel against me.[u]
10 But you, O LORD, have mercy on me;
raise me up,[v] that I may repay them.
11 I know that you are pleased with me,[w]
for my enemy does not triumph over
me.[x]
12 In my integrity you uphold me[y]
and set me in your presence forever.[z]
13 Praise be to the LORD, the God of Israel,[a]
from everlasting to everlasting.
Amen and Amen.[b]

41:7 [s]Ps 56:5; 71:10-11
41:9 [t]2Sa 15:12; Ps 55:12 [u]Job 19:19; Ps 55:20; Mt 26:23; Jn 13:18*
41:10 [v]Ps 3:3
41:11 [w]Ps 147:11 [x]Ps 25:2
41:12 [y]Ps 37:17 [z]Job 36:7
41:13 [a]Ps 72:18 [b]Ps 89:52; 106:48

BOOK II

Psalms 42–72

Psalm 42[a]

For the director of music. A *maskil*[b] of the Sons of Korah.

1 As the deer pants for streams of water,
so my soul pants[c] for you, O God.
2 My soul thirsts[d] for God, for the living
God.[e]
When can I go[f] and meet with God?
3 My tears[g] have been my food
day and night,
while men say to me all day long,
"Where is your God?"[h]
4 These things I remember
as I pour out my soul:
how I used to go with the multitude,
leading the procession to the house of
God,[i]
with shouts of joy and thanksgiving[j]
among the festive throng.
5 Why are you downcast,[k] O my soul?
Why so disturbed within me?
Put your hope in God,[l]
for I will yet praise him,
my Savior[m] and 6my God.
My[c] soul is downcast within me;
therefore I will remember you
from the land of the Jordan,

42:1 [c]Ps 119:131
42:2 [d]Ps 63:1 [e]Jer 10:10 [f]Ps 43:4
42:3 [g]Ps 80:5 [h]Ps 79:10
42:4 [i]Isa 30:29 [j]Ps 100:4
42:5 [k]Ps 38:6; 77:3 [l]La 3:24 [m]Ps 44:3

[a] In many Hebrew manuscripts Psalms 42 and 43 constitute one psalm. [b] Title: Probably a literary or musical term [c] *5,6* A few Hebrew manuscripts, Septuagint and Syriac; most Hebrew manuscripts *praise him for his saving help. / 6O my God, my*

Week 15

Spiritual Depression

It's a foggy place, a place of dark uncertainty. You slide further and further down, but you're helpless to stop the descent. You'd love to climb up and out of this pit, but at this point just stopping the fall would be enough. You look at the past and see what you've lost, but you don't know how to get it back. You're discouraged, heavy, hopeless and alone. You wonder where God is. Why is he so far away? If you could just hear his voice . . .

Can you relate? Then you've experienced a form of spiritual depression. Psalm 42 expresses the cry of the psalmist's heart in the midst of spiritual depression.

What does the psalmist remember (Ps 42:4,6)? Recall your past experiences of God's presence. Was your spiritual condition then due to your great achievements for God? What produced those special times?

What place does praise have in the midst of spiritual depression (Ps 42:5)?

How is God's sovereignty involved in your struggle (Ps 42:7)? Do you think he has allowed this experience? Why? Though the experience may be difficult, even terrifying, what has God promised you (Jos 1:9)?

How honest is the psalmist with God (Ps 42:9–10)? Can you be that honest with God? Why or why not? Can you identify who the "foes" are in your life?

What is the psalmist's final assertion (Ps 42:11)?

Enjoying God THROUGH the Word

Read 1 Kings 19:1–18 (page 562). Elijah has experienced the supernatural power of God at Mount Carmel (1Ki 18:16–40). But now Jezebel is after him. So Elijah runs for his life. He is emotionally, physically and spiritually drained. At this point Elijah says, "I have had enough" (1Ki 19:4). Then God steps in. Elijah thinks he is the only God-fearing person left (1Ki 19:14), but actually there are 7,000 godly people in Israel (1Ki 19:18).

Is it possible that your spiritual depression is due to a lack of faith? Is your perception accurate? Perhaps you are simply exhausted and you need refreshing. You need to say, "I've had enough." God will step in, like he did with Elijah, to provide what you need (Php 4:19; 1Pe 5:7).

Enjoying God THROUGH Experience

In a time of prayer, confess your need for God. Be honest with him. The Holy Spirit can bring hope and peace to your heart. Your spiritual condition may be caused by physical fatigue. Have you confused your commitment to God with your commitment to work for him? Or your spiritual condition may be caused by emotional fatigue. Have you been through a difficult situation in your family or your church? Or your spiritual condition may be the result of an intense spiritual battle. Have your resources been drained by spiritual warfare?

In every aspect of your life, God's grace is sufficient (2Co 12:9). This is a deep truth that you need to put to use again and again in your heart and in your life. It is when you are struggling, when you are weak, that God is strong in you (1Co 1:27–31). Your weakness is God's cue to step in and help, not hurt. "A bruised reed he will not break, and a smoldering wick he will not snuff out" (Isa 42:3).

Go to page 921 for your next weekly study.

Clara Tear Williams wrote the moving words to this hymn in response to a request from a friend who needed it for a book he was writing.

Satisfied

All my life I had a longing
For a drink from some clear spring,
That I hoped would quench the burning
Of the thirst I felt within.

Hallelujah! I have found Him
Whom my soul so long has craved!
Jesus satisfies my longings,
Through His blood I now am saved.

Feeding on the husks around me,
Till my strength was almost gone,
Longed my soul for something better,
Only still to hunger on.

Poor I was, and sought for riches,
Something that would satisfy,
But the dust I gathered round me
Only mocked my soul's sad cry.

Well of water, ever springing,
Bread of life so rich and free,
Untold wealth that never faileth,
My Redeemer is to me.

—Clara Tear Williams

the heights of Hermon—from Mount
Mizar.
7 Deep calls to deep
in the roar of your waterfalls;
all your waves and breakers
have swept over me.[n]

8 By day the LORD directs his love,[o]
at night[p] his song[q] is with me—
a prayer to the God of my life.

9 I say to God my Rock,
"Why have you forgotten me?
Why must I go about mourning,[r]
oppressed by the enemy?"
10 My bones suffer mortal agony
as my foes taunt me,
saying to me all day long,
"Where is your God?"

11 Why are you downcast, O my soul?
Why so disturbed within me?
Put your hope in God,
for I will yet praise him,
my Savior and my God.[s]

42:7 [n]Ps 88:7; Jnh 2:3
42:8 [o]Ps 57:3 [p]Job 35:10 [q]Ps 63:6; 149:5
42:9 [r]Ps 38:6
42:11 [s]Ps 43:5

Psalm 43[a]

1 Vindicate me, O God,
and plead my cause[t] against an
ungodly nation;
rescue me from deceitful and wicked
men.[u]
2 You are God my stronghold.
Why have you rejected[v] me?
Why must I go about mourning,
oppressed by the enemy?[w]
3 Send forth your light[x] and your truth,
let them guide me;
let them bring me to your holy
mountain,[y]
to the place where you dwell.[z]
4 Then will I go to the altar[a] of God,
to God, my joy and my delight.
I will praise you with the harp,[b]
O God, my God.

5 Why are you downcast, O my soul?
Why so disturbed within me?
Put your hope in God,
for I will yet praise him,
my Savior and my God.[c]

43:1 [t]1Sa 24:15; Ps 26:1; 35:1 [u]Ps 5:6
43:2 [v]Ps 44:9 [w]Ps 42:9
43:3 [x]Ps 36:9 [y]Ps 42:4 [z]Ps 84:1
43:4 [a]Ps 26:6 [b]Ps 33:2
43:5 [c]Ps 42:6

Psalm 44

For the director of music. Of the Sons of Korah.
A *maskil*.[b]

1 We have heard with our ears, O God;
our fathers have told us[d]
what you did in their days,
in days long ago.

44:1 [d]Ex 12:26; Ps 78:3

[a] In many Hebrew manuscripts Psalms 42 and 43 constitute one psalm. [b] Title: Probably a literary or musical term

44:2 [e]Ps 78:55 [f]Ex 15:17 [g]Ps 80:9 2 With your hand you drove out[e] the
nations
and planted[f] our fathers;
you crushed the peoples
and made our fathers flourish.[g]
44:3 [h]Dt 8:17; Jos 24:12 [i]Ps 77:15 [j]Dt 4:37; 7:7-8 3 It was not by their sword[h] that they won
the land,
nor did their arm bring them victory;
it was your right hand, your arm,[i]
and the light of your face, for you
loved[j] them.

44:4 [k]Ps 74:12 4 You are my King[k] and my God,
who decrees[a] victories for Jacob.
44:5 [l]Ps 108:13 5 Through you we push back our enemies;
through your name we trample[l] our
foes.
44:6 [m]Ps 33:16 6 I do not trust in my bow,[m]
my sword does not bring me victory;
44:7 [n]Ps 136:24 [o]Ps 53:5 7 but you give us victory[n] over our
enemies,
you put our adversaries to shame.[o]
44:8 [p]Ps 34:2 [q]Ps 30:12 8 In God we make our boast[p] all day long,
and we will praise your name
forever.[q] *Selah*

44:9 [r]Ps 74:1 [s]Ps 60:1,10 9 But now you have rejected[r] and
humbled us;
you no longer go out with our armies.[s]
44:10 [t]Lev 26:17; Jos 7:8; Ps 89:41 10 You made us retreat[t] before the enemy,
and our adversaries have plundered us.
44:11 [u]Ro 8:36 [v]Dt 4:27; 28:64; Ps 106:27 11 You gave us up to be devoured like
sheep[u]
and have scattered us among the
nations.[v]
44:12 [w]Isa 52:3; Jer 15:13; 52:3; Jer 15:13 12 You sold your people for a pittance,[w]
gaining nothing from their sale.

44:13 [x]Ps 79:4; 80:6 [y]Dt 28:37 13 You have made us a reproach to our
neighbors,[x]
the scorn[y] and derision of those
around us.
14 You have made us a byword among the
nations;
44:14 [z]Ps 109:25; Jer 24:9 the peoples shake their heads[z] at us.
15 My disgrace is before me all day long,
and my face is covered with shame
44:16 [a]Ps 74:10 16 at the taunts of those who reproach and
revile[a] me,
because of the enemy, who is bent on
revenge.

44:17 [b]Ps 78:7,57; Da 9:13 17 All this happened to us,
though we had not forgotten[b] you
or been false to your covenant.
44:18 [c]Job 23:11 18 Our hearts had not turned[c] back;
our feet had not strayed from your
path.
44:19 [d]Ps 51:8 19 But you crushed[d] us and made us a
haunt for jackals

[a] 4 Septuagint, Aquila and Syriac; Hebrew *King, O God;* / *command*

Adelaide Anne Procter wrote a number of hymns during her short 39 years. This one was first published only two years before her death.

I Do Not Ask, O Lord

I do not ask, O Lord, that life
may be
A pleasant road;
I do not ask that Thou wouldst take
from me
Aught of its load.

I do not ask that flowers should
always spring
Beneath my feet;
I know too well the poison and
the sting
Of things too sweet.

For one thing, only Lord, dear Lord,
I plead:
Lead me aright,
Though strength should falter and
though heart should bleed,
Through peace to light.

I do not ask, O Lord, that Thou
shouldst shed
Full radiance here
Give but a ray of peace, that I may
tread
Without a fear.

Joy is like restless day; but peace
divine
Like quiet night:
Lead me, O Lord, till perfect day
shall shine,
Through peace to light.

—*Adelaide Anne Procter (1825–1864)*

Does God Sleep?

PS 44:23

In Psalm 121:3-4, the psalmist confidently asserts that the Lord watches around the clock over those he loves. Never does God close his eyes or tune out the needy. But the Psalms as a whole express the full gamut of human emotion: confidence, despair, praise, anger. Here the poet blasts God in frustration and impatience, accusing him of nodding off while his servants are facing death for his sake (Ps 44:22). How dare God just leave them in their misery!

Jesus' disciples level a similar accusation at the Lord during a deadly storm at sea (Mk 4:35-41). "Don't you care about us?" they wail in fear. Jesus' response can give us confidence in our personal storms today. Not only does he still the storm with one authoritative word, but he also assures his friends that they need never be afraid. Even when God appears to be asleep, he is wide awake, watching over his people.

and covered us over with deep
darkness.[e]
20 If we had forgotten[f] the name of our God
or spread out our hands to a foreign
god,[g]
21 would not God have discovered it,
since he knows the secrets of the
heart?[h]
22 Yet for your sake we face death all day
long;
we are considered as sheep to be
slaughtered.[i]
23 Awake,[j] O Lord! Why do you sleep?[k]
Rouse yourself! Do not reject us
forever.[l]
24 Why do you hide your face[m]
and forget our misery and oppression?[n]
25 We are brought down to the dust;[o]
our bodies cling to the ground.
26 Rise up[p] and help us;
redeem[q] us because of your unfailing
love.

44:19 [e]Job 3:5
44:20 [f]Ps 78:11 [g]Dt 6:14; Ps 81:9
44:21 [h]Ps 139:1-2; Jer 17:10
44:22 [i]Isa 53:7; Ro 8:36*
44:23 [j]Ps 7:6 [k]Ps 78:65 [l]Ps 77:7
44:24 [m]Job 13:24 [n]Ps 42:9
44:25 [o]Ps 119:25
44:26 [p]Ps 35:2 [q]Ps 25:22

Psalm 45

For the director of music. To ˻the tune of˼ "Lilies." Of the Sons of Korah. A *maskil.*[a] A wedding song.

1 My heart is stirred by a noble theme
as I recite my verses for the king;
my tongue is the pen of a skillful
writer.

2 You are the most excellent of men
and your lips have been anointed
with grace,[r]
since God has blessed you forever.
3 Gird your sword[s] upon your side,
O mighty one;[t]
clothe yourself with splendor and
majesty.
4 In your majesty ride forth victoriously[u]
in behalf of truth, humility and
righteousness;
let your right hand display awesome
deeds.
5 Let your sharp arrows pierce the hearts
of the king's enemies;
let the nations fall beneath your feet.
6 Your throne, O God, will last for ever
and ever;[v]
a scepter of justice will be the scepter
of your kingdom.
7 You love righteousness[w] and hate
wickedness;
therefore God, your God, has set you
above your companions
by anointing[x] you with the oil of joy.[y]

45:2 [r]Lk 4:22
45:3 [s]Heb 4:12; Rev 1:16 [t]Isa 9:6
45:4 [u]Rev 6:2
45:6 [v]Ps 93:2; 98:9
45:7 [w]Ps 33:5 [x]Isa 61:1 [y]Ps 21:6; Heb 1:8-9*

[a] Title: Probably a literary or musical term

45:8 [8] All your robes are fragrant[z] with myrrh
zSS 1:3 and aloes and cassia;
from palaces adorned with ivory
the music of the strings makes you
45:9 glad.
aSS 6:8 [9] Daughters of kings[a] are among your
b1Ki 2:19 honored women;
at your right hand[b] is the royal bride
in gold of Ophir.

45:10 [10] Listen, O daughter, consider and give ear:
cDt 21:13 Forget your people[c] and your father's
house.
45:11 [11] The king is enthralled by your beauty;
dPs 95:6 honor[d] him, for he is your lord.[e]
eIsa 54:5 [12] The Daughter of Tyre will come with a
45:12 gift,[a][f]
fPs 22:29; Isa 49:23 men of wealth will seek your favor.

45:13 [13] All glorious[g] is the princess within ⌊her
gIsa 61:10 chamber⌋;
her gown is interwoven with gold.
45:14 [14] In embroidered garments she is led to
hSS 1:4 the king;[h]
her virgin companions follow her
and are brought to you.
[15] They are led in with joy and gladness;
they enter the palace of the king.

[16] Your sons will take the place of your
fathers;
you will make them princes
throughout the land.
45:17 [17] I will perpetuate your memory through
iMal 1:11 all generations;[i]
jPs 138:4 therefore the nations will praise you[j]
for ever and ever.

Psalm 46

For the director of music. Of the Sons of Korah. According to *alamoth*.[b] A song.

46:1 kPs 9:9; 14:6 [1] God is our refuge[k] and strength,
lDt 4:7 an ever-present[l] help in trouble.
46:2 [2] Therefore we will not fear,[m] though the
mPs 23:4 earth give way[n]
nPs 82:5 and the mountains fall[o] into the heart
oPs 18:7 of the sea,
46:3 [3] though its waters roar[p] and foam
pPs 93:3 and the mountains quake with their
surging. *Selah*

46:4 [4] There is a river whose streams make
qPs 48:1,8; Isa 60:14 glad the city of God,[q]
46:5 the holy place where the Most High
rIsa 12:6; dwells.
Eze 43:7 [5] God is within her,[r] she will not fall;
sPs 37:40 God will help[s] her at break of day.
46:6 [6] Nations[t] are in uproar, kingdoms[u] fall;
tPs 2:1 he lifts his voice, the earth melts.[v]
uPs 68:32
vMic 1:4

[a] 12 *Or A Tyrian robe is among the gifts* [b] Title: Probably a musical term

A Wedding Song

PS 45:8-15

Most brides and grooms want their weddings to be graced with music—beautiful music with meaningful words. In ancient Israel it was no different, especially when the wedding was between a king and a princess. Pomp and ceremony, lavish ornamentation, and great expense characterized this opulent event.

The song that is sung at the royal wedding depicted in this psalm is a clear foreshadowing of the eternal union between Christ the Messiah-King and his royal bride, the church (Rev 19:6-8; 21:2). While we wait for that glorious wedding day, we can rejoice in the truth that our Lord, our husband forever, is "enthralled" by our beauty (Ps 45:11). He sees us, mere sinful human beings, through an adoring lover's eyes!

Y*ou don't have to get burned to slow down and listen. You can stop and listen to God every day, quiet your spirit before him, ask him to communicate with you. God has plenty to say to you, but he requires your undivided attention. Psalm 46:10 tells us that we will* know *God and his sovereignty when we are "still." Be still and know his will for you today.*

—Thelma Wells

[7]The LORD Almighty is with us;[w]
the God of Jacob is our fortress.[x] *Selah*

[8]Come and see the works of the LORD,[y]
the desolations[z] he has brought on the earth.
[9]He makes wars[a] cease to the ends of the earth;
he breaks the bow[b] and shatters the spear,
he burns the shields[a] with fire.[c]
[10]"Be still, and know that I am God;[d]
I will be exalted[e] among the nations,
I will be exalted in the earth."

[11]The LORD Almighty is with us;
the God of Jacob is our fortress. *Selah*

46:7 [w]2Ch 13:12 [x]Ps 9:9
46:8 [y]Ps 66:5 [z]Isa 61:4
46:9 [a]Isa 2:4 [b]Ps 76:3 [c]Eze 39:9
46:10 [d]Ps 100:3 [e]Isa 2:11

Psalm 47

For the director of music. Of the Sons of Korah. A psalm.

[1]Clap your hands,[f] all you nations;
shout to God with cries of joy.[g]
[2]How awesome[h] is the LORD Most High,
the great King[i] over all the earth!
[3]He subdued[j] nations under us,
peoples under our feet.
[4]He chose our inheritance[k] for us,
the pride of Jacob, whom he loved.
Selah
[5]God has ascended amid shouts of joy,
the LORD amid the sounding of trumpets.[l]
[6]Sing praises[m] to God, sing praises;
sing praises to our King, sing praises.

[7]For God is the King of all the earth;[n]
sing to him a psalm[b][o] of praise.
[8]God reigns[p] over the nations;
God is seated on his holy throne.
[9]The nobles of the nations assemble
as the people of the God of Abraham,
for the kings[c] of the earth belong to God;[q]
he is greatly exalted.[r]

47:1 [f]Ps 98:8; Isa 55:12 [g]Ps 106:47
47:2 [h]Dt 7:21 [i]Mal 1:14
47:3 [j]Ps 18:39,47
47:4 [k]1Pe 1:4
47:5 [l]Ps 68:33; 98:6
47:6 [m]Ps 68:4; 89:18
47:7 [n]Zec 14:9 [o]Col 3:16
47:8 [p]1Ch 16:31
47:9 [q]Ps 72:11; 89:18 [r]Ps 97:9

Psalm 48

A song. A psalm of the Sons of Korah.

[1]Great is the LORD,[s] and most worthy of praise,
in the city of our God,[t] his holy mountain.[u]
[2]It is beautiful[v] in its loftiness,
the joy of the whole earth.
Like the utmost heights of Zaphon[d] is Mount Zion,
the[e] city of the Great King.[w]

48:1 [s]Ps 96:4 [t]Ps 46:4 [u]Isa 2:2-3; Mic 4:1; Zec 8:3
48:2 [v]Ps 50:2; La 2:15 [w]Mt 5:35

[a] 9 Or *chariots* [b] 7 Or *a maskil* (probably a literary or musical term) [c] 9 Or *shields* [d] 2 *Zaphon* can refer to a sacred mountain or the direction north. [e] 2 Or *earth, / Mount Zion, on the northern side / of the*

3 God is in her citadels;
he has shown himself to be her fortress.[x]
4 When the kings joined forces,
when they advanced together,[y]
5 they saw ⌞her⌟ and were astounded;
they fled in terror.[z]
6 Trembling seized them there,
pain like that of a woman in labor.
7 You destroyed them like ships of Tarshish
shattered by an east wind.[a]

8 As we have heard,
so have we seen
in the city of the LORD Almighty,
in the city of our God:
God makes her secure forever.[b] *Selah*
9 Within your temple, O God,
we meditate on your unfailing love.[c]
10 Like your name,[d] O God,
your praise reaches to the ends of the earth;[e]
your right hand is filled with righteousness.
11 Mount Zion rejoices,
the villages of Judah are glad
because of your judgments.[f]
12 Walk about Zion, go around her,
count her towers,
13 consider well her ramparts,
view her citadels,[g]
that you may tell of them to the next generation.[h]
14 For this God is our God for ever and ever;
he will be our guide[i] even to the end.

Psalm 49

For the director of music. Of the Sons of Korah. A psalm.

1 Hear this, all you peoples;[j]
listen, all who live in this world,[k]
2 both low and high,
rich and poor alike:
3 My mouth will speak words of wisdom;[l]
the utterance from my heart will give understanding.[m]
4 I will turn my ear to a proverb;[n]
with the harp I will expound my riddle:[o]

5 Why should I fear[p] when evil days come,
when wicked deceivers surround me—
6 those who trust in their wealth[q]
and boast of their great riches?
7 No man can redeem the life of another
or give to God a ransom for him—
8 the ransom for a life is costly,
no payment is ever enough—[r]

48:3 [x]Ps 46:7
48:4 [y]2Sa 10:1-19
48:5 [z]Ex 15:16
48:7 [a]Jer 18:17; Eze 27:26
48:8 [b]Ps 87:5
48:9 [c]Ps 26:3
48:10 [d]Dt 28:58; Jos 7:9 [e]Isa 41:10
48:11 [f]Ps 97:8
48:13 [g]ver 3; Ps 122:7 [h]Ps 78:6
48:14 [i]Ps 23:4
49:1 [j]Ps 78:1 [k]Ps 33:8
49:3 [l]Ps 37:30 [m]Ps 119:130
49:4 [n]Ps 78:2 [o]Nu 12:8
49:5 [p]Ps 23:4
49:6 [q]Job 31:24
49:8 [r]Mt 16:26

The City of God

PS 48

The sons of Korah compose this ode to the city of Jerusalem, their national and religious capital, applauding its beauty and security. This tribute echoes Isaiah's prophecy in Isaiah 2:1-5. The city of God, the new Jerusalem, is where all followers of Jesus Christ will one day live forever. This city will be filled with the presence of the King; his love will be its overwhelming reality. In that forever home, believers will be completely safe and secure—their eternal perch will be lofty, high above all danger, and their fortress will be impenetrable to any outside threat. Beauty, joy and love will surround them for the rest of time.

Wealth

PS 49:16-17

The psalmist realizes that wealth is not the "be all and end all" so many make it out to be. Yes, having a lot of money can give a person certain freedoms and pleasures, and it can enable him or her to be lavish in their generosity. However, as the psalmist reminds us, when our earthly life ends, the externals cease to make any difference at all. We truly can't take our riches with us!

That's why Jesus urges us not to spend our energy on accumulating material goods at the expense of spiritual riches (Mt 6:19-21). He tells us to guard our hearts from envy and covetousness, for life is not found in our *stuff* (Lk 12:15). Regardless of our material lot in life, each of us faces the same choice: Will we place the highest value on imperishable riches so that, when we leave our *stuff* behind, we will live forever with Jesus Christ (1Pe 1:17-25)?

9 that he should live on[s] forever
and not see decay.

10 For all can see that wise men die;[t]
the foolish and the senseless alike perish
and leave their wealth to others.[u]
11 Their tombs will remain their houses[a] forever,
their dwellings for endless generations,
though they had[b] named[v] lands after themselves.

12 But man, despite his riches, does not endure;
he is[c] like the beasts that perish.
13 This is the fate of those who trust in themselves,[w]
and of their followers, who approve their sayings. *Selah*
14 Like sheep they are destined for the grave,[d x]
and death will feed on them.
The upright will rule[y] over them in the morning;
their forms will decay in the grave,[d]
far from their princely mansions.
15 But God will redeem my life[e] from the grave;[z]
he will surely take me to himself.[a] *Selah*

16 Do not be overawed when a man grows rich,
when the splendor of his house increases;
17 for he will take nothing with him when he dies,
his splendor will not descend with him.[b]
18 Though while he lived he counted himself blessed—[c]
and men praise you when you prosper—
19 he will join the generation of his fathers,[d]
who will never see the light[e] ⌞of life⌟.

20 A man who has riches without understanding
is like the beasts that perish.[f]

Psalm 50

A psalm of Asaph.

1 The Mighty One, God, the LORD,[g]
speaks and summons the earth

49:9 [s]Ps 22:29; 89:48
49:10 [t]Ecc 2:16 [u]Ecc 2:18,21
49:11 [v]Ge 4:17; Dt 3:14
49:13 [w]Lk 12:20
49:14 [x]Job 24:19; Ps 9:17 [y]Da 7:18; Mal 4:3; 1Co 6:2; Rev 2:26
49:15 [z]Ps 56:13; Hos 13:14 [a]Ps 73:24
49:17 [b]Ps 17:14; 1Ti 6:7
49:18 [c]Dt 29:19; Lk 12:19
49:19 [d]Ge 15:15 [e]Job 33:30
49:20 [f]Ecc 3:19
50:1 [g]Jos 22:22

[a] 11 Septuagint and Syriac; Hebrew *In their thoughts their houses will remain* [b] 11 Or / *for they have* [c] 12 Hebrew; Septuagint and Syriac read verse 12 the same as verse 20. [d] 14 Hebrew *Sheol*; also in verse 15 [e] 15 Or *soul*

from the rising of the sun to the place
50:1 [h]Ps 113:3 where it sets.[h]
[2] From Zion, perfect in beauty,[i]
50:2 [i]Ps 48:2 God shines forth.[j]
[j]Dt 33:2; Ps 80:1 [3] Our God comes[k] and will not be silent;
a fire devours before him,[l]
50:3 and around him a tempest rages.
[k]Ps 96:13 [4] He summons the heavens above,
[l]Ps 97:3; Da 7:10 and the earth,[m] that he may judge his
people:
50:4 [m]Dt 4:26; Isa 1:2 [5] "Gather to me my consecrated ones,[n]
who made a covenant[o] with me by
sacrifice."
50:5 [n]Ps 30:4 [6] And the heavens proclaim[p] his
[o]Ex 24:7 righteousness,
for God himself is judge.[q] *Selah*
50:6 [p]Ps 89:5 [7] "Hear, O my people, and I will speak,
[q]Ps 75:7 O Israel, and I will testify[r] against
50:7 you:
[r]Ps 81:8 I am God, your God.[s]
[s]Ex 20:2 [8] I do not rebuke you for your sacrifices
50:8 or your burnt offerings,[t] which are
[t]Ps 40:6; Hos 6:6 ever before me.
[9] I have no need of a bull[u] from your stall
50:9 [u]Ps 69:31 or of goats from your pens,
[10] for every animal of the forest is mine,
50:10 [v]Ps 104:24 and the cattle on a thousand hills.[v]
[11] I know every bird in the mountains,
and the creatures of the field are
mine.
[12] If I were hungry I would not tell you,
50:12 [w]Ex 19:5 for the world[w] is mine, and all that is
in it.
[13] Do I eat the flesh of bulls
or drink the blood of goats?
50:14 [x]Heb 13:15 [14] Sacrifice thank offerings[x] to God,
[y]Dt 23:21 fulfill your vows[y] to the Most High,
50:15 [15] and call[z] upon me in the day of trouble;
[z]Ps 81:7 I will deliver you, and you will honor[a]
[a]Ps 22:23 me."

[16] But to the wicked, God says:

"What right have you to recite my laws
50:16 [b]Isa 29:13 or take my covenant on your lips?[b]
[17] You hate my instruction
50:17 [c]Ne 9:26; and cast my words behind[c] you.
Ro 2:21-22 [18] When you see a thief, you join[d] with
him;
50:18 [d]Ro 1:32; you throw in your lot with adulterers.
1Ti 5:22 [19] You use your mouth for evil
50:19 and harness your tongue to deceit.[e]
[e]Ps 10:7; 52:2 [20] You speak continually against your
brother[f]
50:20 and slander your own mother's son.
[f]Mt 10:21 [21] These things you have done and I kept
silent;[g]
50:21 [g]Ecc 8:11; you thought I was altogether[a] like you.
Isa 42:14 But I will rebuke you

[a] 21 Or *thought the 'I AM' was*

It All Belongs to God

PS 50:9-12

Asaph's psalm reminds us that God, as Creator and Owner of all things, is absolutely self-sufficient. He does not *need* the sacrifices of his people any more than he *needs* our offerings. It is all his. But what he does need and what he does want and what he does deserve is his people's consecration to him. If the Israelites sacrifice without heart involvement, God doesn't need or even want it (1Sa 15:22; Mic 6:6-8).

How easy it is for us to work hard, save "our" money, accumulate things that give us a sense of self-sufficiency and security—only to be brought up short by the realization that none of what we use or hoard belongs to us at all! The whole world belongs to our Father. When we let that reality infuse our motivation and decisions in regard to material things, we will be released from the stress of depending on anything other than God. As his children, we can trust his loving provision (Mt 6:25-33).

Wholehearted Devotion

PS 51:1–17

The events that precede this heartfelt confession of sin are recorded in 2 Samuel 11:1—12:13. When Nathan confronts him, David could have defended himself, lied, made excuses or even condemned the prophet to death. But because David, though a sinner, is wholeheartedly devoted to God (1Ki 15:3), he immediately owns up not only to his wretched behavior but also to his sinful nature. He knows he is thoroughly stained with sin and that only God can cleanse him. His plea for mercy is rooted securely in God's character, not in his own righteousness. He recognizes that his behavior hurts God more than anyone else. He prays that a willing and obedient spirit will replace his wayward one. David perceives the truth that nothing but brokenhearted, humble confession and repentance will please the Lord. When we become aware of our sin, David's prayer of contrition can become our own, restoring our joy in God's presence.

and accuse[h] you to your face.

22 "Consider this, you who forget God,[i]
or I will tear you to pieces, with none to rescue:[j]
23 He who sacrifices thank offerings honors me,
and he prepares the way[k]
so that I may show him[a] the salvation of God.[l]"

Psalm 51

For the director of music. A psalm of David. When the prophet Nathan came to him after David had committed adultery with Bathsheba.

1 Have mercy on me, O God,
according to your unfailing love;
according to your great compassion
blot out[m] my transgressions.[n]
2 Wash away[o] all my iniquity
and cleanse[p] me from my sin.

3 For I know my transgressions,
and my sin is always before me.[q]
4 Against you, you only, have I sinned
and done what is evil in your sight,[r]
so that you are proved right when you speak
and justified when you judge.[s]
5 Surely I was sinful[t] at birth,
sinful from the time my mother conceived me.
6 Surely you desire truth in the inner parts[b];
you teach[c] me wisdom[u] in the inmost place.[v]

7 Cleanse me with hyssop,[w] and I will be clean;
wash me, and I will be whiter than snow.[x]
8 Let me hear joy and gladness;[y]
let the bones you have crushed rejoice.
9 Hide your face from my sins[z]
and blot out all my iniquity.
10 Create in me a pure heart,[a] O God,
and renew a steadfast spirit within me.[b]
11 Do not cast me from your presence
or take your Holy Spirit[c] from me.
12 Restore to me the joy of your salvation[d]
and grant me a willing spirit, to sustain me.

13 Then I will teach transgressors your ways,[e]
and sinners will turn back to you.[f]
14 Save me from bloodguilt,[g] O God,

50:21 [h]Ps 90:8
50:22 [i]Job 8:13; Ps 9:17 [j]Ps 7:2
50:23 [k]Ps 85:13 [l]Ps 91:16
51:1 [m]Ac 3:19 [n]Isa 43:25; Col 2:14
51:2 [o]1Jn 1:9 [p]Heb 9:14
51:3 [q]Isa 59:12
51:4 [r]Ge 20:6; Lk 15:21 [s]Ro 3:4*
51:5 [t]Job 14:4
51:6 [u]Pr 2:6 [v]Ps 15:2
51:7 [w]Lev 14:4; Heb 9:19 [x]Isa 1:18
51:8 [y]Isa 35:10
51:9 [z]Jer 16:17
51:10 [a]Ps 78:37; Ac 15:9 [b]Eze 18:31
51:11 [c]Eph 4:30
51:12 [d]Ps 13:5
51:13 [e]Ac 9:21-22 [f]Ps 22:27
51:14 [g]2Sa 12:9

[a] 23 Or *and to him who considers his way / I will show*
[b] 6 The meaning of the Hebrew for this phrase is uncertain.
[c] 6 Or *you desired . . . ; / you taught*

51:14 the God who saves me,[h]
[h]Ps 25:5 and my tongue will sing of your
[i]Ps 35:28 righteousness.[i]
51:15 [15] O Lord, open my lips,[j]
[j]Ps 9:14 and my mouth will declare your
praise.
51:16 [16] You do not delight in sacrifice,[k] or I
[k]1Sa 15:22; would bring it;
Ps 40:6
you do not take pleasure in burnt
offerings.
51:17 [17] The sacrifices of God are[a] a broken
[l]Ps 34:18 spirit;
a broken and contrite heart,[l]
O God, you will not despise.

51:18 [18] In your good pleasure make Zion[m]
[m]Ps 102:16; prosper;
Isa 51:3 build up the walls of Jerusalem.
51:19 [19] Then there will be righteous sacrifices,[n]
[n]Ps 4:5 whole burnt offerings[o] to delight you;
[o]Ps 66:13 then bulls[p] will be offered on your
[p]Ps 66:15 altar.

Psalm 52

52:1 For the director of music. A *maskil*[b] of David. When Doeg the Edomite[q] had gone to Saul and told him:
[q]1Sa 22:9
[r]Ps 94:4 "David has gone to the house of Ahimelech."

[1] Why do you boast of evil, you mighty
man?
Why do you boast[r] all day long,
you who are a disgrace in the eyes of
God?
52:2 [2] Your tongue plots destruction;
[s]Ps 57:4 it is like a sharpened razor,[s]
[t]Ps 50:19 you who practice deceit.[t]
52:3 [3] You love evil rather than good,
[u]Jer 9:5 falsehood[u] rather than speaking the
truth. *Selah*
52:4 [4] You love every harmful word,
[v]Ps 120:2,3 O you deceitful tongue![v]

[5] Surely God will bring you down to
52:5 everlasting ruin:
[w]Isa 22:19 He will snatch you up and tear[w] you
[x]Pr 2:22 from your tent;
[y]Ps 27:13 he will uproot[x] you from the land of
the living.[y] *Selah*
52:6 [6] The righteous will see and fear;
[z]Job 22:19; they will laugh[z] at him, saying,
Ps 37:34; [7] "Here now is the man
40:3 who did not make God his stronghold
52:7 but trusted in his great wealth[a]
[a]Ps 49:6 and grew strong by destroying
others!"
52:8
[b]Jer 11:16 [8] But I am like an olive tree[b]
[c]Ps 13:5 flourishing in the house of God;
I trust[c] in God's unfailing love
for ever and ever.

[a] 17 Or *My sacrifice, O God, is* [b] Title: Probably a literary or musical term

The Lord continues to heal and restore the wounded places in me as I allow him access. The process is at times so painful that I want to just ignore it and live my life as best I can. But I do believe that we are as sick as our secrets. The places of hurt we bury deep inside, the wounds that seem to open and close according to the circumstances—these things hinder all that we can become in Jesus, all that he desires for our lives. They affect us both relationally and emotionally. They affect us spiritually and morally.

In Psalm 51:6, [David] says [the Lord] desires truth in our inner parts; this is where he can move in power and healing. The psalm goes on to say that he teaches us wisdom in our inmost place. He uproots the bad and pours in his best as we let him.

Don't hide from him. Don't hide from yourself. Jesus is gentle yet strong and will walk you through to victorious beginnings.

You'll be amazed at the miracle you will become.

—Kathy Troccoli

A Fool

PS 53:1

The fools described in this psalm are those whose whole moral sense is twisted and misdirected. They may or may not be obviously "bad" in their behavior, but if we could see into their hearts, we would find no acknowledgment of divine authority. Arrogant fools are their own higher power; "in all [their] thoughts there is no room for God" (Ps 10:4). Throughout Scripture this kind of human pride is denounced because it can lead only to destruction (Pr 16:18).

The words of this psalm are repeated almost word for word in Psalm 14. Why such a repetition is included is uncertain; however, the truth of the message is certainly worth repeating!

9 I will praise you forever[d] for what you
have done;
in your name I will hope, for your
name is good.[e]
I will praise you in the presence of
your saints.

52:9 [d]Ps 30:12 [e]Ps 54:6

Psalm 53

For the director of music. According to *mahalath.*[a] A *maskil*[b] of David.

1 The fool[f] says in his heart,
"There is no God."[g]
They are corrupt, and their ways are
vile;
there is no one who does good.

53:1 [f]Ps 14:1-7; Ro 3:10 [g]Ps 10:4

2 God looks down from heaven[h]
on the sons of men
to see if there are any who understand,
any who seek God.[i]

53:2 [h]Ps 33:13 [i]2Ch 15:2

3 Everyone has turned away,
they have together become corrupt;
there is no one who does good,
not even one.[j]

53:3 [j]Ro 3:10-12*

4 Will the evildoers never learn—
those who devour my people as men
eat bread
and who do not call on God?
5 There they were, overwhelmed with
dread,
where there was nothing to dread.[k]
God scattered the bones[l] of those who
attacked you;
you put them to shame, for God
despised them.

53:5 [k]Lev 26:17 [l]Eze 6:5

6 Oh, that salvation for Israel would come
out of Zion!
When God restores the fortunes of his
people,
let Jacob rejoice and Israel be glad!

Psalm 54

For the director of music. With stringed instruments. A *maskil*[b] of David. When the Ziphites had gone to Saul and said, "Is not David hiding among us?"

1 Save me, O God, by your name;[m]
vindicate me by your might.[n]

54:1 [m]Ps 20:1 [n]2Ch 20:6

2 Hear my prayer, O God;[o]
listen to the words of my mouth.

54:2 [o]Ps 5:1; 55:1

3 Strangers are attacking me;[p]
ruthless men seek my life[q]—
men without regard for God.[r] *Selah*

54:3 [p]Ps 86:14 [q]Ps 40:14 [r]Ps 36:1

4 Surely God is my help;[s]
the Lord is the one who sustains me.[t]

54:4 [s]Ps 118:7 [t]Ps 41:12

5 Let evil recoil[u] on those who slander me;

54:5 [u]Ps 94:23

[a] Title: Probably a musical term [b] Title: Probably a literary or musical term

in your faithfulness[v] destroy them.
6 I will sacrifice a freewill offering[w] to you;
I will praise your name, O LORD,
for it is good.[x]
7 For he has delivered me[y] from all my
troubles,
and my eyes have looked in triumph
on my foes.[z]

Psalm 55

For the director of music. With stringed instruments.
A *maskil*[a] of David.

1 Listen to my prayer, O God,
do not ignore my plea;[a]
2 hear me and answer me.[b]
My thoughts trouble me and I am
distraught[c]
3 at the voice of the enemy,
at the stares of the wicked;
for they bring down suffering upon me[d]
and revile me in their anger.[e]

4 My heart is in anguish within me;
the terrors[f] of death assail me.
5 Fear and trembling[g] have beset me;
horror has overwhelmed me.
6 I said, "Oh, that I had the wings of a
dove!
I would fly away and be at rest—
7 I would flee far away
and stay in the desert; *Selah*
8 I would hurry to my place of shelter,
far from the tempest and storm.[h]"

9 Confuse the wicked, O Lord, confound
their speech,
for I see violence and strife[i] in the
city.
10 Day and night they prowl about on its
walls;
malice and abuse are within it.
11 Destructive forces[j] are at work in the
city;
threats and lies[k] never leave its streets.

12 If an enemy were insulting me,
I could endure it;
if a foe were raising himself against me,
I could hide from him.
13 But it is you, a man like myself,
my companion, my close friend,[l]
14 with whom I once enjoyed sweet
fellowship
as we walked with the throng at the
house of God.[m]

15 Let death take my enemies by surprise;[n]
let them go down alive to the grave,[b][o]
for evil finds lodging among them.

[a] Title: Probably a literary or musical term [b] *15* Hebrew *Sheol*

54:5 [v]Ps 89:49; 143:12
54:6 [w]Ps 50:14 [x]Ps 52:9
54:7 [y]Ps 34:6 [z]Ps 59:10
55:1 [a]Ps 27:9; 61:1
55:2 [b]Ps 66:19 [c]Ps 77:3; Isa 38:14
55:3 [d]2Sa 16:6-8; Ps 17:9 [e]Ps 71:11
55:4 [f]Ps 116:3
55:5 [g]Job 21:6; Ps 119:120
55:8 [h]Isa 4:6
55:9 [i]Jer 6:7
55:11 [j]Ps 5:9 [k]Ps 10:7
55:13 [l]2Sa 15:12; Ps 41:9
55:14 [m]Ps 42:4
55:15 [n]Ps 64:7 [o]Nu 16:30, 33

Fly Away

PS 55:6–8

We can almost hear David's deep sigh of weary longing. His enemies press in around him (Ps 55:3), he's unsure who can be trusted and he's terrified (Ps 55:5). All he wants is to get away from it all!

How often have we felt exactly the same way—perhaps even used similar words? "Oh, if only I could just run away from it all!" To fantasize about escaping from the difficult or demanding aspects of our reality is a human response Jesus understands completely. That's why he offers his own presence and way of life as the refuge we crave (Mt 11:28–30). The Lord never gets tired, and those who rely on his strength will always find renewal (Isa 40:28–31). In the midst of whatever challenges life presents, we can run to Jesus and find rest for our weary souls.

Letting Go

PS 55:22

David brings his concerns and fears to God, asking him to take over and take care of the problems he's facing. He knows he can trust God with the outcome. God has proven himself before and will do so again (Ps 55:16–17).

Much of the time, what we care about is not entirely within our control. We can't dictate the results of our best efforts; we can't force our hopes to materialize; and we definitely can't make someone we love healthy and happy by the sheer force of our will. When we try to control outcomes, we carry a burden too heavy for human shoulders to bear. What a relief it is to finally let go, to heave our heavy burden onto the strong back of the Lord. He promises to sustain our hearts and minds with his peace (Php 4:6–7). And no matter what he chooses to do with what concerns us, we have the assurance that his decisions are guided by his love for us (1Pe 5:7).

16 But I call to God,
and the LORD saves me.
17 Evening,[p] morning[q] and noon
I cry out in distress,
and he hears my voice.
18 He ransoms me unharmed
from the battle waged against me,
even though many oppose me.
19 God, who is enthroned forever,[r]
will hear[s] them and afflict them—
Selah
men who never change their ways
and have no fear of God.

55:17 [p]Ps 141:2; Ac 3:1 [q]Ps 5:3
55:19 [r]Dt 33:27 [s]Ps 78:59

20 My companion attacks his friends;[t]
he violates his covenant.[u]
21 His speech is smooth as butter,
yet war is in his heart;
his words are more soothing than oil,[v]
yet they are drawn swords.[w]
22 Cast your cares on the LORD
and he will sustain you;[x]
he will never let the righteous fall.[y]
23 But you, O God, will bring down the wicked
into the pit[z] of corruption;
bloodthirsty and deceitful men[a]
will not live out half their days.[b]

But as for me, I trust in you.[c]

55:20 [t]Ps 7:4 [u]Ps 89:34
55:21 [v]Pr 5:3 [w]Ps 28:3; Ps 57:4; 59:7
55:22 [x]Ps 37:5; Mt 6:25-34; 1Pe 5:7 [y]Ps 37:24
55:23 [z]Ps 73:18 [a]Ps 5:6 [b]Job 15:32; Pr 10:27 [c]Ps 25:2

Psalm 56

For the director of music. To ⌊the tune of⌋ "A Dove on Distant Oaks." Of David. A *miktam.*[a] When the Philistines had seized him in Gath.

1 Be merciful to me, O God, for men hotly
pursue me;[d]
all day long they press their attack.
2 My slanderers pursue me all day long;[e]
many are attacking me in their pride.[f]

3 When I am afraid,[g]
I will trust in you.
4 In God, whose word I praise,
in God I trust; I will not be afraid.
What can mortal man do to me?[h]

5 All day long they twist my words;[i]
they are always plotting to harm me.
6 They conspire,[j] they lurk,
they watch my steps,
eager to take my life.[k]

7 On no account let them escape;
in your anger, O God, bring down the
nations.[l]
8 Record my lament;
list my tears on your scroll[b]—
are they not in your record?[m]

56:1 [d]Ps 57:1-3
56:2 [e]Ps 57:3 [f]Ps 35:1
56:3 [g]Ps 55:4-5
56:4 [h]Ps 118:6; Heb 13:6
56:5 [i]Ps 41:7
56:6 [j]Ps 59:3 [k]Ps 71:10
56:7 [l]Ps 36:12; 55:23
56:8 [m]Mal 3:16

[a] Title: Probably a literary or musical term [b] 8 Or / *put my tears in your wineskin*

56:9 [n]Ps 9:3 [o]Ps 102:2 [p]Ro 8:31

9 Then my enemies will turn back[n]
when I call for help.[o]
By this I will know that God is for me.[p]
10 In God, whose word I praise,
in the LORD, whose word I praise—
11 in God I trust; I will not be afraid.
What can man do to me?

56:12 [q]Ps 50:14

12 I am under vows[q] to you, O God;
I will present my thank offerings to you.

56:13 [r]Ps 116:8 [s]Job 33:30

13 For you have delivered me[a] from death[r]
and my feet from stumbling,
that I may walk before God
in the light of life.[b][s]

Psalm 57

For the director of music. ⌞To the tune of⌟ "Do Not Destroy." Of David. A *miktam.*[c] When he had fled from Saul into the cave.

57:1 [t]Ps 2:12 [u]Ps 17:8 [v]Isa 26:20

1 Have mercy on me, O God, have mercy on me,
for in you my soul takes refuge.[t]
I will take refuge in the shadow of your wings[u]
until the disaster has passed.[v]

57:2 [w]Ps 138:8

2 I cry out to God Most High,
to God, who fulfills ⌞his purpose⌟ for me.[w]

57:3 [x]Ps 18:9,16 [y]Ps 56:1 [z]Ps 40:11

3 He sends from heaven and saves me,[x]
rebuking those who hotly pursue me;[y] *Selah*
God sends his love and his faithfulness.[z]

57:4 [a]Ps 35:17 [b]Ps 55:21; Pr 30:14

4 I am in the midst of lions;[a]
I lie among ravenous beasts—
men whose teeth are spears and arrows,
whose tongues are sharp swords.[b]

57:5 [c]Ps 108:5

5 Be exalted, O God, above the heavens;
let your glory be over all the earth.[c]

57:6 [d]Ps 145:14 [e]Ps 35:7 [f]Ps 7:15; Pr 28:10

6 They spread a net for my feet—
I was bowed down[d] in distress.
They dug a pit[e] in my path—
but they have fallen into it themselves.[f] *Selah*

57:7 [g]Ps 108:1

7 My heart is steadfast, O God,
my heart is steadfast;[g]
I will sing and make music.

57:8 [h]Ps 16:9; 30:12; 150:3

8 Awake, my soul!
Awake, harp and lyre![h]
I will awaken the dawn.

9 I will praise you, O Lord, among the nations;
I will sing of you among the peoples.

[a] 13 Or *my soul* [b] 13 Or *the land of the living* [c] Title: Probably a literary or musical term

The wisdom and doctrine of Scripture teach that the experience of celebrating God is the core of worship. It is the quintessence of praise and thanksgiving—the most perfect manifestation of a heart that gratefully fellowships with the One who provides life and all the gifts of living. In fact, a grateful heart is not only the greatest virtue, it is the seed bed for all other virtues. When we are caught up into the celebration of God, there is neither room nor time for the invasion of negative living. As we rejoice before the Lord, as we serve him in the area of our calling, as we enter joyfully into our daily journey, as we give thanks to him for his kindness and faithfulness, we celebrate God.

—Luci Swindoll

The Venom of a Snake

PS 58:4–5

Romans 3:10–18 gives a vivid description of what unredeemed human beings are like. Among other things, "The poison of vipers is on their lips" (Ro 3:13). Their words can be deadly, and, deep down, they're mean as snakes.

We may not want to own up to having such qualities before we were saved through faith in Jesus Christ. But this is how, according to the psalmist, our holy God sees the wicked. Unwilling to open their hearts and minds to his counsel, they are like deaf and deadly serpents, refusing to be subdued by even the most heavenly tune. Wise Solomon tells us that fools despise godly instruction (Pr 1:7). If you are trying to get through to a fool, beware. Not only will you probably fail, but you may also get a nasty bite in the process.

[10] For great is your love, reaching to the
heavens; 57:10
your faithfulness reaches to the skies.[i] [i]Ps 36:5; 103:11
[11] Be exalted, O God, above the heavens; 57:11
let your glory be over all the earth.[j] [j]ver 5

Psalm 58

For the director of music. ⌞To the tune of⌟ "Do Not Destroy." Of David. A *miktam*.[a]

[1] Do you rulers indeed speak justly?[k] 58:1 [k]Ps 82:2
Do you judge uprightly among men?
[2] No, in your heart you devise injustice,
and your hands mete out violence on
the earth.[l] 58:2 [l]Ps 94:20; Mal 3:15
[3] Even from birth the wicked go astray;
from the womb they are wayward and
speak lies.
[4] Their venom is like the venom of a
snake,[m] 58:4 [m]Ps 140:3; Ecc 10:11
like that of a cobra that has stopped
its ears,
[5] that will not heed the tune of the
charmer,
however skillful the enchanter may be. 58:6
[6] Break the teeth in their mouths, O God;[n] [n]Ps 3:7
tear out, O LORD, the fangs of the [o]Job 4:10
lions![o]
[7] Let them vanish like water that flows
away;[p] 58:7 [p]Jos 7:5; Ps 112:10
when they draw the bow, let their [q]Ps 64:3
arrows be blunted.[q]
[8] Like a slug melting away as it moves
along,
like a stillborn child,[r] may they not 58:8 [r]Job 3:16
see the sun.

[9] Before your pots can feel ⌞the heat of⌟
the thorns[s]— 58:9 [s]Ps 118:12
whether they be green or dry—the [t]Pr 10:25
wicked will be swept away.[b][t]
[10] The righteous will be glad when they
are avenged,[u] 58:10 [u]Ps 64:10; 91:8
when they bathe their feet in the
blood of the wicked.[v] [v]Ps 68:23
[11] Then men will say,
"Surely the righteous still are
rewarded;
surely there is a God who judges the 58:11 [w]Ps 9:8; 18:20
earth."[w]

Psalm 59

For the director of music. ⌞To the tune of⌟ "Do Not Destroy." Of David. A *miktam*.[a] When Saul had sent men to watch David's house in order to kill him.

[1] Deliver me from my enemies, O God;[x] 59:1 [x]Ps 143:9

[a] Title: Probably a literary or musical term [b] 9 The meaning of the Hebrew for this verse is uncertain.

protect me from those who rise up
against me.
[2]Deliver me from evildoers

59:2 [y]Ps 139:19

and save me from bloodthirsty men.[y]

59:3 [z]Ps 56:6

[3]See how they lie in wait for me!
Fierce men conspire[z] against me
for no offense or sin of mine, O LORD.

59:4 [a]Ps 35:19,23

[4]I have done no wrong, yet they are
ready to attack me.[a]
Arise to help me; look on my plight!
[5]O LORD God Almighty, the God of Israel,
rouse yourself to punish all the
nations;

59:5 [b]Jer 18:23

show no mercy to wicked traitors.[b]
Selah

59:6 [c]ver 14

[6]They return at evening,
snarling like dogs,[c]
and prowl about the city.
[7]See what they spew from their
mouths—

59:7 [d]Ps 57:4 [e]Ps 10:11

they spew out swords[d] from their lips,
and they say, "Who can hear us?"[e]

59:8 [f]Ps 37:13; Pr 1:26 [g]Ps 2:4

[8]But you, O LORD, laugh at them;[f]
you scoff at all those nations.[g]
[9]O my Strength, I watch for you;

59:9 [h]Ps 9:9; 62:2

you, O God, are my fortress,[h] [10]my
loving God.

God will go before me
and will let me gloat over those who
slander me.

59:11 [i]Ps 84:9 [j]Dt 4:9 [k]Ps 106:27

[11]But do not kill them, O Lord our
shield,[a][i]
or my people will forget.[j]
In your might make them wander
about,
and bring them down.[k]

59:12 [l]Ps 10:7 [m]Pr 12:13 [n]Zep 3:11

[12]For the sins of their mouths,[l]
for the words of their lips,[m]
let them be caught in their pride.[n]
For the curses and lies they utter,

59:13 [o]Ps 104:35 [p]Ps 83:18

[13]consume them in wrath,
consume them till they are no more.[o]
Then it will be known to the ends of the
earth
that God rules over Jacob.[p] *Selah*

[14]They return at evening,
snarling like dogs,
and prowl about the city.

59:15 [q]Job 15:23

[15]They wander about for food[q]
and howl if not satisfied.

59:16 [r]Ps 21:13 [s]Ps 88:13 [t]Ps 101:1 [u]Ps 46:1

[16]But I will sing of your strength,[r]
in the morning[s] I will sing of your
love;[t]
for you are my fortress,
my refuge in times of trouble.[u]

[17]O my Strength, I sing praise to you;

[a] 11 Or *sovereign*

The Awareness of God

PS 59:7-8

People who pay no heed to God and his righteousness often take their foolishness a step further: They think that God isn't paying attention to them and that they will get away with their rebellion. But God is all ears and all eyes, and he is fully aware of the futility of wicked schemes (Ps 94:7-11). David expresses confidence in the inevitable humiliation of his enemies. They will be brought low, not necessarily by a dramatic sweep of God's sword, but by the thunder of his scornful laughter. Those who refuse to bow to God's authority may think they're getting away with something, but God will have the last laugh. He knows their day is coming (Ps 10:13-16).

This isn't by any means a call from David for personal revenge on his enemies. It is a call for God's justice to be meted out. God the judge, God the righteous One, will eventually pass judgment on those who rebel against him, not only in David's time, but in our time also (2Th 1:8).

The Sovereign God

PS 60:6–8

The territories referred to here include both the Lord's beloved Israel as well as its surrounding enemies. Even though Israel is perpetually under siege, this song is David's cry of the sure victory to come. The two tribes of Israel represent God's "helmet" of powerful protection (Ephraim) and "scepter" of sovereign rule (Judah). The wicked Moabites will be reduced to God's menial servants, left with nothing but the dirty water from the warrior Lord's bath. He will claim rebel Edom as his own with the conventional sandal-for-land swap (Ru 4:7). And the oppressive Philistines will ultimately be vanquished. These references to territories either conquered by, or in perpetual turmoil with, Israel form a metaphorical reference to God's absolute dominion and sovereignty, not just over these particular physical places, but over the whole earth (Ex 19:5–6).

you, O God, are my fortress, my
loving God.

Psalm 60

For the director of music. To ˌthe tune ofˌ "The Lily of the Covenant." A *miktam*[a] of David. For teaching. When he fought Aram Naharaim[b] and Aram Zobah,[c] and when Joab returned and struck down twelve thousand Edomites in the Valley of Salt.

1 You have rejected us,[v] O God, and burst
forth upon us;
you have been angry[w]—now restore
us![x]
2 You have shaken the land[y] and torn it
open;
mend its fractures,[z] for it is quaking.
3 You have shown your people desperate
times;[a]
you have given us wine that makes us
stagger.[b]

4 But for those who fear you, you have
raised a banner
to be unfurled against the bow. *Selah*

5 Save us and help us with your right
hand,[c]
that those you love[d] may be delivered.
6 God has spoken from his sanctuary:
"In triumph I will parcel out
Shechem[e]
and measure off the Valley of Succoth.
7 Gilead[f] is mine, and Manasseh is mine;
Ephraim is my helmet,
Judah[g] my scepter.[h]
8 Moab is my washbasin,
upon Edom I toss my sandal;
over Philistia I shout in triumph.[i]"

9 Who will bring me to the fortified city?
Who will lead me to Edom?
10 Is it not you, O God, you who have
rejected us
and no longer go out with our armies?[j]
11 Give us aid against the enemy,
for the help of man is worthless.[k]
12 With God we will gain the victory,
and he will trample down our
enemies.[l]

Psalm 61

For the director of music. With stringed instruments. Of David.

1 Hear my cry, O God;[m]
listen to my prayer.[n]

2 From the ends of the earth I call to you,
I call as my heart grows faint;[o]

60:1 [v]2Sa 5:20; Ps 44:9 [w]Ps 79:5 [x]Ps 80:3
60:2 [y]Ps 18:7 [z]2Ch 7:14
60:3 [a]Ps 71:20 [b]Isa 51:17; Jer 25:16
60:5 [c]Ps 17:7; 108:6 [d]Ps 127:2
60:6 [e]Ge 12:6
60:7 [f]Jos 13:31 [g]Dt 33:17 [h]Ge 49:10
60:8 [i]2Sa 8:1
60:10 [j]Jos 7:12; Ps 44:9; 108:11
60:11 [k]Ps 146:3
60:12 [l]Nu 24:18; Ps 44:5
61:1 [m]Ps 64:1 [n]Ps 86:6
61:2 [o]Ps 77:3

[a] Title: Probably a literary or musical term [b] Title: That is, Arameans of Northwest Mesopotamia [c] Title: That is, Arameans of central Syria

61:2 [p]Ps 18:2
lead me to the rock[p] that is higher
than I.

61:3 [q]Ps 62:7 [r]Pr 18:10
3 For you have been my refuge,[q]
a strong tower against the foe.[r]

61:4 [s]Ps 23:6 [t]Ps 91:4
4 I long to dwell[s] in your tent forever
and take refuge in the shelter of your
wings.[t] *Selah*

61:5 [u]Ps 56:12 [v]Ps 86:11
5 For you have heard my vows,[u] O God;
you have given me the heritage of
those who fear your name.[v]

61:6 [w]Ps 21:4
6 Increase the days of the king's life,
his years for many generations.[w]

61:7 [x]Ps 41:12 [y]Ps 40:11
7 May he be enthroned in God's presence
forever;[x]
appoint your love and faithfulness to
protect him.[y]

61:8 [z]Ps 65:1; 71:22
8 Then will I ever sing praise to your
name[z]
and fulfill my vows day after day.

Psalm 62

For the director of music. For Jeduthun. A psalm of David.

62:1 [a]Ps 33:20
1 My soul finds rest[a] in God alone;
my salvation comes from him.

62:2 [b]Ps 89:26
2 He alone is my rock[b] and my salvation;
he is my fortress, I will never be
shaken.

3 How long will you assault a man?
Would all of you throw him down—

62:3 [c]Isa 30:13
this leaning wall,[c] this tottering fence?
4 They fully intend to topple him
from his lofty place;
they take delight in lies.
With their mouths they bless,

62:4 [d]Ps 28:3
but in their hearts they curse.[d] *Selah*

5 Find rest, O my soul, in God alone;
my hope comes from him.
6 He alone is my rock and my salvation;
he is my fortress, I will not be shaken.
7 My salvation and my honor depend on
God[a];

62:7 [e]Ps 46:1; 85:9; Jer 3:23
he is my mighty rock, my refuge.[e]
8 Trust in him at all times, O people;
pour out your hearts to him,[f]
for God is our refuge. *Selah*

62:8 [f]1Sa 1:15; Ps 42:4; La 2:19
9 Lowborn men are but a breath,[g]
the highborn are but a lie;
if weighed on a balance,[h] they are
nothing;

62:9 [g]Ps 39:5,11 [h]Isa 40:15
together they are only a breath.

62:10 [i]Isa 61:8 [j]Job 31:25; 1Ti 6:6-10
10 Do not trust in extortion
or take pride in stolen goods;[i]
though your riches increase,
do not set your heart on them.[j]

A Spiritual Heritage

PS 61:5

Those who have loved and honored the Lord from generation to generation pave the way for countless others to find their way to the promised land. David's heritage goes back from one generation to the next of those who feared and served God in the past and prepared the way for David to follow in their footsteps after a mighty God.

Because we have the record of God's awesome power and unwavering faithfulness to previous generations, we can be confident that everything he promised to those who came before us will be ours as well. God has called each one of us to be distinctly his own. We all have a godly heritage we can follow—those who have gone before us and have feared God's name, whether family, writer, speaker, pastor, Bible character or friend.

[a] 7 Or / *God Most High is my salvation and my honor*

Raging Thirst

PS 63:1

The Psalms are full of earthy, palpable descriptions of intense longings. Here David uses the metaphor of raging thirst to describe how desperately he wants to experience God's refreshing presence. He takes his soul's longing up a notch by articulating it in physical terms—his soul* and *his body long for God: a desire so intense that only an encounter with the lover of his soul will revive him. God's love for us is just as intense; he longs for communion with us (Isa 30:18) as we long for communion with him. Like David, we can bring any need to him, trust he will meet it and then go forth praising him (Ps 63:11).

11 One thing God has spoken,
two things have I heard:
that you, O God, are strong,
12 and that you, O Lord, are loving.
Surely you will reward each person
according to what he has done.[k]

Psalm 63

A psalm of David. When he was in the Desert of Judah.

1 O God, you are my God,
earnestly I seek you;
my soul thirsts for you,[l]
my body longs for you,
in a dry and weary land
where there is no water.

2 I have seen you in the sanctuary[m]
and beheld your power and your glory.
3 Because your love is better than life,[n]
my lips will glorify you.
4 I will praise you as long as I live,[o]
and in your name I will lift up my hands.[p]
5 My soul will be satisfied as with the richest of foods;[q]
with singing lips my mouth will praise you.
6 On my bed I remember you;
I think of you through the watches of the night.[r]
7 Because you are my help,[s]
I sing in the shadow of your wings.
8 My soul clings to you;
your right hand upholds me.[t]
9 They who seek my life will be destroyed;[u]
they will go down to the depths of the earth.[v]
10 They will be given over to the sword
and become food for jackals.
11 But the king will rejoice in God;
all who swear by God's name will praise him,[w]
while the mouths of liars will be silenced.

Psalm 64

For the director of music. A psalm of David.

1 Hear me, O God, as I voice my complaint;[x]
protect my life from the threat of the enemy.[y]
2 Hide me from the conspiracy of the wicked,[z]
from that noisy crowd of evildoers.

3 They sharpen their tongues like swords

62:12 [k]Job 34:11; Mt 16:27
63:1 [l]Ps 42:2; 84:2
63:2 [m]Ps 27:4
63:3 [n]Ps 69:16
63:4 [o]Ps 104:33 [p]Ps 28:2
63:5 [q]Ps 36:8
63:6 [r]Ps 42:8
63:7 [s]Ps 27:9
63:8 [t]Ps 18:35
63:9 [u]Ps 40:14 [v]Ps 55:15
63:11 [w]Dt 6:13; Ps 21:1; Isa 45:23
64:1 [x]Ps 55:2 [y]Ps 140:1
64:2 [z]Ps 56:6; 59:2

Week 16

Thirsting for God

The words of Psalm 63:1-8 are the words of one who has been in God's presence, has tasted the spiritual beauty of God and has no other desire than to be in God's presence again. David, the writer of this psalm, declares, "My soul thirsts for you . . . I have seen you in the sanctuary and beheld your . . . glory" (Ps 63:1-2). To behold God's glory is an awesome and life-changing event. How has it changed David?

What has David discovered about God's love and what is his response (Ps 63:3-4)? Once you have experienced the depth of God's love, you realize that life is empty and worthless without it (Ac 20:24).

What has David discovered about the spiritual food God provides and how does he respond (Ps 63:5)? God's words spoken to your soul are sweet as honey (Ps 119:103); nothing satisfies you like God does (Ps 103:1-5; 107:8-9).

What does David do during the night (Ps 63:6)? Remembering what God has done in the past (Dt 4:9; Ps 77:11; 103:2) will strengthen and encourage you in times of weakness and woundedness.

Why is David able to rejoice in song (Ps 63:7)? The surest way to find the Lord is to seek him through praise (Ps 105:1-4). When Solomon finishes building the temple, all the priests and Levites come to dedicate it to the Lord. But it isn't until the singers lift their voices in praise to God that his glory comes down and his presence fills the temple (2Ch 5:11-14).

What is the key to David's success in seeking God (Ps 63:8)? When you cling to God, when you refuse to let go, God *will* be found (Pr 8:17; Jer 29:13).

Enjoying God THROUGH the Word

Read Isaiah 55:1-13 (pages 1200-1201). This invitation is for every hungry, thirsty soul. No human resource can purchase these waters of refreshment (Isa 55:1). No amount of work can earn these life-giving streams (Isa 55:2). These waters are free because the price has already been paid for them (Ro 6:23). If your soul is thirsty, your spirit starving, come to the Lord and "your soul will delight in the richest of fare" (Isa 55:2).

Jesus says, "If anyone is thirsty, let him come to me and drink . . . [and] streams of living water will flow from within him" (Jn 7:37-38). If you seek to quench your thirst with anything or anyone else, your soul will languish and your spirit will dry up like a desert. Perhaps you already feel that your spirit is a desert. God has a promise for you: "I will make rivers flow on barren heights, and springs within the valleys. I will turn the desert into pools of water, and the parched ground into springs" (Isa 41:18).

Enjoying God THROUGH Experience

If you desire to enter God's presence, go to him in prayer. He is longing to come to you, to refresh you, to love you. Do as David does: remember. In a journal or a notebook or a personal computer file, record times in the past when God seemed near; list his blessings to you; record reasons to rejoice and to praise him for who he is and for what he has done. Build up your faith by writing about who Jesus is and who you are in him. It is in Jesus that you will have confidence to approach the throne of God (Eph 3:12; Heb 10:19-23) and enjoy the sweetness of his presence.

Go to page 967 for your next weekly study.

All Will Fear God

PS 64:9

Those who plan their lives with no heed to God's will and authority may think they're really getting somewhere. They may even prosper and appear to have it made, with no credit given to God at all. But this psalm of David clearly states that a day will come when all creation will bow before God, acknowledging his supremacy and praising his works (Ro 14:11; Php 2:9–11). In his great mercy God extends grace after grace so that everyone is given the opportunity to honor and praise him. God does not want anyone to perish but, instead, wants everyone to repent and become his own (2Pe 3:9).

and aim their words like deadly
arrows.[a] 64:3 [a]Ps 58:7
4 They shoot from ambush at the
innocent man;[b] 64:4 [b]Ps 11:2
they shoot at him suddenly, without [c]Ps 55:19
fear.[c]

5 They encourage each other in evil plans,
they talk about hiding their snares;
they say, "Who will see them*[a]*?"[d] 64:5 [d]Ps 10:11
6 They plot injustice and say,
"We have devised a perfect plan!"
Surely the mind and heart of man are
cunning.
7 But God will shoot them with arrows;
suddenly they will be struck down.
8 He will turn their own tongues against 64:8
them[e] [e]Ps 9:3;
and bring them to ruin; Pr 18:7
all who see them will shake their [f]Ps 22:7
heads[f] in scorn.

9 All mankind will fear;
they will proclaim the works of God
and ponder what he has done.[g] 64:9 [g]Jer 51:10
10 Let the righteous rejoice in the LORD
and take refuge in him;[h] 64:10 [h]Ps 25:20
let all the upright in heart praise him![i] [i]Ps 32:11

Psalm 65

For the director of music. A psalm of David. A song.

1 Praise awaits*[b]* you, O God, in Zion;
to you our vows will be fulfilled.[j] 65:1 [j]Ps 116:18
2 O you who hear prayer,
to you all men will come.[k] 65:2 [k]Isa 66:23
3 When we were overwhelmed by sins,[l]
you forgave*[c]* our transgressions.[m] 65:3 [l]Ps 38:4 [m]Heb 9:14
4 Blessed are those you choose[n]
and bring near to live in your courts!
We are filled with the good things of 65:4 [n]Ps 4:3;
your house,[o] 33:12
of your holy temple. [o]Ps 36:8
5 You answer us with awesome deeds of
righteousness,
O God our Savior,[p] 65:5 [p]Ps 85:4
the hope of all the ends of the earth [q]Ps 107:23
and of the farthest seas,[q]
6 who formed the mountains by your
power,
having armed yourself with strength,[r] 65:6 [r]Ps 93:1
7 who stilled the roaring of the seas,[s]
the roaring of their waves, 65:7 [s]Mt 8:26
and the turmoil of the nations.[t] [t]Isa 17:12-13
8 Those living far away fear your
wonders;
where morning dawns and evening
fades

[a] 5 Or *us* *[b]* 1 Or *befits*; the meaning of the Hebrew for this word is uncertain. *[c]* 3 Or *made atonement for*

you call forth songs of joy.

65:9 9 You care for the land and water it;[u]
[u]Ps 68:9-10 you enrich it abundantly.
[v]Ps 46:4; The streams of God are filled with water
104:14 to provide the people with grain,[v]
for so you have ordained it.[a]
10 You drench its furrows
and level its ridges;
you soften it with showers
and bless its crops.
11 You crown the year with your bounty,
and your carts overflow with
abundance.
65:12 [w]Job 28:26 12 The grasslands of the desert overflow;[w]
the hills are clothed with gladness.
65:13 [x]Ps 144:13 13 The meadows are covered with flocks[x]
[y]Ps 72:16 and the valleys are mantled with
[z]Ps 98:8; grain;[y]
Isa 55:12 they shout for joy and sing.[z]

Psalm 66

For the director of music. A song. A psalm.

66:1 [a]Ps 100:1 1 Shout with joy to God, all the earth![a]
2 Sing the glory of his name;[b]
66:2 [b]Ps 79:9 make his praise glorious!
3 Say to God, "How awesome are your
66:3 deeds![c]
[c]Ps 65:5 So great is your power
[d]Ps 18:44 that your enemies cringe[d] before you.
66:4 4 All the earth bows down[e] to you;
[e]Ps 22:27 they sing praise[f] to you,
[f]Ps 67:3 they sing praise to your name." *Selah*
66:5 5 Come and see what God has done,
[g]Ps 106:22 how awesome his works[g] in man's
66:6 behalf!
[h]Ex 14:22 6 He turned the sea into dry land,[h]
they passed through the waters on
foot—
66:7 come, let us rejoice in him.
[i]Ps 145:13 7 He rules forever[i] by his power,
[j]Ps 11:4 his eyes watch[j] the nations—
[k]Ps 140:8 let not the rebellious[k] rise up against
him. *Selah*

66:8 [l]Ps 98:4 8 Praise[l] our God, O peoples,
let the sound of his praise be heard;
66:9 9 he has preserved our lives
[m]Ps 121:3 and kept our feet from slipping.[m]
66:10 10 For you, O God, tested us;
[n]Ps 17:3; you refined us like silver.[n]
Isa 48:10; 11 You brought us into prison
Zec 13:9; and laid burdens[o] on our backs.
1Pe 1:6-7 12 You let men ride over our heads;[p]
66:11 [o]La 1:13 we went through fire and water,
66:12 but you brought us to a place of
[p]Isa 51:23 abundance.[q]
[q]Isa 43:2

[a] 9 Or *for that is how you prepare the land*

God's Provision

PS 65:9–13

The wonder of God's bountiful provision is the theme of this joyful psalm of praise. God literally tends and blesses the land, sending rain and healthy crops so that the harvest carts are filled with "abundance" (Ps 65:11). Picture such a cart if you can: the golden grain hangs heavily over the sides; the crisp green onions, succulent squashes and nourishing beans are heaped on top; grapes and melons crown the mound of food.

Now take that picture of abundance and use it to visualize God's spiritual, as well as physical, provision. This expression of God's expert care of the earth can also be a metaphorical expression for the way he cares for us: " 'My people will be filled with my bounty,' declares the LORD" (Jer 31:14). He is a God of abundance, whose love enriches, drenches, softens, blesses and gladdens our hearts until we overflow with joy.

A Listening God

PS 66:18–19

God can hear everything, but sometimes he won't hear (Isa 59:1–2; Jn 9:31). God's love for us is unconditional, but our fellowship with him is not. In any relationship, good communication happens only when both parties are fully present and sincere. When we communicate with the God who sees into the depths of our heart, we can't fool him with false devotion. If we're talking out of both sides of our mouth—praying in one breath and pursuing our own selfish interests in the other—then our communication with God will be short-circuited. We can't expect to enjoy sweet fellowship with him while we're holding on to our own agenda, planning to disobey him or disregarding his will. The good news is that, because of Christ's sacrifice for our sins, all it takes to reopen the lines of communication with our Father is a sincere, simple prayer of repentance (1Jn 1:9).

13 I will come to your temple with burnt
offerings
and fulfill my vows[r] to you—
14 vows my lips promised and my mouth
spoke
when I was in trouble.
15 I will sacrifice fat animals to you
and an offering of rams;
I will offer bulls and goats.[s] *Selah*
16 Come and listen,[t] all you who fear God;
let me tell[u] you what he has done for
me.
17 I cried out to him with my mouth;
his praise was on my tongue.
18 If I had cherished sin in my heart,
the Lord would not have listened;[v]
19 but God has surely listened
and heard my voice[w] in prayer.
20 Praise be to God,
who has not rejected[x] my prayer
or withheld his love from me!

Psalm 67

For the director of music. With stringed instruments. A psalm. A song.

1 May God be gracious to us and bless us
and make his face shine upon us,[y]
Selah
2 that your ways may be known on earth,
your salvation[z] among all nations.[a]
3 May the peoples praise you, O God;
may all the peoples praise you.
4 May the nations be glad and sing for joy,
for you rule the peoples justly[b]
and guide the nations of the earth.
Selah
5 May the peoples praise you, O God;
may all the peoples praise you.

6 Then the land will yield its harvest,[c]
and God, our God, will bless us.
7 God will bless us,
and all the ends of the earth will fear
him.[d]

Psalm 68

For the director of music. Of David. A psalm. A song.

1 May God arise, may his enemies be
scattered;
may his foes flee[e] before him.
2 As smoke[f] is blown away by the wind,
may you blow them away;
as wax melts[g] before the fire,
may the wicked perish before God.
3 But may the righteous be glad
and rejoice[h] before God;
may they be happy and joyful.

4 Sing to God, sing praise to his name,[i]

66:13 [r]Ecc 5:4
66:15 [s]Nu 6:14; Ps 51:19
66:16 [t]Ps 34:11 [u]Ps 71:15,24
66:18 [v]Job 36:21; Isa 1:15; Jas 4:3
66:19 [w]Ps 116:1-2
66:20 [x]Ps 22:24; 68:35
67:1 [y]Nu 6:24-26; Ps 4:6
67:2 [z]Isa 52:10 [a]Tit 2:11
67:4 [b]Ps 96:10-13
67:6 [c]Lev 26:4; Ps 85:12; Eze 34:27
67:7 [d]Ps 33:8
68:1 [e]Nu 10:35; Isa 33:3
68:2 [f]Hos 13:3 [g]Isa 9:18; Mic 1:4
68:3 [h]Ps 32:11
68:4 [i]Ps 66:2

extol him who rides on the clouds[a][j]—
his name is the LORD[k]—
and rejoice before him.
5 A father to the fatherless,[l] a defender of widows,[m]
is God in his holy dwelling.[n]
6 God sets the lonely in families,[b][o]
he leads forth the prisoners[p] with singing;
but the rebellious live in a sun-scorched land.[q]

7 When you went out[r] before your people, O God,
when you marched through the wasteland, *Selah*
8 the earth shook,
the heavens poured down rain,[s]
before God, the One of Sinai,[t]
before God, the God of Israel.
9 You gave abundant showers,[u] O God;
you refreshed your weary inheritance.
10 Your people settled in it,
and from your bounty, O God, you provided[v] for the poor.

11 The Lord announced the word,
and great was the company of those who proclaimed it:
12 "Kings and armies flee[w] in haste;
in the camps men divide the plunder.
13 Even while you sleep among the campfires,[c][x]
the wings of ⌞my⌟ dove are sheathed with silver,
its feathers with shining gold."
14 When the Almighty[d] scattered[y] the kings in the land,
it was like snow fallen on Zalmon.

15 The mountains of Bashan are majestic mountains;
rugged are the mountains of Bashan.
16 Why gaze in envy, O rugged mountains,
at the mountain where God chooses[z] to reign,
where the LORD himself will dwell forever?
17 The chariots of God are tens of thousands
and thousands of thousands;[a]
the Lord ⌞has come⌟ from Sinai into his sanctuary.
18 When you ascended on high,
you led captives[b] in your train;
you received gifts from men,[c]
even from[e] the rebellious—
that you,[f] O LORD God, might dwell there.

68:4 [j]Dt 33:26 [k]Ex 6:3; Ps 83:18
68:5 [l]Ps 10:14 [m]Dt 10:18 [n]Dt 26:15
68:6 [o]Ps 113:9 [p]Ac 12:6 [q]Ps 107:34
68:7 [r]Ex 13:21; Jdg 4:14
68:8 [s]Jdg 5:4 [t]Ex 19:16,18
68:9 [u]Dt 11:11
68:10 [v]Ps 74:19
68:12 [w]Jos 10:16
68:13 [x]Ge 49:14
68:14 [y]Jos 10:10
68:16 [z]Dt 12:5
68:17 [a]Dt 33:2; Da 7:10
68:18 [b]Jdg 5:12 [c]Eph 4:8*

[a] 4 Or / *prepare the way for him who rides through the deserts*
[b] 6 Or *the desolate in a homeland*
[c] 13 Or *saddlebags*
[d] 14 Hebrew *Shaddai*
[e] 18 Or *gifts for men, / even*
[f] 18 Or *they*

Sometimes this salvation business becomes confusing because people have so many different opinions. Some believe that a person has to stop doing any kind of wrong before she can receive salvation. Others think they can do enough good works, such as helping people and being kind, to earn salvation. Still others think that because they were raised in a religious home, they are automatically saved. But Scripture clearly teaches that salvation is a personal relationship with God granted only to those who sincerely ask Christ into their hearts and believe by faith what the Scriptures say about him.

—Thelma Wells

A Worship Parade

PS 68:24–27

This victory parade, honoring the Lord's triumph in battle, is not an uncommon sight in Israel's history. Joyous processions mark other momentous occasions, including the ark of the covenant's journey to Jerusalem (2Sa 6:12–15) and Jesus' humble entrance there (Jn 12:12–15). These parades are far more than merely fun and exciting events however; they are a tangible expression of the Hebrews' heartfelt worship of the King of glory. "Who is this King of glory? The LORD strong and mighty, the LORD mighty in battle . . . He is the King of glory" (Ps 24:8–10).

19 Praise be to the Lord, to God our Savior,[d]
who daily bears our burdens.[e] *Selah*
20 Our God is a God who saves;
from the Sovereign LORD comes escape
from death.[f]
21 Surely God will crush the heads[g] of his
enemies,
the hairy crowns of those who go on
in their sins.
22 The Lord says, "I will bring them from
Bashan;
I will bring them from the depths of
the sea,[h]
23 that you may plunge your feet in the
blood of your foes,[i]
while the tongues of your dogs[j] have
their share."

24 Your procession has come into view,
O God,
the procession of my God and King
into the sanctuary.[k]
25 In front are the singers, after them the
musicians;
with them are the maidens playing
tambourines.[l]
26 Praise God in the great congregation;
praise the LORD in the assembly of
Israel.[m]
27 There is the little tribe[n] of Benjamin,
leading them,
there the great throng of Judah's
princes,
and there the princes of Zebulun and
of Naphtali.

28 Summon your power, O God[a];
show us your strength, O God, as you
have done before.
29 Because of your temple at Jerusalem
kings will bring you gifts.[o]
30 Rebuke the beast among the reeds,
the herd of bulls[p] among the calves of
the nations.
Humbled, may it bring bars of silver.
Scatter the nations[q] who delight in
war.
31 Envoys will come from Egypt;[r]
Cush[b] will submit herself to God.

32 Sing to God, O kingdoms of the earth,
sing praise to the Lord, *Selah*
33 to him who rides[s] the ancient skies
above,
who thunders with mighty voice.[t]
34 Proclaim the power[u] of God,
whose majesty is over Israel,
whose power is in the skies.

68:19 [d]Ps 65:5 [e]Ps 55:22
68:20 [f]Ps 56:13
68:21 [g]Ps 110:5; Hab 3:13
68:22 [h]Nu 21:33
68:23 [i]Ps 58:10 [j]1Ki 21:19
68:24 [k]Ps 63:2
68:25 [l]Jdg 11:34; 1Ch 13:8
68:26 [m]Ps 26:12; Isa 48:1
68:27 [n]1Sa 9:21
68:29 [o]Ps 72:10
68:30 [p]Ps 22:12 [q]Ps 89:10
68:31 [r]Isa 19:19; 45:14
68:33 [s]Ps 18:10 [t]Ps 29:4
68:34 [u]Ps 29:1

[a] *28* Many Hebrew manuscripts, Septuagint and Syriac; most Hebrew manuscripts *Your God has summoned power for you*
[b] *31* That is, the upper Nile region

35 You are awesome, O God, in your sanctuary;
the God of Israel gives power and strength to his people.[v]

Praise be to God![w]

68:35 [v]Ps 29:11 [w]Ps 66:20

Psalm 69

For the director of music. To ⌞the tune of⌟ "Lilies." Of David.

1 Save me, O God,
for the waters have come up to my neck.[x]
2 I sink in the miry depths,[y]
where there is no foothold.
I have come into the deep waters;
the floods engulf me.
3 I am worn out calling for help;[z]
my throat is parched.
My eyes fail,[a]
looking for my God.
4 Those who hate me without reason[b]
outnumber the hairs of my head;
many are my enemies without cause,[c]
those who seek to destroy me.
I am forced to restore
what I did not steal.

5 You know my folly,[d] O God;
my guilt is not hidden from you.[e]

6 May those who hope in you
not be disgraced because of me,
O Lord, the LORD Almighty;
may those who seek you
not be put to shame because of me,
O God of Israel.
7 For I endure scorn for your sake,[f]
and shame covers my face.[g]
8 I am a stranger to my brothers,
an alien to my own mother's sons;[h]
9 for zeal for your house consumes me,[i]
and the insults of those who insult you fall on me.[j]
10 When I weep and fast,[k]
I must endure scorn;
11 when I put on sackcloth,[l]
people make sport of me.
12 Those who sit at the gate mock me,
and I am the song of the drunkards.[m]

13 But I pray to you, O LORD,
in the time of your favor;[n]
in your great love,[o] O God,
answer me with your sure salvation.
14 Rescue me from the mire,
do not let me sink;
deliver me from those who hate me,
from the deep waters.[p]
15 Do not let the floodwaters[q] engulf me
or the depths swallow me up[r]
or the pit close its mouth over me.

69:1 [x]Jnh 2:5
69:2 [y]Ps 40:2
69:3 [z]Ps 6:6 [a]Ps 119:82; Isa 38:14
69:4 [b]Jn 15:25* [c]Ps 35:19; 38:19
69:5 [d]Ps 38:5 [e]Ps 44:21
69:7 [f]Jer 15:15 [g]Ps 44:15
69:8 [h]Ps 31:11; Isa 53:3
69:9 [i]Jn 2:17* [j]Ps 89:50-51; Ro 15:3*
69:10 [k]Ps 35:13
69:11 [l]Ps 35:13
69:12 [m]Job 30:9
69:13 [n]Isa 49:8; 2Co 6:2 [o]Ps 51:1
69:14 [p]ver 2; Ps 144:7
69:15 [q]Ps 124:4-5 [r]Nu 16:33

But I Pray . . .

PS 69:13

David has just finished recounting a long list of horrendous sufferings—more than enough to land the average person in abject despair. "But I pray to you, O LORD," David decides. Not only does he have nowhere else to turn as he feels himself sinking beneath the mire, but he also knows that the God who loves him will answer his prayer in divinely perfect timing. God can be trusted because he is loving and merciful (Ps 69:16). David is absolutely confident, in spite of his overwhelmingly bleak circumstances, that God will hear him and rescue him. When we feel ourselves sinking fast, we need not resign ourselves to our fate. Rather, we can choose to pray to God in humble faith, as our Lord did (Heb 5:7). His salvation is sure!

A Cry for Justice

PS 69:27–28

David's merciless curse on the wicked is probably not so much a reflection of his personal desire for revenge as it is a cry for justice and the glory of God's name (see the note on Ps 59:7–8, page 917). Devout Jews in David's day were deeply concerned about how their own public suffering at the hands of their enemies would reflect on God's reputation (Ps 69:6–9).

David finds it unbearable that those who have held him up to public scorn (and thus mocked God himself) will be allowed to go merrily on their way. God's righteous justice demands that these sinners be dealt with mercilessly. They shouldn't even be allowed to keep living in this life, much less in the next! David's sense of divine justice is correct: The wages of sin is death (Ro 6:23). But through the gift of grace in Jesus Christ, even sinners can be saved from what they deserve (Eph 2:12–13).

16 Answer me, O LORD, out of the goodness
of your love;[s]
in your great mercy turn to me.
17 Do not hide your face[t] from your
servant;
answer me quickly, for I am in
trouble.[u]
18 Come near and rescue me;
redeem[v] me because of my foes.

19 You know how I am scorned,[w] disgraced
and shamed;
all my enemies are before you.
20 Scorn has broken my heart
and has left me helpless;
I looked for sympathy, but there was
none,
for comforters,[x] but I found none.[y]
21 They put gall in my food
and gave me vinegar for my thirst.[z]

22 May the table set before them become a
snare;
may it become retribution and[a] a trap.
23 May their eyes be darkened so they
cannot see,
and their backs be bent forever.[a]
24 Pour out your wrath[b] on them;
let your fierce anger overtake them.
25 May their place be deserted;[c]
let there be no one to dwell in their
tents.[d]
26 For they persecute those you wound
and talk about the pain of those you
hurt.[e]
27 Charge them with crime upon crime;[f]
do not let them share in your
salvation.[g]
28 May they be blotted out of the book of
life[h]
and not be listed with the righteous.[i]

29 I am in pain and distress;
may your salvation, O God, protect
me.[j]

30 I will praise God's name in song[k]
and glorify him[l] with thanksgiving.
31 This will please the LORD more than an
ox,
more than a bull with its horns and
hoofs.[m]
32 The poor will see and be glad[n]—
you who seek God, may your hearts
live![o]
33 The LORD hears the needy[p]
and does not despise his captive
people.

34 Let heaven and earth praise him,
the seas and all that move in them,[q]

69:16 [s]Ps 63:3
69:17 [t]Ps 27:9 [u]Ps 66:14
69:18 [v]Ps 49:15
69:19 [w]Ps 22:6
69:20 [x]Job 16:2 [y]Isa 63:5
69:21 [z]Mt 27:34; Mk 15:23; Jn 19:28-30
69:23 [a]Isa 6:9-10; Ro 11:9-10*
69:24 [b]Ps 79:6
69:25 [c]Mt 23:38 [d]Ac 1:20*
69:26 [e]Isa 53:4; Zec 1:15
69:27 [f]Ne 4:5 [g]Ps 109:14; Isa 26:10
69:28 [h]Ex 32:32-33; Lk 10:20; Php 4:3 [i]Eze 13:9
69:29 [j]Ps 59:1; 70:5
69:30 [k]Ps 28:7 [l]Ps 34:3
69:31 [m]Ps 50:9-13
69:32 [n]Ps 34:2 [o]Ps 22:26
69:33 [p]Ps 12:5; 68:6
69:34 [q]Ps 96:11; 148:1; Isa 44:23; 49:13; 55:12

[a] 22 Or *snare / and their fellowship become*

35 for God will save Zion[r]
and rebuild the cities of Judah.[s]
Then people will settle there and
possess it;
36 the children of his servants will
inherit it,
and those who love his name will
dwell there.[t]

Psalm 70

For the director of music. Of David. A petition.

1 Hasten, O God, to save me;
O LORD, come quickly to help me.[u]
2 May those who seek my life[v]
be put to shame and confusion;
may all who desire my ruin
be turned back in disgrace.[w]
3 May those who say to me, "Aha! Aha!"
turn back because of their shame.
4 But may all who seek you
rejoice and be glad in you;
may those who love your salvation
always say,
"Let God be exalted!"

5 Yet I am poor and needy;[x]
come quickly to me,[y] O God.
You are my help and my deliverer;
O LORD, do not delay.

Psalm 71

1 In you, O LORD, I have taken refuge;
let me never be put to shame.[z]
2 Rescue me and deliver me in your
righteousness;
turn your ear[a] to me and save me.
3 Be my rock of refuge,
to which I can always go;
give the command to save me,
for you are my rock and my fortress.[b]
4 Deliver me, O my God, from the hand of
the wicked,[c]
from the grasp of evil and cruel men.

5 For you have been my hope,
O Sovereign LORD,
my confidence[d] since my youth.
6 From birth[e] I have relied on you;
you brought me forth from my
mother's womb.[f]
I will ever praise[g] you.
7 I have become like a portent[h] to many,
but you are my strong refuge.[i]
8 My mouth[j] is filled with your praise,
declaring your splendor[k] all day long.

9 Do not cast[l] me away when I am old;[m]
do not forsake me when my strength
is gone.
10 For my enemies speak against me;

69:35 [r]Ob 1:17 [s]Ps 51:18; Isa 44:26
69:36 [t]Ps 37:29; 102:28
70:1 [u]Ps 40:13
70:2 [v]Ps 35:4 [w]Ps 35:26
70:5 [x]Ps 40:17 [y]Ps 141:1
71:1 [z]Ps 25:2-3; 31:1
71:2 [a]Ps 17:6
71:3 [b]Ps 18:2; 31:2-3; 44:4
71:4 [c]Ps 140:4
71:5 [d]Job 4:6; Jer 17:7
71:6 [e]Ps 22:10 [f]Ps 22:9; Isa 46:3 [g]Ps 9:1; 34:1; 52:9; 119:164; 145:2
71:7 [h]Isa 8:18; 1Co 4:9 [i]2Sa 22:3; Ps 61:3
71:8 [j]Ps 51:15; 63:5 [k]Ps 35:28; 96:6; 104:1
71:9 [l]Ps 51:11 [m]ver 18; Ps 92:14; Isa 46:4

Hurry!

PS 70:1

Pressing needs call for fervent prayers, and David doesn't hesitate to add a sense of urgency to his requests for help. His "Hurry up, God!" is not a frantic, fearful demand, but a proclamation of his faith that God, his sure help and deliverer (Ps 70:5), will indeed come through for him. David *knows* help is on its way; he is bursting with the anticipation of certain rescue.

***When we are in urgent need, we can cry out in vulnerability and faith, "Lord, come quickly!" as David did so many times before us* (Ps 22:19; 31:2; 38:22; 40:13; 141:1). *And we can be confident in the Lord's promise of ultimate deliverance, "Behold, I am coming soon!"* (Rev 22:7).**

Even When I Am Old

PS 71:9,18

All his life the psalmist has experienced God's unwavering faithfulness, and he is full of praise (Ps 71:8). So why the sudden plea that God continue to be faithful, as if God needs to be reminded that the psalmist will no doubt need him even more as he grows old and frail? When we feel particularly weak and vulnerable, we naturally have moments of fear and doubt. A sudden shadow can appear on the sunny landscape of our faith, causing our spiritual hearts to skip a beat. Will everything continue to be all right? Will God be there for us if we become more and more helpless? The psalmist's answer to his own momentary fears is full of faith in a righteous, powerful and loving God (Ps 71:19–24). Not only will God continue to honor and help him, but the Holy One of Israel will also continue to use him, throughout his final days, to declare God's power to others.

those who wait to kill[n] me conspire[o]
together.
11 They say, "God has forsaken him;
pursue him and seize him,
for no one will rescue[p] him."
12 Be not far[q] from me, O God;
come quickly, O my God, to help[r] me.
13 May my accusers perish in shame;
may those who want to harm me
be covered with scorn and disgrace.[s]

14 But as for me, I will always have hope;[t]
I will praise you more and more.
15 My mouth will tell[u] of your
righteousness,
of your salvation all day long,
though I know not its measure.
16 I will come and proclaim your mighty
acts,[v] O Sovereign LORD;
I will proclaim your righteousness,
yours alone.
17 Since my youth, O God, you have
taught[w] me,
and to this day I declare your
marvelous deeds.[x]
18 Even when I am old and gray,[y]
do not forsake me, O God,
till I declare your power to the next
generation,
your might to all who are to come.[z]

19 Your righteousness reaches to the skies,[a]
O God,
you who have done great things.[b]
Who, O God, is like you?[c]
20 Though you have made me see
troubles,[d] many and bitter,
you will restore[e] my life again;
from the depths of the earth
you will again bring me up.
21 You will increase my honor[f]
and comfort[g] me once again.

22 I will praise you with the harp[h]
for your faithfulness, O my God;
I will sing praise to you with the lyre,[i]
O Holy One of Israel.[j]
23 My lips will shout for joy
when I sing praise to you—
I, whom you have redeemed.[k]
24 My tongue will tell of your righteous
acts
all day long,[l]
for those who wanted to harm me[m]
have been put to shame and
confusion.

Psalm 72

Of Solomon.

1 Endow the king with your justice,
O God,

71:10 [n]Ps 10:8; 59:3; Pr 1:18 [o]Ps 31:13; 56:6; Mt 12:14
71:11 [p]Ps 7:2
71:12 [q]Ps 35:22; 38:21 [r]Ps 38:22; 70:1
71:13 [s]ver 24
71:14 [t]Ps 130:7
71:15 [u]Ps 35:28; 40:5
71:16 [v]Ps 106:2
71:17 [w]Dt 4:5 [x]Ps 26:7
71:18 [y]ver 9 [z]Ps 22:30,31; 78:4
71:19 [a]Ps 36:5; 57:10 [b]Ps 126:2; Lk 1:49 [c]Ps 35:10
71:20 [d]Ps 60:3 [e]Hos 6:2
71:21 [f]Ps 18:35 [g]Ps 23:4; 86:17; Isa 12:1; 49:13
71:22 [h]Ps 33:2 [i]Ps 92:3; 144:9 [j]2Ki 19:22
71:23 [k]Ps 103:4
71:24 [l]Ps 35:28 [m]ver 13

the royal son with your righteousness.
72:2 [n]Isa 9:7; 11:4-5; 32:1
[2]He will[a] judge your people in
righteousness,[n]
your afflicted ones with justice.
[3]The mountains will bring prosperity to
the people,
the hills the fruit of righteousness.
[4]He will defend the afflicted among the
people
72:4 [o]Isa 11:4
and save the children of the needy;[o]
he will crush the oppressor.

[5]He will endure[b] as long as the sun,
as long as the moon, through all
generations.
72:6 [p]Dt 32:2; Hos 6:3
[6]He will be like rain[p] falling on a mown
field,
like showers watering the earth.
72:7 [q]Ps 92:12; Isa 2:4
[7]In his days the righteous will flourish;[q]
prosperity will abound till the moon
is no more.
72:8 [r]Ex 23:31 [s]Zec 9:10
[8]He will rule from sea to sea
and from the River[c][r] to the ends of the
earth.[d][s]
[9]The desert tribes will bow before him
and his enemies will lick the dust.
[10]The kings of Tarshish and of distant
shores
will bring tribute to him;
72:10 [t]Ge 10:7 [u]2Ch 9:24
the kings of Sheba[t] and Seba
will present him gifts.[u]
[11]All kings will bow down to him
and all nations will serve him.

[12]For he will deliver the needy who cry
out,
the afflicted who have no one to help.
[13]He will take pity on the weak and the
needy
and save the needy from death.
72:14 [v]Ps 69:18 [w]1Sa 26:21; Ps 116:15
[14]He will rescue[v] them from oppression
and violence,
for precious[w] is their blood in his
sight.

[15]Long may he live!
72:15 [x]Isa 60:6
May gold from Sheba[x] be given him.
May people ever pray for him
and bless him all day long.
[16]Let grain abound throughout the land;
on the tops of the hills may it sway.
72:16 [y]Ps 104:16
Let its fruit flourish like Lebanon;[y]
let it thrive like the grass of the field.
72:17 [z]Ex 3:15 [a]Ps 89:36 [b]Ge 12:3; Lk 1:48
[17]May his name endure forever;[z]
may it continue as long as the sun.[a]

All nations will be blessed through him,
and they will call him blessed.[b]

[a] 2 Or *May he*; similarly in verses 3–11 and 17
[b] 5 Septuagint; Hebrew *You will be feared* [c] 8 That is, the Euphrates [d] 8 Or *the end of the land*

A Prophetic Psalm

PS 72

While this prayer is offered for the reigning Hebrew monarch at the time, most commentators agree that it is also clearly prophetic about the kingdom of Jesus Christ. Under the Messiah's righteous rule, God's people will be treated with perfect justice and mercy. They will be blessed with abundance and continually refreshed with his presence. The royal Son's authority will extend to the ends of the earth and will endure forever. All people will bow to his rule, and the masses will praise him. The afflicted will be protected from any further harm, and the whole earth will burst at the seams with the glory of God. "Amen and Amen" (Ps 72:19)!

[18]Praise be to the LORD God, the God of
Israel,[c]
who alone does marvelous deeds.[d]
[19]Praise be to his glorious name forever;
may the whole earth be filled with his
glory.[e]
Amen and Amen.[f]

[20]This concludes the prayers of David son
of Jesse.

72:18 [c]1Ch 29:10; Ps 41:13; 106:48 [d]Job 5:9
72:19 [e]Nu 14:21; Ne 9:5 [f]Ps 41:13

BOOK III

Psalms 73–89

Psalm 73

A psalm of Asaph.

[1]Surely God is good to Israel,
to those who are pure in heart.[g]

[2]But as for me, my feet had almost
slipped;
I had nearly lost my foothold.
[3]For I envied[h] the arrogant
when I saw the prosperity of the
wicked.[i]

[4]They have no struggles;
their bodies are healthy and strong.[a]
[5]They are free[j] from the burdens
common to man;
they are not plagued by human ills.
[6]Therefore pride is their necklace;[k]
they clothe themselves with violence.[l]
[7]From their callous hearts[m] comes
iniquity[b];
the evil conceits of their minds know
no limits.
[8]They scoff, and speak with malice;
in their arrogance[n] they threaten
oppression.
[9]Their mouths lay claim to heaven,
and their tongues take possession of
the earth.
[10]Therefore their people turn to them
and drink up waters in abundance.[c]
[11]They say, "How can God know?
Does the Most High have
knowledge?"

[12]This is what the wicked are like—
always carefree, they increase in
wealth.[o]

[13]Surely in vain[p] have I kept my heart
pure;

73:1 [g]Mt 5:8
73:3 [h]Ps 37:1; Pr 23:17 [i]Job 21:7; Jer 12:1
73:5 [j]Job 21:9
73:6 [k]Ge 41:42 [l]Ps 109:18
73:7 [m]Ps 17:10
73:8 [n]Ps 17:10; Jude 16
73:12 [o]Ps 49:6
73:13 [p]Job 21:15; 34:9

[a] *4* With a different word division of the Hebrew; Masoretic Text *struggles at their death; / their bodies are healthy* [b] *7* Syriac (see also Septuagint); Hebrew *Their eyes bulge with fat* [c] *10* The meaning of the Hebrew for this verse is uncertain.

God promises to deliver us from fear and torment, but that deliverance must be fueled by prayer, Scripture reading, faith in God, and obedience to him. I have suggested this method of dealing with fear to my children, friends, and acquaintances because as simple as it may seem, it gets God's attention. He is the One who told us to humble ourselves as little children as we seek his face.

—Thelma Wells

73:13 in vain have I washed my hands in
[q]Ps 26:6 innocence.[q]
[14] All day long I have been plagued;
I have been punished every morning.

[15] If I had said, "I will speak thus,"
I would have betrayed your children.
73:16 [16] When I tried to understand[r] all this,
[r]Ecc 8:17 it was oppressive to me
73:17 [17] till I entered the sanctuary[s] of God;
[s]Ps 77:13 then I understood their final destiny.[t]
[t]Ps 37:38

73:18 [18] Surely you place them on slippery
[u]Ps 35:6 ground;[u]
you cast them down to ruin.
73:19 [19] How suddenly[v] are they destroyed,
[v]Isa 47:11 completely swept away by terrors!
73:20 [20] As a dream[w] when one awakes,[x]
[w]Job 20:8 so when you arise, O Lord,
[x]Ps 78:65 you will despise them as fantasies.

[21] When my heart was grieved
and my spirit embittered,
73:22 [22] I was senseless[y] and ignorant;
[y]Ps 49:10; 92:6 I was a brute beast[z] before you.
[z]Ecc 3:18

[23] Yet I am always with you;
you hold me by my right hand.
73:24 [24] You guide[a] me with your counsel,[b]
[a]Ps 48:14 and afterward you will take me into
[b]Ps 32:8 glory.
[25] Whom have I in heaven but you?
And earth has nothing I desire besides
73:25 you.[c]
[c]Php 3:8 [26] My flesh and my heart[d] may fail,[e]
73:26 but God is the strength of my heart
[d]Ps 84:2 and my portion forever.
[e]Ps 40:12

73:27 [27] Those who are far from you will perish;[f]
[f]Ps 119:155 you destroy all who are unfaithful to
you.
73:28 [28] But as for me, it is good to be near God.[g]
[g]Heb 10:22; Jas 4:8 I have made the Sovereign LORD my
[h]Ps 40:5 refuge;
I will tell of all your deeds.[h]

Psalm 74

A *maskil*[a] of Asaph.

74:1 [1] Why have you rejected us forever,[i]
[i]Dt 29:20; Ps 44:23 O God?
[j]Ps 79:13; 95:7; 100:3 Why does your anger smolder against
the sheep of your pasture?[j]
74:2 [2] Remember the people you purchased[k] of
[k]Ex 15:16 old,[l]
[l]Dt 32:7 the tribe of your inheritance, whom
[m]Ex 15:13 you redeemed[m]—
[n]Ps 68:16 Mount Zion, where you dwelt.[n]
[3] Turn your steps toward these everlasting
ruins,
all this destruction the enemy has
brought on the sanctuary.

Asaph

PS 74:1

After the ark of the covenant comes to rest at the house of the Lord, King David appoints several Levites to be music ministry leaders. Asaph is one of these men assigned to use his musical gifts to worship the Lord (1Ch 6:31–32,39). Many years later King Hezekiah orders the Levites to praise the Lord with songs written by Asaph and David (2Ch 29:30). In this verse Asaph is also referred to as a "seer," one to whom God gives prophetic messages (1Sa 9:9). Asaph is credited with a dozen psalms (Ps 50; 73–83), although some of these psalms were composed later and evidently refer to descendants of Asaph who wrote under his name.

[a] Title: Probably a literary or musical term

God in his mercy, out of a desire for a real relationship with us, will continue to allow us to fall flat on our faces until all we want is him. He is so committed to our spiritual health and growth that he will do whatever it takes to free us from our selfish nature. But this is no mindless, barbaric endurance test. He knows us well and loves us lavishly.

—Sheila Walsh

4 Your foes roared[o] in the place where you
met with us;
they set up their standards[p] as signs.
5 They behaved like men wielding axes
to cut through a thicket of trees.[q]
6 They smashed all the carved[r] paneling
with their axes and hatchets.
7 They burned your sanctuary to the
ground;
they defiled the dwelling place of your
Name.
8 They said in their hearts, "We will
crush[s] them completely!"
They burned every place where God
was worshiped in the land.
9 We are given no miraculous signs;
no prophets[t] are left,
and none of us knows how long this
will be.

10 How long will the enemy mock you,
O God?
Will the foe revile[u] your name
forever?
11 Why do you hold back your hand, your
right hand?[v]
Take it from the folds of your garment
and destroy them!

12 But you, O God, are my king[w] from of
old;
you bring salvation upon the earth.
13 It was you who split open the sea[x] by
your power;
you broke the heads of the monster[y]
in the waters.
14 It was you who crushed the heads of
Leviathan
and gave him as food to the creatures
of the desert.
15 It was you who opened up springs[z] and
streams;
you dried up[a] the ever flowing rivers.
16 The day is yours, and yours also the
night;
you established the sun and moon.[b]
17 It was you who set all the boundaries[c]
of the earth;
you made both summer and winter.[d]

18 Remember how the enemy has mocked
you, O LORD,
how foolish people[e] have reviled your
name.
19 Do not hand over the life of your dove to
wild beasts;
do not forget the lives of your
afflicted[f] people forever.
20 Have regard for your covenant,[g]
because haunts of violence fill the
dark places of the land.

74:4 [o]La 2:7 [p]Nu 2:2
74:5 [q]Jer 46:22
74:6 [r]1Ki 6:18
74:8 [s]Ps 83:4
74:9 [t]1Sa 3:1
74:10 [u]Ps 44:16
74:11 [v]La 2:3
74:12 [w]Ps 44:4
74:13 [x]Ex 14:21 [y]Isa 51:9; Eze 29:3
74:15 [z]Ex 17:6; Nu 20:11 [a]Jos 2:10; 3:13
74:16 [b]Ge 1:16; Ps 136:7-9
74:17 [c]Dt 32:8; Ac 17:26 [d]Ge 8:22
74:18 [e]Dt 32:6; Ps 39:8
74:19 [f]Ps 9:18
74:20 [g]Ge 17:7; Ps 106:45

74:21 [h]Ps 103:6 [i]Ps 35:10

21 Do not let the oppressed[h] retreat in
disgrace;
may the poor and needy[i] praise your
name.

74:22 [j]Ps 53:1

22 Rise up, O God, and defend your cause;
remember how fools[j] mock you all
day long.

74:23 [k]Ps 65:7

23 Do not ignore the clamor of your
adversaries,[k]
the uproar of your enemies, which
rises continually.

Psalm 75

For the director of music. ⌞To the tune of⌟ "Do Not Destroy." A psalm of Asaph. A song.

1 We give thanks to you, O God,
we give thanks, for your Name is
near;[l]
men tell of your wonderful deeds.[m]

75:1 [l]Ps 145:18 [m]Ps 44:1; 71:16

2 You say, "I choose the appointed time;
it is I who judge uprightly.
3 When the earth and all its people
quake,[n]
it is I who hold its pillars[o] firm. *Selah*

75:3 [n]Isa 24:19 [o]1Sa 2:8

4 To the arrogant I say, 'Boast no more,'
and to the wicked, 'Do not lift up
your horns.[p]

75:4 [p]Zec 1:21

5 Do not lift your horns against heaven;
do not speak with outstretched neck.' "
6 No one from the east or the west
or from the desert can exalt a man.
7 But it is God who judges:[q]
He brings one down, he exalts
another.[r]

75:7 [q]Ps 50:6 [r]1Sa 2:7; Ps 147:6; Da 2:21

8 In the hand of the LORD is a cup
full of foaming wine mixed[s] with
spices;
he pours it out, and all the wicked of the
earth
drink it down to its very dregs.[t]

75:8 [s]Pr 23:30 [t]Job 21:20; Jer 25:15

9 As for me, I will declare[u] this forever;
I will sing praise to the God of Jacob.

75:9 [u]Ps 40:10

10 I will cut off the horns of all the wicked,
but the horns of the righteous will be
lifted up.[v]

75:10 [v]Ps 89:17; 92:10; 148:14

Psalm 76

For the director of music. With stringed instruments. A psalm of Asaph. A song.

1 In Judah God is known;
his name is great in Israel.
2 His tent is in Salem,[w]
his dwelling place in Zion.

76:2 [w]Ge 14:18

3 There he broke the flashing arrows,
the shields and the swords, the
weapons of war.[x] *Selah*

76:3 [x]Ps 46:9

4 You are resplendent with light,

Wine = Wrath

PS 75:8

The cup of wine is a frequent Biblical metaphor for God's wrath. To mix wine with spices makes it even more potent and destructive (Pr 23:29–35). In the final judgment, the rebel Babylon will be given "the cup filled with the wine of the fury of [God's] wrath" (Rev 16:19). God's chosen people have had to drink this "wine" at times themselves (Ps 60:3; Isa 51:17), but God promises that, for the redeemed, his wrath will come to an end (Isa 51:22–23).

more majestic than mountains rich
with game.
5 Valiant men lie plundered,
they sleep their last sleep;[y]
not one of the warriors
can lift his hands.
6 At your rebuke, O God of Jacob,
both horse and chariot[z] lie still.
7 You alone are to be feared.[a]
Who can stand[b] before you when you
are angry?[c]
8 From heaven you pronounced
judgment,
and the land feared[d] and was quiet—
9 when you, O God, rose up to judge,[e]
to save all the afflicted of the land.
Selah
10 Surely your wrath against men brings
you praise,[f]
and the survivors of your wrath are
restrained.[a]
11 Make vows to the LORD your God and
fulfill them;[g]
let all the neighboring lands
bring gifts[h] to the One to be feared.
12 He breaks the spirit of rulers;
he is feared by the kings of the earth.

76:5 [y]Ps 13:3
76:6 [z]Ex 15:1
76:7 [a]1Ch 16:25 [b]Ezr 9:15; Rev 6:17 [c]Ps 2:5; Na 1:6
76:8 [d]1Ch 16:30; 2Ch 20:29-30
76:9 [e]Ps 9:8
76:10 [f]Ex 9:16; Ro 9:17
76:11 [g]Ps 50:14; Ecc 5:4-5 [h]2Ch 32:23; Ps 68:29

Psalm 77

For the director of music. For Jeduthun. Of Asaph. A psalm.

1 I cried out to God[i] for help;
I cried out to God to hear me.
2 When I was in distress,[j] I sought the
Lord;
at night I stretched out untiring hands[k]
and my soul refused to be comforted.[l]

3 I remembered you, O God, and I
groaned;
I mused, and my spirit grew faint.[m]
Selah
4 You kept my eyes from closing;
I was too troubled to speak.
5 I thought about the former days,[n]
the years of long ago;
6 I remembered my songs in the night.
My heart mused and my spirit
inquired:

7 "Will the Lord reject forever?
Will he never show his favor[o] again?
8 Has his unfailing love vanished forever?
Has his promise[p] failed for all time?
9 Has God forgotten to be merciful?[q]
Has he in anger withheld his
compassion?[r]" *Selah*

77:1 [i]Ps 3:4
77:2 [j]Ps 50:15; Isa 26:9,16 [k]Job 11:13 [l]Ge 37:35
77:3 [m]Ps 143:4
77:5 [n]Dt 32:7; Ps 44:1; 143:5; Isa 51:9
77:7 [o]Ps 85:1
77:8 [p]2Pe 3:9
77:9 [q]Ps 25:6; 40:11; 51:1 [r]Isa 49:15

[a] *10* Or *Surely the wrath of men brings you praise, / and with the remainder of wrath you arm yourself*

I find it wonderfully liberating to talk to God with my humanness showing in all its unattractiveness and not have to worry about what is best for him. God is the strong one and not I. He doesn't need my diplomacy, and neither does he fall off his throne when I tell him what he already knows about my feelings—even when that feeling is anger.

—Marilyn Meberg

10 Then I thought, "To this I will appeal:
the years of the right hand[s] of the Most High."
11 I will remember the deeds of the LORD;
yes, I will remember your miracles[t] of long ago.
12 I will meditate on all your works
and consider all your mighty deeds.

13 Your ways, O God, are holy.
What god is so great as our God?[u]
14 You are the God who performs miracles;
you display your power among the peoples.
15 With your mighty arm you redeemed your people,[v]
the descendants of Jacob and Joseph. *Selah*

16 The waters[w] saw you, O God,
the waters saw you and writhed;[x]
the very depths were convulsed.
17 The clouds poured down water,[y]
the skies resounded with thunder;
your arrows flashed back and forth.
18 Your thunder was heard in the whirlwind,
your lightning lit up the world;
the earth trembled and quaked.[z]
19 Your path led through the sea,[a]
your way through the mighty waters,
though your footprints were not seen.

20 You led your people[b] like a flock[c]
by the hand of Moses and Aaron.

Psalm 78

A *maskil*[a] of Asaph.

1 O my people, hear my teaching;[d]
listen to the words of my mouth.
2 I will open my mouth in parables,[e]
I will utter hidden things, things from of old—
3 what we have heard and known,
what our fathers have told us.[f]
4 We will not hide them from their children;[g]
we will tell the next generation
the praiseworthy deeds[h] of the LORD,
his power, and the wonders he has done.
5 He decreed statutes[i] for Jacob[j]
and established the law in Israel,
which he commanded our forefathers
to teach their children,
6 so the next generation would know them,
even the children yet to be born,[k]
and they in turn would tell their children.

77:10 [s]Ps 31:22
77:11 [t]Ps 143:5
77:13 [u]Ex 15:11; Ps 71:19; 86:8
77:15 [v]Ex 6:6; Dt 9:29
77:16 [w]Ex 14:21, 28; Hab 3:8 [x]Ps 114:4; Hab 3:10
77:17 [y]Jdg 5:4
77:18 [z]Jdg 5:4
77:19 [a]Hab 3:15
77:20 [b]Ex 13:21 [c]Ps 78:52; Isa 63:11
78:1 [d]Isa 51:4; 55:3
78:2 [e]Ps 49:4; Mt 13:35*
78:3 [f]Ps 44:1
78:4 [g]Dt 11:19 [h]Ps 26:7; 71:17
78:5 [i]Ps 19:7; 81:5 [j]Ps 147:19
78:6 [k]Ps 22:31; 102:18

[a] Title: Probably a literary or musical term

Repeating History

PS 78:4–6

If people don't learn from their mistakes, the negative aspects of human history are destined to repeat themselves. That's why God ordains that his statutes and principles, along with the stories of his remarkable deeds, be passed from generation to generation. God urges his people to tell others about him during the everyday events of life: "Talk about them when you sit at home and when you walk along the road, when you lie down and when you get up" (Dt 6:7).

Evangelism occurs when a believer passes on his or her knowledge and experience to another person: parent to child, friend to friend, aged to young. In the context of such relationships, the kingdom of God is perpetuated and disciples are made. We all have opportunities to tell others about God's praiseworthy deeds, power and wonders. Wherever we are—at work, at a neighbor's house, at a family reunion—we can spread that word so that one more person can choose loyalty to the King of kings rather than rebellion (Ps 78:7–8).

M y children should know that the road was broken by the sin and disobedience of Adam, in such a way that no one could arrive at Eternal Life . . . Sin had closed Heaven and bolted the doors of mercy . . . Adam transgressed My obedience, and merited eternal death in soul and body. And, as soon as he had sinned, a tempestuous flood arose, which ever buffets him with its waves, bringing him weariness and trouble from himself, the devil, and the world.

Everyone was drowned in the flood, because no one, with his own justice alone, could arrive at Eternal Life. And so, wishing to remedy your great evils, I have given you the Bridge of My Son, in order that, passing across the flood, you may not be drowned.

—Catherine of Siena (1347-1380)

7 Then they would put their trust in God
and would not forget[l] his deeds
but would keep his commands.[m]
8 They would not be like their
forefathers[n]—
a stubborn[o] and rebellious[p]
generation,
whose hearts were not loyal to God,
whose spirits were not faithful to him.

9 The men of Ephraim, though armed
with bows,[q]
turned back on the day of battle;[r]
10 they did not keep God's covenant[s]
and refused to live by his law.
11 They forgot what he had done,[t]
the wonders he had shown them.
12 He did miracles[u] in the sight of their
fathers
in the land of Egypt,[v] in the region of
Zoan.[w]
13 He divided the sea[x] and led them
through;
he made the water stand firm like a
wall.[y]
14 He guided them with the cloud by day
and with light from the fire all night.[z]
15 He split the rocks[a] in the desert
and gave them water as abundant as
the seas;
16 he brought streams out of a rocky crag
and made water flow down like rivers.
17 But they continued to sin[b] against him,
rebelling in the desert against the
Most High.
18 They willfully put God to the test[c]
by demanding the food they craved.[d]
19 They spoke against God,[e] saying,
"Can God spread a table in the desert?
20 When he struck the rock, water gushed
out,[f]
and streams flowed abundantly.
But can he also give us food?
Can he supply meat[g] for his people?"
21 When the LORD heard them, he was very
angry;
his fire broke out[h] against Jacob,
and his wrath rose against Israel,
22 for they did not believe in God
or trust[i] in his deliverance.
23 Yet he gave a command to the skies
above
and opened the doors of the heavens;[j]
24 he rained down manna[k] for the people
to eat,
he gave them the grain of heaven.
25 Men ate the bread of angels;
he sent them all the food they could
eat.
26 He let loose the east wind[l] from the
heavens

78:7 [l]Dt 6:12 [m]Dt 5:29
78:8 [n]2Ch 30:7 [o]Ex 32:9 [p]ver 37; Isa 30:9
78:9 [q]ver 57; 1Ch 12:2 [r]Jdg 20:39
78:10 [s]2Ki 17:15
78:11 [t]Ps 106:13
78:12 [u]Ps 106:22 [v]Ex 7-12 [w]Nu 13:22
78:13 [x]Ex 14:21; Ps 136:13 [y]Ex 15:8
78:14 [z]Ex 13:21; Ps 105:39
78:15 [a]Nu 20:11; 1Co 10:4
78:17 [b]Dt 9:22; Isa 63:10; Heb 3:16
78:18 [c]1Co 10:9 [d]Ex 16:2; Nu 11:4
78:19 [e]Nu 21:5
78:20 [f]Nu 20:11 [g]Nu 11:18
78:21 [h]Nu 11:1
78:22 [i]Dt 1:32; Heb 3:19
78:23 [j]Ge 7:11; Mal 3:10
78:24 [k]Ex 16:4; Jn 6:31*
78:26 [l]Nu 11:31

Bathsheba

Just Say No?

No one could refuse a summons from the king, even when it came late at night. As Bathsheba followed David's servants back to the palace, did she wonder why David had sent for her? It must have been a somewhat flattering experience to be desired by the king, one of the most powerful and respected men of his time.

It is impossible to put ourselves in Bathsheba's place and understand her predicament. She lived in a time when men ruled women's lives absolutely. But did her powerlessness truly extend this far? Would David have raped her, had she refused him? We know only that David sent for her, and Bathsheba went.

It could have ended as a one-night fling. Except Bathsheba was pregnant. The Law required death for their adultery, and now it couldn't be hidden. She left the situation for David to handle, with tragic results. David's midnight passion began a string of heartbreaks that haunted him and his family for years to come.

Nevertheless, God can bring good out of the worst of beginnings. He placed the burden for their sin on David, for David was the anointed king, the leader of his people. David's repentance may well have brought Bathsheba to her knees as well. The child of their sinful liaison was taken in judgment, but their second son, Solomon, pleased God. David trusted Bathsheba's political instincts in key decisions in the latter years of his reign. She was the most powerful of all David's wives. Later, as queen mother, she shared the power of Solomon's throne during the apex of Israel's history as a nation.

Was there ever a time in Bathsheba's life when she reflected on that first night with David and experienced regret? She watched the decimation of David's gifted sons one by one, in judgment on David's house for his sin against Uriah. The early promise and godly character of her son Solomon was later eclipsed by his attraction to foreign wives with pagan gods. Surely in retrospect, she had to concur that their lives would have given greater testimony to God had they not surrendered to their passions.

We always have choices. However, Paul reminds us, "No temptation has seized you except what is common to man. And God is faithful; he will not let you be tempted beyond what you can bear" (1Co 10:13). No matter how beautiful, talented or bright we are, nothing—mark that down—*nothing* is as precious to God as our obedience to him.

Bathsheba
(*daughter of Sheba*)

2 Samuel 11:1–12:25
1 Kings 1:11–2:25
1 Chronicles 3:5
Psalm 51

Candid SNAPSHOT When Bathsheba went to King Solomon to speak to him for Adonijah, the king stood up to meet her, bowed down to her and sat down on his throne. He had a throne brought for the king's mother, and she sat down at his right hand (1 Kings 2:19).

Tamar

Innocence Betrayed

Tamar was beautiful and confident, a daughter of a great king. She was an innocent young woman, full of compassion. Any who want to put the blame on victims of rape will get no help from Tamar. There is absolutely no evidence in Scripture that she shared responsibility for the disaster that befell her.

When David, her father, asked her to help her eldest half brother, she agreed without a murmur. But in one horrific act by Amnon, Tamar's life passed from one of great promise to one of desolation. A man she knew as a brother made her a woman who, in that culture, could no longer marry, a woman stripped of her dignity and made her a desolate woman.

Amnon was not the only man to betray Tamar. His friend Jonadab, a cousin of both Amnon and Tamar, had helped him plot the unspeakable act. Tamar's brother Absalom took her into his home, but he said, "Be quiet now, my sister; he is your brother. Don't take this thing to heart" (2Sa 13:20). He gave the appearance of dismissing this devastating crime against his sister. (Two years later he took revenge on Amnon by killing him.) But how could *any* woman not "take this thing to heart," *especially* when the assailant was a close relative?

And why didn't her father comfort her? "When King David heard all this, he was furious" (2Sa 13:21). He certainly was angry that Amnon, his firstborn, had made him complicit. But no thought for Tamar? Did David's failure to intervene merely reflect the values of his time? Tamar is David's only daughter mentioned by name in Scripture. God wanted us to know her story. As shown in David's response, people prefer to ignore crimes of sexual exploitation, molestation and rape, expecting victims to "just get over it." Tamar was deeply damaged by her experience—the rest of her life was affected by it: "Tamar lived in her brother Absalom's house, a desolate woman" (2Sa 13:20).

Tamar reaped what she did not sow. The people who loved her failed her. But God grieved. He saw; he cared. He recorded the details of the crime against her and vindicated her to all generations. We don't know to what degree she recovered over time. Tamar reminds us of all women who have suffered sexual abuse. Scripture does not minimize her suffering. If you have suffered such abuse, God doesn't minimize your suffering, either. Turn to Jesus Christ for the help and healing you need.

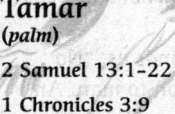

Tamar
(palm)
2 Samuel 13:1-22
1 Chronicles 3:9

Candid SNAPSHOT "Don't, my brother!" she said to him. "Don't force me. Such a thing should not be done in Israel! Don't do this wicked thing. What about me? Where could I get rid of my disgrace? And what about you? You would be like one of the wicked fools in Israel" (2 Samuel 13:12-13).

and led forth the south wind by his
power.
27 He rained meat down on them like dust,
flying birds like sand on the seashore.
28 He made them come down inside their
camp,
all around their tents.
29 They ate till they had more than
enough,[m]
for he had given them what they
craved.
30 But before they turned from the food
they craved,
even while it was still in their
mouths,[n]
31 God's anger rose against them;
he put to death the sturdiest[o] among
them,
cutting down the young men of Israel.

32 In spite of all this, they kept on sinning;
in spite of his wonders,[p] they did not
believe.[q]
33 So he ended their days in futility[r]
and their years in terror.
34 Whenever God slew them, they would
seek[s] him;
they eagerly turned to him again.
35 They remembered that God was their
Rock,[t]
that God Most High was their
Redeemer.[u]
36 But then they would flatter him with
their mouths,[v]
lying to him with their tongues;
37 their hearts were not loyal[w] to him,
they were not faithful to his covenant.
38 Yet he was merciful;[x]
he forgave[y] their iniquities[z]
and did not destroy them.
Time after time he restrained his anger
and did not stir up his full wrath.
39 He remembered that they were but
flesh,[a]
a passing breeze[b] that does not return.

40 How often they rebelled[c] against him in
the desert[d]
and grieved him[e] in the wasteland!
41 Again and again they put God to the
test;[f]
they vexed the Holy One of Israel.[g]
42 They did not remember his power—
the day he redeemed them from the
oppressor,
43 the day he displayed his miraculous
signs in Egypt,
his wonders in the region of Zoan.
44 He turned their rivers to blood;[h]
they could not drink from their
streams.

78:29 [m]Nu 11:20
78:30 [n]Nu 11:33
78:31 [o]Isa 10:16
78:32 [p]ver 11 [q]ver 22
78:33 [r]Nu 14:29,35
78:34 [s]Hos 5:15
78:35 [t]Dt 32:4 [u]Dt 9:26
78:36 [v]Eze 33:31
78:37 [w]ver 8; Ac 8:21
78:38 [x]Ex 34:6 [y]Isa 48:10 [z]Nu 14:18, 20
78:39 [a]Ge 6:3; Ps 103:14 [b]Job 7:7; Jas 4:14
78:40 [c]Heb 3:16 [d]Ps 95:8; 106:14 [e]Eph 4:30
78:41 [f]Nu 14:22 [g]2Ki 19:22; Ps 89:18
78:44 [h]Ex 7:20-21; Ps 105:29

A Beautiful Truth

PS 78:38–39

In the midst of recounting episode after episode of God's faithfulness to his people, their disloyalty to him and his resulting discipline, the psalmist proclaims a beautiful truth: Our just and holy God is also infinitely merciful and tenderly reasonable with sinful people. He deserves our absolute loyalty, and he commands it (Ex 20:3); yet he understands our human limitations and fickle hearts. Instead of giving us the punishment we deserve, he treats us as beloved children (Ps 103:13–14), extending compassion, pity, understanding and mercy (Eze 20:15–17). We need never fear that our mistakes and foolish rebellion will sever our relationship with God or change his faithful nature (2Ti 2:13). Whenever we return to him, he will welcome us, "have mercy" and "freely pardon" (Isa 55:7).

[45]He sent swarms of flies[i] that devoured
them,
and frogs[j] that devastated them.
[46]He gave their crops to the grasshopper,
their produce to the locust.[k]
[47]He destroyed their vines with hail[l]
and their sycamore-figs with sleet.
[48]He gave over their cattle to the hail,
their livestock[m] to bolts of lightning.
[49]He unleashed against them his hot
anger,[n]
his wrath, indignation and hostility—
a band of destroying angels.
[50]He prepared a path for his anger;
he did not spare them from death
but gave them over to the plague.
[51]He struck down all the firstborn of
Egypt,[o]
the firstfruits of manhood in the tents
of Ham.[p]
[52]But he brought his people out like a
flock;[q]
he led them like sheep through the
desert.
[53]He guided them safely, so they were
unafraid;
but the sea engulfed[r] their enemies.[s]
[54]Thus he brought them to the border of
his holy land,
to the hill country his right hand[t] had
taken.
[55]He drove out nations[u] before them
and allotted their lands to them as an
inheritance;[v]
he settled the tribes of Israel in their
homes.

[56]But they put God to the test
and rebelled against the Most High;
they did not keep his statutes.
[57]Like their fathers[w] they were disloyal
and faithless,
as unreliable as a faulty bow.[x]
[58]They angered him[y] with their high
places;[z]
they aroused his jealousy with their
idols.[a]
[59]When God heard them, he was very
angry;
he rejected Israel[b] completely.
[60]He abandoned the tabernacle of Shiloh,[c]
the tent he had set up among men.
[61]He sent ⌊the ark of⌋ his might[d] into
captivity,[e]
his splendor into the hands of the
enemy.
[62]He gave his people over to the sword;
he was very angry with his
inheritance.
[63]Fire consumed[f] their young men,

78:45 [i]Ex 8:24; Ps 105:31 [j]Ex 8:2,6
78:46 [k]Ex 10:13
78:47 [l]Ex 9:23; Ps 105:32
78:48 [m]Ex 9:25
78:49 [n]Ex 15:7
78:51 [o]Ex 12:29; Ps 135:8 [p]Ps 105:23; 106:22
78:52 [q]Ps 77:20
78:53 [r]Ex 14:28 [s]Ps 106:10
78:54 [t]Ex 15:17; Ps 44:3
78:55 [u]Ps 44:2 [v]Jos 13:7
78:57 [w]Eze 20:27 [x]Hos 7:16
78:58 [y]Jdg 2:12 [z]Lev 26:30 [a]Ex 20:4; Dt 32:21
78:59 [b]Dt 32:19
78:60 [c]Jos 18:1
78:61 [d]Ps 132:8 [e]1Sa 4:17
78:63 [f]Nu 11:1

Sometimes allowing *yourself to cry is the scariest thing you'll ever do. And the bravest. It takes a lot of courage to face the facts, stare loss in the face, bare your heart, and let it bleed. But it is the only way to cleanse your wounds and prepare them for healing. God will take care of the rest.*

—Barbara Johnson

and their maidens had no wedding
songs;[g]
64 their priests were put to the sword,[h]
and their widows could not weep.

65 Then the Lord awoke as from sleep,[i]
as a man wakes from the stupor of
wine.
66 He beat back his enemies;
he put them to everlasting shame.[j]
67 Then he rejected the tents of Joseph,
he did not choose the tribe of
Ephraim;
68 but he chose the tribe of Judah,
Mount Zion,[k] which he loved.
69 He built his sanctuary like the heights,
like the earth that he established
forever.
70 He chose David[l] his servant
and took him from the sheep pens;
71 from tending the sheep he brought him
to be the shepherd[m] of his people
Jacob,
of Israel his inheritance.
72 And David shepherded them with
integrity of heart;[n]
with skillful hands he led them.

Psalm 79

A psalm of Asaph.

1 O God, the nations have invaded your
inheritance;[o]
they have defiled your holy temple,
they have reduced Jerusalem to
rubble.[p]
2 They have given the dead bodies of your
servants
as food to the birds of the air,
the flesh of your saints to the beasts
of the earth.[q]
3 They have poured out blood like water
all around Jerusalem,
and there is no one to bury the dead.[r]
4 We are objects of reproach to our
neighbors,
of scorn and derision to those around
us.[s]

5 How long,[t] O LORD? Will you be angry[u]
forever?
How long will your jealousy burn like
fire?[v]
6 Pour out your wrath[w] on the nations
that do not acknowledge[x] you,
on the kingdoms
that do not call on your name;[y]
7 for they have devoured Jacob
and destroyed his homeland.
8 Do not hold against us the sins of the
fathers;[z]

78:63 [g]Jer 7:34; 16:9
78:64 [h]1Sa 4:17; 22:18
78:65 [i]Ps 44:23
78:66 [j]1Sa 5:6
78:68 [k]Ps 87:2
78:70 [l]1Sa 16:1
78:71 [m]2Sa 5:2; Ps 28:9
78:72 [n]1Ki 9:4
79:1 [o]Ps 74:2 [p]2Ki 25:9
79:2 [q]Dt 28:26; Jer 7:33
79:3 [r]Jer 16:4
79:4 [s]Ps 44:13; 80:6
79:5 [t]Ps 74:10 [u]Ps 74:1; 85:5 [v]Dt 29:20; Ps 89:46; Zep 3:8
79:6 [w]Ps 69:24; Rev 16:1 [x]Jer 10:25; 2Th 1:8 [y]Ps 14:4
79:8 [z]Isa 64:9

A Psalm of Exile

PS 79

The attack and destruction referred to in this psalm is most likely the Babylonian invasion of 586 B.C. (2Ki 25:8–11). Many Jews are killed and hundreds are deported by the conquering King Nebuchadnezzar, who also steals sacred temple vessels and valuable palace treasures and sets fire to Jerusalem (2Ch 36:18–19). A new temple isn't completed until 70 years later (Ezr 6:15), as God's people pay a high price in exile and death for their sin.

The person who wrote this psalm is probably in exile himself. The psalm is ascribed to Asaph, but surely was penned by a descendant of this musician from the time of David.

Tears for Food

PS 80:5

When the Israelites grumble and test God in the desert, he mercifully shows them his power and affirms his provision by sending them bread from heaven (Ex 16:14–15) and making fresh water gush forth from solid rock (Ex 17:6–7). But the flock the Lord leads and provides for like a tender shepherd never remains faithful to him; they rebel again and again. Finally God's anger overflows, and he disciplines them by allowing them to be conquered by their enemies. Now their hunger and thirst is not so quickly or mercifully extinguished. They eat "the bread of tears" and drink their own bitter tears "by the bowlful" (Ps 80:5; compare Ps 42:3).

may your mercy come quickly to
meet us,
for we are in desperate need.[a] — **79:8** [a]Ps 116:6; 142:6

9 Help us,[b] O God our Savior, — **79:9** [b]2Ch 14:11 [c]Ps 25:11; 31:3; Jer 14:7
for the glory of your name;
deliver us and forgive our sins
for your name's sake.[c]
10 Why should the nations say,
"Where is their God?"[d] — **79:10** [d]Ps 42:10 [e]Ps 94:1
Before our eyes, make known among
the nations
that you avenge[e] the outpoured blood
of your servants.
11 May the groans of the prisoners come
before you;
by the strength of your arm
preserve those condemned to die.

12 Pay back into the laps[f] of our neighbors — **79:12** [f]Isa 65:6; Jer 32:18 [g]Ge 4:15
seven times[g]
the reproach they have hurled at you,
O Lord.
13 Then we your people, the sheep of your — **79:13** [h]Ps 74:1; 95:7 [i]Ps 44:8
pasture,[h]
will praise you forever;[i]
from generation to generation
we will recount your praise.

Psalm 80

For the director of music. To ˻the tune of˼ "The Lilies of the Covenant." Of Asaph. A psalm.

1 Hear us, O Shepherd of Israel, — **80:1** [j]Ps 77:20 [k]Ex 25:22
you who lead Joseph like a flock;[j]
you who sit enthroned between the
cherubim,[k] shine forth
2 before Ephraim, Benjamin and
Manasseh.[l] — **80:2** [l]Nu 2:18-24 [m]Ps 35:23
Awaken[m] your might;
come and save us.

3 Restore[n] us,[o] O God; — **80:3** [n]Ps 85:4; La 5:21 [o]Nu 6:25
make your face shine upon us,
that we may be saved.

4 O LORD God Almighty,
how long will your anger smolder
against the prayers of your people?
5 You have fed them with the bread of
tears;
you have made them drink tears by
the bowlful.[p] — **80:5** [p]Ps 42:3; Isa 30:20
6 You have made us a source of
contention to our neighbors,
and our enemies mock us.[q] — **80:6** [q]Ps 79:4

7 Restore us, O God Almighty;
make your face shine upon us,
that we may be saved.

8 You brought a vine[r] out of Egypt; — **80:8** [r]Isa 5:1-2; Jer 2:21 [s]Jos 13:6; Ac 7:45
you drove out[s] the nations and
planted it.

9 You cleared the ground for it,
and it took root and filled the land.
10 The mountains were covered with its
shade,
the mighty cedars with its branches.
11 It sent out its boughs to the Sea,[a]
80:11 [t]Ps 72:8 its shoots as far as the River.[b][t]
80:12 [u]Ps 89:40; Isa 5:5 12 Why have you broken down its walls[u]
so that all who pass by pick its
grapes?
80:13 [v]Jer 5:6 13 Boars from the forest ravage[v] it
and the creatures of the field feed
on it.
80:14 [w]Isa 63:15 14 Return to us, O God Almighty!
Look down from heaven and see![w]
Watch over this vine,
15 the root your right hand has planted,
the son[c] you have raised up for
yourself.

16 Your vine is cut down, it is burned with
fire;
80:16 [x]Ps 39:11; 76:6 at your rebuke[x] your people perish.
17 Let your hand rest on the man at your
right hand,
the son of man you have raised up for
yourself.
18 Then we will not turn away from you;
revive us, and we will call on your
name.

19 Restore us, O LORD God Almighty;
make your face shine upon us,
that we may be saved.

Psalm 81

For the director of music. According to *gittith*.[d]
Of Asaph.

1 Sing for joy to God our strength;
81:1 [y]Ps 66:1 shout aloud to the God of Jacob![y]
81:2 [z]Ex 15:20 2 Begin the music, strike the tambourine,[z]
[a]Ps 92:3 play the melodious harp[a] and lyre.

3 Sound the ram's horn at the New Moon,
and when the moon is full, on the day
of our Feast;
4 this is a decree for Israel,
an ordinance of the God of Jacob.
81:5 5 He established it as a statute for Joseph
[b]Ex 11:4 when he went out against Egypt,[b]
[c]Ps 114:1 where we heard a language we did
not understand.[e][c]

6 He says, "I removed the burden from
81:6 [d]Isa 9:4 their shoulders;[d]
their hands were set free from the
basket.

[a] *11* Probably the Mediterranean [b] *11* That is, the Euphrates
[c] *15* Or *branch* [d] Title: Probably a musical term
[e] *5* Or / *and we heard a voice we had not known*

Vine and Branches

PS 80:8–16

The images in these verses of a vine and a branch refer to the nation of Israel (Isa 5:1–7) and eventually to Jesus Christ and his church (Jn 15:5). The psalmist knows that God himself has planted the "vine" of his people, and only God can now tend to it in its distress. A plant cannot survive, much less bear fruit, if it is exposed to the elements and abandoned by the gardener. The psalmist's only hope for his people is that God will take pity on the vine he himself has established (Ps 80:14–15), for without his mercy the whole nation will perish. When we are in distress, paying the price for our sins, our only hope is in the character of God and his commitment to his plan of redemption (Da 9:16–19).

Mouths Open Wide

PS 81:10

Throughout Scripture, all God asks is to be number one in the lives of his people (Ps 81:9). For all he is and does, he simply wants our hearts, our loyalty, our single-minded devotion. As we depend on him alone, he welcomes us to come to him with our deep hunger, opening wide our hearts and souls in expectation of his provision. We need never be ashamed of our raw neediness. Like a mother bird that pours sustenance from her own stomach down the open throats of her babies, God instinctively provides for us. Nothing delights him more than filling us up with his own nourishing, fulfilling, satisfying self.

7 In your distress you called[e] and I
rescued you,
I answered[f] you out of a
thundercloud;
I tested you at the waters of Meribah.[g]
Selah

81:7 [e]Ex 2:23; Ps 50:15 [f]Ex 19:19 [g]Ex 17:7

8 "Hear, O my people,[h] and I will warn
you—
if you would but listen to me,
O Israel!

81:8 [h]Ps 50:7

9 You shall have no foreign god[i] among
you;
you shall not bow down to an alien
god.

81:9 [i]Ex 20:3; Dt 32:12; Isa 43:12

10 I am the LORD your God,
who brought you up out of Egypt.[j]
Open wide your mouth and I will fill[k]
it.

81:10 [j]Ex 20:2 [k]Ps 107:9

11 "But my people would not listen to me;
Israel would not submit to me.[l]

81:11 [l]Ex 32:1-6

12 So I gave them over[m] to their stubborn
hearts
to follow their own devices.

81:12 [m]Ac 7:42; Ro 1:24

13 "If my people would but listen to me,[n]
if Israel would follow my ways,

81:13 [n]Dt 5:29; Isa 48:18

14 how quickly would I subdue[o] their
enemies
and turn my hand against[p] their foes!

81:14 [o]Ps 47:3 [p]Am 1:8

15 Those who hate the LORD would cringe
before him,
and their punishment would last
forever.
16 But you would be fed with the finest of
wheat;[q]
with honey from the rock I would
satisfy you."

81:16 [q]Dt 32:14

Psalm 82

A psalm of Asaph.

1 God presides in the great assembly;
he gives judgment[r] among the "gods":

82:1 [r]Ps 58:11; Isa 3:13

2 "How long will you[a] defend the unjust
and show partiality[s] to the wicked?[t]
Selah

82:2 [s]Dt 1:17 [t]Ps 58:1-2; Pr 18:5

3 Defend the cause of the weak and
fatherless;[u]
maintain the rights of the poor[v] and
oppressed.

82:3 [u]Dt 24:17 [v]Jer 22:16

4 Rescue the weak and needy;
deliver them from the hand of the
wicked.
5 "They know nothing, they understand
nothing.[w]
They walk about in darkness;[x]
all the foundations[y] of the earth are
shaken.

82:5 [w]Ps 14:4; Mic 3:1 [x]Isa 59:9 [y]Ps 11:3

[a] 2 The Hebrew is plural.

6 "I said, 'You are "gods";[z]
you are all sons of the Most High.'
7 But you will die[a] like mere men;
you will fall like every other ruler."

8 Rise up,[b] O God, judge the earth,
for all the nations are your
inheritance.[c]

Psalm 83

A song. A psalm of Asaph.

1 O God, do not keep silent;[d]
be not quiet, O God, be not still.
2 See how your enemies are astir,[e]
how your foes rear their heads.[f]
3 With cunning they conspire[g] against
your people;
they plot against those you cherish.
4 "Come," they say, "let us destroy[h] them
as a nation,
that the name of Israel be
remembered[i] no more."

5 With one mind they plot together;[j]
they form an alliance against you—
6 the tents of Edom[k] and the Ishmaelites,
of Moab[l] and the Hagrites,[m]
7 Gebal,[a][n] Ammon and Amalek,
Philistia, with the people of Tyre.[o]
8 Even Assyria has joined them
to lend strength to the descendants of
Lot.[p] *Selah*
9 Do to them as you did to Midian,[q]
as you did to Sisera and Jabin at the
river Kishon,[r]
10 who perished at Endor
and became like refuse[s] on the
ground.
11 Make their nobles like Oreb and Zeeb,[t]
all their princes like Zebah and
Zalmunna,[u]
12 who said, "Let us take possession[v]
of the pasturelands of God."

13 Make them like tumbleweed, O my God,
like chaff[w] before the wind.
14 As fire consumes the forest
or a flame sets the mountains ablaze,[x]
15 so pursue them with your tempest
and terrify them with your storm.[y]
16 Cover their faces with shame[z]
so that men will seek your name,
O LORD.

17 May they ever be ashamed and
dismayed;
may they perish in disgrace.[a]
18 Let them know that you, whose name is
the LORD—

[a] 7 That is, Byblos

82:6 [z]Jn 10:34*
82:7 [a]Ps 49:12; Eze 31:14
82:8 [b]Ps 12:5 [c]Ps 2:8; Rev 11:15
83:1 [d]Ps 28:1; 35:22
83:2 [e]Ps 2:1; Isa 17:12 [f]Jdg 8:28; Ps 81:15
83:3 [g]Ps 31:13
83:4 [h]Est 3:6 [i]Jer 11:19
83:5 [j]Ps 2:2
83:6 [k]Ps 137:7 [l]2Ch 20:1 [m]Ge 25:16
83:7 [n]Jos 13:5 [o]Eze 27:3
83:8 [p]Dt 2:9
83:9 [q]Jdg 7:1-23 [r]Jdg 4:23-24
83:10 [s]Zep 1:17
83:11 [t]Jdg 7:25 [u]Jdg 8:12,21
83:12 [v]2Ch 20:11
83:13 [w]Ps 35:5; Isa 17:13
83:14 [x]Dt 32:22; Isa 9:18
83:15 [y]Job 9:17
83:16 [z]Ps 109:29; 132:18
83:17 [a]Ps 35:4

If we can keep our minds open to the blessings, humor and education in whatever happens to us—if we can set that little invisible radar dish on top of our heads to constantly search for blessings instead of disasters—our lives will be enriched by the experiences we endure and we can grow from the calamities that fertilize our lives!

—Barbara Johnson

Longing to Be With God

PS 84:10

The writer of this psalm is probably a Levite who once enjoyed serving in some official capacity at the temple. Like a bird that longs to return to its nest, he pines to be in God's presence (Ps 84:3). He'd be happy to return in even the lowliest position: as a humble servant. The privilege of spending even one day where he feels at home would be better than living a thousand days with those who don't love God. When we are truly part of God's family, we don't feel comfortable or fulfilled outside his presence. Because our citizenship is in heaven (Php 3:20), our hearts are programmed for divine fellowship.

that you alone are the Most High over
all the earth.[b] **83:18** [b]Ps 59:13

Psalm 84

For the director of music. According to *gittith*.[a] Of the Sons of Korah. A psalm.

1 How lovely is your dwelling place,[c] **84:1** [c]Ps 27:4; 43:3; 132:5
O LORD Almighty!
2 My soul yearns,[d] even faints, **84:2** [d]Ps 42:1-2
for the courts of the LORD;
my heart and my flesh cry out
for the living God.
3 Even the sparrow has found a home,
and the swallow a nest for herself,
where she may have her young— **84:3** [e]Ps 43:4
a place near your altar,[e] [f]Ps 5:2
O LORD Almighty, my King and my
God.[f]
4 Blessed are those who dwell in your
house;
they are ever praising you. *Selah*
84:5 [g]Ps 81:1 [h]Jer 31:6
5 Blessed are those whose strength[g] is in
you,
who have set their hearts on
pilgrimage.[h]
6 As they pass through the Valley of Baca,
they make it a place of springs;
the autumn[i] rains also cover it with **84:6** [i]Joel 2:23
pools.[b]
7 They go from strength to strength,[j] **84:7** [j]Pr 4:18
till each appears[k] before God in Zion. [k]Dt 16:16
8 Hear my prayer, O LORD God Almighty;
listen to me, O God of Jacob. *Selah*
9 Look upon our shield,[c][l] O God; **84:9** [l]Ps 59:11
look with favor on your anointed [m]1Sa 16:6; Ps 2:2; 132:17
one.[m]
10 Better is one day in your courts
than a thousand elsewhere;
I would rather be a doorkeeper[n] in the **84:10** [n]1Ch 23:5
house of my God
than dwell in the tents of the wicked.
11 For the LORD God is a sun[o] and shield;[p] **84:11** [o]Isa 60:19; Rev 21:23
the LORD bestows favor and honor; [p]Ge 15:1
no good thing does he withhold[q] [q]Ps 34:10
from those whose walk is blameless.
12 O LORD Almighty,
blessed[r] is the man who trusts in you. **84:12** [r]Ps 2:12

Psalm 85

For the director of music. Of the Sons of Korah. **85:1** [s]Ps 14:7; Jer 30:18; Eze 39:25
A psalm.

1 You showed favor to your land, O LORD;
you restored the fortunes[s] of Jacob. **85:2** [t]Nu 14:19
2 You forgave[t] the iniquity[u] of your people [u]Ps 78:38

[a] Title: Probably a musical term [b] 6 Or *blessings* [c] 9 Or *sovereign*

85:3 [v]Ps 106:23 [w]Ex 32:12; Dt 13:17; Ps 78:38; Jnh 3:9
and covered all their sins. *Selah*
[3] You set aside all your wrath[v]
and turned from your fierce anger.[w]

85:4 [x]Ps 80:3,7
[4] Restore[x] us again, O God our Savior,
and put away your displeasure toward us.

85:5 [y]Ps 79:5
[5] Will you be angry with us forever?[y]
Will you prolong your anger through all generations?

85:6 [z]Ps 80:18; Hab 3:2
[6] Will you not revive[z] us again,
that your people may rejoice in you?
[7] Show us your unfailing love, O LORD,
and grant us your salvation.

85:8 [a]Zec 9:10
[8] I will listen to what God the LORD will say;
he promises peace[a] to his people, his saints—
but let them not return to folly.

85:9 [b]Isa 46:13 [c]Zec 2:5
[9] Surely his salvation[b] is near those who fear him,
that his glory[c] may dwell in our land.

85:10 [d]Ps 89:14; Pr 3:3 [e]Ps 72:2-3; Isa 32:17
[10] Love and faithfulness[d] meet together;
righteousness[e] and peace kiss each other.

85:11 [f]Isa 45:8
[11] Faithfulness springs forth from the earth,
and righteousness[f] looks down from heaven.

85:12 [g]Ps 84:11; Jas 1:17 [h]Lev 26:4; Ps 67:6; Zec 8:12
[12] The LORD will indeed give what is good,[g]
and our land will yield[h] its harvest.
[13] Righteousness goes before him
and prepares the way for his steps.

Psalm 86

A prayer of David.

86:1 [i]Ps 17:6
[1] Hear, O LORD, and answer[i] me,
for I am poor and needy.

86:2 [j]Ps 25:2; 31:14
[2] Guard my life, for I am devoted to you.
You are my God; save your servant
who trusts in you.[j]

86:3 [k]Ps 4:1; 57:1 [l]Ps 88:9
[3] Have mercy[k] on me, O Lord,
for I call[l] to you all day long.

86:4 [m]Ps 25:1; 143:8
[4] Bring joy to your servant,
for to you, O Lord,
I lift[m] up my soul.

86:5 [n]Ex 34:6; Ne 9:17; Ps 103:8; 145:8; Joel 2:13; Jnh 4:2
[5] You are forgiving and good, O Lord,
abounding in love[n] to all who call to you.
[6] Hear my prayer, O LORD;
listen to my cry for mercy.

86:7 [o]Ps 50:15
[7] In the day of my trouble[o] I will call to you,
for you will answer me.

86:8 [p]Ex 15:11; Dt 3:24; Ps 89:6
[8] Among the gods there is none like you,[p] O Lord;
no deeds can compare with yours.

Restoration of Harmony

PS 85:10

This verse is a delightful allegory for the restoration and renewal God will bring to his people. The virtues that naturally complement and flow from each other—love and faithfulness, righteousness and peace—have been torn apart by Israel's rebellion. Disharmony has prevailed, and joy has fled. Now the psalmist rejoices in the word he receives from the Lord: God will put everything back together the way he always intended it to be. He will restore morality and harmony in his people and renew his blessing in glorious ways. Because of the Lord's unfailing love, we can always count on his salvation (Ps 85:7).

Give Us a Sign

PS 86:17

Is it wrong to ask God to show himself, to prove himself, to give us a "sign" of his goodness? The Israelites are rebuked and disciplined many times for putting God to the test, for insisting on more evidence of his goodness and power than he's already abundantly provided (Ps 78:41-51). But here the psalmist's motives are clearly not for his own benefit. He is not doubting God or demanding that the Lord demonstrate his character in a tangible way just so he'll feel better. Rather, he wants the evidence of God's loving presence to rebuke and shame the people who have no faith in the Almighty, to whom the psalmist owes his life. Like the prophet Micah, we need not hesitate to pray that God will help and honor us so that his glory will be revealed to the arrogant and unbelieving (Mic 7:8-10).

9 All the nations you have made
will come and worship[q] before you,
O Lord;
they will bring glory[r] to your name.
10 For you are great and do marvelous
deeds;[s]
you alone[t] are God.

11 Teach me your way,[u] O LORD,
and I will walk in your truth;
give me an undivided[v] heart,
that I may fear your name.
12 I will praise you, O Lord my God, with
all my heart;
I will glorify your name forever.
13 For great is your love toward me;
you have delivered me from the
depths of the grave.[a]

14 The arrogant are attacking me, O God;
a band of ruthless men seeks my
life—
men without regard for you.[w]
15 But you, O Lord, are a compassionate
and gracious[x] God,
slow to anger, abounding in love and
faithfulness.[y]
16 Turn to me and have mercy on me;
grant your strength to your servant
and save the son of your
maidservant.[b][z]
17 Give me a sign of your goodness,
that my enemies may see it and be
put to shame,
for you, O LORD, have helped me and
comforted me.

86:9 [q]Ps 66:4; Rev 15:4 [r]Isa 43:7
86:10 [s]Ps 72:18 [t]Dt 6:4; Mk 12:29; 1Co 8:4
86:11 [u]Ps 25:5 [v]Jer 32:39
86:14 [w]Ps 54:3
86:15 [x]Ps 103:8 [y]Ex 34:6; Ne 9:17; Joel 2:13
86:16 [z]Ps 116:16

Psalm 87

Of the Sons of Korah. A psalm. A song.

1 He has set his foundation on the holy
mountain;
2 the LORD loves the gates of Zion[a]
more than all the dwellings of Jacob.
3 Glorious things are said of you,
O city of God:[b] *Selah*
4 "I will record Rahab[c][c] and Babylon
among those who acknowledge me—
Philistia too, and Tyre[d], along with
Cush[d]—
and will say, 'This[e] one was born in
Zion.[e]' "

5 Indeed, of Zion it will be said,
"This one and that one were born in
her,
and the Most High himself will
establish her."

87:2 [a]Ps 78:68
87:3 [b]Ps 46:4; Isa 60:1
87:4 [c]Job 9:13 [d]Ps 45:12 [e]Isa 19:25

[a] 13 Hebrew *Sheol* [b] 16 Or *save your faithful son* [c] 4 A poetic name for Egypt [d] 4 That is, the upper Nile region [e] 4 Or *"O Rahab and Babylon, / Philistia, Tyre and Cush, / I will record concerning those who acknowledge me: / 'This*

6 The LORD will write in the register[f] of
the peoples:
"This one was born in Zion." *Selah*
7 As they make music[g] they will sing,
"All my fountains[h] are in you."

Psalm 88

A song. A psalm of the Sons of Korah. For the director of music. According to *mahalath leannoth.*[a] A *maskil*[b] of Heman the Ezrahite.

1 O LORD, the God who saves me,[i]
day and night I cry out[j] before you.
2 May my prayer come before you;
turn your ear to my cry.

3 For my soul is full of trouble
and my life draws near the grave.[ck]
4 I am counted among those who go
down to the pit;[l]
I am like a man without strength.
5 I am set apart with the dead,
like the slain who lie in the grave,
whom you remember no more,
who are cut off[m] from your care.

6 You have put me in the lowest pit,
in the darkest depths.[n]
7 Your wrath lies heavily upon me;
you have overwhelmed me with all
your waves.[o] *Selah*
8 You have taken from me my closest
friends[p]
and have made me repulsive to them.
I am confined[q] and cannot escape;
9 my eyes[r] are dim with grief.

I call[s] to you, O LORD, every day;
I spread out my hands[t] to you.
10 Do you show your wonders to the dead?
Do those who are dead rise up and
praise you?[u] *Selah*
11 Is your love declared in the grave,
your faithfulness[v] in Destruction[d]?
12 Are your wonders known in the place of
darkness,
or your righteous deeds in the land of
oblivion?

13 But I cry to you for help,[w] O LORD;
in the morning[x] my prayer comes
before you.[y]
14 Why, O LORD, do you reject[z] me
and hide your face[a] from me?

15 From my youth I have been afflicted and
close to death;
I have suffered your terrors[b] and am
in despair.
16 Your wrath has swept over me;

87:6 [f]Ps 69:28; Isa 4:3; Eze 13:9
87:7 [g]Ps 149:3 [h]Ps 36:9
88:1 [i]Ps 51:14 [j]Ps 22:2; 27:9; Lk 18:7
88:3 [k]Ps 107:18, 26
88:4 [l]Ps 28:1
88:5 [m]Ps 31:22; Isa 53:8
88:6 [n]Ps 69:15; La 3:55
88:7 [o]Ps 42:7
88:8 [p]Job 19:13; Ps 31:11 [q]Jer 32:2
88:9 [r]Ps 38:10 [s]Ps 86:3 [t]Job 11:13; Ps 143:6
88:10 [u]Ps 6:5
88:11 [v]Ps 30:9
88:13 [w]Ps 30:2 [x]Ps 5:3 [y]Ps 119:147
88:14 [z]Ps 43:2 [a]Job 13:24; Ps 13:1
88:15 [b]Job 6:4

[a] Title: Possibly a tune, "The Suffering of Affliction" [b] Title: Probably a literary or musical term [c] *3* Hebrew *Sheol* [d] *11* Hebrew *Abaddon*

Korah — PS 88

Korah is the great-grandson of Levi, the head of one of Israel's 12 tribes. The Levites are in charge of worship at the temple, and they take their roles very seriously. When Moses elevates Aaron's family to priestly service, Korah and his followers rebel (Nu 16). The whole group pays the ultimate price for their insolence (see the note on Nu 16:31–33, page 236), but evidently some of Korah's descendants do not participate in the rebellion. Later, Korah's descendants are appointed by David to serve in the temple liturgy (1Ch 6:31–38). These "Sons of Korah" make up the Levitical choir, and 11 psalms are authored by them (Ps 42; 44–49; 84–85; 87–88).

God's Faithfulness

PS 89:2

The highest seat of authority is in heaven itself. No one and nothing is any higher. There even the Lord's divine council worships him in awe (Ps 89:7). The psalmist Ethan declares in this verse that it is at this supreme level of power and authority that God determines his once-and-for-all commitment to his people. No power inside or outside of the heavenly realm can ever change what he establishes. We can have absolute confidence in both the unshakable faithfulness of God and his love. He will be with us, our children and all future generations from everlasting to everlasting (Ps 103:17).

your terrors have destroyed me.
17 All day long they surround me like a flood;[c]
they have completely engulfed me.
18 You have taken my companions[d] and loved ones from me;
the darkness is my closest friend.

Psalm 89

A *maskil*[a] of Ethan the Ezrahite.

1 I will sing[e] of the LORD's great love forever;
with my mouth I will make your faithfulness known[f] through all generations.
2 I will declare that your love stands firm forever,
that you established your faithfulness in heaven itself.[g]
3 You said, "I have made a covenant with my chosen one,
I have sworn to David my servant,
4 'I will establish your line forever
and make your throne firm through all generations.' "[h] *Selah*

5 The heavens[i] praise your wonders, O LORD,
your faithfulness too, in the assembly of the holy ones.
6 For who in the skies above can compare with the LORD?
Who is like the LORD among the heavenly beings?[j]
7 In the council of the holy ones God is greatly feared;
he is more awesome than all who surround him.[k]
8 O LORD God Almighty, who is like you?[l]
You are mighty, O LORD, and your faithfulness surrounds you.

9 You rule over the surging sea;
when its waves mount up, you still them.[m]
10 You crushed Rahab[n] like one of the slain;
with your strong arm you scattered[o] your enemies.
11 The heavens are yours, and yours also the earth;[p]
you founded the world and all that is in it.[q]
12 You created the north and the south;
Tabor[r] and Hermon[s] sing for joy[t] at your name.
13 Your arm is endued with power;
your hand is strong, your right hand exalted.

88:17 [c]Ps 22:16; 124:4
88:18 [d]ver 8; Job 19:13; Ps 38:11
89:1 [e]Ps 59:16; Ps 101:1 [f]Ps 36:5; 40:10
89:2 [g]Ps 36:5
89:4 [h]2Sa 7:12-16; 1Ki 8:16; Ps 132:11-12; Isa 9:7; Lk 1:33
89:5 [i]Ps 19:1
89:6 [j]Ps 113:5
89:7 [k]Ps 47:2
89:8 [l]Ps 71:19
89:9 [m]Ps 65:7
89:10 [n]Ps 87:4 [o]Ps 68:1
89:11 [p]1Ch 29:11; Ps 24:1 [q]Ge 1:1
89:12 [r]Jos 19:22 [s]Dt 3:8; Jos 12:1 [t]Ps 98:8

[a] Title: Probably a literary or musical term

14 Righteousness and justice are the
89:14 [u]Ps 97:2 foundation of your throne;[u]
love and faithfulness go before you.
15 Blessed are those who have learned to
acclaim you,
89:15 [v]Ps 44:3 who walk in the light[v] of your
presence, O LORD.
89:16 [w]Ps 105:3 16 They rejoice in your name[w] all day long;
they exult in your righteousness.
17 For you are their glory and strength,
and by your favor you exalt our
89:17 [x]Ps 75:10; 92:10; 148:14 horn.[a][x]
18 Indeed, our shield[b] belongs to the LORD,
our king[y] to the Holy One of Israel.

89:18 [y]Ps 47:9 19 Once you spoke in a vision,
to your faithful people you said:
"I have bestowed strength on a warrior;
I have exalted a young man from
among the people.
89:20 [z]Ac 13:22 [a]Ps 78:70 [b]1Sa 16:1,12 20 I have found David[z] my servant;[a]
with my sacred oil I have anointed[b]
him.
21 My hand will sustain him;
89:21 [c]Ps 18:35 surely my arm will strengthen him.[c]
22 No enemy will subject him to tribute;
89:22 [d]2Sa 7:10 no wicked man will oppress[d] him.
23 I will crush his foes before him[e]
89:23 [e]Ps 18:40 [f]2Sa 7:9 and strike down his adversaries.[f]
24 My faithful love will be with him,[g]
and through my name his horn[c] will
89:24 [g]2Sa 7:15 be exalted.
25 I will set his hand over the sea,
89:25 [h]Ps 72:8 his right hand over the rivers.[h]
26 He will call out to me, 'You are my
89:26 [i]2Sa 7:14 [j]2Sa 22:47 Father,[i]
my God, the Rock my Savior.'[j]
27 I will also appoint him my firstborn,[k]
89:27 [k]Col 1:18 [l]Nu 24:7 [m]Rev 1:5; 19:16 the most exalted[l] of the kings[m] of the
earth.
28 I will maintain my love to him forever,
and my covenant with him will never
fail.[n]
89:28 [n]ver 33-34; Isa 55:3 29 I will establish his line forever,
his throne as long as the heavens
89:29 [o]ver 4,36; Dt 11:21; Jer 33:17 endure.[o]
30 "If his sons forsake my law
and do not follow my statutes,
31 if they violate my decrees
and fail to keep my commands,
32 I will punish their sin with the rod,
89:32 [p]2Sa 7:14 their iniquity with flogging;[p]
33 but I will not take my love from him,[q]
89:33 [q]2Sa 7:15 nor will I ever betray my faithfulness.
34 I will not violate my covenant
89:34 [r]Nu 23:19 or alter what my lips have uttered.[r]
35 Once for all, I have sworn by my
holiness—

[a] *17* *Horn* here symbolizes strong one. [b] *18* Or *sovereign*
[c] *24* *Horn* here symbolizes strength.

The Fortunate People

PS 89:15-16

Who are the most fortunate people in the world? The psalmist tells us it's those who know the true source of joy and make it a practice to consciously rejoice in what they know. Ethan the Levite models this for us in all the preceding verses. To recall the astounding works of the Lord leads inevitably to spontaneous praise and exultation in his righteousness. We have a choice about where we will place our focus (Php 4:8). The psalmists show us not only that God demonstrates great compassion toward us when we are sunk in the mire of a negative perspective, but also how blessed we are when we learn to focus on God's attributes and works.

𝄞 **The tragedies of life—the death of her mother at age 3, a hip injury that left her an invalid at age 19, and the death of her fiancé just one day before their wedding—produced in Anne Steele's heart a response of songs of praise, most of them published anonymously.**

Father, Whate'er of Earthly Bliss

Father, whate'er of earthly bliss
Thy sovereign will denies,
Accepted at Thy throne, let this
My humble prayer, arise:

Give me a calm and thankful heart,
From every murmur free;
The blessing of Thy grace impart,
And make me live to Thee.

Let the sweet hope that Thou art
mine
My life and death attend,
Thy presence through my journey
shine,
And crown my journey's end.

—Anne Steele (1716–1778)

and I will not lie to David—
36 that his line will continue forever
and his throne endure before me like
the sun;
37 it will be established forever like the
moon,
the faithful witness in the sky." *Selah*
38 But you have rejected,[s] you have spurned,
you have been very angry with your
anointed one.
39 You have renounced the covenant with
your servant
and have defiled his crown in the
dust.[t]
40 You have broken through all his walls[u]
and reduced his strongholds[v] to ruins.
41 All who pass by have plundered him;
he has become the scorn of his
neighbors.[w]
42 You have exalted the right hand of his
foes;
you have made all his enemies
rejoice.[x]
43 You have turned back the edge of his
sword
and have not supported him in
battle.[y]
44 You have put an end to his splendor
and cast his throne to the ground.
45 You have cut short the days of his
youth;
you have covered him with a mantle
of shame.[z] *Selah*
46 How long, O LORD? Will you hide
yourself forever?
How long will your wrath burn like
fire?[a]
47 Remember how fleeting is my life.[b]
For what futility you have created all
men!
48 What man can live and not see death,
or save himself from the power of the
grave*a*?[c] *Selah*
49 O Lord, where is your former great love,
which in your faithfulness you swore
to David?
50 Remember, Lord, how your servant has*b*
been mocked,[d]
how I bear in my heart the taunts of
all the nations,
51 the taunts with which your enemies
have mocked, O LORD,
with which they have mocked every
step of your anointed one.[e]
52 Praise be to the LORD forever!
Amen and Amen.[f]

89:38 [s]Dt 32:19; 1Ch 28:9; Ps 44:9
89:39 [t]La 5:16
89:40 [u]Ps 80:12 [v]La 2:2
89:41 [w]Ps 44:13
89:42 [x]Ps 13:2; 80:6
89:43 [y]Ps 44:10
89:45 [z]Ps 44:15; 109:29
89:46 [a]Ps 79:5
89:47 [b]Job 7:7; Ps 39:5
89:48 [c]Ps 22:29; 49:9
89:50 [d]Ps 69:19
89:51 [e]Ps 74:10
89:52 [f]Ps 41:13; 72:19

a 48 Hebrew *Sheol*   *b* 50 Or *your servants have*

BOOK IV

Psalms 90–106

Psalm 90

A prayer of Moses the man of God.

90:1 [g]Dt 33:27; Eze 11:16
1 Lord, you have been our dwelling place[g]
throughout all generations.
90:2 [h]Job 15:7; Pr 8:25 [i]Ps 102:24-27
2 Before the mountains were born[h]
or you brought forth the earth and the world,
from everlasting to everlasting you are God.[i]

3 You turn men back to dust,
90:3 [j]Ge 3:19; Job 34:15
saying, "Return to dust, O sons of men."[j]
4 For a thousand years in your sight
90:4 [k]2Pe 3:8
are like a day that has just gone by,
or like a watch in the night.[k]
90:5 [l]Ps 73:20; Isa 40:6
5 You sweep men away[l] in the sleep of death;
they are like the new grass of the morning—
6 though in the morning it springs up new,
90:6 [m]Mt 6:30; Jas 1:10
by evening it is dry and withered.[m]

7 We are consumed by your anger
and terrified by your indignation.
8 You have set our iniquities before you,
90:8 [n]Ps 19:12
our secret sins[n] in the light of your presence.
9 All our days pass away under your wrath;
90:9 [o]Ps 78:33
we finish our years with a moan.[o]
10 The length of our days is seventy years—
or eighty, if we have the strength;
yet their span[a] is but trouble and sorrow,
90:10 [p]Job 20:8
for they quickly pass, and we fly away.[p]

11 Who knows the power of your anger?
90:11 [q]Ps 76:7
For your wrath is as great as the fear that is due you.[q]
90:12 [r]Ps 39:4 [s]Dt 32:29
12 Teach us to number our days[r] aright,
that we may gain a heart of wisdom.[s]

13 Relent, O LORD! How long[t] will it be?
90:13 [t]Ps 6:3 [u]Dt 32:36; Ps 135:14
Have compassion on your servants.[u]
14 Satisfy[v] us in the morning with your unfailing love,
90:14 [v]Ps 103:5 [w]Ps 85:6 [x]Ps 31:7
that we may sing for joy[w] and be glad all our days.[x]
15 Make us glad for as many days as you have afflicted us,
for as many years as we have seen trouble.

[a] 10 Or *yet the best of them*

Hiding From God

PS 90:8

Most of us have had the absurd thought that we can somehow hide from God—that we can get away with some secret sin if we just don't let him in on it. But Scripture makes it clear that there is nowhere we can go that is outside of his reach; he will follow us even to the depths of our self-made hell (Ps 139:7–8). The deepest darkness is completely illuminated to him; we cannot hide in it (Ps 139:11–12), nor can we escape his scrutiny anywhere on earth or in heaven (Jer 23:24). This would be bad news indeed if our God dealt with us only according to our sin; none of us could survive his perfect justice. But we serve a God of mercy, who sent his only Son to atone for everything we've tried to get away with in secret. We have nothing to hide! And nothing to fear if we sincerely repent! So let's unload anything we're trying to keep to ourselves and embrace the joyful relief that will surely come with divine forgiveness (Ps 32:3–5).

God's Protection

PS 91

The psalmist's glowing tribute to the Lord's protection and deliverance showcases the kind of faith that dispels fear and allows the soul to rest secure. Anyone who lives in the real world knows from experience that belonging to the Lord is not an insurance policy against earthly trials, dangers, even death. God does not always rescue us from mortal snares. But the believer who places his trust in God to keep his soul secure will never be disappointed. Regardless of what goes on in the world around us, nothing can penetrate the protective shield that God has placed around our spirits. When we trust that we are eternally secure because of God's great love and his ultimate triumph over evil, we can experience an unwavering serenity that transcends our circumstances.

16 May your deeds be shown to your
servants,
your splendor to their children.[y] — 90:16 [y]Ps 44:1; Hab 3:2

17 May the favor[a] of the Lord our God rest
upon us;
establish the work of our hands for
us—
yes, establish the work of our hands.[z] — 90:17 [z]Isa 26:12

Psalm 91

1 He who dwells in the shelter[a] of the
Most High
will rest in the shadow[b] of the
Almighty.[b] — 91:1 [a]Ps 31:20 [b]Ps 17:8

2 I will say[c] of the LORD, "He is my refuge[c]
and my fortress,
my God, in whom I trust." — 91:2 [c]Ps 142:5

3 Surely he will save you from the
fowler's snare[d]
and from the deadly pestilence.[e] — 91:3 [d]Ps 124:7; Pr 6:5 [e]1Ki 8:37

4 He will cover you with his feathers,
and under his wings you will find
refuge;[f]
his faithfulness will be your shield[g]
and rampart. — 91:4 [f]Ps 17:8 [g]Ps 35:2

5 You will not fear[h] the terror of night,
nor the arrow that flies by day, — 91:5 [h]Job 5:21

6 nor the pestilence that stalks in the
darkness,
nor the plague that destroys at
midday.

7 A thousand may fall at your side,
ten thousand at your right hand,
but it will not come near you.

8 You will only observe with your eyes
and see the punishment of the wicked.[i] — 91:8 [i]Ps 37:34; 58:10; Mal 1:5

9 If you make the Most High your
dwelling—
even the LORD, who is my refuge—

10 then no harm[j] will befall you,
no disaster will come near your tent. — 91:10 [j]Pr 12:21

11 For he will command his angels[k]
concerning you
to guard you in all your ways;[l] — 91:11 [k]Heb 1:14 [l]Ps 34:7

12 they will lift you up in their hands,
so that you will not strike your foot
against a stone.[m] — 91:12 [m]Mt 4:6*; Lk 4:10-11*

13 You will tread upon the lion and the
cobra;
you will trample the great lion and
the serpent.[n] — 91:13 [n]Da 6:22; Lk 10:19

14 "Because he loves me," says the LORD, "I
will rescue him;
I will protect him, for he
acknowledges my name.

[a] 17 Or *beauty* [b] 1 Hebrew *Shaddai* [c] 2 Or *He says*

15 He will call upon me, and I will answer
 him;
 I will be with him in trouble,
 I will deliver him and honor him.[o]
16 With long life[p] will I satisfy him
 and show him my salvation.[q]"

Psalm 92

A psalm. A song. For the Sabbath day.

1 It is good to praise the LORD
 and make music to your name,[r]
 O Most High,[s]
2 to proclaim your love in the morning[t]
 and your faithfulness at night,
3 to the music of the ten-stringed lyre
 and the melody of the harp.[u]

4 For you make me glad by your deeds,
 O LORD;
 I sing for joy at the works of your
 hands.[v]
5 How great are your works,[w] O LORD,
 how profound your thoughts![x]
6 The senseless man[y] does not know,
 fools do not understand,
7 that though the wicked spring up like
 grass
 and all evildoers flourish,
 they will be forever destroyed.

8 But you, O LORD, are exalted forever.
9 For surely your enemies, O LORD,
 surely your enemies will perish;
 all evildoers will be scattered.[z]
10 You have exalted my horn[a][a] like that of
 a wild ox;
 fine oils[b] have been poured upon me.
11 My eyes have seen the defeat of my
 adversaries;
 my ears have heard the rout of my
 wicked foes.[c]

12 The righteous will flourish like a palm
 tree,
 they will grow like a cedar of
 Lebanon;[d]
13 planted in the house of the LORD,
 they will flourish in the courts of our
 God.[e]
14 They will still bear fruit[f] in old age,
 they will stay fresh and green,
15 proclaiming, "The LORD is upright;
 he is my Rock, and there is no
 wickedness in him.[g]"

Psalm 93

1 The LORD reigns,[h] he is robed in
 majesty;[i]
 the LORD is robed in majesty

91:15 [o]1Sa 2:30; Ps 50:15; Jn 12:26
91:16 [p]Dt 6:2; Ps 21:4 [q]Ps 50:23
92:1 [r]Ps 147:1 [s]Ps 135:3
92:2 [t]Ps 89:1
92:3 [u]1Sa 10:5; Ne 12:27; Ps 33:2
92:4 [v]Ps 8:6; 143:5
92:5 [w]Rev 15:3 [x]Ps 40:5; 139:17; Isa 28:29; Ro 11:33
92:6 [y]Ps 73:22
92:9 [z]Ps 68:1; 89:10
92:10 [a]Ps 89:17 [b]Ps 23:5
92:11 [c]Ps 54:7; 91:8
92:12 [d]Ps 1:3; 52:8; Jer 17:8; Hos 14:6
92:13 [e]Ps 100:4
92:14 [f]Jn 15:2
92:15 [g]Job 34:10
93:1 [h]Ps 97:1 [i]Ps 104:1

[a] 10 *Horn* here symbolizes strength.

Getting Old

PS 92:12–15

Getting old can be disconcerting, even frightening, to many of us. It's easy to focus on what we think we might lack in old age: strength, vitality, status, usefulness. How encouraging it is to be reminded by the psalmist that those of us whom the Lord has established as his own will never wither or be marginalized in his kingdom. Rather, we will continue to bear spiritual fruit throughout our old age, and our joy and security will be in the goodness and steadfastness of God. Regardless of the changes our bodies go through, our spirits can remain fresh, even flourish and grow stronger.

God's Justice

PS 94:1-2

Justice is a major theme in the Psalms. The psalmists praise God for his just nature and trust him to intervene wherever the wicked oppress the righteous. As those who have been declared righteous by the Judge of the earth, we can confidently take our case to him and ask him to intervene on our behalf. God promises that those who don't honor him or trust in his mercy alone will have their day in court—and it won't be pretty (Ps 10:15-16). *God does not stand idly by while his children are injured. Rather, he takes note of every crime against them and makes plans for how and when he will avenge them* (Dt 32:43; Isa 35:4). *We need not take vengeance into our own hands because divine retribution belongs to God; he will execute justice perfectly* (Heb 10:30).

and is armed with strength.[j]
The world is firmly established;
it cannot be moved.[k]
2 Your throne was established long ago;
you are from all eternity.[l]
3 The seas[m] have lifted up, O LORD,
the seas have lifted up their voice;
the seas have lifted up their pounding waves.
4 Mightier than the thunder[n] of the great waters,
mightier than the breakers of the sea—
the LORD on high is mighty.
5 Your statutes stand firm;
holiness[o] adorns your house
for endless days, O LORD.

Psalm 94

1 O LORD, the God who avenges,[p]
O God who avenges, shine forth.[q]
2 Rise up, O Judge[r] of the earth;
pay back[s] to the proud what they deserve.
3 How long will the wicked, O LORD,
how long will the wicked be jubilant?
4 They pour out arrogant[t] words;
all the evildoers are full of boasting.[u]
5 They crush your people,[v] O LORD;
they oppress your inheritance.
6 They slay the widow and the alien;
they murder the fatherless.
7 They say, "The LORD does not see;[w]
the God of Jacob pays no heed."
8 Take heed, you senseless ones[x] among the people;
you fools, when will you become wise?
9 Does he who implanted the ear not hear?
Does he who formed the eye not see?[y]
10 Does he who disciplines nations not punish?
Does he who teaches[z] man lack knowledge?
11 The LORD knows the thoughts of man;
he knows that they are futile.[a]
12 Blessed is the man you discipline,[b] O LORD,
the man you teach[c] from your law;
13 you grant him relief from days of trouble,
till a pit[d] is dug for the wicked.
14 For the LORD will not reject his people;[e]
he will never forsake his inheritance.
15 Judgment will again be founded on righteousness,[f]

93:1 [j]Ps 65:6 [k]Ps 96:10
93:2 [l]Ps 45:6
93:3 [m]Ps 96:11
93:4 [n]Ps 65:7
93:5 [o]Ps 29:2
94:1 [p]Na 1:2; Ro 12:19 [q]Ps 80:1
94:2 [r]Ge 18:25 [s]Ps 31:23
94:4 [t]Ps 31:18 [u]Ps 52:1
94:5 [v]Isa 3:15
94:7 [w]Job 22:14; Ps 10:11
94:8 [x]Ps 92:6
94:9 [y]Ex 4:11; Pr 20:12
94:10 [z]Job 35:11; Isa 28:26
94:11 [a]1Co 3:20*
94:12 [b]Job 5:17; Heb 12:5 [c]Dt 8:3
94:13 [d]Ps 55:23
94:14 [e]1Sa 12:22; Ps 37:28; Ro 11:2
94:15 [f]Ps 97:2

and all the upright in heart will
follow it.

94:16 [g]Nu 10:35; Ps 17:13 [h]Ps 59:2

16 Who will rise up[g] for me against the
wicked?
Who will take a stand for me against
evildoers?[h]

94:17 [i]Ps 124:2

17 Unless the LORD had given me help,[i]
I would soon have dwelt in the
silence of death.

94:18 [j]Ps 38:16

18 When I said, "My foot is slipping,[j]"
your love, O LORD, supported me.
19 When anxiety was great within me,
your consolation brought joy to my
soul.

20 Can a corrupt throne be allied with
you—
one that brings on misery by its
decrees?[k]

94:20 [k]Ps 58:2

21 They band together[l] against the
righteous
and condemn the innocent[m] to death.

94:21 [l]Ps 56:6 [m]Ps 106:38; Pr 17:15,26

22 But the LORD has become my fortress,
and my God the rock in whom I take
refuge.[n]

94:22 [n]Ps 18:2; 59:9

23 He will repay[o] them for their sins
and destroy them for their
wickedness;
the LORD our God will destroy them.

94:23 [o]Ps 7:16

Psalm 95

95:1 [p]Ps 81:1 [q]2Sa 22:47

1 Come, let us sing for joy to the LORD;
let us shout aloud[p] to the Rock[q] of our
salvation.

95:2 [r]Mic 6:6 [s]Ps 81:2; Eph 5:19

2 Let us come before him[r] with
thanksgiving
and extol him with music[s] and song.

95:3 [t]Ps 48:1; 145:3 [u]Ps 96:4; 97:9

3 For the LORD is the great God,[t]
the great King above all gods.[u]
4 In his hand are the depths of the earth,
and the mountain peaks belong to
him.

95:5 [v]Ge 1:9; Ps 146:6

5 The sea is his, for he made it,
and his hands formed the dry land.[v]

95:6 [w]Php 2:10 [x]2Ch 6:13 [y]Ps 100:3; 149:2; Isa 17:7; Da 6:10-11; Hos 8:14

6 Come, let us bow down[w] in worship,
let us kneel[x] before the LORD our
Maker;[y]
7 for he is our God
and we are the people of his pasture,[z]
the flock under his care.

95:7 [z]Ps 74:1; 79:13

Today, if you hear his voice,
8 do not harden your hearts as you did
at Meribah,[a a]

95:8 [a]Ex 17:7

as you did that day at Massah[b] in the
desert,

95:9 [b]Nu 14:22; Ps 78:18; 1Co 10:9

9 where your fathers tested[b] and tried me,
though they had seen what I did.

[a] 8 *Meribah* means *quarreling.* [b] 8 *Massah* means *testing.*

Relief From Anxiety

PS 94:19

Anxious thoughts weigh the psalmist down. The best way to lighten his burden, he's discovered, is to receive the Lord's consolation—the comfort that ***comes from knowing the truth about his loving nature and his*** **perfect justice. Anxiety is the** ***result of forgetting where our security really is. When we meditate on the goodness and faithfulness of God, we experience the "inexpressible and glorious joy" that comes only through faith*** **(1Pe 1:8). Because he cares so** ***deeply for us, we can turn over all our fears to him, trusting that he will take care of whatever concerns us*** **(Ps 56:3–4; 1Pe 5:7).**

Above All Gods

PS 96:4

Throughout Jewish history, both the Israelites and the pagan people around them have made and worshiped idols. This is strictly forbidden (Ex 20:4–5), but human beings have always had an inherent bent toward trusting in something they have made or can control, rather than trusting in God Almighty. The Old Testament pagan cultures worshiped several false gods: the Canaanites followed Baal, the Moabites honored Chemosh, the Ammonites worshiped the detestable Molech. The Israelites were supposed to steer clear of these people and their gods, but they were repeatedly seduced and they continually committed spiritual adultery.

Regardless of how many times we go astray and put our trust in something or someone other than God, he still will, both now and forever, have dominion over every other power and authority (1Ch 29:11; Eph 1:18–22). He alone is "the true God . . . the living God, the eternal King" (Jer 10:10).

10 For forty years[c] I was angry with that generation;
I said, "They are a people whose hearts go astray,
and they have not known my ways."
11 So I declared on oath[d] in my anger,
"They shall never enter my rest."[e]

95:10 [c]Ac 7:36; Heb 3:17
95:11 [d]Nu 14:23 [e]Dt 1:35; Heb 4:3*

Psalm 96

1 Sing to the LORD[f] a new song;
sing to the LORD, all the earth.
2 Sing to the LORD, praise his name;
proclaim his salvation[g] day after day.
3 Declare his glory among the nations,
his marvelous deeds among all peoples.

4 For great is the LORD and most worthy of praise;[h]
he is to be feared[i] above all gods.[j]
5 For all the gods of the nations are idols,
but the LORD made the heavens.[k]
6 Splendor and majesty are before him;
strength and glory[l] are in his sanctuary.

7 Ascribe to the LORD,[m] O families of nations,[n]
ascribe to the LORD glory and strength.
8 Ascribe to the LORD the glory due his name;
bring an offering[o] and come into his courts.
9 Worship the LORD in the splendor of his[a] holiness;[p]
tremble[q] before him, all the earth.[r]

10 Say among the nations, "The LORD reigns.[s]"
The world is firmly established, it cannot be moved;[t]
he will judge the peoples with equity.[u]
11 Let the heavens rejoice, let the earth be glad;[v]
let the sea resound, and all that is in it;
12 let the fields be jubilant, and everything in them.
Then all the trees of the forest[w] will sing for joy;[x]
13 they will sing before the LORD, for he comes,
he comes to judge[y] the earth.
He will judge the world in righteousness
and the peoples in his truth.

96:1 [f]1Ch 16:23
96:2 [g]Ps 71:15
96:4 [h]Ps 18:3; 145:3 [i]Ps 89:7 [j]Ps 95:3
96:5 [k]Ps 115:15
96:6 [l]Ps 29:1
96:7 [m]Ps 29:1 [n]Ps 22:27
96:8 [o]Ps 45:12; 72:10
96:9 [p]Ps 29:2 [q]Ps 114:7 [r]Ps 33:8
96:10 [s]Ps 97:1 [t]Ps 93:1 [u]Ps 67:4
96:11 [v]Ps 97:1; 98:7; Isa 49:13
96:12 [w]Isa 44:23 [x]Ps 65:13
96:13 [y]Rev 19:11

Psalm 97

1 The LORD reigns,[z] let the earth be glad;[a]

97:1 [z]Ps 96:10 [a]Ps 96:11

[a] 9 Or *LORD with the splendor of*

let the distant shores rejoice.

2 Clouds and thick darkness[b] surround
him;
righteousness and justice are the
foundation of his throne.[c]
3 Fire[d] goes before[e] him
and consumes[f] his foes on every side.
4 His lightning lights up the world;
the earth sees and trembles.[g]
5 The mountains melt[h] like wax before
the LORD,
before the Lord of all the earth.[i]
6 The heavens proclaim his
righteousness,[j]
and all the peoples see his glory.[k]

7 All who worship images[l] are put to
shame,[m]
those who boast in idols—
worship him,[n] all you gods!

8 Zion hears and rejoices
and the villages of Judah are glad
because of your judgments,[o] O LORD.
9 For you, O LORD, are the Most High over
all the earth;[p]
you are exalted[q] far above all gods.

10 Let those who love the LORD hate evil,[r]
for he guards the lives of his faithful
ones[s]
and delivers[t] them from the hand of
the wicked.[u]
11 Light is shed[v] upon the righteous
and joy on the upright in heart.
12 Rejoice in the LORD, you who are
righteous,
and praise his holy name.[w]

Psalm 98

A psalm.

1 Sing to the LORD a new song,[x]
for he has done marvelous things;[y]
his right hand[z] and his holy arm[a]
have worked salvation for him.
2 The LORD has made his salvation
known[b]
and revealed his righteousness to the
nations.
3 He has remembered[c] his love
and his faithfulness to the house of
Israel;
all the ends of the earth have seen
the salvation of our God.

4 Shout for joy[d] to the LORD, all the earth,
burst into jubilant song with music;
5 make music to the LORD with the harp,[e]
with the harp and the sound of
singing,[f]

97:2 [b]Ex 19:9; Ps 18:11 [c]Ps 89:14
97:3 [d]Da 7:10 [e]Hab 3:5 [f]Ps 18:8
97:4 [g]Ps 104:32
97:5 [h]Ps 46:2,6; Mic 1:4 [i]Jos 3:11
97:6 [j]Ps 50:6 [k]Ps 19:1
97:7 [l]Lev 26:1 [m]Jer 10:14 [n]Heb 1:6
97:8 [o]Ps 48:11
97:9 [p]Ps 83:18; 95:3 [q]Ex 18:11
97:10 [r]Ps 34:14; Am 5:15; Ro 12:9 [s]Pr 2:8 [t]Da 3:28 [u]Ps 37:40; Jer 15:21
97:11 [v]Job 22:28
97:12 [w]Ps 30:4
98:1 [x]Ps 96:1 [y]Ps 96:3 [z]Ex 15:6 [a]Isa 52:10
98:2 [b]Isa 52:10
98:3 [c]Lk 1:54
98:4 [d]Isa 44:23
98:5 [e]Ps 92:3 [f]Isa 51:3

God's Hand and Arm

PS 98:1

References to God's "hand" and "arm" are abundant in the Old Testament, paying tribute to the Lord's mighty acts, his loving protection, authority, guidance and correction. Repeatedly, credit for victory is given not to God's people, but to the strong "right hand" of the Lord (Ex 15:6; Ps 17:7). His right hand is "filled with righteousness" (Ps 48:10); his right hand takes hold of his enemies (Ps 21:8); he uses his right hand to "spread out the heavens" (Isa 48:13); his hand holds the scepter of his divine rule (Ps 110:2; Rev 19:15). In the final day, the whole earth will see his triumph when he bares his "holy arm," revealing fully the majesty of his holiness and the might of his power (Isa 52:10).

God's Footstool

PS 99:5

This unnamed psalmist speaks of worshiping at God's footstool. King David had wanted to build a temple that would house the ark of the covenant, which represents the presence and glory of the Lord. David referred to the ark symbolically as God's footstool (see the note on 1Ch 28:2, page 674), the place where God's presence rests, and therefore a fitting place to worship him (Ps 99:5; 132:7).

Scripture also refers to the king's enemies as his footstool, implying that he will trample them under foot in conquest (Ps 110:1; Heb 10:13). Finally, God's footstool also refers to the earth, as heaven represents his throne (Isa 66:1; Mt 5:34–35). We give the Lord his proper due by recognizing his authority over all and bowing in reverent worship at his footstool.

6 with trumpets[g] and the blast of the ram's horn—
shout for joy before the LORD, the King.[h]

7 Let the sea resound, and everything in it,
the world, and all who live in it.[i]
8 Let the rivers clap their hands,
let the mountains[j] sing together for joy;
9 let them sing before the LORD,
for he comes to judge the earth.
He will judge the world in righteousness
and the peoples with equity.[k]

Psalm 99

1 The LORD reigns,[l]
let the nations tremble;
he sits enthroned between the cherubim,[m]
let the earth shake.
2 Great is the LORD[n] in Zion;
he is exalted[o] over all the nations.
3 Let them praise your great and awesome name[p]—
he is holy.

4 The King is mighty, he loves justice[q]—
you have established equity;[r]
in Jacob you have done
what is just and right.
5 Exalt[s] the LORD our God
and worship at his footstool;
he is holy.

6 Moses[t] and Aaron were among his priests,
Samuel[u] was among those who called on his name;
they called on the LORD
and he answered[v] them.
7 He spoke to them from the pillar of cloud;[w]
they kept his statutes and the decrees he gave them.

8 O LORD our God,
you answered them;
you were to Israel[a] a forgiving God,[x]
though you punished their misdeeds.[b]
9 Exalt the LORD our God
and worship at his holy mountain,
for the LORD our God is holy.

Psalm 100

A psalm. For giving thanks.

1 Shout for joy[y] to the LORD, all the earth.
2 Worship the LORD with gladness;

98:6 [g]Nu 10:10 [h]Ps 47:7
98:7 [i]Ps 24:1
98:8 [j]Isa 55:12
98:9 [k]Ps 96:10
99:1 [l]Ps 97:1 [m]Ex 25:22
99:2 [n]Ps 48:1 [o]Ps 97:9; 113:4
99:3 [p]Ps 76:1
99:4 [q]Ps 11:7 [r]Ps 98:9
99:5 [s]Ps 132:7
99:6 [t]Ex 24:6 [u]Jer 15:1 [v]1Sa 7:9
99:7 [w]Ex 33:9
99:8 [x]Nu 14:20
100:1 [y]Ps 98:4

[a] 8 Hebrew *them* [b] 8 Or / *an avenger of the wrongs done to them*

100:2 [z]Ps 95:2

come before him[z] with joyful songs.
3 Know that the LORD is God.[a]

100:3 [a]Ps 46:10 [b]Job 10:3 [c]Ps 74:1; Eze 34:31

It is he who made us,[b] and we are his[a];
we are his people, the sheep of his pasture.[c]

4 Enter his gates with thanksgiving
and his courts with praise;
give thanks to him and praise his name.[d]

100:4 [d]Ps 116:17

100:5 [e]1Ch 16:34; Ps 25:8 [f]Ezr 3:11; Ps 106:1 [g]Ps 119:90

5 For the LORD is good[e] and his love endures forever;[f]
his faithfulness[g] continues through all generations.

Psalm 101

Of David. A psalm.

101:1 [h]Ps 51:14; 89:1; 145:7

1 I will sing of your love[h] and justice;
to you, O LORD, I will sing praise.
2 I will be careful to lead a blameless life—
when will you come to me?

I will walk in my house
with blameless heart.
3 I will set before my eyes
no vile thing.[i]

101:3 [i]Dt 15:9 [j]Ps 40:4

The deeds of faithless men I hate;[j]
they will not cling to me.

101:4 [k]Pr 11:20

4 Men of perverse heart[k] shall be far from me;
I will have nothing to do with evil.

101:5 [l]Ps 50:20 [m]Ps 10:5; Pr 6:17

5 Whoever slanders his neighbor[l] in secret,
him will I put to silence;
whoever has haughty eyes[m] and a proud heart,
him will I not endure.

6 My eyes will be on the faithful in the land,
that they may dwell with me;

101:6 [n]Ps 119:1

he whose walk is blameless[n]
will minister to me.

7 No one who practices deceit
will dwell in my house;
no one who speaks falsely
will stand in my presence.

101:8 [o]Jer 21:12 [p]Ps 75:10 [q]Ps 118:10-12 [r]Ps 46:4

8 Every morning[o] I will put to silence
all the wicked[p] in the land;
I will cut off every evildoer[q]
from the city of the LORD.[r]

[a] 3 Or *and not we ourselves*

Personal Resolution

PS 101:2

The psalmist David's personal resolution can be a model for our own. He makes a conscious decision to be faithful and obedient to the Lord and to keep his heart pure. The Hebrews perceived the heart to be the center of the human spirit, from which springs emotions, thoughts, motivations and actions—"the wellspring of life" (Pr 4:23). The psalmist understands how important it is to be "careful" (Ps 101:2) in the way he directs his life because from his heartfelt vows will flow his behavior in private, at home and in the community.

After making his resolution, without skipping a beat, the psalmist then asks if the Lord will go with him. He realizes that he has no power to keep his resolution apart from the presence of the Lord. Only in him do we have the resources to accomplish our goals and be all that he has in mind for us to be.

Our Eternal Home

PS 102:25-27

The psalmist declares that the earth and the heavens will someday "perish." One day the earth God created will literally "melt" (Ps 97:5; 2Pe 3:12). Everything visible to us now will fall apart and disappear. But God is so much greater than the tallest mountain or the deepest sea! He has no need of anything on earth; he transcends it all. Neither do we need to depend on anything we may now think we can't live without. None of it will last; it will all wear out like a threadbare garment. God himself is "clothed" with honor and majesty, adorned with "glory and splendor" (Job 40:10), dressed in garments that will never wear out—he is the same forever (Ps 102:27; Heb 13:8). Because he is building us "an eternal house in heaven" where we will live with him in glory, we need not lose heart no matter what changes we see on this earth (2Co 4:16–5:1).

Psalm 102

A prayer of an afflicted man. When he is faint and pours out his lament before the LORD.

1 Hear my prayer, O LORD; **102:1**
let my cry for help[s] come to you. [s]Ex 2:23
2 Do not hide your face[t] from me **102:2**
when I am in distress. [t]Ps 69:17
Turn your ear to me;
when I call, answer me quickly.

3 For my days vanish like smoke;[u] **102:3**
my bones burn like glowing embers. [u]Jas 4:14
4 My heart is blighted and withered like **102:4**
grass;[v] [v]Ps 37:2
I forget to eat my food.
5 Because of my loud groaning
I am reduced to skin and bones. **102:6**
6 I am like a desert owl,[w] [w]Job 30:29;
like an owl among the ruins. Isa 34:11
7 I lie awake;[x] I have become **102:7**
like a bird alone[y] on a roof. [x]Ps 77:4
8 All day long my enemies taunt me; [y]Ps 38:11
those who rail against me use my
name as a curse.
9 For I eat ashes as my food **102:9**
and mingle my drink with tears[z] [z]Ps 42:3
10 because of your great wrath,[a] **102:10**
for you have taken me up and thrown [a]Ps 38:3
me aside.
11 My days are like the evening shadow;[b] **102:11**
I wither away like grass. [b]Job 14:2
102:12
12 But you, O LORD, sit enthroned forever;[c] [c]Ps 9:7
your renown endures[d] through all [d]Ps 135:13
generations. **102:13**
13 You will arise and have compassion[e] on [e]Isa 60:10
Zion,
for it is time to show favor to her;
the appointed time has come.
14 For her stones are dear to your servants;
her very dust moves them to pity. **102:15**
15 The nations will fear[f] the name of the [f]1Ki 8:43
LORD, [g]Ps 138:4
all the kings[g] of the earth will revere
your glory.
16 For the LORD will rebuild Zion **102:16**
and appear in his glory.[h] [h]Isa 60:1-2
17 He will respond to the prayer[i] of the
destitute; **102:17**
he will not despise their plea. [i]Ne 1:6

18 Let this be written[j] for a future **102:18**
generation, [j]Ro 15:4
that a people not yet created[k] may [k]Ps 22:31
praise the LORD: **102:19**
19 "The LORD looked down[l] from his [l]Dt 26:15
sanctuary on high,
from heaven he viewed the earth, **102:20**
20 to hear the groans of the prisoners[m] [m]Ps 79:11
and release those condemned to
death."

102:21 [n]Ps 22:22

21 So the name of the LORD will be
declared[n] in Zion
and his praise in Jerusalem
22 when the peoples and the kingdoms
assemble to worship the LORD.

23 In the course of my life[a] he broke my
strength;
he cut short my days.
24 So I said:
"Do not take me away, O my God, in
the midst of my days;
your years go on[o] through all
generations.
25 In the beginning[p] you laid the
foundations of the earth,
and the heavens are the work of your
hands.
26 They will perish,[q] but you remain;
they will all wear out like a garment.
Like clothing you will change them
and they will be discarded.
27 But you remain the same,[r]
and your years will never end.
28 The children of your servants[s] will live
in your presence;
their descendants[t] will be established
before you."

102:24 [o]Ps 90:2; Isa 38:10
102:25 [p]Ge 1:1; Heb 1:10-12*
102:26 [q]Isa 34:4; Mt 24:35; 2Pe 3:7-10; Rev 20:11
102:27 [r]Mal 3:6; Heb 13:8; Jas 1:17
102:28 [s]Ps 69:36 [t]Ps 89:4

Psalm 103

Of David.

1 Praise the LORD, O my soul;[u]
all my inmost being, praise his holy
name.
2 Praise the LORD, O my soul,
and forget not all his benefits—
3 who forgives all your sins[v]
and heals[w] all your diseases,
4 who redeems your life from the pit
and crowns you with love and
compassion,
5 who satisfies your desires with good
things
so that your youth is renewed like the
eagle's.[x]

6 The LORD works righteousness
and justice for all the oppressed.

7 He made known[y] his ways[z] to Moses,
his deeds[a] to the people of Israel:
8 The LORD is compassionate and
gracious,[b]
slow to anger, abounding in love.
9 He will not always accuse,
nor will he harbor his anger forever;[c]
10 he does not treat us as our sins deserve[d]
or repay us according to our
iniquities.

103:1 [u]Ps 104:1
103:3 [v]Ps 130:8 [w]Ex 15:26
103:5 [x]Isa 40:31
103:7 [y]Ps 99:7; 147:19 [z]Ex 33:13 [a]Ps 106:22
103:8 [b]Ex 34:6; Ps 86:15; Jas 5:11
103:9 [c]Ps 30:5; Isa 57:16; Jer 3:5,12; Mic 7:18
103:10 [d]Ezr 9:13

[a] 23 Or *By his power*

God is reported as being angry several hundred times in the Old Testament. But God's anger is a justifiable and righteous reaction to the unrighteousness of his creation. However, God's anger is not removed from his nature of love. Psalm 103:8 states, "The LORD is compassionate and gracious, slow to anger, abounding in love.

—Marilyn Meberg

God's Grace

PS 103:8–10

The grace of God could not be more beautifully described. As sinners we cause him pain, yet he responds to us so entirely unlike how we are inclined to respond to those who hurt us. When someone treats us badly, we feel justified in treating them badly in return. **They deserve it!** ***we think. We too deserve God's wrath, but he gives us his compassion and abundant love instead. He treats us the very opposite way of how we deserve to be treated. In Romans 12:9–21 the apostle Paul gives us a tall order of how this kind of God-like, "sincere" love should be lived out in our human relationships. Study that passage and try to list at least 20 ways you can aim to love others the way God loves you.***

11 For as high as the heavens are above the
earth,
so great is his love[e] for those who fear
him;
12 as far as the east is from the west,
so far has he removed our
transgressions[f] from us.
13 As a father has compassion[g] on his
children,
so the LORD has compassion on those
who fear him;
14 for he knows how we are formed,[h]
he remembers that we are dust.
15 As for man, his days are like grass,[i]
he flourishes like a flower[j] of the
field;
16 the wind blows[k] over it and it is gone,
and its place[l] remembers it no more.
17 But from everlasting to everlasting
the LORD's love is with those who fear
him,
and his righteousness with their
children's children—
18 with those who keep his covenant
and remember to obey his precepts.[m]

19 The LORD has established his throne in
heaven,
and his kingdom rules[n] over all.

20 Praise the LORD, you his angels,[o]
you mighty ones[p] who do his bidding,
who obey his word.
21 Praise the LORD, all his heavenly hosts,[q]
you his servants who do his will.
22 Praise the LORD, all his works[r]
everywhere in his dominion.

Praise the LORD, O my soul.

Psalm 104

1 Praise the LORD, O my soul.[s]

O LORD my God, you are very great;
you are clothed with splendor and
majesty.
2 He wraps[t] himself in light as with a
garment;
he stretches out the heavens[u] like a
tent
3 and lays the beams[v] of his upper
chambers on their waters.
He makes the clouds[w] his chariot
and rides on the wings of the wind.[x]
4 He makes winds his messengers,[a][y]
flames of fire[z] his servants.

5 He set the earth[a] on its foundations;
it can never be moved.
6 You covered it[b] with the deep[c] as with a
garment;

103:11 [e]Ps 57:10
103:12 [f]2Sa 12:13
103:13 [g]Mal 3:17
103:14 [h]Isa 29:16
103:15 [i]Ps 90:5 [j]Job 14:2; Jas 1:10; 1Pe 1:24
103:16 [k]Isa 40:7 [l]Job 7:10
103:18 [m]Dt 7:9
103:19 [n]Ps 47:2
103:20 [o]Ps 148:2; Heb 1:14 [p]Ps 29:1
103:21 [q]1Ki 22:19
103:22 [r]Ps 145:10
104:1 [s]Ps 103:22
104:2 [t]Da 7:9 [u]Isa 40:22
104:3 [v]Am 9:6 [w]Isa 19:1 [x]Ps 18:10
104:4 [y]Ps 148:8; Heb 1:7* [z]2Ki 2:11
104:5 [a]Job 26:7; Ps 24:1-2
104:6 [b]Ge 7:19 [c]Ge 1:2

[a] 4 Or *angels*

Week 17

Your Crown of Love and Compassion

Did you know that you have a crown? God has crowned you with love and compassion (Ps 103:4). Your crown hasn't been given to you as a reward but as a mark and as a symbol of your royalty. You have God's mark, the Holy Spirit (Eph 1:13), and you are God's child (1Jn 3:1)—that makes you royalty. Your Father wants to help you when you are in need and to forgive you when you sin.

Forgiveness, whether human or divine, is an indescribable gift. And it isn't cheap.

What did it cost God to forgive you (Heb 10:10; 1Jn 2:1-2)? Because the price is so high (and has already been paid), is there anything you can humanly do to earn forgiveness?

What step do you need to take to be forgiven (1Jn 1:9)? What happens to your sin when you are forgiven (Ps 103:12; Jer 31:34; Mic 7:19)?

What does receiving God's forgiveness require of you (Mt 6:14-15; Eph 4:32)? How does God's forgiveness change your attitude toward people who need your forgiveness?

Why is it important for you to forgive others (2Co 2:7,11)? How far do you have to go in forgiving those who hurt you (Mt 18:21-35)? Is there someone in your life you find you can't forgive?

Enjoying God THROUGH the Word

Read Luke 15:11-32 (pages 1718-1719). This is the familiar parable of the lost son. Which person in the story best describes you today? Perhaps your inner life has been so transformed by God's forgiveness that you can empathize with others' weaknesses and easily forgive them, like the father in the story. Or perhaps, like the younger son, you've demanded God's gifts and then run your own way toward destruction. Perhaps you yearn to return to God, but you're fearful of rejection. Or perhaps, like the elder son, you look at others and say, "After all the horrible things they've done, how can God use them instead of me?" No matter which person you identify with, no matter what your circumstance, God wants to meet you in your need.

Enjoying God THROUGH Experience

If you need to forgive someone, recall your own weaknesses and failings. Your own need for forgiveness may help you to forgive that person. Forgiveness is a choice. You can choose to hold on to your hurt, but it will leave only bitterness and anger. Forgiving frees you as much as it frees the person who is forgiven. If there is someone you feel you cannot forgive, admit to God that you cannot forgive, and ask him to help you follow his example (Lk 23:34; 1Pe 2:21-23) and to do what he commands (Mt 6:12,14-15; 18:21-35).

If you need to be forgiven by someone, a spirit of brokenness and humility is necessary before you can seek that forgiveness. Allow the Holy Spirit to soften your heart. You may find that a simple "I'm sorry" is not enough. An act of contrition or restitution may be necessary. Remember that you cannot force someone to forgive you. Forgiveness is a gift.

Sometimes it's hard to accept forgiveness from God. You simply can't forgive yourself—even when God already has. Remember that God "does not treat [you] as [your] sins deserve" (Ps 103:10). When you confess your sin, it's gone (Ps 103:12). If you have not asked for forgiveness, why not do so now? If you have already sought forgiveness but you lack assurance, ask for God's grace to be able to accept what he has given you.

Go to page 999 for your next weekly study.

Bursting With Praise

PS 104:10–18

Throughout this song the psalmist is bursting with praise for the majesty and goodness of God. The Lord is "very great . . . clothed with splendor" (Ps 104:1), yet how tenderly he cares for even the lowly creatures he has made: donkeys, birds and cattle (Ps 104:11–12,14). He makes sure that the grass grows (Ps 104:14), the trees get plenty to drink (Ps 104:16), and the badgers ("coneys") have a place to hide in the cliffs (Ps 104:18). For human beings he provides not only food to sustain their physical bodies (Ps 104:14) but also wine to cheer them, oil to bring them health and honor, and the bread of life to sustain them spiritually (Ps 104:15). God is the consummate provider, giving us not just the barest of necessities, but lavishing his bounty on us.

the waters stood above the
mountains.
7 But at your rebuke[d] the waters fled,
at the sound of your thunder they
took to flight;
8 they flowed over the mountains,
they went down into the valleys,
to the place you assigned[e] for them.
9 You set a boundary they cannot cross;
never again will they cover the earth.

10 He makes springs[f] pour water into the
ravines;
it flows between the mountains.
11 They give water to all the beasts of the
field;
the wild donkeys quench their thirst.
12 The birds of the air[g] nest by the waters;
they sing among the branches.
13 He waters the mountains[h] from his
upper chambers;
the earth is satisfied by the fruit of his
work.
14 He makes grass grow[i] for the cattle,
and plants for man to cultivate—
bringing forth food[j] from the earth:
15 wine[k] that gladdens the heart of man,
oil[l] to make his face shine,
and bread that sustains his heart.
16 The trees of the LORD are well watered,
the cedars of Lebanon that he planted.
17 There the birds[m] make their nests;
the stork has its home in the pine
trees.
18 The high mountains belong to the wild
goats;
the crags are a refuge for the coneys.[a][n]
19 The moon marks off the seasons,[o]
and the sun[p] knows when to go
down.
20 You bring darkness,[q] it becomes night,[r]
and all the beasts of the forest[s] prowl.
21 The lions roar for their prey
and seek their food from God.[t]
22 The sun rises, and they steal away;
they return and lie down in their
dens.[u]
23 Then man goes out to his work,[v]
to his labor until evening.

24 How many are your works,[w] O LORD!
In wisdom you made[x] them all;
the earth is full of your creatures.
25 There is the sea,[y] vast and spacious,
teeming with creatures beyond
number—
living things both large and small.
26 There the ships[z] go to and fro,

104:7 [d]Ps 18:15
104:8 [e]Ps 33:7
104:10 [f]Ps 107:33; Isa 41:18
104:12 [g]Mt 8:20
104:13 [h]Ps 147:8; Jer 10:13
104:14 [i]Job 38:27; Ps 147:8 [j]Ge 1:30; Job 28:5
104:15 [k]Jdg 9:13 [l]Ps 23:5; 92:10; Lk 7:46
104:17 [m]ver 12
104:18 [n]Pr 30:26
104:19 [o]Ge 1:14 [p]Ps 19:6
104:20 [q]Isa 45:7 [r]Ps 74:16 [s]Ps 50:10
104:21 [t]Job 38:39; Ps 145:15; Joel 1:20
104:22 [u]Job 37:8
104:23 [v]Ge 3:19
104:24 [w]Ps 40:5 [x]Pr 3:19
104:25 [y]Ps 69:34
104:26 [z]Ps 107:23; Eze 27:9

[a] *18* That is, the hyrax or rock badger

and the leviathan,[a] which you formed
to frolic there.

27 These all look to you
to give them their food[b] at the proper time.
28 When you give it to them,
they gather it up;
when you open your hand,
they are satisfied[c] with good things.
29 When you hide your face,[d]
they are terrified;
when you take away their breath,
they die and return to the dust.[e]
30 When you send your Spirit,
they are created,
and you renew the face of the earth.

31 May the glory of the LORD endure forever;
may the LORD rejoice in his works[f]—
32 he who looks at the earth, and it trembles,[g]
who touches the mountains,[h] and they smoke.[i]

33 I will sing[j] to the LORD all my life;
I will sing praise to my God as long as I live.
34 May my meditation be pleasing to him,
as I rejoice[k] in the LORD.
35 But may sinners vanish[l] from the earth
and the wicked be no more.

Praise the LORD, O my soul.

Praise the LORD.[a][m]

Psalm 105

1 Give thanks to the LORD,[n] call on his name;[o]
make known among the nations what he has done.
2 Sing to him,[p] sing praise to him;
tell of all his wonderful acts.
3 Glory in his holy name;
let the hearts of those who seek the LORD rejoice.
4 Look to the LORD and his strength;
seek his face[q] always.

5 Remember the wonders[r] he has done,
his miracles, and the judgments he pronounced,[s]
6 O descendants of Abraham his servant,[t]
O sons of Jacob, his chosen[u] ones.
7 He is the LORD our God;
his judgments are in all the earth.

8 He remembers his covenant[v] forever,

104:26 [a]Job 41:1
104:27 [b]Job 36:31; Ps 136:25; 145:15; 147:9
104:28 [c]Ps 145:16
104:29 [d]Dt 31:17 [e]Job 34:14; Ecc 12:7
104:31 [f]Ge 1:31
104:32 [g]Ps 97:4 [h]Ex 19:18 [i]Ps 144:5
104:33 [j]Ps 63:4
104:34 [k]Ps 9:2
104:35 [l]Ps 37:38 [m]Ps 105:45; 106:48
105:1 [n]1Ch 16:34 [o]Ps 99:6
105:2 [p]Ps 96:1
105:4 [q]Ps 27:8
105:5 [r]Ps 40:5 [s]Ps 77:11
105:6 [t]ver 42 [u]Ps 106:5
105:8 [v]Ps 106:45; Lk 1:72

[a] *35* Hebrew *Hallelu Yah*; in the Septuagint this line stands at the beginning of Psalm 105.

Sing to the Lord

PS 104:33

When life isn't going the way we'd like it to, do we sing and praise the Lord? If we give God praise only when everything seems perfect, then we won't do it very often. But if we make a choice that we will remain faithful to our God until we die and thank him all along the way, we can change our whole approach to life. Rather than praising him only when we "feel" like it, we can make a vow, as this psalmist does, to praise the Lord as a sacrifice that honors him (Heb 13:15). If we cannot find the words, we can borrow from the "expert praisers" of the Psalms, making exaltations like Psalm 104 our own.

Recall God's Faithfulness

PS 105

This psalm and others that recount Israel's history (Ps 78; 106; 136) were probably used as exhortations to God's people, reminding them of God's faithfulness over time, so they would be encouraged to stay true to him. Perhaps nothing encourages our hearts more than recalling events in which we clearly see the power and love of God. The psalmists knew this. During annual religious festivals, they sang songs celebrating God's past works.

The writer of Lamentations remarks on the power of positive memories when he says, "Yet this I call to mind and therefore I have hope" (La 3:21). He is deeply discouraged by his current circumstances, so he chooses to focus instead on God's faithfulness in the past. His affirmations of God's past goodness and his certain future rescue are some of the most beautiful words in Scripture (La 3:22-26).

the word he commanded, for a
thousand generations,
9 the covenant he made with Abraham,[w]
the oath he swore to Isaac.
10 He confirmed it[x] to Jacob as a decree,
to Israel as an everlasting covenant:
11 "To you I will give the land of Canaan[y]
as the portion you will inherit."

12 When they were but few in number,[z]
few indeed, and strangers in it,[a]
13 they wandered from nation to nation,
from one kingdom to another.
14 He allowed no one to oppress[b] them;
for their sake he rebuked kings:[c]
15 "Do not touch[d] my anointed ones;
do my prophets no harm."

16 He called down famine[e] on the land
and destroyed all their supplies of
food;
17 and he sent a man before them—
Joseph, sold as a slave.[f]
18 They bruised his feet with shackles,[g]
his neck was put in irons,
19 till what he foretold[h] came to pass,
till the word of the LORD proved him
true.
20 The king sent and released him,
the ruler of peoples set him free.[i]
21 He made him master of his household,
ruler over all he possessed,
22 to instruct his princes[j] as he pleased
and teach his elders wisdom.

23 Then Israel entered Egypt;[k]
Jacob lived as an alien in the land of
Ham.
24 The LORD made his people very fruitful;
he made them too numerous[l] for their
foes,
25 whose hearts he turned[m] to hate his
people,
to conspire[n] against his servants.
26 He sent Moses[o] his servant,
and Aaron, whom he had chosen.[p]
27 They performed[q] his miraculous signs
among them,
his wonders in the land of Ham.
28 He sent darkness[r] and made the land
dark—
for had they not rebelled against his
words?
29 He turned their waters into blood,[s]
causing their fish to die.[t]
30 Their land teemed with frogs,[u]
which went up into the bedrooms of
their rulers.
31 He spoke, and there came swarms of
flies,[v]
and gnats[w] throughout their country.
32 He turned their rain into hail,[x]

105:9 [w]Ge 12:7; 17:2; 22:16-18; Gal 3:15-18
105:10 [x]Ge 28:13-15
105:11 [y]Ge 13:15; 15:18
105:12 [z]Ge 34:30; Dt 7:7 [a]Ge 23:4; Heb 11:9
105:14 [b]Ge 35:5 [c]Ge 12:17-20
105:15 [d]Ge 26:11
105:16 [e]Ge 41:54; Lev 26:26; Isa 3:1; Eze 4:16
105:17 [f]Ge 37:28; 45:5; Ac 7:9
105:18 [g]Ge 40:15
105:19 [h]Ge 40:20-22
105:20 [i]Ge 41:14
105:22 [j]Ge 41:43-44
105:23 [k]Ge 46:6; Ac 13:17
105:24 [l]Ex 1:7,9
105:25 [m]Ex 4:21 [n]Ex 1:6-10; Ac 7:19
105:26 [o]Ex 3:10 [p]Nu 16:5; 17:5-8
105:27 [q]Ex 7:8-12:51
105:28 [r]Ex 10:22
105:29 [s]Ps 78:44 [t]Ex 7:21
105:30 [u]Ex 8:2,6
105:31 [v]Ex 8:21-24 [w]Ex 8:16-18
105:32 [x]Ex 9:22-25

with lightning throughout their land;
105:33 [y]Ps 78:47
[33]he struck down their vines[y] and fig trees
and shattered the trees of their
country.
105:34 [z]Ex 10:4,12-15
[34]He spoke, and the locusts came,[z]
grasshoppers without number;
[35]they ate up every green thing in their
land,
ate up the produce of their soil.
105:36 [a]Ex 12:29
[36]Then he struck down all the firstborn[a]
in their land,
the firstfruits of all their manhood.
105:37 [b]Ex 12:35
[37]He brought out Israel, laden with silver
and gold,[b]
and from among their tribes no one
faltered.
105:38 [c]Ex 12:33; 15:16
[38]Egypt was glad when they left,
because dread of Israel[c] had fallen on
them.
105:39 [d]Ex 13:21 [e]Ne 9:12; Ps 78:14
[39]He spread out a cloud[d] as a covering,
and a fire to give light at night.[e]
105:40 [f]Ps 78:18,24 [g]Ex 16:13 [h]Jn 6:31
[40]They asked,[f] and he brought them
quail[g]
and satisfied them with the bread of
heaven.[h]
105:41 [i]Ex 17:6; Nu 20:11; Ps 78:15-16; 1Co 10:4
[41]He opened the rock,[i] and water gushed
out;
like a river it flowed in the desert.
105:42 [j]Ge 15:13-16
[42]For he remembered his holy promise[j]
given to his servant Abraham.
105:43 [k]Ex 15:1-18; Ps 106:12
[43]He brought out his people with
rejoicing,[k]
his chosen ones with shouts of joy;
105:44 [l]Jos 13:6-7
[44]he gave them the lands of the nations,[l]
and they fell heir to what others had
toiled for—
105:45 [m]Dt 4:40; 6:21-24
[45]that they might keep his precepts
and observe his laws.[m]

Praise the LORD.[a]

Psalm 106

106:1 [n]Ps 100:5; 105:1
[1]Praise the LORD.[b]

Give thanks to the LORD, for he is good;[n]
his love endures forever.
106:2 [o]Ps 145:4,12
[2]Who can proclaim the mighty acts[o] of
the LORD
or fully declare his praise?
106:3 [p]Ps 15:2
[3]Blessed are they who maintain justice,
who constantly do what is right.[p]
106:4 [q]Ps 119:132
[4]Remember me,[q] O LORD, when you
show favor to your people,
come to my aid when you save them,
106:5 [r]Ps 1:3 [s]Ps 118:15
[5]that I may enjoy the prosperity[r] of your
chosen ones,
that I may share in the joy[s] of your
nation

[a] *45* Hebrew *Hallelu Yah* [b] *1* Hebrew *Hallelu Yah*; also in verse 48

O love, of pure and heavenly birth!
O simple truth, scarce known on earth!
Whom men resist with stubborn will;
And, more perverse and daring still,
Smother and quench, with *reasonings vain,*
While error and deception reign.

Then, let the price be what it may,
Though poor, I am prepared to pay;
Come shame, come sorrow; spite of tears,
Weakness, and heart-oppressing fears;
One soul, at least, shall not repine,
To give you room; come, reign in mine!

—Madame Guyon (1647-1717)

YET

PS 106:8

***Yet.* Such a small word, but what a huge difference it makes in our destiny! From the beginning of God's relationship with the people he created, we have rebelled against his will and run from his love. *Yet* he pursues us, preserves us, blesses us and saves us! Why? Because our destiny is wrapped up in his.**

Revelation 19:1–8 *gives an awesome picture of the glory in store for our God. Because he desires for every human being to praise him on that glorious day, he will stop at nothing to show us his mercy. "For you know the grace of our Lord Jesus Christ, that though he was rich, yet for your sakes he became poor, so that you through his poverty might become rich" (2Co 8:9, emphasis added).*

**and join your inheritance in giving
praise.**

**6 We have sinned,[t] even as our fathers
did;
we have done wrong and acted
wickedly.
7 When our fathers were in Egypt,
they gave no thought to your
miracles;
they did not remember[u] your many
kindnesses,
and they rebelled by the sea,[v] the Red
Sea.[a]
8 Yet he saved them for his name's sake,[w]
to make his mighty power known.
9 He rebuked[x] the Red Sea, and it dried
up;[y]
he led them through[z] the depths as
through a desert.
10 He saved them[a] from the hand of the
foe;
from the hand of the enemy he
redeemed them.[b]
11 The waters covered[c] their adversaries;
not one of them survived.
12 Then they believed his promises
and sang his praise.[d]
13 But they soon forgot[e] what he had done
and did not wait for his counsel.
14 In the desert they gave in to their
craving;
in the wasteland they put God to the
test.[f]
15 So he gave them[g] what they asked for,
but sent a wasting disease[h] upon
them.
16 In the camp they grew envious[i] of
Moses
and of Aaron, who was consecrated to
the LORD.
17 The earth opened[j] up and swallowed
Dathan;
it buried the company of Abiram.
18 Fire blazed[k] among their followers;
a flame consumed the wicked.
19 At Horeb they made a calf[l]
and worshiped an idol cast from
metal.
20 They exchanged their Glory[m]
for an image of a bull, which eats
grass.
21 They forgot the God[n] who saved them,
who had done great things[o] in Egypt,
22 miracles in the land of Ham[p]
and awesome deeds by the Red Sea.
23 So he said he would destroy[q] them—**

106:6 [t]Da 9:5
106:7 [u]Ps 78:11,42 [v]Ex 14:11-12
106:8 [w]Ex 9:16
106:9 [x]Ps 18:15 [y]Ex 14:21; Na 1:4 [z]Isa 63:11-14
106:10 [a]Ex 14:30 [b]Ps 107:2
106:11 [c]Ex 14:28; 15:5
106:12 [d]Ex 15:1-21
106:13 [e]Ex 15:24
106:14 [f]1Co 10:9
106:15 [g]Nu 11:31 [h]Isa 10:16
106:16 [i]Nu 16:1-3
106:17 [j]Dt 11:6
106:18 [k]Nu 16:35
106:19 [l]Ex 32:4
106:20 [m]Jer 2:11; Ro 1:23
106:21 [n]Ps 78:11 [o]Dt 10:21
106:22 [p]Ps 105:27
106:23 [q]Ex 32:10

[a] *7* Hebrew *Yam Suph*; that is, Sea of Reeds; also in verses 9 and 22

had not Moses, his chosen one,
stood in the breach[r] before him
to keep his wrath from destroying
them.

24 Then they despised the pleasant land;[s]
they did not believe[t] his promise.
25 They grumbled[u] in their tents
and did not obey the LORD.
26 So he swore[v] to them with uplifted hand
that he would make them fall in the
desert,[w]
27 make their descendants fall among the
nations
and scatter[x] them throughout the
lands.

28 They yoked themselves to the Baal of
Peor[y]
and ate sacrifices offered to lifeless
gods;
29 they provoked the LORD to anger by their
wicked deeds,
and a plague broke out among them.
30 But Phinehas stood up and intervened,
and the plague was checked.[z]
31 This was credited to him[a] as
righteousness
for endless generations to come.

32 By the waters of Meribah[b] they angered
the LORD,
and trouble came to Moses because of
them;
33 for they rebelled against the Spirit of
God,
and rash words came from Moses'
lips.[a][c]

34 They did not destroy[d] the peoples
as the LORD had commanded[e] them,
35 but they mingled[f] with the nations
and adopted their customs.
36 They worshiped their idols,[g]
which became a snare to them.
37 They sacrificed their sons[h]
and their daughters to demons.
38 They shed innocent blood,
the blood of their sons[i] and daughters,
whom they sacrificed to the idols of
Canaan,
and the land was desecrated by their
blood.
39 They defiled themselves[j] by what they
did;
by their deeds they prostituted[k]
themselves.

40 Therefore the LORD was angry[l] with his
people
and abhorred his inheritance.[m]

106:23 [r]Ex 32:11-14
106:24 [s]Dt 8:7; Eze 20:6 [t]Heb 3:18-19
106:25 [u]Nu 14:2
106:26 [v]Eze 20:15; Heb 3:11 [w]Nu 14:28-35
106:27 [x]Lev 26:33; Ps 44:11
106:28 [y]Nu 25:2-3; Hos 9:10
106:30 [z]Nu 25:8
106:31 [a]Nu 25:11-13
106:32 [b]Nu 20:2-13; Ps 81:7
106:33 [c]Nu 20:8-12
106:34 [d]Jdg 1:21 [e]Dt 7:16
106:35 [f]Jdg 3:5-6
106:36 [g]Jdg 2:12
106:37 [h]2Ki 16:3; 17:17
106:38 [i]Nu 35:33
106:39 [j]Eze 20:18 [k]Lev 17:7; Nu 15:39
106:40 [l]Jdg 2:14; Ps 78:59 [m]Dt 9:29

Standing in the Gap

PS 106:23

A righteous person mediating for the unrighteous in God's court is a familiar image in the Old Testament and a powerful foreshadowing of the supreme Mediator to come. When God is poised to destroy his "stiff-necked" people after they fashion and worship the golden calf, Moses intercedes, praying for God's favor, and God relents (Ex 32:9–14). On another occasion when his people disobey, God actively looks for someone to stand "in the gap" on behalf of the nation; but when he finds no one righteous, the result is ruin (Eze 22:24–31). Because our God is holy and cannot tolerate sin, we need a perfect intercessor to mediate on our behalf so we will be spared the divine wrath our imperfection demands. Jesus Christ became that mediator (1Ti 2:5), offering his own life as a ransom to set us free from the consequences of our sin (Heb 9:11–15).

[a] 33 Or *against his spirit, / and rash words came from his lips*

When We Suffer

PS 107:1–9

While it is true that God loves a "cheerful giver" (2Co 9:7) and blesses the righteous (Ps 5:12), many stories in Scripture demonstrate that the righteous are not spared from trials. Consider Job, the "blameless and upright" (Job 1:1) servant of God who becomes Satan's target and suffers as few ever will. The apostle Peter tells us not to be surprised at our suffering (1Pe 4:12). Jesus himself tells us that in this fallen world we *will* have trouble (Jn 16:33). But as Jesus overcomes the world and its suffering and sin, so believers in him will stand firm spiritually no matter what the circumstances. We may have many problems, but our deepest sense of well-being and spiritual security can never be threatened. Our emotions in response to suffering may, like Job's, run the gamut; but our abiding faith will glorify God and be remembered by those who watch us overcome.

41 He handed them over[n] to the nations,
and their foes ruled over them.
42 Their enemies oppressed them
and subjected them to their power.
43 Many times he delivered them,
but they were bent on rebellion[o]
and they wasted away in their sin.

44 But he took note of their distress
when he heard their cry;[p]
45 for their sake he remembered his
covenant[q]
and out of his great love[r] he relented.
46 He caused them to be pitied[s]
by all who held them captive.

47 Save us, O LORD our God,
and gather us[t] from the nations,
that we may give thanks to your holy
name
and glory in your praise.

48 Praise be to the LORD, the God of Israel,
from everlasting to everlasting.
Let all the people say, "Amen!"[u]

Praise the LORD.

106:41 [n]Jdg 2:14; Ne 9:27
106:43 [o]Jdg 2:16-19
106:44 [p]Jdg 3:9; 10:10
106:45 [q]Lev 26:42; Ps 105:8 [r]Jdg 2:18
106:46 [s]Ezr 9:9; Jer 42:12
106:47 [t]Ps 147:2
106:48 [u]Ps 41:13

BOOK V

Psalms 107–150

Psalm 107

1 Give thanks to the LORD,[v] for he is good;
his love endures forever.
2 Let the redeemed[w] of the LORD say this—
those he redeemed from the hand of
the foe,
3 those he gathered[x] from the lands,
from east and west, from north and
south.[a]

4 Some wandered in desert[y] wastelands,
finding no way to a city where they
could settle.
5 They were hungry and thirsty,
and their lives ebbed away.
6 Then they cried out[z] to the LORD in their
trouble,
and he delivered them from their
distress.
7 He led them by a straight way[a]
to a city where they could settle.
8 Let them give thanks to the LORD for his
unfailing love
and his wonderful deeds for men,
9 for he satisfies[b] the thirsty
and fills the hungry with good
things.[c]

107:1 [v]Ps 106:1
107:2 [w]Ps 106:10
107:3 [x]Ps 106:47; Isa 43:5-6
107:4 [y]Nu 14:33; 32:13
107:6 [z]Ps 50:15
107:7 [a]Ezr 8:21
107:9 [b]Ps 22:26; Lk 1:53 [c]Ps 34:10

[a] 3 Hebrew *north and the sea*

10 Some sat in darkness[d] and the deepest
gloom,
prisoners suffering in iron chains,[e]
11 for they had rebelled[f] against the words
of God
and despised the counsel[g] of the Most
High.
12 So he subjected them to bitter labor;
they stumbled, and there was no one
to help.[h]
13 Then they cried to the LORD in their
trouble,
and he saved them from their distress.
14 He brought them out of darkness and
the deepest gloom
and broke away their chains.[i]
15 Let them give thanks to the LORD for his
unfailing love
and his wonderful deeds for men,
16 for he breaks down gates of bronze
and cuts through bars of iron.

17 Some became fools through their
rebellious ways
and suffered affliction[j] because of
their iniquities.
18 They loathed all food[k]
and drew near the gates of death.[l]
19 Then they cried to the LORD in their
trouble,
and he saved them from their distress.
20 He sent forth his word[m] and healed
them;[n]
he rescued[o] them from the grave.[p]
21 Let them give thanks to the LORD for his
unfailing love
and his wonderful deeds for men.
22 Let them sacrifice thank offerings[q]
and tell of his works[r] with songs of
joy.

23 Others went out on the sea in ships;
they were merchants on the mighty
waters.
24 They saw the works of the LORD,
his wonderful deeds in the deep.
25 For he spoke[s] and stirred up a tempest[t]
that lifted high the waves.[u]
26 They mounted up to the heavens and
went down to the depths;
in their peril their courage melted[v]
away.
27 They reeled and staggered like drunken
men;
they were at their wits' end.
28 Then they cried out to the LORD in their
trouble,
and he brought them out of their
distress.
29 He stilled the storm[w] to a whisper;
the waves[x] of the sea were hushed.
30 They were glad when it grew calm,

107:10 [d]Lk 1:79 [e]Job 36:8
107:11 [f]Ps 106:7; La 3:42 [g]2Ch 36:16
107:12 [h]Ps 22:11
107:14 [i]Ps 116:16; Lk 13:16; Ac 12:7
107:17 [j]Isa 65:6-7; La 3:39
107:18 [k]Job 33:20 [l]Job 33:22; Ps 9:13; 88:3
107:20 [m]Mt 8:8 [n]Ps 103:3 [o]Job 33:28 [p]Ps 30:3; 49:15
107:22 [q]Lev 7:12; Ps 50:14; 116:17 [r]Ps 9:11; 73:28; 118:17
107:25 [s]Ps 105:31 [t]Jnh 1:4 [u]Ps 93:3
107:26 [v]Ps 22:14
107:29 [w]Mt 8:26 [x]Ps 89:9

God's Discipline

PS 107:10

Because of the Israelites' disobedience to God's commands, he allows them to lose some of their battles and be carried off into captivity in foreign lands, where the treatment they receive in bondage is harsh. God's discipline of his children today is sometimes similar: When we rebel against being "home" with him, we often find ourselves in bondage and in "the deepest gloom" (Ps 107:10). We become trapped in emotional, relational, financial or spiritual prisons of our own making, and there is "no one to help" (Ps 107:12). The good news is that supernatural help is just a prayer away. When we become imprisoned as a result of our own poor choices, we need only to cry out to God. In his power and mercy, he will break our chains and bring us out of darkness into the light of day (Ps 107:13–14).

A Perpetual Cycle

PS 107:33-43

The perpetual cycle of disobedience and discipline, repentance and restoration is poetically described here. Time after time, sinful human beings become proud and rebellious, pay the consequences, humble themselves again, and are divinely blessed. God is in control of this whole process—powerful enough to stop the flow of blessing in an instant, loving enough to refresh the most parched soul at the first sign of repentance. How fortunate we are to serve a God who "longs to be gracious" (Isa 30:18), who never runs out of patience and mercy, and always answers the cry of the humble.

and he guided them to their desired
haven.
31 Let them give thanks to the LORD for his
unfailing love
and his wonderful deeds for men. 107:32
32 Let them exalt him in the assembly[y] of [y]Ps 22:22,
the people 25; 35:18
and praise him in the council of the
elders.

33 He turned rivers into a desert,[z] 107:33
flowing springs into thirsty ground, [z]1Ki 17:1; Ps 74:15
34 and fruitful land into a salt waste,[a]
because of the wickedness of those 107:34
who lived there. [a]Ge 13:10; 14:3; 19:25
35 He turned the desert into pools of water[b] 107:35
and the parched ground into flowing [b]Ps 114:8;
springs; Isa 41:18
36 there he brought the hungry to live,
and they founded a city where they
could settle.
37 They sowed fields and planted
vineyards[c] 107:37 [c]Isa 65:21
that yielded a fruitful harvest;
38 he blessed them, and their numbers
greatly increased,[d] 107:38 [d]Ge 12:2;
and he did not let their herds 17:16,20;
diminish. Ex 1:7
39 Then their numbers decreased,[e] and 107:39 [e]2Ki 10:32;
they were humbled Eze 5:12
by oppression, calamity and sorrow; 107:40
40 he who pours contempt on nobles[f] [f]Job 12:21
made them wander in a trackless [g]Job 12:24
waste.[g] 107:41
41 But he lifted the needy[h] out of their [h]1Sa 2:8;
affliction Ps 113:7-9
and increased their families like
flocks. 107:42
42 The upright see and rejoice,[i] [i]Job 22:19
but all the wicked shut their mouths.[j] [j]Job 5:16; Ps 63:11; Ro 3:19
43 Whoever is wise,[k] let him heed these
things 107:43
and consider the great love[l] of the [k]Jer 9:12;
LORD. Hos 14:9 [l]Ps 64:9

Psalm 108

A song. A psalm of David.

1 My heart is steadfast, O God;
I will sing and make music with all
my soul.
2 Awake, harp and lyre!
I will awaken the dawn.
3 I will praise you, O LORD, among the
nations;
I will sing of you among the peoples.
4 For great is your love, higher than the
heavens;
your faithfulness reaches to the skies.
5 Be exalted, O God, above the heavens,

108:5 and let your glory be over all the
[m]Ps 57:5 earth.[m]

6 Save us and help us with your right
hand,
that those you love may be delivered.
7 God has spoken from his sanctuary:
"In triumph I will parcel out Shechem
and measure off the Valley of Succoth.
8 Gilead is mine, Manasseh is mine;
108:8 Ephraim is my helmet,
[n]Ge 49:10 Judah[n] my scepter.
9 Moab is my washbasin,
upon Edom I toss my sandal;
over Philistia I shout in triumph."

10 Who will bring me to the fortified city?
Who will lead me to Edom?
11 Is it not you, O God, you who have
rejected us
and no longer go out with our
108:11 armies?[o]
[o]Ps 44:9 12 Give us aid against the enemy,
for the help of man is worthless.
13 With God we will gain the victory,
and he will trample down our
enemies.

Psalm 109

For the director of music. Of David. A psalm.

1 O God, whom I praise,
109:1 do not remain silent,[p]
[p]Ps 83:1 2 for wicked and deceitful men
have opened their mouths against me;
they have spoken against me with
109:2 lying tongues.[q]
[q]Ps 52:4; 120:2 3 With words of hatred[r] they surround
me;
109:3 they attack me without cause.[s]
[r]Ps 69:4 [s]Ps 35:7; Jn 15:25 4 In return for my friendship they accuse
me,
109:4 but I am a man of prayer.[t]
[t]Ps 69:13 5 They repay me evil for good,[u]
109:5 and hatred for my friendship.
[u]Ps 35:12; 38:20 6 Appoint[a] an evil man[b] to oppose him;
109:6 let an accuser[c][v] stand at his right
[v]Zec 3:1 hand.
109:7 7 When he is tried, let him be found guilty,
[w]Pr 28:9 and may his prayers condemn[w] him.
109:8 8 May his days be few;
[x]Ac 1:20* may another take his place[x] of
leadership.
109:9 9 May his children be fatherless
[y]Ex 22:24 and his wife a widow.[y]
10 May his children be wandering beggars;
may they be driven[d] from their ruined
homes.

[a] 6 Or ⌊*They say:*⌋ *"Appoint* (with quotation marks at the end of verse 19) [b] 6 Or *the Evil One* [c] 6 Or *let Satan*
[d] *10* Septuagint; Hebrew *sought*

Blessings and Curses

PS 109:9-10

In Hebrew culture it was understood that God hands down both blessings and curses from generation to generation (Ex 20:5-6). The offspring of the righteous will inherit blessing (Ps 103:17), and the descendants of the wicked will pay the price for the sin of their ancestors (Jer 2:9). When David prays curses on the relatives of his enemies, he is not maliciously wishing harm to innocent women and children. Rather, he is asking that God execute his promised judgment of the wicked, which includes terrible and inevitable consequences for their families. David's call for justice is not a personal vendetta but a passionate plea for God's righteousness to reign.

Cursing the Righteous

PS 109:17–19

Unlike curses on the wicked, which reflect God's righteous will, the heathen practice of cursing the righteous, hoping to call down the power of their own gods, did not. Those who wish ill on God's people will be poisoned by their own evil intentions. This is perhaps a principle we should heed in our interactions with others. When we take pleasure in criticizing others, our actions may boomerang; the venom we spew out may come back to poison us. When we intentionally withhold praise and blessing, we will find ourselves short on both. How much better to put our energy into being a blessing, encouraging others and treating them as we would like to be treated (Mt 7:12).

11 May a creditor seize all he has;
may strangers plunder the fruits of his labor.[z]
12 May no one extend kindness to him
or take pity[a] on his fatherless children.
13 May his descendants be cut off,[b]
their names blotted out[c] from the next generation.
14 May the iniquity of his fathers[d] be remembered before the LORD;
may the sin of his mother never be blotted out.
15 May their sins always remain before the LORD,
that he may cut off the memory[e] of them from the earth.

16 For he never thought of doing a kindness,
but hounded to death the poor
and the needy[f] and the brokenhearted.[g]
17 He loved to pronounce a curse—
may it[a] come on him;[h]
he found no pleasure in blessing—
may it be[b] far from him.
18 He wore cursing[i] as his garment;
it entered into his body like water,[j]
into his bones like oil.
19 May it be like a cloak wrapped about him,
like a belt tied forever around him.
20 May this be the LORD's payment[k] to my accusers,
to those who speak evil[l] of me.

21 But you, O Sovereign LORD,
deal well with me for your name's sake;[m]
out of the goodness of your love,[n]
deliver me.
22 For I am poor and needy,
and my heart is wounded within me.
23 I fade away like an evening shadow;[o]
I am shaken off like a locust.
24 My knees give[p] way from fasting;
my body is thin and gaunt.
25 I am an object of scorn[q] to my accusers;
when they see me, they shake their heads.[r]

26 Help me,[s] O LORD my God;
save me in accordance with your love.
27 Let them know[t] that it is your hand,
that you, O LORD, have done it.
28 They may curse,[u] but you will bless;
when they attack they will be put to shame,
but your servant will rejoice.[v]

109:11 [z]Job 5:5
109:12 [a]Isa 9:17
109:13 [b]Job 18:19; Ps 37:28 [c]Pr 10:7
109:14 [d]Ex 20:5; Ne 4:5; Jer 18:23
109:15 [e]Job 18:17; Ps 34:16
109:16 [f]Ps 37:14,32 [g]Ps 34:18
109:17 [h]Pr 14:14; Eze 35:6
109:18 [i]Ps 73:6 [j]Nu 5:22
109:20 [k]Ps 94:23; 2Ti 4:14 [l]Ps 71:10
109:21 [m]Ps 79:9 [n]Ps 69:16
109:23 [o]Ps 102:11
109:24 [p]Heb 12:12
109:25 [q]Ps 22:6 [r]Mt 27:39; Mk 15:29
109:26 [s]Ps 119:86
109:27 [t]Job 37:7
109:28 [u]2Sa 16:12 [v]Isa 65:14

[a] *17* Or *curse, / and it has* [b] *17* Or *blessing, / and it is*

29 My accusers will be clothed with
disgrace
and wrapped in shame[w] as in a cloak.
30 With my mouth I will greatly extol the
LORD;
in the great throng[x] I will praise him.
31 For he stands at the right hand[y] of the
needy one,
to save his life from those who
condemn him.

Psalm 110

Of David. A psalm.

1 The LORD says[z] to my Lord:
"Sit at my right hand
until I make your enemies
a footstool for your feet."[a]
2 The LORD will extend your mighty
scepter[b] from Zion;
you will rule in the midst of your
enemies.
3 Your troops will be willing
on your day of battle.
Arrayed in holy majesty,[c]
from the womb of the dawn
you will receive the dew of your
youth.[a]
4 The LORD has sworn
and will not change his mind:[d]
"You are a priest forever,[e]
in the order of Melchizedek.[f]"
5 The Lord is at your right hand;[g]
he will crush kings[h] on the day of his
wrath.[i]
6 He will judge the nations,[j] heaping up
the dead[k]
and crushing the rulers[l] of the whole
earth.
7 He will drink from a brook beside the
way[b];
therefore he will lift up his head.[m]

Psalm 111[c]

1 Praise the LORD.[d]

I will extol the LORD with all my heart
in the council of the upright and in
the assembly.

2 Great are the works[n] of the LORD;
they are pondered by all who delight
in them.
3 Glorious and majestic are his deeds,

109:29 [w]Ps 35:26; 132:18
109:30 [x]Ps 35:18; 111:1
109:31 [y]Ps 16:8; 73:23; 121:5
110:1 [z]Mt 22:44*; Mk 12:36*; Lk 20:42*; Ac 2:34* [a]1Co 15:25
110:2 [b]Ps 45:6
110:3 [c]Jdg 5:2; Ps 96:9
110:4 [d]Nu 23:19 [e]Heb 5:6*; 7:21* [f]Heb 7:15-17*
110:5 [g]Ps 16:8 [h]Ps 2:12 [i]Ps 2:5; Ro 2:5
110:6 [j]Isa 2:4 [k]Isa 66:24 [l]Ps 68:21
110:7 [m]Ps 27:6
111:2 [n]Ps 92:5; 143:5

[a] *3* Or / *your young men will come to you like the dew* [b] *7* Or / *The One who grants succession will set him in authority* [c] This psalm is an acrostic poem, the lines of which begin with the successive letters of the Hebrew alphabet. [d] *1* Hebrew *Hallelu Yah*

Melchizedek

PS 110:4

In the Jewish culture of David's time, only descendants of Aaron were designated as priests, and none of Israel's kings were allowed to usurp priestly roles. (Read 2Ch 26:16-21 to see what happens to King Uzziah when he tries it!) However, there was a king during Abraham's time—before the Law of Moses and the Aaronic priesthood—whom God installed as the "priest of God Most High" (Ge 14:18; Heb 7:1-2).

Melchizedek is the forerunner of the only other king-priest of all time, Jesus Christ himself (Zec 6:13; Heb 6:20). Christ's priestly role is not dependent on his ancestors but on "the power of an indestructible life" (Heb 7:16). For a glorious description of the value of having the High Priest as our King and Savior, read Hebrews 7:17–8:13.

and his righteousness endures forever.
[4] He has caused his wonders to be
remembered;
the LORD is gracious and
compassionate.[o]
[5] He provides food[p] for those who fear him;
he remembers his covenant forever.
[6] He has shown his people the power of
his works,
giving them the lands of other nations.
[7] The works of his hands are faithful and
just;
all his precepts are trustworthy.[q]
[8] They are steadfast for ever[r] and ever,
done in faithfulness and uprightness.
[9] He provided redemption[s] for his people;
he ordained his covenant forever—
holy and awesome[t] is his name.
[10] The fear of the LORD is the beginning of
wisdom;[u]
all who follow his precepts have good
understanding.[v]
To him belongs eternal praise.[w]

Psalm 112[a]

[1] Praise the LORD.[b]

Blessed is the man who fears the LORD,[x]
who finds great delight[y] in his
commands.

[2] His children will be mighty in the land;
the generation of the upright will be
blessed.
[3] Wealth and riches are in his house,
and his righteousness endures forever.
[4] Even in darkness light dawns[z] for the
upright,
for the gracious and compassionate
and righteous[a] man.[c]
[5] Good will come to him who is generous
and lends freely,[b]
who conducts his affairs with justice.
[6] Surely he will never be shaken;
a righteous man will be remembered[c]
forever.
[7] He will have no fear of bad news;
his heart is steadfast,[d] trusting in the
LORD.
[8] His heart is secure, he will have no fear;
in the end he will look in triumph on
his foes.[e]
[9] He has scattered abroad his gifts to the
poor,[f]
his righteousness endures forever;
his horn[d] will be lifted[g] high in honor.

111:4 [o]Ps 103:8
111:5 [p]Mt 6:26,31-33
111:7 [q]Ps 19:7; Rev 15:3
111:8 [r]Isa 40:8; Mt 5:18
111:9 [s]Lk 1:68 [t]Ps 99:3; Lk 1:49
111:10 [u]Pr 9:10 [v]Ecc 12:13 [w]Ps 145:2
112:1 [x]Ps 128:1 [y]Ps 119:14, 16,47,92
112:4 [z]Job 11:17 [a]Ps 97:11
112:5 [b]Ps 37:21,26
112:6 [c]Pr 10:7
112:7 [d]Ps 57:7; Pr 1:33
112:8 [e]Ps 59:10
112:9 [f]2Co 9:9* [g]Ps 75:10

[a] This psalm is an acrostic poem, the lines of which begin with the successive letters of the Hebrew alphabet. [b] 1 Hebrew *Hallelu Yah* [c] 4 Or / *for* ⌞*the LORD*⌟ *is gracious and compassionate and righteous* [d] 9 *Horn* here symbolizes dignity.

Questioning God sounds blasphemous to some people. They might say, "How dare you? Who do you think you are, that you can come before God and question him?" But I don't think being honest with God is blasphemous at all. I believe God wants us to be honest because he wants a real relationship with us, not something plastic or halfhearted . . . I believe God much prefers to have his children come before him and say, "God, this makes no sense to me. I hurt so badly. I just don't understand. I don't think I'll ever understand, but, God, I love and trust You, and I rest in the fact that You know how I feel . . . I can't understand what is happening to me, but help me to glorify You through it all.*

—Sheila Walsh

10 The wicked man will see[h] and be vexed,
he will gnash his teeth[i] and waste away;[j]
the longings of the wicked will come to nothing.[k]

Psalm 113

1 Praise the LORD.[a]

Praise, O servants of the LORD,[l]
praise the name of the LORD.
2 Let the name of the LORD be praised,
both now and forevermore.[m]
3 From the rising of the sun[n] to the place where it sets,
the name of the LORD is to be praised.

4 The LORD is exalted[o] over all the nations,
his glory above the heavens.[p]
5 Who is like the LORD our God,[q]
the One who sits enthroned[r] on high,
6 who stoops down to look[s]
on the heavens and the earth?

7 He raises the poor[t] from the dust
and lifts the needy[u] from the ash heap;
8 he seats them[v] with princes,
with the princes of their people.
9 He settles the barren[w] woman in her home
as a happy mother of children.

Praise the LORD.

Psalm 114

1 When Israel came out of Egypt,[x]
the house of Jacob from a people of foreign tongue,
2 Judah became God's sanctuary,
Israel his dominion.

3 The sea looked and fled,[y]
the Jordan turned back;[z]
4 the mountains skipped like rams,
the hills like lambs.

5 Why was it, O sea, that you fled,
O Jordan, that you turned back,
6 you mountains, that you skipped like rams,
you hills, like lambs?

7 Tremble, O earth,[a] at the presence of the Lord,
at the presence of the God of Jacob,
8 who turned the rock into a pool,
the hard rock into springs of water.[b]

112:10 [h]Ps 86:17 [i]Ps 37:12 [j]Ps 58:7-8 [k]Pr 11:7
113:1 [l]Ps 135:1
113:2 [m]Da 2:20
113:3 [n]Isa 59:19; Mal 1:11
113:4 [o]Ps 99:2 [p]Ps 8:1; 97:9
113:5 [q]Ps 89:6 [r]Ps 103:19
113:6 [s]Ps 11:4; 138:6; Isa 57:15
113:7 [t]1Sa 2:8 [u]Ps 107:41
113:8 [v]Job 36:7
113:9 [w]1Sa 2:5; Ps 68:6; Isa 54:1
114:1 [x]Ex 13:3
114:3 [y]Ex 14:21; Ps 77:16 [z]Jos 3:16
114:7 [a]Ps 96:9
114:8 [b]Ex 17:6; Nu 20:11; Ps 107:35

[a] *1* Hebrew *Hallelu Yah*; also in verse 9

God of Great Reversals

PS 113:9

In ancient Jewish society, being infertile and childless was the ultimate disgrace and tragedy for a woman. Rachel was filled with such despair over her barrenness that she felt like she would die from the pain (Ge 30:1). Several Old Testament stories follow desperate women like Rachel from barrenness to divine intervention and motherhood, so the psalmist's listeners are familiar with the miraculous turn of events celebrated by families in days gone by. As an illustration for how God can, and does, turn despair into jubilation, this picture of the barren woman becoming the "happy mother" resonates with the psalmist's culture. When we feel empty and hopeless, we too can be encouraged by the fact that God is a God of great reversals: "As surely as the sun rises, he will appear," bringing refreshment and renewal (Hos 6:3, emphasis added).

Increasing

PS 115:14

In the Israelites' minds, having descendants is directly correlated with having God's blessing. Several times God promises to sustain and perpetuate his chosen people by making them "as countless as the stars" and "like the sand on the seashore" (Ge 22:15–18; Jer 33:22; Hos 1:10). To wish that someone will "increase" is to wish great blessing on him or her, for to have children and grandchildren and great-grandchildren is to have the greatest wealth and strength as a people. Today God "increases" us in many other ways besides perpetuating our bloodlines. Make a list of some ways he has made *you* increase—both you and, if you have them, your children.

Psalm 115

[1] Not to us, O LORD, not to us
but to your name be the glory,[c]
because of your love and faithfulness.

[2] Why do the nations say,
"Where is their God?"[d]
[3] Our God is in heaven;[e]
he does whatever pleases him.[f]
[4] But their idols are silver and gold,
made by the hands of men.[g]
[5] They have mouths, but cannot speak,[h]
eyes, but they cannot see;
[6] they have ears, but cannot hear,
noses, but they cannot smell;
[7] they have hands, but cannot feel,
feet, but they cannot walk;
nor can they utter a sound with their throats.
[8] Those who make them will be like them,
and so will all who trust in them.

[9] O house of Israel, trust in the LORD—
he is their help and shield.
[10] O house of Aaron,[i] trust in the LORD—
he is their help and shield.
[11] You who fear him, trust in the LORD—
he is their help and shield.

[12] The LORD remembers us and will bless us:
He will bless the house of Israel,
he will bless the house of Aaron,
[13] he will bless those who fear[j] the LORD—
small and great alike.

[14] May the LORD make you increase,[k]
both you and your children.
[15] May you be blessed by the LORD,
the Maker of heaven[l] and earth.
[16] The highest heavens belong to the LORD,[m]
but the earth he has given[n] to man.
[17] It is not the dead[o] who praise the LORD,
those who go down to silence;
[18] it is we who extol the LORD,
both now and forevermore.[p]

Praise the LORD.[a]

Psalm 116

[1] I love the LORD,[q] for he heard my voice;
he heard my cry[r] for mercy.
[2] Because he turned his ear[s] to me,
I will call on him as long as I live.

[3] The cords of death[t] entangled me,
the anguish of the grave[b] came upon me;

115:1 [c]Ps 96:8; Isa 48:11; Eze 36:32
115:2 [d]Ps 42:3; 79:10
115:3 [e]Ps 103:19 [f]Ps 135:6; Da 4:35
115:4 [g]Dt 4:28; Jer 10:3-5
115:5 [h]Jer 10:5
115:10 [i]Ps 118:3
115:13 [j]Ps 128:1,4
115:14 [k]Dt 1:11
115:15 [l]Ge 1:1; 14:19; Ps 96:5
115:16 [m]Ps 89:11 [n]Ps 8:6-8
115:17 [o]Ps 6:5; 88:10-12; Isa 38:18
115:18 [p]Ps 113:2; Da 2:20
116:1 [q]Ps 18:1 [r]Ps 66:19
116:2 [s]Ps 40:1
116:3 [t]Ps 18:4-5

[a] 18 Hebrew *Hallelu Yah* [b] 3 Hebrew *Sheol*

I was overcome by trouble and
sorrow.
4 Then I called on the name[u] of the LORD:
"O LORD, save me!"[v]

5 The LORD is gracious and righteous;[w]
our God is full of compassion.
6 The LORD protects the simplehearted;
when I was in great need,[x] he saved
me.

7 Be at rest[y] once more, O my soul,
for the LORD has been good[z] to you.

8 For you, O LORD, have delivered my
soul[a] from death,
my eyes from tears,
my feet from stumbling,
9 that I may walk before the LORD
in the land of the living.[b]
10 I believed;[c] therefore[a] I said,
"I am greatly afflicted."
11 And in my dismay I said,
"All men are liars."[d]
12 How can I repay the LORD
for all his goodness to me?
13 I will lift up the cup of salvation
and call on the name[e] of the LORD.
14 I will fulfill my vows[f] to the LORD
in the presence of all his people.
15 Precious in the sight[g] of the LORD
is the death of his saints.
16 O LORD, truly I am your servant;[h]
I am your servant, the son of your
maidservant[b];[i]
you have freed me from my chains.
17 I will sacrifice a thank offering[j] to you
and call on the name of the LORD.
18 I will fulfill my vows to the LORD
in the presence of all his people,
19 in the courts[k] of the house of the LORD—
in your midst, O Jerusalem.

Praise the LORD.[c]

Psalm 117

1 Praise the LORD, all you nations;[l]
extol him, all you peoples.
2 For great is his love toward us,
and the faithfulness of the LORD[m]
endures forever.

Praise the LORD.[c]

Psalm 118

1 Give thanks to the LORD,[n] for he is good;
his love endures forever.[o]

2 Let Israel say:[p]

116:4 [u]Ps 118:5 [v]Ps 22:20
116:5 [w]Ezr 9:15; Ne 9:8; Ps 103:8; 145:17
116:6 [x]Ps 19:7; 79:8
116:7 [y]Jer 6:16; Mt 11:29 [z]Ps 13:6
116:8 [a]Ps 56:13
116:9 [b]Ps 27:13
116:10 [c]2Co 4:13*
116:11 [d]Ro 3:4
116:13 [e]Ps 16:5; 80:18
116:14 [f]Ps 22:25; Jnh 2:9
116:15 [g]Ps 72:14
116:16 [h]Ps 119:125; 143:12 [i]Ps 86:16
116:17 [j]Lev 7:12; Ps 50:14
116:19 [k]Ps 96:8; 135:2
117:1 [l]Ro 15:11*
117:2 [m]Ps 100:5
118:1 [n]1Ch 16:8 [o]Ps 106:1; 136:1
118:2 [p]Ps 115:9

[a] 10 Or *believed even when* [b] 16 Or *servant, your faithful son* [c] 19,2 Hebrew *Hallelu Yah*

Precious in God's Sight

PS 116:15

Even though the Lord eagerly welcomes his children who have died into his eternal presence, he does not take their deaths lightly. God places high value on mortal life, knitting us together in our mother's wombs (Ps 139:13) and faithfully sustaining us with his presence throughout our days on earth (Ps 3:5). Many times he saves us from death, and he rescues us from oppression because he takes our suffering and bloodshed very seriously (Ps 72:13–14). But when death finally comes for those of us who are "his saints," we can be sure—and reassure others—that God watches over the final passage with great attention and loving-kindness.

"His love endures forever."
3 Let the house of Aaron say:
"His love endures forever."
4 Let those who fear the LORD say:
"His love endures forever."
5 In my anguish[q] I cried to the LORD,
and he answered[r] by setting me free.
6 The LORD is with me;[s] I will not be afraid.
What can man do to me?[t]
7 The LORD is with me; he is my helper.[u]
I will look in triumph on my enemies.[v]
8 It is better to take refuge in the LORD[w]
than to trust in man.[x]
9 It is better to take refuge in the LORD
than to trust in princes.[y]
10 All the nations surrounded me,
but in the name of the LORD I cut them off.[z]
11 They surrounded me[a] on every side,[b]
but in the name of the LORD I cut them off.
12 They swarmed around me like bees,[c]
but they died out as quickly as burning thorns;[d]
in the name of the LORD I cut them off.
13 I was pushed back and about to fall,
but the LORD helped me.[e]
14 The LORD is my strength[f] and my song;
he has become my salvation.[g]
15 Shouts of joy[h] and victory
resound in the tents of the righteous:
"The LORD's right hand[i] has done mighty things!
16 The LORD's right hand is lifted high;
the LORD's right hand has done mighty things!"
17 I will not die[j] but live,
and will proclaim[k] what the LORD has done.
18 The LORD has chastened me severely,
but he has not given me over to death.[l]
19 Open for me the gates[m] of righteousness;
I will enter and give thanks to the LORD.
20 This is the gate of the LORD
through which the righteous may enter.[n]
21 I will give you thanks, for you answered me;[o]
you have become my salvation.
22 The stone the builders rejected
has become the capstone;[p]

118:5 [q]Ps 120:1 [r]Ps 18:19
118:6 [s]Heb 13:6* [t]Ps 27:1; 56:4
118:7 [u]Ps 54:4 [v]Ps 59:10
118:8 [w]Ps 40:4 [x]Jer 17:5
118:9 [y]Ps 146:3
118:10 [z]Ps 18:40
118:11 [a]Ps 88:17 [b]Ps 3:6
118:12 [c]Dt 1:44 [d]Ps 58:9
118:13 [e]Ps 86:17; 140:4
118:14 [f]Ex 15:2 [g]Isa 12:2
118:15 [h]Ps 68:3 [i]Ps 89:13
118:17 [j]Ps 6:5; Hab 1:12 [k]Ex 15:6; Ps 73:28
118:18 [l]2Co 6:9
118:19 [m]Isa 26:2
118:20 [n]Ps 24:7; Isa 35:8; Rev 22:14
118:21 [o]Ps 116:1
118:22 [p]Mt 21:42; Mk 12:10; Lk 20:17*; Ac 4:11*; 1Pe 2:7*

The Capstone

PS 118:22

This metaphor has both a historical and prophetic meaning. A capstone, or cornerstone, refers to the most important part of a building—a crucial part of the foundation that anchors the whole structure. The capstone here refers historically either to Israel or her king, despised by other political powers but honored by God. Prophetically it refers to Jesus, the one rejected by his own people, who becomes the "chosen and precious cornerstone" of the church (1Pe 2:6–7).

[23]the LORD has done this,
and it is marvelous in our eyes.
[24]This is the day the LORD has made;
let us rejoice and be glad in it.

[25]O LORD, save us;
O LORD, grant us success.
118:26 [q]Mt 21:9*; Mk 11:9*; Lk 13:35*; 19:38*; Jn 12:13*
[26]Blessed is he who comes[q] in the name of the LORD.
From the house of the LORD we bless you.[a]
118:27 [r]1Pe 2:9
[27]The LORD is God,
and he has made his light shine[r] upon us.
With boughs in hand, join in the festal procession
up[b] to the horns of the altar.

118:28 [s]Isa 25:1 [t]Ex 15:2
[28]You are my God, and I will give you thanks;
you are my God,[s] and I will exalt[t] you.

[29]Give thanks to the LORD, for he is good;
his love endures forever.

Psalm 119[c]

א Aleph

119:1 [u]Ps 128:1
[1]Blessed are they whose ways are blameless,
who walk[u] according to the law of the LORD.
119:2 [v]Dt 6:5
[2]Blessed are they who keep his statutes
and seek him with all their heart.[v]
119:3 [w]1Jn 3:9; 5:18
[3]They do nothing wrong;[w]
they walk in his ways.
[4]You have laid down precepts
that are to be fully obeyed.
[5]Oh, that my ways were steadfast
in obeying your decrees!
[6]Then I would not be put to shame
when I consider all your commands.
[7]I will praise you with an upright heart
as I learn your righteous laws.
[8]I will obey your decrees;
do not utterly forsake me.

ב Beth

119:9 [x]2Ch 6:16
[9]How can a young man keep his way pure?
By living according to your word.[x]
119:10 [y]2Ch 15:15 [z]ver 21,118
[10]I seek you with all my heart;[y]
do not let me stray from your commands.[z]
119:11 [a]Ps 37:31; Lk 2:19,51
[11]I have hidden your word in my heart[a]
that I might not sin against you.
[12]Praise be to you, O LORD;

[a] *26* The Hebrew is plural. [b] *27* Or *Bind the festal sacrifice with ropes / and take it* [c] This psalm is an acrostic poem; the verses of each stanza begin with the same letter of the Hebrew alphabet.

The Longest Psalm

PS 119

The longest psalm (and the longest chapter in the Bible) is a repetitive meditation on the beauty and value of God's Word. God is addressed or referred to in nearly all of its 176 verses. Constructed as an acrostic, the psalm devotes 8 verses to each of the 22 letters of the Hebrew alphabet. Because the psalm is intended to function as an "instruction manual" on living a godly life, the acrostic style was probably useful in ancient oral tradition as the instructions were memorized and passed from generation to generation. The unnamed author of this poetic achievement was an Israelite who was passionately devoted to aligning his life with God's Word.

Joy in God's Ways

PS 119:32

Have you ever felt so full of energy and delight that you just had to run and skip for joy? If it's been awhile since you felt such an urge, perhaps you've observed it in children; they naturally express with their bodies what they feel in their hearts. The psalmist describes the joy and vitality of heart that comes from understanding and following the ways of God. To be set free from folly and sin is to have the shackles removed from our limbs and the heavy burden lifted from our hearts. If we want to run unencumbered toward the "prize" of our heavenly crown (1Co 9:24–25), we must "throw off everything that hinders and the sin that so easily entangles" (Heb 12:1).

teach me your decrees.[b]
13 With my lips I recount
all the laws that come from your mouth.[c]
14 I rejoice in following your statutes
as one rejoices in great riches.
15 I meditate on your precepts[d]
and consider your ways.
16 I delight[e] in your decrees;
I will not neglect your word.

ג Gimel

17 Do good to your servant,[f] and I will live;
I will obey your word.
18 Open my eyes that I may see
wonderful things in your law.
19 I am a stranger on earth;[g]
do not hide your commands from me.
20 My soul is consumed[h] with longing
for your laws[i] at all times.
21 You rebuke the arrogant, who are cursed
and who stray[j] from your commands.
22 Remove from me scorn[k] and contempt,
for I keep your statutes.
23 Though rulers sit together and slander me,
your servant will meditate on your decrees.
24 Your statutes are my delight;
they are my counselors.

ד Daleth

25 I am laid low in the dust;[l]
preserve my life[m] according to your word.
26 I recounted my ways and you answered me;
teach me your decrees.[n]
27 Let me understand the teaching of your precepts;
then I will meditate on your wonders.[o]
28 My soul is weary with sorrow;[p]
strengthen me[q] according to your word.
29 Keep me from deceitful ways;
be gracious to me through your law.
30 I have chosen the way of truth;
I have set my heart on your laws.
31 I hold fast[r] to your statutes, O LORD;
do not let me be put to shame.
32 I run in the path of your commands,
for you have set my heart free.

ה He

33 Teach me,[s] O LORD, to follow your decrees;
then I will keep them to the end.
34 Give me understanding, and I will keep your law
and obey it with all my heart.

119:12 [b]ver 26
119:13 [c]Ps 40:9
119:15 [d]Ps 1:2
119:16 [e]Ps 1:2
119:17 [f]Ps 13:6; 116:7
119:19 [g]1Ch 29:15; Ps 39:12; 2Co 5:6; Heb 11:13
119:20 [h]Ps 42:2; 84:2 [i]Ps 63:1
119:21 [j]ver 10
119:22 [k]Ps 39:8
119:25 [l]Ps 44:25 [m]Ps 143:11
119:26 [n]Ps 25:4; 27:11; 86:11
119:27 [o]Ps 145:5
119:28 [p]Ps 107:26 [q]Ps 20:2; 1Pe 5:10
119:31 [r]Dt 11:22
119:33 [s]ver 12

35 Direct me in the path of your
commands,
for there I find delight.
36 Turn my heart[t] toward your statutes
and not toward selfish gain.[u]
37 Turn my eyes away from worthless
things;
preserve my life[v] according to your
word.[a]
38 Fulfill your promise[w] to your servant,
so that you may be feared.
39 Take away the disgrace I dread,
for your laws are good.
40 How I long[x] for your precepts!
Preserve my life in your
righteousness.

ו Waw

41 May your unfailing love come to me,
O LORD,
your salvation according to your
promise;
42 then I will answer[y] the one who taunts
me,
for I trust in your word.
43 Do not snatch the word of truth from
my mouth,
for I have put my hope in your laws.
44 I will always obey your law,
for ever and ever.
45 I will walk about in freedom,
for I have sought out your precepts.
46 I will speak of your statutes before
kings[z]
and will not be put to shame,
47 for I delight in your commands
because I love them.
48 I lift up my hands to[b] your commands,
which I love,
and I meditate on your decrees.

ז Zayin

49 Remember your word to your servant,
for you have given me hope.
50 My comfort in my suffering is this:
Your promise preserves my life.[a]
51 The arrogant mock me[b] without
restraint,
but I do not turn[c] from your law.
52 I remember[d] your ancient laws, O LORD,
and I find comfort in them.
53 Indignation grips me[e] because of the
wicked,
who have forsaken your law.[f]
54 Your decrees are the theme of my song
wherever I lodge.

119:36 [t]1Ki 8:58 [u]Eze 33:31; Mk 7:21-22; Lk 12:15; Heb 13:5
119:37 [v]Ps 71:20; Isa 33:15
119:38 [w]2Sa 7:25
119:40 [x]ver 20
119:42 [y]Pr 27:11
119:46 [z]Mt 10:18; Ac 26:1-2
119:50 [a]Ro 15:4
119:51 [b]Jer 20:7 [c]ver 157; Job 23:11; Ps 44:18
119:52 [d]Ps 103:18
119:53 [e]Ezr 9:3 [f]Ps 89:30

[a] *37* Two manuscripts of the Masoretic Text and Dead Sea Scrolls; most manuscripts of the Masoretic Text *life in your way* [b] *48* Or *for*

My Comfort

PS 119:50

The psalmist's simple statement highlights in bold relief the bottom line for believers during trials. We may look for comfort in many places, but one unshakable fact is all we really need to sustain us: the Lord is true to his word. No matter what happens to us, no matter what we go through, we can be confident that our God is ultimately in control.

The writer of Hebrews exhorts us to cling to our confidence in the promises of God because our faith will be "richly rewarded" when we see the fulfillment of his Word (Heb 10:35–36). Because all his statutes are "fully trustworthy" (Ps 119:138), we can set our eyes on the future with confidence and a firm hope in God's grace, protection and care.

Good to Be Afflicted?

PS 119:71

No one likes to suffer. If it were up to us, we would probably choose to enjoy nothing but ease and prosperity. If lessons need to be learned, don't make us learn them the hard way! But the inescapable truth, in principle as well as in our experience, is that the pain of life can be a great teacher. When we're in pain, we're more likely to look beyond ourselves for help. Our neediness can drive us to God, both for comfort and for his wise solutions to our problems. A sincere follower of the Lord is willing to be taught wisdom and to look for the lessons in affliction. When we're open to the hidden gifts of coming to the end of our rope, we can actually be grateful for our trials (Ro 5:3–5).

55 In the night I remember[g] your name,
O LORD,
and I will keep your law.
56 This has been my practice:
I obey your precepts.

ח Heth

57 You are my portion,[h] O LORD;
I have promised to obey your words.
58 I have sought your face with all my
heart;
be gracious to me[i] according to your
promise.[j]
59 I have considered my ways[k]
and have turned my steps to your
statutes.
60 I will hasten and not delay
to obey your commands.
61 Though the wicked bind me with ropes,
I will not forget[l] your law.
62 At midnight[m] I rise to give you thanks
for your righteous laws.
63 I am a friend to all who fear you,[n]
to all who follow your precepts.
64 The earth is filled with your love,[o]
O LORD;
teach me your decrees.

ט Teth

65 Do good to your servant
according to your word, O LORD.
66 Teach me knowledge and good
judgment,
for I believe in your commands.
67 Before I was afflicted I went astray,[p]
but now I obey your word.
68 You are good,[q] and what you do is good;
teach me your decrees.[r]
69 Though the arrogant have smeared me
with lies,[s]
I keep your precepts with all my
heart.
70 Their hearts are callous[t] and unfeeling,
but I delight in your law.
71 It was good for me to be afflicted
so that I might learn your decrees.
72 The law from your mouth is more
precious to me
than thousands of pieces of silver and
gold.[u]

י Yodh

73 Your hands made me[v] and formed me;
give me understanding to learn your
commands.
74 May those who fear you rejoice[w] when
they see me,
for I have put my hope in your word.
75 I know, O LORD, that your laws are
righteous,

119:55 [g]Ps 63:6
119:57 [h]Ps 16:5; La 3:24
119:58 [i]1Ki 13:6 [j]ver 41
119:59 [k]Lk 15:17-18
119:61 [l]Ps 140:5
119:62 [m]Ac 16:25
119:63 [n]Ps 101:6-7
119:64 [o]Ps 33:5
119:67 [p]Jer 31:18-19; Heb 12:11
119:68 [q]Ps 106:1; 107:1; Mt 19:17 [r]ver 12
119:69 [s]Job 13:4; Ps 109:2
119:70 [t]Ps 17:10; Isa 6:10; Ac 28:27
119:72 [u]Ps 19:10; Pr 8:10-11,19
119:73 [v]Job 10:8; Ps 100:3; 138:8; 139:13-16
119:74 [w]Ps 34:2

119:75 [x]Heb 12:5-11
and in faithfulness[x] you have afflicted
me.
76 May your unfailing love be my comfort,
according to your promise to your
servant.
119:77 [y]ver 41
77 Let your compassion[y] come to me that I
may live,
for your law is my delight.
119:78 [z]Jer 50:32 [a]ver 86,161
78 May the arrogant[z] be put to shame for
wronging me without cause;[a]
but I will meditate on your precepts.
79 May those who fear you turn to me,
those who understand your statutes.
80 May my heart be blameless toward your
decrees,
that I may not be put to shame.

ℶ Kaph

119:81 [b]Ps 84:2
81 My soul faints[b] with longing for your
salvation,
but I have put my hope in your word.
119:82 [c]Ps 69:3; La 2:11
82 My eyes fail,[c] looking for your promise;
I say, "When will you comfort me?"
83 Though I am like a wineskin in the
smoke,
I do not forget your decrees.
119:84 [d]Ps 39:4; Rev 6:10
84 How long[d] must your servant wait?
When will you punish my
persecutors?
119:85 [e]Ps 35:7; Jer 18:20,22
85 The arrogant dig pitfalls[e] for me,
contrary to your law.
119:86 [f]Ps 35:19 [g]Ps 109:26 [h]ver 78
86 All your commands are trustworthy;[f]
help me,[g] for men persecute me
without cause.[h]
119:87 [i]Isa 58:2
87 They almost wiped me from the earth,
but I have not forsaken[i] your precepts.
88 Preserve my life according to your love,
and I will obey the statutes of your
mouth.

ל Lamedh

119:89 [j]Mt 24:34-35; 1Pe 1:25
89 Your word, O LORD, is eternal;[j]
it stands firm in the heavens.
119:90 [k]Ps 36:5 [l]Ps 148:6; Ecc 1:4
90 Your faithfulness[k] continues through all
generations;
you established the earth, and it
endures.[l]
119:91 [m]Jer 33:25
91 Your laws endure[m] to this day,
for all things serve you.
92 If your law had not been my delight,
I would have perished in my
affliction.
93 I will never forget your precepts,
for by them you have preserved my
life.
94 Save me, for I am yours;
I have sought out your precepts.
95 The wicked are waiting to destroy me,
but I will ponder your statutes.
96 To all perfection I see a limit;
but your commands are boundless.

Sooty Wineskins

PS 119:83

Wineskins, leather containers used as bottles, were often stored in the cooking areas of Israelite homes, where smoke from the cooking fires left them sooty and blackened, even dried out and shriveled. The psalmist is saying that he has so much faith in God's Word that even when he feels like he's cast aside, gathering dust or defaced and made ugly by his circumstances, he won't lose confidence in the rightness of God's ways.

Do you recollect the delicious sense of rest with which you have sometimes gone to bed at night, after a day of great exertion and weariness? How delightful was the sensation of relaxing every muscle, and letting your body go in a perfect abandonment of ease and comfort. The strain of the day had ceased for a few hours at least, and the work of the day had been thrown off. You no longer had to hold up an aching head or a weary back. You trusted yourself to the bed in an absolute confidence, and it held you up, without effort, or strain, or even thought on your part. You rested.

Let this analogy teach you what it means to rest in the Lord. Let your souls lie down upon His sweet will, as your bodies lie down in your beds at night. Relax every strain and lay off every burden. Let yourselves go in perfect abandonment of ease and comfort, sure that when He holds you up you are perfectly safe.

—Hannah Whitall Smith (1832-1911)

מ Mem

97 Oh, how I love your law!
I meditate[n] on it all day long.
98 Your commands make me wiser[o] than my enemies,
for they are ever with me.
99 I have more insight than all my teachers,
for I meditate on your statutes.
100 I have more understanding than the elders,
for I obey your precepts.[p]
101 I have kept my feet[q] from every evil path
so that I might obey your word.
102 I have not departed from your laws,
for you yourself have taught me.
103 How sweet are your words to my taste,
sweeter than honey[r] to my mouth![s]
104 I gain understanding from your precepts;
therefore I hate every wrong path.[t]

נ Nun

105 Your word is a lamp to my feet
and a light[u] for my path.
106 I have taken an oath[v] and confirmed it,
that I will follow your righteous laws.
107 I have suffered much;
preserve my life, O LORD, according to your word.
108 Accept, O LORD, the willing praise of my mouth,[w]
and teach me your laws.
109 Though I constantly take my life in my hands,[x]
I will not forget your law.
110 The wicked have set a snare[y] for me,
but I have not strayed[z] from your precepts.
111 Your statutes are my heritage forever;
they are the joy of my heart.
112 My heart is set on keeping your decrees
to the very end.[a]

ס Samekh

113 I hate double-minded men,[b]
but I love your law.
114 You are my refuge and my shield;[c]
I have put my hope[d] in your word.
115 Away from me,[e] you evildoers,
that I may keep the commands of my God!
116 Sustain me[f] according to your promise,
and I will live;
do not let my hopes be dashed.[g]
117 Uphold me, and I will be delivered;
I will always have regard for your decrees.
118 You reject all who stray from your decrees,

119:97 [n]Ps 1:2
119:98 [o]Dt 4:6
119:100 [p]Job 32:7-9
119:101 [q]Pr 1:15
119:103 [r]Ps 19:10; Pr 8:11 [s]Pr 24:13-14
119:104 [t]ver 128
119:105 [u]Pr 6:23
119:106 [v]Ne 10:29
119:108 [w]Hos 14:2; Heb 13:15
119:109 [x]Jdg 12:3; Job 13:14
119:110 [y]Ps 140:5; 141:9 [z]ver 10
119:112 [a]ver 33
119:113 [b]Jas 1:8
119:114 [c]Ps 32:7; 91:1 [d]ver 74
119:115 [e]Ps 6:8; 139:19; Mt 7:23
119:116 [f]Ps 54:4 [g]Ps 25:2; Ro 5:5; 9:33

for their deceitfulness is in vain.
119 All the wicked of the earth you discard
like dross;[h]
therefore I love your statutes.
120 My flesh trembles[i] in fear of you;
I stand in awe of your laws.

ע Ayin

121 I have done what is righteous and just;
do not leave me to my oppressors.
122 Ensure your servant's well-being;[j]
let not the arrogant oppress me.
123 My eyes fail, looking for your salvation,
looking for your righteous promise.[k]
124 Deal with your servant according to
your love
and teach me your decrees.[l]
125 I am your servant;[m] give me
discernment
that I may understand your statutes.
126 It is time for you to act, O LORD;
your law is being broken.
127 Because I love your commands
more than gold,[n] more than pure
gold,
128 and because I consider all your precepts
right,
I hate every wrong path.[o]

פ Pe

129 Your statutes are wonderful;
therefore I obey them.
130 The unfolding of your words gives
light;[p]
it gives understanding to the simple.[q]
131 I open my mouth and pant,[r]
longing for your commands.[s]
132 Turn to me and have mercy[t] on me,
as you always do to those who love
your name.
133 Direct my footsteps according to your
word;[u]
let no sin rule[v] over me.
134 Redeem me from the oppression of
men,[w]
that I may obey your precepts.
135 Make your face shine[x] upon your
servant
and teach me your decrees.
136 Streams of tears[y] flow from my eyes,
for your law is not obeyed.[z]

צ Tsadhe

137 Righteous are you,[a] O LORD,
and your laws are right.[b]
138 The statutes you have laid down are
righteous;[c]
they are fully trustworthy.
139 My zeal wears me out,[d]
for my enemies ignore your words.

119:119 [h]Eze 22:18, 19
119:120 [i]Hab 3:16
119:122 [j]Job 17:3
119:123 [k]ver 82
119:124 [l]ver 12
119:125 [m]Ps 116:16
119:127 [n]Ps 19:10
119:128 [o]ver 104,163
119:130 [p]Pr 6:23 [q]Ps 19:7
119:131 [r]Ps 42:1 [s]ver 20
119:132 [t]Ps 25:16; 106:4
119:133 [u]Ps 17:5 [v]Ps 19:13; Ro 6:12
119:134 [w]Ps 142:6; Lk 1:74
119:135 [x]Nu 6:25; Ps 4:6
119:136 [y]Jer 9:1,18 [z]Eze 9:4
119:137 [a]Ezr 9:15; Jer 12:1 [b]Ne 9:13
119:138 [c]Ps 19:7
119:139 [d]Ps 69:9; Jn 2:17

God created us to have fellowship with him. When you make a habit of talking to him often, you'll make him happy, and he'll make you content. There is joy in the presence of the Lord.

—Thelma Wells

Let us look at our own shortcomings and leave other people's alone; for those who live carefully ordered lives are apt to be shocked at everything and we might well learn very important lessons from the persons who shock us. Our outward comportment and behavior may be better than theirs, but this, though good, is not the most important thing: there is no reason why we should expect everyone else to travel by our own road.

—Teresa of Avila (1515-1582)

140 Your promises have been thoroughly
tested,[e]
and your servant loves them.
141 Though I am lowly and despised,[f]
I do not forget your precepts.
142 Your righteousness is everlasting
and your law is true.[g]
143 Trouble and distress have come
upon me,
but your commands are my delight.
144 Your statutes are forever right;
give me understanding[h] that I may
live.

ק Qoph

145 I call with all my heart; answer me,
O LORD,
and I will obey your decrees.
146 I call out to you; save me
and I will keep your statutes.
147 I rise before dawn[i] and cry for help;
I have put my hope in your word.
148 My eyes stay open through the watches
of the night,[j]
that I may meditate on your promises.
149 Hear my voice in accordance with your
love;
preserve my life, O LORD, according to
your laws.
150 Those who devise wicked schemes are
near,
but they are far from your law.
151 Yet you are near,[k] O LORD,
and all your commands are true.[l]
152 Long ago I learned from your statutes
that you established them to last
forever.[m]

ר Resh

153 Look upon my suffering[n] and
deliver me,
for I have not forgotten[o] your law.
154 Defend my cause[p] and redeem me;[q]
preserve my life according to your
promise.
155 Salvation is far from the wicked,
for they do not seek out[r] your decrees.
156 Your compassion is great, O LORD;
preserve my life[s] according to your
laws.
157 Many are the foes who persecute me,[t]
but I have not turned from your
statutes.
158 I look on the faithless with loathing,[u]
for they do not obey your word.
159 See how I love your precepts;
preserve my life, O LORD, according to
your love.
160 All your words are true;
all your righteous laws are eternal.

119:140 [e]Ps 12:6
119:141 [f]Ps 22:6
119:143 [g]Ps 19:7
119:144 [h]Ps 19:9
119:147 [i]Ps 5:3; 57:8; 108:2
119:148 [j]Ps 63:6
119:151 [k]Ps 34:18; 145:18 [l]ver 142
119:152 [m]Lk 21:33
119:153 [n]La 5:1 [o]Pr 3:1
119:154 [p]Mic 7:9 [q]1Sa 24:15
119:155 [r]Job 5:4
119:156 [s]2Sa 24:14
119:157 [t]Ps 7:1
119:158 [u]Ps 139:21

ש Sin and Shin

161 Rulers persecute me[v] without cause,
but my heart trembles at your word.
162 I rejoice in your promise
like one who finds great spoil.[w]
163 I hate and abhor falsehood
but I love your law.
164 Seven times a day I praise you
for your righteous laws.
165 Great peace[x] have they who love your law,
and nothing can make them stumble.
166 I wait for your salvation,[y] O LORD,
and I follow your commands.
167 I obey your statutes,
for I love them greatly.
168 I obey your precepts and your statutes,
for all my ways are known[z] to you.

ת Taw

169 May my cry come[a] before you, O LORD;
give me understanding according to your word.
170 May my supplication come[b] before you;
deliver me[c] according to your promise.
171 May my lips overflow with praise,[d]
for you teach me[e] your decrees.
172 May my tongue sing of your word,
for all your commands are righteous.
173 May your hand be ready to help[f] me,
for I have chosen[g] your precepts.
174 I long for your salvation,[h] O LORD,
and your law is my delight.
175 Let me live[i] that I may praise you,
and may your laws sustain me.
176 I have strayed like a lost sheep.[j]
Seek your servant,
for I have not forgotten your commands.

119:161 [v]1Sa 24:11
119:162 [w]1Sa 30:16
119:165 [x]Pr 3:2; Isa 26:3,12; 32:17
119:166 [y]Ge 49:18
119:168 [z]Pr 5:21
119:169 [a]Ps 18:6
119:170 [b]Ps 28:2 [c]Ps 31:2
119:171 [d]Ps 51:15 [e]Ps 94:12
119:173 [f]Ps 37:24 [g]Jos 24:22
119:174 [h]ver 166
119:175 [i]Isa 55:3
119:176 [j]Isa 53:6

Psalm 120

A song of ascents.

1 I call on the LORD in my distress,[k]
and he answers me.
2 Save me, O LORD, from lying lips[l]
and from deceitful tongues.[m]

3 What will he do to you,
and what more besides, O deceitful tongue?
4 He will punish you with a warrior's sharp arrows,[n]
with burning coals of the broom tree.

5 Woe to me that I dwell in Meshech,
that I live among the tents of Kedar![o]
6 Too long have I lived
among those who hate peace.
7 I am a man of peace;
but when I speak, they are for war.

120:1 [k]Ps 102:2; Jnh 2:2
120:2 [l]Pr 12:22 [m]Ps 52:4
120:4 [n]Ps 45:5
120:5 [o]Ge 25:13; Jer 49:28

A Song of Ascents

PS 120

To ascend—to step up—is implied by the title of this psalm, as well as of psalms 121–134. Some believe that the word *ascents* refers to the actual temple stairs and that these songs were part of the liturgy of worship, perhaps sung on the steps of the temple. Others think the word *ascents* refers to the trips to Jerusalem taken three times a year by Hebrew men, normally accompanied by their families, for special festivals (Ex 23:14–17). Still others suggest the word *ascents* is more general and symbolic, representing the pilgrimage all believers make in pursuit of the living God (Ps 84).

Pray for Jerusalem

PS 122:6–7

In the psalmist's day, Jerusalem was the physical place that God had set apart for himself and in which he promised to live among his people (2Ch 6:6; Ps 135:21). The name Jerusalem means "city of peace," so it is only fitting that the psalmist asks worshipers to pray for peace to reign there.

In the Bible, Jerusalem can also refer symbolically to the salvation available in Jesus Christ's church on earth (Heb 12:22–24) and to his glorified church ("the new Jerusalem") in heaven (Rev 3:12; 21:2). In this context, to pray for "the peace of Jerusalem" is not only to pray for the literal city, it is a prayer that peace will reign within God's visible church and his eternal rule over heaven and earth will be sure and will come soon (Rev 22:20).

Psalm 121

A song of ascents.

1 I lift up my eyes to the hills—
where does my help come from?
2 My help comes from the LORD,
the Maker of heaven and earth.[p]

3 He will not let your foot slip—
he who watches over you will not slumber;
4 indeed, he who watches over Israel
will neither slumber nor sleep.

5 The LORD watches over[q] you—
the LORD is your shade at your right hand;
6 the sun[r] will not harm you by day,
nor the moon by night.

7 The LORD will keep you from all harm[s]—
he will watch over your life;
8 the LORD will watch over your coming and going
both now and forevermore.[t]

Psalm 122

A song of ascents. Of David.

1 I rejoiced with those who said to me,
"Let us go to the house of the LORD."
2 Our feet are standing
in your gates, O Jerusalem.

3 Jerusalem is built like a city
that is closely compacted together.
4 That is where the tribes go up,
the tribes of the LORD,
to praise the name of the LORD
according to the statute given to Israel.
5 There the thrones for judgment stand,
the thrones of the house of David.

6 Pray for the peace of Jerusalem:
"May those who love[u] you be secure.
7 May there be peace within your walls
and security within your citadels."
8 For the sake of my brothers and friends,
I will say, "Peace be within you."
9 For the sake of the house of the LORD our God,
I will seek your prosperity.[v]

Psalm 123

A song of ascents.

1 I lift up my eyes to you,
to you whose throne[w] is in heaven.
2 As the eyes of slaves look to the hand of their master,

121:2 [p]Ps 115:15; 124:8
121:5 [q]Isa 25:4
121:6 [r]Ps 91:5; Isa 49:10; Rev 7:16
121:7 [s]Ps 41:2; 91:10-12
121:8 [t]Dt 28:6
122:6 [u]Ps 51:18
122:9 [v]Ne 2:10
123:1 [w]Ps 11:4; 121:1; 141:8

as the eyes of a maid look to the hand
of her mistress,
123:2 [x]Ps 25:15
so our eyes look to the LORD[x] our God,
till he shows us his mercy.

3 Have mercy on us, O LORD, have mercy
on us,
for we have endured much contempt.
4 We have endured much ridicule from
the proud,
much contempt from the arrogant.

Psalm 124

A song of ascents. Of David.

1 If the LORD had not been on our side—
124:1 [y]Ps 129:1
let Israel say[y]—
2 if the LORD had not been on our side
when men attacked us,
3 when their anger flared against us,
they would have swallowed us alive;
4 the flood would have engulfed us,
the torrent would have swept over us,
5 the raging waters
would have swept us away.

6 Praise be to the LORD,
who has not let us be torn by their
teeth.
7 We have escaped like a bird
124:7 [z]Ps 91:3; Pr 6:5
out of the fowler's snare;[z]
the snare has been broken,
and we have escaped.
124:8 [a]Ge 1:1; Ps 121:2; 134:3
8 Our help is in the name of the LORD,
the Maker of heaven[a] and earth.

Psalm 125

A song of ascents.

1 Those who trust in the LORD are like
Mount Zion,
125:1 [b]Ps 46:5
which cannot be shaken[b] but endures
forever.
2 As the mountains surround Jerusalem,
125:2 [c]Ps 121:8; Zec 2:4-5
so the LORD surrounds[c] his people
both now and forevermore.

125:3 [d]Ps 89:22; Pr 22:8; Isa 14:5 [e]1Sa 24:10; Ps 55:20
3 The scepter of the wicked will not
remain[d]
over the land allotted to the righteous,
for then the righteous might use
their hands to do evil.[e]

125:4 [f]Ps 119:68 [g]Ps 7:10; 36:10; 94:15
4 Do good, O LORD,[f] to those who are
good,
to those who are upright in heart.[g]
125:5 [h]Job 23:11 [i]Pr 2:15; Isa 59:8 [j]Ps 128:6
5 But those who turn[h] to crooked ways[i]
the LORD will banish with the
evildoers.

Peace be upon Israel.[j]

Snares

PS 124:7

The kind of trap used to catch tasty birds in the psalmist's day was constructed of two wooden frames, between which a net was stretched. The hunter laid the contraption flat on the ground, and when a bird wandered into it, the frames sprang closed and trapped the creature in the net.

The psalmist is using the snare metaphorically in this psalm to celebrate the fact that the Lord has broken the "frames" of the traps enemies have set for his people, allowing his chosen ones to escape like free birds. By all human calculations and predictions, the Lord's people should have been utterly destroyed by this point in history. They have had countless enemies and so many close calls. But the Lord's love has preserved them. That same love will continue to preserve us until we stand whole and radiant before Jesus Christ himself (Eph 5:25-27).

The Blessing of Family

PS 127:3—128:6

Since the human race began, a clear sign of God's blessing has been its proliferation. God has the power to wipe out life at any time, but he chooses instead to preserve it, nurture it and cherish it. The family structure is crucial to the security and well-being of individuals (Ps 68:6), and Scripture is packed with stories about families and lessons about how to conduct family affairs.

For the Israelites, having family is especially important, as the inheritance God secures for them in the promised land will be lost unless they have heirs to receive it (Nu 27:8–11). Thus, children are especially prized as gifts from God; close family ties are considered a reward for obedience to God's ways.

Psalm 126

A song of ascents.

1 When the LORD brought back[k] the
captives to[a] Zion,
we were like men who dreamed.[b]
2 Our mouths were filled with laughter,
our tongues with songs of joy.[l]
Then it was said among the nations,
"The LORD has done great things[m] for
them."
3 The LORD has done great things for us,
and we are filled with joy.[n]
4 Restore our fortunes,[c] O LORD,
like streams in the Negev.[o]
5 Those who sow in tears
will reap with songs of joy.[p]
6 He who goes out weeping,
carrying seed to sow,
will return with songs of joy,
carrying sheaves with him.

126:1 [k]Ps 85:1; Hos 6:11
126:2 [l]Job 8:21; Ps 51:14 [m]Ps 71:19
126:3 [n]Isa 25:9
126:4 [o]Isa 35:6; 43:19
126:5 [p]Isa 35:10

Psalm 127

A song of ascents. Of Solomon.

1 Unless the LORD builds[q] the house,
its builders labor in vain.
Unless the LORD watches[r] over the city,
the watchmen stand guard in vain.
2 In vain you rise early
and stay up late,
toiling for food[s] to eat—
for he grants sleep[t] to[d] those he loves.
3 Sons are a heritage from the LORD,
children a reward[u] from him.
4 Like arrows in the hands of a warrior
are sons born in one's youth.
5 Blessed is the man
whose quiver is full of them.
They will not be put to shame
when they contend with their
enemies[v] in the gate.

127:1 [q]Ps 78:69 [r]Ps 121:4
127:2 [s]Ge 3:17 [t]Job 11:18
127:3 [u]Ge 33:5
127:5 [v]Pr 27:11

Psalm 128

A song of ascents.

1 Blessed are all who fear the LORD,[w]
who walk in his ways.[x]
2 You will eat the fruit of your labor;[y]
blessings and prosperity[z] will be
yours.
3 Your wife will be like a fruitful vine[a]
within your house;
your sons will be like olive shoots[b]
around your table.
4 Thus is the man blessed
who fears the LORD.

128:1 [w]Ps 112:1 [x]Ps 119:1-3
128:2 [y]Isa 3:10 [z]Ecc 8:12
128:3 [a]Eze 19:10 [b]Ps 52:8; 144:12

[a] *1* Or *LORD restored the fortunes of* [b] *1* Or *men restored to health* [c] *4* Or *Bring back our captives* [d] *2* Or *eat— / for while they sleep he provides for*

128:5 [c]Ps 20:2; 134:3

5 May the LORD bless you from Zion[c]
all the days of your life;
may you see the prosperity of
Jerusalem,
6 and may you live to see your
children's children.[d]

128:6 [d]Ge 50:23; Job 42:16 [e]Ps 125:5

Peace be upon Israel.[e]

Psalm 129

A song of ascents.

129:1 [f]Ps 88:15; Hos 2:15 [g]Ps 124:1

1 They have greatly oppressed me from
my youth[f]—
let Israel say[g]—
2 they have greatly oppressed me from my
youth,

129:2 [h]Mt 16:18

but they have not gained the victory[h]
over me.
3 Plowmen have plowed my back
and made their furrows long.

129:4 [i]Ps 119:137

4 But the LORD is righteous;[i]
he has cut me free from the cords of
the wicked.

129:5 [j]Mic 4:11 [k]Ps 71:13

5 May all who hate Zion[j]
be turned back in shame.[k]
6 May they be like grass on the roof,

129:6 [l]Ps 37:2

which withers[l] before it can grow;
7 with it the reaper cannot fill his hands,
nor the one who gathers fill his arms.
8 May those who pass by not say,
"The blessing of the LORD be upon
you;

129:8 [m]Ru 2:4; Ps 118:26

we bless you[m] in the name of the
LORD."

130:1 [n]Ps 42:7; 69:2; La 3:55

Psalm 130

A song of ascents.

130:2 [o]Ps 28:2 [p]2Ch 6:40; Ps 64:1

1 Out of the depths[n] I cry to you, O LORD;
2 O Lord, hear my voice.[o]
Let your ears be attentive[p]
to my cry for mercy.

130:3 [q]Ps 76:7; 143:2

3 If you, O LORD, kept a record of sins,
O Lord, who could stand?[q]

130:4 [r]Ex 34:7; Isa 55:7; Jer 33:8 [s]1Ki 8:40

4 But with you there is forgiveness;[r]
therefore you are feared.[s]

130:5 [t]Ps 27:14; 33:20; Isa 8:17 [u]Ps 119:81

5 I wait for the LORD,[t] my soul waits,
and in his word[u] I put my hope.
6 My soul waits for the Lord
more than watchmen[v] wait for the
morning,

130:6 [v]Ps 63:6 [w]Ps 119:147

more than watchmen wait for the
morning.[w]

130:7 [x]Ps 131:3

7 O Israel, put your hope[x] in the LORD,
for with the LORD is unfailing love
and with him is full redemption.

130:8 [y]Lk 1:68

8 He himself will redeem[y] Israel
from all their sins.

A Record of Sins

PS 130:3

Have you ever felt like someone was keeping score in their relationship with you—making note of your every "failure" so they could bring it up later in order to berate you? Unfortunately, some of us see God that way—as the great record keeper in the sky, who keeps constant tabs on us and remembers everything we've ever done wrong so he can confront us on judgment day and make us pay. God is certainly aware of our every thought and deed, and, in the end, all will be revealed and perfect justice will be executed (Rev 20:12). But those whose sins are paid for by the shed blood of Jesus Christ have nothing to fear (Heb 9:11–15). If God gives us what we deserve, we will perish; but because of his great mercy, he chooses not to hold our sin against us (Ps 103:10–12).

A Weaned Child

PS 131:2

Every nursing mother knows the distress and restlessness of her child when he or she is hungry—and how quickly it is alleviated the moment her little one is held to her breast for feeding and comfort. Similarly, children who are weaned, who no longer clamor for the breast but trust that they will be fed and cared for by the mother who once nursed them, are content simply to be in their mother's presence. Such imagery, both primal and feminine, is easily understood in light of our relationship with God. Like a tender, dependable mother, God assures us of his presence and reliable provision. In turn we can reassure our shaky souls that all is well, choosing to place childlike trust in the One who is always there for us.

Psalm 131

A song of ascents. Of David.

1 My heart is not proud,[z] O LORD,
my eyes are not haughty;
I do not concern myself with great matters
or things too wonderful for me.
2 But I have stilled and quieted my soul;
like a weaned child with its mother,
like a weaned child is my soul[a] within me.

3 O Israel, put your hope[b] in the LORD
both now and forevermore.

131:1 [z]Ps 101:5; Ro 12:16
131:2 [a]Mt 18:3; 1Co 14:20
131:3 [b]Ps 130:7

Psalm 132

A song of ascents.

1 O LORD, remember David
and all the hardships he endured.

2 He swore an oath to the LORD
and made a vow to the Mighty One of Jacob:[c]
3 "I will not enter my house
or go to my bed—
4 I will allow no sleep to my eyes,
no slumber to my eyelids,
5 till I find a place[d] for the LORD,
a dwelling for the Mighty One of Jacob."

6 We heard it in Ephrathah,[e]
we came upon it in the fields of Jaar[a]:[b][f]
7 "Let us go to his dwelling place;[g]
let us worship at his footstool[h]—
8 arise, O LORD,[i] and come to your resting place,
you and the ark of your might.
9 May your priests be clothed with righteousness;[j]
may your saints sing for joy."

10 For the sake of David your servant,
do not reject your anointed one.

11 The LORD swore an oath to David,[k]
a sure oath that he will not revoke:
"One of your own descendants[l]
I will place on your throne—
12 if your sons keep my covenant
and the statutes I teach them,
then their sons will sit
on your throne[m] for ever and ever."

13 For the LORD has chosen Zion,[n]
he has desired it for his dwelling:

132:2 [c]Ge 49:24
132:5 [d]Ac 7:46
132:6 [e]1Sa 17:12 [f]1Sa 7:2
132:7 [g]Ps 5:7 [h]Ps 99:5
132:8 [i]Nu 10:35; Ps 78:61
132:9 [j]Job 29:14; Isa 61:3, 10
132:11 [k]Ps 89:3-4, 35 [l]2Sa 7:12
132:12 [m]Lk 1:32; Ac 2:30
132:13 [n]Ps 48:1-2

[a] 6 That is, Kiriath Jearim [b] 6 Or *heard of it in Ephrathah, / we found it in the fields of Jaar.* (And no quotes around verses 7–9)

Week 18

Stilling Your Soul Before God

Rush, rush, rush. Your day is bursting at the seams. There's never enough time to accomplish everything on your to-do list. There's no time to enjoy a sunset, to stand for even five minutes simply feeling the wind on your face. So who has the time to just sit before God with no words, no agenda, no schedule?

In recent years meditation has become increasingly popular. But it's nothing new. Christian meditation is different from all other forms. Most forms, such as New Age or Eastern meditation, require the person to empty her or his mind. The goal is to commune either with the inner self or with spiritual energies or entities. Christian meditation involves fixing your eyes on Jesus and filling your mind with the things of God; the goal is to commune with God, submitting your will to his. Although there are counterfeit forms, don't be afraid to use God's gift of meditation to deepen your relationship with him.

- How important is meditation (Ps 46:10; Mk 6:31)?
- What is the first step in meditation (Psalm 131:1–2)? How often do you take time to quiet your soul in awareness of God's presence?
- What does Elisha use to quiet his soul (2Ki 3:15)? What aids can you use to quiet your soul?
- What sort of environment is conducive to meditation (Mk 1:35)? What in your life might hinder it?
- How should you begin your meditation (Heb 12:2)?
- How will you benefit from meditation (Php 4:6–9)?
- What are some things you can meditate on (Jos 1:8; Ps 48:9; 77:12; 119:15,23,27,148)?

Enjoying God THROUGH the Word

Read Psalm 23 (page 879). This psalm is a wonderful example of true meditation. Jesus, the shepherd, leads you into a beautiful pasture near a quiet stream. It is here, in this tranquil setting, that Jesus refreshes you spiritually. He guides you in his ways and walks with you through even the darkest, most difficult times. You have no need to fear—his authority and power are a comfort to you. He prepares a lavish banquet for you under the shade of the trees. He seats you in a place of honor and sends goodness your way for as long as you live. And with your death will come the joy of living in his presence forever.

Meditation can be a wonderful way to enjoy God and to listen to his voice. God has chosen to reveal his thoughts to his people (Am 4:13). But often the noise of the world dulls your spiritual ears to the whispers of God. Meditation is an excellent way to still your spirit so that you can be receptive to the Holy Spirit's voice.

Enjoying God THROUGH Experience

Find a place where you can be alone. Still your heart and mind by using the scene in Psalm 23. Be very quiet; put aside the noise, busyness and duties of your day, and allow the Spirit of God to refresh your spirit. Take your wounded, battle-weary heart to Jesus and just sit with him awhile. This can be a time to bask in God's presence and to enjoy who he is and who you are in him.

Go to page 1057 for your next weekly study.

Unity

PS 133:1

We have all experienced the sense of rightness and pleasure that results from getting along with others—as well as the anxiety and friction that knots up our stomachs when we're at odds with others. Not only do we enjoy peace of mind when we live in harmony with fellow believers, but we also make a statement to the world around us. Jesus' new commandment is that we love one another as he has loved us, so that everyone who observes our loving interaction with each other will know that we belong to Jesus Christ (Jn 13:34–35). We will not always agree with each other on everything, but we are exhorted by Jesus and the apostles to "make every effort to keep the unity of the Spirit through the bond of peace" (Eph 4:3). We may have our differences, but our common purpose and destiny unites our hearts (Eph 4:4–6; Php 2:2).

14 "This is my resting place for ever and ever;[o]
here I will sit enthroned, for I have desired it—
15 I will bless her with abundant provisions;
her poor will I satisfy with food.[p]
16 I will clothe her priests[q] with salvation,
and her saints will ever sing for joy.

17 "Here I will make a horn[a] grow[r] for David
and set up a lamp[s] for my anointed one.
18 I will clothe his enemies with shame,[t]
but the crown on his head will be resplendent."

Psalm 133

A song of ascents. Of David.

1 How good and pleasant it is
when brothers live together[u] in unity!
2 It is like precious oil poured on the head,[v]
running down on the beard,
running down on Aaron's beard,
down upon the collar of his robes.
3 It is as if the dew of Hermon[w]
were falling on Mount Zion.
For there the LORD bestows his blessing,[x]
even life forevermore.[y]

Psalm 134

A song of ascents.

1 Praise the LORD, all you servants[z] of the LORD
who minister by night[a] in the house of the LORD.
2 Lift up your hands[b] in the sanctuary
and praise the LORD.

3 May the LORD, the Maker of heaven[c] and earth,
bless you from Zion.[d]

Psalm 135

1 Praise the LORD.[b]

Praise the name of the LORD;
praise him, you servants[e] of the LORD,
2 you who minister in the house[f] of the LORD,
in the courts[g] of the house of our God.

3 Praise the LORD, for the LORD is good;[h]
sing praise to his name, for that is pleasant.[i]

132:14 [o]Ps 68:16
132:15 [p]Ps 107:9; 147:14
132:16 [q]2Ch 6:41
132:17 [r]Eze 29:21; Lk 1:69 [s]1Ki 11:36; 2Ch 21:7
132:18 [t]Ps 35:26; 109:29
133:1 [u]Ge 13:8; Heb 13:1
133:2 [v]Ex 30:25
133:3 [w]Dt 4:48 [x]Lev 25:21; Dt 28:8 [y]Ps 42:8
134:1 [z]Ps 135:1-2 [a]1Ch 9:33
134:2 [b]Ps 28:2; 1Ti 2:8
134:3 [c]Ps 124:8 [d]Ps 128:5
135:1 [e]Ps 113:1; 134:1
135:2 [f]Lk 2:37 [g]Ps 116:19
135:3 [h]Ps 119:68 [i]Ps 147:1

[a] 17 *Horn* here symbolizes strong one, that is, king.
[b] 1 Hebrew *Hallelu Yah*; also in verses 3 and 21

4 For the LORD has chosen Jacob[j] to be his
own,
Israel to be his treasured possession.[k]

5 I know that the LORD is great,[l]
that our Lord is greater than all gods.[m]
6 The LORD does whatever pleases him,[n]
in the heavens and on the earth,
in the seas and all their depths.
7 He makes clouds rise from the ends of
the earth;
he sends lightning with the rain[o]
and brings out the wind[p] from his
storehouses.[q]

8 He struck down the firstborn[r] of Egypt,
the firstborn of men and animals.
9 He sent his signs[s] and wonders into
your midst, O Egypt,
against Pharaoh and all his servants.[t]
10 He struck down many[u] nations
and killed mighty kings—
11 Sihon[v] king of the Amorites,
Og king of Bashan
and all the kings of Canaan[w]—
12 and he gave their land as an
inheritance,[x]
an inheritance to his people Israel.

13 Your name, O LORD, endures forever,[y]
your renown,[z] O LORD, through all
generations.
14 For the LORD will vindicate his people
and have compassion on his
servants.[a]

15 The idols of the nations are silver and
gold,
made by the hands of men.
16 They have mouths, but cannot speak,
eyes, but they cannot see;
17 they have ears, but cannot hear,
nor is there breath in their mouths.
18 Those who make them will be like
them,
and so will all who trust in them.

19 O house of Israel, praise the LORD;
O house of Aaron, praise the LORD;
20 O house of Levi, praise the LORD;
you who fear him, praise the LORD.
21 Praise be to the LORD from Zion,[b]
to him who dwells in Jerusalem.

Praise the LORD.

Psalm 136

1 Give thanks to the LORD, for he is good.[c]
His love endures forever.[d]
2 Give thanks to the God of gods.[e]
His love endures forever.
3 Give thanks to the Lord of lords:
His love endures forever.

135:4 [j]Dt 10:15; 1Pe 2:9 [k]Ex 19:5; Dt 7:6
135:5 [l]Ps 48:1 [m]Ps 97:9
135:6 [n]Ps 115:3
135:7 [o]Jer 10:13; Zec 10:1 [p]Job 28:25 [q]Job 38:22
135:8 [r]Ex 12:12; Ps 78:51
135:9 [s]Dt 6:22 [t]Ps 136:10-15
135:10 [u]Nu 21:21-25; Ps 136:17-21
135:11 [v]Nu 21:21 [w]Jos 12:7-24
135:12 [x]Ps 78:55
135:13 [y]Ex 3:15 [z]Ps 102:12
135:14 [a]Dt 32:36
135:21 [b]Ps 134:3
136:1 [c]Ps 106:1 [d]1Ch 16:34; 2Ch 20:21
136:2 [e]Dt 10:17

There are times when, oh, what we wouldn't give for a little direction. Desperately we long for God's guidance. How many times have I heard people say, "I really want to do what God wants me to do, but what is it? What is his will anyway?" . . . I've always believed that those who want to know God's will *can* know it . . . I think God has straightforward ways to lead his children:

1. His Word. The Bible is very definitive about the responsibility of a disciple of Christ.

2. Circumstance. God opens some doors and closes others.

3. Wise counsel. Proverbs 13:10 tells us, "Pride only breeds quarrels, but wisdom is found in those who take advice."

And consider this as a rule of thumb: God never calls without enabling us. In other words, if he calls you to do something, *he* makes it possible for you to do it.

—Luci Swindoll

A Poetic Refrain

PS 136

In response to a worship leader's reading or singing of the liturgy, the refrain "His love endures forever" is most likely chanted or sung in unison, either by a Levitical choir (1Ch 16:41) or by the congregation of worshipers (2Ch 7:3). The repetition of such a phrase drives home a great truth, like the divine mercy celebrated in this song. The repetition also serves to unite large groups of people in praise.

4 to him who alone does great wonders,[f]
His love endures forever.
5 who by his understanding[g] made the heavens,[h]
His love endures forever.
6 who spread out the earth[i] upon the waters,[j]
His love endures forever.
7 who made the great lights[k]—
His love endures forever.
8 the sun to govern[l] the day,
His love endures forever.
9 the moon and stars to govern the night;
His love endures forever.

10 to him who struck down the firstborn[m] of Egypt
His love endures forever.
11 and brought Israel out[n] from among them
His love endures forever.
12 with a mighty hand and outstretched arm;[o]
His love endures forever.

13 to him who divided the Red Sea[a][p] asunder
His love endures forever.
14 and brought Israel through[q] the midst of it,
His love endures forever.
15 but swept Pharaoh and his army into the Red Sea;[r]
His love endures forever.

16 to him who led his people through the desert,[s]
His love endures forever.
17 who struck down great kings,[t]
His love endures forever.
18 and killed mighty kings[u]—
His love endures forever.
19 Sihon king of the Amorites[v]
His love endures forever.
20 and Og king of Bashan—
His love endures forever.
21 and gave their land[w] as an inheritance,
His love endures forever.
22 an inheritance to his servant Israel;
His love endures forever.

23 to the One who remembered us[x] in our low estate
His love endures forever.
24 and freed us from our enemies,[y]
His love endures forever.
25 and who gives food[z] to every creature.
His love endures forever.

26 Give thanks to the God of heaven.
His love endures forever.

136:4 [f]Ps 72:18
136:5 [g]Pr 3:19; Jer 51:15 [h]Ge 1:1
136:6 [i]Ge 1:9; Jer 10:12 [j]Ps 24:2
136:7 [k]Ge 1:14,16
136:8 [l]Ge 1:16
136:10 [m]Ex 12:29; Ps 135:8
136:11 [n]Ex 6:6; 12:51
136:12 [o]Dt 4:34; Ps 44:3
136:13 [p]Ex 14:21; Ps 78:13
136:14 [q]Ex 14:22
136:15 [r]Ex 14:27; Ps 135:9
136:16 [s]Ex 13:18
136:17 [t]Ps 135:9-12
136:18 [u]Dt 29:7
136:19 [v]Nu 21:21-25
136:21 [w]Jos 12:1
136:23 [x]Ps 113:7
136:24 [y]Ps 107:2
136:25 [z]Ps 104:27; 145:15

[a] *13* Hebrew *Yam Suph*; that is, Sea of Reeds; also in verse 15

Psalm 137

137:1 [a]Eze 1:1,3 [b]Ne 1:4

[1]By the rivers of Babylon[a] we sat and wept[b]
when we remembered Zion.
[2]There on the poplars
we hung our harps,
[3]for there our captors asked us for songs,
our tormentors demanded[c] songs of joy;
they said, "Sing us one of the songs of Zion!"

137:3 [c]Ps 80:6

[4]How can we sing the songs of the LORD
while in a foreign land?
[5]If I forget you, O Jerusalem,
may my right hand forget ⌊its skill⌋.
[6]May my tongue cling to the roof[d] of my mouth
if I do not remember you,
if I do not consider Jerusalem
my highest joy.

137:6 [d]Eze 3:26

[7]Remember, O LORD, what the Edomites[e] did
on the day Jerusalem fell.[f]
"Tear it down," they cried,
"tear it down to its foundations!"

137:7 [e]Jer 49:7; La 4:21-22; Eze 25:12 [f]Ob 1:11

[8]O Daughter of Babylon, doomed to destruction,[g]
happy is he who repays you
for what you have done to us—
[9]he who seizes your infants
and dashes them[h] against the rocks.

137:8 [g]Isa 13:1,19; Jer 25:12,26; Jer 50:15; Rev 18:6
137:9 [h]2Ki 8:12; Isa 13:16

Psalm 138

Of David.

[1]I will praise you, O LORD, with all my heart;
before the "gods"[i] I will sing your praise.
[2]I will bow down toward your holy temple[j]
and will praise your name
for your love and your faithfulness,
for you have exalted above all things
your name and your word.[k]
[3]When I called, you answered me;
you made me bold and stouthearted.[l]

138:1 [i]Ps 95:3; 96:4
138:2 [j]1Ki 8:29; Ps 5:7; 28:2 [k]Isa 42:21
138:3 [l]Ps 28:7

[4]May all the kings of the earth[m] praise you, O LORD,
when they hear the words of your mouth.
[5]May they sing of the ways of the LORD,
for the glory of the LORD is great.

138:4 [m]Ps 102:15

[6]Though the LORD is on high, he looks upon the lowly,[n]
but the proud[o] he knows from afar.
[7]Though I walk[p] in the midst of trouble,
you preserve my life;

138:6 [n]Ps 113:6; Isa 57:15 [o]Pr 3:34; Jas 4:6
138:7 [p]Ps 23:4

Hanging Up Their Harps

PS 137:1-3

When the Israelites are taken from their homeland by the Babylonians, they are overcome with grief. Singing in praise to the God of Zion is second nature to the Hebrews (2Ch 30:21). But while they are in exile, the last thing they feel like doing is making music. Figuratively—as well as literally—the exiles hang their harps in the branches of the trees on their enemy's land, too sad to even consider playing a tune about their homeland and their God. Their poignant sorrow pierces God's heart, however, and moves him to compassion (Isa 51:3). Through the prophet the promise is given: "The ransomed of the LORD will return. They will enter Zion with singing; everlasting joy will crown their heads. Gladness and joy will overtake them, and sorrow and sighing will flee away" (Isa 51:11).

Our All-Knowing God

PS 139

How often have we thought, "If they *really knew me*, they wouldn't love me"? In our moments of shame and insecurity, we doubt that there is really such a thing as unconditional love. Sometimes we spend enormous amounts of energy trying to hide our "true self" from probing eyes; the risk of rejection seems too great.

While it's true that in human relationships genuine love is hard to find, in the eyes of the God who created us we are both completely known and unconditionally loved. There is absolutely nothing about us that God doesn't know; therefore, nothing we think or do can surprise him or cause him to abandon us. He's constantly thinking about us—with love! And because of the unflinching, undying devotion he has for us, he is committed to searching our hearts and revealing to us "any offensive way" (Ps 139:24) so we can walk a straight path toward our eternal home.

you stretch out your hand against the
anger of my foes,[q]
with your right hand[r] you save me.[s]
8 The LORD will fulfill ⌞his purpose⌟[t] for me;
your love, O LORD, endures forever—
do not abandon the works of your
hands.[u]

Psalm 139

For the director of music. Of David. A psalm.

1 O LORD, you have searched me[v]
and you know[w] me.
2 You know when I sit and when I rise;[x]
you perceive my thoughts[y] from afar.
3 You discern my going out and my lying
down;
you are familiar with all my ways.[z]
4 Before a word is on my tongue
you know it completely,[a] O LORD.

5 You hem me in[b]—behind and before;
you have laid your hand upon me.
6 Such knowledge is too wonderful for
me,
too lofty[c] for me to attain.

7 Where can I go from your Spirit?
Where can I flee[d] from your presence?
8 If I go up to the heavens,[e] you are there;
if I make my bed[f] in the depths,[a] you
are there.
9 If I rise on the wings of the dawn,
if I settle on the far side of the sea,
10 even there your hand will guide me,[g]
your right hand will hold me fast.

11 If I say, "Surely the darkness will hide
me
and the light become night around
me,"
12 even the darkness will not be dark[h] to
you;
the night will shine like the day,
for darkness is as light to you.

13 For you created my inmost being;[i]
you knit me together[j] in my mother's
womb.
14 I praise you because I am fearfully and
wonderfully made;
your works are wonderful,[k]
I know that full well.
15 My frame was not hidden from you
when I was made in the secret place.
When I was woven together[l] in the
depths of the earth,[m]
16 your eyes saw my unformed body.
All the days ordained for me
were written in your book
before one of them came to be.

138:7 [q]Jer 51:25 [r]Ps 20:6 [s]Ps 71:20
138:8 [t]Ps 57:2; Php 1:6 [u]Job 10:3,8; 14:15
139:1 [v]Ps 17:3 [w]Jer 12:3
139:2 [x]2Ki 19:27 [y]Mt 9:4; Jn 2:24
139:3 [z]Job 31:4
139:4 [a]Heb 4:13
139:5 [b]Ps 34:7
139:6 [c]Job 42:3; Ro 11:33
139:7 [d]Jer 23:24; Jnh 1:3
139:8 [e]Am 9:2-3 [f]Pr 15:11
139:10 [g]Ps 23:3
139:12 [h]Job 34:22; Da 2:22
139:13 [i]Ps 119:73 [j]Job 10:11
139:14 [k]Ps 40:5
139:15 [l]Job 10:11 [m]Ps 63:9

[a] 8 Hebrew *Sheol*

139:17 [n]Ps 40:5
[17] How precious to[a] me are your thoughts, O God![n]
How vast is the sum of them!
[18] Were I to count them,
they would outnumber the grains of sand.
When I awake,
I am still with you.

139:19 [o]Isa 11:4 [p]Ps 119:115
[19] If only you would slay the wicked,[o] O God!
Away from me,[p] you bloodthirsty men!
[20] They speak of you with evil intent;
139:20 [q]Jude 15
your adversaries misuse your name.[q]
[21] Do I not hate those[r] who hate you, O LORD,
139:21 [r]2Ch 19:2; Ps 31:6; 119:113, 158
and abhor those who rise up against you?
[22] I have nothing but hatred for them;
I count them my enemies.
139:23 [s]Job 31:6; Ps 26:2 [t]Jer 11:20
[23] Search me,[s] O God, and know my heart;[t]
test me and know my anxious thoughts.
[24] See if there is any offensive way in me,
139:24 [u]Ps 5:8; 143:10; Pr 15:9
and lead me[u] in the way everlasting.

Psalm 140

For the director of music. A psalm of David.

140:1 [v]Ps 17:13 [w]Ps 18:48
[1] Rescue me,[v] O LORD, from evil men;
protect me from men of violence,[w]
140:2 [x]Ps 36:4; 56:6
[2] who devise evil plans[x] in their hearts
and stir up war every day.
[3] They make their tongues as sharp as[y] a serpent's;
140:3 [y]Ps 57:4 [z]Ps 58:4; Jas 3:8
the poison of vipers[z] is on their lips. *Selah*

140:4 [a]Ps 141:9 [b]Ps 71:4
[4] Keep me,[a] O LORD, from the hands of the wicked;[b]
protect me from men of violence
who plan to trip my feet.
[5] Proud men have hidden a snare for me;
they have spread out the cords of their net
140:5 [c]Ps 31:4; 35:7
and have set traps[c] for me along my path. *Selah*
140:6 [d]Ps 16:2 [e]Ps 116:1; 143:1
[6] O LORD, I say to you, "You are my God."[d]
Hear, O LORD, my cry for mercy.[e]
[7] O Sovereign LORD,[f] my strong deliverer,
140:7 [f]Ps 28:8
who shields my head in the day of battle—
140:8 [g]Ps 10:2-3
[8] do not grant the wicked[g] their desires, O LORD;
do not let their plans succeed,
or they will become proud. *Selah*
[9] Let the heads of those who surround me

[a] 17 Or *concerning*

I used to have an answer for most problems in life. I had a lot to say on almost any subject. I now have fewer answers, and they might be reduced to the simple phrase, God is faithful. I don't say that lightly or without thought; I say it because I know it is true, and I have discovered that it is true no matter what is happening in my life . . . I don't mean that he will wave a magic wand and everything will fall into place; far from it. What I mean is that if in the darkest times in our lives we will learn to keep turning our face toward him, he is faithful. Faithful to be with us, faithful to watch over us, faithful to work in us to make us the men and women we are called to be.

—Sheila Walsh

A Mouth Guard

PS 141:3

Have you ever wanted to retrieve words you just heard come out of your mouth—words better left unsaid, or even unthought? We've all experienced the discomfort, embarrassment and repercussions of speaking when we should have kept our mouths shut. Sometimes our words have stung others with their poison, causing pain and destruction we later regret. The New Testament writer James calls the tongue "a restless evil, full of deadly poison" (Jas 3:8). James takes the believer's speech so seriously that he says our religion is "worthless" if we fail to keep our tongues under control (Jas 1:26). The psalmist's prayer here is clearly wise, a prayer we'd do well to emulate. Since we never know when foolish or sinful words will rush to the "door" of our lips, we need a divine sentry to keep constant watch. James agrees with the psalmist that we cannot tame our own tongues (Jas 3:8); therefore, we must rely on God to guard our mouths.

be covered with the trouble their lips
have caused.[h]
[10] Let burning coals fall upon them;
may they be thrown into the fire,[i]
into miry pits, never to rise.
[11] Let slanderers not be established in the
land;
may disaster hunt down men of
violence.[j]
[12] I know that the LORD secures justice for
the poor
and upholds the cause[k] of the needy.[l]
[13] Surely the righteous will praise your
name[m]
and the upright will live[n] before you.

Psalm 141

A psalm of David.

[1] O LORD, I call to you; come quickly[o] to
me.
Hear my voice[p] when I call to you.
[2] May my prayer be set before you like
incense;[q]
may the lifting up of my hands[r] be
like the evening sacrifice.[s]

[3] Set a guard over my mouth, O LORD;
keep watch over the door of my lips.
[4] Let not my heart be drawn to what is
evil,
to take part in wicked deeds
with men who are evildoers;
let me not eat of their delicacies.[t]

[5] Let a righteous man[a] strike me—it is a
kindness;
let him rebuke me[u]—it is oil on my
head.[v]
My head will not refuse it.
Yet my prayer is ever against the deeds
of evildoers;
[6] their rulers will be thrown down from
the cliffs,
and the wicked will learn that my
words were well spoken.
[7] ⌊They will say,⌋ "As one plows and
breaks up the earth,
so our bones have been scattered at
the mouth[w] of the grave.[b]"
[8] But my eyes are fixed[x] on you,
O Sovereign LORD;
in you I take refuge[y]—do not give me
over to death.
[9] Keep me[z] from the snares they have laid
for me,
from the traps set[a] by evildoers.
[10] Let the wicked fall[b] into their own nets,
while I pass by in safety.

140:9 [h]Ps 7:16
140:10 [i]Ps 11:6; 21:9
140:11 [j]Ps 34:21
140:12 [k]Ps 9:4 [l]Ps 35:10
140:13 [m]Ps 97:12 [n]Ps 11:7
141:1 [o]Ps 22:19; 70:5 [p]Ps 143:1
141:2 [q]Rev 5:8; 8:3 [r]1Ti 2:8 [s]Ex 29:39,41
141:4 [t]Pr 23:6
141:5 [u]Pr 9:8 [v]Ps 23:5
141:7 [w]Ps 53:5
141:8 [x]Ps 25:15 [y]Ps 2:12
141:9 [z]Ps 140:4 [a]Ps 38:12
141:10 [b]Ps 35:8

[a] 5 Or *Let the Righteous One* [b] 7 Hebrew *Sheol*

Psalm 142

A *maskil*[a] of David. When he was in the cave. A prayer.

1 I cry aloud to the LORD;
  I lift up my voice to the LORD for mercy.[c]
2 I pour out my complaint[d] before him;
  before him I tell my trouble.

3 When my spirit grows faint[e] within me,
  it is you who know my way.
In the path where I walk
  men have hidden a snare for me.
4 Look to my right and see;
  no one is concerned for me.
I have no refuge;
  no one cares[f] for my life.

5 I cry to you, O LORD;
  I say, "You are my refuge,[g]
  my portion[h] in the land of the living."[i]
6 Listen to my cry,[j]
  for I am in desperate need;[k]
rescue me from those who pursue me,
  for they are too strong for me.
7 Set me free from my prison,[l]
  that I may praise your name.

Then the righteous will gather about me
  because of your goodness to me.[m]

Psalm 143

A psalm of David.

1 O LORD, hear my prayer,
  listen to my cry for mercy;[n]
in your faithfulness[o] and righteousness[p]
  come to my relief.
2 Do not bring your servant into judgment,
  for no one living is righteous[q] before you.

3 The enemy pursues me,
  he crushes me to the ground;
he makes me dwell in darkness
  like those long dead.
4 So my spirit grows faint within me;
  my heart within me is dismayed.[r]
5 I remember[s] the days of long ago;
  I meditate on all your works
  and consider what your hands have done.
6 I spread out my hands[t] to you;
  my soul thirsts for you like a parched land. *Selah*

7 Answer me quickly,[u] O LORD;
  my spirit fails.
Do not hide your face[v] from me

142:1 [c]Ps 30:8
142:2 [d]Isa 26:16
142:3 [e]Ps 140:5; 143:4,7
142:4 [f]Ps 31:11; Jer 30:17
142:5 [g]Ps 46:1 [h]Ps 16:5 [i]Ps 27:13
142:6 [j]Ps 17:1 [k]Ps 79:8; 116:6
142:7 [l]Ps 146:7 [m]Ps 13:6
143:1 [n]Ps 140:6 [o]Ps 89:1-2 [p]Ps 71:2
143:2 [q]Ps 14:3; Ecc 7:20; Ro 3:20
143:4 [r]Ps 142:3
143:5 [s]Ps 77:6
143:6 [t]Ps 63:1; 88:9
143:7 [u]Ps 69:17 [v]Ps 27:9; 28:1

[a] Title: Probably a literary or musical term

God Sees the Way

PS 142:3

When we're feeling overwhelmed, frightened, uncertain of which way to turn, David's words assure us that God is in control of our journey. Even if there are hidden obstacles along the way, we need not stay paralyzed with fear. While we can see only the next step in front of us, God sees the whole path. He knows what's up ahead, and he will be our faithful guide till the end of our days (Ps 48:14). Just as he led the Israelites through the desert by pillars of both cloud and fire, in his compassion he will shine his light on the way we are to take (Ne 9:19). We will never be abandoned in our times of desperate need (Ps 142:6).

Training for War

PS 144:1

The psalmist David lives during a time when surrounding nations are thirsty for the blood of God's people. Israel's enemies are constantly threatening to conquer and loot the country, and David, as king and commander of Israel's army, is dependent on the divine warrior for victory (Ps 60:12). Part of God's strategy for protecting his people and glorifying his name is to make his warriors victorious in battle. He equips them with the resources they need to defend themselves and demonstrate the Lord's superiority over all pagan gods. Today our battles in God's name are not with flesh and blood, but with the spiritual forces of evil. We are just as dependent on the "armor of God" to stand firm against our enemies (Eph 6:10–17) as the Israelites were. The weapons we fight with now are not "the weapons of the world," but spiritual weapons that "have divine power to demolish strongholds" (2Co 10:4).

or I will be like those who go down to
the pit.
8 Let the morning bring me word of your
unfailing love,[w]
for I have put my trust in you.
Show me the way[x] I should go,
for to you I lift up my soul.[y]
9 Rescue me from my enemies,[z] O LORD,
for I hide myself in you.
10 Teach me to do your will,
for you are my God;
may your good Spirit
lead[a] me on level ground.

11 For your name's sake, O LORD, preserve
my life;[b]
in your righteousness,[c] bring me out
of trouble.
12 In your unfailing love, silence my
enemies;
destroy all my foes,[d]
for I am your servant.[e]

143:8 [w]Ps 46:5; 90:14 [x]Ps 27:11 [y]Ps 25:1-2
143:9 [z]Ps 31:15
143:10 [a]Ne 9:20; Ps 23:3; 25:4-5
143:11 [b]Ps 119:25 [c]Ps 31:1
143:12 [d]Ps 52:5; 54:5 [e]Ps 116:16

Psalm 144

Of David.

1 Praise be to the LORD my Rock,[f]
who trains my hands for war,
my fingers for battle.
2 He is my loving God and my fortress,[g]
my stronghold and my deliverer,
my shield,[h] in whom I take refuge,
who subdues peoples[a] under me.

3 O LORD, what is man[i] that you care for
him,
the son of man that you think of him?
4 Man is like a breath;
his days are like a fleeting shadow.[j]

5 Part your heavens,[k] O LORD, and come
down;
touch the mountains, so that they
smoke.[l]
6 Send forth lightning and scatter ⌞the
enemies⌟;
shoot your arrows[m] and rout them.
7 Reach down your hand from on high;
deliver me and rescue me
from the mighty waters,[n]
from the hands of foreigners[o]
8 whose mouths are full of lies,[p]
whose right hands are deceitful.

9 I will sing a new song to you, O God;
on the ten-stringed lyre[q] I will make
music to you,
10 to the One who gives victory to kings,

144:1 [f]Ps 18:2,34
144:2 [g]Ps 59:9; 91:2 [h]Ps 84:9
144:3 [i]Ps 8:4; Heb 2:6
144:4 [j]Ps 39:11; 102:11
144:5 [k]Ps 18:9; Isa 64:1 [l]Ps 104:32
144:6 [m]Ps 7:12-13; 18:14
144:7 [n]Ps 69:2 [o]Ps 18:44
144:8 [p]Ps 12:2
144:9 [q]Ps 33:2-3

[a] *2* Many manuscripts of the Masoretic Text, Dead Sea Scrolls, Aquila, Jerome and Syriac; most manuscripts of the Masoretic Text *subdues my people*

Woman of Abel Beth Maacah

The View From the Wall

A woman stood on the wall of the city and studied the frenzied activity. It looked like an anthill below. Outside, Joab and his army began battering the wall. She and others had watched their preparations. They had sharpened their weapons, had cut trees for battering rams, and had lugged huge mounds of earth to make a siege ramp, which now leaned against the outer fortifications. Inside the wall, the townspeople scrambled to gather food and water. They had already called their children and corralled their livestock in their homes. Terror filled their eyes.

Abel Beth Maacah was under siege, and death was in the air. The woman could hardly believe her eyes. This could go on for *months.* The whole confrontation was caused by one man, Sheba, who was only interested in stirring up trouble to make a name for himself. He had raised a rebellion against King David. Was she the only one to see the pointlessness of the battle underway?

This woman had not studied politics or warfare. She had lived her entire life in an obscure town in northern Israel. Nevertheless, she had a history here and knew the townspeople personally. They were honest, hardworking, loyal citizens who loved the Lord. So she was confident in her assessment: This siege was wrong!

She did not merely shake her head and run for cover. She took the responsibility to do what she could to turn them from their folly. The townspeople trusted her to speak for them. Courageously, she called to Joab from the wall. What would it take to satisfy his demands? The solution was so simple and made so much sense. Hand over Sheba and save the lives of hundreds. *Done.*

Sometimes people become so focused on battle that they lose sight of why they are fighting or how they can accomplish their goals in better ways. When we see a conflict in a different way from others around us, it is our responsibility to express that point of view to them—respectfully. Jesus said, "Blessed are the peacemakers, for they will be called sons of God" (Mt 5:9). Who knows? God may use you to save the lives of hundreds—or at least to redirect their energies to something more useful.

Woman of Abel Beth Maacah
2 Samuel 20

Candid SNAPSHOT [The woman said,] "We are the peaceful and faithful in Israel. You are trying to destroy a city that is a mother in Israel. Why do you want to swallow up the LORD's inheritance?" (2 Samuel 20:19).

Two Mothers

Half Is Better Than None

Father unknown. The two prostitutes shared a house. There were no attendants at the births, no neighbors to share their joy, no witness to identify which child belonged to which woman. It was a case of she said/she said.

Both mothers were outcasts from society. Though most of "normal" life was out of reach, at least motherhood was not. Children—especially sons—proved a woman's worth. It meant that God had not forsaken her.

One mother rolled on her newborn in her sleep. When she found her baby dead in the night, there was no wailing in grief and remorse. She silently traded him for another, like exchanging a torn dress at the mall!

The other mother cherished her son as an irreplaceable gift from the Lord. We'd like to think she considered leaving her lifestyle for his sake. Better to glean in the fields and live hand-to-mouth than to bring a child up in such a place. At any rate, when she woke and found a dead little one at her breast, she was horror-stricken—but wait. She knew her child intimately, had pored over every feature and behavior. That was not his nose. His hair was too thin. This was *not* her son!

The mothers appealed to the court to settle their dispute. It was not an easy matter. Either woman could be lying. Maybe there never were two children, only one lusty child to fight over. How could anyone be sure? One of these women had a baby. The other had an attitude. Only Solomon could unravel the deception.

Solomon was an astute observer. With God's wisdom, perhaps he knew the answer before he took the sword. He only needed to prove the truth to the others in court. With royal authority, he ordered that the living son be cut in two, knowing full well that the child's mother would rather give him up than see him die.

God's love for each of us is fiercer even than that of the good mother. He knows us intimately, and we are irreplaceable in *his* heart. He created our inmost being and knit us together in our mothers' wombs (Ps 139). He surrendered his own happiness on the cross rather than abandon us to death. He has only good in mind for us . . . for our children . . . and for our children's children.

Two Mothers
1 Kings 3:16–28

Candid SNAPSHOT The woman whose son was alive was filled with compassion for her son and said to the king, "Please, my lord, give her the living baby! Don't kill him!" But the other said, "Neither I nor you shall have him. Cut him in two!" (1 Kings 3:26).

144:10 [r]Ps 18:50
who delivers his servant David[r] from
the deadly sword.

[11] Deliver me and rescue me
from the hands of foreigners
144:11 [s]Ps 12:2; Isa 44:20
whose mouths are full of lies,
whose right hands are deceitful.[s]

144:12 [t]Ps 128:3
[12] Then our sons in their youth
will be like well-nurtured plants,[t]
and our daughters will be like pillars
carved to adorn a palace.
[13] Our barns will be filled
with every kind of provision.
Our sheep will increase by thousands,
by tens of thousands in our fields;
[14] our oxen will draw heavy loads.[a]
There will be no breaching of walls,
no going into captivity,
no cry of distress in our streets.
144:15 [u]Ps 33:12
[15] Blessed are the people[u] of whom this is
true;
blessed are the people whose God is
the LORD.

Psalm 145[b]

A psalm of praise. Of David.

145:1 [v]Ps 30:1; 34:1 [w]Ps 5:2
[1] I will exalt you,[v] my God the King;[w]
I will praise your name for ever and
ever.
145:2 [x]Ps 71:6
[2] Every day I will praise[x] you
and extol your name for ever and
ever.

[3] Great is the LORD and most worthy of
145:3 [y]Job 5:9; Ps 147:5; Ro 11:33
praise;
his greatness no one can fathom.[y]
145:4 [z]Isa 38:19
[4] One generation[z] will commend your
works to another;
they will tell of your mighty acts.
[5] They will speak of the glorious splendor
of your majesty,
145:5 [a]Ps 119:27
and I will meditate on your wonderful
works.[c][a]
145:6 [b]Ps 66:3 [c]Dt 32:3
[6] They will tell of the power of your
awesome works,[b]
and I will proclaim[c] your great deeds.
[7] They will celebrate your abundant
145:7 [d]Isa 63:7 [e]Ps 51:14
goodness[d]
and joyfully sing of your
righteousness.[e]

145:8 [f]Ps 86:15 [g]Ex 34:6; Nu 14:18
[8] The LORD is gracious and
compassionate,[f]
slow to anger and rich in love.[g]

[a] *14* Or *our chieftains will be firmly established* [b] This psalm is an acrostic poem, the verses of which (including verse 13b) begin with the successive letters of the Hebrew alphabet. [c] *5* Dead Sea Scrolls and Syriac (see also Septuagint); Masoretic Text *On the glorious splendor of your majesty / and on your wonderful works I will meditate*

Our Children

PS 144:12

David's confident hope for his country's children is similar to what most parents today wish for their own kids. We want our sons to be firmly established—confident and vital and fruitful, "like well-nurtured plants" that are tended by the Lord himself. We long for our daughters to be stable and strong, yet lovely in their femininity and elegant and valuable in the eyes of others. David recognizes that such a heritage for his nation's children is not his to accomplish. He cannot bring it about by the force of his will. The only way it can be accomplished is through the gracious work of God. As parents, we work hard to bring up our children rightly, dressing them, keeping them clean and fed, teaching them and making sure they're spiritually nourished. But ultimately, the best thing we can do for our children is just what David does here: pray for them!

An Everlasting Kingdom

PS 145:13

Do you know anyone who has never broken a single promise—who is *always* reliable, *always* loving, *always* there? No one but God is so steadfast and dependable. And we need never fear that our Lord will change his ways. "Jesus Christ is the same yesterday and today and forever" (Heb 13:8). From creation to the rise and fall of the kingdom of Israel, from the Dark Ages to the electronic age, from the Crusades to World War II, God has been there. His kingdom has prospered and grown through the entire sweep of historical events. As Isaiah prophesied: "Of the increase of his government and peace there will be no end" (Isa 9:7). His reign is forever, and his faithfulness and sovereignty will endure through all generations. "Now to the King eternal, immortal, invisible, the only God, be honor and glory for ever and ever. Amen" (1Ti 1:17).

9 The LORD is good[h] to all; — **145:9** [h]Ps 100:5
he has compassion on all he has made.
10 All you have made will praise you,[i] O LORD; — **145:10** [i]Ps 19:1 [j]Ps 68:26
your saints will extol you.[j]
11 They will tell of the glory of your kingdom
and speak of your might,
12 so that all men may know of your mighty acts[k] — **145:12** [k]Ps 105:1
and the glorious splendor of your kingdom.
13 Your kingdom is an everlasting kingdom,[l] — **145:13** [l]1Ti 1:17; 2Pe 1:11
and your dominion endures through all generations.

The LORD is faithful to all his promises
and loving toward all he has made.[a]
14 The LORD upholds[m] all those who fall — **145:14** [m]Ps 37:24
and lifts up all[n] who are bowed down. — [n]Ps 146:8
15 The eyes of all look to you, — **145:15** [o]Ps 104:27; 136:25
and you give them their food[o] at the proper time.
16 You open your hand — **145:16** [p]Ps 104:28
and satisfy the desires[p] of every living thing.

17 The LORD is righteous in all his ways
and loving toward all he has made.
18 The LORD is near[q] to all who call on him,[r] — **145:18** [q]Dt 4:7 [r]Jn 4:24
to all who call on him in truth.
19 He fulfills the desires[s] of those who fear him; — **145:19** [s]Ps 37:4 [t]Pr 15:29
he hears their cry[t] and saves them.
20 The LORD watches over all who love him,[u] — **145:20** [u]Ps 31:23; 97:10 [v]Ps 9:5
but all the wicked he will destroy.[v]

21 My mouth will speak[w] in praise of the LORD. — **145:21** [w]Ps 71:8 [x]Ps 65:2
Let every creature[x] praise his holy name
for ever and ever.

Psalm 146

1 Praise the LORD.[b]

Praise the LORD,[y] O my soul. — **146:1** [y]Ps 103:1
2 I will praise the LORD all my life;[z] — **146:2** [z]Ps 104:33
I will sing praise to my God as long as I live.

3 Do not put your trust in princes,[a] — **146:3** [a]Ps 118:9 [b]Isa 2:22
in mortal men,[b] who cannot save.

[a] *13* One manuscript of the Masoretic Text, Dead Sea Scrolls and Syriac (see also Septuagint); most manuscripts of the Masoretic Text do not have the last two lines of verse 13.
[b] *1* Hebrew *Hallelu Yah*; also in verse 10

4 When their spirit departs, they return to
the ground;[c]
on that very day their plans come to
nothing.[d]
5 Blessed is he[e] whose help[f] is the God of
Jacob,
whose hope is in the LORD his God,
6 the Maker of heaven[g] and earth,
the sea, and everything in them—
the LORD, who remains faithful[h]
forever.
7 He upholds the cause of the oppressed[i]
and gives food to the hungry.[j]
The LORD sets prisoners free,[k]
8 the LORD gives sight to the blind,[l]
the LORD lifts up those who are bowed
down,
the LORD loves the righteous.
9 The LORD watches over the alien
and sustains the fatherless and the
widow,[m]
but he frustrates the ways of the
wicked.

10 The LORD reigns[n] forever,
your God, O Zion, for all generations.

Praise the LORD.

Psalm 147

1 Praise the LORD.[a]

How good it is to sing praises to our
God,
how pleasant[o] and fitting to praise
him![p]

2 The LORD builds up Jerusalem;[q]
he gathers the exiles[r] of Israel.
3 He heals the brokenhearted
and binds up their wounds.

4 He determines the number of the stars[s]
and calls them each by name.
5 Great is our Lord[t] and mighty in power;
his understanding has no limit.[u]
6 The LORD sustains the humble[v]
but casts the wicked to the ground.

7 Sing to the LORD[w] with thanksgiving;
make music to our God on the harp.
8 He covers the sky with clouds;
he supplies the earth with rain[x]
and makes grass grow[y] on the hills.
9 He provides food[z] for the cattle
and for the young ravens[a] when they
call.

10 His pleasure is not in the strength[b] of
the horse,[c]
nor his delight in the legs of a man;

146:4 [c]Ps 104:29; Ecc 12:7 [d]Ps 33:10; 1Co 2:6
146:5 [e]Ps 144:15; Jer 17:7 [f]Ps 71:5
146:6 [g]Ps 115:15; Ac 14:15; Rev 14:7 [h]Ps 117:2
146:7 [i]Ps 103:6 [j]Ps 107:9 [k]Ps 68:6
146:8 [l]Mt 9:30
146:9 [m]Ex 22:22; Dt 10:18; Ps 68:5
146:10 [n]Ex 15:18; Ps 10:16
147:1 [o]Ps 135:3 [p]Ps 33:1
147:2 [q]Ps 102:16 [r]Dt 30:3
147:4 [s]Isa 40:26
147:5 [t]Ps 48:1 [u]Isa 40:28
147:6 [v]Ps 146:8-9
147:7 [w]Ps 33:3
147:8 [x]Job 38:26 [y]Ps 104:14
147:9 [z]Ps 104:27-28; Mt 6:26 [a]Job 38:41
147:10 [b]1Sa 16:7 [c]Ps 33:16-17

[a] *1* Hebrew *Hallelu Yah*; also in verse 20

Naming the Stars

PS 147:4–5

Ancient understanding of the vastness of the cosmos does not compare to what we know of space today or to what people years from now will know about the universe. As far as we know, the stars could number into mathematical values yet to be understood. The psalmist no doubt shares the belief of his contemporaries that to give something a name is to validate, even initiate, its existence. In determining the birth of each star, God demonstrates that he alone has infinite power, and only he is great and understanding enough to rule such a vast creation. Surely a God who is personally aware of each star in the universe knows what he's doing as he directs the course of our lives on earth.

All Earth Praises Him

PS 148

Every aspect of God's creation, both animate and inanimate, both in heaven and on earth, is directed to praise the Lord. Though only human beings claimed by the Lord can praise God for redemption, all created things point to his splendor and supremacy simply by their existence. Who but a creative, all-powerful God could adorn the heavens, populate the ocean depths, control the weather, form the mountains, bud the trees and fill the earth with a vast array of creatures from centipedes to elephants, bumblebees to eagles? The beauty, variety and majesty of God's creation are a deafening proclamation of his praiseworthy nature.

11 the LORD delights in those who fear him,
who put their hope in his unfailing
love.

12 Extol the LORD, O Jerusalem;
praise your God, O Zion,
13 for he strengthens the bars of your gates
and blesses your people within you.
14 He grants peace[d] to your borders
and satisfies you[e] with the finest of
wheat.

15 He sends his command[f] to the earth;
his word runs swiftly.
16 He spreads the snow[g] like wool
and scatters the frost[h] like ashes.
17 He hurls down his hail like pebbles.
Who can withstand his icy blast?
18 He sends his word[i] and melts them;
he stirs up his breezes, and the waters
flow.

19 He has revealed his word to Jacob,
his laws and decrees[j] to Israel.
20 He has done this for no other nation;[k]
they do not know his laws.

Praise the LORD.

Psalm 148

1 Praise the LORD.[a]

Praise the LORD from the heavens,
praise him in the heights above.
2 Praise him, all his angels,[l]
praise him, all his heavenly hosts.
3 Praise him, sun and moon,
praise him, all you shining stars.
4 Praise him, you highest heavens
and you waters above the skies.[m]
5 Let them praise the name of the LORD,
for he commanded[n] and they were
created.
6 He set them in place for ever and ever;
he gave a decree[o] that will never pass
away.

7 Praise the LORD from the earth,
you great sea creatures[p] and all ocean
depths,
8 lightning and hail, snow and clouds,
stormy winds that do his bidding,[q]
9 you mountains and all hills,[r]
fruit trees and all cedars,
10 wild animals and all cattle,
small creatures and flying birds,
11 kings of the earth and all nations,
you princes and all rulers on earth,
12 young men and maidens,
old men and children.

13 Let them praise the name of the LORD,[s]

147:14 [d]Isa 60:17-18 [e]Ps 132:15
147:15 [f]Job 37:12
147:16 [g]Job 37:6 [h]Job 38:29
147:18 [i]Ps 33:9
147:19 [j]Dt 33:4; Mal 4:4
147:20 [k]Dt 4:7-8,32-34
148:2 [l]Ps 103:20
148:4 [m]Ge 1:7; 1Ki 8:27
148:5 [n]Ge 1:1,6; Ps 33:6,9
148:6 [o]Job 38:33; Ps 89:37; Jer 33:25
148:7 [p]Ps 74:13-14
148:8 [q]Ps 147:15-18
148:9 [r]Isa 44:23; 49:13; 55:12
148:13 [s]Isa 12:4

[a] *1* Hebrew *Hallelu Yah*; also in verse 14

for his name alone is exalted;
148:13 [t]Ps 8:1; 113:4 his splendor is above the earth and
the heavens.[t]
148:14 [u]Ps 75:10 14 He has raised up for his people a horn,[a][u]
the praise of all his saints,
of Israel, the people close to his heart.

Praise the LORD.

Psalm 149

149:1 [v]Ps 33:2 [w]Ps 35:18 1 Praise the LORD.[b][v]

Sing to the LORD a new song,
149:2 [x]Ps 95:6 [y]Ps 47:6; Zec 9:9 his praise in the assembly[w] of the
saints.
2 Let Israel rejoice in their Maker;[x]
let the people of Zion be glad in their
King.[y]
3 Let them praise his name with dancing
149:3 [z]Ps 81:2; 150:4 and make music to him with
tambourine and harp.[z]
4 For the LORD takes delight[a] in his people;
149:4 [a]Ps 35:27 [b]Ps 132:16 he crowns the humble with salvation.[b]
5 Let the saints rejoice[c] in this honor
and sing for joy on their beds.[d]
149:5 [c]Ps 132:16 [d]Job 35:10 6 May the praise of God be in their mouths[e]
and a double-edged[f] sword in their
hands,
149:6 [e]Ps 66:17 [f]Heb 4:12; Rev 1:16 7 to inflict vengeance on the nations
and punishment on the peoples,
8 to bind their kings with fetters,
their nobles with shackles of iron,
9 to carry out the sentence written against
149:9 [g]Dt 7:1; Eze 28:26 [h]Ps 148:14 them.[g]
This is the glory of all his saints.[h]
Praise the LORD.

Psalm 150

1 Praise the LORD.[c]
150:1 [i]Ps 102:19 [j]Ps 19:1 Praise God in his sanctuary;[i]
praise him in his mighty heavens.[j]
150:2 [k]Dt 3:24 [l]Ps 145:5-6 2 Praise him for his acts of power;[k]
praise him for his surpassing
greatness.[l]
3 Praise him with the sounding of the
trumpet,
150:3 [m]Ps 149:3 praise him with the harp and lyre,[m]
150:4 [n]Ex 15:20 [o]Isa 38:20 4 praise him with tambourine and dancing,[n]
praise him with the strings[o] and flute,
5 praise him with the clash of cymbals,[p]
praise him with resounding cymbals.
150:5 [p]1Ch 13:8; 15:16 6 Let everything[q] that has breath praise
the LORD.

150:6 [q]Ps 145:21 Praise the LORD.

[a] *14* *Horn* here symbolizes strong one, that is, king.
[b] *1* Hebrew *Hallelu Yah;* also in verse 9 [c] *1* Hebrew *Hallelu Yah;* also in verse 6

We Praise Him

PS 150

When we praise God, we should go all out! God wants not only the praise of individuals, but also that of the whole orchestra in unison. Sometimes God's people have gotten the idea that reverence equals quiet, being worshipful means being subdued. The psalmist's call to worship encourages passionate, loud, active and harmonious praise, inviting us to use every means we can come up with to celebrate our God's powerful acts and supreme greatness. All our praise here is just a practice run for the awesome celebration in heaven when the multitudes will sound like "the roar of rushing waters and like loud peals of thunder, shouting: 'Hallelujah! For our Lord God Almighty reigns' " (Rev 19:6).

Proverbs

Wise words for living.

Filled with snippets of wisdom and observations about life, the book of Proverbs is a marvelous source of insight on a variety of topics that affect daily living. Compiled by King Solomon and others, this book provides timeless counsel encapsulated in easy-to-remember maxims.

The Israelites used the book of Proverbs as a teaching tool to warn young people against sinful behaviors and ungodly practices as they learned about God's wisdom. Since the majority of the proverbs relate to everyday life, Solomon reminds us that we can only make sense of life when we make the Lord our foundation for wisdom (Pr 1–2). As students of this book, we will find warnings against sexual immorality and its path to tragedy (Pr 5–7). We learn timeless truths about friendship (Pr 16–19; 22; 27) and money (Pr 13; 17). Perhaps we'll even find ourselves in the description of the grumpy and growly wife who surfaces occasionally (Pr 12; 19; 21; 25), and, we hope, also in the description of a godly wife (Pr 31).

The book of Proverbs closes by highlighting a wife of noble character. She is unnamed, an ideal who sets a standard for strength, industry, organization and compassion (Pr 31). A close study of her life can help us start on the path to a fear of God that is the beginning of wisdom.

Quick Study

Author
Primarily Solomon, but several others contributed as well.

Date Written
Most were written in the tenth century B.C., the time of Solomon.

Setting
Israel.

Key Passage
Proverbs 1:7 "The fear of the LORD is the beginning of knowledge, but fools despise wisdom and discipline.

Outline

Introduction.
Pr 1:1-7

Wisdom's way.
Pr 1:8–4:27

Warnings.
Pr 5:1–7:27

The call of wisdom.
Pr 8:1–9:18

Solomon's proverbs.
Pr 10:1–22:16

Wise words.
Pr 22:17–24:34

More of Solomon's proverbs.
Pr 25:1–29:27

Agur's wise sayings.
Pr 30:1-33

King Lemuel's wise sayings.
Pr 31:1-9

A noble wife.
Pr 31:10-31

The Women of Proverbs

A mother	*Her teaching should not be forsaken.* Pr 1:8; 6:20; 23:22; 30:17
The adulteress	*Her way led to death.* Pr 2:16-19; 5:3-6; 22:14
The wife of your youth	*Rejoice in her and be satisfied with her.* Pr 5:15-19
The wayward wife	*She never stayed at home.* Pr 6:24-35; 7
A kindhearted woman	*She gains respect.* Pr 11:16
A beauty with no discretion	*She's like a gold ring in a pig's nose.* Pr 11:22
A disgraceful wife	*Decays her husband's bones.* Pr 12:4
A wise woman	*Builds rather than destroys.* Pr 14:1
The widow	*The Lord protects her rights.* Pr 15:25
A wife	*Finding one is finding good and receiving God's favor.* Pr 18:22
A quarrelsome wife	*A constant drip that can't be stopped.* Pr 19:13; 21:9; 27:15
A prudent wife	*A gift from God.* Pr 19:14
Lemuel's mother	*A wise woman.* Pr 31:1
♀ **A wife of noble character**	*A woman worth imitating.* Pr 12:4; 31:10-31 (page 1412)

♀ Denotes a sketch written about this character

A Mother's Teaching

PR 1:8

In the Jewish society of Biblical times, instructing children in the *Torah* and the ways of God were traditionally the responsibility of fathers, from one generation to the next (Pr 4:1–4). Therefore, it is significant that Solomon also urged his listeners to take their mothers' teaching equally to heart. In fact, the book of Proverbs pays tribute to a mother's teaching more than any other book in the Bible. King Lemuel, who most likely wrote Proverbs 31:1–9, credited his own mother with much of the wisdom that guided his life (Pr 31).

Prologue: Purpose and Theme

1 The proverbs of Solomon[a] son of David, king of Israel:[b]

[2] for attaining wisdom and discipline;
for understanding words of insight;
[3] for acquiring a disciplined and prudent life,
doing what is right and just and fair;
[4] for giving prudence to the simple,[c]
knowledge and discretion[d] to the young—
[5] let the wise listen and add to their learning,[e]
and let the discerning get guidance—
[6] for understanding proverbs and parables,[f]
the sayings and riddles[g] of the wise.

[7] The fear of the LORD[h] is the beginning of knowledge,
but fools[a] despise wisdom and discipline.

Exhortations to Embrace Wisdom

Warning Against Enticement

[8] Listen, my son,[i] to your father's instruction
and do not forsake your mother's teaching.[j]
[9] They will be a garland to grace your head
and a chain to adorn your neck.[k]

[10] My son, if sinners entice[l] you,
do not give in[m] to them.[n]
[11] If they say, "Come along with us;
let's lie in wait[o] for someone's blood,
let's waylay some harmless soul;
[12] let's swallow them alive, like the grave,[b]
and whole, like those who go down to the pit;[p]
[13] we will get all sorts of valuable things
and fill our houses with plunder;
[14] throw in your lot with us,
and we will share a common purse"—
[15] my son, do not go along with them,
do not set foot[q] on their paths;[r]
[16] for their feet rush into sin,
they are swift to shed blood.[s]
[17] How useless to spread a net
in full view of all the birds!
[18] These men lie in wait for their own blood;
they waylay only themselves!
[19] Such is the end of all who go after ill-gotten gain;

1:1 [a]1Ki 4:29-34 [b]Pr 10:1; 25:1; Ecc 1:1
1:4 [c]Pr 8:5 [d]Pr 2:10-11; 8:12
1:5 [e]Pr 9:9
1:6 [f]Ps 49:4; 78:2 [g]Nu 12:8
1:7 [h]Job 28:28; Ps 111:10; Pr 9:10; 15:33; Ecc 12:13
1:8 [i]Pr 4:1 [j]Pr 6:20
1:9 [k]Pr 4:1-9
1:10 [l]Ge 39:7 [m]Dt 13:8 [n]Pr 16:29; Eph 5:11
1:11 [o]Ps 10:8
1:12 [p]Ps 28:1
1:15 [q]Ps 119:101 [r]Ps 1:1; Pr 4:14
1:16 [s]Pr 6:18; Isa 59:7

[a] *7* The Hebrew words rendered *fool* in Proverbs, and often elsewhere in the Old Testament, denote one who is morally deficient. [b] *12* Hebrew *Sheol*

it takes away the lives of those who
get it.[t]

Warning Against Rejecting Wisdom

20 Wisdom calls aloud[u] in the street,
she raises her voice in the public
squares;
21 at the head of the noisy streets[a] she cries
out,
in the gateways of the city she makes
her speech:
22 "How long will you simple ones[b][v] love
your simple ways?
How long will mockers delight in
mockery
and fools hate knowledge?
23 If you had responded to my rebuke,
I would have poured out my heart to
you
and made my thoughts known to you.
24 But since you rejected me when I
called[w]
and no one gave heed when I
stretched out my hand,
25 since you ignored all my advice
and would not accept my rebuke,
26 I in turn will laugh[x] at your disaster;
I will mock when calamity overtakes
you[y]—
27 when calamity overtakes you like a
storm,
when disaster sweeps over you like a
whirlwind,
when distress and trouble overwhelm
you.

28 "Then they will call to me but I will not
answer;[z]
they will look for me but will not find
me.[a]
29 Since they hated knowledge
and did not choose to fear the LORD,[b]
30 since they would not accept my advice
and spurned my rebuke,[c]
31 they will eat the fruit of their ways
and be filled with the fruit of their
schemes.[d]
32 For the waywardness of the simple will
kill them,
and the complacency of fools will
destroy them;[e]
33 but whoever listens to me will live in
safety[f]
and be at ease, without fear of
harm."[g]

1:19 [t]Pr 15:27
1:20 [u]Pr 8:1; 9:1-3,13-15
1:22 [v]Pr 8:5; 9:4,16
1:24 [w]Isa 65:12; 66:4; Jer 7:13; Zec 7:11
1:26 [x]Ps 2:4 [y]Pr 6:15; 10:24
1:28 [z]1Sa 8:18; Isa 1:15; Jer 11:11; Mic 3:4 [a]Job 27:9; Pr 8:17; Eze 8:18; Zec 7:13
1:29 [b]Job 21:14
1:30 [c]ver 25; Ps 81:11
1:31 [d]Job 4:8; Pr 14:14; Isa 3:11; Jer 6:19
1:32 [e]Jer 2:19
1:33 [f]Ps 25:12; Pr 3:23 [g]Ps 112:8

[a] *21* Hebrew; Septuagint / *on the tops of the walls* [b] *22* The Hebrew word rendered *simple* in Proverbs generally denotes one without moral direction and inclined to evil.

Wisdom As a Woman

PR 1:20-21

Personifying important truths is a literary device used elsewhere in Scripture. Here in Proverbs, wisdom is portrayed *as a woman who calls out to the young men in the public square, just as prostitutes do* (Pr 7:10–12). Which voice will they heed: wisdom or folly? Both voices are sweet, but only one leads to life *and godliness.* The implication is *that we will always be pulled in opposing directions—toward sin by our culture, toward righteousness by the Word of God.* Our job is to *discern the path to life, personified here as a wise woman we can trust.* Some of the pagan cultures *in Biblical times mistakenly deified this feminine image rather than recognizing it as an attribute of God himself.*

Folly As a Woman

PR 2:16-19

Following the ways of wisdom protects its adherents from "wicked men" and their perverse and crooked ways (Pr 2:12-15). But the ways of wisdom can also provide protection against "the adulteress" (Pr 2:16), literally "stranger" or "foreigner." She is a married woman who has forgotten her marriage vows and will work her seductions on anyone who is foolish enough to give her attention. Her appeal is subtle and alluring (Pr 7:14-21), and following her will only bring disaster.

In a culture as permissive and pervasively sexual as ours is today, following Lady Folly rather than Lady Wisdom is as seductive and disastrous a course as it was in Biblical times. The way to her house still leads "down to death" (Pr 2:18), the death of marriages, faithfulness and trust.

Moral Benefits of Wisdom

2 My son, if you accept my words
and store up my commands within you,
2 turning your ear to wisdom
and applying your heart to
understanding,[h]
3 and if you call out for insight
and cry aloud for understanding,
4 and if you look for it as for silver
and search for it as for hidden
treasure,[i]
5 then you will understand the fear of the
LORD
and find the knowledge of God.[j]
6 For the LORD gives wisdom,[k]
and from his mouth come knowledge
and understanding.
7 He holds victory in store for the upright,
he is a shield[l] to those whose walk is
blameless,[m]
8 for he guards the course of the just
and protects the way of his faithful
ones.[n]

9 Then you will understand what is right
and just
and fair—every good path.
10 For wisdom will enter your heart,[o]
and knowledge will be pleasant to
your soul.
11 Discretion will protect you,
and understanding will guard you.[p]

12 Wisdom will save you from the ways of
wicked men,
from men whose words are perverse,
13 who leave the straight paths
to walk in dark ways,[q]
14 who delight in doing wrong
and rejoice in the perverseness of evil,[r]
15 whose paths are crooked[s]
and who are devious in their ways.[t]

16 It will save you also from the
adulteress,[u]
from the wayward wife with her
seductive words,
17 who has left the partner of her youth
and ignored the covenant she made
before God.[a][v]
18 For her house leads down to death
and her paths to the spirits of the
dead.[w]
19 None who go to her return
or attain the paths of life.[x]

20 Thus you will walk in the ways of good
men
and keep to the paths of the righteous.
21 For the upright will live in the land,[y]
and the blameless will remain in it;

2:2 [h]Pr 22:17
2:4 [i]Job 3:21; Pr 3:14; Mt 13:44
2:5 [j]Pr 1:7
2:6 [k]1Ki 3:9,12; Jas 1:5
2:7 [l]Pr 30:5-6 [m]Ps 84:11
2:8 [n]1Sa 2:9; Ps 66:9
2:10 [o]Pr 14:33
2:11 [p]Pr 4:6; 6:22
2:13 [q]Pr 4:19; Jn 3:19
2:14 [r]Pr 10:23; Jer 11:15
2:15 [s]Ps 125:5 [t]Pr 21:8
2:16 [u]Pr 5:1-6; 6:20-29; 7:5-27
2:17 [v]Mal 2:14
2:18 [w]Pr 7:27
2:19 [x]Ecc 7:26
2:21 [y]Ps 37:29

[a] 17 Or *covenant of her God*

22 but the wicked will be cut off from the
 land,[z]
 and the unfaithful will be torn from it.[a]

Further Benefits of Wisdom

3 My son, do not forget my teaching,[b]
 but keep my commands in your heart,
2 for they will prolong your life many
 years[c]
 and bring you prosperity.

3 Let love and faithfulness never leave you;
 bind them around your neck,
 write them on the tablet of your heart.[d]
4 Then you will win favor and a good
 name
 in the sight of God and man.[e]

5 Trust in the LORD[f] with all your heart
 and lean not on your own
 understanding;
6 in all your ways acknowledge him,
 and he will make your paths[g]
 straight.[a][h]

7 Do not be wise in your own eyes;[i]
 fear the LORD and shun evil.[j]
8 This will bring health to your body[k]
 and nourishment to your bones.[l]

9 Honor the LORD with your wealth,
 with the firstfruits[m] of all your crops;
10 then your barns will be filled[n] to
 overflowing,
 and your vats will brim over with
 new wine.[o]

11 My son, do not despise the LORD's
 discipline[p]
 and do not resent his rebuke,
12 because the LORD disciplines those he
 loves,[q]
 as a father[b] the son he delights in.[r]

13 Blessed is the man who finds wisdom,
 the man who gains understanding,
14 for she is more profitable than silver
 and yields better returns than gold.[s]
15 She is more precious than rubies;[t]
 nothing you desire can compare with
 her.[u]
16 Long life is in her right hand;
 in her left hand are riches and honor.[v]
17 Her ways are pleasant ways,
 and all her paths are peace.[w]
18 She is a tree of life[x] to those who
 embrace her;
 those who lay hold of her will be
 blessed.

19 By wisdom the LORD laid the earth's
 foundations,[y]

2:22 [z]Job 18:17; Ps 37:38 [a]Dt 28:63; Pr 10:30
3:1 [b]Pr 4:5
3:2 [c]Pr 4:10
3:3 [d]Ex 13:9; Pr 6:21; 7:3; 2Co 3:3
3:4 [e]1Sa 2:26; Lk 2:52
3:5 [f]Ps 37:3,5
3:6 [g]1Ch 28:9 [h]Pr 16:3; Isa 45:13
3:7 [i]Ro 12:16 [j]Job 1:1; Pr 16:6
3:8 [k]Pr 4:22 [l]Job 21:24
3:9 [m]Ex 22:29; 23:19; Dt 26:1-15
3:10 [n]Dt 28:8 [o]Joel 2:24
3:11 [p]Job 5:17
3:12 [q]Pr 13:24; Rev 3:19 [r]Dt 8:5; Heb 12:5-6*
3:14 [s]Job 28:15; Pr 8:19; 16:16
3:15 [t]Job 28:18 [u]Pr 8:11
3:16 [v]Pr 8:18
3:17 [w]Pr 16:7; Mt 11:28-30
3:18 [x]Ge 2:9; Pr 11:30; Rev 2:7
3:19 [y]Ps 104:24

[a] 6 Or *will direct your paths* [b] 12 Hebrew; Septuagint / *and he punishes*

Down to Brass Tacks

Ever wish you could start over? Probably all of us have longed for another chance in some area of our lives. We wouldn't necessarily have done things differently, just more or perhaps less . . . The truth is we can't go back, only forward into uncharted territory. To sit in our sorrow would lead to misery. Although regret that leads to change is a dear friend, regret that leads to shame is a treacherous enemy.

So how do we live without allowing regret to rob us of our joy? How about this insight to prompt us on: "And lean not on your own understanding" (Pr 3:5) . . . There is no guarantee that if we had done a part of our lives differently things would end up any different. We have to trust the God of the universe who directs the outcome of all things that he will do that which ultimately needs to be done (in spite of us, if necessary).

—Patsy Clairmont

Down to Brass Tacks

PR 3:27-31

Solomon's discourse has so far covered the personal and spiritual benefits of acquiring wisdom. For example, the wise person will enjoy God's protection (Pr 1:33), long life and prosperity (Pr 3:2) and a good reputation (Pr 3:4). But here the teacher gets down to brass tacks: the nitty-gritty of how to get along with other people. The implication could be that even the most knowledgeable person can demonstrate a lack of wisdom in how he or she deals with others. These verses are the first of many that clearly spell out good rules to live by: be generous, be a good neighbor, be fair, be gentle. The book of Proverbs is chock full of practical nuggets of wisdom we can carry into everyday life.

by understanding he set the heavens[z]
in place;
20 by his knowledge the deeps were
divided,
and the clouds let drop the dew.

21 My son, preserve sound judgment and
discernment,
do not let them out of your sight;[a]
22 they will be life for you,
an ornament to grace your neck.[b]
23 Then you will go on your way in safety,
and your foot will not stumble;[c]
24 when you lie down,[d] you will not be
afraid;
when you lie down, your sleep[e] will
be sweet.
25 Have no fear of sudden disaster
or of the ruin that overtakes the
wicked,
26 for the LORD will be your confidence
and will keep your foot[f] from being
snared.

27 Do not withhold good from those who
deserve it,
when it is in your power to act.
28 Do not say to your neighbor,
"Come back later; I'll give it
tomorrow"—
when you now have it with you.[g]
29 Do not plot harm against your neighbor,
who lives trustfully near you.
30 Do not accuse a man for no reason—
when he has done you no harm.
31 Do not envy[h] a violent man
or choose any of his ways,
32 for the LORD detests a perverse man[i]
but takes the upright into his
confidence.[j]
33 The LORD's curse[k] is on the house of the
wicked,[l]
but he blesses the home of the
righteous.[m]
34 He mocks proud mockers
but gives grace to the humble.[n]
35 The wise inherit honor,
but fools he holds up to shame.

Wisdom Is Supreme

4 Listen, my sons,[o] to a father's instruction;
pay attention and gain understanding.
2 I give you sound learning,
so do not forsake my teaching.
3 When I was a boy in my father's house,
still tender, and an only child of my
mother,
4 he taught me and said,
"Lay hold of my words with all your
heart;

3:19 [z]Pr 8:27-29
3:21 [a]Pr 4:20-22
3:22 [b]Pr 1:8-9
3:23 [c]Ps 37:24; Pr 4:12
3:24 [d]Lev 26:6; Ps 3:5 [e]Job 11:18
3:26 [f]1Sa 2:9
3:28 [g]Lev 19:13; Dt 24:15
3:31 [h]Ps 37:1; Pr 24:1-2
3:32 [i]Pr 11:20 [j]Job 29:4; Ps 25:14
3:33 [k]Dt 11:28; Mal 2:2 [l]Zec 5:4 [m]Ps 1:3
3:34 [n]Jas 4:6*; 1Pe 5:5*
4:1 [o]Pr 1:8

keep my commands and you will
live.[p]
5 Get wisdom,[q] get understanding;
do not forget my words or swerve
from them.
6 Do not forsake wisdom, and she will
protect you;[r]
love her, and she will watch over you.
7 Wisdom is supreme; therefore get
wisdom.
Though it cost all[s] you have,[a] get
understanding.[t]
8 Esteem her, and she will exalt you;
embrace her, and she will honor you.[u]
9 She will set a garland of grace on your
head
and present you with a crown of
splendor.[v]"

10 Listen, my son, accept what I say,
and the years of your life will be
many.[w]
11 I guide[x] you in the way of wisdom
and lead you along straight paths.
12 When you walk, your steps will not be
hampered;
when you run, you will not stumble.[y]
13 Hold on to instruction, do not let it go;
guard it well, for it is your life.[z]
14 Do not set foot on the path of the
wicked
or walk in the way of evil men.[a]
15 Avoid it, do not travel on it;
turn from it and go on your way.
16 For they cannot sleep till they do evil;[b]
they are robbed of slumber till they
make someone fall.
17 They eat the bread of wickedness
and drink the wine of violence.

18 The path of the righteous[c] is like the
first gleam of dawn,
shining ever brighter till the full light
of day.[d]
19 But the way of the wicked is like deep
darkness;[e]
they do not know what makes them
stumble.

20 My son, pay attention to what I say;
listen closely to my words.[f]
21 Do not let them out of your sight,[g]
keep them within your heart;
22 for they are life to those who find them
and health to a man's whole body.[h]
23 Above all else, guard your heart,
for it is the wellspring of life.[i]
24 Put away perversity from your mouth;
keep corrupt talk far from your lips.
25 Let your eyes look straight ahead,

4:4 [p]Pr 7:2
4:5 [q]Pr 16:16
4:6 [r]2Th 2:10
4:7 [s]Mt 13:44-46 [t]Pr 23:23
4:8 [u]1Sa 2:30; Pr 3:18
4:9 [v]Pr 1:8-9
4:10 [w]Pr 3:2
4:11 [x]1Sa 12:23
4:12 [y]Job 18:7; Pr 3:23
4:13 [z]Pr 3:22
4:14 [a]Ps 1:1; Pr 1:15
4:16 [b]Ps 36:4; Mic 2:1
4:18 [c]Isa 26:7 [d]2Sa 23:4; Da 12:3; Mt 5:14; Php 2:15
4:19 [e]Job 18:5; Pr 2:13; Isa 59:9-10; Jn 12:35
4:20 [f]Pr 5:1
4:21 [g]Pr 3:21; 7:1-2
4:22 [h]Pr 3:8; 12:18
4:23 [i]Mt 12:34; Lk 6:45

What Wisdom Is

PR 4:7-9

Wisdom as Solomon describes it is so much more than mere knowledge, good intuition, cleverness or business acumen. What ranks above all else in God's economy is not a sharp mind but a discerning heart, the only thing Solomon asks God for when he becomes king. God praises and blesses Solomon for choosing such a spiritually meaningful gift (1Ki 3:5-14), and here Solomon assures his listeners that they, too, will receive honor, grace and joy if they diligently pursue wisdom no matter what the cost.

[a] 7 Or *Whatever else you get*

Drink From Your Own Cistern

PR 5:15-19

In the arid land where the Hebrews live, water is precious. To steal water from someone else's well is a criminal act. In comparing marriage to a private cistern, Solomon is exhorting his listeners to place the highest possible value on their chosen spouse—and to respect the covenant made between other husbands and wives by not "drinking" from a "well" that is not their own. Here the teacher goes beyond the "don't touch" admonition concerning adultery in Proverbs 5:8 and encourages his listeners to embrace and rejoice in the marital relationship, to drink deeply of the satisfying pleasures of married love and sexual expression. Only a covenant relationship free from adultery can be fully satisfying. Because Scripture repeatedly makes the point that Israel should have such a relationship with God, these verses can also probably refer to the importance of spiritual, as well as marital, fidelity.

fix your gaze directly before you.
26 Make level[a] paths for your feet[j]
and take only ways that are firm.
27 Do not swerve to the right or the left;[k]
keep your foot from evil.

Warning Against Adultery

5 My son, pay attention to my wisdom,
listen well to my words[l] of insight,
2 that you may maintain discretion
and your lips may preserve
knowledge.
3 For the lips of an adulteress drip honey,
and her speech is smoother than oil;[m]
4 but in the end she is bitter as gall,[n]
sharp as a double-edged sword.
5 Her feet go down to death;
her steps lead straight to the grave.[b o]
6 She gives no thought to the way of life;
her paths are crooked, but she knows
it not.[p]

7 Now then, my sons, listen[q] to me;
do not turn aside from what I say.
8 Keep to a path far from her,[r]
do not go near the door of her house,
9 lest you give your best strength to others
and your years to one who is cruel,
10 lest strangers feast on your wealth
and your toil enrich another man's
house.
11 At the end of your life you will groan,
when your flesh and body are spent.
12 You will say, "How I hated discipline!
How my heart spurned correction![s]
13 I would not obey my teachers
or listen to my instructors.
14 I have come to the brink of utter ruin
in the midst of the whole assembly."

15 Drink water from your own cistern,
running water from your own well.
16 Should your springs overflow in the
streets,
your streams of water in the public
squares?
17 Let them be yours alone,
never to be shared with strangers.
18 May your fountain[t] be blessed,
and may you rejoice in the wife of
your youth.[u]
19 A loving doe, a graceful deer[v]—
may her breasts satisfy you always,
may you ever be captivated by her
love.
20 Why be captivated, my son, by an
adulteress?
Why embrace the bosom of another
man's wife?

4:26 [j]Heb 12:13*
4:27 [k]Dt 5:32; 28:14
5:1 [l]Pr 4:20; 22:17
5:3 [m]Ps 55:21; Pr 2:16; 7:5
5:4 [n]Ecc 7:26
5:5 [o]Pr 7:26-27
5:6 [p]Pr 30:20
5:7 [q]Pr 7:24
5:8 [r]Pr 7:1-27
5:12 [s]Pr 1:29; 12:1
5:18 [t]SS 4:12-15 [u]Ecc 9:9; Mal 2:14
5:19 [v]SS 2:9; 4:5

[a] 26 Or *Consider the* [b] 5 Hebrew *Sheol*

21 For a man's ways are in full view[w] of the
LORD,
and he examines all his paths.[x]
22 The evil deeds of a wicked man ensnare
him;[y]
the cords of his sin hold him fast.[z]
23 He will die for lack of discipline,[a]
led astray by his own great folly.

Warnings Against Folly

6 My son, if you have put up security for
your neighbor,[b]
if you have struck hands in pledge[c]
for another,
2 if you have been trapped by what you
said,
ensnared by the words of your mouth,
3 then do this, my son, to free yourself,
since you have fallen into your
neighbor's hands:
Go and humble yourself;
press your plea with your neighbor!
4 Allow no sleep to your eyes,
no slumber to your eyelids.[d]
5 Free yourself, like a gazelle from the
hand of the hunter,
like a bird from the snare of the
fowler.[e]
6 Go to the ant, you sluggard;[f]
consider its ways and be wise!
7 It has no commander,
no overseer or ruler,
8 yet it stores its provisions in summer
and gathers its food at harvest.[g]

9 How long will you lie there, you
sluggard?[h]
When will you get up from your
sleep?
10 A little sleep, a little slumber,
a little folding of the hands to rest[i]—
11 and poverty[j] will come on you like a
bandit
and scarcity like an armed man.[a]

12 A scoundrel and villain,
who goes about with a corrupt
mouth,
13 who winks with his eye,[k]
signals with his feet
and motions with his fingers,
14 who plots evil[l] with deceit in his
heart—
he always stirs up dissension.[m]
15 Therefore disaster will overtake him in
an instant;
he will suddenly be destroyed—
without remedy.[n]

16 There are six things the LORD hates,

5:21 [w]Ps 119:168; Hos 7:2 [x]Job 14:16; Job 31:4; 34:21; Pr 15:3; Jer 16:17; 32:19; Heb 4:13
5:22 [y]Ps 9:16 [z]Nu 32:23; Ps 7:15-16; Pr 1:31-32
5:23 [a]Job 4:21; 36:12
6:1 [b]Pr 17:18 [c]Pr 11:15; 22:26-27
6:4 [d]Ps 132:4
6:5 [e]Ps 91:3
6:6 [f]Pr 20:4
6:8 [g]Pr 10:4
6:9 [h]Pr 24:30-34
6:10 [i]Pr 24:33
6:11 [j]Pr 24:30-34
6:13 [k]Ps 35:19
6:14 [l]Mic 2:1 [m]ver 16-19
6:15 [n]2Ch 36:16

The Dangers of Inertia

PR 6:9-11

Some people are just simply "dreamers." We might admire their vision, but we notice that some of these individuals are all talk and no action. Even worse, says Solomon, are those who lie around procrastinating, fantasizing about getting things done instead of actually doing them (Pr 28:19). Those foolish souls will reap what they have sown: nothing. The maxim "God helps those who help themselves" has more than a little truth to it. Those who cave in to the "lazybones" within will eventually pay a price for their inertia and passivity. By the time they wake up and think about taking action, it may be too late.

[a] 11 Or *like a vagrant / and scarcity like a beggar*

Six Things, Seven Things

PR 6:16-19

Solomon uses a numerical poetic device here that is common in the Old Testament and useful in driving home a point or perhaps causing the reader to pause and carefully consider what is about to be said (compare Job 5:19; Pr 30:15–31; Am 1:11). In this case, Solomon draws attention to a brief catalog of attitudes and behaviors that are particularly heinous in God's eyes. Note that, unlike the sloth condemned in previous verses, these sins directly affect other people and cause them harm. Throughout Scripture God comes down particularly hard on those who hurt others and cause dissension.

seven that are detestable to him:
17 haughty eyes,
a lying tongue,[o]
hands that shed innocent blood,[p]
18 a heart that devises wicked
schemes,
feet that are quick to rush into
evil,[q]
19 a false witness[r] who pours out lies
and a man who stirs up dissension
among brothers.[s]

Warning Against Adultery

20 My son, keep your father's commands
and do not forsake your mother's
teaching.[t]
21 Bind them upon your heart forever;
fasten them around your neck.[u]
22 When you walk, they will guide you;
when you sleep, they will watch over
you;
when you awake, they will speak to
you.
23 For these commands are a lamp,
this teaching is a light,[v]
and the corrections of discipline
are the way to life,
24 keeping you from the immoral woman,
from the smooth tongue of the
wayward wife.[w]
25 Do not lust in your heart after her
beauty
or let her captivate you with her eyes,
26 for the prostitute reduces you to a loaf of
bread,
and the adulteress preys upon your
very life.[x]
27 Can a man scoop fire into his lap
without his clothes being burned?
28 Can a man walk on hot coals
without his feet being scorched?
29 So is he who sleeps[y] with another man's
wife;[z]
no one who touches her will go
unpunished.

30 Men do not despise a thief if he steals
to satisfy his hunger when he is
starving.
31 Yet if he is caught, he must pay
sevenfold,[a]
though it costs him all the wealth of
his house.
32 But a man who commits adultery[b] lacks
judgment;[c]
whoever does so destroys himself.
33 Blows and disgrace are his lot,
and his shame will never[d] be wiped
away;
34 for jealousy[e] arouses a husband's fury,[f]

6:17 [o]Ps 120:2; Pr 12:22 [p]Dt 19:10; Isa 1:15; 59:7
6:18 [q]Ge 6:5
6:19 [r]Ps 27:12 [s]ver 12-15
6:20 [t]Pr 1:8
6:21 [u]Pr 3:3; 7:1-3
6:23 [v]Ps 19:8; 119:105
6:24 [w]Pr 2:16; 7:5
6:26 [x]Pr 7:22-23; 29:3
6:29 [y]Ex 20:14 [z]Pr 2:16-19; 5:8
6:31 [a]Ex 22:1-14
6:32 [b]Ex 20:14 [c]Pr 7:7; 9:4, 16
6:33 [d]Pr 5:9-14
6:34 [e]Nu 5:14 [f]Ge 34:7

and he will show no mercy when he
takes revenge.
35 He will not accept any compensation;
he will refuse the bribe, however
great it is.[g]

Warning Against the Adulteress

7 My son,[h] keep my words
and store up my commands within you.
2 Keep my commands and you will live;[i]
guard my teachings as the apple of
your eye.
3 Bind them on your fingers;
write them on the tablet of your
heart.[j]
4 Say to wisdom, "You are my sister,"
and call understanding your kinsman;
5 they will keep you from the adulteress,
from the wayward wife with her
seductive words.[k]

6 At the window of my house
I looked out through the lattice.
7 I saw among the simple,
I noticed among the young men,
a youth who lacked judgment.[l]
8 He was going down the street near her
corner,
walking along in the direction of her
house
9 at twilight,[m] as the day was fading,
as the dark of night set in.

10 Then out came a woman to meet him,
dressed like a prostitute and with
crafty intent.
11 (She is loud[n] and defiant,
her feet never stay at home;
12 now in the street, now in the squares,
at every corner she lurks.)[o]
13 She took hold of him[p] and kissed him
and with a brazen face she said:[q]
14 "I have fellowship offerings[a][r] at home;
today I fulfilled my vows.
15 So I came out to meet you;
I looked for you and have found you!
16 I have covered my bed
with colored linens from Egypt.
17 I have perfumed my bed[s]
with myrrh,[t] aloes and cinnamon.
18 Come, let's drink deep of love till
morning;
let's enjoy ourselves with love![u]
19 My husband is not at home;
he has gone on a long journey.
20 He took his purse filled with money
and will not be home till full moon."
21 With persuasive words she led him
astray;

6:35 g Job 31:9-11; SS 8:7
7:1 h Pr 1:8; 2:1
7:2 i Pr 4:4
7:3 j Dt 6:8; Pr 3:3
7:5 k ver 21; Job 31:9; Pr 2:16; 6:24
7:7 l Pr 1:22; 6:32
7:9 m Job 24:15
7:11 n Pr 9:13; 1Ti 5:13
7:12 o Pr 8:1-36; 23:26-28
7:13 p Ge 39:12 q Pr 1:20
7:14 r Lev 7:11-18
7:17 s Est 1:6; Isa 57:7; Eze 23:41; Am 6:4 t Ge 37:25
7:18 u Ge 39:7

The Simple

PR 7:7–9

The Hebrew word for *simple* here indicates a person who is "open," who is vulnerable to influence, whether it be to the wise or the foolish. The aimless, foolish wanderer described here thoughtlessly and naively walks right into the snare of evil. It's easy to do. The foolish walk along with their heads in the clouds and, as the apostle Peter reminds us in 1 Peter 5:8, the devil is always prowling around looking for an easy target. In order to avoid wandering into the wrong spiritual neighborhoods at night, we need to move alertly and purposefully through life, aiming squarely at the goal of knowing and becoming like Jesus Christ (Php 3:10–14).

[a] 14 Traditionally *peace offerings*

What's Valuable

PR 8:10-11

It's easy to get our priorities out of alignment, to lose sight of what is most valuable. So many goals vie for our attention: professional success, domestic happiness, financial security, good health, intimacy with God. Even when we think we know how to "rank" our priorities properly, balancing them can be difficult. That's why we need wisdom so desperately—so we can have the insight to discern what's most important in a world of competing demands.

In 1926, Reinhold Niebuhr first invoked the famous prayer: "God, grant me the serenity to accept the things I cannot change, courage to change the things I can, and wisdom to know the difference." Perhaps the reason Solomon ascribes such high value to wisdom is because, without it, we could waste our lives focusing on the wrong things. Wisdom enables us to know the difference between what gives life and what leads to death (Pr 8:35-36).

she seduced him with her smooth
talk.[v]
22 All at once he followed her
like an ox going to the slaughter,
like a deer[a] stepping into a noose[b][w]
23 till an arrow pierces[x] his liver,
like a bird darting into a snare,
little knowing it will cost him his
life.[y]

24 Now then, my sons, listen[z] to me;
pay attention to what I say.
25 Do not let your heart turn to her ways
or stray into her paths.[a]
26 Many are the victims she has brought
down;
her slain are a mighty throng.
27 Her house is a highway to the grave,[c]
leading down to the chambers of
death.[b]

Wisdom's Call

8 Does not wisdom call out?[c]
Does not understanding raise her voice?
2 On the heights along the way,
where the paths meet, she takes her
stand;
3 beside the gates leading into the city,
at the entrances, she cries aloud:[d]
4 "To you, O men, I call out;
I raise my voice to all mankind.
5 You who are simple,[e] gain prudence;[f]
you who are foolish, gain
understanding.
6 Listen, for I have worthy things to say;
I open my lips to speak what is right.
7 My mouth speaks what is true,[g]
for my lips detest wickedness.
8 All the words of my mouth are just;
none of them is crooked or perverse.
9 To the discerning all of them are right;
they are faultless to those who have
knowledge.
10 Choose my instruction instead of silver,
knowledge rather than choice gold,[h]
11 for wisdom is more precious[i] than
rubies,
and nothing you desire can compare
with her.[j]

12 "I, wisdom, dwell together with
prudence;
I possess knowledge and discretion.[k]
13 To fear the LORD is to hate evil;[l]
I hate[m] pride and arrogance,
evil behavior and perverse speech.
14 Counsel and sound judgment are mine;
I have understanding and power.[n]

7:21 [v]Pr 5:3
7:22 [w]Job 18:10
7:23 [x]Job 15:22; 16:13 [y]Pr 6:26; Ecc 7:26; 9:12
7:24 [z]Pr 1:8-9; 5:7; 8:32
7:25 [a]Pr 5:7-8
7:27 [b]Pr 2:18; 5:5; 9:18; Rev 22:15
8:1 [c]Pr 1:20; 9:3
8:3 [d]Job 29:7
8:5 [e]Pr 1:22 [f]Pr 1:4
8:7 [g]Ps 37:30; Jn 8:14
8:10 [h]Pr 3:14-15
8:11 [i]Job 28:17-19 [j]Pr 3:13-15
8:12 [k]Pr 1:4
8:13 [l]Pr 16:6 [m]Jer 44:4
8:14 [n]Pr 21:22; Ecc 7:19

[a] *22* Syriac (see also Septuagint); Hebrew *fool* [b] *22* The meaning of the Hebrew for this line is uncertain.
[c] *27* Hebrew *Sheol*

[15]By me kings reign
and rulers[o] make laws that are just;
[16]by me princes govern,
and all nobles who rule on earth.[a]
[17]I love those who love me,[p]
and those who seek me find me.[q]
[18]With me are riches and honor,[r]
enduring wealth and prosperity.[s]
[19]My fruit is better than fine gold;
what I yield surpasses choice silver.[t]
[20]I walk in the way of righteousness,
along the paths of justice,
[21]bestowing wealth on those who love me
and making their treasuries full.[u]

[22]"The LORD brought me forth as the first
of his works,[b,c]
before his deeds of old;
[23]I was appointed[d] from eternity,
from the beginning, before the world
began.
[24]When there were no oceans, I was given
birth,
when there were no springs
abounding with water;[v]
[25]before the mountains were settled in
place,
before the hills, I was given birth,[w]
[26]before he made the earth or its fields
or any of the dust of the world.[x]
[27]I was there when he set the heavens in
place,[y]
when he marked out the horizon on
the face of the deep,
[28]when he established the clouds above
and fixed securely the fountains of the
deep,
[29]when he gave the sea its boundary[z]
so the waters would not overstep his
command,[a]
and when he marked out the
foundations of the earth.[b]
[30] Then I was the craftsman at his side.[c]
I was filled with delight day after day,
rejoicing always in his presence,
[31]rejoicing in his whole world
and delighting in mankind.[d]

[32]"Now then, my sons, listen to me;
blessed are[e] those who keep my ways.[f]
[33]Listen to my instruction and be wise;
do not ignore it.
[34]Blessed is the man who listens[g] to me,
watching daily at my doors,
waiting at my doorway.
[35]For whoever finds me[h] finds life
and receives favor from the LORD.[i]

8:15 [o]Da 2:21; Ro 13:1
8:17 [p]1Sa 2:30; Ps 91:14; Jn 14:21-24 [q]Pr 1:28; Jas 1:5
8:18 [r]Pr 3:16 [s]Dt 8:18; Mt 6:33
8:19 [t]Pr 3:13-14; 10:20
8:21 [u]Pr 24:4
8:24 [v]Ge 7:11
8:25 [w]Job 15:7
8:26 [x]Ps 90:2
8:27 [y]Pr 3:19
8:29 [z]Ge 1:9; Job 38:10; Ps 16:6 [a]Ps 104:9 [b]Job 38:5
8:30 [c]Jn 1:1-3
8:31 [d]Ps 16:3; 104:1-30
8:32 [e]Lk 11:28 [f]Ps 119:1-2
8:34 [g]Pr 3:13,18
8:35 [h]Pr 3:13-18 [i]Pr 12:2

[a] *16* Many Hebrew manuscripts and Septuagint; most Hebrew manuscripts *and nobles—all righteous rulers* [b] *22* Or *way;* or *dominion* [c] *22* Or *The LORD possessed me at the beginning of his work*; or *The LORD brought me forth at the beginning of his work* [d] *23* Or *fashioned*

I never saw a moor,
I never saw the sea;
Yet know I how the heather looks,
And what a wave must be.

I never spoke with God,
Nor visited in heaven;
Yet certain am I of the spot
As if the chart were given.

—Emily Dickinson (1830–1886)

Deceitful Lady Folly

PR 9:17

Perhaps the most dangerous aspect of Lady Folly is her deceitfulness. She lies through her teeth while honey drips off her lips (Pr 5:3). To those who lack good judgment and fail to pursue wisdom diligently, Folly's lies are alluring and even sound true. But the wise person knows that stealing water from another person's well yields anything but sweet results (see the note on Pr 5:15–19, page 1024), and having to secretly "eat" from Folly's table cannot possibly lead to freedom and joy. Read John 8:12–47, where Jesus himself makes clear in his discourse with the Jews that there is only one truth (from God the Father) and many lies (from the father of lies, the devil). Each of us must choose whom we will believe and follow.

36 But whoever fails to find me harms
himself;[j]
all who hate me love death."

Invitations of Wisdom and of Folly

9 Wisdom has built[k] her house;
she has hewn out its seven pillars.
2 She has prepared her meat and mixed
her wine;
she has also set her table.[l]
3 She has sent out her maids, and she calls[m]
from the highest point of the city.[n]
4 "Let all who are simple come in here!"
she says to those who lack judgment.[o]
5 "Come, eat my food
and drink the wine I have mixed.[p]
6 Leave your simple ways and you will
live;[q]
walk in the way of understanding.
7 "Whoever corrects a mocker invites
insult;
whoever rebukes a wicked man
incurs abuse.[r]
8 Do not rebuke a mocker[s] or he will hate
you;
rebuke a wise man and he will love
you.[t]
9 Instruct a wise man and he will be
wiser still;
teach a righteous man and he will add
to his learning.[u]
10 "The fear of the LORD[v] is the beginning
of wisdom,
and knowledge of the Holy One is
understanding.
11 For through me your days will be many,
and years will be added to your life.[w]
12 If you are wise, your wisdom will
reward you;
if you are a mocker, you alone will
suffer."
13 The woman Folly is loud;[x]
she is undisciplined and without
knowledge.[y]
14 She sits at the door of her house,
on a seat at the highest point of the
city,[z]
15 calling out to those who pass by,
who go straight on their way.
16 "Let all who are simple come in here!"
she says to those who lack judgment.
17 "Stolen water is sweet;
food eaten in secret is delicious![a]"
18 But little do they know that the dead are
there,
that her guests are in the depths of
the grave.[a][b]

8:36 [j]Pr 15:32
9:1 [k]Eph 2:20-22; 1Pe 2:5
9:2 [l]Lk 14:16-23
9:3 [m]Pr 8:1-3 [n]ver 14
9:4 [o]Pr 6:32
9:5 [p]Isa 55:1
9:6 [q]Pr 8:35
9:7 [r]Pr 23:9
9:8 [s]Pr 15:12 [t]Ps 141:5
9:9 [u]Pr 1:5,7
9:10 [v]Job 28:28; Pr 1:7
9:11 [w]Pr 3:16; 10:27
9:13 [x]Pr 7:11 [y]Pr 5:6
9:14 [z]ver 3
9:17 [a]Pr 20:17
9:18 [b]Pr 2:18; 7:26-27

[a] *18* Hebrew *Sheol*

Proverbs of Solomon

10 The proverbs of Solomon:[c]

A wise son brings joy to his father,[d]
but a foolish son grief to his mother.

2 Ill-gotten treasures are of no value,[e]
but righteousness delivers from death.[f]

3 The LORD does not let the righteous go hungry[g]
but he thwarts the craving of the wicked.

4 Lazy hands make a man poor,[h]
but diligent hands bring wealth.[i]

5 He who gathers crops in summer is a wise son,
but he who sleeps during harvest is a disgraceful son.

6 Blessings crown the head of the righteous,
but violence overwhelms the mouth of the wicked.[a][j]

7 The memory of the righteous[k] will be a blessing,
but the name of the wicked[l] will rot.[m]

8 The wise in heart accept commands,
but a chattering fool comes to ruin.[n]

9 The man of integrity[o] walks securely,[p]
but he who takes crooked paths will be found out.[q]

10 He who winks maliciously[r] causes grief,
and a chattering fool comes to ruin.

11 The mouth of the righteous is a fountain of life,[s]
but violence overwhelms the mouth of the wicked.[t]

12 Hatred stirs up dissension,
but love covers over all wrongs.[u]

13 Wisdom is found on the lips of the discerning,[v]
but a rod is for the back of him who lacks judgment.[w]

14 Wise men store up knowledge,
but the mouth of a fool invites ruin.[x]

15 The wealth of the rich is their fortified city,[y]
but poverty is the ruin of the poor.[z]

16 The wages of the righteous bring them life,
but the income of the wicked brings them punishment.[a]

10:1 [c]Pr 1:1 [d]Pr 15:20; 29:3
10:2 [e]Pr 21:6 [f]Pr 11:4,19
10:3 [g]Mt 6:25-34
10:4 [h]Pr 19:15 [i]Pr 12:24; 13:4; 21:5
10:6 [j]ver 8,11,14
10:7 [k]Ps 112:6 [l]Ps 109:13 [m]Ps 9:6
10:8 [n]Mt 7:24-27
10:9 [o]Isa 33:15 [p]Ps 23:4 [q]Pr 28:18
10:10 [r]Ps 35:19
10:11 [s]Ps 37:30; Pr 13:12,14,19 [t]ver 6
10:12 [u]Pr 17:9; 1Co 13:4-7; 1Pe 4:8
10:13 [v]ver 31 [w]Pr 26:3
10:14 [x]Pr 18:6,7
10:15 [y]Pr 18:11 [z]Pr 19:7
10:16 [a]Pr 11:18-19

Never Hungry?

PR 10:3

It can be tempting to take words like these as a guarantee that God will never let righteous people suffer. But we don't have to look far to see that this isn't true; godly people do sometimes starve, suffer greatly and even die prematurely, while wicked people seem to flourish (Ps 73:12–14). God himself gives Satan permission to torment Job, the most righteous man on earth at the time (Job 1:8).

While a proverb like this one may appear to be an absolute promise we can bank on, its intention is to highlight a generally prevailing truth. In this case, the principle is that, in general, God's people will be blessed and he will fill them with himself (Ps 16:11). We can exercise trust rather than worry in regard to our circumstances, because our heavenly Father knows what we need and will take care of us (Mt 6:25–34).

[a] 6 Or *but the mouth of the wicked conceals violence*; also in verse 11

Ultimate Prospects

PR 10:28

People who don't love God sometimes enjoy a lot of "goodies" here on earth; they may even become convinced that it is worth investing their all in this temporal life. But the Bible repeatedly states that even the most prosperous, satisfied, godless people will be disappointed in the end. They will realize too late that their hope is misplaced (Ps 49:12–14; Pr 11:7). Godly people, on the other hand, can rejoice in the fact that no matter what their earthly life holds, whether it be destitution or abundance, their ultimate prospects are bright. Jesus himself promised, "Blessed are the poor in spirit, for theirs is the kingdom of heaven" (Mt 5:3) and "Blessed are those who hunger and thirst for righteousness, for they will be filled" (Mt 5:6).

17 He who heeds discipline shows the way
to life,[b]
but whoever ignores correction leads
others astray.

18 He who conceals his hatred has lying
lips,
and whoever spreads slander is a fool.

19 When words are many, sin is not absent,
but he who holds his tongue is wise.[c]

20 The tongue of the righteous is choice
silver,
but the heart of the wicked is of little
value.

21 The lips of the righteous nourish many,
but fools die for lack of judgment.[d]

22 The blessing of the LORD brings wealth,[e]
and he adds no trouble to it.

23 A fool finds pleasure in evil conduct,[f]
but a man of understanding delights
in wisdom.

24 What the wicked dreads[g] will overtake
him;
what the righteous desire will be
granted.[h]

25 When the storm has swept by, the
wicked are gone,
but the righteous stand firm[i] forever.[j]

26 As vinegar to the teeth and smoke to the
eyes,
so is a sluggard to those who send
him.[k]

27 The fear of the LORD adds length to life,[l]
but the years of the wicked are cut
short.[m]

28 The prospect of the righteous is joy,
but the hopes of the wicked come to
nothing.[n]

29 The way of the LORD is a refuge for the
righteous,
but it is the ruin of those who do evil.[o]

30 The righteous will never be uprooted,
but the wicked will not remain in the
land.[p]

31 The mouth of the righteous brings forth
wisdom,[q]
but a perverse tongue will be cut out.

32 The lips of the righteous know what is
fitting,[r]
but the mouth of the wicked only
what is perverse.

11 The LORD abhors dishonest scales,[s]
but accurate weights are his delight.[t]

10:17 [b]Pr 6:23
10:19 [c]Pr 17:28; Ecc 5:3; Jas 1:19; 3:2-12
10:21 [d]Pr 5:22-23; Hos 4:1,6,14
10:22 [e]Ge 24:35; Ps 37:22
10:23 [f]Pr 2:14; 15:21
10:24 [g]Isa 66:4 [h]Ps 145:17-19; Mt 5:6; 1Jn 5:14-15
10:25 [i]Ps 15:5 [j]Pr 12:3,7; Mt 7:24-27
10:26 [k]Pr 26:6
10:27 [l]Pr 9:10-11 [m]Job 15:32
10:28 [n]Job 8:13; Pr 11:7
10:29 [o]Pr 21:15
10:30 [p]Ps 37:9,28-29; Pr 2:20-22
10:31 [q]Ps 37:30
10:32 [r]Ecc 10:12
11:1 [s]Lev 19:36; Dt 25:13-16; Pr 20:10,23 [t]Pr 16:11

2 When pride comes, then comes disgrace,[u]
but with humility comes wisdom.[v]

3 The integrity of the upright guides them,
but the unfaithful are destroyed by their duplicity.[w]

4 Wealth is worthless in the day of wrath,[x]
but righteousness delivers from death.[y]

5 The righteousness of the blameless makes a straight way for them,
but the wicked are brought down by their own wickedness.[z]

6 The righteousness of the upright delivers them,
but the unfaithful are trapped by evil desires.

7 When a wicked man dies, his hope perishes;
all he expected from his power comes to nothing.[a]

8 The righteous man is rescued from trouble,
and it comes on the wicked instead.[b]

9 With his mouth the godless destroys his neighbor,
but through knowledge the righteous escape.

10 When the righteous prosper, the city rejoices;[c]
when the wicked perish, there are shouts of joy.

11 Through the blessing of the upright a city is exalted,
but by the mouth of the wicked it is destroyed.[d]

12 A man who lacks judgment derides his neighbor,[e]
but a man of understanding holds his tongue.

13 A gossip betrays a confidence,[f]
but a trustworthy man keeps a secret.

14 For lack of guidance a nation falls,[g]
but many advisers make victory sure.[h]

15 He who puts up security[i] for another will surely suffer,
but whoever refuses to strike hands in pledge is safe.

16 A kindhearted woman gains respect,[j]
but ruthless men gain only wealth.

17 A kind man benefits himself,

11:2 [u]Pr 16:18 [v]Pr 18:12; 29:23
11:3 [w]Pr 13:6
11:4 [x]Eze 7:19; Zep 1:18 [y]Ge 7:1; Pr 10:2
11:5 [z]Pr 5:21-23
11:7 [a]Pr 10:28
11:8 [b]Pr 21:18
11:10 [c]Pr 28:12
11:11 [d]Pr 29:8
11:12 [e]Pr 14:21
11:13 [f]Lev 19:16; Pr 20:19; 1Ti 5:13
11:14 [g]Pr 20:18 [h]Pr 15:22; 24:6
11:15 [i]Pr 6:1
11:16 [j]Pr 31:31

A Kindhearted Woman

PR 11:16

Solomon states that a kindhearted woman *(though she clearly has a lower social status in his day) will gain more respect than any number of wealthy, but ruthless men. But women can be equally rancorous when they lose sight of what is most important.* In Proverbs 31:30-31, *a woman who loves God is credited with the highest reward: the public praise of God and others for the way her noble character has directed her heart and actions. To be a God-fearing, gracious and kindhearted woman is the ultimate victory for a woman in God's kingdom. A woman who makes it her goal to be gentle and kind like Jesus Christ will have a far greater influence for good in the world than anyone who ruthlessly pursues worldly goals.*

A Ring in a Pig's Snout

PR 11:22

What an entertaining picture—a fat and dirty sow with a shiny gold ring in her nose! The meaning of Solomon's proverb here isn't difficult to figure out. In Solomon's time, nose rings on women were considered beautiful ornamentation. And Old Testament law prohibited God's people from eating pork or even touching a pig (Lev 11:7–8). By contrasting a beautiful woman who lacks discretion with the most unclean of animals, Solomon makes a clear point: A woman who is considered beautiful by society's standards may or may not be beautiful in God's eyes. If she doesn't use her head or keep her behavior in line with godly wisdom, then she might as well be an ugly pig with a pretty ring in her snout!

but a cruel man brings trouble on
himself.

18 The wicked man earns deceptive wages,
but he who sows righteousness reaps
a sure reward.[k]

19 The truly righteous man attains life,
but he who pursues evil goes to his
death.

20 The LORD detests men of perverse heart
but he delights in those whose ways
are blameless.[l]

21 Be sure of this: The wicked will not go
unpunished,
but those who are righteous will go
free.[m]

22 Like a gold ring in a pig's snout
is a beautiful woman who shows no
discretion.

23 The desire of the righteous ends only in
good,
but the hope of the wicked only in
wrath.

24 One man gives freely, yet gains even
more;
another withholds unduly, but comes
to poverty.

25 A generous man will prosper;
he who refreshes others will himself
be refreshed.[n]

26 People curse the man who hoards grain,
but blessing crowns him who is
willing to sell.

27 He who seeks good finds goodwill,
but evil comes to him who searches
for it.[o]

28 Whoever trusts in his riches will fall,[p]
but the righteous will thrive like a
green leaf.[q]

29 He who brings trouble on his family
will inherit only wind,
and the fool will be servant to the
wise.[r]

30 The fruit of the righteous is a tree of
life,[s]
and he who wins souls is wise.

31 If the righteous receive their due[t] on
earth,
how much more the ungodly and the
sinner!

12

Whoever loves discipline loves knowledge,
but he who hates correction is stupid.[u]

2 A good man obtains favor from the
LORD,

11:18 [k]Hos 10:12-13
11:20 [l]1Ch 29:17; Ps 119:1; Pr 12:2,22
11:21 [m]Pr 16:5
11:25 [n]Mt 5:7; 2Co 9:6-9
11:27 [o]Est 7:10; Ps 7:15-16
11:28 [p]Job 31:24-28; Ps 49:6; 52:7; Mk 10:25; 1Ti 6:17 [q]Ps 1:3; 92:12-14; Jer 17:8
11:29 [r]Pr 14:19
11:30 [s]Jas 5:20
11:31 [t]Pr 13:21; Jer 25:29; 1Pe 4:18
12:1 [u]Pr 9:7-9; 15:5,10,12, 32

but the LORD condemns a crafty man.

3 A man cannot be established through
wickedness,
but the righteous cannot be
12:3 [v]Pr 10:25 uprooted.[v]

4 A wife of noble character is her
husband's crown,
12:4 but a disgraceful wife is like decay in
[w]Pr 14:30 his bones.[w]

5 The plans of the righteous are just,
but the advice of the wicked is
deceitful.

6 The words of the wicked lie in wait for
blood,
but the speech of the upright rescues
12:6 [x]Pr 14:3 them.[x]

7 Wicked men are overthrown and are no
12:7 [y]Ps 37:36 more,[y]
[z]Pr 10:25 but the house of the righteous stands
firm.[z]

8 A man is praised according to his
wisdom,
but men with warped minds are
despised.

9 Better to be a nobody and yet have a
servant
than pretend to be somebody and
have no food.

10 A righteous man cares for the needs of
his animal,
but the kindest acts of the wicked are
cruel.

11 He who works his land will have
abundant food,
but he who chases fantasies lacks
12:11 [a]Pr 28:19 judgment.[a]

12 The wicked desire the plunder of evil
men,
but the root of the righteous
flourishes.

13 An evil man is trapped by his sinful
12:13 [b]Pr 18:7 talk,[b]
[c]Pr 21:23; 2Pe 2:9 but a righteous man escapes trouble.[c]

12:14 14 From the fruit of his lips a man is filled
[d]Pr 13:2; 15:23; 18:20 with good things[d]
[e]Isa 3:10-11 as surely as the work of his hands
rewards him.[e]

12:15 15 The way of a fool seems right to him,[f]
[f]Pr 14:12; 16:2,25; Lk 18:11 but a wise man listens to advice.

16 A fool shows his annoyance at once,
12:16 but a prudent man overlooks an
[g]Pr 29:11 insult.[g]

A Wife of Noble Character

PR 12:4

The Hebrew word for *noble* is used in relation to women only two other times in the Old Testament (Pr 31:10; Ru 3:11). Read Ruth's story in the book of Ruth and consider what character qualities she demonstrates that earn her such high regard. Do the same for the noble wife described in Proverbs 31. A man who is fortunate enough to marry such a woman will be much more likely to reach his potential and be admired by others, suggesting that a good wife is far more than a social appendage or domestic helper. A wife who pursues wisdom and godly character can be the most important influence in her husband's life. A wife who doesn't, can be his downfall.

The Power of Speech

PR 13:3

Scripture makes countless references to the power people's words have to either bring blessing or pain to others as well as to themselves. What comes out of people's mouths can heal and give life when they are guided by wisdom; but when people speak without thinking, they can do enormous harm (Pr 12:18). In James 3:3–6, we find a description of the life-altering destructiveness of a tongue left unchecked. Many proverbs remind us of the wisdom of keeping our mouths shut (Pr 10:19; 11:12; 21:23). When we speak rashly, we will almost always regret it, and we may even destroy our lives. The tongue literally has "the power of life and death" (Pr 18:21).

17 A truthful witness gives honest
testimony,
but a false witness tells lies.[h] **12:17** [h]Pr 14:5,25

18 Reckless words pierce like a sword,[i] **12:18** [i]Ps 57:4
but the tongue of the wise brings [j]Pr 15:4
healing.[j]

19 Truthful lips endure forever,
but a lying tongue lasts only a
moment.

20 There is deceit in the hearts of those
who plot evil,
but joy for those who promote peace.

21 No harm befalls the righteous,[k] **12:21** [k]Ps 91:10
but the wicked have their fill of
trouble.

22 The LORD detests lying lips,[l] **12:22** [l]Pr 6:17;
but he delights in men who are Rev 22:15
truthful.[m] [m]Pr 11:20

23 A prudent man keeps his knowledge to **12:23**
himself,[n] [n]Pr 10:14;
but the heart of fools blurts out folly. 13:16

24 Diligent hands will rule,
but laziness ends in slave labor.[o] **12:24** [o]Pr 10:4

25 An anxious heart weighs a man down,[p] **12:25**
but a kind word cheers him up. [p]Pr 15:13; Isa 50:4

26 A righteous man is cautious in
friendship,[a]
but the way of the wicked leads them
astray.

27 The lazy man does not roast[b] his game,
but the diligent man prizes his
possessions.

28 In the way of righteousness there is **12:28**
life;[q] [q]Dt 30:15
along that path is immortality.

13

1 A wise son heeds his father's instruction,
but a mocker does not listen to rebuke.[r] **13:1** [r]Pr 10:1

2 From the fruit of his lips a man enjoys
good things,[s] **13:2** [s]Pr 12:14
but the unfaithful have a craving for
violence.

3 He who guards his lips[t] guards his life,[u] **13:3** [t]Jas 3:2
but he who speaks rashly will come [u]Pr 21:23
to ruin.[v] [v]Pr 18:7,20-21

4 The sluggard craves and gets nothing,
but the desires of the diligent are fully
satisfied.

5 The righteous hate what is false,
but the wicked bring shame and
disgrace.

[a] 26 Or *man is a guide to his neighbor* [b] 27 The meaning of the Hebrew for this word is uncertain.

6 Righteousness guards the man of
integrity,
13:6 but wickedness overthrows the
[w]Pr 11:3,5 sinner.[w]

7 One man pretends to be rich, yet has
nothing;
13:7 another pretends to be poor, yet has
[x]2Co 6:10 great wealth.[x]

8 A man's riches may ransom his life,
but a poor man hears no threat.

9 The light of the righteous shines brightly,
13:9 but the lamp of the wicked is snuffed
[y]Job 18:5; Pr 4:18-19; 24:20 out.[y]

10 Pride only breeds quarrels,
but wisdom is found in those who
take advice.

13:11 11 Dishonest money dwindles away,[z]
[z]Pr 10:2 but he who gathers money little by
little makes it grow.

12 Hope deferred makes the heart sick,
but a longing fulfilled is a tree of life.

13 He who scorns instruction will pay for
13:13 it,[a]
[a]Nu 15:31; 2Ch 36:16 but he who respects a command is
rewarded.

14 The teaching of the wise is a fountain of
13:14 life,[b]
[b]Pr 10:11 [c]Pr 14:27 turning a man from the snares of
death.[c]

15 Good understanding wins favor,
but the way of the unfaithful is hard.[a]

16 Every prudent man acts out of
13:16 knowledge,
[d]Pr 12:23 but a fool exposes his folly.[d]

17 A wicked messenger falls into trouble,
13:17 but a trustworthy envoy brings
[e]Pr 25:13 healing.[e]

18 He who ignores discipline comes to
poverty and shame,
but whoever heeds correction is
13:18 honored.[f]
[f]Pr 15:5,31-32

19 A longing fulfilled is sweet to the soul,
but fools detest turning from evil.

20 He who walks with the wise grows wise,
13:20 but a companion of fools suffers
[g]Pr 15:31 harm.[g]

21 Misfortune pursues the sinner,
13:21 but prosperity is the reward of the
[h]Ps 32:10 righteous.[h]

22 A good man leaves an inheritance for
his children's children,

[a] 15 Or *unfaithful does not endure*

Unfulfilled Longings

PR 13:12

Unfulfilled longings are familiar to every woman. Sometimes when a woman must wait for her deepest hopes to be realized she can become heartsick, despondent, even desperate. Consider Rachel, whose longing to have children not only caused her to feel like she would die from the pain of waiting, but also led her to take matters into her own hands in order to get what she wanted (Ge 30:1–5). In a woman's quest for relief from disappointment, she can be tempted to manipulate and demand that her desires be satisfied according to her timetable. Or she can suppress her dreams and desires and settle for much less than God has planned. Either way, she loses. How much better off a woman will be when she trusts God to fulfill her dreams, when she waits on him instead of manipulating or giving up. Only he sees the whole picture, and only he has the power to fulfill her heart's desires (Ge 30:22–23).

A Wise Woman Builds

PR 14:1

Some people who are unfamiliar with the whole of Scripture believe that women are depicted in the Bible as second-class citizens, or that their personal power is minimized. Here is one of many examples of how God views a wise, righteous woman. Not only does she exert enormous influence over her family, but she has also been given the strength and resources with which to build an enduring home and life, "brick by brick." Each time she acts in wisdom, making daily decisions that build up her family and community rather than tear it down, she secures her foundation for the future. If, on the other hand, she lets folly dictate her behavior, she undermines her own best interests as well as her family's and her community's. Any woman (or man) who fails to pursue wisdom or fails to let God determine proper priorities will be destructive rather than life-giving.

but a sinner's wealth is stored up for
the righteous.[i]

23 A poor man's field may produce
abundant food,
but injustice sweeps it away.

24 He who spares the rod hates his son,
but he who loves him is careful to
discipline him.[j]

25 The righteous eat to their hearts' content,
but the stomach of the wicked goes
hungry.[k]

14 The wise woman builds her house,[l]
but with her own hands the foolish one
tears hers down.

2 He whose walk is upright fears the
LORD,
but he whose ways are devious
despises him.

3 A fool's talk brings a rod to his back,
but the lips of the wise protect them.[m]

4 Where there are no oxen, the manger is
empty,
but from the strength of an ox comes
an abundant harvest.

5 A truthful witness does not deceive,
but a false witness pours out lies.[n]

6 The mocker seeks wisdom and finds
none,
but knowledge comes easily to the
discerning.

7 Stay away from a foolish man,
for you will not find knowledge on
his lips.

8 The wisdom of the prudent is to give
thought to their ways,
but the folly of fools is deception.[o]

9 Fools mock at making amends for sin,
but goodwill is found among the
upright.

10 Each heart knows its own bitterness,
and no one else can share its joy.

11 The house of the wicked will be
destroyed,
but the tent of the upright will
flourish.[p]

12 There is a way that seems right to a
man,[q]
but in the end it leads to death.[r]

13 Even in laughter[s] the heart may ache,
and joy may end in grief.

13:22 [i]Job 27:17; Ecc 2:26
13:24 [j]Pr 19:18; 22:15; 23:13-14; 29:15, 17; Heb 12:7
13:25 [k]Ps 34:10; Pr 10:3
14:1 [l]Pr 24:3
14:3 [m]Pr 12:6
14:5 [n]Pr 6:19; 12:17
14:8 [o]ver 24
14:11 [p]Pr 3:33; 12:7
14:12 [q]Pr 12:15 [r]Pr 16:25
14:13 [s]Ecc 2:2

14 The faithless will be fully repaid for
their ways,[t]
and the good man rewarded for his.[u]
15 A simple man believes anything,
but a prudent man gives thought to
his steps.
16 A wise man fears the LORD and shuns
evil,[v]
but a fool is hotheaded and reckless.
17 A quick-tempered man does foolish
things,[w]
and a crafty man is hated.
18 The simple inherit folly,
but the prudent are crowned with
knowledge.
19 Evil men will bow down in the presence
of the good,
and the wicked at the gates of the
righteous.[x]
20 The poor are shunned even by their
neighbors,
but the rich have many friends.[y]
21 He who despises his neighbor sins,[z]
but blessed is he who is kind to the
needy.[a]
22 Do not those who plot evil go astray?
But those who plan what is good find[a]
love and faithfulness.
23 All hard work brings a profit,
but mere talk leads only to poverty.
24 The wealth of the wise is their crown,
but the folly of fools yields folly.
25 A truthful witness saves lives,
but a false witness is deceitful.[b]
26 He who fears the LORD has a secure
fortress,[c]
and for his children it will be a refuge.
27 The fear of the LORD is a fountain of life,
turning a man from the snares of
death.[d]
28 A large population is a king's glory,
but without subjects a prince is
ruined.
29 A patient man has great understanding,
but a quick-tempered man displays
folly.[e]
30 A heart at peace gives life to the body,
but envy rots the bones.[f]
31 He who oppresses the poor shows
contempt for their Maker,[g]

14:14 [t]Pr 1:31 [u]Pr 12:14
14:16 [v]Pr 22:3
14:17 [w]ver 29
14:19 [x]Pr 11:29
14:20 [y]Pr 19:4,7
14:21 [z]Pr 11:12 [a]Ps 41:1; Pr 19:17
14:25 [b]ver 5
14:26 [c]Pr 18:10; 19:23; Isa 33:6
14:27 [d]Pr 13:14
14:29 [e]Ecc 7:8-9; Jas 1:19
14:30 [f]Pr 12:4
14:31 [g]Pr 17:5

[a] 22 Or *show*

Envy's Destructiveness

PR 14:30

What a clear picture this verse gives! Envy is like a vicious cancer; it literally eats away at people's well-being, including their physical health. Directing energy toward craving what others have instead of appreciating what God has given can be a miserable, even spiritually lethal, activity. And it can literally make a person sick in mind, heart and body. Envy brings with it "rot"—decay and pollution of the spirit.

Being a wise woman means also being a content woman—one who puts her trust in God's will and provision rather than in her own. The apostle Paul is one example to follow when considering a life of contentment. Read Philippians 4:4-13 and note his secrets to living at peace with himself, with others and with God.

The Eyes of the LORD

PR 15:3

When evil seems to triumph over good in the world around us, or even in our own families, our faith in God's presence and justice can waver. Here Solomon reminds us of a faith-enhancing truth: God is fully aware, every moment, of what is going on in the world he created as well as in the heart of every person (Pr 15:11). No deed or motive, whether good or evil, escapes his notice. For those whose sin is covered by the atoning blood of Jesus Christ, this is good news indeed. Not only is God diligently keeping loving watch over us, but he is keeping tabs on those who have rejected him. While he wants every person to bow in repentance and become his own (2Pe 3:9), we have his word that those who have no regard for his ways will be dealt with justly and those who love him will be blessed (2Th 2:10–17; Rev 21:6–8).

but whoever is kind to the needy
honors God.

32 When calamity comes, the wicked are brought down,[h]
but even in death the righteous have a refuge.[i]

33 Wisdom reposes in the heart of the discerning[j]
and even among fools she lets herself be known.[a]

34 Righteousness exalts a nation,[k]
but sin is a disgrace to any people.

35 A king delights in a wise servant,
but a shameful servant incurs his wrath.[l]

15

1 A gentle answer turns away wrath,[m]
but a harsh word stirs up anger.

2 The tongue of the wise commends knowledge,
but the mouth of the fool gushes folly.[n]

3 The eyes[o] of the LORD are everywhere,[p]
keeping watch on the wicked and the good.[q]

4 The tongue that brings healing is a tree of life,
but a deceitful tongue crushes the spirit.

5 A fool spurns his father's discipline,
but whoever heeds correction shows prudence.[r]

6 The house of the righteous contains great treasure,[s]
but the income of the wicked brings them trouble.

7 The lips of the wise spread knowledge;
not so the hearts of fools.

8 The LORD detests the sacrifice of the wicked,[t]
but the prayer of the upright pleases him.[u]

9 The LORD detests the way of the wicked
but he loves those who pursue righteousness.[v]

10 Stern discipline awaits him who leaves the path;
he who hates correction will die.[w]

11 Death and Destruction[b] lie open before the LORD[x]—
how much more the hearts of men![y]

14:32 [h]Pr 6:15 [i]Job 13:15; 2Ti 4:18
14:33 [j]Pr 2:6-10
14:34 [k]Pr 11:11
14:35 [l]Mt 24:45-51; 25:14-30
15:1 [m]Pr 25:15
15:2 [n]Pr 12:23
15:3 [o]2Ch 16:9 [p]Job 31:4; Heb 4:13 [q]Job 34:21; Jer 16:17
15:5 [r]Pr 13:1
15:6 [s]Pr 8:21
15:8 [t]Pr 21:27; Isa 1:11; Jer 6:20 [u]ver 29
15:9 [v]Pr 21:21; 1Ti 6:11
15:10 [w]Pr 1:31-32; 5:12
15:11 [x]Job 26:6; Ps 139:8 [y]2Ch 6:30; Ps 44:21

[a] 33 Hebrew; Septuagint and Syriac / *but in the heart of fools she is not known* [b] 11 Hebrew *Sheol and Abaddon*

15:12 [z]Am 5:10

12 A mocker resents correction;[z]
he will not consult the wise.

15:13 [a]Pr 12:25; 17:22; 18:14

13 A happy heart makes the face cheerful,
but heartache crushes the spirit.[a]

15:14 [b]Pr 18:15

14 The discerning heart seeks knowledge,[b]
but the mouth of a fool feeds on folly.

15:15 [c]ver 13

15 All the days of the oppressed are wretched,
but the cheerful heart has a continual feast.[c]

15:16 [d]Ps 37:16-17; Pr 16:8; 1Ti 6:6

16 Better a little with the fear of the LORD
than great wealth with turmoil.[d]

15:17 [e]Pr 17:1

17 Better a meal of vegetables where there is love
than a fattened calf with hatred.[e]

15:18 [f]Pr 26:21 [g]Ge 13:8

18 A hot-tempered man stirs up dissension,[f]
but a patient man calms a quarrel.[g]

15:19 [h]Pr 22:5

19 The way of the sluggard is blocked with thorns,[h]
but the path of the upright is a highway.

15:20 [i]Pr 10:1

20 A wise son brings joy to his father,[i]
but a foolish man despises his mother.

15:21 [j]Pr 10:23

21 Folly delights a man who lacks judgment,[j]
but a man of understanding keeps a straight course.

15:22 [k]Pr 11:14

22 Plans fail for lack of counsel,
but with many advisers they succeed.[k]

15:23 [l]Pr 12:14 [m]Pr 25:11

23 A man finds joy in giving an apt reply[l]—
and how good is a timely word![m]

24 The path of life leads upward for the wise
to keep him from going down to the grave.[a]

15:25 [n]Pr 12:7 [o]Dt 19:14; Ps 68:5-6; Pr 23:10-11

25 The LORD tears down the proud man's house[n]
but he keeps the widow's boundaries intact.[o]

15:26 [p]Pr 6:16

26 The LORD detests the thoughts of the wicked,[p]
but those of the pure are pleasing to him.

15:27 [q]Ex 23:8; Isa 33:15

27 A greedy man brings trouble to his family,
but he who hates bribes will live.[q]

15:28 [r]1Pe 3:15

28 The heart of the righteous weighs its answers,[r]

[a] 24 Hebrew *Sheol*

"If Only" Thinking

PR 15:17

In a world that values money and power above most everything else, it's easy to fall into the trap of "if only" thinking: if only we had more money, we would be happy; if only we had all the goodies and influence that the Smiths have, our family would have it all. But just because someone else has more in terms of wealth or position than we do doesn't mean they are better off. Human beings are created for relationship, so when their relationships with others are at odds, they really can't be happy, no matter what they possess. Without love, they might as well be starving. Better veggies with love than steak with strife.

At Peace

PR 16:7

A mark of people who fear God and live wisely is often peace (Pr 12:20; 29:17), peace in all their ways (Pr 3:17). Now Solomon takes the promise one step further: People who love and please God can even live in peace with those who consider them an enemy. Second Chronicles 14:1–7 describes this phenomenon in King Asa's life. To discover that people's actions and heart attitudes can have a profound and practical effect for good on those around them (even on their enemies!) is liberating and empowering. Often one of the by-products of choosing to live rightly is receiving the peace and rest that everyone longs to experience.

but the mouth of the wicked gushes
evil.

29 The LORD is far from the wicked
but he hears the prayer of the
righteous.[s] 15:29 [s]Ps 145:18-19
30 A cheerful look brings joy to the heart,
and good news gives health to the
bones.

31 He who listens to a life-giving rebuke
will be at home among the wise.[t] 15:31 [t]ver 5

32 He who ignores discipline despises
himself,[u] 15:32 [u]Pr 1:7
but whoever heeds correction gains
understanding.

33 The fear of the LORD[v] teaches a man
wisdom,[a] 15:33 [v]Pr 1:7 [w]Pr 18:12
and humility comes before honor.[w]

16 To man belong the plans of the heart,
but from the LORD comes the reply of the
tongue.[x] 16:1 [x]Pr 19:21

2 All a man's ways seem innocent to him,
but motives are weighed by the LORD.[y] 16:2 [y]Pr 21:2

3 Commit to the LORD whatever you do,
and your plans will succeed.[z] 16:3 [z]Ps 37:5-6; Pr 3:5-6

4 The LORD works out everything for his
own ends[a]— 16:4 [a]Isa 43:7 [b]Ro 9:22
even the wicked for a day of disaster.[b]

5 The LORD detests all the proud of heart.[c] 16:5 [c]Pr 6:16 [d]Pr 11:20-21
Be sure of this: They will not go
unpunished.[d]

6 Through love and faithfulness sin is
atoned for;
through the fear of the LORD a man
avoids evil.[e] 16:6 [e]Pr 14:16

7 When a man's ways are pleasing to the
LORD,
he makes even his enemies live at
peace with him.

8 Better a little with righteousness
than much gain[f] with injustice. 16:8 [f]Ps 37:16
9 In his heart a man plans his course,
but the LORD determines his steps.[g] 16:9 [g]Jer 10:23
10 The lips of a king speak as an oracle,
and his mouth should not betray
justice.

11 Honest scales and balances are from the
LORD;
all the weights in the bag are of his
making.[h] 16:11 [h]Pr 11:1

12 Kings detest wrongdoing,

[a] 33 Or *Wisdom teaches the fear of the LORD*

16:12 [i]Pr 25:5

for a throne is established through
righteousness.[i]

16:13 [j]Pr 14:35

13 Kings take pleasure in honest lips;
they value a man who speaks the
truth.[j]

16:14 [k]Pr 19:12

14 A king's wrath is a messenger of death,[k]
but a wise man will appease it.

16:15 [l]Job 29:24

15 When a king's face brightens, it means
life;[l]
his favor is like a rain cloud in spring.

16:16 [m]Pr 8:10,19

16 How much better to get wisdom than
gold,
to choose understanding rather than
silver![m]

17 The highway of the upright avoids evil;
he who guards his way guards his
life.

16:18 [n]Pr 11:2; 18:12

18 Pride goes before destruction,
a haughty spirit before a fall.[n]

19 Better to be lowly in spirit and among
the oppressed
than to share plunder with the proud.

16:20 [o]Ps 2:12; 34:8; Pr 19:8; Jer 17:7

20 Whoever gives heed to instruction
prospers,
and blessed is he who trusts in the
LORD.[o]

16:21 [p]ver 23

21 The wise in heart are called discerning,
and pleasant words promote
instruction.[a][p]

16:22 [q]Pr 13:14

22 Understanding is a fountain of life to
those who have it,[q]
but folly brings punishment to fools.

23 A wise man's heart guides his mouth,
and his lips promote instruction.[b]

16:24 [r]Pr 24:13-14

24 Pleasant words are a honeycomb,
sweet to the soul and healing to the
bones.[r]

16:25 [s]Pr 12:15 [t]Pr 14:12

25 There is a way that seems right to a
man,[s]
but in the end it leads to death.[t]

26 The laborer's appetite works for him;
his hunger drives him on.

16:27 [u]Jas 3:6

27 A scoundrel plots evil,
and his speech is like a scorching
fire.[u]

16:28 [v]Pr 15:18 [w]Pr 17:9

28 A perverse man stirs up dissension,[v]
and a gossip separates close friends.[w]

16:29 [x]Pr 1:10; 12:26

29 A violent man entices his neighbor
and leads him down a path that is not
good.[x]

[a] 21 Or *words make a man persuasive* [b] 23 Or *mouth / and makes his lips persuasive*

Where Pride Leads

PR 16:18

Feeling good about ourselves and our accomplishments is not sinful, and there is no virtue in putting ourselves down or belittling our gifts. The kind of pride Solomon renounces here is the kind Nebuchadnezzar, king of Babylon, demonstrated. Read about his arrogance, humiliation and restoration in Daniel 4:28–37. The monarch's mistake was not in enjoying his position and the splendor of his kingdom, but in taking all the credit for it and forgetting that everything he was and had was a gift from a sovereign God. When the king came to his senses, he gave God the glory and took his proper place in the scheme of things. Wisdom and humility go hand in hand (Pr 11:2), and a humble person will be honored by God (Pr 29:23).

Gray Hair

PR 16:31

Today the sight of their first gray hair dismays most women. The natural aging process is often met with fear and loathing because modern culture does not value the elderly as ancient Hebrew culture did **(Lev 19:32).** *But because God's truth is timeless, modern women can take great comfort from a Biblical perspective on aging. While youth has its benefits, so does old age—and the young and the old are equally valued by God* **(Pr 20:29).** *Rather than a curse, gray hair can be considered a sign of God's favor on the person who has lived long in pleasing him. The fountain of youth can never compare to the fountain of life* **(Pr 14:27).**

30 He who winks with his eye is plotting
perversity;
he who purses his lips is bent on evil.

31 Gray hair is a crown of splendor;[y]
it is attained by a righteous life.

32 Better a patient man than a warrior,
a man who controls his temper than
one who takes a city.

33 The lot is cast into the lap,
but its every decision is from the
LORD.[z]

17 Better a dry crust with peace and quiet
than a house full of feasting,[a] with strife.[a]

2 A wise servant will rule over a
disgraceful son,
and will share the inheritance as one
of the brothers.

3 The crucible for silver and the furnace
for gold,[b]
but the LORD tests the heart.[c]

4 A wicked man listens to evil lips;
a liar pays attention to a malicious
tongue.

5 He who mocks the poor shows
contempt for their Maker;[d]
whoever gloats over disaster[e] will not
go unpunished.[f]

6 Children's children[g] are a crown to the
aged,
and parents are the pride of their
children.

7 Arrogant[b] lips are unsuited to a fool—
how much worse lying lips to a ruler!

8 A bribe is a charm to the one who gives
it;
wherever he turns, he succeeds.

9 He who covers over an offense promotes
love,[h]
but whoever repeats the matter
separates close friends.[i]

10 A rebuke impresses a man of
discernment
more than a hundred lashes a fool.

11 An evil man is bent only on rebellion;
a merciless official will be sent
against him.

12 Better to meet a bear robbed of her cubs
than a fool in his folly.

13 If a man pays back evil[j] for good,
evil will never leave his house.

16:31 [y]Pr 20:29
16:33 [z]Pr 18:18; 29:26
17:1 [a]Pr 15:16,17
17:3 [b]Pr 27:21 [c]1Ch 29:17; Ps 26:2; Jer 17:10
17:5 [d]Pr 14:31 [e]Job 31:29 [f]Ob 1:12
17:6 [g]Pr 13:22
17:9 [h]Pr 10:12 [i]Pr 16:28
17:13 [j]Ps 109:4-5; Jer 18:20

[a] *1* Hebrew *sacrifices* [b] *7* Or *Eloquent*

14 Starting a quarrel is like breaching a dam;
so drop the matter before a dispute breaks out.[k]

15 Acquitting the guilty and condemning the innocent[l]—
the LORD detests them both.[m]

16 Of what use is money in the hand of a fool,
since he has no desire to get wisdom?[n]

17 A friend loves at all times,
and a brother is born for adversity.

18 A man lacking in judgment strikes hands in pledge
and puts up security for his neighbor.[o]

19 He who loves a quarrel loves sin;
he who builds a high gate invites destruction.

20 A man of perverse heart does not prosper;
he whose tongue is deceitful falls into trouble.

21 To have a fool for a son brings grief;
there is no joy for the father of a fool.[p]

22 A cheerful heart is good medicine,
but a crushed spirit dries up the bones.[q]

23 A wicked man accepts a bribe[r] in secret
to pervert the course of justice.

24 A discerning man keeps wisdom in view,
but a fool's eyes[s] wander to the ends of the earth.

25 A foolish son brings grief to his father
and bitterness to the one who bore him.[t]

26 It is not good to punish an innocent man,[u]
or to flog officials for their integrity.

27 A man of knowledge uses words with restraint,
and a man of understanding is even-tempered.[v]

28 Even a fool is thought wise if he keeps silent,
and discerning if he holds his tongue.[w]

18 An unfriendly man pursues selfish ends;
he defies all sound judgment.

2 A fool finds no pleasure in understanding

17:14 [k]Pr 20:3
17:15 [l]Pr 18:5 [m]Ex 23:6-7; Isa 5:23
17:16 [n]Pr 23:23
17:18 [o]Pr 6:1-5; 11:15; 22:26-27
17:21 [p]Pr 10:1
17:22 [q]Ps 22:15; Pr 15:13
17:23 [r]Ex 23:8
17:24 [s]Ecc 2:14
17:25 [t]Pr 10:1
17:26 [u]Pr 18:5
17:27 [v]Pr 14:29; Jas 1:19
17:28 [w]Job 13:5

The Choice to Be Happy

PR 17:22

The adage "Happiness is a choice" could be applied here. When circumstances threaten to crush people's spirits and sink them in gloom, they need the powerful "medicine" of joy more than ever. Solomon is probably not advocating a superficial "grin and bear it" or "put on a happy face" mentality, but instead, a deep, abiding faith that all will be well for those who trust God.

Life's trials and disappointments can indeed feel crushing at times, but we need not roll over in despair. Rather, the prescription for happiness is at our fingertips. We can cultivate our faith in the profoundly good news of the One who encourages us with these words: "I have told you these things, so that in me you may have peace. In this world you will have trouble. But take heart! I have overcome the world" (Jn 16:33).

but delights in airing his own opinions.[x]

[3] When wickedness comes, so does contempt,
and with shame comes disgrace.

[4] The words of a man's mouth are deep waters,
but the fountain of wisdom is a bubbling brook.

[5] It is not good to be partial to the wicked[y]
or to deprive the innocent of justice.[z]

[6] A fool's lips bring him strife,
and his mouth invites a beating.

[7] A fool's mouth is his undoing,
and his lips are a snare[a] to his soul.[b]

[8] The words of a gossip are like choice morsels;
they go down to a man's inmost parts.[c]

[9] One who is slack in his work
is brother to one who destroys.[d]

[10] The name of the LORD is a strong tower;[e]
the righteous run to it and are safe.

[11] The wealth of the rich is their fortified city;[f]
they imagine it an unscalable wall.

[12] Before his downfall a man's heart is proud,
but humility comes before honor.[g]

[13] He who answers before listening—
that is his folly and his shame.[h]

[14] A man's spirit sustains him in sickness,
but a crushed spirit who can bear?[i]

[15] The heart of the discerning acquires knowledge;[j]
the ears of the wise seek it out.

[16] A gift[k] opens the way for the giver
and ushers him into the presence of the great.

[17] The first to present his case seems right,
till another comes forward and questions him.

[18] Casting the lot settles disputes[l]
and keeps strong opponents apart.

[19] An offended brother is more unyielding than a fortified city,
and disputes are like the barred gates of a citadel.

[20] From the fruit of his mouth a man's stomach is filled;

18:2 [x]Pr 12:23
18:5 [y]Lev 19:15; Pr 24:23-25; 28:21 [z]Ps 82:2; Pr 17:15
18:7 [a]Ps 140:9 [b]Ps 64:8; Pr 10:14; 12:13; 13:3; Ecc 10:12
18:8 [c]Pr 26:22
18:9 [d]Pr 28:24
18:10 [e]2Sa 22:3; Ps 61:3
18:11 [f]Pr 10:15
18:12 [g]Pr 11:2; 15:33; 16:18
18:13 [h]Pr 20:25; Jn 7:51
18:14 [i]Pr 15:13; 17:22
18:15 [j]Pr 15:14
18:16 [k]Ge 32:20
18:18 [l]Pr 16:33

An atheist's most embarrassing moment is when he feels profoundly thankful for something, but can't think of anybody to thank for it.

—Mary Ann Vincent (1819-1887)

18:20 [m]Pr 12:14

with the harvest from his lips he is
satisfied.[m]

18:21 [n]Pr 13:2-3; Mt 12:37

21 The tongue has the power of life and
death,
and those who love it will eat its
fruit.[n]

18:22 [o]Pr 12:4 [p]Pr 19:14; 31:10

22 He who finds a wife finds what is good[o]
and receives favor from the LORD.[p]

23 A poor man pleads for mercy,
but a rich man answers harshly.

18:24 [q]Pr 17:17; Jn 15:13-15

24 A man of many companions may come
to ruin,
but there is a friend who sticks closer
than a brother.[q]

19:1 [r]Pr 28:6

19 Better a poor man whose walk is blameless
than a fool whose lips are perverse.[r]

19:2 [s]Pr 29:20

2 It is not good to have zeal without
knowledge,
nor to be hasty and miss the way.[s]

3 A man's own folly ruins his life,
yet his heart rages against the LORD.

19:4 [t]Pr 14:20

4 Wealth brings many friends,
but a poor man's friend deserts him.[t]

19:5 [u]Ex 23:1 [v]Dt 19:19; Pr 21:28

5 A false witness[u] will not go unpunished,
and he who pours out lies will not go
free.[v]

19:6 [w]Pr 29:26 [x]Pr 17:8; 18:16

6 Many curry favor with a ruler,[w]
and everyone is the friend of a man
who gives gifts.[x]

19:7 [y]ver 4; Ps 38:11

7 A poor man is shunned by all his
relatives—
how much more do his friends avoid
him!
Though he pursues them with pleading,
they are nowhere to be found.[a][y]

19:8 [z]Pr 16:20

8 He who gets wisdom loves his own
soul;
he who cherishes understanding
prospers.[z]

19:9 [a]ver 5

9 A false witness will not go unpunished,
and he who pours out lies will
perish.[a]

19:10 [b]Pr 26:1 [c]Pr 30:21-23; Ecc 10:5-7

10 It is not fitting for a fool[b] to live in
luxury—
how much worse for a slave to rule
over princes![c]

19:11 [d]Pr 16:32

11 A man's wisdom gives him patience;[d]
it is to his glory to overlook an
offense.

19:12 [e]Ps 133:3 [f]Pr 16:14-15

12 A king's rage is like the roar of a lion,
but his favor is like dew[e] on the grass.[f]

[a] 7 The meaning of the Hebrew for this sentence is uncertain.

Godly Wives

PR 18:22

This promise is nearly identical to the one in Proverbs 8:35, where God's favor is connected with finding the ultimate prize of wisdom. Here is one more example of how highly God views women—and godly wives in particular. A good wife is not happened on by chance, nor is she a man's due; rather, she is a gift from God (Ge 2:21–24; Pr 19:14). The apostle Paul calls the spiritual union between husband and wife a profound mystery, comparing it to Jesus Christ's relationship with the church (Eph 5:31–32). Clearly, the husband-wife relationship is a holy thing—a mystery blessed by God that transcends cultural mores and ever-changing roles.

Maybe I'm just a cockeyed optimist, but I think life is to be experienced joyfully rather than endured grudgingly. We know it brings complexities and trouble. Scripture affirms that. But why do we take minor irritations so seriously? Why do we act as though it's the end of the world? Think of the pain and conflict we would spare ourselves, the stress we would forego, if we just realized mere inconveniences can be survived.

This is all part of resting "content, untouched by trouble," as Proverbs 19:23 describes it. It's believing when you trust God, regardless of the circumstances, you have life [and happiness].

—Luci Swindoll

13 A foolish son is his father's ruin,[g]
and a quarrelsome wife is like a constant dripping.[h]

14 Houses and wealth are inherited from parents,[i]
but a prudent wife is from the LORD.[j]

15 Laziness brings on deep sleep,
and the shiftless man goes hungry.[k]

16 He who obeys instructions guards his life,
but he who is contemptuous of his ways will die.[l]

17 He who is kind to the poor lends to the LORD,
and he will reward him for what he has done.[m]

18 Discipline your son, for in that there is hope;
do not be a willing party to his death.[n]

19 A hot-tempered man must pay the penalty;
if you rescue him, you will have to do it again.

20 Listen to advice and accept instruction,[o]
and in the end you will be wise.[p]

21 Many are the plans in a man's heart,
but it is the LORD's purpose that prevails.[q]

22 What a man desires is unfailing love[a];
better to be poor than a liar.

23 The fear of the LORD leads to life:
Then one rests content, untouched by trouble.[r]

24 The sluggard buries his hand in the dish;
he will not even bring it back to his mouth![s]

25 Flog a mocker, and the simple will learn prudence;
rebuke a discerning man, and he will gain knowledge.[t]

26 He who robs his father and drives out his mother[u]
is a son who brings shame and disgrace.

27 Stop listening to instruction, my son,
and you will stray from the words of knowledge.

28 A corrupt witness mocks at justice,
and the mouth of the wicked gulps down evil.[v]

19:13 [g]Pr 10:1 [h]Pr 21:9
19:14 [i]2Co 12:14 [j]Pr 18:22
19:15 [k]Pr 6:9; 10:4
19:16 [l]Pr 16:17; Lk 10:28
19:17 [m]Mt 10:42; 2Co 9:6-8
19:18 [n]Pr 13:24; 23:13-14
19:20 [o]Pr 4:1 [p]Pr 12:15
19:21 [q]Ps 33:11; Pr 16:9; Isa 14:24,27
19:23 [r]Ps 25:13; Pr 12:21; 1Ti 4:8
19:24 [s]Pr 26:15
19:25 [t]Pr 9:9; 21:11
19:26 [u]Pr 28:24
19:28 [v]Job 15:16

[a] 22 Or *A man's greed is his shame*

19:29 [w]Pr 26:3
[29] Penalties are prepared for mockers,
and beatings for the backs of fools.[w]

20 Wine is a mocker and beer a brawler;
whoever is led astray by them is not wise.[x]

20:1 [x]Pr 31:4

20:2 [y]Pr 19:12 [z]Pr 8:36
[2] A king's wrath is like the roar of a lion;[y]
he who angers him forfeits his life.[z]

20:3 [a]Pr 17:14
[3] It is to a man's honor to avoid strife,
but every fool is quick to quarrel.[a]

[4] A sluggard does not plow in season;
so at harvest time he looks but finds nothing.

[5] The purposes of a man's heart are deep waters,
but a man of understanding draws them out.

[6] Many a man claims to have unfailing love,
but a faithful man who can find?[b]

20:6 [b]Ps 12:1

[7] The righteous man leads a blameless life;
blessed are his children after him.[c]

20:7 [c]Ps 37:25-26; 112:2

[8] When a king sits on his throne to judge,
he winnows out all evil with his eyes.[d]

20:8 [d]ver 26; Pr 25:4-5

[9] Who can say, "I have kept my heart pure;
I am clean and without sin"?[e]

20:9 [e]1Ki 8:46; Ecc 7:20; 1Jn 1:8

[10] Differing weights and differing measures—
the LORD detests them both.[f]

20:10 [f]ver 23; Pr 11:1

[11] Even a child is known by his actions,
by whether his conduct is pure[g] and right.

20:11 [g]Mt 7:16

[12] Ears that hear and eyes that see—
the LORD has made them both.[h]

20:12 [h]Ps 94:9

[13] Do not love sleep or you will grow poor;[i]
stay awake and you will have food to spare.

20:13 [i]Pr 6:11; 19:15

[14] "It's no good, it's no good!" says the buyer;
then off he goes and boasts about his purchase.

[15] Gold there is, and rubies in abundance,
but lips that speak knowledge are a rare jewel.

[16] Take the garment of one who puts up security for a stranger;
hold it in pledge[j] if he does it for a wayward woman.[k]

20:16 [j]Ex 22:26 [k]Pr 27:13

Deep Waters

PR 20:5

One of the many benefits of obtaining wisdom is the *almost uncanny ability to discern what is going on in another person's mind and heart.* God alone *can accurately judge a person's deepest motives* (Pr 16:2; 20:27; 21:2), but the closer people get to *seeing things from God's perspective, the more likely they are to be persons of deep understanding.* Those who lack wisdom not only *can't be discerning and prudent in relationships, but they also can't be of much help to others.* Spiritual *understanding, however, can be used by God to draw another person's thoughts and intentions to the surface—like water from a deep well.* By helping others discover what is deep within, the *spiritually discerning can provide a tremendous service to others, revealing hidden truths and pointing them in the right direction.*

Getting Even

PR 20:22

The drive to get even with those who have hurt us can be all-consuming. We can spend inordinate amounts of energy ruminating on old wounds, plotting payback and executing our own brand of justice. The reason such behavior is condemned in Scripture is probably threefold: (1) it derails our energy from positive to negative goals; (2) it is a foolish pursuit, because no finite human being can possibly execute perfect justice; and (3) it demonstrates a lack of faith in the God who promises to deliver us and contend with those who treat us unjustly. Rather than taking matters into our own hands, we are to "wait for the LORD" (Pr 20:22)—not in passive weakness, as a victim, but in strong faith that God will come through on our behalf (Ps 27:14; 37:34; Ro 12:19).

17 Food gained by fraud tastes sweet to a man,[l]
but he ends up with a mouth full of gravel.
18 Make plans by seeking advice;
if you wage war, obtain guidance.[m]
19 A gossip betrays a confidence;[n]
so avoid a man who talks too much.
20 If a man curses his father or mother,[o]
his lamp will be snuffed out in pitch darkness.[p]
21 An inheritance quickly gained at the beginning
will not be blessed at the end.

22 Do not say, "I'll pay you back for this wrong!"[q]
Wait for the LORD, and he will deliver you.[r]
23 The LORD detests differing weights,
and dishonest scales do not please him.[s]
24 A man's steps are directed by the LORD.
How then can anyone understand his own way?[t]
25 It is a trap for a man to dedicate something rashly
and only later to consider his vows.[u]
26 A wise king winnows out the wicked;
he drives the threshing wheel over them.[v]
27 The lamp of the LORD searches the spirit of a man[a];
it searches out his inmost being.
28 Love and faithfulness keep a king safe;
through love his throne is made secure.[w]
29 The glory of young men is their strength,
gray hair the splendor of the old.[x]
30 Blows and wounds cleanse[y] away evil,
and beatings purge the inmost being.

21 The king's heart is in the hand of the LORD;
he directs it like a watercourse wherever he pleases.
2 All a man's ways seem right to him,
but the LORD weighs the heart.[z]
3 To do what is right and just
is more acceptable to the LORD than sacrifice.[a]
4 Haughty eyes[b] and a proud heart,

20:17 [l]Pr 9:17
20:18 [m]Pr 11:14; 24:6
20:19 [n]Pr 11:13
20:20 [o]Pr 30:11 [p]Ex 21:17; Job 18:5
20:22 [q]Pr 24:29 [r]Ro 12:19
20:23 [s]ver 10
20:24 [t]Jer 10:23
20:25 [u]Ecc 5:2,4-5
20:26 [v]ver 8
20:28 [w]Pr 29:14
20:29 [x]Pr 16:31
20:30 [y]Pr 22:15
21:2 [z]Pr 16:2; 24:12; Lk 16:15
21:3 [a]1Sa 15:22; Pr 15:8; Isa 1:11; Hos 6:6; Mic 6:6-8
21:4 [b]Pr 6:17

[a] 27 Or *The spirit of man is the LORD's lamp*

the lamp of the wicked, are sin!

21:5 [c]Pr 10:4; 28:22
5 The plans of the diligent lead to profit[c]
as surely as haste leads to poverty.

6 A fortune made by a lying tongue
is a fleeting vapor and a deadly
snare.[a][d]
21:6 [d]2Pe 2:3

7 The violence of the wicked will drag
them away,
for they refuse to do what is right.

21:8 [e]Pr 2:15
8 The way of the guilty is devious,[e]
but the conduct of the innocent is
upright.

9 Better to live on a corner of the roof
than share a house with a
quarrelsome wife.[f]
21:9 [f]Pr 25:24

10 The wicked man craves evil;
his neighbor gets no mercy from him.

11 When a mocker is punished, the simple
gain wisdom;
when a wise man is instructed, he
gets knowledge.[g]
21:11 [g]Pr 19:25

12 The Righteous One[b] takes note of the
house of the wicked
and brings the wicked to ruin.[h]
21:12 [h]Pr 14:11

13 If a man shuts his ears to the cry of the
poor,
he too will cry out and not be
answered.[i]
21:13 [i]Mt 18:30-34; Jas 2:13

14 A gift given in secret soothes anger,
and a bribe concealed in the cloak
pacifies great wrath.[j]
21:14 [j]Pr 18:16; 19:6

15 When justice is done, it brings joy to the
righteous
but terror to evildoers.[k]
21:15 [k]Pr 10:29

16 A man who strays from the path of
understanding
comes to rest in the company of the
dead.[l]
21:16 [l]Ps 49:14

17 He who loves pleasure will become
poor;
whoever loves wine and oil will never
be rich.[m]
21:17 [m]Pr 23:20-21,29-35

18 The wicked become a ransom[n] for the
righteous,
and the unfaithful for the upright.
21:18 [n]Pr 11:8; Isa 43:3

19 Better to live in a desert
than with a quarrelsome and ill-
tempered wife.[o]
21:19 [o]ver 9

[a] 6 Some Hebrew manuscripts, Septuagint and Vulgate; most Hebrew manuscripts *vapor for those who seek death* [b] 12 Or *The righteous man*

A Quarrelsome Wife

PR 21:9

Anyone who is married knows that maintaining harmony and the ideal of "one-ness" 24 hours a day is impossible. But Solomon has a much greater challenge than the average person. He has not just one wife, but 700—along with 300 concubines (1Ki 11:3)! His frustration with those who are hard to get along with is palpable in Proverbs 19:13, where he compares a quarrelsome wife with "a constant dripping." While it may appear that the king is picking on women, his statements that it's better to live outside the palace or out in the desert (Pr 21:19) than amidst luxury with a contentious wife simply reflect a general truth. There's nothing worse than strife at home—no matter who creates it. Home is the place God intends for us to enjoy intimacy, safety and peace. We each have the responsibility to follow Paul's advice in Romans 12:18: "If it is possible, as far as it depends on you, live at peace with everyone."

A Good Reputation

PR 22:1

In Solomon's day, a good reputation, like wisdom, is considered more valuable than any material thing. Modern society puts much less value on a good name; but for Christians, who are to be salt and light (Mt 5:13–16), it remains crucial. Proverbs as a whole could be considered a primer for those who want to live in a way that inspires the respect and trust of those around them. While no imperfect human being can live out every piece of advice that the wise writers have to offer, the instructions for good living are nevertheless priceless.

20 In the house of the wise are stores of
choice food and oil,
but a foolish man devours all he has.

21 He who pursues righteousness and love
finds life, prosperity[a] and honor.[p]

22 A wise man attacks the city of the
mighty[q]
and pulls down the stronghold in
which they trust.

23 He who guards his mouth[r] and his
tongue
keeps himself from calamity.[s]

24 The proud and arrogant[t] man—
"Mocker" is his name;
he behaves with overweening pride.

25 The sluggard's craving will be the death
of him,[u]
because his hands refuse to work.

26 All day long he craves for more,
but the righteous give without
sparing.[v]

27 The sacrifice of the wicked is
detestable[w]—
how much more so when brought
with evil intent![x]

28 A false witness will perish,[y]
and whoever listens to him will be
destroyed forever.[b]

29 A wicked man puts up a bold front,
but an upright man gives thought to
his ways.

30 There is no wisdom,[z] no insight, no
plan
that can succeed against the LORD.[a]

31 The horse is made ready for the day of
battle,
but victory rests with the LORD.[b]

22 A good name is more desirable than
great riches;
to be esteemed is better than silver or
gold.[c]

2 Rich and poor have this in common:
The LORD is the Maker of them all.[d]

3 A prudent man sees danger and takes
refuge,[e]
but the simple keep going and suffer
for it.[f]

4 Humility and the fear of the LORD
bring wealth and honor and life.

5 In the paths of the wicked lie thorns and
snares,[g]

21:21 [p]Mt 5:6
21:22 [q]Ecc 9:15-16
21:23 [r]Jas 3:2 [s]Pr 12:13; 13:3
21:24 [t]Ps 1:1; Pr 1:22; Isa 16:6; Jer 48:29
21:25 [u]Pr 13:4
21:26 [v]Ps 37:26; Mt 5:42; Eph 4:28
21:27 [w]Isa 66:3; Jer 6:20; Am 5:22 [x]Pr 15:8
21:28 [y]Pr 19:5
21:30 [z]Jer 9:23 [a]Isa 8:10; Ac 5:39
21:31 [b]Ps 3:8; 33:12-19; Isa 31:1
22:1 [c]Ecc 7:1
22:2 [d]Job 31:15
22:3 [e]Pr 14:16 [f]Pr 27:12
22:5 [g]Pr 15:19

[a] *21* Or *righteousness* [b] *28* Or *| but the words of an obedient man will live on*

but he who guards his soul stays far
from them.

22:6 [h]Eph 6:4 — 6 Train[a] a child in the way he should go,[h]
and when he is old he will not turn
from it.

7 The rich rule over the poor,
and the borrower is servant to the
lender.

22:8 [i]Job 4:8 [j]Ps 125:3 — 8 He who sows wickedness reaps trouble,[i]
and the rod of his fury will be
destroyed.[j]

9 A generous man will himself be
22:9 [k]2Co 9:6 [l]Pr 19:17 — blessed,[k]
for he shares his food with the poor.[l]

10 Drive out the mocker, and out goes
strife;
22:10 [m]Pr 18:6; 26:20 — quarrels and insults are ended.[m]

11 He who loves a pure heart and whose
22:11 [n]Pr 16:13; Mt 5:8 — speech is gracious
will have the king for his friend.[n]

12 The eyes of the LORD keep watch over
knowledge,
but he frustrates the words of the
unfaithful.

13 The sluggard says, "There is a lion
22:13 [o]Pr 26:13 — outside!"[o]
or, "I will be murdered in the streets!"

14 The mouth of an adulteress is a deep
22:14 [p]Pr 2:16; 5:3-5; 7:5; 23:27 [q]Ecc 7:26 — pit;[p]
he who is under the LORD's wrath will
fall into it.[q]

15 Folly is bound up in the heart of a child,
but the rod of discipline will drive it
22:15 [r]Pr 13:24; 23:14 — far from him.[r]

16 He who oppresses the poor to increase
his wealth
and he who gives gifts to the rich—
both come to poverty.

Sayings of the Wise

22:17 [s]Pr 5:1 — 17 Pay attention and listen to the sayings of
the wise;[s]
apply your heart to what I teach,
18 for it is pleasing when you keep them in
your heart
and have all of them ready on your
lips.
19 So that your trust may be in the LORD,
I teach you today, even you.
20 Have I not written thirty[b] sayings for
you,
22:21 [t]Lk 1:3-4; 1Pe 3:15 — sayings of counsel and knowledge,
21 teaching you true and reliable words,[t]

[a] 6 Or *Start*
[b] 20 Or *not formerly written*; or *not written excellent*

Train a Child

PR 22:6

Like all the other proverbs, this one offers a wise principle to embrace, not a guarantee that those who follow it will get predictable results every time. No parent, regardless of dedication or skill, can control a child's every move. All individuals, children included, are given freedom by God to make choices about how they use their will. Even if parents could control a child's behavior, they could not determine the course of his or her hidden thoughts. Still, parents are given a mandate to exert strong positive influence over their children. The word train in this verse includes a Hebrew connotation of "dedicate." Parents are to throw themselves wholeheartedly into the task of raising their children. Parents can't fix or control everything and every situation involving their children. But the general principle holds true: Parents are responsible to shape their children's wills and to direct their children in God's ways so they will know the truth and be equipped to make wise choices throughout life.

A Blind Spot

PR 23:4-5

Although Solomon may not have written the proverbs in this section of the book, these verses reveal one of his blind spots. He should be wise enough to know that wealth doesn't satisfy and greed is foolish, yet that doesn't stop him from pursuing fame and luxury. He grabs all the "goodies" he can, often at the expense of his own people, whom he taxes and works excessively (1Ki 12:4). Apparently the king didn't discover until he was old and embittered by the results of his own foolish choices that "nothing was gained" by all his striving (Ecc 2:4-11).

There is nothing inherently wrong with having material wealth; it is a blessing from God. However, we are not to wear ourselves out and spend our energies foolishly in order to acquire more and more. The wise person is a generous peron who restrains greed and stores spiritual, rather than material, wealth (Lk 12:33-34).

so that you can give sound answers
to him who sent you?

22 Do not exploit the poor[u] because they are poor
and do not crush the needy in court,[v]
23 for the LORD will take up their case[w]
and will plunder those who plunder them.[x]

24 Do not make friends with a hot-tempered man,
do not associate with one easily angered,
25 or you may learn his ways
and get yourself ensnared.[y]
26 Do not be a man who strikes hands in pledge[z]
or puts up security for debts;
27 if you lack the means to pay,
your very bed will be snatched from under you.[a]

28 Do not move an ancient boundary stone[b]
set up by your forefathers.
29 Do you see a man skilled in his work?
He will serve[c] before kings;
he will not serve before obscure men.

23 When you sit to dine with a ruler,
note well what[a] is before you,
2 and put a knife to your throat
if you are given to gluttony.
3 Do not crave his delicacies,[d]
for that food is deceptive.

4 Do not wear yourself out to get rich;
have the wisdom to show restraint.
5 Cast but a glance at riches, and they are gone,
for they will surely sprout wings
and fly off to the sky like an eagle.[e]

6 Do not eat the food of a stingy man,
do not crave his delicacies;[f]
7 for he is the kind of man
who is always thinking about the cost.[b]
"Eat and drink," he says to you,
but his heart is not with you.
8 You will vomit up the little you have eaten
and will have wasted your compliments.

9 Do not speak to a fool,
for he will scorn the wisdom of your words.[g]

22:22 [u]Zec 7:10 [v]Ex 23:6; Mal 3:5
22:23 [w]Ps 12:5 [x]1Sa 25:39; Pr 23:10-11
22:25 [y]1Co 15:33
22:26 [z]Pr 11:15
22:27 [a]Pr 17:18
22:28 [b]Dt 19:14; Pr 23:10
22:29 [c]Ge 41:46
23:3 [d]ver 6-8
23:5 [e]Pr 27:24
23:6 [f]Ps 141:4
23:9 [g]Pr; 1:7; 9:7; Mt 7:6

[a] 1 Or *who* [b] 7 Or *for as he thinks within himself, / so he is;* or *for as he puts on a feast, / so he is*

10 Do not move an ancient boundary stone[h]
or encroach on the fields of the fatherless,
11 for their Defender[i] is strong;
he will take up their case against you.[j]

12 Apply your heart to instruction
and your ears to words of knowledge.

13 Do not withhold discipline from a child;
if you punish him with the rod, he will not die.
14 Punish him with the rod
and save his soul from death.[a]

15 My son, if your heart is wise,
then my heart will be glad;
16 my inmost being will rejoice
when your lips speak what is right.[k]

17 Do not let your heart envy[l] sinners,
but always be zealous for the fear of the LORD.
18 There is surely a future hope for you,
and your hope will not be cut off.[m]

19 Listen, my son, and be wise,
and keep your heart on the right path.
20 Do not join those who drink too much wine[n]
or gorge themselves on meat,
21 for drunkards and gluttons become poor,[o]
and drowsiness clothes them in rags.

22 Listen to your father, who gave you life,
and do not despise your mother when she is old.[p]
23 Buy the truth and do not sell it;
get wisdom, discipline and understanding.[q]
24 The father of a righteous man has great joy;
he who has a wise son delights in him.[r]
25 May your father and mother be glad;
may she who gave you birth rejoice!

26 My son,[s] give me your heart
and let your eyes keep to my ways,[t]
27 for a prostitute is a deep pit[u]
and a wayward wife is a narrow well.
28 Like a bandit she lies in wait,[v]
and multiplies the unfaithful among men.
29 Who has woe? Who has sorrow?
Who has strife? Who has complaints?
Who has needless bruises? Who has bloodshot eyes?
30 Those who linger over wine,[w]

23:10 [h]Dt 19:14; Pr 22:28
23:11 [i]Job 19:25 [j]Pr 22:22-23
23:16 [k]ver 24; Pr 27:11
23:17 [l]Ps 37:1; Pr 28:14
23:18 [m]Ps 9:18; Pr 24:14,19-20
23:20 [n]Isa 5:11,22; Ro 13:13; Eph 5:18
23:21 [o]Pr 21:17
23:22 [p]Lev 19:32; Pr 1:8; 30:17; Eph 6:1-2
23:23 [q]Pr 4:7
23:24 [r]ver 15-16; Pr 10:1; 15:20
23:26 [s]Pr 3:1; 5:1-6 [t]Ps 18:21; Pr 4:4
23:27 [u]Pr 22:14
23:28 [v]Pr 7:11-12; Ecc 7:26
23:30 [w]Ps 75:8; Isa 5:11; Eph 5:18

[a] 14 Hebrew *Sheol*

Honor Parents

PR 23:22

The fifth of God's Ten Commandments tells his people to honor their parents, and it is the only commandment that includes a promise of blessing (Ex 20:12). Many centuries later, the apostle Paul instructs us to heed the same commandment (Eph 6:1–3). Obviously, being respectful of our parents is very important to God. Scripture doesn't tell us to do everything our parents say; some parents' guidance is not in line with God's will and should not be followed. However, it is never appropriate to treat our parents with disregard or contempt. We don't have to agree with everything they say and do. We are only told to honor them (Mt 19:19). We can listen to them, honor them for giving us life and be kind to them throughout their old age.

A House of Wisdom

PR 24:3–4

The symbolic "house" in these verses represents the life of an individual or family. The book of Proverbs reminds readers yet again that a meaningful life and enduring legacy are not built by collecting material or intellectual property but by acquiring wisdom and understanding. The "rare and beautiful treasures" (Pr 24:4) that fill the spiritually rich soul are far more priceless than the finest jewels on earth (Pr 3:13–15; 20:15). In building a wise and worthy "house," we follow the example of our own Creator, who "founded the world by his wisdom and stretched out the heavens by his understanding" (Jer 10:12).

who go to sample bowls of mixed
wine.
31 Do not gaze at wine when it is red,
when it sparkles in the cup,
when it goes down smoothly!
32 In the end it bites like a snake
and poisons like a viper.
33 Your eyes will see strange sights
and your mind imagine confusing
things.
34 You will be like one sleeping on the
high seas,
lying on top of the rigging.
35 "They hit me," you will say, "but I'm
not hurt!
They beat me, but I don't feel it!
When will I wake up
so I can find another drink?"

24 Do not envy[x] wicked men,
do not desire their company;
2 for their hearts plot violence,
and their lips talk about making
trouble.[y]

3 By wisdom a house is built,[z]
and through understanding it is
established;
4 through knowledge its rooms are filled
with rare and beautiful treasures.[a]

5 A wise man has great power,
and a man of knowledge increases
strength;
6 for waging war you need guidance,
and for victory many advisers.[b]

7 Wisdom is too high for a fool;
in the assembly at the gate he has
nothing to say.

8 He who plots evil
will be known as a schemer.
9 The schemes of folly are sin,
and men detest a mocker.

10 If you falter in times of trouble,
how small is your strength![c]
11 Rescue those being led away to death;
hold back those staggering toward
slaughter.[d]
12 If you say, "But we knew nothing about
this,"
does not he who weighs[e] the heart
perceive it?
Does not he who guards your life know
it?
Will he not repay each person
according to what he has done?[f]

13 Eat honey, my son, for it is good;
honey from the comb is sweet to your
taste.

24:1 [x]Ps 37:1; 73:3; Pr 3:31-32; 23:17-18
24:2 [y]Ps 10:7
24:3 [z]Pr 14:1
24:4 [a]Pr 8:21
24:6 [b]Pr 11:14; 20:18; Lk 14:31
24:10 [c]Job 4:5; Jer 51:46; Heb 12:3
24:11 [d]Ps 82:4; Isa 58:6-7
24:12 [e]Pr 21:2 [f]Job 34:11; Ps 62:12; Ro 2:6*

Week 19

Construction and Interior Design

Imagine you are planning to build a new home. First you go to a good architect—one you trust to draw up a good plan. Next you find qualified builders to do the construction and artisans to finish the work. After the building is completed, you furnish it with your personal treasures to make your house your home.

Each day you are in the process of building a spiritual house. What determines your plans and influences your decisions? Is your life built on a solid foundation, or have you haphazardly thrown pieces of construction material together? It's never too late to do some remodeling.

Plan and build your house by wisdom (Pr 24:3). People have desired wisdom since the Garden of Eden (Ge 3:6). Its value is beyond comprehension (Job 28:13). What exactly is wisdom (Ps 111:10; Pr 9:10) and to whom does it belong (Job 12:13)? Where can you find wisdom (Job 28:12,23,28)?

Establish your house through understanding (Pr 24:3). What is understanding (Ps 111:10; Pr 9:10)? How valuable is it (Pr 16:16)? What will understanding cost you personally (Pr 4:7)?

Fill the rooms of your house through knowledge (Pr 24:4). What is the beginning of knowledge (Pr 1:7)? Where does knowledge come from (Pr 2:6)? What will result from a lack of knowledge (Hos 4:6)?

Build a solid foundation for your house (Mt 7:24-25). You can build a great house, but if the foundation is weak, all will be lost. Who or what is your foundation (Isa 33:5-6; 1Co 3:10-13)?

Make wisdom the basis for all that is planned, built and done in your life. Do you feel incapable of building anything of value? You can ask the master builder and architect of the universe to help you (Heb 3:4; 11:10). He has given you Jesus Christ, "in whom are hidden all the treasures of wisdom and knowledge" (Col 2:3).

Enjoying God THROUGH the Word

Read Proverbs 2:1-11 (page 1020). These verses contain a road map to wisdom. As you read, note the terminology used: *turning, applying, call, cry, look, search.* The writer's use of these particular words reveals that seeking wisdom and understanding is a choice. It is a pursuit that you resolutely select, a course you willfully undertake.

God delights in giving wisdom (1Ki 3:9-10). When you seek it, you will find it, and it "will enter your heart, and knowledge will be pleasant to your soul. Discretion will protect you, and understanding will guard you" (Pr 2:10-11). What beautiful promises!

Enjoying God THROUGH Experience

When you go to God for wisdom, discernment and understanding, he will generously give you what you desire (Jas 1:5). As you grow in wisdom, it is important that you confirm your growth by your actions (Jas 3:13). "Wisdom that comes from heaven is first of all pure; then peace-loving, considerate, submissive, full of mercy and good fruit, impartial and sincere" (Jas 3:17). That's quite an assignment. But God makes his power available to you (Eph 1:19-20), and with him all things *are* possible!

Go to page 1095 for your next weekly study.

A Kiss on the Lips

PR 24:26

Don't the words of this proverb bring a captivating picture to mind? The picture is one of the beauty of an honest answer and the charm of a kiss on the lips. A kiss is not necessarily considered a romantic act in Biblical times, but rather a sign of true friendship. Those who genuinely love others will be honest with them; their lips will speak truth for their benefit and enrichment. Judas gives the supreme twist on this sign of devotion by pretending to be an intimate friend of Jesus when he kisses him in the moment of betrayal (Mt 26:49). So the next time you get together with a true friend, give him or her the ultimate kiss on the lips—give your friend an honest answer.

14 Know also that wisdom is sweet to your
soul;
if you find it, there is a future hope
for you,
and your hope will not be cut off.[g][h]
15 Do not lie in wait like an outlaw against
a righteous man's house,
do not raid his dwelling place;
16 for though a righteous man falls seven
times, he rises again,
but the wicked are brought down by
calamity.[i]

17 Do not gloat[j] when your enemy falls;
when he stumbles, do not let your
heart rejoice,[k]
18 or the LORD will see and disapprove
and turn his wrath away from him.

19 Do not fret[l] because of evil men
or be envious of the wicked,
20 for the evil man has no future hope,
and the lamp of the wicked will be
snuffed out.[m]

21 Fear the LORD and the king,[n] my son,
and do not join with the rebellious,
22 for those two will send sudden
destruction upon them,
and who knows what calamities they
can bring?

Further Sayings of the Wise

23 These also are sayings of the wise:[o]

To show partiality[p] in judging is not
good:[q]
24 Whoever says to the guilty, "You are
innocent"[r]—
peoples will curse him and nations
denounce him.
25 But it will go well with those who
convict the guilty,
and rich blessing will come upon
them.

26 An honest answer
is like a kiss on the lips.

27 Finish your outdoor work
and get your fields ready;
after that, build your house.

28 Do not testify against your neighbor
without cause,[s]
or use your lips to deceive.
29 Do not say, "I'll do to him as he has
done to me;
I'll pay that man back for what he
did."[t]

30 I went past the field of the sluggard,[u]
past the vineyard of the man who
lacks judgment;

24:14 [g]Ps 119:103; Pr 16:24 [h]Pr 23:18
24:16 [i]Job 5:19; Ps 34:19; Mic 7:8
24:17 [j]Ob 1:12 [k]Job 31:29
24:19 [l]Ps 37:1
24:20 [m]Job 18:5; Pr 13:9; 23:17-18
24:21 [n]Ro 13:1-5; 1Pe 2:17
24:23 [o]Pr 1:6 [p]Lev 19:15 [q]Pr 28:21
24:24 [r]Pr 17:15
24:28 [s]Ps 7:4; Pr 25:18; Eph 4:25
24:29 [t]Pr 20:22; Mt 5:38-41; Ro 12:17
24:30 [u]Pr 6:6-11; 26:13-16

31 thorns had come up everywhere,
the ground was covered with weeds,
and the stone wall was in ruins.
32 I applied my heart to what I observed
and learned a lesson from what I saw:
33 A little sleep, a little slumber,
a little folding of the hands to rest[v]—
34 and poverty will come on you like a bandit
and scarcity like an armed man.[aw]

More Proverbs of Solomon

25 These are more proverbs[x] of Solomon, copied by the men of Hezekiah king of Judah:[y]

2 It is the glory of God to conceal a matter;
to search out a matter is the glory of kings.[z]

3 As the heavens are high and the earth is deep,
so the hearts of kings are unsearchable.

4 Remove the dross from the silver,
and out comes material for[b] the silversmith;
5 remove the wicked from the king's presence,[a]
and his throne will be established[b] through righteousness.[c]

6 Do not exalt yourself in the king's presence,
and do not claim a place among great men;
7 it is better for him to say to you, "Come up here,"[d]
than for him to humiliate you before a nobleman.

What you have seen with your eyes
8 do not bring[c] hastily to court,
for what will you do in the end
if your neighbor puts you to shame?[e]

9 If you argue your case with a neighbor,
do not betray another man's confidence,
10 or he who hears it may shame you
and you will never lose your bad reputation.

11 A word aptly spoken
is like apples of gold in settings of silver.[f]

12 Like an earring of gold or an ornament of fine gold

24:33 [v]Pr 6:10
24:34 [w]Pr 10:4; Ecc 10:18
25:1 [x]1Ki 4:32 [y]Pr 1:1
25:2 [z]Pr 16:10-15
25:5 [a]Pr 20:8 [b]2Sa 7:13 [c]Pr 16:12; 29:14
25:7 [d]Lk 14:7-10
25:8 [e]Mt 5:25-26
25:11 [f]ver 12; Pr 15:23

[a] 34 Or *like a vagrant / and scarcity like a beggar* [b] 4 Or *comes a vessel from* [c] 7,8 Or *nobleman / on whom you had set your eyes. / 8Do not go*

Apples of Gold

PR 25:11

Picture ripe, golden apples, polished to a luster, placed artistically in the finest sterling bowl. Or a 24-karat gold inlay of apples on an exquisite silver platter. This word picture highlights again the beauty and value of wise words spoken at the right time. The wise teachers of Proverbs don't consider it hyperbole to aim to make one's speech a work of art.

Superficial Cheer

PR 25:20

Mixing vinegar with soda produces a fizzy chemical reaction. Being effervescent and bubbly around someone who is downhearted is hardly appropriate. In fact, Solomon implies that offering superficial cheer to those in pain only exposes them to yet more pain. Taking away the coat of those in pain, those out in the cold, so to speak, only exposes them to more pain, more cold. When people are discouraged or depressed, they need to be wrapped in a coat of love and tenderness, not "comforted" with insensitive platitudes, jovial words or cheery songs. The apostle Paul exhorts us to enter into and share the burden of each other's sorrows and struggles (Ro 12:15; Gal 6:2), not pretend things are better than they are.

is a wise man's rebuke to a listening
ear.[g]
13 Like the coolness of snow at harvest time
is a trustworthy messenger to those
who send him;
he refreshes the spirit of his masters.[h]
14 Like clouds and wind without rain
is a man who boasts of gifts he does
not give.

15 Through patience a ruler can be
persuaded,[i]
and a gentle tongue can break a bone.[j]
16 If you find honey, eat just enough—
too much of it, and you will vomit.[k]
17 Seldom set foot in your neighbor's
house—
too much of you, and he will hate you.

18 Like a club or a sword or a sharp arrow
is the man who gives false testimony
against his neighbor.[l]
19 Like a bad tooth or a lame foot
is reliance on the unfaithful in times
of trouble.
20 Like one who takes away a garment on
a cold day,
or like vinegar poured on soda,
is one who sings songs to a heavy
heart.

21 If your enemy is hungry, give him food
to eat;
if he is thirsty, give him water to drink.
22 In doing this, you will heap burning
coals[m] on his head,
and the LORD will reward you.[n]
23 As a north wind brings rain,
so a sly tongue brings angry looks.

24 Better to live on a corner of the roof
than share a house with a
quarrelsome wife.[o]
25 Like cold water to a weary soul
is good news from a distant land.[p]
26 Like a muddied spring or a polluted well
is a righteous man who gives way to
the wicked.

27 It is not good to eat too much honey,[q]
nor is it honorable to seek one's own
honor.[r]
28 Like a city whose walls are broken down
is a man who lacks self-control.

26

Like snow in summer or rain[s] in harvest,
honor is not fitting for a fool.[t]
2 Like a fluttering sparrow or a darting
swallow,

25:12 [g]ver 11; Ps 141:5; Pr 13:18; 15:31
25:13 [h]Pr 10:26; 13:17
25:15 [i]Ecc 10:4 [j]Pr 15:1
25:16 [k]ver 27
25:18 [l]Ps 57:4; Pr 12:18
25:22 [m]Ps 18:8 [n]2Sa 16:12; 2Ch 28:15; Mt 5:44; Ro 12:20*
25:24 [o]Pr 21:9
25:25 [p]Pr 15:30
25:27 [q]ver 16 [r]Pr 27:2; Mt 23:12
26:1 [s]1Sa 12:17 [t]ver 8; Pr 19:10

26:2 [u]Nu 23:8; Dt 23:5

an undeserved curse does not come to
rest.[u]

26:3 [v]Ps 32:9 [w]Pr 10:13

3 A whip for the horse, a halter for the
donkey,[v]
and a rod for the backs of fools![w]

26:4 [x]ver 5; Isa 36:21

4 Do not answer a fool according to his
folly,
or you will be like him yourself.[x]

26:5 [y]ver 4; Pr 3:7

5 Answer a fool according to his folly,
or he will be wise in his own eyes.[y]

26:6 [z]Pr 10:26

6 Like cutting off one's feet or drinking
violence
is the sending of a message by the
hand of a fool.[z]

26:7 [a]ver 9

7 Like a lame man's legs that hang limp
is a proverb in the mouth of a fool.[a]

26:8 [b]ver 1

8 Like tying a stone in a sling
is the giving of honor to a fool.[b]

26:9 [c]ver 7

9 Like a thornbush in a drunkard's hand
is a proverb in the mouth of a fool.[c]

10 Like an archer who wounds at random
is he who hires a fool or any passer-by.

26:11 [d]2Pe 2:22* [e]Ex 8:15; Ps 85:8

11 As a dog returns to its vomit,[d]
so a fool repeats his folly.[e]

26:12 [f]Pr 3:7 [g]Pr 29:20

12 Do you see a man wise in his own eyes?[f]
There is more hope for a fool than for
him.[g]

26:13 [h]Pr 6:6-11; 24:30-34 [i]Pr 22:13

13 The sluggard says,[h] "There is a lion in
the road,
a fierce lion roaming the streets!"[i]

26:14 [j]Pr 6:9

14 As a door turns on its hinges,
so a sluggard turns on his bed.[j]

26:15 [k]Pr 19:24

15 The sluggard buries his hand in the dish;
he is too lazy to bring it back to his
mouth.[k]

16 The sluggard is wiser in his own eyes
than seven men who answer
discreetly.

17 Like one who seizes a dog by the ears
is a passer-by who meddles in a
quarrel not his own.

18 Like a madman shooting
firebrands or deadly arrows
19 is a man who deceives his neighbor
and says, "I was only joking!"

26:20 [l]Pr 22:10

20 Without wood a fire goes out;
without gossip a quarrel dies down.[l]

26:21 [m]Pr 14:17; 15:18

21 As charcoal to embers and as wood to
fire,
so is a quarrelsome man for kindling
strife.[m]

Fools

PR 26:3-12

There are several types of fools referred to in the book of Proverbs—from the naive or simpleminded to the shameless and contemptible. The fool referred to in these verses is one who is obtuse, insensible and even averse to truth. Such people must be controlled by force, like dumb animals. They can't be reasoned with or trusted; wisdom is useless to them, and honor is wasted on them. They are likely to be know-it-alls, high on their own list but low on everyone else's. They don't learn from their mistakes but repeat them over and over. Fools who read these verses will deny they have a problem; therefore, the wisdom here is for those who must live with a fool. In order to operate wisely in relationships, we need to know with whom we're dealing—and act accordingly.

Those Who Are Hungry

PR 27:7

Here Solomon taps the self-sufficient and the self-satisfied, those who are too full of themselves to be hungry for spiritual things. When we are clueless about our own state of need or too satiated by worldly pleasures, we miss out on the sweetness of wisdom and God's sustenance for our souls. Jesus implies the same thing when he says, "Blessed are those who hunger and thirst for righteousness, for they will be filled" (Mt 5:6). In order to maintain our appetite for spiritual things—and receive the blessing of God's rich fare—we need to resist filling ourselves up with foolish and illegitimate things.

22 The words of a gossip are like choice
morsels;
they go down to a man's inmost parts.[n]
23 Like a coating of glaze[a] over
earthenware
are fervent lips with an evil heart.
24 A malicious man disguises himself with
his lips,[o]
but in his heart he harbors deceit.[p]
25 Though his speech is charming,[q] do not
believe him,
for seven abominations fill his heart.[r]
26 His malice may be concealed by
deception,
but his wickedness will be exposed in
the assembly.
27 If a man digs a pit,[s] he will fall into it;[t]
if a man rolls a stone, it will roll back
on him.[u]
28 A lying tongue hates those it hurts,
and a flattering mouth[v] works ruin.

27 Do not boast[w] about tomorrow,
for you do not know what a day may
bring forth.[x]
2 Let another praise you, and not your
own mouth;
someone else, and not your own lips.[y]
3 Stone is heavy and sand[z] a burden,
but provocation by a fool is heavier
than both.
4 Anger is cruel and fury overwhelming,
but who can stand before jealousy?[a]
5 Better is open rebuke
than hidden love.
6 Wounds from a friend can be trusted,
but an enemy multiplies kisses.[b]
7 He who is full loathes honey,
but to the hungry even what is bitter
tastes sweet.
8 Like a bird that strays from its nest[c]
is a man who strays from his home.
9 Perfume[d] and incense bring joy to the
heart,
and the pleasantness of one's friend
springs from his earnest counsel.
10 Do not forsake your friend and the
friend of your father,
and do not go to your brother's house
when disaster[e] strikes you—
better a neighbor nearby than a
brother far away.

26:22 [n]Pr 18:8
26:24 [o]Ps 31:18 [p]Ps 41:6; Pr 10:18; 12:20
26:25 [q]Ps 28:3 [r]Jer 9:4-8
26:27 [s]Ps 7:15 [t]Est 6:13 [u]Est 2:23; 7:9; Ps 35:8; 141:10; Pr 28:10; 29:6; Isa 50:11
26:28 [v]Ps 12:3; Pr 29:5
27:1 [w]1Ki 20:11 [x]Mt 6:34; Lk 12:19-20; Jas 4:13-16
27:2 [y]Pr 25:27
27:3 [z]Job 6:3
27:4 [a]Nu 5:14
27:6 [b]Ps 141:5; Pr 28:23
27:8 [c]Isa 16:2
27:9 [d]Est 2:12; Ps 45:8
27:10 [e]Pr 17:17; 18:24

[a] *23* With a different word division of the Hebrew; Masoretic Text *of silver dross*

[11]Be wise, my son, and bring joy to my
heart;[f]
then I can answer anyone who treats
me with contempt.[g]

[12]The prudent see danger and take refuge,
but the simple keep going and suffer
for it.[h]

[13]Take the garment of one who puts up
security for a stranger;
hold it in pledge if he does it for a
wayward woman.[i]

[14]If a man loudly blesses his neighbor
early in the morning,
it will be taken as a curse.

[15]A quarrelsome wife is like
a constant dripping[j] on a rainy day;
[16]restraining her is like restraining the
wind
or grasping oil with the hand.

[17]As iron sharpens iron,
so one man sharpens another.

[18]He who tends a fig tree will eat its fruit,[k]
and he who looks after his master
will be honored.[l]

[19]As water reflects a face,
so a man's heart reflects the man.

[20]Death and Destruction[a] are never
satisfied,[m]
and neither are the eyes of man.[n]

[21]The crucible for silver and the furnace
for gold,[o]
but man is tested by the praise he
receives.

[22]Though you grind a fool in a mortar,
grinding him like grain with a pestle,
you will not remove his folly from
him.

[23]Be sure you know the condition of your
flocks,[p]
give careful attention to your herds;
[24]for riches do not endure forever,[q]
and a crown is not secure for all
generations.
[25]When the hay is removed and new
growth appears
and the grass from the hills is
gathered in,
[26]the lambs will provide you with clothing,
and the goats with the price of a field.
[27]You will have plenty of goats' milk
to feed you and your family
and to nourish your servant girls.

27:11 [f]Pr 10:1; 23:15-16 [g]Ge 24:60
27:12 [h]Pr 22:3
27:13 [i]Pr 20:16
27:15 [j]Est 1:18; Pr 19:13
27:18 [k]1Co 9:7 [l]Lk 19:12-27
27:20 [m]Pr 30:15-16; Hab 2:5 [n]Ecc 1:8; 6:7
27:21 [o]Pr 17:3
27:23 [p]Pr 12:10
27:24 [q]Pr 23:5

[a]20 Hebrew *Sheol and Abaddon*

Iron Sharpens Iron

PR 27:17

In Ecclesiastes, a treatise most ascribe to Solomon, the king in his twilight years reflects on the value of true friendship. "Two are better than one," he says, and the person who tries to forge through life alone is to be pitied (Ecc 4:9–12). Those who isolate themselves or become too self-reliant only make life harder and put themselves in danger. On top of that, they miss out on the incalculable commodity of other people's wisdom and experience. Humans are not meant to figure everything out for themselves but to put their collective heads together and help each other deal with whatever life presents. In the process of discussion and problem solving, valuable constructive criticism and differences of opinion can sometimes make the sparks fly, even among close friends. But the results of "sharpening" each other through this process are greater wisdom, better decisions and encouraging camaraderie.

Hard Hearts

PR 28:14

To fear the Lord is to humbly submit one's whole being to the loving control of God. To "harden" any part of oneself—the mind, heart or will—is to resist that sovereign control and try to go one's own way, like a horse that won't take to a bridle. In order to keep ourselves spiritually flexible and out of self-made trouble, we need to recognize resistance for what it is—rebellion—and deal with it at its root. Humility and trust are the antidotes to resistance. When we meditate on the fact that our God bought our souls at the price of his Son's life (1Co 6:20) and on the fact that he cares for us (1Pe 5:7), we can let go of our self-will and our defiant responses. The result of submitting to God is great blessing.

28

The wicked man flees[r] though no one
pursues,[s]
but the righteous are as bold as a lion.[t]

[2] When a country is rebellious, it has
many rulers,
but a man of understanding and
knowledge maintains order.

[3] A ruler[a] who oppresses the poor
is like a driving rain that leaves no
crops.

[4] Those who forsake the law praise the
wicked,
but those who keep the law resist
them.

[5] Evil men do not understand justice,
but those who seek the LORD
understand it fully.

[6] Better a poor man whose walk is
blameless
than a rich man whose ways are
perverse.[u]

[7] He who keeps the law is a discerning
son,
but a companion of gluttons disgraces
his father.[v]

[8] He who increases his wealth by
exorbitant interest[w]
amasses it for another,[x] who will be
kind to the poor.[y]

[9] If anyone turns a deaf ear to the law,
even his prayers are detestable.[z]

[10] He who leads the upright along an evil
path
will fall into his own trap,[a]
but the blameless will receive a good
inheritance.

[11] A rich man may be wise in his own eyes,
but a poor man who has discernment
sees through him.

[12] When the righteous triumph, there is
great elation;[b]
but when the wicked rise to power,
men go into hiding.[c]

[13] He who conceals his sins[d] does not
prosper,
but whoever confesses and renounces
them finds mercy.[e]

[14] Blessed is the man who always fears the
LORD,
but he who hardens his heart falls
into trouble.

[15] Like a roaring lion or a charging bear

28:1 [r]2Ki 7:7 [s]Lev 26:17; Ps 53:5 [t]Ps 138:3
28:6 [u]Pr 19:1
28:7 [v]Pr 23:19-21
28:8 [w]Ex 18:21 [x]Job 27:17; Pr 13:22 [y]Ps 112:9; Pr 14:31; Lk 14:12-14
28:9 [z]Ps 66:18; 109:7; Pr 15:8; Isa 1:13
28:10 [a]Pr 26:27
28:12 [b]2Ki 11:20 [c]Pr 11:10; 29:2
28:13 [d]Job 31:33 [e]Ps 32:1-5; 1Jn 1:9

[a] 3 Or *A poor man*

is a wicked man ruling over a helpless
people.

[16] A tyrannical ruler lacks judgment,
but he who hates ill-gotten gain will
enjoy a long life.

[17] A man tormented by the guilt of murder
will be a fugitive[f] till death;
let no one support him.

[18] He whose walk is blameless is kept safe,
but he whose ways are perverse will
suddenly fall.[g]

[19] He who works his land will have
abundant food,
but the one who chases fantasies will
have his fill of poverty.[h]

[20] A faithful man will be richly blessed,
but one eager to get rich will not go
unpunished.[i]

[21] To show partiality is not good[j]—
yet a man will do wrong for a piece of
bread.[k]

[22] A stingy man is eager to get rich
and is unaware that poverty awaits
him.[l]

[23] He who rebukes a man will in the end
gain more favor
than he who has a flattering tongue.[m]

[24] He who robs his father or mother[n]
and says, "It's not wrong"—
he is partner to him who destroys.[o]

[25] A greedy man stirs up dissension,
but he who trusts in the LORD[p] will
prosper.

[26] He who trusts in himself is a fool,[q]
but he who walks in wisdom is kept
safe.

[27] He who gives to the poor will lack
nothing,[r]
but he who closes his eyes to them
receives many curses.

[28] When the wicked rise to power, people
go into hiding;[s]
but when the wicked perish, the
righteous thrive.

29

[1] A man who remains stiff-necked after
many rebukes
will suddenly be destroyed—without
remedy.[t]

[2] When the righteous thrive, the people
rejoice;[u]
when the wicked rule, the people
groan.[v]

28:17 [f]Ge 9:6
28:18 [g]Pr 10:9
28:19 [h]Pr 12:11
28:20 [i]ver 22; Pr 10:6; 1Ti 6:9
28:21 [j]Pr 18:5 [k]Eze 13:19
28:22 [l]ver 20; Pr 23:6
28:23 [m]Pr 27:5-6
28:24 [n]Pr 19:26 [o]Pr 18:9
28:25 [p]Pr 29:25
28:26 [q]Ps 4:5; Pr 3:5
28:27 [r]Dt 15:7; 24:19; Pr 19:17; 22:9
28:28 [s]ver 12
29:1 [t]2Ch 36:16; Pr 6:15
29:2 [u]Est 8:15 [v]Pr 28:12

Keeping the Peace

PR 28:23

For those who like to "keep the peace," dishonesty can become a way of life. They're afraid to rock the boat, reluctant to tell people what they really think—especially if the truth might make someone uncomfortable or defensive. But a wise woman will commit herself to the good of others, even if that requires her to correct or rebuke someone she loves. "Tough love" in a relationship can be costly, and anger or retribution can result. But Solomon's wise principle here is that the person who is willing to love others well, no matter what the cost, will be appreciated more in the end than the friend who takes the easy route of flattery and dishonesty. "Wounds from a friend can be trusted," Solomon says in Proverbs 27:6. When our hearts are in the right place, we can "wound" someone in a way that heals and restores.

Rod of Correction

PR 29:15

Every parent knows that finding the right balance between discipline and permissiveness is a continual challenge when guiding children in the ways of wisdom and righteousness. It's easy to go overboard in laying down the law or executing punishment for misdeeds; using the "rod" of correction does not mean physically or emotionally beating children into submission. However, busy, overwhelmed or discouraged parents can be tempted to take an even "easier" route by being lax in providing guidance or by failing to be consistent with consequences. To leave children to themselves is considered by the wise teacher of Proverbs to be the antithesis of love (Pr 13:24). Such children are likely to go off track and bring disgrace to the parent who has avoided responsible parenting. While there are no guarantees that effective discipline will produce model children, a lack of it has some predictable, negative results for both child and parent.

3 A man who loves wisdom brings joy to
his father,[w]
but a companion of prostitutes
squanders his wealth.[x]
4 By justice a king gives a country
stability,[y]
but one who is greedy for bribes tears
it down.
5 Whoever flatters his neighbor
is spreading a net for his feet.
6 An evil man is snared by his own sin,[z]
but a righteous one can sing and be
glad.
7 The righteous care about justice for the
poor,[a]
but the wicked have no such concern.
8 Mockers stir up a city,
but wise men turn away anger.[b]
9 If a wise man goes to court with a fool,
the fool rages and scoffs, and there is
no peace.
10 Bloodthirsty men hate a man of integrity
and seek to kill the upright.[c]
11 A fool gives full vent to his anger,
but a wise man keeps himself under
control.[d]
12 If a ruler listens to lies,
all his officials become wicked.
13 The poor man and the oppressor have
this in common:
The LORD gives sight to the eyes of
both.[e]
14 If a king judges the poor with fairness,
his throne will always be secure.[f]
15 The rod of correction imparts wisdom,
but a child left to himself disgraces
his mother.[g]
16 When the wicked thrive, so does sin,
but the righteous will see their
downfall.[h]
17 Discipline your son, and he will give
you peace;
he will bring delight to your soul.[i]
18 Where there is no revelation, the people
cast off restraint;
but blessed is he who keeps the law.[j]
19 A servant cannot be corrected by mere
words;
though he understands, he will not
respond.
20 Do you see a man who speaks in haste?

29:3 [w]Pr 10:1 [x]Pr 5:8-10; Lk 15:11-32
29:4 [y]Pr 8:15-16
29:6 [z]Ecc 9:12
29:7 [a]Job 29:16; Ps 41:1; Pr 31:8-9
29:8 [b]Pr 11:11; 16:14
29:10 [c]1Jn 3:12
29:11 [d]Pr 12:16; 19:11
29:13 [e]Pr 22:2; Mt 5:45
29:14 [f]Ps 72:1-5; Pr 16:12
29:15 [g]Pr 10:1; 13:24; 17:21, 25
29:16 [h]Ps 37:35-36; 58:10; 91:8; 92:11
29:17 [i]ver 15; Pr 10:1
29:18 [j]Ps 1:1-2; 119:1-2; Jn 13:17

29:20 [k]Pr 26:12; Jas 1:19

There is more hope for a fool than for
him.[k]

[21] If a man pampers his servant from
youth,
he will bring grief[a] in the end.

29:22 [l]Pr 14:17; 15:18; 26:21

[22] An angry man stirs up dissension,
and a hot-tempered one commits
many sins.[l]

29:23 [m]Pr 11:2; 15:33; 16:18; Isa 66:2; Mt 23:12

[23] A man's pride brings him low,
but a man of lowly spirit gains
honor.[m]

29:24 [n]Lev 5:1

[24] The accomplice of a thief is his own
enemy;
he is put under oath and dare not
testify.[n]

29:25 [o]Pr 28:25

[25] Fear of man will prove to be a snare,
but whoever trusts in the LORD[o] is
kept safe.

29:26 [p]Pr 19:6

[26] Many seek an audience with a ruler,[p]
but it is from the LORD that man gets
justice.

29:27 [q]ver 10

[27] The righteous detest the dishonest;
the wicked detest the upright.[q]

Sayings of Agur

30 The sayings of Agur son of Jakeh—an
oracle[b]:

This man declared to Ithiel,
to Ithiel and to Ucal:[c]

[2] "I am the most ignorant of men;
I do not have a man's understanding.

30:3 [r]Pr 9:10

[3] I have not learned wisdom,
nor have I knowledge of the Holy
One.[r]

30:4 [s]Ps 24:1-2; Jn 3:13; Eph 4:7-10 [t]Ps 104:3; Isa 40:12 [u]Job 26:8; 38:8-9 [v]Ge 1:2 [w]Rev 19:12

[4] Who has gone up[s] to heaven and come
down?
Who has gathered up the wind in the
hollow[t] of his hands?
Who has wrapped up the waters[u] in his
cloak?[v]
Who has established all the ends of
the earth?
What is his name,[w] and the name of his
son?
Tell me if you know!

30:5 [x]Ps 12:6; 18:30 [y]Ge 15:1; Ps 84:11

[5] "Every word of God is flawless;[x]
he is a shield[y] to those who take
refuge in him.

30:6 [z]Dt 4:2; 12:32; Rev 22:18

[6] Do not add[z] to his words,
or he will rebuke you and prove you a
liar.

[a] *21* The meaning of the Hebrew for this word is uncertain.
[b] *1* Or *Jakeh of Massa* [c] *1* Masoretic Text; with a different word division of the Hebrew *declared, "I am weary, O God; / I am weary, O God, and faint.*

Anger PR 29:22

Sometimes anger is an appropriate response to injustice and sin, but when anger is unchecked or misdirected, it can cause great destruction. Jesus goes so far as to say that unresolved anger and resentment are no less serious than murder (Mt 5:21–22)! Stewing over resentments takes people's focus off God and sets them on a course toward evil (Ps 37:8–9). Venting frustration, whether through silent, seething rage or explosive temper tantrums injects the whole situation with negative tension. There certainly are much more productive ways to expend one's energy! Consider the advice in Hebrews 10:24 and come up with some specific ways you could invest your energy more positively in the lives of those around you.

Agur's Prayer

PR 30:7-9

This prayer, offered by the wise man Agur, is one we all could use daily to keep our focus on God and our priorities in balance. How many of us pray with such humility and surrender . . . "God, don't give me any more or less than I need, for I know my own frailty of character: I'm likely to be self-satisfied with excess and self-seeking with lack. Therefore, give me only what you know I need in order to love and serve you well." Such a posture in prayer requires trust in the goodness and generosity of God and will, without a doubt, be honored and rewarded by him (Mt 7:9–11; Jas 4:10).

7 "Two things I ask of you, O LORD;
do not refuse me before I die:
8 Keep falsehood and lies far from me;
give me neither poverty nor riches,
but give me only my daily bread.[a]
9 Otherwise, I may have too much and
disown[b] you
and say, 'Who is the LORD?'[c]
Or I may become poor and steal,
and so dishonor the name of my God.[d]

10 "Do not slander a servant to his master,
or he will curse you, and you will pay
for it.

11 "There are those who curse their fathers
and do not bless their mothers;[e]
12 those who are pure in their own eyes[f]
and yet are not cleansed of their filth;[g]
13 those whose eyes are ever so haughty,[h]
whose glances are so disdainful;
14 those whose teeth[i] are swords
and whose jaws are set with knives[j]
to devour[k] the poor[l] from the earth,
the needy from among mankind.[m]

15 "The leech has two daughters.
'Give! Give!' they cry.

"There are three things that are never
satisfied,[n]
four that never say, 'Enough!':
16 the grave,[a][o] the barren womb,
land, which is never satisfied with
water,
and fire, which never says, 'Enough!'

17 "The eye that mocks[p] a father,
that scorns obedience to a mother,
will be pecked out by the ravens of the
valley,
will be eaten by the vultures.[q]

18 "There are three things that are too
amazing for me,
four that I do not understand:
19 the way of an eagle in the sky,
the way of a snake on a rock,
the way of a ship on the high seas,
and the way of a man with a maiden.

20 "This is the way of an adulteress:
She eats and wipes her mouth
and says, 'I've done nothing wrong.'[r]

21 "Under three things the earth trembles,
under four it cannot bear up:
22 a servant who becomes king,[s]
a fool who is full of food,
23 an unloved woman who is married,
and a maidservant who displaces her
mistress.

30:8 [a]Mt 6:11
30:9 [b]Jos 24:27; Isa 1:4; 59:13 [c]Dt 6:12; 8:10-14; Hos 13:6 [d]Dt 8:12
30:11 [e]Pr 20:20
30:12 [f]Pr 16:2; Lk 18:11 [g]Jer 2:23,35
30:13 [h]2Sa 22:28; Job 41:34; Ps 131:1; Pr 6:17
30:14 [i]Job 4:11; 29:17; Ps 3:7 [j]Ps 57:4 [k]Job 24:9; Ps 14:4 [l]Am 8:4; Mic 2:2 [m]Job 19:22
30:15 [n]Pr 27:20
30:16 [o]Pr 27:20; Isa 5:14; 14:9,11; Hab 2:5
30:17 [p]Dt 21:18-21; Pr 23:22 [q]Job 15:23
30:20 [r]Pr 5:6
30:22 [s]Pr 19:10; 29:2

[a] 16 Hebrew *Sheol*

24 "Four things on earth are small,
yet they are extremely wise:
25 Ants are creatures of little strength,
yet they store up their food in the summer;[t]
26 coneys[a][u] are creatures of little power,
yet they make their home in the crags;
27 locusts[v] have no king,
yet they advance together in ranks;
28 a lizard can be caught with the hand,
yet it is found in kings' palaces.

29 "There are three things that are stately in their stride,
four that move with stately bearing:
30 a lion, mighty among beasts,
who retreats before nothing;
31 a strutting rooster, a he-goat,
and a king with his army around him.[b]

32 "If you have played the fool and exalted yourself,
or if you have planned evil,
clap your hand over your mouth![w]
33 For as churning the milk produces butter,
and as twisting the nose produces blood,
so stirring up anger produces strife."

30:25 [t]Pr 6:6-8
30:26 [u]Ps 104:18
30:27 [v]Ex 10:4
30:32 [w]Job 21:5; 29:9

Sayings of King Lemuel

31 The sayings[x] of King Lemuel—an oracle[c] his mother taught him:

2 "O my son, O son of my womb,
O son of my vows,[d][y]
3 do not spend your strength on women,
your vigor on those who ruin kings.[z]

4 "It is not for kings, O Lemuel—
not for kings to drink wine,[a]
not for rulers to crave beer,
5 lest they drink[b] and forget what the law decrees,[c]
and deprive all the oppressed of their rights.
6 Give beer to those who are perishing,
wine[d] to those who are in anguish;
7 let them drink[e] and forget their poverty
and remember their misery no more.

8 "Speak[f] up for those who cannot speak for themselves,
for the rights of all who are destitute.
9 Speak up and judge fairly;
defend the rights of the poor and needy."[g]

31:1 [x]Pr 22:17
31:2 [y]Jdg 11:30; Isa 49:15
31:3 [z]Dt 17:17; 1Ki 11:3; Ne 13:26; Pr 5:1-14
31:4 [a]Pr 20:1; Ecc 10:16-17; Isa 5:22
31:5 [b]1Ki 16:9 [c]Pr 16:12; Hos 4:11
31:6 [d]Ge 14:18
31:7 [e]Est 1:10
31:8 [f]1Sa 19:4; Job 29:12-17
31:9 [g]Lev 19:15; Dt 1:16; Pr 24:23; 29:7; Isa 1:17; Jer 22:16

[a] *26* That is, the hyrax or rock badger [b] *31* Or *king secure against revolt* [c] *1* Or *of Lemuel king of Massa, which* [d] *2* Or */ the answer to my prayers*

Sometimes life's heartaches and disappointments look like cannonballs—heading straight toward us . . . Every week I talk with people who are battling the heavy artillery of life. Depression, oppression, loneliness, barrenness. In fact, I have recorded over forty "Woes of Hurting Women" . . .

When we see a clown being shot out of a cannon at the circus, we laugh because we know it's not reality. When we're the ones being shot out or shot at, however, it's no laughing matter. It can be thanksgiving matter, though. Not about what's happening to us, but for who protects us in the line of fire. When we take refuge in God, he promises us peace beyond human comprehension. Every situation is included. So don't be afraid, There's no battle too fierce for God.

—Thelma Wells

Wife of Noble Character

PR 31:10-31

If we read this detailed description of the ideal wife and mother as the point-by-point standard God expects us to live up to, we're bound to feel overwhelmed and exhausted before we even begin! The intention of this epilogue to the book of Proverbs wasn't to give women an impossible to-do list, but to spread out before them the many opportunities they have to use their gifts, talents and wisdom in fulfilling and productive ways. Rather than limiting women's roles, they are expanded endlessly. As women we are created to have a positive and profound impact on everyone around us—whether it be our husbands, children, parents, friends, clients, customers or society in general. Being a woman is a blessing, and being a wise, strong and dignified woman blesses others in ways that can't be calculated. (See character sketch for the Wife of Noble Character on page 1412.)

Epilogue: The Wife of Noble Character

10[a] A wife of noble character[h] who can find?[i]
She is worth far more than rubies.
11 Her husband[j] has full confidence in her
and lacks nothing of value.[k]
12 She brings him good, not harm,
all the days of her life.
13 She selects wool and flax
and works with eager hands.[l]
14 She is like the merchant ships,
bringing her food from afar.
15 She gets up while it is still dark;
she provides food for her family
and portions for her servant girls.
16 She considers a field and buys it;
out of her earnings she plants a vineyard.
17 She sets about her work vigorously;
her arms are strong for her tasks.
18 She sees that her trading is profitable,
and her lamp does not go out at night.
19 In her hand she holds the distaff
and grasps the spindle with her fingers.
20 She opens her arms to the poor
and extends her hands to the needy.[m]
21 When it snows, she has no fear for her household;
for all of them are clothed in scarlet.
22 She makes coverings for her bed;
she is clothed in fine linen and purple.
23 Her husband is respected at the city gate,
where he takes his seat among the elders[n] of the land.
24 She makes linen garments and sells them,
and supplies the merchants with sashes.
25 She is clothed with strength and dignity;
she can laugh at the days to come.
26 She speaks with wisdom,
and faithful instruction is on her tongue.[o]
27 She watches over the affairs of her household
and does not eat the bread of idleness.
28 Her children arise and call her blessed;
her husband also, and he praises her:
29 "Many women do noble things,
but you surpass them all."
30 Charm is deceptive, and beauty is fleeting;
but a woman who fears the LORD is to be praised.
31 Give her the reward she has earned,
and let her works bring her praise[p] at the city gate.

31:10 [h]Ru 3:11; Pr 12:4; 18:22 [i]Pr 8:35; 19:14
31:11 [j]Ge 2:18 [k]Pr 12:4
31:13 [l]1Ti 2:9-10
31:20 [m]Dt 15:11; Eph 4:28; Heb 13:16
31:23 [n]Ex 3:16; Ru 4:1,11; Pr 12:4
31:26 [o]Pr 10:31
31:31 [p]Pr 11:16

[a] *10* Verses 10–31 are an acrostic, each verse beginning with a successive letter of the Hebrew alphabet.

Ecclesiastes

Life is meaningless without God.

Examining life from every possible angle and searching through every earthly option to find significance, the Teacher of Ecclesiastes comes up empty, finding only bitterness, futility and meaninglessness. However, when the Teacher changes his focus and centers his energies on pursuing a relationship with God, life takes on new meaning and purpose.

Ecclesiastes explores the spiritual significance of life, revealing the folly of searching for knowledge, wisdom and pleasure without acknowledging God's timing and involvement in everything (Ecc 1–3). We discover the loneliness of the workaholic who places possessions, status or power before God and others (Ecc 4–6). We are transformed as we embrace the practicalities of godly wisdom (Ecc 7). The Teacher's admonition that death comes to all shakes us out of our lethargy (Ecc 9–10) and stirs us to seek God early in life (Ecc 11–12).

The book of Ecclesiastes resounds with the message that life is not a puzzle to be solved. It reminds us to view life as God's good gift to us, rather than to bog down in the analysis of life and our situations and circumstances. God wants us to enjoy life and to find purpose and meaning in it. But the only way he can accomplish his purpose is when we allow him to fill the emptiness of our searching hearts with himself.

Quick Study

Author
Possibly Solomon wrote this book late in his life, or perhaps another unknown "teacher."

Date Written
Authorship by Solomon dictates a date of the tenth century B.C. If an unknown teacher wrote it, a later date is likely.

Setting
Israel.

Key Passage
Ecclesiastes 12:1
"Remember your Creator
in the days of your
youth,
before the days of
trouble come
and the years approach
when you will say,
'I find no pleasure in
them.' "

Outline

No happiness in possessions.
Ecc 1:1-11

Everything is meaningless.
Ecc 1:1–2:26

A time for everything.
Ecc 3:1-22

The bad and the good of life.
Ecc 4:1–8:17

Wisdom's way.
Ecc 9:1–11:6

Remembering God while young.
Ecc 11:7–12:14

The Women of Ecclesiastes

Women singers	*A king's possession.* Ecc 2:8
A deceitful woman	*A man's downfall.* Ecc 7:26

Everything Is Meaningless

1 The words of the Teacher,[a][a] son of David, king
in Jerusalem:[b]

2 "Meaningless! Meaningless!"
says the Teacher.
"Utterly meaningless!
Everything is meaningless."[c]

3 What does man gain from all his labor
at which he toils under the sun?[d]
4 Generations come and generations go,
but the earth remains forever.[e]
5 The sun rises and the sun sets,
and hurries back to where it rises.[f]
6 The wind blows to the south
and turns to the north;
round and round it goes,
ever returning on its course.
7 All streams flow into the sea,
yet the sea is never full.
To the place the streams come from,
there they return again.[g]
8 All things are wearisome,
more than one can say.
The eye never has enough of seeing,[h]
nor the ear its fill of hearing.
9 What has been will be again,
what has been done will be done
again;[i]
there is nothing new under the sun.
10 Is there anything of which one can say,
"Look! This is something new"?
It was here already, long ago;
it was here before our time.
11 There is no remembrance of men of old,
and even those who are yet to come
will not be remembered
by those who follow.[j]

Wisdom Is Meaningless

12 I, the Teacher,[k] was king over Israel in Jerusalem. 13 I devoted myself to study and to explore
by wisdom all that is done under heaven. What
a heavy burden God has laid on men![l] 14 I have
seen all the things that are done under the sun;
all of them are meaningless, a chasing after the
wind.[m]

15 What is twisted cannot be straightened;[n]
what is lacking cannot be counted.

16 I thought to myself, "Look, I have grown and
increased in wisdom more than anyone who has
ruled over Jerusalem before me;[o] I have experienced much of wisdom and knowledge." 17 Then I
applied myself to the understanding of wisdom,[p]
and also of madness and folly,[q] but I learned that
this, too, is a chasing after the wind.

1:1 [a]ver 12; Ecc 7:27; 12:10 [b]Pr 1:1
1:2 [c]Ps 39:5-6; 62:9; 144:4; Ecc 12:8; Ro 8:20-21
1:3 [d]Ecc 2:11,22; 3:9; 5:15-16
1:4 [e]Ps 104:5; 119:90
1:5 [f]Ps 19:5-6
1:7 [g]Job 36:28
1:8 [h]Pr 27:20
1:9 [i]Ecc 2:12; 3:15
1:11 [j]Ecc 2:16
1:12 [k]ver 1
1:13 [l]Ge 3:17; Ecc 3:10
1:14 [m]Ecc 2:11,17
1:15 [n]Ecc 7:13
1:16 [o]1Ki 3:12; 4:30; Ecc 2:9
1:17 [p]Ecc 7:23 [q]Ecc 2:3,12; 7:25

Meaningless

ECC 1:2

Does the Teacher actually mean what he says? Why would a book in the Bible—the Book by the Creator of life—declare repeatedly that life is meaningless? As you make your way through Ecclesiastes, you will see the word *meaningless* repeated about 30 times. The word speaks of things being empty, transitory, unsatisfying. The writer refers to one thing after another as having no meaning. How does this depressing view of things fit in with the rest of Scripture? We are called to praise, thanksgiving and joy (Ps 100). Paul says in 1 Timothy 6:17 that God richly supplies us with "everything for our enjoyment." Here in Ecclesiastes the mood is very different. To solve the puzzle, look for another repeated phrase: "under the sun" (Ecc 1:3, 9,14; 2:11,17,18,19,20,22; 3:16; 4:1,3,7,15; 5:13; 6:1,12; 8:9,15, 17; 9:3,6,9,11,13; 10:5). The Teacher is on a quest to understand what makes life worth living. Feel what he feels and be alert for the answer he finally gives.

[a] *1* Or *leader of the assembly*; also in verses 2 and 12

18 For with much wisdom comes much
sorrow;
the more knowledge, the more grief.[r]

Pleasures Are Meaningless

2 I thought in my heart, "Come now, I will test
you with pleasure[s] to find out what is good."
But that also proved to be meaningless. 2 "Laughter,"[t] I said, "is foolish. And what does pleasure
accomplish?" 3 I tried cheering myself with wine,[u]
and embracing folly[v]—my mind still guiding me
with wisdom. I wanted to see what was worthwhile for men to do under heaven during the few
days of their lives.
4 I undertook great projects: I built houses for
myself[w] and planted vineyards.[x] 5 I made gardens
and parks and planted all kinds of fruit trees in
them. 6 I made reservoirs to water groves of flourishing trees. 7 I bought male and female slaves and
had other slaves who were born in my house. I also
owned more herds and flocks than anyone in
Jerusalem before me. 8 I amassed silver and gold[y]
for myself, and the treasure of kings and provinces.
I acquired men and women singers,[z] and a harem[a]
as well—the delights of the heart of man. 9 I became
greater by far than anyone in Jerusalem before me.[a]
In all this my wisdom stayed with me.

10 I denied myself nothing my eyes
desired;
I refused my heart no pleasure.
My heart took delight in all my work,
and this was the reward for all my
labor.
11 Yet when I surveyed all that my hands
had done
and what I had toiled to achieve,
everything was meaningless, a chasing
after the wind;[b]
nothing was gained under the sun.[c]

Wisdom and Folly Are Meaningless

12 Then I turned my thoughts to consider
wisdom,
and also madness and folly.[d]
What more can the king's successor do
than what has already been done?[e]
13 I saw that wisdom[f] is better than folly,[g]
just as light is better than darkness.
14 The wise man has eyes in his head,
while the fool walks in the darkness;
but I came to realize
that the same fate overtakes them
both.[h]
15 Then I thought in my heart,

"The fate of the fool will overtake me
also.
What then do I gain by being wise?"[i]

1:18 [r]Ecc 2:23; 12:12
2:1 [s]Ecc 7:4; 8:15; Lk 12:19
2:2 [t]Pr 14:13; Ecc 7:6
2:3 [u]ver 24-25; Ecc 3:12-13 [v]Ecc 1:17
2:4 [w]1Ki 7:1-12 [x]SS 8:11
2:8 [y]1Ki 9:28; 10:10,14,21 [z]2Sa 19:35
2:9 [a]1Ch 29:25; Ecc 1:16
2:11 [b]Ecc 1:14 [c]Ecc 1:3
2:12 [d]Ecc 1:17 [e]Ecc 1:9; 7:25
2:13 [f]Ecc 7:19; 9:18 [g]Ecc 7:11-12
2:14 [h]Ps 49:10; Pr 17:24; Ecc 3:19; 6:6; 7:2; 9:3, 11-12
2:15 [i]Ecc 6:8

[a] 8 The meaning of the Hebrew for this phrase is uncertain.

Under the Sun

ECC 2:4-11

Time and money. Opportunity and ability. We never seem to have enough of these things. It's easy to believe that if we did, we could accomplish all the things we long to accomplish and life would be satisfying. The Teacher has everything a person needs for success, and he becomes one of the greatest, wisest, richest men who ever lived. Yet look at his response in Ecclesiastes 2:11 to all he managed to do: "Everything was meaningless, a chasing after the wind; nothing was gained under the sun." His conclusion that experiences and accomplishments will not satisfy forces us to examine our own lives. Is there anything under the sun that can fill our hearts? Or do we have to look beyond this life for answers? Is "the Teacher" King Solomon? Read the story of King Solomon's life found in 1 Kings, especially chapters 3–11, and note the similarities between the Teacher and King Solomon.

The Queen of Sheba

The Fame of the Lord

The queen of Sheba was not one to sit around and rest on her laurels. She was a mover and a shaker—a ruling monarch of a prosperous nation. She made it her business to keep tabs on what was happening around her, and she had heard about Solomon's wisdom and his relationship to God.

She was the queen. She could have sent an ambassador to Solomon for an eyewitness report. Instead, she went to Jerusalem herself, to see and hear firsthand. It was not an easy journey—probably around 1000 miles—with a great caravan on camelback. There were no motels, no indoor plumbing, no air conditioning. But people were traveling to Jerusalem to witness the wonders of God. She had to be one of them.

The queen arrived during the zenith of Solomon's reign. He had amassed great wealth and had surrounded himself with astounding beauty. The visiting queen was overwhelmed by his wealth and even more by the presence of God in his court. Solomon went to his God with childlike trust. This was something new in her experience of gods. Solomon's officials lived like family, in peace and order under Solomon's tutelage. This queen understood what few pagans did—that the Lord was responsible for Solomon's rise to power and that the Lord loved Jerusalem.

The queen of Sheba was Solomon's female counterpart, for she valued God's wisdom above all else. "She came to Solomon and talked with him about all that she had on her mind" (1Ki 10:2). Solomon answered her questions. He freely shared his wisdom, his inventions, and most important, his love for God. He gave her everything she asked for—and more.

Centuries later, Jesus commended her for her passion for truth: "The Queen of the South will rise at the judgment with this generation and condemn it; for she came from the ends of the earth to listen to Solomon's wisdom, and now one greater than Solomon is here" (Mt 12:42). The queen longed for wisdom, and the Lord gave her wealth, honor and fame as well—including a place in his Word.

People came to Jerusalem to see Solomon and his riches and wisdom and found the Lord. The Lord dwells with his people. Today, Christ lives in his people. Others will judge Jesus by the way that *we* live. If they like what they see, they will want it for themselves.

Queen of Sheba

1 Kings 10:1-13

2 Chronicles 9:1-12

Matthew 12:42

Candid SNAPSHOT She said to the king, "The report I heard in my own country about your achievements and your wisdom is true. But I did not believe what they said until I came and saw with my own eyes. Indeed, not even half the greatness of your wisdom was told me; you have far exceeded the report I heard" (2 Chronicles 9:5-6).

Jezebel

Bent on Evil

Jezebel ordered her own life and destiny—or so she thought. But her final destination leaves little to envy: cursed by a prophet, thrown from a palace window, trampled by horses and eaten by dogs (2Ki 9:35-36). There was nothing left to bury but her skull, her feet and her hands. Power is not always worth its cost!

Jezebel's life began in Sidon, a city on the Mediterranean coast known for its vice and idolatry. Idolatry was in her blood and well entrenched in her lifestyle when she married Ahab, the king of Israel. Ahab totally disregarded the law when he married such a woman, and he began to worship Baal. Jezebel quickly promoted Baal worship throughout Israel, convincing Ahab to build a temple to Baal even in Samaria, the capital of his kingdom. She and Ahab made an evil duo.

Jezebel had no morals or goals, apart from getting what she wanted. She worshiped the wrong gods, had the wrong priorities and used any method she needed to get her own way. She lived for power. And she always had another evil scheme in her heart.

Jezebel massacred the prophets of the Lord who opposed her. She threatened to kill Elijah in revenge for his victory on Mount Carmel. But the Lord always balances the scales of justice though evil may triumph for a season.

After the deaths of her husband and of both her sons, Jehu came to confront her in Jezreel. Jezebel painted her face and did her hair as if she were going to a party to dazzle her guests. She meant to taunt Jehu with bitter sarcasm, but her own servants rebelled and threw her out the window (2Ki 9:32-33). For such an intelligent woman, Jezebel hadn't a clue what people really thought of her.

Certainly no Christian woman could be as bent on evil as Jezebel. But we all know women who think they need to control others. Things must be done the way they think is best, and they can make others miserable in accomplishing this. Perhaps it's a mother who runs her daughter's wedding. Perhaps it's someone on a committee at church or someone you work with. Maybe—yes, it's possible—you and I are among these controlling women. Whether motivated by stress, frustration, fear or hurt, we can make life miserable for those around us. How much better for us and for others if we relax and trust the God of heaven with our needs. We will likely find, quite remarkably, that things go okay even if they don't go the way we think they should, and we might even enjoy life. If we give up trying to control, the Lord may take us to destinations better than we could ever devise on our own.

Jezebel
(unexalted, unhusbanded)

1 Kings 16:31; 18:4-19; 19:1-2; 21:5-25

2 Kings 9

Candid SNAPSHOT There was never a man like Ahab, who sold himself to do evil in the eyes of the LORD, urged on by Jezebel his wife (1 Kings 21:25).

I said in my heart,
"This too is meaningless."
16 For the wise man, like the fool, will not
be long remembered;
2:16
in days to come both will be
[j]Ecc 1:11; 9:5
forgotten.[j]
Like the fool, the wise man too must
die!

Toil Is Meaningless

17 So I hated life, because the work that is done
2:17
under the sun was grievous to me. All of it is
[k]Ecc 4:2
meaningless, a chasing after the wind.[k] 18 I hated
all the things I had toiled for under the sun,
2:18
because I must leave them to the one who comes
[l]Ps 39:6;
after me.[l] 19 And who knows whether he will be a
49:10
wise man or a fool? Yet he will have control over
all the work into which I have poured my effort
and skill under the sun. This too is meaningless.
20 So my heart began to despair over all my toilsome labor under the sun. 21 For a man may do his
work with wisdom, knowledge and skill, and
then he must leave all he owns to someone who
has not worked for it. This too is meaningless and
a great misfortune. 22 What does a man get for all
2:22
the toil and anxious striving with which he labors
[m]Ecc 1:3; 3:9
under the sun?[m] 23 All his days his work is pain
2:23
and grief;[n] even at night his mind does not rest.
[n]Job 5:7;
This too is meaningless.
14:1;
24 A man can do nothing better than to eat and
Ecc 1:18
drink[o] and find satisfaction in his work.[p] This too,
2:24
I see, is from the hand of God,[q] 25 for without him,
[o]Ecc 8:15;
who can eat or find enjoyment? 26 To the man who
1Co 15:32
pleases him, God gives wisdom, knowledge and
[p]Ecc 3:22
[q]Ecc 3:12-13;
happiness, but to the sinner he gives the task of
5:17-19; 9:7-
gathering and storing up wealth[r] to hand it over to
10
the one who pleases God.[s] This too is meaning-
2:26
less, a chasing after the wind.
[r]Job 27:17
[s]Pr 13:22

A Time for Everything

3:1
[t]ver 11,17;
Ecc 8:6

3 There is a time[t] for everything,
and a season for every activity under
heaven:

2 a time to be born and a time to die,
a time to plant and a time to uproot,
3 a time to kill and a time to heal,
a time to tear down and a time to
build,
4 a time to weep and a time to laugh,
a time to mourn and a time to dance,
5 a time to scatter stones and a time to
gather them,
a time to embrace and a time to
refrain,
6 a time to search and a time to give up,
a time to keep and a time to throw
away,
7 a time to tear and a time to mend,
3:7
[u]Am 5:13
a time to be silent[u] and a time to
speak,

Enjoy Life

ECC 2:24

This is one of the first positive conclusions in a book that often seems to be a litany of all the things that don't satisfy the heart. The Teacher will repeat this resolution—that life is to be enjoyed—a number of other times (Ecc 3:12-13,22; 5:19; 8:15; 9:7-9). Scripture states clearly that contentment is the key to a satisfying and godly life (Php 4:11-12; 1Ti 6:6).

However, the Teacher is unsatisfied with his own conclusions. Injustice, randomness, the feebleness of our efforts to make life secure—all these things haunt him. And beyond all looms death. The Teacher argues that death's inevitability seems to bleed the meaning out of life (Ecc 2:18-21; 8:8; 9:2-4). The answer in Ecclesiastes 2:24 is a good answer, but it is only a partial one. Something bigger is needed to fill the aching vacuum in the Teacher's soul. We have to keep reading to find his answer.

8 a time to love and a time to hate,
a time for war and a time for peace.

9 What does the worker gain from his toil?[v] 10 I
have seen the burden God has laid on men.[w] 11 He
has made everything beautiful in its time.[x] He has
also set eternity in the hearts of men; yet they cannot fathom[y] what God has done from beginning to
end.[z] 12 I know that there is nothing better for men
than to be happy and do good while they live.
13 That everyone may eat and drink,[a] and find satisfaction[b] in all his toil—this is the gift of God.[c] 14 I
know that everything God does will endure forever; nothing can be added to it and nothing taken
from it. God does it so that men will revere him.[d]

15 Whatever is has already been,[e]
and what will be has been before;[f]
and God will call the past to account.[a]

16 And I saw something else under the sun:

In the place of judgment—wickedness
was there,
in the place of justice—wickedness
was there.

17 I thought in my heart,

"God will bring to judgment[g]
both the righteous and the wicked,
for there will be a time for every
activity,
a time for every deed."[h]

18 I also thought, "As for men, God tests them so
that they may see that they are like the animals.[i]
19 Man's fate[j] is like that of the animals; the same
fate awaits them both: As one dies, so dies the
other. All have the same breath[b]; man has no
advantage over the animal. Everything is meaningless. 20 All go to the same place; all come from
dust, and to dust all return.[k] 21 Who knows if the
spirit of man rises upward[l] and if the spirit of the
animal[c] goes down into the earth?"
22 So I saw that there is nothing better for a man
than to enjoy his work,[m] because that is his lot.[n]
For who can bring him to see what will happen
after him?

Oppression, Toil, Friendlessness

4 Again I looked and saw all the oppression[o]
that was taking place under the sun:

I saw the tears of the oppressed—
and they have no comforter;
power was on the side of their
oppressors—
and they have no comforter.[p]
2 And I declared that the dead,[q]
who had already died,

3:9 [v]Ecc 1:3
3:10 [w]Ecc 1:13
3:11 [x]ver 1 [y]Job 11:7; Ecc 8:17 [z]Job 28:23; Ro 11:33
3:13 [a]Ecc 2:3 [b]Ps 34:12 [c]Dt 12:7,18; Ecc 2:24; 5:19
3:14 [d]Job 23:15; Ecc 5:7; 7:18; 8:12-13; Jas 1:17
3:15 [e]Ecc 6:10 [f]Ecc 1:9
3:17 [g]Job 19:29; Ecc 11:9; Mt 16:27; Ro 2:6-8; 2Th 1:6-7 [h]ver 1
3:18 [i]Ps 73:22
3:19 [j]Ecc 2:14
3:20 [k]Ge 2:7; 3:19; Job 34:15
3:21 [l]Ecc 12:7
3:22 [m]Ecc 2:24; 5:18 [n]Job 31:2
4:1 [o]Ps 12:5; Ecc 3:16 [p]La 1:16
4:2 [q]Jer 20:17-18; 22:10

[a] 15 Or *God calls back the past* [b] 19 Or *spirit* [c] 21 Or *Who knows the spirit of man, which rises upward, or the spirit of the animal, which*

In Ecclesiastes 3, the wisest man who ever lived, Solomon, expounds on the times and seasons of our lives and how they all fit together. Life is not some vague process of subtle, illogical patterns placed willy-nilly in our path for us to puzzle over. It's a composite of definitives: joys and sorrows, gains and losses, giving and keeping, laughing and grieving, loving and losing . . . on and on until the last numbered day arrives.

—Luci Swindoll

4:2 [r]Job 3:17; 10:18
are happier than the living,
who are still alive.[r]
[3]But better than both
4:3 [s]Job 3:16; Ecc 6:3 [t]Job 3:22
is he who has not yet been,[s]
who has not seen the evil
that is done under the sun.[t]

[4]And I saw that all labor and all achievement
4:4 [u]Ecc 1:14
spring from man's envy of his neighbor. This too
is meaningless, a chasing after the wind.[u]

4:5 [v]Pr 6:10
[5]The fool folds his hands[v]
and ruins himself.
[6]Better one handful with tranquillity
4:6 [w]Pr 15:16-17; 16:8
than two handfuls with toil[w]
and chasing after the wind.

[7]Again I saw something meaningless under the
sun:

[8]There was a man all alone;
he had neither son nor brother.
There was no end to his toil,
4:8 [x]Pr 27:20
yet his eyes were not content[x] with
his wealth.
"For whom am I toiling," he asked,
"and why am I depriving myself of
enjoyment?"
This too is meaningless—
a miserable business!

[9]Two are better than one,
because they have a good return for
their work:
[10]If one falls down,
his friend can help him up.
But pity the man who falls
and has no one to help him up!
[11]Also, if two lie down together, they will
keep warm.
But how can one keep warm alone?
[12]Though one may be overpowered,
two can defend themselves.
A cord of three strands is not quickly
broken.

Advancement Is Meaningless

[13]Better a poor but wise youth than an old but
foolish king who no longer knows how to take
warning. [14]The youth may have come from prison
to the kingship, or he may have been born in
poverty within his kingdom. [15]I saw that all who
lived and walked under the sun followed the youth,
the king's successor. [16]There was no end to all the
people who were before them. But those who came
later were not pleased with the successor. This too
is meaningless, a chasing after the wind.

Stand in Awe of God

5 Guard your steps when you go to the house of
God. Go near to listen rather than to offer the
sacrifice of fools, who do not know that they do
wrong.

In Ecclesiastes 4:9–12, *Solomon expounds on the virtues of teamwork. He says when two work together, they have a better reward for their labor. He makes it very practical, acknowledging that when one falls the other can help him [or her] up; when two lie down they keep each other warm. He says that one can be overpowered, but two can defend themselves. This could not be more clear, and I could not agree more. One of the reasons I like these verses is because the implication is that teamwork is not reserved for challenges of a world-changing nature, but is beneficial in the course of everyday living . . . In God's economy you will be hard-pressed to find many examples of successful "Lone Rangers" . . . Connect with a friend, a companion of your heart. You might be amazed at what you'll discover and enjoy together.*

—Luci Swindoll

Keep Quiet

ECC 5:1-7

Embedded within the questions and perplexities of this book are bits of wisdom that speak to the issues of the heart. In Ecclesiastes 5:1–5 the Teacher instructs his listeners in how they should worship. First, he says listen. The Hebrew word *listen* carries with it the responsibility to hear and obey. In 1 Samuel 15:22 Samuel says to Saul, "To obey is better than sacrifice, and to heed is better than the fat of rams." The Teacher makes the same point. Worship without obedience to God in everyday life is inadequate, feeble and offensive to him.

Second, the Teacher says, be careful what you promise God. Following through on what you vow, not the vow itself, is the true act of true worship. The Teacher wants his readers to remember who they are coming to when they worship. He is the Holy One, the Sovereign God, and we should stand in awe and obedience before him.

2 Do not be quick with your mouth,
do not be hasty in your heart
to utter anything before God.[y]
God is in heaven
and you are on earth,
so let your words be few.[z]
3 As a dream[a] comes when there are
many cares,
so the speech of a fool when there are
many words.[b]

4 When you make a vow to God, do not delay in
fulfilling it.[c] He has no pleasure in fools; fulfill your
vow.[d] 5 It is better not to vow than to make a vow
and not fulfill it.[e] 6 Do not let your mouth lead you
into sin. And do not protest to the ⌞temple⌟ messenger, "My vow was a mistake." Why should God
be angry at what you say and destroy the work of
your hands? 7 Much dreaming and many words are
meaningless. Therefore stand in awe of God.[f]

Riches Are Meaningless

8 If you see the poor oppressed[g] in a district, and
justice and rights denied, do not be surprised at
such things; for one official is eyed by a higher
one, and over them both are others higher still.
9 The increase from the land is taken by all; the
king himself profits from the fields.

10 Whoever loves money never has money
enough;
whoever loves wealth is never
satisfied with his income.
This too is meaningless.
11 As goods increase,
so do those who consume them.
And what benefit are they to the owner
except to feast his eyes on them?

12 The sleep of a laborer is sweet,
whether he eats little or much,
but the abundance of a rich man
permits him no sleep.[h]

13 I have seen a grievous evil under the sun:[i]

wealth hoarded to the harm of its
owner,
14 or wealth lost through some
misfortune,
so that when he has a son
there is nothing left for him.
15 Naked a man comes from his mother's
womb,
and as he comes, so he departs.[j]
He takes nothing from his labor[k]
that he can carry in his hand.[l]

16 This too is a grievous evil:

As a man comes, so he departs,
and what does he gain,
since he toils for the wind?[m]
17 All his days he eats in darkness,

5:2 [y]Jdg 11:35 [z]Job 6:24; Pr 10:19; 20:25
5:3 [a]Job 20:8 [b]Ecc 10:14
5:4 [c]Dt 23:21; Jdg 11:35; Ps 119:60 [d]Nu 30:2; Ps 66:13-14; 76:11
5:5 [e]Nu 30:2-4; Pr 20:25; Jnh 2:9; Ac 5:4
5:7 [f]Ecc 3:14; 12:13
5:8 [g]Ps 12:5; Ecc 4:1
5:12 [h]Job 20:20
5:13 [i]Ecc 6:1-2
5:15 [j]Job 1:21 [k]Ps 49:17; 1Ti 6:7 [l]Ecc 1:3
5:16 [m]Pr 11:29; Ecc 1:3

with great frustration, affliction and
anger.

5:18 18 Then I realized that it is good and proper for a
nEcc 2:3 man to eat and drink,[n] and to find satisfaction in
oEcc 2:10,24 his toilsome labor[o] under the sun during the few
days of life God has given him—for this is his lot.
19 Moreover, when God gives any man wealth and
5:19 possessions,[p] and enables him to enjoy them,[q] to
p1Ch 29:12; 2Ch 1:12 accept his lot[r] and be happy in his work—this is a
qEcc 6:2 rJob 31:2 gift of God.[s] 20 He seldom reflects on the days of
sEcc 2:24; 3:13 his life, because God keeps him occupied with
gladness of heart.[t]

5:20 tDt 12:7,18 **6** I have seen another evil under the sun, and it
weighs heavily on men: 2 God gives a man
wealth, possessions and honor, so that he lacks
nothing his heart desires, but God does not enable
6:2 him to enjoy them,[u] and a stranger enjoys them
uPs 17:14; Ecc 5:19 instead. This is meaningless, a grievous evil.[v]
vEcc 5:13 3 A man may have a hundred children and live
many years; yet no matter how long he lives, if he
6:3 cannot enjoy his prosperity and does not receive
wJob 3:16; proper burial, I say that a stillborn[w] child is better
Ecc 4:3 xJob 3:3 off than he.[x] 4 It comes without meaning, it departs
in darkness, and in darkness its name is shrouded.
5 Though it never saw the sun or knew anything, it
has more rest than does that man— 6 even if he
lives a thousand years twice over but fails to enjoy
his prosperity. Do not all go to the same place?

6:7 7 All man's efforts are for his mouth,
yPr 16:26; 27:20 yet his appetite is never satisfied.[y]
8 What advantage has a wise man
6:8 over a fool?[z]
zEcc 2:15 What does a poor man gain
by knowing how to conduct himself
before others?
9 Better what the eye sees
than the roving of the appetite.
This too is meaningless,
6:9 aEcc 1:14 a chasing after the wind.[a]

10 Whatever exists has already been
named,
and what man is has been known;
no man can contend
with one who is stronger than he.
11 The more the words,
the less the meaning,
and how does that profit anyone?

6:12 12 For who knows what is good for a man in life,
bJob 10:20 during the few and meaningless days[b] he passes
cJob 14:2; through like a shadow?[c] Who can tell him what
Ps 39:6; Jas 4:14 will happen under the sun after he is gone?

Wisdom

7:1 dPr 22:1; **7** A good name is better than fine perfume,[d]
SS 1:3 and the day of death better than the day
of birth.
2 It is better to go to a house of mourning
7:2 than to go to a house of feasting,
ePr 11:19 fPs 90:12 for death[e] is the destiny[f] of every man;

Sorrow's Better Than Laughter

Many of us are slow to learn the obvious. We continually fall into the trap of thinking, *If I just had . . . I would be much more content.* Possessions and life itself have meaning only when I come to terms with the God who created all things. When he is my foundation, the Being around whom my life revolves, only then will I have a sense of purpose. When that purpose becomes well defined, I recognize that everything I strive for is limited in its potential to produce fulfillment. That does not mean I can't, shouldn't, or won't seek after those experiences . . . But it does mean I must realize that my ultimate joy will never come from things or persons. It will only come from a personal knowledge of and commitment to God.

In the midst of all his resplendent living, the writer of Ecclesiastes concludes: "I know that everything God does will endure forever; nothing can be added to it and nothing taken from it" (Ecc 3:14). The lack of permanence so common to the affairs of the heart directly contrasts with the longevity of the love we receive from God. We experience the joy that [lasts forever] only as we commune with the divine. "Everything God does will [endure] forever."

—Marilyn Meberg

Sorrow's Better Than Laughter?

ECC 7:3

In what sense is sorrow better than laughter? How can "a sad face" help the heart? The Teacher says that true joy only comes as we honestly face the facts: Death is inevitable; life is brief; most human pleasure is fickle and fleeting. But as we let those realities touch us, we have the opportunity to discover what is eternal, what cannot be taken from us because it is a good gift from God. The sadness encouraged here is not a contradiction of the encouragement in Proverbs 15:30 that joy is good for the heart and body; rather, it is an invitation to explore what the real source of joy is. Paul knows the answer. Find out what he says in Romans 5:3–5 and 2 Corinthians 4:16–18.

the living should take this to heart.
3 Sorrow is better than laughter,[g]
because a sad face is good for the heart.
4 The heart of the wise is in the house of mourning,
but the heart of fools is in the house of pleasure.[h]
5 It is better to heed a wise man's rebuke[i]
than to listen to the song of fools.
6 Like the crackling of thorns[j] under the pot,
so is the laughter[k] of fools.
This too is meaningless.
7 Extortion turns a wise man into a fool,
and a bribe[l] corrupts the heart.

8 The end of a matter is better than its beginning,
and patience[m] is better than pride.
9 Do not be quickly provoked[n] in your spirit,
for anger resides in the lap of fools.
10 Do not say, "Why were the old days better than these?"
For it is not wise to ask such questions.

11 Wisdom, like an inheritance, is a good thing[o]
and benefits those who see the sun.[p]
12 Wisdom is a shelter
as money is a shelter,
but the advantage of knowledge is this:
that wisdom preserves the life of its possessor.

13 Consider what God has done:[q]

Who can straighten
what he has made crooked?[r]
14 When times are good, be happy;
but when times are bad, consider:
God has made the one
as well as the other.
Therefore, a man cannot discover
anything about his future.

15 In this meaningless life[s] of mine I have seen
both of these:

a righteous man perishing in his righteousness,
and a wicked man living long in his wickedness.[t]
16 Do not be overrighteous,
neither be overwise—
why destroy yourself?
17 Do not be overwicked,
and do not be a fool—
why die before your time?[u]
18 It is good to grasp the one
and not let go of the other.

7:3 [g]Pr 14:13
7:4 [h]Ecc 2:1; Jer 16:8
7:5 [i]Ps 141:5; Pr 13:18; 15:31-32
7:6 [j]Ps 58:9; 118:12 [k]Ecc 2:2
7:7 [l]Ex 18:21; 23:8; Dt 16:19
7:8 [m]Pr 14:29; Gal 5:22; Eph 4:2
7:9 [n]Mt 5:22; Pr 14:17; Jas 1:19
7:11 [o]Pr 8:10-11; Ecc 2:13 [p]Ecc 11:7
7:13 [q]Ecc 2:24 [r]Ecc 1:15
7:15 [s]Job 7:7 [t]Ecc 8:12-14; Jer 12:1
7:17 [u]Job 15:32; Ps 55:23

7:18 The man who fears God[v] will avoid all
vEcc 3:14 ⌊extremes⌋.[a]

7:19 [19] Wisdom[w] makes one wise man more
wEcc 2:13 powerful[x]
xEcc 9:13-18 than ten rulers in a city.

7:20 [20] There is not a righteous man[y] on earth
yPs 14:3 who does what is right and never
z1Ki 8:46; 2Ch 6:36; Pr 20:9; Ro 3:23 sins.[z]

[21] Do not pay attention to every word
people say,
7:21 or you[a] may hear your servant cursing
aPr 30:10 you—
[22] for you know in your heart
that many times you yourself have
cursed others.

[23] All this I tested by wisdom and I said,
7:23 "I am determined to be wise"[b]—
bEcc 1:17; Ro 1:22 but this was beyond me.
[24] Whatever wisdom may be,
7:24 it is far off and most profound—
cJob 28:12 who can discover it?[c]
[25] So I turned my mind to understand,
to investigate and to search out
7:25 wisdom and the scheme of things[d]
dJob 28:3 and to understand the stupidity of
eEcc 1:17 wickedness
and the madness of folly.[e]

[26] I find more bitter than death
7:26 the woman who is a snare,[f]
fEx 10:7; Jdg 14:15 whose heart is a trap
gPr 2:16-19; 5:3-5; 7:23; 22:14 and whose hands are chains.
The man who pleases God will escape
her,
but the sinner she will ensnare.[g]

7:27 [27] "Look," says the Teacher,[bh] "this is what I have
hEcc 1:1 discovered:

"Adding one thing to another to discover
the scheme of things—
[28] while I was still searching
but not finding—
I found one ⌊upright⌋ man among a
thousand,
7:28 but not one ⌊upright⌋ woman[i] among
i1Ki 11:3 them all.
[29] This only have I found:
God made mankind upright,
but men have gone in search of many
schemes."

8 Who is like the wise man?
Who knows the explanation of things?
Wisdom brightens a man's face
and changes its hard appearance.

[a] 18 Or *will follow them both* [b] 27 Or *leader of the assembly*

Where Is Wisdom?

ECC 7:23–25

Where can we get wisdom? If the Teacher is frustrated in his attempt to become wise, what hope do we have? To solve this riddle we need to remember that the Teacher has been on a quest for wisdom (Ecc 1:12–18), but everything he has explored has frustrated him. His intense efforts have turned up nothing. Why? The answer lies in the last verse of this chapter: God originally made humanity righteous, but humans have gone their own way "in search of many schemes" (Ecc 7:29). Furthermore, the Teacher's quest has been a search that has taken place "under the sun." He has not turned at this point in the book to the God who made him to find the answers. He has not yet recognized what the rest of the Scriptures teach: "The fear of the LORD is the beginning of wisdom, and knowledge of the Holy One is understanding" (Pr 9:10).

Life Isn't Fair

ECC 8:14

Why isn't life fair? Why don't people get what they deserve? These questions haunt the Teacher. The hardest question arises from the Teacher's observation in Ecclesiastes 8:10: Why does God let wicked people go in and out of his holy place (the temple in Jerusalem)? Why does he let them receive praise, then be buried with dignity? Twice the Teacher repeats his conclusion: This is meaningless (Ecc 8:10,14). Yet he does give us a bigger perspective in Ecclesiastes 8:12–13: Eventually everything will even out. Eventually, life will be fair for both God-fearing people and the wicked. The Teacher is probably referring to a day of judgment when God settles all accounts (1Co 4:5). The Teacher also reveals another part of the answer to life's unfairness (Ecc 8:15). Everyone has a choice to live in anger and despair over all the inequities of life or choose joy. The everyday blessings of God are just as real as the difficulties and questions.

Obey the King

2 Obey the king's command, I say, because you
took an oath before God. 3 Do not be in a hurry to
leave the king's presence.[j] Do not stand up for a
bad cause, for he will do whatever he pleases.
4 Since a king's word is supreme, who can say to
him, "What are you doing?[k]"

5 Whoever obeys his command will come
to no harm,
and the wise heart will know the
proper time and procedure.
6 For there is a proper time and procedure
for every matter,[l]
though a man's misery weighs
heavily upon him.

7 Since no man knows the future,
who can tell him what is to come?
8 No man has power over the wind to
contain it[a];
so no one has power over the day of
his death.
As no one is discharged in time of war,
so wickedness will not release those
who practice it.

9 All this I saw, as I applied my mind to everything done under the sun. There is a time when a
man lords it over others to his own[b] hurt. 10 Then
too, I saw the wicked buried[m]—those who used
to come and go from the holy place and receive
praise[c] in the city where they did this. This too is
meaningless.
11 When the sentence for a crime is not quickly
carried out, the hearts of the people are filled with
schemes to do wrong. 12 Although a wicked man
commits a hundred crimes and still lives a long
time, I know that it will go better[n] with God-fearing men,[o] who are reverent before God.[p] 13 Yet
because the wicked do not fear God,[q] it will not go
well with them, and their days[r] will not lengthen
like a shadow.
14 There is something else meaningless that
occurs on earth: righteous men who get what the
wicked deserve, and wicked men who get what
the righteous deserve.[s] This too, I say, is meaningless.[t] 15 So I commend the enjoyment of life[u],
because nothing is better for a man under the sun
than to eat and drink[v] and be glad.[w] Then joy will
accompany him in his work all the days of the life
God has given him under the sun.
16 When I applied my mind to know wisdom[x]
and to observe man's labor on earth[y]—his eyes
not seeing sleep day or night— 17 then I saw all
that God has done.[z] No one can comprehend what
goes on under the sun. Despite all his efforts to
search it out, man cannot discover its meaning.

8:3 [j]Ecc 10:4
8:4 [k]Job 9:12; Est 1:19; Da 4:35
8:6 [l]Ecc 3:1
8:10 [m]Ecc 1:11
8:12 [n]Dt 12:28; Ps 37:11,18-19; Pr 1:32-33; Isa 3:10-11 [o]Ex 1:20 [p]Ecc 3:14
8:13 [q]Ecc 3:14; Isa 3:11 [r]Dt 4:40; Job 5:26; Ps 34:12; Isa 65:20
8:14 [s]Job 21:7; Ps 73:14; Mal 3:15 [t]Ecc 7:15
8:15 [u]Ps 42:8 [v]Ex 32:6; Ecc 2:3 [w]Ecc 2:24; 3:12-13; 5:18; 9:7
8:16 [x]Ecc 1:17 [y]Ecc 1:13
8:17 [z]Job 28:3

[a] *8* Or *over his spirit to retain it* [b] *9* Or *to their* [c] *10* Some Hebrew manuscripts and Septuagint (Aquila); most Hebrew manuscripts *and are forgotten*

Even if a wise man claims he knows, he cannot
really comprehend it.[a]

A Common Destiny for All

9 So I reflected on all this and concluded that
the righteous and the wise and what they do
are in God's hands, but no man knows whether
love or hate awaits him.[b] 2 All share a common
destiny—the righteous and the wicked, the good
and the bad,*[a]* the clean and the unclean, those
who offer sacrifices and those who do not.

As it is with the good man,
so with the sinner;
as it is with those who take oaths,
so with those who are afraid to take
them.[c]

3 This is the evil in everything that happens
under the sun: The same destiny overtakes all.[d]
The hearts of men, moreover, are full of evil and
there is madness in their hearts while they live,[e]
and afterward they join the dead.[f] 4 Anyone who is
among the living has hope*[b]*—even a live dog is
better off than a dead lion!

5 For the living know that they will die,
but the dead know nothing;[g]
they have no further reward,
and even the memory of them[h] is
forgotten.[i]
6 Their love, their hate
and their jealousy have long since
vanished;
never again will they have a part
in anything that happens under the
sun.[j]

7 Go, eat your food with gladness, and drink
your wine[k] with a joyful heart,[l] for it is now that
God favors what you do. 8 Always be clothed in
white,[m] and always anoint your head with oil.
9 Enjoy life with your wife,[n] whom you love, all the
days of this meaningless life that God has given
you under the sun— all your meaningless days.
For this is your lot[o] in life and in your toilsome
labor under the sun. 10 Whatever[p] your hand finds
to do, do it with all your might,[q] for in the grave,*[c]*[r]
where you are going, there is neither working nor
planning nor knowledge nor wisdom.[s]

11 I have seen something else under the sun:

The race is not to the swift
or the battle to the strong,[t]
nor does food come to the wise[u]
or wealth to the brilliant
or favor to the learned;
but time and chance[v] happen to them
all.[w]

8:17 [a]Job 5:9; 28:23; Ecc 3:11; Ro 11:33
9:1 [b]Dt 33:3; Job 12:10; Ecc 10:14
9:2 [c]Job 9:22; Ecc 2:14; 6:6; 7:2
9:3 [d]Job 9:22; Ecc 2:14 [e]Jer 11:8; 13:10; 16:12; 17:9 [f]Job 21:26
9:5 [g]Job 14:21 [h]Ps 9:6 [i]Ecc 1:11; 2:16; Isa 26:14
9:6 [j]Job 21:21
9:7 [k]Nu 6:20 [l]Ecc 2:24; 8:15
9:8 [m]Ps 23:5; Rev 3:4
9:9 [n]Pr 5:18 [o]Job 31:2
9:10 [p]1Sa 10:7 [q]Ecc 11:6; Ro 12:11; Col 3:23 [r]Nu 16:33 [s]Ecc 2:24
9:11 [t]Am 2:14-15 [u]Job 32:13; Isa 47:10; Jer 9:23 [v]Ecc 2:14 [w]Dt 8:18

Time and Chance

ECC 9:11

Swift, strong, wise, brilliant, learned—we look at the list and envision instant success for the lucky person possessing these qualities. Furthermore, when we look at our own lives and do not see those abilities, we assume we are doomed to mediocrity. The Teacher upsets our assumptions and strips away our fears and excuses. "Time and chance" affect everything. We can despair at that and think it doesn't matter what we do because we cannot control life, or we can see it as an opportunity. Abilities are not all there is to success. God is orchestrating the events of life, the very things that look to us like time and chance. In his plan he will use us as he wills and as we are willing.

a 2 Septuagint (Aquila), Vulgate and Syriac; Hebrew does not have *and the bad.* *b* 4 Or *What then is to be chosen? With all who live, there is hope* *c* 10 Hebrew *Sheol*

Quiet Words

ECC 9:13–18

In his search for wisdom, the Teacher observes that much opposes it. Wisdom can save a city, yet the wise man who helps it happen is forgotten. Wisdom is better than strength, yet it often seems that wisdom has little influence. Ecclesiastes 9:18 affirms this thought: "Wisdom is better than weapons of war, but one sinner [can] destroy [the] good" that wisdom accomplishes. Why then be wise? The answer is found in Ecclesiastes 9:17. No matter how things turn out, no matter how fiercely other people play the power game, quiet wise words still have the most to offer. Wise words quietly spoken will have an influence. Other things may temporarily look more powerful, but they won't last. For a better understanding of how wisdom and quietness fit together for a powerful effect, see James 3:13–18.

12 Moreover, no man knows when his hour will
come:

As fish are caught in a cruel net,
or birds are taken in a snare,
so men are trapped by evil times[x]
that fall unexpectedly upon them.[y]

Wisdom Better Than Folly

13 I also saw under the sun this example of wisdom[z] that greatly impressed me: 14 There was once
a small city with only a few people in it. And a
powerful king came against it, surrounded it and
built huge siegeworks against it. 15 Now there lived
in that city a man poor but wise, and he saved the
city by his wisdom. But nobody remembered that
poor man.[a] 16 So I said, "Wisdom is better than
strength." But the poor man's wisdom is despised,
and his words are no longer heeded.[b]

17 The quiet words of the wise are more to
be heeded
than the shouts of a ruler of fools.
18 Wisdom[c] is better than weapons of war,
but one sinner destroys much good.

10 As dead flies give perfume a bad smell,
so a little folly[d] outweighs wisdom and
honor.
2 The heart of the wise inclines to the
right,
but the heart of the fool to the left.
3 Even as he walks along the road,
the fool lacks sense
and shows everyone[e] how stupid
he is.
4 If a ruler's anger rises against you,
do not leave your post;[f]
calmness can lay great errors to rest.[g]
5 There is an evil I have seen under the
sun,
the sort of error that arises from a
ruler:
6 Fools are put in many high positions,[h]
while the rich occupy the low ones.
7 I have seen slaves on horseback,
while princes go on foot like slaves.[i]
8 Whoever digs a pit may fall into it;[j]
whoever breaks through a wall may
be bitten by a snake.[k]
9 Whoever quarries stones may be injured
by them;
whoever splits logs may be
endangered by them.[l]
10 If the ax is dull
and its edge unsharpened,
more strength is needed
but skill will bring success.
11 If a snake bites before it is charmed,
there is no profit for the charmer.[m]

9:12 [x]Pr 29:6 [y]Ps 73:22; Ecc 2:14; 8:7
9:13 [z]2Sa 20:22
9:15 [a]Ge 40:14; Ecc 1:11; 2:16; 4:13
9:16 [b]Pr 21:22; Ecc 7:19
9:18 [c]ver 16
10:1 [d]Pr 13:16; 18:2
10:3 [e]Pr 13:16; 18:2
10:4 [f]Ecc 8:3 [g]Pr 16:14; 25:15
10:6 [h]Pr 29:2
10:7 [i]Pr 19:10
10:8 [j]Ps 7:15; 57:6; Pr 26:27 [k]Est 2:23; Ps 9:16; Am 5:19
10:9 [l]Pr 26:27
10:11 [m]Ps 58:5; Isa 3:3

10:12
[n]Pr 10:32
[o]Pr 10:14; 14:3; 15:2; 18:7

12 Words from a wise man's mouth are
gracious,[n]
but a fool is consumed by his own
lips.[o]
13 At the beginning his words are folly;
at the end they are wicked madness—
14 and the fool multiplies words.[p]

10:14
[p]Pr 15:2; Ecc 5:3; 6:12; 8:7
[q]Ecc 9:1

No one knows what is coming—
who can tell him what will happen
after him?[q]

15 A fool's work wearies him;
he does not know the way to town.

10:16
[r]Isa 3:4-5,12

16 Woe to you, O land whose king was a
servant[a][r]
and whose princes feast in the
morning.
17 Blessed are you, O land whose king is of
noble birth
and whose princes eat at a proper
time—
for strength and not for drunkenness.[s]

10:17
[s]Dt 14:26; 1Sa 25:36; Pr 31:4

18 If a man is lazy, the rafters sag;
if his hands are idle, the house leaks.[t]

10:18
[t]Pr 20:4; 24:30-34

19 A feast is made for laughter,
and wine[u] makes life merry,
but money is the answer for
everything.

10:19
[u]Ge 14:18; Jdg 9:13

10:20
[v]Ex 22:28

20 Do not revile the king[v] even in your
thoughts,
or curse the rich in your bedroom,
because a bird of the air may carry your
words,
and a bird on the wing may report
what you say.

Bread Upon the Waters

11:1
[w]ver 6; Isa 32:20; Hos 10:12
[x]Dt 24:19; Pr 19:17; Mt 10:42

11

Cast[w] your bread upon the waters,
for after many days you will find it
again.[x]
2 Give portions to seven, yes to eight,
for you do not know what disaster
may come upon the land.

3 If clouds are full of water,
they pour rain upon the earth.
Whether a tree falls to the south or to
the north,
in the place where it falls, there will it
lie.
4 Whoever watches the wind will not
plant;
whoever looks at the clouds will not
reap.
5 As you do not know the path of the
wind,[y]

11:5
[y]Jn 3:8-10

[a] 16 Or *king is a child*

Bread on the Waters

ECC 11:1

What is the Teacher talking about as Ecclesiastes 11 begins? Soggy bread? Probably not! Since Ecclesiastes 9:1, the Teacher has been reminding his readers that life is often unpredictable. Now in this chapter, the Teacher repeats his theme (note the phrase "you do not [or cannot] know" in Ecc 11:2,5,6). There is a lot we don't know about life, but that should not paralyze us. Part of wisdom is moving out, taking risks. Is the Teacher talking about generosity in Ecclesiastes 11:1–2 or the business risks of seafaring trade (see 1Ki 9:26–28)? Bible students see both possibilities in these verses. In either case, the application is the same. Live life; seize opportunities; don't wait for perfect assurances about everything, for they will never come. The choice to live fully is its own reward.

Remember Your Creator

ECC 12:1

Finally, the Teacher is beginning to answer the question of where we can find true joy, a reason for living. Meaning cannot be found under the sun. We must look past creation to the God who made it all. It is important to note that meaning does not come from merely acknowledging God, but from remembering *him. The Hebrew word* remember *is packed with life. It means that we realize every blessing is from him (Dt 8:17–18), we obey him (Ps 119:55) and we delight in thinking about him (Ps 63:6–7). The time to begin that remembering is in our youth. The Teacher says we are to set a template for our lives, to shape our souls by referencing all of life back to God. That way, no matter what the future brings, we will know that the best choice in life is always to choose to be near to God.*

or how the body is formed[a] in a
mother's womb,[z]
so you cannot understand the work of
God,
the Maker of all things.

6 Sow your seed in the morning,
and at evening let not your hands be
idle,[a]
for you do not know which will
succeed,
whether this or that,
or whether both will do equally well.

Remember Your Creator While Young

7 Light is sweet,
and it pleases the eyes to see the sun.[b]
8 However many years a man may live,
let him enjoy them all.
But let him remember[c] the days of
darkness,
for they will be many.
Everything to come is meaningless.

9 Be happy, young man, while you are
young,
and let your heart give you joy in the
days of your youth.
Follow the ways of your heart
and whatever your eyes see,
but know that for all these things
God will bring you to judgment.[d]
10 So then, banish anxiety[e] from your heart
and cast off the troubles of your body,
for youth and vigor are meaningless.[f]

12 Remember[g] your Creator
in the days of your youth,
before the days of trouble[h] come
and the years approach when you will
say,
"I find no pleasure in them"—
2 before the sun and the light
and the moon and the stars grow
dark,
and the clouds return after the rain;
3 when the keepers of the house tremble,
and the strong men stoop,
when the grinders cease because they
are few,
and those looking through the
windows grow dim;
4 when the doors to the street are closed
and the sound of grinding fades;
when men rise up at the sound of birds,
but all their songs grow faint;[i]
5 when men are afraid of heights
and of dangers in the streets;
when the almond tree blossoms

11:5 [z]Ps 139:14-16
11:6 [a]Ecc 9:10
11:7 [b]Ecc 7:11
11:8 [c]Ecc 12:1
11:9 [d]Job 19:29; Ecc 2:24; 3:17; 12:14; Ro 14:10
11:10 [e]Ps 94:19 [f]Ecc 2:24
12:1 [g]Ecc 11:8 [h]2Sa 19:35
12:4 [i]Jer 25:10

[a] 5 Or *know how life* (or *the spirit*) / *enters the body being formed*

and the grasshopper drags himself
along
and desire no longer is stirred.
12:5 Then man goes to his eternal home[j]
[j]Job 17:13; 10:21 and mourners[k] go about the streets.
[k]Jer 9:17; Am 5:16

6 Remember him—before the silver cord
is severed,
or the golden bowl is broken;
before the pitcher is shattered at the
spring,
12:7 or the wheel broken at the well,
[l]Ge 3:19; 7 and the dust returns[l] to the ground it
Job 34:15; came from,
Ps 146:4 [m]Ecc 3:21 and the spirit returns to God[m] who
[n]Job 20:8; gave it.[n]
Zec 12:1

8 "Meaningless! Meaningless!" says the
12:8 Teacher.[a]
[o]Ecc 1:2 "Everything is meaningless![o]"

The Conclusion of the Matter

9 Not only was the Teacher wise, but also he
imparted knowledge to the people. He pondered
12:9 and searched out and set in order many proverbs.[p]
[p]1Ki 4:32 10 The Teacher searched to find just the right
12:10 words, and what he wrote was upright and true.[q]
[q]Pr 22:20-21 11 The words of the wise are like goads, their col-
12:11 lected sayings like firmly embedded nails[r]—giv-
[r]Ezr 9:8 en by one Shepherd. 12 Be warned, my son, of any-
12:12 thing in addition to them.
[s]Ecc 1:18 Of making many books there is no end, and
much study wearies the body.[s]

13 Now all has been heard;
here is the conclusion of the matter:
12:13 Fear God and keep his commandments,[t]
[t]Dt 4:2; 10:12 for this is the whole ⌞duty⌟ of man.[u]
[u]Mic 6:8 14 For God will bring every deed into
12:14 judgment,[v]
[v]Ecc 3:17 including every hidden thing,[w]
[w]Mt 10:26; 1Co 4:5 whether it is good or evil.

Fear and Obey God

ECC 12:13

At last the Teacher brings his questions to an end. The meaninglessness of life, the injustices we experience, the sad truth that wisdom cannot always protect us are cast aside. When all is said and done, our duty as God's creatures is simply to fear and obey God. The reason is given in the next verse. God notices everything and will judge everything (Ecc 12:14). Is that a big enough answer for our emptiness? Yes and no. The New Testament also speaks of an all-encompassing judgment (2Co 5:10), yet it proclaims with even greater clarity the awesome love of God (Jn 3:16). Because of Jesus Christ, love, forgiveness and relationship are at the core of meaning. True obedience flows most freely out of that love, not out of duty.

[a] 8 Or *the leader of the assembly*; also in verses 9 and 10

Song of Songs

A love song.

The Song of Songs celebrates the joy and intimacy of the romantic love relationship between a man and a woman. This tender yet passionate picture of physical love affirms the sanctity of marriage and has often been seen as mirroring God's unconditional love for his people.

Using at times deeply sensual word pictures, and phrases that unveil the joys of physical love, the Song of Songs introduces us to the bride, called "Beloved," who is beautiful and deeply loved and who responds to her "Lover" with affection and passion. The groom, called "Lover," is revealed as a handsome, virile male, who praises his bride's beauty using delicate yet sensuous pictures from nature. The "Friends" of the bride and groom encourage their love and offer them advice and instruction. Song of Songs reaches its literary and emotional climax in chapter 8 when the Beloved passionately describes the intensity and the eternal nature of the love that she and her Lover share.

The lyrical beauty of Song of Songs gives the reader a pleasurable picture of love in its most intimate form. The sensuous images of the physical side of love are paired with passionate declarations of the strength and intensity of love. They combine to reveal like no other passage of Scripture the love between a man and a woman expressed and experienced as God intended. Historically, many commentators have drawn a parallel between the Lover and the Bride in Song of Songs and Jesus Christ and his bride, the church.

Quick Study

Author
Authorship is uncertain, but possibly Solomon.

Date Written
Authorship by Solomon calls for a date during the tenth century B.C.

Setting
Israel.

Key Passage
Song of Songs 8:6–7
"Place me like a seal
over your heart,
like a seal on your arm;
for love is as strong as
death,
its jealousy unyielding as
the grave.
It burns like blazing fire,
like a mighty flame.
Many waters cannot
quench love;
rivers cannot wash it
away.

Outline

The courtship.
SS 1:1–3:5

The wedding.
SS 3:6-11

Vivid expressions of love.
SS 4:1–5:1

Conflict and solutions.
SS 5:2–6:13

More expressions of love.
SS 7:1–8:4

Never-ending love.
SS 8:5-14

The Women of Song of Songs

The Shulammite woman	*The bride.* SS 6:13
The maidens	*They pale in comparison to the bride.* SS 1:3; 2:2; 6:9

A Song of Love

SS 1:1-10

Part of understanding the Song of Songs is discerning who is speaking. This book is a song collection with a unified theme that tells of the beauty of romantic love as it progresses from courtship to marriage to a maturing relationship. Although the Hebrew text does not identify the speakers, we can detect who is speaking by the context and by the Hebrew words, which reflect either the masculine or the feminine. The story revolves around the Beloved (very much in love herself), the Lover (the man pursuing a relationship with her), and the Friends (sometimes called the "daughters of Jerusalem"). Song of Songs is a poem that gives beauty and reality to the love of a bride and her groom. Their thoughts, emotions and longings are revealed, giving us not only a picture of an ancient couple's love but also a picture of ideal wedded love today.

1 Solomon's Song of Songs.[a]

Beloved[a]

2 Let him kiss me with the kisses of his mouth—
for your love[b] is more delightful than wine.
3 Pleasing is the fragrance of your perfumes;[c]
your name[d] is like perfume poured out.
No wonder the maidens[e] love you!
4 Take me away with you—let us hurry!
Let the king bring me into his chambers.[f]

Friends

We rejoice and delight in you[b];
we will praise your love more than wine.

Beloved

How right they are to adore you!

5 Dark am I, yet lovely,[g]
O daughters of Jerusalem,[h]
dark like the tents of Kedar,
like the tent curtains of Solomon.[c]
6 Do not stare at me because I am dark,
because I am darkened by the sun.
My mother's sons were angry with me
and made me take care of the vineyards;[i]
my own vineyard I have neglected.
7 Tell me, you whom I love, where you graze your flock
and where you rest your sheep[j] at midday.
Why should I be like a veiled woman
beside the flocks of your friends?

Friends

8 If you do not know, most beautiful of women,[k]
follow the tracks of the sheep
and graze your young goats
by the tents of the shepherds.

Lover

9 I liken you, my darling, to a mare
harnessed to one of the chariots[l] of Pharaoh.
10 Your cheeks[m] are beautiful with earrings,

1:1 [a]1Ki 4:32
1:2 [b]SS 4:10
1:3 [c]SS 4:10 [d]Ecc 7:1 [e]Ps 45:14
1:4 [f]Ps 45:15
1:5 [g]SS 2:14; 4:3 [h]SS 2:7; 5:8; 5:16
1:6 [i]Ps 69:8; SS 8:12
1:7 [j]SS 3:1-4; Isa 13:20
1:8 [k]SS 5:9; 6:1
1:9 [l]2Ch 1:17
1:10 [m]SS 5:13

[a] Primarily on the basis of the gender of the Hebrew pronouns used, male and female speakers are indicated in the margins by the captions *Lover* and *Beloved* respectively. The words of others are marked *Friends*. In some instances the divisions and their captions are debatable. [b] 4 The Hebrew is masculine singular. [c] 5 Or *Salma*

1:10 [n]Isa 61:10

your neck with strings of jewels.[n]
11 We will make you earrings of gold,
studded with silver.

Beloved

1:12 [o]SS 4:11-14

12 While the king was at his table,
my perfume spread its fragrance.[o]
13 My lover is to me a sachet of myrrh
resting between my breasts.

1:14 [p]SS 4:13 [q]1Sa 23:29

14 My lover is to me a cluster of henna[p] blossoms
from the vineyards of En Gedi.[q]

Lover

1:15 [r]SS 4:7 [s]SS 2:14; 4:1; 5:2,12; 6:9

15 How beautiful[r] you are, my darling!
Oh, how beautiful!
Your eyes are doves.[s]

Beloved

16 How handsome you are, my lover!
Oh, how charming!
And our bed is verdant.

Lover

1:17 [t]1Ki 6:9

17 The beams of our house are cedars;[t]
our rafters are firs.

Beloved[a]

2:1 [u]Isa 35:1 [v]1Ch 27:29 [w]SS 5:13; Hos 14:5

2 I am a rose[b][u] of Sharon,[v]
a lily[w] of the valleys.

Lover

2 Like a lily among thorns
is my darling among the maidens.

Beloved

2:3 [x]SS 1:14 [y]SS 1:4 [z]SS 4:16

3 Like an apple tree among the trees of the forest
is my lover[x] among the young men.
I delight[y] to sit in his shade,
and his fruit is sweet to my taste.[z]

2:4 [a]Est 1:11 [b]Nu 1:52

4 He has taken me to the banquet hall,[a]
and his banner[b] over me is love.

2:5 [c]SS 7:8 [d]SS 5:8

5 Strengthen me with raisins,
refresh me with apples,[c]
for I am faint with love.[d]

2:6 [e]SS 8:3

6 His left arm is under my head,
and his right arm embraces me.[e]

2:7 [f]SS 5:8 [g]SS 3:5; 8:4

7 Daughters of Jerusalem, I charge you[f]
by the gazelles and by the does of the field:
Do not arouse or awaken love
until it so desires.[g]

8 Listen! My lover!
Look! Here he comes,

2:8 [h]ver 17; SS 8:14

leaping across the mountains,
bounding over the hills.[h]

[a] Or *Lover* [b] *1* Possibly a member of the crocus family

She Praises Him

SS 2:3–4

The Beloved is praising her Lover. He is as delightful and unique as an apple tree in a forest; nearness to him is both protection and joy. She says his banner over her is love. Why the introduction of a military motif into a love scene? (A banner is the standard, or flag, that troops carry as they march so that they can identify themselves to others.) The woman is saying, "My Lover lets the whole world know of his love for me." As women, we delight in that kind of romantic love. But we can take this one step further. If this book also pictures the love of Jesus Christ for his church, we realize that this means that Jesus identifies himself to all of creation as the One who loves us. As women, we can delight in his love also.

Springtime

SS 2:10-13

Spring has come and the Lover is inviting his Beloved to leave the confines of her home and join him in an exhilarating walk in the country. God has designed our souls to respond to spring, to the fresh beauty of the world coming to life again. Romantic love does feel like spring. Dreariness disappears; beauty, joy and life seem to be exploding at every turn. Life feels new and fresh again.

On a spiritual level, these verses about spring also have a message for us. As we personally respond to the love of Jesus Christ, we realize that God wants to infuse our tired and dreary souls with life. He wants to fill them with beauty and joy. In Revelation 21:5 he proclaims, "I am making everything new!"

9 My lover is like a gazelle[i] or a young
stag.[j]
Look! There he stands behind our
wall,
gazing through the windows,
peering through the lattice.
10 My lover spoke and said to me,
"Arise, my darling,
my beautiful one, and come with me.
11 See! The winter is past;
the rains are over and gone.
12 Flowers appear on the earth;
the season of singing has come,
the cooing of doves
is heard in our land.
13 The fig tree forms its early fruit;[k]
the blossoming[l] vines spread their
fragrance.
Arise, come, my darling;
my beautiful one, come with me."

Lover

14 My dove[m] in the clefts of the rock,
in the hiding places on the
mountainside,
show me your face,
let me hear your voice;
for your voice is sweet,
and your face is lovely.[n]
15 Catch for us the foxes,[o]
the little foxes
that ruin the vineyards,[p]
our vineyards that are in bloom.[q]

Beloved

16 My lover is mine and I am his;[r]
he browses among the lilies.[s]
17 Until the day breaks
and the shadows flee,[t]
turn, my lover,[u]
and be like a gazelle
or like a young stag[v]
on the rugged hills.[a][w]

3 All night long on my bed
I looked[x] for the one my heart loves;
I looked for him but did not find him.
2 I will get up now and go about the city,
through its streets and squares;
I will search for the one my heart loves.
So I looked for him but did not find
him.
3 The watchmen found me
as they made their rounds in the city.[y]
"Have you seen the one my heart
loves?"
4 Scarcely had I passed them
when I found the one my heart loves.
I held him and would not let him go

2:9 [i]2Sa 2:18 [j]ver 17; SS 8:14
2:13 [k]Isa 28:4; Jer 24:2; Hos 9:10; Mic 7:1; Na 3:12 [l]SS 7:12
2:14 [m]Ge 8:8; SS 1:15 [n]SS 1:5; 8:13
2:15 [o]Jdg 15:4 [p]SS 1:6 [q]SS 7:12
2:16 [r]SS 7:10 [s]SS 4:5; 6:3
2:17 [t]SS 4:6 [u]SS 1:14 [v]ver 9 [w]ver 8
3:1 [x]SS 5:6; Isa 26:9
3:3 [y]SS 5:7

[a] 17 Or *the hills of Bether*

Week 20

Intimacy With God

Does the idea of intimacy with God frighten you? "Who could be intimate with a holy, righteous God?" you ask. Yes, God is holy and righteous, and he is also loving and compassionate. God reveals himself in Scripture as a father and as a husband. He provides for you and protects you as a loving father. As your husband he desires to meet your need for intimacy.

The most intimate human experience is the relationship between a husband and a wife. The Bible reveals God's desire for that type of intimacy through allegories like that in the book of Hosea and through individual passages like Isaiah 54:5: "For your Maker is your husband—the LORD Almighty is his name." Today, Bible scholars emphasize the need to take Song of Songs at face value—as clear and unapologetic love poetry. But historically this book has been viewed as God comparing intimacy with his people to the all-consuming adoration between two lovers.

Song of Songs 2:1-3 expresses the delight lovers find in each other. Who does God delight in (Ps 147:11)? What does God give to those who delight in him (Ps 37:4)?

The lover sees the beloved as unique and more desirable than others (SS 2:2). How does God see you (Eph 1:4-6; 1Pe 2:9)?

The lover proclaims to all that the beloved is his and he loves her (SS 2:4). How does God proclaim his love for you (Eph 1:7-14)?

The beloved finds strength, refreshment and tenderness in her lover (SS 2:5-6). What needs do you have that Jesus can supply?

The beloved longs for her lover's presence and rejoices when he is near (SS 2:8-9). Do you long for God's presence? What can you experience in God's presence (Ps 16:11; 1Jn 3:19-20)?

The lover calls to the beloved, drawing her with promises of love and fulfillment (SS 2:10-13). How does God call to you (Jer 31:3)?

What is the beloved's warning (SS 2:7)? Love for God cannot be feigned or invented. When your love for God and your desire to be in his presence become a hunger and longing, you are approaching the depth of intimacy that God desires to have with you.

Enjoying God through the Word

Read Hosea 2:14-23 (page 1459). God says that Israel has acted like a prostitute because she "went after her lovers, but me she forgot" (Hos 2:13). God is a jealous God (Ex 34:14); he will not share his people's love with anyone. So he determines to "allure her . . . lead her into the desert and speak tenderly to her" (Hos 2:14). God says that Israel "will call me 'my husband' " (Hos 2:16). These are the words of a lover—God—in pursuit of his beloved—Israel.

God is in pursuit of you too. He wants an intimate relationship with you—one that will last forever, one that will satisfy your deepest needs. You can respond to God by allowing him to draw you into his loving arms. Your life, your relationships, your reactions—all will be affected by God's embrace.

Enjoying God through Experience

If you desire intimacy with God, go to him in prayer. He is waiting. He will rejoice, and he will treat you with tenderness and compassion (Isa 40:11). He is the perfect lover of your soul, one who will never disappoint (Ro 5:5), one who will be faithful, true and loving (Ps 145:13; Rev 19:11). How long before you say, "My lover is mine and I am his" (SS 2:16)?

Go to page 1176 for your next weekly study.

till I had brought him to my mother's
house,[z]
to the room of the one who conceived
me.[a]
5 Daughters of Jerusalem, I charge you[b]
by the gazelles and by the does of the
field:
Do not arouse or awaken love
until it so desires.[c]

6 Who is this coming up from the desert[d]
like a column of smoke,
perfumed with myrrh[e] and incense
made from all the spices[f] of the
merchant?
7 Look! It is Solomon's carriage,
escorted by sixty warriors,[g]
the noblest of Israel,
8 all of them wearing the sword,
all experienced in battle,
each with his sword at his side,
prepared for the terrors of the night.[h]
9 King Solomon made for himself the
carriage;
he made it of wood from Lebanon.
10 Its posts he made of silver,
its base of gold.
Its seat was upholstered with purple,
its interior lovingly inlaid
by[a] the daughters of Jerusalem.
11 Come out, you daughters of Zion,[i]
and look at King Solomon wearing
the crown,
the crown with which his mother
crowned him
on the day of his wedding,
the day his heart rejoiced.[j]

Lover

4 How beautiful you are, my darling!
Oh, how beautiful!
Your eyes behind your veil are doves.[k]
Your hair is like a flock of goats
descending from Mount Gilead.[l]
2 Your teeth are like a flock of sheep just
shorn,
coming up from the washing.
Each has its twin;
not one of them is alone.[m]
3 Your lips are like a scarlet ribbon;
your mouth[n] is lovely.
Your temples behind your veil
are like the halves of a pomegranate.[o]
4 Your neck is like the tower[p] of David,
built with elegance[b];
on it hang a thousand shields,[q]
all of them shields of warriors.
5 Your two breasts[r] are like two fawns,
like twin fawns of a gazelle[s]

3:4 [z]SS 8:2 [a]SS 6:9
3:5 [b]SS 2:7 [c]SS 8:4
3:6 [d]SS 8:5 [e]SS 1:13; 4:6,14 [f]Ex 30:34
3:7 [g]1Sa 8:11
3:8 [h]Job 15:22; Ps 91:5
3:11 [i]Isa 4:4 [j]Isa 62:5
4:1 [k]SS 1:15; 5:12 [l]SS 6:5; Mic 7:14
4:2 [m]SS 6:6
4:3 [n]SS 5:16 [o]SS 6:7
4:4 [p]SS 7:4 [q]Eze 27:10
4:5 [r]SS 7:3 [s]Pr 5:19

Beauty is fragile and temporary. A life built on beauty alone will disappear as quickly as a home built of ice when the summer is coming. A life built on the love of God, however, will flourish and will weather loneliness and trials because the love of God lasts forever.

—Sheila Walsh

[a] 10 *Or its inlaid interior a gift of love / from* [b] 4 The meaning of the Hebrew for this word is uncertain.

4:5 [t]SS 2:16; 6:2-3
4:6 [u]SS 2:17 [v]ver 14
4:7 [w]SS 1:15
4:8 [x]SS 5:1 [y]Dt 3:9 [z]1Ch 5:23
4:9 [a]Ge 41:42
4:10 [b]SS 7:6 [c]SS 1:2
4:11 [d]Ps 19:10; SS 5:1 [e]Hos 14:6
4:12 [f]Pr 5:15-18
4:13 [g]SS 6:11; 7:12 [h]SS 1:14
4:14 [i]Ex 30:23 [j]SS 3:6 [k]SS 1:12
4:16 [l]SS 2:3; 5:1

that browse among the lilies.[t]
6 Until the day breaks
and the shadows flee,[u]
I will go to the mountain of myrrh[v]
and to the hill of incense.
7 All beautiful[w] you are, my darling;
there is no flaw in you.

8 Come with me from Lebanon, my bride,[x]
come with me from Lebanon.
Descend from the crest of Amana,
from the top of Senir,[y] the summit of Hermon,[z]
from the lions' dens
and the mountain haunts of the leopards.
9 You have stolen my heart, my sister, my bride;
you have stolen my heart
with one glance of your eyes,
with one jewel of your necklace.[a]
10 How delightful[b] is your love[c], my sister, my bride!
How much more pleasing is your love than wine,
and the fragrance of your perfume than any spice!
11 Your lips drop sweetness as the honeycomb, my bride;
milk and honey are under your tongue.[d]
The fragrance of your garments is like that of Lebanon.[e]
12 You are a garden locked up, my sister, my bride;
you are a spring enclosed, a sealed fountain.[f]
13 Your plants are an orchard of pomegranates[g]
with choice fruits,
with henna[h] and nard,
14 nard and saffron,
calamus and cinnamon,[i]
with every kind of incense tree,
with myrrh[j] and aloes
and all the finest spices.[k]
15 You are[a] a garden fountain,
a well of flowing water
streaming down from Lebanon.

Beloved

16 Awake, north wind,
and come, south wind!
Blow on my garden,
that its fragrance may spread abroad.
Let my lover come into his garden
and taste its choice fruits.[l]

[a] 15 Or *I am* (spoken by the *Beloved*)

You Are a Garden

SS 4:12

Metaphors can speak of sexual romance without becoming lewd or clinical. The beauty and intensity of the sexual love in this book is heightened because the songs are poetic, not graphic. As the Lover describes his Beloved as a garden filled with delight, we see the power of both his love and his desire in the images he uses. Most telling, he delights that she is a locked garden, an enclosed spring, a sealed fountain. She has kept herself a virgin. So now as she gives herself to him, their delight will be even greater because of the exclusivity of their relationship. The beauty of sexual purity before marriage is emphasized. Song of Songs 8:8–9 speaks of the need for a girl's purity to be guarded until the time of her marriage. Likewise, Proverbs 5:15–20 calls men to sexual purity and faithfulness.

Consummation of Love

SS 5:1

The opening lines of Song of Songs 5 express the consummation of the lovers' relationship. The Lover is here expressing the exhilaration and joy of their union, but the pleasure is not his alone. The Beloved also expresses her pleasure (SS 6:2–3). The love they share is not just emotional or physical. The Lover calls his Beloved "my sister, my bride" (SS 5:1), and the Beloved says, "This is my lover, this [is] my friend" (SS 5:16). These two are experiencing what is meant to be one of the significant blessings of marriage: deep, intimate friendship with each other. When the foundation of a marriage is an abiding friendship, which includes mutual respect and care, a marriage can weather most any storm.

Lover

5

I have come into my garden, my sister,
my bride;[m]
I have gathered my myrrh with my
spice.
I have eaten my honeycomb and my
honey;
I have drunk my wine and my milk.[n]

Friends

Eat, O friends, and drink;
drink your fill, O lovers.

Beloved

2 I slept but my heart was awake.
Listen! My lover is knocking:
"Open to me, my sister, my darling,
my dove, my flawless[o] one.[p]
My head is drenched with dew,
my hair with the dampness of the
night."
3 I have taken off my robe—
must I put it on again?
I have washed my feet—
must I soil them again?
4 My lover thrust his hand through the
latch-opening;
my heart began to pound for him.
5 I arose to open for my lover,
and my hands dripped with myrrh,[q]
my fingers with flowing myrrh,
on the handles of the lock.
6 I opened for my lover,[r]
but my lover had left; he was gone.[s]
My heart sank at his departure.[a]
I looked[t] for him but did not find him.
I called him but he did not answer.
7 The watchmen found me
as they made their rounds in the city.[u]
They beat me, they bruised me;
they took away my cloak,
those watchmen of the walls!
8 O daughters of Jerusalem, I charge
you[v]—
if you find my lover,
what will you tell him?
Tell him I am faint with love.[w]

Friends

9 How is your beloved better than others,
most beautiful of women?[x]
How is your beloved better than others,
that you charge us so?

Beloved

10 My lover is radiant and ruddy,
outstanding among ten thousand.[y]
11 His head is purest gold;

5:1 [m]SS 4:8 [n]SS 4:11; Isa 55:1
5:2 [o]SS 4:7 [p]SS 6:9
5:5 [q]ver 13
5:6 [r]SS 6:1 [s]SS 6:2 [t]SS 3:1
5:7 [u]SS 3:3
5:8 [v]SS 2:7; 3:5 [w]SS 2:5
5:9 [x]SS 1:8; 6:1
5:10 [y]Ps 45:2

[a] 6 Or *heart had gone out to him when he spoke*

his hair is wavy
and black as a raven.
12 His eyes are like doves[z]
by the water streams,
washed in milk,[a]
mounted like jewels.
13 His cheeks[b] are like beds of spice[c]
yielding perfume.
His lips are like lilies[d]
dripping with myrrh.
14 His arms are rods of gold
set with chrysolite.
His body is like polished ivory
decorated with sapphires.[a][e]
15 His legs are pillars of marble
set on bases of pure gold.
His appearance is like Lebanon,[f]
choice as its cedars.
16 His mouth[g] is sweetness itself;
he is altogether lovely.
This is my lover,[h] this my friend,
O daughters of Jerusalem.[i]

Friends

6 Where has your lover[j] gone,
most beautiful of women?[k]
Which way did your lover turn,
that we may look for him with you?

Beloved

2 My lover has gone[l] down to his
garden,[m]
to the beds of spices,[n]
to browse in the gardens
and to gather lilies.
3 I am my lover's and my lover is mine;[o]
he browses among the lilies.[p]

Lover

4 You are beautiful, my darling, as
Tirzah,[q]
lovely as Jerusalem,[r]
majestic as troops with banners.[s]
5 Turn your eyes from me;
they overwhelm me.
Your hair is like a flock of goats
descending from Gilead.[t]
6 Your teeth are like a flock of sheep
coming up from the washing.
Each has its twin,
not one of them is alone.[u]
7 Your temples behind your veil[v]
are like the halves of a pomegranate.[w]
8 Sixty queens[x] there may be,
and eighty concubines,[y]
and virgins beyond number;
9 but my dove,[z] my perfect one,[a] is
unique,
the only daughter of her mother,

Lover and Friend

SS 5:16

Again and again the Lover and his Beloved praise each other. She is truly captivated by his appearance and goes to great lengths to explain the delight she finds in every aspect of his physical beauty (SS 5:10–16). What are we to make of such extravagant praise? First, the enjoyment of the physical body of one's spouse is a gift from God. Within the secure covenant of marriage, the bodies of a husband and wife can be seen, touched, enjoyed and admired. Second, with this couple, praise and enjoyment flow both ways. Each one is free to enjoy and be enjoyed. Third, beyond the enjoyment of another's body is the steadfast heart connection they share. They are united to each other, as ever-loyal, ever-loving friends.

5:12 [z]SS 1:15; 4:1 [a]Ge 49:12
5:13 [b]SS 1:10 [c]SS 6:2 [d]SS 2:1
5:14 [e]Job 28:6
5:15 [f]1Ki 4:33; SS 7:4
5:16 [g]SS 4:3 [h]SS 7:9 [i]SS 1:5
6:1 [j]SS 5:6 [k]SS 1:8
6:2 [l]SS 5:6 [m]SS 4:12 [n]SS 5:13
6:3 [o]SS 7:10 [p]SS 2:16
6:4 [q]Jos 12:24 [r]Ps 48:2; 50:2 [s]ver 10
6:5 [t]SS 4:1
6:6 [u]SS 4:2
6:7 [v]Ge 24:65 [w]SS 4:3
6:8 [x]Ps 45:9 [y]Ge 22:24
6:9 [z]SS 1:15 [a]SS 5:2

[a] 14 Or *lapis lazuli*

the favorite of the one who bore her.[b] 6:9 [b]SS 3:4
The maidens saw her and called her
blessed;
the queens and concubines praised
her.

Friends

10 Who is this that appears like the dawn,
fair as the moon, bright as the sun,
majestic as the stars in procession?

Lover

11 I went down to the grove of nut trees
to look at the new growth in the
valley,
to see if the vines had budded
or the pomegranates were in bloom.[c] 6:11 [c]SS 7:12
12 Before I realized it,
my desire set me among the royal
chariots of my people.[a]

Friends

13 Come back, come back, O Shulammite;
come back, come back, that we may
gaze on you!

Lover

Why would you gaze on the
Shulammite
as on the dance[d] of Mahanaim? 6:13 [d]Ex 15:20

7

How beautiful your sandaled feet, 7:1
O prince's[e] daughter! [e]Ps 45:13
Your graceful legs are like jewels,
the work of a craftsman's hands.
2 Your navel is a rounded goblet
that never lacks blended wine.
Your waist is a mound of wheat
encircled by lilies.
3 Your breasts[f] are like two fawns, 7:3 [f]SS 4:5
twins of a gazelle.
4 Your neck is like an ivory tower.[g] 7:4 [g]Ps 144:12;
Your eyes are the pools of Heshbon[h] SS 4:4
by the gate of Bath Rabbim. [h]Nu 21:26
Your nose is like the tower of Lebanon[i] [i]SS 5:15
looking toward Damascus.
5 Your head crowns you like Mount 7:5
Carmel.[j] [j]Isa 35:2
Your hair is like royal tapestry;
the king is held captive by its tresses.
6 How beautiful[k] you are and how 7:6
pleasing, [k]SS 1:15
O love, with your delights![l] [l]SS 4:10
7 Your stature is like that of the palm, 7:7
and your breasts[m] like clusters of [m]SS 4:5
fruit.
8 I said, "I will climb the palm tree;
I will take hold of its fruit."

[a] 12 Or *among the chariots of Amminadab*; or *among the chariots of the people of the prince*

Two Puzzling Words

SS 6:13

Song of Songs 6:13 contains two puzzling words, *Shulammite* and *Mahanaim*. *Shulammite* may mean "a girl from Shunem," a town in northern Israel. Or it may be a feminine form of Solomon. The Beloved refers to her Lover as the king and as King Solomon (SS 1:12; 3:11), so it is fitting for him to return the tribute and say she is queenly and a compliment to him.

***The dance of Mahanaim* is equally puzzling. The name *Mahanaim* first appears in Genesis 32:2. When Jacob leaves Laban and returns to the promised land, he is met by angels. He names the location "Mahanaim." The dance of Mahanaim may be a traditional wedding dance in which the bride dances her way through two long lines of men. The friends' invitation for the bride to "come back, come back" (SS 6:13) may indicate that she is a little shy of all the attention. Her Lover (now husband) responds to the crowd by saying, "Don't look at my beloved too long or too hard. She's mine!"**

May your breasts be like the clusters of
the vine,
7:8 the fragrance of your breath like
[n]SS 2:5 apples,[n]
[9] and your mouth like the best wine.

Beloved

7:9 May the wine go straight to my lover,[o]
[o]SS 5:16 flowing gently over lips and teeth.[a]
[10] I belong to my lover,
7:10 and his desire[p] is for me.[q]
[p]Ps 45:11 [11] Come, my lover, let us go to the
[q]SS 2:16; 6:3 countryside,
7:12 let us spend the night in the villages.[b]
[r]SS 1:6 [12] Let us go early to the vineyards[r]
[s]SS 2:15 to see if the vines have budded,[s]
[t]SS 2:13 if their blossoms[t] have opened,
[u]SS 4:13 and if the pomegranates[u] are in
[v]SS 6:11 bloom[v]—
there I will give you my love.
7:13 [13] The mandrakes[w] send out their
[w]Ge 30:14 fragrance,
[x]SS 4:16 and at our door is every delicacy,
both new and old,
that I have stored up for you, my
lover.[x]

8 If only you were to me like a brother,
who was nursed at my mother's breasts!
Then, if I found you outside,
I would kiss you,
and no one would despise me.
[2] I would lead you
8:2 and bring you to my mother's
[y]SS 3:4 house[y]—
she who has taught me.
I would give you spiced wine to drink,
the nectar of my pomegranates.
8:3 [3] His left arm is under my head
[z]SS 2:6 and his right arm embraces me.[z]
[4] Daughters of Jerusalem, I charge you:
8:4 Do not arouse or awaken love
[a]SS 2:7; 3:5 until it so desires.[a]

Friends

8:5 [5] Who is this coming up from the desert[b]
[b]SS 3:6 leaning on her lover?
[c]SS 3:4

Beloved

Under the apple tree I roused you;
there your mother conceived[c] you,
there she who was in labor gave you
birth.
[6] Place me like a seal over your heart,
like a seal on your arm;
8:6 for love[d] is as strong as death,
[d]SS 1:2 its jealousy[ce] unyielding as the grave.[d]
[e]Nu 5:14 It burns like blazing fire,

[a] 9 Septuagint, Aquila, Vulgate and Syriac; Hebrew *lips of sleepers* [b] 11 Or *henna bushes* [c] 6 Or *ardor* [d] 6 Hebrew *Sheol*

Dorothy Frances Blomfield Gurney wrote the words to this song for her sister's wedding, using a melody that was a favorite. It has been a part of thousands of weddings since.

O Perfect Love

O perfect Love, all human thought
transcending,
Lowly we kneel in prayer before Thy
throne,
That theirs may be the love which
knows no ending,
Whom Thou forevermore dost join
in one.

O perfect Life, be Thou their full
assurance,
Of tender charity and steadfast
faith,
Of patient hope and quiet, brave
endurance,
With childlike trust that fears not
pain nor death.

Grant them the joy which brightens
earthly sorrow;
Grant them the peace which calms
all earthly strife,
And to life's day the glorious
unknown morrow
That dawns upon eternal love and
life.

—Dorothy Gurney (1858–1932)

The Power of Love

SS 8:6–7

These verses are perhaps some of the finest ever written on the beauty and power of love. Love is as relentless, as never ending, as death and the grave. Love is strong enough to withstand the flood of "many waters," the onset of troubles, the difficulties of everyday living, the unexpected, the unplanned. The Beloved is right: Love can survive any onslaught. But it is also true that love can be quenched. In order to survive, love must be nurtured. The loved one must be esteemed and appreciated. How? The book of Proverbs is full of practical advice on how to keep love flourishing. Its advice touches many aspects of our behavior in relationships. Complaining, arguing, self-centeredness, anger, untrustworthiness and unkindness all have the potential to quench love. It is sobering to realize that adversity does not have the power to destroy love but our sinful choices do.

like a mighty flame.[a]
7 Many waters cannot quench love;
rivers cannot wash it away.
If one were to give
all the wealth of his house for love,
it[b] would be utterly scorned.[f]

8:7 [f]Pr 6:35

Friends

8 We have a young sister,
and her breasts are not yet grown.
What shall we do for our sister
for the day she is spoken for?
9 If she is a wall,
we will build towers of silver on her.
If she is a door,
we will enclose her with panels of
cedar.

Beloved

10 I am a wall,
and my breasts are like towers.
Thus I have become in his eyes
like one bringing contentment.
11 Solomon had a vineyard[g] in Baal
Hamon;
he let out his vineyard to tenants.
Each was to bring for its fruit
a thousand shekels[c h] of silver.
12 But my own vineyard[i] is mine to give;
the thousand shekels are for you,
O Solomon,
and two hundred[d] are for those who
tend its fruit.

8:11 [g]Ecc 2:4 [h]Isa 7:23
8:12 [i]SS 1:6

Lover

13 You who dwell in the gardens
with friends in attendance,
let me hear your voice!

Beloved

14 Come away, my lover,
and be like a gazelle[j]
or like a young stag[k]
on the spice-laden mountains.[l]

8:14 [j]Pr 5:19 [k]SS 2:9 [l]SS 2:8,17

[a] *6* Or */ like the very flame of the* LORD [b] *7* Or *he*
[c] *11* That is, about 25 pounds (about 11.5 kilograms); also in verse 12 [d] *12* That is, about 5 pounds (about 2.3 kilograms)

Isaiah

Judgment and salvation.

Quick Study

Author
The prophet Isaiah.

Date Written
Around 700 B.C.

Setting
Judah.

Key Passage
Isaiah 6:8 "Then I heard the voice of the Lord saying, 'Whom shall I send? And who will go for us?' And I said, 'Here am I. Send me!' "

Isaiah discusses problems that are as troublesome today as they were in ancient Israel and Judah. With Israel (the northern kingdom) living in slavery and exile, the inhabitants of Judah (the southern kingdom) stand at a crossroads. Lacking a strong leader to point them back to God, the people slip into idolatry and indifference, extortion and excess, depravity and deceit. In the midst of this spiritual decline, Isaiah brings a message of confrontation to the people of Judah as well as a message of hope for the exiles of Israel.

Isaiah, a well-educated prophet, maintains direct access to the king and to the leaders of Judah. He speaks God's words clearly, denouncing the idolatry and sinful practices of the people (Isa 1–5). He vividly recounts his vision of God, revealing God's holiness (Isa 6). He demonstrates God's awesome power over seemingly insurmountable obstacles when Sennacherib threatens Jerusalem (Isa 36–37). Using a compelling poetic style, Isaiah offers peace and strength to those who follow God (Isa 40).

The book of Isaiah also includes the most vivid portrayal of the Messiah found in the Old Testament. We learn of his birth (Isa 9) and his supremacy over everything (Isa 41–48). We weep as Isaiah portrays the Messiah as the suffering servant and unveils the horrors of his ultimate sacrifice (Isa 49–53). Yet Isaiah's prophecy does not end with horror but with victory, with promises of hope and restoration in God's future kingdom (Isa 60–61).

Outline

A rebellious nation.
Isa 1-5

Isaiah's commissioning.
Isa 6

Several prophecies.
Isa 7-12

Prophecies about specific nations.
Isa 13-23

Devastation.
Isa 24

Praises.
Isa 25-27

Woes.
Isa 28-31

Warnings and restoration.
Isa 32-35

Sennacherib and Hezekiah.
Isa 36-39

Sin, repentance and deliverance.
Isa 40—56:8

Accusations.
Isa 56:9—57:13

Comfort.
Isa 57:14-21

Returning to the Lord.
Isa 58-59

Glory returning to Zion.
Isa 60-66

The Women of Isaiah

Women of Zion	*Spoiled rotten.* Isa 3:16—4:6
The virgin	*Mother of Immanuel.* Isa 7:14
Isaiah's wife	*Wife and prophetess.* Isa 8:1-4
Complacent women	*Change predicted.* Isa 32:9-20
A mother	*She never forgot her child.* Isa 49:15

1 The vision[a] concerning Judah and Jerusalem[b] that Isaiah son of Amoz saw[c] during the reigns of Uzziah,[d] Jotham, Ahaz[e] and Hezekiah, kings of Judah.

A Rebellious Nation

2 Hear, O heavens! Listen, O earth!
For the LORD has spoken:[f]
"I reared children and brought them up,
but they have rebelled[g] against me.
3 The ox knows his master,
the donkey his owner's manger,
but Israel does not know,[h]
my people do not understand."

4 Ah, sinful nation,
a people loaded with guilt,
a brood of evildoers,[i]
children given to corruption!
They have forsaken the LORD;
they have spurned the Holy One[j] of Israel
and turned their backs on him.

5 Why should you be beaten anymore?
Why do you persist in rebellion?[k]
Your whole head is injured,
your whole heart afflicted.[l]
6 From the sole of your foot to the top of your head
there is no soundness[m]—
only wounds and welts
and open sores,
not cleansed or bandaged[n]
or soothed with oil.[o]
7 Your country is desolate,[p]
your cities burned with fire;
your fields are being stripped by foreigners
right before you,
laid waste as when overthrown by strangers.
8 The Daughter of Zion is left
like a shelter in a vineyard,
like a hut[q] in a field of melons,
like a city under siege.
9 Unless the LORD Almighty
had left us some survivors,[r]
we would have become like Sodom,
we would have been like Gomorrah.[s]

10 Hear the word of the LORD,[t]
you rulers of Sodom;[u]
listen to the law[v] of our God,
you people of Gomorrah!
11 "The multitude of your sacrifices—
what are they to me?" says the LORD.
"I have more than enough of burnt offerings,
of rams and the fat of fattened animals;[w]
I have no pleasure

1:1 [a]Nu 12:6 [b]Isa 40:9 [c]Isa 2:1 [d]2Ch 26:22 [e]2Ki 16:1
1:2 [f]Mic 1:2 [g]Isa 30:1,9; 65:2
1:3 [h]Jer 8:7; 9:3,6
1:4 [i]Isa 14:20 [j]Isa 5:19,24
1:5 [k]Isa 31:6 [l]Isa 33:6,24
1:6 [m]Ps 38:3 [n]Isa 30:26; Jer 8:22 [o]Lk 10:34
1:7 [p]Lev 26:34
1:8 [q]Job 27:18
1:9 [r]Isa 10:20-22; 37:4,31-32 [s]Ge 19:24; Ro 9:29*
1:10 [t]Isa 28:14 [u]Isa 3:9; Eze 16:49; Ro 9:29; Rev 11:8 [v]Isa 8:20
1:11 [w]Ps 50:8

About Vision

ISA 1:1

The Lord honors Isaiah by visiting him with a supernatural vision. Biblical people who receive visions gain a special consciousness and understanding of God and his will, especially for the future (for example, Daniel, Ezekiel and John in the book of Revelation). Often a vision "speaks" to the individual(s) through images and metaphors that need interpretation to be fully understood. A vision functions similarly to a dream but occurs when a person is awake.

Though infrequent and sometimes misunderstood, visions can still occur today through brief flashes or prolonged images in the mind's eye. They communicate encouragement as well as warnings. But God is the initiator, not us. Our part is to be open to their occurrence, receive them by faith and hold them up for confirmation from godly people, the Scriptures and the Lord himself. Then when we understand God's words to us, we have the privilege of following his direction and participating in his eternal purposes.

Heart Matters

ISA 1:13–14

The divided kingdom of Israel and Judah dishonors God with their spiritual attitudes and actions. Ruled by King Ahaz of Judah and an assortment of evil, short-lived kings from Israel, the people worship idols and even sacrifice children. Yet at the same time, many continue the feasts and sacrifices required by the Lord. Practiced with brittle hearts and sinful lifestyles, these God-ward sacrifices and celebrations weary the Lord. He's had enough! Instead of outward expressions of ritual, God wants a people with pure, obedient hearts.

Though God isn't abolishing his guidelines for religious practice, he is warning his people to look within. They are not to forsake important traditions and avenues for spiritual growth. Yet most crucial is the condition of their hearts as they approach God. Who they are outweighs the religious rituals they practice.

in the blood of bulls[x] and lambs and
goats.[y]
12 When you come to appear before me,
who has asked this of you,[z]
this trampling of my courts?
13 Stop bringing meaningless offerings![a]
Your incense[b] is detestable to me.
New Moons, Sabbaths and
convocations[c]—
I cannot bear your evil assemblies.
14 Your New Moon festivals and your
appointed feasts[d]
my soul hates.
They have become a burden to me;
I am weary[e] of bearing them.
15 When you spread out your hands in
prayer,
I will hide[f] my eyes from you;
even if you offer many prayers,
I will not listen.
Your hands are full of blood;[g]
16 wash and make yourselves clean.
Take your evil deeds
out of my sight![h]
Stop doing wrong,[i]
17 learn to do right!
Seek justice,[j]
encourage the oppressed.[a]
Defend the cause of the fatherless,[k]
plead the case of the widow.

18 "Come now, let us reason together,"[l]
says the LORD.
"Though your sins are like scarlet,
they shall be as white as snow;[m]
though they are red as crimson,
they shall be like wool.
19 If you are willing and obedient,
you will eat the best from the land;[n]
20 but if you resist and rebel,
you will be devoured by the sword."[o]
For the mouth of the LORD
has spoken.[p]

21 See how the faithful city
has become a harlot![q]
She once was full of justice;
righteousness used to dwell in her—
but now murderers!
22 Your silver has become dross,
your choice wine is diluted with water.
23 Your rulers are rebels,
companions of thieves;
they all love bribes[r]
and chase after gifts.
They do not defend the cause of the
fatherless;
the widow's case does not come
before them.[s]
24 Therefore the Lord, the LORD Almighty,

1:11 [x]Jer 6:20 [y]1Sa 15:22; Mal 1:10
1:12 [z]Ex 23:17
1:13 [a]Isa 66:3 [b]Jer 7:9 [c]1Ch 23:31
1:14 [d]Lev 23:1-44; Nu 28:11-29:39; Isa 29:1 [e]Isa 7:13; 43:22,24
1:15 [f]Isa 8:17; 59:2; Mic 3:4 [g]Isa 59:3
1:16 [h]Isa 52:11 [i]Isa 55:7; Jer 25:5
1:17 [j]Zep 2:3 [k]Ps 82:3
1:18 [l]Isa 41:1; 43:9,26 [m]Ps 51:7; Rev 7:14
1:19 [n]Dt 30:15-16; Isa 55:2
1:20 [o]Isa 3:25; 65:12 [p]Isa 34:16; 40:5; 58:14; Mic 4:4
1:21 [q]Isa 57:3-9; Jer 2:20
1:23 [r]Ex 23:8 [s]Isa 10:2; Jer 5:28; Eze 22:6-7; Zec 7:10

[a] 17 Or / *rebuke the oppressor*

the Mighty One of Israel, declares:
"Ah, I will get relief from my foes
and avenge[t] myself on my enemies.
25 I will turn my hand against you;
I will thoroughly purge away your dross
and remove all your impurities.[u]
26 I will restore your judges as in days of old,[v]
your counselors as at the beginning.
Afterward you will be called
the City of Righteousness,[w]
the Faithful City.[x]"
27 Zion will be redeemed with justice,
her penitent ones with righteousness.[y]
28 But rebels and sinners will both be broken,
and those who forsake the LORD will perish.[z]

29 "You will be ashamed because of the sacred oaks[a]
in which you have delighted;
you will be disgraced because of the gardens[b]
that you have chosen.
30 You will be like an oak with fading leaves,
like a garden without water.
31 The mighty man will become tinder
and his work a spark;
both will burn together,
with no one to quench the fire.[c]"

The Mountain of the LORD

2 This is what Isaiah son of Amoz saw concerning Judah and Jerusalem:[d]

2 In the last days

the mountain[e] of the LORD's temple will be established
as chief among the mountains;
it will be raised above the hills,
and all nations will stream to it.

3 Many peoples will come and say,

"Come, let us go up to the mountain of the LORD,
to the house of the God of Jacob.
He will teach us his ways,
so that we may walk in his paths."
The law[f] will go out from Zion,
the word of the LORD from Jerusalem.[g]
4 He will judge between the nations
and will settle disputes for many peoples.
They will beat their swords into plowshares
and their spears into pruning hooks.[h]
Nation will not take up sword against nation,[i]

1:24 [t]Isa 35:4; 59:17; 61:2; 63:4
1:25 [u]Eze 22:22; Mal 3:3
1:26 [v]Jer 33:7,11 [w]Isa 33:5; 62:1; Zec 8:3 [x]Isa 60:14; 62:2
1:27 [y]Isa 35:10; 62:12; 63:4
1:28 [z]Ps 9:5; Isa 24:20; 66:24; 2Th 1:8-9
1:29 [a]Isa 57:5 [b]Isa 65:3; 66:17
1:31 [c]Isa 5:24; 9:18-19; 26:11; 33:14; 66:15-16,24
2:1 [d]Isa 1:1
2:2 [e]Isa 27:13; 56:7; 66:20; Mic 4:7
2:3 [f]Isa 51:4,7 [g]Lk 24:47
2:4 [h]Joel 3:10 [i]Ps 46:9; Isa 9:5; 11:6-9; 32:18; Hos 2:18; Zec 9:10

Shady Gardens

ISA 1:29

We think of shaded gardens as places of rest and beauty, but in Isaiah's day they represented apostasy. Gardens shaded by oak trees frequently harbored idol worship and rituals that involved sexual intercourse. To God, these were not "sacred gardens" at all. They were abominations.

In an interesting contrast, when people repent, obey and worship God, they will be called "oaks of righteousness, a planting of the LORD for the display of his splendor" (Isa 61:3). No "fading leaves," no "garden without water" (Isa 1:30), the redeemed (Isa 1:27) will instead walk where there are "streams in the desert" and "bubbling springs" (Isa 35:6–7).

The Last Days

ISA 2:2–5

When are the last days? It's a question that's challenged Bible scholars for centuries. Some believe the last days began with Jesus Christ's birth and will continue until his second coming. Others say this time refers to the time of God's judgments, followed by Christ's rule.

Whatever the case, in the last days God will do marvelous things. According to this text, the Lord will establish his temple, teach us his ways, settle disputes and end wars (Isa 2:2–4). So rather than fearing the last days, if our names are written in the Lamb's book of life (Rev 3:5), we can joyfully anticipate them.

nor will they train for war anymore.

5 Come, O house of Jacob,[j]
let us walk in the light[k] of the LORD.

The Day of the LORD

6 You have abandoned[l] your people,
the house of Jacob.
They are full of superstitions from the East;
they practice divination like the Philistines[m]
and clasp hands[n] with pagans.[o]
7 Their land is full of silver and gold;
there is no end to their treasures.
Their land is full of horses;[p]
there is no end to their chariots.[q]
8 Their land is full of idols;[r]
they bow down to the work of their hands,
to what their fingers[s] have made.
9 So man will be brought low[t]
and mankind humbled[u]—
do not forgive them.[a][v]

10 Go into the rocks,
hide in the ground
from dread of the LORD
and the splendor of his majesty![w]
11 The eyes of the arrogant man will be humbled
and the pride[x] of men brought low;
the LORD alone will be exalted in that day.

12 The LORD Almighty has a day in store
for all the proud and lofty,
for all that is exalted[y]
(and they will be humbled),[z]
13 for all the cedars of Lebanon, tall and lofty,
and all the oaks of Bashan,[a]
14 for all the towering mountains
and all the high hills,[b]
15 for every lofty tower
and every fortified wall,[c]
16 for every trading ship[b][d]
and every stately vessel.
17 The arrogance of man will be brought low
and the pride of men humbled;
the LORD alone will be exalted in that day,[e]
18 and the idols will totally disappear.[f]

19 Men will flee to caves in the rocks
and to holes in the ground
from dread of the LORD
and the splendor of his majesty,
when he rises to shake the earth.[g]
20 In that day men will throw away
to the rodents and bats[h]

2:5 [j]Isa 58:1 [k]Isa 60:1,19-20; 1Jn 1:5,7
2:6 [l]Dt 31:17 [m]2Ki 1:2 [n]Pr 6:1 [o]2Ki 16:7
2:7 [p]Dt 17:16 [q]Isa 31:1; Mic 5:10
2:8 [r]Isa 10:9-11 [s]Isa 17:8
2:9 [t]Ps 62:9 [u]Isa 5:15 [v]Ne 4:5
2:10 [w]2Th 1:9; Rev 6:15-16
2:11 [x]Isa 5:15; 37:23
2:12 [y]Isa 24:4,21; Mal 4:1 [z]Job 40:11
2:13 [a]Zec 11:2
2:14 [b]Isa 30:25; 40:4
2:15 [c]Isa 25:2,12
2:16 [d]1Ki 10:22
2:17 [e]ver 11
2:18 [f]Isa 21:9
2:19 [g]Heb 12:26
2:20 [h]Lev 11:19

[a] 9 Or *not raise them up* [b] 16 Hebrew *every ship of Tarshish*

their idols of silver and idols of gold,
which they made to worship.
21 They will flee to caverns in the rocks
and to the overhanging crags
from dread of the LORD
and the splendor of his majesty,
when he rises to shake the earth.[i]
22 Stop trusting in man,[j]
who has but a breath in his nostrils.
Of what account is he?[k]

Judgment on Jerusalem and Judah

3 See now, the Lord,
the LORD Almighty,
is about to take from Jerusalem and Judah
both supply and support:
all supplies of food[l] and all supplies of water,[m]
2 the hero and warrior,[n]
the judge and prophet,
the soothsayer and elder,[o]
3 the captain of fifty and man of rank,
the counselor, skilled craftsman and clever enchanter.

4 I will make boys their officials;
mere children will govern them.[p]
5 People will oppress each other—
man against man, neighbor against neighbor.[q]
The young will rise up against the old,
the base against the honorable.
6 A man will seize one of his brothers
at his father's home, and say,
"You have a cloak, you be our leader;
take charge of this heap of ruins!"
7 But in that day he will cry out,
"I have no remedy.[r]
I have no food or clothing in my house;
do not make me the leader of the people."

8 Jerusalem staggers,
Judah is falling;[s]
their words[t] and deeds are against the LORD,
defying[u] his glorious presence.
9 The look on their faces testifies against them;
they parade their sin like Sodom;[v]
they do not hide it.
Woe to them!
They have brought disaster[w] upon themselves.

10 Tell the righteous it will be well[x] with them,
for they will enjoy the fruit of their deeds.[y]

2:21 [i]ver 19
2:22 [j]Ps 146:3; Jer 17:5 [k]Ps 8:4; 144:3; Isa 40:15; Jas 4:14
3:1 [l]Lev 26:26 [m]Isa 5:13; Eze 4:16
3:2 [n]Eze 17:13 [o]2Ki 24:14; Isa 9:14-15
3:4 [p]Ecc 10:16 *fn*
3:5 [q]Isa 9:19; Jer 9:8; Mic 7:2,6
3:7 [r]Eze 34:4; Hos 5:13
3:8 [s]Isa 1:7 [t]Isa 9:15,17 [u]Ps 73:9,11
3:9 [v]Ge 13:13 [w]Pr 8:36; Ro 6:23
3:10 [x]Dt 28:1-14 [y]Ps 128:2

Whom Do We Trust?

ISA 2:22

When we're depressed, when we're busy beyond belief, when life dishes out its challenges, where do we turn? Where do we place our trust? Often it's a friend, a parent, a husband, a colleague. Or it's food, drink, sex or other quick fixes that dull our senses. Unfortunately these painkillers—whether they're labeled "good" or "bad" for us—don't offer lasting peace and satisfaction. If we place our trust in them they will eventually disappoint or destroy us.

The Lord told Judah to stop trusting in people and the work of their hands. Humans are mortal, and things are temporary. Idols melt in the heat of the day. In contrast, God is immortal, permanent and eternally trustworthy. He is a safe haven for his people's trust in good times and bad.

Women Rulers

ISA 3:12

If we don't know the cultural context, this verse may lead us to think that God disapproves of young or female leaders. The lives of two very young kings (Joash, 2Ki 11:1–3; Josiah, 2Ki 22:1, as well as Deborah (Jdg 4) and Esther (Est 2:1—9:32) reveal the opposite. Still, in this ancient patriarchal society, female leadership indicated a nation in chaos. Isaiah paints a vivid picture for the wayward people; one their minds can easily comprehend.

The prophet may also be pointing to future war. If women and children rule, it means the men have been killed in battle. Or perhaps Isaiah is simply saying that the male leadership of Israel is immature, unfit for leadership. Whatever his intention, we should never forget that the great message of Isaiah is that if people turn from their sin, God will forgive, heal and bless. There is hope for every person, every nation!

11 Woe to the wicked! Disaster[z] is upon
them!
They will be paid back for what their
hands have done.

12 Youths[a] oppress my people,
women rule over them.
O my people, your guides lead you
astray;[b]
they turn you from the path.

13 The LORD takes his place in court;
he rises to judge[c] the people.
14 The LORD enters into judgment[d]
against the elders and leaders of his
people:
"It is you who have ruined my vineyard;
the plunder[e] from the poor is in your
houses.
15 What do you mean by crushing my
people[f]
and grinding the faces of the poor?"
declares the Lord,
the LORD Almighty.

16 The LORD says,
"The women of Zion[g] are haughty,
walking along with outstretched necks,
flirting with their eyes,
tripping along with mincing steps,
with ornaments jingling on their
ankles.
17 Therefore the Lord will bring sores on
the heads of the women of Zion;
the LORD will make their scalps bald."

18 In that day the Lord will snatch away their finery: the bangles and headbands and crescent
necklaces,[h] 19 the earrings and bracelets and veils,
20 the headdresses[i] and ankle chains and sashes,
the perfume bottles and charms, 21 the signet rings
and nose rings, 22 the fine robes and the capes and
cloaks, the purses 23 and mirrors, and the linen
garments and tiaras and shawls.

24 Instead of fragrance[j] there will be a
stench;
instead of a sash,[k] a rope;
instead of well-dressed hair, baldness;[l]
instead of fine clothing, sackcloth;[m]
instead of beauty,[n] branding.
25 Your men will fall by the sword,[o]
your warriors in battle.
26 The gates of Zion will lament and
mourn;[p]
destitute, she will sit on the ground.[q]

4 In that day seven women
will take hold of one man[r]
and say, "We will eat our own food[s]
and provide our own clothes;
only let us be called by your name.
Take away our disgrace!"[t]

3:11 [z]Dt 28:15-68
3:12 [a]ver 4 [b]Isa 9:16
3:13 [c]Mic 6:2
3:14 [d]Job 22:4 [e]Job 24:9; Jas 2:6
3:15 [f]Ps 94:5
3:16 [g]SS 3:11
3:18 [h]Jdg 8:21
3:20 [i]Ex 39:28
3:24 [j]Est 2:12 [k]Pr 31:24 [l]Isa 22:12 [m]La 2:10; Eze 27:30-31 [n]1Pe 3:3
3:25 [o]Isa 1:20
3:26 [p]Jer 14:2 [q]La 2:10
4:1 [r]Isa 13:12 [s]2Th 3:12 [t]Ge 30:23

The Branch of the LORD

[2]In that day the Branch of the LORD[u] will be beautiful and glorious, and the fruit[v] of the land will be the pride and glory of the survivors in Israel. [3]Those who are left in Zion, who remain[w] in Jerusalem, will be called holy,[x] all who are recorded[y] among the living in Jerusalem. [4]The Lord will wash away the filth[z] of the women of Zion; he will cleanse the bloodstains[a] from Jerusalem by a spirit[a] of judgment[b] and a spirit[a] of fire.[c] [5]Then the LORD will create over all of Mount Zion and over those who assemble there a cloud of smoke by day and a glow of flaming fire by night;[d] over all the glory[e] will be a canopy. [6]It will be a shelter[f] and shade from the heat of the day, and a refuge[g] and hiding place from the storm and rain.

The Song of the Vineyard

5 I will sing for the one I love
a song about his vineyard:[h]
My loved one had a vineyard
on a fertile hillside.
[2]He dug it up and cleared it of stones
and planted it with the choicest vines.[i]
He built a watchtower in it
and cut out a winepress as well.
Then he looked for a crop of good grapes,
but it yielded only bad fruit.[j]

[3]"Now you dwellers in Jerusalem and men of Judah,
judge between me and my vineyard.[k]
[4]What more could have been done for my vineyard
than I have done for it?[l]
When I looked for good grapes,
why did it yield only bad?
[5]Now I will tell you
what I am going to do to my vineyard:
I will take away its hedge,
and it will be destroyed;
I will break down its wall,[m]
and it will be trampled.[n]
[6]I will make it a wasteland,
neither pruned nor cultivated,
and briers and thorns[o] will grow there.
I will command the clouds
not to rain on it."

[7]The vineyard[p] of the LORD Almighty
is the house of Israel,
and the men of Judah
are the garden of his delight.
And he looked for justice,[q] but saw bloodshed;
for righteousness, but heard cries of distress.

4:2 [u]Isa 11:1-5; 53:2; Jer 23:5-6; Zec 3:8; 6:12 [v]Ps 72:16
4:3 [w]Ro 11:5 [x]Isa 52:1; 60:21 [y]Lk 10:20
4:4 [z]Isa 3:24 [a]Isa 1:15 [b]Isa 28:6 [c]Isa 1:31; Mt 3:11
4:5 [d]Ex 13:21 [e]Isa 60:1
4:6 [f]Ps 27:5 [g]Isa 25:4
5:1 [h]Ps 80:8-9
5:2 [i]Jer 2:21 [j]Mt 21:19; Mk 11:13; Lk 13:6
5:3 [k]Mt 21:40
5:4 [l]2Ch 36:15; Jer 2:5-7; Mic 6:3-4; Mt 23:37
5:5 [m]Ps 80:12 [n]Isa 28:3,18; La 1:15; Lk 21:24
5:6 [o]Isa 7:23,24; Heb 6:8
5:7 [p]Ps 80:8 [q]Isa 59:15

[a] 4 Or *the Spirit*

The way to his holy habitat is a path of light. That can be a problem if our eyes have become acclimated to the shadows . . . We will tend to pull back from the first painful light of illumination. But just as we adjusted to the deception, so we can choose to adapt to the light and thereby move closer to the Truth . . . There is One who . . . longs for us to know his rest. He understands our desire for a hiding place. He woos us to his soothing side—even when it's him we've foolishly been hiding from—so that we might find the refuge we so desperately need.

—Patsy Clairmont

Land Grabbers

ISA 5:8

In ancient times property served as the primary inheritance of most Israelites, with specified land belonging to families for generations. Property held a spiritual and national significance for these people because, through Abraham, God promised the land of Canaan to their nation (Ge 12:7; Nu 33:53). The Lord told Moses and Joshua to divide the land among the tribes "as an inheritance," according to each group's population (Nu 26:52–53; Jos 13:6–7). So land was considered a sacred gift from God to be treasured and kept indefinitely.

Those who "join field to field" are landowners who profit off the poor, taking another family's inheritance and amassing large blocks of land through unscrupulous business practices. Because God is the true owner of the land, and he's parceled it out carefully, those who gobble up property gather his disfavor. God despises the self-indulgent who swindle the weak and defraud the disadvantaged.

Woes and Judgments

8 Woe[r] to you who add house to house
and join field to field[s]
till no space is left
and you live alone in the land.

9 The LORD Almighty has declared in my hearing:[t]

"Surely the great houses will become
desolate,[u]
the fine mansions left without
occupants.
10 A ten-acre[a] vineyard will produce only a
bath[b] of wine,
a homer[c] of seed only an ephah[d] of
grain."[v]

11 Woe to those who rise early in the
morning
to run after their drinks,
who stay up late at night
till they are inflamed with wine.[w]
12 They have harps and lyres at their
banquets,
tambourines and flutes and wine,
but they have no regard[x] for the deeds
of the LORD,
no respect for the work of his hands.[y]
13 Therefore my people will go into exile[z]
for lack of understanding;[a]
their men of rank will die of hunger
and their masses will be parched with
thirst.
14 Therefore the grave[e][b] enlarges its
appetite
and opens its mouth[c] without limit;
into it will descend their nobles and
masses
with all their brawlers and revelers.
15 So man will be brought low[d]
and mankind humbled,[e]
the eyes of the arrogant[f] humbled.
16 But the LORD Almighty will be exalted
by his justice,[g]
and the holy God will show himself
holy[h] by his righteousness.
17 Then sheep will graze as in their own
pasture;[i]
lambs will feed[f] among the ruins of
the rich.

18 Woe to those who draw sin along with
cords of deceit,
and wickedness[j] as with cart ropes,
19 to those who say, "Let God hurry,

5:8 [r]Jer 22:13 [s]Mic 2:2; Hab 2:9-12
5:9 [t]Isa 22:14 [u]Isa 6:11-12; Mt 23:38
5:10 [v]Lev 26:26
5:11 [w]Pr 23:29-30
5:12 [x]Job 34:27 [y]Ps 28:5; Am 6:5-6
5:13 [z]Hos 4:6 [a]Isa 1:3; Hos 4:6
5:14 [b]Pr 30:16 [c]Nu 16:30
5:15 [d]Isa 10:33 [e]Isa 2:9 [f]Isa 2:11
5:16 [g]Isa 28:17; 30:18; 33:5; 61:8 [h]Isa 29:23
5:17 [i]Isa 7:25; Zep 2:6,14
5:18 [j]Isa 59:4-8; Jer 23:14

[a] *10* Hebrew *ten-yoke,* that is, the land plowed by 10 yoke of oxen in one day [b] *10* That is, probably about 6 gallons (about 22 liters) [c] *10* That is, probably about 6 bushels (about 220 liters) [d] *10* That is, probably about 3/5 bushel (about 22 liters) [e] *14* Hebrew *Sheol* [f] *17* Septuagint; Hebrew / *strangers will eat*

let him hasten his work
so we may see it.
Let it approach,
let the plan of the Holy One of Israel
come,
so we may know it."[k]
20 Woe to those who call evil good
and good evil,
who put darkness for light
and light for darkness,[l]
who put bitter for sweet
and sweet for bitter.[m]
21 Woe to those who are wise in their own
eyes[n]
and clever in their own sight.

22 Woe to those who are heroes at drinking
wine[o]
and champions at mixing drinks,
23 who acquit the guilty for a bribe,[p]
but deny justice[q] to the innocent.[r]
24 Therefore, as tongues of fire lick up
straw
and as dry grass sinks down in the
flames,
so their roots will decay[s]
and their flowers blow away like dust;
for they have rejected the law of the
LORD Almighty
and spurned the word[t] of the Holy
One of Israel.
25 Therefore the LORD's anger[u] burns
against his people;
his hand is raised and he strikes them
down.
The mountains shake,
and the dead bodies are like refuse[v] in
the streets.

Yet for all this, his anger is not turned
away,[w]
his hand is still upraised.[x]

26 He lifts up a banner for the distant
nations,
he whistles[y] for those at the ends of
the earth.[z]
Here they come,
swiftly and speedily!
27 Not one of them grows tired or
stumbles,
not one slumbers or sleeps;
not a belt is loosened at the waist,[a]
not a sandal thong is broken.[b]
28 Their arrows are sharp,[c]
all their bows[d] are strung;
their horses' hoofs seem like flint,
their chariot wheels like a whirlwind.
29 Their roar is like that of the lion,[e]
they roar like young lions;
they growl as they seize[f] their prey

5:19 [k]Jer 17:15; Eze 12:22; 2Pe 3:4
5:20 [l]Mt 6:22-23; Lk 11:34-35 [m]Am 5:7
5:21 [n]Pr 3:7; Ro 12:16; 1Co 3:18-20
5:22 [o]Pr 23:20
5:23 [p]Ex 23:8 [q]Isa 10:2 [r]Ps 94:21; Jas 5:6
5:24 [s]Job 18:16 [t]Isa 8:6; 30:9,12
5:25 [u]2Ki 22:13 [v]2Ki 9:37 [w]Jer 4:8; Da 9:16 [x]Isa 9:12,17, 21; 10:4
5:26 [y]Isa 7:18; Zec 10:8 [z]Dt 28:49; Isa 13:5; 18:3
5:27 [a]Job 12:18 [b]Joel 2:7-8
5:28 [c]Ps 45:5 [d]Ps 7:12
5:29 [e]Jer 51:38; Zep 3:3; Zec 11:3 [f]Isa 10:6; 49:24-25

Woe Are You

ISA 5:20-22

Israelites use the word woe when mourning the death of a friend or relative. Isaiah's emphasis of the word foretells the nation's death via their sins and God's judgment. In this chapter the prophet employs the literary device of repetition to underscore the impending doom. Maybe if he keeps repeating his "woe are you" message, someone might actually listen. Interestingly, Jesus also uses the "woe" approach when he condemns the Pharisees (see the note on Mt 23:5-27, page 1624). Using the word woe turns a speech into a not-to-be-missed message.

In this passage Isaiah's "woe" speeches denounce six sins. Underline them in your Bible. As God's children, we can turn the woe-are-we warning into a we-are-blessed celebration. For each of the six sins, name an opposite action that will elicit God's blessing. Which one of these blessed actions could you practice this week?

Dulled Senses

ISA 6:9–10

God is long-suffering, but, in this case, the people's chronic rebellion has withered his patience. These verses sound as though God wants to make his people's hearts calloused. However, look at the NIV footnote. The essence of these verses is that the Lord looks into the future and sees a nation that has grown even more hard-hearted. Isaiah is commissioned, and his message will cause the people's hearts to grow even more calloused.

So why does the Lord keep pursuing them? God's love for his children is unending, and perhaps a remnant within the nation will hear and obey. Or perhaps the people will remember his words and repent after calamity has struck. Even in his wrath, God exercises mercy.

Thankfully, those who keep their hearts open to the Lord will know only his love and mercy. God sometimes disciplines his children, but the faithful need not fear the exasperated anger he turns toward these defiant sinners.

and carry it off with no one to
rescue.[g]
30 In that day they will roar over it
like the roaring of the sea.[h]
And if one looks at the land,
he will see darkness and distress;[i]
even the light will be darkened[j] by the
clouds.

Isaiah's Commission

6 In the year that King Uzziah[k] died,[l] I saw the
Lord[m] seated on a throne,[n] high and exalted,
and the train of his robe filled the temple. 2 Above
him were seraphs,[o] each with six wings: With two
wings they covered their faces, with two they covered their feet,[p] and with two they were flying.
3 And they were calling to one another:

"Holy, holy, holy is the LORD Almighty;
the whole earth is full of his glory."[q]

4 At the sound of their voices the doorposts and
thresholds shook and the temple was filled with
smoke.
5 "Woe to me!" I cried. "I am ruined! For I am a
man of unclean lips, and I live among a people of
unclean lips,[r] and my eyes have seen the King,[s]
the LORD Almighty."
6 Then one of the seraphs flew to me with a live
coal in his hand, which he had taken with tongs
from the altar. 7 With it he touched my mouth and
said, "See, this has touched your lips;[t] your guilt
is taken away and your sin atoned for.[u]"
8 Then I heard the voice[v] of the Lord saying,
"Whom shall I send? And who will go for us?"
And I said, "Here am I. Send me!"
9 He said, "Go[w] and tell this people:

" 'Be ever hearing, but never
understanding;
be ever seeing, but never perceiving.'[x]
10 Make the heart of this people calloused;[y]
make their ears dull
and close their eyes.[a]
Otherwise they might see with their
eyes,
hear with their ears,[z]
understand with their hearts,
and turn and be healed."[a]

11 Then I said, "For how long, O Lord?"[b]
And he answered:

"Until the cities lie ruined[c]
and without inhabitant,
until the houses are left deserted
and the fields ruined and ravaged,
12 until the LORD has sent everyone far
away[d]

5:29 [g]Isa 42:22; Mic 5:8
5:30 [h]Lk 21:25 [i]Isa 8:22; Jer 4:23-28 [j]Joel 2:10
6:1 [k]2Ch 26:22, 23 [l]2Ki 15:7 [m]Jn 12:41 [n]Rev 4:2
6:2 [o]Rev 4:8 [p]Eze 1:11
6:3 [q]Ps 72:19; Rev 4:8
6:5 [r]Jer 9:3-8 [s]Jer 51:57
6:7 [t]Jer 1:9 [u]1Jn 1:7
6:8 [v]Ac 9:4
6:9 [w]Eze 3:11 [x]Mt 13:15*; Lk 8:10*
6:10 [y]Dt 32:15; Ps 119:70 [z]Jer 5:21 [a]Mt 13:13-15; Mk 4:12*; Ac 28:26-27*
6:11 [b]Ps 79:5 [c]Lev 26:31
6:12 [d]Dt 28:64

[a] 9,10 Hebrew; Septuagint *'You will be ever hearing, but never understanding; / you will be ever seeing, but never perceiving.' / 10 This people's heart has become calloused; / they hardly hear with their ears, / and they have closed their eyes*

6:12 and the land is utterly forsaken.[e]
eJer 4:29 [13]And though a tenth remains[f] in the land,
6:13 it will again be laid waste.
fIsa 1:9 But as the terebinth and oak
gJob 14:7 leave stumps when they are cut down,
so the holy seed will be the stump in
the land."[g]

The Sign of Immanuel

7:1 **7** When Ahaz son of Jotham, the son of Uzziah,
hKi 15:37 was king of Judah, King Rezin[h] of Aram[i] and
i2Ch 28:5 Pekah[j] son of Remaliah king of Israel marched up
j2Ki 15:25 to fight against Jerusalem, but they could not
7:2 overpower it.
kver 13; [2]Now the house of David[k] was told, "Aram has
Isa 22:22 allied itself with[a] Ephraim[l]"; so the hearts of Ahaz
lIsa 9:9 and his people were shaken, as the trees of the
forest are shaken by the wind.
[3]Then the LORD said to Isaiah, "Go out, you and
7:3 your son Shear-Jashub,[b] to meet Ahaz at the end
m2Ki 18:17; of the aqueduct of the Upper Pool, on the road to
Isa 36:2 the Washerman's Field.[m] [4]Say to him, 'Be careful,
7:4 keep calm[n] and don't be afraid.[o] Do not lose
nIsa 30:15 oIsa 35:4 heart[p] because of these two smoldering stubs[q] of
pDt 20:3 firewood—because of the fierce anger[r] of Rezin
qZec 3:2 rIsa 10:24 and Aram and of the son of Remaliah. [5]Aram,
Ephraim and Remaliah's son have plotted your
ruin, saying, [6]"Let us invade Judah; let us tear it
apart and divide it among ourselves, and make
the son of Tabeel king over it." [7]Yet this is what
the Sovereign LORD says:

" 'It will not take place,
7:7 it will not happen,[s]
sIsa 8:10; [8]for the head of Aram is Damascus,[t]
Ac 4:25 and the head of Damascus is only
Rezin.
Within sixty-five years
7:8 Ephraim will be too shattered[u] to be a
tGe 14:15 uIsa 17:1-3 people.
[9]The head of Ephraim is Samaria,
and the head of Samaria is only
Remaliah's son.
7:9 If you do not stand firm in your faith,[v]
v2Ch 20:20 wIsa 8:6-8; 30:12-14 you will not stand at all.' "[w]

[10]Again the LORD spoke to Ahaz, [11]"Ask the LORD
your God for a sign, whether in the deepest
depths or in the highest heights."
[12]But Ahaz said, "I will not ask; I will not put
the LORD to the test."
[13]Then Isaiah said, "Hear now, you house of
7:13 David! Is it not enough to try the patience of men?
xIsa 25:1 Will you try the patience of my God[x] also? [14]There-
7:14 fore the Lord himself will give you[c] a sign: The vir-
yLk 1:31 zIsa 8:8,10; gin will be with child and will give birth to a son,[y]
Mt 1:23* and[d] will call him Immanuel.[ez] [15]He will eat curds

[a] 2 Or *has set up camp in* [b] 3 *Shear-Jashub* means *a remnant will return.* [c] 14 The Hebrew is plural.
[d] 14 Masoretic Text; Dead Sea Scrolls *and he* or *and they*
[e] 14 *Immanuel* means *God with us.*

The Sign

ISA 7:14

When Ahaz refuses to ask God for a sign (Isa 7:12), the Lord gives him a prophecy with a double meaning. First, a young woman, possibly Isaiah's wife, will bear a son. When the boy has grown, Judah's two enemies, Israel and Aram, will be destroyed. Second, a virgin will be miraculously impregnated and bear Jesus, the Messiah. He will be called Immanuel, "God with us" (Mt 1:23).

The virgin birth is a crucial sign of the coming Messiah and later becomes an important part of Christian doctrine. Conceived by the Holy Spirit, Jesus is wholly God. Born of a human mother, he is wholly man. With both qualifications, he perfectly fits the role of intermediary between God and humanity. He can, and does, redeem the world.

and honey[a] when he knows enough to reject the
wrong and choose the right. 16But before the boy
knows[b] enough to reject the wrong and choose the
right, the land of the two kings you dread will be
laid waste.[c] 17The LORD will bring on you and on
your people and on the house of your father a time
unlike any since Ephraim broke away[d] from
Judah—he will bring the king of Assyria.[e]"

18In that day the LORD will whistle[f] for flies from
the distant streams of Egypt and for bees from the
land of Assyria.[g] 19They will all come and settle in
the steep ravines and in the crevices[h] in the rocks,
on all the thornbushes and at all the water holes.
20In that day the Lord will use[i] a razor hired from
beyond the River*[a]*—the king of Assyria[j]—to shave
your head and the hair of your legs, and to take
off your beards also. 21In that day, a man will keep
alive a young cow and two goats. 22And because
of the abundance of the milk they give, he will
have curds to eat. All who remain in the land will
eat curds and honey. 23In that day, in every place
where there were a thousand vines worth a thousand silver shekels,*[b]* there will be only briers and
thorns.[k] 24Men will go there with bow and arrow,
for the land will be covered with briers and thorns.
25As for all the hills once cultivated by the hoe, you
will no longer go there for fear of the briers and
thorns; they will become places where cattle are
turned loose and where sheep run.[l]

Assyria, the LORD's Instrument

8 The LORD said to me, "Take a large scroll[m] and
write on it with an ordinary pen: Maher-Shalal-Hash-Baz.*[c]*[n] 2And I will call in Uriah[o] the priest
and Zechariah son of Jeberekiah as reliable witnesses for me."

3Then I went to the prophetess, and she conceived and gave birth to a son. And the LORD said to
me, "Name him Maher-Shalal-Hash-Baz. 4Before
the boy knows[p] how to say 'My father' or 'My
mother,' the wealth of Damascus and the plunder of
Samaria will be carried off by the king of Assyria.[q]"

5The LORD spoke to me again:

6"Because this people has rejected[r]
the gently flowing waters of Shiloah[s]
and rejoices over Rezin
and the son of Remaliah,[t]
7therefore the Lord is about to bring
against them
the mighty floodwaters[u] of the
River*[a]*—
the king of Assyria[v] with all his
pomp.
It will overflow all its channels,
run over all its banks
8and sweep on into Judah, swirling
over it,

7:15 [a]ver 22
7:16 [b]Isa 8:4 [c]Isa 17:3; Hos 5:9,13; Am 1:3-5
7:17 [d]1Ki 12:16 [e]2Ch 28:20
7:18 [f]Isa 5:26 [g]Isa 13:5
7:19 [h]Isa 2:19
7:20 [i]Isa 10:15 [j]Isa 8:7; 10:5
7:23 [k]Isa 5:6
7:25 [l]Isa 5:17
8:1 [m]Isa 30:8; Hab 2:2 [n]ver 3; Hab 2:2
8:2 [o]2Ki 16:10
8:4 [p]Isa 7:16 [q]Isa 7:8
8:6 [r]Isa 5:24 [s]Jn 9:7 [t]Isa 7:1
8:7 [u]Isa 17:12-13 [v]Isa 7:20

[a] *20,7* That is, the Euphrates *[b]* *23* That is, about 25 pounds (about 11.5 kilograms) *[c]* *1 Maher-Shalal-Hash-Baz* means *quick to the plunder, swift to the spoil*; also in verse 3.

The Boy Child

ISA 8:3

The birth of a son to the prophetess (Isaiah's wife) marks the fulfillment of the prophecy in Isaiah 7:14—or at least the first half of it. Though this child isn't called Immanuel, his name and life are significant to Judah's future. To the Israelites, names often describe an event or characteristic, and the name *Maher-Shalal-Hash-Baz* means "quick to the plunder, swift to the spoil." Before the boy can say his parents' names, Assyria will plunder Judah's enemies, the Arameans and the northern kingdom (Israel). But Judah isn't exempt from the destruction.

Judah's demise occurs after years of God's pursuit and entreaty that they turn from sin and follow him. Throughout history the Lord has waited patiently and given warning about what will happen if the wicked don't repent. We can take comfort in this as we pray for, and interact with, those who don't know him. The Lord offers many chances, many signs and messages, to the rebellious. He tarries so all have opportunity to repent (2Pe 3:9).

passing through it and reaching up to
the neck.
Its outspread wings will cover the
breadth of your land,
O Immanuel[a]!"[w]
9 Raise the war cry,[b][x] you nations, and be
shattered!
Listen, all you distant lands.
Prepare[y] for battle, and be shattered!
Prepare for battle, and be shattered!
10 Devise your strategy, but it will be
thwarted;[z]
propose your plan, but it will not
stand,[a]
for God is with us.[c][b]

Fear God

11 The LORD spoke to me with his strong hand
upon me,[c] warning me not to follow[d] the way of
this people. He said:

12 "Do not call conspiracy[e]
everything that these people call
conspiracy[d];
do not fear what they fear,
and do not dread it.[f]
13 The LORD Almighty is the one you are
to regard as holy,[g]
he is the one you are to fear,
he is the one you are to dread,[h]
14 and he will be a sanctuary;[i]
but for both houses of Israel he
will be
a stone that causes men to stumble
and a rock that makes them fall.[j]
And for the people of Jerusalem he
will be
a trap and a snare.[k]
15 Many of them will stumble;[l]
they will fall and be broken,
they will be snared and captured."

16 Bind up the testimony
and seal[m] up the law among my
disciples.
17 I will wait[n] for the LORD,
who is hiding[o] his face from the
house of Jacob.
I will put my trust in him.

18 Here am I, and the children the LORD has giv-
en me.[p] We are signs[q] and symbols in Israel from
the LORD Almighty, who dwells on Mount Zion.[r]
19 When men tell you to consult[s] mediums and
spiritists, who whisper and mutter,[t] should not a
people inquire of their God? Why consult the dead
on behalf of the living? 20 To the law[u] and to the testimony! If they do not speak according to this

8:8 [w]Isa 7:14
8:9 [x]Isa 17:12-13 [y]Joel 3:9
8:10 [z]Job 5:12 [a]Isa 7:7 [b]Isa 7:14; Ro 8:31
8:11 [c]Eze 3:14 [d]Eze 2:8
8:12 [e]Isa 7:2; 30:1 [f]1Pe 3:14*
8:13 [g]Nu 20:12 [h]Isa 29:23
8:14 [i]Isa 4:6; Eze 11:16 [j]Lk 2:34; Ro 9:33*; 1Pe 2:8* [k]Isa 24:17-18
8:15 [l]Isa 28:13; 59:10; Lk 20:18; Ro 9:32
8:16 [m]Isa 29:11-12
8:17 [n]Hab 2:3 [o]Dt 31:17; Isa 54:8
8:18 [p]Heb 2:13* [q]Lk 2:34 [r]Ps 9:11
8:19 [s]1Sa 28:8 [t]Isa 29:4
8:20 [u]Isa 1:10; Lk 16:29

[a] 8 *Immanuel* means *God with us.* [b] 9 Or *Do your worst* [c] 10 Hebrew *Immanuel* [d] 12 Or *Do not call for a treaty / every time these people call for a treaty*

God With Us

ISA 8:8

The name Immanuel, meaning "God with us," *expresses two sides of God's presence. He is with us to destroy evil, as in the name assigned to Maher-Shalal-Hash-Baz* (Isa 8:3); *and he is with us to redeem those who repent, as in the name given to Jesus, which means "the Lord saves"* (Mt 1:21 *and footnote*). *God's presence never yields complacency. It divides believers from unbelievers.*

Light and Dark

ISA 9:2

"The people walking in darkness" refer to those steeped in the darkness of sin, those without God. Isaiah foretells that God will not leave his people in the dark, but will shine his saving light on them. He will release them from bondage if they're willing to forsake their sin.

Some scholars believe this light metaphor refers to future kings of Judah, such as Hezekiah and Josiah, who would later lead the people back to serving God. Other scholars see this as a reference to the Messiah. He came, offering the light of forgiveness and restoration to sinners: "When Jesus spoke again to the people, he said, 'I am the light of the world. Whoever follows me will never walk in darkness, but will have the light of life' " (Jn 8:12).

As those who now know the Messiah, we too can look forward to God's light shining on our dark world. When Jesus Christ returns, he will banish sin's darkness once and for all, and we will bask in the light of his presence.

word, they have no light[v] of dawn. 21 Distressed and
hungry, they will roam through the land; when
they are famished, they will become enraged and,
looking upward, will curse[w] their king and their
God. 22 Then they will look toward the earth and
see only distress and darkness and fearful gloom,
and they will be thrust into utter darkness.[x]

To Us a Child Is Born

9 Nevertheless, there will be no more gloom for
those who were in distress. In the past he humbled the land of Zebulun and the land of Naphtali,[y] but in the future he will honor Galilee of the
Gentiles, by the way of the sea, along the Jordan—

2 The people walking in darkness
have seen a great light;[z]
on those living in the land of the shadow of death[a][a]
a light has dawned.[b]
3 You have enlarged the nation
and increased their joy;
they rejoice before you
as people rejoice at the harvest,
as men rejoice
when dividing the plunder.
4 For as in the day of Midian's defeat,[c]
you have shattered
the yoke[d] that burdens them,
the bar across their shoulders,[e]
the rod of their oppressor.[f]
5 Every warrior's boot used in battle
and every garment rolled in blood
will be destined for burning,[g]
will be fuel for the fire.
6 For to us a child is born,[h]
to us a son is given,[i]
and the government[j] will be on his shoulders.
And he will be called
Wonderful Counselor,[b][k] Mighty God,[l]
Everlasting Father, Prince of Peace.[m]
7 Of the increase of his government and peace
there will be no end.[n]
He will reign on David's throne
and over his kingdom,
establishing and upholding it
with justice[o] and righteousness
from that time on and forever.
The zeal[p] of the LORD Almighty
will accomplish this.

The LORD's Anger Against Israel

8 The Lord has sent a message against Jacob;
it will fall on Israel.
9 All the people will know it—

8:20 [v]Mic 3:6
8:21 [w]Rev 16:11
8:22 [x]ver 20; Isa 5:30
9:1 [y]2Ki 15:29
9:2 [z]Eph 5:8 [a]Lk 1:79 [b]Mt 4:15-16*
9:4 [c]Jdg 7:25 [d]Isa 14:25 [e]Isa 10:27 [f]Isa 14:4; 49:26; 51:13; 54:14
9:5 [g]Isa 2:4
9:6 [h]Isa 53:2; Lk 2:11 [i]Jn 3:16 [j]Mt 28:18 [k]Isa 28:29 [l]Isa 10:21; 11:2 [m]Isa 26:3,12; 66:12
9:7 [n]Da 2:44; Lk 1:33 [o]Isa 11:4; 16:5; 32:1, 16 [p]Isa 37:32; 59:17

[a] 2 Or *land of darkness* [b] 6 Or *Wonderful, Counselor*

Ephraim and the inhabitants of
Samaria[q]—
who say with pride
and arrogance[r] of heart,
10 "The bricks have fallen down,
but we will rebuild with dressed stone;
the fig trees have been felled,
but we will replace them with cedars."
11 But the LORD has strengthened Rezin's[s]
foes against them
and has spurred their enemies on.
12 Arameans[t] from the east and Philistines[u]
from the west
have devoured[v] Israel with open mouth.

Yet for all this, his anger is not turned
away,
his hand is still upraised.[w]

13 But the people have not returned to him
who struck[x] them,
nor have they sought[y] the LORD
Almighty.
14 So the LORD will cut off from Israel both
head and tail,
both palm branch and reed[z] in a
single day;[a]
15 the elders[b] and prominent men are the
head,
the prophets who teach lies are the
tail.
16 Those who guide[c] this people mislead
them,
and those who are guided are led
astray.[d]
17 Therefore the Lord will take no pleasure
in the young men,[e]
nor will he pity[f] the fatherless and
widows,
for everyone is ungodly[g] and wicked,[h]
every mouth speaks vileness.[i]

Yet for all this, his anger is not turned
away,
his hand is still upraised.[j]

18 Surely wickedness burns like a fire;[k]
it consumes briers and thorns,
it sets the forest thickets ablaze,[l]
so that it rolls upward in a column of
smoke.
19 By the wrath[m] of the LORD Almighty
the land will be scorched
and the people will be fuel for the fire;[n]
no one will spare his brother.[o]
20 On the right they will devour,
but still be hungry;[p]
on the left they will eat,[q]
but not be satisfied.
Each will feed on the flesh of his own
offspring[a]:

9:9 [q]Isa 7:9 [r]Isa 46:12
9:11 [s]Isa 7:8
9:12 [t]2Ki 16:6 [u]2Ch 28:18 [v]Ps 79:7 [w]Isa 5:25
9:13 [x]Jer 5:3 [y]Isa 31:1; Hos 7:7,10
9:14 [z]Isa 19:15 [a]Rev 18:8
9:15 [b]Isa 3:2-3
9:16 [c]Mt 15:14; 23:16,24 [d]Isa 3:12
9:17 [e]Jer 18:21 [f]Isa 27:11 [g]Isa 10:6 [h]Isa 1:4 [i]Mt 12:34 [j]Isa 5:25
9:18 [k]Mal 4:1 [l]Ps 83:14
9:19 [m]Isa 13:9,13 [n]Isa 1:31 [o]Mic 7:2,6
9:20 [p]Lev 26:26 [q]Isa 49:26

[a] 20 Or *arm*

Even the Orphans

ISA 9:17

God especially cares for orphans and widows and defends their cause (Dt 10:18). Yet at this point, even they suffer because of Judah's wickedness. When sin prevails, not just the perpetrators, but even the defenseless, bear the brunt of its punishment. It's hard to think of babies as being wicked, but the Lord says everyone in Judah is "ungodly and wicked" (Isa 9:17). The wicked had earned a death sentence for them all.

On the other hand, "righteousness exalts a nation" (Pr 14:34), and the Lord "loves those who pursue righteousness" (Pr 15:9). One righteous person can save a family (Lot, Cornelius) or a nation (Abraham, Moses). God offers deep satisfaction to those who live righteously among the unconverted.

21 Manasseh will feed on Ephraim, and
Ephraim on Manasseh;
together they will turn against Judah.[r]

Yet for all this, his anger is not turned
away,
his hand is still upraised.[s]

10 Woe to those who make unjust laws,
to those who issue oppressive decrees,[t]
2 to deprive[u] the poor of their rights
and withhold justice from the
oppressed of my people,[v]
making widows their prey
and robbing the fatherless.
3 What will you do on the day of
reckoning,[w]
when disaster[x] comes from afar?
To whom will you run for help?[y]
Where will you leave your riches?
4 Nothing will remain but to cringe
among the captives[z]
or fall among the slain.[a]
Yet for all this, his anger is not turned
away,[b]
his hand is still upraised.

God's Judgment on Assyria

5 "Woe to the Assyrian,[c] the rod of my
anger,
in whose hand is the club[d] of my
wrath![e]
6 I send him against a godless[f] nation,
I dispatch him against a people who
anger me,[g]
to seize loot and snatch plunder,[h]
and to trample them down like mud
in the streets.
7 But this is not what he intends,[i]
this is not what he has in mind;
his purpose is to destroy,
to put an end to many nations.
8 'Are not my commanders[j] all kings?' he
says.
9 'Has not Calno[k] fared like
Carchemish?[l]
Is not Hamath like Arpad,
and Samaria[m] like Damascus?[n]
10 As my hand seized the kingdoms of the
idols,[o]
kingdoms whose images excelled
those of Jerusalem and Samaria—
11 shall I not deal with Jerusalem and her
images
as I dealt with Samaria and her idols?' "

12 When the Lord has finished all his work[p]
against Mount Zion[q] and Jerusalem, he will say, "I
will punish the king of Assyria[r] for the willful
pride of his heart and the haughty look in his
eyes. 13 For he says:

9:21 [r]2Ch 28:6 [s]Isa 5:25
10:1 [t]Ps 58:2
10:2 [u]Isa 3:14 [v]Isa 5:23
10:3 [w]Job 31:14; Hos 9:7 [x]Lk 19:44 [y]Isa 20:6
10:4 [z]Isa 24:22 [a]Isa 22:2; 34:3; 66:16 [b]Isa 5:25
10:5 [c]Isa 14:25; Zep 2:13 [d]Jer 51:20 [e]Isa 13:3,5, 13; 30:30; 66:14
10:6 [f]Isa 9:17 [g]Isa 9:19 [h]Isa 5:29
10:7 [i]Ge 50:20; Ac 4:23-28
10:8 [j]2Ki 18:24
10:9 [k]Ge 10:10 [l]2Ch 35:20 [m]2Ki 17:6 [n]2Ki 16:9
10:10 [o]2Ki 19:18
10:12 [p]Isa 28:21-22; 65:7 [q]2Ki 19:31 [r]Jer 50:18

More Woe

ISA 10:1-3

"If justice prevails, good faith is found in treaties, truth in transactions, order in government, the earth is at peace, and heaven itself sheds over us its beneficent light and radiates down to us its blessed influence."*

God blesses the just, but he says "woe" to those who are unjust (Isa 10:1). He hates injustice and wants his people to fight against it. What injustices do you see in the world today? Jot down a list. How can you contribute to making justice prevail? Describe one practical and immediate thing you can do.

**J. B. Bossuet, 1627-1704, "Sermon on Justice."*

10:13 [s]Isa 37:24; Da 4:30 [t]Eze 28:4

" 'By the strength of my hand I have
done this,[s]
and by my wisdom, because I have
understanding.
I removed the boundaries of nations,
I plundered their treasures;[t]
like a mighty one I subdued[a] their
kings.

10:14 [u]Jer 49:16; Ob 1:4 [v]Job 31:25

14 As one reaches into a nest,[u]
so my hand reached for the wealth[v] of
the nations;
as men gather abandoned eggs,
so I gathered all the countries;
not one flapped a wing,
or opened its mouth to chirp.' "

15 Does the ax raise itself above him who
swings it,
or the saw boast against him who
uses it?[w]

10:15 [w]Isa 45:9; Ro 9:20-21 [x]ver 5

As if a rod were to wield him who lifts it
up,
or a club[x] brandish him who is not
wood!

10:16 [y]ver 18; Isa 17:4 [z]Isa 8:7

16 Therefore, the Lord, the LORD Almighty,
will send a wasting disease[y] upon his
sturdy warriors;
under his pomp[z] a fire will be kindled
like a blazing flame.

10:17 [a]Isa 31:9 [b]Isa 37:23 [c]Nu 11:1-3 [d]Isa 9:18

17 The Light of Israel will become a fire,[a]
their Holy One[b] a flame;
in a single day it will burn and consume
his thorns[c] and his briers.[d]

10:18 [e]2Ki 19:23

18 The splendor of his forests[e] and fertile
fields
it will completely destroy,
as when a sick man wastes away.
19 And the remaining trees of his forests
will be so few[f]
that a child could write them down.

10:19 [f]Isa 21:17

The Remnant of Israel

10:20 [g]Isa 11:10,11 [h]2Ki 16:7 [i]2Ch 28:20 [j]Isa 17:7

20 In that day[g] the remnant of Israel,
the survivors of the house of Jacob,
will no longer rely[h] on him
who struck them down[i]
but will truly rely[j] on the LORD,
the Holy One of Israel.

10:21 [k]Isa 6:13 [l]Isa 9:6

21 A remnant[k] will return,[b] a remnant of
Jacob
will return to the Mighty God.[l]
22 Though your people, O Israel, be like
the sand by the sea,
only a remnant will return.[m]

10:22 [m]Ro 9:27-28 [n]Isa 28:22; Da 9:27

Destruction has been decreed,[n]
overwhelming and righteous.
23 The Lord, the LORD Almighty, will carry
out

[a] 13 Or / *I subdued the mighty,* [b] 21 Hebrew *shear-jashub;* also in verse 22

True Reliance

ISA 10:20

Scholars hold three different viewpoints about who are "the remnant" of the Jewish people. They are (1) survivors of the northern kingdom's demise; (2) survivors of Nebuchadnezzar's later invasion; or (3) future Jewish people who return to complete trust in God. Whoever they are, the Lord declares they will "truly rely" on him.

Whenever God disciplines or passes judgment on his children, his objective is to bring them back to himself. He wants his people to truly rely on him, not on things or people or accomplishments. Instead of living in pain and frustration, he wants his people to live in, and depend on, him (Jn 15:1-8) and know the peace of righteousness (Heb 12:11). With this in mind, we can receive God's correction as an act of his love and mercy, releasing us from bondage so we can live free and unfettered.

Spirit of the LORD

ISA 11:2

In the Old Testament God's Spirit, called "the Spirit of the LORD," comes on people for a specified time so they can accomplish a task. For example, the Spirit of the Lord empowers the barehanded Samson to kill a lion (Jdg 14:5–6). In the New Testament the Spirit of the Lord rests on Jesus. As the Messiah—the "shoot . . . from the stump of Jesse" (Isa 11:1)—he carries the full power of God with him, not for a singular task, but for his entire ministry. His death, resurrection and ascension open the way for God's Spirit, called "the Holy Spirit" (Ac 2:4), to indwell believers. Since then Christians have benefited from the constant presence of the Spirit within, rather than occasionally being endowed with the Spirit for a particular task, as in the Old Testament.

the destruction decreed upon the
whole land.[o]

24 Therefore, this is what the Lord, the LORD
Almighty, says:
"O my people who live in Zion,[p]
do not be afraid of the Assyrians,
who beat[q] you with a rod
and lift up a club against you, as
Egypt did.
25 Very soon[r] my anger against you will end
and my wrath[s] will be directed to
their destruction."

26 The LORD Almighty will lash[t] them with
a whip,
as when he struck down Midian[u] at
the rock of Oreb;
and he will raise his staff over the
waters,[v]
as he did in Egypt.
27 In that day their burden will be lifted
from your shoulders,
their yoke[w] from your neck;[x]
the yoke will be broken
because you have grown so fat.[a]

28 They enter Aiath;
they pass through Migron;[y]
they store supplies at Micmash.[z]
29 They go over the pass, and say,
"We will camp overnight at Geba."
Ramah[a] trembles;
Gibeah of Saul flees.
30 Cry out, O Daughter of Gallim![b]
Listen, O Laishah!
Poor Anathoth![c]
31 Madmenah is in flight;
the people of Gebim take cover.
32 This day they will halt at Nob;[d]
they will shake their fist
at the mount of the Daughter of Zion,[e]
at the hill of Jerusalem.

33 See, the Lord, the LORD Almighty,
will lop off the boughs with great
power.
The lofty trees will be felled,
the tall[f] ones will be brought low.
34 He will cut down the forest thickets
with an ax;
Lebanon will fall before the Mighty
One.

The Branch From Jesse

11 A shoot will come up from the stump of
Jesse;[g]
from his roots a Branch[h] will bear
fruit.
2 The Spirit[i] of the LORD will rest on him—

10:23 [o]Isa 28:22; Ro 9:27-28*
10:24 [p]Ps 87:5-6 [q]Ex 5:14
10:25 [r]Isa 17:14 [s]ver 5; Da 11:36
10:26 [t]Isa 37:36-38 [u]Isa 9:4 [v]Ex 14:16
10:27 [w]Isa 9:4 [x]Isa 14:25
10:28 [y]1Sa 14:2 [z]1Sa 13:2
10:29 [a]Jos 18:25
10:30 [b]1Sa 25:44 [c]Ne 11:32
10:32 [d]1Sa 21:1 [e]Jer 6:23
10:33 [f]Am 2:9
11:1 [g]ver 10; Isa 9:7; Rev 5:5 [h]Isa 4:2
11:2 [i]Isa 42:1; 48:16; 61:1; Mt 3:16; Jn 1:32-33

[a] *27* Hebrew; Septuagint *broken / from your shoulders*

the Spirit of wisdom[j] and of
understanding,
the Spirit of counsel and of power,[k]
the Spirit of knowledge and of the fear
of the LORD—
3 and he will delight in the fear of the
LORD.

He will not judge by what he sees with
his eyes,[l]
or decide by what he hears with his
ears;[m]
4 but with righteousness[n] he will judge
the needy,
with justice[o] he will give decisions for
the poor[p] of the earth.
He will strike[q] the earth with the rod of
his mouth;
with the breath[r] of his lips he will
slay the wicked.
5 Righteousness will be his belt
and faithfulness[s] the sash around his
waist.[t]

6 The wolf will live with the lamb,[u]
the leopard will lie down with the
goat,
the calf and the lion and the yearling[a]
together;
and a little child will lead them.
7 The cow will feed with the bear,
their young will lie down together,
and the lion will eat straw like the ox.
8 The infant will play near the hole of the
cobra,
and the young child put his hand into
the viper's nest.
9 They will neither harm nor destroy[v]
on all my holy mountain,
for the earth[w] will be full of the
knowledge[x] of the LORD
as the waters cover the sea.

10 In that day the Root of Jesse will stand as a banner[y] for the peoples; the nations[z] will rally to him,[a]
and his place of rest[b] will be glorious. 11 In that day[c]
the Lord will reach out his hand a second time to
reclaim the remnant that is left of his people from
Assyria,[d] from Lower Egypt, from Upper Egypt,[b]
from Cush,[c] from Elam,[e] from Babylonia,[d] from
Hamath and from the islands[f] of the sea.

12 He will raise a banner for the nations
and gather the exiles of Israel;
he will assemble the scattered people[g] of
Judah
from the four quarters of the earth.
13 Ephraim's jealousy will vanish,
and Judah's enemies[e] will be cut off;

11:2 [j]Eph 1:17 [k]2Ti 1:7
11:3 [l]Jn 7:24 [m]Jn 2:25
11:4 [n]Ps 72:2 [o]Isa 9:7 [p]Isa 3:14 [q]Mal 4:6 [r]Job 4:9; 2Th 2:8
11:5 [s]Isa 25:1 [t]Eph 6:14
11:6 [u]Isa 65:25
11:9 [v]Job 5:23 [w]Ps 98:2-3; Isa 52:10 [x]Isa 45:6, 14; Hab 2:14
11:10 [y]Jn 12:32 [z]Isa 49:23; Lk 2:32 [a]Ro 15:12* [b]Isa 14:3; 28:12; 32:17-18
11:11 [c]Isa 10:20 [d]Isa 19:24; Hos 11:11; Mic 7:12; Zec 10:10 [e]Ge 10:22 [f]Isa 42:4, 10, 12; 66:19
11:12 [g]Zep 3:10

[a] *6* Hebrew; Septuagint *lion will feed* [b] *11* Hebrew *from Pathros* [c] *11* That is, the upper Nile region [d] *11* Hebrew *Shinar* [e] *13* Or *hostility*

Peaceable Kingdom

ISA 11:6-9

Isaiah depicts a remarkable time when natural predators live in peace together. They feel no need to destroy; they don't fear being destroyed. When will this be? Some say it's during the Millennium when Jesus Christ sets up his kingdom on earth and rules for a thousand years (Rev 20:1-10). During this time the world will be at peace. Some believe this occurs when God establishes the new heaven and new earth at the end of the age (Rev 21:1-4). Others believe Isaiah's peaceable kingdom is a metaphor for sinners who turn to God and live at peace with his children, the lambs. In each of these scenarios, God's people live in a God-generated peace. Even now—when wolves don't lie down with lambs and when children don't play with snakes and when wars do still happen—we can possess peace within.

Thankful Praise

ISA 12:1

Isaiah wants to give hope and meaning to the people as they experience suffering, so he explains how they'll feel once God's judgment has passed and they again live in righteousness. After enduring hardship and allowing it to reshape them, they will be relieved and grateful for what God has accomplished to transform them. Their natural response will be to break out in praise to God: "Surely God is my salvation . . . The LORD, the LORD, is my strength and my song" (Isa 12:2). Their song of praise resounds with the knowledge that God is the source of all good in their lives. Their spiritual perspective changes, and they know joy again.

Ephraim will not be jealous of Judah,
nor Judah hostile toward Ephraim.[h]
14 They will swoop down on the slopes of Philistia to the west;
together they will plunder the people to the east.
They will lay hands on Edom[i] and Moab,[j]
and the Ammonites will be subject to them.
15 The LORD will dry up
the gulf of the Egyptian sea;
with a scorching wind he will sweep his hand[k]
over the Euphrates River.[a][l]
He will break it up into seven streams
so that men can cross over in sandals.
16 There will be a highway[m] for the remnant of his people
that is left from Assyria,
as there was for Israel
when they came up from Egypt.[n]

Songs of Praise

12 In that day you will say:

"I will praise[o] you, O LORD.
Although you were angry with me,
your anger has turned away
and you have comforted me.
2 Surely God is my salvation;
I will trust[p] and not be afraid.
The LORD, the LORD, is my strength and my song;
he has become my salvation.[q]"
3 With joy you will draw water[r]
from the wells of salvation.

4 In that day you will say:

"Give thanks to the LORD, call on his name;[s]
make known among the nations what he has done,
and proclaim that his name is exalted.
5 Sing[t] to the LORD, for he has done glorious things;[u]
let this be known to all the world.
6 Shout aloud and sing for joy, people of Zion,
for great is the Holy One of Israel[v]
among you.[w]"

A Prophecy Against Babylon

13 An oracle concerning Babylon that Isaiah son of Amoz saw:

2 Raise a banner[x] on a bare hilltop,
shout to them;
beckon to them
to enter the gates of the nobles.

11:13 [h]Jer 3:18; Eze 37:16-17,22; Hos 1:11
11:14 [i]Da 11:41; Joel 3:19 [j]Isa 16:14; 25:10
11:15 [k]Isa 19:16 [l]Isa 7:20
11:16 [m]Isa 19:23; 62:10 [n]Ex 14:26-31
12:1 [o]Isa 25:1
12:2 [p]Isa 26:3 [q]Ex 15:2; Ps 118:14
12:3 [r]Jn 4:10,14
12:4 [s]Ps 105:1; Isa 24:15
12:5 [t]Ex 15:1 [u]Ps 98:1
12:6 [v]Isa 49:26 [w]Zep 3:14-17
13:2 [x]Jer 50:2; 51:27

[a] 15 Hebrew *the River*

13:3 [y]Joel 3:11 [z]Ps 149:2

3 I have commanded my holy ones;
I have summoned my warriors[y] to
carry out my wrath—
those who rejoice[z] in my triumph.

13:4 [a]Joel 3:14

4 Listen, a noise on the mountains,
like that of a great multitude![a]
Listen, an uproar among the kingdoms,
like nations massing together!
The LORD Almighty is mustering
an army for war.

13:5 [b]Isa 5:26 [c]Isa 24:1

5 They come from faraway lands,
from the ends of the heavens[b]—
the LORD and the weapons of his
wrath—
to destroy[c] the whole country.

13:6 [d]Eze 30:2 [e]Isa 2:12; Joel 1:15

6 Wail,[d] for the day[e] of the LORD is near;
it will come like destruction from the
Almighty.[a]

13:7 [f]Eze 21:7

7 Because of this, all hands will go limp,
every man's heart will melt.[f]

13:8 [g]Isa 21:4 [h]Na 2:10

8 Terror[g] will seize them,
pain and anguish will grip them;
they will writhe like a woman in
labor.
They will look aghast at each other,
their faces aflame.[h]

9 See, the day of the LORD is coming
—a cruel day, with wrath and fierce
anger—
to make the land desolate
and destroy the sinners within it.

13:10 [i]Isa 24:23 [j]Isa 5:30; Rev 8:12 [k]Eze 32:7; Mt 24:29*; Mk 13:24*

10 The stars of heaven and their
constellations
will not show their light.
The rising sun[i] will be darkened[j]
and the moon will not give its light.[k]

13:11 [l]Isa 3:11; 11:4; 26:21

11 I will punish[l] the world for its evil,
the wicked for their sins.
I will put an end to the arrogance of the
haughty
and will humble the pride of the
ruthless.

13:12 [m]Isa 4:1

12 I will make man[m] scarcer than pure
gold,
more rare than the gold of Ophir.

13:13 [n]Isa 34:4; 51:6; Hag 2:6

13 Therefore I will make the heavens
tremble;[n]
and the earth will shake from its place
at the wrath of the LORD Almighty,
in the day of his burning anger.

13:14 [o]1Ki 22:17 [p]Jer 50:16

14 Like a hunted gazelle,
like sheep without a shepherd,[o]
each will return to his own people,
each will flee to his native land.[p]
15 Whoever is captured will be thrust
through;

[a] 6 Hebrew *Shaddai*

Day of the LORD

ISA 13:6-11

The first 12 chapters of Isaiah speak of God's judgment against the northern and southern kingdoms of Israel. In chapter 13 Isaiah begins his prophecies against pagan nations, particularly Babylon. The day of the LORD is "a cruel day" (Isa 13:9) when God finally punishes the wicked. This prophecy is fulfilled when Medo-Persian forces conquer Babylon. However, many believe that, in addition, there is a day of the LORD yet to come. It will be a time of both judgment and restoration. The enemies of God will receive eternal condemnation when Jesus Christ returns and fulfills God's purposes. The friends of God—those who have accepted Jesus as Savior—will receive God's eternal reward.

Only Animals

ISA 13:21–22

The animal inhabitants listed in these verses represent the complete devastation brought on Babylon. The people are dead. The cities are ruined. Wild animals move in, for they are the only ones capable of living in the rubble.

Babylon's animal-infested ruins remind us that when people reject God, life doesn't just continue indefinitely the way it always has. Souls and lives become the target for Satan and his forces to move in to steal and destroy. The devastation of these verses underscores the truth that disobedience isn't worth it. When we obey the Lord, we protect ourselves from the devourer (1Pe 5:8).

all who are caught will fall[q] by the
sword.[r]
16 Their infants[s] will be dashed to pieces
before their eyes;
their houses will be looted and their
wives ravished.
17 See, I will stir up[t] against them the
Medes,
who do not care for silver
and have no delight in gold.[u]
18 Their bows will strike down the young
men;
they will have no mercy on infants
nor will they look with compassion
on children.
19 Babylon, the jewel of kingdoms,
the glory[v] of the Babylonians'[a] pride,
will be overthrown[w] by God
like Sodom and Gomorrah.[x]
20 She will never be inhabited[y]
or lived in through all generations;
no Arab[z] will pitch his tent there,
no shepherd will rest his flocks there.
21 But desert creatures[a] will lie there,
jackals will fill her houses;
there the owls will dwell,
and there the wild goats will leap
about.
22 Hyenas will howl in her strongholds,[b]
jackals[c] in her luxurious palaces.
Her time is at hand,[d]
and her days will not be prolonged.

14 The LORD will have compassion[e] on Jacob;
once again he will choose[f] Israel
and will settle them in their own
land.
Aliens[g] will join them
and unite with the house of Jacob.
2 Nations will take them
and bring[h] them to their own place.
And the house of Israel will possess the
nations[i]
as menservants and maidservants in
the LORD's land.
They will make captives of their captors
and rule over their oppressors.[j]

3 On the day the LORD gives you relief[k] from suffering and turmoil and cruel bondage, 4 you will
take up this taunt[l] against the king of Babylon:

How the oppressor[m] has come to an
end!
How his fury[b] has ended!
5 The LORD has broken the rod of the
wicked,[n]
the scepter of the rulers,

13:15 [q]Jer 51:4 [r]Isa 14:19; Jer 50:25
13:16 [s]Ps 137:9
13:17 [t]Jer 51:1 [u]Pr 6:34-35
13:19 [v]Da 4:30 [w]Rev 14:8 [x]Ge 19:24
13:20 [y]Isa 14:23; 34:10-15 [z]2Ch 17:11
13:21 [a]Rev 18:2
13:22 [b]Isa 25:2 [c]Isa 34:13 [d]Jer 51:33
14:1 [e]Ps 102:13; Isa 49:10,13; 54:7-8,10 [f]Isa 41:8; 44:1; 49:7; Zec 1:17; 2:12 [g]Eph 2:12-19
14:2 [h]Isa 60:9 [i]Isa 49:7,23 [j]Isa 60:14; 61:5
14:3 [k]Isa 11:10
14:4 [l]Hab 2:6 [m]Isa 9:4
14:5 [n]Ps 125:3

[a] 19 Or *Chaldeans'* [b] 4 Dead Sea Scrolls, Septuagint and Syriac; the meaning of the word in the Masoretic Text is uncertain.

6 which in anger struck down peoples[o]
with unceasing blows,
and in fury subdued nations
with relentless aggression.[p]
7 All the lands are at rest and at peace;
they break into singing.[q]
8 Even the pine trees[r] and the cedars of Lebanon
exult over you and say,
"Now that you have been laid low,
no woodsman comes to cut us down."

9 The grave[a][s] below is all astir
to meet you at your coming;
it rouses the spirits of the departed to greet you—
all those who were leaders in the world;
it makes them rise from their thrones—
all those who were kings over the nations.
10 They will all respond,
they will say to you,
"You also have become weak, as we are;
you have become like us."[t]
11 All your pomp has been brought down to the grave,
along with the noise of your harps;
maggots are spread out beneath you
and worms[u] cover you.

12 How you have fallen[v] from heaven,
O morning star,[w] son of the dawn!
You have been cast down to the earth,
you who once laid low the nations!
13 You said in your heart,
"I will ascend[x] to heaven;
I will raise my throne[y]
above the stars of God;
I will sit enthroned on the mount of assembly,
on the utmost heights of the sacred mountain.[b]
14 I will ascend above the tops of the clouds;
I will make myself like the Most High."[z]
15 But you are brought down to the grave,
to the depths[a] of the pit.
16 Those who see you stare at you,
they ponder your fate:[b]
"Is this the man who shook the earth
and made kingdoms tremble,
17 the man who made the world a desert,[c]
who overthrew its cities
and would not let his captives go home?"
18 All the kings of the nations lie in state,

14:6 [o]Isa 10:14 [p]Isa 47:6
14:7 [q]Ps 98:1; 126:1-3
14:8 [r]Eze 31:16
14:9 [s]Eze 32:21
14:10 [t]Eze 32:21
14:11 [u]Isa 51:8
14:12 [v]Isa 34:4; Lk 10:18 [w]2Pe 1:19; Rev 2:28; 8:10; 9:1
14:13 [x]Da 5:23; 8:10; Mt 11:23 [y]Eze 28:2; 2Th 2:4
14:14 [z]Isa 47:8; 2Th 2:4
14:15 [a]Mt 11:23; Lk 10:15
14:16 [b]Jer 50:23
14:17 [c]Joel 2:3

Babylon or Satan?

ISA 14:12-15

Some think this passage describes the fall of Satan (Lk 10:18). Others see it as a description of the fall of Babylon's king. Some think both interpretations are accurate. Whatever the interpretation, these verses describe the devastating fall of the "morning star" (Isa 14:12), who once lived in splendor. Satan, as a fallen angel, had lived in the splendor of God's presence. The king of Babylon lived in the splendor of his palace with the plunder of those he conquered. Whichever one is referred to here, the reason for the fall is the same: pride. God hates pride (Pr 8:13) and crushes the plans and self-promotion of the proud.

[a] 9 Hebrew *Sheol*; also in verses 11 and 15 [b] *13* Or *the north*; Hebrew *Zaphon*

Slaughter of Sons

ISA 14:18-22

Old Testament law states that fathers are not to be put to death for their children's sin nor children, for their fathers'. Each person dies for his or her own sin (Dt 24:16). So why this reference to sons dying for the sins of their forefathers? The king of Babylon is hungry for power and prestige. His greatest legacy will be the sons he leaves behind to rule, his grand tomb and the cities he builds as he takes over one nation after another. God's punishment here is complete. The king of Babylon will pay for his aggression and pride by receiving none of the accoutrements of greatness. He will die on the battlefield, along with the soldiers he leads to their deaths in order to gratify his lust for power. No great tomb will be erected in his memory. His sons will be killed in his throne's overthrow, and the cities he wishes to build will not be his.

each in his own tomb.
19 But you are cast out[d] of your tomb
like a rejected branch;
you are covered with the slain,
with those pierced by the sword,
those who descend to the stones of
the pit.[e]
Like a corpse trampled underfoot,
20 you will not join them in burial,
for you have destroyed your land
and killed your people.

The offspring[f] of the wicked[g]
will never be mentioned[h] again.
21 Prepare a place to slaughter his sons
for the sins of their forefathers;[i]
they are not to rise to inherit the land
and cover the earth with their cities.
22 "I will rise up against them,"
declares the LORD Almighty.
"I will cut off from Babylon her name
and survivors,
her offspring and descendants,[j]"
declares the LORD.
23 "I will turn her into a place for owls[k]
and into swampland;
I will sweep her with the broom of
destruction,"
declares the LORD Almighty.

A Prophecy Against Assyria

24 The LORD Almighty has sworn,[l]

"Surely, as I have planned, so it will be,
and as I have purposed, so it will
stand.[m]
25 I will crush the Assyrian[n] in my land;
on my mountains I will trample him
down.
His yoke[o] will be taken from my people,
and his burden removed from their
shoulders.[p]"
26 This is the plan[q] determined for the
whole world;
this is the hand[r] stretched out over all
nations.
27 For the LORD Almighty has purposed,
and who can thwart him?
His hand is stretched out, and who
can turn it back?[s]

A Prophecy Against the Philistines

28 This oracle[t] came in the year King Ahaz[u] died:

29 Do not rejoice, all you Philistines,[v]
that the rod that struck you is broken;
from the root of that snake will spring
up a viper,[w]
its fruit will be a darting, venomous
serpent.

14:19 [d]Isa 22:16-18 [e]Jer 41:7-9
14:20 [f]Job 18:19 [g]Isa 1:4 [h]Ps 21:10
14:21 [i]Ex 20:5; Lev 26:39
14:22 [j]1Ki 14:10; Job 18:19
14:23 [k]Isa 34:11-15; Zep 2:14
14:24 [l]Isa 45:23 [m]Ac 4:28
14:25 [n]Isa 10:5,12 [o]Isa 9:4 [p]Isa 10:27
14:26 [q]Isa 23:9 [r]Ex 15:12
14:27 [s]2Ch 20:6; Isa 43:13; Da 4:35
14:28 [t]Isa 13:1 [u]2Ki 16:20
14:29 [v]2Ch 26:6 [w]Isa 11:8

14:30 [x]Isa 3:15 [y]Isa 7:21-22 [z]Isa 8:21; 9:20; 51:19 [a]Jer 25:16
14:31 [b]Isa 3:26 [c]Jer 1:14
14:32 [d]Isa 37:9 [e]Ps 87:2,5; Isa 44:28; 54:11 [f]Isa 4:6; Jas 2:5

30 The poorest of the poor will find pasture,
and the needy[x] will lie down in safety.[y]
But your root I will destroy by famine;[z]
it will slay[a] your survivors.

31 Wail, O gate![b] Howl, O city!
Melt away, all you Philistines!
A cloud of smoke comes from the north,[c]
and there is not a straggler in its ranks.
32 What answer shall be given
to the envoys[d] of that nation?
"The LORD has established Zion,[e]
and in her his afflicted people will
find refuge.[f]"

A Prophecy Against Moab

15:1 [g]Isa 11:14 [h]Jer 48:24, 41
15:2 [i]Jer 48:35 [j]Lev 21:5
15:3 [k]Jer 48:38 [l]Isa 22:4
15:4 [m]Nu 32:3
15:5 [n]Jer 48:31 [o]Jer 48:3,34 [p]Jer 4:20; 48:5
15:6 [q]Isa 19:5-7; Jer 48:34 [r]Joel 1:12
15:7 [s]Isa 30:6; Jer 48:36

15 An oracle concerning Moab:[g]

Ar in Moab is ruined,[h]
destroyed in a night!
Kir in Moab is ruined,
destroyed in a night!
2 Dibon goes up to its temple,
to its high places[i] to weep;
Moab wails over Nebo and Medeba.
Every head is shaved[j]
and every beard cut off.
3 In the streets they wear sackcloth;
on the roofs and in the public squares[k]
they all wail,
prostrate with weeping.[l]
4 Heshbon and Elealeh[m] cry out,
their voices are heard all the way to
Jahaz.
Therefore the armed men of Moab cry
out,
and their hearts are faint.

5 My heart cries out over Moab;[n]
her fugitives flee as far as Zoar,
as far as Eglath Shelishiyah.
They go up the way to Luhith,
weeping as they go;
on the road to Horonaim[o]
they lament their destruction.[p]
6 The waters of Nimrim are dried up[q]
and the grass is withered;[r]
the vegetation is gone
and nothing green is left.
7 So the wealth they have acquired[s] and
stored up
they carry away over the Ravine of
the Poplars.
8 Their outcry echoes along the border of
Moab;
their wailing reaches as far as Eglaim,
their lamentation as far as Beer Elim.
9 Dimon's[a] waters are full of blood,

[a] 9 Masoretic Text; Dead Sea Scrolls, some Septuagint manuscripts and Vulgate *Dibon*

Shaved heads

ISA 15:2–3

Beards and longish hair were common in Old Testament Jewish culture. Shaving the head and beard were often a sign of mourning. Pulling hairs out of one's head and beard was an expression of extreme grief (Ezr 9:3). Mourners wore sackcloth, simple clothing made of coarsely woven fabrics, rather than their ordinary robes. Grief was not expressed quietly or politely, but loudly and with fervor.

God is punishing Moab, a small nation east of the Salt Sea or Dead Sea (see Map 7: Prophets in Israel and Judah at the back of this Bible), for its harsh treatment of Israel. Those who survive the destruction mourn their losses.

The Faithful Throne

ISA 16:1-5

Though insignificant when compared to Assyria and nearby countries, Moab still considers itself a contender among the powerful nations. Now defeated, probably by Assyria, refugees from its cities flee to Judah. These refugees, mostly women and children, request aid from Jerusalem and send lambs (Moab is known for its huge flocks of sheep—2Ki 3:4) with their message.

Israel's redemptive act points to a future time when Israel's Messiah will sit in faithfulness on his throne (Isa 16:5) and bring salvation to everyone, including the Moabite fugitives. The Messiah will also be a "light to the nations" (Isa 51:4), for he is "the light of the world" (Jn 8:12; 9:5).

but I will bring still more upon
Dimon[a]—
a lion[t] upon the fugitives of Moab
and upon those who remain in the land.

15:9 [t]2Ki 17:25

16 Send lambs[u] as tribute
to the ruler of the land,
from Sela,[v] across the desert,
to the mount of the Daughter of Zion.[w]
2 Like fluttering birds
pushed from the nest,[x]
so are the women of Moab
at the fords of the Arnon.[y]

16:1 [u]2Ki 3:4 [v]2Ki 14:7 [w]Isa 10:32
16:2 [x]Pr 27:8 [y]Nu 21:13-14; Jer 48:20

3 "Give us counsel,
render a decision.
Make your shadow like night—
at high noon.
Hide the fugitives,[z]
do not betray the refugees.
4 Let the Moabite fugitives stay with you;
be their shelter from the destroyer."

16:3 [z]1Ki 18:4

The oppressor[a] will come to an end,
and destruction will cease;
the aggressor will vanish from the land.
5 In love a throne[b] will be established;
in faithfulness a man will sit on it—
one from the house[b] of David[c]—
one who in judging seeks justice[d]
and speeds the cause of righteousness.

16:4 [a]Isa 9:4
16:5 [b]Da 7:14; Mic 4:7 [c]Lk 1:32 [d]Isa 9:7

6 We have heard of Moab's[e] pride[f]—
her overweening pride and conceit,
her pride and her insolence—
but her boasts are empty.
7 Therefore the Moabites wail,[g]
they wail together for Moab.
Lament and grieve
for the men[c][h] of Kir Hareseth.[i]
8 The fields of Heshbon wither,
the vines of Sibmah also.
The rulers of the nations
have trampled down the choicest vines,
which once reached Jazer
and spread toward the desert.
Their shoots spread out
and went as far as the sea.
9 So I weep,[j] as Jazer weeps,
for the vines of Sibmah.
O Heshbon, O Elealeh,
I drench you with tears!
The shouts of joy over your ripened fruit
and over your harvests[k] have been stilled.

16:6 [e]Am 2:1; Zep 2:8 [f]Ob 1:3; Zep 2:10
16:7 [g]Jer 48:20 [h]1Ch 16:3 [i]2Ki 3:25
16:9 [j]Isa 15:3 [k]Jer 40:12

[a] 9 Masoretic Text; Dead Sea Scrolls, some Septuagint manuscripts and Vulgate *Dibon* [b] 5 Hebrew *tent*
[c] 7 Or "*raisin cakes*," a wordplay

16:10 [l]Isa 24:7-8 [m]Jdg 9:27 [n]Job 24:11

10 Joy and gladness are taken away from
the orchards;[l]
no one sings or shouts in the
vineyards;
no one treads[m] out wine at the presses,[n]
for I have put an end to the shouting.

16:11 [o]Isa 15:5 [p]Isa 63:15; Hos 11:8; Php 2:1

11 My heart laments for Moab[o] like a harp,
my inmost being[p] for Kir Hareseth.

16:12 [q]Isa 15:2 [r]1Ki 18:29

12 When Moab appears at her high place,
she only wears herself out;
when she goes to her shrine[q] to pray,
it is to no avail.[r]

16:14 [s]Isa 25:10; Jer 48:42 [t]Isa 21:17

13 This is the word the LORD has already spoken
concerning Moab. 14 But now the LORD says:
"Within three years, as a servant bound by contract would count them, Moab's splendor and all
her many people will be despised,[s] and her survivors will be very few and feeble."[t]

An Oracle Against Damascus

17:1 [u]Ge 14:15; Jer 49:23; Ac 9:2 [v]Isa 25:2; Am 1:3; Zec 9:1

17 An oracle concerning Damascus:[u]

"See, Damascus will no longer be a city
but will become a heap of ruins.[v]

17:2 [w]Isa 7:21; Eze 25:5 [x]Jer 7:33; Mic 4:4

2 The cities of Aroer will be deserted
and left to flocks,[w] which will lie
down,
with no one to make them afraid.[x]
3 The fortified city will disappear from
Ephraim,
and royal power from Damascus;
the remnant of Aram will be

17:3 [y]ver 4; Hos 9:11 [z]Isa 7:8,16; 8:4

like the glory[y] of the Israelites,"[z]
declares the LORD Almighty.

17:4 [a]Isa 10:16

4 "In that day the glory of Jacob will fade;
the fat of his body will waste[a] away.
5 It will be as when a reaper gathers the
standing grain

17:5 [b]ver 11; Jer 51:33; Joel 3:13; Mt 13:30

and harvests[b] the grain with his
arm—
as when a man gleans heads of grain
in the Valley of Rephaim.

17:6 [c]Dt 4:27; Isa 24:13 [d]Isa 27:12

6 Yet some gleanings will remain,[c]
as when an olive tree is beaten,[d]
leaving two or three olives on the
topmost branches,
four or five on the fruitful boughs,"
declares the LORD,
the God of Israel.

17:7 [e]Isa 10:20 [f]Mic 7:7

7 In that day men will look[e] to their
Maker
and turn their eyes to the Holy One[f] of
Israel.

17:8 [g]Isa 2:18,20; 30:22

8 They will not look to the altars,
the work of their hands,[g]
and they will have no regard for the
Asherah poles[a]

[a] 8 That is, symbols of the goddess Asherah

Ancient Oracles

ISA 17:1

In the Hebrew language an oracle refers to a word or utterance from God. The word suggests judgment or at least an unwelcome message. Through the prophet Isaiah, God delivers oracles to nations and cities that grieve him, including Babylon, Moab, Damascus, Egypt, Arabia, Tyre and others.

So what can we learn from these oracles, delivered thousands of years ago? First, God communicates with people. He may use messengers or he may speak to us directly in order to tell us about himself and his ways. Second, the Lord is holy and righteous, and he must eventually punish sin. There will be a reckoning and judgment for the unrepentant. Third, though God delivers messages of punishment, he also offers hope for those who repent. He loves us and offers us many chances to forsake sin. Fourth, the Lord speaks through and fulfills his prophetic word. When he promises something, we can count on it happening.

and the incense altars their fingers
have made.

[9]In that day their strong cities, which they left
because of the Israelites, will be like places abandoned to thickets and undergrowth. And all will
be desolation.

[10]You have forgotten[h] God your Savior;[i]
you have not remembered the Rock,
your fortress.
Therefore, though you set out the finest
plants
and plant imported vines,
[11]though on the day you set them out,
you make them grow,
and on the morning[j] when you plant
them, you bring them to bud,
yet the harvest will be as nothing[k]
in the day of disease and incurable
pain.[l]

[12]Oh, the raging of many nations—
they rage like the raging sea![m]
Oh, the uproar of the peoples—
they roar like the roaring of great
waters!
[13]Although the peoples roar like the roar
of surging waters,
when he rebukes[n] them they flee[o] far
away,
driven before the wind like chaff[p] on the
hills,
like tumbleweed before a gale.[q]
[14]In the evening, sudden terror!
Before the morning, they are gone![r]
This is the portion of those who loot us,
the lot of those who plunder us.

A Prophecy Against Cush

18 Woe to the land of whirring wings[a]
along the rivers of Cush,[b][s]
[2]which sends envoys by sea
in papyrus[t] boats over the water.

Go, swift messengers,
to a people tall and smooth-skinned,
to a people feared far and wide,
an aggressive[u] nation of strange speech,
whose land is divided by rivers.[v]

[3]All you people of the world,
you who live on the earth,
when a banner[w] is raised on the
mountains,
you will see it,
and when a trumpet sounds,
you will hear it.
[4]This is what the LORD says to me:
"I will remain quiet and will look on
from my dwelling place,[x]

17:10 [h]Isa 51:13 [i]Ps 68:19; Isa 12:2
17:11 [j]Ps 90:6 [k]Hos 8:7 [l]Job 4:8
17:12 [m]Ps 18:4; Jer 6:23; Lk 21:25
17:13 [n]Ps 9:5 [o]Isa 13:14 [p]Isa 41:2,15-16 [q]Job 21:18
17:14 [r]2Ki 19:35
18:1 [s]Isa 20:3-5; Eze 30:4-5, 9; Zep 2:12; 3:10
18:2 [t]Ex 2:3 [u]Ge 10:8-9; 2Ch 12:3 [v]ver 7
18:3 [w]Isa 5:26
18:4 [x]Isa 26:21; Hos 5:15

There is one single fact which we may oppose to all the wit and argument of infidelity, namely, that no man ever repented of being a Christian on his death-bed.

—Hannah More (1745–1833)

[a] *1* Or *of locusts*   [b] *1* That is, the upper Nile region

like shimmering heat in the sunshine,
like a cloud of dew[y] in the heat of harvest."
5 For, before the harvest, when the blossom is gone
and the flower becomes a ripening grape,
he will cut off the shoots with pruning knives,
and cut down and take away the spreading branches.[z]
6 They will all be left to the mountain birds of prey
and to the wild animals;[a]
the birds will feed on them all summer,
the wild animals all winter.

7 At that time gifts will be brought to the LORD
Almighty

from a people tall and smooth-skinned,
from a people feared far and wide,
an aggressive nation of strange speech,
whose land is divided by rivers—

the gifts will be brought to Mount Zion, the place
of the Name of the LORD Almighty.[b]

A Prophecy About Egypt

19 An oracle[c] concerning Egypt:[de]

See, the LORD rides on a swift cloud[f]
and is coming to Egypt.
The idols of Egypt tremble before him,
and the hearts of the Egyptians melt[g] within them.

2 "I will stir up Egyptian against Egyptian—
brother will fight against brother,[h]
neighbor against neighbor,
city against city,
kingdom against kingdom.[i]
3 The Egyptians will lose heart,
and I will bring their plans to nothing;
they will consult the idols and the spirits of the dead,
the mediums and the spiritists.[j]
4 I will hand the Egyptians over
to the power of a cruel master,
and a fierce king[k] will rule over them,"
declares the Lord, the LORD Almighty.

5 The waters of the river will dry up,[l]
and the riverbed will be parched and dry.
6 The canals will stink;[m]
the streams of Egypt will dwindle and dry up.[n]
The reeds and rushes will wither,[o]
7 also the plants along the Nile,
at the mouth of the river.

18:4 [y]Isa 26:19; Hos 14:5
18:5 [z]Isa 17:10-11; Eze 17:6
18:6 [a]Isa 56:9; Jer 7:33; Eze 32:4; 39:17
18:7 [b]Ps 68:31
19:1 [c]Isa 13:1; Jer 43:12 [d]Joel 3:19 [e]Ex 12:12 [f]Ps 18:10; 104:3; Rev 1:7 [g]Jos 2:11
19:2 [h]Jdg 7:22; Mt 10:21,36 [i]2Ch 20:23
19:3 [j]Isa 8:19; 47:13; Da 2:2,10
19:4 [k]Isa 20:4; Jer 46:26; Eze 29:19
19:5 [l]Jer 51:36
19:6 [m]Ex 7:18 [n]Isa 37:25; Eze 30:12 [o]Isa 15:6

Gifts to God

ISA 18:2,7

These foreigners bring gifts to God because they are grateful to him for the defeat of the Assyrian army. They recognize him as the source of power. These gifts resemble a tribute, which a defeated nation submits to the conquering nation. In this case, the "tall and smooth-skinned" people offer gifts in submission to God.

It's difficult to identify these foreigners because the Hebrew is not easily deciphered. Some say they're people along the Nile River in what is Ethiopia today, or the Medes, or perhaps this is a figure of speech that refers to kingdoms in general. Whoever they are, these people recognize the true source of power and bow to him.

Shuddering Egyptians

ISA 19:16

Isaiah describes the Egyptians as women who "shudder with fear at the uplifted hand." This description doesn't necessarily depict a low view of women, but it does expose an awful truth. In this ancient culture women, without men to protect them, fell prey to abuse from conquering armies. When one nation toppled another, there was great reason for women of the defeated nation to fear. They knew atrocities could lie ahead.

Likewise, in this passage, the Egyptians will shudder at the Lord's wrath. These arrogant warriors probably take offense at this "shuddering" prophecy. They don't like being compared to defenseless females, or for that matter, anyone who loses in battle. But if God moves in anger against a nation, the appropriate emotion is terror, and the correct action is repentance.

Every sown field[p] along the Nile
will become parched, will blow away
and be no more.
8 The fishermen[q] will groan and lament,
all who cast hooks[r] into the Nile;
those who throw nets on the water
will pine away.
9 Those who work with combed flax will
despair,
the weavers of fine linen[s] will lose
hope.
10 The workers in cloth will be dejected,
and all the wage earners will be sick
at heart.

11 The officials of Zoan[t] are nothing but
fools;
the wise counselors of Pharaoh give
senseless advice.
How can you say to Pharaoh,
"I am one of the wise men,[u]
a disciple of the ancient kings"?
12 Where are your wise men[v] now?
Let them show you and make known
what the LORD Almighty
has planned[w] against Egypt.
13 The officials of Zoan have become fools,
the leaders of Memphis[a][x] are
deceived;
the cornerstones of her peoples
have led Egypt astray.
14 The LORD has poured into them
a spirit of dizziness;[y]
they make Egypt stagger in all that she
does,
as a drunkard staggers around in his
vomit.
15 There is nothing Egypt can do—
head or tail, palm branch or reed.[z]

16 In that day the Egyptians will be like women.[a]
They will shudder with fear[b] at the uplifted hand[c]
that the LORD Almighty raises against them. 17 And
the land of Judah will bring terror to the Egyptians; everyone to whom Judah is mentioned will
be terrified, because of what the LORD Almighty is
planning[d] against them.
18 In that day five cities in Egypt will speak the
language of Canaan and swear allegiance[e] to the
LORD Almighty. One of them will be called the City
of Destruction.[b]
19 In that day there will be an altar[f] to the LORD
in the heart of Egypt, and a monument[g] to the
LORD at its border. 20 It will be a sign and witness to
the LORD Almighty in the land of Egypt. When
they cry out to the LORD because of their oppressors, he will send them a savior and defender, and
he will rescue[h] them. 21 So the LORD will make

19:7 [p]Isa 23:3
19:8 [q]Eze 47:10 [r]Hab 1:15
19:9 [s]Pr 7:16; Eze 27:7
19:11 [t]Nu 13:22 [u]1Ki 4:30; Ac 7:22
19:12 [v]1Co 1:20 [w]Isa 14:24; Ro 9:17
19:13 [x]Jer 2:16; Eze 30:13,16
19:14 [y]Mt 17:17
19:15 [z]Isa 9:14
19:16 [a]50:37; 51:30; Na 3:13 [b]Heb 10:31 [c]Isa 11:15
19:17 [d]Isa 14:24
19:18 [e]Zep 3:9
19:19 [f]Jos 22:10 [g]Ge 28:18
19:20 [h]Isa 49:24-26

[a] *13* Hebrew *Noph* [b] *18* Most manuscripts of the Masoretic Text; some manuscripts of the Masoretic Text, Dead Sea Scrolls and Vulgate *City of the Sun* (that is, Heliopolis)

himself known to the Egyptians, and in that day
they will acknowledge[i] the LORD. They will worship[j] with sacrifices and grain offerings; they will
make vows to the LORD and keep them. 22 The LORD
will strike[k] Egypt with a plague; he will strike
them and heal them. They will turn[l] to the LORD,
and he will respond to their pleas and heal[m] them.
23 In that day there will be a highway[n] from
Egypt to Assyria. The Assyrians will go to Egypt
and the Egyptians to Assyria. The Egyptians and
Assyrians will worship[o] together. 24 In that day
Israel will be the third, along with Egypt and
Assyria, a blessing on the earth. 25 The LORD
Almighty will bless them, saying, "Blessed be
Egypt my people,[p] Assyria my handiwork,[q] and
Israel my inheritance.[r]"

A Prophecy Against Egypt and Cush

20 In the year that the supreme commander,[s]
sent by Sargon king of Assyria, came to
Ashdod and attacked and captured it— 2 at that
time the LORD spoke through Isaiah son of Amoz.[t]
He said to him, "Take off the sackcloth[u] from your
body and the sandals[v] from your feet." And he did
so, going around stripped[w] and barefoot.[x]
3 Then the LORD said, "Just as my servant Isaiah
has gone stripped and barefoot for three years, as
a sign[y] and portent against Egypt and Cush,[a][z] 4 so
the king[a] of Assyria will lead away stripped and
barefoot the Egyptian captives and Cushite exiles,
young and old, with buttocks bared—to Egypt's
shame.[b] 5 Those who trusted in Cush and boasted
in Egypt[c] will be afraid and put to shame. 6 In that
day the people who live on this coast will say, 'See
what has happened to those we relied on, those
we fled to for help[d] and deliverance from the king
of Assyria! How then can we escape?[e]' "

A Prophecy Against Babylon

21 An oracle concerning the Desert[f] by the Sea:

Like whirlwinds sweeping through the
    southland,[g]
  an invader comes from the desert,
  from a land of terror.

2 A dire[h] vision has been shown to me:
  The traitor betrays,[i] the looter takes
    loot.
Elam,[j] attack! Media, lay siege!
  I will bring to an end all the groaning
    she caused.

3 At this my body is racked with pain,
  pangs seize me, like those of a
    woman in labor;[k]
I am staggered by what I hear,
  I am bewildered by what I see.
4 My heart falters,
  fear makes me tremble;

[a] 3 That is, the upper Nile region; also in verse 5

19:21 [i]Isa 11:9 [j]Isa 56:7; Mal 1:11
19:22 [k]Heb 12:11 [l]Isa 45:14; Hos 14:1 [m]Dt 32:39
19:23 [n]Isa 11:16 [o]Isa 27:13
19:25 [p]Ps 100:3 [q]Isa 29:23; 45:11; 60:21; 64:8; Eph 2:10 [r]Hos 2:23
20:1 [s]2Ki 18:17
20:2 [t]Isa 13:1 [u]Zec 13:4; Mt 3:4 [v]Eze 24:17, 23 [w]1Sa 19:24 [x]Mic 1:8
20:3 [y]Isa 8:18 [z]Isa 37:9; 43:3
20:4 [a]Isa 19:4 [b]Isa 47:3; Jer 13:22,26
20:5 [c]2Ki 18:21; Isa 30:5
20:6 [d]Isa 10:3 [e]Jer 30:15-17; Mt 23:33; 1Th 5:3; Heb 2:3
21:1 [f]Isa 13:21; Jer 51:43 [g]Zec 9:14
21:2 [h]Ps 60:3 [i]Isa 33:1 [j]Isa 22:6; Jer 49:34
21:3 [k]Ps 48:6; Isa 26:17

Stripped and Shamed

ISA 20

In this chapter Isaiah role-plays according to the Lord's instructions. He discards his sackcloth and sandals, the characteristic garb of prophets, to depict how the enemy will subdue Egypt and Cush. This visual message represents how these spiritually rebellious nations will be stripped and taken into captivity. Though Isaiah probably isn't completely nude, his drama clearly reveals how these warriors will walk with "buttocks barred"—a sign of shame and defeat. When God finally punishes an evil nation, he's thorough. He leaves people empty of hope, full of humiliation.

Get the Oil!

ISA 21:5

Isaiah staggers at the indifference of the Babylonians. They eat and drink when they should be preparing to defend themselves against the enemy's attack. He instructs officers to "oil the shields," a common practice before battle. Their shields were wooden frames covered with animal hides. Oiling shields kept the leather from growing brittle and becoming more vulnerable to piercing from a sword or an arrow. However, in the end, no amount of oil can rescue these men. It is complacency—not the enemy's blows—that eventually kills them. Spiritual neglect isn't static; it slithers ever downward.

the twilight I longed for
has become a horror to me.

5 They set the tables,
they spread the rugs,
they eat, they drink![l]
Get up, you officers,
oil the shields!

6 This is what the Lord says to me:

"Go, post a lookout
and have him report what he sees.
7 When he sees chariots[m]
with teams of horses,
riders on donkeys
or riders on camels,
let him be alert,
fully alert."

8 And the lookout[a][n] shouted,

"Day after day, my lord, I stand on the watchtower;
every night I stay at my post.
9 Look, here comes a man in a chariot
with a team of horses.
And he gives back the answer:
'Babylon[o] has fallen,[p] has fallen!
All the images of its gods[q]
lie shattered on the ground!' "
10 O my people, crushed on the threshing floor,[r]
I tell you what I have heard
from the LORD Almighty,
from the God of Israel.

A Prophecy Against Edom

11 An oracle concerning Dumah[b]:[s]

Someone calls to me from Seir,[t]
"Watchman, what is left of the night?
Watchman, what is left of the night?"
12 The watchman replies,
"Morning is coming, but also the night.
If you would ask, then ask;
and come back yet again."

A Prophecy Against Arabia

13 An oracle[u] concerning Arabia:

You caravans of Dedanites,
who camp in the thickets of Arabia,
14 bring water for the thirsty;
you who live in Tema,[v]
bring food for the fugitives.
15 They flee[w] from the sword,
from the drawn sword,
from the bent bow
and from the heat of battle.

21:5 [l]Jer 51:39, 57; Da 5:2
21:7 [m]ver 9
21:8 [n]Hab 2:1
21:9 [o]Rev 14:8 [p]Jer 51:8; Rev 18:2 [q]Isa 46:1; Jer 50:2; 51:44
21:10 [r]Jer 51:33
21:11 [s]Ge 25:14 [t]Ge 32:3
21:13 [u]Isa 13:1
21:14 [v]Ge 25:15
21:15 [w]Isa 13:14

[a] 8 Dead Sea Scrolls and Syriac; Masoretic Text *A lion*
[b] 11 *Dumah* means *silence* or *stillness,* a wordplay on *Edom.*

21:16 [x]Isa 16:14 [y]Isa 17:3 [z]Ps 120:5; Isa 60:7
21:17 [a]Isa 10:19

16This is what the Lord says to me: "Within one
year, as a servant bound by contract[x] would count
it, all the pomp[y] of Kedar[z] will come to an end.
17The survivors of the bowmen, the warriors of
Kedar, will be few.[a]" The LORD, the God of Israel,
has spoken.

A Prophecy About Jerusalem

22:1 [b]Isa 13:1 [c]Ps 125:2; Jer 21:13; Joel 3:2,12,14
22:2 [d]Isa 32:13

22 An oracle[b] concerning the Valley[c] of Vision:

What troubles you now,
that you have all gone up on the roofs,
2O town full of commotion,
O city of tumult and revelry?[d]
Your slain were not killed by the sword,
nor did they die in battle.
3All your leaders have fled together;
they have been captured without
using the bow.
All you who were caught were taken
prisoner together,
having fled while the enemy was still
far away.
4Therefore I said, "Turn away from me;
let me weep[e] bitterly.
Do not try to console me
over the destruction of my people."[f]

22:4 [e]Isa 15:3; Lk 19:41 [f]Jer 9:1

5The Lord, the LORD Almighty, has a day
of tumult and trampling and terror[g]
in the Valley of Vision,
a day of battering down walls
and of crying out to the mountains.
6Elam[h] takes up the quiver,[i]
with her charioteers and horses;
Kir[j] uncovers the shield.
7Your choicest valleys are full of chariots,
and horsemen are posted at the city
gates;[k]
8 the defenses of Judah are stripped
away.

22:5 [g]La 1:5
22:6 [h]Isa 21:2 [i]Jer 49:35 [j]2Ki 16:9
22:7 [k]2Ch 32:1-2

And you looked in that day
to the weapons[l] in the Palace of the
Forest;[m]
9you saw that the City of David
had many breaches in its defenses;
you stored up water
in the Lower Pool.[n]
10You counted the buildings in Jerusalem
and tore down houses to strengthen
the wall.
11You built a reservoir between the two
walls[o]
for the water of the Old Pool,[p]
but you did not look to the One who
made it,
or have regard for the One who
planned it long ago.

22:8 [l]2Ch 32:5 [m]1Ki 7:2
22:9 [n]2Ch 32:4
22:11 [o]2Ki 25:4; Jer 39:4 [p]2Ch 32:4

12The Lord, the LORD Almighty,
called you on that day

A Fortified Jerusalem

ISA 22:8–10

The people of Jerusalem trust more in their fortified city than in God. Isaiah specifically mentions the palace and its weapons, water supplies and reinforced walls. Isaiah cites these fortifications not in admiration for so ingeniously fortifying Jerusalem, but as an indictment for trusting in these fortifications instead of in God. Still, none of these fortifications deter the living God. At his command the city will collapse like precariously propped matchsticks. This anguishes Isaiah, who pleads with the people to repent. But his call falls on deaf ears.

Eat and Drink

ISA 22:13

Instead of mourning their apostasy, the people cultivate a "don't think about tomorrow" attitude. This isn't the "do not worry about tomorrow" approach taught by Jesus, which promotes trust in God for daily needs (Mt 6:34). It is instead a rebellious denial that declares, "If we don't think about it, maybe it won't happen." However, they can't forever ignore the living God, who has grown tired of their indifference toward him.

In Luke 12:18–20 Jesus teaches that the wealthy person is a fool for eating, drinking and making merry without growing "rich toward God" (Lk 12:21). Paul says if Christ's teaching is false, then everything is a lost cause, and we should drown ourselves in food and drink because we'll die without hope (1Co 15:32). The apostle believes Jesus is the way and heaven is certain for believers; however, what he says is true: If we don't believe these truths, then what's left but to live for the moment?

to weep[q] and to wail,
to tear out your hair[r] and put on sackcloth.[s]
13 But see, there is joy and revelry,
slaughtering of cattle and killing of sheep,
eating of meat and drinking of wine![t]
"Let us eat and drink," you say,
"for tomorrow we die!"[u]

14 The LORD Almighty has revealed this in my
hearing:[v] "Till your dying day this sin will not be
atoned[w] for," says the Lord, the LORD Almighty.

15 This is what the Lord, the LORD Almighty,
says:

"Go, say to this steward,
to Shebna,[x] who is in charge of the palace:
16 What are you doing here and who gave you permission
to cut out a grave[y] for yourself here,
hewing your grave on the height
and chiseling your resting place in the rock?
17 "Beware, the LORD is about to take firm hold of you
and hurl you away, O you mighty man.
18 He will roll you up tightly like a ball
and throw[z] you into a large country.
There you will die
and there your splendid chariots will remain—
you disgrace to your master's house!
19 I will depose you from your office,
and you will be ousted from your position.

20 "In that day I will summon my servant, Eliakim[a] son of Hilkiah. 21 I will clothe him with your
robe and fasten your sash around him and hand
your authority over to him. He will be a father to
those who live in Jerusalem and to the house of
Judah. 22 I will place on his shoulder the key[b] to
the house of David;[c] what he opens no one can
shut, and what he shuts no one can open.[d] 23 I will
drive him like a peg[e] into a firm place;[f] he will be
a seat[a] of honor[g] for the house of his father. 24 All
the glory of his family will hang on him: its offspring and offshoots—all its lesser vessels, from
the bowls to all the jars.

25 "In that day," declares the LORD Almighty, "the
peg[h] driven into the firm place will give way; it
will be sheared off and will fall, and the load
hanging on it will be cut down." The LORD has
spoken.[i]

22:12 [q]Joel 2:17 [r]Mic 1:16 [s]Joel 1:13
22:13 [t]Isa 5:22; 28:7-8; 56:12; Lk 17:26-29 [u]1Co 15:32*
22:14 [v]Isa 5:9 [w]Isa 13:11; 26:21; 30:13-14; Eze 24:13
22:15 [x]2Ki 18:18; Isa 36:3
22:16 [y]Mt 27:60
22:18 [z]Isa 17:13
22:20 [a]2Ki 18:18; Isa 36:3
22:22 [b]Rev 3:7 [c]Isa 7:2 [d]Job 12:14
22:23 [e]Zec 10:4 [f]Ezr 9:8 [g]1Sa 2:7-8; Job 36:7
22:25 [h]ver 23 [i]Isa 46:11; Mic 4:4

[a] 23 Or *throne*

A Prophecy About Tyre

23:1
[j]Jos 19:29; 1Ki 5:1; Jer 47:4; Eze 26,27,28; Joel 3:4-8; Am 1:9-10; Zec 9:2-4
[k]1Ki 10:22
[l]Ge 10:4; Isa 2:16 *fn*

23 An oracle concerning Tyre:[j]

Wail, O ships[k] of Tarshish![l]
For Tyre is destroyed
and left without house or harbor.
From the land of Cyprus[a]
word has come to them.

[2]Be silent, you people of the island
and you merchants of Sidon,
whom the seafarers have enriched.
[3]On the great waters
came the grain of the Shihor;
the harvest of the Nile[b][m] was the
revenue of Tyre,[n]
and she became the marketplace of
the nations.

23:3
[m]Isa 19:7
[n]Eze 27:3

[4]Be ashamed, O Sidon,[o] and you,
O fortress of the sea,
for the sea has spoken:
"I have neither been in labor nor given
birth;
I have neither reared sons nor brought
up daughters."
[5]When word comes to Egypt,
they will be in anguish at the report
from Tyre.

23:4
[o]Ge 10:15,19

[6]Cross over to Tarshish;
wail, you people of the island.
[7]Is this your city of revelry,[p]
the old, old city,
whose feet have taken her
to settle in far-off lands?
[8]Who planned this against Tyre,
the bestower of crowns,
whose merchants are princes,
whose traders are renowned in the
earth?
[9]The LORD Almighty planned it,
to bring low[q] the pride of all glory
and to humble[r] all who are renowned[s]
on the earth.

23:7
[p]Isa 22:2; 32:13

23:9
[q]Job 40:11
[r]Isa 13:11
[s]Isa 5:13; 9:15

[10]Till[c] your land as along the Nile,
O Daughter of Tarshish,
for you no longer have a harbor.
[11]The LORD has stretched out his hand[t]
over the sea
and made its kingdoms tremble.
He has given an order concerning
Phoenicia[d]
that her fortresses be destroyed.[u]
[12]He said, "No more of your reveling,[v]

23:11
[t]Ex 14:21
[u]Isa 25:2; Zec 9:3-4

23:12
[v]Rev 18:22

[a] *1* Hebrew *Kittim* [b] *2,3* Masoretic Text; one Dead Sea Scroll *Sidon, / who cross over the sea; / your envoys [3]are on the great waters. / The grain of the Shihor, / the harvest of the Nile,* [c] *10* Dead Sea Scrolls and some Septuagint manuscripts; Masoretic Text *Go through* [d] *11* Hebrew *Canaan*

The Great Tyre

ISA 23:1

In ancient times the city-state of Tyre boasted a large seaport (see Map 7: Prophets in Israel and Judah at the back of this Bible), and many surrounding areas depended on it for trade. Two harbors—one on the mainland and another on an offshore island—kept the location thriving with business. Tyre prospered during the reigns of David and Solomon because its king provided wood and labor for building palaces and the temple.

The psalmists and the prophets mention Tyre, with the latter condemning its pride and extravagance. Because of these excesses, God allows a succession of enemies to capture Tyre: the Assyrians, Babylonians and Alexander the Great with his Greek army (see the note on Eze 27, page 1387). Jesus visited Tyre a number of times. Today it's a small town of about 5,000 inhabitants.

Wasting the Earth

ISA 24:1-2

So far Isaiah warns of God's judgment on certain cities and nations, but now he prophesies a devastation of the entire earth. The Lord will "lay waste the earth" because of all of its inhabitants' sins (Isa 24:5). The judgment will not only affect the entire earth, it will also affect every race, economic strata and position of its people. Many interpret this destruction as taking place in the last days of human history. The good news is that after crushing the earth, God will create something new—a magnificent city—for the righteous (Isa 26:1-2).

O Virgin Daughter[w] of Sidon, now
crushed!

"Up, cross over to Cyprus[a];
even there you will find no rest."
13 Look at the land of the Babylonians,[b]
this people that is now of no account!
The Assyrians[x] have made it
a place for desert creatures;
they raised up their siege towers,
they stripped its fortresses bare
and turned it into a ruin.[y]

14 Wail, you ships of Tarshish;[z]
your fortress is destroyed!

15 At that time Tyre[a] will be forgotten for seventy years, the span of a king's life. But at the end of
these seventy years, it will happen to Tyre as in
the song of the prostitute:

16 "Take up a harp, walk through the city,
O prostitute forgotten;
play the harp well, sing many a song,
so that you will be remembered."

17 At the end of seventy years, the LORD will deal
with Tyre. She will return to her hire as a prostitute[b] and will ply her trade with all the kingdoms
on the face of the earth. 18 Yet her profit and her
earnings will be set apart for the LORD;[c] they will
not be stored up or hoarded. Her profits will go to
those who live before the LORD,[d] for abundant
food and fine clothes.

The LORD's Devastation of the Earth

24 See, the LORD is going to lay waste the
earth[e]
and devastate it;
he will ruin its face
and scatter its inhabitants—
2 it will be the same
for priest as for people,[f]
for master as for servant,
for mistress as for maid,
for seller as for buyer,[g]
for borrower as for lender,
for debtor as for creditor.[h]
3 The earth will be completely laid waste
and totally plundered.[i]
The LORD has spoken this word.

4 The earth dries up and withers,
the world languishes and withers,
the exalted[j] of the earth languish.
5 The earth is defiled[k] by its people;
they have disobeyed[l] the laws,
violated the statutes
and broken the everlasting covenant.
6 Therefore a curse consumes the earth;
its people must bear their guilt.

23:12 [w]Isa 47:1
23:13 [x]Isa 10:5 [y]Isa 10:7
23:14 [z]Isa 2:16 *fn*
23:15 [a]Jer 25:22
23:17 [b]Eze 16:26; Na 3:4; Rev 17:1
23:18 [c]Ex 28:36; Ps 72:10 [d]Isa 60:5-9; Mic 4:13
24:1 [e]ver 20; Isa 2:19-21; 33:9
24:2 [f]Hos 4:9 [g]Eze 7:12 [h]Lev 25:35-37; Dt 23:19-20
24:3 [i]Isa 6:11-12
24:4 [j]Isa 2:12
24:5 [k]Ge 3:17; Nu 35:33 [l]Isa 10:6; 59:12

[a] 12 Hebrew *Kittim* [b] 13 Or *Chaldeans*

24:6 [m]Isa 1:31 Therefore earth's inhabitants are burned
up,[m]
and very few are left.
24:7 [n]Joel 1:10-12 [o]Isa 16:8-10 7 The new wine dries up and the vine
withers;[n]
all the merrymakers groan.[o]
24:8 [p]Isa 5:12 [q]Jer 7:34; 16:9; 25:10; Hos 2:11 [r]Rev 18:22 [s]Eze 26:13 8 The gaiety of the tambourines[p] is stilled,
the noise[q] of the revelers has stopped,
the joyful harp[r] is silent.[s]
9 No longer do they drink wine[t] with a
song;
the beer is bitter[u] to its drinkers.
24:9 [t]Isa 5:11,22 [u]Isa 5:20 10 The ruined city lies desolate;
the entrance to every house is barred.
11 In the streets they cry out for wine;
24:11 [v]Isa 16:10; 32:13; Jer 14:3 all joy turns to gloom,[v]
all gaiety is banished from the earth.
12 The city is left in ruins,
its gate is battered to pieces.
13 So will it be on the earth
and among the nations,
24:13 [w]Isa 17:6 as when an olive tree is beaten,[w]
or as when gleanings are left after the
grape harvest.

14 They raise their voices, they shout for
24:14 [x]Isa 12:6 joy;[x]
from the west they acclaim the LORD's
majesty.
24:15 [y]Isa 66:19 [z]Isa 25:3; Mal 1:11 15 Therefore in the east give glory[y] to the
LORD;
exalt[z] the name of the LORD, the God
of Israel,
in the islands of the sea.
16 From the ends of the earth we hear
singing:
24:16 [a]Isa 28:5 [b]Isa 21:2; Jer 5:11 "Glory[a] to the Righteous One."

But I said, "I waste away, I waste away!
Woe to me!
The treacherous betray!
With treachery the treacherous
betray![b]"
24:17 [c]Jer 48:43 17 Terror and pit and snare[c] await you,
O people of the earth.
18 Whoever flees at the sound of terror
will fall into a pit;
whoever climbs out of the pit
will be caught in a snare.

24:18 [d]Ge 7:11 [e]Ps 18:7 The floodgates of the heavens[d] are
opened,
the foundations of the earth shake.[e]
19 The earth is broken up,
24:19 [f]Dt 11:6 the earth is split asunder,[f]
the earth is thoroughly shaken.
24:20 [g]Isa 19:14 [h]Isa 1:2,28; 43:27 20 The earth reels like a drunkard,[g]
it sways like a hut in the wind;
so heavy upon it is the guilt of its
rebellion[h]
that it falls—never to rise again.
24:21 [i]Isa 10:12 21 In that day the LORD will punish[i]

Who Are These People?

ISA 24:14–16

Though the earth crumbles and many tremble, a group of people shouts and praises God. They're the righteous who know they'll soon live forever with the Lord. They don't rejoice because the wicked face calamity. They celebrate because they anticipate God's coming kingdom and his eternal glory. The 18th-century Puritan preacher Jonathan Edwards explains: "The saints highly value the Lord on earth; how much more they will value him in the world to come! They will greatly rejoice in all that contributes to his glory."*

**From his sermon, "The End of the Wicked Contemplated by the Righteous."*

Mountain Feast

Who Are These People?

ISA 25:6-8

Like a king hosting his coronation feast or like a great wedding feast, the Lord calls his people to Mount Zion for a celebration. He spares nothing: They eat rich food and drink the best wine. The king also removes the shroud of death from the world, wipes away tears and erases the hostility toward believers. The apostle Paul refers to this time and claims, "Death has been swallowed up in victory. Where, O death, is your victory? Where, O death, is your sting? . . . Thanks be to God! He gives us the victory through our Lord Jesus Christ" (1Co 15:54-55,57). The apostle John also talks about the great feast of the "wedding supper of the Lamb" (Rev 19:9). These Mount Zion guests celebrate the final victory through Jesus, God's Son and our Savior.

the powers in the heavens above
and the kings on the earth below.
22 They will be herded together
like prisoners[j] bound in a dungeon;[k]
they will be shut up in prison
and be punished[a] after many days.[l]
23 The moon will be abashed, the sun[m] ashamed;
for the LORD Almighty will reign[n]
on Mount Zion[o] and in Jerusalem,
and before its elders, gloriously.[p]

Praise to the LORD

25 O LORD, you are my God;
I will exalt you and praise your name,
for in perfect faithfulness
you have done marvelous things,[q]
things planned[r] long ago.
2 You have made the city a heap of rubble,[s]
the fortified[t] town a ruin,
the foreigners' stronghold[u] a city no more;
it will never be rebuilt.
3 Therefore strong peoples will honor you;
cities of ruthless[v] nations will revere you.
4 You have been a refuge[w] for the poor,
a refuge for the needy in his distress,
a shelter from the storm
and a shade from the heat.
For the breath of the ruthless[x]
is like a storm driving against a wall
5 and like the heat of the desert.
You silence[y] the uproar of foreigners;
as heat is reduced by the shadow of a cloud,
so the song of the ruthless is stilled.

6 On this mountain[z] the LORD Almighty will prepare
a feast[a] of rich food for all peoples,
a banquet of aged wine—
the best of meats and the finest of wines.[b]
7 On this mountain he will destroy
the shroud[c] that enfolds all peoples,
the sheet that covers all nations;
8 he will swallow up death[d] forever.
The Sovereign LORD will wipe away the tears[e]
from all faces;
he will remove the disgrace[f] of his people
from all the earth.
The LORD has spoken.

9 In that day they will say,

"Surely this is our God;[g]
we trusted in him, and he saved[h] us.

24:22 [j]Isa 10:4 [k]Isa 42:7,22 [l]Eze 38:8
24:23 [m]Isa 13:10 [n]Rev 22:5 [o]Heb 12:22 [p]Isa 60:19
25:1 [q]Ps 98:1 [r]Nu 23:19
25:2 [s]Isa 17:1 [t]Isa 17:3 [u]Isa 13:22
25:3 [v]Isa 13:11
25:4 [w]Isa 4:6; 17:10; 27:5; 33:16 [x]Isa 29:5; 49:25
25:5 [y]Jer 51:55
25:6 [z]Isa 2:2 [a]Isa 1:19; Mt 8:11; 22:4 [b]Pr 9:2
25:7 [c]2Co 3:15-16; Eph 4:18
25:8 [d]Hos 13:14; 1Co 15:54-55* [e]Isa 30:19; 35:10; 51:11; 65:19; Rev 7:17; 21:4 [f]Mt 5:11; 1Pe 4:14
25:9 [g]Isa 40:9 [h]Ps 20:5; Isa 33:22; 35:4; 49:25-26; 60:16

[a] 22 Or *released*

Widow of Zarephath

Even When We Doubt

She did not have any bread or any means of getting what she needed. There was a famine in the land. There was nothing to harvest, much less glean. She had no family to protect her or to provide for her. She was resigned that she and her son were not going to survive—until Elijah came to stay.

Jezebel was killing the prophets of the Lord, and Elijah was at the top of the most-wanted list. Zarephath was near Jezebel's hometown. Yet the Lord entrusted Elijah's well-being to this widow in enemy territory.

This wasn't hard for Elijah to accept. If ravens could supply his needs, surely a widow in a famine would have the resources. But it was a surprise for the widow. Her cup was more than half empty; it was down to the dregs. She was ready to succumb to the bitter circumstances of her poverty. She could not guess that God was about to do a major work in her heart, as well as in her pantry.

Elijah gave her God's word: Your flour and oil will not run out until the rains come on the land. Did she recognize Elijah as the prophet who had declared this drought to King Ahab (1Ki 17:1)? She decided to trust him—just once. There was a miracle, day after day. The jar of flour and the jug of oil never were full; they just never were empty.

After some time, however, the widow's son became ill and died. This son was the only family she had. And he represented her security in old age—he would have taken care of her. She had seen a miracle of God's provision daily, but in the face of this loss, she accused Elijah and the Lord of turning on her.

Did her attitude shake even Elijah's confidence? Perhaps. But his prayers produced a miracle on the widow's behalf. Her son was raised from death. The Lord pierced the crust around her heart, and, finally, she believed that Elijah—and God—could be trusted.

The Lord loved this woman and went to great lengths to prove it. We know nothing of her background or of her relationship to the Lord before Elijah's stay. But God knew her address and the state of her heart. He loved her too much to leave her stranded in unbelief.

Even when we see God at work in our lives every day, it is possible to doubt him when a crisis comes. But our fearful doubts don't alter his loving care for us.

Widow of Zarephath
1 Kings 17:8-24
Luke 4:25-26

Candid SNAPSHOT "As surely as the LORD your God lives," she replied, "I don't have any bread—only a handful of flour in a jar and a little oil in a jug. I am gathering a few sticks to take home and make a meal for myself and my son, that we may eat it—and die" (1 Kings 17:12).

Widow With Jars of Oil

Generous Provision

While most of us know what it feels like to be desperate for money at some time in our lives, it's hard to imagine the prospect of our children becoming slaves to pay our debts. But that was exactly what this woman faced.

Seeing Elisha in a crowd, she laid her desperation at his feet. Her husband too had been a prophet, perhaps one of those Jezebel had killed, and she was familiar with God's working. If only Elisha would help her find God's solution to her problem.

Instead of giving her solutions, Elisha asked her, "How can I help you? Tell me, what do you have in your house?" (2Ki 4:2). His response must have puzzled her. If she had anything of value in her house, she already would have sold it. She needed money—and he started talking about pouring oil from one jar to another! It didn't make sense, but she may have seen her husband do and say peculiar things, too. She already had tried everything else she knew to solve her problem. She did what Elisha said.

The Lord was stretching her faith. He knew she needed to look at him rather than at her problem. Elisha had said to close the doors. There must be no manipulation, no neighbors to guess her plan and contribute from their stores. This was to be a pure work of God on her behalf.

Imagine her surprise and delight when she began pouring, and the oil kept flowing. A jar with no bottom! God's provision was as abundant as her faith was to obey. When she ran out of jars, the oil stopped flowing. Surely, she fell on her face in thanksgiving. God was real *and all-sufficient.*

Only then did Elisha unveil the next step: Sell the oil. Of course! Oil had great value. She received enough to pay off the debt and she and her sons lived on the rest. God's provision had gone beyond her immediate crisis to meet her daily need. Her sons, who also had witnessed the miracle, felt a huge burden fall from their shoulders that day. They would not be enslaved—God had saved them all.

We often become so fixed on our dilemma that we lose sight of our Deliverer. Then, when we're ready to give up, our generous, compassionate God pours out more than we asked for.

Widow With Jars of Oil
2 Kings 4:1–7

Candid SNAPSHOT The wife of a man from the company of the prophets cried out to Elisha, "Your servant my husband is dead, and you know that he revered the LORD. But now his creditor is coming to take my two boys as his slaves" (2 Kings 4:1).

This is the LORD, we trusted in him;
let us rejoice[i] and be glad in his salvation."
10 The hand of the LORD will rest on this mountain;
but Moab[j] will be trampled under him
as straw is trampled down in the manure.
11 They will spread out their hands in it,
as a swimmer spreads out his hands to swim.
God will bring down[k] their pride[l]
despite the cleverness[a] of their hands.
12 He will bring down your high fortified walls
and lay them low;[m]
he will bring them down to the ground,
to the very dust.

A Song of Praise

26 In that day this song will be sung in the land of Judah:

We have a strong city;[n]
God makes salvation
its walls[o] and ramparts.
2 Open the gates
that the righteous[p] nation may enter,
the nation that keeps faith.
3 You will keep in perfect peace
him whose mind is steadfast,
because he trusts in you.
4 Trust[q] in the LORD forever,
for the LORD, the LORD, is the Rock eternal.
5 He humbles those who dwell on high,
he lays the lofty city low;
he levels it to the ground[r]
and casts it down to the dust.
6 Feet trample it down—
the feet of the oppressed,
the footsteps of the poor.[s]
7 The path of the righteous is level;
O upright One, you make the way of the righteous smooth.[t]
8 Yes, LORD, walking in the way of your laws,[b][u]
we wait for you;
your name[v] and renown
are the desire of our hearts.
9 My soul yearns for you in the night;
in the morning my spirit longs[w] for you.
When your judgments come upon the earth,
the people of the world learn righteousness.[x]
10 Though grace is shown to the wicked,

25:9 [i]Isa 35:2,10
25:10 [j]Am 2:1-3
25:11 [k]Isa 5:25; 14:26; 16:14 [l]Job 40:12
25:12 [m]Isa 15:1
26:1 [n]Isa 14:32 [o]Isa 60:18
26:2 [p]Isa 54:14; 58:8; 62:2
26:4 [q]Isa 12:2; 50:10
26:5 [r]Isa 25:12
26:6 [s]Isa 3:15
26:7 [t]Isa 42:16
26:8 [u]Isa 56:1 [v]Isa 12:4
26:9 [w]Ps 63:1; 78:34; Isa 55:6 [x]Mt 6:33

[a] *11* The meaning of the Hebrew for this word is uncertain.
[b] *8* Or *judgments*

Judgment Versus Grace

ISA 26:9–10

The Lord continually offers us grace, but at times we still need his judgment. That may sound contradictory, but sometimes we take God's grace for granted. Hardship and discipline catch our attention and cause us to change our sinful ways and grow in righteousness. Hebrews 12:11 explains: "No discipline seems pleasant at the time, but painful. Later on, however, it produces a harvest of righteousness and peace for those who have been trained by it." Judgment requires discipline and discipline creates righteousness. Viewed this way, judgment can be seen as a type of grace.

Useless Labor

ISA 26:18

Though the Jews metaphorically feel the agony of labor, with its terrible pain and constant pushing, they don't give birth to spiritual children. Instead of seeking God in their distress, they rely on their own wiles and pagan resources. Neither yields the desired result of bringing the news of salvation to the world, a calling God intends for them. They fail, like a woman who struggles to give birth but delivers nothing. When we neglect God's spiritual path for us, we find ourselves giving birth to the wind. In other words, we become spiritually barren not only in terms of spiritual children, but also in terms of the fruit of the Spirit (Gal 5:22–23).

they do not learn righteousness;
even in a land of uprightness they go on
doing evil[y]
and regard[z] not the majesty of the
LORD.
[11] O LORD, your hand is lifted high,
but they do not see[a] it.
Let them see your zeal for your people
and be put to shame;
let the fire[b] reserved for your enemies
consume them.

[12] LORD, you establish peace for us;
all that we have accomplished you
have done for us.
[13] O LORD, our God, other lords[c] besides
you have ruled over us,
but your name alone do we honor.[d]
[14] They are now dead,[e] they live no more;
those departed spirits do not rise.
You punished them and brought them to
ruin;[f]
you wiped out all memory of them.
[15] You have enlarged the nation, O LORD;
you have enlarged the nation.
You have gained glory for yourself;
you have extended all the borders[g] of
the land.
[16] LORD, they came to you in their distress;[h]
when you disciplined them,
they could barely whisper a prayer.[a]
[17] As a woman with child and about to
give birth[i]
writhes and cries out in her pain,
so were we in your presence, O LORD.
[18] We were with child, we writhed in pain,
but we gave birth[j] to wind.
We have not brought salvation[k] to the
earth;
we have not given birth to people of
the world.

[19] But your dead[l] will live;
their bodies will rise.
You who dwell in the dust,
wake up and shout for joy.
Your dew is like the dew of the morning;
the earth will give birth to her dead.[m]

[20] Go, my people, enter your rooms
and shut the doors[n] behind you;
hide[o] yourselves for a little while
until his wrath has passed by.[p]
[21] See, the LORD is coming[q] out of his
dwelling[r]
to punish[s] the people of the earth for
their sins.
The earth will disclose the blood[t] shed
upon her;
she will conceal her slain no longer.

26:10 [y]Isa 32:6 [z]Isa 22:12-13; Hos 11:7; Jn 5:37-38; Ro 2:4
26:11 [a]Isa 44:9,18 [b]Heb 10:27
26:13 [c]Isa 2:8; 10:5,11 [d]Isa 63:7
26:14 [e]Dt 4:28 [f]Isa 10:3
26:15 [g]Isa 33:17
26:16 [h]Hos 5:15
26:17 [i]Jn 16:21
26:18 [j]Isa 33:11; 59:4 [k]Ps 17:14
26:19 [l]Isa 25:8; Eph 5:14 [m]Eze 37:1-14; Da 12:2
26:20 [n]Ex 12:23 [o]Ps 91:1,4 [p]Ps 30:5; Isa 54:7-8
26:21 [q]Jude 1:14 [r]Mic 1:3 [s]Isa 13:9,11; 30:12-14 [t]Job 16:18; Lk 11:50-51

[a] *16* The meaning of the Hebrew for this clause is uncertain.

Deliverance of Israel

27 In that day,

27:1 [u]Isa 34:6; 66:16 [v]Job 3:8 [w]Ps 74:13

the LORD will punish with his sword,[u]
his fierce, great and powerful sword,
Leviathan[v] the gliding serpent,
Leviathan the coiling serpent;
he will slay the monster[w] of the sea.

[2]In that day—

27:2 [x]Jer 2:21

"Sing about a fruitful vineyard:[x]
[3] I, the LORD, watch over it;

27:3 [y]Isa 58:11

I water[y] it continually.
I guard it day and night
so that no one may harm it.
[4] I am not angry.
If only there were briers and thorns
confronting me!
I would march against them in battle;

27:4 [z]Isa 10:17; Mt 3:12; Heb 6:8

I would set them all on fire.[z]
[5]Or else let them come to me for refuge;[a]
let them make peace[b] with me,

27:5 [a]Isa 25:4 [b]Job 22:21; Ro 5:1; 2Co 5:20

yes, let them make peace with me."

[6]In days to come Jacob will take root,
Israel will bud and blossom[c]
and fill all the world with fruit.[d]

27:6 [c]Hos 14:5-6 [d]Isa 37:31

[7]Has ⌊the LORD⌋ struck her
as he struck[e] down those who struck
her?

27:7 [e]Isa 37:36-38

Has she been killed
as those were killed who killed her?
[8]By warfare[a] and exile[f] you contend with
her—

27:8 [f]Isa 50:1; 54:7

with his fierce blast he drives her out,
as on a day the east wind blows.
[9]By this, then, will Jacob's guilt be
atoned for,
and this will be the full fruitage of the
removal of his sin:[g]

27:9 [g]Ro 11:27* [h]Ex 34:13

When he makes all the altar stones
to be like chalk stones crushed to
pieces,
no Asherah poles[b][h] or incense altars
will be left standing.

27:10 [i]Isa 32:14; Jer 26:6 [j]Isa 17:2

[10]The fortified city stands desolate,[i]
an abandoned settlement, forsaken
like the desert;
there the calves graze,
there they lie down;[j]
they strip its branches bare.
[11]When its twigs are dry, they are broken
off
and women come and make fires with
them.

27:11 [k]Dt 32:28; Isa 1:3; Jer 8:7

For this is a people without
understanding;[k]

[a] *8* See Septuagint; the meaning of the Hebrew for this word is uncertain. [b] *9* That is, symbols of the goddess Asherah

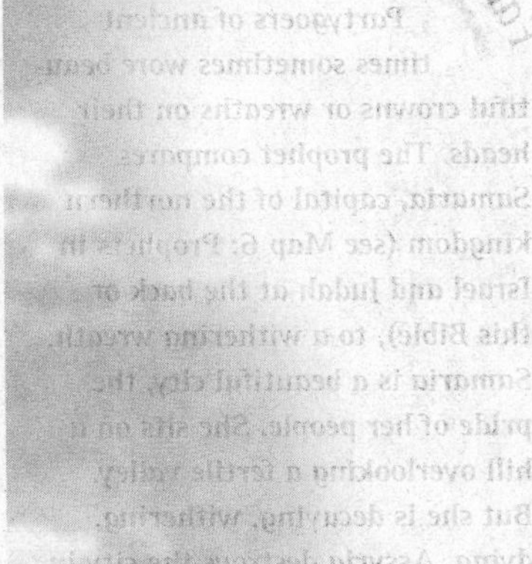

I need to be reminded of *Satan's deceptions and hidden agendas,* not only because they hurt me . . . but also because I soon forget his long-term commitment to my destruction. Understanding that Satan is the author of *hidden agendas,* that his language is lies, and that his motive is our demise prepares us for his attacks.

—Patsy Clairmont

Fading Beauty

ISA 28:1-3

Partygoers of ancient times sometimes wore beautiful crowns or wreaths on their heads. The prophet compares Samaria, capital of the northern kingdom (see Map 6: Prophets in Israel and Judah at the back of this Bible), to a withering wreath. Samaria is a beautiful city, the pride of her people. She sits on a hill overlooking a fertile valley. But she is decaying, withering, dying. Assyria destroys the city in 722 B.C. and takes its inhabitants into captivity.

so their Maker has no compassion on
them,
and their Creator[l] shows them no
favor.[m]

12 In that day the LORD will thresh from the flowing Euphrates[a] to the Wadi of Egypt,[n] and you, O
Israelites, will be gathered[o] up one by one. 13 And
in that day a great trumpet[p] will sound. Those
who were perishing in Assyria and those who
were exiled in Egypt[q] will come and worship the
LORD on the holy mountain in Jerusalem.

Woe to Ephraim

28 Woe to that wreath, the pride of
Ephraim's[r] drunkards,
to the fading flower, his glorious
beauty,
set on the head of a fertile valley[s]—
to that city, the pride of those laid low
by wine![t]
2 See, the Lord has one who is powerful[u]
and strong.
Like a hailstorm[v] and a destructive
wind,[w]
like a driving rain and a flooding[x]
downpour,
he will throw it forcefully to the
ground.
3 That wreath, the pride of Ephraim's[y]
drunkards,
will be trampled underfoot.
4 That fading flower, his glorious beauty,
set on the head of a fertile valley,[z]
will be like a fig[a] ripe before harvest—
as soon as someone sees it and takes
it in his hand,
he swallows it.

5 In that day the LORD Almighty
will be a glorious crown,[b]
a beautiful wreath
for the remnant of his people.
6 He will be a spirit of justice[c]
to him who sits in judgment,[d]
a source of strength
to those who turn back the battle[e] at
the gate.

7 And these also stagger from wine[f]
and reel[g] from beer:
Priests[h] and prophets[i] stagger from beer
and are befuddled with wine;
they reel from beer,
they stagger when seeing visions,[j]
they stumble when rendering
decisions.
8 All the tables are covered with vomit[k]
and there is not a spot without filth.

9 "Who is it he is trying to teach?[l]

27:11 [l]Dt 32:18; Isa 43:1,7, 15; 44:1-2, 21,24 [m]Isa 9:17
27:12 [n]Ge 15:18 [o]Dt 30:4; Isa 11:12; 17:6
27:13 [p]Lev 25:9; Mt 24:31 [q]Isa 19:21,25
28:1 [r]ver 3; Isa 9:9 [s]ver 4 [t]Hos 7:5
28:2 [u]Isa 40:10 [v]Isa 30:30; Eze 13:11 [w]Isa 29:6 [x]Isa 8:7
28:3 [y]ver 1
28:4 [z]ver 1 [a]Hos 9:10; Na 3:12
28:5 [b]Isa 62:3
28:6 [c]Isa 11:2-4; 32:1,16 [d]Jn 5:30 [e]2Ch 32:8
28:7 [f]Isa 22:13 [g]Isa 56:10-12 [h]Isa 24:2 [i]Isa 9:15 [j]Isa 29:11; Hos 4:11
28:8 [k]Jer 48:26
28:9 [l]ver 26; Isa 30:20; 48:17; 50:4; 54:13

[a] *12* Hebrew *River*

28:9 [m]Ps 131:2 [n]Heb 5:12-13

[9]To whom is he explaining his message?
To children weaned[m] from their milk,[n]
to those just taken from the breast?
[10]For it is:
Do and do, do and do,
rule on rule, rule on rule[a];
a little here, a little there."

28:11 [o]Isa 33:19 [p]1Co 14:21*
28:12 [q]Isa 11:10; Mt 11:28-29

[11]Very well then, with foreign lips and
strange tongues[o]
God will speak to this people,[p]
[12]to whom he said,
"This is the resting place, let the
weary rest";[q]
and, "This is the place of repose"—
but they would not listen.
[13]So then, the word of the LORD to them
will become:
Do and do, do and do,
rule on rule, rule on rule;
a little here, a little there—
so that they will go and fall backward,
be injured[r] and snared and captured.[s]

28:13 [r]Mt 21:44 [s]Isa 8:15
28:14 [t]Isa 1:10

[14]Therefore hear the word of the LORD,[t]
you scoffers
who rule this people in Jerusalem.
[15]You boast, "We have entered into a
covenant with death,
with the grave[b] we have made an
agreement.
When an overwhelming scourge sweeps
by,[u]
it cannot touch us,
for we have made a lie[v] our refuge
and falsehood[c] our hiding place.[w]"

28:15 [u]ver 2,18; Isa 8:7-8; 30:28; Da 11:22 [v]Isa 9:15 [w]Isa 29:15

[16]So this is what the Sovereign LORD says:

28:16 [x]Ps 118:22; Isa 8:14-15; Mt 21:42; Ac 4:11; Eph 2:20 [y]Ro 9:33*; 10:11*; 1Pe 2:6*
28:17 [z]Isa 5:16 [a]2Ki 21:13
28:18 [b]Isa 7:7 [c]ver 15 [d]Da 8:13

"See, I lay a stone in Zion,
a tested stone,[x]
a precious cornerstone for a sure
foundation;
the one who trusts will never be
dismayed.[y]
[17]I will make justice[z] the measuring line
and righteousness the plumb line;[a]
hail will sweep away your refuge, the lie,
and water will overflow your hiding
place.
[18]Your covenant with death will be
annulled;
your agreement with the grave will
not stand.[b]
When the overwhelming scourge
sweeps by,[c]
you will be beaten down[d] by it.

[a] *10* Hebrew / *sav lasav sav lasav* / *kav lakav kav lakav* (possibly meaningless sounds; perhaps a mimicking of the prophet's words); also in verse 13 [b] *15* Hebrew *Sheol*; also in verse 18 [c] *15* Or *false gods*

Mocking Priests

ISA 28:9-10

The priests ridicule Isaiah's message of doom, claiming it's too elementary, like someone who teaches the alphabet to children—a little here, a little there. These spiritual leaders claim to know the difference between right and wrong, but they miss God's warnings altogether. Consequently, God says, with a little here and a little there, the Jews will lose their freedom to Assyria (Isa 28:13). What began as the priests mocking Isaiah turns into God mocking the priests.

The wicked often mock God's messengers. Even Jesus knew he would be mocked by unbelievers (Mk 10:33-34; Lk 18:31-33). But mocking the Lord's words or his servants is a dangerous business. Isaiah proclaims, "The ruthless will vanish, the mockers will disappear, and all who have an eye for evil will be cut down" (Isa 29:20).

Zion's Cornerstone

ISA 28:16

The Lord uses metaphors familiar to builders. A cornerstone can be a large stone in the foundation of a building that, because of its enormous size, joins together two or more rows of stones. Or it can refer to the final stone that completes an arch or a top corner of a building. In this passage it probably represents the massive rock on which the temple is built. That rock had been a threshing floor (1Ch 21:28—22:1) and, since threshing is a metaphor for God's judgment, could be seen as a symbol of God's testing and judgment.

The New Testament refers to Jesus Christ as the "chief cornerstone" on which an unshakable faith can be built (Eph 2:20). Peter quotes this passage from Isaiah and explains, "Now to you who believe, this stone is precious. But to those who do not believe," this stone becomes a stumbling block (1Pe 2:7-8).

19 As often as it comes it will carry you
away;[e]
morning after morning, by day and by
night,
it will sweep through."

The understanding of this message
will bring sheer terror.[f]
20 The bed is too short to stretch out on,
the blanket too narrow to wrap
around you.[g]
21 The LORD will rise up as he did at Mount
Perazim,[h]
he will rouse himself as in the Valley
of Gibeon[i]—
to do his work,[j] his strange work,
and perform his task, his alien task.
22 Now stop your mocking,
or your chains will become heavier;
the Lord, the LORD Almighty, has told
me
of the destruction decreed[k] against the
whole land.[l]

23 Listen and hear my voice;
pay attention and hear what I say.
24 When a farmer plows for planting, does
he plow continually?
Does he keep on breaking up and
harrowing the soil?
25 When he has leveled the surface,
does he not sow caraway and scatter
cummin?[m]
Does he not plant wheat in its place,[a]
barley in its plot,[a]
and spelt[n] in its field?
26 His God instructs him
and teaches him the right way.

27 Caraway is not threshed with a sledge,
nor is a cartwheel rolled over
cummin;
caraway is beaten out with a rod,
and cummin with a stick.
28 Grain must be ground to make bread;
so one does not go on threshing it
forever.
Though he drives the wheels of his
threshing cart over it,
his horses do not grind it.
29 All this also comes from the LORD
Almighty,
wonderful in counsel[o] and
magnificent in wisdom.[p]

Woe to David's City

29 Woe[q] to you, Ariel, Ariel,[r]
the city where David settled!
Add year to year
and let your cycle of festivals[s] go on.

28:19 [e]2Ki 24:2 [f]Job 18:11
28:20 [g]Isa 59:6
28:21 [h]1Ch 14:11 [i]Jos 10:10, 12; 1Ch 14:16 [j]Isa 10:12; Lk 19:41-44
28:22 [k]Isa 10:22 [l]Isa 10:23
28:25 [m]Mt 23:23 [n]Ex 9:32
28:29 [o]Isa 9:6 [p]Ro 11:33
29:1 [q]Isa 22:12-13 [r]2Sa 5:9 [s]Isa 1:14

[a] *25* The meaning of the Hebrew for this word is uncertain.

2 Yet I will besiege Ariel;
she will mourn and lament,[t]
she will be to me like an altar hearth.[a]
3 I will encamp against you all around;
I will encircle[u] you with towers
and set up my siege works against you.
4 Brought low, you will speak from the ground;
your speech will mumble[v] out of the dust.
Your voice will come ghostlike from the earth;
out of the dust your speech will whisper.
5 But your many enemies will become like fine dust,
the ruthless hordes like blown chaff.[w]
Suddenly,[x] in an instant,
6 the LORD Almighty will come
with thunder and earthquake[y] and great noise,
with windstorm and tempest and flames of a devouring fire.
7 Then the hordes of all the nations[z] that fight against Ariel,
that attack her and her fortress and besiege her,
will be as it is with a dream,[a]
with a vision in the night—
8 as when a hungry man dreams that he is eating,
but he awakens,[b] and his hunger remains;
as when a thirsty man dreams that he is drinking,
but he awakens faint, with his thirst unquenched.
So will it be with the hordes of all the nations
that fight against Mount Zion.

9 Be stunned and amazed,
blind yourselves and be sightless;
be drunk,[c] but not from wine,[d]
stagger, but not from beer.
10 The LORD has brought over you a deep sleep:
He has sealed your eyes[e] (the prophets);[f]
he has covered your heads (the seers).[g]

11 For you this whole vision is nothing but words
sealed[h] in a scroll. And if you give the scroll to
someone who can read, and say to him, "Read
this, please," he will answer, "I can't; it is sealed."
12 Or if you give the scroll to someone who cannot

29:2 [t]Isa 3:26; La 2:5
29:3 [u]Lk 19:43-44
29:4 [v]Isa 8:19
29:5 [w]Isa 17:13 [x]Isa 17:14; 1Th 5:3
29:6 [y]Mt 24:7; Mk 13:8; Lk 21:11; Rev 11:19
29:7 [z]Mic 4:11-12; Zec 12:9 [a]Job 20:8
29:8 [b]Ps 73:20
29:9 [c]Isa 51:17 [d]Isa 51:21-22
29:10 [e]Ps 69:23; Isa 6:9-10; Ro 11:8* [f]Mic 3:6 [g]1Sa 9:9
29:11 [h]Isa 8:16; Mt 13:11; Rev 5:1-2

[a] 2 The Hebrew for *altar hearth* sounds like the Hebrew for *Ariel.*

Sealed Scroll

ISA 29:9–12

Religious leaders have ignored the Lord's warnings for so long that God finally lets them wallow in their rebellion. He compares them to being blind, drunk or in a deep sleep—unable to comprehend what's happening around them, ignorant of the encroaching destruction. God also likens their lack of understanding to a person who can't read a scroll because it's sealed. Or to someone who can't read, even though the scroll lies open. To all of these people, Isaiah's visions and prophecies mean nothing because they're too spiritually calloused for the messages to penetrate their hearts.

How true this is even today. God never forces himself on us. When we continually resist him (either as a society or as individuals), God gives us over to our sinful desires (Ro 1:24) and hardened hearts (Zec 7:12).

Lips Versus Hearts

ISA 29:13

It's not enough just to practice spiritual rituals. Even if God establishes the religious rules, as he does with the Israelites, they mean nothing to him if his people are cold-hearted when they observe them. They are to worship God with their hearts as well as their mouths. Otherwise, they're counted among the hypocrites.

Jesus quotes this verse when he condemns the religious hypocrites of his day (Mt 15:8–9; Mk 7:6–7). Like their ancestors, the Jews around Jesus don't understand the meaning of true worship. King David explained the worship that God accepts: "You do not delight in sacrifice, or I would bring it; you do not take pleasure in burnt offerings. The sacrifices of God are a broken spirit; a broken and contrite heart, O God, you will not despise" (Ps 51:16–17).

read, and say, "Read this, please," he will answer,
"I don't know how to read."

13 The Lord says:

"These people come near to me with
their mouth
and honor me with their lips,
but their hearts are far from me.[i]
Their worship of me
is made up only of rules taught by
men.[a][j]
14 Therefore once more I will astound
these people
with wonder upon wonder;[k]
the wisdom of the wise[l] will perish,
the intelligence of the intelligent will
vanish.[m]"
15 Woe to those who go to great depths
to hide their plans from the LORD,
who do their work in darkness and
think,
"Who sees us?[n] Who will know?"[o]
16 You turn things upside down,
as if the potter were thought to be like
the clay!
Shall what is formed say to him who
formed it,
"He did not make me"?
Can the pot say of the potter,[p]
"He knows nothing"?

17 In a very short time, will not Lebanon
be turned into a fertile field[q]
and the fertile field seem like a
forest?[r]
18 In that day the deaf[s] will hear the words
of the scroll,
and out of gloom and darkness
the eyes of the blind will see.[t]
19 Once more the humble[u] will rejoice in
the LORD;
the needy[v] will rejoice in the Holy
One of Israel.
20 The ruthless will vanish,
the mockers[w] will disappear,
and all who have an eye for evil[x] will
be cut down—
21 those who with a word make a man out
to be guilty,
who ensnare the defender in court[y]
and with false testimony deprive the
innocent of justice.[z]

22 Therefore this is what the LORD, who
redeemed Abraham,[a] says to the house of Jacob:

"No longer will Jacob be ashamed;[b]
no longer will their faces grow pale.
23 When they see among them their
children,[c]

29:13 [i]Eze 33:31 [j]Mt 15:8-9*; Mk 7:6-7*; Col 2:22
29:14 [k]Hab 1:5 [l]Jer 8:9; 49:7 [m]Isa 6:9-10; 1Co 1:19*
29:15 [n]Ps 10:11-13; 94:7; Isa 57:12 [o]Job 22:13
29:16 [p]Isa 45:9; 64:8; Ro 9:20-21*
29:17 [q]Ps 84:6 [r]Isa 32:15
29:18 [s]Mk 7:37 [t]Isa 32:3; 35:5; Mt 11:5
29:19 [u]Isa 61:1; Mt 5:5; 11:29 [v]Isa 14:30; Mt 11:5; Jas 1:9; 2:5
29:20 [w]Isa 28:22 [x]Isa 59:4; Mic 2:1
29:21 [y]Am 5:10,15 [z]Isa 32:7
29:22 [a]Isa 41:8; 63:16 [b]Isa 49:23
29:23 [c]Isa 49:20-26

[a] 13 Hebrew; Septuagint *They worship me in vain; / their teachings are but rules taught by men*

the work of my hands,[d]
they will keep my name holy;
they will acknowledge the holiness of the Holy One of Jacob,
and will stand in awe of the God of Israel.
24 Those who are wayward[e] in spirit will gain understanding;[f]
those who complain will accept instruction."[g]

Woe to the Obstinate Nation

30 "Woe[h] to the obstinate children,"[i]
declares the LORD,
"to those who carry out plans that are not mine,
forming an alliance,[j] but not by my Spirit,
heaping sin upon sin;
2 who go down to Egypt[k]
without consulting[l] me;
who look for help to Pharaoh's protection,[m]
to Egypt's shade for refuge.
3 But Pharaoh's protection will be to your shame,
Egypt's shade will bring you disgrace.[n]
4 Though they have officials in Zoan[o]
and their envoys have arrived in Hanes,
5 everyone will be put to shame
because of a people[p] useless to them,
who bring neither help nor advantage,
but only shame and disgrace."

6 An oracle concerning the animals of the Negev:

Through a land of hardship and distress,[q]
of lions and lionesses,
of adders and darting snakes,[r]
the envoys carry their riches on donkeys' backs,
their treasures[s] on the humps of camels,
to that unprofitable nation,
7 to Egypt, whose help is utterly useless.
Therefore I call her
Rahab the Do-Nothing.

8 Go now, write it on a tablet for them,
inscribe it on a scroll,[t]
that for the days to come
it may be an everlasting witness.
9 These are rebellious people, deceitful[u] children,
children unwilling to listen to the LORD's instruction.[v]
10 They say to the seers,
"See no more visions[w]!"
and to the prophets,

29:23 [d]Isa 19:25
29:24 [e]Isa 28:7; Heb 5:2 [f]Isa 41:20; 60:16 [g]Isa 30:21
30:1 [h]Isa 29:15 [i]Isa 1:2 [j]Isa 8:12
30:2 [k]Isa 31:1 [l]Nu 27:21 [m]Isa 36:9
30:3 [n]Isa 20:4-5; 36:6
30:4 [o]Isa 19:11
30:5 [p]ver 7
30:6 [q]Ex 5:10,21; Isa 8:22; Jer 11:4 [r]Dt 8:15 [s]Isa 15:7
30:8 [t]Isa 8:1; Hab 2:2
30:9 [u]Isa 28:15; 59:3-4 [v]Isa 1:10
30:10 [w]Jer 11:21; Am 7:13

Rahab the Do-Nothing

ISA 30:6–7

According to Hebrew mythology God subdued Rahab, the female monster of chaos, when he moved across the waters to begin creation. Rahab is used here as a poetic synonym for Egypt, whose armies God destroyed when they pursued the Israelites across the Red Sea. During Isaiah's time foreign armies threaten the Israelites, and they make a treaty with Egypt for protection. This displeases God, who calls Egypt "utterly useless" and a "Do-Nothing" (Isa 30:7). Only God can truly protect his people and keep them secure.

"Give us no more visions of what is
right!
Tell us pleasant things,[x]
prophesy illusions.[y]
11 Leave this way,
get off this path,
and stop confronting[z] us
with the Holy One of Israel!"

12 Therefore, this is what the Holy One of Israel
says:

"Because you have rejected this
message,[a]
relied on oppression[b]
and depended on deceit,
13 this sin will become for you
like a high wall,[c] cracked and
bulging,
that collapses[d] suddenly,[e] in an
instant.
14 It will break in pieces like pottery,[f]
shattered so mercilessly
that among its pieces not a fragment
will be found
for taking coals from a hearth
or scooping water out of a cistern."

15 This is what the Sovereign LORD, the Holy One
of Israel, says:

"In repentance and rest is your
salvation,
in quietness and trust[g] is your
strength,
but you would have none of it.
16 You said, 'No, we will flee on horses.'[h]
Therefore you will flee!
You said, 'We will ride off on swift
horses.'
Therefore your pursuers will be swift!
17 A thousand will flee
at the threat of one;
at the threat of five[i]
you will all flee[j] away,
till you are left
like a flagstaff on a mountaintop,
like a banner on a hill."

18 Yet the LORD longs[k] to be gracious to you;
he rises to show you compassion.
For the LORD is a God of justice.[l]
Blessed are all who wait for him![m]

19 O people of Zion, who live in Jerusalem, you
will weep no more.[n] How gracious he will be
when you cry for help! As soon as he hears, he
will answer[o] you. 20 Although the Lord gives you
the bread[p] of adversity and the water of affliction,
your teachers will be hidden[q] no more; with your
own eyes you will see them. 21 Whether you turn
to the right or to the left, your ears will hear a
voice[r] behind you, saying, "This is the way; walk
in it." 22 Then you will defile your idols[s] overlaid

30:10 [x]1Ki 22:8 [y]Eze 13:7; Ro 16:18
30:11 [z]Job 21:14
30:12 [a]Isa 5:24 [b]Isa 5:7
30:13 [c]Ps 62:3 [d]1Ki 20:30 [e]Isa 29:5
30:14 [f]Ps 2:9; Jer 19:10-11
30:15 [g]Isa 32:17
30:16 [h]Isa 31:1,3
30:17 [i]Lev 26:8; Jos 23:10 [j]Lev 26:36; Dt 28:25
30:18 [k]Isa 42:14; 2Pe 3:9,15 [l]Isa 5:16 [m]Isa 25:9
30:19 [n]Isa 60:20; 61:3 [o]Ps 50:15; Isa 58:9; 65:24; Mt 7:7-11
30:20 [p]1Ki 22:27 [q]Ps 74:9; Am 8:11
30:21 [r]Isa 29:24
30:22 [s]Ex 32:4

This beautiful hymn written in 1752 by Katharina von Schlege speaks to our troubled souls as much now as it did to those who sang it in the 18th and 19th centuries.

Be Still My Soul

Be still, my soul: the Lord is on
thy side.
Bear patiently the cross of grief
or pain.
Leave to your God to order
and provide;
In every change, He faithful
will remain.
Be still, my soul: your best,
your heavenly Friend
Through thorny ways leads to
a joyful end.

Be still, my soul: your God will
undertake
To guide the future, as He has
the past.
Your hope, your confidence let
nothing shake;
All now mysterious shall be
bright at last.
Be still, my soul: the waves
and winds shall know
His voice Who ruled them
while He dwelt below.

—Katharina von Schlege

with silver and your images covered with gold;
you will throw them away like a menstrual cloth
and say to them, "Away with you!"

[23]He will also send you rain[t] for the seed you
sow in the ground, and the food that comes from
the land will be rich and plentiful. In that day
your cattle will graze in broad meadows.[u] [24]The
oxen and donkeys that work the soil will eat fodder and mash, spread out with fork[v] and shovel.
[25]In the day of great slaughter, when the towers[w]
fall, streams of water will flow[x] on every high
mountain and every lofty hill. [26]The moon will
shine like the sun,[y] and the sunlight will be sev-
en times brighter, like the light of seven full days,
when the LORD binds up the bruises of his people
and heals[z] the wounds he inflicted.

[27]See, the Name[a] of the LORD comes from
afar,
with burning anger[b] and dense clouds
of smoke;
his lips are full of wrath,[c]
and his tongue is a consuming fire.
[28]His breath[d] is like a rushing torrent,
rising up to the neck.[e]
He shakes the nations in the sieve[f] of
destruction;
he places in the jaws of the peoples
a bit[g] that leads them astray.
[29]And you will sing
as on the night you celebrate a holy
festival;
your hearts will rejoice
as when people go up with flutes
to the mountain[h] of the LORD,
to the Rock of Israel.
[30]The LORD will cause men to hear his
majestic voice
and will make them see his arm
coming down
with raging anger and consuming fire,
with cloudburst, thunderstorm and
hail.
[31]The voice of the LORD will shatter
Assyria;[i]
with his scepter he will strike[j] them
down.
[32]Every stroke the LORD lays on them
with his punishing rod
will be to the music of tambourines and
harps,
as he fights them in battle with the
blows of his arm.[k]
[33]Topheth[l] has long been prepared;
it has been made ready for the king.
Its fire pit has been made deep and
wide,
with an abundance of fire and wood;
the breath of the LORD,
like a stream of burning sulfur,[m]
sets it ablaze.

30:23 [t]Isa 65:21-22 [u]Ps 65:13
30:24 [v]Mt 3:12; Lk 3:17
30:25 [w]Isa 2:15 [x]Isa 41:18
30:26 [y]Isa 24:23; 60:19-20; Rev 21:23; 22:5 [z]Dt 32:39; Isa 1:5
30:27 [a]Isa 59:19 [b]Isa 66:14 [c]Isa 10:5
30:28 [d]Isa 11:4 [e]Isa 8:8 [f]Am 9:9 [g]2Ki 19:28; Isa 37:29
30:29 [h]Ps 42:4
30:31 [i]Isa 10:5,12 [j]Isa 11:4
30:32 [k]Isa 11:15; Eze 32:10
30:33 [l]2Ki 23:10 [m]Ge 19:24

Castaway Cloths

ISA 30:22

According to Old Testament law, a woman was considered ceremonially unclean during her period, and anyone who touched her was also unclean until evening that day (see the note on Lev 15:19–24, page 179). Menstrual cloths were, naturally, also unclean, and women threw them away.

When God's people return to him, they will throw away their idols, much like abandoned menstrual cloths. Their idols will be as repugnant to them as soiled menstrual rags. Everything about these idols and everyone associated with them is unacceptable to the Lord. God wants a pure and holy people to walk with him.

There is something exhilarating about variety. Don't you love to see a garden of flowers aglow with myriad colors, shapes, and size? The garden would lose much of its appeal if it were all one species, one color and one shape. Can you imagine a symphony performed only by tubas? We need some tubas, but we need cellos, violins, french horns, clarinets, oboes, drums, cymbals, etc., for a rich, full sound. By the same token, I think we achieve a full, rich sound in life when there is variety among us; when our uniqueness is encouraged so that we make a different sound or look from that of everyone around us.

The inevitable result of rigid conformity is a lack of personal authenticity—a phony rather than real approach to ourselves, to others and to life's experiences. God did not create any duplicates in nature or in humankind.

—Marilyn Meberg

Woe to Those Who Rely on Egypt

31 Woe to those who go down to Egypt[n] for help,
who rely on horses,
who trust in the multitude of their chariots[o]
and in the great strength of their horsemen,
but do not look to the Holy One of Israel,
or seek help from the LORD.[p]
2 Yet he too is wise[q] and can bring disaster;[r]
he does not take back his words.[s]
He will rise up against the house of the wicked,[t]
against those who help evildoers.
3 But the Egyptians[u] are men and not God;[v]
their horses are flesh and not spirit.
When the LORD stretches out his hand,[w]
he who helps will stumble,
he who is helped[x] will fall;
both will perish together.

4 This is what the LORD says to me:

"As a lion[y] growls,
a great lion over his prey—
and though a whole band of shepherds
is called together against him,
he is not frightened by their shouts
or disturbed by their clamor—
so the LORD Almighty will come down[z]
to do battle on Mount Zion and on its heights.
5 Like birds hovering overhead,
the LORD Almighty will shield[a] Jerusalem;
he will shield it and deliver[b] it,
he will 'pass over' it and will rescue it."

6 Return to him you have so greatly revolted
against, O Israelites. 7 For in that day every one of
you will reject the idols of silver and gold[c] your
sinful hands have made.

8 "Assyria[d] will fall by a sword that is not of man;
a sword, not of mortals, will devour[e] them.
They will flee before the sword
and their young men will be put to forced labor.[f]
9 Their stronghold[g] will fall because of terror;
at sight of the battle standard their commanders will panic,"
declares the LORD,
whose fire[h] is in Zion,
whose furnace is in Jerusalem.

31:1 [n]Dt 17:16; Isa 30:2,5 [o]Isa 2:7 [p]Ps 20:7; Da 9:13
31:2 [q]Ro 16:27 [r]Isa 45:7 [s]Nu 23:19 [t]Isa 32:6
31:3 [u]Isa 36:9 [v]Eze 28:9; 2Th 2:4 [w]Isa 9:17,21 [x]Isa 30:5-7
31:4 [y]Nu 24:9; Hos 11:10; Am 3:8 [z]Isa 42:13
31:5 [a]Ps 91:4 [b]Isa 37:35; 38:6
31:7 [c]Isa 2:20; 30:22
31:8 [d]Isa 10:12 [e]Isa 14:25; 37:7 [f]Ge 49:15
31:9 [g]Dt 32:31,37 [h]Isa 10:17

The Kingdom of Righteousness

32:1 **32** See, a king[i] will reign in righteousness
[i]Eze 37:24; [j]Ps 72:1-4; and rulers will rule with justice.[j]
Isa 9:7 [2] Each man will be like a shelter[k] from
the wind
32:2 [k]Isa 4:6 and a refuge from the storm,
like streams of water in the desert
and the shadow of a great rock in a
thirsty land.
32:3 [3] Then the eyes of those who see will no
[l]Isa 29:18 longer be closed,[l]
and the ears of those who hear will
listen.
[4] The mind of the rash will know and
32:4 understand,[m]
[m]Isa 29:24 and the stammering tongue will be
fluent and clear.
32:5 [n]1Sa 25:25 [5] No longer will the fool[n] be called noble
nor the scoundrel be highly respected.
32:6 [o]Pr 19:3 [6] For the fool speaks folly,[o]
[p]Isa 9:17 his mind is busy with evil:
[q]Isa 9:16 [r]Isa 3:15 He practices ungodliness[p]
and spreads error[q] concerning the
LORD;
the hungry he leaves empty[r]
and from the thirsty he withholds
water.
32:7 [s]Jer 5:26-28 [7] The scoundrel's methods are wicked,[s]
[t]Mic 7:3 he makes up evil schemes[t]
[u]Isa 61:1 to destroy the poor with lies,
even when the plea of the needy[u] is
just.
[8] But the noble man makes noble plans,
32:8 [v]Pr 11:25 and by noble deeds[v] he stands.

The Women of Jerusalem

[9] You women who are so complacent,
32:9 [w]Isa 28:23 rise up and listen[w] to me;
[x]Isa 47:8; Am 6:1; you daughters who feel secure,[x]
Zep 2:15 hear what I have to say!
[10] In little more than a year
32:10 you who feel secure will tremble;
[y]Isa 5:5-6; the grape harvest will fail,[y]
24:7 and the harvest of fruit will not come.
[11] Tremble, you complacent women;
shudder, you daughters who feel
32:11 secure!
[z]Isa 47:2 Strip off your clothes,[z]
put sackcloth around your waists.
32:12 [a]Na 2:7 [12] Beat your breasts[a] for the pleasant
fields,
for the fruitful vines
[13] and for the land of my people,
32:13 a land overgrown with thorns and
[b]Isa 5:6 [c]Isa 22:2 briers[b]—
yes, mourn for all houses of merriment
32:14 and for this city of revelry.[c]
[d]Isa 13:22; [e]Isa 6:11; [14] The fortress[d] will be abandoned,
27:10 the noisy city deserted;[e]

Complacent Women

ISA 32:9-13

Jerusalem's wealthy class is self-indulgent, living for their own comfort and pleasure. The rich Israelite women particularly exemplify this attitude, and Isaiah vehemently protests the way they go "walking along with outstretched necks, flirting with their eyes, tripping along with mincing steps, with ornaments jingling on their ankles" (Isa 3:16). These wealthy, self-satisfied women consider themselves immune to judgment, but the Lord reminds them that calamity can hit at any time. Within a year (Isa 32:10) the land will turn desolate, their security will wither along with the fruit on the vines. Their laughter will turn to laments; and their silk, to sackcloth.

Though they enjoy life's blessings, they mistakenly place their trust and security in them. People change and circumstances can shift at any time. But "he who fears the LORD has a secure fortress, and for his children it will be a refuge" (Pr 14:26).

Fruit of Righteousness

ISA 32:17

Proverbs 28:1 says, "The wicked man flees though no one pursues." The wicked, because of their sinful ways and guilty consciences, live fearfully and "on guard." They suspect those who might expose their actions. In contrast, the righteous live peacefully, unafraid because they live according to God's laws. No one can accuse them.

Even when the righteous stumble, the Lord will hold them up (Ps 37:24), even if they fall "seven times" (Pr 24:16). Why? Because the righteous confess their sins and receive God's forgiveness (Ps 103:3). On the other hand, the unrepentant wicked are "brought down by calamity" (Pr 24:16). How much "better the little that the righteous have than the wealth of many wicked; for the power of the wicked will be broken, but the LORD upholds the righteous" (Ps 37:16–17).

citadel and watchtower[f] will become a
wasteland forever,
the delight of donkeys,[g] a pasture for
flocks,
15 till the Spirit[h] is poured upon us from on
high,
and the desert becomes a fertile field,[i]
and the fertile field seems like a forest.[j]
16 Justice will dwell in the desert
and righteousness live in the fertile
field.
17 The fruit of righteousness will be peace;[k]
the effect of righteousness will be
quietness and confidence[l] forever.
18 My people will live in peaceful dwelling
places,
in secure homes,
in undisturbed places of rest.[m]
19 Though hail[n] flattens the forest[o]
and the city is leveled[p] completely,
20 how blessed you will be,
sowing[q] your seed by every stream,
and letting your cattle and donkeys
range free.[r]

Distress and Help

33 Woe to you, O destroyer,
you who have not been destroyed!
Woe to you, O traitor,
you who have not been betrayed!
When you stop destroying,
you will be destroyed;[s]
when you stop betraying,
you will be betrayed.[t]

2 O LORD, be gracious to us;
we long for you.
Be our strength[u] every morning,
our salvation[v] in time of distress.
3 At the thunder of your voice, the
peoples flee;
when you rise up,[w] the nations scatter.
4 Your plunder, O nations, is harvested as
by young locusts;
like a swarm of locusts men pounce
on it.
5 The LORD is exalted,[x] for he dwells on
high;
he will fill Zion with justice[y] and
righteousness.[z]
6 He will be the sure foundation for your
times,
a rich store of salvation[a] and wisdom
and knowledge;
the fear[b] of the LORD is the key to this
treasure.[a]

7 Look, their brave men cry aloud in the
streets;

32:14 [f]Isa 34:13 [g]Ps 104:11
32:15 [h]Isa 11:2; Joel 2:28 [i]Ps 107:35; Isa 35:1-2 [j]Isa 29:17
32:17 [k]Ps 119:165; Ro 14:17; Jas 3:18 [l]Isa 30:15
32:18 [m]Hos 2:18-23
32:19 [n]Isa 28:17; 30:30 [o]Isa 10:19; Zec 11:2 [p]Isa 24:10; 27:10
32:20 [q]Ecc 11:1 [r]Isa 30:24
33:1 [s]Hab 2:8; Mt 7:2 [t]Isa 21:2
33:2 [u]Isa 40:10; 51:9; 59:16 [v]Isa 25:9
33:3 [w]Isa 59:16-18
33:5 [x]Ps 97:9 [y]Isa 28:6 [z]Isa 1:26
33:6 [a]Isa 51:6 [b]Isa 11:2-3; Mt 6:33

[a] 6 Or *is a treasure from him*

the envoys[c] of peace weep bitterly.
8 The highways are deserted,
no travelers are on the roads.[d]
The treaty is broken,
its witnesses[a] are despised,
no one is respected.
9 The land mourns[b][e] and wastes away,
Lebanon[f] is ashamed and withers;[g]
Sharon is like the Arabah,
and Bashan and Carmel drop their leaves.

10 "Now will I arise,[h]" says the LORD.
"Now will I be exalted;
now will I be lifted up.
11 You conceive[i] chaff,
you give birth[j] to straw;
your breath is a fire[k] that consumes you.
12 The peoples will be burned as if to lime;
like cut thornbushes they will be set ablaze.[l]"

13 You who are far away,[m] hear[n] what I have done;
you who are near, acknowledge my power!
14 The sinners in Zion are terrified;
trembling[o] grips the godless:
"Who of us can dwell with the consuming fire?[p]
Who of us can dwell with everlasting burning?"
15 He who walks righteously[q]
and speaks what is right,[r]
who rejects gain from extortion
and keeps his hand from accepting bribes,
who stops his ears against plots of murder
and shuts his eyes[s] against contemplating evil—
16 this is the man who will dwell on the heights,
whose refuge[t] will be the mountain fortress.[u]
His bread will be supplied,
and water will not fail[v] him.

17 Your eyes will see the king[w] in his beauty
and view a land that stretches afar.[x]
18 In your thoughts you will ponder the former terror:[y]
"Where is that chief officer?
Where is the one who took the revenue?
Where is the officer in charge of the towers?"

33:7 [c]2Ki 18:37
33:8 [d]Jdg 5:6; Isa 35:8
33:9 [e]Isa 3:26 [f]Isa 2:13; 35:2 [g]Isa 24:4
33:10 [h]Ps 12:5; Isa 2:21
33:11 [i]Ps 7:14; Isa 59:4; Jas 1:15 [j]Isa 26:18 [k]Isa 1:31
33:12 [l]Isa 10:17
33:13 [m]Ps 48:10; 49:1 [n]Isa 49:1
33:14 [o]Isa 32:11 [p]Isa 30:30; Heb 12:29
33:15 [q]Isa 58:8 [r]Ps 15:2; 24:4 [s]Ps 119:37
33:16 [t]Isa 25:4 [u]Isa 26:1 [v]Isa 49:10
33:17 [w]Isa 6:5 [x]Isa 26:15
33:18 [y]Isa 17:14

[a] 8 Dead Sea Scrolls; Masoretic Text / *the cities*
[b] 9 Or *dries up*

Our Consuming God

ISA 33:14

In this context the "consuming fire" and "everlasting burning" refer to God, not the fires of hell. When God led the Israelites through the desert, his glory looked like a "consuming fire" (Ex 24:17). Hebrews 12:29 claims that "God is a consuming fire." God's presence is an all-consuming fire that destroys the sinner and purifies the saint. Without the security of God's salvation, sinners tremble in the fire's presence. For them it means judgment and a hopeless eternity. But saints can look forward to being tested and purified, knowing the result will be their purification, that they will "come forth as gold" (Job 23:10).

[19] You will see those arrogant people no more,
those people of an obscure speech,
with their strange, incomprehensible tongue.[z]

[20] Look upon Zion, the city of our festivals;
your eyes will see Jerusalem,
a peaceful abode,[a] a tent that will not be moved;[b]
its stakes will never be pulled up,
nor any of its ropes broken.
[21] There the LORD will be our Mighty One.
It will be like a place of broad rivers and streams.[c]
No galley with oars will ride them,
no mighty ship will sail them.
[22] For the LORD is our judge,[d]
the LORD is our lawgiver,[e]
the LORD is our king;[f]
it is he who will save[g] us.
[23] Your rigging hangs loose:
The mast is not held secure,
the sail is not spread.
Then an abundance of spoils will be divided
and even the lame[h] will carry off plunder.[i]
[24] No one living in Zion will say, "I am ill";[j]
and the sins of those who dwell there will be forgiven.[k]

Judgment Against the Nations

34 Come near, you nations, and listen;
pay attention, you peoples![l]
Let the earth[m] hear, and all that is in it,
the world, and all that comes out of it![n]
[2] The LORD is angry with all nations;
his wrath is upon all their armies.
He will totally destroy[a][o] them,
he will give them over to slaughter.[p]
[3] Their slain will be thrown out,
their dead bodies will send up a stench;[q]
the mountains will be soaked with their blood.[r]
[4] All the stars of the heavens will be dissolved[s]
and the sky rolled up[t] like a scroll;
all the starry host will fall[u]
like withered leaves from the vine,
like shriveled figs from the fig tree.
[5] My sword[v] has drunk its fill in the heavens;
see, it descends in judgment on Edom,[w]
the people I have totally destroyed.[x]

[a] 2 The Hebrew term refers to the irrevocable giving over of things or persons to the LORD, often by totally destroying them; also in verse 5.

33:19 [z]Isa 28:11; Jer 5:15
33:20 [a]Isa 32:18 [b]Ps 46:5; 125:1-2
33:21 [c]Isa 41:18; 48:18; 66:12
33:22 [d]Isa 11:4 [e]Isa 2:3; Jas 4:12 [f]Ps 89:18 [g]Isa 25:9
33:23 [h]2Ki 7:8 [i]2Ki 7:16
33:24 [j]Isa 30:26 [k]Jer 50:20; 1Jn 1:7-9
34:1 [l]Isa 41:1; 43:9 [m]Ps 49:1 [n]Dt 32:1
34:2 [o]Isa 13:5 [p]Isa 30:25
34:3 [q]Joel 2:20; Am 4:10 [r]ver 7; Eze 14:19; 35:6; 38:22
34:4 [s]Isa 13:13; 2Pe 3:10 [t]Eze 32:7-8 [u]Joel 2:31; Mt 24:29*; Rev 6:13
34:5 [v]Dt 32:41-42; Jer 46:10; Eze 21:5 [w]Am 1:11-12 [x]Isa 24:6; Mal 1:4

Did anyone ever tell you how beautiful you look when you're looking for what's beautiful in someone else?

—Barbara Johnson

6 The sword of the LORD is bathed in
blood,
it is covered with fat—
the blood of lambs and goats,
fat from the kidneys of rams.
For the LORD has a sacrifice in Bozrah
and a great slaughter in Edom.
7 And the wild oxen will fall with them,
the bull calves and the great bulls.[y]
Their land will be drenched with blood,
and the dust will be soaked with fat.

8 For the LORD has a day of vengeance,[z]
a year of retribution, to uphold Zion's
cause.
9 Edom's streams will be turned into
pitch,
her dust into burning sulfur;
her land will become blazing pitch!
10 It will not be quenched night and day;
its smoke will rise forever.[a]
From generation to generation it will lie
desolate;[b]
no one will ever pass through it again.
11 The desert owl[ac] and screech owl[a] will
possess it;
the great owl[a] and the raven will nest
there.
God will stretch out over Edom
the measuring line of chaos
and the plumb line[d] of desolation.
12 Her nobles will have nothing there to be
called a kingdom,
all her princes[e] will vanish[f] away.
13 Thorns will overrun her citadels,
nettles and brambles her
strongholds.[g]
She will become a haunt for jackals,[h]
a home for owls.
14 Desert creatures will meet with hyenas,[i]
and wild goats will bleat to each other;
there the night creatures will also repose
and find for themselves places of rest.
15 The owl will nest there and lay eggs,
she will hatch them, and care for her
young under the shadow of her
wings;
there also the falcons[j] will gather,
each with its mate.

16 Look in the scroll[k] of the LORD and read:
None of these will be missing,
not one will lack her mate.
For it is his mouth[l] that has given the
order,
and his Spirit will gather them
together.
17 He allots their portions;[m]
his hand distributes them by measure.

34:7 [y]Ps 68:30
34:8 [z]Isa 63:4
34:10 [a]Rev 14:10-11; 19:3 [b]Isa 13:20; 24:1; Eze 29:12; Mal 1:3
34:11 [c]Zep 2:14; Rev 18:2 [d]2Ki 21:13; La 2:8
34:12 [e]Jer 27:20; 39:6 [f]Isa 41:11-12
34:13 [g]Isa 13:22; 32:13 [h]Ps 44:19; Jer 9:11; 10:22
34:14 [i]Isa 13:22
34:15 [j]Dt 14:13
34:16 [k]Isa 30:8 [l]Isa 1:20; 58:14
34:17 [m]Isa 17:14; Jer 13:25

[a] *11* The precise identification of these birds is uncertain.

Evil Takeover

ISA 34:16

Most likely the scroll referred to in this verse represents the recorded prophecies of Isaiah. The scroll indicates that these prophecies will be realized, that not one fulfillment will be missing. The prophecies against the nations include pictures from nature. Isaiah 34:13–15 describes the plants and animals that inhabit wastelands and represent the desolation of heathen countries. No one but the animals will roam these deserted places. According to ancient mythology, the "night creatures" (Isa 34:14) are demons that frequent abandoned areas.

This word picture could also depict a devastated life without God. Spiritually nothing remains static. If we refuse the Lord's presence, we create a vacuum for Satan to move into. Evil takes over and traps us. But where the Spirit of the Lord is, there is life and freedom (2Co 3:17).

Ultimate Healing

ISA 35:5–6

The judgments of Isaiah 34 usher in the Messianic kingdom of Jesus Christ. When Jesus returns he will lift the curse from creation and heal the sick and disabled. Though God heals people while they live on earth (Ex 15:26; Jas 5:16; 1Pe 2:24), this also is a beautiful promise for a final, once-and-for-all restoration. All the everyday illnesses, the disabling sicknesses, the wounds from the past and the pains of life will be over. We won't need healing in heaven, for no one there is sick, broken or wounded.

They will possess it forever
and dwell there from generation to generation.[n]

Joy of the Redeemed

35 The desert[o] and the parched land will be glad;
the wilderness will rejoice and blossom.[p]
Like the crocus, 2 it will burst into bloom;
it will rejoice greatly and shout for joy.[q]
The glory of Lebanon[r] will be given to it,
the splendor of Carmel[s] and Sharon;
they will see the glory of the LORD,
the splendor of our God.[t]

3 Strengthen the feeble hands,
steady the knees[u] that give way;
4 say to those with fearful hearts,
"Be strong, do not fear;
your God will come,
he will come with vengeance;[v]
with divine retribution
he will come to save you."

5 Then will the eyes of the blind be opened[w]
and the ears of the deaf[x] unstopped.
6 Then will the lame[y] leap like a deer,
and the mute tongue[z] shout for joy.
Water will gush forth in the wilderness
and streams[a] in the desert.
7 The burning sand will become a pool,
the thirsty ground bubbling springs.[b]
In the haunts where jackals[c] once lay,
grass and reeds and papyrus will grow.

8 And a highway[d] will be there;
it will be called the Way of Holiness.[e]
The unclean[f] will not journey on it;
it will be for those who walk in that Way;
wicked fools will not go about on it.[a]
9 No lion[g] will be there,
nor will any ferocious beast[h] get up on it;
they will not be found there.
But only the redeemed[i] will walk there,
10 and the ransomed of the LORD will return.
They will enter Zion with singing;
everlasting joy[j] will crown their heads.
Gladness and joy will overtake them,
and sorrow and sighing will flee away.[k]

34:17 [n]ver 10
35:1 [o]Isa 27:10; 41:18-19 [p]Isa 51:3
35:2 [q]Isa 25:9; 55:12 [r]Isa 32:15 [s]SS 7:5 [t]Isa 25:9
35:3 [u]Job 4:4; Heb 12:12
35:4 [v]Isa 1:24; 34:8
35:5 [w]Mt 11:5; Jn 9:6-7 [x]Isa 29:18; 50:4
35:6 [y]Mt 15:30; Jn 5:8-9; Ac 3:8 [z]Isa 32:4; Mt 9:32-33; 12:22; Lk 11:14 [a]Isa 41:18; Jn 7:38
35:7 [b]Isa 49:10 [c]Isa 13:22
35:8 [d]Isa 11:16; 33:8; Mt 7:13-14 [e]Isa 4:3; 1Pe 1:15 [f]Isa 52:1
35:9 [g]Isa 30:6 [h]Isa 34:14 [i]Isa 51:11; 62:12; 63:4
35:10 [j]Isa 25:9 [k]Isa 30:19; 51:11; Rev 7:17; 21:4

[a] 8 Or / *the simple will not stray from it*

Sennacherib Threatens Jerusalem

36:1 36 In the fourteenth year of King Hezekiah's
[l]2Ch 32:1 reign, Sennacherib[l] king of Assyria attacked
all the fortified cities of Judah and captured them.
²Then the king of Assyria sent his field commander with a large army from Lachish to King Hezekiah at Jerusalem. When the commander stopped at
36:2 the aqueduct of the Upper Pool, on the road to the
[m]Isa 7:3 Washerman's Field,[m] ³Eliakim[n] son of Hilkiah the
36:3 palace administrator, Shebna[o] the secretary, and
[n]Isa 22:20-21 Joah son of Asaph the recorder went out to him.
[o]2Ki 18:18 ⁴The field commander said to them, "Tell
Hezekiah,

" 'This is what the great king, the king of
Assyria, says: On what are you basing this
confidence of yours? ⁵You say you have strategy and military strength—but you speak
only empty words. On whom are you
36:5 [p]2Ki 18:7 depending, that you rebel[p] against me? ⁶Look
now, you are depending on Egypt,[q] that splin-
36:6 [q]Isa 30:2,5 tered reed[r] of a staff, which pierces a man's
[r]Eze 29:6-7 hand and wounds him if he leans on it! Such
is Pharaoh king of Egypt to all who depend
on him. ⁷And if you say to me, "We are
depending on the LORD our God"—isn't he
36:7 the one whose high places and altars Heze-
[s]2Ki 18:4 kiah removed,[s] saying to Judah and Jerusa-
[t]Dt 12:2-5 lem, "You must worship before this altar"?[t]
⁸" 'Come now, make a bargain with my
master, the king of Assyria: I will give you
two thousand horses—if you can put riders
on them! ⁹How then can you repulse one offi-
36:9 cer of the least of my master's officials, even
[u]Isa 31:3 though you are depending on Egypt[u] for
[v]Isa 30:2-5 chariots and horsemen?[v] ¹⁰Furthermore, have
I come to attack and destroy this land with-
36:10 out the LORD? The LORD himself told[w] me to
[w]1Ki 13:18 march against this country and destroy it.' "

¹¹Then Eliakim, Shebna and Joah said to the field
commander, "Please speak to your servants in Ara-
36:11 maic,[x] since we understand it. Don't speak to us in
[x]Ezr 4:7 Hebrew in the hearing of the people on the wall."
¹²But the commander replied, "Was it only to
your master and you that my master sent me to
say these things, and not to the men sitting on the
wall—who, like you, will have to eat their own
filth and drink their own urine?"
¹³Then the commander stood and called out in
36:13 [y]2Ch 32:18 Hebrew,[y] "Hear the words of the great king, the
king of Assyria! ¹⁴This is what the king says: Do
not let Hezekiah deceive you. He cannot deliver
you! ¹⁵Do not let Hezekiah persuade you to trust
in the LORD when he says, 'The LORD will surely
36:15 deliver us; this city will not be given into the hand
[z]Isa 37:10 of the king of Assyria.'[z]
¹⁶"Do not listen to Hezekiah. This is what the
king of Assyria says: Make peace with me and
36:16 come out to me. Then every one of you will eat
[a]1Ki 4:25; Zec 3:10 from his own vine and fig tree[a] and drink water

Every formula which expresses a law of nature is a hymn of praise to God.

—Maria Mitchell (1818-1889)

from his own cistern,[b] 17until I come and take you 36:16 [b]Pr 5:15
to a land like your own—a land of grain and new
wine, a land of bread and vineyards.
18"Do not let Hezekiah mislead you when he
says, 'The LORD will deliver us.' Has the god of any
nation ever delivered his land from the hand of
the king of Assyria? 19Where are the gods of Hamath and Arpad? Where are the gods of Sepharvaim? Have they rescued Samaria from my hand?
20Who of all the gods[c] of these countries has been 36:20 [c]1Ki 20:23
able to save his land from me? How then can the
LORD deliver Jerusalem from my hand?"
21But the people remained silent and said nothing in reply, because the king had commanded,
"Do not answer him."[d] 36:21 [d]Pr 9:7-8; 26:4
22Then Eliakim son of Hilkiah the palace
administrator, Shebna the secretary, and Joah son
of Asaph the recorder went to Hezekiah, with
their clothes torn, and told him what the field
commander had said.

Jerusalem's Deliverance Foretold

37 When King Hezekiah heard this, he tore his
clothes and put on sackcloth and went into
the temple of the LORD. 2He sent Eliakim the palace
administrator, Shebna the secretary, and the lead-
ing priests, all wearing sackcloth, to the prophet 37:2 [e]Isa 1:1
Isaiah son of Amoz.[e] 3They told him, "This is what
Hezekiah says: This day is a day of distress and
rebuke and disgrace, as when children come to the 37:3 [f]Isa 26:18; 66:9; Hos 13:13
point of birth[f] and there is no strength to deliver
them. 4It may be that the LORD your God will hear
the words of the field commander, whom his master, the king of Assyria, has sent to ridicule the liv-
ing God, and that he will rebuke him for the words 37:4 [g]Isa 36:13, 18-20 [h]Isa 1:9
the LORD your God has heard.[g] Therefore pray for
the remnant[h] that still survives."
5When King Hezekiah's officials came to Isaiah,
6Isaiah said to them, "Tell your master, 'This is 37:6 [i]Isa 7:4
what the LORD says: Do not be afraid[i] of what you
have heard—those words with which the under-
lings of the king of Assyria have blasphemed me.
7Listen! I am going to put a spirit in him so that 37:7 [j]ver 9
when he hears a certain report,[j] he will return to
his own country, and there I will have him cut
down with the sword.' "
8When the field commander heard that the king
of Assyria had left Lachish, he withdrew and
found the king fighting against Libnah.[k] 37:8 [k]Nu 33:20
9Now Sennacherib received a report[l] that Tir-
hakah, the Cushite[a] king ⌞of Egypt⌟, was march- 37:9 [l]ver 7
ing out to fight against him. When he heard it, he
sent messengers to Hezekiah with this word:
10"Say to Hezekiah king of Judah: Do not let the
god you depend on deceive you when he says, 'Jerusalem will not be handed over to the king of
Assyria.'[m] 11Surely you have heard what the kings 37:10 [m]Isa 36:15
of Assyria have done to all the countries, destroy-
ing them completely. And will you be delivered?[n] 37:11 [n]Isa 36:18-20

[a] 9 That is, from the upper Nile region

> Although today He prunes my twigs with pain,
> Yet doth His blood nourish and warm my root;
> Tomorrow I shall put forth buds again
> And clothe myself with fruit.
>
> —*Christina Georgina Rossetti (1830–1894)*

37:12 [12]Did the gods of the nations that were destroyed
[o]2Ki 18:11 by my forefathers[o] deliver them—the gods of
[p]Ge 11:31; Gozan, Haran,[p] Rezeph and the people of Eden
12:1-4; who were in Tel Assar? [13]Where is the king of
Ac 7:2 Hamath, the king of Arpad, the king of the city of
Sepharvaim, or of Hena or Ivvah?"

Hezekiah's Prayer

[14]Hezekiah received the letter from the messengers and read it. Then he went up to the temple of
the LORD and spread it out before the LORD. [15]And
Hezekiah prayed to the LORD: [16]"O LORD Almighty,
God of Israel, enthroned between the cherubim,
37:16 [q]Dt 10:17; you alone are God[q] over all the kingdoms of the
Ps 86:10; earth. You have made heaven and earth. [17]Give
136:2-3 ear, O LORD, and hear;[r] open your eyes, O LORD,
37:17 and see;[s] listen to all the words Sennacherib has
[r]2Ch 6:40 sent to insult the living God.
[s]Da 9:18 [18]"It is true, O LORD, that the Assyrian kings
37:18 have laid waste all these peoples and their lands.[t]
[t]2Ki 15:29; [19]They have thrown their gods into the fire and
Na 2:11-12 destroyed them,[u] for they were not gods[v] but only
37:19 wood and stone, fashioned by human hands.
[u]Isa 26:14 [20]Now, O LORD our God, deliver us from his hand,
[v]Isa 41:24,29 so that all kingdoms on earth may know that you
37:20 [w]Ps 46:10 alone, O LORD, are God.[a][w]"

Sennacherib's Fall

37:21 [x]ver 2 [21]Then Isaiah son of Amoz[x] sent a message to
Hezekiah: "This is what the LORD, the God of Israel, says: Because you have prayed to me concerning Sennacherib king of Assyria, [22]this is the word
the LORD has spoken against him:

"The Virgin Daughter of Zion
despises and mocks you.
The Daughter of Jerusalem
37:22 [y]Job 16:4 tosses her head[y] as you flee.
[23]Who is it you have insulted and
37:23 [z]ver 4 blasphemed?[z]
[a]Isa 2:11 Against whom have you raised your
voice
and lifted your eyes in pride?[a]
Against the Holy One of Israel!
[24]By your messengers
you have heaped insults on the Lord.
And you have said,
'With my many chariots
I have ascended the heights of the
mountains,
37:24 [b]Isa 14:8 the utmost heights of Lebanon.[b]
I have cut down its tallest cedars,
the choicest of its pines.
I have reached its remotest heights,
the finest of its forests.
[25]I have dug wells in foreign lands[b]
and drunk the water there.
With the soles of my feet

Other Gods

ISA 37:12-13

Pagan peoples worship idols of their own creation, gods who obviously aren't able to save them from warring armies. Historical evidence proves that these gods didn't protect the cities listed in Isaiah 37:12 from the Assyrians. Arrogant King Sennacherib of Assyria mixes the one true God into the same pot with all the other "gods." Those gods couldn't save, he claims, and neither can the "god" (Isa 37:10) of Hezekiah.

But what Sennacherib doesn't realize is that his *gods can't protect him either, especially not from the judgment of the Lord, the one true God of the Israelites. The prophecy in Isaiah 37:7 is miraculously fulfilled in Isaiah 37:36-38. Human beings continue today to create gods of their own that usurp the Lord's place in their hearts. They may not be cast of iron or carved from stone or wood, but they are false gods nonetheless and will prove as untrustworthy as the gods of the Assyrian king.*

[a] *20* Dead Sea Scrolls (see also 2 Kings 19:19); Masoretic Text *alone are the LORD* [b] *25* Dead Sea Scrolls (see also 2 Kings 19:24); Masoretic Text does not have *in foreign lands.*

Long-Ago Plans

ISA 37:26

Did God plan all this destruction and judgment? Well, yes and no. God is omniscient. His nature is all-knowing. The people have a chance to avert judgment. God will gladly turn aside from punishing them if they repent. But God, who knows the future, knows what they'll choose and the outcome of those decisions. From our standpoint this characteristic of God is difficult to grasp. Though he communicates with us, in many ways he remains a mystery and beyond our finite human comprehension.

Better that we should focus on the fact that, as believers, God has good plans for us (Jer 29:11)—we can repent, change our course and be restored (Jer 15:19). When we keep our faces turned toward God, our hearts will be soft and sensitive to the Holy Spirit, who will help us discern sin and be aware of those things that lead us from God's path.

I have dried up all the streams of
Egypt.[c]'

26 "Have you not heard?
Long ago I ordained[d] it.
In days of old I planned[e] it;
now I have brought it to pass,
that you have turned fortified cities
into piles of stone.[f]
27 Their people, drained of power,
are dismayed and put to shame.
They are like plants in the field,
like tender green shoots,
like grass sprouting on the roof,[g]
scorched[a] before it grows up.

28 "But I know where you stay
and when you come and go[h]
and how you rage[i] against me.
29 Because you rage against me
and because your insolence[j] has
reached my ears,
I will put my hook in your nose[k]
and my bit in your mouth,
and I will make you return
by the way you came.[l]

30 "This will be the sign for you, O Hezekiah:

"This year you will eat what grows by
itself,
and the second year what springs
from that.
But in the third year sow and reap,
plant vineyards and eat their fruit.
31 Once more a remnant of the house of
Judah
will take root below and bear fruit[m]
above.
32 For out of Jerusalem will come a
remnant,
and out of Mount Zion a band of
survivors.
The zeal[n] of the LORD Almighty
will accomplish this.

33 "Therefore this is what the LORD says concerning the king of Assyria:

"He will not enter this city
or shoot an arrow here.
He will not come before it with shield
or build a siege ramp against it.
34 By the way that he came he will return;[o]
he will not enter this city,"
declares the LORD.
35 "I will defend[p] this city and save it,
for my sake[q] and for the sake of
David[r] my servant!"

36 Then the angel of the LORD went out and put to

37:25 [c]Dt 11:10
37:26 [d]Ac 2:23; 4:27-28; 1Pe 2:8 [e]Isa 10:6; 25:1 [f]Isa 25:2
37:27 [g]Ps 129:6
37:28 [h]Ps 139:1-3 [i]Ps 2:1
37:29 [j]Isa 10:12 [k]Isa 30:28; Eze 38:4 [l]ver 34
37:31 [m]Isa 27:6
37:32 [n]Isa 9:7
37:34 [o]ver 29
37:35 [p]Isa 31:5; 38:6 [q]Isa 43:25; 48:9,11 [r]2Ki 20:6

[a] *27* Some manuscripts of the Masoretic Text, Dead Sea Scrolls and some Septuagint manuscripts (see also 2 Kings 19:26); most manuscripts of the Masoretic Text *roof / and terraced fields*

death a hundred and eighty-five thousand men in
37:36 [s]Isa 10:12 the Assyrian[s] camp. When the people got up the
next morning—there were all the dead bodies! 37So
Sennacherib king of Assyria broke camp and with-
37:37 [t]Ge 10:11 drew. He returned to Nineveh[t] and stayed there.
38One day, while he was worshiping in the tem-
ple of his god Nisroch, his sons Adrammelech and
Sharezer cut him down with the sword, and they
37:38 [u]Ge 8:4; escaped to the land of Ararat.[u] And Esarhaddon
Jer 51:27 his son succeeded him as king.

Hezekiah's Illness

38 In those days Hezekiah became ill and was
38:1 at the point of death. The prophet Isaiah
[v]Isa 37:2 son of Amoz[v] went to him and said, "This is what
[w]2Sa 17:23 the LORD says: Put your house in order,[w] because
you are going to die; you will not recover."
2Hezekiah turned his face to the wall and
38:3 prayed to the LORD, 3"Remember, O LORD, how I
[x]Ne 13:14; Ps 26:3 have walked[x] before you faithfully and with
[y]1Ch 29:19 wholehearted devotion[y] and have done what is
[z]Dt 6:18 good in your eyes.[z]" And Hezekiah wept[a] bitterly.
[a]Ps 6:8 4Then the word of the LORD came to Isaiah: 5"Go
and tell Hezekiah, 'This is what the LORD, the God
of your father David, says: I have heard your
38:5 prayer and seen your tears; I will add fifteen
[b]2Ki 18:2 years[b] to your life. 6And I will deliver you and this
38:6 city from the hand of the king of Assyria. I will
[c]Isa 31:5; defend[c] this city.
37:35 7" 'This is the LORD's sign[d] to you that the LORD
38:7 will do what he has promised: 8I will make the
[d]Isa 7:11,14 shadow cast by the sun go back the ten steps it
has gone down on the stairway of Ahaz.' " So the
38:8 sunlight went back the ten steps it had gone
[e]Jos 10:13 down.[e]

9A writing of Hezekiah king of Judah after his
illness and recovery:

38:10 [f]Ps 102:24 10I said, "In the prime of my life[f]
[g]Ps 107:18; 2Co 1:9 must I go through the gates of death[a][g]
[h]Job 17:11 and be robbed of the rest of my
years?[h]"
38:11 11I said, "I will not again see the LORD,
[i]Ps 27:13; 116:9 the LORD, in the land of the living;[i]
no longer will I look on mankind,
or be with those who now dwell in
this world.[b]
38:12 12Like a shepherd's tent[j] my house
[j]2Co 5:1,4; 2Pe 1:13-14 has been pulled down[k] and taken
[k]Job 4:21 from me.
[l]Heb 1:12 Like a weaver I have rolled[l] up my life,
[m]Job 7:6 and he has cut me off from the loom;[m]
[n]Ps 73:14 day and night[n] you made an end of
me.
13I waited patiently till dawn,
38:13 [o]Ps 51:8 but like a lion he broke[o] all my
[p]Job 10:16; bones;[p]
Da 6:24 day and night you made an end of me.

[a] 10 Hebrew *Sheol* [b] 11 A few Hebrew manuscripts; most Hebrew manuscripts *in the place of cessation*

A Change of Mind

ISA 38:2-8

The old adage says, "Prayer changes things." Indeed, God relents after Hezekiah pleads for his life. When we pray, we touch the heart of God. Overall, God's will for humanity doesn't change. He won't back away from certain decrees and promises he's made. But when we pray, he may change the course of lives and nations within the limits of his overall will.

It's not possible to understand fully God's control versus our choices and prayers. But he does invite us to "pray continually" (1Th 5:17)—for his will, our desires, the needs and salvation of others. Jesus himself prays (Mt 14:23; Heb 7:25) and teaches his disciples to pray and not give up (Lk 18:1). Why would we do any less?

Poultice Healing

ISA 38:21

To the Israelites figs represent peace and divine favor (Isa 36:16), so it's intriguing that God uses this fruit to heal Hezekiah. The Lord could miraculously heal the king, but he chooses a medicinal route instead. God uses many ways to heal us. We can't presume which way he'll choose; we can only humbly receive and be thankful for his blessing.

14 I cried like a swift or thrush,
I moaned like a mourning dove.[q]
My eyes grew weak as I looked to the heavens.
I am troubled; O Lord, come to my aid!"[r]
15 But what can I say?
He has spoken to me, and he himself has done this.[s]
I will walk humbly[t] all my years
because of this anguish of my soul.[u]
16 Lord, by such things men live;
and my spirit finds life in them too.
You restored me to health
and let me live.[v]
17 Surely it was for my benefit
that I suffered such anguish.
In your love you kept me
from the pit[w] of destruction;
you have put all my sins[x]
behind your back.[y]
18 For the grave[a][z] cannot praise you,
death cannot sing your praise;[a]
those who go down to the pit[b]
cannot hope for your faithfulness.
19 The living, the living—they praise[c] you,
as I am doing today;
fathers tell their children[d]
about your faithfulness.
20 The LORD will save me,
and we will sing[e] with stringed instruments[f]
all the days of our lives[g]
in the temple[h] of the LORD.

21 Isaiah had said, "Prepare a poultice of figs and apply it to the boil, and he will recover."
22 Hezekiah had asked, "What will be the sign that I will go up to the temple of the LORD?"

Envoys From Babylon

39 At that time Merodach-Baladan son of Baladan king of Babylon[i] sent Hezekiah letters
and a gift, because he had heard of his illness and
recovery. 2 Hezekiah received the envoys[j] gladly
and showed them what was in his storehouses—
the silver, the gold,[k] the spices, the fine oil, his
entire armory and everything found among his
treasures. There was nothing in his palace or in
all his kingdom that Hezekiah did not show them.
3 Then Isaiah the prophet went to King Hezekiah and asked, "What did those men say, and
where did they come from?"
"From a distant land,[l]" Hezekiah replied. "They
came to me from Babylon."
4 The prophet asked, "What did they see in your
palace?"
"They saw everything in my palace," Hezekiah

38:14 [q]Isa 59:11 [r]Job 17:3
38:15 [s]Ps 39:9 [t]1Ki 21:27 [u]Job 7:11
38:16 [v]Ps 119:25
38:17 [w]Ps 30:3 [x]Jer 31:34 [y]Isa 43:25; Mic 7:19
38:18 [z]Ecc 9:10 [a]Ps 6:5; 88:10-11; 115:17 [b]Ps 30:9
38:19 [c]Dt 6:7; Ps 118:17; 119:175 [d]Dt 11:19
38:20 [e]Ps 68:25 [f]Ps 33:2 [g]Ps 116:2 [h]Ps 116:17-19
39:1 [i]2Ch 32:31
39:2 [j]2Ch 32:31 [k]2Ki 18:15
39:3 [l]Dt 28:49

[a] 18 Hebrew *Sheol*

said. "There is nothing among my treasures that I
did not show them."
5 Then Isaiah said to Hezekiah, "Hear the word
of the LORD Almighty: 6 The time will surely come
when everything in your palace, and all that your
fathers have stored up until this day, will be carried off to Babylon.[m] Nothing will be left, says the
LORD. 7 And some of your descendants, your own
flesh and blood who will be born to you, will be
taken away, and they will become eunuchs in the
palace of the king of Babylon.[n]"
8 "The word of the LORD you have spoken is
good," Hezekiah replied. For he thought, "There
will be peace and security in my lifetime.[o]"

Comfort for God's People

40 Comfort, comfort[p] my people,
says your God.
2 Speak tenderly[q] to Jerusalem,
and proclaim to her
that her hard service has been
completed,[r]
that her sin has been paid for,
that she has received from the LORD's
hand
double[s] for all her sins.
3 A voice of one calling:
"In the desert prepare
the way[t] for the LORD[a];
make straight in the wilderness
a highway for our God.[b][u]
4 Every valley shall be raised up,
every mountain and hill made low;
the rough ground shall become level,[v]
the rugged places a plain.
5 And the glory of the LORD will be
revealed,
and all mankind together will see it.[w]
For the mouth of the LORD
has spoken."[x]
6 A voice says, "Cry out."
And I said, "What shall I cry?"

"All men are like grass,[y]
and all their glory is like the flowers
of the field.
7 The grass withers and the flowers fall,
because the breath[z] of the LORD blows
on them.
Surely the people are grass.
8 The grass withers and the flowers fall,
but the word[a] of our God stands
forever.[b]"
9 You who bring good tidings[c] to Zion,
go up on a high mountain.

39:6 [m]2Ki 24:13; Jer 20:5
39:7 [n]2Ki 24:15; Da 1:1-7
39:8 [o]2Ch 32:26
40:1 [p]Isa 12:1; 49:13; 51:3, 12; 52:9; 61:2; 66:13; Jer 31:13; Zep 3:14-17; 2Co 1:3
40:2 [q]Isa 35:4 [r]Isa 41:11-13; 49:25 [s]Isa 61:7; Jer 16:18; Zec 9:12; Rev 18:6
40:3 [t]Mal 3:1 [u]Mt 3:3*; Mk 1:3*; Jn 1:23*
40:4 [v]Isa 45:2,13
40:5 [w]Isa 52:10; Lk 3:4-6* [x]Isa 1:20; 58:14
40:6 [y]Job 14:2
40:7 [z]Job 41:21
40:8 [a]Isa 55:11; 59:21 [b]Mt 5:18; 1Pe 1:24-25*
40:9 [c]Isa 52:7-10; 61:1; Ro 10:15

[a] 3 Or *A voice of one calling in the desert: / "Prepare the way for the LORD* [b] 3 Hebrew; Septuagint *make straight the paths of our God*

Another Prophet

ISA 40:3,6

Who is this voice in the desert? It's yet another prophet, John the Baptist. He appears in the New Testament as the forerunner of Jesus (Mt 3:3). John preaches repentance for sin, preparing the way for the Lord's salvation. Not only does Isaiah prophesy about the Messiah, he also describes the Savior's earthly cousin, who acts as his messenger. God is amazingly specific about paving the way for his Son, both in the Old and New Testaments.

Good News

ISA 40:9

The good tidings for Jerusalem center on a God who restores and redeems his people. In Matthew the angel announces that the good news resides in the birth of Mary's Son, Jesus, who will save people from their sins (Mt 1:21). The Messiah is good news not just for Israel but for the whole world (Jn 3:16).

Elsewhere, Isaiah exclaims, "How beautiful on the mountains are the feet of those who bring good news" (Isa 52:7). God calls beautiful all those who proclaim the good news of salvation to others. In Isaiah 40:9 the bearer of this good news is so excited and overwhelmed by it that he or she shouts it out from a high mountain. There is no restraint. Such great news can't be contained. It spills out onto friends, family, neighbors, co-workers. Christ's love and our joy compel us (2Co 5:14) to run to the mountains so others can hear about God's salvation.

You who bring good tidings to
Jerusalem,[a]
lift up your voice with a shout,
lift it up, do not be afraid;
say to the towns of Judah,
"Here is your God!"[d]
10 See, the Sovereign LORD comes[e] with
power,
and his arm[f] rules[g] for him.
See, his reward[h] is with him,
and his recompense accompanies him.
11 He tends his flock like a shepherd:[i]
He gathers the lambs in his arms
and carries them close to his heart;
he gently leads those that have young.

12 Who has measured the waters[j] in the
hollow of his hand,[k]
or with the breadth of his hand
marked off the heavens?[l]
Who has held the dust of the earth in a
basket,
or weighed the mountains on the
scales
and the hills in a balance?
13 Who has understood the mind[b] of the
LORD,
or instructed him as his counselor?[m]
14 Whom did the LORD consult to enlighten
him,
and who taught him the right way?
Who was it that taught him knowledge[n]
or showed him the path of
understanding?
15 Surely the nations are like a drop in a
bucket;
they are regarded as dust on the
scales;
he weighs the islands as though they
were fine dust.
16 Lebanon is not sufficient for altar fires,
nor its animals[o] enough for burnt
offerings.
17 Before him all the nations[p] are as
nothing;[q]
they are regarded by him as worthless
and less than nothing.[r]

18 To whom, then, will you compare God?[s]
What image[t] will you compare him to?
19 As for an idol,[u] a craftsman casts it,
and a goldsmith[v] overlays it with gold[w]
and fashions silver chains for it.
20 A man too poor to present such an
offering
selects wood that will not rot.
He looks for a skilled craftsman
to set up an idol that will not topple.[x]

40:9 [d]Isa 25:9
40:10 [e]Rev 22:7 [f]Isa 59:16 [g]Isa 9:6-7 [h]Isa 62:11; Rev 22:12
40:11 [i]Eze 34:23; Mic 5:4; Jn 10:11
40:12 [j]Job 38:10 [k]Pr 30:4 [l]Heb 1:10-12
40:13 [m]Ro 11:34*; 1Co 2:16*
40:14 [n]Job 21:22; Col 2:3
40:16 [o]Ps 50:9-11; Mic 6:7; Heb 10:5-9
40:17 [p]Isa 30:28 [q]Isa 29:7 [r]Da 4:35
40:18 [s]Ex 8:10; 1Sa 2:2; Isa 46:5 [t]Ac 17:29
40:19 [u]Ps 115:4 [v]Isa 41:7; Jer 10:3 [w]Isa 2:20
40:20 [x]1Sa 5:3

[a] *9* Or *O Zion, bringer of good tidings, / go up on a high mountain. / O Jerusalem, bringer of good tidings*
[b] *13* Or *Spirit;* or *spirit*

21 Do you not know?
Have you not heard?
Has it not been told[y] you from the beginning?
Have you not understood[z] since the earth was founded?[a]
22 He sits enthroned above the circle of the earth,
and its people are like grasshoppers.[b]
He stretches out the heavens like a canopy,[c]
and spreads them out like a tent[d] to live in.
23 He brings princes[e] to naught
and reduces the rulers of this world to nothing.[f]
24 No sooner are they planted,
no sooner are they sown,
no sooner do they take root in the ground,
than he blows[g] on them and they wither,
and a whirlwind sweeps them away like chaff.

25 "To whom will you compare me?[h]
Or who is my equal?" says the Holy One.
26 Lift your eyes and look to the heavens:[i]
Who created[j] all these?
He who brings out the starry host[k] one by one,
and calls them each by name.
Because of his great power and mighty strength,
not one of them is missing.[l]

27 Why do you say, O Jacob,
and complain, O Israel,
"My way is hidden from the LORD;
my cause is disregarded by my God"?[m]
28 Do you not know?
Have you not heard?[n]
The LORD is the everlasting[o] God,
the Creator of the ends of the earth.
He will not grow tired or weary,
and his understanding no one can fathom.[p]
29 He gives strength to the weary[q]
and increases the power of the weak.
30 Even youths grow tired and weary,
and young men[r] stumble and fall;
31 but those who hope[s] in the LORD
will renew their strength.[t]
They will soar on wings like eagles;[u]
they will run and not grow weary,
they will walk and not be faint.[v]

The Helper of Israel

41 "Be silent[w] before me, you islands![x]
Let the nations renew their strength!
Let them come forward[y] and speak;

40:21 [y]Ps 19:1; 50:6; Ac 14:17 [z]Ro 1:19 [a]Isa 48:13; 51:13
40:22 [b]Nu 13:33; Ps 104:2; Isa 42:5 [c]Job 22:14 [d]Job 36:29
40:23 [e]Isa 34:12 [f]Job 12:21; Ps 107:40
40:24 [g]Isa 41:16
40:25 [h]ver 18
40:26 [i]Isa 51:6 [j]Ps 89:11-13; Isa 42:5 [k]Ps 147:4 [l]Isa 34:16
40:27 [m]Job 27:2; Lk 18:7-8
40:28 [n]ver 21 [o]Ps 90:2 [p]Ps 147:5; Ro 11:33
40:29 [q]Isa 50:4; Jer 31:25
40:30 [r]Isa 9:17; Jer 6:11; 9:21
40:31 [s]Lk 18:1 [t]2Co 4:16 [u]Ex 19:4; Ps 103:5 [v]2Co 4:1; Heb 12:1-3
41:1 [w]Hab 2:20; Zec 2:13 [x]Isa 11:11 [y]Isa 48:16

Eagle Imagery

ISA 40:31

Isaiah claims that those who hope in the Lord will "soar on wings like eagles" (Isa 40:31). Majestic in appearance, with superb aerial skills, the eagle has served as a symbol of strength and courage since ancient times. Amazingly, an eagle's wingspan can reach up to eight feet. Though it weighs 10-14 pounds, an eagle can average up to 30 miles (50 kilometers) per hour in flight. The eagle's wing feathers are designed to reduce turbulence. When its long and broad wings catch a thermal wind, this bird can soar for significant distances with minimal flapping. Thus, it saves precious energy.

When we hope in the Lord—trusting his promises and timing—we soar above difficulties, reduce the turbulence and manage our energy so we can run and not grow weary, walk and not feel faint. What a reassuring promise!

False Encouragement

ISA 41:5-7

Though the world trembles at the presence of the one true God, the idol makers conjure up their best denial tactics and console one another. They rally the goldsmith to keep creating handmade gods. Even more absurd, they nail down their idols so the Lord can't topple them. But none of their tactics will work. Nothing can stand up to God's wrath.

In essence, the idol makers set up a foolish, false reality by comparing themselves with themselves, as Paul explains in 2 Corinthians 10:12: "When they measure themselves by themselves and compare themselves with themselves, they are not wise." The only true standard is God's standard. Even today we try to create our own codes to live by, our own standards instead of God's, our own sets of rules and regulations. What foolishness we too practice when we go our own way instead of God's.

let us meet together[z] at the place of
judgment.

2 "Who has stirred[a] up one from the east,[b]
calling him in righteousness to his
service[a]?
He hands nations over to him
and subdues kings before him.
He turns them to dust[c] with his sword,
to windblown chaff[d] with his bow.
3 He pursues them and moves on
unscathed,
by a path his feet have not traveled
before.
4 Who has done this and carried it
through,
calling forth the generations from the
beginning?[e]
I, the LORD—with the first of them
and with the last[f]—I am he."

5 The islands[g] have seen it and fear;
the ends of the earth tremble.
They approach and come forward;
6 each helps the other
and says to his brother, "Be strong!"
7 The craftsman encourages the
goldsmith,[h]
and he who smooths with the hammer
spurs on him who strikes the anvil.
He says of the welding, "It is good."
He nails down the idol so it will not
topple.

8 "But you, O Israel, my servant,
Jacob, whom I have chosen,
you descendants of Abraham[i] my
friend,[j]
9 I took you from the ends of the earth,[k]
from its farthest corners I called you.
I said, 'You are my servant';
I have chosen[l] you and have not
rejected you.
10 So do not fear, for I am with you;[m]
do not be dismayed, for I am your God.
I will strengthen you and help[n] you;
I will uphold you with my righteous
right hand.

11 "All who rage[o] against you
will surely be ashamed and
disgraced;[p]
those who oppose[q] you
will be as nothing and perish.[r]
12 Though you search for your enemies,
you will not find them.[s]
Those who wage war against you
will be as nothing[t] at all.
13 For I am the LORD, your God,
who takes hold of your right hand[u]
and says to you, Do not fear;

41:1 [z]Isa 1:18; 34:1; 50:8
41:2 [a]Ezr 1:2 [b]ver 25; Isa 45:1,13 [c]2Sa 22:43 [d]Isa 40:24
41:4 [e]ver 26; Isa 46:10 [f]Isa 44:6; 48:12; Rev 1:8,17; 22:13
41:5 [g]Eze 26:17-18
41:7 [h]Isa 40:19
41:8 [i]Isa 29:22; 51:2; 63:16 [j]2Ch 20:7; Jas 2:23
41:9 [k]Isa 11:12 [l]Dt 7:6
41:10 [m]Jos 1:9; Isa 43:2,5; Ro 8:31 [n]ver 13-14; Isa 44:2; 49:8
41:11 [o]Isa 17:12 [p]Isa 45:24 [q]Ex 23:22 [r]Isa 29:8
41:12 [s]Ps 37:35-36 [t]Isa 17:14
41:13 [u]Isa 42:6; 45:1

[a] 2 Or / *whom victory meets at every step*

41:13 [v]ver 10
I will help[v] you.
14 Do not be afraid, O worm Jacob,
O little Israel,
for I myself will help you," declares the LORD,
your Redeemer, the Holy One of Israel.
15 "See, I will make you into a threshing sledge,[w]
41:15 [w]Mic 4:13
new and sharp, with many teeth.
You will thresh the mountains and crush them,
and reduce the hills to chaff.
16 You will winnow[x] them, the wind will pick them up,
41:16 [x]Jer 51:2 [y]Isa 45:25
and a gale will blow them away.
But you will rejoice in the LORD
and glory[y] in the Holy One of Israel.

17 "The poor and needy search for water,[z]
41:17 [z]Isa 43:20 [a]Isa 30:19
but there is none;
their tongues are parched with thirst.
But I the LORD will answer[a] them;
I, the God of Israel, will not forsake them.
18 I will make rivers flow[b] on barren heights,
41:18 [b]Isa 30:25 [c]Isa 43:19 [d]Isa 35:7
and springs within the valleys.
I will turn the desert[c] into pools of water,
and the parched ground into springs.[d]
19 I will put in the desert
the cedar and the acacia, the myrtle and the olive.
I will set pines in the wasteland,
41:19 [e]Isa 60:13
the fir and the cypress together,[e]
20 so that people may see and know,
may consider and understand,
that the hand of the LORD has done this,
that the Holy One of Israel has
41:20 [f]Job 12:9
created[f] it.

21 "Present your case," says the LORD.
"Set forth your arguments," says
41:21 [g]Isa 43:15
Jacob's King.[g]
22 "Bring in ⌊your idols⌋ to tell us
41:22 [h]Isa 43:9; 45:21 [i]Isa 46:10
what is going to happen.[h]
Tell us what the former things were,
so that we may consider them
and know their final outcome.
Or declare to us the things to come,[i]
23 tell us what the future holds,
41:23 [j]Isa 42:9; 44:7-8; 45:3 [k]Jer 10:5
so we may know[j] that you are gods.
Do something, whether good or bad,[k]
so that we will be dismayed and filled with fear.
24 But you are less than nothing[l]
41:24 [l]Isa 37:19; 44:9; 1Co 8:4 [m]Ps 115:8
and your works are utterly worthless;
he who chooses you is detestable.[m]

25 "I have stirred up one from the north,[n]
41:25 [n]ver 2
and he comes—

The Threshing Sledge

ISA 41:15–16

God used images familiar to his listeners in these verses. They understood the role of a threshing sledge during harvest time. Harvesters cut and dried the grain, then laid it on a threshing floor so the threshing sledge could crush it. This sledge, drawn by animals, raked its sharp teeth across the grain, separating the stalks and husks from the kernels. It was a powerful winnowing process that divided the inedible and edible parts of the grain.

The Lord says he will be Israel's strength and make her into a mighty threshing sledge. This contrasts with God calling Israel an insignificant "worm" in Isaiah 41:14. When we separate the worthless from the worthy, winnowing our own souls and claiming God as our source, we become powerful spiritual instruments in his hands.

High Praise

ISA 42:1

Scripture's prophecies often contain multiple *meanings, which may be the case in this verse. During this time in history, the servant could refer to Cyrus, ruler of Persia, who frees the people of Judah from exile to restore their homeland. He is the "one from the east" mentioned in Isaiah 41:2. Jewish scholars interpret the servant as Israel itself, suffering for humanity's sins. Christians understand the servant to be Jesus (Mt 12:15–21), Savior of the Jews, but also a "light for the Gentiles" (Isa 42:6).*

When John baptizes Jesus, the Father's voice from heaven echoes the words in Isaiah: "This is my Son, whom I love; with him I am well pleased" (Mt 3:17). As children of God, we all hope to hear these words from our heavenly Father. It's the highest praise possible: "These are my children . . . I love them . . . They please me."

one from the rising sun who calls on
my name.
He treads[o] on rulers as if they were
mortar,
as if he were a potter treading the clay.
26 Who told of this from the beginning, so
we could know,
or beforehand, so we could say, 'He
was right'?
No one told of this,
no one foretold it,
no one heard any words[p] from you.
27 I was the first to tell[q] Zion, 'Look, here
they are!'
I gave to Jerusalem a messenger of
good tidings.[r]
28 I look but there is no one[s]—
no one among them to give counsel,[t]
no one to give answer when I ask
them.
29 See, they are all false!
Their deeds amount to nothing;[u]
their images are but wind[v] and
confusion.

The Servant of the LORD

42 "Here is my servant, whom I uphold,
my chosen one[w] in whom I delight;
I will put my Spirit[x] on him
and he will bring justice to the
nations.
2 He will not shout or cry out,
or raise his voice in the streets.
3 A bruised reed he will not break,
and a smoldering wick he will not
snuff out.
In faithfulness he will bring forth
justice;[y]
4 he will not falter or be discouraged
till he establishes justice on earth.
In his law the islands will put their
hope."[z]

5 This is what God the LORD says—
he who created the heavens and
stretched them out,
who spread out the earth and all that
comes out of it,[a]
who gives breath[b] to its people,
and life to those who walk on it:
6 "I, the LORD, have called[c] you in
righteousness;[d]
I will take hold of your hand.
I will keep[e] you and will make you
to be a covenant[f] for the people
and a light for the Gentiles,[g]
7 to open eyes that are blind,[h]
to free[i] captives from prison[j]
and to release from the dungeon those
who sit in darkness.
8 "I am the LORD; that is my name![k]

41:25 [o]2Sa 22:43
41:26 [p]Hab 2:18-19
41:27 [q]Isa 48:3,16 [r]Isa 40:9
41:28 [s]Isa 50:2; 59:16; 63:5 [t]Isa 40:13-14
41:29 [u]ver 24 [v]Jer 5:13
42:1 [w]Isa 43:10; Lk 9:35; 1Pe 2:4,6 [x]Isa 11:2; Mt 3:16-17; Jn 3:34
42:3 [y]Ps 72:2
42:4 [z]Ge 49:10; Mt 12:18-21*
42:5 [a]Ps 24:2 [b]Ac 17:25
42:6 [c]Isa 43:1 [d]Jer 23:6 [e]Isa 26:3 [f]Isa 49:8 [g]Lk 2:32; Ac 13:47
42:7 [h]Isa 35:5 [i]Isa 49:9; 61:1 [j]Lk 4:19; 2Ti 2:26; Heb 2:14-15
42:8 [k]Ex 3:15

42:8 [l]Isa 48:11

I will not give my glory to another[l]
or my praise to idols.
9 See, the former things have taken place,
and new things I declare;
before they spring into being
I announce them to you."

Song of Praise to the LORD

42:10 [m]Ps 33:3; 40:3; 98:1 [n]Isa 49:6 [o]1Ch 16:32; Ps 96:11

10 Sing to the LORD a new song,[m]
his praise from the ends of the earth,[n]
you who go down to the sea, and all
that is in it,[o]
you islands, and all who live in them.

42:11 [p]Isa 32:16 [q]Isa 60:7 [r]Isa 52:7; Na 1:15

11 Let the desert[p] and its towns raise their
voices;
let the settlements where Kedar[q] lives
rejoice.
Let the people of Sela sing for joy;
let them shout from the
mountaintops.[r]

42:12 [s]Isa 24:15

12 Let them give glory[s] to the LORD
and proclaim his praise in the islands.

42:13 [t]Isa 9:6 [u]Isa 26:11 [v]Hos 11:10 [w]Isa 66:14

13 The LORD will march out like a mighty[t]
man,
like a warrior he will stir up his zeal;[u]
with a shout[v] he will raise the battle cry
and will triumph over his enemies.[w]

14 "For a long time I have kept silent,
I have been quiet and held myself
back.
But now, like a woman in childbirth,
I cry out, I gasp and pant.

42:15 [x]Eze 38:20 [y]Isa 50:2; Na 1:4-6

15 I will lay waste[x] the mountains and hills
and dry up all their vegetation;
I will turn rivers into islands
and dry up[y] the pools.

42:16 [z]Lk 1:78-79 [a]Isa 32:3 [b]Lk 3:5 [c]Heb 13:5

16 I will lead[z] the blind[a] by ways they have
not known,
along unfamiliar paths I will guide
them;
I will turn the darkness into light before
them
and make the rough places smooth.[b]
These are the things I will do;
I will not forsake[c] them.
17 But those who trust in idols,
who say to images, 'You are our gods,'
will be turned back in utter shame.[d]

42:17 [d]Ps 97:7; Isa 1:29; 44:11; 45:16

Israel Blind and Deaf

42:18 [e]Isa 35:5

18 "Hear, you deaf;[e]
look, you blind, and see!

42:19 [f]Isa 43:8; Eze 12:2 [g]Isa 41:8-9 [h]Isa 44:26 [i]Isa 26:3

19 Who is blind[f] but my servant,[g]
and deaf like the messenger[h] I send?
Who is blind like the one committed[i] to
me,
blind like the servant of the LORD?
20 You have seen many things, but have
paid no attention;

***N**ails were not enough to hold God-and-man nailed and fastened on the cross, had not love held him there.*

—Catherine of Siena (1347-1380)

Week 21

Something New

Living in this world is hard: The poor are neglected, the innocent are abused, injustice seems to rule and problems weigh on your heart. Sometimes it just seems too much. Discouragement sets in. But there is comfort. There is hope. His name is Jesus.

Jesus is the only One who can give you true comfort and hope. You've probably heard it before, yet do you continue to seek comfort and happiness from other people and other things? Why? Hope that endures can be found in no other.

Isaiah 42:1-4 is quoted in Matthew 12:18-21 as a reference to Jesus. What can you learn about Jesus' qualifications from Isaiah 42:1?

What picture of gentleness is painted in Isaiah 42:3? What is Jesus willing to do for you (Isa 40:11)?

What amazing things does God say Jesus will do (Isa 42:6-7)? Jesus is your rescuer and warrior (2Sa 22:4; Isa 42:13). What are your greatest needs? Can you trust him with them?

What warning is given in Isaiah 42:8? If God rescues you, how will you respond? Who will get the credit when you are rescued from some illness or calamity or hardship? Your doctor? Your bank? Your friends or family? Or God?

God says through Isaiah that he will do "new things" (Isa 42:9). Those new things are available to you in Jesus. What song can you sing in response (Isa 42:10)?

Enjoying God THROUGH the Word

Read Isaiah 40:25-31 (page 1171). Do you want to soar like an eagle? A soaring eagle doesn't flap its wings frantically in a struggle to stay aloft. It glides on, enjoying the wind, sweeping effortlessly through the sky. That is what God has in mind for you. He wants you to soar on the wind of his Holy Spirit. He wants you to enjoy the adventure and the scenery.

Don't think you can get up that high? Think you're too wounded to fly? Listen to what God did for Jacob (a rotten liar and a deceiver, by the way): "In a desert land [God] found him, in a barren and howling waste. He shielded him and cared for him; he guarded him as the apple of his eye, like an eagle that stirs up its nest and hovers over its young, that spreads its wings to catch them and carries them on its pinions" (Dt 32:10-11). That's your God! Can't fly? Let him carry you. Enjoy the ride—it's glorious!

Enjoying God THROUGH Experience

Trust Jesus. Just trust him. What have you got to lose? Haven't you already tried everything else anyway? He is able to help you. And he is willing (Mk 1:40-41). Are you ready to let him gather you in his arms (Mt 23:37)? In prayer, lay everything before God—your problems, your discouragement, your broken heart. Don't hold back. Take as long as you need—minutes, hours, days. But give it all to him. He requires all of you. Then he will lift you up, and you will fly with him on his wings of love.

Go to page 1259 for your next weekly study.

your ears are open, but you hear
nothing."[j]
21 It pleased the LORD
for the sake of his righteousness
to make his law[k] great and glorious.
22 But this is a people plundered and looted,
all of them trapped in pits[l]
or hidden away in prisons.[m]
They have become plunder,
with no one to rescue them;
they have been made loot,
with no one to say, "Send them back."

23 Which of you will listen to this
or pay close attention[n] in time to
come?
24 Who handed Jacob over to become loot,
and Israel to the plunderers?
Was it not the LORD,
against whom we have sinned?
For they would not follow[o] his ways;
they did not obey his law.
25 So he poured out on them his burning
anger,
the violence of war.
It enveloped them in flames,[p] yet they
did not understand;
it consumed them, but they did not
take it to heart.[q]

Israel's Only Savior

43 But now, this is what the LORD says—
he who created you, O Jacob,
he who formed[r] you, O Israel:[s]
"Fear not, for I have redeemed[t] you;
I have summoned you by name;[u] you
are mine.
2 When you pass through the waters,[v]
I will be with you;[w]
and when you pass through the rivers,
they will not sweep over you.
When you walk through the fire,[x]
you will not be burned;
the flames will not set you ablaze.[y]
3 For I am the LORD, your God,[z]
the Holy One of Israel, your Savior;
I give Egypt for your ransom,
Cush[a][a] and Seba in your stead.[b]
4 Since you are precious and honored in
my sight,
and because I love[c] you,
I will give men in exchange for you,
and people in exchange for your life.
5 Do not be afraid,[d] for I am with you;[e]
I will bring your children[f] from the
east
and gather you from the west.
6 I will say to the north, 'Give them up!'

42:20 [j]Jer 6:10
42:21 [k]ver 4
42:22 [l]Isa 24:18 [m]Isa 24:22
42:23 [n]Isa 48:18
42:24 [o]Isa 30:15
42:25 [p]2Ki 25:9 [q]Isa 29:13; 47:7; 57:1, 11; Hos 7:9
43:1 [r]ver 7 [s]Ge 32:28; Isa 44:21 [t]Isa 44:2,6 [u]Isa 42:6; 45:3-4
43:2 [v]Isa 8:7 [w]Dt 31:6,8 [x]Isa 29:6; 30:27 [y]Ps 66:12; Da 3:25-27
43:3 [z]Ex 20:2 [a]Isa 20:3 [b]Pr 21:18
43:4 [c]Isa 63:9
43:5 [d]Isa 44:2 [e]Jer 30:10-11 [f]Isa 41:8

Called by Name

ISA 43:1

We all love to hear people call us by name, especially if it's done in a loving fashion. A "hey, you" or even a nickname doesn't carry the same impact as hearing our real name specifically and tenderly called by a loved one. A name is our identity and using that name gives us value and a sense of belonging. How wonderful that God, with his vast responsibilities, calls us by name and says, "You are mine." Jesus reinforces this truth in John 10:3. Referring to himself as the shepherd, he says, "He calls his own sheep by name and leads them out." The Lord individually notices, names and nurtures us.

[a] 3 That is, the upper Nile region

God's Witnesses

ISA 43:10

God seems to be setting up a courtroom filled with the nations (Isa 43:5-9), and a repentant Israel is the primary witness. Israel will testify that the Lord is God, not the nation's idols. In the Old Testament God repeats the claim "I am the Lord" 156 times, usually when he gives instructions to his people. In Leviticus 19:4 he states, "Do not turn to idols or make gods of cast metal for yourselves. I am the LORD *your God." In Isaiah he thunders this command to the wayward nations. He allows no other gods before him (Ex 20:3; Dt 5:7).*

and to the south,[g] 'Do not hold them back.'
Bring my sons from afar
and my daughters[h] from the ends of the earth—
7 everyone who is called by my name,[i]
whom I created for my glory,
whom I formed and made.[j]"

8 Lead out those who have eyes but are blind,[k]
who have ears but are deaf.[l]
9 All the nations gather together[m]
and the peoples assemble.
Which of them foretold[n] this
and proclaimed to us the former things?
Let them bring in their witnesses to prove they were right,
so that others may hear and say, "It is true."
10 "You are my witnesses," declares the LORD,
"and my servant[o] whom I have chosen,
so that you may know and believe me
and understand that I am he.
Before me no god[p] was formed,
nor will there be one after me.
11 I, even I, am the LORD,
and apart from me there is no savior.[q]
12 I have revealed and saved and proclaimed—
I, and not some foreign god[r] among you.
You are my witnesses,[s]" declares the LORD, "that I am God.
13 Yes, and from ancient days[t] I am he.
No one can deliver out of my hand.
When I act, who can reverse it?"[u]

God's Mercy and Israel's Unfaithfulness

14 This is what the LORD says—
your Redeemer, the Holy One of Israel:
"For your sake I will send to Babylon
and bring down as fugitives[v] all the Babylonians,[a][w]
in the ships in which they took pride.
15 I am the LORD, your Holy One,
Israel's Creator, your King."

16 This is what the LORD says—
he who made a way through the sea,
a path through the mighty waters,[x]
17 who drew out[y] the chariots and horses,
the army and reinforcements together,[z]
and they lay there, never to rise again,
extinguished, snuffed out like a wick:

43:6 [g] Ps 107:3 [h] 2Co 6:18
43:7 [i] Isa 56:5; 63:19; Jas 2:7 [j] ver 1,21; Ps 100:3; Eph 2:10
43:8 [k] Isa 6:9-10 [l] Isa 42:20; Eze 12:2
43:9 [m] Isa 41:1 [n] Isa 41:26
43:10 [o] Isa 41:8-9 [p] Isa 44:6,8
43:11 [q] Isa 45:21
43:12 [r] Dt 32:12; Ps 81:9 [s] Isa 44:8
43:13 [t] Ps 90:2 [u] Job 9:12; Isa 14:27
43:14 [v] Isa 13:14-15 [w] Isa 23:13
43:16 [x] Ps 77:19; Isa 11:15; 51:10
43:17 [y] Ps 118:12; Isa 1:31 [z] Ex 14:9

[a] 14 Or *Chaldeans*

18 “Forget the former things;
do not dwell on the past.
19 See, I am doing a new thing![a]
Now it springs up; do you not
perceive it?
I am making a way in the desert[b]
and streams in the wasteland.
20 The wild animals honor me,
the jackals[c] and the owls,
because I provide water[d] in the desert
and streams in the wasteland,
to give drink to my people, my chosen,
21 the people I formed for myself
that they may proclaim my praise.[e]

22 “Yet you have not called upon me,
O Jacob,
you have not wearied yourselves for
me, O Israel.[f]
23 You have not brought me sheep for
burnt offerings,
nor honored[g] me with your
sacrifices.[h]
I have not burdened you with grain
offerings
nor wearied you with demands[i] for
incense.[j]
24 You have not bought any fragrant
calamus[k] for me,
or lavished on me the fat of your
sacrifices.
But you have burdened me with your
sins
and wearied[l] me with your offenses.[m]

25 “I, even I, am he who blots out
your transgressions,[n] for my own
sake,[o]
and remembers your sins no more.[p]
26 Review the past for me,
let us argue the matter together;[q]
state the case[r] for your innocence.
27 Your first father sinned;
your spokesmen[s] rebelled against me.
28 So I will disgrace the dignitaries of your
temple,
and I will consign Jacob to
destruction[a]
and Israel to scorn.[t]

Israel the Chosen

44 “But now listen, O Jacob, my servant,[u]
Israel, whom I have chosen.
2 This is what the LORD says—
he who made you, who formed you in
the womb,
and who will help[v] you:
Do not be afraid, O Jacob, my servant,
Jeshurun,[w] whom I have chosen.

[a] 28 The Hebrew term refers to the irrevocable giving over of things or persons to the LORD, often by totally destroying them.

43:19 [a] 2Co 5:17; Rev 21:5 [b] Ex 17:6; Nu 20:11
43:20 [c] Isa 13:22 [d] Isa 48:21
43:21 [e] Ps 102:18; 1Pe 2:9
43:22 [f] Isa 30:11
43:23 [g] Zec 7:5-6; Mal 1:6-8 [h] Am 5:25 [i] Jer 7:22 [j] Ex 30:35; Lev 2:1
43:24 [k] Ex 30:23 [l] Isa 1:14; 7:13 [m] Mal 2:17
43:25 [n] Ac 3:19 [o] Isa 37:35; Eze 36:22 [p] Isa 38:17; Jer 31:34
43:26 [q] Isa 1:18 [r] Isa 41:1; 50:8
43:27 [s] Isa 9:15; 28:7; Jer 5:31
43:28 [t] Jer 24:9; Eze 5:15
44:1 [u] ver 21; Jer 30:10; 46:27-28
44:2 [v] Isa 41:10 [w] Dt 32:15

The test of whether we have forgiven someone is not whether we remember the incident but in the attitudes and behaviors we exhibit. We know we have forgiven someone when we are no longer controlled by the pain . . . In other words, we remember the occurrence, but it no longer has power over our thinking and behavior.

Forgiving is better than forgetting, but God does both. Micah 7:18–19 describes God's style of forgiving. Don't you love it? God doesn't stay mad at us because he loves to show mercy and compassion. Instead he stomps on our confessed sins and flings them into the ocean. What vivid and liberating images! And then he does what we can't do: "I, even I, am he who blots out your transgressions, for my own sake, and remembers your sins no more" (Isa 43:25).

God's style of forgiveness serves as a model for us as we attempt to forgive with mercy and compassion; we don't need to worry about forgetting.

—Marilyn Meberg

Hand Writing

ISA 44:5

Branding a slave's hand with the owner's name was an ancient practice. This branding clearly defined who was the master and who was the servant. Who that slave belonged to could never be forgotten or concealed. In a similar fashion, God instructs the Israelites to place reminders of God's laws on their foreheads and hands (Ex 13:9,16; Dt 6:8), so they won't forget his laws or him. In a role reversal in Isaiah 49:16, God reveals that he's written his people's names on the palms of his hands. Just as they are not to forget the Lord, he inscribes their names upon his hands as a sign that he will never forget them. Actually, it's not possible for God to forget his children, but this remains a powerful image of comfort and security to the Israelites, and to us.

3 For I will pour water[x] on the thirsty land,
and streams on the dry ground;
I will pour out my Spirit[y] on your offspring,
and my blessing on your descendants.[z]
4 They will spring up like grass in a meadow,
like poplar trees[a] by flowing streams.[b]
5 One will say, 'I belong to the LORD';
another will call himself by the name of Jacob;
still another will write on his hand,[c] 'The LORD's,'[d]
and will take the name Israel.

The LORD, Not Idols

6 "This is what the LORD says—
Israel's King[e] and Redeemer,[f] the LORD Almighty:
I am the first and I am the last;[g]
apart from me there is no God.
7 Who then is like me? Let him proclaim it.
Let him declare and lay out before me
what has happened since I established my ancient people,
and what is yet to come—
yes, let him foretell[h] what will come.
8 Do not tremble, do not be afraid.
Did I not proclaim this and foretell it long ago?
You are my witnesses. Is there any God[i] besides me?
No, there is no other Rock;[j] I know not one."

9 All who make idols are nothing,
and the things they treasure are worthless.[k]
Those who would speak up for them are blind;
they are ignorant, to their own shame.
10 Who shapes a god and casts an idol,
which can profit him nothing?[l]
11 He and his kind will be put to shame;[m]
craftsmen are nothing but men.
Let them all come together and take their stand;
they will be brought down to terror and infamy.[n]

12 The blacksmith[o] takes a tool
and works with it in the coals;
he shapes an idol with hammers,
he forges it with the might of his arm.[p]
He gets hungry and loses his strength;
he drinks no water and grows faint.
13 The carpenter[q] measures with a line
and makes an outline with a marker;
he roughs it out with chisels
and marks it with compasses.
He shapes it in the form of man,[r]

44:3 [x]Joel 3:18 [y]Joel 2:28; Ac 2:17 [z]Isa 61:9; 65:23
44:4 [a]Lev 23:40 [b]Job 40:22
44:5 [c]Ex 13:9 [d]Zec 8:20-22
44:6 [e]Isa 41:21 [f]Isa 43:1 [g]Isa 41:4; Rev 1:8,17; 22:13
44:7 [h]Isa 41:22,26
44:8 [i]Isa 43:10 [j]Dt 4:35; 1Sa 2:2
44:9 [k]Isa 41:24
44:10 [l]Isa 41:29; Jer 10:5; Ac 19:26
44:11 [m]Isa 1:29 [n]Isa 42:17
44:12 [o]Isa 40:19; 41:6-7 [p]Jer 10:3-5; Ac 17:29
44:13 [q]Isa 41:7 [r]Ps 115:4-7

of man in all his glory,
that it may dwell in a shrine.[s]
14 He cut down cedars,
or perhaps took a cypress or oak.
He let it grow among the trees of the forest,
or planted a pine, and the rain made it grow.
15 It is man's fuel[t] for burning;
some of it he takes and warms himself,
he kindles a fire and bakes bread.
But he also fashions a god and worships it;
he makes an idol and bows[u] down to it.
16 Half of the wood he burns in the fire;
over it he prepares his meal,
he roasts his meat and eats his fill.
He also warms himself and says,
"Ah! I am warm; I see the fire."
17 From the rest he makes a god, his idol;
he bows down to it and worships.
He prays[v] to it and says,
"Save[w] me; you are my god."
18 They know nothing, they understand[x] nothing;
their eyes[y] are plastered over so they cannot see,
and their minds closed so they cannot understand.
19 No one stops to think,
no one has the knowledge or understanding[z] to say,
"Half of it I used for fuel;
I even baked bread over its coals,
I roasted meat and I ate.
Shall I make a detestable[a] thing from what is left?
Shall I bow down to a block of wood?"
20 He feeds on ashes,[b] a deluded[c] heart misleads him;
he cannot save himself, or say,
"Is not this thing in my right hand a lie?[d]"

21 "Remember[e] these things, O Jacob,
for you are my servant, O Israel.
I have made you, you are my servant;[f]
O Israel, I will not forget you.[g]
22 I have swept away[h] your offenses like a cloud,
your sins like the morning mist.
Return[i] to me,
for I have redeemed[j] you."

23 Sing for joy,[k] O heavens, for the LORD has done this;
shout aloud, O earth[l] beneath.
Burst into song, you mountains,[m]
you forests and all your trees,

44:13 [s]Jdg 17:4-5
44:15 [t]ver 19 [u]2Ch 25:14
44:17 [v]1Ki 18:26 [w]Isa 45:20
44:18 [x]Isa 1:3 [y]Isa 6:9-10
44:19 [z]Isa 5:13; 27:11; 45:20 [a]Dt 27:15
44:20 [b]Ps 102:9 [c]Job 15:31; Ro 1:21-23, 28; 2Th 2:11; 2Ti 3:13 [d]Isa 59:3,4, 13; Ro 1:25
44:21 [e]Isa 46:8; Zec 10:9 [f]ver 1-2 [g]Isa 49:15
44:22 [h]Isa 43:25; Ac 3:19 [i]Isa 55:7 [j]1Co 6:20
44:23 [k]Isa 42:10 [l]Ps 148:7 [m]Ps 98:8

Everyday Idols

ISA 44:15-17

Isaiah describes the absurdity of creating idols and worshiping them. People use some of their wood to build a fire to warm themselves and cook their food and then use the rest to fashion an idol. There is a hint of ridicule in Isaiah's description. How can a powerless people create powerful gods? They can't; and this practice, if it weren't so pitiful, would be laughable. People can't save themselves with something that's even less capable than they are. Salvation occurs when the stronger rescues the weaker. Only the powerful God can save his people from sin's mire and destruction. Yet, even today, people try to save and satisfy themselves with everyday idols. What examples come to mind?

for the LORD has redeemed Jacob,
he displays his glory[n] in Israel.

44:23 [n]Isa 61:3

Lord of Everything

ISA 44:24–28

From forming us in the womb to establishing the earth, the Lord is the Maker of all things. His creative résumé can't be exceeded, and he wants us to remember that—not just because he is the Lord and worthy of our worship, but also because it is a comforting reminder that he's in control and won't forget us.

Jerusalem to Be Inhabited

24 "This is what the LORD says—
your Redeemer,[o] who formed you in the womb:

I am the LORD,
who has made all things,
who alone stretched out the heavens,[p]
who spread out the earth by myself,
25 who foils[q] the signs of false prophets
and makes fools of diviners,[r]
who overthrows the learning of the wise[s]
and turns it into nonsense,[t]
26 who carries out the words[u] of his servants
and fulfills[v] the predictions of his messengers,

who says of Jerusalem, 'It shall be inhabited,'
of the towns of Judah, 'They shall be built,'
and of their ruins, 'I will restore them,'[w]
27 who says to the watery deep, 'Be dry,
and I will dry up your streams,'
28 who says of Cyrus,[x] 'He is my shepherd
and will accomplish all that I please;
he will say of Jerusalem,[y] "Let it be rebuilt,"
and of the temple,[z] "Let its foundations be laid." '

44:24 [o]Isa 43:14 [p]Isa 42:5
44:25 [q]Ps 33:10 [r]Isa 47:13 [s]1Co 1:27 [t]2Sa 15:31; 1Co 1:19-20
44:26 [u]Zec 1:6 [v]Isa 55:11; Mt 5:18 [w]Isa 49:8-21
44:28 [x]2Ch 36:22 [y]Isa 14:32 [z]Ezr 1:2-4

45

"This is what the LORD says to his anointed,
to Cyrus, whose right hand I take hold[a] of
to subdue nations[b] before him
and to strip kings of their armor,
to open doors before him
so that gates will not be shut:
2 I will go before you
and will level[c] the mountains[a];
I will break down gates of bronze
and cut through bars of iron.[d]
3 I will give you the treasures[e] of darkness,
riches stored in secret places,[f]
so that you may know[g] that I am the LORD,
the God of Israel, who summons you by name.[h]
4 For the sake of Jacob my servant,[i]
of Israel my chosen,
I summon you by name
and bestow on you a title of honor,

45:1 [a]Ps 73:23; Isa 41:13; 42:6 [b]Jer 50:35
45:2 [c]Isa 40:4 [d]Ps 107:16; Jer 51:30
45:3 [e]Jer 50:37 [f]Jer 41:8 [g]Isa 41:23 [h]Ex 33:12; Isa 43:1
45:4 [i]Isa 41:8-9

[a] *2* Dead Sea Scrolls and Septuagint; the meaning of the word in the Masoretic Text is uncertain.

though you do not acknowledge[j] me.
5 I am the LORD, and there is no other;[k]
apart from me there is no God.[l]
I will strengthen you,[m]
though you have not acknowledged me,
6 so that from the rising of the sun
to the place of its setting[n]
men may know there is none besides me.[o]
I am the LORD, and there is no other.
7 I form the light and create darkness,
I bring prosperity and create disaster;[p]
I, the LORD, do all these things.

8 "You heavens above, rain[q] down righteousness;[r]
let the clouds shower it down.
Let the earth open wide,
let salvation[s] spring up,
let righteousness grow with it;
I, the LORD, have created it.

9 "Woe to him who quarrels[t] with his Maker,
to him who is but a potsherd among the potsherds on the ground.
Does the clay say to the potter,[u]
'What are you making?'
Does your work say,
'He has no hands'?
10 Woe to him who says to his father,
'What have you begotten?'
or to his mother,
'What have you brought to birth?'

11 "This is what the LORD says—
the Holy One of Israel, and its Maker:
Concerning things to come,
do you question me about my children,
or give me orders about the work of my hands?[v]
12 It is I who made the earth
and created mankind upon it.
My own hands stretched out the heavens;[w]
I marshaled their starry hosts.[x]
13 I will raise up Cyrus[a][y] in my righteousness:
I will make all his ways straight.
He will rebuild my city
and set my exiles free,
but not for a price or reward,[z]
says the LORD Almighty."
14 This is what the LORD says:

"The products of Egypt and the merchandise of Cush,[b]
and those tall Sabeans—

45:4 [j]Ac 17:23
45:5 [k]Isa 44:8 [l]Ps 18:31 [m]Ps 18:39
45:6 [n]Isa 43:5; Mal 1:11 [o]ver 5,18
45:7 [p]Isa 31:2; Am 3:6
45:8 [q]Ps 72:6; Joel 3:18 [r]Ps 85:11; Isa 60:21; 61:10,11; Hos 10:12 [s]Isa 12:3
45:9 [t]Job 15:25 [u]Isa 29:16; Ro 9:20-21*
45:11 [v]Isa 19:25
45:12 [w]Ge 2:1; Isa 42:5 [x]Ne 9:6
45:13 [y]2Ch 36:22; Isa 41:2 [z]Isa 52:3

[a] *13* Hebrew *him* [b] *14* That is, the upper Nile region

Broken Pottery

ISA 45:9

God calls his complaining people "potsherds," broken pieces of clay. These broken bits rank as the least valuable materials for pottery making and are usually thrown into a potter's field and abandoned. Or they're used as scrapers, scoops or pieces of scratch paper. The Lord says these clay shards scarcely compare to the potter, who masterminds the creative process.

King David calls himself a piece of "broken pottery" when he feels worthless and fears that people disrespect him (Ps 31:12). Being a potsherd is as far as someone can crumble. That's who we are compared to God, but it's not our final identity. Our relationship with God is a balance between realizing we're unworthy without him (Ps 14:3) but worthy because of him through Jesus Christ (2Co 5:21). Though we're only bits of clay, when we reverence who he is versus who we are, he can remold us into vessels full of his power (2Co 4:7).

A Hidden God?

ISA 45:15-19

To the pagan nations who worship gods of wood and stone, the Lord seems hidden because he's spirit and invisible to the eye. However, God insists that he doesn't speak in secret, nor does anyone seek him in vain. He speaks and reveals himself to those who seek him with their whole heart (Jer 29:13). The psalmist assures us: "Those who know your name will trust in you, for you, LORD, have never forsaken those who seek you" (Psalm 9:10).

they will come over to you
and will be yours;
they will trudge behind you,
coming over to you in chains.[a]
They will bow down before you
and plead[b] with you, saying,
'Surely God is with you,[c] and there is no other;
there is no other god.' "

15 Truly you are a God who hides[d] himself,
O God and Savior of Israel.
16 All the makers of idols will be put to shame and disgraced;[e]
they will go off into disgrace together.
17 But Israel will be saved[f] by the LORD
with an everlasting salvation;[g]
you will never be put to shame or disgraced,
to ages everlasting.

18 For this is what the LORD says—
he who created the heavens,
he is God;
he who fashioned and made the earth,
he founded it;
he did not create it to be empty,[h]
but formed it to be inhabited[i]—
he says:
"I am the LORD,
and there is no other.[j]
19 I have not spoken in secret,[k]
from somewhere in a land of darkness;
I have not said to Jacob's descendants,[l]
'Seek me in vain.'
I, the LORD, speak the truth;
I declare what is right.[m]

20 "Gather together[n] and come;
assemble, you fugitives from the nations.
Ignorant[o] are those who carry[p] about idols of wood,
who pray to gods that cannot save.[q]
21 Declare what is to be, present it—
let them take counsel together.
Who foretold[r] this long ago,
who declared it from the distant past?
Was it not I, the LORD?
And there is no God apart from me,[s]
a righteous God and a Savior;
there is none but me.

22 "Turn[t] to me and be saved,[u]
all you ends of the earth;[v]
for I am God, and there is no other.
23 By myself I have sworn,[w]
my mouth has uttered in all integrity[x]
a word that will not be revoked:[y]
Before me every knee will bow;
by me every tongue will swear.[z]
24 They will say of me, 'In the LORD alone

45:14 [a]Isa 14:1-2 [b]Jer 16:19; Zec 8:20-23 [c]1Co 14:25
45:15 [d]Ps 44:24
45:16 [e]Isa 44:9,11
45:17 [f]Ro 11:26 [g]Isa 26:4
45:18 [h]Ge 1:2 [i]Ge 1:26; Isa 42:5 [j]ver 5
45:19 [k]Isa 48:16 [l]Isa 41:8 [m]Dt 30:11
45:20 [n]Isa 43:9 [o]Isa 44:19 [p]Isa 46:1; Jer 10:5 [q]Isa 44:17; 46:6-7
45:21 [r]Isa 41:22 [s]ver 5
45:22 [t]Zec 12:10 [u]Nu 21:8-9; 2Ch 20:12 [v]Isa 49:6,12
45:23 [w]Ge 22:16 [x]Heb 6:13 [y]Isa 55:11 [z]Ps 63:11; Isa 19:18; Ro 14:11*; Php 2:10-11

are righteousness[a] and strength.’ ”
All who have raged against him
will come to him and be put to
shame.[b]
25 But in the LORD all the descendants of
Israel
will be found righteous and will exult.[c]

Gods of Babylon

46 Bel[d] bows down, Nebo stoops low;
their idols are borne by beasts of burden.[a]
The images that are carried[e] about are
burdensome,
a burden for the weary.
2 They stoop and bow down together;
unable to rescue the burden,
they themselves go off into captivity.[f]

3 “Listen[g] to me, O house of Jacob,
all you who remain of the house of
Israel,
you whom I have upheld since you were
conceived,
and have carried since your birth.
4 Even to your old age and gray hairs[h]
I am he,[i] I am he who will sustain you.
I have made you and I will carry you;
I will sustain you and I will rescue
you.

5 “To whom will you compare me or
count me equal?
To whom will you liken me that we
may be compared?[j]
6 Some pour out gold from their bags
and weigh out silver on the scales;
they hire a goldsmith[k] to make it into a
god,
and they bow down and worship it.[l]
7 They lift it to their shoulders and carry[m]
it;
they set it up in its place, and there it
stands.
From that spot it cannot move.
Though one cries out to it, it does not
answer;
it cannot save[n] him from his troubles.
8 “Remember[o] this, fix it in mind,
take it to heart, you rebels.
9 Remember the former things, those of
long ago;[p]
I am God, and there is no other;
I am God, and there is none like me.[q]
10 I make known the end from the
beginning,
from ancient times,[r] what is still to
come.
I say: My purpose will stand,[s]
and I will do all that I please.

45:24 [a]Jer 33:16 [b]Isa 41:11
45:25 [c]Isa 41:16
46:1 [d]Isa 21:9; Jer 50:2; 51:44 [e]Isa 45:20
46:2 [f]Jdg 18:17-18; 2Sa 5:21
46:3 [g]ver 12
46:4 [h]Ps 71:18 [i]Isa 43:13
46:5 [j]Isa 40:18,25
46:6 [k]Isa 40:19 [l]Isa 44:17
46:7 [m]ver 1 [n]Isa 44:17; Isa 45:20
46:8 [o]Isa 44:21
46:9 [p]Dt 32:7 [q]Isa 45:5,21
46:10 [r]Isa 45:21 [s]Pr 19:21; Ac 5:39

[a] 1 Or *are but beasts and cattle*

Lifetime Guarantee

ISA 46:1-4

God here compares the care he gives with that given by the idols of Babylon. These idols must themselves be carried. Instead of being a supporter of their people, they must themselves be supported. The weary people are made more weary by their gods.

Not so with the one true God of Israel. He is the great sustainer. He offers a lifetime guarantee. He'll carry and support his people through old age and into eternity. Gray hairs and wrinkles don't diminish their value to him, nor do slowing faculties or illness. Rather than needing to be carried, like the gods of Babylon, he carries his people, lovingly and carefully, from birth to death—and beyond.

Someone's Watching

ISA 47:8–10

Who are we when nobody's watching? That's the true test of character. The residents of Babylon mistakenly think that as long as nobody sees their wicked deeds, they're safe to keep sinning. But they forget one thing: Although people may not observe them, God sees everything they do. "Nothing in all creation is hidden from God's sight. Everything is uncovered and laid bare before the eyes of him to whom we must give account" (Heb 4:13).

God's watchful eye can be either disturbing or comforting. The sinner is disturbed to know that God's sees everything. The forgiven believer is comforted to know that God sees and controls everything. With sincere confession there is always forgiveness for sinners with God. We can pray with David, "Forgive my hidden faults" (Ps 19:12). That's the way to freedom.

11 From the east I summon a bird of prey;
from a far-off land, a man to fulfill my purpose.
What I have said, that will I bring about;
what I have planned, that will I do.
12 Listen[t] to me, you stubborn-hearted,
you who are far from righteousness.[u]
13 I am bringing my righteousness near,
it is not far away;
and my salvation will not be delayed.
I will grant salvation to Zion,
my splendor[v] to Israel.

The Fall of Babylon

47 "Go down, sit in the dust,
Virgin Daughter[w] of Babylon;
sit on the ground without a throne,
Daughter of the Babylonians.[a][x]
No more will you be called
tender or delicate.[y]
2 Take millstones[z] and grind[a] flour;
take off your veil.[b]
Lift up your skirts,[c] bare your legs,
and wade through the streams.
3 Your nakedness[d] will be exposed
and your shame[e] uncovered.
I will take vengeance;[f]
I will spare no one."

4 Our Redeemer—the LORD Almighty is his name[g]—
is the Holy One of Israel.

5 "Sit in silence, go into darkness,[h]
Daughter of the Babylonians;
no more will you be called
queen of kingdoms.[i]
6 I was angry[j] with my people
and desecrated my inheritance;
I gave them into your hand,[k]
and you showed them no mercy.
Even on the aged
you laid a very heavy yoke.
7 You said, 'I will continue forever—
the eternal queen!'[l]
But you did not consider these things
or reflect[m] on what might happen.[n]

8 "Now then, listen, you wanton creature,
lounging in your security[o]
and saying to yourself,
'I am, and there is none besides me.[p]
I will never be a widow[q]
or suffer the loss of children.'
9 Both of these will overtake you
in a moment,[r] on a single day:
loss of children[s] and widowhood.
They will come upon you in full measure,

46:12 [t]ver 3 [u]Ps 119:150; Isa 48:1; Jer 2:5
46:13 [v]Isa 44:23
47:1 [w]Isa 23:12 [x]Ps 137:8; Jer 50:42; 51:33; Zec 2:7 [y]Dt 28:56
47:2 [z]Ex 11:5; Mt 24:41 [a]Jdg 16:21 [b]Ge 24:65 [c]Isa 32:11
47:3 [d]Eze 16:37; Na 3:5 [e]Isa 20:4 [f]Isa 34:8
47:4 [g]Jer 50:34
47:5 [h]Isa 13:10 [i]Isa 13:19
47:6 [j]2Ch 28:9 [k]Isa 10:13
47:7 [l]ver 5; Rev 18:7 [m]Isa 42:23, 25 [n]Dt 32:29
47:8 [o]Isa 32:9 [p]Isa 45:6; Zep 2:15 [q]Rev 18:7
47:9 [r]Ps 73:19; 1Th 5:3; Rev 18:8-10 [s]Isa 13:18

[a] *1* Or *Chaldeans*; also in verse 5

in spite of your many sorceries[t]
and all your potent spells.[u]
10 You have trusted[v] in your wickedness
and have said, 'No one sees me.'[w]
Your wisdom[x] and knowledge mislead[y]
you
when you say to yourself,
'I am, and there is none besides me.'
11 Disaster will come upon you,
and you will not know how to
conjure it away.
A calamity will fall upon you
that you cannot ward off with a
ransom;
a catastrophe you cannot foresee
will suddenly[z] come upon you.
12 "Keep on, then, with your magic spells
and with your many sorceries,[a]
which you have labored at since
childhood.
Perhaps you will succeed,
perhaps you will cause terror.
13 All the counsel you have received has
only worn you out![b]
Let your astrologers[c] come forward,
those stargazers who make predictions
month by month,
let them save[d] you from what is
coming upon you.
14 Surely they are like stubble;[e]
the fire will burn them up.
They cannot even save themselves
from the power of the flame.[f]
Here are no coals to warm anyone;
here is no fire to sit by.
15 That is all they can do for you—
these you have labored with
and trafficked[g] with since childhood.
Each of them goes on in his error;
there is not one that can save you.

Stubborn Israel

48 "Listen to this, O house of Jacob,
you who are called by the name of Israel
and come from the line of Judah,
you who take oaths in the name of the
LORD
and invoke[h] the God of Israel—
but not in truth[i] or righteousness—
2 you who call yourselves citizens of the
holy city[j]
and rely[k] on the God of Israel—
the LORD Almighty is his name:
3 I foretold the former things[l] long ago,
my mouth announced[m] them and I
made them known;
then suddenly I acted, and they came
to pass.
4 For I knew how stubborn[n] you were;
the sinews of your neck[o] were iron,

47:9 [t]Na 3:4 [u]Rev 18:23
47:10 [v]Ps 52:7; 62:10 [w]Isa 29:15 [x]Isa 5:21 [y]Isa 44:20
47:11 [z]1Th 5:3
47:12 [a]ver 9
47:13 [b]Isa 57:10; Jer 51:58 [c]Isa 44:25 [d]ver 15
47:14 [e]Isa 5:24; Na 1:10 [f]Isa 10:17; Jer 51:30,32, 58
47:15 [g]Rev 18:11
48:1 [h]Isa 58:2 [i]Jer 4:2
48:2 [j]Isa 52:1 [k]Isa 10:20; Mic 3:11; Ro 2:17
48:3 [l]Isa 41:22 [m]Isa 45:21
48:4 [n]Dt 31:27 [o]Ex 32:9; Ac 7:51

The Star Maker

ISA 47:13

Babylon abounds in the magic arts, and astrologers study the stars and advise its leaders. Yet God laughs at their predictions. He designed the heavens and hung the stars, so how can mere humans interpret the universe? Without the Creator, how can they receive sound guidance? Charting stars won't save the Babylonians from the coming destruction because it springs from God's hand. Babylon needs to forsake the stargazers' forecasts and listen to the original star Maker. He is mightier than their magic.

What about astrology today? Is it any different from what the Babylonians practiced? Astrological charts, though popular and generally accepted in our culture, have their roots in the evil spirit world. Reading horoscopes isn't just the "harmless fun" it's purported to be. Believers need to beware, steer clear and seek their guidance from the Lord.

Am I a stone, and not a sheep,
That I can stand, O Christ, beneath Thy cross,
To number drop by drop Thy Blood's slow loss,
And yet not weep?

Not so those women loved
Who with exceeding grief lamented Thee;
Not so fallen Peter weeping bitterly;
Not so the thief was moved;

Not so the Sun and Moon
Which hid their faces in a starless sky:
A horror of great darkness at broad noon
I only I.

Yet give not o'er
But seek Thy sheep, true Shepherd of the flock;
Greater than Moses, turn and look once more
And smite a rock.

—*Christina Rossetti (1830–1894)*

your forehead[p] was bronze.
5 Therefore I told you these things long
ago;
before they happened I announced
them to you
so that you could not say,
'My idols did them;[q]
my wooden image and metal god
ordained them.'
6 You have heard these things; look at
them all.
Will you not admit them?

"From now on I will tell you of new
things,
of hidden things unknown to you.
7 They are created now, and not long ago;
you have not heard of them before
today.
So you cannot say,
'Yes, I knew of them.'
8 You have neither heard nor understood;
from of old your ear has not been
open.
Well do I know how treacherous you are;
you were called a rebel[r] from birth.
9 For my own name's sake I delay my
wrath;[s]
for the sake of my praise I hold it
back from you,
so as not to cut you off.[t]
10 See, I have refined you, though not as
silver;
I have tested you in the furnace[u] of
affliction.
11 For my own sake,[v] for my own sake, I
do this.
How can I let myself be defamed?[w]
I will not yield my glory to another.[x]

Israel Freed

12 "Listen[y] to me, O Jacob,
Israel, whom I have called:
I am he;
I am the first and I am the last.[z]
13 My own hand laid the foundations of
the earth,[a]
and my right hand spread out the
heavens;[b]
when I summon them,
they all stand up together.[c]

14 "Come together,[d] all of you, and listen:
Which of ⌊the idols⌋ has foretold these
things?
The LORD's chosen ally
will carry out his purpose[e] against
Babylon;
his arm will be against the
Babylonians.[a]

48:4 [p]Eze 3:9
48:5 [q]Jer 44:15-18
48:8 [r]Dt 9:7,24; Ps 58:3
48:9 [s]Ps 78:38; Isa 30:18 [t]Ne 9:31
48:10 [u]1Ki 8:51
48:11 [v]1Sa 12:22; Isa 37:35 [w]Dt 32:27; Jer 14:7,21; Eze 20:9,14, 22,44 [x]Isa 42:8
48:12 [y]Isa 46:3 [z]Isa 41:4; Rev 1:17; 22:13
48:13 [a]Heb 1:10-12 [b]Ex 20:11 [c]Isa 40:26
48:14 [d]Isa 43:9 [e]Isa 46:10-11

[a] 14 Or *Chaldeans*; also in verse 20

48:15 [f]Isa 45:1

15 I, even I, have spoken;
yes, I have called[f] him.
I will bring him,
and he will succeed in his mission.

48:16 [g]Isa 41:1 [h]Isa 45:19 [i]Zec 2:9,11

16 "Come near[g] me and listen to this:

"From the first announcement I have not spoken in secret;[h]
at the time it happens, I am there."

And now the Sovereign LORD has sent[i] me,
with his Spirit.

48:17 [j]Isa 49:7 [k]Isa 43:14 [l]Isa 49:10 [m]Ps 32:8

17 This is what the LORD says—
your Redeemer,[j] the Holy One[k] of Israel:
"I am the LORD your God,
who teaches you what is best for you,
who directs[l] you in the way[m] you should go.

48:18 [n]Dt 32:29 [o]Ps 119:165; Isa 66:12 [p]Isa 45:8

18 If only you had paid attention[n] to my commands,
your peace[o] would have been like a river,
your righteousness[p] like the waves of the sea.
19 Your descendants would have been like the sand,
your children like its numberless grains;[q]
their name would never be cut off[r]
nor destroyed from before me."

48:19 [q]Ge 22:17 [r]Isa 56:5; 66:22

48:20 [s]Jer 50:8; 51:6,45; Zec 2:6-7; Rev 18:4 [t]Isa 49:13 [u]Isa 52:9; 63:9

20 Leave Babylon,
flee[s] from the Babylonians!
Announce this with shouts of joy[t]
and proclaim it.
Send it out to the ends of the earth;
say, "The LORD has redeemed[u] his servant Jacob."

48:21 [v]Isa 41:17 [w]Isa 30:25 [x]Ex 17:6; Nu 20:11; Ps 105:41; Isa 35:6

21 They did not thirst[v] when he led them through the deserts;
he made water flow[w] for them from the rock;
he split the rock
and water gushed out.[x]

48:22 [y]Isa 57:21

22 "There is no peace," says the LORD, "for the wicked."[y]

The Servant of the LORD

49:1 [z]Isa 44:24; 46:3; Mt 1:20 [a]Isa 7:14; 9:6; 44:2; Jer 1:5; Gal 1:15

49 Listen to me, you islands;
hear this, you distant nations:
Before I was born[z] the LORD called[a] me;
from my birth he has made mention of my name.

49:2 [b]Isa 11:4; Rev 1:16

2 He made my mouth like a sharpened sword,[b]
in the shadow of his hand he hid me;
he made me into a polished arrow
and concealed me in his quiver.

49:3 [c]Zec 3:8

3 He said to me, "You are my servant,[c]

Our Teacher

ISA 48:17

Good teachers inspire, motivate, guide and correct their students without crushing their identity and creativity. They care about their students' welfare, give them their best, applaud successes and forgive failures. They listen more than they speak and love more than they demand. They dispense wisdom and discard vanity. Good teachers impart more than knowledge; they participate in, and shape, lives.

God does all of these things for us. He is the greatest teacher of all: "I will instruct you and teach you in the way you should go; I will counsel you and watch over you" (Ps 32:8). "Teach me your way, O LORD, and I will walk in your truth; give me an undivided heart, that I may fear your name" (Ps 86:11).

God's Timing

ISA 49:8

The time of God's favor probably has its roots in the Year of Jubilee. Leviticus 25:10 announces that this is a year to "proclaim liberty throughout the land." Isaiah announces that "the year of the LORD's favor" is when God will "proclaim freedom for the captives" (Isa 61:1–2). Isaiah 49 describes the time of God's favor as a time of restoration and blessing for Israel, when God will redeem his people, set them free from exile and restore them to their homeland. But the Israelites must wait for the time of God's favor.

However, in the New Testament Paul writes, "I tell you, now *is the time of God's favor,* now *is the day of salvation" (2Co 6:2, emphasis added). We don't need to wait for our salvation. Jesus has already paid the price for our sin (1Co 7:23). We can be part of the redeemed, the forgiven, the blessed—right now.*

Israel, in whom I will display my
splendor.[d]"
4 But I said, "I have labored to no
purpose;
I have spent my strength in vain[e] and
for nothing.
Yet what is due me is in the LORD's
hand,
and my reward[f] is with my God."

5 And now the LORD says—
he who formed me in the womb to be
his servant
to bring Jacob back to him
and gather Israel[g] to himself,
for I am honored[h] in the eyes of the
LORD
and my God has been my strength—
6 he says:
"It is too small a thing for you to be my
servant
to restore the tribes of Jacob
and bring back those of Israel I have
kept.
I will also make you a light for the
Gentiles,[i]
that you may bring my salvation to
the ends of the earth."[j]

7 This is what the LORD says—
the Redeemer and Holy One of
Israel[k]—
to him who was despised[l] and abhorred
by the nation,
to the servant of rulers:
"Kings[m] will see you and rise up,
princes will see and bow down,
because of the LORD, who is faithful,
the Holy One of Israel, who has
chosen you."

Restoration of Israel

8 This is what the LORD says:
"In the time of my favor[n] I will answer
you,
and in the day of salvation I will help
you;[o]
I will keep[p] you and will make you
to be a covenant for the people,[q]
to restore the land[r]
and to reassign its desolate
inheritances,
9 to say to the captives,[s] 'Come out,'
and to those in darkness, 'Be free!'
"They will feed beside the roads
and find pasture on every barren hill.[t]
10 They will neither hunger nor thirst,[u]
nor will the desert heat or the sun
beat upon them.[v]
He who has compassion[w] on them will
guide them

49:3 [d]Isa 44:23
49:4 [e]Isa 65:23 [f]Isa 35:4
49:5 [g]Isa 11:12 [h]Isa 43:4
49:6 [i]Lk 2:32 [j]Ac 13:47*
49:7 [k]Isa 48:17 [l]Ps 22:6; 69:7-9 [m]Isa 52:15
49:8 [n]Ps 69:13 [o]2Co 6:2* [p]Isa 26:3 [q]Isa 42:6 [r]Isa 44:26
49:9 [s]Isa 42:7; 61:1; Lk 4:19 [t]Isa 41:18
49:10 [u]Isa 33:16 [v]Ps 121:6; Rev 7:16 [w]Isa 14:1

and lead them beside springs[x] of
water.
11 I will turn all my mountains into roads,
and my highways[y] will be raised up.[z]
12 See, they will come from afar[a]—
some from the north, some from the
west,
some from the region of Aswan.[a]"

13 Shout for joy, O heavens;
rejoice, O earth;
burst into song, O mountains![b]
For the LORD comforts[c] his people
and will have compassion on his
afflicted ones.

14 But Zion said, "The LORD has forsaken
me,
the Lord has forgotten me."

15 "Can a mother forget the baby at her
breast
and have no compassion on the child
she has borne?
Though she may forget,
I will not forget you![d]
16 See, I have engraved[e] you on the palms
of my hands;
your walls[f] are ever before me.
17 Your sons hasten back,
and those who laid you waste[g] depart
from you.
18 Lift up your eyes and look around;
all your sons gather[h] and come to you.
As surely as I live,[i]" declares the LORD,
"you will wear[j] them all as
ornaments;
you will put them on, like a bride.

19 "Though you were ruined and made
desolate[k]
and your land laid waste,[l]
now you will be too small for your
people,[m]
and those who devoured you will be
far away.
20 The children born during your
bereavement
will yet say in your hearing,
'This place is too small for us;
give us more space to live in.'[n]
21 Then you will say in your heart,
'Who bore me these?
I was bereaved and barren;
I was exiled and rejected.[o]
Who brought these up?
I was left[p] all alone,
but these—where have they come
from?' "
22 This is what the Sovereign LORD says:

49:10 [x]Isa 35:7
49:11 [y]Isa 11:16 [z]Isa 40:4
49:12 [a]Isa 43:5-6
49:13 [b]Isa 44:23 [c]Isa 40:1
49:15 [d]Isa 44:21
49:16 [e]SS 8:6 [f]Ps 48:12-13; Isa 62:6
49:17 [g]Isa 10:6
49:18 [h]Isa 43:5; 54:7; Isa 60:4 [i]Isa 45:23 [j]Isa 52:1
49:19 [k]Isa 54:1,3 [l]Isa 5:6 [m]Zec 10:10
49:20 [n]Isa 54:1-3
49:21 [o]Isa 5:13 [p]Isa 1:8

Isaiah 49:15 asks a poignant question about forgetfulness. "Can a mother forget the baby at her breast and have no compassion on the child she has borne? Though she may forget, I will not forget you!" Hallelujah, we are never forgotten! Even when our very own mother might not remember us, God can be depended on . . . How wonderful, how beautiful, how comforting to know we have a God who is always near to console and cheer, just when we need him most.

—Thelma Wells

[a] *12* Dead Sea Scrolls; Masoretic Text *Sinim*

Extreme Measures

ISA 49:26

If God is love, why does he promise to accomplish such terrible deeds? The answer is quite distressing in its simplicity: It seems to be the only way he can get everyone's attention. If the nations squander God's goodness, perhaps they'll respect his fury. Like a wild lover, the Lord proves his passion by taking extreme measures. His flesh-and-blood approach proves, conclusively, that he is the Mighty One. The wicked can't escape his wrath, nor can the chosen ones cast off his love.

"See, I will beckon to the Gentiles,
I will lift up my banner[q] to the peoples;
they will bring your sons in their arms
and carry your daughters on their shoulders.[r]
23 Kings[s] will be your foster fathers,
and their queens your nursing mothers.[t]
They will bow down before you with their faces to the ground;
they will lick the dust[u] at your feet.
Then you will know that I am the LORD;[v]
those who hope in me will not be disappointed."
24 Can plunder be taken from warriors,[w]
or captives rescued from the fierce[a]?

25 But this is what the LORD says:

"Yes, captives[x] will be taken from warriors,[y]
and plunder retrieved from the fierce;
I will contend with those who contend with you,
and your children I will save.[z]
26 I will make your oppressors[a] eat[b] their own flesh;
they will be drunk on their own blood,[c] as with wine.
Then all mankind will know[d]
that I, the LORD, am your Savior,
your Redeemer, the Mighty One of Jacob."

Israel's Sin and the Servant's Obedience

50 This is what the LORD says:

"Where is your mother's certificate of divorce[e]
with which I sent her away?
Or to which of my creditors
did I sell[f] you?
Because of your sins you were sold;[g]
because of your transgressions your mother was sent away.
2 When I came, why was there no one?
When I called, why was there no one to answer?[h]
Was my arm too short[i] to ransom you?
Do I lack the strength[j] to rescue you?
By a mere rebuke I dry up the sea,[k]
I turn rivers into a desert;
their fish rot for lack of water
and die of thirst.
3 I clothe the sky with darkness
and make sackcloth[l] its covering."

49:22 [q]Isa 11:10 [r]Isa 60:4
49:23 [s]Isa 60:3, 10-11 [t]Isa 60:16 [u]Ps 72:9 [v]Mic 7:17
49:24 [w]Mt 12:29; Lk 11:21
49:25 [x]Isa 14:2 [y]Jer 50:33-34 [z]Isa 25:9; 35:4
49:26 [a]Isa 9:4 [b]Isa 9:20 [c]Rev 16:6 [d]Eze 39:7
50:1 [e]Dt 24:1; Jer 3:8; Hos 2:2 [f]Ne 5:5; Mt 18:25 [g]Dt 32:30; Isa 52:3
50:2 [h]Isa 41:28 [i]Nu 11:23; Isa 59:1 [j]Ge 18:14 [k]Ex 14:22; Jos 3:16
50:3 [l]Rev 6:12

[a] *24* Dead Sea Scrolls, Vulgate and Syriac (see also Septuagint and verse 25); Masoretic Text *righteous*

4 The Sovereign LORD has given me an
instructed tongue,[m]
to know the word that sustains the
weary.[n]
He wakens me morning by morning,[o]
wakens my ear to listen like one
being taught.
5 The Sovereign LORD has opened my
ears,[p]
and I have not been rebellious;[q]
I have not drawn back.
6 I offered my back to those who beat[r]
me,
my cheeks to those who pulled out
my beard;
I did not hide my face
from mocking and spitting.[s]
7 Because the Sovereign LORD helps[t] me,
I will not be disgraced.
Therefore have I set my face like flint,[u]
and I know I will not be put to shame.
8 He who vindicates me is near.
Who then will bring charges against
me?[v]
Let us face each other![w]
Who is my accuser?
Let him confront me!
9 It is the Sovereign LORD who helps[x] me.
Who is he that will condemn me?
They will all wear out like a garment;
the moths[y] will eat them up.

10 Who among you fears the LORD
and obeys the word of his servant?[z]
Let him who walks in the dark,
who has no light,
trust[a] in the name of the LORD
and rely on his God.
11 But now, all you who light fires
and provide yourselves with flaming
torches,[b]
go, walk in the light of your fires[c]
and of the torches you have set
ablaze.
This is what you shall receive from my
hand:
You will lie down in torment.[d]

Everlasting Salvation for Zion

51 "Listen[e] to me, you who pursue
righteousness[f]
and who seek the LORD:
Look to the rock from which you were
cut
and to the quarry from which you
were hewn;
2 look to Abraham,[g] your father,
and to Sarah, who gave you birth.
When I called him he was but one,
and I blessed him and made him
many.[h]

50:4 [m]Ex 4:12 [n]Mt 11:28 [o]Ps 5:3; 119:147; 143:8
50:5 [p]Isa 35:5 [q]Mt 26:39; Jn 8:29; 14:31; 15:10; Ac 26:19; Heb 5:8
50:6 [r]Isa 53:5; Mt 27:30; Mk 14:65; 15:19; Lk 22:63 [s]La 3:30; Mt 26:67
50:7 [t]Isa 42:1 [u]Eze 3:8-9
50:8 [v]Isa 43:26; Ro 8:32-34 [w]Isa 41:1
50:9 [x]Isa 41:10 [y]Job 13:28; Isa 51:8
50:10 [z]Isa 49:3 [a]Isa 26:4
50:11 [b]Pr 26:18 [c]Jas 3:6 [d]Isa 65:13-15
51:1 [e]Isa 46:3 [f]ver 7; Ps 94:15; Ro 9:30-31
51:2 [g]Isa 29:22; Ro 4:16; Heb 11:11 [h]Ge 12:2

Mocking the Messiah

ISA 50:6

This abuse—beating, mocking, spitting—looks ahead to the Messiah's treatment before he is crucified. Matthew records, "They stripped [Jesus] and put a scarlet robe on him, and then twisted together a crown of thorns and set it on his head. They put a staff in his right hand and knelt in front of him and *mocked him*. 'Hail, king of the Jews,' they said. *They spit on him,* and took the staff and *struck him on the head again and again*" (Mt 27:28-30; emphasis added). The Savior doesn't merely put up with this treatment, he obediently and willingly *offers* himself (Isa 50:6). His obedience is in stark contrast to the rebellion of Israel.

Everlasting Salvation

ISA 51:6

Everlasting salvation is a revolutionary concept to the Israelites. Old Testament Jewish law required that people repeatedly make atonement for their sins. Only a priest could offer a lamb's blood to request forgiveness for the people; they couldn't obtain it for themselves. But when Jesus shed his blood for humanity, he personally and finally atoned for sin and provided salvation for those who believe in him. Individually, we can confess our sin and accept this gift (1Jn 1:9). Christ's salvation lasts beyond the confines of time, beyond a world worn out. It's a guarantee for eternity.

3 The LORD will surely comfort[i] Zion
and will look with compassion on all her ruins;[j]
he will make her deserts like Eden,[k]
her wastelands like the garden of the LORD.
Joy and gladness[l] will be found in her,
thanksgiving and the sound of singing.

4 "Listen to me, my people;[m]
hear me, my nation:
The law will go out from me;
my justice[n] will become a light to the nations.[o]
5 My righteousness draws near speedily,
my salvation is on the way,[p]
and my arm[q] will bring justice to the nations.
The islands will look to me
and wait in hope for my arm.
6 Lift up your eyes to the heavens,
look at the earth beneath;
the heavens will vanish like smoke,[r]
the earth will wear out like a garment[s]
and its inhabitants die like flies.
But my salvation will last forever,
my righteousness will never fail.
7 "Hear me, you who know what is right,[t]
you people who have my law in your hearts:[u]
Do not fear the reproach of men
or be terrified by their insults.[v]
8 For the moth will eat them up like a garment;[w]
the worm will devour them like wool.
But my righteousness will last forever,[x]
my salvation through all generations."

9 Awake, awake! Clothe yourself with strength,[y]
O arm of the LORD;
awake, as in days gone by,
as in generations of old.[z]
Was it not you who cut Rahab to pieces,
who pierced that monster[a] through?
10 Was it not you who dried up the sea,[b]
the waters of the great deep,
who made a road in the depths of the sea
so that the redeemed might cross over?
11 The ransomed[c] of the LORD will return.
They will enter Zion with singing;
everlasting joy will crown their heads.
Gladness and joy[d] will overtake them,
and sorrow and sighing will flee away.[e]
12 "I, even I, am he who comforts[f] you.
Who are you that you fear mortal men,[g]
the sons of men, who are but grass,[h]
13 that you forget[i] the LORD your Maker,[j]
who stretched out the heavens[k]

51:3 [i]Isa 40:1 [j]Isa 52:9 [k]Ge 2:8 [l]Isa 25:9; 66:10
51:4 [m]Ps 50:7 [n]Isa 2:4 [o]Isa 42:4,6
51:5 [p]Isa 46:13 [q]Isa 40:10; 63:1,5
51:6 [r]Mt 24:35; 2Pe 3:10 [s]Ps 102:25-26
51:7 [t]ver 1 [u]Ps 37:31 [v]Mt 5:11; Ac 5:41
51:8 [w]Isa 50:9 [x]ver 6
51:9 [y]Isa 52:1 [z]Dt 4:34 [a]Ps 74:13
51:10 [b]Ex 14:22
51:11 [c]Isa 35:9 [d]Jer 33:11 [e]Rev 7:17
51:12 [f]2Co 1:4 [g]Ps 118:6; Isa 2:22 [h]Isa 40:6-7; 1Pe 1:24
51:13 [i]Isa 17:10 [j]Isa 45:11 [k]Ps 104:2; Isa 48:13

51:13 [l]Isa 7:4

and laid the foundations of the earth,
that you live in constant terror[l] every day
because of the wrath of the oppressor,
who is bent on destruction?
For where is the wrath of the oppressor?
14 The cowering prisoners will soon be set free;
they will not die in their dungeon,
nor will they lack bread.[m]
15 For I am the LORD your God,
who churns up the sea[n] so that its waves roar—
the LORD Almighty is his name.
16 I have put my words in your mouth[o]
and covered you with the shadow of my hand[p]—
I who set the heavens in place,
who laid the foundations of the earth,
and who say to Zion, 'You are my people.' "

51:14 [m]Isa 49:10
51:15 [n]Jer 31:35
51:16 [o]Dt 18:18; Isa 59:21 [p]Ex 33:22

The Cup of the LORD*'s Wrath*

17 Awake, awake![q]
Rise up, O Jerusalem,
you who have drunk from the hand of the LORD
the cup of his wrath,[r]
you who have drained to its dregs
the goblet that makes men stagger.[s]
18 Of all the sons[t] she bore
there was none to guide her;[u]
of all the sons she reared
there was none to take her by the hand.
19 These double calamities[v] have come upon you—
who can comfort you?—
ruin and destruction, famine[w] and sword—
who can[a] console you?
20 Your sons have fainted;
they lie at the head of every street,[x]
like antelope caught in a net.
They are filled with the wrath of the LORD
and the rebuke of your God.

21 Therefore hear this, you afflicted one,
made drunk,[y] but not with wine.
22 This is what your Sovereign LORD says,
your God, who defends[z] his people:
"See, I have taken out of your hand
the cup[a] that made you stagger;
from that cup, the goblet of my wrath,
you will never drink again.
23 I will put it into the hands of your tormentors,[b]
who said to you,

51:17 [q]Isa 52:1 [r]Job 21:20; Rev 14:10; 16:19 [s]Ps 60:3
51:18 [t]Ps 88:18 [u]Isa 49:21
51:19 [v]Isa 47:9 [w]Isa 14:30
51:20 [x]Isa 5:25; Jer 14:16
51:21 [y]ver 17; Isa 29:9
51:22 [z]Isa 49:25 [a]ver 17
51:23 [b]Isa 49:26; Jer 25:15-17, 26,28; 49:12

[a] *19* Dead Sea Scrolls, Septuagint, Vulgate and Syriac; Masoretic Text / *how can I*

Cup of Wrath

ISA 51:17,22

God likens his anger to pouring out a cup of wine that causes those who drink it to stagger (see the note on Jer 25:15–16, *page* 1273). He usually keeps his wrath contained, but now it will flow uncontrollably, destroying all in its path. Yet God says that for his people, those who truly follow him (Isa 51:22), he'll relent and remove the cup of wrath and serve it to their "tormentors" (Isa 51:23). God's redemption is as radical as his wrath.

Joyful Watchmen

ISA 52:8

In the Old Testament, watchtowers fulfilled two purposes. In earliest times they stood in the middle of sheep pastures or vineyards, and watchmen scanned the horizon for predators and thieves. Later watchtowers served as a defense for a city, with watchmen keeping guard against enemy attacks. Watchmen in capital cities sent word to the king about any who approached the city walls. In this metaphor the watchmen have no reason to fear; they rejoice because they see the Lord returning to Zion.

'Fall prostrate[c] that we may walk[d]
over you.'
And you made your back like the ground,
like a street to be walked over."

52 Awake, awake,[e] O Zion,
clothe yourself with strength.[f]
Put on your garments of splendor,[g]
O Jerusalem, the holy city.[h]
The uncircumcised and defiled
will not enter you again.[i]
2 Shake off your dust;[j]
rise up, sit enthroned, O Jerusalem.
Free yourself from the chains on your
neck,
O captive Daughter of Zion.

3 For this is what the LORD says:

"You were sold for nothing,[k]
and without money[l] you will be
redeemed."

4 For this is what the Sovereign LORD says:

"At first my people went down to Egypt[m]
to live;
lately, Assyria has oppressed them.

5 "And now what do I have here?" declares the
LORD.

"For my people have been taken away
for nothing,
and those who rule them mock,[a]"
declares the LORD.
"And all day long
my name is constantly blasphemed.[n]
6 Therefore my people will know[o] my
name;
therefore in that day they will know
that it is I who foretold it.
Yes, it is I."

7 How beautiful on the mountains
are the feet of those who bring good
news,[p]
who proclaim peace,[q]
who bring good tidings,
who proclaim salvation,
who say to Zion,
"Your God reigns!"[r]
8 Listen! Your watchmen[s] lift up their
voices;
together they shout for joy.
When the LORD returns to Zion,
they will see it with their own eyes.
9 Burst into songs of joy[t] together,
you ruins[u] of Jerusalem,
for the LORD has comforted his people,
he has redeemed Jerusalem.[v]
10 The LORD will lay bare his holy arm

51:23 [c]Zec 12:2 [d]Jos 10:24
52:1 [e]Isa 51:17 [f]Isa 51:9 [g]Ex 28:2,40; Ps 110:3; Zec 3:4 [h]Ne 11:1; Mt 4:5; Rev 21:2 [i]Na 1:15; Rev 21:27
52:2 [j]Isa 29:4
52:3 [k]Ps 44:12 [l]Isa 45:13
52:4 [m]Ge 46:6
52:5 [n]Eze 36:20; Ro 2:24*
52:6 [o]Isa 49:23
52:7 [p]Isa 40:9; Ro 10:15* [q]Na 1:15; Eph 6:15 [r]Ps 93:1
52:8 [s]Isa 62:6
52:9 [t]Ps 98:4 [u]Isa 51:3 [v]Isa 48:20

[a] 5 Dead Sea Scrolls and Vulgate; Masoretic Text *wail*

52:10 [w]Isa 66:18 [x]Ps 98:2-3; Lk 3:6

in the sight of all the nations,[w]
and all the ends of the earth will see
the salvation[x] of our God.

52:11 [y]Isa 48:20 [z]Isa 1:16; 2Co 6:17* [a]2Ti 2:19

11 Depart,[y] depart, go out from there!
Touch no unclean thing![z]
Come out from it and be pure,[a]
you who carry the vessels of the LORD.

52:12 [b]Ex 12:11 [c]Mic 2:13 [d]Ex 14:19

12 But you will not leave in haste[b]
or go in flight;
for the LORD will go before you,[c]
the God of Israel will be your rear
guard.[d]

The Suffering and Glory of the Servant

52:13 [e]Isa 42:1 [f]Isa 57:15; Php 2:9

13 See, my servant[e] will act wisely[a];
he will be raised and lifted up and
highly exalted.[f]

52:15 [g]Ro 15:21*; Eph 3:4-5

14 Just as there were many who were
appalled at him[b]—
his appearance was so disfigured
beyond that of any man
and his form marred beyond human
likeness—
15 so will he sprinkle many nations,[c]
and kings will shut their mouths
because of him.
For what they were not told, they will
see,
and what they have not heard, they
will understand.[g]

53:1 [h]Ro 10:16* [i]Jn 12:38*

53 Who has believed our message[h]
and to whom has the arm of the LORD
been revealed?[i]
2 He grew up before him like a tender
shoot,
and like a root out of dry ground.
He had no beauty or majesty to attract
us to him,

53:2 [j]Isa 52:14

nothing in his appearance[j] that we
should desire him.
3 He was despised and rejected by men,
a man of sorrows, and familiar with
suffering.[k]

53:3 [k]ver 4,10; Lk 18:31-33 [l]Ps 22:6; Jn 1:10-11

Like one from whom men hide their
faces
he was despised,[l] and we esteemed
him not.

53:4 [m]Mt 8:17* [n]Jn 19:7

4 Surely he took up our infirmities
and carried our sorrows,[m]
yet we considered him stricken by God,[n]
smitten by him, and afflicted.

53:5 [o]Ro 4:25; 1Co 15:3; Heb 9:28 [p]1Pe 2:24-25

5 But he was pierced for our
transgressions,[o]
he was crushed for our iniquities;
the punishment that brought us peace
was upon him,
and by his wounds we are healed.[p]

[a] 13 Or *will prosper* [b] 14 Hebrew *you* [c] 15 Hebrew; Septuagint *so will many nations marvel at him*

Front and Back

ISA 52:11-12

The migration described in these verses resembles the first exodus when the cloud led them by day and the pillar of fire by night (Ex 13:21). However, this time the people begin the journey joyfully and purposefully, rather than fearfully and frantically. The Lord acts as both their leader and their rear guard, ensuring safety both before and behind them.

When the omnipresent God leads, he securely hems us in, moving both before and behind us. Isaiah presents comforting descriptions of (1) how the Lord leads: "I will lead the blind by ways they have not known, along unfamiliar paths I will guide them; I will turn the darkness into light before them and make the rough places smooth. These are the things I will do; I will not forsake them" (Isa 42:16); and (2) how the Lord follows: "Whether you turn to the right or to the left, your ears will hear a voice behind you, saying, 'This is the way; walk in it' " (Isa 30:21).

Wandering Sheep

ISA 53:6

The Bible often pictures human beings as sheep. *And the analogy is an accurate one. We're natural wanderers. We would rather go our own way—even if it leads to destruction. But the beauty of the picture is that as sheep we have a shepherd, a leader who is wholly loving, compassionate and willing to suffer on our behalf. Just as a shepherd will put himself in danger in order to fight off the wild beasts that threaten his flock, so our shepherd was willingly "oppressed and afflicted"* (Isa 53:7) *so that we might be saved. Jesus himself used the sheep/shepherd analogy when he told his disciples,* "I am the good shepherd. The good shepherd lays down his life for the sheep" (Jn 10:11).

6 We all, like sheep, have gone astray,
each of us has turned to his own way;
and the LORD has laid on him
the iniquity of us all.
7 He was oppressed and afflicted,
yet he did not open his mouth;[q]
he was led like a lamb to the slaughter,
and as a sheep before her shearers is silent,
so he did not open his mouth.
8 By oppression[a] and judgment he was taken away.
And who can speak of his descendants?
For he was cut off from the land of the living;[r]
for the transgression[s] of my people he was stricken.[b]
9 He was assigned a grave with the wicked,
and with the rich[t] in his death,
though he had done no violence,[u]
nor was any deceit in his mouth.[v]
10 Yet it was the LORD's will[w] to crush[x] him and cause him to suffer,[y]
and though the LORD makes[c] his life a guilt offering,
he will see his offspring[z] and prolong his days,
and the will of the LORD will prosper in his hand.
11 After the suffering[a] of his soul,
he will see the light ⌞of life⌟[d] and be satisfied[e];
by his knowledge[f] my righteous servant will justify[b] many,
and he will bear their iniquities.
12 Therefore I will give him a portion among the great,[g][c]
and he will divide the spoils with the strong,[h]
because he poured out his life unto death,[d]
and was numbered with the transgressors.[e]
For he bore the sin of many,
and made intercession for the transgressors.

53:7 [q]Mk 14:61
53:8 [r]Da 9:26; Ac 8:32-33* [s]ver 12
53:9 [t]Mt 27:57-60 [u]Isa 42:1-3 [v]1Pe 2:22*
53:10 [w]Isa 46:10 [x]ver 5 [y]ver 3 [z]Ps 22:30
53:11 [a]Jn 10:14-18 [b]Ro 5:18-19
53:12 [c]Php 2:9 [d]Mt 26:28, 38,39,42 [e]Mk 15:27*; Lk 22:37*; 23:32

The Future Glory of Zion

54 "Sing, O barren woman,
you who never bore a child;

[a] 8 Or *From arrest* [b] 8 Or *away. / Yet who of his generation considered / that he was cut off from the land of the living / for the transgression of my people, / to whom the blow was due?* [c] 10 Hebrew *though you make* [d] 11 Dead Sea Scrolls (see also Septuagint); Masoretic Text does not have *the light ⌞of life⌟.* [e] 11 Or (with Masoretic Text) [11] *He will see the result of the suffering of his soul / and be satisfied* [f] 11 Or *by knowledge of him* [g] 12 Or *many* [h] 12 Or *numerous*

burst into song, shout for joy,
you who were never in labor;

54:1 [f]Isa 49:20 [g]1Sa 2:5; Gal 4:27*

because more are the children[f] of the
desolate woman
than of her who has a husband,[g]"
says the LORD.

54:2 [h]Isa 49:19-20 [i]Ex 35:18; 39:40

2 "Enlarge the place of your tent,[h]
stretch your tent curtains wide,
do not hold back;
lengthen your cords,
strengthen your stakes.[i]
3 For you will spread out to the right and
to the left;
your descendants will dispossess
nations

54:3 [j]Isa 49:19

and settle in their desolate[j] cities.

4 "Do not be afraid; you will not suffer
shame.
Do not fear disgrace; you will not be
humiliated.
You will forget the shame of your youth

54:4 [k]Isa 51:7

and remember no more the reproach[k]
of your widowhood.

54:5 [l]Jer 3:14 [m]Isa 48:17 [n]Isa 6:3

5 For your Maker is your husband[l]—
the LORD Almighty is his name—
the Holy One of Israel is your
Redeemer;[m]
he is called the God of all the earth.[n]

54:6 [o]Isa 49:14-21 [p]Isa 50:1-2; 62:4,12

6 The LORD will call you back[o]
as if you were a wife deserted[p] and
distressed in spirit—
a wife who married young,
only to be rejected," says your God.

54:7 [q]Isa 26:20 [r]Isa 49:18

7 "For a brief moment[q] I abandoned you,
but with deep compassion I will bring
you back.[r]

54:8 [s]Isa 60:10 [t]ver 10

8 In a surge of anger[s]
I hid my face from you for a moment,
but with everlasting kindness[t]
I will have compassion on you,"
says the LORD your Redeemer.

9 "To me this is like the days of Noah,
when I swore that the waters of Noah
would never again cover the

54:9 [u]Ge 8:21 [v]Isa 12:1

earth.[u]
So now I have sworn not to be angry[v]
with you,
never to rebuke you again.

54:10 [w]Ps 46:2 [x]Isa 51:6 [y]Ps 89:34 [z]ver 8

10 Though the mountains be shaken[w]
and the hills be removed,
yet my unfailing love for you will not be
shaken[x]
nor my covenant[y] of peace be
removed,"
says the LORD, who has compassion[z]
on you.

54:11 [a]Isa 14:32 [b]Isa 28:2; 29:6 [c]Isa 51:19

11 "O afflicted[a] city, lashed by storms[b] and
not comforted,[c]

Like a Barren Woman

ISA 54:1-6

In the culture of Isaiah's day, an unmarried woman or a barren wife sat at the bottom of the social hierarchy. To be husbandless or childless disgraced a woman and her family, and a husband could divorce his wife if she was infertile. Even a widow who once bore children could become an outcast, with people suggesting that her widowed state was a result of sin. For women, success and acceptance equaled a husband and lots of children.

Isaiah compares God's people to a barren woman, but he promises they'll not always be ashamed. For a time Jerusalem will be desolate, but later it will be populated and filled with rich and powerful resources. God fulfills this prophecy when the Jews taken captive by the Babylonians return to Jerusalem under the leadership of Ezra and Nehemiah.

Real Riches

ISA 55:2

Somebody once asked a multi-millionaire, "How much money is enough?" He replied, "Always a little more than what I have." The writer of Ecclesiastes gained extraordinary wealth to accomplish great projects and claimed it was "meaningless, a chasing after the wind" (Ecc 2:11). If we scramble after riches, we can wind up feeling empty, especially if we've left our souls unfed.

God says "the richest of fare" (Isa 55:2) can be found in him. Only in him will we find deep satisfaction for our souls. If we "delight" in his Word (Ps 119:16), remain in him (Jn 15:4), "seek first his kingdom and his righteousness," then "all these things" will be ours as well (Mt 6:33). When we seek God first, provision, and even prosperity, can follow in a way that satisfies, rather than saps, us.

I will build you with stones of
turquoise,[a][d]
your foundations[e] with sapphires.[b]
12 I will make your battlements of rubies,
your gates of sparkling jewels,
and all your walls of precious stones.
13 All your sons will be taught by the
LORD,[f]
and great will be your children's
peace.[g]
14 In righteousness you will be
established:
Tyranny[h] will be far from you;
you will have nothing to fear.
Terror will be far removed;
it will not come near you.
15 If anyone does attack you, it will not be
my doing;
whoever attacks you will surrender[i]
to you.

16 "See, it is I who created the blacksmith
who fans the coals into flame
and forges a weapon fit for its work.
And it is I who have created the
destroyer to work havoc;
17 no weapon forged against you will
prevail,[j]
and you will refute[k] every tongue that
accuses you.
This is the heritage of the servants of
the LORD,
and this is their vindication from me,"
declares the LORD.

Invitation to the Thirsty

55 "Come, all you who are thirsty,[l]
come to the waters;
and you who have no money,
come, buy[m] and eat!
Come, buy wine and milk[n]
without money and without cost.[o]
2 Why spend money on what is not bread,
and your labor on what does not
satisfy?[p]
Listen, listen to me, and eat what is
good,[q]
and your soul will delight in the
richest of fare.
3 Give ear and come to me;
hear me, that your soul may live.[r]
I will make an everlasting covenant[s]
with you,
my faithful love[t] promised to David.[u]
4 See, I have made him a witness to the
peoples,
a leader and commander[v] of the
peoples.

54:11 [d]1Ch 29:2; Rev 21:18 [e]Isa 28:16; Rev 21:19-20
54:13 [f]Jn 6:45* [g]Isa 48:18
54:14 [h]Isa 9:4
54:15 [i]Isa 41:11-16
54:17 [j]Isa 29:8 [k]Isa 45:24-25
55:1 [l]Jn 4:14; 7:37 [m]La 5:4; Mt 13:44; Rev 3:18 [n]SS 5:1 [o]Hos 14:4; Mt 10:8; Rev 21:6
55:2 [p]Ps 22:26; Ecc 6:2; Hos 8:7 [q]Isa 1:19
55:3 [r]Lev 18:5; Ro 10:5 [s]Isa 61:8 [t]Isa 54:8 [u]Ac 13:34*
55:4 [v]Jer 30:9; Eze 34:23-24

[a] *11* The meaning of the Hebrew for this word is uncertain.
[b] *11* Or *lapis lazuli*

55:5 [w]Isa 49:6 [x]Isa 60:9

[5]Surely you will summon nations[w] you
know not,
and nations that do not know you will
hasten to you,
because of the LORD your God,
the Holy One of Israel,
for he has endowed you with
splendor."[x]

55:6 [y]Ps 32:6; Isa 49:8; 2Co 6:1-2 [z]Isa 65:24

[6]Seek the LORD while he may be found;[y]
call[z] on him while he is near.
[7]Let the wicked forsake his way
and the evil man his thoughts.[a]
Let him turn[b] to the LORD, and he will
have mercy[c] on him,
and to our God, for he will freely
pardon.[d]

55:7 [a]Isa 32:7; 59:7 [b]Isa 44:22 [c]Isa 54:10 [d]Isa 1:18; 40:2

[8]"For my thoughts are not your thoughts,
neither are your ways my ways,"[e]
declares the LORD.

55:8 [e]Isa 53:6

[9]"As the heavens are higher than the
earth,[f]
so are my ways higher than your
ways
and my thoughts than your thoughts.

55:9 [f]Ps 103:11

[10]As the rain[g] and the snow
come down from heaven,
and do not return to it
without watering the earth
and making it bud and flourish,
so that it yields seed for the sower and
bread for the eater,[h]
[11]so is my word that goes out from my
mouth:
It will not return to me empty,[i]
but will accomplish what I desire
and achieve the purpose[j] for which I
sent it.

55:10 [g]Isa 30:23 [h]2Co 9:10

55:11 [i]Isa 45:23 [j]Isa 44:26

[12]You will go out in joy
and be led forth in peace;[k]
the mountains and hills
will burst into song before you,
and all the trees[l] of the field
will clap their hands.[m]
[13]Instead of the thornbush will grow the
pine tree,
and instead of briers[n] the myrtle[o] will
grow.
This will be for the LORD's renown,[p]
for an everlasting sign,
which will not be destroyed."

55:12 [k]Isa 54:10,13 [l]1Ch 16:33 [m]Ps 98:8

55:13 [n]Isa 5:6 [o]Isa 41:19 [p]Isa 63:12

Salvation for Others

56 This is what the LORD says:

"Maintain justice[q]
and do what is right,
for my salvation[r] is close at hand
and my righteousness will soon be
revealed.
[2]Blessed[s] is the man who does this,

56:1 [q]Isa 1:17 [r]Ps 85:9

56:2 [s]Ps 119:2

The God Above

ISA 55:9

While God dwells far above us, he's not inaccessible to humans. Elsewhere in the pages of Isaiah, the Lord declares that his arm is long and ready to save (Isa 50:2), that he guides (Isa 42:6), that he loves unfailingly (Isa 43:4; 54:10), and that he acts on behalf of those who wait for him (Isa 64:4). This isn't a picture of a God who distances himself from his people. The evidence points to a Father who hovers over his children, a God who lives in a "high and holy place," but who also lives with those who are "contrite and lowly in spirit" (Isa 57:15).

So what does Isaiah 55:9 mean? Although God reveals himself to us, we can't understand everything about him or his ways. After all, he is the master of the universe, and we are his subjects. Yet because of his great love and care for us, we can trust him even when we don't understand him.

House of Prayer

ISA 56:6–7

Isaiah in this chapter gives consolation to two groups of people formerly excluded from worship. Foreigners (Ex 12:43) and eunuchs (Dt 23:1) were forbidden to join the people when they assembled to worship. However, in this chapter, their position of exclusion is now changed to one of inclusion. To eunuchs (Isa 56:4) and foreigners (Isa 56:6) who obey God's laws and follow him contritely and wholeheartedly, God promises joy and acceptance (Isa 56:7). The "holy mountain" (Isa 56:7) refers to Mount Zion, the location of the Jewish temple in Jerusalem. In the last days God's house won't shelter just the Jews, but it will be a place for people from all nations (Isa 2:2–4).

Today our places of worship can also be houses of prayer for people of all nationalities, races and needs. Together we look forward to the day when worshipers of all races, languages and nationalities will gather to worship the Lamb in heaven (Rev 7:9).

the man who holds it fast,
who keeps the Sabbath[t] without
desecrating it,
and keeps his hand from doing any
evil."

[3] Let no foreigner who has bound himself
to the LORD say,
"The LORD will surely exclude me
from his people."
And let not any eunuch[u] complain,
"I am only a dry tree."

[4] For this is what the LORD says:

"To the eunuchs who keep my Sabbaths,
who choose what pleases me
and hold fast to my covenant—
[5] to them I will give within my temple
and its walls[v]
a memorial and a name
better than sons and daughters;
I will give them an everlasting name
that will not be cut off.[w]
[6] And foreigners who bind themselves to
the LORD
to serve[x] him,
to love the name of the LORD,
and to worship him,
all who keep the Sabbath[y] without
desecrating it
and who hold fast to my covenant—
[7] these I will bring to my holy mountain[z]
and give them joy in my house of
prayer.
Their burnt offerings and sacrifices[a]
will be accepted on my altar;
for my house will be called
a house of prayer for all nations.[b]"[c]
[8] The Sovereign LORD declares—
he who gathers the exiles of Israel:
"I will gather[d] still others to them
besides those already gathered."

God's Accusation Against the Wicked

[9] Come, all you beasts of the field,[e]
come and devour, all you beasts of the
forest!
[10] Israel's watchmen[f] are blind,
they all lack knowledge;
they are all mute dogs,
they cannot bark;
they lie around and dream,
they love to sleep.[g]
[11] They are dogs with mighty appetites;
they never have enough.
They are shepherds[h] who lack
understanding;[i]
they all turn to their own way,
each seeks his own gain.[j]
[12] "Come," each one cries, "let me get
wine!

56:2 [t]Ex 20:8,10; Isa 58:13
56:3 [u]Jer 38:7 *fn*; Ac 8:27
56:5 [v]Isa 26:1; 60:18 [w]Isa 48:19; 55:13
56:6 [x]Isa 60:7,10; 61:5 [y]ver 2,4
56:7 [z]Isa 2:2 [a]Ro 12:1; Heb 13:15 [b]Mt 21:13*; Lk 19:46* [c]Mk 11:17*
56:8 [d]Isa 11:12; 60:3-11; Jn 10:16
56:9 [e]Isa 18:6; Jer 12:9
56:10 [f]Eze 3:17 [g]Na 3:18
56:11 [h]Eze 34:2 [i]Isa 1:3 [j]Isa 57:17; Eze 13:19; Mic 3:11

Let us drink our fill of beer!
And tomorrow will be like today,
or even far better."[k]

57

The righteous perish,[l]
and no one ponders it in his heart;[m]
devout men are taken away,
and no one understands
that the righteous are taken away
to be spared from evil.[n]
2 Those who walk uprightly[o]
enter into peace;
they find rest as they lie in death.

3 "But you—come here, you sons of a sorceress,
you offspring of adulterers[p] and prostitutes![q]
4 Whom are you mocking?
At whom do you sneer
and stick out your tongue?
Are you not a brood of rebels,
the offspring of liars?
5 You burn with lust among the oaks
and under every spreading tree;[r]
you sacrifice your children[s] in the ravines
and under the overhanging crags.
6 ⌊The idols⌋[t] among the smooth stones of the ravines are your portion;
they, they are your lot.
Yes, to them you have poured out drink offerings[u]
and offered grain offerings.
In the light of these things, should I relent?[v]
7 You have made your bed on a high and lofty hill;[w]
there you went up to offer your sacrifices.
8 Behind your doors and your doorposts
you have put your pagan symbols.
Forsaking me, you uncovered your bed,
you climbed into it and opened it wide;
you made a pact with those whose beds you love,[x]
and you looked on their nakedness.[y]
9 You went to Molech[a] with olive oil
and increased your perfumes.
You sent your ambassadors[b][z] far away;
you descended to the grave[c] itself!
10 You were wearied by all your ways,
but you would not say, 'It is hopeless.'[a]
You found renewal of your strength,
and so you did not faint.

11 "Whom have you so dreaded and feared[b]
that you have been false to me,
and have neither remembered[c] me
nor pondered this in your hearts?

56:12 [k]Ps 10:6; Lk 12:18-19
57:1 [l]Ps 12:1 [m]Isa 42:25 [n]2Ki 22:20
57:2 [o]Isa 26:7
57:3 [p]Mt 16:4 [q]Isa 1:21
57:5 [r]2Ki 16:4 [s]Lev 18:21; Ps 106:37-38; Eze 16:20
57:6 [t]Jer 3:9 [u]Jer 7:18 [v]Jer 5:9,29; 9:9
57:7 [w]Jer 3:6; Eze 16:16
57:8 [x]Eze 16:26; 23:7 [y]Eze 23:18
57:9 [z]Eze 23:16, 40
57:10 [a]Jer 2:25; 18:12
57:11 [b]Pr 29:25 [c]Jer 2:32; 3:21

Peace in Death

ISA 57:1-2

Scripture honors the sanctity of life, and only God holds the right to begin or end a person's time on earth. So ***these verses aren't a justification for suicide, euthanasia or mercy killing.*** **However, they do underscore that the peace of our afterlife with God will far exceed the peace of our days on earth. Death releases believers from evil, pain and suffering. We can look forward to rest and peace in God's arms.**

[a] 9 Or *to the king* [b] 9 Or *idols* [c] 9 Hebrew *Sheol*

God's Home

ISA 57:15

Both the Old and New Testaments describe God as living in heaven, but also dwelling with or within his people. Actually both of these abodes are possible because God is omnipresent. In that sense he dwells everywhere. This diversity can comfort us, for God lives "above" and controls the universe, but also "below" with the humble of heart.

The psalmist wonderfully expresses this omnipresence of God when he says, "Where can I go from your Spirit? Where can I flee from your presence? If I go up to the heavens, you are there; if I make my bed in the depths, you are there. If I rise on the wings of the dawn, if I settle on the far side of the sea, even there your hand will guide me, your right hand will hold me fast" (Ps 139:7–10).

Is it not because I have long been silent[d]
that you do not fear me?
12 I will expose your righteousness and
your works,[e]
and they will not benefit you.
13 When you cry out[f] for help,
let your collection ⌊of idols⌋ save you!
The wind will carry all of them off,
a mere breath will blow them away.
But the man who makes me his refuge
will inherit the land[g]
and possess my holy mountain."[h]

Comfort for the Contrite

14 And it will be said:

"Build up, build up, prepare the road!
Remove the obstacles out of the way
of my people."[i]
15 For this is what the high and lofty[j] One
says—
he who lives forever,[k] whose name is
holy:
"I live in a high and holy place,
but also with him who is contrite[l] and
lowly in spirit,[m]
to revive the spirit of the lowly
and to revive the heart of the
contrite.[n]
16 I will not accuse forever,
nor will I always be angry,[o]
for then the spirit of man would grow
faint before me—
the breath of man that I have created.
17 I was enraged by his sinful greed;[p]
I punished him, and hid my face in
anger,
yet he kept on in his willful ways.[q]
18 I have seen his ways, but I will heal[r]
him;
I will guide him and restore comfort[s]
to him,
19 creating praise on the lips[t] of the
mourners in Israel.
Peace, peace,[u] to those far and near,"[v]
says the LORD. "And I will heal them."
20 But the wicked[w] are like the tossing sea,
which cannot rest,
whose waves cast up mire and mud.
21 "There is no peace,"[x] says my God, "for
the wicked."[y]

True Fasting

58 "Shout it aloud,[z] do not hold back.
Raise your voice like a trumpet.
Declare to my people their rebellion[a]
and to the house of Jacob their sins.
2 For day after day they seek[b] me out;
they seem eager to know my ways,
as if they were a nation that does what
is right

57:11 [d]Ps 50:21
57:12 [e]Isa 29:15; Mic 3:2-4,8
57:13 [f]Jer 22:20; 30:15 [g]Ps 37:9 [h]Isa 65:9-11
57:14 [i]Isa 62:10; Jer 18:15
57:15 [j]Isa 52:13 [k]Dt 33:27 [l]Ps 147:3 [m]Ps 34:18; 51:17; Isa 66:2 [n]Isa 61:1
57:16 [o]Ps 85:5; 103:9; Mic 7:18
57:17 [p]Isa 56:11 [q]Isa 1:4
57:18 [r]Isa 30:26 [s]Isa 61:1-3
57:19 [t]Isa 6:7; Heb 13:15 [u]Eph 2:17 [v]Ac 2:39
57:20 [w]Job 18:5-21
57:21 [x]Isa 59:8 [y]Isa 48:22
58:1 [z]Isa 40:6 [a]Isa 48:8
58:2 [b]Isa 48:1; Tit 1:16; Jas 4:8

and has not forsaken the commands
of its God.
They ask me for just decisions
58:2 [c]Isa 29:13
and seem eager for God to come near[c]
them.
58:3 [d]Lev 16:29 [e]Mal 3:14 [f]Isa 22:13; Zec 7:5-6
[3]'Why have we fasted,'[d] they say,
'and you have not seen it?
Why have we humbled ourselves,
and you have not noticed?'[e]

"Yet on the day of your fasting, you do
as you please[f]
and exploit all your workers.
[4]Your fasting ends in quarreling and
58:4 [g]1Ki 21:9-13; Isa 59:6 [h]Isa 59:2
strife,[g]
and in striking each other with
wicked fists.
You cannot fast as you do today
and expect your voice to be heard[h] on
high.
58:5 [i]Zec 7:5 [j]1Ki 21:27 [k]Job 2:8
[5]Is this the kind of fast[i] I have chosen,
only a day for a man to humble[j]
himself?
Is it only for bowing one's head like a
reed
and for lying on sackcloth and ashes?[k]
Is that what you call a fast,
a day acceptable to the LORD?
[6]"Is not this the kind of fasting I have
chosen:
58:6 [l]Ne 5:10-11 [m]Jer 34:9
to loose the chains of injustice[l]
and untie the cords of the yoke,
to set the oppressed[m] free
and break every yoke?
[7]Is it not to share your food with the
58:7 [n]Eze 18:16; Lk 3:11 [o]Isa 16:4; Heb 13:2 [p]Job 31:19-20; Mt 25:36 [q]Ge 29:14; Lk 10:31-32
hungry[n]
and to provide the poor wanderer
with shelter[o]—
when you see the naked, to clothe[p] him,
and not to turn away from your own
flesh and blood?[q]
[8]Then your light will break forth like the
58:8 [r]Job 11:17 [s]Isa 30:26 [t]Ex 14:19
dawn,[r]
and your healing[s] will quickly appear;
then your righteousness[a] will go before
you,
and the glory of the LORD will be your
rear guard.[t]
58:9 [u]Ps 50:15 [v]Pr 6:13 [w]Ps 12:2; Isa 59:13
[9]Then you will call,[u] and the LORD will
answer;
you will cry for help, and he will say:
Here am I.

"If you do away with the yoke of
oppression,
with the pointing finger[v] and
malicious talk,[w]
[10]and if you spend yourselves in behalf of
the hungry

For when all is said and done, there is only this to say: No matter how sweet the event, how consoling the moment, there is always a deep longing within us that cuts like a knife. It is a yearning that stirs even when (or perhaps most often when) the air is flooded with sunshine and the sky dazzles us with color and light . . . Yet in the midst of our gratitude for the beauty of created things, we know in our very bones that there is something yet to be given. The emptiness is the mark and reminder of God. By this sense of what is not, we know what is and what is yet to be.

—Nicole Johnson

[a] 8 Or *your righteous One*

Keeping the Sabbath

ISA 58:13–14

Hebrew law clearly commands God's people to love him wholeheartedly and to put him first (Dt 6:5). They're to give him the firstfruits of their labor (Ex 23:19), and observing the Sabbath honors God with the firstfruits or best of their week. A day to worship and rest keeps their focus on who and what matters most. At the same time, a day of rest spiritually and physically replenishes their souls and bodies.

These verses are another of the beautiful if-then proposals of God. "If" (Isa 58:13) his people obey his Sabbath laws, setting aside the mundane and the everyday, spending time resting and focusing on him, "then" (Isa 58:14) God will in turn focus on his people and provide the joy and the exhilaration of riding with him on "the heights" (Isa 58:14).

and satisfy the needs of the oppressed,[x]
then your light[y] will rise in the darkness,
and your night will become like the noonday.[z]
11 The LORD will guide you always;
he will satisfy your needs[a] in a sun-scorched land
and will strengthen your frame.
You will be like a well-watered garden,[b]
like a spring[c] whose waters never fail.
12 Your people will rebuild the ancient ruins[d]
and will raise up the age-old foundations;[e]
you will be called Repairer of Broken Walls,
Restorer of Streets with Dwellings.

13 "If you keep your feet from breaking the Sabbath[f]
and from doing as you please on my holy day,
if you call the Sabbath a delight[g]
and the LORD's holy day honorable,
and if you honor it by not going your own way
and not doing as you please or speaking idle words,
14 then you will find your joy[h] in the LORD,
and I will cause you to ride on the heights[i] of the land
and to feast on the inheritance of your father Jacob."
The mouth of the LORD has spoken.[j]

Sin, Confession and Redemption

59 Surely the arm of the LORD is not too short[k] to save,
nor his ear too dull to hear.[l]
2 But your iniquities have separated you from your God;
your sins have hidden his face from you,
so that he will not hear.[m]
3 For your hands are stained with blood,[n]
your fingers with guilt.
Your lips have spoken lies,
and your tongue mutters wicked things.
4 No one calls for justice;
no one pleads his case with integrity.
They rely on empty arguments and speak lies;
they conceive trouble and give birth to evil.[o]
5 They hatch the eggs of vipers
and spin a spider's web.[p]
Whoever eats their eggs will die,
and when one is broken, an adder is hatched.
6 Their cobwebs are useless for clothing;

58:10 [x]Dt 15:7-8 [y]Isa 42:16 [z]Job 11:17
58:11 [a]Ps 107:9 [b]SS 4:15 [c]Jn 4:14
58:12 [d]Isa 49:8 [e]Isa 44:28
58:13 [f]Isa 56:2 [g]Ps 84:2,10
58:14 [h]Job 22:26 [i]Dt 32:13 [j]Isa 1:20
59:1 [k]Nu 11:23; Isa 50:2 [l]Isa 58:9; 65:24
59:2 [m]Isa 1:15; 58:4
59:3 [n]Isa 1:15
59:4 [o]Job 15:35; Ps 7:14
59:5 [p]Job 8:14

they cannot cover themselves with
what they make.[q]
Their deeds are evil deeds,
and acts of violence[r] are in their hands.
7 Their feet rush into sin;
they are swift to shed innocent blood.[s]
Their thoughts are evil thoughts;[t]
ruin and destruction mark their
ways.[u]
8 The way of peace they do not know;
there is no justice in their paths.
They have turned them into crooked
roads;
no one who walks in them will know
peace.[v]

9 So justice is far from us,
and righteousness does not reach us.
We look for light, but all is darkness;[w]
for brightness, but we walk in deep
shadows.
10 Like the blind[x] we grope along the wall,
feeling our way like men without
eyes.
At midday we stumble[y] as if it were
twilight;
among the strong, we are like the
dead.[z]
11 We all growl like bears;
we moan mournfully like doves.[a]
We look for justice, but find none;
for deliverance, but it is far away.

12 For our offenses[b] are many in your sight,
and our sins testify[c] against us.
Our offenses are ever with us,
and we acknowledge our iniquities:
13 rebellion and treachery against the LORD,
turning our backs[d] on our God,
fomenting oppression[e] and revolt,
uttering lies[f] our hearts have
conceived.
14 So justice is driven back,
and righteousness[g] stands at a
distance;
truth[h] has stumbled in the streets,
honesty cannot enter.
15 Truth is nowhere to be found,
and whoever shuns evil becomes a
prey.

The LORD looked and was displeased
that there was no justice.
16 He saw that there was no one,[i]
he was appalled that there was no one
to intervene;
so his own arm worked salvation[j] for
him,
and his own righteousness sustained
him.
17 He put on righteousness as his
breastplate,[k]

59:6 [q]Isa 28:20 [r]Isa 58:4
59:7 [s]Pr 6:17 [t]Mk 7:21-22 [u]Ro 3:15-17*
59:8 [v]Isa 57:21; Lk 1:79
59:9 [w]Isa 5:30; 8:20
59:10 [x]Dt 28:29 [y]Isa 8:15 [z]La 3:6
59:11 [a]Isa 38:14; Eze 7:16
59:12 [b]Ezr 9:6 [c]Isa 3:9
59:13 [d]Pr 30:9; Mt 10:33; Tit 1:16 [e]Isa 5:7 [f]Mk 7:21-22
59:14 [g]Isa 1:21 [h]Isa 48:1
59:16 [i]Isa 41:28 [j]Ps 98:1; Isa 63:5
59:17 [k]Eph 6:14

No Intervention

ISA 59:16

When the people and leaders don't stand up against injustice, an appalled God intervenes. The injustices of the people include violence, lying, hostility, rebellion, treachery, oppressing the weak and ignoring God (Isa 59:3-9). These sins place a barrier between God and the people (Isa 59:1-2), so in a sense they can no longer dispense true and holy justice. Only the Lord himself is able to do so. And he doesn't hesitate to step in where his people fail to offer salvation, restoration and justice.

Returning Home

ISA 60:4–5

Sons and daughters live "afar" off because Babylon overtakes God's people and forces them into exile. Isaiah looks beyond their captivity, though, and predicts a later time when the Israelites return to Jerusalem. He paints a jubilant picture of men marching home, carrying children on their shoulders. This return marks the beginning of new wealth and prosperity for a beleaguered nation.

and the helmet[l] of salvation on his
 head;
he put on the garments[m] of vengeance
 and wrapped himself in zeal[n] as in a
 cloak.
18 According to what they have done,
 so will he repay
wrath to his enemies
 and retribution to his foes;
 he will repay the islands their due.
19 From the west,[o] men will fear the name
 of the LORD,
 and from the rising of the sun,[p] they
 will revere his glory.
For he will come like a pent-up flood
 that the breath of the LORD drives
 along.[a]

20 "The Redeemer will come to Zion,
 to those in Jacob who repent of their
 sins,"[q]
 declares the LORD.

21 "As for me, this is my covenant with them,"
says the LORD. "My Spirit,[r] who is on you, and my
words that I have put in your mouth will not
depart from your mouth, or from the mouths of
your children, or from the mouths of their descendants from this time on and forever," says the
LORD.

The Glory of Zion

60 "Arise,[s] shine, for your light[t] has come,
 and the glory of the LORD rises upon you.
2 See, darkness covers the earth
 and thick darkness[u] is over the
 peoples,
but the LORD rises upon you
 and his glory appears over you.
3 Nations[v] will come to your light,
 and kings[w] to the brightness of your
 dawn.

4 "Lift up your eyes and look about you:
 All assemble[x] and come to you;
your sons come from afar,
 and your daughters[y] are carried on
 the arm.[z]
5 Then you will look and be radiant,
 your heart will throb and swell with
 joy;
the wealth on the seas will be brought
 to you,
 to you the riches of the nations will
 come.
6 Herds of camels will cover your land,
 young camels of Midian[a] and Ephah.[b]
And all from Sheba[c] will come,
 bearing gold and incense[d]

[a] 19 Or *When the enemy comes in like a flood, / the Spirit of the LORD will put him to flight*

59:17 [l]Eph 6:17; 1Th 5:8 [m]Isa 63:3 [n]Isa 9:7

59:19 [o]Isa 49:12 [p]Ps 113:3

59:20 [q]Ac 2:38-39; Ro 11:26-27*

59:21 [r]Isa 11:2; 44:3

60:1 [s]Isa 52:2 [t]Eph 5:14

60:2 [u]Jer 13:16; Col 1:13

60:3 [v]Isa 45:14; Rev 21:24 [w]Isa 49:23

60:4 [x]Isa 11:12 [y]Isa 43:6 [z]Isa 49:20-22

60:6 [a]Ge 25:2 [b]Ge 25:4 [c]Ps 72:10 [d]Isa 43:23; Mt 2:11

60:6 [e]Isa 42:10

and proclaiming the praise[e] of the
LORD.

60:7 [f]Ge 25:13 [g]ver 13; Hag 2:3,7,9

7 All Kedar's[f] flocks will be gathered to
you,
the rams of Nebaioth will serve you;
they will be accepted as offerings on my
altar,
and I will adorn my glorious temple.[g]

60:8 [h]Isa 49:21

8 "Who are these[h] that fly along like
clouds,
like doves to their nests?

60:9 [i]Isa 11:11 [j]Isa 2:16 *fn* [k]Isa 14:2; 43:6 [l]Isa 55:5

9 Surely the islands[i] look to me;
in the lead are the ships of Tarshish,[a][j]
bringing[k] your sons from afar,
with their silver and gold,
to the honor of the LORD your God,
the Holy One of Israel,
for he has endowed you with
splendor.[l]

60:10 [m]Isa 14:1-2 [n]Isa 49:23; Rev 21:24 [o]Isa 54:8

10 "Foreigners[m] will rebuild your walls,
and their kings[n] will serve you.
Though in anger I struck you,
in favor I will show you compassion.[o]

60:11 [p]ver 18; Isa 62:10; Rev 21:25 [q]ver 5; Rev 21:26 [r]Ps 149:8

11 Your gates[p] will always stand open,
they will never be shut, day or night,
so that men may bring you the wealth
of the nations[q]—
their kings[r] led in triumphal
procession.

60:12 [s]Isa 14:2

12 For the nation or kingdom that will not
serve[s] you will perish;
it will be utterly ruined.

60:13 [t]Isa 35:2 [u]Isa 41:19 [v]1Ch 28:2; Ps 132:7

13 "The glory of Lebanon[t] will come to
you,
the pine, the fir and the cypress
together,[u]
to adorn the place of my sanctuary;
and I will glorify the place of my
feet.[v]

60:14 [w]Isa 14:2 [x]Isa 49:23; Rev 3:9 [y]Heb 12:22

14 The sons of your oppressors[w] will come
bowing before you;
all who despise you will bow down[x]
at your feet
and will call you the City of the LORD,
Zion[y] of the Holy One of Israel.

60:15 [z]Isa 1:7-9; 6:12 [a]Isa 33:8 [b]Isa 4:2 [c]Isa 65:18

15 "Although you have been forsaken[z] and
hated,
with no one traveling[a] through,
I will make you the everlasting pride[b]
and the joy[c] of all generations.

60:16 [d]Isa 49:23; 66:11,12 [e]Isa 59:20

16 You will drink the milk of nations
and be nursed[d] at royal breasts.
Then you will know that I, the LORD, am
your Savior,
your Redeemer,[e] the Mighty One of
Jacob.

[a] 9 Or *the trading ships*

Royal Breasts

ISA 60:16

God promises his people luxurious fare. The metaphor "royal breasts" (Isa 60:16) indicates the best nurturing that anyone can offer—all the provision a child (or a nation) could possibly need or want. God sometimes compares himself to a mother because motherhood symbolizes tender love and protection—qualities he offers to his children. In Isaiah 49:15 he asks, "Can a mother forget the baby at her breast and have no compassion on the child she has borne? Though she may forget, I will not forget you!" (see quote on page 1191). In Isaiah 66:13 he promises, "As a mother comforts her child, so will I comfort you; and you will be comforted over Jerusalem."

The Least of You

ISA 60:22

The Lord specializes in turning a little into a lot. Numbers don't matter when he infuses people and situations with his power. With only 300 men Gideon defeated a Midianite army as "thick as locusts" (Jdg 7:7,12). Young David, with only a sling and a stone, "struck down" the enormous Goliath with his giant sword (1Sa 17:50). Later in Israel's history, Queen Esther courageously stepped out alone and saved a nation (Est 8:5). To turn the least person into "a thousand" and "the smallest [into] a mighty nation" (Isa 60:22) may be metaphorical, but it also represents the reality of what God is able and willing to do for his people.

17 Instead of bronze I will bring you gold,
and silver in place of iron.
Instead of wood I will bring you bronze,
and iron in place of stones.
I will make peace your governor
and righteousness your ruler.
18 No longer will violence be heard in your land,
nor ruin or destruction within your borders,
but you will call your walls Salvation[f]
and your gates Praise.
19 The sun will no more be your light by day,
nor will the brightness of the moon shine on you,
for the LORD will be your everlasting light,[g]
and your God will be your glory.[h]
20 Your sun[i] will never set again,
and your moon will wane no more;
the LORD will be your everlasting light,
and your days of sorrow[j] will end.
21 Then will all your people be righteous[k]
and they will possess[l] the land forever.
They are the shoot I have planted,[m]
the work of my hands,[n]
for the display of my splendor.[o]
22 The least of you will become a thousand,
the smallest a mighty nation.
I am the LORD;
in its time I will do this swiftly."

The Year of the LORD's Favor

61 The Spirit[p] of the Sovereign LORD is on me,
because the LORD has anointed[q] me
to preach good news to the poor.[r]
He has sent me to bind up[s] the brokenhearted,
to proclaim freedom for the captives[t]
and release from darkness for the prisoners,[a]
2 to proclaim the year of the LORD's favor[u]
and the day of vengeance[v] of our God,
to comfort[w] all who mourn,
3 and provide for those who grieve in Zion—
to bestow on them a crown of beauty
instead of ashes,
the oil of gladness
instead of mourning,
and a garment of praise
instead of a spirit of despair.
They will be called oaks of righteousness,
a planting of the LORD
for the display of his splendor.[x]

60:18 [f]Isa 26:1
60:19 [g]Rev 22:5 [h]Zec 2:5; Rev 21:23
60:20 [i]Isa 30:26 [j]Isa 35:10
60:21 [k]Rev 21:27 [l]Ps 37:11,22; Isa 57:13; 61:7 [m]Mt 15:13 [n]Isa 19:25; 29:23; Eph 2:10 [o]Isa 52:1
61:1 [p]Isa 11:2 [q]Ps 45:7 [r]Mt 11:5; Lk 7:22 [s]Isa 57:15 [t]Isa 42:7; 49:9
61:2 [u]Isa 49:8; Lk 4:18-19* [v]Isa 34:8 [w]Isa 57:18; Mt 5:4
61:3 [x]Isa 60:20-21

[a] *1* Hebrew; Septuagint *the blind*

Woman of Shunem

I Can Do It Myself

Elisha had longed for a place like this. It suited him perfectly. The woman of Shunem had seen to that. What could he do to repay her kindness? She met his question with unexpected resistance. She needed nothing.

The woman was well-to-do and very generous. She was also afraid, afraid to need others. No, it was better to be self-sufficient. She would give but ask nothing in return.

It was Gehazi's suggestion to Elisha: pray for her to have a son. With all her wealth, this was something the Shunammite could not provide for herself. She burst into tears and begged Elisha not to tease her. Surely, she had prayed for a child before, but the Lord had not answered. She was resigned to her barrenness. But, a year later, a son was born to her, through Elisha's faith, not her own.

When the child was old enough to go to the fields with his father, he was struck with a violent headache. His mother held him, doing everything in her power to help him hold on to life. Yet he died in her arms. Once again, she was confronted with her own insufficiency. Could she trust others to help? Could she trust *God?* Perhaps Elisha could help her. But no one else must know. They might think she was foolish to hope for such a thing.

She hurried to Elisha at Mount Carmel. Falling at his feet, she clung to him and would not let him go. He had to come *personally*. Nothing else would do. God used her love for her son to crack her shell of self-sufficiency. She needed Elisha. She needed the Lord. This time *her* faith brought life to her son.

Could she allow the Lord to take her even deeper, to trust him and his people for everything she needed? We know she did. At Elisha's warning, she and her husband left their home and land for seven years to live among the Philistines during a famine in Israel. They had abandoned their property and might have difficulty getting it back. But the Shunammite just happened to speak to the king when Gahazi, Elisha's servant, just happened to be telling the king about Elisha's deeds, including raising the Shunammite's dead son! The king returned her family's land.

The Lord designed us to need him and to need others in our lives. If we only give and never receive, we should not be surprised when we come to the end of our own resources. The Lord is softening our hearts to let him—and others—in.

Woman of Shunem
2 Kings 4:8–37; 8:1–6

Candid SNAPSHOT But the child's mother said, "As surely as the LORD lives and as you live, I will not leave you." So he got up and followed her (2 Kings 4:30).

Servant Girl

Speaking Up for God Wherever We Are

The young Israelite girl was a mere statistic, a captive of war taken to Aram. She could expect to remain a servant there all her life. When they were old enough, girls in her situation often became concubines to the husbands of the women they served. Her master, Naaman, was a valiant and successful soldier; he was well liked by those he served and by those who served him. But the young captive felt sorry for him, for Naaman had leprosy. Only a miracle of God could make him whole.

One day the girl mentioned a prophet in Israel to Naaman's wife. If only Naaman would go to him. Elisha was not known for curing lepers, but this young girl knew that he was a prophet of God. And God could heal *anything*, including leprosy. She had simple yet profound faith. No one else had any answers for Naaman, so his king thought it was worth a try.

In Israel, Naaman came in contact with the living God. He was not only healed of his leprosy, he was cured of his unbelief. He even carried two bags of soil from the promised land back to Aram to build an altar for God. Who knows how many lives Naaman touched in his zeal for God in his high position in government?

It all came about because one young slave cared about a foreigner who had carried her captive away from her home and her family—because she saw his life as important to God. She did not have anything to gain. She did not withhold her insight or bargain for release. She gave freely the faith she had and left the rest in God's hands. Certainly she experienced the joy of knowing that God had used her to bring about a mighty work. The One who counted most was pleased with her.

We never know where the Lord might use us. There are many around us who are spiritually sick and need the touch of the ultimate Healer. Take any opportunity God gives, no matter what circumstance you are in, to tell others that Jesus Christ is the One they need.

Servant Girl

2 Kings 5:1–19

Candid SNAPSHOT Now bands from Aram had gone out and had taken captive a young girl from Israel, and she served Naaman's wife. She said to her mistress, "If only my master would see the prophet who is in Samaria! He would cure him of his leprosy" (2 Kings 5:2–3).

61:4 [y]Isa 49:8; Eze 36:33; Am 9:14

4 They will rebuild the ancient ruins[y]
and restore the places long devastated;
they will renew the ruined cities
that have been devastated for
generations.

61:5 [z]Isa 14:1-2

5 Aliens[z] will shepherd your flocks;
foreigners will work your fields and
vineyards.

61:6 [a]Ex 19:6; 1Pe 2:5 [b]Isa 60:11

6 And you will be called priests[a] of the
LORD,
you will be named ministers of our
God.
You will feed on the wealth[b] of nations,
and in their riches you will boast.

61:7 [c]Isa 40:2; Zec 9:12

7 Instead of their shame
my people will receive a double[c]
portion,
and instead of disgrace
they will rejoice in their inheritance;
and so they will inherit a double portion
in their land,
and everlasting joy will be theirs.

61:8 [d]Ps 11:7; Isa 5:16 [e]Isa 55:3

8 "For I, the LORD, love justice;[d]
I hate robbery and iniquity.
In my faithfulness I will reward them
and make an everlasting covenant[e]
with them.
9 Their descendants will be known
among the nations
and their offspring among the
peoples.
All who see them will acknowledge
that they are a people the LORD has
blessed."

61:10 [f]Isa 25:9; Hab 3:18 [g]Ps 132:9; Isa 52:1 [h]Isa 49:18; Rev 21:2

10 I delight greatly in the LORD;
my soul rejoices[f] in my God.
For he has clothed me with garments of
salvation
and arrayed me in a robe of
righteousness,[g]
as a bridegroom adorns his head like a
priest,
and as a bride[h] adorns herself with
her jewels.

61:11 [i]Ps 85:11

11 For as the soil makes the sprout come up
and a garden causes seeds to grow,
so the Sovereign LORD will make
righteousness[i] and praise
spring up before all nations.

Zion's New Name

62:1 [j]Isa 1:26

62 For Zion's sake I will not keep silent,
for Jerusalem's sake I will not remain
quiet,
till her righteousness[j] shines out like the
dawn,
her salvation like a blazing torch.

62:2 [k]Isa 52:10; 60:3

2 The nations[k] will see your righteousness,

Restoration

ISA 61:1–4

God promises that those who grieve in Zion will "rebuild the ancient ruins" of cities and "restore the places long devastated" (Isa 61:4). This is likely a reference to the restoration of the ruins created by the successive invasions of Assyria and Babylon. Though this is a remarkable commitment, God focuses first on the restoration of people. He will bind up the brokenhearted, proclaim freedom for the captives, and release prisoners from their dark cells (Isa 61:1). The outer restoration symbolizes an inner healing of hearts. The inner person matters most to God, and his motto could be, "People, then places." So the physical rebuilding of torn-down dwelling places reveals a Comforter who cares about his people's every need and desire. He travels the extra mile to restore their dignity and security.

When Jesus begins his ministry in Nazareth, he enters the synagogue and reads Isaiah 61:1–2 to the congregation. Then he claims, "Today this scripture is fulfilled in your hearing" (Lk 4:21). Like his Father, the Son's first priority is soul restoration (Ps 23:3).

and all kings your glory;
you will be called by a new name[l]
that the mouth of the LORD will bestow.
3 You will be a crown[m] of splendor in the LORD's hand,
a royal diadem in the hand of your God.
4 No longer will they call you Deserted,[n]
or name your land Desolate.
But you will be called Hephzibah,[a]
and your land Beulah[b];
for the LORD will take delight[o] in you,
and your land will be married.[p]
5 As a young man marries a maiden,
so will your sons[c] marry you;
as a bridegroom rejoices over his bride,
so will your God rejoice[q] over you.

6 I have posted watchmen[r] on your walls, O Jerusalem;
they will never be silent day or night.
You who call on the LORD,
give yourselves no rest,
7 and give him no rest[s] till he establishes Jerusalem
and makes her the praise of the earth.

8 The LORD has sworn by his right hand
and by his mighty arm:
"Never again will I give your grain[t]
as food for your enemies,
and never again will foreigners drink the new wine
for which you have toiled;
9 but those who harvest it will eat it
and praise the LORD,
and those who gather the grapes will drink it
in the courts of my sanctuary."

10 Pass through, pass through the gates![u]
Prepare the way for the people.
Build up, build up the highway![v][w]
Remove the stones.
Raise a banner[x] for the nations.
11 The LORD has made proclamation
to the ends of the earth:
"Say to the Daughter of Zion,[y]
'See, your Savior comes![z]
See, his reward is with him,
and his recompense accompanies him.' "[a]
12 They will be called[b] the Holy People,[c]
the Redeemed[d] of the LORD;
and you will be called Sought After,
the City No Longer Deserted.[e]

62:2 [l]ver 4, 12
62:3 [m]Isa 28:5; Zec 9:16; 1Th 2:19
62:4 [n]Isa 54:6 [o]Jer 32:41; Zep 3:17 [p]Jer 3:14; Hos 2:19
62:5 [q]Isa 65:19
62:6 [r]Isa 52:8; Eze 3:17
62:7 [s]Mt 15:21-28; Lk 18:1-8
62:8 [t]Dt 28:30-33; Isa 1:7; Jer 5:17
62:10 [u]Isa 60:11 [v]Isa 57:14 [w]Isa 11:16 [x]Isa 11:10
62:11 [y]Zec 9:9; Mt 21:5 [z]Rev 22:12 [a]Isa 40:10
62:12 [b]ver 4 [c]1Pe 2:9 [d]Isa 35:9 [e]Isa 42:16

[a] 4 *Hephzibah* means *my delight is in her.* [b] 4 *Beulah* means *married.* [c] 5 Or *Builder*

New Names

ISA 62:12

As if to underscore the point of Isaiah 62:11, God *assigns new names to his people* (Holy People, Redeemed of the Lord, Sought After, City No Longer Deserted). *These names not only reflect Israel's history* (Holy People), *spiritual salvation* (Redeemed) *and physical restoration* (City No Longer Deserted), *but the title "Sought After" seems to indicate that other nations will revere and seek to be like them.* God stamps his irrevocable ownership on the Jews. He claims them as his own—forever.

God's Day of Vengeance and Redemption

63:1 [f]Am 1:12 [g]Zep 3:17

63 Who is this coming from Edom,
from Bozrah,[f] with his garments stained
crimson?
Who is this, robed in splendor,
striding forward in the greatness of
his strength?

"It is I, speaking in righteousness,
mighty to save."[g]

2 Why are your garments red,
like those of one treading the
winepress?

63:3 [h]Rev 14:20; 19:15 [i]Isa 22:5 [j]Rev 19:13

3 "I have trodden the winepress[h] alone;
from the nations no one was with me.
I trampled them in my anger
and trod them down in my wrath;[i]
their blood spattered my garments,[j]
and I stained all my clothing.
4 For the day of vengeance was in my
heart,
and the year of my redemption has
come.

63:5 [k]Isa 41:28 [l]Ps 44:3; 98:1 [m]Isa 59:16

5 I looked, but there was no one[k] to help,
I was appalled that no one gave
support;
so my own arm[l] worked salvation for
me,
and my own wrath sustained me.[m]

63:6 [n]Isa 29:9 [o]Isa 34:3

6 I trampled the nations in my anger;
in my wrath I made them drunk[n]
and poured their blood[o] on the
ground."

Praise and Prayer

63:7 [p]Isa 54:8 [q]Ps 51:1; Eph 2:4

7 I will tell of the kindnesses[p] of the LORD,
the deeds for which he is to be
praised,
according to all the LORD has done for
us—
yes, the many good things he has done
for the house of Israel,
according to his compassion[q] and
many kindnesses.

63:8 [r]Isa 51:4

8 He said, "Surely they are my people,[r]
sons who will not be false to me";
and so he became their Savior.

63:9 [s]Ex 33:14 [t]Dt 7:7-8 [u]Dt 1:31

9 In all their distress he too was
distressed,
and the angel of his presence[s] saved
them.
In his love and mercy he redeemed[t]
them;
he lifted them up and carried[u] them
all the days of old.

63:10 [v]Ps 78:40 [w]Ps 51:11; Ac 7:51; Eph 4:30 [x]Ps 106:40

10 Yet they rebelled[v]
and grieved his Holy Spirit.[w]
So he turned and became their enemy[x]
and he himself fought against them.

What wonders a bit of encouragement can do! It's one of the most awesome treasures God has given us—the ability to inspire, motivate, and reassure others.

—Barbara Johnson

Challenging God

ISA 63:15-17

The praise in this chapter turns into frustration as Isaiah struggles to understand why God would allow his people to wander. Why would the Creator harden their hearts? Perhaps the prophet expresses how he feels, not what he knows to be true. God isn't the author of sin, but he allows humans the privilege of free choice. It may seem like the Lord hardens people's hearts, but they actually turn their own hearts to stone (see the note on Ex 7:3, page 98). Heartbroken people don't always discern the difference between what God causes and what God allows.

11 Then his people recalled[a] the days of old,
the days of Moses and his people—
where is he who brought them through
the sea,[y]
with the shepherd of his flock?
Where is he who set
his Holy Spirit[z] among them, 63:11 [y]Ex 14:22,30
12 who sent his glorious arm of power [z]Nu 11:17
to be at Moses' right hand,
who divided the waters[a] before them, 63:12 [a]Ex 14:21-
to gain for himself everlasting renown, 22; Isa 11:15
13 who led[b] them through the depths?
Like a horse in open country, 63:13 [b]Dt 32:12
they did not stumble;[c] [c]Jer 31:9
14 like cattle that go down to the plain,
they were given rest by the Spirit of
the LORD.
This is how you guided your people
to make for yourself a glorious name.

15 Look down from heaven[d] and see 63:15 [d]Dt 26:15;
from your lofty throne,[e] holy and Ps 80:14
glorious. [e]Ps 123:1
Where are your zeal[f] and your might? [f]Isa 9:7;
Your tenderness and compassion[g] are 26:11
withheld from us. [g]Jer 31:20; Hos 11:8
16 But you are our Father,
though Abraham does not know us
or Israel acknowledge[h] us; 63:16 [h]Job 14:21
you, O LORD, are our Father, [i]Isa 41:14;
our Redeemer[i] from of old is your 44:6
name.
17 Why, O LORD, do you make us wander
from your ways
and harden our hearts so we do not
revere[j] you? 63:17 [j]Isa 29:13
Return[k] for the sake of your servants, [k]Nu 10:36
the tribes that are your inheritance.
18 For a little while your people possessed
your holy place,
but now our enemies have trampled
down your sanctuary.[l] 63:18 [l]Ps 74:3-8
19 We are yours from of old;
but you have not ruled over them,
they have not been called by your
name.[b]

64

Oh, that you would rend the heavens[m] 64:1 [m]Ps 18:9;
and come down,[n] 144:5
that the mountains[o] would tremble [n]Mic 1:3
before you! [o]Ex 19:18
2 As when fire sets twigs ablaze
and causes water to boil,
come down to make your name known
to your enemies 64:2
and cause the nations to quake[p] [p]Ps 99:1;
before you! Jer 5:22; 33:9
3 For when you did awesome[q] things that
we did not expect, 64:3 [q]Ps 65:5

[a] 11 Or *But may he recall* [b] 19 Or *We are like those you have never ruled, / like those never called by your name*

you came down, and the mountains
trembled before you.
4 Since ancient times no one has heard,
no ear has perceived,
no eye has seen any God besides you,
who acts on behalf of those who wait
for him.[r]
5 You come to the help of those who
gladly do right,[s]
who remember your ways.
But when we continued to sin against
them,
you were angry.
How then can we be saved?
6 All of us have become like one who is
unclean,
and all our righteous[t] acts are like
filthy rags;
we all shrivel up like a leaf,[u]
and like the wind our sins sweep us
away.
7 No one[v] calls on your name
or strives to lay hold of you;
for you have hidden[w] your face from us
and made us waste away[x] because of
our sins.

8 Yet, O LORD, you are our Father.[y]
We are the clay, you are the potter;[z]
we are all the work of your hand.
9 Do not be angry[a] beyond measure,
O LORD;
do not remember our sins[b] forever.
Oh, look upon us, we pray,
for we are all your people.
10 Your sacred cities have become a desert;
even Zion is a desert, Jerusalem a
desolation.
11 Our holy and glorious temple,[c] where
our fathers praised you,
has been burned with fire,
and all that we treasured[d] lies in
ruins.
12 After all this, O LORD, will you hold
yourself back?[e]
Will you keep silent[f] and punish us
beyond measure?

Judgment and Salvation

65 "I revealed myself to those who did not
ask for me;
I was found by those who did not
seek me.[g]
To a nation[h] that did not call on my
name,
I said, 'Here am I, here am I.'
2 All day long I have held out my hands
to an obstinate people,[i]
who walk in ways not good,
pursuing their own imaginations[j]—
3 a people who continually provoke me

64:4 [r]Isa 30:18; 1Co 2:9*
64:5 [s]Isa 26:8
64:6 [t]Isa 46:12; 48:1 [u]Ps 90:5-6
64:7 [v]Isa 59:4 [w]Dt 31:18; Isa 1:15; 54:8 [x]Isa 9:18
64:8 [y]Isa 63:16 [z]Isa 29:16
64:9 [a]Isa 57:17; 60:10 [b]Isa 43:25
64:11 [c]Ps 74:3-7 [d]La 1:7,10
64:12 [e]Ps 74:10-11; Isa 42:14 [f]Ps 83:1
65:1 [g]Hos 1:10; Ro 9:24-26; 10:20* [h]Eph 2:12
65:2 [i]Isa 1:2,23; Ro 10:21* [j]Ps 81:11-12; Isa 66:18

First Move

ISA 65:1

As if to answer Isaiah's complaint in the previous chapter, God confirms that he reveals himself to people, even to those who don't seek him. He initiates the first move in his contact with humans. If he didn't, we sinners wouldn't even look for a way out of our darkness (Ro 3:10–11). The light of his presence awakens us spiritually and exposes our need for salvation and for the Lord himself.

to my very face,[k]
offering sacrifices in gardens[l]
and burning incense on altars of brick;
4 who sit among the graves
and spend their nights keeping secret vigil;
who eat the flesh of pigs,[m]
and whose pots hold broth of unclean meat;
5 who say, 'Keep away; don't come near me,
for I am too sacred[n] for you!'
Such people are smoke in my nostrils,
a fire that keeps burning all day.
6 "See, it stands written before me:
I will not keep silent[o] but will pay back[p] in full;
I will pay it back into their laps[q]—
7 both your sins[r] and the sins of your fathers,"[s]
says the LORD.
"Because they burned sacrifices on the mountains
and defied me on the hills,[t]
I will measure into their laps
the full payment for their former deeds."

8 This is what the LORD says:
"As when juice is still found in a cluster of grapes
and men say, 'Don't destroy it,
there is yet some good in it,'
so will I do in behalf of my servants;
I will not destroy them all.
9 I will bring forth descendants[u] from Jacob,
and from Judah those who will possess[v] my mountains;
my chosen people will inherit them,
and there will my servants live.[w]
10 Sharon[x] will become a pasture for flocks,
and the Valley of Achor[y] a resting place for herds,
for my people who seek[z] me.

11 "But as for you who forsake[a] the LORD
and forget my holy mountain,
who spread a table for Fortune
and fill bowls of mixed wine for Destiny,
12 I will destine you for the sword,[b]
and you will all bend down for the slaughter;
for I called but you did not answer,[c]
I spoke but you did not listen.[d]
You did evil in my sight
and chose what displeases me."

65:3 [k]Job 1:11 [l]Isa 1:29
65:4 [m]Lev 11:7
65:5 [n]Mt 9:11; Lk 7:39; 18:9-12
65:6 [o]Ps 50:3 [p]Jer 16:18 [q]Ps 79:12
65:7 [r]Isa 22:14 [s]Ex 20:5 [t]Isa 57:7
65:9 [u]Isa 45:19 [v]Am 9:11-15 [w]Isa 32:18
65:10 [x]Isa 35:2 [y]Jos 7:26 [z]Isa 51:1
65:11 [a]Dt 29:24-25; Isa 1:28
65:12 [b]Isa 27:1 [c]Pr 1:24-25; Isa 41:28; 66:4 [d]2Ch 36:15-16; Jer 7:13

Hope uncovers new possibilities *and shows us what can be done. It wrestles with angels, looks impossibilities in the eye and winks. Hope springs eternal. Hope supersedes all good intentions.*

Positive thinking, on the other hand, can get you only so far. When that train of thought won't get you further, jump track and keep going by the power of God's grace. After all, you know Immanuel, God who is with us. Dare to believe that he has planned greater things right around the corner for the ones you love. Hold your loved ones before the throne and count on God's answer in their lives. Don't let your ability or inability to think your way around circumstances hold you back. Pray and rest. Then pray some more.

—Barbara Johnson

13 Therefore this is what the Sovereign LORD says:

"My servants will eat,[e]
but you will go hungry;
my servants will drink,
but you will go thirsty;[f]
my servants will rejoice,
but you will be put to shame.[g]
14 My servants will sing
out of the joy of their hearts,
but you will cry out[h]
from anguish of heart
and wail in brokenness of spirit.
15 You will leave your name
to my chosen ones as a curse;[i]
the Sovereign LORD will put you to death,
but to his servants he will give
another name.
16 Whoever invokes a blessing in the land
will do so by the God of truth;[j]
he who takes an oath in the land
will swear[k] by the God of truth.
For the past troubles will be forgotten
and hidden from my eyes.

65:13 [e]Isa 1:19 [f]Isa 41:17 [g]Isa 44:9
65:14 [h]Mt 8:12; Lk 13:28
65:15 [i]Zec 8:13
65:16 [j]Ps 31:5 [k]Isa 19:18

New Heavens and a New Earth

17 "Behold, I will create
new heavens and a new earth.[l]
The former things will not be
remembered,[m]
nor will they come to mind.
18 But be glad and rejoice[n] forever
in what I will create,
for I will create Jerusalem to be a
delight
and its people a joy.
19 I will rejoice[o] over Jerusalem
and take delight in my people;
the sound of weeping and of crying[p]
will be heard in it no more.
20 "Never again will there be in it
an infant who lives but a few days,
or an old man who does not live out
his years;[q]
he who dies at a hundred
will be thought a mere youth;
he who fails to reach[a] a hundred
will be considered accursed.
21 They will build houses[r] and dwell in
them;
they will plant vineyards and eat their
fruit.[s]
22 No longer will they build houses and
others live in them,
or plant and others eat.
For as the days of a tree,[t]
so will be the days[u] of my people;

65:17 [l]Isa 66:22; 2Pe 3:13 [m]Isa 43:18; Jer 3:16
65:18 [n]Ps 98:1-9; Isa 25:9
65:19 [o]Isa 35:10; 62:5 [p]Isa 25:8; Rev 7:17
65:20 [q]Ecc 8:13
65:21 [r]Isa 32:18 [s]Isa 37:30; Am 9:14
65:22 [t]Ps 92:12-14 [u]Ps 21:4; 91:16

[a] 20 Or / *the sinner who reaches*

New Everything

ISA 65:17

Though some read this verse as the end of the world, others interpret it as a metaphor for God's reformation of his people's lives. Either way the transformation is both beautiful and complete. God promises to change the world, as if beginning over again with a new heaven and earth. The new Jerusalem will be filled with rejoicing (Isa 65:18–19), and people won't die prematurely (Isa 65:20). Residents will own property and workers will enjoy the fruits of their labor (Isa 65:21–22). The Lord will bless them, and they will bless the Lord. As always, God's salvation produces a complete transformation.

Whom God Esteems

ISA 66:2

God clearly explains how to be esteemed by him. First, be humble. Second, respect his Word. It's a simple formula, but many of us take a lifetime to learn it. We like to make our spirituality more "showy" and complicated than this. But once again, God cares about what's in our hearts. In his upside-down kingdom, power resides with the humble; wisdom dwells in his Word. These qualities not only please God, but they draw others to him.

my chosen ones will long enjoy
the works of their hands.
23 They will not toil in vain
or bear children doomed to
misfortune;
for they will be a people blessed[v] by the
LORD,
they and their descendants[w] with
them.
24 Before they call[x] I will answer;
while they are still speaking[y] I will
hear.
25 The wolf and the lamb[z] will feed
together,
and the lion will eat straw like the ox,
but dust will be the serpent's[a] food.
They will neither harm nor destroy
on all my holy mountain,"
says the LORD.

65:23 [v]Dt 28:3-12; Isa 61:9 [w]Ac 2:39
65:24 [x]Isa 55:6 [y]Da 9:20-23; 10:12
65:25 [z]Isa 11:6 [a]Ge 3:14; Mic 7:17

Judgment and Hope

66 This is what the LORD says:

"Heaven is my throne,[b]
and the earth is my footstool.[c]
Where is the house[d] you will build for
me?
Where will my resting place be?
2 Has not my hand made all these things,[e]
and so they came into being?"
declares the LORD.

"This is the one I esteem:
he who is humble and contrite in
spirit,[f]
and trembles at my word.[g]
3 But whoever sacrifices a bull[h]
is like one who kills a man,
and whoever offers a lamb,
like one who breaks a dog's neck;
whoever makes a grain offering
is like one who presents pig's blood,
and whoever burns memorial incense,[i]
like one who worships an idol.
They have chosen their own ways,[j]
and their souls delight in their
abominations;
4 so I also will choose harsh treatment for
them
and will bring upon them what they
dread.[k]
For when I called, no one answered,[l]
when I spoke, no one listened.
They did evil[m] in my sight
and chose what displeases me."[n]

5 Hear the word of the LORD,
you who tremble at his word:
"Your brothers who hate[o] you,
and exclude you because of my name,
have said,
'Let the LORD be glorified,

66:1 [b]Mt 23:22 [c]1Ki 8:27; Mt 5:34-35 [d]2Sa 7:7; Jn 4:20-21; Ac 7:49*; 17:24
66:2 [e]Isa 40:26; Ac 7:50* [f]Isa 57:15; Mt 5:3-4; Lk 18:13-14 [g]Ezr 9:4
66:3 [h]Isa 1:11 [i]Lev 2:2 [j]Isa 57:17
66:4 [k]Pr 10:24 [l]Pr 1:24; Jer 7:13 [m]2Ki 21:2, 4,6 [n]Isa 65:12
66:5 [o]Ps 38:20; Isa 60:15

that we may see your joy!'
66:5 [p]Lk 13:17
Yet they will be put to shame.[p]
6 Hear that uproar from the city,
hear that noise from the temple!
It is the sound of the LORD
66:6 [q]Isa 65:6; Joel 3:7
repaying[q] his enemies all they
deserve.

66:7 [r]Isa 54:1 [s]Rev 12:5
7 "Before she goes into labor,[r]
she gives birth;
before the pains come upon her,
she delivers a son.[s]
8 Who has ever heard of such a thing?
66:8 [t]Isa 64:4
Who has ever seen[t] such things?
Can a country be born in a day
or a nation be brought forth in a
moment?
Yet no sooner is Zion in labor
than she gives birth to her children.
66:9 [u]Isa 37:3
9 Do I bring to the moment of birth[u]
and not give delivery?" says the LORD.
"Do I close up the womb
when I bring to delivery?" says your
God.
66:10 [v]Dt 32:43; Ro 15:10 [w]Ps 26:8
10 "Rejoice[v] with Jerusalem and be glad for
her,
all you who love[w] her;
rejoice greatly with her,
all you who mourn over her.
66:11 [x]Isa 60:16
11 For you will nurse[x] and be satisfied
at her comforting breasts;
you will drink deeply
and delight in her overflowing
abundance."

12 For this is what the LORD says:

66:12 [y]Isa 48:18 [z]Ps 72:3; Isa 60:5; 61:6 [a]Isa 60:4
"I will extend peace to her like a river,[y]
and the wealth[z] of nations like a
flooding stream;
you will nurse and be carried[a] on her
arm
and dandled on her knees.
13 As a mother comforts her child,
66:13 [b]Isa 40:1; 2Co 1:4
so will I comfort[b] you;
and you will be comforted over
Jerusalem."

14 When you see this, your heart will
rejoice
and you will flourish like grass;
the hand of the LORD will be made
known to his servants,
66:14 [c]Isa 10:5
but his fury[c] will be shown to his
foes.
15 See, the LORD is coming with fire,
66:15 [d]Ps 68:17 [e]Ps 9:5
and his chariots[d] are like a whirlwind;
he will bring down his anger with fury,
and his rebuke[e] with flames of fire.
66:16 [f]Isa 30:30 [g]Isa 27:1
16 For with fire[f] and with his sword[g]
the LORD will execute judgment upon
all men,

Childlike Protection

ISA 66:12

Nothing is as sweet as an innocent, trusting baby, and maternal instincts prompt us to protect and cuddle these small ones. Isaiah 66:12 depicts the motherly side of God, who nurses, carries and bounces a child on his knees. Though God is neither male nor female, he expresses the qualities of both genders. This tender description wraps his people in the comfort and security of his eternal love.

Abominable Things

ISA 66:17

These abominable things violate the laws of God and involve idol worship and immorality (see the note on Isaiah 1:29, page 1107). The Lord detests these actions and punishes those who commit them. He allows these sinners to "meet their end together" (Isa 66:17). This verse doesn't reveal how these people will self-destruct. But when we flagrantly disobey God, we often create our own demise without much help from anyone else.

and many will be those slain by the
LORD.

17"Those who consecrate and purify themselves
to go into the gardens,[h] following the one in the
midst of[a] those who eat the flesh of pigs[i] and rats
and other abominable things—they will meet
their end[j] together," declares the LORD.
18"And I, because of their actions and their
imaginations, am about to come[b] and gather all
nations and tongues, and they will come and see
my glory.
19"I will set a sign[k] among them, and I will send
some of those who survive to the nations—to Tarshish,[l] to the Libyans[c] and Lydians[m] (famous as
archers), to Tubal[n] and Greece, and to the distant
islands[o] that have not heard of my fame or seen
my glory.[p] They will proclaim my glory among
the nations. 20And they will bring all your brothers, from all the nations, to my holy mountain in
Jerusalem as an offering to the LORD—on horses,
in chariots and wagons, and on mules and
camels," says the LORD. "They will bring them, as
the Israelites bring their grain offerings, to the
temple of the LORD in ceremonially clean vessels.[q]
21And I will select some of them also to be priests[r]
and Levites," says the LORD.

22"As the new heavens and the new earth[s] that
I make will endure before me," declares the LORD,
"so will your name and descendants endure.[t]
23From one New Moon to another and from one
Sabbath[u] to another, all mankind will come and
bow down[v] before me," says the LORD. 24"And they
will go out and look upon the dead bodies of
those who rebelled against me; their worm[w] will
not die, nor will their fire be quenched,[x] and they
will be loathsome to all mankind."

66:17 [h]Isa 1:29 [i]Lev 11:7 [j]Ps 37:20; Isa 1:28

66:19 [k]Isa 11:10; 49:22 [l]Isa 2:16 [m]Eze 27:10 [n]Ge 10:2 [o]Isa 11:11 [p]1Ch 16:24; Isa 24:15

66:20 [q]Isa 52:11

66:21 [r]Ex 19:6; Isa 61:6; 1Pe 2:5,9

66:22 [s]Isa 65:17; Heb 12:26-27; 2Pe 3:13; Rev 21:1 [t]Jn 10:27-29; 1Pe 1:4-5

66:23 [u]Eze 46:1-3 [v]Isa 19:21

66:24 [w]Isa 14:11 [x]Isa 1:31; Mk 9:48*

[a] *17* Or *gardens behind one of your temples, and* [b] *18* The meaning of the Hebrew for this clause is uncertain.
[c] *19* Some Septuagint manuscripts *Put* (Libyans); Hebrew *Pul*

Jeremiah

Words of warning rejected.

Quick Study

Author
The prophet Jeremiah.

Date Written
Around 600 B.C.

Setting
Judah.

Key Passage
Jeremiah 31:33 " 'This is the covenant I will make with the house of Israel
after that time," declares the LORD.
"I will put my law in their minds
and write it on their hearts.
I will be their God,
and they will be my people.' "

The book of Jeremiah sounds a warning to God's people that those who do not turn from evil will face severe consequences. With passionate prose and poetry, Jeremiah mingles his tears of compassion with God's sober message of judgment to the nation of Judah. For over forty years the prophet stands virtually alone urging his people to repent before it is too late. Despite his emotional appeals, Jeremiah's words fall on deaf ears, and he lives to see God's judgment fall.

Woven throughout Jeremiah's message of doom and destruction are some surprising passages. The sanctity of human life is established in Jeremiah's appointment as a prophet while still in his mother's womb (Jer 1). Jeremiah establishes that God's justice requires us to answer to him for how we live (Jer 5). We are horrified at the descriptions of child sacrifice and obscene religious practices (Jer 7). We recognize the pitfalls of pride and arrogance (Jer 13). We are surprised at Jeremiah's strident honesty with God (Jer 20). And we quickly realize that God will deal harshly with those who lie and lead others astray (Jer 28).

Yet Jeremiah's words are not only words of discouragement; there are also nuggets of encouragement. God is our potter; he is in control of our circumstances (Jer 18). He will provide for our needs even in disastrous situations (Jer 29). And he will renew us by restoring our hearts (Jer 31–32). Jeremiah's words ultimately remind us that faithfulness to God's way will always overcome the failures of sin in our lives.

Outline

The call of Jeremiah.
Jer 1

The sinful condition of Judah.
Jer 2–6

The temple and the law.
Jer 7–12

Messages on the coming disaster.
Jer 13–18

Jeremiah's confrontation of the leaders.
Jer 19–29

Restoration promised.
Jer 30–33

The nation's collapse.
Jer 34–38

The fall of Jerusalem foretold.
Jer 39

Jeremiah's flight.
Jer 40–45

Messages about specific nations.
Jer 46–51

Jerusalem's collapse.
Jer 52

The Women of Jeremiah

Queen of Heaven	*Babylonian god.* Jer 7:18; 44:17–19,25
Jeremiah's mother	*Jeremiah wished she hadn't borne him.* Jer 15:10
Queen mother	*Jehoiachin's mother.* Jer 13:18; 29:2
Rachel	*Jacob's favorite wife.* Jer 31:15
Zedekiah's daughters	*Taken captive.* Jer 41:10; 43:6
Wives	*They burned incense to false gods.* Jer 44:7–10,15–30
Hamutal	*Mother of King Zedekiah.* Jer 52:1

1

1 The words of Jeremiah son of Hilkiah, one of
the priests at Anathoth[a] in the territory of Benjamin. 2 The word of the LORD came to him in the
thirteenth year of the reign of Josiah son of Amon
king of Judah, 3 and through the reign of
Jehoiakim[b] son of Josiah king of Judah, down to
the fifth month of the eleventh year of Zedekiah[c]
son of Josiah king of Judah, when the people of
Jerusalem went into exile.[d]

The Call of Jeremiah

4 The word of the LORD came to me, saying,

> 5 "Before I formed you in the womb I
> knew[ae] you,
> before you were born[f] I set you apart;
> I appointed you as a prophet to the
> nations.[g]"

6 "Ah, Sovereign LORD," I said, "I do not know
how to speak;[h] I am only a child."[i]
7 But the LORD said to me, "Do not say, 'I am
only a child.' You must go to everyone I send you
to and say whatever I command you. 8 Do not be
afraid[j] of them, for I am with you[k] and will rescue
you," declares the LORD.
9 Then the LORD reached out his hand and
touched[l] my mouth and said to me, "Now, I have
put my words in your mouth.[m] 10 See, today I
appoint you over nations and kingdoms to uproot
and tear down, to destroy and overthrow, to build
and to plant."[n]
11 The word of the LORD came to me: "What do
you see, Jeremiah?"[o]
"I see the branch of an almond tree," I replied.
12 The LORD said to me, "You have seen correctly, for I am watching[b] to see that my word is
fulfilled."
13 The word of the LORD came to me again:
"What do you see?"[p]
"I see a boiling pot, tilting away from the
north," I answered.
14 The LORD said to me, "From the north disaster will be poured out on all who live in the land.
15 I am about to summon all the peoples of the
northern kingdoms," declares the LORD.

> "Their kings will come and set up their
> thrones
> in the entrance of the gates of
> Jerusalem;
> they will come against all her
> surrounding walls
> and against all the towns of Judah.[q]
> 16 I will pronounce my judgments on my
> people
> because of their wickedness[r] in
> forsaking me,[s]
> in burning incense to other gods[t]

1:1 [a]Jos 21:18; 1Ch 6:60; Jer 32:7-9
1:3 [b]2Ki 23:34 [c]2Ki 24:17; Jer 39:2 [d]Jer 52:15
1:5 [e]Ps 139:16 [f]Isa 49:1 [g]ver 10; Jer 25:15-26
1:6 [h]Ex 4:10; 6:12 [i]1Ki 3:7
1:8 [j]Eze 2:6 [k]Jos 1:5; Jer 15:20
1:9 [l]Isa 6:7 [m]Ex 4:12
1:10 [n]Jer 18:7-10; 24:6; 31:4,28
1:11 [o]Jer 24:3; Am 7:8
1:13 [p]Zec 4:2
1:15 [q]Jer 4:16; 9:11
1:16 [r]Dt 28:20 [s]Jer 17:13 [t]Jer 7:9; 19:4

[a] 5 Or *chose* [b] 12 The Hebrew for *watching* sounds like the Hebrew for *almond tree.*

Called by God

JER 1:4-10

Jeremiah prepares to follow his father into the priesthood (Jer 1:1) until his heavenly Father calls him to a different mission, one with greater responsibility—prophet of God. Timid by nature, young Jeremiah believes he is too young and inadequate in public speaking to be God's messenger. But God has dismissed similar rationales from past prophets: Moses (Ex 3:11; 4:10) and Isaiah (Isa 6:5).

Notice how many times God reminds Jeremiah of the power that undergirds his ministry. "I formed you . . . I knew you . . . I set you apart . . . I appointed you . . . I am with you and will rescue you . . . I have put my words in your mouth." When God appoints a person to a specific task or life calling, he provides the resources for success.

First Love

JER 2:2

God's relationship with Israel is often described as a husband's with his bride (Isa 54:5–7; Hos 2:2–20). In Israel's honeymoon stage, the people devote themselves to God and please him. But over the years Israel slips in her commitment as the people mix with the surrounding nations and evil kings defile God's laws with idolatry and heathen activities. During the reign of Josiah, Judah's last good king, God directs Jeremiah to call the people back to their love relationship with him.

God's same earnest plea for a restored relationship appears in Revelation 2:4: "You have forsaken your first love." Temptations to follow society's ways challenge us today just as they did the Israelites. Everyday distractions, large and small, keep us from our original commitment to love and follow God. What do we need to do each day to rekindle our first love for our bridegroom?

and in worshiping what their hands
have made.

17“Get yourself ready! Stand up and say to them
whatever I command you. Do not be terrified[u] by
them, or I will terrify you before them. 18Today I
have made you[v] a fortified city, an iron pillar and a
bronze wall to stand against the whole land—
against the kings of Judah, its officials, its priests
and the people of the land. 19They will fight against
you but will not overcome you, for I am with you[w]
and will rescue[x] you,” declares the LORD.

Israel Forsakes God

2 The word of the LORD came to me: 2“Go and
proclaim in the hearing of Jerusalem:

“ ‘I remember the devotion of your
youth,[y]
how as a bride you loved me
and followed me through the desert,[z]
through a land not sown.
3Israel was holy[a] to the LORD,[b]
the firstfruits[c] of his harvest;
all who devoured[d] her were held guilty,[e]
and disaster overtook them,’ ”
declares the LORD.

4Hear the word of the LORD, O house of
Jacob,
all you clans of the house of Israel.

5This is what the LORD says:

“What fault did your fathers find in me,
that they strayed so far from me?
They followed worthless idols
and became worthless[f] themselves.
6They did not ask, ‘Where is the LORD,
who brought us up out of Egypt[g]
and led us through the barren
wilderness,
through a land of deserts[h] and rifts,[i]
a land of drought and darkness,[a]
a land where no one travels and no
one lives?’
7I brought you into a fertile land
to eat its fruit and rich produce.[j]
But you came and defiled my land
and made my inheritance detestable.[k]
8The priests did not ask,
‘Where is the LORD?’
Those who deal with the law did not
know me;[l]
the leaders rebelled against me.
The prophets prophesied by Baal,[m]
following worthless idols.[n]
9“Therefore I bring charges[o] against you
again,”
declares the LORD.

1:17 [u]Eze 2:6
1:18 [v]Isa 50:7
1:19 [w]Jer 20:11 [x]ver 8
2:2 [y]Eze 16:8-14,60; Hos 2:15 [z]Dt 2:7
2:3 [a]Dt 7:6 [b]Ex 19:6 [c]Jas 1:18; Rev 14:4 [d]Isa 41:11; Jer 30:16 [e]Jer 50:7
2:5 [f]2Ki 17:15
2:6 [g]Hos 13:4 [h]Dt 8:15 [i]Dt 32:10
2:7 [j]Nu 13:27; Dt 8:7-9; 11:10-12 [k]Ps 106:34-39; Jer 16:18
2:8 [l]Jer 4:22 [m]Jer 23:13 [n]Jer 16:19
2:9 [o]Eze 20:35-36; Mic 6:2

[a]6 Or *and the shadow of death*

"And I will bring charges against your
children's children.
10 Cross over to the coasts of Kittim[a] and
look,
send to Kedar[b] and observe closely;
see if there has ever been anything
like this:
11 Has a nation ever changed its gods?
(Yet they are not gods[p] at all.)
But my people have exchanged their[c]
Glory[q]
for worthless idols.
12 Be appalled at this, O heavens,
and shudder with great horror,"
declares the LORD.
13 "My people have committed two sins:
They have forsaken me,
the spring of living water,[r]
and have dug their own cisterns,
broken cisterns that cannot hold water.
14 Is Israel a servant, a slave[s] by birth?
Why then has he become plunder?
15 Lions[t] have roared;
they have growled at him.
They have laid waste[u] his land;
his towns are burned and deserted.
16 Also, the men of Memphis[d][v] and
Tahpanhes[w]
have shaved the crown of your head.[e]
17 Have you not brought this on
yourselves[x]
by forsaking the LORD your God
when he led you in the way?
18 Now why go to Egypt[y]
to drink water from the Shihor[f]?[z]
And why go to Assyria
to drink water from the River[g]?
19 Your wickedness will punish you;
your backsliding[a] will rebuke[b] you.
Consider then and realize
how evil and bitter[c] it is for you
when you forsake the LORD your God
and have no awe[d] of me,"
declares the Lord,
the LORD Almighty.
20 "Long ago you broke off your yoke[e]
and tore off your bonds;
you said, 'I will not serve you!'
Indeed, on every high hill[f]
and under every spreading tree[g]
you lay down as a prostitute.
21 I had planted[h] you like a choice vine[i]
of sound and reliable stock.
How then did you turn against me
into a corrupt,[j] wild vine?

2:11 [p]Isa 37:19; Jer 16:20 [q]Ps 106:20; Ro 1:23
2:13 [r]Ps 36:9; Jn 4:14
2:14 [s]Ex 4:22
2:15 [t]Jer 4:7; 50:17 [u]Isa 1:7
2:16 [v]Isa 19:13 [w]Jer 43:7-9
2:17 [x]Jer 4:18
2:18 [y]Isa 30:2 [z]Jos 13:3
2:19 [a]Jer 3:11,22 [b]Isa 3:9; Hos 5:5 [c]Job 20:14; Am 8:10 [d]Ps 36:1
2:20 [e]Lev 26:13 [f]Isa 57:7; Jer 17:2 [g]Dt 12:2
2:21 [h]Ex 15:17 [i]Ps 80:8 [j]Isa 5:4

[a] *10* That is, Cyprus and western coastlands [b] *10* The home of Bedouin tribes in the Syro-Arabian desert [c] *11* Masoretic Text; an ancient Hebrew scribal tradition *my* [d] *16* Hebrew *Noph* [e] *16* Or *have cracked your skull* [f] *18* That is, a branch of the Nile [g] *18* That is, the Euphrates

Reap What You Sow

JER 2:19

Jeremiah begins his unpopular preaching to Judah with this warning: Your wickedness and backsliding will catch up with you. He urges them to "consider then and realize" (Jer 2:19) that punishment is unavoidable for those who forsake and disrespect their Creator.

While it seems those who frolic with the world engage in endless fun, God reminds them that, in time, everyone reaps what he or she sows. "The one who sows to please his sinful nature, from that nature will reap destruction; the one who sows to please the Spirit, from the Spirit will reap eternal life" (Gal 6:8). While evil seems to triumph, it's reassuring to know that sowing to please God will someday result in rewards beyond measure.

22 Although you wash yourself with soda
and use an abundance of soap,
the stain of your guilt is still before
me,"
declares the Sovereign LORD.
23 "How can you say, 'I am not defiled;[k]
I have not run after the Baals'?[l]
See how you behaved in the valley;[m]
consider what you have done.
You are a swift she-camel
running[n] here and there,
24 a wild donkey[o] accustomed to the desert,
sniffing the wind in her craving—
in her heat who can restrain her?
Any males that pursue her need not tire
themselves;
at mating time they will find her.
25 Do not run until your feet are bare
and your throat is dry.
But you said, 'It's no use!
I love foreign gods,[p]
and I must go after them.'

26 "As a thief is disgraced[q] when he is
caught,
so the house of Israel is disgraced—
they, their kings and their officials,
their priests and their prophets.
27 They say to wood, 'You are my father,'
and to stone,[r] 'You gave me birth.'
They have turned their backs to me
and not their faces;[s]
yet when they are in trouble,[t] they say,
'Come and save us!'
28 Where then are the gods[u] you made for
yourselves?
Let them come if they can save you
when you are in trouble![v]
For you have as many gods
as you have towns,[w] O Judah.

29 "Why do you bring charges against me?
You have all[x] rebelled against me,"
declares the LORD.
30 "In vain I punished your people;
they did not respond to correction.
Your sword has devoured your prophets[y]
like a ravening lion.

31 "You of this generation, consider the word of
the LORD:

"Have I been a desert to Israel
or a land of great darkness?[z]
Why do my people say, 'We are free to
roam;
we will come to you no more'?
32 Does a maiden forget her jewelry,
a bride her wedding ornaments?
Yet my people have forgotten me,
days without number.
33 How skilled you are at pursuing love!

2:23 [k]Pr 30:12 [l]Jer 9:14 [m]Jer 7:31 [n]ver 33; Jer 31:22
2:24 [o]Jer 14:6
2:25 [p]Dt 32:16; Jer 3:13; 14:10
2:26 [q]Jer 48:27
2:27 [r]Jer 3:9 [s]Jer 18:17; 32:33 [t]Jdg 10:10; Isa 26:16
2:28 [u]Isa 45:20 [v]Dt 32:37 [w]2Ki 17:29; Jer 11:13
2:29 [x]Jer 5:1; 6:13; Da 9:11
2:30 [y]Ne 9:26; Ac 7:52; 1Th 2:15
2:31 [z]Isa 45:19

The highest earthly enjoyments are but a shadow of the joy I find in reading God's word.

—Lady Jane Grey (1537-1554)

Even the worst of women can learn
from your ways.
34 On your clothes men find
2:34 a2Ki 21:16 the lifeblood[a] of the innocent poor,
bEx 22:2 though you did not catch them
breaking in.[b]
Yet in spite of all this
35 you say, 'I am innocent;
he is not angry with me.'
2:35 But I will pass judgment[c] on you
cJer 25:31 dJn 1:8,10 because you say, 'I have not sinned.'[d]
36 Why do you go about so much,
2:36 eJer 31:22 changing[e] your ways?
fIsa 30:2,3,7 You will be disappointed by Egypt[f]
as you were by Assyria.
37 You will also leave that place
2:37 with your hands on your head,[g]
g2Sa 13:19 hJer 37:7 for the LORD has rejected those you
trust;
you will not be helped[h] by them.

3:1 iDt 24:1-4 jJer 2:20,25; Eze 16:26,29 3 "If a man divorces[i] his wife
and she leaves him and marries another
man,
should he return to her again?
Would not the land be completely
defiled?
But you have lived as a prostitute with
many lovers[j]—
would you now return to me?"
declares the LORD.
2 "Look up to the barren heights and see.
Is there any place where you have not
been ravished?
3:2 kGe 38:14; Eze 16:25 By the roadside[k] you sat waiting for
lovers,
lJer 2:7 sat like a nomad[a] in the desert.
You have defiled the land[l]
with your prostitution and
wickedness.
3 Therefore the showers have been
3:3 mLev 26:19 withheld,[m]
nJer 14:4 and no spring rains[n] have fallen.
oJer 6:15; 8:12; Zep 3:5 Yet you have the brazen look of a
prostitute;
you refuse to blush with shame.[o]
4 Have you not just called to me:
3:4 pver 19 'My Father,[p] my friend from my
qJer 2:2 youth,[q]
5 will you always be angry?[r]
3:5 rPs 103:9; Isa 57:16 Will your wrath continue forever?'
This is how you talk,
but you do all the evil you can."

Unfaithful Israel

6 During the reign of King Josiah, the LORD said
to me, "Have you seen what faithless Israel has
done? She has gone up on every high hill and
3:6 sJer 17:2 under every spreading tree[s] and has committed

Looking for Love

JER 2:33

God's people run from his love into the arms of pagan religions and human power. Moral depravity, political corruption and spiritual idolatry mar the nation and its people. The people of Judah pursue love in all the wrong places, refusing the power of God to fill their emptiness and satisfy their cravings.

[a] 2 Or *an Arab*

Our Husband

JER 3:14

Throughout Scripture God compares himself to a tender husband, a joyful bridegroom who cares for his people, his bride. Like any adoring husband, God rightfully grows angry when his bride (Judah) strays.

Scripture also repeatedly reminds us of God's jealous love for his people (Ex 20:5; 34:14; Zec 8:2). When they ignore their divine lover or flirt with the world, they hurt and disappoint their heavenly husband. He wants them, like Judah, to live pure lives as they prepare to join him in heaven. "As a bridegroom rejoices over his bride, so will your God rejoice over you" (Isa 62:5).

adultery[t] there. 7I thought that after she had done
all this she would return to me but she did not,
and her unfaithful sister[u] Judah saw it. 8I gave
faithless Israel her certificate of divorce and sent
her away because of all her adulteries. Yet I saw
that her unfaithful sister Judah had no fear;[v] she
also went out and committed adultery. 9Because
Israel's immorality mattered so little to her, she
defiled the land[w] and committed adultery with
stone[x] and wood.[y] 10In spite of all this, her unfaithful sister Judah did not return to me with all her
heart, but only in pretense,[z]" declares the LORD.
11The LORD said to me, "Faithless Israel is more
righteous[a] than unfaithful[b] Judah. 12Go, proclaim
this message toward the north:[c]

" 'Return,[d] faithless Israel,' declares the
LORD,
'I will frown on you no longer,
for I am merciful,' declares the LORD,
'I will not be angry[e] forever.
13 Only acknowledge[f] your guilt—
you have rebelled against the LORD
your God,
you have scattered your favors to foreign
gods[g]
under every spreading tree,[h]
and have not obeyed[i] me,' "
declares the LORD.

14"Return,[j] faithless people," declares the LORD,
"for I am your husband. I will choose you—one
from a town and two from a clan—and bring you
to Zion. 15Then I will give you shepherds[k] after
my own heart, who will lead you with knowledge
and understanding. 16In those days, when your
numbers have increased greatly in the land,"
declares the LORD, "men will no longer say, 'The
ark of the covenant of the LORD.' It will never enter
their minds or be remembered;[l] it will not be
missed, nor will another one be made. 17At that
time they will call Jerusalem The Throne[m] of the
LORD, and all nations will gather in Jerusalem to
honor[n] the name of the LORD. No longer will they
follow the stubbornness of their evil hearts.[o] 18In
those days the house of Judah will join the house
of Israel,[p] and together[q] they will come from a
northern[r] land to the land[s] I gave your forefathers
as an inheritance.
19"I myself said,

" 'How gladly would I treat you like sons
and give you a desirable land,
the most beautiful inheritance of any
nation.'
I thought you would call me 'Father'[t]
and not turn away from following me.
20 But like a woman unfaithful to her
husband,
so you have been unfaithful to me,
O house of Israel,"
declares the LORD.

3:6 [t]Jer 2:20
3:7 [u]Eze 16:46
3:8 [v]Eze 16:47; 23:11
3:9 [w]ver 2 [x]Isa 57:6 [y]Jer 2:27
3:10 [z]Jer 12:2
3:11 [a]Eze 16:52; 23:11 [b]ver 7
3:12 [c]2Ki 17:3-6 [d]ver 14; Jer 31:21,22; Eze 33:11 [e]Ps 86:15
3:13 [f]Dt 30:1-3; Jer 14:20; 1Jn 1:9 [g]Jer 2:25 [h]Dt 12:2 [i]ver 25
3:14 [j]Hos 2:19
3:15 [k]Ac 20:28
3:16 [l]Isa 65:17
3:17 [m]Jer 17:12; Eze 43:7 [n]Isa 60:9 [o]Jer 11:8
3:18 [p]Hos 1:11 [q]Isa 11:13; Jer 50:4 [r]Jer 16:15; 31:8 [s]Am 9:15
3:19 [t]ver 4; Isa 63:16

3:21 [u]ver 2
[21] A cry is heard on the barren heights,[u]
the weeping and pleading of the people of Israel,
because they have perverted their ways
and have forgotten the LORD their God.

3:22 [v]Hos 14:4 [w]Jer 33:6; Hos 6:1
[22] "Return,[v] faithless people;
I will cure[w] you of backsliding."

"Yes, we will come to you,
for you are the LORD our God.
[23] Surely the ⌊idolatrous⌋ commotion on the hills
and mountains is a deception;
surely in the LORD our God
3:23 [x]Ps 3:8; Jer 17:14
is the salvation[x] of Israel.
[24] From our youth shameful[y] gods have consumed
3:24 [y]Hos 9:10
the fruits of our fathers' labor—
their flocks and herds,
their sons and daughters.
3:25 [z]Ezr 9:6 [a]Jer 22:21
[25] Let us lie down in our shame,[z]
and let our disgrace cover us.
We have sinned against the LORD our God,
both we and our fathers;
from our youth[a] till this day
we have not obeyed the LORD our God."

4:1 [b]Jer 3:1,22; Joel 2:12 [c]Jer 35:15
4 "If you will return[b], O Israel,
return to me,"
declares the LORD.
"If you put your detestable idols[c] out of my sight
and no longer go astray,
[2] and if in a truthful, just and righteous way
4:2 [d]Dt 10:20; Isa 65:16 [e]Jer 12:16 [f]Ge 22:18; Gal 3:8
you swear,[d] 'As surely as the LORD lives,'[e]
then the nations will be blessed[f] by him
and in him they will glory."

[3] This is what the LORD says to the men of Judah
and to Jerusalem:
4:3 [g]Hos 10:12 [h]Mk 4:18
"Break up your unplowed ground[g]
and do not sow among thorns.[h]
4:4 [i]Dt 10:16; Jer 9:26; Ro 2:28-29 [j]Zep 2:2 [k]Am 5:6
[4] Circumcise yourselves to the LORD,
circumcise your hearts,[i]
you men of Judah and people of Jerusalem,
or my wrath[j] will break out and burn like fire
because of the evil you have done—
burn with no one to quench[k] it.

Disaster From the North

[5] "Announce in Judah and proclaim in Jerusalem and say:
'Sound the trumpet throughout the land!'

Promised Blessing

JER 4:1-2

God offers Israel a blessing in exchange for its renewed devotion. This conditional blessing divides into two parts: if the people return to God, then he promises to bless them.

God first offers a blessing to Israel through his covenant with Abraham in Genesis 12:1-3. This unconditional blessing rests solely on God's grace. In this Jeremiah passage, God offers a conditional blessing to point the people to right conduct. If the people obey God, he will shower them with material and spiritual rewards. The obedience of the individual affects the condition of the entire nation. When God's people follow him, he will bless them. But his temporal gifts pale when compared to the spiritual rewards of peace, forgiveness and eternal life through Abraham's son, the Messiah.

Honest Prayer

JER 4:10

The prophet Jeremiah calls God a deceiver in this verse because he allows false prophets to lull the people into greater spiritual apathy. He grieves that Babylon from the north will overtake Judah like a destructive sirocco, an unbearably hot desert wind. As intercessor for the people, Jeremiah sympathizes with his fellow citizens. God's words of judgment upset him, and he cries out in deep sorrow.

Because Jeremiah trusts God's goodness in spite of the approaching judgments, he boldly and honestly shares his disappointment over the Almighty's decision. He is free to cry out honestly and boldly to God. We too can approach God honestly and boldly, practicing the words of Psalm 62:8: "Trust in him at all times, O people; pour out your hearts to him, for God is our refuge."

Cry aloud and say:
'Gather together!
Let us flee to the fortified cities!'[l]
6 Raise the signal to go to Zion!
Flee for safety without delay!
For I am bringing disaster from the north,[m]
even terrible destruction."
7 A lion[n] has come out of his lair;
a destroyer of nations has set out.
He has left his place
to lay waste[o] your land.
Your towns will lie in ruins[p]
without inhabitant.
8 So put on sackcloth,[q]
lament and wail,
for the fierce anger[r] of the LORD
has not turned away from us.
9 "In that day," declares the LORD,
"the king and the officials will lose heart,
the priests will be horrified,
and the prophets will be appalled."[s]

10 Then I said, "Ah, Sovereign LORD, how completely you have deceived[t] this people and Jerusalem by saying, 'You will have peace,'[u] when the
sword is at our throats."
11 At that time this people and Jerusalem will be
told, "A scorching wind[v] from the barren heights
in the desert blows toward my people, but not to
winnow or cleanse; 12 a wind too strong for that
comes from me.[a] Now I pronounce my judgments[w] against them."

13 Look! He advances like the clouds,[x]
his chariots[y] come like a whirlwind,[z]
his horses are swifter than eagles.[a]
Woe to us! We are ruined!
14 O Jerusalem, wash[b] the evil from your heart and be saved.
How long will you harbor wicked thoughts?
15 A voice is announcing from Dan,[c]
proclaiming disaster from the hills of Ephraim.
16 "Tell this to the nations,
proclaim it to Jerusalem:
'A besieging army is coming from a distant land,
raising a war cry[d] against the cities of Judah.
17 They surround[e] her like men guarding a field,
because she has rebelled[f] against me,' "
declares the LORD.
18 "Your own conduct and actions[g]
have brought this upon you.[h]

4:5 [l] Jos 10:20; Jer 8:14
4:6 [m] Jer 1:13-15; 50:3
4:7 [n] 2Ki 24:1; Jer 2:15 [o] Isa 1:7 [p] Jer 25:9
4:8 [q] Isa 22:12; Jer 6:26 [r] Jer 30:24
4:9 [s] Isa 29:9
4:10 [t] 2Th 2:11 [u] Jer 14:13
4:11 [v] Eze 17:10; Hos 13:15
4:12 [w] Jer 1:16
4:13 [x] Isa 19:1 [y] Isa 66:15 [z] Isa 5:28 [a] Dt 28:49; Hab 1:8
4:14 [b] Jas 4:8
4:15 [c] Jer 8:16
4:16 [d] Eze 21:22
4:17 [e] 2Ki 25:1,4 [f] Jer 5:23
4:18 [g] Ps 107:17; Isa 50:1 [h] Jer 2:17

[a] 12 Or *comes at my command*

This is your punishment.
How bitter[i] it is!
How it pierces to the heart!"

19 Oh, my anguish, my anguish![j]
I writhe in pain.
Oh, the agony of my heart!
My heart pounds within me,
I cannot keep silent.[k]
For I have heard the sound of the trumpet;
I have heard the battle cry.[l]
20 Disaster follows disaster;[m]
the whole land lies in ruins.
In an instant my tents[n] are destroyed,
my shelter in a moment.
21 How long must I see the battle standard
and hear the sound of the trumpet?

22 "My people are fools;[o]
they do not know me.[p]
They are senseless children;
they have no understanding.
They are skilled in doing evil;[q]
they know not how to do good."[r]

23 I looked at the earth,
and it was formless and empty;[s]
and at the heavens,
and their light was gone.
24 I looked at the mountains,
and they were quaking;[t]
all the hills were swaying.
25 I looked, and there were no people;
every bird in the sky had flown away.[u]
26 I looked, and the fruitful land was a desert;
all its towns lay in ruins
before the LORD, before his fierce anger.

27 This is what the LORD says:

"The whole land will be ruined,
though I will not destroy[v] it completely.
28 Therefore the earth will mourn[w]
and the heavens above grow dark,[x]
because I have spoken and will not relent,[y]
I have decided and will not turn back.[z]"

29 At the sound of horsemen and archers[a]
every town takes to flight.[b]
Some go into the thickets;
some climb up among the rocks.
All the towns are deserted;[c]
no one lives in them.

30 What are you doing,[d] O devastated one?
Why dress yourself in scarlet
and put on jewels[e] of gold?
Why shade your eyes with paint?[f]

4:18 [i]Jer 2:19
4:19 [j]Isa 16:11; 22:4; Jer 9:10 [k]Jer 20:9 [l]Nu 10:9
4:20 [m]Ps 42:7; Eze 7:26 [n]Jer 10:20
4:22 [o]Jer 10:8 [p]Jer 2:8 [q]Jer 13:23; 1Co 14:20 [r]Ro 16:19
4:23 [s]Ge 1:2
4:24 [t]Isa 5:25; Eze 38:20
4:25 [u]Jer 9:10; 12:4; Zep 1:3
4:27 [v]Jer 5:10,18; 12:12; 30:11; 46:28
4:28 [w]Jer 12:4,11; 14:2; Hos 4:3 [x]Isa 5:30; 50:3 [y]Nu 23:19 [z]Jer 23:20; 30:24
4:29 [a]Jer 6:23 [b]2Ki 25:4 [c]ver 7
4:30 [d]Isa 10:3-4 [e]Eze 23:40 [f]2Ki 9:30

Heart Cries

JER 4:19-21

A gentle man of candor and passion, Jeremiah's personality doesn't match his strident role as God's spokesperson. The prophet endures nearly 50 years of ridicule and abuse by the people he tries to help. He is placed in stocks, beaten, cursed, starved and thrown in a pit for delivering God's message. Even the men in his own hometown of Anathoth—possibly his own family and friends—plan to murder him (Jer 11:18-23). Except for his one companion, Baruch, Jeremiah remains a loner. God even instructs him not to marry or raise a family (Jer 16:1-4). This "weeping prophet" stays keenly sensitive to the plight of his people and grieves over their rebelliousness.

Labor Pains

JER 4:31

Judah must endure the final stages of destruction. Jeremiah compares the death throes of the nation with a woman agonizing during the birth of her first child. Just as a woman groans and gasps for breath during delivery, Jerusalem will cry out during her final hours at the hands of mighty Babylon. While the pain of childbirth results in the joy of new life, the pain of disobeying God causes Jerusalem increased misery and eventual destruction.

You adorn yourself in vain.
Your lovers[g] despise you;
they seek your life.

31 I hear a cry as of a woman in labor,[h]
a groan as of one bearing her first child—
the cry of the Daughter of Zion gasping for breath,[i]
stretching out her hands[j] and saying,
"Alas! I am fainting;
my life is given over to murderers."

Not One Is Upright

5 "Go up and down[k] the streets of Jerusalem,
look around and consider,
search through her squares.
If you can find but one person[l]
who deals honestly and seeks the truth,
I will forgive[m] this city.
2 Although they say, 'As surely as the LORD lives,'[n]
still they are swearing falsely."

3 O LORD, do not your eyes[o] look for truth?
You struck[p] them, but they felt no pain;
you crushed them, but they refused correction.[q]
They made their faces harder than stone[r]
and refused to repent.
4 I thought, "These are only the poor;
they are foolish,
for they do not know[s] the way of the LORD,
the requirements of their God.
5 So I will go to the leaders[t]
and speak to them;
surely they know the way of the LORD,
the requirements of their God."
But with one accord they too had broken off the yoke
and torn off the bonds.[u]
6 Therefore a lion from the forest will attack them,
a wolf from the desert will ravage them,
a leopard[v] will lie in wait near their towns
to tear to pieces any who venture out,
for their rebellion is great
and their backslidings many.[w]

7 "Why should I forgive you?
Your children have forsaken me
and sworn[x] by gods that are not gods.[y]
I supplied all their needs,
yet they committed adultery[z]

4:30 [g]La 1:2; Eze 23:9,22
4:31 [h]Jer 13:21 [i]Isa 42:14 [j]Isa 1:15; La 1:17
5:1 [k]2Ch 16:9; Eze 22:30 [l]Ge 18:32 [m]Ge 18:24
5:2 [n]Jer 4:2
5:3 [o]2Ch 16:9 [p]Isa 9:13 [q]Jer 2:30; Zep 3:2 [r]Jer 7:26; 19:15; Eze 3:8-9
5:4 [s]Jer 8:7
5:5 [t]Mic 3:1,9 [u]Ps 2:3; Jer 2:20
5:6 [v]Hos 13:7 [w]Jer 30:14
5:7 [x]Jos 23:7; Zep 1:5 [y]Dt 32:21; Jer 2:11; Gal 4:8 [z]Nu 25:1

and thronged to the houses of
prostitutes.
8 They are well-fed, lusty stallions,
each neighing for another man's wife.[a]
9 Should I not punish them for this?"[b]
declares the LORD.
"Should I not avenge myself
on such a nation as this?

10 "Go through her vineyards and ravage
them,
but do not destroy them completely.[c]
Strip off her branches,
for these people do not belong to the
LORD.
11 The house of Israel and the house of
Judah
have been utterly unfaithful[d] to me,"
declares the LORD.

12 They have lied about the LORD;
they said, "He will do nothing!
No harm will come to us;[e]
we will never see sword or famine.[f]
13 The prophets[g] are but wind
and the word is not in them;
so let what they say be done to them."

14 Therefore this is what the LORD God Almighty
says:

"Because the people have spoken these
words,
I will make my words in your mouth[h]
a fire[i]
and these people the wood it
consumes.
15 O house of Israel," declares the LORD,
"I am bringing a distant nation[j]
against you—
an ancient and enduring nation,
a people whose language[k] you do not
know,
whose speech you do not understand.
16 Their quivers are like an open grave;
all of them are mighty warriors.
17 They will devour[l m] your harvests and
food,
devour[n o] your sons and daughters;
they will devour[p] your flocks and herds,
devour your vines and fig trees.
With the sword they will destroy
the fortified cities in which you trust.[q]

18 "Yet even in those days," declares the LORD, "I
will not destroy[r] you completely. 19 And when the
people ask,[s] 'Why has the LORD our God done all
this to us?' you will tell them, 'As you have forsaken me and served foreign gods[t] in your own
land, so now you will serve foreigners[u] in a land
not your own.'

20 "Announce this to the house of Jacob
and proclaim it in Judah:

5:8 [a]Jer 29:23; Eze 22:11
5:9 [b]ver 29; Jer 9:9
5:10 [c]Jer 4:27
5:11 [d]Jer 3:20
5:12 [e]Jer 23:17 [f]2Ch 36:16; Jer 14:13
5:13 [g]Jer 14:15
5:14 [h]Jer 1:9; Hos 6:5 [i]Jer 23:29
5:15 [j]Dt 28:49; Isa 5:26; Jer 4:16 [k]Isa 28:11
5:17 [l]Jer 8:16 [m]Lev 26:16 [n]Jer 50:7,17 [o]Dt 28:32 [p]Dt 28:31 [q]Dt 28:33
5:18 [r]Jer 4:27
5:19 [s]Dt 29:24-26; 1Ki 9:9 [t]Jer 16:13 [u]Dt 28:48

The Real Enemy

JER 5:15-16

In the early days of Jeremiah's ministry, Judah primarily fears the threats of Egypt and Assyria. But Judah focuses on the wrong enemy. In this passage God warns of attack by a distant, ancient nation. Soon Babylon defeats Assyria and gains world power. Babylon becomes the prophesied foe with "mighty warriors" (Jer 5:16). Eventually, they will come to Judah, destroy Jerusalem and take captive to foreign countries those who survive the devastation.

I am still amazed at my lack of grace and kindness in the most simple of situations. I can go from speaking to a crowd about the love of God, feeling so close to heaven that it seems as if I have gold dust on my shoes to . . . driving in traffic and having someone cut me off—and I become a maniac.

All I know to do is (1) to keep bringing this rip in my soul to the foot of the cross and (2) whenever my unkindness touches the life of another to go to that person and ask forgiveness. It is my calling to treat every human being with grace and dignity, to treat every person, whether encountered in a palace or a gas station as a life made in the image of God.

—Sheila Walsh

21 Hear this, you foolish and senseless
people,
who have eyes[v] but do not see,
who have ears but do not hear:[w]
22 Should you not fear[x] me?" declares the
LORD.
"Should you not tremble in my
presence?
I made the sand a boundary for the sea,
an everlasting barrier it cannot cross.
The waves may roll, but they cannot
prevail;
they may roar, but they cannot cross it.
23 But these people have stubborn and
rebellious[y] hearts;
they have turned aside and gone away.
24 They do not say to themselves,
'Let us fear the LORD our God,
who gives autumn and spring rains[z] in
season,
who assures us of the regular weeks
of harvest.'[a]
25 Your wrongdoings have kept these
away;
your sins have deprived you of good.
26 "Among my people are wicked men
who lie in wait[b] like men who snare
birds
and like those who set traps to catch
men.
27 Like cages full of birds,
their houses are full of deceit;[c]
they have become rich[d] and powerful
28 and have grown fat[e] and sleek.
Their evil deeds have no limit;
they do not plead the case of the
fatherless[f] to win it,
they do not defend the rights of the
poor.[g]
29 Should I not punish them for this?"
declares the LORD.
"Should I not avenge myself
on such a nation as this?
30 "A horrible[h] and shocking thing
has happened in the land:
31 The prophets prophesy lies,[i]
the priests rule by their own
authority,
and my people love it this way.
But what will you do in the end?

Jerusalem Under Siege

6 "Flee for safety, people of Benjamin!
Flee from Jerusalem!
Sound the trumpet in Tekoa![j]
Raise the signal over Beth
Hakkerem![k]
For disaster looms out of the north,[l]
even terrible destruction.
2 I will destroy the Daughter of Zion,

5:21 [v]Isa 6:10; Eze 12:2 [w]Mt 13:15; Mk 8:18
5:22 [x]Dt 28:58
5:23 [y]Dt 21:18
5:24 [z]Ps 147:8; Joel 2:23 [a]Ge 8:22; Ac 14:17
5:26 [b]Ps 10:8; Pr 1:11
5:27 [c]Jer 9:6 [d]Jer 12:1
5:28 [e]Dt 32:15 [f]Zec 7:10 [g]Isa 1:23; Jer 7:6
5:30 [h]Jer 23:14; Hos 6:10
5:31 [i]Eze 13:6; Mic 2:11
6:1 [j]2Ch 11:6 [k]Ne 3:14 [l]Jer 4:6

so beautiful and delicate.
3 Shepherds[m] with their flocks will come
against her;
they will pitch their tents around[n] her,
each tending his own portion."

4 "Prepare for battle against her!
Arise, let us attack at noon![o]
But, alas, the daylight is fading,
and the shadows of evening grow long.
5 So arise, let us attack at night
and destroy her fortresses!"

6 This is what the LORD Almighty says:

"Cut down the trees[p]
and build siege ramps[q] against
Jerusalem.
This city must be punished;
it is filled with oppression.
7 As a well pours out its water,
so she pours out her wickedness.
Violence[r] and destruction[s] resound in
her;
her sickness and wounds are ever
before me.
8 Take warning, O Jerusalem,
or I will turn away[t] from you
and make your land desolate
so no one can live in it."

9 This is what the LORD Almighty says:

"Let them glean the remnant of Israel
as thoroughly as a vine;
pass your hand over the branches again,
like one gathering grapes."

10 To whom can I speak and give warning?
Who will listen to me?
Their ears are closed[a][u]
so they cannot hear.
The word[v] of the LORD is offensive to
them;
they find no pleasure in it.
11 But I am full of the wrath[w] of the LORD,
and I cannot hold it in.[x]

"Pour it out on the children in the street
and on the young men[y] gathered
together;
both husband and wife will be caught in
it,
and the old, those weighed down with
years.
12 Their houses will be turned over to
others,[z]
together with their fields and their
wives,[a]
when I stretch out my hand[b]
against those who live in the land,"
declares the LORD.

6:3 [m]Jer 12:10 [n]2Ki 25:4; Lk 19:43
6:4 [o]Jer 15:8
6:6 [p]Dt 20:19-20 [q]Jer 32:24
6:7 [r]Ps 55:9; Eze 7:11,23 [s]Jer 20:8
6:8 [t]Eze 23:18; Hos 9:12
6:10 [u]Ac 7:51 [v]Jer 20:8
6:11 [w]Jer 7:20 [x]Job 32:20; Jer 20:9 [y]Jer 9:21
6:12 [z]Dt 28:30 [a]Jer 8:10; 38:22 [b]Isa 5:25

[a] 10 Hebrew *uncircumcised*

Sheep's Clothing

JER 6:3

Sheep are the most familiar animal mentioned in the Bible, and keeping flocks is the first occupation listed in Scripture (Ge 4:2). The people of Judah are well acquainted with flocks roaming the countryside, and they depend on these ceremonially clean animals (Dt 14:6) for meat and wool. They have an innate trust in shepherds, who protect these animals and who can call each member of their flocks by name.

So when God warns that shepherds will attack the Daughter of Zion, the people question his troubling words. The picture surprises them: How can a shepherd, one known for being loving and kind, wreak such havoc on their nation? The evil shepherds represent enemy kings; and the flocks, their legions of soldiers—wolves in sheep's clothing, so to speak. We too need to watch for those in "sheep's clothing," those who may appear peaceful and safe on the outside, "but inwardly they are ferocious wolves" (Mt 7:15).

Looking Back

JER 6:16

Jeremiah tells the people to look back at the ways of their ancestors, who saw God deliver them from the hands of Egypt. He begs them to ask for "where the good way is, and walk in it" (Jer 6:16). He doesn't want the people to rely on ancient traditions but on the Lord, who has guided the nation of Israel from its inception.

Sometimes looking back to the past reminds us of what God has done for us and makes us confident of his involvement in our present and future. In Joshua 4:1–9, God directs the 12 tribes of Israel to set up memorial stones as a reminder of his safe guidance across the Jordan River. Make a list of your own "memorial stones." How has God, who is sovereign over the past, the present and the future, provided for you step by step in your life's journey?

13 "From the least to the greatest,
all are greedy for gain;[c]
prophets and priests alike,
all practice deceit.[d]
14 They dress the wound of my people
as though it were not serious.
'Peace, peace,' they say,
when there is no peace.[e]
15 Are they ashamed of their loathsome conduct?
No, they have no shame at all;
they do not even know how to blush.[f]
So they will fall among the fallen;
they will be brought down when I punish them,"
says the LORD.

16 This is what the LORD says:

"Stand at the crossroads and look;
ask for the ancient paths,[g]
ask where the good way[h] is, and walk in it,
and you will find rest[i] for your souls.
But you said, 'We will not walk in it.'
17 I appointed watchmen[j] over you and said,
'Listen to the sound of the trumpet!'
But you said, 'We will not listen.'[k]
18 Therefore hear, O nations;
observe, O witnesses,
what will happen to them.
19 Hear, O earth:[l]
I am bringing disaster on this people,
the fruit of their schemes,[m]
because they have not listened to my words
and have rejected my law.[n]
20 What do I care about incense from Sheba
or sweet calamus[o] from a distant land?
Your burnt offerings are not acceptable;[p]
your sacrifices[q] do not please me."[r]

21 Therefore this is what the LORD says:

"I will put obstacles before this people.
Fathers and sons alike will stumble[s] over them;
neighbors and friends will perish."

22 This is what the LORD says:

"Look, an army is coming
from the land of the north;[t]
a great nation is being stirred up
from the ends of the earth.
23 They are armed with bow and spear;
they are cruel and show no mercy.[u]
They sound like the roaring sea
as they ride on their horses;[v]
they come like men in battle formation
to attack you, O Daughter of Zion."

6:13 [c]Isa 56:11 [d]Jer 8:10
6:14 [e]Jer 4:10; 8:11; Eze 13:10
6:15 [f]Jer 3:3; 8:10-12
6:16 [g]Jer 18:15 [h]Ps 119:3 [i]Mt 11:29
6:17 [j]Eze 3:17 [k]Jer 11:7-8; 25:4
6:19 [l]Isa 1:2; Jer 22:29 [m]Pr 1:31 [n]Jer 8:9
6:20 [o]Ex 30:23 [p]Am 5:22 [q]Ps 50:8-10; Jer 7:21; Mic 6:7-8 [r]Isa 1:11
6:21 [s]Isa 8:14
6:22 [t]Jer 1:15; 10:22
6:23 [u]Isa 13:18 [v]Jer 4:29

24 We have heard reports about them,
and our hands hang limp.
Anguish[w] has gripped us,
pain like that of a woman in labor.[x]
25 Do not go out to the fields
or walk on the roads,
for the enemy has a sword,
and there is terror on every side.[y]
26 O my people, put on sackcloth[z]
and roll in ashes;[a]
mourn with bitter wailing
as for an only son,[b]
for suddenly the destroyer
will come upon us.
27 "I have made you a tester[c] of metals
and my people the ore,
that you may observe
and test their ways.
28 They are all hardened rebels,[d]
going about to slander.[e]
They are bronze and iron;[f]
they all act corruptly.
29 The bellows blow fiercely
to burn away the lead with fire,
but the refining goes on in vain;
the wicked are not purged out.
30 They are called rejected silver,
because the LORD has rejected them."[g]

False Religion Worthless

7 This is the word that came to Jeremiah from
the LORD: 2 "Stand[h] at the gate of the LORD's
house and there proclaim this message:
" 'Hear the word of the LORD, all you people of
Judah who come through these gates to worship
the LORD. 3 This is what the LORD Almighty, the
God of Israel, says: Reform your ways[i] and your
actions, and I will let you live in this place. 4 Do
not trust in deceptive[j] words and say, "This is the
temple of the LORD, the temple of the LORD, the
temple of the LORD!" 5 If you really change your
ways and your actions and deal with each other
justly,[k] 6 if you do not oppress the alien, the fatherless or the widow and do not shed innocent blood[l]
in this place, and if you do not follow other gods[m]
to your own harm, 7 then I will let you live in this
place, in the land[n] I gave your forefathers for ever
and ever. 8 But look, you are trusting in deceptive
words that are worthless.
9 " 'Will you steal and murder, commit adultery
and perjury,[a] burn incense to Baal[o] and follow
other gods[p] you have not known, 10 and then come
and stand before me in this house,[q] which bears
my Name, and say, "We are safe"—safe to do all
these detestable things? 11 Has this house,[r] which
bears my Name, become a den of robbers[s] to you?
But I have been watching![t] declares the LORD.
12 " 'Go now to the place in Shiloh[u] where I first

[a] 9 Or *and swear by false gods*

6:24 [w]Jer 4:19 [x]Jer 4:31; 50:41-43
6:25 [y]Jer 49:29
6:26 [z]Jer 4:8 [a]Jer 25:34; Mic 1:10 [b]Zec 12:10
6:27 [c]Jer 9:7
6:28 [d]Jer 5:23 [e]Jer 9:4 [f]Eze 22:18
6:30 [g]Ps 119:119; Jer 7:29; Hos 9:17
7:2 [h]Jer 17:19
7:3 [i]Jer 18:11; 26:13
7:4 [j]Mic 3:11
7:5 [k]Jer 22:3
7:6 [l]Jer 2:34; 19:4 [m]Dt 8:19
7:7 [n]Dt 4:40
7:9 [o]Jer 11:13,17 [p]Ex 20:3
7:10 [q]Jer 32:34; Eze 23:38-39
7:11 [r]Isa 56:7 [s]Mt 21:13*; Mk 11:17*; Lk 19:46* [t]Jer 29:23
7:12 [u]Jos 18:1

Under Fire

Authentic Worship

JER 6:28–29

Heat tests and purifies metal. Under fire, impurities burn away until only the pure metal remains. At times, metal is tested and found to contain too little valuable ore to be worth working. It is then thrown out. When God tests the people of Judah, he finds lives filled with impurities. Judah has been tested and fired and, just like poor metal, is too impure to be worth working. The people are hardened rebels who refuse to turn from their sinful ways. They are rejected, just as poor metal is rejected. God will toss them out to the Babylonians. Willing hearts are those that are not spiritually hardened but rather are purified by the master refiner, "who gave himself for us to redeem us from all wickedness and to purify for himself a people that are his very own, eager to do what is good" (Tit 2:14).

Family Worship

JER 7:18

Jeremiah describes a family preparing ceremonial cakes for the Queen of Heaven, Ishtar, the Mesopotamian fertility goddess. As a goddess of fertility, her worship involved cultic prostitution. Not only in the towns of Judah, but also in the streets of Jerusalem, God's appointed holy city, the people worshiped Ishtar and other foreign gods. Even after the fall of Jerusalem, Judah's inhabitants fled to Egypt and continued worshiping her there (Jer 44:15–17). No wonder God is angry with his people! He is pleased when families honor him—the King of kings (1Ti 6:15)—not a man-made goddess or religious symbol.

made a dwelling for my Name, and see what I
did[v] to it because of the wickedness of my people
Israel. 13While you were doing all these things,
declares the LORD, I spoke to you again and
again,[w] but you did not listen;[x] I called you, but
you did not answer.[y] 14Therefore, what I did to
Shiloh I will now do to the house that bears my
Name,[z] the temple you trust in, the place I gave
to you and your fathers. 15I will thrust you from
my presence, just as I did all your brothers, the
people of Ephraim.'[a]

16"So do not pray for this people nor offer any
plea[b] or petition for them; do not plead with me,
for I will not listen to you. 17Do you not see what
they are doing in the towns of Judah and in the
streets of Jerusalem? 18The children gather wood,
the fathers light the fire, and the women knead the
dough and make cakes of bread for the Queen of
Heaven.[c] They pour out drink offerings[d] to other
gods to provoke[e] me to anger. 19But am I the one
they are provoking? declares the LORD. Are they not
rather harming themselves, to their own shame?[f]

20" 'Therefore this is what the Sovereign LORD
says: My anger[g] and my wrath will be poured out
on this place, on man and beast, on the trees of
the field and on the fruit of the ground, and it will
burn and not be quenched.

21" 'This is what the LORD Almighty, the God of
Israel, says: Go ahead, add your burnt offerings to
your other sacrifices[h] and eat[i] the meat yourselves! 22For when I brought your forefathers out
of Egypt and spoke to them, I did not just give
them commands about burnt offerings and sacrifices,[j] 23but I gave them this command: Obey[k] me,
and I will be your God and you will be my people.[l] Walk in all the ways I command you, that it
may go well[m] with you. 24But they did not listen
or pay attention;[n] instead, they followed the stubborn inclinations of their evil hearts. They went
backward and not forward. 25From the time your
forefathers left Egypt until now, day after day,
again and again I sent you my servants the prophets.[o] 26But they did not listen to me or pay attention. They were stiff-necked and did more evil
than their forefathers.'[p]

27"When you tell[q] them all this, they will not
listen[r] to you; when you call to them, they will
not answer. 28Therefore say to them, 'This is the
nation that has not obeyed the LORD its God or
responded to correction. Truth has perished; it has
vanished from their lips. 29Cut off[s] your hair and
throw it away; take up a lament on the barren
heights, for the LORD has rejected and abandoned[t]
this generation that is under his wrath.

The Valley of Slaughter

30" 'The people of Judah have done evil in my
eyes, declares the LORD. They have set up their
detestable idols[u] in the house that bears my Name
and have defiled[v] it. 31They have built the high
places of Topheth[w] in the Valley of Ben Hinnom

7:12 [v]1Sa 4:10-11, 22; Ps 78:60-64
7:13 [w]2Ch 36:15 [x]Isa 65:12 [y]Jer 35:17
7:14 [z]1Ki 9:7
7:15 [a]Ps 78:67
7:16 [b]Ex 32:10; Dt 9:14; Jer 15:1
7:18 [c]Jer 44:17-19 [d]Jer 19:13 [e]1Ki 14:9
7:19 [f]Jer 9:19
7:20 [g]Jer 42:18; La 2:3-5
7:21 [h]Isa 1:11; Am 5:21-22 [i]Hos 8:13
7:22 [j]1Sa 15:22; Ps 51:16; Hos 6:6
7:23 [k]Ex 19:5 [l]Lev 26:12 [m]Ex 15:26
7:24 [n]Ps 81:11-12; Jer 11:8
7:25 [o]Jer 25:4
7:26 [p]Jer 16:12
7:27 [q]Eze 2:7 [r]Eze 3:7
7:29 [s]Job 1:20; Isa 15:2; Mic 1:16 [t]Jer 6:30
7:30 [u]Eze 7:20-22 [v]Jer 32:34
7:31 [w]2Ki 23:10

7:31 to burn their sons and daughters[x] in the fire—
[x]Ps 106:38 something I did not command, nor did it enter my
[y]Jer 19:5 mind.[y] 32 So beware, the days are coming, declares
the LORD, when people will no longer call it
7:32 Topheth or the Valley of Ben Hinnom, but the Val-
[z]Jer 19:6 ley of Slaughter,[z] for they will bury[a] the dead in
[a]Jer 19:11 Topheth until there is no more room. 33 Then the
7:33 carcasses of this people will become food[b] for the
[b]Dt 28:26 birds of the air and the beasts of the earth, and
7:34 there will be no one to frighten them away. 34 I will
[c]Isa 24:8; bring an end to the sounds[c] of joy and gladness
Eze 26:13 [d]Rev 18:23 and to the voices of bride and bridegroom[d] in the
[e]Lev 26:34 towns of Judah and the streets of Jerusalem, for
the land will become desolate.[e]

8 " 'At that time, declares the LORD, the bones of
the kings and officials of Judah, the bones of
the priests and prophets, and the bones of the people of Jerusalem will be removed from their
graves. 2 They will be exposed to the sun and the
8:2 moon and all the stars of the heavens, which they
[f]2Ki 23:5; have loved and served[f] and which they have fol-
Ac 7:42 lowed and consulted and worshiped. They will
not be gathered up or buried, but will be like
refuse lying on the ground. 3 Wherever I banish
8:3 them, all the survivors of this evil nation will pre-
[g]Job 3:22; fer death to life,[g] declares the LORD Almighty.'
Rev 9:6

Sin and Punishment

4 "Say to them, 'This is what the LORD says:

" 'When men fall down, do they not get
8:4 up?[h]
[h]Pr 24:16 When a man turns away, does he not
return?
5 Why then have these people turned
away?
Why does Jerusalem always turn
8:5 away?
[i]Jer 5:27 They cling to deceit;[i]
[j]Jer 7:24; 9:6 they refuse to return.[j]
6 I have listened attentively,
8:6 but they do not say what is right.
[k]Rev 9:20 No one repents[k] of his wickedness,
[l]Ps 14:1-3 saying, "What have I done?"
Each pursues his own course[l]
like a horse charging into battle.
7 Even the stork in the sky
knows her appointed seasons,
and the dove, the swift and the thrush
8:7 observe the time of their migration.
[m]Isa 1:3; But my people do not know[m]
Jer 5:4-5 the requirements of the LORD.
8:8 8 " 'How can you say, "We are wise,
[n]Ro 2:17 for we have the law[n] of the LORD,"
when actually the lying pen of the
scribes
8:9 has handled it falsely?
[o]Jer 6:15 9 The wise[o] will be put to shame;
[p]Jer 6:19 they will be dismayed and trapped.
Since they have rejected the word[p] of
the LORD,

Need Directions?

JER 8:7–9

The people keep turning away from God, heading in the wrong direction toward deeper sinfulness. Instead of seeking or changing direction, they totally lose perspective on following God's will. The leaders twist the law to suit themselves, rationalizing behavior that is horrifying to God. God points out that even migrating wild birds know when and where to fly, but his people fly in the opposite direction, ignoring the course God has given them.

Our Comforter

JER 8:18–19

Again Jeremiah cries out in anguish as he watches the people rebel against God. The saddened prophet laments their wickedness and weeps for their upcoming destruction. The Hebrew meaning for faint *reveals that Jeremiah is severely or loathsomely ill with grief. Yet in his heartache, Jeremiah boldly calls God his "Comforter in sorrow." Though God must pronounce judgment, the Comforter still compassionately longs for his people.*

The words of Jeremiah's predecessor, Isaiah, also confirm God's desire to show compassion to his disobedient children (Isa 51:3; 57:18). Even when God's people disappoint him with their selfish ways, "the Father of compassion and the God of all comfort" (2Co 1:3) wants to embrace and restore them to himself.

what kind of wisdom do they have?
10 Therefore I will give their wives to other men
and their fields to new owners.[q]
From the least to the greatest,
all are greedy for gain;[r]
prophets and priests alike,
all practice deceit.
11 They dress the wound of my people
as though it were not serious.
"Peace, peace," they say,
when there is no peace.[s]
12 Are they ashamed of their loathsome conduct?
No, they have no shame[t] at all;
they do not even know how to blush.
So they will fall among the fallen;
they will be brought down when they are punished,[u]
says the LORD.[v]

13 " 'I will take away their harvest,
declares the LORD.
There will be no grapes on the vine.[w]
There will be no figs[x] on the tree,
and their leaves will wither.[y]
What I have given them
will be taken[z] from them.[a]' "

14 "Why are we sitting here?
Gather together!
Let us flee to the fortified cities[a]
and perish there!
For the LORD our God has doomed us to perish
and given us poisoned water[b] to drink,
because we have sinned[c] against him.
15 We hoped for peace[d]
but no good has come,
for a time of healing
but there was only terror.[e]
16 The snorting of the enemy's horses
is heard from Dan;[f]
at the neighing of their stallions
the whole land trembles.
They have come to devour
the land and everything in it,
the city and all who live there."

17 "See, I will send venomous snakes[g]
among you,
vipers that cannot be charmed,[h]
and they will bite you,"
declares the LORD.

18 O my Comforter[b] in sorrow,
my heart is faint[i] within me.
19 Listen to the cry of my people
from a land far away:[j]

8:10 [q]Jer 6:12 [r]Isa 56:11
8:11 [s]Jer 6:14
8:12 [t]Jer 3:3 [u]Ps 52:5-7; Isa 3:9 [v]Jer 6:15
8:13 [w]Joel 1:7 [x]Lk 13:6 [y]Mt 21:19 [z]Jer 5:17
8:14 [a]Jer 4:5; Jer 35:11 [b]Dt 29:18; Jer 9:15; 23:15 [c]Jer 14:7,20
8:15 [d]ver 11 [e]Jer 14:19
8:16 [f]Jer 4:15
8:17 [g]Nu 21:6; Dt 32:24 [h]Ps 58:5
8:18 [i]La 5:17
8:19 [j]Jer 9:16

[a] *13* The meaning of the Hebrew for this sentence is uncertain.
[b] *18* The meaning of the Hebrew for this word is uncertain.

"Is the LORD not in Zion?
  Is her King no longer there?"

"Why have they provoked me to anger
  with their images,
  with their worthless foreign idols?"[k]

8:19 [k]Dt 32:21

20 "The harvest is past,
  the summer has ended,
  and we are not saved."

21 Since my people are crushed, I am
    crushed;
  I mourn,[l] and horror grips me.
22 Is there no balm in Gilead?[m]
  Is there no physician there?
Why then is there no healing[n]
  for the wound of my people?

8:21 [l]Jer 14:17
8:22 [m]Ge 37:25 [n]Jer 30:12

9

1 Oh, that my head were a spring of water
  and my eyes a fountain of tears!
I would weep[o] day and night
  for the slain of my people.[p]
2 Oh, that I had in the desert
  a lodging place for travelers,
so that I might leave my people
  and go away from them;
for they are all adulterers,[q]
  a crowd of unfaithful people.

9:1 [o]Jer 13:17; La 2:11,18 [p]Isa 22:4
9:2 [q]Jer 5:7-8; 23:10; Hos 4:2

3 "They make ready their tongue
  like a bow, to shoot lies;[r]
it is not by truth
  that they triumph[a] in the land.
They go from one sin to another;
  they do not acknowledge me,"
    declares the LORD.

9:3 [r]Ps 64:3

4 "Beware of your friends;
  do not trust your brothers.[s]
For every brother is a deceiver,[b][t]
  and every friend a slanderer.
5 Friend deceives friend,
  and no one speaks the truth.
They have taught their tongues to lie;
  they weary themselves with sinning.
6 You[c] live in the midst of deception;[u]
  in their deceit they refuse to
    acknowledge me,"
    declares the LORD.

9:4 [s]Mic 7:5-6 [t]Ge 27:35
9:6 [u]Jer 5:27

7 Therefore this is what the LORD Almighty says:

"See, I will refine[v] and test[w] them,
  for what else can I do
  because of the sin of my people?
8 Their tongue[x] is a deadly arrow;
  it speaks with deceit.
With his mouth each speaks cordially to
    his neighbor,
  but in his heart he sets a trap[y] for
    him.
9 Should I not punish them for this?"

9:7 [v]Isa 1:25 [w]Jer 6:27
9:8 [x]ver 3 [y]Jer 5:26

[a] 3 Or *lies; / they are not valiant for truth* [b] 4 Or *a deceiving Jacob* [c] 6 That is, Jeremiah (the Hebrew is singular)

Healing Balm

JER 8:22

Gilead is the mountainous country north of the Dead Sea (see Map 7: Prophets in Israel and Judah at the back of this Bible). The region is covered with numerous springs and shrubs and produces balsam trees with an intensely fragrant resin extract. It's likely this bushy evergreen tree, native to Arabia, is the source of the medicinal balm referred to in this verse. People crush the plants' leaves, berries and bark to extract a pale yellow gum, which is then mixed with water to make an ointment.

The Bible first mentions this balm of Gilead in Genesis 37:25 and later in Jeremiah 46:11. In Jeremiah 8:22 the balm symbolizes spiritual healing. Judah's people suffer from severe sickness of soul. God offers a cure, but they refuse to accept it. Today God offers Jesus, the Great Physician, as the cure for our spiritual ailments (Mk 2:17).

Mourners for Hire

JER 9:17–18

With a dash of irony the disheartened Jeremiah calls on professional mourners to join him in lamenting over Judah. In Israelite culture, families hired mourners (usually women) to weep and wail over their dead loved ones (see the note on Lk 8:52, page 1702). Halfhearted wailing over the deceased was a sign of disgrace and disrespect.

With the approaching death of Judah climbing "through our windows" (Jer 9:21), Jeremiah calls for help from fellow mourners. But no one appears. Instead, he and God seem to be the only ones grieving over Judah's sin and the coming destruction.

declares the LORD.
"Should I not avenge[z] myself
on such a nation as this?"
[10] I will weep and wail for the mountains
and take up a lament concerning the desert pastures.
They are desolate and untraveled,
and the lowing of cattle is not heard.
The birds of the air[a] have fled
and the animals are gone.

[11] "I will make Jerusalem a heap of ruins,
a haunt of jackals;[b]
and I will lay waste the towns of Judah
so no one can live there."[c]

[12] What man is wise[d] enough to understand
this? Who has been instructed by the LORD and
can explain it? Why has the land been ruined and
laid waste like a desert that no one can cross?
[13] The LORD said, "It is because they have forsaken my law, which I set before them; they have
not obeyed me or followed my law.[e] [14] Instead,
they have followed[f] the stubbornness of their
hearts;[g] they have followed the Baals, as their
fathers taught them." [15] Therefore, this is what the
LORD Almighty, the God of Israel, says: "See, I will
make this people eat bitter food[h] and drink poisoned water.[i] [16] I will scatter them among nations[j]
that neither they nor their fathers have known,[k]
and I will pursue them with the sword[l] until I
have destroyed them."[m]

[17] This is what the LORD Almighty says:

"Consider now! Call for the wailing
women[n] to come;
send for the most skillful of them.
[18] Let them come quickly
and wail over us
till our eyes overflow with tears
and water streams from our eyelids.[o]
[19] The sound of wailing is heard from
Zion:
'How ruined[p] we are!
How great is our shame!
We must leave our land
because our houses are in ruins.' "
[20] Now, O women, hear the word of the
LORD;
open your ears to the words of his
mouth.
Teach your daughters how to wail;
teach one another a lament.[q]
[21] Death has climbed in through our
windows
and has entered our fortresses;
it has cut off the children from the
streets
and the young men[r] from the public
squares.

9:9 [z] Jer 5:9,29
9:10 [a] Jer 4:25; 12:4; Hos 4:3
9:11 [b] Isa 34:13 [c] Isa 25:2; Jer 26:9
9:12 [d] Ps 107:43; Hos 14:9
9:13 [e] 2Ch 7:19; Ps 89:30-32
9:14 [f] Jer 2:8,23 [g] Jer 7:24
9:15 [h] La 3:15 [i] Jer 8:14
9:16 [j] Lev 26:33 [k] Dt 28:64 [l] Eze 5:2 [m] Jer 44:27; Eze 5:12
9:17 [n] 2Ch 35:25; Ecc 12:5; Am 5:16
9:18 [o] Jer 14:17
9:19 [p] Jer 4:13
9:20 [q] Isa 32:9-13
9:21 [r] 2Ch 36:17

22 Say, "This is what the LORD declares:

" 'The dead bodies of men will lie
like refuse[s] on the open field,
like cut grain behind the reaper,
with no one to gather them.' "

23 This is what the LORD says:

"Let not the wise man boast of his
wisdom[t]
or the strong man boast of his
strength[u]
or the rich man boast of his riches,[v]
24 but let him who boasts boast[w] about
this:
that he understands and knows me,
that I am the LORD,[x] who exercises
kindness,[y]
justice and righteousness[z] on earth,
for in these I delight,"
declares the LORD.

25 "The days are coming," declares the LORD,
"when I will punish all who are circumcised only
in the flesh[a]— 26 Egypt, Judah, Edom, Ammon,
Moab and all who live in the desert in distant
places.[ab] For all these nations are really uncircumcised, and even the whole house of Israel is
uncircumcised in heart.[c]"

God and Idols

10 Hear what the LORD says to you, O house of
Israel. 2 This is what the LORD says:

"Do not learn the ways of the nations[d]
or be terrified by signs in the sky,
though the nations are terrified by
them.
3 For the customs of the peoples are
worthless;
they cut a tree out of the forest,
and a craftsman[e] shapes it with his
chisel.
4 They adorn it with silver and gold;
they fasten it with hammer and nails
so it will not totter.[f]
5 Like a scarecrow in a melon patch,
their idols cannot speak;[g]
they must be carried
because they cannot walk.[h]
Do not fear them;
they can do no harm
nor can they do any good."[i]

6 No one is like you, O LORD;
you are great,[j]
and your name is mighty in power.
7 Who should not revere you,
O King of the nations?[k]
This is your due.
Among all the wise men of the nations

9:22 [s]Jer 8:2
9:23 [t]Ecc 9:11 [u]1Ki 20:11 [v]Eze 28:4-5
9:24 [w]1Co 1:31*; Gal 6:14 [x]2Co 10:17* [y]Ps 51:1; Mic 7:18 [z]Ps 36:6
9:25 [a]Ro 2:8-9
9:26 [b]Jer 25:23 [c]Lev 26:41; Ac 7:51; Ro 2:28
10:2 [d]Lev 20:23
10:3 [e]Isa 40:19
10:4 [f]Isa 41:7
10:5 [g]1Co 12:2 [h]Ps 115:5,7 [i]Isa 41:24; 46:7
10:6 [j]Ps 48:1
10:7 [k]Ps 22:28; Rev 15:4

[a] 26 Or *desert and who clip the hair by their foreheads*

Bragging Rights

JER 9:23–24

Jeremiah notes that people take pride in their wisdom, power and riches. After all these centuries they still boast about their intellect, personal prowess and wealth. They still think they can save themselves with their own skills and abilities. But God firmly rejects their boasting. He says they can, and should, boast in only one thing: him. They should boast that they know God, not that their heads are filled with knowledge; boast that they rely on God, not on their own abilities or strength; and boast that they are a compassionate and just people, not that they are rich and powerful. While humanity looks at the outward appearance and earthly gains, God calls his people to a higher responsibility of reflecting his kindness, justice and righteousness to the self-glorifying world around them.

Measure of Worth

JER 10:14–16

Foolish individuals measure their worth by the *work they produce or the material things they accumulate. Jeremiah says that even the ornate idol masterpieces a goldsmith crafts are "a fraud"* (Jer 10:14) *and "worthless"* (Jer 10:15). *In contrast, God, "the Portion of Jacob . . . is the Maker of all things"* (Jer 10:16), *including the people who preen about their artistry.*

In a society that esteems performance and financial success, it's a challenge not to seek significance in what we accomplish or acquire in life. It's not a sin to work hard and be rewarded for good work, but it is more important that we remember "we are God's workmanship, created in Christ Jesus to do good works, which God prepared in advance for us to do" (Eph 2:10). *Our worth rests on who we belong to, not what we do.*

and in all their kingdoms,
there is no one like you.
8 They are all senseless and foolish;[l]
they are taught by worthless wooden
idols.
9 Hammered silver is brought from
Tarshish
and gold from Uphaz.
What the craftsman and goldsmith have
made[m]
is then dressed in blue and purple—
all made by skilled workers.
10 But the LORD is the true God;
he is the living God, the eternal King.
When he is angry, the earth trembles;
the nations cannot endure his wrath.[n]

11 "Tell them this: 'These gods, who did not
make the heavens and the earth, will perish[o] from
the earth and from under the heavens.' "[a]

12 But God made the earth by his power;
he founded the world by his wisdom
and stretched out the heavens[p] by his
understanding.
13 When he thunders,[q] the waters in the
heavens roar;
he makes clouds rise from the ends of
the earth.
He sends lightning with the rain[r]
and brings out the wind from his
storehouses.

14 Everyone is senseless and without
knowledge;
every goldsmith is shamed by his
idols.
His images are a fraud;
they have no breath in them.
15 They are worthless,[s] the objects of
mockery;
when their judgment comes, they will
perish.
16 He who is the Portion[t] of Jacob is not
like these,
for he is the Maker of all things,[u]
including Israel, the tribe of his
inheritance[v]—
the LORD Almighty is his name.[w]

Coming Destruction

17 Gather up your belongings[x] to leave the
land,
you who live under siege.
18 For this is what the LORD says:
"At this time I will hurl[y] out
those who live in this land;
I will bring distress on them
so that they may be captured."

19 Woe to me because of my injury!

10:8 [l]Isa 40:19; Jer 4:22
10:9 [m]Ps 115:4; Isa 40:19
10:10 [n]Ps 76:7
10:11 [o]Ps 96:5; Isa 2:18
10:12 [p]Ge 1:1,8; Job 9:8; Isa 40:22
10:13 [q]Job 36:29 [r]Ps 135:7
10:15 [s]Isa 41:24; Jer 14:22
10:16 [t]Dt 32:9; Ps 119:57 [u]ver 12 [v]Ps 74:2 [w]Jer 31:35; 32:18
10:17 [x]Eze 12:3-12
10:18 [y]1Sa 25:29

[a] *11* The text of this verse is in Aramaic.

My wound[z] is incurable!
Yet I said to myself,
"This is my sickness, and I must
endure[a] it."
20 My tent[b] is destroyed;
all its ropes are snapped.
My sons are gone from me and are no
more;[c]
no one is left now to pitch my tent
or to set up my shelter.
21 The shepherds are senseless
and do not inquire of the LORD;
so they do not prosper
and all their flock is scattered.[d]
22 Listen! The report is coming—
a great commotion from the land of
the north!
It will make the towns of Judah
desolate,
a haunt of jackals.[e]

Jeremiah's Prayer

23 I know, O LORD, that a man's life is not
his own;
it is not for man to direct his steps.[f]
24 Correct me, LORD, but only with
justice—
not in your anger,[g]
lest you reduce me to nothing.[h]
25 Pour out your wrath on the nations[i]
that do not acknowledge you,
on the peoples who do not call on
your name.[j]
For they have devoured[k] Jacob;
they have devoured him completely
and destroyed his homeland.[l]

The Covenant Is Broken

11 This is the word that came to Jeremiah from
the LORD: 2"Listen to the terms of this covenant and tell them to the people of Judah and to
those who live in Jerusalem. 3Tell them that this is
what the LORD, the God of Israel, says: 'Cursed[m]
is the man who does not obey the terms of this
covenant— 4the terms I commanded your forefathers when I brought them out of Egypt, out of
the iron-smelting furnace.[n]' I said, 'Obey[o] me and
do everything I command you, and you will be
my people,[p] and I will be your God. 5Then I will
fulfill the oath I swore[q] to your forefathers, to give
them a land flowing with milk and honey'—the
land you possess today."

I answered, "Amen, LORD."

6The LORD said to me, "Proclaim all these words
in the towns of Judah and in the streets of Jerusalem: 'Listen to the terms of this covenant and follow[r] them. 7From the time I brought your forefathers up from Egypt until today, I warned them
again and again,[s] saying, "Obey me." 8But they
did not listen or pay attention;[t] instead, they fol-

10:19 [z]Jer 14:17 [a]Mic 7:9
10:20 [b]Jer 4:20 [c]Jer 31:15; La 1:5
10:21 [d]Jer 23:2
10:22 [e]Jer 9:11
10:23 [f]Pr 20:24
10:24 [g]Ps 6:1; 38:1 [h]Jer 30:11
10:25 [i]Zep 3:8 [j]Job 18:21; Ps 14:4 [k]Ps 79:7; Jer 8:16 [l]Ps 79:6-7
11:3 [m]Dt 27:26; Gal 3:10
11:4 [n]Dt 4:20; 1Ki 8:51 [o]Ex 24:8 [p]Jer 7:23; 31:33
11:5 [q]Ex 13:5; Dt 7:12; Ps 105:8-11
11:6 [r]Dt 15:5; Ro 2:13; Jas 1:22
11:7 [s]2Ch 36:15
11:8 [t]Jer 7:26

Correcting Our Course

JER 10:24

A contrite man aware of his own sinfulness, Jeremiah humbly prays for God to correct him. The prophet knows God can crush him into nothing. As punishment for sin, we all deserve total destruction by God. Instead God pours out his loving-kindness because "his mercy extends to those who fear him, from generation to generation" (Lk 1:50). If only Judah would run to God's mercy!

Drawing the Line

JER 11:14

At first read, this verse sounds like an outrageous action by God. How could God tell Jeremiah not to intercede for the people? Why wouldn't God listen to their cries of distress? After all, he listened to Moses' petitions for the Israelites when they sinned (Ex 32:11–14; Nu 14:11–20).

But as Moses and Jeremiah learned, God does draw the line concerning sin. Rebellion reaps consequences. When God's people refuse to repent and turn from their defiant ways to a holy God, he gives them their bitter reward. Fortunately, "The LORD is slow to anger, abounding in love and forgiving sin and rebellion" (Nu 14:18), but that does not give his people license to blatantly disobey him. As Judah finds out, their sin eventually catches up with them, and God refuses to listen to their cries.

lowed the stubbornness of their evil hearts. So I
brought on them all the curses[u] of the covenant I
had commanded them to follow but that they did
not keep.' "

9Then the LORD said to me, "There is a conspiracy[v] among the people of Judah and those who live
in Jerusalem. 10They have returned to the sins of
their forefathers,[w] who refused to listen to my
words. They have followed other gods[x] to serve
them. Both the house of Israel and the house of
Judah have broken the covenant I made with their
forefathers. 11Therefore this is what the LORD says:
'I will bring on them a disaster[y] they cannot escape.
Although they cry[z] out to me, I will not listen[a] to
them. 12The towns of Judah and the people of Jerusalem will go and cry out to the gods to whom they
burn incense,[b] but they will not help them at all
when disaster[c] strikes. 13You have as many gods as
you have towns, O Judah; and the altars you have
set up to burn incense[d] to that shameful[e] god Baal
are as many as the streets of Jerusalem.'

14"Do not pray[f] for this people nor offer any plea
or petition for them, because I will not listen[g]
when they call to me in the time of their distress.

> 15"What is my beloved doing in my temple
> as she works out her evil schemes with many?
> Can consecrated meat avert ⌊your punishment⌋?
> When you engage in your wickedness,
> then you rejoice.[a]"
>
> 16The LORD called you a thriving olive tree
> with fruit beautiful in form.
> But with the roar of a mighty storm
> he will set it on fire,[h]
> and its branches will be broken.[i]

17The LORD Almighty, who planted[j] you, has
decreed disaster for you, because the house of
Israel and the house of Judah have done evil and
provoked me to anger by burning incense to
Baal.[k]

Plot Against Jeremiah

18Because the LORD revealed their plot to me, I
knew it, for at that time he showed me what they
were doing. 19I had been like a gentle lamb led to
the slaughter; I did not realize that they had plotted[l] against me, saying,

> "Let us destroy the tree and its fruit;
> let us cut him off from the land of the living,[m]
> that his name be remembered[n] no more."
> 20But, O LORD Almighty, you who judge righteously

11:8 [u]Lev 26:14-43
11:9 [v]Eze 22:25
11:10 [w]Dt 9:7 [x]Jdg 2:12-13
11:11 [y]2Ki 22:16 [z]Jer 14:12; Eze 8:18 [a]ver 14; Pr 1:28; Isa 1:15; Zec 7:13
11:12 [b]Jer 44:17 [c]Dt 32:37
11:13 [d]Jer 7:9 [e]Jer 3:24
11:14 [f]Ex 32:10 [g]ver 11
11:16 [h]Jer 21:14 [i]Isa 27:11; Ro 11:17-24
11:17 [j]Isa 5:2; Jer 12:2 [k]Jer 7:9
11:19 [l]Jer 18:18; 20:10 [m]Job 28:13; Isa 53:8 [n]Ps 83:4

[a] 15 Or *Could consecrated meat avert your punishment? / Then you would rejoice*

and test the heart and mind,[o]
let me see your vengeance upon them,
for to you I have committed my cause.

21 "Therefore this is what the LORD says about
the men of Anathoth who are seeking your life[p]
and saying, 'Do not prophesy in the name of the
LORD or you will die[q] by our hands'— 22 therefore
this is what the LORD Almighty says: 'I will punish
them. Their young men[r] will die by the sword,
their sons and daughters by famine. 23 Not even a
remnant[s] will be left to them, because I will bring
disaster on the men of Anathoth in the year of
their punishment.[t]' "

Jeremiah's Complaint

12 You are always righteous,[u] O LORD,
when I bring a case before you.
Yet I would speak with you about your
justice:
Why does the way of the wicked
prosper?[v]
Why do all the faithless live at ease?
2 You have planted[w] them, and they have
taken root;
they grow and bear fruit.
You are always on their lips
but far from their hearts.[x]
3 Yet you know me, O LORD;
you see me and test[y] my thoughts
about you.
Drag them off like sheep to be
butchered!
Set them apart for the day of
slaughter![z]
4 How long will the land lie parched[a][a]
and the grass in every field be
withered?[b]
Because those who live in it are wicked,
the animals and birds have perished.[c]
Moreover, the people are saying,
"He will not see what happens to us."

God's Answer

5 "If you have raced with men on foot
and they have worn you out,
how can you compete with horses?
If you stumble in safe country,[b]
how will you manage in the thickets[d]
by[c] the Jordan?
6 Your brothers, your own family—
even they have betrayed you;
they have raised a loud cry against
you.[e]
Do not trust them,
though they speak well of you.[f]

7 "I will forsake my house,
abandon[g] my inheritance;

11:20 [o]Ps 7:9
11:21 [p]Jer 12:6 [q]Jer 26:8,11; 38:4
11:22 [r]Jer 18:21
11:23 [s]Jer 6:9 [t]Jer 23:12
12:1 [u]Ezr 9:15 [v]Jer 5:27-28
12:2 [w]Jer 11:17 [x]Isa 29:13; Jer 3:10; Mt 15:8; Tit 1:16
12:3 [y]Ps 7:9; 11:5; 139:1-4; Jer 11:20 [z]Jer 17:18
12:4 [a]Jer 4:28 [b]Joel 1:10-12 [c]Jer 4:25; 9:10
12:5 [d]Jer 49:19; 50:44
12:6 [e]Pr 26:24-25; Jer 9:4 [f]Ps 12:2
12:7 [g]Jer 7:29

[a] 4 Or *land mourn* [b] 5 Or *If you put your trust in a land of safety* [c] 5 Or *the flooding of*

Why, God?

JER 12:1

The prophet asks some insightful questions: Why do the wicked prosper? Why do the faithless live easy lives? He is not alone in his wondering. Job and David interrogate God with similar questions (Job 21:7-21; Ps 73), as does Habakkuk when he asks, "Why then do you tolerate the treacherous?" (Hab 1:13). We may be asking the same questions today.

Jeremiah knows God's justice will eventually prevail, but he's growing impatient as he watches the wicked get away with lawlessness. God responds to Jeremiah with his own question: If you can't run the race now, how will you endure against even greater injustices (Jer 12:5)? It's natural for us to expect God to straighten out the wicked, but our ways are not his ways (Isa 55:9). God accomplishes his justice on his own timetable, not ours.

Staying Useful

JER 13:1–5

God uses this object lesson to illustrate how the people of Judah once were close to God and played an important role among the nations. Like the linen belt or loincloth, Judah was once a healthy, prosperous nation that honored God's laws. But Judah's pride and willingness to mix with the surrounding nations rot away her usefulness, and she becomes like the belt ruined among the rocks.

Pride, compromise and indifference eat away at our hearts too. We lose our usefulness and are "no longer good for anything, except to be thrown out and trampled by men" (Mt 5:13). But humility and repentance—as modeled by the prophet Jeremiah—can keep us effective servants for God.

I will give the one I love
into the hands of her enemies.
8 My inheritance has become to me
like a lion in the forest.
She roars at me;
therefore I hate her.[h]
9 Has not my inheritance become to me
like a speckled bird of prey
that other birds of prey surround and attack?
Go and gather all the wild beasts;
bring them to devour.[i]
10 Many shepherds[j] will ruin my vineyard
and trample down my field;
they will turn my pleasant field
into a desolate wasteland.[k]
11 It will be made a wasteland,
parched and desolate before me;[l]
the whole land will be laid waste
because there is no one who cares.
12 Over all the barren heights in the desert
destroyers will swarm,
for the sword of the LORD[m] will devour
from one end of the land to the other;[n]
no one will be safe.
13 They will sow wheat but reap thorns;
they will wear themselves out but gain nothing.[o]
So bear the shame of your harvest
because of the LORD's fierce anger."[p]

14 This is what the LORD says: "As for all my
wicked neighbors who seize the inheritance I
gave my people Israel, I will uproot[q] them from
their lands and I will uproot the house of Judah
from among them. 15 But after I uproot them, I will
again have compassion and will bring[r] each of
them back to his own inheritance and his own
country. 16 And if they learn well the ways of my
people and swear by my name, saying, 'As surely
as the LORD lives'[s]—even as they once taught my
people to swear by Baal[t]—then they will be established among my people.[u] 17 But if any nation does
not listen, I will completely uproot and destroy[v]
it," declares the LORD.

A Linen Belt

13 This is what the LORD said to me: "Go and buy a linen belt and put it around your waist, but do not let it touch water." 2 So I bought a belt, as the LORD directed, and put it around my waist.

3 Then the word of the LORD came to me a second time: 4 "Take the belt you bought and are
wearing around your waist, and go now to Perath[a]
and hide it there in a crevice in the rocks." 5 So I
went and hid it at Perath, as the LORD told me.[w]
6 Many days later the LORD said to me, "Go now

[a] 4 Or possibly *the Euphrates*; also in verses 5–7

12:8 [h] Hos 9:15; Am 6:8
12:9 [i] Isa 56:9; Jer 15:3; Eze 23:25
12:10 [j] Jer 23:1 [k] Isa 5:1-7
12:11 [l] ver 4; Isa 42:25; Jer 23:10
12:12 [m] Jer 47:6 [n] Jer 3:2
12:13 [o] Lev 26:20; Dt 28:38; Mic 6:15; Hag 1:6 [p] Jer 4:26
12:14 [q] Zec 2:7-9
12:15 [r] Am 9:14-15
12:16 [s] Jer 4:2 [t] Jos 23:7 [u] Isa 49:6; Jer 3:17
12:17 [v] Isa 60:12
13:5 [w] Ex 40:16

to Perath and get the belt I told you to hide there."
7So I went to Perath and dug up the belt and took
it from the place where I had hidden it, but now it
was ruined and completely useless.
8Then the word of the LORD came to me: 9"This
is what the LORD says: 'In the same way I will ruin
the pride of Judah and the great pride[x] of Jerusalem. 10These wicked people, who refuse to listen
to my words, who follow the stubbornness of
their hearts[y] and go after other gods[z] to serve and
worship them, will be like this belt—completely
useless! 11For as a belt is bound around a man's
waist, so I bound the whole house of Israel and
the whole house of Judah to me,' declares the
LORD, 'to be my people for my renown[a] and praise
and honor.[b] But they have not listened.'[c]

Wineskins

12"Say to them: 'This is what the LORD, the God
of Israel, says: Every wineskin should be filled
with wine.' And if they say to you, 'Don't we
know that every wineskin should be filled with
wine?' 13then tell them, 'This is what the LORD
says: I am going to fill with drunkenness[d] all who
live in this land, including the kings who sit on
David's throne, the priests, the prophets and all
those living in Jerusalem. 14I will smash them one
against the other, fathers and sons alike, declares
the LORD. I will allow no pity or mercy or compassion[e] to keep me from destroying[f] them.' "

Threat of Captivity

15Hear and pay attention,
do not be arrogant,
for the LORD has spoken.
16Give glory[g] to the LORD your God
before he brings the darkness,
before your feet stumble[h]
on the darkening hills.
You hope for light,
but he will turn it to thick darkness
and change it to deep gloom.[i]
17But if you do not listen,[j]
I will weep in secret
because of your pride;
my eyes will weep bitterly,
overflowing with tears,[k]
because the LORD's flock[l] will be taken
captive.[m]

18Say to the king and to the queen
mother,
"Come down from your thrones,
for your glorious crowns
will fall from your heads."
19The cities in the Negev will be shut up,
and there will be no one to open
them.
All Judah[n] will be carried into exile,
carried completely away.

13:9 [x]Lev 26:19
13:10 [y]Jer 11:8; 16:12 [z]Jer 9:14
13:11 [a]Jer 32:20; 33:9 [b]Ex 19:5-6 [c]Jer 7:26
13:13 [d]Ps 60:3; 75:8; Isa 51:17; 63:6; Jer 51:57
13:14 [e]Jer 16:5 [f]Dt 29:20; Eze 5:10
13:16 [g]Jos 7:19 [h]Jer 23:12 [i]Isa 59:9
13:17 [j]Mal 2:2 [k]Jer 9:1 [l]Ps 80:1; Jer 23:1 [m]Jer 14:18
13:19 [n]Jer 20:4; 52:30

I was too ambitious in my
deed,
And thought to distance all
men in success.
Till God came to me, marked
the place, and said,
"Ill doer, henceforth keep
within this line,
Attempting less than others"—
and I stand
And work among Christ's little
ones, content.

—Elizabeth Barrett Browning (1806-1861)

Dry Times

JER 14:3

Judah depends on wells and underground reservoirs called cisterns for its water supply. The people dig cisterns out of solid rock or line clay reservoirs with cement to prevent seepage and evaporation. Women regularly gather around the cisterns to fill household water jugs and visit with each other. Irrigation trenches from the cisterns also nourish elaborate palace and city gardens.

In a land of little rainfall, cisterns provide water for the people's survival and their social well-being. A drought impacts rich and poor, young and old, alike. The Israelites fear the droughts that have plagued their land over the centuries, realizing that God often uses such dryness as a judgment (1Ki 8:35).

20 Lift up your eyes and see
those who are coming from the north.[o]
Where is the flock[p] that was entrusted to you,
the sheep of which you boasted?
21 What will you say when ⌞the LORD⌟ sets over you
those you cultivated as your special allies?[q]
Will not pain grip you
like that of a woman in labor?[r]
22 And if you ask yourself,
"Why has this happened to me?"—
it is because of your many sins[s]
that your skirts have been torn off
and your body mistreated.[t]
23 Can the Ethiopian[a] change his skin
or the leopard its spots?
Neither can you do good
who are accustomed to doing evil.

24 "I will scatter you like chaff[u]
driven by the desert wind.[v]
25 This is your lot,
the portion[w] I have decreed for you,"
declares the LORD,
"because you have forgotten me
and trusted in false gods.
26 I will pull up your skirts over your face
that your shame may be seen[x]—
27 your adulteries and lustful neighings,
your shameless prostitution![y]
I have seen your detestable acts
on the hills and in the fields.[z]
Woe to you, O Jerusalem!
How long will you be unclean?"[a]

Drought, Famine, Sword

14 This is the word of the LORD to Jeremiah concerning the drought:

2 "Judah mourns,[b]
her cities languish;
they wail for the land,
and a cry goes up from Jerusalem.
3 The nobles send their servants for water;
they go to the cisterns
but find no water.[c]
They return with their jars unfilled;
dismayed and despairing,
they cover their heads.[d]
4 The ground is cracked
because there is no rain in the land;[e]
the farmers are dismayed
and cover their heads.
5 Even the doe in the field
deserts her newborn fawn

13:20 [o]Jer 6:22; Hab 1:6 [p]Jer 23:2
13:21 [q]Jer 38:22 [r]Jer 4:31
13:22 [s]Jer 9:2-6; 16:10-12 [t]Eze 16:37; Na 3:5-6
13:24 [u]Ps 1:4 [v]Lev 26:33
13:25 [w]Job 20:29; Mt 24:51
13:26 [x]La 1:8; Eze 16:37; Hos 2:10
13:27 [y]Jer 2:20 [z]Eze 6:13 [a]Hos 8:5
14:2 [b]Isa 3:26; Jer 8:21
14:3 [c]2Ki 18:31; Job 6:19-20 [d]2Sa 15:30
14:4 [e]Jer 3:3

[a] *23* Hebrew *Cushite* (probably a person from the upper Nile region)

because there is no grass.[f]
6 Wild donkeys stand on the barren
heights[g]
and pant like jackals;
their eyesight fails
for lack of pasture."

7 Although our sins testify[h] against us,
O LORD, do something for the sake of
your name.
For our backsliding[i] is great;
we have sinned[j] against you.
8 O Hope[k] of Israel,
its Savior in times of distress,
why are you like a stranger in the land,
like a traveler who stays only a night?
9 Why are you like a man taken by
surprise,
like a warrior powerless to save?[l]
You are among[m] us, O LORD,
and we bear your name;[n]
do not forsake us!

10 This is what the LORD says about this people:

"They greatly love to wander;
they do not restrain their feet.[o]
So the LORD does not accept[p] them;
he will now remember[q] their
wickedness
and punish them for their sins."[r]

11 Then the LORD said to me, "Do not pray[s] for
the well-being of this people. 12 Although they fast,
I will not listen to their cry;[t] though they offer
burnt offerings[u] and grain offerings, I will not
accept[v] them. Instead, I will destroy them with the
sword, famine and plague."
13 But I said, "Ah, Sovereign LORD, the prophets
keep telling them, 'You will not see the sword or
suffer famine.[w] Indeed, I will give you lasting
peace in this place.' "
14 Then the LORD said to me, "The prophets are
prophesying lies[x] in my name. I have not sent[y]
them or appointed them or spoken to them. They
are prophesying to you false visions,[z] divinations,[a]
idolatries[a] and the delusions of their own minds.
15 Therefore, this is what the LORD says about the
prophets who are prophesying in my name: I did
not send them, yet they are saying, 'No sword or
famine will touch this land.' Those same prophets will perish[b] by sword and famine.[c] 16 And the
people they are prophesying to will be thrown out
into the streets of Jerusalem because of the famine
and sword. There will be no one to bury[d] them or
their wives, their sons or their daughters.[e] I will
pour out on them the calamity they deserve.[f]

17 "Speak this word to them:

" 'Let my eyes overflow with tears[g]
night and day without ceasing;

14:5 [f]Isa 15:6
14:6 [g]Job 39:5-6; Jer 2:24
14:7 [h]Hos 5:5 [i]Jer 5:6 [j]Jer 8:14
14:8 [k]Jer 17:13
14:9 [l]Isa 50:2 [m]Jer 8:19 [n]Isa 63:19; Jer 15:16
14:10 [o]Ps 119:101; Jer 2:25 [p]Jer 6:20; Am 5:22 [q]Hos 9:9 [r]Jer 44:21-23; Hos 8:13
14:11 [s]Ex 32:10
14:12 [t]Isa 1:15; Jer 11:11 [u]Jer 7:21 [v]Jer 6:20
14:13 [w]Jer 5:12
14:14 [x]Jer 27:14 [y]Jer 23:21,32 [z]Jer 23:16 [a]Eze 12:24
14:15 [b]Eze 14:9 [c]Jer 5:12-13
14:16 [d]Ps 79:3 [e]Jer 7:33 [f]Pr 1:31
14:17 [g]Jer 9:1

[a] *14* Or *visions, worthless divinations*

Forgetting Sin

JER 14:10-11

Again God instructs Jeremiah to cease praying for the people (see note on Jer 11:14). They cry out to God when drought hits, but they don't sincerely repent. Their empty sacrifices do not appease God's anger. His patience has worn thin, and he vows to "remember their wickedness" (Jer 14:10). This is in contrast to his more familiar promise later in Jeremiah 31:34: "I will forgive their wickedness and will remember their sins no more."

Under the old covenant, God uses his prophets, like Jeremiah, to encourage the people to forsake their wickedness, follow God's laws and be forgiven for their sins. Unfortunately, Judah does not listen. God sends Babylon to overthrow and punish them. The promise of forgiveness God gives Jeremiah in chapter 31 speaks of the new covenant in Jesus Christ (Heb 8:6-12). All those who repent and forsake their sins will find forgiveness and restoration through Christ.

Lip Service

JER 14:21; 15:1

In a flurry of words, Jeremiah speaks on behalf of the people, asking God not to condemn them. He even pleads with God "for the sake of [his] name" (Jer 14:21), reminding him of his merciful character, hoping thereby to win his grace. But God says that even if the great intercessors Moses and Samuel (Ex 32:11–14; 1Sa 7:9; 12:17–18) were to plead Judah's case, he would still refuse their request. God sees past the people's words to the insincerity of their hearts. Judah wants God to act, but they stubbornly refuse to change their actions. The only way to stay God's judgment—for Judah and for us—is to not only express sorrow for our wrong deeds, but to also forsake our sinful ways and obey God. When we offer God not just our words, but our hearts, "he is faithful and just and will forgive us our sins and purify us from all unrighteousness" (1Jn 1:9).

for my virgin daughter—my people—
has suffered a grievous wound,
a crushing blow.[h]
18 If I go into the country,
I see those slain by the sword;
if I go into the city,
I see the ravages of famine.[i]
Both prophet and priest
have gone to a land they know not.' "

19 Have you rejected Judah completely?[j]
Do you despise Zion?
Why have you afflicted us
so that we cannot be healed?[k]
We hoped for peace
but no good has come,
for a time of healing
but there is only terror.[l]
20 O LORD, we acknowledge our
wickedness
and the guilt of our fathers;
we have indeed sinned[m] against you.
21 For the sake of your name[n] do not
despise us;
do not dishonor your glorious
throne.[o]
Remember your covenant with us
and do not break it.
22 Do any of the worthless idols of the
nations bring rain?[p]
Do the skies themselves send down
showers?
No, it is you, O LORD our God.
Therefore our hope is in you,
for you are the one who does all this.

15 Then the LORD said to me: "Even if Moses[q]
and Samuel[r] were to stand before me, my
heart would not go out to this people.[s] Send them
away from my presence![t] Let them go! 2 And if
they ask you, 'Where shall we go?' tell them,
'This is what the LORD says:

" 'Those destined for death, to death;
those for the sword, to the sword;[u]
those for starvation, to starvation;[v]
those for captivity, to captivity.'[w]

3 "I will send four kinds of destroyers[x] against
them," declares the LORD, "the sword to kill and
the dogs to drag away and the birds[y] of the air and
the beasts of the earth to devour and destroy.[z] 4 I
will make them abhorrent[a] to all the kingdoms of
the earth[b] because of what Manasseh[c] son of Hezekiah king of Judah did in Jerusalem.

5 "Who will have pity[d] on you,
O Jerusalem?
Who will mourn for you?
Who will stop to ask how you are?
6 You have rejected[e] me," declares the
LORD.
"You keep on backsliding.

14:17 [h]Jer 8:21
14:18 [i]Eze 7:15
14:19 [j]Jer 7:29 [k]Jer 30:12-13 [l]Jer 8:15
14:20 [m]Da 9:7-8
14:21 [n]ver 7 [o]Jer 3:17
14:22 [p]Ps 135:7
15:1 [q]Ex 32:11; Nu 14:13-20 [r]1Sa 7:9 [s]Jer 7:16; Eze 14:14,20 [t]2Ki 17:20
15:2 [u]Jer 43:11 [v]Jer 14:12 [w]Rev 13:10
15:3 [x]Lev 26:16 [y]Dt 28:26 [z]Lev 26:22; Eze 14:21
15:4 [a]Jer 24:9; 29:18 [b]Dt 28:25 [c]2Ki 21:2; 23:26-27
15:5 [d]Isa 51:19; Jer 13:14; 21:7; Na 3:7
15:6 [e]Jer 6:19; 7:24

So I will lay hands[f] on you and destroy
you;
I can no longer show compassion.
7 I will winnow them with a winnowing
fork
at the city gates of the land.
I will bring bereavement and
destruction on my people,[g]
for they have not changed their ways.
8 I will make their widows more
numerous
than the sand of the sea.
At midday I will bring a destroyer[h]
against the mothers of their young
men;
suddenly I will bring down on them
anguish and terror.
9 The mother of seven will grow faint[i]
and breathe her last.
Her sun will set while it is still day;
she will be disgraced and humiliated.
I will put the survivors to the sword[j]
before their enemies,"
declares the LORD.

10 Alas, my mother, that you gave me
birth,[k]
a man with whom the whole land
strives and contends![l]
I have neither lent[m] nor borrowed,
yet everyone curses me.

11 The LORD said,

"Surely I will deliver you[n] for a good
purpose;
surely I will make your enemies
plead[o] with you
in times of disaster and times of
distress.
12 "Can a man break iron—
iron from the north[p]—or bronze?
13 Your wealth and your treasures
I will give as plunder, without
charge,[q]
because of all your sins
throughout your country.[r]
14 I will enslave you to your enemies
in[a] a land you do not know,[s]
for my anger will kindle a fire[t]
that will burn against you."

15 You understand, O LORD;
remember me and care for me.
Avenge me on my persecutors.[u]
You are long-suffering—do not take me
away;
think of how I suffer reproach for
your sake.[v]

15:6 [f]Zep 1:4
15:7 [g]Jer 18:21
15:8 [h]Jer 6:4
15:9 [i]1Sa 2:5 [j]Jer 21:7
15:10 [k]Job 3:1 [l]Jer 1:19 [m]Lev 25:36
15:11 [n]Jer 40:4 [o]Jer 21:1-2; 37:3; 42:1-3
15:12 [p]Jer 28:14
15:13 [q]Ps 44:12 [r]Jer 17:3
15:14 [s]Dt 28:36; Jer 16:13 [t]Dt 32:22; Ps 21:9
15:15 [u]Jer 12:3 [v]Ps 69:7-9

[a] *14* Some Hebrew manuscripts, Septuagint and Syriac (see also Jer. 17:4); most Hebrew manuscripts *I will cause your enemies to bring you / into*

Mighty Warrior

JER 15:8

In Exodus 14:14 God reassures his people, "The LORD will fight for you." But now in Jeremiah, God turns from protecting his people to punishing them. God's judgment—to *"make their widows more numerous than the sand of the sea"* (Jer 15:8)—is *a disturbing reversal of his promise to Abraham—to "make [his] descendants like the sand on the sea"* (Ge 32:12). Regardless of social status, no woman will escape the impending disaster. Even the royal women will be exiled (Jer 38:22-23) and the wives of landowners handed over to enemies (Jer 6:12). Hebrew family structure, the center of Hebrew society, will be destroyed when Babylon conquers them. The progressive destruction of Judah is pictured in the killing of the men, then the widows and mothers. God, the "mighty warrior" (Jer 20:11), exasperated by persistent sin, fights *against*, rather than *for*, his people.

Hunger for the Word

JER 15:16

In lamenting the doom that hangs like a dark cloud over Judah, Jeremiah declares that God's words are his sufficiency, his strength. He eats them—meaning he makes them a part of his heart and soul. Both Ezekiel and John share a similar experience of eating the words of God before taking God's message to the people (Eze 3:1–3; Rev 10:8–11). Ezekiel and John describe God's words as "sweet as honey" (Eze 3:3; Rev 10:9). Certainly they would agree with the psalmist: "How sweet are your words to my taste, sweeter than honey to my mouth!" (Ps 119:103).

16 When your words came, I ate[w] them;
they were my joy and my heart's delight,[x]
for I bear your name,[y]
O LORD God Almighty.
17 I never sat[z] in the company of revelers,
never made merry with them;
I sat alone because your hand was on me
and you had filled me with indignation.
18 Why is my pain unending
and my wound grievous and incurable?[a]
Will you be to me like a deceptive brook,
like a spring that fails?[b]

19 Therefore this is what the LORD says:

"If you repent, I will restore you
that you may serve[c] me;
if you utter worthy, not worthless, words,
you will be my spokesman.
Let this people turn to you,
but you must not turn to them.
20 I will make you a wall to this people,
a fortified wall of bronze;
they will fight against you
but will not overcome you,
for I am with you
to rescue and save you,"[d]
declares the LORD.
21 "I will save you from the hands of the wicked
and redeem[e] you from the grasp of the cruel."[f]

15:16 [w]Eze 3:3; Rev 10:10 [x]Ps 119:72, 103 [y]Jer 14:9
15:17 [z]Ps 1:1; 26:4-5; Jer 16:8
15:18 [a]Jer 30:15; Mic 1:9 [b]Job 6:15
15:19 [c]Zec 3:7
15:20 [d]Jer 20:11; Eze 3:8
15:21 [e]Jer 50:34 [f]Ge 48:16

Day of Disaster

16 Then the word of the LORD came to me:
2 "You must not marry[g] and have sons or
daughters in this place." 3 For this is what the LORD
says about the sons and daughters born in this
land and about the women who are their mothers
and the men who are their fathers:[h] 4 "They will
die of deadly diseases. They will not be mourned
or buried[i] but will be like refuse lying on the
ground.[j] They will perish by sword and famine,
and their dead bodies will become food for the
birds of the air and the beasts of the earth."[k]
5 For this is what the LORD says: "Do not enter a
house where there is a funeral meal; do not go to
mourn or show sympathy, because I have withdrawn my blessing, my love and my pity from this
people," declares the LORD. 6 "Both high and low
will die in this land.[l] They will not be buried or
mourned, and no one will cut[m] himself or shave[n]
his head for them. 7 No one will offer food to comfort those who mourn[o] for the dead—not even for
a father or a mother—nor will anyone give them
a drink to console them.
8 "And do not enter a house where there is feasting and sit down to eat and drink.[p] 9 For this is
what the LORD Almighty, the God of Israel, says:

16:2 [g]1Co 7:26-27
16:3 [h]Jer 6:21
16:4 [i]Jer 25:33 [j]Ps 83:10; Jer 9:22 [k]Ps 79:1-3; Jer 15:3; 34:20
16:6 [l]Eze 9:5-6 [m]Lev 19:28 [n]Jer 41:5; 47:5
16:7 [o]Eze 24:17; Hos 9:4
16:8 [p]Ecc 7:2-4; Jer 15:17

Before your eyes and in your days I will bring an
end to the sounds[q] of joy and gladness and to the
voices of bride and bridegroom in this place.[r]
10 "When you tell these people all this and they
ask you, 'Why has the LORD decreed such a great
disaster against us? What wrong have we done?
What sin have we committed against the LORD our
God?'[s] 11 then say to them, 'It is because your
fathers forsook me,' declares the LORD, 'and followed other gods and served and worshiped them.
They forsook me and did not keep my law.[t] 12 But
you have behaved more wickedly than your
fathers.[u] See how each of you is following the
stubbornness of his evil heart[v] instead of obeying
me. 13 So I will throw you out of this land into a
land neither you nor your fathers have known,[w]
and there you will serve other gods[x] day and
night, for I will show you no favor.'[y]
14 "However, the days are coming," declares the
LORD, "when men will no longer say, 'As surely as
the LORD lives, who brought the Israelites up out
of Egypt,'[z] 15 but they will say, 'As surely as the
LORD lives, who brought the Israelites up out of
the land of the north and out of all the countries
where he had banished them.'[a] For I will restore[b]
them to the land I gave their forefathers.
16 "But now I will send for many fishermen,"
declares the LORD, "and they will catch them.[c]
After that I will send for many hunters, and they
will hunt[d] them down on every mountain and hill
and from the crevices of the rocks.[e] 17 My eyes are
on all their ways; they are not hidden[f] from me,
nor is their sin concealed from my eyes.[g] 18 I will
repay them double[h] for their wickedness and their
sin, because they have defiled my land[i] with the
lifeless forms of their vile images and have filled
my inheritance with their detestable idols."

19 O LORD, my strength and my fortress,
  my refuge in time of distress,
to you the nations will come[j]
  from the ends of the earth and say,
"Our fathers possessed nothing but false
  gods,[k]
  worthless idols that did them no good.
20 Do men make their own gods?
  Yes, but they are not gods!"[l]

21 "Therefore I will teach them—
  this time I will teach them
  my power and might.
Then they will know
  that my name is the LORD.

17 "Judah's sin is engraved with an iron tool,[m]
  inscribed with a flint point,
on the tablets of their hearts[n]
  and on the horns of their altars.
2 Even their children remember
  their altars and Asherah poles[a][o]

16:9 [q] Isa 24:8; Eze 26:13; Hos 2:11 [r] Rev 18:23
16:10 [s] Dt 29:24; Jer 5:19
16:11 [t] Dt 29:25-26; 1Ki 9:9; Ps 106:35-43; Jer 22:9
16:12 [u] Jer 7:26 [v] Ecc 9:3; Jer 13:10
16:13 [w] Dt 28:36; Jer 5:19 [x] Dt 4:28 [y] Jer 15:5
16:14 [z] Dt 15:15; Jer 23:7-8
16:15 [a] Isa 11:11; Jer 23:8 [b] Jer 24:6
16:16 [c] Am 4:2; Hab 1:14-15 [d] Am 9:3; Mic 7:2 [e] 1Sa 26:20
16:17 [f] 1Co 4:5; Heb 4:13 [g] Pr 15:3
16:18 [h] Isa 40:2; Rev 18:6 [i] Nu 35:34; Jer 2:7
16:19 [j] Isa 2:2; Jer 3:17 [k] Ps 4:2
16:20 [l] Ps 115:4-7; Isa 37:19; Jer 2:11
17:1 [m] Job 19:24 [n] Pr 3:3; 2Co 3:3
17:2 [o] 2Ch 24:18

[a] 2 That is, symbols of the goddess Asherah

Famed author of the anti-slavery novel, *Uncle Tom's Cabin*, Harriet Beecher Stowe also wrote numerous hymns.

Abide in Me

Abide in me, O Lord, and I in Thee,
From this good hour, oh, leave me nevermore;
Then shall the discord cease, the wound be healed,
The lifelong bleeding of the soul be o'er.

Abide in me; o'ershadowed by Thy love
Each half formed purpose and dark thought of sin;
Quench ere it rise each selfish, low desire,
And keep my soul as Thine, calm and divine.

Abide in me; there have been moments blest
When I have heard Thy voice and felt Thy power;
Then evil lost its grasp; and passion, hushed,
Owned the divine enchantment of the hour.

These were but seasons beautiful and rare;
Abide in me, and they shall ever be;
Fulfill at once Thy precept and my prayer,
Come, and abide in me, and I in Thee.

—Harriet Beecher Stowe (1812-1896)

Heart Checkup

JER 17:10-11

Jeremiah reminds the people that the Almighty *looks past outward appearances and performance to test hearts and minds "to reward a man according to his conduct"* (Jer 17:10). The prophet also *warns that those who gain wealth through deceitful practices eventually end up poor fools and those who do good deeds to cover up a sin-filled heart will be judged.* Judah fails God's heart exam *because deceit clogs their relationship with God. The lesson for all of us is that sin blocks the our lifeline to God—no matter how good our deeds—and keeps us from enjoying vibrant spiritual health.*

beside the spreading trees
and on the high hills.[p]
3 My mountain in the land
and your[a] wealth and all your
treasures
I will give away as plunder,[q]
together with your high places,[r]
because of sin throughout your
country.[s]
4 Through your own fault you will lose
the inheritance[t] I gave you.
I will enslave you to your enemies[u]
in a land[v] you do not know,
for you have kindled my anger,
and it will burn[w] forever."

5 This is what the LORD says:

"Cursed is the one who trusts in man,[x]
who depends on flesh for his strength
and whose heart turns away from the
LORD.
6 He will be like a bush in the wastelands;
he will not see prosperity when it
comes.
He will dwell in the parched places of
the desert,
in a salt[y] land where no one lives.

7 "But blessed is the man who trusts[z] in
the LORD,
whose confidence is in him.
8 He will be like a tree planted by the
water
that sends out its roots by the stream.
It does not fear when heat comes;
its leaves are always green.
It has no worries in a year of drought[a]
and never fails to bear fruit."[b]

9 The heart[c] is deceitful above all things
and beyond cure.
Who can understand it?
10 "I the LORD search the heart[d]
and examine the mind,[e]
to reward[f] a man according to his
conduct,
according to what his deeds deserve."[g]

11 Like a partridge that hatches eggs it did
not lay
is the man who gains riches by unjust
means.
When his life is half gone, they will
desert him,
and in the end he will prove to be a
fool.[h]

12 A glorious throne,[i] exalted from the
beginning,
is the place of our sanctuary.

17:2 [p]Jer 2:20
17:3 [q]2Ki 24:13 [r]Jer 26:18; Mic 3:12 [s]Jer 15:13
17:4 [t]La 5:2 [u]Dt 28:48; Jer 12:7 [v]Jer 16:13 [w]Jer 7:20; 15:14
17:5 [x]Isa 2:22; 30:1-3
17:6 [y]Dt 29:23; Job 39:6
17:7 [z]Ps 34:8; 40:4; Pr 16:20
17:8 [a]Jer 14:1-6 [b]Ps 1:3; 92:12-14
17:9 [c]Ecc 9:3; Mt 13:15; Mk 7:21-22
17:10 [d]1Sa 16:7; Rev 2:23 [e]Ps 17:3; 139:23; Jer 11:20; 20:12; Ro 8:27 [f]Ps 62:12; Jer 32:19 [g]Ro 2:6
17:11 [h]Lk 12:20
17:12 [i]Jer 3:17

[a] 2,3 Or *hills* / [3]*and the mountains of the land. / Your*

Week 22

Are You a Bush or a Tree?

Imagine you are walking in a wasteland. The heat is oppressive; the sun is scorching your back and your mouth is dry. Up ahead is a squat, dried-up bush sitting on the flat, sandy plain. In another direction is a tall, fully leafed tree near a stream; it is heavy with ripe fruit. Where would you go for shade and refreshment? It's not a tough choice. God says that a person can be either like a bush or like a tree. Look at Jeremiah 17:5-8 to discover some differences between the bush and the tree.

To what does God compare people who trust in themselves or the world (Jer 17:5-6)? To what does God compare people who trust in him (Jer 17:7-8)?

What are the locations of the bush (Jer 17:6) and the tree (Jer 17:8), and why are they important?

What are hidden from view that will allow the tree to benefit from the stream (Jer 17:8)? Why is the bush unable to benefit from the stream (Jer 17:6)?

Why is the tree unafraid of drought (Jer 17:8)? How consistently does it bear fruit (Jer 17:8)?

If you want to be a tree that lives, your roots should be connected to water. What do you think the stream represents (Eze 47:1-11; Jn 7:37-39)?

The word *planted* in Jeremiah 17:8 could also be translated "transplanted." That means there is hope for every bush out on the sandy plain. When you are transplanted, you are lifted out of your present place and replanted in a new location. To be spiritually transplanted, a person must be "born again" (Jn 3:3-7). Your refreshment will be the "living water" that only God provides (Jn 4:10), water that gives "eternal life" (Jn 4:13-14).

Enjoying God THROUGH the Word

Read John 15:1-17 (pages 1774-1775). Even people uneducated in horticulture know that only a healthy, living branch can produce fruit and that a sickly branch may produce fruit but it won't be good fruit. If a branch is cut off of the vine, it can't produce fruit at all.

If you are trying to produce spiritual fruit or good works on your own, forget it. You can only produce when you are connected to Jesus (Jn 15:4). Jesus places great priority on your relationship with him. Without him, you will wither and die spiritually (Jn 15:6). But Jesus makes a marvelous promise: If you stay close to him, you will bear "much fruit" (Jn 15:7-8).

Enjoying God THROUGH Experience

On a piece of paper draw a dry bush, then over and around it draw a lush tree. Spend some time thinking about your relationship with Jesus. How are you still like a bush? How have you grown more treelike? You can't grow and *remain* in Jesus if you aren't already *in* him. Have you made that choice? If not, give your heart to him today by confessing your need for him. Be honest with the Lord about your need for a closer relationship with him. Confess to him your bushlike qualities and ask him to help you become more like a healthy, fruitful tree. He longs to fill you with the "inexpressible and glorious joy" (1Pe 1:8) that comes only from life in him.

Go to page 1340 for your next weekly study.

Rest Up

JER 17:19–27

The people view the Sabbath, God's established day of rest (Dt 5:12–15), as an ordinary day of work. They place work and making money above keeping God's law. Breaking God's Sabbath laws is another way Judah exercises a rebellious spirit. Their defiance shouts, "Who is God to tell us how to live?"

God promises to bless his people if they put him first in their lives. Later the Messiah challenges Sabbath rituals (Mt 12:3–13), and debate still exists today over how to regard or observe the Sabbath. But the principle of putting God first remains constant. Regardless of when and how we observe a time of rest, as "Lord of the Sabbath" (Lk 6:5), God deserves our honor. We will find rest for our body and soul as we put him first in everything.

13 O LORD, the hope[j] of Israel,
all who forsake[k] you will be put to shame.
Those who turn away from you will be written in the dust
because they have forsaken the LORD,
the spring of living water.

14 Heal me, O LORD, and I will be healed;
save me and I will be saved,
for you are the one I praise.[l]
15 They keep saying to me,
"Where is the word of the LORD?
Let it now be fulfilled!"[m]
16 I have not run away from being your shepherd;
you know I have not desired the day of despair.
What passes my lips is open before you.
17 Do not be a terror[n] to me;
you are my refuge[o] in the day of disaster.
18 Let my persecutors be put to shame,
but keep me from shame;
let them be terrified,
but keep me from terror.
Bring on them the day of disaster;
destroy them with double destruction.[p]

Keeping the Sabbath Holy

19 This is what the LORD said to me: "Go and
stand at the gate of the people, through which the
kings of Judah go in and out; stand also at all the
other gates of Jerusalem.[q] 20 Say to them, 'Hear the
word of the LORD, O kings of Judah and all people
of Judah and everyone living in Jerusalem[r] who
come through these gates.[s] 21 This is what the LORD
says: Be careful not to carry a load on the Sabbath[t]
day or bring it through the gates of Jerusalem.
22 Do not bring a load out of your houses or do any
work on the Sabbath, but keep the Sabbath day
holy, as I commanded your forefathers.[u] 23 Yet they
did not listen or pay attention;[v] they were stiff-
necked[w] and would not listen or respond to discipline.[x] 24 But if you are careful to obey me, declares
the LORD, and bring no load through the gates of
this city on the Sabbath, but keep the Sabbath day
holy by not doing any work on it, 25 then kings
who sit on David's throne[y] will come through the
gates of this city with their officials. They and
their officials will come riding in chariots and on
horses, accompanied by the men of Judah and
those living in Jerusalem, and this city will be
inhabited forever. 26 People will come from the
towns of Judah and the villages around Jerusalem, from the territory of Benjamin and the western foothills, from the hill country and the Negev,[z] bringing burnt offerings and sacrifices, grain
offerings, incense and thank offerings to the

17:13 [j]Jer 14:8 [k]Isa 1:28; Jer 2:17
17:14 [l]Ps 109:1
17:15 [m]Isa 5:19; 2Pe 3:4
17:17 [n]Ps 88:15-16 [o]Jer 16:19; Na 1:7
17:18 [p]Ps 35:1-8
17:19 [q]Jer 7:2; 26:2
17:20 [r]Jer 19:3 [s]Jer 22:2
17:21 [t]Nu 15:32-36; Ne 13:15-21; Jn 5:10
17:22 [u]Ex 20:8; 31:13; Isa 56:2-6; Eze 20:12
17:23 [v]Jer 7:26 [w]Jer 19:15 [x]Jer 7:28
17:25 [y]2Sa 7:13; Isa 9:7; Jer 22:2,4; Lk 1:32
17:26 [z]Jer 32:44; 33:13; Zec 7:7

house of the LORD. 27But if you do not obey[a] me to
keep the Sabbath day holy by not carrying any
load as you come through the gates of Jerusalem
on the Sabbath day, then I will kindle an
unquenchable fire[b] in the gates of Jerusalem that
will consume her fortresses.' "[c]

At the Potter's House

18 This is the word that came to Jeremiah from
the LORD: 2"Go down to the potter's house,
and there I will give you my message." 3So I went
down to the potter's house, and I saw him working at the wheel. 4But the pot he was shaping
from the clay was marred in his hands; so the potter formed it into another pot, shaping it as
seemed best to him.

5Then the word of the LORD came to me: 6"O
house of Israel, can I not do with you as this potter does?" declares the LORD. "Like clay[d] in the
hand of the potter, so are you in my hand, O
house of Israel. 7If at any time I announce that a
nation or kingdom is to be uprooted,[e] torn down
and destroyed, 8and if that nation I warned
repents of its evil, then I will relent[f] and not inflict
on it the disaster[g] I had planned. 9And if at another time I announce that a nation or kingdom is to
be built[h] up and planted, 10and if it does evil[i] in
my sight and does not obey me, then I will reconsider[j] the good I had intended to do for it.

11"Now therefore say to the people of Judah and
those living in Jerusalem, 'This is what the LORD
says: Look! I am preparing a disaster[k] for you and
devising a plan against you. So turn[l] from your evil
ways,[m] each one of you, and reform your ways and
your actions.' 12But they will reply, 'It's no use.[n]
We will continue with our own plans; each of us
will follow the stubbornness of his evil heart.' "

13Therefore this is what the LORD says:

"Inquire among the nations:
  Who has ever heard anything like
    this?[o]
A most horrible[p] thing has been done
  by Virgin Israel.
14Does the snow of Lebanon
  ever vanish from its rocky slopes?
Do its cool waters from distant sources
  ever cease to flow?[a]
15Yet my people have forgotten me;
  they burn incense to worthless idols,[q]
which made them stumble in their ways
  and in the ancient paths.[r]
They made them walk in bypaths
  and on roads not built up.[s]
16Their land will be laid waste,[t]
  an object of lasting scorn;[u]
all who pass by will be appalled
  and will shake their heads.[v]
17Like a wind[w] from the east,

17:27 [a]Jer 22:5 [b]Jer 7:20 [c]2Ki 25:9; Am 2:5
18:6 [d]Isa 45:9; Ro 9:20-21
18:7 [e]Jer 1:10
18:8 [f]Jer 26:13; Jnh 3:8-10 [g]Eze 18:21; Hos 11:8-9
18:9 [h]Jer 1:10; 31:28
18:10 [i]Eze 33:18 [j]1Sa 2:29-30
18:11 [k]Jer 4:6 [l]2Ki 17:13; Isa 1:16-19 [m]Jer 7:3
18:12 [n]Isa 57:10; Jer 2:25
18:13 [o]Isa 66:8; Jer 2:10 [p]Jer 5:30
18:15 [q]Jer 10:15 [r]Jer 6:16 [s]Isa 57:14; 62:10
18:16 [t]Jer 25:9 [u]Jer 19:8 [v]Ps 22:7
18:17 [w]Jer 13:24

[a] *14* The meaning of the Hebrew for this sentence is uncertain.

The Potter's Hands

JER 18:3-4

In Biblical times virtually every village or town marketplace featured a potter's wheel. Since clay abounded in Judah, every home contained clay pottery for carrying, storing and serving water, wine or other household goods. Pots were also used for preparing sacrifices (Lev 6:24-28), and hand-painted pottery decorated royal palaces.

These verses illustrate the master potter's sovereignty in shaping the nation of Judah into a vessel that is pleasing to him. Just as a potter kneads clay to remove impurities and air bubbles, God removes impurities to make people useful for his service. Just as a potter turns the wheel and shapes the clay into a useful vessel, so God uses the turning of events to shape his people. In light of the new covenant God has established with us through Jesus Christ, we can trust the master potter to work out our imperfections and gently mold us into the likeness of his Son (Ro 8:29).

I will scatter them before their
enemies;
I will show them my back and not my
face[x]
in the day of their disaster."

[18]They said, "Come, let's make plans[y] against
Jeremiah; for the teaching of the law by the priest[z]
will not be lost, nor will counsel from the wise,
nor the word from the prophets.[a] So come, let's
attack him with our tongues[b] and pay no attention to anything he says."

[19] Listen to me, O LORD;
hear what my accusers are saying!
[20] Should good be repaid with evil?
Yet they have dug a pit[c] for me.
Remember that I stood before you
and spoke in their behalf[d]
to turn your wrath away from them.
[21] So give their children over to famine;[e]
hand them over to the power of the
sword.
Let their wives be made childless and
widows;[f]
let their men be put to death,
their young men slain by the sword in
battle.
[22] Let a cry[g] be heard from their houses
when you suddenly bring invaders
against them,
for they have dug a pit to capture me
and have hidden snares[h] for my feet.
[23] But you know, O LORD,
all their plots to kill[i] me.
Do not forgive[j] their crimes
or blot out their sins from your sight.
Let them be overthrown before you;
deal with them in the time of your
anger.

19 This is what the LORD says: "Go and buy a
clay jar from a potter.[k] Take along some of
the elders[l] of the people and of the priests [2]and go
out to the Valley of Ben Hinnom,[m] near the
entrance of the Potsherd Gate. There proclaim the
words I tell you, [3]and say, 'Hear the word of the
LORD, O kings[n] of Judah and people of Jerusalem.
This is what the LORD Almighty, the God of Israel,
says: Listen! I am going to bring a disaster[o] on this
place that will make the ears of everyone who
hears of it tingle.[p] [4]For they have forsaken[q] me
and made this a place of foreign gods; they have
burned sacrifices[r] in it to gods that neither they
nor their fathers nor the kings of Judah ever
knew, and they have filled this place with the
blood of the innocent.[s] [5]They have built the high
places of Baal to burn their sons[t] in the fire as
offerings to Baal—something I did not command
or mention, nor did it enter my mind.[u] [6]So
beware, the days are coming, declares the LORD,
when people will no longer call this place Topheth

Then be content, poor heart!
God's plans, like lilies pure and white, unfold:
We must not tear the close-knit leaves apart—
Time will reveal the calyxes of gold!

—May Louise Riley Smith (1842-1927)

18:17 [x]Jer 2:27
18:18 [y]Jer 11:19 [z]Mal 2:7 [a]Jer 5:13 [b]Ps 52:2
18:20 [c]Ps 35:7; 57:6 [d]Ps 106:23
18:21 [e]Jer 11:22 [f]Ps 109:9
18:22 [g]Jer 6:26 [h]Ps 140:5
18:23 [i]Jer 11:21 [j]Ps 109:14
19:1 [k]Jer 18:2 [l]Nu 11:17
19:2 [m]Jos 15:8
19:3 [n]Jer 17:20 [o]Jer 6:19 [p]1Sa 3:11
19:4 [q]Dt 28:20; Isa 65:11 [r]Lev 18:21 [s]2Ki 21:16; Jer 2:34
19:5 [t]Lev 18:21; Ps 106:37-38 [u]Jer 7:31; 32:35

or the Valley of Ben Hinnom,[v] but the Valley of Slaughter.[w]

7" 'In this place I will ruin[a] the plans of Judah and Jerusalem. I will make them fall by the sword before their enemies,[x] at the hands of those who seek their lives, and I will give their carcasses[y] as food[z] to the birds of the air and the beasts of the earth. 8I will devastate this city and make it an object of scorn;[a] all who pass by will be appalled and will scoff because of all its wounds. 9I will make them eat[b] the flesh of their sons and daughters, and they will eat one another's flesh during the stress of the siege imposed on them by the enemies[c] who seek their lives.'

10"Then break the jar[d] while those who go with you are watching, 11and say to them, 'This is what the LORD Almighty says: I will smash[e] this nation and this city just as this potter's jar is smashed and cannot be repaired. They will bury[f] the dead in Topheth until there is no more room. 12This is what I will do to this place and to those who live here, declares the LORD. I will make this city like Topheth. 13The houses[g] in Jerusalem and those of the kings of Judah will be defiled like this place, Topheth—all the houses where they burned incense on the roofs to all the starry hosts[h] and poured out drink offerings[i] to other gods.' "

14Jeremiah then returned from Topheth, where the LORD had sent him to prophesy, and stood in the court[j] of the LORD's temple and said to all the people, 15"This is what the LORD Almighty, the God of Israel, says: 'Listen! I am going to bring on this city and the villages around it every disaster I pronounced against them, because they were stiff-necked[k] and would not listen to my words.' "

Jeremiah and Pashhur

20 When the priest Pashhur son of Immer,[l] the chief officer[m] in the temple of the LORD, heard Jeremiah prophesying these things, 2he had Jeremiah the prophet beaten[n] and put in the stocks[o] at the Upper Gate of Benjamin[p] at the LORD's temple. 3The next day, when Pashhur released him from the stocks, Jeremiah said to him, "The LORD's name for you is not Pashhur, but Magor-Missabib.[b][q] 4For this is what the LORD says: 'I will make you a terror to yourself and to all your friends; with your own eyes[r] you will see them fall by the sword of their enemies. I will hand[s] all Judah over to the king of Babylon, who will carry[t] them away to Babylon or put them to the sword. 5I will hand over to their enemies all the wealth[u] of this city—all its products, all its valuables and all the treasures of the kings of Judah. They will take it away[v] as plunder and carry it off to Babylon. 6And you, Pashhur, and all who live in your house will go into exile to Babylon. There you will die

19:6 [v]Jos 15:8 [w]Jer 7:32
19:7 [x]Lev 26:17; Dt 28:25 [y]Jer 16:4; 34:20 [z]Ps 79:2
19:8 [a]Jer 18:16
19:9 [b]Lev 26:29; Dt 28:49-57; La 4:10 [c]Isa 9:20
19:10 [d]ver 1
19:11 [e]Ps 2:9; Isa 30:14 [f]Jer 7:32
19:13 [g]Jer 32:29; 52:13 [h]Dt 4:19; Ac 7:42 [i]Jer 7:18; Eze 20:28
19:14 [j]2Ch 20:5; Jer 26:2
19:15 [k]Ne 9:16; Jer 7:26; 17:23
20:1 [l]1Ch 24:14 [m]2Ki 25:18
20:2 [n]Jer 1:19 [o]Job 13:27 [p]Jer 37:13; 38:7; Zec 14:10
20:3 [q]ver 10
20:4 [r]Jer 29:21 [s]Jer 21:10 [t]Jer 52:27
20:5 [u]Jer 17:3 [v]2Ki 20:17

[a] 7 The Hebrew for *ruin* sounds like the Hebrew for *jar* (see verses 1 and 10). [b] 3 *Magor-Missabib* means *terror on every side.*

Cruel Punishment

JER 20:2

Pashhur, the priestly insider, is incensed by Jeremiah's doomsday prophecies and decides to punish him. Jeremiah's punishment is threefold: First he is beaten, perhaps even by the priest himself out of his anger. Second, Jeremiah is placed in the stocks. Stocks held a victim in a contorted, doubled-over position, a painful and sometimes crippling posture. Last, the stocks are located at the Upper Gate of Benjamin, a well-traveled area where Jeremiah's punishment will be the most public and the most humiliating. Pashhur could confine Jeremiah in jail. Instead, he wants the whole city to see the prophet shamed outside the temple where he preaches. Perhaps Pashhur hopes to intimidate Jeremiah into softening his convicting message. Far from softening, however, Jeremiah courageously turns his address from the nation to Pashhur himself, prophesying exile and death for the priest (Jer 20:6).

Honesty With God

JER 20:7-18

This passage is the last recording of Jeremiah's confessions. His intensely honest prayer reveals the tremendous cost he's paid for serving God. Comfortable in his relationship with his Maker, Jeremiah complains that God has deceived him and that everyone mocks him (Jer 20:7). He even curses the day of his birth (Jer 20:14-18). Yet in the midst of his soul-anguish, Jeremiah praises his God (Jer 20:11-13). He remembers to acknowledge God as the Sovereign Lord, even if his feelings scream the opposite.

King David shares similar candid prayers throughout the Psalms. In Psalm 22 David cries out, "I am a worm . . . Dogs have surrounded me" (Ps 22:6,16). But he also praises God, like Jeremiah, saying, "In the congregation I will praise you" (Ps 22:22). Our God, who knows our troubled thoughts before we even articulate them, invites us to come to him, regardless of how we feel. He is not appalled by our raw emotions or perplexed by our questions.

and be buried, you and all your friends to whom
you have prophesied[w] lies.' "

Jeremiah's Complaint

7 O LORD, you deceived[a] me, and I was
deceived[a];
you overpowered me and prevailed.
I am ridiculed all day long;
everyone mocks me.
8 Whenever I speak, I cry out
proclaiming violence and
destruction.[x]
So the word of the LORD has brought me
insult and reproach[y] all day long.
9 But if I say, "I will not mention him
or speak any more in his name,"
his word is in my heart like a fire,[z]
a fire shut up in my bones.
I am weary of holding it in;[a]
indeed, I cannot.
10 I hear many whispering,
"Terror[b] on every side!
Report[c] him! Let's report him!"
All my friends[d]
are waiting for me to slip,[e] saying,
"Perhaps he will be deceived;
then we will prevail[f] over him
and take our revenge on him."

11 But the LORD[g] is with me like a mighty
warrior;
so my persecutors[h] will stumble and
not prevail.[i]
They will fail and be thoroughly
disgraced;[j]
their dishonor will never be forgotten.
12 O LORD Almighty, you who examine the
righteous
and probe the heart and mind,[k]
let me see your vengeance[l] upon them,
for to you I have committed[m] my
cause.
13 Sing to the LORD!
Give praise to the LORD!
He rescues[n] the life of the needy
from the hands of the wicked.

14 Cursed be the day I was born![o]
May the day my mother bore me not
be blessed!
15 Cursed be the man who brought my
father the news,
who made him very glad, saying,
"A child is born to you—a son!"
16 May that man be like the towns[p]
the LORD overthrew without pity.
May he hear wailing in the morning,
a battle cry at noon.
17 For he did not kill me in the womb,[q]

20:6 [w]Jer 14:15; La 2:14
20:8 [x]Jer 6:7 [y]2Ch 36:16; Jer 6:10
20:9 [z]Ps 39:3 [a]Job 32:18-20; Ac 4:20
20:10 [b]Ps 31:13; Jer 6:25 [c]Isa 29:21 [d]Ps 41:9 [e]Lk 11:53-54 [f]1Ki 19:2
20:11 [g]Jer 1:8; Ro 8:31 [h]Jer 17:18 [i]Jer 15:20 [j]Jer 23:40
20:12 [k]Jer 17:10 [l]Ps 54:7; 59:10 [m]Ps 62:8; Jer 11:20
20:13 [n]Ps 35:10
20:14 [o]Job 3:3; Jer 15:10
20:16 [p]Ge 19:25
20:17 [q]Job 10:18-19

[a] 7 Or *persuaded*

with my mother as my grave,
her womb enlarged forever.
18 Why did I ever come out of the womb
to see trouble and sorrow
and to end my days in shame?[r]

God Rejects Zedekiah's Request

21 The word came to Jeremiah from the LORD
when King Zedekiah[s] sent to him Pashhur[t]
son of Malkijah and the priest Zephaniah[u] son of
Maaseiah. They said: 2"Inquire[v] now of the LORD
for us because Nebuchadnezzar[a][w] king of Babylon
is attacking us. Perhaps the LORD will perform
wonders[x] for us as in times past so that he will
withdraw from us."
3But Jeremiah answered them, "Tell Zedekiah,
4'This is what the LORD, the God of Israel, says: I
am about to turn[y] against you the weapons of war
that are in your hands, which you are using to
fight the king of Babylon and the Babylonians[b]
who are outside the wall besieging[z] you. And I
will gather them inside this city. 5I myself will
fight against you with an outstretched hand[a] and
a mighty arm in anger and fury and great wrath.
6I will strike down those who live in this city—
both men and animals—and they will die of a terrible plague.[b] 7After that, declares the LORD, I will
hand over Zedekiah[c] king of Judah, his officials
and the people in this city who survive the plague,
sword and famine, to Nebuchadnezzar king of
Babylon[d] and to their enemies who seek their
lives. He will put them to the sword; he will show
them no mercy or pity or compassion.'[e]
8"Furthermore, tell the people, 'This is what the
LORD says: See, I am setting before you the way of
life and the way of death. 9Whoever stays in this
city will die by the sword, famine or plague.[f] But
whoever goes out and surrenders to the Babylonians who are besieging you will live; he will
escape with his life.[g] 10I have determined to do
this city harm[h] and not good, declares the LORD. It
will be given into the hands[i] of the king of Babylon, and he will destroy it with fire.'[j]
11"Moreover, say to the royal house[k] of Judah,
'Hear the word of the LORD; 12O house of David,
this is what the LORD says:

" 'Administer justice[l] every morning;
rescue from the hand of his oppressor
the one who has been robbed,
or my wrath will break out and burn
like fire
because of the evil you have done—
burn with no one to quench[m] it.
13 I am against[n] you, ⌞Jerusalem,⌟
you who live above this valley[o]
on the rocky plateau,
declares the LORD—

20:18 [r]Ps 90:9
21:1 [s]2Ki 24:18; Jer 52:1 [t]Jer 38:1 [u]2Ki 25:18; Jer 29:25; 37:3
21:2 [v]Jer 37:3,7 [w]2Ki 25:1 [x]Ps 44:1-4; Jer 32:17
21:4 [y]Jer 32:5 [z]Jer 37:8-10
21:5 [a]Jer 6:12
21:6 [b]Jer 14:12
21:7 [c]2Ki 25:7; Jer 52:9 [d]Jer 37:17; 39:5 [e]2Ch 36:17; Eze 7:9; Hab 1:6
21:9 [f]Jer 14:12 [g]Jer 38:2,17; 39:18; 45:5
21:10 [h]Jer 44:11, 27; Am 9:4 [i]Jer 32:28; 38:2-3 [j]Jer 52:13
21:11 [k]Jer 13:18
21:12 [l]Jer 22:3 [m]Isa 1:31
21:13 [n]Eze 13:8 [o]Ps 125:2

[a] *2* Hebrew *Nebuchadrezzar,* of which *Nebuchadnezzar* is a variant; here and often in Jeremiah and Ezekiel [b] *4* Or *Chaldeans*; also in verse 9

The Way

JER 21:8

Jeremiah's words describe the same life choices Moses gave to Judah's ancestors: life and prosperity or death and destruction (Dt 30:15). Walking in God's way brings blessings and life, but choosing a self-centered path yields death. Way, *meaning "path," "journey," "manner" or "road," is used throughout Scripture to contrast the difference between those following God and those following their own sinful natures.*

The early Christians were collectively called "the Way" (Ac 9:2) because their lives pointed to the one who calls himself "the way and the truth and the life" (Jn 14:6). Jesus is not just one of many ways to reach God; he is the *way. He leads us on the "narrow . . . road that leads to life" (Mt 7:14).*

When God Swears

JER 22:5

God calls on the king and the people to show mercy to others, especially to the poor and needy. God takes this directive so seriously that he pledges himself by a solemn oath to destroy the king's house for disobeying this command.

The Bible is replete with people making pledges, using common phrases such as "as the LORD lives" (1Sa 14:45), "God is a witness" (Ge 31:50), and "God . . . judge between us" (Ge 31:53). But when God swears by himself, humans need to take notice. Hebrew 6:13 says, "When God made his promise to Abraham, since there was no one greater for him to swear by, he swore by himself." God is the ultimate authority to back any oath. When he makes a commitment, we can trust his word no matter what.

you who say, "Who can come against
us?
Who can enter our refuge?"[p]
14 I will punish you as your deeds[q]
deserve,
declares the LORD.
I will kindle a fire[r] in your forests[s]
that will consume everything around
you.' "

Judgment Against Evil Kings

22 This is what the LORD says: "Go down to the
palace of the king of Judah and proclaim this
message there: 2'Hear the word of the LORD, O king
of Judah, you who sit on David's throne[t]—you,
your officials and your people who come through
these gates.[u] 3This is what the LORD says: Do what
is just[v] and right. Rescue from the hand of his
oppressor[w] the one who has been robbed. Do no
wrong or violence to the alien, the fatherless or the
widow,[x] and do not shed innocent blood in this
place. 4For if you are careful to carry out these commands, then kings[y] who sit on David's throne will
come through the gates of this palace, riding in
chariots and on horses, accompanied by their officials and their people. 5But if you do not obey[z]
these commands, declares the LORD, I swear[a] by
myself that this palace will become a ruin.' "
6For this is what the LORD says about the palace
of the king of Judah:

"Though you are like Gilead to me,
like the summit of Lebanon,
I will surely make you like a desert,[b]
like towns not inhabited.
7 I will send destroyers[c] against you,
each man with his weapons,
and they will cut[d] up your fine cedar
beams
and throw them into the fire.

8"People from many nations will pass by this
city and will ask one another, 'Why has the LORD
done such a thing to this great city?'[e] 9And the
answer will be: 'Because they have forsaken the
covenant of the LORD their God and have worshiped and served other gods.[f]' "

10 Do not weep for the dead[g] ⌊king⌋ or
mourn[h] his loss;
rather, weep bitterly for him who is
exiled,
because he will never return
nor see his native land again.

11 For this is what the LORD says about Shallum[a][i]
son of Josiah, who succeeded his father as king
of Judah but has gone from this place: "He will
never return. 12He will die[j] in the place where
they have led him captive; he will not see this
land again."

21:13 [p]Jer 49:4; Ob 1:3-4
21:14 [q]Isa 3:10-11 [r]2Ch 36:19; Jer 52:13 [s]Eze 20:47
22:2 [t]Jer 17:25; Lk 1:32 [u]Jer 17:20
22:3 [v]Mic 6:8; Zec 7:9 [w]Ps 72:4; Jer 21:12 [x]Ex 22:22
22:4 [y]Jer 17:25
22:5 [z]Jer 17:27 [a]Heb 6:13
22:6 [b]Mic 3:12
22:7 [c]Jer 4:7 [d]Isa 10:34
22:8 [e]Dt 29:25-26; 1Ki 9:8-9; Jer 16:10-11
22:9 [f]2Ki 22:17; 2Ch 34:25
22:10 [g]Ecc 4:2 [h]ver 18
22:11 [i]2Ki 23:31
22:12 [j]2Ki 23:34

[a] 11 Also called *Jehoahaz*

22:13 [k]Mic 3:10; Hab 2:9 [l]Lev 19:13; Jas 5:4

[13] "Woe to him who builds[k] his palace by
unrighteousness,
his upper rooms by injustice,
making his countrymen work for
nothing,
not paying[l] them for their labor.
[14] He says, 'I will build myself a great
palace[m]
with spacious upper rooms.'
So he makes large windows in it,
panels it with cedar[n]
and decorates it in red.

22:14 [m]Isa 5:8-9 [n]2Sa 7:2

[15] "Does it make you a king
to have more and more cedar?
Did not your father have food and drink?
He did what was right and just,[o]
so all went well[p] with him.
[16] He defended the cause of the poor and
needy,[q]
and so all went well.
Is that not what it means to know me?"
declares the LORD.

22:15 [o]2Ki 23:25 [p]Ps 128:2; Isa 3:10
22:16 [q]Ps 72:1-4, 12-13

[17] "But your eyes and your heart
are set only on dishonest gain,
on shedding innocent blood[r]
and on oppression and extortion."

22:17 [r]2Ki 24:4

[18] Therefore this is what the LORD says about
Jehoiakim son of Josiah king of Judah:

"They will not mourn for him:
'Alas, my brother! Alas, my sister!'
They will not mourn for him:
'Alas, my master! Alas, his splendor!'
[19] He will have the burial of a donkey—
dragged away and thrown[s]
outside the gates of Jerusalem."

22:19 [s]Jer 36:30

[20] "Go up to Lebanon and cry out,
let your voice be heard in Bashan,
cry out from Abarim,[t]
for all your allies are crushed.
[21] I warned you when you felt secure,
but you said, 'I will not listen!'
This has been your way from your
youth;[u]
you have not obeyed[v] me.
[22] The wind will drive all your shepherds
away,
and your allies will go into exile.
Then you will be ashamed and
disgraced
because of all your wickedness.
[23] You who live in 'Lebanon,'[a]
who are nestled in cedar buildings,
how you will groan when pangs come
upon you,
pain[w] like that of a woman in labor!

22:20 [t]Nu 27:12
22:21 [u]Jer 3:25; 32:30 [v]Jer 7:23-28
22:23 [w]Jer 4:31

[24] "As surely as I live," declares the LORD, "even if

[a] 23 That is, the palace in Jerusalem (see 1 Kings 7:2)

Worthy Workers

JER 22:13

King Jehoahaz ("Shallum") rebels against the righteous ways of his father, King Josiah. Jehoahaz lasts only three months as king before he's exiled to Egypt in 609 B.C. (2Ki 23:30-34). Now Judah looks to Jehoahaz's brother, Jehoiakim, to lead them to prosperity, but his selfish heart pushes him to snub God and the people.

Jeremiah's charge against Jehoiakim is one of his most caustic. The prophet blasts the king for building his palace with forced labor. Jehoiakim oppresses the workers much like Pharaoh had in Moses' day. Wealthy Jehoiakim withholds just wages from his citizens and profits at the expense of others. This displeases God who says, "The worker deserves his wages" (1Ti 5:18) *and "I will be quick to testify against . . . those who defraud laborers of their wages"* (Mal 3:5)*—serious words from God, warning to employers to be fair to their employees.*

The Survivors

JER 23:3

The Israelites who have endured wars, pestilence and famine fully understand the remnant (survivor) concept. Though burdened with catastrophes to the point of near extinction, God continually preserves them. The prophets clearly speak of Israel's remnant: 2 Kings 19:31 and Isaiah 37:32 refer to the survivors after the Assyrian invasion; Amos 9:11–15 and Micah 2:12 mention the survivors after the Babylonian exile.

Here Jeremiah also predicts that the Shepherd will reunite his people after their Babylonian captivity. God will even bring back "a few fugitives" who scatter to Egypt (Jer 44:14). No matter how often they disobey, or how far they stray, God compassionately longs to gather wanderers back to himself.

you, Jehoiachin[a][x] son of Jehoiakim king of Judah,
were a signet ring on my right hand, I would still
pull you off. 25 I will hand you over[y] to those who
seek your life, those you fear—to Nebuchadnezzar
king of Babylon and to the Babylonians.[b] 26 I will
hurl[z] you and the mother who gave you birth into
another country, where neither of you was born,
and there you both will die. 27 You will never come
back to the land you long to return to."

28 Is this man Jehoiachin a despised,
 broken pot,[a]
 an object no one wants?
Why will he and his children be hurled[b]
 out,
 cast into a land[c] they do not know?
29 O land,[d] land, land,
 hear the word of the LORD!
30 This is what the LORD says:
"Record this man as if childless,[e]
 a man who will not prosper[f] in his
 lifetime,
for none of his offspring will prosper,
 none will sit on the throne[g] of David
 or rule anymore in Judah."

The Righteous Branch

23 "Woe to the shepherds[h] who are destroying
and scattering[i] the sheep of my pasture!"[j]
declares the LORD. 2 Therefore this is what the LORD,
the God of Israel, says to the shepherds who tend
my people: "Because you have scattered my flock
and driven them away and have not bestowed care
on them, I will bestow punishment on you for the
evil[k] you have done," declares the LORD. 3 "I myself
will gather the remnant[l] of my flock out of all the
countries where I have driven them and will bring
them back to their pasture, where they will be
fruitful and increase in number. 4 I will place shepherds[m] over them who will tend them, and they
will no longer be afraid[n] or terrified, nor will any
be missing,[o]" declares the LORD.

5 "The days are coming," declares the
 LORD,
 "when I will raise up to David[c] a
 righteous Branch,[p]
a King who will reign[q] wisely
 and do what is just and right[r] in the
 land.
6 In his days Judah will be saved
 and Israel will live in safety.
This is the name[s] by which he will be
 called:
 The LORD Our Righteousness.[t]

7 "So then, the days are coming," declares the
LORD, "when people will no longer say, 'As surely
as the LORD lives, who brought the Israelites up
out of Egypt,'[u] 8 but they will say, 'As surely as the

[a] *24* Hebrew *Coniah,* a variant of *Jehoiachin;* also in verse 28
[b] *25* Or *Chaldeans* [c] *5* Or *up from David's line*

22:24 [x]2Ki 24:6,8; Jer 37:1
22:25 [y]2Ki 24:16; Jer 34:20
22:26 [z]2Ki 24:8; 2Ch 36:10
22:28 [a]Ps 31:12; Jer 48:38; Hos 8:8 [b]Jer 15:1 [c]Jer 17:4
22:29 [d]Jer 6:19; Mic 1:2
22:30 [e]1Ch 3:18; Mt 1:12 [f]Jer 10:21 [g]Ps 94:20
23:1 [h]Jer 10:21; Eze 34:1-10; Zec 11:15-17 [i]Isa 56:11 [j]Eze 34:31
23:2 [k]Jer 21:12
23:3 [l]Isa 11:10-12; Jer 32:37; Eze 34:11-16
23:4 [m]Jer 3:15; 31:10; Eze 34:23 [n]Jer 30:10; 46:27-28 [o]Jn 6:39
23:5 [p]Isa 4:2 [q]Isa 9:7 [r]Isa 11:1; Zec 6:12
23:6 [s]Jer 33:16; Mt 1:21-23 [t]Ro 3:21-22; 1Co 1:30
23:7 [u]Jer 16:14

LORD lives, who brought the descendants of Israel up out of the land of the north and out of all the countries where he had banished them.' Then they will live in their own land."[v]

23:8 [v]Isa 43:5-6; Am 9:14-15

Lying Prophets

9 Concerning the prophets:

My heart is broken within me;
all my bones tremble.
I am like a drunken man,
like a man overcome by wine,
because of the LORD
and his holy words.[w]
10 The land is full of adulterers;[x]
because of the curse[a] the land lies
parched[b]
and the pastures[y] in the desert are
withered.[z]
The ⌊prophets⌋ follow an evil course
and use their power unjustly.

23:9 [w]Jer 20:8-9
23:10 [x]Jer 9:2 [y]Ps 107:34; Jer 9:10 [z]Hos 4:2-3

11 "Both prophet and priest are godless;[a]
even in my temple[b] I find their
wickedness,"
declares the LORD.
12 "Therefore their path will become
slippery;[c]
they will be banished to darkness
and there they will fall.
I will bring disaster on them
in the year they are punished,[d]"
declares the LORD.

23:11 [a]Jer 6:13; 8:10; Zep 3:4 [b]Jer 7:10
23:12 [c]Ps 35:6; Jer 13:16 [d]Jer 11:23

13 "Among the prophets of Samaria
I saw this repulsive thing:
They prophesied by Baal[e]
and led my people Israel astray.
14 And among the prophets of Jerusalem
I have seen something horrible:[f]
They commit adultery and live a lie.[g]
They strengthen the hands of evildoers,[h]
so that no one turns from his
wickedness.
They are all like Sodom[i] to me;
the people of Jerusalem are like
Gomorrah."[j]

23:13 [e]Jer 2:8
23:14 [f]Jer 5:30 [g]Jer 29:23 [h]Eze 13:22 [i]Ge 18:20 [j]Isa 1:9-10; Jer 20:16

15 Therefore, this is what the LORD Almighty says concerning the prophets:

"I will make them eat bitter food
and drink poisoned water,[k]
because from the prophets of Jerusalem
ungodliness has spread throughout
the land."

23:15 [k]Jer 8:14; 9:15

16 This is what the LORD Almighty says:

"Do not listen[l] to what the prophets are
prophesying to you;
they fill you with false hopes.

23:16 [l]Jer 27:9-10, 14; Mt 7:15

[a] *10* Or *because of these things* [b] *10* Or *land mourns*

True or False?

JER 23:9-22

Several false prophets promise the people peace and prosperity. These prophets are popular; Jeremiah is not. He declares the purity of God's Word while these religious forecasters "follow an evil course" (Jer 23:10). God warns the people to discern between the message of these immoral deceivers and that of his chosen spokesperson.

God's Word gives several guidelines to follow in discerning true from false prophets. First, no matter what a prophet may accomplish, if he or she tells the people something contrary to God's Word, that prophet is false (Ro 16:17; 2Pe 2:1). Also God tells his people to judge whether a prophet's words come true or not, using that measure to discern truth from falsehood (Dt 18:21-22). Finally, the character and the fruits of the prophets' lives will reveal who is a true prophet of God and who is not (1Sa 3:19-20). God assures us that we can rely on "the Spirit of truth" to "guide [us] into all truth" (Jn 16:13).

Near and Far

JER 23:23–24

God declares that false prophets cannot escape his punishment. He reminds the people that he is both nearby and far away. God fills heaven and earth, and no one can hide from his presence. The words of the false prophets do not escape him, no matter where the prophets go to hide.

David speaks of God's guiding omnipresence in Psalm 139:7–10: "Where can I go from your Spirit? Where can I flee from your presence? . . . If I rise on the wings of the dawn, if I settle on the far side of the sea, even there your hand will guide me, your right hand will hold me fast." God hovers near at all times. His guiding hand corrects us when we stray and upholds us when we're weak.

They speak visions[m] from their own
  minds,
  not from the mouth[n] of the LORD.
17 They keep saying to those who despise
  me,
  'The LORD says: You will have peace.'[o]
And to all who follow the stubbornness[p]
  of their hearts
  they say, 'No harm[q] will come to you.'
18 But which of them has stood in the
  council of the LORD
  to see or to hear his word?
  Who has listened and heard his word?
19 See, the storm[r] of the LORD
  will burst out in wrath,
a whirlwind swirling down
  on the heads of the wicked.
20 The anger[s] of the LORD will not turn
  back[t]
  until he fully accomplishes
  the purposes of his heart.
In days to come
  you will understand it clearly.
21 I did not send[u] these prophets,
  yet they have run with their message;
I did not speak to them,
  yet they have prophesied.
22 But if they had stood in my council,
  they would have proclaimed my
  words to my people
and would have turned[v] them from their
  evil ways
  and from their evil deeds.

23 "Am I only a God nearby,[w]"
  declares the LORD,
  "and not a God far away?
24 Can anyone hide[x] in secret places
  so that I cannot see him?"
  declares the LORD.
  "Do not I fill heaven and earth?"[y]
  declares the LORD.

25 "I have heard what the prophets say who
prophesy lies[z] in my name. They say, 'I had a
dream![a] I had a dream!' 26 How long will this continue in the hearts of these lying prophets, who
prophesy the delusions[b] of their own minds?
27 They think the dreams they tell one another will
make my people forget[c] my name, just as their
fathers forgot[d] my name through Baal worship.
28 Let the prophet who has a dream tell his dream,
but let the one who has my word speak it faithfully. For what has straw to do with grain?"
declares the LORD. 29 "Is not my word like fire,"[e]
declares the LORD, "and like a hammer that breaks
a rock in pieces?

30 "Therefore," declares the LORD, "I am against[f]
the prophets[g] who steal from one another words
supposedly from me. 31 Yes," declares the LORD, "I
am against the prophets who wag their own
tongues and yet declare, 'The LORD declares.'[h]

23:16 [m] Jer 14:14 [n] Jer 9:20
23:17 [o] Jer 8:11 [p] Jer 13:10 [q] Jer 5:12; Am 9:10; Mic 3:11
23:19 [r] Jer 25:32; 30:23
23:20 [s] 2Ki 23:26 [t] Jer 30:24
23:21 [u] Jer 14:14; 27:15
23:22 [v] Jer 25:5; Zec 1:4
23:23 [w] Ps 139:1-10
23:24 [x] Job 22:12-14 [y] 1Ki 8:27
23:25 [z] Jer 14:14 [a] ver 28,32; Jer 29:8
23:26 [b] 1Ti 4:1-2
23:27 [c] Dt 13:1-3; Jer 29:8 [d] Jdg 3:7; 8:33-34
23:29 [e] Jer 5:14
23:30 [f] Ps 34:16 [g] Dt 18:20; Jer 14:15
23:31 [h] ver 17

32 Indeed, I am against those who prophesy false
dreams,[i]" declares the LORD. "They tell them and
lead my people astray with their reckless lies, yet
I did not send or appoint them. They do not benefit[j] these people in the least," declares the LORD.

False Oracles and False Prophets

33 "When these people, or a prophet or a priest,
ask you, 'What is the oracle[a][k] of the LORD?' say to
them, 'What oracle?[b] I will forsake[l] you, declares
the LORD.' 34 If a prophet or a priest or anyone else
claims, 'This is the oracle[m] of the LORD,' I will punish[n] that man and his household. 35 This is what
each of you keeps on saying to his friend or relative: 'What is the LORD's answer?'[o] or 'What has
the LORD spoken?' 36 But you must not mention
'the oracle of the LORD' again, because every
man's own word becomes his oracle and so you
distort[p] the words of the living God, the LORD
Almighty, our God. 37 This is what you keep saying
to a prophet: 'What is the LORD's answer to you?'
or 'What has the LORD spoken?' 38 Although you
claim, 'This is the oracle of the LORD,' this is what
the LORD says: You used the words, 'This is the
oracle of the LORD,' even though I told you that
you must not claim, 'This is the oracle of the
LORD.' 39 Therefore, I will surely forget you and
cast[q] you out of my presence along with the city I
gave to you and your fathers. 40 I will bring upon
you everlasting disgrace[r]—everlasting shame that
will not be forgotten."

Two Baskets of Figs

24 After Jehoiachin[c][s] son of Jehoiakim king of
Judah and the officials, the craftsmen and
the artisans of Judah were carried into exile from
Jerusalem to Babylon by Nebuchadnezzar king of
Babylon, the LORD showed me two baskets of figs[t]
placed in front of the temple of the LORD. 2 One
basket had very good figs, like those that ripen
early; the other basket had very poor[u] figs, so bad
they could not be eaten.

3 Then the LORD asked me, "What do you see,[v]
Jeremiah?"

"Figs," I answered. "The good ones are very
good, but the poor ones are so bad they cannot be
eaten."

4 Then the word of the LORD came to me: 5 "This
is what the LORD, the God of Israel, says: 'Like
these good figs, I regard as good the exiles from
Judah, whom I sent away from this place to the
land of the Babylonians.[d] 6 My eyes will watch
over them for their good, and I will bring them
back[w] to this land. I will build[x] them up and not
tear them down; I will plant them and not uproot
them. 7 I will give them a heart to know me, that I

23:32 [i]ver 25 [j]Jer 7:8; La 2:14
23:33 [k]Mal 1:1 [l]ver 39
23:34 [m]La 2:14 [n]Zec 13:3
23:35 [o]Jer 33:3; 42:4
23:36 [p]Gal 1:7-8; 2Pe 3:16
23:39 [q]Jer 7:15
23:40 [r]Jer 20:11; Eze 5:14-15
24:1 [s]2Ki 24:16; 2Ch 36:9; Jer 29:2 [t]Am 8:1-2
24:2 [u]Isa 5:4
24:3 [v]Jer 1:11; Am 8:2
24:6 [w]Jer 29:10; Eze 11:17 [x]Jer 33:7; 42:10

[a] *33* Or *burden* (see Septuagint and Vulgate) [b] *33* Hebrew; Septuagint and Vulgate '*You are the burden.* (The Hebrew for *oracle* and *burden* is the same.) [c] *1* Hebrew *Jeconiah,* a variant of *Jehoiachin* [d] *5* Or *Chaldeans*

Lasting Fruit

JER 24:1-10

In 597 B.C. Jehoiachin succeeds his wicked father and reigns only three months until he's captured by the Babylonians (2Ki 24:8-12). Jeremiah's vision portrays the good figs as the exiles who are taken to Babylon and the bad figs as those who remain in Jerusalem under Zedekiah, the new king appointed by Nebuchadnezzar.

The exiles (good figs) are not necessarily righteous people, but God sustains them and brings them back to the land after their hearts are purified through their captivity. The people who stay (bad figs) think they have been lucky to escape and have no further need of God; but God will destroy them. As is true throughout Scripture, this is a heart matter. The returning exiles will have a heart to know and follow God (Jer 24:7), and he will allow them to return to their homeland and will bless them there.

Everyday Life

JER 25:10–11

This significant passage foretells Judah's 70-year captivity in Babylon. Jeremiah predicts the captivity just before it begins. Babylon and its allies will soon overpower Judah and the joys of everyday life will cease. The enemy will rob Judah of wedding feasts and business success; homes will remain in silent darkness. The punishment for Judah's sin will affect all of society, all parts of personal and community life.

am the LORD. They will be my people,[y] and I will
be their God, for they will return[z] to me with all
their heart.[a]
8" 'But like the poor[b] figs, which are so bad they
cannot be eaten,' says the LORD, 'so will I deal
with Zedekiah king of Judah, his officials[c] and the
survivors[d] from Jerusalem, whether they remain
in this land or live in Egypt.[e] 9I will make them
abhorrent[f] and an offense to all the kingdoms of
the earth, a reproach and a byword,[g] an object of
ridicule and cursing,[h] wherever I banish[i] them. 10I
will send the sword,[j] famine and plague[k] against
them until they are destroyed from the land I gave
to them and their fathers.' "

Seventy Years of Captivity

25 The word came to Jeremiah concerning all
the people of Judah in the fourth year of
Jehoiakim[l] son of Josiah king of Judah, which
was the first year of Nebuchadnezzar[m] king of
Babylon. 2So Jeremiah the prophet said to all the
people of Judah[n] and to all those living in Jerusalem: 3For twenty-three years—from the thirteenth
year of Josiah[o] son of Amon king of Judah until
this very day—the word of the LORD has come to
me and I have spoken to you again and again,[p]
but you have not listened.[q]
4And though the LORD has sent all his servants
the prophets[r] to you again and again, you have not
listened or paid any attention. 5They said, "Turn
now, each of you, from your evil ways and your
evil practices, and you can stay in the land the
LORD gave to you and your fathers for ever and
ever. 6Do not follow other gods[s] to serve and worship them; do not provoke me to anger with what
your hands have made. Then I will not harm you."
7"But you did not listen to me," declares the
LORD, "and you have provoked me with what your
hands have made,[t] and you have brought harm[u]
to yourselves."
8Therefore the LORD Almighty says this: "Because
you have not listened to my words, 9I will summon[v] all the peoples of the north[w] and my servant[x]
Nebuchadnezzar king of Babylon," declares the
LORD, "and I will bring them against this land and
its inhabitants and against all the surrounding
nations. I will completely destroy[*a*] them and make
them an object of horror and scorn,[y] and an everlasting ruin. 10I will banish from them the sounds[z]
of joy and gladness, the voices of bride and bridegroom,[a] the sound of millstones[b] and the light of
the lamp.[c] 11This whole country will become a desolate wasteland,[d] and these nations will serve the
king of Babylon seventy years.[e]
12"But when the seventy years[f] are fulfilled, I
will punish the king of Babylon and his nation, the
land of the Babylonians,[*b*] for their guilt," declares

a 9 The Hebrew term refers to the irrevocable giving over of things or persons to the LORD, often by totally destroying them.
b 12 Or *Chaldeans*

24:7 [y]Isa 51:16; Jer 31:33; Heb 8:10 [z]Jer 32:40 [a]Eze 11:19
24:8 [b]Jer 29:17 [c]Jer 39:6 [d]Jer 39:9 [e]Jer 44:1,26
24:9 [f]Jer 15:4; 34:17 [g]Dt 28:25; 1Ki 9:7 [h]Jer 29:18 [i]Dt 28:37
24:10 [j]Isa 51:19 [k]Jer 27:8
25:1 [l]2Ki 24:2; Jer 36:1 [m]2Ki 24:1
25:2 [n]Jer 18:11
25:3 [o]Jer 1:2 [p]Jer 11:7; 26:5 [q]Jer 7:26
25:4 [r]Jer 7:25
25:6 [s]Dt 8:19
25:7 [t]Dt 32:21 [u]2Ki 21:15
25:9 [v]Isa 13:3-5 [w]Jer 1:15 [x]Jer 27:6 [y]Jer 18:16
25:10 [z]Isa 24:8; Eze 26:13 [a]Jer 7:34 [b]Ecc 12:3-4 [c]Rev 18:22-23
25:11 [d]Jer 4:26-27; 12:11-12 [e]2Ch 36:21
25:12 [f]Jer 29:10

the LORD, "and will make it desolate[g] forever. 13 I
will bring upon that land all the things I have spoken against it, all that are written in this book and
prophesied by Jeremiah against all the nations.
14 They themselves will be enslaved[h] by many
nations[i] and great kings; I will repay[j] them according to their deeds and the work of their hands."

The Cup of God's Wrath

15 This is what the LORD, the God of Israel, said
to me: "Take from my hand this cup[k] filled with
the wine of my wrath and make all the nations to
whom I send you drink it. 16 When they drink it,
they will stagger[l] and go mad[m] because of the
sword I will send among them."

17 So I took the cup from the LORD's hand and
made all the nations to whom he sent[n] me drink it:
18 Jerusalem and the towns of Judah, its kings and
officials, to make them a ruin and an object of horror and scorn and cursing,[o] as they are today;[p]
19 Pharaoh king of Egypt, his attendants, his officials
and all his people, 20 and all the foreign people
there; all the kings of Uz;[q] all the kings of the Philistines (those of Ashkelon,[r] Gaza, Ekron, and the
people left at Ashdod); 21 Edom, Moab and
Ammon;[s] 22 all the kings of Tyre and Sidon;[t] the
kings of the coastlands[u] across the sea; 23 Dedan,
Tema, Buz and all who are in distant places[a];[v] 24 all
the kings of Arabia[w] and all the kings of the foreign people who live in the desert; 25 all the kings of
Zimri, Elam[x] and Media; 26 and all the kings of the
north,[y] near and far, one after the other—all the
kingdoms on the face of the earth. And after all of
them, the king of Sheshach[b][z] will drink it too.

27 "Then tell them, 'This is what the LORD Almighty, the God of Israel, says: Drink, get drunk[a]
and vomit, and fall to rise no more because of the
sword[b] I will send among you.' 28 But if they refuse
to take the cup from your hand and drink, tell
them, 'This is what the LORD Almighty says: You
must drink it! 29 See, I am beginning to bring
disaster[c] on the city that bears my Name,[d] and
will you indeed go unpunished?[e] You will not go
unpunished, for I am calling down a sword upon
all[f] who live on the earth, declares the LORD Almighty.'

30 "Now prophesy all these words against them
and say to them:

" 'The LORD will roar[g] from on high;
he will thunder[h] from his holy
dwelling
and roar mightily against his land.
He will shout like those who tread the
grapes,
shout against all who live on the
earth.
31 The tumult will resound to the ends of
the earth,

25:12 [g]Isa 13:19-22; 14:22-23
25:14 [h]Jer 27:7 [i]Jer 50:9; 51:27-28 [j]Jer 51:6
25:15 [k]Isa 51:17; Ps 75:8; Rev 14:10
25:16 [l]Na 3:11 [m]Jer 51:7
25:17 [n]Jer 1:10
25:18 [o]Jer 24:9 [p]Jer 44:22
25:20 [q]Job 1:1 [r]Jer 47:5
25:21 [s]Jer 49:1
25:22 [t]Jer 47:4 [u]Jer 31:10
25:23 [v]Jer 9:26; 49:32
25:24 [w]2Ch 9:14
25:25 [x]Ge 10:22
25:26 [y]Jer 50:3,9 [z]Jer 51:41
25:27 [a]ver 16,28; Hab 2:16 [b]Eze 21:4
25:29 [c]Jer 13:12-14 [d]1Pe 4:17 [e]Pr 11:31 [f]ver 30-31
25:30 [g]Isa 16:10; 42:13 [h]Joel 3:16; Am 1:2

[a] *23* Or *who clip the hair by their foreheads* [b] *26* *Sheshach* is a cryptogram for Babylon.

Cup of Wrath

JER 25:15-16

Because of the people's waywardness, God holds the cup filled with his fury (see the note on Isa 51:17,21, page 1195) *and prepares to make the nations drink it.* Judah and the surrounding nations will experience God's *wrath as they slip under Babylon's domination as if in a drunken stupor, as if they have gone mad* (Jer 25:16; 51:7).

God's punishment prophesied *here is severe.* This is no mere slap *on the hand or divine spanking.* The nations will drink the cup of *God's wrath, become sick, stagger,* vomit, and then fall down, *never to rise again* (Jer 25:27). The nations conquered by the mighty Babylonians are devastated, *destroyed.* Many of them never *again rise to their former prominence.*

for the LORD will bring charges[i]
against the nations;
he will bring judgment on all mankind
and put the wicked to the sword,' "
declares the LORD.

32 This is what the LORD Almighty says:

"Look! Disaster is spreading
from nation to nation;[j]
a mighty storm[k] is rising
from the ends of the earth."

33 At that time those slain[l] by the LORD will be
everywhere—from one end of the earth to the
other. They will not be mourned or gathered[m] up
or buried,[n] but will be like refuse lying on the
ground.

34 Weep and wail, you shepherds;
roll[o] in the dust, you leaders of the
flock.
For your time to be slaughtered[p] has
come;
you will fall and be shattered like fine
pottery.
35 The shepherds will have nowhere to flee,
the leaders of the flock no place to
escape.[q]
36 Hear the cry of the shepherds,
the wailing of the leaders of the flock,
for the LORD is destroying their pasture.
37 The peaceful meadows will be laid waste
because of the fierce anger of the LORD.
38 Like a lion[r] he will leave his lair,
and their land will become desolate
because of the sword[a] of the oppressor
and because of the LORD's fierce anger.

Jeremiah Threatened With Death

26 Early in the reign of Jehoiakim[s] son of Josiah king of Judah, this word came from the
LORD: 2 "This is what the LORD says: Stand in the
courtyard[t] of the LORD's house and speak to all the
people of the towns of Judah who come to worship in the house of the LORD. Tell[u] them everything I command you; do not omit[v] a word. 3 Perhaps they will listen and each will turn[w] from his
evil way. Then I will relent[x] and not bring on them
the disaster I was planning because of the evil they
have done. 4 Say to them, 'This is what the LORD
says: If you do not listen[y] to me and follow my
law,[z] which I have set before you, 5 and if you do
not listen to the words of my servants the prophets, whom I have sent to you again and again
(though you have not listened[a]), 6 then I will make
this house like Shiloh[b] and this city an object of
cursing[c] among all the nations of the earth.' "

7 The priests, the prophets and all the people
heard Jeremiah speak these words in the house of

25:31 [i]Hos 4:1; Joel 3:2; Mic 6:2
25:32 [j]Isa 34:2 [k]Jer 23:19
25:33 [l]Isa 66:16; Eze 39:17-20 [m]Jer 16:4 [n]Ps 79:3
25:34 [o]Jer 6:26 [p]Isa 34:6; Jer 50:27
25:35 [q]Job 11:20
25:38 [r]Jer 4:7
26:1 [s]2Ki 23:36
26:2 [t]Jer 19:14 [u]Jer 1:17; Mt 28:20; Ac 20:27 [v]Dt 4:2
26:3 [w]Jer 36:7 [x]Jer 18:8
26:4 [y]Lev 26:14 [z]1Ki 9:6
26:5 [a]Jer 25:4
26:6 [b]Jos 18:1 [c]2Ki 22:19

[a] *38* Some Hebrew manuscripts and Septuagint (see also Jer. 46:16 and 50:16); most Hebrew manuscripts *anger*

Any fool can count *the seeds in an apple. But only God can count the apples in a seed.*

—Barbara Johnson

the LORD. 8 But as soon as Jeremiah finished telling
all the people everything the LORD had commanded him to say, the priests, the prophets and all the
people seized him and said, "You must die! 9 Why
do you prophesy in the LORD's name that this
house will be like Shiloh and this city will be des-
26:9 olate and deserted?"[d] And all the people crowded
[d]Jer 9:11 around Jeremiah in the house of the LORD.
10 When the officials of Judah heard about these
things, they went up from the royal palace to the
house of the LORD and took their places at the
entrance of the New Gate of the LORD's house.
11 Then the priests and the prophets said to the offi-
26:11 cials and all the people, "This man should be sen-
[e]Dt 18:20; tenced to death[e] because he has prophesied against
Jer 18:23; this city. You have heard it with your own ears!"
38:4; Mt 26:66; 12 Then Jeremiah said to all the officials[f] and all
Ac 6:11 the people: "The LORD sent me to prophesy[g]
26:12 against this house and this city all the things you
[f]Jer 1:18 have heard.[h] 13 Now reform[i] your ways and your
[g]Am 7:15; actions and obey the LORD your God. Then the
Ac 4:18-20; 5:29 LORD will relent and not bring the disaster he has
[h]ver 2,15 pronounced against you. 14 As for me, I am in your
hands;[j] do with me whatever you think is good
26:13 [i]Jer 7:5; and right. 15 Be assured, however, that if you put
Joel 2:12-14 me to death, you will bring the guilt of innocent
blood on yourselves and on this city and on those
26:14 [j]Jer 38:5 who live in it, for in truth the LORD has sent me to
26:16 you to speak all these words in your hearing."
[k]Ac 23:9 16 Then the officials[k] and all the people said to
[l]Ac 5:34-39; the priests and the prophets, "This man should
23:29 not be sentenced to death![l] He has spoken to us in
the name of the LORD our God."
17 Some of the elders of the land stepped forward
and said to the entire assembly of people,
26:18 [m]Mic 1:1 18 "Micah[m] of Moresheth prophesied in the days of
[n]Isa 2:3 Hezekiah king of Judah. He told all the people of
[o]Ne 4:2; Jer 9:11 Judah, 'This is what the LORD Almighty says:

[p]Mic 4:1; Zec 8:3 " 'Zion[n] will be plowed like a field,
[q]Jer 17:3 Jerusalem will become a heap of
rubble,[o]
the temple hill[p] a mound overgrown
with thickets.'[a][q]

26:19 19 "Did Hezekiah king of Judah or anyone else in
[r]2Ch 32:24-26; Judah put him to death? Did not Hezekiah[r] fear
Isa 37:14-20 the LORD and seek his favor? And did not the LORD
[s]Ex 32:14; relent,[s] so that he did not bring the disaster[t] he
2Sa 24:16 [t]Jer 44:7 pronounced against them? We are about to bring
[u]Hab 2:10 a terrible disaster[u] on ourselves!"
20 (Now Uriah son of Shemaiah from Kiriath Jea-
26:20 [v]Jos 9:17 rim[v] was another man who prophesied in the
name of the LORD; he prophesied the same things
26:21 against this city and this land as Jeremiah did.
[w]1Ki 19:2 21 When King Jehoiakim[w] and all his officers and
[x]Mt 10:23 officials heard his words, the king sought to put
him to death. But Uriah heard of it and fled[x] in
26:22 fear to Egypt. 22 King Jehoiakim, however, sent
[y]Jer 36:12, 25 Elnathan[y] son of Acbor to Egypt, along with some

[a] 18 Micah 3:12

The Truth Hurts

JER 26:7-9

The people want to kill Jeremiah for speaking the painful truth. He infuriates the priests, false prophets and the temple mob: How dare he claim that the Lord will desert the temple and city, that God will make them "like Shiloh" (Jer 26:9)!

During the time of the judges, God established his tabernacle in Shiloh, a town north of Bethel. Samuel grew up in the Shiloh tabernacle (1Sa 1:24), which housed the holy ark of the covenant.

While the Bible doesn't specifically mention the fall of Shiloh, it does refer to God "abandon[ing] the tabernacle of Shiloh, the tent he had set up among men" (Ps 78:60). The people's idolatry and lasciviousness spurred God to destroy the house that bore his name in Shiloh (Jer 7:12-14), and now history is about to repeat itself in Jerusalem.

Yoke-Mates

JER 27:8-11

God at times asks his prophets to do something symbolic, something that is a picture of a future event or judgment to come. Jeremiah is told to wear a yoke (Jer 27:2). A yoke is a wooden frame that joins two cattle or oxen together to work in unison. Jeremiah actually wears a yoke around his neck for an undisclosed period of time, until the false prophet Hananiah removes it from Jeremiah's neck and breaks it (Jer 28:10). Jeremiah's yoke symbolizes Judah's inevitable bondage to the Babylonians.

The Bible mentions yoke *more than 50 times. Most of the Old Testament references describe the oppressive bondage that results from disobeying God (Isa 10:27; Eze 34:27). The New Testament symbolically uses the word to exhort believers not to be "burdened again by a yoke of slavery" to sin (Gal 5:1), not to be "yoked together with unbelievers" (2Co 6:14) and to bear the light and easy yoke of the Savior (Mt 11:29-30).*

other men. 23They brought Uriah out of Egypt and
took him to King Jehoiakim, who had him struck
down with a sword and his body thrown into the
burial place of the common people.) 26:24
24Furthermore, Ahikam[z] son of Shaphan sup- [z]2Ki 22:12
ported Jeremiah, and so he was not handed over
to the people to be put to death.

Judah to Serve Nebuchadnezzar

27 Early in the reign of Zedekiah[a][a] son of Josi- 27:1 [a]2Ch 36:11
ah king of Judah, this word came to Jeremi-
ah from the LORD: 2This is what the LORD said to
me: "Make a yoke[b] out of straps and crossbars and 27:2
put it on your neck. 3Then send word to the kings [b]Jer 28:10, 13
of Edom, Moab, Ammon,[c] Tyre and Sidon through 27:3
the envoys who have come to Jerusalem to Zede- [c]Jer 25:21
kiah king of Judah. 4Give them a message for their
masters and say, 'This is what the LORD Almighty,
the God of Israel, says: "Tell this to your masters: 27:5
5With my great power and outstretched arm[d] I [d]Dt 9:29
made the earth and its people and the animals that [e]Ps 115:16
are on it, and I give[e] it to anyone I please. 6Now I 27:6
will hand all your countries over to my servant[f] [f]Jer 25:9
Nebuchadnezzar[g] king of Babylon; I will make [g]Jer 21:7; Eze 29:18-20
even the wild animals subject to him.[h] 7All nations [h]Jer 28:14;
will serve[i] him and his son and his grandson until Da 2:37-38
the time[j] for his land comes; then many nations 27:7
and great kings will subjugate[k] him. [i]2Ch 36:20
8" ' "If, however, any nation or kingdom will [j]Jer 25:12 [k]Jer 25:14;
not serve Nebuchadnezzar king of Babylon or Da 5:28
bow its neck under his yoke, I will punish that
nation with the sword, famine and plague,
declares the LORD, until I destroy it by his hand.
9So do not listen to your prophets, your diviners,
your interpreters of dreams, your mediums[l] or 27:9 [l]Dt 18:11
your sorcerers who tell you, 'You will not serve
the king of Babylon.' 10They prophesy lies[m] to you 27:10
that will only serve to remove you far from your [m]Jer 23:25
lands; I will banish you and you will perish. 11But 27:11
if any nation will bow its neck under the yoke[n] of [n]Jer 21:9
the king of Babylon and serve him, I will let that
nation remain in its own land to till it and to live
there, declares the LORD." ' "

12I gave the same message to Zedekiah king of
Judah. I said, "Bow your neck under the yoke of
the king of Babylon; serve him and his people, and 27:13
you will live. 13Why will you and your people die[o] [o]Eze 18:31
by the sword, famine and plague with which the
LORD has threatened any nation that will not serve
the king of Babylon? 14Do not listen to the words of
the prophets who say to you, 'You will not serve 27:14
the king of Babylon,' for they are prophesying lies[p] [p]Jer 14:14
to you. 15'I have not sent[q] them,' declares the LORD. 27:15
'They are prophesying lies in my name.[r] Therefore, [q]Jer 23:21
I will banish you and you will perish,[s] both you [r]Jer 29:9
and the prophets who prophesy to you.' " [s]Jer 6:15

16Then I said to the priests and all these people,

[a] *1* A few Hebrew manuscripts and Syriac (see also Jer. 27:3, 12 and 28:1); most Hebrew manuscripts *Jehoiakim* (Most Septuagint manuscripts do not have this verse.)

Athaliah

Evil Ambition

We see the signs on bumpers of RVs on the highway, in national parks and at small-town restaurants: "Ask me about my grandkids!" If you give them even a moment, out come the photos and all the stories. Grandchildren—the reward of our later years. Warm kisses, tight hugs, shining eyes, new adventures. But unfortunately not everyone appreciates these precious ones as they should.

Consider Athaliah. She was a daughter of Ahab, one of the most wicked kings of Israel. She worshiped Baal, hated God and likely turned her husband, Jehoram, and her son Ahaziah (both kings of Judah) away from the Lord (2Ki 8:18). Athaliah was also a grandmother. But when she had to choose between her grandsons and assuming the throne herself at her son's death, she chose the throne.

Athaliah murdered her grandchildren, nearly destroying the family line of David—all except one. And one is all God needed to keep his oath to David. Joash, a tiny babe hidden in the temple by his courageous aunt, kept alive David's line and would prove to be Athaliah's undoing. Athaliah was so out of touch with her own family, she apparently did not even miss him in the slaughter!

Athaliah ruled for six years, the only woman in Judah's history to reign as queen. Under other circumstances, this might have been a great accomplishment. But she was a cruel monarch. When Joash—the true heir to the throne—was revealed to the people, they clapped and cheered in delight. Athaliah shrieked in outrage at the sight of him and tried to muster her supporters. She had none. She was killed on the palace grounds.

Athaliah completely bypassed the greatest treasures of life in exchange for a few years of power. She left behind a trail of intimate friends and family members dead before their time. She did not notice or care, because her values were so distorted.

Jesus said, "What good will it be for a man if he gains the whole world, yet forfeits his soul? Or what can a man give in exchange for his soul?" (Mt 16:26). We could ask Athaliah. In the end, what did she gain?

Athaliah
(afflicted of the LORD)
2 Kings 8:26; 11
2 Chronicles 22; 23:12-21

Candid SNAPSHOT When Athaliah heard the noise made by the guards and the people, she went to the people at the temple of the LORD. She looked and there was the king, standing by the pillar, as the custom was. The officers and the trumpeters were beside the king, and all the people of the land were rejoicing and blowing trumpets. Then Athaliah tore her robes and called out, "Treason! Treason!" (2 Kings 11:13-14).

Jehosheba

Marching to a Different Drummer

Sometimes, in the midst of a really rotten family there is one amazingly good kid. The suffering and evil this child sees at home apparently drives him or her *to* the Lord rather than *away*. There were some heavyweight sinners on her family tree, but Jehosheba came out unpredictably whole and righteous.

Jehoram, the king of Judah, was her father. Jehoram had married Athaliah, a daughter of Ahab, the wicked king of Israel. Ahaziah, Jehosheba's half brother, was the child of that union, and he became the king of Judah. Ahab had led Israel into apostasy and Baal worship. Now his wickedness was infecting Judah as well.

Jehosheba was married to the high priest, Jehoiada. Jehosheba is the only royalty recorded to have married into the priesthood. Her husband was a devout and godly man. When Jehu killed Jezebel's son Joram, who was king of Israel after Ahab, Jehu also killed Ahaziah, who had been visiting Joram. When Athaliah, in Jerusalem, heard about her son's death, she prepared to kill all the potential heirs to the throne of Judah, her grandchildren. When Jehosheba saw Athaliah about to kill them, she moved quickly. She couldn't save them all, but she could save one. So she hid the infant Joash in a bedroom with his nurse to keep him from being killed. God also hid Joash from Athaliah's memory. In her haste to claim the throne for herself, she apparently forgot to keep count of her grandchildren. In this way, Jehosheba and her husband saved the line of David—and God's Messianic plan of redemption—from extinction.

Jehosheba hid Joash in the temple for six years. Joash learned the ways of God there. Jehosheba's and Jehoiada's long-term investment in her brother's child paid big dividends to the kingdom of Judah when Joash assumed the crown. He was the first king in many years to seek the Lord and to lead Judah away from apostasy.

Jehosheba was loyal to a family who did not deserve her loyalty, and she placed her life in great danger to save a child not her own. As God had preserved and raised up Moses, he raised up Joash to lead his people and to keep his promise to David. Not only was the line of David preserved, but also God himself was served by Jehosheba's selfless act.

The enemy of our souls is snatching little children daily. Perhaps the Lord is calling you to save one, to cover a life in truth and to nurture a soul so it will be in heaven one day with Jesus Christ.

Jehosheba
(the oath of Jehovah)

2 Kings 11:2

2 Chronicles 22:11

Candid SNAPSHOT But Jehosheba, the daughter of King Jehoram and sister of Ahaziah, took Joash son of Ahaziah and stole him away from among the royal princes, who were about to be murdered. She put him and his nurse in a bedroom to hide him from Athaliah; so he was not killed (2 Kings 11:2).

"This is what the LORD says: Do not listen to the prophets who say, 'Very soon now the articles[t] from the LORD's house will be brought back from Babylon.' They are prophesying lies to you. 17Do not listen to them. Serve the king of Babylon, and you will live. Why should this city become a ruin? 18If they are prophets and have the word of the LORD, let them plead[u] with the LORD Almighty that the furnishings remaining in the house of the LORD and in the palace of the king of Judah and in Jerusalem not be taken to Babylon. 19For this is what the LORD Almighty says about the pillars, the Sea,[v] the movable stands and the other furnishings[w] that are left in this city, 20which Nebuchadnezzar king of Babylon did not take away when he carried[x] Jehoiachin[a][y] son of Jehoiakim king of Judah into exile from Jerusalem to Babylon, along with all the nobles of Judah and Jerusalem— 21yes, this is what the LORD Almighty, the God of Israel, says about the things that are left in the house of the LORD and in the palace of the king of Judah and in Jerusalem: 22'They will be taken[z] to Babylon and there they will remain until the day[a] I come for them,' declares the LORD. 'Then I will bring[b] them back and restore them to this place.' "

The False Prophet Hananiah

28 In the fifth month of that same year, the fourth year, early in the reign of Zedekiah[c] king of Judah, the prophet Hananiah son of Azzur, who was from Gibeon,[d] said to me in the house of the LORD in the presence of the priests and all the people: 2"This is what the LORD Almighty, the God of Israel, says: 'I will break the yoke[e] of the king of Babylon. 3Within two years I will bring back to this place all the articles[f] of the LORD's house that Nebuchadnezzar king of Babylon removed from here and took to Babylon. 4I will also bring back to this place Jehoiachin[a][g] son of Jehoiakim king of Judah and all the other exiles from Judah who went to Babylon,' declares the LORD, 'for I will break the yoke of the king of Babylon.' "

5Then the prophet Jeremiah replied to the prophet Hananiah before the priests and all the people who were standing in the house of the LORD. 6He said, "Amen! May the LORD do so! May the LORD fulfill the words you have prophesied by bringing the articles of the LORD's house and all the exiles back to this place from Babylon. 7Nevertheless, listen to what I have to say in your hearing and in the hearing of all the people: 8From early times the prophets who preceded you and me have prophesied war, disaster and plague[h] against many countries and great kingdoms. 9But the prophet who prophesies peace will be recognized as one truly sent by the LORD only if his prediction comes true.[i]"

10Then the prophet Hananiah took the yoke[j] off the neck of the prophet Jeremiah and broke it, 11and he said[k] before all the people, "This is what

27:16 [t]2Ki 24:13; 2Ch 36:7,10; Jer 28:3; Da 1:2
27:18 [u]1Sa 7:8
27:19 [v]2Ki 25:13 [w]Jer 52:17-23
27:20 [x]2Ch 36:10; Jer 24:1 [y]Jer 22:24
27:22 [z]2Ki 25:13 [a]2Ch 36:21 [b]Ezr 1:7; 7:19
28:1 [c]Jer 27:1,3 [d]Jos 9:3
28:2 [e]Jer 27:12
28:3 [f]2Ki 24:13
28:4 [g]Jer 22:24-27
28:8 [h]Lev 26:14-17; Isa 5:5-7
28:9 [i]Dt 18:22
28:10 [j]Jer 27:2
28:11 [k]Jer 14:14; 27:10

Sacred Vessels

JER 28:6

Nebuchadnezzar invades Jerusalem in 597 B.C. and carries off priceless articles from the temple (2Ki 24:13). Jeremiah foresees that, in another invasion, Babylon will confiscate even more temple valuables. Some of these valuables are expensive treasures given to God; others are sacred articles used in sacrifices for sin (2Ki 25:13–15). These aren't just tools or expensive collectibles. These articles signify God's presence and offer the people a means of true worship. Removing these holy vessels from the temple represents how the Lord is, step-by-step, cutting off communion with his people.

[a] *20,4* Hebrew *Jeconiah,* a variant of *Jehoiachin*

When you pray with other Christians, believing in faith, and God doesn't show up when you think he should, don't get discouraged. Many times I have prayed believing that my prayer was part of God's perfect will, yet he didn't move as quickly as I wanted him to. One time I had to wait sixteen years for him to answer. But when he did, it was the right answer at the right time. While I was waiting on him, I wondered what was happening. Sometimes I asked if he really heard me. Was I praying right? What else could I do? But deep within he assured me that he would see me through. He'll do the same for you.

—Thelma Wells

the LORD says: 'In the same way will I break the
yoke of Nebuchadnezzar king of Babylon off the
neck of all the nations within two years.' " At this,
the prophet Jeremiah went on his way.
12Shortly after the prophet Hananiah had broken the yoke off the neck of the prophet Jeremiah,
the word of the LORD came to Jeremiah: 13"Go and
tell Hananiah, 'This is what the LORD says: You
have broken a wooden yoke, but in its place you
will get a yoke of iron. 14This is what the LORD
Almighty, the God of Israel, says: I will put an iron
yoke[l] on the necks of all these nations to make 28:14 [l]Dt 28:48
them serve[m] Nebuchadnezzar king of Babylon, [m]Jer 25:11
and they will serve him. I will even give him con- [n]Jer 27:6
trol over the wild animals.[n]' "
15Then the prophet Jeremiah said to Hananiah
the prophet, "Listen, Hananiah! The LORD has not 28:15
sent[o] you, yet you have persuaded this nation to [o]Jer 29:31
trust in lies.[p] 16Therefore, this is what the LORD [p]Jer 20:6;
says: 'I am about to remove you from the face of 29:21;
the earth.[q] This very year you are going to die, La 2:14; Eze 13:6
because you have preached rebellion[r] against the 28:16
LORD.' " [q]Ge 7:4
17In the seventh month of that same year, Han- [r]Dt 13:5;
aniah the prophet died. Jer 29:32

A Letter to the Exiles

29 This is the text of the letter that the prophet
Jeremiah sent from Jerusalem to the surviving elders among the exiles and to the priests, the
prophets and all the other people Nebuchadnezzar 29:1
had carried into exile from Jerusalem to Babylon.[s] [s]2Ch 36:10
2(This was after King Jehoiachin[a][t] and the queen
mother, the court officials and the leaders of Judah 29:2
and Jerusalem, the craftsmen and the artisans had [t]2Ki 24:12;
gone into exile from Jerusalem.) 3He entrusted the Jer 22:24-28
letter to Elasah son of Shaphan and to Gemariah
son of Hilkiah, whom Zedekiah king of Judah sent
to King Nebuchadnezzar in Babylon. It said:

4This is what the LORD Almighty, the God
of Israel, says to all those I carried[u] into exile 29:4
from Jerusalem to Babylon: 5"Build[v] houses [u]Jer 24:5
and settle down; plant gardens and eat what 29:5
they produce. 6Marry and have sons and [v]ver 28
daughters; find wives for your sons and give
your daughters in marriage, so that they too
may have sons and daughters. Increase in
number there; do not decrease. 7Also, seek
the peace and prosperity of the city to which 29:7
I have carried you into exile. Pray[w] to the [w]Ezr 6:10;
LORD for it, because if it prospers, you too will 1Ti 2:1-2
prosper." 8Yes, this is what the LORD Al-
mighty, the God of Israel, says: "Do not let
the prophets and diviners among you 29:8
deceive[x] you. Do not listen to the dreams you [x]Jer 37:9
encourage them to have.[y] 9They are prophe- [y]Jer 23:27
sying lies[z] to you in my name. I have not sent 29:9
them," declares the LORD. [z]Jer 14:14; 27:15

[a] 2 Hebrew *Jeconiah,* a variant of *Jehoiachin*

10 This is what the LORD says: "When seven-
29:10 [a]2Ch 36:21; ty years[a] are completed for Babylon, I will
Jer 25:12; come to you and fulfill my gracious promise
Da 9:2 to bring you back[b] to this place. 11 For I know
[b]Jer 21:22 the plans[c] I have for you," declares the LORD,
29:11 "plans to prosper you and not to harm you,
[c]Ps 40:5 plans to give you hope and a future. 12 Then
you will call upon me and come and pray to
29:12 me, and I will listen[d] to you. 13 You will seek[e]
[d]Ps 145:19 me and find me when you seek me with all
29:13 [e]Mt 7:7 your heart.[f] 14 I will be found by you," declares
[f]Dt 4:29; the LORD, "and will bring you back[g] from cap-
Jer 24:7 tivity.[a] I will gather you from all the nations
and places where I have banished you,"
29:14 [g]Dt 30:3; declares the LORD, "and will bring you back to
Jer 30:3 [h]Jer 23:3-4 the place from which I carried you into exile."[h]
15 You may say, "The LORD has raised up
prophets for us in Babylon," 16 but this is what
the LORD says about the king who sits on
David's throne and all the people who remain
in this city, your countrymen who did not go
with you into exile— 17 yes, this is what the
LORD Almighty says: "I will send the sword,
29:17 [i]Jer 27:8 famine and plague[i] against them and I will
[j]Jer 24:8-10 make them like poor figs[j] that are so bad they
cannot be eaten. 18 I will pursue them with
29:18 the sword, famine and plague and will make
[k]Jer 15:4 them abhorrent[k] to all the kingdoms of the
[l]Dt 28:25; earth and an object of cursing and horror,[l] of
Jer 42:18 scorn and reproach, among all the nations
where I drive them. 19 For they have not lis-
29:19 [m]Jer 6:19 tened to my words,"[m] declares the LORD,
[n]Jer 25:4 "words that I sent to them again and again by
my servants the prophets.[n] And you exiles
have not listened either," declares the LORD.
20 Therefore, hear the word of the LORD, all
29:20 [o]Jer 24:5 you exiles whom I have sent[o] away from Jerusalem to Babylon. 21 This is what the LORD
Almighty, the God of Israel, says about Ahab
son of Kolaiah and Zedekiah son of Maase-
29:21 iah, who are prophesying lies[p] to you in my
[p]ver 9; Jer 14:14 name: "I will hand them over to Nebuchadnezzar king of Babylon, and he will put them
to death before your very eyes. 22 Because of
them, all the exiles from Judah who are in
Babylon will use this curse: 'The LORD treat
29:22 you like Zedekiah and Ahab, whom the king
[q]Da 3:6 of Babylon burned[q] in the fire.' 23 For they
29:23 have done outrageous things in Israel; they
[r]Jer 23:14 have committed adultery[r] with their neigh-
[s]Heb 4:13 bors' wives and in my name have spoken
lies, which I did not tell them to do. I know[s]
it and am a witness to it," declares the LORD.

Message to Shemaiah

24 Tell Shemaiah the Nehelamite, 25 "This is what
the LORD Almighty, the God of Israel, says: You sent
29:25 letters in your own name to all the people in Jeru-
[t]2Ki 25:18; Jer 21:1 salem, to Zephaniah[t] son of Maseiah the priest,

Hopeful Future

JER 29:11-13

Jeremiah sends a letter to the Babylonian exiles. These Hebrews are sent into exile when Nebuchadnezzar takes Jehoiachin captive to Babylon (2Ki 24:15). They are primarily the leaders of the land, royalty, the rich, artisans, priests and soldiers (2Ki 24:14,16; Jer 29:1-2). Jeremiah has heard that false prophets are predicting a speedy end to the exile and to the Babylonian Empire. He has other words from God.

Jeremiah exhorts the people to settle in the land and move ahead with their lives. He doesn't guarantee a speedy release like some of the exiled prophets, but he does give them hope. After 70 years God will return his people to their homeland (Jer 29:10). In the meantime, he gives them the dazzling words of Jeremiah 29:11-13, words of comfort and confidence, words that offer hope not only to the captives, but also to us today. God knows the future and wants us to trust him for the journey ahead. When we feel like abandoned captives, he promises his presence. When we tire of waiting for distant dreams, he promises strength. No matter how bleak our circumstances, God promises "hope and a future" (Jer 29:11).

[a] 14 Or *will restore your fortunes*

End Times

JER 30:6–7

Jeremiah writes this section of his prophecy approximately one year before the final destruction of Jerusalem and the exportation of yet more exiles to Babylon. It is a grim time in Judah's history. But Jeremiah now looks past the events of this near judgment to the end-times judgment. In his prophetic vision, the day of the Lord begins with severe distress for Judah and the nations. Amos 5:18–20 and Zechariah 14:1–8,12–15 also describe this time of Jacob's trouble. The picture of men agonizing in childbirth expresses the intense anguish of that time. This unusual imagery points to "how awful that day will be!" (Jer 30:7). Thankfully, this is not the end of the story. Restoration and redemption are promised as well as judgment (Jer 30:3,8–9).

and to all the other priests. You said to Zephaniah,
26 'The LORD has appointed you priest in place of
Jehoiada to be in charge of the house of the LORD;
you should put any madman[u] who acts like a
prophet into the stocks[v] and neck-irons. 27 So why
have you not reprimanded Jeremiah from Anathoth, who poses as a prophet among you? 28 He has
sent this message[w] to us in Babylon: It will be a
long time.[x] Therefore build[y] houses and settle
down; plant gardens and eat what they produce.' "
29 Zephaniah the priest, however, read the letter
to Jeremiah the prophet. 30 Then the word of the
LORD came to Jeremiah: 31 "Send this message to
all the exiles: 'This is what the LORD says about
Shemaiah[z] the Nehelamite: Because Shemaiah has
prophesied to you, even though I did not send[a]
him, and has led you to believe a lie, 32 this is what
the LORD says: I will surely punish Shemaiah the
Nehelamite and his descendants.[b] He will have no
one left among this people, nor will he see the
good[c] things I will do for my people, declares
the LORD, because he has preached rebellion[d]
against me.' "

Restoration of Israel

30 This is the word that came to Jeremiah from
the LORD: 2 "This is what the LORD, the God
of Israel, says: 'Write[e] in a book all the words I
have spoken to you. 3 The days are coming,'
declares the LORD, 'when I will bring[f] my people
Israel and Judah back from captivity[a] and restore[g]
them to the land I gave their forefathers to possess,' says the LORD."
4 These are the words the LORD spoke concerning Israel and Judah: 5 "This is what the LORD says:

" 'Cries of fear[h] are heard—
terror, not peace.
6 Ask and see:
Can a man bear children?
Then why do I see every strong man
with his hands on his stomach like a
woman in labor,[i]
every face turned deathly pale?
7 How awful that day[j] will be!
None will be like it.
It will be a time of trouble[k] for Jacob,
but he will be saved[l] out of it.

8 " 'In that day,' declares the LORD
Almighty,
'I will break the yoke[m] off their necks
and will tear off their bonds;
no longer will foreigners enslave
them.[n]
9 Instead, they will serve the LORD their
God
and David[o] their king,[p]
whom I will raise up for them.

29:26 [u]2Ki 9:11; Hos 9:7; Jn 10:20 [v]Jer 20:2
29:28 [w]ver 1 [x]ver 10 [y]ver 5
29:31 [z]ver 24 [a]Jer 14:14; 28:15
29:32 [b]1Sa 2:30-33 [c]ver 10 [d]Jer 28:16
30:2 [e]Isa 30:8
30:3 [f]Jer 29:14 [g]Jer 16:15
30:5 [h]Jer 6:25
30:6 [i]Jer 4:31
30:7 [j]Isa 2:12; Joel 2:11 [k]Zep 1:15 [l]ver 10
30:8 [m]Isa 9:4 [n]Eze 34:27
30:9 [o]Isa 55:3-4; Lk 1:69; Ac 2:30; 13:23 [p]Eze 34:23-24; 37:24; Hos 3:5

[a] 3 Or *will restore the fortunes of my people Israel and Judah*

30:10
[q]Isa 43:5; Jer 46:27-28
[r]Isa 44:2
[s]Jer 29:14
[t]Isa 35:9

10 " 'So do not fear,[q] O Jacob my servant;[r]
do not be dismayed, O Israel,'
declares the LORD.
'I will surely save[s] you out of a distant
place,
your descendants from the land of
their exile.
Jacob will again have peace and
security,[t]
and no one will make him afraid.
11 I am with you and will save you,'
declares the LORD.
'Though I completely destroy all the
nations
among which I scatter you,
I will not completely destroy[u] you.
I will discipline[v] you but only with
justice;
I will not let you go entirely
unpunished.'[w]

30:11
[u]Jer 4:27; 46:28
[v]Jer 10:24
[w]Am 9:8

12 "This is what the LORD says:

" 'Your wound is incurable,
your injury beyond healing.[x]
13 There is no one to plead your cause,
no remedy for your sore,
no healing[y] for you.
14 All your allies[z] have forgotten you;
they care nothing for you.
I have struck you as an enemy[a] would
and punished you as would the
cruel,[b]
because your guilt is so great
and your sins[c] so many.
15 Why do you cry out over your wound,
your pain that has no cure?
Because of your great guilt and many
sins
I have done these things to you.

30:12
[x]Jer 15:18

30:13
[y]Jer 8:22; 14:19; 46:11

30:14
[z]Jer 22:20; La 1:2
[a]Job 13:24
[b]Job 30:21
[c]Jer 5:6

16 " 'But all who devour[d] you will be
devoured;
all your enemies will go into exile.[e]
Those who plunder[f] you will be
plundered;
all who make spoil of you I will
despoil.
17 But I will restore you to health
and heal your wounds,'
declares the LORD,
'because you are called an outcast,[g]
Zion for whom no one cares.'

30:16
[d]Isa 33:1; Jer 2:3; 10:25
[e]Isa 14:2; Joel 3:4-8
[f]Jer 50:10

30:17
[g]Jer 33:24

18 "This is what the LORD says:

" 'I will restore the fortunes[h] of Jacob's
tents
and have compassion[i] on his
dwellings;
the city will be rebuilt[j] on her ruins,
and the palace will stand in its proper
place.

30:18
[h]ver 3; Jer 31:23
[i]Ps 102:13
[j]Jer 31:4,24, 38

The Cure

JER 30:12-13

Sin is terminal. It cannot be cured by moral living or religious ardor. Judah's festering wound of rebellion is incurable. She has no allies left to plead her cause. No person or nation can effectively bandage her damaged spirit. Only the Lord can heal her injured soul. This is the essence of God's redeeming love for Judah and for us.

At times we might feel helpless like Judah. Maybe our sinful past is hurling accusations our way. Maybe we've turned our backs on a God who seems slow to answer. Whether we are restless and limping or broken and alone, our healer lovingly waits to bind up our wounds (Ps 147:3). Our Savior Christ Jesus is the only cure for our spiritual malaise.

Everlasting Love

JER 30:24; 31:3–4

God never wavers from his purposes for Israel and Judah. Their stubborn rebellion requires justice. Their punishment and captivity are part of his design to soften the people's hearts and restore them to himself. Even when the people despise God, his steadfast love continues to woo them to himself. Sometimes our waywardness requires God's correction. If we stubbornly refuse to listen and continue to go off course, he applies more pressure. But throughout the entire process, he never stops loving us and longing for our best.

19 From them will come songs[k] of
thanksgiving[l]
and the sound of rejoicing.[m]
I will add to their numbers,[n]
and they will not be decreased;
I will bring them honor,[o]
and they will not be disdained.
20 Their children[p] will be as in days of old,
and their community will be
established[q] before me;
I will punish all who oppress them.
21 Their leader[r] will be one of their own;
their ruler will arise from among
them.
I will bring him near[s] and he will come
close to me,
for who is he who will devote himself
to be close to me?'
declares the LORD.
22 " 'So you will be my people,
and I will be your God.' "

23 See, the storm[t] of the LORD
will burst out in wrath,
a driving wind swirling down
on the heads of the wicked.
24 The fierce anger[u] of the LORD will not
turn back[v]
until he fully accomplishes
the purposes of his heart.
In days to come
you will understand[w] this.

31 "At that time," declares the LORD, "I will be
the God[x] of all the clans of Israel, and they
will be my people."
2 This is what the LORD says:

"The people who survive the sword
will find favor[y] in the desert;
I will come to give rest[z] to Israel."
3 The LORD appeared to us in the past,[a] saying:

"I have loved[a] you with an everlasting
love;
I have drawn[b] you with loving-
kindness.
4 I will build you up again
and you will be rebuilt, O Virgin
Israel.
Again you will take up your
tambourines
and go out to dance with the joyful.[c]
5 Again you will plant vineyards
on the hills of Samaria;[d]
the farmers will plant them
and enjoy their fruit.[e]
6 There will be a day when watchmen cry
out
on the hills of Ephraim,

30:19 [k]Isa 35:10; 51:11 [l]Isa 51:3 [m]Ps 126:1-2; Jer 31:4 [n]Jer 33:22 [o]Isa 60:9
30:20 [p]Isa 54:13; Jer 31:17 [q]Isa 54:14
30:21 [r]ver 9 [s]Nu 16:5
30:23 [t]Jer 23:19
30:24 [u]Jer 4:8 [v]Jer 4:28 [w]Jer 23:19-20
31:1 [x]Jer 30:22
31:2 [y]Nu 14:20 [z]Ex 33:14
31:3 [a]Dt 4:37 [b]Hos 11:4
31:4 [c]Jer 30:19
31:5 [d]Jer 50:19 [e]Isa 65:21; Am 9:14

[a] 3 Or *LORD has appeared to us from afar*

'Come, let us go up to Zion,
to the LORD our God.' "[f]

7 This is what the LORD says:

"Sing with joy for Jacob;
shout for the foremost[g] of the nations.
Make your praises heard, and say,
'O LORD, save[h] your people,
the remnant[i] of Israel.'
8 See, I will bring them from the land of
the north[j]
and gather[k] them from the ends of the
earth.
Among them will be the blind[l] and the
lame,[m]
expectant mothers and women in
labor;
a great throng will return.
9 They will come with weeping;[n]
they will pray as I bring them back.
I will lead[o] them beside streams of water
on a level[p] path where they will not
stumble,
because I am Israel's father,[q]
and Ephraim is my firstborn son.

10 "Hear the word of the LORD, O nations;
proclaim it in distant coastlands:[r]
'He who scattered Israel will gather[s]
them
and will watch over his flock like a
shepherd.'[t]
11 For the LORD will ransom Jacob
and redeem[u] them from the hand of
those stronger[v] than they.
12 They will come and shout for joy on the
heights[w] of Zion;
they will rejoice in the bounty[x] of the
LORD—
the grain, the new wine and the oil,[y]
the young of the flocks and herds.
They will be like a well-watered
garden,[z]
and they will sorrow[a] no more.
13 Then maidens will dance and be glad,
young men and old as well.
I will turn their mourning[b] into
gladness;
I will give them comfort and joy[c]
instead of sorrow.
14 I will satisfy[d] the priests with abundance,
and my people will be filled with my
bounty,"
declares the LORD.

15 This is what the LORD says:

"A voice is heard in Ramah,[e]
mourning and great weeping,
Rachel weeping for her children
and refusing to be comforted,[f]
because her children are no more."[g]

31:6 [f]Isa 2:3; Jer 50:4-5; Mic 4:2
31:7 [g]Dt 28:13; Isa 61:9 [h]Ps 14:7; 28:9 [i]Isa 37:31
31:8 [j]Jer 3:18; 23:8 [k]Dt 30:4; Eze 34:12-14 [l]Isa 42:16 [m]Eze 34:16; Mic 4:6
31:9 [n]Ps 126:5 [o]Isa 63:13 [p]Isa 49:11 [q]Ex 4:22; Jer 3:4
31:10 [r]Isa 66:19; Jer 25:22 [s]Jer 50:19 [t]Isa 40:11; Eze 34:12
31:11 [u]Isa 44:23; 48:20 [v]Ps 142:6
31:12 [w]Eze 17:23; Mic 4:1 [x]Joel 3:18 [y]Hos 2:21-22 [z]Isa 58:11 [a]Isa 65:19; Jn 16:22; Rev 7:17
31:13 [b]Isa 61:3 [c]Ps 30:11; Isa 51:11
31:14 [d]ver 25
31:15 [e]Jos 18:25 [f]Ge 37:35 [g]Jer 10:20; Mt 2:17-18*

Mighty Defender

JER 31:8

Like many of Jeremiah's prophecies, this one finds fulfillment in Israel's near future as well as in the distant future. The exiles see the places in Assyria and Babylon as "the ends of the earth" (Jer 31:8). The Lord will one day gather his disenfranchised people: the now extinct northern kingdom of Israel scattered between Samaria and Assyria as well as the exiles from the southern kingdom of Judah now living in Babylon.

In the millennial kingdom, Israel will be restored as God's people. From the ends of the earth, God will call his children to return to him, to return home in a noble procession that includes the weak and vulnerable. Why does God specifically list these defenseless people? Perhaps our mighty Defender wants to remind us of his compassionate guidance. He isn't just a God of outspoken leaders and determined survivalists. He cares for those slowed by physical limitations. He cares for those unable to read his Word or speak his name.

Women Surround Men

JER 31:22

Using incisive language, Jeremiah presents an unusual picture in this verse. This is something new, he says, something not seen before on the earth: "A woman will surround a man" (Jer 31:22). The Hebrew word for surround could also be translated "protect" (see the NIV footnote on Jer 31:22). In Hebrew culture, the men "surround" and "protect" the women. But women are now in a new position—that of being the protector instead of the protected. Some scholars think this verse points to the role of Mary as the mother of Jesus, a virgin who bore a human/divine being. Others say it refers to the love that Israel will finally have for her Lord after years of unfaithfulness. Whatever the interpretation, it serves to splendidly underscore the value the Lord places on women. No second-class citizens, no afterthought, no unnecessary appendage—women play an important role in the story of God's plan of salvation.

16 This is what the LORD says:

"Restrain your voice from weeping
and your eyes from tears,[h]
for your work will be rewarded,[i]"
declares the LORD.
"They will return[j] from the land of the enemy.
17 So there is hope for your future,"
declares the LORD.
"Your children will return to their own land.

31:16 [h]Isa 25:8; 30:19 [i]Ru 2:12 [j]Jer 30:3; Eze 11:17

18 "I have surely heard Ephraim's moaning:
'You disciplined[k] me like an unruly calf,[l]
and I have been disciplined.
Restore[m] me, and I will return,
because you are the LORD my God.
19 After I strayed,[n]
I repented;
after I came to understand,
I beat[o] my breast.
I was ashamed and humiliated
because I bore the disgrace of my youth.'
20 Is not Ephraim my dear son,
the child in whom I delight?
Though I often speak against him,
I still remember[p] him.
Therefore my heart yearns for him;
I have great compassion[q] for him,"
declares the LORD.

31:18 [k]Job 5:17 [l]Hos 4:16 [m]Ps 80:3
31:19 [n]Eze 36:31 [o]Eze 21:12; Lk 18:13
31:20 [p]Hos 4:4; 11:8 [q]Isa 55:7; 63:15; Mic 7:18

21 "Set up road signs;
put up guideposts.
Take note of the highway,[r]
the road that you take.
Return,[s] O Virgin[t] Israel,
return to your towns.
22 How long will you wander,[u]
O unfaithful[v] daughter?
The LORD will create a new thing on earth—
a woman will surround[a] a man."

31:21 [r]Jer 50:5 [s]Isa 52:11 [t]ver 4
31:22 [u]Jer 2:23 [v]Jer 3:6

23 This is what the LORD Almighty, the God of
Israel, says: "When I bring them back from captivity,[b][w] the people in the land of Judah and in its
towns will once again use these words: 'The LORD
bless you, O righteous dwelling,[x] O sacred mountain.'[y] 24 People will live[z] together in Judah and all
its towns—farmers and those who move about
with their flocks. 25 I will refresh the weary and
satisfy the faint."[a]
26 At this I awoke[b] and looked around. My sleep
had been pleasant to me.
27 "The days are coming," declares the LORD,
"when I will plant[c] the house of Israel and the

31:23 [w]Jer 30:18 [x]Isa 1:26 [y]Ps 48:1; Zec 8:3
31:24 [z]Zec 8:4-8
31:25 [a]Jn 4:14
31:26 [b]Zec 4:1
31:27 [c]Eze 36:9-11; Hos 2:23

[a] 22 Or *will go about* ⌞*seeking*⌟; or *will protect* [b] 23 Or *I restore their fortunes*

house of Judah with the offspring of men and of
animals. [28]Just as I watched over them to uproot
and tear down, and to overthrow, destroy and
31:28 [d]Jer 18:8; 44:27 [e]Jer 1:10
bring disaster,[d] so I will watch over them to build
and to plant,"[e] declares the LORD. [29]"In those days
people will no longer say,

31:29 [f]La 5:7 [g]Eze 18:2

'The fathers[f] have eaten sour grapes,
and the children's teeth are set on
edge.'[g]

31:30 [h]Isa 3:11; Gal 6:7

[30]Instead, everyone will die for his own sin;[h] whoever eats sour grapes—his own teeth will be set
on edge.

31:31 [i]Jer 32:40; Eze 37:26; Lk 22:20; Heb 8:8-12*; 10:16-17

[31]"The time is coming," declares the LORD,
"when I will make a new covenant[i]
with the house of Israel
and with the house of Judah.
[32]It will not be like the covenant[j]
I made with their forefathers[k]

31:32 [j]Ex 24:8 [k]Dt 5:3

when I took them by the hand
to lead them out of Egypt,
because they broke my covenant,
though I was a husband to[a] them,[b]"
declares the LORD.
[33]"This is the covenant I will make with
the house of Israel
after that time," declares the LORD.
"I will put my law in their minds
and write it on their hearts.[l]

31:33 [l]2Co 3:3 [m]Jer 24:7; Heb 10:16

I will be their God,
and they will be my people.[m]
[34]No longer will a man teach[n] his
neighbor,

31:34 [n]1Jn 2:27 [o]Jn 6:45 [p]Isa 54:13; Jer 33:8; 50:20 [q]Ro 11:27; Mic 7:19; Heb 10:17*

or a man his brother, saying, 'Know
the LORD,'
because they will all know[o] me,
from the least of them to the greatest,"
declares the LORD.
"For I will forgive[p] their wickedness
and will remember their sins[q] no
more."

[35]This is what the LORD says,

31:35 [r]Ps 136:7-9 [s]Ge 1:16 [t]Jer 10:16

he who appoints[r] the sun
to shine by day,
who decrees the moon and stars
to shine by night,[s]
who stirs up the sea
so that its waves roar—
the LORD Almighty is his name:[t]

31:36 [u]Isa 54:9-10; Jer 33:20-26 [v]Ps 89:36-37

[36]"Only if these decrees[u] vanish from my
sight,"
declares the LORD,
"will the descendants[v] of Israel ever
cease
to be a nation before me."

[37]This is what the LORD says:

[a] *32* Hebrew; Septuagint and Syriac / *and I turned away from*
[b] *32* Or *was their master*

New Beginnings

JER 31:31–33

Israel and Judah break God's covenant, rebelling and ignoring God and his commandments (Ex 19:5–6; 24:3–8; Dt 29:1–29). Now Jeremiah declares that one day God will make a new covenant with his people. Instead of laws inscribed on stone, God promises to write his laws on people's hearts and minds.

The writer to the Hebrews quotes this passage of Jeremiah when he describes the fulfillment of this new covenant (Heb 8:7–13). Jesus Christ is its foundation, and grace and forgiveness flow from him. Jeremiah looks forward to the arrival of this new covenant. Today we have the privilege of looking back at Christ's atoning death, which ratifies the covenant for us. Through the gift of his Son, God offers us a direct and personal relationship with himself. Under this new covenant, our obedience is motivated by our God-conscious hearts rather than by laws written on stone.

The Invincible City

JER 31:38–40

God declares that "the days are coming" (Jer 31:38) when Jerusalem, the capital city of his favored nation, will be rebuilt. He gives specific details of the reconstruction from one location of the wall to another.

The "valley where dead bodies and ashes are thrown" (Jer 31:40) is generally understood to be the Hinnom Valley (Jer 7:31–32). Throughout their history, the Israelites use this area as a dumping ground and a place to burn trash. During the time of the kings it is also used as a place of idol worship, where apostate Israelites offer their children as sacrifices (2Ki 23:10). Even these polluted and defiled areas where the dead lie and trash is thrown will be consecrated to the Lord.

This prophecy cannot be about the Jerusalem temple rebuilt during the time of Ezra and Nehemiah because it was "demolished" (Jer 31:40) in A.D. *70, which Jesus predicted (Mt 24:1–2; Lk 21:5–6). This prophecy of a rebuilt, invincible city points to a future Jerusalem (Rev 21:2,10).*

"Only if the heavens above can be
measured[w]
and the foundations of the earth
below be searched out
will I reject[x] all the descendants of Israel
because of all they have done,"
declares the LORD.

38"The days are coming," declares the LORD,
"when this city will be rebuilt[y] for me from the
Tower of Hananel[z] to the Corner Gate.[a] 39The
measuring line will stretch from there straight to
the hill of Gareb and then turn to Goah. 40The
whole valley[b] where dead bodies[c] and ashes are
thrown, and all the terraces out to the Kidron Valley[d] on the east as far as the corner of the Horse
Gate,[e] will be holy[f] to the LORD. The city will never again be uprooted or demolished."

Jeremiah Buys a Field

32 This is the word that came to Jeremiah from
the LORD in the tenth[g] year of Zedekiah king
of Judah, which was the eighteenth[h] year of Nebuchadnezzar. 2The army of the king of Babylon
was then besieging Jerusalem, and Jeremiah the
prophet was confined in the courtyard of the
guard[i] in the royal palace of Judah.
3Now Zedekiah king of Judah had imprisoned
him there, saying, "Why do you prophesy[j] as you
do? You say, 'This is what the LORD says: I am
about to hand this city over to the king of Babylon,
and he will capture[k] it. 4Zedekiah king of Judah
will not escape[l] out of the hands of the Babylonians[a] but will certainly be handed over to the king
of Babylon, and will speak with him face to face
and see him with his own eyes. 5He will take[m]
Zedekiah to Babylon, where he will remain until I
deal with him, declares the LORD. If you fight
against the Babylonians, you will not succeed.' "[n]
6Jeremiah said, "The word of the LORD came to
me: 7Hanamel son of Shallum your uncle is going
to come to you and say, 'Buy my field at Anathoth, because as nearest relative it is your right
and duty[o] to buy it.'
8"Then, just as the LORD had said, my cousin
Hanamel came to me in the courtyard of the guard
and said, 'Buy my field at Anathoth in the territory of Benjamin. Since it is your right to redeem it
and possess it, buy it for yourself.'
"I knew that this was the word of the LORD; 9so
I bought the field at Anathoth from my cousin
Hanamel and weighed out for him seventeen
shekels[b] of silver.[p] 10I signed and sealed the deed,
had it witnessed,[q] and weighed out the silver on
the scales. 11I took the deed of purchase—the
sealed copy containing the terms and conditions,
as well as the unsealed copy— 12and I gave this
deed to Baruch[r] son of Neriah,[s] the son of Mahse-
iah, in the presence of my cousin Hanamel and of

31:37 [w]Jer 33:22 [x]Jer 33:24-26; Ro 11:1-5
31:38 [y]Jer 30:18 [z]Ne 3:1 [a]2Ki 14:13; Zec 14:10
31:40 [b]Jer 7:31-32 [c]Jer 8:2 [d]2Sa 15:23; Jn 18:1 [e]2Ki 11:16 [f]Joel 3:17; Zec 14:21
32:1 [g]2Ki 25:1 [h]Jer 25:1; 39:1
32:2 [i]Ne 3:25; Jer 37:21
32:3 [j]Jer 26:8-9 [k]ver 28; Jer 34:2-3
32:4 [l]Jer 38:18, 23; 39:5-7; 52:9
32:5 [m]Jer 39:7; Eze 12:13 [n]Jer 21:4
32:7 [o]Lev 25:24-25; Ru 4:3-4; Mt 27:10*
32:9 [p]Ge 23:16
32:10 [q]Ru 4:9
32:12 [r]ver 16; Jer 36:4; 43:3,6; 45:1 [s]Jer 51:59

[a] 4 Or *Chaldeans*; also in verses 5, 24, 25, 28, 29 and 43
[b] 9 That is, about 7 ounces (about 200 grams)

the witnesses who had signed the deed and of all
the Jews sitting in the courtyard of the guard.
13“In their presence I gave Baruch these instructions: 14‘This is what the LORD Almighty, the God
of Israel, says: Take these documents, both the
sealed and unsealed copies of the deed of purchase, and put them in a clay jar so they will last
a long time. 15For this is what the LORD Almighty,
the God of Israel, says: Houses, fields and vine-
32:15 [t]ver 43-44; yards will again be bought in this land.’[t]
Jer 30:18; 16“After I had given the deed of purchase to Bar-
Am 9:14-15 uch son of Neriah, I prayed to the LORD:

32:17 [u]Jer 1:6 17“Ah, Sovereign LORD,[u] you have made the
[v]2Ki 19:15; heavens and the earth by your great power
Ps 102:25 and outstretched arm.[v] Nothing is too hard[w]
[w]Mt 19:26 for you. 18You show love[x] to thousands but
32:18 [x]Dt 5:10 bring the punishment for the fathers’ sins
[y]Ex 20:5 into the laps of their children[y] after them.
[z]Jer 10:16 O great and powerful God, whose name is the
LORD Almighty,[z] 19great are your purposes
32:19 and mighty are your deeds.[a] Your eyes are
[a]Isa 28:29 [b]Pr 5:21; open to all the ways of men;[b] you reward
Jer 16:17 everyone according to his conduct and as his
[c]Jer 17:10; Mt 16:27 deeds deserve.[c] 20You performed miraculous
signs and wonders in Egypt[d] and have con-
32:20 [d]Ex 9:16 tinued them to this day, both in Israel and
among all mankind, and have gained the
renown that is still yours. 21You brought your
people Israel out of Egypt with signs and
32:21 wonders, by a mighty hand[e] and an out-
[e]Ex 6:6; stretched arm and with great terror.[f] 22You
1Ch 17:21; Da 9:15 gave them this land you had sworn to give
[f]Dt 26:8 their forefathers, a land flowing with milk
32:22 and honey.[g] 23They came in and took posses-
[g]Ex 3:8; sion[h] of it, but they did not obey you or fol-
Jer 11:5 low your law;[i] they did not do what you com-
32:23 manded them to do. So you brought all this
[h]Ps 44:2; disaster[j] upon them.
78:54-55 24“See how the siege ramps are built up to
[i]Ne 9:26; Jer 11:8 take the city. Because of the sword, famine
[j]Da 9:14 and plague,[k] the city will be handed over to
32:24 the Babylonians who are attacking it. What
[k]Jer 14:12 you said[l] has happened, as you now see.
[l]Dt 4:25-26; 25And though the city will be handed over to
Jos 23:15-16 the Babylonians, you, O Sovereign LORD, say
to me, ‘Buy the field with silver and have the
transaction witnessed.’ ”

26Then the word of the LORD came to Jeremiah:
32:27 [m]Nu 16:22 27“I am the LORD, the God of all mankind.[m] Is anything too hard for me? 28Therefore, this is what
32:28 the LORD says: I am about to hand this city over
[n]2Ch 36:17 to the Babylonians and to Nebuchadnezzar[n] king
[o]ver 3 of Babylon, who will capture it.[o] 29The Babyloni-
32:29 ans who are attacking this city will come in and
[p]2Ch 36:19; Jer 21:10; set it on fire; they will burn it down,[p] along with
37:8,10; the houses[q] where the people provoked me to
52:13 anger by burning incense on the roofs to Baal and
[q]Jer 19:13 [r]Jer 44:18 by pouring out drink offerings[r] to other gods.
32:30 30“The people of Israel and Judah have done
[s]Jer 22:21 nothing but evil in my sight from their youth;[s]

An Inheritance Preserved

JER 32:14

Despite the impending invasion of the Babylonian army encamped around the city gate, Jeremiah obeys God’s command to purchase a field outside of Jerusalem. Why would he buy a field that is already controlled by an enemy he knows will soon overtake the entire country? But by faith Jeremiah goes ahead and does what God asks. Although he is a prisoner in the palace courtyard, Jeremiah buys land to demonstrate that God intends his people to return from exile and rebuild Jerusalem.

Jeremiah 32:12 is the first mention of Baruch, Jeremiah’s secretary and loyal friend. Jeremiah asks Baruch to safeguard the land’s purchase deed in a clay jar. Jeremiah’s secured documents give him the right to reclaim his land after the exile. Storing documents in an earthenware jar, sealed with pitch, is much like using a safety deposit box. Archaeologists have discovered ancient clay storage jars in Elephantine, Egypt, and Qumran (west of the Dead Sea), many containing ancient documents, some more than 2000 years old.

Single-Hearted

JER 32:39

For years the people's hearts have wandered from the Lord. Through Jeremiah, God pledges to focus their hearts and actions on him again. He vows to make them single-hearted, sincere and concentrated in purpose. He will restore them to a wholehearted love relationship with their Creator. The people will realign their purposes and desires toward God, serving him with "wholehearted devotion and with a willing mind" (1Ch 28:9).

We face the same challenge. The "foreign gods" of power, prestige and popularity call to our hearts every day. Ask God to help your heart and mind stay focused on him. Thank him that he can be found and deserves our devotion.

indeed, the people of Israel have done nothing but
provoke[t] me with what their hands have made,[u]
declares the LORD. 31 From the day it was built until
now, this city has so aroused my anger and wrath
that I must remove[v] it from my sight. 32 The people
of Israel and Judah have provoked me by all the
evil[w] they have done—they, their kings and officials,
their priests and prophets, the men of Judah
and the people of Jerusalem. 33 They turned their
backs[x] to me and not their faces; though I taught[y]
them again and again, they would not listen or
respond to discipline. 34 They set up their abominable
idols in the house that bears my Name and
defiled[z] it. 35 They built high places for Baal in the
Valley of Ben Hinnom to sacrifice their sons and
daughters[a] to Molech,[a] though I never commanded,
nor did it enter my mind,[b] that they should do
such a detestable thing and so make Judah sin.

36 "You are saying about this city, 'By the sword,
famine and plague[c] it will be handed over to the
king of Babylon'; but this is what the LORD, the God
of Israel, says: 37 I will surely gather[d] them from all
the lands where I banish them in my furious anger
and great wrath; I will bring them back to this
place and let them live in safety.[e] 38 They will be my
people,[f] and I will be their God. 39 I will give them
singleness[g] of heart and action, so that they will
always fear me for their own good and the good of
their children after them. 40 I will make an everlasting
covenant[h] with them: I will never stop doing
good to them, and I will inspire them to fear me, so
that they will never turn away from me.[i] 41 I will
rejoice in doing them good[j] and will assuredly
plant[k] them in this land with all my heart and soul.

42 "This is what the LORD says: As I have brought
all this great calamity on this people, so I will give
them all the prosperity I have promised[l] them.
43 Once more fields will be bought[m] in this land of
which you say, 'It is a desolate waste, without
men or animals, for it has been handed over to
the Babylonians.' 44 Fields will be bought for silver,
and deeds[n] will be signed, sealed and witnessed
in the territory of Benjamin, in the villages
around Jerusalem, in the towns of Judah and in
the towns of the hill country, of the western
foothills and of the Negev,[o] because I will restore[p]
their fortunes,[b] declares the LORD."

Promise of Restoration

33 While Jeremiah was still confined in the
courtyard[q] of the guard, the word of the
LORD came to him a second time: 2 "This is what
the LORD says, he who made the earth,[r] the LORD
who formed it and established it—the LORD is his
name:[s] 3 'Call[t] to me and I will answer you and tell
you great and unsearchable things you do not
know.' 4 For this is what the LORD, the God of Israel,
says about the houses in this city and the roy-

32:30 [t]Jer 8:19 [u]Jer 25:7
32:31 [v]2Ki 23:27; 24:3
32:32 [w]Isa 1:4-6; Da 9:8
32:33 [x]Jer 2:27; Eze 8:16 [y]Jer 7:13
32:34 [z]Jer 7:30
32:35 [a]Lev 18:21 [b]Jer 7:31; 19:5
32:36 [c]ver 24
32:37 [d]Jer 23:3,6 [e]Dt 30:3; Eze 34:28
32:38 [f]Jer 24:7; 2Co 6:16*
32:39 [g]Eze 11:19
32:40 [h]Isa 55:3 [i]Jer 24:7
32:41 [j]Dt 30:9 [k]Jer 24:6; 31:28; Am 9:15
32:42 [l]Jer 31:28
32:43 [m]ver 15
32:44 [n]ver 10 [o]Jer 17:26 [p]Jer 33:7,11, 26
33:1 [q]Jer 32:2-3; 37:21; 38:28
33:2 [r]Jer 10:16 [s]Ex 3:15; 15:3
33:3 [t]Isa 55:6; Jer 29:12

[a] 35 Or *to make their sons and daughters pass through* ⌞*the fire*⌟ [b] 44 Or *will bring them back from captivity*

al palaces of Judah that have been torn down to
be used against the siege[u] ramps[v] and the sword
5 in the fight with the Babylonians[a]: 'They will be
filled with the dead bodies of the men I will slay
in my anger and wrath.[w] I will hide my face[x] from
this city because of all its wickedness.
6 " 'Nevertheless, I will bring health and healing
to it; I will heal my people and will let them enjoy
abundant peace and security. 7 I will bring Judah[y]
and Israel back from captivity[b][z] and will rebuild
them as they were before.[a] 8 I will cleanse[b] them
from all the sin they have committed against me
and will forgive[c] all their sins of rebellion against
me. 9 Then this city will bring me renown, joy,
praise[d] and honor[e] before all nations on earth that
hear of all the good things I do for it; and they will
be in awe and will tremble at the abundant prosperity and peace I provide for it.'
10 "This is what the LORD says: 'You say about
this place, "It is a desolate waste, without men or
animals."[f] Yet in the towns of Judah and the
streets of Jerusalem that are deserted, inhabited
by neither men nor animals, there will be heard
once more 11 the sounds of joy and gladness,[g] the
voices of bride and bridegroom, and the voices of
those who bring thank offerings[h] to the house of
the LORD, saying,

"Give thanks to the LORD Almighty,
for the LORD is good;[i]
his love endures forever."[j]

For I will restore the fortunes of the land as they
were before,' says the LORD.
12 "This is what the LORD Almighty says: 'In this
place, desolate[k] and without men or animals—in
all its towns there will again be pastures for shepherds to rest their flocks.[l] 13 In the towns of the hill
country, of the western foothills and of the Negev,[m] in the territory of Benjamin, in the villages
around Jerusalem and in the towns of Judah,
flocks will again pass under the hand[n] of the one
who counts them,' says the LORD.
14 " 'The days are coming,' declares the LORD,
'when I will fulfill the gracious promise[o] I made to
the house of Israel and to the house of Judah.

15 " 'In those days and at that time
I will make a righteous[p] Branch[q]
sprout from David's line;
he will do what is just and right in
the land.
16 In those days Judah will be saved[r]
and Jerusalem will live in safety.
This is the name by which it[c] will be
called:
The LORD Our Righteousness.'[s]

17 For this is what the LORD says: 'David will never
fail[t] to have a man to sit on the throne of the

33:4 [u]Eze 4:2 [v]Jer 32:24; Hab 1:10
33:5 [w]Jer 21:4-7 [x]Isa 8:17
33:7 [y]Jer 32:44 [z]Jer 30:3; Am 9:14 [a]Isa 1:26
33:8 [b]Heb 9:13-14 [c]Jer 31:34; Mic 7:18; Zec 13:1
33:9 [d]Jer 13:11 [e]Isa 62:7; Jer 3:17
33:10 [f]Jer 32:43
33:11 [g]Isa 51:3 [h]Lev 7:12 [i]1Ch 16:8; Ps 136:1 [j]1Ch 16:34; 2Ch 5:13; Ps 100:4-5
33:12 [k]Jer 32:43 [l]Isa 65:10; Eze 34:11-15
33:13 [m]Jer 17:26 [n]Lev 27:32
33:14 [o]Jer 29:10
33:15 [p]Ps 72:2 [q]Isa 4:2; 11:1; Jer 23:5
33:16 [r]Isa 45:17 [s]1Co 1:30
33:17 [t]2Sa 7:13; 1Ki 2:4; Ps 89:29-37; Lk 1:33

[a]5 Or *Chaldeans* [b]7 Or *will restore the fortunes of Judah and Israel* [c]16 Or *he*

Righteous Ruler

JER 33:15-16

From the time of King David to the exile, many kings rule over Judah. Most do not match David's devotion to God. *Jeremiah now prophesies that a Branch will grow from David's line to rule with righteousness.* King David himself and the prophet *Isaiah speak of this future ruler* (Ps 9:7-8; Isa 9:6-7). In Jeremiah 23:5-6, Jeremiah calls this righteous ruler "The LORD Our Righteousness," but in this verse *Jerusalem bears this title.* Under this righteous ruler, the Holy City *will finally attain righteousness.*

"The days are coming" (Jer 33:14), declares Jeremiah, when the King of kings will reign over heaven and earth.* Matthew's *Gospel opens with the lineage of this mighty son of King David. We can look forward to his glorious kingdom, a kingdom that will have no end.

Burial Rites

JER 34:1–5

The following chapters of Jeremiah deal with the siege and subsequent destruction of Jerusalem and other fortified cities in Judah. They are not in strict chronological order, but they give a clear picture of the conditions and events of that time.

Through Jeremiah, God gives a conditional promise to King Zedekiah. If he surrenders to Nebuchadnezzar, God will let him die peacefully (Jer 38:17). Zedekiah will receive the full royal honors of a funeral fire, in which aromatic spices burn during the burial ceremony. The Israelites don't practice cremation, so the fire refers to this incense-burning custom. However, if Zedekiah does not surrender to Nebuchadnezzar, his end will not be so peaceful.

Zedekiah doesn't surrender to the Babylonians. Therefore, rather than dying peacefully, his eyes are gouged out and he is taken to prison in Babylon (2Ki 25:5–7; Jer 39:7; Eze 12:13), where he dies.

house of Israel, 18nor will the priests, who are 33:18
Levites,[u] ever fail to have a man to stand before [u]Dt 18:1
me continually to offer burnt offerings, to burn [v]Heb 13:15
grain offerings and to present sacrifices.[v]' "
19The word of the LORD came to Jeremiah: 20"This
is what the LORD says: 'If you can break my covenant with the day[w] and my covenant with the 33:20
night, so that day and night no longer come at their [w]Ps 89:36
appointed time, 21then my covenant[x] with David 33:21
my servant—and my covenant with the Levites [x]Ps 89:34
who are priests ministering before me—can be bro- [y]2Ch 7:18
ken and David will no longer have a descendant to
reign on his throne.[y] 22I will make the descendants
of David my servant and the Levites who minister
before me as countless[z] as the stars of the sky and 33:22
as measureless as the sand on the seashore.' " [z]Ge 15:5
23The word of the LORD came to Jeremiah:
24"Have you not noticed that these people are say- 33:24
ing, 'The LORD has rejected the two kingdoms[aa] he [a]Eze 37:22
chose'? So they despise[b] my people and no longer [b]Ne 4:4
regard them as a nation.[c] 25This is what the LORD [c]Jer 30:17
says: 'If I have not established my covenant with 33:25
day and night[d] and the fixed laws of heaven and [d]Jer 31:35-36
earth,[e] 26then I will reject[f] the descendants of [e]Ps 74:16-17
Jacob[g] and David my servant and will not choose 33:26
one of his sons to rule over the descendants of [f]Jer 31:37
Abraham, Isaac and Jacob. For I will restore their [g]Isa 14:1
fortunes[bh] and have compassion on them.' " [h]ver 7

Warning to Zedekiah

34 While Nebuchadnezzar king of Babylon
and all his army and all the kingdoms and 34:1
peoples[i] in the empire he ruled were fighting [i]Jer 27:7
against Jerusalem[j] and all its surrounding towns, [j]2Ki 25:1;
this word came to Jeremiah from the LORD: 2"This Jer 39:1
is what the LORD, the God of Israel, says: Go to
Zedekiah[k] king of Judah and tell him, 'This is 34:2
what the LORD says: I am about to hand this city [k]2Ch 36:11
over to the king of Babylon, and he will burn it [l]ver 22;
down.[l] 3You will not escape from his grasp but Jer 32:29; 37:8
will surely be captured and handed over[m] to him. 34:3
You will see the king of Babylon with your own [m]2Ki 25:7;
eyes, and he will speak with you face to face. And Jer 21:7;
you will go to Babylon. 32:4
4" 'Yet hear the promise of the LORD, O Zedekiah king of Judah. This is what the LORD says concerning you: You will not die by the sword; 5you 34:5
will die peacefully. As people made a funeral fire[n] [n]2Ch 16:14;
in honor of your fathers, the former kings who 21:19
preceded you, so they will make a fire in your [o]Jer 22:18
honor and lament, "Alas,[o] O master!" I myself
make this promise, declares the LORD.' "
6Then Jeremiah the prophet told all this to Zedekiah king of Judah, in Jerusalem, 7while the
army of the king of Babylon was fighting against
Jerusalem and the other cities of Judah that were 34:7
still holding out—Lachish[p] and Azekah.[q] These [p]Jos 10:3
were the only fortified cities left in Judah. [q]Jos 10:10; 2Ch 11:9

[a] 24 Or *families* [b] 26 Or *will bring them back from captivity*

Freedom for Slaves

8The word came to Jeremiah from the LORD
after King Zedekiah had made a covenant with all
the people[r] in Jerusalem to proclaim freedom[s] for
the slaves. 9Everyone was to free his Hebrew
slaves, both male and female; no one was to hold
a fellow Jew in bondage.[t] 10So all the officials and
people who entered into this covenant agreed that
they would free their male and female slaves and
no longer hold them in bondage. They agreed,
and set them free. 11But afterward they changed
their minds and took back the slaves they had
freed and enslaved them again.

12Then the word of the LORD came to Jeremiah:
13"This is what the LORD, the God of Israel, says: I
made a covenant with your forefathers[u] when I
brought them out of Egypt, out of the land of slavery. I said, 14'Every seventh year each of you must
free any fellow Hebrew who has sold himself to
you. After he has served you six years, you must
let him go free.'[a][v] Your fathers, however, did not
listen to me or pay attention[w] to me. 15Recently
you repented and did what is right in my sight:
Each of you proclaimed freedom to his countrymen.[x] You even made a covenant before me in the
house that bears my Name.[y] 16But now you have
turned around[z] and profaned[a] my name; each of
you has taken back the male and female slaves
you had set free to go where they wished. You
have forced them to become your slaves again.

17"Therefore, this is what the LORD says: You
have not obeyed me; you have not proclaimed
freedom for your fellow countrymen. So I now
proclaim 'freedom' for you,[b] declares the LORD—
'freedom' to fall by the sword, plague and famine.
I will make you abhorrent to all the kingdoms of
the earth.[c] 18The men who have violated my covenant and have not fulfilled the terms of the covenant they made before me, I will treat like the
calf they cut in two and then walked between its
pieces.[d] 19The leaders of Judah and Jerusalem, the
court officials,[e] the priests and all the people of
the land who walked between the pieces of the
calf, 20I will hand over[f] to their enemies who seek
their lives.[g] Their dead bodies will become food
for the birds of the air and the beasts of the earth.[h]

21"I will hand Zedekiah[i] king of Judah and his
officials[j] over to their enemies who seek their
lives, to the army of the king of Babylon, which
has withdrawn[k] from you. 22I am going to give the
order, declares the LORD, and I will bring them
back to this city. They will fight against it, take[l] it
and burn[m] it down. And I will lay waste the towns
of Judah so no one can live there."

The Recabites

35 This is the word that came to Jeremiah from
the LORD during the reign of Jehoiakim[n] son

34:8 [r]2Ki 11:17 [s]Ex 21:2; Lev 25:10, 39-41; Ne 5:5-8
34:9 [t]Lev 25:39-46
34:13 [u]Ex 24:8
34:14 [v]Ex 21:2 [w]Dt 15:12; 2Ki 17:14
34:15 [x]ver 8 [y]Jer 7:10-11; 32:34
34:16 [z]Eze 3:20; 18:24 [a]Ex 20:7; Lev 19:12
34:17 [b]Mt 7:2; Gal 6:7 [c]Dt 28:25, 64; Jer 29:18
34:18 [d]Ge 15:10
34:19 [e]Zep 3:3-4
34:20 [f]Jer 21:7 [g]Jer 11:21 [h]Dt 28:26; Jer 7:33; 19:7
34:21 [i]Jer 32:4 [j]Jer 39:6; 52:24-27 [k]Jer 37:5
34:22 [l]Jer 39:1-2 [m]Jer 39:8
35:1 [n]2Ch 36:5

[a] *14* Deut. 15:12

Empty Promises

JER 34:12-16

Jewish law limited the bondage of a Hebrew slave to six years. If a slave wanted to serve his master longer, he could sign up for a lifetime of service (Ex 21:5-6), but the choice was his, not the master's. Hebrew slaves were considered a part of their master's family and were usually treated fairly.

Over time the Israelites, especially the affluent, have ignored God's six-year limit on slavery. Attempting to appease God when the Babylonians threaten, King Zedekiah orders the release of these slaves (Jer 34:8). But when Babylon turns away from Jerusalem to fight off Egyptian forces, the Hebrew slave owners force their former slaves back into bondage. They break their pledge to God and earn his displeasure. Their empty promises do not satisfy God. In a cutting turn of phrase, God promises them the freedom they had taken from their slaves: freedom to die (Jer 34:17-20).

God's Object Lesson

JER 35:6–11

The Recabites are puritan followers of Jonadab son of Recab. Jonadab helped purge the northern kingdom of Baal worship, and his ancestors model his devotion to righteousness (2Ki 10:15–28). The Recabites live as desert nomads and, like the Nazirites (Nu 6:1–3), vow to abstain from wine, probably because it is abused in Baal worship.

The Recabites move to Jerusalem when Nebuchadnezzar's armies pillage the countryside. God uses their refusal of Jeremiah's wine as an object lesson for Judah. For years the Recabites had carefully regarded the rules of their ancestor, while the people of Judah had recklessly disregarded God's commands.

of Josiah king of Judah: 2"Go to the Recabite[o] family and invite them to come to one of the side rooms[p] of the house of the LORD and give them wine to drink."

3So I went to get Jaazaniah son of Jeremiah, the son of Habazziniah, and his brothers and all his sons—the whole family of the Recabites. 4I brought them into the house of the LORD, into the room of the sons of Hanan son of Igdaliah the man of God.[q] It was next to the room of the officials, which was over that of Maaseiah son of Shallum[r] the doorkeeper.[s] 5Then I set bowls full of wine and some cups before the men of the Recabite family and said to them, "Drink some wine."

6But they replied, "We do not drink wine, because our forefather Jonadab[t] son of Recab gave us this command: 'Neither you nor your descendants must ever drink wine.[u] 7Also you must never build houses, sow seed or plant vineyards; you must never have any of these things, but must always live in tents.[v] Then you will live a long time in the land[w] where you are nomads.' 8We have obeyed everything our forefather[x] Jonadab son of Recab commanded us. Neither we nor our wives nor our sons and daughters have ever drunk wine 9or built houses to live in or had vineyards, fields or crops.[y] 10We have lived in tents and have fully obeyed everything our forefather Jonadab commanded us. 11But when Nebuchadnezzar king of Babylon invaded[z] this land, we said, 'Come, we must go to Jerusalem[a] to escape the Babylonian[a] and Aramean armies.' So we have remained in Jerusalem."

12Then the word of the LORD came to Jeremiah, saying: 13"This is what the LORD Almighty, the God of Israel, says: Go and tell the men of Judah and the people of Jerusalem, 'Will you not learn a lesson[b] and obey my words?' declares the LORD. 14'Jonadab son of Recab ordered his sons not to drink wine and this command has been kept. To this day they do not drink wine, because they obey their forefather's command. But I have spoken to you again and again,[c] yet you have not obeyed[d] me. 15Again and again I sent all my servants the prophets[e] to you. They said, "Each of you must turn[f] from your wicked ways and reform[g] your actions; do not follow other gods to serve them. Then you will live in the land[h] I have given to you and your fathers." But you have not paid attention or listened[i] to me. 16The descendants of Jonadab son of Recab have carried out the command their forefather[j] gave them, but these people have not obeyed me.'

17"Therefore, this is what the LORD God Almighty, the God of Israel, says: 'Listen! I am going to bring on Judah and on everyone living in Jerusalem every disaster[k] I pronounced against them. I spoke to them, but they did not listen;[l] I called to them, but they did not answer.'"[m]

35:2 [o]2Ki 10:15; 1Ch 2:55 [p]1Ki 6:5
35:4 [q]Dt 33:1 [r]1Ch 9:19 [s]2Ki 12:9
35:6 [t]2Ki 10:15 [u]Lev 10:9; Nu 6:2-4; Lk 1:15
35:7 [v]Heb 11:9 [w]Ex 20:12; Eph 6:2-3
35:8 [x]Pr 1:8; Col 3:20
35:9 [y]1Ti 6:6
35:11 [z]2Ki 24:1 [a]Jer 8:14
35:13 [b]Jer 6:10; 32:33
35:14 [c]Jer 7:13; 25:3 [d]Isa 30:9
35:15 [e]Jer 7:25 [f]Jer 26:3 [g]Isa 1:16-17; Jer 4:1; 18:11; Eze 18:30 [h]Jer 25:5 [i]Jer 7:26
35:16 [j]Mal 1:6
35:17 [k]Jos 23:15; Jer 21:4-7 [l]Pr 1:24; Ro 10:21 [m]Isa 65:12; 66:4; Jer 7:13

[a] *11* Or *Chaldean*

18Then Jeremiah said to the family of the Recabites, "This is what the LORD Almighty, the God of
Israel, says: 'You have obeyed the command of
your forefather Jonadab and have followed all his
instructions and have done everything he ordered.'
19Therefore, this is what the LORD Almighty, the
35:19 God of Israel, says: 'Jonadab son of Recab will nev-
[n]Jer 33:17 [o]Jer 15:19 er fail[n] to have a man to serve[o] me.' "

Jehoiakim Burns Jeremiah's Scroll

36:1 **36** In the fourth year of Jehoiakim[p] son of Josi-
[p]2Ch 36:5 ah king of Judah, this word came to Jere-
36:2 miah from the LORD: 2"Take a scroll[q] and write on
[q]Ex 17:14; it all the words I have spoken to you concerning
Jer 30:2; Hab 2:2 Israel, Judah and all the other nations from the
[r]Jer 1:2; 25:3 time I began speaking to you in the reign of Josi-
36:3 ah[r] till now. 3Perhaps[s] when the people of Judah
[s]ver 7; hear[t] about every disaster I plan to inflict on them,
Eze 12:3 [t]Mk 4:12 each of them will turn[u] from his wicked way; then
[u]Jer 26:3; I will forgive[v] their wickedness and their sin."
Jnh 3:8; 4So Jeremiah called Baruch[w] son of Neriah, and
Ac 3:19 [v]Jer 18:8 while Jeremiah dictated[x] all the words the LORD
had spoken to him, Baruch wrote them on the
36:4 [w]Jer 32:12 scroll.[y] 5Then Jeremiah told Baruch, "I am restrict-
[x]ver 18 ed; I cannot go to the LORD's temple. 6So you go to
[y]Eze 2:9 the house of the LORD on a day of fasting[z] and read
36:6 to the people from the scroll the words of the LORD
[z]ver 9 that you wrote as I dictated. Read them to all the
people of Judah who come in from their towns.
36:7 7Perhaps they will bring their petition before the
[a]Jer 26:3 LORD, and each will turn[a] from his wicked ways,
[b]Dt 31:17 for the anger[b] and wrath pronounced against this
people by the LORD are great."
8Baruch son of Neriah did everything Jeremiah
the prophet told him to do; at the LORD's temple he
read the words of the LORD from the scroll. 9In the
36:9 [c]ver 22 ninth month[c] of the fifth year of Jehoiakim son of
[d]2Ch 20:3 Josiah king of Judah, a time of fasting[d] before the
LORD was proclaimed for all the people in Jerusa-
lem and those who had come from the towns of
Judah. 10From the room of Gemariah son of Sha-
36:10 [e]Jer 52:25 phan the secretary,[e] which was in the upper court-
[f]Jer 26:10 yard at the entrance of the New Gate[f] of the temple, Baruch read to all the people at the LORD's
temple the words of Jeremiah from the scroll.
11When Micaiah son of Gemariah, the son of
Shaphan, heard all the words of the LORD from the
scroll, 12he went down to the secretary's room in
the royal palace, where all the officials were sit-
36:12 ting: Elishama the secretary, Delaiah son of She-
[g]Jer 26:22 maiah, Elnathan[g] son of Acbor, Gemariah son of
Shaphan, Zedekiah son of Hananiah, and all the
other officials. 13After Micaiah told them everything he had heard Baruch read to the people from
36:14 [h]ver 21 the scroll, 14all the officials sent Jehudi[h] son of
Nethaniah, the son of Shelemiah, the son of
Cushi, to say to Baruch, "Bring the scroll from
which you have read to the people and come." So
Baruch son of Neriah went to them with the scroll
in his hand. 15They said to him, "Sit down, please,
and read it to us."

Up in Smoke

JER 36:1-26

Jeremiah dictates his prophecies to Baruch, his secretary and confidant. Since most people in ancient times couldn't read or write, scribes like Baruch were valuable. This chapter gives the only Old Testament description of recording a prophetic book.

King Josiah "tore his robes" when God's Law was read to him (2Ki 22:11). Now, however, his son Jehoiakim scorns and scorches God's words. The vindictive king burns Jeremiah's scroll bit by bit. His calculated and painstaking destruction of God's written message serves as a dramatic warning to Jeremiah.

Imagine how Jeremiah and Baruch felt when the king turned the Lord's words into ashes. Yet note also Jeremiah's unflappable reaction. He starts over with no saved notes, remaining composed and determined when his work goes up in smoke.

Leisure Moments

JER 36:22

The king's winter apartment is a warm palace room that faces the winter sun. Since December in Israel can be cold and rainy, even with some light snowfall, Jehoiakim snuggles up to his charcoal-burning firepot, a portable brazier or metal pot that can be carried wherever he goes. He sits by his fire while one of his men reads Jeremiah's scroll to him. With contempt for the truth of God's Word, he burns the entire scroll in his firepot, then heaps one offense on another and orders the arrest of Jeremiah and Baruch.

So Baruch read it to them. 16When they heard all these words, they looked at each other in fear and said to Baruch, "We must report all these words to the king." 17Then they asked Baruch, "Tell us, how did you come to write all this? Did Jeremiah dictate it?"

18"Yes," Baruch replied, "he dictated[i] all these words to me, and I wrote them in ink on the scroll."

19Then the officials said to Baruch, "You and Jeremiah, go and hide.[j] Don't let anyone know where you are."

20After they put the scroll in the room of Elishama the secretary, they went to the king in the courtyard and reported everything to him. 21The king sent Jehudi[k] to get the scroll, and Jehudi brought it from the room of Elishama the secretary and read it to the king[l] and all the officials standing beside him. 22It was the ninth month and the king was sitting in the winter apartment,[m] with a fire burning in the firepot in front of him. 23Whenever Jehudi had read three or four columns of the scroll, the king cut them off with a scribe's knife and threw them into the firepot, until the entire scroll was burned in the fire.[n] 24The king and all his attendants who heard all these words showed no fear,[o] nor did they tear their clothes.[p] 25Even though Elnathan, Delaiah and Gemariah urged the king not to burn the scroll, he would not listen to them. 26Instead, the king commanded Jerahmeel, a son of the king, Seraiah son of Azriel and Shelemiah son of Abdeel to arrest[q] Baruch the scribe and Jeremiah the prophet. But the LORD had hidden[r] them.

27After the king burned the scroll containing the words that Baruch had written at Jeremiah's dictation,[s] the word of the LORD came to Jeremiah: 28"Take another scroll and write on it all the words that were on the first scroll, which Jehoiakim king of Judah burned up. 29Also tell Jehoiakim king of Judah, 'This is what the LORD says: You burned that scroll and said, "Why did you write on it that the king of Babylon would certainly come and destroy this land and cut off both men and animals from it?"[t] 30Therefore, this is what the LORD says about Jehoiakim king of Judah: He will have no one to sit on the throne of David; his body will be thrown out[u] and exposed to the heat by day and the frost by night. 31I will punish him and his children and his attendants for their wickedness; I will bring on them and those living in Jerusalem and the people of Judah every disaster[v] I pronounced against them, because they have not listened.' "

32So Jeremiah took another scroll and gave it to the scribe Baruch son of Neriah, and as Jeremiah dictated,[w] Baruch wrote[x] on it all the words of the scroll that Jehoiakim king of Judah had burned[y] in the fire. And many similar words were added to them.

36:18 [i]ver 4
36:19 [j]1Ki 17:3
36:21 [k]ver 14 [l]2Ki 22:10
36:22 [m]Am 3:15
36:23 [n]1Ki 22:8
36:24 [o]Ps 36:1 [p]Ge 37:29; 2Ki 22:11; Isa 37:1
36:26 [q]Mt 23:34 [r]Jer 15:21
36:27 [s]ver 4
36:29 [t]Isa 30:10
36:30 [u]Jer 22:19
36:31 [v]Pr 29:1
36:32 [w]ver 4 [x]Ex 34:1 [y]ver 23

Jeremiah in Prison

37 Zedekiah[z] son of Josiah was made king[a] of Judah by Nebuchadnezzar king of Babylon; he reigned in place of Jehoiachin[a][b] son of Jehoiakim. [2]Neither he nor his attendants nor the people of the land paid any attention[c] to the words the LORD had spoken through Jeremiah the prophet.

[3]King Zedekiah, however, sent Jehucal son of Shelemiah with the priest Zephaniah[d] son of Maaseiah to Jeremiah the prophet with this message: "Please pray[e] to the LORD our God for us."

[4]Now Jeremiah was free to come and go among the people, for he had not yet been put in prison.[f] [5]Pharaoh's army had marched out of Egypt,[g] and when the Babylonians[b] who were besieging Jerusalem heard the report about them, they withdrew[h] from Jerusalem.[i]

[6]Then the word of the LORD came to Jeremiah the prophet: [7]"This is what the LORD, the God of Israel, says: Tell the king of Judah, who sent you to inquire[j] of me, 'Pharaoh's army, which has marched out to support you, will go back to its own land, to Egypt.[k] [8]Then the Babylonians will return and attack this city; they will capture it and burn[l] it down.'

[9]"This is what the LORD says: Do not deceive[m] yourselves, thinking, 'The Babylonians will surely leave us.' They will not! [10]Even if you were to defeat the entire Babylonian[c] army that is attacking you and only wounded men were left in their tents, they would come out and burn this city down."

[11]After the Babylonian army had withdrawn[n] from Jerusalem because of Pharaoh's army, [12]Jeremiah started to leave the city to go to the territory of Benjamin to get his share of the property[o] among the people there. [13]But when he reached the Benjamin Gate, the captain of the guard, whose name was Irijah son of Shelemiah, the son of Hananiah, arrested him and said, "You are deserting to the Babylonians!"

[14]"That's not true!" Jeremiah said. "I am not deserting to the Babylonians." But Irijah would not listen to him; instead, he arrested[p] Jeremiah and brought him to the officials. [15]They were angry with Jeremiah and had him beaten[q] and imprisoned in the house[r] of Jonathan the secretary, which they had made into a prison.

[16]Jeremiah was put into a vaulted cell in a dungeon, where he remained a long time. [17]Then King Zedekiah sent for him and had him brought to the palace, where he asked[s] him privately,[t] "Is there any word from the LORD?"

"Yes," Jeremiah replied, "you will be handed over[u] to the king of Babylon."

[18]Then Jeremiah said to King Zedekiah, "What crime[v] have I committed against you or your offi-

Panic Prayers

JER 37:3

King Zedekiah is a weak-willed ruler, swayed by the wicked officials who surround him. He is like his brother Jehoiakim in one respect: He refuses to pay "any attention to the words the LORD [has] spoken through Jeremiah the prophet" (Jer 37:2).

However, Zedekiah changes his thinking a bit when the heat is on from Babylon. Instead of ignoring God, he asks Jeremiah to pray for him. Many people offer "panic prayers" in times of crisis, and King Zedekiah is no exception. Through Jeremiah's prayers, Zedekiah and his officials seek God's blessings but not God himself. Like Judah, these leaders want a superficial religion without personal cost.

37:1 [z]2Ki 24:17 [a]Eze 17:13 [b]2Ki 24:8, 12; 2Ch 36:10; Jer 22:24
37:2 [c]2Ki 24:19; 2Ch 36:12, 14
37:3 [d]Jer 29:25; 52:24 [e]1Ki 13:6; Jer 21:1-2; 42:2
37:4 [f]ver 15; Jer 32:2
37:5 [g]Eze 17:15 [h]Jer 34:21 [i]2Ki 24:7
37:7 [j]2Ki 22:18 [k]Jer 2:36; La 4:17
37:8 [l]Jer 34:22; 39:8
37:9 [m]Jer 29:8
37:11 [n]ver 5
37:12 [o]Jer 32:9
37:14 [p]Jer 40:4
37:15 [q]Jer 20:2 [r]Jer 38:26
37:17 [s]Jer 15:11 [t]Jer 38:16 [u]Jer 21:7
37:18 [v]1Sa 26:18; Jn 10:32; Ac 25:8

[a] *1* Hebrew *Coniah,* a variant of *Jehoiachin* [b] *5* Or *Chaldeans*; also in verses 8, 9, 13 and 14 [c] *10* Or *Chaldean*; also in verse 11

Extending Mercy

JER 37:21

King Zedekiah releases Jeremiah from his "vaulted" (Jer 37:16) dungeon cell and secretly asks him, "Is there any word from the LORD?" (Jer 37:17). Jeremiah answers the king concisely and directly, then goes on to plead for freedom from his squalid prison cell. Zedekiah extends mercy. He transfers Jeremiah to the courtyard of the guard next to the palace. The king orders that Jeremiah be fed from the city's rapidly decreasing food supply.

This is the only place in Scripture where a specific Jerusalem street is named. The "street of the bakers" (Jer 27:21), or Baker's Street, is an example of the Near Eastern practice of naming a street after the businesses or professions that line it.

cials or this people, that you have put me in
prison? 19 Where are your prophets who prophesied to you, 'The king of Babylon will not attack
you or this land'? 20 But now, my lord the king,
please listen. Let me bring my petition before you:
Do not send me back to the house of Jonathan the
secretary, or I will die there."

21 King Zedekiah then gave orders for Jeremiah
to be placed in the courtyard of the guard and giv-
en bread from the street of the bakers each day
until all the bread[w] in the city was gone.[x] So Jeremiah remained in the courtyard of the guard.[y]

Jeremiah Thrown Into a Cistern

38 Shephatiah son of Mattan, Gedaliah son of
Pashhur, Jehucal[a][z] son of Shelemiah, and
Pashhur son of Malkijah heard what Jeremiah
was telling all the people when he said, 2 "This is
what the LORD says: 'Whoever stays in this city
will die by the sword, famine or plague,[a] but
whoever goes over to the Babylonians[b] will live.
He will escape with his life; he will live.'[b] 3 And
this is what the LORD says: 'This city will certainly be handed over to the army of the king of Babylon, who will capture it.' "[c]

4 Then the officials[d] said to the king, "This man
should be put to death.[e] He is discouraging the
soldiers who are left in this city, as well as all the
people, by the things he is saying to them. This
man is not seeking the good of these people but
their ruin."

5 "He is in your hands," King Zedekiah
answered. "The king can do nothing to oppose
you."

6 So they took Jeremiah and put him into the cistern of Malkijah, the king's son, which was in the
courtyard of the guard.[f] They lowered Jeremiah
by ropes into the cistern; it had no water in it,
only mud, and Jeremiah sank down into the mud.

7 But Ebed-Melech,[g] a Cushite,[c] an official[d][h] in
the royal palace, heard that they had put Jeremiah
into the cistern. While the king was sitting in the
Benjamin Gate,[i] 8 Ebed-Melech went out of the
palace and said to him, 9 "My lord the king, these
men have acted wickedly in all they have done to
Jeremiah the prophet. They have thrown him into
a cistern, where he will starve to death when
there is no longer any bread[j] in the city."

10 Then the king commanded Ebed-Melech the
Cushite, "Take thirty men from here with you and
lift Jeremiah the prophet out of the cistern before
he dies."

11 So Ebed-Melech took the men with him and
went to a room under the treasury in the palace.
He took some old rags and worn-out clothes from
there and let them down with ropes to Jeremiah
in the cistern. 12 Ebed-Melech the Cushite said to

37:21 [w]Isa 33:16; Jer 38:9 [x]2Ki 25:3; Jer 52:6 [y]Jer 32:2; 38:6,13,28
38:1 [z]Jer 37:3
38:2 [a]Jer 34:17 [b]Jer 21:9; 39:18; 45:5
38:3 [c]Jer 21:4,10; 32:3
38:4 [d]Jer 36:12 [e]Jer 26:11
38:6 [f]Jer 37:21
38:7 [g]Jer 39:16 [h]Ac 8:27 [i]Job 29:7
38:9 [j]Jer 37:21

[a] *1* Hebrew *Jucal,* a variant of *Jehucal* [b] *2* Or *Chaldeans;* also in verses 18, 19 and 23 [c] *7* Probably from the upper Nile region [d] *7* Or *a eunuch*

Jeremiah, "Put these old rags and worn-out
clothes under your arms to pad the ropes." Jeremiah did so, 13and they pulled him up with the
ropes and lifted him out of the cistern. And Jeremiah remained in the courtyard of the guard.[k]

Zedekiah Questions Jeremiah Again

14Then King Zedekiah sent for Jeremiah the
prophet and had him brought to the third
entrance to the temple of the LORD. "I am going to
ask you something," the king said to Jeremiah.
"Do not hide[l] anything from me."
15Jeremiah said to Zedekiah, "If I give you an
answer, will you not kill me? Even if I did give
you counsel, you would not listen to me."
16But King Zedekiah swore this oath secretly[m]
to Jeremiah: "As surely as the LORD lives, who has
given us breath,[n] I will neither kill you nor hand
you over to those who are seeking your life."[o]
17Then Jeremiah said to Zedekiah, "This is what
the LORD God Almighty, the God of Israel, says: 'If
you surrender to the officers of the king of Babylon, your life will be spared and this city will not
be burned down; you and your family will live.[p]
18But if you will not surrender to the officers of
the king of Babylon, this city will be handed over[q]
to the Babylonians and they will burn[r] it down;
you yourself will not escape[s] from their hands.' "
19King Zedekiah said to Jeremiah, "I am afraid[t]
of the Jews who have gone over[u] to the Babylonians, for the Babylonians may hand me over to
them and they will mistreat me."
20"They will not hand you over," Jeremiah
replied. "Obey[v] the LORD by doing what I tell you.
Then it will go well with you, and your life[w] will
be spared. 21But if you refuse to surrender, this is
what the LORD has revealed to me: 22All the
women[x] left in the palace of the king of Judah
will be brought out to the officials of the king of
Babylon. Those women will say to you:

" 'They misled you and overcame you—
those trusted friends of yours.
Your feet are sunk in the mud;
your friends have deserted you.'

23"All your wives and children[y] will be brought
out to the Babylonians. You yourself will not escape
from their hands but will be captured[z] by the king
of Babylon; and this city will[a] be burned down."
24Then Zedekiah said to Jeremiah, "Do not let
anyone know about this conversation, or you may
die. 25If the officials hear that I talked with you,
and they come to you and say, 'Tell us what you
said to the king and what the king said to you; do
not hide it from us or we will kill you,' 26then tell
them, 'I was pleading with the king not to send
me back to Jonathan's house[a] to die there.' "
27All the officials did come to Jeremiah and
question him, and he told them everything the

38:13 [k]Jer 37:21
38:14 [l]1Sa 3:17
38:16 [m]Jer 37:17 [n]Isa 42:5; 57:16 [o]ver 4
38:17 [p]2Ki 24:12; Jer 21:9
38:18 [q]ver 3; Jer 34:3 [r]Jer 37:8 [s]Jer 24:8; 32:4
38:19 [t]Isa 51:12; Jn 12:42 [u]Jer 39:9
38:20 [v]Jer 11:4 [w]Isa 55:3
38:22 [x]Jer 6:12
38:23 [y]2Ki 25:6 [z]Jer 41:10
38:26 [a]Jer 37:15

[a] 23 Or *and you will cause this city to*

Intimate Details

JER 38:7-13

Ebed-Melech, a native of Cush, thought perhaps to be the Upper Nile area south of Egypt, fears God more than human power (Jer 39:18). He is the only palace official to back away from the murder plot against Jeremiah. Many people detest the prophet, and only this foreigner comes to his rescue.

In Jeremiah 38:12 we catch a glimpse of the tender details God includes in his Word. Ebed-Melech and his men could simply have yanked Jeremiah out of the cistern, but instead, they gave him old clothing to pad his underarms and prevent rope burns. Why does God mention the old rags and clothes? Perhaps to help us vividly picture this compassionate recovery effort. And perhaps to remind us that he cares about the intimate details of our everyday lives. Nothing in our lives escapes his notice.

The Conqueror's Policy

JER 39:8–10

In this final siege of Judah, Jerusalem is totally destroyed and all the remaining people fall captive except for a small remnant. Babylon's cunning foreign policy toward conquered lands calls for deporting the powerful and wealthy, leaving a few destitute citizens in charge of the land. This policy assures that the gratefully indebted poor—too fearful to revolt—remain loyal to their conquerors and that the devastated exiles remain too weak to rebel.

king had ordered him to say. So they said no more
to him, for no one had heard his conversation
with the king.
28And Jeremiah remained in the courtyard of
the guard[b] until the day Jerusalem was captured. **38:28** [b]Jer 37:21; 39:14

The Fall of Jerusalem

39 This is how Jerusalem was taken: 1In the
ninth year of Zedekiah king of Judah, in the
tenth month, Nebuchadnezzar king of Babylon
marched against Jerusalem with his whole army
and laid siege[c] to it. 2And on the ninth day of the **39:1** [c]2Ki 25:1; Jer 52:4; Eze 24:2
fourth month of Zedekiah's eleventh year, the city
wall was broken through. 3Then all the officials[d]
of the king of Babylon came and took seats in the **39:3** [d]Jer 21:4
Middle Gate: Nergal-Sharezer of Samgar, Nebo-
Sarsekim[a] a chief officer, Nergal-Sharezer a high
official and all the other officials of the king of
Babylon. 4When Zedekiah king of Judah and all
the soldiers saw them, they fled; they left the city
at night by way of the king's garden, through the
gate between the two walls, and headed toward
the Arabah.[b]
5But the Babylonian[c] army pursued them and **39:5** [e]Jer 32:4
overtook Zedekiah[e] in the plains of Jericho. They [f]2Ki 23:33
captured him and took him to Nebuchadnezzar
king of Babylon at Riblah[f] in the land of Hamath,
where he pronounced sentence on him. 6There at
Riblah the king of Babylon slaughtered the sons of
Zedekiah before his eyes and also killed all the
nobles of Judah. 7Then he put out Zedekiah's
eyes[g] and bound him with bronze shackles to take **39:7** [g]Eze 12:13
him to Babylon.[h] [h]Jer 32:5
8The Babylonians[d] set fire[i] to the royal palace **39:8**
and the houses of the people and broke down the [i]Jer 38:18
walls[j] of Jerusalem. 9Nebuzaradan commander of [j]Ne 1:3
the imperial guard carried into exile to Babylon
the people who remained in the city, along with
those who had gone over to him, and the rest of **39:9**
the people.[k] 10But Nebuzaradan the commander [k]Jer 40:1
of the guard left behind in the land of Judah some
of the poor people, who owned nothing; and at
that time he gave them vineyards and fields.
11Now Nebuchadnezzar king of Babylon had
given these orders about Jeremiah through Nebuzaradan commander of the imperial guard: **39:12**
12"Take him and look after him; don't harm[l] him [l]Pr 16:7;
but do for him whatever he asks." 13So Neb- 1Pe 3:13
uzaradan the commander of the guard, Nebus-
hazban a chief officer, Nergal-Sharezer a high official and all the other officers of the king of
Babylon 14sent and had Jeremiah taken out of the
courtyard of the guard.[m] They turned him over to **39:14**
Gedaliah son of Ahikam,[n] the son of Shaphan, to [m]Jer 38:28 [n]2Ki 22:12
take him back to his home. So he remained [o]Jer 40:5
among his own people.[o]
15While Jeremiah had been confined in the
courtyard of the guard, the word of the LORD came

[a] 3 Or *Nergal-Sharezer, Samgar-Nebo, Sarsekim* [b] 4 Or *the Jordan Valley* [c] 5 Or *Chaldean* [d] 8 Or *Chaldeans*

39:16 to him: 16“Go and tell Ebed-Melech[p] the Cushite,
[p]Jer 38:7 [q]Jer 21:10; ‘This is what the LORD Almighty, the God of Isra-
Da 9:12 el, says: I am about to fulfill my words against this
city through disaster,[q] not prosperity. At that time
they will be fulfilled before your eyes. 17But I will
39:17 rescue[r] you on that day, declares the LORD; you
[r]Ps 41:1-2 will not be handed over to those you fear. 18I will
39:18 save you; you will not fall by the sword[s] but will
[s]Jer 45:5 escape with your life,[t] because you trust[u] in me,
[t]Jer 21:9; 38:2 [u]Jer 17:7 declares the LORD.’ ”

Jeremiah Freed

40 The word came to Jeremiah from the LORD
after Nebuzaradan commander of the imperial guard had released him at Ramah. He had
found Jeremiah bound in chains among all the
captives from Jerusalem and Judah who were
being carried into exile to Babylon. 2When the
commander of the guard found Jeremiah, he said
to him, “The LORD your God decreed this disaster
40:2 for this place.[v] 3And now the LORD has brought it
[v]Jer 50:7 40:3 about; he has done just as he said he would. All
[w]Da 9:11 [x]Dt 29:24- this happened because you people sinned[w] against
28; Ro 2:5-9 the LORD and did not obey[x] him. 4But today I am
freeing you from the chains on your wrists. Come
with me to Babylon, if you like, and I will look
after you; but if you do not want to, then don’t
40:4 come. Look, the whole country lies before you; go
[y]Ge 13:9; Jer 39:11-12 wherever you please.”[y] 5However, before Jeremiah turned to go,[a] Nebuzaradan added, “Go back to
40:5 Gedaliah[z] son of Ahikam, the son of Shaphan,
[z]2Ki 25:22 [a]Jer 39:14 whom the king of Babylon has appointed over the
towns of Judah, and live with him among the peo-
ple, or go anywhere else you please.”[a]
Then the commander gave him provisions and
a present and let him go. 6So Jeremiah went to
40:6 [b]Jdg 20:1; Gedaliah son of Ahikam at Mizpah[b] and stayed
1Sa 7:5-17 with him among the people who were left behind
in the land.

Gedaliah Assassinated

7When all the army officers and their men who
were still in the open country heard that the king
of Babylon had appointed Gedaliah son of Ahikam as governor over the land and had put him in
40:7 charge of the men, women and children who
[c]Jer 39:10 were the poorest[c] in the land and who had not
40:8 been carried into exile to Babylon, 8they came to
[d]ver 13 Gedaliah at Mizpah[d]—Ishmael[e] son of Nethaniah,
[e]ver 14; Jer 41:1,2 Johanan and Jonathan the sons of Kareah, Seraiah
[f]2Sa 23:28 son of Tanhumeth, the sons of Ephai the Netoph-
[g]Dt 3:14 athite,[f] and Jaazaniah[b] the son of the Maacathite,[g]
and their men. 9Gedaliah son of Ahikam, the son
40:9 of Shaphan, took an oath to reassure them and
[h]Jer 27:11 their men. “Do not be afraid to serve[h] the Babylo-
[i]Jer 38:20 nians,[c]” he said. “Settle down in the land and
serve the king of Babylon, and it will go well with
40:10 [j]ver 6 you.[i] 10I myself will stay at Mizpah[j] to represent

[a] 5 Or *Jeremiah answered* [b] 8 Hebrew *Jezaniah,* a variant of *Jaazaniah* [c] 9 Or *Chaldeans*; also in verse 10

Holy moments come to us daily if we will ask for eyes to see. It may be the sun streaming through the window as you fold laundry. Or maybe it’s lifting your friends to God [in prayer] while you vacuum. We can’t always withdraw to quiet hillsides to pray, but Christ will meet with us in the quiet places of our hearts.

—Sheila Walsh

you before the Babylonians who come to us, but
you are to harvest the wine, summer fruit and oil,
and put them in your storage jars, and live in the
towns you have taken over."[k] 40:10
11When all the Jews in Moab,[l] Ammon, Edom [k]Dt 1:39
and all the other countries heard that the king of 40:11
Babylon had left a remnant in Judah and had [l]Nu 25:1
appointed Gedaliah son of Ahikam, the son of
Shaphan, as governor over them, 12they all came
back to the land of Judah, to Gedaliah at Mizpah,
from all the countries where they had been scattered.[m] And they harvested an abundance of wine 40:12
and summer fruit. [m]Jer 43:5

13Johanan son of Kareah and all the army officers still in the open country came to Gedaliah at
Mizpah[n] 14and said to him, "Don't you know that 40:13
Baalis king of the Ammonites[o] has sent Ishmael [n]ver 8
son of Nethaniah to take your life?" But Gedaliah 40:14
son of Ahikam did not believe them. [o]2Sa 10:1-19;
15Then Johanan son of Kareah said privately to Jer 25:21;
Gedaliah in Mizpah, "Let me go and kill Ishmael 41:10
son of Nethaniah, and no one will know it. Why
should he take your life and cause all the Jews
who are gathered around you to be scattered and
the remnant of Judah to perish?"

16But Gedaliah son of Ahikam said to Johanan
son of Kareah, "Don't do such a thing! What you
are saying about Ishmael is not true."

41 In the seventh month Ishmael[p] son of Neth- 41:1
aniah, the son of Elishama, who was of roy- [p]Jer 40:8
al blood and had been one of the king's officers,
came with ten men to Gedaliah son of Ahikam at
Mizpah. While they were eating together there, 41:2
2Ishmael[q] son of Nethaniah and the ten men who [q]Ps 41:9;
were with him got up and struck down Gedaliah 109:5
son of Ahikam, the son of Shaphan, with the [r]Jer 40:5
sword, killing the one whom the king of Babylon [s]2Sa 3:27;
had appointed[r] as governor over the land.[s] 3Ish- 20:9-10
mael also killed all the Jews who were with Gedaliah at Mizpah, as well as the Babylonian[a] soldiers who were there.

4The day after Gedaliah's assassination, before
anyone knew about it, 5eighty men who had
shaved off their beards,[t] torn their clothes and cut 41:5
themselves came from Shechem,[u] Shiloh[v] and [t]Lev 19:27
Samaria,[w] bringing grain offerings and incense [u]Ge 33:18; Jdg 9:1-57;
with them to the house of the LORD.[x] 6Ishmael son 1Ki 12:1
of Nethaniah went out from Mizpah to meet them, [v]Jos 18:1 [w]1Ki 16:24
weeping[y] as he went. When he met them, he said, [x]2Ki 25:9
"Come to Gedaliah son of Ahikam." 7When they 41:6
went into the city, Ishmael son of Nethaniah and [y]2Sa 3:16
the men who were with him slaughtered them
and threw them into a cistern. 8But ten of them
said to Ishmael, "Don't kill us! We have wheat 41:8
and barley, oil and honey, hidden in a field."[z] So [z]Isa 45:3
he let them alone and did not kill them with the
others. 9Now the cistern where he threw all the
bodies of the men he had killed along with Geda- 41:9
liah was the one King Asa[a] had made as part of [a]1Ki 15:22; 2Ch 16:6

[a] 3 Or *Chaldean*

Vengeful Hearts

JER 41:1-3

The king of Babylon appoints Gedaliah governor over Judah. He helps the remnant poor settle in the land (Jer 40:7-12). He is a good leader, and it appears Jeremiah supports him (Jer 40:5-6).

Ishmael is a rebel leader of royal descent. He and ten of his men assassinate Gedaliah. Ishmael scorns Babylonian rule and may be trying to exact revenge against the Babylonians for the indignities committed against his relative King Zedekiah (Jer 39:6-7).

Hatred and revenge have ravaged the hearts of humanity since the fall (Ge 4:4-8). But instead of revenge, the Prince of Peace calls us to a higher standard—to love and pray for our enemies and to turn the other cheek (Lk 6:27-31).

his defense[b] against Baasha[c] king of Israel. Ishmael son of Nethaniah filled it with the dead.
10 Ishmael made captives of all the rest of the
people[d] who were in Mizpah—the king's daughters along with all the others who were left there,
over whom Nebuzaradan commander of the imperial guard had appointed Gedaliah son of Ahikam.
Ishmael son of Nethaniah took them captive and
set out to cross over to the Ammonites.[e]
11 When Johanan[f] son of Kareah and all the
army officers who were with him heard about all
the crimes Ishmael son of Nethaniah had committed, 12 they took all their men and went to fight
Ishmael son of Nethaniah. They caught up with
him near the great pool[g] in Gibeon. 13 When all the
people[h] Ishmael had with him saw Johanan son
of Kareah and the army officers who were with
him, they were glad. 14 All the people Ishmael had
taken captive at Mizpah turned and went over to
Johanan son of Kareah. 15 But Ishmael son of Nethaniah and eight of his men escaped[i] from Johanan and fled to the Ammonites.

Flight to Egypt

16 Then Johanan son of Kareah and all the army
officers who were with him led away all the survivors[j] from Mizpah whom he had recovered from
Ishmael son of Nethaniah after he had assassinated Gedaliah son of Ahikam: the soldiers, women,
children and court officials he had brought from
Gibeon. 17 And they went on, stopping at Geruth
Kimham[k] near Bethlehem on their way to Egypt[l]
18 to escape the Babylonians.[a] They were afraid[m] of
them because Ishmael son of Nethaniah had killed
Gedaliah[n] son of Ahikam, whom the king of Babylon had appointed as governor over the land.

42 Then all the army officers, including Johanan[o] son of Kareah and Jezaniah[b] son of
Hoshaiah, and all the people from the least to the
greatest[p] approached 2 Jeremiah the prophet and
said to him, "Please hear our petition and pray[q]
to the LORD your God for this entire remnant.[r] For
as you now see, though we were once many, now
only a few[s] are left. 3 Pray that the LORD your God
will tell us where we should go and what we
should do."[t]
4 "I have heard you," replied Jeremiah the
prophet. "I will certainly pray[u] to the LORD your
God as you have requested; I will tell you everything the LORD says and will keep nothing back
from you."[v]
5 Then they said to Jeremiah, "May the LORD be
a true and faithful witness[w] against us if we do
not act in accordance with everything the LORD
your God sends you to tell us. 6 Whether it is favorable or unfavorable, we will obey the LORD our
God, to whom we are sending you, so that it will

41:9 [b]Jdg 6:2 [c]2Ch 16:1
41:10 [d]Jer 40:7,12 [e]Jer 40:14
41:11 [f]Jer 40:8
41:12 [g]2Sa 2:13
41:13 [h]ver 10
41:15 [i]Job 21:30; Pr 28:17
41:16 [j]Jer 43:4
41:17 [k]2Sa 19:37 [l]Jer 42:14
41:18 [m]Isa 51:12; Jer 42:16; Lk 12:4-5 [n]Jer 40:5
42:1 [o]Jer 40:13; 41:11 [p]Jer 6:13; 44:12
42:2 [q]Jer 36:7; Ac 8:24; Jas 5:16 [r]Isa 1:9 [s]Lev 26:22; La 1:1
42:3 [t]Ps 86:11; Pr 3:6
42:4 [u]Ex 8:29; 1Sa 12:23 [v]1Ki 22:14; 1Sa 3:17
42:5 [w]Ge 31:50

[a] *18* Or *Chaldeans* [b] *1* Hebrew; Septuagint (see also 43:2) *Azariah*

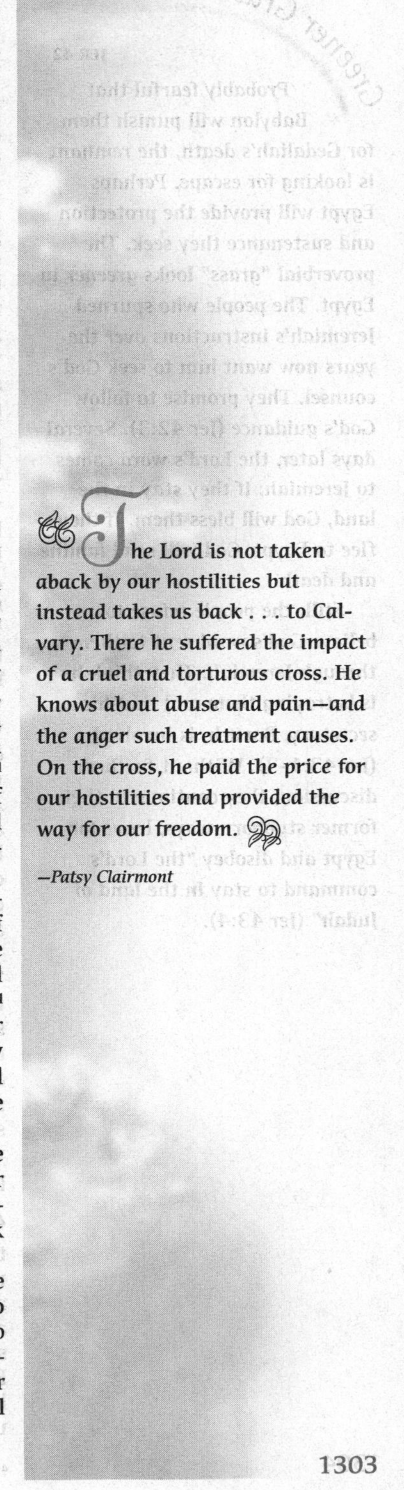

The Lord is not taken aback by our hostilities but instead takes us back . . . to Calvary. There he suffered the impact of a cruel and torturous cross. He knows about abuse and pain—and the anger such treatment causes. On the cross, he paid the price for our hostilities and provided the way for our freedom.

—Patsy Clairmont

Greener Grass?

JER 42

Probably fearful that Babylon will punish them for Gedaliah's death, the remnant is looking for escape. Perhaps Egypt will provide the protection and sustenance they seek. The proverbial "grass" looks greener in Egypt. The people who spurned Jeremiah's instructions over the years now want him to seek God's counsel. They promise to follow God's guidance (Jer 42:3). Several days later, the Lord's word comes to Jeremiah: If they stay in the land, God will bless them. If they flee to Egypt, God will send famine and death.

Still, the people refuse to believe God's word sent to them through Jeremiah. They think he is betraying them and that his secretary, Baruch, is involved (Jer 43:1–3). Without further discussion, they continue in their former stubborn ways, leave for Egypt and disobey "the Lord's command to stay in the land of Judah" (Jer 43:4).

go well[x] with us, for we will obey[y] the LORD our God."

7 Ten days later the word of the LORD came to Jeremiah. 8 So he called together Johanan son of Kareah and all the army officers[z] who were with him and all the people from the least to the greatest. 9 He said to them, "This is what the LORD, the God of Israel, to whom you sent me to present your petition, says:[a] 10 'If you stay in this land, I will build[b] you up and not tear you down; I will plant[c] you and not uproot you,[d] for I am grieved over the disaster I have inflicted on you.[e] 11 Do not be afraid of the king of Babylon,[f] whom you now fear.[g] Do not be afraid of him, declares the LORD, for I am with you and will save[h] you and deliver you from his hands.[i] 12 I will show you compassion so that he will have compassion on you and restore you to your land.'[j]

13 "However, if you say, 'We will not stay in this land,' and so disobey[k] the LORD your God, 14 and if you say, 'No, we will go and live in Egypt,[l] where we will not see war or hear the trumpet or be hungry for bread,' 15 then hear the word of the LORD, O remnant of Judah. This is what the LORD Almighty, the God of Israel, says: 'If you are determined to go to Egypt and you do go to settle there, 16 then the sword[m] you fear will overtake you there, and the famine you dread will follow you into Egypt, and there you will die. 17 Indeed, all who are determined to go to Egypt to settle there will die by the sword, famine and plague;[n] not one of them will survive or escape the disaster I will bring on them.' 18 This is what the LORD Almighty, the God of Israel, says: 'As my anger and wrath[o] have been poured out on those who lived in Jerusalem,[p] so will my wrath be poured out on you when you go to Egypt. You will be an object of cursing and horror,[q] of condemnation and reproach; you will never see this place again.'[r]

19 "O remnant of Judah, the LORD has told you, 'Do not go to Egypt.'[s] Be sure of this: I warn you today 20 that you made a fatal mistake[a] when you sent me to the LORD your God and said, 'Pray to the LORD our God for us; tell us everything he says and we will do it.'[t] 21 I have told you today, but you still have not obeyed the LORD your God in all he sent me to tell you.[u] 22 So now, be sure of this: You will die by the sword, famine and plague[v] in the place where you want to go to settle."[w]

43 When Jeremiah finished telling the people all the words of the LORD their God—everything the LORD had sent him to tell them[x]— 2 Azariah son of Hoshaiah and Johanan[y] son of Kareah and all the arrogant men said to Jeremiah, "You are lying! The LORD our God has not sent you to say, 'You must not go to Egypt to settle there.' 3 But Baruch son of Neriah is inciting you against us to hand us over to the Babylonians,[b] so they may kill us or carry us into exile to Babylon."[z]

42:6 [x]Dt 5:29; 6:3; Jer 7:23 [y]Ex 24:7; Jos 24:24
42:8 [z]ver 1
42:9 [a]2Ki 22:15
42:10 [b]Jer 24:6 [c]Jer 31:28 [d]Eze 36:36 [e]Jer 18:8
42:11 [f]Jer 27:11 [g]Nu 14:9 [h]Isa 43:5 [i]Jer 1:8; Ro 8:31
42:12 [j]Ps 106:44-46
42:13 [k]Jer 44:16
42:14 [l]Nu 11:4-5
42:16 [m]Eze 11:8
42:17 [n]ver 22; Jer 44:13
42:18 [o]Dt 29:18-20; Jer 7:20 [p]2Ch 36:19; Jer 39:1-9 [q]Jer 29:18 [r]Jer 22:10
42:19 [s]Dt 17:16; Isa 30:7
42:20 [t]ver 2
42:21 [u]Eze 2:7; Zec 7:11-12
42:22 [v]ver 17; Eze 6:11 [w]Hos 9:6
43:1 [x]Jer 26:8; 42:9-22
43:2 [y]Jer 42:1
43:3 [z]Jer 38:4

[a] 20 Or *you erred in your hearts* [b] 3 Or *Chaldeans*

4So Johanan son of Kareah and all the army
officers and all the people disobeyed the LORD's
command[a] to stay in the land of Judah.[b] 5Instead,
Johanan son of Kareah and all the army officers
led away all the remnant of Judah who had come
back to live in the land of Judah from all the
nations where they had been scattered.[c] 6They
also led away all the men, women and children
and the king's daughters whom Nebuzaradan
commander of the imperial guard had left with
Gedaliah son of Ahikam, the son of Shaphan, and
Jeremiah the prophet and Baruch son of Neriah.
7So they entered Egypt in disobedience to the LORD
and went as far as Tahpanhes.[d]
8In Tahpanhes[e] the word of the LORD came to
Jeremiah: 9"While the Jews are watching, take
some large stones with you and bury them in clay
in the brick pavement at the entrance to Pharaoh's
palace in Tahpanhes. 10Then say to them, 'This is
what the LORD Almighty, the God of Israel, says: I
will send for my servant[f] Nebuchadnezzar king of
Babylon, and I will set his throne over these stones
I have buried here; he will spread his royal canopy
above them. 11He will come and attack Egypt,[g]
bringing death to those destined for death, captivity to those destined for captivity, and the sword
to those destined for the sword.[h] 12He[a] will set fire
to the temples of the gods[i] of Egypt; he will burn
their temples and take their gods captive. As a
shepherd wraps[j] his garment around him, so will
he wrap Egypt around himself and depart from
there unscathed. 13There in the temple of the sun[b]
in Egypt he will demolish the sacred pillars and
will burn down the temples of the gods of Egypt.' "

Disaster Because of Idolatry

44 This word came to Jeremiah concerning all
the Jews living in Lower Egypt—in Migdol,[k]
Tahpanhes[l] and Memphis[c][m]—and in Upper
Egypt[d]:[n] 2"This is what the LORD Almighty, the God
of Israel, says: You saw the great disaster I brought
on Jerusalem and on all the towns of Judah. Today
they lie deserted and in ruins[o] 3because of the evil
they have done. They provoked me to anger by
burning incense and by worshiping other gods[p]
that neither they nor you nor your fathers[q] ever
knew. 4Again and again[r] I sent my servants the
prophets,[s] who said, 'Do not do this detestable
thing that I hate!' 5But they did not listen or pay
attention; they did not turn from their wickedness
or stop burning incense to other gods.[t] 6Therefore,
my fierce anger was poured out; it raged against
the towns of Judah and the streets of Jerusalem
and made them the desolate ruins they are today.
7"Now this is what the LORD God Almighty, the
God of Israel, says: Why bring such great disaster[u]
on yourselves by cutting off from Judah the men
and women,[v] the children and infants, and so leave

43:4 [a]Jer 42:5-6 [b]Jer 42:10
43:5 [c]Jer 40:12
43:7 [d]Jer 2:16; 44:1
43:8 [e]Jer 2:16
43:10 [f]Isa 44:28; Jer 25:9; 27:6
43:11 [g]Jer 46:13-26; Eze 29:19-20 [h]Jer 15:2; 44:13; Zec 11:9
43:12 [i]Jer 46:25; Eze 30:13 [j]Ps 104:2; 109:18-19
44:1 [k]Ex 14:2 [l]Jer 43:7,8 [m]Isa 19:13 [n]Isa 11:11; Jer 46:14
44:2 [o]Isa 6:11; Jer 9:11; 34:22
44:3 [p]ver 8; Dt 13:6-11; 29:26 [q]Dt 32:17; Jer 19:4
44:4 [r]Jer 7:13 [s]Jer 7:25; 25:4; 26:5
44:5 [t]Jer 11:8-10
44:7 [u]Jer 26:19 [v]Jer 51:22

[a] *12* Or *I* [b] *13* Or *in Heliopolis* [c] *1* Hebrew *Noph*
[d] *1* Hebrew *in Pathros*

Crippled by Sin

JER 43

Rejecting God's directive, the remnant leaves Judah and goes to northeastern Egypt. It appears that they force Jeremiah and Baruch to flee with them. In this land of opportunity and plenty, the Hebrews begin to blend into Egyptian culture and join the Egyptians in pagan worship (Jer 44:7-8). Their penchant for worshiping false gods only grows in this Egyptian environment, and God's judgment, instead of blessing, is their destiny again.

The blatant idolatry of the Egyptians and the Israelites leads also to Egypt's downfall, which Jeremiah predicts in these verses. Nebuchadnezzar invades Egypt in 568 B.C., killing the Hebrew refugees and allowing only a few to join the captives in Babylon. The once grand nation never regains its strength or prominence.

Pagan Prosperity

JER 44:15-19

The complaints of the remnant sound just like the complaints of their ancestors who fled Egypt under Moses' leadership (Ex 14:11-12; 16:3). "In the old days, we had prosperity and plenty of food. What are you doing, God? Leave us alone!" The people again blame God for the death and famine they experience. They reason that worshiping their own gods will secure their well-being. To them, the spiritual reforms of their last righteous king (Josiah) led to their ruin. The people continue to blow pagan incense in God's face and refuse to repent.

It's a mistake to associate prosperity and comfort with righteousness. Judah thinks following God's ways should guarantee material security. But God sees through their feeble attempts to honor him. While God often prospers the righteous, walking with God does not safeguard us from troubling times. But when hard times knock, "the Lord is faithful, and he will strengthen and protect [us]" (2Th 3:3).

yourselves without a remnant? 8 Why provoke me
to anger with what your hands have made,[w] burning incense to other gods in Egypt, where you have
come to live?[x] You will destroy yourselves and
make yourselves an object of cursing and reproach[y]
among all the nations on earth. 9 Have you forgotten the wickedness committed by your fathers and
by the kings and queens of Judah and the wickedness committed by you and your wives in the land
of Judah and the streets of Jerusalem?[z] 10 To this day
they have not humbled themselves or shown reverence, nor have they followed my law[a] and the
decrees I set before you and your fathers.[b]

11 "Therefore, this is what the LORD Almighty, the
God of Israel, says: I am determined to bring
disaster[c] on you and to destroy all Judah. 12 I will
take away the remnant[d] of Judah who were determined to go to Egypt to settle there. They will all
perish in Egypt; they will fall by the sword or die
from famine. From the least to the greatest, they
will die by sword or famine.[e] They will become
an object of cursing and horror, of condemnation
and reproach.[f] 13 I will punish those who live in
Egypt with the sword, famine and plague,[g] as I
punished Jerusalem. 14 None of the remnant of
Judah who have gone to live in Egypt will escape
or survive to return to the land of Judah, to which
they long to return and live; none will return
except a few fugitives."[h]

15 Then all the men who knew that their wives
were burning incense to other gods, along with
all the women who were present—a large assembly—and all the people living in Lower and Upper
Egypt,[a] said to Jeremiah, 16 "We will not listen[i] to
the message you have spoken to us in the name of
the LORD! 17 We will certainly do everything we
said we would:[j] We will burn incense to the
Queen of Heaven[k] and will pour out drink offerings to her just as we and our fathers, our kings
and our officials did in the towns of Judah and in
the streets of Jerusalem. At that time we had plenty of food and were well off and suffered no
harm.[l] 18 But ever since we stopped burning
incense to the Queen of Heaven and pouring out
drink offerings to her, we have had nothing and
have been perishing by sword and famine.[m]"

19 The women added, "When we burned incense
to the Queen of Heaven[n] and poured out drink
offerings to her, did not our husbands know that
we were making cakes like her image and pouring
out drink offerings to her?"

20 Then Jeremiah said to all the people, both men
and women, who were answering him, 21 "Did not
the LORD remember[o] and think about the incense[p]
burned in the towns of Judah and the streets of Jerusalem[q] by you and your fathers,[r] your kings and
your officials and the people of the land? 22 When
the LORD could no longer endure your wicked
actions and the detestable things you did, your

44:8 [w]Jer 25:6-7 [x]1Co 10:22 [y]Jer 42:18
44:9 [z]ver 17,21
44:10 [a]Jos 1:7 [b]1Ki 9:6-9
44:11 [c]Jer 21:10; Am 9:4
44:12 [d]ver 7 [e]Isa 1:28 [f]Jer 29:18; 42:15-18
44:13 [g]Jer 42:17
44:14 [h]ver 28; Jer 22:24-27; Ro 9:27
44:16 [i]Jer 11:8-10
44:17 [j]Dt 23:23 [k]ver 25; Jer 7:18 [l]Hos 2:5-13
44:18 [m]Mal 3:13-15
44:19 [n]Jer 7:18
44:21 [o]Isa 64:9; Jer 14:10 [p]Jer 11:13 [q]ver 9 [r]Ps 79:8

[a] 15 Hebrew *in Egypt and Pathros*

land became an object of cursing[s] and a desolate
waste without inhabitants, as it is today.[t] 23Because
you have burned incense and have sinned against
the LORD and have not obeyed him or followed his
law or his decrees or his stipulations, this disaster[u] has come upon you, as you now see."[v]
24Then Jeremiah said to all the people, including the women,[w] "Hear the word of the LORD, all
you people of Judah in Egypt.[x] 25This is what the
LORD Almighty, the God of Israel, says: You and
your wives have shown by your actions what you
promised when you said, 'We will certainly carry
out the vows we made to burn incense and pour
out drink offerings to the Queen of Heaven.'[y]
"Go ahead then, do what you promised! Keep
your vows![z] 26But hear the word of the LORD, all
Jews living in Egypt: 'I swear[a] by my great name,'
says the LORD, 'that no one from Judah living anywhere in Egypt will ever again invoke my name
or swear, "As surely as the Sovereign LORD lives."[b]
27For I am watching over them for harm,[c] not for
good; the Jews in Egypt will perish by sword and
famine until they are all destroyed. 28Those who
escape the sword and return to the land of Judah
from Egypt will be very few.[d] Then the whole
remnant of Judah who came to live in Egypt will
know whose word will stand—mine or theirs.[e]
29" 'This will be the sign to you that I will punish you in this place,' declares the LORD, 'so that
you will know that my threats of harm against
you will surely stand.'[f] 30This is what the LORD
says: 'I am going to hand Pharaoh[g] Hophra king
of Egypt over to his enemies who seek his life, just
as I handed Zedekiah[h] king of Judah over to Nebuchadnezzar king of Babylon, the enemy who
was seeking his life.' "[i]

A Message to Baruch

45 This is what Jeremiah the prophet told Baruch[j] son of Neriah in the fourth year of
Jehoiakim[k] son of Josiah king of Judah, after Baruch had written on a scroll the words Jeremiah
was then dictating: 2"This is what the LORD, the
God of Israel, says to you, Baruch: 3You said, 'Woe
to me! The LORD has added sorrow to my pain; I
am worn out with groaning[l] and find no rest.' "
4⌊The LORD said,⌋ "Say this to him: 'This is what
the LORD says: I will overthrow what I have built
and uproot what I have planted,[m] throughout the
land.[n] 5Should you then seek great things for
yourself? Seek them not.[o] For I will bring disaster
on all people, declares the LORD, but wherever you
go I will let you escape with your life.' "[p]

A Message About Egypt

46 This is the word of the LORD that came to
Jeremiah the prophet concerning the
nations:[q]

2Concerning Egypt:

44:22 [s]Jer 25:18 [t]Ge 19:13; Ps 107:33-34
44:23 [u]Jer 40:2 [v]1Ki 9:9; Jer 7:13-15; Da 9:11-12
44:24 [w]ver 15 [x]Jer 43:7
44:25 [y]ver 17 [z]Eze 20:39
44:26 [a]Ge 22:16; Isa 48:1; Heb 6:13-17 [b]Dt 32:40; Ps 50:16
44:27 [c]Jer 31:28
44:28 [d]ver 13-14; Isa 10:19 [e]ver 17,25-26
44:29 [f]Pr 19:21
44:30 [g]Jer 46:26; Eze 30:21 [h]2Ki 25:1-7 [i]Jer 39:5
45:1 [j]Jer 32:12; 36:4,18,32 [k]2Ch 36:5
45:3 [l]Ps 69:3
45:4 [m]Jer 11:17 [n]Isa 5:5-7; Jer 18:7-10
45:5 [o]Mt 6:25-27, 33 [p]Jer 21:9; 38:2; 39:18
46:1 [q]Jer 1:10; 25:15-38

Nothing in this lost and ruined world bears the meek impress of the Son of God so surely as forgiveness.

—Alice Cary (1820-1871)

The Mighty Nile

JER 46:7-10

Jeremiah compares the Egyptian armies to the Nile River during its annual flood stage. The Nile River flows from south to north through Egypt (see Map 13: Paul's Missionary Journeys at the back of this Bible), and the civilization of Egypt lies almost exclusively along the narrow strips of watered land on each side of the river. Every June the rains and snowmelt of central Africa push waters of the Nile more than 15 feet over its banks. The waters leave behind a layer of rich, fertile silt, excellent soil for growing all the produce of the land. Too large a rise in the river can destroy homes and carry away, rather than deposit, the fertile soil; too small a rise in the river can produce a lean agricultural year. The unpredictable flooding has been brought under control in recent years by building dams at strategic points along the river.

This is the message against the army of Pharaoh Neco[r] king of Egypt, which was defeated at Carchemish[s] on the Euphrates River by Nebuchadnezzar king of Babylon in the fourth year of Jehoiakim[t] son of Josiah king of Judah:

3 "Prepare your shields,[u] both large and small,
and march out for battle!
4 Harness the horses,
mount the steeds!
Take your positions
with helmets on!
Polish[v] your spears,
put on your armor![w]
5 What do I see?
They are terrified,
they are retreating,
their warriors are defeated.
They flee[x] in haste
without looking back,
and there is terror[y] on every side,"
declares the LORD.
6 "The swift cannot flee[z]
nor the strong escape.
In the north by the River Euphrates
they stumble and fall.[a]
7 "Who is this that rises like the Nile,
like rivers of surging waters?[b]
8 Egypt rises like the Nile,
like rivers of surging waters.
She says, 'I will rise and cover the earth;
I will destroy cities and their people.'
9 Charge, O horses!
Drive furiously, O charioteers![c]
March on, O warriors—
men of Cush[a] and Put who carry shields,
men of Lydia[d] who draw the bow.
10 But that day[e] belongs to the Lord, the LORD Almighty—
a day of vengeance, for vengeance on his foes.
The sword will devour[f] till it is satisfied,
till it has quenched its thirst with blood.
For the Lord, the LORD Almighty, will offer sacrifice[g]
in the land of the north by the River Euphrates.
11 "Go up to Gilead and get balm,[h]
O Virgin[i] Daughter of Egypt.
But you multiply remedies in vain;
there is no healing[j] for you.
12 The nations will hear of your shame;
your cries will fill the earth.
One warrior will stumble over another;
both will fall[k] down together."

46:2 [r]2Ki 23:29 [s]2Ch 35:20 [t]Jer 45:1
46:3 [u]Isa 21:5; Jer 51:11-12
46:4 [v]Eze 21:9-11 [w]1Sa 17:5, 38; 2Ch 26:14; Ne 4:16
46:5 [x]ver 21 [y]Jer 49:29
46:6 [z]Isa 30:16 [a]ver 12,16; Da 11:19
46:7 [b]Jer 47:2
46:9 [c]Jer 47:3 [d]Isa 66:19
46:10 [e]Joel 1:15 [f]Dt 32:42 [g]Zep 1:7
46:11 [h]Jer 8:22 [i]Isa 47:1 [j]Jer 30:13; Mic 1:9
46:12 [k]Isa 19:4; Na 3:8-10

[a] 9 That is, the upper Nile region

13 This is the message the LORD spoke to Jeremi-
46:13 ah the prophet about the coming of Nebuchad-
[l]Isa 19:1 nezzar king of Babylon to attack Egypt:[l]

14 "Announce this in Egypt, and proclaim
46:14 it in Migdol;
[m]Jer 43:8 proclaim it also in Memphis[a] and
Tahpanhes:[m]
'Take your positions and get ready,
for the sword devours those around
you.'
15 Why will your warriors be laid low?
They cannot stand, for the LORD will
46:15 push them down.[n]
[n]Isa 66:15-16 16 They will stumble[o] repeatedly;
46:16 they will fall[p] over each other.
[o]Lev 26:37 [p]ver 6 They will say, 'Get up, let us go back
to our own people and our native
lands,
away from the sword of the oppressor.'
17 There they will exclaim,
'Pharaoh king of Egypt is only a loud
46:17 noise;
[q]Isa 19:11-16 he has missed his opportunity.[q]'

46:18 18 "As surely as I live," declares the King,[r]
[r]Jer 48:15 whose name is the LORD Almighty,
[s]Jos 19:22 "one will come who is like Tabor[s]
[t]1Ki 18:42 among the mountains,
like Carmel[t] by the sea.
46:19 19 Pack your belongings for exile,[u]
[u]Isa 20:4 you who live in Egypt,
for Memphis will be laid waste
and lie in ruins without inhabitant.

20 "Egypt is a beautiful heifer,
but a gadfly is coming
46:20 against her from the north.[v]
[v]ver 24; Jer 47:2 21 The mercenaries[w] in her ranks
are like fattened calves.
46:21 They too will turn and flee[x] together,
[w]2Ki 7:6 [x]ver 5 they will not stand their ground,
[y]Ps 37:13 for the day[y] of disaster is coming upon
them,
the time for them to be punished.
22 Egypt will hiss like a fleeing serpent
as the enemy advances in force;
they will come against her with axes,
like men who cut down trees.
23 They will chop down her forest,"
declares the LORD,
46:23 "dense though it be.
[z]Jdg 7:12 They are more numerous than locusts,[z]
they cannot be counted.
24 The Daughter of Egypt will be put to
shame,
46:24 handed over to the people of the
[a]Jer 1:15 north.[a]"

25 The LORD Almighty, the God of Israel, says: "I
am about to bring punishment on Amon god of

[a] *14* Hebrew *Noph*; also in verse 19

Little Pests

JER 46:20-24

Jeremiah uses imaginative language in these verses to describe the downfall of the mighty nation of Egypt. He compares her to a heifer, an animal that ancient people viewed as evidence of the wealth of a person or a nation. Jeremiah warns that this beautiful heifer will be destroyed, not quickly by a death blow, but little by little by a "gadfly" (Jer 46:20). Nebuchadnezzar and his armies are the gadfly. They come to sting and bite the heifer Egypt, slowly pestering her and wearing her down until she is destroyed.

Thebes,[a][b] on Pharaoh, on Egypt and her gods[c] and
her kings, and on those who rely[d] on Pharaoh. 26 I
will hand them over[e] to those who seek their
lives, to Nebuchadnezzar king[f] of Babylon and his
officers. Later, however, Egypt will be inhabited[g]
as in times past," declares the LORD.

27 "Do not fear,[h] O Jacob my servant;
do not be dismayed, O Israel.
I will surely save you out of a distant place,
your descendants from the land of their exile.[i]
Jacob will again have peace and security,
and no one will make him afraid.
28 Do not fear, O Jacob my servant,
for I am with you,"[j] declares the LORD.
"Though I completely destroy[k] all the nations
among which I scatter you,
I will not completely destroy you.
I will discipline you but only with justice;
I will not let you go entirely unpunished."

A Message About the Philistines

47 This is the word of the LORD that came to
Jeremiah the prophet concerning the Philistines before Pharaoh attacked Gaza:[l]

2 This is what the LORD says:
"See how the waters are rising in the north;[m]
they will become an overflowing torrent.
They will overflow the land and everything in it,
the towns and those who live in them.
The people will cry out;
all who dwell in the land will wail
3 at the sound of the hoofs of galloping steeds,
at the noise of enemy chariots
and the rumble of their wheels.
Fathers will not turn to help their children;
their hands will hang limp.
4 For the day has come
to destroy all the Philistines
and to cut off all survivors
who could help Tyre[n] and Sidon.[o]
The LORD is about to destroy the Philistines,[p]
the remnant from the coasts of Caphtor.[b][q]
5 Gaza will shave[r] her head in mourning;

46:25 [b]Eze 30:14; Na 3:8 [c]Jer 43:12 [d]Isa 20:6
46:26 [e]Jer 44:30 [f]Eze 32:11 [g]Eze 29:11-16
46:27 [h]Isa 41:13; 43:5 [i]Isa 11:11; Jer 50:19
46:28 [j]Isa 8:9-10 [k]Jer 4:27
47:1 [l]Ge 10:19; Am 1:6; Zec 9:5-7
47:2 [m]Isa 8:7; 14:31
47:4 [n]Am 1:9-10; Zec 9:2-4 [o]Jer 25:22 [p]Ge 10:14; Joel 3:4 [q]Dt 2:23
47:5 [r]Jer 41:5; Mic 1:16

Limp Arms — JER 47:3

It's a natural instinct for fathers and mothers to protect their children. Even wild animals safeguard their young. Yet Jeremiah says that Babylon's invasion from the north will so terrify the Philistines that the strong arms of fathers will "hang limp," defenseless to help their needy children. What a devastating picture of total abandonment!

[a] 25 Hebrew *No* [b] 4 That is, Crete

47:5 Ashkelon[s] will be silenced.
[s]Jer 25:20 O remnant on the plain,
how long will you cut yourselves?

47:6 [6]"'Ah, sword[t] of the LORD,' ⌞you cry,⌟
[t]Jer 12:12 'how long till you rest?
Return to your scabbard;
cease and be still.'
[7]But how can it rest
when the LORD has commanded it,
when he has ordered it
to attack Ashkelon and the coast?"

A Message About Moab

48

Concerning Moab:

This is what the LORD Almighty, the God of Israel, says:

48:1 "Woe to Nebo,[u] for it will be ruined.
[u]Nu 32:38 [v]Nu 32:37 Kiriathaim[v] will be disgraced and captured;
the stronghold[a] will be disgraced and shattered.
48:2 [2]Moab will be praised[w] no more;
[w]Isa 16:14 [x]Nu 21:25 in Heshbon[b x] men will plot her downfall:
'Come, let us put an end to that nation.'
You too, O Madmen,[c] will be silenced;
the sword will pursue you.
48:3 [3]Listen to the cries from Horonaim,[y]
[y]Isa 15:5 cries of great havoc and destruction.
[4]Moab will be broken;
her little ones will cry out.[d]
48:5 [z]Isa 15:5 [5]They go up the way to Luhith,[z]
weeping bitterly as they go;
on the road down to Horonaim
anguished cries over the destruction are heard.
48:6 [6]Flee! Run for your lives;
[a]Jer 17:6 become like a bush[e] in the desert.[a]
[7]Since you trust in your deeds and riches,
48:7 you too will be taken captive,
[b]Nu 21:29 and Chemosh[b] will go into exile,[c]
[c]Isa 46:1-2; Jer 49:3 together with his priests and officials.
[8]The destroyer will come against every town,
and not a town will escape.
The valley will be ruined
and the plateau destroyed,
because the LORD has spoken.
[9]Put salt on Moab,
for she will be laid waste[f];
her towns will become desolate,
with no one to live in them.

[a] *1* Or / *Misgab* [b] *2* The Hebrew for *Heshbon* sounds like the Hebrew for *plot*. [c] *2* The name of the Moabite town Madmen sounds like the Hebrew for *be silenced*.
[d] *4* Hebrew; Septuagint / *proclaim it to Zoar* [e] *6* Or *like Aroer* [f] *9* Or *Give wings to Moab, / for she will fly away*

Desert Bush

JER 48:6

The meaning of "bush in the desert" is not clear. The Hebrew word used here denotes nakedness, which would suggest a sparse shrub. The NIV footnote on this word indicates that it could also refer to** Aroer**, meaning "naked," the name of several Israelite towns. Other than its use as a name for a town, this Hebrew word is translated "bush" only here and in Jeremiah 17:6. In Psalm 102:17 it is translated "destitute." Whatever the translation, this phrase clearly symbolizes isolation, loneliness and destruction. The meaning behind the words is clear: The Moabites will be captured and stripped of their good life.

Wholehearted Service

JER 48:10

Jeremiah speaks out against the Moabites, long-time enemies of the Hebrews. Descendants of the son of Lot's older daughter (Ge 19:36–37), the Moabites seduce Israel into idolatry (Nu 25:1–3). Because Moab relies on its own strength, rather than on the Lord, God orchestrates the nation's demise under Nebuchadnezzar's hand (Jer 48:7). God has endured enough of Moab's wicked influence over his chosen people. Jeremiah's oracle curses those who fall back from carrying out God's plan to punish the Moabites.

10 "A curse on him who is lax in doing the LORD's work!
A curse on him who keeps his sword[d] from bloodshed![e]
11 "Moab has been at rest[f] from youth,
like wine left on its dregs,[g]
not poured from one jar to another—
she has not gone into exile.
So she tastes as she did,
and her aroma is unchanged.
12 But days are coming,"
declares the LORD,
"when I will send men who pour from jars,
and they will pour her out;
they will empty her jars
and smash her jugs.
13 Then Moab will be ashamed[h] of Chemosh,
as the house of Israel was ashamed
when they trusted in Bethel.

14 "How can you say, 'We are warriors,[i]
men valiant in battle'?
15 Moab will be destroyed and her towns invaded;
her finest young men will go down in the slaughter,[j]"
declares the King,[k] whose name is the LORD Almighty.[l]
16 "The fall of Moab is at hand;[m]
her calamity will come quickly.
17 Mourn for her, all who live around her,
all who know her fame;
say, 'How broken is the mighty scepter,
how broken the glorious staff!'

18 "Come down from your glory
and sit on the parched ground,[n]
O inhabitants of the Daughter of Dibon,[o]
for he who destroys Moab
will come up against you
and ruin your fortified cities.[p]
19 Stand by the road and watch,
you who live in Aroer.[q]
Ask the man fleeing and the woman escaping,
ask them, 'What has happened?'
20 Moab is disgraced, for she is shattered.
Wail[r] and cry out!
Announce by the Arnon[s]
that Moab is destroyed.
21 Judgment has come to the plateau—
to Holon, Jahzah[t] and Mephaath,[u]
22 to Dibon,[v] Nebo and Beth Diblathaim,
23 to Kiriathaim, Beth Gamul and Beth Meon,[w]
24 to Kerioth[x] and Bozrah—
to all the towns of Moab, far and near.

48:10 [d]Jer 47:6 [e]1Ki 20:42; 2Ki 13:15-19
48:11 [f]Zec 1:15 [g]Zep 1:12
48:13 [h]Hos 10:6
48:14 [i]Ps 33:16
48:15 [j]Jer 50:27 [k]Jer 46:18 [l]Jer 51:57
48:16 [m]Isa 13:22
48:18 [n]Isa 47:1 [o]Nu 21:30; Jos 13:9 [p]ver 8
48:19 [q]Dt 2:36
48:20 [r]Isa 16:7 [s]Nu 21:13
48:21 [t]Nu 21:23; Isa 15:4 [u]Jos 13:18
48:22 [v]Jos 13:9,17
48:23 [w]Jos 13:17
48:24 [x]Am 2:2

[25] Moab's horn[a][y] is cut off;
her arm[z] is broken,"
declares the LORD.
[26] "Make her drunk,[a]
for she has defied the LORD.
Let Moab wallow in her vomit;
let her be an object of ridicule.
[27] Was not Israel the object of your
ridicule?[b]
Was she caught among thieves,
that you shake your head[c] in scorn[d]
whenever you speak of her?
[28] Abandon your towns and dwell among
the rocks,
you who live in Moab.
Be like a dove[e] that makes its nest
at the mouth of a cave.[f]

[29] "We have heard of Moab's pride[g]—
her overweening pride and conceit,
her pride and arrogance
and the haughtiness of her heart.
[30] I know her insolence but it is futile,"
declares the LORD,
"and her boasts accomplish nothing.
[31] Therefore I wail[h] over Moab,
for all Moab I cry out,
I moan for the men of Kir Hareseth.[i]
[32] I weep for you, as Jazer weeps,
O vines of Sibmah.[j]
Your branches spread as far as the sea;
they reached as far as the sea of Jazer.
The destroyer has fallen
on your ripened fruit and grapes.
[33] Joy and gladness are gone
from the orchards and fields of Moab.
I have stopped the flow of wine[k] from
the presses;
no one treads them with shouts of
joy.[l]
Although there are shouts,
they are not shouts of joy.

[34] "The sound of their cry rises
from Heshbon to Elealeh[m] and Jahaz,[n]
from Zoar[o] as far as Horonaim[p] and
Eglath Shelishiyah,
for even the waters of Nimrim are
dried up.[q]
[35] In Moab I will put an end
to those who make offerings on the
high places[r]
and burn incense[s] to their gods,"
declares the LORD.
[36] "So my heart laments[t] for Moab like a
flute;
it laments like a flute for the men of
Kir Hareseth.
The wealth they acquired[u] is gone.

48:25 [y]Ps 75:10 [z]Ps 10:15; Eze 30:21
48:26 [a]Jer 25:16, 27
48:27 [b]Jer 2:26 [c]Job 16:4; Jer 18:16 [d]Mic 7:8-10
48:28 [e]Ps 55:6-7 [f]Jdg 6:2
48:29 [g]Job 40:12; Isa 16:6
48:31 [h]Isa 15:5-8 [i]2Ki 3:25
48:32 [j]Isa 16:8-9
48:33 [k]Isa 16:10 [l]Joel 1:12
48:34 [m]Nu 32:3 [n]Isa 15:4 [o]Ge 13:10 [p]Isa 15:5 [q]Isa 15:6
48:35 [r]Isa 15:2; 16:12 [s]Jer 11:13
48:36 [t]Isa 16:11 [u]Isa 15:7

[a] *25* *Horn* here symbolizes strength.

***O** sad estate*
Of human wretchedness; so weak
is man,
So ignorant and blind, that did
not God
Sometimes withhold in mercy
what we ask,
We should be ruined at our own
request.

—Hannah More (1745-1833)

In Mourning

JER 48:37

God's punishment of the Moabites for their wickedness gives him no pleasure. Jeremiah says God's heart "laments for Moab like a flute" (Jer 48:36). (Flutes were traditional instruments used in mourning and at funerals.) Jeremiah says other traditional forms of mourning will be present: shaving the hair and beard and wearing sackcloth (see the note on Job 2:12, page 799). He also mentions the mourning practice of cutting skin. This extreme expression of grief was common in pagan cultures and was forbidden by God (Lev 19:28; Dt 14:1).

37 Every head is shaved[v]
and every beard cut off;
every hand is slashed
and every waist is covered with sackcloth.[w]
38 On all the roofs in Moab
and in the public squares
there is nothing but mourning,
for I have broken Moab
like a jar[x] that no one wants,"
declares the LORD.
39 "How shattered she is! How they wail!
How Moab turns her back in shame!
Moab has become an object of ridicule,
an object of horror to all those around her."

40 This is what the LORD says:

"Look! An eagle is swooping[y] down,
spreading its wings[z] over Moab.
41 Kerioth[a] will be captured
and the strongholds taken.
In that day the hearts of Moab's warriors
will be like the heart of a woman in labor.[a]
42 Moab will be destroyed[b] as a nation[c]
because she defied[d] the LORD.
43 Terror and pit and snare[e] await you,
O people of Moab,"
declares the LORD.
44 "Whoever flees[f] from the terror
will fall into a pit,
whoever climbs out of the pit
will be caught in a snare;
for I will bring upon Moab
the year[g] of her punishment,"
declares the LORD.

45 "In the shadow of Heshbon
the fugitives stand helpless,
for a fire has gone out from Heshbon,
a blaze from the midst of Sihon;[h]
it burns the foreheads of Moab,
the skulls[i] of the noisy boasters.
46 Woe to you, O Moab![j]
The people of Chemosh are destroyed;
your sons are taken into exile
and your daughters into captivity.

47 "Yet I will restore[k] the fortunes of Moab
in days to come,"
declares the LORD.

Here ends the judgment on Moab.

A Message About Ammon

49 Concerning the Ammonites:[l]

This is what the LORD says:

48:37 [v]Isa 15:2; Jer 41:5 [w]Ge 37:34
48:38 [x]Jer 22:28
48:40 [y]Dt 28:49; Hab 1:8 [z]Isa 8:8
48:41 [a]Isa 21:3
48:42 [b]Ps 83:4; Isa 16:14 [c]ver 2 [d]ver 26
48:43 [e]Isa 24:17
48:44 [f]1Ki 19:17; Isa 24:18 [g]Jer 11:23
48:45 [h]Nu 21:21, 26-28 [i]Nu 24:17
48:46 [j]Nu 21:29
48:47 [k]Jer 12:15; 49:6,39
49:1 [l]Am 1:13; Zep 2:8-9

[a] 41 Or *The cities*

"Has Israel no sons?
Has she no heirs?
Why then has Molech[a] taken possession
of Gad?
Why do his people live in its towns?
2 But the days are coming,"
declares the LORD,
"when I will sound the battle cry[m]
against Rabbah[n] of the Ammonites;
it will become a mound of ruins,
and its surrounding villages will be
set on fire.
Then Israel will drive out
those who drove her out,[o]"
says the LORD.

49:2 [m]Jer 4:19 [n]Dt 3:11 [o]Isa 14:2; Eze 21:28-32; 25:2-11

3 "Wail, O Heshbon, for Ai[p] is destroyed!
Cry out, O inhabitants of Rabbah!
Put on sackcloth and mourn;
rush here and there inside the walls,
for Molech will go into exile,[q]
together with his priests and officials.
4 Why do you boast of your valleys,
boast of your valleys so fruitful?
O unfaithful daughter,
you trust in your riches[r] and say,
'Who will attack me?'[s]
5 I will bring terror on you
from all those around you,"
declares the Lord,
the LORD Almighty.
"Every one of you will be driven away,
and no one will gather the fugitives.

49:3 [p]Jos 8:28 [q]Jer 48:7
49:4 [r]Jer 9:23; 1Ti 6:17 [s]Jer 21:13

6 "Yet afterward, I will restore[t] the
fortunes of the Ammonites,"
declares the LORD.

49:6 [t]ver 39; Jer 48:47

A Message About Edom

7 Concerning Edom:[u]

This is what the LORD Almighty says:

"Is there no longer wisdom in Teman?[v]
Has counsel perished from the prudent?
Has their wisdom decayed?
8 Turn and flee, hide in deep caves,
you who live in Dedan,[w]
for I will bring disaster on Esau
at the time I punish him.
9 If grape pickers came to you,
would they not leave a few grapes?
If thieves came during the night,
would they not steal only as much as
they wanted?
10 But I will strip Esau bare;
I will uncover his hiding places,
so that he cannot conceal himself.
His children, relatives and neighbors
will perish,
and he will be no more.[x]

49:7 [u]Ge 25:30; Eze 25:12 [v]Ge 36:11, 15,34
49:8 [w]Jer 25:23
49:10 [x]Mal 1:2-5

[a] *1* Or *their king;* Hebrew *malcam;* also in verse 3

When you decided to become *a* mother, you *gave* your heart permission to forever walk around outside your body.

—Barbara Johnson

God's Care

JER 49:9–11

Hebrew law required grape harvesters to leave behind some produce for widows and orphans (Lev 19:10; Dt 24:21). These poor of the land would come behind the harvesters to "glean" what had been left behind. Ruth is probably the Bible's most memorable gleaner (Ru 2:2). Jeremiah reminds the people of this provision of God for the needy. By contrast, however, God vows to "strip Esau bare" (Jer 49:10), leaving nothing behind. The nation of Ammon will be completely destroyed.

Some view Jeremiah 49:11 as a threat from God. If Edom (another name for the people of Ammon) turns their children over to God, he will do with them as he wills. An interpretation that is more in line with God's character would be to see this verse as an expression of God's compassion for the defenseless.

11 Leave your orphans;[y] I will protect their
lives.
Your widows too can trust in me."

12 This is what the LORD says: "If those who do
not deserve to drink the cup[z] must drink it, why
should you go unpunished?[a] You will not go
unpunished, but must drink it. 13 I swear[b] by
myself," declares the LORD, "that Bozrah[c] will
become a ruin and an object of horror, of reproach
and of cursing; and all its towns will be in ruins
forever."

14 I have heard a message from the LORD:
An envoy was sent to the nations to
say,
"Assemble yourselves to attack it!
Rise up for battle!"

15 "Now I will make you small among the
nations,
despised among men.
16 The terror you inspire
and the pride of your heart have
deceived you,
you who live in the clefts of the rocks,
who occupy the heights of the hill.
Though you build your nest[d] as high as
the eagle's,
from there I will bring you down,"
declares the LORD.
17 "Edom will become an object of horror;[e]
all who pass by will be appalled and
will scoff
because of all its wounds.[f]
18 As Sodom and Gomorrah[g] were
overthrown,
along with their neighboring towns,"
says the LORD,
"so no one will live there;
no man will dwell[h] in it.

19 "Like a lion coming up from Jordan's
thickets[i]
to a rich pastureland,
I will chase Edom from its land in an
instant.
Who is the chosen one I will appoint
for this?
Who is like me and who can challenge
me?[j]
And what shepherd can stand against
me?"
20 Therefore, hear what the LORD has
planned against Edom,
what he has purposed[k] against those
who live in Teman:
The young of the flock[l] will be dragged
away;
he will completely destroy[m] their
pasture because of them.
21 At the sound of their fall the earth will
tremble;[n]

49:11 [y]Hos 14:3
49:12 [z]Jer 25:15 [a]Jer 25:28-29
49:13 [b]Ge 22:16 [c]Ge 36:33; Isa 34:6
49:16 [d]Job 39:27; Am 9:2
49:17 [e]ver 13 [f]Jer 50:13; Eze 35:7
49:18 [g]Ge 19:24; Dt 29:23 [h]ver 33
49:19 [i]Jer 12:5 [j]Jer 50:44
49:20 [k]Isa 14:27 [l]Jer 50:45 [m]Mal 1:3-4
49:21 [n]Eze 26:15

49:21 [o]Jer 50:46; Eze 26:18
49:22 [p]Hos 8:1 [q]Isa 13:8; Jer 48:40-41

their cry[o] will resound to the Red
Sea.[a]
22 Look! An eagle will soar and swoop[p]
down,
spreading its wings over Bozrah.
In that day the hearts of Edom's
warriors
will be like the heart of a woman in
labor.[q]

A Message About Damascus

49:23 [r]Ge 14:15; 2Ch 16:2; Ac 9:2 [s]Isa 10:9; Am 6:2; Zec 9:2 [t]2Ki 18:34 [u]Ge 49:4; Isa 57:20

23 Concerning Damascus:[r]

"Hamath[s] and Arpad[t] are dismayed,
for they have heard bad news.
They are disheartened,
troubled like[b] the restless sea.[u]
24 Damascus has become feeble,
she has turned to flee
and panic has gripped her;
anguish and pain have seized her,
pain like that of a woman in labor.
25 Why has the city of renown not been
abandoned,
the town in which I delight?
26 Surely, her young men will fall in the
streets;
all her soldiers will be silenced[v] in
that day,"
declares the LORD Almighty.
27 "I will set fire[w] to the walls of
Damascus;
it will consume the fortresses of Ben-
Hadad.[x]"

49:26 [v]Jer 50:30
49:27 [w]Jer 43:12; Am 1:4 [x]1Ki 15:18

A Message About Kedar and Hazor

49:28 [y]Ge 25:13 [z]Jdg 6:3

28 Concerning Kedar[y] and the kingdoms of
Hazor, which Nebuchadnezzar king of Babylon
attacked:

This is what the LORD says:

"Arise, and attack Kedar
and destroy the people of the East.[z]
29 Their tents and their flocks will be
taken;
their shelters will be carried off
with all their goods and camels.
Men will shout to them,
'Terror[a] on every side!'

49:29 [a]Jer 6:25; 46:5

30 "Flee quickly away!
Stay in deep caves, you who live in
Hazor,"
declares the LORD.
"Nebuchadnezzar king of Babylon has
plotted against you;
he has devised a plan against you.
31 "Arise and attack a nation at ease,

[a] *21* Hebrew *Yam Suph*; that is, Sea of Reeds [b] *23* Hebrew *on* or *by*

Swooping Eagle

JER 49:22

The Edomites, descendants of Esau, rejoice when Jerusalem falls and they cry, "Tear it down to its foundations!" (Ps 137:7). God notices their gloating and promises to punish them for their arrogance. While Edom may seem like an unimportant nation, Jeremiah 49:21 says that "the earth will tremble" when Edom falls to the swooping eagle.

The eagle metaphor is used often in the Bible, sometimes as a symbol of destruction. Eagles dive down and, with razor-sharp talons, rip apart their prey. Jeremiah 48:40–41 speaks of Nebuchadnezzar as the attacking eagle, and he is probably the same eagle mentioned here. God later punishes Nebuchadnezzar by literally turning him into this feared bird—"his hair grew like the feathers of an eagle and his nails like the claws of a bird" (Da 4:33).

Four Winds

JER 49:36

Elam, an ancient nation descended from Noah's son Shem (Ge 10:22), lies east of Babylon. According to Genesis 14:1-11, Elam was once a powerful kingdom. But Assyria conquers Elam about 640 B.C., and Nebuchadnezzar later defeats it. Susa, Elam's capital, is more than 700 miles from Jerusalem (see Map 8b: Babylonian Empire at the back of this Bible), yet Jeremiah and the exiles keep their eyes on it. Even this nation will not be able to stand against its enemies' onslaught. Like a mighty wind blowing from the four corners of heaven, God will invade Elam. Yet, as promised in Jeremiah 49:39, Elam later rises to power again. Daniel 8:2 records the nation and its capital as the center of the Persian Empire.

which lives in confidence,"
declares the LORD,
"a nation that has neither gates nor
bars;[b] 49:31 [b]Eze 38:11
its people live alone.
32 Their camels will become plunder,
and their large herds will be booty.
I will scatter to the winds those who are
in distant places[a][c] 49:32 [c]Jer 9:26
and will bring disaster on them from
every side,"
declares the LORD.
33 "Hazor will become a haunt of jackals, 49:33
a desolate[d] place forever. [d]Jer 10:22
No one will live there; [e]ver 18; Jer 51:37
no man will dwell[e] in it."

A Message About Elam

34 This is the word of the LORD that came to Jer- 49:34
emiah the prophet concerning Elam,[f] early in the [f]Ge 10:22
reign of Zedekiah[g] king of Judah: [g]2Ki 24:18
35 This is what the LORD Almighty says:

"See, I will break the bow[h] of Elam, 49:35 [h]Isa 22:6
the mainstay of their might.
36 I will bring against Elam the four winds[i] 49:36 [i]ver 32
from the four quarters of the heavens;
I will scatter them to the four winds,
and there will not be a nation
where Elam's exiles do not go.
37 I will shatter Elam before their foes,
before those who seek their lives;
I will bring disaster upon them,
even my fierce anger,"[j] 49:37 [j]Jer 30:24
declares the LORD. [k]Jer 9:16
"I will pursue them with the sword[k]
until I have made an end of them.
38 I will set my throne in Elam
and destroy her king and officials,"
declares the LORD.
39 "Yet I will restore[l] the fortunes of Elam 49:39 [l]Jer 48:47
in days to come,"
declares the LORD.

A Message About Babylon

50 This is the word the LORD spoke through
Jeremiah the prophet concerning Babylon[m] 50:1 [m]Ge 10:10; Isa 13:1
and the land of the Babylonians[b]:

2 "Announce and proclaim[n] among the 50:2 [n]Jer 4:16
nations, [o]Jer 51:31
lift up a banner and proclaim it; [p]Isa 46:1
keep nothing back, but say, [q]Jer 51:47
'Babylon will be captured;[o]
Bel[p] will be put to shame,
Marduk[q] filled with terror.
Her images will be put to shame
and her idols filled with terror.'

[a] 32 Or *who clip the hair by their foreheads*
[b] 1 Or *Chaldeans*; also in verses 8, 25, 35 and 45

[3]A nation from the north will attack her
and lay waste her land.
No one will live[r] in it;
both men and animals[s] will flee away.

[4]"In those days, at that time,"
declares the LORD,
"the people of Israel and the people of Judah together[t]
will go in tears[u] to seek[v] the LORD their God.
[5]They will ask the way to Zion
and turn their faces toward it.
They will come[w] and bind themselves to the LORD
in an everlasting covenant[x]
that will not be forgotten.

[6]"My people have been lost sheep;[y]
their shepherds have led them astray
and caused them to roam on the mountains.
They wandered over mountain and hill[z]
and forgot their own resting place.[a]
[7]Whoever found them devoured them;
their enemies said, 'We are not guilty,[b]
for they sinned against the LORD, their true pasture,
the LORD, the hope[c] of their fathers.'

[8]"Flee[d] out of Babylon;
leave the land of the Babylonians,
and be like the goats that lead the flock.
[9]For I will stir up and bring against Babylon
an alliance of great nations from the land of the north.
They will take up their positions against her,
and from the north she will be captured.
Their arrows will be like skilled warriors
who do not return empty-handed.
[10]So Babylonia[a] will be plundered;
all who plunder her will have their fill,"
declares the LORD.

[11]"Because you rejoice and are glad,
you who pillage my inheritance,[e]
because you frolic like a heifer threshing grain
and neigh like stallions,
[12]your mother will be greatly ashamed;
she who gave you birth will be disgraced.
She will be the least of the nations—
a wilderness, a dry land, a desert.

[a] 10 Or *Chaldea*

50:3 [r]ver 13; Isa 14:22-23 [s]Zep 1:3
50:4 [t]Jer 3:18; Hos 1:11 [u]Ezr 3:12; Jer 31:9 [v]Hos 3:5
50:5 [w]Jer 33:7 [x]Isa 55:3; Jer 32:40; Heb 8:6-10
50:6 [y]Isa 53:6; Mt 9:36; 10:6 [z]Jer 3:6; Eze 34:6 [a]ver 19
50:7 [b]Jer 2:3 [c]Jer 14:8
50:8 [d]Isa 48:20; Jer 51:6; Rev 18:4
50:11 [e]Isa 47:6

Mother of Nations

JER 50:12

Jeremiah predicts the punishment of the heathen nation Babylon. As God's instrument of discipline against Judah and surrounding nations, Babylon must now pay for its own pride, idolatry and rebellion. In 539 B.C. Babylon falls to Cyrus the Persian. Jeremiah describes Babylon as the embarrassed mother of its citizens. The once-proud nation will now be "the least of the nations" (Jer 50:12).

Scripture often metaphorically describes nations as mothers. In Genesis 17:15–16 God promises that the barren Sarai "will be the mother of nations." Ezekiel refers to Israel as a "mother among the lions" (Eze 19:2), and the apostle Paul declares that Jerusalem "is our mother" (Gal 4:26). Perhaps God uses women to symbolize nations because women bring forth children to inhabit and lead the land. No nation can stand without the influence of its women.

13 Because of the LORD's anger she will not
be inhabited
but will be completely desolate.
All who pass Babylon will be horrified
and scoff[f]
because of all her wounds.[g]

14 "Take up your positions around
Babylon,
all you who draw the bow.[h]
Shoot at her! Spare no arrows,
for she has sinned against the LORD.
15 Shout[i] against her on every side!
She surrenders, her towers fall,
her walls[j] are torn down.
Since this is the vengeance[k] of the LORD,
take vengeance on her;
do to her[l] as she has done to others.
16 Cut off from Babylon the sower,
and the reaper with his sickle at
harvest.
Because of the sword[m] of the oppressor
let everyone return to his own
people,[n]
let everyone flee to his own land.[o]

17 "Israel is a scattered flock
that lions[p] have chased away.
The first to devour him
was the king[q] of Assyria;
the last to crush his bones
was Nebuchadnezzar[r] king[s] of
Babylon."

18 Therefore this is what the LORD Almighty, the God of Israel, says:

"I will punish the king of Babylon and
his land
as I punished the king[t] of Assyria.[u]
19 But I will bring[v] Israel back to his own
pasture
and he will graze on Carmel and
Bashan;
his appetite will be satisfied
on the hills[w] of Ephraim and Gilead.
20 In those days, at that time,"
declares the LORD,
"search will be made for Israel's guilt,
but there will be none,
and for the sins[x] of Judah,
but none will be found,
for I will forgive[y] the remnant[z] I
spare.

21 "Attack the land of Merathaim
and those who live in Pekod.[a]
Pursue, kill and completely destroy[a]
them,"
declares the LORD.

50:13 [f]Jer 18:16 [g]Jer 49:17
50:14 [h]ver 29,42
50:15 [i]Jer 51:14 [j]Jer 51:44,58 [k]Jer 51:6 [l]Ps 137:8; Rev 18:6
50:16 [m]Jer 25:38 [n]Isa 13:14 [o]Jer 51:9
50:17 [p]Jer 2:15 [q]2Ki 17:6 [r]2Ki 24:10, 14 [s]2Ki 25:7
50:18 [t]Isa 10:12 [u]Eze 31:3
50:19 [v]Jer 31:10; Eze 34:13 [w]Jer 31:5; 33:12
50:20 [x]Mic 7:18,19 [y]Jer 31:34 [z]Isa 1:9
50:21 [a]Eze 23:23

[a] *21* The Hebrew term refers to the irrevocable giving over of things or persons to the LORD, often by totally destroying them; also in verse 26.

To pray together, in whatever tongue or ritual, is the most tender brotherhood of hope and sympathy that man can contract in this life.

—Madame Anne-Louise-Germaine de Staël (1766–1817)

"Do everything I have commanded
50:22 you.
[b]Jer 4:19-21; 22 The noise[b] of battle is in the land,
51:54 the noise of great destruction!
23 How broken and shattered
50:23 is the hammer of the whole earth!
[c]Isa 14:16 How desolate[c] is Babylon
50:24 among the nations!
[d]Da 5:30-31 24 I set a trap[d] for you, O Babylon,
[e]Jer 51:31 and you were caught before you knew
[f]Job 9:4 it;
you were found and captured[e]
because you opposed[f] the LORD.
25 The LORD has opened his arsenal
50:25
[g]Isa 13:5 and brought out the weapons[g] of his
[h]Jer 51:25,55 wrath,
for the Sovereign LORD Almighty has
work to do
in the land of the Babylonians.[h]
26 Come against her from afar.
Break open her granaries;
50:26 pile her up like heaps of grain.
[i]Isa 14:22-23 Completely destroy[i] her
and leave her no remnant.
27 Kill all her young bulls;
let them go down to the slaughter!
Woe to them! For their day has come,
the time for them to be punished.
28 Listen to the fugitives and refugees from
Babylon
50:28 declaring in Zion[j]
[j]Isa 48:20; how the LORD our God has taken
Jer 51:10
[k]ver 15 vengeance,[k]
vengeance for his temple.

50:29 29 "Summon archers against Babylon,
[l]ver 14 all those who draw the bow.[l]
[m]Rev 18:6 Encamp all around her;
[n]Jer 51:56 let no one escape.
[o]Isa 47:10 Repay[m] her for her deeds;[n]
do to her as she has done.
For she has defied[o] the LORD,
50:30 the Holy One of Israel.
[p]Isa 13:18; 30 Therefore, her young men[p] will fall in
Jer 49:26 the streets;
all her soldiers will be silenced in that
day,"
50:31 declares the LORD.
[q]Jer 21:13 31 "See, I am against[q] you, O arrogant
one,"
declares the Lord, the LORD Almighty,
"for your day has come,
the time for you to be punished.
32 The arrogant one will stumble and fall
50:32 and no one will help her up;
[r]Jer 21:14; I will kindle a fire[r] in her towns
49:27 that will consume all who are around
her."
33 This is what the LORD Almighty says:

50:33
[s]Isa 58:6 "The people of Israel are oppressed,[s]

Draw Your Bows

JER 50:29

Early civilizations relied on a variety of warfare weapons, from axes and daggers to swords and spears. Bows and slings were the long-range weapons of choice. The first archer mentioned in the Bible is Abram's son Ishmael (Ge 21:20). The Assyrians mastered the skill of military archery, and the Babylonians followed with their own bow and arrow commandos. Archery sharpshooters could attack from virtually anywhere—from open fields to narrow rock crevices.

Now God calls for the Persians to give the Babylonians some of their own warfare medicine: "Take up your positions around Babylon, all you who draw the bow. Shoot at her! Spare no arrows, for she has sinned against the LORD" (Jer 50:14). No super power—no matter what its weapons or skills—can defeat God's purposes.

Our Redeemer

JER 50:34

The Babylonians meet their match in Cyrus and mighty Persia. After defeating Babylon, Cyrus allows Judah's exiles to return to their land and rebuild Jerusalem. Yet the Lord Almighty declares himself, not Cyrus, as the people's strong Redeemer.

To redeem means to "buy back" or "set free from distress or harm." God is described as our Redeemer 17 times—all in the Old Testament. Job, in his agony, declares, "I know that my Redeemer lives" (Job 19:25); troubled David, in Psalm 19:14, calls out, "O LORD, my Rock and my Redeemer." The prophet Isaiah proclaims the Lord as Israel's Redeemer 13 times (Isa 41:14; 43:14; 44:6,24; 47:4; 48:17; 49:7,26; 54:5,8; 59:20; 60:16; 63:16). The Redeemer who rescues Israel from the confines of exile is the same Redeemer who frees us from the confines of sin (Tit 2:13–14).

and the people of Judah as well.
All their captors hold them fast,
refusing to let them go.[t]
34 Yet their Redeemer is strong;
the LORD Almighty[u] is his name.
He will vigorously defend their cause[v]
so that he may bring rest[w] to their land,
but unrest to those who live in Babylon.

35 "A sword[x] against the Babylonians!"
declares the LORD—
"against those who live in Babylon
and against her officials and wise[y] men!
36 A sword against her false prophets!
They will become fools.
A sword against her warriors![z]
They will be filled with terror.
37 A sword against her horses and chariots[a]
and all the foreigners in her ranks!
They will become women.[b]
A sword against her treasures!
They will be plundered.
38 A drought on[a] her waters!
They will dry[c] up.
For it is a land of idols,[d]
idols that will go mad with terror.

39 "So desert creatures and hyenas will live there,
and there the owl will dwell.
It will never again be inhabited
or lived in from generation to generation.[e]
40 As God overthrew Sodom and Gomorrah[f]
along with their neighboring towns,"
declares the LORD,
"so no one will live there;
no man will dwell in it.

41 "Look! An army is coming from the north;[g]
a great nation and many kings
are being stirred up from the ends of the earth.[h]
42 They are armed with bows[i] and spears;
they are cruel and without mercy.[j]
They sound like the roaring sea[k]
as they ride on their horses;
they come like men in battle formation
to attack you, O Daughter of Babylon.[l]
43 The king of Babylon has heard reports about them,
and his hands hang limp.
Anguish has gripped him,
pain like that of a woman in labor.

50:33 [t]Isa 14:17
50:34 [u]Jer 51:19 [v]Jer 15:21; 51:36 [w]Isa 14:7
50:35 [x]Jer 47:6 [y]Da 5:7
50:36 [z]Jer 49:22
50:37 [a]Jer 51:21 [b]Jer 51:30; Na 3:13
50:38 [c]Jer 51:36 [d]ver 2
50:39 [e]Isa 13:19-22; 34:13-15; Jer 51:37; Rev 18:2
50:40 [f]Ge 19:24
50:41 [g]Jer 6:22 [h]Isa 13:4; Jer 51:22-28
50:42 [i]ver 14 [j]Isa 13:18 [k]Isa 5:30 [l]Jer 6:23

[a] 38 Or *A sword against*

44 Like a lion coming up from Jordan's
thickets
to a rich pastureland,
I will chase Babylon from its land in an
instant.
Who is the chosen[m] one I will appoint
for this?
Who is like me and who can challenge
me?[n]
And what shepherd can stand against
me?"
45 Therefore, hear what the LORD has
planned against Babylon,
what he has purposed[o] against the
land of the Babylonians:
The young of the flock will be dragged
away;
he will completely destroy their
pasture because of them.
46 At the sound of Babylon's capture the
earth will tremble;
its cry[p] will resound among the
nations.

51

This is what the LORD says:

"See, I will stir up the spirit of a
destroyer
against Babylon and the people of Leb
Kamai.[a]
2 I will send foreigners to Babylon
to winnow[q] her and to devastate her
land;
they will oppose her on every side
in the day of her disaster.
3 Let not the archer string his bow,[r]
nor let him put on his armor.[s]
Do not spare her young men;
completely destroy[b] her army.
4 They will fall[t] down slain in Babylon,[c]
fatally wounded in her streets.[u]
5 For Israel and Judah have not been
forsaken[v]
by their God, the LORD Almighty,
though their land[d] is full of guilt[w]
before the Holy One of Israel.
6 "Flee[x] from Babylon!
Run for your lives!
Do not be destroyed because of her
sins.[y]
It is time for the LORD's vengeance;[z]
he will pay[a] her what she deserves.
7 Babylon was a gold cup[b] in the LORD's
hand;
she made the whole earth drunk.
The nations drank her wine;

50:44 [m]Nu 16:5 [n]Job 41:10; Isa 46:9; Jer 49:19
50:45 [o]Ps 33:11; Isa 14:24; Jer 51:11
50:46 [p]Rev 18:9-10
51:2 [q]Isa 41:16; Jer 15:7; Mt 3:12
51:3 [r]Jer 50:29 [s]Jer 46:4
51:4 [t]Isa 13:15 [u]Jer 49:26; 50:30
51:5 [v]Isa 54:6-8 [w]Hos 4:1
51:6 [x]Jer 50:8 [y]Nu 16:26; Rev 18:4 [z]Jer 50:15 [a]Jer 25:14
51:7 [b]Jer 25:15-16; Rev 14:8-10; 17:4

[a] *1 Leb Kamai* is a cryptogram for Chaldea, that is, Babylonia.
[b] *3* The Hebrew term refers to the irrevocable giving over of things or persons to the LORD, often by totally destroying them.
[c] *4* Or *Chaldea*
[d] *5* Or / *and the land* ⌞*of the Babylonians*⌟

Lion Attack

JER 50:44

Jeremiah prophesies that the Persians, like a silent stalking lion, will pounce on and chase the Babylonians from their land. The lions of Israel stalked the hills and thickets bordering the Jordan River and the people feared them, although many also probably knew the story of mighty Samson, who killed one of these wild beasts in individual combat (Jdg 14:5-6). Near Eastern kings reveled in the sport of lion hunting, and the officials of Persian King Darius punished Daniel by throwing him into a dangerous den of lions (Da 6:16).

The lion is the wild animal mentioned most often in Scripture, probably because it represents power, courage and loyalty. For the same reason:

- *Judah, Gad and Dan (Ge 49:9; Dt 33:20,22) chose the lion as their tribal symbol.*
- *The Egyptians built mammoth sphinxes depicting a lion's body and a king's head.*
- *Finally, the conquering Christ is described as "the Lion of the tribe of Judah" (Rev 5:5).*

Senseless Devotion

JER 51:17

Jeremiah blasts the Babylonians' reliance on their man-made idols. A polytheistic nation, Babylon worshiped their chief god, Marduk, and other gods including Ishtar (the goddess of love and war), Sin (the moon god) and Shemesh (the sun god). Open courts were the sites of sacrificial ceremonies and the burning of incense. An elaborate temple for Marduk towered in Babylon's capital, and the people continually prayed and sacrificed to these idol gods for blessing, protection and forgiveness.

Yet God says these lifeless images "are worthless, the objects of mockery" (Jer 51:18). Sometimes it's easy to think that the things and people we see and touch can offer us more than God does. But it's foolish to devote ourselves to material objects or any path of spirituality beside "the great King above all gods" (Ps 95:3).

therefore they have now gone mad.
8 Babylon will suddenly fall[c] and be broken.
Wail over her!
Get balm[d] for her pain;
perhaps she can be healed.

9 " 'We would have healed Babylon,
but she cannot be healed;
let us leave[e] her and each go to his own land,
for her judgment[f] reaches to the skies,
it rises as high as the clouds.'

10 " 'The LORD has vindicated[g] us;
come, let us tell in Zion
what the LORD our God has done.'[h]

11 "Sharpen the arrows,[i]
take up the shields![j]
The LORD has stirred up the kings of the Medes,[k]
because his purpose[l] is to destroy Babylon.
The LORD will take vengeance,
vengeance for his temple.[m]
12 Lift up a banner against the walls of Babylon!
Reinforce the guard,
station the watchmen,
prepare an ambush!
The LORD will carry out his purpose,
his decree against the people of Babylon.
13 You who live by many waters[n]
and are rich in treasures,[o]
your end has come,
the time for you to be cut off.
14 The LORD Almighty has sworn by himself:[p]
I will surely fill you with men, as with a swarm of locusts,[q]
and they will shout[r] in triumph over you.

15 "He made the earth by his power;
he founded the world by his wisdom
and stretched[s] out the heavens by his understanding.
16 When he thunders,[t] the waters in the heavens roar;
he makes clouds rise from the ends of the earth.
He sends lightning with the rain
and brings out the wind from his storehouses.[u]

17 "Every man is senseless and without knowledge;
every goldsmith is shamed by his idols.
His images are a fraud;[v]
they have no breath in them.

51:8 [c]Isa 21:9; Rev 14:8 [d]Jer 46:11
51:9 [e]Isa 13:14; Jer 50:16 [f]Rev 18:4-5
51:10 [g]Mic 7:9 [h]Jer 50:28
51:11 [i]Jer 50:9 [j]Jer 46:4 [k]ver 28 [l]Jer 50:45 [m]Jer 50:28
51:13 [n]Rev 17:1,15 [o]Isa 45:3; Hab 2:9
51:14 [p]Am 6:8 [q]ver 27; Na 3:15 [r]Jer 50:15
51:15 [s]Ge 1:1; Job 9:8; Ps 104:2
51:16 [t]Ps 18:11-13 [u]Ps 135:7; Jnh 1:4
51:17 [v]Isa 44:20; Hab 2:18-19

51:18 [w]Jer 18:15

18 They are worthless,[w] the objects of
mockery;
when their judgment comes, they will
perish.
19 He who is the Portion of Jacob is not
like these,
for he is the Maker of all things,
including the tribe of his inheritance—
the LORD Almighty is his name.

51:20 [x]Isa 10:5 [y]Mic 4:13

20 "You are my war club,[x]
my weapon for battle—
with you I shatter[y] nations,
with you I destroy kingdoms,

51:21 [z]Ex 15:1

21 with you I shatter horse and rider,[z]
with you I shatter chariot and driver,
22 with you I shatter man and woman,
with you I shatter old man and youth,

51:22 [a]2Ch 36:17; Isa 13:17-18

with you I shatter young man and
maiden,[a]
23 with you I shatter shepherd and flock,
with you I shatter farmer and oxen,
with you I shatter governors and

51:23 [b]ver 57

officials.[b]

51:24 [c]Jer 50:15

24 "Before your eyes I will repay[c] Babylon and
all who live in Babylonia[a] for all the wrong they
have done in Zion," declares the LORD.

25 "I am against you, O destroying
mountain,
you who destroy the whole earth,"
declares the LORD.
"I will stretch out my hand against you,
roll you off the cliffs,
and make you a burned-out

51:25 [d]Zec 4:7

mountain.[d]
26 No rock will be taken from you for a
cornerstone,

51:26 [e]ver 29; Isa 13:19-22; Jer 50:12

nor any stone for a foundation,
for you will be desolate[e] forever,"
declares the LORD.

51:27 [f]Isa 13:2; Jer 50:2 [g]Jer 25:14 [h]Ge 8:4 [i]Ge 10:3

27 "Lift up a banner[f] in the land!
Blow the trumpet among the nations!
Prepare the nations for battle against
her;
summon against her these kingdoms:[g]
Ararat,[h] Minni and Ashkenaz.[i]
Appoint a commander against her;
send up horses like a swarm of
locusts.
28 Prepare the nations for battle against
her—

51:28 [j]ver 11

the kings of the Medes,[j]
their governors and all their officials,
and all the countries they rule.
29 The land trembles and writhes,
for the LORD's purposes against
Babylon stand—
to lay waste the land of Babylon

[a] 24 Or *Chaldea*; also in verse 35

Our Inheritance

JER 51:19

Jeremiah mentions the "Portion of Jacob" twice in his writings (here and in Jer 10:16). Jacob here is synonymous with Israel. The Hebrew word *cheleq,* or *portion,* means "share" or "possession" and has legal inheritance connotations. God is a possession or the inheritance of his people.

The Levites have no inheritance among the other tribes. Instead, Deuteronomy 10:9 says, "The LORD is their inheritance." The psalmist declares, "You are my portion, O LORD" (Ps 119:57) and "my portion forever" (Ps 73:26). As our inheritance, God is our provider and life-source. He adopts us into his kingdom and makes us his royal heirs (Gal 4:7).

But God is not just our portion or inheritance, we are also his possession, his inheritance. "For the LORD's portion is his people," says Deuteronomy 32:9. The Father appointed his Son the "heir of all things" (Heb 1:2)—and that includes us!

so that no one will live there.[k]
[30]Babylon's warriors[l] have stopped
fighting;
they remain in their strongholds.
Their strength is exhausted;
they have become like women.[m]
Her dwellings are set on fire;
the bars[n] of her gates are broken.
[31]One courier[o] follows another
and messenger follows messenger
to announce to the king of Babylon
that his entire city is captured,
[32]the river crossings seized,
the marshes set on fire,
and the soldiers terrified.[p]"

[33]This is what the LORD Almighty, the God of
Israel, says:

"The Daughter of Babylon is like a
threshing floor[q]
at the time it is trampled;
the time to harvest[r] her will soon
come."

[34]"Nebuchadnezzar[s] king of Babylon has
devoured us,
he has thrown us into confusion,
he has made us an empty jar.
Like a serpent he has swallowed us
and filled his stomach with our
delicacies,
and then has spewed us out.
[35]May the violence done to our flesh[a] be
upon Babylon,"
say the inhabitants of Zion.
"May our blood be on those who live in
Babylonia,"
says Jerusalem.[t]

[36]Therefore, this is what the LORD says:

"See, I will defend your cause[u]
and avenge[v] you;
I will dry up[w] her sea
and make her springs dry.
[37]Babylon will be a heap of ruins,
a haunt[x] of jackals,
an object of horror and scorn,
a place where no one lives.[y]
[38]Her people all roar like young lions,
they growl like lion cubs.
[39]But while they are aroused,
I will set out a feast for them
and make them drunk,
so that they shout with laughter—
then sleep forever and not awake,"
declares the LORD.[z]
[40]"I will bring them down
like lambs to the slaughter,
like rams and goats.

51:29 [k]ver 43; Isa 13:20
51:30 [l]Jer 50:36 [m]Isa 19:16 [n]Isa 45:2; La 2:9; Na 3:13
51:31 [o]2Sa 18:19-31
51:32 [p]Jer 50:36
51:33 [q]Isa 21:10 [r]Isa 17:5; Hos 6:11
51:34 [s]Jer 50:17
51:35 [t]ver 24; Ps 137:8
51:36 [u]Ps 140:12; Jer 50:34; La 3:58 [v]ver 6; Ro 12:19 [w]Jer 50:38
51:37 [x]Isa 13:22; Rev 18:2 [y]Jer 50:13, 39
51:39 [z]ver 57

[a] 35 Or *done to us and to our children*

***I** know that, as a human being, I am made in the image of God. That truth is like a river that steers me through my life. Because of the sacrifice of Christ, I am forgiven for my sins and restored to fellowship with God. This covenant engraved into the hand of God is secure; it is eternal. As a child of God and a member of the body of Christ, I belong with the fellowship of believers. We are family forever.*

People were made for community. While it is wonderful to have a home to love, a place of peace, we often use that place of rest as a place to hide, to isolate ourselves from one another. But homes are not eternal. Relationships are the only things that have eternity written all over them. We need to "find ourselves" in Christ and in relationship with one another. It is in relationship that we see our strengths and our weaknesses and find the courage to change.

—Sheila Walsh

51:41 [a]Jer 25:26 [b]Isa 13:19

41 "How Sheshach[a][a] will be captured,[b]
the boast of the whole earth seized!
What a horror Babylon will be
among the nations!

51:42 [c]Isa 8:7

42 The sea will rise over Babylon;
its roaring waves[c] will cover her.

51:43 [d]ver 29,62; Isa 13:20; Jer 2:6

43 Her towns will be desolate,
a dry and desert land,
a land where no one lives,
through which no man travels.[d]

51:44 [e]Isa 46:1 [f]ver 34 [g]ver 58; Jer 50:15

44 I will punish Bel[e] in Babylon
and make him spew out[f] what he has
swallowed.
The nations will no longer stream to
him.
And the wall[g] of Babylon will fall.

51:45 [h]Rev 18:4 [i]ver 6; Isa 48:20; Jer 50:8

45 "Come out[h] of her, my people!
Run[i] for your lives!
Run from the fierce anger of the LORD.

51:46 [j]Jer 46:27 [k]2Ki 19:7

46 Do not lose heart or be afraid[j]
when rumors[k] are heard in the land;
one rumor comes this year, another the
next,
rumors of violence in the land
and of ruler against ruler.

51:47 [l]ver 52; Isa 46:1-2; Jer 50:2 [m]Jer 50:12

47 For the time will surely come
when I will punish the idols[l] of
Babylon;
her whole land will be disgraced[m]
and her slain will all lie fallen within
her.

51:48 [n]Isa 44:23; Rev 18:20 [o]ver 11

48 Then heaven and earth and all that is in
them
will shout[n] for joy over Babylon,
for out of the north[o]
destroyers will attack her,"
declares the LORD.

51:49 [p]Ps 137:8; Jer 50:29

49 "Babylon must fall because of Israel's
slain,
just as the slain in all the earth
have fallen because of Babylon.[p]

51:50 [q]ver 45 [r]Ps 137:6

50 You who have escaped the sword,
leave[q] and do not linger!
Remember[r] the LORD in a distant land,
and think on Jerusalem."

51:51 [s]Ps 44:13-16; 79:4 [t]La 1:10

51 "We are disgraced,[s]
for we have been insulted
and shame covers our faces,
because foreigners have entered
the holy places of the LORD's house."[t]

51:52 [u]ver 47

52 "But days are coming," declares the
LORD,
"when I will punish her idols,[u]
and throughout her land
the wounded will groan.

51:53 [v]Ge 11:4; Isa 14:13-14

53 Even if Babylon reaches the sky[v]
and fortifies her lofty stronghold,

[a] 41 *Sheshach* is a cryptogram for Babylon.

Raised a Quaker and involved in charitable work throughout her life, Anna Laetitia Waring wrote numerous hymns.

In Heavenly Love Abiding

In heavenly love abiding, no change
my heart shall fear.
And safe in such confiding, for
nothing changes here.
The storm may roar without me, my
heart may low be laid,
But God is round about me, and can
I be dismayed?

Wherever He may guide me, no
want shall turn me back.
My Shepherd is beside me, and
nothing can I lack.
His wisdom ever waking, His sight
is never dim.
He knows the way He's taking, and
I will walk with Him.

Green pastures are before me, which
yet I have not seen.
Bright skies will soon be over me,
where darkest clouds have been.
My hope I cannot measure, my path
to life is free.
My Savior has my treasure, and He
will walk with me.

—*Anna Laetitia Waring* (1823-1910)

A Ruined Nation

JER 51:64

The Babylonian Empire reached its height of glory under Nebuchadnezzar, who turned the city of Babylon into the most magnificent capital of his time. Beautiful hanging gardens and grand architecture filled this expansive city of about 200 square miles. But the political dominance of Babylon ended with the Persian invasion in 539 B.C. Belshazzar served as the last king of Babylon (Da 5), and Babylon's final revolt against Darius in 514 B.C. only hastened its destruction. Subsequent conquerors, including the Greeks, the Romans and the Parthians, ruled a weakened Babylon, which Jeremiah said would "rise no more" (Jer 51:64).

In Jeremiah 51:37 Jeremiah prophesies that Babylon "will be a heap of ruins . . . a place where no one lives." Today the city exists only as three ancient archaeological mounds. The once famed nation is now an unproductive wasteland.

I will send destroyers[w] against her,"
declares the LORD.

54 "The sound of a cry comes from
Babylon,
the sound of great destruction[x]
from the land of the Babylonians.[a]
55 The LORD will destroy Babylon;
he will silence her noisy din.
Waves[y] ⌞of enemies⌟ will rage like great
waters;
the roar of their voices will resound.
56 A destroyer[z] will come against Babylon;
her warriors will be captured,
and their bows will be broken.[a]
For the LORD is a God of retribution;
he will repay[b] in full.
57 I will make her officials and wise men
drunk,
her governors, officers and warriors as
well;
they will sleep[c] forever and not awake,"
declares the King,[d] whose name is the
LORD Almighty.

58 This is what the LORD Almighty says:

"Babylon's thick wall[e] will be leveled
and her high gates set on fire;
the peoples[f] exhaust themselves for
nothing,
the nations' labor is only fuel for the
flames."[g]

59 This is the message Jeremiah gave to the staff
officer Seraiah son of Neriah,[h] the son of Mahse-
iah, when he went to Babylon with Zedekiah[i]
king of Judah in the fourth[j] year of his reign.
60 Jeremiah had written on a scroll[k] about all the
disasters that would come upon Babylon—all that
had been recorded concerning Babylon. 61 He said
to Seraiah, "When you get to Babylon, see that
you read all these words aloud. 62 Then say,
'O LORD, you have said you will destroy this place,
so that neither man nor animal will live in it; it
will be desolate[l] forever.' 63 When you finish reading this scroll, tie a stone to it and throw it into
the Euphrates. 64 Then say, 'So will Babylon sink to
rise no more because of the disaster I will bring
upon her. And her people[m] will fall.' "

The words of Jeremiah end[n] here.

The Fall of Jerusalem

52 Zedekiah[o] was twenty-one years old when
he became king, and he reigned in Jerusalem eleven years. His mother's name was Hamutal daughter of Jeremiah; she was from Libnah.[p]
2 He did evil in the eyes of the LORD, just as
Jehoiakim[q] had done. 3 It was because of the
LORD's anger that all this happened to Jerusalem

51:53 [w]Jer 49:16
51:54 [x]Jer 50:22
51:55 [y]Ps 18:4
51:56 [z]ver 48 [a]Ps 46:9 [b]ver 6; Ps 94:1-2; Hab 2:8
51:57 [c]Ps 76:5; Jer 25:27 [d]Jer 46:18; 48:15
51:58 [e]ver 44 [f]ver 64 [g]Hab 2:13
51:59 [h]Jer 36:4 [i]Jer 52:1 [j]Jer 28:1
51:60 [k]Jer 30:2; 36:2
51:62 [l]Isa 13:20; Jer 50:13,39
51:64 [m]ver 58 [n]Job 31:40
52:1 [o]2Ki 24:17 [p]Jos 10:29; 2Ki 8:22
52:2 [q]Jer 36:30

[a] 54 Or *Chaldeans*

52:3 and Judah,[r] and in the end he thrust them from
[r]Isa 3:1 his presence.
[s]Eze 17:12-16 Now Zedekiah rebelled[s] against the king of
Babylon.
52:4 4So in the ninth year of Zedekiah's reign, on the
[t]Zec 8:19 tenth[t] day of the tenth month, Nebuchadnezzar
[u]2Ki 25:1-7; Jer 39:1 king of Babylon marched against Jerusalem[u] with
[v]Eze 24:1-2 his whole army. They camped outside the city and
built siege works all around it.[v] 5The city was kept
under siege until the eleventh year of King
Zedekiah.
6By the ninth day of the fourth month the
famine in the city had become so severe that there
52:6 was no food for the people to eat.[w] 7Then the city
[w]Isa 3:1 wall was broken through, and the whole army
fled. They left the city at night through the gate
between the two walls near the king's garden,
though the Babylonians[a] were surrounding the
city. They fled toward the Arabah,[b] 8but the Babylonian[c] army pursued King Zedekiah and overtook him in the plains of Jericho. All his soldiers
52:9 were separated from him and scattered, 9and he
[x]Jer 32:4 was captured.[x]
[y]Nu 34:11 He was taken to the king of Babylon at Riblah[y]
[z]Nu 13:21 in the land of Hamath,[z] where he pronounced sen-
52:10 tence on him. 10There at Riblah the king of Bab-
[a]Jer 22:30 ylon slaughtered the sons[a] of Zedekiah before his
eyes; he also killed all the officials of Judah. 11Then
he put out Zedekiah's eyes, bound him with
bronze shackles and took him to Babylon, where
52:11 [b]Eze 12:13 he put him in prison till the day of his death.[b]
12On the tenth day of the fifth[c] month, in the
52:12 nineteenth year of Nebuchadnezzar king of Bab-
[c]Zec 7:5; 8:19 ylon, Nebuzaradan[d] commander of the imperial
[d]Jer 39:9 guard, who served the king of Babylon, came to
52:13 Jerusalem. 13He set fire[e] to the temple[f] of the LORD,
[e]2Ch 36:19; the royal palace and all the houses of Jerusalem.
Ps 74:8; La 2:6 Every important building he burned down. 14The
[f]Ps 79:1; Mic 3:12 whole Babylonian army under the commander of
the imperial guard broke down all the walls[g]
52:14 around Jerusalem. 15Nebuzaradan the commander
[g]Ne 1:3 of the guard carried into exile some of the poorest
people and those who remained in the city, along
with the rest of the craftsmen[d] and those who had
gone over to the king of Babylon. 16But Neb-
52:16 [h]Jer 40:6 uzaradan left behind[h] the rest of the poorest people
of the land to work the vineyards and fields.
52:17 17The Babylonians broke up the bronze pillars,[i]
[i]1Ki 7:15 [j]1Ki 7:27-37 the movable stands[j] and the bronze Sea[k] that were
[k]1Ki 7:23 at the temple of the LORD and they carried all the
[l]Jer 27:19-22 bronze to Babylon.[l] 18They also took away the
pots, shovels, wick trimmers, sprinkling bowls,
dishes and all the bronze articles used in the tem-
52:18 ple service.[m] 19The commander of the imperial
[m]Ex 27:3; 1Ki 7:45 guard took away the basins, censers,[n] sprinkling
52:19 bowls, pots, lampstands, dishes and bowls used
[n]1Ki 7:50 for drink offerings—all that were made of pure
gold or silver.

[a] *7* Or *Chaldeans*; also in verse 17 [b] *7* Or *the Jordan Valley*
[c] *8* Or *Chaldean*; also in verse 14 [d] *15* Or *populace*

Keeping His Word

JER 52

Jeremiah 52 is a historical appendix to the book of Jeremiah and essentially repeats* 2 Kings 24:18—25:30. *Information that is not included in* 2 Kings *is given in* Jeremiah 40-43. *Some think this final chapter was added to Jeremiah's writings, but this possibility does not discredit Jeremiah's authorship of the major portion of the book* (Jer 1:1; 51:64). *The appendix reveals that Jerusalem's destruction and the Babylonian captivity did take place as Jeremiah had faithfully prophesied.

***Knowing that God keeps and fulfills his word can encourage us to hold on to his truths, especially when we face opposition and doubts. God says, "My word that goes out from my mouth: It will not return to me empty, but will accomplish what I desire and achieve the purpose for which I sent it"* (Isa 55:11).**

Head Count

JER 52:30

Three deportations of Judah are listed in this passage. The first is during Nebuchadnezzar's seventh year (or eighth year as described in 2Ki 24:12–16). The one-year discrepancy between Jeremiah and 2 Kings emerges from the differences between the Hebrew and Babylonian dating systems. The 2 Kings passage says that 18,000 are taken from Jerusalem, while Jeremiah lists only 3,023. Some believe Jeremiah only reported how many survived the journey to Babylon or that Jeremiah did not include women and children in his count (Mt 14:21).

The second wave of exiles departs in Nebuchadnezzar's 18th or 19th year when Jerusalem is destroyed (2Ki 25:8–9). The final deportation is not mentioned anywhere else. This attack is probably in retaliation for Gedaliah's assassination (Jer 41:2). But as Jeremiah foretells (Jer 25:11), God is faithful to his people and ends the exile 70 years later.

20The bronze from the two pillars, the Sea and
the twelve bronze bulls under it, and the movable
stands, which King Solomon had made for the
temple of the LORD, was more than could be
weighed.[o] 21Each of the pillars was eighteen cubits 52:20
high and twelve cubits in circumference[a]; each [o]1Ki 7:47
was four fingers thick, and hollow.[p] 22The bronze 52:21
capital[q] on top of the one pillar was five cubits[b] [p]1Ki 7:15
high and was decorated with a network and 52:22
pomegranates of bronze all around. The other pil- [q]1Ki 7:16
lar, with its pomegranates, was similar. 23There
were ninety-six pomegranates on the sides; the 52:23
total number of pomegranates[r] above the sur- [r]1Ki 7:20
rounding network was a hundred.

24The commander of the guard took as prison- 52:24
ers Seraiah[s] the chief priest, Zephaniah[t] the priest [s]2Ki 25:18
next in rank and the three doorkeepers. 25Of those [t]Jer 21:1;
still in the city, he took the officer in charge of the 37:3
fighting men, and seven royal advisers. He also
took the secretary who was chief officer in charge
of conscripting the people of the land and sixty of
his men who were found in the city. 26Nebuzar- 52:26
adan[u] the commander took them all and brought [u]ver 12
them to the king of Babylon at Riblah. 27There at
Riblah, in the land of Hamath, the king had them
executed.

So Judah went into captivity, away[v] from her 52:27
land. 28This is the number of the people Nebu- [v]Jer 20:4
chadnezzar carried into exile:[w] 52:28

in the seventh year, 3,023 Jews; [w]2Ki 24:14-16;
29 in Nebuchadnezzar's eighteenth year, 2Ch 36:20
832 people from Jerusalem;
30 in his twenty-third year,
745 Jews taken into exile by Nebuzaradan
the commander of the imperial guard.
There were 4,600 people in all.

Jehoiachin Released

31In the thirty-seventh year of the exile of Jehoiachin king of Judah, in the year Evil-Merodach[c]
became king of Babylon, he released Jehoiachin
king of Judah and freed him from prison on the
twenty-fifth day of the twelfth month. 32He spoke
kindly to him and gave him a seat of honor higher than those of the other kings who were with
him in Babylon. 33So Jehoiachin put aside his
prison clothes and for the rest of his life ate regu- 52:33
larly at the king's table.[x] 34Day by day the king of [x]2Sa 9:7
Babylon gave Jehoiachin a regular allowance[y] as 52:34
long as he lived, till the day of his death. [y]2Sa 9:10

[a] *21* That is, about 27 feet (about 8.1 meters) high and 18 feet (about 5.4 meters) in circumference [b] *22* That is, about 7 1/2 feet (about 2.3 meters) [c] *31* Also called *Amel-Marduk*

Lamentations

Weeping for a lost city.

The book of Lamentations is Jeremiah's eyewitness account of the disaster that befalls Jerusalem when the city is invaded by the Babylonian army. Jeremiah had predicted the devastation of his homeland, and he writes this funeral poem to express his grief. Masterfully written, each verse in each chapter begins with a successive letter of the Hebrew alphabet. The book of Lamentations is a vivid reminder that God keeps his promises—even the promises of judgment and destruction.

Lamentations likens the city of Jerusalem to a woman who was once a princess and is now a slave; once a woman full of many children, now a widow, bereft and alone (La 1). She wears rough clothing and is slowly starving to death (La 2). Her children fall prey to sickness and cannibalism (La 4). The city is in ruins.

Yet embedded in the middle of this small book is a jewel of hope for the ruined city and for the devastated nation. Because of God's character there are new mercies with every sunrise, justice in all of his judgments, and full grace and love available to all those who seek his forgiveness (La 3). Jeremiah ends his lament with the reminder that only God can restore what has been shattered (La 5). Even as Jeremiah expresses his terrible grief over the destruction he's seen, he also expresses his hope for restoration. His lesson can be ours. When we face tremendous loss, when life overwhelms us, there is One we can trust to restore. Jeremiah's God is our God: a God of grace as well as judgment.

Quick Study

Author
Anonymous, but probably Jeremiah.

Date Written
Sometime between Jerusalem's destruction and restoration, between 586 and 516 B.C.

Setting
Judah.

Key Passage
Lamentations 3:22–23
"Because of the LORD's
great love we are not
consumed,
for his compassions
never fail.
They are new every
morning;
great is your
faithfulness."

Outline

Mourning Jerusalem.
La 1

God's anger with his people.
La 2

Judah's complaint and God's consolation.
La 3

Zion's past and present.
La 4

Repentance and forgiveness.
La 5

The Women of Lamentations

Maidens	*Overwhelmed by grief.* La 1:4,18
Young women of Jerusalem	*Heads bowed in grief.* La 2:10
Mothers	*Their children starve in their arms.* La 2:12
Young maidens	*They lie dead in the dust of the streets.* La 2:21
Compassionate women	*But they commit desperate acts.* La 2:20; 4:10
Women and virgins	*Both are raped.* La 5:11

1:1 [a]Isa 47:8 [b]1Ki 4:21 [c]Isa 3:26; Jer 40:9

1[a]

How deserted lies the city,
once so full of people!
How like a widow[a] is she,
who once was great[b] among the nations!
She who was queen among the provinces
has now become a slave.[c]

1:2 [d]Ps 6:6 [e]Jer 3:1 [f]Jer 4:30; Mic 7:5 [g]ver 16

2 Bitterly she weeps[d] at night,
tears are upon her cheeks.
Among all her lovers[e]
there is none to comfort her.
All her friends have betrayed[f] her;
they have become her enemies.[g]

1:3 [h]Jer 13:19 [i]Dt 28:65

3 After affliction and harsh labor,
Judah has gone into exile.[h]
She dwells among the nations;
she finds no resting place.[i]
All who pursue her have overtaken her
in the midst of her distress.

1:4 [j]Jer 9:11 [k]Joel 1:8-13

4 The roads to Zion mourn,
for no one comes to her appointed feasts.
All her gateways are desolate,[j]
her priests groan,
her maidens grieve,
and she is in bitter anguish.[k]

1:5 [l]Jer 30:15 [m]Jer 39:9; 52:28-30

5 Her foes have become her masters;
her enemies are at ease.
The LORD has brought her grief[l]
because of her many sins.
Her children have gone into exile,[m]
captive before the foe.

1:6 [n]Jer 13:18

6 All the splendor has departed
from the Daughter of Zion.[n]
Her princes are like deer
that find no pasture;
in weakness they have fled
before the pursuer.

1:7 [o]Jer 37:7; La 4:17

7 In the days of her affliction and wandering
Jerusalem remembers all the treasures
that were hers in days of old.
When her people fell into enemy hands,
there was no one to help her.[o]
Her enemies looked at her
and laughed at her destruction.

1:8 [p]ver 20; Isa 59:2-13 [q]Jer 13:22, 26 [r]ver 21,22

8 Jerusalem has sinned[p] greatly
and so has become unclean.
All who honored her despise her,
for they have seen her nakedness;[q]
she herself groans[r]
and turns away.

9 Her filthiness clung to her skirts;

[a] This chapter is an acrostic poem, the verses of which begin with the successive letters of the Hebrew alphabet.

God can take your trouble and change it into treasure. Your sorrow can become joy—not just a momentary smile but a deep, new joy. It will be a bubbling experience of new hope that puts a brightness in your eyes and a song in your heart.

In the midst of the darkness you will learn lessons you might never have learned in the day. We all have seen dreams turn to ashes—ugly things, hopeless experiences—but beauty for ashes is God's exchange. Offer yourself to God and ask for a spirit of praise so your whole being will be restored.

—Barbara Johnson

Mourning Jerusalem

LA 1:9

In the first of five sorrowful poems (laments), the writer of Lamentations mourns the destruction of Jerusalem. After an 18-month siege, Jerusalem falls to King Nebuchadnezzar of Babylon in 586 B.C. Nebuchadnezzar's army wrecks the temple, desecrates the Most Holy Place, murders young and old and drags the survivors to Babylon. Jerusalem, once the capital of a strong nation known for its ability to capture surrounding nations and gain respect, is now the captive.

The writer personifies Jerusalem as a woman who dirties her own skirts by her willful sin (La 1:9). She does not think beyond the moment's sinful pleasure to what her rebellious behavior will mean to her sons and daughters. She plunges from the mountaintop of power and respect into the gutter of despair and humiliation, finding no one to console her there. However, she realizes that her humiliating dilemma results from her own bad choices, and she cries, "O Lord, see me here."

she did not consider her future.[s]
Her fall[t] was astounding;
there was none to comfort[u] her.
"Look, O LORD, on my affliction,[v]
for the enemy has triumphed."

10 The enemy laid hands
on all her treasures;[w]
she saw pagan nations
enter her sanctuary[x]—
those you had forbidden[y]
to enter your assembly.

11 All her people groan[z]
as they search for bread;[a]
they barter their treasures for food
to keep themselves alive.
"Look, O LORD, and consider,
for I am despised."

12 "Is it nothing to you, all you who pass by?[b]
Look around and see.
Is any suffering like my suffering[c]
that was inflicted on me,
that the LORD brought on me
in the day of his fierce anger?[d]

13 "From on high he sent fire,
sent it down into my bones.[e]
He spread a net for my feet
and turned me back.
He made me desolate,[f]
faint[g] all the day long.

14 "My sins have been bound into a yoke[a];[h]
by his hands they were woven together.
They have come upon my neck
and the Lord has sapped my strength.
He has handed me over[i]
to those I cannot withstand.

15 "The Lord has rejected
all the warriors in my midst;[j]
he has summoned an army[k] against me
to[b] crush my young men.[l]
In his winepress the Lord has trampled
the Virgin Daughter of Judah.

16 "This is why I weep
and my eyes overflow with tears.[m]
No one is near to comfort[n] me,
no one to restore my spirit.
My children are destitute
because the enemy has prevailed."[o]

17 Zion stretches out her hands,[p]
but there is no one to comfort her.
The LORD has decreed for Jacob
that his neighbors become his foes;

1:9 [s]Dt 32:28-29; Isa 47:7; Eze 24:13 [t]Jer 13:18 [u]Ecc 4:1; Jer 16:7 [v]Ps 25:18
1:10 [w]Isa 64:11 [x]Ps 74:7-8; Jer 51:51 [y]Dt 23:3
1:11 [z]Ps 38:8 [a]Jer 52:6
1:12 [b]Jer 18:16 [c]ver 18 [d]Isa 13:13; Jer 30:24
1:13 [e]Job 30:30 [f]Jer 44:6 [g]Hab 3:16
1:14 [h]Dt 28:48; Isa 47:6 [i]Jer 32:5
1:15 [j]Jer 37:10 [k]Isa 41:2 [l]Isa 28:18; Jer 18:21
1:16 [m]La 2:11,18; 3:48-49 [n]Ps 69:20; Ecc 4:1 [o]ver 2; Jer 13:17; 14:17
1:17 [p]Jer 4:31

[a] 14 Most Hebrew manuscripts; Septuagint *He kept watch over my sins* [b] 15 Or *has set a time for me / when he will*

Jerusalem has become
an unclean thing among them.

1:18 [q]1Sa 12:14 [r]ver 12 [s]Dt 28:32,41

18 "The LORD is righteous,
yet I rebelled[q] against his command.
Listen, all you peoples;
look upon my suffering.[r]
My young men and maidens
have gone into exile.[s]

1:19 [t]Jer 14:15; La 2:20

19 "I called to my allies
but they betrayed me.
My priests and my elders
perished[t] in the city
while they searched for food
to keep themselves alive.

1:20 [u]Jer 4:19 [v]La 2:11 [w]Dt 32:25; Eze 7:15

20 "See, O LORD, how distressed[u] I am!
I am in torment[v] within,
and in my heart I am disturbed,
for I have been most rebellious.
Outside, the sword bereaves;
inside, there is only death.[w]

1:21 [x]ver 8 [y]ver 4 [z]La 2:15 [a]Isa 47:11; Jer 30:16

21 "People have heard my groaning,[x]
but there is no one to comfort me.[y]
All my enemies have heard of my distress;
they rejoice[z] at what you have done.
May you bring the day[a] you have announced
so they may become like me.

1:22 [b]Ne 4:5

22 "Let all their wickedness come before you;
deal with them
as you have dealt with me
because of all my sins.[b]
My groans are many
and my heart is faint."

2:1 [c]La 3:44 [d]Ps 99:5; 132:7

2[a] How the Lord has covered the Daughter of Zion
with the cloud of his anger[b]![c]
He has hurled down the splendor of Israel
from heaven to earth;
he has not remembered his footstool[d]
in the day of his anger.

2:2 [e]La 3:43 [f]Ps 21:9 [g]Ps 89:39-40; Mic 5:11 [h]Isa 25:12

2 Without pity[e] the Lord has swallowed[f] up
all the dwellings of Jacob;
in his wrath he has torn down
the strongholds[g] of the Daughter of Judah.
He has brought her kingdom and its princes
down to the ground[h] in dishonor.

[a] This chapter is an acrostic poem, the verses of which begin with the successive letters of the Hebrew alphabet. [b] *1* Or *How the Lord in his anger / has treated the Daughter of Zion with contempt*

Daughter of Zion

LA 2:1-2

The phrase "Daughter of Zion" is used eight times in Lamentations and "Daughter of Judah," three times. These phrases are essentially the same thing: a personification of Jerusalem and its residents.

Zion is another name for the Jebusite area that King David conquered at the beginning of his reign (1Ch 11:4–5). Although Zion proper was originally only the southeast hill of Jerusalem, eventually it expanded to include the temple and then all of Jerusalem. Over the centuries Zion has been applied figuratively to the nation of Judah and "all Israel." In the Old Testament, Zion had religious overtones, highlighting Jerusalem as the city of God and the Israelites as God's people.

In the New Testament the spiritual significance of Zion expanded to include God's people of all nations and ages (Heb 12:22–23; 1Pe 2:4–6). Zion now refers to the new Jerusalem, where the Messiah will appear and reign at the end of time (Rev 14:1).

A Measuring Line

LA 2:8

A measuring line is a cord of a specific length used for calculating the exact dimensions necessary for building specifications. In Lamentations 2:8 the "measuring line" is a metaphor for God's exacting criteria used in implementing punishment on Jerusalem for disobeying him. The Israelites sin against God and then return to him many times. Eventually, however, they remain unrepentant, and God's justice cannot allow their sin and rebellion to go unpunished.

God is consistent about his "measuring line" of righteousness and justice. He gives the Israelites specific rules that protect them and help them know how to live. When they follow these guidelines, their relationship with God flourishes. But when they ignore his loving boundaries, they pay the consequences of his "stretched out . . . measuring line."

3 In fierce anger he has cut off
every horn[a][i] of Israel.
He has withdrawn his right hand[j]
at the approach of the enemy.
He has burned in Jacob like a flaming fire
that consumes everything around it.[k]

4 Like an enemy he has strung his bow;[l]
his right hand is ready.
Like a foe he has slain
all who were pleasing to the eye;[m]
he has poured out his wrath like fire[n]
on the tent of the Daughter of Zion.

5 The Lord is like an enemy;[o]
he has swallowed up Israel.
He has swallowed up all her palaces
and destroyed her strongholds.[p]
He has multiplied mourning and lamentation
for the Daughter of Judah.[q]

6 He has laid waste his dwelling like a garden;
he has destroyed his place of meeting.[r]
The LORD has made Zion forget
her appointed feasts and her Sabbaths;[s]
in his fierce anger he has spurned
both king and priest.[t]

7 The Lord has rejected his altar
and abandoned his sanctuary.
He has handed over to the enemy
the walls of her palaces;[u]
they have raised a shout in the house of the LORD
as on the day of an appointed feast.

8 The LORD determined to tear down
the wall around the Daughter of Zion.
He stretched out a measuring line[v]
and did not withhold his hand from destroying.
He made ramparts and walls lament;
together they wasted away.[w]

9 Her gates[x] have sunk into the ground;
their bars he has broken and destroyed.
Her king and her princes are exiled[y]
among the nations,
the law[z] is no more,
and her prophets no longer find
visions[a] from the LORD.

10 The elders of the Daughter of Zion
sit on the ground in silence;
they have sprinkled dust on their heads[b]
and put on sackcloth.[c]
The young women of Jerusalem
have bowed their heads to the ground.[d]

2:3 [i]Ps 75:5,10 [j]Ps 74:11 [k]Isa 42:25; Jer 21:4-5,14
2:4 [l]Job 16:13; La 3:12-13 [m]Eze 24:16, 25 [n]Isa 42:25; Jer 7:20
2:5 [o]Jer 30:14 [p]ver 2 [q]Jer 9:17-20
2:6 [r]Jer 52:13 [s]La 1:4; Zep 3:18 [t]La 4:16
2:7 [u]Ps 74:7-8; Isa 64:11; Jer 33:4-5
2:8 [v]2Ki 21:13; Isa 34:11 [w]Isa 3:26
2:9 [x]Ne 1:3 [y]Dt 28:36; 2Ki 24:15 [z]2Ch 15:3 [a]Jer 14:14
2:10 [b]Job 2:12 [c]Isa 15:3 [d]Job 2:13; Isa 3:26

[a] 3 Or / *all the strength*; or *every king*; *horn* here symbolizes strength.

2:11 [e]La 1:16; 3:48-51 [f]La 1:20 [g]ver 19; Ps 22:14 [h]La 4:4

11 My eyes fail from weeping,[e]
I am in torment within,[f]
my heart is poured out[g] on the ground
because my people are destroyed,
because children and infants faint[h]
in the streets of the city.

2:12 [i]La 4:4

12 They say to their mothers,
"Where is bread and wine?"
as they faint like wounded men
in the streets of the city,
as their lives ebb away
in their mothers' arms.[i]

2:13 [j]Isa 37:22 [k]Jer 14:17; La 1:12

13 What can I say for you?
With what can I compare you,
O Daughter of Jerusalem?
To what can I liken you,
that I may comfort you,
O Virgin Daughter of Zion?[j]
Your wound is as deep as the sea.[k]
Who can heal you?

2:14 [l]Isa 58:1 [m]Jer 2:8; 23:25-32,33-40; 29:9; Eze 13:3; 22:28

14 The visions of your prophets
were false and worthless;
they did not expose your sin
to ward off your captivity.[l]
The oracles they gave you
were false and misleading.[m]

2:15 [n]Eze 25:6 [o]Jer 19:8 [p]Ps 50:2 [q]Ps 48:2

15 All who pass your way
clap their hands at you;[n]
they scoff[o] and shake their heads
at the Daughter of Jerusalem:
"Is this the city that was called
the perfection of beauty,[p]
the joy of the whole earth?"[q]

2:16 [r]Ps 56:2; La 3:46 [s]Job 16:9 [t]Ps 35:25

16 All your enemies open their mouths
wide against you;[r]
they scoff and gnash their teeth[s]
and say, "We have swallowed her up.[t]
This is the day we have waited for;
we have lived to see it."

2:17 [u]Dt 28:15-45 [v]ver 2; Eze 5:11 [w]Ps 89:42

17 The LORD has done what he planned;
he has fulfilled his word,
which he decreed long ago.[u]
He has overthrown you without pity,[v]
he has let the enemy gloat over you,
he has exalted the horn[a] of your
foes.[w]

2:18 [x]Ps 119:145 [y]La 1:16 [z]Jer 9:1 [a]La 3:49

18 The hearts of the people
cry out to the Lord.[x]
O wall of the Daughter of Zion,
let your tears[y] flow like a river
day and night;[z]
give yourself no relief,
your eyes no rest.[a]

19 Arise, cry out in the night,
as the watches of the night begin;

[a] 17 *Horn* here symbolizes strength.

Clapping Hands

LA 2:15-17

For years Jerusalem's residents experience the respect of surrounding nations. They are called "the joy of the whole earth" (La 2:15). Ezekiel writes that their "fame spread among the nations on account of [their] beauty . . . [and] splendor" (Eze 16:14). But the people sell out to idols and exploitation in the name of religion, and God allows them to experience the consequences.

Instead of applauding their glory, the neighboring nations clap as the Babylonians lead Jerusalem's inhabitants away in chains. The author of Lamentations (probably Jeremiah) expresses the shame of this situation in poetic form. Although he never participates in their sinful acts, he feels their humiliation. He warns the Israelites that destruction and dishonor will come, but they do not listen. Jeremiah could have said, "I told you so." Instead, he shares their sorrow and describes their grief in these laments. The people of nations who once paid homage to the splendor of Jerusalem now scoff.

Ineffective Prayer

LA 3:8–9

Jeremiah writes about the pain of the Israelites' sin-produced destruction as if it were his own. Although he does not turn on God as the people have, he identifies with their shame—for he is one of them. The prophet's despair is genuine: He feels alienated from God. As the people's representative, he understands the sad results of persistent disobedience. He knows that consistently neglecting God's ways renders prayer ineffective.

Jeremiah watches as the wayward Israelites stop calling on God and then conclude God is impotent—or at least uninterested. He begs the people to repent and reestablish their connection to God. They do not. The people's decisions lead them into isolation and despair. They need to pray, but their sin alienates them from God. Jeremiah expresses the sad results in this lament.

pour out your heart[b] like water
in the presence of the Lord.[c]
Lift up your hands to him
for the lives of your children,
who faint[d] from hunger
at the head of every street.

20 "Look, O LORD, and consider:
Whom have you ever treated like this?
Should women eat their offspring,[e]
the children they have cared for?[f]
Should priest and prophet be killed[g]
in the sanctuary of the Lord?

21 "Young and old lie together
in the dust of the streets;
my young men and maidens
have fallen by the sword.[h]
You have slain them in the day of your anger;
you have slaughtered them without pity.[i]

22 "As you summon to a feast day,
so you summoned against me terrors[j]
on every side.
In the day of the LORD's anger
no one escaped or survived;
those I cared for and reared,[k]
my enemy has destroyed."

3[a]

I am the man who has seen affliction
by the rod of his wrath.[l]
2 He has driven me away and made me walk
in darkness[m] rather than light;
3 indeed, he has turned his hand against me[n]
again and again, all day long.

4 He has made my skin and my flesh grow old
and has broken my bones.[o]
5 He has besieged me and surrounded me
with bitterness[p] and hardship.[q]
6 He has made me dwell in darkness
like those long dead.[r]

7 He has walled me in so I cannot escape;[s]
he has weighed me down with chains.[t]
8 Even when I call out or cry for help,
he shuts out my prayer.[u]
9 He has barred my way with blocks of stone;
he has made my paths crooked.[v]

10 Like a bear lying in wait,
like a lion in hiding,
11 he dragged me from the path and mangled[w] me

2:19 [b]1Sa 1:15; Ps 62:8 [c]Isa 26:9 [d]Isa 51:20
2:20 [e]Dt 28:53; Jer 19:9 [f]La 4:10 [g]Ps 78:64; Jer 14:15
2:21 [h]2Ch 36:17; Ps 78:62-63; Jer 6:11 [i]Jer 13:14; La 3:43; Zec 11:6
2:22 [j]Ps 31:13; Jer 6:25 [k]Hos 9:13
3:1 [l]Job 19:21; Ps 88:7
3:2 [m]Jer 4:23
3:3 [n]Isa 5:25
3:4 [o]Ps 51:8; Isa 38:13; Jer 50:17
3:5 [p]ver 19 [q]Jer 23:15
3:6 [r]Ps 88:5-6
3:7 [s]Job 3:23 [t]Jer 40:4
3:8 [u]Job 30:20; Ps 22:2
3:9 [v]Isa 63:17; Hos 2:6
3:11 [w]Hos 6:1

[a] This chapter is an acrostic poem; the verses of each stanza begin with the successive letters of the Hebrew alphabet, and the verses within each stanza begin with the same letter.

and left me without help.
12 He drew his bow[x]
and made me the target[y] for his arrows.[z]
13 He pierced my heart
with arrows from his quiver.[a]
14 I became the laughingstock[b] of all my people;
they mock me in song[c] all day long.
15 He has filled me with bitter herbs
and sated me with gall.[d]
16 He has broken my teeth with gravel;[e]
he has trampled me in the dust.
17 I have been deprived of peace;
I have forgotten what prosperity is.
18 So I say, "My splendor is gone
and all that I had hoped from the Lord."[f]
19 I remember my affliction and my wandering,
the bitterness and the gall.
20 I well remember them,
and my soul is downcast[g] within me.[h]
21 Yet this I call to mind
and therefore I have hope:
22 Because of the Lord's great love we are not consumed,
for his compassions never fail.[i]
23 They are new every morning;
great is your faithfulness.[j]
24 I say to myself, "The Lord is my portion;[k]
therefore I will wait for him."
25 The Lord is good to those whose hope is in him,
to the one who seeks him;[l]
26 it is good to wait quietly
for the salvation of the Lord.[m]
27 It is good for a man to bear the yoke
while he is young.
28 Let him sit alone in silence,[n]
for the Lord has laid it on him.
29 Let him bury his face in the dust—
there may yet be hope.[o]
30 Let him offer his cheek to one who would strike him,[p]
and let him be filled with disgrace.
31 For men are not cast off
by the Lord forever.[q]
32 Though he brings grief, he will show compassion,
so great is his unfailing love.[r]
33 For he does not willingly bring affliction
or grief to the children of men.[s]
34 To crush underfoot
all prisoners in the land,
35 to deny a man his rights

3:12 [x]La 2:4 [y]Job 7:20 [z]Ps 7:12-13; 38:2
3:13 [a]Job 6:4
3:14 [b]Jer 20:7 [c]Job 30:9
3:15 [d]Jer 9:15
3:16 [e]Pr 20:17
3:18 [f]Job 17:15
3:20 [g]Ps 42:5 [h]Ps 42:11
3:22 [i]Ps 78:38; Mal 3:6
3:23 [j]Zep 3:5
3:24 [k]Ps 16:5
3:25 [l]Isa 25:9; 30:18
3:26 [m]Ps 37:7; 40:1
3:28 [n]Jer 15:17
3:29 [o]Jer 31:17
3:30 [p]Job 16:10; Isa 50:6
3:31 [q]Ps 94:14; Isa 54:7
3:32 [r]Ps 78:38; Hos 11:8
3:33 [s]Eze 33:11

Bitter Herbs

LA 3:15

The meaning behind the Hebrew phrase "filled me with bitter herbs" (La 3:15) is "overwhelmed me with misery." The Israelites readily identify with the phrase because God had instructed Moses and Aaron to use "bitter herbs" on the meat roasted during Passover (Ex 12:8). The bitter herbs (sorrel, dandelions, horse radish, endive and chicory) remind the people of their "bitter" years as Egyptian slaves.

During the Babylonian captivity, Jeremiah feels that God is feeding him bitter herbs again. Though depressed (La 3:18–20), the prophet turns from his bitterness to hope with one word: "yet" (La 3:21). Though their situation is dismal, "yet" they can have hope: "Because of the Lord's great love we are not consumed, for his compassions never fail. They are new every morning" (La 3:22–23). Then he adds the spontaneous acclamation, "Great is your faithfulness" (La 3:23).

Thomas Chisholm wrote a poem that became the well-known hymn "Great Is Thy Faithfulness." Underline this phrase in your Bible, and jot a few words in the margin that remind you of God's faithful love and care.

Week 23

A Heart Filled With Bitterness

It is slow and subtle, growing undetected until you find yourself drowning in it. It taints your body, your soul and your spirit. It saturates your heart. It overflows and infects those around you. It colors every part of your life until you finally recognize the darkness you're living in. It is an ancient enemy called bitterness. Bitterness can be caused by circumstances: the death of a child or other loved one (Ru 1:20; 2Ki 4:27,32), injustice (Am 5:7), the overwhelming troubles of life (Ps 71:20), foolish children (Pr 17:25), or your own sin and rebellion against God (Jer 4:17-18).

Yet the circumstance doesn't produce your bitterness; your reaction to it does. Refusing to forgive a sin or a hurt committed against you gives bitterness fertile ground in which to grow. Refusing to repent will give bitterness a foothold and will result in a scarred relationship with God. But you can have freedom from bitterness; you can enjoy God and life again.

Read Lamentations 3:1-18. With which part of Jeremiah's lament do you most identify?

The book of Lamentations expresses the bitterness and grief associated with the destruction of Jerusalem. God destroys Jerusalem as an act of judgment for the rebellion of his people (La 2:1-8). If your bitterness is a reaction to the consequences of your own sin, what is the only way to escape it (La 3:40-42)? God does not willingly bring grief (La 3:31-33). But his discipline is meant to bring a sorrow that leads to repentance (2Co 7:9-10).

Hannah is tormented because of infertility, something she has no control over (1Sa 1:6-7). Her reaction produces bitterness (1Sa 1:10). Do you have a hurtful circumstance in your life in which you allow bitterness to grow?

What does bitterness prevent you from enjoying (Job 21:25)? How have you experienced this in your own life?

Where is the only place to go to restore a bitter heart (Ps 71:20-21)?

Enjoying God THROUGH the Word

Read Ruth 1:1-22 (page 413). Naomi is a beaten woman. She returns to Judah with nothing. Her husband and her two sons are dead. On her arrival, she tells the people, "Don't call me Naomi . . . Call me Mara ['Bitter'], because the Almighty has made my life very bitter" (Ru 1:20). What Naomi needs—and receives—is a redeemer.

In the Old Testament a kinsman-redeemer is a blood relative (Lev 25:47-49) with the necessary resources and the willingness to provide for needy members of the extended family (Jer 32:6-9). You also have a kinsman-redeemer to rescue you in your need. His name is Jesus. He meets all the requirements: he is your brother (Gal 4:4-5; Heb 2:17) and has willingly (Jn 10:17-18) paid the required price (1Co 6:20; 1Pe 1:18-19) for your redemption (Jn 8:34-36).

Enjoying God THROUGH Experience

You have all you need in Jesus! If you have a bitter heart, go to the feet of Jesus. Lie at his feet as Ruth lay at the feet of Boaz (Ru 3:7-14). Jesus is your provider and healer, the only One who can redeem your heart and life, the only One who can bring enjoyment back into your life. If you need healing from an emotional wound, take your pain to him in prayer. If you need to repent, confess your sin to him and seek his forgiveness. He'll cut off your bitterness at the root. Do not settle for a partial healing of your spiritual ailments. Allow him to finish the work he has begun.

Go to page 1403 for your next weekly study.

before the Most High,
36 to deprive a man of justice—
would not the Lord see such things?[t]

37 Who can speak and have it happen
if the Lord has not decreed it?[u]
38 Is it not from the mouth of the Most High
that both calamities and good things come?[v]
39 Why should any living man complain
when punished for his sins?[w]

40 Let us examine our ways and test them,[x]
and let us return to the LORD.[y]
41 Let us lift up our hearts and our hands
to God in heaven,[z] and say:
42 "We have sinned and rebelled[a]
and you have not forgiven.[b]

43 "You have covered yourself with anger
and pursued us;
you have slain without pity.[c]
44 You have covered yourself with a cloud[d]
so that no prayer[e] can get through.
45 You have made us scum[f] and refuse
among the nations.

46 "All our enemies have opened their mouths
wide against us.[g]
47 We have suffered terror and pitfalls,[h]
ruin and destruction.[i]"
48 Streams of tears flow from my eyes[j]
because my people are destroyed.[k]

49 My eyes will flow unceasingly,
without relief,[l]
50 until the LORD looks down
from heaven and sees.[m]
51 What I see brings grief to my soul
because of all the women of my city.

52 Those who were my enemies without cause
hunted me like a bird.[n]
53 They tried to end my life in a pit[o]
and threw stones at me;
54 the waters closed over my head,[p]
and I thought I was about to be cut off.

55 I called on your name, O LORD,
from the depths of the pit.[q]
56 You heard my plea:[r] "Do not close your ears
to my cry for relief."
57 You came near when I called you,
and you said, "Do not fear."[s]

58 O Lord, you took up my case;[t]
you redeemed my life.[u]
59 You have seen, O LORD, the wrong done to me.[v]
Uphold my cause!

3:36 [t]Jer 22:3; Hab 1:13
3:37 [u]Ps 33:9-11
3:38 [v]Job 2:10; Isa 45:7; Jer 32:42
3:39 [w]Jer 30:15; Mic 7:9
3:40 [x]2Co 13:5 [y]Ps 119:59; 139:23-24
3:41 [z]Ps 25:1; 28:2
3:42 [a]Da 9:5 [b]Jer 5:7-9
3:43 [c]La 2:2,17, 21
3:44 [d]Ps 97:2 [e]ver 8
3:45 [f]1Co 4:13
3:46 [g]La 2:16
3:47 [h]Jer 48:43 [i]Isa 24:17-18; 51:19
3:48 [j]La 1:16 [k]La 2:11
3:49 [l]Jer 14:17
3:50 [m]Isa 63:15
3:52 [n]Ps 35:7
3:53 [o]Jer 37:16
3:54 [p]Ps 69:2; Jnh 2:3-5
3:55 [q]Ps 130:1; Jnh 2:2
3:56 [r]Ps 55:1
3:57 [s]Isa 41:10
3:58 [t]Jer 51:36 [u]Ps 34:22; Jer 50:34
3:59 [v]Jer 18:19-20

Affliction

LA 3:58

"I am the man who has seen affliction" (La 3:1). Jeremiah understands how intense inner pain can lead a person to the brink of despair, and he wants to help his readers—whether a hurting Israelite of his time or a heartbroken woman of today—regain faith.

Jeremiah knows his God is trustworthy and that gives him hope (La 3:21). The Lord is his source (La 3:24), and he waits for God to show him fresh love and faithfulness each morning (La 3:22-23). Though the prophet cannot stop crying, he expects God to respond to his pleas (La 3:49-50). He may be referring to his imprisonment in a cistern (Jer 38:6-13) when he testifies that he called on God "from the depths of the pit" (La 3:55). Jeremiah wants every reader to know how God responded to his need and faithfully restored his life (La 3:58).

Punishment

LA 4:6

Although both Sodom and Jerusalem experience death and destruction, the ongoing suffering of the residents of Jerusalem seems greater than the swift judgment pronounced on the men and women of Sodom (Ge 19:24–25). Each day reminds the Babylonian captives that their own sin has caused their current anguish. God had given them repeated opportunities to repent, but they had ignored the prophets' warnings and turned their backs on God's love (2Ch 36:15–16).

The Israelites lose everything: their reputation as a powerful nation, their freedom, their health, their livelihoods, their family units, their self-esteem. Circumstances become so devastating during the siege of Jerusalem that starvation-crazed mothers resort to eating their own children (La 4:10.) The wicked citizens of Sodom experienced swift and absolute annihilation, but the captured Israelites know the prolonged agony of feeling powerless and unprotected by God.

60 You have seen the depth of their
vengeance,
all their plots against me.[w]

61 O LORD, you have heard their insults,
all their plots against me—
62 what my enemies whisper and mutter
against me all day long.[x]
63 Look at them! Sitting or standing,
they mock me in their songs.
64 Pay them back what they deserve, O LORD,
for what their hands have done.[y]
65 Put a veil over their hearts,[z]
and may your curse be on them!
66 Pursue them in anger and destroy them
from under the heavens of the LORD.

4[a]

How the gold has lost its luster,
the fine gold become dull!
The sacred gems are scattered
at the head of every street.[a]

2 How the precious sons of Zion,
once worth their weight in gold,
are now considered as pots of clay,
the work of a potter's hands!

3 Even jackals offer their breasts
to nurse their young,
but my people have become heartless
like ostriches in the desert.[b]

4 Because of thirst the infant's tongue
sticks to the roof of its mouth;[c]
the children beg for bread,
but no one gives it to them.[d]

5 Those who once ate delicacies
are destitute in the streets.
Those nurtured in purple[e]
now lie on ash heaps.[f]

6 The punishment of my people
is greater than that of Sodom,[g]
which was overthrown in a moment
without a hand turned to help her.

7 Their princes were brighter than snow
and whiter than milk,
their bodies more ruddy than rubies,
their appearance like sapphires.[b]

8 But now they are blacker[h] than soot;
they are not recognized in the streets.
Their skin has shriveled on their bones;[i]
it has become as dry as a stick.

9 Those killed by the sword are better off
than those who die of famine;
racked with hunger, they waste away
for lack of food from the field.[j]

[a] This chapter is an acrostic poem, the verses of which begin with the successive letters of the Hebrew alphabet. [b] 7 Or *lapis lazuli*

3:60 [w]Jer 11:20; 18:18
3:62 [x]Eze 36:3
3:64 [y]Ps 28:4
3:65 [z]Isa 6:10
4:1 [a]Eze 7:19
4:3 [b]Job 39:16
4:4 [c]Ps 22:15 [d]La 2:11,12
4:5 [e]Jer 6:2 [f]Am 6:3-7
4:6 [g]Ge 19:25
4:8 [h]Job 30:28 [i]Ps 102:3-5
4:9 [j]Jer 15:2; 16:4

Vashti

Sovereign Over All

There was a lot of drinking going on—for seven days, in fact. Nobody at the feast was still sober. The king had pulled out all the stops—quite literally.

For a full six months, Xerxes, king of Persia, had shown off his kingdom, his vast wealth and "the splendor and glory of his majesty" (Est 1:4). The king, muddled with drunkenness, now wanted to show off his queen, to put her beauty on display. Vashti was too dignified and perhaps even too shy to entertain a room full of drunken men. The king dishonored her with his request, so she declined. Surely he would understand.

Unfortunately, Xerxes chose to take her rebuff personally. Vashti had refused an order of the *king!* His counselors were right. She had set a bad example for other women.

Vashti must be publicly disciplined, for the good of the kingdom *and* for the good of men. Her response to her husband was so outrageous that it would encourage other women to disobey their husbands. The issue was considered so critical that letters concerning the king's decision and edict were sent throughout the entire kingdom. The king had acted in anger. What if he had waited and talked to Vashti first? However, his counselors had advised that "Vashti is never again to enter the presence of King Xerxes" (Est 1:19). The ruling men of Persia were so threatened by Vashti's show of independence that they feared social chaos.

Vashti might have been wiser to grant her husband's request. After all, everyone was drunk and would quickly forget her "performance." However, even in the middle of a vast, pagan festival, God's hand acted to set the course of future events. He was gentle with Vashti—her offense could have earned her a much harsher penalty. God removed her nonetheless, so he could raise up Esther, whose heroic acts later saved the Jews from extermination.

Our God is sovereign. There is nothing too big, too small, too imminent or too distant to escape his notice and control. Sometimes events in life that seem catastrophic at the moment can be seen in retrospect as blessings from God. When we suffer such seeming setbacks, then is the time our faith in him must be strongest, whether or not we ever understand his reasons.

Vashti
(beautiful woman)
Esther 1:1–2:4,17

Candid SNAPSHOT But when the attendants delivered the king's command, Queen Vashti refused to come. Then the king became furious and burned with anger. (Esther 1:12)

Esther

Beauty That Doesn't Fade

Think of the most beautiful woman's face you have ever seen. Queen Esther looked like *that*. She easily could have been self-absorbed, pursuing all the benefits of a stunning appearance. But her loveliness would have faded with time, at best forgotten in one generation. It is Esther's *inner* beauty that has been immortalized in Scripture and in the history of her people. For Esther was beautiful inside and out.

It was a Cinderella story. Esther, orphaned at a young age, had been taken in by her cousin, Mordecai. They were Jews, alien exiles, a distrusted minority in the hands of fierce captors. But Esther grew in grace and beauty, encouraged by Mordecai to see her worth in God's eyes. When King Xerxes decided to find a new queen to replace the headstrong Vashti, many young women were brought to his harem to be groomed for the position—including Esther. When she appeared before Xerxes, "the king was attracted to Esther more than to any of the other women . . . So he set a royal crown on her head and made her queen instead of Vashti" (Est 2:17).

Then came dreadful news from Mordecai to Esther. It seemed almost beyond belief. All the Jews in Persia were to be exterminated by edict of the king! Esther was the queen, but what could *she* do? King Xerxes had absolute power over his people; they existed—or died—at his whim. Even the queen.

Mordecai's wisdom and his love for Esther could not be denied, but the stakes were extreme. *Go to the king on behalf of my people? The king does not even know I am a Jew.* Esther's mind must have searched for an easier solution. But Mordecai's counsel pierced her heart: "And who knows but that you have come to royal position for such a time as this?" (Est 4:14). With inestimable courage, Esther seized her destiny.

Esther's beautiful face and form alone could not have stayed Xerxes' hand. But her courage and wisdom won his compassion, and he granted her request. Esther's *true* beauty had prepared her to be an instrument in God's hand for saving the Jews in a time of great peril.

Every woman is beautiful. *She is.* Oh, she may not have the classic features of this year's fashionable face, but she has a unique, God-given beauty and strength. There will be circumstances in our lives when we will need to exercise character and courage, as did Esther. Let's not settle for beauty that fades but instead ask the Lord to help us develop an inner beauty, the "forever" beauty by which we will be known in heaven.

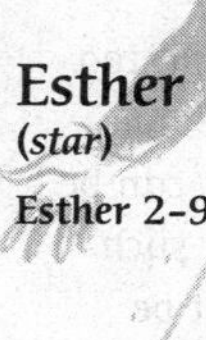

Esther
(*star*)
Esther 2-9

Candid SNAPSHOT Go, gather together all the Jews who are in Susa, and fast for me. Do not eat or drink for three days, night or day. I and my maids will fast as you do. When this is done, I will go to the king, even though it is against the law. And if I perish, I perish (Esther 4:16).

10 With their own hands compassionate
women
have cooked their own children,[k]
who became their food
when my people were destroyed.

11 The LORD has given full vent to his wrath;
he has poured out his fierce anger.
He kindled a fire[l] in Zion
that consumed her foundations.[m]

12 The kings of the earth did not believe,
nor did any of the world's people,
that enemies and foes could enter
the gates of Jerusalem.[n]

13 But it happened because of the sins of
her prophets
and the iniquities of her priests,[o]
who shed within her
the blood of the righteous.

14 Now they grope through the streets
like men who are blind.[p]
They are so defiled with blood[q]
that no one dares to touch their
garments.

15 "Go away! You are unclean!" men cry to
them.
"Away! Away! Don't touch us!"
When they flee and wander about,
people among the nations say,
"They can stay here no longer."[r]

16 The LORD himself has scattered them;
he no longer watches over them.[s]
The priests are shown no honor,
the elders[t] no favor.

17 Moreover, our eyes failed,
looking in vain[u] for help;[v]
from our towers we watched
for a nation[w] that could not save us.

18 Men stalked us at every step,
so we could not walk in our streets.
Our end was near, our days were
numbered,
for our end had come.[x]

19 Our pursuers were swifter
than eagles[y] in the sky;
they chased us[z] over the mountains
and lay in wait for us in the desert.

20 The LORD's anointed,[a] our very life breath,
was caught in their traps.[b]
We thought that under his shadow
we would live among the nations.

21 Rejoice and be glad, O Daughter of Edom,
you who live in the land of Uz.
But to you also the cup[c] will be passed;
you will be drunk and stripped naked.[d]

4:10 [k]Lev 26:29; Dt 28:53-57; Jer 19:9; La 2:20; Eze 5:10
4:11 [l]Jer 17:27 [m]Dt 32:22; Jer 7:20; Eze 22:31
4:12 [n]1Ki 9:9; Jer 21:13
4:13 [o]Jer 5:31; 6:13; Eze 22:28; Mic 3:11
4:14 [p]Isa 59:10 [q]Jer 2:34; 19:4
4:15 [r]Lev 13:46
4:16 [s]Isa 9:14-16 [t]La 5:12
4:17 [u]Isa 20:5; Eze 29:16 [v]La 1:7 [w]Jer 37:7
4:18 [x]Eze 7:2-12; Am 8:2
4:19 [y]Dt 28:49 [z]Isa 5:26-28
4:20 [a]2Sa 19:21 [b]Jer 39:5; Eze 12:12-13; 19:4,8
4:21 [c]Jer 25:15 [d]Isa 34:6-10; Am 1:11-12; Ob 1:16

I am constantly reminded of the faithfulness of God and that his mercies are new every morning. *What I was yesterday, what I felt yesterday, what I did yesterday is covered by his grace. He remembers it no more. He throws it as far as the east is from the west—as I turn, as I repent, as I offer him my sins, my failures and even the consequences of my choices. There is so much beauty to the morning, and there is so much beauty in a heart filled with the certainty that the Lord has once again come to fill, restore and heal.*

His steadfast love never ceases. His mercies never end.

—Kathy Troccoli

Point of No Return?

LA 5:21–22

The last verses of Lamentations seem to suggest a hopeless scenario. The poet totters on the brink of despair as he begs God to respond to his inquiries: "Have you utterly rejected us? Is your anger with us beyond redemption?" (author's paraphrase).

However, the writer knows God, which is evidenced by his preceding plea: "Lord, restore us to experience your presence anew." He believes God is in the business of giving second chances. Indeed, the Lord gives the Israelites many opportunities to change their rebellious ways and return to his protective care (Jer 44:4–6).

Is there a point of no return? As long as someone refuses God's invitation of love, there is no hope. But the moment that person reaches out to God in faith, hope comes alive. God proves this repeatedly through the Biblical history of his people. Today he offers all people of all nations hope through his son, Jesus Christ.

22 O Daughter of Zion, your punishment
will end;[e]
he will not prolong your exile.
But, O Daughter of Edom, he will
punish your sin
and expose your wickedness.[f]

5

Remember, O LORD, what has happened
to us;
look, and see our disgrace.[g]
2 Our inheritance[h] has been turned over
to aliens,
our homes[i] to foreigners.
3 We have become orphans and
fatherless,
our mothers like widows.[j]
4 We must buy the water we drink;
our wood can be had only at a price.[k]
5 Those who pursue us are at our heels;
we are weary[l] and find no rest.
6 We submitted to Egypt and Assyria[m]
to get enough bread.
7 Our fathers sinned and are no more,
and we bear their punishment.[n]
8 Slaves[o] rule over us,
and there is none to free us from their
hands.[p]
9 We get our bread at the risk of our lives
because of the sword in the desert.
10 Our skin is hot as an oven,
feverish from hunger.[q]
11 Women have been ravished[r] in Zion,
and virgins in the towns of Judah.
12 Princes have been hung up by their
hands;
elders are shown no respect.[s]
13 Young men toil at the millstones;
boys stagger under loads of wood.
14 The elders are gone from the city gate;
the young men have stopped their
music.[t]
15 Joy is gone from our hearts;
our dancing has turned to mourning.[u]
16 The crown[v] has fallen from our head.
Woe to us, for we have sinned![w]
17 Because of this our hearts[x] are faint,
because of these things our eyes[y]
grow dim
18 for Mount Zion, which lies desolate,[z]
with jackals prowling over it.
19 You, O LORD, reign forever;
your throne endures[a] from generation
to generation.
20 Why do you always forget us?[b]
Why do you forsake us so long?
21 Restore[c] us to yourself, O LORD, that we
may return;
renew our days as of old
22 unless you have utterly rejected us
and are angry with us beyond measure.[d]

4:22 [e]Isa 40:2; Jer 33:8 [f]Ps 137:7; Mal 1:4
5:1 [g]Ps 44:13-16; 89:50
5:2 [h]Ps 79:1 [i]Zep 1:13
5:3 [j]Jer 15:8; 18:21
5:4 [k]Isa 3:1
5:5 [l]Ne 9:37
5:6 [m]Hos 9:3
5:7 [n]Jer 14:20; 16:12
5:8 [o]Ne 5:15 [p]Zec 11:6
5:10 [q]La 4:8-9
5:11 [r]Zec 14:2
5:12 [s]La 4:16
5:14 [t]Isa 24:8; Jer 7:34
5:15 [u]Jer 25:10
5:16 [v]Ps 89:39 [w]Isa 3:11
5:17 [x]Isa 1:5 [y]Ps 6:7
5:18 [z]Mic 3:12
5:19 [a]Ps 45:6; 102:12,24-27
5:20 [b]Ps 13:1; 44:24
5:21 [c]Ps 80:3
5:22 [d]Isa 64:9

Ezekiel

A watchman warns and encourages.

Strange visions and powerful dramas fill the chapters of Ezekiel, bringing God's messages of condemnation and consolation to the Jews living in exile in Babylon. Much of the book falls into two distinct sections: alarming words of divine judgment and encouraging words of hope and restoration. Ezekiel reminds the discouraged captives that their spiritual blindness brought about their captivity, yet his words also assure them that God will restore them to their homeland.

Vivid imagery and object lessons empower Ezekiel's message to the captives. He likens the city of Jerusalem to an adulterous woman who is abused by her sinful partners (Eze 16; 23). He reminds his audience that Babylon is merely a sword in God's hand, executing God's judgment (Eze 21). And he compares the hearts of the unrepentant people to a valley of dry bones (Eze 37). Ezekiel also helps bring a balanced perspective to the people's suffering. Though he describes a ruined, desecrated temple (Eze 8–10), he also paints a picture of a glorious, restored temple (Eze 40–43). God's anger against the wickedness of Judah (Eze 11) is tempered by God's mercy in restoring Judah to her homeland (Eze 47–48). Ezekiel's calling as a watchman of judgment (Eze 3) is balanced against his appointment as a watchman of restoration (Eze 33).

Throughout his message, Ezekiel emphasizes again and again God's declaration that all the things that happen do so in order that the Israelites "may know that I am the LORD." In everything that God does, whether in grace or in judgment, his aim is to reveal himself—no less today than in Ezekiel's day.

Quick Study

Author
The prophet-priest Ezekiel.

Date Written
Between 593 and 571 B.C.

Setting
Babylon.

Key Passage
Ezekiel 16:59–60, 62 "This is what the Sovereign LORD says: I will deal with you as you deserve, because you have despised my oath by breaking the covenant. Yet I will remember the covenant I made with you in the days of your youth, and I will establish an everlasting covenant with you . . . and you will know that I am the LORD."

Outline

Ezekiel's call and first vision.
Eze 1–3

Acts portraying the siege of Jerusalem.
Eze 4–5

Words of divine judgment.
Eze 6–7

God's glory leaving the temple.
Eze 8–11

Acts portraying the exile.
Eze 12

More words of divine judgment.
Eze 13–24

Words of judgment against specific nations.
Eze 25–32

Ezekiel as a watchman.
Eze 33:1–20

Jerusalem's fall.
Eze 33:21–33

Shepherds and sheep.
Eze 34

Words of judgment against Edom.
Eze 35

Consolation for Israel.
Eze 36

A valley of dry bones.
Eze 37

Words of judgment against Gog.
Eze 38–39

Restoration of the temple and worship.
Eze 40–48

The Women of Ezekiel

Women who mourned Tammuz	*Mourning a false god.* Eze 8:14
Daughters who prophesy	*Not true prophecies but pure imagination.* Eze 13:17–18
Oholah, Oholibah	*Symbolic women of Samaria and Jerusalem.* Eze 23
Ezekiel's wife	*Ezekiel couldn't mourn her death.* Eze 24:15–27

The Living Creatures and the Glory
1:1 ### of the LORD

[a]Eze 11:24- 1 In the[a] thirtieth year, in the fourth month on
25 [b]Mt 3:16; Ac 7:56 the fifth day, while I was among the exiles[a] by
[c]Ex 24:10 the Kebar River, the heavens were opened[b] and I
saw visions[c] of God.
1:2 2 On the fifth of the month—it was the fifth year
[d]2Ki 24:15 of the exile of King Jehoiachin[d]— 3 the word of the
1:3 LORD came to Ezekiel the priest, the son of Buzi,[b]
[e]2Ki 3:15; by the Kebar River in the land of the Babylonians.[c]
Eze 3:14,22 There the hand of the LORD was upon him.[e]
1:4 4 I looked, and I saw a windstorm coming out of
[f]Jer 1:14 the north[f]—an immense cloud with flashing light-
[g]Eze 8:2 ning and surrounded by brilliant light. The center
1:5 of the fire looked like glowing metal,[g] 5 and in the
[h]Rev 4:6 [i]ver 26 fire was what looked like four living creatures.[h] In
1:6 appearance their form was that of a man,[i] 6 but each
[j]Eze 10:14 of them had four faces[j] and four wings. 7 Their legs
1:7 were straight; their feet were like those of a calf and
[k]Da 10:6; gleamed like burnished bronze.[k] 8 Under their
Rev 1:15 wings on their four sides they had the hands of a
man.[l] All four of them had faces and wings, 9 and
1:8 [l]Eze 10:8 their wings touched one another. Each one went
straight ahead; they did not turn as they moved.[m]
1:9 10 Their faces looked like this: Each of the four
[m]Eze 10:22 had the face of a man, and on the right side each
1:10 had the face of a lion, and on the left the face of an
[n]Eze 10:14; ox; each also had the face of an eagle.[n] 11 Such
Rev 4:7 were their faces. Their wings[o] were spread out
1:11 upward; each had two wings, one touching the
[o]Isa 6:2 wing of another creature on either side, and two
wings covering its body. 12 Each one went straight
ahead. Wherever the spirit would go, they would
go, without turning as they went. 13 The appearance of the living creatures was like burning coals
1:13 of fire or like torches. Fire moved back and forth
[p]Rev 4:5 among the creatures; it was bright, and lightning[p]
1:14 flashed out of it. 14 The creatures sped back and
[q]Ps 29:7 forth like flashes of lightning.[q]
15 As I looked at the living creatures, I saw a
wheel on the ground beside each creature with its
1:16 four faces. 16 This was the appearance and struc-
[r]Eze 10:9-11; ture of the wheels: They sparkled like chrysolite,[r]
Da 10:6 and all four looked alike. Each appeared to be
made like a wheel intersecting a wheel. 17 As they
moved, they would go in any one of the four
1:17 directions the creatures faced; the wheels did not
[s]ver 9 turn[s] about[d] as the creatures went. 18 Their rims
1:18 were high and awesome, and all four rims were
[t]Eze 10:12; full of eyes[t] all around.
Rev 4:6 19 When the living creatures moved, the wheels
beside them moved; and when the living creatures
1:20 rose from the ground, the wheels also rose.
[u]ver 12 20 Wherever the spirit would go, they would go,[u]
and the wheels would rise along with them,
because the spirit of the living creatures was in the
wheels. 21 When the creatures moved, they also
moved; when the creatures stood still, they also

[a] *1* Or ⌊*my*⌋ [b] *3* Or *Ezekiel son of Buzi the priest*
[c] *3* Or *Chaldeans* [d] *17* Or *aside*

Ezekiel's Message

EZE 1:1

With little fanfare Ezekiel announces his year, the point in history, his location—and then these fantastic words: "the heavens were opened and I saw visions of God."

Ezekiel's visions, though bizarre and difficult to visualize, have messages that are pertinent to us today as well as to the exiles to whom he preached. Had he been in Jerusalem rather than in exile in Babylon, Ezekiel would probably have begun his priestly duties in this, his thirtieth year. Instead, God calls him into a ministry of prophecy to proclaim to the captives the message that God will judge Jerusalem—it will be destroyed. But after that message of despair, when word was received that Jerusalem had fallen, the rest of the book of Ezekiel offers a message of hope: Though the people are judged, they are not forsaken; though they have sinned, there is forgiveness and a dazzling promise for their future: "I will make a covenant of peace with them . . . I will send down showers . . . of blessing" (Eze 34:25–26), and the people will live in a city with an extraordinary name:* THE LORD IS THERE *(Eze 48:35).

Falling Facedown

EZE 1:25–28

Obviously, what Ezekiel sees here is only an image. There is nothing unreal about it, however. What he sees is very real, so real that he falls facedown in awe and worship. But it is only a representation ***of God himself—"the*** appearance ***of the*** likeness ***of the glory of the Lord" (Eze 1:28, emphasis added).***

This majestic vision of God is given to Ezekiel as preparation for his time of ministry. God at other times revealed himself in a stunning display in order to prepare other servants for ministry: Moses faced a burning bush (Ex 3:2), Isaiah saw God's glory fill the temple (Isa 6:1–4), and, later in history, a blinding light quickly got Saul's attention (Ac 9:3). The response of each one is the same: a recognition of who is revealing himself (God's presence is unmistakable); a response of worship (God's presence demands it); and a willingness to serve (God's invitation is irresistible).

stood still; and when the creatures rose from the
ground, the wheels rose along with them, because
the spirit of the living creatures was in the wheels.[v]
22 Spread out above the heads of the living creatures was what looked like an expanse,[w] sparkling
like ice, and awesome. 23 Under the expanse their
wings were stretched out one toward the other, and
each had two wings covering its body. 24 When the
creatures moved, I heard the sound of their wings,
like the roar of rushing waters, like the voice[x] of
the Almighty,[a] like the tumult of an army.[y] When
they stood still, they lowered their wings.
25 Then there came a voice from above the
expanse over their heads as they stood with lowered wings. 26 Above the expanse over their heads
was what looked like a throne of sapphire,[b][z] and
high above on the throne was a figure like that of
a man.[a] 27 I saw that from what appeared to be his
waist up he looked like glowing metal, as if full of
fire, and that from there down he looked like fire;
and brilliant light surrounded him.[b] 28 Like the
appearance of a rainbow[c] in the clouds on a rainy
day, so was the radiance around him.[d]
This was the appearance of the likeness of the
glory[e] of the LORD. When I saw it, I fell facedown,[f]
and I heard the voice of one speaking.

Ezekiel's Call

2 He said to me, "Son of man, stand[g] up on your
feet and I will speak to you." 2 As he spoke, the
Spirit came into me and raised me[h] to my feet,
and I heard him speaking to me.
3 He said: "Son of man, I am sending you to the
Israelites, to a rebellious nation that has rebelled
against me; they and their fathers have been in
revolt against me to this very day.[i] 4 The people to
whom I am sending you are obstinate and stubborn.[j] Say to them, 'This is what the Sovereign
LORD says.' 5 And whether they listen or fail to listen[k]—for they are a rebellious house[l]—they will
know that a prophet has been among them.[m] 6 And
you, son of man, do not be afraid[n] of them or their
words. Do not be afraid, though briers and thorns[o]
are all around you and you live among scorpions.
Do not be afraid of what they say or terrified by
them, though they are a rebellious house.[p] 7 You
must speak my words to them, whether they listen
or fail to listen, for they are rebellious.[q] 8 But you,
son of man, listen to what I say to you. Do not
rebel like that rebellious house;[r] open your mouth
and eat[s] what I give you."
9 Then I looked, and I saw a hand[t] stretched out
to me. In it was a scroll, 10 which he unrolled
before me. On both sides of it were written words
of lament and mourning and woe.[u]

3 And he said to me, "Son of man, eat what is
before you, eat this scroll; then go and speak
to the house of Israel." 2 So I opened my mouth,
and he gave me the scroll to eat.

1:21 [v]Eze 10:17
1:22 [w]Eze 10:1
1:24 [x]Eze 10:5; 43:2; Da 10:6; Rev 1:15; 19:6 [y]2Ki 7:6
1:26 [z]Ex 24:10; Eze 10:1 [a]Rev 1:13
1:27 [b]Eze 8:2
1:28 [c]Ge 9:13; Rev 10:1 [d]Rev 4:2 [e]Eze 8:4 [f]Eze 3:23; Da 8:17; Rev 1:17
2:1 [g]Da 10:11
2:2 [h]Eze 3:24; Da 8:18
2:3 [i]Jer 3:25; Eze 20:8-24
2:4 [j]Eze 3:7
2:5 [k]Eze 3:11 [l]Eze 3:27 [m]Eze 33:33
2:6 [n]Jer 1:8,17 [o]Isa 9:18; Mic 7:4 [p]Eze 3:9
2:7 [q]Jer 1:7; Eze 3:10-11
2:8 [r]Isa 50:5 [s]Jer 15:16; Rev 10:9
2:9 [t]Eze 8:3
2:10 [u]Rev 8:13

[a] 24 Hebrew *Shaddai* [b] 26 Or *lapis lazuli*

3 Then he said to me, "Son of man, eat this scroll
I am giving you and fill your stomach with it." So
I ate[v] it, and it tasted as sweet as honey[w] in my
mouth.
4 He then said to me: "Son of man, go now to the
house of Israel and speak my words to them. 5 You
are not being sent to a people of obscure speech
and difficult language,[x] but to the house of Israel— 6 not to many peoples of obscure speech and
difficult language, whose words you cannot understand. Surely if I had sent you to them, they would
have listened to you.[y] 7 But the house of Israel is
not willing to listen to you because they are not
willing to listen to me, for the whole house of Israel is hardened and obstinate.[z] 8 But I will make you
as unyielding and hardened as they are.[a] 9 I will
make your forehead like the hardest stone, harder
than flint. Do not be afraid of them or terrified by
them, though they are a rebellious house.[b]"
10 And he said to me, "Son of man, listen carefully and take to heart all the words I speak to you.
11 Go now to your countrymen in exile and speak to
them. Say to them, 'This is what the Sovereign
LORD says,' whether they listen or fail to listen.[c]"
12 Then the Spirit lifted me up,[d] and I heard
behind me a loud rumbling sound—May the glory
of the LORD be praised in his dwelling place!— 13 the
sound of the wings of the living creatures brush-
ing against each other and the sound of the wheels
beside them, a loud rumbling sound.[e] 14 The Spirit
then lifted me up and took me away, and I went in
bitterness and in the anger of my spirit, with the
strong hand of the LORD upon me. 15 I came to the
exiles who lived at Tel Abib near the Kebar River.[f]
And there, where they were living, I sat among
them for seven days[g]—overwhelmed.

Warning to Israel

16 At the end of seven days the word of the LORD
came to me:[h] 17 "Son of man, I have made you a
watchman[i] for the house of Israel; so hear the
word I speak and give them warning from me.
18 When I say to a wicked man, 'You will surely
die,' and you do not warn him or speak out to dissuade him from his evil ways in order to save his
life, that wicked man will die for[a] his sin, and I
will hold you accountable for his blood.[j] 19 But if
you do warn the wicked man and he does not
turn from his wickedness or from his evil ways,
he will die for his sin; but you will have saved
yourself.[k]
20 "Again, when a righteous man turns from his
righteousness and does evil, and I put a stumbling
block before him, he will die. Since you did not
warn him, he will die for his sin. The righteous
things he did will not be remembered, and I will
hold you accountable for his blood.[l] 21 But if you
do warn the righteous man not to sin and he does

3:3 [v]Jer 15:16 [w]Ps 19:10; Ps 119:103; Rev 10:9-10
3:5 [x]Isa 28:11; Jnh 1:2
3:6 [y]Mt 11:21-23
3:7 [z]Eze 2:4; Jn 15:20-23
3:8 [a]Jer 1:18
3:9 [b]Isa 50:7; Eze 2:6; Mic 3:8
3:11 [c]Eze 2:4-5,7
3:12 [d]Eze 8:3; Ac 8:39
3:13 [e]Eze 1:24; 10:5,16-17
3:15 [f]Ps 137:1 [g]Job 2:13
3:16 [h]Jer 42:7
3:17 [i]Isa 52:8; Jer 6:17; Eze 33:7-9
3:18 [j]ver 20; Eze 33:6
3:19 [k]2Ki 17:13; Eze 14:14, 20; Ac 18:6; 20:26; 1Ti 4:14-16
3:20 [l]Ps 125:5; Eze 18:24; 33:12,18

[a] *18* Or *in*; also in verses 19 and 20

Anger and Bitterness

EZE 3:3-15

As part of Ezekiel's call, God tells him to eat a scroll. The scroll contains words of "lament and mourning and woe" (Eze 2:10). Surprisingly, when Ezekiel eats the scroll, it tastes sweet, revealing to him and his listeners that even God's words of bitter judgment can be sweet because they are a last call to turn to him and be saved.

After eating the scroll, Ezekiel recognizes the troublesome task ahead of him. He must relay a discouraging message to the people in exile. These are his *people, people he belongs to and loves. And he must tell them that God has decided to destroy Jerusalem, the city they adore. God's judgment is now inescapable. But worse than the message itself is the sure knowledge that the people will not listen. Ezekiel's heart is broken. He grieves for seven days; he is "overwhelmed" (Eze 3:15) by what he's seen and heard. Only after those seven days of agitation and mourning does he respond to God's call and begin his ministry.*

not sin, he will surely live because he took warning, and you will have saved yourself.[m]"
22 The hand of the LORD[n] was upon me there,
and he said to me, "Get up and go[o] out to the
plain,[p] and there I will speak to you." 23 So I got
up and went out to the plain. And the glory of the
LORD was standing there, like the glory I had seen
by the Kebar River,[q] and I fell facedown.[r]
24 Then the Spirit came into me and raised me[s]
to my feet. He spoke to me and said: "Go, shut
yourself inside your house. 25 And you, son of
man, they will tie with ropes; you will be bound
so that you cannot go out among the people.[t] 26 I
will make your tongue stick to the roof of your
mouth so that you will be silent and unable to
rebuke them, though they are a rebellious house.[u]
27 But when I speak to you, I will open your mouth
and you shall say to them, 'This is what the Sovereign LORD says.'[v] Whoever will listen let him listen, and whoever will refuse let him refuse; for
they are a rebellious house.[w]

Siege of Jerusalem Symbolized

4 "Now, son of man, take a clay tablet, put it in
front of you and draw the city of Jerusalem on
it. 2 Then lay siege to it: Erect siege works against
it, build a ramp[x] up to it, set up camps against it
and put battering rams around it.[y] 3 Then take an
iron pan, place it as an iron wall between you and
the city and turn your face toward it. It will be
under siege, and you shall besiege it. This will be
a sign[z] to the house of Israel.[a]
4 "Then lie on your left side and put the sin of
the house of Israel upon yourself.[a] You are to bear
their sin for the number of days you lie on your
side. 5 I have assigned you the same number of
days as the years of their sin. So for 390 days you
will bear the sin of the house of Israel.
6 "After you have finished this, lie down again,
this time on your right side, and bear the sin of
the house of Judah. I have assigned you 40 days,
a day for each year.[b] 7 Turn your face toward the
siege of Jerusalem and with bared arm prophesy
against her. 8 I will tie you up with ropes so that
you cannot turn from one side to the other until
you have finished the days of your siege.[c]
9 "Take wheat and barley, beans and lentils, mil-
let and spelt;[d] put them in a storage jar and use
them to make bread for yourself. You are to eat it
during the 390 days you lie on your side. 10 Weigh
out twenty shekels[b] of food to eat each day and
eat it at set times. 11 Also measure out a sixth of a
hin[c] of water and drink it at set times. 12 Eat the
food as you would a barley cake; bake it in the
sight of the people, using human excrement[e] for
fuel." 13 The LORD said, "In this way the people of
Israel will eat defiled food among the nations
where I will drive them."[f]

Mute and Tied With Ropes

EZE 3:24–27

The Spirit of God now tells Ezekiel to go to his own home. There he is tied with ropes and is unable to speak. Figuratively, Ezekiel is God's slave, "tied" to God's will, mute unless God opens his mouth. He is totally dependent on God's timing and location for his message to be relayed to the people. Ezekiel will be free to publicly speak and move about only when God's divine message comes to him.

God's message will have its designated outcome: "Whoever will listen let him listen, and whoever will refuse let him refuse" (Eze 3:27). Individual responsibility to respond to God's message is emphasized here, mirrored by Christ's call to his contemporaries and to us: "He who has ears to hear, let him hear" (Mk 4:9).

3:21 [m]Ac 20:31
3:22 [n]Eze 1:3 [o]Ac 9:6 [p]Eze 8:4
3:23 [q]Eze 1:1 [r]Eze 1:28
3:24 [s]Eze 2:2
3:25 [t]Eze 4:8
3:26 [u]Eze 2:5; 24:27; 33:22
3:27 [v]ver 11 [w]Eze 12:3; 24:27; 33:22
4:2 [x]Jer 6:6 [y]Eze 21:22
4:3 [z]Isa 8:18; 20:3; Eze 12:3-6; 24:24,27 [a]Jer 39:1
4:6 [b]Nu 14:34; Da 9:24-26; 12:11-12
4:8 [c]Eze 3:25
4:9 [d]Isa 28:25
4:12 [e]Isa 36:12
4:13 [f]Hos 9:3

[a] *4* Or *your side* [b] *10* That is, about 8 ounces (about 0.2 kilogram) [c] *11* That is, about 2/3 quart (about 0.6 liter)

[14]Then I said, "Not so, Sovereign LORD![g] I have never defiled myself. From my youth until now I have never eaten anything found dead[h] or torn by wild animals. No unclean meat has ever entered my mouth.[i]"

[15]"Very well," he said, "I will let you bake your bread over cow manure instead of human excrement."

[16]He then said to me: "Son of man, I will cut off[j] the supply of food in Jerusalem. The people will eat rationed food in anxiety and drink rationed water in despair,[k] [17]for food and water will be scarce. They will be appalled at the sight of each other and will waste away because of[a] their sin.[l]

5

"Now, son of man, take a sharp sword and use it as a barber's razor[m] to shave[n] your head and your beard.[o] Then take a set of scales and divide up the hair. [2]When the days of your siege come to an end, burn a third of the hair with fire inside the city. Take a third and strike it with the sword all around the city. And scatter a third to the wind. For I will pursue them with drawn sword.[p] [3]But take a few strands of hair and tuck them away in the folds of your garment.[q] [4]Again, take a few of these and throw them into the fire and burn them up. A fire will spread from there to the whole house of Israel.

[5]"This is what the Sovereign LORD says: This is Jerusalem, which I have set in the center of the nations, with countries all around her. [6]Yet in her wickedness she has rebelled against my laws and decrees more than the nations and countries around her. She has rejected my laws and has not followed my decrees.[r]

[7]"Therefore this is what the Sovereign LORD says: You have been more unruly than the nations around you and have not followed my decrees or kept my laws. You have not even[b] conformed to the standards of the nations around you.[s]

[8]"Therefore this is what the Sovereign LORD says: I myself am against you, Jerusalem, and I will inflict punishment on you in the sight of the nations.[t] [9]Because of all your detestable idols, I will do to you what I have never done before and will never do again.[u] [10]Therefore in your midst fathers will eat their children, and children will eat their fathers.[v] I will inflict punishment on you and will scatter all your survivors to the winds.[w] [11]Therefore as surely as I live, declares the Sovereign LORD, because you have defiled my sanctuary with all your vile images[x] and detestable practices,[y] I myself will withdraw my favor; I will not look on you with pity or spare you.[z] [12]A third of your people will die of the plague or perish by famine inside you; a third will fall by the sword outside your walls; and a third I will scatter to the winds and pursue with drawn sword.[a]

[13]"Then my anger will cease and my wrath[b]

4:14 [g]Jer 1:6; Eze 9:8; 20:49 [h]Lev 11:39 [i]Ex 22:31; Dt 14:3; Ac 10:14
4:16 [j]Ps 105:16; Eze 5:16 [k]ver 10-11; Lev 26:26; Isa 3:1; Eze 12:19
4:17 [l]Lev 26:39; Eze 24:23; 33:10
5:1 [m]Isa 7:20 [n]Eze 44:20 [o]Lev 21:5
5:2 [p]ver 12; Lev 26:33
5:3 [q]Jer 39:10
5:6 [r]Jer 11:10; Eze 16:47-51; Zec 7:11
5:7 [s]2Ch 33:9; Jer 2:10-11; Eze 16:47
5:8 [t]Eze 15:7
5:9 [u]Da 9:12; Mt 24:21
5:10 [v]Lev 26:29; La 2:20 [w]Lev 26:33; Ps 44:11; Eze 12:14; Zec 2:6
5:11 [x]Eze 7:20 [y]2Ch 36:14; Eze 8:6 [z]Eze 7:4,9
5:12 [a]ver 2,17; Jer 15:2; 21:9; Eze 6:11-12; 12:14
5:13 [b]Eze 21:17; 36:6

[a] 17 Or *away in* [b] 7 Most Hebrew manuscripts; some Hebrew manuscripts and Syriac *You have*

Ezekiel's Protest

EZE 4:14-15

Throughout his book Ezekiel willingly obeys the Lord's commands to perform the most outlandish behavior in order to teach the people divine truths. He lies on one side for 390 days and on the other side for 40 days (Eze 4:4-6). He shaves his head and beard with a sword (Eze 5:1). He digs holes through walls (Eze 12:5). But when God tells Ezekiel to cook his food over human excrement, Ezekiel protests. Not because it's too hard or indecent, but because it will make him unclean, unholy before God, something he's spent his life guarding himself against.

Something foolish? Yes, Lord. Something embarrassing? Sure, Lord. Something that will make the people think I'm crazy? OK, Lord. Something that will make me unclean before you, Lord? Please, no, Lord! And God honors his request. Ezekiel's desire to be pleasing to God—and his lack of concern with his image before others—is a beautiful example to us of wholehearted, sold-out, never-turning-back commitment to God.

against them will subside, and I will be avenged.[c] And when I have spent my wrath upon them, they will know that I the LORD have spoken in my zeal.

14“I will make you a ruin and a reproach among the nations around you, in the sight of all who pass by.[d] 15You will be a reproach and a taunt, a warning and an object of horror to the nations around you when I inflict punishment on you in anger and in wrath and with stinging rebuke.[e] I the LORD have spoken.[f] 16When I shoot at you with my deadly and destructive arrows of famine, I will shoot to destroy you. I will bring more and more famine upon you and cut off your supply of food.[g] 17I will send famine and wild beasts against you, and they will leave you childless. Plague and bloodshed[h] will sweep through you, and I will bring the sword against you. I the LORD have spoken.[i]”

A Prophecy Against the Mountains of Israel

6 The word of the LORD came to me: 2“Son of man, set your face against the mountains[j] of Israel; prophesy against them 3and say: ‘O mountains of Israel, hear the word of the Sovereign LORD. This is what the Sovereign LORD says to the mountains and hills, to the ravines and valleys:[k] I am about to bring a sword against you, and I will destroy your high places.[l] 4Your altars will be demolished and your incense altars[m] will be smashed; and I will slay your people in front of your idols. 5I will lay the dead bodies of the Israelites in front of their idols, and I will scatter your bones[n] around your altars. 6Wherever you live, the towns will be laid waste and the high places demolished, so that your altars will be laid waste and devastated, your idols[o] smashed and ruined, your incense altars[p] broken down, and what you have made wiped out.[q] 7Your people will fall slain among you, and you will know that I am the LORD.

8“ ‘But I will spare some, for some of you will escape[r] the sword when you are scattered among the lands and nations.[s] 9Then in the nations where they have been carried captive, those who escape will remember me—how I have been grieved[t] by their adulterous hearts, which have turned away from me, and by their eyes, which have lusted after their idols.[u] They will loathe themselves for the evil they have done and for all their detestable practices.[v] 10And they will know that I am the LORD; I did not threaten in vain to bring this calamity on them.

11“ ‘This is what the Sovereign LORD says: Strike your hands together and stamp your feet and cry out “Alas!” because of all the wicked and detestable practices of the house of Israel, for they will fall by the sword, famine and plague.[w] 12He that is far away will die of the plague, and he that is near will fall by the sword, and he that survives and is spared will die of famine. So will I spend

5:13 [c]Isa 1:24
5:14 [d]Lev 26:32; Ne 2:17; Ps 74:3-10; 79:1-4
5:15 [e]1Ki 9:7; Jer 22:8-9; 24:9 [f]Eze 25:17
5:16 [g]Dt 32:24
5:17 [h]Eze 38:22 [i]Eze 14:21
6:2 [j]Eze 36:1
6:3 [k]Eze 36:4 [l]Lev 26:30
6:4 [m]2Ch 14:5
6:5 [n]Jer 8:1-2
6:6 [o]Mic 1:7; Zec 13:2 [p]Lev 26:30 [q]Isa 6:11; Eze 5:14
6:8 [r]Jer 44:28 [s]Isa 6:13; Jer 44:14; Eze 12:16; 14:22
6:9 [t]Ps 78:40; Isa 7:13 [u]Eze 20:7,24 [v]Eze 20:43; 36:31
6:11 [w]Eze 5:12; 21:14,17; 25:6

No matter how old they grow, some people never lose their beauty. They merely move it from their faces into their hearts.

—Barbara Johnson

[a] *14* Most Hebrew manuscripts; a few Hebrew manuscripts *Riblah*

6:12 my wrath upon them.[x] 13And they will know that
[x]Eze 5:12 I am the LORD, when their people lie slain among
their idols around their altars, on every high hill
and on all the mountaintops, under every spread-
6:13 [y]Isa 57:5 ing tree and every leafy oak[y]—places where they
[z]1Ki 14:23; offered fragrant incense to all their idols.[z] 14And I
Jer 2:20; Eze 20:28; will stretch out my hand[a] against them and make
Hos 4:13 the land a desolate waste from the desert to Dib-
lah[a]—wherever they live. Then they will know
6:14 [a]Isa 5:25 that I am the LORD.[b]' "
[b]Eze 14:13

The End Has Come

7 The word of the LORD came to me: 2"Son of
7:2 man, this is what the Sovereign LORD says to
[c]Am 8:2,10 the land of Israel: The end![c] The end has come
[d]Rev 7:1; 20:8 upon the four corners[d] of the land. 3The end is
now upon you and I will unleash my anger
against you. I will judge you according to your
7:4 conduct and repay you for all your detestable
[e]Eze 5:11 practices. 4I will not look on you with pity[e] or
spare you; I will surely repay you for your conduct and the detestable practices among you.
Then you will know that I am the LORD.
7:5 5"This is what the Sovereign LORD says: Disas-
[f]2Ki 21:12 ter![f] An unheard-of[a] disaster is coming. 6The end
has come! The end has come! It has roused itself
against you. It has come! 7Doom has come upon
7:7 you—you who dwell in the land. The time has
[g]Eze 12:23; Zep 1:14 come, the day is near;[g] there is panic, not joy,
upon the mountains. 8I am about to pour out my
7:8 wrath[h] on you and spend my anger against you; I
[h]Isa 42:25; will judge you according to your conduct and
Eze 9:8; 14:19; repay you for all your detestable practices.[i] 9I will
Na 1:6 [i]Eze 20:8,21; not look on you with pity or spare you; I will
36:19 repay you in accordance with your conduct and
the detestable practices among you. Then you will
7:10 [j]Ps 89:32; know that it is I the LORD who strikes the blow.
Isa 10:5 10"The day is here! It has come! Doom has burst
7:11 forth, the rod[j] has budded, arrogance has blos-
[k]Jer 16:6; Zep 1:18 somed! 11Violence has grown into[b] a rod to punish
wickedness; none of the people will be left, none
7:12 of that crowd—no wealth, nothing of value.[k] 12The
[l]ver 7; time has come, the day has arrived. Let not the
Isa 5:13-14; Eze 30:3 buyer rejoice nor the seller grieve, for wrath is
upon the whole crowd.[l] 13The seller will not recov-
7:13 er the land he has sold as long as both of them live,
[m]Lev 25:24-28 for the vision concerning the whole crowd will not
be reversed. Because of their sins, not one of them
7:15 [n]Dt 32:25; will preserve his life.[m] 14Though they blow the
Jer 14:18; trumpet and get everything ready, no one will go
La 1:20; Eze 5:12 into battle, for my wrath is upon the whole crowd.
15"Outside is the sword, inside are plague and
7:16 famine; those in the country will die by the
[o]Isa 59:11 [p]Ezr 9:15; sword, and those in the city will be devoured by
Eze 6:8 famine and plague.[n] 16All who survive and escape
7:17 will be in the mountains, moaning like doves[o] of
[q]Isa 13:7; Eze 21:7; the valleys, each because of his sins.[p] 17Every
22:14 hand will go limp,[q] and every knee will become

[a] *5* Most Hebrew manuscripts; some Hebrew manuscripts and Syriac *Disaster after*   [b] *11* Or *The violent one has become*

The End! The End!

EZE 7:1-4

Ezekiel's message takes on a special urgency in these verses. With a poetic force, he calls to the people, "The end, the end, the end." With these words spoken through Ezekiel, God tries one more time to get the attention of his people. No longer using words to describe this punishment or that punishment, the people are now forced to look at the final *end* of all that is familiar, the end of all they love, the end of Jerusalem.

God's people have proven over and over again their stubbornness and their unwillingness to listen. They ignore Ezekiel's words of judgment, just as they've ignored all the prophets before him. *Surely God won't destroy Jerusalem*, they think. *After all, this is his dwelling place on earth.* But they don't comprehend the depth of their sin or the righteousness of their God. He not only *will* judge, but he *must* judge.

Utterly Detestable

EZE 8:6

A total of 42 times Ezekiel calls the things done by Israel and other nations "detestable" in God's sight. In this one verse alone he calls their deeds "utterly detestable" and "even more detestable." Extreme language. But what exactly does he mean?

The word "detestable" is used to translate the Hebrew word toevah. *The word can refer to idols, the gods idols represent, the practice of worshiping idols, and the sometimes lewd, sometimes unclean, sometimes horrifying practices that go along with the worship of false gods. Anything that turns the people's heads and hearts away from God is* detestable *to him. He is a God who jealously guards our loyalties, wanting only that we follow him wholeheartedly and not get involved in anything that is* detestable *to him.*

as weak as water. 18They will put on sackcloth
and be clothed with terror.[r] Their faces will be
covered with shame and their heads will be
shaved.[s] 19They will throw their silver into the
streets, and their gold will be an unclean thing.
Their silver and gold will not be able to save them
in the day of the LORD's wrath.[t] They will not satisfy
their hunger or fill their stomachs with it, for
it has made them stumble[u] into sin.[v] 20They were
proud of their beautiful jewelry and used it to
make their detestable idols and vile images.[w]
Therefore I will turn these into an unclean thing
for them. 21I will hand it all over as plunder to foreigners
and as loot to the wicked of the earth, and
they will defile it.[x] 22I will turn my face[y] away
from them, and they will desecrate my treasured
place; robbers will enter it and desecrate it.
23"Prepare chains, because the land is full of
bloodshed[z] and the city is full of violence. 24I will
bring the most wicked of the nations to take possession
of their houses; I will put an end to the
pride of the mighty, and their sanctuaries[a] will be
desecrated.[b] 25When terror comes, they will seek
peace, but there will be none.[c] 26Calamity upon
calamity[d] will come, and rumor upon rumor.
They will try to get a vision from the prophet; the
teaching of the law by the priest will be lost, as
will the counsel of the elders.[e] 27The king will
mourn, the prince will be clothed with despair,[f]
and the hands of the people of the land will tremble.
I will deal with them according to their conduct,[g]
and by their own standards I will judge
them. Then they will know that I am the LORD.[h]"

Idolatry in the Temple

8 In the sixth year, in the sixth month on the fifth
day, while I was sitting in my house and the
elders[i] of Judah were sitting before[j] me, the hand of
the Sovereign LORD came upon me there.[k] 2I looked,
and I saw a figure like that of a man.[a] From what
appeared to be his waist down he was like fire, and
from there up his appearance was as bright as
glowing metal.[l] 3He stretched out what looked like
a hand and took me by the hair of my head. The
Spirit lifted me up[m] between earth and heaven and
in visions of God he took me to Jerusalem, to the
entrance to the north gate of the inner court, where
the idol that provokes to jealousy[n] stood. 4And
there before me was the glory[o] of the God of Israel,
as in the vision I had seen in the plain.[p]
5Then he said to me, "Son of man, look toward
the north." So I looked, and in the entrance north
of the gate of the altar I saw this idol[q] of jealousy.
6And he said to me, "Son of man, do you see
what they are doing—the utterly detestable[r]
things the house of Israel is doing here, things
that will drive me far from my sanctuary? But you
will see things that are even more detestable."
7Then he brought me to the entrance to the

7:18 [r]Ps 55:5 [s]Isa 15:2-3; Eze 27:31; Am 8:10
7:19 [t]Eze 13:5; Zep 1:7,18 [u]Eze 14:3 [v]Pr 11:4
7:20 [w]Jer 7:30
7:21 [x]2Ki 24:13
7:22 [y]Eze 39:23-24
7:23 [z]2Ki 21:16
7:24 [a]Eze 24:21 [b]2Ch 7:20; Eze 28:7
7:25 [c]Eze 13:10, 16
7:26 [d]Jer 4:20 [e]Isa 47:11; Eze 20:1-3; Mic 3:6
7:27 [f]Ps 109:19; Eze 26:16 [g]Eze 18:20 [h]ver 4
8:1 [i]Eze 14:1 [j]Eze 33:31 [k]Eze 1:1-3
8:2 [l]Eze 1:4,26-27
8:3 [m]Eze 3:12; 11:1 [n]Ex 20:5; Dt 32:16
8:4 [o]Eze 1:28 [p]Eze 3:22
8:5 [q]Ps 78:58; Jer 32:34
8:6 [r]Eze 5:11

[a] 2 Or *saw a fiery figure*

court. I looked, and I saw a hole in the wall. 8He
said to me, "Son of man, now dig into the wall."
So I dug into the wall and saw a doorway there.
9And he said to me, "Go in and see the wicked
and detestable things they are doing here." 10So I
went in and looked, and I saw portrayed all over
the walls all kinds of crawling things and
8:10 detestable animals and all the idols of the house of
[s]Ex 20:4 Israel.[s] 11In front of them stood seventy elders of the
8:11 house of Israel, and Jaazaniah son of Shaphan was
[t]Nu 16:17 standing among them. Each had a censer[t] in his
[u]Nu 16:35 hand, and a fragrant cloud of incense[u] was rising.
12He said to me, "Son of man, have you seen
what the elders of the house of Israel are doing in
8:12 the darkness, each at the shrine of his own idol?
[v]Ps 10:11; They say, 'The LORD does not see[v] us; the LORD has
Isa 29:15; forsaken the land.' " 13Again, he said, "You will see
Eze 9:9 them doing things that are even more detestable."
14Then he brought me to the entrance to the
north gate of the house of the LORD, and I saw
women sitting there, mourning for Tammuz. 15He
said to me, "Do you see this, son of man? You will
see things that are even more detestable than this."
16He then brought me into the inner court of the
8:16 house of the LORD, and there at the entrance to the
[w]Joel 2:17 temple, between the portico and the altar,[w] were
[x]Dt 4:19; about twenty-five men. With their backs toward the
17:3; Job 31:28; temple of the LORD and their faces toward the east,
Jer 2:27; Eze 11:1,12 they were bowing down to the sun in the east.[x]
17He said to me, "Have you seen this, son of
man? Is it a trivial matter for the house of Judah
8:17 to do the detestable things they are doing here?
[y]Eze 9:9 [z]Eze 16:26 Must they also fill the land with violence[y] and
continually provoke me to anger?[z] Look at them
putting the branch to their nose! 18Therefore I will
8:18 deal with them in anger; I will not look on them
[a]Eze 9:10; 24:14 with pity[a] or spare them. Although they shout in
[b]Isa 1:15; Jer 11:11; Mic 3:4; Zec 7:13 my ears, I will not listen[b] to them."

Idolaters Killed

9 Then I heard him call out in a loud voice,
"Bring the guards of the city here, each with a
weapon in his hand." 2And I saw six men coming
from the direction of the upper gate, which faces
9:2 north, each with a deadly weapon in his hand.
[c]Lev 16:4; With them was a man clothed in linen[c] who had
Eze 10:2; a writing kit at his side. They came in and stood
Rev 15:6 beside the bronze altar.
9:3 3Now the glory[d] of the God of Israel went up
[d]Eze 10:4 [e]Eze 11:22 from above the cherubim,[e] where it had been, and
moved to the threshold of the temple. Then the
LORD called to the man clothed in linen who had
9:4 the writing kit at his side 4and said to him, "Go
[f]Ex 12:7; throughout the city of Jerusalem and put a mark[f]
2Co 1:22; on the foreheads of those who grieve and lament[g]
Rev 7:3; 9:4 [g]Ps 119:136; over all the detestable things that are done in it.[h]"
Jer 13:17; 5As I listened, he said to the others, "Follow him
Eze 21:6 [h]Ps 119:53 through the city and kill, without showing pity[i]
or compassion. 6Slaughter old men, young men
9:5 and maidens, women and children, but do not
[i]Eze 5:11 touch anyone who has the mark. Begin at my

Mourning Tammuz

EZE 8:14

How much more detestable can it get? Israelite women sit at the entrance to the temple of the true God and mourn a false god. Such a futile activity—to mourn for someone who doesn't even exist!

Tammuz was a well-known fertility god of the ancient Near East, worshiped in many of the nations surrounding Israel. While taking care of his sheep (so the myth surrounding this god goes), Tammuz was killed by a wild boar. His death symbolizes the start of the winter season, when plants die and the leaves fall from the trees. Female worshipers participate in ceremonial mourning rites at this same time each year. This is just one of many detestable acts God shows Ezekiel in his visionary tour of Jerusalem.

Cherubim

EZE 10:3–12

The word cherubim occurs more times in this chapter of Ezekiel than in any other single location in Scripture. More than just ethereal, unearthly beings, the cherubim are very real beings, as Ezekiel 1 makes clear when it calls them "living creatures" (Eze 1:5) and clearly—though with difficulty—describes their appearance. Two cherubim are placed as guardians outside of Eden (Ge 3:24). Cherubim are placed on each side of the mercy seat of the ark to represent the protection of God's holiness and as a "throne" for his presence (Ex 25:18–22). Cherubim symbolize worship of a holy God, as is revealed when they are placed throughout Solomon's temple (1Ki 6–8). Scripture speaks of God sitting "enthroned" between the cherubim (Ps 80:1; 99:1). The cherubim appear again in the book of Revelation as "living creatures." They are the guardians of the throne of God, and they never stop—day or night—praising God with these mighty and so "truth-full" words: "Holy, holy, holy is the Lord God Almighty, who was, and is, and is to come" (Rev 4:8).

sanctuary." So they began with the elders[j] who were in front of the temple.[k]

7 Then he said to them, "Defile the temple and fill the courts with the slain. Go!" So they went out and began killing throughout the city. 8 While they were killing and I was left alone, I fell facedown,[l] crying out, "Ah, Sovereign LORD! Are you going to destroy the entire remnant of Israel in this outpouring of your wrath on Jerusalem?[m]"

9 He answered me, "The sin of the house of Israel and Judah is exceedingly great; the land is full of bloodshed and the city is full of injustice.[n] They say, 'The LORD has forsaken the land; the LORD does not see.'[o] 10 So I will not look on them with pity[p] or spare them, but I will bring down on their own heads what they have done.[q]"

11 Then the man in linen with the writing kit at his side brought back word, saying, "I have done as you commanded."

The Glory Departs From the Temple

10 I looked, and I saw the likeness of a throne[r] of sapphire[a][s] above the expanse[t] that was over the heads of the cherubim. 2 The LORD said to the man clothed in linen,[u] "Go in among the wheels[v] beneath the cherubim. Fill[w] your hands with burning coals from among the cherubim and scatter them over the city." And as I watched, he went in.

3 Now the cherubim were standing on the south side of the temple when the man went in, and a cloud filled the inner court. 4 Then the glory of the LORD[x] rose from above the cherubim and moved to the threshold of the temple. The cloud filled the temple, and the court was full of the radiance of the glory of the LORD. 5 The sound of the wings of the cherubim could be heard as far away as the outer court, like the voice[y] of God Almighty[b] when he speaks.

6 When the LORD commanded the man in linen, "Take fire from among the wheels, from among the cherubim," the man went in and stood beside a wheel. 7 Then one of the cherubim reached out his hand to the fire that was among them. He took up some of it and put it into the hands of the man in linen, who took it and went out. 8 (Under the wings of the cherubim could be seen what looked like the hands of a man.)[z]

9 I looked, and I saw beside the cherubim four wheels, one beside each of the cherubim; the wheels sparkled like chrysolite.[a] 10 As for their appearance, the four of them looked alike; each was like a wheel intersecting a wheel. 11 As they moved, they would go in any one of the four directions the cherubim faced; the wheels did not turn about[c] as the cherubim went. The cherubim went in whatever direction the head faced, without turning as they went. 12 Their entire bodies, including their backs, their hands and their

9:6 [j]Eze 8:11-13, 16 [k]2Ch 36:17; Jer 25:29; 1Pe 4:17
9:8 [l]Jos 7:6 [m]Eze 11:13; Am 7:1-6
9:9 [n]Eze 22:29 [o]Job 22:13; Eze 8:12
9:10 [p]Eze 7:4; 8:18 [q]Isa 65:6; Eze 11:21
10:1 [r]Rev 4:2 [s]Ex 24:10 [t]Eze 1:22
10:2 [u]Eze 9:2 [v]Eze 1:15 [w]Rev 8:5
10:4 [x]Eze 1:28; 9:3
10:5 [y]Job 40:9; Eze 1:24
10:8 [z]Eze 1:8
10:9 [a]Eze 1:15-16; Rev 21:20

[a] 1 Or *lapis lazuli* [b] 5 Hebrew *El-Shaddai* [c] 11 Or *aside*

wings, were completely full of eyes,[b] as were their
four wheels.[c] 13I heard the wheels being called
"the whirling wheels." 14Each of the cherubim[d]
had four faces:[e] One face was that of a cherub, the
second the face of a man, the third the face of a
lion, and the fourth the face of an eagle.[f]
15Then the cherubim rose upward. These were
the living creatures[g] I had seen by the Kebar River. 16When the cherubim moved, the wheels
beside them moved; and when the cherubim
spread their wings to rise from the ground, the
wheels did not leave their side. 17When the cherubim stood still, they also stood still; and when
the cherubim rose, they rose with them, because
the spirit of the living creatures was in them.[h]
18Then the glory of the LORD departed from over
the threshold of the temple and stopped above the
cherubim.[i] 19While I watched, the cherubim
spread their wings and rose from the ground, and
as they went, the wheels went with them.[j] They
stopped at the entrance to the east gate of the
LORD's house, and the glory of the God of Israel
was above them.
20These were the living creatures I had seen
beneath the God of Israel by the Kebar River,[k] and
I realized that they were cherubim. 21Each had
four faces[l] and four wings,[m] and under their
wings was what looked like the hands of a man.
22Their faces had the same appearance as those I
had seen by the Kebar River. Each one went
straight ahead.

Judgment on Israel's Leaders

11 Then the Spirit lifted me up and brought me
to the gate of the house of the LORD that
faces east. There at the entrance to the gate were
twenty-five men, and I saw among them Jaazaniah son of Azzur and Pelatiah son of Benaiah, leaders of the people.[n] 2The LORD said to me, "Son of
man, these are the men who are plotting evil and
giving wicked advice in this city. 3They say, 'Will
it not soon be time to build houses?[a] This city is a
cooking pot,[o] and we are the meat.'[p] 4Therefore
prophesy[q] against them; prophesy, son of man."
5Then the Spirit of the LORD came upon me, and
he told me to say: "This is what the LORD says:
That is what you are saying, O house of Israel, but
I know what is going through your mind.[r] 6You
have killed many people in this city and filled its
streets with the dead.[s]
7"Therefore this is what the Sovereign LORD
says: The bodies you have thrown there are the
meat and this city is the pot, but I will drive you
out of it.[t] 8You fear the sword, and the sword is
what I will bring against you, declares the Sovereign LORD.[u] 9I will drive you out of the city and
hand you over[v] to foreigners and inflict punishment on you.[w] 10You will fall by the sword, and I
will execute judgment on you at the borders of

[a] 3 Or *This is not the time to build houses.*

10:12 [b]Rev 4:6-8 [c]Eze 1:15-21
10:14 [d]1Ki 7:36 [e]Eze 1:6 [f]Eze 1:10; Rev 4:7
10:15 [g]Eze 1:3,5
10:17 [h]Eze 1:20-21
10:18 [i]Ps 18:10
10:19 [j]Eze 11:1,22
10:20 [k]Eze 1:1
10:21 [l]Eze 41:18 [m]Eze 1:6
11:1 [n]Eze 8:16; 10:19; 43:4-5
11:3 [o]Jer 1:13; Eze 24:3 [p]ver 7,11
11:4 [q]Eze 3:4,17
11:5 [r]Jer 17:10
11:6 [s]Eze 7:23; 22:6
11:7 [t]Eze 24:3-13; Mic 3:2-3
11:8 [u]Pr 10:24
11:9 [v]Ps 106:41 [w]Dt 28:36; Eze 5:8

The Glory of the LORD

EZE 10:18

God's glory—his presence in all his abilities, attributes, holiness, goodness and mercy—comes to inhabit the tabernacle (Ex 40:34-35) and then the temple (1Ki 8:10-11) in the form of a "glory cloud" that covers each edifice at its dedication. Now Ezekiel again sees God's glory over the temple. This time, however, it is not coming, but going. The people's sins have grieved God so excessively that he is now rejecting the temple (Eze 11:23), just as he promised he would do if they rejected him (1Ki 9:6-7). Ezekiel sees God go and mourns (Eze 11:13).

A Sanctuary

EZE 11:16

The symbol of God's presence with his people Israel has been the sanctuary, the temple in Jerusalem. There, between the cherubim on the mercy seat of the ark, God has dwelt with his people (Ex 30:6). The Jews at that time perceived God's presence with them in a more physical sense than we perceive it today. Although God had revealed that his presence was unlimited (1Ki 8:27; Ps 139:7–12), the Jews in exile likely found it hard to believe that God was with them in Babylon since they were so distant from the temple in Jerusalem.

These words from God through Ezekiel must have been a great comfort to these exiles, who were not only separated from their homes and families but thought they were also separated from their God. He consoles them by assuring them that he is still with them—he *himself* is now their sanctuary, their place of refuge, their home away from home.

Israel.[x] Then you will know that I am the LORD.
11This city will not be a pot[y] for you, nor will you
be the meat in it; I will execute judgment on you
at the borders of Israel. 12And you will know that
I am the LORD, for you have not followed my
decrees[z] or kept my laws but have conformed to
the standards of the nations around you.[a]"
13Now as I was prophesying, Pelatiah[b] son of
Benaiah died. Then I fell facedown and cried out
in a loud voice, "Ah, Sovereign LORD! Will you
completely destroy the remnant of Israel?[c]"
14The word of the LORD came to me: 15"Son of
man, your brothers—your brothers who are your
blood relatives[a] and the whole house of Israel—
are those of whom the people of Jerusalem have
said, 'They are[b] far away from the LORD; this land
was given to us as our possession.'[d]

Promised Return of Israel

16"Therefore say: 'This is what the Sovereign
LORD says: Although I sent them far away among
the nations and scattered them among the countries, yet for a little while I have been a sanctuary[e]
for them in the countries where they have gone.'
17"Therefore say: 'This is what the Sovereign
LORD says: I will gather you from the nations and
bring you back from the countries where you
have been scattered, and I will give you back the
land of Israel again.'[f]
18"They will return to it and remove all its vile
images[g] and detestable idols.[h] 19I will give them
an undivided heart[i] and put a new spirit in them;
I will remove from them their heart of stone[j] and
give them a heart of flesh.[k] 20Then they will follow my decrees and be careful to keep my laws.[l]
They will be my people, and I will be their God.[m]
21But as for those whose hearts are devoted to
their vile images and detestable idols, I will bring
down on their own heads what they have done,
declares the Sovereign LORD.[n]"
22Then the cherubim, with the wheels beside
them, spread their wings, and the glory of the God
of Israel was above them.[o] 23The glory[p] of the
LORD went up from within the city and stopped
above the mountain[q] east of it. 24The Spirit[r] lifted
me up and brought me to the exiles in Babylonia[c]
in the vision[s] given by the Spirit of God.
Then the vision I had seen went up from me,
25and I told the exiles everything the LORD had
shown me.[t]

The Exile Symbolized

12 The word of the LORD came to me: 2"Son of
man, you are living among a rebellious people. They have eyes to see but do not see and ears
to hear but do not hear, for they are a rebellious
people.[u]

[a] 15 Or *are in exile with you* (see Septuagint and Syriac)
[b] 15 Or *those to whom the people of Jerusalem have said, 'Stay*
[c] 24 Or *Chaldea*

11:10 [x] 2Ki 14:25
11:11 [y] ver 3
11:12 [z] Lev 18:4; Eze 18:9 [a] Eze 8:10
11:13 [b] ver 1 [c] Eze 9:8
11:15 [d] Eze 33:24
11:16 [e] Ps 90:1; 91:9; Isa 8:14
11:17 [f] Jer 3:18; 24:5-6; Eze 28:25; 34:13
11:18 [g] Eze 5:11 [h] Eze 37:23
11:19 [i] Jer 32:39 [j] Zec 7:12 [k] Eze 18:31; 36:26; 2Co 3:3
11:20 [l] Ps 105:45 [m] Eze 14:11; 36:26-28
11:21 [n] Eze 9:10; 16:43
11:22 [o] Eze 10:19
11:23 [p] Eze 8:4; 10:4 [q] Zec 14:4
11:24 [r] Eze 8:3 [s] 2Co 12:2-4
11:25 [t] Eze 3:4,11
12:2 [u] Isa 6:10; Eze 2:6-8; Mt 13:15

3“Therefore, son of man, pack your belongings
for exile and in the daytime, as they watch, set out
and go from where you are to another place. Perhaps[v] they will understand,[w] though they are a
rebellious house.[x] 4During the daytime, while they
watch, bring out your belongings packed for exile.
Then in the evening, while they are watching, go
out like those who go into exile.[y] 5While they
watch, dig through the wall and take your belongings out through it. 6Put them on your shoulder as
they are watching and carry them out at dusk.
Cover your face so that you cannot see the land,
for I have made you a sign[z] to the house of Israel.”
7So I did as I was commanded.[a] During the day
I brought out my things packed for exile. Then in
the evening I dug through the wall with my
hands. I took my belongings out at dusk, carrying them on my shoulders while they watched.
8In the morning the word of the LORD came to
me: 9“Son of man, did not that rebellious house
of Israel ask you, ‘What are you doing?’[b]
10“Say to them, ‘This is what the Sovereign LORD
says: This oracle concerns the prince in Jerusalem
and the whole house of Israel who are there.’ 11Say
to them, ‘I am a sign to you.’
“As I have done, so it will be done to them.
They will go into exile as captives.[c]
12“The prince among them will put his things
on his shoulder at dusk[d] and leave, and a hole will
be dug in the wall for him to go through. He will
cover his face so that he cannot see the land.[e] 13I
will spread my net[f] for him, and he will be caught
in my snare;[g] I will bring him to Babylonia, the
land of the Chaldeans, but he will not see[h] it, and
there he will die.[i] 14I will scatter to the winds all
those around him—his staff and all his troops—
and I will pursue them with drawn sword.[j]
15“They will know that I am the LORD, when I
disperse them among the nations and scatter them
through the countries. 16But I will spare a few of
them from the sword, famine and plague, so that
in the nations where they go they may acknowledge all their detestable practices. Then they will
know that I am the LORD.[k]”
17The word of the LORD came to me: 18“Son of
man, tremble as you eat your food,[l] and shudder
in fear as you drink your water. 19Say to the people of the land: ‘This is what the Sovereign LORD
says about those living in Jerusalem and in the
land of Israel: They will eat their food in anxiety
and drink their water in despair, for their land will
be stripped of everything[m] in it because of the violence of all who live there.[n] 20The inhabited towns
will be laid waste and the land will be desolate.
Then you will know that I am the LORD.[o]’ ”
21The word of the LORD came to me: 22“Son of
man, what is this proverb you have in the land of
Israel: ‘The days go by and every vision comes to
nothing’?[p] 23Say to them, ‘This is what the Sovereign LORD says: I am going to put an end to this
proverb, and they will no longer quote it in Israel.’

12:3 [v]Jer 36:3 [w]Jer 26:3 [x]2Ti 2:25-26
12:4 [y]ver 12; Jer 39:4
12:6 [z]ver 12; Isa 8:18; 20:3; Eze 4:3; 24:24
12:7 [a]Eze 24:18; 37:10
12:9 [b]Eze 17:12; 20:49; 24:19
12:11 [c]2Ki 25:7; Jer 15:2; 52:15
12:12 [d]Jer 39:4 [e]Jer 52:7
12:13 [f]Eze 17:20; 19:8; Hos 7:12 [g]Isa 24:17-18 [h]Jer 39:7 [i]Jer 52:11; Eze 17:16
12:14 [j]2Ki 25:5; Eze 5:10,12
12:16 [k]Jer 22:8-9; Eze 6:8-10; 14:22
12:18 [l]La 5:9; Eze 4:16
12:19 [m]Eze 6:6-14; Mic 7:13; Zec 7:14 [n]Eze 4:16; 23:33
12:20 [o]Isa 7:23-24; Jer 4:7
12:22 [p]Eze 11:3; Am 6:3; 2Pe 3:4

What a lavish God we serve. His expressions of love and commitment to us are limitless. He keeps every promise he makes. His giving is never-ending—an eternal fountain, flowing forever. His life pours into us as we open ourselves to him. His love is unconditional. Faithful.

—Kathy Troccoli

False Prophets

EZE 13

Ezekiel denounces the prophets of Israel who are prophesying "out of their own imagination" (Eze 13:2). Their words do not come from God but from their own minds and imaginations. The Old Testament provides three tests to determine if a prophet is from God or is a false prophet. First, if a prophet's words do not come true, he or she is a false prophet (Dt 18:21–22). Second, if a prophet speaks words, even with accompanying signs and wonders, that encourage idolatry, that contradict or invalidate some known commandment or understanding about God, that prophet is false and not to be trusted (Dt 13:1–3). Third, the prophets themselves must live lives that evidence their trust in God and their adherence to his commandments (Jer 23:14). False prophets are not only a sad reproach on Israelite society, but they are also a danger to God's people. Jesus calls them "ferocious wolves" (Mt 7:15).

Say to them, 'The days are near when every vision
will be fulfilled.[q] 24For there will be no more false
visions or flattering divinations[r] among the people
of Israel. 25But I the LORD will speak what I will,
and it shall be fulfilled without delay. For in your
days, you rebellious house, I will fulfill whatever
I say, declares the Sovereign LORD.[s]' "
26The word of the LORD came to me: 27"Son of
man, the house of Israel is saying, 'The vision he
sees is for many years from now, and he prophesies about the distant future.'[t]
28"Therefore say to them, 'This is what the Sovereign LORD says: None of my words will be
delayed any longer; whatever I say will be fulfilled, declares the Sovereign LORD.' "

False Prophets Condemned

13 The word of the LORD came to me: 2"Son of
man, prophesy against the prophets of Israel who are now prophesying. Say to those who
prophesy out of their own imagination: 'Hear the
word of the LORD![u] 3This is what the Sovereign
LORD says: Woe to the foolish[a] prophets[v] who follow their own spirit and have seen nothing![w] 4Your
prophets, O Israel, are like jackals among ruins.
5You have not gone up to the breaks in the wall to
repair[x] it for the house of Israel so that it will stand
firm in the battle on the day of the LORD.[y] 6Their
visions are false and their divinations a lie. They
say, "The LORD declares," when the LORD has not
sent them; yet they expect their words to be fulfilled.[z] 7Have you not seen false visions and
uttered lying divinations when you say, "The LORD
declares," though I have not spoken?
8" 'Therefore this is what the Sovereign LORD
says: Because of your false words and lying
visions, I am against you, declares the Sovereign
LORD. 9My hand will be against the prophets who
see false visions and utter lying divinations. They
will not belong to the council of my people or be
listed in the records[a] of the house of Israel, nor
will they enter the land of Israel. Then you will
know that I am the Sovereign LORD.[b]
10" 'Because they lead my people astray,[c] saying,
"Peace," when there is no peace, and because,
when a flimsy wall is built, they cover it with
whitewash,[d] 11therefore tell those who cover it with
whitewash that it is going to fall. Rain will come
in torrents, and I will send hailstones hurtling
down, and violent winds will burst forth.[e] 12When
the wall collapses, will people not ask you, "Where
is the whitewash you covered it with?"
13" 'Therefore this is what the Sovereign LORD
says: In my wrath I will unleash a violent wind,
and in my anger hailstones[f] and torrents of rain
will fall with destructive fury.[g] 14I will tear down
the wall you have covered with whitewash and
will level it to the ground so that its foundation[h]
will be laid bare. When it[b] falls,[i] you will be

[a] 3 Or *wicked* [b] 14 Or *the city*

12:23 [q]Ps 37:13; Joel 2:1; Zep 1:14
12:24 [r]Jer 14:14; Eze 13:23; Zec 13:2-4
12:25 [s]Isa 14:24; Hab 1:5
12:27 [t]Da 10:14
13:2 [u]ver 17; Jer 23:16; 37:19
13:3 [v]La 2:14 [w]Jer 23:25-32
13:5 [x]Isa 58:12; Eze 22:30 [y]Eze 7:19
13:6 [z]Jer 28:15; Eze 22:28
13:9 [a]Jer 17:13 [b]Eze 20:38
13:10 [c]Jer 50:6 [d]Eze 7:25; 22:28
13:11 [e]Eze 38:22
13:13 [f]Rev 11:19; 16:21 [g]Ex 9:25; Isa 30:30
13:14 [h]Mic 1:6 [i]Jer 6:15

destroyed in it; and you will know that I am the
LORD. [15]So I will spend my wrath against the wall
and against those who covered it with whitewash.
I will say to you, "The wall is gone and so are
those who whitewashed it, [16]those prophets of
Israel who prophesied to Jerusalem and saw
13:16 visions of peace for her when there was no peace,
declares the Sovereign LORD.[j]" '
[17]"Now, son of man, set your face against the
13:17 daughters[k] of your people who prophesy out of
their own imagination. Prophesy against them[l]
[18]and say, 'This is what the Sovereign LORD says:
Woe to the women who sew magic charms on all
their wrists and make veils of various lengths for
their heads in order to ensnare people. Will you
13:19 ensnare the lives of my people but preserve your
own? [19]You have profaned[m] me among my people
for a few handfuls of barley and scraps of bread.
By lying to my people, who listen to lies, you have
killed those who should not have died and have
spared those who should not live.[n]
[20]" 'Therefore this is what the Sovereign LORD
says: I am against your magic charms with which
you ensnare people like birds and I will tear them
from your arms; I will set free the people that you
ensnare like birds. [21]I will tear off your veils and
save my people from your hands, and they will no
13:21 longer fall prey to your power. Then you will
know that I am the LORD.[o] [22]Because you disheartened the righteous with your lies, when I
had brought them no grief, and because you
encouraged the wicked not to turn from their evil
13:22 ways and so save their lives,[p] [23]therefore you will
no longer see false visions or practice divination.[q]
13:23 I will save my people from your hands. And then
you will know that I am the LORD.[r]' "

Idolaters Condemned

14:1 **14** Some of the elders of Israel came to me and
sat down in front of me.[s] [2]Then the word of
the LORD came to me: [3]"Son of man, these men
have set up idols in their hearts and put wicked
14:3 stumbling blocks[t] before their faces. Should I let
them inquire of me at all?[u] [4]Therefore speak to
them and tell them, 'This is what the Sovereign
LORD says: When any Israelite sets up idols in his
heart and puts a wicked stumbling block before
his face and then goes to a prophet, I the LORD will
answer him myself in keeping with his great idolatry. [5]I will do this to recapture the hearts of the
14:5 people of Israel, who have all deserted[v] me for
their idols.'[w]
[6]"Therefore say to the house of Israel, 'This is
what the Sovereign LORD says: Repent! Turn from
your idols and renounce all your detestable
14:6 practices![x]
[7]" 'When any Israelite or any alien[y] living in Isra-
14:7 el separates himself from me and sets up idols in
his heart and puts a wicked stumbling block before
his face and then goes to a prophet to inquire of
me, I the LORD will answer him myself. [8]I will set

13:16 [j]Isa 57:21; Jer 6:14
13:17 [k]Rev 2:20 [l]ver 2
13:19 [m]Eze 20:39; 22:26 [n]Pr 28:21
13:21 [o]Ps 91:3
13:22 [p]Jer 23:14; Eze 33:14-16
13:23 [q]ver 6; Eze 12:24 [r]Mic 3:6
14:1 [s]Eze 8:1; 20:1
14:3 [t]ver 7; Eze 7:19 [u]Isa 1:15; Eze 20:31
14:5 [v]Zec 11:8 [w]Jer 2:11
14:6 [x]Isa 2:20; 30:22
14:7 [y]Ex 12:48; 20:10

Magic Charms

EZE 13:20

The "daughters of your people" (Eze 13:17) are involved in using "magic charms" (Eze 13:20) to influence the people of Israel to follow their own wicked ways rather than the ways of God. These "charms" are probably sewn bracelets and veils (Eze 13:18) worn by these women when they prophesy or speak incantations. Isaiah also speaks of the women of his day wearing charms (Isa 3:20). Ezekiel rebukes these women for their activities.

my face against[z] that man and make him an example and a byword.[a] I will cut him off from my people. Then you will know that I am the LORD.
9“ ‘And if the prophet[b] is enticed[c] to utter a
prophecy, I the LORD have enticed that prophet,
and I will stretch out my hand against him and
destroy him from among my people Israel.[d] 10They
will bear their guilt—the prophet will be as guilty
as the one who consults him. 11Then the people
of Israel will no longer stray[e] from me, nor will
they defile themselves anymore with all their sins.
They will be my people, and I will be their God,
declares the Sovereign LORD.[f] ’ ”

Judgment Inescapable

12The word of the LORD came to me: 13“Son of
man, if a country sins against me by being
unfaithful and I stretch out my hand against it to
cut off its food supply[g] and send famine upon it
and kill its men and their animals,[h] 14even if these
three men—Noah,[i] Daniel[a][j] and Job[k]—were in it,
they could save only themselves by their righteousness,[l] declares the Sovereign LORD.
15“Or if I send wild beasts[m] through that country
and they leave it childless and it becomes desolate
so that no one can pass through it because of the
beasts,[n] 16as surely as I live, declares the Sovereign
LORD, even if these three men were in it, they could
not save their own sons or daughters. They alone
would be saved, but the land would be desolate.[o]
17“Or if I bring a sword[p] against that country and
say, ‘Let the sword pass throughout the land,’ and
I kill its men and their animals,[q] 18as surely as I
live, declares the Sovereign LORD, even if these
three men were in it, they could not save their own
sons or daughters. They alone would be saved.
19“Or if I send a plague into that land and pour
out my wrath[r] upon it through bloodshed, killing
its men and their animals,[s] 20as surely as I live,
declares the Sovereign LORD, even if Noah, Daniel
and Job were in it, they could save neither son nor
daughter. They would save only themselves by
their righteousness.[t]
21“For this is what the Sovereign LORD says:
How much worse will it be when I send against
Jerusalem my four dreadful judgments—sword
and famine and wild beasts and plague—to kill its
men and their animals![u] 22Yet there will be some
survivors—sons and daughters who will be
brought out of it.[v] They will come to you, and
when you see their conduct[w] and their actions,
you will be consoled regarding the disaster I have
brought upon Jerusalem—every disaster I have
brought upon it. 23You will be consoled when you
see their conduct and their actions, for you will
know that I have done nothing in it without
cause, declares the Sovereign LORD.[x]”

This life is but the passage of a day,
This life is but a pang and all is over;
But in the life to come which fades not away
Every love shall abide and every lover.

—*Christina Georgina Rossetti* (1830-1894)

14:8 [z]Eze 15:7 [a]Eze 5:15
14:9 [b]Jer 14:15 [c]Jer 4:10 [d]1Ki 22:23
14:11 [e]Eze 48:11 [f]Eze 11:19-20; 37:23
14:13 [g]Lev 26:26 [h]Eze 5:16; 6:14; 15:8
14:14 [i]Ge 6:8 [j]ver 20; Eze 28:3; Da 1:6; 6:13 [k]Job 1:1 [l]Job 42:9; Jer 15:1; Eze 18:20
14:15 [m]Eze 5:17 [n]Lev 26:22
14:16 [o]Eze 18:20
14:17 [p]Lev 26:25; Eze 5:12; 21:3-4 [q]Eze 25:13; Zep 1:3
14:19 [r]Eze 7:8 [s]Eze 38:22
14:20 [t]ver 14
14:21 [u]Jer 15:3; Eze 5:17; 33:27; Am 4:6-10; Rev 6:8
14:22 [v]Eze 12:16 [w]Eze 20:43
14:23 [x]Jer 22:8-9

[a] *14* Or *Danel;* the Hebrew spelling may suggest a person other than the prophet Daniel; also in verse 20.

Jerusalem, A Useless Vine

15 The word of the LORD came to me: 2“Son of
15:2 [y]Isa 5:1-7; Jer 2:21; Hos 10:1 man, how is the wood of a vine[y] better than
that of a branch on any of the trees in the forest?
3Is wood ever taken from it to make anything useful? Do they make pegs from it to hang things on?
4And after it is thrown on the fire as fuel and the
15:4 [z]Eze 19:14; Jn 15:6 fire burns both ends and chars the middle, is it
then useful for anything?[z] 5If it was not useful for
anything when it was whole, how much less can
it be made into something useful when the fire
has burned it and it is charred?
6“Therefore this is what the Sovereign LORD
says: As I have given the wood of the vine among
the trees of the forest as fuel for the fire, so will I
15:7 [a]Ps 34:16; Eze 14:8 [b]Isa 24:18; Am 9:1-4 treat the people living in Jerusalem. 7I will set my
face against[a] them. Although they have come out
of the fire, the fire will yet consume them. And
when I set my face against them, you will know
that I am the LORD.[b] 8I will make the land deso-
15:8 [c]Eze 14:13 [d]Eze 17:20 late[c] because they have been unfaithful,[d] declares
the Sovereign LORD.”

An Allegory of Unfaithful Jerusalem

16:2 [e]Eze 20:4; 22:2 16 The word of the LORD came to me: 2“Son of
man, confront Jerusalem with her detestable
16:3 [f]Eze 21:30 [g]ver 45 practices[e] 3and say, ‘This is what the Sovereign
LORD says to Jerusalem: Your ancestry[f] and birth
were in the land of the Canaanites; your father was
16:4 [h]Hos 2:3 an Amorite and your mother a Hittite.[g] 4On the day
you were born[h] your cord was not cut, nor were
you washed with water to make you clean, nor
were you rubbed with salt or wrapped in cloths.
5No one looked on you with pity or had compassion enough to do any of these things for you.
Rather, you were thrown out into the open field,
for on the day you were born you were despised.
16:6 [i]Ex 19:4 6“ ‘Then I passed by and saw you kicking about
in your blood, and as you lay there in your blood
16:7 [j]Dt 1:10 [k]Ex 1:7 I said to you, “Live!”[a][i] 7I made you grow[j] like a
plant of the field. You grew up and developed and
became the most beautiful of jewels.[b] Your breasts
were formed and your hair grew, you who were
naked and bare.[k]
16:8 [l]Ru 3:9 [m]Jer 2:2; Hos 2:7,19-20 8“ ‘Later I passed by, and when I looked at you
and saw that you were old enough for love, I spread
the corner of my garment[l] over you and covered
your nakedness. I gave you my solemn oath and
16:9 [n]Ru 3:3 entered into a covenant with you, declares the Sovereign LORD, and you became mine.[m]
16:10 [o]Ex 26:36 [p]Eze 27:16 [q]ver 18 9“ ‘I bathed[c] you with water and washed[n] the
blood from you and put ointments on you. 10I
clothed you with an embroidered[o] dress and put
16:11 [r]Eze 23:40 [s]Isa 3:19; Eze 23:42 leather sandals on you. I dressed you in fine
linen[p] and covered you with costly garments.[q] 11I
adorned you with jewelry:[r] I put bracelets[s] on

[a] 6 A few Hebrew manuscripts, Septuagint and Syriac; most Hebrew manuscripts *“Live!” And as you lay there in your blood I said to you, “Live!”* [b] 7 Or *became mature*
[c] 9 Or *I had bathed*

Jerusalem

EZEKIEL 16

Ezekiel allegorically describes Jerusalem as a woman. She is born of pagan parents—Jerusalem was originally settled by pagan nations. She is dressed and taken care of as a young groom would care for his young bride—David conquered Jerusalem and made it his capital, fashioning it into a beautiful and major city of the Near East. Solomon continued that beautification project, using enormous amounts of gold and silver. Jerusalem, however, comes to depend on her beauty rather than on God—her people turned to idols and turned away from God. For that Ezekiel charges her with the crime of prostitution, she has used all that God has given her for her own glory and pleasure rather than for his.

How easy it is to draw a clear lesson for today from such a passage! We too have been “bought at a price” (1Co 7:23), freed from our “pagan” roots, made to glorify God. We can either use what he’s given us to honor him, or we can go our own way into selfishness and corruption.

your arms and a necklace[t] around your neck,
12and I put a ring on your nose,[u] earrings on your
ears and a beautiful crown[v] on your head. 13So
you were adorned with gold and silver; your
clothes were of fine linen and costly fabric and
embroidered cloth. Your food was fine flour, honey and olive oil.[w] You became very beautiful and
rose to be a queen.[x] 14And your fame[y] spread
among the nations on account of your beauty,[z]
because the splendor I had given you made your
beauty perfect, declares the Sovereign LORD.

15" 'But you trusted in your beauty and used
your fame to become a prostitute. You lavished
your favors on anyone who passed by[a] and your
beauty became his.[a][b] 16You took some of your garments to make gaudy high places, where you carried on your prostitution.[c] Such things should not
happen, nor should they ever occur. 17You also took
the fine jewelry I gave you, the jewelry made of my
gold and silver, and you made for yourself male
idols and engaged in prostitution with them.[d]
18And you took your embroidered clothes to put on
them, and you offered my oil and incense before
them. 19Also the food I provided for you—the fine
flour, olive oil and honey I gave you to eat—you
offered as fragrant incense before them. That is
what happened, declares the Sovereign LORD.[e]

20" 'And you took your sons and daughters[f]
whom you bore to me[g] and sacrificed them as food
to the idols. Was your prostitution not enough?[h]
21You slaughtered my children and sacrificed
them[b] to the idols.[i] 22In all your detestable practices and your prostitution you did not remember
the days of your youth,[j] when you were naked and
bare, kicking about in your blood.[k]

23" 'Woe! Woe to you, declares the Sovereign
LORD. In addition to all your other wickedness,
24you built a mound for yourself and made a lofty
shrine[l] in every public square.[m] 25At the head of
every street you built your lofty shrines and
degraded your beauty, offering your body with
increasing promiscuity to anyone who passed by.[n]
26You engaged in prostitution with the Egyptians,
your lustful neighbors, and provoked[o] me to anger
with your increasing promiscuity.[p] 27So I stretched
out my hand[q] against you and reduced your territory; I gave you over to the greed of your enemies,
the daughters of the Philistines,[r] who were
shocked by your lewd conduct. 28You engaged in
prostitution with the Assyrians[s] too, because you
were insatiable; and even after that, you still were
not satisfied. 29Then you increased your promiscuity to include Babylonia,[c][t] a land of merchants,
but even with this you were not satisfied.

30" 'How weak-willed you are, declares the Sovereign LORD, when you do all these things, acting

***S**eek some silence. Balance your busyness with moments of meditation. Don't allow all the flashing lights on the outside to distract you from the inner light of his presence. Even a short silence each day will give a greater semblance of order to your emotions and schedule.*

—Patsy Clairmont

16:11 [t]Ge 41:42
16:12 [u]Isa 3:21 [v]Isa 28:5; Jer 13:18
16:13 [w]1Sa 10:1 [x]Dt 32:13-14; 1Ki 4:21
16:14 [y]1Ki 10:24 [z]La 2:15
16:15 [a]ver 25 [b]Isa 57:8; Jer 2:20; Eze 23:3; 27:3
16:16 [c]2Ki 23:7
16:17 [d]Eze 7:20
16:19 [e]Hos 2:8
16:20 [f]Jer 7:31 [g]Ex 13:2 [h]Ps 106:37-38; Isa 57:5; Eze 23:37
16:21 [i]2Ki 17:17; Jer 19:5
16:22 [j]Jer 2:2; Hos 11:1 [k]ver 6
16:24 [l]ver 31; Isa 57:7 [m]Ps 78:58; Jer 2:20; 3:2; Eze 20:28
16:25 [n]ver 15; Pr 9:14
16:26 [o]Eze 8:17 [p]Eze 20:8; 23:19-21
16:27 [q]Eze 20:33 [r]2Ch 28:18
16:28 [s]2Ki 16:7
16:29 [t]Eze 23:14-17

[a] *15* Most Hebrew manuscripts; one Hebrew manuscript (see some Septuagint manuscripts) *by. Such a thing should not happen* [b] *21* Or *and made them pass through* ⌞*the fire*⌟ [c] *29* Or *Chaldea*

16:30 like a brazen prostitute![u] 31 When you built your
[u]Jer 3:3 mounds at the head of every street and made your
16:31 lofty shrines[v] in every public square, you were
[v]ver 24 unlike a prostitute, because you scorned payment.
32 " 'You adulterous wife! You prefer strangers to
16:33 your own husband! 33 Every prostitute receives a
[w]Isa 30:6; fee, but you give gifts[w] to all your lovers, bribing
57:9 them to come to you from everywhere for your
[x]Hos 8:9-10 illicit favors.[x] 34 So in your prostitution you are the
opposite of others; no one runs after you for your
favors. You are the very opposite, for you give payment and none is given to you.
35 " 'Therefore, you prostitute, hear the word of
the LORD! 36 This is what the Sovereign LORD says:
Because you poured out your wealth[a] and exposed
your nakedness in your promiscuity with your
16:36 lovers, and because of all your detestable idols,
[y]Jer 19:5; and because you gave them your children's blood,[y]
Eze 23:10 37 therefore I am going to gather all your lovers,
with whom you found pleasure, those you loved
as well as those you hated. I will gather them
against you from all around and will strip you in
16:37 front of them, and they will see all your naked-
[z]Jer 13:22 ness.[z] 38 I will sentence you to the punishment of
16:38 women who commit adultery and who shed
[a]Eze 23:45 blood;[a] I will bring upon you the blood vengeance
[b]Lev 20:10; of my wrath and jealous anger.[b] 39 Then I will hand
Eze 23:25 you over to your lovers, and they will tear down
your mounds and destroy your lofty shrines. They
16:39 will strip you of your clothes and take your fine
[c]Eze 23:26; jewelry and leave you naked and bare.[c] 40 They will
Hos 2:3 bring a mob against you, who will stone[d] you and
16:40 hack you to pieces with their swords. 41 They will
[d]Jn 8:5,7 burn down[e] your houses and inflict punishment
16:41 on you in the sight of many women.[f] I will put a
[e]Dt 13:16 stop[g] to your prostitution, and you will no longer
[f]Eze 23:10 [g]Eze 23:27, pay your lovers. 42 Then my wrath against you will
48 subside and my jealous anger will turn away from
you; I will be calm and no longer angry.[h]
16:42 [h]Isa 54:9; 43 " 'Because you did not remember[i] the days of
Eze 5:13; your youth but enraged me with all these things,
39:29 I will surely bring down[j] on your head what you
16:43 have done, declares the Sovereign LORD. Did you
[i]Ps 78:42 not add lewdness to all your other detestable
[j]Eze 22:31 [k]ver 22; practices?[k]
Eze 11:21 44 " 'Everyone who quotes proverbs will quote
this proverb about you: "Like mother, like daughter." 45 You are a true daughter of your mother,
who despised her husband and her children; and
you are a true sister of your sisters, who despised
their husbands and their children. Your mother
16:45 was a Hittite and your father an Amorite.[l] 46 Your
[l]Eze 23:2 older sister was Samaria, who lived to the north of
you with her daughters; and your younger sister,
16:46 who lived to the south of you with her daughters,
[m]Ge 13:10- was Sodom.[m] 47 You not only walked in their ways
13; Eze 23:4 and copied their detestable practices, but in all
16:47 your ways you soon became more depraved than
[n]2Ki 21:9; Eze 5:7 they.[n] 48 As surely as I live, declares the Sovereign

[a] 36 Or *lust*

Like Mother, Like Daughter

EZE 16:44–58

Ezekiel goes on to compare Jerusalem with her two "sisters," Samaria (the capital of the northern kingdom of Israel) and Sodom. Both of these cities had long since been destroyed (Ge 19:24–25; 2Ki 17:5–6). But these wicked cities, filled with promiscuity and injustice, almost appear righteous in comparison to the sin-filled city of Jerusalem (Eze 16:52). She has not only acted like a prostitute by going after false gods; she, like Sodom, is "arrogant, overfed and unconcerned," not helping "the poor and needy" (Eze 16:49). Sodom and Samaria's sins had not gone unpunished. Neither will Jerusalem's.

An Everlasting Covenant

EZE 16:59-63

God is not ignoring the desperate wickedness he sees in his royal city Jerusalem. He will punish; he will deal with the sins of the city. But after Ezekiel lists all the sins and the impending punishments, he inserts one little, very important word: "yet" (Eze 16:60). Although God sees his people's sin and promises to punish it, he also remembers his promise to be their God forever. His people have broken and forgotten their covenant with him, but he will remember forever his covenant with them and will establish it as an "everlasting covenant" (Eze 16:60) ultimately through Jesus, our Savior and "the mediator of a new covenant" (Heb 12:24).

LORD, your sister Sodom and her daughters never
did what you and your daughters have done.[o]
49" 'Now this was the sin of your sister Sodom:[p]
She and her daughters were arrogant,[q] overfed
and unconcerned; they did not help the poor and
needy.[r] 50They were haughty and did detestable
things before me. Therefore I did away with them
as you have seen.[s] 51Samaria did not commit half
the sins you did. You have done more detestable
things than they, and have made your sisters seem
righteous by all these things you have done.[t]
52Bear your disgrace, for you have furnished some
justification for your sisters. Because your sins
were more vile than theirs, they appear more righteous than you. So then, be ashamed and bear
your disgrace, for you have made your sisters
appear righteous.
53" 'However, I will restore[u] the fortunes of Sodom and her daughters and of Samaria and her
daughters, and your fortunes along with them,
54so that you may bear your disgrace[v] and be
ashamed of all you have done in giving them
comfort. 55And your sisters, Sodom with her
daughters and Samaria with her daughters, will
return to what they were before; and you and
your daughters will return to what you were
before.[w] 56You would not even mention your sister
Sodom in the day of your pride, 57before your
wickedness was uncovered. Even so, you are now
scorned by the daughters of Edom[a][x] and all her
neighbors and the daughters of the Philistines—
all those around you who despise you. 58You will
bear the consequences of your lewdness and your
detestable practices, declares the LORD.[y]
59" 'This is what the Sovereign LORD says: I will
deal with you as you deserve, because you have
despised my oath by breaking the covenant.[z] 60Yet
I will remember the covenant I made with you in
the days of your youth, and I will establish an
everlasting covenant[a] with you. 61Then you will
remember your ways and be ashamed[b] when you
receive your sisters, both those who are older than
you and those who are younger. I will give them
to you as daughters, but not on the basis of my
covenant with you. 62So I will establish my covenant with you, and you will know that I am the
LORD.[c] 63Then, when I make atonement[d] for you
for all you have done, you will remember and be
ashamed and never again open your mouth[e]
because of your humiliation, declares the Sovereign LORD.[f] ' "

Two Eagles and a Vine

17 The word of the LORD came to me: 2"Son of
man, set forth an allegory and tell the house
of Israel a parable.[g] 3Say to them, 'This is what the
Sovereign LORD says: A great eagle[h] with powerful
wings, long feathers and full plumage of varied

16:48 [o]Mt 10:15; 11:23-24
16:49 [p]Ge 13:13 [q]Ps 138:6 [r]Eze 18:7, 12,16; Lk 12:16-20
16:50 [s]Ge 18:20-21; 19:5
16:51 [t]Jer 3:8-11
16:53 [u]Isa 19:24-25
16:54 [v]Jer 2:26; Eze 14:22
16:55 [w]Mal 3:4
16:57 [x]2Ki 16:6
16:58 [y]Eze 23:49
16:59 [z]Eze 17:19
16:60 [a]Jer 32:40; Eze 37:26
16:61 [b]Eze 20:43
16:62 [c]Jer 24:7; Eze 20:37, 43-44; Hos 2:19-20
16:63 [d]Ps 65:3; 79:9 [e]Ro 3:19 [f]Ps 39:9; Da 9:7-8
17:2 [g]Eze 20:49
17:3 [h]Hos 8:1

[a] *57* Many Hebrew manuscripts and Syriac; most Hebrew manuscripts, Septuagint and Vulgate *Aram*

17:3 colors came to Lebanon.[i] Taking hold of the top
[i]Jer 22:23 of a cedar, 4he broke off its topmost shoot and carried it away to a land of merchants, where he
planted it in a city of traders.
5" 'He took some of the seed of your land and
17:5 put it in fertile soil. He planted it like a willow by
[j]Dt 8:7-9; abundant water,[j] 6and it sprouted and became a
Isa 44:4 low, spreading vine. Its branches turned toward
him, but its roots remained under it. So it became
a vine and produced branches and put out leafy
boughs.
7" 'But there was another great eagle with powerful wings and full plumage. The vine now sent
out its roots toward him from the plot where it
17:7 was planted and stretched out its branches to him
[k]Eze 31:4 for water.[k] 8It had been planted in good soil by
abundant water so that it would produce
branches, bear fruit and become a splendid vine.'
9"Say to them, 'This is what the Sovereign LORD
says: Will it thrive? Will it not be uprooted and
stripped of its fruit so that it withers? All its new
growth will wither. It will not take a strong arm or
17:10 many people to pull it up by the roots. 10Even if
[l]Hos 13:15 it[l] is transplanted, will it thrive? Will it not wither completely when the east wind strikes it—
wither away in the plot where it grew?' "
11Then the word of the LORD came to me: 12"Say
17:12 to this rebellious house, 'Do you not know what
[m]Eze 12:9 these things mean?[m]' Say to them: 'The king of
[n]2Ki 24:15 Babylon went to Jerusalem and carried off her
[o]Eze 24:19 king and her nobles,[n] bringing them back with
him to Babylon.[o] 13Then he took a member of the
17:13 royal family and made a treaty with him, putting
[p]2Ch 36:13 him under oath.[p] He also carried away the leading
17:14 men of the land, 14so that the kingdom would be
[q]Eze 29:14 brought low,[q] unable to rise again, surviving only
17:15 by keeping his treaty. 15But the king rebelled[r]
[r]Jer 52:3 against him by sending his envoys to Egypt to get
[s]Dt 17:16 horses and a large army.[s] Will he succeed? Will
[t]Jer 34:3; he who does such things escape? Will he break
38:18 the treaty and yet escape?[t]
17:16 16" 'As surely as I live, declares the Sovereign
[u]Jer 52:11; Eze 12:13 LORD, he shall die[u] in Babylon, in the land of the
[v]2Ki 24:17 king who put him on the throne, whose oath he
17:17 despised and whose treaty he broke.[v] 17Pharaoh[w]
[w]Jer 37:7 with his mighty army and great horde will be of
[x]Eze 4:2 no help to him in war, when ramps[x] are built and
[y]Isa 36:6; Jer 37:5; siege works erected to destroy many lives.[y] 18He
Eze 29:6-7 despised the oath by breaking the covenant.
17:18 Because he had given his hand in pledge[z] and yet
[z]1Ch 29:24 did all these things, he shall not escape.
19" 'Therefore this is what the Sovereign LORD
17:19 [a]Eze 16:59 says: As surely as I live, I will bring down on his
head my oath that he despised and my covenant
17:20 that he broke.[a] 20I will spread my net[b] for him,
[b]Eze 12:13; and he will be caught in my snare. I will bring
32:3 [c]Jer 2:35; him to Babylon and execute judgment[c] upon him
Eze 20:36 there because he was unfaithful to me. 21All his
17:21 fleeing troops will fall by the sword,[d] and the sur-
[d]Eze 12:14 [e]2Ki 25:11 vivors[e] will be scattered to the winds.[f] Then you
[f]2Ki 25:5 will know that I the LORD have spoken.

I f you are blessed with a creative imagination, use it. Celebrate it! Keep it alive and well-oiled by constantly dreaming of inventions from which others will benefit. You don't have to build a Disneyland, but you can produce creative accomplishments in your own realm. Be imaginative and creative in your planning, during vacations, on your days off, at mealtimes, at parties, in your dress, in your decor. Make your own gift-wraps and greeting cards. Invent new recipes. Don't be afraid to let your mind try new ideas. Constantly look for the hidden possibilities in the obvious.

—Luci Swindoll

A New Tree

EZE 17:22–24

The tree (Judah and Israel) has proven to be unfaithful and unfruitful. Therefore, the Lord declares that he will grow a new tree. The new tree will grow from a shoot of the old tree, so it, while new, is still part of the old.

The shoot that the new tree grows from is referred to as a "tender sprig" (Eze 17:22), terms that have Messianic connotations (Isa 11:1; 53:2). "Birds of every kind" (Eze 17:23) may be a reference to the Messiah's offer of salvation to Jews and Gentiles alike, "men from every nation" (Ac 10:35; see also Mk 4:30–32).

22" 'This is what the Sovereign LORD says: I
myself will take a shoot from the very top of a
cedar and plant it; I will break off a tender sprig
from its topmost shoots and plant it on a high and
lofty mountain.[g] 23On the mountain heights of
Israel I will plant it; it will produce branches and
bear fruit and become a splendid cedar. Birds of
every kind will nest in it; they will find shelter in
the shade of its branches.[h] 24All the trees of the
field[i] will know that I the LORD bring down the
tall tree and make the low tree grow tall. I dry up
the green tree and make the dry tree flourish.

" 'I the LORD have spoken, and I will do it.[j]' "

The Soul Who Sins Will Die

18 The word of the LORD came to me: 2"What
do you people mean by quoting this proverb about the land of Israel:

" 'The fathers eat sour grapes,
and the children's teeth are set on edge'?[k]

3"As surely as I live, declares the Sovereign
LORD, you will no longer quote this proverb in
Israel. 4For every living soul belongs to me, the
father as well as the son—both alike belong to me.
The soul who sins is the one who will die.[l]

5"Suppose there is a righteous man
who does what is just and right.
6He does not eat at the mountain[m] shrines
or look to the idols[n] of the house of Israel.
He does not defile his neighbor's wife
or lie with a woman during her period.
7He does not oppress[o] anyone,
but returns what he took in pledge[p] for a loan.
He does not commit robbery
but gives his food to the hungry
and provides clothing for the naked.[q]
8He does not lend at usury
or take excessive interest.[a][r]
He withholds his hand from doing wrong
and judges fairly[s] between man and man.
9He follows my decrees
and faithfully keeps my laws.
That man is righteous;[t]
he will surely live,[u]
declares the Sovereign LORD.

10"Suppose he has a violent son, who sheds
blood[v] or does any of these other things[b] 11(though
the father has done none of them):

"He eats at the mountain shrines.

[a] 8 Or *take interest*; similarly in verses 13 and 17
[b] 10 Or *things to a brother*

17:22 [g]Jer 23:5; Eze 20:40; 36:1,36; 37:22
17:23 [h]Ps 92:12; Isa 2:2; Eze 31:6; Da 4:12; Hos 14:5-7; Mt 13:32
17:24 [i]Ps 96:12 [j]Eze 19:12; 21:26; 22:14; Am 9:11
18:2 [k]Isa 3:15; Jer 31:29; La 5:7
18:4 [l]ver 20; Isa 42:5; Ro 6:23
18:6 [m]Eze 22:9 [n]Dt 4:19; Eze 6:13; 20:24
18:7 [o]Ex 22:21 [p]Ex 22:26; Dt 24:12 [q]Dt 15:11; Mt 25:36
18:8 [r]Ex 22:25; Lev 25:35-37; Dt 23:19-20 [s]Zec 8:16
18:9 [t]Hab 2:4 [u]Lev 18:5; Eze 20:11; Am 5:4
18:10 [v]Ex 21:12

He defiles his neighbor's wife.
[12]He oppresses the poor[w] and needy.
He commits robbery.
He does not return what he took in
pledge.
He looks to the idols.
He does detestable things.[x]
[13]He lends at usury and takes excessive
interest.[y]

Will such a man live? He will not! Because he has
done all these detestable things, he will surely be
put to death and his blood will be on his own
head.[z]
[14]"But suppose this son has a son who sees all
the sins his father commits, and though he sees
them, he does not do such things:[a]

[15]"He does not eat at the mountain
shrines
or look to the idols of the house of
Israel.
He does not defile his neighbor's wife.
[16]He does not oppress anyone
or require a pledge for a loan.
He does not commit robbery
but gives his food to the hungry
and provides clothing for the naked.[b]
[17]He withholds his hand from sin[a]
and takes no usury or excessive
interest.
He keeps my laws and follows my
decrees.

He will not die for his father's sin; he will surely
live. [18]But his father will die for his own sin,
because he practiced extortion, robbed his brother and did what was wrong among his people.
[19]"Yet you ask, 'Why does the son not share the
guilt of his father?' Since the son has done what is
just and right and has been careful to keep all my
decrees, he will surely live.[c] [20]The soul who sins is
the one who will die. The son will not share the
guilt of the father, nor will the father share the
guilt of the son. The righteousness of the righteous
man will be credited to him, and the wickedness
of the wicked will be charged against him.[d]
[21]"But if a wicked man turns away from all the
sins he has committed and keeps all my decrees
and does what is just and right, he will surely live;
he will not die.[e] [22]None of the offenses he has committed will be remembered against him. Because
of the righteous things he has done, he will live.[f]
[23]Do I take any pleasure in the death of the wicked?
declares the Sovereign LORD. Rather, am I not
pleased[g] when they turn from their ways and live?[h]
[24]"But if a righteous man turns from his righteousness and commits sin and does the same
detestable things the wicked man does, will he
live? None of the righteous things he has done

18:12 [w]Am 4:1 [x]2Ki 21:11; Isa 59:6-7; Jer 22:17; Eze 8:6,17
18:13 [y]Ex 22:25 [z]Eze 33:4-5
18:14 [a]2Ch 34:21; Pr 23:24
18:16 [b]Ps 41:1; Isa 58:10
18:19 [c]Ex 20:5; Dt 5:9; Jer 15:4; Zec 1:3-6
18:20 [d]Dt 24:16; 1Ki 8:32; 2Ki 14:6; Isa 3:11; Mt 16:27; Ro 2:9
18:21 [e]Eze 33:12, 19
18:22 [f]Ps 18:20-24; Isa 43:25; Mic 7:19
18:23 [g]Ps 147:11 [h]Eze 33:11; 1Ti 2:4

[a] *17* Septuagint (see also verse 8); Hebrew *from the poor*

Breaking the Cycle

EZE 18:20

Here, through Ezekiel, God makes it clear that he judges and rewards people only for their own sin or their own faithfulness, not for that of their parents. This seems to contradict earlier Biblical statements: "I, the LORD your God, am a jealous God, punishing the children for the sin of the fathers to the third and fourth generation of those who hate me" (Ex 20:5).

There is a distinction, however, between these two passages. In Exodus, God is saying that the rebellious person's punishment will affect his or her children. Israelite society had stronger familial ties than we, in modern society, can even comprehend—people were not viewed so much as individuals, but as part of the larger entity of the family. We still see the effects of sin passing from one generation to another today. The amazing message of Ezekiel is that wickedness does not have to be generational. God's grace and forgiveness, which have the power to break the cycle, are available to anyone who seeks him.

God's Pleasure

EZE 18:31-32

God is a righteous and holy God who must *punish sin and rebellion. But he certainly takes no pleasure in it. God is also a righteous and loving God who* willingly *rewards faithfulness. He offers Israel again and again his mercy and grace. When they accept it, he is happy to offer them his goodness. However, when they reject him and willfully rebel against him, his holiness demands punishment.*

The New Testament declares this same truth in the words of Paul in Romans 6:23: "For the wages of sin is death, but the gift of God is eternal life in Christ Jesus our Lord." God offers us a "new heart and a new spirit" (Eze 18:31). His grace gives us the power to reject rebellion and turn to him in love and faithfulness, which in turn allows us to receive not only his goodness here on earth, but also the blessing of eternal life with him in heaven.

will be remembered. Because of the unfaithfulness he is guilty of and because of the sins he has
committed, he will die.[i]
25 "Yet you say, 'The way of the Lord is not just.'
Hear, O house of Israel: Is my way unjust?[j] Is it not
your ways that are unjust? 26 If a righteous man
turns from his righteousness and commits sin, he
will die for it; because of the sin he has committed
he will die. 27 But if a wicked man turns away from
the wickedness he has committed and does what
is just and right, he will save his life.[k] 28 Because
he considers all the offenses he has committed and
turns away from them, he will surely live; he will
not die. 29 Yet the house of Israel says, 'The way of
the Lord is not just.' Are my ways unjust, O house
of Israel? Is it not your ways that are unjust?
30 "Therefore, O house of Israel, I will judge you,
each one according to his ways, declares the Sovereign LORD. Repent![l] Turn away from all your
offenses; then sin will not be your downfall.[m]
31 Rid yourselves of all the offenses you have committed, and get a new heart[n] and a new spirit.
Why will you die, O house of Israel?[o] 32 For I take
no pleasure in the death of anyone, declares the
Sovereign LORD. Repent and live![p]

A Lament for Israel's Princes

19 "Take up a lament[q] concerning the princes[r]
of Israel 2 and say:

" 'What a lioness was your mother
among the lions!
She lay down among the young lions
and reared her cubs.
3 She brought up one of her cubs,
and he became a strong lion.
He learned to tear the prey
and he devoured men.
4 The nations heard about him,
and he was trapped in their pit.
They led him with hooks
to the land of Egypt.[s]

5 " 'When she saw her hope unfulfilled,
her expectation gone,
she took another of her cubs
and made him a strong lion.[t]
6 He prowled among the lions,
for he was now a strong lion.
He learned to tear the prey
and he devoured men.[u]
7 He broke down[a] their strongholds
and devastated[v] their towns.
The land and all who were in it
were terrified by his roaring.
8 Then the nations[w] came against him,
those from regions round about.
They spread their net for him,
and he was trapped in their pit.[x]
9 With hooks they pulled him into a cage

18:24 [i]1Sa 15:11; 2Ch 24:17-20; Eze 3:20; 20:27; 2Pe 2:20-22
18:25 [j]Ge 18:25; Jer 12:1; Eze 33:17; Zep 3:5; Mal 2:17; 3:13-15
18:27 [k]Isa 1:18
18:30 [l]Mt 3:2 [m]Eze 7:3; 33:20; Hos 12:6
18:31 [n]Ps 51:10 [o]Isa 1:16-17; Eze 11:19; 36:26
18:32 [p]Eze 33:11
19:1 [q]Eze 26:17; 27:2,32 [r]2Ki 24:6
19:4 [s]2Ki 23:33-34; 2Ch 36:4
19:5 [t]2Ki 23:34
19:6 [u]2Ki 24:9; 2Ch 36:9
19:7 [v]Eze 30:12
19:8 [w]2Ki 24:2 [x]2Ki 24:11

[a] 7 Targum (see Septuagint); Hebrew *He knew*

19:9 and brought him to the king of
y2Ch 36:6 Babylon.[y]
z2Ki 24:15 They put him in prison,
so his roar was heard no longer
on the mountains of Israel.[z]

19:10 10 " 'Your mother was like a vine in your
aPs 80:8-11 vineyard[a]
planted by the water;
it was fruitful and full of branches
because of abundant water.[a]
11 Its branches were strong,
fit for a ruler's scepter.
It towered high
above the thick foliage,
19:11 conspicuous for its height
bEze 31:3; and for its many branches.[b]
Da 4:11 12 But it was uprooted[c] in fury
19:12 and thrown to the ground.
cEze 17:10 The east wind made it shrivel,
dIsa 27:11; it was stripped of its fruit;
Eze 28:17; its strong branches withered
Hos 13:15 and fire consumed them.[d]
19:13 eEze 20:35 13 Now it is planted in the desert,[e]
fHos 2:3 in a dry and thirsty land.[f]
19:14 14 Fire spread from one of its main[b]
gEze 20:47 branches
hEze 15:4 and consumed[g] its fruit.
No strong branch is left on it
fit for a ruler's scepter.'[h]

This is a lament and is to be used as a lament."

Rebellious Israel

20 In the seventh year, in the fifth month on
the tenth day, some of the elders of Israel
came to inquire of the LORD, and they sat down in
20:1 iEze 8:1 front of me.[i]
2 Then the word of the LORD came to me: 3 "Son
of man, speak to the elders of Israel and say to
20:3 them, 'This is what the Sovereign LORD says: Have
jEze 14:3 you come to inquire[j] of me? As surely as I live, I
kMic 3:7 will not let you inquire of me, declares the Sovereign LORD.'[k]
4 "Will you judge them? Will you judge them,
20:4 son of man? Then confront them with the
lEze 16:2; detestable practices of their fathers[l] 5 and say to
22:2; Mt 23:32 them: 'This is what the Sovereign LORD says: On
the day I chose[m] Israel, I swore with uplifted hand
20:5 to the descendants of the house of Jacob and
mDt 7:6 nEx 6:7 revealed myself to them in Egypt. With uplifted
hand I said to them, "I am the LORD your God."[n]
6 On that day I swore to them that I would bring
20:6 them out of Egypt into a land I had searched out
oEx 3:8; Jer 32:22 for them, a land flowing with milk and honey,[o] the
pDt 8:7; Ps 48:2; most beautiful of all lands.[p] 7 And I said to them,
Da 8:9 "Each of you, get rid of the vile images[q] you have
set your eyes on, and do not defile yourselves with
20:7 the idols of Egypt. I am the LORD your God."[r]'
qEx 20:4 rEx 20:2; Lev 18:3; Dt 29:18

[a] 10 Two Hebrew manuscripts; most Hebrew manuscripts *your blood* [b] 14 Or *from under its*

This Is a Lament

EZE 19:14

The official language of mourning, laments were eulogies or songs that were sung for those who had died. Official mourners sang laments during the grieving time, both before the burial and at the burial. Laments were also songs used to express grief over national sin and rebellion against God.

Ezekiel's words, which he specifically identifies as a lament and states are to be used as such, mourn Israel's princes. The lioness and cub imagery in the first part of Ezekiel 19, as well as the vine imagery in the latter verses, demonstrate the foolhardiness of trusting in the kings of Israel, who only lead the people further into wickedness and closer to final judgment. Therefore, the only response can be to mourn the kings who bring Israel down.

Sometimes we just don't want to let go of our grudges and heartaches. We want to hold on to them and watch our enemies suffer. We look for opportunities to bring up the past and rub the guilty persons' faces in what they've done. But while we're in the "get back at them" stage, we are constantly rehashing their actions toward us, our reactions toward them, and our hopes for their destruction. Resentment spreads like a cancer, eating away at the soul. It destroys our hopes and relationships. I know. I've been there.

Have you been there? Are you there now? . . . If this is true, you can ask God to help you become willing to forgive, and ultimately to speak forgiveness to those who have hurt you.

Jesus told us that if we are unwilling to forgive, we will not be forgiven. Friend don't miss out on God's precious grace. Allow the Holy Spirit to administer the healing medicine of forgiveness.

—Thelma Wells

8" 'But they rebelled against me and would not listen to me; they did not get rid of the vile images they had set their eyes on, nor did they forsake the idols of Egypt.[s] So I said I would pour out my wrath on them and spend my anger against them in Egypt.[t] 9But for the sake of my name I did what would keep it from being profaned in the eyes of the nations they lived among and in whose sight I had revealed myself to the Israelites by bringing them out of Egypt.[u] 10Therefore I led them out of Egypt and brought them into the desert.[v] 11I gave them my decrees and made known to them my laws, for the man who obeys them will live by them.[w] 12Also I gave them my Sabbaths as a sign[x] between us, so they would know that I the LORD made them holy.

13" 'Yet the people of Israel rebelled[y] against me in the desert. They did not follow my decrees but rejected my laws—although the man who obeys them will live by them—and they utterly desecrated my Sabbaths. So I said I would pour out my wrath[z] on them and destroy them in the desert.[a] 14But for the sake of my name I did what would keep it from being profaned in the eyes of the nations in whose sight I had brought them out.[b] 15Also with uplifted hand I swore to them in the desert that I would not bring them into the land I had given them—a land flowing with milk and honey, most beautiful of all lands[c]— 16because they rejected my laws and did not follow my decrees and desecrated my Sabbaths. For their hearts[d] were devoted to their idols.[e] 17Yet I looked on them with pity and did not destroy them or put an end to them in the desert. 18I said to their children in the desert, "Do not follow the statutes of your fathers[f] or keep their laws or defile yourselves with their idols. 19I am the LORD your God;[g] follow my decrees and be careful to keep my laws.[h] 20Keep my Sabbaths holy, that they may be a sign between us. Then you will know that I am the LORD your God.[i]"

21" 'But the children rebelled against me: They did not follow my decrees, they were not careful to keep my laws—although the man who obeys them will live by them—and they desecrated my Sabbaths. So I said I would pour out my wrath on them and spend my anger against them in the desert. 22But I withheld[j] my hand, and for the sake of my name I did what would keep it from being profaned in the eyes of the nations in whose sight I had brought them out. 23Also with uplifted hand I swore to them in the desert that I would disperse them among the nations and scatter[k] them through the countries, 24because they had not obeyed my laws but had rejected my decrees and desecrated my Sabbaths,[l] and their eyes ⌞lusted⌟ after[m] their fathers' idols.[n] 25I also gave them over[o] to statutes that were not good and laws they could not live by;[p] 26I let them become defiled through their gifts—the sacrifice of every firstborn[a]—that I

20:8 [s]Eze 7:8 [t]Isa 63:10
20:9 [u]Eze 36:22; 39:7
20:10 [v]Ex 13:18
20:11 [w]Lev 18:5; Dt 4:7-8; Ro 10:5
20:12 [x]Ex 31:13
20:13 [y]Ps 78:40 [z]Dt 9:8 [a]Nu 14:29; Ps 95:8-10; Isa 56:6
20:14 [b]Eze 36:23
20:15 [c]Ps 95:11; 106:26
20:16 [d]Nu 15:39 [e]Am 5:26
20:18 [f]Zec 1:4
20:19 [g]Ex 20:2 [h]Dt 5:32-33; 6:1-2; 8:1; 11:1; 12:1
20:20 [i]Jer 17:22
20:22 [j]Ps 78:38
20:23 [k]Lev 26:33; Dt 28:64
20:24 [l]ver 13 [m]Eze 6:9 [n]ver 16
20:25 [o]Ps 81:12 [p]2Th 2:11

[a] 26 Or *—making every firstborn pass through ⌞the fire⌟*

might fill them with horror so they would know that I am the LORD.[q]'

27"Therefore, son of man, speak to the people of Israel and say to them, 'This is what the Sovereign LORD says: In this also your fathers blasphemed[r] me by forsaking me:[s] 28When I brought them into the land[t] I had sworn to give them and they saw any high hill or any leafy tree, there they offered their sacrifices, made offerings that provoked me to anger, presented their fragrant incense and poured out their drink offerings.[u] 29Then I said to them: What is this high place you go to?' " (It is called Bamah[a] to this day.)

Judgment and Restoration

30"Therefore say to the house of Israel: 'This is what the Sovereign LORD says: Will you defile yourselves[v] the way your fathers did and lust after their vile images?[w] 31When you offer your gifts—the sacrifice of your sons[x] in[b] the fire—you continue to defile yourselves with all your idols to this day. Am I to let you inquire of me, O house of Israel? As surely as I live, declares the Sovereign LORD, I will not let you inquire of me.[y]

32" 'You say, "We want to be like the nations, like the peoples of the world, who serve wood and stone." But what you have in mind will never happen. 33As surely as I live, declares the Sovereign LORD, I will rule over you with a mighty hand and an outstretched arm and with outpoured wrath.[z] 34I will bring you from the nations[a] and gather you from the countries where you have been scattered—with a mighty hand and an outstretched arm and with outpoured wrath.[b] 35I will bring you into the desert of the nations and there, face to face, I will execute judgment[c] upon you. 36As I judged your fathers in the desert of the land of Egypt, so I will judge you, declares the Sovereign LORD.[d] 37I will take note of you as you pass under my rod,[e] and I will bring you into the bond of the covenant.[f] 38I will purge[g] you of those who revolt and rebel against me. Although I will bring them out of the land where they are living, yet they will not enter the land of Israel. Then you will know that I am the LORD.[h]

39" 'As for you, O house of Israel, this is what the Sovereign LORD says: Go and serve your idols,[i] every one of you! But afterward you will surely listen to me and no longer profane my holy name with your gifts and idols.[j] 40For on my holy mountain, the high mountain of Israel, declares the Sovereign LORD, there in the land the entire house of Israel will serve me, and there I will accept them. There I will require your offerings[k] and your choice gifts,[c] along with all your holy sacrifices.[l] 41I will accept you as fragrant incense when I bring you out from the nations and gather you from the countries where you have been scattered,

20:26 [q]2Ki 17:17
20:27 [r]Ro 2:24 [s]Eze 18:24
20:28 [t]Ps 78:55,58 [u]Eze 6:13
20:30 [v]ver 43 [w]Jer 16:12
20:31 [x]Eze 16:20 [y]Ps 106:37-39; Jer 7:31
20:33 [z]Jer 21:5
20:34 [a]2Co 6:17* [b]Isa 27:12-13; S Jer 44:6; La 2:4
20:35 [c]Jer 2:35
20:36 [d]Nu 11:1-35; 1Co 10:5-10
20:37 [e]Lev 27:32; Jer 33:13 [f]Eze 16:62
20:38 [g]Eze 34:17-22; Am 9:9-10 [h]Ps 95:11; Jer 44:14; Eze 13:9; Mal 3:3; Heb 4:3
20:39 [i]Jer 44:25 [j]Isa 1:13; Eze 43:7; Am 4:4
20:40 [k]Isa 60:7 [l]Isa 56:7; Mal 3:4

[a] 29 *Bamah* means *high place.* [b] 31 Or *—making your sons pass through* [c] 40 Or *and the gifts of your firstfruits*

High Hills, Leafy Trees

EZE 20:28

When the Israelites entered the promised land, God told them they were to worship him at a centralized location, which he would choose (Dt 12:5). They were also to destroy the "high places" of worship of the inhabitants of the land. Instead, the Israelites quickly became enamored with the pagan places of worship. Pagan gods were worshiped in high, exposed places in the land, ostensibly so that the god could see the people's worship and respond. The Canaanite god Baal was worshiped in these high places. His worship was primarily marked by fertility rites, sexual acts with priests and priestesses. The prophets, including Ezekiel, therefore, used the imagery of prostitution when describing—in surprisingly graphic terms—Israel's unfaithfulness to God (Jer 2:20; 13:27; Eze 16:16; Hos 4:13).

Groan in Grief and Fear

EZE 21:6–7

Ezekiel follows God's instructions and groans and sighs with grief over the news that Israel is about to be destroyed. When the people hear him crying, they ask him why. He has a ready answer, given to him by God.

Using descriptive language, Ezekiel describes the fear that will penetrate the land in the end. God is judging the people for their rebellion, and the sight is not pretty. In fact it is horrifying—so horrifying that their hearts melt, their hands are limp, their spirits grow faint, and they are weak-kneed with fear.

and I will show myself holy[m] among you in the
sight of the nations.[n] 42 Then you will know that I
am the LORD,[o] when I bring you into the land of
Israel,[p] the land I had sworn with uplifted hand
to give to your fathers. 43 There you will remember your conduct and all the actions by which you
have defiled yourselves, and you will loathe yourselves for all the evil you have done.[q] 44 You will
know that I am the LORD, when I deal with you
for my name's sake[r] and not according to your
evil ways and your corrupt practices, O house of
Israel, declares the Sovereign LORD.[s]' "

Prophecy Against the South

45 The word of the LORD came to me: 46 "Son of
man, set your face toward the south; preach
against the south and prophesy against[t] the forest
of the southland.[u] 47 Say to the southern forest:
'Hear the word of the LORD. This is what the Sovereign LORD says: I am about to set fire to you, and
it will consume all your trees, both green and dry.
The blazing flame will not be quenched, and
every face from south to north will be scorched
by it.[v] 48 Everyone will see that I the LORD have
kindled it; it will not be quenched.[w]' "

49 Then I said, "Ah, Sovereign LORD! They are
saying of me, 'Isn't he just telling parables?[x]' "

Babylon, God's Sword of Judgment

21 The word of the LORD came to me: 2 "Son of
man, set your face against Jerusalem and
preach against the sanctuary. Prophesy against[y]
the land of Israel 3 and say to her: 'This is what the
LORD says: I am against you.[z] I will draw my
sword from its scabbard and cut off from you both
the righteous and the wicked.[a] 4 Because I am
going to cut off the righteous and the wicked, my
sword will be unsheathed against everyone from
south to north.[b] 5 Then all people will know that I
the LORD have drawn my sword from its scabbard;
it will not return[c] again.'[d]

6 "Therefore groan, son of man! Groan before
them with broken heart and bitter grief.[e] 7 And
when they ask you, 'Why are you groaning?' you
shall say, 'Because of the news that is coming.
Every heart will melt and every hand go limp;[f]
every spirit will become faint and every knee
become as weak as water.' It is coming! It will
surely take place, declares the Sovereign LORD."

8 The word of the LORD came to me: 9 "Son of
man, prophesy and say, 'This is what the Lord
says:

" 'A sword, a sword,
sharpened and polished—
10 sharpened for the slaughter,[g]
polished to flash like lightning!

" 'Shall we rejoice in the scepter of my son
⌊Judah⌋? The sword despises every such stick.

20:41 [m]Eze 28:25; 36:23 [n]Eze 11:17
20:42 [o]Eze 38:23 [p]Eze 34:13; 36:24
20:43 [q]Eze 6:9; 16:61; Hos 5:15
20:44 [r]Eze 36:22 [s]Eze 24:24
20:46 [t]Eze 21:2; Am 7:16 [u]Isa 30:6; Jer 13:19
20:47 [v]Isa 9:18-19; 13:8; Jer 21:14
20:48 [w]Jer 7:20
20:49 [x]Mt 13:13; Jn 16:25
21:2 [y]Eze 20:46
21:3 [z]Jer 21:13 [a]ver 9-11; Job 9:22
21:4 [b]Eze 20:47
21:5 [c]ver 30 [d]Na 1:9
21:6 [e]Isa 22:4
21:7 [f]Eze 22:14; 7:17
21:10 [g]Ps 110:5-6; Isa 34:5-6

11“ ‘The sword is appointed to be
21:11 [h]Jer 46:4 polished,[h]
to be grasped with the hand;
it is sharpened and polished,
made ready for the hand of the slayer.
12 Cry out and wail, son of man,
for it is against my people;
it is against all the princes of Israel.
They are thrown to the sword
21:12 along with my people.
[i]Jer 31:19 Therefore beat your breast.[i]

13“ ‘Testing will surely come. And what if the
scepter ⌊of Judah⌋, which the sword despises, does
not continue? declares the Sovereign LORD.’

21:14 14“So then, son of man, prophesy
[j]Nu 24:10 and strike your hands[j] together.
[k]Eze 6:11; Let the sword strike twice,
30:24 even three times.
It is a sword for slaughter—
a sword for great slaughter,
closing in on them from every side.[k]
21:15 [l]2Sa 17:10 15 So that hearts may melt[l]
[m]Ps 22:14 and the fallen be many,
I have stationed the sword for slaughter[a]
at all their gates.
Oh! It is made to flash like lightning,
it is grasped for slaughter.[m]
16 O sword, slash to the right,
then to the left,
21:17 wherever your blade is turned.
[n]ver 14; 17 I too will strike my hands[n] together,
Eze 22:13 [o]Eze 5:13 and my wrath[o] will subside.
I the LORD have spoken.”

18 The word of the LORD came to me: 19“Son of
man, mark out two roads for the sword of the
king of Babylon to take, both starting from the
same country. Make a signpost where the road
branches off to the city. 20 Mark out one road for
21:20 [p]Dt 3:11; the sword to come against Rabbah of the
Jer 49:2; Ammonites[p] and another against Judah and forti-
Am 1:14 fied Jerusalem. 21 For the king of Babylon will stop
21:21 at the fork in the road, at the junction of the two
[q]Pr 16:33 roads, to seek an omen: He will cast lots[q] with
[r]Nu 22:7; arrows, he will consult his idols, he will examine
23:23 the liver.[r] 22 Into his right hand will come the lot
for Jerusalem, where he is to set up battering
rams, to give the command to slaughter, to sound
21:22 the battle cry, to set battering rams against the
[s]Eze 4:2; 26:9 gates, to build a ramp and to erect siege works.[s]
23 It will seem like a false omen to those who have
21:23 sworn allegiance to him, but he will remind[t] them
[t]Nu 5:15 of their guilt and take them captive.

24“Therefore this is what the Sovereign LORD
says: ‘Because you people have brought to mind
your guilt by your open rebellion, revealing your
sins in all that you do—because you have done
this, you will be taken captive.

[a] 15 Septuagint; the meaning of the Hebrew for this word is uncertain.

Looking for an Omen

EZE 21:21

The king of Babylon, according to Ezekiel, will stop at a fork in the road and use omens to decide which way to proceed. All three forms of looking for omens listed in this verse were in common use in Biblical times. A number of arrows, each marked with one of the decisions to be made, were put into a quiver and then spun. The arrow that was drawn out of the quiver provided the answer. Household gods were thought to have special abilities in giving guidance to their owners. One of the most common forms of divination was to examine a sheep liver and make a decision based on its color or structure. None of these forms of discovering the future or making a decision were (or are) accurate in any way. However, the Creator God can use any form of human folly to bring about his perfect will.

The Greek word *koinonia* is used in Scripture for our word *fellowship* and is defined as "that which is in common." *The International Dictionary of the Bible* defines *fellowship* as "that heavenly love that fills the hearts of believers one for another and for God. This fellowship is deeper and more satisfying than any mere human love whether social, parental, conjugal or other." I love that definition, and of course, when I say I love the word *fellowship,* what I really love is the experience of fellowship . . . How about you? Are you pining for the fellowship that surpasses all others? Get yourself to the nearest Christian and connect. Spend time with fellow believers rejoicing over what you have in Jesus. Sing some songs. Laugh together. Pray for one another. Hug each other. Celebrate the blessed tie that binds you to one another in Christian love.

—Marilyn Meberg

25" 'O profane and wicked prince of Israel,
whose day has come, whose time of punishment
has reached its climax,[u] 26this is what the Sovereign LORD says: Take off the turban, remove the
crown.[v] It will not be as it was: The lowly will be
exalted and the exalted will be brought low.[w] 27A
ruin! A ruin! I will make it a ruin! It will not be
restored until he comes to whom it rightfully
belongs; to him I will give it.'[x]

28"And you, son of man, prophesy and say, 'This
is what the Sovereign LORD says about the
Ammonites[y] and their insults:

" 'A sword,[z] a sword,
drawn for the slaughter,
polished to consume
and to flash like lightning!
29 Despite false visions concerning you
and lying divinations about you,
it will be laid on the necks
of the wicked who are to be slain,
whose day has come,
whose time of punishment has
reached its climax.[a]
30 Return the sword to its scabbard.[b]
In the place where you were created,
in the land of your ancestry,[c]
I will judge you.
31 I will pour out my wrath upon you
and breathe out my fiery anger[d]
against you;
I will hand you over to brutal men,
men skilled in destruction.[e]
32 You will be fuel for the fire,[f]
your blood will be shed in your land,
you will be remembered[g] no more;
for I the LORD have spoken.' "

Jerusalem's Sins

22 The word of the LORD came to me: 2"Son of
man, will you judge her? Will you judge
this city of bloodshed?[h] Then confront her with
all her detestable practices[i] 3and say: 'This is what
the Sovereign LORD says: O city that brings on herself doom by shedding blood[j] in her midst and
defiles herself by making idols, 4you have become
guilty because of the blood you have shed[k] and
have become defiled by the idols you have made.
You have brought your days to a close, and the
end of your years has come.[l] Therefore I will
make you an object of scorn to the nations and a
laughingstock to all the countries.[m] 5Those who
are near and those who are far away will mock
you, O infamous city, full of turmoil.

6" 'See how each of the princes of Israel who
are in you uses his power to shed blood.[n] 7In you
they have treated father and mother with contempt;[o] in you they have oppressed the alien and
mistreated the fatherless and the widow.[p] 8You
have despised my holy things and desecrated my
Sabbaths.[q] 9In you are slanderous men[r] bent on

21:25 [u]Eze 35:5
21:26 [v]Jer 13:18 [w]Ps 75:7; Eze 17:24
21:27 [x]Ps 2:6; Jer 23:5-6; Eze 37:24; Hag 2:21-22
21:28 [y]Zep 2:8 [z]Jer 12:12
21:29 [a]ver 25; Eze 22:28; 35:5
21:30 [b]Jer 47:6 [c]Eze 16:3
21:31 [d]Eze 22:20-21 [e]Jer 51:20-23
21:32 [f]Mal 4:1 [g]Eze 25:10
22:2 [h]Eze 24:6,9; Na 3:1 [i]Eze 16:2
22:3 [j]ver 6,13,27; Eze 23:37,45
22:4 [k]2Ki 21:16 [l]Eze 21:25 [m]Eze 5:14
22:6 [n]Isa 1:23
22:7 [o]Dt 5:16; 27:16 [p]Ex 22:21-22
22:8 [q]Eze 23:38-39
22:9 [r]Lev 19:16

shedding blood; in you are those who eat at the
mountain shrines[s] and commit lewd acts.[t] 10In you
are those who dishonor their fathers' bed; in you
are those who violate women during their period,
when they are ceremonially unclean.[u] 11In you
one man commits a detestable offense with his
neighbor's wife, another shamefully defiles his
daughter-in-law,[v] and another violates his sister,[w]
his own father's daughter. 12In you men accept
bribes[x] to shed blood; you take usury and excessive interest[a] and make unjust gain from your
neighbors[y] by extortion. And you have forgotten
me, declares the Sovereign LORD.

13" 'I will surely strike my hands[z] together at
the unjust gain[a] you have made and at the blood[b]
you have shed in your midst. 14Will your courage
endure or your hands be strong in the day I deal
with you? I the LORD have spoken,[c] and I will do
it.[d] 15I will disperse you among the nations and
scatter[e] you through the countries; and I will put
an end to your uncleanness.[f] 16When you have
been defiled[b] in the eyes of the nations, you will
know that I am the LORD.' "

17Then the word of the LORD came to me: 18"Son
of man, the house of Israel has become dross[g] to
me; all of them are the copper, tin, iron and lead
left inside a furnace. They are but the dross of silver.[h] 19Therefore this is what the Sovereign LORD
says: 'Because you have all become dross, I will
gather you into Jerusalem. 20As men gather silver,
copper, iron, lead and tin into a furnace to melt it
with a fiery blast, so will I gather you in my anger
and my wrath and put you inside the city and melt
you.[i] 21I will gather you and I will blow on you
with my fiery wrath, and you will be melted inside
her. 22As silver is melted[j] in a furnace, so you will
be melted inside her, and you will know that I the
LORD have poured out my wrath upon you.' "[k]

23Again the word of the LORD came to me:
24"Son of man, say to the land, 'You are a land that
has had no rain or showers[c] in the day of wrath.'[l]
25There is a conspiracy[m] of her princes[d] within her
like a roaring lion tearing its prey; they devour
people,[n] take treasures and precious things and
make many widows[o] within her. 26Her priests do
violence to my law[p] and profane my holy things;
they do not distinguish between the holy and the
common;[q] they teach that there is no difference
between the unclean and the clean;[r] and they shut
their eyes to the keeping of my Sabbaths, so that
I am profaned among them.[s] 27Her officials within her are like wolves tearing their prey; they shed
blood and kill people to make unjust gain.[t] 28Her
prophets whitewash[u] these deeds for them by
false visions and lying divinations. They say, 'This
is what the Sovereign LORD says'—when the LORD
has not spoken.[v] 29The people of the land practice

22:9 [s]Eze 18:11 [t]Hos 4:10,14
22:10 [u]Lev 18:8,19
22:11 [v]Lev 18:15 [w]Lev 18:9; 2Sa 13:14
22:12 [x]Dt 27:25; Mic 7:3 [y]Lev 19:13
22:13 [z]Eze 21:17 [a]Isa 33:15 [b]ver 3
22:14 [c]Eze 24:14 [d]Eze 17:24; 21:7
22:15 [e]Dt 4:27; Zec 7:14 [f]Eze 23:27
22:18 [g]Ps 119:119; Isa 1:22 [h]Jer 6:28-30
22:20 [i]Mal 3:2
22:22 [j]Isa 1:25 [k]Eze 20:8,33
22:24 [l]Eze 24:13
22:25 [m]Jer 11:9 [n]Hos 6:9 [o]Jer 15:8
22:26 [p]Mal 2:7-8 [q]Eze 44:23 [r]Lev 10:10 [s]1Sa 2:12-17; Jer 2:8,26; Hag 2:11-14
22:27 [t]Isa 1:23
22:28 [u]Eze 13:10 [v]Eze 13:2, 6-7

[a] 12 Or *usury and interest* [b] 16 Or *When I have allotted you your inheritance* [c] 24 Septuagint; Hebrew *has not been cleansed or rained on* [d] 25 Septuagint; Hebrew *prophets*

Stand in the Gap

I am old and blind!
Men point at me as smitten by
God's frown;
Afflicted and deserted of my kind,
Yet I am not cast down.
I am weak, yet strong;
I murmur not that I no longer see;
Poor, old, and helpless, I the more
belong,
Father Supreme! to Thee.

All-merciful One!
When men are furthest, then art
Thou most near,
When friends pass by, my weak-
nesses to shun,
Thy chariot I hear.

Thy glorious face
Is leaning toward me, and its holy
light
Shines in upon my lonely
dwelling-place,—
And there is no more night.

—Elizabeth Lloyd Howell (1811-1896)

Stand in the Gap

EZE 22:30–31

When the Israelites disobey God in the desert and worship a golden calf, God determines that he will destroy them. Moses quickly "stands in the gap" and begs God to reconsider. When God sees Moses' faithfulness, he relents (Ex 32:9–14). Now God is again looking for a leader for the Israelites, a righteous leader who will lead the people to repentance and true faith in God, a faithful follower of God who will intercede before the Almighty on their behalf. Unfortunately, no one can be found. All of the leaders of Israel are corrupt and rebellious. So a sad pronunciation of judgment follows: God "will pour out [his] wrath" and "consume" the people (Eze 22:31). There is no longer any hope of a reprieve.

Who "stands in the gap" for our country? Our churches? Our communities? Our families? God is still looking for faithful leaders to stand and intercede before him, leaders who will call people to a faithful way of life through following our faithful God.

extortion and commit robbery; they oppress the
poor and needy and mistreat the alien,[w] denying
them justice.[x]
30"I looked for a man among them who would
build up the wall[y] and stand before me in the gap
on behalf of the land so I would not have to
destroy it, but I found none.[z] 31So I will pour out
my wrath on them and consume them with my
fiery anger, bringing down[a] on their own heads
all they have done, declares the Sovereign LORD.[b]"

Two Adulterous Sisters

23 The word of the LORD came to me: 2"Son of
man, there were two women, daughters of
the same mother.[c] 3They became prostitutes in
Egypt,[d] engaging in prostitution[e] from their youth.
In that land their breasts were fondled and their
virgin bosoms caressed. 4The older was named
Oholah, and her sister was Oholibah. They were
mine and gave birth to sons and daughters. Oholah is Samaria, and Oholibah is Jerusalem.
5"Oholah engaged in prostitution while she was
still mine; and she lusted after her lovers, the
Assyrians[f]—warriors[g] 6clothed in blue, governors
and commanders, all of them handsome young
men, and mounted horsemen. 7She gave herself
as a prostitute to all the elite of the Assyrians and
defiled herself with all the idols of everyone she
lusted after.[h] 8She did not give up the prostitution
she began in Egypt,[i] when during her youth men
slept with her, caressed her virgin bosom and
poured out their lust upon her.[j]
9"Therefore I handed her over[k] to her lovers, the
Assyrians, for whom she lusted.[l] 10They stripped[m]
her naked, took away her sons and daughters and
killed her with the sword. She became a byword
among women,[n] and punishment was inflicted on
her.[o]
11"Her sister Oholibah saw this, yet in her lust
and prostitution she was more depraved than her
sister.[p] 12She too lusted after the Assyrians—governors and commanders, warriors in full dress,
mounted horsemen, all handsome young men.[q]
13I saw that she too defiled herself; both of them
went the same way.
14"But she carried her prostitution still further.
She saw men portrayed on a wall,[r] figures of
Chaldeans[a] portrayed in red,[s] 15with belts around
their waists and flowing turbans on their heads;
all of them looked like Babylonian chariot officers,
natives of Chaldea.[b] 16As soon as she saw them,
she lusted after them and sent messengers to them
in Chaldea. 17Then the Babylonians came to her,
to the bed of love, and in their lust they defiled
her. After she had been defiled by them, she
turned away from them in disgust. 18When she
carried on her prostitution openly and exposed
her nakedness, I turned away[t] from her in disgust,
just as I had turned away from her sister.[u] 19Yet

a 14 Or *Babylonians* *b* 15 Or *Babylonia*; also in verse 16

22:29 [w]Ex 22:21; 23:9 [x]Isa 5:7
22:30 [y]Eze 13:5 [z]Ps 106:23; Jer 5:1
22:31 [a]Eze 16:43 [b]Eze 7:8-9; 9:10; Ro 2:8
23:2 [c]Jer 3:7; Eze 16:45
23:3 [d]Jos 24:14 [e]Lev 17:7
23:5 [f]2Ki 16:7; Hos 5:13 [g]Hos 8:9
23:7 [h]Hos 5:3; 6:10
23:8 [i]Ex 32:4 [j]Eze 16:15
23:9 [k]2Ki 18:11 [l]Hos 11:5
23:10 [m]Hos 2:10 [n]Eze 16:41 [o]Eze 16:36
23:11 [p]Jer 3:8-11; Eze 16:51
23:12 [q]2Ki 16:7-15; 2Ch 28:16
23:14 [r]Eze 8:10 [s]Jer 22:14
23:18 [t]Ps 78:59; 106:40; Jer 6:8 [u]Jer 12:8; Am 5:21

she became more and more promiscuous as she
recalled the days of her youth, when she was a
prostitute in Egypt. 20There she lusted after her
lovers, whose genitals were like those of donkeys
and whose emission was like that of horses. 21So
you longed for the lewdness of your youth, when
in Egypt your bosom was caressed and your
young breasts fondled.[a][v]
22"Therefore, Oholibah, this is what the Sovereign LORD says: I will stir up your lovers against
you, those you turned away from in disgust, and
I will bring them against you from every side[w]—
23the Babylonians[x] and all the Chaldeans, the men
of Pekod[y] and Shoa and Koa, and all the Assyrians with them, handsome young men, all of
them governors and commanders, chariot officers
and men of high rank, all mounted on horses.[z]
24They will come against you with weapons,[b]
chariots and wagons[a] and with a throng of people; they will take up positions against you on
every side with large and small shields and with
helmets. I will turn you over to them for punishment,[b] and they will punish you according to
their standards. 25I will direct my jealous anger
against you, and they will deal with you in fury.
They will cut off your noses and your ears, and
those of you who are left will fall by the sword.
They will take away your sons and daughters,[c]
and those of you who are left will be consumed
by fire.[d] 26They will also strip[e] you of your clothes
and take your fine jewelry.[f] 27So I will put a stop[g]
to the lewdness and prostitution you began in
Egypt. You will not look on these things with
longing or remember Egypt anymore.
28"For this is what the Sovereign LORD says: I
am about to hand you over[h] to those you hate,
to those you turned away from in disgust. 29They
will deal with you in hatred and take away
everything you have worked for. They will leave
you naked and bare, and the shame of your prostitution will be exposed. Your lewdness and
promiscuity[i] 30have brought this upon you,
because you lusted after the nations and defiled
yourself with their idols.[j] 31You have gone the
way of your sister; so I will put her cup[k] into
your hand.[l]
32"This is what the Sovereign LORD says:

"You will drink your sister's cup,
a cup large and deep;
it will bring scorn and derision,
for it holds so much.[m]
33You will be filled with drunkenness and
sorrow,
the cup of ruin and desolation,
the cup of your sister Samaria.[n]
34You will drink it[o] and drain it dry;
you will dash it to pieces

23:21 [v]Eze 16:26
23:22 [w]Eze 16:37
23:23 [x]2Ki 20:14-18 [y]Jer 50:21 [z]2Ki 24:2
23:24 [a]Jer 47:3; Eze 26:7,10; Na 2:4 [b]Jer 39:5-6
23:25 [c]ver 47 [d]Eze 20:47-48
23:26 [e]Jer 13:22 [f]Isa 3:18-23; Eze 16:39
23:27 [g]Eze 16:41
23:28 [h]Jer 34:20
23:29 [i]Dt 28:48
23:30 [j]Eze 6:9
23:31 [k]Jer 25:15 [l]2Ki 21:13
23:32 [m]Ps 60:3; Isa 51:17; Jer 25:15
23:33 [n]Jer 25:15-16
23:34 [o]Ps 75:8; Isa 51:17

[a] 21 Syriac (see also verse 3); Hebrew *caressed because of your young breasts* [b] 24 The meaning of the Hebrew for this word is uncertain.

An Obscene Picture

EZE 23:20-21

It's offensive to our ears, something we'd rather not even read. This picture of Jerusalem's alliance with Egypt has more than sexual overtones. It is blatantly and repulsively sexual. Why would God and Ezekiel use such language?

If we find this lusty, sexual picture grossly offensive, we begin to understand how repulsive God finds the relationship between Jerusalem and Egypt. Rather than trusting in him, they turn to Egypt and look to that country to defend them against invasion. After all these years, after all the miraculous interventions by God, the people have still failed to learn that their only true security rests in God. No country, no person, no relationship can give them the protection God is willing, and waiting, to provide.

Today we still look in all the wrong places for our security and fulfillment. Our finances, our families, our jobs and even our churches cannot provide anything close to the shelter and contentment God is waiting to provide for us.

Spiritual Prostitution

EZE 23:35–49

Because they have turned from God to worship idols, even sacrificing their own children to them, God accuses—and now judges—the people for their spiritual prostitution. Their behavior is repugnant to him. He has waited for them to turn away from their unfaithful ways, but they have refused. Now he pronounces judgment. He promises that they will "suffer the penalty" and "bear the consequences" (Eze 23:49) for their rebellion. A faithful God is faithful not only to his people, but also to himself. Injustice, rebellion and sin must be punished. His holiness demands it. Only repentance can bring reprieve. But no repentance comes. So instead, the Israelites experience God's judgment.

and tear your breasts.
I have spoken, declares the Sovereign LORD.
35"Therefore this is what the Sovereign LORD
says: Since you have forgotten[p] me and thrust me
behind your back,[q] you must bear the consequences
of your lewdness and prostitution."
36The LORD said to me: "Son of man, will you
judge Oholah and Oholibah? Then confront[r] them
with their detestable practices,[s] 37for they have
committed adultery and blood is on their hands.
They committed adultery with their idols; they
even sacrificed their children, whom they bore to
me,[a] as food for them.[t] 38They have also done this
to me: At that same time they defiled my sanctuary
and desecrated my Sabbaths. 39On the very
day they sacrificed their children to their idols,
they entered my sanctuary and desecrated[u] it.
That is what they did in my house.[v]
40"They even sent messengers for men who
came from far away,[w] and when they arrived you
bathed yourself for them, painted your eyes[x] and
put on your jewelry.[y] 41You sat on an elegant
couch,[z] with a table[a] spread before it on which
you had placed the incense and oil that belonged
to me.
42"The noise of a carefree crowd was around
her; Sabeans[b] were brought from the desert along
with men from the rabble, and they put bracelets[b]
on the arms of the woman and her sister and
beautiful crowns on their heads.[c] 43Then I said
about the one worn out by adultery, 'Now let
them use her as a prostitute,[d] for that is all she is.'
44And they slept with her. As men sleep with a
prostitute, so they slept with those lewd women,
Oholah and Oholibah. 45But righteous men will
sentence them to the punishment of women who
commit adultery and shed blood, because they are
adulterous and blood is on their hands.[e]
46"This is what the Sovereign LORD says: Bring a
mob[f] against them and give them over to terror
and plunder. 47The mob will stone them and cut
them down with their swords; they will kill their
sons and daughters and burn[g] down their houses.[h]
48"So I will put an end to lewdness in the land,
that all women may take warning and not imitate
you.[i] 49You will suffer the penalty for your lewdness
and bear the consequences of your sins of
idolatry. Then you will know that I am the Sovereign
LORD.[j]"

The Cooking Pot

24 In the ninth year, in the tenth month on the
tenth day, the word of the LORD came to
me:[k] 2"Son of man, record this date, this very date,
because the king of Babylon has laid siege to Jerusalem
this very day.[l] 3Tell this rebellious house[m] a
parable[n] and say to them: 'This is what the Sovereign
LORD says:

23:35 [p]Isa 17:10; Jer 3:21 [q]1Ki 14:9
23:36 [r]Eze 16:2 [s]Isa 58:1; Eze 22:2; Mic 3:8
23:37 [t]Eze 16:36
23:39 [u]2Ki 21:4 [v]Jer 7:10
23:40 [w]Isa 57:9 [x]2Ki 9:30 [y]Jer 4:30; Eze 16:13-19
23:41 [z]Est 1:6; Pr 7:17; Am 6:4 [a]Isa 65:11; Eze 44:16
23:42 [b]Ge 24:30 [c]Eze 16:11-12
23:43 [d]ver 3
23:45 [e]Lev 20:10; Eze 16:38; Hos 6:5
23:46 [f]Eze 16:40
23:47 [g]2Ch 36:19 [h]2Ch 36:17; Eze 16:40-41
23:48 [i]2Pe 2:6
23:49 [j]Eze 7:4; 9:10; 20:38
24:1 [k]Eze 8:1
24:2 [l]2Ki 25:1; Jer 39:1; 52:4
24:3 [m]Isa 1:2; Eze 2:3,6

[a] 37 Or *even made the children they bore to me pass through* ⌊*the fire*⌋ [b] 42 Or *drunkards*

24:3 [n]Eze 17:2; 20:49 [o]Jer 1:13; Eze 11:3

" 'Put on the cooking pot;[o] put it on
and pour water into it.
4 Put into it the pieces of meat,
all the choice pieces—the leg and the shoulder.
Fill it with the best of these bones;
5 take the pick of the flock.[p]
Pile wood beneath it for the bones;
bring it to a boil
and cook the bones in it.[q]

24:5 [p]Jer 52:10 [q]Jer 52:24-27

6 " 'For this is what the Sovereign LORD says:

24:6 [r]Eze 22:2 [s]Ob 1:11; Na 3:10

" 'Woe to the city of bloodshed,[r]
to the pot now encrusted,
whose deposit will not go away!
Empty it piece by piece
without casting lots[s] for them.

7 " 'For the blood she shed is in her midst:
She poured it on the bare rock;
she did not pour it on the ground,
where the dust would cover it.[t]
8 To stir up wrath and take revenge
I put her blood on the bare rock,
so that it would not be covered.

24:7 [t]Lev 17:13

9 " 'Therefore this is what the Sovereign LORD says:

" 'Woe to the city of bloodshed!
I, too, will pile the wood high.
10 So heap on the wood
and kindle the fire.
Cook the meat well,
mixing in the spices;
and let the bones be charred.
11 Then set the empty pot on the coals
till it becomes hot and its copper glows
so its impurities may be melted
and its deposit burned away.[u]
12 It has frustrated all efforts;
its heavy deposit has not been removed,
not even by fire.

24:11 [u]Jer 21:10; Eze 22:15

13 " 'Now your impurity is lewdness. Because I
tried to cleanse you but you would not be cleansed
from your impurity, you will not be clean again
until my wrath against you has subsided.[v]

24:13 [v]Jer 6:28-30; Eze 16:42; 22:24

14 " 'I the LORD have spoken. The time has come
for me to act. I will not hold back; I will not have
pity, nor will I relent. You will be judged according to your conduct and your actions,[w] declares
the Sovereign LORD.[x]' "

24:14 [w]Eze 36:19 [x]Eze 18:30

Ezekiel's Wife Dies

15 The word of the LORD came to me: 16 "Son of
man, with one blow I am about to take away from
you the delight of your eyes. Yet do not lament or
weep or shed any tears.[y] 17 Groan quietly; do not
mourn for the dead. Keep your turban fastened

24:16 [y]Jer 13:17; 16:5; 22:10

A Cooking Pot

EZE 24:1-14

Ezekiel continues his words of judgment by comparing Jerusalem to a cooking pot. It has been put on the fire—*the city is under siege.* Choice pieces of meat have been put into it—*those who thought they escaped the earlier exile because they were "good."* Wood is placed under the pot in order to cook the contents—*the Babylonians bring in their war equipment and tighten the siege around Jerusalem.* The cooked meat is taken out, piece by piece—*exiles are sent away from the captured city.* The pot is emptied—*everyone goes into exile and Jerusalem is emptied of inhabitants.* The empty pot is left on the coals until it becomes red hot—*the empty city of Jerusalem is burned down.*

An Unnatural Response

EZE 24:15-27

God now asks something totally unnatural of Ezekiel. His wife—a wife he must have cherished since she is referred to as "the delight of [his] eyes" (Eze 24:16)—will die, and Ezekiel will not be allowed to mourn. In the culture of that day, mourning for a loved one was a very public affair. The mourners moaned and wailed, ripped their clothing, fasted and went without shoes.

Ezekiel's lack of display does not go unnoticed. The people ask him why he isn't mourning, which is just the opening Ezekiel—and God—are looking for. Ezekiel explains that his situation is a foreshadowing of theirs. (In fact, Exekiel's wife died the same day the temple was burned.) Jerusalem will be destroyed. The way of life they cherish, the city they love, the temple that is the "delight" of their eyes (Eze 24:21)—all will be taken away. And they, too, will go through this "death" without grieving, because as exiles in Babylon they are far from Jerusalem and because they will be forced to recognize that this is God's just judgment on them.

and your sandals on your feet; do not cover the lower part of your face or eat the customary food ⌊of mourners⌋.[z]"

18So I spoke to the people in the morning, and in the evening my wife died. The next morning I did as I had been commanded.

19Then the people asked me, "Won't you tell us what these things have to do with us?[a]"

20So I said to them, "The word of the LORD came to me: 21Say to the house of Israel, 'This is what the Sovereign LORD says: I am about to desecrate my sanctuary—the stronghold in which you take pride, the delight of your eyes,[b] the object of your affection. The sons and daughters[c] you left behind will fall by the sword.[d] 22And you will do as I have done. You will not cover the lower part of your face or eat the customary food ⌊of mourners⌋.[e] 23You will keep your turbans on your heads and your sandals on your feet. You will not mourn[f] or weep but will waste away because of[a] your sins and groan among yourselves.[g] 24Ezekiel will be a sign[h] to you; you will do just as he has done. When this happens, you will know that I am the Sovereign LORD.'

25"And you, son of man, on the day I take away their stronghold, their joy and glory, the delight of their eyes, their heart's desire, and their sons and daughters[i] as well— 26on that day a fugitive will come to tell you[j] the news. 27At that time your mouth will be opened; you will speak with him and will no longer be silent. So you will be a sign to them, and they will know that I am the LORD.[k]"

A Prophecy Against Ammon

25 The word of the LORD came to me: 2"Son of man, set your face against the Ammonites[l] and prophesy against them.[m] 3Say to them, 'Hear the word of the Sovereign LORD. This is what the Sovereign LORD says: Because you said "Aha![n]" over my sanctuary when it was desecrated and over the land of Israel when it was laid waste and over the people of Judah when they went into exile,[o] 4therefore I am going to give you to the people of the East[p] as a possession. They will set up their camps and pitch their tents among you; they will eat your fruit and drink your milk.[q] 5I will turn Rabbah[r] into a pasture for camels and Ammon into a resting place for sheep.[s] Then you will know that I am the LORD. 6For this is what the Sovereign LORD says: Because you have clapped your hands and stamped your feet, rejoicing with all the malice of your heart against the land of Israel,[t] 7therefore I will stretch out my hand[u] against you and give you as plunder to the nations. I will cut you off from the nations and exterminate you from the countries. I will destroy[v] you, and you will know that I am the LORD.[w]' "

A Prophecy Against Moab

8"This is what the Sovereign LORD says:

24:17 [z]Jer 16:7
24:19 [a]Eze 12:9; 37:18
24:21 [b]Ps 27:4 [c]Eze 23:25 [d]Jer 7:14,15; Eze 23:47
24:22 [e]Jer 16:7
24:23 [f]Job 27:15 [g]Ps 78:64
24:24 [h]Isa 20:3; Eze 4:3; 12:11
24:25 [i]Jer 11:22
24:26 [j]1Sa 4:12; Job 1:15-19
24:27 [k]Eze 3:26; 33:22
25:2 [l]Eze 21:28; Zep 2:8-9 [m]Jer 49:1-6
25:3 [n]Eze 26:2; 36:2 [o]Pr 17:5
25:4 [p]Jdg 6:3 [q]Dt 28:33, 51; Jdg 6:33
25:5 [r]Dt 3:11; Eze 21:20 [s]Isa 17:2
25:6 [t]Ob 1:12; Zep 2:8
25:7 [u]Zep 1:4 [v]Eze 21:31 [w]Am 1:14-15

25:8 xJer 48:1; Am 2:1 ‘Because Moab[x] and Seir said, “Look, the house
of Judah has become like all the other nations,”
[9]therefore I will expose the flank of Moab, begin-
25:9 yNu 33:49 zNu 32:3; Jos 13:17 aNu 32:37; Jos 13:19 ning at its frontier towns—Beth Jeshimoth[y], Baal
Meon[z] and Kiriathaim[a]—the glory of that land. [10]I
will give Moab along with the Ammonites to the
people of the East as a possession, so that the
Ammonites will not be remembered[b] among the
25:10 bEze 21:32 nations; [11]and I will inflict punishment on Moab.
Then they will know that I am the LORD.’ ”

A Prophecy Against Edom

[12]“This is what the Sovereign LORD says: ‘Because
25:12 c2Ch 28:17 Edom[c] took revenge on the house of Judah and
became very guilty by doing so, [13]therefore this is
what the Sovereign LORD says: I will stretch out my
25:13 dEze 29:8 eJer 25:23 hand against Edom and kill its men and their animals.[d] I will lay it waste, and from Teman to
Dedan[e] they will fall by the sword. [14]I will take
vengeance on Edom by the hand of my people Israel, and they will deal with Edom in accordance
25:14 fEze 35:11 with my anger[f] and my wrath; they will know my
vengeance, declares the Sovereign LORD.’ ”

A Prophecy Against Philistia

[15]“This is what the Sovereign LORD says:
25:15 g2Ch 28:18 ‘Because the Philistines[g] acted in vengeance and
took revenge with malice in their hearts, and with
ancient hostility sought to destroy Judah, [16]there-
fore this is what the Sovereign LORD says: I am
about to stretch out my hand against the Philis-
25:16 hJer 47:1-7 i1Sa 30:14; Zep 2:4-5 tines,[h] and I will cut off the Kerethites[i] and destroy
those remaining along the coast. [17]I will carry out
great vengeance on them and punish them in my
wrath. Then they will know that I am the LORD,
when I take vengeance on them.’ ”

A Prophecy Against Tyre

26 In the eleventh year, on the first day of the
month, the word of the LORD came to me:
26:2 j2Sa 5:11; Isa 23 kEze 25:3 [2]“Son of man, because Tyre[j] has said of Jerusalem,
‘Aha![k] The gate to the nations is broken, and its
doors have swung open to me; now that she lies in
ruins I will prosper,’ [3]therefore this is what the Sovereign LORD says: I am against you, O Tyre, and I
26:3 lIsa 5:30; Jer 50:42; 51:42 will bring many nations against you, like the sea[l]
casting up its waves. [4]They will destroy[m] the walls
of Tyre[n] and pull down her towers; I will scrape
away her rubble and make her a bare rock. [5]Out in
26:4 mIsa 23:1,11 nAm 1:10 the sea[o] she will become a place to spread fishnets,
for I have spoken, declares the Sovereign LORD. She
26:5 oEze 27:32 pEze 29:19 will become plunder[p] for the nations, [6]and her settlements on the mainland will be ravaged by the
sword. Then they will know that I am the LORD.
[7]“For this is what the Sovereign LORD says: From
26:7 qJer 27:6 rEzr 7:12; Da 2:37 the north I am going to bring against Tyre Nebuchadnezzar[b][q] king of Babylon, king of kings,[r]

[a] 23 Or *away in* [b] 7 Hebrew *Nebuchadrezzar,* of which *Nebuchadnezzar* is a variant; here and often in Ezekiel and Jeremiah

Aha!

EZE 26:1-6

“Aha!” That one word tersely expresses Tyre’s response when Jerusalem is conquered. They gloat. They are thrilled. Now that Jerusalem is destroyed and her gates lie open, they will have free rein to enter her and gain plunder for themselves. With no thought of the devastation to their neighbors, the inhabitants of Jerusalem, the inhabitants of Tyre think only of adding wealth to their personal coffers.

God does not take their attitude toward his people or his holy city lightly. Through Ezekiel he pronounces judgment on Tyre, stating that wave after wave of nations will come in to conquer and destroy the city. Their judgment begins with Nebuchadnezzar, who besieges the city for 15 years, beginning shortly after the destruction of Jerusalem. Throughout the history of Tyre, she has been under the rule of one nation after another—God’s judgment fulfilled.

with horses and chariots,[s] with horsemen and a great army. 8He will ravage your settlements on the mainland with the sword; he will set up siege works[t] against you, build a ramp[u] up to your walls and raise his shields against you. 9He will direct the blows of his battering rams against your walls and demolish your towers with his weapons. 10His horses will be so many that they will cover you with dust. Your walls will tremble at the noise of the war horses, wagons and chariots[v] when he enters your gates as men enter a city whose walls have been broken through. 11The hoofs[w] of his horses will trample all your streets; he will kill your people with the sword, and your strong pillars[x] will fall to the ground.[y] 12They will plunder your wealth and loot your merchandise; they will break down your walls and demolish your fine houses and throw your stones, timber and rubble into the sea.[z] 13I will put an end[a] to your noisy songs, and the music of your harps[b] will be heard no more.[c] 14I will make you a bare rock, and you will become a place to spread fishnets. You will never be rebuilt,[d] for I the LORD have spoken, declares the Sovereign LORD.

15"This is what the Sovereign LORD says to Tyre: Will not the coastlands[e] tremble[f] at the sound of your fall, when the wounded groan and the slaughter takes place in you? 16Then all the princes of the coast will step down from their thrones and lay aside their robes and take off their embroidered garments. Clothed[g] with terror, they will sit on the ground, trembling[h] every moment, appalled[i] at you. 17Then they will take up a lament[j] concerning you and say to you:

" 'How you are destroyed, O city of
    renown,
  peopled by men of the sea!
You were a power on the seas,
  you and your citizens;
you put your terror
  on all who lived there.[k]
18Now the coastlands tremble
  on the day of your fall;
the islands in the sea
  are terrified at your collapse.'[l]

19"This is what the Sovereign LORD says: When I make you a desolate city, like cities no longer inhabited, and when I bring the ocean depths over you and its vast waters cover you,[m] 20then I will bring you down with those who go down to the pit,[n] to the people of long ago. I will make you dwell in the earth below, as in ancient ruins, with those who go down to the pit, and you will not return or take your place[a] in the land of the living.[o] 21I will bring you to a horrible end and you will be no more. You will be sought, but you will never again be found, declares the Sovereign LORD."[p]

[a] 20 Septuagint; Hebrew *return, and I will give glory*

26:7 [s]Eze 23:24; Na 2:3-4
26:8 [t]Jer 6:6 [u]Eze 21:22
26:10 [v]Jer 4:13
26:11 [w]Isa 5:28 [x]Jer 43:13 [y]Isa 26:5
26:12 [z]Isa 23:8; Eze 27:3-27; 28:8
26:13 [a]Jer 7:34 [b]Isa 14:11 [c]Jer 25:10; Rev 18:22
26:14 [d]Job 12:14; Mal 1:4
26:15 [e]Eze 27:35 [f]Jer 49:21
26:16 [g]Job 8:22 [h]Hos 11:10 [i]Eze 32:10
26:17 [j]Eze 19:1; 27:32 [k]Isa 14:12
26:18 [l]Isa 23:5; 41:5; Eze 27:35
26:19 [m]Isa 8:7-8
26:20 [n]Eze 32:18; Am 9:2; Jnh 2:2,6 [o]Eze 32:24, 30
26:21 [p]Eze 27:36; 28:19; Rev 18:21

I want to live a passionate life. I want to live a life that recognizes the fears but moves out with courage. I want to show the world the eternal mystery of what God can do through a miserable sinner sold out to him. Why would I settle for anything less?

—Sheila Walsh

A Lament for Tyre

27 The word of the LORD came to me: 2"Son of
27:3 [q]ver 33 [r]Eze 28:2 — man, take up a lament concerning Tyre.
3Say to Tyre, situated at the gateway to the sea,[q]
merchant of peoples on many coasts, 'This is what
the Sovereign LORD says:

" 'You say, O Tyre,
"I am perfect in beauty.[r]"
4Your domain was on the high seas;
your builders brought your beauty to perfection.
5They made all your timbers
27:5 [s]Dt 3:9 — of pine trees from Senir[a];[s]
they took a cedar from Lebanon
to make a mast for you.
27:6 [t]Nu 21:33; Jer 22:20; Zec 11:2 [u]Ge 10:4; Isa 23:12 — 6Of oaks[t] from Bashan
they made your oars;
of cypress wood[b] from the coasts of Cyprus[c][u]
they made your deck, inlaid with ivory.
7Fine embroidered linen from Egypt was your sail
27:7 [v]Ex 25:4; Jer 10:9 — and served as your banner;
your awnings were of blue and purple[v]
from the coasts of Elishah.
27:8 [w]Ge 10:18 [x]1Ki 9:27 — 8Men of Sidon and Arvad[w] were your oarsmen;
your skilled men, O Tyre, were aboard
as your seamen.[x]
27:9 [y]Jos 13:5; 1Ki 5:18 — 9Veteran craftsmen of Gebal[d][y] were on board
as shipwrights to caulk your seams.
All the ships of the sea and their sailors
came alongside to trade for your wares.

27:10 [z]Eze 38:5 [a]Eze 30:5 — 10" 'Men of Persia,[z] Lydia and Put[a]
served as soldiers in your army.
They hung their shields and helmets on your walls,
bringing you splendor.
11Men of Arvad and Helech
manned your walls on every side;
men of Gammad
were in your towers.
They hung their shields around your walls;
27:12 [b]Ge 10:4 [c]ver 18,33 — they brought your beauty to perfection.

12" 'Tarshish[b] did business with you because of
27:13 [d]Ge 10:2; Isa 66:19; Eze 38:2 [e]Rev 18:13 — your great wealth of goods;[c] they exchanged silver, iron, tin and lead for your merchandise.
13" 'Greece, Tubal and Meshech[d] traded with
you; they exchanged slaves[e] and articles of bronze
27:14 [f]Ge 10:3; Eze 38:6 — for your wares.
14" 'Men of Beth Togarmah[f] exchanged work

[a] 5 That is, Hermon [b] 6 Targum; the Masoretic Text has a different division of the consonants. [c] 6 Hebrew *Kittim* [d] 9 That is, Byblos

Tyre

EZE 27

A beautiful and rich city during this time period, Tyre was one of the two major cities of Phoenicia, the other one being Sidon, about 25 miles to the north (see Map 7: Prophets in Israel and Judah at the back of this Bible). Tyre was an island city with harbors that promoted her shipping endeavors (see the note on Isa 23:1, page 1139). King Solomon participated with Tyre in the shipping trades, bringing wealth to Israel as well as to Phoenicia.

One of the great military stories of history is Alexander the Great's long siege of the island city in 332 B.C. He used the rubble from the conquered mainland city to build a causeway to the island fortress in order to enter and destroy it. Although the ancient city no longer exists, the causeway still remains today.

Sharing the Wealth

EZE 27:12-24

Tyre's trading and shipping business made her, as well as many other nations, wealthy. She traded with most of the nations in the known world at that time and shipped almost every rich commodity imaginable.

Ezekiel lists the nations and cities and their goods in detail in these verses. His point is to draw a picture of the immensity of Tyre's riches and therefore the enormous repercussions of her destruction. All the neighboring nations and city states are affected by Tyre's fall. Their wealth is controlled by hers. With her destruction, those around her are also destroyed, and they "wail and mourn" (Eze 27:32) their loss.

horses, war horses and mules for your merchandise.
15" 'The men of Rhodes[a][g] traded with you, and
many coastlands[h] were your customers; they paid
you with ivory[i] tusks and ebony.
16" 'Aram[b][j] did business with you because of
your many products; they exchanged turquoise,[k]
purple fabric, embroidered work, fine linen, coral
and rubies for your merchandise.
17" 'Judah and Israel traded with you; they
exchanged wheat from Minnith[l] and confections,[c]
honey, oil and balm for your wares.
18" 'Damascus,[m] because of your many products
and great wealth of goods, did business with you
in wine from Helbon and wool from Zahar.
19" 'Danites and Greeks from Uzal bought your
merchandise; they exchanged wrought iron, cassia and calamus for your wares.
20" 'Dedan traded in saddle blankets with you.
21" 'Arabia and all the princes of Kedar[n] were
your customers; they did business with you in
lambs, rams and goats.
22" 'The merchants of Sheba[o] and Raamah traded with you; for your merchandise they
exchanged the finest of all kinds of spices[p] and
precious stones, and gold.
23" 'Haran,[q] Canneh and Eden[r] and merchants
of Sheba, Asshur and Kilmad traded with you.
24In your marketplace they traded with you beautiful garments, blue fabric, embroidered work and
multicolored rugs with cords twisted and tightly
knotted.

25" 'The ships of Tarshish[s] serve
as carriers for your wares.
You are filled with heavy cargo
in the heart of the sea.
26Your oarsmen take you
out to the high seas.
But the east wind[t] will break you to pieces
in the heart of the sea.
27Your wealth,[u] merchandise and wares,
your mariners, seamen and shipwrights,
your merchants and all your soldiers,
and everyone else on board
will sink into the heart of the sea
on the day of your shipwreck.
28The shorelands will quake[v]
when your seamen cry out.
29All who handle the oars
will abandon their ships;
the mariners and all the seamen
will stand on the shore.
30They will raise their voice
and cry bitterly over you;
they will sprinkle dust[w] on their heads

27:15 [g]Ge 10:7 [h]Jer 25:22 [i]1Ki 10:22; Rev 18:12
27:16 [j]Jdg 10:6; Isa 7:1-8 [k]Eze 28:13
27:17 [l]Jdg 11:33
27:18 [m]Ge 14:15; Eze 47:16-18
27:21 [n]Ge 25:13; Isa 60:7
27:22 [o]Ge 10:7,28; 1Ki 10:1-2; Isa 60:6 [p]Ge 43:11
27:23 [q]2Ki 19:12 [r]Isa 37:12
27:25 [s]Isa 2:16 *fn*
27:26 [t]Ps 48:7; Jer 18:17
27:27 [u]Pr 11:4
27:28 [v]Eze 26:15
27:30 [w]2Sa 1:2

[a] *15* Septuagint; Hebrew *Dedan* [b] *16* Most Hebrew manuscripts; some Hebrew manuscripts and Syriac *Edom* [c] *17* The meaning of the Hebrew for this word is uncertain.

and roll[x] in ashes.[y]
31 They will shave their heads because of you
and will put on sackcloth.
They will weep[z] over you with anguish of soul
and with bitter mourning.[a]
32 As they wail and mourn over you,
they will take up a lament[b] concerning you:
"Who was ever silenced like Tyre,
surrounded by the sea?"
33 When your merchandise went out on the seas,
you satisfied many nations;
with your great wealth[c] and your wares
you enriched the kings of the earth.
34 Now you are shattered by the sea
in the depths of the waters;
your wares and all your company
have gone down with you.[d]
35 All who live in the coastlands[e]
are appalled at you;
their kings shudder with horror
and their faces are distorted with fear.
36 The merchants among the nations hiss at you;[f]
you have come to a horrible end
and will be no more.[g]' "

A Prophecy Against the King of Tyre

28 The word of the LORD came to me: 2 "Son of man, say to the ruler of Tyre, 'This is what the Sovereign LORD says:

" 'In the pride of your heart
you say, "I am a god;
I sit on the throne[h] of a god
in the heart of the seas."
But you are a man and not a god,
though you think you are as wise as a god.[i]
3 Are you wiser than Daniel[a]?[j]
Is no secret hidden from you?
4 By your wisdom and understanding
you have gained wealth for yourself
and amassed gold and silver
in your treasuries.[k]
5 By your great skill in trading
you have increased your wealth,
and because of your wealth
your heart has grown proud.[l]

6 " 'Therefore this is what the Sovereign LORD says:

" 'Because you think you are wise,
as wise as a god,
7 I am going to bring foreigners against you,

27:30 [x]Jer 6:26 [y]Rev 18:18-19
27:31 [z]Isa 16:9 [a]Isa 22:12; Eze 7:18
27:32 [b]Eze 26:17
27:33 [c]ver 12; Eze 28:4-5
27:34 [d]Zec 9:4
27:35 [e]Eze 26:15
27:36 [f]Jer 18:16; 19:8; 49:17; 50:13; Zep 2:15 [g]Ps 37:10,36; Eze 26:21
28:2 [h]Isa 14:13 [i]Ps 9:20; 82:6-7; Isa 31:3; 2Th 2:4
28:3 [j]Da 1:20; 5:11-12
28:4 [k]Zec 9:3
28:5 [l]Job 31:25; Ps 52:7; 62:10; Hos 12:8; 13:6

I sit and think, when the sunset's gold
Is flushing river, and hill, and shore,
I shall one day stand by the water cold,
And list for the sound of the boatman's oar;
I shall watch for a gleam of the flapping sail;
I shall hear the boat as it gains the strand;
I shall pass from sight, with the boatman pale,
To the better shore of the spirit land;
I shall know the loved who have gone before,—
And joyfully sweet will the meeting be,
When over the river, the peaceful river,
The Angel of Death shall carry me.

—Nancy Priest Wakefield (1836-1870)

[a] 3 Or *Danel*; the Hebrew spelling may suggest a person other than the prophet Daniel.

King of Tyre

EZE 28:6-10

The king of Tyre proclaims himself a god (Eze 28:2,6). Pagan cultures had a variety of gods of greater and lesser powers, and the king of Tyre arrogantly places himself among this divine company. For this arrogance, God will judge him. While he's declaring his divinity, "foreigners" (Eze 28:10) will kill him, and "he will die the death of the uncircumcised" (Eze 28:10). Phoenicians (inhabitants of the region which included Tyre) practiced circumcision, and to die "the death of the uncircumcised" was considered shameful and dishonorable.

the most ruthless of nations;[m]
they will draw their swords against your
beauty and wisdom
and pierce your shining splendor.
8 They will bring you down to the pit,[n]
and you will die a violent death
in the heart of the seas.[o]
9 Will you then say, "I am a god,"
in the presence of those who kill you?
You will be but a man, not a god,
in the hands of those who slay you.
10 You will die the death of the
uncircumcised[p]
at the hands of foreigners.

I have spoken, declares the Sovereign LORD.' "

11 The word of the LORD came to me: 12 "Son of
man, take up a lament[q] concerning the king of
Tyre and say to him: 'This is what the Sovereign
LORD says:

" 'You were the model of perfection,
full of wisdom and perfect in beauty.[r]
13 You were in Eden,[s]
the garden of God;[t]
every precious stone adorned you:
ruby, topaz and emerald,
chrysolite, onyx and jasper,
sapphire,[a] turquoise[u] and beryl.[b]
Your settings and mountings[c] were
made of gold;
on the day you were created they
were prepared.
14 You were anointed[v] as a guardian
cherub,[w]
for so I ordained you.
You were on the holy mount of God;
you walked among the fiery stones.
15 You were blameless in your ways
from the day you were created
till wickedness was found in you.
16 Through your widespread trade
you were filled with violence,[x]
and you sinned.
So I drove you in disgrace from the
mount of God,
and I expelled you, O guardian
cherub,[y]
from among the fiery stones.
17 Your heart became proud[z]
on account of your beauty,
and you corrupted your wisdom
because of your splendor.
So I threw you to the earth;
I made a spectacle of you before
kings.
18 By your many sins and dishonest trade
you have desecrated your sanctuaries.

28:7 [m]Eze 30:11; 31:12; 32:12; Hab 1:6
28:8 [n]Eze 32:30 [o]Eze 27:27
28:10 [p]Eze 31:18; 32:19,24
28:12 [q]Eze 19:1 [r]Eze 27:2-4
28:13 [s]Ge 2:8 [t]Eze 31:8-9 [u]Eze 27:16
28:14 [v]Ex 30:26; 40:9 [w]Ex 25:17-20
28:16 [x]Hab 2:17 [y]Ge 3:24
28:17 [z]Eze 31:10

[a] 13 Or *lapis lazuli* [b] 13 The precise identification of some of these precious stones is uncertain. [c] 13 The meaning of the Hebrew for this phrase is uncertain.

So I made a fire come out from you,
  and it consumed you,
and I reduced you to ashes[a] on the
    ground
  in the sight of all who were watching.
19 All the nations who knew you
  are appalled at you;
you have come to a horrible end
  and will be no more.[b]' "

A Prophecy Against Sidon

20 The word of the LORD came to me: 21 "Son of
man, set your face against[c] Sidon;[d] prophesy
against her 22 and say: 'This is what the Sovereign
LORD says:

" 'I am against you, O Sidon,
  and I will gain glory[e] within you.
They will know that I am the LORD,
  when I inflict punishment[f] on her
  and show myself holy within her.
23 I will send a plague upon her
  and make blood flow in her streets.
The slain will fall within her,
  with the sword against her on every
    side.
Then they will know that I am the
  LORD.[g]

24 " 'No longer will the people of Israel have
malicious neighbors who are painful briers and
sharp thorns.[h] Then they will know that I am the
Sovereign LORD.

25 " 'This is what the Sovereign LORD says: When
I gather[i] the people of Israel from the nations where
they have been scattered,[j] I will show myself holy[k]
among them in the sight of the nations. Then they
will live in their own land, which I gave to my servant Jacob.[l] 26 They will live there in safety[m] and
will build houses and plant vineyards; they will
live in safety when I inflict punishment on all their
neighbors who maligned them. Then they will
know that I am the LORD their God.[n]' "

A Prophecy Against Egypt

29 In the tenth year, in the tenth month on the
twelfth day, the word of the LORD came to
me:[o] 2 "Son of man, set your face against Pharaoh
king of Egypt[p] and prophesy against him and
against all Egypt.[q] 3 Speak to him and say: 'This is
what the Sovereign LORD says:

" 'I am against you, Pharaoh[r] king of
    Egypt,
  you great monster[s] lying among your
    streams.
You say, "The Nile is mine;
  I made it for myself."
4 But I will put hooks[t] in your jaws
  and make the fish of your streams
    stick to your scales.

28:18 [a]Mal 4:3
28:19 [b]Jer 51:64; Eze 26:21; 27:36
28:21 [c]Eze 6:2 [d]Ge 10:15; Jer 25:22
28:22 [e]Eze 39:13 [f]Eze 30:19
28:23 [g]Eze 38:22
28:24 [h]Nu 33:55; Jos 23:13; Eze 2:6
28:25 [i]Ps 106:47; Jer 32:37 [j]Isa 11:12 [k]Eze 20:41 [l]Jer 23:8; Eze 11:17; 34:27; 37:25
28:26 [m]Jer 23:6 [n]Isa 65:21; Jer 32:15; Eze 38:8; Am 9:14-15
29:1 [o]ver 17; Eze 26:1
29:2 [p]Jer 25:19 [q]Isa 19:1-17; Jer 46:2; Eze 30:1-26; 31:1-18; 32:1-32
29:3 [r]Jer 44:30 [s]Ps 74:13; Isa 27:1; Eze 32:2
29:4 [t]2Ki 19:28

Israel's Neighbors

EZE 28:24

Ezekiel 25–28 catalogs God's judgment of the near neighbors of Israel. Ammon, Moab, Edom, Philistia, Tyre and Sidon (see Map 7: Prophets in Israel and Judah at the back of this Bible) will all bear God's judgment for their "malicious" (Eze 28:24) behaviors toward God's people. Their actions toward Israel are the very actions threatened in Joshua 23:12–13. God warned the Israelites that if they didn't drive these nations out of the promised land, if they instead allied themselves with them, these nations would cause misery and disaster for Israel. Now, because of their part in Israel's rebellion and demise, these nations also fall under God's judgment. His punishment of these people will have the effect of not only removing these "painful briers and sharp thorns" (Eze 28:24) from Israel's side, but also proving God's holiness to his people. When they realize what he has done, they will recognize him as Lord.

Judgment on Egypt

EZE 29:16

The judgments of God now turn toward Egypt, the nation that has played a major role in Israel's history. For her capriciousness in her support of Israel, God will judge her. For taking the refugee family of Jacob in and allowing the nation of Israel to develop within her borders, and then turning that nation into slaves; for one time supporting Israel, and the next, moving to conquer her—God pronounces the same judgment on Egypt as on Judah. She will lie desolate for 40 years, her people dispersed throughout the nations; then her people will be allowed to return (Eze 29:11–13), just as Judah will be allowed to return to Jerusalem.

Babylonian historical records show Egypt's demise at their hands as occurring at about the same time as Judah's. Although no historical record exists evidencing their exile or return, 40 years would bring them (historically) to the Persian takeover of the Babylonian kingdom. Persia's policy of returning exiles to their homelands brought the Jews back to Israel and perhaps also brought the Egyptians back to Egypt.

I will pull you out from among your
    streams,
  with all the fish sticking to your
    scales.[u]
5I will leave you in the desert,
  you and all the fish of your streams.
You will fall on the open field
  and not be gathered or picked up.
I will give you as food
  to the beasts of the earth and the birds
    of the air.[v]

6Then all who live in Egypt will know that I am the LORD.

" 'You have been a staff of reed[w] for the house of Israel. 7When they grasped you with their hands, you splintered[x] and you tore open their shoulders; when they leaned on you, you broke and their backs were wrenched.[a][y]

8" 'Therefore this is what the Sovereign LORD says: I will bring a sword against you and kill your men and their animals.[z] 9Egypt will become a desolate wasteland. Then they will know that I am the LORD.

" 'Because you said, "The Nile is mine; I made it,[a]" 10therefore I am against you and against your streams, and I will make the land of Egypt a ruin and a desolate waste from Migdol to Aswan,[b] as far as the border of Cush.[b] 11No foot of man or animal will pass through it; no one will live there for forty years.[c] 12I will make the land of Egypt desolate among devastated lands, and her cities will lie desolate forty years among ruined cities. And I will disperse the Egyptians among the nations and scatter them through the countries.[d]

13" 'Yet this is what the Sovereign LORD says: At the end of forty years I will gather the Egyptians from the nations where they were scattered. 14I will bring them back from captivity and return them to Upper Egypt,[c][e] the land of their ancestry. There they will be a lowly[f] kingdom. 15It will be the lowliest of kingdoms and will never again exalt itself above the other nations.[g] I will make it so weak that it will never again rule over the nations. 16Egypt will no longer be a source of confidence[h] for the people of Israel but will be a reminder of their sin in turning to her for help. Then they will know that I am the Sovereign LORD.[i] ' "

17In the twenty-seventh year, in the first month on the first day, the word of the LORD came to me:[j] 18"Son of man, Nebuchadnezzar[k] king of Babylon drove his army in a hard campaign against Tyre; every head was rubbed bare[l] and every shoulder made raw. Yet he and his army got no reward from the campaign he led against Tyre. 19Therefore this is what the Sovereign LORD says: I am going to give Egypt to Nebuchadnezzar king of

29:4 [u]Eze 38:4
29:5 [v]Jer 7:33; 34:20; Eze 32:4-6; 39:4
29:6 [w]2Ki 18:21; Isa 36:6
29:7 [x]Isa 36:6 [y]Eze 17:15-17
29:8 [z]Eze 14:17; 32:11-13
29:9 [a]Eze 30:7-8, 13-19
29:10 [b]Eze 30:6
29:11 [c]Eze 32:13
29:12 [d]Jer 46:19; Eze 30:7,23, 26
29:14 [e]Eze 30:14 [f]Eze 17:14
29:15 [g]Zec 10:11
29:16 [h]Isa 36:4,6 [i]Isa 30:2; Hos 8:13
29:17 [j]Eze 24:1
29:18 [k]Jer 27:6; Eze 26:7-8 [l]Jer 48:37

[a] 7 Syriac (see also Septuagint and Vulgate); Hebrew *and you caused their backs to stand* [b] 10 That is, the upper Nile region [c] 14 Hebrew *to Pathros*

Babylon, and he will carry off its wealth. He will
loot and plunder the land as pay for his army.[m] 20 I
have given him Egypt as a reward for his efforts
because he and his army did it for me, declares
the Sovereign LORD.[n]

21 "On that day I will make a horn[a][o] grow for the
house of Israel, and I will open your mouth[p]
among them. Then they will know that I am the
LORD.[q]"

A Lament for Egypt

30 The word of the LORD came to me: 2 "Son of
man, prophesy and say: 'This is what the
Sovereign LORD says:

" 'Wail[r] and say,
"Alas for that day!"
3 For the day is near,[s]
the day of the LORD[t] is near—
a day of clouds,
a time of doom for the nations.
4 A sword will come against Egypt,
and anguish will come upon Cush.[b]
When the slain fall in Egypt,
her wealth will be carried away
and her foundations torn down.[u]

5 Cush and Put,[v] Lydia and all Arabia, Libya[c] and
the people[w] of the covenant land will fall by the
sword along with Egypt.

6 " 'This is what the LORD says:

" 'The allies of Egypt will fall
and her proud strength will fail.
From Migdol to Aswan[x]
they will fall by the sword within her,
declares the Sovereign LORD.
7 " 'They will be desolate
among desolate lands,
and their cities will lie
among ruined cities.[y]
8 Then they will know that I am the LORD,
when I set fire to Egypt
and all her helpers are crushed.

9 " 'On that day messengers will go out from me
in ships to frighten Cush[z] out of her complacency.
Anguish[a] will take hold of them on the day of
Egypt's doom, for it is sure to come.[b]

10 " 'This is what the Sovereign LORD says:

" 'I will put an end to the hordes of
Egypt
by the hand of Nebuchadnezzar king
of Babylon.[c]
11 He and his army—the most ruthless of
nations[d]—
will be brought in to destroy the land.
They will draw their swords against
Egypt

29:19 [m] Jer 43:10-13; Eze 30:4, 10,24-25
29:20 [n] Isa 10:6-7; 45:1; Jer 25:9
29:21 [o] Ps 132:17 [p] Eze 33:22 [q] Eze 24:27
30:2 [r] Isa 13:6
30:3 [s] Eze 7:7; Joel 2:1,11; Ob 1:15 [t] ver 18; Eze 7:12,19
30:4 [u] Eze 29:19
30:5 [v] Eze 27:10 [w] Jer 25:20
30:6 [x] Eze 29:10
30:7 [y] Eze 29:12
30:9 [z] Isa 18:1-2 [a] Isa 23:5 [b] Eze 32:9-10
30:10 [c] Eze 29:19
30:11 [d] Eze 28:7

[a] 21 *Horn* here symbolizes strength. [b] 4 That is, the upper Nile region; also in verses 5 and 9 [c] 5 Hebrew *Cub*

All in the April morning,
April airs were abroad;
The sheep with their little lambs
Pass'd me by on the road.

The sheep with their little lambs
Pass'd me by on the road;
All in an April evening
I thought on the Lamb of God.

The lambs were weary, and crying
With a weak human cry,
I thought on the Lamb of God
Going meekly to die.

Up in the blue, blue mountains
Dewy pastures are sweet:
Rest for the little bodies,
Rest for the little feet.

Rest for the Lamb of God
Up on the hill-top green,
Only a cross of shame
Two stark crosses between.

All in the April evening,
April airs were abroad;
I saw the sheep with their lambs,
And thought on the Lamb of God.

—*Katharine Tynan Hinkson (1861-1937)*

Great Cities of Egypt

EZE 30:13–19

A world power for centuries, Egypt was a mighty nation with a number of great cities. Ezekiel lists specific judgments on eight of them. Memphis, situated on the Nile River near the modern-day city of Cairo, was united Egypt's first capital. Zoan, a capital in Egypt's early history and an important religious center, eventually became the city of Alexandria. Renowned for its huge city of the dead, Thebes, also known as No, was the center for worship of the god Amon. Located on the northeastern border of Egypt, Pelusium was the residence of the ruling dynasty of Egypt in Ezekiel's day. The ancient city of Heliopolis, also called On, was the religious center of the sun god. Shishak, an upstart king of Egypt, invaded Israel during the time of Rehoboam from his capital city of Bubastis. Tahpanhes was situated on the eastern edge of the Nile delta and was the city to which many Jews fled after Jerusalem fell to the Babylonians. All these cities shared a common fate in God's judgment of Egypt.

and fill the land with the slain.
12 I will dry up[e] the streams of the Nile[f]
and sell the land to evil men;
by the hand of foreigners
I will lay waste the land and
everything in it.

I the LORD have spoken.

13 " 'This is what the Sovereign LORD says:

" 'I will destroy the idols[g]
and put an end to the images in
Memphis.[a][h]
No longer will there be a prince in
Egypt,[i]
and I will spread fear throughout the
land.
14 I will lay[j] waste Upper Egypt,[b]
set fire to Zoan[k]
and inflict punishment on Thebes.[c][l]
15 I will pour out my wrath on Pelusium,[d]
the stronghold of Egypt,
and cut off the hordes of Thebes.
16 I will set fire to Egypt;
Pelusium will writhe in agony.
Thebes will be taken by storm;
Memphis will be in constant distress.
17 The young men of Heliopolis[e][m] and
Bubastis[f]
will fall by the sword,
and the cities themselves will go into
captivity.
18 Dark will be the day at Tahpanhes
when I break the yoke of Egypt;[n]
there her proud strength will come to
an end.
She will be covered with clouds,
and her villages will go into
captivity.[o]
19 So I will inflict punishment on Egypt,
and they will know that I am the
LORD.' "

20 In the eleventh year, in the first month on the
seventh day, the word of the LORD came to me:[p]
21 "Son of man, I have broken the arm[q] of Pharaoh
king of Egypt. It has not been bound up for healing[r] or put in a splint so as to become strong
enough to hold a sword. 22 Therefore this is what
the Sovereign LORD says: I am against Pharaoh
king of Egypt.[s] I will break both his arms, the
good arm as well as the broken one, and make the
sword fall from his hand.[t] 23 I will disperse the
Egyptians among the nations and scatter them
through the countries.[u] 24 I will strengthen[v] the
arms of the king of Babylon and put my sword[w] in
his hand, but I will break the arms of Pharaoh,

30:12 [e]Isa 19:6 [f]Eze 29:9
30:13 [g]Jer 43:12 [h]Isa 19:13 [i]Zec 10:11
30:14 [j]Eze 29:14 [k]Ps 78:12,43 [l]Jer 46:25
30:17 [m]Ge 41:45
30:18 [n]Lev 26:13 [o]ver 3
30:20 [p]Eze 26:1; 29:17; 31:1
30:21 [q]Jer 48:25 [r]Jer 30:13; 46:11
30:22 [s]Jer 46:25 [t]Ps 37:17
30:23 [u]Eze 29:12
30:24 [v]Zec 10:6,12 [w]Eze 21:14; Zep 2:12

[a] *13* Hebrew *Noph*; also in verse 16 [b] *14* Hebrew *waste Pathros* [c] *14* Hebrew *No*; also in verses 15 and 16 [d] *15* Hebrew *Sin*; also in verse 16 [e] *17* Hebrew *Awen* (or *On*) [f] *17* Hebrew *Pi Beseth*

and he will groan before him like a mortally
wounded man. 25I will strengthen the arms of the
king of Babylon, but the arms of Pharaoh will fall
limp. Then they will know that I am the LORD,
when I put my sword into the hand of the king of
Babylon and he brandishes it against Egypt. 26I
will disperse the Egyptians among the nations and
scatter them through the countries. Then they will
know that I am the LORD.[x]"

30:26 [x]Eze 29:12

A Cedar in Lebanon

31 In the eleventh year,[y] in the third month on
the first day, the word of the LORD came to
me:[z] 2"Son of man, say to Pharaoh king of Egypt
and to his hordes:

31:1 [y]Jer 52:5 [z]Eze 30:20

" 'Who can be compared with you in
majesty?
3Consider Assyria, once a cedar in
Lebanon,
with beautiful branches
overshadowing the forest;
it towered on high,
its top above the thick foliage.[a]
4The waters nourished it,
deep springs made it grow tall;
their streams flowed
all around its base
and sent their channels
to all the trees of the field.
5So it towered higher
than all the trees of the field;
its boughs increased
and its branches grew long,
spreading because of abundant
waters.[b]
6All the birds of the air
nested in its boughs,
all the beasts of the field
gave birth under its branches;
all the great nations
lived in its shade.[c]
7It was majestic in beauty,
with its spreading boughs,
for its roots went down
to abundant waters.
8The cedars[d] in the garden of God
could not rival it,
nor could the pine trees
equal its boughs,
nor could the plane trees
compare with its branches—
no tree in the garden of God
could match its beauty.[e]
9I made it beautiful
with abundant branches,
the envy of all the trees of Eden[f]
in the garden of God.[g]

31:3 [a]Isa 10:34
31:5 [b]Eze 17:5
31:6 [c]Eze 17:23; Mt 13:32
31:8 [d]Ps 80:10 [e]Ge 2:8-9
31:9 [f]Ge 2:8 [g]Ge 13:10; Eze 28:13

10" 'Therefore this is what the Sovereign LORD
says: Because it towered on high, lifting its top
above the thick foliage, and because it was proud[h]

31:10 [h]Isa 14:13-14; Eze 28:17

A Cedar in Lebanon

EZE 31:3-9

Ezekiel likens the nation of Assyria to a "cedar in Lebanon" (Eze 31:3). In a land where few trees grow to any size, a particular form of cedar tree grows to great heights because of its large root system, which extends down to underground water supplies. Towering over other trees, a reference to Assyria's domination of the world, this tree grows arrogant because of its height (Eze 31:10). Therefore God destroys it, allowing Babylon, "the most ruthless of foreign nations" (Eze 31:12), to conquer it. Though Egypt may consider herself a large and beautiful tree, God's judgment on her will be the same as on the great tree of Assyria (Eze 31:18).

of its height, 11I handed it over to the ruler of the
nations, for him to deal with according to its
wickedness. I cast it aside,[i] 12and the most ruthless of foreign nations[j] cut it down and left it. Its
boughs fell on the mountains and in all the valleys;[k] its branches lay broken in all the ravines of
the land. All the nations of the earth came out
from under its shade and left it.[l] 13All the birds of
the air settled on the fallen tree, and all the beasts
of the field were among its branches.[m] 14Therefore
no other trees by the waters are ever to tower
proudly on high, lifting their tops above the thick
foliage. No other trees so well-watered are ever to
reach such a height; they are all destined for
death,[n] for the earth below, among mortal men,
with those who go down to the pit.[o]

15" 'This is what the Sovereign LORD says: On the
day it was brought down to the grave[a] I covered the
deep springs with mourning for it; I held back its
streams, and its abundant waters were restrained.
Because of it I clothed Lebanon with gloom, and
all the trees of the field withered away. 16I made the
nations tremble[p] at the sound of its fall when I
brought it down to the grave with those who go
down to the pit. Then all the trees[q] of Eden, the
choicest and best of Lebanon, all the trees that were
well-watered, were consoled[r] in the earth below.[s]
17Those who lived in its shade, its allies among the
nations, had also gone down to the grave with it,
joining those killed by the sword.[t]

18" 'Which of the trees of Eden can be compared
with you in splendor and majesty? Yet you, too,
will be brought down with the trees of Eden to the
earth below; you will lie among the uncircumcised,[u] with those killed by the sword.

" 'This is Pharaoh and all his hordes, declares
the Sovereign LORD.' "

31:11 [i]Da 5:20
31:12 [j]Eze 28:7 [k]Eze 32:5; 35:8 [l]Eze 32:11-12; Da 4:14
31:13 [m]Isa 18:6; Eze 29:5; 32:4
31:14 [n]Ps 82:7 [o]Ps 63:9; Eze 26:20; 32:24
31:16 [p]Eze 26:15 [q]Isa 14:8 [r]Eze 14:22; 32:31 [s]Isa 14:15; Eze 32:18
31:17 [t]Ps 9:17
31:18 [u]Jer 9:26; Eze 32:19,21

The dying words of Queen Elizabeth I:

All my possessions for a moment of time.

—*Queen Elizabeth I (1533-1603)*

A Lament for Pharaoh

32 In the twelfth year, in the twelfth month on
the first day, the word of the LORD came to
me:[v] 2"Son of man, take up a lament[w] concerning
Pharaoh king of Egypt and say to him:

" 'You are like a lion[x] among the
nations;
you are like a monster in the seas
thrashing about in your streams,
churning the water with your feet
and muddying the streams.[y]

3" 'This is what the Sovereign LORD says:

" 'With a great throng of people
I will cast my net over you,
and they will haul you up in my net.[z]
4I will throw you on the land
and hurl you on the open field.
I will let all the birds of the air settle on
you

32:1 [v]Eze 31:1; 33:21
32:2 [w]Eze 19:1; 27:2 [x]Eze 19:3,6; Na 2:11-13 [y]Eze 29:3; 34:18
32:3 [z]Eze 12:13

[a] *15* Hebrew *Sheol;* also in verses 16 and 17

and all the beasts of the earth gorge
themselves on you.[a]

32:4 [a]Isa 18:6; Eze 31:12-13

5 I will spread your flesh on the
mountains
and fill the valleys[b] with your
remains.

32:5 [b]Eze 31:12

6 I will drench the land with your flowing
blood[c]
all the way to the mountains,
and the ravines will be filled with
your flesh.

32:6 [c]Isa 34:3

7 When I snuff you out, I will cover the
heavens
and darken their stars;
I will cover the sun with a cloud,
and the moon will not give its light.[d]

32:7 [d]Isa 13:10; 34:4; Eze 30:3; Joel 2:2,31; 3:15; Mt 24:29; Rev 8:12

8 All the shining lights in the heavens
I will darken over you;
I will bring darkness over your land,
declares the Sovereign LORD.
9 I will trouble the hearts of many peoples
when I bring about your destruction
among the nations,
among[*a*] lands you have not known.
10 I will cause many peoples to be appalled
at you,
and their kings will shudder with
horror because of you
when I brandish my sword before
them.
On the day[e] of your downfall
each of them will tremble
every moment for his life.[f]

32:10 [e]Jer 46:10 [f]Eze 26:16; 27:35

11 " 'For this is what the Sovereign LORD says:

" 'The sword of the king of Babylon[g]
will come against you.

32:11 [g]Jer 46:26

12 I will cause your hordes to fall
by the swords of mighty men—
the most ruthless of all nations.[h]
They will shatter the pride of Egypt,
and all her hordes will be
overthrown.[i]

32:12 [h]Eze 28:7 [i]Eze 31:11-12

13 I will destroy all her cattle
from beside abundant waters
no longer to be stirred by the foot of
man
or muddied by the hoofs of cattle.[j]

32:13 [j]Eze 29:8,11

14 Then I will let her waters settle
and make her streams flow like oil,
declares the Sovereign LORD.
15 When I make Egypt desolate
and strip the land of everything in it,
when I strike down all who live there,
then they will know that I am the
LORD.[k]'

32:15 [k]Ex 7:5; 14:4,18; Ps 107:33-34; Eze 6:7

16 "This is the lament[l] they will chant for her.
The daughters of the nations will chant it; for

32:16 [l]2Sa 1:17; 2Ch 35:25; Eze 26:17

[*a*] 9 Hebrew; Septuagint *bring you into captivity among the nations, / to*

Like Oil

EZE 32:14

Egypt's future is no different from any other nation that has disdained God and treated God's people violently. Although Egypt has had a powerful and prominent past, her future is dark. In describing all that will happen to the once mighty nation, Ezekiel describes her streams in a strange, almost spooky, manner. Egypt's streams will no longer flow freely and vigorously. The water in them will instead "flow like oil" (Eze 32:14). This picture of a future drought in Egypt is part of God's judgment of the nation. Egypt's glory is the mighty Nile River. But it too will be affected; there will be so little water in it that it will flow sluggishly. Without water, the nation will be defeated. God's purpose is clear, as it is for the judgments he delivers to every rebellious nation: "They will know that I am the LORD" (Eze 32:15).

Uncircumcised

EZE 32:25-30

The word uncircumcised is used here in the sense of "barbarian." Anyone who was uncircumcised was thought to be from a backward and crude nation. Those who died uncircumcised, died as barbarically as they lived. Those who were circumcised but laid dead among the uncircumcised, died a dishonorable and uncivilized death. All of these—circumcised and uncircumcised—civilized and uncivilized—faced the same judgment of God for their wickedness.

Egypt and all her hordes they will chant it, declares the Sovereign LORD."

17 In the twelfth year, on the fifteenth day of the month, the word of the LORD came to me:[m] 18 "Son of man, wail for the hordes of Egypt and consign[n] to the earth below both her and the daughters of mighty nations, with those who go down to the pit.[o] 19 Say to them, 'Are you more favored than others? Go down and be laid among the uncircumcised.'[p] 20 They will fall among those killed by the sword. The sword is drawn; let her be dragged[q] off with all her hordes. 21 From within the grave[a][r] the mighty leaders will say of Egypt and her allies, 'They have come down and they lie with the uncircumcised, with those killed by the sword.'

22 "Assyria is there with her whole army; she is surrounded by the graves of all her slain, all who have fallen by the sword. 23 Their graves are in the depths of the pit[s] and her army lies around her grave. All who had spread terror in the land of the living are slain, fallen by the sword.

24 "Elam[t] is there, with all her hordes around her grave. All of them are slain, fallen by the sword.[u] All who had spread terror in the land of the living[v] went down uncircumcised to the earth below. They bear their shame with those who go down to the pit.[w] 25 A bed is made for her among the slain, with all her hordes around her grave. All of them are uncircumcised, killed by the sword. Because their terror had spread in the land of the living, they bear their shame with those who go down to the pit; they are laid among the slain.

26 "Meshech and Tubal[x] are there, with all their hordes around their graves. All of them are uncircumcised, killed by the sword because they spread their terror in the land of the living. 27 Do they not lie with the other uncircumcised warriors who have fallen, who went down to the grave with their weapons of war, whose swords were placed under their heads? The punishment for their sins rested on their bones, though the terror of these warriors had stalked through the land of the living.

28 "You too, O Pharaoh, will be broken and will lie among the uncircumcised, with those killed by the sword.

29 "Edom[y] is there, her kings and all her princes; despite their power, they are laid with those killed by the sword. They lie with the uncircumcised, with those who go down to the pit.[z]

30 "All the princes of the north[a] and all the Sidonians[b] are there; they went down with the slain in disgrace despite the terror caused by their power. They lie uncircumcised with those killed by the sword and bear their shame with those who go down to the pit.

31 "Pharaoh—he and all his army—will see them and he will be consoled[c] for all his hordes that were killed by the sword, declares the Sovereign

32:17 [m] ver 1
32:18 [n] Jer 1:10 [o] Eze 31:14, 16; Mic 1:8
32:19 [p] ver 29-30; Eze 28:10; 31:18
32:20 [q] Ps 28:3
32:21 [r] Isa 14:9
32:23 [s] Isa 14:15
32:24 [t] Ge 10:22 [u] Jer 49:37 [v] Job 28:13 [w] Eze 26:20
32:26 [x] Ge 10:2; Eze 27:13
32:29 [y] Isa 34:5-15; Jer 49:7; Eze 35:15; Ob 1:1 [z] Eze 25:12-14
32:30 [a] Jer 25:26; Eze 38:6; 39:2 [b] Jer 25:22; Eze 28:21
32:31 [c] Eze 14:22; 31:16

[a] 21 Hebrew *Sheol*; also in verse 27

LORD. 32Although I had him spread terror in the
land of the living, Pharaoh and all his hordes will
be laid among the uncircumcised, with those
killed by the sword, declares the Sovereign LORD."

Ezekiel a Watchman

33 The word of the LORD came to me: 2"Son of
man, speak to your countrymen and say to
33:2 [d]Jer 12:12 [e]Eze 3:11 them: 'When I bring the sword[d] against a land,
and the people of the land choose one of their
men and make him their watchman,[e] 3and he sees
33:3 [f]Hos 8:1 the sword coming against the land and blows the
trumpet[f] to warn the people, 4then if anyone hears
33:4 [g]2Ch 25:16 [h]Jer 6:17; Eze 18:13; Zec 1:4; Ac 18:6 the trumpet but does not take warning[g] and the
sword comes and takes his life, his blood will be
on his own head.[h] 5Since he heard the sound of
the trumpet but did not take warning, his blood
will be on his own head. If he had taken warning,
he would have saved himself. 6But if the watchman sees the sword coming and does not blow the
trumpet to warn the people and the sword comes
and takes the life of one of them, that man will be
taken away because of his sin, but I will hold the
33:6 [i]Eze 3:18 watchman accountable for his blood.'[i]
7"Son of man, I have made you a watchman for
the house of Israel; so hear the word I speak and
33:7 [j]Jer 26:2; Eze 3:17 give them warning from me.[j] 8When I say to the
wicked, 'O wicked man, you will surely die,[k]' and
you do not speak out to dissuade him from his
33:8 [k]ver 14 [l]Eze 18:4 ways, that wicked man will die for[a] his sin, and I
will hold you accountable for his blood.[l] 9But if
you do warn the wicked man to turn from his
ways and he does not do so, he will die for his sin,
33:9 [m]Eze 3:17-19 but you will have saved yourself.[m]
10"Son of man, say to the house of Israel, 'This
is what you are saying: "Our offenses and sins
33:10 [n]Eze 24:23 [o]Lev 26:39; Eze 4:17 weigh us down, and we are wasting away[n]
because of[b] them. How then can we live?[o]" ' 11Say
to them, 'As surely as I live, declares the Sovereign LORD, I take no pleasure in the death of the
33:11 [p]Eze 18:32; 2Pe 3:9 [q]Eze 18:23 wicked, but rather that they turn from their ways
and live.[p] Turn! Turn from your evil ways! Why
will you die, O house of Israel?'[q]
12"Therefore, son of man, say to your countrymen, 'The righteousness of the righteous man will
not save him when he disobeys, and the wickedness of the wicked man will not cause him to fall
when he turns from it. The righteous man, if he
33:12 [r]2Ch 7:14; Eze 3:20 sins, will not be allowed to live because of his former righteousness.'[r] 13If I tell the righteous man
that he will surely live, but then he trusts in his
righteousness and does evil, none of the righteous
things he has done will be remembered; he will die
33:13 [s]Eze 18:24; Heb 10:38; 2Pe 2:20-21 for the evil he has done.[s] 14And if I say to the
wicked man, 'You will surely die,' but he then turns
away from his sin and does what is just[t] and
33:14 [t]Eze 18:27 right— 15if he gives back what he took in pledge
for a loan, returns what he has stolen,[u] follows the
decrees that give life, and does no evil, he will sure-
33:15 [u]Ex 22:1-4;

[a] 8 Or *in*; also in verse 9 [b] 10 Or *away in*

Ezekiel the Watchman

EZE 33:1-4

Watchmen stood on the walls of a city and watched for the enemy. Their job was to warn the inhabitants of any impending danger. Then it was up to the inhabitants to take cover.

Ezekiel is Judah's watchman and God's spokesman (Eze 33:7). He has the words of warning from God, and it is his responsibility to communicate those words to the people. Then it's up to the people to take appropriate action, which, in this case, would be to repent for their sin and rebellion. Ezekiel's job is to faithfully fulfill his duty as watchman. Only the people can decide how they will respond.

We also have a duty as "watchmen" today. God's message of love and forgiveness must be communicated. Our responsibility is to communicate the message. We cannot control how people will respond. Only they can decide to believe in God's message and be saved, or turn from him and be lost.

Ezekiel's Silence

EZE 33:22

It is not altogether clear how long Ezekiel is silent or what purpose is behind his inability to speak. It seems he only speaks when he has a word of prophecy from God to give to the people (Eze 24:26–27).

Ezekiel 24:25–27 records the prophecy that Ezekiel will regain his speech when Jerusalem falls. This passage records the fulfillment of that prophecy. An Israelite escapes the devastation of Jerusalem and brings the news of the destruction to the exiles in Babylon. When he hears the words, Ezekiel's vocal abilities are restored.

ly live; he will not die.[v] 16None of the sins he has
committed will be remembered against him. He
has done what is just and right; he will surely live.[w]
17"Yet your countrymen say, 'The way of the
Lord is not just.' But it is their way that is not just.
18If a righteous man turns from his righteousness
and does evil, he will die for it.[x] 19And if a wicked
man turns away from his wickedness and does
what is just and right, he will live by doing so.
20Yet, O house of Israel, you say, 'The way of the
Lord is not just.' But I will judge each of you
according to his own ways."

Jerusalem's Fall Explained

21In the twelfth year of our exile, in the tenth
month on the fifth day, a man who had escaped[y]
from Jerusalem came to me and said, "The city
has fallen![z]" 22Now the evening before the man
arrived, the hand of the LORD was upon me,[a] and
he opened my mouth[b] before the man came to me
in the morning. So my mouth was opened and I
was no longer silent.[c]
23Then the word of the LORD came to me: 24"Son
of man, the people living in those ruins[d] in the
land of Israel are saying, 'Abraham was only one
man, yet he possessed the land. But we are many;
surely the land has been given to us as our possession.'[e]
25Therefore say to them, 'This is what
the Sovereign LORD says: Since you eat meat with
the blood[f] still in it and look to your idols and
shed blood, should you then possess the land?[g]
26You rely on your sword, you do detestable
things, and each of you defiles his neighbor's
wife.[h] Should you then possess the land?'
27"Say this to them: 'This is what the Sovereign
LORD says: As surely as I live, those who are left in
the ruins will fall by the sword, those out in the
country I will give to the wild animals to be
devoured, and those in strongholds and caves will
die of a plague.[i] 28I will make the land a desolate
waste, and her proud strength will come to an
end, and the mountains of Israel will become desolate
so that no one will cross them. 29Then they
will know that I am the LORD, when I have made
the land a desolate waste because of all the
detestable things they have done.'
30"As for you, son of man, your countrymen are
talking together about you by the walls and at the
doors of the houses, saying to each other, 'Come
and hear the message that has come from the
LORD.' 31My people come to you, as they usually
do, and sit before[j] you to listen to your words, but
they do not put them into practice. With their
mouths they express devotion, but their hearts are
greedy for unjust gain.[k] 32Indeed, to them you are
nothing more than one who sings love songs with
a beautiful voice and plays an instrument well, for
they hear your words but do not put them into
practice.[l]
33"When all this comes true—and it surely

33:15 Lev 6:2-5 [v]Eze 20:11; Lk 19:8
33:16 [w]Isa 43:25; Eze 18:22
33:18 [x]Eze 3:20; Eze 18:26
33:21 [y]Eze 24:26 [z]2Ki 25:4,10; Jer 39:1-2; Eze 32:1
33:22 [a]Eze 1:3 [b]Lk 1:64 [c]Eze 3:26-27; 24:27
33:24 [d]Eze 36:4 [e]Isa 51:2; Jer 40:7; Eze 11:15; Ac 7:5
33:25 [f]Ge 9:4; Dt 12:16 [g]Jer 7:9-10; Eze 22:6,27
33:26 [h]Eze 22:11
33:27 [i]1Sa 13:6; Isa 2:19; Jer 42:22; Eze 39:4
33:31 [j]Eze 8:1 [k]Ps 78:36-37; Isa 29:13; Eze 22:27; Mt 13:22; 1Jn 3:18
33:32 [l]Mk 6:20

will—then they will know that a prophet has been
among them.[m]"

Shepherds and Sheep

34 The word of the LORD came to me: 2"Son of
man, prophesy against the shepherds of
Israel; prophesy and say to them: 'This is what the
Sovereign LORD says: Woe to the shepherds of Israel who only take care of themselves! Should not
shepherds take care of the flock?[n] 3You eat the
curds, clothe yourselves with the wool and
slaughter the choice animals, but you do not take
care of the flock.[o] 4You have not strengthened the
weak or healed the sick or bound up the injured.
You have not brought back the strays or searched
for the lost. You have ruled them harshly and brutally.[p] 5So they were scattered because there was
no shepherd,[q] and when they were scattered they
became food for all the wild animals.[r] 6My sheep
wandered over all the mountains and on every
high hill. They were scattered over the whole
earth, and no one searched or looked for them.[s]

7" 'Therefore, you shepherds, hear the word of
the LORD: 8As surely as I live, declares the Sovereign LORD, because my flock lacks a shepherd and
so has been plundered and has become food for
all the wild animals, and because my shepherds
did not search for my flock but cared for themselves rather than for my flock, 9therefore, O shepherds, hear the word of the LORD: 10This is what
the Sovereign LORD says: I am against[t] the shepherds and will hold them accountable for my
flock. I will remove them from tending the flock
so that the shepherds can no longer feed themselves. I will rescue[u] my flock from their mouths,
and it will no longer be food for them.[v]

11" 'For this is what the Sovereign LORD says: I
myself will search for my sheep and look after
them. 12As a shepherd[w] looks after his scattered
flock when he is with them, so will I look after my
sheep. I will rescue them from all the places where
they were scattered on a day of clouds and darkness.[x] 13I will bring them out from the nations and
gather them from the countries, and I will bring
them into their own land. I will pasture them on
the mountains of Israel, in the ravines and in all
the settlements in the land.[y] 14I will tend them in
a good pasture, and the mountain heights of Israel[z] will be their grazing land. There they will lie
down in good grazing land, and there they will
feed in a rich pasture[a] on the mountains of Israel.[b]
15I myself will tend my sheep and have them lie
down, declares the Sovereign LORD.[c] 16I will search
for the lost and bring back the strays. I will bind
up the injured and strengthen the weak,[d] but the
sleek and the strong I will destroy. I will shepherd
the flock with justice.[e]

17" 'As for you, my flock, this is what the Sovereign LORD says: I will judge between one sheep and
another, and between rams and goats.[f] 18Is it not
enough for you to feed on the good pasture? Must

33:33 [m]1Sa 3:20; Jer 28:9; Eze 2:5
34:2 [n]Ps 78:70-72; Isa 40:11; Jer 3:15; 23:1; Mic 3:11; Jn 10:11; 21:15-17
34:3 [o]Isa 56:11; Eze 22:27; Zec 11:16
34:4 [p]Zec 11:15-17
34:5 [q]Nu 27:17 [r]ver 28; Isa 56:9
34:6 [s]Ps 142:4; 1Pe 2:25
34:10 [t]Jer 21:13 [u]Ps 72:14 [v]1Sa 2:29-30; Zec 10:3
34:12 [w]Isa 40:11; Jer 31:10; Lk 19:10 [x]Eze 30:3
34:13 [y]Jer 23:3
34:14 [z]Eze 20:40 [a]Ps 23:2 [b]Eze 36:29-30
34:15 [c]Ps 23:1-2
34:16 [d]Mic 4:6 [e]Isa 10:16; Lk 5:32
34:17 [f]Mt 25:32-33

Shepherds and Sheep

EZE 34

Using clear and condemning imagery, Ezekiel denounces the "shepherds" of Israel (the leaders of the nation), who lead the "sheep" (the people of Israel) astray. These shepherds have selfishly used their power and position for their own gain and protection rather than for the good of their flock. They have left the flock without a leader, and the flock is now scattered in exile. God declares that he will himself become the people's shepherd, gathering them back to himself, an affirmation of the end of the exile and the return of the Jews to Israel (Eze 34:11-16).

My Servant David

EZE 34:23–24

God promises to gather Israel back to himself and to place over her a righteous leader, not one like the wicked leaders of her past. This leader will be like his servant David, "a man after [God's] own heart" (Ac 13:22). This is not, of course, a reference to the historical King David, but to the Messiah, the true servant of God (Ac 3:13). This servant will come to lead his people out of sin and into a righteousness gained through his own magnificent willingness to put his people's needs above his own—to the point of death.

you also trample the rest of your pasture with your
feet? Is it not enough for you to drink clear water?
Must you also muddy the rest with your feet?
19 Must my flock feed on what you have trampled
and drink what you have muddied with your feet?
20 " 'Therefore this is what the Sovereign LORD
says to them: See, I myself will judge between the
fat sheep and the lean sheep. 21 Because you shove
with flank and shoulder, butting all the weak sheep
with your horns[g] until you have driven them away,
22 I will save my flock, and they will no longer be
plundered. I will judge between one sheep and
another.[h] 23 I will place over them one shepherd, my
servant David, and he will tend[i] them; he will tend
them and be their shepherd. 24 I the LORD will be
their God,[j] and my servant David will be prince
among them. I the LORD have spoken.[k]
25 " 'I will make a covenant of peace with them
and rid the land of wild beasts[l] so that they may
live in the desert and sleep in the forests in safety.[m]
26 I will bless[n] them and the places surrounding my
hill.[a] I will send down showers in season;[o] there
will be showers of blessing.[p] 27 The trees of the field
will yield their fruit and the ground will yield its
crops; the people will be secure in their land. They
will know that I am the LORD, when I break the
bars of their yoke[q] and rescue them from the
hands of those who enslaved them.[r] 28 They will no
longer be plundered by the nations, nor will wild
animals devour them. They will live in safety, and
no one will make them afraid.[s] 29 I will provide for
them a land renowned[t] for its crops, and they will
no longer be victims of famine[u] in the land or bear
the scorn[v] of the nations.[w] 30 Then they will know
that I, the LORD their God, am with them and that
they, the house of Israel, are my people, declares
the Sovereign LORD.[x] 31 You my sheep, the sheep of
my pasture,[y] are people, and I am your God,
declares the Sovereign LORD.' "

A Prophecy Against Edom

35 The word of the LORD came to me: 2 "Son of
man, set your face against Mount Seir;
prophesy against it 3 and say: 'This is what the
Sovereign LORD says: I am against you, Mount
Seir, and I will stretch out my hand[z] against you
and make you a desolate waste.[a] 4 I will turn your
towns into ruins and you will be desolate. Then
you will know that I am the LORD.[b]
5 " 'Because you harbored an ancient hostility
and delivered the Israelites over to the sword at
the time of their calamity, the time their punishment reached its climax,[c] 6 therefore as surely as I
live, declares the Sovereign LORD, I will give you
over to bloodshed and it will pursue you.[d] Since
you did not hate bloodshed, bloodshed will pursue you. 7 I will make Mount Seir a desolate waste
and cut off from it all who come and go. 8 I will

34:21 [g]Dt 33:17
34:22 [h]Ps 72:12-14; Jer 23:2-3
34:23 [i]Isa 40:11
34:24 [j]Eze 36:28 [k]Jer 30:9
34:25 [l]Lev 26:6 [m]Isa 11:6-9; Hos 2:18
34:26 [n]Ge 12:2 [o]Ps 68:9 [p]Dt 11:13-15; Isa 44:3
34:27 [q]Lev 26:13 [r]Jer 30:8
34:28 [s]Jer 30:10; Eze 39:26
34:29 [t]Isa 4:2 [u]Eze 36:29 [v]Eze 36:6 [w]Eze 36:15
34:30 [x]Eze 14:11; 37:27
34:31 [y]Ps 100:3; Jer 23:1
35:3 [z]Jer 6:12 [a]Eze 25:12-14
35:4 [b]ver 9
35:5 [c]Ps 137:7; Eze 21:29
35:6 [d]Isa 63:2-6

[a] 26 Or *I will make them and the places surrounding my hill a blessing*

Week 24

Wounded Saints

Churches are not perfect places. Most Christians have, at one time or another, been deeply wounded by a pastor or a church leader. It's painful and distressing when a respected and honorable person acts in a hurtful and unloving way. Has this happened to you? Then God has some things to say to you.

What things do the leaders ("shepherds") of God's people do to cause God's wrath (Eze 34:1-6)? When have you experienced a church leader's lack of concern in one of these areas?

What does God say he will do regarding these types of leaders (Eze 34:10)? Of course, your response shouldn't be to gloat because the leader who hurt you will one day be called to account. Why not instead pray for this leader, who needs your mercy as well as God's?

What are some things the Lord, the Good Shepherd, will do to make things right (Eze 34:11-16)? How can you interpret these things for your present situation?

How has another church member wounded you (Eze 34:17-19)? When have you felt the sting of a sharp rebuke that came from a haughty heart? What promises does God have for you (Eze 34:20-31)?

What is God's ultimate goal regarding these warnings and judgments (Eze 34:30-31)?

If you are a wounded saint, take heart. Jesus, your Good Shepherd (Jn 10:11), is watching over you. He will protect and care for you and will make provision for your needs. Don't allow bitterness and anger to eat away at your soul. They prevent you from enjoying all the goodness God has for you (Job 21:25).

Enjoying God THROUGH the Word

Read Numbers 11:10-17 (pages 226-227). Moses has had it! He has led the rebellious, complaining Israelites long enough. It has only been one year since they left Egypt (Nu 10:11), but these people have been a terrible thorn in Moses' side. In desperation, Moses tells God, "I cannot carry all these people by myself; the burden is too heavy for me. If this is how you are going to treat me, put me to death right now" (Nu 11:14-15).

Leadership is a weighty responsibility and, at times, an overwhelming burden. Church leaders are often overworked and under appreciated. Do you pray for your leaders? Do you offer to help them? Do you encourage them with a word, a card or another expression of appreciation? Your leaders need you. They need your prayers. You have a responsibility to care for them (Eze 44:30) as they go about caring for you.

Enjoying God THROUGH Experience

If a church leader or a church member has wounded you, go to God as *El Roi*, the "God who sees." He is aware of what has happened. Ask him to heal your hurting heart of the wounds inflicted by those in authority over you. Let him heal the wounds and dry your tears (Isa 40:11).

Now turn the tables. Instead of dwelling on how you've been hurt, pray for the one who hurt you. Greater healing is yours in praying for this person than in any other action. Pray that God will help you forgive this person, and pray that God will give this leader the wisdom, courage, compassion and gentleness needed each day.

Go to page 1451 for your next weekly study.

fill your mountains with the slain; those killed by
the sword will fall on your hills and in your valleys and in all your ravines.[e] 9 I will make you desolate forever; your towns will not be inhabited.
Then you will know that I am the LORD.[f]
10 " 'Because you have said, "These two nations
and countries will be ours and we will take possession[g] of them," even though I the LORD was
there, 11 therefore as surely as I live, declares the
Sovereign LORD, I will treat you in accordance with
the anger[h] and jealousy you showed in your hatred
of them and I will make myself known among
them when I judge you.[i] 12 Then you will know
that I the LORD have heard all the contemptible
things you have said against the mountains of Israel. You said, "They have been laid waste and have
been given over to us to devour.[j]" 13 You boasted
against me and spoke against me without restraint,
and I heard it.[k] 14 This is what the Sovereign LORD
says: While the whole earth rejoices, I will make
you desolate.[l] 15 Because you rejoiced[m] when the
inheritance of the house of Israel became desolate,
that is how I will treat you. You will be desolate,
O Mount Seir,[n] you and all of Edom.[o] Then they
will know that I am the LORD.' "

A Prophecy to the Mountains of Israel

36 "Son of man, prophesy to the mountains of
Israel and say, 'O mountains of Israel, hear
the word of the LORD. 2 This is what the Sovereign
LORD says: The enemy said of you, "Aha![p] The
ancient heights[q] have become our possession.[r]" '
3 Therefore prophesy and say, 'This is what the
Sovereign LORD says: Because they ravaged and
hounded you from every side so that you became
the possession of the rest of the nations and the
object of people's malicious talk and slander,[s]
4 therefore, O mountains of Israel, hear the word
of the Sovereign LORD: This is what the Sovereign
LORD says to the mountains and hills, to the
ravines and valleys,[t] to the desolate ruins and the
deserted towns that have been plundered and
ridiculed by the rest of the nations around you[u]—
5 this is what the Sovereign LORD says: In my burning zeal I have spoken against the rest of the
nations, and against all Edom, for with glee and
with malice in their hearts they made my land
their own possession so that they might plunder
its pastureland.'[v] 6 Therefore prophesy concerning
the land of Israel and say to the mountains and
hills, to the ravines and valleys: 'This is what the
Sovereign LORD says: I speak in my jealous wrath
because you have suffered the scorn of the
nations.[w] 7 Therefore this is what the Sovereign
LORD says: I swear with uplifted hand that the
nations around you will also suffer scorn.
8 " 'But you, O mountains of Israel, will produce
branches and fruit[x] for my people Israel, for they
will soon come home. 9 I am concerned for you
and will look on you with favor; you will be
plowed and sown, 10 and I will multiply the num-

35:8 [e]Eze 31:12
35:9 [f]Jer 49:13
35:10 [g]Ps 83:12; Eze 36:2,5
35:11 [h]Eze 25:14 [i]Ps 9:16; Mt 7:2
35:12 [j]Jer 50:7
35:13 [k]Da 11:36
35:14 [l]Jer 51:48
35:15 [m]Ob 1:12 [n]ver 3 [o]Isa 34:5-6, 11; Jer 50:11-13; La 4:21
36:2 [p]Eze 25:3 [q]Dt 32:13 [r]Eze 35:10
36:3 [s]Ps 44:13-14
36:4 [t]Eze 6:3 [u]Dt 11:11; Ps 79:4; Eze 34:28
36:5 [v]Jer 50:11; Eze 25:12-14; 35:10,15
36:6 [w]Ps 123:3-4; Eze 34:29
36:8 [x]Isa 27:6

Nobody is so far from God that he can't get back to the Lord. Our responsibility is to keep knocking at God's door about that person, to keep believing God will answer our prayers. Thank God for what he will do. Patiently but expectantly wait on the Lord. Renew your hope!

—Thelma Wells

ber of people upon you, even the whole house of
36:10 Israel. The towns will be inhabited and the ruins
yver 33; rebuilt.[y] 11 I will increase the number of men and
Isa 49:17-23 animals upon you, and they will be fruitful and
36:11 become numerous. I will settle people on you as
zMic 7:14 in the past[z] and will make you prosper more than
aJer 31:28; before.[a] Then you will know that I am the LORD.
Eze 16:55 12 I will cause people, my people Israel, to walk
upon you. They will possess you, and you will be
36:12 bEze 47:14, their inheritance;[b] you will never again deprive
22 them of their children.
36:13 13 " 'This is what the Sovereign LORD says:
cNu 13:32 Because people say to you, "You devour men[c] and
deprive your nation of its children," 14 therefore
you will no longer devour men or make your
nation childless, declares the Sovereign LORD. 15 No
longer will I make you hear the taunts of the
nations, and no longer will you suffer the scorn
of the peoples or cause your nation to fall,
36:15 dPs 89:50-51; declares the Sovereign LORD.[d] ' "
Eze 34:29 16 Again the word of the LORD came to me:
17 "Son of man, when the people of Israel were
living in their own land, they defiled it by their
conduct and their actions. Their conduct was
36:17 eJer 2:7 like a woman's monthly uncleanness in my
sight.[e] 18 So I poured out[f] my wrath on them
36:18 because they had shed blood in the land and
f2Ch 34:21 because they had defiled it with their idols. 19 I
dispersed them among the nations, and they
36:19 gDt 28:64 were scattered[g] through the countries; I judged
hEze 39:24 them according to their conduct and their
actions.[h] 20 And wherever they went among the
36:20 iRo 2:24 nations they profaned[i] my holy name, for it was
jIsa 52:5; said of them, 'These are the LORD's people, and
Jer 33:24; yet they had to leave his land.'[j] 21 I had concern
Eze 12:16 for my holy name, which the house of Israel
profaned among the nations where they had
36:21 kPs 74:18; gone.[k]
Isa 48:9 22 "Therefore say to the house of Israel, 'This is
what the Sovereign LORD says: It is not for your
sake, O house of Israel, that I am going to do
36:22 these things, but for the sake of my holy name,
lRo 2:24* which you have profaned[l] among the nations
mPs 106:8 where you have gone.[m] 23 I will show the holiness
of my great name, which has been profaned
36:23 among the nations, the name you have profaned
nEze 20:41 among them. Then the nations will know that I
oPs 126:2; am the LORD, declares the Sovereign LORD, when
Isa 5:16 I show myself holy[n] through you before their
36:24 eyes.[o]
pEze 34:13; 24 " 'For I will take you out of the nations; I will
37:21 gather you from all the countries and bring you
36:25 qHeb 9:13; back into your own land.[p] 25 I will sprinkle[q] clean
10:22 water on you, and you will be clean; I will
rPs 51:2,7 cleanse[r] you from all your impurities and from
sZec 13:2 all your idols.[s] 26 I will give you a new heart[t] and
36:26 put a new spirit in you; I will remove from you
tJer 24:7 uPs 51:10; your heart of stone and give you a heart of flesh.[u]
Eze 11:19 27 And I will put my Spirit[v] in you and move you
36:27 to follow my decrees and be careful to keep my
vEze 37:14 laws. 28 You will live in the land I gave your fore-

Menstrual Uncleanness

EZE 36:17

When a Hebrew woman was menstruating, she was ceremonially unclean. She could not participate in the worship functions of the community, and everything she sat or laid on, as well as anyone who touched her, became unclean also (Lev 15:19–23). As any menstruating woman knows, the flow of menstruation is a messy, at times bothersome, fact of life.

God uses this image of menstruation to depict his people's unfaithfulness to him. While they were living in Israel before their exile, their rebellion and idolatry made them unclean in God's sight. Their actions contaminated the promised land. Therefore, their punishment was inevitable. Just as a Hebrew woman had a certain prescribed pattern to follow in order to cleanse herself after her period, so Israel must be cleansed. God is in the midst of accomplishing that cleansing through the exile.

A Valley of Dry Bones

EZE 37:1–14

Ezekiel's next vision takes him to a valley full of dried-up human bones—a gruesome picture, but one with a beautiful outcome. These dried-up, old bones represent the spiritual condition of Israel. Their hope is gone. They are in exile. Jerusalem is destroyed. The temple is gone. At this point in their history, it is hard for them to imagine that God will ever restore them as a nation. Ezekiel's vision reveals to them the promise of the future. With a "breath" (Eze 37:10) the bones rattle together and grow muscle and tendon and flesh, becoming living human beings once again. Just as God can raise dead bones to life, his people must believe he can raise their nation again to life and restore them to their homeland—and to himself.

fathers; you will be my people,[w] and I will be
your God.[x] 29I will save you from all your
uncleanness. I will call for the grain and make it
plentiful and will not bring famine[y] upon you. 30I
will increase the fruit of the trees and the crops of
the field, so that you will no longer suffer disgrace among the nations because of famine.[z]
31Then you will remember your evil ways and
wicked deeds, and you will loathe yourselves for
your sins and detestable practices.[a] 32I want you
to know that I am not doing this for your sake,
declares the Sovereign LORD. Be ashamed and disgraced for your conduct, O house of Israel![b]
33" 'This is what the Sovereign LORD says: On the
day I cleanse you from all your sins, I will resettle
your towns, and the ruins will be rebuilt. 34The desolate land will be cultivated instead of lying desolate in the sight of all who pass through it. 35They
will say, "This land that was laid waste has become
like the garden of Eden;[c] the cities that were lying
in ruins, desolate and destroyed, are now fortified
and inhabited.[d]" 36Then the nations around you
that remain will know that I the LORD have rebuilt
what was destroyed and have replanted what was
desolate. I the LORD have spoken, and I will do it.'[e]
37"This is what the Sovereign LORD says: Once
again I will yield to the plea of the house of Israel
and do this for them: I will make their people as
numerous as sheep, 38as numerous as the flocks for
offerings[f] at Jerusalem during her appointed feasts.
So will the ruined cities be filled with flocks of people. Then they will know that I am the LORD."

The Valley of Dry Bones

37 The hand of the LORD was upon me,[g] and
he brought me out by the Spirit[h] of the LORD
and set me in the middle of a valley;[i] it was full of
bones.[j] 2He led me back and forth among them,
and I saw a great many bones on the floor of the
valley, bones that were very dry. 3He asked me,
"Son of man, can these bones live?"
I said, "O Sovereign LORD, you alone know.[k]"
4Then he said to me, "Prophesy to these bones
and say to them, 'Dry bones, hear the word of the
LORD![l] 5This is what the Sovereign LORD says to
these bones: I will make breath[a] enter you, and you
will come to life.[m] 6I will attach tendons to you and
make flesh come upon you and cover you with
skin; I will put breath in you, and you will come to
life. Then you will know that I am the LORD.[n]' "
7So I prophesied as I was commanded. And as I
was prophesying, there was a noise, a rattling
sound, and the bones came together, bone to
bone. 8I looked, and tendons and flesh appeared
on them and skin covered them, but there was no
breath in them.
9Then he said to me, "Prophesy to the breath;[o]
prophesy, son of man, and say to it, 'This is what

36:28 [w]Jer 30:22 [x]Eze 14:11; 37:14,27
36:29 [y]Eze 34:29
36:30 [z]Lev 26:4-5; Eze 34:27; Hos 2:21-22
36:31 [a]Eze 6:9; 20:43
36:32 [b]Dt 9:5
36:35 [c]Joel 2:3 [d]Isa 51:3
36:36 [e]Eze 17:22; 22:14; 37:14; 39:27-28
36:38 [f]1Ki 8:63; 2Ch 35:7-9
37:1 [g]Eze 1:3; 8:3 [h]Eze 11:24; Lk 4:1; Ac 8:39 [i]Jer 7:32 [j]Jer 8:2; Eze 40:1
37:3 [k]Dt 32:39; 1Sa 2:6; Isa 26:19
37:4 [l]Jer 22:29
37:5 [m]Ge 2:7; Ps 104:29-30
37:6 [n]Eze 38:23; Joel 2:27; 3:17
37:9 [o]Ps 104:30

[a] 5 The Hebrew for this word can also mean *wind* or *spirit* (see verses 6–14).

the Sovereign LORD says: Come from the four winds, O breath, and breathe into these slain, that they may live.' " 10So I prophesied as he commanded me, and breath entered them; they came to life and stood up on their feet—a vast army.[p]

11Then he said to me: "Son of man, these bones are the whole house of Israel. They say, 'Our bones are dried up and our hope is gone; we are cut off.'[q] 12Therefore prophesy and say to them: 'This is what the Sovereign LORD says: O my people, I am going to open your graves and bring you up from them; I will bring you back to the land of Israel.[r] 13Then you, my people, will know that I am the LORD, when I open your graves and bring you up from them. 14I will put my Spirit[s] in you and you will live, and I will settle you in your own land. Then you will know that I the LORD have spoken, and I have done it, declares the LORD.[t]' "

One Nation Under One King

15The word of the LORD came to me: 16"Son of man, take a stick of wood and write on it, 'Belonging to Judah and the Israelites[u] associated with him.[v]' Then take another stick of wood, and write on it, 'Ephraim's stick, belonging to Joseph and all the house of Israel associated with him.' 17Join them together into one stick so that they will become one in your hand.[w]

18"When your countrymen ask you, 'Won't you tell us what you mean by this?'[x] 19say to them, 'This is what the Sovereign LORD says: I am going to take the stick of Joseph—which is in Ephraim's hand—and of the Israelite tribes associated with him, and join it to Judah's stick, making them a single stick of wood, and they will become one in my hand.'[y] 20Hold before their eyes the sticks you have written on 21and say to them, 'This is what the Sovereign LORD says: I will take the Israelites out of the nations where they have gone. I will gather them from all around and bring them back into their own land.[z] 22I will make them one nation in the land, on the mountains of Israel. There will be one king over all of them and they will never again be two nations or be divided into two kingdoms.[a] 23They will no longer defile[b] themselves with their idols and vile images or with any of their offenses, for I will save them from all their sinful backsliding,[a] and I will cleanse them. They will be my people, and I will be their God.[c]

24" 'My servant David[d] will be king over them, and they will all have one shepherd.[e] They will follow my laws and be careful to keep my decrees.[f] 25They will live in the land I gave to my servant Jacob, the land where your fathers lived.[g] They and their children and their children's children will live there forever,[h] and David my servant will be their prince forever.[i] 26I will make a covenant of peace[j] with them; it will be an everlasting covenant. I will

37:10 [p]Rev 11:11
37:11 [q]La 3:54
37:12 [r]Dt 32:39; 1Sa 2:6; Isa 26:19; Hos 13:14; Am 9:14-15
37:14 [s]Joel 2:28-29 [t]Eze 36:27-28,36
37:16 [u]1Ki 12:20; 2Ch 10:17-19 [v]Nu 17:2-3; 2Ch 15:9
37:17 [w]ver 24; Isa 11:13; Jer 50:4; Hos 1:11
37:18 [x]Eze 24:19
37:19 [y]Zec 10:6
7:21 [z]Isa 43:5-6; Eze 36:24; 39:27
37:22 [a]Isa 11:13; Jer 3:18; Hos 1:11
37:23 [b]Eze 36:25; 43:7 [c]Eze 11:18; 36:28
37:24 [d]Hos 3:5 [e]Isa 40:11; Eze 34:23 [f]Ps 78:70-71
37:25 [g]Eze 28:25 [h]Am 9:15 [i]Isa 11:1
37:26 [j]Isa 55:3

[a] 23 Many Hebrew manuscripts (see also Septuagint); most Hebrew manuscripts *all their dwelling places where they sinned*

One Nation, One King

EZE 37:22

In their future restoration, divided Israel will be reunited under one king. Since the reign of Rehoboam, Solomon's son, Israel has been divided into two rival nations, Israel (also known as Ephraim, as in this passage) and Judah (1Ki 12:16-17). Under the Messiah, her final and forever king, this new spiritual Israel will be one nation, as Ezekiel's image of two joined sticks illustrates (Eze 37:16-17). Under their king, the "Israel of God" (Gal 6:16), made up of both Jews and Gentiles, will finally be the nation God had originally called them to be—a holy people, fully committed to him.

Gog and Magog

EZE 38:2

The identities of these two names, Gog and Magog, have been researched and disputed heartily over the centuries. No definite identifications can be made, although Gog (1Ch 5:4; Rev 20:8) and Magog (Ge 10:2; 1Ch 1:5; Rev 20:8) both appear elsewhere in Scripture. The identifications of the names isn't necessary, however, in order to understand the passage. A judgment from God will arrive from the north to punish the people for their rejection of God and for their sins against his holiness. No such judgment coming from the north is recorded in history—at least nothing as severe as Ezekiel depicts here. Therefore, most scholars agree that this prophecy has yet to be fulfilled.

establish them and increase their numbers,[k] and I
will put my sanctuary among them forever.[l] 27My
dwelling place[m] will be with them; I will be their
God, and they will be my people.[n] 28Then the
nations will know that I the LORD make Israel holy,[o]
when my sanctuary is among them forever.' "

A Prophecy Against Gog

38 The word of the LORD came to me: 2"Son of
man, set your face against Gog, of the land
of Magog,[p] the chief prince of[a] Meshech and
Tubal;[q] prophesy against him 3and say: 'This is
what the Sovereign LORD says: I am against you,
O Gog, chief prince of[b] Meshech and Tubal.[r] 4I will
turn you around, put hooks[s] in your jaws and
bring you out with your whole army—your
horses, your horsemen fully armed, and a great
horde with large and small shields, all of them
brandishing their swords.[t] 5Persia, Cush[c][u] and
Put[v] will be with them, all with shields and helmets, 6also Gomer[w] with all its troops, and Beth
Togarmah[x] from the far north with all its troops—
the many nations with you.

7" 'Get ready; be prepared,[y] you and all the
hordes gathered about you, and take command of
them. 8After many days[z] you will be called to
arms. In future years you will invade a land that
has recovered from war, whose people were gathered from many nations[a] to the mountains of Israel, which had long been desolate. They had been
brought out from the nations, and now all of them
live in safety.[b] 9You and all your troops and the
many nations with you will go up, advancing like
a storm;[c] you will be like a cloud[d] covering the
land.

10" 'This is what the Sovereign LORD says: On
that day thoughts will come into your mind and
you will devise an evil scheme.[e] 11You will say, "I
will invade a land of unwalled villages; I will
attack a peaceful and unsuspecting people—all of
them living without walls and without gates and
bars.[f] 12I will plunder and loot and turn my hand
against the resettled ruins and the people gathered
from the nations, rich in livestock and goods, living at the center of the land." 13Sheba[g] and Dedan
and the merchants of Tarshish and all her villages[d] will say to you, "Have you come to plunder? Have you gathered your hordes to loot, to
carry off silver and gold, to take away livestock
and goods and to seize much plunder?[h]" '

14"Therefore, son of man, prophesy and say to
Gog: 'This is what the Sovereign LORD says: In that
day, when my people Israel are living in safety,[i]
will you not take notice of it? 15You will come from
your place in the far north, you and many nations
with you, all of them riding on horses, a great
horde, a mighty army.[j] 16You will advance against
my people Israel like a cloud[k] that covers the land.

37:26 [k]Jer 30:19 [l]Eze 16:62
37:27 [m]Lev 26:11; Jn 1:14 [n]2Co 6:16*
37:28 [o]Ex 31:13; Eze 20:12
38:2 [p]Ge 10:2 [q]Rev 20:8
38:3 [r]Eze 39:1
38:4 [s]2Ki 19:28 [t]Eze 29:4; Da 11:40
38:5 [u]Ge 10:6 [v]Eze 27:10
38:6 [w]Ge 10:2 [x]Eze 27:14
38:7 [y]Isa 8:9
38:8 [z]Isa 24:22 [a]Isa 11:11 [b]Jer 23:6
38:9 [c]Isa 28:2 [d]Jer 4:13; Joel 2:2
38:10 [e]Ps 36:4; Mic 2:1
38:11 [f]Jer 49:31; Zec 2:4
38:13 [g]Eze 27:22 [h]Isa 10:6; Jer 15:13
38:14 [i]ver 8; Zec 2:5
38:15 [j]Eze 39:2
38:16 [k]ver 9

[a] *2* Or *the prince of Rosh,* [b] *3* Or *Gog, prince of Rosh,*
[c] *5* That is, the upper Nile region [d] *13* Or *her strong lions*

In days to come, O Gog, I will bring you against
38:16 [l]Isa 29:23; Eze 39:21 my land, so that the nations may know me when
I show myself holy through you before their eyes.[l]
17 “ ‘This is what the Sovereign LORD says: Are
you not the one I spoke of in former days by my
servants the prophets of Israel? At that time they
prophesied for years that I would bring you
against them. 18 This is what will happen in that
day: When Gog attacks the land of Israel, my hot
anger will be aroused, declares the Sovereign
LORD. 19 In my zeal and fiery wrath I declare that at
that time there shall be a great earthquake in the
38:19 [m]Ps 18:7; Eze 5:13; Hag 2:6,21 land of Israel.[m] 20 The fish of the sea, the birds of
the air, the beasts of the field, every creature that
moves along the ground, and all the people on the
face of the earth will tremble at my presence. The
mountains will be overturned, the cliffs will
38:20 [n]Hos 4:3; Na 1:5 crumble and every wall will fall to the ground.[n]
21 I will summon a sword[o] against Gog on all my
mountains, declares the Sovereign LORD. Every
38:21 [o]Eze 14:17 [p]1Sa 14:20; 2Ch 20:23; Hag 2:22 man's sword will be against his brother.[p] 22 I will
execute judgment[q] upon him with plague and
bloodshed; I will pour down torrents of rain, hailstones[r] and burning sulfur on him and on his
38:22 [q]Isa 66:16; Jer 25:31 [r]Ps 18:12; Rev 16:21 troops and on the many nations with him. 23 And
so I will show my greatness and my holiness, and
I will make myself known in the sight of many
nations. Then they will know that I am the LORD.[s]’

38:23 [s]Eze 36:23 **39** “Son of man, prophesy against Gog and say:
‘This is what the Sovereign LORD says: I am
against you, O Gog, chief prince of[a] Meshech and
39:1 [t]Eze 38:2,3 Tubal.[t] 2 I will turn you around and drag you along.
I will bring you from the far north and send you
against the mountains of Israel. 3 Then I will strike
39:3 [u]Hos 1:5 [v]Ps 76:3 your bow[u] from your left hand and make your
arrows[v] drop from your right hand. 4 On the moun-
tains of Israel you will fall, you and all your troops
and the nations with you. I will give you as food to
all kinds of carrion birds and to the wild animals.[w]
39:4 [w]ver 17-20; Eze 29:5; 33:27 5 You will fall in the open field, for I have spoken,
declares the Sovereign LORD. 6 I will send fire[x] on
Magog and on those who live in safety in the coastlands,[y] and they will know that I am the LORD.
39:6 [x]Eze 30:8; Am 1:4 [y]Jer 25:22 7 “ ‘I will make known my holy name among
my people Israel. I will no longer let my holy
name be profaned,[z] and the nations will know
39:7 [z]Ex 20:7 [a]Isa 12:6; Eze 36:16,23 that I the LORD am the Holy One in Israel.[a] 8 It is
coming! It will surely take place, declares the Sov-
ereign LORD. This is the day I have spoken of.
9 “ ‘Then those who live in the towns of Israel
will go out and use the weapons for fuel and burn
them up—the small and large shields, the bows
and arrows, the war clubs and spears. For seven
39:9 [b]Ps 46:9 years they will use them for fuel.[b] 10 They will not
need to gather wood from the fields or cut it from
the forests, because they will use the weapons for
fuel. And they will plunder those who plundered
39:10 [c]Isa 14:2; 33:1; Hab 2:8 them and loot those who looted them, declares
the Sovereign LORD.[c]

[a] 1 Or *Gog, prince of Rosh,*

In this unforgettable image of bones coming together and life being breathed back into them, God promised his children that he, the giver of all life, the preserver of his chosen people, would reestablish them as a nation: “Son of man, these bones are the whole house of Israel” (Ezekiel 37:11) . . . This passage in Ezekiel suggests a pattern God seems to use as he introduces us to his extraordinary ways. First he gets our attention; then he tells us his purpose: “[that you] will know that I am the LORD” [Eze 37:13] . . . God does the unusual so that we recognize his unmistakable hand. Why? I cannot take the credit for how things work out in my life. I cannot brag about my fine insights, good judgment or special ability. God makes sure that his accomplishments are performed by him; it is his insight, his good judgment and his ability that brings extraordinary results out of ordinary circumstances.

—Marilyn Meberg

A Judgment Supper

EZE 39:17-20

Ezekiel continues his depiction of judgment on those who have ignored God's call to repentance with a gory description of the carnage that will take place. Ezekiel calls the slaughter of that day a "great sacrifice" (Eze 39:17), one that the animals and birds of the earth are called to eat. Those killed are not weaklings but strong soldiers and princes, which Ezekiel reveals by comparing them to the well-fed animals that are raised on the plains of Bashan (Eze 39:18).

A similar slaughter and feast also takes place in Revelation 19:11-21, where birds of prey are invited to feast on the "flesh" (Rev 19:18) of those who have fought against God and his purposes and been defeated. The similarities of these two passages cause most scholars to see the fulfillment of Ezekiel in Revelation, and both in the future at the second coming of Christ.

11" 'On that day I will give Gog a burial place in
Israel, in the valley of those who travel east toward[a]
the Sea.[b] It will block the way of travelers, because
Gog and all his hordes will be buried there. So it
will be called the Valley of Hamon Gog.[c][d]
12" 'For seven months the house of Israel will
be burying them in order to cleanse the land.[e]
13All the people of the land will bury them, and
the day I am glorified[f] will be a memorable day
for them, declares the Sovereign LORD.
14" 'Men will be regularly employed to cleanse
the land. Some will go throughout the land and,
in addition to them, others will bury those that
remain on the ground. At the end of the seven
months they will begin their search. 15As they go
through the land and one of them sees a human
bone, he will set up a marker beside it until the
gravediggers have buried it in the Valley of
Hamon Gog. 16(Also a town called Hamonah[d] will
be there.) And so they will cleanse the land.'
17"Son of man, this is what the Sovereign LORD
says: Call out to every kind of bird[g] and all the wild
animals: 'Assemble and come together from all
around to the sacrifice I am preparing for you, the
great sacrifice on the mountains of Israel. There
you will eat flesh and drink blood. 18You will eat
the flesh of mighty men and drink the blood of the
princes of the earth as if they were rams and lambs,
goats and bulls—all of them fattened animals from
Bashan.[h] 19At the sacrifice I am preparing for you,
you will eat fat till you are glutted and drink blood
till you are drunk. 20At my table you will eat your
fill of horses and riders, mighty men and soldiers of
every kind,' declares the Sovereign LORD.[i]
21"I will display my glory among the nations,
and all the nations will see the punishment I
inflict and the hand I lay upon them.[j] 22From that
day forward the house of Israel will know that I
am the LORD their God. 23And the nations will
know that the people of Israel went into exile for
their sin, because they were unfaithful to me. So
I hid my face from them and handed them over to
their enemies, and they all fell by the sword.[k] 24I
dealt with them according to their uncleanness
and their offenses, and I hid my face from them.[l]
25"Therefore this is what the Sovereign LORD
says: I will now bring Jacob back from captivity[e][m]
and will have compassion[n] on all the people of
Israel, and I will be zealous for my holy name.[o]
26They will forget their shame and all the unfaithfulness they showed toward me when they lived
in safety[p] in their land with no one to make them
afraid.[q] 27When I have brought them back from
the nations and have gathered them from the
countries of their enemies, I will show myself
holy through them in the sight of many nations.[r]
28Then they will know that I am the LORD their

39:11 [d]Eze 38:2
39:12 [e]Dt 21:23
39:13 [f]Eze 28:22
39:17 [g]Rev 19:17
39:18 [h]Ps 22:12; Jer 51:40
39:20 [i]Rev 19:17-18
39:21 [j]Ex 9:16; Isa 37:20; Eze 38:16
39:23 [k]Isa 1:15; 59:2; Jer 22:8-9; 44:23
39:24 [l]Jer 2:17,19; 4:18; Eze 36:19
39:25 [m]Jer 33:7; Eze 34:13 [n]Jer 30:18 [o]Isa 27:12-13
39:26 [p]1Ki 4:25 [q]Isa 17:2; Eze 34:28; Mic 4:4
39:27 [r]Eze 36:23-24; 37:21; 38:16

[a] *11* Or *of* [b] *11* That is, the Dead Sea [c] *11* *Hamon Gog* means *hordes of Gog.* [d] *16* *Hamonah* means *horde.*
[e] *25* Or *now restore the fortunes of Jacob*

Job's Wife

Wise Enough to Wait

She couldn't stand it any longer. As she watched Job sit in ashes of mourning and scrape his boils with a piece of broken pottery, she was overwhelmed. She held her hands to her head—she felt as if it was about to burst—and she shrieked at Job. He had to do *something* to end the siege—even if it meant dying.

She loved him deeply. Job was a good man and loved God with his whole heart. God had blessed everything Job touched. She loved their life and was ready for their golden years together, now that the children were grown.

Then, in one day, they lost all their wealth, their servants and their children. They were devastated, to say the least. But she still had Job. Together they would start over and make it through. But now even Job was going down. What had they done to deserve this? What had *Job* done? She was terrified and *angry*. Their life was broken, and she didn't know how to put things back together. She didn't know how to be strong for Job. He had always been the strong one. So she yelled.

Her anger and pain frustrated Job. He had enough to contend with! He shot back: "Stop being foolish!" But he also comforted her. God was still God. Job knew in his heart that sin was not the cause of their suffering. They had to do the best they could to accept the circumstances and continue to seek God for answers.

Job's wife had the wisdom—and the grace—to stop talking. She could only wait and see what God would do. God's wisdom prevailed, and when Job learned what he needed to learn, their fortunes were restored. But what if they had not been? What if their lives had improved only a little or not at all? Had their encounter with God taught them a new way to communicate their pain and fear? They certainly would need it. They would also need true friends to stand by them and help them work through the rough times. Despair could become a daily battle.

Suffering and loss profoundly test a relationship. Marriages have foundered and friendships have collapsed when familiar roles are reversed. The people we love cannot always make us feel secure in the eye of the storm. There are no pat answers for tragedy, pain and suffering. We have to read the end of the Book: "He will wipe every tear from their eyes. There will be no more death or mourning or crying or pain, for the old order of things has passed away" (Rev. 21:4).

Job's Wife
Job 2:9-10

Candid SNAPSHOT Then Job took a piece of broken pottery and scraped himself with it as he sat among the ashes. His wife said to him, "Are you still holding on to your integrity? Curse God and die!" (Job 2:8-9).

A Wife of Noble Character

Late to Bed, Early to Rise

Ahh, the noble wife. Busy, busy, busy. How does one woman find time for so much?

That's it! She is not one woman. She's all of us—and none of us. In a time when most women were not taken very seriously apart from childbearing, the writer of this proverb dared to present a picture of a woman as a glorious, vibrant, competent and intelligent creation of God. The imagery is as relevant today as the day he wrote it. As we put some of the noble wife's talents into a modern context, we recognize her in ourselves and our sisters.

Some women might go after quality clothing for their families and shop at several supermarkets to find the best buys. They fill their houses with plants. Their pantries are well stocked, their bathrooms are laden with plenty of toilet paper and fresh towels.

Some women contribute clean used clothing and food to the poor. They give birthday parties for disadvantaged children and tutor slow learners. They rock newborn babies at the hospital, wash windows for the elderly and take in foster children. Their homes are gathering places for neighborhood kids.

There are women for whom no job is too challenging or too niggling. They chop wood for the fireplace, mow the lawn and shovel snow. They repair the toaster, put up shelving, balance the budget and debug the computer. They also dress attractively, quilt and sew and sell homemade gift items on consignment.

A godly wife may impress her workplace with her good judgment and reliability. She plans the week's activities to make sure the important things come first, both at work and at home. She prays and sets family goals with her husband. She encourages him, asks about his day and shares her insight. On special occasions she may invite friends from his or her work to dinner.

A wife of noble character wears many faces and fills many roles—roles that can change with the seasons of her life. In essence, she draws her strength from the Lord to lay down her life for those she loves. Her creative industry may fill her day with countless activities or only one or two to which she gives herself deeply. Her reward? Her children adore her. Her husband cherishes her company, trusts her judgment and brags about her to all his friends. She will be remembered—long after she is gone—not as a woman who beautifully knit a sweater or successfully balanced a budget but as a woman who sought the Lord first of all.

A Wife of Noble Character
Proverbs 31:10-31

Candid SNAPSHOT *Charm is deceptive, and beauty is fleeting; but a woman who fears the* LORD *is to be praised. Give her the reward she has earned, and let her works bring her praise at the city gate* (Proverbs 31:30-31).

God, for though I sent them into exile among the
nations, I will gather them to their own land, not
leaving any behind. [29]I will no longer hide my
39:29 [s]Joel 2:28; face from them, for I will pour out my Spirit[s] on
Ac 2:17 the house of Israel, declares the Sovereign LORD."

The New Temple Area

40 In the twenty-fifth year of our exile, at the
beginning of the year, on the tenth of the
month, in the fourteenth year after the fall of the
40:1 [t]2Ki 25:7; city[t]—on that very day the hand of the LORD was
Jer 39:1-10; upon me[u] and he took me there. [2]In visions[v] of
52:4-11; God he took me to the land of Israel and set me on
Eze 33:21 a very high mountain,[w] on whose south side were
[u]Eze 1:3 some buildings that looked like a city. [3]He took
40:2 [v]Da 7:1,7 me there, and I saw a man whose appearance was
[w]Eze 17:22; like bronze;[x] he was standing in the gateway with
Rev 21:10 a linen cord and a measuring rod[y] in his hand.
40:3 [4]The man said to me, "Son of man, look with your
[x]Eze 1:7; eyes and hear with your ears and pay attention to
Da 10:6; everything I am going to show you, for that is
Rev 1:15 [y]Eze 47:3; why you have been brought here. Tell[z] the house
Zec 2:1-2; of Israel everything you see.[a]"
Rev 11:1; 21:15

The East Gate to the Outer Court

40:4 [z]Jer 26:2 [5]I saw a wall completely surrounding the temple
[a]Eze 44:5 area. The length of the measuring rod in the man's
hand was six long cubits, each of which was a
40:5 [b]Eze 42:20 cubit[a] and a handbreadth.[b] He measured[b] the wall;
it was one measuring rod thick and one rod high.
40:6 [6]Then he went to the gate facing east.[c] He
[c]Eze 8:16 climbed its steps and measured the threshold of the
40:7 gate; it was one rod deep.[c] [7]The alcoves[d] for the
[d]ver 36 guards were one rod long and one rod wide, and
the projecting walls between the alcoves were five
cubits thick. And the threshold of the gate next to
the portico facing the temple was one rod deep.
[8]Then he measured the portico of the gateway;
[9]it[d] was eight cubits deep and its jambs were two
cubits thick. The portico of the gateway faced the
temple.
[10]Inside the east gate were three alcoves on each
side; the three had the same measurements, and
the faces of the projecting walls on each side had
the same measurements. [11]Then he measured the
width of the entrance to the gateway; it was ten
cubits and its length was thirteen cubits. [12]In front
of each alcove was a wall one cubit high, and the
alcoves were six cubits square. [13]Then he measured the gateway from the top of the rear wall of
one alcove to the top of the opposite one; the distance was twenty-five cubits from one parapet
opening to the opposite one. [14]He measured along
the faces of the projecting walls all around the

[a] 5 The common cubit was about 1 1/2 feet (about 0.5 meter).
[b] 5 That is, about 3 inches (about 8 centimeters)
[c] 6 Septuagint; Hebrew *deep, the first threshold, one rod deep*
[d] 8,9 Many Hebrew manuscripts, Septuagint, Vulgate and Syriac; most Hebrew manuscripts *gateway facing the temple; it was one rod deep. [9]Then he measured the portico of the gateway; it*

Outpouring of God's Spirit

EZE 39:29

God promises that in the future he will pour his Spirit out on all those willing to turn to him, follow him and obey him. That Spirit will give them the power they need to remain faithful. When Jesus comes, fulfilling the law through his life and death, he inaugurates the new covenant; now God's commands are no longer written on harsh and hard stone tablets but are written on the living flesh of the human heart (Jer 31:33). God accomplishes this through the outpouring of his Holy Spirit on believers' hearts, making them attuned to his authority and his direction, causing them to respond with love and tenderness rather than with rebellion.

God promises this outpouring of the Holy Spirit several times throughout the Old Testament, most noticeably in Joel 2:28 when he says, "I will pour out my Spirit on all people." Peter quotes this verse on the day of Pentecost when he explains to the crowd the amazing events they have witnessed (Ac 2:17).

Palm Tree Decorations

EZE 40:16,22,26,31,34,37

Palm trees are tropical trees that grow in some of Israel's warmer areas. The city of Jericho was known as "the City of Palms" (Dt 34:3).

Solomon decorated the walls of the temple with carved palm trees that had been carefully covered with beaten gold (1Ki 6:29–35).

Ezekiel describes in this chapter a number of places in the temple of his vision where palm trees are used for decorations.

When Jesus entered Jerusalem, the celebrants carried palm branches and shouted praises to him (Jn 12:13). Revelation depicts another celebration of Jesus in which the participants carry palm branches (Rev 7:9).

The significance of the use of the palm tree in religious buildings and events is somewhat uncertain, but may be a reminder of the beauty of the Garden of Eden.

inside of the gateway—sixty cubits. The measure- 40:14
ment was up to the portico[a] facing the courtyard.[b][e] [e]Ex 27:9
[15]The distance from the entrance of the gateway to
the far end of its portico was fifty cubits. [16]The
alcoves and the projecting walls inside the gateway were surmounted by narrow parapet openings all around, as was the portico; the openings
all around faced inward. The faces of the project- 40:16
ing walls were decorated with palm trees.[f] [f]ver 21-22; 2Ch 3:5; Eze 41:26

The Outer Court

[17]Then he brought me into the outer court.[g] 40:17
There I saw some rooms and a pavement that had [g]Rev 11:2
been constructed all around the court; there were [h]Eze 41:6
thirty rooms[h] along the pavement.[i] [18]It abutted the [i]Eze 42:1
sides of the gateways and was as wide as they
were long; this was the lower pavement. [19]Then
he measured the distance from the inside of the
lower gateway to the outside of the inner court;[j] it 40:19 [j]Eze 46:1
was a hundred cubits[k] on the east side as well as [k]ver 23,27
on the north.

The North Gate

[20]Then he measured the length and width of the
gate facing north, leading into the outer court.
[21]Its alcoves[l]—three on each side—its projecting 40:21
walls and its portico had the same measurements [l]ver 7
as those of the first gateway. It was fifty cubits
long and twenty-five cubits wide. [22]Its openings, 40:22
its portico[m] and its palm tree decorations had the [m]ver 49
same measurements as those of the gate facing
east. Seven steps led up to it, with its portico
opposite them. [23]There was a gate to the inner
court facing the north gate, just as there was on
the east. He measured from one gate to the oppo- 40:23
site one; it was a hundred cubits.[n] [n]ver 19

The South Gate

[24]Then he led me to the south side and I saw a
gate facing south. He measured its jambs and its
portico, and they had the same measurements as
the others. [25]The gateway and its portico had narrow openings all around, like the openings of the
others. It was fifty cubits long and twenty-five 40:25
cubits wide.[o] [26]Seven steps led up to it, with its [o]ver 33
portico opposite them; it had palm tree decora-
tions on the faces of the projecting walls on each 40:26
side.[p] [27]The inner court[q] also had a gate facing [p]ver 22
south, and he measured from this gate to the out- 40:27
er gate on the south side; it was a hundred cubits. [q]ver 32

Gates to the Inner Court

[28]Then he brought me into the inner court
through the south gate, and he measured the 40:28
south gate; it had the same measurements[r] as the [r]ver 35
others. [29]Its alcoves, its projecting walls and its
portico had the same measurements as the others.
The gateway and its portico had openings all

[a] 14 Septuagint; Hebrew *projecting wall* [b] 14 The meaning of the Hebrew for this verse is uncertain.

around. It was fifty cubits long and twenty-five
40:30 [s]ver 21 cubits wide. 30 (The porticoes[s] of the gateways
around the inner court were twenty-five cubits
40:31 [t]ver 22 wide and five cubits deep.) 31 Its portico[t] faced the
outer court; palm trees decorated its jambs, and
eight steps led up to it.

32 Then he brought me to the inner court on the
east side, and he measured the gateway; it had the
same measurements as the others. 33 Its alcoves,
its projecting walls and its portico had the same
measurements as the others. The gateway and its
portico had openings all around. It was fifty cubits
40:34 [u]ver 22 long and twenty-five cubits wide. 34 Its portico[u]
faced the outer court; palm trees decorated the
jambs on either side, and eight steps led up to it.
40:35 [v]Eze 44:4; 47:2 35 Then he brought me to the north gate[v] and
measured it. It had the same measurements as the
40:36 [w]ver 7 others, 36 as did its alcoves,[w] its projecting walls
and its portico, and it had openings all around. It
was fifty cubits long and twenty-five cubits wide.
37 Its portico[a] faced the outer court; palm trees decorated the jambs on either side, and eight steps
led up to it.

The Rooms for Preparing Sacrifices

38 A room with a doorway was by the portico in
each of the inner gateways, where the burnt offer-
40:38 [x]2Ch 4:6; Eze 42:13 ings[x] were washed. 39 In the portico of the gateway
were two tables on each side, on which the burnt
offerings,[y] sin offerings[z] and guilt offerings[a] were
40:39 [y]Eze 46:2 [z]Lev 4:3,28 [a]Lev 7:1 slaughtered. 40 By the outside wall of the portico
of the gateway, near the steps at the entrance to
the north gateway were two tables, and on the
other side of the steps were two tables. 41 So there
were four tables on one side of the gateway and
four on the other—eight tables in all—on which
the sacrifices were slaughtered. 42 There were also
40:42 [b]Ex 20:25 [c]ver 39 four tables of dressed stone[b] for the burnt offerings, each a cubit and a half long, a cubit and a
half wide and a cubit high. On them were placed
the utensils for slaughtering the burnt offerings
and the other sacrifices.[c] 43 And double-pronged
hooks, each a handbreadth long, were attached to
the wall all around. The tables were for the flesh
of the offerings.

Rooms for the Priests

44 Outside the inner gate, within the inner court,
were two rooms, one[b] at the side of the north gate
and facing south, and another at the side of the
40:45 [d]1Ch 9:23 south[c] gate and facing north. 45 He said to me,
"The room facing south is for the priests who
40:46 [e]Eze 42:13 [f]Nu 18:5 [g]1Ki 2:35 [h]Nu 16:5; Eze 43:19; 44:15; 45:4; 48:11 have charge of the temple,[d] 46 and the room facing
north[e] is for the priests who have charge of the
altar.[f] These are the sons of Zadok,[g] who are the
only Levites who may draw near to the LORD to
minister before him.[h]"

[a] *37* Septuagint (see also verses 31 and 34); Hebrew *jambs*
[b] *44* Septuagint; Hebrew *were rooms for singers, which were*
[c] *44* Septuagint; Hebrew *east*

Everybody experiences difficult situations in life. Everybody. Things that make us want to scream out or give up. Deprivations. Sacrifices. Losses. Misunderstandings. But isn't there some way for the Christian to respond without getting mad at God? Otherwise, what's the good of our faith? There has to be some key to being joyful in the midst of discouraging circumstances and crabby people. What is it?

It's taking God at his Word. It's believing he will do what he says, no matter how things look or how we feel . . . Trusting God with everything we have, everything we are, every problem that is ours, every loss we endure, every battle we face, every person who disappoints us—with thanksgiving—gives us the grace to come through it with flying colors.

—Luci Swindoll

Ezekiel's Temple

EZE 40–48

Various interpretations have been offered as to exactly which temple Ezekiel is describing here. Some look to one of the actual historical temples—Solomon's, Zerubbabel's or Herod's. Others look for a future temple to be built in the final Messianic age. Still others prefer a spiritual interpretation, saying the temple described here is the future blessing and perfection of God's plan for the church.

47Then he measured the court: It was square—
a hundred cubits long and a hundred cubits wide.
And the altar was in front of the temple.

The Temple **40:48**

48He brought me to the portico of the temple[i] [i]1Ki 6:2
and measured the jambs of the portico; they were
five cubits wide on either side. The width of the
entrance was fourteen cubits and its projecting
walls were[a] three cubits wide on either side. 49The **40:49**
portico[j] was twenty cubits wide, and twelve[b] [j]ver 22;
cubits from front to back. It was reached by a 1Ki 6:3
flight of stairs,[c] and there were pillars[k] on each [k]1Ki 7:15
side of the jambs.

41 Then the man brought me to the outer sanc- **41:1**
tuary[l] and measured the jambs; the width [l]ver 23
of the jambs was six cubits[d] on each side.[e] 2The
entrance was ten cubits wide, and the projecting
walls on each side of it were five cubits wide. He
also measured the outer sanctuary; it was forty **41:2**
cubits long and twenty cubits wide.[m] [m]2Ch 3:3

3Then he went into the inner sanctuary and
measured the jambs of the entrance; each was two
cubits wide. The entrance was six cubits wide,
and the projecting walls on each side of it were
seven cubits wide. 4And he measured the length
of the inner sanctuary; it was twenty cubits, and
its width was twenty cubits across the end of the
outer sanctuary.[n] He said to me, "This is the Most **41:4**
Holy Place.[o]" [n]1Ki 6:20

5Then he measured the wall of the temple; it [o]Ex 26:33;
was six cubits thick, and each side room around Heb 9:3-8
the temple was four cubits wide. 6The side rooms **41:6**
were on three levels, one above another, thirty[p] [p]Eze 40:17
on each level. There were ledges all around the [q]1Ki 6:5
wall of the temple to serve as supports for the side
rooms, so that the supports were not inserted into
the wall of the temple.[q] 7The side rooms all
around the temple were wider at each successive
level. The structure surrounding the temple was
built in ascending stages, so that the rooms
widened as one went upward. A stairway[r] went **41:7**
up from the lowest floor to the top floor through [r]1Ki 6:8
the middle floor.

8I saw that the temple had a raised base all
around it, forming the foundation of the side
rooms. It was the length of the rod, six long
cubits. 9The outer wall of the side rooms was five
cubits thick. The open area between the side
rooms of the temple 10and the ⌊priests'⌋ rooms was
twenty cubits wide all around the temple. 11There
were entrances to the side rooms from the open
area, one on the north and another on the south;
and the base adjoining the open area was five
cubits wide all around.

12The building facing the temple courtyard on

[a] *48* Septuagint; Hebrew *entrance was* [b] *49* Septuagint; Hebrew *eleven* [c] *49* Hebrew; Septuagint *Ten steps led up to it* [d] *1* The common cubit was about 1 1/2 feet (about 0.5 meter). [e] *1* One Hebrew manuscript and Septuagint; most Hebrew manuscripts *side, the width of the tent*

the west side was seventy cubits wide. The wall of
the building was five cubits thick all around, and
its length was ninety cubits.
13Then he measured the temple; it was a hundred cubits long, and the temple courtyard and
the building with its walls were also a hundred
cubits long. 14The width of the temple courtyard
on the east, including the front of the temple, was
41:14 [s]Eze 40:47 a hundred cubits.[s]
15Then he measured the length of the building
41:15 facing the courtyard at the rear of the temple,
[t]Eze 42:3 including its galleries[t] on each side; it was a hundred cubits.
The outer sanctuary, the inner sanctuary and
41:16 the portico facing the court, 16as well as the
[u]1Ki 6:4 thresholds and the narrow windows[u] and galleries
[v]ver 25-26; around the three of them—everything beyond and
1Ki 6:15; Eze 42:3 including the threshold was covered with wood.
The floor, the wall up to the windows, and the
windows were covered.[v] 17In the space above the
outside of the entrance to the inner sanctuary and
on the walls at regular intervals all around the
41:18 inner and outer sanctuary 18were carved[w] cheru-
[w]1Ki 6:18 bim[x] and palm trees.[y] Palm trees alternated with
[x]Ex 37:7; 2Ch 3:7 cherubim. Each cherub had two faces:[z] 19the face
[y]1Ki 6:29; 7:36 of a man toward the palm tree on one side and the
[z]Eze 10:21 face of a lion toward the palm tree on the other.
41:19 They were carved all around the whole temple.[a]
[a]Eze 10:14 20From the floor to the area above the entrance,
cherubim and palm trees were carved on the wall
of the outer sanctuary.
41:21 [b]ver 1 21The outer sanctuary[b] had a rectangular doorframe, and the one at the front of the Most Holy
41:22 Place was similar. 22There was a wooden altar[c]
[c]Ex 30:1 three cubits high and two cubits square[a]; its cor-
[d]Ex 25:23; ners, its base[b] and its sides were of wood. The
Eze 23:41; man said to me, "This is the table[d] that is before
44:16; Mal 1:7,12 the LORD." 23Both the outer sanctuary[e] and the
41:23 Most Holy Place had double doors.[f] 24Each door
[e]ver 1 had two leaves—two hinged leaves[g] for each door.
[f]1Ki 6:32 25And on the doors of the outer sanctuary were
41:24 carved cherubim and palm trees like those carved
[g]1Ki 6:34 on the walls, and there was a wooden overhang
on the front of the portico. 26On the sidewalls of
the portico were narrow windows with palm trees
41:26 carved on each side. The side rooms of the temple
[h]ver 15-16; Eze 40:16 also had overhangs.[h]

Rooms for the Priests

42 Then the man led me northward into the
42:1 [i]ver 13 outer court and brought me to the rooms[i]
[j]Eze 41:12-14 opposite the temple courtyard[j] and opposite the
[k]Eze 40:17 outer wall on the north side.[k] 2The building
whose door faced north was a hundred cubits[c]
long and fifty cubits wide. 3Both in the section
twenty cubits from the inner court and in the section opposite the pavement of the outer court,

[a] *22* Septuagint; Hebrew *long* [b] *22* Septuagint; Hebrew *length* [c] *2* The common cubit was about 1 1/2 feet (about 0.5 meter).

Most Holy Place

EZE 41:21

Each of the historical temples in Jerusalem (Solomon's, built during the time of the kings; Zerubbabel's, built when the exiles return to Jerusalem; and Herod's, begun shortly before the birth of Christ) have similar designs and include a Most Holy Place, as does the temple Ezekiel describes here. The tabernacle built by Moses in the desert also had such a room.

The Most Holy Place is the inner sanctuary of the temple, the place where God's presence dwells with his people. A curtain separates the Most Holy Place from the other rooms of the temple, shielding God from the sin of the people and shielding the people from God's holiness. When Christ dies on the cross, this curtain is violently torn in two from the top to the bottom (Mt 27:51; Mk 15:38; Lk 23:45), a glorious event that reveals, probably more than any other event, the fullness and finality of Jesus Christ's death. Direct access to God is now available to every believer (Heb 10:19–22).

Measuring

EZE 42:15-20

Ezekiel's vision of the temple continues when the holy messenger takes him outside. They measure the entire temple structure on the outside. The measurements Ezekiel gives form a perfect square, "five hundred cubits long and five hundred cubits wide" (Eze 42:20). The outer wall separates "the holy from the common" (Eze 42:20). Often throughout Israel's history they ignored God's holiness and profaned his "holy name" by their actions (Lev 20:3; Jer 34:16; Eze 20:39). The wall of this new temple, whether seen as actual or spiritual in nature, emphasizes again the need for God's people to recognize, protect and worship his holiness.

gallery[l] faced gallery at the three levels.[m] 4 In front
of the rooms was an inner passageway ten cubits
wide and a hundred cubits[a] long. Their doors
were on the north.[n] 5 Now the upper rooms were
narrower, for the galleries took more space from
them than from the rooms on the lower and middle floors of the building. 6 The rooms on the third
floor had no pillars, as the courts had; so they
were smaller in floor space than those on the lower and middle floors. 7 There was an outer wall
parallel to the rooms and the outer court; it
extended in front of the rooms for fifty cubits.
8 While the row of rooms on the side next to the
outer court was fifty cubits long, the row on the
side nearest the sanctuary was a hundred cubits
long. 9 The lower rooms had an entrance[o] on the
east side as one enters them from the outer court.
10 On the south side[b] along the length of the wall
of the outer court, adjoining the temple courtyard
and opposite the outer wall, were rooms[p] 11 with a
passageway in front of them. These were like the
rooms on the north; they had the same length and
width, with similar exits and dimensions. Similar
to the doorways on the north 12 were the doorways
of the rooms on the south. There was a doorway
at the beginning of the passageway that was parallel to the corresponding wall extending eastward, by which one enters the rooms.
13 Then he said to me, "The north[q] and south
rooms facing the temple courtyard are the priests'
rooms, where the priests who approach the LORD
will eat the most holy offerings. There they will
put the most holy offerings—the grain offerings,
the sin offerings[r] and the guilt offerings[s]—for the
place is holy.[t] 14 Once the priests enter the holy
precincts, they are not to go into the outer court
until they leave behind the garments[u] in which
they minister, for these are holy. They are to put
on other clothes before they go near the places
that are for the people.[v]"
15 When he had finished measuring what was
inside the temple area, he led me out by the east
gate[w] and measured the area all around: 16 He
measured the east side with the measuring rod; it
was five hundred cubits.[c] 17 He measured the north
side; it was five hundred cubits[d] by the measuring rod. 18 He measured the south side; it was five
hundred cubits by the measuring rod. 19 Then he
turned to the west side and measured; it was five
hundred cubits by the measuring rod. 20 So he
measured[x] the area on all four sides. It had a wall
around it,[y] five hundred cubits long and five hundred cubits wide,[z] to separate the holy from the
common.[a]

42:3 [l]Eze 41:15 [m]Eze 41:16
42:4 [n]Eze 46:19
42:9 [o]Eze 44:5; 46:19
42:10 [p]ver 1
42:13 [q]Eze 40:46 [r]Lev 10:17; 6:25 [s]Lev 14:13 [t]Ex 29:31; Lev 6:29; 7:6; 10:12-13; Nu 18:9-10
42:14 [u]Eze 44:19 [v]Ex 29:9; Lev 8:7-9
42:15 [w]Eze 43:1
42:20 [x]Eze 40:5 [y]Zec 2:5 [z]Eze 45:2; Rev 21:16 [a]Eze 22:26

[a] *4* Septuagint and Syriac; Hebrew *and one cubit*
[b] *10* Septuagint; Hebrew *Eastward* [c] *16* See Septuagint of verse 17; Hebrew *rods*; also in verses 18 and 19.
[d] *17* Septuagint; Hebrew *rods*

The Glory Returns to the Temple

43 Then the man brought me to the gate fac-
43:1 [b]Eze 10:19; ing east,[b] [2]and I saw the glory of the God of
42:15; 44:1; Israel coming from the east. His voice was like the
46:1 roar of rushing waters,[c] and the land was radiant
43:2 with his glory.[d] [3]The vision I saw was like the
[c]Rev 1:15 vision I had seen when he[a] came to destroy the
[d]Isa 6:3; city and like the visions I had seen by the Kebar
Eze 11:23; Rev 18:1 River, and I fell facedown. [4]The glory[e] of the LORD
entered the temple through the gate facing east.[f]
43:4 [e]Eze 1:28 [5]Then the Spirit[g] lifted me up[h] and brought me
[f]Eze 10:19 into the inner court, and the glory of the LORD
43:5 filled the temple.
[g]Eze 11:24 [6]While the man was standing beside me, I
[h]Eze 3:12; 8:3 heard someone speaking to me from inside the
temple. [7]He said: "Son of man, this is the place of
my throne and the place for the soles of my feet.
This is where I will live among the Israelites forever. The house of Israel will never again defile
my holy name—neither they nor their kings—by
43:7 their prostitution[b] and the lifeless idols[c] of their
[i]Lev 26:30 kings at their high places.[i] [8]When they placed
their threshold next to my threshold and their
doorposts beside my doorposts, with only a wall
between me and them, they defiled my holy name
by their detestable practices. So I destroyed them
in my anger. [9]Now let them put away from me
43:9 their prostitution and the lifeless idols of their
[j]Eze 37:26-28 kings, and I will live among them forever.[j]
[10]"Son of man, describe the temple to the people
43:10 [k]Eze 16:61 of Israel, that they may be ashamed[k] of their sins.
Let them consider the plan, [11]and if they are
ashamed of all they have done, make known to
them the design of the temple—its arrangement,
its exits and entrances—its whole design and all
its regulations[d] and laws. Write these down before
them so that they may be faithful to its design and
43:11 [l]Eze 44:5 follow all its regulations.[l]
[12]"This is the law of the temple: All the sur-
43:12 rounding area[m] on top of the mountain will be
[m]Eze 40:2 most holy. Such is the law of the temple.

The Altar

43:13 [13]"These are the measurements of the altar[n] in
[n]2Ch 4:1 long cubits, that cubit being a cubit[e] and a handbreadth[f]: Its gutter is a cubit deep and a cubit wide,
with a rim of one span[g] around the edge. And this
is the height of the altar: [14]From the gutter on the
ground up to the lower ledge it is two cubits high
and a cubit wide, and from the smaller ledge up to
the larger ledge it is four cubits high and a cubit
wide. [15]The altar hearth is four cubits high, and
43:15 [o]Ex 27:2 four horns[o] project upward from the hearth. [16]The

[a] *3* Some Hebrew manuscripts and Vulgate; most Hebrew manuscripts *I* [b] *7* Or *their spiritual adultery*; also in verse 9 [c] *7* Or *the corpses*; also in verse 9 [d] *11* Some Hebrew manuscripts and Septuagint; most Hebrew manuscripts *regulations and its whole design* [e] *13* The common cubit was about 1 1/2 feet (about 0.5 meter). [f] *13* That is, about 3 inches (about 8 centimeters) [g] *13* That is, about 9 inches (about 22 centimeters)

Radiant Glory

EZE 43:2

Ezekiel's vision reaches its high point with the glory of God returning to this new temple. Ezekiel has previously recorded seeing the glory of God leave the temple (Eze 10:18). Now, from the same direction, the east, the glory of God returns (Eze 10:19; 11:23; 43:1). Throughout the Scriptures the words used to describe God's glory are consistently words of brightness and light (Ex 24:17; Lev 9:23–24; 2Ch 7:3; Eze 10:4; Lk 2:9; 2Co 4:6; Rev 21:11,23).

altar hearth is square, twelve cubits long and twelve cubits wide. 17 The upper ledge also is square, fourteen cubits long and fourteen cubits wide, with a rim of half a cubit and a gutter of a cubit all around. The steps[p] of the altar face east."

18 Then he said to me, "Son of man, this is what the Sovereign LORD says: These will be the regulations for sacrificing burnt offerings[q] and sprinkling blood[r] upon the altar when it is built: 19 You are to give a young bull[s] as a sin offering to the priests, who are Levites, of the family of Zadok,[t] who come near[u] to minister before me, declares the Sovereign LORD. 20 You are to take some of its blood and put it on the four horns of the altar and on the four corners of the upper ledge[v] and all around the rim, and so purify the altar[w] and make atonement for it. 21 You are to take the bull for the sin offering and burn it in the designated part of the temple area outside the sanctuary.[x]

22 "On the second day you are to offer a male goat without defect for a sin offering, and the altar is to be purified as it was purified with the bull. 23 When you have finished purifying it, you are to offer a young bull and a ram from the flock, both without defect.[y] 24 You are to offer them before the LORD, and the priests are to sprinkle salt[z] on them and sacrifice them as a burnt offering to the LORD.

25 "For seven days[a] you are to provide a male goat daily for a sin offering; you are also to provide a young bull and a ram from the flock, both without defect.[b] 26 For seven days they are to make atonement for the altar and cleanse it; thus they will dedicate it. 27 At the end of these days, from the eighth day[c] on, the priests are to present your burnt offerings and fellowship offerings[a][d] on the altar. Then I will accept you, declares the Sovereign LORD."

The Prince, the Levites, the Priests

44 Then the man brought me back to the outer gate of the sanctuary, the one facing east,[e] and it was shut. 2 The LORD said to me, "This gate is to remain shut. It must not be opened; no one may enter through it.[f] It is to remain shut because the LORD, the God of Israel, has entered through it. 3 The prince himself is the only one who may sit inside the gateway to eat in the presence[g] of the LORD. He is to enter by way of the portico of the gateway and go out the same way.[h]"

4 Then the man brought me by way of the north gate to the front of the temple. I looked and saw the glory of the LORD filling the temple[i] of the LORD, and I fell facedown.[j]

5 The LORD said to me, "Son of man, look carefully, listen closely and give attention to everything I tell you concerning all the regulations regarding the temple of the LORD. Give attention to the entrance of the temple and all the exits of the sanctuary.[k] 6 Say to the rebellious house[l] of Israel, 'This is what the Sovereign LORD says: Enough of your

[a] 27 Traditionally *peace offerings*

43:17 [p]Ex 20:26
43:18 [q]Ex 40:29 [r]Lev 1:5,11; Heb 9:21-22
43:19 [s]Lev 4:3; Eze 45:18-19 [t]Eze 44:15 [u]Nu 16:40; Eze 40:46
43:20 [v]ver 17 [w]Lev 16:19
43:21 [x]Ex 29:14; Heb 13:11
43:23 [y]Ex 29:1
43:24 [z]Lev 2:13; Mk 9:49-50
43:25 [a]Lev 8:33 [b]Ex 29:37
43:27 [c]Lev 9:1 [d]Lev 17:5
44:1 [e]Eze 43:1
44:2 [f]Eze 43:4-5
44:3 [g]Ex 24:9-11 [h]Eze 46:2,8
44:4 [i]Isa 6:4; Rev 15:8 [j]Eze 1:28; 3:23
44:5 [k]Eze 40:4; 43:10-11
44:6 [l]Eze 3:9

I'm very lonely now, Mary,
For the poor make no new friends;
But oh they love the better still
The few our Father sends!

—Lady Dufferin (1807–1867)

detestable practices, O house of Israel! 7 In addition to all your other detestable practices, you brought foreigners uncircumcised in heart[m] and flesh into my sanctuary, desecrating my temple while you offered me food, fat and blood, and you broke my covenant.[n] 8 Instead of carrying out your duty in regard to my holy things, you put others in charge of my sanctuary.[o] 9 This is what the Sovereign LORD says: No foreigner uncircumcised in heart and flesh is to enter my sanctuary, not even the foreigners who live among the Israelites.[p]

10 " 'The Levites who went far from me when Israel went astray[q] and who wandered from me after their idols must bear the consequences of their sin.[r] 11 They may serve in my sanctuary, having charge of the gates of the temple and serving in it; they may slaughter the burnt offerings[s] and sacrifices for the people and stand before the people and serve them.[t] 12 But because they served them in the presence of their idols and made the house of Israel fall into sin, therefore I have sworn with uplifted hand[u] that they must bear the consequences of their sin, declares the Sovereign LORD.[v] 13 They are not to come near to serve me as priests or come near any of my holy things or my most holy offerings; they must bear the shame[w] of their detestable practices.[x] 14 Yet I will put them in charge of the duties of the temple and all the work that is to be done in it.[y]

15 " 'But the priests, who are Levites and descendants of Zadok and who faithfully carried out the duties of my sanctuary when the Israelites went astray from me, are to come near to minister before me; they are to stand before me to offer sacrifices of fat and blood, declares the Sovereign LORD.[z] 16 They alone are to enter my sanctuary; they alone are to come near my table[a] to minister before me and perform my service.[b]

17 " 'When they enter the gates of the inner court, they are to wear linen clothes;[c] they must not wear any woolen garment while ministering at the gates of the inner court or inside the temple. 18 They are to wear linen turbans[d] on their heads and linen undergarments[e] around their waists. They must not wear anything that makes them perspire.[f] 19 When they go out into the outer court where the people are, they are to take off the clothes they have been ministering in and are to leave them in the sacred rooms, and put on other clothes, so that they do not consecrate[g] the people by means of their garments.[h]

20 " 'They must not shave their heads or let their hair grow long, but they are to keep the hair of their heads trimmed.[i] 21 No priest is to drink wine when he enters the inner court.[j] 22 They must not marry widows or divorced women; they may marry only virgins of Israelite descent or widows of priests.[k] 23 They are to teach my people the difference between the holy and the common[l] and show them how to distinguish between the unclean and the clean.[m]

44:7 [m]Lev 26:41 [n]Ge 17:14; Ex 12:48; Lev 22:25
44:8 [o]Lev 22:2; Nu 18:7
44:9 [p]Joel 3:17; Zec 14:21
44:10 [q]2Ki 23:8 [r]Nu 18:23
44:11 [s]2Ch 29:34 [t]Nu 3:5-37; 16:9; 1Ch 26:12-19
44:12 [u]Ps 106:26 [v]2Ki 16:10-16
44:13 [w]Eze 16:61 [x]Nu 18:3
44:14 [y]Nu 18:4; 1Ch 23:28-32
44:15 [z]Jer 33:18; Eze 40:46; Zec 3:7
44:16 [a]Eze 41:22 [b]Nu 18:5
44:17 [c]Ex 39:27-28; Rev 19:8
44:18 [d]Ex 28:39; Isa 3:20 [e]Ex 28:42 [f]Lev 16:4
44:19 [g]Lev 6:27; Eze 46:20 [h]Lev 6:10-11; Eze 42:14
44:20 [i]Lev 21:5; Nu 6:5
44:21 [j]Lev 10:9
44:22 [k]Lev 21:7
44:23 [l]Eze 22:26 [m]Mal 2:7

Linen Garments

EZE 44:17–19

Just as the Levitical priests earlier in Israel's history (Ex 28), the priests in Ezekiel's prophecy are commanded to wear special linen garments when ministering in the temple. Linen is a finer cloth than what is usually worn by most people of that day during their everyday duties. Its fineness as well as its whiteness is a sign of the purity required of the priests. The lighter weight of the fabric also keeps the priests from perspiring as they go about their duties.

No Inheritance

EZE 44:28

Ezekiel reiterates earlier commands that priests are not to own land (see the note on Nu 18:20, page 239). Their focus is not to be on providing for their own comfort or for that of their families, or on tilling the land and reaping crops, but their focus is to be on the Lord and his provision for them.

Not a bad thought for any of God's people, is it? How often do we get caught up in what we're doing to get ahead, or just trying to stay even? How much time is consumed thinking about paying bills or gathering enough to make the next purchase? God's ideal for his people is much different. As the "priesthood" (1Pe 2:9) of believers, our inheritance is to share in God and his kingdom, just as it was the inheritance of the Levitical priests.

24" 'In any dispute, the priests are to serve as judges[n] and decide it according to my ordinances. They are to keep my laws and my decrees for all my appointed feasts, and they are to keep my Sabbaths holy.[o]

25" 'A priest must not defile himself by going near a dead person; however, if the dead person was his father or mother, son or daughter, brother or unmarried sister, then he may defile himself.[p] 26After he is cleansed, he must wait seven days.[q] 27On the day he goes into the inner court of the sanctuary to minister in the sanctuary, he is to offer a sin offering for himself, declares the Sovereign LORD.

28" 'I am to be the only inheritance[r] the priests have. You are to give them no possession in Israel; I will be their possession. 29They will eat the grain offerings, the sin offerings and the guilt offerings; and everything in Israel devoted[a] to the LORD[s] will belong to them.[t] 30The best of all the firstfruits[u] and of all your special gifts will belong to the priests. You are to give them the first portion of your ground meal[v] so that a blessing[w] may rest on your household.[x] 31The priests must not eat anything, bird or animal, found dead or torn by wild animals.[y]

Division of the Land

45 " 'When you allot the land as an inheritance,[z] you are to present to the LORD a portion of the land as a sacred district, 25,000 cubits long and 20,000[b] cubits wide; the entire area will be holy.[a] 2Of this, a section 500 cubits square[b] is to be for the sanctuary, with 50 cubits around it for open land. 3In the sacred district, measure off a section 25,000 cubits[c] long and 10,000 cubits[d] wide. In it will be the sanctuary, the Most Holy Place. 4It will be the sacred portion of the land for the priests,[c] who minister in the sanctuary and who draw near to minister before the LORD. It will be a place for their houses as well as a holy place for the sanctuary.[d] 5An area 25,000 cubits long and 10,000 cubits wide will belong to the Levites, who serve in the temple, as their possession for towns to live in.[e][e]

6" 'You are to give the city as its property an area 5,000 cubits wide and 25,000 cubits long, adjoining the sacred portion; it will belong to the whole house of Israel.[f]

7" 'The prince will have the land bordering each side of the area formed by the sacred district and the property of the city. It will extend westward from the west side and eastward from the east side, running lengthwise from the western to the eastern border parallel to one of the tribal por-

44:24 [n]Dt 17:8-9; 1Ch 23:4 [o]2Ch 19:8
44:25 [p]Lev 21:1-4
44:26 [q]Nu 19:14
44:28 [r]Nu 18:20; Dt 10:9; 18:1-2; Jos 13:33
44:29 [s]Lev 27:21 [t]Nu 18:9,14
44:30 [u]Nu 18:12-13 [v]Nu 15:18-21 [w]Mal 3:10 [x]Ne 10:35-37
44:31 [y]Ex 22:31; Lev 22:8
45:1 [z]Eze 47:21-22 [a]Eze 48:8-9, 29
45:2 [b]Eze 42:20
45:4 [c]Eze 40:46 [d]Eze 48:10-11
45:5 [e]Eze 48:13
45:6 [f]Eze 48:15-18

[a] *29* The Hebrew term refers to the irrevocable giving over of things or persons to the LORD. [b] *1* Septuagint (see also verses 3 and 5 and 48:9); Hebrew *10,000* [c] *3* That is, about 7 miles (about 12 kilometers) [d] *3* That is, about 3 miles (about 5 kilometers) [e] *5* Septuagint; Hebrew *temple; they will have as their possession 20 rooms*

tions.[g] 8This land will be his possession in Israel.
And my princes will no longer oppress my people
but will allow the house of Israel to possess the
land according to their tribes.[h]
9" 'This is what the Sovereign LORD says: You
have gone far enough, O princes of Israel! Give up
your violence and oppression and do what is just
and right.[i] Stop dispossessing my people, declares
the Sovereign LORD. 10You are to use accurate
scales,[j] an accurate ephah[a][k] and an accurate bath.[b]
11The ephah[l] and the bath are to be the same size,
the bath containing a tenth of a homer[c] and the
ephah a tenth of a homer; the homer is to be the
standard measure for both. 12The shekel[d] is to consist of twenty gerahs.[m] Twenty shekels plus twenty-
five shekels plus fifteen shekels equal one mina.[e]

Offerings and Holy Days

13" 'This is the special gift you are to offer: a
sixth of an ephah from each homer of wheat and
a sixth of an ephah from each homer of barley.
14The prescribed portion of oil, measured by the
bath, is a tenth of a bath from each cor (which
consists of ten baths or one homer, for ten baths
are equivalent to a homer). 15Also one sheep is to
be taken from every flock of two hundred from
the well-watered pastures of Israel. These will be
used for the grain offerings, burnt offerings[n] and
fellowship offerings[f] to make atonement[o] for the
people, declares the Sovereign LORD. 16All the people of the land will participate in this special gift
for the use of the prince in Israel. 17It will be the
duty of the prince to provide the burnt offerings,
grain offerings and drink offerings at the festivals,
the New Moons and the Sabbaths[p]—at all the
appointed feasts of the house of Israel. He will
provide the sin offerings, grain offerings, burnt
offerings and fellowship offerings to make atonement for the house of Israel.[q]
18" 'This is what the Sovereign LORD says: In the
first month[r] on the first day you are to take a
young bull without defect[s] and purify the sanctuary.[t] 19The priest is to take some of the blood of
the sin offering and put it on the doorposts of the
temple, on the four corners of the upper ledge[u] of
the altar[v] and on the gateposts of the inner court.
20You are to do the same on the seventh day of the
month for anyone who sins unintentionally[w] or
through ignorance; so you are to make atonement
for the temple.
21" 'In the first month on the fourteenth day you
are to observe the Passover,[x] a feast lasting seven
days, during which you shall eat bread made
without yeast. 22On that day the prince is to provide a bull as a sin offering for himself and for all
the people of the land.[y] 23Every day during the

[a] *10* An ephah was a dry measure. [b] *10* A bath was a liquid measure. [c] *11* A homer was a dry measure. [d] *12* A shekel weighed about 2/5 ounce (about 11.5 grams). [e] *12* That is, 60 shekels; the common mina was 50 shekels.
[f] *15* Traditionally *peace offerings*; also in verse 17

45:7 [g]Eze 48:21
45:8 [h]Nu 26:53; Eze 46:18
45:9 [i]Jer 22:3; Zec 7:9-10; 8:16
45:10 [j]Dt 25:15; Pr 11:1; Am 8:4-6; Mic 6:10-11 [k]Lev 19:36
45:11 [l]Isa 5:10
45:12 [m]Ex 30:13; Lev 27:25; Nu 3:47
45:15 [n]Lev 1:4 [o]Lev 6:30
45:17 [p]Lev 23:38; Isa 66:23 [q]1Ki 8:62; 2Ch 31:3; Eze 46:4-12
45:18 [r]Ex 12:2 [s]Lev 22:20; Heb 9:14 [t]Lev 16:16, 33
45:19 [u]Eze 43:17 [v]Lev 16:18-19; Eze 43:20
45:20 [w]Lev 4:27
45:21 [x]Ex 12:11; Lev 23:5-6
45:22 [y]Lev 4:14

Honest Weights

EZE 45:10

"Honesty is the best policy," the old adage goes. God not only agrees, but is also the author of honesty, the Creator of integrity. He is concerned throughout the Old Testament with honesty, and he commands his people to use accurate scales and measures when dealing with each other* (Dt 25:15; Pr 11:1). *The prophets rebuke the people again and again for their inaccurate weights and scales* (Mic 6:10–11) *and for their injustice when dealing with each other, especially with those who are most helpless* (Isa 1:17). *Their dishonesty is one of the reasons they are now in exile, and Ezekiel wants to be sure they don't return to their former ways of injustice.

The Eastern Gates

EZE 46:1

The eastern gate of the inner court is to be closed on the six working days of the week, but it is to be opened on the Sabbath and during the New Moon Festival, obviously so the people can enter the temple for worship on those days.

In contrast, the eastern gate of the outer court is to be permanently closed according to Ezekiel 44:2. Ezekiel not only saw God's glory leave the temple through this gate (Eze 10:18–19), but he also saw God's glory return through this gate (Eze 43:1–4). Perhaps this gate is now to remain closed because God's entrance through it has made it holy. Perhaps the gate is to remain closed because God will never again vacate the temple; or perhaps it is to be closed to prevent worship of the sun. Interestingly, the eastern gate into the Moslem mosque that now resides on the temple mount is also permanently closed because of a tradition that is perhaps related to this one in Ezekiel.

seven days of the Feast he is to provide seven bulls
and seven rams[z] without defect as a burnt offering
to the LORD, and a male goat for a sin offering.[a]
24 He is to provide as a grain offering[b] an ephah for
each bull and an ephah for each ram, along with
a hin[a] of oil for each ephah.[c]
25 " 'During the seven days of the Feast,[d] which
begins in the seventh month on the fifteenth day,
he is to make the same provision for sin offerings,
burnt offerings, grain offerings and oil.[e]

46

" 'This is what the Sovereign LORD says:
The gate of the inner court[f] facing east[g] is
to be shut on the six working days, but on the
Sabbath day and on the day of the New Moon[h] it
is to be opened. 2 The prince is to enter from the
outside through the portico[i] of the gateway and
stand by the gatepost. The priests are to sacrifice
his burnt offering and his fellowship offerings.[b]
He is to worship at the threshold of the gateway
and then go out, but the gate will not be shut
until evening.[j] 3 On the Sabbaths and New Moons
the people of the land are to worship in the presence
of the LORD at the entrance to that gateway.[k]
4 The burnt offering the prince brings to the LORD
on the Sabbath day is to be six male lambs and a
ram, all without defect. 5 The grain offering given
with the ram is to be an ephah,[c] and the grain
offering with the lambs is to be as much as he
pleases, along with a hin[a] of oil for each ephah.[l]
6 On the day of the New Moon[m] he is to offer a
young bull, six lambs and a ram, all without
defect. 7 He is to provide as a grain offering one
ephah with the bull, one ephah with the ram,
and with the lambs as much as he wants to give,
along with a hin of oil with each ephah.[n] 8 When
the prince enters, he is to go in through the portico[o]
of the gateway, and he is to come out the
same way.[p]
9 " 'When the people of the land come before the
LORD at the appointed feasts,[q] whoever enters by
the north gate to worship is to go out the south
gate; and whoever enters by the south gate is to go
out the north gate. No one is to return through the
gate by which he entered, but each is to go out
the opposite gate. 10 The prince is to be among
them, going in when they go in and going out
when they go out.[r]
11 " 'At the festivals and the appointed feasts, the
grain offering is to be an ephah with a bull, an
ephah with a ram, and with the lambs as much
as one pleases, along with a hin of oil for each
ephah.[s] 12 When the prince provides[t] a freewill
offering[u] to the LORD—whether a burnt offering or
fellowship offerings—the gate facing east is to be
opened for him. He shall offer his burnt offering
or his fellowship offerings as he does on the Sab-

45:23 [z]Job 42:8 [a]Nu 28:16-25
45:24 [b]Nu 28:12-13 [c]Eze 46:5-7
45:25 [d]Dt 16:13 [e]Lev 23:34-43; Nu 29:12-38
46:1 [f]Eze 40:19 [g]1Ch 9:18 [h]ver 6; Isa 66:23
46:2 [i]ver 8 [j]ver 12; Eze 44:3
46:3 [k]Lk 1:10
46:5 [l]ver 11; Eze 45:24
46:6 [m]ver 1; Nu 10:10
46:7 [n]Eze 45:24
46:8 [o]ver 2 [p]Eze 44:3
46:9 [q]Ex 23:14; 34:20
46:10 [r]2Sa 6:14-15; Ps 42:4
46:11 [s]ver 5
46:12 [t]Eze 45:17 [u]Lev 7:16

[a] *24* That is, probably about 4 quarts (about 4 liters)
[b] *2* Traditionally *peace offerings*; also in verse 12
[c] *5* That is, probably about 3/5 bushel (about 22 liters)

46:12 bath day. Then he shall go out, and after he has
[v]ver 2 gone out, the gate will be shut.[v]
13" 'Every day you are to provide a year-old
46:13 lamb without defect for a burnt offering to the
[w]Ex 29:38; LORD; morning by morning you shall provide it.[w]
Nu 28:3 14You are also to provide with it morning by morning a grain offering, consisting of a sixth of an
ephah with a third of a hin of oil to moisten the
46:14 flour. The presenting of this grain offering to the
[x]Da 8:11 LORD is a lasting ordinance.[x] 15So the lamb and the
46:15 grain offering and the oil shall be provided morn-
[y]Ex 29:42 ing by morning for a regular[y] burnt offering.[z]
[z]Ex 29:38; 16" 'This is what the Sovereign LORD says: If the
Nu 28:5-6 prince makes a gift from his inheritance to one of
46:16 his sons, it will also belong to his descendants; it
[a]2Ch 21:3 is to be their property by inheritance.[a] 17If, however, he makes a gift from his inheritance to one
46:17 of his servants, the servant may keep it until the
[b]Lev 25:10 year of freedom;[b] then it will revert to the prince.
His inheritance belongs to his sons only; it is
46:18 theirs. 18The prince must not take any of the
[c]Lev 25:23; inheritance[c] of the people, driving them off their
Eze 45:8; property. He is to give his sons their inheritance
Mic 2:1-2 out of his own property, so that none of my people
will be separated from his property.' "
19Then the man brought me through the
46:19 entrance[d] at the side of the gate to the sacred
[d]Eze 42:9 rooms facing north, which belonged to the priests,
and showed me a place at the western end. 20He
said to me, "This is the place where the priests will
cook the guilt offering and the sin offering and
46:20 bake the grain offering, to avoid bringing them
[e]Lev 6:27 into the outer court and consecrating[e] the people."[f]
[f]Zec 14:20 21He then brought me to the outer court and led
me around to its four corners, and I saw in each
corner another court. 22In the four corners of the
outer court were enclosed[a] courts, forty cubits
long and thirty cubits wide; each of the courts in
the four corners was the same size. 23Around the
inside of each of the four courts was a ledge of
stone, with places for fire built all around under
the ledge. 24He said to me, "These are the kitchens
where those who minister at the temple will cook
the sacrifices of the people."

The River From the Temple

47:1 **47** The man brought me back to the entrance
[g]Isa 55:1 of the temple, and I saw water[g] coming out
[h]Ps 46:4; Joel 3:18; from under the threshold of the temple toward the
Rev 22:1 east (for the temple faced east). The water was
coming down from under the south side of the
temple, south of the altar.[h] 2He then brought me
out through the north gate and led me around the
outside to the outer gate facing east, and the water
was flowing from the south side.
47:3 3As the man went eastward with a measuring
[i]Eze 40:3 line[i] in his hand, he measured off a thousand
cubits[b] and then led me through water that was

[a] *22* The meaning of the Hebrew for this word is uncertain.
[b] *3* That is, about 1,500 feet (about 450 meters)

The River

EZE 47:1-3

Ezekiel's divine messenger now leads him on an exploration of an amazing river. This river flows from beneath the south side of the temple all the way east to the Dead Sea (Eze 47:8). Trees grow in healthy numbers all along the river, and they bear fruit on a monthly cycle (Eze 47:12). When the river's waters empty into the Dead Sea, that water comes to life with fish of many kinds (Eze 47:9), a wonderful picture of God's fruitful and healthy future provision.

More on the River

EZE 47:7–12

The river Ezekiel describes here can be compared to the river that flows from the throne of God in John's revelation (Rev 22:1–2). Both are pictures of the life-giving nature of God. He will come in the last days, heal the land and make it new. The refreshing waters, the leafy trees, the healthy crops of fruit—all are pictures of God's eternal provision for his people.

ankle-deep. 4 He measured off another thousand
cubits and led me through water that was knee-
deep. He measured off another thousand and led
me through water that was up to the waist. 5 He
measured off another thousand, but now it was a
river that I could not cross, because the water had
risen and was deep enough to swim in—a river
that no one could cross.[j] 6 He asked me, "Son of
man, do you see this?"

Then he led me back to the bank of the river.
7 When I arrived there, I saw a great number of
trees on each side of the river.[k] 8 He said to me,
"This water flows toward the eastern region and
goes down into the Arabah,[a][l] where it enters the
Sea.[b] When it empties into the Sea,[d] the water
there becomes fresh.[m] 9 Swarms of living creatures
will live wherever the river flows. There will be
large numbers of fish, because this water flows
there and makes the salt water fresh; so where the
river flows everything will live.[n] 10 Fishermen[o] will
stand along the shore; from En Gedi[p] to En Eglaim
there will be places for spreading nets.[q] The fish
will be of many kinds[r]—like the fish of the Great
Sea.[c][s] 11 But the swamps and marshes will not
become fresh; they will be left for salt.[t] 12 Fruit trees
of all kinds will grow on both banks of the river.[u]
Their leaves will not wither, nor will their fruit[v]
fail. Every month they will bear, because the water
from the sanctuary flows to them. Their fruit will
serve for food and their leaves for healing.[w]"

The Boundaries of the Land

13 This is what the Sovereign LORD says: "These
are the boundaries[x] by which you are to divide
the land for an inheritance among the twelve
tribes of Israel, with two portions for Joseph.[y]
14 You are to divide it equally among them.
Because I swore with uplifted hand to give it to
your forefathers, this land will become your
inheritance.[z]

15 "This is to be the boundary of the land:

"On the north side it will run from the Great Sea
by the Hethlon road[a] past Lebo[d] Hamath to
Zedad, 16 Berothah[e][b] and Sibraim (which lies
on the border between Damascus and
Hamath),[c] as far as Hazer Hatticon, which is
on the border of Hauran. 17 The boundary will
extend from the sea to Hazar Enan,[f] along the
northern border of Damascus, with the border of Hamath to the north. This will be the
north boundary.[d]

18 "On the east side the boundary will run
between Hauran and Damascus, along the
Jordan between Gilead and the land of Israel,

47:5 [j]Isa 11:9; Hab 2:14
47:7 [k]ver 12; Rev 22:2
47:8 [l]Dt 3:17; Jos 3:16 [m]Isa 41:18
47:9 [n]Isa 12:3; 55:1; Jn 4:14; 7:37-38
47:10 [o]Mt 4:19 [p]Jos 15:62 [q]Eze 26:5 [r]Ps 104:25; Mt 13:47 [s]Nu 34:6
47:11 [t]Dt 29:23
47:12 [u]ver 7; Rev 22:2 [v]Ps 1:3 [w]Ge 2:9; Jer 17:8
47:13 [x]Nu 34:2-12 [y]Ge 48:5
47:14 [z]Ge 12:7; Dt 1:8; Eze 20:5-6
47:15 [a]Eze 48:1
47:16 [b]2Sa 8:8 [c]Nu 13:21; Eze 48:1
47:17 [d]Eze 48:1

[a] 8 Or *the Jordan Valley* [b] 8 That is, the Dead Sea
[c] 10 That is, the Mediterranean; also in verses 15, 19 and 20
[d] 15 Or *past the entrance to* [e] 15,16 See Septuagint and Ezekiel 48:1; Hebrew *road to go into Zedad, 16 Hamath, Berothah* [f] 17 Hebrew *Enon,* a variant of *Enan*

to the eastern sea and as far as Tamar.[a] This
will be the east boundary.
19“On the south side it will run from Tamar as far
as the waters of Meribah Kadesh,[e] then along
the Wadi ⌊of Egypt⌋[f] to the Great Sea.[g] This
will be the south boundary.
20“On the west side, the Great Sea will be the
boundary to a point opposite Lebo[b] Hamath.[h]
This will be the west boundary.[i]

21“You are to distribute this land among yourselves according to the tribes of Israel. 22You are to
allot it as an inheritance for yourselves and for the
aliens[j] who have settled among you and who have
children. You are to consider them as native-born
Israelites; along with you they are to be allotted an
inheritance among the tribes of Israel.[k] 23In whatever tribe the alien settles, there you are to give
him his inheritance,” declares the Sovereign LORD.

The Division of the Land

48 “These are the tribes, listed by name: At the
northern frontier, Dan[l] will have one portion; it will follow the Hethlon road[m] to Lebo[c]
Hamath;[n] Hazar Enan and the northern border of
Damascus next to Hamath will be part of its border from the east side to the west side.
2“Asher[o] will have one portion; it will border
the territory of Dan from east to west.
3“Naphtali[p] will have one portion; it will border
the territory of Asher from east to west.
4“Manasseh[q] will have one portion; it will border the territory of Naphtali from east to west.
5“Ephraim[r] will have one portion; it will border
the territory of Manasseh[s] from east to west.[t]
6“Reuben[u] will have one portion; it will border
the territory of Ephraim from east to west.
7“Judah[v] will have one portion; it will border
the territory of Reuben from east to west.
8“Bordering the territory of Judah from east to
west will be the portion you are to present as a
special gift. It will be 25,000 cubits[d] wide, and its
length from east to west will equal one of the tribal portions; the sanctuary will be in the center
of it.[w]
9“The special portion you are to offer to the
LORD will be 25,000 cubits long and 10,000 cubits[e]
wide.[x] 10This will be the sacred portion for the
priests. It will be 25,000 cubits long on the north
side, 10,000 cubits wide on the west side, 10,000
cubits wide on the east side and 25,000 cubits
long on the south side. In the center of it will be
the sanctuary of the LORD.[y] 11This will be for the
consecrated priests, the Zadokites,[z] who were
faithful in serving me[a] and did not go astray as
the Levites did when the Israelites went astray.[b]
12It will be a special gift to them from the sacred

47:19 [e]Dt 32:51 [f]Isa 27:12 [g]Eze 48:28
47:20 [h]Eze 48:1 [i]Nu 34:6
47:22 [j]Isa 14:1 [k]Nu 26:55-56; Isa 56:6-7; Ro 10:12; Eph 2:12-16; 3:6; Col 3:11
48:1 [l]Ge 30:6 [m]Eze 47:15-17 [n]Eze 47:20
48:2 [o]Jos 19:24-31
48:3 [p]Jos 19:32-39
48:4 [q]Jos 17:1-11
48:5 [r]Jos 16:5-9 [s]Jos 17:7-10 [t]Jos 17:17
48:6 [u]Jos 13:15-21
48:7 [v]Jos 15:1-63
48:8 [w]ver 21
48:9 [x]Eze 45:1
48:10 [y]ver 21; Eze 45:3-4
48:11 [z]2Sa 8:17 [a]Lev 8:35 [b]Eze 14:11; 44:15

[a] *18* Septuagint and Syriac; Hebrew *Israel. You will measure to the eastern sea* [b] *20* Or *opposite the entrance to* [c] *1* Or *to the entrance to* [d] *8* That is, about 7 miles (about 12 kilometers) [e] *9* That is, about 3 miles (about 5 kilometers)

Little deeds of kindness, little words of love,
Help to make earth happy like the heaven above.

—Julia A. Fletcher Carney (1824-1908)

portion of the land, a most holy portion, bordering the territory of the Levites.

13 "Alongside the territory of the priests, the Levites will have an allotment 25,000 cubits long and 10,000 cubits wide. Its total length will be 25,000 cubits and its width 10,000 cubits.[c] 14 They must not sell or exchange any of it. This is the best of the land and must not pass into other hands, because it is holy to the LORD.[d]

15 "The remaining area, 5,000 cubits wide and 25,000 cubits long, will be for the common use of the city, for houses and for pastureland. The city will be in the center of it 16 and will have these measurements: the north side 4,500 cubits, the south side 4,500 cubits, the east side 4,500 cubits, and the west side 4,500 cubits.[e] 17 The pastureland for the city will be 250 cubits on the north, 250 cubits on the south, 250 cubits on the east, and 250 cubits on the west. 18 What remains of the area, bordering on the sacred portion and running the length of it, will be 10,000 cubits on the east side and 10,000 cubits on the west side. Its produce will supply food for the workers of the city.[f] 19 The workers from the city who farm it will come from all the tribes of Israel. 20 The entire portion will be a square, 25,000 cubits on each side. As a special gift you will set aside the sacred portion, along with the property of the city.

21 "What remains on both sides of the area formed by the sacred portion and the city property will belong to the prince. It will extend eastward from the 25,000 cubits of the sacred portion to the eastern border, and westward from the 25,000 cubits to the western border. Both these areas running the length of the tribal portions will belong to the prince, and the sacred portion with the temple sanctuary will be in the center of them.[g] 22 So the property of the Levites and the property of the city will lie in the center of the area that belongs to the prince. The area belonging to the prince will lie between the border of Judah and the border of Benjamin.

23 "As for the rest of the tribes: Benjamin[h] will have one portion; it will extend from the east side to the west side.

24 "Simeon[i] will have one portion; it will border the territory of Benjamin from east to west.

25 "Issachar[j] will have one portion; it will border the territory of Simeon from east to west.

26 "Zebulun[k] will have one portion; it will border the territory of Issachar from east to west.

27 "Gad[l] will have one portion; it will border the territory of Zebulun from east to west.

28 "The southern boundary of Gad will run south from Tamar[m] to the waters of Meribah Kadesh, then along the Wadi ⌊of Egypt⌋ to the Great Sea.[a][n]

29 "This is the land you are to allot as an inheri-

48:13 [c]Eze 45:5
48:14 [d]Lev 25:34; 27:10,28
48:16 [e]Rev 21:16
48:18 [f]Eze 45:6
48:21 [g]ver 8, 10; Eze 45:7
48:23 [h]Jos 18:11-28
48:24 [i]Ge 29:33; Jos 19:1-9
48:25 [j]Jos 19:17-23
48:26 [k]Jos 19:10-16
48:27 [l]Jos 13:24-28
48:28 [m]Ge 14:7 [n]Eze 47:19

In the trials we've faced, something good has happened: God has fine-tuned us so we are more compassionate, more caring, more loving, more aware of others' pain.

—Barbara Johnson

[a] *28* That is, the Mediterranean

tance to the tribes of Israel, and these will be their
portions," declares the Sovereign LORD.

The Gates of the City

30"These will be the exits of the city: Beginning
on the north side, which is 4,500 cubits long, 31the
gates of the city will be named after the tribes of
Israel. The three gates on the north side will be
the gate of Reuben, the gate of Judah and the gate
of Levi.

32"On the east side, which is 4,500 cubits long,
will be three gates: the gate of Joseph, the gate of
Benjamin and the gate of Dan.

33"On the south side, which measures 4,500
cubits, will be three gates: the gate of Simeon, the
gate of Issachar and the gate of Zebulun.

34"On the west side, which is 4,500 cubits long,
will be three gates: the gate of Gad, the gate of
Asher and the gate of Naphtali.

35"The distance all around will be 18,000 cubits.

"And the name of the city from that time on
will be:

THE LORD IS THERE.[o]"

48:35 [o]Isa 12:6; 24:23; Jer 3:17; 14:9; Jer 33:16; Joel 3:21; Zec 2:10; Rev 21:3

THE LORD IS THERE

EZE 48:35

What more needs to be said? "THE LORD IS THERE." ***The city has a new name, one that brings up images of peace, fulfillment, contentment and excitement. What a wonderful place God will eventually call his people to share with him. No more separation. No more striving. No more wondering if we measure up. Everything is finalized and beautifully fulfilled, just as he has promised. The Lord is there. We'll be there too. Praise him!***

God's ultimate sovereignty.

Written to encourage the exiles in Babylon, the book of Daniel reminds God's people of God's ultimate control over human history. Daniel, exiled to Babylon while still a young man, rises through the ranks of the royal court to become a trusted adviser to several Babylonian (and Persian) kings. A man of flawless integrity, Daniel also becomes a significant prophet in Israel's history, recording God's plan for the rise and fall of several empires, demonstrating God's power over human government while protecting those who trust in him.

Daniel begins this book by detailing his life in Babylon and relating the importance of obeying God in all details of life (Da 1). In response to Daniel's faithfulness, God gives him the ability to interpret one king's dreams and a mysterious, handwritten message that appears on another king's palace wall (Da 2; 4; 5). Yet even this supernatural skill does not remove Daniel and his friends from situations that test their faith in God (Da 3; 6). The book ends with Daniel's visions of God's power and sovereignty over Gentile nations and with visions of a righteous kingdom that will last forever (Da 7–12).

The many Jews exiled in Babylon feared that God had forgotten them, that he was no longer in control of the swirl of human events. Daniel's life and prophecies gave them—and us—hope and restored their faith in the sovereignty of their God. Life may appear to be running out of control, but Daniel's words assure us that is not the case. God *is* in control, and we can safely frame our lives on resolute trust in his care.

Quick Study

Author
The prophet Daniel.

Date Written
Daniel probably wrote near the end of his life, around 530 B.C.

Setting
Babylon.

Key Passage
Daniel 9:18–19 "Give ear, O God, and hear; open your eyes and see the desolation of the city that bears your Name. We do not make requests of you because we are righteous, but because of your great mercy. O Lord, listen! O Lord, forgive! O Lord, hear and act! For your sake, O my God, do not delay, because your city and your people bear your Name."

Outline

The Women of Daniel

⚘ Denotes a sketch written about this character

From Hostages to Princes

DA 1:3-7

King Nebuchadnezzar enlists Ashpenaz, principal of the royal academy, to instruct and transform promising young Jewish boys into cultured Babylonian princes. Daniel and his three companions excel above all the others (Da 1:19). King Nebuchadnezzar questions them, and they have answers that are far better than anything the king can get from the most respected "magicians and enchanters" (Da 1:20) in his kingdom—ten times better in fact. What the king doesn't know, however, is that the God of Israel is the One who gives these young men all their knowledge and wisdom and understanding. Future events will, however, reveal this truth to him.

Daniel's Training in Babylon

1 In the third year of the reign of Jehoiakim king
of Judah, Nebuchadnezzar[a] king of Babylon
came to Jerusalem and besieged it.[b] 2And the Lord
delivered Jehoiakim king of Judah into his hand,
along with some of the articles from the temple of
God. These he carried off to the temple of his god
in Babylonia[a] and put in the treasure house of his
god.[c]
3Then the king ordered Ashpenaz, chief of his
court officials, to bring in some of the Israelites
from the royal family and the nobility[d]— 4young
men without any physical defect, handsome,
showing aptitude for every kind of learning, well
informed, quick to understand, and qualified to
serve in the king's palace. He was to teach them
the language and literature of the Babylonians.[b]
5The king assigned them a daily amount of food
and wine[e] from the king's table. They were to be
trained for three years, and after that they were to
enter the king's service.[f]
6Among these were some from Judah: Daniel,[g]
Hananiah, Mishael and Azariah. 7The chief official gave them new names: to Daniel, the name
Belteshazzar;[h] to Hananiah, Shadrach; to Mishael,
Meshach; and to Azariah, Abednego.[i]
8But Daniel resolved not to defile[j] himself with
the royal food and wine, and he asked the chief
official for permission not to defile himself this
way. 9Now God had caused the official to show
favor[k] and sympathy[l] to Daniel, 10but the official
told Daniel, "I am afraid of my lord the king, who
has assigned your[c] food and drink. Why should
he see you looking worse than the other young
men your age? The king would then have my
head because of you."
11Daniel then said to the guard whom the chief
official had appointed over Daniel, Hananiah,
Mishael and Azariah, 12"Please test your servants
for ten days: Give us nothing but vegetables to eat
and water to drink. 13Then compare our appearance with that of the young men who eat the royal food, and treat your servants in accordance
with what you see." 14So he agreed to this and
tested them for ten days.
15At the end of the ten days they looked health-
ier and better nourished than any of the young
men who ate the royal food.[m] 16So the guard took
away their choice food and the wine they were to
drink and gave them vegetables instead.[n]
17To these four young men God gave knowledge
and understanding[o] of all kinds of literature and
learning.[p] And Daniel could understand visions
and dreams of all kinds.[q]
18At the end of the time[r] set by the king to bring
them in, the chief official presented them to Nebuchadnezzar. 19The king talked with them, and he
found none equal to Daniel, Hananiah, Mishael

1:1 [a]2Ki 24:1 [b]2Ch 36:6
1:2 [c]2Ch 36:7; Jer 27:19-20; Zec 5:5-11
1:3 [d]2Ki 20:18; 24:15; Isa 39:7
1:5 [e]ver 8,10 [f]ver 19
1:6 [g]Eze 14:14
1:7 [h]Da 4:8; 5:12 [i]Da 2:49; 3:12
1:8 [j]Eze 4:13-14
1:9 [k]Ge 39:21; Pr 16:7 [l]1Ki 8:50; Ps 106:46
1:15 [m]Ex 23:25
1:16 [n]ver 12-13
1:17 [o]1Ki 3:12 [p]Da 2:23; Jas 1:5 [q]Da 2:19,30; 7:1; 8:1
1:18 [r]ver 5

[a] 2 Hebrew *Shinar* [b] 4 Or *Chaldeans* [c] 10 The Hebrew for *your* and *you* in this verse is plural.

1:19 and Azariah; so they entered the king's service.[s]
[s]Ge 41:46 20 In every matter of wisdom and understanding
about which the king questioned them, he found
1:20 them ten times better than all the magicians and
[t]1Ki 4:30; enchanters in his whole kingdom.[t]
Da 2:13,28 21 And Daniel remained there until the first year
1:21 of King Cyrus.[u]
[u]Da 6:28; 10:1

Nebuchadnezzar's Dream

2 In the second year of his reign, Nebuchadnez-
2:1 zar had dreams;[v] his mind was troubled[w] and
[v]Job 33:15, 18; Da 4:5 he could not sleep.[x] 2 So the king summoned the
[w]Ge 41:8 magicians,[y] enchanters, sorcerers[z] and astrolo-
[x]Est 6:1; Da 6:18 gers[a][a] to tell him what he had dreamed.[b] When
they came in and stood before the king, 3 he said
2:2 to them, "I have had a dream that troubles[c] me
[y]Ge 41:8 and I want to know what it means.[b]"
[z]Ex 7:11 4 Then the astrologers answered the king in Ara-
[a]ver 10; Da 5:7 maic,[c][d] "O king, live forever![e] Tell your servants
[b]Da 4:6 the dream, and we will interpret it."
2:3 5 The king replied to the astrologers, "This is
[c]Da 4:5 what I have firmly decided: If you do not tell me
2:4 what my dream was and interpret it, I will have
[d]Ezr 4:7 you cut into pieces[f] and your houses turned into
[e]Da 3:9; 5:10 piles of rubble.[g] 6 But if you tell me the dream and
2:5 explain it, you will receive from me gifts and
[f]ver 12 rewards and great honor.[h] So tell me the dream
[g]Ezr 6:11; Da 3:29 and interpret it for me."
2:6 7 Once more they replied, "Let the king tell his
[h]ver 48; Da 5:7,16 servants the dream, and we will interpret it."
8 Then the king answered, "I am certain that you
are trying to gain time, because you realize that
this is what I have firmly decided: 9 If you do not
2:9 tell me the dream, there is just one penalty[i] for
[i]Est 4:11 you. You have conspired to tell me misleading and
[j]Isa 41:22-24 wicked things, hoping the situation will change.
So then, tell me the dream, and I will know that
you can interpret it for me."[j]
10 The astrologers answered the king, "There is
not a man on earth who can do what the king
asks! No king, however great and mighty, has
ever asked such a thing of any magician or
2:10 enchanter or astrologer.[k] 11 What the king asks is
[k]ver 27 too difficult. No one can reveal it to the king
2:11 except the gods,[l] and they do not live among
[l]Da 5:11 men."
2:12 12 This made the king so angry and furious[m] that
[m]Da 3:13,19 he ordered the execution[n] of all the wise men of
[n]ver 5 Babylon. 13 So the decree was issued to put the
2:13 wise men to death, and men were sent to look for
[o]Da 1:20 Daniel and his friends to put them to death.[o]
14 When Arioch, the commander of the king's
guard, had gone out to put to death the wise men
of Babylon, Daniel spoke to him with wisdom and
tact. 15 He asked the king's officer, "Why did the
king issue such a harsh decree?" Arioch then
explained the matter to Daniel. 16 At this, Daniel

[a] *2* Or *Chaldeans;* also in verses 4, 5 and 10 [b] *3* Or *was*
[c] *4* The text from here through chapter 7 is in Aramaic.

Dreams

DA 2:5

In ancient times, dreams were considered important as a means of foretelling the future and communicating the will of the gods. Interpreting dreams was the responsibility of the magicians, sorcerers and astrologers in the king's court. Formulas, books, astrological signs and discussions all played a part in determining the meaning of a dream.

The king's threat to kill all the wise men of Babylon if his dream isn't revealed and interpreted extends to Daniel and his friends. In order to stay the execution order, they turn to God, the only One who has the ability to do what the king asks.

Revealer of Dreams

DA 2:26–30

Daniel acknowledges God in heaven as the One who reveals mysteries and interprets dreams. Daniel knows this with certainty because he and his friends cried out to God in the night asking for wisdom to interpret the king's dream (Da 2:18) and received it. When Daniel's prayer is answered, he willingly praises God—both alone (Da 2:19) and before the king (Da 2:28)—as the One who "reveals deep and hidden things" (Da 2:22).

went in to the king and asked for time, so that he might interpret the dream for him.

17 Then Daniel returned to his house and explained the matter to his friends Hananiah, Mishael and Azariah.[p] 18 He urged them to plead for mercy[q] from the God of heaven concerning this mystery,[r] so that he and his friends might not be executed with the rest of the wise men of Babylon. 19 During the night the mystery[s] was revealed to Daniel in a vision.[t] Then Daniel praised the God of heaven 20 and said:

"Praise be to the name of God for ever
and ever;[u]
wisdom and power[v] are his.
21 He changes times and seasons;[w]
he sets up kings and deposes[x] them.
He gives wisdom[y] to the wise
and knowledge to the discerning.
22 He reveals deep and hidden things;[z]
he knows what lies in darkness,[a]
and light[b] dwells with him.
23 I thank and praise you, O God of my
fathers:[c]
You have given me wisdom[d] and
power,
you have made known to me what we
asked of you,
you have made known to us the
dream of the king."

Daniel Interprets the Dream

24 Then Daniel went to Arioch,[e] whom the king had appointed to execute the wise men of Babylon, and said to him, "Do not execute the wise men of Babylon. Take me to the king, and I will interpret his dream for him."

25 Arioch took Daniel to the king at once and said, "I have found a man among the exiles from Judah[f] who can tell the king what his dream means."

26 The king asked Daniel (also called Belteshazzar),[g] "Are you able to tell me what I saw in my dream and interpret it?"

27 Daniel replied, "No wise man, enchanter, magician or diviner can explain to the king the mystery he has asked about,[h] 28 but there is a God in heaven who reveals mysteries.[i] He has shown King Nebuchadnezzar what will happen in days to come.[j] Your dream and the visions that passed through your mind[k] as you lay on your bed are these:

29 "As you were lying there, O king, your mind turned to things to come, and the revealer of mysteries showed you what is going to happen. 30 As for me, this mystery has been revealed[l] to me, not because I have greater wisdom than other living men, but so that you, O king, may know the interpretation and that you may understand what went through your mind.

31 "You looked, O king, and there before you stood a large statue—an enormous, dazzling stat-

2:17 [p]Da 1:6
2:18 [q]Isa 37:4 [r]Jer 33:3
2:19 [s]ver 28 [t]Job 33:15; Da 1:17
2:20 [u]Ps 113:2; 145:1-2 [v]Jer 32:19
2:21 [w]Da 7:25 [x]Job 12:19; Ps 75:6-7 [y]Jas 1:5
2:22 [z]Job 12:22; Ps 25:14; Da 5:11 [a]Ps 139:11-12; Jer 23:24; Heb 4:13 [b]Isa 45:7; Jas 1:17
2:23 [c]Ex 3:15 [d]Da 1:17
2:24 [e]ver 14
2:25 [f]Da 1:6; 5:13; 6:13
2:26 [g]Da 1:7
2:27 [h]ver 10
2:28 [i]Ge 40:8; Am 4:13 [j]Ge 49:1; Da 10:14 [k]Da 4:5
2:30 [l]Isa 45:3; Da 1:17; Am 4:13

2:31 [m]Hab 1:7 ue,[m] awesome in appearance. 32The head of the
statue was made of pure gold, its chest and arms of
silver, its belly and thighs of bronze, 33its legs of
iron, its feet partly of iron and partly of baked clay.
2:34 [n]Zec 4:6 [o]ver 44-45; Ps 2:9; Isa 60:12; Da 8:25 34While you were watching, a rock was cut out,
but not by human hands.[n] It struck the statue on
its feet of iron and clay and smashed them.[o] 35Then
the iron, the clay, the bronze, the silver and the
gold were broken to pieces at the same time and
2:35 [p]Ps 1:4; 37:10; Isa 17:13 [q]Isa 2:3; Mic 4:1 became like chaff on a threshing floor in the summer. The wind swept them away[p] without leaving
a trace. But the rock that struck the statue became
a huge mountain[q] and filled the whole earth.
36"This was the dream, and now we will inter-
2:37 [r]Eze 26:7 [s]Jer 27:7 pret it to the king. 37You, O king, are the king of
kings.[r] The God of heaven has given you domin-
ion[s] and power and might and glory; 38in your
hands he has placed mankind and the beasts of
the field and the birds of the air. Wherever they
2:38 [t]Jer 27:6; Da 4:21-22 live, he has made you ruler over them all.[t] You are
that head of gold.
39"After you, another kingdom will rise, inferior
to yours. Next, a third kingdom, one of bronze,
will rule over the whole earth. 40Finally, there will
be a fourth kingdom, strong as iron—for iron
breaks and smashes everything—and as iron
breaks things to pieces, so it will crush and break
2:40 [u]Da 7:7,23 all the others.[u] 41Just as you saw that the feet and
toes were partly of baked clay and partly of iron,
so this will be a divided kingdom; yet it will have
some of the strength of iron in it, even as you saw
iron mixed with clay. 42As the toes were partly
iron and partly clay, so this kingdom will be partly strong and partly brittle. 43And just as you saw
the iron mixed with baked clay, so the people will
be a mixture and will not remain united, any
more than iron mixes with clay.
44"In the time of those kings, the God of heaven
2:44 [v]Ps 2:9; 1Co 15:24 [w]Isa 60:12 [x]Ps 145:13; Isa 9:7; Da 4:34; 6:26; 7:14, 27; Mic 4:7, 13; Lk 1:33 will set up a kingdom that will never be destroyed, nor will it be left to another people. It will
crush[v] all those kingdoms[w] and bring them to an
end, but it will itself endure forever.[x] 45This is the
meaning of the vision of the rock[y] cut out of a
mountain, but not by human hands[z]—a rock that
broke the iron, the bronze, the clay, the silver and
the gold to pieces.
2:45 [y]Isa 28:16 [z]Da 8:25 "The great God has shown the king what will
take place in the future. The dream is true and the
interpretation is trustworthy."
46Then King Nebuchadnezzar fell prostrate[a]
2:46 [a]Da 8:17; Ac 10:25 [b]Ac 14:13 before Daniel and paid him honor and ordered that
an offering[b] and incense be presented to him. 47The
king said to Daniel, "Surely your God is the God of
2:47 [c]Da 11:36 [d]Da 4:25 [e]ver 22,28 gods[c] and the Lord of kings[d] and a revealer of mysteries,[e] for you were able to reveal this mystery."
48Then the king placed Daniel in a high position and lavished many gifts on him. He made
2:48 [f]ver 6; Da 4:9; 5:11 him ruler over the entire province of Babylon and
placed him in charge of all its wise men.[f] 49More-
over, at Daniel's request the king appointed Shadrach, Meshach and Abednego administrators

The Dream Fulfilled

DA 2:36–45

Daniel foretells events that are to come to pass during and following the reign of King Nebuchadnezzar. Looking back, we can see that the gold head is the Babylonian kingdom of Nebuchadnezzar, which is conquered by the silver chest and arms of the Persian Empire. The bronze belly and thighs represent the Greek kingdom, followed by the iron legs of the Roman Empire. The identities of the kingdoms of the toes are disputed, with some scholars thinking they represent kingdoms after the Roman Empire and others thinking they represent ten kingdoms that will be united under one ruler shortly before the end of time.

The most important element of the dream is the eternal kingdom God will one day establish, a kingdom that will never be destroyed and never end (Da 2:44). We don't know the exact hour, but we do know God will reign supreme at the end of the age after the second coming of his Son Jesus.

Music DA 3:5

Babylonians play music at royal ceremonies and at worship rites, using instruments that come from Greek traders. The music described here is made by the six instruments listed as well as by "all kinds of music," referring probably to other instruments and perhaps voice. An orchestra, then, heralds the moment when all those present are to bow down to the idol erected by King Nebuchadnezzar.

Music has been an integral part of worship throughout the centuries. Moses and Miriam led the people in worship through singing and dancing and tambourine music after they passed through the Red Sea on dry ground (Ex 15). King David worshiped exuberantly with many musical instruments (2Sa 6:5) and commissioned singers for worship (1Ch 15:16). King Solomon wrote "a thousand and five" songs (1Ki 4:32) and employed hundreds of musicians in the dedication of the temple (2Ch 5:12–13). Today, as well, we continue to use music in a variety of forms to worship God.

over the province of Babylon,[g] while Daniel himself remained at the royal court.

The Image of Gold and the Fiery Furnace

3 King Nebuchadnezzar made an image[h] of gold, ninety feet high and nine feet[a] wide, and set it up on the plain of Dura in the province of Babylon. 2He then summoned the satraps, prefects, governors, advisers, treasurers, judges, magistrates and all the other provincial officials[i] to come to the dedication of the image he had set up. 3So the satraps, prefects, governors, advisers, treasurers, judges, magistrates and all the other provincial officials assembled for the dedication of the image that King Nebuchadnezzar had set up, and they stood before it.

4Then the herald loudly proclaimed, "This is what you are commanded to do, O peoples, nations and men of every language:[j] 5As soon as you hear the sound of the horn, flute, zither, lyre, harp, pipes and all kinds of music, you must fall down and worship the image of gold that King Nebuchadnezzar has set up.[k] 6Whoever does not fall down and worship will immediately be thrown into a blazing furnace."[l]

7Therefore, as soon as they heard the sound of the horn, flute, zither, lyre, harp and all kinds of music, all the peoples, nations and men of every language fell down and worshiped the image of gold that King Nebuchadnezzar had set up.[m]

8At this time some astrologers[b][n] came forward and denounced the Jews. 9They said to King Nebuchadnezzar, "O king, live forever![o] 10You have issued a decree,[p] O king, that everyone who hears the sound of the horn, flute, zither, lyre, harp, pipes and all kinds of music must fall down and worship the image of gold,[q] 11and that whoever does not fall down and worship will be thrown into a blazing furnace. 12But there are some Jews whom you have set over the affairs of the province of Babylon—Shadrach, Meshach and Abednego[r]—who pay no attention[s] to you, O king. They neither serve your gods nor worship the image of gold you have set up."[t]

13Furious[u] with rage, Nebuchadnezzar summoned Shadrach, Meshach and Abednego. So these men were brought before the king, 14and Nebuchadnezzar said to them, "Is it true, Shadrach, Meshach and Abednego, that you do not serve my gods[v] or worship the image[w] of gold I have set up? 15Now when you hear the sound of the horn, flute, zither, lyre, harp, pipes and all kinds of music, if you are ready to fall down and worship the image I made, very good. But if you do not worship it, you will be thrown immediately into a blazing furnace. Then what god[x] will be able to rescue[y] you from my hand?"

16Shadrach, Meshach and Abednego[z] replied to

2:49 [g]Da 1:7
3:1 [h]Isa 46:6; Jer 16:20; Hab 2:19
3:2 [i]ver 27; Da 6:7
3:4 [j]Da 4:1; 6:25
3:5 [k]ver 10,15
3:6 [l]ver 11,15, 21; Jer 29:22; Da 6:7; Mt 13:42,50; Rev 13:15
3:7 [m]ver 5
3:8 [n]Da 2:10
3:9 [o]Ne 2:3; Da 5:10; 6:6
3:10 [p]Da 6:12 [q]ver 4-6
3:12 [r]Da 2:49 [s]Da 6:13 [t]Est 3:3
3:13 [u]Da 2:12
3:14 [v]Isa 46:1; Jer 50:2 [w]ver 1
3:15 [x]Isa 36:18-20 [y]Ex 5:2; 2Ch 32:15
3:16 [z]Da 1:7

[a] *1* Aramaic *sixty cubits high and six cubits wide* (about 27 meters high and 2.7 meters wide) [b] *8* Or *Chaldeans*

the king, "O Nebuchadnezzar, we do not need to
defend ourselves before you in this matter. 17 If we
3:17 [a]Ps 27:1-2 [b]Job 5:19; Jer 1:8 are thrown into the blazing furnace, the God we
serve is able to save[a] us from it, and he will res-
cue[b] us from your hand, O king. 18 But even if he
does not, we want you to know, O king, that we
3:18 [c]ver 28; Jos 24:15 will not serve your gods or worship the image of
gold you have set up.[c]"
19 Then Nebuchadnezzar was furious with Shadrach, Meshach and Abednego, and his attitude
3:19 [d]Lev 26:18-28 toward them changed. He ordered the furnace
heated seven[d] times hotter than usual 20 and commanded some of the strongest soldiers in his army
to tie up Shadrach, Meshach and Abednego and
throw them into the blazing furnace. 21 So these
men, wearing their robes, trousers, turbans and
other clothes, were bound and thrown into the
blazing furnace. 22 The king's command was so
urgent and the furnace so hot that the flames of
3:22 [e]Da 1:7 the fire killed the soldiers who took up Shadrach,
Meshach and Abednego,[e] 23 and these three men,
firmly tied, fell into the blazing furnace.
24 Then King Nebuchadnezzar leaped to his feet
in amazement and asked his advisers, "Weren't
there three men that we tied up and threw into
the fire?"
They replied, "Certainly, O king."
25 He said, "Look! I see four men walking
around in the fire, unbound and unharmed, and
the fourth looks like a son of the gods."
26 Nebuchadnezzar then approached the opening of the blazing furnace and shouted, "Sha-
3:26 [f]Da 4:2,34 drach, Meshach and Abednego, servants of the
Most High God,[f] come out! Come here!"
So Shadrach, Meshach and Abednego came out
3:27 [g]ver 2 [h]Isa 43:2; Heb 11:32-34 [i]Da 6:23 of the fire, 27 and the satraps, prefects, governors
and royal advisers[g] crowded around them.[h] They
saw that the fire[i] had not harmed their bodies, nor
was a hair of their heads singed; their robes were
not scorched, and there was no smell of fire on
them.
28 Then Nebuchadnezzar said, "Praise be to the
3:28 [j]Ps 34:7; Da 6:22; Ac 5:19 [k]Job 13:15; Ps 26:1; 84:12; Jer 17:7 [l]ver 18 God of Shadrach, Meshach and Abednego, who
has sent his angel[j] and rescued his servants! They
trusted[k] in him and defied the king's command
and were willing to give up their lives rather than
serve or worship any god except their own God.[l]
29 Therefore I decree[m] that the people of any
nation or language who say anything against the
3:29 [m]Da 6:26 [n]Ezr 6:11 [o]Da 6:27 God of Shadrach, Meshach and Abednego be cut
into pieces and their houses be turned into piles
of rubble,[n] for no other god can save[o] in this
way."
30 Then the king promoted Shadrach, Meshach
3:30 [p]Da 2:49 and Abednego in the province of Babylon.[p]

Nebuchadnezzar's Dream of a Tree

4 King Nebuchadnezzar,

To the peoples, nations and men of every
4:1 [q]Da 3:4 language,[q] who live in all the world:

True Bravery

DA 3:18

Consider the bravery of these three young men. They respect their king and are willing to carry out their courtly duties, even to receive new pagan names. But they draw the line when it comes to **worshiping** ***false gods. They believe the God of heaven will protect them from the fiery furnace. Even if he does not, they will not back down. They would rather die than betray him. What a witness to believers throughout the centuries!***

A Messenger

DA 4:13-14

In the Old Testament God often used angels as his messengers. We can assume that the "holy one" (Da 4:13) spoken of here is an angel sent by God with a warning for King Nebuchadnezzar: If he does not acknowledge the God of heaven as sovereign, he will be cut down like the tree in his dream.

May you prosper greatly![r]

[2]It is my pleasure to tell you about the
miraculous signs[s] and wonders that the Most
High God[t] has performed for me.

[3] How great are his signs,
how mighty his wonders![u]
His kingdom is an eternal kingdom;
his dominion endures[v] from
generation to generation.

[4]I, Nebuchadnezzar, was at home in my
palace, contented[w] and prosperous. [5]I had a
dream[x] that made me afraid. As I was lying
in my bed, the images and visions that
passed through my mind[y] terrified me. [6]So I
commanded that all the wise men of Babylon
be brought before me to interpret[z] the dream
for me. [7]When the magicians,[a] enchanters,
astrologers[a] and diviners[b] came, I told them
the dream, but they could not interpret it for
me.[c] [8]Finally, Daniel came into my presence
and I told him the dream. (He is called Belteshazzar,[d] after the name of my god, and the
spirit of the holy gods[e] is in him.)

[9]I said, "Belteshazzar, chief[f] of the magicians, I know that the spirit of the holy gods[g]
is in you, and no mystery is too difficult for
you. Here is my dream; interpret it for me.
[10]These are the visions I saw while lying in
my bed:[h] I looked, and there before me stood
a tree in the middle of the land. Its height
was enormous.[i] [11]The tree grew large and
strong and its top touched the sky; it was visible to the ends of the earth. [12]Its leaves were
beautiful, its fruit abundant, and on it was
food for all. Under it the beasts of the field
found shelter, and the birds of the air lived
in its branches;[j] from it every creature was
fed.

[13]"In the visions I saw while lying in my
bed,[k] I looked, and there before me was a
messenger,[b] a holy one,[l] coming down from
heaven. [14]He called in a loud voice: 'Cut
down the tree and trim off its branches; strip
off its leaves and scatter its fruit. Let the animals flee from under it and the birds from its
branches.[m] [15]But let the stump and its roots,
bound with iron and bronze, remain in the
ground, in the grass of the field.

" 'Let him be drenched with the dew of
heaven, and let him live with the animals
among the plants of the earth. [16]Let his mind
be changed from that of a man and let him
be given the mind of an animal, till seven
times[c] pass by for him.[n]

[17]" 'The decision is announced by messengers, the holy ones declare the verdict, so that
the living may know that the Most High[o] is

[a] *7* Or *Chaldeans* [b] *13* Or *watchman;* also in verses 17 and 23 [c] *16* Or *years;* also in verses 23, 25 and 32

4:1 [r]Da 6:25
4:2 [s]Ps 74:9 [t]Da 3:26
4:3 [u]Ps 105:27; Da 6:27 [v]Da 2:44
4:4 [w]Ps 30:6
4:5 [x]Da 2:1 [y]Da 2:28
4:6 [z]Da 2:2
4:7 [a]Ge 41:8 [b]Isa 44:25; Da 2:2 [c]Da 2:10
4:8 [d]Da 1:7 [e]Da 5:11,14
4:9 [f]Da 2:48 [g]Da 5:11-12
4:10 [h]ver 5 [i]Eze 31:3-4
4:12 [j]Eze 17:23; Mt 13:32
4:13 [k]Da 7:1 [l]ver 23; Dt 33:2; Da 8:13
4:14 [m]Eze 31:12; Mt 3:10
4:16 [n]ver 23,32
4:17 [o]ver 2,25; Ps 83:18

4:17 [p]Jer 27:5-7; Da 2:21; 5:18-21 [q]Da 11:21
sovereign[p] over the kingdoms of men and
gives them to anyone he wishes and sets over
them the lowliest[q] of men.'
18"This is the dream that I, King Nebuchad-
4:18 [r]Ge 41:8; Da 5:8,15 [s]Ge 41:15 [t]ver 7-9
nezzar, had. Now, Belteshazzar, tell me what it
means, for none of the wise men in my kingdom can interpret it for me.[r] But you can,[s]
because the spirit of the holy gods is in you."[t]

Daniel Interprets the Dream

19Then Daniel (also called Belteshazzar)
4:19 [u]Da 7:15,28; 8:27; 10:16-17
was greatly perplexed for a time, and his
thoughts terrified[u] him. So the king said,
"Belteshazzar, do not let the dream or its
meaning alarm you."
Belteshazzar answered, "My lord, if only
the dream applied to your enemies and its
meaning to your adversaries! 20The tree you
saw, which grew large and strong, with its top
touching the sky, visible to the whole earth,
21with beautiful leaves and abundant fruit,
providing food for all, giving shelter to the
4:22 [v]2Sa 12:7 [w]Jer 27:7; Da 2:37-38; 5:18-19
beasts of the field, and having nesting places
in its branches for the birds of the air— 22you,
O king, are that tree![v] You have become great
and strong; your greatness has grown until it
reaches the sky, and your dominion extends
to distant parts of the earth.[w]
4:23 [x]ver 13 [y]Da 5:21
23"You, O king, saw a messenger, a holy
one,[x] coming down from heaven and saying,
'Cut down the tree and destroy it, but leave
the stump, bound with iron and bronze, in
the grass of the field, while its roots remain in
the ground. Let him be drenched with the
dew of heaven; let him live like the wild animals, until seven times pass by for him.'[y]
4:24 [z]Job 40:12; Ps 107:40
24"This is the interpretation, O king, and
this is the decree[z] the Most High has issued
against my lord the king: 25You will be driven
away from people and will live with the wild
animals; you will eat grass like cattle and be
4:25 [a]ver 17; Ps 83:18 [b]Jer 27:5; Da 5:21
drenched with the dew of heaven. Seven
times will pass by for you until you acknowledge that the Most High[a] is sovereign over the
kingdoms of men and gives them to anyone
4:26 [c]ver 15 [d]Da 2:37
he wishes.[b] 26The command to leave the
stump of the tree with its roots[c] means that
your kingdom will be restored to you when
you acknowledge that Heaven rules.[d]
27Therefore, O king, be pleased to accept my
4:27 [e]Isa 55:6-7 [f]1Ki 21:29; Ps 41:3; Eze 18:22
advice: Renounce your sins by doing what is
right, and your wickedness by being kind to
the oppressed.[e] It may be that then your prosperity will continue.[f]"

The Dream Is Fulfilled

4:28 [g]Nu 23:19
28All this happened[g] to King Nebuchadnezzar. 29Twelve months later, as the king
was walking on the roof of the royal palace
of Babylon, 30he said, "Is not this the great

There is nothing average about the God we know, the Father we long to serve. He's unconventional and exorbitant. He's extravagant in his giving. He's unrestrained in his love for us. In fact, God is extraordinary in every way. He's outrageous! If you and I were to catch even a glimpse of who he is, our lives would never be the same. And yet, he's shown us who he is. His truth and glory are revealed in his Son, Jesus Christ . . .

God's whole plan to reconcile the human race to himself was outrageous. It was inevitable that his own Son would be outrageous too! Jesus was a man of paradoxes who shocked, surprised, incensed or delighted everyone he met. As his followers, we shouldn't be surprised that our lives will take some outrageous twists and turns, or that we will sometimes stand out as "circus freaks" in a world that doesn't recognize our glorious nature in Christ. As my friend Thelma Wells puts it, to be a woman of faith means that "your elevator doesn't go to the top floor. Your clock ticks in a counterclockwise direction. Your cart is before the horse. And your joy is always ignited in spite of your delicate condition.

—Luci Swindoll

The Sin of Pride

DA 4:31-33

King Nebuchadnezzar has so much to be proud of! He has built Babylon into a city of great power and has constructed magnificent buildings and flowering gardens. During his reign Babylon is probably the most important city in the ancient world. And Nebuchadnezzar knows it. But his heart is still cold toward God. The king claims that the wealth and beauty of his kingdom are for **his** ***glory and majesty. His pride pushes him over the edge. Now he will suffer the consequences.***

Insidious pride still corrupts people today, just as it did Nebuchadnezzar. Without flinching, we think of all we've accomplished, all we've gained, and we fail to give the glory to whom it is due. The road's the same as the one Nebuchadnezzar walked. It doesn't lead to life but to destruction.

Babylon I have built as the royal residence,
by my mighty power and for the glory of my
majesty?"[h]
31 The words were still on his lips when a
voice came from heaven, "This is what is
decreed for you, King Nebuchadnezzar: Your
royal authority has been taken from you.
32 You will be driven away from people and
will live with the wild animals; you will eat
grass like cattle. Seven times will pass by for
you until you acknowledge that the Most
High is sovereign over the kingdoms of men
and gives them to anyone he wishes."
33 Immediately what had been said about
Nebuchadnezzar was fulfilled. He was driven
away from people and ate grass like cattle.
His body was drenched with the dew of heav-
en until his hair grew like the feathers of an
eagle and his nails like the claws of a bird.[i]

34 At the end of that time, I, Nebuchadnezzar, raised my eyes toward heaven, and my
sanity was restored. Then I praised the Most
High; I honored and glorified him who lives
forever.[j]

> His dominion is an eternal dominion;
> his kingdom endures from generation
> to generation.[k]
> 35 All the peoples of the earth
> are regarded as nothing.[l]
> He does as he pleases[m]
> with the powers of heaven
> and the peoples of the earth.
> No one can hold back his hand
> or say to him: "What have you
> done?"[n]

36 At the same time that my sanity was
restored, my honor and splendor were
returned to me for the glory of my kingdom.[o]
My advisers and nobles sought me out, and I
was restored to my throne and became even
greater than before. 37 Now I, Nebuchadnezzar, praise and exalt and glorify the King of
heaven, because everything he does is right
and all his ways are just.[p] And those who
walk in pride he is able to humble.[q]

The Writing on the Wall

5 King Belshazzar gave a great banquet[r] for a
thousand of his nobles and drank wine with
them. 2 While Belshazzar was drinking his wine,
he gave orders to bring in the gold and silver goblets[s] that Nebuchadnezzar his father[a] had taken
from the temple in Jerusalem, so that the king and
his nobles, his wives and his concubines might
drink from them.[t] 3 So they brought in the gold
goblets that had been taken from the temple of
God in Jerusalem, and the king and his nobles,

4:30 [h]Isa 37:24-25; Da 5:20; Hab 2:4
4:33 [i]Da 5:20-21
4:34 [j]Da 12:7; Rev 4:10 [k]Ps 145:13; Da 2:44; 5:21; 6:26; Lk 1:33
4:35 [l]Isa 40:17 [m]Ps 115:3; 135:6 [n]Isa 45:9; Ro 9:20
4:36 [o]Pr 22:4
4:37 [p]Dt 32:4; Ps 33:4-5 [q]Ex 18:11; Job 40:11-12; Da 5:20,23
5:1 [r]Est 1:3
5:2 [s]2Ki 24:13; Jer 52:19 [t]Est 1:7; Da 1:2

[a] 2 Or *ancestor*; or *predecessor*; also in verses 11, 13 and 18

his wives and his concubines drank from them.
4As they drank the wine, they praised the gods of
gold and silver, of bronze, iron, wood and stone.[u]
5Suddenly the fingers of a human hand
appeared and wrote on the plaster of the wall,
near the lampstand in the royal palace. The king
watched the hand as it wrote. 6His face turned
pale and he was so frightened[v] that his knees
knocked together and his legs gave way.[w]
7The king called out for the enchanters,
astrologers[a] and diviners[x] to be brought and said
to these wise[y] men of Babylon, "Whoever reads
this writing and tells me what it means will be
clothed in purple and have a gold chain placed
around his neck,[z] and he will be made the third
highest ruler in the kingdom."[a]
8Then all the king's wise men came in, but they
could not read the writing or tell the king what it
meant.[b] 9So King Belshazzar became even more
terrified[c] and his face grew more pale. His nobles
were baffled.
10The queen,[b] hearing the voices of the king and
his nobles, came into the banquet hall. "O king,
live forever!"[d] she said. "Don't be alarmed! Don't
look so pale! 11There is a man in your kingdom
who has the spirit of the holy gods[e] in him. In the
time of your father he was found to have insight
and intelligence and wisdom[f] like that of the gods.
King Nebuchadnezzar your father—your father
the king, I say—appointed him chief of the magicians, enchanters, astrologers and diviners.[g] 12This
man Daniel, whom the king called Belteshazzar,[h]
was found to have a keen mind and knowledge
and understanding, and also the ability to interpret dreams, explain riddles and solve difficult
problems.[i] Call for Daniel, and he will tell you
what the writing means."
13So Daniel was brought before the king, and
the king said to him, "Are you Daniel, one of the
exiles my father the king brought from Judah?[j] 14I
have heard that the spirit of the gods is in you and
that you have insight, intelligence and outstanding wisdom. 15The wise men and enchanters were
brought before me to read this writing and tell me
what it means, but they could not explain it.
16Now I have heard that you are able to give interpretations and to solve difficult problems. If you
can read this writing and tell me what it means,
you will be clothed in purple and have a gold
chain placed around your neck, and you will be
made the third highest ruler in the kingdom."
17Then Daniel answered the king, "You may
keep your gifts for yourself and give your rewards
to someone else.[k] Nevertheless, I will read the
writing for the king and tell him what it means.
18"O king, the Most High God gave your father
Nebuchadnezzar sovereignty and greatness and
glory and splendor.[l] 19Because of the high position
he gave him, all the peoples and nations and men

5:4 [u]Ps 135:15-18; Hab 2:19; Rev 9:20
5:6 [v]Da 4:5 [w]Eze 7:17
5:7 [x]Isa 44:25 [y]Da 4:6-7 [z]Ge 41:42 [a]Da 2:5-6, 48; 6:2-3
5:8 [b]Da 2:10,27
5:9 [c]Isa 21:4
5:10 [d]Da 3:9
5:11 [e]Da 4:8-9,19 [f]ver 14; Da 1:17 [g]Da 2:47-48
5:12 [h]Da 1:7 [i]ver 14-16; Da 6:3
5:13 [j]Da 6:13
5:17 [k]2Ki 5:16
5:18 [l]Jer 27:7; Da 2:37-38

[a] 7 Or *Chaldeans*; also in verse 11 [b] 10 Or *queen mother*

Daniel's Humility

DA 5:17

Daniel's humility is in distinct contrast here to the pride of the king. Belshazzar tries to bribe Daniel with purple clothing, a gold chain and a royal title. But Daniel doesn't want such gifts. He knows the true King—the God of heaven. He also knows that soon Babylon will fall because of King Belshazzar's pride and idol worship. Daniel has no need for the trappings of success. Where he finds his true success and fulfillment are evident from his attitudes throughout the book. His unswerving loyalty to his God is a foundation that provides more satisfaction than any title or gift.

Pride Versus Humility

DA 5:22–24

Daniel speaks with humility and poignancy as he confronts the king with his pride and flagrancy. Belshazzar has publicly praised man-made idols of gold and silver, stone and wood, idols that cannot hear or speak or understand. He's taken holy vessels from the Jerusalem temple and used them as everyday wineglasses. Consequently, he completely misses the God who holds his very life in his hands. It appears from Daniel's speech in Daniel 5:18–21, in which he recalls the demise of King Nebuchadnezzar, that King Belshazzar has not learned from his predecessor's experience. God's judgment is swift. "That very night" (Da 5:30) Belshazzar dies and his kingdom goes to Darius the Mede.

of every language dreaded and feared him. Those the king wanted to put to death, he put to death;[m] those he wanted to spare, he spared; those he wanted to promote, he promoted; and those he wanted to humble, he humbled. 20 But when his heart became arrogant and hardened with pride,[n] he was deposed from his royal throne and stripped[o] of his glory.[p] 21 He was driven away from people and given the mind of an animal; he lived with the wild donkeys and ate grass like cattle; and his body was drenched with the dew of heaven, until he acknowledged that the Most High God is sovereign[q] over the kingdoms of men and sets over them anyone he wishes.[r]

22 "But you his son,[a] O Belshazzar, have not humbled[s] yourself, though you knew all this. 23 Instead, you have set yourself up against[t] the Lord of heaven. You had the goblets from his temple brought to you, and you and your nobles, your wives and your concubines drank wine from them. You praised the gods of silver and gold, of bronze, iron, wood and stone, which cannot see or hear or understand.[u] But you did not honor the God who holds in his hand your life[v] and all your ways.[w] 24 Therefore he sent the hand that wrote the inscription.

25 "This is the inscription that was written:

MENE, MENE, TEKEL, PARSIN[b]

26 "This is what these words mean:

Mene[c]: God has numbered the days[x] of your reign and brought it to an end.[y]
27 *Tekel*[d]: You have been weighed on the scales and found wanting.[z]
28 *Peres*[e]: Your kingdom is divided and given to the Medes[a] and Persians."[b]

29 Then at Belshazzar's command, Daniel was clothed in purple, a gold chain was placed around his neck, and he was proclaimed the third highest ruler in the kingdom.

30 That very night Belshazzar,[c] king of the Babylonians,[f] was slain,[d] 31 and Darius[e] the Mede took over the kingdom, at the age of sixty-two.

Daniel in the Den of Lions

6 It pleased Darius[f] to appoint 120 satraps[g] to rule throughout the kingdom, 2 with three administrators over them, one of whom was Daniel.[h] The satraps were made accountable[i] to them so that the king might not suffer loss. 3 Now Daniel so distinguished himself among the administrators and the satraps by his exceptional qualities that the king planned to set him over the whole kingdom.[j] 4 At this, the administrators and the satraps tried to find grounds for charges against

5:19 [m]Da 2:12-13; 3:6
5:20 [n]Da 4:30 [o]Jer 13:18 [p]Job 40:12; Isa 14:13-15
5:21 [q]Eze 17:24 [r]Da 4:16-17, 35
5:22 [s]Ex 10:3; 2Ch 33:23
5:23 [t]Jer 50:29 [u]Ps 115:4-8; Hab 2:19 [v]Job 12:10 [w]Job 31:4; Jer 10:23
5:26 [x]Jer 27:7 [y]Isa 13:6
5:27 [z]Ps 62:9
5:28 [a]Isa 13:17 [b]Da 6:28
5:30 [c]ver 1 [d]Isa 21:9; Jer 51:31
5:31 [e]Da 6:1; 9:1
6:1 [f]Da 5:31 [g]Est 1:1
6:2 [h]Da 2:48-49 [i]Ezr 4:22
6:3 [j]Ge 41:41; Est 10:3; Da 5:12-14

[a] 22 Or *descendant*; or *successor* [b] 25 Aramaic *UPARSIN* (that is, *AND PARSIN*) [c] 26 *Mene* can mean *numbered* or *mina* (a unit of money). [d] 27 *Tekel* can mean *weighed* or *shekel.* [e] 28 *Peres* (the singular of *Parsin*) can mean *divided* or *Persia* or *a half mina* or *a half shekel.* [f] 30 Or *Chaldeans*

Daniel in his conduct of government affairs, but they were unable to do so. They could find no corruption in him, because he was trustworthy and neither corrupt nor negligent. 5 Finally these men said, "We will never find any basis for charges against this man Daniel unless it has something to do with the law of his God."[k]

6 So the administrators and the satraps went as a group to the king and said: "O King Darius, live forever![l] 7 The royal administrators, prefects, satraps, advisers and governors[m] have all agreed that the king should issue an edict and enforce the decree that anyone who prays to any god or man during the next thirty days, except to you, O king, shall be thrown into the lions' den.[n] 8 Now, O king, issue the decree and put it in writing so that it cannot be altered—in accordance with the laws of the Medes and Persians, which cannot be repealed."[o] 9 So King Darius put the decree in writing.

10 Now when Daniel learned that the decree had been published, he went home to his upstairs room where the windows opened toward[p] Jerusalem. Three times a day he got down on his knees[q] and prayed, giving thanks to his God, just as he had done before.[r] 11 Then these men went as a group and found Daniel praying and asking God for help. 12 So they went to the king and spoke to him about his royal decree: "Did you not publish a decree that during the next thirty days anyone who prays to any god or man except to you, O king, would be thrown into the lions' den?"

The king answered, "The decree stands—in accordance with the laws of the Medes and Persians, which cannot be repealed."[s]

13 Then they said to the king, "Daniel, who is one of the exiles from Judah,[t] pays no attention[u] to you, O king, or to the decree you put in writing. He still prays three times a day." 14 When the king heard this, he was greatly distressed;[v] he was determined to rescue Daniel and made every effort until sundown to save him.

15 Then the men went as a group to the king and said to him, "Remember, O king, that according to the law of the Medes and Persians no decree or edict that the king issues can be changed."[w]

16 So the king gave the order, and they brought Daniel and threw him into the lions' den.[x] The king said to Daniel, "May your God, whom you serve continually, rescue[y] you!"

17 A stone was brought and placed over the mouth of the den, and the king sealed[z] it with his own signet ring and with the rings of his nobles, so that Daniel's situation might not be changed. 18 Then the king returned to his palace and spent the night without eating[a] and without any entertainment being brought to him. And he could not sleep.[b]

19 At the first light of dawn, the king got up and hurried to the lions' den. 20 When he came near the den, he called to Daniel in an anguished voice, "Daniel, servant of the living God, has your God,

6:5 [k]Ac 24:13-16
6:6 [l]Ne 2:3; Da 2:4
6:7 [m]Da 3:2 [n]Ps 59:3; 64:2-6; Da 3:6
6:8 [o]Est 1:19
6:10 [p]1Ki 8:48-49 [q]Ps 95:6 [r]Ac 5:29
6:12 [s]Est 1:19; Da 3:8-12
6:13 [t]Da 2:25; 5:13 [u]Est 3:8; Da 3:12
6:14 [v]Mk 6:26
6:15 [w]Est 8:8
6:16 [x]ver 7 [y]Job 5:19; Ps 37:39-40
6:17 [z]Mt 27:66
6:18 [a]2Sa 12:17 [b]Est 6:1; Da 2:1

A Trap for Daniel

DA 6:5-18

Daniel's fellow administrators, jealous of his governmental success and his relationship with the king, look for a way to trip him up. But they quickly realize that no ordinary means will accomplish their task. Somehow they have to fabricate a way to make obeying his God illegal for Daniel. By suggesting to the king that for 30 days no one should worship any other god but the king himself, they cause Daniel to disobey the law. And since the law takes precedence over friendship and feelings, even the king is trapped. He has to carry out the dictum, regardless of his affection for Daniel.

Dreams and Visions

DA 7

Daniel's vision of four beasts in Daniel 7 has a definite correlation to the dream of Nebuchadnezzar in Daniel 2. The first beast, the lion, represents the kingdom of Babylon, just as the head of gold in the first dream. The second beast, a bear, corresponding to the chest of silver, depicts the kingdom of the Medes and the Persians. The third beast, a leopard, parallels the bronze belly and thighs of the image and is the kingdom of Greece. The fourth beast, unnamed but "terrifying and frightening and very powerful" (Da 7:7), relates to the iron legs of the image and represents Rome. The ten horns correlate to the ten toes of the image. One upon another, the dreams and visions build a picture of future events and God's hand in them.

whom you serve continually, been able to rescue
you from the lions?"[c]
21 Daniel answered, "O king, live forever![d] 22 My
God sent his angel,[e] and he shut the mouths of
the lions.[f] They have not hurt me, because I was
found innocent in his sight.[g] Nor have I ever done
any wrong before you, O king."
23 The king was overjoyed and gave orders to lift
Daniel out of the den. And when Daniel was lifted from the den, no wound[h] was found on him,
because he had trusted[i] in his God.
24 At the king's command, the men who had
falsely accused Daniel were brought in and
thrown into the lions' den,[j] along with their wives
and children.[k] And before they reached the floor
of the den, the lions overpowered them and
crushed all their bones.[l]
25 Then King Darius wrote to all the peoples,
nations and men of every language throughout
the land:

"May you prosper greatly![m]

26 "I issue a decree that in every part of my
kingdom people must fear and reverence the
God of Daniel.[n]

"For he is the living God
and he endures forever;
his kingdom will not be destroyed,
his dominion will never end.[o]
27 He rescues and he saves;
he performs signs and wonders[p]
in the heavens and on the earth.
He has rescued Daniel
from the power of the lions."[q]

28 So Daniel prospered during the reign of Darius and the reign of Cyrus[a][r] the Persian.

Daniel's Dream of Four Beasts

7 In the first year of Belshazzar[s] king of Babylon, Daniel had a dream, and visions passed
through his mind[t] as he was lying on his bed. He
wrote[u] down the substance of his dream.
2 Daniel said: "In my vision at night I looked, and
there before me were the four winds of heaven[v]
churning up the great sea. 3 Four great beasts,[w] each
different from the others, came up out of the sea.
4 "The first was like a lion,[x] and it had the wings
of an eagle.[y] I watched until its wings were torn
off and it was lifted from the ground so that it
stood on two feet like a man, and the heart of a
man was given to it.
5 "And there before me was a second beast,
which looked like a bear. It was raised up on one
of its sides, and it had three ribs in its mouth
between its teeth. It was told, 'Get up and eat your
fill of flesh!'[z]
6 "After that, I looked, and there before me was
another beast, one that looked like a leopard.[a]

6:20 [c]Da 3:17
6:21 [d]Da 2:4
6:22 [e]Da 3:28 [f]Ps 91:11-13; Heb 11:33 [g]Ac 12:11; 2Ti 4:17
6:23 [h]Da 3:27 [i]1Ch 5:20
6:24 [j]Dt 19:18-19; Est 7:9-10; Ps 54:5 [k]Dt 24:16; 2Ki 14:6 [l]Isa 38:13
6:25 [m]Da 4:1
6:26 [n]Ps 99:1-3; Da 3:29 [o]Da 2:44; 4:34
6:27 [p]Da 4:3 [q]ver 22
6:28 [r]2Ch 36:22; Da 1:21
7:1 [s]Da 5:1 [t]Da 1:17 [u]Jer 36:4
7:2 [v]Rev 7:1
7:3 [w]Rev 13:1
7:4 [x]Jer 4:7 [y]Eze 17:3
7:5 [z]Da 2:39
7:6 [a]Rev 13:2

[a] 28 Or *Darius, that is, the reign of Cyrus*

And on its back it had four wings like those of a
bird. This beast had four heads, and it was given
authority to rule.
7“After that, in my vision at night I looked, and
there before me was a fourth beast—terrifying and
frightening and very powerful. It had large iron[b]
teeth; it crushed and devoured its victims and trampled underfoot whatever was left. It was different
from all the former beasts, and it had ten horns.[c]
8“While I was thinking about the horns, there
before me was another horn, a little[d] one, which
came up among them; and three of the first horns
were uprooted before it. This horn had eyes like
the eyes of a man[e] and a mouth that spoke
boastfully.[f]
9“As I looked,

“thrones were set in place,
and the Ancient of Days took his seat.
His clothing was as white as snow;
the hair of his head was white like
wool.[g]
His throne was flaming with fire,
and its wheels[h] were all ablaze.
10A river of fire[i] was flowing,
coming out from before him.[j]
Thousands upon thousands attended
him;
ten thousand times ten thousand
stood before him.
The court was seated,
and the books[k] were opened.

11“Then I continued to watch because of the
boastful words the horn was speaking. I kept
looking until the beast was slain and its body
destroyed and thrown into the blazing fire.[l] 12(The
other beasts had been stripped of their authority,
but were allowed to live for a period of time.)
13“In my vision at night I looked, and there
before me was one like a son of man,[m] coming
with the clouds of heaven.[n] He approached the
Ancient of Days and was led into his presence.
14He was given authority,[o] glory and sovereign
power; all peoples, nations and men of every language worshiped him.[p] His dominion is an everlasting dominion that will not pass away, and his
kingdom is one that will never be destroyed.[q]

The Interpretation of the Dream

15“I, Daniel, was troubled in spirit, and the
visions that passed through my mind disturbed
me.[r] 16I approached one of those standing there
and asked him the true meaning of all this.
“So he told me and gave me the interpretation[s]
of these things: 17‘The four great beasts are four
kingdoms that will rise from the earth. 18But the
saints of the Most High will receive the kingdom
and will possess it forever—yes, for ever and
ever.’[t]
19“Then I wanted to know the true meaning of
the fourth beast, which was different from all the

7:7 [b]Da 2:40 [c]Rev 12:3
7:8 [d]Da 8:9 [e]Rev 9:7 [f]Ps 12:3; Rev 13:5-6
7:9 [g]Rev 1:14 [h]Eze 1:15; 10:6
7:10 [i]Ps 50:3; 97:3; Isa 30:27 [j]Dt 33:2; Ps 68:17; Rev 5:11 [k]Rev 20:11-15
7:11 [l]Rev 19:20
7:13 [m]Mt 8:20*; Rev 1:13* [n]Mt 24:30; Rev 1:7
7:14 [o]Mt 28:18 [p]Ps 72:11; 102:22; 1Co 15:27; Eph 1:22 [q]Da 2:44; Heb 12:28; Rev 11:15
7:15 [r]Da 4:19
7:16 [s]Da 8:16; 9:22; Zec 1:9
7:18 [t]Isa 60:12-14; Rev 2:26; 20:4

The Ancient of Days

DA 7:9

The title “Ancient of Days” refers to God the Father and his eternal existence. Daniel describes God in great detail. He includes word pictures of God’s appearance (Da 7:9–10) as he comes in glory to judge all people. Similar descriptions can be found in Isaiah 6:1–5 and in Ezekiel 1:15–21.

Daniel's Response

DA 7:28

Daniel's visions are so troubling to him that he can only consider one response: silence. With a face pale from what he has seen, he recognizes the difficulty and the horror of the events to come. In Daniel 8:27 he has another, similar experience. In this case, the angel Gabriel interprets another of Daniel's visions (Da 8:16) and that interpretation exhausts Daniel to the point of fainting and sickness.

others and most terrifying, with its iron teeth and
bronze claws—the beast that crushed and
devoured its victims and trampled underfoot
whatever was left. 20 I also wanted to know about
the ten horns on its head and about the other horn
that came up, before which three of them fell—
the horn that looked more imposing than the others and that had eyes and a mouth that spoke
boastfully. 21 As I watched, this horn was waging
war against the saints and defeating them,[u] 22 until
the Ancient of Days came and pronounced judgment in favor of the saints of the Most High, and
the time came when they possessed the kingdom.
23 "He gave me this explanation: 'The fourth
beast is a fourth kingdom that will appear on
earth. It will be different from all the other kingdoms and will devour the whole earth, trampling
it down and crushing it.[v] 24 The ten horns[w] are ten
kings who will come from this kingdom. After
them another king will arise, different from the
earlier ones; he will subdue three kings. 25 He will
speak against the Most High[x] and oppress his
saints and try to change the set times[y] and the
laws. The saints will be handed over to him for a
time, times and half a time.[a][z]
26 " 'But the court will sit, and his power will be
taken away and completely destroyed forever.
27 Then the sovereignty, power and greatness of the
kingdoms under the whole heaven will be handed over to the saints, the people of the Most High.
His kingdom will be an everlasting[a] kingdom, and
all rulers will worship[b] and obey him.'
28 "This is the end of the matter. I, Daniel, was
deeply troubled[c] by my thoughts, and my face
turned pale, but I kept the matter to myself."

Daniel's Vision of a Ram and a Goat

8 In the third year of King Belshazzar's reign, I,
Daniel, had a vision, after the one that had
already appeared to me. 2 In my vision I saw
myself in the citadel of Susa[d] in the province of
Elam;[e] in the vision I was beside the Ulai Canal. 3 I
looked up,[f] and there before me was a ram with
two horns, standing beside the canal, and the
horns were long. One of the horns was longer
than the other but grew up later. 4 I watched the
ram as he charged toward the west and the north
and the south. No animal could stand against
him, and none could rescue from his power. He
did as he pleased[g] and became great.
5 As I was thinking about this, suddenly a goat
with a prominent horn between his eyes came
from the west, crossing the whole earth without
touching the ground. 6 He came toward the two-
horned ram I had seen standing beside the canal
and charged at him in great rage. 7 I saw him attack
the ram furiously, striking the ram and shattering
his two horns. The ram was powerless to stand
against him; the goat knocked him to the ground

7:21 [u]Rev 13:7
7:23 [v]Da 2:40
7:24 [w]Rev 17:12
7:25 [x]Isa 37:23; Da 11:36 [y]Da 2:21 [z]Da 8:24; 12:7; Rev 12:14
7:27 [a]Da 2:44; 4:34; Lk 1:33; Rev 11:15; 22:5 [b]Ps 22:27; 72:11; 86:9
7:28 [c]Da 4:19
8:2 [d]Est 1:2 [e]Ge 10:22
8:3 [f]Da 10:5
8:4 [g]Da 11:3,16

[a] 25 Or *for a year, two years and half a year*

and trampled on him,[h] and none could rescue the
ram from his power. 8The goat became very great,
but at the height of his power his large horn was
broken off,[i] and in its place four prominent horns
grew up toward the four winds of heaven.[j]
9Out of one of them came another horn, which
started small but grew in power to the south and
to the east and toward the Beautiful Land.[k] 10It
grew until it reached[l] the host of the heavens, and
it threw some of the starry host down to the
earth[m] and trampled[n] on them. 11It set itself up to
be as great as the Prince of the host;[o] it took away
the daily sacrifice[p] from him, and the place of his
sanctuary was brought low.[q] 12Because of rebellion, the host ⌞of the saints⌟[a] and the daily sacrifice
were given over to it. It prospered in everything it
did, and truth was thrown to the ground.
13Then I heard a holy one[r] speaking, and another holy one said to him, "How long will it take for
the vision to be fulfilled[s]—the vision concerning
the daily sacrifice, the rebellion that causes desolation, and the surrender of the sanctuary and of
the host that will be trampled[t] underfoot?"
14He said to me, "It will take 2,300 evenings and
mornings; then the sanctuary will be reconse-
crated."[u]

The Interpretation of the Vision

15While I, Daniel, was watching the vision[v] and
trying to understand it, there before me stood one
who looked like a man.[w] 16And I heard a man's
voice from the Ulai calling, "Gabriel,[x] tell this
man the meaning of the vision."
17As he came near the place where I was standing, I was terrified and fell prostrate.[y] "Son of
man," he said to me, "understand that the vision
concerns the time of the end."[z]
18While he was speaking to me, I was in a deep
sleep, with my face to the ground.[a] Then he
touched me and raised me to my feet.[b]
19He said: "I am going to tell you what will happen later in the time of wrath, because the vision
concerns the appointed time of the end.[b][c] 20The
two-horned ram that you saw represents the kings
of Media and Persia. 21The shaggy goat is the king
of Greece,[d] and the large horn between his eyes is
the first king.[e] 22The four horns that replaced the
one that was broken off represent four kingdoms
that will emerge from his nation but will not have
the same power.
23"In the latter part of their reign, when rebels
have become completely wicked, a stern-faced
king, a master of intrigue, will arise. 24He will
become very strong, but not by his own power.
He will cause astounding devastation and will
succeed in whatever he does. He will destroy the
mighty men and the holy people.[f] 25He will cause
deceit to prosper, and he will consider himself

8:7 [h]Da 7:7
8:8 [i]2Ch 26:16-21; Da 5:20 [j]Da 7:2; Rev 7:1
8:9 [k]Da 11:16
8:10 [l]Isa 14:13 [m]Rev 12:4 [n]Da 7:7
8:11 [o]Da 11:36-37 [p]Eze 46:13-14 [q]Da 11:31; 12:11
8:13 [r]Da 4:23 [s]Da 12:6 [t]Lk 21:24; Rev 11:2
8:14 [u]Da 12:11-12
8:15 [v]ver 1 [w]Da 10:16-18
8:16 [x]Da 9:21; Lk 1:19
8:17 [y]Eze 1:28; Da 2:46; Rev 1:17 [z]Hab 2:3
8:18 [a]Da 10:9 [b]Eze 2:2; Da 10:16-18
8:19 [c]Hab 2:3
8:21 [d]Da 10:20 [e]Da 11:3
8:24 [f]Da 7:25; 11:36

[a] 12 Or *rebellion, the armies* [b] 19 Or *because the end will be at the appointed time*

Beautiful Land

DA 8:9

"The Beautiful Land." You can almost hear the longing in Daniel's voice as he calls Israel "the Beautiful Land." From his position in exile, away from his homeland, Daniel refers to the promised land in nostalgic terms. Daniel knows it's a homeland they lost by their own rebellion and waywardness. If they had only obeyed God as he had asked, he would gladly have given them this "desirable land, the most beautiful inheritance of any nation" (Jer 3:19).

Phoebe Hinsdale Brown wrote the words to this hymn while living with four small children and a sick sister in a small, unfinished house. She had nowhere to go for prayer and devotion, so in the evening, when all was quiet, she would slip away to stand outside her wealthy neighbor's garden for prayer and communion with God.

I Love to Steal Awhile Away

I love to steal awhile away
From ev'ry cumbering care,
And spend the hours of closing day
In humble, grateful, prayer.

I love to think on mercies past,
And future good implore,
And all my cares and sorrows cast
On God, Whom I adore.

I love by faith to take a view
Of brighter scenes in heaven;
The prospect doth my strength
renew,
While here by tempests driven.

Thus, when life's toilsome day
is o'er,
May its departing ray,
Be calm at this impressive hour,
And lead to endless day.

—Phoebe Hinsdale Brown (1783-1861)

superior. When they feel secure, he will destroy
many and take his stand against the Prince of
princes.[g] Yet he will be destroyed, but not by
human power.[h]
26 "The vision of the evenings and mornings that
has been given you is true,[i] but seal[j] up the vision,
for it concerns the distant future."[k]
27 I, Daniel, was exhausted and lay ill for several days. Then I got up and went about the king's
business.[l] I was appalled[m] by the vision; it was
beyond understanding.

Daniel's Prayer

9 In the first year of Darius[n] son of Xerxes[a] (a
Mede by descent), who was made ruler over
the Babylonian[b] kingdom— 2 in the first year of his
reign, I, Daniel, understood from the Scriptures,
according to the word of the LORD given to Jeremiah the prophet, that the desolation of Jerusalem would last seventy[o] years. 3 So I turned to the
Lord God and pleaded with him in prayer and
petition, in fasting, and in sackcloth and ashes.[p]
4 I prayed to the LORD my God and confessed:

"O Lord, the great and awesome God,[q] who
keeps his covenant of love[r] with all who love
him and obey his commands, 5 we have
sinned and done wrong.[s] We have been
wicked and have rebelled; we have turned
away[t] from your commands and laws.[u] 6 We
have not listened to your servants the prophets,[v] who spoke in your name to our kings,
our princes and our fathers, and to all the
people of the land.

7 "Lord, you are righteous, but this day we
are covered with shame[w]—the men of Judah
and people of Jerusalem and all Israel, both
near and far, in all the countries where you
have scattered[x] us because of our unfaithfulness to you.[y] 8 O LORD, we and our kings, our
princes and our fathers are covered with
shame because we have sinned against you.
9 The Lord our God is merciful and forgiving,[z]
even though we have rebelled against him;[a]
10 we have not obeyed the LORD our God or kept
the laws he gave us through his servants the
prophets.[b] 11 All Israel has transgressed your
law and turned away, refusing to obey you.

"Therefore the curses and sworn judgments
written in the Law of Moses, the servant of
God, have been poured out on us, because we
have sinned[c] against you. 12 You have fulfilled[d]
the words spoken against us and against our
rulers by bringing upon us great disaster.
Under the whole heaven nothing has ever
been done like what has been done to Jerusalem.[e] 13 Just as it is written in the Law of
Moses, all this disaster has come upon us, yet
we have not sought the favor of the LORD our

8:25 [g]Da 11:36 [h]Da 2:34; 11:21
8:26 [i]Da 10:1 [j]Rev 22:10 [k]Da 10:14
8:27 [l]Da 2:48 [m]Da 7:28
9:1 [n]Da 5:31
9:2 [o]2Ch 36:21; Jer 29:10; Zec 7:5
9:3 [p]Ne 1:4; Jer 29:12
9:4 [q]Dt 7:21 [r]Dt 7:9
9:5 [s]Ps 106:6 [t]Isa 53:6 [u]ver 11; La 1:20
9:6 [v]2Ch 36:16; Jer 44:5
9:7 [w]Ps 44:15 [x]Dt 4:27; Am 9:9 [y]Jer 3:25
9:9 [z]Ps 130:4 [a]Ne 9:17; Jer 14:7
9:10 [b]2Ki 17:13-15; 18:12
9:11 [c]Isa 1:4-6; Jer 8:5-10
9:12 [d]Isa 44:26; Zec 1:6 [e]Jer 44:2-6; Eze 5:9

[a] 1 Hebrew *Ahasuerus* [b] 1 Or *Chaldean*

9:13 [f]Isa 9:13; God by turning from our sins and giving
Jer 2:30 attention to your truth.[f] 14The LORD did not
hesitate to bring the disaster[g] upon us, for the
9:14 [g]Jer 44:27 LORD our God is righteous in everything he
[h]Ne 9:33 does; yet we have not obeyed him.[h]
15"Now, O Lord our God, who brought your
9:15 [i]Jer 32:21 people out of Egypt with a mighty hand[i] and
[j]Ne 9:10 who made for yourself a name[j] that endures
to this day, we have sinned, we have done
9:16 [k]Ps 31:1 wrong. 16O Lord, in keeping with all your
[l]Jer 32:32 righteous acts,[k] turn away your anger and
[m]Zec 8:3 your wrath from Jerusalem,[l] your city, your
[n]Eze 5:14 holy hill.[m] Our sins and the iniquities of our
fathers have made Jerusalem and your peo-
ple an object of scorn[n] to all those around us.
17"Now, our God, hear the prayers and peti-
9:17 tions of your servant. For your sake, O Lord,
[o]Nu 6:24-26; look with favor[o] on your desolate sanctuary.
Ps 80:19 18Give ear, O God, and hear; open your eyes
9:18 [p]Ps 80:14 and see[p] the desolation of the city that bears
[q]Isa 37:17; your Name.[q] We do not make requests of you
Jer 7:10-12; because we are righteous, but because of
25:29 your great mercy. 19O Lord, listen! O Lord,
9:19 [r]Ps 44:23 forgive![r] O Lord, hear and act! For your sake,
O my God, do not delay, because your city
and your people bear your Name."

The Seventy "Sevens"

20While I was speaking and praying, confessing
my sin and the sin of my people Israel and mak-
9:20 ing my request to the LORD my God for his holy
[s]ver 3; hill[s]— 21while I was still in prayer, Gabriel,[t] the
Ps 145:18; man I had seen in the earlier vision, came to me
Isa 58:9 in swift flight about the time of the evening sacri-
9:21 [t]Da 8:16; fice.[u] 22He instructed me and said to me, "Daniel,
Lk 1:19 I have now come to give you insight and under-
[u]Ex 29:39 standing. 23As soon as you began to pray, an
9:23 [v]Da 10:19; answer was given, which I have come to tell you,
Lk 1:28 for you are highly esteemed.[v] Therefore, consider
[w]Da 10:11- the message and understand the vision:[w]
12; Mt 24:15 24"Seventy 'sevens'[a] are decreed for your people
9:24 and your holy city to finish[b] transgression, to put
[x]Isa 53:10 an end to sin, to atone[x] for wickedness, to bring in
[y]Isa 56:1 everlasting righteousness,[y] to seal up vision and
prophecy and to anoint the most holy.[c]
9:25 25"Know and understand this: From the issuing
[z]Ezr 4:24 of the decree[d] to restore and rebuild[z] Jerusalem
[a]Jn 4:25 until the Anointed One,[e][a] the ruler, comes, there
will be seven 'sevens,' and sixty-two 'sevens.' It will
be rebuilt with streets and a trench, but in times of
9:26 trouble. 26After the sixty-two 'sevens,' the Anointed
[b]Isa 53:8 One will be cut off[b] and will have nothing.[f] The
[c]Na 1:8 people of the ruler who will come will destroy the
city and the sanctuary. The end will come like a
flood:[c] War will continue until the end, and desolations have been decreed. 27He will confirm a cov-

[a] 24 Or *'weeks'*; also in verses 25 and 26 [b] 24 Or *restrain*
[c] 24 Or *Most Holy Place*; or *most holy One* [d] 25 Or *word*
[e] 25 Or *an anointed one*; also in verse 26 [f] 26 Or *off and will have no one*; or *off, but not for himself*

Confession

DA 9:20

Daniel, aware that the Lord has decreed the end of Babylon, goes to God in prayer. He confesses his own sin (though the nature of his sin is not revealed) and the sins of the Israelites; then he pleads for the swift restoration of his people and their land. He trusts God to be faithful to his promises. The moment Daniel begins to pray, the angel Gabriel appears to tell him of God's plan. Gabriel begins by encouraging Daniel, telling him he is "highly esteemed" (Da 9:23) and his faithfulness is recognized. It's a beautiful expression of God's deep love for his servant Daniel.

Spiritual Battles

DA 10:12–14

Here God pulls back the curtain for a moment to give Daniel insight into the ongoing spiritual warfare that occurs between the agents of darkness and the agents of peace. The "king of Persia" is probably not a human king or he'd have been no match for one of God's angels. More likely, this king is a demon, one of Satan's emissaries. This demon's commission is to thwart God's messenger, who has been sent to Daniel to bring encouragement and hope. The powers of the unseen world are at work today also. That is why Paul warns us in the New Testament to put on the full armor of God (Eph 6:11–12). When we are fully equipped for battle, we can have the victory in Christ Jesus!

enant with many for one 'seven.'[a] In the middle of
the 'seven'[a] he will put an end to sacrifice and
offering. And on a wing ⌞of the temple⌟ he will set
up an abomination that causes desolation, until the
end that is decreed[d] is poured out on him.[b]"[c]

Daniel's Vision of a Man

10 In the third year of Cyrus[e] king of Persia, a
revelation was given to Daniel (who was
called Belteshazzar).[f] Its message was true[g] and
it concerned a great war.[d] The understanding of
the message came to him in a vision.
2 At that time I, Daniel, mourned[h] for three
weeks. 3 I ate no choice food; no meat or wine
touched my lips; and I used no lotions at all until
the three weeks were over.
4 On the twenty-fourth day of the first month, as
I was standing on the bank of the great river, the
Tigris,[i] 5 I looked up and there before me was a
man dressed in linen,[j] with a belt of the finest
gold[k] around his waist. 6 His body was like chrysolite, his face like lightning,[l] his eyes like flaming
torches,[m] his arms and legs like the gleam of burnished bronze,[n] and his voice like the sound of a
multitude.
7 I, Daniel, was the only one who saw the
vision; the men with me did not see it,[o] but such
terror overwhelmed them that they fled and hid
themselves. 8 So I was left alone,[p] gazing at this
great vision; I had no strength left,[q] my face
turned deathly pale and I was helpless.[r] 9 Then I
heard him speaking, and as I listened to him, I fell
into a deep sleep, my face to the ground.[s]
10 A hand touched me[t] and set me trembling on
my hands and knees.[u] 11 He said, "Daniel, you who
are highly esteemed,[v] consider carefully the words
I am about to speak to you, and stand up,[w] for I
have now been sent to you." And when he said
this to me, I stood up trembling.
12 Then he continued, "Do not be afraid, Daniel.
Since the first day that you set your mind to gain
understanding and to humble[x] yourself before
your God, your words were heard, and I have
come in response to them.[y] 13 But the prince of the
Persian kingdom resisted me twenty-one days.
Then Michael,[z] one of the chief princes, came to
help me, because I was detained there with the
king of Persia. 14 Now I have come to explain[a] to
you what will happen to your people in the future,
for the vision concerns a time yet to come.[b]"
15 While he was saying this to me, I bowed with
my face toward the ground and was speechless.[c]
16 Then one who looked like a man[e] touched my
lips, and I opened my mouth and began to speak.[d]

[a] 27 Or *'week'* [b] 27 Or *it* [c] 27 Or *And one who causes desolation will come upon the pinnacle of the abominable ⌞temple⌟, until the end that is decreed is poured out on the desolated ⌞city⌟* [d] 1 Or *true and burdensome* [e] 16 Most manuscripts of the Masoretic Text; one manuscript of the Masoretic Text, Dead Sea Scrolls and Septuagint *Then something that looked like a man's hand*

9:27 [d] Isa 10:22
10:1 [e] Da 1:21 [f] Da 1:7 [g] Da 8:26
10:2 [h] Ezr 9:4
10:4 [i] Ge 2:14
10:5 [j] Eze 9:2; Rev 15:6 [k] Jer 10:9
10:6 [l] Mt 17:2 [m] Rev 19:12 [n] Rev 1:15
10:7 [o] 2Ki 6:17-20; Ac 9:7
10:8 [p] Ge 32:24 [q] Da 8:27 [r] Hab 3:16
10:9 [s] Da 8:18
10:10 [t] Jer 1:9 [u] Rev 1:17
10:11 [v] Da 9:23 [w] Eze 2:1
10:12 [x] Da 9:3 [y] Da 9:20
10:13 [z] ver 21; Da 12:1; Jude 1:9
10:14 [a] Da 9:22 [b] Da 2:28; 8:26; Hab 2:3
10:15 [c] Eze 24:27; Lk 1:20
10:16 [d] Isa 6:7; Jer 1:9; Da 8:15-18

Week 25

Prayer

For three weeks Daniel prays and fasts and mourns (Da 10:2-3)—three full weeks of abstaining from choice meats and wines and "lotions" (what an interesting window into that culture). He has had a revelation from God, and he is seeking to understand it (Da 10:1). Then he experiences a breakthrough. And what a breakthrough it is! A man appears to Daniel in a vision and tells him, "Your words were heard" (Da 10:12).

Do you ever pray and pray and feel like no one is listening—like your prayers go no farther than the walls or ceiling of the room? Does God hear, even when you feel like he doesn't? Is he *always* listening? Let's look at what Scripture says about prayer.

Prayer is a means of communication with God (Ps 54:2). When have you felt like words could not express what was in your heart? What is God's provision for you in such times (Ro 8:26-27)?

Jesus makes prayer a high priority during his earthly ministry (Lk 6:12; Heb 5:7). What type of environment does he seek out for extended times of prayer (Mt 14:23; Mk 1:35)? Where does Jesus suggest people pray (Mt 6:5-6)? Why would this be important?

How can your spiritual condition hinder your prayers (Isa 59:2; Jas 1:6-7; 4:3)? How can your relationships with other people hinder your prayers (Pr 21:13; Mt 5:23-24; 1Pe 3:7)?

What makes prayer effective (Jas 5:16; 1Pe 3:10-12)?

What are some of the benefits of prayer (Lk 22:46; Ac 28:8; Jas 5:13-15)? What does God want to reveal to you when you pray (Jer 33:3)?

Why is intercession—prayer for others—important (Ge 18:16-33; Ps 106:23; Eze 22:29-31)?

Enjoying God through the Word

Read Luke 18:9-14 (page 1723). The parable of the tax collector and the Pharisee reveals that the prayers of the humble are heard by God and that righteousness comes through humility. The Pharisee stands up—probably in the center of the temple area where he can be clearly seen—and proceeds to pray "about himself" (Lk 18:11). He is quick to compare himself to others, lifting himself up and listing all his good deeds. The tax collector, on the other hand, stands at a distance, away from the center of attention. He compares himself to God's holiness, and, seeing his unworthiness, he cries out for God's mercy. Which man leaves the temple justified? The tax collector. "For everyone who exalts himself will be humbled, and he who humbles himself will be exalted" (Lk 18:14). Humility is the key to righteousness and to answered prayers.

Enjoying God through Experience

When you pray, you approach God himself. That knowledge alone should make you humble. The wonderful result of humility is that God's *grace* is released (Pr 3:34). God's grace, offered through Jesus, gives you the confidence you need to approach God's holy throne (Heb 4:16). God desires to hear you and answer you. Go to him in prayer right now. Throw off everything that hinders humility. Enjoy God's presence, and believe that he hears and will answer you when you call out to him (2Ch 7:14; Ps 6:9).

Go to page 1471 for your next weekly study.

Who Are These Kings?

DA 11:2–6

The "mighty king" refers to Alexander the Great, the Greek king who conquered Persia. After his death, his kingdom was divided into four parts, each one ruled by one of his *generals*. The "king of the South" (Da 11:5) refers to the Ptolemies of Egypt, while the "king of the North" (Da 11:6) refers to the Seleucids of Syria. Daniel outlines in *great* detail the intrigue in the courts of these two family lines. What he predicts comes true.

I said to the one standing before me, "I am overcome with anguish[e] because of the vision, my lord, and I am helpless. 17 How can I, your servant, talk with you, my lord? My strength is gone and I can hardly breathe."[f]

18 Again the one who looked like a man touched[g] me and gave me strength. 19 "Do not be afraid, O man highly esteemed," he said. "Peace![h] Be strong now; be strong."[i]

When he spoke to me, I was strengthened and said, "Speak, my lord, since you have given me strength."[j]

20 So he said, "Do you know why I have come to you? Soon I will return to fight against the prince of Persia, and when I go, the prince of Greece[k] will come; 21 but first I will tell you what is written in the Book of Truth.[l] (No one supports me against them except Michael,[m] your prince.

11 1 And in the first year of Darius[n] the Mede, I took my stand to support and protect him.)

The Kings of the South and the North

2 "Now then, I tell you the truth:[o] Three more kings will appear in Persia, and then a fourth, who will be far richer than all the others. When he has gained power by his wealth, he will stir up everyone against the kingdom of Greece.[p] 3 Then a mighty king will appear, who will rule with great power and do as he pleases.[q] 4 After he has appeared, his empire will be broken up and parceled out toward the four winds of heaven.[r] It will not go to his descendants, nor will it have the power he exercised, because his empire will be uprooted and given to others.

5 "The king of the South will become strong, but one of his commanders will become even stronger than he and will rule his own kingdom with great power. 6 After some years, they will become allies. The daughter of the king of the South will go to the king of the North to make an alliance, but she will not retain her power, and he and his power[a] will not last. In those days she will be handed over, together with her royal escort and her father[b] and the one who supported her.

7 "One from her family line will arise to take her place. He will attack the forces of the king of the North[s] and enter his fortress; he will fight against them and be victorious. 8 He will also seize their gods,[t] their metal images and their valuable articles of silver and gold and carry them off to Egypt.[u] For some years he will leave the king of the North alone. 9 Then the king of the North will invade the realm of the king of the South but will retreat to his own country. 10 His sons will prepare for war and assemble a great army, which will sweep on like an irresistible flood[v] and carry the battle as far as his fortress.

11 "Then the king of the South will march out in a rage and fight against the king of the North,

10:16 [e]Isa 21:3
10:17 [f]Da 4:19
10:18 [g]ver 16
10:19 [h]Jdg 6:23; Isa 35:4 [i]Jos 1:9 [j]Isa 6:1-8
10:20 [k]Da 8:21; 11:2
10:21 [l]Da 11:2 [m]ver 13; Jude 1:9
11:1 [n]Da 5:31
11:2 [o]Da 10:21 [p]Da 10:20
11:3 [q]Da 8:4,21
11:4 [r]Da 7:2; 8:22
11:7 [s]ver 6
11:8 [t]Isa 37:19; 46:1-2 [u]Jer 43:12
11:10 [v]Isa 8:8; Jer 46:8; Da 9:26

[a] 6 Or *offspring* [b] 6 Or *child* (see Vulgate and Syriac)

11:11 who will raise a large army, but it will be defeat-
[w]Da 8:7-8 ed.[w] [12]When the army is carried off, the king of
the South will be filled with pride and will slaughter many thousands, yet he will not remain triumphant. [13]For the king of the North will muster
another army, larger than the first; and after several years, he will advance with a huge army fully equipped.

[14]"In those times many will rise against the king
of the South. The violent men among your own
people will rebel in fulfillment of the vision, but
11:15 without success. [15]Then the king of the North will
[x]Eze 4:2 come and build up siege ramps[x] and will capture a
fortified city. The forces of the South will be powerless to resist; even their best troops will not have
11:16 the strength to stand. [16]The invader will do as he
[y]Da 8:4 pleases;[y] no one will be able to stand against him.[z]
[z]Jos 1:5; Da 8:7 He will establish himself in the Beautiful Land and
[a]Da 8:9 will have the power to destroy it.[a] [17]He will determine to come with the might of his entire king-
dom and will make an alliance with the king of
the South. And he will give him a daughter in
11:17 marriage in order to overthrow the kingdom, but
[b]Ps 20:4 his plans[a] will not succeed[b] or help him. [18]Then
11:18 he will turn his attention to the coastlands[c] and
[c]Isa 66:19; will take many of them, but a commander will put
Jer 25:22 an end to his insolence and will turn his insolence
[d]Hos 12:14 back upon him.[d] [19]After this, he will turn back
11:19 [e]Ps 27:2 toward the fortresses of his own country but will
[f]Ps 37:36; stumble and fall,[e] to be seen no more.[f]

Eze 26:21 [20]"His successor will send out a tax collector to
maintain the royal splendor.[g] In a few years, how-
11:20 [g]Isa 60:17 ever, he will be destroyed, yet not in anger or in
battle.

11:21 [21]"He will be succeeded by a contemptible[h] per-
[h]Da 4:17 [i]Da 8:25 son who has not been given the honor of royalty.[i]
He will invade the kingdom when its people feel
secure, and he will seize it through intrigue.
[22]Then an overwhelming army will be swept away
11:22 before him; both it and a prince of the covenant
[j]Da 8:10-11 will be destroyed.[j] [23]After coming to an agreement
11:23 with him, he will act deceitfully,[k] and with only a
[k]Da 8:25 few people he will rise to power. [24]When the richest provinces feel secure, he will invade them and
will achieve what neither his fathers nor his fore-
11:24 fathers did. He will distribute plunder, loot and
[l]Ne 9:25 wealth among his followers.[l] He will plot the overthrow of fortresses—but only for a time.

[25]"With a large army he will stir up his strength
and courage against the king of the South. The
king of the South will wage war with a large and
very powerful army, but he will not be able to
stand because of the plots devised against him.
[26]Those who eat from the king's provisions will try
to destroy him; his army will be swept away, and
11:27 many will fall in battle. [27]The two kings, with their
[m]Ps 64:6 hearts bent on evil,[m] will sit at the same table and
[n]Ps 12:2; lie[n] to each other, but to no avail, because an end
Jer 9:5 [o]Hab 2:3 will still come at the appointed time.[o] [28]The king of

[a] 17 Or *but she*

Belshazzar had a
letter—
He never had but one;
Belshazzar's correspondence
Concluded and begun
In that immortal copy
The conscience of us all
Can read without its glasses
On revelation's wall.

—Emily Dickinson (1830-1886)

the North will return to his own country with great wealth, but his heart will be set against the holy covenant. He will take action against it and then return to his own country.

29 "At the appointed time he will invade the South again, but this time the outcome will be different from what it was before. 30 Ships of the western coastlands[a][p] will oppose him, and he will lose heart. Then he will turn back and vent his fury against the holy covenant. He will return and show favor to those who forsake the holy covenant.

31 "His armed forces will rise up to desecrate the temple fortress and will abolish the daily sacrifice. Then they will set up the abomination that causes desolation.[q] 32 With flattery he will corrupt those who have violated the covenant, but the people who know their God will firmly resist[r] him.

33 "Those who are wise will instruct[s] many, though for a time they will fall by the sword or be burned or captured or plundered.[t] 34 When they fall, they will receive a little help, and many who are not sincere[u] will join them. 35 Some of the wise will stumble, so that they may be refined,[v] purified and made spotless until the time of the end, for it will still come at the appointed time.

The King Who Exalts Himself

36 "The king will do as he pleases. He will exalt and magnify himself above every god and will say unheard-of things[w] against the God of gods.[x] He will be successful until the time of wrath[y] is completed, for what has been determined must take place. 37 He will show no regard for the gods of his fathers or for the one desired by women, nor will he regard any god, but will exalt himself above them all. 38 Instead of them, he will honor a god of fortresses; a god unknown to his fathers he will honor with gold and silver, with precious stones and costly gifts. 39 He will attack the mightiest fortresses with the help of a foreign god and will greatly honor those who acknowledge him. He will make them rulers over many people and will distribute the land at a price.[b]

40 "At the time of the end the king of the South[z] will engage him in battle, and the king of the North will storm[a] out against him with chariots and cavalry and a great fleet of ships. He will invade many countries and sweep through them like a flood.[b] 41 He will also invade the Beautiful Land. Many countries will fall, but Edom,[c] Moab[d] and the leaders of Ammon will be delivered from his hand. 42 He will extend his power over many countries; Egypt will not escape. 43 He will gain control of the treasures of gold and silver and all the riches of Egypt,[e] with the Libyans[f] and Nubians in submission. 44 But reports from the east and the north will alarm him, and he will set out in a great rage to destroy and annihilate many. 45 He will pitch his royal tents between the seas

11:30 [p]Ge 10:4
11:31 [q]Da 8:11-13; 9:27; Mt 24:15*; Mk 13:14*
11:32 [r]Mic 5:7-9
11:33 [s]Mal 2:7 [t]Mt 24:9; Jn 16:2; Heb 11:32-38
11:34 [u]Mt 7:15; Ro 16:18
11:35 [v]Ps 78:38; Da 12:10; Zec 13:9; Jn 15:2
11:36 [w]Rev 13:5-6 [x]Dt 10:17; Isa 14:13-14; Da 7:25; 8:11-12,25; 2Th 2:4 [y]Isa 10:25; 26:20
11:40 [z]Isa 21:1 [a]Isa 5:28 [b]Eze 38:4
11:41 [c]Isa 11:14 [d]Jer 48:47
11:43 [e]Eze 30:4 [f]2Ch 12:3; Na 3:9

A Christian will find it cheaper to pardon than to resent. *Forgiveness saves the expense of anger, the cost of hatred, the waste of spirits.*

—Hannah More (1745–1833)

[a] 30 Hebrew *of Kittim* [b] 39 Or *land for a reward*

at[a] the beautiful holy mountain. Yet he will come
to his end, and no one will help him.

The End Times

12 "At that time Michael,[g] the great prince who
protects your people, will arise. There will
be a time of distress[h] such as has not happened
from the beginning of nations until then. But at
that time your people—everyone whose name is
found written in the book[i]—will be delivered.[j]
[2]Multitudes who sleep in the dust of the earth will
awake: some to everlasting life, others to shame
and everlasting contempt.[k] [3]Those who are wise[b][l]
will shine[m] like the brightness of the heavens, and
those who lead many to righteousness, like the
stars for ever and ever.[n] [4]But you, Daniel, close up
and seal[o] the words of the scroll until the time of
the end.[p] Many will go here and there to increase
knowledge."

[5]Then I, Daniel, looked, and there before me
stood two others, one on this bank of the river and
one on the opposite bank.[q] [6]One of them said to
the man clothed in linen,[r] who was above the
waters of the river, "How long will it be before
these astonishing things are fulfilled?"[s]

[7]The man clothed in linen, who was above the
waters of the river, lifted his right hand and his
left hand toward heaven, and I heard him swear
by him who lives forever,[t] saying, "It will be for a
time, times and half a time.[c][u] When the power of
the holy people[v] has been finally broken, all these
things will be completed.[w]"

[8]I heard, but I did not understand. So I asked,
"My lord, what will the outcome of all this be?"

[9]He replied, "Go your way, Daniel, because the
words are closed up and sealed until the time of
the end.[x] [10]Many will be purified, made spotless
and refined,[y] but the wicked will continue to be
wicked.[z] None of the wicked will understand, but
those who are wise will understand.[a]

[11]"From the time that the daily sacrifice is abolished
and the abomination that causes desolation[b]
is set up, there will be 1,290 days. [12]Blessed is the
one who waits[c] for and reaches the end of the
1,335 days.[d]

[13]"As for you, go your way till the end. You will
rest,[e] and then at the end of the days you will rise
to receive your allotted inheritance.[f]"

12:1 [g]Da 10:13 [h]Da 9:12; Mt 24:21; Mk 13:19; Rev 16:18 [i]Ex 32:32; Ps 56:8 [j]Jer 30:7
12:2 [k]Isa 26:19; Mt 25:46; Jn 5:28-29
12:3 [l]Da 11:33 [m]Mt 13:43; Jn 5:35 [n]1Co 15:42
12:4 [o]Isa 8:16 [p]ver 9,13; Rev 22:10
12:5 [q]Da 10:4
12:6 [r]Eze 9:2 [s]Da 8:13
12:7 [t]Rev 10:5-6 [u]Da 7:25 [v]Da 8:24 [w]Lk 21:24; Rev 10:7
12:9 [x]ver 4
12:10 [y]Da 11:35 [z]Isa 32:7; Rev 22:11 [a]Hos 14:9
12:11 [b]Da 8:11; 9:27; Mt 24:15*; Mk 13:14*
12:12 [c]Isa 30:18 [d]Da 8:14
12:13 [e]Isa 57:2 [f]Ps 16:5; Rev 14:13

Daniel's Prophecy

DA 12:5-13

Daniel's prophecy has both immediate and future fulfillment. As Daniel 11 reveals, *his prophecy is fulfilled down to the last detail in the rise and fall of the kingdoms that follow the Medes and the Persians.* But there are also prophecies in Daniel that *have yet to find fulfillment.* Exactly how that fulfillment will take place and what Daniel's words mean are disputed. But the basic truth stands: Those who remain faithful will be rewarded with everlasting life with God; the ungodly will be condemned to eternal punishment (Da 12:1-2). Though no one knows the day or the hour, believers can rest assured that God will fully establish his kingdom on earth. In the meantime, this prophecy and God's promise to the faithful will fortify us against evil and bring fresh hope and joyful anticipation of what is to come if we persevere.

[a] 45 Or *the sea and* [b] 3 Or *who impart wisdom* [c] 7 Or *a year, two years and half a year*

Loving pursuit of the unfaithful.

Quick Study

Author
The prophet Hosea.

Date Written
The middle of the eighth century B.C.

Setting
The northern kingdom of Israel.

Key Passage
Hosea 2:23 "I will show my love to the one I called 'Not my loved one.'
I will say to those called 'Not my people,' 'You are my people,'
and they will say, 'You are my God.' "

Hosea delivers this message of warning to the northern kingdom of Israel just a few short years before they are sent into exile. Israel has made unwise alliances with Assyria and Egypt (Hos 7:11) and adopted their idolatrous practices. The events of Hosea's personal life parallel the sins of the people and God's unconditional love for them, as well as reminding the people of God's promised judgment for disobedience.

Hosea's story is a painful tale of love and unfaithfulness. At God's command, Hosea takes Gomer as his wife. She is unfaithful to him, paralleling Israel's unfaithfulness to God. The children born of their union are given names dictated by God. Our hearts break when Hosea names one of his children "Lo-Ruhamah," meaning *not loved,* and another "Lo-Ammi," meaning *not my people.* Yet as we follow the book to its conclusion, we also find reason for hope. When Hosea lovingly brings Gomer home following her descent into prostitution, God reveals his loving restoration of his people (Hos 3). And God announces to Hosea that he will not always call his people "not loved" and "not my people." When they turn to him, he will show them his love and restore them (Hos 2:23).

Hosea ends his book with a series of sermons that declare God's holiness, justice and love. Though God will discipline his people for disobedience, his compassion for them will never cease. As Hosea seeks out his unfaithful wife and brings her back home, we are assured that, like Gomer and the Israelites, we are never too far gone for God's grace. Repentance always brings restoration and blessing (Hos 14).

Outline

Hosea's wife and children.
Hos 1:1–2:1

Israel's punishment and restoration.
Hos 2:2–23

Reconciliation.
Hos 3:1–5

Israel's unfaithfulness.
Hos 4:1–6:3

Israel's punishment.
Hos 6:4–10:15

The Lord's faithful love.
Hos 11:1–14:9

The Women of Hosea

⚘ **Gomer**	***An unfaithful wife.*** Hos 1:2–11; 3:1–5 (page 1476)
Lo-Ruhamah	***Her name meant "not loved."*** Hos 1:6,8
Mother and wife	***Symbolic of unfaithful Israel.*** Hos 2:2–23; 4:1–10:15

⚘ ***Denotes a sketch written about this character***

God's Workings and Ways

HOS 1:2–11

Hosea obeys God's instruction to marry Gomer, a prostitute. Although difficult—even repulsive—Hosea does not hesitate. Just as the Lord reveals himself to Job through his suffering and gains a more intimate relationship with him, the Lord uses Hosea's marriage to Gomer to mirror the people of Israel's unfaithful relationship with him. And Hosea, like Job, remains faithful to God throughout his suffering. He honors his marital commitment, just as the Lord honors his commitment to Israel despite her persistent disobedience. What cause for hope this is for us today! God is always ready to forgive and restore us when we repent—regardless of our sin or the events in our lives that challenge our faith. (See character sketch for Gomer on page 1476.)

1 The word of the LORD that came to Hosea son
of Beeri during the reigns of Uzziah, Jotham,
Ahaz and Hezekiah, kings of Judah,[a] and during
the reign of Jeroboam[b] son of Jehoash[a] king of
Israel:[c]

Hosea's Wife and Children

2 When the LORD began to speak through Hosea,
the LORD said to him, "Go, take to yourself an
adulterous[d] wife and children of unfaithfulness,
because the land is guilty of the vilest adultery[e]
in departing from the LORD." 3 So he married
Gomer daughter of Diblaim, and she conceived
and bore him a son.
4 Then the LORD said to Hosea, "Call him Jezreel,[f] because I will soon punish the house of Jehu
for the massacre at Jezreel, and I will put an end
to the kingdom of Israel. 5 In that day I will break
Israel's bow in the Valley of Jezreel.[g]"
6 Gomer[h] conceived again and gave birth to a
daughter. Then the LORD said to Hosea, "Call her
Lo-Ruhamah,[b] for I will no longer show love to the
house of Israel,[i] that I should at all forgive them.
7 Yet I will show love to the house of Judah; and I
will save them—not by bow,[j] sword or battle, or by
horses and horsemen, but by the LORD their God.[k]"
8 After she had weaned Lo-Ruhamah, Gomer
had another son. 9 Then the LORD said, "Call him
Lo-Ammi,[c] for you are not my people, and I am
not your God.
10 "Yet the Israelites will be like the sand on the
seashore, which cannot be measured or counted.[l]
In the place where it was said to them, 'You are
not my people,' they will be called 'sons of the living God.'[m] 11 The people of Judah and the people of
Israel will be reunited,[n] and they will appoint one
leader[o] and will come up out of the land,[p] for
great will be the day of Jezreel.

2 "Say of your brothers, 'My people,' and of your
sisters, 'My loved one.'[q]

Israel Punished and Restored

2 "Rebuke your mother,[r] rebuke her,
for she is not my wife,
and I am not her husband.
Let her remove the adulterous[s] look
from her face
and the unfaithfulness from between
her breasts.
3 Otherwise I will strip her naked
and make her as bare as on the day
she was born;[t]
I will make her like a desert,[u]
turn her into a parched land,
and slay her with thirst.
4 I will not show my love to her children,[v]
because they are the children of
adultery.

1:1 [a]Isa 1:1; Mic 1:1 [b]2Ki 13:13 [c]Am 1:1
1:2 [d]Jer 3:1; Hos 2:2,5; 3:1 [e]Dt 31:16; Jer 3:14; Eze 23:3-21; Hos 5:3
1:4 [f]2Ki 10:1-14; Hos 2:22
1:5 [g]2Ki 15:29
1:6 [h]ver 3 [i]Hos 2:4
1:7 [j]Ps 44:6 [k]Zec 4:6
1:10 [l]Ge 22:17; Jer 33:22 [m]ver 9; Ro 9:26*
1:11 [n]Isa 11:12,13 [o]Jer 23:5-8 [p]Eze 37:15-28
2:1 [q]ver 23
2:2 [r]ver 5; Isa 50:1; Hos 1:2 [s]Eze 23:45
2:3 [t]Eze 16:4,22 [u]Isa 32:13-14
2:4 [v]Eze 8:18

[a] *1* Hebrew *Joash,* a variant of *Jehoash* [b] *6* *Lo-Ruhamah* means *not loved.* [c] *9* *Lo-Ammi* means *not my people.*

5 Their mother has been unfaithful
and has conceived them in disgrace.
She said, 'I will go after my lovers,[w]
who give me my food and my water,
my wool and my linen, my oil and my drink.'[x]
6 Therefore I will block her path with thornbushes;
I will wall her in so that she cannot find her way.[y]
7 She will chase after her lovers but not catch them;
she will look for them but not find them.[z]
Then she will say,
'I will go back to my husband as at first,[a]
for then I was better off[b] than now.'
8 She has not acknowledged[c] that I was the one
who gave her the grain, the new wine and oil,
who lavished on her the silver and gold—
which they used for Baal.[d]

9 "Therefore I will take away my grain[e]
when it ripens,
and my new wine[f] when it is ready.
I will take back my wool and my linen,
intended to cover her nakedness.
10 So now I will expose her lewdness
before the eyes of her lovers;
no one will take her out of my hands.[g]
11 I will stop[h] all her celebrations:
her yearly festivals, her New Moons,
her Sabbath days—all her appointed feasts.[i]
12 I will ruin her vines[j] and her fig trees,
which she said were her pay from her lovers;
I will make them a thicket,[k]
and wild animals will devour them.[l]
13 I will punish her for the days
she burned incense to the Baals;[m]
she decked herself with rings and jewelry,[n]
and went after her lovers,[o]
but me she forgot,[p]"
declares the LORD.

14 "Therefore I am now going to allure her;
I will lead her into the desert
and speak tenderly to her.
15 There I will give her back her vineyards,
and will make the Valley of Achor[a][q] a door of hope.
There she will sing[b][r] as in the days of her youth,[s]

2:5 [w]Jer 3:6 [x]Jer 44:17-18
2:6 [y]Job 3:23; 19:8; La 3:9
2:7 [z]Hos 5:13 [a]Jer 2:2; 3:1 [b]Eze 16:8
2:8 [c]Isa 1:3 [d]Eze 16:15-19; Hos 8:4
2:9 [e]Hos 8:7 [f]Hos 9:2
2:10 [g]Eze 16:37
2:11 [h]Jer 7:34 [i]Isa 1:14; Jer 16:9; Hos 3:4; Am 8:10
2:12 [j]Isa 7:23; Jer 8:13 [k]Isa 5:6 [l]Hos 13:8
2:13 [m]Hos 11:2 [n]Eze 16:17 [o]Hos 4:13 [p]Hos 4:6; 8:14; 13:6
2:15 [q]Jos 7:24,26 [r]Ex 15:1-18 [s]Jer 2:2

[a] 15 *Achor* means *trouble.* [b] 15 Or *respond*

Spiritual Unfaithfulness

HOS 2:2–23

Gomer is unfaithful to her marriage vows, a mirror of Israel's unfaithfulness to the Lord. The picture in these verses is one of blatant unfaithfulness. Without thought God's people go their own way into licentiousness and worship of false gods. They forget who has given them every past blessing. They run from God to indulge in all kinds of wickedness.

But it is not God's intention to leave them in their sin. Continuing the metaphor of marriage, God says he will "allure her" and "speak tenderly to her" (Hos 2:14). She will again call him her "husband" (Hos 2:16), and he will show his love to her (Hos 2:23). Without fail, the God who is righteously disturbed and angered at his people's unfaithfulness still works to draw them lovingly back to himself. The picture is one of comfort and reassurance for all those who have wandered.

Reconciliation

HOS 3:2-3

It is hard to imagine that Hosea would even want to take Gomer back after she has run away from him and their children. But he does as the Lord instructs. Evidently Gomer has sold herself into slavery, possibly as a temple prostitute. Hosea has to pay the man who has bought his wife at least the price her owner had originally paid. The picture gets clearer and clearer of a God who is faithful to Israel—and to us, even when we don't deserve it.

as in the day she came up out of
Egypt.[t]

16 "In that day," declares the LORD,
"you will call me 'my husband';
you will no longer call me 'my
master.[a]'
17 I will remove the names of the Baals
from her lips;[u]
no longer will their names be
invoked.[v]
18 In that day I will make a covenant for
them
with the beasts of the field and the
birds of the air
and the creatures that move along the
ground.[w]
Bow and sword and battle
I will abolish[x] from the land,
so that all may lie down in safety.[y]
19 I will betroth[z] you to me forever;
I will betroth you in[b] righteousness
and justice,[a]
in[c] love and compassion.
20 I will betroth you in faithfulness,
and you will acknowledge[b] the LORD.

21 "In that day I will respond,"
declares the LORD—
"I will respond[c] to the skies,
and they will respond to the earth;
22 and the earth will respond to the grain,
the new wine and oil,[a]
and they will respond to Jezreel.[d]
23 I will plant[e] her for myself in the land;
I will show my love to the one I called
'Not my loved one.[e][f]'
I will say to those called 'Not my
people,[f]' 'You are my people';[g]
and they will say, 'You are my
God.[h]' "

Hosea's Reconciliation With His Wife

3 The LORD said to me, "Go, show your love to
your wife again, though she is loved by another and is an adulteress.[i] Love her as the LORD loves
the Israelites, though they turn to other gods and
love the sacred raisin cakes.[j]"
2 So I bought her for fifteen shekels[g] of silver
and about a homer and a lethek[h] of barley. 3 Then
I told her, "You are to live with[i] me many days;
you must not be a prostitute or be intimate with
any man, and I will live with[i] you."
4 For the Israelites will live many days without
king or prince,[k] without sacrifice[l] or sacred
stones, without ephod or idol.[m] 5 Afterward the
Israelites will return and seek the LORD their God

2:15 [t]Hos 12:9
2:17 [u]Ex 23:13; Ps 16:4 [v]Jos 23:7
2:18 [w]Job 5:22 [x]Isa 2:4 [y]Jer 23:6; Eze 34:25
2:19 [z]Isa 62:4 [a]Isa 1:27
2:20 [b]Jer 31:34; Hos 6:6; 13:4
2:21 [c]Isa 55:10; Zec 8:12
2:22 [d]Jer 31:12; Joel 2:19
2:23 [e]Jer 31:27 [f]Hos 1:6 [g]Hos 1:10 [h]Ro 9:25*; 1Pe 2:10
3:1 [i]Hos 1:2 [j]2Sa 6:19
3:4 [k]Hos 13:11 [l]Da 11:31; Hos 2:11 [m]Jdg 17:5-6; Zec 10:2

[a] *16* Hebrew *baal* [b] *19* Or *with*; also in verse 20 [c] *19* Or *with* [d] *22* *Jezreel* means *God plants.* [e] *23* Hebrew *Lo-Ruhamah* [f] *23* Hebrew *Lo-Ammi* [g] *2* That is, about 6 ounces (about 170 grams) [h] *2* That is, probably about 10 bushels (about 330 liters) [i] *3* Or *wait for*

and David their king.[n] They will come trembling
to the LORD and to his blessings in the last days.[o]

The Charge Against Israel

4 Hear the word of the LORD, you Israelites,
because the LORD has a charge to bring
against you who live in the land:
"There is no faithfulness, no love,
no acknowledgment[p] of God in the
land.
[2] There is only cursing,[a] lying[q] and
murder,[r]
stealing[s] and adultery;
they break all bounds,
and bloodshed follows bloodshed.
[3] Because of this the land mourns,[b][t]
and all who live in it waste away;[u]
the beasts of the field and the birds of
the air
and the fish of the sea are dying.[v]

[4] "But let no man bring a charge,
let no man accuse another,
for your people are like those
who bring charges against a priest.[w]
[5] You stumble[x] day and night,
and the prophets stumble with you.
So I will destroy your mother[y]—
[6] my people are destroyed from lack of
knowledge.[z]

"Because you have rejected knowledge,
I also reject you as my priests;
because you have ignored the law[a] of
your God,
I also will ignore your children.
[7] The more the priests increased,
the more they sinned against me;
they exchanged[c] their[d] Glory[b] for
something disgraceful.[c]
[8] They feed on the sins of my people
and relish their wickedness.[d]
[9] And it will be: Like people, like priests.[e]
I will punish both of them for their
ways
and repay them for their deeds.[f]
[10] "They will eat but not have enough;[g]
they will engage in prostitution but
not increase,
because they have deserted[h] the LORD
to give themselves [11] to prostitution,[i]
to old wine and new,
which take away the understanding[j]
[12] of my people.
They consult a wooden idol[k]
and are answered by a stick of wood.[l]

[a] 2 That is, to pronounce a curse upon [b] 3 Or *dries up*
[c] 7 Syriac and an ancient Hebrew scribal tradition; Masoretic Text *I will exchange* [d] 7 Masoretic Text; an ancient Hebrew scribal tradition *my*

3:5 [n] Eze 34:23-24 [o] Jer 50:4-5
4:1 [p] Jer 7:28
4:2 [q] Hos 7:3; 10:4 [r] Hos 6:9 [s] Hos 7:1
4:3 [t] Jer 4:28 [u] Isa 33:9 [v] Jer 4:25; Zep 1:3
4:4 [w] Dt 17:12; Eze 3:26
4:5 [x] Eze 14:7 [y] Hos 2:2
4:6 [z] Hos 2:13; Mal 2:7-8 [a] Hos 8:1,12
4:7 [b] Hab 2:16 [c] Hos 10:1,6; 13:6
4:8 [d] Isa 56:11; Mic 3:11
4:9 [e] Isa 24:2 [f] Jer 5:31; Hos 8:13; 9:9,15
4:10 [g] Lev 26:26; Mic 6:14 [h] Hos 7:14; 9:17
4:11 [i] Hos 5:4 [j] Pr 20:1
4:12 [k] Jer 2:27 [l] Hab 2:19

The entire book of Hosea gives us a metaphorical picture of God (Hosea) loving his people (Gomer) in spite of their unfaithfulness . . . The Israelites, with their unstable, willful disobedience to God, are at an all-time low. The nation is a mess. They live in civil revolt, anarchy and bloodshed that has gone on for more than three hundred years . . . The homes are corrupt, the courts are corrupt and even the priests are corrupt. There is no spiritual health to be found.

Into this societal cesspool God drops Hosea to be a prophet to illustrate God's love for his unworthy, faithless bride, the Israelite people. God does this by having the people watch Hosea as he stands by the wayward Gomer, buys her out of slavery, and ultimately brings her home to himself. She didn't deserve that love from Hosea, and neither did the Israelites deserve that love from God. But love he did and love he still does . . . That's not to say that God was not also furious with these people . . . Yet in spite of their godless indifference, sin-seeking preferences and revolting practices of idolatry, God still said: "I will heal their waywardness and love them freely" (Hos 14:4).

—Marilyn Meberg

Spiritual Prostitution

HOS 4:12–14

The people's "spirit of prostitution leads them astray" (Hos 4:12). They have a bent toward unfaithfulness to God. God refers in Hosea 4:13–14 to the cultural/historical connection between prostitution and idolatry. Men worshiped at pagan shrines on hills and mountains. Part of the ritual of worship included sexual intercourse with shrine prostitutes. These practices had an immoral influence on their daughters and daughters-in-law so that they sold themselves into shrine prostitution at these same pagan temples.

People today have this same bent toward unfaithfulness. The act of prostitution may not be involved, but anytime we turn to our culture for gratification or consolation instead of turning to God, we exhibit that same dangerous "spirit of prostitution."

A spirit of prostitution leads them
astray;[m]
they are unfaithful to their God.
13 They sacrifice on the mountaintops
and burn offerings on the hills,
under oak,[n] poplar and terebinth,
where the shade is pleasant.[o]
Therefore your daughters turn to
prostitution[p]
and your daughters-in-law to
adultery.[q]

14 "I will not punish your daughters
when they turn to prostitution,
nor your daughters-in-law
when they commit adultery,
because the men themselves consort
with harlots[r]
and sacrifice with shrine prostitutes—
a people without understanding will
come to ruin!

15 "Though you commit adultery, O Israel,
let not Judah become guilty.

"Do not go to Gilgal;[s]
do not go up to Beth Aven.[a]
And do not swear, 'As surely as the
LORD lives!'
16 The Israelites are stubborn,
like a stubborn heifer.
How then can the LORD pasture them
like lambs[t] in a meadow?
17 Ephraim is joined to idols;
leave him alone!
18 Even when their drinks are gone,
they continue their prostitution;
their rulers dearly love shameful
ways.
19 A whirlwind[u] will sweep them away,
and their sacrifices will bring them
shame.[v]

Judgment Against Israel

5 "Hear this, you priests!
Pay attention, you Israelites!
Listen, O royal house!
This judgment is against you:
You have been a snare[w] at Mizpah,
a net spread out on Tabor.
2 The rebels are deep in slaughter.[x]
I will discipline all of them.[y]
3 I know all about Ephraim;
Israel is not hidden from me.
Ephraim, you have now turned to
prostitution;
Israel is corrupt.[z]

4 "Their deeds do not permit them
to return to their God.

4:12 [m]Isa 44:20
4:13 [n]Isa 1:29 [o]Jer 3:6; Hos 11:2 [p]Jer 2:20; Am 7:17 [q]Hos 2:13
4:14 [r]ver 11
4:15 [s]Hos 9:15; 12:11; Am 4:4
4:16 [t]Isa 5:17; 7:25
4:19 [u]Hos 12:1; 13:15 [v]Isa 1:29
5:1 [w]Hos 6:9; 9:8
5:2 [x]Hos 4:2 [y]Hos 9:15
5:3 [z]Hos 6:10

[a] 15 *Beth Aven* means *house of wickedness* (a name for Bethel, which means *house of God*).

A spirit of prostitution[a] is in their heart;
  they do not acknowledge[b] the LORD.
5 Israel's arrogance testifies[c] against them;
  the Israelites, even Ephraim, stumble
    in their sin;
  Judah also stumbles with them.
6 When they go with their flocks and
    herds
  to seek the LORD,[d]
they will not find him;
  he has withdrawn[e] himself from
    them.
7 They are unfaithful[f] to the LORD;
  they give birth to illegitimate[g]
    children.
Now their New Moon festivals
  will devour[h] them and their fields.

8 "Sound the trumpet in Gibeah,[i]
  the horn in Ramah.[j]
Raise the battle cry in Beth Aven[a];[k]
  lead on, O Benjamin.
9 Ephraim will be laid waste
  on the day of reckoning.[l]
Among the tribes of Israel
  I proclaim what is certain.[m]
10 Judah's leaders are like those
  who move boundary stones.[n]
I will pour out my wrath[o] on them
  like a flood of water.
11 Ephraim is oppressed,
  trampled in judgment,
  intent on pursuing idols.[b][p]
12 I am like a moth[q] to Ephraim,
  like rot to the people of Judah.

13 "When Ephraim saw his sickness,
  and Judah his sores,
then Ephraim turned to Assyria,[r]
  and sent to the great king for help.[s]
But he is not able to cure[t] you,
  not able to heal your sores.[u]
14 For I will be like a lion[v] to Ephraim,
  like a great lion to Judah.
I will tear them to pieces and go away;
  I will carry them off, with no one to
    rescue them.[w]
15 Then I will go back to my place
  until they admit their guilt.
And they will seek my face;[x]
  in their misery[y] they will earnestly
    seek me.[z]"

Israel Unrepentant

6 "Come, let us return to the LORD.
He has torn us to pieces[a]
  but he will heal us;
he has injured us

5:4 [a]Hos 4:11 [b]Hos 4:6
5:5 [c]Hos 7:10
5:6 [d]Mic 6:6-7 [e]Pr 1:28; Isa 1:15; Eze 8:6
5:7 [f]Hos 6:7 [g]Hos 2:4 [h]Hos 2:11-12
5:8 [i]Hos 9:9; 10:9 [j]Isa 10:29 [k]Hos 4:15
5:9 [l]Isa 37:3; Hos 9:11-17 [m]Isa 46:10; Zec 1:6
5:10 [n]Dt 19:14 [o]Eze 7:8
5:11 [p]Hos 9:16; Mic 6:16
5:12 [q]Isa 51:8
5:13 [r]Hos 7:11; 8:9 [s]Hos 10:6 [t]Hos 14:3 [u]Jer 30:12
5:14 [v]Am 3:4 [w]Mic 5:8
5:15 [x]Hos 3:5 [y]Jer 2:27 [z]Isa 64:9
6:1 [a]Hos 5:14

[a] *8 Beth Aven* means *house of wickedness* (a name for Bethel, which means *house of God*). [b] *11* The meaning of the Hebrew for this word is uncertain.

Does God Hide?

HOS 5:6

God does *hide* himself from us when we blatantly and consistently disobey him (Isa 59:2). But he never *abandons* us. He has promised, "I will not leave you as orphans; I will come to you" (Jn 14:18). It is frightening to consider ever being separated from the love of God—even for a moment. But we never have to. He is always there to receive us when we come to him in sincere repentance.

Like the Spring Rains

HOS 6:1–3

Think for a moment of the wonderful feeling of a soft spring rain. It's fresh and warm. It cleans, brightens and restores. That's how God comes to his people when they repent. Though God deals with his people harshly when they break their covenant with him, he does not withhold himself. When they cry out to him, he comes like the spring rains. Unfortunately, in Hosea's time—as well as often throughout Israel's history—that repentance is short-lived. The cycle recorded so often in the book of Judges repeats itself throughout Israel's history: "The Israelites did evil in the eyes of the LORD . . . But when they cried out to the LORD, he raised up for them a deliverer" (Jdg 3:7,9). When the people sin and then repent, a faithful God is there with forgiveness and the restoration of soft spring rains. But his patience will not last forever. Judgment is coming.

but he will bind up our wounds.[b]
2 After two days he will revive us;[c]
on the third day he will restore us,
that we may live in his presence.
3 Let us acknowledge the LORD;
let us press on to acknowledge him.
As surely as the sun rises,
he will appear;
he will come to us like the winter rains,[d]
like the spring rains that water the earth.[e]"

4 "What can I do with you, Ephraim?[f]
What can I do with you, Judah?
Your love is like the morning mist,
like the early dew that disappears.[g]
5 Therefore I cut you in pieces with my prophets,
I killed you with the words of my mouth;[h]
my judgments flashed like lightning upon you.[i]
6 For I desire mercy, not sacrifice,[j]
and acknowledgment[k] of God rather than burnt offerings.
7 Like Adam,[a] they have broken the covenant[l]—
they were unfaithful[m] to me there.
8 Gilead is a city of wicked men,
stained with footprints of blood.
9 As marauders lie in ambush for a man,
so do bands of priests;
they murder on the road to Shechem,
committing shameful crimes.[n]
10 I have seen a horrible[o] thing
in the house of Israel.
There Ephraim is given to prostitution
and Israel is defiled.[p]

11 "Also for you, Judah,
a harvest[q] is appointed.

"Whenever I would restore the fortunes of my people,
7 1 whenever I would heal Israel,
the sins of Ephraim are exposed
and the crimes of Samaria revealed.[r]
They practice deceit,[s]
thieves break into houses,[t]
bandits rob in the streets;
2 but they do not realize
that I remember[u] all their evil deeds.
Their sins engulf them;[v]
they are always before me.

3 "They delight the king with their wickedness,
the princes with their lies.[w]
4 They are all adulterers,[x]
burning like an oven
whose fire the baker need not stir

6:1 [b]Dt 32:39; Jer 30:17; Hos 14:4
6:2 [c]Ps 30:5
6:3 [d]Joel 2:23 [e]Ps 72:6
6:4 [f]Hos 11:8 [g]Hos 7:1; 13:3
6:5 [h]Jer 1:9-10; 23:29 [i]Heb 4:12
6:6 [j]Isa 1:11; Mt 9:13*; 12:7* [k]Hos 2:20
6:7 [l]Hos 8:1 [m]Hos 5:7
6:9 [n]Jer 7:9-10; Eze 22:9; Hos 7:1
6:10 [o]Jer 5:30 [p]Hos 5:3
6:11 [q]Jer 51:33; Joel 3:13
7:1 [r]Hos 6:4 [s]ver 13 [t]Hos 4:2
7:2 [u]Jer 14:10; Hos 8:13 [v]Jer 2:19
7:3 [w]Hos 4:2; Mic 7:3
7:4 [x]Jer 9:2

[a] 7 Or *As at Adam*; or *Like men*

from the kneading of the dough till it
rises.
5 On the day of the festival of our king
7:5 the princes become inflamed with
[y]Isa 28:1,7 wine,[y]
and he joins hands with the mockers.
7:6 [z]Ps 21:9 6 Their hearts are like an oven;[z]
they approach him with intrigue.
Their passion smolders all night;
in the morning it blazes like a flaming
fire.
7 All of them are hot as an oven;
they devour their rulers.
7:7 All their kings fall,
[a]ver 16 and none of them calls[a] on me.

7:8 8 "Ephraim mixes[b] with the nations;
[b]ver 11; Ps 106:35; Ephraim is a flat cake not turned over.
Hos 5:13 9 Foreigners sap his strength,[c]
7:9 but he does not realize it.
[c]Isa 1:7; His hair is sprinkled with gray,
Hos 8:7 but he does not notice.
7:10 10 Israel's arrogance testifies against him,[d]
[d]Hos 5:5 but despite all this
[e]Isa 9:13 he does not return to the LORD his God
or search[e] for him.

7:11 [f]Hos 11:11 11 "Ephraim is like a dove,[f]
[g]Hos 5:13; easily deceived and senseless—
12:1 now calling to Egypt,
7:12 now turning to Assyria.[g]
[h]Eze 12:13 12 When they go, I will throw my net[h] over
them;
I will pull them down like birds of the
air.
When I hear them flocking together,
I will catch them.
7:13 [i]Hos 9:12 13 Woe[i] to them,
[j]Jer 14:10; because they have strayed[j] from me!
Eze 34:4-6; Destruction to them,
Hos 9:17 [k]ver 1; because they have rebelled against
Mt 23:37 me!
I long to redeem them
but they speak lies against me.[k]
7:14 14 They do not cry out to me from their
[l]Jer 3:10 hearts[l]
[m]Am 2:8 [n]Hos 13:16 but wail upon their beds.
They gather together[a] for grain and new
wine[m]
but turn away from me.[n]
7:15 15 I trained them and strengthened them,
[o]Na 1:9,11 but they plot evil[o] against me.
7:16 16 They do not turn to the Most High;
[p]Ps 78:9,57 they are like a faulty bow.[p]
[q]Eze 23:32 Their leaders will fall by the sword
[r]Hos 9:3 because of their insolent words.
For this they will be ridiculed[q]
in the land of Egypt.[r]

[a] *14* Most Hebrew manuscripts; some Hebrew manuscripts and Septuagint *They slash themselves*

Like an Oven

HOS 7:6

Lust—for power as well as other vices—threatens to consume the people of Israel. God likens the intensity of their emotion to a burning-hot oven. The heat is already so high there is no need for a baker to stoke the fire (Hos 7:4)! Passion, intrigue, immorality and debauchery flame within each one, and there is none among them willing to turn from the flame. The lust for power causes the princes of the land to assassinate their kings. Hosea does not mention any one king specifically, but several kings of Israel are killed just before judgment falls on the nation (2Ki 15:10,14,25,30).

Sowing and Reaping

HOS 8:7

Sow the wind, reap a whirlwind! As the people of Israel continue to plant the seeds of idolatry and lust, the result is a whirlwind of instability and chaos in their personal lives and in the life of their nation. Stalks have no heads and the few that remain are stolen by foreigners seeking to trample their land and destroy everything in sight. The truth of Hosea is the same for us today. If we sow the wind, putting comfort, money, career or other people before God, we too will reap a whirlwind. If we sow the Spirit of God, we reap the harvest of his love, protection and eternal life (Gal 6:7–8).

Israel to Reap the Whirlwind

8 "Put the trumpet to your lips!
An eagle[s] is over the house of the LORD
because the people have broken my covenant
and rebelled against my law.[t]
2 Israel cries out to me,
'O our God, we acknowledge you!'
3 But Israel has rejected what is good;
an enemy will pursue him.
4 They set up kings without my consent;
they choose princes without my approval.[u]
With their silver and gold
they make idols[v] for themselves
to their own destruction.
5 Throw out your calf-idol, O Samaria![w]
My anger burns against them.
How long will they be incapable of purity?[x]
6 They are from Israel!
This calf—a craftsman has made it;
it is not God.
It will be broken in pieces,
that calf of Samaria.

7 "They sow the wind
and reap the whirlwind.[y]
The stalk has no head;
it will produce no flour.
Were it to yield grain,
foreigners would swallow it up.[z]
8 Israel is swallowed up;[a]
now she is among the nations
like a worthless[b] thing.
9 For they have gone up to Assyria
like a wild donkey wandering alone.
Ephraim has sold herself to lovers.
10 Although they have sold themselves
among the nations,
I will now gather them together.[c]
They will begin to waste away[d]
under the oppression of the mighty king.

11 "Though Ephraim built many altars for sin offerings,
these have become altars for sinning.[e]
12 I wrote for them the many things of my law,
but they regarded them as something alien.
13 They offer sacrifices given to me
and they eat[f] the meat,
but the LORD is not pleased with them.
Now he will remember[g] their wickedness
and punish their sins:[h]
They will return to Egypt.[i]
14 Israel has forgotten[j] his Maker
and built palaces;

8:1 [s]Dt 28:49; Jer 4:13 [t]Hos 4:6; 6:7
8:4 [u]Hos 13:10 [v]Hos 2:8
8:5 [w]Hos 10:5 [x]Jer 13:27
8:7 [y]Pr 22:8; Isa 66:15; Hos 10:12-13; Na 1:3 [z]Hos 2:9
8:8 [a]Jer 51:34 [b]Jer 22:28
8:10 [c]Eze 16:37; 22:20 [d]Jer 42:2
8:11 [e]Hos 10:1; 12:11
8:13 [f]Jer 7:21 [g]Hos 7:2 [h]Hos 4:9 [i]Hos 9:3,6
8:14 [j]Dt 32:18; Hos 2:13

Judah has fortified many towns.
But I will send fire upon their cities
that will consume their fortresses."[k]

Punishment for Israel

9 Do not rejoice, O Israel;
do not be jubilant[l] like the other nations.
For you have been unfaithful[m] to your God;
you love the wages of a prostitute
at every threshing floor.
2 Threshing floors and winepresses will not feed the people;
the new wine[n] will fail them.
3 They will not remain[o] in the LORD's land;
Ephraim will return to Egypt[p]
and eat unclean[a] food in Assyria.[q]
4 They will not pour out wine offerings to the LORD,
nor will their sacrifices please[r] him.
Such sacrifices will be to them like the bread of mourners;
all who eat them will be unclean.[s]
This food will be for themselves;
it will not come into the temple of the LORD.

5 What will you do[t] on the day of your appointed feasts,[u]
on the festival days of the LORD?
6 Even if they escape from destruction,
Egypt will gather them,
and Memphis[v] will bury them.
Their treasures of silver will be taken over by briers,
and thorns[w] will overrun their tents.
7 The days of punishment[x] are coming,
the days of reckoning are at hand.
Let Israel know this.
Because your sins[y] are so many
and your hostility so great,
the prophet is considered a fool,[z]
the inspired man a maniac.
8 The prophet, along with my God,
is the watchman over Ephraim,[b]
yet snares[a] await him on all his paths,
and hostility in the house of his God.
9 They have sunk deep into corruption,
as in the days of Gibeah.[b]
God will remember[c] their wickedness
and punish them for their sins.

10 "When I found Israel,
it was like finding grapes in the desert;
when I saw your fathers,
it was like seeing the early fruit on the fig tree.

8:14 [k]Jer 17:27
9:1 [l]Isa 22:12-13 [m]Hos 10:5
9:2 [n]Hos 2:9
9:3 [o]Lev 25:23 [p]Hos 8:13 [q]Eze 4:13; Hos 7:11
9:4 [r]Jer 6:20; Hos 8:13 [s]Hag 2:13-14
9:5 [t]Isa 10:3; Jer 5:31 [u]Hos 2:11
9:6 [v]Isa 19:13 [w]Isa 5:6; Hos 10:8
9:7 [x]Isa 34:8; Jer 10:15; Mic 7:4 [y]Jer 16:18 [z]Isa 44:25; La 2:14; Eze 14:9-10
9:8 [a]Hos 5:1
9:9 [b]Jdg 19:16-30; Hos 5:8; 10:9 [c]Hos 8:13

[a] 3 That is, ceremonially unclean [b] 8 Or *The prophet is the watchman over Ephraim, / the people of my God*

On the Threshing Floor

HOS 9:1-2

At the end of the harvest, a feast was held on the threshing floor, where the reapers then slept to guard the grain from thieves. Women were not encouraged to attend, but prostitutes took advantage of the occasion. By contrast, Ruth went to the threshing floor to meet Boaz as he guarded the grain (Ru 3:1–15). She waited until the men were asleep in order to avoid being recognized and to protect Boaz's reputation. Her purpose, unlike a prostitute's, was to remind Boaz that he was the "redeeming relative" God had selected for her to marry, since her first husband had died.

God sometimes directs us to take an action that goes against custom or, at times, may even be illegal (Mt 12:11–12). But when we have an intimate relationship with God, we trust that he will work out the details. We need not be afraid.

Judgment

HOS 9:10–14

God tells the Israelites, very directly, what a bitter disappointment they are. Their dedication to idol worship, immorality and the sexual orgies of the festivals has earned his wrath. Ephraim, one of Hosea's primary designations for the northern kingdom of Israel, has come under the Lord's judgment. All the glory of the past will vanish! Women will be struck barren. And the children they are rearing will live with sorrow and death. Hosea echoes God's outrage in his impassioned plea to the Lord to cause the women to miscarry and their breasts to dry up. Even the God of mercy eventually withdraws his hand when his people continually defy his will and his generosity.

But when they came to Baal Peor,[d]
they consecrated themselves to that
shameful idol[e]
and became as vile as the thing they
loved.
[11] Ephraim's glory will fly away like a
bird[f]—
no birth, no pregnancy, no
conception.[g]
[12] Even if they rear children,
I will bereave them of every one.
Woe[h] to them
when I turn away from them![i]
[13] I have seen Ephraim, like Tyre,
planted in a pleasant place.[j]
But Ephraim will bring out
their children to the slayer."

[14] Give them, O LORD—
what will you give them?
Give them wombs that miscarry
and breasts that are dry.[k]
[15] "Because of all their wickedness in
Gilgal,[l]
I hated them there.
Because of their sinful deeds,[m]
I will drive them out of my house.
I will no longer love them;
all their leaders are rebellious.[n]
[16] Ephraim[o] is blighted,
their root is withered,
they yield no fruit.[p]
Even if they bear children,
I will slay[q] their cherished offspring."
[17] My God will reject them
because they have not obeyed[r] him;
they will be wanderers among the
nations.[s]

10 Israel was a spreading vine;[t]
he brought forth fruit for himself.
As his fruit increased,
he built more altars;[u]
as his land prospered,
he adorned his sacred stones.[v]
[2] Their heart is deceitful,[w]
and now they must bear their guilt.[x]
The LORD will demolish their altars[y]
and destroy their sacred stones.[z]

[3] Then they will say, "We have no king
because we did not revere the LORD.
But even if we had a king,
what could he do for us?"
[4] They make many promises,
take false oaths[a]
and make agreements;[b]
therefore lawsuits spring up
like poisonous weeds in a plowed
field.
[5] The people who live in Samaria fear

9:10 [d]Nu 25:1-5; Ps 106:28-29 [e]Jer 11:13; Hos 4:14
9:11 [f]Hos 4:7; 10:5 [g]ver 14
9:12 [h]Hos 7:13 [i]Dt 31:17
9:13 [j]Eze 27:3
9:14 [k]ver 11; Lk 23:29
9:15 [l]Hos 4:15 [m]Hos 7:2 [n]Isa 1:23; Hos 4:9; 5:2
9:16 [o]Hos 5:11 [p]Hos 8:7 [q]ver 12
9:17 [r]Hos 4:10 [s]Dt 28:65; Hos 7:13
10:1 [t]Eze 15:2 [u]1Ki 14:23 [v]Hos 8:11; 12:11
10:2 [w]1Ki 18:21 [x]Hos 13:16 [y]ver 8 [z]Mic 5:13
10:4 [a]Hos 4:2 [b]Eze 17:19; Am 5:7

for the calf-idol of Beth Aven.[a][c]
Its people will mourn over it,
and so will its idolatrous priests,[d]
those who had rejoiced over its
splendor,
because it is taken from them into
exile.[e]
6 It will be carried to Assyria[f]
as tribute for the great king.[g]
Ephraim will be disgraced;[h]
Israel will be ashamed of its wooden
idols.[b]
7 Samaria and its king will float away[i]
like a twig on the surface of the
waters.
8 The high places of wickedness[c][j] will be
destroyed—
it is the sin of Israel.
Thorns[k] and thistles will grow up
and cover their altars.[l]
Then they will say to the mountains,
"Cover us!"
and to the hills, "Fall on us!"[m]
9 "Since the days of Gibeah,[n] you have
sinned, O Israel,
and there you have remained.[d]
Did not war overtake
the evildoers in Gibeah?
10 When I please, I will punish[o] them;
nations will be gathered against them
to put them in bonds for their double
sin.
11 Ephraim is a trained heifer
that loves to thresh;
so I will put a yoke
on her fair neck.
I will drive Ephraim,
Judah must plow,
and Jacob must break up the ground.
12 Sow for yourselves righteousness,[p]
reap the fruit of unfailing love,
and break up your unplowed ground;[q]
for it is time to seek[r] the LORD,
until he comes
and showers righteousness[s] on you.
13 But you have planted wickedness,
you have reaped evil,[t]
you have eaten the fruit of deception.
Because you have depended on your
own strength
and on your many warriors,[u]
14 the roar of battle will rise against your
people,
so that all your fortresses will be
devastated[v]—

10:5 [c]Hos 5:8 [d]2Ki 23:5 [e]Hos 8:5; 9:1,3,11
10:6 [f]Hos 11:5 [g]Hos 5:13 [h]Isa 30:3; Hos 4:7
10:7 [i]Hos 13:11
10:8 [j]1Ki 12:28-30; Hos 4:13 [k]Hos 9:6 [l]ver 2; Isa 32:13 [m]Lk 23:30*; Rev 6:16
10:9 [n]Hos 5:8
10:10 [o]Eze 5:13; Hos 4:9
10:12 [p]Pr 11:18 [q]Jer 4:3 [r]Hos 12:6 [s]Isa 45:8
10:13 [t]Job 4:8; Hos 7:3; 11:12; Gal 6:7-8 [u]Ps 33:16
10:14 [v]Isa 17:3

[a] 5 *Beth Aven* means *house of wickedness* (a name for Bethel, which means *house of God*). [b] 6 Or *its counsel*
[c] 8 Hebrew *aven*, a reference to Beth Aven (a derogatory name for Bethel) [d] 9 Or *there a stand was taken*

Say to the Mountains . . .

HOS 10:8

When the Israelites finally wake up to the magnitude of their sin against God, they will be filled with shame. The very land where they worship idols and practice sexual immorality will be brought down, exposing their betrayal of the Lord. At that time they will want the mountains and hills to fall on them rather than have to stand before God and receive his judgment. Revelation 6:16 *echoes this passage.* Those who recognize their sin at the end of the world will prefer to have the mountains crush them than to have to face the God of judgment.

God As Parent

HOS 11:1-4

The image of God taking his chosen people by the hand—nurturing, leading, teaching and loving them as a parent would a child—is all the more poignant when we consider the outcome. Instead of growing in grace and power at the hand of their heavenly Father, the Israelites embrace the fleeting, sensual pleasures that lead them away from his protection and guidance. He leads them with "cords of human kindness" (Hos 11:4). Although the meaning of this phrase is somewhat uncertain, it could refer to a rope used to lift the heavy yoke from the neck of oxen so they can eat more comfortably or a father lifting his son to his cheek. Either way, the image is one of concern and tenderness.

This beautiful imagery includes a sobering message for us today. Will we walk under the guidance and protection of our Father God, or will we run from him to the passing pleasures of the world?

as Shalman devastated Beth Arbel on
the day of battle,
when mothers were dashed to the
ground with their children.[w] **10:14** [w]Hos 13:16
15 Thus will it happen to you, O Bethel,
because your wickedness is great.
When that day dawns,
the king of Israel will be completely **10:15**
destroyed.[x] [x]ver 7

God's Love for Israel

11 "When Israel was a child, I loved him, **11:1**
and out of Egypt I called my son.[y] [y]Ex 4:22;
2 But the more I[a] called Israel, Hos 12:9,13;
the further they went from me.[b] 13:4;
They sacrificed to the Baals[z] Mt 2:15*
and they burned incense to images.[a] **11:2**
3 It was I who taught Ephraim to walk, [z]Hos 2:13
taking them by the arms;[b] [a]2Ki 17:15;
but they did not realize Isa 65:7;
it was I who healed[c] them. Jer 18:15
4 I led them with cords of human **11:3**
kindness, [b]Dt 1:31;
with ties of love;[d] Hos 7:15
I lifted the yoke[e] from their neck [c]Jer 30:17
and bent down to feed[f] them. **11:4**
5 "Will they not return to Egypt[g] [d]Jer 31:2-3
and will not Assyria[h] rule over them [e]Lev 26:13
because they refuse to repent? [f]Ex 16:32;
6 Swords[i] will flash in their cities, Ps 78:25
will destroy the bars of their gates **11:5**
and put an end to their plans. [g]Hos 7:16
7 My people are determined to turn from [h]Hos 10:6
me.[j] **11:6** [i]Hos 13:16
Even if they call to the Most High, **11:7** [j]Jer 3:6-7;
he will by no means exalt them. 8:5

8 "How can I give you up, Ephraim?[k] **11:8** [k]Hos 6:4
How can I hand you over, Israel? [l]Ge 14:8
How can I treat you like Admah?
How can I make you like Zeboiim?[l]
My heart is changed within me;
all my compassion is aroused.
9 I will not carry out my fierce anger,[m] **11:9** [m]Dt 13:17;
nor will I turn and devastate[n] Ephraim. Jer 30:11
For I am God, and not man[o]— [n]Mal 3:6
the Holy One among you. [o]Nu 23:19
I will not come in wrath.[c]
10 They will follow the LORD;
he will roar like a lion.
When he roars,
his children will come trembling from **11:10**
the west.[p] [p]Hos 6:1-3
11 They will come trembling
like birds from Egypt,
like doves from Assyria.[q] **11:11**
I will settle them in their homes,"[r] [q]Isa 11:11
declares the LORD. [r]Eze 28:26

[a] 2 Some Septuagint manuscripts; Hebrew *they*
[b] 2 Septuagint; Hebrew *them* [c] 9 Or *come against any city*

Week 26

God's Love for the Wanderer

Israel, God's chosen people, wander so far and their unfaithfulness is so blatant that God compares them to "adulterers, burning like an oven" (Hos 7:4) who "love the wages of a prostitute" (Hos 9:1). That's harsh! In Hosea 11, Israel is compared to a wayward son who is loved by his father in spite of everything.

You can probably see a little of Israel in yourself (Isa 53:6). What is God's response to your wandering? What will your response to him be?

Describe God's attitude toward "young" Israel (Hos 11:1). What has God's attitude been toward you since before time began (Eph 1:4-6)?

Where was Israel when God called (Hos 11:1)? Where were you when God called you (Eph 5:8; 1Pe 2:9)?

Israel does not realize how God constantly has led her, cared for her and lifted her burdens (Hos 11:3-4). As you think back on your life, how has God faithfully "led [you] with cords of human kindness, with ties of love" (Hos 11:4)?

God's righteous anger flares at Israel's unfaithfulness (Hos 11:5-7), but it is quickly dispelled by his compassion (Hos 11:8-9). Though Israel will be punished, God will bring her safely home again (Hos 11:10-11). Think of a time when you have experienced God's discipline after a time of wandering and having felt his restoring love when the discipline was over.

Enjoying God THROUGH the Word

Read Luke 15:3-7 (page 1718). This parable is often interpreted as follows: Jesus goes out looking for unbelievers, and when they come to salvation, he and the angels rejoice. But think about this parable from a different perspective. The lost sheep is already one of Jesus' sheep. It is not from a different pen and does not belong to a different shepherd. This sheep belongs to Jesus, yet it wanders away and becomes temporarily lost. Jesus' response to lost sheep is always the same: "I myself will search for my sheep and look after them . . . I will rescue them . . . and gather them . . . and I will bring them into their own land" (Eze 34:11-13). Jesus sees wandering sheep as a priority (Lk 19:10).

Do you know a wandering sheep? Are you one yourself? Jesus will never throw up his hands in frustration and leave you to your own devices. He will come running to find you. "He tends his flock like a shepherd: He gathers the lambs in his arms and carries them close to his heart; he gently leads those that have young" (Isa 40:11). This is your Savior, your shepherd, your friend.

Enjoying God THROUGH Experience

If you are wandering from God, return to him through repentance (Hos 14:1-2). He will receive you with open arms, will draw you to himself and will rejoice. God's compassion and love are far greater than your sins (Ps 103:8-14). He is saying even now, "I have swept away your offenses like a cloud, your sins like the morning mist. Return to me, for I have redeemed you" (Isa 44:22).

Go to page 1483 for your next weekly study.

Israel's Sin

[12] Ephraim has surrounded me with lies,[s]
the house of Israel with deceit.
And Judah is unruly against God,
even against the faithful Holy One.

12 [1] Ephraim feeds on the wind;[t]
he pursues the east wind all day
and multiplies lies and violence.
He makes a treaty with Assyria
and sends olive oil to Egypt.[u]
[2] The LORD has a charge[v] to bring against Judah;
he will punish Jacob[a] according to his ways
and repay him according to his deeds.[w]
[3] In the womb he grasped his brother's heel;[x]
as a man he struggled[y] with God.
[4] He struggled with the angel and overcame him;
he wept and begged for his favor.
He found him at Bethel[z]
and talked with him there—
[5] the LORD God Almighty,
the LORD is his name[a] of renown!
[6] But you must return to your God;
maintain love and justice,[b]
and wait for your God always.[c]

[7] The merchant uses dishonest scales;[d]
he loves to defraud.
[8] Ephraim boasts,
"I am very rich; I have become wealthy.[e]
With all my wealth they will not find in me
any iniquity or sin."

[9] "I am the LORD your God,
⌞who brought you⌟ out of[b] Egypt;[f]
I will make you live in tents[g] again,
as in the days of your appointed feasts.
[10] I spoke to the prophets,
gave them many visions
and told parables[h] through them."[i]
[11] Is Gilead wicked?[j]
Its people are worthless!
Do they sacrifice bulls in Gilgal?[k]
Their altars will be like piles of stones
on a plowed field.[l]
[12] Jacob fled to the country of Aram[c];[m]
Israel served to get a wife,
and to pay for her he tended sheep.[n]
[13] The LORD used a prophet to bring Israel
up from Egypt,

11:12 [s]Hos 4:2
12:1 [t]Eze 17:10 [u]2Ki 17:4
12:2 [v]Mic 6:2 [w]Hos 4:9
12:3 [x]Ge 25:26 [y]Ge 32:24-29
12:4 [z]Ge 28:12-15; 35:15
12:5 [a]Ex 3:15
12:6 [b]Mic 6:8 [c]Hos 6:1-3; 10:12; Mic 7:7
12:7 [d]Am 8:5
12:8 [e]Ps 62:10; Rev 3:17
12:9 [f]Lev 23:43; Hos 11:1 [g]Ne 8:17
12:10 [h]Eze 20:49 [i]2Ki 17:13; Jer 7:25
12:11 [j]Hos 6:8 [k]Hos 4:15 [l]Hos 8:11
12:12 [m]Ge 28:5 [n]Ge 29:18

[a] *2 Jacob* means *he grasps the heel* (figuratively, *he deceives*).
[b] *9* Or *God / ever since you were in*
[c] *12* That is, Northwest Mesopotamia

Rocked in the cradle of the deep
I lay me down in peace to sleep;
Secure I rest upon the wave,
For Thou, O Lord! hast power to save.
I know Thou wilt not slight my call,
For Thou dost mark the sparrow's fall;
And calm and peaceful shall I sleep,
Rocked in the cradle of the deep.

—*Emma (Hart) Willard (1787-1870)*

by a prophet he cared for him.[o]
14 But Ephraim has bitterly provoked him
to anger;
his Lord will leave upon him the guilt
of his bloodshed[p]
and will repay him for his contempt.[q]

The LORD's Anger Against Israel

13 When Ephraim spoke, men trembled;[r]
he was exalted[s] in Israel.
But he became guilty of Baal worship[t]
and died.
2 Now they sin more and more;
they make idols for themselves from
their silver,[u]
cleverly fashioned images,
all of them the work of craftsmen.
It is said of these people,
"They offer human sacrifice
and kiss[a] the calf-idols.[v]"
3 Therefore they will be like the morning
mist,
like the early dew that disappears,[w]
like chaff[x] swirling from a threshing
floor,[y]
like smoke[z] escaping through a
window.

4 "But I am the LORD your God,
⌊who brought you⌋ out of[b] Egypt.[a]
You shall acknowledge no God but me,[b]
no Savior[c] except me.
5 I cared for you in the desert,
in the land of burning heat.
6 When I fed them, they were satisfied;
when they were satisfied, they
became proud;
then they forgot me.[d]
7 So I will come upon them like a lion,
like a leopard I will lurk by the path.
8 Like a bear robbed of her cubs,[e]
I will attack them and rip them open.
Like a lion I will devour them;
a wild animal will tear them apart.[f]

9 "You are destroyed, O Israel,
because you are against me,[g] against
your helper.[h]
10 Where is your king,[i] that he may save
you?
Where are your rulers in all your
towns,
of whom you said,
'Give me a king and princes'?[j]
11 So in my anger I gave you a king,
and in my wrath I took him away.[k]
12 The guilt of Ephraim is stored up,
his sins are kept on record.[l]

12:13 [o]Ex 13:3; Isa 63:11-14
12:14 [p]Eze 18:13 [q]Da 11:18
13:1 [r]Jdg 12:1 [s]Jdg 8:1 [t]Hos 11:2
13:2 [u]Isa 46:6; Jer 10:4 [v]Isa 44:17-20
13:3 [w]Hos 6:4 [x]Isa 17:13 [y]Da 2:35 [z]Ps 68:2
13:4 [a]Hos 12:9 [b]Ex 20:3 [c]Isa 43:11; 45:21-22
13:6 [d]Dt 32:12-15; Hos 2:13
13:8 [e]2Sa 17:8 [f]Ps 50:22
13:9 [g]Jer 2:17-19 [h]Dt 33:29
13:10 [i]2Ki 17:4 [j]1Sa 8:6; Hos 8:4
13:11 [k]1Ki 14:10; Hos 10:7
13:12 [l]Dt 32:34

[a] 2 Or *"Men who sacrifice / kiss* [b] 4 Or *God / ever since you were in*

What you need to do then, dear Christian, if you are in bondage, is to put your will over completely into the hands of your Lord, surrendering to Him the entire control of it. Say, "Yes, Lord, YES!" to everything; and trust Him so to work in you to will, as to bring your whole wishes and affections into conformity with His own sweet and lovable and most lovely will . . . It is wonderful what miracles God works in wills that are utterly surrendered to Him. He turns hard things into easy, and bitter things into sweet. It is not that He puts easy things in the place of the hard, but He actually changes the hard thing into an easy one. And this is salvation. It is grand. Do try it, you who are going about your daily Christian living as to a hard and weary task, and see if your divine Master will not transform the very life you live now as a bondage, into the most delicious liberty!

—Hannah Whitall Smith (1832-1911)

The Fruit of Our Lips

HOS 14:2

As Hosea instructs his people to repent of their sin, he reminds them that it is not enough simply to turn toward God. They must confess their sorrow and their commitment to obey the Lord with words, the "fruit" of their lips. God isn't looking for empty words or ritual but for a genuine expression of repentance and praise.

13 Pains as of a woman in childbirth[m]
come to him,
but he is a child without wisdom;
when the time arrives,
he does not come to the opening of
the womb.[n]

14 "I will ransom them from the power of
the grave[a];[o]
I will redeem them from death.
Where, O death, are your plagues?
Where, O grave,[a] is your destruction?[p]

"I will have no compassion,
15 even though he thrives[q] among his
brothers.
An east wind[r] from the LORD will come,
blowing in from the desert;
his spring will fail
and his well dry up.[s]
His storehouse will be plundered[t]
of all its treasures.

16 The people of Samaria must bear their
guilt,[u]
because they have rebelled[v] against
their God.
They will fall by the sword;[w]
their little ones will be dashed[x] to the
ground,
their pregnant women[y] ripped open."

Repentance to Bring Blessing

14 Return, O Israel, to the LORD your God.
Your sins have been your downfall![z]
2 Take words with you
and return to the LORD.
Say to him:
"Forgive all our sins
and receive us graciously,[a]
that we may offer the fruit of our
lips.[b][b]
3 Assyria cannot save us;
we will not mount war-horses.[c]
We will never again say 'Our gods'[d]
to what our own hands have made,
for in you the fatherless[e] find
compassion."

4 "I will heal[f] their waywardness
and love them freely,[g]
for my anger has turned away from
them.
5 I will be like the dew to Israel;
he will blossom like a lily.[h]
Like a cedar of Lebanon[i]
he will send down his roots;[j]
6 his young shoots will grow.
His splendor will be like an olive tree,[k]
his fragrance like a cedar of Lebanon.[l]
7 Men will dwell again in his shade.[m]

13:13 [m]Isa 13:8; Mic 4:9-10 [n]Isa 66:9
13:14 [o]Ps 49:15; Eze 37:12-13 [p]1Co 15:55*
13:15 [q]Hos 10:1 [r]Eze 19:12 [s]Jer 51:36 [t]Jer 20:5
13:16 [u]Hos 10:2 [v]Hos 7:14 [w]Hos 11:6 [x]2Ki 8:12; Hos 10:14 [y]2Ki 15:16; Isa 13:16
14:1 [z]Hos 5:5
14:2 [a]Mic 7:18-19 [b]Heb 13:15
14:3 [c]Ps 33:17; Isa 31:1 [d]Hos 8:6 [e]Ps 10:14; 68:5
14:4 [f]Hos 6:1 [g]Zep 3:17
14:5 [h]SS 2:1 [i]Isa 35:2 [j]Job 29:19
14:6 [k]Ps 52:8; Jer 11:16 [l]SS 4:11
14:7 [m]Ps 91:1-4

[a] 14 Hebrew *Sheol* [b] 2 Or *offer our lips as sacrifices of bulls*

Belshazzar's Queen

So Close, Yet So Far

The wild party grew suddenly silent as a disembodied hand wrote strange words on the wall. Mocking the God of Israel by drinking from goblets taken from his temple in Jerusalem was no longer the sport it had seemed a few minutes before. Belshazzar, king of Babylon, felt sick. He was so frightened his legs gave way. What did the words mean? He called for all his wise men—enchanters, astrologers and diviners—but none could read the writing or tell him what it meant.

The queen, hearing the news, entered the banquet hall. Perhaps she had been waiting for such a moment. The king had not followed in the ways of his repentant predecessor, Nebuchadnezzar. Belshazzar not only refused to acknowledge the God of Israel, but also scorned his very existence. What would it take to turn Belshazzar around? The powerful kingdom that had been left in his charge was crumbling. Still, he considered himself invincible—until now.

"Call for Daniel," the queen advised, "and he will tell you what the writing means." It is possible that she only dabbled in spiritual things, loving the excitement of mystery. Perhaps she only wanted to call Daniel as a court magician, not caring how he gained his wisdom.

It is also possible, however, that she witnessed the trials and successes of Nebuchadnezzar's reign, and she didn't want to repeat his predecessor's mistakes. Unlike Belshazzar, the queen recognized wisdom when she saw it. Could Daniel's God possibly win over a king one more time?

To her great sorrow, Belshazzar was a fool. He only wanted to know the content of the message. He had no interest in reform or repairing the damage of his gross offense toward God. Belshazzar died, unrepentant, by an assassin's hand that very night.

What a tragedy, to be so close yet so far, to see God's final warning written on the wall and yet refuse to repent. Perhaps, if Belshazzar had humbled himself, the disaster might have been averted, as it was in Nineveh in the days of Jonah.

It is difficult to watch the ones we love make foolish choices. It is almost unbearable to see them scorn the Water of Life. But our hope in God helps us to keep trying, to look for every opportunity to show the reason for our faith. Pray. Be sensitive, be persistent and be patient. While they still live, the final sentence hasn't been written over them.

Belshazzar's Queen

Daniel 5:10-12

Candid SNAPSHOT The queen, hearing the voices of the king and his nobles, came into the banquet hall. "O king, live forever!" she said. "Don't be alarmed! Don't look so pale! There is a man in your kingdom who has the spirit of the holy gods in him" (Daniel 5:10-11).

Gomer

True Love

If you like love stories, this one's the real deal. Hosea cupped Gomer's face in his hands, looked deeply into her eyes and told her to come home. Pulling her into his arms, he said, *"You are to live with me many days; you must not be a prostitute or be intimate with any man, and I will live with you"* (Hos 3:3)—such tender words to a harlot wife whose very essence was unfaithfulness, words that could only come from the heart of God.

Hosea loved Gomer, even though her repeated betrayals caused him great pain. Apparently Gomer thought Hosea did not provide the things she "needed" in order to be happy, so she looked elsewhere. *Everywhere* else. Other men gave her fine clothing, jewels, rich food and drink for her favors. But through it all, Hosea remained faithful.

Yet Gomer continued down her customary path. Eventually she became a slave. Perhaps only then did she begin to appreciate what she had scorned in the past. Hosea had been good to her, and she missed her children. When she was at her lowest, Hosea redeemed her, buying her freedom for fifteen pieces of silver, half the going price of a slave. God had told him to take her back, as a symbol of God's love for Israel. Hosea obeyed.

Everyone in town knew about Gomer. It wasn't the kind of thing she or Hosea could hide. People probably thought Hosea was a fool to forgive her and still want her as his wife. But that is exactly how God responds to us. Hosea shared God's pain firsthand. When *he* prophesied of God's covenant love, no one could question his sincerity: *"I will betroth you in righteousness and justice, in love and compassion. I will betroth you in faithfulness, and you will acknowledge the* LORD*"* (Hos 2:19–20). A prophet called to speak for God to the people often paid a high price to understand God's heart.

Gomer
(completion)
Hosea 1:2–11; 3:1–3

Gomer shows us that no matter how low we get, God does not cease to love and care for us. There is a way back, a home in him to return to. He has purchased us out of slavery with the blood of his only Son Jesus. The greatness of our sin or degradation is the best reason to go to him, not a reason to stay away from him, for Jesus said, *"It is not the healthy who need a doctor, but the sick. I have not come to call the righteous, but sinners to repentance"* (Lu 5:31).

Candid SNAPSHOT The LORD said to [Hosea], *"Go, show your love to your wife again, though she is loved by another and is an adulteress. Love her as the* LORD *loves the Israelites, though they turn to other gods"* (Hosea 3:1).

He will flourish like the grain.
He will blossom like a vine,
14:7 [n]Hos 2:22 [o]Eze 17:23 — and his fame will be like the wine[n]
from Lebanon.[o]
14:8 [p]ver 3 — 8 O Ephraim, what more have I[a] to do
with idols?[p]
I will answer him and care for him.
I am like a green pine tree;
your fruitfulness comes from me."

14:9 [q]Ps 107:43 [r]Pr 10:29; Isa 1:28 [s]Ps 111:7-8; Zep 3:5; Ac 13:10 [t]Isa 26:7 — 9 Who is wise?[q] He will realize these
things.
Who is discerning? He will
understand them.[r]
The ways of the LORD are right;[s]
the righteous walk[t] in them,
but the rebellious stumble in them.

Wisdom's Response

HOS 14:9

Those who are in relationship with God will have the eyes to see and the ears to hear (Mt 13:16) the difference between good and evil in social and moral matters. Those who walk with the Lord gain a marvelous ability to discern truth and to then make choices that reflect that understanding. When we lack understanding, we only have to ask the Lord in prayer for it, and he will generously give us that gift (Jas 1:5) so that we may walk in his way without faltering.

[a] 8 Or *What more has Ephraim*

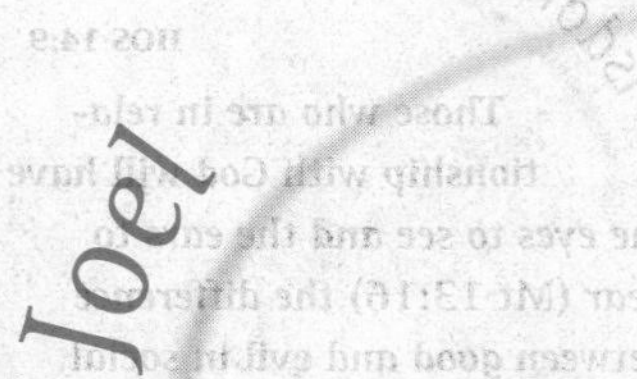

Repentance needed for revival.

The prophet Joel shares a vision of ruin, a call to repentance and a glorious promise of restoration in this brief prophecy about the coming "day of the LORD." The nation of Judah has wandered. Using a locust plague as an object lesson of God's impending judgment, Joel urges the people of Judah to repent, turn back to God and find hope for the future.

Joel tempers his frightening words about God's dreadful and unavoidable punishment with words that inspire repentance because of the promised outpouring of the Holy Spirit on all people (Joel 1–2). Joel assures his readers that God's power is unlimited and that God's forgiveness is always available. Even if catastrophe and calamity come because of sin, Joel promises that repentance will bring restoration and such joy that sorrow and pain will be more than made up for (Joel 2).

Joel's appeal for a change of heart touches us deeply. Judah's example exposes our own tendency to wander away from God when life seems to be going well, when affluence, friends and family surround us. Joel reminds us that a close relationship with God is vital in both good times and bad. God loves us so much that he will use whatever he can to get our attention and bring us closer to him—even a plague of locusts.

Quick Study

Author
The prophet Joel.

Date Written
Although Joel contains no information that makes firm dating possible, a good possibility is about 830 B.C.

Setting
Probably Judah.

Key Passage
Joel 2:13 "Rend your heart
and not your garments.
Return to the LORD your God,
for he is gracious and compassionate,
slow to anger and abounding in love,
and he relents from sending calamity."

Outline

Locust invasion.
Joel 1:1–12

A call to repentance.
Joel 1:13–20

Warnings and promises.
Joel 2

God's final judgment and blessing.
Joel 3

The Women of Joel

A virgin	*She mourned for her husband.* Joel 1:8
A bride	*Called from the bridal chamber.* Joel 2:16
Spirit-filled women	*Recipients of God's Spirit.* Joel 2:29
Girls	*Sold for wine.* Joel 3:3

Army of Locusts

JOEL 1:4–7

The southern kingdom of Judah suffered a devastating plague of locusts. This "army" of insects, swarming for miles, blocked the sunlight by their sheer numbers and devoured every green thing in their path, including grain, precious fig trees and grape vines—staples of the men, women, children and animals of the land. The insects even stripped the bark from trees, "leaving their branches white." There had never been a plague like it before.

Joel uses this opportunity to call his people to repentance before an even greater judgment comes. Joel's "call" speaks to us even today. God still uses natural disasters to get our attention. He is patient. He is merciful. He is forgiving. But he will not always be so if we continue to ignore him.

1 The word of the LORD that came[a] to Joel[b] son of Pethuel.

An Invasion of Locusts

2 Hear this,[c] you elders;
listen, all who live in the land.[d]
Has anything like this ever happened in your days
or in the days of your forefathers?[e]
3 Tell it to your children,[f]
and let your children tell it to their children,
and their children to the next generation.
4 What the locust swarm has left
the great locusts have eaten;
what the great locusts have left
the young locusts have eaten;
what the young locusts have left
other locusts[a] have eaten.[g]

5 Wake up, you drunkards, and weep!
Wail, all you drinkers of wine;[h]
wail because of the new wine,
for it has been snatched from your lips.
6 A nation has invaded my land,
powerful and without number;[i]
it has the teeth[j] of a lion,
the fangs of a lioness.
7 It has laid waste[k] my vines
and ruined my fig trees.[l]
It has stripped off their bark
and thrown it away,
leaving their branches white.

8 Mourn like a virgin[b] in sackcloth[m]
grieving for the husband[c] of her youth.
9 Grain offerings and drink offerings[n]
are cut off from the house of the LORD.
The priests are in mourning,
those who minister before the LORD.
10 The fields are ruined,
the ground is dried up[d];[o]
the grain is destroyed,
the new wine[p] is dried up,
the oil fails.
11 Despair, you farmers,[q]
wail, you vine growers;
grieve for the wheat and the barley,
because the harvest of the field is destroyed.[r]
12 The vine is dried up
and the fig tree is withered;
the pomegranate, the palm and the apple tree—

1:1 [a]Jer 1:2 [b]Ac 2:16
1:2 [c]Hos 5:1 [d]Hos 4:1 [e]Joel 2:2
1:3 [f]Ex 10:2; Ps 78:4
1:4 [g]Dt 28:39; Na 3:15
1:5 [h]Joel 3:3
1:6 [i]Joel 2:2, 11, 25 [j]Rev 9:8
1:7 [k]Isa 5:6 [l]Am 4:9
1:8 [m]ver 13; Isa 22:12; Am 8:10
1:9 [n]Hos 9:4; Joel 2:14, 17
1:10 [o]Isa 24:4 [p]Hos 9:2
1:11 [q]Jer 14:3-4; Am 5:16 [r]Isa 17:11

[a] *4* The precise meaning of the four Hebrew words used here for locusts is uncertain. [b] *8* Or *young woman* [c] *8* Or *betrothed* [d] *10* Or *ground mourns*

1:12 [s]Hag 2:19

all the trees of the field—are dried
up.[s]
Surely the joy of mankind
is withered away.

A Call to Repentance

1:13 [t]Jer 4:8 [u]Joel 2:17 [v]ver 9

13 Put on sackcloth,[t] O priests, and mourn;
wail, you who minister[u] before the
altar.
Come, spend the night in sackcloth,
you who minister before my God;
for the grain offerings and drink
offerings[v]
are withheld from the house of your
God.

1:14 [w]2Ch 20:3 [x]Jnh 3:8

14 Declare a holy fast;[w]
call a sacred assembly.
Summon the elders
and all who live in the land
to the house of the LORD your God,
and cry out[x] to the LORD.

1:15 [y]Jer 30:7 [z]Isa 13:6,9; Joel 2:1,11, 31

15 Alas for that[y] day!
For the day of the LORD[z] is near;
it will come like destruction from the
Almighty.[a]

1:16 [a]Isa 3:7 [b]Dt 12:7

16 Has not the food been cut off[a]
before our very eyes—
joy and gladness
from the house of our God?[b]

1:17 [c]Isa 17:10-11

17 The seeds are shriveled
beneath the clods.[b][c]
The storehouses are in ruins,
the granaries have been broken down,
for the grain has dried up.
18 How the cattle moan!
The herds mill about
because they have no pasture;
even the flocks of sheep are suffering.

1:19 [d]Ps 50:15 [e]Am 7:4 [f]Jer 9:10

19 To you, O LORD, I call,[d]
for fire[e] has devoured the open
pastures[f]
and flames have burned up all the
trees of the field.

1:20 [g]Ps 104:21 [h]1Ki 17:7

20 Even the wild animals pant for you;[g]
the streams of water have dried up[h]
and fire has devoured the open
pastures.

An Army of Locusts

2:1 [i]Jer 4:5 [j]ver 15 [k]Joel 1:15; Zep 1:14-16 [l]Ob 1:15

2 Blow the trumpet[i] in Zion;[j]
sound the alarm on my holy hill.
Let all who live in the land tremble,
for the day of the LORD[k] is coming.
It is close at hand[l]—

2:2 [m]Am 5:18 [n]Da 9:12

2 a day of darkness[m] and gloom,[n]
a day of clouds and blackness.

[a] *15* Hebrew *Shaddai* [b] *17* The meaning of the Hebrew for this word is uncertain.

Holy Fast

JOEL 1:14

The term "holy fast" in the Old Testament denotes a time of public abstinence from food or drink to demonstrate sorrow for sin and recommitment to God. Joel urgently calls together a "sacred assembly" with the elders and people of the land. The plague of locusts is only a warning call of the judgment that is coming. If God's people cry out to him in sincere repentance, God will be merciful. But their repentance must be true and heartfelt. God is not satisfied with people merely going through the motions of fasting. The fast must be an outward expression of an inward repentance (Zec 7:4-5). Today, followers of Jesus Christ also fast during times of danger, personal distress, repentance from sin or when seeking the Lord's will for a particular situation. And God's desire is the same today: for a people whose hearts are involved and affected by their outward action.

Rend Your Hearts

JOEL 2:13

Joel uses a graphic word picture here to describe a sincere, heartfelt repentance. He tells the people to tear their hearts, not their clothing, in sorrow. Outward religious expression is useless unless the people turn wholeheartedly to God. Some people use fasting purely to display their "righteousness" publicly, hoping to gain the admiration of friends and strangers by appearing weak, unkempt and drawn. But God is not interested in public demonstrations (Mt 6:16–18). He is looking for people who turn their hearts to him in humility and meekness so they may receive his forgiveness and be restored.

True repentance, however, does not guarantee that we will not suffer or face calamity. Suffering will come and go throughout our lives. It is one of the consequences of our sinful condition. But as long as we are "right" with God, we can be at peace, regardless of the circumstances.

Like dawn spreading across the
mountains
a large and mighty army[o] comes,
such as never was of old[p]
nor ever will be in ages to come.

3 Before them fire devours,
behind them a flame blazes.
Before them the land is like the garden
of Eden,[q]
behind them, a desert waste[r]—
nothing escapes them.
4 They have the appearance of horses;[s]
they gallop along like cavalry.
5 With a noise like that of chariots[t]
they leap over the mountaintops,
like a crackling fire[u] consuming stubble,
like a mighty army drawn up for
battle.

6 At the sight of them, nations are in
anguish;[v]
every face turns pale.[w]
7 They charge like warriors;
they scale walls like soldiers.
They all march in line,
not swerving[x] from their course.
8 They do not jostle each other;
each marches straight ahead.
They plunge through defenses
without breaking ranks.
9 They rush upon the city;
they run along the wall.
They climb into the houses;
like thieves they enter through the
windows.[y]

10 Before them the earth shakes,[z]
the sky trembles,
the sun and moon are darkened,[a]
and the stars no longer shine.[b]
11 The LORD[c] thunders
at the head of his army;
his forces are beyond number,
and mighty are those who obey his
command.
The day of the LORD is great;[d]
it is dreadful.
Who can endure it?[e]

Rend Your Heart

12 "Even now," declares the LORD,
"return[f] to me with all your heart,
with fasting and weeping and
mourning."

13 Rend your heart[g]
and not your garments.[h]
Return to the LORD your God,
for he is gracious and compassionate,
slow to anger and abounding in love,[i]
and he relents from sending calamity.[j]

2:2 [o]Joel 1:6 [p]Joel 1:2
2:3 [q]Ge 2:8 [r]Ps 105:34-35
2:4 [s]Rev 9:7
2:5 [t]Rev 9:9 [u]Isa 5:24; 30:30
2:6 [v]Isa 13:8 [w]Na 2:10
2:7 [x]Isa 5:27
2:9 [y]Jer 9:21
2:10 [z]Ps 18:7 [a]Mt 24:29 [b]Isa 13:10; Eze 32:8
2:11 [c]Joel 1:15 [d]Zep 1:14; Rev 18:8 [e]Eze 22:14
2:12 [f]Jer 4:1; Hos 12:6
2:13 [g]Ps 34:18; Isa 57:15 [h]Job 1:20 [i]Ex 34:6 [j]Jer 18:8

Week 27

God's Love and Mercy

The Hebrew and Greek words for *mercy* are often translated "love" or "compassion." The words convey a concern that moves a person to help. It's more than a feeling; it is a feeling that prompts action—an action that is *undeserved* by the one who benefits from it. In this passage, the prophet Joel characterizes God as "compassionate . . . and abounding in love."

How is God described in Psalm 103:8–14? When do you confuse the attributes of your heavenly Father with those of your earthly father, thinking that God will respond to you as your earthly father has?

Psalm 78 lists some of the many things the Israelites do to deserve God's wrath. How does God respond? Their rebellion brings God's discipline, but God's judgment is mixed with mercy.

When have you experienced God's discipline? Remember that God disciplines those he loves (Rev 3:19), his mercy outlives his anger (Ps 103:10–11; Isa 54:8).

Do you ever fear rejection from God? If you return to him, how will he respond (2Ch 30:9; Jer 3:12–13; Joel 2:13)?

God is holy and righteous. That causes fear. But Jesus has paid the debt incurred by your sin (Ro 5:8–9). He has saved you from God's wrath. Even your salvation is accomplished because of God's mercy (1Pe 1:3). And he delights to show you his mercy (Mic 7:18)!

Enjoying God THROUGH the Word

Read Matthew 18:21–35 (page 1615). Have you ever wondered what you would do if you were in the shoes of the unmerciful servant? This servant was forgiven a huge debt; one he could never hope to repay. Yet, despite the mercy shown to him by his master, he refused to forgive another servant of a debt that amounted to a pittance.

How will you respond to those who need mercy from you? God requires that you extend justice, mercy and compassion to others (Mic 6:8; Zec 7:9). When Jesus walked this earth, he reminded his listeners that the important matters of the law are justice, mercy and faithfulness (Mt 23:23).

The opposite of mercy is judgment. When you are judgmental or refuse to show mercy, as the servant does in this parable, you will face judgment because "judgment without mercy will be shown to anyone who has not been merciful" (Jas 2:13). When you realize the extent of God's mercy toward you, your heart will overflow with love and gratitude. The greater the debt canceled, the greater the love and gratitude in response (Lk 7:42–43). If you are having trouble forgiving others or being merciful, perhaps you have yet to discover the depth of God's mercy toward you.

Enjoying God THROUGH Experience

Honestly examine your heart. Are you the rebellious child needing to return to your Father? Are you the unmerciful servant denying others the mercy they need so much? "Have mercy on me, O God, according to your unfailing love; according to your great compassion blot out my transgressions" (Ps 51:1). Rebellion, an unrepentant heart or disobedience will keep you from feeling the love and mercy of God. Stop going through the motions—"Rend your heart and not your garments. Return to the LORD your God, for he is gracious and compassionate" (Joel 2:13).

Go to page 1521 for your next weekly study.

The God who is behind His promises and is infinitely greater than His promises, can never fail us in any emergency, and the soul that is stayed on Him cannot know anything but perfect peace.

The little child does not always understand its mother's promises, but it knows its mother, and its childlike trust is founded not on her word, but upon herself. And just so it is with us . . . There may not be a prayer answered or a promise fulfilled to our own consciousness, but what of that? Behind the prayers and behind the promises, there is God, and He is enough. And to such a soul the simple words, GOD IS, answer every question and solve every doubt.

—Hannah Whitall Smith (1832-1911)

14 Who knows? He may turn[k] and have pity
and leave behind a blessing[l]—
grain offerings and drink offerings[m]
for the LORD your God.

15 Blow the trumpet[n] in Zion,
declare a holy fast,[o]
call a sacred assembly.[p]
16 Gather the people,
consecrate[q] the assembly;
bring together the elders,
gather the children,
those nursing at the breast.
Let the bridegroom[r] leave his room
and the bride her chamber.
17 Let the priests, who minister before the LORD,
weep between the temple porch and the altar.[s]
Let them say, "Spare your people, O LORD.
Do not make your inheritance an object of scorn,[t]
a byword among the nations.
Why should they say among the peoples,
'Where is their God?[u]' "

The LORD's Answer

18 Then the LORD will be jealous[v] for his land
and take pity on his people.

19 The LORD will reply[a] to them:
"I am sending you grain, new wine and oil,[w]
enough to satisfy you fully;
never again will I make you
an object of scorn[x] to the nations.

20 "I will drive the northern army[y] far from you,
pushing it into a parched and barren land,
with its front columns going into the eastern[z] sea[b]
and those in the rear into the western sea.[c]
And its stench[a] will go up;
its smell will rise."

Surely he has done great things.[d]
21 Be not afraid,[b] O land;
be glad and rejoice.
Surely the LORD has done great things.[c]
22 Be not afraid, O wild animals,

2:14 [k]Jer 26:3 [l]Hag 2:19 [m]Joel 1:13
2:15 [n]Nu 10:2 [o]Jer 36:9 [p]Joel 1:14
2:16 [q]Ex 19:10,22 [r]Ps 19:5
2:17 [s]Eze 8:16; Mt 23:35 [t]Dt 9:26-29; Ps 44:13 [u]Ps 42:3
2:18 [v]Zec 1:14
2:19 [w]Jer 31:12 [x]Eze 34:29
2:20 [y]Jer 1:14-15 [z]Zec 14:8 [a]Isa 34:3
2:21 [b]Isa 54:4; Zep 3:16-17 [c]Ps 126:3

[a] *18,19* Or *LORD was jealous . . . / and took pity . . . / [19]The LORD replied* [b] *20* That is, the Dead Sea [c] *20* That is, the Mediterranean [d] *20* Or *rise. / Surely it has done great things."*

2:22 [d]Ps 65:12 [e]Joel 1:18-20
for the open pastures are becoming
green.[d]
The trees are bearing their fruit;
the fig tree and the vine yield their
riches.[e]
23 Be glad, O people of Zion,
2:23 [f]Ps 149:2; Isa 12:6; 41:16; Hab 3:18; Zec 10:7 [g]Lev 26:4
rejoice[f] in the LORD your God,
for he has given you
the autumn rains in righteousness.[a]
He sends you abundant showers,
both autumn and spring rains,[g] as
before.
24 The threshing floors will be filled with
grain;
2:24 [h]Lev 26:10; Mal 3:10 [i]Am 9:13
the vats will overflow[h] with new
wine[i] and oil.

25 "I will repay you for the years the
locusts have eaten—
the great locust and the young locust,
the other locusts and the locust
swarm[b]—
my great army that I sent among you.
26 You will have plenty to eat, until you
2:26 [j]Lev 26:5 [k]Isa 62:9 [l]Ps 126:3; Isa 25:1
are full,[j]
and you will praise[k] the name of the
LORD your God,
who has worked wonders[l] for you;
never again will my people be shamed.
27 Then you will know that I am in Israel,
2:27 [m]Joel 3:17
that I am the LORD[m] your God,
and that there is no other;
never again will my people be shamed.

The Day of the LORD

28 "And afterward,
2:28 [n]Eze 39:29
I will pour out my Spirit[n] on all people.
Your sons and daughters will prophesy,
your old men will dream dreams,
your young men will see visions.
2:29 [o]1Co 12:13; Gal 3:28
29 Even on my servants,[o] both men and
women,
I will pour out my Spirit in those days.
2:30 [p]Lk 21:11 [q]Mk 13:24-25
30 I will show wonders in the heavens[p]
and on the earth,[q]
blood and fire and billows of smoke.
2:31 [r]Mt 24:29 [s]Isa 13:9-10; Mal 4:1,5
31 The sun will be turned to darkness[r]
and the moon to blood
before the coming of the great and
dreadful day of the LORD.[s]
32 And everyone who calls
on the name of the LORD will be
2:32 [t]Ac 2:17-21*; Ro 10:13* [u]Isa 46:13 [v]Ob 1:17 [w]Isa 11:11; Mic 4:7; Ro 9:27
saved;[t]
for on Mount Zion[u] and in Jerusalem
there will be deliverance,[v]
as the LORD has said,
among the survivors[w]
whom the LORD calls.

[a] 23 Or / *the teacher for righteousness:* [b] 25 The precise meaning of the four Hebrew words used here for locusts is uncertain.

The Day of the LORD

JOEL 2:28-32

These beautiful and then frightening words speak of a time when God will pour out his Spirit on all people, regardless of race, age or gender. Peter quotes these verses, claiming that the events of Pentecost fulfill Joel's prophecy (Ac 2:16-21).

The horrors spoken of in Joel 2:30-31 have a future fulfillment. The "day of the LORD," a phrase Joel uses five times in his book, speaks of a day of judgment, a time of distress that will encompass natural and social disasters and will end only when Christ returns to rule (Mt 24:29-30). Since no one knows the hour or the day of God's judgment, followers of Jesus Christ must be ready at all times. God is merciful now, but there will come a time when he will no longer extend his mercy to those who reject him.

Swords and Plowshares

JOEL 3:10

In an interesting reversal of the prophecies of Isaiah and Micah—"plowshares into swords" rather than "swords into plowshares" (Isa 2:4; Mic 4:3)—Joel warns his listeners that the time of peace has not yet arrived. Judgment still awaits. Joel is speaking of the final struggle before the end of history. The followers of the "beast" (Rev 19:19) will go to war against the Lord and his army. Until Christ reigns supreme after this day of the Lord, there will be those who oppose God and righteousness. Despite the conflict, however, there is nothing to fear because our Sovereign Lord will be the final victor.

The Nations Judged

3 "In those days and at that time,
when I restore the fortunes[x] of Judah
and Jerusalem,
[2] I will gather all nations
and bring them down to the Valley of
Jehoshaphat.[a]
There I will enter into judgment[y]
against them
concerning my inheritance, my people
Israel,
for they scattered my people among the
nations
and divided up my land.
[3] They cast lots for my people
and traded boys for prostitutes;
they sold girls for wine[z]
that they might drink.

[4] "Now what have you against me, O Tyre and
Sidon[a] and all you regions of Philistia? Are you
repaying me for something I have done? If you are
paying me back, I will swiftly and speedily return
on your own heads what you have done.[b] [5] For
you took my silver and my gold and carried off
my finest treasures to your temples.[c] [6] You sold the
people of Judah and Jerusalem to the Greeks, that
you might send them far from their homeland.

[7] "See, I am going to rouse them out of the
places to which you sold them,[d] and I will return
on your own heads what you have done. [8] I will
sell your sons[e] and daughters to the people of
Judah,[f] and they will sell them to the Sabeans, a
nation far away." The LORD has spoken.

[9] Proclaim this among the nations:
Prepare for war![g]
Rouse the warriors![h]
Let all the fighting men draw near
and attack.
[10] Beat your plowshares into swords
and your pruning hooks[i] into spears.
Let the weakling[j] say,
"I am strong!"
[11] Come quickly, all you nations from
every side,
and assemble[k] there.

Bring down your warriors,[l] O LORD!
[12] "Let the nations be roused;
let them advance into the Valley of
Jehoshaphat,
for there I will sit
to judge[m] all the nations on every
side.
[13] Swing the sickle,
for the harvest[n] is ripe.
Come, trample the grapes,
for the winepress[o] is full
and the vats overflow—

3:1 [x]Jer 16:15
3:2 [y]Eze 36:5
3:3 [z]Am 2:6
3:4 [a]Mt 11:21 [b]Isa 34:8
3:5 [c]2Ch 21:16-17
3:7 [d]Isa 43:5-6; Jer 23:8
3:8 [e]Isa 60:14 [f]Isa 14:2
3:9 [g]Isa 8:9 [h]Jer 46:4
3:10 [i]Isa 2:4; Mic 4:3 [j]Zec 12:8
3:11 [k]Eze 38:15-16; Zep 3:8 [l]Isa 13:3
3:12 [m]Isa 2:4
3:13 [n]Hos 6:11; Mt 13:39; Rev 14:15-19 [o]Rev 14:20

[a] 2 *Jehoshaphat* means *the LORD judges*; also in verse 12.

so great is their wickedness!"

[14]Multitudes, multitudes
in the valley of decision!
3:14 [p]Isa 34:2-8; Joel 1:15
For the day of the LORD[p] is near
in the valley of decision.
[15]The sun and moon will be darkened,
and the stars no longer shine.
3:16 [q]Am 1:2 [r]Eze 38:19 [s]Jer 16:19
[16]The LORD will roar from Zion
and thunder from Jerusalem;[q]
the earth and the sky will tremble.[r]
But the LORD will be a refuge for his
people,
a stronghold[s] for the people of Israel.

Blessings for God's People

3:17 [t]Joel 2:27 [u]Isa 4:3
[17]"Then you will know that I, the LORD
your God,[t]
dwell in Zion,[u] my holy hill.
Jerusalem will be holy;
never again will foreigners invade her.

[18]"In that day the mountains will drip
new wine,
3:18 [v]Ex 3:8 [w]Isa 30:25; 35:6 [x]Rev 22:1-2 [y]Eze 47:1; Am 9:13
and the hills will flow with milk;[v]
all the ravines of Judah will run with
water.[w]
A fountain will flow out of the LORD's
house[x]
and will water the valley of acacias.[a][y]
[19]But Egypt will be desolate,
Edom a desert waste,
3:19 [z]Ob 1:10
because of violence[z] done to the people
of Judah,
in whose land they shed innocent
blood.
3:20 [a]Am 9:15
[20]Judah will be inhabited forever[a]
and Jerusalem through all
generations.
[21]Their bloodguilt, which I have not
pardoned,
3:21 [b]Eze 36:25
I will pardon.[b]"

The LORD dwells in Zion!

The Holy City

JOEL 3:17

After Satan and his cohorts have been defeated and Jesus Christ has judged the nations, he will establish his everlasting kingdom and rule for all eternity. His people will reside with him in Zion. At that time Jerusalem will be the golden and holy city. Enemies will never again pass through her gates. What encouragement this is for believers today. We have so much to anticipate! The God of the universe will reign supreme. All sorrow and suffering will end. And peace and blessing will be our inheritance.

[a] 18 Or *Valley of Shittim*

Amos

A stand against materialism.

The nation of Israel, the northern kingdom, experiences economic and political successes that foster a false sense of optimism, comfort and security. Deluded by their own sense of self-importance, the people become complacent, greedy and corrupt, allowing slavery, cruelty and injustice to flourish. Amos courageously confronts them with God's perspective on their materialistic society and challenges them to stand against immorality by lives of justice and righteousness.

Fearless, Amos begins by declaring God's judgment on Israel's neighbors for their cruelty (Am 1–2). He then moves to point the finger of judgment at Israel itself for its idolatry, for its exploitation of the poor, for its abuse of the righteous and for overlooking injustice (Am 3–6). In the opening verses of chapter 4, Amos focuses on the women of Israel for their selfish, self-indulgent lives. Amos relates his conversation with God, who is holding a plumb line. The plumb line swings down among the people of Israel and shows them to be seriously flawed (Am 7). Finally, Amos compares Israel to a basket of ripe fruit, ripe for plucking and for judgment (Am 8–9).

Amos boldly speaks God's words and denounces the sins of the people. His example is an excellent one for us today, encouraging us to speak up when we see injustice, to change our ways that conflict with God's ways, and to find hope in the knowledge that God will honor those who are willing to walk with him in righteousness.

Quick Study

Author
The shepherd-prophet Amos.

Date Written
About 760–750 B.C.

Setting
Although Amos was from Judah, he prophesied to the northern kingdom of Israel and probably spent the years of his ministry there.

Key Passage
Amos 5:14 "Seek good,
not evil,
that you may live.
Then the LORD God
Almighty will be with
you,
just as you say he is."

Outline

Judgments on Israel's neighbors.
Am 1:1–2:5

Judgment on Israel.
Am 2:6-16

Oracles against Israel.
Am 3:1–4:13

A lament and a call to repent.
Am 5:1-17

Announcement of the coming exile.
Am 5:18–6:14

Visions of locusts, fire and a plumb line.
Am 7

Vision of a basket of fruit.
Am 8

Israel's destruction.
Am 9:1-10

Israel's restoration.
Am 9:11-15

The Women of Amos

Oppressive women	*Amos called them cows.* Am 4:1
Wife	*Will become a prostitute.* Am 7:17
Daughters	*Dying by the sword.* Am 7:17
Young women	*Fainting with thirst.* Am 8:13

The Calling

AM 1:1

An earthquake (also recorded in Zec 14:5) hits Israel sometime between 760 and 750 B.C., during Amos's ministry. It must have been severe, but just as jolting is the prophecy of this ordinary shepherd, who addresses Israel during a time of economic growth. Armed with a vision from God, Amos is confident of his calling (Am 7:14–15) and speaks out against mighty and wealthy kings. When God unmistakably says, "Go, prophesy to my people Israel" (Am 7:15), Amos joins the ranks of other simple people, like Elisha the farmer (1Ki 19:19), and becomes God's voice to his people. Through Amos God proves once again that the station of life doesn't matter nearly as much as the station of the heart.

1 The words of Amos, one of the shepherds of
Tekoa[a]—what he saw concerning Israel two
years before the earthquake,[b] when Uzziah[c] was
king of Judah and Jeroboam[d] son of Jehoash[a] was
king of Israel.[e]
2 He said:

"The LORD roars[f] from Zion
  and thunders from Jerusalem;[g]
the pastures of the shepherds dry up,[b]
  and the top of Carmel[h] withers."[i]

Judgment on Israel's Neighbors

3 This is what the LORD says:

"For three sins of Damascus,[j]
  even for four, I will not turn back ⌊my wrath⌋.[k]
Because she threshed Gilead
  with sledges having iron teeth,
4 I will send fire[l] upon the house of Hazael
  that will consume the fortresses[m] of Ben-Hadad.[n]
5 I will break down the gate[o] of Damascus;
  I will destroy the king who is in[c] the Valley of Aven[d]
and the one who holds the scepter in Beth Eden.
  The people of Aram will go into exile to Kir,[p]"
says the LORD.

6 This is what the LORD says:

"For three sins of Gaza,[q]
  even for four, I will not turn back ⌊my wrath⌋.
Because she took captive whole communities
  and sold them to Edom,[r]
7 I will send fire upon the walls of Gaza
  that will consume her fortresses.
8 I will destroy the king[e] of Ashdod[s]
  and the one who holds the scepter in Ashkelon.
I will turn my hand[t] against Ekron,
  till the last of the Philistines[u] is dead,"
says the Sovereign LORD.[v]

9 This is what the LORD says:

"For three sins of Tyre,[w]
  even for four, I will not turn back ⌊my wrath⌋.
Because she sold whole communities of captives to Edom,
  disregarding a treaty of brotherhood,

1:1 [a] 2Sa 14:2 [b] Zec 14:5 [c] 2Ch 26:23 [d] 2Ki 14:23 [e] Hos 1:1
1:2 [f] Isa 42:13 [g] Joel 3:16 [h] Am 9:3 [i] Jer 12:4
1:3 [j] Isa 8:4; 17:1-3 [k] Am 2:6
1:4 [l] Jer 49:27 [m] Jer 17:27 [n] 1Ki 20:1; 2Ki 6:24
1:5 [o] Jer 51:30 [p] 2Ki 16:9
1:6 [q] 1Sa 6:17; Zep 2:4 [r] Ob 1:11
1:8 [s] 2Ch 26:6 [t] Ps 81:14 [u] Eze 25:16 [v] Isa 14:28-32; Zep 2:4-7
1:9 [w] 1Ki 5:1; 9:11-14; Isa 23:1-18; Jer 25:22; Joel 3:4; Mt 11:21

[a] *1* Hebrew *Joash,* a variant of *Jehoash* [b] *2* Or *shepherds mourn* [c] *5* Or *the inhabitants of* [d] *5* *Aven* means *wickedness.* [e] *8* Or *inhabitants*

10 I will send fire upon the walls of Tyre
that will consume her fortresses.[x]"

11 This is what the LORD says:

"For three sins of Edom,[y]
even for four, I will not turn back ⌞my wrath⌟.
Because he pursued his brother with a sword,
stifling all compassion,[a]
because his anger raged continually
and his fury flamed unchecked,[z]
12 I will send fire upon Teman[a]
that will consume the fortresses of Bozrah."

13 This is what the LORD says:

"For three sins of Ammon,[b]
even for four, I will not turn back ⌞my wrath⌟.
Because he ripped open the pregnant women[c] of Gilead
in order to extend his borders,
14 I will set fire to the walls of Rabbah[d]
that will consume her fortresses
amid war cries[e] on the day of battle,
amid violent winds on a stormy day.
15 Her king[b] will go into exile,
he and his officials together,"
says the LORD.

2 This is what the LORD says:

"For three sins of Moab,
even for four, I will not turn back ⌞my wrath⌟.
Because he burned, as if to lime,
the bones of Edom's king,
2 I will send fire upon Moab
that will consume the fortresses of Kerioth.[c]
Moab will go down in great tumult
amid war cries and the blast of the trumpet.
3 I will destroy her ruler[f]
and kill all her officials with him,"[g]
says the LORD.

4 This is what the LORD says:

"For three sins of Judah,[h]
even for four, I will not turn back ⌞my wrath⌟.
Because they have rejected the law[i] of the LORD
and have not kept his decrees,[j]
because they have been led astray[k] by false gods,[e][l]
the gods[e] their ancestors followed,[m]

1:10 [x]Zec 9:1-4
1:11 [y]Nu 20:14-21; 2Ch 28:17; Jer 49:7-22 [z]Eze 25:12-14
1:12 [a]Ob 1:9-10
1:13 [b]Jer 49:1-6; Eze 21:28; 25:2-7 [c]Hos 13:16
1:14 [d]Dt 3:11 [e]Am 2:2
2:3 [f]Ps 2:10 [g]Isa 40:23
2:4 [h]2Ki 17:19; Hos 12:2 [i]Jer 6:19 [j]Eze 20:24 [k]Isa 9:16 [l]Isa 28:15 [m]2Ki 22:13; Jer 16:12

a 11 Or *sword / and destroyed his allies* *b 15* Or / *Molech;* Hebrew *malcam* *c 2* Or *of her cities* *d 4* Or *by lies* *e 4* Or *lies*

Three, Even Four

AM 1:11,13; 2:1,4

Amos is set not only on getting his message across, but in doing so with style. In this book he makes a point to use words with strong, poetic imagery. "For three sins of Edom, even for four," Amos says, "I [God] will not turn back my wrath" (Am 1:11). This three/four literary device is typical of Old Testament writing in which numbers are used for rhetorical impact. Amos employs this formula to build progression and anticipation. By making bold statements, Amos proves that God is serious about these offenses and will no longer allow the nations to sweep their sins under the rug. A similar use of this literary style is found in Proverbs 30:15, 18, 21, 29.

5 I will send fire upon Judah
that will consume the fortresses of
Jerusalem.[n]"

Judgment on Israel

6 This is what the LORD says:

"For three sins of Israel,
even for four, I will not turn back ⌊my
wrath⌋.
They sell the righteous for silver,
and the needy for a pair of sandals.[o]
7 They trample on the heads of the poor
as upon the dust of the ground
and deny justice to the oppressed.
Father and son use the same girl
and so profane my holy name.[p]
8 They lie down beside every altar
on garments taken in pledge.[q]
In the house of their god
they drink wine[r] taken as fines.

9 "I destroyed the Amorite[s] before them,
though he was tall as the cedars
and strong as the oaks.
I destroyed his fruit above
and his roots[t] below.

10 "I brought you up out of Egypt,[u]
and I led you forty years in the desert[v]
to give you the land of the Amorites.[w]
11 I also raised up prophets[x] from among
your sons
and Nazirites[y] from among your
young men.
Is this not true, people of Israel?"
declares the LORD.
12 "But you made the Nazirites drink wine
and commanded the prophets not to
prophesy.[z]

13 "Now then, I will crush you
as a cart crushes when loaded with
grain.
14 The swift will not escape,
the strong[a] will not muster their
strength,
and the warrior will not save his life.[b]
15 The archer[c] will not stand his ground,
the fleet-footed soldier will not get
away,
and the horseman will not save his life.
16 Even the bravest warriors[d]
will flee naked on that day,"
declares the LORD.

Witnesses Summoned Against Israel

3 Hear this word the LORD has spoken against
you, O people of Israel—against the whole
family I brought up out of Egypt:[e]

2 "You only have I chosen[f]
of all the families of the earth;

2:5 [n]Jer 17:27; Hos 8:14
2:6 [o]Joel 3:3; Am 8:6
2:7 [p]Am 5:11-12; 8:4
2:8 [q]Ex 22:26 [r]Am 4:1; 6:6
2:9 [s]Nu 21:23-26; Jos 10:12 [t]Eze 17:9; Mal 4:1
2:10 [u]Ex 20:2; Am 3:1 [v]Dt 2:7 [w]Ex 3:8; Am 9:7
2:11 [x]Dt 18:18; Jer 7:25 [y]Nu 6:2-3; Jdg 13:5
2:12 [z]Isa 30:10; Jer 11:21; Am 7:12-13; Mic 2:6
2:14 [a]Jer 9:23 [b]Ps 33:16; Isa 30:16-17
2:15 [c]Eze 39:3
2:16 [d]Jer 48:41
3:1 [e]Am 2:10
3:2 [f]Dt 7:6; Lk 12:47

Something about injustice convinces us of our right to hold onto our anger and even embrace it. *I'm learning anger is not necessarily a wrong response . . . until I choose to harbor and nurture it. When I enfold anger, it drains my energy and takes up valuable inner space. Brewing anger taxes my physical, mental and emotional well-being. It also hampers my close relationships with others and God.*

—Patsy Clairmont

therefore I will punish you
for all your sins.[g]"

3 Do two walk together
unless they have agreed to do so?
4 Does a lion roar in the thicket
when he has no prey?[h]
Does he growl in his den
when he has caught nothing?
5 Does a bird fall into a trap on the ground
where no snare has been set?
Does a trap spring up from the earth
when there is nothing to catch?
6 When a trumpet sounds in a city,
do not the people tremble?
When disaster comes to a city,
has not the LORD caused it?[i]

7 Surely the Sovereign LORD does nothing
without revealing his plan[j]
to his servants the prophets.[k]

8 The lion has roared—
who will not fear?
The Sovereign LORD has spoken—
who can but prophesy?[l]

9 Proclaim to the fortresses of Ashdod
and to the fortresses of Egypt:
"Assemble yourselves on the mountains of Samaria;[m]
see the great unrest within her
and the oppression among her people."

10 "They do not know how to do right,[n]"
declares the LORD,
"who hoard plunder[o] and loot in their fortresses."[p]

11 Therefore this is what the Sovereign LORD
says:

"An enemy will overrun the land;
he will pull down your strongholds
and plunder your fortresses.[q]"

12 This is what the LORD says:

"As a shepherd saves from the lion's[r] mouth
only two leg bones or a piece of an ear,
so will the Israelites be saved,
those who sit in Samaria
on the edge of their beds
and in Damascus on their couches.[a][s]"

13 "Hear this and testify[t] against the house of
Jacob," declares the Lord, the LORD God Almighty.

14 "On the day I punish Israel for her sins,
I will destroy the altars of Bethel;[u]

[a] 12 The meaning of the Hebrew for this line is uncertain.

3:2 [g]Jer 14:10
3:4 [h]Ps 104:21; Hos 5:14
3:6 [i]Isa 14:24-27; 45:7
3:7 [j]Ge 18:17; Da 9:22; Jn 15:15; Rev 10:7 [k]Jer 23:22
3:8 [l]Jer 20:9; Jnh 1:1-3; 3:1-3; Ac 4:20
3:9 [m]Am 4:1; 6:1
3:10 [n]Jer 4:22; Am 5:7; 6:12 [o]Hab 2:8 [p]Zep 1:9
3:11 [q]Am 2:5; 6:14
3:12 [r]1Sa 17:34 [s]Am 6:4
3:13 [t]Eze 2:7
3:14 [u]Am 5:5-6

Wake Up

AM 3:3–6

How do the questions in this passage relate to each other? There is a method to Amos's seemingly absurd questioning. He is telling Israel, "Wake up!" The signs of disaster are all around them, and the people should easily see the warnings and realize what they mean.

Taken individually, Amos's rhetorical questions also hold deeper meanings and speak of God's heart. Amos 3:3 describes Israel's broken communion with God. God is reminding the people that he cannot be present unless they reconcile with him and walk in his ways. In Amos 3:4 God states that his approaching judgments are not without cause. And in Amos 3:5, God reflects that, though he prepares trouble for sinners, it is because of their own offenses that they are snared. If rewritten today, the passage might read something like this: "You've made a bad move. Wake up and smell the coffee. Get a grip, before the grip of sin gets a stranglehold on you."

Cows of Bashan

AM 4:1

Even if the cows of Bashan are the finest around, it is doubtful any woman would consider being compared to one a compliment! We must remember that Amos has been a herdsman, and he is familiar with these animals. Obviously, he sees something in the women of Israel that reminds him of them. Perhaps it is their size—all these women care about is filling their bellies. Perhaps it is their careless and callous attitudes. Cattle are known to have a difficult time keeping within the bounds of their pasture, trampling anyone weaker and smaller who happens to get in their way. Or perhaps it is a combination of both. It seems these women have an unquenchable passion for pampering and pleasure, no matter what the cost, no matter who is in their way. This is completely unacceptable to a God who promises to satisfy those who help the needy (Isa 58:6–11).

the horns of the altar will be cut off
and fall to the ground.
15 I will tear down the winter house[v]
along with the summer house;[w]
the houses adorned with ivory[x] will be
destroyed
and the mansions will be
demolished,"
declares the LORD.

Israel Has Not Returned to God

4 Hear this word, you cows of Bashan[y] on
Mount Samaria,[z]
you women who oppress the poor and
crush the needy
and say to your husbands, "Bring us
some drinks![a]"
2 The Sovereign LORD has sworn by his
holiness:
"The time will surely come
when you will be taken away[b] with
hooks,
the last of you with fishhooks.
3 You will each go straight out
through breaks in the wall,[c]
and you will be cast out toward
Harmon,[a]"
declares the LORD.

4 "Go to Bethel and sin;
go to Gilgal[d] and sin yet more.
Bring your sacrifices every morning,[e]
your tithes[f] every three years.[b][g]
5 Burn leavened bread[h] as a thank
offering
and brag about your freewill
offerings[i]—
boast about them, you Israelites,
for this is what you love to do,"
declares the Sovereign LORD.

6 "I gave you empty stomachs[c] in every
city
and lack of bread in every town,
yet you have not returned to me,"
declares the LORD.[j]

7 "I also withheld rain from you
when the harvest was still three
months away.
I sent rain on one town,
but withheld it from another.[k]
One field had rain;
another had none and dried up.
8 People staggered from town to town for
water[l]
but did not get enough to drink,
yet you have not returned[m] to me,"
declares the LORD.[n]

3:15 [v]Jer 36:22 [w]Jdg 3:20 [x]1Ki 22:39
4:1 [y]Ps 22:12; Eze 39:18 [z]Am 3:9 [a]Am 2:8; 5:11; 8:6
4:2 [b]Am 6:8
4:3 [c]Eze 12:5
4:4 [d]Hos 4:15 [e]Nu 28:3 [f]Dt 14:28 [g]Eze 20:39; Am 5:21-22
4:5 [h]Lev 7:13 [i]Lev 22:18-21
4:6 [j]Isa 3:1; Jer 5:3; Hag 2:17
4:7 [k]Ex 9:4,26; Dt 11:17; 2Ch 7:13
4:8 [l]Eze 4:16-17 [m]Jer 3:7 [n]Jer 14:4

[a] *3* Masoretic Text; with a different word division of the Hebrew (see Septuagint) *out, O mountain of oppression* [b] *4* Or *tithes on the third day* [c] *6* Hebrew *you cleanness of teeth*

4:9 [o]Dt 28:22 [p]Joel 1:7 [q]Jer 3:10; Hag 2:17

9 "Many times I struck your gardens and vineyards,
I struck them with blight and mildew.[o]
Locusts devoured your fig and olive trees,[p]
yet you have not returned[q] to me,"
declares the LORD.

4:10 [r]Ex 9:3; Dt 28:27 [s]Isa 9:13

10 "I sent plagues[r] among you
as I did to Egypt.
I killed your young men with the sword,
along with your captured horses.
I filled your nostrils with the stench of your camps,
yet you have not returned to me,"
declares the LORD.[s]

4:11 [t]Ge 19:24; Jer 23:14

11 "I overthrew some of you
as I[a] overthrew Sodom and Gomorrah.[t]
You were like a burning stick snatched from the fire,
yet you have not returned to me,"
declares the LORD.

12 "Therefore this is what I will do to you, Israel,
and because I will do this to you,
prepare to meet your God, O Israel."

4:13 [u]Ps 65:6 [v]Da 2:28 [w]Mic 1:3 [x]Isa 47:4; Am 5:8,27; 9:6

13 He who forms the mountains,[u]
creates the wind,
and reveals his thoughts[v] to man,
he who turns dawn to darkness,
and treads the high places of the earth[w]—
the LORD God Almighty is his name.[x]

A Lament and Call to Repentance

5:1 [y]Eze 19:1

5 Hear this word, O house of Israel, this lament[y]
I take up concerning you:

5:2 [z]Jer 14:17 [a]Jer 50:32; Am 8:14

2 "Fallen is Virgin[z] Israel,
never to rise again,
deserted in her own land,
with no one to lift her up.[a]"

3 This is what the Sovereign LORD says:

"The city that marches out a thousand strong for Israel
will have only a hundred left;
the town that marches out a hundred strong
will have only ten left.[b]"

5:3 [b]Isa 6:13; Am 6:9

5:4 [c]Isa 55:3; Jer 29:13

4 This is what the LORD says to the house of Israel:

"Seek me and live;[c]
5 do not seek Bethel,
do not go to Gilgal,[d]

5:5 [d]1Sa 11:14; Am 4:4

[a] 11 Hebrew *God*

Virgin Israel

AM 5:2

The term "Virgin Israel" is a word picture to show how far God's chosen nation has fallen. This term is used several times in Scripture, including Jeremiah 18:13, which says, "A most horrible thing has been done by Virgin Israel." Once a chaste bride, favored by God, Israel has prostituted herself to other gods. No one is offering to rescue her . . . no one except God, that is. Even in her weary and tattered state, God calls out to her, "Seek me and live" (Am 5:4). This proves again that no matter what state we're in, no matter how far we've fallen from purity and grace, God still desires to cleanse us and renew us to the position of his beloved bride.

A Heart for the Poor

AM 5:11

God shows his heart by speaking out for the poor and needy more than 200 times in the Bible. He also uses treatment of the poor as a measuring stick to test whether a person, or a nation, is righteous in his sight. According to God, righteous people care for others (Ac 10:2) and promote peace and well-being (Mt 5:9). Obviously, the rich in Israel do not measure up to God's standard. For the sake of indulgence, they take from the poor what little they have and cause even more suffering. "Seek good," Amos says, "Then the LORD God Almighty will be with you" (Am 5:14). Underline this verse in your Bible; then consider ways you can care for those in need. Inch by inch, kindness by kindness, each of us can measure up to God's expectations of his people.

do not journey to Beersheba.[e]
For Gilgal will surely go into exile,
and Bethel will be reduced to nothing.[a][f]"
6 Seek[g] the LORD and live,[h]
or he will sweep through the house of Joseph like a fire;[i]
it will devour,
and Bethel[j] will have no one to quench it.

7 You who turn justice into bitterness[k]
and cast righteousness to the ground
8 (he who made the Pleiades and Orion,[l]
who turns blackness into dawn[m]
and darkens day into night,[n]
who calls for the waters of the sea
and pours them out over the face of the land—
the LORD is his name[o]—
9 he flashes destruction on the stronghold
and brings the fortified city to ruin),[p]
10 you hate the one who reproves in court[q]
and despise him who tells the truth.[r]
11 You trample on the poor[s]
and force him to give you grain.
Therefore, though you have built stone mansions,[t]
you will not live in them;
though you have planted lush vineyards,
you will not drink their wine.[u]
12 For I know how many are your offenses
and how great your sins.

You oppress the righteous and take bribes
and you deprive the poor of justice in the courts.[v]
13 Therefore the prudent man keeps quiet in such times,
for the times are evil.

14 Seek good, not evil,
that you may live.
Then the LORD God Almighty will be with you,
just as you say he is.
15 Hate evil,[w] love good;
maintain justice in the courts.
Perhaps the LORD God Almighty will have mercy[x]
on the remnant[y] of Joseph.

16 Therefore this is what the Lord, the LORD God Almighty, says:

"There will be wailing[z] in all the streets
and cries of anguish in every public square.

5:5 [e]Am 8:14 [f]1Sa 7:16
5:6 [g]Isa 55:6 [h]ver 14 [i]Dt 4:24 [j]Am 3:14
5:7 [k]Am 6:12
5:8 [l]Job 9:9 [m]Isa 42:16 [n]Ps 104:20; Am 8:9 [o]Ps 104:6-9; Am 4:13
5:9 [p]Mic 5:11
5:10 [q]Isa 29:21 [r]1Ki 22:8
5:11 [s]Am 8:6 [t]Am 3:15 [u]Mic 6:15
5:12 [v]Isa 5:23; Am 2:6-7
5:15 [w]Ps 97:10; Ro 12:9 [x]Joel 2:14 [y]Mic 5:7,8
5:16 [z]Jer 9:17

[a] 5 Or *grief*; or *wickedness*; Hebrew *aven*, a reference to Beth Aven (a derogatory name for Bethel)

The farmers[a] will be summoned to weep
and the mourners to wail.
17 There will be wailing in all the
vineyards,
for I will pass through[b] your midst,"
says the LORD.[c]

The Day of the LORD

18 Woe to you who long
for the day of the LORD![d]
Why do you long for the day of the
LORD?
That day will be darkness,[e] not light.[f]
19 It will be as though a man fled from a
lion
only to meet a bear,
as though he entered his house
and rested his hand on the wall
only to have a snake bite him.[g]
20 Will not the day of the LORD be
darkness, not light—
pitch-dark, without a ray of
brightness?[h]

21 "I hate, I despise your religious feasts;[i]
I cannot stand your assemblies.[j]
22 Even though you bring me burnt
offerings and grain offerings,
I will not accept them.
Though you bring choice fellowship
offerings,[a]
I will have no regard for them.[k][l]
23 Away with the noise of your songs!
I will not listen to the music of your
harps.[m]
24 But let justice[n] roll on like a river,
righteousness like a never-failing
stream![o]

25 "Did you bring me sacrifices[p] and
offerings
forty years[q] in the desert, O house of
Israel?
26 You have lifted up the shrine of your
king,
the pedestal of your idols,
the star of your god[b]—
which you made for yourselves.
27 Therefore I will send you into exile
beyond Damascus,"
says the LORD, whose name is God
Almighty.[r]

Woe to the Complacent

6 Woe to you[s] who are complacent in Zion,
and to you who feel secure on Mount
Samaria,

5:16 [a]Joel 1:11
5:17 [b]Ex 12:12; [c]Isa 16:10; Jer 48:33
5:18 [d]Joel 1:15 [e]Joel 2:2 [f]Isa 5:19,30; Jer 30:7
5:19 [g]Job 20:24; Isa 24:17-18; Jer 15:2-3; 48:44
5:20 [h]Isa 13:10; Zep 1:15
5:21 [i]Lev 26:31 [j]Isa 1:11-16
5:22 [k]Am 4:4; Mic 6:6-7 [l]Isa 66:3
5:23 [m]Am 6:5
5:24 [n]Jer 22:3 [o]Mic 6:8
5:25 [p]Isa 43:23 [q]Dt 32:17
5:27 [r]Am 4:13; Ac 7:42-43*
6:1 [s]Lk 6:24

[a] 22 Traditionally *peace offerings* [b] 26 Or *lifted up Sakkuth your king / and Kaiwan your idols, / your star-gods*; Septuagint *lifted up the shrine of Molech / and the star of your god Rephan, / their idols*

Ignoring God

AM 5:21

The feasts of the Jewish nation were times of celebration. They included music, food and dancing and were designed by God to be outward expressions of the people's faith in, and love for, him. So why would God hate the very festivals he had instituted? Like an extravagant birthday party where the guest of honor is uninvited (and no one even notices or cares), the festivals and worship ceremonies of the Israelites look good but are insincere. The Israelites of Amos's day attend the necessary feasts and offer the necessary sacrifices, but God is not fooled. He clearly sees the lack of devotion behind the hoopla.

Complacency

AM 6:1–7

The Israelites eat, drink and make merry, and God is angry—not because of their prosperity but because they are set on satisfying themselves rather than seeking God for satisfaction. Look closely at the verbs listed in Amos 6:3–7. They show complacency at its finest. The people are lying on beds of ivory and dining on the finest of foods when, really, God says, they should be grieving over the state of their nation (Am 6:6).

Complacency is not confined to that time or people. In good times, smugness and pride can creep in, and people forget God. Yet, God warns, the "feasting and lounging will end" (Am 6:7). God's favor will then be extended only to those who have learned to dine on his love and rest in his mercy.

you notable men of the foremost nation,
to whom the people of Israel come![t]
2 Go to Calneh[u] and look at it;
go from there to great Hamath,[v]
and then go down to Gath[w] in
Philistia.
Are they better off than[x] your two
kingdoms?
Is their land larger than yours?
3 You put off the evil day
and bring near a reign of terror.[y]
4 You lie on beds inlaid with ivory
and lounge on your couches.
You dine on choice lambs
and fattened calves.[z]
5 You strum away on your harps[a] like
David
and improvise on musical
instruments.[b]
6 You drink wine[c] by the bowlful
and use the finest lotions,
but you do not grieve[d] over the ruin of
Joseph.
7 Therefore you will be among the first to
go into exile;
your feasting and lounging will end.

The LORD Abhors the Pride of Israel

8 The Sovereign LORD has sworn by himself[e]—
the LORD God Almighty declares:

"I abhor[f] the pride of Jacob[g]
and detest his fortresses;
I will deliver up[h] the city
and everything in it.[i]"

9 If ten[j] men are left in one house, they too will
die. 10 And if a relative who is to burn the bodies[k]
comes to carry them out of the house and asks
anyone still hiding there, "Is anyone with you?"
and he says, "No," then he will say, "Hush![l] We
must not mention the name of the LORD."

11 For the LORD has given the command,
and he will smash the great house[m]
into pieces
and the small house into bits.[n]

12 Do horses run on the rocky crags?
Does one plow there with oxen?
But you have turned justice into poison[o]
and the fruit of righteousness into
bitterness[p]—
13 you who rejoice in the conquest of Lo
Debar[a]
and say, "Did we not take Karnaim[b]
by our own strength?[q]"
14 For the LORD God Almighty declares,
"I will stir up a nation[r] against you,
O house of Israel,

6:1 [t]Isa 32:9-11
6:2 [u]Ge 10:10 [v]2Ki 18:34 [w]2Ch 26:6 [x]Na 3:8
6:3 [y]Isa 56:12; Am 9:10
6:4 [z]Eze 34:2-3; Am 3:12
6:5 [a]Isa 5:12; Am 5:23 [b]1Ch 15:16
6:6 [c]Am 2:8 [d]Eze 9:4
6:8 [e]Ge 22:16; Heb 6:13 [f]Lev 26:30 [g]Ps 47:4 [h]Am 4:2 [i]Dt 32:19
6:9 [j]Am 5:3
6:10 [k]1Sa 31:12 [l]Am 8:3
6:11 [m]Am 3:15 [n]Isa 55:11
6:12 [o]Hos 10:4 [p]Am 5:7
6:13 [q]Job 8:15; Isa 28:14-15
6:14 [r]Jer 5:15

[a] 13 *Lo Debar* means *nothing.* [b] 13 *Karnaim* means *horns; horn* here symbolizes strength.

that will oppress you all the way
from Lebo[a] Hamath[s] to the valley of
the Arabah.[t]"

Locusts, Fire and a Plumb Line

7 This is what the Sovereign LORD showed me:[u]
He was preparing swarms of locusts[v] after the
king's share had been harvested and just as the second crop was coming up. 2When they had stripped
the land clean,[w] I cried out, "Sovereign LORD, forgive! How can Jacob survive?[x] He is so small![y]"
3So the LORD relented.[z]
"This will not happen," the LORD said.[a]
4This is what the Sovereign LORD showed me:
The Sovereign LORD was calling for judgment by
fire;[b] it dried up the great deep and devoured[c] the
land. 5Then I cried out, "Sovereign LORD, I beg
you, stop! How can Jacob survive? He is so
small![d]"
6So the LORD relented.[e]
"This will not happen either," the Sovereign
LORD said.

7This is what he showed me: The Lord was
standing by a wall that had been built true to
plumb, with a plumb line in his hand. 8And the
LORD asked me, "What do you see,[f] Amos?[g]"
"A plumb line,[h]" I replied.
Then the Lord said, "Look, I am setting a plumb
line among my people Israel; I will spare them no
longer.[i]

9"The high places of Isaac will be
destroyed
and the sanctuaries[j] of Israel will be
ruined;
with my sword I will rise against the
house of Jeroboam.[k]"

Amos and Amaziah

10Then Amaziah the priest of Bethel[l] sent a message to Jeroboam[m] king of Israel: "Amos is raising
a conspiracy[n] against you in the very heart of Israel. The land cannot bear all his words.[o] 11For this
is what Amos is saying:

" 'Jeroboam will die by the sword,
and Israel will surely go into exile,
away from their native land.' "

12Then Amaziah said to Amos, "Get out, you
seer! Go back to the land of Judah. Earn your bread
there and do your prophesying there.[p] 13Don't
prophesy anymore at Bethel, because this is the
king's sanctuary and the temple of the kingdom.[q]"
14Amos answered Amaziah, "I was neither a
prophet[r] nor a prophet's son, but I was a shepherd, and I also took care of sycamore-fig trees.
15But the LORD took me from tending the flock[s]
and said to me, 'Go, prophesy to my people Isra-

6:14 [s]1Ki 8:65 [t]Am 3:11
7:1 [u]Am 8:1 [v]Joel 1:4
7:2 [w]Ex 10:15 [x]Isa 37:4 [y]Eze 11:13
7:3 [z]Dt 32:36; Jer 26:19; Jnh 3:10 [a]Hos 11:8
7:4 [b]Isa 66:16 [c]Dt 32:22
7:5 [d]ver 1-2; Joel 2:17
7:6 [e]Jnh 3:10
7:8 [f]Jer 1:11,13 [g]Isa 28:17; La 2:8; Am 8:2 [h]2Ki 21:13 [i]Jer 15:6; Eze 7:2-9
7:9 [j]Lev 26:31 [k]2Ki 15:9; Isa 63:18; Hos 10:8
7:10 [l]1Ki 12:32 [m]2Ki 14:23 [n]Jer 38:4 [o]Jer 26:8-11
7:12 [p]Mt 8:34
7:13 [q]Am 2:12; Ac 4:18
7:14 [r]2Ki 2:5; 4:38
7:15 [s]2Sa 7:8

Whether we say just the right thing or can't think of *anything* that seems right, all we can do is open our mouths and trust God to use us. That doesn't mean we shouldn't be prepared to offer *a* reasoned explanation for our faith, but it does take the pressure off of us. We are the instruments, but God is the one who must make the music through us.

—Thelma Wells

[a] 14 Or *from the entrance to*

el.'[t] 16Now then, hear the word of the LORD. You
say,

> " 'Do not prophesy against[u] Israel,
> and stop preaching against the house
> of Isaac.'

17"Therefore this is what the LORD says:

> " 'Your wife will become a prostitute[v] in
> the city,
> and your sons and daughters will fall
> by the sword.
> Your land will be measured and divided
> up,
> and you yourself will die in a pagan[a]
> country.
> And Israel will certainly go into exile,
> away from their native land.[w]' "

A Basket of Ripe Fruit

8 This is what the Sovereign LORD showed me: a
basket of ripe fruit. 2"What do you see,[x]
Amos?[y]" he asked.
"A basket of ripe fruit," I answered.
Then the LORD said to me, "The time is ripe for
my people Israel; I will spare them no longer.[z]
3"In that day," declares the Sovereign LORD, "the
songs in the temple will turn to wailing.[b][a] Many,
many bodies—flung everywhere! Silence![b]"

> 4Hear this, you who trample the needy
> and do away with the poor[c] of the
> land,[d]

5saying,

> "When will the New Moon be over
> that we may sell grain,
> and the Sabbath be ended
> that we may market wheat?"—
> skimping the measure,
> boosting the price
> and cheating with dishonest scales,[e]
> 6buying the poor with silver
> and the needy for a pair of sandals,
> selling even the sweepings with the
> wheat.[f]

7The LORD has sworn by the Pride of Jacob:[g] "I
will never forget[h] anything they have done.

> 8"Will not the land tremble[i] for this,
> and all who live in it mourn?
> The whole land will rise like the Nile;
> it will be stirred up and then sink
> like the river of Egypt.[j]

> 9"In that day," declares the Sovereign LORD,
> "I will make the sun go down at noon
> and darken the earth in broad
> daylight.[k]

7:15 [t]Jer 7:1-2; Eze 2:3-4
7:16 [u]Eze 20:46; Mic 2:6
7:17 [v]Hos 4:13 [w]2Ki 17:6; Eze 4:13; Hos 9:3
8:2 [x]Jer 24:3 [y]Am 7:8 [z]Eze 7:2-9
8:3 [a]Am 5:16 [b]Am 5:23; 6:10
8:4 [c]Pr 30:14 [d]Ps 14:4; Am 2:7
8:5 [e]2Ki 4:23; Ne 13:15-16; Hos 12:7; Mic 6:10-11
8:6 [f]Am 2:6
8:7 [g]Am 6:8 [h]Hos 8:13
8:8 [i]Hos 4:3 [j]Ps 18:7; Jer 46:8; Am 9:5
8:9 [k]Job 5:14; Isa 59:9-10; Jer 15:9; Am 5:8; Mic 3:6

[a] 17 Hebrew *an unclean* [b] 3 Or *"the temple singers will wail*

> ***A**s we offer our small*
> ***rejoicing***
> ***For the love that surrounds***
> ***our days,***
> ***All the wonderful works of***
> ***Thy goodness***
> ***Shall open before our gaze;***
> ***Through the gates of our***
> ***narrow thanksgiving***
> ***We shall enter Thy courts***
> ***of praise.***

—Annie Johnson Flint (1862–1932)

[10]I will turn your religious feasts into
mourning
and all your singing into weeping.
8:10 [l]Jer 48:37 [m]Jer 6:26; Zec 12:10 [n]Eze 7:18
I will make all of you wear sackcloth[l]
and shave your heads.
I will make that time like mourning for
an only son[m]
and the end of it like a bitter day.[n]

[11]"The days are coming," declares the
Sovereign LORD,
"when I will send a famine through
the land—
not a famine of food or a thirst for
water,
but a famine of hearing the words of
8:11 [o]1Sa 3:1; 2Ch 15:3; Eze 7:26
the LORD.[o]
[12]Men will stagger from sea to sea
and wander from north to east,
8:12 [p]Eze 20:3,31
searching for the word of the LORD,
but they will not find it.[p]

[13]"In that day

"the lovely young women and strong
young men
8:13 [q]Isa 41:17; Hos 2:3
will faint because of thirst.[q]
[14]They who swear by the shame[a] of
Samaria,
8:14 [r]1Ki 12:29 [s]Am 5:5 [t]Am 5:2
or say, 'As surely as your god lives,
O Dan,'[r]
or, 'As surely as the god[b] of
Beersheba[s] lives'—
they will fall,
never to rise again.[t]"

Israel to Be Destroyed

9 I saw the Lord standing by the altar, and he
said:

"Strike the tops of the pillars
so that the thresholds shake.
9:1 [u]Ps 68:21
Bring them down on the heads[u] of all
the people;
those who are left I will kill with the
sword.
Not one will get away,
none will escape.
[2]Though they dig down to the depths of
9:2 [v]Ps 139:8 [w]Jer 51:53 [x]Ob 1:4
the grave,[c][v]
from there my hand will take them.
Though they climb up to the heavens,[w]
from there I will bring them down.[x]
[3]Though they hide themselves on the top
9:3 [y]Am 1:2 [z]Ps 139:8-10
of Carmel,[y]
there I will hunt them down and seize
them.[z]
Though they hide from me at the
bottom of the sea,

[a] 14 Or *by Ashima;* or *by the idol* [b] 14 Or *power*
[c] 2 Hebrew *to Sheol*

Dry, Cracked Souls

AM 8:11

When we think of a famine, we imagine dry hillsides and cracked streambeds. Yet the famine Amos describes is of an entirely different sort—"a famine of hearing the words of the LORD" (Am 8:11). This is, in fact, a state the people bring on themselves. They refuse to listen to the prophets (God's voice during that time), so God promises that prophecies will cease. The Israelites starve their souls by chasing after other gods, as well as their own comfort and prosperity, so no hope of refreshment waits on the horizon. Instead, God inflicts his greatest judgment on them—the absence of his words and the absence of his presence.

Sometimes life becomes so complicated we feel as if we've gone as far as we can down this stressful highway. We imagine ourselves smashed up against a brick wall, unable to answer one more call, hear one more complaint and take one more breath. When that's the image that fills your mind, change the brick wall to God. Imagine yourself pressed tightly against his heart, wrapped in his everlasting arms, soothed by his life-giving breath. Picture yourself encircled in God's love, soaked in his strength. Then step out onto the highway once more.

—Barbara Johnson

there I will command the serpent to
bite them.[a] 9:3 [a]Jer 16:16-17
4 Though they are driven into exile by
their enemies,
there I will command the sword[b] to 9:4 [b]Lev 26:33; Eze 5:12
slay them.
I will fix my eyes upon them [c]Jer 21:10
for evil[c] and not for good.[d]"[e] [d]Jer 39:16 [e]Jer 44:11

5 The Lord, the LORD Almighty,
he who touches the earth and it
melts,[f] 9:5 [f]Ps 46:2; Mic 1:4
and all who live in it mourn—
the whole land rises like the Nile, [g]Am 8:8
then sinks like the river of
Egypt[g]—
6 he who builds his lofty palace[a] in the
heavens
and sets its foundation[b] on the earth,
who calls for the waters of the sea
and pours them out over the face of
the land—
the LORD is his name.[h] 9:6 [h]Ps 104:1-3, 5-6,13; Am 5:8

7 "Are not you Israelites
the same to me as the Cushites[c]?"[i]
declares the LORD. 9:7 [i]Isa 20:4; 43:3
"Did I not bring Israel up from Egypt,
the Philistines from Caphtor[d][j] [j]Dt 2:23; Jer 47:4
and the Arameans from Kir?[k] [k]2Ki 16:9; Isa 22:6; Am 1:5; 2:10

8 "Surely the eyes of the Sovereign LORD
are on the sinful kingdom.
I will destroy it
from the face of the earth—
yet I will not totally destroy
the house of Jacob,"
declares the LORD.[l] 9:8 [l]Jer 44:27
9 "For I will give the command,
and I will shake the house of Israel
among all the nations
as grain[m] is shaken in a sieve,[n] 9:9 [m]Lk 22:31
and not a pebble will reach the [n]Isa 30:28
ground.
10 All the sinners among my people
will die by the sword,
all those who say,
'Disaster will not overtake or meet
us.'[o] 9:10 [o]Am 6:3

Israel's Restoration

11 "In that day I will restore
David's fallen tent.
I will repair its broken places,
restore its ruins,
and build it as it used to be,[p] 9:11 [p]Ps 80:12
12 so that they may possess the remnant of 9:12
Edom[q] [q]Nu 24:18

[a]6 The meaning of the Hebrew for this phrase is uncertain.
[b]6 The meaning of the Hebrew for this word is uncertain.
[c]7 That is, people from the upper Nile region [d]7 That is, Crete

9:12 [r]Isa 43:7 [s]Ac 15:16-17*

and all the nations that bear my
name,[a][r]"
declares the LORD,
who will do these things.[s]

[13]"The days are coming," declares the LORD,

9:13 [t]Lev 26:5 [u]Joel 3:18

"when the reaper will be overtaken by
the plowman[t]
and the planter by the one treading
grapes.
New wine will drip from the mountains
and flow from all the hills.[u]
[14]I will bring back my exiled[b] people
Israel;

9:14 [v]Isa 61:4 [w]Jer 30:18; 31:28; Eze 28:25-26

they will rebuild the ruined cities[v]
and live in them.
They will plant vineyards and drink
their wine;
they will make gardens and eat their
fruit.[w]

9:15 [x]Isa 60:21 [y]Jer 24:6; Eze 34:25-28; 37:12,25

[15]I will plant[x] Israel in their own land,
never again to be uprooted
from the land I have given them,"
says the LORD your God.[y]

New Wine, New Hope

AM 9:13

In Scripture, new wine signifies the earth's richness. It is the fruit of a blessed land. When Isaac gave Jacob the blessing of birthright, he prayed for "an abundance of grain and new wine" (Ge 27:28). When Moses gave his last address as the Israelites prepared to enter the promised land, he said God would bless them by giving them "grain, new wine and oil" (Dt 7:13). In this passage, by telling the people that "new wine will drip from the mountains and flow from all the hills" (Am 9:13), God promises fruitfulness once again. His threats of doom are followed by words of promise.

[a] 12 Hebrew; Septuagint *so that the remnant of men / and all the nations that bear my name may seek ⌊the Lord⌋* [b] 14 Or *will restore the fortunes of my*

Obadiah

Pride goes before destruction.

The shortest book in the Old Testament, the prophecy of Obadiah is directed not to Israel but to Edom, the descendants of Esau, who were long-standing enemies of Israel. Though distant relatives of the Israelites, the people of Edom take every opportunity to inflict pain and suffering on God's children. Obadiah condemns their treachery and declares God's intent to wipe Edom, who has been gloating over Jerusalem's devastation at the hands of the Babylonian army, off the map. While most of the other prophetic books in the Old Testament offer a word of hope or the promise of eventual restoration, Obadiah's words pronounce only judgment and God's pledge to humble this proud, deceitful nation.

Though short on words, Obadiah is long on meaning. Woven throughout these few verses are reminders that proud hearts that thrive on self-centeredness will reap the bitter fruit of judgment (Ob 2–7). We hear the ringing condemnation and promise of failure for those who find pleasure in someone else's tragedy (Ob 10–14). And the certainty of destruction is revealed for those who hold grudges or take revenge on others (Ob 15–17). Obadiah resoundingly proclaims that no situation, nation or circumstance can be truly secure unless God is in the center of it, for justice ultimately belongs to him.

Quick Study

Author
The prophet Obadiah.

Date Written
The dates are not certain, but probably sometime between 605 and 586 B.C.

Setting
Judah.

Key Passage
Obadiah 18 "The house of Jacob will be a fire
and the house of Joseph a flame;
the house of Esau will be stubble,
and they will set it on fire and consume it.
There will be no survivors
from the house of Esau."

Outline

Edom's doom.
Ob 1–14
Edom in the day of the Lord.
Ob 15–21

The Women of Obadiah

No women are mentioned in the book of Obadiah.

Edom's Heartlessness

OB 10

The descendants of Esau, the Edomites, act heartlessly toward the descendants of Jacob, God's people. They revel in Judah's destruction, loot Jerusalem and return to the conquering Babylonians those citizens of Judah who try to escape (Ob 12–14). God will not allow such behavior to go unpunished. Centuries earlier, he had promised Abraham (then Abram): "I will bless those who bless you, and whoever curses you I will curse" (Ge 12:3). While that blessing might have continued through the line of Abraham's grandson Esau, it was instead transferred to the descendants of Jacob after Esau sold his birthright for a bowl of stew (Ge 25:29–34).

Though his promise to Abraham had been made long before, God remembers it clearly—and honors it. God's memory is perfect—and, in his perfect timing, he deals with those who commit injustices against his people.

OBADIAH

[1]The vision of Obadiah.

This is what the Sovereign LORD says about Edom[a]—

We have heard a message from the LORD:
An envoy[b] was sent to the nations to say,
"Rise, and let us go against her for battle"[c]—

1:1 [a]Isa 63:1-6; Jer 49:7-22; Eze 25:12-14; Am 1:11-12 [b]Isa 18:2 [c]Jer 6:4-5

[2]"See, I will make you small among the nations;
you will be utterly despised.
[3]The pride[d] of your heart has deceived you,
you who live in the clefts of the rocks[a]
and make your home on the heights,
you who say to yourself,
'Who can bring me down to the ground?'[e]

1:3 [d]Isa 16:6 [e]Isa 14:13-15; Rev 18:7

[4]Though you soar like the eagle
and make your nest[f] among the stars,
from there I will bring you down,"[g]
declares the LORD.[h]

1:4 [f]Hab 2:9 [g]Isa 14:13 [h]Job 20:6

[5]"If thieves came to you,
if robbers in the night—
Oh, what a disaster awaits you—
would they not steal only as much as they wanted?
If grape pickers came to you,
would they not leave a few grapes?[i]

1:5 [i]Dt 24:21

[6]But how Esau will be ransacked,
his hidden treasures pillaged!
[7]All your allies[j] will force you to the border;
your friends will deceive and overpower you;
those who eat your bread[k] will set a trap for you,[b]
but you will not detect it.

1:7 [j]Jer 30:14 [k]Ps 41:9

[8]"In that day," declares the LORD,
"will I not destroy[l] the wise men of Edom,
men of understanding in the mountains of Esau?

1:8 [l]Job 5:12; Isa 29:14

[9]Your warriors, O Teman,[m] will be terrified,
and everyone in Esau's mountains
will be cut down in the slaughter.

1:9 [m]Ge 36:11, 34

[10]Because of the violence[n] against your brother Jacob,[o]
you will be covered with shame;
you will be destroyed forever.[p]

1:10 [n]Joel 3:19 [o]Ps 137:7; Am 1:11-12 [p]Eze 35:9

[11]On the day you stood aloof
while strangers carried off his wealth
and foreigners entered his gates
and cast lots[q] for Jerusalem,
you were like one of them.

1:11 [q]Na 3:10

[a] 3 Or *of Sela* [b] 7 The meaning of the Hebrew for this clause is uncertain.

[12]You should not look down on your
brother
in the day of his misfortune,
1:12 [r]Eze 35:15 [s]Pr 17:5 [t]Mic 4:11
nor rejoice[r] over the people of Judah
in the day of their destruction,[s]
nor boast so much
in the day of their trouble.[t]
[13]You should not march through the gates
of my people
in the day of their disaster,
nor look down on them in their
1:13 [u]Eze 35:5
calamity[u]
in the day of their disaster,
nor seize their wealth
in the day of their disaster.
[14]You should not wait at the crossroads
to cut down their fugitives,
nor hand over their survivors
in the day of their trouble.
1:15 [v]Eze 30:3 [w]Jer 50:29; Hab 2:8
[15]"The day of the LORD is near[v]
for all nations.
As you have done, it will be done to you;
your deeds[w] will return upon your
own head.
1:16 [x]Jer 25:15; 49:12
[16]Just as you drank on my holy hill,
so all the nations will drink[x]
continually;
they will drink and drink
and be as if they had never been.
1:17 [y]Am 9:11-15 [z]Isa 4:3
[17]But on Mount Zion will be deliverance;[y]
it will be holy,[z]
and the house of Jacob
will possess its inheritance.
[18]The house of Jacob will be a fire
and the house of Joseph a flame;
the house of Esau will be stubble,
1:18 [a]Zec 12:6
and they will set it on fire and
consume[a] it.
There will be no survivors
from the house of Esau."
The LORD has spoken.

[19]People from the Negev will occupy
the mountains of Esau,
and people from the foothills will possess
1:19 [b]Isa 11:14 [c]Jer 31:5
the land of the Philistines.[b]
They will occupy the fields of Ephraim
and Samaria,[c]
and Benjamin will possess Gilead.
[20]This company of Israelite exiles who are
in Canaan
1:20 [d]1Ki 17:9-10 [e]Jer 33:13
will possess ⌊the land⌋ as far as
Zarephath;[d]
the exiles from Jerusalem who are in
Sepharad
will possess the towns of the Negev.[e]
[21]Deliverers will go up on[a] Mount Zion
1:21 [f]Ps 22:28; Zec 14:9,16; Rev 11:15
to govern the mountains of Esau.
And the kingdom will be the LORD's.[f]

My Holy Hill

OB 16

"My holy hill" refers here to the city of Jerusalem, Zion. The place where God has chosen to dwell with his people, and the place where the temple, the symbol of God's presence, is located. Those who defile Jerusalem and torment God's chosen ones incur the wrath of the Lord, who vows that Judah's enemies will be destroyed "as if they had never been." Though the Edomites drink wine while rejoicing in the suffering of Judah, they will soon drink of God's cup of sorrow, which accompanies the elimination of their people.

[a] *21* Or *from*

Jonah

A reluctant missionary.

The book of Jonah contrasts the mercy of God with the deeply ingrained prejudices of his people. Nineveh has long been a wicked, barbaric thorn in Israel's side, inflicting terror and cruelty. When God tells Jonah to go to Nineveh and preach a message of judgment, Jonah flatly refuses (Jnh 1), because, he says in 4:2, "I knew that you are a gracious and compassionate God, . . . who relents from sending calamity." Jonah's attitude is that Nineveh is too wicked for God's grace; Nineveh should be destroyed. In his refusal to yield his prejudice to God's mercy, Jonah runs away from God, suffering the consequences of his rebellion (Jnh 2). Yet God ultimately uses this reluctant prophet to bring the people of Nineveh to repentance, and God forgives them (Jnh 3).

Jonah ends his story with a complaint to God about Nineveh's repentance and God's forgiveness (Jnh 4). This final dialogue exposes Jonah's narrowness of heart. God is quick to remind Jonah that God's compassion and concern extend far beyond what Jonah expects or desires. In fact, no one is beyond God's forgiveness and love. God will deliver all who call out to him, regardless of background, nationality, way of life or ethnic group.

The message of the book of Jonah also clearly demonstrates that running away from God is never a good idea. The God of Jonah and of Nineveh is our God today, and he is a God of second chances (Jnh 3:1). Just as he saved Jonah when he called to God from the stomach of the great fish and Nineveh when they heard Jonah's message of judgment, he offers us today a second, a third, even a fourth opportunity to call on him and be saved.

Quick Study

Author
The prophet Jonah.

Date Written
While there is some dispute, the book was probably written sometime between 785 and 750 B.C.

Setting
Israel, Joppa and Nineveh.

Key Passage
Jonah 2:1 "In my distress I called to the LORD,
and he answered me.
From the depths of the grave I called for help,
and you listened to my cry."

Outline

Jonah's call and flight.
Jnh 1
Jonah's prayer and deliverance.
Jnh 2
Jonah's work in Nineveh.
Jnh 3
Jonah's anger and God's response.
Jnh 4

The Women of Jonah

No women are mentioned in the book of Jonah.

I Am Jonah

JNH 1:9

When we ask people about themselves, we usually ask questions similar to what the mariners sailing with Jonah asked: Where are you from? What do you do for a living? What is your family like? In answering the sailors, Jonah's simple and straightforward description of himself is rich with meaning. He focuses only on the fact that he belongs to God. He is a Hebrew, a descriptor first attributed to Abram (Ge 14:13), the father of God's chosen people, the Israelites. Not only is Jonah aligning himself with the God of Abraham, and thus distinguishing himself from the culture around him, but he is also informing the sailors of who is causing the storm—"the God of heaven, who made the sea and the land." Immediately, the people around him are terrified because they understand that the cargo they are carrying—Jonah—is endangering everyone else on the ship.

Jonah Flees From the LORD

1 The word of the LORD came to Jonah[a] son of
Amittai:[b] 2"Go to the great city of Nineveh[c]
and preach against it, because its wickedness has
come up before me."
3But Jonah ran[d] away from the LORD and headed for Tarshish. He went down to Joppa,[e] where
he found a ship bound for that port. After paying
the fare, he went aboard and sailed for Tarshish
to flee from the LORD.
4Then the LORD sent a great wind on the sea, and
such a violent storm arose that the ship threatened
to break up.[f] 5All the sailors were afraid and each
cried out to his own god. And they threw the cargo into the sea to lighten the ship.[g]
But Jonah had gone below deck, where he lay
down and fell into a deep sleep. 6The captain went
to him and said, "How can you sleep? Get up and
call[h] on your god! Maybe he will take notice of
us, and we will not perish."[i]
7Then the sailors said to each other, "Come, let
us cast lots to find out who is responsible for this
calamity."[j] They cast lots and the lot fell on Jonah.
8So they asked him, "Tell us, who is responsible
for making all this trouble for us? What do you
do? Where do you come from? What is your country? From what people are you?"
9He answered, "I am a Hebrew and I worship
the LORD, the God of heaven,[k] who made the sea
and the land.[l]"
10This terrified them and they asked, "What
have you done?" (They knew he was running
away from the LORD, because he had already told
them so.)
11The sea was getting rougher and rougher. So
they asked him, "What should we do to you to
make the sea calm down for us?"
12"Pick me up and throw me into the sea," he
replied, "and it will become calm. I know that it is
my fault that this great storm has come upon
you."[m]
13Instead, the men did their best to row back to
land. But they could not, for the sea grew even
wilder than before.[n] 14Then they cried to the LORD,
"O LORD, please do not let us die for taking this
man's life. Do not hold us accountable for killing
an innocent man,[o] for you, O LORD, have done as
you pleased."[p] 15Then they took Jonah and threw
him overboard, and the raging sea grew calm.[q]
16At this the men greatly feared[r] the LORD, and
they offered a sacrifice to the LORD and made vows
to him.
17But the LORD provided a great fish to swallow
Jonah,[s] and Jonah was inside the fish three days
and three nights.

Jonah's Prayer

2 From inside the fish Jonah prayed to the LORD
his God. 2He said:

"In my distress I called to the LORD,[t]

1:1 [a]Mt 12:39-41 [b]2Ki 14:25
1:2 [c]Ge 10:11
1:3 [d]Ps 139:7 [e]Jos 19:46; Ac 9:36,43
1:4 [f]Ps 107:23-26
1:5 [g]Ac 27:18-19
1:6 [h]Jnh 3:8 [i]Ps 107:28
1:7 [j]Jos 7:10-18; 1Sa 14:42
1:9 [k]Ac 17:24 [l]Ps 146:6
1:12 [m]2Sa 24:17; 1Ch 21:17
1:13 [n]Pr 21:30
1:14 [o]Dt 21:8 [p]Ps 115:3
1:15 [q]Ps 107:29; Lk 8:24
1:16 [r]Mk 4:41
1:17 [s]Mt 12:40; 16:4; Lk 11:30
2:2 [t]Ps 18:6; 120:1

and he answered me.
From the depths of the grave[a] I called
for help,
and you listened to my cry.
2:3 [u]Ps 88:6 [v]Ps 42:7
3You hurled me into the deep,[u]
into the very heart of the seas,
and the currents swirled about me;
all your waves and breakers
swept over me.[v]
4I said, 'I have been banished
from your sight;[w]
2:4 [w]Ps 31:22
yet I will look again
toward your holy temple.'
5The engulfing waters threatened me,[b]
the deep surrounded me;
seaweed was wrapped around my
head.[x]
2:5 [x]Ps 69:1-2
6To the roots of the mountains I sank
down;
the earth beneath barred me in
forever.
But you brought my life up from the pit,
O LORD my God.

7"When my life was ebbing away,
2:7 [y]Ps 77:11-12 [z]2Ch 30:27 [a]Ps 11:4; 18:6
I remembered[y] you, LORD,
and my prayer[z] rose to you,
to your holy temple.[a]
2:8 [b]2Ki 17:15; Jer 10:8
8"Those who cling to worthless idols[b]
forfeit the grace that could be theirs.
9But I, with a song of thanksgiving,
2:9 [c]Ps 50:14,23; Hos 14:2 [d]Ecc 5:4-5 [e]Ps 3:8
will sacrifice[c] to you.
What I have vowed[d] I will make good.
Salvation[e] comes from the LORD."

10And the LORD commanded the fish, and it
vomited Jonah onto dry land.

Jonah Goes to Nineveh

3:1 [f]Jnh 1:1
3 Then the word of the LORD came to Jonah[f] a
second time: 2"Go to the great city of Nineveh
and proclaim to it the message I give you."
3Jonah obeyed the word of the LORD and went to
Nineveh. Now Nineveh was a very important
city—a visit required three days. 4On the first day,
Jonah started into the city. He proclaimed: "Forty
more days and Nineveh will be overturned." 5The
Ninevites believed God. They declared a fast, and
all of them, from the greatest to the least, put on
3:5 [g]Da 9:3; Lk 11:32
sackcloth.[g]
6When the news reached the king of Nineveh,
he rose from his throne, took off his royal robes,
covered himself with sackcloth and sat down in
3:6 [h]Job 2:8,13; Eze 27:30-31
the dust.[h] 7Then he issued a proclamation in
Nineveh:

"By the decree of the king and his nobles:

Do not let any man or beast, herd or flock,
3:7 [i]2Ch 20:3
taste anything; do not let them eat or drink.[i]

[a] 2 Hebrew *Sheol* [b] 5 Or *waters were at my throat*

Sheol

JNH 2:2

The Hebrew word *Sheol* (see the NIV footnote on "*grave*") occurs in the Old Testament more than 60 times and is translated in a variety of ways, primarily "grave." Sheol is described in the book of Job as a place of no return (Job 7:9), a place to hide (Job 14:13)—a deep (Job 11:8), dark (Job 17:13) and enclosed (Job 17:16) place. No wonder Jonah likens being in the fish's belly to being in Sheol! But Jonah is not complaining. His full statement is actually a burst of praise to the God who has, so far, spared him from Sheol's fate. Jonah feels buried at the moment, but he is buried *alive*.

When we feel like we're at death's door emotionally, spiritually or even physically, we can take heart from the experience of Jonah and others who have received God's mercy. Next time you are "swallowed" by overwhelming emotion, meditate on Psalm 30 and rejoice with David that while "*weeping may remain for a night . . . rejoicing comes in the morning*" (Ps 30:5).

8But let man and beast be covered with sackcloth. Let everyone call[j] urgently on God. Let
them give up their evil ways and their violence. 9Who knows?[k] God may yet relent and
with compassion turn[l] from his fierce anger
so that we will not perish."

10When God saw what they did and how they
turned from their evil ways, he had compassion[m]
and did not bring upon them the destruction[n] he
had threatened.[o]

Jonah's Anger at the LORD's Compassion

4 But Jonah was greatly displeased and became
angry.[p] 2He prayed to the LORD, "O LORD, is this
not what I said when I was still at home? That is
why I was so quick to flee to Tarshish. I knew[q]
that you are a gracious and compassionate God,
slow to anger and abounding in love,[r] a God who
relents from sending calamity.[s] 3Now, O LORD,
take away my life,[t] for it is better for me to die[u]
than to live."

4But the LORD replied, "Have you any right to be
angry?"[v]

5Jonah went out and sat down at a place east of
the city. There he made himself a shelter, sat in
its shade and waited to see what would happen to
the city. 6Then the LORD God provided a vine and
made it grow up over Jonah to give shade for his
head to ease his discomfort, and Jonah was very
happy about the vine. 7But at dawn the next day
God provided a worm, which chewed the vine so
that it withered.[w] 8When the sun rose, God provided a scorching east wind, and the sun blazed
on Jonah's head so that he grew faint. He wanted
to die, and said, "It would be better for me to die
than to live."

9But God said to Jonah, "Do you have a right to
be angry about the vine?"

"I do," he said. "I am angry enough to die."

10But the LORD said, "You have been concerned
about this vine, though you did not tend it or
make it grow. It sprang up overnight and died
overnight. 11But Nineveh[x] has more than a hundred and twenty thousand people who cannot tell
their right hand from their left, and many cattle
as well. Should I not be concerned[y] about that
great city?"

3:8 [j]Ps 130:1; Jnh 1:6
3:9 [k]2Sa 12:22 [l]Joel 2:14
3:10 [m]Am 7:6 [n]Jer 18:8 [o]Ex 32:14
4:1 [p]ver 4; Lk 15:28
4:2 [q]Jer 20:7-8 [r]Ex 34:6; Ps 86:5,15 [s]Joel 2:13
4:3 [t]1Ki 19:4 [u]Job 7:15
4:4 [v]Mt 20:11-15
4:7 [w]Joel 1:12
4:11 [x]Jnh 1:2; 3:2 [y]Jnh 3:10

Adelaide Addison Pollard felt the Lord's call to mission work in Africa but was unable to raise the money to go. She wrote this song in response to encouraging words she heard at an evening prayer meeting when one of the attendees prayed, "It's all right, Lord. It doesn't matter what you bring into our lives, just have your own way with us."

Have Thine Own Way

Have Thine own way, Lord! Have Thine own way!
Thou art the Potter, I am the clay.
Mold me and make me after Thy will,
While I am waiting, yielded and still.

Have Thine own way, Lord! Have Thine own way!
Search me and try me, Master, today!
Whiter than snow, Lord, wash me just now,
As in Thy presence humbly I bow.

Have Thine own way, Lord! Have Thine own way!
Wounded and weary, help me, I pray!
Power, all power, surely is Thine!
Touch me and heal me, Savior divine.

Have Thine own way, Lord! Have Thine own way!
Hold o'er my being absolute sway!
Fill with Thy Spirit 'till all shall see
Christ only, always, living in me.

—Adelaide Addison Pollard (1862-1934)

Micah

God's matchless mercy.

Micah proclaims the downfall of the prosperous and the deliverance of the powerless in this message of warning to Israel, the northern kingdom, and Judah, the southern kingdom. A contemporary of Isaiah, Micah champions the cause of the poor as he warns God's people of the destructive consequences of disobedience. Because corruption and exploitation run rampant among the wealthy, Micah's message of imminent judgment is not popular.

Using poetry, metaphors and vivid figures of speech, this powerful preacher from the country prophesies against Samaria and Jerusalem, the capital cities of Israel and Judah (Mic 1). His short speeches document the dangers of pretense and the coming judgment on false prophets and corrupt leaders (Mic 2–3). Yet Micah balances God's judgment against God's deliverance as he foretells the birth of the Messiah in Bethlehem (Mic 5). Micah ends his book with an encouraging note, assuring the people that God's judgment will not permanently destroy the nation but will rather bring a life of peace to those who willingly obey God (Mic 6–7).

Warnings are a part of everyday life. We find them on bridges and boxes and helmets and hot cups of coffee. Although most people pay little attention to these repeated warnings, the book of Micah is one repeated warning that deserves attention. We hear Micah proclaim the terrible judgment awaiting all who ignore God. We wonder how long God's patience with our society will last. But we are assured that God's greatest desire for us is a faith that shows itself in love, justice and obedience to God's plan. We can heed Micah's warnings and rejoice in God's acceptance and forgiveness.

Quick Study

Author
The prophet Micah.

Date Written
Micah prophesied and wrote his book sometime between 750 and 686 B.C.

Setting
Judah.

Key Passage
Micah 6:8 "He has showed you, O man, what is good.
And what does the LORD require of you?
To act justly and to love mercy
and to walk humbly with your God."

Outline

Judgment of Israel and Judah.
Mic 1–3

Hope for Israel and Judah.
Mic 4–5

The Lord's case against Israel.
Mic 6

Misery and triumph.
Mic 7

The Women of Micah

Women of my people	*Driven away.* Mic 2:9
Wife, daughter, mother, daughter-in-law, mother-in-law	*None of them can be trusted.* Mic 7:5–6

1 The word of the LORD that came to Micah of Moresheth[a] during the reigns of Jotham,[b] Ahaz[c] and Hezekiah, kings of Judah[d]—the vision[e] he saw concerning Samaria and Jerusalem.

2 Hear, O peoples, all of you,[f]
listen, O earth[g] and all who are in it,
that the Sovereign LORD may witness[h]
against you,
the Lord from his holy temple.[i]

Judgment Against Samaria and Jerusalem

3 Look! The LORD is coming from his
dwelling[j] place;
he comes down and treads the high
places of the earth.[k]
4 The mountains melt[l] beneath him
and the valleys split apart,[m]
like wax before the fire,
like water rushing down a slope.
5 All this is because of Jacob's
transgression,
because of the sins of the house of
Israel.
What is Jacob's transgression?
Is it not Samaria?[n]
What is Judah's high place?
Is it not Jerusalem?

6 "Therefore I will make Samaria a heap
of rubble,
a place for planting vineyards.
I will pour her stones[o] into the valley
and lay bare her foundations.[p]
7 All her idols[q] will be broken to pieces;
all her temple gifts will be burned
with fire;
I will destroy all her images.[r]
Since she gathered her gifts from the
wages of prostitutes,[s]
as the wages of prostitutes they will
again be used."

Weeping and Mourning

8 Because of this I will weep[t] and wail;
I will go about barefoot and naked.
I will howl like a jackal
and moan like an owl.
9 For her wound[u] is incurable;
it has come to Judah.[v]
It[a] has reached the very gate[w] of my
people,
even to Jerusalem itself.
10 Tell it not in Gath[b];
weep not at all.[c]
In Beth Ophrah[d]
roll in the dust.

1:1 [a]Jer 26:18 [b]1Ch 3:12 [c]1Ch 3:13 [d]Hos 1:1 [e]Isa 1:1
1:2 [f]Ps 50:7 [g]Jer 6:19 [h]Ge 31:50; Dt 4:26; Isa 1:2 [i]Ps 11:4
1:3 [j]Isa 18:4 [k]Am 4:13
1:4 [l]Ps 46:2,6 [m]Nu 16:31; Na 1:5
1:5 [n]Am 8:14
1:6 [o]Am 5:11 [p]Eze 13:14
1:7 [q]Eze 6:6 [r]Dt 9:21 [s]Dt 23:17-18
1:8 [t]Isa 15:3
1:9 [u]Jer 46:11 [v]2Ki 18:13 [w]Isa 3:26

[a] *9* Or *He* [b] *10* *Gath* sounds like the Hebrew for *tell.*
[c] *10* Hebrew; Septuagint may suggest *not in Acco.* The Hebrew for *in Acco* sounds like the Hebrew for *weep.* [d] *10* *Beth Ophrah* means *house of dust.*

The Carpenter of Galilee
Comes down the street again,
In every land, in every age,
He still is building men.
On Christmas Eve we hear him
knock;
He goes from door to door:
"Are any workmen out of work?
The Carpenter needs more.

—Hilda W. Smith (b. 1888)

God's Plans

MIC 2:1,3

Humans love to make plans. We plan our day, plan our meals, even plan our vacations a year in advance. God must chuckle at our efforts. No matter how many plans we make, he knows who's ultimately in charge. It seems the people of Judah need to be reminded of this. God makes it clear that though they lie awake at night plotting wicked schemes, they cannot save themselves from what he has in store. Like a thunderstorm, God's dark clouds are mounting on the horizon. He knows that the people of Judah are indifferent to the storm that is building, but judgment is still on the way. The plans of people may go awry, but God's plans cannot be thwarted.

11 Pass on in nakedness[x] and shame,
you who live in Shaphir.[a]
Those who live in Zaanan[b]
will not come out.
Beth Ezel is in mourning;
its protection is taken from you.
12 Those who live in Maroth[c] writhe in pain,
waiting for relief,[y]
because disaster has come from the LORD,
even to the gate of Jerusalem.
13 You who live in Lachish,[d][z]
harness the team to the chariot.
You were the beginning of sin
to the Daughter of Zion,
for the transgressions of Israel
were found in you.
14 Therefore you will give parting gifts[a]
to Moresheth Gath.
The town of Aczib[e][b] will prove deceptive[c]
to the kings of Israel.
15 I will bring a conqueror against you
who live in Mareshah.[f][d]
He who is the glory of Israel
will come to Adullam.[e]
16 Shave[f] your heads in mourning
for the children in whom you delight;
make yourselves as bald as the vulture,
for they will go from you into exile.

Man's Plans and God's

2 Woe to those who plan iniquity,
to those who plot evil on their beds![g]
At morning's light they carry it out
because it is in their power to do it.
2 They covet fields[h] and seize them,
and houses, and take them.
They defraud[i] a man of his home,
a fellowman of his inheritance.

3 Therefore, the LORD says:

"I am planning disaster[j] against this people,
from which you cannot save yourselves.
You will no longer walk proudly,[k]
for it will be a time of calamity.
4 In that day men will ridicule you;
they will taunt you with this mournful song:
'We are utterly ruined;[l]
my people's possession is divided up.
He takes it from me!
He assigns our fields to traitors.' "

1:11 [x]Eze 23:29
1:12 [y]Jer 14:19
1:13 [z]Jos 10:3
1:14 [a]2Ki 16:8 [b]Jos 15:44 [c]Jer 15:18
1:15 [d]Jos 15:44 [e]Jos 12:15
1:16 [f]Job 1:20
2:1 [g]Ps 36:4
2:2 [h]Isa 5:8 [i]Jer 22:17
2:3 [j]Jer 18:11; Am 3:1-2 [k]Isa 2:12
2:4 [l]Jer 4:13

[a] 11 *Shaphir* means *pleasant.* [b] 11 *Zaanan* sounds like the Hebrew for *come out.* [c] 12 *Maroth* sounds like the Hebrew for *bitter.* [d] 13 *Lachish* sounds like the Hebrew for *team.* [e] 14 *Aczib* means *deception.* [f] 15 *Mareshah* sounds like the Hebrew for *conqueror.*

5 Therefore you will have no one in the
assembly of the LORD
2:5 [m]Jos 18:4 to divide the land[m] by lot.

False Prophets

6 "Do not prophesy," their prophets say.
"Do not prophesy about these things;
2:6 [n]Mic 6:16 [o]Am 2:12 disgrace[n] will not overtake us.[o]"
7 Should it be said, O house of Jacob:
"Is the Spirit of the LORD angry?
Does he do such things?"

2:7 [p]Ps 119:65 [q]Ps 15:2; 84:11 "Do not my words do good[p]
to him whose ways are upright?[q]
8 Lately my people have risen up
like an enemy.
You strip off the rich robe
from those who pass by without a
care,
like men returning from battle.
2:9 [r]Jer 10:20 9 You drive the women of my people
from their pleasant homes.[r]
You take away my blessing
from their children forever.
10 Get up, go away!
2:10 [s]Dt 12:9 [t]Lev 18:25-29; Ps 106:38-39 For this is not your resting place,[s]
because it is defiled,[t]
it is ruined, beyond all remedy.
11 If a liar and deceiver[u] comes and says,
2:11 [u]Jer 5:31 [v]Isa 30:10 'I will prophesy for you plenty of
wine and beer,'
he would be just the prophet for this
people![v]

Deliverance Promised

12 "I will surely gather all of you, O Jacob;
I will surely bring together the
2:12 [w]Mic 4:7; 5:7; 7:18 remnant[w] of Israel.
I will bring them together like sheep in
a pen,
like a flock in its pasture;
the place will throng with people.
2:13 [x]Isa 52:12 13 One who breaks open the way will go
up before[x] them;
they will break through the gate and
go out.
Their king will pass through before
them,
the LORD at their head."

Leaders and Prophets Rebuked

3 Then I said,

3:1 [y]Jer 5:5 "Listen, you leaders[y] of Jacob,
you rulers of the house of Israel.
Should you not know justice,
2 you who hate good and love evil;
3:2 [z]Ps 53:4; Eze 22:27 who tear the skin from my people
and the flesh from their bones;[z]
3:3 [a]Ps 14:4 3 who eat my people's flesh,[a]
strip off their skin

Blessing Robbers

MIC 2:9

Often we think of God's blessings as being untouchable by others, but here we see that evildoers can exercise their oppression even to the point of taking away God's benefits. God promised the people of Israel an inheritance of land on which they could live and flourish (Lev 20:24). But the "Joneses," the rich neighbors down the street, steal God's blessings by evicting families from their land through any means possible—exorbitant interest rates, extreme economic regulations, high taxes and judicial decisions based on bribes. In addition to the injustice of the situation, the orphans and widows, who are the most defenseless, are also the most abused. God does not take such inequity lightly.

and break their bones in pieces;[b]
who chop them up like meat for the pan,
like flesh for the pot?[c]"

[4] Then they will cry out to the LORD,
but he will not answer them.[d]
At that time he will hide his face[e] from them
because of the evil they have done.

[5] This is what the LORD says:

"As for the prophets
who lead my people astray,[f]
if one feeds them,
they proclaim 'peace';
if he does not,
they prepare to wage war against him.
[6] Therefore night will come over you,
without visions,
and darkness, without divination.[g]
The sun will set for the prophets,[h]
and the day will go dark for them.
[7] The seers will be ashamed[i]
and the diviners disgraced.[j]
They will all cover their faces
because there is no answer from God."

[8] But as for me, I am filled with power,
with the Spirit of the LORD,
and with justice and might,
to declare to Jacob his transgression,
to Israel his sin.[k]
[9] Hear this, you leaders of the house of Jacob,
you rulers of the house of Israel,
who despise justice
and distort all that is right;[l]
[10] who build[m] Zion with bloodshed,[n]
and Jerusalem with wickedness.[o]
[11] Her leaders judge for a bribe,
her priests teach for a price,
and her prophets tell fortunes for money.[p]
Yet they lean upon the LORD and say,
"Is not the LORD among us?
No disaster will come upon us."[q]
[12] Therefore because of you,
Zion will be plowed like a field,
Jerusalem will become a heap of rubble,[r]
the temple hill a mound overgrown with thickets.

The Mountain of the LORD

4 In the last days

the mountain[s] of the LORD's temple will be established
as chief among the mountains;
it will be raised above the hills,[t]
and peoples will stream to it.[u]

3:3 [b]Zep 3:3 [c]Eze 11:7
3:4 [d]Ps 18:41; Isa 1:15 [e]Dt 31:17
3:5 [f]Isa 3:12; 9:16
3:6 [g]Isa 8:19-22 [h]Isa 29:10
3:7 [i]Mic 7:16 [j]Isa 44:25
3:8 [k]Isa 58:1
3:9 [l]Ps 58:1-2; Isa 1:23
3:10 [m]Jer 22:13 [n]Hab 2:12 [o]Eze 22:27
3:11 [p]Isa 1:23; Jer 6:13; Hos 4:8,18 [q]Jer 7:4
3:12 [r]Jer 26:18
4:1 [s]Zec 8:3 [t]Eze 17:22 [u]Ps 22:27; 86:9; Jer 3:17

Knowledge by suffering entereth,
And life is perfected by death.

—Elizabeth Barrett Browning (1809-1961)

[2]Many nations will come and say,

4:2 [v]Jer 31:6 [w]Zec 2:11; 14:16 [x]Ps 25:8-9; Isa 54:13

"Come, let us go up to the mountain of
the LORD,[v]
to the house of the God of Jacob.[w]
He will teach us his ways,[x]
so that we may walk in his paths."
The law will go out from Zion,
the word of the LORD from Jerusalem.
[3]He will judge between many peoples
and will settle disputes for strong
nations far and wide.[y]

4:3 [y]Isa 11:4 [z]Joel 3:10 [a]Isa 2:4

They will beat their swords into
plowshares
and their spears into pruning hooks.[z]
Nation will not take up sword against
nation,
nor will they train for war anymore.[a]
[4]Every man will sit under his own vine
and under his own fig tree,[b]
and no one will make them afraid,[c]
for the LORD Almighty has spoken.[d]

4:4 [b]1Ki 4:25 [c]Lev 26:6 [d]Isa 1:20; Zec 3:10

[5]All the nations may walk
in the name of their gods;[e]
we will walk in the name of the LORD
our God for ever and ever.[f]

4:5 [e]2Ki 17:29 [f]Jos 24:14-15; Isa 26:8; Zec 10:12

The LORD's Plan

[6]"In that day," declares the LORD,

"I will gather the lame;
I will assemble the exiles[g]
and those I have brought to grief.[h]
[7]I will make the lame a remnant,[i]
those driven away a strong nation.
The LORD will rule over them in Mount
Zion
from that day and forever.[j]

4:6 [g]Ps 147:2 [h]Eze 34:13, 16; 37:21; Zep 3:19

4:7 [i]Mic 2:12 [j]Da 7:14; Lk 1:33; Rev 11:15

[8]As for you, O watchtower of the flock,
O stronghold[a] of the Daughter of
Zion,
the former dominion will be restored[k] to
you;
kingship will come to the Daughter of
Jerusalem."

4:8 [k]Isa 1:26

[9]Why do you now cry aloud—
have you no king?[l]
Has your counselor perished,
that pain seizes you like that of a
woman in labor?[m]
[10]Writhe in agony, O Daughter of Zion,
like a woman in labor,
for now you must leave the city
to camp in the open field.
You will go to Babylon;[n]
there you will be rescued.
There the LORD will redeem[o] you
out of the hand of your enemies.

4:9 [l]Jer 8:19 [m]Jer 30:6

4:10 [n]2Ki 20:18; Isa 43:14 [o]Isa 48:20

[11]But now many nations

[a]8 Or *hill*

Many Nations Will Come

MIC 4:2

A prophecy is given. In the days when God will rule the world, the nation of God's people, which has been Israel, will become the nation of people for God. In Scripture, the word *nations* usually means "Gentiles" (in contrast with the Jews). These are the same people Jesus spoke of in the Great Commission when he said, "Make disciples of all nations" (Mt 28:19). From these nations an eternal temple will be established, and believers will stream in to learn and worship (Mic 4:1). These nations will live in peace because God will have destroyed his enemies (Mic 4:4). In the four words "many nations will come" (Mic 4:2), the purpose of the Bible is given, and the climax of Scripture unfolds.

The House of Bread

MIC 5:2

Using many voices over thousands of years, God sprinkles promises of the coming Messiah throughout Scripture. Here and there, God scatters hope as he points to the Redeemer of Israel. In Micah 5:2, we discover that Bethlehem, whose name means "house of bread," will be the birthplace of Christ, "the bread of life" (Jn 6:48). This passage reveals that the King of kings will take his first human breath in a city that is "small" in comparison to those around it. Reread Micah 5:2, along with 1 Corinthians 1:27. Through these passages we see that God's best work often comes from feeble things overlooked by humans. It was true for Bethlehem. It is true for us too.

are gathered against you.
They say, "Let her be defiled,
let our eyes gloat[p] over Zion!"
12 But they do not know
the thoughts of the LORD;
they do not understand his plan,[q]
he who gathers them like sheaves to
the threshing floor.
13 "Rise and thresh, O Daughter of Zion,
for I will give you horns of iron;
I will give you hoofs of bronze
and you will break to pieces many
nations."[r]
You will devote their ill-gotten gains to
the LORD,
their wealth to the Lord of all the
earth.

A Promised Ruler From Bethlehem

5 Marshal your troops, O city of troops,[a]
for a siege is laid against us.
They will strike Israel's ruler
on the cheek[s] with a rod.
2 "But you, Bethlehem[t] Ephrathah,[u]
though you are small among the
clans[b] of Judah,
out of you will come for me
one who will be ruler over Israel,
whose origins[c] are from of old,[v]
from ancient times.[d]"[w]
3 Therefore Israel will be abandoned
until the time when she who is in
labor gives birth
and the rest of his brothers return
to join the Israelites.
4 He will stand and shepherd his flock[x]
in the strength of the LORD,
in the majesty of the name of the
LORD his God.
And they will live securely, for then his
greatness[y]
will reach to the ends of the earth.
5 And he will be their peace.[z]

Deliverance and Destruction

When the Assyrian invades[a] our land
and marches through our fortresses,
we will raise against him seven
shepherds,
even eight leaders of men.[b]
6 They will rule[e] the land of Assyria with
the sword,
the land of Nimrod[c] with drawn
sword.[f][d]
He will deliver us from the Assyrian

4:11 [p]La 2:16; Ob 1:12
4:12 [q]Isa 55:8; Ro 11:33-34
4:13 [r]Da 2:44
5:1 [s]La 3:30
5:2 [t]Jn 7:42 [u]Ge 48:7 [v]Ps 102:25 [w]Mt 2:6*
5:4 [x]Isa 40:11; 49:9; Eze 34:11-15,23; Mic 7:14 [y]Isa 52:13; Lk 1:32
5:5 [z]Isa 9:6; Lk 2:14; Col 1:19-20 [a]Isa 8:7 [b]Isa 10:24-27
5:6 [c]Ge 10:8 [d]Zep 2:13

[a] 1 Or *Strengthen your walls, O walled city* [b] 2 Or *rulers* [c] 2 Hebrew *goings out* [d] 2 Or *from days of eternity* [e] 6 Or *crush* [f] 6 Or *Nimrod in its gates*

Week 28

Jesus, Prince of Peace

In a world filled with strife, peace often seems too elusive to even hope for. But Scripture makes it clear that peace is indeed possible. God is a God of peace (Ro 15:33; 1Co 14:33), and peace comes from him (Isa 26:12; Jer 33:6). How can you have peace?

The traditional Hebrew understanding of peace included completeness, soundness and well-being of the total person, which is reflected in their greeting one another that continues to this day: *Shalom* (the Hebrew word for peace). Through Jesus we find the fulfillment of this hope as well as a sense of trust that God is in control (Phil 4:6-7).

What is the first step toward peace (Ps 34:14; 2Ti 2:22)? How can you make this a daily goal? How is peace a calling for believers (Col 3:15)?

Who will never be at peace (Isa 57:20-21)? Why not (Ro 3:10-18)? Who will *enjoy peace (Ps 37:11; 85:8; 119:165)?*

What is the pathway to peace with God (Ro 5:1)? What did your peace with God cost Jesus (Isa 53:5; Col 1:19-20)?

The peace that Jesus gives is different from the peace the world offers (Jn 14:27). What makes God's peace better (Isa 54:10)? Where have you seen evidence of false peace and where have you found the peace that only comes from God?

What are some things you can do to be at peace (Isa 26:3; Ro 15:13; Heb 12:11; 2Pe 1:2)? It is clear from these passages that peace comes through your relationship with Jesus. It is based on your close friendship with him, on consistent—steadfast—time spent with him, on your acceptance of his discipline and, most important, on your trusting him.

What should be your goal in your personal relationships (Ro 12:18; Heb 12:14)? How far should you go in your attempts to promote peace with others (Ro 14:19)? Does it seem like an impossible goal? How is it possible to be at peace with even your enemies (Pr 16:7; Eph 2:14)?

Enjoying God THROUGH the Word

Read Colossians 3:12-15 (page 1952). No one enjoys living in a home filled with fighting and bickering, and no one wants to be part of a church family in which there is backbiting and quarreling. Proverbs 17:1 says, "Better a dry crust with peace and quiet than a house full of feasting, with strife." How true! This passage in Colossians gives clear, practical advice for promoting peace in your family and in your fellowship with other believers. Notice the qualities mentioned: compassion, kindness, humility, gentleness, patience, forgiveness and love.

Unity of the Spirit cannot be achieved without the bond of peace (Eph 4:3). Choose to make every effort today to live at peace with those around you. And remember that God will strengthen you in your endeavor. Who knows, your peace-loving attitude may even catch on!

Enjoying God THROUGH Experience

Are you embroiled in strife? Does life always seem turbulent? Peace will come when you embrace the presence of God in your life. Jesus is the Prince of Peace (Isa 9:6). He has promised to meet your needs (Php 4:19), shelter you (Ps 27:5) and rescue you (Ps 91:14). If you have no peace, perhaps you have taken your eyes off Jesus (Heb 12:2). Trust him. He is always with you. In the midst of turmoil, do your best to turn your eyes to him. "And the peace of God, which transcends all understanding, will guard your hearts and your minds in Christ Jesus" (Php 4:7).

Go to page 1539 for your next weekly study.

when he invades our land
and marches into our borders.[e]

5:6 [e]Na 2:11-13

7 The remnant[f] of Jacob will be
in the midst of many peoples
like dew from the LORD,
like showers on the grass,[g]
which do not wait for man
or linger for mankind.

5:7 [f]Mic 2:12 [g]Isa 44:4

8 The remnant of Jacob will be among the
nations,
in the midst of many peoples,
like a lion among the beasts of the forest,[h]
like a young lion among flocks of
sheep,
which mauls and mangles[i] as it goes,
and no one can rescue.[j]

5:8 [h]Ge 49:9 [i]Mic 4:13; Zec 10:5 [j]Ps 50:22; Hos 5:14

9 Your hand will be lifted up[k] in triumph
over your enemies,
and all your foes will be destroyed.

5:9 [k]Ps 10:12

10 "In that day," declares the LORD,

"I will destroy your horses from among
you
and demolish your chariots.[l]
11 I will destroy the cities[m] of your land
and tear down all your strongholds.[n]
12 I will destroy your witchcraft
and you will no longer cast spells.[o]
13 I will destroy your carved images
and your sacred stones from among
you;
you will no longer bow down
to the work of your hands.[p]
14 I will uproot from among you your
Asherah poles[a][q]
and demolish your cities.
15 I will take vengeance[r] in anger and
wrath
upon the nations that have not obeyed
me."

5:10 [l]Hos 14:3; Zec 9:10
5:11 [m]Isa 6:11 [n]Hos 10:14; Am 5:9
5:12 [o]Dt 18:10-12; Isa 2:6; 8:19
5:13 [p]Eze 6:9; Zec 13:2
5:14 [q]Ex 34:13
5:15 [r]Isa 65:12

Little drops of water,
little grains of sand,
Make the mighty ocean and
the pleasant land.
So the little minutes, humble
though they be,
Make the mighty ages of
eternity.

—Julia A. Fletcher Carney (1824-1908)

The LORD's Case Against Israel

6 Listen to what the LORD says:

"Stand up, plead your case before the
mountains;[s]
let the hills hear what you have to say.
2 Hear,[t] O mountains, the LORD's
accusation;[u]
listen, you everlasting foundations of
the earth.
For the LORD has a case against his
people;
he is lodging a charge[v] against Israel.

6:1 [s]Ps 50:1; Eze 6:2
6:2 [t]Dt 32:1 [u]Hos 12:2 [v]Ps 50:7

3 "My people, what have I done to you?
How have I burdened[w] you? Answer
me.
4 I brought you up out of Egypt

6:3 [w]Jer 2:5

[a] *14* That is, symbols of the goddess Asherah

and redeemed you from the land of
slavery.[x]
I sent Moses[y] to lead you,
also Aaron[z] and Miriam.[a]
5 My people, remember
what Balak[b] king of Moab counseled
and what Balaam son of Beor answered.
Remember ⌞your journey⌟ from Shittim[c]
to Gilgal,[d]
that you may know the righteous
acts[e] of the LORD."

6 With what shall I come before the LORD
and bow down before the exalted God?
Shall I come before him with burnt
offerings,
with calves a year old?[f]
7 Will the LORD be pleased with thousands
of rams,[g]
with ten thousand rivers of oil?[h]
Shall I offer my firstborn[i] for my
transgression,
the fruit of my body for the sin of my
soul?[j]
8 He has showed you, O man, what is
good.
And what does the LORD require of you?
To act justly[k] and to love mercy
and to walk humbly[l] with your God.[m]

Israel's Guilt and Punishment

9 Listen! The LORD is calling to the city—
and to fear your name is wisdom—
"Heed the rod and the One who
appointed it.[a]
10 Am I still to forget, O wicked house,
your ill-gotten treasures
and the short ephah,[b] which is
accursed?[n]
11 Shall I acquit a man with dishonest
scales,[o]
with a bag of false weights?
12 Her rich men are violent;[p]
her people are liars[q]
and their tongues speak deceitfully.[r]
13 Therefore, I have begun to destroy[s] you,
to ruin you because of your sins.
14 You will eat but not be satisfied;[t]
your stomach will still be empty.[c]
You will store up but save nothing,[u]
because what you save I will give to
the sword.
15 You will plant but not harvest;[v]
you will press olives but not use the
oil on yourselves,
you will crush grapes but not drink
the wine.[w]

6:4 [x]Dt 7:8 [y]Ex 4:16 [z]Ps 77:20 [a]Ex 15:20
6:5 [b]Nu 22:5-6 [c]Nu 25:1 [d]Jos 5:9-10 [e]Jdg 5:11; 1Sa 12:7
6:6 [f]Ps 40:6-8; 51:16-17
6:7 [g]Isa 40:16 [h]Ps 50:8-10 [i]Lev 18:21 [j]2Ki 16:3
6:8 [k]Isa 1:17; Jer 22:3 [l]Isa 57:15 [m]Dt 10:12-13; 1Sa 15:22; Hos 6:6
6:10 [n]Eze 45:9-10; Am 3:10; 8:4-6
6:11 [o]Lev 19:36; Hos 12:7
6:12 [p]Isa 1:23 [q]Isa 3:8 [r]Jer 9:3
6:13 [s]Isa 1:7; 6:11
6:14 [t]Isa 9:20 [u]Isa 30:6
6:15 [v]Dt 28:38; Jer 12:13 [w]Am 5:11; Zep 1:13

[a] *9* The meaning of the Hebrew for this line is uncertain.
[b] *10* An ephah was a dry measure.
[c] *14* The meaning of the Hebrew for this word is uncertain.

An Upright Walk

MIC 6:6-8

Micah is speaking to a people God delivered from Egypt and through whom he wants to establish a model society. His plan is that, through the Israelites' moral and noble living, other nations will be attracted to him (Dt 4:5-6). But the people are quick to perform the rituals while neglecting the right lifestyle (Mic 6:8). Here, Micah explains that even "thousands of rams" and "ten thousand rivers of oil" (Mic 6:7) do not satisfy God. Instead, he desires a lifestyle of love in action—an upright walk that draws others to him.

"To Hope"

MIC 7:5–7

Someone once said, "As the home goes, so goes the nation." If this statement is true, Micah's portrait of family decay proves that the very existence of Israel is threatened. These verses speak of more unfaithfulness than a bad soap opera. However, the prophet ends this passage with a glimmer of hope. Even when all his trust in humanity is shattered, Micah watches and waits for his God. By definition, *to wait* literally means "to hope." In our society, waiting is ranked right up there with having a root canal. We are told, "Get going. Get busy. Do something!" But according to the Bible, "waiting" has definite merit.

16 You have observed the statutes of
Omri[x]
and all the practices of Ahab's[y] house,
and you have followed their
traditions.[z]
Therefore I will give you over to ruin[a]
and your people to derision;
you will bear the scorn[b] of the
nations.[a]"

6:16 [x]1Ki 16:25 [y]1Ki 16:29-33 [z]Jer 7:24 [a]Jer 25:9 [b]Jer 51:51

Israel's Misery

7 What misery is mine!
I am like one who gathers summer fruit
at the gleaning of the vineyard;
there is no cluster of grapes to eat,
none of the early figs that I crave.
2 The godly have been swept from the
land;[c]
not one upright man remains.
All men lie in wait to shed blood;[d]
each hunts his brother with a net.[e]
3 Both hands are skilled in doing evil;[f]
the ruler demands gifts,
the judge accepts bribes,
the powerful dictate what they desire—
they all conspire together.
4 The best of them is like a brier,[g]
the most upright worse than a thorn
hedge.
The day of your watchmen has come,
the day God visits you.
Now is the time of their confusion.[h]
5 Do not trust a neighbor;
put no confidence in a friend.[i]
Even with her who lies in your embrace
be careful of your words.
6 For a son dishonors his father,
a daughter rises up against her
mother,[j]
a daughter-in-law against her mother-in-
law—
a man's enemies are the members of
his own household.[k]

7 But as for me, I watch in hope[l] for the
LORD,
I wait for God my Savior;
my God will hear[m] me.

7:2 [c]Ps 12:1 [d]Mic 3:10 [e]Jer 5:26
7:3 [f]Pr 4:16
7:4 [g]Eze 2:6 [h]Isa 22:5; Hos 9:7
7:5 [i]Jer 9:4
7:6 [j]Eze 22:7 [k]Mt 10:35-36*
7:7 [l]Ps 130:5; Isa 25:9 [m]Ps 4:3

Israel Will Rise

8 Do not gloat over me,[n] my enemy!
Though I have fallen, I will rise.[o]
Though I sit in darkness,
the LORD will be my light.[p]
9 Because I have sinned against him,
I will bear the LORD's wrath,[q]
until he pleads my case
and establishes my right.
He will bring me out into the light;

7:8 [n]Pr 24:17 [o]Ps 37:24; Am 9:11 [p]Isa 9:2
7:9 [q]La 3:39-40

[a] 16 Septuagint; Hebrew *scorn due my people*

7:9 [r]Isa 46:13

I will see his righteousness.[r]
10 Then my enemy will see it
and will be covered with shame,[s]
she who said to me,
"Where is the LORD your God?"
My eyes will see her downfall;[t]
even now she will be trampled[u]
underfoot
like mire in the streets.

7:10 [s]Ps 35:26 [t]Isa 51:23 [u]Zec 10:5

11 The day for building your walls[v] will
come,
the day for extending your
boundaries.

7:11 [v]Isa 54:11

12 In that day people will come to you
from Assyria and the cities of Egypt,
even from Egypt to the Euphrates
and from sea to sea
and from mountain to mountain.[w]

7:12 [w]Isa 19:23-25

13 The earth will become desolate because
of its inhabitants,
as the result of their deeds.[x]

7:13 [x]Isa 3:10-11

Prayer and Praise

14 Shepherd[y] your people with your staff,[z]
the flock of your inheritance,
which lives by itself in a forest,
in fertile pasturelands.[a]
Let them feed in Bashan and Gilead[a]
as in days long ago.

7:14 [y]Mic 5:4 [z]Ps 23:4 [a]Jer 50:19

15 "As in the days when you came out of
Egypt,
I will show them my wonders.[b]"

7:15 [b]Ex 3:20; Ps 78:12

16 Nations will see and be ashamed,[c]
deprived of all their power.
They will lay their hands on their
mouths
and their ears will become deaf.

7:16 [c]Isa 26:11

17 They will lick dust like a snake,
like creatures that crawl on the ground.
They will come trembling out of their
dens;
they will turn in fear[d] to the LORD our
God
and will be afraid of you.

7:17 [d]Isa 25:3; 49:23; 59:19

18 Who is a God like you,
who pardons sin[e] and forgives[f] the
transgression
of the remnant[g] of his inheritance?[h]
You do not stay angry[i] forever
but delight to show mercy.[j]

7:18 [e]Isa 43:25; Jer 50:20 [f]Ps 103:8-13 [g]Mic 2:12 [h]Ex 34:9 [i]Ps 103:9 [j]Jer 32:41

19 You will again have compassion on us;
you will tread our sins underfoot
and hurl all our iniquities[k] into the
depths of the sea.[l]

7:19 [k]Isa 43:25 [l]Jer 31:34

20 You will be true to Jacob,
and show mercy to Abraham,
as you pledged on oath to our fathers[m]
in days long ago.

7:20 [m]Dt 7:8; Lk 1:72

[a] 14 Or *in the middle of Carmel*

Who?

MIC 7:18

"Who is a God like you?" is not only the praise of Micah's mouth, but also the praise of Micah's very name, which means "Who is like the LORD?" What distinguishes our God from other gods? The Bible is the only religious book that presents a God who completely forgives sin, a God who does not retain his anger but shows mercy. Mercy is said to be the aspect of God's love that causes him to help the miserable, and the people of Israel are certainly that. The people suffer due to their own corruption. Anyone else would have remained distant and uninvolved, but God wishes to restore. Through his words, Micah helps God's people hope again, and in the process, he must have developed a greater understanding of the truth behind his name—the truth of God's glorious uniqueness.

Nahum

Who?

Evil will not last forever.

Nahum delivers this message to the people of Judah though most of his words concern the future of the Assyrians. A little over a hundred years earlier, the people of Nineveh had responded to God's warning of judgment delivered by the prophet Jonah. However, those who had heeded God's call to repentance fail to pass their knowledge of God on to their descendants, and the city of Nineveh gradually slides back into its old routines of cruelty and wickedness. Assyria and the people of Nineveh now threaten to invade Judah. This grim reality causes God to declare that judgment cannot be averted any longer—Nineveh is doomed.

Nahum paints an inspiring portrait of God as he presents God's case against Nineveh (Na 1). With vivid images of a draining pool, a den full of bones and a wanton prostitute, Nahum describes the destruction about to befall the city (Na 2–3). And, in a final comparison with the Egyptian city of Thebes, Nahum warns the Assyrians that their pride and strength will not save them from God's wrath (Na 3).

Nahum's message firmly asserts that we can stand in respect and reverence before God, knowing that evildoers will have their day of reckoning no matter how powerful or persuasive they may seem to be right now. God will not tolerate business as usual when he has called for repentance. He is the ultimate power and authority, and he calls us to live life his way.

Quick Study

Author
The prophet Nahum.

Date Written
Nahum wrote his book sometime shortly before the fall of Nineveh in 612 B.C.

Setting
Judah.

Key Passage
Nahum 1:7–8 "The LORD
is good,
a refuge in times of
trouble.
He cares for those who
trust in him,
but with an
overwhelming flood
he will make an end of
Nineveh;
he will pursue his foes
into darkness."

Outline

Nineveh's judge.
Na 1

Nineveh's judgment.
Na 2

Nineveh's total destruction.
Na 3

The Women of Nahum

Harlot	*Nineveh was compared to one.* Na 3:4

Our Jealous God

NA 1:2

What does the word jealous make you think of? A ranting boyfriend? A co-worker who "talks down" another person's success to make herself look good? These are examples of the sinful trait of jealousy, but they couldn't be further from the kind of jealousy God displays.

Godly jealousy is untainted by selfishness or lack of control. Rather, God's jealousy is consistent with his love. Because of his love, he grieves when his people look to other things for security and happiness. He wants his people to be as faithful to him as a bride is to her husband (2Co 11:2), and his jealousy (which is related to the Hebrew word for zealous) moves him to do all he can to keep that relationship pure. His holy jealousy will even express itself as vengeance on those who harm his bride. This holy jealousy is his motive for the actions depicted in the book of Nahum.

1 An oracle[a] concerning Nineveh.[b] The book of the vision of Nahum the Elkoshite.

The LORD's Anger Against Nineveh

2 The LORD is a jealous[c] and avenging God;
the LORD takes vengeance[d] and is filled with wrath.
The LORD takes vengeance on his foes
and maintains his wrath against his enemies.
3 The LORD is slow to anger[e] and great in power;
the LORD will not leave the guilty unpunished.[f]
His way is in the whirlwind and the storm,
and clouds[g] are the dust of his feet.
4 He rebukes the sea and dries it up;
he makes all the rivers run dry.
Bashan and Carmel[h] wither
and the blossoms of Lebanon fade.
5 The mountains quake[i] before him
and the hills melt away.[j]
The earth trembles at his presence,
the world and all who live in it.
6 Who can withstand his indignation?
Who can endure[k] his fierce anger?
His wrath is poured out like fire;[l]
the rocks are shattered[m] before him.

7 The LORD is good,[n]
a refuge in times of trouble.
He cares for[o] those who trust in him,
8 but with an overwhelming flood
he will make an end of ⌊Nineveh⌋;
he will pursue his foes into darkness.

9 Whatever they plot against the LORD
he[a] will bring to an end;
trouble will not come a second time.
10 They will be entangled among thorns[p]
and drunk from their wine;
they will be consumed like dry stubble.[b][q]
11 From you, ⌊O Nineveh,⌋ has one come forth
who plots evil against the LORD
and counsels wickedness.

12 This is what the LORD says:

"Although they have allies and are numerous,
they will be cut off[r] and pass away.
Although I have afflicted you, ⌊O Judah,⌋
I will afflict you no more.[s]
13 Now I will break their yoke[t] from your neck
and tear your shackles away."

14 The LORD has given a command
concerning you, ⌊Nineveh⌋:

1:1 [a]Isa 13:1; 19:1; Jer 23:33-34 [b]Jnh 1:2; Na 2:8; Zep 2:13
1:2 [c]Ex 20:5 [d]Dt 32:41; Ps 94:1
1:3 [e]Ne 9:17 [f]Ex 34:7 [g]Ps 104:3
1:4 [h]Isa 33:9
1:5 [i]Ex 19:18 [j]Mic 1:4
1:6 [k]Mal 3:2 [l]Jer 10:10 [m]1Ki 19:11
1:7 [n]Jer 33:11 [o]Ps 1:6
1:10 [p]2Sa 23:6 [q]Isa 5:24; Mal 4:1
1:12 [r]Isa 10:34 [s]Isa 54:6-8; La 3:31-32
1:13 [t]Isa 9:4

[a] *9* Or *What do you foes plot against the LORD? / He* [b] *10* The meaning of the Hebrew for this verse is uncertain.

1:14 [u]Isa 14:22 [v]Mic 5:13 [w]Eze 32:22-23

"You will have no descendants to bear
your name.[u]
I will destroy the carved images[v] and
cast idols
that are in the temple of your gods.
I will prepare your grave,[w]
for you are vile."

1:15 [x]Isa 40:9; Ro 10:15 [y]Isa 52:7 [z]Lev 23:2-4 [a]Isa 52:1

15 Look, there on the mountains,
the feet of one who brings good news,[x]
who proclaims peace![y]
Celebrate your festivals,[z] O Judah,
and fulfill your vows.
No more will the wicked invade you;[a]
they will be completely destroyed.

Nineveh to Fall

2:1 [b]Jer 51:20

2 An attacker[b] advances against you, ⌊Nineveh⌋.
Guard the fortress,
watch the road,
brace yourselves,
marshal all your strength!

2:2 [c]Eze 37:23 [d]Isa 60:15

2 The LORD will restore[c] the splendor[d] of
Jacob
like the splendor of Israel,
though destroyers have laid them waste
and have ruined their vines.

2:3 [e]Eze 23:14-15

3 The shields of his soldiers are red;
the warriors are clad in scarlet.[e]
The metal on the chariots flashes
on the day they are made ready;
the spears of pine are brandished.[a]

2:4 [f]Jer 4:13

4 The chariots[f] storm through the streets,
rushing back and forth through the
squares.
They look like flaming torches;
they dart about like lightning.

2:5 [g]Jer 46:12

5 He summons his picked troops,
yet they stumble[g] on their way.
They dash to the city wall;
the protective shield is put in place.

2:6 [h]Na 3:13

6 The river gates[h] are thrown open
and the palace collapses.
7 It is decreed[b] that ⌊the city⌋
be exiled and carried away.

2:7 [i]Isa 59:11 [j]Isa 32:12

Its slave girls moan[i] like doves
and beat upon their breasts.[j]
8 Nineveh is like a pool,
and its water is draining away.
"Stop! Stop!" they cry,
but no one turns back.
9 Plunder the silver!
Plunder the gold!
The supply is endless,
the wealth from all its treasures!
10 She is pillaged, plundered, stripped!

[a] 3 Hebrew; Septuagint and Syriac / *the horsemen rush to and fro* [b] 7 The meaning of the Hebrew for this word is uncertain.

**While Thee I seek,
protecting Power,
Be my vain wishes stilled;
And may this consecrated hour
With better hopes be filled.**

—Helen Maria Williams (1762-1827)

A Harlot's Punishment

NA 3:1–7

Read this passage aloud, with expression. Shocking, isn't it? Why is this prophecy so graphic, so disgusting and so horrifying? First, God wants to make it clear that he is fed up with prostitution. During the time of Jonah, the people of Nineveh had repented of their wicked ways (Jnh 3:7–10). But then Nineveh blatantly bequeathed the love she had vowed to God to her other lovers. Second, the prophecy depicts a common practice of this time and culture: a harlot or an adulteress was punished by being publicly stripped (Eze 16:37–39). God intends Nineveh to receive this same punishment, claiming in Nahum 3:5, that he will "show the nations [her] nakedness and the kingdoms [her] shame." Finally, this description could be a play on words since the Hebrew term for "nakedness" also means "exile." God's point is clear—wanton lusts will not only lead to being disrobed of honor but will also lead to the loss of homelands.

Hearts melt, knees give way,
bodies tremble, every face grows pale.[k]

[11] Where now is the lions' den,[l]
the place where they fed their young,
where the lion and lioness went,
and the cubs, with nothing to fear?
[12] The lion killed[m] enough for his cubs
and strangled the prey for his mate,
filling his lairs with the kill
and his dens with the prey.

[13] "I am against[n] you,"
declares the LORD Almighty.
"I will burn up your chariots in smoke,[o]
and the sword will devour your young
lions.
I will leave you no prey on the earth.
The voices of your messengers
will no longer be heard."

Woe to Nineveh

3 Woe to the city of blood,[p]
full of lies,
full of plunder,
never without victims!
[2] The crack of whips,
the clatter of wheels,
galloping horses
and jolting chariots!
[3] Charging cavalry,
flashing swords
and glittering spears!
Many casualties,
piles of dead,
bodies without number,
people stumbling over the corpses[q]—
[4] all because of the wanton lust of a harlot,
alluring, the mistress of sorceries,[r]
who enslaved nations by her prostitution[s]
and peoples by her witchcraft.

[5] "I am against[t] you," declares the LORD
Almighty.
"I will lift your skirts[u] over your face.
I will show the nations your nakedness[v]
and the kingdoms your shame.
[6] I will pelt you with filth,[w]
I will treat you with contempt[x]
and make you a spectacle.[y]
[7] All who see you will flee from you and
say,
'Nineveh[z] is in ruins—who will
mourn for her?'[a]
Where can I find anyone to comfort[b]
you?"

[8] Are you better than[c] Thebes,[a][d]
situated on the Nile,[e]
with water around her?
The river was her defense,

2:10 [k]Isa 29:22
2:11 [l]Isa 5:29
2:12 [m]Jer 51:34
2:13 [n]Jer 21:13; Na 3:5 [o]Ps 46:9
3:1 [p]Eze 22:2; Mic 3:10
3:3 [q]2Ki 19:35; Isa 34:3
3:4 [r]Isa 47:9 [s]Isa 23:17; Eze 16:25-29
3:5 [t]Na 2:13 [u]Jer 13:22 [v]Isa 47:3
3:6 [w]Job 9:31 [x]1Sa 2:30; Jer 51:37 [y]Isa 14:16
3:7 [z]Na 1:1 [a]Jer 15:5 [b]Isa 51:19
3:8 [c]Am 6:2 [d]Jer 46:25 [e]Isa 19:6-9

[a] 8 Hebrew *No Amon*

the waters her wall.
9 Cush[a][f] and Egypt were her boundless
strength;
Put[g] and Libya[h] were among her allies.
10 Yet she was taken captive[i]
and went into exile.
Her infants were dashed[j] to pieces
at the head of every street.
Lots were cast for her nobles,
and all her great men were put in
chains.
11 You too will become drunk;[k]
you will go into hiding[l]
and seek refuge from the enemy.

12 All your fortresses are like fig trees
with their first ripe fruit;
when they are shaken,
the figs[m] fall into the mouth of the
eater.
13 Look at your troops—
they are all women![n]
The gates[o] of your land
are wide open to your enemies;
fire has consumed their bars.[p]
14 Draw water for the siege,[q]
strengthen your defenses![r]
Work the clay,
tread the mortar,
repair the brickwork!
15 There the fire will devour you;
the sword will cut you down
and, like grasshoppers, consume you.
Multiply like grasshoppers,
multiply like locusts![s]
16 You have increased the number of your
merchants
till they are more than the stars of the
sky,
but like locusts they strip the land
and then fly away.
17 Your guards are like locusts,[t]
your officials like swarms of locusts
that settle in the walls on a cold day—
but when the sun appears they fly away,
and no one knows where.

18 O king of Assyria, your shepherds[b]
slumber;[u]
your nobles lie down to rest.[v]
Your people are scattered[w] on the
mountains
with no one to gather them.
19 Nothing can heal your wound;[x]
your injury is fatal.
Everyone who hears the news about you
claps his hands[y] at your fall,
for who has not felt
your endless cruelty?

3:9 [f]2Ch 12:3 [g]Eze 27:10 [h]Eze 30:5
3:10 [i]Isa 20:4 [j]Isa 13:16; Hos 13:16
3:11 [k]Isa 49:26 [l]Isa 2:10
3:12 [m]Isa 28:4
3:13 [n]Isa 19:16; Jer 50:37 [o]Na 2:6 [p]Isa 45:2
3:14 [q]2Ch 32:4 [r]Na 2:1
3:15 [s]Joel 1:4
3:17 [t]Jer 51:27
3:18 [u]Ps 76:5-6 [v]Isa 56:10 [w]1Ki 22:17
3:19 [x]Jer 30:13; Mic 1:9 [y]Job 27:23; La 2:15; Zep 2:15

Why Children Suffer

NA 3:9-10

One of the toughest questions we face is why a loving God allows children to suffer. The problem arises when we try to make God accountable for the actions of vile people. From nations and people untouched by the peace of Jesus Christ, we can expect to see Satan's murderous devises in full swing (Jn 8:44). Consequently, innocents, such as children and infants, are often caught in the crossfire of unforgiveness and escalating revenge.

In this passage God reminds Assyria that her act of murdering infants has not gone unnoticed. During their hostilities with Egypt, Assyrian soldiers killed innocent children. The atrocities of war will soon be seen within Assyria's own ranks—not due to any unfairness on God's part, but because it is the way of sinful people, living in a sinful world.

[a] 9 That is, the upper Nile region [b] 18 Or *rulers*

Habakkuk

Honest questions about injustice.

The nation of Judah faces a time of turmoil and struggle because of persistent sin. The king terrorizes God's prophets and encourages idolatry. Habakkuk worries about his nation's spiritual decline and calls out to God, wondering if God is listening and if God will put an end to the injustice (Hab 1). But the message Habakkuk receives troubles him.

God assures his puzzled prophet that he is still in control. Yet he warns Habakkuk of Judah's impending destruction at the hands of the Babylonians (Hab 1). Though Judah's sin is great, Babylon's sin is greater still, and we share Habakkuk's incredulity as the prophet questions God's unusual means of bringing about justice in Judah. We find reassurance in God's promise that Babylon will itself one day face judgment, and we share Habakkuk's relief as God grants him a vision of Judah's future restoration (Hab 2). Trusting God to bring good out of Judah's imminent disaster, Habakkuk shares his song of hope as he receives a glimpse of God's glory and a clearer understanding of God's plan (Hab 3).

This short book packs a mighty message. God is at work in the lives of his people even when it seems evil has triumphed. Because God is sovereign, he will not let injustice continue forever. God's ways may seem unfathomable, but he was in control in Habakkuk's day, and he is still in control today. Habakkuk's song of hope and faith is a song we can join in singing.

Quick Study

Author
The prophet Habakkuk.

Date Written
Sometime around the battle of Carchemish in 605 B.C.

Setting
Judah.

Key Passage
Habakkuk 3:17-18

"Though the fig tree
does not bud
and there are no grapes
on the vines,
though the olive crop
fails
and the fields produce no
food,
though there are no
sheep in the pen
and no cattle in the
stalls,
yet I will rejoice in the
LORD,
I will be joyful in God my
Savior."

Outline

Habakkuk's first complaint.
Hab 1:1-4

God's answer.
Hab 1:5-11

Habakkuk's second complaint.
Hab 1:12–2:1

God's answer.
Hab 2:2-20

Habakkuk's prayer of confession.
Hab 3

The Women of Habakkuk

No women are mentioned in the book of Habakkuk.

1 The oracle[a] that Habakkuk the prophet received.

Habakkuk's Complaint

2 How long, O LORD, must I call for help,
but you do not listen?[b]
Or cry out to you, "Violence!"
but you do not save?[c]
3 Why do you make me look at injustice?
Why do you tolerate[d] wrong?
Destruction and violence[e] are before me;
there is strife,[f] and conflict abounds.
4 Therefore the law[g] is paralyzed,
and justice never prevails.
The wicked hem in the righteous,
so that justice is perverted.[h]

The LORD's Answer

5 "Look at the nations and watch—
and be utterly amazed.[i]
For I am going to do something in your days
that you would not believe,
even if you were told.[j]
6 I am raising up the Babylonians,[a][k]
that ruthless and impetuous people,
who sweep across the whole earth
to seize dwelling places not their own.[l]
7 They are a feared and dreaded people;[m]
they are a law to themselves
and promote their own honor.
8 Their horses are swifter[n] than leopards,
fiercer than wolves at dusk.
Their cavalry gallops headlong;
their horsemen come from afar.
They fly like a vulture swooping to devour;
9 they all come bent on violence.
Their hordes[b] advance like a desert wind
and gather prisoners[o] like sand.
10 They deride kings
and scoff at rulers.[p]
They laugh at all fortified cities;
they build earthen ramps and capture them.
11 Then they sweep past like the wind[q] and go on—
guilty men, whose own strength is their god."[r]

Habakkuk's Second Complaint

12 O LORD, are you not from everlasting?
My God, my Holy One,[s] we will not die.
O LORD, you have appointed[t] them to execute judgment;

1:1 [a]Na 1:1
1:2 [b]Ps 13:1-2; 22:1-2 [c]Jer 14:9
1:3 [d]ver 13 [e]Jer 20:8 [f]Ps 55:9
1:4 [g]Ps 119:126 [h]Job 19:7; Isa 1:23; 5:20; Eze 9:9
1:5 [i]Isa 29:9 [j]Ac 13:41*
1:6 [k]2Ki 24:2 [l]Jer 13:20
1:7 [m]Isa 18:7; Jer 39:5-9
1:8 [n]Jer 4:13
1:9 [o]Hab 2:5
1:10 [p]2Ch 36:6
1:11 [q]Jer 4:11-12 [r]Da 4:30
1:12 [s]Isa 31:1 [t]Isa 10:6

Oh that it were my chief delight
To do the things I ought!
Then let me try with all my might
To mind what I am taught.

—Jane Taylor (1783-1824)

[a] *6* Or *Chaldeans* [b] *9* The meaning of the Hebrew for this word is uncertain.

O Rock, you have ordained them to
punish.
13 Your eyes are too pure to look on evil;
you cannot tolerate wrong.[u]
Why then do you tolerate the
treacherous?
Why are you silent while the wicked
swallow up those more righteous than
themselves?
14 You have made men like fish in the sea,
like sea creatures that have no ruler.
15 The wicked foe pulls all of them up with
hooks,[v]
he catches them in his net,[w]
he gathers them up in his dragnet;
and so he rejoices and is glad.
16 Therefore he sacrifices to his net
and burns incense[x] to his dragnet,
for by his net he lives in luxury
and enjoys the choicest food.
17 Is he to keep on emptying his net,
destroying nations without mercy?[y]

2 I will stand at my watch[z]
and station myself on the ramparts;[a]
I will look to see what he will say[b] to
me,
and what answer I am to give to this
complaint.[ac]

The LORD's Answer

2 Then the LORD replied:

"Write[d] down the revelation
and make it plain on tablets
so that a herald[b] may run with it.
3 For the revelation awaits an appointed
time;
it speaks of the end[e]
and will not prove false.
Though it linger, wait[f] for it;
it[c] will certainly come and will not
delay.[g]

4 "See, he is puffed up;
his desires are not upright—
but the righteous will live by his
faith[dh]—
5 indeed, wine[i] betrays him;
he is arrogant and never at rest.
Because he is as greedy as the grave[e]
and like death is never satisfied,[j]
he gathers to himself all the nations
and takes captive all the peoples.

6 "Will not all of them taunt[k] him with ridicule
and scorn, saying,

"'Woe to him who piles up stolen goods

1:13 [u]La 3:34-36
1:15 [v]Isa 19:8 [w]Jer 16:16
1:16 [x]Jer 44:8
1:17 [y]Isa 14:6; 19:8
2:1 [z]Isa 21:8 [a]Ps 48:13 [b]Ps 85:8 [c]Ps 5:3
2:2 [d]Rev 1:19
2:3 [e]Da 8:17; 10:14 [f]Ps 27:14 [g]Eze 12:25; Heb 10:37-38
2:4 [h]Ro 1:17*; Gal 3:11*; Heb 10:37-38*
2:5 [i]Pr 20:1 [j]Pr 27:20; 30:15-16
2:6 [k]Isa 14:4

[a] 1 Or *and what to answer when I am rebuked* [b] 2 Or *so that whoever reads it* [c] 3 Or *Though he linger, wait for him; / he* [d] 4 Or *faithfulness* [e] 5 Hebrew *Sheol*

God Cannot Tolerate Evil

HAB 1:13

The prophet Habakkuk, like us, wonders how a loving God can use evil nations to bring judgment on his people. The answer: God's justice, purity and holiness cannot tolerate wrongdoing; and, yes, he will even use the "bad guys" to discipline the "good guys." Though God has found a way through Jesus Christ to be reconciled to sinners, he never will, and never can, be reconciled to sin. God hates sin and literally cannot live with it (Ps 5:4–5). To a lesser degree, God puts this need for justice inside each of us. We are offended when the wicked seem to win at the expense of what Habakkuk calls the "more righteous" (Hab 1:13). God may allow wickedness for a time—he is patient and wishes for all to repent—but someday the time will come when he will tolerate evil no more.

and makes himself wealthy by
extortion![l]
How long must this go on?'
7 Will not your debtors[a] suddenly arise?
Will they not wake up and make you
tremble?
Then you will become their victim.[m]
8 Because you have plundered many
nations,
the peoples who are left will plunder
you.[n]
For you have shed man's blood;[o]
you have destroyed lands and cities
and everyone in them.

9 "Woe to him who builds[p] his realm by
unjust gain
to set his nest on high,
to escape the clutches of ruin!
10 You have plotted the ruin[q] of many
peoples,
shaming[r] your own house and
forfeiting your life.
11 The stones[s] of the wall will cry out,
and the beams of the woodwork will
echo it.

12 "Woe to him who builds a city with
bloodshed[t]
and establishes a town by crime!
13 Has not the LORD Almighty determined
that the people's labor is only fuel for
the fire,[u]
that the nations exhaust themselves
for nothing?[v]
14 For the earth will be filled with the
knowledge of the glory[w] of the
LORD,
as the waters cover the sea.[x]

15 "Woe to him who gives drink to his
neighbors,
pouring it from the wineskin till they
are drunk,
so that he can gaze on their naked
bodies.
16 You will be filled with shame[y] instead of
glory.
Now it is your turn! Drink and be
exposed[b]![z]
The cup[a] from the LORD's right hand is
coming around to you,
and disgrace will cover your glory.
17 The violence[b] you have done to
Lebanon will overwhelm you,
and your destruction of animals will
terrify you.[c]
For you have shed man's blood;[d]
you have destroyed lands and cities
and everyone in them.

2:6 [l]Am 2:8
2:7 [m]Pr 29:1
2:8 [n]Isa 33:1; Zec 2:8-9 [o]ver 17
2:9 [p]Jer 22:13
2:10 [q]Jer 26:19 [r]ver 16
2:11 [s]Jos 24:27; Lk 19:40
2:12 [t]Mic 3:10
2:13 [u]Isa 50:11 [v]Isa 47:13
2:14 [w]Nu 14:21 [x]Isa 11:9
2:16 [y]ver 10 [z]La 4:21 [a]Isa 51:22
2:17 [b]Jer 51:35 [c]Jer 50:15 [d]ver 8

To become tenderhearted, insightful and responsive to the Lord and others, we must first wade through our [own] losses. That means a willingness to feel the effects of our loss, to examine our hearts under the tutelage of the Holy Spirit, to release tears and to relinquish our rights to understand. In doing so, we will feel the pain, but we'll learn appropriate ways to express it. Sometimes it will be through the healing release of tears, prayer, some form of art, or words (spoken or written).

—Patsy Clairmont

[a] 7 Or *creditors* [b] 16 Masoretic Text; Dead Sea Scrolls, Aquila, Vulgate and Syriac (see also Septuagint) *and stagger*

2:18 [e]Jer 5:21 [f]Ps 115:4-5; Jer 10:14

18 "Of what value is an idol,[e] since a man
has carved it?
Or an image that teaches lies?
For he who makes it trusts in his own
creation;
he makes idols that cannot speak.[f]

2:19 [g]1Ki 18:27 [h]Jer 10:4

19 Woe to him who says to wood, 'Come to
life!'
Or to lifeless stone, 'Wake up!'[g]
Can it give guidance?
It is covered with gold and silver;[h]
there is no breath in it.

2:20 [i]Ps 11:4 [j]Isa 41:1

20 But the LORD is in his holy temple;[i]
let all the earth be silent[j] before him."

Habakkuk's Prayer

3 A prayer of Habakkuk the prophet. On
shigionoth.[a]

3:2 [k]Ps 44:1 [l]Ps 119:120 [m]Ps 85:6 [n]Isa 54:8

2 LORD, I have heard[k] of your fame;
I stand in awe[l] of your deeds, O LORD.
Renew[m] them in our day,
in our time make them known;
in wrath remember mercy.[n]

3 God came from Teman,
the Holy One from Mount Paran.
Selah[b]

3:3 [o]Ps 48:10

His glory covered the heavens
and his praise filled the earth.[o]
4 His splendor was like the sunrise;
rays flashed from his hand,
where his power was hidden.
5 Plague went before him;
pestilence followed his steps.

3:6 [p]Ps 114:1-6

6 He stood, and shook the earth;
he looked, and made the nations
tremble.
The ancient mountains crumbled
and the age-old hills collapsed.[p]
His ways are eternal.

3:7 [q]Jdg 7:24-25 [r]Ex 15:14

7 I saw the tents of Cushan in distress,
the dwellings of Midian[q] in anguish.[r]

3:8 [s]Ex 7:20 [t]Ps 68:17

8 Were you angry with the rivers,[s]
O LORD?
Was your wrath against the streams?
Did you rage against the sea
when you rode with your horses
and your victorious chariots?[t]

3:9 [u]Ps 7:12-13

9 You uncovered your bow,
you called for many arrows.[u] *Selah*
You split the earth with rivers;
10 the mountains saw you and writhed.

3:10 [v]Ps 98:7 [w]Ps 93:3

Torrents of water swept by;
the deep roared[v]
and lifted its waves[w] on high.

[a] *1* Probably a literary or musical term [b] *3* A word of uncertain meaning; possibly a musical term; also in verses 9 and 13

Silence

HAB 2:19-20

Habakkuk poses a hard question to God in chapter 1: How can he use the despicable Babylonians to punish his people? In chapter 2, God acknowledges the importance of asking questions and receiving answers by providing Habakkuk with a response. But his reply is disturbing: He will mete out terrible punishment on Babylon. The despicable Babylonians will themselves be punished.

Then, in Habakkuk 2:19, God sets up a sharp contrast between the silence of the Babylonian idols, which cannot speak because they are lifeless, and the silence that befalls all God's creatures in the face of his power and sovereignty. The world around us might be in chaos and our specific questions might not be answered as we wish, but our God is very much alive and capable of speaking through his actions—and our rightful response to such a mighty Lord is to be worshipfully silent.

The words of this hymn by Englishwoman Anna Laetitia Aikin Barbauld beautifully echo those of the prophet Habakkuk in chapter 3:17-19.

Praise to God, Immortal Praise

Praise to God, immortal praise,
For the love that crowns our days;
Bounteous Source of every joy,
Let Thy praise our tongues employ.

These to Thee, my God, we owe,
Source whence all our blessings flow;
And for these my soul shall raise
Grateful vows and solemn praise.

Yet, should rising whirlwinds tear
From its stem the ripening ear;
Should the fig tree's blasted shoot
Drop her green untimely fruit,

Should the vine put forth no more,
Nor the olive yield her store;
Though the sickening flocks should fall,
And the herds desert the stall,

Yet to Thee my soul shall raise
Grateful vows and solemn praise;
And, when every blessing's flown
Love Thee for Thyself alone.

—Anna Laetitia Aikin Barbauld (1743-1825)

11 Sun and moon stood still[x] in the heavens
at the glint of your flying arrows,[y]
at the lightning of your flashing spear.
12 In wrath you strode through the earth
and in anger you threshed[z] the nations.
13 You came out to deliver[a] your people,
to save your anointed one.
You crushed[b] the leader of the land of wickedness,
you stripped him from head to foot.
Selah
14 With his own spear you pierced his head
when his warriors stormed out to scatter us,[c]
gloating as though about to devour
the wretched[d] who were in hiding.
15 You trampled the sea with your horses,
churning the great waters.[e]

16 I heard and my heart pounded,
my lips quivered at the sound;
decay crept into my bones,
and my legs trembled.
Yet I will wait patiently for the day of calamity
to come on the nation invading us.
17 Though the fig tree does not bud
and there are no grapes on the vines,
though the olive crop fails
and the fields produce no food,[f]
though there are no sheep in the pen
and no cattle in the stalls,[g]
18 yet I will rejoice in the LORD,[h]
I will be joyful in God my Savior.
19 The Sovereign LORD is my strength;[i]
he makes my feet like the feet of a deer,
he enables me to go on the heights.[j]

For the director of music. On my stringed instruments.

3:11 [x]Jos 10:13 [y]Ps 18:14
3:12 [z]Isa 41:15
3:13 [a]Ps 20:6; 28:8 [b]Ps 68:21; 110:6
3:14 [c]Jdg 7:22 [d]Ps 64:2-5
3:15 [e]Ex 15:8; Ps 77:19
3:17 [f]Joel 1:10-12, 18 [g]Jer 5:17
3:18 [h]Isa 61:10; Php 4:4
3:19 [i]Dt 33:29; Ps 46:1-5 [j]Dt 32:13; 2Sa 22:34; Ps 18:33

Week 29

Trusting When Tested

The prophet Habakkuk lives in a time of distress and desperation. Wickedness and oppression surround him. In frustration Habakkuk asks God, "Where are you in all this?" God then reveals his plan to punish Judah for its rebellion and refusal to repent: the Babylonian invasion and resulting exile. Despite Habakkuk's circumstances and the coming calamity, he chooses to rejoice.

When you are in the midst of a distressing situation or are weary of the wickedness surrounding you, do you, like Habakkuk, wonder, *Where are you, God?* Perhaps your faith is being tested and you need to learn what Habakkuk comes to understand.

What two areas within you does God test (1Ch 29:17; Jer 11:20; 12:3)? How have you experienced testing in these areas of your life?

God uses circumstances, things and people to test you. How does God use manna to test the Israelites in the desert (Ex 16:4)? What are some other reasons why God would test you (Jer 9:7; Zec 13:9)? What is God's ultimate purpose in testing you (Dt 8:16; Jas 1:3-4)? What reward will you receive if you stand the test (Jas 1:12)? How have you grown as a result of the tests you have faced?

God allows counterfeit religions to exist side by side with Christianity to test your faith. What will this testing prove (Dt 13:1-4)? What impact does a need to understand and defend your beliefs have on your faith?

Do all tests come from God (Job 1:6-9; Mt 4:1-11)? How do you know when the test you're experiencing comes from God (Jas 1:13-14)? What hope do you have to overcome your trials and temptations (Hab 3:19)? When have *you* experienced "the feet of a deer"?

Enjoying God THROUGH the Word

Read Deuteronomy 8:2-5 (page 288). The Israelites' entire 40-year desert experience is a test with a twofold purpose: to humble them and to discipline them for their disobedience. God promises them the land of Canaan, but they rebel against him by refusing to enter. They refuse because they do "not trust him or obey him" (Dt 9:23). Hebrews 3:7-19 makes it even more clear: "So we see that they [are] not able to enter [the promised land], because of their unbelief" (Heb 3:19). They face a test—and fail. They can trust God for victory or they can trust themselves and run. They run.

When you face trials and testing, you also have a choice. You can choose to trust the strength of the Lord, as Habakkuk does, or you can choose to rely on yourself (as the Israelites do). Depending on self results in corruption and deception (Hos 10:13). Depending on God results in the ability to rejoice regardless of circumstances (Hab 3:18).

Enjoying God THROUGH Experience

If you are enduring testing, be aware of the clear choices before you. If you trust in worldly power (Ps 20:7), weapons (Ps 44:6-7), wealth (Ps 49:12-13), friends or family (Jer 9:4; 12:6), neighbors (Mic 7:5) or your own understanding (Pr 3:5), you will be disappointed. But "the LORD is good, a refuge in times of trouble. He cares for those who trust in him" (Na 1:7). Trust him, and be filled with joy, peace and hope (Ro 15:13).

Go to page 1547 for your next weekly study.

Zephaniah

From judgment to joy.

Using a poetic style, vivid figures of speech and emotionally charged language, Zephaniah paints a picture of doom to shake the people of Judah out of their complacency and direct them back to obedience to God. During Zephaniah's time young King Josiah institutes well-intentioned reforms, but the king's efforts are not enough to turn the people away from their idolatry and corruption. God's demands for righteous living seem irrelevant to a people who find their security in wealth and possessions.

Zephaniah warns of God's terrible judgment on the nations and recounts the depressing list of sins that God holds against Judah (Zep 1–2). Though gloomy predictions of a worldwide catastrophe fill most of the book, Zephaniah also sings a song of joy as he envisions a time of repentance and restoration for God's people (Zep 3).

Blunt and hard-hitting in its portrayal of sin and judgment, Zephaniah calls us to action: Irresponsibility and complacency will lead to spiritual downfall. There are consequences for wrongdoing though those consequences may be delayed for a while. Material comforts should never become a barrier to commitment to God. And faith and hope in God can still burn brightly even in the darkness of a corrupt and sinful world.

Quick Study

Author
The prophet Zephaniah.

Date Written
Early in the reign of Josiah between 640 and 627 B.C.

Setting
Judah.

Key Passage
Zephaniah 2:3 "Seek the LORD, all you humble of the land,
you who do what he commands.
Seek righteousness, seek humility;
perhaps you will be sheltered
on the day of the LORD's anger."

Outline

Warning of coming judgment.
Zep 1:1–2:3

Warnings against specific nations.
Zep 2:4–15

Warnings against Jerusalem.
Zep 3:1–8

Redemption of the remnant.
Zep 3:9–20

The Women of Zephaniah

No women are mentioned in the book of Zephaniah.

Prophecy and Fulfillment

ZEP 1:2-3

Zephaniah prophesies to a country whose affections are divided. Judah does not intend to quit its service to God—it is the religion of the people. Yet they are also attracted to what they see around them and begin to worship the idols of surrounding nations. Zephaniah's prophecy of their coming punishment—the fall of Jerusalem—is fulfilled in 586 B.C.

Similar to other Old Testament warnings, however, this passage also speaks of destruction yet to come. Zephaniah's words prophesy events that will take place at the end of the world (Rev 6:17). At that point, God's judgment will be experienced again, only then it will be a global judgment. Those holy and set apart for God will be spared. All others will be destroyed or, as Zephaniah says, swept "from the face of the earth" (Zep 1:2). God has made it clear that he's not interested in sharing his people's affection with any other god —never has been, never will be.

1 The word of the LORD that came to Zephaniah son of Cushi, the son of Gedaliah, the son of Amariah, the son of Hezekiah, during the reign of Josiah[a] son of Amon king of Judah:

Warning of Coming Destruction

2 "I will sweep away everything
from the face of the earth,"[b]
declares the LORD.
3 "I will sweep away both men and animals;
I will sweep away the birds of the air[c]
and the fish of the sea.
The wicked will have only heaps of rubble[a]
when I cut off man from the face of the earth,"[d]
declares the LORD.

Against Judah

4 "I will stretch out my hand[e] against Judah
and against all who live in Jerusalem.
I will cut off from this place every remnant of Baal,[f]
the names of the pagan and the idolatrous priests[g]—
5 those who bow down on the roofs
to worship the starry host,
those who bow down and swear by the LORD
and who also swear by Molech,[b][h]
6 those who turn back from following[i] the LORD
and neither seek[j] the LORD nor inquire[k] of him.
7 Be silent[l] before the Sovereign LORD,
for the day of the LORD[m] is near.
The LORD has prepared a sacrifice;[n]
he has consecrated those he has invited.
8 On the day of the LORD's sacrifice
I will punish[o] the princes
and the king's sons[p]
and all those clad
in foreign clothes.
9 On that day I will punish
all who avoid stepping on the threshold,[c]
who fill the temple of their gods
with violence and deceit.[q]

10 "On that day," declares the LORD,
"a cry will go up from the Fish Gate,[r]
wailing from the New Quarter,
and a loud crash from the hills.
11 Wail,[s] you who live in the market district[d];

1:1 [a]2Ki 22:1; 2Ch 34:1-35:25
1:2 [b]Ge 6:7
1:3 [c]Jer 4:25 [d]Hos 4:3
1:4 [e]Jer 6:12 [f]Mic 5:13 [g]Hos 10:5
1:5 [h]Jer 5:7
1:6 [i]Isa 1:4; Jer 2:13 [j]Isa 9:13 [k]Hos 7:7
1:7 [l]Hab 2:20; Zec 2:13 [m]ver 14; Isa 13:6 [n]Isa 34:6; Jer 46:10
1:8 [o]Isa 24:21 [p]Jer 39:6
1:9 [q]Am 3:10
1:10 [r]2Ch 33:14
1:11 [s]Jas 5:1

[a] *3* The meaning of the Hebrew for this line is uncertain.
[b] *5* Hebrew *Malcam,* that is, Milcom
[c] *9* See 1 Samuel 5:5.
[d] *11* Or *the Mortar*

all your merchants will be wiped out,
all who trade with[a] silver will be ruined.[t]
12 At that time I will search Jerusalem with lamps
and punish those who are complacent,[u]
who are like wine left on its dregs,[v]
who think, 'The LORD will do nothing,[w]
either good or bad.'
13 Their wealth will be plundered,[x]
their houses demolished.
They will build houses
but not live in them;
they will plant vineyards
but not drink the wine.[y]

The Great Day of the LORD

14 "The great day of the LORD[z] is near[a]—
near and coming quickly.
Listen! The cry on the day of the LORD will be bitter,
the shouting of the warrior there.
15 That day will be a day of wrath,
a day of distress and anguish,
a day of trouble and ruin,
a day of darkness and gloom,
a day of clouds and blackness,[b]
16 a day of trumpet and battle cry[c]
against the fortified cities
and against the corner towers.[d]
17 I will bring distress on the people
and they will walk like blind[e] men,
because they have sinned against the LORD.
Their blood will be poured out[f] like dust
and their entrails like filth.[g]
18 Neither their silver nor their gold
will be able to save them
on the day of the LORD's wrath.[h]
In the fire of his jealousy
the whole world will be consumed,[i]
for he will make a sudden end
of all who live in the earth.[j]"

2 Gather together,[k] gather together,
O shameful[l] nation,
2 before the appointed time arrives
and that day sweeps on like chaff,[m]
before the fierce anger[n] of the LORD
comes upon you,
before the day of the LORD's wrath
comes upon you.
3 Seek[o] the LORD, all you humble of the land,
you who do what he commands.
Seek righteousness, seek humility;[p]
perhaps you will be sheltered[q]
on the day of the LORD's anger.

1:11 [t]Hos 9:6
1:12 [u]Am 6:1 [v]Jer 48:11 [w]Eze 8:12
1:13 [x]Jer 15:13 [y]Dt 28:30, 39; Am 5:11; Mic 6:15
1:14 [z]ver 7; Joel 1:15 [a]Eze 7:7
1:15 [b]Isa 22:5; Joel 2:2
1:16 [c]Jer 4:19 [d]Isa 2:15
1:17 [e]Isa 59:10 [f]Ps 79:3 [g]Jer 9:22
1:18 [h]Eze 7:19 [i]ver 2-3; Zep 3:8 [j]Ge 6:7
2:1 [k]2Ch 20:4; Joel 1:14 [l]Jer 3:3; 6:15
2:2 [m]Isa 17:13; Hos 13:3 [n]La 4:11
2:3 [o]Am 5:6 [p]Ps 45:4; Am 5:14-15 [q]Ps 57:1

[a] 11 Or *in*

In every situation, *whether ordinary or life threatening, God assures us that he keeps his eye on us and knows the number of hairs on our heads. Absolutely everything that can happen to us—good, bad or indifferent—God knows and cares about. God is concerned about us all the time, in every area of our lives, even if nobody else is. He promises that we are never away from his presence.*

Does that mean nothing bad will ever happen to us? No. But *it does mean that we can have inner peace in this dangerous world.*

—Thelma Wells

Our Awesome God

ZEP 2:11

At some moments in our lives we all find ourselves overwhelmed. We may become speechless after receiving a grand, unexpected gift. Or we might be stunned by an overwhelming loss. As opposite as these two situations are, they both can be described with the word *awesome*. Recently, *awesome* has been used as slang for "cool" or "exciting." *Awesome* is used in such a way (but to an even greater extent) in Psalm 47:2: "How awesome is the LORD Most High, the great King over all the earth!"

In Zephaniah 2:11 the word *awesome* expresses an overwhelming, even terrorizing, reverence for the Lord. God promises that one day all the people on the face of the earth will "tremble at [his] presence" (Eze 38:20). All will be overwhelmed. All will be awed—either in utter panic or in complete joy—as they find themselves on their knees before the living God (Ro 14:11).

Against Philistia

4 Gaza[r] will be abandoned
and Ashkelon left in ruins.
At midday Ashdod will be emptied
and Ekron uprooted.
5 Woe to you who live by the sea,
O Kerethite[s] people;
the word of the LORD is against you,[t]
O Canaan, land of the Philistines.

"I will destroy you,
and none will be left."[u]

6 The land by the sea, where the
Kerethites[a] dwell,
will be a place for shepherds and
sheep pens.[v]
7 It will belong to the remnant of the
house of Judah;
there they will find pasture.
In the evening they will lie down
in the houses of Ashkelon.
The LORD their God will care for them;
he will restore their fortunes.[b][w]

Against Moab and Ammon

8 "I have heard the insults[x] of Moab
and the taunts of the Ammonites,
who insulted[y] my people
and made threats against their land.
9 Therefore, as surely as I live,"
declares the LORD Almighty, the God
of Israel,
"surely Moab[z] will become like Sodom,[a]
the Ammonites[b] like Gomorrah—
a place of weeds and salt pits,
a wasteland forever.
The remnant of my people will plunder[c]
them;
the survivors of my nation will inherit
their land.[d]"

10 This is what they will get in return for
their pride,[e]
for insulting[f] and mocking the people
of the LORD Almighty.
11 The LORD will be awesome[g] to them
when he destroys all the gods[h] of the
land.
The nations on every shore will worship
him,[i]
every one in its own land.

Against Cush

12 "You too, O Cushites,[c][j]
will be slain by my sword.[k]"

2:4 [r]Am 1:6,7-8; Zec 9:5-7
2:5 [s]Eze 25:16 [t]Am 3:1 [u]Isa 14:30
2:6 [v]Isa 5:17
2:7 [w]Ps 126:4; Jer 32:44
2:8 [x]Jer 48:27 [y]Eze 25:3
2:9 [z]Isa 15:1-16:14; Jer 48:1-47 [a]Dt 29:23 [b]Jer 49:1-6; Eze 25:1-7 [c]Isa 11:14 [d]Am 2:1-3
2:10 [e]Isa 16:6 [f]Jer 48:27
2:11 [g]Joel 2:11 [h]Zep 1:4 [i]Zep 3:9
2:12 [j]Isa 18:1; 20:4 [k]Jer 46:10

[a] 6 The meaning of the Hebrew for this word is uncertain.
[b] 7 Or *will bring back their captives*
[c] 12 That is, people from the upper Nile region

Against Assyria

13 He will stretch out his hand against the north
2:13 and destroy Assyria,
[l]Na 1:1 leaving Nineveh[l] utterly desolate
[m]Mic 5:6 and dry as the desert.[m]
14 Flocks and herds will lie down there,
2:14 creatures of every kind.
[n]Isa 14:23 The desert owl[n] and the screech owl
will roost on her columns.
Their calls will echo through the windows,
rubble will be in the doorways,
2:15 the beams of cedar will be exposed.
[o]Isa 32:9 15 This is the carefree[o] city
[p]Isa 47:8 that lived in safety.[p]
[q]Eze 28:2
[r]Na 3:19 She said to herself,
"I am, and there is none besides me."[q]
What a ruin she has become,
a lair for wild beasts!
All who pass by her scoff[r]
and shake their fists.

The Future of Jerusalem

3:1
[s]Jer 6:6 **3** Woe to the city of oppressors,[s]
[t]Eze 23:30 rebellious and defiled![t]
3:2 2 She obeys[u] no one,
[u]Jer 22:21 she accepts no correction.[v]
[v]Jer 7:28
[w]Ps 73:28; She does not trust in the LORD,
Jer 5:3 she does not draw near[w] to her God.
3:3 3 Her officials are roaring lions,
[x]Eze 22:27 her rulers are evening wolves,[x]
who leave nothing for the morning.
3:4 4 Her prophets are arrogant;
[y]Jer 9:4 they are treacherous[y] men.
[z]Eze 22:26 Her priests profane the sanctuary
and do violence to the law.[z]
3:5 5 The LORD within her is righteous;
[a]Dt 32:4 he does no wrong.[a]
Morning by morning he dispenses his justice,
and every new day he does not fail,
yet the unrighteous know no shame.

6 "I have cut off nations;
their strongholds are demolished.
I have left their streets deserted,
3:6 with no one passing through.
[b]Lev 26:31 Their cities are destroyed;[b]
no one will be left—no one at all.
7 I said to the city,
'Surely you will fear me
and accept correction!'
Then her dwelling would not be cut off,
nor all my punishments come upon her.
3:7 But they were still eager
[c]Hos 9:9 to act corruptly[c] in all they did.
3:8 8 Therefore wait[d] for me," declares the
[d]Ps 27:14 LORD,

Nineveh's Desolation

ZEP 2:13–14

Ghost towns are remnants of glory days gone by. In our mind's eye we picture windowless, empty buildings lining dusty streets. Yet can you imagine a magnificent city, once home to splendid temples, palaces, gardens and fortifications, so completely destroyed that scholars for a time question its very existence? Nineveh, the capital of Assyria, was at one time home to 120,000 people (Jnh 4:11), but it wasn't until its ruins began to be explored in 1845 that many finally admitted it had existed at all.

During the time of Zephaniah, Nineveh is so strong that she fears no evil (Zep 2:15). This pompous attitude leads to her ruin. In Zephaniah 2:14 God declares that Nineveh will be home to screech owls. The Hebrew people considered the owl an unclean bird (Lev 11:13–18) and associated it with a scene of desolation. That's exactly what becomes of Nineveh—the palaces of kings become roosts for owls.

When God Sings

ZEP 3:14–17

This passage, written for the Daughter of Zion—Jerusalem (Zep 3:14)—is also written for us as God's daughters. When we come through times of pain or shame, God is there to rejoice over us. In fact, the mere thought of us brings a song to his lips! The Hebrew word translated "singing" can also mean shouting with joy or laughing cheerfully. Perhaps even more precious is the knowledge that God is there during difficult times—during the times we feel exiled from "home," as are the people of Jerusalem in this passage. As a caring Father, God walks beside us, and his whispers of assurance ease our sorrows and quiet our fears. Write out and memorize Zephaniah 3:17. Then, rejoice that he is your God and sing a song of praise to him!

"for the day I will stand up to testify.[a]
I have decided to assemble the nations,[e]
to gather the kingdoms
and to pour out my wrath on them—
all my fierce anger.
The whole world will be consumed[f]
by the fire of my jealous anger.

9 "Then will I purify the lips of the peoples,
that all of them may call[g] on the name of the LORD
and serve[h] him shoulder to shoulder.
10 From beyond the rivers of Cush[b][i]
my worshipers, my scattered people,
will bring me offerings.[j]
11 On that day you will not be put to shame[k]
for all the wrongs you have done to me,
because I will remove from this city
those who rejoice in their pride.
Never again will you be haughty
on my holy hill.
12 But I will leave within you
the meek[l] and humble,
who trust[m] in the name of the LORD.
13 The remnant[n] of Israel will do no wrong;[o]
they will speak no lies,[p]
nor will deceit be found in their mouths.
They will eat and lie down[q]
and no one will make them afraid.[r]"
14 Sing, O Daughter of Zion;[s]
shout aloud,[t] O Israel!
Be glad and rejoice with all your heart,
O Daughter of Jerusalem!
15 The LORD has taken away your punishment,
he has turned back your enemy.
The LORD, the King of Israel, is with you;[u]
never again will you fear[v] any harm.
16 On that day they will say to Jerusalem,
"Do not fear, O Zion;
do not let your hands hang limp.[w]
17 The LORD your God is with you,
he is mighty to save.[x]
He will take great delight[y] in you,
he will quiet you with his love,
he will rejoice over you with singing."

18 "The sorrows for the appointed feasts
I will remove from you;
they are a burden and a reproach to you.[c]

3:8 [e]Joel 3:2 [f]Zep 1:18
3:9 [g]Zep 2:11 [h]Isa 19:18
3:10 [i]Ps 68:31 [j]Isa 60:7
3:11 [k]Joel 2:26-27
3:12 [l]Isa 14:32 [m]Na 1:7
3:13 [n]Isa 10:21; Mic 4:7 [o]Ps 119:3 [p]Rev 14:5 [q]Eze 34:15; Zep 2:7 [r]Eze 34:25-28
3:14 [s]Zec 2:10 [t]Isa 12:6
3:15 [u]Eze 37:26-28 [v]Isa 54:14
3:16 [w]Job 4:3; Isa 35:3-4; Heb 12:12
3:17 [x]Isa 63:1 [y]Isa 62:4

[a] *8* Septuagint and Syriac; Hebrew *will rise up to plunder*
[b] *10* That is, the upper Nile region
[c] *18* Or *"I will gather you who mourn for the appointed feasts; / your reproach is a burden to you*

Week 30

The Singing God

Imagine hearing God sing. Does it sound like the mighty roar of thunder (Joel 3:16), or like a soft and gentle whisper (1Ki 19:12)? It is powerful and strong, yet unimaginably beautiful, pure and sweet. And he is singing that glorious song over you! Why does God sing over you? Because he delights in you. *You* make his heart sing with joy.

Do you believe this? If not, why not? There are obstacles, you say—your sin and guilt, your constant wandering from God, the enemy's accusations that you are unworthy, and your fear of rejection. Let's look at each of these obstacles so you can grasp the fact that all you need you already possess. God's mercy, grace, love and presence are already yours.

Yes, you're a sinner. That is the very reason for you to go to him. What has God done for you and why did he do it (1Ti 1:15; Tit 3:4-7)?

God is delighted when you obey (Dt 30:9-10). If you wander from him, he will discipline you (Pr 3:11-12; Heb 12:5-11). What is God's goal in discipline (2Co 7:9-10)?

How does God quiet your feelings of rejection and unworthiness (Zep 3:17)? It is not his power or his majesty that quiets your fears; it is his unfailing love (Ps 36:7-8; Isa 54:10).

What is God's promise to you (Jer 32:38-41)? Do you believe this? God rejoices when he can do good things for you (Jer 32:41). He delights in your well-being (Ps 35:27).

What about your enemy, the accuser (Isa 50:7-9; 54:16-17; Zep 3:15; Ro 8:31-34)?

Why will God never reject you (1Sa 12:22; Ps 94:14)? God's name is glorified when he pours out love and good on his people. For his own name's sake—his glory—he will never forsake you (Isa 48:9-11).

God's love for you is deep and strong. It will never be shaken (Isa 54:10). You are secure in him. Knowing that he delights in you can give you freedom to delight in him and in all that he has for you.

Enjoying God THROUGH the Word

Read Ezekiel 36:24-32 (pages 1405-1406). This beautiful passage has meaning for every believer. God rejoices over you and desires to bless you with these things: freedom (Eze 36:24), cleansing (Eze 36:25), a new—not remodeled—heart and spirit (Eze 36:26), his very own Spirit within you to enable you to obey (Eze 36:27), personal relationship with him (Eze 36:28) and prosperity (Eze 36:29-30). God will remove your impurities (Eze 36:25), your heart of stone (Eze 36:26), your uncleanness (Eze 36:29) and your disgrace (Eze 36:30). In all of this, God's holy name is glorified (Eze 36:22). Your transformation brings him glory. You are an example of his grace, mercy, love and power!

Enjoying God THROUGH Experience

Read Ezekiel 36:24-32 again, this time out loud as a prayer of declaration of what God will do for you. Rejoice in knowing that God is glorified as you are spiritually transformed. When you take a step of faith, when you grow and mature, he is singing over you from a heart bursting with joy and pride. He is your loving Father. Listen to the special love song he is singing just for you.

Go to page 1593 for your next weekly study.

From Rags to Riches

ZEP 3:20

At one time, Judah was praised above all nations. Her beauty and majesty testified to the favor granted her. Then, because of sinful choices, she became like a princess turned peasant. Like a peasant, she wandered, troubled and penniless. Yet even then she was neither alone nor forgotten. At her darkest moment, a happily-ever-after ending is promised. Someday, Zephaniah prophesies, Judah will be restored to her former glory.

This scenario is not only for Judah but also for the Christian church. One day the church, too, will be restored and presented to Jesus Christ as his bride (Rev 19:7). As members of the church, we can know that God will heal any shame we encounter, bring a balm for any pain and forget our poor choices when we repent of them. And he will welcome us home, into his kingdom. That makes this the ultimate rags-to-riches tale.

19 At that time I will deal
with all who oppressed you;
I will rescue the lame
and gather those who have been
scattered.[z]
I will give them praise[a] and honor
in every land where they were put to
shame.
20 At that time I will gather you;
at that time I will bring[b] you home.
I will give you honor[c] and praise
among all the peoples of the earth
when I restore your fortunes[a][d]
before your very eyes,"
says the LORD.

3:19 [z]Eze 34:16; Mic 4:6 [a]Isa 60:18

3:20 [b]Jer 29:14; Eze 37:12 [c]Isa 56:5; 66:22 [d]Joel 3:1

[a] 20 Or *I bring back your captives*

Haggai

Proper priorities ensure success.

Several years pass after the first group of Jewish exiles return to their homeland to rebuild the temple. After completing the temple's foundation, the people face opposition to the rebuilding project. Judah is a wasteland and resources are limited, so the people turn their attention to constructing homes for themselves, leaving God's temple in ruins. Haggai stirs the people to resume building the temple. His message is simple: Put God first and God will bless you. The people respond enthusiastically to Haggai's message, begin rebuilding the temple and experience God's blessings.

Haggai's words hit their mark as he reminds the exiles of the close connection between obedience and blessing. We hear Haggai's call to rebuild the temple (Hag 1). We rejoice when we see the enthusiastic response of the people (Hag 1:14). And we are awed by God's desire to give his people not just good, but the best, not just a partially rebuilt temple but a glorious new place of worship (Hag 2).

God's challenge to the Jews through Haggai is our challenge. If we obey, his Spirit will encourage and help us. If we rebel and turn away, only God's judgment will be our due. Haggai's encouragement to the Jews to get their priorities in order is ours as well. God must come first.

Quick Study

Author
The prophet Haggai.

Date Written
520 B.C.

Setting
Judah.

Key Passage
Haggai 1:5 "Now this is what the LORD Almighty says: 'Give careful thought to your ways.' "

Outline

The call to rebuild the temple.
Hag 1:1-11

The response of the people.
Hag 1:12-15

The temple to be filled with glory.
Hag 2:1-9

A defiled people purified and blessed.
Hag 2:10-19

God's promise to Zerubbabel.
Hag 2:20-23

The Women of Haggai

No women are mentioned in the book of Haggai.

A Call to Build the House of the LORD

1 In the second year of King Darius,[a] on the first
day of the sixth month, the word of the LORD
came through the prophet Haggai[b] to Zerubbabel[c]
son of Shealtiel, governor[d] of Judah, and to Joshua[a][e] son of Jehozadak,[f] the high priest:
2This is what the LORD Almighty says: "These
people say, 'The time has not yet come for the
LORD's house to be built.'"
3Then the word of the LORD came through the
prophet Haggai:[g] 4"Is it a time for you yourselves
to be living in your paneled houses,[h] while this
house remains a ruin?[i]"
5Now this is what the LORD Almighty says:
"Give careful thought[j] to your ways. 6You have
planted much, but have harvested little.[k] You eat,
but never have enough. You drink, but never have
your fill. You put on clothes, but are not warm.
You earn wages,[l] only to put them in a purse with
holes in it."
7This is what the LORD Almighty says: "Give
careful thought to your ways. 8Go up into the
mountains and bring down timber and build the
house, so that I may take pleasure[m] in it and be
honored," says the LORD. 9"You expected much,
but see, it turned out to be little. What you
brought home, I blew away. Why?" declares the
LORD Almighty. "Because of my house, which
remains a ruin,[n] while each of you is busy with
his own house. 10Therefore, because of you the
heavens have withheld their dew and the earth its
crops.[o] 11I called for a drought[p] on the fields and
the mountains, on the grain, the new wine, the oil
and whatever the ground produces, on men and
cattle, and on the labor of your hands.[q]"

12Then Zerubbabel[r] son of Shealtiel, Joshua son
of Jehozadak, the high priest, and the whole remnant[s] of the people obeyed[t] the voice of the LORD
their God and the message of the prophet Haggai,
because the LORD their God had sent him. And the
people feared[u] the LORD.
13Then Haggai, the LORD's messenger, gave this
message of the LORD to the people: "I am with[v]
you," declares the LORD. 14So the LORD stirred up
the spirit of Zerubbabel[w] son of Shealtiel, governor of Judah, and the spirit of Joshua son of
Jehozadak, the high priest, and the spirit of the
whole remnant[x] of the people. They came and
began to work on the house of the LORD Almighty,
their God, 15on the twenty-fourth day of the sixth
month[y] in the second year of King Darius.

The Promised Glory of the New House

2 On the twenty-first day of the seventh month,
the word of the LORD came through the prophet Haggai: 2"Speak to Zerubbabel son of Shealtiel,
governor of Judah, to Joshua son of Jehozadak,

1:1 [a]Ezr 4:24 [b]Ezr 5:1 [c]Mt 1:12-13 [d]Ezr 5:3 [e]Ezr 2:2 [f]1Ch 6:15; Ezr 3:2
1:3 [g]Ezr 5:1
1:4 [h]2Sa 7:2 [i]ver 9; Jer 33:12
1:5 [j]La 3:40
1:6 [k]Dt 28:38 [l]Hag 2:16; Zec 8:10
1:8 [m]Ps 132:13-14
1:9 [n]ver 4
1:10 [o]Lev 26:19; Dt 28:23
1:11 [p]Dt 28:22; 1Ki 17:1 [q]Hag 2:17
1:12 [r]ver 1 [s]ver 14; Isa 1:9; Hag 2:2 [t]Isa 50:10 [u]Dt 31:12
1:13 [v]Mt 28:20; Ro 8:31
1:14 [w]Ezr 5:2 [x]ver 12
1:15 [y]ver 1

[a] *1* A variant of *Jeshua*; here and elsewhere in Haggai

Misguided Priorities

HAG 1:3–7

Haggai attributes a neglected commitment to the misguided priorities of the people. They had built and enjoyed their homes before building the Lord's temple. The returning exiles started rebuilding the temple as soon as they returned to Jerusalem. But when neighboring nations opposed their efforts, they abandoned the work and instead began to build their own homes, neglecting the house of God. Now, 18 years later, they are suffering the consequences of their misplaced priorities. God's blessing has been withheld from them.

"Give careful thought to your ways," the Lord says to Haggai's contemporaries (Hag 1:5,7). He similarly nudges us to review our priorities. Are they in line with God's?

the high priest, and to the remnant of the people.
Ask them, [3]'Who of you is left who saw this
house[z] in its former glory? How does it look to
you now? Does it not seem to you like nothing?[a]
[4]But now be strong, O Zerubbabel,' declares the
LORD. 'Be strong,[b] O Joshua son of Jehozadak, the
high priest. Be strong, all you people of the land,'
declares the LORD, 'and work. For I am with[c] you,'
declares the LORD Almighty. [5]'This is what I covenanted with you when you came out of Egypt.[d]
And my Spirit[e] remains among you. Do not fear.'
[6]"This is what the LORD Almighty says: 'In a little while[f] I will once more shake the heavens and
the earth,[g] the sea and the dry land. [7]I will shake
all nations, and the desired of all nations will
come, and I will fill this house[h] with glory,' says
the LORD Almighty. [8]'The silver is mine and the
gold is mine,' declares the LORD Almighty. [9]'The
glory[i] of this present house will be greater than
the glory of the former house,' says the LORD
Almighty. 'And in this place I will grant peace,'
declares the LORD Almighty."

Blessings for a Defiled People

[10]On the twenty-fourth day of the ninth month,[j]
in the second year of Darius, the word of the LORD
came to the prophet Haggai: [11]"This is what the
LORD Almighty says: 'Ask the priests[k] what the
law says: [12]If a person carries consecrated meat in
the fold of his garment, and that fold touches
some bread or stew, some wine, oil or other food,
does it become consecrated?'"
The priests answered, "No."
[13]Then Haggai said, "If a person defiled by contact with a dead body touches one of these things,
does it become defiled?"
"Yes," the priests replied, "it becomes defiled.[m]"
[14]Then Haggai said, "'So it is with this people
and this nation in my sight,' declares the LORD.
'Whatever they do and whatever they offer[n] there
is defiled.
[15]"'Now give careful thought[o] to this from this
day on[a]—consider how things were before one
stone was laid[p] on another in the LORD's temple.[q]
[16]When anyone came to a heap of twenty measures, there were only ten. When anyone went to
a wine vat to draw fifty measures, there were only
twenty.[r] [17]I struck all the work of your hands[s]
with blight,[t] mildew and hail, yet you did not turn
to me,' declares the LORD.[u] [18]'From this day on,
from this twenty-fourth day of the ninth month,
give careful thought to the day when the foundation[v] of the LORD's temple was laid. Give careful
thought: [19]Is there yet any seed left in the barn?
Until now, the vine and the fig tree, the pomegranate and the olive tree have not borne fruit.
"'From this day on I will bless you.'"

[a] *15* Or *to the days past*

2:3 [z]Ezr 3:12 [a]Zec 4:10
2:4 [b]1Ch 28:20; Zec 8:9; Eph 6:10 [c]2Sa 5:10; Ac 7:9
2:5 [d]Ex 29:46 [e]Ne 9:20; Isa 63:11
2:6 [f]Isa 10:25 [g]Heb 12:26*
2:7 [h]Isa 60:7
2:9 [i]Ps 85:9
2:10 [j]ver 1
2:11 [k]Lev 10:10-11; Dt 17:8-11; Mal 2:7
2:12 [l]Lev 6:27; Mt 23:19
2:13 [m]Lev 22:4-6
2:14 [n]Isa 1:13
2:15 [o]Hag 1:5 [p]Ezr 3:10 [q]Ezr 4:24
2:16 [r]Hag 1:6
2:17 [s]Hag 1:11 [t]Dt 28:22; 1Ki 8:37; Am 4:9 [u]Am 4:6
2:18 [v]Zec 8:9

A Greater Glory

HAG 2:3–9

A few older people returning from exile remember from childhood the physical splendor of Solomon's great temple (Ezr 3:12): its size, its carvings, its walls covered with gold, its rich tapestries. The new temple will lack the lavish adornments of Solomon's, although amazingly the exiles do bring some of the original temple articles back with them from Babylon (Ezr 1:7–11). However, the ark of the covenant and other important furnishings are now lost. Yet God, Creator and controller of the world's silver and gold, assures his people that the glory of the new temple will be greater than that of the old. Previously the glory of God was limited to a few select, anointed individuals and the Most Holy Place in the temple (1Ki 8:11). But now, through Jesus Christ, God's glory abides in the hearts of his people (1Co 3:16).

Zerubbabel the LORD's Signet Ring

[20]The word of the LORD came to Haggai a second time on the twenty-fourth day of the month:
2:21 [w]Ezr 5:2 [21]"Tell Zerubbabel[w] governor of Judah that I will
shake the heavens and the earth. [22]I will overturn
2:22 royal thrones and shatter the power of the foreign
[x]Da 2:44 kingdoms.[x] I will overthrow chariots[y] and their
[y]Mic 5:10 drivers; horses and their riders will fall, each by
[z]Jdg 7:22 the sword of his brother.[z]

[23]" 'On that day,' declares the LORD Almighty, 'I
2:23 [a]Isa 43:10 will take you, my servant[a] Zerubbabel son of
Shealtiel,' declares the LORD, 'and I will make you
like my signet ring, for I have chosen you,'
declares the LORD Almighty."

God's Signet Ring

HAG 2:23

A descendant of David listed in the New Testament genealogy of Jesus (Mt 1:12–13), Governor Zerubbabel starts to rebuild the Lord's house—what has been called "Zerubbabel's temple." As God's chosen agent on earth, Zerubbabel is called God's "signet ring" (Hag 2:23). The mark made by a signet ring—a personal insignia—was used to establish the authenticity of a document and the authority of the owner of the ring (see the note on Est 3:9–10, 13, page 787). As God's signet ring, Zerubbabel is deemed important—especially in light of the fact that he is part of the lineage of the Messiah—Jesus Christ, who also has God's seal of approval (Jn 6:27).

Similarly, Ephesians 1:13 teaches that the Holy Spirit is the "seal" that marks us as belonging to Christ. In Haggai's time, as well as today, the Lord does not forget his people.

Zechariah

The hope of a future deliverer.

Zechariah, a prophet and a priest, writes this message to motivate the returning exiles to turn to the Lord and finish rebuilding the temple. Though Haggai and Zechariah are contemporaries, Haggai stirs the people to action with his sermons while Zechariah motivates the people by sharing his visions and dreams of the future. Though the people are discouraged, Zechariah's words rouse them to action when they realize that God's glory will only return to Jerusalem if the temple is complete.

Though the book of Zechariah is filled with unusual visions and difficult language, the underlying message of this prophecy is that God has a future plan for his people. Zechariah points out the people's sin and urges them to repent (Zec 1). The vision of Joshua's clean garments reminds Zechariah's readers of the righteousness available to those who turn to God for cleansing (Zec 3). The dreams of a scroll and a basket are a vivid assurance that God is sovereign and will carry out his plan (Zec 5). And Zechariah's prophecies about the Messiah offer hope and encouragement that our King is coming to rescue his people and to reign in power and glory (Zec 6; 9; 11).

Zechariah spoke the right word at the right time to inspire God's people. His words continue to inspire us today as we remember that nothing we do for God is unimportant or meaningless. God is in control of everything, and the future holds no fear when we remain obedient to him.

Quick Study

Author
The prophet-priest Zechariah.

Date Written
520 B.C.

Setting
Judah.

Key Passage
Zechariah 1:3 "Therefore tell the people: This is what the LORD Almighty says: 'Return to me,' declares the LORD Almighty, 'and I will return to you,' says the LORD Almighty."

Outline

Call to repentance.
Zec 1:1-6

A man in the trees.
Zec 1:7-17

Four horns and four horsemen.
Zec 1:18-20

A man with a measuring line.
Zec 2

Clean garments for the high priest.
Zec 3

A lampstand and olive trees.
Zec 4

A flying scroll.
Zec 5:1-4

A woman in a basket.
Zec 5:5-11

Four chariots.
Zec 6:1-8

Crowning Joshua.
Zec 6:9-15

Fasting and the future.
Zec 7-8

The coming and the rejection of the Messiah.
Zec 9:1–11:17

The coming and the redemption of the Messiah.
Zec 12:1–14:21

The Women of Zechariah

Woman in a basket — *Part of an unusual vision.* Zec 5:7

Old women — *A sign of blessing.* Zec 8:4

Girls — *Playing again.* Zec 8:5

Young women — *Refreshed and renewed.* Zec 9:17

Myrtle Trees

ZEC 1:8-11

Three times Zechariah notes that the heavenly messenger stands among myrtle trees. Myrtle is a common but beautiful bush adorned with starry white flowers bursting with many yellow stamens. *Myrtle* comes from the Greek word for "perfume." Myrtle blossoms emit a scent more exquisite than that of a rose. Myrtle's dark berries have medicinal properties. Its shiny leaves add flavor to food, and its branches are used to construct the booths for the Feast of Tabernacles. On barren hillsides, the shrub grows plentifully but is often small. When well-tended, deep-rooted and well-watered, the evergreen can grow to 18 feet in height. Queen Esther's Hebrew name, Hadassah, is from *hadas,* meaning "myrtle."

A Call to Return to the LORD

1 In the eighth month of the second year of Darius,[a] the word of the LORD came to the prophet Zechariah[b] son of Berekiah,[c] the son of Iddo:[d]

2"The LORD was very angry[e] with your forefathers. 3Therefore tell the people: This is what the LORD Almighty says: 'Return to me,' declares the LORD Almighty, 'and I will return to you,'[f] says the LORD Almighty. 4Do not be like your forefathers,[g] to whom the earlier prophets proclaimed: This is what the LORD Almighty says: 'Turn from your evil ways[h] and your evil practices.' But they would not listen or pay attention to me,[i] declares the LORD. 5Where are your forefathers now? And the prophets, do they live forever? 6But did not my words and my decrees, which I commanded my servants the prophets, overtake your forefathers?

"Then they repented and said, 'The LORD Almighty has done to us what our ways and practices deserve,[j] just as he determined to do.'"

The Man Among the Myrtle Trees

7On the twenty-fourth day of the eleventh month, the month of Shebat, in the second year of Darius, the word of the LORD came to the prophet Zechariah son of Berekiah, the son of Iddo.

8During the night I had a vision—and there before me was a man riding a red[k] horse! He was standing among the myrtle trees in a ravine. Behind him were red, brown and white horses.[l]

9I asked, "What are these, my lord?"

The angel[m] who was talking with me answered, "I will show you what they are."

10Then the man standing among the myrtle trees explained, "They are the ones the LORD has sent to go throughout the earth."[n]

11And they reported to the angel of the LORD, who was standing among the myrtle trees, "We have gone throughout the earth and found the whole world at rest and in peace."[o]

12Then the angel of the LORD said, "LORD Almighty, how long will you withhold mercy from Jerusalem and from the towns of Judah, which you have been angry with these seventy[p] years?" 13So the LORD spoke kind and comforting words to the angel who talked with me.[q]

14Then the angel who was speaking to me said, "Proclaim this word: This is what the LORD Almighty says: 'I am very jealous[r] for Jerusalem and Zion, 15but I am very angry with the nations that feel secure.[s] I was only a little angry, but they added to the calamity.'[t]

16"Therefore, this is what the LORD says: 'I will return[u] to Jerusalem with mercy, and there my house will be rebuilt. And the measuring line[v] will be stretched out over Jerusalem,' declares the LORD Almighty.

17"Proclaim further: This is what the LORD Almighty says: 'My towns will again overflow

1:1 [a]Ezr 4:24; 6:15 [b]Ezr 5:1 [c]Mt 23:35; Lk 11:51 [d]ver 7; Ne 12:4
1:2 [e]2Ch 36:16
1:3 [f]Mal 3:7; Jas 4:8
1:4 [g]2Ch 36:15 [h]Ps 106:6 [i]2Ch 24:19; Ps 78:8; Jer 6:17
1:6 [j]Jer 12:14-17; La 2:17
1:8 [k]Rev 6:4 [l]Zec 6:2-7
1:9 [m]Zec 4:1,4-5
1:10 [n]Zec 6:5-8
1:11 [o]Isa 14:7
1:12 [p]Da 9:2
1:13 [q]Zec 4:1
1:14 [r]Joel 2:18; Zec 8:2
1:15 [s]Jer 48:11 [t]Ps 123:3-4; Am 1:11
1:16 [u]Zec 8:3 [v]Zec 2:1-2

1:17 wIsa 51:3 with prosperity, and the LORD will again comfort[w]
xIsa 14:1 yZec 2:12 Zion and choose[x] Jerusalem.' "[y]

Four Horns and Four Craftsmen

[18]Then I looked up—and there before me were
four horns! [19]I asked the angel who was speaking
1:19 to me, "What are these?"
zAm 6:13 He answered me, "These are the horns[z] that
scattered Judah, Israel and Jerusalem."
[20]Then the LORD showed me four craftsmen. [21]I
asked, "What are these coming to do?"
He answered, "These are the horns that scattered Judah so that no one could raise his head,
but the craftsmen have come to terrify them and
throw down these horns of the nations who lifted
1:21 up their horns[a] against the land of Judah to scat-
aPs 75:4 bPs 75:10 ter its people."[b]

A Man With a Measuring Line

2 Then I looked up—and there before me was a
man with a measuring line in his hand! [2]I
2:2 asked, "Where are you going?"
cEze 40:3; He answered me, "To measure Jerusalem, to
Rev 21:15 find out how wide and how long it is."[c]
[3]Then the angel who was speaking to me left,
2:4 and another angel came to meet him [4]and said to
dEze 38:11 him: "Run, tell that young man, 'Jerusalem will
eIsa 49:20; Jer 30:19; be a city without walls[d] because of the great num-
33:22 ber[e] of men and livestock in it. [5]And I myself will
2:5 be a wall[f] of fire around it,' declares the LORD, 'and
fIsa 26:1 gRev 21:23 I will be its glory[g] within.'
[6]"Come! Come! Flee from the land of the north,"
2:6 declares the LORD, "for I have scattered you to the
hEze 17:21 four winds of heaven,"[h] declares the LORD.
2:7 [7]"Come, O Zion! Escape, you who live in the
iIsa 48:20 Daughter of Babylon!"[i] [8]For this is what the LORD
Almighty says: "After he has honored me and has
2:8 sent me against the nations that have plundered
jDt 32:10 you—for whoever touches you touches the apple
2:9 of his eye[j]— [9]I will surely raise my hand against
kIsa 14:2 lZec 4:9 them so that their slaves will plunder them.[ak] Then
you will know that the LORD Almighty has sent me.[l]
2:10 [10]"Shout and be glad, O Daughter of Zion.[m] For
mZep 3:14 nZec 9:9 I am coming,[n] and I will live among you,"[o]
oLev 26:12; declares the LORD. [11]"Many nations will be joined
Zec 8:3 with the LORD in that day and will become my
2:12 people. I will live among you and you will know
pDt 32:9; that the LORD Almighty has sent me to you. [12]The
Ps 33:12; LORD will inherit[p] Judah as his portion in the holy
Jer 10:16 qZec 1:17 land and will again choose[q] Jerusalem. [13]Be still[r]
2:13 before the LORD, all mankind, because he has
rHab 2:20 roused himself from his holy dwelling."

Clean Garments for the High Priest

3 Then he showed me Joshua[bs] the high priest
3:1 sHag 1:1; standing before the angel of the LORD, and
Zec 6:11 tPs 109:6 Satan[ct] standing at his right side to accuse him.

[a] 8,9 Or *says after . . . eye:* [9]*"I . . . plunder them."* [b] 1 A variant of *Jeshua;* here and elsewhere in Zechariah
[c] 1 *Satan* means *accuser.*

Divine Protection

ZEC 2:1-8

With a tape measure in hand, a man on a mission appears, ready to measure the city of God. Where are the walled borders so necessary for defense? Where is the rocky fortress that will protect God's people? An angel says that God himself, as a wall of roaring fire, will surround and protect his people. A tape measure suddenly seems a ridiculously inadequate tool for calculating the size and security of the flamed fortress.

God's people are precious to him. They are the "apple [pupil] of his eye" (Zec 2:8), that body part so carefully protected by nature—by a deep eye socket and eyebrows and lids and lashes—and by instinct, as we hurl an arm to our face if threatened. God is as protective of his people as we are of our eyes. His love and protection are an intrinsic part of his very being.

Small Things

ZEC 4:6–10

It seems that Governor Zerubbabel, a descendant of King David, faces "mountainous" obstacles in rebuilding the temple. Perhaps those obstacles are the neighboring nations who oppose the rebuilding or the reluctant exiles themselves. Zerubbabel is a political leader, bringing back to Jerusalem a beleaguered group of exiled Jews, setting up a city, laying the foundation of the new temple. The Lord tells him that any victories he experiences will come by the Spirit of God, not by human might or muscle. And yet Zerubbabel's hard, persistent work to reestablish the kingdom isn't discounted, nor is ours. In our daily tasks of faithfulness, we serve a Lord who does not despise "small things" (Zec 4:10).

2The LORD said to Satan, "The LORD rebuke you,[u] Satan! The LORD, who has chosen[v] Jerusalem, rebuke you! Is not this man a burning stick snatched from the fire?"[w]

3Now Joshua was dressed in filthy clothes as he stood before the angel. 4The angel said to those who were standing before him, "Take off his filthy clothes."

Then he said to Joshua, "See, I have taken away your sin,[x] and I will put rich garments[y] on you."

5Then I said, "Put a clean turban[z] on his head." So they put a clean turban on his head and clothed him, while the angel of the LORD stood by.

6The angel of the LORD gave this charge to Joshua: 7"This is what the LORD Almighty says: 'If you will walk in my ways and keep my requirements, then you will govern my house[a] and have charge of my courts, and I will give you a place among these standing here.

8" 'Listen, O high priest Joshua and your associates seated before you, who are men symbolic[b] of things to come: I am going to bring my servant, the Branch.[c] 9See, the stone I have set in front of Joshua! There are seven eyes[a] on that one stone,[d] and I will engrave an inscription on it,' says the LORD Almighty, 'and I will remove the sin[e] of this land in a single day.

10" 'In that day each of you will invite his neighbor to sit under his vine and fig tree,[f]' declares the LORD Almighty."

The Gold Lampstand and the Two Olive Trees

4 Then the angel who talked with me returned and wakened[g] me, as a man is wakened from his sleep.[h] 2He asked me, "What do you see?"[i]

I answered, "I see a solid gold lampstand[j] with a bowl at the top and seven lights[k] on it, with seven channels to the lights. 3Also there are two olive trees[l] by it, one on the right of the bowl and the other on its left."

4I asked the angel who talked with me, "What are these, my lord?"

5He answered, "Do you not know what these are?"

"No, my lord," I replied.[m]

6So he said to me, "This is the word of the LORD to Zerubbabel:[n] 'Not by might nor by power, but by my Spirit,'[o] says the LORD Almighty.

7"What[b] are you, O mighty mountain? Before Zerubbabel you will become level ground.[p] Then he will bring out the capstone[q] to shouts of 'God bless it! God bless it!' "

8Then the word of the LORD came to me: 9"The hands of Zerubbabel have laid the foundation[r] of this temple; his hands will also complete it.[s] Then you will know that the LORD Almighty has sent me[t] to you.

10"Who despises the day of small things?[u] Men

3:2 [u]Jude 1:9 [v]Isa 14:1 [w]Am 4:11; Jude 1:23
3:4 [x]Eze 36:25; Mic 7:18 [y]Isa 52:1; Rev 19:8
3:5 [z]Ex 29:6
3:7 [a]Dt 17:8-11; Eze 44:15-16
3:8 [b]Eze 12:11 [c]Isa 4:2
3:9 [d]Isa 28:16 [e]Jer 50:20
3:10 [f]1Ki 4:25; Mic 4:4
4:1 [g]Da 8:18 [h]Jer 31:26
4:2 [i]Jer 1:13 [j]Ex 25:31; Rev 1:12 [k]Rev 4:5
4:3 [l]ver 11; Rev 11:4
4:5 [m]Zec 1:9
4:6 [n]Ezr 5:2 [o]Isa 11:2-4; Hos 1:7
4:7 [p]Jer 51:25 [q]Ps 118:22
4:9 [r]Ezr 3:11 [s]Ezr 3:8; 6:15; Zec 6:12 [t]Zec 2:9
4:10 [u]Hag 2:3

[a] 9 Or *facets* [b] 7 Or *Who*

will rejoice when they see the plumb line in the
4:10 hand of Zerubbabel.
[v]Zec 3:9; “(These seven are the eyes[v] of the LORD, which
Rev 5:6 range throughout the earth.)”
11 Then I asked the angel, “What are these two
4:11 [w]ver 3; olive trees[w] on the right and the left of the
Rev 11:4 lampstand?”
12 Again I asked him, “What are these two olive
branches beside the two gold pipes that pour out
golden oil?”
13 He replied, “Do you not know what these
are?”
“No, my lord,” I said.
14 So he said, “These are the two who are anoint-
4:14 [x]Ex 29:7; ed[x] to[a] serve the Lord of all the earth.”
40:15;
Da 9:24-26; *The Flying Scroll*
Zec 3:1-7
5:1 **5** I looked again—and there before me was a fly-
[y]Eze 2:9; ing scroll![y]
Rev 5:1 2 He asked me, “What do you see?”
I answered, “I see a flying scroll, thirty feet long
and fifteen feet wide.[b]”
5:3 3 And he said to me, “This is the curse[z] that is
[z]Isa 24:6; going out over the whole land; for according to
43:28;
Mal 3:9; 4:6 what it says on one side, every thief[a] will be ban-
[a]Ex 20:15; ished, and according to what it says on the other,
Mal 3:8
[b]Isa 48:1 everyone who swears falsely[b] will be banished.
4 The LORD Almighty declares, ‘I will send it out,
and it will enter the house of the thief and the
house of him who swears falsely by my name. It
will remain in his house and destroy it, both its
5:4 [c]Lev 14:34-45; Hab 2:9- timbers and its stones.[c]’ ”
11; Mal 3:5 *The Woman in a Basket*

5 Then the angel who was speaking to me came
forward and said to me, “Look up and see what
this is that is appearing.”
6 I asked, “What is it?”
He replied, “It is a measuring basket.[c]” And he
added, “This is the iniquity[d] of the people
throughout the land.”
7 Then the cover of lead was raised, and there in
the basket sat a woman! 8 He said, “This is wicked-
5:8 ness,” and he pushed her back into the basket and
[d]Mic 6:11 pushed the lead cover down over its mouth.[d]
9 Then I looked up—and there before me were
5:9 two women, with the wind in their wings! They
[e]Lev 11:19 had wings like those of a stork,[e] and they lifted
up the basket between heaven and earth.
10 “Where are they taking the basket?” I asked
5:11 the angel who was speaking to me.
[f]Ge 10:10 11 He replied, “To the country of Babylonia[e][f] to
[g]Jer 29:5,28 build a house[g] for it. When it is ready, the basket
[h]Da 1:2 will be set there in its place.”[h]

[a] 14 Or *two who bring oil and* [b] 2 Hebrew *twenty cubits long and ten cubits wide* (about 9 meters long and 4.5 meters wide) [c] 6 Hebrew *an ephah*; also in verses 7–11 [d] 6 Or *appearance* [e] 11 Hebrew *Shinar*

Two Visions

ZEC 5:1-11

Zechariah sees two visions, one of a flying scroll, the other of a woman in a basket. These two visions show the Lord purifying the land before the establishment of his kingdom. Evil is removed by spiritual means, without direct human intervention. Those who disobey God's laws are cursed or punished and then destroyed. Wickedness itself is borne away on the wind. God's holy land is being cleansed of evil, prepared for his righteousness.

Both Priest and King

ZEC 6:9–15

Here a crown is molded for, and worn by, Joshua, the high priest in Zechariah's day. There is no precedent for crowning a high priest as king. Levitical priests and Davidic kings were from two separate family lines, from two different tribes. This scene foreshadows the Messiah, "the Branch" (Zec 6:12), who will be both our priest and our king as Joshua's name, Yeshua, is the same word we use for Jesus.

Four Chariots

6 I looked up again—and there before me were
four chariots[i] coming out from between two
mountains—mountains of bronze! [2]The first chariot had red horses, the second black,[j] [3]the third
white,[k] and the fourth dappled—all of them powerful. [4]I asked the angel who was speaking to me,
"What are these, my lord?"
[5]The angel answered me, "These are the four
spirits[a][l] of heaven, going out from standing in the
presence of the Lord of the whole world. [6]The one
with the black horses is going toward the north
country, the one with the white horses toward the
west,[b] and the one with the dappled horses
toward the south."
[7]When the powerful horses went out, they were
straining to go throughout the earth.[m] And he
said, "Go throughout the earth!" So they went
throughout the earth.
[8]Then he called to me, "Look, those going
toward the north country have given my Spirit[c]
rest[n] in the land of the north."

A Crown for Joshua

[9]The word of the LORD came to me: [10]"Take ⌊sil-
ver and gold⌋ from the exiles Heldai, Tobijah and
Jedaiah, who have arrived from Babylon.[o] Go the
same day to the house of Josiah son of Zephaniah.
[11]Take the silver and gold and make a crown,[p] and
set it on the head of the high priest, Joshua[q] son of
Jehozadak.[r] [12]Tell him this is what the LORD
Almighty says: 'Here is the man whose name is
the Branch,[s] and he will branch out from his place
and build the temple of the LORD.[t] [13]It is he who
will build the temple of the LORD, and he will be
clothed with majesty and will sit and rule on his
throne. And he will be a priest[u] on his throne.
And there will be harmony between the two.'
[14]The crown will be given to Heldai,[d] Tobijah,
Jedaiah and Hen[e] son of Zephaniah as a memorial in the temple of the LORD. [15]Those who are far
away will come and help to build the temple of
the LORD,[v] and you will know that the LORD
Almighty has sent me to you.[w] This will happen if
you diligently obey[x] the LORD your God."

Justice and Mercy, Not Fasting

7 In the fourth year of King Darius, the word of
the LORD came to Zechariah on the fourth day
of the ninth month, the month of Kislev.[y] [2]The
people of Bethel had sent Sharezer and Regem-
Melech, together with their men, to entreat[z] the
LORD [3]by asking the priests of the house of the
LORD Almighty and the prophets, "Should I
mourn[a] and fast in the fifth[b] month, as I have
done for so many years?"
[4]Then the word of the LORD Almighty came to
me: [5]"Ask all the people of the land and the

6:1 [i]ver 5
6:2 [j]Rev 6:5
6:3 [k]Rev 6:2
6:5 [l]Eze 37:9; Mt 24:31; Rev 7:1
6:7 [m]Zec 1:10
6:8 [n]Eze 5:13; 24:13
6:10 [o]Ezr 7:14-16; Jer 28:6
6:11 [p]Ps 21:3 [q]Zec 3:1 [r]Ezr 3:2
6:12 [s]Isa 4:2; Zec 3:8 [t]Ezr 3:8-10; Zec 4:6-9
6:13 [u]Ps 110:4
6:15 [v]Isa 60:10 [w]Zec 2:9-11 [x]Isa 58:12; Jer 7:23; Zec 3:7
7:1 [y]Ne 1:1
7:2 [z]Jer 26:19; Zec 8:21
7:3 [a]Zec 12:12-14 [b]Jer 52:12-14; Zec 8:19

[a] 5 Or *winds* [b] 6 Or *horses after them* [c] 8 Or *spirit*
[d] 14 Syriac; Hebrew *Helem* [e] 14 Or *and the gracious one, the*

priests, 'When you fasted[c] and mourned in the fifth and seventh months for the past seventy years, was it really for me that you fasted? 6And when you were eating and drinking, were you not just feasting for yourselves? 7Are these not the words the LORD proclaimed through the earlier prophets[d] when Jerusalem and its surrounding towns were at rest[e] and prosperous, and the Negev and the western foothills[f] were settled?' "

8And the word of the LORD came again to Zechariah: 9"This is what the LORD Almighty says: 'Administer true justice;[g] show mercy and compassion to one another. 10Do not oppress the widow or the fatherless, the alien[h] or the poor. In your hearts do not think evil of each other.'[i]

11"But they refused to pay attention; stubbornly they turned their backs and stopped up their ears.[j] 12They made their hearts as hard as flint[k] and would not listen to the law or to the words that the LORD Almighty had sent by his Spirit through the earlier prophets.[l] So the LORD Almighty was very angry.[m]

13" 'When I called, they did not listen;[n] so when they called, I would not listen,'[o] says the LORD Almighty.[p] 14'I scattered[q] them with a whirlwind[r] among all the nations, where they were strangers. The land was left so desolate behind them that no one could come or go. This is how they made the pleasant land desolate.[s]' "

The LORD Promises to Bless Jerusalem

8 Again the word of the LORD Almighty came to me. 2This is what the LORD Almighty says: "I am very jealous for Zion; I am burning with jealousy for her."

3This is what the LORD says: "I will return[t] to Zion and dwell in Jerusalem.[u] Then Jerusalem will be called the City of Truth, and the mountain of the LORD Almighty will be called the Holy Mountain."

4This is what the LORD Almighty says: "Once again men and women of ripe old age will sit in the streets of Jerusalem,[v] each with cane in hand because of his age. 5The city streets will be filled with boys and girls playing there.[w]"

6This is what the LORD Almighty says: "It may seem marvelous to the remnant of this people at that time,[x] but will it seem marvelous to me?[y]" declares the LORD Almighty.

7This is what the LORD Almighty says: "I will save my people from the countries of the east and the west.[z] 8I will bring them back[a] to live in Jerusalem; they will be my people,[b] and I will be faithful and righteous to them as their God."

9This is what the LORD Almighty says: "You who now hear these words spoken by the prophets[c] who were there when the foundation was laid for the house of the LORD Almighty, let your hands be strong[d] so that the temple may be built. 10Before that time there were no wages[e] for man or beast. No one could go about his business safely because

7:5 [c]Isa 58:5
7:7 [d]Zec 1:4 [e]Jer 22:21 [f]Jer 17:26
7:9 [g]Zec 8:16
7:10 [h]Ex 22:21 [i]Ex 22:22; Isa 1:17
7:11 [j]Jer 8:5; 11:10; 17:23
7:12 [k]Jer 17:1; Eze 11:19 [l]Ne 9:29 [m]Da 9:12
7:13 [n]Pr 1:24 [o]Isa 1:15; Jer 11:11; 14:12; Mic 3:4 [p]Pr 1:28
7:14 [q]Dt 4:27; 28:64-67 [r]Jer 23:19 [s]Jer 44:6
8:3 [t]Zec 1:16 [u]Zec 2:10
8:4 [v]Isa 65:20
8:5 [w]Jer 30:20; 31:13
8:6 [x]Ps 118:23; 126:1-3 [y]Jer 32:17, 27
8:7 [z]Ps 107:3; Isa 11:11; 43:5
8:8 [a]Zec 10:10 [b]Eze 11:19-20; 36:28; Zec 2:11
8:9 [c]Ezr 5:1 [d]Hag 2:4
8:10 [e]Hag 1:6

Citizens of All Ages

ZEC 8:4–5

A God-blessed city will respect and give protection and comfort to its most vulnerable citizens. The old, leaning on canes, will sit safely on curbside benches. The young will play, happy and carefree, on sidewalks and in parks. They will be protected and provided for—neither begging nor laboring for their upkeep. The scene is one of tranquillity and prosperity. The complete fulfillment of this prophecy awaits the second coming of Christ. However, we can glimpse a bit of this future promise as we work together to live out the commands recorded in Zechariah 7:9–10. How can we show mercy to someone of "ripe old age" (Zec 8:4) or to a child?

of his enemy, for I had turned every man against
his neighbor. 11 But now I will not deal with the
remnant of this people as I did in the past,"[f]
declares the LORD Almighty.

12 "The seed will grow well, the vine will yield
its fruit,[g] the ground will produce its crops,[h] and
the heavens will drop their dew.[i] I will give all
these things as an inheritance[j] to the remnant of
this people. 13 As you have been an object of cursing[k] among the nations, O Judah and Israel, so
will I save you, and you will be a blessing.[l] Do not
be afraid, but let your hands be strong."

14 This is what the LORD Almighty says: "Just as
I had determined to bring disaster[m] upon you and
showed no pity when your fathers angered me,"
says the LORD Almighty, 15 "so now I have determined to do good[n] again to Jerusalem and Judah.
Do not be afraid. 16 These are the things you are to
do: Speak the truth[o] to each other, and render true
and sound judgment in your courts;[p] 17 do not plot
evil[q] against your neighbor, and do not love to
swear falsely.[r] I hate all this," declares the LORD.

18 Again the word of the LORD Almighty came to
me. 19 This is what the LORD Almighty says: "The
fasts of the fourth,[s] fifth,[t] seventh[u] and tenth[v]
months will become joyful[w] and glad occasions
and happy festivals for Judah. Therefore love
truth[x] and peace."

20 This is what the LORD Almighty says: "Many
peoples and the inhabitants of many cities will yet
come, 21 and the inhabitants of one city will go to
another and say, 'Let us go at once to entreat[y] the
LORD and seek the LORD Almighty. I myself am
going.' 22 And many peoples and powerful nations
will come to Jerusalem to seek the LORD Almighty
and to entreat him."[z]

23 This is what the LORD Almighty says: "In those
days ten men from all languages and nations will
take firm hold of one Jew by the hem of his robe
and say, 'Let us go with you, because we have
heard that God is with you.' "[a]

Judgment on Israel's Enemies

An Oracle

9 The word of the LORD is against the land
of Hadrach
and will rest upon Damascus[b]—
for the eyes of men and all the tribes of
Israel
are on the LORD—[a]
2 and upon Hamath[c] too, which borders
on it,
and upon Tyre[d] and Sidon, though
they are very skillful.
3 Tyre has built herself a stronghold;
she has heaped up silver like dust,
and gold like the dirt of the streets.[e]

[a] 1 Or *Damascus. / For the eye of the LORD is on all mankind, / as well as on the tribes of Israel,*

8:11 [f]Isa 12:1
8:12 [g]Joel 2:22 [h]Ps 67:6 [i]Ge 27:28 [j]Ob 1:17
8:13 [k]Jer 42:18 [l]Ge 12:2
8:14 [m]Jer 31:28; Eze 24:14
8:15 [n]ver 13; Jer 29:11; Mic 7:18-20
8:16 [o]Ps 15:2; Eph 4:25 [p]Zec 7:9
8:17 [q]Pr 3:29 [r]Pr 6:16-19
8:19 [s]Jer 39:2 [t]Jer 52:12 [u]2Ki 25:25 [v]Jer 52:4 [w]Ps 30:11 [x]ver 16
8:21 [y]Zec 7:2
8:22 [z]Ps 117:1; Isa 60:3; Zec 2:11
8:23 [a]Isa 45:14; 1Co 14:25
9:1 [b]Isa 17:1
9:2 [c]Jer 49:23 [d]Eze 28:1-19
9:3 [e]Job 27:16; Eze 28:4

I thank the goodness and the grace
Which on my birth have smiled,
And made me, in these Christian days,
A happy Christian child.

—Jane Taylor (1783–1824)

4 But the Lord will take away her
possessions
and destroy her power on the sea,
9:4
[f]Isa 23:1; Eze 26:3-5; 28:18
and she will be consumed by fire.[f]
5 Ashkelon will see it and fear;
Gaza will writhe in agony,
and Ekron too, for her hope will
wither.
Gaza will lose her king
and Ashkelon will be deserted.
6 Foreigners will occupy Ashdod,
and I will cut off the pride of the
Philistines.
7 I will take the blood from their mouths,
the forbidden food from between their
teeth.
Those who are left will belong to our
God
and become leaders in Judah,
and Ekron will be like the Jebusites.
8 But I will defend my house
against marauding forces.
Never again will an oppressor overrun
my people,
9:8
[g]Isa 52:1; 54:14
for now I am keeping watch.[g]

The Coming of Zion's King

9 Rejoice greatly, O Daughter of Zion!
Shout, Daughter of Jerusalem!
9:9
[h]Isa 9:6-7; 43:3-11; Jer 23:5-6; Zep 3:14-15; Zec 2:10
[i]Mt 21:5*; Jn 12:15*
See, your king[a] comes to you,
righteous and having salvation,[h]
gentle and riding on a donkey,
on a colt, the foal of a donkey.[i]
10 I will take away the chariots from
Ephraim
9:10
[j]Hos 1:7; 2:18; Mic 4:3; 5:10; Zec 10:4
[k]Ps 72:8
and the war-horses from Jerusalem,
and the battle bow will be broken.[j]
He will proclaim peace to the nations.
His rule will extend from sea to sea
and from the River[b] to the ends of the
earth.[ck]
9:11
[l]Ex 24:8
[m]Isa 42:7
11 As for you, because of the blood of my
covenant[l] with you,
I will free your prisoners[m] from the
waterless pit.
9:12
[n]Joel 3:16
12 Return to your fortress,[n] O prisoners of
hope;
even now I announce that I will
restore twice as much to you.
13 I will bend Judah as I bend my bow
9:13
[o]Isa 49:2
[p]Joel 3:6
[q]Jer 51:20
and fill it with Ephraim.[o]
I will rouse your sons, O Zion,
against your sons, O Greece,[p]
and make you like a warrior's sword.[q]

The Lord Will Appear

9:14
[r]Isa 31:5
[s]Ps 18:14; Hab 3:11
14 Then the Lord will appear over them;[r]
his arrow will flash like lightning.[s]

[a] *9* Or *King* [b] *10* That is, the Euphrates [c] *10* Or *the end of the land*

Prisoners of Hope

ZEC 9:11-12

The Holy Land is spotted with cisterns to save rainy-season water for use in dry months (see the note on Jer 14:3, page 1252). They are generally lined with stone (or hewn out of solid rock), sealed with plaster and covered. Many have stairs winding down to the bottom for water retrieval. Occasionally a dry or muddy cistern confines a prisoner. Joseph was held captive by his brothers in a cistern (Ge 37:24), and Jeremiah was held prisoner in a muddy cistern (Jer 38:6). The Lord promises his people deliverance from such prisons. As "prisoners of hope" (Zec 9:12), they are to return to God, their true and eternal fortress. God calls his people to be hopeful, confident of their sovereign's final victory. He even now draws us out of the cistern prisons that confine us—emotionally, spiritually, physically, materially—and calls us instead to be "prisoners of hope."

The Messiah

ZEC 10:3–7

The Lord will punish the shepherds who have oppressed his flock. He will care for his flock himself, and from the tribe of Judah he will raise up the Messiah. The Messiah is here presented in several key images: the cornerstone that provides the foundational stone for a structure, the peg that secures a tent, the bow that hurls an arrow, the King of kings.

God promises to be with Judah and make them mighty and strong. As a compassionate God, he promises to reunite the southern kingdom (synonymous with Judah—Zec 10:6) and the northern kingdom (synonymous with Ephraim—Zec 10:7).

The Sovereign LORD will sound the
trumpet;
he will march in the storms[t] of the
south,
15 and the LORD Almighty will shield[u]
them.
They will destroy
and overcome with slingstones.
They will drink and roar as with wine;
they will be full like a bowl
used for sprinkling[a] the corners[v] of
the altar.
16 The LORD their God will save them on
that day
as the flock of his people.
They will sparkle in his land
like jewels in a crown.[w]
17 How attractive and beautiful they will
be!
Grain will make the young men
thrive,
and new wine the young women.

The LORD Will Care for Judah

10 Ask the LORD for rain in the springtime;
it is the LORD who makes the storm clouds.
He gives showers of rain to men,
and plants of the field to everyone.
2 The idols[x] speak deceit,
diviners see visions that lie;
they tell dreams that are false,
they give comfort in vain.
Therefore the people wander like sheep
oppressed for lack of a shepherd.[y]

3 "My anger burns against the shepherds,
and I will punish the leaders;[z]
for the LORD Almighty will care
for his flock, the house of Judah,
and make them like a proud horse in
battle.
4 From Judah will come the cornerstone,
from him the tent peg,[a]
from him the battle bow,[b]
from him every ruler.
5 Together they[b] will be like mighty men
trampling the muddy streets in battle.[c]
Because the LORD is with them,
they will fight and overthrow the
horsemen.[d]

6 "I will strengthen the house of Judah
and save the house of Joseph.
I will restore them
because I have compassion on them.[e]
They will be as though
I had not rejected them,
for I am the LORD their God
and I will answer[f] them.

9:14 [t]Isa 21:1; 66:15
9:15 [u]Isa 37:35; Zec 12:8 [v]Ex 27:2
9:16 [w]Isa 62:3; Jer 31:11
10:2 [x]Eze 21:21 [y]Eze 34:5; Hos 3:4; Mt 9:36
10:3 [z]Jer 25:34
10:4 [a]Isa 22:23 [b]Zec 9:10
10:5 [c]2Sa 22:43 [d]Am 2:15; Hag 2:22
10:6 [e]Zec 8:7-8 [f]Zec 13:9

[a] 15 Or *bowl, / like* [b] 4,5 Or *ruler, all of them together. / 5They*

7 The Ephraimites will become like
mighty men,
10:7 [g]Zec 9:15 — and their hearts will be glad as with
wine.[g]
Their children will see it and be joyful;
their hearts will rejoice in the LORD.
10:8 [h]Isa 5:26 — 8 I will signal[h] for them
[i]Jer 33:22; Eze 36:11 — and gather them in.
Surely I will redeem them;
they will be as numerous[i] as before.
9 Though I scatter them among the
peoples,
10:9 [j]Eze 6:9 — yet in distant lands they will
remember me.[j]
They and their children will survive,
and they will return.
10 I will bring them back from Egypt
10:10 [k]Isa 11:11 — and gather them from Assyria.[k]
[l]Jer 50:19 — I will bring them to Gilead[l] and
[m]Isa 49:19 — Lebanon,
and there will not be room[m] enough
for them.
11 They will pass through the sea of
trouble;
the surging sea will be subdued
10:11 [n]Isa 19:5-7; 51:10 — and all the depths of the Nile will dry
up.[n]
[o]Zep 2:13 — Assyria's pride[o] will be brought down
[p]Eze 30:13 — and Egypt's scepter[p] will pass away.
10:12 [q]Mic 4:5 — 12 I will strengthen them in the LORD
and in his name they will walk,[q]"
declares the LORD.

11:1 [r]Eze 31:3 — **11** Open your doors, O Lebanon,[r]
so that fire may devour your cedars!
2 Wail, O pine tree, for the cedar has
fallen;
the stately trees are ruined!
11:2 [s]Isa 32:19 — Wail, oaks of Bashan;
the dense forest[s] has been cut down!
3 Listen to the wail of the shepherds;
their rich pastures are destroyed!
Listen to the roar of the lions;
11:3 [t]Jer 2:15; 50:44 — the lush thicket of the Jordan is
ruined![t]

Two Shepherds

4 This is what the LORD my God says: "Pasture
the flock marked for slaughter. 5 Their buyers
slaughter them and go unpunished. Those who
11:5 [u]Jer 50:7; Eze 34:2-3 — sell them say, 'Praise the LORD, I am rich!' Their
own shepherds do not spare them.[u] 6 For I will no
longer have pity on the people of the land,"
declares the LORD. "I will hand everyone over to
11:6 [v]Zec 14:13 [w]Isa 9:19-21; Jer 13:14; Mic 5:8; 7:2-6 — his neighbor[v] and his king. They will oppress the
land, and I will not rescue them from their
hands."[w]
7 So I pastured the flock marked for slaughter,
particularly the oppressed of the flock. Then I
took two staffs and called one Favor and the oth-

I love the fact that God is a God who encourages relationship not just with himself, but with each other. Jesus modeled that for us in the richness of his relationships with the twelve disciples. We are indeed rich when we have many friends, and I'm thoroughly convinced that God loves us, encourages, us, nurtures us and supports us through other human beings. They can almost become to us Jesus with skin.

May we not become so busy, harried and overcommitted that we neglect that part of our soul that is fed and sustained by friendship.

—Marilyn Meberg

er Union, and I pastured the flock. [8]In one month
I got rid of the three shepherds.
The flock detested me, and I grew weary of
them [9]and said, "I will not be your shepherd. Let
the dying die, and the perishing perish.[x] Let those
who are left eat one another's flesh."
[10]Then I took my staff called Favor[y] and broke
it, revoking[z] the covenant I had made with all the
nations. [11]It was revoked on that day, and so the
afflicted of the flock who were watching me knew
it was the word of the LORD.
[12]I told them, "If you think it best, give me my
pay; but if not, keep it." So they paid me thirty
pieces of silver.[a]
[13]And the LORD said to me, "Throw it to the potter"—the handsome price at which they priced
me! So I took the thirty pieces of silver and threw
them into the house of the LORD to the potter.[b]
[14]Then I broke my second staff called Union,
breaking the brotherhood between Judah and
Israel.
[15]Then the LORD said to me, "Take again the
equipment of a foolish shepherd. [16]For I am going
to raise up a shepherd over the land who will not
care for the lost, or seek the young, or heal the
injured, or feed the healthy, but will eat the meat
of the choice sheep, tearing off their hoofs.

[17]"Woe to the worthless shepherd,[c]
who deserts the flock!
May the sword strike his arm[d] and his
right eye!
May his arm be completely withered,
his right eye totally blinded!"[e]

Jerusalem's Enemies to Be Destroyed

An Oracle

12 This is the word of the LORD concerning
Israel. The LORD, who stretches out the
heavens,[f] who lays the foundation of the earth,[g]
and who forms the spirit of man[h] within him,
declares: [2]"I am going to make Jerusalem a cup[i]
that sends all the surrounding peoples reeling.[j]
Judah[k] will be besieged as well as Jerusalem. [3]On
that day, when all the nations[l] of the earth are
gathered against her, I will make Jerusalem an
immovable rock[m] for all the nations. All who try
to move it will injure[n] themselves. [4]On that day I
will strike every horse with panic and its rider
with madness," declares the LORD. "I will keep a
watchful eye over the house of Judah, but I will
blind all the horses of the nations.[o] [5]Then the
leaders of Judah will say in their hearts, 'The people of Jerusalem are strong, because the LORD
Almighty is their God.'
[6]"On that day I will make the leaders of Judah
like a firepot[p] in a woodpile, like a flaming torch
among sheaves. They will consume[q] right and left
all the surrounding peoples, but Jerusalem will
remain intact in her place.
[7]"The LORD will save the dwellings of Judah

Thirty Pieces of Silver

ZEC 11:12-13

Exodus 21:32 records 30 pieces of silver as the price for a slave. The shepherd in these verses sarcastically calls the payment a "handsome price" (Zec 11:13). The amount paid is certainly not commesurate with the work accomplished. This price is the same amount Judas receives to betray Jesus (Mt 26:14-15). Matthew repeats these words, crediting them to Jeremiah (Mt 27:9-10). Zechariah says the coins are to be thrown to the potter (Zec 11:13), possibly foreshadowing the potter's field the chief priests of the temple buy with Judas's discarded money (Mt 27:6-7).

11:9 [x]Jer 15:2; 43:11
11:10 [y]ver 7 [z]Ps 89:39; Jer 14:21
11:12 [a]Ex 21:32; Mt 26:15
11:13 [b]Mt 27:9-10*; Ac 1:18-19
11:17 [c]Jer 23:1 [d]Eze 30:21-22 [e]Jer 23:1
12:1 [f]Isa 42:5; Jer 51:15 [g]Ps 102:25; Heb 1:10 [h]Isa 57:16
12:2 [i]Ps 75:8 [j]Isa 51:23 [k]Zec 14:14
12:3 [l]Zec 14:2 [m]Da 2:34-35 [n]Mt 21:44
12:4 [o]Ps 76:6
12:6 [p]Isa 10:17-18; Zec 11:1 [q]Ob 1:18

first, so that the honor of the house of David and
12:7 [r]Jer 30:18; Am 9:11 of Jerusalem's inhabitants may not be greater
than that of Judah.[r] 8 On that day the LORD will
shield[s] those who live in Jerusalem, so that the
12:8 [s]Joel 3:16; Zec 9:15 [t]Ps 82:6 [u]Mic 7:8 feeblest among them will be like David, and the
house of David will be like God,[t] like the Angel of
the LORD going before[u] them. 9 On that day I will
set out to destroy all the nations that attack
12:9 [v]Zec 14:2-3 Jerusalem.[v]

Mourning for the One They Pierced

10 "And I will pour out on the house of David and
12:10 [w]Isa 44:3; Eze 39:29; Joel 2:28-29 [x]Jn 19:34, 37*; Rev 1:7 the inhabitants of Jerusalem a spirit[a] of grace and
supplication.[w] They will look on[b] me, the one they
have pierced,[x] and they will mourn for him as one
mourns for an only child, and grieve bitterly for
him as one grieves for a firstborn son. 11 On that
day the weeping in Jerusalem will be great, like
the weeping of Hadad Rimmon in the plain of
12:11 [y]2Ki 23:29 Megiddo.[y] 12 The land will mourn,[z] each clan by
itself, with their wives by themselves: the clan of
12:12 [z]Mt 24:30; Rev 1:7 the house of David and their wives, the clan of the
house of Nathan and their wives, 13 the clan of the
house of Levi and their wives, the clan of Shimei
and their wives, 14 and all the rest of the clans and
their wives.

Cleansing From Sin

13:1 [a]Jer 17:13 [b]Ps 51:2; Heb 9:14 **13** "On that day a fountain[a] will be opened to
the house of David and the inhabitants of
Jerusalem, to cleanse[b] them from sin and impurity.
13:2 [c]Ex 23:13; Eze 36:25; Hos 2:17 [d]1Ki 22:22; Jer 23:14-15 2 "On that day, I will banish the names of the
idols[c] from the land, and they will be remembered
no more," declares the LORD Almighty. "I will
remove both the prophets[d] and the spirit of impurity from the land. 3 And if anyone still prophesies,
his father and mother, to whom he was born, will
say to him, 'You must die, because you have told
lies in the LORD's name.' When he prophesies, his
13:3 [e]Dt 13:6-11; 18:20; Jer 23:34; Eze 14:9 own parents will stab him.[e]
4 "On that day every prophet will be ashamed[f]
of his prophetic vision. He will not put on a
prophet's garment[g] of hair[h] in order to deceive.
13:4 [f]Jer 6:15; Mic 3:6-7 [g]Mt 3:4 [h]2Ki 1:8; Isa 20:2 5 He will say, 'I am not a prophet. I am a farmer;
the land has been my livelihood since my youth.[c]'[i]
6 If someone asks him, 'What are these wounds on
your body[d]?' he will answer, 'The wounds I was
13:5 [i]Am 7:14 given at the house of my friends.'

The Shepherd Struck, the Sheep Scattered

13:7 [j]Jer 47:6 [k]Isa 40:11; 53:4; Eze 37:24 [l]Mt 26:31*; Mk 14:27* 7 "Awake, O sword,[j] against my
shepherd,[k]
against the man who is close to me!"
declares the LORD Almighty.
"Strike the shepherd,
and the sheep will be scattered,[l]

[a] 10 Or *the Spirit* [b] 10 Or *to* [c] 5 Or *farmer; a man sold me in my youth* [d] 6 Or *wounds between your hands*

Pierced

ZEC 12:10-14

God's people will mourn "the one they have pierced" (Zec 12:10) with the intensity of a parent grieving over the death of an only child or a firstborn son—the child of special hope and blessing. Zechariah notes that each clan will grieve separately, and he lists the women apart from the men, perhaps to represent personal heartfelt grief rather than crowd-contagious hysteria. These verses depict the depth of grief that accompanies the realization of the significance of Jesus Christ's atoning death—pierced by our own sins.

That Great Day

ZEC 14:6-9

On this unique future day, the patterns of nature will be interrupted. Water—meaning either literal H_2O or spiritual refreshment—will flow from Jerusalem, half to the "eastern sea" (Zec 14:8), the Dead Sea, and the other half to the "western sea" (Zec 14:8), the Mediterranean Sea. On this day the Lord will reign as king over all the earth, and the foundational prayer of the Jewish people will prevail: "The LORD *our God, the* LORD *is one" (Dt 6:4).*

and I will turn my hand against the
little ones.
8 In the whole land," declares the LORD,
"two-thirds will be struck down and
perish;
yet one-third will be left in it.[m]
9 This third I will bring into the fire;[n]
I will refine them like silver[o]
and test them like gold.
They will call[p] on my name
and I will answer[q] them;
I will say, 'They are my people,'[r]
and they will say, 'The LORD is our
God.[s]' "

The LORD Comes and Reigns

14 A day of the LORD[t] is coming when your
plunder will be divided among you.
2 I will gather all the nations to Jerusalem to
fight against it; the city will be captured, the
houses ransacked, and the women raped. Half of
the city will go into exile, but the rest of the people will not be taken from the city.[u]
3 Then the LORD will go out and fight[v] against
those nations, as he fights in the day of battle. 4 On
that day his feet will stand on the Mount of
Olives,[w] east of Jerusalem, and the Mount of
Olives will be split in two from east to west, forming a great valley, with half of the mountain moving north and half moving south. 5 You will flee by
my mountain valley, for it will extend to Azel. You
will flee as you fled from the earthquake[a][x] in the
days of Uzziah king of Judah. Then the LORD my
God will come,[y] and all the holy ones with him.[z]
6 On that day there will be no light,[a] no cold or
frost. 7 It will be a unique[b] day, without daytime
or nighttime[c]—a day known to the LORD. When
evening comes, there will be light.[d]
8 On that day living water[e] will flow out from
Jerusalem, half to the eastern[f] sea[b] and half to the
western sea,[c] in summer and in winter.
9 The LORD will be king over the whole earth.[g]
On that day there will be one LORD, and his name
the only name.[h]
10 The whole land, from Geba[i] to Rimmon, south
of Jerusalem, will become like the Arabah. But
Jerusalem will be raised up[j] and remain in its
place,[k] from the Benjamin Gate to the site of the
First Gate, to the Corner Gate, and from the Tower of Hananel to the royal winepresses. 11 It will be
inhabited; never again will it be destroyed. Jerusalem will be secure.[l]
12 This is the plague with which the LORD will
strike all the nations that fought against Jerusalem: Their flesh will rot while they are still
standing on their feet, their eyes will rot in their

13:8 [m]Eze 5:2-4, 12
13:9 [n]Mal 3:2 [o]Isa 48:10; 1Pe 1:6-7 [p]Ps 50:15 [q]Zec 10:6 [r]Jer 30:22 [s]Jer 29:12
14:1 [t]Isa 13:9; Mal 4:1
14:2 [u]Isa 13:6; Zec 13:8
14:3 [v]Zec 9:14-15
14:4 [w]Eze 11:23
14:5 [x]Am 1:1 [y]Isa 29:6; 66:15-16 [z]Mt 16:27; 25:31
14:6 [a]Isa 13:10; Jer 4:23
14:7 [b]Jer 30:7 [c]Rev 21:23-25; 22:5 [d]Isa 30:26
14:8 [e]Eze 47:1-12; Jn 7:38; Rev 22:1-2 [f]Joel 2:20
14:9 [g]Dt 6:4; Isa 45:24; Rev 11:15 [h]Eph 4:5-6
14:10 [i]1Ki 15:22 [j]Jer 30:18; Am 9:11 [k]Zec 12:6
14:11 [l]Eze 34:25-28

[a] 5 Or *5 My mountain valley will be blocked and will extend to Azel. It will be blocked as it was blocked because of the earthquake* [b] 8 That is, the Dead Sea [c] 8 That is, the Mediterranean

sockets, and their tongues will rot in their
14:12 [m]Lev 26:16; mouths.[m] [13]On that day men will be stricken by
Dt 28:22 the LORD with great panic. Each man will seize the
hand of another, and they will attack each other.[n]
14:13 [n]Zec 11:6 [14]Judah[o] too will fight at Jerusalem. The wealth
of all the surrounding nations will be collected[p]—
14:14 [o]Zec 12:2 great quantities of gold and silver and clothing.
[p]Isa 23:18 [15]A similar plague[q] will strike the horses and
mules, the camels and donkeys, and all the ani-
14:15 [q]ver 12 mals in those camps.
[16]Then the survivors from all the nations that
have attacked Jerusalem will go up year after year
14:16 to worship the King, the LORD Almighty, and to
[r]Isa 60:6-9 celebrate the Feast of Tabernacles.[r] [17]If any of the
peoples of the earth do not go up to Jerusalem to
worship the King, the LORD Almighty, they will
14:17 have no rain.[s] [18]If the Egyptian people do not go
[s]Jer 14:4; Am 4:7 up and take part, they will have no rain. The
LORD[a] will bring on them the plague he inflicts on
14:18 the nations that do not go up to celebrate the Feast
[t]ver 12 of Tabernacles.[t] [19]This will be the punishment of
Egypt and the punishment of all the nations that
do not go up to celebrate the Feast of Tabernacles.
[20]On that day HOLY TO THE LORD will be inscribed
14:20 [u]Eze 46:20 on the bells of the horses, and the cooking pots[u]
[v]Zec 9:15 in the LORD's house will be like the sacred bowls[v]
in front of the altar. [21]Every pot in Jerusalem and
14:21 [w]Ro 14:6-7; Judah will be holy[w] to the LORD Almighty, and all
1Co 10:31 who come to sacrifice will take some of the pots
[x]Ne 8:10 [y]Zec 9:8 and cook in them. And on that day[x] there will no
[z]Eze 44:9 longer be a Canaanite[b][y] in the house of the LORD
Almighty.[z]

HOLY TO THE LORD

ZEC 14:20-21

Exodus 28:36-37 gives instructions for "HOLY TO THE LORD" to be engraved on a gold plate and attached to the turban of the high priest. Zechariah prophesies about a glorious future day when even such common items as horse bells and cooking pots will be inscribed with these words. On that day God's original purpose for the Israelite nation will be fulfilled (Ex 19:6): they will be a holy people established for his glory. Even the most ordinary of utensils will be hallowed in that day when used for the glory of God. "This includes you" (2Th 1:10), single woman, lonely housewife, harried mother—you are one of God's "Holy People, the Redeemed of the LORD" (Isa 62:12).

[a] 18 Or *part, then the LORD* [b] 21 Or *merchant*

Apathy results in faithless ritual.

The last of the Old Testament prophets brings a message designed to shake people out of their religious routines and ignite a new passion for God in their hearts. Malachi delivers this brief prophecy during a time of national indifference to God. Though the people of Israel recommit themselves to God on returning to their homeland, compromise and corruption cool their devotion, and the people slip back into old patterns of complacency. What once was a meaningful relationship with God has become a meaningless ritual. Only repentance can cure Israel's spirit of skepticism and carelessness in worship.

Using a question-and-answer format, Malachi raises several complaints from the people that are answered by God in forceful prose. Malachi begins by scolding the Jews for doubting God's love for them: "How have you loved us?" (Mal 1:2). When asked, "How have we wearied [the Lord]?" Malachi's answer rings with accusation (Mal 2:17). The people's very words, because they are untrue and apathetic, weary the Lord. Malachi accuses the people of robbing God by bringing only partial tithes to him (Mal 3:6–12). Then the final question is asked: "What have we said against you?" The people have complained to each other and said "harsh things" about God, and Malachi censures them for it (Mal 3:13–15). Each question is itself an indictment, because their spiritual sensitivity is so dulled and their awareness of God's presence is so impaired.

With calculated sensitivity Malachi confronts spiritual complacency by focusing attention on God's presence. As each question is asked and then answered, Malachi offers not only judgment for complacency and injustice, but also blessing for repentance and a return to following the Lord.

Quick Study

Author
The prophet Malachi.

Date Written
Some time around 433 B.C.

Setting
Judah.

Key Passage
Malachi 3:16–17 "Then those who feared the LORD talked with each other, and the LORD listened and heard . . . 'They will be mine,' says the LORD Almighty, 'in the day when I make up my treasured possession.' "

Outline

God's love for Israel.
Mal 1:1–5

Admonition for the priests and the Jewish people.
Mal 1:6–2:16

Wearying the Lord.
Mal 2:17–3:5

Robbing the Lord.
Mal 3:6–18

The Lord's coming.
Mal 4

The Women of Malachi

The daughters of a foreign god	*Jewish men married them.* Mal 2:11
The wives of their youth	*Jewish men divorced them.* Mal 2:14–15

1 An oracle:[a] The word[b] of the LORD to Israel through Malachi.[a]

Jacob Loved, Esau Hated

2 "I have loved[c] you," says the LORD.

"But you ask, 'How have you loved us?'

"Was not Esau Jacob's brother?" the LORD says. "Yet I have loved Jacob,[d] 3 but Esau I have hated, and I have turned his mountains into a wasteland[e] and left his inheritance to the desert jackals.[f]"

4 Edom may say, "Though we have been crushed, we will rebuild[g] the ruins."

But this is what the LORD Almighty says: "They may build, but I will demolish. They will be called the Wicked Land, a people always under the wrath of the LORD.[h] 5 You will see it with your own eyes and say, 'Great[i] is the LORD—even beyond the borders of Israel!'[j]

Blemished Sacrifices

6 "A son honors his father, and a servant his master. If I am a father, where is the honor due me? If I am a master, where is the respect[k] due me?" says the LORD Almighty.[l] "It is you, O priests, who show contempt for my name.

"But you ask, 'How have we shown contempt for your name?'

7 "You place defiled food[m] on my altar.

"But you ask, 'How have we defiled you?'

"By saying that the LORD's table is contemptible. 8 When you bring blind animals for sacrifice, is that not wrong? When you sacrifice crippled or diseased animals,[n] is that not wrong? Try offering them to your governor! Would he be pleased with you? Would he accept you?" says the LORD Almighty.[o]

9 "Now implore God to be gracious to us. With such offerings[p] from your hands, will he accept you?"—says the LORD Almighty.

10 "Oh, that one of you would shut the temple doors, so that you would not light useless fires on my altar! I am not pleased[q] with you," says the LORD Almighty, "and I will accept no offering[r] from your hands. 11 My name will be great among the nations, from the rising to the setting of the sun. In every place incense[s] and pure offerings will be brought to my name, because my name will be great among the nations," says the LORD Almighty.

12 "But you profane it by saying of the Lord's table, 'It is defiled,' and of its food,[t] 'It is contemptible.' 13 And you say, 'What a burden!'[u] and you sniff at it contemptuously," says the LORD Almighty.

"When you bring injured, crippled or diseased animals and offer them as sacrifices, should I accept them from your hands?" says the LORD. 14 "Cursed is the cheat who has an acceptable male in his flock and vows to give it, but then sacrifices

1:1 [a]Na 1:1 [b]1Pe 4:11
1:2 [c]Dt 4:37 [d]Ro 9:13*
1:3 [e]Isa 34:10 [f]Eze 35:3-9
1:4 [g]Isa 9:10 [h]Eze 25:12-14
1:5 [i]Ps 35:27; Mic 5:4 [j]Am 1:11-12
1:6 [k]Isa 1:2 [l]Job 5:17
1:7 [m]ver 12; Lev 21:6
1:8 [n]Lev 22:22; Dt 15:21 [o]Isa 43:23
1:9 [p]Lev 23:33-44
1:10 [q]Hos 5:6 [r]Isa 1:11-14; Jer 14:12
1:11 [s]Isa 60:6-7; Rev 8:3
1:12 [t]ver 7
1:13 [u]Isa 43:22-24

[a] *1 Malachi* means *my messenger.*

Hate Versus Love

MAL 1:2-3

This passage raises the difficult question of how God could possibly hate a person or a nation. The word *hate* here is a strong one that literally means "enemy." Esau refers to Jacob's twin brother Esau and to Edom, the nation of Esau's descendants. Some scholars believe the word *hate* is used here to contrast the special love God has for Jacob. Only one of the brothers, Jacob or Esau, could provide the family line through which the Messiah would come. While both men were deeply flawed, God chose Jacob.

Romans 9:10-24 further explains that God makes choices we humans won't ever understand. At such times, when our limited understanding doesn't allow us to comprehend God's vastness, our only sensible response can be to simply bow before him and recognize his sovereignty over the entire world and over each of us individually.

1:14 a blemished animal[v] to the Lord. For I am a great
[v]Lev 22:18-21 king,[w]" says the LORD Almighty, "and my name is
[w]1Ti 6:15 to be feared among the nations.

Admonition for the Priests

2:1 **2** "And now this admonition is for you,
[x]ver 7 O priests.[x] [2]If you do not listen, and if you do
2:2 not set your heart to honor my name," says the
[y]Dt 28:20 LORD Almighty, "I will send a curse[y] upon you,
and I will curse your blessings. Yes, I have already
cursed them, because you have not set your heart
2:3 to honor me.
[z]Ex 29:14 [3]"Because of you I will rebuke[a] your descen-
[a]1Ki 14:10 dants[b]; I will spread on your faces the offal[z] from
your festival sacrifices, and you will be carried off
2:4 with it.[a] [4]And you will know that I have sent you
[b]Nu 3:12 this admonition so that my covenant with Levi[b]
2:5 may continue," says the LORD Almighty. [5]"My cov-
[c]Dt 33:9 enant was with him, a covenant[c] of life and
[d]Nu 25:12 peace,[d] and I gave them to him; this called for reverence and he revered me and stood in awe of my
2:6 name. [6]True instruction[e] was in his mouth and
[e]Dt 33:10 nothing false was found on his lips. He walked
[f]Jer 23:22; Jas 5:19-20 with me in peace and uprightness, and turned
many from sin.[f]
[7]"For the lips of a priest[g] ought to preserve
2:7 knowledge, and from his mouth men should seek
[g]Jer 18:18 instruction[h]—because he is the messenger[i] of the
[h]Lev 10:11 LORD Almighty. [8]But you have turned from the
[i]Nu 27:21 way and by your teaching have caused many to
2:8 stumble;[j] you have violated the covenant with
[j]Jer 18:15 Levi," says the LORD Almighty. [9]"So I have caused
2:9 you to be despised[k] and humiliated before all the
[k]1Sa 2:30 people, because you have not followed my ways
but have shown partiality in matters of the law."

Judah Unfaithful

2:10 [10]Have we not all one Father[c]?[l] Did not one God
[l]1Co 8:6 [m]Ex 19:5 create us? Why do we profane the covenant[m] of
our fathers by breaking faith with one another?
[11]Judah has broken faith. A detestable thing has
been committed in Israel and in Jerusalem: Judah
2:11 has desecrated the sanctuary the LORD loves, by
[n]Ne 13:23 marrying[n] the daughter of a foreign god.[o] [12]As for
[o]Ezr 9:1; Jer 3:7-9 the man who does this, whoever he may be, may
2:12 the LORD cut him off[p] from the tents of Jacob[d]—
[p]Eze 24:21 even though he brings offerings[q] to the LORD
[q]Mal 1:10 Almighty.
[13]Another thing you do: You flood the LORD's
2:13 altar with tears. You weep and wail because he no
[r]Jer 14:12 longer pays attention[r] to your offerings or accepts
them with pleasure from your hands. [14]You ask,
"Why?" It is because the LORD is acting as the wit-
2:14 ness between you and the wife of your youth,[s]
[s]Pr 5:18 because you have broken faith with her, though

We rest on Thee, our shield and our defender!
Thine is the battle, Thine shall be the praise;
When passing through the gates of pearly splendor,
Victors, we rest with Thee, through endless days.

—Edith Gilling Cherry (1872-1897)

[a] 3 Or *cut off* (see Septuagint) [b] 3 Or *will blight your grain*
[c] 10 Or *father* [d] 12 Or *[12]May the LORD cut off from the tents of Jacob anyone who gives testimony in behalf of the man who does this*

Marriage Versus Divorce

MAL 2:14–16

The men of Judah are smashing into bits God's ideal of marriage. They are divorcing their wives to marry pagan women. While this passage depicts such behavior as unfaithfulness to the original wives and to God, the verses also remind us of God's ideal for marriage. It is God's design that both partners strive to keep their promise to be faithful and that each endeavors to become one with the other in "flesh and spirit" (Mal 2:15), signifying their physical and spiritual intimacy. Out of this union, God wants "godly offspring" (Mal 2:15)—both the children who are born to a couple and the couple themselves are God's offspring (Ac 17:28–29). As God's and as godly, they are inclined toward a strong relationship with the Lord. The passage closes with a statement of how damaging divorce is to the spirit. Regardless of how justifiable the reasons for divorce may seem, divorce does violence to everyone involved.

she is your partner, the wife of your marriage
covenant.
15Has not ⌊the LORD⌋ made them one?[t] In flesh
and spirit they are his. And why one? Because he
was seeking godly offspring.[a][u] So guard yourself
in your spirit, and do not break faith with the wife
of your youth.
16"I hate divorce,[v]" says the LORD God of Israel,
"and I hate a man's covering himself[b] with violence as well as with his garment," says the LORD
Almighty.
So guard yourself in your spirit, and do not
break faith.

The Day of Judgment

17You have wearied[w] the LORD with your words.
"How have we wearied him?" you ask.
By saying, "All who do evil are good in the eyes
of the LORD, and he is pleased with them" or
"Where is the God of justice?"

3 "See, I will send my messenger, who will prepare the way before me.[x] Then suddenly the
Lord you are seeking will come to his temple; the
messenger of the covenant, whom you desire, will
come," says the LORD Almighty.
2But who can endure[y] the day of his coming?
Who can stand when he appears? For he will be
like a refiner's fire[z] or a launderer's soap. 3He will
sit as a refiner and purifier of silver;[a] he will purify[b] the Levites and refine them like gold and silver. Then the LORD will have men who will bring
offerings in righteousness, 4and the offerings[c] of
Judah and Jerusalem will be acceptable to the
LORD, as in days gone by, as in former years.[d]
5"So I will come near to you for judgment. I will
be quick to testify against sorcerers, adulterers
and perjurers,[e] against those who defraud laborers
of their wages,[f] who oppress the widows[g] and the
fatherless, and deprive aliens of justice, but do not
fear me," says the LORD Almighty.

Robbing God

6"I the LORD do not change.[h] So you, O descendants of Jacob, are not destroyed. 7Ever since the
time of your forefathers you have turned away[i]
from my decrees and have not kept them. Return
to me, and I will return to you,"[j] says the LORD
Almighty.
"But you ask, 'How are we to return?'
8"Will a man rob God? Yet you rob me.
"But you ask, 'How do we rob you?'
"In tithes[k] and offerings. 9You are under a
curse—the whole nation of you—because you are
robbing me. 10Bring the whole tithe into the storehouse,[l] that there may be food in my house. Test
me in this," says the LORD Almighty, "and see if I
will not throw open the floodgates[m] of heaven and

2:15 [t]Ge 2:24; Mt 19:4-6 [u]1Co 7:14
2:16 [v]Dt 24:1; Mt 5:31-32; 19:4-9
2:17 [w]Isa 43:24
3:1 [x]Isa 40:3; Mt 11:10*; Mk 1:2*; Lk 7:27*
3:2 [y]Eze 22:14; Rev 6:17 [z]Zec 13:9; Mt 3:10-12
3:3 [a]Da 12:10 [b]Isa 1:25
3:4 [c]2Ch 7:12; Ps 51:19; Mal 1:11 [d]2Ch 7:3
3:5 [e]Jer 7:9 [f]Lev 19:13; Jas 5:4 [g]Ex 22:22
3:6 [h]Nu 23:19; Jas 1:17
3:7 [i]Jer 7:26; Ac 7:51 [j]Zec 1:3
3:8 [k]Ne 13:10-12
3:10 [l]Ne 13:12 [m]2Ki 7:2

[a] 15 Or [15]*But the one ⌊who is our father⌋ did not do this, not as long as life remained in him. And what was he seeking? An offspring from God* [b] 16 Or *his wife*

pour out so much blessing that you will not have
room enough for it. 11I will prevent pests from
devouring your crops, and the vines in your fields
3:12 will not cast their fruit," says the LORD Almighty.
[n]Isa 61:9 12"Then all the nations will call you blessed,[n] for
[o]Isa 62:4 yours will be a delightful land,"[o] says the LORD
3:13 Almighty.
[p]Mal 2:17 13"You have said harsh things[p] against me," says
the LORD.
3:14 "Yet you ask, 'What have we said against you?'
[q]Ps 73:13 14"You have said, 'It is futile[q] to serve God.
[r]Isa 58:3 What did we gain by carrying out his requirements and going about like mourners[r] before the
LORD Almighty? 15But now we call the arrogant
3:15 [s]Jer 7:10 blessed. Certainly the evildoers[s] prosper, and even
those who challenge God escape.' "
3:16 16Then those who feared the LORD talked with
[t]Ps 34:15 each other, and the LORD listened and heard.[t] A
[u]Ps 56:8 scroll[u] of remembrance was written in his presence concerning those who feared the LORD and
honored his name.
17"They will be mine," says the LORD Almighty,
3:17 "in the day when I make up my treasured posses-
[v]Dt 7:6 sion.[a][v] I will spare[w] them, just as in compassion a
[w]Ps 103:13; Isa 26:20 man spares his son who serves him. 18And you
will again see the distinction between the righ-
3:18 [x]Ge 18:25 teous[x] and the wicked, between those who serve
God and those who do not.

The Day of the LORD

4:1 [y]Joel 2:31 4 "Surely the day is coming;[y] it will burn like a
[z]Isa 5:24; Ob 1:18 furnace. All the arrogant and every evildoer
will be stubble,[z] and that day that is coming will
4:2 set them on fire," says the LORD Almighty. "Not a
[a]Lk 1:78; root or a branch will be left to them. 2But for you
Eph 5:14 [b]Isa 30:26 who revere my name, the sun of righteousness[a]
[c]Isa 35:6 will rise with healing[b] in its wings. And you will
4:3 go out and leap[c] like calves released from the stall.
[d]Job 40:12 3Then you will trample[d] down the wicked; they
[e]Eze 28:18 will be ashes[e] under the soles of your feet on the
day when I do these things," says the LORD Al-
4:4 [f]Ps 147:19 mighty.
4"Remember the law[f] of my servant Moses, the
4:5 decrees and laws I gave him at Horeb for all Israel.
[g]Mt 11:14; Lk 1:17 5"See, I will send you the prophet Elijah[g] before
[h]Joel 2:31 that great and dreadful day of the LORD comes.[h]
4:6 6He will turn the hearts of the fathers to their chil-
[i]Lk 1:17 dren,[i] and the hearts of the children to their
[j]Isa 11:4; Rev 19:15 fathers; or else I will come and strike[j] the land
[k]Zec 5:3 with a curse."[k]

Robbed!

MAL 3:6-18

Anyone who has ever been robbed knows how invasive that experience is. What belongs to you is taken away by someone who did nothing to earn it and who has no right to it. So, too, God says, he has been robbed. His children now hoard for themselves what truly belongs to him. And worst of all, the heartfelt love that should be behind each gift is absent.

But along with God's condemnation of the stinginess of his people, he also offers a promise of blessing. Isn't this an amazing God? All the while denouncing those who withhold what rightfully belongs to him, God offers a promise of blessing—greater than they can imagine—if they will only give him his tithes and offerings. If they are generous with God, he will be doubly generous with them. Circle each blessing listed in these verses; then make a bold promise to give generously to God, not out of expectation of blessing, but out of a heart of love.

[a] *17* Or *Almighty, "my treasured possession, in the day when I act*

New Testament

Matthew

The Messiah has come.

For centuries the Jewish community longed for its promised king, the Messiah. Matthew, a former tax collector, announces in his book that Jesus is the long-awaited King of glory. Drawing on Old Testament prophecies and recording the amazing words and deeds of Jesus of Nazareth, Matthew offers proof that the Messiah has come to bring God's kingdom and to offer salvation.

Because Jesus' message and methods shatter the cultural traditions of the religious community, many of the Jewish leaders refuse to accept him as Messiah. But Matthew identifies several women who recognize who Jesus is: a Canaanite woman (Mt 15), an unnamed woman who pours out her love and devotion along with an alabaster bottle of perfume (Mt 26), and Pilate's wife, who realizes that Jesus is not someone to be lightly dismissed (Mt 27).

Matthew also records distinct teachings of Jesus that cover topics like how the blessed will live (Mt 5), the dangers of spiritual blindness (Mt 16), God's concerns about divorce (Mt 19) and the importance of personal preparation for the coming of God's kingdom (Mt 25). As we read through Matthew's Gospel and rightly understand its message, we learn the beginning steps of faith and bow before King Jesus, the promised Messiah of Israel.

Quick Study

Author
The apostle Matthew.

Date Written
Sometime before the destruction of Jerusalem in A.D. 70.

Setting
Israel, primarily the regions of Galilee and Jerusalem.

Key Passage
Matthew 1:23 " 'The virgin will be with child and will give birth to a son, and they will call him Immanuel'—which means, 'God with us.' "

Outline

Jesus' genealogy.
Mt 1:1-17

Jesus' birth.
Mt 1:18-25

Jesus' early life.
Mt 2

Jesus' baptism by John.
Mt 3

Beginning of Jesus' ministry.
Mt 4

The Sermon on the Mount.
Mt 5:1–7:29

Teaching and healing.
Mt 8:1–12:50

Parables.
Mt 13

Teaching and miracles.
Mt 14:1–20:34

The Triumphal Entry.
Mt 21:1-17

Final teachings.
Mt 21:18–25:46

Jesus' anointing, betrayal and arrest.
Mt 26:1-56

Jesus' trial.
Mt 26:57–27:31

Jesus' death and burial.
Mt 27:32-66

Jesus' resurrection.
Mt 28:1-15

The commissioning.
Mt 28:16-20

The Women of Matthew

⚘ **Mary, mother of Jesus**	*Virgin who gave birth to Jesus.* Mt 1-2; 12:46-50 (page 1613)
⚘ **Simon Peter's mother-in-law**	*Healed by Jesus.* Mt 8:14-15 (page 1687)
⚘ **Woman subject to bleeding**	*Twelve years of suffering ended.* Mt 9:20-22 (page 1745)
⚘ **A ruler's daughter**	*A dead girl brought to life.* Mt 9:18-25 (page 1746)
Woman with dough	*An example of the kingdom.* Mt 13:33
Jesus' sisters	*Not known if they believed in him.* Mt 13:55-56
⚘ **Herodias**	*Married her brother-in-law.* Mt 14:3-12 (page 1779)
⚘ **Daughter of Herodias**	*Danced for Herod.* Mt 14:6-11 (page 1780)
⚘ **Canaanite woman**	*Persistence personified.* Mt 15:21-28 (page 1811)
Wife sold for debt	*An inhumane practice.* Mt 18:25
⚘ **Mother of the Zebedees**	*She asked a favor of Jesus.* Mt 20:20-24; 27:56 (page 1878)
Woman with seven husbands	*Each husband died before she did.* Mt 22:25-32
Women at the mill	*One taken, one left.* Mt 24:41
The ten virgins	*Some wise, some foolish.* Mt 25:1-13
⚘ **A woman at a banquet (Mary of Bethany)**	*She anointed Jesus.* Mt 26:6-13 (page 1843)
Servant girls	*They confronted Peter.* Mt 26:69-71
⚘ **Pilate's wife**	*She warned her husband.* Mt 27:19 (page 1912)
⚘ **Women at Calvary**	*They watched from a distance.* Mt 27:55-56 (page 1941)
⚘ **Mary Magdalene**	*She watched Jesus die.* Mt 27:56,61; 28:1 (page 1714)
⚘ **Mary, mother of James and Joses**	*She was at the cross.* Mt 27:56,61; 28:1 (page 1941)

⚘ Denotes a sketch written about this character

The Genealogy of Jesus

1 A record of the genealogy of Jesus Christ the son of David,[a] the son of Abraham:[b]

2 Abraham was the father of Isaac,[c]
Isaac the father of Jacob,[d]
Jacob the father of Judah and his brothers,[e]
3 Judah the father of Perez and Zerah, whose mother was Tamar,[f]
Perez the father of Hezron,
Hezron the father of Ram,
4 Ram the father of Amminadab,
Amminadab the father of Nahshon,
Nahshon the father of Salmon,
5 Salmon the father of Boaz, whose mother was Rahab,
Boaz the father of Obed, whose mother was Ruth,
Obed the father of Jesse,
6 and Jesse the father of King David.[g]

David was the father of Solomon, whose mother had been Uriah's wife,[h]
7 Solomon the father of Rehoboam,
Rehoboam the father of Abijah,
Abijah the father of Asa,
8 Asa the father of Jehoshaphat,
Jehoshaphat the father of Jehoram,
Jehoram the father of Uzziah,
9 Uzziah the father of Jotham,
Jotham the father of Ahaz,
Ahaz the father of Hezekiah,
10 Hezekiah the father of Manasseh,[i]
Manasseh the father of Amon,
Amon the father of Josiah,
11 and Josiah the father of Jeconiah[a] and his brothers at the time of the exile to Babylon.[j]

12 After the exile to Babylon:
Jeconiah was the father of Shealtiel,[k]
Shealtiel the father of Zerubbabel,[l]
13 Zerubbabel the father of Abiud,
Abiud the father of Eliakim,
Eliakim the father of Azor,
14 Azor the father of Zadok,
Zadok the father of Akim,
Akim the father of Eliud,
15 Eliud the father of Eleazar,
Eleazar the father of Matthan,
Matthan the father of Jacob,
16 and Jacob the father of Joseph, the husband of Mary,[m] of whom was born Jesus, who is called Christ.[n]

17 Thus there were fourteen generations in all from Abraham to David, fourteen from David to the exile to Babylon, and fourteen from the exile to the Christ.[b]

1:1 [a]2Sa 7:12-16; Isa 9:6,7; 11:1; Jer 23:5,6; Mt 9:27; Lk 1:32,69; Ro 1:3; Rev 22:16 [b]Ge 22:18; Gal 3:16
1:2 [c]Ge 21:3,12 [d]Ge 25:26 [e]Ge 29:35
1:3 [f]Ge 38:27-30
1:6 [g]1Sa 16:1; 17:12 [h]2Sa 12:24
1:10 [i]2Ki 20:21
1:11 [j]2Ki 24:14-16; Jer 27:20; Da 1:1,2
1:12 [k]1Ch 3:17 [l]1Ch 3:19; Ezr 3:2
1:16 [m]Lk 1:27 [n]Mt 27:17

[a] *11* That is, Jehoiachin; also in verse 12 [b] *17* Or *Messiah.* "The Christ" (Greek) and "the Messiah" (Hebrew) both mean "the Anointed One."

Anne Brontë, one of the famous literary Brontë sisters of Great Britain, composed many poems and wrote two novels. This song expresses her joy on Christmas morning.

Music on Christmas Morning

Music I love—but ne'er a strain
Could kindle raptures so divine,
So grief assuage, so conquer pain,
And rouse this pensive heart of mine;
As that we hear on Christmas morn,
Upon the wintry breezes borne.

To greet with joy the glorious morn,
Which angels welcomed long ago,
When our redeeming Lord was born,
To bring the light of Heaven below . . .

With them, I celebrate His birth;
Glory to God, in highest Heaven,
Good will to men, and peace on Earth,
To us a Savior King is given;
Our God is come to claim His own,
And Satan's power is overthrown!

A sinless God, for sinful men,
Descends to suffer and to bleed;
Hell must renounce its empire then;
The price is paid, the world is freed,
And Satan's self must now confess,
That Christ has earned a right to bless.

—Anne Brontë (1820-1849)

Joseph's Reaction

MT 1:19

Joseph's remarkable response to Mary's announcement of her pregnancy can be better understood in light of the marriage customs of the day. According to Hebrew custom, parents arranged marriages. After the contract was settled, the two individuals were considered married, though they did not live together as husband and wife. Instead, each lived at home for a certain period of time with his or her parents. If conception occurred during this time, the marriage could be annulled. After the waiting period, the husband then went to the home of the bride's parents in a grand processional march to lead his bride back to his home, where they would live together as husband and wife.

So when Mary is found to be pregnant during the betrothal period, Joseph plans to quietly divorce her, until the angel intervenes and explains that neither the conception nor the child she carries are ordinary but are, instead, extraordinary, supernatural and the fulfillment of God's great redemptive plan.

The Birth of Jesus Christ

18 This is how the birth of Jesus Christ came about: His mother Mary was pledged to be married to Joseph, but before they came together, she was found to be with child through the Holy Spirit.[o] 19 Because Joseph her husband was a righteous man and did not want to expose her to public disgrace, he had in mind to divorce[p] her quietly.

20 But after he had considered this, an angel of the Lord appeared to him in a dream and said, "Joseph son of David, do not be afraid to take Mary home as your wife, because what is conceived in her is from the Holy Spirit. 21 She will give birth to a son, and you are to give him the name Jesus,[a][q] because he will save his people from their sins."[r]

22 All this took place to fulfill what the Lord had said through the prophet: 23 "The virgin will be with child and will give birth to a son, and they will call him Immanuel"[b][s]—which means, "God with us."

24 When Joseph woke up, he did what the angel of the Lord had commanded him and took Mary home as his wife. 25 But he had no union with her until she gave birth to a son. And he gave him the name Jesus.[t]

The Visit of the Magi

2 After Jesus was born in Bethlehem in Judea,[u] during the time of King Herod,[v] Magi[c] from the east came to Jerusalem 2 and asked, "Where is the one who has been born king of the Jews?[w] We saw his star[x] in the east[d] and have come to worship him."

3 When King Herod heard this he was disturbed, and all Jerusalem with him. 4 When he had called together all the people's chief priests and teachers of the law, he asked them where the Christ[e] was to be born. 5 "In Bethlehem[y] in Judea," they replied, "for this is what the prophet has written:

> 6 " 'But you, Bethlehem, in the land of Judah,
> are by no means least among the rulers of Judah;
> for out of you will come a ruler
> who will be the shepherd of my people Israel.'[f]"[z]

7 Then Herod called the Magi secretly and found out from them the exact time the star had appeared. 8 He sent them to Bethlehem and said, "Go and make a careful search for the child. As soon as you find him, report to me, so that I too may go and worship him."

9 After they had heard the king, they went on their way, and the star they had seen in the east[g]

1:18 [o]Lk 1:35
1:19 [p]Dt 24:1
1:21 [q]Lk 1:31 [r]Lk 2:11; Ac 5:31; 13:23,28
1:23 [s]Isa 7:14; 8:8,10
1:25 [t]ver 21
2:1 [u]Lk 2:4-7 [v]Lk 1:5
2:2 [w]Jer 23:5; Mt 27:11; Mk 15:2; Jn 1:49; 18:33-37 [x]Nu 24:17
2:5 [y]Jn 7:42
2:6 [z]Mic 5:2; 2Sa 5:2

[a] *21* *Jesus* is the Greek form of *Joshua,* which means *the LORD saves.* [b] *23* Isaiah 7:14 [c] *1* Traditionally *Wise Men* [d] *2* Or *star when it rose* [e] *4* Or *Messiah* [f] *6* Micah 5:2 [g] *9* Or *seen when it rose*

went ahead of them until it stopped over the place
where the child was. [10]When they saw the star,
they were overjoyed. [11]On coming to the house,
they saw the child with his mother Mary, and they
bowed down and worshiped him.[a] Then they
opened their treasures and presented him with
gifts[b] of gold and of incense and of myrrh. [12]And
having been warned[c] in a dream[d] not to go back
to Herod, they returned to their country by another route.

The Escape to Egypt

[13]When they had gone, an angel[e] of the Lord
appeared to Joseph in a dream.[f] "Get up," he said,
"take the child and his mother and escape to
Egypt. Stay there until I tell you, for Herod is
going to search for the child to kill him."

[14]So he got up, took the child and his mother
during the night and left for Egypt, [15]where he
stayed until the death of Herod. And so was fulfilled what the Lord had said through the prophet:
"Out of Egypt I called my son."[a][g]

[16]When Herod realized that he had been out-
witted by the Magi, he was furious, and he gave
orders to kill all the boys in Bethlehem and its
vicinity who were two years old and under, in
accordance with the time he had learned from the
Magi. [17]Then what was said through the prophet
Jeremiah was fulfilled:

> [18]"A voice is heard in Ramah,
> weeping and great mourning,
> Rachel weeping for her children
> and refusing to be comforted,
> because they are no more."[b][h]

The Return to Nazareth

[19]After Herod died, an angel of the Lord
appeared in a dream[i] to Joseph in Egypt [20]and
said, "Get up, take the child and his mother and
go to the land of Israel, for those who were trying
to take the child's life are dead."

[21]So he got up, took the child and his mother
and went to the land of Israel. [22]But when he
heard that Archelaus was reigning in Judea in
place of his father Herod, he was afraid to go
there. Having been warned in a dream,[j] he withdrew to the district of Galilee,[k] [23]and he went and
lived in a town called Nazareth.[l] So was fulfilled[m]
what was said through the prophets: "He will be
called a Nazarene."[n]

John the Baptist Prepares the Way

3 In those days John the Baptist[o] came, preaching in the Desert of Judea [2]and saying,
"Repent, for the kingdom of heaven[p] is near."
[3]This is he who was spoken of through the prophet Isaiah:

> "A voice of one calling in the desert,

2:11 [a]Isa 60:3 [b]Ps 72:10
2:12 [c]Heb 11:7 [d]ver 13,19, 22; Mt 27:19
2:13 [e]Ac 5:19 [f]ver 12,19, 22
2:15 [g]Hos 11:1; Ex 4:22,23
2:18 [h]Jer 31:15
2:19 [i]ver 12,13, 22
2:22 [j]ver 12,13, 19; Mt 27:19 [k]Lk 2:39
2:23 [l]Lk 1:26; Jn 1:45,46 [m]Mt 1:22 [n]Mk 1:24
3:1 [o]Lk 1:13,57-66; 3:2-19
3:2 [p]Da 2:44; Mt 4:17; 6:10; Lk 11:20; 21:31; Jn 3:3,5; Ac 1:3,6

a 15 Hosea 11:1 *b 18* Jer. 31:15

They Come Bearing Gifts

MT 2:10–12

In the ancient East, one always brought gifts to a superior. So the wise men bring to Jesus gifts worthy of a king—gold, incense and myrrh. Gold has continued to be valuable throughout the centuries. The incense frankincense likely consisted of a fragrant gum obtained by making incisions in various tree barks. Myrrh was a highly valued spice and perfume. These gifts may have provided the means by which Joseph took his family to Egypt and supported them there until Herod, who wished to kill the child, died.

Some commentators see these gifts as symbolic: the gold represents Christ's deity, purity or royalty; the incense is associated with priestly worship; and myrrh, used for embalming, signifies his sacrifice and death.

> 'Prepare the way for the Lord,
> make straight paths for him.' "[a][q]

4John's clothes were made of camel's hair, and he had a leather belt around his waist.[r] His food was locusts[s] and wild honey. 5People went out to him from Jerusalem and all Judea and the whole region of the Jordan. 6Confessing their sins, they were baptized by him in the Jordan River.

7But when he saw many of the Pharisees and Sadducees coming to where he was baptizing, he said to them: "You brood of vipers![t] Who warned you to flee from the coming wrath?[u] 8Produce fruit in keeping with repentance.[v] 9And do not think you can say to yourselves, 'We have Abraham as our father.' I tell you that out of these stones God can raise up children for Abraham. 10The ax is already at the root of the trees, and every tree that does not produce good fruit will be cut down and thrown into the fire.[w]

11"I baptize you with[b] water for repentance. But after me will come one who is more powerful than I, whose sandals I am not fit to carry. He will baptize you with the Holy Spirit[x] and with fire.[y] 12His winnowing fork is in his hand, and he will clear his threshing floor, gathering his wheat into the barn and burning up the chaff with unquenchable fire."[z]

The Baptism of Jesus

13Then Jesus came from Galilee to the Jordan to be baptized by John.[a] 14But John tried to deter him, saying, "I need to be baptized by you, and do you come to me?"

15Jesus replied, "Let it be so now; it is proper for us to do this to fulfill all righteousness." Then John consented.

16As soon as Jesus was baptized, he went up out of the water. At that moment heaven was opened, and he saw the Spirit of God[b] descending like a dove and lighting on him. 17And a voice from heaven[c] said, "This is my Son,[d] whom I love; with him I am well pleased."[e]

The Temptation of Jesus

4 Then Jesus was led by the Spirit into the desert to be tempted by the devil. 2After fasting forty days and forty nights,[f] he was hungry. 3The tempter[g] came to him and said, "If you are the Son of God,[h] tell these stones to become bread."

4Jesus answered, "It is written: 'Man does not live on bread alone, but on every word that comes from the mouth of God.'[c]"[i]

5Then the devil took him to the holy city[j] and had him stand on the highest point of the temple. 6"If you are the Son of God," he said, "throw yourself down. For it is written:

> " 'He will command his angels
> concerning you,

3:3 [q]Isa 40:3; Mal 3:1; Lk 1:76; Jn 1:23
3:4 [r]2Ki 1:8 [s]Lev 11:22
3:7 [t]Mt 12:34; 23:33 [u]Ro 1:18; 1Th 1:10
3:8 [v]Ac 26:20
3:10 [w]Mt 7:19; Lk 13:6-9; Jn 15:2,6
3:11 [x]Mk 1:8 [y]Isa 4:4; Ac 2:3,4
3:12 [z]Mt 13:30
3:13 [a]Mk 1:4
3:16 [b]Isa 11:2; 42:1
3:17 [c]Mt 17:5; Jn 12:28 [d]Ps 2:7; 2Pe 1:17,18 [e]Isa 42:1; Mt 12:18; 17:5; Mk 1:11; 9:7; Lk 9:35
4:2 [f]Ex 34:28; 1Ki 19:8
4:3 [g]1Th 3:5 [h]Mt 3:17; Jn 5:25; Ac 9:20
4:4 [i]Dt 8:3
4:5 [j]Ne 11:1; Da 9:24; Mt 27:53

[a] *3* Isaiah 40:3 [b] *11* Or *in* [c] *4* Deut. 8:3

Baptism

MT 3:11-17

John the Baptist recognizes that his role is to prepare the way for the Messiah. Those who hear his words probably are reminded of two Old Testament prophecies: Joel 2:28-29 and Malachi 3:2-5. John knows that he is unworthy to baptize Jesus. However, John steps into the water with Jesus and baptizes him in order for Jesus to be identified with the sinners he has come to save.

In this marvelous event, God the Father expresses in an audible voice two hallmarks of blessing: He claims Jesus as his Son and reveals his pleasure in him. In Jesus' baptism, all three persons of the Godhead appear. The Son is baptized, the Father speaks a confirmation of his Son, and the Spirit descends on Jesus like a dove (see the note on Mk 1:9-13, page 1641). Surely the spectators of this event must realize that this is no ordinary man and no ordinary baptism taking place on the banks of the Jordan.

> and they will lift you up in their
> hands,
> so that you will not strike your foot
> against a stone.'[a]"[k]

7 Jesus answered him, "It is also written: 'Do not put the Lord your God to the test.'[b]"[l]

8 Again, the devil took him to a very high mountain and showed him all the kingdoms of the world and their splendor. 9 "All this I will give you," he said, "if you will bow down and worship me."

10 Jesus said to him, "Away from me, Satan![m] For it is written: 'Worship the Lord your God, and serve him only.'[c]"[n]

11 Then the devil left him, and angels came and attended him.[o]

Jesus Begins to Preach

12 When Jesus heard that John had been put in prison,[p] he returned to Galilee.[q] 13 Leaving Nazareth, he went and lived in Capernaum,[r] which was by the lake in the area of Zebulun and Naphtali— 14 to fulfill what was said through the prophet Isaiah:

> 15 "Land of Zebulun and land of Naphtali,
> the way to the sea, along the Jordan,
> Galilee of the Gentiles—
> 16 the people living in darkness
> have seen a great light;
> on those living in the land of the
> shadow of death
> a light has dawned."[d][s]

17 From that time on Jesus began to preach, "Repent, for the kingdom of heaven[t] is near."

The Calling of the First Disciples

18 As Jesus was walking beside the Sea of Galilee,[u] he saw two brothers, Simon called Peter[v] and his brother Andrew. They were casting a net into the lake, for they were fishermen. 19 "Come, follow me,"[w] Jesus said, "and I will make you fishers of men." 20 At once they left their nets and followed him.

21 Going on from there, he saw two other brothers, James son of Zebedee and his brother John.[x] They were in a boat with their father Zebedee, preparing their nets. Jesus called them, 22 and immediately they left the boat and their father and followed him.

Jesus Heals the Sick

23 Jesus went throughout Galilee,[y] teaching in their synagogues,[z] preaching the good news[a] of the kingdom,[b] and healing every disease and sickness among the people.[c] 24 News about him spread all over Syria,[d] and people brought to him all who

4:6 [k]Ps 91:11,12
4:7 [l]Dt 6:16
4:10 [m]1Ch 21:1 [n]Dt 6:13
4:11 [o]Mt 26:53; Lk 22:43; Heb 1:14
4:12 [p]Mt 14:3 [q]Mk 1:14
4:13 [r]Mk 1:21; Lk 4:23,31; Jn 2:12; 4:46,47
4:16 [s]Isa 9:1,2; Lk 2:32
4:17 [t]Mt 3:2
4:18 [u]Mt 15:29; Mk 7:31; Jn 6:1 [v]Mt 16:17,18
4:19 [w]Mk 10:21, 28,52
4:21 [x]Mt 20:20
4:23 [y]Mk 1:39; Lk 4:15,44 [z]Mt 9:35; 13:54; Mk 1:21; Lk 4:15; Jn 6:59 [a]Mk 1:14 [b]Mt 3:2; Ac 20:25 [c]Mt 8:16; 15:30; Ac 10:38
4:24 [d]Lk 2:2

[a] *6* Psalm 91:11,12 [b] *7* Deut. 6:16 [c] *10* Deut. 6:13
[d] *16* Isaiah 9:1,2

Jesus Is Tested

MT 4:1-11

Jesus moves quickly from the spiritual heights—his baptism and the confirmation by the Father and Spirit on his ministry—to the spiritual depths—testing and temptation by Satan in the desert. These temptations are part of Jesus' preparation for ministry. The first test pertains to his relationship with God. Satan attempts to use Jesus' hunger to persuade him to act independently of his Father. The second test builds on the first and focuses on the temptation for popularity and personal display. Common belief at that time held that the Messiah would appear suddenly in the sky, standing on the pinnacle of the temple. In Satan's final test, he offers Jesus the kingdoms of the world if only Jesus will worship him. If Jesus succumbs to Satan's ploys, he will avoid the cross—but God's great plan of salvation will be thwarted. Praise God that Jesus overcame Satan, and that the story does not end in defeat, but in victory, for Christ and all who follow him!

Beautiful Beatitudes

MT 5:3–11

The Sermon on the Mount is the first of five major discourses found in Matthew's Gospel and is the longest of the five. While the Beatitudes, found in Matthew 5:3–11, are beautiful poetry and often quoted, their true value is found in their description of what it means to live a commendable life in God's kingdom. The guidelines that Jews in Jesus' day had for righteous living were the minutiae of the rules of the scribes and Pharisees. The Sermon on the Mount shows what the life of a person who is rightly related to God looks like. The qualities Jesus highlights—being poor in spirit, meek, pure in heart, merciful—contrast sharply with the pride of the Pharisees. Jesus calls us to a higher standard of life and a righteousness that can only come from walking closely with him (Mt 5:20).

were ill with various diseases, those suffering
severe pain, the demon-possessed,[e] those having
seizures,[f] and the paralyzed,[g] and he healed them.
25 Large crowds from Galilee, the Decapolis,[a] Jerusalem, Judea and the region across the Jordan followed him.[h]

The Beatitudes

5 Now when he saw the crowds, he went up on
a mountainside and sat down. His disciples
came to him, 2 and he began to teach them, saying:

3 "Blessed are the poor in spirit,
  for theirs is the kingdom of heaven.[i]
4 Blessed are those who mourn,
  for they will be comforted.[j]
5 Blessed are the meek,
  for they will inherit the earth.[k]
6 Blessed are those who hunger and thirst
    for righteousness,
  for they will be filled.[l]
7 Blessed are the merciful,
  for they will be shown mercy.
8 Blessed are the pure in heart,[m]
  for they will see God.[n]
9 Blessed are the peacemakers,
  for they will be called sons of God.[o]
10 Blessed are those who are persecuted
    because of righteousness,[p]
  for theirs is the kingdom of heaven.

11 "Blessed are you when people insult you,[q] persecute you and falsely say all kinds of evil against
you because of me. 12 Rejoice and be glad,[r]
because great is your reward in heaven, for in the
same way they persecuted the prophets who were
before you.[s]

Salt and Light

13 "You are the salt of the earth. But if the salt
loses its saltiness, how can it be made salty again?
It is no longer good for anything, except to be
thrown out and trampled by men.[t]
14 "You are the light of the world.[u] A city on a
hill cannot be hidden. 15 Neither do people light a
lamp and put it under a bowl. Instead they put it
on its stand, and it gives light to everyone in the
house.[v] 16 In the same way, let your light shine
before men, that they may see your good deeds
and praise[w] your Father in heaven.

The Fulfillment of the Law

17 "Do not think that I have come to abolish the
Law or the Prophets; I have not come to abolish
them but to fulfill them.[x] 18 I tell you the truth,
until heaven and earth disappear, not the smallest letter, not the least stroke of a pen, will by any
means disappear from the Law until everything is
accomplished.[y] 19 Anyone who breaks one of the
least of these commandments[z] and teaches others

[a] *25* That is, the Ten Cities

4:24 [e] Mt 8:16,28; 9:32; 15:22; Mk 1:32; 5:15,16,18 [f] Mt 17:15 [g] Mt 8:6; 9:2; Mk 2:3
4:25 [h] Mk 3:7,8; Lk 6:17
5:3 [i] ver 10,19; Mt 25:34
5:4 [j] Isa 61:2,3; Rev 7:17
5:5 [k] Ps 37:11; Ro 4:13
5:6 [l] Isa 55:1,2
5:8 [m] Ps 24:3,4 [n] Heb 12:14; Rev 22:4
5:9 [o] ver 44,45; Ro 8:14
5:10 [p] 1Pe 3:14
5:11 [q] 1Pe 4:14
5:12 [r] Ac 5:41; 1Pe 4:13,16 [s] Mt 23:31,37; Ac 7:52; 1Th 2:15
5:13 [t] Mk 9:50; Lk 14:34,35
5:14 [u] Jn 8:12
5:15 [v] Mk 4:21; Lk 8:16
5:16 [w] Mt 9:8
5:17 [x] Ro 3:31
5:18 [y] Lk 16:17
5:19 [z] Jas 2:10

to do the same will be called least in the kingdom of heaven, but whoever practices and teaches these commands will be called great in the kingdom of heaven. [20]For I tell you that unless your righteousness surpasses that of the Pharisees and the teachers of the law, you will certainly not enter the kingdom of heaven.

Murder

[21]"You have heard that it was said to the people long ago, 'Do not murder,[a][a] and anyone who murders will be subject to judgment.' [22]But I tell you that anyone who is angry with his brother[b] will be subject to judgment.[b] Again, anyone who says to his brother, 'Raca,[c]' is answerable to the Sanhedrin.[c] But anyone who says, 'You fool!' will be in danger of the fire of hell.[d]

[23]"Therefore, if you are offering your gift at the altar and there remember that your brother has something against you, [24]leave your gift there in front of the altar. First go and be reconciled to your brother; then come and offer your gift.

[25]"Settle matters quickly with your adversary who is taking you to court. Do it while you are still with him on the way, or he may hand you over to the judge, and the judge may hand you over to the officer, and you may be thrown into prison. [26]I tell you the truth, you will not get out until you have paid the last penny.[d]

Adultery

[27]"You have heard that it was said, 'Do not commit adultery.'[e][e] [28]But I tell you that anyone who looks at a woman lustfully has already committed adultery with her in his heart.[f] [29]If your right eye causes you to sin,[g] gouge it out and throw it away. It is better for you to lose one part of your body than for your whole body to be thrown into hell. [30]And if your right hand causes you to sin, cut it off and throw it away. It is better for you to lose one part of your body than for your whole body to go into hell.

Divorce

[31]"It has been said, 'Anyone who divorces his wife must give her a certificate of divorce.'[f][h] [32]But I tell you that anyone who divorces his wife, except for marital unfaithfulness, causes her to become an adulteress, and anyone who marries the divorced woman commits adultery.[i]

Oaths

[33]"Again, you have heard that it was said to the people long ago, 'Do not break your oath,[j] but keep the oaths you have made to the Lord.'[k] [34]But I tell you, Do not swear at all:[l] either by heaven, for it is God's throne;[m] [35]or by the earth, for it is

5:21 [a]Ex 20:13; Dt 5:17
5:22 [b]1Jn 3:15 [c]Mt 26:59 [d]Jas 3:6
5:27 [e]Ex 20:14; Dt 5:18
5:28 [f]Pr 6:25
5:29 [g]Mt 18:6,8,9; Mk 9:42-47
5:31 [h]Dt 24:1-4
5:32 [i]Lk 16:18
5:33 [j]Lev 19:12 [k]Nu 30:2; Dt 23:21; Mt 23:16-22
5:34 [l]Jas 5:12 [m]Isa 66:1; Mt 23:22

[a] *21* Exodus 20:13 [b] *22* Some manuscripts *brother without cause* [c] *22* An Aramaic term of contempt [d] *26* Greek *kodrantes* [e] *27* Exodus 20:14 [f] *31* Deut. 24:1

But I Tell You

MT 5:21-48

Jesus rejects the tradition of the Pharisees. Six times in this passage he says, "You have heard that it was said . . . But I tell you . . ." (Mt 5:21-22,27-28,31-32,33-34,38-39,43-44). Jesus teaches that the true intent of God's law is, in many cases, different from what the Pharisees maintain. Jesus instructs his followers to heed the spirit of the law, not just the letter of the law. Murder is more than taking someone's life, as the Pharisees teach; murder is also allowing hatred to take root in one's heart, calling another a "fool." Adultery is more than illicit sex; adultery begins with, and includes, an attitude of lust. We cannot read Jesus' interpretation of the law without hearing his call to a right heart attitude.

The Sermon Continues

MT 6:1-24

Jesus continues his sermon, breaking down piece by piece the Pharisee's notion of truth and replacing it with his own. The Pharisees make a great show of giving to the needy; Jesus says that giving should be done in secret and the reward for it will come in heaven. The "hypocrites" (Mt 6:5) love to pray loudly and publicly; Jesus says prayers should be private, quiet, secret. He rebukes those same hypocrites for their long faces as they fast, hoping others will notice their piety; Jesus tells his listeners to fast without trying to gain recognition. In every case, Jesus makes it clear that he is ushering in a new order, calling his followers to a higher standard.

his footstool; or by Jerusalem, for it is the city of the Great King.[n] 36 And do not swear by your head, for you cannot make even one hair white or black. 37 Simply let your 'Yes' be 'Yes,' and your 'No,' 'No';[o] anything beyond this comes from the evil one.[p]

An Eye for an Eye

38 "You have heard that it was said, 'Eye for eye, and tooth for tooth.'[a][q] 39 But I tell you, Do not resist an evil person. If someone strikes you on the right cheek, turn to him the other also.[r] 40 And if someone wants to sue you and take your tunic, let him have your cloak as well. 41 If someone forces you to go one mile, go with him two miles. 42 Give to the one who asks you, and do not turn away from the one who wants to borrow from you.[s]

Love for Enemies

43 "You have heard that it was said, 'Love your neighbor[b][t] and hate your enemy.'[u] 44 But I tell you: Love your enemies[c] and pray for those who persecute you,[v] 45 that you may be sons[w] of your Father in heaven. He causes his sun to rise on the evil and the good, and sends rain on the righteous and the unrighteous.[x] 46 If you love those who love you, what reward will you get?[y] Are not even the tax collectors doing that? 47 And if you greet only your brothers, what are you doing more than others? Do not even pagans do that? 48 Be perfect, therefore, as your heavenly Father is perfect.[z]

Giving to the Needy

6 "Be careful not to do your 'acts of righteousness' before men, to be seen by them.[a] If you do, you will have no reward from your Father in heaven.

2 "So when you give to the needy, do not announce it with trumpets, as the hypocrites do in the synagogues and on the streets, to be honored by men. I tell you the truth, they have received their reward in full. 3 But when you give to the needy, do not let your left hand know what your right hand is doing, 4 so that your giving may be in secret. Then your Father, who sees what is done in secret, will reward you.[b]

Prayer

5 "And when you pray, do not be like the hypocrites, for they love to pray standing[c] in the synagogues and on the street corners to be seen by men. I tell you the truth, they have received their reward in full. 6 But when you pray, go into your room, close the door and pray to your Father,[d] who is unseen. Then your Father, who sees what is done in secret, will reward you. 7 And when you pray, do not keep on babbling[e] like pagans, for

5:35 [n]Ps 48:2
5:37 [o]Jas 5:12 [p]Mt 6:13; 13:19,38; Jn 17:15; 2Th 3:3; 1Jn 2:13,14; 3:12; 5:18, 19
5:38 [q]Ex 21:24; Lev 24:20; Dt 19:21
5:39 [r]Lk 6:29; Ro 12:17,19; 1Co 6:7; 1Pe 3:9
5:42 [s]Dt 15:8; Lk 6:30
5:43 [t]Lev 19:18 [u]Dt 23:6
5:44 [v]Lk 6:27,28; 23:34; Ac 7:60; Ro 12:14; 1Co 4:12; 1Pe 2:23
5:45 [w]ver 9 [x]Job 25:3
5:46 [y]Lk 6:32
5:48 [z]Lev 19:2; 1Pe 1:16
6:1 [a]Mt 23:5
6:4 [b]ver 6,18; Col 3:23,24
6:5 [c]Mk 11:25; Lk 18:10-14
6:6 [d]2Ki 4:33
6:7 [e]Ecc 5:2

[a] *38* Exodus 21:24; Lev. 24:20; Deut. 19:21 [b] *43* Lev. 19:18
[c] *44* Some late manuscripts *enemies, bless those who curse you, do good to those who hate you*

they think they will be heard because of their
many words.[f] 8Do not be like them, for your
Father knows what you need[g] before you ask him.
9"This, then, is how you should pray:

" 'Our Father in heaven,
hallowed be your name,
10your kingdom[h] come,
your will be done[i]
on earth as it is in heaven.
11Give us today our daily bread.[j]
12Forgive us our debts,
as we also have forgiven our debtors.[k]
13And lead us not into temptation,[l]
but deliver us from the evil one.[a][m]

14For if you forgive men when they sin against
you, your heavenly Father will also forgive you.[n]
15But if you do not forgive men their sins, your
Father will not forgive your sins.[o]

Fasting

16"When you fast, do not look somber[p] as the
hypocrites do, for they disfigure their faces to
show men they are fasting. I tell you the truth,
they have received their reward in full. 17But
when you fast, put oil on your head and wash
your face, 18so that it will not be obvious to men
that you are fasting, but only to your Father, who
is unseen; and your Father, who sees what is done
in secret, will reward you.[q]

Treasures in Heaven

19"Do not store up for yourselves treasures on
earth,[r] where moth and rust destroy,[s] and where
thieves break in and steal. 20But store up for yourselves treasures in heaven,[t] where moth and rust
do not destroy, and where thieves do not break in
and steal.[u] 21For where your treasure is, there your
heart will be also.[v]
22"The eye is the lamp of the body. If your eyes
are good, your whole body will be full of light.
23But if your eyes are bad, your whole body will
be full of darkness. If then the light within you is
darkness, how great is that darkness!
24"No one can serve two masters. Either he will
hate the one and love the other, or he will be
devoted to the one and despise the other. You cannot serve both God and Money.[w]

Do Not Worry

25"Therefore I tell you, do not worry[x] about
your life, what you will eat or drink; or about
your body, what you will wear. Is not life more
important than food, and the body more important than clothes? 26Look at the birds of the air;
they do not sow or reap or store away in barns,
and yet your heavenly Father feeds them.[y] Are
you not much more valuable than they?[z] 27Who

6:7 [f]1Ki 18:26-29
6:8 [g]ver 32
6:10 [h]Mt 3:2 [i]Mt 26:39
6:11 [j]Pr 30:8
6:12 [k]Mt 18:21-35
6:13 [l]Jas 1:13 [m]Mt 5:37
6:14 [n]Mt 18:21-35; Mk 11:25,26; Eph 4:32; Col 3:13
6:15 [o]Mt 18:35
6:16 [p]Isa 58:5
6:18 [q]ver 4,6
6:19 [r]Pr 23:4; Heb 13:5 [s]Jas 5:2,3
6:20 [t]Mt 19:21; Lk 12:33; 18:22; 1Ti 6:19 [u]Lk 12:33
6:21 [v]Lk 12:34
6:24 [w]Lk 16:13
6:25 [x]ver 27,28, 31,34; Lk 10:41; 12:11,22; Php 4:6; 1Pe 5:7
6:26 [y]Job 38:41; Ps 147:9 [z]Mt 10:29-31

[a] *13* Or *from evil*; some late manuscripts *one, / for yours is the kingdom and the power and the glory forever. Amen.*

Worry never empties tomorrow of its sorrow, but it does empty it of its strength. Don't let anyone rob you of your confidence in God. Know his Word. Hold on to his hand. He will make your impossible mission possible and your life so much more than bearable.

—Barbara Johnson

Pigs and Pearls

MT 7:6

Jesus' admonition to not "give dogs what is sacred" and to not "throw your pearls to pigs" (Mt 7:6) can be better understood in light of the historical time period and Jewish custom. Dogs were undomesticated, wild and vicious, capable of savage attack. Pigs were ceremonially unclean animals, and Jews could not eat their meat or use them for sacrifices. The phrase "what is sacred" refers to the gospel of the kingdom. Jesus is telling his listeners not to entrust the gospel of the kingdom—not to throw their pearls—to those who give clear evidence of rejecting the gospel with scorn and hardened contempt.

of you by worrying can add a single hour to his
life[a]?[a]
28“And why do you worry about clothes? See
how the lilies of the field grow. They do not labor
or spin. 29Yet I tell you that not even Solomon in
all his splendor[b] was dressed like one of these. 30If
that is how God clothes the grass of the field,
which is here today and tomorrow is thrown into
the fire, will he not much more clothe you, O you
of little faith?[c] 31So do not worry, saying, ‘What
shall we eat?’ or ‘What shall we drink?’ or ‘What
shall we wear?’ 32For the pagans run after all these
things, and your heavenly Father knows that you
need them.[d] 33But seek first his kingdom and his
righteousness, and all these things will be given to
you as well.[e] 34Therefore do not worry about
tomorrow, for tomorrow will worry about itself.
Each day has enough trouble of its own.

Judging Others

7 “Do not judge, or you too will be judged.[f] 2For
in the same way you judge others, you will be
judged, and with the measure you use, it will be
measured to you.[g]
3“Why do you look at the speck of sawdust in
your brother's eye and pay no attention to the
plank in your own eye? 4How can you say to your
brother, ‘Let me take the speck out of your eye,’
when all the time there is a plank in your own
eye? 5You hypocrite, first take the plank out of
your own eye, and then you will see clearly to
remove the speck from your brother's eye.
6“Do not give dogs what is sacred; do not throw
your pearls to pigs. If you do, they may trample
them under their feet, and then turn and tear you
to pieces.

Ask, Seek, Knock

7“Ask and it will be given to you;[h] seek and you
will find; knock and the door will be opened to
you. 8For everyone who asks receives; he who
seeks finds;[i] and to him who knocks, the door
will be opened.
9“Which of you, if his son asks for bread, will
give him a stone? 10Or if he asks for a fish, will give
him a snake? 11If you, then, though you are evil,
know how to give good gifts to your children, how
much more will your Father in heaven give good
gifts to those who ask him! 12So in everything, do
to others what you would have them do to you,[j]
for this sums up the Law and the Prophets.[k]

The Narrow and Wide Gates

13“Enter through the narrow gate.[l] For wide is
the gate and broad is the road that leads to
destruction, and many enter through it. 14But
small is the gate and narrow the road that leads to
life, and only a few find it.

6:27 [a]Ps 39:5
6:29 [b]1Ki 10:4-7
6:30 [c]Mt 8:26; 14:31; 16:8
6:32 [d]ver 8
6:33 [e]Mt 19:29; Mk 10:29-30
7:1 [f]Lk 6:37; Ro 14:4,10, 13; 1Co 4:5; Jas 4:11,12
7:2 [g]Mk 4:24; Lk 6:38
7:7 [h]Mt 21:22; Mk 11:24; Jn 14:13,14; 15:7,16; 16:23,24; Jas 1:5-8; 4:2,3; 1Jn 3:22; 5:14,15
7:8 [i]Pr 8:17; Jer 29:12,13
7:12 [j]Lk 6:31 [k]Ro 13:8-10; Gal 5:14
7:13 [l]Lk 13:24

[a] *27* Or *single cubit to his height*

A Tree and Its Fruit

15“Watch out for false prophets.[m] They come to you in sheep’s clothing, but inwardly they are ferocious wolves.[n] 16By their fruit you will recognize them.[o] Do people pick grapes from thornbushes, or figs from thistles?[p] 17Likewise every good tree bears good fruit, but a bad tree bears bad fruit. 18A good tree cannot bear bad fruit, and a bad tree cannot bear good fruit. 19Every tree that does not bear good fruit is cut down and thrown into the fire.[q] 20Thus, by their fruit you will recognize them.

21“Not everyone who says to me, ‘Lord, Lord,’[r] will enter the kingdom of heaven, but only he who does the will of my Father who is in heaven.[s] 22Many will say to me on that day,[t] ‘Lord, Lord, did we not prophesy in your name, and in your name drive out demons and perform many miracles?’[u] 23Then I will tell them plainly, ‘I never knew you. Away from me, you evildoers!’[v]

The Wise and Foolish Builders

24“Therefore everyone who hears these words of mine and puts them into practice[w] is like a wise man who built his house on the rock. 25The rain came down, the streams rose, and the winds blew and beat against that house; yet it did not fall, because it had its foundation on the rock. 26But everyone who hears these words of mine and does not put them into practice is like a foolish man who built his house on sand. 27The rain came down, the streams rose, and the winds blew and beat against that house, and it fell with a great crash.”

28When Jesus had finished saying these things,[x] the crowds were amazed at his teaching,[y] 29because he taught as one who had authority, and not as their teachers of the law.

The Man With Leprosy

8 When he came down from the mountainside, large crowds followed him. 2A man with leprosy[a][z] came and knelt before him[a] and said, “Lord, if you are willing, you can make me clean.”

3Jesus reached out his hand and touched the man. “I am willing,” he said. “Be clean!” Immediately he was cured[b] of his leprosy. 4Then Jesus said to him, “See that you don’t tell anyone.[b] But go, show yourself to the priest and offer the gift Moses commanded,[c] as a testimony to them.”

The Faith of the Centurion

5When Jesus had entered Capernaum, a centurion came to him, asking for help. 6“Lord,” he said, “my servant lies at home paralyzed and in terrible suffering.”

7Jesus said to him, “I will go and heal him.”

8The centurion replied, “Lord, I do not deserve

[a] 2 The Greek word was used for various diseases affecting the skin—not necessarily leprosy. [b] 3 Greek *made clean*

7:15 [m]Jer 23:16; Mt 24:24; Mk 13:22; Lk 6:26; 2Pe 2:1; 1Jn 4:1; Rev 16:13 [n]Ac 20:29
7:16 [o]Mt 12:33; Lk 6:44 [p]Jas 3:12
7:19 [q]Mt 3:10
7:21 [r]Hos 8:2; Mt 25:11 [s]Ro 2:13; Jas 1:22
7:22 [t]Mt 10:15 [u]1Co 13:1-3
7:23 [v]Ps 6:8; Mt 25:12,41; Lk 13:25-27
7:24 [w]Jas 1:22-25
7:28 [x]Mt 11:1; 13:53; 19:1; 26:1 [y]Mt 13:54; Mk 1:22; 6:2; Lk 4:32; Jn 7:46
8:2 [z]Lk 5:12 [a]Mt 9:18; 15:25; 18:26; 20:20
8:4 [b]Mt 9:30; Mk 5:43; 7:36; 8:30 [c]Lev 14:2-32

False Prophets

MT 7:15–29

Jesus warns his listeners to be wary of false prophets, those who seem as harmless as sheep but are actually “ferocious wolves” (Mt 7:15). He says that the discerning listener will know false messengers by their fruit, meaning that the evidence of their lives and their lack of relationship with Jesus will be observable and telling. Those who build their lives on God’s truth build on a firm foundation, Jesus himself. Those who build on the sand—ignoring Jesus’ teachings—will not be able to withstand the storms of life. If we want our lives to hold up under pressure, our only choice is to build on the rock of God’s truth revealed in Christ.

Jesus teaches with such authority that the crowds are “amazed” (Mt 7:28), which means, literally, “overwhelmed.” His teaching so far surpasses that of the Pharisees that his listeners know he is no ordinary rabbi.

Faith and Healing

MT 8:1-17

In these verses we see Jesus exercising his power and his heart to heal. He heals a man's leprosy with only a touch. He heals the centurion's servant without even being present. He heals Peter's mother-in-law of an incapacitating fever. Many who are possessed by demons come to Peter's home to be healed by Jesus.

Jesus' power to heal is a fulfillment of Isaiah's prophecy that the Messiah will take up our infirmities and carry our sorrows (Isa 53:4). Our eternal future also holds the promise of his healing power: "He will wipe every tear from [our] eyes. There will be no more death or mourning or crying or pain" (Rev 21:4). Now, while we live between the earthly and heavenly reigns of Christ, we may indeed experience his healing power, but our true healing will not be complete until we are with him forever.

to have you come under my roof. But just say the
word, and my servant will be healed.[d] 9For I
myself am a man under authority, with soldiers
under me. I tell this one, 'Go,' and he goes; and
that one, 'Come,' and he comes. I say to my servant, 'Do this,' and he does it."
10When Jesus heard this, he was astonished and
said to those following him, "I tell you the truth, I
have not found anyone in Israel with such great
faith.[e] 11I say to you that many will come from the
east and the west,[f] and will take their places at the
feast with Abraham, Isaac and Jacob in the kingdom of heaven.[g] 12But the subjects of the kingdom[h]
will be thrown outside, into the darkness, where
there will be weeping and gnashing of teeth."[i]
13Then Jesus said to the centurion, "Go! It will
be done just as you believed it would."[j] And his
servant was healed at that very hour.

Jesus Heals Many

14When Jesus came into Peter's house, he saw
Peter's mother-in-law lying in bed with a fever.
15He touched her hand and the fever left her, and
she got up and began to wait on him.
16When evening came, many who were demon-possessed were brought to him, and he drove out
the spirits with a word and healed all the sick.[k]
17This was to fulfill[l] what was spoken through the
prophet Isaiah:

> "He took up our infirmities
> and carried our diseases."[c][m]

The Cost of Following Jesus

18When Jesus saw the crowd around him, he
gave orders to cross to the other side of the lake.[n]
19Then a teacher of the law came to him and said,
"Teacher, I will follow you wherever you go."
20Jesus replied, "Foxes have holes and birds of
the air have nests, but the Son of Man[o] has no
place to lay his head."
21Another disciple said to him, "Lord, first let
me go and bury my father."
22But Jesus told him, "Follow me,[p] and let the
dead bury their own dead."

Jesus Calms the Storm

23Then he got into the boat and his disciples followed him. 24Without warning, a furious storm
came up on the lake, so that the waves swept over
the boat. But Jesus was sleeping. 25The disciples
went and woke him, saying, "Lord, save us! We're
going to drown!"
26He replied, "You of little faith,[q] why are you
so afraid?" Then he got up and rebuked the winds
and the waves, and it was completely calm.[r]
27The men were amazed and asked, "What kind
of man is this? Even the winds and the waves
obey him!"

[c] *17* Isaiah 53:4

8:8 [d]Ps 107:20
8:10 [e]Mt 15:28
8:11 [f]Ps 107:3; Isa 49:12; 59:19; Mal 1:11 [g]Lk 13:29
8:12 [h]Mt 13:38 [i]Mt 13:42, 50; 22:13; 24:51; 25:30; Lk 13:28
8:13 [j]Mt 9:22
8:16 [k]Mt 4:23,24
8:17 [l]Mt 1:22 [m]Isa 53:4
8:18 [n]Mk 4:35
8:20 [o]Da 7:13; Mt 12:8,32, 40; 16:13, 27,28; 17:9; 19:28; Mk 2:10; 8:31
8:22 [p]Mt 4:19
8:26 [q]Mt 6:30 [r]Ps 65:7; 89:9; 107:29

Week 31

Calming the Storm

Some people love the howling winds, flashing lightning and crashing thunder during a storm. Other people cower in fear. It's easy to deride other people's reactions when you feel safe. But when your security is gone and you're staring destruction in the face, it's not so easy to be courageous.

Describe the storm the disciples are experiencing (Mt 8:24; Lk 8:23). They are in great danger. Their fear is not unfounded. What sorts of sudden, furious "storms" have tested your courage?

Jesus is sleeping through all this turmoil and chaos. How long do you think the disciples bail water before they wake him? How do you try to calm your own storms?

In terror, the disciples finally wake Jesus, saying, "Lord, save us! Teacher, don't you care if we drown?" (Mt 8:25; Mk 4:38). In the midst of the storms of life, how are you like the disciples?

What is Jesus' response (Mt 8:26)? Notice that Jesus does not calm the storm before he asks this question; he asks it while the waves are still sweeping over the boat. It's easy to be calm and fearless when the danger is past. Jesus is asking for your trust in the *midst* of the storm. Why do you think Jesus seems surprised by the disciples' fear? Is he surprised by yours?

After Jesus calms the storm, what is the reaction of the disciples (Mt 8:27)? Are you ever astounded when, after you have asked for God's help, he intervenes in your life to calm your storm? How can your feelings of fear be a gauge to measure the level of your faith?

Enjoying God THROUGH the Word

Read 1 Samuel 17:4-50 (pages 447-449). After you read the description of Goliath, you can perhaps better understand Saul's fear and that of the Israelites (1Sa 17:11,24). They see Goliath's threats not only as a physical danger, but also as an attack on their personal reputations and the reputation of their nation (1Sa 17:10,25). But David sees Goliath's threats as an affront to God (1Sa 17:26). Goliath certainly intimidates David, but David isn't trusting his own abilities. He is trusting the power of Almighty God (1Sa 17:37,47).

When you trust God rather than yourself, you can depend on his help. Your courage in difficult circumstances may be misunderstood, as was David's (1Sa 17:28). People may try to dissuade you from trusting God, as they did David (1Sa 17:33). But if you make it clear that your courage comes from your confidence in God's abilities (1Sa 17:37), not your own, then God will receive the glory for the outcome (1Sa 17:47).

Enjoying God THROUGH Experience

Fear is a normal human reaction. When you're afraid, do as David did. He says, "When I am afraid, I will trust in [God]" (Ps 56:3). Fear is an opportunity to expand your faith in God. It is an opportunity to run to the Lord as your shelter. You can find refuge "under his wings" (Ps 91:4). Bring your fears, anxieties and concerns to God, the only One is who fully able to calm your storms and defeat your Goliaths.

Go to page 1605 for your next weekly study.

Mercy, Not Sacrifice

MT 9:12–13

Matthew's dinner party includes tax collectors and sinners—just the sort of people no self-respecting Pharisee will entertain. Jesus' presence at this dinner makes it clear that his ministry is directed to those whose hearts are open, regardless of their station in life. While the Pharisees focus on proper Jewish ceremony and sacrifices, Jesus recites the words of Hosea 6:6 to indicate that the sacrifice he values is a merciful heart ("I desire mercy, not sacrifice"). Jesus longs for us to have compassionate hearts.

The Healing of Two Demon-possessed Men

28When he arrived at the other side in the
region of the Gadarenes,[a] two demon-possessed[s]
men coming from the tombs met him. They were
so violent that no one could pass that way.
29"What do you want with us,[t] Son of God?" they
shouted. "Have you come here to torture us before
the appointed time?"[u]
30Some distance from them a large herd of pigs
was feeding. 31The demons begged Jesus, "If you
drive us out, send us into the herd of pigs."
32He said to them, "Go!" So they came out and
went into the pigs, and the whole herd rushed
down the steep bank into the lake and died in the
water. 33Those tending the pigs ran off, went into
the town and reported all this, including what had
happened to the demon-possessed men. 34Then
the whole town went out to meet Jesus. And
when they saw him, they pleaded with him to
leave their region.[v]

Jesus Heals a Paralytic

9 Jesus stepped into a boat, crossed over and
came to his own town.[w] 2Some men brought
to him a paralytic,[x] lying on a mat. When Jesus
saw their faith,[y] he said to the paralytic, "Take
heart,[z] son; your sins are forgiven."[a]
3At this, some of the teachers of the law said to
themselves, "This fellow is blaspheming!"[b]
4Knowing their thoughts,[c] Jesus said, "Why do
you entertain evil thoughts in your hearts?
5Which is easier: to say, 'Your sins are forgiven,' or
to say, 'Get up and walk'? 6But so that you may
know that the Son of Man[d] has authority on earth
to forgive sins . . ." Then he said to the paralytic,
"Get up, take your mat and go home." 7And the
man got up and went home. 8When the crowd
saw this, they were filled with awe; and they
praised God,[e] who had given such authority to
men.

The Calling of Matthew

9As Jesus went on from there, he saw a man
named Matthew sitting at the tax collector's
booth. "Follow me," he told him, and Matthew got
up and followed him.
10While Jesus was having dinner at Matthew's
house, many tax collectors and "sinners" came
and ate with him and his disciples. 11When the
Pharisees saw this, they asked his disciples, "Why
does your teacher eat with tax collectors and
'sinners'?"[f]
12On hearing this, Jesus said, "It is not the
healthy who need a doctor, but the sick. 13But go
and learn what this means: 'I desire mercy, not
sacrifice.'[b][g] For I have not come to call the righteous, but sinners."[h]

8:28 [s]Mt 4:24
8:29 [t]Jdg 11:12; 2Sa 16:10; 1Ki 17:18; Mk 1:24; Lk 4:34; Jn 2:4 [u]2Pe 2:4
8:34 [v]Lk 5:8; Ac 16:39
9:1 [w]Mt 4:13
9:2 [x]Mt 4:24 [y]ver 22 [z]Jn 16:33 [a]Lk 7:48
9:3 [b]Mt 26:65; Jn 10:33
9:4 [c]Ps 94:11; Mt 12:25; Lk 6:8; 9:47; 11:17
9:6 [d]Mt 8:20
9:8 [e]Mt 5:16; 15:31; Lk 7:16; 13:13; 17:15; 23:47; Jn 15:8; Ac 4:21; 11:18; 21:20
9:11 [f]Mt 11:19; Lk 5:30; 15:2; Gal 2:15
9:13 [g]Hos 6:6; Mic 6:6-8; Mt 12:7 [h]1Ti 1:15

[a] *28* Some manuscripts *Gergesenes*; others *Gerasenes*
[b] *13* Hosea 6:6

Jesus Questioned About Fasting

14 Then John's disciples came and asked him,
9:14 "How is it that we and the Pharisees fast,[i] but
[i]Lk 18:12 your disciples do not fast?"
15 Jesus answered, "How can the guests of the
9:15 [j]Jn 3:29 bridegroom mourn while he is with them?[j] The
[k]Ac 13:2,3; time will come when the bridegroom will be tak-
14:23 en from them; then they will fast.[k]
16 "No one sews a patch of unshrunk cloth on an
old garment, for the patch will pull away from the
garment, making the tear worse. 17 Neither do men
pour new wine into old wineskins. If they do, the
skins will burst, the wine will run out and the
wineskins will be ruined. No, they pour new wine
into new wineskins, and both are preserved."

A Dead Girl and a Sick Woman

9:18 18 While he was saying this, a ruler came and
[l]Mt 8:2 knelt before him[l] and said, "My daughter has just
[m]Mk 5:23 died. But come and put your hand on her,[m] and
she will live." 19 Jesus got up and went with him,
and so did his disciples.
20 Just then a woman who had been subject to
bleeding for twelve years came up behind him
9:20 and touched the edge of his cloak.[n] 21 She said to
[n]Mt 14:36; Mk 3:10 herself, "If I only touch his cloak, I will be
healed."
9:22 22 Jesus turned and saw her. "Take heart, daugh-
[o]Mk 10:52; Lk 7:50; ter," he said, "your faith has healed you."[o] And
17:19; 18:42 the woman was healed from that moment.[p]
[p]Mt 15:28 23 When Jesus entered the ruler's house and saw
9:23 the flute players and the noisy crowd,[q] 24 he said,
[q]2Ch 35:25; Jer 9:17,18 "Go away. The girl is not dead[r] but asleep."[s] But
they laughed at him. 25 After the crowd had been
9:24 put outside, he went in and took the girl by the
[r]Ac 20:10 hand, and she got up. 26 News of this spread
[s]Jn 11:11-14 through all that region.[t]

9:26 [t]Mt 4:24

Jesus Heals the Blind and Mute

27 As Jesus went on from there, two blind men
followed him, calling out, "Have mercy on us, Son
9:27 of David!"[u]
[u]Mt 15:22; 28 When he had gone indoors, the blind men
Mk 10:47; Lk 18:38-39 came to him, and he asked them, "Do you believe
that I am able to do this?"
"Yes, Lord," they replied.
9:29 29 Then he touched their eyes and said, "Accord-
[v]ver 22 ing to your faith will it be done to you";[v] 30 and
9:30 their sight was restored. Jesus warned them stern-
[w]Mt 8:4 ly, "See that no one knows about this."[w] 31 But they
9:31 went out and spread the news about him all over
[x]ver 26; Mk 7:36 that region.[x]
32 While they were going out, a man who was
9:32 [y]Mt 4:24 demon-possessed[y] and could not talk[z] was
[z]Mt 12:22-24 brought to Jesus. 33 And when the demon was
driven out, the man who had been mute spoke.
9:33 [a]Mk 2:12 The crowd was amazed and said, "Nothing like
this has ever been seen in Israel."[a]
9:34 34 But the Pharisees said, "It is by the prince of
[b]Mt 12:24; Lk 11:15 demons that he drives out demons."[b]

Cecil Frances Alexander wrote over 400 hymns in her lifetime. She also founded, with her sister, a school for the deaf.

Jesus Calls Us

Jesus calls us over the tumult
Of our life's wild, restless, sea;
Day by day His sweet voice
soundeth,
Saying, "Christian, follow Me!"

As of old Saint Andrew heard it
By the Galilean lake,
Turned from home and toil and
kindred,
Leaving all for Jesus' sake.

Jesus calls us from the worship
Of the vain world's golden store,
From each idol that would keep us,
Saying, "Christian, love Me more!"

In our joys and in our sorrows,
Days of toil and hours of ease,
Still He calls, in cares and
pleasures,
"Christian, love Me more than
these!"

Jesus calls us! By Thy mercies,
Savior, may we hear Thy call,
Give our hearts to Thine obedience,
Serve and love Thee best of all.

—Cecil Frances Humphreys Alexander

(1818–1895)

The Twelve

MT 10:2–4

In the Gospels' listing of Jesus' 12 disciples, Peter always appears first and Judas Iscariot always last. *Peter*, known for his denial of Christ, went on to become a missionary in Asia Minor. *Andrew*, like his brother Peter, was a fisherman, and first introduced Peter to Jesus (Jn 1:40–42). *James* was the first apostolic martyr (Ac 12:2). *John* ministered into old age. *Philip* came from Bethsaida and was originally a follower of John the Baptist. *Matthew*, a tax collector, was also known as Levi (Mk 2:14). Little is known of *Bartholomew*; he was possibly also called Nathanael, in whom Jesus said was "nothing false" (Jn 1:47). *Thomas* is remembered as the doubter, but he should also be noted for his courage (Jn 11:16) and his confession (Jn 20:28). Little is known about *James* the son of Alphaeus. *Thaddeus* may have also been called "Judas son of James" (Lk 6:16). *Simon the Zealot* was a member of the revolutionary group that sought to overthrow the Roman Empire. *Judas Iscariot* betrayed Jesus.

Jesus chose men of varied temperaments and backgrounds who were bound together by their loyalty to him and their desire to follow him.

The Workers Are Few

35Jesus went through all the towns and villages, teaching in their synagogues, preaching the good news of the kingdom and healing every disease and sickness.[c] 36When he saw the crowds, he had compassion on them,[d] because they were harassed and helpless, like sheep without a shepherd.[e] 37Then he said to his disciples, "The harvest[f] is plentiful but the workers are few.[g] 38Ask the Lord of the harvest, therefore, to send out workers into his harvest field."

Jesus Sends Out the Twelve

10 He called his twelve disciples to him and gave them authority to drive out evil[a] spirits[h] and to heal every disease and sickness.

2These are the names of the twelve apostles: first, Simon (who is called Peter) and his brother Andrew; James son of Zebedee, and his brother John; 3Philip and Bartholomew; Thomas and Matthew the tax collector; James son of Alphaeus, and Thaddaeus; 4Simon the Zealot and Judas Iscariot, who betrayed him.[i]

5These twelve Jesus sent out with the following instructions: "Do not go among the Gentiles or enter any town of the Samaritans.[j] 6Go rather to the lost sheep of Israel.[k] 7As you go, preach this message: 'The kingdom of heaven[l] is near.' 8Heal the sick, raise the dead, cleanse those who have leprosy,[b] drive out demons. Freely you have received, freely give. 9Do not take along any gold or silver or copper in your belts;[m] 10take no bag for the journey, or extra tunic, or sandals or a staff; for the worker is worth his keep.[n]

11"Whatever town or village you enter, search for some worthy person there and stay at his house until you leave. 12As you enter the home, give it your greeting.[o] 13If the home is deserving, let your peace rest on it; if it is not, let your peace return to you. 14If anyone will not welcome you or listen to your words, shake the dust off your feet[p] when you leave that home or town. 15I tell you the truth, it will be more bearable for Sodom and Gomorrah[q] on the day of judgment[r] than for that town.[s] 16I am sending you out like sheep among wolves.[t] Therefore be as shrewd as snakes and as innocent as doves.[u]

17"Be on your guard against men; they will hand you over to the local councils[v] and flog you in their synagogues.[w] 18On my account you will be brought before governors and kings[x] as witnesses to them and to the Gentiles. 19But when they arrest you, do not worry about what to say or how to say it.[y] At that time you will be given what to say, 20for it will not be you speaking, but the Spirit of your Father[z] speaking through you.

21"Brother will betray brother to death, and a father his child; children will rebel against their

9:35 [c]Mt 4:23
9:36 [d]Mt 14:14 [e]Nu 27:17; Eze 34:5,6; Zec 10:2; Mk 6:34
9:37 [f]Jn 4:35 [g]Lk 10:2
10:1 [h]Mk 3:13-15; Lk 9:1
10:4 [i]Mt 26:14-16,25,47; Jn 13:2,26, 27
10:5 [j]2Ki 17:24; Lk 9:52; Jn 4:4-26, 39,40; Ac 8:5,25
10:6 [k]Jer 50:6; Mt 15:24
10:7 [l]Mt 3:2
10:9 [m]Lk 22:35
10:10 [n]1Ti 5:18
10:12 [o]1Sa 25:6
10:14 [p]Ne 5:13; Lk 10:11; Ac 13:51
10:15 [q]2Pe 2:6 [r]Mt 12:36; 2Pe 2:9; 1Jn 4:17 [s]Mt 11:22,24
10:16 [t]Lk 10:3 [u]Ro 16:19
10:17 [v]Mt 5:22 [w]Mt 23:34; Mk 13:9; Ac 5:40; 26:11
10:18 [x]Ac 25:24-26
10:19 [y]Ex 4:12
10:20 [z]Ac 4:8

[a] 1 Greek *unclean* [b] 8 The Greek word was used for various diseases affecting the skin—not necessarily leprosy.

parents[a] and have them put to death. 22 All men
will hate you because of me, but he who stands
firm to the end will be saved.[b] 23 When you are
persecuted in one place, flee to another. I tell you
the truth, you will not finish going through the
cities of Israel before the Son of Man comes.
24 "A student is not above his teacher, nor a servant above his master.[c] 25 It is enough for the student to be like his teacher, and the servant like his
master. If the head of the house has been called
Beelzebub,[a][d] how much more the members of his
household!
26 "So do not be afraid of them. There is nothing
concealed that will not be disclosed, or hidden
that will not be made known.[e] 27 What I tell you in
the dark, speak in the daylight; what is whispered
in your ear, proclaim from the roofs. 28 Do not be
afraid of those who kill the body but cannot kill
the soul. Rather, be afraid of the One[f] who can
destroy both soul and body in hell. 29 Are not two
sparrows sold for a penny[b]? Yet not one of them
will fall to the ground apart from the will of your
Father. 30 And even the very hairs of your head are
all numbered.[g] 31 So don't be afraid; you are worth
more than many sparrows.[h]
32 "Whoever acknowledges me before men,[i] I
will also acknowledge him before my Father in
heaven. 33 But whoever disowns me before men, I
will disown him before my Father in heaven.[j]
34 "Do not suppose that I have come to bring
peace to the earth. I did not come to bring peace,
but a sword. 35 For I have come to turn

" 'a man against his father,
a daughter against her mother,
a daughter-in-law against her mother-in-
law[k]—
36 a man's enemies will be the members
of his own household.'[c][l]

37 "Anyone who loves his father or mother more
than me is not worthy of me; anyone who loves
his son or daughter more than me is not worthy of
me;[m] 38 and anyone who does not take his cross
and follow me is not worthy of me.[n] 39 Whoever
finds his life will lose it, and whoever loses his
life for my sake will find it.[o]
40 "He who receives you receives me,[p] and he
who receives me receives the one who sent me.[q]
41 Anyone who receives a prophet because he is a
prophet will receive a prophet's reward, and anyone who receives a righteous man because he is a
righteous man will receive a righteous man's
reward. 42 And if anyone gives even a cup of cold
water to one of these little ones because he is my
disciple, I tell you the truth, he will certainly not
lose his reward."[r]

10:21 [a]ver 35,36; Mic 7:6
10:22 [b]Mt 24:13; Mk 13:13
10:24 [c]Lk 6:40; Jn 13:16; 15:20
10:25 [d]Mk 3:22
10:26 [e]Mk 4:22; Lk 8:17
10:28 [f]Isa 8:12,13; Heb 10:31
10:30 [g]1Sa 14:45; 2Sa 14:11; Lk 21:18; Ac 27:34
10:31 [h]Mt 12:12
10:32 [i]Ro 10:9
10:33 [j]Mk 8:38; 2Ti 2:12
10:35 [k]ver 21
10:36 [l]Mic 7:6
10:37 [m]Lk 14:26
10:38 [n]Mt 16:24; Lk 14:27
10:39 [o]Lk 17:33; Jn 12:25
10:40 [p]Mt 18:5; Gal 4:14 [q]Lk 9:48; Jn 12:44; 13:20
10:42 [r]Mt 25:40; Mk 9:41; Heb 6:10

The Cost

MT 10:32-39

Jesus is clear about the cost of following him. Not even love for family should be greater than love for him. True disciples will pick up their crosses and follow Jesus, a reference to the Roman practice of requiring criminals to carry their own crosses as a public admission of their guilt. Jesus' followers admit his preeminence in their lives, a submission to his authority—even to death—that they willingly embrace. In the great paradox that believers over the centuries have discovered to be true, Jesus promises that only in losing our lives to him will we truly find ourselves.

[a] *25* Greek *Beezeboul* or *Beelzeboul* [b] *29* Greek *an assarion*
[c] *36* Micah 7:6

The Fulfillment

MT 11:10-15

The prophet Malachi prophesied about the coming of a "messenger" who would prepare the way before the Lord (Mal 3:1), calling him "Elijah" (Mal 4:5). Jesus offers his listeners the opportunity to recognize that John the Baptist is the prophesied "messenger," the "Elijah," who prepares the way for the Messiah. Therefore, John's admissions of Jesus as the Messiah fulfill the Old Testament prophecy. Jesus acknowledges that this truth is difficult to grasp. Nonetheless, the answer to the people's hopes for a Messiah actually stands right there among them. Jesus' listeners, both then and now, are called to believe that he is, indeed, the one promised of God, given for our salvation.

Jesus and John the Baptist

11 After Jesus had finished instructing his
twelve disciples,[s] he went on from there to
teach and preach in the towns of Galilee.[a]
2When John heard in prison[t] what Christ was
doing, he sent his disciples 3to ask him, "Are you
the one who was to come,[u] or should we expect
someone else?"
4Jesus replied, "Go back and report to John
what you hear and see: 5The blind receive sight,
the lame walk, those who have leprosy[b] are cured,
the deaf hear, the dead are raised, and the good
news is preached to the poor.[v] 6Blessed is the man
who does not fall away on account of me."[w]
7As John's[x] disciples were leaving, Jesus began
to speak to the crowd about John: "What did you
go out into the desert to see? A reed swayed by the
wind? 8If not, what did you go out to see? A man
dressed in fine clothes? No, those who wear fine
clothes are in kings' palaces. 9Then what did you
go out to see? A prophet?[y] Yes, I tell you, and more
than a prophet. 10This is the one about whom it is
written:

> " 'I will send my messenger ahead of
> you,
> who will prepare your way before
> you.'[c][z]

11I tell you the truth: Among those born of women
there has not risen anyone greater than John the
Baptist; yet he who is least in the kingdom of
heaven is greater than he. 12From the days of John
the Baptist until now, the kingdom of heaven has
been forcefully advancing, and forceful men lay
hold of it. 13For all the Prophets and the Law
prophesied until John. 14And if you are willing to
accept it, he is the Elijah who was to come.[a] 15He
who has ears, let him hear.[b]
16"To what can I compare this generation? They
are like children sitting in the marketplaces and
calling out to others:

> 17" 'We played the flute for you,
> and you did not dance;
> we sang a dirge,
> and you did not mourn.'

18For John came neither eating[c] nor drinking,[d]
and they say, 'He has a demon.' 19The Son of Man
came eating and drinking, and they say, 'Here is a
glutton and a drunkard, a friend of tax collectors
and "sinners." '[e] But wisdom is proved right by
her actions."

Woe on Unrepentant Cities

20Then Jesus began to denounce the cities in
which most of his miracles had been performed,
because they did not repent. 21"Woe to you, Kora-

11:1 [s]Mt 7:28
11:2 [t]Mt 14:3
11:3 [u]Ps 118:26; Jn 11:27; Heb 10:37
11:5 [v]Isa 35:4-6; 61:1; Lk 4:18,19
11:6 [w]Mt 13:21
11:7 [x]Mt 3:1
11:9 [y]Mt 21:26; Lk 1:76
11:10 [z]Mal 3:1; Mk 1:2
11:14 [a]Mal 4:5; Mt 17:10-13; Mk 9:11-13; Lk 1:17; Jn 1:21
11:15 [b]Mt 13:9,43; Mk 4:23; Lk 14:35; Rev 2:7
11:18 [c]Mt 3:4 [d]Lk 1:15
11:19 [e]Mt 9:11

[a] *1* Greek *in their towns* [b] *5* The Greek word was used for various diseases affecting the skin—not necessarily leprosy. [c] *10* Mal. 3:1

zin! Woe to you, Bethsaida![f] If the miracles that
were performed in you had been performed in
Tyre and Sidon,[g] they would have repented long
ago in sackcloth and ashes.[h] 22But I tell you, it will
be more bearable for Tyre and Sidon on the day of
judgment than for you.[i] 23And you, Capernaum,[j]
will you be lifted up to the skies? No, you will go
down to the depths.[a][k] If the miracles that were
performed in you had been performed in Sodom,
it would have remained to this day. 24But I tell you
that it will be more bearable for Sodom on the day
of judgment than for you."[l]

Rest for the Weary

25At that time Jesus said, "I praise you, Father,[m]
Lord of heaven and earth, because you have hidden these things from the wise and learned, and
revealed them to little children.[n] 26Yes, Father, for
this was your good pleasure.

27"All things have been committed to me[o] by my
Father.[p] No one knows the Son except the Father,
and no one knows the Father except the Son and
those to whom the Son chooses to reveal him.[q]

28"Come to me,[r] all you who are weary and
burdened, and I will give you rest. 29Take my yoke
upon you and learn from me,[s] for I am gentle and
humble in heart, and you will find rest for your
souls.[t] 30For my yoke is easy and my burden is
light."[u]

Lord of the Sabbath

12 At that time Jesus went through the grainfields on the Sabbath. His disciples were
hungry and began to pick some heads of grain[v]
and eat them. 2When the Pharisees saw this, they
said to him, "Look! Your disciples are doing what
is unlawful on the Sabbath."[w]

3He answered, "Haven't you read what David
did when he and his companions were hungry?[x]
4He entered the house of God, and he and his
companions ate the consecrated bread—which
was not lawful for them to do, but only for the
priests.[y] 5Or haven't you read in the Law that on
the Sabbath the priests in the temple desecrate the
day[z] and yet are innocent? 6I tell you that one[b]
greater than the temple is here.[a] 7If you had
known what these words mean, 'I desire mercy,
not sacrifice,'[c][b] you would not have condemned
the innocent. 8For the Son of Man[c] is Lord of the
Sabbath."

9Going on from that place, he went into their
synagogue, 10and a man with a shriveled hand
was there. Looking for a reason to accuse Jesus,
they asked him, "Is it lawful to heal on the
Sabbath?"[d]

11He said to them, "If any of you has a sheep
and it falls into a pit on the Sabbath, will you not
take hold of it and lift it out?[e] 12How much more

11:21 [f]Mk 6:45; Lk 9:10; Jn 12:21 [g]Mt 15:21; Lk 6:17; Ac 12:20 [h]Jnh 3:5-9
11:22 [i]ver 24; Mt 10:15
11:23 [j]Mt 4:13 [k]Isa 14:13-15
11:24 [l]Mt 10:15
11:25 [m]Lk 22:42; Jn 11:41 [n]1Co 1:26-29
11:27 [o]Mt 28:18 [p]Jn 3:35; 13:3; 17:2 [q]Jn 10:15
11:28 [r]Jn 7:37
11:29 [s]Jn 13:15; Php 2:5; 1Pe 2:21; 1Jn 2:6 [t]Jer 6:16
11:30 [u]1Jn 5:3
12:1 [v]Dt 23:25
12:2 [w]ver 10; Lk 13:14; 14:3; Jn 5:10; 7:23; 9:16
12:3 [x]1Sa 21:6
12:4 [y]Lev 24:5,9
12:5 [z]Nu 28:9,10; Jn 7:22,23
12:6 [a]ver 41,42
12:7 [b]Hos 6:6; Mic 6:6-8; Mt 9:13
12:8 [c]Mt 8:20
12:10 [d]ver 2; Lk 13:14; 14:3; Jn 9:16
12:11 [e]Lk 14:5

[a] 23 Greek *Hades* [b] 6 Or *something*; also in verses 41 and 42
[c] 7 Hosea 6:6

Rest for the Weary

MT 11:25-30

The invitation to lay heavy burdens on Jesus is recorded only in Matthew's Gospel. Jesus invites not the "wise and learned" (Mt 11:25), but the "weary and burdened" (Mt 11:28). *Weary* refers here to being tired from difficult struggling or labor; *burden* carries the concept of a beast weighed down with a heavy load. Jesus' *yoke* is a metaphor for the discipline of discipleship. Farmers use yokes to harness their cattle together to work, easing the load for each beast. Jesus is here contrasting the burden of submission to Pharisaic regulations with the easier burden of following him. He is gentle and humble and will not give his followers any burden heavier than they can carry.

Jesus and Satan

MT 12:22–29

Jesus confronts the power of Satan and the challenge of the Pharisees in healing this demon-possessed man, who is also blind and mute. The Pharisees attribute Jesus' ability to heal to the power of Beelzebub, the prince of demons. Jesus refutes their arguments by pointing out that if he were casting out a demon by Satan's power, then Satan would be working against himself. By driving out demons, Jesus proves that he can go into Satan's realm and come away with victory—and thus, his power is a sign that the kingdom of God has come to earth.

valuable is a man than a sheep![f] Therefore it is
lawful to do good on the Sabbath."
13Then he said to the man, "Stretch out your
hand." So he stretched it out and it was completely restored, just as sound as the other. 14But
the Pharisees went out and plotted how they
might kill Jesus.[g]

God's Chosen Servant

15Aware of this, Jesus withdrew from that place.
Many followed him, and he healed all their sick,[h]
16warning them not to tell who he was.[i] 17This
was to fulfill what was spoken through the prophet Isaiah:

18"Here is my servant whom I have
chosen,
the one I love, in whom I delight;[j]
I will put my Spirit on him,
and he will proclaim justice to the
nations.
19He will not quarrel or cry out;
no one will hear his voice in the
streets.
20A bruised reed he will not break,
and a smoldering wick he will not
snuff out,
till he leads justice to victory.
21 In his name the nations will put their
hope."[a][k]

Jesus and Beelzebub

22Then they brought him a demon-possessed
man who was blind and mute, and Jesus healed
him, so that he could both talk and see.[l] 23All the
people were astonished and said, "Could this be
the Son of David?"[m]
24But when the Pharisees heard this, they said,
"It is only by Beelzebub,[b][n] the prince of demons,
that this fellow drives out demons."[o]
25Jesus knew their thoughts[p] and said to them,
"Every kingdom divided against itself will be
ruined, and every city or household divided
against itself will not stand. 26If Satan[q] drives out
Satan, he is divided against himself. How then
can his kingdom stand? 27And if I drive out
demons by Beelzebub, by whom do your people[r]
drive them out? So then, they will be your judges.
28But if I drive out demons by the Spirit of God,
then the kingdom of God has come upon you.
29"Or again, how can anyone enter a strong
man's house and carry off his possessions unless
he first ties up the strong man? Then he can rob
his house.
30"He who is not with me is against me, and he
who does not gather with me scatters.[s] 31And so I
tell you, every sin and blasphemy will be forgiven
men, but the blasphemy against the Spirit will not

12:12 [f]Mt 10:31
12:14 [g]Mt 26:4; 27:1; Mk 3:6; Lk 6:11; Jn 5:18; 11:53
12:15 [h]Mt 4:23
12:16 [i]Mt 8:4
12:18 [j]Mt 3:17
12:21 [k]Isa 42:1-4
12:22 [l]Mt 4:24; 9:32-33
12:23 [m]Mt 9:27
12:24 [n]Mk 3:22 [o]Mt 9:34
12:25 [p]Mt 9:4
12:26 [q]Mt 4:10
12:27 [r]Ac 19:13
12:30 [s]Mk 9:40; Lk 11:23

[a] 21 Isaiah 42:1–4 [b] 24 Greek *Beezeboul* or *Beelzeboul*; also in verse 27

be forgiven.[t] 32 Anyone who speaks a word against the Son of Man will be forgiven, but anyone who speaks against the Holy Spirit will not be forgiven, either in this age[u] or in the age to come.[v]

33 "Make a tree good and its fruit will be good, or make a tree bad and its fruit will be bad, for a tree is recognized by its fruit.[w] 34 You brood of vipers,[x] how can you who are evil say anything good? For out of the overflow of the heart the mouth speaks.[y] 35 The good man brings good things out of the good stored up in him, and the evil man brings evil things out of the evil stored up in him. 36 But I tell you that men will have to give account on the day of judgment for every careless word they have spoken. 37 For by your words you will be acquitted, and by your words you will be condemned."

The Sign of Jonah

38 Then some of the Pharisees and teachers of the law said to him, "Teacher, we want to see a miraculous sign from you."[z]

39 He answered, "A wicked and adulterous generation asks for a miraculous sign! But none will be given it except the sign of the prophet Jonah.[a] 40 For as Jonah was three days and three nights in the belly of a huge fish,[b] so the Son of Man[c] will be three days and three nights in the heart of the earth.[d] 41 The men of Nineveh[e] will stand up at the judgment with this generation and condemn it; for they repented at the preaching of Jonah,[f] and now one[*a*] greater than Jonah is here. 42 The Queen of the South will rise at the judgment with this generation and condemn it; for she came[g] from the ends of the earth to listen to Solomon's wisdom, and now one greater than Solomon is here.

43 "When an evil[*b*] spirit comes out of a man, it goes through arid places seeking rest and does not find it. 44 Then it says, 'I will return to the house I left.' When it arrives, it finds the house unoccupied, swept clean and put in order. 45 Then it goes and takes with it seven other spirits more wicked than itself, and they go in and live there. And the final condition of that man is worse than the first.[h] That is how it will be with this wicked generation."

Jesus' Mother and Brothers

46 While Jesus was still talking to the crowd, his mother[i] and brothers[j] stood outside, wanting to speak to him. 47 Someone told him, "Your mother and brothers are standing outside, wanting to speak to you."[*c*]

48 He replied to him, "Who is my mother, and who are my brothers?" 49 Pointing to his disciples, he said, "Here are my mother and my brothers. 50 For whoever does the will of my Father in heaven[k] is my brother and sister and mother."

12:31 [t]Mk 3:28,29; Lk 12:10
12:32 [u]Tit 2:12 [v]Mk 10:30; Lk 20:34,35; Eph 1:21; Heb 6:5
12:33 [w]Mt 7:16,17; Lk 6:43,44
12:34 [x]Mt 3:7; 23:33 [y]Mt 15:18; Lk 6:45
12:38 [z]Mt 16:1; Mk 8:11,12; Lk 11:16; Jn 2:18; 6:30; 1Co 1:22
12:39 [a]Mt 16:4; Lk 11:29
12:40 [b]Jnh 1:17 [c]Mt 8:20 [d]Mt 16:21
12:41 [e]Jnh 1:2 [f]Jnh 3:5
12:42 [g]1Ki 10:1; 2Ch 9:1
12:45 [h]2Pe 2:20
12:46 [i]Mt 1:18; 2:11,13,14, 20; Lk 1:43; 2:33,34,48, 51; Jn 2:1,5; 19:25,26 [j]Mt 13:55; Jn 2:12; 7:3, 5; Ac 1:14; 1Co 9:5; Gal 1:19
12:50 [k]Jn 15:14

a 41 Or *something*; also in verse 42 *b 43* Greek *unclean*
c 47 Some manuscripts do not have verse 47.

Out of the Heart

MT 12:33-37

This is one of Jesus' most scathing rebukes of the Pharisees. The Pharisees can quote Scripture, but their hearts are corrupt. Jesus likens a person's behavior and speech to the way in which a tree is known by the fruit it produces. In this passage, Jesus teaches that words matter, precisely because they reflect what is in one's heart, "for out of the overflow of the heart the mouth speaks" (Mt 12:34). Other Scriptures confirm the importance of the words we speak: Ephesians 5:3–4; Colossians 3:17; James 1:19; 3:1–12.

Parables MT 13

Jesus uses parables as a teaching tool to communicate truth concerning the kingdom. Behind the word *parable* stands the Hebrew word *mashal*, a word that refers to proverbs, maxims, allegories, comparisons and especially stories containing important truths. Thus, a parable can be a proverb, a profound saying, a nonverbal symbol, an illustrative comparison or a clarifying story. Most parables are extended metaphors or similes.

Rising opposition to the ministry of Jesus encourages his greater and greater use of parables to communicate the message of the kingdom. He often concludes his parables with the admonition that those who have ears should hear and believe his word.

The Parable of the Sower

13 That same day Jesus went out of the house[l]
and sat by the lake. 2Such large crowds
gathered around him that he got into a boat[m] and
sat in it, while all the people stood on the shore.
3Then he told them many things in parables, saying: "A farmer went out to sow his seed. 4As he
was scattering the seed, some fell along the path,
and the birds came and ate it up. 5Some fell on
rocky places, where it did not have much soil. It
sprang up quickly, because the soil was shallow.
6But when the sun came up, the plants were
scorched, and they withered because they had no
root. 7Other seed fell among thorns, which grew
up and choked the plants. 8Still other seed fell on
good soil, where it produced a crop—a hundred,[n]
sixty or thirty times what was sown. 9He who has
ears, let him hear."[o]

10The disciples came to him and asked, "Why
do you speak to the people in parables?"

11He replied, "The knowledge of the secrets of
the kingdom of heaven has been given to you,[p]
but not to them. 12Whoever has will be given
more, and he will have an abundance. Whoever
does not have, even what he has will be taken
from him.[q] 13This is why I speak to them in
parables:

"Though seeing, they do not see;
though hearing, they do not hear or
understand.[r]

14In them is fulfilled the prophecy of Isaiah:

" 'You will be ever hearing but never
understanding;
you will be ever seeing but never
perceiving.
15For this people's heart has become
calloused;
they hardly hear with their ears,
and they have closed their eyes.
Otherwise they might see with their
eyes,
hear with their ears,
understand with their hearts
and turn, and I would heal them.'[a][s]

16But blessed are your eyes because they see, and
your ears because they hear.[t] 17For I tell you the
truth, many prophets and righteous men longed
to see what you see[u] but did not see it, and to hear
what you hear but did not hear it.

18"Listen then to what the parable of the sower
means: 19When anyone hears the message about
the kingdom[v] and does not understand it, the evil
one[w] comes and snatches away what was sown in
his heart. This is the seed sown along the path.
20The one who received the seed that fell on rocky
places is the man who hears the word and at once
receives it with joy. 21But since he has no root, he

13:1 [l]ver 36; Mt 9:28
13:2 [m]Lk 5:3
13:8 [n]Ge 26:12
13:9 [o]Mt 11:15
13:11 [p]Mt 11:25; 16:17; 19:11; Jn 6:65; 1Co 2:10,14; Col 1:27; 1Jn 2:20,27
13:12 [q]Mt 25:29; Lk 19:26
13:13 [r]Dt 29:4; Jer 5:21; Eze 12:2
13:15 [s]Isa 6:9,10; Jn 12:40; Ac 28:26,27; Ro 11:8
13:16 [t]Mt 16:17
13:17 [u]Jn 8:56; Heb 11:13; 1Pe 1:10-12
13:19 [v]Mt 4:23 [w]Mt 5:37

[a] *15* Isaiah 6:9,10

lasts only a short time. When trouble or persecution comes because of the word, he quickly falls
away.[x] 22 The one who received the seed that fell
among the thorns is the man who hears the word,
but the worries of this life and the deceitfulness
of wealth[y] choke it, making it unfruitful. 23 But the
one who received the seed that fell on good soil
is the man who hears the word and understands
it. He produces a crop, yielding a hundred, sixty
or thirty times what was sown."[z]

The Parable of the Weeds

24 Jesus told them another parable: "The kingdom
of heaven is like[a] a man who sowed good seed in
his field. 25 But while everyone was sleeping, his
enemy came and sowed weeds among the wheat,
and went away. 26 When the wheat sprouted and
formed heads, then the weeds also appeared.
27 "The owner's servants came to him and said,
'Sir, didn't you sow good seed in your field?
Where then did the weeds come from?'
28 " 'An enemy did this,' he replied.
"The servants asked him, 'Do you want us to
go and pull them up?'
29 " 'No,' he answered, 'because while you are
pulling the weeds, you may root up the wheat with
them. 30 Let both grow together until the harvest. At
that time I will tell the harvesters: First collect the
weeds and tie them in bundles to be burned; then
gather the wheat and bring it into my barn.' "[b]

The Parables of the Mustard Seed and the Yeast

31 He told them another parable: "The kingdom
of heaven is like[c] a mustard seed,[d] which a man
took and planted in his field. 32 Though it is the
smallest of all your seeds, yet when it grows, it is
the largest of garden plants and becomes a tree,
so that the birds of the air come and perch in its
branches."[e]
33 He told them still another parable: "The kingdom of heaven is like[f] yeast that a woman took
and mixed into a large amount[a] of flour[g] until it
worked all through the dough."[h]
34 Jesus spoke all these things to the crowd in
parables; he did not say anything to them without using a parable.[i] 35 So was fulfilled what was
spoken through the prophet:

> "I will open my mouth in parables,
> I will utter things hidden since the
> creation of the world."[b][j]

The Parable of the Weeds Explained

36 Then he left the crowd and went into the
house. His disciples came to him and said, "Explain
to us the parable[k] of the weeds in the field."
37 He answered, "The one who sowed the good

13:21 [x]Mt 11:6
13:22 [y]Mt 19:23; 1Ti 6:9,10,17
13:23 [z]ver 8
13:24 [a]ver 31,33,45,47; Mt 18:23; 20:1; 22:2; 25:1; Mk 4:26,30
13:30 [b]Mt 3:12
13:31 [c]ver 24 [d]Mt 17:20; Lk 17:6
13:32 [e]Ps 104:12; Eze 17:23; 31:6; Da 4:12
13:33 [f]ver 24 [g]Ge 18:6 [h]Gal 5:9
13:34 [i]Mk 4:33; Jn 16:25
13:35 [j]Ps 78:2; Ro 16:25,26; 1Co 2:7; Eph 3:9; Col 1:26
13:36 [k]Mt 15:15

[a] 33 Greek *three satas* (probably about 1/2 bushel or 22 liters)
[b] 35 Psalm 78:2

Mary Magdalene

. . . never forgot where she came from, what she was saved from, what she was capable of, and where she'd be without God. But Mary became God's woman, his person, his precious and beautiful bride. Jesus loved her, saved her, believed for her when she didn't even know there was another way, another life, a new and holy journey.

We are all Marys in some sort of way. Wretched women but beautiful brides. Sinners but saved. Broken but beloved. All because he lives in us.

—Kathy Troccoli

A Treasure

MT 13:44–46

Jesus likens the kingdom of God to two treasures commonly understood in the culture of the time. The parables of the buried treasure and the expensive pearl reinforce the same truth: the supreme worth of the kingdom of God.

In a land like ancient Israel, frequently ravaged by invading nations, many people would bury their valuables to keep them hidden from the invaders. Actually finding one of these buried treasure troves happens only once in a hundred lifetimes. To find such a treasure, then, makes one willing to purchase at any cost the land where it is buried. The one who buys the land possesses far more than the price of the field itself. Such a treasure is worth every sacrifice; so, too, the kingdom of heaven far surpasses the price and sacrifice of discipleship.

In the second parable the merchant whose job it is to seek pearls happens upon one of incredible value. It so surpasses any other pearl that he considers the sale of everything he owns a fair trade. As in the first parable, Jesus makes the point that those who truly understand the ultimate value of the kingdom of Christ will gladly exchange all else to follow him.

seed is the Son of Man.[l] 38 The field is the world,
and the good seed stands for the sons of the kingdom. The weeds are the sons of the evil one,[m]
39 and the enemy who sows them is the devil. The
harvest[n] is the end of the age,[o] and the harvesters
are angels.[p]
40 "As the weeds are pulled up and burned in the
fire, so it will be at the end of the age. 41 The Son of
Man[q] will send out his angels,[r] and they will weed
out of his kingdom everything that causes sin and
all who do evil. 42 They will throw them into the
fiery furnace, where there will be weeping and
gnashing of teeth.[s] 43 Then the righteous will shine
like the sun[t] in the kingdom of their Father. He
who has ears, let him hear.[u]

The Parables of the Hidden Treasure and the Pearl

44 "The kingdom of heaven is like[v] treasure hidden in a field. When a man found it, he hid it
again, and then in his joy went and sold all he
had and bought that field.[w]
45 "Again, the kingdom of heaven is like[x] a merchant looking for fine pearls. 46 When he found
one of great value, he went away and sold everything he had and bought it.

The Parable of the Net

47 "Once again, the kingdom of heaven is like[y] a
net that was let down into the lake and caught all
kinds[z] of fish. 48 When it was full, the fishermen
pulled it up on the shore. Then they sat down and
collected the good fish in baskets, but threw the
bad away. 49 This is how it will be at the end of the
age. The angels will come and separate the
wicked from the righteous[a] 50 and throw them into
the fiery furnace, where there will be weeping and
gnashing of teeth.[b]
51 "Have you understood all these things?" Jesus
asked.
"Yes," they replied.
52 He said to them, "Therefore every teacher of
the law who has been instructed about the kingdom of heaven is like the owner of a house who
brings out of his storeroom new treasures as well
as old."

A Prophet Without Honor

53 When Jesus had finished these parables,[c] he
moved on from there. 54 Coming to his hometown,
he began teaching the people in their synagogue,[d]
and they were amazed.[e] "Where did this man get
this wisdom and these miraculous powers?" they
asked. 55 "Isn't this the carpenter's son?[f] Isn't his
mother's[g] name Mary, and aren't his brothers
James, Joseph, Simon and Judas? 56 Aren't all his
sisters with us? Where then did this man get all
these things?" 57 And they took offense[h] at him.
But Jesus said to them, "Only in his hometown

13:37 [l]Mt 8:20
13:38 [m]Jn 8:44,45; 1Jn 3:10
13:39 [n]Joel 3:13 [o]Mt 24:3; 28:20 [p]Rev 14:15
13:41 [q]Mt 8:20 [r]Mt 24:31
13:42 [s]ver 50; Mt 8:12
13:43 [t]Da 12:3 [u]Mt 11:15
13:44 [v]ver 24 [w]Isa 55:1; Php 3:7,8
13:45 [x]ver 24
13:47 [y]ver 24 [z]Mt 22:10
13:49 [a]Mt 25:32
13:50 [b]Mt 8:12
13:53 [c]Mt 7:28
13:54 [d]Mt 4:23 [e]Mt 7:28
13:55 [f]Lk 3:23; Jn 6:42 [g]Mt 12:46
13:57 [h]Jn 6:61

Week 32

The Kingdom of Heaven Is Here

A kingdom is the reign or the realm of a king. The kingdom of heaven is the royal reign—kingship—of Jesus Christ. Wherever Jesus reigns, whether physically or spiritually, the kingdom of heaven exists. Jesus says that his kingdom "is not of this world," but "is from another place" (Jn 18:36). But the Bible also speaks of the kingdom of heaven here on earth (Mt 12:28).

Does the state of the world discourage you? Are you tired of struggling with sin? There is hope. You will live in a kingdom of perfection—for all eternity. But even now you may taste that kingdom during times of spiritual communion with Jesus. When you experience and enjoy God, you taste the glory to come.

What does Jesus say the kingdom of heaven is like (Mt 13:44-45)? Why is the man happy to sell all that he has? What could be of such value that you would sell everything you have to buy it? What truth is being expressed?

Matthew 13:44,46 is not implying that you can buy your way into heaven. Eternal life is so valuable that no one can buy it. How then does one obtain it (Jn 3:16; Heb 9:15)? Eternal life is God's gift to give (Rev 22:17) because he has already paid the price for it.

If the kingdom of heaven is eternal, yet can be experienced to a degree here on earth, when does it begin (Jn 3:36; 20:31; Ro 10:9-10)?

Repentance is the pathway to the kingdom (Mt 4:17), and Jesus is the door (Lk 13:22-24; Jn 10:9). To live a "kingdom life," you must leave self-interest behind and walk into life through Jesus. What is your chief hindrance to living a kingdom life?

Enjoying God THROUGH the Word

Read Matthew 19:16-30 (pages 1616-1617). This rich young man knows the value of eternal life, and he wants to have it. But he assumes that eternal life can be purchased by living a good life. He never blinks when Jesus begins listing off the commandments. The young man says he has kept them all.

Jesus knows this young man's heart. The real problem is not the man's wealth but his love of it. "Go, sell your possessions and give to the poor, and you will have treasure in heaven. Then come, follow me" (Mt 19:21). What do you love? Power, status, relationships, career, material things? Is something (even something good) holding you back from a wholehearted love for Jesus? Will you "sell" it to follow Jesus?

Enjoying God THROUGH Experience

Time spent in prayer can be a taste of heaven. Sit quietly for a few minutes. Ask the Holy Spirit to reveal anything that is holding you back from knowing God and the measure of kingdom life that is possible here on earth. If he brings something to your mind, repent and surrender it to Jesus. Allow him to refresh you and give you strength. Thank him for your taste of heaven and that you will be with him eternally to know him even better.

Go to page 1632 for your next weekly study.

Herod Antipas

MT 14:1–12

Herod Antipas ruled for more than 40 years a small region that included Galilee, the setting of John the Baptist's ministry. He despised John the Baptist for reasons both moral and political. John repeatedly exposed the incestuous nature of Herod's marriage to Herodias, who was his half-brother's wife and also his niece.

In this passage, we see that Herod is not only wicked, but also weak. When Salome, the young daughter of Herodias, pleases him with her sensual dance, he plays the pompous ruler and agrees to grant her any request. Her mother, Herodias, uses the opportunity to get rid of the man whose only offense is telling the truth. In Herod's weak acquiescence, he also flagrantly violates Jewish law, which prohibits execution without trial (see character sketches for Salome and Herodias on pages 1780 and 1779).

and in his own house is a prophet without honor."[i]

58 And he did not do many miracles there because of their lack of faith.

John the Baptist Beheaded

14 At that time Herod[j] the tetrarch heard the reports about Jesus,[k] 2 and he said to his attendants, "This is John the Baptist;[l] he has risen from the dead! That is why miraculous powers are at work in him."

3 Now Herod had arrested John and bound him and put him in prison[m] because of Herodias, his brother Philip's wife,[n] 4 for John had been saying to him: "It is not lawful for you to have her."[o] 5 Herod wanted to kill John, but he was afraid of the people, because they considered him a prophet.[p]

6 On Herod's birthday the daughter of Herodias danced for them and pleased Herod so much 7 that he promised with an oath to give her whatever she asked. 8 Prompted by her mother, she said, "Give me here on a platter the head of John the Baptist." 9 The king was distressed, but because of his oaths and his dinner guests, he ordered that her request be granted 10 and had John beheaded[q] in the prison. 11 His head was brought in on a platter and given to the girl, who carried it to her mother. 12 John's disciples came and took his body and buried it.[r] Then they went and told Jesus.

Jesus Feeds the Five Thousand

13 When Jesus heard what had happened, he withdrew by boat privately to a solitary place. Hearing of this, the crowds followed him on foot from the towns. 14 When Jesus landed and saw a large crowd, he had compassion on them[s] and healed their sick.[t]

15 As evening approached, the disciples came to him and said, "This is a remote place, and it's already getting late. Send the crowds away, so they can go to the villages and buy themselves some food."

16 Jesus replied, "They do not need to go away. You give them something to eat."

17 "We have here only five loaves[u] of bread and two fish," they answered.

18 "Bring them here to me," he said. 19 And he directed the people to sit down on the grass. Taking the five loaves and the two fish and looking up to heaven, he gave thanks and broke the loaves.[v] Then he gave them to the disciples, and the disciples gave them to the people. 20 They all ate and were satisfied, and the disciples picked up twelve basketfuls of broken pieces that were left over. 21 The number of those who ate was about five thousand men, besides women and children.

Jesus Walks on the Water

22 Immediately Jesus made the disciples get into the boat and go on ahead of him to the other side,

13:57 [i]Lk 4:24; Jn 4:44
14:1 [j]Mk 8:15; Lk 3:1,19; 13:31; 23:7, 8; Ac 4:27; 12:1 [k]Lk 9:7-9
14:2 [l]Mt 3:1
14:3 [m]Mt 4:12; 11:2 [n]Lk 3:19,20
14:4 [o]Lev 18:16; 20:21
14:5 [p]Mt 11:9
14:10 [q]Mt 17:12
14:12 [r]Ac 8:2
14:14 [s]Mt 9:36 [t]Mt 4:23
14:17 [u]Mt 16:9
14:19 [v]1Sa 9:13; Mt 26:26; Mk 8:6; Lk 24:30; Ac 2:42; 27:35; 1Ti 4:4

while he dismissed the crowd. 23After he had dis-
14:23 missed them, he went up on a mountainside by
[w]Lk 3:21 himself to pray.[w] When evening came, he was
there alone, 24but the boat was already a considerable distance[a] from land, buffeted by the waves
because the wind was against it.
25During the fourth watch of the night Jesus
went out to them, walking on the lake. 26When
14:26 the disciples saw him walking on the lake, they
[x]Lk 24:37 were terrified. "It's a ghost,"[x] they said, and cried
out in fear.
14:27 27But Jesus immediately said to them: "Take
[y]Mt 9:2; courage![y] It is I. Don't be afraid."[z]
Ac 23:11 28"Lord, if it's you," Peter replied, "tell me to
[z]Da 10:12; Mt 17:7; come to you on the water."
28:10; 29"Come," he said.
Lk 1:13,30; 2:10; Then Peter got down out of the boat, walked on
Ac 18:9; the water and came toward Jesus. 30But when he
23:11; saw the wind, he was afraid and, beginning to
Rev 1:17 sink, cried out, "Lord, save me!"
31Immediately Jesus reached out his hand and
14:31 [a]Mt 6:30 caught him. "You of little faith,"[a] he said, "why
did you doubt?"
32And when they climbed into the boat, the
wind died down. 33Then those who were in the
boat worshiped him, saying, "Truly you are the
14:33 [b]Ps 2:7; Son of God."[b]
Mt 4:3 34When they had crossed over, they landed at
Gennesaret. 35And when the men of that place recognized Jesus, they sent word to all the surrounding country. People brought all their sick to
14:36 him 36and begged him to let the sick just touch
[c]Mt 9:20 the edge of his cloak,[c] and all who touched him
were healed.

Clean and Unclean

15 Then some Pharisees and teachers of the
law came to Jesus from Jerusalem and
asked, 2"Why do your disciples break the tradi-
15:2 tion of the elders? They don't wash their hands
[d]Lk 11:38 before they eat!"[d]
3Jesus replied, "And why do you break the command of God for the sake of your tradition? 4For
15:4 God said, 'Honor your father and mother'[b][e] and
[e]Ex 20:12; 'Anyone who curses his father or mother must be
Dt 5:16; Eph 6:2 put to death.'[c][f] 5But you say that if a man says to
[f]Ex 21:17; Lev 20:9 his father or mother, 'Whatever help you might
otherwise have received from me is a gift devoted
to God,' 6he is not to 'honor his father[d]' with it.
Thus you nullify the word of God for the sake of
your tradition. 7You hypocrites! Isaiah was right
when he prophesied about you:

8" 'These people honor me with their lips,
but their hearts are far from me.
15:9 9They worship me in vain;
[g]Col 2:20-22 their teachings are but rules taught by
[h]Isa 29:13; Mal 2:2 men.[g]'[e][h]"

[a] 24 Greek *many stadia* [b] 4 Exodus 20:12; Deut. 5:16
[c] 4 Exodus 21:17; Lev. 20:9 [d] 6 Some manuscripts *father or his mother* [e] 9 Isaiah 29:13

Walking on Water

MT 14:25-33

Peter is the disciple most willing to do what no one else dares to do. That he even attempts to step out of the boat and walk on the water is amazing. His faith is strong enough to get him out of the boat but not strong enough to stand up to a storm. He begins to sink as soon as he takes his eyes off Jesus. Jesus calls him a man "of little faith" (Mt 14:31) and asks him why he doubted.

The story of Peter's life reveals a dramatic change after Jesus' ascension and the ministry of the indwelling Spirit. Once an impetuous man given to bouts of fear, Peter becomes a courageous champion in the early church, the "rock" that Jesus says he will one day be (Mt 16:18).

A Canaanite Woman

MT 15:21-28

This miracle of Jesus, performed for a Gentile woman on Gentile territory, in "the region of Tyre and Sidon" (Mt 15:21), is likely of immense interest to Matthew's Jewish readers. The Canaanite woman appeals to Jesus' Jewishness, calling him "Son of David" (Mt 15:22) when asking for help for her daughter. Jesus' reply underscores that the kingdom will first be offered to the Jews. Jesus has come to offer his own people the kingdom promised through David centuries before. The Canaanite woman asks simply, then, for the "crumbs" of his help (Mt 15:27), that some of his blessing might extend to her in her need. Jesus commends the woman for her great faith and immediately heals her daughter (see the character sketch for this woman on page 1811).

10 Jesus called the crowd to him and said, "Listen and understand. 11 What goes into a man's
mouth does not make him 'unclean,'[i] but what
comes out of his mouth, that is what makes him
'unclean.' "[j]
12 Then the disciples came to him and asked,
"Do you know that the Pharisees were offended
when they heard this?"
13 He replied, "Every plant that my heavenly
Father has not planted[k] will be pulled up by the
roots. 14 Leave them; they are blind guides.[a][l] If a
blind man leads a blind man, both will fall into a
pit."[m]
15 Peter said, "Explain the parable to us."[n]
16 "Are you still so dull?"[o] Jesus asked them.
17 "Don't you see that whatever enters the mouth
goes into the stomach and then out of the body?
18 But the things that come out of the mouth come
from the heart,[p] and these make a man 'unclean.'
19 For out of the heart come evil thoughts, murder,
adultery, sexual immorality, theft, false testimony, slander.[q] 20 These are what make a man
'unclean';[r] but eating with unwashed hands does
not make him 'unclean.' "

The Faith of the Canaanite Woman

21 Leaving that place, Jesus withdrew to the
region of Tyre and Sidon.[s] 22 A Canaanite woman
from that vicinity came to him, crying out, "Lord,
Son of David,[t] have mercy on me! My daughter is
suffering terribly from demon-possession."[u]
23 Jesus did not answer a word. So his disciples
came to him and urged him, "Send her away, for
she keeps crying out after us."
24 He answered, "I was sent only to the lost
sheep of Israel."[v]
25 The woman came and knelt before him.[w]
"Lord, help me!" she said.
26 He replied, "It is not right to take the children's bread and toss it to their dogs."
27 "Yes, Lord," she said, "but even the dogs eat
the crumbs that fall from their masters' table."
28 Then Jesus answered, "Woman, you have
great faith![x] Your request is granted." And her
daughter was healed from that very hour.

Jesus Feeds the Four Thousand

29 Jesus left there and went along the Sea of Galilee. Then he went up on a mountainside and sat
down. 30 Great crowds came to him, bringing the
lame, the blind, the crippled, the mute and many
others, and laid them at his feet; and he healed
them.[y] 31 The people were amazed when they saw
the mute speaking, the crippled made well, the
lame walking and the blind seeing. And they
praised the God of Israel.[z]
32 Jesus called his disciples to him and said, "I
have compassion for these people;[a] they have
already been with me three days and have noth-

15:11 [i]Ac 10:14,15 [j]ver 18
15:13 [k]Isa 60:21; 61:3; Jn 15:2
15:14 [l]Mt 23:16, 24; Ro 2:19 [m]Lk 6:39
15:15 [n]Mt 13:36
15:16 [o]Mt 16:9
15:18 [p]Mt 12:34; Lk 6:45; Jas 3:6
15:19 [q]Gal 5:19-21
15:20 [r]Ro 14:14
15:21 [s]Mt 11:21
15:22 [t]Mt 9:27 [u]Mt 4:24
15:24 [v]Mt 10:6,23; Ro 15:8
15:25 [w]Mt 8:2
15:28 [x]Mt 9:22
15:30 [y]Mt 4:23
15:31 [z]Mt 9:8
15:32 [a]Mt 9:36

[a] *14* Some manuscripts *guides of the blind*

ing to eat. I do not want to send them away hungry, or they may collapse on the way."
33 His disciples answered, "Where could we get
enough bread in this remote place to feed such a
crowd?"
34 "How many loaves do you have?" Jesus asked.
"Seven," they replied, "and a few small fish."
35 He told the crowd to sit down on the ground.
36 Then he took the seven loaves and the fish, and
when he had given thanks, he broke them[b] and
15:36 [b]Mt 14:19 gave them to the disciples, and they in turn to the
people. 37 They all ate and were satisfied. After-
ward the disciples picked up seven basketfuls of
15:37 broken pieces that were left over.[c] 38 The number
[c]Mt 16:10 of those who ate was four thousand, besides
women and children. 39 After Jesus had sent the
crowd away, he got into the boat and went to the
vicinity of Magadan.

The Demand for a Sign

16:1 **16** The Pharisees and Sadducees[d] came to
[d]Ac 4:1 Jesus and tested him by asking him to show
[e]Mt 12:38 them a sign from heaven.[e]
2 He replied,[a] "When evening comes, you say, 'It
will be fair weather, for the sky is red,' 3 and in the
morning, 'Today it will be stormy, for the sky is
red and overcast.' You know how to interpret the
appearance of the sky, but you cannot interpret
16:3 the signs of the times.[f] 4 A wicked and adulterous
[f]Lk 12:54-56 generation looks for a miraculous sign, but none
16:4 will be given it except the sign of Jonah."[g] Jesus
[g]Mt 12:39 then left them and went away.

The Yeast of the Pharisees and Sadducees

5 When they went across the lake, the disciples
forgot to take bread. 6 "Be careful," Jesus said to
them. "Be on your guard against the yeast of the
16:6 Pharisees and Sadducees."[h]
[h]Lk 12:1 7 They discussed this among themselves and
said, "It is because we didn't bring any bread."
8 Aware of their discussion, Jesus asked, "You of
16:8 little faith,[i] why are you talking among yourselves
[i]Mt 6:30 about having no bread? 9 Do you still not understand? Don't you remember the five loaves for the
five thousand, and how many basketfuls you
16:9 gathered?[j] 10 Or the seven loaves for the four thou-
[j]Mt 14:17-21 sand, and how many basketfuls you gathered?[k]
16:10 11 How is it you don't understand that I was not
[k]Mt 15:34-38 talking to you about bread? But be on your guard
against the yeast of the Pharisees and Sadducees."
12 Then they understood that he was not telling
them to guard against the yeast used in bread, but
16:12 against the teaching of the Pharisees and
[l]Ac 4:1 Sadducees.[l]

Peter's Confession of Christ

13 When Jesus came to the region of Caesarea

[a] 2 Some early manuscripts do not have the rest of verse 2 and all of verse 3.

Yeast

MT 16:5-12

The disciples' recollection that they have forgotten to bring bread on their trip prompts a lesson from Jesus on "the yeast of the Pharisees and Sadducees" (Mt 16:6; see the note on Mk 8:15, page 1656). The obtuse disciples are mired in their thoughts of hunger and don't understand what Jesus means.

Jesus doesn't explain. He only repeats his warning, "Be on your guard" (Mt 16:11). He wants the disciples to think deeply and figure out for themselves that just as a little yeast or leaven can permeate the whole loaf of bread, so the "yeast" of the religious leaders, their unwillingness to acknowledge the truth, can spread to others.

Peter was a rough, strong, loud, salt-of-the-earth fisherman, the kind of friend you would lean on in a crisis. He was passionately committed to following Christ, wherever that took him. When Jesus began to talk of a different end to his life than the one Peter had imagined, Peter was confused and hurt. He could never imagine leaving Jesus, let alone deny knowing him. Surely their relationship had come too far for that. And yet one night Jesus said Peter would deny him before morning. In anguish Peter cried out that he would die before letting that happen . . . bold and utterly confident in his own abilities to overcome any obstacle in his way. He knew *Jesus could count on him. Christ gave Peter a glimpse into the horror that lay just around the corner and let him know that, when it was all over, not only would Jesus still love Peter, but he also had a job for him to do: "When you have turned back, strengthen your brothers" (Lk 22:32) . . . Peter was given a second chance. He went on to become a martyr of the early church . . . Peter's life and death fed the church, for from that life-changing confrontation with Christ on the beach, he was a different man, a man who selflessly gave himself to the building up of the body of Christ. "You are Peter, and on this rock I will build my church" (Mt 16:18).*

—Sheila Walsh

Philippi, he asked his disciples, "Who do people
say the Son of Man is?"
14 They replied, "Some say John the Baptist;[m]
others say Elijah; and still others, Jeremiah or one
of the prophets."[n]
15 "But what about you?" he asked. "Who do
you say I am?"
16 Simon Peter answered, "You are the Christ,[a]
the Son of the living God."[o]
17 Jesus replied, "Blessed are you, Simon son of
Jonah, for this was not revealed to you by man,[p]
but by my Father in heaven. 18 And I tell you that
you are Peter,[b][q] and on this rock I will build my
church,[r] and the gates of Hades[c] will not overcome it.[d] 19 I will give you the keys[s] of the kingdom of heaven; whatever you bind on earth will
be[e] bound in heaven, and whatever you loose on
earth will be[e] loosed in heaven."[t] 20 Then he
warned his disciples not to tell anyone[u] that he
was the Christ.

Jesus Predicts His Death

21 From that time on Jesus began to explain to
his disciples that he must go to Jerusalem and suffer many things[v] at the hands of the elders, chief
priests and teachers of the law, and that he must
be killed and on the third day[w] be raised to life.[x]
22 Peter took him aside and began to rebuke
him. "Never, Lord!" he said. "This shall never
happen to you!"
23 Jesus turned and said to Peter, "Get behind
me, Satan![y] You are a stumbling block to me; you
do not have in mind the things of God, but the
things of men."
24 Then Jesus said to his disciples, "If anyone
would come after me, he must deny himself and
take up his cross and follow me.[z] 25 For whoever
wants to save his life[f] will lose it, but whoever
loses his life for me will find it.[a] 26 What good will
it be for a man if he gains the whole world, yet forfeits his soul? Or what can a man give in exchange
for his soul? 27 For the Son of Man[b] is going to
come[c] in his Father's glory with his angels, and
then he will reward each person according to what
he has done.[d] 28 I tell you the truth, some who are
standing here will not taste death before they see
the Son of Man coming in his kingdom."

The Transfiguration

17 After six days Jesus took with him Peter,
James and John the brother of James, and
led them up a high mountain by themselves.
2 There he was transfigured before them. His face
shone like the sun, and his clothes became as
white as the light. 3 Just then there appeared
before them Moses and Elijah, talking with Jesus.

16:14 [m]Mt 3:1; 14:2 [n]Mk 6:15; Jn 1:21

16:16 [o]Mt 4:3; Ps 42:2; Jn 11:27; Ac 14:15; 2Co 6:16; 1Th 1:9; 1Ti 3:15; Heb 10:31; 12:22

16:17 [p]1Co 15:50; Gal 1:16; Eph 6:12; Heb 2:14

16:18 [q]Jn 1:42 [r]Eph 2:20

16:19 [s]Isa 22:22; Rev 3:7 [t]Mt 18:18; Jn 20:23

16:20 [u]Mk 8:30

16:21 [v]Mk 10:34; Lk 17:25 [w]Jn 2:19 [x]Mt 17:22, 23; 27:63; Mk 9:31; Lk 9:22; 18:31-33; 24:6,7

16:23 [y]Mt 4:10

16:24 [z]Mt 10:38; Lk 14:27

16:25 [a]Jn 12:25

16:27 [b]Mt 8:20 [c]Ac 1:11 [d]Job 34:11; Ps 62:12; Jer 17:10; Ro 2:6; 2Co 5:10; Rev 22:12

[a] *16* Or *Messiah*; also in verse 20 [b] *18* *Peter* means *rock.* [c] *18* Or *hell* [d] *18* Or *not prove stronger than it* [e] *19* Or *have been* [f] *25* The Greek word means either *life* or *soul*; also in verse 26.

4Peter said to Jesus, "Lord, it is good for us to be
here. If you wish, I will put up three shelters—
one for you, one for Moses and one for Elijah."
5While he was still speaking, a bright cloud
enveloped them, and a voice from the cloud said,
"This is my Son, whom I love; with him I am well
17:5 [e]Mt 3:17; 2Pe 1:17 [f]Ac 3:22,23 pleased.[e] Listen to him!"[f]
6When the disciples heard this, they fell face-
down to the ground, terrified. 7But Jesus came
17:7 [g]Mt 14:27 and touched them. "Get up," he said. "Don't be
afraid."[g] 8When they looked up, they saw no one
except Jesus.
9As they were coming down the mountain,
17:9 [h]Mk 8:30 [i]Mt 8:20 [j]Mt 16:21 Jesus instructed them, "Don't tell anyone[h] what
you have seen, until the Son of Man[i] has been
raised from the dead."[j]
10The disciples asked him, "Why then do the
teachers of the law say that Elijah must come first?"
11Jesus replied, "To be sure, Elijah comes and
17:11 [k]Mal 4:6; Lk 1:16,17 will restore all things.[k] 12But I tell you, Elijah has
already come,[l] and they did not recognize him,
but have done to him everything they wished.[m] In
17:12 [l]Mt 11:14 [m]Mt 14:3,10 [n]Mt 16:21 the same way the Son of Man is going to suffer[n] at
their hands." 13Then the disciples understood that
he was talking to them about John the Baptist.

The Healing of a Boy With a Demon

14When they came to the crowd, a man
approached Jesus and knelt before him. 15"Lord,
have mercy on my son," he said. "He has sei-
17:15 [o]Mt 4:24 zures[o] and is suffering greatly. He often falls into
the fire or into the water. 16I brought him to your
disciples, but they could not heal him."
17"O unbelieving and perverse generation," Jesus
replied, "how long shall I stay with you? How long
shall I put up with you? Bring the boy here to me."
18Jesus rebuked the demon, and it came out of the
boy, and he was healed from that moment.
19Then the disciples came to Jesus in private
and asked, "Why couldn't we drive it out?"
20He replied, "Because you have so little faith. I
17:20 [p]Mt 21:21 [q]Mt 13:31; Mk 11:23; Lk 17:6 [r]1Co 13:2 tell you the truth, if you have faith[p] as small as a
mustard seed,[q] you can say to this mountain,
'Move from here to there' and it will move.[r] Nothing will be impossible for you.[a]"
22When they came together in Galilee, he said
17:22 [s]Mt 8:20 to them, "The Son of Man[s] is going to be betrayed
into the hands of men. 23They will kill him,[t] and
17:23 [t]Ac 2:23; 3:13 [u]Mt 16:21 [v]Mt 16:21 on the third day[u] he will be raised to life."[v] And
the disciples were filled with grief.

The Temple Tax

24After Jesus and his disciples arrived in Caper-
17:24 [w]Ex 30:13 naum, the collectors of the two-drachma tax[w]
came to Peter and asked, "Doesn't your teacher
pay the temple tax[b]?"
25"Yes, he does," he replied.
When Peter came into the house, Jesus was the

[a] 20 Some manuscripts *you.* 21*But this kind does not go out except by prayer and fasting.* [b] 24 Greek *the two drachmas*

A minister told Charlotte Elliott that she could find the Savior by coming to him as she was. Shortly after her conversion, she wrote this hymn.

Just as I Am

Just as I am, without one plea,
But that Thy blood was shed for me,
And that Thou bidst me come to Thee,
O Lamb of God, I come, I come.

Just as I am, and waiting not
To rid my soul of one dark blot,
To Thee whose blood can cleanse each spot,
O Lamb of God, I come, I come.

Just as I am, though tossed about
With many a conflict, many a doubt,
Fightings and fears within, without,
O Lamb of God, I come, I come . . .

Just as I am, of that free love
The breadth, length, depth, and height to prove,
Here for a season, then above,
O Lamb of God, I come!

—*Charlotte Elliott* (1789–1871)

Angels

MT 18:1–10

Jesus calls a little child to him—can you picture a little one toddling confidently up to the Savior?—and places that child before his listeners as an example of the humble, childlike attitude needed by anyone who will enter his kingdom. He says his followers are not to look down on children, for "their angels in heaven always see the face of my Father in heaven" (Mt 18:10). The most likely explanation for his statement is that these are the guardian angels not only of these little ones but of any of God's people. The sustaining lesson here is that no person—no matter what age or social position—is unworthy of God's notice and care.

first to speak. "What do you think, Simon?" he
asked. "From whom do the kings of the earth col- **17:25**
lect duty and taxes[x]—from their own sons or from [x]Mt 22:17-
others?" 21; Ro 13:7
26"From others," Peter answered.
"Then the sons are exempt," Jesus said to him.
27"But so that we may not offend[y] them, go to the **17:27** [y]Jn 6:61
lake and throw out your line. Take the first fish
you catch; open its mouth and you will find a
four-drachma coin. Take it and give it to them for
my tax and yours."

The Greatest in the Kingdom of Heaven

18 At that time the disciples came to Jesus and
asked, "Who is the greatest in the kingdom
of heaven?"
2He called a little child and had him stand
among them. 3And he said: "I tell you the truth,
unless you change and become like little children,[z] **18:3** [z]Mt 19:14;
you will never enter the kingdom of heaven.[a] 1Pe 2:2
4Therefore, whoever humbles himself like this [a]Mt 3:2
child is the greatest in the kingdom of heaven.[b]
5"And whoever welcomes a little child like this **18:4** [b]Mk 9:35
in my name welcomes me.[c] 6But if anyone causes
one of these little ones who believe in me to sin,[d] **18:5** [c]Mt 10:40
it would be better for him to have a large mill-
stone hung around his neck and to be drowned in **18:6** [d]Mt 5:29
the depths of the sea.[e] [e]Mk 9:42;
7"Woe to the world because of the things that Lk 17:2
cause people to sin! Such things must come, but
woe to the man through whom they come![f] 8If **18:7**
your hand or your foot causes you to sin,[g] cut it [f]Lk 17:1
off and throw it away. It is better for you to enter **18:8**
life maimed or crippled than to have two hands [g]Mt 5:29;
or two feet and be thrown into eternal fire. 9And if Mk 9:43,45
your eye causes you to sin,[h] gouge it out and **18:9** [h]Mt 5:29
throw it away. It is better for you to enter life with [i]Mt 5:22
one eye than to have two eyes and be thrown into
the fire of hell.[i]

The Parable of the Lost Sheep

10"See that you do not look down on one of
these little ones. For I tell you that their angels[j] in **18:10**
heaven always see the face of my Father in [j]Ge 48:16;
heaven.[a] Ps 34:7;
12"What do you think? If a man owns a hundred Ac 12:11,15;
sheep, and one of them wanders away, will he not Heb 1:14
leave the ninety-nine on the hills and go to look
for the one that wandered off? 13And if he finds it,
I tell you the truth, he is happier about that one
sheep than about the ninety-nine that did not
wander off. 14In the same way your Father in
heaven is not willing that any of these little ones
should be lost.

A Brother Who Sins Against You

15"If your brother sins against you,[b] go and show

[a] 10 Some manuscripts *heaven.* [11]*The Son of Man came to save what was lost.* [b] 15 Some manuscripts do not have *against you.*

Mary, the Mother of Jesus

A Faith to Follow

Like a woman covered in veils with only her eyes to convey her heart, Mary is wrapped in mystery. We are left to guess so much: her appearance, her relationship with Joseph, how she mothered Jesus, her widowhood, her death. Yet the glimpses we have—like windows to her soul—sketch a clear image of a woman of great faith. Mary believed God. Completely.

She believed the angel Gabriel. How much did she know about the prophesied virgin birth when only the boys of her time were schooled in Scripture? For that matter, did *anyone* understand? Even so, Mary's answer was a simple, "I am the Lord's servant . . . May it be to me as you have said" (Lk 1:38).

Mary believed God spoke to Joseph in his dreams and gave him wisdom to care for her and her child. She followed him to Egypt in the middle of the night to escape from Herod. About two years later, she followed him home after another dream.

Mary believed that Jesus was the Messiah—even when he was on the cross. But she didn't understand any better than his disciples what the full plan of God was, so she certainly suffered grief and loss and confusion at Jesus' death.

Jesus had grown from the tiny fetus in her womb to the resurrected Lord of glory. Mother became daughter, parent became disciple, but Mary was always a believer. Hers was a simple life—daily faithfulness to menial tasks in a remote part of an obscure nation. Hers was an extraordinary life, with angels, prophecy, Magi and a sword that pierced not only her Son's body but her own heart—a life given to conceiving, birthing and raising the only Son of God.

The tiny band of disciples that grew into a multitude respected Mary not for her position or celebrity but for her faith. "From now on all generations will call me blessed, for the Mighty One has done great things for me—holy is his name" (Lk 1:48-49).

It's hard for us to remember that Mary was a real woman. Through the years, she has been made into an almost magical figure. But she had real problems, fears and failings. God uses real people to accomplish his will. We respect Mary for her faith, but One greater than Mary said, "Whoever does the will of my Father in heaven is my brother and sister and mother" (Mt 12:50). Faithful obedience, like Mary's, is the evidence that we are spiritually related to Christ, just as she was.

Mary
(bitter)

Matthew 1-2; 12:46-50
Mark 3:31-35
Luke 1-2; 8:19-21
John 2:1-11; 19:25-27
Acts 1:14

Candid SNAPSHOT This is how the birth of Jesus Christ came about: His mother Mary was pledged to be married to Joseph, but before they came together, she was found to be with child through the Holy Spirit (Matthew 1:18).

Elizabeth

It Is Written

Elizabeth was puzzled and a little worried when Zechariah, her husband, walked in the door excited and gesturing in frustration. He could not speak. Something extraordinary had happened, but what? She sat down and invited him to join her. It was clear this would take some time to unravel.

Years of sun, smiles and the complex emotions of barrenness may have etched Elizabeth's aging face with "character lines." If Elizabeth felt empty without children, it did not color her countenance. She lived with zest.

The news Zechariah communicated to her was miraculous, amazing. An angel named Gabriel had told Zechariah they were going have a son. They were to name him John. He would fulfill Old Testament prophecy by going before the Lord in the spirit and power of Elijah to prepare a people for the Lord!

As amazing as this news was to an aging couple, Elizabeth took it in stride. The promise sounded familiar. Scripture said, "Abraham fell facedown; he laughed and said to himself, 'Will a son be born to a man a hundred years old? Will Sarah bear a child at the age of ninety?' . . . Then God said, . . . 'your wife Sarah will bear you a son, and you will call him Isaac' " (Ge 17:17,19). Sarah had Isaac in her old age. Elizabeth believed that if it had happened to Sarah, it could happen to her. A son!

Elizabeth was pregnant six months when Mary, her relative, came to visit. Mary—also visited by an angel—had conceived by the Holy Spirit. What incredible spiritual sensitivity Elizabeth possessed! When Mary stepped across her threshold, Elizabeth's baby leaped within her, and she exclaimed, "Blessed are you among women, and blessed is the child you will bear!" (Lk 1:42).

Elizabeth and Zechariah had read Isaiah: "The virgin will be with child and will give birth to a son, and will call him Immanuel" (Isa 7:14). God revealed to her that Mary was the virgin. Elizabeth expected the Messiah. Their son, John, was to be his forerunner. *God's Word* had given her all the pieces of the puzzle she needed in order to understand the events that were happening around her.

Scripture does not just use rules and regulations to tell us how to live. Our merciful Lord gives us flesh-and-blood accounts of his love in action—people like Elizabeth and Sarah, people like us, who learned to follow God by trial and error and who are blessed for their faithfulness.

Elizabeth
(God is [my] oath)
Luke 1:5-80

Candid SNAPSHOT After this his wife Elizabeth became pregnant and for five months remained in seclusion. "The Lord has done this for me," she said. "In these days he has shown his favor and taken away my disgrace among the people" (Luke 1:24-25).

him his fault,[k] just between the two of you. If he listens to you, you have won your brother over. 16 But if he will not listen, take one or two others along, so that 'every matter may be established by the testimony of two or three witnesses.'[a][l] 17 If he refuses to listen to them, tell it to the church;[m] and if he refuses to listen even to the church, treat him as you would a pagan or a tax collector.[n]

18 "I tell you the truth, whatever you bind on earth will be[b] bound in heaven, and whatever you loose on earth will be[b] loosed in heaven.[o]

19 "Again, I tell you that if two of you on earth agree about anything you ask for, it will be done for you[p] by my Father in heaven. 20 For where two or three come together in my name, there am I with them."

The Parable of the Unmerciful Servant

21 Then Peter came to Jesus and asked, "Lord, how many times shall I forgive my brother when he sins against me?[q] Up to seven times?"[r]

22 Jesus answered, "I tell you, not seven times, but seventy-seven times.[c][s]

23 "Therefore, the kingdom of heaven is like[t] a king who wanted to settle accounts[u] with his servants. 24 As he began the settlement, a man who owed him ten thousand talents[d] was brought to him. 25 Since he was not able to pay,[v] the master ordered that he and his wife and his children and all that he had be sold[w] to repay the debt.

26 "The servant fell on his knees before him.[x] 'Be patient with me,' he begged, 'and I will pay back everything.' 27 The servant's master took pity on him, canceled the debt and let him go.

28 "But when that servant went out, he found one of his fellow servants who owed him a hundred denarii.[e] He grabbed him and began to choke him. 'Pay back what you owe me!' he demanded.

29 "His fellow servant fell to his knees and begged him, 'Be patient with me, and I will pay you back.'

30 "But he refused. Instead, he went off and had the man thrown into prison until he could pay the debt. 31 When the other servants saw what had happened, they were greatly distressed and went and told their master everything that had happened.

32 "Then the master called the servant in. 'You wicked servant,' he said, 'I canceled all that debt of yours because you begged me to. 33 Shouldn't you have had mercy on your fellow servant just as I had on you?' 34 In anger his master turned him over to the jailers to be tortured, until he should pay back all he owed.

35 "This is how my heavenly Father will treat each of you unless you forgive your brother from your heart."[y]

18:15 [k]Lev 19:17; Lk 17:3; Gal 6:1; Jas 5:19,20
18:16 [l]Nu 35:30; Dt 17:6; 19:15; Jn 8:17; 2Co 13:1; 1Ti 5:19; Heb 10:28
18:17 [m]1Co 6:1-6 [n]Ro 16:17; 2Th 3:6,14
18:18 [o]Mt 16:19; Jn 20:23
18:19 [p]Mt 7:7
18:21 [q]Mt 6:14 [r]Lk 17:4
18:22 [s]Ge 4:24
18:23 [t]Mt 13:24 [u]Mt 25:19
18:25 [v]Lk 7:42 [w]Lev 25:39; 2Ki 4:1; Ne 5:5,8
18:26 [x]Mt 8:2
18:35 [y]Mt 6:14; Jas 2:13

[a] *16* Deut. 19:15 [b] *18* Or *have been* [c] *22* Or *seventy times seven* [d] *24* That is, millions of dollars [e] *28* That is, a few dollars

Seventy-Seven Times

MT 18:21-35

So begins one of Jesus' most poignant instructions *regarding forgiveness. When Peter asks Jesus how many times he should forgive, Peter is being generous with his suggestion of seven times. Traditional Rabbinic teaching required that an offended person only forgive an offender three times. Jesus answers with hyperbole, essentially saying that no limits on forgiveness apply when we consider the depth and extent to which we have been forgiven by God. Each of us is like the first servant in Jesus' parable whose debt before God is so large—and forgiven—that we have no grounds for withholding forgiveness from anyone.*

It is thought that Karolina Sandell-Berg wrote this hymn in response to a tragic boat trip with her father, during which he fell overboard and drowned before her eyes.

Children of the Heavenly Father

Children of the heavenly Father
Safely in His bosom gather;
Nestling bird nor star in heaven
Such a refuge ever was given.

Neither life nor death shall ever
From the Lord His children sever;
Unto them His grace He showeth,
And their sorrows all He knoweth.

Though He giveth or He taketh,
God His children never forsaketh;
His the loving purpose solely
To preserve them pure and holy.

Lo, their very hairs He numbers,
And no daily care encumbers
Them that share His every blessing
And His help in woes distressing.

Praise the Lord in joyful numbers:
Your Protector never slumbers.
At the will of your Defender
Every foeman must surrender.

—*Karolina Wilhelmina Sandell-Berg*
(1832–1903)

Divorce

19 When Jesus had finished saying these
things,[z] he left Galilee and went into the **19:1**
region of Judea to the other side of the Jordan. [z]Mt 7:28
2 Large crowds followed him, and he healed them[a] **19:2**
there. [a]Mt 4:23
3 Some Pharisees came to him to test him. They
asked, "Is it lawful for a man to divorce his wife[b] **19:3**
for any and every reason?" [b]Mt 5:31
4 "Haven't you read," he replied, "that at the
beginning the Creator 'made them male and
female,'[a][c] 5 and said, 'For this reason a man will **19:4**
leave his father and mother and be united to his [c]Ge 1:27; 5:2
wife, and the two will become one flesh'[b]?[d] 6 So **19:5**
they are no longer two, but one. Therefore what [d]Ge 2:24; 1Co 6:16;
God has joined together, let man not separate." Eph 5:31
7 "Why then," they asked, "did Moses command
that a man give his wife a certificate of divorce **19:7**
and send her away?"[e] [e]Dt 24:1-4;
8 Jesus replied, "Moses permitted you to divorce Mt 5:31
your wives because your hearts were hard. But it
was not this way from the beginning. 9 I tell you
that anyone who divorces his wife, except for
marital unfaithfulness, and marries another **19:9**
woman commits adultery."[f] [f]Mt 5:32;
10 The disciples said to him, "If this is the situa- Lk 16:18
tion between a husband and wife, it is better not
to marry."
11 Jesus replied, "Not everyone can accept this **19:11**
word, but only those to whom it has been given.[g] [g]Mt 13:11;
12 For some are eunuchs because they were born 1Co 7:7-9,17
that way; others were made that way by men; and
others have renounced marriage[c] because of the
kingdom of heaven. The one who can accept this
should accept it."

The Little Children and Jesus

13 Then little children were brought to Jesus for **19:13**
him to place his hands on them[h] and pray for [h]Mk 5:23
them. But the disciples rebuked those who
brought them.
14 Jesus said, "Let the little children come to me,
and do not hinder them, for the kingdom of heav- **19:14**
en belongs[i] to such as these."[j] 15 When he had [i]Mt 25:34
placed his hands on them, he went on from there. [j]Mt 18:3;
1Pe 2:2

The Rich Young Man

16 Now a man came up to Jesus and asked,
"Teacher, what good thing must I do to get eternal **19:16**
life[k]?"[l] [k]Mt 25:46
17 "Why do you ask me about what is good?" [l]Lk 10:25
Jesus replied. "There is only One who is good. If
you want to enter life, obey the command- **19:17**
ments."[m] [m]Lev 18:5
18 "Which ones?" the man inquired.
Jesus replied, " 'Do not murder, do not commit
adultery,[n] do not steal, do not give false testimony, **19:18** [n]Jas 2:11

[a] *4* Gen. 1:27 [b] *5* Gen. 2:24 [c] *12* Or *have made themselves eunuchs*

19 honor your father and mother,'[a][o] and 'love your neighbor as yourself.'[b]"[p]

20 "All these I have kept," the young man said. "What do I still lack?"

21 Jesus answered, "If you want to be perfect,[q] go, sell your possessions and give to the poor,[r] and you will have treasure in heaven.[s] Then come, follow me."

22 When the young man heard this, he went away sad, because he had great wealth.

23 Then Jesus said to his disciples, "I tell you the truth, it is hard for a rich man[t] to enter the kingdom of heaven. 24 Again I tell you, it is easier for a camel to go through the eye of a needle than for a rich man to enter the kingdom of God."

25 When the disciples heard this, they were greatly astonished and asked, "Who then can be saved?"

26 Jesus looked at them and said, "With man this is impossible, but with God all things are possible."[u]

27 Peter answered him, "We have left everything to follow you![v] What then will there be for us?"

28 Jesus said to them, "I tell you the truth, at the renewal of all things, when the Son of Man sits on his glorious throne,[w] you who have followed me will also sit on twelve thrones, judging the twelve tribes of Israel.[x] 29 And everyone who has left houses or brothers or sisters or father or mother[c] or children or fields for my sake will receive a hundred times as much and will inherit eternal life.[y] 30 But many who are first will be last, and many who are last will be first.[z]

The Parable of the Workers in the Vineyard

20 "For the kingdom of heaven is like[a] a landowner who went out early in the morning to hire men to work in his vineyard.[b] 2 He agreed to pay them a denarius for the day and sent them into his vineyard.

3 "About the third hour he went out and saw others standing in the marketplace doing nothing. 4 He told them, 'You also go and work in my vineyard, and I will pay you whatever is right.' 5 So they went.

"He went out again about the sixth hour and the ninth hour and did the same thing. 6 About the eleventh hour he went out and found still others standing around. He asked them, 'Why have you been standing here all day long doing nothing?'

7 " 'Because no one has hired us,' they answered.

"He said to them, 'You also go and work in my vineyard.'

8 "When evening came,[c] the owner of the vineyard said to his foreman, 'Call the workers and pay them their wages, beginning with the last ones hired and going on to the first.'

19:19 [o]Ex 20:12-16; Dt 5:16-20 [p]Lev 19:18; Mt 5:43
19:21 [q]Mt 5:48 [r]Lk 12:33; Ac 2:45; 4:34-35 [s]Mt 6:20
19:23 [t]Mt 13:22; 1Ti 6:9,10
19:26 [u]Ge 18:14; Job 42:2; Jer 32:17; Zec 8:6; Lk 1:37; 18:27; Ro 4:21
19:27 [v]Mt 4:19
19:28 [w]Mt 20:21; 25:31 [x]Lk 22:28-30; Rev 3:21; 4:4; 20:4
19:29 [y]Mt 6:33; 25:46
19:30 [z]Mt 20:16; Mk 10:31; Lk 13:30
20:1 [a]Mt 13:24 [b]Mt 21:28,33
20:8 [c]Lev 19:13; Dt 24:15

[a] *19* Exodus 20:12–16; Deut. 5:16–20 [b] *19* Lev. 19:18
[c] *29* Some manuscripts *mother or wife*

A Rich Young Man

MT 19:16–22

This rich young man has everything except an assurance of entrance into Jesus' kingdom. He wants to know what good thing he can do that will demonstrate he is qualified to enter. Jesus answers with a series of responses designed to show him his need for a righteousness far greater than his own—the righteousness of the Messiah. Jesus points to the commandments: do not murder, do not commit adultery . . . love your neighbor. When the rich young man claims to have kept them all, Jesus puts before him one requirement that exposes the inner workings of his unrighteous heart. He tells the young man to sell all he has, give the money to the poor and follow him. The rich young man goes away sorrowful, unable to let go of his wealth. He does not love his neighbor—or God—to that extent.

Misplaced Pride

MT 20:20-28

The mother of James and John, the sons of Zebedee, might have heard Jesus say that his disciples would one day be seated on thrones (Mt 19:28). In motherly but misplaced pride, she wants her sons to have the best spots, right beside Christ. Jesus uses this request to stress a truth his disciples still find difficult to grasp. The trademark of his kingdom is humility and a servant's spirit. Jesus turns immediately to James and John and asks them if they are willing to "drink the cup [he is] going to drink" (Mt 20:22). He wants to know if they are willing to suffer with him. They promise, perhaps somewhat glibly, that they are, never realizing what lies ahead. (Indeed, James is martyred during the reign of Herod Agrippa; John is banished to the island of Patmos for his testimony to the gospel.) The actual determination as to who will sit at Jesus' side, though, is a prerogative reserved for his Father; he will grant it to those whom he has chosen (see the character sketch for James and John's Mother on page 1878).

9“The workers who were hired about the
eleventh hour came and each received a denarius. 10So when those came who were hired first,
they expected to receive more. But each one of
them also received a denarius. 11When they
received it, they began to grumble[d] against the
landowner. 12‘These men who were hired last
worked only one hour,’ they said, ‘and you have
made them equal to us who have borne the burden of the work and the heat[e] of the day.’
13“But he answered one of them, ‘Friend,[f] I am
not being unfair to you. Didn’t you agree to work
for a denarius? 14Take your pay and go. I want to
give the man who was hired last the same as I
gave you. 15Don’t I have the right to do what I
want with my own money? Or are you envious
because I am generous?’[g]
16“So the last will be first, and the first will be
last.”[h]

Jesus Again Predicts His Death

17Now as Jesus was going up to Jerusalem, he
took the twelve disciples aside and said to them,
18“We are going up to Jerusalem,[i] and the Son of
Man[j] will be betrayed to the chief priests and the
teachers of the law.[k] They will condemn him to
death 19and will turn him over to the Gentiles to
be mocked and flogged[l] and crucified.[m] On the
third day[n] he will be raised to life!”[o]

A Mother’s Request

20Then the mother of Zebedee’s sons[p] came to
Jesus with her sons and, kneeling down,[q] asked a
favor of him.
21“What is it you want?” he asked.
She said, “Grant that one of these two sons of
mine may sit at your right and the other at your
left in your kingdom.”[r]
22“You don’t know what you are asking,” Jesus
said to them. “Can you drink the cup[s] I am going
to drink?”
“We can,” they answered.
23Jesus said to them, “You will indeed drink
from my cup,[t] but to sit at my right or left is not
for me to grant. These places belong to those for
whom they have been prepared by my Father.”
24When the ten heard about this, they were
indignant[u] with the two brothers. 25Jesus called
them together and said, “You know that the rulers
of the Gentiles lord it over them, and their high
officials exercise authority over them. 26Not so
with you. Instead, whoever wants to become great
among you must be your servant,[v] 27and whoever
wants to be first must be your slave— 28just as the
Son of Man[w] did not come to be served, but to
serve,[x] and to give his life as a ransom[y] for many.”

Two Blind Men Receive Sight

29As Jesus and his disciples were leaving Jericho, a large crowd followed him. 30Two blind men

20:11 [d]Jnh 4:1
20:12 [e]Jnh 4:8; Lk 12:55; Jas 1:11
20:13 [f]Mt 22:12; 26:50
20:15 [g]Dt 15:9; Mk 7:22
20:16 [h]Mt 19:30
20:18 [i]Lk 9:51 [j]Mt 8:20 [k]Mt 16:21; 27:1,2
20:19 [l]Mt 16:21 [m]Ac 2:23 [n]Mt 16:21 [o]Mt 16:21
20:20 [p]Mt 4:21 [q]Mt 8:2
20:21 [r]Mt 19:28
20:22 [s]Isa 51:17, 22; Jer 49:12; Mt 26:39,42; Mk 14:36; Lk 22:42; Jn 18:11
20:23 [t]Ac 12:2; Rev 1:9
20:24 [u]Lk 22:24,25
20:26 [v]Mt 23:11; Mk 9:35
20:28 [w]Mt 8:20 [x]Lk 22:27; Jn 13:13-16; 2Co 8:9; Php 2:7 [y]Isa 53:10; Mt 26:28; 1Ti 2:6; Tit 2:14; Heb 9:28; 1Pe 1:18,19

were sitting by the roadside, and when they heard
20:30 that Jesus was going by, they shouted, "Lord, Son
[z]Mt 9:27 of David,[z] have mercy on us!"
[31]The crowd rebuked them and told them to be
quiet, but they shouted all the louder, "Lord, Son
of David, have mercy on us!"
[32]Jesus stopped and called them. "What do you
want me to do for you?" he asked.
[33]"Lord," they answered, "we want our sight."
[34]Jesus had compassion on them and touched
their eyes. Immediately they received their sight
and followed him.

The Triumphal Entry

21:1 [a]Mt 24:3; 26:30; Mk 14:26; Lk 19:37; 21:37; 22:39; Jn 8:1; Ac 1:12
21 As they approached Jerusalem and came to
Bethphage on the Mount of Olives,[a] Jesus
sent two disciples, [2]saying to them, "Go to the village ahead of you, and at once you will find a
donkey tied there, with her colt by her. Untie
them and bring them to me. [3]If anyone says anything to you, tell him that the Lord needs them,
and he will send them right away."
[4]This took place to fulfill what was spoken
through the prophet:

> [5]"Say to the Daughter of Zion,
> 'See, your king comes to you,
> gentle and riding on a donkey,
> 21:5 [b]Zec 9:9; Isa 62:11 on a colt, the foal of a donkey.' "[a][b]

[6]The disciples went and did as Jesus had
instructed them. [7]They brought the donkey and
the colt, placed their cloaks on them, and Jesus
21:8 sat on them. [8]A very large crowd spread their
[c]2Ki 9:13 cloaks[c] on the road, while others cut branches
from the trees and spread them on the road. [9]The
crowds that went ahead of him and those that followed shouted,

21:9 [d]ver 15; Mt 9:27 [e]Ps 118:26; Mt 23:39 [f]Lk 2:14
> "Hosanna[b] to the Son of David!"[d]
> "Blessed is he who comes in the name
> of the Lord!"[c][e]
>
> "Hosanna[b] in the highest!"[f]

[10]When Jesus entered Jerusalem, the whole city
was stirred and asked, "Who is this?"
21:11 [11]The crowds answered, "This is Jesus, the
[g]Lk 7:16,39; 24:19; Jn 1:21,25; 6:14; 7:40 prophet[g] from Nazareth in Galilee."

Jesus at the Temple

21:12 [12]Jesus entered the temple area and drove out all
[h]Dt 14:26 who were buying[h] and selling there. He over-
[i]Ex 30:13 turned the tables of the money changers[i] and the
[j]Lev 1:14 benches of those selling doves.[j] [13]"It is written," he
said to them, " 'My house will be called a house of
21:13 prayer,'[d][k] but you are making it a 'den of rob-
[k]Isa 56:7 [l]Jer 7:11 bers.'[e]"[l]
[14]The blind and the lame came to him at the

[a] 5 Zech. 9:9 [b] 9 A Hebrew expression meaning "Save!" which became an exclamation of praise; also in verse 15
[c] 9 Psalm 118:26 [d] 13 Isaiah 56:7 [e] 13 Jer. 7:11

Everyone is blessed with an imagination. Some just know how to use it better than others. Developing your imagination takes some effort. Don't quench your creativity with thoughts of "I could never do that," or "That's impossible," or "Maybe some other day." Let your mind dream big. Brainstorm, just letting your thoughts run rampant. You may even hit on something that will change the world!

Don't settle for premade, premeasured, prepackaged life. Keep your friends and family guessing what you'll do next. Make life an exciting adventure for you and for them!

—Luci Swindoll

A Fig Tree

MT 21:18–22

Fig trees normally produce leaves and fruit at the same time. Since the fig tree Jesus passes already has leaves, figs should have been on the tree as well. Jesus curses the fig tree, using it as an object lesson; it promises fruit, yet it is bearing none. The fig tree immediately withers. This miracle becomes an opportunity to teach the disciples about faith. Their faith will not only be able to wither a fig tree, Jesus says, but to move mountains.

Many also believe that the fig tree symbolizes the nation of Israel, which professed to be fruitful but was instead fruitless. Within a few days, the people would reject the Messiah. Then they would experience the "withering" judgment of God in **A.D.** ***70 when the Romans demolished the temple and overran the country.***

temple, and he healed them.[m] 15 But when the 21:14 [m]Mt 4:23
chief priests and the teachers of the law saw the
wonderful things he did and the children shouting
in the temple area, "Hosanna to the Son of
David,"[n] they were indignant.[o] 21:15 [n]ver 9; Mt 9:27 [o]Lk 19:39
16 "Do you hear what these children are saying?"
they asked him.
"Yes," replied Jesus, "have you never read,

" 'From the lips of children and infants
you have ordained praise'[a]?"[p] 21:16 [p]Ps 8:2

17 And he left them and went out of the city to 21:17 [q]Mt 26:6; Mk 11:1; Lk 24:50; Jn 11:1,18; 12:1
Bethany,[q] where he spent the night.

The Fig Tree Withers

18 Early in the morning, as he was on his way
back to the city, he was hungry. 19 Seeing a fig tree
by the road, he went up to it but found nothing
on it except leaves. Then he said to it, "May you
never bear fruit again!" Immediately the tree 21:19 [r]Isa 34:4; Jer 8:13
withered.[r]
20 When the disciples saw this, they were
amazed. "How did the fig tree wither so quickly?"
they asked.
21 Jesus replied, "I tell you the truth, if you have
faith and do not doubt,[s] not only can you do what 21:21 [s]Mt 17:20; Lk 17:6; 1Co 13:2; Jas 1:6
was done to the fig tree, but also you can say to
this mountain, 'Go, throw yourself into the sea,'
and it will be done. 22 If you believe, you will
receive whatever you ask for[t] in prayer." 21:22 [t]Mt 7:7

The Authority of Jesus Questioned

23 Jesus entered the temple courts, and, while he
was teaching, the chief priests and the elders of
the people came to him. "By what authority[u] are 21:23 [u]Ac 4:7; 7:27
you doing these things?" they asked. "And who
gave you this authority?"
24 Jesus replied, "I will also ask you one question.
If you answer me, I will tell you by what
authority I am doing these things. 25 John's baptism—where
did it come from? Was it from heaven,
or from men?"
They discussed it among themselves and said,
"If we say, 'From heaven,' he will ask, 'Then why
didn't you believe him?' 26 But if we say, 'From
men'—we are afraid of the people, for they all
hold that John was a prophet."[v] 21:26 [v]Mt 11:9; Mk 6:20
27 So they answered Jesus, "We don't know."
Then he said, "Neither will I tell you by what
authority I am doing these things.

The Parable of the Two Sons

28 "What do you think? There was a man who
had two sons. He went to the first and said, 'Son,
go and work today in the vineyard.'[w] 21:28 [w]ver 33; Mt 20:1
29 " 'I will not,' he answered, but later he
changed his mind and went.
30 "Then the father went to the other son and

[a] *16* Psalm 8:2

said the same thing. He answered, 'I will, sir,' but
he did not go.
31"Which of the two did what his father
wanted?"
"The first," they answered.
21:31 Jesus said to them, "I tell you the truth, the tax
[x]Lk 7:29 collectors[x] and the prostitutes[y] are entering the
[y]Lk 7:50 kingdom of God ahead of you. 32For John came to
21:32 you to show you the way of righteousness,[z] and
[z]Mt 3:1-12 you did not believe him, but the tax collectors[a]
[a]Lk 3:12,13; 7:29 and the prostitutes[b] did. And even after you saw
[b]Lk 7:36-50 this, you did not repent[c] and believe him.
[c]Lk 7:30

The Parable of the Tenants

21:33 33"Listen to another parable: There was a
[d]Ps 80:8 landowner who planted[d] a vineyard. He put a wall
[e]Isa 5:1-7 around it, dug a winepress in it and built a watch-
[f]Mt 25:14,15 tower.[e] Then he rented the vineyard to some farm-
21:34 ers and went away on a journey.[f] 34When the har-
[g]Mt 22:3 vest time approached, he sent his servants[g] to the
tenants to collect his fruit.
21:35 35"The tenants seized his servants; they beat
[h]2Ch 24:21; one, killed another, and stoned a third.[h] 36Then he
Mt 23:34,37; Heb 11:36, sent other servants[i] to them, more than the first
37 time, and the tenants treated them the same way.
21:36 37Last of all, he sent his son to them. 'They will
[i]Mt 22:4 respect my son,' he said.
21:38 38"But when the tenants saw the son, they said
[j]Heb 1:2 to each other, 'This is the heir.[j] Come, let's kill
[k]Mt 12:14 him[k] and take his inheritance.'[l] 39So they took him
[l]Ps 2:8 and threw him out of the vineyard and killed him.
40"Therefore, when the owner of the vineyard
comes, what will he do to those tenants?"
21:41 41"He will bring those wretches to a wretched
[m]Mt 8:11,12 end,"[m] they replied, "and he will rent the vineyard
[n]Ac 13:46; to other tenants,[n] who will give him his share of
18:6; 28:28 the crop at harvest time."
42Jesus said to them, "Have you never read in
the Scriptures:

"'The stone the builders rejected
has become the capstone[a];
21:42 the Lord has done this,
[o]Ps 118:22, and it is marvelous in our eyes'[b]?[o]
23; Ac 4:11; 1Pe 2:7

43"Therefore I tell you that the kingdom of God
21:43 will be taken away from you[p] and given to a peo-
[p]Mt 8:12 ple who will produce its fruit. 44He who falls on
this stone will be broken to pieces, but he on
21:44 whom it falls will be crushed."[c][q]
[q]Lk 2:34
45When the chief priests and the Pharisees
heard Jesus' parables, they knew he was talking
about them. 46They looked for a way to arrest
21:46 him, but they were afraid of the crowd because
[r]ver 11,26 the people held that he was a prophet.[r]

The Parable of the Wedding Banquet

22:2 **22** Jesus spoke to them again in parables, say-
[s]Mt 13:24 ing: 2"The kingdom of heaven is like[s] a king

[a] *42* Or *cornerstone* [b] *42* Psalm 118:22,23 [c] *44* Some manuscripts do not have verse 44.

A Message to Israel

MT 21:28-46

In the parable of the two sons and the parable of the tenants, Jesus makes it clear that the kingdom will be given to those who respond to the Messiah. The self-righteous religious leaders who hear him are stunned to think that God's favor will be taken from them and given to tax collectors, prostitutes and Gentiles. In the parable of the tenants, Jesus gives a poignant picture of rejection. The Jews have rejected the prophets sent by God, and they also reject him as Messiah. Their rejection of the Son means that the kingdom will be taken away from Israel and be given to—in the religious leaders' own words—"other tenants," the Gentiles (Mt 21:41).

The Wedding Feast

MT 22:1–14

A wedding feast is a meal prepared for those invited to share the joy of a newly married bride and groom. In Biblical times large wedding feasts went on for days. Jesus tells a parable about a wedding feast. Many guests are invited, but they spurn their invitations for mundane and unimportant reasons, thereby insulting their host. So the host goes out into the streets and offers the invitation to anyone he can find. The host fills the wedding hall with these unusual guests. Jesus ties up the lesson in a succinct, eight-word explanation: "For many are invited, but few are chosen" (Mt 22:14). *Jesus' invitation to enter his kingdom is a broad one, yet one to be taken seriously and one that requires action.*

who prepared a wedding banquet for his son. 3He
sent his servants[t] to those who had been invited to **22:3** [t]Mt 21:34
the banquet to tell them to come, but they refused
to come.
4"Then he sent some more servants[u] and said, **22:4** [u]Mt 21:36
'Tell those who have been invited that I have prepared my dinner: My oxen and fattened cattle
have been butchered, and everything is ready.
Come to the wedding banquet.'
5"But they paid no attention and went off—one
to his field, another to his business. 6The rest seized
his servants, mistreated them and killed them. 7The
king was enraged. He sent his army and destroyed
those murderers[v] and burned their city. **22:7** [v]Lk 19:27
8"Then he said to his servants, 'The wedding
banquet is ready, but those I invited did not
deserve to come. 9Go to the street corners[w] and **22:9** [w]Eze 21:21
invite to the banquet anyone you find.' 10So the
servants went out into the streets and gathered all
the people they could find, both good and bad,[x] **22:10** [x]Mt 13:47,48
and the wedding hall was filled with guests.
11"But when the king came in to see the guests,
he noticed a man there who was not wearing
wedding clothes. 12'Friend,'[y] he asked, 'how did **22:12** [y]Mt 20:13; 26:50
you get in here without wedding clothes?' The
man was speechless.
13"Then the king told the attendants, 'Tie him
hand and foot, and throw him outside, into the
darkness, where there will be weeping and gnashing of teeth.'[z] **22:13** [z]Mt 8:12
14"For many are invited, but few are chosen."[a] **22:14** [a]Rev 17:14

Paying Taxes to Caesar

15Then the Pharisees went out and laid plans to
trap him in his words. 16They sent their disciples
to him along with the Herodians.[b] "Teacher," they **22:16** [b]Mk 3:6
said, "we know you are a man of integrity and
that you teach the way of God in accordance with
the truth. You aren't swayed by men, because you
pay no attention to who they are. 17Tell us then,
what is your opinion? Is it right to pay taxes[c] to **22:17** [c]Mt 17:25
Caesar or not?"
18But Jesus, knowing their evil intent, said,
"You hypocrites, why are you trying to trap me?
19Show me the coin used for paying the tax." They
brought him a denarius, 20and he asked them,
"Whose portrait is this? And whose inscription?"
21"Caesar's," they replied.
Then he said to them, "Give to Caesar what is
Caesar's,[d] and to God what is God's." **22:21** [d]Ro 13:7
22When they heard this, they were amazed. So
they left him and went away.[e] **22:22** [e]Mk 12:12

Marriage at the Resurrection

23That same day the Sadducees,[f] who say there **22:23** [f]Ac 4:1
is no resurrection,[g] came to him with a question. [g]Ac 23:8; 1Co 15:12
24"Teacher," they said, "Moses told us that if a
man dies without having children, his brother
must marry the widow and have children for
him.[h] 25Now there were seven brothers among us. **22:24** [h]Dt 25:5,6

The first one married and died, and since he had
no children, he left his wife to his brother. 26The
same thing happened to the second and third
brother, right on down to the seventh. 27Finally,
the woman died. 28Now then, at the resurrection,
whose wife will she be of the seven, since all of
them were married to her?"
22:29 29Jesus replied, "You are in error because you
[i]Jn 20:9 do not know the Scriptures[i] or the power of God.
22:30 30At the resurrection people will neither marry nor
[j]Mt 24:38 be given in marriage;[j] they will be like the angels
in heaven. 31But about the resurrection of the
dead—have you not read what God said to you,
22:32 32'I am the God of Abraham, the God of Isaac, and
[k]Ex 3:6; the God of Jacob'[a]?[k] He is not the God of the dead
Ac 7:32 but of the living."
22:33 33When the crowds heard this, they were aston-
[l]Mt 7:28 ished at his teaching.[l]

The Greatest Commandment

22:34 34Hearing that Jesus had silenced the Sad-
[m]Ac 4:1 ducees,[m] the Pharisees got together. 35One of
22:35 them, an expert in the law,[n] tested him with this
[n]Lk 7:30; question: 36"Teacher, which is the greatest com-
10:25; 11:45; mandment in the Law?"
14:3 37Jesus replied: " 'Love the Lord your God with
22:37 all your heart and with all your soul and with all
[o]Dt 6:5 your mind.'[b][o] 38This is the first and greatest com-
22:39 mandment. 39And the second is like it: 'Love your
[p]Lev 19:18; neighbor as yourself.'[c][p] 40All the Law and the
Mt 5:43; Prophets hang on these two commandments."[q]
19:19;
Gal 5:14

Whose Son Is the Christ?

22:40 41While the Pharisees were gathered together,
[q]Mt 7:12 Jesus asked them, 42"What do you think about the
Christ[d]? Whose son is he?"
22:42 "The son of David,"[r] they replied.
[r]Mt 9:27 43He said to them, "How is it then that David,
speaking by the Spirit, calls him 'Lord'? For he
says,

44" 'The Lord said to my Lord:
"Sit at my right hand
22:44 until I put your enemies
[s]Ps 110:1; under your feet." '[e][s]
Ac 2:34,35;
1Co 15:25;
Heb 1:13; 45If then David calls him 'Lord,' how can he be his
10:13 son?" 46No one could say a word in reply, and
22:46 from that day on no one dared to ask him any
[t]Mk 12:34; more questions.[t]
Lk 20:40

Seven Woes

23:2 **23** Then Jesus said to the crowds and to his
[u]Ezr 7:6,25; disciples: 2"The teachers of the law[u] and the
Ne 8:4 Pharisees sit in Moses' seat. 3So you must obey
them and do everything they tell you. But do not
do what they do, for they do not practice what
they preach. 4They tie up heavy loads and put

What Do You Think?

MT 22:41-46

In this confrontation with the Pharisees, Jesus seeks not to start a debate or argument, but to find out from them what they think the Scriptures teach about the Messiah. He refers to Psalm 110, an Old Testament chapter that is quoted most frequently in the New Testament. Jesus appeals to their understanding that the Messiah will come from the Davidic line. If the Christ is merely the earthly son of David, then why would David attribute deity to him by calling him "Lord"? The Messiah must certainly be more than just a human descendant of King David—as the Old Testament Scripture reveals. He is also the divine Lord. The silence of the Pharisees is a tribute to the unanswerable logic of Jesus, who consistently confounds the greatest theologians of his day.

[a] *32* Exodus 3:6 [b] *37* Deut. 6:5 [c] *39* Lev. 19:18 [d] *42* Or *Messiah* [e] *44* Psalm 110:1

Woe to You

MT 23:13-32

The hypocrisy and unbelief of Israel's religious leaders prompt the strongest rebuke from Jesus. He tells his followers to recognize the Pharisees' authority and yet not to follow their hypocritical practices (Mt 23:1-3). He pronounces seven denunciations, each beginning with "Woe to you" (see the note on Isa 5:20-22, page 1113). He denounces the Pharisees for being stumbling blocks who prevent their fellow citizens from entering the kingdom. He rebukes them for appearing to make a binding oath while using fine lines of distinction so they do not have to keep it. He uses the strongest of words in calling them "blind guides," "blind fools" and "blind men" (Mt 23:16,17,19). He exposes the absurdity of meticulous tithing while ignoring the true import of the law—justice, mercy and faithfulness. Jesus calls the Pharisees "whitewashed tombs" (Mt 23:27), likening them to the stench of death covered up by well-decorated appearances. This passage records Jesus' most stinging rebuke of the Jewish religious leaders of his day.

them on men's shoulders, but they themselves are
not willing to lift a finger to move them.[v]
5 "Everything they do is done for men to see:[w]
They make their phylacteries[a][x] wide and the tassels on their garments[y] long; 6 they love the place
of honor at banquets and the most important seats
in the synagogues;[z] 7 they love to be greeted in the
marketplaces and to have men call them 'Rabbi.'[a]
8 "But you are not to be called 'Rabbi,' for you
have only one Master and you are all brothers.
9 And do not call anyone on earth 'father,' for you
have one Father,[b] and he is in heaven. 10 Nor are
you to be called 'teacher,' for you have one
Teacher, the Christ.[b] 11 The greatest among you will
be your servant.[c] 12 For whoever exalts himself will
be humbled, and whoever humbles himself will
be exalted.[d]
13 "Woe to you, teachers of the law and Pharisees,
you hypocrites![e] You shut the kingdom of heaven
in men's faces. You yourselves do not enter, nor
will you let those enter who are trying to.[c][f]
15 "Woe to you, teachers of the law and Pharisees, you hypocrites! You travel over land and sea
to win a single convert,[g] and when he becomes
one, you make him twice as much a son of hell[h]
as you are.
16 "Woe to you, blind guides![i] You say, 'If anyone swears by the temple, it means nothing; but if
anyone swears by the gold of the temple, he is
bound by his oath.'[j] 17 You blind fools! Which is
greater: the gold, or the temple that makes the
gold sacred?[k] 18 You also say, 'If anyone swears by
the altar, it means nothing; but if anyone swears
by the gift on it, he is bound by his oath.' 19 You
blind men! Which is greater: the gift, or the altar
that makes the gift sacred?[l] 20 Therefore, he who
swears by the altar swears by it and by everything
on it. 21 And he who swears by the temple swears
by it and by the one who dwells[m] in it. 22 And he
who swears by heaven swears by God's throne
and by the one who sits on it.[n]
23 "Woe to you, teachers of the law and Pharisees, you hypocrites! You give a tenth[o] of your
spices—mint, dill and cummin. But you have neglected the more important matters of the law—justice, mercy and faithfulness.[p] You should have
practiced the latter, without neglecting the former.
24 You blind guides![q] You strain out a gnat but
swallow a camel.
25 "Woe to you, teachers of the law and Pharisees, you hypocrites! You clean the outside of the
cup and dish,[r] but inside they are full of greed and
self-indulgence.[s] 26 Blind Pharisee! First clean the
inside of the cup and dish, and then the outside
also will be clean.
27 "Woe to you, teachers of the law and Phar-

23:4 [v]Lk 11:46; Ac 15:10; Gal 6:13
23:5 [w]Mt 6:1,2,5, 16 [x]Ex 13:9; Dt 6:8 [y]Nu 15:38; Dt 22:12
23:6 [z]Lk 11:43; 14:7; 20:46
23:7 [a]ver 8; Mk 9:5; 10:51; Jn 1:38,49
23:9 [b]Mal 1:6; Mt 7:11
23:11 [c]Mt 20:26; Mk 9:35
23:12 [d]Lk 14:11
23:13 [e]ver 15,23, 25,27,29 [f]Lk 11:52
23:15 [g]Ac 2:11; 6:5; 13:43 [h]Mt 5:22
23:16 [i]ver 24; Mt 15:14 [j]Mt 5:33-35
23:17 [k]Ex 30:29
23:19 [l]Ex 29:37
23:21 [m]1Ki 8:13; Ps 26:8
23:22 [n]Ps 11:4; Mt 5:34
23:23 [o]Lev 27:30 [p]Mic 6:8; Lk 11:42
23:24 [q]ver 16
23:25 [r]Mk 7:4 [s]Lk 11:39

[a] *5* That is, boxes containing Scripture verses, worn on forehead and arm [b] *10* Or *Messiah* [c] *13* Some manuscripts *to.* [14]*Woe to you, teachers of the law and Pharisees, you hypocrites! You devour widows' houses and for a show make lengthy prayers. Therefore you will be punished more severely.*

isees, you hypocrites! You are like whitewashed tombs,[t] which look beautiful on the outside but on the inside are full of dead men's bones and everything unclean. [28]In the same way, on the outside you appear to people as righteous but on the inside you are full of hypocrisy and wickedness.

[29]"Woe to you, teachers of the law and Pharisees, you hypocrites! You build tombs for the prophets[u] and decorate the graves of the righteous. [30]And you say, 'If we had lived in the days of our forefathers, we would not have taken part with them in shedding the blood of the prophets.' [31]So you testify against yourselves that you are the descendants of those who murdered the prophets.[v] [32]Fill up, then, the measure[w] of the sin of your forefathers!

[33]"You snakes! You brood of vipers![x] How will you escape being condemned to hell?[y] [34]Therefore I am sending you prophets and wise men and teachers. Some of them you will kill and crucify;[z] others you will flog in your synagogues[a] and pursue from town to town.[b] [35]And so upon you will come all the righteous blood that has been shed on earth, from the blood of righteous Abel[c] to the blood of Zechariah son of Berekiah,[d] whom you murdered between the temple and the altar.[e] [36]I tell you the truth, all this will come upon this generation.[f]

[37]"O Jerusalem, Jerusalem, you who kill the prophets and stone those sent to you,[g] how often I have longed to gather your children together, as a hen gathers her chicks under her wings, but you were not willing. [38]Look, your house is left to you desolate.[h] [39]For I tell you, you will not see me again until you say, 'Blessed is he who comes in the name of the Lord.'[a]"[i]

Signs of the End of the Age

24 Jesus left the temple and was walking away when his disciples came up to him to call his attention to its buildings. [2]"Do you see all these things?" he asked. "I tell you the truth, not one stone here will be left on another;[j] every one will be thrown down."

[3]As Jesus was sitting on the Mount of Olives,[k] the disciples came to him privately. "Tell us," they said, "when will this happen, and what will be the sign of your coming and of the end of the age?"

[4]Jesus answered: "Watch out that no one deceives you. [5]For many will come in my name, claiming, 'I am the Christ,[b]' and will deceive many.[l] [6]You will hear of wars and rumors of wars, but see to it that you are not alarmed. Such things must happen, but the end is still to come. [7]Nation will rise against nation, and kingdom against kingdom.[m] There will be famines[n] and earthquakes in various places. [8]All these are the beginning of birth pains.

[9]"Then you will be handed over to be persecut-

23:27 [t]Lk 11:44; Ac 23:3
23:29 [u]Lk 11:47,48
23:31 [v]Ac 7:51-52
23:32 [w]1Th 2:16
23:33 [x]Mt 3:7; 12:34 [y]Mt 5:22
23:34 [z]2Ch 36:15, 16; Lk 11:49 [a]Mt 10:17 [b]Mt 10:23
23:35 [c]Ge 4:8; Heb 11:4 [d]Zec 1:1 [e]2Ch 24:21
23:36 [f]Mt 10:23; 24:34
23:37 [g]2Ch 24:21; Mt 5:12
23:38 [h]1Ki 9:7,8; Jer 22:5
23:39 [i]Ps 118:26; Mt 21:9
24:2 [j]Lk 19:44
24:3 [k]Mt 21:1
24:5 [l]ver 11,23, 24; 1Jn 2:18
24:7 [m]Isa 19:2 [n]Ac 11:28

[a] 39 Psalm 118:26 [b] 5 Or *Messiah*; also in verse 23

Blinded at 6 weeks of age, Fanny Crosby wrote the poignant words of this hymn, one of the nearly 5000 she composed during her lifetime:

I Long to See My Savior First of All

When my life work is ended, and
I cross the swelling tide,
When the bright and glorious
morning I shall see;
I shall know my Redeemer when
I reach the other side,
And His smile will be the first
to welcome me.

Oh, the soul thrilling rapture when
I view His blessed face,
And the luster of His kindly
beaming eye;
How my full heart will praise Him
for the mercy, love and grace,
That prepare for me a mansion
in the sky.

Through the gates to the city
in a robe of spotless white,
He will lead me where no tears will
ever fall;
In the glad song of ages I shall
mingle with delight;
But I long to meet my Savior first
of all.

—*Fanny Crosby* (1820-1915)

The Signs

MT 24:1-35

Throughout the centuries people have wondered how to interpret the signs of the end of the age, the time when Jesus will return. From this passage it is clear that Jesus' appearance will follow great persecution, apostasy and deception. There will probably be physical signs also, just as there were physical signs at Jesus' first Advent (Mt 2:1-10; Lk 2:8-16). The sign that Israel had been set aside as God's chosen nation was the departure of God's glory from the temple when it was destroyed for the final time in A.D. 70.

Some believe that Jesus' return will involve God's glory descending back to earth. His appearance will be visible for all to see, from one end of the heavens to the other. He will come in great power and glory, gathering his children from every corner of the earth.

ed[o] and put to death,[p] and you will be hated by
all nations because of me. 10At that time many will
turn away from the faith and will betray and hate
each other, 11and many false prophets[q] will appear
and deceive many people. 12Because of the
increase of wickedness, the love of most will grow
cold, 13but he who stands firm to the end will be
saved.[r] 14And this gospel of the kingdom[s] will be
preached in the whole world[t] as a testimony to all
nations, and then the end will come.

15"So when you see standing in the holy place[u]
'the abomination that causes desolation,'[a][v] spoken
of through the prophet Daniel—let the reader
understand— 16then let those who are in Judea
flee to the mountains. 17Let no one on the roof of
his house[w] go down to take anything out of the
house. 18Let no one in the field go back to get his
cloak. 19How dreadful it will be in those days for
pregnant women and nursing mothers![x] 20Pray
that your flight will not take place in winter or on
the Sabbath. 21For then there will be great distress,
unequaled from the beginning of the world until
now—and never to be equaled again.[y] 22If those
days had not been cut short, no one would survive,
but for the sake of the elect[z] those days will
be shortened. 23At that time if anyone says to you,
'Look, here is the Christ!' or, 'There he is!' do not
believe it.[a] 24For false Christs and false prophets
will appear and perform great signs and miracles[b]
to deceive even the elect—if that were possible.
25See, I have told you ahead of time.

26"So if anyone tells you, 'There he is, out in the
desert,' do not go out; or, 'Here he is, in the inner
rooms,' do not believe it. 27For as lightning[c] that
comes from the east is visible even in the west, so
will be the coming of the Son of Man.[d] 28Wherever
there is a carcass, there the vultures will gather.[e]

29"Immediately after the distress of those days

" 'the sun will be darkened,
and the moon will not give its light;
the stars will fall from the sky,
and the heavenly bodies will be
shaken.'[b][f]

30"At that time the sign of the Son of Man will
appear in the sky, and all the nations of the earth
will mourn. They will see the Son of Man coming
on the clouds of the sky,[g] with power and great glory.
31And he will send his angels[h] with a loud trumpet
call,[i] and they will gather his elect from the four
winds, from one end of the heavens to the other.

32"Now learn this lesson from the fig tree: As
soon as its twigs get tender and its leaves come
out, you know that summer is near. 33Even so,
when you see all these things, you know that it[c] is
near, right at the door.[j] 34I tell you the truth, this
generation[d] will certainly not pass away until all
these things have happened.[k] 35Heaven and earth

[a] *15* Daniel 9:27; 11:31; 12:11 [b] *29* Isaiah 13:10; 34:4
[c] *33* Or *he* [d] *34* Or *race*

24:9 [o]Mt 10:17 [p]Jn 16:2
24:11 [q]Mt 7:15
24:13 [r]Mt 10:22
24:14 [s]Mt 4:23 [t]Ro 10:18; Col 1:6,23; Lk 2:1; 4:5; Ac 11:28; 17:6; Rev 3:10; 16:14
24:15 [u]Ac 6:13 [v]Da 9:27; 11:31; 12:11
24:17 [w]1Sa 9:25; Mt 10:27; Lk 12:3; Ac 10:9
24:19 [x]Lk 23:29
24:21 [y]Da 12:1; Joel 2:2
24:22 [z]ver 24,31
24:23 [a]Lk 17:23; 1:8
24:24 [b]2Th 2:9-11; Rev 13:13
24:27 [c]Lk 17:24 [d]Mt 8:20
24:28 [e]Lk 17:37
24:29 [f]Isa 13:10; 34:4; Eze 32:7; Joel 2:10,31; Zep 1:15; Rev 6:12,13; 8:12
24:30 [g]Da 7:13; Rev 1:7
24:31 [h]Mt 13:41 [i]Isa 27:13; Zec 9:14; 1Co 15:52; 1Th 4:16; Rev 8:2; 10:7; 11:15
24:33 [j]Jas 5:9
24:34 [k]Mt 16:28; 23:36

24:35 will pass away, but my words will never pass
[l]Mt 5:18 away.[l]

The Day and Hour Unknown

36"No one knows about that day or hour, not
even the angels in heaven, nor the Son,[a] but only
24:36 [m]Ac 1:7 the Father.[m] 37As it was in the days of Noah,[n] so it
will be at the coming of the Son of Man. 38For in
24:37 [n]Ge 6:5; 7:6- the days before the flood, people were eating and
23 drinking, marrying and giving in marriage,[o] up to
24:38 the day Noah entered the ark; 39and they knew
[o]Mt 22:30 nothing about what would happen until the flood
came and took them all away. That is how it will
be at the coming of the Son of Man. 40Two men
24:40 will be in the field; one will be taken and the oth-
[p]Lk 17:34 er left.[p] 41Two women will be grinding with a
24:41 hand mill; one will be taken and the other left.[q]
[q]Lk 17:35 42"Therefore keep watch, because you do not
24:42 know on what day your Lord will come.[r] 43But
[r]Mt 25:13; understand this: If the owner of the house had
Lk 12:40 known at what time of night the thief was com-
24:43 ing,[s] he would have kept watch and would not
[s]Lk 12:39 have let his house be broken into. 44So you also
24:44 must be ready,[t] because the Son of Man will come
[t]1Th 5:6 at an hour when you do not expect him.
24:45 45"Who then is the faithful and wise servant,[u]
[u]Mt 25:21,23 whom the master has put in charge of the servants
in his household to give them their food at the
24:46 proper time? 46It will be good for that servant
[v]Rev 16:15 whose master finds him doing so when he returns.[v]
24:47 47I tell you the truth, he will put him in charge of all
[w]Mt 25:21, his possessions.[w] 48But suppose that servant is
23 wicked and says to himself, 'My master is staying
away a long time,' 49and he then begins to beat his
24:49 fellow servants and to eat and drink with drunk-
[x]Lk 21:34 ards.[x] 50The master of that servant will come on a
day when he does not expect him and at an hour
he is not aware of. 51He will cut him to pieces and
24:51 assign him a place with the hypocrites, where there
[y]Mt 8:12 will be weeping and gnashing of teeth.[y]

The Parable of the Ten Virgins

25:1 **25** "At that time the kingdom of heaven will be
[z]Mt 13:24 [a]Lk 12:35- like[z] ten virgins who took their lamps[a] and
38; Ac 20:8; went out to meet the bridegroom.[b] 2Five of them
Rev 4:5 [b]Rev 19:7; were foolish and five were wise.[c] 3The foolish
21:2 ones took their lamps but did not take any oil
with them. 4The wise, however, took oil in jars
25:2 [c]Mt 24:45 along with their lamps. 5The bridegroom was a
long time in coming, and they all became drowsy
25:5 [d]1Th 5:6 and fell asleep.[d]
6"At midnight the cry rang out: 'Here's the
bridegroom! Come out to meet him!'
7"Then all the virgins woke up and trimmed
25:8 their lamps. 8The foolish ones said to the wise,
[e]Lk 12:35 'Give us some of your oil; our lamps are going out.'[e]
9" 'No,' they replied, 'there may not be enough
for both us and you. Instead, go to those who sell
oil and buy some for yourselves.'

Be Ready!

MT 24:36–51

Only the Father knows the moment of Jesus' return. *The days that precede his coming are likened to the days of Noah, when people ate and drank, married and gave their children in marriage, as though judgment was the furthest thing from their minds. They were unprepared and thus were suddenly swept away.* **So, too, Jesus' return will happen when people least expect it. His followers are told, then, to "keep watch" (Mt 24:42),** *or be alert.* **Be ready to meet him.** *The apostle John gives perhaps the best explanation of being prepared:* **"Continue in him, so that when he appears we may be confident and unashamed before him at his coming" (1Jn 2:28).**

[a] 36 Some manuscripts do not have *nor the Son.*

Talents

MT 25:14-30

The parable of the talents emphasizes the need to serve the master while he is away. This parable focuses on the use of "talents." (A talent was a unit of measure, weighing about 75 pounds and worth more than a thousand dollars.) Two of the servants invest wisely and are rewarded. The third servant hides his talent. He is rebuked as lazy and wicked because he fails to invest his talent wisely. This parable is often used to emphasize the need to use our "talents" wisely—by investing our time, money and gifts for the kingdom so that when the Lord comes again, we will hear his words, "Well done, good and faithful servant!" (Mt 25:21).

10"But while they were on their way to buy the
oil, the bridegroom arrived. The virgins who were
ready went in with him to the wedding banquet.[f]
And the door was shut.
11"Later the others also came. 'Sir! Sir!' they
said. 'Open the door for us!'
12"But he replied, 'I tell you the truth, I don't
know you.'
13"Therefore keep watch, because you do not
know the day or the hour.[g]

The Parable of the Talents

14"Again, it will be like a man going on a journey,[h] who called his servants and entrusted his
property to them. 15To one he gave five talents[a] of
money, to another two talents, and to another one
talent, each according to his ability.[i] Then he went
on his journey. 16The man who had received the
five talents went at once and put his money to
work and gained five more. 17So also, the one with
the two talents gained two more. 18But the man
who had received the one talent went off, dug a
hole in the ground and hid his master's money.
19"After a long time the master of those servants
returned and settled accounts with them.[j] 20The
man who had received the five talents brought the
other five. 'Master,' he said, 'you entrusted me
with five talents. See, I have gained five more.'
21"His master replied, 'Well done, good and
faithful servant! You have been faithful with a few
things; I will put you in charge of many things.[k]
Come and share your master's happiness!'
22"The man with the two talents also came.
'Master,' he said, 'you entrusted me with two talents; see, I have gained two more.'
23"His master replied, 'Well done, good and
faithful servant! You have been faithful with a few
things; I will put you in charge of many things.[l]
Come and share your master's happiness!'
24"Then the man who had received the one talent came. 'Master,' he said, 'I knew that you are a
hard man, harvesting where you have not sown
and gathering where you have not scattered seed.
25So I was afraid and went out and hid your talent
in the ground. See, here is what belongs to you.'
26"His master replied, 'You wicked, lazy servant! So you knew that I harvest where I have not
sown and gather where I have not scattered seed?
27Well then, you should have put my money on
deposit with the bankers, so that when I returned
I would have received it back with interest.
28" 'Take the talent from him and give it to the
one who has the ten talents. 29For everyone who
has will be given more, and he will have an abundance. Whoever does not have, even what he has
will be taken from him.[m] 30And throw that worthless servant outside, into the darkness, where
there will be weeping and gnashing of teeth.'[n]

25:10 [f]Rev 19:9
25:13 [g]Mt 24:42, 44; Mk 13:35; Lk 12:40
25:14 [h]Mt 21:33; Lk 19:12
25:15 [i]Mt 18:24,25
25:19 [j]Mt 18:23
25:21 [k]ver 23; Mt 24:45,47; Lk 16:10
25:23 [l]ver 21
25:29 [m]Mt 13:12; Mk 4:25; Lk 8:18; 19:26
25:30 [n]Mt 8:12

[a] *15* A talent was worth more than a thousand dollars.

The Sheep and the Goats

31 “When the Son of Man comes[o] in his glory,
and all the angels with him, he will sit on his
throne[p] in heavenly glory. 32 All the nations will
be gathered before him, and he will separate[q] the
people one from another as a shepherd separates
the sheep from the goats.[r] 33 He will put the sheep
on his right and the goats on his left.
34 “Then the King will say to those on his right,
‘Come, you who are blessed by my Father; take
your inheritance, the kingdom[s] prepared for you
since the creation of the world.[t] 35 For I was hungry and you gave me something to eat, I was
thirsty and you gave me something to drink, I was
a stranger and you invited me in,[u] 36 I needed
clothes and you clothed me,[v] I was sick and you
looked after me,[w] I was in prison and you came
to visit me.’[x]
37 “Then the righteous will answer him, ‘Lord,
when did we see you hungry and feed you, or
thirsty and give you something to drink? 38 When
did we see you a stranger and invite you in, or
needing clothes and clothe you? 39 When did we
see you sick or in prison and go to visit you?’
40 “The King will reply, ‘I tell you the truth,
whatever you did for one of the least of these
brothers of mine, you did for me.’[y]
41 “Then he will say to those on his left, ‘Depart
from me,[z] you who are cursed, into the eternal
fire[a] prepared for the devil and his angels.[b] 42 For I
was hungry and you gave me nothing to eat, I was
thirsty and you gave me nothing to drink, 43 I was
a stranger and you did not invite me in, I needed
clothes and you did not clothe me, I was sick and
in prison and you did not look after me.’
44 “They also will answer, ‘Lord, when did we
see you hungry or thirsty or a stranger or needing clothes or sick or in prison, and did not help
you?’
45 “He will reply, ‘I tell you the truth, whatever
you did not do for one of the least of these, you
did not do for me.’[c]
46 “Then they will go away to eternal punishment, but the righteous to eternal life.[d]”[e]

The Plot Against Jesus

26 When Jesus had finished saying all these
things,[f] he said to his disciples, 2 “As you
know, the Passover[g] is two days away—and the
Son of Man will be handed over to be crucified.”
3 Then the chief priests and the elders of the people assembled[h] in the palace of the high priest,
whose name was Caiaphas,[i] 4 and they plotted to
arrest Jesus in some sly way and kill him.[j] 5 “But
not during the Feast,” they said, “or there may be
a riot[k] among the people.”

Jesus Anointed at Bethany

6 While Jesus was in Bethany[l] in the home of a
man known as Simon the Leper, 7 a woman came

25:31 [o]Mt 16:27; Lk 17:30 [p]Mt 19:28
25:32 [q]Mal 3:18 [r]Eze 34:17, 20
25:34 [s]Mt 3:2; 5:3, 10,19; 19:14; Ac 20:32; 1Co 15:50; Gal 5:21; Jas 2:5 [t]Heb 4:3; 9:26; Rev 13:8; 17:8
25:35 [u]Job 31:32; Isa 58:7; Eze 18:7; Heb 13:2
25:36 [v]Isa 58:7; Eze 18:7; Jas 2:15,16 [w]Jas 1:27 [x]2Ti 1:16
25:40 [y]Pr 19:17; Mt 10:40,42; Heb 6:10; 13:2
25:41 [z]Mt 7:23 [a]Isa 66:24; Mt 3:12; 5:22; Mk 9:43,48; Lk 3:17; Jude 7 [b]2Pe 2:4
25:45 [c]Pr 14:31; 17:5
25:46 [d]Mt 19:29; Jn 3:15,16, 36; 17:2,3; Ro 2:7; Gal 6:8; 5:11, 13,20 [e]Da 12:2; Jn 5:29; Ac 24:15; Ro 2:7,8; Gal 6:8
26:1 [f]Mt 7:28
26:2 [g]Jn 11:55; 13:1
26:3 [h]Ps 2:2 [i]ver 57; Jn 11:47-53; 18:13,14,24, 28
26:4 [j]Mt 12:14
26:5 [k]Mt 27:24
26:6 [l]Mt 21:17

The Face of Christ

MT 25:31–46

Jesus speaks these challenging words only three days before his suffering begins. He describes a scene that will occur at the end of the ages, when the Son of Man will sit on his throne in all his glory. Those before him will be judged on the basis of their response to human need—whatever they offered to “the least of these” (Mt 25:40, 45), they offered to him! No gift is unimportant—a cup of cold water, a coat, a visit to prison. As we listen to Jesus’ words here, we begin to realize that as we move about our day and occupation, we see the face of Jesus in everyone we meet. We minister to the lowliest as if he or she were the Christ. What we do for anyone in need, we do for him.

to him with an alabaster jar of very expensive perfume, which she poured on his head as he was
reclining at the table.
8When the disciples saw this, they were indignant. "Why this waste?" they asked. 9"This perfume could have been sold at a high price and the
money given to the poor."
10Aware of this, Jesus said to them, "Why are
you bothering this woman? She has done a beautiful thing to me. 11The poor you will always have
with you,[m] but you will not always have me.
12When she poured this perfume on my body, she
did it to prepare me for burial.[n] 13I tell you the
truth, wherever this gospel is preached throughout the world, what she has done will also be
told, in memory of her."

Judas Agrees to Betray Jesus

14Then one of the Twelve—the one called Judas
Iscariot[o]—went to the chief priests 15and asked,
"What are you willing to give me if I hand him
over to you?" So they counted out for him thirty
silver coins.[p] 16From then on Judas watched for
an opportunity to hand him over.

The Lord's Supper

17On the first day of the Feast of Unleavened
Bread,[q] the disciples came to Jesus and asked,
"Where do you want us to make preparations for
you to eat the Passover?"
18He replied, "Go into the city to a certain man
and tell him, 'The Teacher says: My appointed
time[r] is near. I am going to celebrate the Passover
with my disciples at your house.' " 19So the disciples did as Jesus had directed them and prepared
the Passover.
20When evening came, Jesus was reclining at
the table with the Twelve. 21And while they were
eating, he said, "I tell you the truth, one of you
will betray me."[s]
22They were very sad and began to say to him
one after the other, "Surely not I, Lord?"
23Jesus replied, "The one who has dipped his
hand into the bowl with me will betray me.[t] 24The
Son of Man will go just as it is written about him.[u]
But woe to that man who betrays the Son of Man!
It would be better for him if he had not been born."
25Then Judas, the one who would betray him,
said, "Surely not I, Rabbi?"[v]
Jesus answered, "Yes, it is you."[a]
26While they were eating, Jesus took bread,
gave thanks and broke it,[w] and gave it to his disciples, saying, "Take and eat; this is my body."
27Then he took the cup, gave thanks and offered
it to them, saying, "Drink from it, all of you.
28This is my blood of the[b] covenant,[x] which is
poured out for many for the forgiveness of sins.[y]
29I tell you, I will not drink of this fruit of the vine

26:11 [m]Dt 15:11
26:12 [n]Jn 19:40
26:14 [o]ver 25,47; Mt 10:4
26:15 [p]Ex 21:32; Zec 11:12
26:17 [q]Ex 12:18-20
26:18 [r]Jn 7:6,8,30; 12:23; 13:1; 17:1
26:21 [s]Lk 22:21-23; Jn 13:21
26:23 [t]Ps 41:9; Jn 13:18
26:24 [u]Isa 53; Da 9:26; Mk 9:12; Lk 24:25-27, 46; Ac 17:2, 3; 26:22,23
26:25 [v]Mt 23:7
26:26 [w]Mt 14:19; 1Co 10:16
26:28 [x]Ex 24:6-8; Heb 9:20 [y]Mt 20:28; Mk 1:4

[a] *25* Or *"You yourself have said it"* [b] *28* Some manuscripts *the new*

The Anointing

MT 26:6-13

The scene radiates extravagant love. We know from John's Gospel that the unnamed woman here is Mary, the sister of Martha and Lazarus. Mary's act is one of transparent, unselfish adoration for her Savior. The event takes place during the final week of Jesus' life, in the home of Simon the Leper in Bethany. Mary anoints Jesus' head with an expensive, fragrant perfume (Jn 12:3; see also the note on Mk 14:1-11, page 1669). In Jewish culture the bodies of the dead were prepared for burial in a similar fashion—unless the person had died the death of a criminal. Thus, as Jesus notes, Mary is preparing his body for burial, foreshadowing his death on the cross. The perfume she used comes from the nard plant, native to India and costing approximately a year's salary for an average working person (Jn 12:5). Jesus praises Mary's act of extravagant, costly love and commends her deed as one that will be remembered wherever the gospel is preached (see the character sketch for this woman on page 1843).

26:29 from now on until that day when I drink it anew
[z]Ac 10:41 with you[z] in my Father's kingdom."
30 When they had sung a hymn, they went out
26:30 [a]Mt 21:1; to the Mount of Olives.[a]
Mk 14:26

Jesus Predicts Peter's Denial

26:31 [b]Mt 11:6 31 Then Jesus told them, "This very night you
[c]Zec 13:7; will all fall away on account of me,[b] for it is
Jn 16:32 written:

> " 'I will strike the shepherd,
> and the sheep of the flock will be
> scattered.'[ac]

32 But after I have risen, I will go ahead of you into
26:32 [d]Mt 28:7,10, 16 Galilee."[d]
33 Peter replied, "Even if all fall away on account
of you, I never will."
34 "I tell you the truth," Jesus answered, "this
26:34 very night, before the rooster crows, you will dis-
[e]ver 75; own me three times."[e]
Jn 13:38 35 But Peter declared, "Even if I have to die with
26:35 you,[f] I will never disown you." And all the other
[f]Jn 13:37 disciples said the same.

Gethsemane

36 Then Jesus went with his disciples to a place
called Gethsemane, and he said to them, "Sit here
while I go over there and pray." 37 He took Peter
26:37 [g]Mt 4:21 and the two sons of Zebedee[g] along with him, and
he began to be sorrowful and troubled. 38 Then he
said to them, "My soul is overwhelmed with sor-
26:38 [h]Jn 12:27 row[h] to the point of death. Stay here and keep
[i]ver 40,41 watch with me."[i]
39 Going a little farther, he fell with his face to
26:39 the ground and prayed, "My Father, if it is possi-
[j]Mt 20:22 ble, may this cup[j] be taken from me. Yet not as I
[k]ver 42; Ps 40:6-8; will, but as you will."[k]
Isa 50:5; 40 Then he returned to his disciples and found
Jn 5:30; 6:38 them sleeping. "Could you men not keep watch
26:40 with me[l] for one hour?" he asked Peter. 41 "Watch
[l]ver 38 and pray so that you will not fall into tempta-
26:41 [m]Mt 6:13 tion.[m] The spirit is willing, but the body is weak."
42 He went away a second time and prayed, "My
Father, if it is not possible for this cup to be taken
away unless I drink it, may your will be done."
43 When he came back, he again found them
sleeping, because their eyes were heavy. 44 So he
left them and went away once more and prayed
the third time, saying the same thing.
45 Then he returned to the disciples and said to
them, "Are you still sleeping and resting? Look,
26:45 [n]ver 18 the hour[n] is near, and the Son of Man is betrayed
into the hands of sinners. 46 Rise, let us go! Here
comes my betrayer!"

Jesus Arrested

47 While he was still speaking, Judas, one of the
Twelve, arrived. With him was a large crowd armed
with swords and clubs, sent from the chief priests

[a] *31* Zech. 13:7

33 The Garden

MT 26:36–46

Jesus takes his disciples to the Garden of Gethsemane (Gethsemane means "oil press"), a garden they frequent on the western slopes of the Mount of Olives. Jesus is deeply troubled and shares his anguish with his disciples: "My soul is overwhelmed with sorrow" (Mt 26:38). His words speak of an intense, devastating grief (see the note on Mk 14:36, page 1671). As their Savior suffers, the disciples sleep, leaving him alone in his suffering, strengthened only by an angel (Lk 22:43). Jesus asks the Father to forestall, if possible, the suffering he is about to undergo; yet he willingly submits himself to the Father's will. Jesus does not die a martyr's death, for his life is not taken from him but is freely given by him for the sake of those who will inherit eternal life in his name.

Week 33

The Cup of Suffering

At the close of his life here on earth, Jesus suffered more than we can comprehend. He chose to accept his suffering in order to do his Father's will. Jesus' suffering is far more amazing than his miracles, for to follow God's will when the sacrifice is extreme is the greatest test of faith. You will never reach the depth of suffering to which your Lord was subjected, but at times you may feel as though you are sharing it. How can you find courage and hope to help you endure?

How does Jesus describe his suffering (Mt 26:38)? What is his request of God and how many times does he make it (Mt 26:39,42,44)? How is Jesus' submission to his Father revealed through his request (Mt 26:39)?

Jesus says, "If it is possible, may this cup be taken from me" (Mt 26:39). Who will also drink from Jesus' cup (Mt 20:22-23)? What do you think this means (Ro 8:17)? How does it apply to you?

What is the purpose of suffering (Job 23:10)? Your suffering can either purify you—or petrify you. Will you allow God's consuming fire to soften and cleanse you, or will you harden yourself against suffering and, in the process, miss its refining purpose? The very trial you are enduring is the tool God is using to refine you.

What does Jesus do when faced with suffering (Isa 53:7; Heb 12:2)? What does the psalmist do in the midst of suffering (Ps 119:50)? What should you do when you suffer (1Pe 4:12-19)?

Have your dreams been crushed? Are your daily burdens too heavy? Are you suffering physically, financially, emotionally or spiritually? Will you accept the part of your suffering that comes from God (Php 1:29), looking to his promises and to the glory to come, or will you harden yourself against it and miss its transforming power?

Enjoying God THROUGH the Word

Read Mark 14:22-24 (page 1670). The Lord's Supper is celebrated by Christians around the world, a significant image of Jesus' broken body and shed blood. Notice that Jesus "offered [the cup] to them, and they all drank from it" (Mk 14:23). Jesus suffered willingly, paying the price of your sin (Jn 10:17-18) even though he could have refused the cup (Jn 18:11). Because of his sacrifice, your sin is forever paid for (Heb 7:27).

The cup of the Lord's Supper is the symbol of your fellowship with Jesus and his suffering; it is your "participation in the blood of Christ" and "in the body of Christ" (1Co 10:16). You may accept his fellowship and the suffering that comes with it (Php 3:10), or you can turn away from it. The choice is yours. But the promise stands: We are God's children and heirs, "if indeed we share in his sufferings in order that we may also share in his glory" (Ro 8:17). Paul makes his choice clear: "I consider that our present sufferings are not worth comparing with the glory that will be revealed in us" (Ro 8:18). In times of suffering, hold on to his promises.

Enjoying God THROUGH Experience

Ask the Holy Spirit to enable you to accept your sufferings. Willingly offer them to God as a sacrifice. Then ask God to purify and renew you through them. "We do not lose heart. Though outwardly we are wasting away, yet inwardly we are being renewed day by day. For our light and momentary troubles are achieving for us an eternal glory that far outweighs them all" (2Co 4:16-17).

Go to page 1659 for your next weekly study.

and the elders of the people. 48Now the betrayer
had arranged a signal with them: "The one I kiss is
26:49 the man; arrest him." 49Going at once to Jesus,
[o]ver 25 Judas said, "Greetings, Rabbi!"[o] and kissed him.
26:50 50Jesus replied, "Friend,[p] do what you came
[p]Mt 20:13; for."[a]
22:12 Then the men stepped forward, seized Jesus
and arrested him. 51With that, one of Jesus' com-
26:51 panions reached for his sword,[q] drew it out and
[q]Lk 22:36,38 [r]Jn 18:10 struck the servant of the high priest, cutting off
his ear.[r]
52"Put your sword back in its place," Jesus said
to him, "for all who draw the sword will die by
26:52 the sword.[s] 53Do you think I cannot call on my
[s]Ge 9:6; Rev 13:10 Father, and he will at once put at my disposal
26:53 more than twelve legions of angels?[t] 54But how
[t]2Ki 6:17; then would the Scriptures be fulfilled[u] that say it
Da 7:10; must happen in this way?"
Mt 4:11 55At that time Jesus said to the crowd, "Am I
26:54 leading a rebellion, that you have come out with
[u]ver 24 swords and clubs to capture me? Every day I sat in
26:55 the temple courts teaching,[v] and you did not
[v]Mk 12:35; arrest me. 56But this has all taken place that the
Lk 21:37; writings of the prophets might be fulfilled."[w] Then
Jn 7:14,28; 18:20 all the disciples deserted him and fled.

26:56 [w]ver 24

Before the Sanhedrin

26:57 57Those who had arrested Jesus took him to
[x]ver 3 Caiaphas,[x] the high priest, where the teachers of
the law and the elders had assembled. 58But Peter
26:58 followed him at a distance, right up to the court-
[y]Jn 18:15 yard of the high priest.[y] He entered and sat down
[z]Jn 7:32,45, 46 with the guards[z] to see the outcome.
59The chief priests and the whole Sanhedrin[a]
26:59 were looking for false evidence against Jesus so
[a]Mt 5:22 that they could put him to death. 60But they did
26:60 not find any, though many false witnesses[b] came
[b]Ps 27:12; forward.
35:11; Ac 6:13 Finally two[c] came forward 61and declared, "This
[c]Dt 19:15 fellow said, 'I am able to destroy the temple of
God and rebuild it in three days.' "[d]
26:61 [d]Jn 2:19 62Then the high priest stood up and said to
Jesus, "Are you not going to answer? What is this
26:63 testimony that these men are bringing against
[e]Mt 27:12,14 you?" 63But Jesus remained silent.[e]
[f]Lev 5:1 [g]Mt 16:16 The high priest said to him, "I charge you under
oath[f] by the living God:[g] Tell us if you are the
Christ,[b] the Son of God."
64"Yes, it is as you say," Jesus replied. "But I say
to all of you: In the future you will see the Son of
26:64 Man sitting at the right hand of the Mighty One[h]
[h]Ps 110:1 [i]Da 7:13; and coming on the clouds of heaven."[i]
Rev 1:7 65Then the high priest tore his clothes[j] and said,
26:65 "He has spoken blasphemy! Why do we need any
[j]Mk 14:63 more witnesses? Look, now you have heard the
26:66 blasphemy. 66What do you think?"
[k]Lev 24:16; "He is worthy of death,"[k] they answered.
Jn 19:7 67Then they spit in his face and struck him with

[a] 50 Or *"Friend, why have you come?"* [b] 63 Or *Messiah;* also in verse 68

The Sanhedrin

MT 26:57–68

Jesus is tried before the Sanhedrin, the council of highest Jewish authority. The purpose of his trial is to find some legal basis by which to convict and execute him, although the Sanhedrin had no legal authority to order Jesus' death (see the note on Lk 19:47–48, page 1727). That is why his trial later moves into the Roman court system. Many irregularities occur in the trial. Jesus declines to answer any of the charges brought against him until the high priest places him under sacred oath: "by the living God" (Mt 26:63). Caiaphas demands that Jesus tell them if he is the Christ, the Son of God. Jesus answers in the affirmative and adds that in the future they will see him sitting at the right hand of God. With Jesus' clear assertion of his deity, Caiaphas tears his clothes (an act that is ordinarily forbidden by Levitical law—Lev 21:10) and declares Jesus guilty of blasphemy, a charge worthy of death under Levitical law (Lev 24:16).

King of the Jews

MT 27:11

Pilate asks Jesus a question designed to uncover the source of his authority and position. "Are you the king of the Jews?" Jesus answers in the affirmative—although his kingdom is different from the type of kingdom Pilate is referring to, since it is "not of this world" (Jn 18:36). Jesus' claim to be the king of the Jews results in a charge of treason from the Jewish Sanhedrin and is displayed above Jesus' head as he hangs on the cross (Mt 27:37). Jesus' assertion builds a foundation for Christianity, which rests on the conviction that Jesus is indeed the promised Messiah, risen from the dead, the true King of the Jews.

their fists.[l] Others slapped him 68and said, "Prophesy to us, Christ. Who hit you?"[m]

Peter Disowns Jesus

69Now Peter was sitting out in the courtyard,
and a servant girl came to him. "You also were
with Jesus of Galilee," she said.
70But he denied it before them all. "I don't know
what you're talking about," he said.
71Then he went out to the gateway, where
another girl saw him and said to the people there,
"This fellow was with Jesus of Nazareth."
72He denied it again, with an oath: "I don't
know the man!"
73After a little while, those standing there went
up to Peter and said, "Surely you are one of them,
for your accent gives you away."
74Then he began to call down curses on himself
and he swore to them, "I don't know the man!"
Immediately a rooster crowed. 75Then Peter
remembered the word Jesus had spoken: "Before
the rooster crows, you will disown me three
times."[n] And he went outside and wept bitterly.

Judas Hangs Himself

27 Early in the morning, all the chief priests
and the elders of the people came to the
decision to put Jesus to death.[o] 2They bound him,
led him away and handed him over[p] to Pilate, the
governor.[q]
3When Judas, who had betrayed him,[r] saw that
Jesus was condemned, he was seized with
remorse and returned the thirty silver coins[s] to the
chief priests and the elders. 4"I have sinned," he
said, "for I have betrayed innocent blood."
"What is that to us?" they replied. "That's your
responsibility."[t]
5So Judas threw the money into the temple[u] and
left. Then he went away and hanged himself.[v]
6The chief priests picked up the coins and said,
"It is against the law to put this into the treasury,
since it is blood money." 7So they decided to use
the money to buy the potter's field as a burial
place for foreigners. 8That is why it has been
called the Field of Blood[w] to this day. 9Then what
was spoken by Jeremiah the prophet was fulfilled:[x] "They took the thirty silver coins, the price
set on him by the people of Israel, 10and they used
them to buy the potter's field, as the Lord commanded me."[a][y]

Jesus Before Pilate

11Meanwhile Jesus stood before the governor,
and the governor asked him, "Are you the king of
the Jews?"[z]
"Yes, it is as you say," Jesus replied.
12When he was accused by the chief priests and
the elders, he gave no answer.[a] 13Then Pilate
asked him, "Don't you hear the testimony they

26:67 [l]Mt 16:21; 27:30
26:68 [m]Lk 22:63-65
26:75 [n]ver 34; Jn 13:38
27:1 [o]Mt 12:14; Mk 15:1; Lk 22:66
27:2 [p]Mt 20:19 [q]Mk 15:1; Lk 13:1; Ac 3:13; 1Ti 6:13
27:3 [r]Mt 10:4 [s]Mt 26:14,15
27:4 [t]ver 24
27:5 [u]Lk 1:9,21 [v]Ac 1:18
27:8 [w]Ac 1:19
27:9 [x]Mt 1:22
27:10 [y]Zec 11:12,13; Jer 32:6-9
27:11 [z]Mt 2:2
27:12 [a]Mt 26:63; Mk 14:61; Jn 19:9

[a] *10* See Zech. 11:12,13; Jer. 19:1–13; 32:6–9.

are bringing against you?"[b] 14But Jesus made no
reply,[c] not even to a single charge—to the great
amazement of the governor.
15Now it was the governor's custom at the Feast
to release a prisoner[d] chosen by the crowd. 16At
that time they had a notorious prisoner, called
Barabbas. 17So when the crowd had gathered,
Pilate asked them, "Which one do you want me
to release to you: Barabbas, or Jesus who is called
Christ?"[e] 18For he knew it was out of envy that
they had handed Jesus over to him.
19While Pilate was sitting on the judge's seat,[f] his
wife sent him this message: "Don't have anything
to do with that innocent[g] man, for I have suffered
a great deal today in a dream[h] because of him."
20But the chief priests and the elders persuaded
the crowd to ask for Barabbas and to have Jesus
executed.[i]
21"Which of the two do you want me to release
to you?" asked the governor.
"Barabbas," they answered.
22"What shall I do, then, with Jesus who is
called Christ?"[j] Pilate asked.
They all answered, "Crucify him!"
23"Why? What crime has he committed?" asked
Pilate.
But they shouted all the louder, "Crucify him!"
24When Pilate saw that he was getting nowhere,
but that instead an uproar[k] was starting, he took
water and washed his hands[l] in front of the
crowd. "I am innocent of this man's blood,"[m] he
said. "It is your responsibility!"[n]
25All the people answered, "Let his blood be on
us and on our children!"[o]
26Then he released Barabbas to them. But he
had Jesus flogged,[p] and handed him over to be
crucified.

The Soldiers Mock Jesus

27Then the governor's soldiers took Jesus into
the Praetorium[q] and gathered the whole company of soldiers around him. 28They stripped him
and put a scarlet robe on him,[r] 29and then twisted
together a crown of thorns and set it on his head.
They put a staff in his right hand and knelt in
front of him and mocked him. "Hail, king of the
Jews!" they said.[s] 30They spit on him, and took
the staff and struck him on the head again and
again.[t] 31After they had mocked him, they took off
the robe and put his own clothes on him. Then
they led him away to crucify him.[u]

The Crucifixion

32As they were going out,[v] they met a man from
Cyrene,[w] named Simon, and they forced him to
carry the cross.[x] 33They came to a place called
Golgotha (which means The Place of the Skull).[y]
34There they offered Jesus wine to drink, mixed
with gall;[z] but after tasting it, he refused to drink
it. 35When they had crucified him, they divided

27:13 [b]Mt 26:62
27:14 [c]Mk 14:61
27:15 [d]Jn 18:39
27:17 [e]ver 22; Mt 1:16
27:19 [f]Jn 19:13 [g]ver 24 [h]Ge 20:6; Nu 12:6; 1Ki 3:5; Job 33:14-16; Mt 1:20; 2:12,13,19, 22
27:20 [i]Ac 3:14
27:22 [j]Mt 1:16
27:24 [k]Mt 26:5 [l]Ps 26:6 [m]Dt 21:6-8 [n]ver 4
27:25 [o]Jos 2:19; Ac 5:28
27:26 [p]Isa 53:5; Jn 19:1
27:27 [q]Jn 18:28, 33; 19:9
27:28 [r]Jn 19:2
27:29 [s]Isa 53:3; Jn 19:2,3
27:30 [t]Mt 16:21; 26:67
27:31 [u]Isa 53:7
27:32 [v]Heb 13:12 [w]Ac 2:10; 6:9; 11:20; 13:1 [x]Mk 15:21; Lk 23:26
27:33 [y]Jn 19:17
27:34 [z]ver 48; Ps 69:21

Crucifixion

MT 27:32–44

In the ancient world, death by crucifixion was universally regarded with horror. The Romans reserved it for their worst criminals and for the lowest classes. No Roman citizen could be crucified without a direct edict from Caesar. Among the Jews, the stigma was even greater. The one crucified was thought to be under the curse of God: "Anyone who is hung on a tree is under God's curse" (Dt 21:23).

Executions normally took place outside the city walls. It seems that Jesus managed to carry his cross as far as the city gates, where Simon was enlisted to continue the task. Death by crucifixion is both unspeakably painful and acutely shameful. Jesus endured physical agony, public humiliation and spiritual separation from the Father that was beyond the human mind to grasp. John's Revelation describes the result of the act: "Worthy is the Lamb, who was slain, to receive power and wealth and wisdom and strength and honor and glory and praise!" (Rev 5:12).

The Women

MT 27:55–56

The Galilean women, who watch Jesus' death from a distance, whether from timidity or modesty, stand with Jesus until the bitter end. Women are last at the cross and first at the tomb. At the cross, Matthew mentions three women in particular: Mary Magdalene, Mary the mother of James and Joses, and the mother of James and John (probably Salome of Mk 15:40). They were among those women who traveled with Jesus and his disciples throughout his preaching ministry, contributing to their needs out of their own resources.

In Jewish culture, women were considered second-class citizens. But Jesus transcends culture and honors women—he teaches them, welcomes their presence and appears first to women at his resurrection (see the character study for these women on page 1941).

up his clothes by casting lots.[a][a] 36 And sitting down, they kept watch[b] over him there. 37 Above his head they placed the written charge against him: THIS IS JESUS, THE KING OF THE JEWS. 38 Two robbers were crucified with him,[c] one on his right and one on his left. 39 Those who passed by hurled insults at him, shaking their heads[d] 40 and saying, "You who are going to destroy the temple and build it in three days,[e] save yourself![f] Come down from the cross, if you are the Son of God!"[g]

41 In the same way the chief priests, the teachers of the law and the elders mocked him. 42 "He saved others," they said, "but he can't save himself! He's the King of Israel![h] Let him come down now from the cross, and we will believe[i] in him. 43 He trusts in God. Let God rescue him[j] now if he wants him, for he said, 'I am the Son of God.' " 44 In the same way the robbers who were crucified with him also heaped insults on him.

The Death of Jesus

45 From the sixth hour until the ninth hour darkness[k] came over all the land. 46 About the ninth hour Jesus cried out in a loud voice, *"Eloi, Eloi,*[b] *lama sabachthani?"*—which means, "My God, my God, why have you forsaken me?"[c][l]

47 When some of those standing there heard this, they said, "He's calling Elijah."

48 Immediately one of them ran and got a sponge. He filled it with wine vinegar,[m] put it on a stick, and offered it to Jesus to drink. 49 The rest said, "Now leave him alone. Let's see if Elijah comes to save him."

50 And when Jesus had cried out again in a loud voice, he gave up his spirit.[n]

51 At that moment the curtain of the temple[o] was torn in two from top to bottom. The earth shook and the rocks split.[p] 52 The tombs broke open and the bodies of many holy people who had died were raised to life. 53 They came out of the tombs, and after Jesus' resurrection they went into the holy city[q] and appeared to many people.

54 When the centurion and those with him who were guarding[r] Jesus saw the earthquake and all that had happened, they were terrified, and exclaimed, "Surely he was the Son[d] of God!"[s]

55 Many women were there, watching from a distance. They had followed Jesus from Galilee to care for his needs.[t] 56 Among them were Mary Magdalene, Mary the mother of James and Joses, and the mother of Zebedee's sons.[u]

The Burial of Jesus

57 As evening approached, there came a rich man from Arimathea, named Joseph, who had himself become a disciple of Jesus. 58 Going to

27:35 [a]Ps 22:18
27:36 [b]ver 54
27:38 [c]Isa 53:12
27:39 [d]Ps 22:7; 109:25; La 2:15
27:40 [e]Mt 26:61; Jn 2:19 [f]ver 42 [g]Mt 4:3,6
27:42 [h]Jn 1:49; 12:13 [i]Jn 3:15
27:43 [j]Ps 22:8
27:45 [k]Am 8:9
27:46 [l]Ps 22:1
27:48 [m]ver 34; Ps 69:21
27:50 [n]Jn 19:30
27:51 [o]Ex 26:31-33; Heb 9:3,8 [p]ver 54
27:53 [q]Mt 4:5
27:54 [r]ver 36 [s]Mt 4:3; 17:5
27:55 [t]Lk 8:2,3
27:56 [u]Mk 15:47; Lk 24:10; Jn 19:25

[a] *35* A few late manuscripts *lots that the word spoken by the prophet might be fulfilled: "They divided my garments among themselves and cast lots for my clothing"* (Psalm 22:18)
[b] *46* Some manuscripts *Eli, Eli* [c] *46* Psalm 22:1
[d] *54* Or *a son*

Pilate, he asked for Jesus' body, and Pilate ordered that it be given to him. 59 Joseph took the body, wrapped it in a clean linen cloth, 60 and placed it in his own new tomb[v] that he had cut out of the rock. He rolled a big stone in front of the entrance to the tomb and went away. 61 Mary Magdalene and the other Mary were sitting there opposite the tomb.

The Guard at the Tomb

62 The next day, the one after Preparation Day, the chief priests and the Pharisees went to Pilate. 63 "Sir," they said, "we remember that while he was still alive that deceiver said, 'After three days I will rise again.'[w] 64 So give the order for the tomb to be made secure until the third day. Otherwise, his disciples may come and steal the body and tell the people that he has been raised from the dead. This last deception will be worse than the first."

65 "Take a guard,"[x] Pilate answered. "Go, make the tomb as secure as you know how." 66 So they went and made the tomb secure by putting a seal[y] on the stone[z] and posting the guard.[a]

The Resurrection

28 After the Sabbath, at dawn on the first day of the week, Mary Magdalene and the other Mary[b] went to look at the tomb.

2 There was a violent earthquake,[c] for an angel[d] of the Lord came down from heaven and, going to the tomb, rolled back the stone and sat on it. 3 His appearance was like lightning, and his clothes were white as snow.[e] 4 The guards were so afraid of him that they shook and became like dead men.

5 The angel said to the women, "Do not be afraid,[f] for I know that you are looking for Jesus, who was crucified. 6 He is not here; he has risen, just as he said.[g] Come and see the place where he lay. 7 Then go quickly and tell his disciples: 'He has risen from the dead and is going ahead of you into Galilee.[h] There you will see him.' Now I have told you."

8 So the women hurried away from the tomb, afraid yet filled with joy, and ran to tell his disciples. 9 Suddenly Jesus met them.[i] "Greetings," he said. They came to him, clasped his feet and worshiped him. 10 Then Jesus said to them, "Do not be afraid. Go and tell my brothers[j] to go to Galilee; there they will see me."

The Guards' Report

11 While the women were on their way, some of the guards[k] went into the city and reported to the chief priests everything that had happened. 12 When the chief priests had met with the elders and devised a plan, they gave the soldiers a large sum of money, 13 telling them, "You are to say, 'His disciples came during the night and stole him away while we were asleep.' 14 If this report gets

27:60 [v]Mt 27:66; 28:2; Mk 16:4
27:63 [w]Mt 16:21
27:65 [x]ver 66; Mt 28:11
27:66 [y]Da 6:17 [z]ver 60; Mt 28:2 [a]Mt 28:11
28:1 [b]Mt 27:56
28:2 [c]Mt 27:51 [d]Jn 20:12
28:3 [e]Da 10:6; Mk 9:3; Jn 20:12
28:5 [f]ver 10; Mt 14:27
28:6 [g]Mt 16:21
28:7 [h]ver 10,16; Mt 26:32
28:9 [i]Jn 20:14-18
28:10 [j]Jn 20:17; Ro 8:29; Heb 2:11-13, 17
28:11 [k]Mt 27:65,66

First to Women

MT 28:1-10

With the attention of a Jewish scribe, Matthew records many details necessary to verify the accuracy and truth of the Messiah's resurrection. He is the only Gospel writer to record that soldiers kept watch over Jesus as he died, eliminating any suspicion that Jesus was removed from the cross while still alive (Mt 27:36). Only Matthew mentions that Joseph, who lends Jesus his own tomb and prepares him for burial, is rich, as Isaiah prophesied (Isa 53:9; Mt 27:57-60). Matthew also notes that the women watch Jesus' burial (Mt 27:61). The actuality of burial becomes an integral part of the gospel proclamation (1Co 15:4). Guards are posted at Jesus' tomb, and the stone over the opening is sealed, which also helps to authenticate his true death and resurrection (Mt 27:66). Matthew also notes that an angel announces that Jesus is risen, "just as he said" (compare Mt 28:6 with Mt 16:21; 17:23; 20:18-19; 27:63). Evidence of Jesus' death and resurrection are important to verify Jesus' claim that he is indeed the Messiah, the Savior.

The Great Commission

MT 28:16-20

The last passage in Matthew's Gospel, known as "the Great Commission," records Jesus' final instructions just before his ascension. These verses are dominated by the word all: all authority, all nations, all things (here translated "everything"), all days (here translated "always"). His command to "go" is based on his sovereign authority. In his resurrection Jesus becomes the One through whom all God's sovereign authority is presented. He is the King! Resting on his authority and power, we go to the nations, baptizing them in the name of the triune God and teaching them all that Jesus said. His commands will not change; they will remain until the end of the age. But marvelously surpassing his command is his promise that he will be with us as we fulfill it.

to the governor,[l] we will satisfy him and keep you
out of trouble." 15 So the soldiers took the money
and did as they were instructed. And this story
has been widely circulated among the Jews to this
very day.

The Great Commission

16 Then the eleven disciples went to Galilee, to
the mountain where Jesus had told them to go.[m]
17 When they saw him, they worshiped him; but
some doubted. 18 Then Jesus came to them and
said, "All authority in heaven and on earth has
been given to me.[n] 19 Therefore go and make disciples of all nations,[o] baptizing them in[a] the name
of the Father and of the Son and of the Holy Spirit,[p] 20 and teaching[q] them to obey everything I have
commanded you. And surely I am with you[r]
always, to the very end of the age."[s]

28:14 [l]Mt 27:2

28:16 [m]ver 7,10; Mt 26:32

28:18 [n]Da 7:13,14; Lk 10:22; Jn 3:35; 17:2; 1Co 15:27; Eph 1:20-22; Php 2:9,10

28:19 [o]Mk 16:15, 16; Lk 24:47; Ac 1:8; 14:21 [p]Ac 2:38; 8:16; Ro 6:3,4

28:20 [q]Ac 2:42 [r]Mt 18:20; Ac 18:10 [s]Mt 13:39

[a] *19* Or *into*; see Acts 8:16; 19:5; Romans 6:3; 1 Cor. 1:13; 10:2 and Gal. 3:27.

The suffering servant as Savior.

With a fast-paced style and practical appeal, the book of Mark paints a compelling portrait of the Savior serving others. The briefest of the four Gospels, Mark provides snapshots of Jesus' ministry, giving scant attention to his teachings but recording many of his miracles. Almost half of the book focuses on the events surrounding Jesus' final week on earth, drawing attention to his suffering and sacrifice on the cross as the Savior of the world.

Because Mark's underlying purpose is to present Jesus as the Messiah and Son of God, many of the other characters in this account are noted but not named. We meet four determined friends who find a novel way to bring a loved one to Jesus (Mk 2). We come upon an unknown woman who has been hemorrhaging for twelve years and sense her desperate search to find healing (Mk 5). We witness the miracle of a daughter brought back to life (Mk 5). We applaud a widow's generosity and trust in God's provision as she gives a great gift to his work (Mk 12). And we encounter a servant girl whose tenacious questioning reveals an unsettling weakness in one of the disciples (Mk 14).

One of the greatest messages of the book of Mark is the call for us to serve others even as Jesus served (Mk 10:45). Through his words and actions Jesus portrays service and self-sacrifice as the hallmarks of true greatness.

Quick Study

Author
Mark, who traveled with Paul and Barnabas, wrote his Gospel based on his association with Peter.

Date Written
The book of Mark was probably the first Gospel written and therefore is most likely dated around A.D. 55.

Setting
Israel, primarily the regions of Galilee, Judea and Perea.

Key Passage
Mark 1:14–15 "Jesus went into Galilee, proclaiming the good news of God. 'The time has come,' he said. 'The kingdom of God is near. Repent and believe the good news!' "

Outline

Baptism and temptation.
Mk 1:1-13

The beginning of Jesus' ministry.
Mk 1:14—3:35

Various parables.
Mk 4:1-34

Miracles and healings.
Mk 4:35—5:43

Jesus' ministry continues.
Mk 6:1-29

Miracles and teachings.
Mk 6:30—10:52

Entering Jerusalem.
Mk 11

More teachings.
Mk 12:1—13:37

Jesus anointed, betrayed and arrested.
Mk 14:1-52

Jesus' trial.
Mk 14:53—15:20

Jesus' death.
Mk 15:21-47

Jesus' resurrection.
Mk 16

The Women of Mark

✤	**Simon Peter's mother-in-law**	*Jesus took her hand and healed her.* Mk 1:29-31 (page 1687)
✤	**Mary, mother of Jesus**	*Jesus' mother.* Mk 3:31-35 (page 1613)
✤	**Woman subject to bleeding**	*Healing brought joy and relief.* Mk 5:25-34 (page 1745)
✤	**Jairus's daughter**	*A dead girl brought to life.* Mk 5:21-43 (page 1746)
	Jesus' sisters	*They lived in Nazareth.* Mk 6:3
✤	**Herodias**	*She hated John the Baptist.* Mk 6:14-29 (page 1779)
✤	**Daughter of Herodias**	*She danced for Herod.* Mk 6:22-28 (page 1780)
✤	**Syrophoenician woman**	*Her perseverance was rewarded.* Mk 7:24-30 (page 1811)
✤	**Widow with two coins**	*She gave all she had.* Mk 12:41-44 (page 1911)
✤	**A woman with a jar of perfume (Mary of Bethany)**	*She anointed Jesus.* Mk 14:1-11 (page 1843)
	Servant girls	*Peter lied to them.* Mk 14:66-69
✤	**Salome**	*She was at Jesus' crucifixion and resurrection.* Mk 15:40-41; 16:1-8 (page 1878)
✤	**Mary Magdalene**	*She cared for Jesus.* Mk 15:40-41,47; 16:1-11 (page 1714)
✤	**Women who followed Jesus**	*True disciples.* Mk 15:40-41,47; 16:1-8 (page 1941)

✤ Denotes a sketch written about this character

John the Baptist Prepares the Way

1:1 1 The beginning of the gospel about Jesus
[a]Mt 4:3 Christ, the Son of God.[a][a]

2It is written in Isaiah the prophet:
"I will send my messenger ahead of you,
1:2 who will prepare your way"[b][b]—
[b]Mal 3:1; 3"a voice of one calling in the desert,
Mt 11:10; Lk 7:27 'Prepare the way for the Lord,
1:3 make straight paths for him.' "[c][c]
[c]Isa 40:3; Jn 1:23 4And so John[d] came, baptizing in the desert
1:4 region and preaching a baptism of repentance[e] for
[d]Mt 3:1 the forgiveness of sins.[f] 5The whole Judean coun-
[e]Ac 13:24 tryside and all the people of Jerusalem went out to
[f]Lk 1:77 him. Confessing their sins, they were baptized by
him in the Jordan River. 6John wore clothing
1:6 made of camel's hair, with a leather belt around
[g]Lev 11:22 his waist, and he ate locusts[g] and wild honey.
7And this was his message: "After me will come
one more powerful than I, the thongs of whose
sandals I am not worthy to stoop down and
1:7 [h]Ac 13:25 untie.[h] 8I baptize you with[d] water, but he will bap-
1:8 tize you with the Holy Spirit."[i]

[i]Isa 44:3; Joel 2:28;

The Baptism and Temptation of Jesus

Ac 1:5; 2:4; 9At that time Jesus came from Nazareth[j] in Gal-
11:16; 19:4-6 ilee and was baptized by John in the Jordan. 10As
1:9 Jesus was coming up out of the water, he saw
[j]Mt 2:23 heaven being torn open and the Spirit descending
1:10 on him like a dove.[k] 11And a voice came from
[k]Jn 1:32 heaven: "You are my Son,[l] whom I love; with you
I am well pleased."
1:11 [l]Mt 3:17 12At once the Spirit sent him out into the desert,
13and he was in the desert forty days, being tempt-
1:13 [m]Mt 4:10 ed by Satan.[m] He was with the wild animals, and
angels attended him.

The Calling of the First Disciples

14After John was put in prison, Jesus went into
1:14 [n]Mt 4:12 Galilee,[n] proclaiming the good news of God.[o]
[o]Mt 4:23 15"The time has come,"[p] he said. "The kingdom of
1:15 God is near. Repent and believe the good news!"[q]
[p]Gal 4:4; 16As Jesus walked beside the Sea of Galilee, he
Eph 1:10 saw Simon and his brother Andrew casting a net
[q]Ac 20:21 into the lake, for they were fishermen. 17"Come,
follow me," Jesus said, "and I will make you fishers of men." 18At once they left their nets and followed him.
19When he had gone a little farther, he saw
James son of Zebedee and his brother John in a
boat, preparing their nets. 20Without delay he
called them, and they left their father Zebedee in
the boat with the hired men and followed him.

Jesus Drives Out an Evil Spirit

21They went to Capernaum, and when the Sabbath came, Jesus went into the synagogue and

[a] *1* Some manuscripts do not have *the Son of God.* [b] *2* Mal. 3:1 [c] *3* Isaiah 40:3 [d] *8* Or *in*

The Spirit's Inauguration

MK 1:9-13

On the inauguration day of Jesus' ministry, an unknown carpenter walks into the water to be baptized. He knows that each step takes him away from common living and into public ministry.

The triune family is present: Father, Son and Spirit (see the note on Mt 3:11-17, page 1584). The Spirit's role in Jesus' baptism is that of anointing and confirming. The Spirit descends "like a dove" (Mk 1:10) and anoints Jesus, an act of setting him apart for a particular work. The Holy Spirit's presence also confirms Old Testament prophecies of this event (Isa 11:2; 42:1; 61:1). On a separate piece of paper, list the specific works Isaiah says the "chosen one" will accomplish under the Holy Spirit's guidance (Isa 42:1; 61:1-3). Then take time to thank Jesus for the ways he has accomplished these works in your life.

began to teach.[r] 22 The people were amazed at his teaching, because he taught them as one who had authority, not as the teachers of the law.[s] 23 Just then a man in their synagogue who was possessed by an evil[a] spirit cried out, 24 "What do you want with us,[t] Jesus of Nazareth?[u] Have you come to destroy us? I know who you are—the Holy One of God!"[v]

25 "Be quiet!" said Jesus sternly. "Come out of him!"[w] 26 The evil spirit shook the man violently and came out of him with a shriek.[x]

27 The people were all so amazed[y] that they asked each other, "What is this? A new teaching—and with authority! He even gives orders to evil spirits and they obey him." 28 News about him spread quickly over the whole region[z] of Galilee.

Jesus Heals Many

29 As soon as they left the synagogue,[a] they went with James and John to the home of Simon and Andrew. 30 Simon's mother-in-law was in bed with a fever, and they told Jesus about her. 31 So he went to her, took her hand and helped her up.[b] The fever left her and she began to wait on them.

32 That evening after sunset the people brought to Jesus all the sick and demon-possessed.[c] 33 The whole town gathered at the door, 34 and Jesus healed many who had various diseases.[d] He also drove out many demons, but he would not let the demons speak because they knew who he was.[e]

Jesus Prays in a Solitary Place

35 Very early in the morning, while it was still dark, Jesus got up, left the house and went off to a solitary place, where he prayed.[f] 36 Simon and his companions went to look for him, 37 and when they found him, they exclaimed: "Everyone is looking for you!"

38 Jesus replied, "Let us go somewhere else—to the nearby villages—so I can preach there also. That is why I have come."[g] 39 So he traveled throughout Galilee, preaching in their synagogues[h] and driving out demons.[i]

A Man With Leprosy

40 A man with leprosy[b] came to him and begged him on his knees,[j] "If you are willing, you can make me clean."

41 Filled with compassion, Jesus reached out his hand and touched the man. "I am willing," he said. "Be clean!" 42 Immediately the leprosy left him and he was cured.

43 Jesus sent him away at once with a strong warning: 44 "See that you don't tell this to anyone.[k] But go, show yourself to the priest[l] and offer the sacrifices that Moses commanded for your cleansing,[m] as a testimony to them." 45 Instead he went out and began to talk freely, spreading the news.

[a] *23* Greek *unclean;* also in verses 26 and 27 [b] *40* The Greek word was used for various diseases affecting the skin—not necessarily leprosy.

1:21 [r]Mt 4:23; Mk 10:1
1:22 [s]Mt 7:28,29
1:24 [t]Mt 8:29 [u]Mt 2:23; Lk 24:19; Ac 24:5 [v]Lk 1:35; Jn 6:69; Ac 3:14
1:25 [w]ver 34
1:26 [x]Mk 9:20
1:27 [y]Mk 10:24, 32
1:28 [z]Mt 9:26
1:29 [a]ver 21,23
1:31 [b]Lk 7:14
1:32 [c]Mt 4:24
1:34 [d]Mt 4:23 [e]Mk 3:12; Ac 16:17,18
1:35 [f]Lk 3:21
1:38 [g]Isa 61:1
1:39 [h]Mt 4:23 [i]Mt 4:24
1:40 [j]Mk 10:17
1:44 [k]Mt 8:4 [l]Lev 13:49 [m]Lev 14:1-32

Guidelines for Prayer

MK 1:35-39

Jesus' day unfolds as follows: It starts with teaching at the synagogue (Mk 1:21), includes casting out an evil spirit (Mk 1:25-26) and healing a family friend (Mk 1:31), then ends with ministering to an entire town (Mk 1:32-34). No one would have thought any less of Jesus if he had slept in the next morning, but instead we find him up early, meeting his Father in prayer.

Mark 1:35 suggests a model we can apply to our own prayer lives. Jesus prays in the morning, while his spirit is still fresh from sleep and unencumbered with the cares of his day. While others snore, his soul soars in communion with God. Jesus shows us the importance of giving our first and our best to God. Jesus prays alone, in a quiet and "solitary" place (Mk 1:35). He knows the importance of limiting distractions in order to spend time with his Father.

1:45 As a result, Jesus could no longer enter a town
[n]Lk 5:15,16 openly but stayed outside in lonely places.[n] Yet
[o]Mk 2:13; Lk 5:17; Jn 6:2 the people still came to him from everywhere.[o]

Jesus Heals a Paralytic

2 A few days later, when Jesus again entered
2:2 Capernaum, the people heard that he had
[p]ver 13; Mk 1:45 come home. 2So many[p] gathered that there was
no room left, not even outside the door, and he
preached the word to them. 3Some men came,
2:3 bringing to him a paralytic,[q] carried by four of
[q]Mt 4:24 them. 4Since they could not get him to Jesus
because of the crowd, they made an opening in
the roof above Jesus and, after digging through it,
lowered the mat the paralyzed man was lying on.
2:5 5When Jesus saw their faith, he said to the para-
[r]Lk 7:48 lytic, "Son, your sins are forgiven."[r]
6Now some teachers of the law were sitting
there, thinking to themselves, 7"Why does this fellow talk like that? He's blaspheming! Who can
2:7 [s]Isa 43:25 forgive sins but God alone?"[s]
8Immediately Jesus knew in his spirit that this
was what they were thinking in their hearts, and
he said to them, "Why are you thinking these
things? 9Which is easier: to say to the paralytic,
'Your sins are forgiven,' or to say, 'Get up, take
your mat and walk'? 10But that you may know
2:10 [t]Mt 8:20 that the Son of Man[t] has authority on earth to forgive sins . . ." He said to the paralytic, 11"I tell you,
get up, take your mat and go home." 12He got up,
2:12 took his mat and walked out in full view of them
[u]Mt 9:8 all. This amazed everyone and they praised God,[u]
[v]Mt 9:33 saying, "We have never seen anything like this!"[v]

The Calling of Levi

2:13 13Once again Jesus went out beside the lake. A
[w]Mk 1:45; Lk 5:15; Jn 6:2 large crowd came to him,[w] and he began to teach
them. 14As he walked along, he saw Levi son of
Alphaeus sitting at the tax collector's booth. "Fol-
2:14 [x]Mt 4:19 low me,"[x] Jesus told him, and Levi got up and followed him.
15While Jesus was having dinner at Levi's
house, many tax collectors and "sinners" were
eating with him and his disciples, for there were
2:16 many who followed him. 16When the teachers of
[y]Ac 23:9 the law who were Pharisees[y] saw him eating with
[z]Mt 9:11 the "sinners" and tax collectors, they asked his
disciples: "Why does he eat with tax collectors
and 'sinners'?"[z]
17On hearing this, Jesus said to them, "It is not
the healthy who need a doctor, but the sick. I have
2:17 [a]Lk 19:10; 1Ti 1:15 not come to call the righteous, but sinners."[a]

Jesus Questioned About Fasting

2:18 18Now John's disciples and the Pharisees were
[b]Mt 6:16-18; Ac 13:2 fasting.[b] Some people came and asked Jesus,
"How is it that John's disciples and the disciples
of the Pharisees are fasting, but yours are not?"
19Jesus answered, "How can the guests of the
bridegroom fast while he is with them? They can-

Loving, Faithful Friends

MK 2:1–12

The friends of the paralytic show a great love for him and a great faith in Jesus. If T-shirts could be printed for these men, a perfect slogan would be, "Actions speak louder than words." No obstacle—even a roof—can slow them down. But even greater than their love is their faith. Just as we wouldn't waste time cracking open a nut if we didn't have hope of finding "treasure" inside, these men wouldn't have ripped open a ceiling unless they had believed the treasure of healing for their friend could be found inside. In the end, Jesus provides a healing because he "saw** their **faith" (Mk 2:5, emphasis added)—the faith of the friends! The beauty of their role doesn't start with their muscles; it starts with their hearts.

Jesus' Anger and Distress

MK 3:4–5

Jesus isn't asking a trick question. He simply wants the people in the synagogue to realize how their infatuation with the technicalities of the law has severed them from the laws of love. Anger flares in Jesus, and the people's stubborn hearts distress him. While these emotions are very human, they are also godly—Jesus' anger is directed toward the bondage of sin. As Jesus looks around, he takes note of the locked jaws and chained hearts. But instead of flying into a fit of rage, his distress causes him to set his own jaw with determination. While human anger is usually caused by self-motivation, Jesus' anger is a selfless expression of his holy love—so selfless that it takes him all the way to the cross.

not, so long as they have him with them. 20But the
time will come when the bridegroom will be tak-
en from them,[c] and on that day they will fast.
21"No one sews a patch of unshrunk cloth on an
old garment. If he does, the new piece will pull
away from the old, making the tear worse. 22And
no one pours new wine into old wineskins. If he
does, the wine will burst the skins, and both the
wine and the wineskins will be ruined. No, he
pours new wine into new wineskins."

Lord of the Sabbath

23One Sabbath Jesus was going through the
grainfields, and as his disciples walked along,
they began to pick some heads of grain.[d] 24The
Pharisees said to him, "Look, why are they doing
what is unlawful on the Sabbath?"[e]
25He answered, "Have you never read what
David did when he and his companions were
hungry and in need? 26In the days of Abiathar the
high priest,[f] he entered the house of God and ate
the consecrated bread, which is lawful only for
priests to eat.[g] And he also gave some to his
companions."[h]
27Then he said to them, "The Sabbath was made
for man,[i] not man for the Sabbath.[j] 28So the Son of
Man[k] is Lord even of the Sabbath."

3 Another time he went into the synagogue,[l]
and a man with a shriveled hand was there.
2Some of them were looking for a reason to accuse
Jesus, so they watched him closely[m] to see if he
would heal him on the Sabbath.[n] 3Jesus said to
the man with the shriveled hand, "Stand up in
front of everyone."
4Then Jesus asked them, "Which is lawful on
the Sabbath: to do good or to do evil, to save life
or to kill?" But they remained silent.
5He looked around at them in anger and, deeply
distressed at their stubborn hearts, said to the
man, "Stretch out your hand." He stretched it out,
and his hand was completely restored. 6Then the
Pharisees went out and began to plot with the
Herodians[o] how they might kill Jesus.[p]

Crowds Follow Jesus

7Jesus withdrew with his disciples to the lake,
and a large crowd from Galilee followed.[q] 8When
they heard all he was doing, many people came
to him from Judea, Jerusalem, Idumea, and the
regions across the Jordan and around Tyre and
Sidon.[r] 9Because of the crowd he told his disciples
to have a small boat ready for him, to keep the
people from crowding him. 10For he had healed
many,[s] so that those with diseases were pushing
forward to touch him.[t] 11Whenever the evil[a] spirits saw him, they fell down before him and cried
out, "You are the Son of God."[u] 12But he gave them
strict orders not to tell who he was.[v]

2:20 [c]Lk 17:22
2:23 [d]Dt 23:25
2:24 [e]Mt 12:2
2:26 [f]1Ch 24:6; 2Sa 8:17 [g]Lev 24:5-9 [h]1Sa 21:1-6
2:27 [i]Ex 23:12; Dt 5:14 [j]Col 2:16
2:28 [k]Mt 8:20
3:1 [l]Mt 4:23; Mk 1:21
3:2 [m]Mt 12:10 [n]Lk 14:1
3:6 [o]Mt 22:16; Mk 12:13 [p]Mt 12:14
3:7 [q]Mt 4:25
3:8 [r]Mt 11:21
3:10 [s]Mt 4:23 [t]Mt 9:20
3:11 [u]Mt 4:3; Mk 1:23,24
3:12 [v]Mt 8:4; Mk 1:24,25, 34; Ac 16:17, 18

[a] *11* Greek *unclean*; also in verse 30

Anna

Worth the Wait

Anna got up and put on her clothes. God had given her another day of life—another day to worship him and to pray! She was the most fortunate woman she knew. What would he tell her today? Whom would she meet in the temple? Every day was an adventure. Anna loved God, and she loved life.

She was very old; her hair was white and her body bent. But her wrinkled face shone with God's light. Anna heard *his* voice. She was a prophetess in an age noted for God's silence. *Could this be the day?* She wondered. Anna knew the Messiah was coming soon. Would she meet him face to face? She prayed fervently day and night that she might see him before she died.

Anna saw Simeon as she entered the temple. He had a child in his arms—could this be the One? What would it be like to gaze into *his* eyes? She hurried to Simeon's side. They had often talked about the Messiah. Her eyes closed in bliss as she listened to Simeon's words. It *was* the child they had been looking for. Anna's spirit confirmed it. His name was Jesus—*Yahweh saves.*

She must tell the others who also waited for the news: Messiah is here! The Son of the Most High has come to redeem his people! She had a mission to last her the rest of her days. She was fulfilled.

Those who live for God bear fruit even in old age. Anna had seven short years with her husband and never remarried. She lived celibate, spending her days in the temple of the Almighty. The time that others spent in caring for homes and children and spouses Anna devoted to the Lord.

Some, like Anna, are called by God or by circumstance to celibacy. Our culture teaches us that this is something we should dread. But Anna *thrived* in God's presence. She quiets our fears of abandonment and loneliness, for her life does not reveal a state to be avoided but a gift to be embraced. Anna would say with the psalmist: "And I—in righteousness I will see your face; when I awake, I will be satisfied with seeing your likeness" (Ps 17:15).

Anna
(*grace*)

Luke 2:36-38

Candid SNAPSHOT *She was very old; she had lived with her husband seven years after her marriage, and then was a widow until she was eighty-four. She never left the temple but worshiped night and day, fasting and praying (Luke 2:36-37).*

Woman at the Well

Everyday Meetings

The clay jar felt heavy even when it was empty, she thought, as she trudged to the well. It would be even heavier on her return, but she was used to it. She had been coming to this well since she was a young girl. Getting water was women's work. She noticed a man sitting at the edge of the well but averted her eyes. He was a Jew. He would never talk to her, a Samaritan woman. It was better to pretend he wasn't even there.

When Jesus asked her for a drink, she was startled. He didn't have a cup, and she—a Samaritan—was unclean as far as Jews were concerned. But it was the middle of the day, and he looked hot and tired. Well, let *him* worry about it.

This man unnerved her. He made such peculiar comments, about "living water." However, she was good at questions, too. She could just change the subject when he got too close with his personal questions. But when he brought up the subject of husbands, she stopped cold. The best thing to do was tell the truth. She suspected he could see through a lie anyway. How could he know so much about her? She panicked. She needed to grab control again, ask another question . . .

Jesus knew her Samaritan upbringing had confused the woman theologically. He understood her reticence and fear of exposure. Most important, he saw her thirst for more than water and her hunger for more than food. Despite her sharp edge, she consistently spoke the truth. The others would believe her.

She left her jar and ran to tell her friends. She was in a hurry, but she wanted Jesus to understand that she would be back. He couldn't leave yet!

The people in Sychar saw a change in her—perhaps an air of peace and hope that shone in her eyes. And she was talking about the Christ! This must be something real, for she would never lie.

Many people were saved that day. Samaritans! And they asked Jesus to stay so they could learn from him and end their confusion. The woman had met the Messiah, just doing what she always did. She'd held him off, but he won her heart anyway. In the end, he even answered all her questions.

Woman at the Well

John 4

Jesus is waiting for us, too. He wants to talk to us in our everyday activities—putting on makeup, changing diapers, driving to work or taking a walk. He'll listen to all our questions and opinions and put up with our attitudes. Then—when we stop our chatter for just a moment—he'll reveal our deepest need—and meet it.

Candid SNAPSHOT The woman said to him, "Sir, give me this water so that I won't get thirsty and have to keep coming here to draw water." He told her, "Go, call your husband and come back."

"I have no husband," she replied (John 4:15-17).

The Appointing of the Twelve Apostles

13 Jesus went up on a mountainside and called
3:13 [w]Mt 5:1 to him those he wanted, and they came to him.[w]
14 He appointed twelve—designating them apos-
3:14 [x]Mk 6:30 tles[a][x]—that they might be with him and that he
might send them out to preach 15 and to have
3:15 [y]Mt 10:1 authority to drive out demons.[y] 16 These are the
twelve he appointed: Simon (to whom he gave the
3:16 [z]Jn 1:42 name Peter);[z] 17 James son of Zebedee and his
brother John (to them he gave the name Boaner-
ges, which means Sons of Thunder); 18 Andrew,
Philip, Bartholomew, Matthew, Thomas, James
son of Alphaeus, Thaddaeus, Simon the Zealot
19 and Judas Iscariot, who betrayed him.

Jesus and Beelzebub

20 Then Jesus entered a house, and again a
3:20 [a]ver 7 [b]Mk 6:31 crowd gathered,[a] so that he and his disciples were
not even able to eat.[b] 21 When his family heard
about this, they went to take charge of him, for
3:21 [c]Jn 10:20; Ac 26:24 they said, "He is out of his mind."[c]
22 And the teachers of the law who came down
3:22 [d]Mt 15:1 [e]Mt 10:25; 11:18; 12:24; Jn 7:20; 8:48,52; 10:20 [f]Mt 9:34 from Jerusalem[d] said, "He is possessed by Beelzebub[b]![e] By the prince of demons he is driving out
demons."[f]
23 So Jesus called them and spoke to them in
parables:[g] "How can Satan[h] drive out Satan? 24 If a
kingdom is divided against itself, that kingdom
cannot stand. 25 If a house is divided against itself,
3:23 [g]Mk 4:2 [h]Mt 4:10 that house cannot stand. 26 And if Satan opposes
himself and is divided, he cannot stand; his end
has come. 27 In fact, no one can enter a strong
man's house and carry off his possessions unless
3:27 [i]Isa 49:24,25 he first ties up the strong man. Then he can rob
his house.[i] 28 I tell you the truth, all the sins and
blasphemies of men will be forgiven them. 29 But
3:29 [j]Mt 12:31, 32; Lk 12:10 whoever blasphemes against the Holy Spirit will
never be forgiven; he is guilty of an eternal sin."[j]
30 He said this because they were saying, "He
has an evil spirit."

Jesus' Mother and Brothers

3:31 [k]ver 21 31 Then Jesus' mother and brothers arrived.[k]
Standing outside, they sent someone in to call
him. 32 A crowd was sitting around him, and they
told him, "Your mother and brothers are outside
looking for you."
33 "Who are my mother and my brothers?" he
asked.
34 Then he looked at those seated in a circle
around him and said, "Here are my mother and
my brothers! 35 Whoever does God's will is my
brother and sister and mother."

The Parable of the Sower

4:1 [l]Mk 2:13; 3:7 4 Again Jesus began to teach by the lake.[l] The
crowd that gathered around him was so large
that he got into a boat and sat in it out on the lake,

[a] 14 Some manuscripts do not have *designating them apostles.*
[b] 22 Greek *Beezeboul* or *Beelzeboul*

Given, not lent,
And not withdrawn,
once sent,
This Infant of mankind, this One,
Is still the little welcome Son.

New every year,
New-born and newly dear,
He comes with tidings and a song,
The ages long, the ages long.

—Alice Meynell (1847–1922)

Secrets Shared

MK 4:21-25

Jesus communicates God's truth through parables to the crowds. But to his chosen disciples, he explains the secrets behind the stories (Mk 4:11). Were these secrets for the disciples' benefit only? Not at all. Share the secrets, Jesus says. Make these private truths public (Mk 4:22). But before the disciples do so, Jesus urges them to "consider carefully what [they] hear" (Mk 4:24). These truths are meant to be pondered, remembered and only then acted on. In fact, Jesus tacks on a promise for those who are faithful in doing this (Mk 4:25), in essence saying, "The amount you act on these truths and share them, that same amount I will share with you—and even more." This is a promise each of us can take to heart.

while all the people were along the shore at the
water's edge. 2He taught them many things by
parables,[m] and in his teaching said: 3"Listen! A
farmer went out to sow his seed.[n] 4As he was scattering the seed, some fell along the path, and the
birds came and ate it up. 5Some fell on rocky
places, where it did not have much soil. It sprang
up quickly, because the soil was shallow. 6But
when the sun came up, the plants were scorched,
and they withered because they had no root.
7Other seed fell among thorns, which grew up and
choked the plants, so that they did not bear grain.
8Still other seed fell on good soil. It came up, grew
and produced a crop, multiplying thirty, sixty, or
even a hundred times."[o]

9Then Jesus said, "He who has ears to hear, let
him hear."[p]

10When he was alone, the Twelve and the others
around him asked him about the parables. 11He
told them, "The secret of the kingdom of God[q] has
been given to you. But to those on the outside[r]
everything is said in parables 12so that,

" 'they may be ever seeing but never
perceiving,
and ever hearing but never
understanding;
otherwise they might turn and be
forgiven!'[a]"[s]

13Then Jesus said to them, "Don't you understand this parable? How then will you understand
any parable? 14The farmer sows the word.[t] 15Some
people are like seed along the path, where the
word is sown. As soon as they hear it, Satan[u]
comes and takes away the word that was sown in
them. 16Others, like seed sown on rocky places,
hear the word and at once receive it with joy.
17But since they have no root, they last only a
short time. When trouble or persecution comes
because of the word, they quickly fall away. 18Still
others, like seed sown among thorns, hear the
word; 19but the worries of this life, the deceitfulness of wealth[v] and the desires for other things
come in and choke the word, making it unfruitful. 20Others, like seed sown on good soil, hear the
word, accept it, and produce a crop—thirty, sixty
or even a hundred times what was sown."

A Lamp on a Stand

21He said to them, "Do you bring in a lamp to
put it under a bowl or a bed? Instead, don't you
put it on its stand?[w] 22For whatever is hidden is
meant to be disclosed, and whatever is concealed
is meant to be brought out into the open.[x] 23If anyone has ears to hear, let him hear."[y]

24"Consider carefully what you hear," he continued. "With the measure you use, it will be
measured to you—and even more.[z] 25Whoever has

4:2 [m]ver 11; Mk 3:23
4:3 [n]ver 26
4:8 [o]Jn 15:5; Col 1:6
4:9 [p]ver 23; Mt 11:15
4:11 [q]Mt 3:2 [r]1Co 5:12, 13; Col 4:5; 1Th 4:12; 1Ti 3:7
4:12 [s]Isa 6:9,10; Mt 13:13-15
4:14 [t]Mk 16:20; Lk 1:2; Ac 4:31; 8:4; 16:6; 17:11; Php 1:14
4:15 [u]Mt 4:10
4:19 [v]Mt 19:23; 1Ti 6:9,10, 17; 1Jn 2:15-17
4:21 [w]Mt 5:15
4:22 [x]Jer 16:17; Mt 10:26; Lk 8:17; 12:2
4:23 [y]ver 9; Mt 11:15
4:24 [z]Mt 7:2; Lk 6:38

[a] *12* Isaiah 6:9,10

will be given more; whoever does not have, even
4:25 [a]Mt 13:12; 25:29 what he has will be taken from him."[a]

The Parable of the Growing Seed

[26]He also said, "This is what the kingdom of
4:26 [b]Mt 13:24 God is like.[b] A man scatters seed on the ground.
[27]Night and day, whether he sleeps or gets up, the
seed sprouts and grows, though he does not know
how. [28]All by itself the soil produces grain—first
the stalk, then the head, then the full kernel in
4:29 the head. [29]As soon as the grain is ripe, he puts
[c]Rev 14:15 the sickle to it, because the harvest has come."[c]

The Parable of the Mustard Seed

[30]Again he said, "What shall we say the king-
4:30 [d]Mt 13:24 dom of God is like,[d] or what parable shall we use
to describe it? [31]It is like a mustard seed, which is
the smallest seed you plant in the ground. [32]Yet
when planted, it grows and becomes the largest
of all garden plants, with such big branches that
the birds of the air can perch in its shade."
4:33 [33]With many similar parables Jesus spoke the
[e]Jn 16:12 word to them, as much as they could understand.[e]
4:34 [34]He did not say anything to them without using a
[f]Jn 16:25 parable.[f] But when he was alone with his own disciples, he explained everything.

Jesus Calms the Storm

[35]That day when evening came, he said to his
disciples, "Let us go over to the other side." [36]Leav-
4:36 ing the crowd behind, they took him along, just as
[g]ver 1; Mk 3:9; 5:2, he was, in the boat.[g] There were also other boats
21; 6:32,45 with him. [37]A furious squall came up, and the
waves broke over the boat, so that it was nearly
swamped. [38]Jesus was in the stern, sleeping on a
cushion. The disciples woke him and said to him,
"Teacher, don't you care if we drown?"
[39]He got up, rebuked the wind and said to the
waves, "Quiet! Be still!" Then the wind died down
and it was completely calm.
4:40 [40]He said to his disciples, "Why are you so
[h]Mt 14:31; afraid? Do you still have no faith?"[h]
Mk 16:14 [41]They were terrified and asked each other,
"Who is this? Even the wind and the waves obey
him!"

The Healing of a Demon-possessed Man

5 They went across the lake to the region of the
5:2 [i]Mk 4:1 Gerasenes.[a] [2]When Jesus got out of the boat,[i]
[j]Mk 1:23 a man with an evil[b] spirit[j] came from the tombs to
meet him. [3]This man lived in the tombs, and no
one could bind him any more, not even with a
chain. [4]For he had often been chained hand and
foot, but he tore the chains apart and broke the
irons on his feet. No one was strong enough to
subdue him. [5]Night and day among the tombs and
in the hills he would cry out and cut himself with
stones.

[a] *1* Some manuscripts *Gadarenes*; other manuscripts *Gergesenes* [b] *2* Greek *unclean*; also in verses 8 and 13

Small Beginnings

MK 4:30-34

Jesus discusses God's kingdom by comparing it to something his listeners can literally grasp—if they are careful. The mustard seed was the smallest cultivated seed in Jesus' day. It is 1/20th of an inch in size—about the size of a pinhead. The remarkable thing is that this herb can grow as large as 10-12 feet in height, with a stem the size of a man's arm. Jesus uses this analogy to illustrate the point that God delights in small beginnings. One man, Abraham, fathers many nations (Ge 17:5). One Savior, Jesus Christ, offers salvation to all people (Ro 10:12). One roomful of believers changes the world (Ac 1:13-14). In God's kingdom, simple truth takes hold, small faith flourishes and phenomenal growth takes place.

Weak Body, Strong Faith

MK 5:25-34

We know this woman's bleeding is a longstanding problem and incurable (Mk 5:25–26). The flow has drained her of vitality, health and finances. Most likely it is an excessive menstrual flow caused by a fibroid tumor in her womb. This condition produces a flooding flow of blood with large clots and results in severe anemia. In addition to these physical problems, she experiences social barriers. According to Mosaic Law, a woman suffering from menstrual disorders is ceremonially unclean. "Any bed she lies on while her discharge continues will be unclean . . . and anything she sits on will be unclean . . . Whoever touches them will be unclean" (Lev 15:26–27). Actually, anyone who touches her ***will be unclean (Lev 15:19). What disgrace! Yet she carries her weak body through a pressing crowd and stretches out her "unclean" hand to touch Jesus. The result? Her body is healed, and her faith is commended (Mk 5:34; see the character sketch for this woman on page 1745).***

6 When he saw Jesus from a distance, he ran and
fell on his knees in front of him. 7 He shouted at
the top of his voice, "What do you want with me,[k]
Jesus, Son of the Most High God?[l] Swear to God
that you won't torture me!" 8 For Jesus had said to
him, "Come out of this man, you evil spirit!"
9 Then Jesus asked him, "What is your name?"
"My name is Legion,"[m] he replied, "for we are
many." 10 And he begged Jesus again and again not
to send them out of the area.
11 A large herd of pigs was feeding on the nearby hillside. 12 The demons begged Jesus, "Send us
among the pigs; allow us to go into them." 13 He
gave them permission, and the evil spirits came
out and went into the pigs. The herd, about two
thousand in number, rushed down the steep bank
into the lake and were drowned.
14 Those tending the pigs ran off and reported this
in the town and countryside, and the people went
out to see what had happened. 15 When they came
to Jesus, they saw the man who had been possessed by the legion[n] of demons,[o] sitting there,
dressed and in his right mind; and they were afraid.
16 Those who had seen it told the people what had
happened to the demon-possessed man—and told
about the pigs as well. 17 Then the people began to
plead with Jesus to leave their region.
18 As Jesus was getting into the boat, the man
who had been demon-possessed begged to go
with him. 19 Jesus did not let him, but said, "Go
home to your family and tell them[p] how much the
Lord has done for you, and how he has had mercy on you." 20 So the man went away and began to
tell in the Decapolis[a][q] how much Jesus had done
for him. And all the people were amazed.

A Dead Girl and a Sick Woman

21 When Jesus had again crossed over by boat to
the other side of the lake,[r] a large crowd gathered
around him while he was by the lake.[s] 22 Then one
of the synagogue rulers,[t] named Jairus, came
there. Seeing Jesus, he fell at his feet 23 and pleaded earnestly with him, "My little daughter is
dying. Please come and put your hands on[u] her
so that she will be healed and live." 24 So Jesus
went with him.
A large crowd followed and pressed around him.
25 And a woman was there who had been subject to
bleeding[v] for twelve years. 26 She had suffered a
great deal under the care of many doctors and had
spent all she had, yet instead of getting better she
grew worse. 27 When she heard about Jesus, she
came up behind him in the crowd and touched his
cloak, 28 because she thought, "If I just touch his
clothes,[w] I will be healed." 29 Immediately her
bleeding stopped and she felt in her body that she
was freed from her suffering.[x]
30 At once Jesus realized that power[y] had gone

5:7 [k]Mt 8:29 [l]Mt 4:3; Lk 1:32; 6:35; Ac 16:17; Heb 7:1
5:9 [m]ver 15
5:15 [n]ver 9 [o]ver 16,18; Mt 4:24
5:19 [p]Mt 8:4
5:20 [q]Mt 4:25; Mk 7:31
5:21 [r]Mt 9:1 [s]Mk 4:1
5:22 [t]ver 35,36, 38; Lk 13:14; Ac 13:15; 18:8,17
5:23 [u]Mt 19:13; Mk 6:5; 7:32; 8:23; 16:18; Lk 4:40; 13:13; Ac 6:6
5:25 [v]Lev 15:25-30
5:28 [w]Mt 9:20
5:29 [x]ver 34
5:30 [y]Lk 5:17; 6:19

[a] *20* That is, the Ten Cities

out from him. He turned around in the crowd and
asked, "Who touched my clothes?"
31"You see the people crowding against you,"
his disciples answered, "and yet you can ask,
'Who touched me?' "
32But Jesus kept looking around to see who had
done it. 33Then the woman, knowing what had
happened to her, came and fell at his feet and,
5:34 trembling with fear, told him the whole truth. 34He
[z]Mt 9:22 said to her, "Daughter, your faith has healed you.[z]
[a]Ac 15:33 Go in peace[a] and be freed from your suffering."
35While Jesus was still speaking, some men
came from the house of Jairus, the synagogue
5:35 ruler.[b] "Your daughter is dead," they said. "Why
[b]ver 22 bother the teacher any more?"
36Ignoring what they said, Jesus told the synagogue ruler, "Don't be afraid; just believe."
37He did not let anyone follow him except Peter,
5:37 James and John the brother of James.[c] 38When
[c]Mt 4:21 they came to the home of the synagogue ruler,[d]
5:38 Jesus saw a commotion, with people crying and
[d]ver 22 wailing loudly. 39He went in and said to them,
"Why all this commotion and wailing? The child is
5:39 not dead but asleep."[e] 40But they laughed at him.
[e]Mt 9:24 After he put them all out, he took the child's
father and mother and the disciples who were
5:41 with him, and went in where the child was. 41He
[f]Mk 1:31 took her by the hand[f] and said to her, *"Talitha*
[g]Lk 7:14; *koum!"* (which means, "Little girl, I say to you,
Ac 9:40 get up!").[g] 42Immediately the girl stood up and
walked around (she was twelve years old). At this
5:43 they were completely astonished. 43He gave strict
[h]Mt 8:4 orders not to let anyone know about this,[h] and
told them to give her something to eat.

A Prophet Without Honor

6:1 [i]Mt 2:23 6 Jesus left there and went to his hometown,[i]
6:2 accompanied by his disciples. 2When the Sab-
[j]Mk 1:21 [k]Mt 4:23 bath came,[j] he began to teach in the synagogue,[k]
[l]Mt 7:28 and many who heard him were amazed.[l]
"Where did this man get these things?" they
asked. "What's this wisdom that has been given
him, that he even does miracles! 3Isn't this the
6:3 carpenter? Isn't this Mary's son and the brother of
[m]Mt 12:46 James, Joseph,[a] Judas and Simon?[m] Aren't his sis-
[n]Mt 11:6; ters here with us?" And they took offense at him.[n]
Jn 6:61 4Jesus said to them, "Only in his hometown,
among his relatives and in his own house is a
6:4 prophet without honor."[o] 5He could not do any
[o]Lk 4:24; miracles there, except lay his hands on[p] a few sick
Jn 4:44 people and heal them. 6And he was amazed at
6:5 their lack of faith.
[p]Mk 5:23

Jesus Sends Out the Twelve

6:6 [q]Mt 9:35; Mk 1:39; Then Jesus went around teaching from village
Lk 13:22 to village.[q] 7Calling the Twelve to him,[r] he sent
6:7 them out two by twos[s] and gave them authority
[r]Mk 3:13 over evil[b] spirits.[t]
[s]Dt 17:6; Lk 10:1 8These were his instructions: "Take nothing for
[t]Mt 10:1

[a] 3 Greek *Joses,* a variant of *Joseph* [b] 7 Greek *unclean*

Anonymous Savior

MK 5:43

Is Jesus using reverse psychology when he orders the witnesses to be silent about bringing Jairus's daughter back to life? How could he expect them to keep this miracle a secret? And why? This is not the only instance when Jesus attempts to stay anonymous (Mk 1:44; 8:30). Yet his words speak of honesty, not trickery. Jesus is the Christ. He needs neither people's awe nor demons' exclamations to prove it (Lk 4:41). He has God's "seal of approval" (Jn 6:27). Jesus also has a perfect plan and a perfect timetable. He knows that if word of his deeds spreads too quickly, the people will expect him to live up to their expectations of the Messiah—a political hero who will free them from the Romans. His mission is contrary to their image. The freedom he has planned is more sweeping than anything they can imagine (Ro 8:1-2).

Dance of Death

MK 6:22

In Biblical times, the Hebrews saw dancing as an expression of joy. Women danced after a military victory (1Sa 18:6). As an act of worship, David danced "before the LORD *with all his might" (2Sa 6:14). Yet Salome's dancing (her name comes from historical documents, not the Gospels), which wins her John the Baptist's head on a platter, is believed to be in the tradition of Greek dancing. This is a sensual art form rather than an act of worship. Whether Salome is overtly malicious herself or is merely a pawn in her mother's hands or whether Herod is simply weak, we cannot be certain—probably all are at least somewhat accurate (see the character sketch for Salome on page 1780).*

In other portions of Scripture, women are exploited for entertainment purposes (Est 1:10–12). Such services are generally rewarded, although the expression, "I'll give you up to half of my kingdom" (Est 5:6, author's paraphrase), is most likely a stock promise, not intended to be taken literally.

the journey except a staff—no bread, no bag, no
money in your belts. [9]Wear sandals but not an
extra tunic. [10]Whenever you enter a house, stay
there until you leave that town. [11]And if any place
will not welcome you or listen to you, shake the 6:11
dust off your feet[u] when you leave, as a testimony [u]Mt 10:14
against them."
[12]They went out and preached that people
should repent.[v] [13]They drove out many demons 6:12 [v]Lk 9:6
and anointed many sick people with oil[w] and
healed them. 6:13 [w]Jas 5:14

John the Baptist Beheaded

[14]King Herod heard about this, for Jesus' name
had become well known. Some were saying,[a]
"John the Baptist[x] has been raised from the dead, 6:14 [x]Mt 3:1
and that is why miraculous powers are at work in
him."
[15]Others said, "He is Elijah."[y] 6:15 [y]Mal 4:5
And still others claimed, "He is a prophet,[z] like [z]Mt 21:11
one of the prophets of long ago."[a] [a]Mt 16:14; Mk 8:28
[16]But when Herod heard this, he said, "John,
the man I beheaded, has been raised from the
dead!"
[17]For Herod himself had given orders to have
John arrested, and he had him bound and put in
prison.[b] He did this because of Herodias, his 6:17 [b]Mt 4:12; 11:2; Lk 3:19,20
brother Philip's wife, whom he had married. [18]For
John had been saying to Herod, "It is not lawful
for you to have your brother's wife."[c] [19]So Hero- 6:18 [c]Lev 18:16; 20:21
dias nursed a grudge against John and wanted to
kill him. But she was not able to, [20]because Herod
feared John and protected him, knowing him to
be a righteous and holy man.[d] When Herod heard 6:20 [d]Mt 11:9; 21:26
John, he was greatly puzzled[b]; yet he liked to lis-
ten to him.
[21]Finally the opportune time came. On his birth-
day Herod gave a banquet[e] for his high officials and 6:21 [e]Est 1:3; 2:18
military commanders and the leading men of Gali-
lee.[f] [22]When the daughter of Herodias came in and [f]Lk 3:1
danced, she pleased Herod and his dinner guests.
The king said to the girl, "Ask me for anything
you want, and I'll give it to you." [23]And he promised her with an oath, "Whatever you ask I will 6:23
give you, up to half my kingdom."[g] [g]Est 5:3,6; 7:2
[24]She went out and said to her mother, "What
shall I ask for?"
"The head of John the Baptist," she answered.
[25]At once the girl hurried in to the king with the
request: "I want you to give me right now the
head of John the Baptist on a platter."
[26]The king was greatly distressed, but because
of his oaths and his dinner guests, he did not want
to refuse her. [27]So he immediately sent an execu-
tioner with orders to bring John's head. The man
went, beheaded John in the prison, [28]and brought
back his head on a platter. He presented it to the
girl, and she gave it to her mother. [29]On hearing of

[a] *14* Some early manuscripts *He was saying* [b] *20* Some early manuscripts *he did many things*

this, John's disciples came and took his body and
laid it in a tomb.

Jesus Feeds the Five Thousand

6:30 [h]Mt 10:2; [30]The apostles[h] gathered around Jesus and
Lk 9:10; reported to him all they had done and taught.[i]
17:5; 22:14; [31]Then, because so many people were coming and
24:10; Ac 1:2,26 going that they did not even have a chance to eat,[j]
[i]Lk 9:10 he said to them, "Come with me by yourselves to
6:31 a quiet place and get some rest."
[j]Mk 3:20 [32]So they went away by themselves in a boat[k]
6:32 to a solitary place. [33]But many who saw them
[k]ver 45; leaving recognized them and ran on foot from all
Mk 4:36 the towns and got there ahead of them. [34]When
Jesus landed and saw a large crowd, he had com-
6:34 passion on them, because they were like sheep
[l]Mt 9:36 without a shepherd.[l] So he began teaching them
many things.

[35]By this time it was late in the day, so his disciples came to him. "This is a remote place," they
said, "and it's already very late. [36]Send the people
away so they can go to the surrounding countryside and villages and buy themselves something
to eat."

6:37 [37]But he answered, "You give them something
[m]2Ki 4:42-44 to eat."[m]

They said to him, "That would take eight
months of a man's wages[a]! Are we to go and
spend that much on bread and give it to them to
eat?"

[38]"How many loaves do you have?" he asked.
"Go and see."

When they found out, they said, "Five—and
6:38 two fish."[n]

[n]Mt 15:34; [39]Then Jesus directed them to have all the peo-
Mk 8:5 ple sit down in groups on the green grass. [40]So
they sat down in groups of hundreds and fifties.
[41]Taking the five loaves and the two fish and look-
6:41 ing up to heaven, he gave thanks and broke the
[o]Mt 14:19 loaves.[o] Then he gave them to his disciples to set
before the people. He also divided the two fish
among them all. [42]They all ate and were satisfied,
[43]and the disciples picked up twelve basketfuls of
broken pieces of bread and fish. [44]The number of
the men who had eaten was five thousand.

Jesus Walks on the Water

6:45 [45]Immediately Jesus made his disciples get into
[p]ver 32 the boat[p] and go on ahead of him to Bethsaida,[q]
[q]Mt 11:21 while he dismissed the crowd. [46]After leaving
6:46 them, he went up on a mountainside to pray.[r]
[r]Lk 3:21 [47]When evening came, the boat was in the middle of the lake, and he was alone on land. [48]He
saw the disciples straining at the oars, because the
wind was against them. About the fourth watch
of the night he went out to them, walking on the
lake. He was about to pass by them, [49]but when
they saw him walking on the lake, they thought

Little Is Much

MK 6:30-44

A young boy is not spoken of in this passage, but he is mentioned in the parallel story in John 6:9. And although he is unnamed, we can learn a lot from him—namely his willingness to give a little so that Jesus can accomplish a lot. The boy could have kept the food for himself. After all, what good would such a little lunch be for such a large group? Yet he doesn't focus on the gift's size. In themselves, five coarse barley loaves and two small fish are useless to the crowd. Instead, the boy focuses on the Savior. The boy's gifts are meager and ordinary; yet they speak volumes about his expansive heart. Now, take a moment and think about what you can offer to the masses. Is it meager and ordinary? Perfect! Hand it over to God and expect a miracle.

[a] 37 Greek *take two hundred denarii*

Objects of Healing

MK 6:56

Obviously the story has spread: A woman has been healed by simply touching Jesus' cloak (Mk 5:25–34). Now, as the crowds press in, there is not just one outstretched hand, but many. There are other times in Scripture when God's power was exhibited through an object. One man was brought back to life when his body touched Elisha's bones (2Ki 13:21). In the early church, many experienced healing when the handkerchiefs and aprons touched by Paul were brought to them (Ac 19:11–12). Still, we must remember that these were only objects. The miracles happened because of the power behind them—God's power (Lk 6:19). In this passage, the people press in, eager for a miracle, and perhaps some stay to listen to the miracle worker. The masses show concern for their bodies, but Jesus plans to touch their hearts.

he was a ghost.[s] They cried out, [50]because they all **6:49**
saw him and were terrified. [s]Lk 24:37
Immediately he spoke to them and said, "Take
courage! It is I. Don't be afraid."[t] [51]Then he **6:50**
climbed into the boat[u] with them, and the wind [t]Mt 14:27
died down.[v] They were completely amazed, [52]for **6:51**
they had not understood about the loaves; their [u]ver 32
hearts were hardened.[w] [v]Mk 4:39
[53]When they had crossed over, they landed at **6:52**
Gennesaret and anchored there.[x] [54]As soon as they [w]Mk 8:17-21
got out of the boat, people recognized Jesus. **6:53**
[55]They ran throughout that whole region and car- [x]Jn 6:24,25
ried the sick on mats to wherever they heard he
was. [56]And wherever he went—into villages,
towns or countryside—they placed the sick in the
marketplaces. They begged him to let them touch **6:56**
even the edge of his cloak,[y] and all who touched [y]Mt 9:20
him were healed.

Clean and Unclean

7 The Pharisees and some of the teachers of the
law who had come from Jerusalem gathered
around Jesus and [2]saw some of his disciples eat- **7:2**
ing food with hands that were "unclean,"[z] that is, [z]Ac 10:14,
unwashed. [3](The Pharisees and all the Jews do 28; 11:8;
not eat unless they give their hands a ceremonial Ro 14:14
washing, holding to the tradition of the elders.[a] **7:3**
[4]When they come from the marketplace they do [a]ver 5,8,9,
not eat unless they wash. And they observe many 13; Lk 11:38
other traditions, such as the washing of cups,
pitchers and kettles.[a]) [b] **7:4**
[5]So the Pharisees and teachers of the law asked [b]Mt 23:25; Lk 11:39
Jesus, "Why don't your disciples live according to
the tradition of the elders[c] instead of eating their **7:5** [c]ver 3;
food with 'unclean' hands?" Gal 1:14;
[6]He replied, "Isaiah was right when he prophe- Col 2:8
sied about you hypocrites; as it is written:

" 'These people honor me with their
lips,
but their hearts are far from me.
[7]They worship me in vain;
their teachings are but rules taught by **7:7**
men.'[b][d] [d]Isa 29:13

[8]You have let go of the commands of God and are
holding on to the traditions of men."[e] **7:8** [e]ver 3
[9]And he said to them: "You have a fine way of **7:9**
setting aside the commands of God in order to [f]ver 3
observe[c] your own traditions![f] [10]For Moses said,
'Honor your father and your mother,'[d][g] and, 'Any- **7:10** [g]Ex 20:12;
one who curses his father or mother must be put Dt 5:16
to death.'[e][h] [11]But you say[i] that if a man says to his [h]Ex 21:17;
father or mother: 'Whatever help you might oth- Lev 20:9
erwise have received from me is Corban' (that is, **7:11**
a gift devoted to God), [12]then you no longer let [i]Mt 23:16,18
him do anything for his father or mother. [13]Thus **7:13**
you nullify the word of God[j] by your tradition[k] [j]Heb 4:12 [k]ver 3

[a] *4* Some early manuscripts *pitchers, kettles and dining couches*   [b] *6,7* Isaiah 29:13   [c] *9* Some manuscripts *set up*
[d] *10* Exodus 20:12; Deut. 5:16   [e] *10* Exodus 21:17; Lev. 20:9

that you have handed down. And you do many
things like that."
14Again Jesus called the crowd to him and said,
"Listen to me, everyone, and understand this.
15Nothing outside a man can make him 'unclean'
by going into him. Rather, it is what comes out of
a man that makes him 'unclean.'[a]"
17After he had left the crowd and entered the
7:17 [l]Mk 9:28 house, his disciples asked him[l] about this parable.
18"Are you so dull?" he asked. "Don't you see that
nothing that enters a man from the outside can
make him 'unclean'? 19For it doesn't go into his
heart but into his stomach, and then out of his
7:19 [m]Ro 14:1-12; Col 2:16; 1Ti 4:3-5 [n]Ac 10:15 body." (In saying this, Jesus declared all foods[m]
"clean.")[n]
20He went on: "What comes out of a man is
what makes him 'unclean.' 21For from within, out
of men's hearts, come evil thoughts, sexual
7:22 [o]Mt 20:15 immorality, theft, murder, adultery, 22greed,[o] malice, deceit, lewdness, envy, slander, arrogance and
folly. 23All these evils come from inside and make
a man 'unclean.'"

The Faith of a Syrophoenician Woman

24Jesus left that place and went to the vicinity of
7:24 [p]Mt 11:21 Tyre.[b][p] He entered a house and did not want anyone to know it; yet he could not keep his presence
secret. 25In fact, as soon as she heard about him, a
7:25 [q]Mt 4:24 woman whose little daughter was possessed by an
evil[c] spirit[q] came and fell at his feet. 26The woman
was a Greek, born in Syrian Phoenicia. She begged
Jesus to drive the demon out of her daughter.
27"First let the children eat all they want," he
told her, "for it is not right to take the children's
bread and toss it to their dogs."
28"Yes, Lord," she replied, "but even the dogs
under the table eat the children's crumbs."
29Then he told her, "For such a reply, you may
go; the demon has left your daughter."
30She went home and found her child lying on
7:31 [r]ver 24; Mt 11:21 [s]Mt 4:18 [t]Mt 4:25; Mk 5:20 the bed, and the demon gone.

The Healing of a Deaf and Mute Man

31Then Jesus left the vicinity of Tyre[r] and went
7:32 [u]Mt 9:32; Lk 11:14 [v]Mk 5:23 through Sidon, down to the Sea of Galilee[s] and
into the region of the Decapolis.[d][t] 32There some
people brought to him a man who was deaf and
could hardly talk,[u] and they begged him to place
7:33 [w]Mk 8:23 his hand on[v] the man.
33After he took him aside, away from the crowd,
7:34 [x]Mk 6:41; Jn 11:41 [y]Mk 8:12 Jesus put his fingers into the man's ears. Then he
spit[w] and touched the man's tongue. 34He looked
up to heaven[x] and with a deep sigh[y] said to him,
"Ephphatha!" (which means, "Be opened!"). 35At
7:35 [z]Isa 35:5,6 this, the man's ears were opened, his tongue was
loosened and he began to speak plainly.[z]
7:36 [a]Mt 8:4 36Jesus commanded them not to tell anyone.[a] But

[a] *15* Some early manuscripts *'unclean.' 16If anyone has ears to hear, let him hear.* [b] *24* Many early manuscripts *Tyre and Sidon* [c] *25* Greek *unclean* [d] *31* That is, the Ten Cities

Internal Examination

MK 7:20-23

Summing up his teaching on the laws on being clean and unclean, Jesus states plainly, "It's what's on the inside that counts." And according to the Son of Man, the inside isn't too pretty. The word ***unclean*** ***here could literally be translated "profane." Jesus is not speaking about slightly muddied issues but about stinky, putrid "heart" problems. This is contrary to the Pharisees' understanding of the law. The Pharisees not only take these laws of clean and unclean to extremes (Mk 7:3–4), but they also consider themselves self-righteous by following them. Instead of being awed by their diligence, Jesus points out their diseased hearts. His notion is so contrary to the mandate of their society that even the disciples have a hard time understanding it (Mk 7:17–18).***

Intimate Examination

Yeast MK 8:15

Yeast is spoken of throughout the Bible. The Israelites celebrated the Feast of Unleavened Bread (bread that doesn't rise because there is no yeast in it) by removing all yeast from their homes (Ex 12:17-20). Grain offerings to the Lord throughout the year were to be made without yeast (Lev 2:11). But now Jesus speaks of "the yeast of the Pharisees and that of Herod" (Mk 8:15; *see the note on Mt 16:5-12, page 1609*).

To understand Jesus' use of the word "yeast" here, consider what yeast does to a loaf of bread. Yeast puffs bread up, giving it an inflated shape and filling it with hot air—an apropos image of the Pharisees and of Herod. Both were puffed up with pride and corrupt attitudes. And while they swayed to two extremes—the Pharisees to legalism and Herod to passion and vice—both not only exhibited their corrupt lifestyles and attitudes but also, like yeast, spread their dangerous views throughout society—even going so far as to potentially influence the disciples' thinking.

the more he did so, the more they kept talking
about it. 37People were overwhelmed with amazement. "He has done everything well," they said.
"He even makes the deaf hear and the mute speak."

Jesus Feeds the Four Thousand

8 During those days another large crowd gathered. Since they had nothing to eat, Jesus
called his disciples to him and said, 2"I have com- **8:2**
passion for these people;[b] they have already been [b]Mt 9:36
with me three days and have nothing to eat. 3If I
send them home hungry, they will collapse on the
way, because some of them have come a long
distance."

4His disciples answered, "But where in this
remote place can anyone get enough bread to feed
them?"

5"How many loaves do you have?" Jesus asked.
"Seven," they replied.

6He told the crowd to sit down on the ground.
When he had taken the seven loaves and given
thanks, he broke them and gave them to his disciples to set before the people, and they did so.
7They had a few small fish as well; he gave thanks
for them also and told the disciples to distribute **8:7**
them.[c] 8The people ate and were satisfied. After- [c]Mt 14:19
ward the disciples picked up seven basketfuls of
broken pieces that were left over.[d] 9About four **8:8** [d]ver 20
thousand men were present. And having sent
them away, 10he got into the boat with his disciples and went to the region of Dalmanutha.

11The Pharisees came and began to question
Jesus. To test him, they asked him for a sign from **8:11**
heaven.[e] 12He sighed deeply[f] and said, "Why does [e]Mt 12:38
this generation ask for a miraculous sign? I tell **8:12**
you the truth, no sign will be given to it." 13Then [f]Mk 7:34
he left them, got back into the boat and crossed
to the other side.

The Yeast of the Pharisees and Herod

14The disciples had forgotten to bring bread,
except for one loaf they had with them in the
boat. 15"Be careful," Jesus warned them. "Watch **8:15**
out for the yeast[g] of the Pharisees[h] and that of [g]1Co 5:6-8
Herod."[i] [h]Lk 12:1 [i]Mt 14:1;
16They discussed this with one another and Mk 12:13
said, "It is because we have no bread."

17Aware of their discussion, Jesus asked them:
"Why are you talking about having no bread? Do
you still not see or understand? Are your hearts **8:17**
hardened?[j] 18Do you have eyes but fail to see, and [j]Isa 6:9,10;
ears but fail to hear? And don't you remember? Mk 6:52
19When I broke the five loaves for the five thousand, how many basketfuls of pieces did you **8:19**
pick up?" [k]Mt 14:20;

"Twelve,"[k] they replied. Mk 6:41-44;
20"And when I broke the seven loaves for the Lk 9:17; Jn 6:13
four thousand, how many basketfuls of pieces did
you pick up?" **8:20**

They answered, "Seven."[l] [l]ver 6-9; Mt 15:37

8:21 21 He said to them, "Do you still not under-
[m]Mk 6:52 stand?"[m]

8:22 *The Healing of a Blind Man at Bethsaida*

[n]Mt 11:21 22 They came to Bethsaida,[n] and some people
[o]Mk 10:46; brought a blind man[o] and begged Jesus to touch
Jn 9:1 him. 23 He took the blind man by the hand and led
8:23 him outside the village. When he had spit[p] on the
[p]Mk 7:33 [q]Mk 5:23 man's eyes and put his hands on[q] him, Jesus
asked, "Do you see anything?"
24 He looked up and said, "I see people; they
look like trees walking around."
25 Once more Jesus put his hands on the man's
eyes. Then his eyes were opened, his sight was
restored, and he saw everything clearly. 26 Jesus
sent him home, saying, "Don't go into the village.[a]"

Peter's Confession of Christ

27 Jesus and his disciples went on to the villages
around Caesarea Philippi. On the way he asked
8:28 them, "Who do people say I am?"
[r]Mt 3:1 28 They replied, "Some say John the Baptist;[r]
[s]Mal 4:5 others say Elijah;[s] and still others, one of the
prophets."
29 "But what about you?" he asked. "Who do
8:29 you say I am?"
[t]Jn 6:69; Peter answered, "You are the Christ.[b]"[t]
11:27 30 Jesus warned them not to tell anyone about
8:30 him.[u]
[u]Mt 8:4; 16:20; 17:9; Mk 9:9; *Jesus Predicts His Death*

Lk 9:21 31 He then began to teach them that the Son of
8:31 Man[v] must suffer many things[w] and be rejected by
[v]Mt 8:20 [w]Mt 16:21 the elders, chief priests and teachers of the law,[x]
[x]Mt 27:1,2 and that he must be killed[y] and after three days[z]
[y]Ac 2:23; rise again.[a] 32 He spoke plainly[b] about this, and
3:13 Peter took him aside and began to rebuke him.
[z]Mt 16:21 [a]Mt 16:21 33 But when Jesus turned and looked at his disciples, he rebuked Peter. "Get behind me, Satan!"[c]
8:32 he said. "You do not have in mind the things of
[b]Jn 18:20 God, but the things of men."
8:33 34 Then he called the crowd to him along with
[c]Mt 4:10 his disciples and said: "If anyone would come
after me, he must deny himself and take up his
8:34 [d]Mt 10:38; cross and follow me.[d] 35 For whoever wants to save
Lk 14:27 his life[c] will lose it, but whoever loses his life for
8:35 me and for the gospel will save it.[e] 36 What good is
[e]Jn 12:25 it for a man to gain the whole world, yet forfeit
his soul? 37 Or what can a man give in exchange
for his soul? 38 If anyone is ashamed of me and my
words in this adulterous and sinful generation,
8:38 [f]Mt 8:20 the Son of Man[f] will be ashamed of him[g] when he
[g]Mt 10:33; comes[h] in his Father's glory with the holy angels."
Lk 12:9 [h]1Th 2:19 **9** And he said to them, "I tell you the truth,
some who are standing here will not taste

[a] 26 Some manuscripts *Don't go and tell anyone in the village*
[b] 29 Or *Messiah.* "The Christ" (Greek) and "the Messiah" (Hebrew) both mean "the Anointed One." [c] 35 The Greek word means either *life* or *soul*; also in verse 36.

The Christ

MK 8:29

Peter's answer is short, but it is sweet to Jesus' ears. "You are the Christ," Peter says. Those four words contain mountains of meaning. When Peter calls Jesus "the Christ," he is stating that Jesus is the Anointed One of God, the Messiah. While others consider Jesus a good man or a prophet (Mk 8:28), Peter testifies that Jesus is the Savior their nation has been seeking. This is a moving confession—one that generations of believers have proclaimed since Peter's time. This is also a confession that at some point every person will utter. As Philippians 2:10-11 states, "At the name of Jesus every knee should bow, in heaven and on earth and under the earth, and every tongue confess that Jesus Christ is Lord." Take a moment and think back to the day when you first believed Jesus was the Christ. Now, say a prayer for someone who has yet to utter that confession.

The Transfiguration

MK 9:2-13

Through Jesus' transfiguration, God's kingdom is seen and experienced as never before. Three disciples watch as Elijah and Moses appear and talk to Jesus about his death (Lk 9:31). Their visit is for the disciples' benefit. This marvel not only verifies to the three disciples who Jesus is but also confirms that their Messiah's mission on earth is nearing completion. Moses the law-giver is present to testify of the fulfillment of the Law, and Elijah the great prophet is present to testify to the fulfillment of prophecy. The disciples are awed and tongue-tied (Mk 9:6). The visit is also for Jesus' benefit, to give him strength and support for the task ahead.

Let's not forget, however, that the disciples are not the only ones to witness God's miracle of transformation. What began on the mountain continues today in each believer: "And we . . . are being transformed into his likeness with ever-increasing glory" (2Co 3:18).

death before they see the kingdom of God come[i]
with power."[j]

The Transfiguration

2 After six days Jesus took Peter, James and
John[k] with him and led them up a high mountain,
where they were all alone. There he was transfigured before them. 3 His clothes became dazzling
white,[l] whiter than anyone in the world could
bleach them. 4 And there appeared before them
Elijah and Moses, who were talking with Jesus.
5 Peter said to Jesus, "Rabbi,[m] it is good for us
to be here. Let us put up three shelters—one for
you, one for Moses and one for Elijah." 6 (He did
not know what to say, they were so frightened.)
7 Then a cloud appeared and enveloped them,
and a voice came from the cloud:[n] "This is my
Son, whom I love. Listen to him!"[o]
8 Suddenly, when they looked around, they no
longer saw anyone with them except Jesus.
9 As they were coming down the mountain,
Jesus gave them orders not to tell anyone[p] what
they had seen until the Son of Man[q] had risen from
the dead. 10 They kept the matter to themselves,
discussing what "rising from the dead" meant.
11 And they asked him, "Why do the teachers of
the law say that Elijah must come first?"
12 Jesus replied, "To be sure, Elijah does come
first, and restores all things. Why then is it written
that the Son of Man[r] must suffer much[s] and be
rejected?[t] 13 But I tell you, Elijah has come,[u] and
they have done to him everything they wished,
just as it is written about him."

The Healing of a Boy With an Evil Spirit

14 When they came to the other disciples, they
saw a large crowd around them and the teachers
of the law arguing with them. 15 As soon as all the
people saw Jesus, they were overwhelmed with
wonder and ran to greet him.
16 "What are you arguing with them about?" he
asked.
17 A man in the crowd answered, "Teacher, I
brought you my son, who is possessed by a spirit
that has robbed him of speech. 18 Whenever it
seizes him, it throws him to the ground. He foams
at the mouth, gnashes his teeth and becomes
rigid. I asked your disciples to drive out the spirit, but they could not."
19 "O unbelieving generation," Jesus replied,
"how long shall I stay with you? How long shall I
put up with you? Bring the boy to me."
20 So they brought him. When the spirit saw
Jesus, it immediately threw the boy into a convulsion. He fell to the ground and rolled around,
foaming at the mouth.[v]
21 Jesus asked the boy's father, "How long has
he been like this?"
"From childhood," he answered. 22 "It has often

9:1 [i]Mk 13:30; Lk 22:18 [j]Mt 24:30; 25:31
9:2 [k]Mt 4:21
9:3 [l]Mt 28:3
9:5 [m]Mt 23:7
9:7 [n]Ex 24:16 [o]Mt 3:17
9:9 [p]Mk 8:30 [q]Mt 8:20
9:12 [r]Mt 8:20 [s]Mt 16:21 [t]Lk 23:11
9:13 [u]Mt 11:14
9:20 [v]Mk 1:26

Week 34

Can You Believe the Unbelievable?

"I believe God can do the unbelievable." That's quite a statement! What is unbelievable to your finite, human mind becomes believable when faith steps in. Do you believe God can do even what others say is impossible? Do you believe God can give you faith to believe what seems unbelievable?

Jesus gives the disciples authority to drive out demons (Mk 3:14-15). Yet the disciples cannot heal a boy with an evil spirit. Why (Mk 9:29; Mt 17:19-20)?

The boy's father has obviously heard of Jesus, his disciples and the many people they have healed. By using the words "if you can" (Mk 9:22), he shows that his "hope" is only wishful thinking. His unbelief is cloaked with hope, but it is unbelief nonetheless. What is Jesus' response (Mk 9:23)?

How often do you come to God with more hope than faith? Is this kind of hope actually unbelief? Faith produces true, trusting hope. Faith then takes hope and makes it a certainty (Heb 11:1).

How does the father respond to Jesus' statement (Mk 9:24)? When has unbelief prevented your faith from growing? When have you hoped God would heal or help you while you still harbored doubt or conflict? Here is the answer to your doubt: Ask Jesus to help you overcome your unbelief.

What is possible if you believe (Mt 17:20; Mk 9:23)?

Enjoying God THROUGH the Word

Read Joshua 6:1-20 (pages 340-341). No doubt the people of Jericho are surprised when forty thousand armed Israelites march around their city (Jos 4:13; 6:3). With soldiers in front of them and behind them, seven priests blowing trumpets accompany the ark of the covenant. They circle the city once a day for six days. This is certainly not typical military strategy! On the seventh day, they march around the city seven times. The seventh time around, the Israelites give a tremendous shout—and Jericho's walls collapse.

Do you think the Israelites simply hope God will come through as he has promised? If so, they are taking a very big risk. Why do they have such confidence? They have just seen God part the Jordan River, allowing them to cross on dry ground (Jos 3:1-18). They have true, trusting hope, not mere wishful-thinking hope. It is their faith, not just their hope, that makes the walls of Jericho fall (Heb 11:30).

What can you accomplish with faith? Anything! Thankfully, it takes only a little faith to do incredible things (Mt 17:20). Amazing, isn't it? Your great God has chosen to use your "little faith" to do mighty things.

Enjoying God THROUGH Experience

What are you experiencing today? Guilt, because what you think is hope is really unbelief? Or joy that your "little faith" can be used so mightily by God? Print the words *hope* and *faith* on a piece of paper and hang it where you can see it every day. Seek Jesus' help to overcome your unbelief. He will respond as lovingly to you as he did to the father in Mark 9. Praise him for his work in you. "Now to him who is able to do immeasurably more than all we ask or imagine, according to his power that is at work within us, to him be glory in the church and in Christ Jesus throughout all generations, for ever and ever! Amen" (Eph 3:20-21).

Go to page 1682 for your next weekly study.

Christ Preached

MK 9:38–41

The disciples enjoy being on the "inside track" with Christ—so much so that John assumes anyone else performing miracles in Jesus' name is in the wrong. Jesus quickly straightens out John's thinking by, in effect, saying, "You may not know him, but if he's furthering my kingdom, you can assume he's on my side." Paul expounds on this concept in Philippians 1:18. "The important thing is that in every way, whether from false motives or true, Christ is preached." We, too, should think this way, realizing that Jesus not only accepts those who do the smallest acts of kindness in his name, but he also rewards them (Mk 9:41). The word reward here actually means "wages." While we may not know the exact nature of these rewards, Jesus promises that all people—not only those similar to us but also those very different from us—will be paid for their services to God's kingdom.

thrown him into fire or water to kill him. But if
you can do anything, take pity on us and help us."
23" 'If you can'?" said Jesus. "Everything is possible for him who believes."[w]
24Immediately the boy's father exclaimed, "I do
believe; help me overcome my unbelief!"
25When Jesus saw that a crowd was running to
the scene,[x] he rebuked the evil[a] spirit. "You deaf
and mute spirit," he said, "I command you, come
out of him and never enter him again."
26The spirit shrieked, convulsed him violently
and came out. The boy looked so much like a
corpse that many said, "He's dead." 27But Jesus
took him by the hand and lifted him to his feet,
and he stood up.
28After Jesus had gone indoors, his disciples
asked him privately,[y] "Why couldn't we drive it
out?"
29He replied, "This kind can come out only by
prayer.[b]"
30They left that place and passed through Galilee. Jesus did not want anyone to know where
they were, 31because he was teaching his disciples. He said to them, "The Son of Man[z] is going
to be betrayed into the hands of men. They will
kill him,[a] and after three days[b] he will rise."[c] 32But
they did not understand what he meant[d] and were
afraid to ask him about it.

Who Is the Greatest?

33They came to Capernaum.[e] When he was in
the house,[f] he asked them, "What were you arguing about on the road?" 34But they kept quiet
because on the way they had argued about who
was the greatest.[g]
35Sitting down, Jesus called the Twelve and
said, "If anyone wants to be first, he must be the
very last, and the servant of all."[h]
36He took a little child and had him stand
among them. Taking him in his arms,[i] he said to
them, 37"Whoever welcomes one of these little
children in my name welcomes me; and whoever
welcomes me does not welcome me but the one
who sent me."[j]

Whoever Is Not Against Us Is for Us

38"Teacher," said John, "we saw a man driving
out demons in your name and we told him to
stop, because he was not one of us."[k]
39"Do not stop him," Jesus said. "No one who
does a miracle in my name can in the next
moment say anything bad about me, 40for whoever is not against us is for us.[l] 41I tell you the truth,
anyone who gives you a cup of water in my name
because you belong to Christ will certainly not
lose his reward.[m]

9:23 [w]Mt 21:21; Mk 11:23; Jn 11:40
9:25 [x]ver 15
9:28 [y]Mk 7:17
9:31 [z]Mt 8:20 [a]ver 12; Ac 2:23; 3:13 [b]Mt 16:21 [c]Mt 16:21
9:32 [d]Lk 2:50; 9:45; 18:34; Jn 12:16
9:33 [e]Mt 4:13 [f]Mk 1:29
9:34 [g]Lk 22:24
9:35 [h]Mt 18:4; 20:26; Mk 10:43; Lk 22:26
9:36 [i]Mk 10:16
9:37 [j]Mt 10:40
9:38 [k]Nu 11:27-29
9:40 [l]Mt 12:30; Lk 11:23
9:41 [m]Mt 10:42

[a] 25 Greek *unclean* [b] 29 Some manuscripts *prayer and fasting*

Causing to Sin

42“And if anyone causes one of these little ones
who believe in me to sin,[n] it would be better for
him to be thrown into the sea with a large millstone tied around his neck.[o] 43If your hand causes
you to sin,[p] cut it off. It is better for you to enter
life maimed than with two hands to go into hell,[q]
where the fire never goes out.[a][r] 45And if your foot
causes you to sin,[s] cut it off. It is better for you to
enter life crippled than to have two feet and be
thrown into hell.[b][t] 47And if your eye causes you to
sin,[u] pluck it out. It is better for you to enter the
kingdom of God with one eye than to have two
eyes and be thrown into hell,[v] 48where

“ ‘their worm does not die,
and the fire is not quenched.’[c][w]

49Everyone will be salted[x] with fire.
50“Salt is good, but if it loses its saltiness, how
can you make it salty again?[y] Have salt in yourselves,[z] and be at peace with each other.”[a]

Divorce

10 Jesus then left that place and went into the
region of Judea and across the Jordan.[b]
Again crowds of people came to him, and as was
his custom, he taught them.[c]
2Some Pharisees[d] came and tested him by asking, “Is it lawful for a man to divorce his wife?”
3“What did Moses command you?” he replied.
4They said, “Moses permitted a man to write a
certificate of divorce and send her away.”[e]
5“It was because your hearts were hard[f] that
Moses wrote you this law,” Jesus replied. 6“But at
the beginning of creation God ‘made them male
and female.’[d][g] 7‘For this reason a man will leave
his father and mother and be united to his wife,[e]
8and the two will become one flesh.’[f][h] So they are
no longer two, but one. 9Therefore what God has
joined together, let man not separate.”
10When they were in the house again, the disciples asked Jesus about this. 11He answered, “Anyone who divorces his wife and marries another
woman commits adultery against her.[i] 12And if
she divorces her husband and marries another
man, she commits adultery.”[j]

The Little Children and Jesus

13People were bringing little children to Jesus to
have him touch them, but the disciples rebuked
them. 14When Jesus saw this, he was indignant.
He said to them, “Let the little children come to
me, and do not hinder them, for the kingdom of
God belongs to such as these.[k] 15I tell you the

9:42 [n]Mt 5:29 [o]Mt 18:6; Lk 17:2
9:43 [p]Mt 5:29 [q]Mt 5:30; 18:8 [r]Mt 25:41
9:45 [s]Mt 5:29 [t]Mt 18:8
9:47 [u]Mt 5:29 [v]Mt 5:29; 18:9
9:48 [w]Isa 66:24; Mt 25:41
9:49 [x]Lev 2:13
9:50 [y]Mt 5:13; Lk 14:34,35 [z]Col 4:6 [a]Ro 12:18; 2Co 13:11; 1Th 5:13
10:1 [b]Mk 1:5; Jn 10:40; 11:7 [c]Mt 4:23; Mk 2:13; 4:2; 6:6,34
10:2 [d]Mk 2:16
10:4 [e]Dt 24:1-4; Mt 5:31
10:5 [f]Ps 95:8; Heb 3:15
10:6 [g]Ge 1:27; 5:2
10:8 [h]Ge 2:24; 1Co 6:16
10:11 [i]Mt 5:32; Lk 16:18
10:12 [j]Ro 7:3; 1Co 7:10,11
10:14 [k]Mt 25:34

[a] 43 Some manuscripts *out,* 44*where / “ ‘their worm does not die, / and the fire is not quenched.’* [b] 45 Some manuscripts *hell,* 46*where / “ ‘their worm does not die, / and the fire is not quenched.’* [c] 48 Isaiah 66:24 [d] 6 Gen. 1:27 [e] 7 Some early manuscripts do not have *and be united to his wife.* [f] 8 Gen. 2:24

It is interesting that Jesus said it is impossible to enter the *kingdom* unless we become as little children (Mk 10:15). I believe he recognized the need for adults to be jolted out of their dull, wooden mind-sets and assume the trusting unpretentiousness so characteristic of a child. Jesus placed a very high premium upon that childlike quality. The most profound truth in the universe is that God loves me; yet many miss that truth because of its simplicity. When Jesus said, “I praise you, Father, Lord of heaven and earth, because you have hidden these things from the wise and learned, and revealed them to little children” (Mt 11:25), he once again reminds us of how preferable it is at times to be childlike.

—Marilyn Meberg

Unwilling to Sell All?

MK 10:17–31

Jesus, with perfect vision, looks into this young man's heart and discovers his true love—money. While the man sees himself as diligently keeping God's commandments, Jesus knows the fellow has not given God his whole heart. This is confirmed by his response. When Jesus asks him to "sell everything," the man's "face fell" (Mk 10:21–22). It's too much to ask. God may come in a close second, but money still holds the lead.

This statement of Jesus is not a command to all believers to rid themselves of their material possessions. Instead, it is an encouragement for us to seriously consider what holds our hearts. Wealth *here can refer to anything we take pleasure in. For some it may be money, but for others it's food, fame or even shopping. Anything in our lives that is more important to us than our Savior needs to be closely examined and then appropriate action needs to be taken. Today, take a moment to consider what holds your heart. Is there something you're unwilling to "sell" for Jesus?*

truth, anyone who will not receive the kingdom of
God like a little child will never enter it."[l] 16 And
he took the children in his arms,[m] put his hands
on them and blessed them.

The Rich Young Man

17 As Jesus started on his way, a man ran up to
him and fell on his knees[n] before him. "Good
teacher," he asked, "what must I do to inherit eternal life?"[o]

18 "Why do you call me good?" Jesus answered.
"No one is good—except God alone. 19 You know
the commandments: 'Do not murder, do not commit adultery, do not steal, do not give false testimony, do not defraud, honor your father and
mother.'[a]"[p]

20 "Teacher," he declared, "all these I have kept
since I was a boy."

21 Jesus looked at him and loved him. "One
thing you lack," he said. "Go, sell everything you
have and give to the poor,[q] and you will have
treasure in heaven.[r] Then come, follow me."[s]

22 At this the man's face fell. He went away sad,
because he had great wealth.

23 Jesus looked around and said to his disciples,
"How hard it is for the rich[t] to enter the kingdom
of God!"

24 The disciples were amazed at his words. But
Jesus said again, "Children, how hard it is[b] to
enter the kingdom of God![u] 25 It is easier for a
camel to go through the eye of a needle than for a
rich man to enter the kingdom of God."[v]

26 The disciples were even more amazed, and
said to each other, "Who then can be saved?"

27 Jesus looked at them and said, "With man this
is impossible, but not with God; all things are possible with God."[w]

28 Peter said to him, "We have left everything to
follow you!"[x]

29 "I tell you the truth," Jesus replied, "no one
who has left home or brothers or sisters or mother or father or children or fields for me and the
gospel 30 will fail to receive a hundred times as
much[y] in this present age (homes, brothers, sisters, mothers, children and fields—and with them,
persecutions) and in the age to come,[z] eternal
life.[a] 31 But many who are first will be last, and the
last first."[b]

Jesus Again Predicts His Death

32 They were on their way up to Jerusalem, with
Jesus leading the way, and the disciples were
astonished, while those who followed were afraid.
Again he took the Twelve[c] aside and told them
what was going to happen to him. 33 "We are going
up to Jerusalem,"[d] he said, "and the Son of Man[e]
will be betrayed to the chief priests and teachers
of the law.[f] They will condemn him to death and

10:15 [l]Mt 18:3
10:16 [m]Mk 9:36
10:17 [n]Mk 1:40 [o]Lk 10:25; Ac 20:32
10:19 [p]Ex 20:12-16; Dt 5:16-20
10:21 [q]Ac 2:45 [r]Mt 6:20; Lk 12:33 [s]Mt 4:19
10:23 [t]Ps 52:7; 62:10; 1Ti 6:9,10,17
10:24 [u]Mt 7:13,14
10:25 [v]Lk 12:16-20
10:27 [w]Mt 19:26
10:28 [x]Mt 4:19
10:30 [y]Mt 6:33 [z]Mt 12:32 [a]Mt 25:46
10:31 [b]Mt 19:30
10:32 [c]Mk 3:16-19
10:33 [d]Lk 9:51 [e]Mt 8:20 [f]Mt 27:1,2

[a] *19* Exodus 20:12–16; Deut. 5:16–20 [b] *24* Some manuscripts *is for those who trust in riches*

10:34 will hand him over to the Gentiles, 34who will
[g]Mt 16:21 mock him and spit on him, flog him[g] and kill
[h]Ac 2:23; 3:13 him.[h] Three days later[i] he will rise."[j]

[i]Mt 16:21 [j]Mt 16:21

The Request of James and John

35Then James and John, the sons of Zebedee,
came to him. "Teacher," they said, "we want you
to do for us whatever we ask."
36"What do you want me to do for you?" he
asked.
10:37 37They replied, "Let one of us sit at your right
[k]Mt 19:28 and the other at your left in your glory."[k]
10:38 38"You don't know what you are asking,"[l] Jesus
[l]Job 38:2 said. "Can you drink the cup[m] I drink or be bap-
[m]Mt 20:22 tized with the baptism I am baptized with?"[n]
[n]Lk 12:50 39"We can," they answered.
Jesus said to them, "You will drink the cup I
10:39 drink and be baptized with the baptism I am bap-
[o]Ac 12:2; tized with,[o] 40but to sit at my right or left is not
Rev 1:9 for me to grant. These places belong to those for
whom they have been prepared."
41When the ten heard about this, they became
indignant with James and John. 42Jesus called
them together and said, "You know that those
who are regarded as rulers of the Gentiles lord it
over them, and their high officials exercise authority over them. 43Not so with you. Instead, whoev-
10:43 er wants to become great among you must be
[p]Mk 9:35 your servant,[p] 44and whoever wants to be first
10:45 must be slave of all. 45For even the Son of Man did
[q]Mt 20:28 not come to be served, but to serve,[q] and to give
[r]Mt 20:28 his life as a ransom for many."[r]

Blind Bartimaeus Receives His Sight

46Then they came to Jericho. As Jesus and his
disciples, together with a large crowd, were leaving the city, a blind man, Bartimaeus (that is, the
Son of Timaeus), was sitting by the roadside beg-
10:47 ging. 47When he heard that it was Jesus of Naza-
[s]Mk 1:24 reth,[s] he began to shout, "Jesus, Son of David,[t]
[t]Mt 9:27 have mercy on me!"
48Many rebuked him and told him to be quiet,
but he shouted all the more, "Son of David, have
mercy on me!"
49Jesus stopped and said, "Call him."
So they called to the blind man, "Cheer up! On
your feet! He's calling you." 50Throwing his cloak
aside, he jumped to his feet and came to Jesus.
51"What do you want me to do for you?" Jesus
10:51 asked him.
[u]Mt 23:7 The blind man said, "Rabbi,[u] I want to see."
10:52 52"Go," said Jesus, "your faith has healed you."[v]
[v]Mt 9:22 Immediately he received his sight and followed[w]
[w]Mt 4:19 Jesus along the road.

The Triumphal Entry

11:1 11 As they approached Jerusalem and came to
[x]Mt 21:17 Bethphage and Bethany[x] at the Mount of
[y]Mt 21:1 Olives,[y] Jesus sent two of his disciples, 2saying to
them, "Go to the village ahead of you, and just as

Servant Leadership

MK 10:42–45

Most women know about servant leadership. Their days are spent in service—to spouses, children, parents, bosses, churches and friends. The key in this verse is not that they serve, but that—like Jesus—they joyfully *choose* to serve. That joyful choice is the heart of true servant leadership.

Let's look at Jesus' own example as a servant-leader: (1) he stoops and labors during his time on earth, for he comes not to be ministered to, but to minister; (2) he completes his service through love, for though the need is great, Jesus' love is greater; (3) he not only serves a few, but he also gives his life "for many" (Mk 10:45). Jesus asks the same of us: that we not work for our own gain or position, but that we work with the benefit of others in mind. In turn, Jesus promises that we will be "great"—not through our own authority or works, but through his.

Perfect Anger

MK 11:15–19

Unlike human anger, which is often selfish, fitful or malicious, God's anger is perfect. It is the response of his holiness in the face of sin. In this case Jesus angrily clears the temple. His point is not to destroy the temple, but to purify it. He does so with authority since he is the Son in his own house. He does so with good reason, stating that his house should be a house of prayer and not a den of robbers (Mk 11:17).

As Christians, however, we need to be cautious in expressing our anger. Our anger can often be self-regarding and vindictive. The Scriptures encourage us to be "slow" to anger (Jas 1:19). When we do become angry, we should "not sin" (Eph 4:26) in how we express our feelings. God is pleased when we follow his commands for peace, stating it is to our "glory to overlook an offense" (Pr 19:11).

you enter it, you will find a colt tied there, which
no one has ever ridden.[z] Untie it and bring it here.
3If anyone asks you, 'Why are you doing this?' tell
him, 'The Lord needs it and will send it back here
shortly.' "
4They went and found a colt outside in the
street, tied at a doorway.[a] As they untied it, 5some
people standing there asked, "What are you
doing, untying that colt?" 6They answered as
Jesus had told them to, and the people let them
go. 7When they brought the colt to Jesus and
threw their cloaks over it, he sat on it. 8Many people spread their cloaks on the road, while others
spread branches they had cut in the fields. 9Those
who went ahead and those who followed shouted,

> "Hosanna![*a*]"
>
> "Blessed is he who comes in the name
> of the Lord!"[*b*][b]
>
> 10"Blessed is the coming kingdom of our
> father David!"
>
> "Hosanna in the highest!"[c]

11Jesus entered Jerusalem and went to the temple. He looked around at everything, but since it
was already late, he went out to Bethany with the
Twelve.[d]

Jesus Clears the Temple

12The next day as they were leaving Bethany,
Jesus was hungry. 13Seeing in the distance a fig
tree in leaf, he went to find out if it had any fruit.
When he reached it, he found nothing but leaves,
because it was not the season for figs.[e] 14Then he
said to the tree, "May no one ever eat fruit from
you again." And his disciples heard him say it.
15On reaching Jerusalem, Jesus entered the temple area and began driving out those who were
buying and selling there. He overturned the tables
of the money changers and the benches of those
selling doves, 16and would not allow anyone to
carry merchandise through the temple courts.
17And as he taught them, he said, "Is it not
written:

> " 'My house will be called
> a house of prayer for all nations'[*c*]?[f]

But you have made it 'a den of robbers.'[*d*]"[g]
18The chief priests and the teachers of the law
heard this and began looking for a way to kill
him, for they feared him,[h] because the whole
crowd was amazed at his teaching.[i]
19When evening came, they[*e*] went out of the
city.[j]

11:2 [z]Nu 19:2; Dt 21:3; 1Sa 6:7
11:4 [a]Mk 14:16
11:9 [b]Ps 118:25, 26; Mt 23:39
11:10 [c]Lk 2:14
11:11 [d]Mt 21:12,17
11:13 [e]Lk 13:6-9
11:17 [f]Isa 56:7 [g]Jer 7:11
11:18 [h]Mt 21:46; Mk 12:12; Lk 20:19 [i]Mt 7:28
11:19 [j]Lk 21:37

[*a*] *9* A Hebrew expression meaning "Save!" which became an exclamation of praise; also in verse 10 [*b*] *9* Psalm 118:25,26 [*c*] *17* Isaiah 56:7 [*d*] *17* Jer. 7:11 [*e*] *19* Some early manuscripts *he*

The Withered Fig Tree

20 In the morning, as they went along, they saw
11:21 [k]Mt 23:7 the fig tree withered from the roots. 21 Peter
remembered and said to Jesus, "Rabbi,[k] look! The
fig tree you cursed has withered!"
22 "Have[a] faith in God," Jesus answered. 23 "I tell
you the truth, if anyone says to this mountain,
'Go, throw yourself into the sea,' and does not
doubt in his heart but believes that what he says
11:23 [l]Mt 21:21 will happen, it will be done for him.[l] 24 Therefore
I tell you, whatever you ask for in prayer, believe
11:24 [m]Mt 7:7 that you have received it, and it will be yours.[m]
25 And when you stand praying, if you hold any-
11:25 [n]Mt 6:14 thing against anyone, forgive him, so that your
Father in heaven may forgive you your sins.[b]"[n]

The Authority of Jesus Questioned

27 They arrived again in Jerusalem, and while
Jesus was walking in the temple courts, the chief
priests, the teachers of the law and the elders
came to him. 28 "By what authority are you doing
these things?" they asked. "And who gave you
authority to do this?"
29 Jesus replied, "I will ask you one question.
Answer me, and I will tell you by what authority
I am doing these things. 30 John's baptism—was it
from heaven, or from men? Tell me!"
31 They discussed it among themselves and said,
"If we say, 'From heaven,' he will ask, 'Then why
didn't you believe him?' 32 But if we say, 'From
11:32 [o]Mt 11:9 men' . . ." (They feared the people, for everyone
held that John really was a prophet.)[o]
33 So they answered Jesus, "We don't know."
Jesus said, "Neither will I tell you by what
authority I am doing these things."

The Parable of the Tenants

12:1 [p]Isa 5:1-7 **12** He then began to speak to them in parables:
"A man planted a vineyard.[p] He put a wall
around it, dug a pit for the winepress and built a
watchtower. Then he rented the vineyard to some
farmers and went away on a journey. 2 At harvest
time he sent a servant to the tenants to collect
from them some of the fruit of the vineyard. 3 But
they seized him, beat him and sent him away
empty-handed. 4 Then he sent another servant to
them; they struck this man on the head and treated him shamefully. 5 He sent still another, and that
one they killed. He sent many others; some of
them they beat, others they killed.
12:6 [q]Heb 1:1-3 6 "He had one left to send, a son, whom he
loved. He sent him last of all,[q] saying, 'They will
respect my son.'
7 "But the tenants said to one another, 'This is
the heir. Come, let's kill him, and the inheritance
will be ours.' 8 So they took him and killed him,
and threw him out of the vineyard.

[a] 22 Some early manuscripts *If you have* [b] 25 Some manuscripts *sins.* 26 *But if you do not forgive, neither will your Father who is in heaven forgive your sins.*

Jessie Brown Pounds published her first material at age 15. In her life as a minister's wife she published 50 cantatas and operettas, 9 books, and more than 400 gospel songs.

Anywhere With Jesus

Anywhere with Jesus I can safely go,
Anywhere He leads me in this world below;
Anywhere without Him dearest joys would fade;
Anywhere with Jesus I am not afraid.

Anywhere, anywhere! Fear I cannot know;
Anywhere with Jesus I can safely go.

Anywhere with Jesus I am not alone;
Other friends may fail me, He is still my own;
Though His hand may lead me over drearest ways,
Anywhere with Jesus is a house of praise.

—Jessie Brown Pounds (1861-1921)

Led Astray

MK 12:24

Not knowing the Scriptures or the power of God has been called the sin of American Christianity. Yet it's not a new problem. Jesus tells the Sadducees, members of a powerful religious and political sect originating in the priestly line of Israel, that they are in error in these same areas. The word *error* here means "to lead astray." The Sadducees do not deny the truth outright; instead, they allow their thinking to be led astray by unanswered questions. They deny any truth they cannot "prove," such as the resurrection or angels. They also claim to believe in God's power, but they do not live as though they do.

Has such thinking crept into your mind? Such negative thought patterns can be eradicated by studying the Scriptures in light of God's miraculous power. Doing so will help you trust in God's ability, abundance and provision. And soon, you, too, will be "fully persuaded that God [has] power to do what he [has] promised" (Ro 4:21).

9"What then will the owner of the vineyard do?
He will come and kill those tenants and give the
vineyard to others. 10Haven't you read this
scripture:

> " 'The stone the builders rejected 12:10
> has become the capstone[a];[r] [r]Ac 4:11
> 11the Lord has done this,
> and it is marvelous in our eyes'[b]?"[s] 12:11 [s]Ps 118:22, 23

12Then they looked for a way to arrest him
because they knew he had spoken the parable
against them. But they were afraid of the crowd;[t] 12:12
so they left him and went away.[u] [t]Mk 11:18 [u]Mt 22:22

Paying Taxes to Caesar

13Later they sent some of the Pharisees and 12:13
Herodians[v] to Jesus to catch him[w] in his words. [v]Mt 22:16;
14They came to him and said, "Teacher, we know Mk 3:6
you are a man of integrity. You aren't swayed by [w]Mt 12:10
men, because you pay no attention to who they
are; but you teach the way of God in accordance
with the truth. Is it right to pay taxes to Caesar or
not? 15Should we pay or shouldn't we?"

But Jesus knew their hypocrisy. "Why are you
trying to trap me?" he asked. "Bring me a denarius and let me look at it." 16They brought the coin,
and he asked them, "Whose portrait is this? And
whose inscription?"

"Caesar's," they replied.

17Then Jesus said to them, "Give to Caesar what 12:17
is Caesar's and to God what is God's."[x] [x]Ro 13:7

And they were amazed at him.

Marriage at the Resurrection

18Then the Sadducees,[y] who say there is no res- 12:18
urrection,[z] came to him with a question. 19"Teach- [y]Ac 4:1 [z]Ac 23:8;
er," they said, "Moses wrote for us that if a man's 1Co 15:12
brother dies and leaves a wife but no children, the
man must marry the widow and have children for
his brother.[a] 20Now there were seven brothers. The 12:19
first one married and died without leaving any [a]Dt 25:5
children. 21The second one married the widow,
but he also died, leaving no child. It was the same
with the third. 22In fact, none of the seven left any
children. Last of all, the woman died too. 23At the
resurrection[c] whose wife will she be, since the
seven were married to her?"

24Jesus replied, "Are you not in error because 12:24
you do not know the Scriptures[b] or the power of [b]2Ti 3:15-17
God? 25When the dead rise, they will neither mar-
ry nor be given in marriage; they will be like the 12:25
angels in heaven.[c] 26Now about the dead rising— [c]1Co 15:42,
have you not read in the book of Moses, in the 49,52
account of the bush, how God said to him, 'I am
the God of Abraham, the God of Isaac, and the 12:26
God of Jacob'[d]?[d] 27He is not the God of the dead, [d]Ex 3:6
but of the living. You are badly mistaken!"

[a] 10 Or *cornerstone* [b] 11 Psalm 118:22,23 [c] 23 Some manuscripts *resurrection, when men rise from the dead,* [d] 26 Exodus 3:6

The Greatest Commandment

12:28 [e]Lk 10:25-28; 20:39 28 One of the teachers of the law[e] came and
heard them debating. Noticing that Jesus had giv-
en them a good answer, he asked him, "Of all the
commandments, which is the most important?"
29 "The most important one," answered Jesus,
"is this: 'Hear, O Israel, the Lord our God, the Lord
is one.[a] 30 Love the Lord your God with all your
heart and with all your soul and with all your
12:30 [f]Dt 6:4,5 mind and with all your strength.'[b][f] 31 The second
is this: 'Love your neighbor as yourself.'[c][g] There
12:31 [g]Lev 19:18; Mt 5:43 is no commandment greater than these."
32 "Well said, teacher," the man replied. "You are
right in saying that God is one and there is no
12:32 [h]Dt 4:35,39; Isa 45:6,14; 46:9 other but him.[h] 33 To love him with all your heart,
with all your understanding and with all your
strength, and to love your neighbor as yourself is
more important than all burnt offerings and
12:33 [i]1Sa 15:22; Hos 6:6; Mic 6:6-8; Heb 10:8 sacrifices."[i]
34 When Jesus saw that he had answered wisely,
he said to him, "You are not far from the kingdom
of God."[j] And from then on no one dared ask him
12:34 [j]Mt 3:2 [k]Mt 22:46; Lk 20:40 any more questions.[k]

Whose Son Is the Christ?

35 While Jesus was teaching in the temple
12:35 [l]Mt 26:55 [m]Mt 9:27 courts,[l] he asked, "How is it that the teachers of
the law say that the Christ[d] is the son of David?[m]
36 David himself, speaking by the Holy Spirit,[n]
12:36 [n]2Sa 23:2 [o]Ps 110:1; Mt 22:44 declared:

> " 'The Lord said to my Lord:
> "Sit at my right hand
> until I put your enemies
> under your feet." '[e][o]

37 David himself calls him 'Lord.' How then can he
be his son?"
12:37 [p]Jn 12:9 The large crowd[p] listened to him with delight.
38 As he taught, Jesus said, "Watch out for the
teachers of the law. They like to walk around in
flowing robes and be greeted in the marketplaces,
39 and have the most important seats in the syna-
12:39 [q]Lk 11:43 gogues and the places of honor at banquets.[q]
40 They devour widows' houses and for a show
make lengthy prayers. Such men will be punished
most severely."

The Widow's Offering

41 Jesus sat down opposite the place where the
12:41 [r]2Ki 12:9; Jn 8:20 offerings were put[r] and watched the crowd putting their money into the temple treasury. Many
rich people threw in large amounts. 42 But a poor
widow came and put in two very small copper
coins,[f] worth only a fraction of a penny.[g]
43 Calling his disciples to him, Jesus said, "I tell
you the truth, this poor widow has put more into
the treasury than all the others. 44 They all gave

[a] 29 Or *the Lord our God is one Lord* [b] 30 Deut. 6:4,5
[c] 31 Lev. 19:18 [d] 35 Or *Messiah* [e] 36 Psalm 110:1
[f] 42 Greek *two lepta* [g] 42 Greek *kodrantes*

Less Is More

MK 12:41-44

Jesus watches the temple crowd as people give their offerings. He hears—everyone can—the sound of the precious metals dropping into the temple treasury. Yet he doesn't take much notice of the coins. He is intent on the people's hearts. The rich give plenty, and Jesus nods. It is good they do so out of their abundance. Then he sees a peasant widow who gives from her scarcity. She gives two coins worth less than a penny. These are the smallest of coins, equal to about one-eighth of a cent. Contrary to all human reasoning, the Savior commends her. The woman is stretching herself, even denying herself. And Jesus sees her heart. The widow knows that her source of provision is not the coins. Her source is God. She gives all, confident that he will provide. In Jesus' eyes, her less is more. So is yours (see the character sketch for this woman on page 1911).

Signs of the Times

MK 13

The disciples are curious about signs of the end of the age and Jesus' return (Mk 13:3–4; Mt 24:3). Reading Jesus' answers to their questions can be overwhelming; yet three promises rest among these "signs": (1) God never sends judgment without previous warning (Mk 13:23); (2) even if believers are required to face opposition, God will be near them, giving them courage and providing them with the words to speak (Mk 13:11); (3) false prophets will appear, showing signs and wonders, but the elect will be guarded by God (Mk 13:22). This passage assures us that, although we don't always understand everything about future events, we can trust that God will tell us what we need to know and will strengthen us for what we need to face.

As you read these verses, your response may be one of confusion or fright. But read them through to the end—Jesus returns, victory for him and his followers is assured, and he begins his forever reign in his new and peaceful kingdom.

out of their wealth; but she, out of her poverty,
put in everything—all she had to live on."[s]

Signs of the End of the Age

13 As he was leaving the temple, one of his
disciples said to him, "Look, Teacher! What
massive stones! What magnificent buildings!"
2"Do you see all these great buildings?" replied
Jesus. "Not one stone here will be left on another;
every one will be thrown down."[t]
3As Jesus was sitting on the Mount of Olives[u]
opposite the temple, Peter, James, John[v] and
Andrew asked him privately, 4"Tell us, when will
these things happen? And what will be the sign
that they are all about to be fulfilled?"
5Jesus said to them: "Watch out that no one
deceives you.[w] 6Many will come in my name,
claiming, 'I am he,' and will deceive many. 7When
you hear of wars and rumors of wars, do not be
alarmed. Such things must happen, but the end is
still to come. 8Nation will rise against nation, and
kingdom against kingdom. There will be earthquakes in various places, and famines. These are
the beginning of birth pains.
9"You must be on your guard. You will be handed over to the local councils and flogged in the
synagogues.[x] On account of me you will stand
before governors and kings as witnesses to them.
10And the gospel must first be preached to all
nations. 11Whenever you are arrested and brought
to trial, do not worry beforehand about what to
say. Just say whatever is given you at the time, for
it is not you speaking, but the Holy Spirit.[y]
12"Brother will betray brother to death, and a
father his child. Children will rebel against their
parents and have them put to death.[z] 13All men
will hate you because of me,[a] but he who stands
firm to the end will be saved.[b]
14"When you see 'the abomination that causes
desolation'[a][c] standing where it[b] does not belong—
let the reader understand—then let those who are
in Judea flee to the mountains. 15Let no one on
the roof of his house go down or enter the house
to take anything out. 16Let no one in the field go
back to get his cloak. 17How dreadful it will be in
those days for pregnant women and nursing
mothers![d] 18Pray that this will not take place in
winter, 19because those will be days of distress
unequaled from the beginning, when God created
the world,[e] until now—and never to be equaled
again.[f] 20If the Lord had not cut short those days,
no one would survive. But for the sake of the
elect, whom he has chosen, he has shortened
them. 21At that time if anyone says to you, 'Look,
here is the Christ[c]!' or, 'Look, there he is!' do not
believe it.[g] 22For false Christs and false prophets[h]
will appear and perform signs and miracles[i] to
deceive the elect—if that were possible. 23So be on

12:44 [s]2Co 8:12
13:2 [t]Lk 19:44
13:3 [u]Mt 21:1 [v]Mt 4:21
13:5 [w]ver 22; Jer 29:8; Eph 5:6; 2Th 2:3, 10-12; 1Ti 4:1; 2Ti 3:13; 1Jn 4:6
13:9 [x]Mt 10:17
13:11 [y]Mt 10:19, 20; Lk 12:11, 12
13:12 [z]Mic 7:6; Mt 10:21; Lk 12:51-53
13:13 [a]Jn 15:21 [b]Mt 10:22
13:14 [c]Da 9:27; 11:31; 12:11
13:17 [d]Lk 23:29
13:19 [e]Mk 10:6 [f]Da 9:26; 12:1; Joel 2:2
13:21 [g]Lk 17:23; 21:8
13:22 [h]Mt 7:15 [i]Jn 4:48; 2Th 2:9, 10

[a] *14* Daniel 9:27; 11:31; 12:11 [b] *14* Or *he*; also in verse 29
[c] *21* Or *Messiah*

13:23 your guard;[j] I have told you everything ahead of
j2Pe 3:17 time.
[24]"But in those days, following that distress,

" 'the sun will be darkened,
and the moon will not give its light;
[25]the stars will fall from the sky,
13:25 and the heavenly bodies will be
kIsa 13:10; 34:4; shaken.'[a][k]

Mt 24:29 [26]"At that time men will see the Son of Man
13:26 coming in clouds[l] with great power and glory.
lDa 7:13; [27]And he will send his angels and gather his elect
Mt 16:27; from the four winds, from the ends of the earth to
Rev 1:7 the ends of the heavens.[m]
13:27 [28]"Now learn this lesson from the fig tree: As soon
mZec 2:6 as its twigs get tender and its leaves come out, you
know that summer is near. [29]Even so, when you see
these things happening, you know that it is near,
13:30 right at the door. [30]I tell you the truth, this genera-
nLk 17:25 tion[b][n] will certainly not pass away until all these
oMk 9:1 things have happened.[o] [31]Heaven and earth will
13:31 pass away, but my words will never pass away.[p]
pMt 5:18

The Day and Hour Unknown

[32]"No one knows about that day or hour, not
13:32 even the angels in heaven, nor the Son, but only
qAc 1:7; the Father.[q] [33]Be on guard! Be alert[c]![r] You do not
1Th 5:1,2 know when that time will come. [34]It's like a man
13:33 going away: He leaves his house and puts his ser-
r1Th 5:6 vants[s] in charge, each with his assigned task, and
13:34 tells the one at the door to keep watch.
sMt 25:14 [35]"Therefore keep watch because you do not
know when the owner of the house will come
back—whether in the evening, or at midnight, or
when the rooster crows, or at dawn. [36]If he comes
suddenly, do not let him find you sleeping. [37]What
13:37 I say to you, I say to everyone: 'Watch!' "[t]
tLk 12:35-40

Jesus Anointed at Bethany

14:1 **14** Now the Passover[u] and the Feast of Unleav-
uJn 11:55; 13:1 ened Bread were only two days away, and
vMt 12:14 the chief priests and the teachers of the law were
looking for some sly way to arrest Jesus and kill
him.[v] [2]"But not during the Feast," they said, "or
14:3 the people may riot."
wMt 21:17 [3]While he was in Bethany,[w] reclining at the
xLk 7:37-39 table in the home of a man known as Simon the
Leper, a woman came with an alabaster jar of very
expensive perfume, made of pure nard. She broke
the jar and poured the perfume on his head.[x]
[4]Some of those present were saying indignantly
to one another, "Why this waste of perfume? [5]It
could have been sold for more than a year's
wages[d] and the money given to the poor." And
they rebuked her harshly.
[6]"Leave her alone," said Jesus. "Why are you
bothering her? She has done a beautiful thing to

[a] *25* Isaiah 13:10; 34:4 [b] *30* Or *race* [c] *33* Some manuscripts *alert and pray* [d] *5* Greek *than three hundred denarii*

A Beautiful Thing

MK 14:1-11

A woman approaches and breaks an alabaster jar of expensive perfume (see the note on Mt 26:6-13, page 1630). We know from John's Gospel that the unnamed woman here is Mary, the sister of Martha and Lazarus. The word broke *here literally means "to shatter completely." This woman doesn't hold anything back. She pours all of the fragrant oil on Jesus' head. To some of those present, her actions seem foolish and wasteful. But Jesus sees a beautiful thing; he sees a complete outpouring of her love.*

Today, each of us can be like that woman if we are willing to break our most precious gift—the gift of ourselves—and pour all we have before our Savior (see the character sketch for this woman on page 1843).

Heavenly Wine

MK 14:25

Most of us are familiar with Leonardo da Vinci's famous painting The Last Supper. *It displays the disciples with frozen expressions on their faces. In reality, that night must have been very different. It is Jesus' last meal. The sadness of the occasion is overwhelming as Jesus tells his disciples that this is the last time he'll drink from the fruit of the vine in this lifetime. Yet Jesus ends his statement with an exclamation of hope. He speaks of his second coming, the reality of life beyond death, and of the kingdom of God. Many of us picture heaven as a vague, dreamy place. This is neither Jesus' vision nor what he tries to communicate to us. In truth and reality, we, the redeemed, will celebrate with our Redeemer as he drinks new, fresh, heavenly wine.*

me. 7The poor you will always have with you, and
you can help them any time you want.[y] But you 14:7 [y]Dt 15:11
will not always have me. 8She did what she could.
She poured perfume on my body beforehand to
prepare for my burial.[z] 9I tell you the truth, wher- 14:8 [z]Jn 19:40
ever the gospel is preached throughout the world,[a]
what she has done will also be told, in memory 14:9 [a]Mt 24:14;
of her.” Mk 16:15
10Then Judas Iscariot, one of the Twelve,[b] went 14:10
to the chief priests to betray Jesus to them.[c] 11They [b]Mk 3:16-19
were delighted to hear this and promised to give [c]Mt 10:4
him money. So he watched for an opportunity to
hand him over.

The Lord's Supper

12On the first day of the Feast of Unleavened
Bread, when it was customary to sacrifice the
Passover lamb,[d] Jesus' disciples asked him, 14:12
“Where do you want us to go and make prepara- [d]Ex 12:1-11;
tions for you to eat the Passover?” Dt 16:1-4;
13So he sent two of his disciples, telling them, 1Co 5:7
“Go into the city, and a man carrying a jar of
water will meet you. Follow him. 14Say to the
owner of the house he enters, ‘The Teacher asks:
Where is my guest room, where I may eat the
Passover with my disciples?’ 15He will show you a 14:15
large upper room,[e] furnished and ready. Make [e]Ac 1:13
preparations for us there.”
16The disciples left, went into the city and found
things just as Jesus had told them. So they prepared the Passover.
17When evening came, Jesus arrived with the
Twelve. 18While they were reclining at the table
eating, he said, “I tell you the truth, one of you
will betray me—one who is eating with me.”
19They were saddened, and one by one they
said to him, “Surely not I?”
20“It is one of the Twelve,” he replied, “one who 14:20
dips bread into the bowl with me.[f] 21The Son of [f]Jn 13:18-27
Man[g] will go just as it is written about him. But 14:21
woe to that man who betrays the Son of Man! It [g]Mt 8:20
would be better for him if he had not been born.”
22While they were eating, Jesus took bread, 14:22
gave thanks and broke it,[h] and gave it to his dis- [h]Mt 14:19
ciples, saying, “Take it; this is my body.”
23Then he took the cup, gave thanks and offered 14:23
it to them, and they all drank from it.[i] [i]1Co 10:16
24“This is my blood of the[a] covenant,[j] which is 14:24
poured out for many,” he said to them. 25“I tell [j]Mt 26:28
you the truth, I will not drink again of the fruit of
the vine until that day when I drink it anew in the 14:25
kingdom of God.”[k] [k]Mt 3:2
26When they had sung a hymn, they went out 14:26
to the Mount of Olives.[l] [l]Mt 21:1

Jesus Predicts Peter's Denial

27“You will all fall away,” Jesus told them, “for
it is written:

[a] *24* Some manuscripts *the new*

" 'I will strike the shepherd,
14:27 [m]Zec 13:7 — and the sheep will be scattered.'[a][m]

14:28 [n]Mk 16:7 — 28 But after I have risen, I will go ahead of you into
Galilee."[n]
29 Peter declared, "Even if all fall away, I will not."
30 "I tell you the truth," Jesus answered,
"today—yes, tonight—before the rooster crows
14:30 [o]ver 66-72; Lk 22:34; Jn 13:38 — twice[b] you yourself will disown me three times."[o]
31 But Peter insisted emphatically, "Even if I have
to die with you,[p] I will never disown you." And
14:31 [p]Lk 22:33; Jn 13:37 — all the others said the same.

Gethsemane

32 They went to a place called Gethsemane, and
Jesus said to his disciples, "Sit here while I pray."
14:33 [q]Mt 4:21 — 33 He took Peter, James and John[q] along with him,
and he began to be deeply distressed and trou-
bled. 34 "My soul is overwhelmed with sorrow to
14:34 [r]Jn 12:27 — the point of death,"[r] he said to them. "Stay here
and keep watch."
35 Going a little farther, he fell to the ground and
14:35 [s]ver 41; Mt 26:18 — prayed that if possible the hour[s] might pass from
him. 36 "*Abba*,[c] Father,"[t] he said, "everything is
14:36 [t]Ro 8:15; Gal 4:6 [u]Mt 20:22 [v]Mt 26:39 — possible for you. Take this cup[u] from me. Yet not
what I will, but what you will."[v]
37 Then he returned to his disciples and found
them sleeping. "Simon," he said to Peter, "are you
asleep? Could you not keep watch for one hour?
38 Watch and pray so that you will not fall into
14:38 [w]Mt 6:13 [x]Ro 7:22,23 — temptation.[w] The spirit is willing, but the body is
weak."[x]
39 Once more he went away and prayed the same
thing. 40 When he came back, he again found them
sleeping, because their eyes were heavy. They did
not know what to say to him.
41 Returning the third time, he said to them, "Are
14:41 [y]ver 35; Mt 26:18 — you still sleeping and resting? Enough! The hour[y]
has come. Look, the Son of Man is betrayed into
the hands of sinners. 42 Rise! Let us go! Here
comes my betrayer!"

Jesus Arrested

14:43 [z]Mt 10:4 — 43 Just as he was speaking, Judas,[z] one of the
Twelve, appeared. With him was a crowd armed
with swords and clubs, sent from the chief priests,
the teachers of the law, and the elders.
44 Now the betrayer had arranged a signal with
them: "The one I kiss is the man; arrest him and
lead him away under guard." 45 Going at once to
14:45 [a]Mt 23:7 — Jesus, Judas said, "Rabbi!"[a] and kissed him.
46 The men seized Jesus and arrested him. 47 Then
one of those standing near drew his sword and
struck the servant of the high priest, cutting off
his ear.
48 "Am I leading a rebellion," said Jesus, "that
you have come out with swords and clubs to capture me? 49 Every day I was with you, teaching in

[a] *27* Zech. 13:7 [b] *30* Some early manuscripts do not have *twice.* [c] *36* Aramaic for *Father*

Abba

MK 14:36

Jesus cries out, Abba, which means "Father," in a beautiful and intimate way. It's an expression that the Jews of that day would never have dreamed of using toward God. With that word, Jesus expresses his close relationship with God as his Father. Abba is a title used only by a child to his or her daddy. Jesus' heart is breaking, and he is asking for a change of plans, not as a disgruntled worker but as a son (see the note on Mt 26:36–46, page 1631).

Paul encourages believers to approach God with the same sort of intimacy: "For you did not receive a spirit that makes you a slave again to fear, but you received the Spirit of sonship. And by him we cry, 'Abba, Father'" (Ro 8:15). Today, take a moment to speak to God—not as you would speak to a commander or superior, but as you would speak to your daddy.

Blasphemy!

MK 14:55-65

Jesus claims, as he stands before the high priest, that he will sit at God's right hand and journey through the clouds. "Blasphemy!" the high priest cries, meaning that Jesus is insulting and defaming God. This is no ordinary man who is outraged by Jesus' claims. The high priest was established by God as the one allowed to enter into God's presence. He was the most important religious leader of the day. And blasphemy was a crime worthy of the death penalty according to Mosaic Law (Lev 24:16). The false accusers at Jesus' trial do not need to make an accusation that warrants a sentence of death for Jesus. He himself makes a claim that automatically does so, evidence of his amazing willingness to suffer and die for us.

Think of all Jesus has said and done, and then put yourself at that trial. You hear Jesus make this claim about himself. Would you believe Jesus' claim any more than those present at his trial? When Jesus was on earth, even the elite and learned did not see him for who he is. Ponder this, and praise God for opening your eyes to the truth of Jesus.

the temple courts,[b] and you did not arrest me. But
the Scriptures must be fulfilled."[c] 50Then everyone
deserted him and fled.[d]
51A young man, wearing nothing but a linen
garment, was following Jesus. When they seized
him, 52he fled naked, leaving his garment behind.

Before the Sanhedrin

53They took Jesus to the high priest, and all the
chief priests, elders and teachers of the law came
together. 54Peter followed him at a distance, right
into the courtyard of the high priest.[e] There he sat
with the guards and warmed himself at the fire.[f]
55The chief priests and the whole Sanhedrin[g]
were looking for evidence against Jesus so that
they could put him to death, but they did not find
any. 56Many testified falsely against him, but their
statements did not agree.
57Then some stood up and gave this false testimony against him: 58"We heard him say, 'I will
destroy this man-made temple and in three days
will build another,[h] not made by man.' " 59Yet
even then their testimony did not agree.
60Then the high priest stood up before them and
asked Jesus, "Are you not going to answer? What
is this testimony that these men are bringing
against you?" 61But Jesus remained silent and gave
no answer.[i]
Again the high priest asked him, "Are you the
Christ,[a] the Son of the Blessed One?"[j]
62"I am," said Jesus. "And you will see the Son
of Man sitting at the right hand of the Mighty One
and coming on the clouds of heaven."[k]
63The high priest tore his clothes.[l] "Why do we
need any more witnesses?" he asked. 64"You have
heard the blasphemy. What do you think?"
They all condemned him as worthy of death.[m]
65Then some began to spit at him; they blindfolded him, struck him with their fists, and said,
"Prophesy!" And the guards took him and beat
him.[n]

Peter Disowns Jesus

66While Peter was below in the courtyard,[o] one
of the servant girls of the high priest came by.
67When she saw Peter warming himself,[p] she
looked closely at him.
"You also were with that Nazarene, Jesus,"[q] she
said.
68But he denied it. "I don't know or understand
what you're talking about,"[r] he said, and went out
into the entryway.[b]
69When the servant girl saw him there, she said
again to those standing around, "This fellow is
one of them." 70Again he denied it.[s]
After a little while, those standing near said to
Peter, "Surely you are one of them, for you are a
Galilean."[t]

14:49 [b]Mt 26:55 [c]Isa 53:7-12; Mt 1:22
14:50 [d]ver 27
14:54 [e]Mt 26:3 [f]Jn 18:18
14:55 [g]Mt 5:22
14:58 [h]Mk 15:29; Jn 2:19
14:61 [i]Isa 53:7; Mt 27:12,14; Mk 15:5; Lk 23:9; Jn 19:9 [j]Mt 16:16; Jn 4:25,26
14:62 [k]Rev 1:7
14:63 [l]Lev 10:6; 21:10; Nu 14:6; Ac 14:14
14:64 [m]Lev 24:16
14:65 [n]Mt 16:21
14:66 [o]ver 54
14:67 [p]ver 54 [q]Mk 1:24
14:68 [r]ver 30,72
14:70 [s]ver 30,68, 72 [t]Ac 2:7

[a] *61* Or *Messiah* [b] *68* Some early manuscripts *entryway and the rooster crowed*

71He began to call down curses on himself, and
14:71 he swore to them, “I don’t know this man you’re
[u]ver 30,72 talking about.”[u]
72Immediately the rooster crowed the second
time.[a] Then Peter remembered the word Jesus had
14:72 spoken to him: “Before the rooster crows twice[b]
[v]ver 30,68 you will disown me three times.”[v] And he broke
down and wept.

Jesus Before Pilate

15:1 15 Very early in the morning, the chief priests,
[w]Mt 27:1; with the elders, the teachers of the law[w] and
Lk 22:66 [x]Mt 5:22 the whole Sanhedrin,[x] reached a decision. They
[y]Mt 27:2 bound Jesus, led him away and handed him over
to Pilate.[y]
15:2 [z]ver 9,12,18, 2“Are you the king of the Jews?”[z] asked Pilate.
26; Mt 2:2 “Yes, it is as you say,” Jesus replied.
3The chief priests accused him of many things.
4So again Pilate asked him, “Aren’t you going to
answer? See how many things they are accusing
you of.”
15:5 5But Jesus still made no reply,[a] and Pilate was
[a]Mk 14:61 amazed.
6Now it was the custom at the Feast to release a
prisoner whom the people requested. 7A man
called Barabbas was in prison with the insurrec-
tionists who had committed murder in the uprising. 8The crowd came up and asked Pilate to do
for them what he usually did.
15:9 9“Do you want me to release to you the king of
[b]ver 2 the Jews?”[b] asked Pilate, 10knowing it was out of
envy that the chief priests had handed Jesus over
15:11 to him. 11But the chief priests stirred up the crowd
[c]Ac 3:14 to have Pilate release Barabbas[c] instead.
12“What shall I do, then, with the one you call
the king of the Jews?” Pilate asked them.
13“Crucify him!” they shouted.
14“Why? What crime has he committed?” asked
Pilate.
But they shouted all the louder, “Crucify him!”
15:15 15Wanting to satisfy the crowd, Pilate released
[d]Isa 53:6 Barabbas to them. He had Jesus flogged,[d] and
handed him over to be crucified.

The Soldiers Mock Jesus

15:16 16The soldiers led Jesus away into the palace[e]
[e]Jn 18:28, 33; 19:9 (that is, the Praetorium) and called together the
whole company of soldiers. 17They put a purple
robe on him, then twisted together a crown of
15:18 thorns and set it on him. 18And they began to call
[f]ver 2 out to him, “Hail, king of the Jews!”[f] 19Again and
again they struck him on the head with a staff and
spit on him. Falling on their knees, they paid
homage to him. 20And when they had mocked
15:20 him, they took off the purple robe and put his
[g]Heb 13:12 own clothes on him. Then they led him out[g] to
crucify him.

[a] 72 Some early manuscripts do not have *the second time.*
[b] 72 Some early manuscripts do not have *twice.*

Peter’s Denial

MK 14:66–72

In Mark 14:29 Peter insists, “Even if all fall away, I will not.” Later he tells Jesus, “Even if I have to die with you, I will never disown you” (Mk 14:31). These words are typical for Peter, who is zealous and vocal. But soon after, with the same vigor he uses to proclaim his devotion, Peter denies his Lord (Mk 14:71). Peter’s faith is strong enough to take him into the courtyard near where Jesus is being tried, but not strong enough to get him through the test of recognition as a follower. And while it’s easy to condemn Peter, perhaps we should instead consider how we, too, have at times failed to recognize our Lord or stand up for our faith. Peter’s confident assurance that he will never deny Jesus is based on his own strength, which is too weak to stand the test. Not until the day of Pentecost does Peter receive the power that allows him not only to profess his love for Christ but also to courageously address thousands with the message of a risen Lord (Ac 2:14–41).

The Curtain

MK 15:38

The curtain spoken of in *Mark 15:38 refers to the* curtain of the temple that con-*cealed* the Most Holy Place. *Estab-lished* by God *when Moses built* the tabernacle in the desert (Ex 26:31–33) *and when* Solomon built the temple (2Ch 3:14), *it separated* God's presence *from humanity.*

This heavy curtain *is miracu-lously* torn in two from top to bot-tom *at the very* moment Jesus *dies.* Its *tearing opens up a new way* to approach God. Hebrews 10:19–20 says, *"We have confi-dence* to enter the Most Holy Place *by the blood of Jesus, by a new and living way opened for us* through the curtain, that is, his *body."* Because of Jesus' *sacrifice and because the temple's curtain was torn in two, each believer can* now enter God's holy presence *through Jesus, the new, everlast-ing high priest* (Heb 2:17).

The Crucifixion

21 A certain man from Cyrene,[h] Simon, the father
of Alexander and Rufus,[i] was passing by on his
way in from the country, and they forced him to
carry the cross.[j] 22 They brought Jesus to the place
called Golgotha (which means The Place of the
Skull). 23 Then they offered him wine mixed with
myrrh,[k] but he did not take it. 24 And they crucified him. Dividing up his clothes, they cast lots[l]
to see what each would get.
25 It was the third hour when they crucified him.
26 The written notice of the charge against him
read: THE KING OF THE JEWS.[m] 27 They crucified two
robbers with him, one on his right and one on his
left.[a] 29 Those who passed by hurled insults at him,
shaking their heads[n] and saying, "So! You who
are going to destroy the temple and build it in
three days,[o] 30 come down from the cross and save
yourself!"
31 In the same way the chief priests and the
teachers of the law mocked him[p] among themselves. "He saved others," they said, "but he can't
save himself! 32 Let this Christ,[b][q] this King of Israel,[r] come down now from the cross, that we may
see and believe." Those crucified with him also
heaped insults on him.

The Death of Jesus

33 At the sixth hour darkness came over the
whole land until the ninth hour.[s] 34 And at the
ninth hour Jesus cried out in a loud voice, *"Eloi,
Eloi, lama sabachthani?"*—which means, "My
God, my God, why have you forsaken me?"[c][t]
35 When some of those standing near heard this,
they said, "Listen, he's calling Elijah."
36 One man ran, filled a sponge with wine vinegar,[u] put it on a stick, and offered it to Jesus to
drink. "Now leave him alone. Let's see if Elijah
comes to take him down," he said.
37 With a loud cry, Jesus breathed his last.[v]
38 The curtain of the temple was torn in two
from top to bottom.[w] 39 And when the centurion,[x]
who stood there in front of Jesus, heard his cry
and[d] saw how he died, he said, "Surely this man
was the Son[e] of God!"[y]
40 Some women were watching from a distance.[z]
Among them were Mary Magdalene, Mary the
mother of James the younger and of Joses, and
Salome.[a] 41 In Galilee these women had followed
him and cared for his needs. Many other women
who had come up with him to Jerusalem were
also there.[b]

The Burial of Jesus

42 It was Preparation Day (that is, the day before
the Sabbath).[c] So as evening approached, 43 Joseph

15:21 [h]Mt 27:32 [i]Ro 16:13 [j]Mt 27:32; Lk 23:26
15:23 [k]ver 36; Ps 69:21; Pr 31:6
15:24 [l]Ps 22:18
15:26 [m]ver 2
15:29 [n]Ps 22:7; 109:25 [o]Mk 14:58; Jn 2:19
15:31 [p]Ps 22:7
15:32 [q]Mk 14:61 [r]ver 2
15:33 [s]Am 8:9
15:34 [t]Ps 22:1
15:36 [u]ver 23; Ps 69:21
15:37 [v]Jn 19:30
15:38 [w]Heb 10:19, 20
15:39 [x]ver 45 [y]Mk 1:1,11; 9:7; Mt 4:3
15:40 [z]Ps 38:11 [a]Mk 16:1; Lk 24:10; Jn 19:25
15:41 [b]Mt 27:55, 56; Lk 8:2,3
15:42 [c]Mt 27:62; Jn 19:31

[a] 27 Some manuscripts *left,* 28 *and the scripture was fulfilled which says, "He was counted with the lawless ones"* (Isaiah 53:12) [b] 32 Or *Messiah* [c] 34 Psalm 22:1 [d] 39 Some manuscripts do not have *heard his cry and* [e] 39 Or *a son*

of Arimathea, a prominent member of the Coun-
15:43 [d]Mt 5:22 cil,[d] who was himself waiting for the kingdom of
[e]Mt 3:2; God,[e] went boldly to Pilate and asked for Jesus'
Lk 2:25,38 body. 44Pilate was surprised to hear that he was
already dead. Summoning the centurion, he asked
him if Jesus had already died. 45When he learned
15:45 [f]ver 39 from the centurion[f] that it was so, he gave the
body to Joseph. 46So Joseph bought some linen
cloth, took down the body, wrapped it in the
linen, and placed it in a tomb cut out of rock.
Then he rolled a stone against the entrance of the
15:46 [g]Mk 16:3 tomb.[g] 47Mary Magdalene and Mary the mother of
Joses[h] saw where he was laid.

15:47 [h]ver 40

The Resurrection

16 When the Sabbath was over, Mary Magda-
16:1 lene, Mary the mother of James, and Salo-
[i]Lk 23:56; me bought spices[i] so that they might go to anoint
Jn 19:39,40 Jesus' body. 2Very early on the first day of the
week, just after sunrise, they were on their way
to the tomb 3and they asked each other, "Who will
roll the stone away from the entrance of the
16:3 [j]Mk 15:46 tomb?"[j]
4But when they looked up, they saw that the
stone, which was very large, had been rolled
away. 5As they entered the tomb, they saw a
16:5 young man dressed in a white robe[k] sitting on the
[k]Jn 20:12 right side, and they were alarmed.
6"Don't be alarmed," he said. "You are looking
16:6 [l]Mk 1:24 for Jesus the Nazarene,[l] who was crucified. He
has risen! He is not here. See the place where they
laid him. 7But go, tell his disciples and Peter, 'He
16:7 is going ahead of you into Galilee. There you will
[m]Jn 21:1-23 see him,[m] just as he told you.' "[n]
[n]Mk 14:28 8Trembling and bewildered, the women went
out and fled from the tomb. They said nothing to
anyone, because they were afraid.

[The earliest manuscripts and some other ancient witnesses do not have Mark 16:9–20.]

9When Jesus rose early on the first day of the
16:9 [o]Jn 20:11-18 week, he appeared first to Mary Magdalene,[o] out
of whom he had driven seven demons. 10She went
and told those who had been with him and who
were mourning and weeping. 11When they heard
16:11 that Jesus was alive and that she had seen him,
[p]ver 13,14; they did not believe it.[p]
Lk 24:11 12Afterward Jesus appeared in a different form
to two of them while they were walking in the
16:12 [q]Lk 24:13-32 country.[q] 13These returned and reported it to the
rest; but they did not believe them either.
14Later Jesus appeared to the Eleven as they
were eating; he rebuked them for their lack of
16:14 faith and their stubborn refusal to believe those
[r]Lk 24:36-43 who had seen him after he had risen.[r]
16:15 15He said to them, "Go into all the world and
[s]Mt 28:18- preach the good news to all creation.[s] 16Whoever
20; Lk 24:47, 48 believes and is baptized will be saved, but whoever

Faithful Women

MK 16:1-8

Three women travel to Jesus' tomb, not because they expect him to be alive, but because they are his faithful friends and desire to care for his body. They worry about getting into the tomb (Mk 16:3), but what must trouble them even more is the thought of looking on their Lord's lifeless face. Still, love carries them forward, step by step. They arrive at the tomb and look up (Mk 16:4), astonished by what they see. Because they were willing to honor the "dead" Jesus, God allows them to be the first to learn of the resurrection of Jesus Christ and to experience the greatest moment in history (see the character sketch for these women on page 1941).

Miracles Happen

MK 16:17-20

Although Mark 16:9-20 quite likely wasn't part of Mark's original Gospel, these verses serve as a valuable testimony to the vitality of the early church.

As the disciples travel and preach, Jesus is with them. He is their co-worker, laboring beside them and making their efforts successful. He works with them (Mk 16:20). Yet how can Jesus possibly be working with the disciples after *he has ascended? The key is in three little words in Mark 16:17: "In my name . . ." As the disciples share their lives and experiences, they use Jesus' name—which, in fact, is calling on the power behind that name. Consequently, miracles happen. Lives are changed. By these miracles, Jesus' words while here on earth are confirmed.*

Today we see the miracle of redemption, but we do not as often see some of the miracles listed in Mark 16:17-18. However, the power of Jesus is still here among us (Mt 28:20) and his words still sustain us (Heb 1:3). Thank God for Jesus, your co-worker, as you set out today. And pray that you will discover more of the power behind his name.

does not believe will be condemned.[t] 17And these
signs will accompany those who believe: In my
name they will drive out demons;[u] they will speak
in new tongues;[v] 18they will pick up snakes[w] with
their hands; and when they drink deadly poison,
it will not hurt them at all; they will place their
hands on[x] sick people, and they will get well."
19After the Lord Jesus had spoken to them, he
was taken up into heaven[y] and he sat at the right
hand of God.[z] 20Then the disciples went out and
preached everywhere, and the Lord worked with
them and confirmed his word by the signs that
accompanied it.

16:16 [t]Jn 3:16,18, 36; Ac 16:31

16:17 [u]Mk 9:38; Lk 10:17; Ac 5:16; 8:7; 16:18; 19:13-16 [v]Ac 2:4; 10:46; 19:6; 1Co 12:10, 28,30

16:18 [w]Lk 10:19; Ac 28:3-5 [x]Ac 6:6

16:19 [y]Lk 24:50, 51; Jn 6:62; Ac 1:9-11; 1Ti 3:16 [z]Ps 110:1; Ro 8:34; Col 3:1; Heb 1:3; 12:2

The compassion of Jesus Christ.

This historical account of the life of Jesus is addressed to an individual, Theophilus, who was probably a new convert and a friend of its author, Luke. As a physician Luke was skilled in the observation and assessment of people's needs. His gospel account reflects this skill as he records Jesus' compassion for those who needed his healing touch and caring words.

Luke calls special attention to Jesus' concern for the outcasts of society, primarily women, children and the poor. We meet Mary and Elizabeth, two women who worship God, and our hearts warm as we watch them willingly follow God's plan for their lives (Lk 1). We long to live like Anna, who never stops growing in her faith (Lk 2). We witness a widow's only son come back to life (Lk 7) and catch a glimpse of the many women who follow Jesus faithfully and provide for his needs (Lk 8). We learn the importance of balanced priorities as we encounter Martha's harried hospitality (Lk 10). We rejoice in the healing of an unnamed woman with a damaging disability (Lk 13). In reading two of Jesus' many parables, we celebrate with the woman who finds her lost coin (Lk 15) and cheer for the persistent widow whose request is granted by the unjust judge (Lk 18).

Through the parable of the Good Samaritan (Lk 10) and Jesus' encounter with Zacchaeus (Lk 19), Luke reinforces our need to show love. This underlying principle is the life-changing message of Luke: God loves his people and offers the gift of salvation to all regardless of age, sex or race.

Quick Study

Author
Luke, a physician, a Gentile and a companion of Paul.

Date Written
Probably between A.D. 59 and 63, although some think it may have been written in the 70s or 80s.

Setting
Israel, primarily the regions of Galilee, Judea and Perea.

Key Passage
Luke 9:20 " 'But what about you?' he asked. 'Who do you say I am?' Peter answered, 'The Christ of God.' "

Outline

Jesus and John the Baptist's births foretold.
Lk 1:1-56

John the Baptist's birth.
Lk 1:57-80

Jesus' birth and early life.
Lk 2

Jesus' baptism and genealogy.
Lk 3

Jesus' temptation.
Lk 4:1-13

Teachings, healings and miracles.
Lk 4:14–10:24

Stories and teachings.
Lk 10:25–21:38

The Last Supper and the betrayal.
Lk 22:1-62

Jesus' trial.
Lk 22:63–23:25

Jesus' death and burial.
Lk 23:26-56

Jesus' resurrection.
Lk 24:1-49

Jesus' ascension.
Lk 24:50-53

The Women of Luke

✢	**Mary, mother of Jesus**	*A faithful young woman.* Lk 1-2; 8:19-21 (page 1613)
✢	**Elizabeth**	*Finally! A son!* Lk 1:5-80 (page 1614)
✢	**Anna**	*Widow and prophet.* Lk 2:36-38 (page 1645)
✢	**Herodias**	*John the Baptist condemned her actions.* Lk 3:19-20 (page 1779)
✢	**Simon Peter's mother-in-law**	*Healed of a fever.* Lk 4:38-39 (page 1687)
✢	**Widow of Nain**	*Her son was raised.* Lk 7:11-17 (page 1688)
✢	**Sinful woman at Simon's house**	*She lavished her love on Jesus.* Lk 7:36-50 (page 1713)
	Joanna	*One of Herod's household.* Lk 8:1-3; 24:10
✢	**Mary Magdalene**	*Seven demons were cast out of her.* Lk 8:1-3; 24:10 (page 1714)
	Susanna	*Supported Jesus out of her own means.* Lk 8:1-3
✢	**Woman subject to bleeding**	*Healed after 12 years of suffering.* Lk 8:43-48 (page 1745)
✢	**Jairus's daughter**	*A dead girl brought back to life.* Lk 8:41-56 (page 1746)
✢	**Mary of Bethany**	*She hung on all of Jesus' words.* Lk 10:38-41 (page 1843)
✢	**Martha**	*Confused priorities.* Lk 10:38-41 (page 1844)
	A woman in the crowd	*She called Jesus' mother blessed.* Lk 11:27-28
✢	**Crippled woman**	*Made whole!* Lk 13:10-17 (page 1877)
	Woman with dough	*Jesus uses her as a comparison.* Lk 13:20-21
	Woman who lost a coin	*A time to rejoice.* Lk 15:8-10
	Importunate widow	*Persistence pays off.* Lk 18:1-8
	Woman with seven husbands	*A lesson about heaven.* Lk 20:27-40
✢	**Widow with two coins**	*Cheerful giver of all she had.* Lk 21:1-4 (page 1911)
	Servant girl	*Recognized Peter.* Lk 22:56-59
✢	**Mary, mother of James**	*Told the disciples that Jesus had risen.* Lk 24:10 (page 1941)

✢ Denotes a sketch written about this character

Introduction

1 Many have undertaken to draw up an account
of the things that have been fulfilled[a] among
us, 2 just as they were handed down to us by those
who from the first[a] were eyewitnesses[b] and servants of the word.[c] 3 Therefore, since I myself have
carefully investigated everything from the beginning, it seemed good also to me to write an orderly account[d] for you, most excellent[e] Theophilus,[f]
4 so that you may know the certainty of the things
you have been taught.[g]

The Birth of John the Baptist Foretold

5 In the time of Herod king of Judea[h] there was a
priest named Zechariah, who belonged to the
priestly division of Abijah;[i] his wife Elizabeth was
also a descendant of Aaron. 6 Both of them were
upright in the sight of God, observing all the Lord's
commandments and regulations blamelessly.[j] 7 But
they had no children, because Elizabeth was barren; and they were both well along in years.
8 Once when Zechariah's division was on duty
and he was serving as priest before God,[k] 9 he was
chosen by lot, according to the custom of the
priesthood, to go into the temple of the Lord and
burn incense.[l] 10 And when the time for the burning of incense came, all the assembled worshipers
were praying outside.[m]
11 Then an angel[n] of the Lord appeared to him,
standing at the right side of the altar of incense.[o]
12 When Zechariah saw him, he was startled and
was gripped with fear.[p] 13 But the angel said to
him: "Do not be afraid,[q] Zechariah; your prayer
has been heard. Your wife Elizabeth will bear you
a son, and you are to give him the name John.[r]
14 He will be a joy and delight to you, and many
will rejoice because of his birth,[s] 15 for he will be
great in the sight of the Lord. He is never to take
wine or other fermented drink,[t] and he will be
filled with the Holy Spirit even from birth.[b][u]
16 Many of the people of Israel will he bring back
to the Lord their God. 17 And he will go on before
the Lord,[v] in the spirit and power of Elijah,[w] to
turn the hearts of the fathers to their children[x] and
the disobedient to the wisdom of the righteous—
to make ready a people prepared for the Lord."
18 Zechariah asked the angel, "How can I be sure
of this? I am an old man and my wife is well along
in years."[y]
19 The angel answered, "I am Gabriel.[z] I stand in
the presence of God, and I have been sent to speak
to you and to tell you this good news. 20 And now
you will be silent and not able to speak[a] until the
day this happens, because you did not believe my
words, which will come true at their proper time."
21 Meanwhile, the people were waiting for
Zechariah and wondering why he stayed so long
in the temple. 22 When he came out, he could not

1:2 [a]Mk 1:1; Jn 15:27; Ac 1:21,22 [b]Heb 2:3; 1Pe 5:1; 2Pe 1:16; 1Jn 1:1 [c]Mk 4:14
1:3 [d]Ac 11:4 [e]Ac 24:3; 26:25 [f]Ac 1:1
1:4 [g]Jn 20:31
1:5 [h]Mt 2:1 [i]1Ch 24:10
1:6 [j]Ge 7:1; 1Ki 9:4
1:8 [k]1Ch 24:19; 2Ch 8:14
1:9 [l]Ex 30:7,8; 1Ch 23:13; 2Ch 29:11
1:10 [m]Lev 16:17
1:11 [n]Ac 5:19 [o]Ex 30:1-10
1:12 [p]Jdg 6:22, 23; 13:22
1:13 [q]ver 30; Mt 14:27 [r]ver 60,63
1:14 [s]ver 58
1:15 [t]Nu 6:3; Jdg 13:4; Lk 7:33 [u]Jer 1:5; Gal 1:15
1:17 [v]ver 76 [w]Mt 11:14 [x]Mal 4:5,6
1:18 [y]ver 34; Ge 17:17
1:19 [z]ver 26; Mt 18:10; Da 8:16; 9:21
1:20 [a]Eze 3:26

Consider the Virgin Mary's response to the angel's visitation. A maiden with her whole life before her is asked to risk *scandal, misunderstanding, lunacy charges, and possibly stoning.* Mary, however, doesn't see it as a risk but as an honor to be chosen (even if it included scandal, misunderstanding, and so forth). We read her powerful "Whatever, Lord" in the gospel of Luke: "I am the Lord's servant . . . May it be to me as you have said." (Lk 1:38).

Now that's trust. How impressive that *such a young woman would respond immediately to a request never before made of anyone.* It wasn't as if others had ever been in this situation and Mary could use their experience to guide her. When the angel Gabriel extended God's incredible invitation, Mary was flying solo with no previous experience.

—Patsy Clairmont

[a] 1 Or *been surely believed* [b] 15 Or *from his mother's womb*

The Mystery

LK 1:35

How the Holy Spirit impregnates Mary is one of the Bible's great mysteries. The word overshadow means "to throw a shadow over" and here the word carries the sense of the power of the Most High that overcomes Mary. Somehow, God's glory infuses her with his presence. The same word that is translated "overshadow" here is also used in Matthew 17:5 when Jesus is transfigured and a bright cloud "enveloped" the disciples. We also learn a little of the effects of being exposed to God's glory by observing Moses after he received the Ten Commandments (Ex 34:29). His face glowed like a neon bulb for several days after his encounter with God.

The author of this book, Luke, is a medical doctor. Since he fails to give us a specific description of how the conception takes place, we can assume he is conveying that this action transcends natural law.

speak to them. They realized he had seen a vision 1:22
in the temple, for he kept making signs[b] to them [b]ver 62
but remained unable to speak.
23 When his time of service was completed, he
returned home. 24 After this his wife Elizabeth
became pregnant and for five months remained in
seclusion. 25 "The Lord has done this for me," she
said. "In these days he has shown his favor and
taken away my disgrace[c] among the people." 1:25 [c]Ge 30:23; Isa 4:1

The Birth of Jesus Foretold

26 In the sixth month, God sent the angel Gabri- 1:26
el[d] to Nazareth,[e] a town in Galilee, 27 to a virgin [d]ver 19 [e]Mt 2:23
pledged to be married to a man named Joseph,[f] a
descendant of David. The virgin's name was Mary. 1:27 [f]Mt 1:16,18, 20; Lk 2:4
28 The angel went to her and said, "Greetings, you
who are highly favored! The Lord is with you."
29 Mary was greatly troubled at his words and
wondered what kind of greeting this might be.
30 But the angel said to her, "Do not be afraid,[g] 1:30 [g]ver 13;
Mary, you have found favor with God. 31 You will Mt 14:27
be with child and give birth to a son, and you are 1:31 [h]Isa 7:14;
to give him the name Jesus.[h] 32 He will be great Mt 1:21,25;
and will be called the Son of the Most High.[i] The Lk 2:21
Lord God will give him the throne of his father
David, 33 and he will reign over the house of Jacob 1:32 [i]ver 35,76;
forever; his kingdom[j] will never end."[k] Mk 5:7
34 "How will this be," Mary asked the angel,
"since I am a virgin?" 1:33 [j]Mt 28:18
35 The angel answered, "The Holy Spirit will [k]Da 2:44;
come upon you,[l] and the power of the Most High[m] 7:14,27;
will overshadow you. So the holy one[n] to be born Mic 4:7;
will be called[a] the Son of God.[o] 36 Even Elizabeth Heb 1:8
your relative is going to have a child in her old age, 1:35 [l]Mt 1:18
and she who was said to be barren is in her sixth [m]ver 32,76
month. 37 For nothing is impossible with God."[p] [n]Mk 1:24 [o]Mt 4:3
38 "I am the Lord's servant," Mary answered.
"May it be to me as you have said." Then the 1:37 [p]Mt 19:26
angel left her.

Mary Visits Elizabeth

39 At that time Mary got ready and hurried to a
town in the hill country of Judea,[q] 40 where she 1:39 [q]ver 65
entered Zechariah's home and greeted Elizabeth.
41 When Elizabeth heard Mary's greeting, the baby
leaped in her womb, and Elizabeth was filled with
the Holy Spirit. 42 In a loud voice she exclaimed:
"Blessed are you among women,[r] and blessed is 1:42 [r]Jdg 5:24
the child you will bear! 43 But why am I so favored,
that the mother of my Lord should come to me?
44 As soon as the sound of your greeting reached
my ears, the baby in my womb leaped for joy.
45 Blessed is she who has believed that what the
Lord has said to her will be accomplished!"

Mary's Song

46 And Mary said:

"My soul glorifies the Lord[s] 1:46 [s]Ps 34:2,3

[a] 35 Or *So the child to be born will be called holy,*

47 and my spirit rejoices in God my
Savior,[t]
48 for he has been mindful
of the humble state of his servant.[u]
From now on all generations will call
me blessed,[v]
49 for the Mighty One has done great
things[w] for me—
holy is his name.[x]
50 His mercy extends to those who fear him,
from generation to generation.[y]
51 He has performed mighty deeds with his
arm;[z]
he has scattered those who are proud
in their inmost thoughts.
52 He has brought down rulers from their
thrones
but has lifted up the humble.
53 He has filled the hungry with good
things[a]
but has sent the rich away empty.
54 He has helped his servant Israel,
remembering to be merciful[b]
55 to Abraham and his descendants[c]
forever,
even as he said to our fathers."

56 Mary stayed with Elizabeth for about three
months and then returned home.

The Birth of John the Baptist

57 When it was time for Elizabeth to have her
baby, she gave birth to a son. 58 Her neighbors and
relatives heard that the Lord had shown her great
mercy, and they shared her joy.
59 On the eighth day they came to circumcise[d]
the child, and they were going to name him after
his father Zechariah, 60 but his mother spoke up
and said, "No! He is to be called John."[e]
61 They said to her, "There is no one among your
relatives who has that name."
62 Then they made signs[f] to his father, to find out
what he would like to name the child. 63 He asked
for a writing tablet, and to everyone's astonishment
he wrote, "His name is John."[g] 64 Immediately his
mouth was opened and his tongue was loosed, and
he began to speak,[h] praising God. 65 The neighbors
were all filled with awe, and throughout the hill
country of Judea[i] people were talking about all
these things. 66 Everyone who heard this wondered
about it, asking, "What then is this child going to
be?" For the Lord's hand was with him.[j]

Zechariah's Song

67 His father Zechariah was filled with the Holy
Spirit and prophesied:[k]

68 "Praise be to the Lord, the God of Israel,[l]
because he has come and has
redeemed his people.[m]

1:47 [t]1Ti 1:1; 2:3
1:48 [u]Ps 138:6 [v]Lk 11:27
1:49 [w]Ps 71:19 [x]Ps 111:9
1:50 [y]Ex 20:6; Ps 103:17
1:51 [z]Ps 98:1; Isa 40:10
1:53 [a]Ps 107:9
1:54 [b]Ps 98:3
1:55 [c]Ge 17:19; Ps 132:11; Gal 3:16
1:59 [d]Ge 17:12; Lev 12:3; Lk 2:21; Php 3:5
1:60 [e]ver 13,63
1:62 [f]ver 22
1:63 [g]ver 13,60
1:64 [h]ver 20
1:65 [i]ver 39
1:66 [j]Ge 39:2; Ac 11:21
1:67 [k]Joel 2:28
1:68 [l]Ps 72:18 [m]Ps 111:9; Lk 7:16

Mary Macdougall Macdonald originally wrote this hymn in Gaelic. It was translated into English after her death.

Child in the Manger

Child in the manger, infant
of Mary,
Outcast and Stranger, Lord of
us all,
Child Who inherits all our
transgressions,
All our demerits upon Him fall.

Once the most holy Child
of salvation
Gently and lowly lived here below.
Now as our glorious mighty
Redeemer,
See Him victorious over each foe.

Prophets foretold Him, Infant
of wonder;
Angels behold Him on His throne.
Worthy our Savior of all our
praises;
Happy forever are His own.

—Mary Macdougall Macdonald (1789-1872)

Week 35

Food for the Hungry

A man comes into a meeting room carrying a tray. On the tray are glasses of water. He says to the people in the room, "If you're thirsty, feel free to take a glass of water." Those who are thirsty take a glass; those who are not, shake their heads no. Those who take the water are refreshed; those who are not thirsty do not feel they are missing out on anything.

But consider this: What if someone who is not thirsty says, "Sorry, mister, you can't come in here with that water. We don't want any water, and you're interrupting our meeting"? How would you feel if you were one of the thirsty people? Jesus has some things to say both to those who are thirsty and to those who are not.

What does Jesus call those who are hungry and thirsty for righteousness (Mt 5:6)? What is his promise to them? God is looking for people who hunger and thirst after him (Ps 14:2).

Everyone has a void within that only God can fill. People often try to fill that void with things that do not satisfy. Name some things you have tasted in hopes of easing your hunger. What does God say about the ability of riches to satisfy your hunger (Eze 7:19)? What does he say about materialism (Hag 1:6)?

There are many belief systems in today's society that claim to fill the void in people. What does God say about the "fool" who spreads error concerning God (Isa 32:6)? Do those beliefs satisfy?

What does Jesus claim about himself (Jn 4:10–14; 6:35)? With what will God fill the hungry (Ro 15:13; Col 1:9)?

Enjoying God THROUGH the Word

Read John 6:35–66 (pages 1755–1756). This teaching of Jesus brings about a parting of the ways: "From this time many of his disciples turned back and no longer followed him" (Jn 6:66). What is so offensive about this teaching? Jesus says he is the only food and the only drink that brings life (Jn 6:53–55). Without Jesus you cannot have eternal life. You must go beyond intellectual belief to a life-sustaining relationship. Your relationship with Jesus *is* your life. Unfortunately, this is where many refuse to follow.

If you are hungry for Jesus, praise God! He is drawing you to himself. Be thankful for your thirst—God is working in your life! Danger comes from those who are not thirsty. Because they have no desire for water, they wish to send the man with the water out of the room. Jesus says to the Pharisees, "You shut the kingdom of heaven in men's faces. You yourselves do not enter, nor will you let those enter who are trying to" (Mt 23:13). If you are hungry for Jesus, reach out to him. Don't allow anyone or anything to stand between you and the One who can satisfy.

Enjoying God THROUGH Experience

Go to God in prayer. If you are hungry for him, cry out to be filled. He will fill you "with an inexpressible and glorious joy" (1Pe 1:8). Thank God that he is drawing you to himself. If you do not have this hunger, ask God to fill you with a desire for him, to extend your intellectual beliefs about him from your head to your heart. Pray that you may "grasp how wide and long and high and deep is the love of Christ . . . [so] that you may be filled to the measure of all the fullness of God" (Eph 3:18–19).

Go to page 1738 for your next weekly study.

69 He has raised up a horn[d][n] of salvation
for us
in the house of his servant David[o]
70 (as he said through his holy prophets of
long ago),[p]
71 salvation from our enemies
and from the hand of all who hate
us—
72 to show mercy to our fathers[q]
and to remember his holy covenant,[r]
73 the oath he swore to our father
Abraham:[s]
74 to rescue us from the hand of our
enemies,
and to enable us to serve him[t]
without fear
75 in holiness and righteousness[u] before
him all our days.

76 And you, my child, will be called a
prophet[v] of the Most High;[w]
for you will go on before the Lord to
prepare the way for him,[x]
77 to give his people the knowledge of
salvation
through the forgiveness of their sins,[y]
78 because of the tender mercy of our God,
by which the rising sun[z] will come to
us from heaven
79 to shine on those living in darkness
and in the shadow of death,[a]
to guide our feet into the path of peace."

80 And the child grew and became strong in spirit;[b] and he lived in the desert until he appeared
publicly to Israel.

The Birth of Jesus

2 In those days Caesar Augustus[c] issued a
decree that a census should be taken of the
entire Roman world.[d] 2 (This was the first census
that took place while Quirinius was governor of
Syria.)[e] 3 And everyone went to his own town to
register.
4 So Joseph also went up from the town of Nazareth in Galilee to Judea, to Bethlehem[f] the town
of David, because he belonged to the house and
line of David. 5 He went there to register with
Mary, who was pledged to be married to him and
was expecting a child. 6 While they were there, the
time came for the baby to be born, 7 and she gave
birth to her firstborn, a son. She wrapped him in
cloths and placed him in a manger, because there
was no room for them in the inn.

The Shepherds and the Angels

8 And there were shepherds living out in the
fields nearby, keeping watch over their flocks at
night. 9 An angel[g] of the Lord appeared to them,

1:69 [n]1Sa 2:1,10; Ps 18:2; 89:17; 132:17; Eze 29:21 [o]Mt 1:1
1:70 [p]Jer 23:5
1:72 [q]Mic 7:20 [r]Ps 105:8,9; 106:45; Eze 16:60
1:73 [s]Ge 22:16-18
1:74 [t]Heb 9:14
1:75 [u]Eph 4:24
1:76 [v]Mt 11:9 [w]ver 32,35 [x]ver 17; Mal 3:1
1:77 [y]Jer 31:34; Mk 1:4
1:78 [z]Mal 4:2
1:79 [a]Isa 9:2; 59:9; Mt 4:16; Ac 26:18
1:80 [b]Lk 2:40,52
2:1 [c]Lk 3:1; Mt 22:17 [d]Mt 24:14
2:2 [e]Mt 4:24
2:4 [f]Jn 7:42
2:9 [g]Lk 1:11; Ac 5:19

[d] 69 *Horn* here symbolizes strength.

Expectations

LK 1:76–80

The words that spill from Zechariah's lips must have thrilled his own heart. Yet what Zechariah envisions that day is probably very different from what God has in mind. John will live in the desert. (*Why not raise him in a city, a seat of power?*) And he will live there until he is about 30 years old. (*What about all that wasted time?*) And his lifestyle will be that of one who lives very simply off the land. (*What about rich food and robes of fine cloth?*) And he will die a criminal's death. (*What about receiving honor for his actions?*)

All parents have visions of good things for their children. But few parents dream of the sacrifices that might be asked of their children. Most of us struggle to temper our dreams with the reality of who our children are and what God intends for them. We would choose all the good and none of the difficult. God often has other plans.

and the glory of the Lord shone around them, and
they were terrified. 10But the angel said to them,
"Do not be afraid.[h] I bring you good news of great
joy that will be for all the people. 11Today in the
town of David a Savior[i] has been born to you; he
is Christ[a][j] the Lord. 12This will be a sign[k] to you:
You will find a baby wrapped in cloths and lying
in a manger."

13Suddenly a great company of the heavenly
host appeared with the angel, praising God and
saying,

> 14"Glory to God in the highest,
> and on earth peace[l] to men on whom
> his favor rests."

15When the angels had left them and gone into
heaven, the shepherds said to one another, "Let's
go to Bethlehem and see this thing that has happened, which the Lord has told us about."

16So they hurried off and found Mary and
Joseph, and the baby, who was lying in the
manger. 17When they had seen him, they spread
the word concerning what had been told them
about this child, 18and all who heard it were
amazed at what the shepherds said to them. 19But
Mary treasured up all these things and pondered
them in her heart.[m] 20The shepherds returned, glorifying and praising God[n] for all the things they
had heard and seen, which were just as they had
been told.

Jesus Presented in the Temple

21On the eighth day, when it was time to circumcise him,[o] he was named Jesus, the name the
angel had given him before he had been conceived.[p]

22When the time of their purification according
to the Law of Moses[q] had been completed, Joseph
and Mary took him to Jerusalem to present him
to the Lord 23(as it is written in the Law of the
Lord, "Every firstborn male is to be consecrated
to the Lord"[b]),[r] 24and to offer a sacrifice in keeping
with what is said in the Law of the Lord: "a pair of
doves or two young pigeons."[c][s]

25Now there was a man in Jerusalem called
Simeon, who was righteous and devout.[t] He was
waiting for the consolation of Israel,[u] and the
Holy Spirit was upon him. 26It had been revealed
to him by the Holy Spirit that he would not die
before he had seen the Lord's Christ. 27Moved by
the Spirit, he went into the temple courts. When
the parents brought in the child Jesus to do for
him what the custom of the Law required,[v] 28Simeon took him in his arms and praised God,
saying:

> 29"Sovereign Lord, as you have
> promised,[w]

2:10 [h]Mt 14:27
2:11 [i]Mt 1:21; Jn 4:42; Ac 5:31 [j]Mt 1:16; 16:16,20; Jn 11:27; Ac 2:36
2:12 [k]1Sa 2:34; 2Ki 19:29; Isa 7:14
2:14 [l]Lk 1:79; Ro 5:1; Eph 2:14,17
2:19 [m]ver 51
2:20 [n]Mt 9:8
2:21 [o]Lk 1:59 [p]Lk 1:31
2:22 [q]Lev 12:2-8
2:23 [r]Ex 13:2,12, 15; Nu 3:13
2:24 [s]Lev 12:8
2:25 [t]Lk 1:6 [u]ver 38; Isa 52:9; Lk 23:51
2:27 [v]ver 22
2:29 [w]ver 26

I can imagine Elizabeth, soon-to-be mom of John the Baptist, drawing Mary, soon-to-be mother of Jesus, onto her aging shoulder. Two women, the old and the young, embracing in mutual identification. Two women seeking solace in each other's company. Two women honorably connecting to one another. Sisters of divine circumstance shouldering the future of humanity.

—Patsy Clairmont

[a] *11* Or *Messiah.* "The Christ" (Greek) and "the Messiah" (Hebrew) both mean "the Anointed One"; also in verse 26.
[b] *23* Exodus 13:2,12 [c] *24* Lev. 12:8

2:29 you now dismiss[a] your servant in
[x]Ac 2:24 peace.[x]
30 For my eyes have seen your salvation,[y]
2:30 [y]Isa 52:10; 31 which you have prepared in the sight
Lk 3:6 of all people,
2:32 32 a light for revelation to the Gentiles
[z]Isa 42:6; 49:6; and for glory to your people Israel."[z]
Ac 13:47; 33 The child's father and mother marveled at
26:23 what was said about him. 34 Then Simeon blessed
2:34 them and said to Mary, his mother:[a] "This child
[a]Mt 12:46 is destined to cause the falling[b] and rising of many
[b]Isa 8:14; Mt 21:44; in Israel, and to be a sign that will be spoken
1Co 1:23; against, 35 so that the thoughts of many hearts will
2Co 2:16; be revealed. And a sword will pierce your own
1Pe 2:7,8 soul too."
2:36 36 There was also a prophetess,[c] Anna, the
[c]Ac 21:9 daughter of Phanuel, of the tribe of Asher. She
was very old; she had lived with her husband sev-
en years after her marriage, 37 and then was a wid-
2:37 ow until she was eighty-four.[b][d] She never left the
[d]1Ti 5:9 [e]Ac 13:3; temple but worshiped night and day, fasting and
14:23; 1Ti 5:5 praying.[e] 38 Coming up to them at that very
moment, she gave thanks to God and spoke about
the child to all who were looking forward to the
2:38 [f]ver 25; redemption of Jerusalem.[f]
Isa 40:2; 39 When Joseph and Mary had done everything
Lk 1:68; required by the Law of the Lord, they returned to
24:21 Galilee to their own town of Nazareth.[g] 40 And the
2:39 child grew and became strong; he was filled with
[g]ver 51; Mt 2:23 wisdom, and the grace of God was upon him.[h]

The Boy Jesus at the Temple

2:40 [h]ver 52; 41 Every year his parents went to Jerusalem for
Lk 1:80 2:41 the Feast of the Passover.[i] 42 When he was twelve
[i]Ex 23:15; years old, they went up to the Feast, according to
Dt 16:1-8 the custom. 43 After the Feast was over, while his
parents were returning home, the boy Jesus
stayed behind in Jerusalem, but they were
unaware of it. 44 Thinking he was in their company, they traveled on for a day. Then they began
looking for him among their relatives and friends.
45 When they did not find him, they went back to
Jerusalem to look for him. 46 After three days they
found him in the temple courts, sitting among the
teachers, listening to them and asking them ques-
2:47 tions. 47 Everyone who heard him was amazed[j] at
[j]Mt 7:28 his understanding and his answers. 48 When his
parents saw him, they were astonished. His moth-
2:48 er[k] said to him, "Son, why have you treated us
[k]Mt 12:46 like this? Your father[l] and I have been anxiously
[l]Lk 3:23; 4:22 searching for you."
2:49 49 "Why were you searching for me?" he asked.
[m]Jn 2:16 "Didn't you know I had to be in my Father's
house?"[m] 50 But they did not understand what he
2:50 was saying to them.[n]
[n]Mk 9:32 51 Then he went down to Nazareth with them[o]
2:51 and was obedient to them. But his mother trea-
[o]ver 39; Mt 2:23 [p]ver 19 sured all these things in her heart.[p] 52 And Jesus

[a] *29* Or *promised, / now dismiss* [b] *37* Or *widow for eighty-four years*

Just a Regular Boy

LK 2:40

Jesus, who recognizes his special relationship with God while still young (Lk 2:49), is *in many ways just an ordinary* boy. Like his playmates, he physi*cally matures, gains insights into* life, *grows intellectually, and makes himself a student of God. We struggle to understand this seemingly normal childhood in light of his actually* being *God, but that is part of the wonder of the incarnation (God made flesh).* Jesus truly is *a boy, a boy who understands he has a mission and a purpose and a relatedness to* God that others don't. And yet he, too, skins his knee, *is expected to* obey his mother and needs to *learn addition and subtraction,* just like any other child. Where the "dividing line" exists between *his godly nature and his human nature we comprehend no more than we understand where it exists between our physical and spiritual natures. Some aspects are obvious; others are blurred.* But the beauty and purpose resi*dent in this God-man is apparent to any who will scrutinize his* life—and his death.

grew in wisdom and stature, and in favor with God and men.[q]

John the Baptist Prepares the Way

3 In the fifteenth year of the reign of Tiberius Caesar—when Pontius Pilate[r] was governor of Judea, Herod[s] tetrarch of Galilee, his brother Philip tetrarch of Iturea and Traconitis, and Lysanias tetrarch of Abilene— 2during the high priesthood of Annas and Caiaphas,[t] the word of God came to John[u] son of Zechariah[v] in the desert. 3He went into all the country around the Jordan, preaching a baptism of repentance for the forgiveness of sins.[w] 4As is written in the book of the words of Isaiah the prophet:

"A voice of one calling in the desert,
'Prepare the way for the Lord,
make straight paths for him.
5Every valley shall be filled in,
every mountain and hill made low.
The crooked roads shall become straight,
the rough ways smooth.
6And all mankind will see God's salvation.' "[a][x]

7John said to the crowds coming out to be baptized by him, "You brood of vipers![y] Who warned you to flee from the coming wrath?[z] 8Produce fruit in keeping with repentance. And do not begin to say to yourselves, 'We have Abraham as our father.'[a] For I tell you that out of these stones God can raise up children for Abraham. 9The ax is already at the root of the trees, and every tree that does not produce good fruit will be cut down and thrown into the fire."[b]

10"What should we do then?"[c] the crowd asked.

11John answered, "The man with two tunics should share with him who has none, and the one who has food should do the same."[d]

12Tax collectors also came to be baptized.[e] "Teacher," they asked, "what should we do?"

13"Don't collect any more than you are required to,"[f] he told them.

14Then some soldiers asked him, "And what should we do?"

He replied, "Don't extort money and don't accuse people falsely[g]—be content with your pay."

15The people were waiting expectantly and were all wondering in their hearts if John[h] might possibly be the Christ.[b][i] 16John answered them all, "I baptize you with[c] water.[j] But one more powerful than I will come, the thongs of whose sandals I am not worthy to untie. He will baptize you with the Holy Spirit and with fire.[k] 17His winnowing fork[l] is in his hand to clear his threshing floor and to gather the wheat into his barn, but he will burn up the chaff with unquenchable fire."[m] 18And with

---

Good News?

LK 3:7-18

The crowd's response to John's message might strike us as odd at first. The people seem to soak up his words of judgment and wrath as if they are honey and cream. It's not that they don't understand the image of winnowing (Lk 3:17). They have seen a farmer use a large, wooden fork to toss grain into the air so the lightweight chaff blows away while the grain falls to the ground. This crowd understands that the Messiah will separate those who are to receive punishment from those who are to receive reward. Apparently, John's straightforward message pierces his audience's heart like an arrow, convicting each person of his or her shortcomings and need to repent. The people recognize the truth of what he says and conclude that, if they repent (which includes specific lifestyle changes—Lk 3:11-14), his message is indeed good news, for salvation is at last at hand.

2:52 [q]ver 40; 1Sa 2:26; Lk 1:80
3:1 [r]Mt 27:2 [s]Mt 14:1
3:2 [t]Mt 26:3; Jn 18:13; Ac 4:6 [u]Mt 3:1 [v]Lk 1:13
3:3 [w]ver 16; Mk 1:4
3:6 [x]Isa 40:3-5; Ps 98:2; Isa 42:16; 52:10; Lk 2:30
3:7 [y]Mt 12:34; 23:33 [z]Ro 1:18
3:8 [a]Isa 51:2; Lk 19:9; Jn 8:33,39; Ac 13:26; Ro 4:1,11, 12,16,17; Gal 3:7
3:9 [b]Mt 3:10
3:10 [c]ver 12,14; Ac 2:37; 16:30
3:11 [d]Isa 58:7
3:12 [e]Lk 7:29
3:13 [f]Lk 19:8
3:14 [g]Ex 23:1; Lev 19:11
3:15 [h]Mt 3:1 [i]Jn 1:19,20; Ac 13:25
3:16 [j]ver 3; Mk 1:4 [k]Jn 1:26,33; Ac 1:5; 11:16; 19:4
3:17 [l]Isa 30:24 [m]Mt 13:30; 25:41

[a] 6 Isaiah 40:3-5 [b] 15 Or *Messiah* [c] 16 Or *in*

Simon Peter's Mother-in-Law

Down but Not Out

Thoughts flooded her feverish brain as she lay on her mat. She didn't think so highly of this Jesus everyone was talking about. Simon had taken to following this Jesus—days at a time—throughout the countryside, leaving her daughter to have to manage everything at home. Simon was a very good man, but he was also a very impulsive man.

How inconvenient to be ill when company was expected. She heard voices at the door—Jesus, Simon and others. Oh, if only she weren't sick! But wait, were they talking about her? She heard Simon tell Jesus that she was ill, then Jesus walked over to her mat.

He touched her hand—but it was more than a touch. She felt love and an indefinable sweetness infuse her entire body. It seemed like a dream, but she knew she wasn't asleep. In fact, she felt more awake than she had ever felt in her entire life. It was like being a young girl again. Her fever broke immediately and her energy returned. Clearly, there was something extraordinary about this Jesus, something of God was within him. Perhaps Simon's involvement with him wasn't such a bad thing after all.

She got up off her mat. How could she repay—no, it was more than repay—how could she *honor* this man of God? How could she express her gratitude and, yes, love? She did what she knew best. She went to her daughter and helped cook for their guests. She served them with great joy and reverence.

After the meal, neighbors and townspeople came to their door to see the Master. He healed all their diseases. Her own healing had been no fluke. God was among them, working in power. Some said he was the Messiah. All she knew was that God was with Jesus. She never forgot that day.

Something extraordinary happens when Jesus touches us. We are never the same. Serving him and others is no longer a duty; it is an expression of love and joy. If Jesus has not yet come personally to your home and taken your hand to heal you and make you whole, why not invite him in? He's standing just outside your door.

Simon Peter's Mother-in-law

Matthew 8:14–15

Mark 1:29–31

Luke 4:38–39

Candid SNAPSHOT When Jesus came into Peter's house, he saw Peter's mother-in-law lying in bed with a fever. He touched her hand and the fever left her, and she got up and began to wait on him (Matthew 8:14–15).

Widow of Nain

Unexpected Mercy

She was pale with shock—a widow surrounded by her friends, with her only son on a funeral bier. Within a few minutes, they would give him back to the earth. She still couldn't take it in. He had been such a loving son, moving her into his own home when her husband died. Now he too was dead. Not only did she grieve her son, but also soon she would be destitute.

Jesus watched the drama unfold as he entered the gate of the village. He had seen it played out in the lives of countless poor. Crowds of the dispossessed filled every city—the blind, the insane, the demon-possessed, widows, orphans, runaways, castaways and refugees. There were no social safety nets, no pension checks, public shelters or food pantries. The unfortunate became the unnamed and invisible as they slid through the cracks of their culture. Many resorted to begging, stealing, selling themselves as slaves or prostitutes—merely to survive. They were the "little ones" Jesus loved and came to save.

This widow faced desperate straits for the rest of her days. She did not know Jesus or ask for his help. He merely saw her walking, with her tear-stained face focused on the ground to keep from stumbling. He *saw* her and had compassion. Perhaps in her he saw his own mother, or all the mothers on earth who suffer pain and loss. He had compassion and told her not to cry, and he raised her son from the dead!

Could this woman ever have imagined such a gift from God? Eight hundred years had passed since Elisha raised the son of the Shunammite (2 Ki 4:8-37). Surely God no longer worked that way. That was for the old times, the days of the prophets. Besides, the Shunammite was wealthy and important, but this woman was poor and of no consequence. Did the widow know that one greater than the prophets walked among her neighbors and friends? That her loss was as important to him as the death of any king? Probably not. She only knew that her son had died, and she had nowhere to turn for help—until Jesus saw her.

Widow of Nain
Luke 7:11-17

Sometimes the Lord works miracles on our behalf. Sometimes he looks on us in simple mercy and intervenes to give us back a son, or whatever else it is that is causing our suffering. We can do nothing to earn such favor. When it happens, rejoice *greatly*. Jesus is very much alive. He still dwells among his people.

Candid SNAPSHOT As he approached the town gate, a dead person was being carried out—the only son of his mother, and she was a widow. And a large crowd from the town was with her. When the Lord saw her, his heart went out to her and he said, "Don't cry" (Luke 7:12-13).

many other words John exhorted the people and
3:19 preached the good news to them.
[n]ver 1 19 But when John rebuked Herod[n] the tetrarch
because of Herodias, his brother's wife, and all the
other evil things he had done, 20 Herod added this
3:20 [o]Mt 14:3,4; Mk 6:17-18 to them all: He locked John up in prison.[o]

The Baptism and Genealogy of Jesus

3:21 21 When all the people were being baptized,
[p]Mt 14:23; Mk 1:35; Jesus was baptized too. And as he was praying,[p]
6:46; heaven was opened 22 and the Holy Spirit descend-
Lk 5:16; ed on him[q] in bodily form like a dove. And a voice
6:12; 9:18, came from heaven: "You are my Son,[r] whom I
28; 11:1 love; with you I am well pleased."[s]
3:22 [q]Isa 42:1; 23 Now Jesus himself was about thirty years old
Jn 1:32,33; when he began his ministry.[t] He was the son, so
Ac 10:38 [r]Mt 3:17 it was thought, of Joseph,[u]
[s]Mt 3:17

the son of Heli, 24 the son of Matthat,
3:23 the son of Levi, the son of Melki,
[t]Mt 4:17; the son of Jannai, the son of Joseph,
Ac 1:1
[u]Lk 1:27 25 the son of Mattathias, the son of Amos,
the son of Nahum, the son of Esli,
the son of Naggai, 26 the son of Maath,
the son of Mattathias, the son of Semein,
the son of Josech, the son of Joda,
27 the son of Joanan, the son of Rhesa,
3:27 [v]Mt 1:12 the son of Zerubbabel,[v] the son of Shealtiel,
the son of Neri, 28 the son of Melki,
the son of Addi, the son of Cosam,
the son of Elmadam, the son of Er,
29 the son of Joshua, the son of Eliezer,
the son of Jorim, the son of Matthat,
the son of Levi, 30 the son of Simeon,
the son of Judah, the son of Joseph,
the son of Jonam, the son of Eliakim,
31 the son of Melea, the son of Menna,
3:31 [w]2Sa 5:14; the son of Mattatha, the son of Nathan,[w]
1Ch 3:5 the son of David, 32 the son of Jesse,
the son of Obed, the son of Boaz,
the son of Salmon,[a] the son of Nahshon,
33 the son of Amminadab, the son of Ram,[b]
3:33 [x]Ru 4:18-22; the son of Hezron, the son of Perez,[x]
1Ch 2:10-12 the son of Judah, 34 the son of Jacob,
the son of Isaac, the son of Abraham,
3:34 [y]Ge 11:24,26 the son of Terah, the son of Nahor,[y]
35 the son of Serug, the son of Reu,
the son of Peleg, the son of Eber,
the son of Shelah, 36 the son of Cainan,
3:36 [z]Ge 11:12 the son of Arphaxad,[z] the son of Shem,
[a]Ge 5:28-32 the son of Noah, the son of Lamech,[a]
37 the son of Methuselah, the son of Enoch,
the son of Jared, the son of Mahalalel,
the son of Kenan, 38 the son of Enosh,
3:38 the son of Seth, the son of Adam,
[b]Ge 5:1,2, 6-9 the son of God.[b]

[a] 32 Some early manuscripts *Sala* [b] 33 Some manuscripts *Amminadab, the son of Admin, the son of Arni*; other manuscripts vary widely.

The Blessing

LK 3:22

Jesus is about to begin his ministry. He isn't a sinner, so he doesn't need to be baptized. However, he willingly submits to John's baptism in order to identify with those he has come to save. As the act takes place, God sends his affirmation and blessing. In one sentence, God says, "I identify myself as related to you; you are my Son; I love you; I am so pleased with you." In this way, God blesses Jesus' ministry as he begins to proclaim the truth and prepares to offer himself as a sacrifice. How gracious of God to give Jesus this special "send-off."

If you haven't told your children lately how you feel about them, take a minute to say, "I'm so glad I'm your parent; I love you; I'm so pleased with you." And if you don't have children to deliver that message to, consider who in your life (your spouse? your best friend?) would love to hear those words. Now, go give a blessing.

Tempted

LK 4:1-13

Jesus goes from the high of receiving his Father's affirmation to the low of being tempted by Satan. Note that the devil doesn't tempt Jesus with anything that is beyond Jesus' power to obtain for himself. It's just that the devil asks Jesus to obtain these things in the wrong way and at the wrong time. The devil tempts Jesus to fulfill his natural desire to eat even though this is a time to fast. He tempts Jesus to assume a position of power through self-assertion rather than through reliance on God.

Jesus uses Scripture to counteract each of Satan's enticements. And each Scripture points to God—and nothing else—as the center of life. Not giving God his rightful place in our lives—that is the crux behind each temptation Satan sets before Jesus; it is the heart of Satan's approach to Eve (Ge 3:1-6); and it is at the center of his seduction of us as well.

The Temptation of Jesus

4 Jesus, full of the Holy Spirit,[c] returned from
the Jordan[d] and was led by the Spirit[e] in the
desert, 2where for forty days[f] he was tempted by
the devil. He ate nothing during those days, and at
the end of them he was hungry.
3The devil said to him, "If you are the Son of
God, tell this stone to become bread."
4Jesus answered, "It is written: 'Man does not
live on bread alone.'[a]"[g]
5The devil led him up to a high place and
showed him in an instant all the kingdoms of the
world.[h] 6And he said to him, "I will give you all
their authority and splendor, for it has been given
to me,[i] and I can give it to anyone I want to. 7So if
you worship me, it will all be yours."
8Jesus answered, "It is written: 'Worship the
Lord your God and serve him only.'[b]"[j]
9The devil led him to Jerusalem and had him
stand on the highest point of the temple. "If you
are the Son of God," he said, "throw yourself
down from here. 10For it is written:

" 'He will command his angels
 concerning you
 to guard you carefully;
11 they will lift you up in their hands,
 so that you will not strike your foot
 against a stone.'[c]"[k]

12Jesus answered, "It says: 'Do not put the Lord
your God to the test.'[d]"[l]
13When the devil had finished all this tempting,[m] he left him[n] until an opportune time.

Jesus Rejected at Nazareth

14Jesus returned to Galilee[o] in the power of the
Spirit, and news about him spread through the
whole countryside.[p] 15He taught in their synagogues,[q] and everyone praised him.
16He went to Nazareth,[r] where he had been
brought up, and on the Sabbath day he went into
the synagogue,[s] as was his custom. And he stood
up to read. 17The scroll of the prophet Isaiah was
handed to him. Unrolling it, he found the place
where it is written:

18 "The Spirit of the Lord is on me,[t]
 because he has anointed me
 to preach good news to the poor.
He has sent me to proclaim freedom for
 the prisoners
 and recovery of sight for the blind,
to release the oppressed,
19 to proclaim the year of the Lord's
 favor."[e][u]

20Then he rolled up the scroll, gave it back to
the attendant and sat down.[v] The eyes of everyone in the synagogue were fastened on him, 21and

4:1 [c]ver 14,18 [d]Lk 3:3,21 [e]Lk 2:27
4:2 [f]Ex 34:28; 1Ki 19:8
4:4 [g]Dt 8:3
4:5 [h]Mt 24:14
4:6 [i]Jn 12:31; 14:30; 1Jn 5:19
4:8 [j]Dt 6:13
4:11 [k]Ps 91:11,12
4:12 [l]Dt 6:16
4:13 [m]Heb 4:15 [n]Jn 14:30
4:14 [o]Mt 4:12 [p]Mt 9:26
4:15 [q]Mt 4:23
4:16 [r]Mt 2:23 [s]Mt 13:54
4:18 [t]Jn 3:34
4:19 [u]Isa 61:1,2; Lev 25:10
4:20 [v]ver 17; Mt 26:55

[a] *4* Deut. 8:3 [b] *8* Deut. 6:13 [c] *11* Psalm 91:11,12
[d] *12* Deut. 6:16 [e] *19* Isaiah 61:1,2

he began by saying to them, "Today this scripture
is fulfilled in your hearing."
22 All spoke well of him and were amazed at the
gracious words that came from his lips. "Isn't this
Joseph's son?" they asked.[w]
23 Jesus said to them, "Surely you will quote this
proverb to me: 'Physician, heal yourself! Do here
in your hometown[x] what we have heard that you
did in Capernaum.' "[y]
24 "I tell you the truth," he continued, "no prophet is accepted in his hometown.[z] 25 I assure you that
there were many widows in Israel in Elijah's time,
when the sky was shut for three and a half years
and there was a severe famine throughout the
land.[a] 26 Yet Elijah was not sent to any of them, but
to a widow in Zarephath in the region of Sidon.[b]
27 And there were many in Israel with leprosy[a] in
the time of Elisha the prophet, yet not one of them
was cleansed—only Naaman the Syrian."[c]
28 All the people in the synagogue were furious
when they heard this. 29 They got up, drove him
out of the town,[d] and took him to the brow of the
hill on which the town was built, in order to
throw him down the cliff. 30 But he walked right
through the crowd and went on his way.[e]

Jesus Drives Out an Evil Spirit

31 Then he went down to Capernaum,[f] a town in
Galilee, and on the Sabbath began to teach the
people. 32 They were amazed at his teaching,[g]
because his message had authority.[h]
33 In the synagogue there was a man possessed
by a demon, an evil[b] spirit. He cried out at the top
of his voice, 34 "Ha! What do you want with us,[i]
Jesus of Nazareth?[j] Have you come to destroy us?
I know who you are[k]—the Holy One of God!"[l]
35 "Be quiet!" Jesus said sternly.[m] "Come out of
him!" Then the demon threw the man down before
them all and came out without injuring him.
36 All the people were amazed[n] and said to each
other, "What is this teaching? With authority[o] and
power he gives orders to evil spirits and they come
out!" 37 And the news about him spread throughout the surrounding area.[p]

Jesus Heals Many

38 Jesus left the synagogue and went to the home
of Simon. Now Simon's mother-in-law was suffering from a high fever, and they asked Jesus to
help her. 39 So he bent over her and rebuked[q] the
fever, and it left her. She got up at once and began
to wait on them.
40 When the sun was setting, the people brought
to Jesus all who had various kinds of sickness,
and laying his hands on each one,[r] he healed
them.[s] 41 Moreover, demons came out of many
people, shouting, "You are the Son of God!"[t] But

4:22 [w]Mt 13:54, 55; Jn 6:42; 7:15
4:23 [x]ver 16 [y]Mk 1:21-28; 2:1-12
4:24 [z]Mt 13:57; Jn 4:44
4:25 [a]1Ki 17:1; 18:1; Jas 5:17,18
4:26 [b]1Ki 17:8-16; Mt 11:21
4:27 [c]2Ki 5:1-14
4:29 [d]Nu 15:35; Ac 7:58; Heb 13:12
4:30 [e]Jn 8:59; 10:39
4:31 [f]ver 23; Mt 4:13
4:32 [g]Mt 7:28 [h]ver 36; Mt 7:29
4:34 [i]Mt 8:29 [j]Mk 1:24 [k]Jas 2:19 [l]ver 41; Mk 1:24
4:35 [m]ver 39,41; Mt 8:26; Lk 8:24
4:36 [n]Mt 7:28 [o]ver 32; Mt 7:29; Mt 10:1
4:37 [p]ver 14; Mt 9:26
4:39 [q]ver 35,41
4:40 [r]Mk 5:23 [s]Mt 4:23
4:41 [t]Mt 4:3

a *27* The Greek word was used for various diseases affecting the skin—not necessarily leprosy. *b* *33* Greek *unclean*; also in verse 36

The Proclamation

LK 4:24-27

Part of Jesus' plan to begin his ministry includes proclaiming who he is in his hometown synagogue. Those in attendance move from pride that such an eloquent fellow should spring from their very midst to outrage at his words. For he tells them that they are as faithless as the Jews in Elijah and Elisha's time (1Ki 17:7-16; 2Ki 5:1-15). *He reminds them that both of these prophets performed miracles for Gentiles, who sometimes experienced God's blessing while God's recalcitrant people experienced famine. This comparison was highly offensive because the Jews viewed themselves as God's specially chosen people. They viewed other nations as unclean and unworthy of God's touch.*

Jesus seems willing to accept the mantle of a prophet, including being rejected by those he is appointed to prophesy among. Elijah certainly played that role as he strove to return God's people to worship of the true God (as opposed to worship of Baal) and to righteous living (1Ki 18:20-40). *Now Jesus picks up the mantle and calls the people to the same holy living.*

he rebuked[u] them and would not allow them to
speak,[v] because they knew he was the Christ.[a]
42 At daybreak Jesus went out to a solitary place.
The people were looking for him and when they
came to where he was, they tried to keep him from
leaving them. 43 But he said, "I must preach the
good news of the kingdom of God[w] to the other
towns also, because that is why I was sent." 44 And
he kept on preaching in the synagogues of Judea.[b][x]

The Calling of the First Disciples

5 One day as Jesus was standing by the Lake of
Gennesaret,[c] with the people crowding around
him and listening to the word of God,[y] 2 he saw at
the water's edge two boats, left there by the fishermen, who were washing their nets. 3 He got into
one of the boats, the one belonging to Simon, and
asked him to put out a little from shore. Then he
sat down and taught the people from the boat.[z]
4 When he had finished speaking, he said to
Simon, "Put out into deep water, and let down[d]
the nets for a catch."[a]
5 Simon answered, "Master,[b] we've worked hard
all night and haven't caught anything.[c] But
because you say so, I will let down the nets."
6 When they had done so, they caught such a
large number of fish that their nets began to
break.[d] 7 So they signaled their partners in the other boat to come and help them, and they came
and filled both boats so full that they began to
sink.
8 When Simon Peter saw this, he fell at Jesus'
knees and said, "Go away from me, Lord; I am a
sinful man!"[e] 9 For he and all his companions were
astonished at the catch of fish they had taken,
10 and so were James and John, the sons of Zebedee, Simon's partners.
Then Jesus said to Simon, "Don't be afraid;[f]
from now on you will catch men." 11 So they
pulled their boats up on shore, left everything and
followed him.[g]

The Man With Leprosy

12 While Jesus was in one of the towns, a man
came along who was covered with leprosy.[e][h]
When he saw Jesus, he fell with his face to the
ground and begged him, "Lord, if you are willing,
you can make me clean."
13 Jesus reached out his hand and touched the
man. "I am willing," he said. "Be clean!" And
immediately the leprosy left him.
14 Then Jesus ordered him, "Don't tell anyone,[i]
but go, show yourself to the priest and offer the
sacrifices that Moses commanded[j] for your cleansing, as a testimony to them."
15 Yet the news about him spread all the more,[k]

4:41 [u]ver 35 [v]Mt 8:4
4:43 [w]Mt 3:2
4:44 [x]Mt 4:23
5:1 [y]Mk 4:14; Heb 4:12
5:3 [z]Mt 13:2
5:4 [a]Jn 21:6
5:5 [b]Lk 8:24,45; 9:33,49; 17:13 [c]Jn 21:3
5:6 [d]Jn 21:11
5:8 [e]Ge 18:27; Job 42:6; Isa 6:5
5:10 [f]Mt 14:27
5:11 [g]ver 28; Mt 4:19
5:12 [h]Mt 8:2
5:14 [i]Mt 8:4 [j]Lev 14:2-32
5:15 [k]Mt 9:26

[a] 41 Or *Messiah* [b] 44 Or *the land of the Jews*; some manuscripts *Galilee* [c] 1 That is, Sea of Galilee [d] 4 The Greek verb is plural. [e] 12 The Greek word was used for various diseases affecting the skin—not necessarily leprosy.

Living on an island near the U.S. Military Academy at West Point, Anna Bartlett Warner and her sister regularly conducted Bible study classes for the cadets in attendance there. She is buried at the Academy. She wrote perhaps one of the simplest, but best-loved and best-known Bible songs of all time.

Jesus Loves Me

Jesus loves me! This I know,
For the Bible tells me so,
Little ones to Him belong;
They are weak, but He is strong.

Jesus loves me! He who died
Heaven's gate to open wide;
He will wash away my sin,
Let His little child come in.

Jesus loves me! He will stay
Close beside me all the way;
Thou hast bled and died for me,
I will henceforth live for Thee.

—*Anna Bartlett Warner (1820-1915)*

so that crowds of people came to hear him and to
5:16 be healed of their sicknesses. 16But Jesus often
[l]Mt 14:23; withdrew to lonely places and prayed.[l]
Lk 3:21

Jesus Heals a Paralytic

17One day as he was teaching, Pharisees and
5:17 [m]Mt 15:1; teachers of the law,[m] who had come from every
Lk 2:46 village of Galilee and from Judea and Jerusalem,
[n]Mk 5:30; were sitting there. And the power of the Lord was
Lk 6:19 present for him to heal the sick.[n] 18Some men
came carrying a paralytic on a mat and tried to
take him into the house to lay him before Jesus.
19When they could not find a way to do this
because of the crowd, they went up on the roof
and lowered him on his mat through the tiles into
the middle of the crowd, right in front of Jesus.
20When Jesus saw their faith, he said, "Friend,
5:20 [o]Lk 7:48,49 your sins are forgiven."[o]
21The Pharisees and the teachers of the law
began thinking to themselves, "Who is this fellow
5:21 who speaks blasphemy? Who can forgive sins but
[p]Isa 43:25 God alone?"[p]
22Jesus knew what they were thinking and
asked, "Why are you thinking these things in your
hearts? 23Which is easier: to say, 'Your sins are for-
5:24 given,' or to say, 'Get up and walk'? 24But that you
[q]Mt 8:20 may know that the Son of Man[q] has authority on
earth to forgive sins . . ." He said to the paralyzed
man, "I tell you, get up, take your mat and go
home." 25Immediately he stood up in front of
them, took what he had been lying on and went
home praising God. 26Everyone was amazed and
5:26 [r]Mt 9:8 gave praise to God.[r] They were filled with awe and
said, "We have seen remarkable things today."

The Calling of Levi

27After this, Jesus went out and saw a tax col-
5:27 lector by the name of Levi sitting at his tax booth.
[s]Mt 4:19 "Follow me,"[s] Jesus said to him, 28and Levi got up,
5:28 left everything and followed him.[t]
[t]ver 11; 29Then Levi held a great banquet for Jesus at his
Mt 4:19 house, and a large crowd of tax collectors[u] and
5:29 others were eating with them. 30But the Pharisees
[u]Lk 15:1 and the teachers of the law who belonged to their
5:30 sect[v] complained to his disciples, "Why do you eat
[v]Ac 23:9 and drink with tax collectors and 'sinners'?"[w]
[w]Mt 9:11 31Jesus answered them, "It is not the healthy
5:32 who need a doctor, but the sick. 32I have not come
[x]Jn 3:17 to call the righteous, but sinners to repentance."[x]

5:33

Jesus Questioned About Fasting

[y]Lk 7:18; Jn 1:35; 33They said to him, "John's disciples[y] often fast
3:25,26 and pray, and so do the disciples of the Pharisees,
but yours go on eating and drinking."
5:34 34Jesus answered, "Can you make the guests of
[z]Jn 3:29 the bridegroom[z] fast while he is with them? 35But
5:35 the time will come when the bridegroom will be
[a]Lk 9:22; taken from them;[a] in those days they will fast."
17:22; 36He told them this parable: "No one tears a
Jn 16:5-7 patch from a new garment and sews it on an old

The Company of Sinners

LK 5:27-32

The Jews considered tax collectors low-down, no-good traitors. Tax collectors collaborated with the Romans, who paid them for the privilege of pursuing the tax-collecting profession. Tax collectors were also regarded as swindlers for their practice of charging their fellow citizens higher taxes and skimming off a portion for themselves.

The Pharisees, unable to see beyond their prejudice, can't figure out what Jesus is doing with these lowlifes. Of course, the Pharisees view these sinners as "sick" while regarding themselves as the picture of health. Jesus, as a spiritual "doctor," knows his mission is to those who are sick. The Pharisees don't recognize their illness, while the tax collectors and "sinners" do. Jesus' focus provides clear guidelines for us today. Our mission, too, is to the sick. Who is willing to acknowledge a spiritual ailment? Who is open to hearing how to be made well? As in Jesus' time, the answer might surprise—and appall—us.

Lord of the Sabbath

LK 6:1–11

As a result of the loss of Israel's nationhood and temple worship, due to the exile, the Israelites turned their focus to the observance of the law. Consequently, the Sabbath became increasingly important, and rules were added to distinguish the observant Jew from the lax Jew. The rules became increasingly refined—and minute—until the Sabbath became a burden rather than a blessing. God the Father provided the precedent for Sabbath observance at creation (Ge 2:2–3). Therefore, it's not too difficult to understand why the Pharisees are infuriated when Jesus asserts that he, as the "Son of Man," is Lord of the Sabbath. They don't see or understand Jesus' special relationship with the Father. But Jesus' words are not meant to bring division. They are meant to bring perspective. The Lord of the Sabbath has the right to declare what is honoring to God. Doing good is honoring, doing evil is not; saving a life is, destroying a life is not (Lk 6:9). Those same criteria can serve us well today. Are our "day of rest" activities good deeds? Are we adding to someone's life or taking away from it?

one. If he does, he will have torn the new garment,
and the patch from the new will not match the old.
37And no one pours new wine into old wineskins.
If he does, the new wine will burst the skins, the
wine will run out and the wineskins will be
ruined. 38No, new wine must be poured into new
wineskins. 39And no one after drinking old wine
wants the new, for he says, 'The old is better.' "

Lord of the Sabbath

6 One Sabbath Jesus was going through the
grainfields, and his disciples began to pick
some heads of grain, rub them in their hands and
eat the kernels.[b] 2Some of the Pharisees asked, **6:1** [b]Dt 23:25
"Why are you doing what is unlawful on the
Sabbath?"[c] **6:2** [c]Mt 12:2
3Jesus answered them, "Have you never read
what David did when he and his companions
were hungry?[d] 4He entered the house of God, and **6:3** [d]1Sa 21:6
taking the consecrated bread, he ate what is law-
ful only for priests to eat.[e] And he also gave some **6:4** [e]Lev 24:5,9
to his companions." 5Then Jesus said to them,
"The Son of Man[f] is Lord of the Sabbath." **6:5** [f]Mt 8:20
6On another Sabbath[g] he went into the syna-
gogue and was teaching, and a man was there **6:6** [g]ver 1
whose right hand was shriveled. 7The Pharisees
and the teachers of the law were looking for a reason to accuse Jesus, so they watched him close-
ly[h] to see if he would heal on the Sabbath.[i] 8But **6:7** [h]Mt 12:10
Jesus knew what they were thinking[j] and said to [i]Mt 12:2
the man with the shriveled hand, "Get up and
stand in front of everyone." So he got up and **6:8** [j]Mt 9:4
stood there.
9Then Jesus said to them, "I ask you, which is
lawful on the Sabbath: to do good or to do evil, to
save life or to destroy it?"
10He looked around at them all, and then said to
the man, "Stretch out your hand." He did so, and
his hand was completely restored. 11But they were
furious[k] and began to discuss with one another **6:11** [k]Jn 5:18
what they might do to Jesus.

The Twelve Apostles

12One of those days Jesus went out to a mountainside to pray, and spent the night praying to
God.[l] 13When morning came, he called his disci- **6:12** [l]Lk 3:21
ples to him and chose twelve of them, whom he
also designated apostles:[m] 14Simon (whom he **6:13** [m]Mk 6:30
named Peter), his brother Andrew, James, John,
Philip, Bartholomew, 15Matthew,[n] Thomas, James **6:15** [n]Mt 9:9
son of Alphaeus, Simon who was called the Zeal-
ot, 16Judas son of James, and Judas Iscariot, who
became a traitor.

Blessings and Woes

17He went down with them and stood on a level place. A large crowd of his disciples was there
and a great number of people from all over Judea, **6:17** [o]Mt 4:25;
from Jerusalem, and from the coast of Tyre and Mt 11:21;
Sidon,[o] 18who had come to hear him and to be Mk 3:7,8

healed of their diseases. Those troubled by evil[a]
spirits were cured, 19and the people all tried to
touch him,[p] because power was coming from him
and healing them all.[q]
20Looking at his disciples, he said:

"Blessed are you who are poor,
for yours is the kingdom of God.[r]
21Blessed are you who hunger now,
for you will be satisfied.[s]
Blessed are you who weep now,
for you will laugh.[t]
22Blessed are you when men hate you,
when they exclude you[u] and insult
you[v]
and reject your name as evil,
because of the Son of Man.[w]

23"Rejoice in that day and leap for joy,[x] because
great is your reward in heaven. For that is how
their fathers treated the prophets.[y]

24"But woe to you who are rich,[z]
for you have already received your
comfort.[a]
25Woe to you who are well fed now,
for you will go hungry.[b]
Woe to you who laugh now,
for you will mourn and weep.[c]
26Woe to you when all men speak well of
you,
for that is how their fathers treated
the false prophets.[d]

Love for Enemies

27"But I tell you who hear me: Love your enemies, do good to those who hate you,[e] 28bless
those who curse you, pray for those who mistreat
you.[f] 29If someone strikes you on one cheek, turn
to him the other also. If someone takes your cloak,
do not stop him from taking your tunic. 30Give to
everyone who asks you, and if anyone takes what
belongs to you, do not demand it back.[g] 31Do to
others as you would have them do to you.[h]
32"If you love those who love you, what credit is
that to you?[i] Even 'sinners' love those who love
them. 33And if you do good to those who are good
to you, what credit is that to you? Even 'sinners'
do that. 34And if you lend to those from whom
you expect repayment, what credit is that to you?[j]
Even 'sinners' lend to 'sinners,' expecting to be
repaid in full. 35But love your enemies, do good to
them,[k] and lend to them without expecting to get
anything back. Then your reward will be great,
and you will be sons[l] of the Most High,[m] because
he is kind to the ungrateful and wicked. 36Be merciful,[n] just as your Father[o] is merciful.

Judging Others

37"Do not judge, and you will not be judged.[p]

[a] 18 Greek *unclean*

6:19 [p]Mt 9:20 [q]Mt 14:36; Mk 5:30; Lk 5:17
6:20 [r]Mt 25:34
6:21 [s]Isa 55:1,2; Mt 5:6 [t]Isa 61:2,3; Mt 5:4; Rev 7:17
6:22 [u]Jn 9:22; 16:2 [v]Isa 51:7 [w]Jn 15:21
6:23 [x]Mt 5:12 [y]Mt 5:12
6:24 [z]Jas 5:1 [a]Lk 16:25
6:25 [b]Isa 65:13 [c]Pr 14:13
6:26 [d]Mt 7:15
6:27 [e]ver 35; Mt 5:44; Ro 12:20
6:28 [f]Mt 5:44
6:30 [g]Dt 15:7,8, 10; Pr 21:26
6:31 [h]Mt 7:12
6:32 [i]Mt 5:46
6:34 [j]Mt 5:42
6:35 [k]ver 27 [l]Ro 8:14 [m]Mk 5:7
6:36 [n]Jas 2:13 [o]Mt 5:48; 6:1; Lk 11:2; 12:32; Ro 8:15; Eph 4:6; 1Pe 1:17; 1Jn 1:3; 3:1
6:37 [p]Mt 7:1

As we consider our role in loving one another rather than judging one another, we need to remember there is a vast difference between acceptance and approval. We are not mandated to approve of wrong behavior. Jesus did not approve of the adulterous behavior of the woman at the well, but he did accept her as one worthy of his love and provision. There is also a distinction to be made between compassion and permissiveness. To feel compassion for the misdeeds of others need not imply that a spirit of permissiveness is eroding our standards. It simply means that we recognize the worth of others and our behavior reflects a caring, warm receptivity to them in spite of what they've done.

—Marilyn Meberg

A Good Measure

LK 6:38

Any cook worth her whisk knows that a lot more flour can be squeezed into a cup if it is pressed down, shaken around and heaped over the top. That's the kind of measure God uses when he gives back to us after we've given generously to others, including to those we are prone to judge and condemn. He even promises to pour out enough so that it will spill into our laps.

Now, if you were shopping in a street market in old Galilee, would you go to the vendor who had a cup with a false bottom so he or she could give you less than you asked for? Or would you go to the vendor you knew would press, shake, heap and pour on some more? Ask God if you've dealt with anyone lately out of a stingy heart. How can you instead be generous beyond expectation?

Do not condemn, and you will not be condemned.
Forgive, and you will be forgiven.[q] 38Give, and it
will be given to you. A good measure, pressed
down, shaken together and running over, will be
poured into your lap.[r] For with the measure you
use, it will be measured to you."[s]
39He also told them this parable: "Can a blind
man lead a blind man? Will they not both fall into
a pit?[t] 40A student is not above his teacher, but
everyone who is fully trained will be like his
teacher.[u]
41"Why do you look at the speck of sawdust in
your brother's eye and pay no attention to the
plank in your own eye? 42How can you say to your
brother, 'Brother, let me take the speck out of your
eye,' when you yourself fail to see the plank in
your own eye? You hypocrite, first take the plank
out of your eye, and then you will see clearly to
remove the speck from your brother's eye.

A Tree and Its Fruit

43"No good tree bears bad fruit, nor does a bad
tree bear good fruit. 44Each tree is recognized by
its own fruit.[v] People do not pick figs from thornbushes, or grapes from briers. 45The good man
brings good things out of the good stored up in
his heart, and the evil man brings evil things out
of the evil stored up in his heart. For out of the
overflow of his heart his mouth speaks.[w]

The Wise and Foolish Builders

46"Why do you call me, 'Lord, Lord,'[x] and do not
do what I say?[y] 47I will show you what he is like
who comes to me and hears my words and puts
them into practice.[z] 48He is like a man building a
house, who dug down deep and laid the foundation on rock. When a flood came, the torrent
struck that house but could not shake it, because
it was well built. 49But the one who hears my
words and does not put them into practice is like
a man who built a house on the ground without a
foundation. The moment the torrent struck that
house, it collapsed and its destruction was
complete."

The Faith of the Centurion

7 When Jesus had finished saying all this[a] in the
hearing of the people, he entered Capernaum.
2There a centurion's servant, whom his master
valued highly, was sick and about to die. 3The
centurion heard of Jesus and sent some elders of
the Jews to him, asking him to come and heal his
servant. 4When they came to Jesus, they pleaded
earnestly with him, "This man deserves to have
you do this, 5because he loves our nation and has
built our synagogue." 6So Jesus went with them.
He was not far from the house when the centurion sent friends to say to him: "Lord, don't trouble yourself, for I do not deserve to have you come
under my roof. 7That is why I did not even con-

6:37 [q]Mt 6:14
6:38 [r]Ps 79:12; Isa 65:6,7 [s]Mt 7:2; Mk 4:24
6:39 [t]Mt 15:14
6:40 [u]Mt 10:24; Jn 13:16
6:44 [v]Mt 12:33
6:45 [w]Pr 4:23; Mt 12:34,35; Mk 7:20
6:46 [x]Jn 13:13 [y]Mal 1:6; Mt 7:21
6:47 [z]Lk 8:21; 11:28; Jas 1:22-25
7:1 [a]Mt 7:28

sider myself worthy to come to you. But say the
7:7 [b]Ps 107:20 word, and my servant will be healed.[b] 8For I
myself am a man under authority, with soldiers
under me. I tell this one, 'Go,' and he goes; and
that one, 'Come,' and he comes. I say to my servant, 'Do this,' and he does it."
9When Jesus heard this, he was amazed at him,
and turning to the crowd following him, he said,
"I tell you, I have not found such great faith even
in Israel." 10Then the men who had been sent
returned to the house and found the servant well.

Jesus Raises a Widow's Son

11Soon afterward, Jesus went to a town called
Nain, and his disciples and a large crowd went
along with him. 12As he approached the town
gate, a dead person was being carried out—the
only son of his mother, and she was a widow. And
7:13 a large crowd from the town was with her.
[c]ver 19; Lk 10:1; 13When the Lord[c] saw her, his heart went out to
13:15; 17:5; her and he said, "Don't cry."
22:61; 24:34; Jn 11:2 14Then he went up and touched the coffin, and
those carrying it stood still. He said, "Young man,
7:14 [d]Mt 9:25; I say to you, get up!"[d] 15The dead man sat up and
Mk 1:31; began to talk, and Jesus gave him back to his
Lk 8:54; Jn 11:43; mother.
Ac 9:40 16They were all filled with awe[e] and praised
God.[f] "A great prophet[g] has appeared among us,"
7:16 [e]Lk 1:65 [f]Mt 9:8 they said. "God has come to help his people."[h]
[g]ver 39; Mt 21:11 17This news about Jesus spread throughout Judea[a]
[h]Lk 1:68 and the surrounding country.[i]

Jesus and John the Baptist

7:17 [i]Mt 9:26 18John's[j] disciples[k] told him about all these
things. Calling two of them, 19he sent them to the
7:18 [j]Mt 3:1 Lord to ask, "Are you the one who was to come, or
[k]Lk 5:33 should we expect someone else?"
20When the men came to Jesus, they said, "John
the Baptist sent us to you to ask, 'Are you the one
who was to come, or should we expect someone
else?' "
21At that very time Jesus cured many who had
7:21 [l]Mt 4:23 diseases, sicknesses[l] and evil spirits, and gave
sight to many who were blind. 22So he replied to
the messengers, "Go back and report to John what
you have seen and heard: The blind receive sight,
the lame walk, those who have leprosy[b] are cured,
7:22 the deaf hear, the dead are raised, and the good
[m]Isa 29:18, news is preached to the poor.[m] 23Blessed is the
19; 35:5,6; man who does not fall away on account of me."
61:1,2; Lk 4:18 24After John's messengers left, Jesus began to
speak to the crowd about John: "What did you go
out into the desert to see? A reed swayed by the
wind? 25If not, what did you go out to see? A man
dressed in fine clothes? No, those who wear
expensive clothes and indulge in luxury are in
palaces. 26But what did you go out to see? A

[a] 17 Or *the land of the Jews* [b] 22 The Greek word was used for various diseases affecting the skin—not necessarily leprosy.

Miracles

LK 7:11-17

From the outset of Jesus' ministry, he uses miracles ***to help explain who he is and to deepen people's understanding of*** **God. When John the Baptist asks Jesus to explain who he is, Jesus points to his miracles (Lk 7:18–22). These physical miracles are** ***symbols or pictures of what Jesus can do spiritually.*** **The spiritually blind will see, the spiritually deaf will hear, the spiritually lame will walk, and the spiritually dead will live.** ***In the case of this particular miracle, Jesus is moved by pure compassion for the widow who has*** **lost her only son (Lk 7:13). The** ***large crowd escorting her and the coffin to the burial site is evidence of the sympathy others felt for her,*** **too. Through this physical act** ***Jesus intends to touch his audience spiritually, and that's exactly the result, as evidenced by their response*** **(Lk 7:16;** ***see the character sketch for this woman on page*** **1688).**

A Topsy-Turvy Kingdom

LK 7:28

Jesus gives John what, at first, appears to be the highest compliment a person can give: "There is no one greater than John" (Lk 7:28). But then Jesus surprises his listeners by saying the person who is the lowest of the low in the kingdom of God is greater than John. How does that add up? John the Baptist was great, yes, but he was only a forerunner of Jesus, who established a new covenant with higher privileges and benefits for its followers. The positions and privileges of kingdom citizens are given, not because of deeds done, but because of God's grace. So all the old formulas are tossed into the trash. Words like *earned, most, best, brightest, prettiest* and *strongest* become meaningless. As Paul so richly depicts in 1 Corinthians 1:26–31, kingdom math works in ways we just aren't used to. Don't pass up the opportunity to turn to those verses and read Paul's description of this topsy-turvy kingdom. John the Baptist's followers found Jesus' news liberating rather than unsettling (Lk 7:29), and so should we.

prophet?[n] Yes, I tell you, and more than a prophet. 27This is the one about whom it is written:

> " 'I will send my messenger ahead of you,
> who will prepare your way before you.'[a][o]

28I tell you, among those born of women there is no one greater than John; yet the one who is least in the kingdom of God[p] is greater than he."

29(All the people, even the tax collectors, when they heard Jesus' words, acknowledged that God's way was right, because they had been baptized by John.[q] 30But the Pharisees and experts in the law[r] rejected God's purpose for themselves, because they had not been baptized by John.)

31"To what, then, can I compare the people of this generation? What are they like? 32They are like children sitting in the marketplace and calling out to each other:

> " 'We played the flute for you,
> and you did not dance;
> we sang a dirge,
> and you did not cry.'

33For John the Baptist came neither eating bread nor drinking wine,[s] and you say, 'He has a demon.' 34The Son of Man came eating and drinking, and you say, 'Here is a glutton and a drunkard, a friend of tax collectors and "sinners." '[t] 35But wisdom is proved right by all her children."

Jesus Anointed by a Sinful Woman

36Now one of the Pharisees invited Jesus to have dinner with him, so he went to the Pharisee's house and reclined at the table. 37When a woman who had lived a sinful life in that town learned that Jesus was eating at the Pharisee's house, she brought an alabaster jar of perfume, 38and as she stood behind him at his feet weeping, she began to wet his feet with her tears. Then she wiped them with her hair, kissed them and poured perfume on them.

39When the Pharisee who had invited him saw this, he said to himself, "If this man were a prophet,[u] he would know who is touching him and what kind of woman she is—that she is a sinner."

40Jesus answered him, "Simon, I have something to tell you."

"Tell me, teacher," he said.

41"Two men owed money to a certain moneylender. One owed him five hundred denarii,[b] and the other fifty. 42Neither of them had the money to pay him back, so he canceled the debts of both. Now which of them will love him more?"

43Simon replied, "I suppose the one who had the bigger debt canceled."

"You have judged correctly," Jesus said.

7:26 [n]Mt 11:9
7:27 [o]Mal 3:1; Mt 11:10; Mk 1:2
7:28 [p]Mt 3:2
7:29 [q]Mt 21:32; Mk 1:5; Lk 3:12
7:30 [r]Mt 22:35
7:33 [s]Lk 1:15
7:34 [t]Lk 5:29,30; 15:1,2
7:39 [u]ver 16; Mt 21:11

[a] *27* Mal. 3:1 [b] *41* A denarius was a coin worth about a day's wages.

44Then he turned toward the woman and said
to Simon, "Do you see this woman? I came into
7:44 [v]Ge 18:4; 19:2; 43:24; Jdg 19:21; Jn 13:4-14; 1Ti 5:10
your house. You did not give me any water for my
feet,[v] but she wet my feet with her tears and
wiped them with her hair. 45You did not give me a
kiss,[w] but this woman, from the time I entered,
has not stopped kissing my feet. 46You did not put
7:45 [w]Lk 22:47, 48; Ro 16:16
oil on my head,[x] but she has poured perfume on
my feet. 47Therefore, I tell you, her many sins
have been forgiven—for she loved much. But he
7:46 [x]Ps 23:5; Ecc 9:8
who has been forgiven little loves little."
48Then Jesus said to her, "Your sins are
forgiven."[y]
7:48 [y]Mt 9:2
49The other guests began to say among themselves, "Who is this who even forgives sins?"
50Jesus said to the woman, "Your faith has
7:50 [z]Mt 9:22; Mk 5:34; Lk 8:48 [a]Ac 15:33
saved you;[z] go in peace."[a]

The Parable of the Sower

8 After this, Jesus traveled about from one town
and village to another, proclaiming the good
8:1 [b]Mt 4:23
news of the kingdom of God.[b] The Twelve were
with him, 2and also some women who had been
cured of evil spirits and diseases: Mary (called
8:2 [c]Mt 27:55,56
Magdalene)[c] from whom seven demons had come
out; 3Joanna the wife of Cuza, the manager of
8:3 [d]Mt 14:1
Herod's[d] household; Susanna; and many others.
These women were helping to support them out
of their own means.
4While a large crowd was gathering and people
were coming to Jesus from town after town, he
told this parable: 5"A farmer went out to sow his
seed. As he was scattering the seed, some fell
along the path; it was trampled on, and the birds
of the air ate it up. 6Some fell on rock, and when it
came up, the plants withered because they had no
moisture. 7Other seed fell among thorns, which
grew up with it and choked the plants. 8Still other
seed fell on good soil. It came up and yielded a
crop, a hundred times more than was sown."
8:8 [e]Mt 11:15
When he said this, he called out, "He who has
ears to hear, let him hear."[e]
9His disciples asked him what this parable
meant. 10He said, "The knowledge of the secrets
8:10 [f]Mt 13:11 [g]Isa 6:9; Mt 13:13,14
of the kingdom of God has been given to you,[f] but
to others I speak in parables, so that,

" 'though seeing, they may not see;
though hearing, they may not
understand.'[a][g]

11"This is the meaning of the parable: The seed
8:11 [h]Heb 4:12
is the word of God.[h] 12Those along the path are
the ones who hear, and then the devil comes and
takes away the word from their hearts, so that
they may not believe and be saved. 13Those on the
rock are the ones who receive the word with joy
when they hear it, but they have no root. They
believe for a while, but in the time of testing they
8:13 [i]Mt 11:6
fall away.[i] 14The seed that fell among thorns

[a] *10* Isaiah 6:9

The Eye of the Beholder

LK 7:36-50

Somehow Simon the Pharisee, who fails in his responsibilities as a host (Lk 7:44-46), misconstrues what is happening before his very eyes. The wealth of this woman's tears and the generosity of her heart leave the Pharisee cold. He even passes judgment on Jesus, deciding he is an undiscerning man (Lk 7:39)! The woman, who may have intended to anoint Jesus' head, which is a sign of hospitality and regard (Lk 7:46) as well as of personal grooming (Mt 6:17), is so overcome by humility and gratitude that she instead bathes his feet with her tears and perfume.

Put yourself in that house that day. How will you react? You can't see into this woman's heart. You only know that she has lived a sinful life. Unfortunately, we often respond like the Pharisee. We think we have the whole picture when, in actuality, we have misjudged another's motives and actions. And we haven't taken even the smallest step toward seeing ourselves as we really are (see the character sketch for this woman on page 1713).

The Thorns

LK 8:14

Jesus describes life's worries, riches and pleasures as thorns that keep those who initially respond to the gospel from reaching spiritual maturity. We tend to think of thorns as ugly things that cry out to be weeded from our lives. And we also tend to think of thorns more as the trials and difficulties of life. But Jesus tells us riches and pleasures—the things we want most out of life—are also true thorns. Using the garden analogy, good things can dominate a garden, taking it over so other plants can't flourish. Even these good things are "thorns." It takes a discerning gardener to know which plants to encourage and which to control. In your own garden patch, have certain plants choked out your good spiritual intentions, blocking the sun and stealing nutrients from other plants you care about? Mere neglect can lead to a crop of thorns.

stands for those who hear, but as they go on their
way they are choked by life's worries, riches[j] and 8:14 [j]Mt 19:23;
pleasures, and they do not mature. 15But the seed 1Ti 6:9,10,
on good soil stands for those with a noble and 17
good heart, who hear the word, retain it, and by
persevering produce a crop.

A Lamp on a Stand

16"No one lights a lamp and hides it in a jar or
puts it under a bed. Instead, he puts it on a stand,
so that those who come in can see the light.[k] 17For 8:16 [k]Mt 5:15;
there is nothing hidden that will not be disclosed, Mk 4:21;
and nothing concealed that will not be known or Lk 11:33
brought out into the open.[l] 18Therefore consider 8:17
carefully how you listen. Whoever has will be [l]Mt 10:26;
given more; whoever does not have, even what he Mk 4:22;
thinks he has will be taken from him."[m] Lk 12:2

8:18 [m]Mt 13:12; 25:29; Lk 19:26

Jesus' Mother and Brothers

19Now Jesus' mother and brothers came to see
him, but they were not able to get near him
because of the crowd. 20Someone told him, "Your 8:20
mother and brothers[n] are standing outside, want- [n]Jn 7:5
ing to see you."
21He replied, "My mother and brothers are those 8:21
who hear God's word and put it into practice."[o] [o]Lk 6:47; 11:28; Jn 14:21

Jesus Calms the Storm

22One day Jesus said to his disciples, "Let's go
over to the other side of the lake." So they got into
a boat and set out. 23As they sailed, he fell asleep.
A squall came down on the lake, so that the boat
was being swamped, and they were in great
danger.
24The disciples went and woke him, saying, 8:24
"Master, Master,[p] we're going to drown!" [p]Lk 5:5
He got up and rebuked[q] the wind and the rag- [q]Lk 4:35,39, 41
ing waters; the storm subsided, and all was calm.[r] [r]Ps 107:29;
25"Where is your faith?" he asked his disciples. Jnh 1:15
In fear and amazement they asked one another,
"Who is this? He commands even the winds and
the water, and they obey him."

The Healing of a Demon-possessed Man

26They sailed to the region of the Gerasenes,[a]
which is across the lake from Galilee. 27When
Jesus stepped ashore, he was met by a demon-
possessed man from the town. For a long time this
man had not worn clothes or lived in a house, but
had lived in the tombs. 28When he saw Jesus, he
cried out and fell at his feet, shouting at the top of 8:28
his voice, "What do you want with me,[s] Jesus, [s]Mt 8:29
Son of the Most High God?[t] I beg you, don't tor- [t]Mk 5:7
ture me!" 29For Jesus had commanded the evil[b]
spirit to come out of the man. Many times it had
seized him, and though he was chained hand and
foot and kept under guard, he had broken his

[a] 26 Some manuscripts *Gadarenes*; other manuscripts *Gergesenes*; also in verse 37 [b] 29 Greek *unclean*

chains and had been driven by the demon into
solitary places.
30 Jesus asked him, "What is your name?"
"Legion," he replied, because many demons
8:31 had gone into him. 31 And they begged him repeat-
[u]Rev 9:1,2, edly not to order them to go into the Abyss.[u]
11; 11:7; 32 A large herd of pigs was feeding there on the
17:8; 20:1,3 hillside. The demons begged Jesus to let them go
into them, and he gave them permission. 33 When
the demons came out of the man, they went into
8:33 the pigs, and the herd rushed down the steep
[v]ver 22,23 bank into the lake[v] and was drowned.
34 When those tending the pigs saw what had
happened, they ran off and reported this in the
town and countryside, 35 and the people went out
to see what had happened. When they came to
8:35 Jesus, they found the man from whom the demons
[w]Lk 10:39 had gone out, sitting at Jesus' feet,[w] dressed and in
his right mind; and they were afraid. 36 Those who
had seen it told the people how the demon-pos-
8:36 sessed[x] man had been cured. 37 Then all the peo-
[x]Mt 4:24 ple of the region of the Gerasenes asked Jesus to
8:37 leave them,[y] because they were overcome with
[y]Ac 16:39 fear. So he got into the boat and left.
38 The man from whom the demons had gone
out begged to go with him, but Jesus sent him
away, saying, 39 "Return home and tell how much
God has done for you." So the man went away
and told all over town how much Jesus had done
for him.

A Dead Girl and a Sick Woman

40 Now when Jesus returned, a crowd welcomed
8:41 him, for they were all expecting him. 41 Then a
[z]ver 49; man named Jairus, a ruler of the synagogue,[z]
Mk 5:22 came and fell at Jesus' feet, pleading with him to
come to his house 42 because his only daughter, a
girl of about twelve, was dying.
As Jesus was on his way, the crowds almost
crushed him. 43 And a woman was there who had
8:43 been subject to bleeding[a] for twelve years,[a] but no
[a]Lev 15:25-30 one could heal her. 44 She came up behind him and
8:44 touched the edge of his cloak,[b] and immediately
[b]Mt 9:20 her bleeding stopped.
8:45 45 "Who touched me?" Jesus asked.
[c]Lk 5:5 When they all denied it, Peter said, "Master,[c]
the people are crowding and pressing against
8:46 you."
[d]Mt 14:36; 46 But Jesus said, "Someone touched me;[d] I
Mk 3:10 [e]Lk 5:17; know that power has gone out from me."[e]
6:19 47 Then the woman, seeing that she could not go
unnoticed, came trembling and fell at his feet. In
the presence of all the people, she told why she
8:48 had touched him and how she had been instantly
[f]Mt 9:22 healed. 48 Then he said to her, "Daughter, your
[g]Ac 15:33 faith has healed you.[f] Go in peace."[g]
8:49 49 While Jesus was still speaking, someone came
[h]ver 41 from the house of Jairus, the synagogue ruler.[h]

[a] *43* Many manuscripts *years, and she had spent all she had on doctors*

***Y**ou can imagine the demand Jesus was in when word spread there was a competent doctor in town. It was not unusual for him to be pressed by crowds as the well-wishers, the curious, and the needy pursued him. Such was the day when, in the midst of the throngs, a slender hand sought out the hem of his garment (Lk 8:44). Immediately, Christ asked who had touched him. His followers were amazed at his question when it was obvious many had been in physical contact with their Master. But Jesus knew something the others didn't—except for the woman with the slender hand. She knew what had happened: She had been healed, and she began to tremble.*

She knelt before him and told him what he already knew—her story. Christ gently affirmed her faith and proclaimed her well. That woman with her unclean illness knew she should not have been in the crowds, much less touch anyone. But she couldn't help herself. She, like many of us, had suffered for so long, and the local doctors had only added to her pain and humiliation. Her healing that day came from a compassionate Christ and had more to do with the issue of her heart than the issue of her blood.

—Patsy Clairmont

Mourning

LK 8:52

The Middle East has long known the tradition of demonstrative mourning. This includes weeping, wailing, beating the breast and employing professional mourners, if one can afford them. Jeremiah explains that these professionals sing evocative funeral songs "till our eyes overflow with tears" (Jer 9:18). A rabbi from A.D. 140–165 says, "Even the poorest in Israel should hire not less than two flutes and a wailing woman." The mourning period is seven days, but the actual internment takes place as soon as possible after death, normally on the same day.

"Your daughter is dead," he said. "Don't bother
the teacher any more."
50Hearing this, Jesus said to Jairus, "Don't be
afraid; just believe, and she will be healed."
51When he arrived at the house of Jairus, he did
not let anyone go in with him except Peter, John
and James,[i] and the child's father and mother.
52Meanwhile, all the people were wailing and
mourning[j] for her. "Stop wailing," Jesus said. "She
is not dead but asleep."[k]
53They laughed at him, knowing that she was
dead. 54But he took her by the hand and said, "My
child, get up!"[l] 55Her spirit returned, and at once
she stood up. Then Jesus told them to give her
something to eat. 56Her parents were astonished,
but he ordered them not to tell anyone what had
happened.[m]

Jesus Sends Out the Twelve

9 When Jesus had called the Twelve together, he
gave them power and authority to drive out all
demons[n] and to cure diseases,[o] 2and he sent them
out to preach the kingdom of God[p] and to heal the
sick. 3He told them: "Take nothing for the journey—no staff, no bag, no bread, no money, no
extra tunic.[q] 4Whatever house you enter, stay
there until you leave that town. 5If people do not
welcome you, shake the dust off your feet when
you leave their town, as a testimony against
them."[r] 6So they set out and went from village to
village, preaching the gospel and healing people
everywhere.
7Now Herod[s] the tetrarch heard about all that
was going on. And he was perplexed, because
some were saying that John[t] had been raised from
the dead,[u] 8others that Elijah had appeared,[v] and
still others that one of the prophets of long ago
had come back to life.[w] 9But Herod said, "I
beheaded John. Who, then, is this I hear such
things about?" And he tried to see him.[x]

Jesus Feeds the Five Thousand

10When the apostles[y] returned, they reported to
Jesus what they had done. Then he took them
with him and they withdrew by themselves to a
town called Bethsaida,[z] 11but the crowds learned
about it and followed him. He welcomed them
and spoke to them about the kingdom of God,[a]
and healed those who needed healing.
12Late in the afternoon the Twelve came to him
and said, "Send the crowd away so they can go to
the surrounding villages and countryside and find
food and lodging, because we are in a remote
place here."
13He replied, "You give them something to eat."
They answered, "We have only five loaves of
bread and two fish—unless we go and buy food
for all this crowd." 14(About five thousand men
were there.)
But he said to his disciples, "Have them sit

8:51 [i]Mt 4:21
8:52 [j]Lk 23:27 [k]Mt 9:24; Jn 11:11,13
8:54 [l]Lk 7:14
8:56 [m]Mt 8:4
9:1 [n]Mt 10:1 [o]Mt 4:23; Lk 5:17
9:2 [p]Mt 3:2
9:3 [q]Lk 10:4; 22:35
9:5 [r]Mt 10:14
9:7 [s]Mt 14:1 [t]Mt 3:1 [u]ver 19
9:8 [v]Mt 11:14 [w]ver 19; Jn 1:21
9:9 [x]Lk 23:8
9:10 [y]Mk 6:30 [z]Mt 11:21
9:11 [a]ver 2; Mt 3:2

down in groups of about fifty each." 15The disciples did so, and everybody sat down. 16Taking the
five loaves and the two fish and looking up to
9:16 [b]Mt 14:19 heaven, he gave thanks and broke them.[b] Then he
gave them to the disciples to set before the peo-
ple. 17They all ate and were satisfied, and the disciples picked up twelve basketfuls of broken
pieces that were left over.

Peter's Confession of Christ

9:18 [c]Lk 3:21 18Once when Jesus was praying[c] in private and
his disciples were with him, he asked them, "Who
do the crowds say I am?"
9:19 [d]Mt 3:1 [e]ver 7,8 19They replied, "Some say John the Baptist;[d]
others say Elijah; and still others, that one of the
prophets of long ago has come back to life."[e]
20"But what about you?" he asked. "Who do
you say I am?"
9:20 [f]Jn 1:49; 6:66-69; 11:27 Peter answered, "The Christ[a] of God."[f]
21Jesus strictly warned them not to tell this to
anyone.[g] 22And he said, "The Son of Man[h] must
9:21 [g]Mt 16:20; Mk 8:30 suffer many things[i] and be rejected by the elders,
chief priests and teachers of the law,[j] and he must
be killed[k] and on the third day[l] be raised to life."[m]
9:22 [h]Mt 8:20 [i]Mt 16:21 [j]Mt 27:1,2 [k]Ac 2:23; 3:13 [l]Mt 16:21 [m]Mt 16:21 23Then he said to them all: "If anyone would
come after me, he must deny himself and take up
his cross daily and follow me.[n] 24For whoever
wants to save his life will lose it, but whoever
loses his life for me will save it.[o] 25What good is it
for a man to gain the whole world, and yet lose or
forfeit his very self? 26If anyone is ashamed of me
9:23 [n]Mt 10:38; Lk 14:27 and my words, the Son of Man will be ashamed of
him[p] when he comes in his glory and in the glo-
9:24 [o]Jn 12:25 ry of the Father and of the holy angels.[q] 27I tell you
the truth, some who are standing here will not
9:26 [p]Mt 10:33; Lk 12:9; 2Ti 2:12 [q]Mt 16:27 taste death before they see the kingdom of God."

The Transfiguration

28About eight days after Jesus said this, he took
Peter, John and James[r] with him and went up
9:28 [r]Mt 4:21 [s]Lk 3:21 onto a mountain to pray.[s] 29As he was praying, the
appearance of his face changed, and his clothes
became as bright as a flash of lightning. 30Two
men, Moses and Elijah, 31appeared in glorious
splendor, talking with Jesus. They spoke about his
9:31 [t]2Pe 1:15 departure,[t] which he was about to bring to fulfillment at Jerusalem. 32Peter and his companions
9:32 [u]Mt 26:43 were very sleepy,[u] but when they became fully
awake, they saw his glory and the two men stand-
9:33 [v]Lk 5:5 ing with him. 33As the men were leaving Jesus,
Peter said to him, "Master,[v] it is good for us to be
here. Let us put up three shelters—one for you,
one for Moses and one for Elijah." (He did not
know what he was saying.)
34While he was speaking, a cloud appeared and
enveloped them, and they were afraid as they
9:35 [w]Isa 42:1 [x]Mt 3:17 entered the cloud. 35A voice came from the cloud,
saying, "This is my Son, whom I have chosen;[w]
listen to him."[x] 36When the voice had spoken,

[a] 20 Or *Messiah*

Health From What? — Meals

LK 9:13

The lunch of bread and fish is no surprise. Bethsaida, where the feeding of the 5,000 takes place, is located close to the Sea of Galilee, which is the center of Israel's fishing industry.

In Jesus' time, bread is *the* ***staple of every Israelite's diet and is made either from wheat or barley flour, with barley most commonly used by the poor. Other food items Israelites eat include grapes, olives, figs and the pods of carob trees (only the poor eat these). Olive oil serves as an important element in everyone's diet. Meat, however, is seldom eaten. Kids, calves and lamb may be offered at festive times. Sparrows might be eaten by the poor. Food is seasoned with salt, mint, dill, cumin and rue. Mustard seeds are ground into powder and used for flavoring as well as for medicinal purposes.***

Healing From What?

LK 9:37–42

The symptoms the boy's father described lead many today to believe the boy experienced epileptic seizures. But Jesus saw more here. When Jesus encounters someone with a physical illness, he usually touches or speaks to the sick person. But when he heals someone possessed by an evil spirit, he speaks to the demon itself, commanding it to depart. Jesus treats this boy's illness as one of demon-possession. Individuals tormented by demons may also experience blindness and muteness (Mt 9:32–33, 12:22). Of course, not everyone with the symptoms of epilepsy, blindness or muteness is demon-possessed.

they found that Jesus was alone. The disciples
kept this to themselves, and told no one at that
time what they had seen.[y] 9:36 [y]Mt 17:9

The Healing of a Boy With an Evil Spirit

37 The next day, when they came down from the
mountain, a large crowd met him. 38 A man in the
crowd called out, "Teacher, I beg you to look at my
son, for he is my only child. 39 A spirit seizes him
and he suddenly screams; it throws him into con-
vulsions so that he foams at the mouth. It scarcely
ever leaves him and is destroying him. 40 I begged
your disciples to drive it out, but they could not."
41 "O unbelieving and perverse generation,"[z] 9:41 [z]Dt 32:5
Jesus replied, "how long shall I stay with you and
put up with you? Bring your son here."
42 Even while the boy was coming, the demon
threw him to the ground in a convulsion. But
Jesus rebuked the evil[a] spirit, healed the boy and
gave him back to his father. 43 And they were all
amazed at the greatness of God.
While everyone was marveling at all that Jesus
did, he said to his disciples, 44 "Listen carefully to
what I am about to tell you: The Son of Man is
going to be betrayed into the hands of men."[a] 9:44 [a]ver 22
45 But they did not understand what this meant. It
was hidden from them, so that they did not grasp
it,[b] and they were afraid to ask him about it. 9:45 [b]Mk 9:32

Who Will Be the Greatest?

46 An argument started among the disciples as
to which of them would be the greatest.[c] 47 Jesus, 9:46 [c]Lk 22:24
knowing their thoughts,[d] took a little child and 9:47 [d]Mt 9:4
had him stand beside him. 48 Then he said to
them, "Whoever welcomes this little child in my
name welcomes me; and whoever welcomes me
welcomes the one who sent me.[e] For he who is 9:48 [e]Mt 10:40
least among you all—he is the greatest."[f] [f]Mk 9:35
49 "Master,"[g] said John, "we saw a man driving 9:49 [g]Lk 5:5
out demons in your name and we tried to stop
him, because he is not one of us."
50 "Do not stop him," Jesus said, "for whoever is
not against you is for you."[h] 9:50 [h]Mt 12:30; Lk 11:23

Samaritan Opposition

51 As the time approached for him to be taken up
to heaven,[i] Jesus resolutely set out for Jerusalem.[j] 9:51 [i]Mk 16:19 [j]Lk 13:22; 17:11; 18:31; 19:28
52 And he sent messengers on ahead, who went
into a Samaritan[k] village to get things ready for 9:52 [k]Mt 10:5
him; 53 but the people there did not welcome him,
because he was heading for Jerusalem. 54 When the
disciples James and John[l] saw this, they asked, 9:54 [l]Mt 4:21
"Lord, do you want us to call fire down from heav-
en to destroy them[b]?"[m] 55 But Jesus turned and [m]2Ki 1:10,12
rebuked them, 56 and[c] they went to another village.

[a] 42 Greek *unclean* [b] 54 Some manuscripts *them, even as Elijah did* [c] 55,56 Some manuscripts *them. And he said, "You do not know what kind of spirit you are of, for the Son of Man did not come to destroy men's lives, but to save them."* 56 *And*

The Cost of Following Jesus

9:57 [n]ver 51 57 As they were walking along the road,[n] a man
said to him, "I will follow you wherever you go."
58 Jesus replied, "Foxes have holes and birds of
9:58 [o]Mt 8:20 the air have nests, but the Son of Man[o] has no
place to lay his head."
9:59 59 He said to another man, "Follow me."[p]
[p]Mt 4:19 But the man replied, "Lord, first let me go and
bury my father."
60 Jesus said to him, "Let the dead bury their
9:60 own dead, but you go and proclaim the kingdom
[q]Mt 3:2 of God."[q]
61 Still another said, "I will follow you, Lord; but
9:61 first let me go back and say good-by to my
[r]1Ki 19:20 family."[r]
62 Jesus replied, "No one who puts his hand to
the plow and looks back is fit for service in the
kingdom of God."

Jesus Sends Out the Seventy-two

10:1 [s]Lk 7:13 10 After this the Lord[s] appointed seventy-two[a]
[t]Lk 9:1,2,51, 52 others[t] and sent them two by two[u] ahead of
[u]Mk 6:7 him to every town and place where he was about
[v]Mt 10:1 to go.[v] 2 He told them, "The harvest is plentiful,
but the workers are few. Ask the Lord of the har-
10:2 vest, therefore, to send out workers into his har-
[w]Mt 9:37,38; vest field.[w] 3 Go! I am sending you out like lambs
Jn 4:35 10:3 among wolves.[x] 4 Do not take a purse or bag or
[x]Mt 10:16 sandals; and do not greet anyone on the road.
5 "When you enter a house, first say, 'Peace to
this house.' 6 If a man of peace is there, your peace
will rest on him; if not, it will return to you. 7 Stay
10:7 in that house, eating and drinking whatever they
[y]Mt 10:10; give you, for the worker deserves his wages.[y] Do
1Co 9:14; 1Ti 5:18 not move around from house to house.
8 "When you enter a town and are welcomed,
10:8 eat what is set before you.[z] 9 Heal the sick who are
[z]1Co 10:27 there and tell them, 'The kingdom of God[a] is near
10:9 you.' 10 But when you enter a town and are not
[a]Mt 3:2; 10:7 welcomed, go into its streets and say, 11 'Even the
10:11 dust of your town that sticks to our feet we wipe
[b]Mt 10:14; off against you.[b] Yet be sure of this: The kingdom
Mk 6:11 [c]ver 9 of God is near.'[c] 12 I tell you, it will be more bearable on that day for Sodom[d] than for that town.[e]
10:12 [d]Mt 10:15 13 "Woe to you,[f] Korazin! Woe to you, Bethsai-
[e]Mt 11:24 da! For if the miracles that were performed in you
had been performed in Tyre and Sidon, they
10:13 would have repented long ago, sitting in sack-
[f]Lk 6:24-26 [g]Rev 11:3 cloth[g] and ashes. 14 But it will be more bearable for
10:15 Tyre and Sidon at the judgment than for you.
[h]Mt 4:13 15 And you, Capernaum,[h] will you be lifted up to
the skies? No, you will go down to the depths.[b]
16 "He who listens to you listens to me; he who
10:16 rejects you rejects me; but he who rejects me
[i]Mt 10:40; Jn 13:20 rejects him who sent me."[i]
17 The seventy-two[j] returned with joy and said,
10:17 "Lord, even the demons submit to us in your
[j]ver 1 [k]Mk 16:17 name."[k]

[a] *1* Some manuscripts *seventy*; also in verse 17 [b] *15* Greek *Hades*

I am amazed and humbled to realize that an awesome, omnipotent, sovereign God would want to communicate with me. But that's one of the reasons he created us: he wants us to have fellowship with him. People have tried to explain how to hear the voice of God. In my opinion, nobody has been able to describe it fully. I believe God's sheep know the Shepherd's voice by faith.

—Thelma Wells

Falling From Heaven

LK 10:17-20

Like lightning crashing down from the heavens, Satan falls before Christ's power. Now the disciples, in Jesus' name, also have that power over Satan's minions, the demons (Lk 10:17). Jesus and his disciples carry out a ministry of miracles, proving that God's power is greater than Satan's. But Jesus holds the disciples' sense of mastery in check by reminding them that causing spirits to submit pales in the glorious light of their names being recorded in heaven.

18 He replied, "I saw Satan[l] fall like lightning
from heaven.[m] 19 I have given you authority to
trample on snakes[n] and scorpions and to overcome all the power of the enemy; nothing will
harm you. 20 However, do not rejoice that the spirits submit to you, but rejoice that your names are
written in heaven."[o]
21 At that time Jesus, full of joy through the Holy
Spirit, said, "I praise you, Father, Lord of heaven
and earth, because you have hidden these things
from the wise and learned, and revealed them to
little children.[p] Yes, Father, for this was your good
pleasure.
22 "All things have been committed to me by my
Father.[q] No one knows who the Son is except the
Father, and no one knows who the Father is
except the Son and those to whom the Son
chooses to reveal him."[r]
23 Then he turned to his disciples and said privately, "Blessed are the eyes that see what you see.
24 For I tell you that many prophets and kings
wanted to see what you see but did not see it, and
to hear what you hear but did not hear it."[s]

The Parable of the Good Samaritan

25 On one occasion an expert in the law stood up
to test Jesus. "Teacher," he asked, "what must I do
to inherit eternal life?"[t]
26 "What is written in the Law?" he replied.
"How do you read it?"
27 He answered: " 'Love the Lord your God with
all your heart and with all your soul and with all
your strength and with all your mind'[a];[u] and,
'Love your neighbor as yourself.'[b]"[v]
28 "You have answered correctly," Jesus replied.
"Do this and you will live."[w]
29 But he wanted to justify himself,[x] so he asked
Jesus, "And who is my neighbor?"
30 In reply Jesus said: "A man was going down
from Jerusalem to Jericho, when he fell into the
hands of robbers. They stripped him of his clothes,
beat him and went away, leaving him half dead.
31 A priest happened to be going down the same
road, and when he saw the man, he passed by on
the other side.[y] 32 So too, a Levite, when he came to
the place and saw him, passed by on the other side.
33 But a Samaritan,[z] as he traveled, came where the
man was; and when he saw him, he took pity on
him. 34 He went to him and bandaged his wounds,
pouring on oil and wine. Then he put the man on
his own donkey, took him to an inn and took care
of him. 35 The next day he took out two silver coins[c]
and gave them to the innkeeper. 'Look after him,'
he said, 'and when I return, I will reimburse you
for any extra expense you may have.'
36 "Which of these three do you think was a
neighbor to the man who fell into the hands of
robbers?"

10:18 [l]Mt 4:10 [m]Isa 14:12; Rev 9:1; 12:8,9
10:19 [n]Mk 16:18; Ac 28:3-5
10:20 [o]Ex 32:32; Ps 69:28; Da 12:1; Php 4:3; Heb 12:23; Rev 13:8; 20:12; 21:27
10:21 [p]1Co 1:26-29
10:22 [q]Mt 28:18 [r]Jn 1:18
10:24 [s]1Pe 1:10-12
10:25 [t]Mt 19:16; Lk 18:18
10:27 [u]Dt 6:5 [v]Lev 19:18; Mt 5:43
10:28 [w]Lev 18:5; Ro 7:10
10:29 [x]Lk 16:15
10:31 [y]Lev 21:1-3
10:33 [z]Mt 10:5

[a] *27* Deut. 6:5 [b] *27* Lev. 19:18 [c] *35* Greek *two denarii*

37 The expert in the law replied, "The one who
had mercy on him."
Jesus told him, "Go and do likewise."

At the Home of Martha and Mary

38 As Jesus and his disciples were on their way,
10:38 he came to a village where a woman named Mar-
[a]Jn 11:1; 12:2 tha[a] opened her home to him. 39 She had a sister
called Mary,[b] who sat at the Lord's feet[c] listening
10:39 to what he said. 40 But Martha was distracted by
[b]Jn 11:1; 12:3 all the preparations that had to be made. She came
[c]Lk 8:35 to him and asked, "Lord, don't you care[d] that my
sister has left me to do the work by myself? Tell
10:40 [d]Mk 4:38 her to help me!"
41 "Martha, Martha," the Lord answered, "you
10:41 [e]Mt 6:25-34; Lk 12:11,22 are worried[e] and upset about many things, 42 but
only one thing is needed.[af] Mary has chosen what
is better, and it will not be taken away from her."
10:42 [f]Ps 27:4

Jesus' Teaching on Prayer

11:1 [g]Lk 3:21 [h]Jn 13:13 **11** One day Jesus was praying[g] in a certain
place. When he finished, one of his disciples
said to him, "Lord,[h] teach us to pray, just as John
taught his disciples."
2 He said to them, "When you pray, say:

" 'Father,[b]
hallowed be your name,
11:2 [i]Mt 3:2 your kingdom[i] come.[c]
3 Give us each day our daily bread.
4 Forgive us our sins,
for we also forgive everyone who sins
11:4 [j]Mt 18:35; Mk 11:25 against us.[dj]
[k]Mt 26:41; Jas 1:13 And lead us not into temptation.[e]' "[k]

5 Then he said to them, "Suppose one of you has
a friend, and he goes to him at midnight and says,
'Friend, lend me three loaves of bread, 6 because a
friend of mine on a journey has come to me, and
I have nothing to set before him.'
7 "Then the one inside answers, 'Don't bother
me. The door is already locked, and my children
are with me in bed. I can't get up and give you
anything.' 8 I tell you, though he will not get up
and give him the bread because he is his friend,
yet because of the man's boldness[f] he will get up
11:8 [l]Lk 18:1-6 and give him as much as he needs.[l]
9 "So I say to you: Ask and it will be given to
11:9 [m]Mt 7:7 you;[m] seek and you will find; knock and the door
will be opened to you. 10 For everyone who asks
receives; he who seeks finds; and to him who
knocks, the door will be opened.
11 "Which of you fathers, if your son asks for[g] a
fish, will give him a snake instead? 12 Or if he asks
for an egg, will give him a scorpion? 13 If you then,

[a] 42 Some manuscripts *but few things are needed—or only one*
[b] 2 Some manuscripts *Our Father in heaven* [c] 2 Some manuscripts *come. May your will be done on earth as it is in heaven.* [d] 4 Greek *everyone who is indebted to us*
[e] 4 Some manuscripts *temptation but deliver us from the evil one* [f] 8 Or *persistence* [g] 11 Some manuscripts *for bread, will give him a stone; or if he asks for*

Martha

LK 10:38–42

Will all the Marthas in the room please raise your hands? Yes, God sees all those hands! After all, women are taught to be "do-ers," not "be-ers." When houseguests show up, women shift into fifth gear. When someone stays overnight, women do more laps around the house than a car at the Indy 500.

Unfortunately, this scenario can apply to women spiritually as well as literally. Once women slip into their "doing" gear, many have trouble downshifting—ever. Being quiet and contemplative makes them feel guilty—shouldn't they be doing something for someone somewhere? In Mary-fashion, we need to learn to hear God calling us away from our tasks for a pit stop. At Jesus' feet we'll be refueled. Then we can dash off to "Martha" the world that awaits us (see character sketches for Martha and Mary on pages 1844 and 1843).

Good Gifts

LK 11:11-13

What does God consider a good gift? Jesus uses the analogies of a son asking for a fish or an egg—both food for sustenance—and receiving from his father a snake or a scorpion—both creatures of nature that can kill. Then Jesus says that God, out of his bounty, knows how to give good gifts, just as earthly fathers love giving good gifts to their children. God could give us health or wealth, but these are fleeting presents. Instead, he gives us a greater gift, one that feeds our souls. He gives us a part of himself—the Holy Spirit—to be with us at all times and in all circumstances. What more could we ask of a loving Father?

though you are evil, know how to give good gifts
to your children, how much more will your Father
in heaven give the Holy Spirit to those who ask
him!"

Jesus and Beelzebub

14Jesus was driving out a demon that was mute.
When the demon left, the man who had been
mute spoke, and the crowd was amazed.[n] 15But **11:14** [n]Mt 9:32,33
some of them said, "By Beelzebub,[a][o] the prince of
demons, he is driving out demons."[p] 16Others test- **11:15** [o]Mk 3:22
ed him by asking for a sign from heaven.[q] [p]Mt 9:34
17Jesus knew their thoughts[r] and said to them:
"Any kingdom divided against itself will be **11:16** [q]Mt 12:38
ruined, and a house divided against itself will fall.
18If Satan[s] is divided against himself, how can his **11:17** [r]Mt 9:4
kingdom stand? I say this because you claim that
I drive out demons by Beelzebub. 19Now if I drive **11:18** [s]Mt 4:10
out demons by Beelzebub, by whom do your fol-
lowers drive them out? So then, they will be your
judges. 20But if I drive out demons by the finger of **11:20** [t]Ex 8:19
God,[t] then the kingdom of God[u] has come to you. [u]Mt 3:2
21"When a strong man, fully armed, guards his
own house, his possessions are safe. 22But when
someone stronger attacks and overpowers him, he
takes away the armor in which the man trusted
and divides up the spoils.
23"He who is not with me is against me, and he **11:23** [v]Mt 12:30;
who does not gather with me, scatters.[v] Mk 9:40;
24"When an evil[b] spirit comes out of a man, it Lk 9:50
goes through arid places seeking rest and does not
find it. Then it says, 'I will return to the house I
left.' 25When it arrives, it finds the house swept
clean and put in order. 26Then it goes and takes
seven other spirits more wicked than itself, and
they go in and live there. And the final condition **11:26**
of that man is worse than the first."[w] [w]2Pe 2:20
27As Jesus was saying these things, a woman in
the crowd called out, "Blessed is the mother who **11:27**
gave you birth and nursed you."[x] [x]Lk 23:29
28He replied, "Blessed rather are those who hear
the word of God[y] and obey it."[z] **11:28** [y]Heb 4:12 [z]Pr 8:32; Lk 6:47; 8:21; Jn 14:21

The Sign of Jonah

29As the crowds increased, Jesus said, "This is a
wicked generation. It asks for a miraculous sign,[a] **11:29**
but none will be given it except the sign of Jonah.[b] [a]ver 16;
30For as Jonah was a sign to the Ninevites, so also Mt 12:38
will the Son of Man be to this generation. 31The [b]Jnh 1:17; Mt 16:4
Queen of the South will rise at the judgment with
the men of this generation and condemn them; for
she came from the ends of the earth to listen to
Solomon's wisdom,[c] and now one[c] greater than **11:31** [c]1Ki 10:1;
Solomon is here. 32The men of Nineveh will stand 2Ch 9:1
up at the judgment with this generation and condemn it; for they repented at the preaching of
Jonah,[d] and now one greater than Jonah is here. **11:32** [d]Jnh 3:5

[a] *15* Greek *Beezeboul* or *Beelzeboul*; also in verses 18 and 19
[b] *24* Greek *unclean* [c] *31* Or *something*; also in verse 32

The Lamp of the Body

33“No one lights a lamp and puts it in a place
where it will be hidden, or under a bowl. Instead
he puts it on its stand, so that those who come in
may see the light.[e] 34Your eye is the lamp of your
body. When your eyes are good, your whole body
also is full of light. But when they are bad, your
body also is full of darkness. 35See to it, then, that
the light within you is not darkness. 36Therefore,
if your whole body is full of light, and no part of
it dark, it will be completely lighted, as when the
light of a lamp shines on you.”

Six Woes

37When Jesus had finished speaking, a Pharisee
invited him to eat with him; so he went in and
reclined at the table.[f] 38But the Pharisee, noticing
that Jesus did not first wash before the meal,[g] was
surprised.
39Then the Lord[h] said to him, “Now then, you
Pharisees clean the outside of the cup and dish,
but inside you are full of greed and wickedness.[i]
40You foolish people![j] Did not the one who made
the outside make the inside also? 41But give what
is inside ⌊the dish⌋[a] to the poor,[k] and everything
will be clean for you.[l]
42“Woe to you Pharisees, because you give God
a tenth[m] of your mint, rue and all other kinds of
garden herbs, but you neglect justice and the love
of God.[n] You should have practiced the latter without leaving the former undone.[o]
43“Woe to you Pharisees, because you love the
most important seats in the synagogues and greetings in the marketplaces.[p]
44“Woe to you, because you are like unmarked
graves,[q] which men walk over without knowing it.”
45One of the experts in the law[r] answered him,
“Teacher, when you say these things, you insult
us also.”
46Jesus replied, “And you experts in the law,
woe to you, because you load people down with
burdens they can hardly carry, and you yourselves
will not lift one finger to help them.[s]
47“Woe to you, because you build tombs for the
prophets, and it was your forefathers who killed
them. 48So you testify that you approve of what
your forefathers did; they killed the prophets, and
you build their tombs.[t] 49Because of this, God in
his wisdom[u] said, ‘I will send them prophets and
apostles, some of whom they will kill and others
they will persecute.’[v] 50Therefore this generation
will be held responsible for the blood of all the
prophets that has been shed since the beginning
of the world, 51from the blood of Abel[w] to the
blood of Zechariah,[x] who was killed between the
altar and the sanctuary. Yes, I tell you, this generation will be held responsible for it all.[y]

11:33 [e]Mt 5:15; Mk 4:21; Lk 8:16
11:37 [f]Lk 7:36; 14:1
11:38 [g]Mk 7:3,4
11:39 [h]Lk 7:13 [i]Mt 23:25, 26; Mk 7:20-23
11:40 [j]Lk 12:20; 1Co 15:36
11:41 [k]Lk 12:33 [l]Ac 10:15
11:42 [m]Lk 18:12 [n]Dt 6:5; Mic 6:8 [o]Mt 23:23
11:43 [p]Mt 23:6,7; Mk 12:38-39; Lk 14:7; 20:46
11:44 [q]Mt 23:27
11:45 [r]Mt 22:35
11:46 [s]Mt 23:4
11:48 [t]Mt 23:29-32; Ac 7:51-53
11:49 [u]1Co 1:24, 30; Col 2:3 [v]Mt 23:34
11:51 [w]Ge 4:8 [x]2Ch 24:20, 21 [y]Mt 23:35,36

[a] 41 Or *what you have*

Unmarked Graves

LK 11:44

Tombs in Biblical times were often cut from rocks and were marked, not with the occupants' names, but by being whitewashed once a year. This made them easily visible and prevented individuals from accidentally coming into contact with the dead, which rendered a person ceremonially unclean.

Jesus tells the Pharisees that they are like unclean tombs, but they are the worst kind of tomb—an unmarked one, so anyone coming into contact with them becomes unclean too. The Pharisees, like unmarked tombs, are deceptive because they do not declare what they are. And contact with them can corrupt.

Jesus explains in Luke 11:39 that washing the outside of a cup filled with greed and wickedness does not render that cup clean. We, too, can look good on the outside, masking sinful attitudes on the inside. Take a few minutes to examine the “cup” of your life. Has it been washed outside *and* inside?

Speaking Up

LK 12:11-12

Jesus knows that his followers will be called before authorities to give an account of their faith in him, and he wants them to know that, even when they are under duress, God will be with them. Jesus says the Holy Spirit will "teach" them what to say (Lk 12:12). What a relief! That doesn't mean, however, that Jesus' followers are excused from being students of his words. Instead, 2 Timothy 2:15 reminds us: "Do your best to present yourself to God as one approved, a workman who does not need to be ashamed and who correctly handles the word of truth." Jesus' words assure us that we have the perfect safeguards for those moments that would otherwise render us speechless: the Holy Spirit to prompt us at that moment and our knowledge of the Bible acquired through diligent study and application. Don't neglect either one.

52"Woe to you experts in the law, because you
have taken away the key to knowledge. You yourselves have not entered, and you have hindered 11:52
those who were entering."[z] zMt 23:13
53When Jesus left there, the Pharisees and the
teachers of the law began to oppose him fiercely
and to besiege him with questions, 54waiting to 11:54
catch him in something he might say.[a] aMt 12:10;
Mk 12:13

Warnings and Encouragements

12 Meanwhile, when a crowd of many thousands had gathered, so that they were tramp-
pling on one another, Jesus began to speak first to
his disciples, saying: "Be on your guard against 12:1
the yeast of the Pharisees, which is hypocrisy.[b] bMt 16:6,11,
2There is nothing concealed that will not be dis- 12; Mk 8:15
closed, or hidden that will not be made known.[c] 12:2
3What you have said in the dark will be heard in cMk 4:22;
the daylight, and what you have whispered in the Lk 8:17
ear in the inner rooms will be proclaimed from
the roofs.
4"I tell you, my friends,[d] do not be afraid of 12:4 dJn 15:14,15
those who kill the body and after that can do no
more. 5But I will show you whom you should
fear: Fear him who, after the killing of the body,
has power to throw you into hell. Yes, I tell you,
fear him.[e] 6Are not five sparrows sold for two 12:5 eHeb 10:31
pennies[a]? Yet not one of them is forgotten by God.
7Indeed, the very hairs of your head are all num- 12:7
bered.[f] Don't be afraid; you are worth more than fMt 10:30
many sparrows.[g] gMt 12:12
8"I tell you, whoever acknowledges me before
men, the Son of Man will also acknowledge him
before the angels of God.[h] 9But he who disowns 12:8
me before men will be disowned[i] before the hLk 15:10
angels of God. 10And everyone who speaks a word 12:9
against the Son of Man[j] will be forgiven, but any- iMk 8:38;
one who blasphemes against the Holy Spirit will 2Ti 2:12
not be forgiven.[k] 12:10
11"When you are brought before synagogues, jMt 8:20
rulers and authorities, do not worry about how kMt 12:31, 32; Mk 3:28-
you will defend yourselves or what you will say,[l] 29; 1Jn 5:16
12for the Holy Spirit will teach you at that time 12:11
what you should say."[m] lMt 10:17, 19;

The Parable of the Rich Fool Mk 13:11; Lk 21:12,14

13Someone in the crowd said to him, "Teacher, 12:12
tell my brother to divide the inheritance with me." mEx 4:12;
14Jesus replied, "Man, who appointed me a Mt 10:20;
judge or an arbiter between you?" 15Then he said Mk 13:11; Lk 21:15
to them, "Watch out! Be on your guard against all
kinds of greed; a man's life does not consist in the 12:15
abundance of his possessions."[n] nJob 20:20;
16And he told them this parable: "The ground 31:24;
of a certain rich man produced a good crop. 17He Ps 62:10
thought to himself, 'What shall I do? I have no
place to store my crops.'
18"Then he said, 'This is what I'll do. I will tear
down my barns and build bigger ones, and there

a 6 Greek *two assaria*

I will store all my grain and my goods. 19And I'll
say to myself, "You have plenty of good things laid
up for many years. Take life easy; eat, drink and
12:20 be merry." '
[o]Jer 17:11; 20"But God said to him, 'You fool![o] This very
Lk 11:40 night your life will be demanded from you.[p] Then
[p]Job 27:8 [q]Ps 39:6; who will get what you have prepared for
49:10 yourself?'[q]
12:21 21"This is how it will be with anyone who stores
[r]ver 33 up things for himself but is not rich toward God."[r]

Do Not Worry

22Then Jesus said to his disciples: "Therefore I
tell you, do not worry about your life, what you
will eat; or about your body, what you will wear.
23Life is more than food, and the body more than
clothes. 24Consider the ravens: They do not sow or
reap, they have no storeroom or barn; yet God feeds
12:24 them.[s] And how much more valuable you are than
[s]Job 38:41; Ps 147:9 birds! 25Who of you by worrying can add a single
hour to his life[a]? 26Since you cannot do this very little thing, why do you worry about the rest?
27"Consider how the lilies grow. They do not
12:27 labor or spin. Yet I tell you, not even Solomon in
[t]1Ki 10:4-7 all his splendor[t] was dressed like one of these. 28If
that is how God clothes the grass of the field,
which is here today, and tomorrow is thrown into
the fire, how much more will he clothe you,
12:28 O you of little faith![u] 29And do not set your heart
[u]Mt 6:30 on what you will eat or drink; do not worry about
it. 30For the pagan world runs after all such things,
12:30 and your Father[v] knows that you need them.[w]
[v]Lk 6:36 [w]Mt 6:8 31But seek his kingdom,[x] and these things will be
12:31 given to you as well.[y]
[x]Mt 3:2 32"Do not be afraid,[z] little flock, for your Father
[y]Mt 19:29 has been pleased to give you the kingdom.[a] 33Sell
12:32 your possessions and give to the poor.[b] Provide
[z]Mt 14:27 purses for yourselves that will not wear out, a
[a]Mt 25:34 treasure in heaven[c] that will not be exhausted,
12:33 where no thief comes near and no moth destroys.[d]
[b]Mt 19:21; Ac 2:45 34For where your treasure is, there your heart will
[c]Mt 6:20 be also.[e]
[d]Jas 5:2
12:34 [e]Mt 6:21

Watchfulness

35"Be dressed ready for service and keep your
lamps burning, 36like men waiting for their master to return from a wedding banquet, so that
when he comes and knocks they can immediately open the door for him. 37It will be good for
12:37 those servants whose master finds them watching
[f]Mt 24:42, 46; 25:13 when he comes.[f] I tell you the truth, he will dress
[g]Mt 20:28 himself to serve, will have them recline at the
12:39 table and will come and wait on them.[g] 38It will be
[h]Mt 6:19; good for those servants whose master finds them
1Th 5:2; ready, even if he comes in the second or third
2Pe 3:10; watch of the night. 39But understand this: If the
Rev 3:3; 16:15 owner of the house had known at what hour the
12:40 thief[h] was coming, he would not have let his
[i]Mk 13:33; Lk 21:36 house be broken into. 40You also must be ready,[i]

[a] 25 Or *single cubit to his height*

Civilla Durfee Martin wrote this favorite hymn of singer Ethel Waters after visiting a couple, both of whom were invalids. When asked how they maintained their cheerfulness and positive attitudes in spite of their afflictions, the wife answered, "His eye is on the sparrow, and I know he watches me." Her answer inspired the words of this song.

His Eye Is on the Sparrow

Why should I feel discouraged, why
should the shadows come,
Why should my heart be lonely, and
long for heaven and home,
When Jesus is my portion? My
constant friend is He:
His eye is on the sparrow, and
I know He watches me;
His eye is on the sparrow, and
I know He watches me.

"Let not your heart be troubled,"
His tender word I hear,
And resting on His goodness, I lose
my doubts and fears;
Though by the path He leadeth, but
one step I may see;
His eye is on the sparrow, and
I know He watches me;
His eye is on the sparrow, and
I know He watches me.

Whenever I am tempted, whenever
clouds arise,
When songs give place to sighing,
when hope within me dies,
I draw the closer to Him, from care
He sets me free;
His eye is on the sparrow, and
I know He watches me;
His eye is on the sparrow, and
I know He watches me.

—Civilla Durfee Martin (1866–1948)

Family Divisions

LK 12:51–53

While Christ brings peace to an individual's heart, faith in him at times brings separation to families. Jesus warns us in a straightforward fashion that following him is not all sweetness and light. Some family members will choose to follow him; some will not. These fundamental differences may cause bitterness and darkness in a family. Hearts filled with pride and prejudice will clash with spiritually restored hearts. And that will break everyone's heart.

because the Son of Man will come at an hour
when you do not expect him."
41 Peter asked, "Lord, are you telling this parable to us, or to everyone?"
42 The Lord[j] answered, "Who then is the faith- **12:42** [j]Lk 7:13
ful and wise manager, whom the master puts in
charge of his servants to give them their food
allowance at the proper time? 43 It will be good for
that servant whom the master finds doing so
when he returns. 44 I tell you the truth, he will put
him in charge of all his possessions. 45 But suppose
the servant says to himself, 'My master is taking a
long time in coming,' and he then begins to beat
the menservants and maidservants and to eat and
drink and get drunk. 46 The master of that servant
will come on a day when he does not expect him **12:46**
and at an hour he is not aware of.[k] He will cut [k]ver 40
him to pieces and assign him a place with the
unbelievers.
47 "That servant who knows his master's will
and does not get ready or does not do what his **12:47**
master wants will be beaten with many blows.[l] [l]Dt 25:2
48 But the one who does not know and does things
deserving punishment will be beaten with few
blows.[m] From everyone who has been given **12:48**
much, much will be demanded; and from the one [m]Lev 5:17; Nu 15:27-30
who has been entrusted with much, much more
will be asked.

Not Peace but Division

49 "I have come to bring fire on the earth, and
how I wish it were already kindled! 50 But I have a **12:50**
baptism[n] to undergo, and how distressed I am [n]Mk 10:38
until it is completed![o] 51 Do you think I came to [o]Jn 19:30
bring peace on earth? No, I tell you, but division.
52 From now on there will be five in one family
divided against each other, three against two and
two against three. 53 They will be divided, father
against son and son against father, mother against
daughter and daughter against mother, mother-in-
law against daughter-in-law and daughter-in-law **12:53**
against mother-in-law."[p] [p]Mic 7:6; Mt 10:21

Interpreting the Times

54 He said to the crowd: "When you see a cloud
rising in the west, immediately you say, 'It's going
to rain,' and it does.[q] 55 And when the south wind **12:54**
blows, you say, 'It's going to be hot,' and it is. [q]Mt 16:2
56 Hypocrites! You know how to interpret the
appearance of the earth and the sky. How is it that **12:56**
you don't know how to interpret this present time?[r] [r]Mt 16:3
57 "Why don't you judge for yourselves what is
right? 58 As you are going with your adversary to
the magistrate, try hard to be reconciled to him on
the way, or he may drag you off to the judge, and **12:58**
the judge turn you over to the officer, and the offi- [s]Mt 5:25
cer throw you into prison.[s] 59 I tell you, you will **12:59**
not get out until you have paid the last penny.[a]"[t] [t]Mt 5:26; Mk 12:42

[a] 59 Greek *lepton*

Sinful Woman

Loving With Abandon

Feet are smelly—even today with deodorant soaps, daily showers and fresh socks. How much more so in Jesus' day, when the streets were filled with dust, garbage and animal dung. Add to that open sandals and a lot of walking. It took a fountain of tears to wash away the dirt.

Perhaps she knew one of Simon's servants who let her in when she learned Jesus would be there. The "sinful woman" didn't come to crash a party; she only came to bless the Lord. She had so little concern for herself, so much for Jesus. As she wept and used her long hair as a towel, she kissed his feet in gratitude. Her perfume would make them sweet—anointing the Anointed One.

Her conversion was probably recent, for she was known for her infamous sin. Perhaps in time those around her would see her repentance shape a whole new way of life. Even now her heart was an open book to those who had eyes to read it. This was no elaborate ploy for getting attention—she stood behind Jesus, at his feet as he reclined to eat. She was immersed in love for him, her act the effect, not the cause, of her pardon. She no longer cared how she looked. Her surroundings were irrelevant. Her heart was set to serve the Lord and him only.

Simon had invited Jesus to his home looking for some way to trap him. He thought this woman might be just the ticket. If Jesus were a prophet, he would know her kind. How blind was Simon that he did not see the handiwork of God! How lost to think his judgment carried weight. Jesus exposed Simon's spiritual poverty with these words: "Her many sins have been forgiven—for she loved much. But he who has been forgiven little loves little" (Lk 7:47).

Most Christians know of someone who came to Jesus with a shameful past. How tempting it is to see ourselves better than they, to freeze them in their past sin while at the same time we ignore our own in the present. Be careful. Like the woman who fell at his feet, we all owe Jesus more than we could ever repay.

Sinful Woman
Luke 7:36–50

Candid SNAPSHOT When a woman who had lived a sinful life in that town learned that Jesus was eating at the Pharisee's house, she brought an alabaster jar of perfume, and as she stood behind him at his feet weeping, she began to wet his feet with her tears. Then she wiped them with her hair, kissed them and poured perfume on them (Luke 7:37–38).

Mary Magdalene

One-Track Heart

The disciples did not believe the news. They called it "nonsense" (Lk 24:11). As much as they longed for Jesus to be alive, surely the angel's annoucement of Jesus' resurrection would not be made first to a group of women—especially one with Mary's background.

Mary's grief had been profound. How could she go on? What meaning could life hold with Jesus gone? Her eyes red and swollen from weeping, she thought she saw the gardener. Then he spoke her name: "Mary." Her heart raced again at the memory. "I have seen the Lord!" Her witness was sure, for she knew him well.

Before she met Jesus, life was torture for Mary of Magdala. Imagine *seven* demons. Their effect may have been physical, emotional, moral or all three combined. Undoubtedly, before her healing, Mary had few friends and was greatly misunderstood. We do know she had a reputation among the disciples—the Mary of seven demons.

There are no details of Mary's deliverance, but as the demons' crushing hold was broken, Jesus surely looked into eyes filled with a pure love for God. From that moment on, her sole focus was to follow Jesus.

She was among the women who traveled with Jesus and his disciples, "helping to support them out of their own means" (Lk 8:3). All four Gospels record her at the cross, outside the tomb as Jesus is laid to rest, and among those who came to anoint his body after the Sabbath. Even death could not quench the fire of her love and the constancy of her presence with him.

There was no mistake: Jesus chose Mary Magdalene to be the first of his followers to see him risen from the grave (Jn 20:18). He wanted personally to end her bewilderment at the empty tomb. He waited for her, longing to reward her single-hearted devotion and loyalty. He was glad to see her. Mary's was a love that Jesus trusted, a love that he cherished.

There is a reward for faithfulness far beyond our ability to comprehend or predict. When God calls us to a life of single-hearted devotion to him, we need to hold on to it with everything in us. Anything others might think or say can't begin to touch the wonder we will know when we see him face to face and hear him speak our names.

Mary Magdalene
(bitter)

Matthew 27:56,61; 28:1
Mark 15:40–41,47; 16:1–11
Luke 8:1–3; 23:49; 23:55–24:11
John 19:25; 20:1–18

Candid SNAPSHOT When Jesus rose early on the first day of the week, he appeared first to Mary Magdalene, out of whom he had driven seven demons. She went and told those who had been with him and who were mourning and weeping. When they heard that Jesus was alive and that she had seen him, they did not believe it (Mark 16:9–11).

Repent or Perish

13 Now there were some present at that time
13:1 who told Jesus about the Galileans whose
[u]Mt 27:2 blood Pilate[u] had mixed with their sacrifices. 2Jesus
answered, "Do you think that these Galileans were
13:2 worse sinners than all the other Galileans because
[v]Jn 9:2,3 they suffered this way?[v] 3I tell you, no! But unless
13:4 you repent, you too will all perish. 4Or those eigh-
[w]Jn 9:7,11 teen who died when the tower in Siloam[w] fell on
them—do you think they were more guilty than all
13:5 the others living in Jerusalem? 5I tell you, no! But
[x]Mt 3:2; unless you repent,[x] you too will all perish."
Ac 2:38 6Then he told this parable: "A man had a fig
tree, planted in his vineyard, and he went to look
13:6 [y]Isa 5:2; for fruit on it, but did not find any.[y] 7So he said to
Jer 8:13; the man who took care of the vineyard, 'For three
Mt 21:19 years now I've been coming to look for fruit on
13:7 this fig tree and haven't found any. Cut it down![z]
[z]Mt 3:10 Why should it use up the soil?'
8" 'Sir,' the man replied, 'leave it alone for one
more year, and I'll dig around it and fertilize it. 9If it
bears fruit next year, fine! If not, then cut it down.' "

A Crippled Woman Healed on the Sabbath

13:10 10On a Sabbath Jesus was teaching in one of the
[a]Mt 4:23 synagogues,[a] 11and a woman was there who had
13:11 been crippled by a spirit for eighteen years.[b] She
[b]ver 16 was bent over and could not straighten up at all.
12When Jesus saw her, he called her forward and
13:13 said to her, "Woman, you are set free from your
[c]Mk 5:23 infirmity." 13Then he put his hands on her,[c] and
immediately she straightened up and praised God.
14Indignant because Jesus had healed on the
13:14 Sabbath,[d] the synagogue ruler[e] said to the people,
[d]Mt 12:2; Lk 14:3 "There are six days for work.[f] So come and be
[e]Mk 5:22 [f]Ex 20:9 healed on those days, not on the Sabbath."
15The Lord answered him, "You hypocrites!
Doesn't each of you on the Sabbath untie his ox or
13:15 donkey from the stall and lead it out to give it
[g]Lk 14:5 water?[g] 16Then should not this woman, a daughter
13:16 of Abraham,[h] whom Satan[i] has kept bound for
[h]Lk 3:8; 19:9 eighteen long years, be set free on the Sabbath day
[i]Mt 4:10 from what bound her?"
13:17 17When he said this, all his opponents were
[j]Isa 66:5 humiliated,[j] but the people were delighted with
all the wonderful things he was doing.

The Parables of the Mustard Seed and the Yeast

18Then Jesus asked, "What is the kingdom of
13:18 [k]Mt 3:2 God[k] like?[l] What shall I compare it to? 19It is like
[l]Mt 13:24 a mustard seed, which a man took and planted in
13:19 his garden. It grew and became a tree,[m] and the
[m]Lk 17:6 birds of the air perched in its branches."[n]
[n]Mt 13:32 20Again he asked, "What shall I compare the
kingdom of God to? 21It is like yeast that a woman
took and mixed into a large amount[a] of flour until
13:21 [o]1Co 5:6 it worked all through the dough."[o]

[a] *21* Greek *three satas* (probably about 1/2 bushel or 22 liters)

Humiliated or Delighted

LK 13:10-17

Jesus, in true rabbinic style, debates with the synagogue ruler the appropriateness of a woman being healed on the Sabbath. Those opposed to Jesus can't find fault with his arguments and have nothing to retort. But rather than being won over, they are humiliated, which keeps them from responding to the wonderful news that the Messiah is in their midst. On the other hand, those who come to worship at the synagogue find more reason to rejoice than they ever expected. Here is someone who not only unbinds Satan's 18-year grip on a woman but also someone who unbinds all of them from the stifling rigidity of the rules the religious leaders have laid on the people (see the character sketch for this woman on page 1877).

A Narrow Door

LK 13:24

Most of us would like to think our homes have wide doors that evoke warmth and hospitality. But Jesus tells us the door to God's kingdom is the opposite. It is narrow—meaning that the way into the kingdom is not wide and easy but narrow and demanding. Suffering and self-denial are the austere apparel of the guests who gain admittance rather than the fine evening dress of pride and self-indulgence. In fact, the kingdom's door not only isn't wide, but it also isn't handsome, brightly painted or bedecked with wreaths. Yet, on the other side of the door, Jesus informs us, a feast is going on, attended by people we long to join (Lk 13:27–29). The price of admission is high—but worth it.

The Narrow Door

22Then Jesus went through the towns and vil-
lages, teaching as he made his way to Jerusalem.[p] 13:22 [p]Lk 9:51
23Someone asked him, "Lord, are only a few peo-
ple going to be saved?"
He said to them, 24"Make every effort to enter
through the narrow door,[q] because many, I tell 13:24 [q]Mt 7:13
you, will try to enter and will not be able to.
25Once the owner of the house gets up and closes
the door, you will stand outside knocking and
pleading, 'Sir, open the door for us.'
"But he will answer, 'I don't know you or 13:25
where you come from.'[r] [r]Mt 7:23; 25:10-12
26"Then you will say, 'We ate and drank with
you, and you taught in our streets.'
27"But he will reply, 'I don't know you or where
you come from. Away from me, all you 13:27
evildoers!'[s] [s]Mt 7:23; 25:41
28"There will be weeping there, and gnashing of
teeth,[t] when you see Abraham, Isaac and Jacob 13:28
and all the prophets in the kingdom of God, but [t]Mt 8:12
you yourselves thrown out. 29People will come
from east and west[u] and north and south, and will 13:29
take their places at the feast in the kingdom of [u]Mt 8:11
God. 30Indeed there are those who are last who
will be first, and first who will be last."[v] 13:30 [v]Mt 19:30

Jesus' Sorrow for Jerusalem

31At that time some Pharisees came to Jesus and
said to him, "Leave this place and go somewhere 13:31
else. Herod[w] wants to kill you." [w]Mt 14:1
32He replied, "Go tell that fox, 'I will drive out
demons and heal people today and tomorrow, and 13:32
on the third day I will reach my goal.'[x] 33In any [x]Heb 2:10
case, I must keep going today and tomorrow and 13:33
the next day—for surely no prophet[y] can die out- [y]Mt 21:11
side Jerusalem!
34"O Jerusalem, Jerusalem, you who kill the
prophets and stone those sent to you, how often I
have longed to gather your children together, as a
hen gathers her chicks under her wings,[z] but you 13:34
were not willing! 35Look, your house is left to you [z]Mt 23:37
desolate.[a] I tell you, you will not see me again 13:35
until you say, 'Blessed is he who comes in the [a]Jer 12:17; 22:5
name of the Lord.'[a]"[b] [b]Ps 118:26; Mt 21:9; Lk 19:38

Jesus at a Pharisee's House

14 One Sabbath, when Jesus went to eat in the 14:1
house of a prominent Pharisee,[c] he was [c]Lk 7:36; 11:37
being carefully watched.[d] 2There in front of him [d]Mt 12:10
was a man suffering from dropsy. 3Jesus asked the
Pharisees and experts in the law,[e] "Is it lawful to 14:3
heal on the Sabbath or not?"[f] 4But they remained [e]Mt 22:35 [f]Mt 12:2
silent. So taking hold of the man, he healed him
and sent him away.
5Then he asked them, "If one of you has a son[b]
or an ox that falls into a well on the Sabbath day,

[a] *35* Psalm 118:26 [b] *5* Some manuscripts *donkey*

14:5 will you not immediately pull him out?"[g] 6And
[g]Lk 13:15 they had nothing to say.
14:7 7When he noticed how the guests picked the
[h]Lk 11:43 places of honor at the table,[h] he told them this
parable: 8"When someone invites you to a wed-
ding feast, do not take the place of honor, for a
person more distinguished than you may have
been invited. 9If so, the host who invited both of
you will come and say to you, 'Give this man your
seat.' Then, humiliated, you will have to take the
least important place. 10But when you are invited,
take the lowest place, so that when your host
comes, he will say to you, 'Friend, move up to a
better place.' Then you will be honored in the
presence of all your fellow guests. 11For everyone
14:11 who exalts himself will be humbled, and he who
[i]Mt 23:12; humbles himself will be exalted."[i]
Lk 18:14 12Then Jesus said to his host, "When you give a
luncheon or dinner, do not invite your friends,
your brothers or relatives, or your rich neighbors;
if you do, they may invite you back and so you
14:13 will be repaid. 13But when you give a banquet,
[j]ver 21 invite the poor, the crippled, the lame, the blind,[j]
14and you will be blessed. Although they cannot
repay you, you will be repaid at the resurrection
14:14 of the righteous."[k]
[k]Ac 24:15

The Parable of the Great Banquet

15When one of those at the table with him heard
this, he said to Jesus, "Blessed is the man who
14:15 will eat at the feast[l] in the kingdom of God."[m]
[l]Isa 25:6; 16Jesus replied: "A certain man was preparing a
Mt 26:29; great banquet and invited many guests. 17At the
Lk 13:29; time of the banquet he sent his servant to tell
Rev 19:9 those who had been invited, 'Come, for every-
[m]Mt 3:2 thing is now ready.'
18"But they all alike began to make excuses. The
first said, 'I have just bought a field, and I must go
and see it. Please excuse me.'
19"Another said, 'I have just bought five yoke of
oxen, and I'm on my way to try them out. Please
excuse me.'
20"Still another said, 'I just got married, so I
can't come.'
21"The servant came back and reported this to
his master. Then the owner of the house became
angry and ordered his servant, 'Go out quickly
14:21 into the streets and alleys of the town and bring in
[n]ver 13 the poor, the crippled, the blind and the lame.'[n]
22" 'Sir,' the servant said, 'what you ordered has
been done, but there is still room.'
23"Then the master told his servant, 'Go out to
the roads and country lanes and make them come
in, so that my house will be full. 24I tell you, not
one of those men who were invited will get a taste
14:24 of my banquet.' "[o]
[o]Mt 21:43;
Ac 13:46

The Cost of Being a Disciple

25Large crowds were traveling with Jesus, and
turning to them he said: 26"If anyone comes to me

Excuses, Excuses

LK 14:15-24

In Jesus' day, two invitations were commonly extended to guests. The first was issued well in advance of the event and required a response; the second was to announce that the banquet was ready. Apparently, the invitees in Jesus' parable accepted the first invitation but then declined to come when the food and festivities were ready. Jesus portrays the guests as insincere and seeking the slightest excuse to avoid actually attending. Their responses betrayed their indifference to the host and were far more offensive than if they had said no to begin with.

But then haven't we all been impolite "guests" to God? Haven't we at times said that we would spend solitary time with him, that we would be more devoted to him? And yet, when the time comes to act on each of those decisions, we have new purchases to admire or other relationships that woo us away from the One who has prepared a banquet for us. Jesus' story is fair warning to the Pharisees of his day—and to us.

Lost—and Found

LK 15

Jesus declares that he is the seeker of the lost (Lk 19:10). He tells three stories of lost items in Luke 15: a sheep, a coin and a son. Each is found, and the occasion is a cause for rejoicing.

Lots of items can be lost: our eyeglasses, our car keys, our pets, even our youth and our souls. Sometimes we feel as though we've lost our wits, and at times we know we've lost our sense of humor. We can lose our way, our hope, our sense of ourselves. Time and space can disappear on us. Opportunities can dissipate. A battle can be lost. We can be "lost to the world," as in "forgotten." We can be a lost cause or experience a lost weekend (one spent in dissolute living). Take an inventory of what you have lost in your life recently—or something you lost long ago but still feel emptiness about. Prayerfully ask God what you can find within the loss that will enable you to rejoice, not because of the loss, but because God takes things that have strayed away from us and marvelously restores them to us in ways we might not immediately recognize or appreciate.

and does not hate his father and mother, his wife
and children, his brothers and sisters—yes, even
his own life—he cannot be my disciple.[p] 27And
anyone who does not carry his cross and follow
me cannot be my disciple.[q]

28"Suppose one of you wants to build a tower.
Will he not first sit down and estimate the cost to
see if he has enough money to complete it? 29For
if he lays the foundation and is not able to finish
it, everyone who sees it will ridicule him, 30saying,
'This fellow began to build and was not able
to finish.'

31"Or suppose a king is about to go to war
against another king. Will he not first sit down
and consider whether he is able with ten thousand
men to oppose the one coming against him
with twenty thousand? 32If he is not able, he will
send a delegation while the other is still a long
way off and will ask for terms of peace. 33In the
same way, any of you who does not give up everything
he has cannot be my disciple.[r]

34"Salt is good, but if it loses its saltiness, how
can it be made salty again?[s] 35It is fit neither for
the soil nor for the manure pile; it is thrown out.[t]

"He who has ears to hear, let him hear."[u]

The Parable of the Lost Sheep

15 Now the tax collectors[v] and "sinners" were
all gathering around to hear him. 2But the
Pharisees and the teachers of the law muttered,
"This man welcomes sinners and eats with
them."[w]

3Then Jesus told them this parable:[x] 4"Suppose
one of you has a hundred sheep and loses one of
them. Does he not leave the ninety-nine in the
open country and go after the lost sheep until he
finds it?[y] 5And when he finds it, he joyfully puts it
on his shoulders 6and goes home. Then he calls
his friends and neighbors together and says,
'Rejoice with me; I have found my lost sheep.'[z] 7I
tell you that in the same way there will be more
rejoicing in heaven over one sinner who repents
than over ninety-nine righteous persons who do
not need to repent.[a]

The Parable of the Lost Coin

8"Or suppose a woman has ten silver coins[a] and
loses one. Does she not light a lamp, sweep the
house and search carefully until she finds it? 9And
when she finds it, she calls her friends and neighbors
together and says, 'Rejoice with me; I have
found my lost coin.'[b] 10In the same way, I tell you,
there is rejoicing in the presence of the angels of
God over one sinner who repents."[c]

The Parable of the Lost Son

11Jesus continued: "There was a man who had
two sons.[d] 12The younger one said to his father,

[a] 8 Greek *ten drachmas,* each worth about a day's wages

14:26 [p]Mt 10:37; Jn 12:25
14:27 [q]Mt 10:38; Lk 9:23
14:33 [r]Php 3:7,8
14:34 [s]Mk 9:50
14:35 [t]Mt 5:13 [u]Mt 11:15
15:1 [v]Lk 5:29
15:2 [w]Mt 9:11
15:3 [x]Mt 13:3
15:4 [y]Ps 23; 119:176; Jer 31:10; Eze 34:11-16; Lk 5:32; 19:10
15:6 [z]ver 9
15:7 [a]ver 10
15:9 [b]ver 6
15:10 [c]ver 7
15:11 [d]Mt 21:28

15:12 [e]Dt 21:17 'Father, give me my share of the estate.'[e] So he
[f]ver 30 divided his property[f] between them.
13"Not long after that, the younger son got
15:13 together all he had, set off for a distant country
[g]ver 30; and there squandered his wealth[g] in wild living.
Lk 16:1 14After he had spent everything, there was a
severe famine in that whole country, and he
began to be in need. 15So he went and hired himself out to a citizen of that country, who sent him
15:15 to his fields to feed pigs.[h] 16He longed to fill his
[h]Lev 11:7 stomach with the pods that the pigs were eating,
but no one gave him anything.
17"When he came to his senses, he said, 'How
many of my father's hired men have food to spare,
and here I am starving to death! 18I will set out
15:18 and go back to my father and say to him: Father,
[i]Lev 26:40; I have sinned[i] against heaven and against you. 19I
Mt 3:2 am no longer worthy to be called your son; make
me like one of your hired men.' 20So he got up and
went to his father.
"But while he was still a long way off, his father
saw him and was filled with compassion for him;
he ran to his son, threw his arms around him and
15:20 kissed him.[j]
[j]Ge 45:14, 15; 46:29; 21"The son said to him, 'Father, I have sinned
Ac 20:37 against heaven and against you.[k] I am no longer
15:21 worthy to be called your son.[a]'
[k]Ps 51:4 22"But the father said to his servants, 'Quick!
15:22 [l]Zec 3:4; Bring the best robe[l] and put it on him. Put a ring
Rev 6:11 on his finger[m] and sandals on his feet. 23Bring the
[m]Ge 41:42 fattened calf and kill it. Let's have a feast and cel-
15:24 ebrate. 24For this son of mine was dead and is
[n]Eph 2:1,5; 5:14; 1Ti 5:6 alive again;[n] he was lost and is found.' So they
[o]ver 32 began to celebrate.[o]
25"Meanwhile, the older son was in the field.
When he came near the house, he heard music
and dancing. 26So he called one of the servants
and asked him what was going on. 27'Your brother has come,' he replied, 'and your father has
killed the fattened calf because he has him back
15:28 safe and sound.'
[p]Jnh 4:1 28"The older brother became angry[p] and refused
to go in. So his father went out and pleaded with
him. 29But he answered his father, 'Look! All these
years I've been slaving for you and never disobeyed your orders. Yet you never gave me even a
young goat so I could celebrate with my friends.
30But when this son of yours who has squandered
15:30 [q]ver 12,13 your property[q] with prostitutes[r] comes home, you
[r]Pr 29:3 kill the fattened calf for him!'
31" 'My son,' the father said, 'you are always
with me, and everything I have is yours. 32But we
had to celebrate and be glad, because this brother
15:32 of yours was dead and is alive again; he was lost
[s]ver 24; Mal 3:17 and is found.' "[s]

[a] 21 Some early manuscripts *son. Make me like one of your hired men.*

As [the lost son runs toward him, the father] stretches out his arms in welcome the second he sees the kid approaching. When they rush into each other's arms, the boy begins his prepared speech—but the father wasn't listening. The father has already forgiven him . . .

Of all the parables Jesus told, this is the one that most clearly illustrates the unconditional love and grace of the heavenly Father . . . We see grace extended by the father to this selfish, rebellious, immature, demanding, and utterly self-serving young man. He didn't earn that grace nor did he deserve it, but grace he received. Through that parable, Jesus simply wanted to illustrate dramatically and clearly that we are loved by God the Father—loved beyond measure, loved beyond comprehension, and yes, loved beyond what we deserve.

—Marilyn Meberg

Building on the Old

LK 16:16–17

At first glance, Jesus appears to say, "Things have changed around here, but then again, nothing has changed." In actuality, he is telling us that the coming of the Messiah builds on the foundation the prophets laid. Jesus doesn't abolish the law—he fulfills it. A modern analogy: taking a room that is empty and painted yellow and adding furniture and personal touches. The room appears to be a different place, but it's actually the same place, just changed, magnified. So, too, Jesus' message doesn't cancel out what the prophets have said but adds depth and meaning to it. The law prepares the way for God to show his love through Jesus (Ro 3:21–24). The law cannot bring righteousness or oneness with God (Gal 3:10–13); however, the law shows us our need for a Savior and points us to Christ (Gal 3:19,24), who is the only way (Jn 14:6).

The Parable of the Shrewd Manager

16 Jesus told his disciples: "There was a rich
man whose manager was accused of wast- 16:1
ing his possessions.[t] 2So he called him in and [t]Lk 15:13,30
asked him, 'What is this I hear about you? Give
an account of your management, because you
cannot be manager any longer.'
3"The manager said to himself, 'What shall I do
now? My master is taking away my job. I'm not
strong enough to dig, and I'm ashamed to beg— 4I
know what I'll do so that, when I lose my job
here, people will welcome me into their houses.'
5"So he called in each one of his master's
debtors. He asked the first, 'How much do you
owe my master?'
6" 'Eight hundred gallons[a] of olive oil,' he
replied.
"The manager told him, 'Take your bill, sit
down quickly, and make it four hundred.'
7"Then he asked the second, 'And how much
do you owe?'
" 'A thousand bushels[b] of wheat,' he replied.
"He told him, 'Take your bill and make it eight
hundred.'
8"The master commended the dishonest manager because he had acted shrewdly. For the peo- 16:8
ple of this world[u] are more shrewd[v] in dealing [u]Ps 17:14
with their own kind than are the people of the [v]Ps 18:26
light.[w] 9I tell you, use worldly wealth[x] to gain [w]Jn 12:36; Eph 5:8;
friends for yourselves, so that when it is gone, you 1Th 5:5
will be welcomed into eternal dwellings.[y] 16:9
10"Whoever can be trusted with very little can [x]ver 11,13
also be trusted with much,[z] and whoever is dis- [y]Mt 19:21;
honest with very little will also be dishonest with Lk 12:33
much. 11So if you have not been trustworthy in 16:10
handling worldly wealth,[a] who will trust you with [z]Mt 25:21,
true riches? 12And if you have not been trustwor- 23; Lk 19:17
thy with someone else's property, who will give 16:11
you property of your own? [a]ver 9,13
13"No servant can serve two masters. Either he
will hate the one and love the other, or he will be
devoted to the one and despise the other. You can- 16:13
not serve both God and Money."[b] [b]ver 9,11;
14The Pharisees, who loved money,[c] heard all Mt 6:24
this and were sneering at Jesus.[d] 15He said to 16:14
them, "You are the ones who justify yourselves[e] [c]1Ti 3:3
in the eyes of men, but God knows your hearts.[f] [d]Lk 23:35
What is highly valued among men is detestable 16:15
in God's sight. [e]Lk 10:29 [f]1Sa 16:7; Rev 2:23

Additional Teachings

16"The Law and the Prophets were proclaimed
until John.[g] Since that time, the good news of the 16:16
kingdom of God is being preached,[h] and everyone [g]Mt 11:12,13
is forcing his way into it. 17It is easier for heaven [h]Mt 4:23
and earth to disappear than for the least stroke of 16:17
a pen to drop out of the Law.[i] [i]Mt 5:18
18"Anyone who divorces his wife and marries

[a] 6 Greek *one hundred batous* (probably about 3 kiloliters)
[b] 7 Greek *one hundred korous* (probably about 35 kiloliters)

another woman commits adultery, and the man who marries a divorced woman commits adultery.[j]

The Rich Man and Lazarus

19“There was a rich man who was dressed in purple and fine linen and lived in luxury every day.[k] 20At his gate was laid a beggar[l] named Lazarus, covered with sores 21and longing to eat what fell from the rich man’s table.[m] Even the dogs came and licked his sores.

22“The time came when the beggar died and the angels carried him to Abraham’s side. The rich man also died and was buried. 23In hell,[a] where he was in torment, he looked up and saw Abraham far away, with Lazarus by his side. 24So he called to him, ‘Father Abraham,[n] have pity on me and send Lazarus to dip the tip of his finger in water and cool my tongue, because I am in agony in this fire.’[o]

25“But Abraham replied, ‘Son, remember that in your lifetime you received your good things, while Lazarus received bad things,[p] but now he is comforted here and you are in agony.[q] 26And besides all this, between us and you a great chasm has been fixed, so that those who want to go from here to you cannot, nor can anyone cross over from there to us.’

27“He answered, ‘Then I beg you, father, send Lazarus to my father’s house, 28for I have five brothers. Let him warn them,[r] so that they will not also come to this place of torment.’

29“Abraham replied, ‘They have Moses[s] and the Prophets;[t] let them listen to them.’

30“ ‘No, father Abraham,’[u] he said, ‘but if someone from the dead goes to them, they will repent.’

31“He said to him, ‘If they do not listen to Moses and the Prophets, they will not be convinced even if someone rises from the dead.’ ”

Sin, Faith, Duty

17 Jesus said to his disciples: “Things that cause people to sin[v] are bound to come, but woe to that person through whom they come.[w] 2It would be better for him to be thrown into the sea with a millstone tied around his neck than for him to cause one of these little ones[x] to sin.[y] 3So watch yourselves.

“If your brother sins, rebuke him,[z] and if he repents, forgive him.[a] 4If he sins against you seven times in a day, and seven times comes back to you and says, ‘I repent,’ forgive him.”[b]

5The apostles[c] said to the Lord,[d] “Increase our faith!”

6He replied, “If you have faith as small as a mustard seed,[e] you can say to this mulberry tree, ‘Be uprooted and planted in the sea,’ and it will obey you.[f]

7“Suppose one of you had a servant plowing or looking after the sheep. Would he say to the servant when he comes in from the field, ‘Come

16:18 [j]Mt 5:31,32; 19:9; Mk 10:11; Ro 7:2,3; 1Co 7:10,11
16:19 [k]Eze 16:49
16:20 [l]Ac 3:2
16:21 [m]Mt 15:27
16:24 [n]ver 30; Lk 3:8 [o]Mt 5:22
16:25 [p]Ps 17:14 [q]Lk 6:21,24, 25
16:28 [r]Ac 2:40; 20:23; 1Th 4:6
16:29 [s]Lk 24:27, 44; Jn 5:45-47; Ac 15:21 [t]Lk 4:17; Jn 1:45
16:30 [u]ver 24; Lk 3:8
17:1 [v]Mt 5:29 [w]Mt 18:7
17:2 [x]Mk 10:24; Lk 10:21 [y]Mt 5:29
17:3 [z]Mt 18:15 [a]Eph 4:32; Col 3:13
17:4 [b]Mt 18:21,22
17:5 [c]Mk 6:30 [d]Lk 7:13
17:6 [e]Mt 13:31; 17:20; Lk 13:19 [f]Mt 21:21; Mk 9:23

[a] 23 Greek *Hades*

The Weight of Sin

LK 17:1–5

A millstone is one of two circular stone slabs, each about 18 inches across, which rotate against each other to grind grain. In Jesus’ day some millstones were much larger and were located in millhouses rather than in households. Animals (such as donkeys) turned these larger millstones. Jesus refers to this larger millstone in his teaching, placing enormous responsibility on a person who causes another to sin.

Those who are sinned against don’t get off lightly either. Individuals are asked to forgive the sinner regardless of how many times the sinner does wrong and asks for forgiveness. The disciples, realizing their “forgiveness muscles” would be stretched beyond the weight they could bear, cry out, “Increase our faith!” (Lk 17:5). Their response provides the key to finding within ourselves the capacity to forgive. Our faith in God’s ability to use even evil for our good and improvement (Ro 8:28) softens our hearts, humbles us and gives us the strength to say, “All is forgiven—again.”

The Kingdom Within

LK 17:20-21

The Pharisees quiz Jesus about when the kingdom of God will come. Jesus understands that they are asking about a kingdom that will bring material benefits. That is why he tells them they are thinking about it in the wrong way. The kingdom of God is a spiritual kingdom. It began with Christ's arrival and will be consummated at his second coming. When Jesus says the kingdom is "within" you, that word can also be translated as "among" you (see Lk 17:21 and NIV text note). "I, the King, am standing before you," Jesus is telling his questioners. On other occasions he points to his deeds and his person as manifestations of the kingdom: casting out demons (breaking Satan's power—Lk 11:20), healing (Lk 10:9), and proclaiming salvation through himself (Jn 14:6).

along now and sit down to eat'? 8Would he not
rather say, 'Prepare my supper, get yourself ready
and wait on me[g] while I eat and drink; after that
you may eat and drink'? 9Would he thank the servant because he did what he was told to do? 10So
you also, when you have done everything you
were told to do, should say, 'We are unworthy servants; we have only done our duty.' "[h]

Ten Healed of Leprosy

11Now on his way to Jerusalem,[i] Jesus traveled
along the border between Samaria and Galilee.[j]
12As he was going into a village, ten men who had
leprosy[a][k] met him. They stood at a distance[l] 13and
called out in a loud voice, "Jesus, Master,[m] have
pity on us!"
14When he saw them, he said, "Go, show yourselves to the priests."[n] And as they went, they
were cleansed.
15One of them, when he saw he was healed,
came back, praising God[o] in a loud voice. 16He
threw himself at Jesus' feet and thanked him—
and he was a Samaritan.[p]
17Jesus asked, "Were not all ten cleansed?
Where are the other nine? 18Was no one found to
return and give praise to God except this foreigner?" 19Then he said to him, "Rise and go; your
faith has made you well."[q]

The Coming of the Kingdom of God

20Once, having been asked by the Pharisees
when the kingdom of God would come,[r] Jesus
replied, "The kingdom of God does not come with
your careful observation, 21nor will people say,
'Here it is,' or 'There it is,'[s] because the kingdom
of God is within[b] you."
22Then he said to his disciples, "The time is
coming when you will long to see one of the days
of the Son of Man,[t] but you will not see it.[u] 23Men
will tell you, 'There he is!' or 'Here he is!' Do not
go running off after them.[v] 24For the Son of Man
in his day[c] will be like the lightning,[w] which
flashes and lights up the sky from one end to the
other. 25But first he must suffer many things[x] and
be rejected[y] by this generation.[z]
26"Just as it was in the days of Noah,[a] so also
will it be in the days of the Son of Man. 27People
were eating, drinking, marrying and being given
in marriage up to the day Noah entered the ark.
Then the flood came and destroyed them all.
28"It was the same in the days of Lot.[b] People
were eating and drinking, buying and selling,
planting and building. 29But the day Lot left Sodom, fire and sulfur rained down from heaven and
destroyed them all.
30"It will be just like this on the day the Son of
Man is revealed.[c] 31On that day no one who is on

17:8 [g]Lk 12:37
17:10 [h]1Co 9:16
17:11 [i]Lk 9:51 [j]Lk 9:51,52; Jn 4:3,4
17:12 [k]Mt 8:2 [l]Lev 13:45,46
17:13 [m]Lk 5:5
17:14 [n]Lev 14:2; Mt 8:4
17:15 [o]Mt 9:8
17:16 [p]Mt 10:5
17:19 [q]Mt 9:22
17:20 [r]Mt 3:2
17:21 [s]ver 23
17:22 [t]Mt 8:20 [u]Mt 9:15; Lk 5:35
17:23 [v]Mt 24:23; Mk 13:21; Lk 21:8
17:24 [w]Mt 24:27
17:25 [x]Mt 16:21 [y]Lk 9:22; 18:32 [z]Mk 13:30; Lk 21:32
17:26 [a]Ge 7:6-24
17:28 [b]Ge 19:1-28
17:30 [c]Mt 10:23; 16:27; 24:3,27,37,39; 25:31; 1Co 1:7; 1Th 2:19; 2Th 1:7; 2:8; 2Pe 3:4; Rev 1:7

[a] *12* The Greek word was used for various diseases affecting the skin—not necessarily leprosy. [b] *21* Or *among*
[c] *24* Some manuscripts do not have *in his day.*

the roof of his house, with his goods inside, should go down to get them. Likewise, no one in the field should go back for anything.[d] 32 Remember Lot's wife![e] 33 Whoever tries to keep his life will lose it, and whoever loses his life will preserve it.[f] 34 I tell you, on that night two people will be in one bed; one will be taken and the other left. 35 Two women will be grinding grain together; one will be taken and the other left.[a]"[g]

37 "Where, Lord?" they asked.

He replied, "Where there is a dead body, there the vultures will gather."[h]

The Parable of the Persistent Widow

18 Then Jesus told his disciples a parable to show them that they should always pray and not give up.[i] 2 He said: "In a certain town there was a judge who neither feared God nor cared about men. 3 And there was a widow in that town who kept coming to him with the plea, 'Grant me justice[j] against my adversary.'

4 "For some time he refused. But finally he said to himself, 'Even though I don't fear God or care about men, 5 yet because this widow keeps bothering me, I will see that she gets justice, so that she won't eventually wear me out with her coming!' "[k]

6 And the Lord[l] said, "Listen to what the unjust judge says. 7 And will not God bring about justice for his chosen ones, who cry out[m] to him day and night? Will he keep putting them off? 8 I tell you, he will see that they get justice, and quickly. However, when the Son of Man[n] comes,[o] will he find faith on the earth?"

The Parable of the Pharisee and the Tax Collector

9 To some who were confident of their own righteousness[p] and looked down on everybody else,[q] Jesus told this parable: 10 "Two men went up to the temple to pray,[r] one a Pharisee and the other a tax collector. 11 The Pharisee stood up[s] and prayed about[b] himself: 'God, I thank you that I am not like other men—robbers, evildoers, adulterers—or even like this tax collector. 12 I fast[t] twice a week and give a tenth[u] of all I get.'

13 "But the tax collector stood at a distance. He would not even look up to heaven, but beat his breast[v] and said, 'God, have mercy on me, a sinner.'[w]

14 "I tell you that this man, rather than the other, went home justified before God. For everyone who exalts himself will be humbled, and he who humbles himself will be exalted."[x]

The Little Children and Jesus

15 People were also bringing babies to Jesus to have him touch them. When the disciples saw this, they rebuked them. 16 But Jesus called the

[a] 35 Some manuscripts *left.* 36 *Two men will be in the field; one will be taken and the other left.* [b] 11 Or *to*

17:31 [d]Mt 24:17,18; Mk 13:15-16
17:32 [e]Ge 19:26
17:33 [f]Jn 12:25
17:35 [g]Mt 24:41
17:37 [h]Mt 24:28
18:1 [i]Isa 40:31; Lk 11:5-8; Ac 1:14; Ro 12:12; Eph 6:18; Col 4:2; 1Th 5:17
18:3 [j]Isa 1:17
18:5 [k]Lk 11:8
18:6 [l]Lk 7:13
18:7 [m]Ex 22:23; Ps 88:1; Rev 6:10
18:8 [n]Mt 8:20 [o]Mt 16:27
18:9 [p]Lk 16:15 [q]Isa 65:5
18:10 [r]Ac 3:1
18:11 [s]Mt 6:5; Mk 11:25
18:12 [t]Isa 58:3; Mt 9:14 [u]Mal 3:8; Lk 11:42
18:13 [v]Isa 66:2; Jer 31:19; Lk 23:48 [w]Lk 5:32; 1Ti 1:15
18:14 [x]Mt 23:12; Lk 14:11

Persistence Pays Off

LK 18:1–8

Jesus tells a parable that gives his listeners a glimpse into what type of prayer God approves of: persistent prayer. Persistent prayer is tenacious, constant, even insistent. In the face of difficulty or what appears to be a lack of response, persistent prayer continues and even expands. Jesus encourages us to ask again and again and again in the face of seeming unresponsiveness. He contrasts God, who is caring and tender toward us, with an indifferent and calloused judge who has the power to mete out justice but doesn't care enough to act. God—unlike the lackadaisical judge—will respond eagerly to our persistence.

Jesus ends his story with a hard question worth pondering: Can faith be found anywhere on earth? Those who are persistent enough to hang on to the end will be few.

The essence of beauty is transient, short-lived, fleeting. It is in the eye of the beholder, relative to the correlation of things at hand and our mood at any given moment. It is fairer and better than what we see or hear. It is born out of the commonplace, household life, personal relations, beating heart, meeting eyes, poverty, necessity, hope, and fear. And, finally, the real celebrating of its presence comes as we recall it in our memory, replaying the old records of our thoughts, gazing at the gallery of pictures with the eye of remembrance, and singing the song that is going on within us, a song to which we listen.

These moments are the pinnacles of our experience, lifting us out of the dreary circumstances and giving us pleasure and delight until we fall back and again become our ordinary selves. They must be interwoven into our daily existence in order to make life endurable and sweet.

—Luci Swindoll

children to him and said, "Let the little children
come to me, and do not hinder them, for the kingdom of God belongs to such as these. [17]I tell you
the truth, anyone who will not receive the king- 18:17
dom of God like a little child[y] will never enter it." [y]Mt 11:25;
18:3

The Rich Ruler

[18]A certain ruler asked him, "Good teacher, 18:18
what must I do to inherit eternal life?"[z] [z]Lk 10:25
[19]"Why do you call me good?" Jesus answered.
"No one is good—except God alone. [20]You know
the commandments: 'Do not commit adultery, do
not murder, do not steal, do not give false testi- 18:20
mony, honor your father and mother.'[a][a] [a]Ex 20:12-
[21]"All these I have kept since I was a boy," he 16; Dt 5:16-
said. 20; Ro 13:9
[22]When Jesus heard this, he said to him, "You
still lack one thing. Sell everything you have and
give to the poor,[b] and you will have treasure in 18:22
heaven.[c] Then come, follow me." [b]Ac 2:45
[23]When he heard this, he became very sad, [c]Mt 6:20
because he was a man of great wealth. [24]Jesus
looked at him and said, "How hard it is for the rich 18:24
to enter the kingdom of God![d] [25]Indeed, it is easi- [d]Pr 11:28
er for a camel to go through the eye of a needle
than for a rich man to enter the kingdom of God."
[26]Those who heard this asked, "Who then can
be saved?"
[27]Jesus replied, "What is impossible with men
is possible with God."[e] 18:27
[28]Peter said to him, "We have left all we had to [e]Mt 19:26
follow you!"[f] 18:28
[29]"I tell you the truth," Jesus said to them, "no [f]Mt 4:19
one who has left home or wife or brothers or parents or children for the sake of the kingdom of
God [30]will fail to receive many times as much in 18:30
this age and, in the age to come,[g] eternal life."[h] [g]Mt 12:32
[h]Mt 25:46

Jesus Again Predicts His Death

[31]Jesus took the Twelve aside and told them, 18:31
"We are going up to Jerusalem,[i] and everything [i]Lk 9:51
that is written by the prophets[j] about the Son of [j]Ps 22; Isa 53
Man[k] will be fulfilled. [32]He will be handed over to [k]Mt 8:20
the Gentiles.[l] They will mock him, insult him, spit 18:32
on him, flog him[m] and kill him.[n] [33]On the third [l]Lk 23:1
day[o] he will rise again."[p] [m]Mt 16:21
[34]The disciples did not understand any of this. [n]Ac 2:23
Its meaning was hidden from them, and they did 18:33
not know what he was talking about.[q] [o]Mt 16:21
[p]Mt 16:21
18:34

A Blind Beggar Receives His Sight

[q]Mk 9:32;
[35]As Jesus approached Jericho,[r] a blind man Lk 9:45
was sitting by the roadside begging. [36]When he 18:35
heard the crowd going by, he asked what was [r]Lk 19:1
happening. [37]They told him, "Jesus of Nazareth is 18:37
passing by."[s] [s]Lk 19:4
[38]He called out, "Jesus, Son of David,[t] have mer- 18:38
cy[u] on me!" [t]ver 39;
[39]Those who led the way rebuked him and told Mt 9:27
[u]Mt 17:15;
Lk 18:13

[a] 20 Exodus 20:12–16; Deut. 5:16–20

him to be quiet, but he shouted all the more, "Son
18:39 [v]ver 38 of David, have mercy on me!"[v]
40 Jesus stopped and ordered the man to be
brought to him. When he came near, Jesus asked
him, 41 "What do you want me to do for you?"
"Lord, I want to see," he replied.
18:42 42 Jesus said to him, "Receive your sight; your
[w]Mt 9:22 faith has healed you."[w] 43 Immediately he received
18:43 his sight and followed Jesus, praising God. When
[x]Mt 9:8; Lk 13:17 all the people saw it, they also praised God.[x]

Zacchaeus the Tax Collector

19:1 [y]Lk 18:35 19 Jesus entered Jericho[y] and was passing
through. 2 A man was there by the name of
Zacchaeus; he was a chief tax collector and was
wealthy. 3 He wanted to see who Jesus was, but
being a short man he could not, because of the
19:4 crowd. 4 So he ran ahead and climbed a sycamore-
[z]1Ki 10:27; fig[z] tree to see him, since Jesus was coming that
1Ch 27:28; Isa 9:10 way.[a]
[a]Lk 18:37 5 When Jesus reached the spot, he looked up
and said to him, "Zacchaeus, come down immediately. I must stay at your house today." 6 So he
came down at once and welcomed him gladly.
19:7 7 All the people saw this and began to mutter,
[b]Mt 9:11 "He has gone to be the guest of a 'sinner.' "[b]
19:8 8 But Zacchaeus stood up and said to the Lord,[c]
[c]Lk 7:13 "Look, Lord! Here and now I give half of my pos-
[d]Lk 3:12,13 sessions to the poor, and if I have cheated any-
[e]Ex 22:1; Lev 6:4,5; body out of anything,[d] I will pay back four times
Nu 5:7; the amount."[e]
2Sa 12:6 9 Jesus said to him, "Today salvation has come
to this house, because this man, too, is a son of
19:9 [f]Lk 3:8; Abraham.[f] 10 For the Son of Man came to seek and
13:16; Ro 4:16; to save what was lost."[g]
Gal 3:7

The Parable of the Ten Minas

19:10 11 While they were listening to this, he went on
[g]Eze 34:12, to tell them a parable, because he was near Jeru-
16; Jn 3:17 salem and the people thought that the kingdom
19:11 [h]Mt 3:2 of God[h] was going to appear at once.[i] 12 He said:
[i]Lk 17:20; "A man of noble birth went to a distant country
Ac 1:6 to have himself appointed king and then to return.
19:13 13 So he called ten of his servants[j] and gave them
[j]Mk 13:34 ten minas.[a] 'Put this money to work,' he said,
'until I come back.'
14 "But his subjects hated him and sent a delegation after him to say, 'We don't want this man
to be our king.'
15 "He was made king, however, and returned
home. Then he sent for the servants to whom he
had given the money, in order to find out what
they had gained with it.
16 "The first one came and said, 'Sir, your mina
has earned ten more.'
19:17 [k]Pr 27:18 17 " 'Well done, my good servant!'[k] his master
[l]Lk 16:10 replied. 'Because you have been trustworthy in a
very small matter, take charge of ten cities.'[l]

[a] *13* A mina was about three months' wages.

Does Faith Heal?

LK 18:35–43

The blind man "sees" what others in the crowd miss. By proclaiming Jesus the Son of David, he acknowledges that Jesus is the promised Messiah, and he thereby displays his faith. Because faith involves abandoning all trust in one's own resources and casting oneself unreservedly on God's mercy, the blind man's faith is an emptying of himself.

Faith is rather like a doorknob on a door. The doorknob, by itself, cannot open the door, but it is the means by which the door can be opened. Because of the doorknob (faith), the door to healing can be opened.

Our faith is an act of relinquishment to God, an instrument he uses to accomplish his purposes. But our faith cannot, in and of itself, cause certain action to take place. Instead, just as a door is not able to be opened if no doorknob exists or if we don't reach out to take hold of it, so God can choose not to act when faith is not present.

Nothing to Lose

LK 19:11-27

Jesus is on his way to Jerusalem, where he will enter the city triumphantly but leave by way of the cross. Since the crowd expects him to become their earthly king, he tells this parable to help them understand that his kingdom is spiritual. The people need to remain faithful until the kingdom fully arrives (at Christ's second coming). The parable centers on the servant who is unfaithful. He takes no risks, playing it safe and trying to preserve what he has. Jesus points out that the servant deceives himself, for all he has belongs to the master, who will take it back if it isn't used well. We can sometimes be like this servant and let our insecurities, worries and fears keep us from doing God's will. God calls us, however, to step out, to be faithful, and to trust him.

18“The second came and said, ‘Sir, your mina
has earned five more.’
19“His master answered, ‘You take charge of five
cities.’
20“Then another servant came and said, ‘Sir,
here is your mina; I have kept it laid away in a
piece of cloth. 21I was afraid of you, because you
are a hard man. You take out what you did not put **19:21**
in and reap what you did not sow.’[m] [m]Mt 25:24
22“His master replied, ‘I will judge you by your **19:22**
own words,[n] you wicked servant! You knew, did [n]2Sa 1:16; Job 15:6
you, that I am a hard man, taking out what I did [o]Mt 25:26
not put in, and reaping what I did not sow?[o]
23Why then didn't you put my money on deposit,
so that when I came back, I could have collected
it with interest?’
24“Then he said to those standing by, ‘Take his
mina away from him and give it to the one who
has ten minas.’
25“ ‘Sir,’ they said, ‘he already has ten!’
26“He replied, ‘I tell you that to everyone who
has, more will be given, but as for the one who
has nothing, even what he has will be taken
away.[p] 27But those enemies of mine who did not **19:26**
want me to be king over them—bring them here [p]Mt 13:12; 25:29;
and kill them in front of me.’ ” Lk 8:18

The Triumphal Entry

28After Jesus had said this, he went on ahead, **19:28**
going up to Jerusalem.[q] 29As he approached Beth- [q]Mk 10:32;
phage and Bethany[r] at the hill called the Mount Lk 9:51
of Olives,[s] he sent two of his disciples, saying to **19:29**
them, 30“Go to the village ahead of you, and as [r]Mt 21:17
you enter it, you will find a colt tied there, which [s]Mt 21:1
no one has ever ridden. Untie it and bring it here.
31If anyone asks you, ‘Why are you untying it?’
tell him, ‘The Lord needs it.’ ”
32Those who were sent ahead went and found it **19:32**
just as he had told them.[t] 33As they were untying [t]Lk 22:13
the colt, its owners asked them, “Why are you
untying the colt?”
34They replied, “The Lord needs it.”
35They brought it to Jesus, threw their cloaks
on the colt and put Jesus on it. 36As he went
along, people spread their cloaks[u] on the road. **19:36**
37When he came near the place where the road [u]2Ki 9:13
goes down the Mount of Olives,[v] the whole crowd **19:37**
of disciples began joyfully to praise God in loud [v]Mt 21:1
voices for all the miracles they had seen:

38“Blessed is the king who comes in the
name of the Lord!”[a][w] **19:38**
“Peace in heaven and glory in the [w]Ps 118:26; Lk 13:35
highest!”[x] [x]Lk 2:14

39Some of the Pharisees in the crowd said to
Jesus, “Teacher, rebuke your disciples!”[y] **19:39**
40“I tell you,” he replied, “if they keep quiet, the [y]Mt 21:15,16
stones will cry out.”[z] **19:40** [z]Hab 2:11

[a] *38* Psalm 118:26

41As he approached Jerusalem and saw the city,
he wept over it[a] 42and said, "If you, even you, had
only known on this day what would bring you
peace—but now it is hidden from your eyes. 43The
days will come upon you when your enemies will
build an embankment against you and encircle
you and hem you in on every side.[b] 44They will
dash you to the ground, you and the children
within your walls.[c] They will not leave one stone
on another,[d] because you did not recognize the
time of God's coming[e] to you."

Jesus at the Temple

45Then he entered the temple area and began
driving out those who were selling. 46"It is written," he said to them, " 'My house will be a house
of prayer'[a];[f] but you have made it 'a den of
robbers.'[b]"[g]

47Every day he was teaching at the temple.[h] But
the chief priests, the teachers of the law and the
leaders among the people were trying to kill him.[i]
48Yet they could not find any way to do it, because
all the people hung on his words.

The Authority of Jesus Questioned

20 One day as he was teaching the people in
the temple courts[j] and preaching the
gospel,[k] the chief priests and the teachers of the
law, together with the elders, came up to him.
2"Tell us by what authority you are doing these
things," they said. "Who gave you this authority?"[l]

3He replied, "I will also ask you a question. Tell
me, 4John's baptism[m]—was it from heaven, or
from men?"

5They discussed it among themselves and said,
"If we say, 'From heaven,' he will ask, 'Why didn't
you believe him?' 6But if we say, 'From men,' all
the people[n] will stone us, because they are persuaded that John was a prophet."[o]

7So they answered, "We don't know where it
was from."

8Jesus said, "Neither will I tell you by what
authority I am doing these things."

The Parable of the Tenants

9He went on to tell the people this parable: "A
man planted a vineyard,[p] rented it to some farmers and went away for a long time.[q] 10At harvest
time he sent a servant to the tenants so they
would give him some of the fruit of the vineyard.
But the tenants beat him and sent him away empty-handed. 11He sent another servant, but that one
also they beat and treated shamefully and sent
away empty-handed. 12He sent still a third, and
they wounded him and threw him out.

13"Then the owner of the vineyard said, 'What
shall I do? I will send my son, whom I love;[r] perhaps they will respect him.'

[a] 46 Isaiah 56:7 [b] 46 Jer. 7:11

19:41 [a]Isa 22:4; Lk 13:34,35
19:43 [b]Isa 29:3; Jer 6:6; Eze 4:2; 26:8; Lk 21:20
19:44 [c]Ps 137:9 [d]Mt 24:2; Mk 13:2; Lk 21:6 [e]1Pe 2:12
19:46 [f]Isa 56:7 [g]Jer 7:11
19:47 [h]Mt 26:55 [i]Mt 12:14; Mk 11:18
20:1 [j]Mt 26:55 [k]Lk 8:1
20:2 [l]Jn 2:18; Ac 4:7; 7:27
20:4 [m]Mk 1:4
20:6 [n]Lk 7:29 [o]Mt 11:9
20:9 [p]Isa 5:1-7 [q]Mt 25:14
20:13 [r]Mt 3:17

Who's in Charge Here?

LK 19:47-48

The religious council mentioned in these verses was called the Sanhedrin and was made up of 71 members. During the Greek and Roman period, it was the highest ruling body of the Jews. The government of the country, though under Roman control, was in all practicality under the rule of the Sanhedrin. Its duties included hearing civil and criminal cases and imposing punishment, short of the death penalty. The death penalty required the authorization of the Roman procurator. So the council was held in check by the boundaries the government placed on it and by the people's opinions. These factors kept the Sanhedrin from killing Jesus and from later punishing Peter and John after Jesus' resurrection (Ac 4). Acts 4:21 portrays the group as befuddled and cowed by Peter and John's popularity. If the Sanhedrin responded in such a tenuous way to the disciples, imagine how much more intimidated it was by Jesus, "because the people hung on his words" (Lk 19:48).

Grapes and Gentiles

LK 20:9–19

Obviously, Jesus' audience grasps the meaning of the parable of the tenants, for the crowd is shocked and dismayed when the story concludes (Lk 20:16). The owner of the vineyard represents God; the vineyard is Israel; the tenant farmers are the religious leaders; the servants are the prophets; the son is the Messiah; and the others are the Gentiles. The crowd is stunned by the mistreatment of the servants, the killing of the son, and the judgment against the tenants, but the story's galling climax for them is that God will give his vineyard to the Gentiles. Jesus drives home the point in Luke 20:17 when he says Scripture has prophesied his rejection, but he will become the cornerstone that holds up the building of God's kingdom. And what, according to the parable, will the building consist of? Not Abraham's descendants, but Gentiles. This is a horrifying thought to those who think of themselves as God's chosen people. But their rejection of him and his Son brings about their own rejection by God.

14“But when the tenants saw him, they talked
the matter over. ‘This is the heir,’ they said. ‘Let's
kill him, and the inheritance will be ours.’ 15So
they threw him out of the vineyard and killed him.
“What then will the owner of the vineyard do to
them? 16He will come and kill those tenants[s] and
give the vineyard to others.”
When the people heard this, they said, “May
this never be!”
17Jesus looked directly at them and asked,
“Then what is the meaning of that which is
written:

> “ ‘The stone the builders rejected
> has become the capstone[a][b]’?[t]

18Everyone who falls on that stone will be broken
to pieces, but he on whom it falls will be
crushed.”[u]
19The teachers of the law and the chief priests
looked for a way to arrest him[v] immediately,
because they knew he had spoken this parable
against them. But they were afraid of the people.[w]

20:16 [s]Lk 19:27
20:17 [t]Ps 118:22; Ac 4:11
20:18 [u]Isa 8:14,15
20:19 [v]Lk 19:47 [w]Mk 11:18

Paying Taxes to Caesar

20Keeping a close watch on him, they sent spies,
who pretended to be honest. They hoped to catch
Jesus in something he said[x] so that they might
hand him over to the power and authority of the
governor.[y] 21So the spies questioned him: “Teacher,
we know that you speak and teach what is right,
and that you do not show partiality but teach the
way of God in accordance with the truth.[z] 22Is it
right for us to pay taxes to Caesar or not?”
23He saw through their duplicity and said to
them, 24“Show me a denarius. Whose portrait and
inscription are on it?”
25“Caesar's,” they replied.
He said to them, “Then give to Caesar what is
Caesar's,[a] and to God what is God's.”
26They were unable to trap him in what he had
said there in public. And astonished by his
answer, they became silent.

20:20 [x]Mt 12:10 [y]Mt 27:2
20:21 [z]Jn 3:2
20:25 [a]Lk 23:2; Ro 13:7

The Resurrection and Marriage

27Some of the Sadducees,[b] who say there is no
resurrection,[c] came to Jesus with a question.
28“Teacher,” they said, “Moses wrote for us that if
a man's brother dies and leaves a wife but no children,
the man must marry the widow and have
children for his brother.[d] 29Now there were seven
brothers. The first one married a woman and died
childless. 30The second 31and then the third married
her, and in the same way the seven died, leaving
no children. 32Finally, the woman died too.
33Now then, at the resurrection whose wife will
she be, since the seven were married to her?”
34Jesus replied, “The people of this age marry
and are given in marriage. 35But those who are
considered worthy of taking part in that age[e] and

20:27 [b]Ac 4:1 [c]Ac 23:8; 1Co 15:12
20:28 [d]Dt 25:5
20:35 [e]Mt 12:32

[a] 17 Or *cornerstone* [b] 17 Psalm 118:22

in the resurrection from the dead will neither
marry nor be given in marriage, 36and they can no
20:36 longer die; for they are like the angels. They are
[f]Jn 1:12; God's children,[f] since they are children of the res-
1Jn 3:1-2 urrection. 37But in the account of the bush, even
Moses showed that the dead rise, for he calls the
20:37 Lord 'the God of Abraham, and the God of Isaac,
[g]Ex 3:6 and the God of Jacob.'[a][g] 38He is not the God of the
dead, but of the living, for to him all are alive."
39Some of the teachers of the law responded,
"Well said, teacher!" 40And no one dared to ask
20:40 [h]Mt 22:46; him any more questions.[h]
Mk 12:34

Whose Son Is the Christ?

41Then Jesus said to them, "How is it that they
20:41 say the Christ[b] is the Son of David?[i] 42David him-
[i]Mt 1:1 self declares in the Book of Psalms:

" 'The Lord said to my Lord:
"Sit at my right hand
20:43 43until I make your enemies
[j]Ps 110:1; a footstool for your feet." '[c][j]
Mt 22:44
44David calls him 'Lord.' How then can he be his
son?"
45While all the people were listening, Jesus said
to his disciples, 46"Beware of the teachers of the
law. They like to walk around in flowing robes
and love to be greeted in the marketplaces and
20:46 have the most important seats in the synagogues
[k]Lk 11:43 and the places of honor at banquets.[k] 47They
devour widows' houses and for a show make
lengthy prayers. Such men will be punished most
severely."

The Widow's Offering

21:1 **21** As he looked up, Jesus saw the rich putting
[l]Mt 27:6; their gifts into the temple treasury.[l] 2He also
Jn 8:20 saw a poor widow put in two very small copper
coins.[d] 3"I tell you the truth," he said, "this poor
widow has put in more than all the others. 4All
these people gave their gifts out of their wealth;
21:4 but she out of her poverty put in all she had to
[m]2Co 8:12 live on."[m]

Signs of the End of the Age

5Some of his disciples were remarking about
how the temple was adorned with beautiful
stones and with gifts dedicated to God. But Jesus
said, 6"As for what you see here, the time will
21:6 come when not one stone will be left on anoth-
[n]Lk 19:44 er;[n] every one of them will be thrown down."
7"Teacher," they asked, "when will these things
happen? And what will be the sign that they are
about to take place?"
8He replied: "Watch out that you are not
deceived. For many will come in my name, claiming, 'I am he,' and, 'The time is near.' Do not follow
21:8 them.[o] 9When you hear of wars and revolutions,
[o]Lk 17:23

[a] 37 Exodus 3:6 [b] 41 Or *Messiah* [c] 43 Psalm 110:1
[d] 2 Greek *two lepta*

Marriage in Heaven

LK 20:35

The Bible gives us few glimpses of heaven—just enough for us to know a few details: We will have transformed bodies (Php 3:21); death will die (1Co 15:54–55); we will not cry (Rev 21:4); the sun will not exist (Rev 21:23) and neither will marriage (Lk 20:35). If marriage is not a part of heaven, that means the family unit will not exist as we know it. Just as our bodies will be transformed, so, too, will our relationships be altered. We will experience a closeness and a depth of understanding with each other that is beyond our present capacity or imagination. Such in-depth relationships will be so satisfying, and we'll be capable of that kind of intimacy with so many people all at the same time, that marriage and family will seem like a dim and pleasant memory. It will fade into the shadows compared to the riches of heavenly relationships.

Fear-Filled Times

LK 21:14-19

These verses describe how Jesus wants his disciples to respond during a time of persecution and catastrophe, when life seems to spin out of control. He asks them not to worry because he will give them "words and wisdom" (Lk 21:15) when their adversaries confront them regarding their faith. And the disciples' responses will be so eloquent that they will be irresistible and irrefutable. Also, Jesus tells them they will be betrayed by the very people they love. But not a hair of their heads will perish. Obviously, Jesus isn't promising that a physical shield of protection will drop down to surround them. Instead, he is speaking spiritually—even if they are put to death, they will live unharmed spiritually. Are you facing adversaries and betrayals? Take Jesus' words to heart. He will protect and provide for you as well.

do not be frightened. These things must happen first, but the end will not come right away."

10 Then he said to them: "Nation will rise against nation, and kingdom against kingdom.[p] 11 There will be great earthquakes, famines and pestilences in various places, and fearful events and great signs from heaven.[q]

12 "But before all this, they will lay hands on you and persecute you. They will deliver you to synagogues and prisons, and you will be brought before kings and governors, and all on account of my name. 13 This will result in your being witnesses to them.[r] 14 But make up your mind not to worry beforehand how you will defend yourselves.[s] 15 For I will give you[t] words and wisdom that none of your adversaries will be able to resist or contradict. 16 You will be betrayed even by parents, brothers, relatives and friends,[u] and they will put some of you to death. 17 All men will hate you because of me.[v] 18 But not a hair of your head will perish.[w] 19 By standing firm you will gain life.[x]

20 "When you see Jerusalem being surrounded by armies,[y] you will know that its desolation is near. 21 Then let those who are in Judea flee to the mountains, let those in the city get out, and let those in the country not enter the city.[z] 22 For this is the time of punishment[a] in fulfillment[b] of all that has been written. 23 How dreadful it will be in those days for pregnant women and nursing mothers! There will be great distress in the land and wrath against this people. 24 They will fall by the sword and will be taken as prisoners to all the nations. Jerusalem will be trampled[c] on by the Gentiles until the times of the Gentiles are fulfilled.

25 "There will be signs in the sun, moon and stars. On the earth, nations will be in anguish and perplexity at the roaring and tossing of the sea.[d] 26 Men will faint from terror, apprehensive of what is coming on the world, for the heavenly bodies will be shaken.[e] 27 At that time they will see the Son of Man[f] coming in a cloud[g] with power and great glory. 28 When these things begin to take place, stand up and lift up your heads, because your redemption is drawing near."[h]

29 He told them this parable: "Look at the fig tree and all the trees. 30 When they sprout leaves, you can see for yourselves and know that summer is near. 31 Even so, when you see these things happening, you know that the kingdom of God[i] is near.

32 "I tell you the truth, this generation[a][j] will certainly not pass away until all these things have happened. 33 Heaven and earth will pass away, but my words will never pass away.[k]

34 "Be careful, or your hearts will be weighed down with dissipation, drunkenness and the anxieties of life,[l] and that day will close on you unexpectedly[m] like a trap. 35 For it will come upon all those who live on the face of the whole earth. 36 Be always on the watch, and pray[n] that you may be

21:10 [p]2Ch 15:6; Isa 19:2
21:11 [q]Isa 29:6; Joel 2:30
21:13 [r]Php 1:12
21:14 [s]Lk 12:11
21:15 [t]Lk 12:12
21:16 [u]Lk 12:52,53
21:17 [v]Jn 15:21
21:18 [w]Mt 10:30
21:19 [x]Mt 10:22
21:20 [y]Lk 19:43
21:21 [z]Lk 17:31
21:22 [a]Isa 63:4; Da 9:24-27; Hos 9:7 [b]Mt 1:22
21:24 [c]Isa 5:5; 63:18; Da 8:13; Rev 11:2
21:25 [d]2Pe 3:10,12
21:26 [e]Mt 24:29
21:27 [f]Mt 8:20 [g]Rev 1:7
21:28 [h]Lk 18:7
21:31 [i]Mt 3:2
21:32 [j]Lk 11:50; 17:25
21:33 [k]Mt 5:18
21:34 [l]Mk 4:19 [m]Lk 12:40, 46; 1Th 5:2-7
21:36 [n]Mt 26:41

[a] *32* Or *race*

able to escape all that is about to happen, and that
21:37 you may be able to stand before the Son of Man."
[o]Mt 26:55 37Each day Jesus was teaching at the temple,[o]
[p]Mk 11:19 [q]Mt 21:1 and each evening he went out[p] to spend the night
on the hill called the Mount of Olives,[q] 38and all
21:38 the people came early in the morning to hear him
[r]Jn 8:2 at the temple.[r]

Judas Agrees to Betray Jesus

22:1 22 Now the Feast of Unleavened Bread, called
[s]Jn 11:55 the Passover, was approaching,[s] 2and the
chief priests and the teachers of the law were
22:2 looking for some way to get rid of Jesus,[t] for they
[t]Mt 12:14 were afraid of the people. 3Then Satan[u] entered
22:3 Judas, called Iscariot,[v] one of the Twelve. 4And
[u]Mt 4:10; Jn 13:2 Judas went to the chief priests and the officers of
[v]Mt 10:4 the temple guard[w] and discussed with them how
he might betray Jesus. 5They were delighted and
22:4 [w]ver 52; agreed to give him money.[x] 6He consented, and
Ac 4:1; 5:24 watched for an opportunity to hand Jesus over to
22:5 them when no crowd was present.
[x]Zec 11:12

The Last Supper

7Then came the day of Unleavened Bread on
22:7 [y]Ex 12:18- which the Passover lamb had to be sacrificed.[y]
20; 8Jesus sent Peter and John,[z] saying, "Go and make
Dt 16:5-8; Mk 14:12 preparations for us to eat the Passover."
9"Where do you want us to prepare for it?" they
22:8 asked.
[z]Ac 3:1,11; 4:13,19; 10He replied, "As you enter the city, a man car-
8:14 rying a jar of water will meet you. Follow him to
the house that he enters, 11and say to the owner of
the house, 'The Teacher asks: Where is the guest
22:13 room, where I may eat the Passover with my dis-
[a]Lk 19:32 ciples?' 12He will show you a large upper room,
22:14 all furnished. Make preparations there."
[b]Mk 6:30 [c]Mt 26:20; 13They left and found things just as Jesus had
Mk 14:17,18 told them.[a] So they prepared the Passover.
22:15 14When the hour came, Jesus and his apostles[b]
[d]Mt 16:21 reclined at the table.[c] 15And he said to them, "I have
eagerly desired to eat this Passover with you before
22:16 I suffer.[d] 16For I tell you, I will not eat it again until
[e]Lk 14:15; Rev 19:9 it finds fulfillment in the kingdom of God."[e]
17After taking the cup, he gave thanks and said,
22:19 [f]Mt 14:19 "Take this and divide it among you. 18For I tell you
22:20 I will not drink again of the fruit of the vine until
[g]Ex 24:8; Isa 42:6; the kingdom of God comes."
Jer 31:31-34; 19And he took bread, gave thanks and broke it,[f]
Zec 9:11; 2Co 3:6; and gave it to them, saying, "This is my body giv-
Heb 8:6; en for you; do this in remembrance of me."
9:15 20In the same way, after the supper he took the
cup, saying, "This cup is the new covenant[g] in my
22:21 [h]Ps 41:9 blood, which is poured out for you. 21But the hand
of him who is going to betray me is with mine on
22:22 the table.[h] 22The Son of Man[i] will go as it has been
[i]Mt 8:20 [j]Ac 2:23; decreed,[j] but woe to that man who betrays him."
4:28 23They began to question among themselves
which of them it might be who would do this.
22:24 24Also a dispute arose among them as to which
[k]Mk 9:34; Lk 9:46 of them was considered to be greatest.[k] 25Jesus

Choices

LK 22:3

What does it mean that Satan enters Judas? Is Judas a puppet, fulfilling Satan's desires, or does Judas willingly betray Jesus? While some believe Judas was possessed by a demon, most scholars agree that Judas was vulnerable to Satan and allowed himself to be used as Satan's instrument. Judas may have been frustrated when Jesus did not make a political move to overthrow the Romans. Perhaps he hoped to force Jesus' hand. Or Judas may have been motivated by financial gain. (He already had pilfered the group's money bag, which had been entrusted to him as treasurer—Jn 12:6.)

Whatever his twisted purpose, Judas does not buy into Jesus' spiritual kingdom. The most respectful term he ever uses for Jesus is **Rabbi** ***(Mt 26:25,49), meaning "teacher." He spends three years with Jesus and still finds within himself the capacity to commit the sinister deed of turning Jesus over to his enemies.***

This hymn by Edith Gilling Cherry was sung by five young missionaries as they prepared to make their fateful journey into the jungle to evangelize the Auca Indians of Ecuador. All five were martyred that day in January, 1956.

We Rest on Thee

We rest on Thee, our shield and
our defender!
We go not forth alone against
the foe;
Strong in Thy strength, safe in Thy
keeping tender,
We rest on Thee, and in Thy Name
we go.
Strong in Thy strength, safe in Thy
keeping tender,
We rest on Thee, and in Thy Name
we go . . .

We rest on Thee, our shield and
our defender!
Thine is the battle, Thine shall be
the praise;
When passing through the gates
of pearly splendor,
Victors, we rest with Thee, through
endless days.
When passing through the gates
of pearly splendor,
Victors, we rest with Thee, through
endless days.

—*Edith Gilling Cherry (1895)*

said to them, "The kings of the Gentiles lord it
over them; and those who exercise authority over
them call themselves Benefactors. 26 But you are
not to be like that. Instead, the greatest among
you should be like the youngest,[l] and the one who
rules like the one who serves.[m] 27 For who is
greater, the one who is at the table or the one who
serves? Is it not the one who is at the table? But I
am among you as one who serves.[n] 28 You are
those who have stood by me in my trials. 29 And I
confer on you a kingdom,[o] just as my Father conferred one on me, 30 so that you may eat and drink
at my table in my kingdom[p] and sit on thrones,
judging the twelve tribes of Israel.[q]
31 "Simon, Simon, Satan has asked[r] to sift you[a]
as wheat.[s] 32 But I have prayed for you,[t] Simon,
that your faith may not fail. And when you have
turned back, strengthen your brothers."[u]
33 But he replied, "Lord, I am ready to go with
you to prison and to death."[v]
34 Jesus answered, "I tell you, Peter, before the
rooster crows today, you will deny three times that
you know me."
35 Then Jesus asked them, "When I sent you
without purse, bag or sandals,[w] did you lack
anything?"
"Nothing," they answered.
36 He said to them, "But now if you have a purse,
take it, and also a bag; and if you don't have a
sword, sell your cloak and buy one. 37 It is written: 'And he was numbered with the transgressors'[b];[x] and I tell you that this must be fulfilled in
me. Yes, what is written about me is reaching its
fulfillment."
38 The disciples said, "See, Lord, here are two
swords."
"That is enough," he replied.

Jesus Prays on the Mount of Olives

39 Jesus went out as usual[y] to the Mount of
Olives,[z] and his disciples followed him. 40 On
reaching the place, he said to them, "Pray that you
will not fall into temptation."[a] 41 He withdrew
about a stone's throw beyond them, knelt down[b]
and prayed, 42 "Father, if you are willing, take this
cup[c] from me; yet not my will, but yours be
done."[d] 43 An angel from heaven appeared to him
and strengthened him.[e] 44 And being in anguish,
he prayed more earnestly, and his sweat was like
drops of blood falling to the ground.[c]
45 When he rose from prayer and went back to
the disciples, he found them asleep, exhausted
from sorrow. 46 "Why are you sleeping?" he asked
them. "Get up and pray so that you will not fall
into temptation."[f]

Jesus Arrested

47 While he was still speaking a crowd came up,

22:26 [l]1Pe 5:5 [m]Mk 9:35; Lk 9:48
22:27 [n]Mt 20:28; Lk 12:37
22:29 [o]Mt 25:34; 2Ti 2:12
22:30 [p]Lk 14:15 [q]Mt 19:28
22:31 [r]Job 1:6-12 [s]Am 9:9
22:32 [t]Jn 17:9,15; Ro 8:34 [u]Jn 21:15-17
22:33 [v]Jn 11:16
22:35 [w]Mt 10:9,10; Lk 9:3; 10:4
22:37 [x]Isa 53:12
22:39 [y]Lk 21:37 [z]Mt 21:1
22:40 [a]Mt 6:13
22:41 [b]Lk 18:11
22:42 [c]Mt 20:22 [d]Mt 26:39
22:43 [e]Mt 4:11; Mk 1:13
22:46 [f]ver 40

[a] *31* The Greek is plural. [b] *37* Isaiah 53:12 [c] *44* Some early manuscripts do not have verses 43 and 44.

and the man who was called Judas, one of the
Twelve, was leading them. He approached Jesus
to kiss him, 48 but Jesus asked him, "Judas, are
you betraying the Son of Man with a kiss?"
49 When Jesus' followers saw what was going to
22:49 happen, they said, "Lord, should we strike with
[g]ver 38 our swords?"[g] 50 And one of them struck the servant of the high priest, cutting off his right ear.
51 But Jesus answered, "No more of this!" And
he touched the man's ear and healed him.
22:52 52 Then Jesus said to the chief priests, the offi-
[h]ver 4 cers of the temple guard,[h] and the elders, who had
come for him, "Am I leading a rebellion, that you
22:53 have come with swords and clubs? 53 Every day I
[i]Mt 26:55 was with you in the temple courts,[i] and you did
[j]Jn 12:27 [k]Mt 8:12; not lay a hand on me. But this is your hour[j]—
Jn 1:5; 3:20 when darkness reigns."[k]

Peter Disowns Jesus

54 Then seizing him, they led him away and took
22:54 [l]Mt 26:57; him into the house of the high priest.[l] Peter fol-
Mk 14:53 lowed at a distance.[m] 55 But when they had kindled
[m]Mt 26:58; Mk 14:54; a fire in the middle of the courtyard and had sat
Jn 18:15 down together, Peter sat down with them. 56 A servant girl saw him seated there in the firelight. She
looked closely at him and said, "This man was
with him."
57 But he denied it. "Woman, I don't know him,"
he said.
58 A little later someone else saw him and said,
"You also are one of them."
"Man, I am not!" Peter replied.
59 About an hour later another asserted, "Certainly this fellow was with him, for he is a Gali-
22:59 [n]Lk 23:6 lean."[n]
60 Peter replied, "Man, I don't know what you're
22:61 talking about!" Just as he was speaking, the roos-
[o]Lk 7:13 ter crowed. 61 The Lord[o] turned and looked straight
[p]ver 34 at Peter. Then Peter remembered the word the
Lord had spoken to him: "Before the rooster crows
today, you will disown me three times."[p] 62 And he
went outside and wept bitterly.

The Guards Mock Jesus

63 The men who were guarding Jesus began
mocking and beating him. 64 They blindfolded him
and demanded, "Prophesy! Who hit you?" 65 And
22:65 they said many other insulting things to him.[q]
[q]Mt 16:21

Jesus Before Pilate and Herod

22:66 66 At daybreak the council[r] of the elders of the
[r]Mt 5:22 [s]Mt 27:1; people, both the chief priests and teachers of the
Mk 15:1 law, met together,[s] and Jesus was led before them.
67 "If you are the Christ,[a]" they said, "tell us."
Jesus answered, "If I tell you, you will not
22:68 believe me, 68 and if I asked you, you would not
[t]Lk 20:3-8 answer.[t] 69 But from now on, the Son of Man will
22:69 be seated at the right hand of the mighty God."[u]
[u]Mk 16:19

[a]67 Or *Messiah*

Jesus' Trial

LK 22:66–71

This gathering of Jewish religious leaders is more like a grand jury than an actual trial. The group examines Jesus, hoping his response will be convicting enough to result in the death penalty by the Roman authorities. Jesus' response to their questions is to declare, "I am," which is similar to the way God proclaimed his existence to Moses in Exodus 3:14. The members of the council immediately understand that Jesus is claiming to be God, which is the highest form of blasphemy and is a crime punishable by death according to the law (see the note on Mt 26:57–68, page 1633). The religious leaders are now ready to turn Jesus over to Pilate, the Roman governor. They expect Pilate to construe Jesus' claim to kingship in a political sense and to see Jesus as an insurrectionist who deserves the death penalty.

Barabbas

LK 23:18–19

Barabbas was a revolutionary and, in this politically turbulent time, his case wasn't an unusual one. Because of his insurrectionist posture, he was the perfect person to place next to Jesus, who also was accused of insurrection. Barabbas, who had also committed murder, was probably also sentenced to be crucified for his crimes.

Barabbas's name is Aramaic and means "son of the father," which is ironic considering Jesus' status as Son of the Father. The Passover custom of releasing a prisoner is unknown outside the Gospels.

70They all asked, "Are you then the Son of
God?"[v]
He replied, "You are right in saying I am."[w]
71Then they said, "Why do we need any more
testimony? We have heard it from his own lips."
23 Then the whole assembly rose and led him
off to Pilate.[x] 2And they began to accuse
him, saying, "We have found this man subverting
our nation.[y] He opposes payment of taxes to Caesar[z] and claims to be Christ,[*a*] a king."[a]
3So Pilate asked Jesus, "Are you the king of the
Jews?"
"Yes, it is as you say," Jesus replied.
4Then Pilate announced to the chief priests and
the crowd, "I find no basis for a charge against
this man."[b]
5But they insisted, "He stirs up the people all
over Judea[*b*] by his teaching. He started in Galilee[c]
and has come all the way here."
6On hearing this, Pilate asked if the man was a
Galilean.[d] 7When he learned that Jesus was under
Herod's jurisdiction, he sent him to Herod,[e] who
was also in Jerusalem at that time.
8When Herod saw Jesus, he was greatly
pleased, because for a long time he had been
wanting to see him.[f] From what he had heard
about him, he hoped to see him perform some
miracle. 9He plied him with many questions, but
Jesus gave him no answer.[g] 10The chief priests and
the teachers of the law were standing there, vehemently accusing him. 11Then Herod and his soldiers ridiculed and mocked him. Dressing him in
an elegant robe,[h] they sent him back to Pilate.
12That day Herod and Pilate became friends[i]—
before this they had been enemies.
13Pilate called together the chief priests, the
rulers and the people, 14and said to them, "You
brought me this man as one who was inciting the
people to rebellion. I have examined him in your
presence and have found no basis for your
charges against him.[j] 15Neither has Herod, for he
sent him back to us; as you can see, he has done
nothing to deserve death. 16Therefore, I will punish him[k] and then release him.[*c*]"
18With one voice they cried out, "Away with this
man! Release Barabbas to us!"[l] 19(Barabbas had
been thrown into prison for an insurrection in the
city, and for murder.)
20Wanting to release Jesus, Pilate appealed to
them again. 21But they kept shouting, "Crucify
him! Crucify him!"
22For the third time he spoke to them: "Why?
What crime has this man committed? I have
found in him no grounds for the death penalty.
Therefore I will have him punished and then
release him."[m]
23But with loud shouts they insistently demand-

22:70 [v]Mt 4:3 [w]Mt 27:11; Lk 23:3
23:1 [x]Mt 27:2; Mk 15:1; Jn 18:28
23:2 [y]ver 14 [z]Lk 20:22 [a]Jn 19:12
23:4 [b]ver 14,22, 41; Mt 27:23; Jn 18:38; 1Ti 6:13; 2Co 5:21
23:5 [c]Mk 1:14
23:6 [d]Lk 22:59
23:7 [e]Mt 14:1; Lk 3:1
23:8 [f]Lk 9:9
23:9 [g]Mk 14:61
23:11 [h]Mk 15:17-19; Jn 19:2,3
23:12 [i]Ac 4:27
23:14 [j]ver 4
23:16 [k]ver 22; Mt 27:26; Jn 19:1; Ac 16:37; 2Co 11:23,24
23:18 [l]Ac 3:13,14
23:22 [m]ver 16

[*a*] 2 Or *Messiah*; also in verses 35 and 39 [*b*] 5 Or *over the land of the Jews* [*c*] 16 Some manuscripts *him." 17Now he was obliged to release one man to them at the Feast.*

ed that he be crucified, and their shouts prevailed.
24 So Pilate decided to grant their demand. 25 He
released the man who had been thrown into
prison for insurrection and murder, the one they
asked for, and surrendered Jesus to their will.

The Crucifixion

26 As they led him away, they seized Simon from
Cyrene,[n] who was on his way in from the country,
and put the cross on him and made him carry it
behind Jesus.[o] 27 A large number of people followed him, including women who mourned and
wailed[p] for him. 28 Jesus turned and said to them,
"Daughters of Jerusalem, do not weep for me;
weep for yourselves and for your children.[q] 29 For
the time will come when you will say, 'Blessed are
the barren women, the wombs that never bore
and the breasts that never nursed!'[r] 30 Then

> " 'they will say to the mountains, "Fall
> on us!"
> and to the hills, "Cover us!" '[a][s]

31 For if men do these things when the tree is
green, what will happen when it is dry?"[t]
32 Two other men, both criminals, were also led
out with him to be executed.[u] 33 When they came
to the place called the Skull, there they crucified
him, along with the criminals—one on his right,
the other on his left. 34 Jesus said, "Father,[v] forgive
them, for they do not know what they are
doing."[b][w] And they divided up his clothes by casting lots.[x]
35 The people stood watching, and the rulers
even sneered at him.[y] They said, "He saved others; let him save himself if he is the Christ of God,
the Chosen One."[z]
36 The soldiers also came up and mocked him.[a]
They offered him wine vinegar[b] 37 and said, "If you
are the king of the Jews,[c] save yourself."
38 There was a written notice above him, which
read: THIS IS THE KING OF THE JEWS.[d]
39 One of the criminals who hung there hurled
insults at him: "Aren't you the Christ? Save yourself and us!"[e]
40 But the other criminal rebuked him. "Don't
you fear God," he said, "since you are under the
same sentence? 41 We are punished justly, for we
are getting what our deeds deserve. But this man
has done nothing wrong."[f]
42 Then he said, "Jesus, remember me when you
come into your kingdom.[c]"[g]
43 Jesus answered him, "I tell you the truth,
today you will be with me in paradise."[h]

Jesus' Death

44 It was now about the sixth hour, and darkness
came over the whole land until the ninth hour,[i]

23:26 [n]Mt 27:32 [o]Mk 15:21; Jn 19:17
23:27 [p]Lk 8:52
23:28 [q]Lk 19:41-44; 21:23,24
23:29 [r]Mt 24:19
23:30 [s]Hos 10:8; Isa 2:19; Rev 6:16
23:31 [t]Eze 20:47
23:32 [u]Isa 53:12; Mt 27:38; Mk 15:27; Jn 19:18
23:34 [v]Mt 11:25 [w]Mt 5:44 [x]Ps 22:18
23:35 [y]Ps 22:17 [z]Isa 42:1
23:36 [a]Ps 22:7 [b]Ps 69:21; Mt 27:48
23:37 [c]Lk 4:3,9
23:38 [d]Mt 2:2
23:39 [e]ver 35,37
23:41 [f]ver 4
23:42 [g]Mt 16:27
23:43 [h]2Co 12:3,4; Rev 2:7
23:44 [i]Am 8:9

[a] *30* Hosea 10:8 [b] *34* Some early manuscripts do not have this sentence. [c] *42* Some manuscripts *come with your kingly power*

The Burial

Wouldn't you love to have been in that garden outside Jerusalem two thousand years ago? The trees were budding, the flowers bursting through the ground. That morning as the sun was rising, Jesus wore his new body for the first time. In the hazy light of dawn he was mistaken for the gardener by a woman who had watched him die [Jn 20:10–18]. Surely she never forgot that wonderful encounter in the garden.

—Barbara Johnson

The Burial

LK 23:50–56

Joseph of Arimathea must have surprised everyone (perhaps even himself) when he asked for Jesus' body and offered his own tomb as a burial place. Joseph, who was part of the council that decided Jesus was guilty of blasphemy, disagreed with the Sanhedrin's verdict (see Jn 19:38), but he probably wasn't very vocal or perhaps wasn't present at Jesus' trial. Still, he dares to align himself with Jesus at this point. Jesus' friends follow the traditional burial customs of washing the body and applying a mixture of spices (Jn 19:39), perhaps as a preservative or to ward off the smell of decomposition. The body is then placed in a linen shroud (Lk 23:53). Mourners would typically visit the tomb to re-anoint the body, which is probably the mission of the women who go to Jesus' empty tomb the morning after the Sabbath.

45 for the sun stopped shining. And the curtain of
the temple[j] was torn in two.[k] 46 Jesus called out
with a loud voice,[l] "Father, into your hands I commit my spirit."[m] When he had said this, he
breathed his last.[n]

47 The centurion, seeing what had happened,
praised God[o] and said, "Surely this was a righteous man." 48 When all the people who had gathered to witness this sight saw what took place,
they beat their breasts[p] and went away. 49 But all
those who knew him, including the women who
had followed him from Galilee,[q] stood at a distance,[r] watching these things.

Jesus' Burial

50 Now there was a man named Joseph, a member of the Council, a good and upright man, 51 who
had not consented to their decision and action. He
came from the Judean town of Arimathea and he
was waiting for the kingdom of God.[s] 52 Going to
Pilate, he asked for Jesus' body. 53 Then he took it
down, wrapped it in linen cloth and placed it in a
tomb cut in the rock, one in which no one had yet
been laid. 54 It was Preparation Day,[t] and the Sabbath was about to begin.

55 The women who had come with Jesus from
Galilee[u] followed Joseph and saw the tomb and
how his body was laid in it. 56 Then they went
home and prepared spices and perfumes.[v] But
they rested on the Sabbath in obedience to the
commandment.[w]

The Resurrection

24 On the first day of the week, very early in
the morning, the women took the spices
they had prepared[x] and went to the tomb. 2 They
found the stone rolled away from the tomb, 3 but
when they entered, they did not find the body of
the Lord Jesus.[y] 4 While they were wondering
about this, suddenly two men in clothes that
gleamed like lightning[z] stood beside them. 5 In
their fright the women bowed down with their
faces to the ground, but the men said to them,
"Why do you look for the living among the dead?
6 He is not here; he has risen! Remember how he
told you, while he was still with you in Galilee:[a]
7 'The Son of Man[b] must be delivered into the
hands of sinful men, be crucified and on the third
day be raised again.' "[c] 8 Then they remembered
his words.[d]

9 When they came back from the tomb, they told
all these things to the Eleven and to all the others. 10 It was Mary Magdalene, Joanna, Mary the
mother of James, and the others with them[e] who
told this to the apostles.[f] 11 But they did not
believe[g] the women, because their words seemed
to them like nonsense. 12 Peter, however, got up
and ran to the tomb. Bending over, he saw the
strips of linen lying by themselves,[h] and he went
away,[i] wondering to himself what had happened.

23:45 [j]Ex 26:31-33; Heb 9:3,8 [k]Heb 10:19,20
23:46 [l]Mt 27:50 [m]Ps 31:5; 1Pe 2:23 [n]Jn 19:30
23:47 [o]Mt 9:8
23:48 [p]Lk 18:13
23:49 [q]Lk 8:2 [r]Ps 38:11
23:51 [s]Lk 2:25,38
23:54 [t]Mt 27:62
23:55 [u]ver 49
23:56 [v]Mk 16:1; Lk 24:1 [w]Ex 12:16; 20:10
24:1 [x]Lk 23:56
24:3 [y]ver 23,24
24:4 [z]Jn 20:12
24:6 [a]Mt 17:22,23; Mk 9:30-31; Lk 9:22; 24:44
24:7 [b]Mt 8:20 [c]Mt 16:21
24:8 [d]Jn 2:22
24:10 [e]Lk 8:1-3 [f]Mk 6:30
24:11 [g]Mk 16:11
24:12 [h]Jn 20:3-7 [i]Jn 20:10

On the Road to Emmaus

13 Now that same day two of them were going to
24:13 a village called Emmaus, about seven miles[a] from
[j]Mk 16:12 Jerusalem.[j] 14 They were talking with each other
about everything that had happened. 15 As they
talked and discussed these things with each other,
Jesus himself came up and walked along with
24:15 them;[k] 16 but they were kept from recognizing him.[l]
[k]ver 36 17 He asked them, "What are you discussing
24:16 together as you walk along?"
[l]Jn 20:14; They stood still, their faces downcast. 18 One of
21:4 them, named Cleopas,[m] asked him, "Are you only
24:18 a visitor to Jerusalem and do not know the things
[m]Jn 19:25 that have happened there in these days?"
19 "What things?" he asked.
24:19 [n]Mk 1:24 "About Jesus of Nazareth,"[n] they replied. "He
[o]Mt 21:11 was a prophet,[o] powerful in word and deed before
God and all the people. 20 The chief priests and our
24:20 [p]Lk 23:13 rulers[p] handed him over to be sentenced to death,
and they crucified him; 21 but we had hoped that
24:21 [q]Lk 1:68; he was the one who was going to redeem Israel.[q]
2:38; 21:28 And what is more, it is the third day[r] since all this
[r]Mt 16:21 took place. 22 In addition, some of our women
24:22 amazed us.[s] They went to the tomb early this
[s]ver 1-10 morning 23 but didn't find his body. They came
and told us that they had seen a vision of angels,
who said he was alive. 24 Then some of our companions went to the tomb and found it just as the
24:24 [t]ver 12 women had said, but him they did not see."[t]
25 He said to them, "How foolish you are, and
how slow of heart to believe all that the prophets
have spoken! 26 Did not the Christ[b] have to suffer
24:26 these things and then enter his glory?"[u] 27 And
[u]Heb 2:10; beginning with Moses[v] and all the Prophets,[w] he
1Pe 1:11 explained to them what was said in all the Scrip-
24:27 tures concerning himself.[x]
[v]Ge 3:15; 28 As they approached the village to which they
Nu 21:9; Dt 18:15 were going, Jesus acted as if he were going far-
[w]Isa 7:14; 9:6; 40:10, ther. 29 But they urged him strongly, "Stay with us,
11; 53; for it is nearly evening; the day is almost over."
Eze 34:23; Da 9:24; So he went in to stay with them.
Mic 7:20; 30 When he was at the table with them, he took
Mal 3:1 bread, gave thanks, broke it[y] and began to give it
[x]Jn 1:45 to them. 31 Then their eyes were opened and they
24:30 recognized him,[z] and he disappeared from their
[y]Mt 14:19 sight. 32 They asked each other, "Were not our
24:31 hearts burning within us[a] while he talked with us
[z]ver 16 on the road and opened the Scriptures[b] to us?"
33 They got up and returned at once to Jerusa-
24:32 [a]Ps 39:3 lem. There they found the Eleven and those with
[b]ver 27,45 them, assembled together 34 and saying, "It is true!
24:34 The Lord has risen and has appeared to Simon."[c]
[c]1Co 15:5 35 Then the two told what had happened on the
24:35 way, and how Jesus was recognized by them
[d]ver 30,31 when he broke the bread.[d]

Jesus Appears to the Disciples

36 While they were still talking about this, Jesus

[a] *13* Greek *sixty stadia* (about 11 kilometers)
[b] *26* Or *Messiah*; also in verse 46

Redeeming the Situation

LK 24:13-35

Disappointment, sadness and confusion reign in the lives of Jesus' two followers as they travel down the road. How they must be wrestling with the horrifying events of the last few days—and the astounding report of their leader's resurrection. They explain that they had hoped Jesus would "redeem" Israel (Lk 24:21). A literal translation of that word is "set free." These two men long for Jesus to establish a physical kingdom, to throw off the strangling Roman rule and to free Israel. But they have a shortsighted view of what Jesus ultimately accomplishes. He not only establishes a kingdom over which he still rules today, but, for those who respond to his offer of freedom, he also removes sin's stranglehold and frees them to become citizens of his spiritual kingdom. He redeems in a way that still stuns and awes us today.

Eyes That See

It's difficult to imagine the conflicting emotions in the two men who walk toward Emmaus. They are believers. This very day, they have heard the report of the women regarding the empty tomb. They are discussing it as they walk along. Their anguish at Jesus' death has been replaced with a small glimmer of hope and a lot of confusion.

How do the travelers describe Jesus (Lk 24:19)? Why is it significant that they are reluctant to call Jesus the Messiah (Lk 24:21)?

What is Jesus' response to their doubt and confusion (Lk 24:27)? How do you think Jesus responds to your doubt and confusion?

What is Jesus doing when they recognize him (Lk 24:30–31,35)? Reading between the lines, what can you speculate about the significance of this act?

What is their response to having their eyes opened (Lk 24:31–32)? Why is the condition of their hearts important?

How does God open your eyes to spiritual things (1Co 2:12)? Why are only those with the Holy Spirit able to understand spiritual things (1Co 2:14)? How does this truth explain the confusion unbelievers have regarding Jesus?

Enjoying God THROUGH the Word

Read Luke 24:36–49 (pages 1737,1739). The excited travelers have returned to Jerusalem and have told their story to the other disciples. Jesus appears, startling and frightening all of them. In view of their doubt and confusion, Jesus lovingly says, "Look at my hands and my feet . . . Touch me and see" (Lk 24:39). Yet even with this physical evidence, they have trouble believing (Lk 24:41).

Just as the Israelites saw God's miraculous acts during the exodus, the disciples see the material facts, but their minds and hearts cannot take in the implications of what they see (Dt 29:2–4). Their minds need to be opened so that they can understand the Scriptures (Lk 24:45).

Jesus tells his disciples that those who have spiritual discernment will receive more and more insight into the kingdom of heaven (Mt 13:11–12). Spiritual discernment is not a one-time event. You can ask for greater spiritual understanding each day. Jesus is available "to open eyes that are blind, to free captives from prison and to release from the dungeon those who sit in darkness" (Isa 42:7; see also Lk 4:17–21).

Enjoying God THROUGH Experience

Go into a dark room (or even a walk-in closet) for a minute or two. With no light available, open your eyes and look around. Just as your physical eyes are open but can see nothing, so your spiritual eyes can see nothing without the Light, Jesus. Through the Spirit, your spiritual eyes can be opened "to give [you] the light of the knowledge of the glory of God in the face of Christ" (2Co 4:6). Ask God to give you more understanding of spiritual truths. He promises: "Call to me and I will answer you and tell you great and unsearchable things you do not know" (Jer 33:3).

Go to page 1773 for your next weekly study.

himself stood among them and said to them,
"Peace be with you."[e]
37They were startled and frightened, thinking
they saw a ghost.[f] 38He said to them, "Why are
you troubled, and why do doubts rise in your
minds? 39Look at my hands and my feet. It is I
myself! Touch me and see;[g] a ghost does not have
flesh and bones, as you see I have."
40When he had said this, he showed them his
hands and feet. 41And while they still did not
believe it because of joy and amazement, he asked
them, "Do you have anything here to eat?" 42They
gave him a piece of broiled fish, 43and he took it
and ate it in their presence.[h]
44He said to them, "This is what I told you
while I was still with you:[i] Everything must be
fulfilled[j] that is written about me in the Law of
Moses,[k] the Prophets and the Psalms."[l]
45Then he opened their minds so they could
understand the Scriptures. 46He told them, "This is
what is written: The Christ will suffer and rise
from the dead on the third day, 47and repentance
and forgiveness of sins will be preached in his
name[m] to all nations,[n] beginning at Jerusalem.
48You are witnesses[o] of these things. 49I am going
to send you what my Father has promised;[p] but
stay in the city until you have been clothed with
power from on high."

The Ascension

50When he had led them out to the vicinity of
Bethany,[q] he lifted up his hands and blessed them.
51While he was blessing them, he left them and
was taken up into heaven.[r] 52Then they worshiped
him and returned to Jerusalem with great joy.
53And they stayed continually at the temple,[s]
praising God.

24:36 [e]Jn 20:19,21, 26; 14:27
24:37 [f]Mk 6:49
24:39 [g]Jn 20:27; 1Jn 1:1
24:43 [h]Ac 10:41
24:44 [i]Lk 9:45; 18:34 [j]Mt 16:21; Lk 9:22,44; 18:31-33; 22:37 [k]ver 27 [l]Ps 2; 16; 22; 69; 72; 110; 118
24:47 [m]Ac 5:31; 10:43; 13:38 [n]Mt 28:19
24:48 [o]Ac 1:8; 2:32; 5:32; 13:31; 1Pe 5:1
24:49 [p]Jn 14:16; Ac 1:4
24:50 [q]Mt 21:17
24:51 [r]2Ki 2:11
24:53 [s]Ac 2:46

Open Minds

LK 24:45

On the road to Emmaus, the two disciples are unable to see that the "uninformed" traveler who walks with them is Jesus because God closes their minds to that concept (Lk 24:16). But then God opens their eyes (Lk 24:31), and understanding floods in like water from a broken dam.

Now Jesus' other disciples' eyes are opened as well (Lk 24:45). They see the Old Testament with new eyes. They can look at Scripture and see how Jesus fulfills prophecies spoken hundreds of years before, and they come to understand that his is a kingdom with parameters far exceeding their dammed up hopes and dreams. Even today God lets us go through faith crises, and we don't see how he can bring good out of these situations. But each of us must live through our Good Friday and Silent Saturday to arrive at Easter Sunday, a time of resurrected hopes and dreams.

John

The basics of belief in Jesus Christ.

The apostle John records this unique gospel narrative to introduce who Jesus is and what he came to do. John directs his words to non-Jews, using powerful accounts of Jesus' miracles, vivid images and the "I am" statements of Jesus to prove Jesus' claim to be God's Son. John includes several sermons and miracles not found in the other gospel narratives. While he concentrates on portraying Jesus as God's Son, John doesn't ignore Jesus' humanity, including small bits of information about Jesus being hungry, tired, compassionate and sad.

In his Gospel John records the accounts of several people who accept Jesus' invitation to seek a personal relationship with God. The Samaritan woman at the well overcomes her past to find freedom in a new life of faith (Jn 4). Mary and Martha experience healing of body and spirit as Jesus brings their brother back to life and teaches them how to prioritize their faith and family responsibilities (Jn 11). Mary Magdalene stands with Jesus throughout his ministry, crucifixion, death and resurrection as a model of one whose faith forms a vital part of her life (Jn 19–20).

John repeatedly reminds his readers of the basics of Christianity, alerting us to the dangers of spiritual blindness and assuring us that God's power can reside in us. John affirms that since Jesus is the Son of God, we can trust Jesus' words, we can receive eternal life, and we can actively live in the world and share our faith with others.

Quick Study

Author
John, "the disciple whom Jesus loved" (Jn 13:23; 19:26; 21:7; 21:20).

Date Written
Traditionally thought to have been sometime late in the first century A.D., although more recently some scholars give it an earlier date, perhaps as early as A.D. 50 but no later than A.D. 70.

Setting
Israel.

Key Passage
John 3:16–17 "For God so loved the world that he gave his one and only Son, that whoever believes in him shall not perish but have eternal life. For God did not send his Son into the world to condemn the world, but to save the world through him."

Outline

The Word.
Jn 1:1-18

Jesus' early ministry.
Jn 1:19-51

Miracles, teachings and healings.
Jn 2:1–10:42

Mary, Martha and Lazarus.
Jn 11:1-44

Jesus' last days.
Jn 11:45–13:38

Jesus' last teachings and prayer.
Jn 14:1–17:26

Jesus' arrest and trial.
Jn 18:1–19:16

Jesus' death and burial.
Jn 19:17-42

The resurrection.
Jn 20

The resurrected Christ and his disciples.
Jn 21

The Women of John

⚘ **Mary, mother of Jesus**	*An example of faithfulness.* Jn 2:1-11; 6:42; 19:25 (page 1613)
⚘ **Woman at the well**	*She responded to Jesus' invitation.* Jn 4 (page 1646)
⚘ **Woman caught in adultery**	*Saved from death and charged to leave her sin.* Jn 8:1-11 (page 1812)
⚘ **Mary of Bethany**	*Captivated by Jesus' teachings.* Jn 11; 12:1-3 (page 1843)
⚘ **Martha**	*Believed in Jesus.* Jn 11 (page 1844)
Woman giving birth	*Pain gives way to joy.* Jn 16:20-21
Servant girl	*Questions Peter.* Jn 18:16-17
⚘ **Mary Magdalene**	*Follower and provider.* Jn 19:25; 20:1-18 (page 1714)
⚘ **Mary, the wife of Clopas**	*Faithful follower.* Jn 19:25 (page 1941)

⚘ Denotes a sketch written about this character

The Word

JN 1:1–18

In referring to "the Word," the prologue of the fourth Gospel immediately taps into Christ's identity as God and Creator. These verses testify that before time and before the creation of the world, the Word existed. From the statement "the Word was with God," we gather that his is a distinct personality, distinguishable from that of God the Father. At the same time, "the Word was God," making them coexistent and equal. The author declares that all things were created through the Word, teaches that the Word is the origin of light and life, and proclaims that the Word became human and lived with us. With these dramatic statements, he establishes the foundation on which his entire argument (that Christ is God) is built.

The Word Became Flesh

1 In the beginning was the Word,[a] and the Word
was with God,[b] and the Word was God.[c] 2He
was with God in the beginning.[d]
3Through him all things were made; without
him nothing was made that has been made.[e] 4In
him was life,[f] and that life was the light[g] of men.
5The light shines in the darkness, but the darkness has not understood[a] it.[h]
6There came a man who was sent from God; his
name was John.[i] 7He came as a witness to testify[j]
concerning that light, so that through him all men
might believe.[k] 8He himself was not the light; he
came only as a witness to the light. 9The true
light[l] that gives light to every man[m] was coming
into the world.[b]
10He was in the world, and though the world was
made through him,[n] the world did not recognize
him. 11He came to that which was his own, but his
own did not receive him. 12Yet to all who received
him, to those who believed[o] in his name,[p] he gave
the right to become children of God[q]— 13children
born not of natural descent,[c] nor of human decision or a husband's will, but born of God.[r]
14The Word became flesh[s] and made his
dwelling among us. We have seen his glory, the
glory of the One and Only,[d] who came from the
Father, full of grace and truth.[t]
15John testifies[u] concerning him. He cries out,
saying, "This was he of whom I said, 'He who
comes after me has surpassed me because he was
before me.' "[v] 16From the fullness[w] of his grace we
have all received one blessing after another. 17For
the law was given through Moses;[x] grace and
truth came through Jesus Christ.[y] 18No one has
ever seen God,[z] but God the One and Only,[d,e][a] who
is at the Father's side, has made him known.

John the Baptist Denies Being the Christ

19Now this was John's testimony when the
Jews[b] of Jerusalem sent priests and Levites to ask
him who he was. 20He did not fail to confess, but
confessed freely, "I am not the Christ.[f]"[c]
21They asked him, "Then who are you? Are you
Elijah?"[d]
He said, "I am not."
"Are you the Prophet?"[e]
He answered, "No."
22Finally they said, "Who are you? Give us an
answer to take back to those who sent us. What
do you say about yourself?"
23John replied in the words of Isaiah the prophet, "I am the voice of one calling in the desert,[f]
'Make straight the way for the Lord.' "[g][g]

[a] *5* Or *darkness, and the darkness has not overcome* [b] *9* Or *This was the true light that gives light to every man who comes into the world* [c] *13* Greek *of bloods* [d] *14,18* Or *the Only Begotten* [e] *18* Some manuscripts *but the only* (or *only begotten*) *Son* [f] *20* Or *Messiah.* "The Christ" (Greek) and "the Messiah" (Hebrew) both mean "the Anointed One"; also in verse 25. [g] *23* Isaiah 40:3

1:1 [a]Rev 19:13 [b]Jn 17:5; 1Jn 1:2 [c]Php 2:6
1:2 [d]Ge 1:1
1:3 [e]1Co 8:6; Col 1:16; Heb 1:2
1:4 [f]Jn 5:26; 11:25; 14:6 [g]Jn 8:12
1:5 [h]Jn 3:19
1:6 [i]Mt 3:1
1:7 [j]ver 15,19, 32 [k]ver 12
1:9 [l]1Jn 2:8 [m]Isa 49:6
1:10 [n]Heb 1:2
1:12 [o]ver 7 [p]1Jn 3:23 [q]Gal 3:26
1:13 [r]Jn 3:6; Jas 1:18; 1Pe 1:23; 1Jn 3:9
1:14 [s]Gal 4:4; Php 2:7,8; 1Ti 3:16; Heb 2:14 [t]Jn 14:6
1:15 [u]ver 7 [v]ver 30; Mt 3:11
1:16 [w]Eph 1:23; Col 1:19
1:17 [x]Jn 7:19 [y]ver 14
1:18 [z]Ex 33:20; Jn 6:46; Col 1:15; 1Ti 6:16 [a]Jn 3:16,18; 1Jn 4:9
1:19 [b]Jn 2:18; 5:10,16; 6:41,52
1:20 [c]Jn 3:28; Lk 3:15,16
1:21 [d]Mt 11:14 [e]Dt 18:15
1:23 [f]Mt 3:1 [g]Isa 40:3

[24]Now some Pharisees who had been sent
[25]questioned him, "Why then do you baptize if
you are not the Christ, nor Elijah, nor the
Prophet?"
[26]"I baptize with[a] water," John replied, "but
among you stands one you do not know. [27]He is
1:27 hver 15,30 the one who comes after me,[h] the thongs of whose
sandals I am not worthy to untie."
[28]This all happened at Bethany on the other side
1:28 iJn 3:26; 10:40 of the Jordan,[i] where John was baptizing.

Jesus the Lamb of God

[29]The next day John saw Jesus coming toward
1:29 jver 36; him and said, "Look, the Lamb of God,[j] who takes
Isa 53:7; away the sin of the world! [30]This is the one I
1Pe 1:19; meant when I said, 'A man who comes after me
Rev 5:6 has surpassed me because he was before me.'[k] [31]I
1:30 kver 15,27 myself did not know him, but the reason I came
baptizing with water was that he might be
revealed to Israel."
[32]Then John gave this testimony: "I saw the
1:32 Spirit come down from heaven as a dove and
lMt 3:16; remain on him.[l] [33]I would not have known him,
Mk 1:10 except that the one who sent me to baptize with
1:33 water[m] told me, 'The man on whom you see the
mMk 1:4 Spirit come down and remain is he who will bap-
nMt 3:11; Mk 1:8 tize with the Holy Spirit.'[n] [34]I have seen and I testify that this is the Son of God."[o]

1:34 over 49; Mt 4:3

Jesus' First Disciples

1:35 [35]The next day John[p] was there again with two
pMt 3:1 of his disciples. [36]When he saw Jesus passing by,
he said, "Look, the Lamb of God!"[q]
1:36 qver 29 [37]When the two disciples heard him say this,
they followed Jesus. [38]Turning around, Jesus saw
them following and asked, "What do you want?"
1:38 rver 49; They said, "Rabbi"[r] (which means Teacher),
Mt 23:7 "where are you staying?"
[39]"Come," he replied, "and you will see."
So they went and saw where he was staying,
and spent that day with him. It was about the
tenth hour.
[40]Andrew, Simon Peter's brother, was one of the
two who heard what John had said and who had
1:41 followed Jesus. [41]The first thing Andrew did was
sJn 4:25 to find his brother Simon and tell him, "We have
1:42 found the Messiah" (that is, the Christ).[s] [42]And he
tGe 17:5,15 uMt 16:18 brought him to Jesus.
Jesus looked at him and said, "You are Simon
1:43 son of John. You will be called[t] Cephas" (which,
vMt 10:3; when translated, is Peter[b]).[u]

Jn 6:5-7; 12:21,22; 14:8,9 wMt 4:19

Jesus Calls Philip and Nathanael

[43]The next day Jesus decided to leave for Gali-
1:44 lee. Finding Philip,[v] he said to him, "Follow me."[w]
xMt 11:21; [44]Philip, like Andrew and Peter, was from the
Jn 12:21 town of Bethsaida.[x] [45]Philip found Nathanael[y] and
1:45 yJn 21:2 told him, "We have found the one Moses wrote

[a] *26* Or *in*; also in verses 31 and 33 [b] *42* Both *Cephas* (Aramaic) and *Peter* (Greek) mean *rock*.

Jesus, the Lamb of God

JN 1:29-34

According to Old Testament law, Jewish priests were to daily sacrifice two lambs to atone for the sins of the people (Ex 29:38). Each Israelite family also sacrificed a lamb each year to commemorate the first Passover, when the destroying angel spared the firstborn sons of Israelites whose doorframes were marked with lamb's blood (Ex 12). The prophet Isaiah predicted that the Messiah would sacrifice his own life and be "led like a lamb to the slaughter" (Isa 53:7). After Christ's death and resurrection, Paul compares Jesus to the Passover lamb (1Co 5:7). In the book of Revelation, Jesus is referred to as "the Lamb" 29 times.

John the Baptist urges the people to see Jesus as the Lamb when he cries, "Look, the Lamb of God" as Jesus approaches (Jn 1:29). He knows that Jesus is the fulfillment of all the prophecies and all the former ways of atoning for sin through animal sacrifice. Jesus is the perfect sacrifice, the perfect "Lamb of God, who takes away the sin of the world!" (Jn 1:29).

The Wedding at Cana

JN 2:1–11

Some scholars suggest that the invitation to this wedding comes through Nathanael, who is from Cana (Jn 21:2), and whom Jesus has just called to follow him (Jn 1:43–51). Tradition holds that Mary is the aunt—and Jesus, the cousin—of the bridegroom. Regardless of how Jesus and his mother come to be at the wedding, when the supply of wine dwindles, Mary grows anxious and brings the matter to Jesus.

While few of us in the 21st century would consider it courteous to address our mother as "woman" (Jn 2:4), Jesus is in fact employing a title of respect in his day. Mary honors Jesus' desire to be discreet and tells the servants to do as Jesus bids them. Jesus, in turn, responds to Mary's implied request that he solve the problem. This first miraculous sign remains an isolated incident, however, until Jesus' time for widespread miracles arrives several months later, following the initiation of his public ministry in Jerusalem.

about in the Law,[z] and about whom the prophets
also wrote[a]—Jesus of Nazareth,[b] the son of
Joseph."[c]
46"Nazareth! Can anything good come from
there?"[d] Nathanael asked.
"Come and see," said Philip.
47When Jesus saw Nathanael approaching, he
said of him, "Here is a true Israelite,[e] in whom
there is nothing false."[f]
48"How do you know me?" Nathanael asked.
Jesus answered, "I saw you while you were still
under the fig tree before Philip called you."
49Then Nathanael declared, "Rabbi,[g] you are the
Son of God;[h] you are the King of Israel."[i]
50Jesus said, "You believe[a] because I told you I
saw you under the fig tree. You shall see greater
things than that." 51He then added, "I tell you[b] the
truth, you[b] shall see heaven open,[j] and the angels
of God ascending and descending[k] on the Son of
Man."[l]

Jesus Changes Water to Wine

2 On the third day a wedding took place at Cana
in Galilee.[m] Jesus' mother[n] was there, 2and
Jesus and his disciples had also been invited to
the wedding. 3When the wine was gone, Jesus'
mother said to him, "They have no more wine."
4"Dear woman,[o] why do you involve me?"[p]
Jesus replied. "My time[q] has not yet come."
5His mother said to the servants, "Do whatever
he tells you."[r]
6Nearby stood six stone water jars, the kind
used by the Jews for ceremonial washing,[s] each
holding from twenty to thirty gallons.[c]
7Jesus said to the servants, "Fill the jars with
water"; so they filled them to the brim.
8Then he told them, "Now draw some out and
take it to the master of the banquet."
They did so, 9and the master of the banquet
tasted the water that had been turned into wine.[t]
He did not realize where it had come from,
though the servants who had drawn the water
knew. Then he called the bridegroom aside 10and
said, "Everyone brings out the choice wine first
and then the cheaper wine after the guests have
had too much to drink; but you have saved the
best till now."
11This, the first of his miraculous signs,[u] Jesus
performed at Cana in Galilee. He thus revealed his
glory,[v] and his disciples put their faith in him.[w]

Jesus Clears the Temple

12After this he went down to Capernaum[x] with
his mother and brothers[y] and his disciples. There
they stayed for a few days.
13When it was almost time for the Jewish
Passover,[z] Jesus went up to Jerusalem.[a] 14In the

[a] 50 Or *Do you believe . . . ?* [b] 51 The Greek is plural.
[c] 6 Greek *two to three metretes* (probably about 75 to 115 liters)

1:45 [z]Lk 24:27 [a]Lk 24:27 [b]Mt 2:23; Mk 1:24 [c]Lk 3:23
1:46 [d]Jn 7:41,42, 52
1:47 [e]Ro 9:4,6 [f]Ps 32:2
1:49 [g]ver 38; Mt 23:7 [h]ver 34; Mt 4:3 [i]Mt 2:2; 27:42; Jn 12:13
1:51 [j]Mt 3:16 [k]Ge 28:12 [l]Mt 8:20
2:1 [m]Jn 4:46; 21:2 [n]Mt 12:46
2:4 [o]Jn 19:26 [p]Mt 8:29 [q]Mt 26:18; Jn 7:6
2:5 [r]Ge 41:55
2:6 [s]Mk 7:3,4; Jn 3:25
2:9 [t]Jn 4:46
2:11 [u]ver 23; Jn 3:2; 4:48; 6:2,14,26, 30; 12:37; 20:30 [v]Jn 1:14 [w]Ex 14:31
2:12 [x]Mt 4:13 [y]Mt 12:46
2:13 [z]Jn 11:55 [a]Dt 16:1-6; Lk 2:41

A Woman Subject to Bleeding

No Appointment Needed

She saw the look on Jesus' face. Jairus had an urgent need, and Jesus was going to his home as quickly as he could move through the crowd around him. She had to hurry. She felt too ashamed to tell him her story, but now there was no time anyway. If only she dared touch him . . .

The woman had been bleeding for 12 years and had no more resources to find a cure. She was anemic and exhausted, but worse by far was her unending state of uncleanness. No one could touch her, and she could touch no one. It was the law. She felt dirty and useless. The chairs she sat on, the bed she lay on—all were unclean.

With utter conviction of Jesus' power to heal, she threw off all restraint. She *touched* him, and she felt the bleeding quit. Her heart began to pound when Jesus suddenly stopped. Did he know? Could he possibly distinguish *her* hand on his robe in such a pressing crowd? "At once Jesus realized that power had gone out from him. He turned around in the crowd and asked, 'Who touched my clothes?' " (Mk 5:30). She had been found out!

Trembling, she went forward. Would the crowd beat her for defiling this holy man? Was Jesus angry because she had made him unclean—unclean, when on a mission of greatest urgency? Someone was dying and needed his help. And she had polluted him.

Falling at his feet, she poured out her whole story, her eyes on the ground. Then she looked up and saw his eyes. Jesus wasn't angry, he was *moved.* He called her "Daughter," and said her faith in God had restored her to health.

Jesus began to move on again, but the woman remained on her knees, wrapped in God's presence, weeping with joy and relief. He had not passed her by. Her suffering was over. She was whole again. She was *clean.*

Some of us think that the Lord has so many important things to do that our petty problems can wait. The truth is, we don't need an appointment with him. He is always available. Our faith blesses him, and his foremost purpose for us until he returns is to make us his "pure, spotless bride." Don't hold back. Press in. He *wants* to make us clean and whole.

A Woman Subject to Bleeding

Matthew 9:20-22

Mark 5:25-34

Luke 8:43-48

Candid SNAPSHOT Then the woman, seeing that she could not go unnoticed, came trembling and fell at his feet. In the presence of all the people, she told why she had touched him and how she had been instantly healed (Luke 8:47).

Jairus's Daughter

Only on Pause

The mourners were in full voice when Jairus arrived with Jesus. Mourning did not mean whispered condolences and quiet tears. The mourners shrieked and wailed and played their flutes. While Jairus was bringing Jesus back to his sick child, word came that she had died. There was no use in bothering the teacher any further. But Jesus had said, "Don't be afraid; just believe, and she will be healed." The scene here at home said hope was futile. The house smelled like death. And everyone here confirmed it.

Jesus saw Jairus's shoulders slump. Though Jesus had worked many miracles in that region, the mourners laughed when he said the young girl only slept. They knew what death looked like. It was part of their daily lives. Many had lost children to disease. The daughter of Jairus was *dead*, not asleep. Jesus ordered the mourners to leave. Their behavior was proper for expressing grief, but it was not a fitting climate for the miracle about to happen.

Although the law forbids touching the dead, Jesus did not hesitate to make himself unclean for the sake of another. "He took her by the hand and said, 'My child, get up!'" (Lk 8:54). She was called from death to life with a word, and the first thing she saw was the face of her Savior. What an incredible, unforgettable gift—to her and to her parents.

Before she had gotten sick and died, she probably was like any 12-year-old girl in the village—childish giggles mixed with budding womanhood. After she returned from death, she could never be the same. She knew she was a daughter of the one true God. Could she ever doubt again that her life had great worth in his eyes? "Give her something to eat," Jesus said. Food for the body *and* food for the spirit. Her hunger for God would be great, her desire to please him insatiable.

Those who have looked death in the face and yet live have an indelible sense of security and destiny. They know that they will not die until God ordains it. Each of us is called from death when God births us anew in his Spirit. Yet we await an even greater call from our Savior. Paul addressed our deepest longing when he wrote, "Listen, I tell you a mystery: We will not all sleep, but we will all be changed—in a flash, in the twinkling of an eye, at the last trumpet. For the trumpet will sound, the dead will be raised imperishable, and we will be changed" (1Co 15:51-52). No more tears, no more grief, no more pain.

Jairus's Daughter
Matthew 9:18-26
Mark 5:21-43
Luke 8:41-56

Candid SNAPSHOT But he took her by the hand and said, "My child, get up!" Her spirit returned, and at once she stood up. Then Jesus told them to give her something to eat (Luke 8:54-55).

temple courts he found men selling cattle, sheep
and doves, and others sitting at tables exchanging
money. 15So he made a whip out of cords, and
drove all from the temple area, both sheep and
cattle; he scattered the coins of the money changers and overturned their tables. 16To those who
sold doves he said, "Get these out of here! How
dare you turn my Father's house[b] into a market!"
17His disciples remembered that it is written:
"Zeal for your house will consume me."[ac]
18Then the Jews demanded of him, "What
miraculous sign can you show us to prove your
authority to do all this?"[d]
19Jesus answered them, "Destroy this temple,
and I will raise it again in three days."[e]
20The Jews replied, "It has taken forty-six years
to build this temple, and you are going to raise it
in three days?" 21But the temple he had spoken of
was his body.[f] 22After he was raised from the dead,
his disciples recalled what he had said.[g] Then they
believed the Scripture and the words that Jesus
had spoken.
23Now while he was in Jerusalem at the
Passover Feast,[h] many people saw the miraculous
signs he was doing and believed in his name.[b]
24But Jesus would not entrust himself to them, for
he knew all men. 25He did not need man's testimony about man, for he knew what was in a
man.[i]

Jesus Teaches Nicodemus

3 Now there was a man of the Pharisees named
Nicodemus,[j] a member of the Jewish ruling
council.[k] 2He came to Jesus at night and said,
"Rabbi, we know you are a teacher who has come
from God. For no one could perform the miraculous signs[l] you are doing if God were not with
him."[m]
3In reply Jesus declared, "I tell you the truth, no
one can see the kingdom of God unless he is born
again.[c]"[n]
4"How can a man be born when he is old?" Nicodemus asked. "Surely he cannot enter a second
time into his mother's womb to be born!"
5Jesus answered, "I tell you the truth, no one
can enter the kingdom of God unless he is born
of water and the Spirit.[o] 6Flesh gives birth to flesh,
but the Spirit[d] gives birth to spirit.[p] 7You should
not be surprised at my saying, 'You[e] must be born
again.' 8The wind blows wherever it pleases. You
hear its sound, but you cannot tell where it comes
from or where it is going. So it is with everyone
born of the Spirit."
9"How can this be?"[q] Nicodemus asked.
10"You are Israel's teacher,"[r] said Jesus, "and do
you not understand these things? 11I tell you the
truth, we speak of what we know,[s] and we testify

2:16 [b]Lk 2:49
2:17 [c]Ps 69:9
2:18 [d]Mt 12:38
2:19 [e]Mt 26:61; 27:40; Mk 14:58; 15:29
2:21 [f]1Co 6:19
2:22 [g]Lk 24:5-8; Jn 12:16; 14:26
2:23 [h]ver 13
2:25 [i]Mt 9:4; Jn 6:61,64; 13:11
3:1 [j]Jn 7:50; 19:39 [k]Lk 23:13
3:2 [l]Jn 9:16,33 [m]Ac 2:22; 10:38
3:3 [n]Jn 1:13; 1Pe 1:23
3:5 [o]Tit 3:5
3:6 [p]Jn 1:13; 1Co 15:50
3:9 [q]Jn 6:52,60
3:10 [r]Lk 2:46
3:11 [s]Jn 1:18; 7:16,17

Born Again

JN 3:1–11

As a Pharisee, Nicodemus studied the law and possibly made a connection between Jesus' words and the new spiritual life that the prophets foretold (Jer 31:33; Eze 11:19). Yet Nicodemus, also one of the Sanhedrin (the highest ruling body among the people of Israel at that time), focuses on the physical realities and perhaps the political ramifications of Jesus' presence. He comments on the miracles Jesus has performed and questions how Jesus' words about being "born again" (Jn 3:3) can be applied to the natural world (Jn 3:4).

Viewing Scripture from a 21st century perspective, it is tempting to judge Nicodemus harshly for his failure to understand the spiritual truth Jesus speaks. But all that changes when we place ourselves in Nicodemus's stead. If, having never encountered the concept of a spiritual birth, we were to hear Jesus say that we must be "born again," how would we likely react? What immediate response comes to mind?

[a] 17 Psalm 69:9 [b] 23 Or *and believed in him* [c] 3 Or *born from above*; also in verse 7 [d] 6 Or *but spirit* [e] 7 The Greek is plural.

God So Loved

JN 3:16

Often memorized by both children and adults, John 3:16 is one of the best-known and most-loved verses in Scripture, as well as one of the most significant. Succinctly and eloquently, this familiar verse spells out not just the heart of the teachings in John but also the very essence of the gospel message.

Here is the first time we see the theme of redemption and judgment that is so prevalent in the fourth Gospel. The writer teaches that the consequence for rejecting Christ is to "perish," or to be lost. Yet the emphasis of the passage rests on the hope of salvation, on God's generous compassion not just to Israel, but to the entire "world," and on his promise that "whoever believes" in Christ will be redeemed.

to what we have seen, but still you people do not accept our testimony.[t] 12 I have spoken to you of earthly things and you do not believe; how then will you believe if I speak of heavenly things? 13 No one has ever gone into heaven[u] except the one who came from heaven[v]—the Son of Man.[a] 14 Just as Moses lifted up the snake in the desert,[w] so the Son of Man must be lifted up,[x] 15 that everyone who believes[y] in him may have eternal life.[b]

16 "For God so loved[z] the world that he gave his one and only Son,[c] that whoever believes in him shall not perish but have eternal life.[a] 17 For God did not send his Son into the world[b] to condemn the world, but to save the world through him.[c] 18 Whoever believes in him is not condemned,[d] but whoever does not believe stands condemned already because he has not believed in the name of God's one and only Son.[de] 19 This is the verdict: Light[f] has come into the world, but men loved darkness instead of light because their deeds were evil. 20 Everyone who does evil hates the light, and will not come into the light for fear that his deeds will be exposed.[g] 21 But whoever lives by the truth comes into the light, so that it may be seen plainly that what he has done has been done through God."[e]

John the Baptist's Testimony About Jesus

22 After this, Jesus and his disciples went out into the Judean countryside, where he spent some time with them, and baptized.[h] 23 Now John also was baptizing at Aenon near Salim, because there was plenty of water, and people were constantly coming to be baptized. 24 (This was before John was put in prison.)[i] 25 An argument developed between some of John's disciples and a certain Jew[f] over the matter of ceremonial washing.[j] 26 They came to John and said to him, "Rabbi,[k] that man who was with you on the other side of the Jordan—the one you testified[l] about—well, he is baptizing, and everyone is going to him."

27 To this John replied, "A man can receive only what is given him from heaven. 28 You yourselves can testify that I said, 'I am not the Christ[g] but am sent ahead of him.'[m] 29 The bride belongs to the bridegroom.[n] The friend who attends the bridegroom waits and listens for him, and is full of joy when he hears the bridegroom's voice. That joy is mine, and it is now complete.[o] 30 He must become greater; I must become less.

31 "The one who comes from above[p] is above all; the one who is from the earth belongs to the earth, and speaks as one from the earth.[q] The one who comes from heaven is above all. 32 He testifies to what he has seen and heard,[r] but no one accepts his testimony.[s] 33 The man who has accept-

3:11 [t]ver 32
3:13 [u]Pr 30:4; Ac 2:34; Eph 4:8-10 [v]Jn 6:38,42
3:14 [w]Nu 21:8,9 [x]Jn 8:28; 12:32
3:15 [y]ver 16,36
3:16 [z]Ro 5:8; Eph 2:4; 1Jn 4:9,10 [a]ver 36; Jn 6:29,40; 11:25,26
3:17 [b]Jn 6:29,57; 10:36; 11:42; 17:8,21; 20:21 [c]Jn 12:47; 1Jn 4:14
3:18 [d]Jn 5:24 [e]1Jn 4:9
3:19 [f]Jn 1:4; 8:12
3:20 [g]Eph 5:11,13
3:22 [h]Jn 4:2
3:24 [i]Mt 4:12; 14:3
3:25 [j]Jn 2:6
3:26 [k]Mt 23:7 [l]Jn 1:7
3:28 [m]Jn 1:20,23
3:29 [n]Mt 9:15 [o]Jn 16:24; 17:13; Php 2:2; 1Jn 1:4; 2Jn 12
3:31 [p]ver 13 [q]Jn 8:23; 1Jn 4:5
3:32 [r]Jn 8:26; 15:15 [s]ver 11

[a] *13* Some manuscripts *Man, who is in heaven* [b] *15* Or *believes may have eternal life in him* [c] *16* Or *his only begotten Son* [d] *18* Or *God's only begotten Son* [e] *21* Some interpreters end the quotation after verse 15. [f] *25* Some manuscripts *and certain Jews* [g] *28* Or *Messiah*

ed it has certified that God is truthful. 34For the
one whom God has sent[t] speaks the words of God,
for God[a] gives the Spirit[u] without limit. 35The
Father loves the Son and has placed everything in
his hands.[v] 36Whoever believes in the Son has
eternal life,[w] but whoever rejects the Son will not
see life, for God's wrath remains on him."[b]

Jesus Talks With a Samaritan Woman

4 The Pharisees heard that Jesus was gaining
and baptizing more disciples than John,[x]
2although in fact it was not Jesus who baptized,
but his disciples. 3When the Lord learned of this,
he left Judea[y] and went back once more to Galilee.
4Now he had to go through Samaria. 5So he
came to a town in Samaria called Sychar, near the
plot of ground Jacob had given to his son Joseph.[z]
6Jacob's well was there, and Jesus, tired as he was
from the journey, sat down by the well. It was
about the sixth hour.
7When a Samaritan woman came to draw
water, Jesus said to her, "Will you give me a
drink?" 8(His disciples had gone into the town[a] to
buy food.)
9The Samaritan woman said to him, "You are a
Jew and I am a Samaritan[b] woman. How can you
ask me for a drink?" (For Jews do not associate
with Samaritans.[c])
10Jesus answered her, "If you knew the gift of
God and who it is that asks you for a drink, you
would have asked him and he would have given
you living water."[c]
11"Sir," the woman said, "you have nothing to
draw with and the well is deep. Where can you
get this living water? 12Are you greater than our
father Jacob, who gave us the well[d] and drank
from it himself, as did also his sons and his flocks
and herds?"
13Jesus answered, "Everyone who drinks this
water will be thirsty again, 14but whoever drinks
the water I give him will never thirst.[e] Indeed, the
water I give him will become in him a spring of
water[f] welling up to eternal life."[g]
15The woman said to him, "Sir, give me this
water so that I won't get thirsty[h] and have to keep
coming here to draw water."
16He told her, "Go, call your husband and come
back."
17"I have no husband," she replied.
Jesus said to her, "You are right when you say
you have no husband. 18The fact is, you have had
five husbands, and the man you now have is not
your husband. What you have just said is quite
true."
19"Sir," the woman said, "I can see that you are
a prophet.[i] 20Our fathers worshiped on this mountain,[j] but you Jews claim that the place where we
must worship is in Jerusalem."[k]

3:34 [t]ver 17 [u]Mt 12:18; Lk 4:18; Ac 10:38
3:35 [v]Mt 28:18; Jn 5:20,22; 17:2
3:36 [w]ver 15; Jn 5:24; 6:47
4:1 [x]Jn 3:22,26
4:3 [y]Jn 3:22
4:5 [z]Ge 33:19; 48:22; Jos 24:32
4:8 [a]ver 5,39
4:9 [b]Mt 10:5; Lk 9:52,53
4:10 [c]Isa 44:3; Jer 2:13; Zec 14:8; Jn 7:37,38; Rev 21:6; 22:1,17
4:12 [d]ver 6
4:14 [e]Jn 6:35 [f]Jn 7:38 [g]Mt 25:46
4:15 [h]Jn 6:34
4:19 [i]Mt 21:11
4:20 [j]Dt 11:29; Jos 8:33 [k]Lk 9:53

[a] *34* Greek *he* [b] *36* Some interpreters end the quotation after verse 30. [c] *9* Or *do not use dishes Samaritans have used*

Lucy J. Rider wrote the words and music of this hymn to express for herself, and for all those who sing it, the truth of Christ's words in John 4:14.

Ho, Every One That Is Thirsty

Ho! every one that is thirsty
in spirit,
Ho! every one that is weary and
sad;
Come to the fountain, there's
fullness in Jesus,
All that you're longing for: come
and be glad!

"I will pour water on him that is
thirsty,
I will pour floods upon the dry
ground;
Open your hearts for the gifts I am
bringing;
While ye are seeking Me, I will be
found."

Child of the world, are you tired
of your bondage?
Weary of earth joys, so false,
so untrue?
Thirsting for God and His fullness
of blessing?
List to the promise, a message
for you!

Child of the kingdom, be filled with
the Spirit!
Nothing but "fullness" thy longing
can meet;
'Tis the enduement for life and for
service;
Thine is the promise, so certain,
so sweet.

—Lucy J. Rider (20th century)

The Christ

JN 4:4–26

Prior to his meeting with the woman at the well, Jesus referred to himself as the Son of Man (a phrase that could mean "man," "prophet" or "Messiah") but did not publicly declare his identity as the Christ. This is the first time that Jesus clearly identifies himself as the Christ (Jn 4:25–26), more a title (meaning "anointed one") than a name.

It is significant that Jesus first tells a woman that he is the Christ. In Jewish culture at the time, women were not highly respected and were often ignored. But not only does Jesus reveal his identity to a woman, but also to a non-Jew—this woman is a Samaritan. The people of Samaria, whose Israelite ancestors intermarried with Assyrian colonists seven centuries earlier, were even more culturally devalued than women. Though the Samaritans trusted in the Pentateuch and claimed to worship the God of Israel, they continued in their idolatry and were of mixed race. Because of this, the Jewish people despised them. Jesus' interactions with the Samaritan woman speak volumes about the value he sees in, and compassion he feels toward, *all* people—regardless of gender, race or background (see the character sketch for this woman on page 1646).

21 Jesus declared, "Believe me, woman, a time is coming[l] when you will worship the Father neither on this mountain nor in Jerusalem.[m] 22 You Samaritans worship what you do not know;[n] we worship what we do know, for salvation is from the Jews.[o] 23 Yet a time is coming and has now come[p] when the true worshipers will worship the Father in spirit[q] and truth, for they are the kind of worshipers the Father seeks. 24 God is spirit,[r] and his worshipers must worship in spirit and in truth."

25 The woman said, "I know that Messiah" (called Christ)[s] "is coming. When he comes, he will explain everything to us."

26 Then Jesus declared, "I who speak to you am he."[t]

The Disciples Rejoin Jesus

27 Just then his disciples returned[u] and were surprised to find him talking with a woman. But no one asked, "What do you want?" or "Why are you talking with her?"

28 Then, leaving her water jar, the woman went back to the town and said to the people, 29 "Come, see a man who told me everything I ever did.[v] Could this be the Christ[a]?"[w] 30 They came out of the town and made their way toward him.

31 Meanwhile his disciples urged him, "Rabbi,[x] eat something."

32 But he said to them, "I have food to eat[y] that you know nothing about."

33 Then his disciples said to each other, "Could someone have brought him food?"

34 "My food," said Jesus, "is to do the will[z] of him who sent me and to finish his work.[a] 35 Do you not say, 'Four months more and then the harvest'? I tell you, open your eyes and look at the fields! They are ripe for harvest.[b] 36 Even now the reaper draws his wages, even now he harvests[c] the crop for eternal life,[d] so that the sower and the reaper may be glad together. 37 Thus the saying 'One sows and another reaps'[e] is true. 38 I sent you to reap what you have not worked for. Others have done the hard work, and you have reaped the benefits of their labor."

Many Samaritans Believe

39 Many of the Samaritans from that town[f] believed in him because of the woman's testimony, "He told me everything I ever did."[g] 40 So when the Samaritans came to him, they urged him to stay with them, and he stayed two days. 41 And because of his words many more became believers.

42 They said to the woman, "We no longer believe just because of what you said; now we have heard for ourselves, and we know that this man really is the Savior of the world."[h]

4:21 [l]Jn 5:28; 16:2 [m]Mal 1:11; 1Ti 2:8
4:22 [n]2Ki 17:28-41 [o]Isa 2:3; Ro 3:1,2; 9:4,5
4:23 [p]Jn 5:25; 16:32 [q]Php 3:3
4:24 [r]Php 3:3
4:25 [s]Mt 1:16
4:26 [t]Jn 8:24; 9:35-37
4:27 [u]ver 8
4:29 [v]ver 17,18 [w]Mt 12:23; Jn 7:26,31
4:31 [x]Mt 23:7
4:32 [y]Job 23:12; Mt 4:4; Jn 6:27
4:34 [z]Mt 26:39; Jn 6:38; 17:4; 19:30 [a]Jn 19:30
4:35 [b]Mt 9:37; Lk 10:2
4:36 [c]Ro 1:13 [d]Mt 25:46
4:37 [e]Job 31:8; Mic 6:15
4:39 [f]ver 5 [g]ver 29
4:42 [h]Lk 2:11; 1Jn 4:14

[a] 29 Or *Messiah*

Jesus Heals the Official's Son

43 After the two days[i] he left for Galilee. 44 (Now
Jesus himself had pointed out that a prophet has
no honor in his own country.)[j] 45 When he arrived
in Galilee, the Galileans welcomed him. They had
seen all that he had done in Jerusalem at the
Passover Feast,[k] for they also had been there.
46 Once more he visited Cana in Galilee, where
he had turned the water into wine.[l] And there was
a certain royal official whose son lay sick at
Capernaum. 47 When this man heard that Jesus
had arrived in Galilee from Judea,[m] he went to
him and begged him to come and heal his son,
who was close to death.
48 "Unless you people see miraculous signs and
wonders,"[n] Jesus told him, "you will never
believe."
49 The royal official said, "Sir, come down before
my child dies."
50 Jesus replied, "You may go. Your son will
live."
The man took Jesus at his word and departed.
51 While he was still on the way, his servants met
him with the news that his boy was living.
52 When he inquired as to the time when his son
got better, they said to him, "The fever left him
yesterday at the seventh hour."
53 Then the father realized that this was the
exact time at which Jesus had said to him, "Your
son will live." So he and all his household[o]
believed.
54 This was the second miraculous sign[p] that
Jesus performed, having come from Judea to
Galilee.

The Healing at the Pool

5 Some time later, Jesus went up to Jerusalem
for a feast of the Jews. 2 Now there is in Jerusalem near the Sheep Gate[q] a pool, which in Aramaic[r] is called Bethesda[a] and which is surrounded by five covered colonnades. 3 Here a great
number of disabled people used to lie—the blind,
the lame, the paralyzed.[b] 5 One who was there had
been an invalid for thirty-eight years. 6 When
Jesus saw him lying there and learned that he had
been in this condition for a long time, he asked
him, "Do you want to get well?"
7 "Sir," the invalid replied, "I have no one to help
me into the pool when the water is stirred. While
I am trying to get in, someone else goes down
ahead of me."
8 Then Jesus said to him, "Get up! Pick up your
mat and walk."[s] 9 At once the man was cured; he
picked up his mat and walked.

4:43 [i]ver 40
4:44 [j]Mt 13:57; Lk 4:24
4:45 [k]Jn 2:23
4:46 [l]Jn 2:1-11
4:47 [m]ver 3,54
4:48 [n]Da 4:2,3; Jn 2:11; Ac 2:43; 14:3; Ro 15:19; 2Co 12:12; Heb 2:4
4:53 [o]Ac 11:14
4:54 [p]ver 48; Jn 2:11
5:2 [q]Ne 3:1; 12:39 [r]Jn 19:13, 17,20; 20:16; Ac 21:40; 22:2; 26:14
5:8 [s]Mt 9:5,6; Mk 2:11; Lk 5:24

[a] 2 Some manuscripts *Bethzatha;* other manuscripts *Bethsaida*
[b] 3 Some less important manuscripts *paralyzed—and they waited for the moving of the waters. 4From time to time an angel of the Lord would come down and stir up the waters. The first one into the pool after each such disturbance would be cured of whatever disease he had.*

The woman's story is found in John 4:1-42. The first *miracle was that Jesus talked to this Samaritan woman at all, for* Jews had nothing to do with Samaritans. Not only did Christ talk to this woman, but he also *asked her for a drink, which would have been unheard of in those times.*

This woman knew she was in trouble . . . Relationally, her life *was a mess. She had been married five times and was now living with a man who was not her husband.* I doubt she had many friends. She would have been mistrusted by *women and joked about among men.*

But Jesus looked at her—really looked at her—and talked to her as if she mattered, because to him, she did. Something about that *gaze connected with her, because* the woman came clean with him. *She had no need to step out of her shadows into the sunlight for a stranger, but she revealed to Jesus* that the man she was living with was not her husband. What a gift *Christ gave her in letting her* know that he was aware of this and of all the rest as well. If he had offered her living water without ever revealing that he knew all the truth about her, perhaps she would have let his words of life bypass her, thinking, *If you only knew.* But he loved her enough to let her know, "I know it all, and I still love you." That unfamiliar *and glorious gift changed her life so that, even as she was gulping it down, she was running to tell oth-* ers the Good News.

—Sheila Walsh

The Father and the Son

JN 5:16–30

In response to those who challenge his authority to heal on the Sabbath, Jesus presents an astounding description of his unique relationship with the Father. By claiming God as his own Father, Jesus announces his divinity and his equality with God. He establishes that he himself is the giver of life and the one through whom all judgment will come.

Yet despite the wrath his comments inspire, Jesus' declarations bear no trace of arrogance or competition with the Father. He explains that his authority comes from the Father (Jn 5:27) and humbly declares his dependency on the One who sent him: "The Son can do nothing by himself; he can do only what he sees his Father doing" (Jn 5:19). This theme of unity appears often in John and is best summed up by Jesus' statement, "I and the Father are one" (Jn 10:30).

The day on which this took place was a Sab-
bath,[t] 10 and so the Jews[u] said to the man who had
been healed, "It is the Sabbath; the law forbids
you to carry your mat."[v]
11 But he replied, "The man who made me well
said to me, 'Pick up your mat and walk.' "
12 So they asked him, "Who is this fellow who
told you to pick it up and walk?"
13 The man who was healed had no idea who it
was, for Jesus had slipped away into the crowd
that was there.
14 Later Jesus found him at the temple and said
to him, "See, you are well again. Stop sinning[w] or
something worse may happen to you." 15 The man
went away and told the Jews[x] that it was Jesus
who had made him well.

Life Through the Son

16 So, because Jesus was doing these things on
the Sabbath, the Jews persecuted him. 17 Jesus said
to them, "My Father is always at his work[y] to this
very day, and I, too, am working." 18 For this rea-
son the Jews tried all the harder to kill him;[z] not
only was he breaking the Sabbath, but he was
even calling God his own Father, making himself
equal with God.[a]
19 Jesus gave them this answer: "I tell you the
truth, the Son can do nothing by himself;[b] he can
do only what he sees his Father doing, because
whatever the Father does the Son also does. 20 For
the Father loves the Son[c] and shows him all he
does. Yes, to your amazement he will show him
even greater things than these.[d] 21 For just as the
Father raises the dead and gives them life,[e] even
so the Son gives life[f] to whom he is pleased to give
it. 22 Moreover, the Father judges no one, but has
entrusted all judgment to the Son,[g] 23 that all may
honor the Son just as they honor the Father. He
who does not honor the Son does not honor the
Father, who sent him.[h]
24 "I tell you the truth, whoever hears my word
and believes him who sent me has eternal life and
will not be condemned;[i] he has crossed over from
death to life.[j] 25 I tell you the truth, a time is com-
ing and has now come[k] when the dead will hear[l]
the voice of the Son of God and those who hear
will live. 26 For as the Father has life in himself, so
he has granted the Son to have life in himself.
27 And he has given him authority to judge[m]
because he is the Son of Man.
28 "Do not be amazed at this, for a time is com-
ing[n] when all who are in their graves will hear his
voice 29 and come out—those who have done good
will rise to live, and those who have done evil will
rise to be condemned.[o] 30 By myself I can do noth-
ing;[p] I judge only as I hear, and my judgment is
just,[q] for I seek not to please myself but him who
sent me.[r]

5:9 [t]Jn 9:14
5:10 [u]ver 16 [v]Ne 13:15-22; Jer 17:21; Mt 12:2
5:14 [w]Mk 2:5; Jn 8:11
5:15 [x]Jn 1:19
5:17 [y]Jn 9:4; 14:10
5:18 [z]Jn 7:1 [a]Jn 10:30,33; 19:7
5:19 [b]ver 30; Jn 8:28
5:20 [c]Jn 3:35 [d]Jn 14:12
5:21 [e]Ro 4:17; 8:11 [f]Jn 11:25
5:22 [g]ver 27; Jn 9:39; Ac 10:42; 17:31
5:23 [h]Lk 10:16; 1Jn 2:23
5:24 [i]Jn 3:18 [j]1Jn 3:14
5:25 [k]Jn 4:23 [l]Jn 8:43,47
5:27 [m]ver 22; Ac 10:42; 17:31
5:28 [n]Jn 4:21
5:29 [o]Da 12:2; Mt 25:46
5:30 [p]ver 19 [q]Jn 8:16 [r]Mt 26:39; Jn 4:34; 6:38

Testimonies About Jesus

31“If I testify about myself, my testimony is not
valid.[s] 32There is another who testifies in my
favor,[t] and I know that his testimony about me is
valid.
33“You have sent to John and he has testified[u]
to the truth. 34Not that I accept human testimony;[v] but I mention it that you may be saved.
35John was a lamp that burned and gave light,[w]
and you chose for a time to enjoy his light.
36“I have testimony weightier than that of
John.[x] For the very work that the Father has giv-
en me to finish, and which I am doing,[y] testifies
that the Father has sent me.[z] 37And the Father who
sent me has himself testified concerning me.[a] You
have never heard his voice nor seen his form,[b]
38nor does his word dwell in you,[c] for you do not
believe the one he sent.[d] 39You diligently study[a]
the Scriptures[e] because you think that by them
you possess eternal life. These are the Scriptures
that testify about me,[f] 40yet you refuse to come to
me to have life.
41“I do not accept praise from men,[g] 42but I
know you. I know that you do not have the love
of God in your hearts. 43I have come in my
Father’s name, and you do not accept me; but if
someone else comes in his own name, you will
accept him. 44How can you believe if you accept
praise from one another, yet make no effort to
obtain the praise that comes from the only God[b]?[h]
45“But do not think I will accuse you before the
Father. Your accuser is Moses,[i] on whom your
hopes are set.[j] 46If you believed Moses, you would
believe me, for he wrote about me.[k] 47But since
you do not believe what he wrote, how are you
going to believe what I say?”[l]

Jesus Feeds the Five Thousand

6 Some time after this, Jesus crossed to the far
shore of the Sea of Galilee (that is, the Sea of
Tiberias), 2and a great crowd of people followed
him because they saw the miraculous signs[m] he
had performed on the sick. 3Then Jesus went up
on a mountainside[n] and sat down with his disciples. 4The Jewish Passover Feast[o] was near.
5When Jesus looked up and saw a great crowd
coming toward him, he said to Philip,[p] “Where
shall we buy bread for these people to eat?” 6He
asked this only to test him, for he already had in
mind what he was going to do.
7Philip answered him, “Eight months’ wages[c]
would not buy enough bread for each one to have
a bite!”
8Another of his disciples, Andrew, Simon
Peter’s brother,[q] spoke up, 9“Here is a boy with
five small barley loaves and two small fish, but
how far will they go among so many?”[r]
10Jesus said, “Have the people sit down.” There

5:31 [s]Jn 8:14
5:32 [t]ver 37; Jn 8:18
5:33 [u]Jn 1:7
5:34 [v]1Jn 5:9
5:35 [w]2Pe 1:19
5:36 [x]1Jn 5:9 [y]Jn 14:11; 15:24 [z]Jn 3:17; 10:25
5:37 [a]Jn 8:18 [b]Dt 4:12; 1Ti 1:17; Jn 1:18
5:38 [c]1Jn 2:14 [d]Jn 3:17
5:39 [e]Ro 2:17,18 [f]Lk 24:27, 44; Ac 13:27
5:41 [g]ver 44
5:44 [h]Ro 2:29
5:45 [i]Jn 9:28 [j]Ro 2:17
5:46 [k]Ge 3:15; Lk 24:27,44; Ac 26:22
5:47 [l]Lk 16:29,31
6:2 [m]Jn 2:11
6:3 [n]ver 15
6:4 [o]Jn 2:13; 11:55
6:5 [p]Jn 1:43
6:8 [q]Jn 1:40
6:9 [r]2Ki 4:43

[a] 39 Or *Study diligently* (the imperative) [b] 44 Some early manuscripts *the Only One* [c] 7 Greek *two hundred denarii*

Testimony

JN 5:31-47

According to Old Testament law, a man could not be convicted of a crime based on the testimony of a single witness (Nu 35:30; Dt 17:6; 19:15). In light of this requirement for legal testimony, Jesus cites four sources that support his claim to be the Messiah. Most notable is the divine testimony of God the Father (Jn 5:37). This may refer to the word God speaks at Jesus’ baptism (Mt 3:16-17; Mk 1:9-11; Lk 3:21-22), the witness to Jesus inherent in Mosaic Law (Nu 24:17; Jn 5:46-47), or the Father’s testimony given directly to the hearts of people. Jesus also identifies three other sources to support his claim: the human testimony of John the Baptist (Jn 1:19-34; 3:27-30; 5:33), the evidence of Jesus’ miracles (Jn 2:11; 5:36; 10:25; 14:11), and the testimony of Scripture (Isa 53:7; Lk 24:44; Jn 5:39,40).

Jesus the King

JN 6:15

The people of Israel are expecting both a prophet (Dt 18:18) and a Messiah (Da 9:25–26). Some Jews distinguish between the two identities. Others evidently see the prophet and Messiah as being one. Both groups anticipate that the Messiah will be the king of the Jews. This means, in their minds, that he will be their political leader. They fully expect that, as such, the Messiah will conquer the Romans and usher in a new age of wealth and peace for Israel.

Jesus' kingdom, however, is spiritual in nature; had he publicly admitted to being the Messiah, the people would have seen him as a political figure. For this reason, until the time of his crucifixion (Mk 14:61–62), Jesus accepts the title of "Messiah" (or "the Christ") only from the Samaritan woman (Jn 4:25–26) and from his disciples (Mt 16:16), keeping his identity as Messiah largely a secret (Mk 8:29–30).

was plenty of grass in that place, and the men sat
down, about five thousand of them. 11 Jesus then
took the loaves, gave thanks,[s] and distributed to
those who were seated as much as they wanted.
He did the same with the fish.
12 When they had all had enough to eat, he said
to his disciples, "Gather the pieces that are left over.
Let nothing be wasted." 13 So they gathered them
and filled twelve baskets with the pieces of the five
barley loaves left over by those who had eaten.
14 After the people saw the miraculous sign[t] that
Jesus did, they began to say, "Surely this is the
Prophet who is to come into the world."[u] 15 Jesus,
knowing that they intended to come and make
him king[v] by force, withdrew again to a mountain
by himself.[w]

Jesus Walks on the Water

16 When evening came, his disciples went down
to the lake, 17 where they got into a boat and set
off across the lake for Capernaum. By now it was
dark, and Jesus had not yet joined them. 18 A
strong wind was blowing and the waters grew
rough. 19 When they had rowed three or three and
a half miles,[a] they saw Jesus approaching the
boat, walking on the water;[x] and they were terrified.
20 But he said to them, "It is I; don't be
afraid."[y] 21 Then they were willing to take him into
the boat, and immediately the boat reached the
shore where they were heading.
22 The next day the crowd that had stayed on the
opposite shore of the lake[z] realized that only one
boat had been there, and that Jesus had not
entered it with his disciples, but that they had
gone away alone.[a] 23 Then some boats from Tiberias[b]
landed near the place where the people had
eaten the bread after the Lord had given thanks.[c]
24 Once the crowd realized that neither Jesus nor
his disciples were there, they got into the boats
and went to Capernaum in search of Jesus.

Jesus the Bread of Life

25 When they found him on the other side of the
lake, they asked him, "Rabbi,[d] when did you get
here?"
26 Jesus answered, "I tell you the truth, you are
looking for me,[e] not because you saw miraculous
signs[f] but because you ate the loaves and had
your fill. 27 Do not work for food that spoils, but
for food that endures[g] to eternal life,[h] which the
Son of Man[i] will give you. On him God the Father
has placed his seal[j] of approval."
28 Then they asked him, "What must we do to
do the works God requires?"
29 Jesus answered, "The work of God is this: to
believe[k] in the one he has sent."[l]
30 So they asked him, "What miraculous sign[m]
then will you give that we may see it and believe

6:11 [s]ver 23; Mt 14:19
6:14 [t]Jn 2:11 [u]Dt 18:15, 18; Mt 11:3; 21:11
6:15 [v]Jn 18:36 [w]Mt 14:23; Mk 6:46
6:19 [x]Job 9:8
6:20 [y]Mt 14:27
6:22 [z]ver 2 [a]ver 15-21
6:23 [b]ver 1 [c]ver 11
6:25 [d]Mt 23:7
6:26 [e]ver 24 [f]ver 30; Jn 2:11
6:27 [g]Isa 55:2 [h]ver 54; Mt 25:46; Jn 4:14 [i]Mt 8:20 [j]Ro 4:11; 1Co 9:2; 2Co 1:22; Eph 1:13; 4:30; 2Ti 2:19; Rev 7:3
6:29 [k]1Jn 3:23 [l]Jn 3:17
6:30 [m]Jn 2:11

[a] *19* Greek *rowed twenty-five or thirty stadia* (about 5 or 6 kilometers)

you?[n] What will you do? 31Our forefathers ate the
manna[o] in the desert; as it is written: 'He gave
them bread from heaven to eat.'[a]"[p]
32Jesus said to them, "I tell you the truth, it is
not Moses who has given you the bread from
heaven, but it is my Father who gives you the true
bread from heaven. 33For the bread of God is he
who comes down from heaven[q] and gives life to
the world."
34"Sir," they said, "from now on give us this
bread."[r]
35Then Jesus declared, "I am the bread of life.[s]
He who comes to me will never go hungry, and
he who believes in me will never be thirsty.[t] 36But
as I told you, you have seen me and still you do
not believe. 37All that the Father gives me[u] will
come to me, and whoever comes to me I will never drive away. 38For I have come down from heav-
en not to do my will but to do the will of him who
sent me.[v] 39And this is the will of him who sent
me, that I shall lose none of all that he has given
me,[w] but raise them up at the last day.[x] 40For my
Father's will is that everyone who looks to the Son
and believes in him shall have eternal life,[y] and I
will raise him up at the last day."
41At this the Jews began to grumble about him
because he said, "I am the bread that came down
from heaven." 42They said, "Is this not Jesus, the
son of Joseph,[z] whose father and mother we
know?[a] How can he now say, 'I came down from
heaven'?"[b]
43"Stop grumbling among yourselves," Jesus
answered. 44"No one can come to me unless the
Father who sent me draws him,[c] and I will raise
him up at the last day. 45It is written in the Prophets: 'They will all be taught by God.'[b][d] Everyone
who listens to the Father and learns from him
comes to me. 46No one has seen the Father except
the one who is from God;[e] only he has seen the
Father. 47I tell you the truth, he who believes has
everlasting life. 48I am the bread of life.[f] 49Your
forefathers ate the manna in the desert, yet they
died.[g] 50But here is the bread that comes down
from heaven,[h] which a man may eat and not die.
51I am the living bread that came down from heav-
en. If anyone eats of this bread, he will live forever. This bread is my flesh, which I will give for the
life of the world."[i]
52Then the Jews began to argue sharply among
themselves,[j] "How can this man give us his flesh
to eat?"
53Jesus said to them, "I tell you the truth, unless
you eat the flesh of the Son of Man[k] and drink his
blood, you have no life in you. 54Whoever eats my
flesh and drinks my blood has eternal life, and I
will raise him up at the last day.[l] 55For my flesh is
real food and my blood is real drink. 56Whoever
eats my flesh and drinks my blood remains in me,

6:30 [n]Mt 12:38
6:31 [o]Nu 11:7-9 [p]Ex 16:4,15; Ne 9:15; Ps 78:24; 105:40
6:33 [q]ver 50
6:34 [r]Jn 4:15
6:35 [s]ver 48,51 [t]Jn 4:14
6:37 [u]ver 39; Jn 17:2,6,9, 24
6:38 [v]Jn 4:34; 5:30
6:39 [w]Jn 10:28; 17:12; 18:9 [x]ver 40,44, 54
6:40 [y]Jn 3:15,16
6:42 [z]Lk 4:22 [a]Jn 7:27,28 [b]ver 38,62
6:44 [c]ver 65; Jer 31:3; Jn 12:32
6:45 [d]Isa 54:13; Jer 31:33,34; Heb 8:10,11; 10:16
6:46 [e]Jn 1:18; 5:37; 7:29
6:48 [f]ver 35,51
6:49 [g]ver 31,58
6:50 [h]ver 33
6:51 [i]Heb 10:10
6:52 [j]Jn 7:43; 9:16; 10:19
6:53 [k]Mt 8:20
6:54 [l]ver 39

[a] *31* Exodus 16:4; Neh. 9:15; Psalm 78:24,25 [b] *45* Isaiah 54:13

The Bread of Life

JN 6:26-35

Jesus charges that the crowd has sought him out not because they believe in him, but because they want him to provide nourishment for their bodies as he had at the feeding of the **5,000 (Jn 6:1-13). The crowd** ***responds by asking for a sign on which they can base their faith in him, suggesting something akin to the "bread of heaven" their ances*****tors had received in the wilderness (Ex 16:11-15; Ps 105:40; Jn 6:32).**

The people's focus is on receiving physical sustenance; Jesus' message is that he has come to satisfy their spiritual hunger. He reminds them that God provided manna in the desert and that God is now granting them "true bread from heaven" (Jn 6:32). Identifying himself as this bread, Jesus teaches that eternal life comes, not from something outward that he provides, but from who he is. This bread is available to all who put their trust in him.

True Discipleship

JN 6:60–69

The difference between a student and a disciple can be viewed as a difference in the level of commitment. While a student merely studies a master's teachings, a disciple fully accepts and applies those teachings to his or her life. True disciples of Jesus (not just the 12 disciples) need to not only embrace his teachings but also commit themselves wholeheartedly to Christ.

Within the crowd at Capernaum, many are unwilling to make such a commitment. They find some of Christ's teachings difficult to accept. What is our response when faced with a "hard teaching" (Jn 6:60) that we disagree with or find difficult to accept? Occasionally, like the disciples in this passage, we may be tempted to turn away from Jesus (Jn 6:66). But hopefully, we are more like Peter—so hungry for truth that we follow despite the difficulty. We can achieve true, radical discipleship by following the example of Peter, who chooses to eliminate all of his other spiritual options (Jn 6:68) and put his faith in the "Holy One of God" (Jn 6:69).

and I in him.[m] 57 Just as the living Father sent me[n]
and I live because of the Father, so the one who
feeds on me will live because of me. 58 This is the
bread that came down from heaven. Your forefathers ate manna and died, but he who feeds on
this bread will live forever."[o] 59 He said this while
teaching in the synagogue in Capernaum.

Many Disciples Desert Jesus

60 On hearing it, many of his disciples[p] said,
"This is a hard teaching. Who can accept it?"
61 Aware that his disciples were grumbling about
this, Jesus said to them, "Does this offend you?[q]
62 What if you see the Son of Man ascend to where
he was before![r] 63 The Spirit gives life;[s] the flesh
counts for nothing. The words I have spoken to
you are spirit[a] and they are life. 64 Yet there are
some of you who do not believe." For Jesus had
known[t] from the beginning which of them did not
believe and who would betray him. 65 He went on
to say, "This is why I told you that no one can
come to me unless the Father has enabled him."[u]
66 From this time many of his disciples[v] turned
back and no longer followed him.
67 "You do not want to leave too, do you?" Jesus
asked the Twelve.[w]
68 Simon Peter answered him,[x] "Lord, to whom
shall we go? You have the words of eternal life.
69 We believe and know that you are the Holy One
of God."[y]
70 Then Jesus replied, "Have I not chosen you,[z]
the Twelve? Yet one of you is a devil!"[a] 71 (He
meant Judas, the son of Simon Iscariot, who,
though one of the Twelve, was later to betray
him.)

Jesus Goes to the Feast of Tabernacles

7 After this, Jesus went around in Galilee, pur-
posely staying away from Judea because the
Jews[b] there were waiting to take his life.[c] 2 But
when the Jewish Feast of Tabernacles[d] was near,
3 Jesus' brothers[e] said to him, "You ought to leave
here and go to Judea, so that your disciples may
see the miracles you do. 4 No one who wants to
become a public figure acts in secret. Since you are
doing these things, show yourself to the world."
5 For even his own brothers did not believe in him.[f]
6 Therefore Jesus told them, "The right time[g] for
me has not yet come; for you any time is right.
7 The world cannot hate you, but it hates me[h]
because I testify that what it does is evil.[i] 8 You go
to the Feast. I am not yet[b] going up to this Feast,
because for me the right time[j] has not yet come."
9 Having said this, he stayed in Galilee.
10 However, after his brothers had left for the
Feast, he went also, not publicly, but in secret.
11 Now at the Feast the Jews were watching for
him[k] and asking, "Where is that man?"
12 Among the crowds there was widespread

6:56 [m]Jn 15:4-7; 1Jn 3:24; 4:15
6:57 [n]Jn 3:17
6:58 [o]ver 49-51; Jn 3:36
6:60 [p]ver 66
6:61 [q]Mt 11:6
6:62 [r]Mk 16:19; Jn 3:13; 17:5
6:63 [s]2Co 3:6
6:64 [t]Jn 2:25
6:65 [u]ver 37,44
6:66 [v]ver 60
6:67 [w]Mt 10:2
6:68 [x]Mt 16:16
6:69 [y]Mk 8:29; Lk 9:20
6:70 [z]Jn 15:16,19 [a]Jn 13:27
7:1 [b]Jn 1:19 [c]Jn 5:18
7:2 [d]Lev 23:34; Dt 16:16
7:3 [e]Mt 12:46
7:5 [f]Mk 3:21
7:6 [g]Mt 26:18
7:7 [h]Jn 15:18,19 [i]Jn 3:19,20
7:8 [j]ver 6
7:11 [k]Jn 11:56

[a] 63 Or *Spirit*   [b] 8 Some early manuscripts do not have *yet.*

whispering about him. Some said, "He is a good man."

Others replied, "No, he deceives the people."[l] 13 But no one would say anything publicly about him for fear of the Jews.[m]

Jesus Teaches at the Feast

14 Not until halfway through the Feast did Jesus go up to the temple courts and begin to teach.[n] 15 The Jews[o] were amazed and asked, "How did this man get such learning[p] without having studied?"[q]

16 Jesus answered, "My teaching is not my own. It comes from him who sent me.[r] 17 If anyone chooses to do God's will, he will find out[s] whether my teaching comes from God or whether I speak on my own. 18 He who speaks on his own does so to gain honor for himself,[t] but he who works for the honor of the one who sent him is a man of truth; there is nothing false about him. 19 Has not Moses given you the law?[u] Yet not one of you keeps the law. Why are you trying to kill me?"[v]

20 "You are demon-possessed,"[w] the crowd answered. "Who is trying to kill you?"

21 Jesus said to them, "I did one miracle, and you are all astonished. 22 Yet, because Moses gave you circumcision[x] (though actually it did not come from Moses, but from the patriarchs),[y] you circumcise a child on the Sabbath. 23 Now if a child can be circumcised on the Sabbath so that the law of Moses may not be broken, why are you angry with me for healing the whole man on the Sabbath? 24 Stop judging by mere appearances, and make a right judgment."[z]

Is Jesus the Christ?

25 At that point some of the people of Jerusalem began to ask, "Isn't this the man they are trying to kill? 26 Here he is, speaking publicly, and they are not saying a word to him. Have the authorities[a] really concluded that he is the Christ[a]? 27 But we know where this man is from;[b] when the Christ comes, no one will know where he is from."

28 Then Jesus, still teaching in the temple courts,[c] cried out, "Yes, you know me, and you know where I am from.[d] I am not here on my own, but he who sent me is true.[e] You do not know him, 29 but I know him[f] because I am from him and he sent me."

30 At this they tried to seize him, but no one laid a hand on him,[g] because his time had not yet come. 31 Still, many in the crowd put their faith in him.[h] They said, "When the Christ comes, will he do more miraculous signs[i] than this man?"

32 The Pharisees heard the crowd whispering such things about him. Then the chief priests and the Pharisees sent temple guards to arrest him.

33 Jesus said, "I am with you for only a short time,[j] and then I go to the one who sent me.[k]

7:12 [l]ver 40,43
7:13 [m]Jn 9:22; 12:42; 19:38
7:14 [n]ver 28; Mt 26:55
7:15 [o]Jn 1:19 [p]Ac 26:24 [q]Mt 13:54
7:16 [r]Jn 3:11; 14:24
7:17 [s]Ps 25:14; Jn 8:43
7:18 [t]Jn 5:41; 8:50,54
7:19 [u]Jn 1:17 [v]ver 1; Mt 12:14
7:20 [w]Jn 8:48; 10:20
7:22 [x]Lev 12:3 [y]Ge 17:10-14
7:24 [z]Isa 11:3,4; Jn 8:15
7:26 [a]ver 48
7:27 [b]Mt 13:55; Lk 4:22
7:28 [c]ver 14 [d]Jn 8:14 [e]Jn 8:26,42
7:29 [f]Mt 11:27
7:30 [g]ver 32,44; Jn 10:39
7:31 [h]Jn 8:30 [i]Jn 2:11
7:33 [j]Jn 13:33; 16:16 [k]Jn 16:5,10, 17,28

[a] *26* Or *Messiah*; also in verses 27, 31, 41 and 42

Jesus, the Jew

JN 7:14-24

Throughout the year, the people of Israel gathered to worship the Lord at a number of regularly scheduled assemblies. The Feast of Tabernacles, an important eight-day harvest festival, was held to commemorate Israel's rescue from Egypt and to recall the years the Israelites spent wandering in the wilderness.

It is tempting to look at specific events, such as Christ's interactions with the temple money changers and his rebuke of the Pharisees (Mt 21:12-13; 23:13-36), and conclude that Jesus pitted himself fully against the religious establishment. But here we see that Jesus, a Jew, follows the religious observances of his day (demonstrated by his teaching at the temple during the feast), speaking against the religious leaders only when their spirits are hollow and their behavior arrogant.

From Bethlehem

JN 7:42

The Jewish people believe that the coming Messiah will be born in Bethlehem. Scripture foretells that the Messiah will be a descendant of David and that he will be born in the city of David's youth (1Sa 17:12; Mic 5:2). Unaware of the circumstances surrounding Jesus' birth in Bethlehem, the people of Jerusalem assume that he was born in Nazareth of Galilee. On the basis of this falsehood, many reject outright the possibility that he is the Christ.

34You will look for me, but you will not find me;
and where I am, you cannot come."[l]
35The Jews said to one another, "Where does
this man intend to go that we cannot find him?
Will he go where our people live scattered[m]
among the Greeks,[n] and teach the Greeks? 36What
did he mean when he said, 'You will look for me,
but you will not find me,' and 'Where I am, you
cannot come'?"
37On the last and greatest day of the Feast,[o]
Jesus stood and said in a loud voice, "If anyone is
thirsty, let him come to me and drink.[p] 38Whoev-
er believes in me, as[a] the Scripture has said,[q]
streams of living water[r] will flow from within
him."[s] 39By this he meant the Spirit,[t] whom those
who believed in him were later to receive.[u] Up to
that time the Spirit had not been given, since
Jesus had not yet been glorified.[v]
40On hearing his words, some of the people
said, "Surely this man is the Prophet."[w]
41Others said, "He is the Christ."
Still others asked, "How can the Christ come
from Galilee?[x] 42Does not the Scripture say that
the Christ will come from David's family[b][y] and
from Bethlehem,[z] the town where David lived?"
43Thus the people were divided[a] because of Jesus.
44Some wanted to seize him, but no one laid a
hand on him.[b]

Unbelief of the Jewish Leaders

45Finally the temple guards went back to the
chief priests and Pharisees, who asked them,
"Why didn't you bring him in?"
46"No one ever spoke the way this man does,"[c]
the guards declared.
47"You mean he has deceived you also?"[d] the
Pharisees retorted. 48"Has any of the rulers or of
the Pharisees believed in him?[e] 49No! But this mob
that knows nothing of the law—there is a curse
on them."
50Nicodemus,[f] who had gone to Jesus earlier
and who was one of their own number, asked,
51"Does our law condemn anyone without first
hearing him to find out what he is doing?"
52They replied, "Are you from Galilee, too? Look
into it, and you will find that a prophet[c] does not
come out of Galilee."[g]

[The earliest manuscripts and many other ancient witnesses do not have John 7:53–8:11.]

53Then each went to his own home.
8 But Jesus went to the Mount of Olives.[h] 2At
dawn he appeared again in the temple courts,
where all the people gathered around him, and he

7:34 [l]Jn 8:21; 13:33
7:35 [m]Jas 1:1 [n]Jn 12:20; 1Pe 1:1
7:37 [o]Lev 23:36 [p]Isa 55:1; Rev 22:17
7:38 [q]Isa 58:11 [r]Jn 4:10 [s]Jn 4:14
7:39 [t]Joel 2:28; Ac 2:17,33 [u]Jn 20:22 [v]Jn 12:23; 13:31,32
7:40 [w]Mt 21:11; Jn 1:21
7:41 [x]ver 52; Jn 1:46
7:42 [y]Mt 1:1 [z]Mic 5:2; Mt 2:5,6; Lk 2:4
7:43 [a]Jn 9:16; 10:19
7:44 [b]ver 30
7:46 [c]Mt 7:28
7:47 [d]ver 12
7:48 [e]Jn 12:42
7:50 [f]Jn 3:1; 19:39
7:52 [g]ver 41
8:1 [h]Mt 21:1

[a] 37,38 Or / *If anyone is thirsty, let him come to me. / And let him drink,* 38*who believes in me. / As* [b] 42 Greek *seed*
[c] 52 Two early manuscripts *the Prophet*

sat down to teach them.[i] 3The teachers of the law
and the Pharisees brought in a woman caught in
adultery. They made her stand before the group
4and said to Jesus, "Teacher, this woman was
caught in the act of adultery. 5In the Law Moses
commanded us to stone such women.[j] Now what
do you say?" 6They were using this question as a
trap,[k] in order to have a basis for accusing him.[l]
But Jesus bent down and started to write on the
ground with his finger. 7When they kept on questioning him, he straightened up and said to them,
"If any one of you is without sin, let him be the
first to throw a stone[m] at her."[n] 8Again he stooped
down and wrote on the ground.
9At this, those who heard began to go away one
at a time, the older ones first, until only Jesus was
left, with the woman still standing there. 10Jesus
straightened up and asked her, "Woman, where
are they? Has no one condemned you?"
11"No one, sir," she said.
"Then neither do I condemn you,"[o] Jesus
declared. "Go now and leave your life of sin."[p]

The Validity of Jesus' Testimony

12When Jesus spoke again to the people, he
said, "I am[q] the light of the world.[r] Whoever follows me will never walk in darkness, but will
have the light of life."[s]
13The Pharisees challenged him, "Here you are,
appearing as your own witness; your testimony is
not valid."[t]
14Jesus answered, "Even if I testify on my own
behalf, my testimony is valid, for I know where I
came from and where I am going.[u] But you have
no idea where I come from[v] or where I am going.
15You judge by human standards;[w] I pass judgment on no one.[x] 16But if I do judge, my decisions
are right, because I am not alone. I stand with the
Father, who sent me.[y] 17In your own Law it is
written that the testimony of two men is valid.[z]
18I am one who testifies for myself; my other witness is the Father, who sent me."[a]
19Then they asked him, "Where is your father?"
"You do not know me or my Father,"[b] Jesus
replied. "If you knew me, you would know my
Father also."[c] 20He spoke these words while teaching[d] in the temple area near the place where the
offerings were put.[e] Yet no one seized him,
because his time had not yet come.[f]
21Once more Jesus said to them, "I am going
away, and you will look for me, and you will die[g]
in your sin. Where I go, you cannot come."[h]
22This made the Jews ask, "Will he kill himself?
Is that why he says, 'Where I go, you cannot
come'?"
23But he continued, "You are from below; I am
from above. You are of this world; I am not of this
world.[i] 24I told you that you would die in your

8:2 [i]ver 20; Mt 26:55
8:5 [j]Lev 20:10; Dt 22:22
8:6 [k]Mt 22:15,18 [l]Mt 12:10
8:7 [m]Dt 17:7 [n]Ro 2:1,22
8:11 [o]Jn 3:17 [p]Jn 5:14
8:12 [q]Jn 6:35 [r]Jn 1:4; 12:35 [s]Pr 4:18; Mt 5:14
8:13 [t]Jn 5:31
8:14 [u]Jn 13:3; 16:28 [v]Jn 7:28; 9:29
8:15 [w]Jn 7:24 [x]Jn 3:17
8:16 [y]Jn 5:30
8:17 [z]Dt 17:6; Mt 18:16
8:18 [a]Jn 5:37
8:19 [b]Jn 16:3 [c]Jn 14:7; 1Jn 2:23
8:20 [d]Mt 26:55 [e]Mk 12:41 [f]Mt 26:18; Jn 7:30
8:21 [g]Eze 3:18 [h]Jn 7:34; 13:33
8:23 [i]Jn 3:31; 17:14

I'm so grateful for Jesus' compassionate response to the woman the crowd was about to stone for her adulterous behavior. Imagine an angry mob of people with raised rocks and haughty hearts positioned to pummel you with their judgment. Then Jesus steps into their midst, and with piercing conviction, turns to you, extends undeserved mercy, and proclaims, "Go now and leave your life of sin" (Jn 8:11).

I don't have proof, but I would imagine that the adulterous woman never returned to her former behavior. Not because she feared dying, for she probably wished many times that she could escape her sinful passions and her guilt-ridden self-esteem. But because Jesus had liberated her with his forgiveness. It was her chance for a new beginning, a fresh start, a clean slate.

—Patsy Clairmont

sins; if you do not believe that I am ⌊the one I
claim to be⌋,[a][j] you will indeed die in your sins."
25"Who are you?" they asked.
"Just what I have been claiming all along,"
Jesus replied. 26"I have much to say in judgment
of you. But he who sent me is reliable,[k] and what
I have heard from him I tell the world."[l]
27They did not understand that he was telling
them about his Father. 28So Jesus said, "When you
have lifted up the Son of Man,[m] then you will
know that I am ⌊the one I claim to be⌋ and that I
do nothing on my own but speak just what the
Father has taught me. 29The one who sent me is
with me; he has not left me alone,[n] for I always do
what pleases him."[o] 30Even as he spoke, many put
their faith in him.[p]

The Children of Abraham

31To the Jews who had believed him, Jesus said,
"If you hold to my teaching,[q] you are really my
disciples. 32Then you will know the truth, and the
truth will set you free."[r]
33They answered him, "We are Abraham's
descendants[b][s] and have never been slaves of anyone. How can you say that we shall be set free?"
34Jesus replied, "I tell you the truth, everyone
who sins is a slave to sin.[t] 35Now a slave has no
permanent place in the family, but a son belongs
to it forever.[u] 36So if the Son sets you free, you will
be free indeed. 37I know you are Abraham's
descendants. Yet you are ready to kill me,[v] because
you have no room for my word. 38I am telling you
what I have seen in the Father's presence,[w] and
you do what you have heard from your father.[c]"
39"Abraham is our father," they answered.
"If you were Abraham's children,"[x] said Jesus,
"then you would[d] do the things Abraham did. 40As
it is, you are determined to kill me, a man who
has told you the truth that I heard from God.[y]
Abraham did not do such things. 41You are doing
the things your own father does."[z]
"We are not illegitimate children," they protest-
ed. "The only Father we have is God himself."[a]

The Children of the Devil

42Jesus said to them, "If God were your Father,
you would love me,[b] for I came from God[c] and
now am here. I have not come on my own;[d] but
he sent me.[e] 43Why is my language not clear to
you? Because you are unable to hear what I say.
44You belong to your father, the devil,[f] and you
want to carry out your father's desire.[g] He was a
murderer from the beginning, not holding to the
truth, for there is no truth in him. When he lies,
he speaks his native language, for he is a liar and
the father of lies.[h] 45Yet because I tell the truth,[i]

8:24 [j]Jn 4:26; 13:19
8:26 [k]Jn 7:28 [l]Jn 3:32; 15:15
8:28 [m]Jn 3:14; 5:19; 12:32
8:29 [n]ver 16; Jn 16:32 [o]Jn 4:34; 5:30; 6:38
8:30 [p]Jn 7:31
8:31 [q]Jn 15:7; 2Jn 9
8:32 [r]Ro 8:2; Jas 2:12
8:33 [s]ver 37,39; Mt 3:9
8:34 [t]Ro 6:16; 2Pe 2:19
8:35 [u]Gal 4:30
8:37 [v]ver 39,40
8:38 [w]Jn 5:19,30; 14:10,24
8:39 [x]ver 37; Ro 9:7; Gal 3:7
8:40 [y]ver 26
8:41 [z]ver 38,44 [a]Isa 63:16; 64:8
8:42 [b]1Jn 5:1 [c]Jn 16:27; 17:8 [d]Jn 7:28 [e]Jn 3:17
8:44 [f]1Jn 3:8 [g]ver 38,41 [h]Ge 3:4
8:45 [i]Jn 18:37

[a] *24* Or *I am he*; also in verse 28 [b] *33* Greek *seed*; also in verse 37 [c] *38* Or *presence. Therefore do what you have heard from the Father.* [d] *39* Some early manuscripts *"If you are Abraham's children," said Jesus, "then*

In all of life, study is a faithful friend if we learn its ways. I see that a great deal of damage is done not by evil but by ignorance. Christ tells us that we will know the truth and the truth will set us free (Jn 8:32), but so often we don't know what the truth is. We don't know how to dig it out. In Romans Paul tells us that our lives are to be transformed by the renewing of our minds [Ro 12:2]. But if we have no firm grasp on what God's Word says, how can we be changed by it?

I think we Christians have become lazy. We would rather read a book about how someone else became closer to God than spend time alone with him ourselves. We would rather listen to someone else's interpretation of the Word of God than read it for ourselves. And yet we alone are accountable for what we believe. We can't stand before God on the day of judgment and explain that our incredible ignorance is our pastor's fault. It is our responsibility to access God's Word for ourselves.

—Sheila Walsh

you do not believe me! 46 Can any of you prove me guilty of sin? If I am telling the truth, why don't you believe me? 47 He who belongs to God hears what God says.[j] The reason you do not hear is that you do not belong to God."

The Claims of Jesus About Himself

48 The Jews answered him, "Aren't we right in saying that you are a Samaritan[k] and demon-possessed?"[l]

49 "I am not possessed by a demon," said Jesus, "but I honor my Father and you dishonor me. 50 I am not seeking glory for myself;[m] but there is one who seeks it, and he is the judge. 51 I tell you the truth, if anyone keeps my word, he will never see death."[n]

52 At this the Jews exclaimed, "Now we know that you are demon-possessed! Abraham died and so did the prophets, yet you say that if anyone keeps your word, he will never taste death. 53 Are you greater than our father Abraham?[o] He died, and so did the prophets. Who do you think you are?"

54 Jesus replied, "If I glorify myself,[p] my glory means nothing. My Father, whom you claim as your God, is the one who glorifies me.[q] 55 Though you do not know him,[r] I know him.[s] If I said I did not, I would be a liar like you, but I do know him and keep his word.[t] 56 Your father Abraham[u] rejoiced at the thought of seeing my day; he saw it[v] and was glad."

57 "You are not yet fifty years old," the Jews said to him, "and you have seen Abraham!"

58 "I tell you the truth," Jesus answered, "before Abraham was born,[w] I am!"[x] 59 At this, they picked up stones to stone him,[y] but Jesus hid himself,[z] slipping away from the temple grounds.

Jesus Heals a Man Born Blind

9 As he went along, he saw a man blind from birth. 2 His disciples asked him, "Rabbi,[a] who sinned,[b] this man[c] or his parents,[d] that he was born blind?"

3 "Neither this man nor his parents sinned," said Jesus, "but this happened so that the work of God might be displayed in his life.[e] 4 As long as it is day,[f] we must do the work of him who sent me. Night is coming, when no one can work. 5 While I am in the world, I am the light of the world."[g]

6 Having said this, he spit[h] on the ground, made some mud with the saliva, and put it on the man's eyes. 7 "Go," he told him, "wash in the Pool of Siloam"[i] (this word means Sent). So the man went and washed, and came home seeing.[j]

8 His neighbors and those who had formerly seen him begging asked, "Isn't this the same man who used to sit and beg?"[k] 9 Some claimed that he was.

Others said, "No, he only looks like him."

But he himself insisted, "I am the man."

10 "How then were your eyes opened?" they demanded.

8:47 [j]Jn 18:37; 1Jn 4:6
8:48 [k]Mt 10:5 [l]ver 52; Jn 7:20
8:50 [m]ver 54; Jn 5:41
8:51 [n]Jn 11:26
8:53 [o]Jn 4:12
8:54 [p]ver 50 [q]Jn 16:14; 17:1,5
8:55 [r]ver 19 [s]Jn 7:28,29 [t]Jn 15:10
8:56 [u]ver 37,39 [v]Mt 13:17; Heb 11:13
8:58 [w]Jn 1:2; 17:5,24 [x]Ex 3:14
8:59 [y]Lev 24:16; Jn 10:31; 11:8 [z]Jn 12:36
9:2 [a]Mt 23:7 [b]ver 34; Lk 13:2; Ac 28:4 [c]Eze 18:20 [d]Ex 20:5; Job 21:19
9:3 [e]Jn 11:4
9:4 [f]Jn 11:9; 12:35
9:5 [g]Jn 1:4; 8:12; 12:46
9:6 [h]Mk 7:33; 8:23
9:7 [i]ver 11; 2Ki 5:10; Lk 13:4 [j]Isa 35:5; Jn 11:37
9:8 [k]Ac 3:2,10

I Am!

JN 8:48–59

The question posed by the Jewish people is one of age: How can Jesus, who is in his 30s, have been seen by Abraham, who died hundreds of years earlier? Once again, the people's focus is on the temporal, physical world, while Jesus' response is rooted in the spiritual: "Before Abraham was born, I am!" (Jn 8:58).

Jesus is not claiming that he is older than Abraham in physical years. Rather, he is echoing God's own statement about himself: "I AM WHO I AM" (Ex 3:14). The Jewish people see this declaration for what it is: a claim to deity. Unbelieving, they take Jesus' words as blasphemy and actually pick up the stones to kill him.

11 He replied, "The man they call Jesus made
some mud and put it on my eyes. He told me to go
to Siloam and wash. So I went and washed, and
then I could see."[l]
12 "Where is this man?" they asked him.
"I don't know," he said.

The Pharisees Investigate the Healing

13 They brought to the Pharisees the man who
had been blind. 14 Now the day on which Jesus
had made the mud and opened the man's eyes
was a Sabbath.[m] 15 Therefore the Pharisees also
asked him how he had received his sight.[n] "He
put mud on my eyes," the man replied, "and I
washed, and now I see."
16 Some of the Pharisees said, "This man is not
from God, for he does not keep the Sabbath."[o]
But others asked, "How can a sinner do such
miraculous signs?" So they were divided.[p]
17 Finally they turned again to the blind man,
"What have you to say about him? It was your
eyes he opened."
The man replied, "He is a prophet."[q]
18 The Jews[r] still did not believe that he had
been blind and had received his sight until they
sent for the man's parents. 19 "Is this your son?"
they asked. "Is this the one you say was born
blind? How is it that now he can see?"
20 "We know he is our son," the parents answered,
"and we know he was born blind. 21 But how he can
see now, or who opened his eyes, we don't know.
Ask him. He is of age; he will speak for himself."
22 His parents said this because they were afraid of
the Jews,[s] for already the Jews had decided that
anyone who acknowledged that Jesus was the
Christ[a] would be put out[t] of the synagogue.[u] 23 That
was why his parents said, "He is of age; ask him."[v]
24 A second time they summoned the man who
had been blind. "Give glory to God,[b]"[w] they said.
"We know this man is a sinner."[x]
25 He replied, "Whether he is a sinner or not, I
don't know. One thing I do know. I was blind but
now I see!"
26 Then they asked him, "What did he do to you?
How did he open your eyes?"
27 He answered, "I have told you already[y] and
you did not listen. Why do you want to hear it
again? Do you want to become his disciples, too?"
28 Then they hurled insults at him and said,
"You are this fellow's disciple! We are disciples of
Moses![z] 29 We know that God spoke to Moses, but
as for this fellow, we don't even know where he
comes from."[a]
30 The man answered, "Now that is remarkable!
You don't know where he comes from, yet he
opened my eyes. 31 We know that God does not listen to sinners. He listens to the godly man who
does his will.[b] 32 Nobody has ever heard of open-

9:11 [l]ver 7
9:14 [m]Jn 5:9
9:15 [n]ver 10
9:16 [o]Mt 12:2 [p]Jn 6:52; 7:43; 10:19
9:17 [q]Mt 21:11
9:18 [r]Jn 1:19
9:22 [s]Jn 7:13 [t]ver 34; Lk 6:22 [u]Jn 12:42; 16:2
9:23 [v]ver 21
9:24 [w]Jos 7:19 [x]ver 16
9:27 [y]ver 15
9:28 [z]Jn 5:45
9:29 [a]Jn 8:14
9:31 [b]Ge 18:23-32; Ps 34:15,16; 66:18; 145:19,20; Pr 15:29; Isa 1:15; 59:1,2; Jn 15:7; Jas 5:16-18; 1Jn 5:14,15

One of the best statements about Christianity I've heard was made by *a female evangelist I greatly respect:* "Christianity is not a religion like most people think. Christianity is a life of imitating Jesus.

—Thelma Wells

[a] *22* Or *Messiah* [b] *24* A solemn charge to tell the truth (see Joshua 7:19)

ing the eyes of a man born blind. 33If this man
were not from God,[c] he could do nothing."
34To this they replied, "You were steeped in sin
at birth;[d] how dare you lecture us!" And they
threw him out.[e]

Spiritual Blindness

35Jesus heard that they had thrown him out,
and when he found him, he said, "Do you believe
in the Son of Man?"
36"Who is he, sir?" the man asked. "Tell me so
that I may believe in him."[f]
37Jesus said, "You have now seen him; in fact,
he is the one speaking with you."[g]
38Then the man said, "Lord, I believe," and he
worshiped him.[h]
39Jesus said, "For judgment[i] I have come into
this world,[j] so that the blind will see[k] and those
who see will become blind."[l]
40Some Pharisees who were with him heard
him say this and asked, "What? Are we blind
too?"[m]
41Jesus said, "If you were blind, you would not
be guilty of sin; but now that you claim you can
see, your guilt remains.[n]

The Shepherd and His Flock

10 "I tell you the truth, the man who does not
enter the sheep pen by the gate, but climbs
in by some other way, is a thief and a robber. 2The
man who enters by the gate is the shepherd of his
sheep.[o] 3The watchman opens the gate for him,
and the sheep listen to his voice.[p] He calls his own
sheep by name and leads them out. 4When he has
brought out all his own, he goes on ahead of
them, and his sheep follow him because they
know his voice. 5But they will never follow a
stranger; in fact, they will run away from him
because they do not recognize a stranger's voice."
6Jesus used this figure of speech,[q] but they did not
understand what he was telling them.
7Therefore Jesus said again, "I tell you the
truth, I am the gate for the sheep. 8All who ever
came before me[r] were thieves and robbers, but the
sheep did not listen to them. 9I am the gate; whoever enters through me will be saved.[a] He will
come in and go out, and find pasture. 10The thief
comes only to steal and kill and destroy; I have
come that they may have life, and have it to the
full.
11"I am the good shepherd.[s] The good shepherd
lays down his life for the sheep.[t] 12The hired hand
is not the shepherd who owns the sheep. So when
he sees the wolf coming, he abandons the sheep
and runs away.[u] Then the wolf attacks the flock
and scatters it. 13The man runs away because he is
a hired hand and cares nothing for the sheep.
14"I am the good shepherd;[v] I know my sheep[w]
and my sheep know me— 15just as the Father

[a] 9 Or *kept safe*

9:33 [c]ver 16; Jn 3:2
9:34 [d]ver 2 [e]ver 22,35; Isa 66:5
9:36 [f]Ro 10:14
9:37 [g]Jn 4:26
9:38 [h]Mt 28:9
9:39 [i]Jn 5:22 [j]Jn 3:19 [k]Lk 4:18 [l]Mt 13:13
9:40 [m]Ro 2:19
9:41 [n]Jn 15:22,24
10:2 [o]ver 11,14
10:3 [p]ver 4,5,14, 16,27
10:6 [q]Jn 16:25
10:8 [r]Jer 23:1,2
10:11 [s]ver 14; Isa 40:11; Eze 34:11-16,23; Heb 13:20; 1Pe 5:4; Rev 7:17 [t]Jn 15:13; 1Jn 3:16
10:12 [u]Zec 11:16, 17
10:14 [v]ver 11 [w]ver 27

The Good Shepherd

JN 10:1-15

The people of Israel are well acquainted with the work of a shepherd. The sons of Abraham, Isaac and Jacob tended sheep, as did many other historical Jewish figures, including Rachel, Moses and David. Drawing on the Hebrew people's familiarity with this role, Old Testament texts paint a picture of the Lord as a shepherd who leads, tends, loves and provides for his sheep (Ps 23). In addition to describing the character of God, the image of the shepherd who will come to personally care for his people is prophetic in nature (Isa 40:11; Eze 34:11-16,23). That promise is fulfilled with the coming of the Messiah. In the New Testament, Christ is referred to as the "great Shepherd" (Heb 13:20) and the "Chief Shepherd" (1Pe 5:4). In his own words, describes himself as the "good shepherd" (Jn 10:11, 14). As a shepherd lovingly watches over and cares for his sheep, so Jesus compassionately and kindly guides us on our life's journey.

Other Sheep

JN 10:16

The "other sheep" Jesus cites in this verse are those who are not a part of the Jewish nation. The "sheep pen" is a picture of the people of Israel. This is one of Christ's first and most explicit teachings regarding his acceptance—and welcome—of believing Gentiles into his kingdom.

knows me and I know the Father[x]—and I lay down
my life for the sheep. 16 I have other sheep[y] that are
not of this sheep pen. I must bring them also. They
too will listen to my voice, and there shall be one
flock[z] and one shepherd.[a] 17 The reason my Father
loves me is that I lay down my life[b]—only to take
it up again. 18 No one takes it from me, but I lay it
down of my own accord.[c] I have authority to lay it
down and authority to take it up again. This command I received from my Father."[d]
19 At these words the Jews were again divided.[e]
20 Many of them said, "He is demon-possessed[f] and
raving mad.[g] Why listen to him?"
21 But others said, "These are not the sayings of
a man possessed by a demon.[h] Can a demon open
the eyes of the blind?"[i]

The Unbelief of the Jews

22 Then came the Feast of Dedication[a] at Jerusalem. It was winter, 23 and Jesus was in the temple
area walking in Solomon's Colonnade.[j] 24 The
Jews[k] gathered around him, saying, "How long
will you keep us in suspense? If you are the
Christ,[b] tell us plainly."[l]
25 Jesus answered, "I did tell you,[m] but you do
not believe. The miracles I do in my Father's name
speak for me,[n] 26 but you do not believe because
you are not my sheep.[o] 27 My sheep listen to my
voice; I know them,[p] and they follow me.[q] 28 I give
them eternal life, and they shall never perish; no
one can snatch them out of my hand.[r] 29 My
Father, who has given them to me,[s] is greater than
all[c];[t] no one can snatch them out of my Father's
hand. 30 I and the Father are one."[u]
31 Again the Jews picked up stones to stone
him,[v] 32 but Jesus said to them, "I have shown you
many great miracles from the Father. For which of
these do you stone me?"
33 "We are not stoning you for any of these,"
replied the Jews, "but for blasphemy, because
you, a mere man, claim to be God."[w]
34 Jesus answered them, "Is it not written in your
Law,[x] 'I have said you are gods'[d]?[y] 35 If he called
them 'gods,' to whom the word of God came—and
the Scripture cannot be broken— 36 what about the
one whom the Father set apart[z] as his very own[a]
and sent into the world?[b] Why then do you accuse
me of blasphemy because I said, 'I am God's Son'?[c]
37 Do not believe me unless I do what my Father
does.[d] 38 But if I do it, even though you do not
believe me, believe the miracles, that you may
know and understand that the Father is in me, and
I in the Father."[e] 39 Again they tried to seize him,[f]
but he escaped their grasp.[g]
40 Then Jesus went back across the Jordan[h] to
the place where John had been baptizing in the
early days. Here he stayed 41 and many people

[a] 22 That is, Hanukkah [b] 24 Or *Messiah* [c] 29 Many early manuscripts *What my Father has given me is greater than all*
[d] 34 Psalm 82:6

10:15 [x]Mt 11:27
10:16 [y]Isa 56:8 [z]Jn 11:52; Eph 2:11-19 [a]Eze 37:24; 1Pe 2:25
10:17 [b]ver 11,15, 18
10:18 [c]Mt 26:53 [d]Jn 15:10; Php 2:8; Heb 5:8
10:19 [e]Jn 7:43; 9:16
10:20 [f]Jn 7:20 [g]Mk 3:21
10:21 [h]Mt 4:24 [i]Ex 4:11; Jn 9:32,33
10:23 [j]Ac 3:11; 5:12
10:24 [k]Jn 1:19 [l]Jn 16:25,29
10:25 [m]Jn 8:58 [n]Jn 5:36
10:26 [o]Jn 8:47
10:27 [p]ver 14 [q]ver 4
10:28 [r]Jn 6:39
10:29 [s]Jn 17:2,6,24 [t]Jn 14:28
10:30 [u]Jn 17:21-23
10:31 [v]Jn 8:59
10:33 [w]Lev 24:16; Jn 5:18
10:34 [x]Jn 8:17; Ro 3:19 [y]Ps 82:6
10:36 [z]Jer 1:5 [a]Jn 6:69 [b]Jn 3:17 [c]Jn 5:17,18
10:37 [d]ver 25; Jn 15:24
10:38 [e]Jn 14:10,11, 20; 17:21
10:39 [f]Jn 7:30 [g]Lk 4:30; Jn 8:59
10:40 [h]Jn 1:28

came to him. They said, "Though John never performed a miraculous sign,[i] all that John said
about this man was true."[j] 42And in that place
many believed in Jesus.[k]

The Death of Lazarus

11 Now a man named Lazarus was sick. He
was from Bethany,[l] the village of Mary and
her sister Martha.[m] 2This Mary, whose brother
Lazarus now lay sick, was the same one who
poured perfume on the Lord and wiped his feet
with her hair.[n] 3So the sisters sent word to Jesus,
"Lord, the one you love[o] is sick."
4When he heard this, Jesus said, "This sickness
will not end in death. No, it is for God's glory[p] so
that God's Son may be glorified through it." 5Jesus
loved Martha and her sister and Lazarus. 6Yet
when he heard that Lazarus was sick, he stayed
where he was two more days.
7Then he said to his disciples, "Let us go back to
Judea."[q]
8"But Rabbi,"[r] they said, "a short while ago the
Jews tried to stone you,[s] and yet you are going
back there?"
9Jesus answered, "Are there not twelve hours of
daylight? A man who walks by day will not stumble, for he sees by this world's light.[t] 10It is when
he walks by night that he stumbles, for he has no
light."
11After he had said this, he went on to tell them,
"Our friend[u] Lazarus has fallen asleep;[v] but I am
going there to wake him up."
12His disciples replied, "Lord, if he sleeps, he will
get better." 13Jesus had been speaking of his death,
but his disciples thought he meant natural sleep.[w]
14So then he told them plainly, "Lazarus is dead,
15and for your sake I am glad I was not there, so
that you may believe. But let us go to him."
16Then Thomas[x] (called Didymus) said to the
rest of the disciples, "Let us also go, that we may
die with him."

Jesus Comforts the Sisters

17On his arrival, Jesus found that Lazarus had
already been in the tomb for four days.[y] 18Betha-
ny[z] was less than two miles[a] from Jerusalem,
19and many Jews had come to Martha and Mary to
comfort them in the loss of their brother.[a] 20When
Martha heard that Jesus was coming, she went
out to meet him, but Mary stayed at home.[b]
21"Lord," Martha said to Jesus, "if you had been
here, my brother would not have died.[c] 22But I
know that even now God will give you whatever
you ask."[d]
23Jesus said to her, "Your brother will rise
again."
24Martha answered, "I know he will rise again
in the resurrection[e] at the last day."
25Jesus said to her, "I am the resurrection and

10:41 [i]Jn 2:11; 3:30 [j]Jn 1:26,27, 30,34
10:42 [k]Jn 7:31
11:1 [l]Mt 21:17 [m]Lk 10:38
11:2 [n]Mk 14:3; Lk 7:38; Jn 12:3
11:3 [o]ver 5,36
11:4 [p]ver 40; Jn 9:3
11:7 [q]Jn 10:40
11:8 [r]Mt 23:7 [s]Jn 8:59; 10:31
11:9 [t]Jn 9:4; 12:35
11:11 [u]ver 3 [v]Ac 7:60
11:13 [w]Mt 9:24
11:16 [x]Mt 10:3; Jn 14:5; 20:24-28; 21:2; Ac 1:13
11:17 [y]ver 6,39
11:18 [z]ver 1
11:19 [a]ver 31; Job 2:11
11:20 [b]Lk 10:38-42
11:21 [c]ver 32,37
11:22 [d]ver 41,42; Jn 9:31
11:24 [e]Da 12:2; Jn 5:28,29; Ac 24:15

[a] *18* Greek *fifteen stadia* (about 3 kilometers)

Thomas

JN 11:16

Thomas, one of the 12 disciples, is famous for not believing that Jesus had risen from the dead, even after Jesus appeared to the other disciples (Jn 20:24–25). The term "doubting Thomas" originates from this lack of faith on Thomas's part.

In this verse, however, we see an earlier picture of Thomas as a man enthusiastically devoted to his Lord. When Jesus proposes to his disciples that they return to Jerusalem, Thomas responds first, declaring that he is willing to go—and even to die—with Jesus. Yet despite his noble intentions, Thomas, along with Jesus' other disciples, fails to stand by him in his final hour (Mt 26:56). Later, following Christ's ascension, Thomas is with the other disciples in the upper room when they receive the Holy Spirit. Tradition holds that, empowered by the Spirit, Thomas went on to evangelize in Parthia and Persia, while apocryphal accounts credit him with founding the church in India.

Martha's Confession

JN 11:25–27

When Jesus tells Martha that her brother will rise again, she agrees, citing widely accepted teachings regarding the resurrection of the body on the last day. In telling her, "I am the resurrection and the life" (Jn 11:25), however, Jesus is stating that the resurrection is not just a future, but a *present*, reality. In reply, Martha confesses her faith in Jesus. She is willing to see him as the Christ and as the Son of God, but her subsequent words at Lazarus's tomb demonstrate that she does not fully realize the meaning of his claims (Jn 11:39). By raising Lazarus, Jesus illustrates for Martha, Mary and the crowd of Jews gathered at the tomb the divine truth that he is the source of life itself (see the character sketch on Martha on page 1844).

the life.[f] He who believes in me will live, even
though he dies; 26and whoever lives and believes
in me will never die. Do you believe this?"
27"Yes, Lord," she told him, "I believe that you
are the Christ,[a][g] the Son of God,[h] who was to
come into the world."[i]
28And after she had said this, she went back and
called her sister Mary aside. "The Teacher[j] is here,"
she said, "and is asking for you." 29When Mary
heard this, she got up quickly and went to him.
30Now Jesus had not yet entered the village, but
was still at the place where Martha had met him.[k]
31When the Jews who had been with Mary in the
house, comforting her,[l] noticed how quickly she
got up and went out, they followed her, supposing
she was going to the tomb to mourn there.
32When Mary reached the place where Jesus
was and saw him, she fell at his feet and said,
"Lord, if you had been here, my brother would not
have died."[m]
33When Jesus saw her weeping, and the Jews
who had come along with her also weeping, he
was deeply moved[n] in spirit and troubled.[o]
34"Where have you laid him?" he asked.
"Come and see, Lord," they replied.
35Jesus wept.[p]
36Then the Jews said, "See how he loved him!"[q]
37But some of them said, "Could not he who
opened the eyes of the blind man[r] have kept this
man from dying?"[s]

Jesus Raises Lazarus From the Dead

38Jesus, once more deeply moved,[t] came to the
tomb. It was a cave with a stone laid across the
entrance.[u] 39"Take away the stone," he said.
"But, Lord," said Martha, the sister of the dead
man, "by this time there is a bad odor, for he has
been there four days."[v]
40Then Jesus said, "Did I not tell you that if you
believed,[w] you would see the glory of God?"[x]
41So they took away the stone. Then Jesus
looked up[y] and said, "Father,[z] I thank you that
you have heard me. 42I knew that you always hear
me, but I said this for the benefit of the people
standing here,[a] that they may believe that you
sent me."[b]
43When he had said this, Jesus called in a loud
voice, "Lazarus, come out!"[c] 44The dead man
came out, his hands and feet wrapped with strips
of linen,[d] and a cloth around his face.[e]
Jesus said to them, "Take off the grave clothes
and let him go."

The Plot to Kill Jesus

45Therefore many of the Jews who had come to
visit Mary,[f] and had seen what Jesus did,[g] put
their faith in him.[h] 46But some of them went to the
Pharisees and told them what Jesus had done.

11:25 [f]Jn 1:4
11:27 [g]Lk 2:11 [h]Mt 16:16 [i]Jn 6:14
11:28 [j]Mt 26:18; Jn 13:13
11:30 [k]ver 20
11:31 [l]ver 19
11:32 [m]ver 21
11:33 [n]ver 38 [o]Jn 12:27
11:35 [p]Lk 19:41
11:36 [q]ver 3
11:37 [r]Jn 9:6,7 [s]ver 21,32
11:38 [t]ver 33 [u]Mt 27:60; Lk 24:2; Jn 20:1
11:39 [v]ver 17
11:40 [w]ver 23-25 [x]ver 4
11:41 [y]Jn 17:1 [z]Mt 11:25
11:42 [a]Jn 12:30 [b]Jn 3:17
11:43 [c]Lk 7:14
11:44 [d]Jn 19:40 [e]Jn 20:7
11:45 [f]ver 19 [g]Jn 2:23 [h]Ex 14:31; Jn 7:31

[a] 27 Or *Messiah*

11:47 [i]ver 57 47Then the chief priests and the Pharisees[i] called a
[j]Mt 26:3 meeting[j] of the Sanhedrin.[k]
[k]Mt 5:22 "What are we accomplishing?" they asked.
[l]Jn 2:11 "Here is this man performing many miraculous
signs.[l] 48If we let him go on like this, everyone will
believe in him, and then the Romans will come
11:49 and take away both our place[a] and our nation."
[m]Mt 26:3 49Then one of them, named Caiaphas,[m] who
[n]ver 51; was high priest that year,[n] spoke up, "You know
Jn 18:13,14 nothing at all! 50You do not realize that it is better
11:50 for you that one man die for the people than that
[o]Jn 18:14 the whole nation perish."[o]
51He did not say this on his own, but as high
11:52 [p]Isa 49:6; priest that year he prophesied that Jesus would
Jn 10:16 die for the Jewish nation, 52and not only for that
nation but also for the scattered children of God,
11:53 to bring them together and make them one.[p] 53So
[q]Mt 12:14 from that day on they plotted to take his life.[q]
54Therefore Jesus no longer moved about pub-
11:54 [r]Jn 7:1 licly among the Jews.[r] Instead he withdrew to a
region near the desert, to a village called Ephraim,
where he stayed with his disciples.
55When it was almost time for the Jewish
11:55 [s]Ex 12:13, Passover,[s] many went up from the country to Jeru-
23,27; salem for their ceremonial cleansing[t] before the
Mt 26:1,2; Passover. 56They kept looking for Jesus,[u] and as
Mk 14:1; Jn 13:1 they stood in the temple area they asked one
[t]2Ch 30:17, another, "What do you think? Isn't he coming to
18 the Feast at all?" 57But the chief priests and Phar-
11:56 isees had given orders that if anyone found out
[u]Jn 7:11 where Jesus was, he should report it so that they
might arrest him.

Jesus Anointed at Bethany

12:1 [v]Jn 11:55 **12** Six days before the Passover,[v] Jesus arrived
[w]Mt 21:17 at Bethany,[w] where Lazarus lived, whom
Jesus had raised from the dead. 2Here a dinner was
12:2 [x]Lk 10:38-42 given in Jesus' honor. Martha served,[x] while Lazarus was among those reclining at the table with
him. 3Then Mary took about a pint[b] of pure nard,
12:3 [y]Mk 14:3 an expensive perfume;[y] she poured it on Jesus' feet
[z]Jn 11:2 and wiped his feet with her hair.[z] And the house
was filled with the fragrance of the perfume.
12:4 4But one of his disciples, Judas Iscariot, who was
[a]Mt 10:4 later to betray him,[a] objected, 5"Why wasn't this
perfume sold and the money given to the poor? It
was worth a year's wages.[c]" 6He did not say this
because he cared about the poor but because he
12:6 [b]Jn 13:29 was a thief; as keeper of the money bag,[b] he used to
help himself to what was put into it.
7"Leave her alone," Jesus replied. "⌞It was
intended⌟ that she should save this perfume for
12:7 [c]Jn 19:40 the day of my burial.[c] 8You will always have the
poor among you,[d] but you will not always
12:8 [d]Dt 15:11 have me."
9Meanwhile a large crowd of Jews found out
that Jesus was there and came, not only because
of him but also to see Lazarus, whom he had

[a] *48* Or *temple* [b] *3* Greek *a litra* (probably about 0.5 liter)
[c] *5* Greek *three hundred denarii*

A Decision Is Made

JN 11:45-53

Jesus has already performed numerous miracles. His latest, raising Lazarus from the dead, has caused a new wave of Jewish people to put their faith in him. The members of the Sanhedrin realize that if this trend continues, eventually "everyone will believe in him" as the Christ (Jn 11:48).

At this time, the Jewish people are enjoying various privileges under Roman rule, as they have since the reign of Julius Caesar. The rising popularity of Jesus puts this status in jeopardy. The Jewish people themselves view the coming Messiah as a political figure who will bring about the destruction of Israel's enemies; any movement to follow Jesus is likely to be interpreted by the Romans as a political revolution. Reasoning that this will cause the Romans to seize the temple and disband the nation, the Jewish leaders justify their decision to have Jesus put to death.

The Triumphal Entry

JN 12:12–19

As Jesus approaches Jerusalem, he is met by an enthusiastic crowd of pilgrims who have come to celebrate the Passover. This "Triumphal Entry," recorded in all four Gospels (Mt 21:4–9; Mk 11:7–10; Lk 19:35–38), is a grand entrance fit for a king, which, of course, is exactly what the crowd has determined him to be: the "King of Israel" (Jn 12:13). Shouts of "Hosanna!" meet Jesus' ears: a cry of praise rooted in the Hebrew expression for "Save now, I pray." The people carry palm fronds, which have been present at celebrations and victories since the days of Moses (Lev 23:40), and they publicly acknowledge him as the One "who comes in the name of the Lord!" (Jn 12:13).

Against this backdrop, Jesus fulfills the prophecy that the Messiah will come "gentle and riding on . . . the foal of a donkey" (Zec 9:9). Though his disciples do not yet understand the significance of this act (Jn 12:16), the crowd at this moment joyously hails him as the Christ.

raised from the dead.[e] 10 So the chief priests made plans to kill Lazarus as well, 11 for on account of him[f] many of the Jews were going over to Jesus and putting their faith in him.[g]

The Triumphal Entry

12 The next day the great crowd that had come for the Feast heard that Jesus was on his way to Jerusalem. 13 They took palm branches and went out to meet him, shouting,

> "Hosanna![a]"
>
> "Blessed is he who comes in the name
> of the Lord!"[b][h]
>
> "Blessed is the King of Israel!"[i]

14 Jesus found a young donkey and sat upon it, as it is written,

> 15 "Do not be afraid, O Daughter of Zion;
> see, your king is coming,
> seated on a donkey's colt."[c][j]

16 At first his disciples did not understand all this.[k] Only after Jesus was glorified[l] did they realize that these things had been written about him and that they had done these things to him.

17 Now the crowd that was with him[m] when he called Lazarus from the tomb and raised him from the dead continued to spread the word. 18 Many people, because they had heard that he had given this miraculous sign,[n] went out to meet him. 19 So the Pharisees said to one another, "See, this is getting us nowhere. Look how the whole world has gone after him!"[o]

Jesus Predicts His Death

20 Now there were some Greeks[p] among those who went up to worship at the Feast. 21 They came to Philip, who was from Bethsaida[q] in Galilee, with a request. "Sir," they said, "we would like to see Jesus." 22 Philip went to tell Andrew; Andrew and Philip in turn told Jesus.

23 Jesus replied, "The hour has come for the Son of Man to be glorified.[r] 24 I tell you the truth, unless a kernel of wheat falls to the ground and dies,[s] it remains only a single seed. But if it dies, it produces many seeds. 25 The man who loves his life will lose it, while the man who hates his life in this world will keep it[t] for eternal life. 26 Whoever serves me must follow me; and where I am, my servant also will be.[u] My Father will honor the one who serves me.

27 "Now my heart is troubled,[v] and what shall I say? 'Father,[w] save me from this hour'?[x] No, it was for this very reason I came to this hour. 28 Father, glorify your name!"

Then a voice came from heaven,[y] "I have glori-

12:9 [e]Jn 11:43,44
12:11 [f]ver 17,18; Jn 11:45 [g]Jn 7:31
12:13 [h]Ps 118:25, 26 [i]Jn 1:49
12:15 [j]Zec 9:9
12:16 [k]Mk 9:32 [l]Jn 2:22; 7:39; 14:26
12:17 [m]Jn 11:42
12:18 [n]ver 11
12:19 [o]Jn 11:47,48
12:20 [p]Jn 7:35; Ac 11:20
12:21 [q]Mt 11:21; Jn 1:44
12:23 [r]Jn 13:32; 17:1
12:24 [s]1Co 15:36
12:25 [t]Mt 10:39; Mk 8:35; Lk 14:26
12:26 [u]Jn 14:3; 17:24; 2Co 5:8; 1Th 4:17
12:27 [v]Mt 26:38, 39; Jn 11:33, 38; 13:21 [w]Mt 11:25 [x]ver 23
12:28 [y]Mt 3:17

[a] *13* A Hebrew expression meaning "Save!" which became an exclamation of praise [b] *13* Psalm 118:25,26
[c] *15* Zech. 9:9

fied it, and will glorify it again.” 29The crowd that
was there and heard it said it had thundered; others said an angel had spoken to him.
30Jesus said, “This voice was for your benefit,[z]
not mine. 31Now is the time for judgment on this
world;[a] now the prince of this world[b] will be driv-
en out. 32But I, when I am lifted up from the earth,[c]
will draw all men to myself.”[d] 33He said this to
show the kind of death he was going to die.[e]
34The crowd spoke up, “We have heard from the
Law that the Christ[a] will remain forever,[f] so how
can you say, ‘The Son of Man[g] must be lifted up’?[h]
Who is this ‘Son of Man’?”
35Then Jesus told them, “You are going to have
the light[i] just a little while longer. Walk while you
have the light,[j] before darkness overtakes you.[k]
The man who walks in the dark does not know
where he is going. 36Put your trust in the light
while you have it, so that you may become sons of
light.”[l] When he had finished speaking, Jesus left
and hid himself from them.[m]

The Jews Continue in Their Unbelief

37Even after Jesus had done all these miraculous signs[n] in their presence, they still would not
believe in him. 38This was to fulfill the word of
Isaiah the prophet:

> “Lord, who has believed our message
> and to whom has the arm of the Lord
> been revealed?”[b][o]

39For this reason they could not believe,
because, as Isaiah says elsewhere:

> 40“He has blinded their eyes
> and deadened their hearts,
> so they can neither see with their eyes,
> nor understand with their hearts,
> nor turn—and I would heal them.”[c][p]

41Isaiah said this because he saw Jesus’ glory[q] and
spoke about him.[r]
42Yet at the same time many even among the
leaders believed in him.[s] But because of the Pharisees[t] they would not confess their faith for fear
they would be put out of the synagogue;[u] 43for
they loved praise from men more than praise from
God.[v]
44Then Jesus cried out, “When a man believes
in me, he does not believe in me only, but in the
one who sent me.[w] 45When he looks at me, he
sees the one who sent me.[x] 46I have come into the
world as a light,[y] so that no one who believes in
me should stay in darkness.
47“As for the person who hears my words but
does not keep them, I do not judge him. For I did
not come to judge the world, but to save it.[z]
48There is a judge for the one who rejects me and
does not accept my words; that very word which
I spoke will condemn him[a] at the last day. 49For I

12:30 [z]Jn 11:42
12:31 [a]Jn 16:11 [b]Jn 14:30; 16:11; 2Co 4:4; Eph 2:2; 1Jn 4:4
12:32 [c]ver 34; Jn 3:14; 8:28 [d]Jn 6:44
12:33 [e]Jn 18:32
12:34 [f]Ps 110:4; Isa 9:7; Eze 37:25; Da 7:14 [g]Mt 8:20 [h]Jn 3:14
12:35 [i]ver 46 [j]Eph 5:8 [k]1Jn 2:11
12:36 [l]Lk 16:8 [m]Jn 8:59
12:37 [n]Jn 2:11
12:38 [o]Isa 53:1; Ro 10:16
12:40 [p]Isa 6:10; Mt 13:13,15
12:41 [q]Isa 6:1-4 [r]Lk 24:27
12:42 [s]ver 11; Jn 7:48 [t]Jn 7:13 [u]Jn 9:22
12:43 [v]Jn 5:44
12:44 [w]Mt 10:40; Jn 5:24
12:45 [x]Jn 14:9
12:46 [y]Jn 1:4; 3:19; 8:12; 9:5
12:47 [z]Jn 3:17
12:48 [a]Jn 5:45

[a] 34 Or *Messiah* [b] 38 Isaiah 53:1 [c] 40 Isaiah 6:10

Walking in the Light

JN 12:34–36

When the crowd asks Jesus a question about the Son of Man, meaning the Messiah, he responds by stressing the importance of walking in the light. This is not the shift in subject it first appears to be, for the two are closely connected. The description of the Messiah as a light to the nations was penned by the prophet Isaiah nearly seven centuries earlier (Isa 49:6). Jesus highlights the connection between sight and blindness and light and darkness when he restores sight to a blind man in John 9. In quick succession he refers to himself as “the light of the world” (Jn 9:5), then as “the Son of Man” (Jn 9:35-37). The Son of Man* is *the light. The topic of light and darkness is one that matters to Jesus, for it is an evidence of spiritual sight or blindness and of the choice to be made to follow the light or to continue in darkness (Jn 12:36). Walking in the light isn’t simply about living a moral life; it is a matter of following Christ, who* is *the light.

Washing Feet

JN 13:1–17

Jesus' disciples participated in a petty quarrel among themselves about which of them would be greatest in the kingdom of heaven (Mk 9:34; Lk 9:46). Now the familiar argument is sparked again (Lk 22:24). Stubbornly, the apostles cling to dreams of earthly glory, despite Jesus' repeated explanations that his is not an earthly kingdom.

In the upper room, the preparations for foot washing have been made, but no servant is there to carry out the task. Any one of the disciples could have jumped in, but pride presumably gets in the way. Instead, to their shock, Jesus steps forward and performs this intimate act of service.

Understandably, Peter protests. (Imagine how you would feel if Jesus knelt before you to wash your dirty feet!) Yet Jesus insists and, through his actions, provides an emotionally charged illustration of genuine humility and love (Jn 13:1). Take a moment to think about Jesus' humble example. Jot down on paper or in your journal a few ways you can wash the feet of others.

did not speak of my own accord, but the Father
who sent me commanded me[b] what to say and
how to say it. 50I know that his command leads to
eternal life. So whatever I say is just what the
Father has told me to say."

Jesus Washes His Disciples' Feet

13 It was just before the Passover Feast.[c] Jesus
knew that the time had come[d] for him to
leave this world and go to the Father.[e] Having
loved his own who were in the world, he now
showed them the full extent of his love.[a]
2The evening meal was being served, and the
devil had already prompted Judas Iscariot, son of
Simon, to betray Jesus. 3Jesus knew that the Father
had put all things under his power,[f] and that he
had come from God[g] and was returning to God; 4so
he got up from the meal, took off his outer clothing,
and wrapped a towel around his waist. 5After
that, he poured water into a basin and began to
wash his disciples' feet,[h] drying them with the
towel that was wrapped around him.
6He came to Simon Peter, who said to him,
"Lord, are you going to wash my feet?"
7Jesus replied, "You do not realize now what I
am doing, but later you will understand."[i]
8"No," said Peter, "you shall never wash my
feet."
Jesus answered, "Unless I wash you, you have
no part with me."
9"Then, Lord," Simon Peter replied, "not just
my feet but my hands and my head as well!"
10Jesus answered, "A person who has had a bath
needs only to wash his feet; his whole body is
clean. And you are clean,[j] though not every one of
you." 11For he knew who was going to betray him,
and that was why he said not every one was clean.
12When he had finished washing their feet, he
put on his clothes and returned to his place. "Do
you understand what I have done for you?" he
asked them. 13"You call me 'Teacher'[k] and 'Lord,'[l]
and rightly so, for that is what I am. 14Now that I,
your Lord and Teacher, have washed your feet, you
also should wash one another's feet.[m] 15I have set
you an example that you should do as I have done
for you.[n] 16I tell you the truth, no servant is greater
than his master,[o] nor is a messenger greater than
the one who sent him. 17Now that you know these
things, you will be blessed if you do them.[p]

Jesus Predicts His Betrayal

18"I am not referring to all of you;[q] I know those
I have chosen.[r] But this is to fulfill the scripture:
'He who shares my bread[s] has lifted up his heel[t]
against me.'[b][u]
19"I am telling you now before it happens, so
that when it does happen you will believe[v] that I
am He.[w] 20I tell you the truth, whoever accepts

12:49 [b]Jn 14:31
13:1 [c]Jn 11:55 [d]Jn 12:23 [e]Jn 16:28
13:3 [f]Mt 28:18 [g]Jn 8:42; 16:27,28,30
13:5 [h]Lk 7:44
13:7 [i]ver 12
13:10 [j]Jn 15:3
13:13 [k]Jn 11:28 [l]Lk 6:46; 1Co 12:3; Php 2:11
13:14 [m]1Pe 5:5
13:15 [n]Mt 11:29
13:16 [o]Mt 10:24; Lk 6:40; Jn 15:20
13:17 [p]Mt 7:24,25; Lk 11:28; Jas 1:25
13:18 [q]ver 10 [r]Jn 15:16,19 [s]Mt 26:23 [t]Jn 6:70 [u]Ps 41:9
13:19 [v]Jn 14:29; 16:4 [w]Jn 8:24

[a] *1* Or *he loved them to the last* [b] *18* Psalm 41:9

anyone I send accepts me; and whoever accepts
13:20 [x]Mt 10:40; me accepts the one who sent me."[x]
Lk 10:16 [21]After he had said this, Jesus was troubled in
13:21 spirit[y] and testified, "I tell you the truth, one of
[y]Jn 12:27 you is going to betray me."[z]
[z]Mt 26:21 [22]His disciples stared at one another, at a loss to
13:23 know which of them he meant. [23]One of them, the
[a]Jn 19:26; disciple whom Jesus loved,[a] was reclining next to
20:2; 21:7,20 him. [24]Simon Peter motioned to this disciple and
said, "Ask him which one he means."
[25]Leaning back against Jesus, he asked him,
13:25 [b]Jn 21:20 "Lord, who is it?"[b]
[26]Jesus answered, "It is the one to whom I will
give this piece of bread when I have dipped it in
the dish." Then, dipping the piece of bread, he
gave it to Judas Iscariot, son of Simon. [27]As soon
13:27 [c]Lk 22:3 as Judas took the bread, Satan entered into him.[c]
"What you are about to do, do quickly," Jesus
told him, [28]but no one at the meal understood why
Jesus said this to him. [29]Since Judas had charge of
13:29 the money,[d] some thought Jesus was telling him
[d]Jn 12:6 to buy what was needed for the Feast, or to give
something to the poor. [30]As soon as Judas had tak-
13:30 [e]Lk 22:53 en the bread, he went out. And it was night.[e]

Jesus Predicts Peter's Denial

13:31 [31]When he was gone, Jesus said, "Now is the
[f]Jn 7:39 [g]Jn 14:13; Son of Man glorified[f] and God is glorified in him.[g]
17:4; [32]If God is glorified in him,[a] God will glorify the
1Pe 4:11 Son in himself,[h] and will glorify him at once.
13:32 [33]"My children, I will be with you only a little
[h]Jn 17:1 longer. You will look for me, and just as I told the
Jews, so I tell you now: Where I am going, you
13:33 [i]Jn 7:33,34 cannot come.[i]
[34]"A new command[j] I give you: Love one anoth-
13:34 [j]1Jn 2:7-11; er.[k] As I have loved you, so you must love one
3:11 [k]Lev 19:18; another.[l] [35]By this all men will know that you are
1Th 4:9; my disciples, if you love one another."[m]
1Pe 1:22 [36]Simon Peter asked him, "Lord, where are you
[l]Jn 15:12; Eph 5:2; going?"
1Jn 4:10,11 Jesus replied, "Where I am going, you cannot
follow now,[n] but you will follow later."[o]
13:35 [m]1Jn 3:14; [37]Peter asked, "Lord, why can't I follow you
4:20 now? I will lay down my life for you."
13:36 [38]Then Jesus answered, "Will you really lay
[n]ver 33; down your life for me? I tell you the truth, before
Jn 14:2 the rooster crows, you will disown me three
[o]Jn 21:18, 19; 2Pe 1:14 times![p]

13:38 [p]Jn 18:27

Jesus Comforts His Disciples

14:1 **14** "Do not let your hearts be troubled.[q] Trust
[q]ver 27 in God[b]; trust also in me. [2]In my Father's
14:2 house are many rooms; if it were not so, I would
[r]Jn 13:33,36 have told you. I am going there[r] to prepare a place
14:3 for you. [3]And if I go and prepare a place for you,
[s]Jn 12:26 I will come back and take you to be with me that
you also may be where I am.[s] [4]You know the way
to the place where I am going."

[a] *32* Many early manuscripts do not have *If God is glorified in him.* [b] *1* Or *You trust in God*

Supreme Comfort

JN 14:1–4

The disciples have received a great deal of harsh news in a relatively short period. Jesus has foretold his own betrayal, and he has predicted Peter's denials. Worst of all, he has announced that he will soon leave them. To the apostles, the world probably appears to be spinning out of control.

Yet Jesus tempers his announcements by offering the supreme comfort only the Son of God can provide. He explains that there are many rooms in his Father's house (heaven) and that he is going there to prepare a place for them. He assures them that he will come back to take them to be with him. And though we don't know precisely what the "place" he refers to is like, we can trust that—as he is the One through whom all things were created (Jn 1:3)—it will be far more glorious than anything we can imagine or dream of.

The Way

JN 14:6–7

In the face of Jesus' imminent departure, Thomas expresses the disciples' desire to follow him, but they do not know the way. Jesus responds by announcing that he *is the way, as well as the truth and the life. Jesus is saying that he is the way to God the Father, the truth of God, and the vessel by which eternal life comes to the human race. The Father is the one who sent Jesus.*

Do you see Jesus as your emissary to the Father? Or does worshiping Christ sometimes overshadow your need for the One who sent him? Jesus teaches that he and the Father, while two persons, are one God (Jn 14:9,11). We cannot have one without the other—nor would we want to! We need them both. Each day this week, ask Jesus to reveal truths to you about God the Father that will help you draw closer to him. Then spend several minutes praising the Father and thanking him for sending his Son.

Jesus the Way to the Father

5 Thomas[t] said to him, "Lord, we don't know
where you are going, so how can we know the
way?"
6 Jesus answered, "I am the way[u] and the truth
and the life.[v] No one comes to the Father except
through me. 7 If you really knew me, you would
know[a] my Father as well.[w] From now on, you do
know him and have seen him."
8 Philip said, "Lord, show us the Father and that
will be enough for us."
9 Jesus answered: "Don't you know me, Philip,
even after I have been among you such a long
time? Anyone who has seen me has seen the
Father.[x] How can you say, 'Show us the Father'?
10 Don't you believe that I am in the Father, and
that the Father is in me?[y] The words I say to you
are not just my own.[z] Rather, it is the Father, living in me, who is doing his work. 11 Believe me
when I say that I am in the Father and the Father
is in me; or at least believe on the evidence of the
miracles themselves.[a] 12 I tell you the truth, anyone who has faith[b] in me will do what I have been
doing.[c] He will do even greater things than these,
because I am going to the Father. 13 And I will do
whatever you ask[d] in my name, so that the Son
may bring glory to the Father. 14 You may ask me
for anything in my name, and I will do it.

Jesus Promises the Holy Spirit

15 "If you love me, you will obey what I command.[e] 16 And I will ask the Father, and he will
give you another Counselor[f] to be with you forever— 17 the Spirit of truth.[g] The world cannot accept
him,[h] because it neither sees him nor knows him.
But you know him, for he lives with you and will
be[b] in you. 18 I will not leave you as orphans; I will
come to you.[i] 19 Before long, the world will not see
me anymore, but you will see me.[j] Because I live,
you also will live.[k] 20 On that day you will realize
that I am in my Father,[l] and you are in me, and I
am in you. 21 Whoever has my commands and
obeys them, he is the one who loves me.[m] He who
loves me will be loved by my Father,[n] and I too
will love him and show myself to him."
22 Then Judas[o] (not Judas Iscariot) said, "But,
Lord, why do you intend to show yourself to us
and not to the world?"[p]
23 Jesus replied, "If anyone loves me, he will
obey my teaching.[q] My Father will love him, and
we will come to him and make our home with
him.[r] 24 He who does not love me will not obey my
teaching. These words you hear are not my own;
they belong to the Father who sent me.[s]
25 "All this I have spoken while still with you.
26 But the Counselor,[t] the Holy Spirit, whom the
Father will send in my name,[u] will teach you all
things[v] and will remind you of everything I have

14:5 [t]Jn 11:16
14:6 [u]Jn 10:9 [v]Jn 11:25
14:7 [w]Jn 8:19
14:9 [x]Jn 12:45; Col 1:15; Heb 1:3
14:10 [y]Jn 10:38 [z]Jn 5:19
14:11 [a]Jn 5:36; 10:38
14:12 [b]Mt 21:21 [c]Lk 10:17
14:13 [d]Mt 7:7
14:15 [e]ver 21,23; Jn 15:10; 1Jn 5:3
14:16 [f]Jn 15:26; 16:7
14:17 [g]Jn 15:26; 16:13; 1Jn 4:6 [h]1Co 2:14
14:18 [i]ver 3,28
14:19 [j]Jn 7:33,34; 16:16 [k]Jn 6:57
14:20 [l]Jn 10:38
14:21 [m]1Jn 5:3 [n]1Jn 2:5
14:22 [o]Lk 6:16; Ac 1:13 [p]Ac 10:41
14:23 [q]ver 15 [r]1Jn 2:24; Rev 3:20
14:24 [s]Jn 7:16
14:26 [t]Jn 15:26; 16:7 [u]Ac 2:33 [v]Jn 16:13; 1Jn 2:20,27

[a] *7* Some early manuscripts *If you really have known me, you will know* [b] *17* Some early manuscripts *and is*

Week 37

Jesus: Your Comfort

Does God ever seem too far away, too fearsome, too holy? How can this kind of God be a comfort to you? You know in your mind that God can be trusted, yet your heart resists. Jesus knows your fears and doubts. He came to this earth to show you the Father (Jn 14:9-10; Heb 1:3). He came so you could know him and know the Father's heart—a heart of love, gentleness and compassion (Ps 103:8). When you know Jesus, you also know the Father (Jn 14:7).

Jesus knows the disciples are going to face distressing times (Jn 16:33), so he has a message for them—and for you. *What should you do when faced with troubling circumstances (Jn 14:1)?*

When you trust in something or in someone, you have total confidence in that thing or person. *What are some things you should not trust (Ps 44:6; 49:12-13; Mic 7:5)? What does God say about trusting your education, knowledge or understanding (Pr 3:5)?* Remember that trust is built through having a relationship, not simply through intellectual belief.

Trust is tested and proven by uncertainty. Jesus knows troubles will come, but he says you have a choice. You can choose not to allow your circumstances to trouble your heart because you trust him (Pr 29:25; Hab 3:17-19).

What will come to you when you trust God (Ro 15:13)? What will God do for you if you trust him (Jer 39:18; Na 1:7)?

A person's natural inclination is to want to know what's ahead. Trusting God does not mean he will tell you what's going to happen. It means you know you are safe with him—no matter what happens. You can take on the adventures God has planned because you know he is there to protect you. You can meet your troubles head-on because you know God will provide for you. Trust allows you to accept and appreciate all the surprises of life.

Enjoying God THROUGH the Word

Read 2 Corinthians 1:3-7 (page 1900). In these verses God is called "the Father of compassion and the God of all comfort, who comforts [you] in all [your] troubles" (2Co 1:3-4). As God cares for Israel, his chosen people, he cares for you, his chosen child.

God's comfort has a definite purpose. He comforts you so that you "can comfort those in any trouble with the comfort [you yourself] have received from God" (2Co 1:4). God's comfort to you will be so great that it will overflow to others. Others will be comforted in their sufferings by your example and by your words of empathy and encouragement.

Are you walking a difficult path right now? God is longing to comfort you. He has a plan for you that includes building you up so that you may help others in their times of need.

Enjoying God THROUGH Experience

Find a quiet place where you will not be interrupted and speak with Jesus. Allow this to be a time of slow, thoughtful meditation. You may want to picture taking the pain in your heart and actually handing it to Jesus. His arms are always open, ready to take your pain and offer you comfort.

Go to page 1805 for your next weekly study.

said to you.[w] 27 Peace I leave with you; my peace I
give you.[x] I do not give to you as the world gives.
Do not let your hearts be troubled and do not be
afraid.
28 “You heard me say, ‘I am going away and I am
coming back to you.’[y] If you loved me, you would
be glad that I am going to the Father,[z] for the
Father is greater than I.[a] 29 I have told you now
before it happens, so that when it does happen
you will believe.[b] 30 I will not speak with you
much longer, for the prince of this world[c] is coming. He has no hold on me, 31 but the world must
learn that I love the Father and that I do exactly
what my Father has commanded me.[d]
“Come now; let us leave.

The Vine and the Branches

15 “I am the true vine,[e] and my Father is the
gardener. 2 He cuts off every branch in me
that bears no fruit, while every branch that does
bear fruit he prunes[a] so that it will be even more
fruitful. 3 You are already clean because of the
word I have spoken to you.[f] 4 Remain in me, and I
will remain in you.[g] No branch can bear fruit by
itself; it must remain in the vine. Neither can you
bear fruit unless you remain in me.
5 “I am the vine; you are the branches. If a man
remains in me and I in him, he will bear much
fruit;[h] apart from me you can do nothing. 6 If anyone does not remain in me, he is like a branch
that is thrown away and withers; such branches
are picked up, thrown into the fire and burned.[i] 7 If
you remain in me and my words remain in you,
ask whatever you wish, and it will be given you.[j]
8 This is to my Father’s glory,[k] that you bear much
fruit, showing yourselves to be my disciples.[l]
9 “As the Father has loved me,[m] so have I loved
you. Now remain in my love. 10 If you obey my
commands,[n] you will remain in my love, just as I
have obeyed my Father’s commands and remain
in his love. 11 I have told you this so that my joy
may be in you and that your joy may be complete.[o]
12 My command is this: Love each other as I have
loved you.[p] 13 Greater love has no one than this,
that he lay down his life for his friends.[q] 14 You are
my friends[r] if you do what I command.[s] 15 I no
longer call you servants, because a servant does
not know his master’s business. Instead, I have
called you friends, for everything that I learned
from my Father I have made known to you.[t] 16 You
did not choose me, but I chose you and appointed
you[u] to go and bear fruit—fruit that will last. Then
the Father will give you whatever you ask in my
name. 17 This is my command: Love each other.[v]

The World Hates the Disciples

18 “If the world hates you,[w] keep in mind that it
hated me first. 19 If you belonged to the world, it
would love you as its own. As it is, you do not

14:26 [w]Jn 2:22
14:27 [x]Jn 16:33; Php 4:7; Col 3:15
14:28 [y]ver 2-4,18 [z]Jn 5:18 [a]Jn 10:29; Php 2:6
14:29 [b]Jn 13:19; 16:4
14:30 [c]Jn 12:31
14:31 [d]Jn 10:18; 12:49
15:1 [e]Isa 5:1-7
15:3 [f]Jn 13:10; 17:17; Eph 5:26
15:4 [g]Jn 6:56; 1Jn 2:6
15:5 [h]ver 16
15:6 [i]ver 2
15:7 [j]Mt 7:7
15:8 [k]Mt 5:16 [l]Jn 8:31
15:9 [m]Jn 17:23, 24,26
15:10 [n]Jn 14:15
15:11 [o]Jn 17:13
15:12 [p]Jn 13:34
15:13 [q]Jn 10:11; Ro 5:7,8
15:14 [r]Lk 12:4 [s]Mt 12:50
15:15 [t]Jn 8:26
15:16 [u]Jn 6:70; 13:18
15:17 [v]ver 12
15:18 [w]1Jn 3:13

[a] *2* The Greek for *prunes* also means *cleans.*

I struggle with not knowing where I am going . . . I know my ultimate destination; I know that when my life is over on this earth I will be with Christ forever. But until then . . . where is God leading me?

The disciples had similar questions. Thomas asked Jesus, “Lord, we don’t know where you are going, so how can we know the way?” [Jn 14:5] . . . Christ answered Thomas and he answers us: “You ask for the way, I AM THE WAY.”

It would be so much easier if we were given a road map. It would make so much of the journey more bearable if we could see that the path that is painful for a time is leading somewhere and that it will get better. We don’t have that. No believer who has gone before us has had that. There is no map; Christ is the Way . . . Sometimes we feel so torn in two. Our human flesh cries out for comfort and direction, for some control, and yet we are called to live above that . . . Surely, it is on the path with Christ that we will find rest. And when we are there, we will no longer wonder about God’s will for our lives—we are living it.

—Sheila Walsh

belong to the world, but I have chosen you[x] out of
the world. That is why the world hates you.[y]
20 Remember the words I spoke to you: 'No servant
is greater than his master.'[a][z] If they persecuted me,
they will persecute you also.[a] If they obeyed my
teaching, they will obey yours also. 21 They will
treat you this way because of my name,[b] for they
do not know the One who sent me.[c] 22 If I had not
come and spoken to them, they would not be
guilty of sin. Now, however, they have no excuse
for their sin.[d] 23 He who hates me hates my Father
as well. 24 If I had not done among them what no
one else did,[e] they would not be guilty of sin. But
now they have seen these miracles, and yet they
have hated both me and my Father. 25 But this is
to fulfill what is written in their Law: 'They hated
me without reason.'[b][f]

26 "When the Counselor[g] comes, whom I will
send to you from the Father,[h] the Spirit of truth[i]
who goes out from the Father, he will testify about
me.[j] 27 And you also must testify,[k] for you have
been with me from the beginning.[l]

16 "All this[m] I have told you so that you will
not go astray.[n] 2 They will put you out of the
synagogue;[o] in fact, a time is coming when anyone who kills you will think he is offering a service to God.[p] 3 They will do such things because
they have not known the Father or me.[q] 4 I have
told you this, so that when the time comes you
will remember[r] that I warned you. I did not tell
you this at first because I was with you.

The Work of the Holy Spirit

5 "Now I am going to him who sent me,[s] yet
none of you asks me, 'Where are you going?'[t]
6 Because I have said these things, you are filled
with grief. 7 But I tell you the truth: It is for your
good that I am going away. Unless I go away, the
Counselor[u] will not come to you; but if I go, I will
send him to you.[v] 8 When he comes, he will convict the world of guilt[c] in regard to sin and righteousness and judgment: 9 in regard to sin,[w]
because men do not believe in me; 10 in regard to
righteousness,[x] because I am going to the Father,
where you can see me no longer; 11 and in regard
to judgment, because the prince of this world[y]
now stands condemned.

12 "I have much more to say to you, more than
you can now bear.[z] 13 But when he, the Spirit of
truth,[a] comes, he will guide you into all truth.[b] He
will not speak on his own; he will speak only
what he hears, and he will tell you what is yet to
come. 14 He will bring glory to me by taking from
what is mine and making it known to you. 15 All
that belongs to the Father is mine.[c] That is why I
said the Spirit will take from what is mine and
make it known to you.

15:19 [x]ver 16 [y]Jn 17:14
15:20 [z]Jn 13:16 [a]2Ti 3:12
15:21 [b]Mt 10:22 [c]Jn 16:3
15:22 [d]Jn 9:41; Ro 1:20
15:24 [e]Jn 5:36
15:25 [f]Ps 35:19; 69:4
15:26 [g]Jn 14:16 [h]Jn 14:26 [i]Jn 14:17 [j]1Jn 5:7
15:27 [k]Lk 24:48; 1Jn 1:2; 4:14 [l]Lk 1:2
16:1 [m]Jn 15:18-27 [n]Mt 11:6
16:2 [o]Jn 9:22 [p]Isa 66:5; Ac 26:9,10; Rev 6:9
16:3 [q]Jn 15:21; 17:25; 1Jn 3:1
16:4 [r]Jn 13:19
16:5 [s]Jn 7:33 [t]Jn 13:36; 14:5
16:7 [u]Jn 14:16, 26; 15:26 [v]Jn 7:39
16:9 [w]Jn 15:22
16:10 [x]Ac 3:14; 7:52; 1Pe 3:18
16:11 [y]Jn 12:31
16:12 [z]Mk 4:33
16:13 [a]Jn 14:17 [b]Jn 14:26
16:15 [c]Jn 17:10

[a] *20* John 13:16 [b] *25* Psalms 35:19; 69:4 [c] *8* Or *will expose the guilt of the world*

The Hate of the World

JN 15:19

It isn't easy to be a Christian in this world. At times, our popularity will suffer because of our faith. At times people will misunderstand us. Some may even dislike us. Still others may go out of their way to oppress us or cause us suffering.

In such situations, it is tempting to blame ourselves for some imagined failure or to assume that our circumstances are out of the ordinary. Jesus, however, makes no bones about the destiny of believers. He states clearly that persecution will come to his followers because the world is hostile to those who follow him (Mt 5:11; Jn 15:21).

Persecution is never comfortable. But it may help to remember that the focus of the battle is not on us, but on Christ. Jesus doesn't call us to be liked by everyone. He simply calls us to be faithful. And he reminds us that, when persecution descends, it's simply evidence of the fact we belong to him (Jn 15:18–20).

Like a Woman in Labor

JN 16:19–24

In comparing the disciples' grief to a mother's labor pains, Jesus paints an emotional word picture perfectly suited to touch a woman's heart. Those who have borne a child remember the agony experienced during the hours leading up to the baby's birth; the pain was intense, but the joy felt at the little one's arrival was far greater. Or we may recall hearing our mothers, or a dear friend, talk about the rewards of childbirth: "I was in labor for 39 hours . . . but when I saw my perfect, healthy baby, I knew it was worth every minute."

In the same way, the gift the disciples will ultimately receive is "worth" every moment of their suffering. For though the pain of separation is immediate, a joyous future with Christ is ensured through his sacrifice, resurrection and ascension into heaven, where he goes to prepare a place for them (Jn 14:2–3) . . . and for all those who commit their lives to him.

16 "In a little while[d] you will see me no more,
and then after a little while you will see me."[e]

The Disciples' Grief Will Turn to Joy

17 Some of his disciples said to one another,
"What does he mean by saying, 'In a little while
you will see me no more, and then after a little
while you will see me,'[f] and 'Because I am going
to the Father'?"[g] 18 They kept asking, "What does
he mean by 'a little while'? We don't understand
what he is saying."
19 Jesus saw that they wanted to ask him about
this, so he said to them, "Are you asking one
another what I meant when I said, 'In a little while
you will see me no more, and then after a little
while you will see me'? 20 I tell you the truth, you
will weep and mourn[h] while the world rejoices.
You will grieve, but your grief will turn to joy.[i] 21 A
woman giving birth to a child has pain[j] because
her time has come; but when her baby is born she
forgets the anguish because of her joy that a child
is born into the world. 22 So with you: Now is your
time of grief,[k] but I will see you again[l] and you
will rejoice, and no one will take away your joy.
23 In that day you will no longer ask me anything.
I tell you the truth, my Father will give you whatever you ask in my name.[m] 24 Until now you have
not asked for anything in my name. Ask and you
will receive, and your joy will be complete.[n]
25 "Though I have been speaking figuratively,[o] a
time is coming[p] when I will no longer use this
kind of language but will tell you plainly about
my Father. 26 In that day you will ask in my name.[q]
I am not saying that I will ask the Father on your
behalf. 27 No, the Father himself loves you because
you have loved me[r] and have believed that I came
from God. 28 I came from the Father and entered
the world; now I am leaving the world and going
back to the Father."[s]
29 Then Jesus' disciples said, "Now you are
speaking clearly and without figures of speech.[t]
30 Now we can see that you know all things and
that you do not even need to have anyone ask you
questions. This makes us believe that you came
from God."
31 "You believe at last!"[a] Jesus answered. 32 "But
a time is coming,[u] and has come, when you will
be scattered,[v] each to his own home. You will
leave me all alone. Yet I am not alone, for my
Father is with me.[w]
33 "I have told you these things, so that in me you
may have peace.[x] In this world you will have trouble.[y] But take heart! I have overcome[z] the world."

Jesus Prays for Himself

17 After Jesus said this, he looked toward
heaven[a] and prayed:

"Father, the time has come. Glorify your

16:16 [d]Jn 7:33 [e]Jn 14:18-24
16:17 [f]ver 16 [g]ver 5
16:20 [h]Lk 23:27 [i]Jn 20:20
16:21 [j]Isa 26:17; 1Th 5:3
16:22 [k]ver 6 [l]ver 16
16:23 [m]Mt 7:7; Jn 15:16
16:24 [n]Jn 3:29; 15:11
16:25 [o]Mt 13:34; Jn 10:6 [p]ver 2
16:26 [q]ver 23,24
16:27 [r]Jn 14:21,23
16:28 [s]Jn 13:3
16:29 [t]ver 25
16:32 [u]ver 2,25 [v]Mt 26:31 [w]Jn 8:16,29
16:33 [x]Jn 14:27 [y]Jn 15:18-21 [z]Ro 8:37; 1Jn 4:4
17:1 [a]Jn 11:41

[a] *31* Or *"Do you now believe?"*

Son, that your Son may glorify you.[b] 2For you granted him authority over all people that he might give eternal life to all those you have given him.[c] 3Now this is eternal life: that they may know you, the only true God, and Jesus Christ, whom you have sent.[d] 4I have brought you glory[e] on earth by completing the work you gave me to do.[f] 5And now, Father, glorify me in your presence with the glory I had with you[g] before the world began.[h]

Jesus Prays for His Disciples

6"I have revealed you[a][i] to those whom you gave me[j] out of the world. They were yours; you gave them to me and they have obeyed your word. 7Now they know that everything you have given me comes from you. 8For I gave them the words you gave me[k] and they accepted them. They knew with certainty that I came from you,[l] and they believed that you sent me.[m] 9I pray for them.[n] I am not praying for the world, but for those you have given me, for they are yours. 10All I have is yours, and all you have is mine.[o] And glory has come to me through them. 11I will remain in the world no longer, but they are still in the world,[p] and I am coming to you.[q] Holy Father, protect them by the power of your name—the name you gave me—so that they may be one[r] as we are one.[s] 12While I was with them, I protected them and kept them safe by that name you gave me. None has been lost[t] except the one doomed to destruction[u] so that Scripture would be fulfilled.

13"I am coming to you now, but I say these things while I am still in the world, so that they may have the full measure of my joy[v] within them. 14I have given them your word and the world has hated them,[w] for they are not of the world any more than I am of the world.[x] 15My prayer is not that you take them out of the world but that you protect them from the evil one.[y] 16They are not of the world, even as I am not of it.[z] 17Sanctify[b] them by the truth; your word is truth.[a] 18As you sent me into the world,[b] I have sent them into the world.[c] 19For them I sanctify myself, that they too may be truly sanctified.

Jesus Prays for All Believers

20"My prayer is not for them alone. I pray also for those who will believe in me through their message, 21that all of them may be one, Father, just as you are in me and I am in you.[d] May they also be in us so that the world may believe that you have sent me.[e] 22I have given them the glory that you gave me, that they may be one as we are one:[f] 23I in them

17:1 [b]Jn 12:23; 13:31,32
17:2 [c]ver 6,9,24; Da 7:14; Jn 6:37,39
17:3 [d]ver 8,18,21, 23,25; Jn 3:17
17:4 [e]Jn 13:31 [f]Jn 4:34
17:5 [g]Php 2:6 [h]Jn 1:2
17:6 [i]ver 26 [j]ver 2; Jn 6:37,39
17:8 [k]ver 14,26 [l]Jn 16:27 [m]ver 3,18, 21,23,25; Jn 3:17
17:9 [n]Lk 22:32
17:10 [o]Jn 16:15
17:11 [p]Jn 13:1 [q]Jn 7:33 [r]ver 21-23 [s]Jn 10:30
17:12 [t]Jn 6:39 [u]Jn 6:70
17:13 [v]Jn 3:29
17:14 [w]Jn 15:19 [x]Jn 8:23
17:15 [y]Mt 5:37
17:16 [z]ver 14
17:17 [a]Jn 15:3
17:18 [b]ver 3,8,21, 23,25 [c]Jn 20:21
17:21 [d]Jn 10:38 [e]ver 3,8,18, 23,25; Jn 3:17
17:22 [f]Jn 14:20

[a] 6 Greek *your name*; also in verse 26 [b] 17 Greek *hagiazo* *(set apart for sacred use* or *make holy)*; also in verse 19

Jesus Intercedes for Us

JN 17:20-23

With just hours left to live, Jesus takes the time to pray for his disciples and all those who will believe in him (Jn 17:9, 20). How telling it is that at this crucial moment, Jesus embraces his role as intercessor. Perhaps billions of people throughout history have prayed on behalf of others. In fact, Old Testament priests were engaged in intercession full time. But Scripture testifies that Christ is the greatest intercessor of all.

Jesus' intercession takes many forms. Throughout his ministry, he prayed for his followers (Lk 22:32); in giving his life on the cross, he performed the ultimate act of intercession (Lk 23:34); and today he reigns at the Father's right hand, where he continues to intercede on our behalf (Ro 8:34).

We, too, are called to be intercessors (1Ti 2:1). Do you know someone who needs prayer today? Write down one name in the margin of your Bible, and pray for that person for seven days. Then meditate on how that person's life —and yours—has been impacted.

and you in me. May they be brought to complete unity to let the world know that you sent me[g] and have loved them[h] even as you have loved me.

24 "Father, I want those you have given me to be with me where I am,[i] and to see my glory,[j] the glory you have given me because you loved me before the creation of the world.[k]

25 "Righteous Father, though the world does not know you,[l] I know you, and they know that you have sent me.[m] 26 I have made you known to them,[n] and will continue to make you known in order that the love you have for me may be in them[o] and that I myself may be in them."

Jesus Arrested

18 When he had finished praying, Jesus left with his disciples and crossed the Kidron Valley.[p] On the other side there was an olive grove,[q] and he and his disciples went into it.[r]

2 Now Judas, who betrayed him, knew the place, because Jesus had often met there with his disciples.[s] 3 So Judas came to the grove, guiding[t] a detachment of soldiers and some officials from the chief priests and Pharisees.[u] They were carrying torches, lanterns and weapons.

4 Jesus, knowing all that was going to happen to him,[v] went out and asked them, "Who is it you want?"[w]

5 "Jesus of Nazareth," they replied.

"I am he," Jesus said. (And Judas the traitor was standing there with them.) 6 When Jesus said, "I am he," they drew back and fell to the ground.

7 Again he asked them, "Who is it you want?"[x]

And they said, "Jesus of Nazareth."

8 "I told you that I am he," Jesus answered. "If you are looking for me, then let these men go." 9 This happened so that the words he had spoken would be fulfilled: "I have not lost one of those you gave me."[a][y]

10 Then Simon Peter, who had a sword, drew it and struck the high priest's servant, cutting off his right ear. (The servant's name was Malchus.)

11 Jesus commanded Peter, "Put your sword away! Shall I not drink the cup[z] the Father has given me?"

Jesus Taken to Annas

12 Then the detachment of soldiers with its commander and the Jewish officials[a] arrested Jesus. They bound him 13 and brought him first to Annas, who was the father-in-law of Caiaphas,[b] the high priest that year. 14 Caiaphas was the one who had advised the Jews that it would be good if one man died for the people.[c]

Peter's First Denial

15 Simon Peter and another disciple were fol-

[a] *9* John 6:39

17:23 [g]Jn 3:17 [h]Jn 16:27
17:24 [i]Jn 12:26 [j]Jn 1:14 [k]ver 5; Mt 25:34
17:25 [l]Jn 15:21; 16:3 [m]ver 3,8,18, 21,23; Jn 3:17; 7:29; 16:27
17:26 [n]ver 6 [o]Jn 15:9
18:1 [p]2Sa 15:23 [q]ver 26 [r]Mt 26:36
18:2 [s]Lk 21:37; 22:39
18:3 [t]Ac 1:16 [u]ver 12
18:4 [v]Jn 6:64; 13:1,11 [w]ver 7
18:7 [x]ver 4
18:9 [y]Jn 17:12
18:11 [z]Mt 20:22
18:12 [a]ver 3
18:13 [b]ver 24; Mt 26:3
18:14 [c]Jn 11:49-51

Jesus knows what it's like to suffer; he suffered on our behalf! And he also knows what it's like, late at night, to feel such heartache you think you'll die. On the night before he was crucified, he led his disciples to Gethsemane and told them, "My soul is overwhelmed with sorrow to the point of death" [Mk 14:34]. And certainly he knows what it's like to feel all alone, because those same disciples—his closest friends and followers—suddenly disappeared when the bad times started.

Jesus knows how you feel—hurt, scared, alone—and he's always with you to wrap you in his comfort blanket of love.

—Barbara Johnson

Herodias

Getting Even

Sin makes us foolish; it damages our brains. Herodias was convinced if she could just silence John, people would stop criticizing her for her blatant disregard for God's law. She was wrong.

Herodias and Herod Antipas were two of a kind: They were wicked. Their infamous marriage probably began with an elopement. That sounds romantic. The only problem was that they were both already married to other people. Evil attracts evil. Perhaps that was why they wanted each other so much. No one dared speak out against their sin and lewd desires—except John the Baptist. He publicly condemned their illicit union.

Herod was willing to put John in jail, but even he had enough sense to know he was dealing with a holy man. He thought it was wise to stop there; the people might revolt. Herodias would have none of it; John was a threat. He could ruin their lives! She had risked everything to marry Herod, and no so-called prophet was going to rob her now. She knew there must be some way to convince Herod to do what must be done. She could wait. In time, she would be rid of John. Then no one could stop her from doing what *she* wanted to do!

She saw her chance. She was not blind to Herod's lustful interest in her daughter Salome. Evil desire unleashed has great power. So she devised a plan. When Herod was drunk, she would use Salome to put on the pressure. Yes, that would work. Salome danced with abandon, and her young body proved irresistible. Before witnesses Herod made promises to Salome that Herodias could use to get what she wanted—John the Baptist out of the way.

Herodias got what she thought she wanted: the head of John the Baptist on a platter, his mouth silenced forever. But the talk didn't stop. Neither did the wheels of justice. Herod's conscience so plagued him that he thought Jesus was the reincarnation of John (Mk 6:16). Though Herod sanctioned Jesus' crucifixion, he also heard the stories of his resurrection. Herodias could not stifle truth. In the end, their downfall came and Herodias and Herod—along with their sin—were banished to an obscure Roman outpost for the rest of their lives. Even so, they got better than they deserved.

Persisting in sin is utterly foolish, even stupid. Resisting God's correction is futile. We shouldn't fool ourselves into thinking otherwise.

Herodias
(the female form of Herod)

Matthew 14:3-12

Mark 6:14-28

Luke 3:19-20

Candid SNAPSHOT For Herod himself had given orders to have John arrested, and he had him bound and put in prison. He did this because of Herodias, his brother Philip's wife, whom he had married. For John had been saying to Herod, "It is not lawful for you to have your brother's wife" (Mk 6:17-18).

Salome, Daughter of Herodias

Her Mother's Daughter

We learn the name of Herodias's daughter from the ancient historian Josephus. Salome, though born a child of privilege to the ruling family of Herod, was the unfortunate victim of a broken home. She lived with her mother, whose sin was infamous. Did Salome's cheeks burn with shame when people talked? Or did she close her ears and pretend she didn't hear? There was no way to avoid it. Salome had to work it out, one way or another.

Her mother was hard to please. Herodias was not interested either in children or in mothering. Her focus was satisfying her *own* desires. Salome was desperate to be needed and wanted, as is any child. When Herodias suggested that Salome dance for her stepfather on his birthday, the girl agreed. Finally, she would get some attention. This was her chance to show her mother what she could do, and she knew the way to please Herod—she had watched her mother. So Salome pulled out all the stops.

Most mothers would have been shocked and grieved to see a daughter so sexually precocious. Probably not Herodias. It got her what she wanted. That seems to have been her only moral standard. Instead of hurrying to Salome's side to protect and mentor her, Herodias used her daughter to force Herod's hand and murder a prophet of God.

Children are vulnerable to the enemy. They need parental love and nurturing to choose wisely and to stay on the right path. Children will usually follow what they learn at home. Given good examples and encouragement, most can successfully weather life's disappointments, pain and temptations. Without the positive influence of parents, most perish, giving way to their flesh, the world and the devil. It is a sobering thought and a matter for prayer.

Salome
(the female form of Solomon)

Matthew 14:6-11

Mark 6:22-28

Candid SNAPSHOT On Herod's birthday the daughter of Herodias danced for them and pleased Herod so much that he promised with an oath to give her whatever she asked. Prompted by her mother, she said, "Give me here on a platter the head of John the Baptist" (Matthew 14:6-8).

lowing Jesus. Because this disciple was known to
18:15 [d]Mt 26:3 the high priest,[d] he went with Jesus into the high
[e]Mt 26:58; priest's courtyard,[e] 16but Peter had to wait outside
Mk 14:54; at the door. The other disciple, who was known
Lk 22:54 to the high priest, came back, spoke to the girl on
duty there and brought Peter in.
17"You are not one of his disciples, are you?" the
girl at the door asked Peter.
18:17 He replied, "I am not."[f]
[f]ver 25 18It was cold, and the servants and officials
18:18 stood around a fire[g] they had made to keep warm.
[g]Jn 21:9 [h]Mk 14:54, Peter also was standing with them, warming
67 himself.[h]

The High Priest Questions Jesus

19Meanwhile, the high priest questioned Jesus
about his disciples and his teaching.
20"I have spoken openly to the world," Jesus
18:20 [i]Mt 4:23 replied. "I always taught in synagogues[i] or at the
[j]Mt 26:55 temple,[j] where all the Jews come together. I said
[k]Jn 7:26 nothing in secret.[k] 21Why question me? Ask those
18:22 who heard me. Surely they know what I said."
[l]ver 3 22When Jesus said this, one of the officials[l]
[m]Mt 16:21; nearby struck him in the face.[m] "Is this the way
Jn 19:3 you answer the high priest?" he demanded.
23"If I said something wrong," Jesus replied,
18:23 "testify as to what is wrong. But if I spoke the
[n]Mt 5:39; truth, why did you strike me?"[n] 24Then Annas
Ac 23:2-5 sent him, still bound, to Caiaphas[o] the high
18:24 priest.[a]
[o]ver 13; Mt 26:3

Peter's Second and Third Denials

18:25 25As Simon Peter stood warming himself,[p] he
[p]ver 18 was asked, "You are not one of his disciples, are
[q]ver 17 you?"
He denied it, saying, "I am not."[q]
26One of the high priest's servants, a relative of
18:26 [r]ver 10 the man whose ear Peter had cut off,[r] challenged
[s]ver 1 him, "Didn't I see you with him in the olive
18:27 grove?"[s] 27Again Peter denied it, and at that
[t]Jn 13:38 moment a rooster began to crow.[t]

Jesus Before Pilate

28Then the Jews led Jesus from Caiaphas to the
18:28 [u]Mt 27:2; palace of the Roman governor.[u] By now it was ear-
Mk 15:1; ly morning, and to avoid ceremonial uncleanness
Lk 23:1 the Jews did not enter the palace;[v] they wanted to
[v]ver 33; Jn 19:9 be able to eat the Passover.[w] 29So Pilate came out
[w]Jn 11:55 to them and asked, "What charges are you bringing against this man?"
30"If he were not a criminal," they replied, "we
would not have handed him over to you."
31Pilate said, "Take him yourselves and judge
him by your own law."
"But we have no right to execute anyone," the
18:32 [x]Mt 20:19; Jews objected. 32This happened so that the words
26:2; Jesus had spoken indicating the kind of death he
Jn 3:14; was going to die[x] would be fulfilled.
8:28; 12:32, 33

[a] 24 Or *(Now Annas had sent him, still bound, to Caiaphas the high priest.)*

Elizabeth Cecelia Douglas Clephane lived only 38 short years. All of her hymns, including this favorite of the church, were published after her death.

Beneath the Cross of Jesus

Beneath the cross of Jesus I fain
would take my stand,
The shadow of a mighty rock within
a weary land;
A home within the wilderness,
a rest upon the way,
From the burning of the noontide
heat, and the burden of the day.

Upon that cross of Jesus mine eye at
times can see
The very dying form of One Who
suffered there for me;
And from my stricken heart with
tears two wonders I confess;
The wonders of redeeming love and
my unworthiness.

I take, O cross, thy shadow for my
abiding place;
I ask no other sunshine than the
sunshine of His face;
Content to let the world go by
to know no gain or loss,
My sinful self my only shame,
my glory all the cross.

—Elizabeth Cecelia Douglas Clephane (1830-1869)

Jesus and Pilate

JN 18:33-40

The question Pilate poses to Jesus is a critical one: "Are you the king of the Jews?" (Jn 18:33). If Jesus answers, "Yes," then Pilate has a real problem on his hands. Such a claim might point to a bid for political power, and it is Pilate's responsibility to squelch uprisings against the Roman government.

Jesus answers vaguely, however, turning the question back on Pilate (Jn 18:34). When he finally does accept the title (Jn 18:37), Jesus is careful to point out that his is not a worldly kingdom (Jn 18:36). Though Jesus does not deny that he is the Messiah, Pilate seems to sense he is a man without political aspirations. With no evidence that he is a threat to the government, Pilate is prepared to release him (Jn 18:38-39). He knows in his heart what is right, yet he eventually caves in to outside pressures (Jn 19:8-16).

33Pilate then went back inside the palace,[y] summoned Jesus and asked him, "Are you the king of
the Jews?"[z]
34"Is that your own idea," Jesus asked, "or did
others talk to you about me?"
35"Am I a Jew?" Pilate replied. "It was your people and your chief priests who handed you over
to me. What is it you have done?"
36Jesus said, "My kingdom[a] is not of this world.
If it were, my servants would fight to prevent my
arrest by the Jews.[b] But now my kingdom is from
another place."[c]
37"You are a king, then!" said Pilate.
Jesus answered, "You are right in saying I am a
king. In fact, for this reason I was born, and for
this I came into the world, to testify to the truth.[d]
Everyone on the side of truth listens to me."[e]
38"What is truth?" Pilate asked. With this he
went out again to the Jews and said, "I find no
basis for a charge against him.[f] 39But it is your
custom for me to release to you one prisoner at
the time of the Passover. Do you want me to
release 'the king of the Jews'?"
40They shouted back, "No, not him! Give us
Barabbas!" Now Barabbas had taken part in a
rebellion.[g]

Jesus Sentenced to Be Crucified

19 Then Pilate took Jesus and had him
flogged.[h] 2The soldiers twisted together a
crown of thorns and put it on his head. They
clothed him in a purple robe 3and went up to him
again and again, saying, "Hail, king of the Jews!"[i]
And they struck him in the face.[j]
4Once more Pilate came out and said to the
Jews, "Look, I am bringing him out[k] to you to let
you know that I find no basis for a charge against
him."[l] 5When Jesus came out wearing the crown
of thorns and the purple robe,[m] Pilate said to
them, "Here is the man!"
6As soon as the chief priests and their officials
saw him, they shouted, "Crucify! Crucify!"
But Pilate answered, "You take him and crucify
him.[n] As for me, I find no basis for a charge
against him."[o]
7The Jews insisted, "We have a law, and according to that law he must die,[p] because he claimed
to be the Son of God."[q]
8When Pilate heard this, he was even more
afraid, 9and he went back inside the palace.[r]
"Where do you come from?" he asked Jesus, but
Jesus gave him no answer.[s] 10"Do you refuse to
speak to me?" Pilate said. "Don't you realize I
have power either to free you or to crucify you?"
11Jesus answered, "You would have no power
over me if it were not given to you from above.[t]
Therefore the one who handed me over to you[u] is
guilty of a greater sin."
12From then on, Pilate tried to set Jesus free, but
the Jews kept shouting, "If you let this man go,

18:33 [y]ver 28,29; Jn 19:9 [z]Lk 23:3; Mt 2:2
18:36 [a]Mt 3:2 [b]Mt 26:53 [c]Lk 17:21; Jn 6:15
18:37 [d]Jn 3:32 [e]Jn 8:47; 1Jn 4:6
18:38 [f]Lk 23:4; Jn 19:4,6
18:40 [g]Ac 3:14
19:1 [h]Dt 25:3; Isa 50:6; 53:5; Mt 27:26
19:3 [i]Mt 27:29 [j]Jn 18:22
19:4 [k]Jn 18:38 [l]ver 6; Lk 23:4
19:5 [m]ver 2
19:6 [n]Ac 3:13 [o]ver 4; Lk 23:4
19:7 [p]Lev 24:16 [q]Mt 26:63-66; Jn 5:18; 10:33
19:9 [r]Jn 18:33 [s]Mk 14:61
19:11 [t]Ro 13:1 [u]Jn 18:28-30; Ac 3:13

you are no friend of Caesar. Anyone who claims to
19:12 [v]Lk 23:2 be a king[v] opposes Caesar.”
13When Pilate heard this, he brought Jesus out
19:13 [w]Mt 27:19 and sat down on the judge's seat[w] at a place
[x]Jn 5:2 known as the Stone Pavement (which in Aramaic[x]
is Gabbatha). 14It was the day of Preparation[y] of
19:14 [y]Mt 27:62 Passover Week, about the sixth hour.[z]
[z]Mk 15:25 [a]ver 19,21 “Here is your king,”[a] Pilate said to the Jews.
15But they shouted, “Take him away! Take him
away! Crucify him!”
“Shall I crucify your king?” Pilate asked.
“We have no king but Caesar,” the chief priests
answered.
16Finally Pilate handed him over to them to be
19:16 [b]Mt 27:26; Mk 15:15; Lk 23:25 crucified.[b]

The Crucifixion

So the soldiers took charge of Jesus. 17Carrying
19:17 [c]Ge 22:6; his own cross,[c] he went out to the place of the
Lk 14:27; 23:26 Skull[d] (which in Aramaic[e] is called Golgotha).
[d]Lk 23:33 18Here they crucified him, and with him two oth-
[e]Jn 5:2 ers[f]—one on each side and Jesus in the middle.
19Pilate had a notice prepared and fastened to
19:18 [f]Lk 23:32 the cross. It read: JESUS OF NAZARETH,[g] THE KING OF
THE JEWS.[h] 20Many of the Jews read this sign, for
19:19 [g]Mk 1:24 the place where Jesus was crucified was near the
[h]ver 14,21 city,[i] and the sign was written in Aramaic, Latin
and Greek. 21The chief priests of the Jews protest-
19:20 [i]Heb 13:12 ed to Pilate, “Do not write ‘The King of the Jews,’
but that this man claimed to be king of the Jews.”[j]
19:21 [j]ver 14 22Pilate answered, “What I have written, I have
written.”
23When the soldiers crucified Jesus, they took
his clothes, dividing them into four shares, one
for each of them, with the undergarment remaining. This garment was seamless, woven in one
piece from top to bottom.
24“Let's not tear it,” they said to one another.
“Let's decide by lot who will get it.”
19:24 This happened that the scripture might be ful-
[k]ver 28,36, 37; Mt 1:22 [l]Ps 22:18 filled[k] which said,

> “They divided my garments among
> them
> and cast lots for my clothing.”[a][l]

19:25 So this is what the soldiers did.
[m]Mt 27:55, 56; 25Near the cross[m] of Jesus stood his mother,[n] his
Mk 15:40, mother's sister, Mary the wife of Clopas, and Mary
41; Lk 23:49 [n]Mt 12:46 Magdalene.[o] 26When Jesus saw his mother[p] there,
[o]Lk 24:18 and the disciple whom he loved[q] standing nearby, he said to his mother, “Dear woman, here is
19:26 [p]Mt 12:46 your son,” 27and to the disciple, “Here is your
[q]Jn 13:23 mother.” From that time on, this disciple took her
into his home.

19:28 [r]ver 30; Jn 13:1 [s]ver 24,36, 37

The Death of Jesus

28Later, knowing that all was now completed,[r]
and so that the Scripture would be fulfilled,[s] Jesus
19:29 [t]Ps 69:21 said, “I am thirsty.” 29A jar of wine vinegar[t] was

[a] *24* Psalm 22:18

The Women in Jesus' Life

JN 19:25-27

Throughout the Gospels, women are key participants in Jesus' ministry. Many support him financially and follow him as he travels (Lk 8:1-3). A number serve him, providing for his needs and those of the disciples (Lk 10:38). At Christ's crucifixion, we see one of the most poignant examples of the role women play in Jesus' life. While John is apparently the only disciple present, several of the women remain with him to the end. The women love Jesus. They want to be near him, perhaps even to comfort him. Even in his pain, Jesus responds to the tragic sight of his mother's hurt and helplessness. He purposefully entrusts her to John's care.

Take a moment to thank God for making you the woman you are. Tell him that you, too, want to be near him, and ask how you might serve him today (see the character sketch for these women on page 1941).

The Scriptures Fulfilled

JN 19:28,36–37

Repeatedly, John assures his readers that the details of Christ's death occur in order to bring Scripture to complete fulfillment. The Psalmist wrote that the Messiah, in his time of disgrace and shame would be offered wine vinegar to drink (Ps 69:21). The prophet Zechariah foretold the piercing of the Messiah (Zec 12:10), and the prophecy regarding his bones comes from three different sources (Ex 12:46; Nu 9:12; Ps 34:20).

Thus, the beauty of Scripture is fulfilled in every detail, assuring us that Christ is the One of whom the prophets foretold. This fulfillment is encouraging on multiple levels. We can rejoice in the knowledge that the Messiah has *come. We can trust that God will fulfill his promises. We can know also that, in God's eyes, no detail is too small for him to notice.*

Is there some detail of your life that you believe God has overlooked? Some promise of Scripture you are hesitant to claim? Take those things before God now, and ask him to reveal to you his faithfulness.

there, so they soaked a sponge in it, put the sponge on a stalk of the hyssop plant, and lifted it to Jesus' lips. [30]When he had received the drink, Jesus said, "It is finished."[u] With that, he bowed his head and gave up his spirit.

[31]Now it was the day of Preparation,[v] and the next day was to be a special Sabbath. Because the Jews did not want the bodies left on the crosses[w] during the Sabbath, they asked Pilate to have the legs broken and the bodies taken down. [32]The soldiers therefore came and broke the legs of the first man who had been crucified with Jesus, and then those of the other.[x] [33]But when they came to Jesus and found that he was already dead, they did not break his legs. [34]Instead, one of the soldiers pierced[y] Jesus' side with a spear, bringing a sudden flow of blood and water.[z] [35]The man who saw it[a] has given testimony, and his testimony is true.[b] He knows that he tells the truth, and he testifies so that you also may believe. [36]These things happened so that the scripture would be fulfilled:[c] "Not one of his bones will be broken,"[ad] [37]and, as another scripture says, "They will look on the one they have pierced."[be]

The Burial of Jesus

[38]Later, Joseph of Arimathea asked Pilate for the body of Jesus. Now Joseph was a disciple of Jesus, but secretly because he feared the Jews. With Pilate's permission, he came and took the body away. [39]He was accompanied by Nicodemus,[f] the man who earlier had visited Jesus at night. Nicodemus brought a mixture of myrrh and aloes, about seventy-five pounds.[c] [40]Taking Jesus' body, the two of them wrapped it, with the spices, in strips of linen.[g] This was in accordance with Jewish burial customs.[h] [41]At the place where Jesus was crucified, there was a garden, and in the garden a new tomb, in which no one had ever been laid. [42]Because it was the Jewish day of Preparation[i] and since the tomb was nearby,[j] they laid Jesus there.

The Empty Tomb

20 Early on the first day of the week, while it was still dark, Mary Magdalene[k] went to the tomb and saw that the stone had been removed from the entrance.[l] [2]So she came running to Simon Peter and the other disciple, the one Jesus loved,[m] and said, "They have taken the Lord out of the tomb, and we don't know where they have put him!"[n]

[3]So Peter and the other disciple started for the tomb.[o] [4]Both were running, but the other disciple outran Peter and reached the tomb first. [5]He bent over and looked in[p] at the strips of linen[q] lying there but did not go in. [6]Then Simon Peter, who was behind him, arrived and went into the tomb.

19:30 [u]Lk 12:50; Jn 17:4
19:31 [v]ver 14,42 [w]Dt 21:23; Jos 8:29; 10:26,27
19:32 [x]ver 18
19:34 [y]Zec 12:10 [z]1Jn 5:6,8
19:35 [a]Lk 24:48 [b]Jn 15:27; 21:24
19:36 [c]ver 24,28, 37; Mt 1:22 [d]Ex 12:46; Nu 9:12; Ps 34:20
19:37 [e]Zec 12:10; Rev 1:7
19:39 [f]Jn 3:1; 7:50
19:40 [g]Lk 24:12; Jn 11:44; 20:5,7 [h]Mt 26:12
19:42 [i]ver 14,31 [j]ver 20,41
20:1 [k]ver 18; Jn 19:25 [l]Mt 27:60,66
20:2 [m]Jn 13:23 [n]ver 13
20:3 [o]Lk 24:12
20:5 [p]ver 11 [q]Jn 19:40

[a] *36* Exodus 12:46; Num. 9:12; Psalm 34:20 [b] *37* Zech. 12:10 [c] *39* Greek *a hundred litrai* (about 34 kilograms)

20:7 He saw the strips of linen lying there, 7 as well as
rJn 11:44 the burial cloth that had been around Jesus' head.[r]
The cloth was folded up by itself, separate from
20:8 the linen. 8 Finally the other disciple, who had
sver 4 reached the tomb first,[s] also went inside. He saw
20:9 and believed. 9 (They still did not understand from
tMt 22:29; Jn 2:22 Scripture[t] that Jesus had to rise from the dead.)[u]

uLk 24:26,46 *Jesus Appears to Mary Magdalene*

10 Then the disciples went back to their homes,
20:11 11 but Mary stood outside the tomb crying. As she
vver 5 wept, she bent over to look into the tomb[v] 12 and
20:12 saw two angels in white,[w] seated where Jesus'
wMt 28:2,3; body had been, one at the head and the other at
Mk 16:5; Lk 24:4; the foot.
Ac 5:19 13 They asked her, "Woman, why are you
crying?"[x]
20:13 xver 15 "They have taken my Lord away," she said,
yver 2 "and I don't know where they have put him."[y]
20:14 14 At this, she turned around and saw Jesus stand-
zMt 28:9; ing there,[z] but she did not realize that it was
Mk 16:9 aLk 24:16; Jesus.[a]
Jn 21:4 15 "Woman," he said, "why are you crying?[b]
Who is it you are looking for?"
20:15 Thinking he was the gardener, she said, "Sir, if
bver 13 you have carried him away, tell me where you
have put him, and I will get him."
16 Jesus said to her, "Mary."
20:16 She turned toward him and cried out in Ara-
cJn 5:2 dMt 23:7 maic,[c] "Rabboni!"[d] (which means Teacher).
17 Jesus said, "Do not hold on to me, for I have
not yet returned to the Father. Go instead to my
20:17 brothers[e] and tell them, 'I am returning to my
eMt 28:10 fJn 7:33 Father[f] and your Father, to my God and your God.' "
18 Mary Magdalene[g] went to the disciples[h] with
20:18 the news: "I have seen the Lord!" And she told
gver 1 hLk 24:10, them that he had said these things to her.

22,23 *Jesus Appears to His Disciples*

20:19 iJn 7:13 19 On the evening of that first day of the week,
jJn 14:27 when the disciples were together, with the doors
kver 21,26; Lk 24:36-39 locked for fear of the Jews,[i] Jesus came and stood
among them and said, "Peace[j] be with you!"[k]
20:20 20 After he said this, he showed them his hands
lLk 24:39, 40; Jn 19:34 and side.[l] The disciples were overjoyed[m] when
mJn 16:20, 22 they saw the Lord.
21 Again Jesus said, "Peace be with you![n] As the
20:21 Father has sent me,[o] I am sending you."[p] 22 And
nver 19 oJn 3:17 with that he breathed on them and said, "Receive
pMt 28:19; the Holy Spirit.[q] 23 If you forgive anyone his sins,
Jn 17:18 they are forgiven; if you do not forgive them, they
20:22 are not forgiven."[r]

qJn 7:39; Ac 2:38; 8:15-17; *Jesus Appears to Thomas*

19:2; Gal 3:2 24 Now Thomas[s] (called Didymus), one of the
20:23 Twelve, was not with the disciples when Jesus
rMt 16:19; came. 25 So the other disciples told him, "We have
18:18 seen the Lord!"
20:24 But he said to them, "Unless I see the nail
sJn 11:16 marks in his hands and put my finger where the

Jesus Appears to Mary

JN 20:10-18

From the moment he cast seven demons from her (Mk 16:9), Mary Magdalene was a devoted follower of Jesus. When others abandoned him, she remained near. Now she stands nearby, watching Jesus' crucifixion (Jn 19:25), and she follows Jesus to the burial place (Mt 27:61). On the morning after the Sabbath, she goes to the tomb (Jn 20:1). Perhaps she goes to anoint Jesus' body with oils or to weep. Maybe she just wants to visit the tomb. But what she finds upsets her terribly. While John and Peter come and go, Mary stays, grieving and investigating (Jn 20:11). What appears to be the loss of Jesus' body is painful for her, especially so soon after the heart-wrenching loss of his life. It is at this point of deep distress that Mary becomes the first person to witness the resurrected Christ, an honor granted to a woman who has fully given her life to her Lord (see the character study for Mary on page 1714).

Jesus' Glorified Body

JN 20:26

It is difficult for our finite, human minds to comprehend how Jesus could both walk through walls, as he did at least twice (Jn 20:19,26), and be physically touched (Lk 24:39; Jn 20:27). But the Bible clearly teaches that this is the case. Jesus also eats food given to him (Lk 24:42–43), providing further evidence that he is present in his resurrected body and not simply present in spirit. Such accounts remind us that Jesus is unlike any person who ever walked on this earth—that he was, and is, God.

What is the one truth about Jesus that is hardest for you to grasp? How would you feel if it were possible to understand everything about him? Confess to God any doubts you've harbored or resistance you've felt toward his unknowable nature, and ask him to expand your appreciation for the role of mystery in deepening your faith.

nails were, and put my hand into his side,[t] I will not believe it."[u]

26 A week later his disciples were in the house again, and Thomas was with them. Though the doors were locked, Jesus came and stood among them and said, "Peace[v] be with you!"[w] 27 Then he said to Thomas, "Put your finger here; see my hands. Reach out your hand and put it into my side. Stop doubting and believe."[x]

28 Thomas said to him, "My Lord and my God!"

29 Then Jesus told him, "Because you have seen me, you have believed;[y] blessed are those who have not seen and yet have believed."[z]

30 Jesus did many other miraculous signs[a] in the presence of his disciples, which are not recorded in this book.[b] 31 But these are written that you may[a] believe[c] that Jesus is the Christ, the Son of God,[d] and that by believing you may have life in his name.[e]

Jesus and the Miraculous Catch of Fish

21 Afterward Jesus appeared again to his disciples,[f] by the Sea of Tiberias.[b][g] It happened this way: 2 Simon Peter, Thomas[h] (called Didymus), Nathanael[i] from Cana in Galilee,[j] the sons of Zebedee,[k] and two other disciples were together. 3 "I'm going out to fish," Simon Peter told them, and they said, "We'll go with you." So they went out and got into the boat, but that night they caught nothing.[l]

4 Early in the morning, Jesus stood on the shore, but the disciples did not realize that it was Jesus.[m]

5 He called out to them, "Friends, haven't you any fish?"

"No," they answered.

6 He said, "Throw your net on the right side of the boat and you will find some." When they did, they were unable to haul the net in because of the large number of fish.[n]

7 Then the disciple whom Jesus loved[o] said to Peter, "It is the Lord!" As soon as Simon Peter heard him say, "It is the Lord," he wrapped his outer garment around him (for he had taken it off) and jumped into the water. 8 The other disciples followed in the boat, towing the net full of fish, for they were not far from shore, about a hundred yards.[c] 9 When they landed, they saw a fire[p] of burning coals there with fish on it,[q] and some bread.

10 Jesus said to them, "Bring some of the fish you have just caught."

11 Simon Peter climbed aboard and dragged the net ashore. It was full of large fish, 153, but even with so many the net was not torn. 12 Jesus said to them, "Come and have breakfast." None of the disciples dared ask him, "Who are you?" They knew it was the Lord. 13 Jesus came, took the

[a] *31* Some manuscripts *may continue to* [b] *1* That is, Sea of Galilee [c] *8* Greek *about two hundred cubits* (about 90 meters)

20:25 [t]ver 20 [u]Mk 16:11
20:26 [v]Jn 14:27 [w]ver 21
20:27 [x]ver 25; Lk 24:40
20:29 [y]Jn 3:15 [z]1Pe 1:8
20:30 [a]Jn 2:11 [b]Jn 21:25
20:31 [c]Jn 3:15; 19:35 [d]Mt 4:3 [e]Mt 25:46
21:1 [f]Jn 20:19,26 [g]Jn 6:1
21:2 [h]Jn 11:16 [i]Jn 1:45 [j]Jn 2:1 [k]Mt 4:21
21:3 [l]Lk 5:5
21:4 [m]Lk 24:16; Jn 20:14
21:6 [n]Lk 5:4-7
21:7 [o]Jn 13:23
21:9 [p]Jn 18:18 [q]ver 10,13

bread and gave it to them, and did the same with
21:13 [r]ver 9 the fish.[r] 14This was now the third time Jesus
appeared to his disciples[s] after he was raised from
21:14 [s]Jn 20:19,26 the dead.

Jesus Reinstates Peter

15When they had finished eating, Jesus said to
Simon Peter, "Simon son of John, do you truly
love me more than these?"
21:15 "Yes, Lord," he said, "you know that I love
[t]Mt 26:33, you."[t]
35; Jn 13:37 [u]Lk 12:32 Jesus said, "Feed my lambs."[u]
16Again Jesus said, "Simon son of John, do you
truly love me?"
He answered, "Yes, Lord, you know that I love
you."
21:16 [v]Mt 2:6; Jesus said, "Take care of my sheep."[v]
Ac 20:28; 17The third time he said to him, "Simon son of
1Pe 5:2,3 John, do you love me?"
21:17 Peter was hurt because Jesus asked him the
[w]Jn 13:38 third time, "Do you love me?"[w] He said, "Lord,
[x]Jn 16:30 [y]ver 16 you know all things;[x] you know that I love you."
Jesus said, "Feed my sheep.[y] 18I tell you the
truth, when you were younger you dressed yourself and went where you wanted; but when you
are old you will stretch out your hands, and
someone else will dress you and lead you where
you do not want to go." 19Jesus said this to indi-
21:19 cate the kind of death[z] by which Peter would glo-
[z]Jn 12:33; 18:32 rify God.[a] Then he said to him, "Follow me!"
[a]2Pe 1:14 20Peter turned and saw that the disciple whom
Jesus loved[b] was following them. (This was the
21:20 [b]ver 7; one who had leaned back against Jesus at the sup-
Jn 13:23 per and had said, "Lord, who is going to betray
[c]Jn 13:25 you?")[c] 21When Peter saw him, he asked, "Lord,
what about him?"
22Jesus answered, "If I want him to remain alive
21:22 [d]Mt 16:27; until I return,[d] what is that to you? You must fol-
1Co 4:5; low me."[e] 23Because of this, the rumor spread
Rev 2:25 among the brothers[f] that this disciple would not
[e]ver 19 die. But Jesus did not say that he would not die;
21:23 he only said, "If I want him to remain alive until
[f]Ac 1:16 I return, what is that to you?"
24This is the disciple who testifies to these
21:24 [g]Jn 15:27 things[g] and who wrote them down. We know that
[h]Jn 19:35 his testimony is true.[h]
25Jesus did many other things as well.[i] If every
21:25 [i]Jn 20:30 one of them were written down, I suppose that
even the whole world would not have room for
the books that would be written.

Reinstating Peter

JN 21:15-17

At Jesus' trial Peter publicly denies Christ, not once, but three times (Jn 18:15-26). Now a resurrected Jesus graciously creates an opportunity for Peter to declare his devotion three times: in a sense canceling out, or atoning for, the three previous betrayals.

To each affirmative response, Jesus responds by commanding Peter to participate in active ministry. Through this agonizing yet loving interaction, Jesus fully reinstates Peter as a disciple. If there is a doubt in anyone's mind that Peter has the right to represent him, the Lord effectively and graciously wipes it away.

We, too, can be restored, or established for the first time, as ministers of the gospel after we receive Christ's forgiveness for our sins. No matter what we've done in the past, it cannot *keep us from Jesus once we seek redemption. Nor can it ever disqualify us from ministering in his wonderful name.*

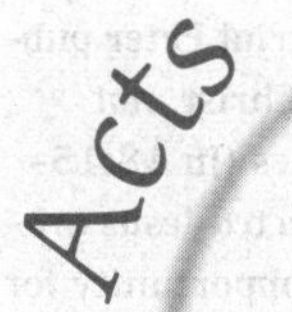

The growth of the church.

As a sequel to Luke's Gospel, the book of Acts tells about the growth of the early church. Although the church begins with only a few believers, the Holy Spirit empowers them to share the life-changing message of Jesus' resurrection with others. As a result, the church experiences explosive growth in spite of severe opposition and persecution.

The book of Acts illustrates the various roles women played in the growth of the early church. We cringe at Sapphira's untimely death (Ac 5). We weep at the death of Dorcas and rejoice when God restores her to life (Ac 9). We chuckle at Rhoda's antics when Peter knocks at the door of Mary's home (Ac 12). We're proud of Lydia and of Priscilla, who use their business resources to further the gospel (Ac 16; 18). We marvel at God's use of Philip's four daughters who speak to the early church (Ac 21). And we grasp the importance of our choices as we watch Damaris embrace Christianity (Ac 17) but Drusilla and Bernice walk away from God's grace (Ac 24; 25).

These women from the book of Acts remind us that we, too, are a part of the story of the church. As we live as Christians in the sight of our children and of our communities, as we show compassion to those around us, as we share the truths of the Good News, we participate in the history of the church, a continuing story of God's love poured out on the world.

Quick Study

Author
Luke, the physician who also wrote the Gospel of Luke.

Date Written
Probably around A.D. 63.

Setting
Many cities in the Roman Empire.

Key Passage
Acts 4:31-33 "After they prayed, the place where they were meeting was shaken. And they were all filled with the Holy Spirit and spoke the word of God boldly. All the believers were one in heart and mind. No one claimed that any of his possessions was his own, but they shared everything they had. With great power the apostles continued to testify to the resurrection of the Lord Jesus, and much grace was upon them all."

Outline

Ascension of Jesus into heaven. Ac 1:1-11

Matthias chosen. Ac 1:12-26

Pentecost. Ac 2:1-47

Peter's early ministry. Ac 3:1-26

Persecution begins. Ac 4:1-22

Believers pray and share together. Ac 4:23-37

Deceit of Ananias and Sapphira. Ac 5:1-11

More persecution. Ac 5:12–8:14

Philip's ministry. Ac 8:15-40

Saul's conversion. Ac 9:1-31

Peter's ministry and vision. Ac 9:32–11:18

First Gentile church. Ac 11:19-30

Peter's escape from prison. Ac 12:1-25

Paul's first missionary journey. Ac 13:1–14:28

The Jerusalem council. Ac 15:1-35

Paul's second missionary journey. Ac 15:36–18:22

Paul's third missionary journey. Ac 18:23–21:16

Paul's arrest and trial in Jerusalem. Ac 21:17–23:35

Paul's trial before Felix. Ac 24:1-27

Paul's trial before Festus. Ac 25:1-22

Paul's trial before Agrippa. Ac 25:23–26:32

On to Rome. Ac 27:1–28:31

The Women of Acts

⚘	**Mary, mother of Jesus**	*Not just mother of, but believer in, Christ.* Ac 1:14 (page 1613)
⚘	**Sapphira**	*Huge consequences for one false act.* Ac 5:1-11 (page 1942)
	Grecian Jewish widows	*They were being overlooked.* Ac 6:1-4
	Candace	*The queen of Ethiopia.* Ac 8:27
⚘	**Dorcas (Tabitha)**	*Dearly loved for her good deeds.* Ac 9:36-43 (page 1977)
	Mary, mother of John Mark	*A prayer meeting for Peter was held in her home.* Ac 12:1-19
⚘	**Rhoda**	*Peter surprised her.* Ac 12:12-16 (page 1978)
	Women of Pisidian Antioch	*Persecutors of Paul and Barnabas.* Ac 13:50
⚘	**Timothy's mother**	*She was Jewish by birth.* Ac 16:1 (page 2080)
⚘	**Lydia**	*A converted businesswoman.* Ac 16:12-15,40 (page 2017)
	Slave girl	*A demonized fortune-teller.* Ac 16:16-21
	Damaris	*A woman of Athens who believed Paul's message.* Ac 17:34
⚘	**Priscilla**	*Tentmaker with Paul and her husband.* Ac 18:2-3,18-19,26 (page 2047)
	Artemis	*A fertility god of Ephesus.* Ac 19:24-41
	Daughters of Philip	*Four unmarried prophets.* Ac 21:8-9
	Paul's sister	*Her son told Paul of a plot to kill him.* Ac 23:16-22
⚘	**Drusilla**	*She turned away from Paul's teaching.* Ac 24:24-27 (page 2018)
	Bernice	*Unbelieving wife of King Agrippa.* Ac 25:13,23; 26:30

⚘ Denotes a sketch written about this character

The Church Is Born

AC 1:14

Something new is about to happen. The womb of history is ready to deliver and the birth of the church will take place. The Holy Spirit of God is descending in power. Take a close look at who is gathered and praying as a preamble to this Spirit-anointed delivery. Women are present along with the disciples. There is even special mention that Mary, the mother of Jesus, is part of this small group. The one who gave birth to the Son of God is also present at the birth of the church.

In a culture where the place of women was downplayed, we see the role of godly women elevated. Women were pivotal in the plan of God at the starting of the church and continue to be part of what God is doing today.

Jesus Taken Up Into Heaven

1 In my former book,[a] Theophilus, I wrote about all that Jesus began to do and to teach[b] 2until the day he was taken up to heaven,[c] after giving instructions[d] through the Holy Spirit to the apostles[e] he had chosen.[f] 3After his suffering, he showed himself to these men and gave many convincing proofs that he was alive. He appeared to them[g] over a period of forty days and spoke about the kingdom of God. 4On one occasion, while he was eating with them, he gave them this command: "Do not leave Jerusalem, but wait for the gift my Father promised, which you have heard me speak about.[h] 5For John baptized with[a] water, but in a few days you will be baptized with the Holy Spirit."

6So when they met together, they asked him, "Lord, are you at this time going to restore[i] the kingdom to Israel?"

7He said to them: "It is not for you to know the times or dates the Father has set by his own authority.[j] 8But you will receive power when the Holy Spirit comes on you;[k] and you will be my witnesses[l] in Jerusalem, and in all Judea and Samaria,[m] and to the ends of the earth."[n]

9After he said this, he was taken up[o] before their very eyes, and a cloud hid him from their sight.

10They were looking intently up into the sky as he was going, when suddenly two men dressed in white[p] stood beside them. 11"Men of Galilee,"[q] they said, "why do you stand here looking into the sky? This same Jesus, who has been taken from you into heaven, will come back[r] in the same way you have seen him go into heaven."

Matthias Chosen to Replace Judas

12Then they returned to Jerusalem[s] from the hill called the Mount of Olives,[t] a Sabbath day's walk[b] from the city. 13When they arrived, they went upstairs to the room[u] where they were staying. Those present were Peter, John, James and Andrew; Philip and Thomas, Bartholomew and Matthew; James son of Alphaeus and Simon the Zealot, and Judas son of James.[v] 14They all joined together constantly in prayer,[w] along with the women[x] and Mary the mother of Jesus, and with his brothers.[y]

15In those days Peter stood up among the believers[c] (a group numbering about a hundred and twenty) 16and said, "Brothers, the Scripture had to be fulfilled[z] which the Holy Spirit spoke long ago through the mouth of David concerning Judas,[a] who served as guide for those who arrested Jesus— 17he was one of our number[b] and shared in this ministry."[c]

18(With the reward[d] he got for his wickedness, Judas bought a field;[e] there he fell headlong, his

1:1 [a]Lk 1:1-4 [b]Lk 3:23
1:2 [c]ver 9,11; Mk 16:19 [d]Mt 28:19,20 [e]Mk 6:30 [f]Jn 13:18
1:3 [g]Mt 28:17; Lk 24:34,36; Jn 20:19,26; 21:1,14; 1Co 15:5-7
1:4 [h]Lk 24:49; Jn 14:16; Ac 2:33
1:6 [i]Mt 17:11
1:7 [j]Mt 24:36
1:8 [k]Ac 2:1-4 [l]Lk 24:48 [m]Ac 8:1-25 [n]Mt 28:19
1:9 [o]ver 2
1:10 [p]Lk 24:4; Jn 20:12
1:11 [q]Ac 2:7 [r]Mt 16:27
1:12 [s]Lk 24:52 [t]Mt 21:1
1:13 [u]Ac 9:37; 20:8 [v]Mt 10:2-4; Mk 3:16-19; Lk 6:14-16
1:14 [w]Ac 2:42; 6:4 [x]Lk 23:49,55 [y]Mt 12:46
1:16 [z]ver 20 [a]Jn 13:18
1:17 [b]Jn 6:70,71 [c]ver 25
1:18 [d]Mt 26:14,15 [e]Mt 27:3-10

[a] *5* Or *in* [b] *12* That is, about 3/4 mile (about 1,100 meters)
[c] *15* Greek *brothers*

body burst open and all his intestines spilled out. 19 Everyone in Jerusalem heard about this, so they called that field in their language Akeldama, that is, Field of Blood.)

20 "For," said Peter, "it is written in the book of Psalms,

> " 'May his place be deserted;
> let there be no one to dwell in it,'[a][f]

and,

> " 'May another take his place of
> leadership.'[b][g]

21 Therefore it is necessary to choose one of the men who have been with us the whole time the Lord Jesus went in and out among us, 22 beginning from John's baptism[h] to the time when Jesus was taken up from us. For one of these must become a witness[i] with us of his resurrection."

23 So they proposed two men: Joseph called Barsabbas (also known as Justus) and Matthias. 24 Then they prayed,[j] "Lord, you know everyone's heart.[k] Show us which of these two you have chosen 25 to take over this apostolic ministry, which Judas left to go where he belongs." 26 Then they cast lots, and the lot fell to Matthias; so he was added to the eleven apostles.[l]

The Holy Spirit Comes at Pentecost

2 When the day of Pentecost[m] came, they were all together[n] in one place. 2 Suddenly a sound like the blowing of a violent wind came from heaven and filled the whole house where they were sitting.[o] 3 They saw what seemed to be tongues of fire that separated and came to rest on each of them. 4 All of them were filled with the Holy Spirit and began to speak in other tongues[c][p] as the Spirit enabled them.

5 Now there were staying in Jerusalem God-fearing[q] Jews from every nation under heaven. 6 When they heard this sound, a crowd came together in bewilderment, because each one heard them speaking in his own language. 7 Utterly amazed,[r] they asked: "Are not all these men who are speaking Galileans?[s] 8 Then how is it that each of us hears them in his own native language? 9 Parthians, Medes and Elamites; residents of Mesopotamia, Judea and Cappadocia,[t] Pontus[u] and Asia,[v] 10 Phrygia[w] and Pamphylia,[x] Egypt and the parts of Libya near Cyrene;[y] visitors from Rome 11 (both Jews and converts to Judaism); Cretans and Arabs—we hear them declaring the wonders of God in our own tongues!" 12 Amazed and perplexed, they asked one another, "What does this mean?"

13 Some, however, made fun of them and said, "They have had too much wine.[d]"[z]

1:20 [f]Ps 69:25 [g]Ps 109:8
1:22 [h]Mk 1:4 [i]ver 8
1:24 [j]Ac 6:6; 14:23 [k]1Sa 16:7; Jer 17:10; Ac 15:8; Rev 2:23
1:26 [l]Ac 2:14
2:1 [m]Lev 23:15, 16; Ac 20:16 [n]Ac 1:14
2:2 [o]Ac 4:31
2:4 [p]Mk 16:17; 1Co 12:10
2:5 [q]Ac 8:2
2:7 [r]ver 12 [s]Ac 1:11
2:9 [t]1Pe 1:1 [u]Ac 18:2 [v]Ac 16:6; Ro 16:5; 1Co 16:19; 2Co 1:8
2:10 [w]Ac 16:6; 18:23 [x]Ac 13:13; 15:38 [y]Mt 27:32
2:13 [z]1Co 14:23

[a] 20 Psalm 69:25 [b] 20 Psalm 109:8 [c] 4 Or *languages*; also in verse 11 [d] 13 Or *sweet wine*

The Spirit's Presence

Pentecost

AC 2:1–13

Pentecost. The birth of the church. The coming of the Holy Spirit. It all begins here. Or does it?

Take a moment and turn back to the second verse of the Bible. You will discover these words: "The Spirit of God was hovering over the waters" (Ge 1:2). The Holy Spirit was present from before the beginning of time. The Old Testament is filled with examples of how the Spirit worked in powerful and amazing ways, in unique situations and through specific people.

How then is the day of Pentecost a dividing line in human history? Because it is on this day that the Holy Spirit of God becomes available to every Christian man, woman and child. Previously, the Spirit revealed himself only occasionally and for unique works of God. Today, the Spirit never leaves. He lives in us (1Co 6:19), is ever with us (Jn 14:16–17) and gives us the "righteousness, peace and joy" (Ro 14:17) that is such a beautiful evidence of his work in our lives.

The Spirit's Presence

AC 2:17-21

The prophet Joel pointed to this day of Pentecost (Joel 2:28-32). He promised the people of Israel that one day the Holy Spirit of God would be poured out in power on all of God's people. Young and old, men and women—no one would be missed! The Holy Spirit would come to believers, and no one would be able to deny his power and presence.

It was promised by Joel. It is realized at Pentecost. The burning question then becomes: Is this a one-time event when the Spirit comes in power, or is this same Holy Spirit ready to work in and through men and women today? The way we answer this question makes all the difference in our lives—and in our world. The Holy Spirit is still active and working among his people, giving us power (Ac 1:8) and hope (Ro 15:13), just as he lived and worked among first-century Christians.

Peter Addresses the Crowd

14 Then Peter stood up with the Eleven, raised
his voice and addressed the crowd: "Fellow Jews
and all of you who live in Jerusalem, let me
explain this to you; listen carefully to what I say.
15 These men are not drunk, as you suppose. It's
only nine in the morning![a] 16 No, this is what was
spoken by the prophet Joel:

17 " 'In the last days, God says,
I will pour out my Spirit on all people.[b]
Your sons and daughters will prophesy,[c]
your young men will see visions,
your old men will dream dreams.
18 Even on my servants, both men and women,
I will pour out my Spirit in those days,
and they will prophesy.[d]
19 I will show wonders in the heaven above
and signs on the earth below,
blood and fire and billows of smoke.
20 The sun will be turned to darkness
and the moon to blood[e]
before the coming of the great and glorious day of the Lord.
21 And everyone who calls
on the name of the Lord will be saved.'[a][f]

22 "Men of Israel, listen to this: Jesus of Nazareth was a man accredited by God to you by miracles, wonders and signs,[g] which God did among
you through him,[h] as you yourselves know. 23 This
man was handed over to you by God's set purpose
and foreknowledge;[i] and you, with the help of
wicked men,[b] put him to death by nailing him to
the cross.[j] 24 But God raised him from the dead,[k]
freeing him from the agony of death, because it
was impossible for death to keep its hold on him.[l]
25 David said about him:

" 'I saw the Lord always before me.
Because he is at my right hand,
I will not be shaken.
26 Therefore my heart is glad and my tongue rejoices;
my body also will live in hope,
27 because you will not abandon me to the grave,
nor will you let your Holy One see decay.[m]
28 You have made known to me the paths of life;
you will fill me with joy in your presence.'[c]

29 "Brothers, I can tell you confidently that the

2:15 [a]1Th 5:7
2:17 [b]Isa 44:3; Jn 7:37-39; Ac 10:45 [c]Ac 21:9
2:18 [d]Ac 21:9-12
2:20 [e]Mt 24:29
2:21 [f]Ro 10:13
2:22 [g]Jn 4:48; Ac 10:38 [h]Jn 3:2
2:23 [i]Lk 22:22; Ac 3:18; 4:28 [j]Lk 24:20; Ac 3:13
2:24 [k]ver 32; 1Co 6:14; 2Co 4:14; Eph 1:20; Col 2:12; Heb 13:20; 1Pe 1:21 [l]Jn 20:9
2:27 [m]ver 31; Ac 13:35

[a] *21* Joel 2:28–32 [b] *23* Or *of those not having the law* (that is, Gentiles) [c] *28* Psalm 16:8–11

patriarch[n] David died and was buried,[o] and his
tomb is here[p] to this day. 30But he was a prophet
and knew that God had promised him on oath
that he would place one of his descendants on his
throne.[q] 31Seeing what was ahead, he spoke of the
resurrection of the Christ,[a] that he was not abandoned to the grave, nor did his body see decay.[r]
32God has raised this Jesus to life,[s] and we are all
witnesses[t] of the fact. 33Exalted[u] to the right hand
of God,[v] he has received from the Father[w] the
promised Holy Spirit[x] and has poured out[y] what
you now see and hear. 34For David did not ascend
to heaven, and yet he said,

" 'The Lord said to my Lord:
"Sit at my right hand
35 until I make your enemies
a footstool for your feet." '[b][z]

36"Therefore let all Israel be assured of this: God
has made this Jesus, whom you crucified, both
Lord and Christ."[a]

37When the people heard this, they were cut to
the heart and said to Peter and the other apostles,
"Brothers, what shall we do?"[b]

38Peter replied, "Repent and be baptized,[c] every
one of you, in the name of Jesus Christ for the forgiveness of your sins.[d] And you will receive the
gift of the Holy Spirit. 39The promise is for you
and your children[e] and for all who are far off[f]—for
all whom the Lord our God will call."

40With many other words he warned them; and
he pleaded with them, "Save yourselves from this
corrupt generation."[g] 41Those who accepted his
message were baptized, and about three thousand
were added to their number that day.

The Fellowship of the Believers

42They devoted themselves to the apostles'
teaching and to the fellowship, to the breaking of
bread and to prayer.[h] 43Everyone was filled with
awe, and many wonders and miraculous signs
were done by the apostles.[i] 44All the believers were
together and had everything in common.[j] 45Selling
their possessions and goods, they gave to anyone
as he had need.[k] 46Every day they continued to
meet together in the temple courts.[l] They broke
bread[m] in their homes and ate together with glad
and sincere hearts, 47praising God and enjoying the
favor of all the people.[n] And the Lord added to
their number[o] daily those who were being saved.

Peter Heals the Crippled Beggar

3 One day Peter and John[p] were going up to the
temple[q] at the time of prayer—at three in the
afternoon.[r] 2Now a man crippled from birth[s] was
being carried to the temple gate[t] called Beautiful,
where he was put every day to beg[u] from those

2:29 [n]Ac 7:8,9 [o]Ac 13:36; 1Ki 2:10 [p]Ne 3:16
2:30 [q]2Sa 7:12; Ps 132:11
2:31 [r]Ps 16:10
2:32 [s]ver 24 [t]Ac 1:8
2:33 [u]Php 2:9 [v]Mk 16:19 [w]Ac 1:4 [x]Jn 7:39; 14:26 [y]Ac 10:45
2:35 [z]Ps 110:1; Mt 22:44
2:36 [a]Lk 2:11
2:37 [b]Lk 3:10,12,14
2:38 [c]Ac 8:12,16,36,38; 22:16 [d]Lk 24:47; Ac 3:19
2:39 [e]Isa 44:3 [f]Ac 10:45; Eph 2:13
2:40 [g]Dt 32:5
2:42 [h]Ac 1:14
2:43 [i]Ac 5:12
2:44 [j]Ac 4:32
2:45 [k]Mt 19:21
2:46 [l]Lk 24:53; Ac 5:21,42 [m]Ac 20:7
2:47 [n]Ro 14:18 [o]ver 41; Ac 5:14
3:1 [p]Lk 22:8 [q]Ac 2:46 [r]Ps 55:17
3:2 [s]Ac 14:8 [t]Lk 16:20 [u]Jn 9:8

[a] 31 Or *Messiah.* "The Christ" (Greek) and "the Messiah" (Hebrew) both mean "the Anointed One"; also in verse 36.
[b] 35 Psalm 110:1

The Family of God

AC 2:42-47

Dependent. Connected. Related. **These are just a few of the words that describe the community life of first-century Christians. In our individualistic culture, the intimacy of the early followers of Christ might surprise us a little and even put us off. These first-century Christians voluntarily share their resources and willingly invest their hard-earned money in the lives of others. They meet in the temple regularly to feed on the heavenly bread of the Word of God. They gather in their homes to break bread and enjoy table fellowship with each other. Their lives are intertwined and interconnected.**

Like the body image used so often by the apostle Paul (Ro 12:4-5; 1Co 12:12-31; Eph 4:4), these believers draw life from each other. They share in each other's joys and sorrows. They are like family to each other. The family of God.

A Transformed Peter

AC 3:11–26

Who is this bold and authoritative preacher? Who is this confrontational, uncompromising warrior? This is Peter, the "rock" (Mt 16:18)!

Only a short time ago there was that unforgettable scene in the courtyard of the high priest. Peter the rock was confronted about his relationship with Jesus. And Peter the rock waffled. Three times he adamantly told his accusers: "I don't know what you're talking about! I don't know the man!" (Mt 26:72–74). Peter the rock was as fickle as shifting sand.

What has happened since that fateful and tear-filled night of Peter's denials? He met the resurrected Christ along the Sea of Galilee and received forgiveness and restoration. And he experienced the filling of the Holy Spirit. In the glow of these experiences Peter's heart has been ignited by the indwelling Spirit. Not because of his own strength or abilities, but because of Christ's touch and the Holy Spirit's filling, Peter is becoming the rock.

going into the temple courts. 3When he saw Peter
and John about to enter, he asked them for money.
4Peter looked straight at him, as did John. Then
Peter said, "Look at us!" 5So the man gave them his
attention, expecting to get something from them.
6Then Peter said, "Silver or gold I do not have,
but what I have I give you. In the name of Jesus
Christ of Nazareth,[v] walk." 7Taking him by the
right hand, he helped him up, and instantly the
man's feet and ankles became strong. 8He jumped
to his feet and began to walk. Then he went with
them into the temple courts, walking and jumping,[w]
and praising God. 9When all the people[x] saw
him walking and praising God, 10they recognized
him as the same man who used to sit begging at
the temple gate called Beautiful,[y] and they were
filled with wonder and amazement at what had
happened to him.

Peter Speaks to the Onlookers

11While the beggar held on to Peter and John,[z]
all the people were astonished and came running
to them in the place called Solomon's Colonnade.[a]
12When Peter saw this, he said to them: "Men of
Israel, why does this surprise you? Why do you
stare at us as if by our own power or godliness we
had made this man walk? 13The God of Abraham,
Isaac and Jacob, the God of our fathers,[b] has glorified
his servant Jesus. You handed him over to
be killed, and you disowned him before Pilate,[c]
though he had decided to let him go.[d] 14You disowned
the Holy[e] and Righteous One[f] and asked
that a murderer be released to you.[g] 15You killed
the author of life, but God raised him from the
dead.[h] We are witnesses of this. 16By faith in the
name of Jesus, this man whom you see and know
was made strong. It is Jesus' name and the faith
that comes through him that has given this complete
healing to him, as you can all see.
17"Now, brothers, I know that you acted in ignorance,[i]
as did your leaders.[j] 18But this is how God
fulfilled what he had foretold[k] through all the
prophets,[l] saying that his Christ[a] would suffer.[m]
19Repent, then, and turn to God, so that your sins
may be wiped out,[n] that times of refreshing may
come from the Lord, 20and that he may send the
Christ, who has been appointed for you—even
Jesus. 21He must remain in heaven[o] until the time
comes for God to restore everything,[p] as he promised
long ago through his holy prophets.[q] 22For
Moses said, 'The Lord your God will raise up for
you a prophet like me from among your own people;
you must listen to everything he tells you.[r]
23Anyone who does not listen to him will be completely
cut off from among his people.'[b][s]
24"Indeed, all the prophets[t] from Samuel on, as
many as have spoken, have foretold these days.
25And you are heirs[u] of the prophets and of the
covenant[v] God made with your fathers. He said to

3:6 [v]ver 16; Ac 4:10
3:8 [w]Ac 14:10
3:9 [x]Ac 4:16,21
3:10 [y]ver 2
3:11 [z]Lk 22:8 [a]Jn 10:23; Ac 5:12
3:13 [b]Ac 5:30 [c]Mt 27:2 [d]Lk 23:4
3:14 [e]Mk 1:24; Ac 4:27 [f]Ac 7:52 [g]Mk 15:11; Lk 23:18-25
3:15 [h]Ac 2:24
3:17 [i]Lk 23:34 [j]Ac 13:27
3:18 [k]Ac 2:23 [l]Lk 24:27 [m]Ac 17:2,3; 26:22,23
3:19 [n]Ac 2:38
3:21 [o]Ac 1:11 [p]Mt 17:11 [q]Lk 1:70
3:22 [r]Dt 18:15, 18; Ac 7:37
3:23 [s]Dt 18:19
3:24 [t]Lk 24:27
3:25 [u]Ac 2:39 [v]Ro 9:4,5

[a] *18* Or *Messiah*; also in verse 20 [b] *23* Deut. 18:15,18,19

Abraham, 'Through your offspring all peoples on
earth will be blessed.'[a][w] 26 When God raised up[x]
his servant, he sent him first[y] to you to bless you
by turning each of you from your wicked ways."

Peter and John Before the Sanhedrin

4 The priests and the captain of the temple
guard[z] and the Sadducees[a] came up to Peter
and John while they were speaking to the people.
2 They were greatly disturbed because the apostles
were teaching the people and proclaiming in Jesus
the resurrection of the dead.[b] 3 They seized Peter
and John, and because it was evening, they put
them in jail[c] until the next day. 4 But many who
heard the message believed, and the number of
men grew[d] to about five thousand.
5 The next day the rulers,[e] elders and teachers of
the law met in Jerusalem. 6 Annas the high priest
was there, and so were Caiaphas,[f] John, Alexander and the other men of the high priest's family.
7 They had Peter and John brought before them
and began to question them: "By what power or
what name did you do this?"
8 Then Peter, filled with the Holy Spirit, said to
them: "Rulers and elders of the people![g] 9 If we are
being called to account today for an act of kindness shown to a cripple[h] and are asked how he
was healed, 10 then know this, you and all the people of Israel: It is by the name of Jesus Christ of
Nazareth, whom you crucified but whom God
raised from the dead,[i] that this man stands before
you healed. 11 He is

" 'the stone you builders rejected,
which has become the capstone.[b]'[c][j]

12 Salvation is found in no one else, for there is no
other name under heaven given to men by which
we must be saved."[k]
13 When they saw the courage of Peter and John[l]
and realized that they were unschooled, ordinary
men,[m] they were astonished and they took note
that these men had been with Jesus. 14 But since
they could see the man who had been healed
standing there with them, there was nothing they
could say. 15 So they ordered them to withdraw
from the Sanhedrin[n] and then conferred together.
16 "What are we going to do with these men?"[o] they
asked. "Everybody living in Jerusalem knows they
have done an outstanding miracle,[p] and we cannot deny it. 17 But to stop this thing from spreading
any further among the people, we must warn these
men to speak no longer to anyone in this name."
18 Then they called them in again and commanded them not to speak or teach at all in the name of
Jesus.[q] 19 But Peter and John replied, "Judge for
yourselves whether it is right in God's sight to obey
you rather than God.[r] 20 For we cannot help speaking about what we have seen and heard."

3:25 [w]Ge 12:3; 22:18; 26:4; 28:14
3:26 [x]ver 22; Ac 2:24 [y]Ac 13:46; Ro 1:16
4:1 [z]Lk 22:4 [a]Mt 3:7
4:2 [b]Ac 17:18
4:3 [c]Ac 5:18
4:4 [d]Ac 2:41
4:5 [e]Lk 23:13
4:6 [f]Mt 26:3; Lk 3:2
4:8 [g]ver 5; Lk 23:13
4:9 [h]Ac 3:6
4:10 [i]Ac 2:24
4:11 [j]Ps 118:22; Isa 28:16; Mt 21:42
4:12 [k]Mt 1:21; Ac 10:43; 1Ti 2:5
4:13 [l]Lk 22:8 [m]Mt 11:25
4:15 [n]Mt 5:22
4:16 [o]Jn 11:47 [p]Ac 3:6-10
4:18 [q]Ac 5:40
4:19 [r]Ac 5:29

[a] *25* Gen. 22:18; 26:4 [b] *11* Or *cornerstone* [c] *11* Psalm 118:22

No Other Name

AC 4:11-12

Look closely at the context of Peter's declaration in Acts 4:12. This is no kindergarten Sunday school class. This is no Basic Doctrine 101 entry-level class. Peter is relating to the Sanhedrin, the rulers and elders of the Jewish nation. He is talking with the religious hierarchy, the ecclesiastical heavyweights of his day. These are the leaders who orchestrated the crucifixion of Jesus.

With razor sharp conviction Peter informs them that the One they have rejected and nailed to a cross is their only hope for salvation. He lets them know that the stone they tossed out in the rubbish heap is actually the capstone that will hold their whole religious structure together. Without him, they have no chance of finding salvation or wholeness. This is no poetic word game to highlight Jesus as some sad martyr. It is a crystal clear declaration that there is one, and only one, way to heaven. There is only one name in all of heaven and earth that has the power to save. That name is Jesus (Ro 10:13).

Delightful views of
nature, dressed by art,
Enchant no longer this
indifferent heart;
The Lord of all things, in his
humble birth,
Makes mean the proud
magnificence of earth;
The straw, the manger, and the
mouldering wall,
Eclipse its lustre; and I scorn
it all.
Canals, and fountains, and
delicious vales,
Green slopes and plains, whose
plenty never fails; . . .
Rocks, lofty mountains,
caverns dark and deep,
And torrents raving down the
rugged steep;
Smooth downs, whose fragrant
herbs the spirits cheer;
Meads crowned with flowers;
streams musical and clear,
Whose silver waters, and
whose murmurs, join
Their artless charms, to make
the scene divine;
The fruitful vineyard, and the
furrowed plain,
That seems a rolling sea
of golden grain:
All, all have lost the charms
they once possessed;
An infant God reigns sovereign
in my breast;
From Bethlehem's bosom I no
more will rove;
There dwells the Savior, and
there rests my love.

—Madame Guyon (1647–1717)

21 After further threats they let them go. They
could not decide how to punish them, because all
the people[s] were praising God[t] for what had happened. 22 For the man who was miraculously
healed was over forty years old.

The Believers' Prayer

23 On their release, Peter and John went back to
their own people and reported all that the chief
priests and elders had said to them. 24 When they
heard this, they raised their voices together in
prayer to God. "Sovereign Lord," they said, "you
made the heaven and the earth and the sea, and
everything in them. 25 You spoke by the Holy Spirit through the mouth of your servant, our father
David:[u]

"'Why do the nations rage
and the peoples plot in vain?
26 The kings of the earth take their stand
and the rulers gather together
against the Lord
and against his Anointed One.[a][b][v]

27 Indeed Herod[w] and Pontius Pilate[x] met together
with the Gentiles and the people[c] of Israel in this
city to conspire against your holy servant Jesus,[y]
whom you anointed. 28 They did what your power
and will had decided beforehand should happen.[z]
29 Now, Lord, consider their threats and enable
your servants to speak your word with great boldness.[a] 30 Stretch out your hand to heal and perform
miraculous signs and wonders[b] through the name
of your holy servant Jesus."[c]

31 After they prayed, the place where they were
meeting was shaken.[d] And they were all filled
with the Holy Spirit and spoke the word of God
boldly.[e]

The Believers Share Their Possessions

32 All the believers were one in heart and mind.
No one claimed that any of his possessions was
his own, but they shared everything they had.[f]
33 With great power the apostles continued to testify[g] to the resurrection[h] of the Lord Jesus, and
much grace was upon them all. 34 There were no
needy persons among them. For from time to time
those who owned lands or houses sold them,[i]
brought the money from the sales 35 and put it at
the apostles' feet,[j] and it was distributed to anyone as he had need.[k]

36 Joseph, a Levite from Cyprus, whom the apostles called Barnabas[l] (which means Son of Encouragement), 37 sold a field he owned and brought the
money and put it at the apostles' feet.[m]

Ananias and Sapphira

5 Now a man named Ananias, together with his
wife Sapphira, also sold a piece of property.

4:21 [s]Ac 5:26 [t]Mt 9:8
4:25 [u]Ac 1:16
4:26 [v]Ps 2:1,2; Da 9:25; Lk 4:18; Ac 10:38; Heb 1:9
4:27 [w]Mt 14:1 [x]Mt 27:2; Lk 23:12 [y]ver 30
4:28 [z]Ac 2:23
4:29 [a]ver 13,31; Ac 9:27; 14:3; Php 1:14
4:30 [b]Jn 4:48 [c]ver 27
4:31 [d]Ac 2:2 [e]ver 29
4:32 [f]Ac 2:44
4:33 [g]Lk 24:48 [h]Ac 1:22
4:34 [i]Mt 19:21; Ac 2:45
4:35 [j]ver 37; Ac 5:2 [k]Ac 2:45; 6:1
4:36 [l]Ac 9:27; 1Co 9:6
4:37 [m]ver 35; Ac 5:2

[a] *26* That is, Christ or Messiah [b] *26* Psalm 2:1,2 [c] *27* The Greek is plural.

2 With his wife's full knowledge he kept back part
5:2 of the money for himself, but brought the rest and
[n]Ac 4:35,37 put it at the apostles' feet.[n]
5:3 3 Then Peter said, "Ananias, how is it that Satan[o]
[o]Mt 4:10 has so filled your heart[p] that you have lied to the
[p]Jn 13:2,27 Holy Spirit[q] and have kept for yourself some of the
[q]ver 9 money you received for the land? 4 Didn't it belong
to you before it was sold? And after it was sold,
wasn't the money at your disposal? What made
you think of doing such a thing? You have not lied
to men but to God."
5:5 5 When Ananias heard this, he fell down and
[r]ver 10 died.[r] And great fear[s] seized all who heard what
[s]ver 11 had happened. 6 Then the young men came for-
5:6 ward, wrapped up his body,[t] and carried him out
[t]Jn 19:40 and buried him.
7 About three hours later his wife came in, not
knowing what had happened. 8 Peter asked her,
"Tell me, is this the price you and Ananias got for
5:8 the land?"
[u]ver 2 "Yes," she said, "that is the price."[u]
5:9 9 Peter said to her, "How could you agree to test
[v]ver 3 the Spirit of the Lord?[v] Look! The feet of the men
who buried your husband are at the door, and
they will carry you out also."
10 At that moment she fell down at his feet and
5:10 died.[w] Then the young men came in and, finding
[w]ver 5 her dead, carried her out and buried her beside
5:11 her husband. 11 Great fear[x] seized the whole
[x]ver 5; Ac 19:17 church and all who heard about these events.

The Apostles Heal Many

12 The apostles performed many miraculous signs
5:12 [y]Ac 2:43 and wonders[y] among the people. And all the believ-
[z]Ac 4:32 ers used to meet together[z] in Solomon's Colon-
[a]Ac 3:11 nade.[a] 13 No one else dared join them, even though
5:13 they were highly regarded by the people.[b] 14 Never-
[b]Ac 2:47; theless, more and more men and women believed
4:21 in the Lord and were added to their number. 15 As a
result, people brought the sick into the streets and
5:15 laid them on beds and mats so that at least Peter's
[c]Ac 19:12 shadow might fall on some of them as he passed
5:16 by.[c] 16 Crowds gathered also from the towns around
[d]Mk 16:17 Jerusalem, bringing their sick and those tormented
5:17 by evil[a] spirits, and all of them were healed.[d]
[e]Ac 15:5 [f]Ac 4:1

The Apostles Persecuted

5:18 17 Then the high priest and all his associates,
[g]Ac 4:3 who were members of the party[e] of the Sad-
5:19 ducees,[f] were filled with jealousy. 18 They arrested
[h]Mt 1:20; the apostles and put them in the public jail.[g] 19 But
Lk 1:11; during the night an angel[h] of the Lord opened the
Ac 8:26; 27:23 doors of the jail[i] and brought them out. 20 "Go,
[i]Ac 16:26 stand in the temple courts," he said, "and tell the
5:20 people the full message of this new life."[j]
[j]Jn 6:63,68 21 At daybreak they entered the temple courts, as
5:21 they had been told, and began to teach the people.
[k]Ac 4:5,6 When the high priest and his associates[k]
[l]ver 27,34, 41; Mt 5:22 arrived, they called together the Sanhedrin[l]—the

[a] 16 Greek *unclean*

Ananias and Sapphira

AC 5:1-11

The crime these early church members commit is a matter of the heart. The act is gracious from all outward appearances, not so different from the gift Barnabas offered (Ac 4:36-37). Barnabas sold a field he owned and brought the money to the apostles. There is no commentary. Apparently the church leaders received the gift with joy. Ananias and Sapphira also sell a piece of their property and voluntarily bring some of the money to the disciples. Sin enters the picture when they lie about their gift. They present it as if they are giving the entire amount, but in reality they are holding some back. In this they sin against God. They act one way, but their hearts harbor deception.

The punishment is immediate and severe, providing a clear message to the young church on the dangers of deception and hypocrisy. Fear grips the whole church, and God's purpose is fulfilled: They understand the message and take seriously the need for truth to reign in the new church (see the character sketch for Sapphira on page 1942).

Good Advice

AC 5:29-39

Gamaliel is an honored teacher of the law, a Pharisee par excellence. He is possibly the grandson of Hillel, a well-known teacher of the law. Gamaliel is also the rabbi under whom Paul receives his teaching in the law (Ac 22:3). Gamaliel gives the Sanhedrin good advice. He counsels the leaders to remember that God's ways are not always obvious. God will, at times, work in ways they may not understand. Let this movement speak for itself, he says. If it is from God, it will continue and flourish. If it is not a sovereign work of God, it will fizzle and fade away. No human plan or strategy, however great, will defeat the purposes of God.

full assembly of the elders of Israel—and sent to the jail for the apostles. 22But on arriving at the jail, the officers did not find them there. So they went back and reported, 23"We found the jail securely locked, with the guards standing at the doors; but when we opened them, we found no one inside." 24On hearing this report, the captain of the temple guard and the chief priests[m] were puzzled, wondering what would come of this.

25Then someone came and said, "Look! The men you put in jail are standing in the temple courts teaching the people." 26At that, the captain went with his officers and brought the apostles. They did not use force, because they feared that the people[n] would stone them.

27Having brought the apostles, they made them appear before the Sanhedrin[o] to be questioned by the high priest. 28"We gave you strict orders not to teach in this name,"[p] he said. "Yet you have filled Jerusalem with your teaching and are determined to make us guilty of this man's blood."[q]

29Peter and the other apostles replied: "We must obey God rather than men![r] 30The God of our fathers[s] raised Jesus from the dead[t]—whom you had killed by hanging him on a tree.[u] 31God exalted him to his own right hand[v] as Prince and Savior[w] that he might give repentance and forgiveness of sins to Israel.[x] 32We are witnesses of these things,[y] and so is the Holy Spirit,[z] whom God has given to those who obey him."

33When they heard this, they were furious[a] and wanted to put them to death. 34But a Pharisee named Gamaliel,[b] a teacher of the law,[c] who was honored by all the people, stood up in the Sanhedrin and ordered that the men be put outside for a little while. 35Then he addressed them: "Men of Israel, consider carefully what you intend to do to these men. 36Some time ago Theudas appeared, claiming to be somebody, and about four hundred men rallied to him. He was killed, all his followers were dispersed, and it all came to nothing. 37After him, Judas the Galilean appeared in the days of the census[d] and led a band of people in revolt. He too was killed, and all his followers were scattered. 38Therefore, in the present case I advise you: Leave these men alone! Let them go! For if their purpose or activity is of human origin, it will fail.[e] 39But if it is from God, you will not be able to stop these men; you will only find yourselves fighting against God."[f]

40His speech persuaded them. They called the apostles in and had them flogged.[g] Then they ordered them not to speak in the name of Jesus, and let them go.

41The apostles left the Sanhedrin, rejoicing[h] because they had been counted worthy of suffering disgrace for the Name.[i] 42Day after day, in the temple courts[j] and from house to house, they never stopped teaching and proclaiming the good news that Jesus is the Christ.[a]

5:24 [m]Ac 4:1
5:26 [n]Ac 4:21
5:27 [o]Mt 5:22
5:28 [p]Ac 4:18 [q]Mt 23:35; 27:25; Ac 2:23,36; 3:14,15; 7:52
5:29 [r]Ac 4:19
5:30 [s]Ac 3:13 [t]Ac 2:24 [u]Ac 10:39; 13:29; Gal 3:13; 1Pe 2:24
5:31 [v]Ac 2:33 [w]Lk 2:11 [x]Mt 1:21; Lk 24:47; Ac 2:38
5:32 [y]Lk 24:48 [z]Jn 15:26
5:33 [a]Ac 2:37; 7:54
5:34 [b]Ac 22:3 [c]Lk 2:46
5:37 [d]Lk 2:1,2
5:38 [e]Mt 15:13
5:39 [f]Pr 21:30; Ac 7:51; 11:17
5:40 [g]Mt 10:17
5:41 [h]Mt 5:12 [i]Jn 15:21
5:42 [j]Ac 2:46

[a] 42 Or *Messiah*

The Choosing of the Seven

6 In those days when the number of disciples was
6:1 [k]Ac 2:41 increasing,[k] the Grecian Jews[l] among them
[l]Ac 9:29 complained against the Hebraic Jews because their
[m]Ac 9:39,41 [n]Ac 4:35 widows[m] were being overlooked in the daily distribution of food.[n] 2So the Twelve gathered all the dis-
ciples together and said, "It would not be right for
6:3 us to neglect the ministry of the word of God in
[o]Ac 1:16 order to wait on tables. 3Brothers,[o] choose seven
men from among you who are known to be full of
the Spirit and wisdom. We will turn this responsibility over to them 4and will give our attention to
6:4 [p]Ac 1:14 prayer[p] and the ministry of the word."
5This proposal pleased the whole group. They
6:5 [q]ver 8; chose Stephen,[q] a man full of faith and of the Holy
Ac 11:19 Spirit;[r] also Philip,[s] Procorus, Nicanor, Timon,
[r]Ac 11:24 [s]Ac 8:5-40; Parmenas, and Nicolas from Antioch, a convert to
21:8 Judaism. 6They presented these men to the apos-
tles, who prayed[t] and laid their hands on them.[u]
6:6 [t]Ac 1:24; 7So the word of God spread.[v] The number of dis-
8:17; 13:3; 2Ti 1:6 ciples in Jerusalem increased rapidly, and a large
[u]Nu 8:10; number of priests became obedient to the faith.

Ac 9:17; 1Ti 4:14

Stephen Seized

6:7 8Now Stephen, a man full of God's grace and
[v]Ac 12:24; 19:20 power, did great wonders and miraculous signs[w]
among the people. 9Opposition arose, however,
6:8 from members of the Synagogue of the Freedmen
[w]Jn 4:48 (as it was called)—Jews of Cyrene[x] and Alexan-
6:9 dria as well as the provinces of Cilicia[y] and Asia.[z]
[x]Mt 27:32 These men began to argue with Stephen, 10but
[y]Ac 15:23, 41; 22:3; they could not stand up against his wisdom or the
23:34 Spirit by whom he spoke.[a]
[z]Ac 2:9 11Then they secretly[b] persuaded some men to
6:10 say, "We have heard Stephen speak words of blas-
[a]Lk 21:15 phemy against Moses and against God."[c]
6:11 12So they stirred up the people and the elders and
[b]1Ki 21:10 the teachers of the law. They seized Stephen and
[c]Mt 26:59-61 brought him before the Sanhedrin.[d] 13They pro-
6:12 duced false witnesses, who testified, "This fellow
[d]Mt 5:22 never stops speaking against this holy place[e] and
against the law. 14For we have heard him say that
6:13 [e]Ac 21:28 this Jesus of Nazareth will destroy this place and
change the customs Moses handed down to us."[f]
6:14 [f]Ac 15:1; 15All who were sitting in the Sanhedrin[g] looked
21:21; 26:3; 28:17 intently at Stephen, and they saw that his face
was like the face of an angel.

6:15 [g]Mt 5:22

Stephen's Speech to the Sanhedrin

7 Then the high priest asked him, "Are these
charges true?"
7:2 [h]Ac 22:1 2To this he replied: "Brothers and fathers,[h] listen
[i]Ps 29:3 [j]Ge 11:31; to me! The God of glory[i] appeared to our father
15:7 Abraham while he was still in Mesopotamia,
before he lived in Haran.[j] 3'Leave your country
7:3 and your people,' God said, 'and go to the land I
[k]Ge 12:1 will show you.'[a][k]
4"So he left the land of the Chaldeans and set-

[a] 3 Gen. 12:1

The Office of Deacon

AC 6:1–4

Wherever people are in fellowship with one another, there is potential for problems, complaints and conflicts. First century . . . twenty-first century, this is always true. In the first-century church, there is a group of needy people being overlooked and neglected. The concern is clearly expressed to the apostles, and the issue is dealt with quickly, fairly and effectively. The leaders hear the complaint, evaluate the situation and recognize the validity of the need. They gather together and do some problem solving.

Notice how these leaders of the early church do not feel they themselves have to meet every need and do every job. They know their gifting and call from God is to prayer and the ministry of the Word. Under the leading of the Spirit, they call out a new group of gifted leaders to meet some of the physical needs that are being neglected. The words "wait on" in Acts 6:2 translate the Greek word from which we derive the word *deacon*. This appears to be the genesis of the office of deacon in the church.

Stephen

AC 6:8-15

The Christian church is born and is now, so to speak, in its toddler years. It is still being formed. Offices are being developed. Every lesson is important. Every step sets the scene for the years ahead. Leadership will be a critical issue. Does character matter? What kind of people will God call to lead, preach and guide his church into the future? Look at Stephen, and you will begin to get an idea of the type of leaders God is calling. What marks Stephen's life? What qualities and attributes does he model? Stephen is full of faith, of the Holy Spirit (Ac 6:5), and of wisdom (Ac 6:10). Filled with God's grace and power, he does amazing signs and wonders (Ac 6:8). He is willing to speak the truth, no matter what the cost (Ac 7). He is so devoted that the Sanhedrin looks at his face and sees "the face of an angel" (Ac 6:15).

Does character really matter in the life of a leader? God seems to think so.

tled in Haran. After the death of his father, God
sent him to this land where you are now living.[l]
5He gave him no inheritance here, not even a foot
of ground. But God promised him that he and his
descendants after him would possess the land,[m]
even though at that time Abraham had no child.
6God spoke to him in this way: 'Your descendants
will be strangers in a country not their own, and
they will be enslaved and mistreated four hundred
years.[n] 7But I will punish the nation they serve as
slaves,' God said, 'and afterward they will come
out of that country and worship me in this place.'[a][o]
8Then he gave Abraham the covenant of circumcision.[p] And Abraham became the father of Isaac
and circumcised him eight days after his birth.[q]
Later Isaac became the father of Jacob,[r] and Jacob
became the father of the twelve patriarchs.[s]
9"Because the patriarchs were jealous of
Joseph,[t] they sold him as a slave into Egypt.[u] But
God was with him[v] 10and rescued him from all his
troubles. He gave Joseph wisdom and enabled
him to gain the goodwill of Pharaoh king of
Egypt; so he made him ruler over Egypt and all
his palace.[w]
11"Then a famine struck all Egypt and Canaan,
bringing great suffering, and our fathers could not
find food.[x] 12When Jacob heard that there was
grain in Egypt, he sent our fathers on their first
visit.[y] 13On their second visit, Joseph told his
brothers who he was,[z] and Pharaoh learned about
Joseph's family. 14After this, Joseph sent for his
father Jacob and his whole family,[a] seventy-five
in all.[b] 15Then Jacob went down to Egypt, where
he and our fathers died.[c] 16Their bodies were
brought back to Shechem and placed in the tomb
that Abraham had bought from the sons of Hamor
at Shechem for a certain sum of money.[d]
17"As the time drew near for God to fulfill his
promise to Abraham, the number of our people in
Egypt greatly increased.[e] 18Then another king,
who knew nothing about Joseph, became ruler of
Egypt.[f] 19He dealt treacherously with our people
and oppressed our forefathers by forcing them to
throw out their newborn babies so that they
would die.[g]
20"At that time Moses was born, and he was no
ordinary child.[b] For three months he was cared for
in his father's house.[h] 21When he was placed outside, Pharaoh's daughter took him and brought
him up as her own son.[i] 22Moses was educated in
all the wisdom of the Egyptians[j] and was powerful in speech and action.
23"When Moses was forty years old, he decided
to visit his fellow Israelites. 24He saw one of them
being mistreated by an Egyptian, so he went to
his defense and avenged him by killing the Egyptian. 25Moses thought that his own people would
realize that God was using him to rescue them,
but they did not. 26The next day Moses came upon

7:4 [l]Ge 12:5
7:5 [m]Ge 12:7; 17:8; 26:3
7:6 [n]Ex 12:40
7:7 [o]Ex 3:12
7:8 [p]Ge 17:9-14 [q]Ge 21:2-4 [r]Ge 25:26 [s]Ge 29:31-35; 30:5-13, 17-24; 35:16-18,22-26
7:9 [t]Ge 37:4,11 [u]Ge 37:28; Ps 105:17 [v]Ge 39:2,21, 23
7:10 [w]Ge 41:37-43
7:11 [x]Ge 41:54
7:12 [y]Ge 42:1,2
7:13 [z]Ge 45:1-4
7:14 [a]Ge 45:9,10 [b]Ge 46:26, 27; Ex 1:5; Dt 10:22
7:15 [c]Ge 46:5-7; 49:33; Ex 1:6
7:16 [d]Ge 23:16-20; 33:18, 19; 50:13; Jos 24:32
7:17 [e]Ex 1:7; Ps 105:24
7:18 [f]Ex 1:8
7:19 [g]Ex 1:10-22
7:20 [h]Ex 2:2; Heb 11:23
7:21 [i]Ex 2:3-10
7:22 [j]1Ki 4:30; Isa 19:11

[a] *7* Gen. 15:13,14 [b] *20* Or *was fair in the sight of God*

two Israelites who were fighting. He tried to reconcile them by saying, 'Men, you are brothers;
why do you want to hurt each other?'
27 "But the man who was mistreating the other
pushed Moses aside and said, 'Who made you
ruler and judge over us? 28 Do you want to kill me
as you killed the Egyptian yesterday?'[a] 29 When
Moses heard this, he fled to Midian, where he set-
7:29 [k]Ex 2:11-15 tled as a foreigner and had two sons.[k]
30 "After forty years had passed, an angel
appeared to Moses in the flames of a burning bush
in the desert near Mount Sinai. 31 When he saw
this, he was amazed at the sight. As he went over
7:31 [l]Ex 3:1-4 to look more closely, he heard the Lord's voice:[l]
32 'I am the God of your fathers, the God of Abra-
ham, Isaac and Jacob.'[b] Moses trembled with fear
7:32 [m]Ex 3:6 and did not dare to look.[m]
33 "Then the Lord said to him, 'Take off your
sandals; the place where you are standing is holy
7:33 [n]Ex 3:5; Jos 5:15 ground.[n] 34 I have indeed seen the oppression of
my people in Egypt. I have heard their groaning
and have come down to set them free. Now come,
7:34 [o]Ex 3:7-10 I will send you back to Egypt.'[c][o]
35 "This is the same Moses whom they had reject-
7:35 [p]ver 27 ed with the words, 'Who made you ruler and
judge?'[p] He was sent to be their ruler and deliverer
by God himself, through the angel who appeared
7:36 [q]Ex 12:41; 33:1 [r]Ex 14:21 to him in the bush. 36 He led them out of Egypt[q] and
did wonders and miraculous signs in Egypt, at the
Red Sea[d][r] and for forty years in the desert.
37 "This is that Moses who told the Israelites,
'God will send you a prophet like me from your
7:37 [s]Dt 18:15, 18; Ac 3:22 own people.'[e][s] 38 He was in the assembly in the
desert, with the angel[t] who spoke to him on
7:38 [t]ver 53 [u]Ex 19:17 [v]Dt 32:45-47; Heb 4:12 [w]Ro 3:2 Mount Sinai, and with our fathers;[u] and he
received living words[v] to pass on to us.[w]
39 "But our fathers refused to obey him. Instead,
they rejected him and in their hearts turned back
to Egypt.[x] 40 They told Aaron, 'Make us gods who
7:39 [x]Nu 14:3,4 will go before us. As for this fellow Moses who
led us out of Egypt—we don't know what has
happened to him!'[f][y] 41 That was the time they
7:40 [y]Ex 32:1,23 made an idol in the form of a calf. They brought
sacrifices to it and held a celebration in honor of
7:41 [z]Ex 32:4-6; Ps 106:19, 20; Rev 9:20 what their hands had made.[z] 42 But God turned
away[a] and gave them over to the worship of the
heavenly bodies.[b] This agrees with what is written
7:42 [a]Jos 24:20; Isa 63:10 [b]Jer 19:13 in the book of the prophets:

" 'Did you bring me sacrifices and
offerings
forty years in the desert, O house of
Israel?
43 You have lifted up the shrine of Molech
and the star of your god Rephan,
the idols you made to worship.
7:43 [c]Am 5:25-27 Therefore I will send you into exile'[g][c]
beyond Babylon.

[a] *28* Exodus 2:14 [b] *32* Exodus 3:6 [c] *34* Exodus 3:5,7,8,10 [d] *36* That is, Sea of Reeds [e] *37* Deut. 18:15 [f] *40* Exodus 32:1 [g] *43* Amos 5:25–27

There is such a need for the healing touch of Christ in our communities. I see this struggle in the body of Christ. I see those who long to serve God with an undivided heart but their heart is broken. I see those who feel pulled in two, torn between the grace and mercy of God and the pain and cruelty of the world. Those of us who have gone through similar experiences can share some of the burden of our wounded brothers and sisters, but only Christ can fully know what any one soul is bearing. So we take the load to him.

Whatever you are carrying, take it to Jesus. That may sound simple and trite, but it is the very best choice that any of us can make. He who knelt in the garden and [sweat drops] of blood, who had his body whipped and ripped on a wooden cross, understands the agony that tears at your soul. As he knelt in Gethsemane, facing the horror of what lay ahead, he prayed, "Father, if you are willing, take this cup from me; yet not my will, but yours be done" (Lk 22:42).

There is healing in the will of God, a pulling together of all the pieces of our lives. It doesn't mean that we will always understand what is happening to us, but we bring our torn edges to him who holds us together.

—Sheila Walsh

Bold Stephen

AC 7:51–53

Passion? You better believe it! Boldness? No doubt! Truth? Stephen speaks it without apology. His final accusations bring some tough words to his hearers. Some may say, “Stephen is not very diplomatic. If he would have only been more sensitive and careful with his words, he might have lived to preach another day.”

Please remember, diplomacy is not what Stephen’s life is about. His life is about truth. The problem is not in the words he speaks. The problem is in the hearts of his listeners. The conflict arises because his words are not palatable to his hearers. Just like his Savior, Stephen speaks the truth, and it costs him his life. His message is loud and clear: The history of the Israelite nation reveals again and again their rejection of the God who is their Father. God seeks them and loves them, but they keep running, refusing his courtship. In Stephen’s accusers we see the same pattern. God wants to extend his grace, but instead of receiving it, the people respond by killing the messenger.

44“Our forefathers had the tabernacle of the Testimony[d] with them in the desert. It had been made as God directed Moses, according to the pattern he had seen.[e] 45Having received the tabernacle, our fathers under Joshua brought it with them when they took the land from the nations God drove out before them.[f] It remained in the land until the time of David, 46who enjoyed God’s favor and asked that he might provide a dwelling place for the God of Jacob.[a][g] 47But it was Solomon who built the house for him.

48“However, the Most High does not live in houses made by men.[h] As the prophet says:

49“ ‘Heaven is my throne,
and the earth is my footstool.[i]
What kind of house will you build for me?
says the Lord.
Or where will my resting place be?
50Has not my hand made all these things?’[b][j]

51“You stiff-necked people,[k] with uncircumcised hearts[l] and ears! You are just like your fathers: You always resist the Holy Spirit! 52Was there ever a prophet your fathers did not persecute?[m] They even killed those who predicted the coming of the Righteous One. And now you have betrayed and murdered him[n]— 53you who have received the law that was put into effect through angels[o] but have not obeyed it.”

The Stoning of Stephen

54When they heard this, they were furious[p] and gnashed their teeth at him. 55But Stephen, full of the Holy Spirit, looked up to heaven and saw the glory of God, and Jesus standing at the right hand of God.[q] 56“Look,” he said, “I see heaven open[r] and the Son of Man[s] standing at the right hand of God.”

57At this they covered their ears and, yelling at the top of their voices, they all rushed at him, 58dragged him out of the city[t] and began to stone him.[u] Meanwhile, the witnesses laid their clothes[v] at the feet of a young man named Saul.[w]

59While they were stoning him, Stephen prayed, “Lord Jesus, receive my spirit.”[x] 60Then he fell on his knees[y] and cried out, “Lord, do not hold this sin against them.”[z] When he had said this, he fell asleep.

8 And Saul[a] was there, giving approval to his death.

The Church Persecuted and Scattered

On that day a great persecution broke out against the church at Jerusalem, and all except the apostles were scattered[b] throughout Judea and Samaria.[c] 2Godly men buried Stephen and

7:44 [d]Ex 38:21 [e]Ex 25:8,9, 40
7:45 [f]Jos 3:14-17; 18:1; 23:9; 24:18; Ps 44:2
7:46 [g]2Sa 7:8-16; Ps 132:1-5
7:48 [h]1Ki 8:27; 2Ch 2:6
7:49 [i]Mt 5:34,35
7:50 [j]Isa 66:1,2
7:51 [k]Ex 32:9; 33:3,5 [l]Lev 26:41; Dt 10:16; Jer 4:4; 9:26
7:52 [m]2Ch 36:16; Mt 5:12 [n]Ac 3:14; 1Th 2:15
7:53 [o]ver 38; Gal 3:19; Heb 2:2
7:54 [p]Ac 5:33
7:55 [q]Mk 16:19
7:56 [r]Mt 3:16 [s]Mt 8:20
7:58 [t]Lk 4:29 [u]Lev 24:14, 16; Dt 13:9 [v]Ac 22:20 [w]Ac 8:1
7:59 [x]Ps 31:5; Lk 23:46
7:60 [y]Ac 9:40 [z]Mt 5:44
8:1 [a]Ac 7:58 [b]Ac 11:19 [c]Ac 9:31

[a] *46* Some early manuscripts *the house of Jacob* [b] *50* Isaiah 66:1,2

mourned deeply for him. 3But Saul[d] began to
destroy the church.[e] Going from house to house,
he dragged off men and women and put them in
prison.

Philip in Samaria

4Those who had been scattered[f] preached the
word wherever they went.[g] 5Philip[h] went down to
a city in Samaria and proclaimed the Christ[a] there.
6When the crowds heard Philip and saw the miraculous signs he did, they all paid close attention to
what he said. 7With shrieks, evil[b] spirits came out
of many,[i] and many paralytics and cripples were
healed.[j] 8So there was great joy in that city.

Simon the Sorcerer

9Now for some time a man named Simon had
practiced sorcery[k] in the city and amazed all the
people of Samaria. He boasted that he was someone great,[l] 10and all the people, both high and low,
gave him their attention and exclaimed, "This
man is the divine power known as the Great Power."[m] 11They followed him because he had amazed
them for a long time with his magic. 12But when
they believed Philip as he preached the good news
of the kingdom of God[n] and the name of Jesus
Christ, they were baptized,[o] both men and
women. 13Simon himself believed and was baptized. And he followed Philip everywhere, astonished by the great signs and miracles[p] he saw.
14When the apostles in Jerusalem heard that
Samaria[q] had accepted the word of God, they sent
Peter and John[r] to them. 15When they arrived,
they prayed for them that they might receive the
Holy Spirit,[s] 16because the Holy Spirit had not yet
come upon any of them;[t] they had simply been
baptized into[c] the name of the Lord Jesus.[u] 17Then
Peter and John placed their hands on them,[v] and
they received the Holy Spirit.
18When Simon saw that the Spirit was given at
the laying on of the apostles' hands, he offered
them money 19and said, "Give me also this ability
so that everyone on whom I lay my hands may
receive the Holy Spirit."
20Peter answered: "May your money perish with
you, because you thought you could buy the gift
of God with money![w] 21You have no part or share
in this ministry, because your heart is not right[x]
before God. 22Repent of this wickedness and pray
to the Lord. Perhaps he will forgive you for having
such a thought in your heart. 23For I see that you
are full of bitterness and captive to sin."
24Then Simon answered, "Pray to the Lord for
me[y] so that nothing you have said may happen
to me."
25When they had testified and proclaimed the
word of the Lord, Peter and John returned to Jerusalem, preaching the gospel in many Samaritan
villages.[z]

8:3 [d]Ac 7:58 [e]Ac 22:4,19; 26:10,11; 1Co 15:9; Gal 1:13,23; Php 3:6; 1Ti 1:13
8:4 [f]ver 1 [g]Ac 15:35
8:5 [h]Ac 6:5
8:7 [i]Mk 16:17 [j]Mt 4:24
8:9 [k]Ac 13:6 [l]Ac 5:36
8:10 [m]Ac 14:11; 28:6
8:12 [n]Ac 1:3 [o]Ac 2:38
8:13 [p]ver 6; Ac 19:11
8:14 [q]ver 1 [r]Lk 22:8
8:15 [s]Ac 2:38
8:16 [t]Ac 19:2 [u]Mt 28:19; Ac 2:38
8:17 [v]Ac 6:6
8:20 [w]2Ki 5:16; Da 5:17; Mt 10:8; Ac 2:38
8:21 [x]Ps 78:37
8:24 [y]Ex 8:8; Nu 21:7; 1Ki 13:6
8:25 [z]ver 40

Persecution

AC 8:1–4

The martyrdom of Stephen brings about a wave of persecution against the church. This eruption of conflict drives the Christians out of Jerusalem into Judea and Samaria. Look closely at what happens: "Those who had been scattered preached the word wherever they went" (Ac 8:4). The early followers of Christ could easily have become discouraged. Instead, they are driven out of their homes by their hardships, forced to settle in unfamiliar places, and react by spreading the gospel wherever they go.

Luke, the author of both the Gospel of Luke and the book of Acts, makes a historical observation in Acts 11:19–21. He looks back and sees the persecution and death of Stephen as the impetus for the spreading of the gospel. Stephen's passion is to see the Good News of Jesus Christ spread to the ends of the earth. His passion is accomplished through both his life and death.

[a] 5 Or *Messiah* [b] 7 Greek *unclean* [c] 16 Or *in*

Gentile Conversion

AC 8:26–40

Luke, the author of Acts, now moves his focus from "the church at Jerusalem" (Ac 8:1) and the movement of the Good News into Samaria (Ac 8:14,25) to the movement of the gospel to "the ends of the earth" (Ac 1:8), that is, to the eunuch from Ethiopia. This minister of finance under Queen Candace had been to Jerusalem to worship and was reading the book of Isaiah as he traveled home. Therefore, either he had abandoned the emptiness of paganism for worship of the one true God and moral living or he was a full-fledged proselyte to Judaism, following all the laws of Moses. Either way, he was open to a fuller understanding of the truth and willing to hear it from a Jew.

This story forms a bridge for Luke from the spread of the gospel within Judaism—those of the Jewish race or those who had converted to the religion of Judaism—to the conversion of Saul and the spread of the gospel to the Gentiles. The circle of those who are receiving the gospel and following Christ is broadening. The church is spreading, both geographically and demographically, reminding us that all people are welcome in the kingdom of God.

Philip and the Ethiopian

26 Now an angel[a] of the Lord said to Philip, "Go
south to the road—the desert road—that goes
down from Jerusalem to Gaza." 27 So he started
out, and on his way he met an Ethiopian[ab]
eunuch,[c] an important official in charge of all the
treasury of Candace, queen of the Ethiopians. This
man had gone to Jerusalem to worship,[d] 28 and on
his way home was sitting in his chariot reading
the book of Isaiah the prophet. 29 The Spirit told[e]
Philip, "Go to that chariot and stay near it."
30 Then Philip ran up to the chariot and heard
the man reading Isaiah the prophet. "Do you
understand what you are reading?" Philip asked.
31 "How can I," he said, "unless someone
explains it to me?" So he invited Philip to come
up and sit with him.
32 The eunuch was reading this passage of
Scripture:

> "He was led like a sheep to the slaughter,
> and as a lamb before the shearer is silent,
> so he did not open his mouth.
> 33 In his humiliation he was deprived of justice.
> Who can speak of his descendants?
> For his life was taken from the earth."[bf]

34 The eunuch asked Philip, "Tell me, please,
who is the prophet talking about, himself or
someone else?" 35 Then Philip began[g] with that
very passage of Scripture[h] and told him the good
news about Jesus.
36 As they traveled along the road, they came to
some water and the eunuch said, "Look, here is
water. Why shouldn't I be baptized?"[ci] 38 And he
gave orders to stop the chariot. Then both Philip
and the eunuch went down into the water and
Philip baptized him. 39 When they came up out of
the water, the Spirit of the Lord suddenly took
Philip away,[j] and the eunuch did not see him
again, but went on his way rejoicing. 40 Philip,
however, appeared at Azotus and traveled about,
preaching the gospel in all the towns[k] until he
reached Caesarea.[l]

Saul's Conversion

9 Meanwhile, Saul was still breathing out murderous threats against the Lord's disciples.[m]
He went to the high priest 2 and asked him for letters to the synagogues in Damascus, so that if he
found any there who belonged to the Way,[n]
whether men or women, he might take them as
prisoners to Jerusalem. 3 As he neared Damascus

8:26 [a]Ac 5:19
8:27 [b]Ps 68:31; 87:4; Zep 3:10 [c]Isa 56:3-5 [d]1Ki 8:41-43; Jn 12:20
8:29 [e]Ac 10:19; 11:12; 13:2; 20:23; 21:11
8:33 [f]Isa 53:7,8
8:35 [g]Mt 5:2 [h]Lk 24:27; Ac 17:2; 18:28; 28:23
8:36 [i]Ac 10:47
8:39 [j]1Ki 18:12; 2Ki 2:16; Eze 3:12,14; 8:3; 11:1,24; 43:5; 2Co 12:2
8:40 [k]ver 25 [l]Ac 10:1,24; 12:19; 21:8, 16; 23:23, 33; 25:1,4,6, 13
9:1 [m]Ac 8:3
9:2 [n]Ac 19:9,23; 22:4; 24:14, 22

[a] 27 That is, from the upper Nile region [b] 33 Isaiah 53:7,8
[c] 36 Some late manuscripts *baptized?" 37 Philip said, "If you believe with all your heart, you may." The eunuch answered, "I believe that Jesus Christ is the Son of God."*

Week 38

A God-Ordained Meeting

The story of Philip and the Ethiopian eunuch teaches that meeting people where they are and allowing God to work is the best approach when sharing your faith. God definitely has an agenda, and simple obedience—even when you don't understand the plan—is the best way to fit into that agenda.

Philip is given a simple command: "Go down the road" (Ac 8:26). What does he do? Do you think he has any inkling of the events that are to follow? Why or why not?

Whether the eunuch is a full-fledged Jewish proselyte or simply a God-fearing Gentile is not known, but he has been to Jerusalem to worship and now sits in his chariot, reading the book of Isaiah (Ac 8:27-28). One thing is clear: God is working in his heart and orchestrating events around him. Can you think of ways God has carefully orchestrated the events of your life? What can you do to increase your awareness of God's hand in the events of your life?

Philip asks the eunuch if he understands what he is reading. The eunuch's response is: "How can I understand this stuff unless someone explains it to me?" Philip doesn't have to push his beliefs on the eunuch. The eunuch *invites* Philip to explain the Scriptures to him. Are there people in your life who want you to explain the Good News to them? Who are they? What will you do?

Philip explains the Good News by beginning with the very passage the eunuch is reading (Ac 8:35). Philip meets the eunuch where he is, and he proceeds from that point. How can you apply Philip's example to situations in which you share your faith?

As they travel along, they come to some water (Ac 8:36). How convenient for God to have water nearby! It is the eunuch who initiates the baptism (Ac 8:36-38). Do you sometimes forget that it is God who does the work in a person's heart, not you? Whose task is it to speak the truth of the gospel (Ro 10:14)? Whose task is it to open blind eyes (Lk 24:45)?

Enjoying God THROUGH the Word

Read Acts 24:24-27 (pages 1837-1838). Paul is in a lot of trouble for preaching the Good News. He is, at this point, under the control and authority of Felix. What does Paul do in this situation? He shares his faith in Christ with Felix and explains the Good News to him (Ac 24:24-25). We don't know if Felix ever becomes a believer. The point is this: Paul is faithful in using his situation to speak the truth to those around him. Paul knows it is up to God to open Felix's spiritual eyes.

Ask God to help you become more sensitive to situations in which you find yourself. Ask him to show you how to gently share your faith with others by meeting them where they are. This week, try to see your life opportunities through God's eyes.

Enjoying God THROUGH Experience

Make a list of your family members, friends and acquaintances who need to hear the gospel. Ask God to give you sensitivity to his Spirit during times of contact with these people. In the coming days and weeks, pray for each person on your list and ask God to make a "divine appointment" with her or with him.

Go to page 1823 for your next weekly study.

The Conversion of Saul

AC 9:1–19

It is probably fair to say that this *passage* contains an account of the most famous conversion in human history. *Conversion* is a word the Christian church uses freely. What exactly does it mean? The English word comes from the Latin *convertere/ conversio*, meaning "to turn around." This is an important starting point. Every conversion involves a turning from sin and self and a turning toward God.

Although every conversion has a turning process at its core, no two conversion stories are the same. They are as different as the people, their backgrounds, their past sins and their new relationships with God. Paul's conversion story is just that—Paul's—just as our conversion stories are uniquely our own.

on his journey, suddenly a light from heaven
flashed around him.[o] 4He fell to the ground and
heard a voice say to him, "Saul, Saul, why do you
persecute me?"
5"Who are you, Lord?" Saul asked.
"I am Jesus, whom you are persecuting," he
replied. 6"Now get up and go into the city, and
you will be told what you must do."[p]
7The men traveling with Saul stood there
speechless; they heard the sound[q] but did not see
anyone.[r] 8Saul got up from the ground, but when
he opened his eyes he could see nothing. So they
led him by the hand into Damascus. 9For three
days he was blind, and did not eat or drink
anything.
10In Damascus there was a disciple named Ananias. The Lord called to him in a vision,[s]
"Ananias!"
"Yes, Lord," he answered.
11The Lord told him, "Go to the house of Judas
on Straight Street and ask for a man from Tarsus[t]
named Saul, for he is praying. 12In a vision he has
seen a man named Ananias come and place his
hands on[u] him to restore his sight."
13"Lord," Ananias answered, "I have heard
many reports about this man and all the harm he
has done to your saints[v] in Jerusalem.[w] 14And he
has come here with authority from the chief
priests[x] to arrest all who call on your name."
15But the Lord said to Ananias, "Go! This man is
my chosen instrument[y] to carry my name before
the Gentiles[z] and their kings[a] and before the people of Israel. 16I will show him how much he must
suffer for my name."[b]
17Then Ananias went to the house and entered
it. Placing his hands on[c] Saul, he said, "Brother
Saul, the Lord—Jesus, who appeared to you on
the road as you were coming here—has sent me
so that you may see again and be filled with the
Holy Spirit." 18Immediately, something like scales
fell from Saul's eyes, and he could see again. He
got up and was baptized, 19and after taking some
food, he regained his strength.

Saul in Damascus and Jerusalem

Saul spent several days with the disciples[d] in
Damascus.[e] 20At once he began to preach in the
synagogues[f] that Jesus is the Son of God.[g] 21All
those who heard him were astonished and asked,
"Isn't he the man who raised havoc in Jerusalem
among those who call on this name?[h] And hasn't
he come here to take them as prisoners to the
chief priests?"[i] 22Yet Saul grew more and more
powerful and baffled the Jews living in Damascus
by proving that Jesus is the Christ.[a][j]
23After many days had gone by, the Jews conspired to kill him, 24but Saul learned of their
plan.[k] Day and night they kept close watch on the
city gates in order to kill him. 25But his followers

9:3 [o]1Co 15:8
9:6 [p]ver 16
9:7 [q]Jn 12:29 [r]Da 10:7; Ac 22:9
9:10 [s]Ac 10:3,17, 19
9:11 [t]ver 30; Ac 21:39; 22:3
9:12 [u]Mk 5:23
9:13 [v]ver 32; Ro 1:7; 16:2, 15 [w]Ac 8:3
9:14 [x]ver 2,21
9:15 [y]Ac 13:2; Ro 1:1; Gal 1:15 [z]Ro 11:13; 15:15,16; Gal 2:7,8; Eph 3:7,8 [a]Ac 25:22, 23; 26:1
9:16 [b]Ac 20:23; 21:11; 2Co 11:23-27
9:17 [c]Ac 6:6
9:19 [d]Ac 11:26 [e]Ac 26:20
9:20 [f]Ac 13:5,14 [g]Mt 4:3
9:21 [h]Ac 8:3 [i]Gal 1:13,23
9:22 [j]Ac 18:5,28
9:24 [k]Ac 20:3,19

[a] 22 Or *Messiah*

9:25 took him by night and lowered him in a basket
[l]1Sa 19:12; through an opening in the wall.[l]
2Co 11:32,33 26When he came to Jerusalem,[m] he tried to join
9:26 the disciples, but they were all afraid of him, not
[m]Ac 22:17; believing that he really was a disciple. 27But Bar-
26:20; nabas[n] took him and brought him to the apostles.
Gal 1:17,18 He told them how Saul on his journey had seen the
9:27 Lord and that the Lord had spoken to him,[o] and
[n]Ac 4:36 how in Damascus he had preached fearlessly in the
[o]ver 3-6 [p]ver 20,22 name of Jesus.[p] 28So Saul stayed with them and
moved about freely in Jerusalem, speaking boldly
9:29 in the name of the Lord. 29He talked and debated
[q]Ac 6:1 with the Grecian Jews,[q] but they tried to kill him.[r]
[r]2Co 11:26 30When the brothers[s] learned of this, they took him
9:30 down to Caesarea[t] and sent him off to Tarsus.[u]
[s]Ac 1:16 31Then the church throughout Judea, Galilee
[t]Ac 8:40 [u]ver 11 and Samaria[v] enjoyed a time of peace. It was
strengthened; and encouraged by the Holy Spirit,
9:31 [v]Ac 8:1 it grew in numbers, living in the fear of the Lord.

Aeneas and Dorcas

9:32 32As Peter traveled about the country, he went
[w]ver 13 to visit the saints[w] in Lydda. 33There he found a
man named Aeneas, a paralytic who had been
9:34 bedridden for eight years. 34"Aeneas," Peter said
[x]Ac 3:6,16; to him, "Jesus Christ heals you.[x] Get up and take
4:10 care of your mat." Immediately Aeneas got up.
9:35 35All those who lived in Lydda and Sharon[y] saw
[y]1Ch 5:16; him and turned to the Lord.[z]
27:29; Isa 33:9; 36In Joppa[a] there was a disciple named Tabitha
35:2; 65:10 [z]Ac 11:21 (which, when translated, is Dorcas[a]), who was
always doing good[b] and helping the poor. 37About
9:36 that time she became sick and died, and her body
[a]Jos 19:46; 2Ch 2:16; was washed and placed in an upstairs room.[c]
Ezr 3:7; 38Lydda was near Joppa; so when the disciples[d]
Jnh 1:3; Ac 10:5 heard that Peter was in Lydda, they sent two men
[b]1Ti 2:10; to him and urged him, "Please come at once!"
Tit 3:8 39Peter went with them, and when he arrived
9:37 he was taken upstairs to the room. All the wid-
[c]Ac 1:13 ows[e] stood around him, crying and showing him
the robes and other clothing that Dorcas had
9:38 [d]Ac 11:26 made while she was still with them.
40Peter sent them all out of the room;[f] then he
9:39 got down on his knees[g] and prayed. Turning
[e]Ac 6:1 toward the dead woman, he said, "Tabitha, get
9:40 up." She opened her eyes, and seeing Peter she sat
[f]Mt 9:25 up. 41He took her by the hand and helped her to
[g]Lk 22:41; Ac 7:60 her feet. Then he called the believers and the widows and presented her to them alive. 42This
became known all over Joppa, and many people
9:43 believed in the Lord. 43Peter stayed in Joppa for
[h]Ac 10:6 some time with a tanner named Simon.[h]

Cornelius Calls for Peter

10:1 [i]Ac 8:40 **10** At Caesarea[i] there was a man named Cornelius, a centurion in what was known as
10:2 the Italian Regiment. 2He and all his family were
[j]ver 22,35; devout and God-fearing;[j] he gave generously to
Ac 13:16,26 those in need and prayed to God regularly. 3One

[a]*36* Both *Tabitha* (Aramaic) and *Dorcas* (Greek) mean *gazelle.*

Healings

AC 9:40-43

The blind can see again. The lame can walk. The lepers are healed. The dead are restored to life. Jesus speaks the word, reaches out his hand, touches those in need and healing power flows. When we read of the signs and wonders Jesus performs, we see exactly what we would expect. He is God in human flesh.

The sick are healed. Demons are cast out. The dead are raised. The apostles speak in the name of Jesus, and the signs and wonders continue. When we read of these historical accounts in the book of Acts, we can't deny that the power of God flows through these first-century believers. The same Jesus who had performed miracles continues to work through the leaders of the early church. It is still Jesus at work, but now it is through the lives of his people.

Clean and Unclean

AC 10:9–23

From his childhood Peter had been taught what was clean and unclean. Certain foods could be eaten with gladness; others were forbidden. Only Jews could enter the home of a devout Jew, sit at the table and enjoy the intimacy of fellowship—Gentiles were not numbered among those people.

Peter is about to have his whole worldview rocked to its foundations. In his vision he sees many animals that are on the "unclean" and "be sure to avoid" list. Yet the Lord says to him, "Get up, Peter. Kill and eat" (Ac 10:13). Moments later he is invited to go to the home of a Gentile. Not only is he expected to enter the home and share fellowship with an "unclean" person, he is called to preach the gospel and offer to this man the table fellowship of the kingdom of God. Peter is learning the same lesson that applies to us today: "Do not call anything impure that God has made clean" (Ac 10:15).

day at about three in the afternoon[k] he had a vision.[l] He distinctly saw an angel[m] of God, who came to him and said, "Cornelius!"

4Cornelius stared at him in fear. "What is it, Lord?" he asked.

The angel answered, "Your prayers and gifts to the poor have come up as a memorial offering[n] before God.[o] 5Now send men to Joppa[p] to bring back a man named Simon who is called Peter. 6He is staying with Simon the tanner,[q] whose house is by the sea."

7When the angel who spoke to him had gone, Cornelius called two of his servants and a devout soldier who was one of his attendants. 8He told them everything that had happened and sent them to Joppa.[r]

Peter's Vision

9About noon the following day as they were on their journey and approaching the city, Peter went up on the roof[s] to pray. 10He became hungry and wanted something to eat, and while the meal was being prepared, he fell into a trance.[t] 11He saw heaven opened and something like a large sheet being let down to earth by its four corners. 12It contained all kinds of four-footed animals, as well as reptiles of the earth and birds of the air. 13Then a voice told him, "Get up, Peter. Kill and eat."

14"Surely not, Lord!"[u] Peter replied. "I have never eaten anything impure or unclean."[v]

15The voice spoke to him a second time, "Do not call anything impure that God has made clean."[w]

16This happened three times, and immediately the sheet was taken back to heaven.

17While Peter was wondering about the meaning of the vision, the men sent by Cornelius[x] found out where Simon's house was and stopped at the gate. 18They called out, asking if Simon who was known as Peter was staying there.

19While Peter was still thinking about the vision, the Spirit said[y] to him, "Simon, three[a] men are looking for you. 20So get up and go downstairs. Do not hesitate to go with them, for I have sent them."[z]

21Peter went down and said to the men, "I'm the one you're looking for. Why have you come?"

22The men replied, "We have come from Cornelius the centurion. He is a righteous and God-fearing man,[a] who is respected by all the Jewish people. A holy angel told him to have you come to his house so that he could hear what you have to say."[b] 23Then Peter invited the men into the house to be his guests.

Peter at Cornelius's House

The next day Peter started out with them, and some of the brothers[c] from Joppa went along.[d] 24The following day he arrived in Caesarea.[e] Cor-

[a] *19* One early manuscript *two*; other manuscripts do not have the number.

10:3 [k]Ac 3:1 [l]Ac 9:10 [m]Ac 5:19
10:4 [n]Mt 26:13 [o]Rev 8:4
10:5 [p]Ac 9:36
10:6 [q]Ac 9:43
10:8 [r]Ac 9:36
10:9 [s]Mt 24:17
10:10 [t]Ac 22:17
10:14 [u]Ac 9:5 [v]Lev 11:4-8, 13-20; 20:25; Dt 14:3-20; Eze 4:14
10:15 [w]Mt 15:11; Ro 14:14,17, 20; 1Co 10:25; 1Ti 4:3,4; Tit 1:15
10:17 [x]ver 7,8
10:19 [y]Ac 8:29
10:20 [z]Ac 15:7-9
10:22 [a]ver 2 [b]Ac 11:14
10:23 [c]Ac 1:16 [d]ver 45; Ac 11:12
10:24 [e]Ac 8:40

nelius was expecting them and had called together his relatives and close friends. 25 As Peter entered the house, Cornelius met him and fell at his feet in reverence. 26 But Peter made him get up. "Stand up," he said, "I am only a man myself."[f]

27 Talking with him, Peter went inside and found a large gathering of people. 28 He said to them: "You are well aware that it is against our law for a Jew to associate with a Gentile or visit him.[g] But God has shown me that I should not call any man impure or unclean.[h] 29 So when I was sent for, I came without raising any objection. May I ask why you sent for me?"

30 Cornelius answered: "Four days ago I was in my house praying at this hour, at three in the afternoon. Suddenly a man in shining clothes stood before me 31 and said, 'Cornelius, God has heard your prayer and remembered your gifts to the poor. 32 Send to Joppa for Simon who is called Peter. He is a guest in the home of Simon the tanner, who lives by the sea.' 33 So I sent for you immediately, and it was good of you to come. Now we are all here in the presence of God to listen to everything the Lord has commanded you to tell us."

34 Then Peter began to speak: "I now realize how true it is that God does not show favoritism[i] 35 but accepts men from every nation who fear him and do what is right.[j] 36 You know the message God sent to the people of Israel, telling the good news[k] of peace[l] through Jesus Christ, who is Lord of all.[m] 37 You know what has happened throughout Judea, beginning in Galilee after the baptism that John preached— 38 how God anointed[n] Jesus of Nazareth with the Holy Spirit and power, and how he went around doing good and healing[o] all who were under the power of the devil, because God was with him.[p]

39 "We are witnesses[q] of everything he did in the country of the Jews and in Jerusalem. They killed him by hanging him on a tree,[r] 40 but God raised him from the dead[s] on the third day and caused him to be seen. 41 He was not seen by all the people,[t] but by witnesses whom God had already chosen—by us who ate[u] and drank with him after he rose from the dead. 42 He commanded us to preach to the people[v] and to testify that he is the one whom God appointed as judge of the living and the dead.[w] 43 All the prophets testify about him[x] that everyone[y] who believes in him receives forgiveness of sins through his name."

44 While Peter was still speaking these words, the Holy Spirit came on[z] all who heard the message. 45 The circumcised believers who had come with Peter[a] were astonished that the gift of the Holy Spirit had been poured out[b] even on the Gentiles.[c] 46 For they heard them speaking in tongues[a][d] and praising God.

Then Peter said, 47 "Can anyone keep these people from being baptized with water?[e] They have

10:26 [f]Ac 14:15; Rev 19:10
10:28 [g]Jn 4:9; 18:28; Ac 11:3 [h]Ac 15:8,9
10:34 [i]Dt 10:17; 2Ch 19:7; Job 34:19; Ro 2:11; Gal 2:6; Eph 6:9; Col 3:25; 1Pe 1:17
10:35 [j]Ac 15:9
10:36 [k]Ac 13:32 [l]Lk 2:14 [m]Mt 28:18; Ro 10:12
10:38 [n]Ac 4:26 [o]Mt 4:23 [p]Jn 3:2
10:39 [q]Lk 24:48 [r]Ac 5:30
10:40 [s]Ac 2:24
10:41 [t]Jn 14:17,22 [u]Lk 24:43; Jn 21:13
10:42 [v]Mt 28:19,20 [w]Jn 5:22; Ac 17:31; Ro 14:9; 2Co 5:10; 2Ti 4:1; 1Pe 4:5
10:43 [x]Isa 53:11 [y]Ac 15:9
10:44 [z]Ac 8:15,16; 11:15; 15:8
10:45 [a]ver 23 [b]Ac 2:33,38 [c]Ac 11:18
10:46 [d]Mk 16:17
10:47 [e]Ac 8:36

[a] 46 Or *other languages*

Even on the Gentiles

AC 10:34-35,45

The familiar old hymn begins, "Amazing grace! how sweet the sound, that saved a wretch like me!" In some ways, the words *like me* express the heart of Peter, the early Christians, and many today. Too often we are attracted only to those who are much like us. We don't mind wretches, as long as they are our kind of wretches.

In the early days of the New Testament church, the followers of Christ were converted Jews. Many of them believed God's grace was only big enough for them . . . or wretches just like them. It was time for their vision to get bigger and their hearts to be expanded. Through Peter's encounter with Cornelius and his family and close friends (see Map 12: Apostles' Early Travels at the back of this Bible), it becomes crystal clear that no one is beyond God's grace, regardless of position or race. Jesus loves all people, the Holy Spirit can fill their lives, and they can be brought into relationship with the heavenly Father.

received the Holy Spirit just as we have."[f] 48So he
ordered that they be baptized in the name of Jesus
Christ.[g] Then they asked Peter to stay with them
for a few days.

Peter Explains His Actions

11 The apostles and the brothers[h] throughout
Judea heard that the Gentiles also had
received the word of God. 2So when Peter went up
to Jerusalem, the circumcised believers[i] criticized
him 3and said, "You went into the house of uncircumcised men and ate with them."[j]

4Peter began and explained everything to them
precisely as it had happened: 5"I was in the city
of Joppa praying, and in a trance I saw a vision.[k]
I saw something like a large sheet being let down
from heaven by its four corners, and it came down
to where I was. 6I looked into it and saw four-footed animals of the earth, wild beasts, reptiles, and
birds of the air. 7Then I heard a voice telling me,
'Get up, Peter. Kill and eat.'

8"I replied, 'Surely not, Lord! Nothing impure
or unclean has ever entered my mouth.'

9"The voice spoke from heaven a second time,
'Do not call anything impure that God has made
clean.'[l] 10This happened three times, and then it
was all pulled up to heaven again.

11"Right then three men who had been sent to
me from Caesarea stopped at the house where I
was staying. 12The Spirit told[m] me to have no hesitation about going with them.[n] These six brothers
also went with me, and we entered the man's
house. 13He told us how he had seen an angel
appear in his house and say, 'Send to Joppa for
Simon who is called Peter. 14He will bring you a
message through which you and all your household[o] will be saved.'

15"As I began to speak, the Holy Spirit came on[p]
them as he had come on us at the beginning.[q]
16Then I remembered what the Lord had said:
'John baptized with[a] water, but you will be baptized with the Holy Spirit.'[r] 17So if God gave them
the same gift as he gave us,[s] who believed in the
Lord Jesus Christ, who was I to think that I could
oppose God?"

18When they heard this, they had no further
objections and praised God, saying, "So then, God
has granted even the Gentiles repentance unto
life."[t]

The Church in Antioch

19Now those who had been scattered by the persecution in connection with Stephen[u] traveled as
far as Phoenicia, Cyprus and Antioch,[v] telling the
message only to Jews. 20Some of them, however,
men from Cyprus[w] and Cyrene,[x] went to Antioch
and began to speak to Greeks also, telling them
the good news about the Lord Jesus. 21The Lord's

[a] 16 Or *in*

10:47 [f]Ac 11:17
10:48 [g]Ac 2:38; 8:16
11:1 [h]Ac 1:16
11:2 [i]Ac 10:45
11:3 [j]Ac 10:25,28; Gal 2:12
11:5 [k]Ac 10:9-32; 9:10
11:9 [l]Ac 10:15
11:12 [m]Ac 8:29 [n]Ac 15:9; Ro 3:22
11:14 [o]Jn 4:53; Ac 16:15,31-34; 1Co 1:11,16
11:15 [p]Ac 10:44 [q]Ac 2:4
11:16 [r]Mk 1:8; Ac 1:5
11:17 [s]Ac 10:45,47
11:18 [t]Ro 10:12,13; 2Co 7:10
11:19 [u]Ac 8:1,4 [v]ver 26,27; Ac 13:1; 18:22; Gal 2:11
11:20 [w]Ac 4:36 [x]Mt 27:32

**When Death bestows the Martyr's crown,
And calls me into Jesus' rest.
Then for my ultimate reward—
Then for the world-rejoicing word—
The voice from Father-Spirit-Son:
"Servant of God, well hast thou done!**

—*Charlotte Brontë (1816–1855)*

Syrophoenician (Canaanite) Woman

A Tenacious Faith

She called him Lord. Who was she kidding? She was a Gentile. The disciples wished she would get lost. Jesus did not want anyone to know he was here, and she was ruining it all. They pleaded with him, "Send her away, for she keeps crying out after us" (Mt 15:23).

Things did not seem to be going well for Jesus lately. Herod had beheaded John the Baptist. The Pharisees had plotted to kill Jesus. His own hometown was offended by his teaching, and his disciples were spiritually thickheaded. The resistance to his ministry grew rapidly, and Jesus needed time to think and pray. He had come from Galilee to be alone with his disciples. Perhaps here the Father might show him the answers he needed in the face of persecution. But first he must handle this new crisis for the disciples.

As he turned to answer her, Jesus saw something in the woman's face. This Gentile was not going to give up—she believed in him! Perhaps Jesus thought aloud as he tested her: "I was sent only to the lost sheep of Israel" (Mt 15:24).

Thinking he might refuse her, she came close and knelt at Jesus' feet, again begging for mercy. She had no claim on Israel's Messiah. Nonetheless, only God could grant her mercy and deliver her daughter from demons. She did not even flinch when Jesus said she was robbing Israel's provision. She knew that Jesus was the answer. Jesus did not have to give her the whole package. Even the crumbs would satisfy her.

When Jesus saw her faith, her tenacity and her humility, he was amazed. She was not the first Gentile that Jesus healed, and she would certainly not be the last.

Faith is a powerful force. It *changes* things. It provides a way when there is no way, an answer when there is no answer. It turns "no" into "yes." Faith touches God. It is a gift of the Spirit and a sign to unbelievers. We pray for faith when we have none, and we keep asking until God answers.

Syrophoenician Woman

Matthew 15:21-28

Mark 7:24-30

Candid SNAPSHOT "Yes, Lord," she said, "but even the dogs eat the crumbs that fall from their masters' table." Then Jesus answered, "Woman, you have great faith! Your request is granted." And her daughter was healed from that very hour (Matthew 15:27-28).

Woman Caught in Adultery

Not Excused but Forgiven

The Pharisees shoved her into the temple court where Jesus was teaching. The crowd around him leered at her and craned their necks to see. The Pharisees were setting a trap for Jesus, and this woman was the bait. She had been caught in adultery. If Jesus said that she should be stoned, he violated Roman law, which prohibited the practice. If he said that she should not be stoned, he violated Moses' law. The woman's shoulders sank, and she began to tremble. She knew she was going to die. The enormity of her crime sank in. Stoning was a horrible death.

Jesus was quiet for some time as the questions and the jeers continued. Then he stated his case. He applied the Law to her *accusers!* Jesus bent down and wrote in the dust. She couldn't see what he was writing, but his silence was having its effect on her accusers. No one wanted to meet Jesus' eyes or anyone else's. Shame overtook them one by one. The woman held her breath as the men left without comment. Finally, she was alone with Jesus, the only one who was perfect enough to condemn her—the only one merciful enough not to.

She wondered what to do. She did not try to run away or argue. She did not gloat over the fact that her accusers were gone.

But wait! She could hardly take it in; Jesus found her guilty, but he *forgave* her. *Yes*, she would change her way of life. Her illicit affair had brought her close to death. Perhaps for the first time in her life things clicked into place. Maybe she finally realized how terrible her adultery was. And perhaps she recognized that today she had encountered Truth. Only Jesus could know that is what she had longed for all along.

Jesus came to bring sinners to repentance. He came to save, not to destroy. No matter how hard we try, we will always be sinners until we are with the Lord. First John 1:9 says, "If we confess our sins, he is faithful and just and will forgive us our sins and purify us from all unrighteousness." When you sin, throw yourself on God's mercy. Confess. Humble yourself. He will not excuse you; he will *forgive* you.

Woman Caught in Adultery

John 8:1–11

Candid SNAPSHOT Jesus straightened up and asked her, "Woman, where are they? Has no one condemned you?"

"No one, sir," she said.

"Then neither do I condemn you," Jesus declared. "Go now and leave your life of sin" (John 8:10–11).

11:21 hand was with them,[y] and a great number of peo-
[y]Lk 1:66 [z]Ac 2:47 ple believed and turned to the Lord.[z]
22News of this reached the ears of the church at
11:22 [a]Ac 4:36 Jerusalem, and they sent Barnabas[a] to Antioch.
23When he arrived and saw the evidence of the
11:23 grace of God,[b] he was glad and encouraged them
[b]Ac 13:43; 14:26; 20:24 all to remain true to the Lord with all their hearts.[c]
[c]Ac 14:22 24He was a good man, full of the Holy Spirit and
11:24 faith, and a great number of people were brought
[d]ver 21; to the Lord.[d]
Ac 5:14 25Then Barnabas went to Tarsus[e] to look for
Saul, 26and when he found him, he brought him
11:25 [e]Ac 9:11 to Antioch. So for a whole year Barnabas and Saul
met with the church and taught great numbers of
11:26 [f]Ac 6:1,2; people. The disciples[f] were called Christians first[g]
13:52 at Antioch.
[g]Ac 26:28; 27During this time some prophets[h] came down
1Pe 4:16 from Jerusalem to Antioch. 28One of them, named
11:27 Agabus,[i] stood up and through the Spirit predict-
[h]Ac 13:1; 15:32; ed that a severe famine would spread over the
1Co 12:28, entire Roman world.[j] (This happened during the
29; Eph 4:11 reign of Claudius.)[k] 29The disciples,[l] each accord-
11:28 ing to his ability, decided to provide help[m] for the
[i]Ac 21:10 [j]Mt 24:14 brothers[n] living in Judea. 30This they did, sending
[k]Ac 18:2 their gift to the elders[o] by Barnabas and Saul.[p]

11:29 [l]ver 26

Peter's Miraculous Escape From Prison

[m]Ro 15:26; 12 It was about this time that King Herod arrest-
2Co 9:2 ed some who belonged to the church, intend-
[n]Ac 1:16 ing to persecute them. 2He had James, the brother
11:30 of John,[q] put to death with the sword. 3When he
[o]Ac 14:23 saw that this pleased the Jews,[r] he proceeded to
[p]Ac 12:25 seize Peter also. This happened during the Feast of
12:2 Unleavened Bread.[s] 4After arresting him, he put
[q]Mt 4:21 him in prison, handing him over to be guarded by
12:3 four squads of four soldiers each. Herod intended
[r]Ac 24:27 to bring him out for public trial after the Passover.
[s]Ex 12:15; 23:15 5So Peter was kept in prison, but the church
was earnestly praying to God for him.[t]
12:5 6The night before Herod was to bring him to tri-
[t]Eph 6:18 al, Peter was sleeping between two soldiers, bound
12:6 with two chains,[u] and sentries stood guard at the
[u]Ac 21:33 entrance. 7Suddenly an angel[v] of the Lord
12:7 appeared and a light shone in the cell. He struck
[v]Ac 5:19 Peter on the side and woke him up. "Quick, get
[w]Ac 16:26 up!" he said, and the chains fell off Peter's wrists.[w]
8Then the angel said to him, "Put on your
clothes and sandals." And Peter did so. "Wrap
your cloak around you and follow me," the angel
told him. 9Peter followed him out of the prison,
but he had no idea that what the angel was doing
12:9 was really happening; he thought he was seeing a
[x]Ac 9:10 vision.[x] 10They passed the first and second guards
12:10 and came to the iron gate leading to the city. It
[y]Ac 5:19; 16:26 opened for them by itself,[y] and they went through
it. When they had walked the length of one street,
12:11 suddenly the angel left him.
[z]Lk 15:17 11Then Peter came to himself[z] and said, "Now I
[a]Ps 34:7; Da 3:28; know without a doubt that the Lord sent his angel
6:22; 2Co 1:10; and rescued me[a] from Herod's clutches and from
2Pe 2:9 everything the Jewish people were anticipating."

Cornerstone of the Church

AC 11:25–26

Teaching has always been a cornerstone in the church. God has given his truth and revealed himself in the Scriptures. From the earliest day, God's people were called to communicate this truth to others through intentional and systematic teaching (Dt 6:6–7).

By the first century, things have not changed. For an entire year Barnabas and Saul (Paul) gather with the believers in the city of Antioch (see Map 12: Apostles' Early Travels at the back of this Bible) and instruct them in the truth of God's Word. It should not surprise us that Antioch is the city where the disciples of Jesus are first called Christians. The term itself means those "belonging to Christ." As Barnabas and Paul teach the Word faithfully, the disciples' devotion to Christ grows deeper and deeper. Everyone can see that these are people belonging to Jesus Christ—the name "Christian" is most fitting.

Herod's Death

AC 12:23

Herod's sudden and shocking death raises two immediate questions: Why? and How?

As for the why, Luke helps us understand by letting us know that this is a divine judgment by the hand of God through an angel. Interestingly, the first-century Jewish historian Josephus gives a similar account of Herod Agrippa's death in A.D. 44. Both Luke and Josephus are clear that his death is a sign of divine judgment against Herod's ungodliness.

Luke is even specific about the way God's righteous judgment falls on Herod, stating that Herod dies from an infestation of some sort of worm, probably intestinal roundworms. If this was the case, Herod's body would have been infested by worms that eventually caused an excruciatingly painful death.

12 When this had dawned on him, he went to the house of Mary the mother of John, also called Mark,[b] where many people had gathered and were praying.[c] 13 Peter knocked at the outer entrance, and a servant girl named Rhoda came to answer the door.[d] 14 When she recognized Peter's voice, she was so overjoyed[e] she ran back without opening it and exclaimed, "Peter is at the door!"

15 "You're out of your mind," they told her. When she kept insisting that it was so, they said, "It must be his angel."[f]

16 But Peter kept on knocking, and when they opened the door and saw him, they were astonished. 17 Peter motioned with his hand[g] for them to be quiet and described how the Lord had brought him out of prison. "Tell James[h] and the brothers[i] about this," he said, and then he left for another place.

18 In the morning, there was no small commotion among the soldiers as to what had become of Peter. 19 After Herod had a thorough search made for him and did not find him, he cross-examined the guards and ordered that they be executed.[j]

Herod's Death

Then Herod went from Judea to Caesarea[k] and stayed there a while. 20 He had been quarreling with the people of Tyre and Sidon;[l] they now joined together and sought an audience with him. Having secured the support of Blastus, a trusted personal servant of the king, they asked for peace, because they depended on the king's country for their food supply.[m]

21 On the appointed day Herod, wearing his royal robes, sat on his throne and delivered a public address to the people. 22 They shouted, "This is the voice of a god, not of a man." 23 Immediately, because Herod did not give praise to God, an angel of the Lord struck him down,[n] and he was eaten by worms and died.

24 But the word of God continued to increase and spread.[o]

25 When Barnabas[p] and Saul had finished their mission,[q] they returned from[a] Jerusalem, taking with them John, also called Mark.[r]

Barnabas and Saul Sent Off

13 In the church at Antioch[s] there were prophets[t] and teachers: Barnabas,[u] Simeon called Niger, Lucius of Cyrene, Manaen (who had been brought up with Herod[v] the tetrarch) and Saul. 2 While they were worshiping the Lord and fasting, the Holy Spirit said,[w] "Set apart for me Barnabas and Saul for the work[x] to which I have called them."[y] 3 So after they had fasted and prayed, they placed their hands on them[z] and sent them off.[a]

[a] 25 Some manuscripts *to*

12:12 [b]ver 25; Ac 15:37,39; Col 4:10; Phm 24; 1Pe 5:13 [c]ver 5
12:13 [d]Jn 18:16,17
12:14 [e]Lk 24:41
12:15 [f]Mt 18:10
12:17 [g]Ac 13:16; 19:33; 21:40 [h]Ac 15:13 [i]Ac 1:16
12:19 [j]Ac 16:27 [k]Ac 8:40
12:20 [l]Mt 11:21 [m]1Ki 5:9,11; Eze 27:17
12:23 [n]1Sa 25:38; 2Sa 24:16,17
12:24 [o]Ac 6:7; 19:20
12:25 [p]Ac 4:36 [q]Ac 11:30 [r]ver 12
13:1 [s]Ac 11:19 [t]Ac 11:27 [u]Ac 4:36; 11:22-26 [v]Mt 14:1
13:2 [w]Ac 8:29 [x]Ac 14:26 [y]Ac 22:21
13:3 [z]Ac 6:6 [a]Ac 14:26

On Cyprus

4 The two of them, sent on their way by the Holy
Spirit,[b] went down to Seleucia and sailed from
there to Cyprus.[c] 5 When they arrived at Salamis,
they proclaimed the word of God in the Jewish
synagogues.[d] John[e] was with them as their helper.
6 They traveled through the whole island until
they came to Paphos. There they met a Jewish sorcerer[f] and false prophet[g] named Bar-Jesus, 7 who
was an attendant of the proconsul,[h] Sergius Pau-
lus. The proconsul, an intelligent man, sent for
Barnabas and Saul because he wanted to hear the
word of God. 8 But Elymas the sorcerer[i] (for that
is what his name means) opposed them and tried
to turn the proconsul[j] from the faith.[k] 9 Then Saul,
who was also called Paul, filled with the Holy
Spirit,[l] looked straight at Elymas and said, 10 "You
are a child of the devil[m] and an enemy of everything that is right! You are full of all kinds of
deceit and trickery. Will you never stop pervert-
ing the right ways of the Lord?[n] 11 Now the hand of
the Lord is against you.[o] You are going to be blind,
and for a time you will be unable to see the light
of the sun."
Immediately mist and darkness came over him,
and he groped about, seeking someone to lead
him by the hand. 12 When the proconsul[p] saw
what had happened, he believed, for he was
amazed at the teaching about the Lord.

In Pisidian Antioch

13 From Paphos,[q] Paul and his companions
sailed to Perga in Pamphylia, where John[r] left
them to return to Jerusalem. 14 From Perga they
went on to Pisidian Antioch.[s] On the Sabbath[t]
they entered the synagogue[u] and sat down. 15 After
the reading from the Law[v] and the Prophets, the
synagogue rulers sent word to them, saying,
"Brothers, if you have a message of encouragement for the people, please speak."
16 Standing up, Paul motioned with his hand[w]
and said: "Men of Israel and you Gentiles who
worship God, listen to me! 17 The God of the people of Israel chose our fathers; he made the people
prosper during their stay in Egypt, with mighty
power he led them out of that country,[x] 18 he
endured their conduct[a][y] for about forty years in
the desert,[z] 19 he overthrew seven nations in
Canaan[a] and gave their land to his people[b] as their
inheritance. 20 All this took about 450 years.
"After this, God gave them judges[c] until the
time of Samuel the prophet.[d] 21 Then the people
asked for a king,[e] and he gave them Saul[f] son of
Kish, of the tribe of Benjamin,[g] who ruled forty
years. 22 After removing Saul,[h] he made David
their king.[i] He testified concerning him: 'I have
found David son of Jesse a man after my own
heart;[j] he will do everything I want him to do.'

13:4 [b]ver 2,3 [c]Ac 4:36
13:5 [d]Ac 9:20 [e]Ac 12:12
13:6 [f]Ac 8:9 [g]Mt 7:15
13:7 [h]ver 8,12; Ac 19:38
13:8 [i]Ac 8:9 [j]ver 7 [k]Ac 6:7
13:9 [l]Ac 4:8
13:10 [m]Mt 13:38; Jn 8:44 [n]Hos 14:9
13:11 [o]Ex 9:3; 1Sa 5:6,7; Ps 32:4
13:12 [p]ver 7
13:13 [q]ver 6 [r]Ac 12:12
13:14 [s]Ac 14:19,21 [t]Ac 16:13 [u]Ac 9:20
13:15 [v]Ac 15:21
13:16 [w]Ac 12:17
13:17 [x]Ex 6:6,7; Dt 7:6-8
13:18 [y]Dt 1:31 [z]Ac 7:36
13:19 [a]Dt 7:1 [b]Jos 19:51
13:20 [c]Jdg 2:16 [d]1Sa 3:19,20
13:21 [e]1Sa 8:5,19 [f]1Sa 10:1 [g]1Sa 9:1,2
13:22 [h]1Sa 15:23,26 [i]1Sa 16:13; Ps 89:20 [j]1Sa 13:14

[a] 18 Some manuscripts *and cared for them*

Paul's Strategy

AC 13:14

Call it a pattern. Call it a strategy. Call it what you will, but Paul makes it a point to start his ministry in new cities by visiting the local Jewish synagogue. Paul starts his ministry in Pisidian Antioch with a visit to the synagogue (Ac 13:14), just as he does in a number of other locations (see Map 12: Apostles' Early Travels at the back of this Bible): Salamis (Ac 13:5), Iconium (Ac 14:1), Thessalonica (Ac 17:1–2), Berea (Ac 17:10), Athens (Ac 17:16–17), Corinth (Ac 18:1–4), and Ephesus (Ac 18:19).

Why this strong commitment to beginning ministry in the gathering place of the Jewish community? There can be many reasons, but the first perhaps is Paul's passionate love and care for his fellow Jews. These are the people for whom Paul said he would be willing to sacrifice his own salvation if only they would come to faith in Christ (Ro 9:1–5). Paul's ministry strategy grows out of love—love for God and love for the lost.

Good News

AC 13:32–33

The apostle Paul is in Pisidian Antioch and is preaching in the synagogue on the Sabbath. He gives the Jews gathered there a review of Biblical history. From Egypt to the desert to the promised land, Paul reminds them that God has been faithful. Paul walks them quickly through the time of the judges and the kings, then moves all the way up to the life of Jesus. Finally, Paul recites all that happened on Calvary's hill and the glorious joy of Easter morning.

To wrap it all up, Paul declares that this is the Good News! This is what God promised centuries before. The Good News, the best news, the greatest news of all history: Jesus Christ is risen! He is risen indeed! This is still the message of the church today. It is the Good News that Christians carry in their hearts and on their lips.

23 “From this man's descendants[k] God has
brought to Israel the Savior[l] Jesus,[m] as he promised.[n] 24 Before the coming of Jesus, John preached
repentance and baptism to all the people of Israel.[o] 25 As John was completing his work,[p] he said:
'Who do you think I am? I am not that one.[q] No,
but he is coming after me, whose sandals I am not
worthy to untie.'[r]
26 “Brothers, children of Abraham, and you God-
fearing Gentiles, it is to us that this message of salvation[s] has been sent. 27 The people of Jerusalem
and their rulers did not recognize Jesus,[t] yet in
condemning him they fulfilled the words of the
prophets[u] that are read every Sabbath. 28 Though
they found no proper ground for a death sentence,
they asked Pilate to have him executed.[v] 29 When
they had carried out all that was written about
him,[w] they took him down from the tree[x] and laid
him in a tomb.[y] 30 But God raised him from the
dead,[z] 31 and for many days he was seen by those
who had traveled with him from Galilee to Jerusalem.[a] They are now his witnesses[b] to our people.
32 “We tell you the good news:[c] What God promised our fathers[d] 33 he has fulfilled for us, their
children, by raising up Jesus. As it is written in
the second Psalm:

> “ 'You are my Son;
> today I have become your Father.'[a][b][e]

34 The fact that God raised him from the dead, never to decay, is stated in these words:

> “ 'I will give you the holy and sure
> blessings promised to David.'[c][f]

35 So it is stated elsewhere:

> “ 'You will not let your Holy One see
> decay.'[d][g]

36 “For when David had served God's purpose in
his own generation, he fell asleep; he was buried
with his fathers[h] and his body decayed. 37 But the
one whom God raised from the dead did not see
decay.
38 “Therefore, my brothers, I want you to know
that through Jesus the forgiveness of sins is proclaimed to you.[i] 39 Through him everyone who
believes is justified from everything you could not
be justified from by the law of Moses.[j] 40 Take care
that what the prophets have said does not happen
to you:

> 41 “ 'Look, you scoffers,
> wonder and perish,
> for I am going to do something in your
> days
> that you would never believe,
> even if someone told you.'[e]”[k]

42 As Paul and Barnabas were leaving the syna-

13:23 [k]Mt 1:1 [l]Lk 2:11 [m]Mt 1:21 [n]ver 32
13:24 [o]Mk 1:4
13:25 [p]Ac 20:24 [q]Jn 1:20 [r]Mt 3:11; Jn 1:27
13:26 [s]Ac 4:12
13:27 [t]Ac 3:17 [u]Lk 24:27
13:28 [v]Mt 27:20-25; Ac 3:14
13:29 [w]Lk 18:31 [x]Ac 5:30 [y]Lk 23:53
13:30 [z]Mt 28:6; Ac 2:24
13:31 [a]Mt 28:16 [b]Lk 24:48
13:32 [c]Ac 5:42 [d]Ac 26:6; Ro 4:13
13:33 [e]Ps 2:7
13:34 [f]Isa 55:3
13:35 [g]Ps 16:10; Ac 2:27
13:36 [h]1Ki 2:10; Ac 2:29
13:38 [i]Lk 24:47; Ac 2:38
13:39 [j]Ro 3:28
13:41 [k]Hab 1:5

[a] *33* Or *have begotten you* [b] *33* Psalm 2:7 [c] *34* Isaiah 55:3 [d] *35* Psalm 16:10 [e] *41* Hab. 1:5

13:42 gogue,[l] the people invited them to speak further
[l]ver 14 about these things on the next Sabbath. 43When
the congregation was dismissed, many of the Jews
and devout converts to Judaism followed Paul and
13:43 Barnabas, who talked with them and urged them
[m]Ac 11:23; to continue in the grace of God.[m]
14:22 44On the next Sabbath almost the whole city
gathered to hear the word of the Lord. 45When the
13:45 Jews saw the crowds, they were filled with jeal-
[n]Ac 18:6; ousy and talked abusively[n] against what Paul was
1Pe 4:4; saying.[o]
Jude 10 [o]1Th 2:16 46Then Paul and Barnabas answered them boldly: "We had to speak the word of God to you first.[p]
13:46 Since you reject it and do not consider yourselves
[p]ver 26; worthy of eternal life, we now turn to the Gen-
Ac 3:26 [q]Ac 18:6; tiles.[q] 47For this is what the Lord has command-
22:21; 28:28 ed us:

13:47 " 'I have made you[a] a light for the
[r]Lk 2:32 Gentiles,[r]
[s]Isa 49:6 that you[a] may bring salvation to the
ends of the earth.'[b]"[s]

48When the Gentiles heard this, they were glad
and honored the word of the Lord; and all who
were appointed for eternal life believed.
49The word of the Lord spread through the
whole region. 50But the Jews incited the God-fearing women of high standing and the leading men
of the city. They stirred up persecution against
Paul and Barnabas, and expelled them from their
13:50 region.[t] 51So they shook the dust from their feet[u]
[t]1Th 2:16 in protest against them and went to Iconium.[v]
13:51 52And the disciples were filled with joy and with
[u]Mt 10:14; Ac 18:6 the Holy Spirit.

[v]Ac 14:1,19, 21; 2Ti 3:11

In Iconium

14:1 **14** At Iconium[w] Paul and Barnabas went as
[w]Ac 13:51 usual into the Jewish synagogue. There they
spoke so effectively that a great number of Jews
and Gentiles believed. 2But the Jews who refused
to believe stirred up the Gentiles and poisoned
their minds against the brothers. 3So Paul and Barnabas spent considerable time there, speaking
14:3 boldly[x] for the Lord, who confirmed the message
[x]Ac 4:29 [y]Jn 4:48; of his grace by enabling them to do miraculous
Heb 2:4 signs and wonders.[y] 4The people of the city were
14:4 divided; some sided with the Jews, others with the
[z]Ac 17:4,5 apostles.[z] 5There was a plot afoot among the Gen-
14:5 tiles and Jews, together with their leaders, to mis-
[a]ver 19 treat them and stone them.[a] 6But they found out
14:6 about it and fled[b] to the Lycaonian cities of Lystra
[b]Mt 10:23 and Derbe and to the surrounding country, 7where
14:7 they continued to preach[c] the good news.[d]
[c]Ac 16:10 [d]ver 15,21

In Lystra and Derbe

14:8 8In Lystra there sat a man crippled in his feet,
[e]Ac 3:2 who was lame from birth[e] and had never walked.
9He listened to Paul as he was speaking. Paul
looked directly at him, saw that he had faith to be

[a]47 The Greek is singular. [b]47 Isaiah 49:6

Cities of Asia Minor

AC 14

When we look at a road map, we see a complex web of highways, toll roads and interstate expressways that crisscross the landscape. Our challenge is deciding which route to take as we decide between our many options.

Not so in the days of the apostle Paul. In the first century there were few options for travel. The apostle Paul often used the most familiar and traveled roads of his day. This was certainly true in his travels from Pisidian Antioch to Iconium, Lystra and Derbe. A great Roman trade route wound its way from Ephesus to the Euphrates and was very likely the road the apostle Paul used on this particular missionary journey (see Map 11: Paul's Missionary Journeys at the back of this Bible).

Paul has a way of using what is available to accomplish the goals God has set before him. The merchants of the day know that the trade route will bring them to the streets of Pisidian Antioch with its thousands of residents and that they can continue south to many other cities. Paul uses the same roads to bring his message.

Only People

AC 14:12

When we read the book of Acts, we can't simply separate all the people into two groups: the Jews, who are religious; and the Gentiles, who are not. This would be a mistake. Many of the people who are not Jewish are still very religious. The people of Lystra worship many gods, and they believe these gods occasionally walk among them. (This was common thought in their mythological worldview.)

So when Barnabas and Paul arrive on the scene and heal a man who has been crippled from birth, the people make a natural deduction: "The gods have come down to us" (Ac 14:11). In their minds, this kind of healing has to be from their gods. They are sincere, but they are sincerely wrong! Paul and Barnabas quickly correct their misconception. They say what we all need to say when anyone puts us on a pedestal: "We too are only people." Only from this posture—one of being among rather than over—can we faithfully bring the message of Jesus.

healed[f] 10and called out, "Stand up on your feet!" At that, the man jumped up and began to walk.[g]

11When the crowd saw what Paul had done, they shouted in the Lycaonian language, "The gods have come down to us in human form!"[h] 12Barnabas they called Zeus, and Paul they called Hermes because he was the chief speaker. 13The priest of Zeus, whose temple was just outside the city, brought bulls and wreaths to the city gates because he and the crowd wanted to offer sacrifices to them.

14But when the apostles Barnabas and Paul heard of this, they tore their clothes[i] and rushed out into the crowd, shouting: 15"Men, why are you doing this? We too are only men,[j] human like you. We are bringing you good news,[k] telling you to turn from these worthless things[l] to the living God,[m] who made heaven and earth[n] and sea and everything in them.[o] 16In the past, he let[p] all nations go their own way.[q] 17Yet he has not left himself without testimony:[r] He has shown kindness by giving you rain from heaven and crops in their seasons;[s] he provides you with plenty of food and fills your hearts with joy." 18Even with these words, they had difficulty keeping the crowd from sacrificing to them.

19Then some Jews[t] came from Antioch and Iconium[u] and won the crowd over. They stoned Paul[v] and dragged him outside the city, thinking he was dead. 20But after the disciples[w] had gathered around him, he got up and went back into the city. The next day he and Barnabas left for Derbe.

The Return to Antioch in Syria

21They preached the good news in that city and won a large number of disciples. Then they returned to Lystra, Iconium[x] and Antioch, 22strengthening the disciples and encouraging them to remain true to the faith.[y] "We must go through many hardships[z] to enter the kingdom of God," they said. 23Paul and Barnabas appointed elders[a][a] for them in each church and, with prayer and fasting,[b] committed them to the Lord,[c] in whom they had put their trust. 24After going through Pisidia, they came into Pamphylia, 25and when they had preached the word in Perga, they went down to Attalia.

26From Attalia they sailed back to Antioch,[d] where they had been committed to the grace of God[e] for the work they had now completed.[f] 27On arriving there, they gathered the church together and reported all that God had done through them[g] and how he had opened the door[h] of faith to the Gentiles. 28And they stayed there a long time with the disciples.

[a] 23 Or *Barnabas ordained elders*; or *Barnabas had elders elected*

14:9 [f]Mt 9:28,29
14:10 [g]Ac 3:8
14:11 [h]Ac 8:10; 28:6
14:14 [i]Mk 14:63
14:15 [j]Ac 10:26; Jas 5:17 [k]ver 7,21; Ac 13:32 [l]1Sa 12:21; 1Co 8:4; 1Th 1:9 [m]Mt 16:16 [n]Ge 1:1; Jer 14:22 [o]Ps 146:6; Rev 14:7
14:16 [p]Ac 17:30 [q]Ps 81:12; Mic 4:5
14:17 [r]Ac 17:27; Ro 1:20 [s]Dt 11:14; Job 5:10; Ps 65:10
14:19 [t]Ac 13:45 [u]Ac 13:51 [v]2Co 11:25; 2Ti 3:11
14:20 [w]ver 22,28; Ac 11:26
14:21 [x]Ac 13:51
14:22 [y]Ac 11:23; 13:43 [z]Jn 16:33; 1Th 3:3; 2Ti 3:12
14:23 [a]Ac 11:30; Tit 1:5 [b]Ac 13:3 [c]Ac 20:32
14:26 [d]Ac 11:19 [e]Ac 15:40 [f]Ac 13:1,3
14:27 [g]Ac 15:4,12; 21:19 [h]1Co 16:9; 2Co 2:12; Col 4:3; Rev 3:8

The Council at Jerusalem

15 Some men[i] came down from Judea to Antioch and were teaching the brothers: "Unless
you are circumcised,[j] according to the custom
taught by Moses,[k] you cannot be saved." 2This
brought Paul and Barnabas into sharp dispute and
debate with them. So Paul and Barnabas were
appointed, along with some other believers, to go
up to Jerusalem[l] to see the apostles and elders[m]
about this question. 3The church sent them on
their way, and as they traveled through Phoenicia
and Samaria, they told how the Gentiles had been
converted.[n] This news made all the brothers very
glad. 4When they came to Jerusalem, they were
welcomed by the church and the apostles and elders, to whom they reported everything God had
done through them.[o]

5Then some of the believers who belonged to
the party of the Pharisees stood up and said, "The
Gentiles must be circumcised and required to
obey the law of Moses."

6The apostles and elders met to consider this
question. 7After much discussion, Peter got up
and addressed them: "Brothers, you know that
some time ago God made a choice among you that
the Gentiles might hear from my lips the message
of the gospel and believe. 8God, who knows the
heart,[p] showed that he accepted them by giving
the Holy Spirit to them,[q] just as he did to us. 9He
made no distinction between us and them,[r] for he
purified their hearts by faith.[s] 10Now then, why do
you try to test God by putting on the necks of the
disciples a yoke[t] that neither we nor our fathers
have been able to bear? 11No! We believe it is
through the grace[u] of our Lord Jesus that we are
saved, just as they are."

12The whole assembly became silent as they listened to Barnabas and Paul telling about the
miraculous signs and wonders[v] God had done
among the Gentiles through them.[w] 13When they
finished, James[x] spoke up: "Brothers, listen to me.
14Simon[a] has described to us how God at first
showed his concern by taking from the Gentiles a
people for himself. 15The words of the prophets
are in agreement with this, as it is written:

16" 'After this I will return
and rebuild David's fallen tent.
Its ruins I will rebuild,
and I will restore it,
17that the remnant of men may seek the
Lord,
and all the Gentiles who bear my
name,
says the Lord, who does these things'[b][y]
18 that have been known for ages.[c]

19"It is my judgment, therefore, that we should

15:1 [i]ver 24; Gal 2:12 [j]ver 5; Gal 5:2,3 [k]Ac 6:14
15:2 [l]Gal 2:2 [m]Ac 11:30
15:3 [n]Ac 14:27
15:4 [o]ver 12; Ac 14:27
15:8 [p]Ac 1:24 [q]Ac 10:44,47
15:9 [r]Ac 10:28, 34; 11:12 [s]Ac 10:43
15:10 [t]Mt 23:4; Gal 5:1
15:11 [u]Ro 3:24; Eph 2:5-8
15:12 [v]Jn 4:48 [w]Ac 14:27
15:13 [x]Ac 12:17
15:17 [y]Am 9:11,12

[a] 14 Greek *Simeon*, a variant of *Simon*; that is, Peter
[b] 17 Amos 9:11,12 [c] *17,18* Some manuscripts *things'— / 18known to the Lord for ages is his work*

The Council at Jerusalem

AC 15

The same question has been asked repeatedly throughout the history of the church: What is necessary for salvation? Do we need to add anything to Christ's sacrifice on the cross? This same issue is at the heart of the argument here. Some people argue that adherence to the Jewish law is a prerequisite for salvation. In particular, some say that circumcision is mandatory.

The council in Jerusalem is a gathering of church leaders who address this critical issue and come to the clear conclusion that salvation is through the grace of Jesus Christ alone. This is true for both Jews and Gentiles. There is serious deliberation and honest debate, but at the end of the day the message is clear. Nothing can, or should, be added to the finished work of Christ on the cross. So it was in the first century and so it is now. We are saved by grace and grace alone.

An Encouraging Word

AC 15:32

We live in a time when an encouraging word can be hard to find—and so it was in the first century. The church leaders review the situation and realize that some overzealous people have disturbed and discouraged many fellow Christians. They may not have been intentionally malicious, but they have done damage through their words. What will the church leaders do to remedy this situation? Will they look the other way? Will they say nothing? No! They fight the problem with words of blessing. They send a letter to the churches with a message that brings gladness and encouragement. Along with the letter they send representatives who add their own verbal words of blessing. They model how Spirit-filled Christians today can fight discouragement and harsh words.

not make it difficult for the Gentiles who are turning to God. 20 Instead we should write to them,
telling them to abstain from food polluted by
idols,[z] from sexual immorality,[a] from the meat of
strangled animals and from blood.[b] 21 For Moses
has been preached in every city from the earliest
times and is read in the synagogues on every
Sabbath."[c]

The Council's Letter to Gentile Believers

22 Then the apostles and elders, with the whole
church, decided to choose some of their own men
and send them to Antioch with Paul and Barnabas. They chose Judas (called Barsabbas) and
Silas,[d] two men who were leaders among the
brothers. 23 With them they sent the following
letter:

The apostles and elders, your brothers,

To the Gentile believers in Antioch,[e] Syria
and Cilicia:[f]

Greetings.[g]

24 We have heard that some went out from
us without our authorization and disturbed
you, troubling your minds by what they
said.[h] 25 So we all agreed to choose some men
and send them to you with our dear friends
Barnabas and Paul— 26 men who have risked
their lives[i] for the name of our Lord Jesus
Christ. 27 Therefore we are sending Judas and
Silas to confirm by word of mouth what we
are writing. 28 It seemed good to the Holy
Spirit[j] and to us not to burden you with anything beyond the following requirements:
29 You are to abstain from food sacrificed to
idols, from blood, from the meat of strangled
animals and from sexual immorality.[k] You
will do well to avoid these things.

Farewell.

30 The men were sent off and went down to Antioch, where they gathered the church together and
delivered the letter. 31 The people read it and were
glad for its encouraging message. 32 Judas and
Silas, who themselves were prophets, said much
to encourage and strengthen the brothers. 33 After
spending some time there, they were sent off by
the brothers with the blessing of peace[l] to return to
those who had sent them.[a] 35 But Paul and Barnabas remained in Antioch, where they and many
others taught and preached[m] the word of the Lord.

Disagreement Between Paul and Barnabas

36 Some time later Paul said to Barnabas, "Let us
go back and visit the brothers in all the towns[n]
where we preached the word of the Lord and see

15:20 [z]1Co 8:7-13; 10:14-28; Rev 2:14,20 [a]1Co 10:7,8 [b]ver 29; Ge 9:4; Lev 3:17; Dt 12:16,23
15:21 [c]Ac 13:15; 2Co 3:14,15
15:22 [d]ver 27,32, 40
15:23 [e]ver 1 [f]ver 41 [g]Ac 23:25, 26; Jas 1:1
15:24 [h]ver 1; Gal 1:7; 5:10
15:26 [i]Ac 9:23-25; 14:19
15:28 [j]Ac 5:32
15:29 [k]ver 20; Ac 21:25
15:33 [l]Mk 5:34; Ac 16:36; 1Co 16:11
15:35 [m]Ac 8:4
15:36 [n]Ac 13:4,13, 14,51; 14:1, 6,24,25

[a] 33 Some manuscripts *them,* 34*but Silas decided to remain there*

how they are doing." 37Barnabas wanted to take John, also called Mark,[o] with them, 38but Paul did not think it wise to take him, because he had deserted them[p] in Pamphylia and had not continued with them in the work. 39They had such a sharp disagreement that they parted company. Barnabas took Mark and sailed for Cyprus, 40but Paul chose Silas[q] and left, commended by the brothers to the grace of the Lord.[r] 41He went through Syria[s] and Cilicia,[t] strengthening the churches.[u]

Timothy Joins Paul and Silas

16 He came to Derbe and then to Lystra,[v] where a disciple named Timothy[w] lived, whose mother was a Jewess and a believer, but whose father was a Greek. 2The brothers[x] at Lystra and Iconium[y] spoke well of him. 3Paul wanted to take him along on the journey, so he circumcised him because of the Jews who lived in that area, for they all knew that his father was a Greek.[z] 4As they traveled from town to town, they delivered the decisions reached by the apostles and elders[a] in Jerusalem[b] for the people to obey.[c] 5So the churches were strengthened[d] in the faith and grew daily in numbers.

Paul's Vision of the Man of Macedonia

6Paul and his companions traveled throughout the region of Phrygia[e] and Galatia,[f] having been kept by the Holy Spirit from preaching the word in the province of Asia.[g] 7When they came to the border of Mysia, they tried to enter Bithynia, but the Spirit of Jesus[h] would not allow them to. 8So they passed by Mysia and went down to Troas.[i] 9During the night Paul had a vision[j] of a man of Macedonia[k] standing and begging him, "Come over to Macedonia and help us." 10After Paul had seen the vision, we[l] got ready at once to leave for Macedonia, concluding that God had called us to preach the gospel[m] to them.

Lydia's Conversion in Philippi

11From Troas[n] we put out to sea and sailed straight for Samothrace, and the next day on to Neapolis. 12From there we traveled to Philippi,[o] a Roman colony and the leading city of that district of Macedonia.[p] And we stayed there several days.

13On the Sabbath[q] we went outside the city gate to the river, where we expected to find a place of prayer. We sat down and began to speak to the women who had gathered there. 14One of those listening was a woman named Lydia, a dealer in purple cloth from the city of Thyatira,[r] who was a worshiper of God. The Lord opened her heart[s] to respond to Paul's message. 15When she and the members of her household[t] were baptized, she invited us to her home. "If you consider me a believer in the Lord," she said, "come and stay at my house." And she persuaded us.

15:37 [o]Ac 12:12
15:38 [p]Ac 13:13
15:40 [q]ver 22 [r]Ac 11:23
15:41 [s]ver 23 [t]Ac 6:9 [u]Ac 16:5
16:1 [v]Ac 14:6 [w]Ac 17:14; 18:5; 19:22; Ro 16:21; 1Co 4:17; 2Co 1:1,19; 1Th 3:2,6; 1Ti 1:2,18; 2Ti 1:2,5,6
16:2 [x]ver 40 [y]Ac 13:51
16:3 [z]Gal 2:3
16:4 [a]Ac 11:30 [b]Ac 15:2 [c]Ac 15:28,29
16:5 [d]Ac 9:31; 15:41
16:6 [e]Ac 18:23 [f]Ac 18:23; Gal 1:2; 3:1 [g]Ac 2:9
16:7 [h]Ro 8:9; Gal 4:6
16:8 [i]ver 11; 2Co 2:12; 2Ti 4:13
16:9 [j]Ac 9:10 [k]Ac 20:1,3
16:10 [l]ver 10-17 [m]Ac 14:7
16:11 [n]ver 8
16:12 [o]Ac 20:6; Php 1:1; 1Th 2:2 [p]ver 9
16:13 [q]Ac 13:14
16:14 [r]Rev 1:11 [s]Lk 24:45
16:15 [t]Ac 11:14

Disagreement

AC 15:36-41

The apostle Paul and Barnabas face a conflict in their relationship. There are past, present and future aspects to this story. In the past, John Mark had left their ministry team and headed back to Jerusalem (Ac 13:13). In Paul's mind it was an untimely desertion. In the present, Barnabas wishes to invite John Mark to join them for the next portion of their mission work. Paul disagrees sharply. They part ways and Barnabas takes Mark as a ministry partner. Paul chooses Silas. In the future, however, Paul and Mark are restored in their friendship and partnership in the gospel (Col 4:10; 2Ti 4:11; Phm 24).

Paul's initial hesitancy and then willingness to leave the past behind and forge a new relationship with Mark offers an excellent lesson for today's believers. No one likes conflict. But when it does arise, there should always be room for restoration and healing, even if it takes time.

What Must I Do?

AC 16:30-31

Can it really be that simple? In a world that grows more and more complex, is the message of Christ still simple enough even for a child to understand (Mt 19:14)? The answer is a resounding "Yes!"

When the jailer realizes that the prison doors are open, he draws his sword and gets ready to impale himself. He knows the penalty for a Roman guard who lets his prisoners escape—death. But, out of the dark comes a voice, "Don't harm yourself! We are all here!" (Ac 16:28). Shaken by the earthquake and his own near death, the jailer cries out and asks what is necessary for him to have the faith that has allowed this persecuted band of missionaries to not only sing while imprisoned, but also to extend grace to the one who has kept them captive.

The answer? Not a list of do's and don'ts. Not a call to memorize pages of doctrine. Not a time of probation to prove sincerity. No, it is the same simple answer given to every seeking heart: "Believe in the Lord Jesus" (Ac 16:31). Not a religion, but a relationship. It really is that simple.

Paul and Silas in Prison

16Once when we were going to the place of
prayer,[u] we were met by a slave girl who had a
spirit[v] by which she predicted the future. She
earned a great deal of money for her owners by
fortune-telling. 17This girl followed Paul and the
rest of us, shouting, "These men are servants of
the Most High God,[w] who are telling you the way
to be saved." 18She kept this up for many days.
Finally Paul became so troubled that he turned
around and said to the spirit, "In the name of
Jesus Christ I command you to come out of her!"
At that moment the spirit left her.[x]
19When the owners of the slave girl realized
that their hope of making money[y] was gone, they
seized Paul and Silas[z] and dragged[a] them into the
marketplace to face the authorities. 20They
brought them before the magistrates and said,
"These men are Jews, and are throwing our city
into an uproar[b] 21by advocating customs unlawful
for us Romans[c] to accept or practice."[d]
22The crowd joined in the attack against Paul
and Silas, and the magistrates ordered them to be
stripped and beaten.[e] 23After they had been severely flogged, they were thrown into prison, and the
jailer[f] was commanded to guard them carefully.
24Upon receiving such orders, he put them in the
inner cell and fastened their feet in the stocks.[g]
25About midnight Paul and Silas were praying
and singing hymns[h] to God, and the other prisoners were listening to them. 26Suddenly there was
such a violent earthquake that the foundations of
the prison were shaken.[i] At once all the prison
doors flew open,[j] and everybody's chains came
loose.[k] 27The jailer woke up, and when he saw the
prison doors open, he drew his sword and was
about to kill himself because he thought the prisoners had escaped.[l] 28But Paul shouted, "Don't
harm yourself! We are all here!"
29The jailer called for lights, rushed in and fell
trembling before Paul and Silas. 30He then brought
them out and asked, "Sirs, what must I do to be
saved?"[m]
31They replied, "Believe in the Lord Jesus, and
you will be saved—you and your household."[n]
32Then they spoke the word of the Lord to him
and to all the others in his house. 33At that hour of
the night[o] the jailer took them and washed their
wounds; then immediately he and all his family
were baptized. 34The jailer brought them into his
house and set a meal before them; he[p] was filled
with joy because he had come to believe in God—
he and his whole family.
35When it was daylight, the magistrates sent
their officers to the jailer with the order: "Release
those men." 36The jailer[q] told Paul, "The magistrates have ordered that you and Silas be released.
Now you can leave. Go in peace."[r]
37But Paul said to the officers: "They beat us
publicly without a trial, even though we are

16:16 [u]ver 13 [v]Dt 18:11; 1Sa 28:3,7
16:17 [w]Mk 5:7
16:18 [x]Mk 16:17
16:19 [y]ver 16; Ac 19:25,26 [z]Ac 15:22 [a]Ac 8:3; 17:6; 21:30; Jas 2:6
16:20 [b]Ac 17:6
16:21 [c]ver 12 [d]Est 3:8
16:22 [e]2Co 11:25; 1Th 2:2
16:23 [f]ver 27,36
16:24 [g]Job 13:27; 33:11; Jer 20:2,3; 29:26
16:25 [h]Eph 5:19
16:26 [i]Ac 4:31 [j]Ac 12:10 [k]Ac 12:7
16:27 [l]Ac 12:19
16:30 [m]Ac 2:37
16:31 [n]Ac 11:14
16:33 [o]ver 25
16:34 [p]Ac 11:14
16:36 [q]ver 23,27 [r]Ac 15:33

Week 39

Uncommon Joy

Talk about a thriller! This event in the lives of Paul and Silas contains all the elements of a great novel: evil (the evil spirit), greed (the owners of the slave girl), unjust torture of the heroes (flogging and imprisonment), natural disaster (the earthquake), supernatural intervention (prison doors opening and chains falling off), emotional distress (the jailer) and a happy outcome (the salvation of the jailer and his family and freedom for the heroes). But this story is something other than a piece of good fiction—it truly happened. What is more amazing (and certainly unlike many novels) is the joy and peace Paul and Silas experience during the entire course of events. What do they have to sing about?

Where does all joy originate (Ne 12:43; Ps 43:4)?

What produces joy in an unbeliever (Ac 14:17)? What produces joy in a believer (Ac 8:5-8; 16:34)?

How is this joy produced in you (1Th 1:6)? Joy is a fruit produced by the presence of the Holy Spirit (Gal 5:22).

Jesus says an intimate relationship with him ("remain in my love") through obedience to God's commands is the way to complete joy (Jn 15:10-11). Is your relationship with Jesus intimate enough to produce complete joy? What can you do to receive this complete joy (Jn 16:24)?

What happens to your joy when troubles come? How can you retain your joy in times of trial (Ps 33:16-22)? Jesus knows life is filled with trouble and suffering (Jn 16:33; 17:13-15). How is joy compatible with suffering (Jas 1:2-4; 1Pe 1:6-9)?

The struggles and tragedies of this life need not affect your joy as a child of God. True joy is based on the spiritual realities of who God is and what he has promised. God *is* good and God *is* faithful—regardless of your situation. Paul and Silas learn this truth, and they have much to sing about.

Enjoying God THROUGH the Word

Read 1 Chronicles 16:8-12,23-36 (pages 654-655). This beautiful psalm of praise expresses the unique joy that belongs to a child of God. You have no need to fear or to be anxious. Your God is powerful and mighty to save (Zep 3:17). Despite your circumstances you can "glory in his holy name" and your heart can rejoice as you seek him and the strength he offers (1Ch 16:10-11).

Linger on the words of this passage from 1 Chronicles. Let them seep into your heart as well as into your mind. You are coming to the great God, in whose presence are splendor, majesty, strength and joy (1Ch 16:27). He is worthy of all praise and glory (1Ch 16:29). Communion with God may or may not change your circumstances, but your heart and your attitude will never be the same.

Enjoying God THROUGH Experience

If your heart is bursting with joy today, give thanks! Speak aloud your joy and thanksgiving to God. Spend time praising and worshiping him through music and prayer. He is worthy of your exuberant praise.

If you are longing for the kind of joy described in this study, ask the Holy Spirit to fill you with his joy. The Spirit is the joy-bringer. "Ask and you will receive, and your joy will be complete" (Jn 16:24). That's a promise from Jesus' own lips, and he is faithful.

Go to page 1855 for your next weekly study.

The Bereans

AC 17:11

As we grow mature in faith, we learn that it is healthy and responsible to ask hard questions and dig deep into God's Word. The Bereans set a marvelous example for us. Their response is twofold. They receive the message gladly and with eagerness. Yet they also examine the Scriptures to be sure that Paul's teachings line up with the truths of God's Word. Their searching, seeking, studying and willingness to dig deep and ask hard questions does not drive them away from the truth. It actually leads many to faith.

We can affirm those who ask honest questions, and we can recognize the value of questioning the teachings of any person to be certain they are consistent with the teachings of Scriptures. The Bereans provide us with an excellent pattern to follow.

Roman citizens,[s] and threw us into prison. And
now do they want to get rid of us quietly? No! Let
them come themselves and escort us out."
38 The officers reported this to the magistrates,
and when they heard that Paul and Silas were
Roman citizens, they were alarmed.[t] 39 They came
to appease them and escorted them from the
prison, requesting them to leave the city.[u] 40 After
Paul and Silas came out of the prison, they went
to Lydia's house,[v] where they met with the brothers[w] and encouraged them. Then they left.

In Thessalonica

17 When they had passed through Amphipolis
and Apollonia, they came to Thessalonica,[x]
where there was a Jewish synagogue. 2 As his custom was, Paul went into the synagogue,[y] and on
three Sabbath[z] days he reasoned with them from
the Scriptures,[a] 3 explaining and proving that the
Christ[*a*] had to suffer[b] and rise from the dead.[c] "This
Jesus I am proclaiming to you is the Christ,[*a*]"[d] he
said. 4 Some of the Jews were persuaded and joined
Paul and Silas,[e] as did a large number of God-fearing Greeks and not a few prominent women.
5 But the Jews were jealous; so they rounded up
some bad characters from the marketplace,
formed a mob and started a riot in the city.[f] They
rushed to Jason's[g] house in search of Paul and
Silas in order to bring them out to the crowd.[*b*]
6 But when they did not find them, they dragged[h]
Jason and some other brothers before the city officials, shouting: "These men who have caused
trouble all over the world[i] have now come here,[j]
7 and Jason has welcomed them into his house.
They are all defying Caesar's decrees, saying that
there is another king, one called Jesus."[k] 8 When
they heard this, the crowd and the city officials
were thrown into turmoil. 9 Then they made Jason[l]
and the others post bond and let them go.

In Berea

10 As soon as it was night, the brothers sent Paul
and Silas away to Berea.[m] On arriving there, they
went to the Jewish synagogue. 11 Now the Bereans
were of more noble character than the Thessalonians,[n] for they received the message with great
eagerness and examined the Scriptures[o] every day
to see if what Paul said was true. 12 Many of the
Jews believed, as did also a number of prominent
Greek women and many Greek men.
13 When the Jews in Thessalonica learned that
Paul was preaching the word of God at Berea, they
went there too, agitating the crowds and stirring
them up. 14 The brothers immediately sent Paul to
the coast, but Silas[p] and Timothy[q] stayed at Berea.
15 The men who escorted Paul brought him to Athens[r] and then left with instructions for Silas and
Timothy to join him as soon as possible.[s]

16:37 [s]Ac 22:25-29
16:38 [t]Ac 22:29
16:39 [u]Mt 8:34
16:40 [v]ver 14 [w]ver 2; Ac 1:16
17:1 [x]ver 11,13; Php 4:16; 1Th 1:1; 2Th 1:1; 2Ti 4:10
17:2 [y]Ac 9:20 [z]Ac 13:14 [a]Ac 8:35
17:3 [b]Lk 24:26; Ac 3:18 [c]Lk 24:46 [d]Ac 9:22; 18:28
17:4 [e]Ac 15:22
17:5 [f]ver 13; 1Th 2:16 [g]Ro 16:21
17:6 [h]Ac 16:19 [i]Mt 24:14 [j]Ac 16:20
17:7 [k]Lk 23:2; Jn 19:12
17:9 [l]ver 5
17:10 [m]ver 13; Ac 20:4
17:11 [n]ver 1 [o]Lk 16:29; Jn 5:39
17:14 [p]Ac 15:22 [q]Ac 16:1
17:15 [r]ver 16,21, 22; Ac 18:1; 1Th 3:1 [s]Ac 18:5

a 3 Or *Messiah* *b* 5 Or *the assembly of the people*

In Athens

16 While Paul was waiting for them in Athens,
17:17 he was greatly distressed to see that the city was
[t]Ac 9:20 full of idols. 17 So he reasoned in the synagogue[t]
with the Jews and the God-fearing Greeks, as well
as in the marketplace day by day with those who
happened to be there. 18 A group of Epicurean and
Stoic philosophers began to dispute with him.
Some of them asked, "What is this babbler trying
to say?" Others remarked, "He seems to be advocating foreign gods." They said this because Paul
17:18 was preaching the good news about Jesus and the
[u]ver 31,32; resurrection.[u] 19 Then they took him and brought
Ac 4:2 him to a meeting of the Areopagus,[v] where they
17:19 said to him, "May we know what this new teach-
[v]ver 22 [w]Mk 1:27 ing[w] is that you are presenting? 20 You are bringing some strange ideas to our ears, and we want
to know what they mean." 21 (All the Athenians
and the foreigners who lived there spent their
time doing nothing but talking about and listening to the latest ideas.)
22 Paul then stood up in the meeting of the Areopagus and said: "Men of Athens! I see that in
17:23 [x]Jn 4:22 every way you are very religious. 23 For as I walked
around and looked carefully at your objects of wor-
17:24 [y]Isa 42:5; ship, I even found an altar with this inscription: TO
Ac 14:15 AN UNKNOWN GOD. Now what you worship as some-
[z]Dt 10:14; Mt 11:25 thing unknown[x] I am going to proclaim to you.
[a]Ac 7:48 24 "The God who made the world and everything
in it[y] is the Lord of heaven and earth[z] and does not
17:25 [b]Ps 50:10-12; live in temples built by hands.[a] 25 And he is not
Isa 42:5 served by human hands, as if he needed anything,
because he himself gives all men life and breath
17:26 [c]Dt 32:8; and everything else.[b] 26 From one man he made
Job 12:23 every nation of men, that they should inhabit the
17:27 whole earth; and he determined the times set for
[d]Dt 4:7; Jer 23:23,24; them and the exact places where they should live.[c]
Ac 14:17 27 God did this so that men would seek him and
perhaps reach out for him and find him, though
17:28 [e]Job 12:10; he is not far from each one of us.[d] 28 'For in him we
Da 5:23 live and move and have our being.'[e] As some of
17:29 your own poets have said, 'We are his offspring.'
[f]Isa 40:18- 29 "Therefore since we are God's offspring, we
20; Ro 1:23 should not think that the divine being is like gold
17:30 or silver or stone—an image made by man's
[g]Ac 14:16; Ro 3:25 design and skill.[f] 30 In the past God overlooked[g]
[h]ver 23; such ignorance,[h] but now he commands all peo-
1Pe 1:14 ple everywhere to repent.[i] 31 For he has set a day
[i]Lk 24:47; Tit 2:11,12 when he will judge[j] the world with justice[k] by the
17:31 man he has appointed.[l] He has given proof of this
[j]Mt 10:15 to all men by raising him from the dead."[m]
[k]Ps 9:8; 96:13; 98:9 32 When they heard about the resurrection of the
[l]Ac 10:42 dead,[n] some of them sneered, but others said, "We
[m]Ac 2:24 want to hear you again on this subject." 33 At that,
17:32 Paul left the Council. 34 A few men became fol-
[n]ver 18,31 lowers of Paul and believed. Among them was
17:34 Dionysius, a member of the Areopagus,[o] also a
[o]ver 19,22 woman named Damaris, and a number of others.

Paul in Athens

AC 17:16-34

Jesus has a wonderful way of meeting people right where they are. When he is by the seashore, his words are about fishing (Mt 4:18-19). When on a mountainside, flowers of the field and birds of the air become the best images to make a point (Mt 5:1; 6:26,28). The apostle Paul follows in the footsteps of Jesus in this respect. In fact, Paul says, "I have become all things to all men so that by all possible means I might save some" (1Co 9:22).

It makes sense then for Paul, when he is in Athens, one of the philosophical centers of the ancient world, to use the natural contours of the intellectual landscape. He affirms the people's seeking and their desire to be religious. This fact becomes the springboard into a conversation about the unknown god to whom they have built an altar. In his conversation with these philosophers, Paul even quotes two of their own poets. Paul's example, modeled after Jesus, still speaks to us today. The best way to reach the lost is to speak their "language."

Aquila and Priscilla

AC 18:1–4

During his second missionary journey, Paul travels through the city of Corinth (see Map 11: Paul's Missionary Journeys at the back of this Bible). There he meets Priscilla and Aquila. They are tentmakers like Paul, so they work together. Over time, they travel and minister in partnership. A friendship is forged that lasts a lifetime. In two of his letters, Paul sends greetings to Aquila and Priscilla (Ro 16:3; 2Ti 4:19). In a letter to Corinth, Paul sends greetings from the couple to the church in Corinth (1Co 16:19). Paul calls them "fellow workers in Christ" (Ro 16:3), and he acknowledges that they actually risked their lives for him and other believers (Ro 16:3–4). Now that's friendship! (See the character sketch for Priscilla on page 2047.)

One of God's greatest gifts is the gift of friendship. Our friends become part of our lives, just as Aquila and Priscilla became part of Paul's life. Our friends rejoice with us in our moments of victory and blessing and weep with us in times of sorrow and pain. Thank God for this wonderful gift!

In Corinth

18 After this, Paul left Athens[p] and went to
Corinth.[q] 2There he met a Jew named Aquila, a native of Pontus, who had recently come
from Italy with his wife Priscilla,[r] because Claudius[s] had ordered all the Jews to leave Rome. Paul
went to see them, 3and because he was a tentmaker as they were, he stayed and worked with
them.[t] 4Every Sabbath[u] he reasoned in the synagogue, trying to persuade Jews and Greeks.

5When Silas[v] and Timothy[w] came from Macedonia,[x] Paul devoted himself exclusively to
preaching, testifying to the Jews that Jesus was
the Christ.[a][y] 6But when the Jews opposed Paul
and became abusive,[z] he shook out his clothes in
protest and said to them, "Your blood be on your
own heads![a] I am clear of my responsibility.[b]
From now on I will go to the Gentiles."[c]

7Then Paul left the synagogue and went next
door to the house of Titius Justus, a worshiper of
God.[d] 8Crispus,[e] the synagogue ruler,[f] and his
entire household[g] believed in the Lord; and many
of the Corinthians who heard him believed and
were baptized.

9One night the Lord spoke to Paul in a vision:
"Do not be afraid; keep on speaking, do not be
silent. 10For I am with you,[h] and no one is going to
attack and harm you, because I have many people
in this city." 11So Paul stayed for a year and a half,
teaching them the word of God.

12While Gallio was proconsul of Achaia,[i] the
Jews made a united attack on Paul and brought
him into court. 13"This man," they charged, "is
persuading the people to worship God in ways
contrary to the law."

14Just as Paul was about to speak, Gallio said to
the Jews, "If you Jews were making a complaint
about some misdemeanor or serious crime, it
would be reasonable for me to listen to you. 15But
since it involves questions about words and
names and your own law[j]—settle the matter yourselves. I will not be a judge of such things." 16So
he had them ejected from the court. 17Then they
all turned on Sosthenes[k] the synagogue ruler and
beat him in front of the court. But Gallio showed
no concern whatever.

Priscilla, Aquila and Apollos

18Paul stayed on in Corinth for some time. Then
he left the brothers[l] and sailed for Syria, accompanied by Priscilla and Aquila. Before he sailed,
he had his hair cut off at Cenchrea[m] because of a
vow he had taken.[n] 19They arrived at Ephesus,[o]
where Paul left Priscilla and Aquila. He himself
went into the synagogue and reasoned with the
Jews. 20When they asked him to spend more time
with them, he declined. 21But as he left, he promised, "I will come back if it is God's will."[p] Then

18:1 [p]Ac 17:15 [q]Ac 19:1; 1Co 1:2; 2Co 1:1,23; 2Ti 4:20
18:2 [r]Ro 16:3; 1Co 16:19; 2Ti 4:19 [s]Ac 11:28
18:3 [t]Ac 20:34; 1Co 4:12; 1Th 2:9; 2Th 3:8
18:4 [u]Ac 13:14
18:5 [v]Ac 15:22 [w]Ac 16:1 [x]Ac 16:9; 17:14,15 [y]ver 28; Ac 17:3
18:6 [z]Ac 13:45 [a]2Sa 1:16; Eze 18:13; 33:4 [b]Ac 20:26 [c]Ac 13:46
18:7 [d]Ac 16:14
18:8 [e]1Co 1:14 [f]Mk 5:22 [g]Ac 11:14
18:10 [h]Mt 28:20
18:12 [i]ver 27
18:15 [j]Ac 23:29; 25:11,19
18:17 [k]1Co 1:1
18:18 [l]Ac 1:16 [m]Ro 16:1 [n]Nu 6:2,5, 18; Ac 21:24
18:19 [o]ver 21,24; 1Co 15:32
18:21 [p]Ro 1:10; 1Co 4:19; Jas 4:15

[a] 5 Or *Messiah;* also in verse 28

he set sail from Ephesus. [22]When he landed at
Caesarea,[q] he went up and greeted the church and
then went down to Antioch.[r]
[23]After spending some time in Antioch, Paul set
out from there and traveled from place to place
throughout the region of Galatia[s] and Phrygia,
strengthening all the disciples.[t]
[24]Meanwhile a Jew named Apollos,[u] a native of
Alexandria, came to Ephesus. He was a learned
man, with a thorough knowledge of the Scriptures. [25]He had been instructed in the way of the
Lord, and he spoke with great fervor[a][v] and taught
about Jesus accurately, though he knew only the
baptism of John.[w] [26]He began to speak boldly in
the synagogue. When Priscilla and Aquila heard
him, they invited him to their home and
explained to him the way of God more adequately.
[27]When Apollos wanted to go to Achaia,[x] the
brothers[y] encouraged him and wrote to the disciples there to welcome him. On arriving, he was a
great help to those who by grace had believed.
[28]For he vigorously refuted the Jews in public
debate, proving from the Scriptures[z] that Jesus
was the Christ.[a]

Paul in Ephesus

19 While Apollos was at Corinth,[b] Paul took
the road through the interior and arrived at
Ephesus.[c] There he found some disciples [2]and
asked them, "Did you receive the Holy Spirit
when[b] you believed?"
They answered, "No, we have not even heard
that there is a Holy Spirit."
[3]So Paul asked, "Then what baptism did you
receive?"
"John's baptism," they replied.
[4]Paul said, "John's baptism was a baptism of
repentance. He told the people to believe in the
one coming after him, that is, in Jesus."[d] [5]On
hearing this, they were baptized into[c] the name of
the Lord Jesus. [6]When Paul placed his hands on
them,[e] the Holy Spirit came on them,[f] and they
spoke in tongues[d][g] and prophesied. [7]There were
about twelve men in all.
[8]Paul entered the synagogue[h] and spoke boldly
there for three months, arguing persuasively about
the kingdom of God.[i] [9]But some of them[j] became
obstinate; they refused to believe and publicly
maligned the Way.[k] So Paul left them. He took the
disciples[l] with him and had discussions daily in the
lecture hall of Tyrannus. [10]This went on for two
years,[m] so that all the Jews and Greeks who lived in
the province of Asia[n] heard the word of the Lord.
[11]God did extraordinary miracles[o] through Paul,
[12]so that even handkerchiefs and aprons that had
touched him were taken to the sick, and their illnesses were cured[p] and the evil spirits left them.
[13]Some Jews who went around driving out evil

18:22 [q]Ac 8:40 [r]Ac 11:19
18:23 [s]Ac 16:6 [t]Ac 14:22; 15:32,41
18:24 [u]Ac 19:1; 1Co 1:12; 3:5,6,22; 4:6; 16:12; Tit 3:13
18:25 [v]Ro 12:11 [w]Ac 19:3
18:27 [x]ver 12 [y]ver 18
18:28 [z]Ac 17:2 [a]ver 5; Ac 9:22
19:1 [b]Ac 18:1 [c]Ac 18:19
19:4 [d]Jn 1:7; Ac 13:24,25
19:6 [e]Ac 6:6; 8:17 [f]Ac 2:4 [g]Mk 16:17; Ac 10:46
19:8 [h]Ac 9:20 [i]Ac 1:3; 28:23
19:9 [j]Ac 14:4 [k]ver 23; Ac 9:2 [l]ver 30; Ac 11:26
19:10 [m]Ac 20:31 [n]ver 22,26, 27
19:11 [o]Ac 8:13
19:12 [p]Ac 5:15

[a]25 Or *with fervor in the Spirit* [b]2 Or *after* [c]5 Or *in*
[d]6 Or *other languages*

Gracious Teaching

AC 18:24-26

Apollos is a scholar, an apologist and a gifted debater. He loves the Lord and is zealous about defending the faith. However, even with all his training and credentials, he still has more to learn. When Apollos teaches in the Jewish synagogue, Priscilla and Aquila hear him. They immediately recognize his love for God, his zeal and his gifts. They also see that he needs to receive additional instruction in the truth. Rather than discussing his deficiency behind his back, looking the other way or hoping someone else will take on the task, Priscilla and Aquila invite Apollos into their home and, with graciousness and openness, begin to teach him more fully the things of God. They open their home, they open their hearts, they open their mouths and they speak the truth. In partnership, this godly couple use their gifts to strengthen Apollos and ultimately bless the whole church (see the character sketch for Priscilla on page 2047).

The Name of Jesus

AC 19:13-16

We need to get one thing absolutely straight. The name of Jesus is not to be used like a lucky rabbit's foot. We can't simply say the name and expect to overpower the demons of hell. In this story, seven men are using the name of Jesus like a lucky charm or some mindless incantation. They use Jesus' name as they would the name of any god, adding Paul's name just for good measure. They do not know Jesus, they are not filled with the Spirit, and they have no right to speak in his holy name. Believers, on the other hand, are empowered by the Holy Spirit and called to operate in the name of Jesus. When we speak in Jesus' name and the power of his shed blood, the demons must obey . . . because Jesus is present!

spirits[q] tried to invoke the name of the Lord Jesus
over those who were demon-possessed. They
would say, "In the name of Jesus,[r] whom Paul
preaches, I command you to come out." 14 Seven
sons of Sceva, a Jewish chief priest, were doing
this. 15 ⌊One day⌋ the evil spirit answered them,
"Jesus I know, and I know about Paul, but who
are you?" 16 Then the man who had the evil spirit
jumped on them and overpowered them all. He
gave them such a beating that they ran out of the
house naked and bleeding.
17 When this became known to the Jews and
Greeks living in Ephesus,[s] they were all seized
with fear,[t] and the name of the Lord Jesus was
held in high honor. 18 Many of those who believed
now came and openly confessed their evil deeds.
19 A number who had practiced sorcery brought
their scrolls together and burned them publicly.
When they calculated the value of the scrolls, the
total came to fifty thousand drachmas.[a] 20 In this
way the word of the Lord spread widely and grew
in power.[u]
21 After all this had happened, Paul decided to go
to Jerusalem,[v] passing through Macedonia[w] and
Achaia.[x] "After I have been there," he said, "I must
visit Rome also."[y] 22 He sent two of his helpers,[z]
Timothy[a] and Erastus,[b] to Macedonia, while he
stayed in the province of Asia[c] a little longer.

The Riot in Ephesus

23 About that time there arose a great disturbance about the Way.[d] 24 A silversmith named
Demetrius, who made silver shrines of Artemis,
brought in no little business for the craftsmen.
25 He called them together, along with the workmen in related trades, and said: "Men, you know
we receive a good income from this business.[e]
26 And you see and hear how this fellow Paul has
convinced and led astray large numbers of people
here in Ephesus[f] and in practically the whole
province of Asia. He says that man-made gods are
no gods at all.[g] 27 There is danger not only that our
trade will lose its good name, but also that the
temple of the great goddess Artemis will be discredited, and the goddess herself, who is worshiped throughout the province of Asia and the
world, will be robbed of her divine majesty."
28 When they heard this, they were furious and
began shouting: "Great is Artemis of the Ephesians!"[h] 29 Soon the whole city was in an uproar.
The people seized Gaius[i] and Aristarchus,[j] Paul's
traveling companions from Macedonia,[k] and
rushed as one man into the theater. 30 Paul wanted
to appear before the crowd, but the disciples
would not let him. 31 Even some of the officials of
the province, friends of Paul, sent him a message
begging him not to venture into the theater.
32 The assembly was in confusion: Some were
shouting one thing, some another.[l] Most of the

19:13 [q]Mt 12:27 [r]Mk 9:38
19:17 [s]Ac 18:19 [t]Ac 5:5,11
19:20 [u]Ac 6:7; 12:24
19:21 [v]Ac 20:16, 22; Ro 15:25 [w]Ac 16:9 [x]Ac 18:12 [y]Ro 15:24,28
19:22 [z]Ac 13:5 [a]Ac 16:1 [b]Ro 16:23; 2Ti 4:20 [c]ver 10,26, 27
19:23 [d]Ac 9:2
19:25 [e]Ac 16:16, 19,20
19:26 [f]Ac 18:19 [g]Dt 4:28; Ps 115:4; Isa 44:10-20; Jer 10:3-5; Ac 17:29; 1Co 8:4; Rev 9:20
19:28 [h]Ac 18:19
19:29 [i]Ac 20:4; Ro 16:23; 1Co 1:14 [j]Ac 20:4; 27:2; Col 4:10; Phm 24 [k]Ac 16:9
19:32 [l]Ac 21:34

[a] *19* A drachma was a silver coin worth about a day's wages.

people did not even know why they were there.
33 The Jews pushed Alexander to the front, and
some of the crowd shouted instructions to him. He
19:33 [m]Ac 12:17 motioned[m] for silence in order to make a defense
before the people. 34 But when they realized he was
a Jew, they all shouted in unison for about two
hours: "Great is Artemis of the Ephesians!"
35 The city clerk quieted the crowd and said:
19:35 [n]Ac 18:19 "Men of Ephesus,[n] doesn't all the world know that
the city of Ephesus is the guardian of the temple of
the great Artemis and of her image, which fell from
heaven? 36 Therefore, since these facts are undeni-
able, you ought to be quiet and not do anything
rash. 37 You have brought these men here, though
19:37 [o]Ro 2:22 they have neither robbed temples[o] nor blasphemed
our goddess. 38 If, then, Demetrius and his fellow
craftsmen have a grievance against anybody, the
courts are open and there are proconsuls.[p] They
19:38 [p]Ac 13:7,8,12 can press charges. 39 If there is anything further you
want to bring up, it must be settled in a legal
assembly. 40 As it is, we are in danger of being
charged with rioting because of today's events. In
that case we would not be able to account for this
commotion, since there is no reason for it." 41 After
he had said this, he dismissed the assembly.

Through Macedonia and Greece

20:1 20 When the uproar had ended, Paul sent for
[q]Ac 11:26 the disciples[q] and, after encouraging them,
[r]Ac 16:9 said good-by and set out for Macedonia.[r] 2 He trav-
20:3 eled through that area, speaking many words of
[s]ver 19; Ac 9:23,24; encouragement to the people, and finally arrived
23:12,15,30; in Greece, 3 where he stayed three months.
25:3; Because the Jews made a plot against him[s] just as
2Co 11:26 he was about to sail for Syria, he decided to go
[t]Ac 16:9 back through Macedonia.[t] 4 He was accompanied
20:4 by Sopater son of Pyrrhus from Berea, Aristar-
[u]Ac 19:29 chus[u] and Secundus from Thessalonica,[v] Gaius[w]
[v]Ac 17:1 [w]Ac 19:29 from Derbe, Timothy[x] also, and Tychicus[y] and
[x]Ac 16:1 Trophimus[z] from the province of Asia. 5 These
[y]Eph 6:21; Col 4:7; men went on ahead and waited for us[a] at Troas.[b]
2Ti 4:12; 6 But we sailed from Philippi[c] after the Feast of
Tit 3:12 [z]Ac 21:29; Unleavened Bread, and five days later joined the
2Ti 4:20 others at Troas,[d] where we stayed seven days.

20:5 [a]Ac 16:10 [b]Ac 16:8

Eutychus Raised From the Dead at Troas

7 On the first day of the week[e] we came togeth-
20:6 er to break bread. Paul spoke to the people and,
[c]Ac 16:12 because he intended to leave the next day, kept on
[d]Ac 16:8 talking until midnight. 8 There were many lamps
20:7 in the upstairs room[f] where we were meeting.
[e]1Co 16:2; 9 Seated in a window was a young man named
Rev 1:10 Eutychus, who was sinking into a deep sleep as
20:8 Paul talked on and on. When he was sound
[f]Ac 1:13 asleep, he fell to the ground from the third story
20:10 and was picked up dead. 10 Paul went down, threw
[g]1Ki 17:21; himself on the young man[g] and put his arms
2Ki 4:34 around him. "Don't be alarmed," he said. "He's
[h]Mt 9:23,24 alive!"[h] 11 Then he went upstairs again and broke
20:11 [i]ver 7 bread[i] and ate. After talking until daylight, he left.

Elizabeth Prentiss wrote the words of this hymn when she was ill. She showed it to no one until 13 years later when her husband encouraged her to have it published.

More Love to Thee

More love to Thee, O Christ, more
love to Thee!
Hear Thou the prayer I make
on bended knee.
This is my earnest plea: More love,
O Christ, to Thee;
More love to Thee, more love
to Thee!

Once earthly joy I craved, sought
peace and rest;
Now Thee alone I seek, give what
is best.
This all my prayer shall be: More
love, O Christ to Thee;
More love to Thee, more love
to Thee!

Let sorrow do its work, come grief
or pain;
Sweet are Thy messengers, sweet
their refrain,
When they can sing with me: More
love, O Christ, to Thee;
More love to Thee, more love
to Thee!

Then shall my latest breath whisper
Thy praise;
This be the parting cry my heart
shall raise;
This still its prayer shall be: More
love, O Christ to Thee;
More love to Thee, more love
to Thee!

—Elizabeth Payson Prentiss (1818–1878)

Paul's Boasting

AC 20:19-24

There is a difference between boasting and speaking the truth. The distinction can sometimes be subtle and hard to discern, but Paul is not lifting up himself in a boastful way in this passage. Rather, he is giving a clear and honest picture of what he has done. Not only does Paul review what God has done through him, but he points to what lies ahead. He is willing to face any hardship for the sake of the gospel. While not trying to lift himself up into the spiritual spotlight, Paul does recognize that his life can be an inspiration and encouragement to others. He is willing to point out some of his own spirit-anointed ministry moments if these examples will strengthen his brothers and sisters in Christ to be faithful in their own lives and ministries.

12 The people took the young man home alive and
were greatly comforted.

Paul's Farewell to the Ephesian Elders

13 We went on ahead to the ship and sailed for
Assos, where we were going to take Paul aboard.
He had made this arrangement because he was
going there on foot. 14 When he met us at Assos,
we took him aboard and went on to Mitylene.
15 The next day we set sail from there and arrived
off Kios. The day after that we crossed over to
Samos, and on the following day arrived at Miletus.[j] 16 Paul had decided to sail past Ephesus[k] to
avoid spending time in the province of Asia, for
he was in a hurry to reach Jerusalem,[l] if possible,
by the day of Pentecost.[m]

17 From Miletus, Paul sent to Ephesus for the
elders[n] of the church. 18 When they arrived, he
said to them: "You know how I lived the whole
time I was with you,[o] from the first day I came
into the province of Asia. 19 I served the Lord with
great humility and with tears, although I was
severely tested by the plots of the Jews.[p] 20 You
know that I have not hesitated to preach anything[q] that would be helpful to you but have
taught you publicly and from house to house. 21 I
have declared to both Jews[r] and Greeks that they
must turn to God in repentance[s] and have faith in
our Lord Jesus.[t]

22 "And now, compelled by the Spirit, I am going
to Jerusalem,[u] not knowing what will happen to
me there. 23 I only know that in every city the Holy
Spirit warns me[v] that prison and hardships are
facing me.[w] 24 However, I consider my life worth
nothing to me,[x] if only I may finish the race and
complete the task[y] the Lord Jesus has given me[z]—
the task of testifying to the gospel of God's grace.

25 "Now I know that none of you among whom
I have gone about preaching the kingdom will
ever see me again.[a] 26 Therefore, I declare to you
today that I am innocent of the blood of all men.[b]
27 For I have not hesitated to proclaim to you the
whole will of God.[c] 28 Keep watch over yourselves
and all the flock of which the Holy Spirit has
made you overseers.[ad] Be shepherds of the church
of God,[b] which he bought with his own blood. 29 I
know that after I leave, savage wolves[e] will come
in among you and will not spare the flock.[f] 30 Even
from your own number men will arise and distort
the truth in order to draw away disciples[g] after
them. 31 So be on your guard! Remember that for
three years[h] I never stopped warning each of you
night and day with tears.[i]

32 "Now I commit you to God[j] and to the word of
his grace, which can build you up and give you
an inheritance[k] among all those who are sanctified.[l] 33 I have not coveted anyone's silver or gold
or clothing.[m] 34 You yourselves know that these

[a] 28 Traditionally *bishops* [b] 28 Many manuscripts *of the Lord*

20:15 [j]ver 17; 2Ti 4:20
20:16 [k]Ac 18:19 [l]Ac 19:21 [m]Ac 2:1; 1Co 16:8
20:17 [n]Ac 11:30
20:18 [o]Ac 18:19-21; 19:1-41
20:19 [p]ver 3
20:20 [q]ver 27
20:21 [r]Ac 18:5 [s]Ac 2:38 [t]Ac 24:24; 26:18; Eph 1:15; Col 2:5; Phm 5
20:22 [u]ver 16
20:23 [v]Ac 21:4 [w]Ac 9:16
20:24 [x]Ac 21:13 [y]2Co 4:1 [z]Gal 1:1; Tit 1:3
20:25 [a]ver 38
20:26 [b]Ac 18:6
20:27 [c]ver 20
20:28 [d]1Pe 5:2
20:29 [e]Mt 7:15 [f]ver 28
20:30 [g]Ac 11:26
20:31 [h]Ac 19:10 [i]ver 19
20:32 [j]Ac 14:23 [k]Eph 1:14; Col 1:12; 3:24; Heb 9:15; 1Pe 1:4 [l]Ac 26:18
20:33 [m]1Sa 12:3; 1Co 9:12; 2Co 7:2; 11:9; 12:14-17

hands of mine have supplied my own needs and
the needs of my companions.[n] 35In everything I
did, I showed you that by this kind of hard work
we must help the weak, remembering the words
the Lord Jesus himself said: 'It is more blessed to
give than to receive.' "
36When he had said this, he knelt down with all
of them and prayed.[o] 37They all wept as they
embraced him and kissed him.[p] 38What grieved
them most was his statement that they would never see his face again.[q] Then they accompanied
him to the ship.

On to Jerusalem

21 After we[r] had torn ourselves away from
them, we put out to sea and sailed straight
to Cos. The next day we went to Rhodes and from
there to Patara. 2We found a ship crossing over to
Phoenicia,[s] went on board and set sail. 3After
sighting Cyprus and passing to the south of it, we
sailed on to Syria. We landed at Tyre, where our
ship was to unload its cargo. 4Finding the disciples[t] there, we stayed with them seven days.
Through the Spirit[u] they urged Paul not to go on
to Jerusalem. 5But when our time was up, we left
and continued on our way. All the disciples and
their wives and children accompanied us out of
the city, and there on the beach we knelt to pray.[v]
6After saying good-by to each other, we went
aboard the ship, and they returned home.
7We continued our voyage from Tyre[w] and landed at Ptolemais, where we greeted the brothers[x]
and stayed with them for a day. 8Leaving the next
day, we reached Caesarea[y] and stayed at the house
of Philip[z] the evangelist,[a] one of the Seven. 9He
had four unmarried daughters who prophesied.[b]
10After we had been there a number of days, a
prophet named Agabus[c] came down from Judea.
11Coming over to us, he took Paul's belt, tied his
own hands and feet with it and said, "The Holy
Spirit says, 'In this way the Jews of Jerusalem will
bind[d] the owner of this belt and will hand him
over to the Gentiles.' "[e]
12When we heard this, we and the people there
pleaded with Paul not to go up to Jerusalem.
13Then Paul answered, "Why are you weeping and
breaking my heart? I am ready not only to be
bound, but also to die[f] in Jerusalem for the name
of the Lord Jesus."[g] 14When he would not be dis-
suaded, we gave up and said, "The Lord's will be
done."
15After this, we got ready and went up to Jerusalem. 16Some of the disciples from Caesarea[h]
accompanied us and brought us to the home of
Mnason, where we were to stay. He was a man
from Cyprus[i] and one of the early disciples.

Paul's Arrival at Jerusalem

17When we arrived at Jerusalem, the brothers
received us warmly.[j] 18The next day Paul and the

20:34 [n]Ac 18:3
20:36 [o]Lk 22:41; Ac 21:5
20:37 [p]Lk 15:20
20:38 [q]ver 25
21:1 [r]Ac 16:10
21:2 [s]Ac 11:19
21:4 [t]Ac 11:26 [u]ver 11; Ac 20:23
21:5 [v]Ac 20:36
21:7 [w]Ac 12:20 [x]Ac 1:16
21:8 [y]Ac 8:40 [z]Ac 6:5; 8:5-40 [a]Eph 4:11; 2Ti 4:5
21:9 [b]Lk 2:36; Ac 2:17
21:10 [c]Ac 11:28
21:11 [d]ver 33 [e]1Ki 22:11
21:13 [f]Ac 20:24 [g]Ac 9:16
21:16 [h]Ac 8:40 [i]ver 3,4
21:17 [j]Ac 15:4

Danger!

AC 21:10-14

When we read of Paul's profound awareness of the risks ahead, we might wonder why he presses forward. The signs are posted: *Danger Ahead!* ***Yet Paul continues on his chosen way. Agabus, a Judean prophet, makes Paul's future painfully clear. He will be bound hand and foot by the Jews in Jerusalem and given to the Gentiles.***

All the people respond naturally. They plead with Paul not to go to Jerusalem. They see the signs and want Paul to be spared. However, Paul makes his decision clear. He sees the warning signs too, but there is no turning back. He will be bound; he will be imprisoned; later, he will even die for Jesus (Ac 21:13; 2Ti 4:6-8). His declaration rings down through the centuries, giving boldness and courage to believers from every age who face discouragement, persecution, even death.

rest of us went to see James,[k] and all the elders[l]
were present. 19 Paul greeted them and reported in
detail what God had done among the Gentiles[m]
through his ministry.[n]
20 When they heard this, they praised God. Then
they said to Paul: "You see, brother, how many
thousands of Jews have believed, and all of them
are zealous[o] for the law.[p] 21 They have been
informed that you teach all the Jews who live
among the Gentiles to turn away from Moses,[q]
telling them not to circumcise their children[r] or
live according to our customs.[s] 22 What shall we
do? They will certainly hear that you have come,
23 so do what we tell you. There are four men with
us who have made a vow.[t] 24 Take these men, join
in their purification rites[u] and pay their expenses,
so that they can have their heads shaved.[v] Then
everybody will know there is no truth in these
reports about you, but that you yourself are living
in obedience to the law. 25 As for the Gentile
believers, we have written to them our decision
that they should abstain from food sacrificed to
idols, from blood, from the meat of strangled animals and from sexual immorality."[w]
26 The next day Paul took the men and purified
himself along with them. Then he went to the
temple to give notice of the date when the days of
purification would end and the offering would be
made for each of them.[x]

Paul Arrested

27 When the seven days were nearly over, some
Jews from the province of Asia saw Paul at the
temple. They stirred up the whole crowd and
seized him,[y] 28 shouting, "Men of Israel, help us!
This is the man who teaches all men everywhere
against our people and our law and this place.
And besides, he has brought Greeks into the temple area and defiled this holy place."[z] 29 (They had
previously seen Trophimus[a] the Ephesian[b] in the
city with Paul and assumed that Paul had brought
him into the temple area.)
30 The whole city was aroused, and the people
came running from all directions. Seizing Paul,[c]
they dragged him[d] from the temple, and immediately the gates were shut. 31 While they were trying
to kill him, news reached the commander of the
Roman troops that the whole city of Jerusalem
was in an uproar. 32 He at once took some officers
and soldiers and ran down to the crowd. When
the rioters saw the commander and his soldiers,
they stopped beating Paul.[e]
33 The commander came up and arrested him
and ordered him to be bound[f] with two[g] chains.[h]
Then he asked who he was and what he had
done. 34 Some in the crowd shouted one thing and
some another,[i] and since the commander could
not get at the truth because of the uproar, he
ordered that Paul be taken into the barracks.[j]
35 When Paul reached the steps,[k] the violence of
the mob was so great he had to be carried by the

21:18 [k]Ac 15:13 [l]Ac 11:30
21:19 [m]Ac 14:27 [n]Ac 1:17
21:20 [o]Ac 22:3; Ro 10:2; Gal 1:14 [p]Ac 15:1,5
21:21 [q]ver 28 [r]Ac 15:19-21; 1Co 7:18,19 [s]Ac 6:14
21:23 [t]Ac 18:18
21:24 [u]ver 26; Ac 24:18 [v]Ac 18:18
21:25 [w]Ac 15:20, 29
21:26 [x]Nu 6:13-20; Ac 24:18
21:27 [y]Ac 24:18; 26:21
21:28 [z]Mt 24:15; Ac 24:5,6
21:29 [a]Ac 20:4 [b]Ac 18:19
21:30 [c]Ac 26:21 [d]Ac 16:19
21:32 [e]Ac 23:27
21:33 [f]ver 11 [g]Ac 12:6 [h]Ac 20:23; Eph 6:20; 2Ti 2:9
21:34 [i]Ac 19:32 [j]ver 37; Ac 23:10,16, 32
21:35 [k]ver 40

When you have a need to know your future, turn to God. Ask for wisdom and guidance. He knows what is in store for you, and he will reassure you that he is in control of your destiny. He has promised to direct your path when you trust in him.

—Thelma Wells

21:36 soldiers. 36 The crowd that followed kept shouting,
[l]Lk 23:18; Jn 19:15; “Away with him!”[l]

Ac 22:22 *Paul Speaks to the Crowd*

21:37 37 As the soldiers were about to take Paul into
[m]ver 34 the barracks,[m] he asked the commander, “May I
say something to you?”
“Do you speak Greek?” he replied. 38 “Aren’t you
21:38 the Egyptian who started a revolt and led four
[n]Mt 24:26 thousand terrorists out into the desert[n] some time
[o]Ac 5:36 ago?”[o]
21:39 39 Paul answered, “I am a Jew, from Tarsus[p] in
[p]Ac 9:11 [q]Ac 22:3 Cilicia,[q] a citizen of no ordinary city. Please let me
speak to the people.”
40 Having received the commander’s permission,
21:40 [r]Ac 12:17 Paul stood on the steps and motioned[r] to the
[s]Jn 5:2 crowd. When they were all silent, he said to them
22:1 **22** in Aramaic[a]:[s] 1 “Brothers and fathers,[t] listen
[t]Ac 7:2 now to my defense.”
22:2 2 When they heard him speak to them in Ara-
[u]Ac 21:40 maic,[u] they became very quiet.
22:3 Then Paul said: 3 “I am a Jew,[v] born in Tarsus[w]
[v]Ac 21:39 of Cilicia, but brought up in this city. Under[x]
[w]Ac 9:11 Gamaliel[y] I was thoroughly trained in the law of
[x]Lk 10:39 [y]Ac 5:34 our fathers[z] and was just as zealous[a] for God as
[z]Ac 26:5 any of you are today. 4 I persecuted[b] the followers
[a]Ac 21:20 of this Way to their death, arresting both men and
22:4 women and throwing them into prison,[c] 5 as also
[b]Ac 8:3 [c]ver 19,20 the high priest and all the Council[d] can testify. I
even obtained letters from them to their brothers[e]
22:5 in Damascus,[f] and went there to bring these peo-
[d]Lk 22:66 [e]Ac 13:26 ple as prisoners to Jerusalem to be punished.
[f]Ac 9:2 6 “About noon as I came near Damascus, suddenly a bright light from heaven flashed around
22:6 [g]Ac 9:3 me.[g] 7 I fell to the ground and heard a voice say to
me, ‘Saul! Saul! Why do you persecute me?’
8 “ ‘Who are you, Lord?’ I asked.
“ ‘I am Jesus of Nazareth, whom you are perse-
22:9 cuting,’ he replied. 9 My companions saw the
[h]Ac 26:13 light,[h] but they did not understand the voice[i] of
[i]Ac 9:7 him who was speaking to me.
10 “ ‘What shall I do, Lord?’ I asked.
“ ‘Get up,’ the Lord said, ‘and go into Damas-
22:10 cus. There you will be told all that you have been
[j]Ac 16:30 assigned to do.’[j] 11 My companions led me by the
hand into Damascus, because the brilliance of the
22:11 [k]Ac 9:8 light had blinded me.[k]
12 “A man named Ananias came to see me.[l] He
22:12 [l]Ac 9:17 was a devout observer of the law and highly
[m]Ac 10:22 respected by all the Jews living there.[m] 13 He stood
beside me and said, ‘Brother Saul, receive your
sight!’ And at that very moment I was able to see
22:14 him.
[n]Ac 3:13 14 “Then he said: ‘The God of our fathers[n] has
[o]1Co 9:1; chosen you to know his will and to see[o] the Righ-
15:8 [p]Ac 7:52 teous One[p] and to hear words from his mouth.
15 You will be his witness[q] to all men of what you
22:15 [q]Ac 23:11; 26:16 have seen and heard. 16 And now what are you

[a] *40* Or possibly *Hebrew*; also in 22:2

Paul’s Training

AC 22:3

Paul has only been in Jerusalem for a few days (Ac 21:27) and already the prophecy about the difficulties he will face (Ac 21:11) is coming true. He is seized by the crowd, and the uproar is so great and the people so inflamed that Paul must be carried away by Roman soldiers for his own safety (Ac 21:35). But Paul wishes to stop and speak to this violent group. One word from Paul in their common language, Aramaic, silences the crowd. His command not only of Greek but also of Aramaic impresses them. But Paul has more than the language to give him credibility with the crowd. He is a student of the famous and wise teacher Gamaliel (see the note on Ac 5:29–39, page 1798) and has an impeccable and impressive educational background. He uses what he has in common with these people to gain an opening for his conversion story and the truth of the gospel.

Paul's Roman Citizenship

AC 22:22-29

Just as he is about to be beaten, Paul turns a sober eye on the Roman centurion in charge and asks him if he thinks he should beat a Roman citizen. The centurion is shocked to find that Paul is a Roman citizen.

There were only three ways to become a Roman citizen. If a person offered some outstanding act of service to Rome, he or she might be given citizenship as a reward. The wealthy could pay a high price and purchase their citizenship. Finally, a person born to parents who were citizens was automatically a Roman citizen by birth. Paul falls into this third category.

A Roman citizen could not be beaten without first being found guilty of a crime in a Roman court of law. In fact, Roman citizens were exempt from all degrading forms of punishment such as beatings with rods, scourging and crucifixion. Paul's citizenship was a wall of protection that he chose to use at this critical moment.

waiting for? Get up, be baptized[r] and wash your
sins away,[s] calling on his name.'[t]
17"When I returned to Jerusalem[u] and was praying at the temple, I fell into a trance[v] 18and saw
the Lord speaking. 'Quick!' he said to me. 'Leave
Jerusalem immediately, because they will not
accept your testimony about me.'
19" 'Lord,' I replied, 'these men know that I
went from one synagogue to another to imprison[w]
and beat[x] those who believe in you. 20And when
the blood of your martyr[a] Stephen was shed, I
stood there giving my approval and guarding the
clothes of those who were killing him.'[y]
21"Then the Lord said to me, 'Go; I will send you
far away to the Gentiles.' "[z]

Paul the Roman Citizen

22The crowd listened to Paul until he said this.
Then they raised their voices and shouted, "Rid
the earth of him![a] He's not fit to live!"[b]
23As they were shouting and throwing off their
cloaks[c] and flinging dust into the air,[d] 24the commander ordered Paul to be taken into the barracks.[e] He directed[f] that he be flogged and questioned in order to find out why the people were
shouting at him like this. 25As they stretched him
out to flog him, Paul said to the centurion standing there, "Is it legal for you to flog a Roman citizen who hasn't even been found guilty?"[g]
26When the centurion heard this, he went to the
commander and reported it. "What are you going
to do?" he asked. "This man is a Roman citizen."
27The commander went to Paul and asked, "Tell
me, are you a Roman citizen?"
"Yes, I am," he answered.
28Then the commander said, "I had to pay a big
price for my citizenship."
"But I was born a citizen," Paul replied.
29Those who were about to question him withdrew immediately. The commander himself was
alarmed when he realized that he had put Paul, a
Roman citizen,[h] in chains.

Before the Sanhedrin

30The next day, since the commander wanted to
find out exactly why Paul was being accused by
the Jews,[i] he released him[j] and ordered the chief
priests and all the Sanhedrin[k] to assemble. Then
he brought Paul and had him stand before them.
23 Paul looked straight at the Sanhedrin[l] and
said, "My brothers,[m] I have fulfilled my
duty to God in all good conscience[n] to this day."
2At this the high priest Ananias[o] ordered those
standing near Paul to strike him on the mouth.[p]
3Then Paul said to him, "God will strike you, you
whitewashed wall![q] You sit there to judge me
according to the law, yet you yourself violate the
law by commanding that I be struck!"[r]

22:16 [r]Ac 2:38 [s]Heb 10:22 [t]Ro 10:13
22:17 [u]Ac 9:26 [v]Ac 10:10
22:19 [w]ver 4; Ac 8:3 [x]Mt 10:17
22:20 [y]Ac 7:57-60; 8:1
22:21 [z]Ac 9:15; 13:46
22:22 [a]Ac 21:36 [b]Ac 25:24
22:23 [c]Ac 7:58 [d]2Sa 16:13
22:24 [e]Ac 21:34 [f]ver 29
22:25 [g]Ac 16:37
22:29 [h]ver 24,25; Ac 16:38
22:30 [i]Ac 23:28 [j]Ac 21:33 [k]Mt 5:22
23:1 [l]Ac 22:30 [m]Ac 22:5 [n]Ac 24:16; 1Co 4:4; 2Co 1:12; 2Ti 1:3; Heb 13:18
23:2 [o]Ac 24:1 [p]Jn 18:22
23:3 [q]Mt 23:27 [r]Lev 19:15; Dt 25:1,2; Jn 7:51

[a] 20 Or *witness*

4Those who were standing near Paul said, "You
dare to insult God's high priest?"
5Paul replied, "Brothers, I did not realize that
he was the high priest; for it is written: 'Do not
speak evil about the ruler of your people.'[a]"[s]
6Then Paul, knowing that some of them were
Sadducees and the others Pharisees, called out in
the Sanhedrin, "My brothers,[t] I am a Pharisee,[u]
the son of a Pharisee. I stand on trial because of
my hope in the resurrection of the dead."[v] 7When
he said this, a dispute broke out between the
Pharisees and the Sadducees, and the assembly
was divided. 8(The Sadducees say that there is no
resurrection,[w] and that there are neither angels
nor spirits, but the Pharisees acknowledge them
all.)
9There was a great uproar, and some of the
teachers of the law who were Pharisees[x] stood up
and argued vigorously. "We find nothing wrong
with this man,"[y] they said. "What if a spirit or an
angel has spoken to him?"[z] 10The dispute became
so violent that the commander was afraid Paul
would be torn to pieces by them. He ordered the
troops to go down and take him away from them
by force and bring him into the barracks.[a]
11The following night the Lord stood near Paul
and said, "Take courage![b] As you have testified
about me in Jerusalem, so you must also testify
in Rome."[c]

The Plot to Kill Paul

12The next morning the Jews formed a conspiracy and bound themselves with an oath not to eat
or drink until they had killed Paul.[d] 13More than
forty men were involved in this plot. 14They went
to the chief priests and elders and said, "We have
taken a solemn oath not to eat anything until we
have killed Paul.[e] 15Now then, you and the Sanhedrin[f] petition the commander to bring him
before you on the pretext of wanting more accurate information about his case. We are ready to
kill him before he gets here."
16But when the son of Paul's sister heard of this
plot, he went into the barracks[g] and told Paul.
17Then Paul called one of the centurions and
said, "Take this young man to the commander; he
has something to tell him." 18So he took him to
the commander.
The centurion said, "Paul, the prisoner,[h] sent
for me and asked me to bring this young man to
you because he has something to tell you."
19The commander took the young man by the
hand, drew him aside and asked, "What is it you
want to tell me?"
20He said: "The Jews have agreed to ask you to
bring Paul before the Sanhedrin[i] tomorrow on the
pretext of wanting more accurate information
about him.[j] 21Don't give in to them, because more
than forty[k] of them are waiting in ambush for

[a] 5 Exodus 22:28

23:5 [s]Ex 22:28
23:6 [t]Ac 22:5 [u]Ac 26:5; Php 3:5 [v]Ac 24:15, 21; 26:8
23:8 [w]Mt 22:23
23:9 [x]Mk 2:16 [y]ver 29; Ac 25:25; 26:31 [z]Ac 22:7,17, 18
23:10 [a]Ac 21:34
23:11 [b]Ac 18:9 [c]Ac 19:21; 28:23
23:12 [d]ver 14,21, 30; Ac 25:3
23:14 [e]ver 12
23:15 [f]ver 1; Ac 22:30
23:16 [g]ver 10; Ac 21:34
23:18 [h]Eph 3:1
23:20 [i]ver 1 [j]ver 14,15
23:21 [k]ver 13

Paul the Pharisee

AC 22:30–23:11

Paul is brought before the supreme court of his day, the Sanhedrin (see the note on Lk 19:47–48, page 1727). This council is comprised of both Pharisees and Sadducees. The Pharisees believe in angels, spirits and the resurrection. The Sadducees deny all of these. In the midst of this theological powder keg, Paul tosses one little match.

He lets them all know that he is a second-generation Pharisee and that he believes in the resurrection. In fact, he declares that he is on trial because of his confidence in the resurrection. Now the sparks begin to fly! Some of the Pharisees come to his side. As things escalate and erupt, the Roman commander has to step in and remove Paul so that he will not be "torn to pieces" (Ac 23:10) in the middle of the dispute.

Paul's Protection

AC 23:23

Why does it take 470 men to escort one man (Paul) from Jerusalem to Caesarea? What makes Paul so special? The answer is simple. He is a Roman citizen. In the first century, Roman citizenship meant everything. So, not only is Paul exempt from cruel and unusual punishment, not only is he given the right to a fair trial before any judgment is made against him, but he also comes under the powerful protecting hand of the Roman Empire. Because a group of more that 40 religious zealots have committed to fast until Paul is dead (Ac 23:12–13), the Roman government takes extreme measures to deliver Paul safely to the next level: Governor Felix.

him. They have taken an oath not to eat or drink
until they have killed him.[l] They are ready now,
waiting for your consent to their request."
22The commander dismissed the young man
and cautioned him, "Don't tell anyone that you
have reported this to me."

Paul Transferred to Caesarea

23Then he called two of his centurions and
ordered them, "Get ready a detachment of two
hundred soldiers, seventy horsemen and two hundred
spearmen[a] to go to Caesarea[m] at nine tonight.[n]
24Provide mounts for Paul so that he may
be taken safely to Governor Felix."[o]
25He wrote a letter as follows:

26Claudius Lysias,

To His Excellency,[p] Governor Felix:
Greetings.[q]

27This man was seized by the Jews and
they were about to kill him,[r] but I came with
my troops and rescued him,[s] for I had learned
that he is a Roman citizen.[t] 28I wanted to
know why they were accusing him, so I
brought him to their Sanhedrin.[u] 29I found
that the accusation had to do with questions
about their law,[v] but there was no charge
against him[w] that deserved death or imprisonment.
30When I was informed[x] of a plot[y] to
be carried out against the man, I sent him to
you at once. I also ordered his accusers[z] to
present to you their case against him.

31So the soldiers, carrying out their orders, took
Paul with them during the night and brought him
as far as Antipatris. 32The next day they let the
cavalry[a] go on with him, while they returned to
the barracks.[b] 33When the cavalry[c] arrived in
Caesarea,[d] they delivered the letter to the governor[e]
and handed Paul over to him. 34The governor
read the letter and asked what province he was
from. Learning that he was from Cilicia,[f] 35he said,
"I will hear your case when your accusers[g] get
here." Then he ordered that Paul be kept under
guard[h] in Herod's palace.

The Trial Before Felix

24 Five days later the high priest Ananias[i] went
down to Caesarea with some of the elders
and a lawyer named Tertullus, and they brought
their charges[j] against Paul before the governor.[k]
2When Paul was called in, Tertullus presented his
case before Felix: "We have enjoyed a long period
of peace under you, and your foresight has
brought about reforms in this nation. 3Everywhere
and in every way, most excellent[l] Felix, we
acknowledge this with profound gratitude. 4But in

23:21 [l]ver 12,14
23:23 [m]Ac 8:40 [n]ver 33
23:24 [o]ver 26,33; Ac 24:1-3, 10; 25:14
23:26 [p]Lk 1:3; Ac 24:3; 26:25 [q]Ac 15:23
23:27 [r]Ac 21:32 [s]Ac 21:33 [t]Ac 22:25-29
23:28 [u]Ac 22:30
23:29 [v]Ac 18:15; 25:19 [w]ver 9; Ac 26:31
23:30 [x]ver 20,21 [y]Ac 20:3 [z]ver 35; Ac 24:19; 25:16
23:32 [a]ver 23 [b]Ac 21:34
23:33 [c]ver 23,24 [d]Ac 8:40 [e]ver 26
23:34 [f]Ac 6:9; 21:39
23:35 [g]ver 30; Ac 24:19; 25:16 [h]Ac 24:27
24:1 [i]Ac 23:2 [j]Ac 23:30,35 [k]Ac 23:24
24:3 [l]Lk 1:3; Ac 23:26; 26:25

[a] *23* The meaning of the Greek for this word is uncertain.

order not to weary you further, I would request
that you be kind enough to hear us briefly.
5 “We have found this man to be a troublemaker, stirring up riots[m] among the Jews[n] all over the
world. He is a ringleader of the Nazarene[o] sect[p]
6 and even tried to desecrate the temple;[q] so we
seized him. 8 By[a] examining him yourself you will
be able to learn the truth about all these charges
we are bringing against him.”
9 The Jews joined in the accusation,[r] asserting
that these things were true.
10 When the governor[s] motioned for him to
speak, Paul replied: “I know that for a number of
years you have been a judge over this nation; so I
gladly make my defense. 11 You can easily verify
that no more than twelve days[t] ago I went up to
Jerusalem to worship. 12 My accusers did not find
me arguing with anyone at the temple,[u] or stirring
up a crowd[v] in the synagogues or anywhere else
in the city. 13 And they cannot prove to you the
charges they are now making against me.[w] 14 However, I admit that I worship the God of our fathers[x]
as a follower of the Way,[y] which they call a sect.[z]
I believe everything that agrees with the Law and
that is written in the Prophets,[a] 15 and I have the
same hope in God as these men, that there will be
a resurrection[b] of both the righteous and the
wicked.[c] 16 So I strive always to keep my conscience clear[d] before God and man.
17 “After an absence of several years, I came to
Jerusalem to bring my people gifts for the poor[e]
and to present offerings. 18 I was ceremonially
clean[f] when they found me in the temple courts
doing this. There was no crowd with me, nor was
I involved in any disturbance.[g] 19 But there are
some Jews from the province of Asia, who ought
to be here before you and bring charges if they
have anything against me.[h] 20 Or these who are
here should state what crime they found in me
when I stood before the Sanhedrin— 21 unless it
was this one thing I shouted as I stood in their
presence: ‘It is concerning the resurrection of the
dead that I am on trial before you today.’ ”[i]
22 Then Felix, who was well acquainted with the
Way, adjourned the proceedings. “When Lysias
the commander comes,” he said, “I will decide
your case.” 23 He ordered the centurion to keep
Paul under guard[j] but to give him some freedom[k]
and permit his friends to take care of his needs.[l]
24 Several days later Felix came with his wife
Drusilla, who was a Jewess. He sent for Paul and
listened to him as he spoke about faith in Christ
Jesus.[m] 25 As Paul discoursed on righteousness,
self-control[n] and the judgment[o] to come, Felix was
afraid and said, “That’s enough for now! You may
leave. When I find it convenient, I will send for

[a] 6–8 Some manuscripts *him and wanted to judge him according to our law.* [7]*But the commander, Lysias, came and with the use of much force snatched him from our hands* [8]*and ordered his accusers to come before you. By*

24:5 [m]Ac 16:20; 17:6 [n]Ac 21:28 [o]Mk 1:24 [p]ver 14; Ac 26:5; 28:22
24:6 [q]Ac 21:28
24:9 [r]1Th 2:16
24:10 [s]Ac 23:24
24:11 [t]Ac 21:27; ver 1
24:12 [u]Ac 25:8; 28:17 [v]ver 18
24:13 [w]Ac 25:7
24:14 [x]Ac 3:13 [y]Ac 9:2 [z]ver 5 [a]Ac 26:6,22; 28:23
24:15 [b]Ac 23:6; 28:20 [c]Da 12:2; Jn 5:28,29
24:16 [d]Ac 23:1
24:17 [e]Ac 11:29, 30; Ro 15:25-28, 31; 1Co 16:1-4,15; 2Co 8:1-4; Gal 2:10
24:18 [f]Ac 21:26 [g]ver 12
24:19 [h]Ac 23:30
24:21 [i]Ac 23:6
24:23 [j]Ac 23:35 [k]Ac 28:16 [l]Ac 23:16; 27:3
24:24 [m]Ac 20:21
24:25 [n]Gal 5:23; 2Pe 1:6 [o]Ac 10:42

People of the Way

AC 24:14

Although no one knows exactly when or where the term originated, the early Christians sometimes referred to themselves as people of “the Way.” Back when Paul was still called Saul and was persecuting the church, he was hunting for those who belonged to “the Way” so that he could imprison them (Ac 9:1-2). Now he himself is a follower of the Way, and he is under fire.

The Jewish leaders see the followers of the Way as a suspiciously strange sect of Judaism. Its followers agree with all of the basic tenets of Judaism and see God as their Father, but they also see Christ as the fulfillment of Jewish law. The early Christians simply see themselves as those who follow “the way” of their Savior. If Jesus is truly “the way and the truth and the life” (Jn 14:6), then early Christians as well as contemporary Christians have “the way” set out for them by Jesus and willingly walk in it daily.

God Brings the Growth

AC 24:24-27

Paul makes it clear that believers can plant the seeds of the gospel and water them, but only God can bring the growth (1Co 3:5–9). For two full years Paul plants and waters. Each time he is given a chance to talk with Felix, Paul proclaims the message of faith in Christ with boldness. Initially, Felix is filled with fear and makes Paul stop speaking. However, he later allows ongoing discussion about faith to continue—although he was at least partially motivated by a desire to receive a bribe from Paul.

We don't know if Felix ever responded to the message. What we do know is that Paul continued to speak the truth even when there was no evidence of change in Felix's life. Our call is to communicate our faith lovingly and clearly. Some will receive the message. Others will reject it outright. We can't control the response. What we can do is water and plant seeds and pray for God to bring the growth. When he does, we give him the credit and the glory.

you." 26 At the same time he was hoping that Paul
would offer him a bribe, so he sent for him frequently and talked with him.
27 When two years had passed, Felix was succeeded by Porcius Festus,[p] but because Felix
wanted to grant a favor to the Jews,[q] he left Paul
in prison.[r]

The Trial Before Festus

25 Three days after arriving in the province,
Festus went up from Caesarea[s] to Jerusalem, 2 where the chief priests and Jewish leaders
appeared before him and presented the charges
against Paul.[t] 3 They urgently requested Festus, as
a favor to them, to have Paul transferred to Jerusalem, for they were preparing an ambush to kill
him along the way. 4 Festus answered, "Paul is
being held[u] at Caesarea, and I myself am going
there soon. 5 Let some of your leaders come with
me and press charges against the man there, if he
has done anything wrong."
6 After spending eight or ten days with them, he
went down to Caesarea, and the next day he convened the court[v] and ordered that Paul be brought
before him. 7 When Paul appeared, the Jews who
had come down from Jerusalem stood around
him, bringing many serious charges against him,[w]
which they could not prove.[x]
8 Then Paul made his defense: "I have done
nothing wrong against the law of the Jews or
against the temple[y] or against Caesar."
9 Festus, wishing to do the Jews a favor,[z] said to
Paul, "Are you willing to go up to Jerusalem and
stand trial before me there on these charges?"[a]
10 Paul answered: "I am now standing before
Caesar's court, where I ought to be tried. I have
not done any wrong to the Jews, as you yourself
know very well. 11 If, however, I am guilty of doing
anything deserving death, I do not refuse to die.
But if the charges brought against me by these
Jews are not true, no one has the right to hand me
over to them. I appeal to Caesar!"[b]
12 After Festus had conferred with his council,
he declared: "You have appealed to Caesar. To Caesar you will go!"

Festus Consults King Agrippa

13 A few days later King Agrippa and Bernice
arrived at Caesarea[c] to pay their respects to Festus. 14 Since they were spending many days there,
Festus discussed Paul's case with the king. He
said: "There is a man here whom Felix left as a
prisoner.[d] 15 When I went to Jerusalem, the chief
priests and elders of the Jews brought charges
against him[e] and asked that he be condemned.
16 "I told them that it is not the Roman custom to
hand over any man before he has faced his accusers and has had an opportunity to defend himself
against their charges.[f] 17 When they came here
with me, I did not delay the case, but convened

24:27 [p]Ac 25:1,4, 9,14 [q]Ac 12:3; 25:9 [r]Ac 23:35; 25:14
25:1 [s]Ac 8:40
25:2 [t]ver 15; Ac 24:1
25:4 [u]Ac 24:23
25:6 [v]ver 17
25:7 [w]Mk 15:3; Lk 23:2,10; Ac 24:5,6 [x]Ac 24:13
25:8 [y]Ac 6:13; 24:12; 28:17
25:9 [z]Ac 24:27 [a]ver 20
25:11 [b]ver 21,25; Ac 26:32; 28:19
25:13 [c]Ac 8:40
25:14 [d]Ac 24:27
25:15 [e]ver 2; Ac 24:1
25:16 [f]ver 4,5; Ac 23:30

the court the next day and ordered the man to be
25:17 [g]ver 6,10 brought in.[g] [18]When his accusers got up to speak,
they did not charge him with any of the crimes I
had expected. [19]Instead, they had some points of
25:19 [h]Ac 18:15; dispute[h] with him about their own religion[i] and
23:29 about a dead man named Jesus who Paul claimed
[i]Ac 17:22 was alive. [20]I was at a loss how to investigate such
matters; so I asked if he would be willing to go to
25:20 [j]ver 9 Jerusalem and stand trial there on these charges.[j]
[21]When Paul made his appeal to be held over for
the Emperor's decision, I ordered him held until I
25:21 [k]ver 11,12 could send him to Caesar."[k]
[22]Then Agrippa said to Festus, "I would like to
hear this man myself."
25:22 [l]Ac 9:15 He replied, "Tomorrow you will hear him."[l]

Paul Before Agrippa

25:23 [m]ver 13; [23]The next day Agrippa and Bernice[m] came with
Ac 26:30 great pomp and entered the audience room with
the high ranking officers and the leading men of
the city. At the command of Festus, Paul was
brought in. [24]Festus said: "King Agrippa, and all
25:24 [n]ver 2,3,7 who are present with us, you see this man! The
[o]Ac 22:22 whole Jewish community[n] has petitioned me
about him in Jerusalem and here in Caesarea,
shouting that he ought not to live any longer.[o] [25]I
25:25 [p]Ac 23:9 found he had done nothing deserving of death,[p]
[q]ver 11 but because he made his appeal to the Emperor[q] I
decided to send him to Rome. [26]But I have nothing
definite to write to His Majesty about him. Therefore I have brought him before all of you, and
especially before you, King Agrippa, so that as a
result of this investigation I may have something
to write. [27]For I think it is unreasonable to send
on a prisoner without specifying the charges
26:1 [r]Ac 9:15; against him."
25:22 **26** Then Agrippa said to Paul, "You have permission to speak for yourself."[r]
26:3 [s]ver 7; So Paul motioned with his hand and began his
Ac 6:14 defense: [2]"King Agrippa, I consider myself fortu-
[t]Ac 25:19 nate to stand before you today as I make my
26:4 defense against all the accusations of the Jews,
[u]Gal 1:13, 14; Php 3:5 [3]and especially so because you are well acquainted with all the Jewish customs[s] and controver-
26:5 [v]Ac 22:3 sies.[t] Therefore, I beg you to listen to me patiently.
[w]Ac 23:6; [4]"The Jews all know the way I have lived ever
Php 3:5 since I was a child,[u] from the beginning of my life
26:6 in my own country, and also in Jerusalem. [5]They
[x]Ac 23:6; 24:15; 28:20 have known me for a long time[v] and can testify, if
[y]Ac 13:32; they are willing, that according to the strictest sect
Ro 15:8 of our religion, I lived as a Pharisee.[w] [6]And now it
26:7 is because of my hope[x] in what God has promised
[z]Jas 1:1 our fathers[y] that I am on trial today. [7]This is the
[a]1Th 3:10; 1Ti 5:5 promise our twelve tribes[z] are hoping to see ful-
[b]ver 2 filled as they earnestly serve God day and night.[a]
26:8 O king, it is because of this hope that the Jews are
[c]Ac 23:6 accusing me.[b] [8]Why should any of you consider
it incredible that God raises the dead?[c]
26:9 [9]"I too was convinced[d] that I ought to do all that
[d]1Ti 1:13 [e]Jn 16:2 was possible to oppose[e] the name of Jesus of Naz-
[f]Jn 15:21 areth.[f] [10]And that is just what I did in Jerusalem.

The Core Issue

AC 25:16–21

The religious leaders of the Jewish people try many tactics to get the Roman government to condemn Paul as a criminal. However, all of their efforts fail. Now they have one more chance. Paul is now under the authority of Festus, who is trying to sort out the charges against Paul. The Jewish leaders again level their charges. But this time something is different. This time all the charges are religious, not political. The charges deal with the resurrection of Jesus Christ.

How often has this happened throughout history? People resist Christ with countless excuses, faulty explanations and smoke screens. They don't want to face the core issue of the faith. But finally, the smoke clears and there is one issue still on the table. Do they believe that Jesus lived, died and rose again in glory? It all comes down to this. Do you believe or don't you?

King Agrippa

AC 26:25-29

Over and over again, Paul tells his story. Every time someone will listen, Paul tells how Jesus broke through Paul's granite heart and made him a new man. Paul boldly invites others, even rulers and kings, to receive this Good News and accept this Jesus who has so transformed his life.

In a straightforward and convicting manner, Paul confronts King Agrippa. Agrippa is a Jew, part of the line of Herodian kings of Judah, who were puppets of the Roman government. Paul knows that Agrippa understands the Old Testament truths and that, if he is willing, he can see Jesus as the fulfillment of those truths. Without wavering Paul confronts him: Will he or will he not believe? Paul does not care if it happens in the snap of a finger or over a great length of time (Ac 26:29). He just wants to see Agrippa come to know Christ. Paul's boldness, as well as his heart and passion for the lost, is part of the unforgettable legacy he left to the Christian church.

On the authority of the chief priests I put many of
the saints[g] in prison,[h] and when they were put to
death, I cast my vote against them.[i] 11Many a time
I went from one synagogue to another to have
them punished,[j] and I tried to force them to blaspheme. In my obsession against them, I even
went to foreign cities to persecute them.
12"On one of these journeys I was going to
Damascus with the authority and commission of
the chief priests. 13About noon, O king, as I was
on the road, I saw a light from heaven, brighter
than the sun, blazing around me and my companions. 14We all fell to the ground, and I heard a
voice[k] saying to me in Aramaic,[a] 'Saul, Saul, why
do you persecute me? It is hard for you to kick
against the goads.'
15"Then I asked, 'Who are you, Lord?'
" 'I am Jesus, whom you are persecuting,' the
Lord replied. 16'Now get up and stand on your
feet.[l] I have appeared to you to appoint you as a
servant and as a witness of what you have seen
of me and what I will show you.[m] 17I will rescue
you[n] from your own people and from the Gentiles.[o] I am sending you to them 18to open their
eyes[p] and turn them from darkness to light,[q] and
from the power of Satan to God, so that they may
receive forgiveness of sins[r] and a place among
those who are sanctified by faith in me.'[s]
19"So then, King Agrippa, I was not disobedient
to the vision from heaven. 20First to those in
Damascus,[t] then to those in Jerusalem[u] and in all
Judea, and to the Gentiles[v] also, I preached that
they should repent[w] and turn to God and prove
their repentance by their deeds.[x] 21That is why the
Jews seized me[y] in the temple courts and tried to
kill me.[z] 22But I have had God's help to this very
day, and so I stand here and testify to small and
great alike. I am saying nothing beyond what the
prophets and Moses said would happen[a]— 23that
the Christ[b] would suffer and, as the first to rise
from the dead,[b] would proclaim light to his own
people and to the Gentiles."[c]
24At this point Festus interrupted Paul's defense.
"You are out of your mind,[d] Paul!" he shouted.
"Your great learning[e] is driving you insane."
25"I am not insane, most excellent[f] Festus," Paul
replied. "What I am saying is true and reasonable.
26The king is familiar with these things,[g] and I can
speak freely to him. I am convinced that none of
this has escaped his notice, because it was not
done in a corner. 27King Agrippa, do you believe
the prophets? I know you do."
28Then Agrippa said to Paul, "Do you think that
in such a short time you can persuade me to be a
Christian?"[h]
29Paul replied, "Short time or long—I pray God
that not only you but all who are listening to me
today may become what I am, except for these
chains."[i]

26:10 [g]Ac 9:13 [h]Ac 8:3; 9:2, 14,21 [i]Ac 22:20
26:11 [j]Mt 10:17
26:14 [k]Ac 9:7
26:16 [l]Eze 2:1; Da 10:11 [m]Ac 22:14, 15
26:17 [n]Jer 1:8,19 [o]Ac 9:15
26:18 [p]Isa 35:5 [q]Isa 42:7,16; Eph 5:8; Col 1:13; 1Pe 2:9 [r]Lk 24:47; Ac 2:38 [s]Ac 20:21,32
26:20 [t]Ac 9:19-25 [u]Ac 9:26-29; 22:17-20 [v]Ac 9:15; 13:46 [w]Ac 3:19 [x]Mt 3:8; Lk 3:8
26:21 [y]Ac 21:27,30 [z]Ac 21:31
26:22 [a]Lk 24:27, 44; Ac 10:43; 24:14
26:23 [b]1Co 15:20, 23; Col 1:18; Rev 1:5 [c]Lk 2:32
26:24 [d]Jn 10:20; 1Co 4:10 [e]Jn 7:15
26:25 [f]Ac 23:26
26:26 [g]ver 3
26:28 [h]Ac 11:26
26:29 [i]Ac 21:33

[a] 14 Or *Hebrew* [b] 23 Or *Messiah*

30 The king rose, and with him the governor and Bernice[j] and those sitting with them. 31 They left the room, and while talking with one another, they said, "This man is not doing anything that deserves death or imprisonment."[k]

32 Agrippa said to Festus, "This man could have been set free[l] if he had not appealed to Caesar."[m]

Paul Sails for Rome

27 When it was decided that we[n] would sail for Italy,[o] Paul and some other prisoners were handed over to a centurion named Julius, who belonged to the Imperial Regiment.[p] 2 We boarded a ship from Adramyttium about to sail for ports along the coast of the province of Asia,[q] and we put out to sea. Aristarchus,[r] a Macedonian[s] from Thessalonica,[t] was with us.

3 The next day we landed at Sidon;[u] and Julius, in kindness to Paul,[v] allowed him to go to his friends so they might provide for his needs.[w] 4 From there we put out to sea again and passed to the lee of Cyprus because the winds were against us.[x] 5 When we had sailed across the open sea off the coast of Cilicia[y] and Pamphylia, we landed at Myra in Lycia. 6 There the centurion found an Alexandrian ship[z] sailing for Italy[a] and put us on board. 7 We made slow headway for many days and had difficulty arriving off Cnidus. When the wind did not allow us to hold our course,[b] we sailed to the lee of Crete,[c] opposite Salmone. 8 We moved along the coast with difficulty and came to a place called Fair Havens, near the town of Lasea.

9 Much time had been lost, and sailing had already become dangerous because by now it was after the Fast.[a][d] So Paul warned them, 10 "Men, I can see that our voyage is going to be disastrous and bring great loss to ship and cargo, and to our own lives also."[e] 11 But the centurion, instead of listening to what Paul said, followed the advice of the pilot and of the owner of the ship. 12 Since the harbor was unsuitable to winter in, the majority decided that we should sail on, hoping to reach Phoenix and winter there. This was a harbor in Crete, facing both southwest and northwest.

The Storm

13 When a gentle south wind began to blow, they thought they had obtained what they wanted; so they weighed anchor and sailed along the shore of Crete. 14 Before very long, a wind of hurricane force,[f] called the "northeaster," swept down from the island. 15 The ship was caught by the storm and could not head into the wind; so we gave way to it and were driven along. 16 As we passed to the lee of a small island called Cauda, we were hardly able to make the lifeboat secure. 17 When the men had hoisted it aboard, they passed ropes under the ship itself to hold it together. Fearing that they would run aground[g] on the sandbars of

26:30 [j]Ac 25:23
26:31 [k]Ac 23:9
26:32 [l]Ac 28:18 [m]Ac 25:11
27:1 [n]Ac 16:10 [o]Ac 18:2; 25:12,25 [p]Ac 10:1
27:2 [q]Ac 2:9 [r]Ac 19:29 [s]Ac 16:9 [t]Ac 17:1
27:3 [u]Mt 11:21 [v]ver 43 [w]Ac 24:23; 28:16
27:4 [x]ver 7
27:5 [y]Ac 6:9
27:6 [z]Ac 28:11 [a]ver 1
27:7 [b]ver 4 [c]ver 12,13, 21
27:9 [d]Lev 16:29-31; 23:27-29; Nu 29:7
27:10 [e]ver 21
27:14 [f]Mk 4:37
27:17 [g]ver 26,39

[a] 9 That is, the Day of Atonement (Yom Kippur)

Paul's Choices

AC 26:32

Paul was between the proverbial rock and hard place. If he allowed himself to be returned to Jerusalem, there was a good chance the Jewish leaders could persuade Festus to hand him over to the Sanhedrin for trial or that an attempt would be made to take his life en route (Ac 23:12–16; 25:3). Paul knew that the charges they would bring against him carried the death sentence. On the other hand, if he appealed to Caesar, he would continue in custody until Emperor Nero could see him in Rome. This could be a very long wait. Neither option was a good one. Paul decided on the second of these tough choices.

Remember that Paul has been confident that his ministry will lead him to Rome (Ac 19:21; 23:11). Appealing to Caesar will make Paul's trip to Rome certain and will give him the opportunity to evangelize there. As the highest court to which he could appeal, Paul's appearance before Caesar could accomplish not only his acquittal of the charges against him, but could also possibly give recognition to Christianity as a separate religion from Judaism.

Traveling by Ship

AC 27

Travel by sea has been around since long before the days of Solomon, who gathered much of his wealth from the far corners of the earth in his fleet of ships. Small fishing boats on the Sea of Galilee carried no more than a dozen fishermen. But there were also huge ships like the Alexandrian grain ship that carried Paul and 275 other people (Ac 27:37) as well as cargo. The first-century historian Josephus wrote of traveling to Rome on a ship with 600 people on board. In the first century much of the world's trade was done on the seas. There were well-developed routes and harbors, as well as dependable seasons for safe travel.

Syrtis, they lowered the sea anchor and let the ship be driven along. [18]We took such a violent battering from the storm that the next day they began to throw the cargo overboard.[h] [19]On the third day, they threw the ship's tackle overboard with their own hands. [20]When neither sun nor stars appeared for many days and the storm continued raging, we finally gave up all hope of being saved.

[21]After the men had gone a long time without food, Paul stood up before them and said: "Men, you should have taken my advice[i] not to sail from Crete;[j] then you would have spared yourselves this damage and loss. [22]But now I urge you to keep up your courage,[k] because not one of you will be lost; only the ship will be destroyed. [23]Last night an angel[l] of the God whose I am and whom I serve[m] stood beside me[n] [24]and said, 'Do not be afraid, Paul. You must stand trial before Caesar;[o] and God has graciously given you the lives of all who sail with you.'[p] [25]So keep up your courage,[q] men, for I have faith in God that it will happen just as he told me.[r] [26]Nevertheless, we must run aground[s] on some island."[t]

The Shipwreck

[27]On the fourteenth night we were still being driven across the Adriatic[a] Sea, when about midnight the sailors sensed they were approaching land. [28]They took soundings and found that the water was a hundred and twenty feet[b] deep. A short time later they took soundings again and found it was ninety feet[c] deep. [29]Fearing that we would be dashed against the rocks, they dropped four anchors from the stern and prayed for daylight. [30]In an attempt to escape from the ship, the sailors let the lifeboat[u] down into the sea, pretending they were going to lower some anchors from the bow. [31]Then Paul said to the centurion and the soldiers, "Unless these men stay with the ship, you cannot be saved."[v] [32]So the soldiers cut the ropes that held the lifeboat and let it fall away.

[33]Just before dawn Paul urged them all to eat. "For the last fourteen days," he said, "you have been in constant suspense and have gone without food—you haven't eaten anything. [34]Now I urge you to take some food. You need it to survive. Not one of you will lose a single hair from his head."[w] [35]After he said this, he took some bread and gave thanks to God in front of them all. Then he broke it[x] and began to eat. [36]They were all encouraged[y] and ate some food themselves. [37]Altogether there were 276 of us on board. [38]When they had eaten as much as they wanted, they lightened the ship by throwing the grain into the sea.[z]

[39]When daylight came, they did not recognize the land, but they saw a bay with a sandy beach,[a] where they decided to run the ship aground if

27:18 [h]ver 19,38; Jnh 1:5
27:21 [i]ver 10 [j]ver 7
27:22 [k]ver 25,36
27:23 [l]Ac 5:19 [m]Ro 1:9 [n]Ac 18:9; 23:11; 2Ti 4:17
27:24 [o]Ac 23:11 [p]ver 44
27:25 [q]ver 22,36 [r]Ro 4:20,21
27:26 [s]ver 17,39 [t]Ac 28:1
27:30 [u]ver 16
27:31 [v]ver 24
27:34 [w]Mt 10:30
27:35 [x]Mt 14:19
27:36 [y]ver 22,25
27:38 [z]ver 18; Jnh 1:5
27:39 [a]Ac 28:1

[a] *27* In ancient times the name referred to an area extending well south of Italy. [b] *28* Greek *twenty orguias* (about 37 meters) [c] *28* Greek *fifteen orguias* (about 27 meters)

Mary of Bethany

One of a Kind

Emily Dickinson always dressed in white. Even a glimpse of her was rare, and gradually just the mention of her name brought shrugs and rolled eyes from her neighbors. After her death, they found the stacks of poems that lined her room—poems that revealed her literary genius and touched millions. No one had ever imagined the creative force driving her life with such passion. No one, not even her family, knew of the well within her that served such rare wine. Single women with unconventional lifestyles are often misunderstood. Perhaps Mary of Bethany was one of them.

When Jesus came to visit, Martha insisted that her sister Mary act the "woman's part" and serve in the kitchen. Instead, Mary sat at the feet of Jesus, learning from him—perhaps the only woman in a crowd of men. Yet Jesus not only defended her choice, he commended her for it. He saw her hunger and passion for truth. He loved that in her.

This same Mary later "took about a pint of pure nard, an expensive perfume" and poured it on the Lord's feet and then wiped them dry with her hair (Jn 12:3). Mary knew nothing about Jesus' imminent betrayal and crucifixion. However, in a way the men around Jesus did not, she perceived and responded to Jesus' pain and need for comfort. Without restraint she gave all she had to the Lord. Her gift was very costly, but she gladly spent it in love for Jesus.

Jesus profoundly honored Mary of Bethany, saying, "Wherever the gospel is preached throughout the world, what she has done will also be told, in memory of her" (Mark 14:9). No small thing: *wherever the gospel is preached.* Her story continues even today.

Jesus calls us to recognize and treasure the "Mary" in our midst, the woman who is single, whether by destiny, choice, divorce or death. We sometimes honor her for what she does but seldom for who she is. And we rarely catch even a glimpse of the intimate love she shares with the Lord. Failing to see the passion that drives her life, we may think of her only as "different." Such a Mary may be sitting next to you at church or behind a desk at the office. She spends herself caring for aging parents or teaching children. She fights battles on behalf of the poor, the dispossessed, the victims of our culture. She intercedes and brings others to Jesus through her witness. Hers is not a romantic life—just daily faithfulness, priceless to the Lord.

Mary of Bethany
(bitter)

Matthew 26:6–13

Mark 14:1–9

Luke 10:38–42

John 11:1–12:3

Candid SNAPSHOT Then Mary took about a pint of pure nard, an expensive perfume; she poured it on Jesus' feet and wiped his feet with her hair. And the house was filled with the fragrance of the perfume (John 12:3).

Martha

Open Home, Open Heart

Martha pursed her lips and clenched her jaw as she watched Mary, her sister, follow the men to sit at Jesus' feet. Martha loved having Jesus in her home. He and his disciples were always welcome. Their visits were one of the joys of her life. But there was a lot to do, cooking and providing for so many men. It made her angry that Mary sneaked off when things were busiest.

Martha was secure in Jesus' love for her. She told him exactly what she thought. Some say he rebuked her, but perhaps it is better called instruction: " 'Martha, Martha,' the Lord answered, 'you are worried and upset about many things, but only one thing is needed. Mary has chosen what is better, and it will not be taken away from her' " (Lk 10:41-42). At that important moment, Mary was seeking the eternal; Martha was not. Martha learned something that day.

The next time we meet Martha, her brother, Lazarus, has just died. "When Martha heard that Jesus was coming, she went out to meet him, but Mary stayed at home" (Jn 11:20). This time Martha dropped everything. She didn't concern herself with the mourners in her home and their needs. She ran to Jesus, expecting him to have the answers to console her. " 'Lord,' Martha said to Jesus, 'if you had been here, my brother would not have died' " (Jn 11:21). This was not a rebuke. To plainspoken Martha, it was a fact. She knew the Lord loved her; she knew he understood her. She said what was on her heart.

This time, Martha addressed eternal issues. "But I know that even now God will give you whatever you ask" (Jn 11:22). Martha had worked hard to change her perspective. Jesus now took her deeper. "I am the resurrection and the life" (Jn 11:25).

Jesus was not just Martha's friend. He was her Messiah. She believed. Jesus prepared her for not only Lazarus's resurrection but also his own. It was important to Jesus that Martha—as well as Mary—understand his lordship. Jesus did not want Martha to stop being Martha. Her warm hospitality and servant's heart blessed him greatly. He loved her for it. But he wanted her to know—beyond any doubt—whom she served and why.

We are often reluctant to share our deepest feelings with the Lord. Irrationally, we believe if we don't say it, he won't know it. The Lord wants us to be totally honest and open with him. He can surely handle our strongest emotions. As we confess our struggles, we lay down our pride and learn from his counsel, like Martha did.

Martha
(lady, mistress)

Luke 10:38-41
John 11:1–12:3

Candid SNAPSHOT "Lord," Martha said to Jesus, "if you had been here, my brother would not have died. But I know that even now God will give you whatever you ask" (John 11:21-22).

27:40 they could. 40Cutting loose the anchors,[b] they left
[b]ver 29 them in the sea and at the same time untied the
ropes that held the rudders. Then they hoisted the
foresail to the wind and made for the beach. 41But
the ship struck a sandbar and ran aground. The
27:41 bow stuck fast and would not move, and the stern
[c]2Co 11:25 was broken to pieces by the pounding of the surf.[c]
42The soldiers planned to kill the prisoners to
prevent any of them from swimming away and
escaping. 43But the centurion wanted to spare
27:43 Paul's life[d] and kept them from carrying out their
[d]ver 3 plan. He ordered those who could swim to jump
overboard first and get to land. 44The rest were to
27:44 get there on planks or on pieces of the ship. In this
[e]ver 22,31 way everyone reached land in safety.[e]

Ashore on Malta

28:1
[f]Ac 16:10 **28** Once safely on shore, we[f] found out that the
[g]Ac 27:26,39 island[g] was called Malta. 2The islanders
showed us unusual kindness. They built a fire and
welcomed us all because it was raining and cold.
3Paul gathered a pile of brushwood and, as he put
it on the fire, a viper, driven out by the heat, fas-
28:4 tened itself on his hand. 4When the islanders saw
[h]Mk 16:18 the snake hanging from his hand,[h] they said to
[i]Lk 13:2,4 each other, "This man must be a murderer; for
though he escaped from the sea, Justice has not
28:5 allowed him to live."[i] 5But Paul shook the snake
[j]Lk 10:19 off into the fire and suffered no ill effects.[j] 6The
people expected him to swell up or suddenly fall
dead, but after waiting a long time and seeing
nothing unusual happen to him, they changed
28:6 their minds and said he was a god.[k]
[k]Ac 14:11 7There was an estate nearby that belonged to
Publius, the chief official of the island. He welcomed us to his home and for three days entertained us hospitably. 8His father was sick in bed,
suffering from fever and dysentery. Paul went in
28:8 to see him and, after prayer,[l] placed his hands on
[l]Jas 5:14,15 [m]Ac 9:40 him and healed him.[m] 9When this had happened,
the rest of the sick on the island came and were
cured. 10They honored us in many ways and when
we were ready to sail, they furnished us with the
supplies we needed.

Arrival at Rome

11After three months we put out to sea in a ship
28:11 that had wintered in the island. It was an Alexan-
[n]Ac 27:6 drian ship[n] with the figurehead of the twin gods
Castor and Pollux. 12We put in at Syracuse and
stayed there three days. 13From there we set sail
and arrived at Rhegium. The next day the south
wind came up, and on the following day we
28:14 reached Puteoli. 14There we found some brothers[o]
[o]Ac 1:16 who invited us to spend a week with them. And
28:15 so we came to Rome. 15The brothers[p] there had
[p]Ac 1:16 heard that we were coming, and they traveled as
far as the Forum of Appius and the Three Taverns
to meet us. At the sight of these men Paul thanked
God and was encouraged. 16When we got to

Snake Handling

AC 28:1-6

God works miracles. The islanders know this particular kind of snake, and they have seen what its bite can do. After Paul is bitten, the people wait to see what his reaction will be and are surprised there is no swelling, no death. A miracle. Even in the strangest places God can choose to reveal his power. This miracle opens the door for Paul to minister to the people on the island of Malta.

Some extremists have taken this passage and others like it as an invitation to handle deadly and poisonous snakes. There does not appear to be anything in this passage that presents this one-time experience of Paul as normative for Christians. It is a miracle. God is at work, protecting his servant Paul. But it is not an example of behavior that followers of Christ ought to intentionally duplicate.

A Radical Shift

AC 28:26-28

It is very difficult for us to imagine what a radical shift is reflected in these few verses. The Jews are God's chosen people. When Jesus sent out his disciples, he called them to go to the lost sheep of Israel. In the early days of the church virtually every believer was a converted Jew. Now Paul declares that God's saving plan has shifted from the Jews to the whole world.

The Gentiles, who are despised by the Jews, have become the objects of God's mercy. Salvation is for all people, of all nations, of all times. Ears will hear, hearts will open, eyes will see, and people from every tribe, nation and people will enter the family of God. What a marvelous ending to the book of Acts! The salvation of God is available to you, to me, to everyone *who will believe in Jesus Christ.*

Rome, Paul was allowed to live by himself, with a
soldier to guard him.[q]

Paul Preaches at Rome Under Guard

17 Three days later he called together the leaders
of the Jews.[r] When they had assembled, Paul said
to them: "My brothers,[s] although I have done
nothing against our people[t] or against the customs
of our ancestors,[u] I was arrested in Jerusalem and
handed over to the Romans. 18 They examined me[v]
and wanted to release me,[w] because I was not
guilty of any crime deserving death.[x] 19 But when
the Jews objected, I was compelled to appeal to
Caesar[y]—not that I had any charge to bring against
my own people. 20 For this reason I have asked to
see you and talk with you. It is because of the hope
of Israel[z] that I am bound with this chain."[a]
21 They replied, "We have not received any letters from Judea concerning you, and none of the
brothers[b] who have come from there has reported
or said anything bad about you. 22 But we want to
hear what your views are, for we know that people everywhere are talking against this sect."[c]
23 They arranged to meet Paul on a certain day,
and came in even larger numbers to the place
where he was staying. From morning till evening
he explained and declared to them the kingdom
of God[d] and tried to convince them about Jesus[e]
from the Law of Moses and from the Prophets.[f]
24 Some were convinced by what he said, but others would not believe.[g] 25 They disagreed among
themselves and began to leave after Paul had
made this final statement: "The Holy Spirit spoke
the truth to your forefathers when he said through
Isaiah the prophet:

26 " 'Go to this people and say,
"You will be ever hearing but never
understanding;
you will be ever seeing but never
perceiving."
27 For this people's heart has become
calloused;[h]
they hardly hear with their ears,
and they have closed their eyes.
Otherwise they might see with their
eyes,
hear with their ears,
understand with their hearts
and turn, and I would heal them.'[a][i]

28 "Therefore I want you to know that God's salvation[j] has been sent to the Gentiles,[k] and they
will listen!"[b]
30 For two whole years Paul stayed there in his
own rented house and welcomed all who came to
see him. 31 Boldly and without hindrance he
preached the kingdom of God[l] and taught about
the Lord Jesus Christ.

28:16 [q]Ac 24:23; 27:3
28:17 [r]Ac 25:2 [s]Ac 22:5 [t]Ac 25:8 [u]Ac 6:14
28:18 [v]Ac 22:24 [w]Ac 26:31,32 [x]Ac 23:9
28:19 [y]Ac 25:11
28:20 [z]Ac 26:6,7 [a]Ac 21:33
28:21 [b]Ac 22:5
28:22 [c]Ac 24:5,14
28:23 [d]Ac 19:8 [e]Ac 17:3 [f]Ac 8:35
28:24 [g]Ac 14:4
28:27 [h]Ps 119:70 [i]Isa 6:9,10
28:28 [j]Lk 2:30 [k]Ac 13:46
28:31 [l]ver 23; Mt 4:23

[a] *27* Isaiah 6:9,10 [b] *28* Some manuscripts *listen!" 29 After he said this, the Jews left, arguing vigorously among themselves.*

Romans

God's power for salvation.

Paul's letter to the Romans provides believers with a strong foundation for faith in Christ. Using this letter to introduce himself to the church in Rome, Paul develops and defends the truth of the gospel, encouraging believers to rely solely on God's grace for salvation. Following a logical progression of thought, Paul begins by stating that all people are sinners but then asserts that believers are free from sin's control, the demands of the law and fear of God's punishment. Armed with such freedom, believers can grow in their relationship with Christ and live in the power of the Holy Spirit.

As Paul recounts our sin and God's righteous judgment, we thankfully acknowledge God's patience and mercy (Ro 1-5). We rejoice that we can establish a righteous relationship with God and are awed that the Creator of the world longs to be our Father (Ro 6-8). The "apostle to the Gentiles" explains that Israel, though the people rejected the Messiah, still has a role in God's plan of redemption (Ro 9-11). Paul admonishes us to behave like God's children in service to one another and respectful submission to authority (Ro 12-15). He also greets a number of believers who work for the Lord in many ways, highlighting Phoebe, Paul's courier to Rome (Ro 16).

Sin and selfishness drive a wedge between us and God that can only be removed by our repentance and God's forgiveness. The book of Romans reminds us that a person living in faith and trust in God will manifest a Christlike spirit of humility, a unity with other believers, and a strength of character that can carry her or him victoriously through tough times.

Quick Study

Author
The apostle Paul.

Date Written
Probably during the early spring of A.D. 57.

Written From
Most likely Corinth.

Key Passage
Romans 3:23-24 "For all have sinned and fall short of the glory of God, and are justified freely by his grace through the redemption that came by Christ Jesus."

Outline

Introductory remarks.
Ro 1:1-15

Theme of the letter.
Ro 1:16-17

Sin and the law.
Ro 1:18—3:20

Justified by faith.
Ro 3:21—5:11

Death and life.
Ro 5:12—7:6

Struggling with sin.
Ro 7:7-25

Living by the Spirit.
Ro 8:1-39

God's plan relative to Israel.
Ro 9:1—11:36

Practicing righteousness.
Ro 12:1—15:13

Paul's ministry and plans.
Ro 15:14-33

Closing greetings.
Ro 16:1-27

The Women of Romans

✿ **Phoebe**	*A servant of the church in Cenchrea.* Ro 16:1-2 (page 2048)
✿ **Priscilla**	*Paul's fellow worker in ministry.* Ro 16:3 (page 2047)
✿ **Mary**	*A hard worker.* Ro 16:6 (page 2048)
✿ **Tryphena, Tryphosa, Persis**	*More hard workers.* Ro 16:12 (page 2048)
Rufus's mother	*She was like a mother to Paul.* Ro 16:13
Julia	*Nothing is known of her except her name.* Ro 16:15
Nereus's sister	*Not even her name is known.* Ro 16:15

✿ Denotes a sketch written about this character

1:1 1 Paul, a servant of Christ Jesus, called to be an
a1Co 1:1 apostle[a] and set apart[b] for the gospel of God[c]—
bAc 9:15 2 the gospel he promised beforehand through his
c2Co 11:7 prophets in the Holy Scriptures[d] 3 regarding his Son,
1:2 who as to his human nature[e] was a descendant of
dGal 3:8 David, 4 and who through the Spirit[a] of holiness
1:3 was declared with power to be the Son of God[b] by
eJn 1:14 his resurrection from the dead: Jesus Christ our
Lord. 5 Through him and for his name's sake, we
1:5 received grace and apostleship to call people from
fAc 9:15 among all the Gentiles[f] to the obedience that comes
gAc 6:7 from faith.[g] 6 And you also are among those who
1:6 are called to belong to Jesus Christ.[h]
hRev 17:14

1:7 7 To all in Rome who are loved by God[i] and
iRo 8:39 called to be saints:
j1Co 1:3

Grace and peace to you from God our Father
and from the Lord Jesus Christ.[j]

Paul's Longing to Visit Rome

1:8 8 First, I thank my God through Jesus Christ for
k1Co 1:4 all of you,[k] because your faith is being reported
lRo 16:19 all over the world.[l] 9 God, whom I serve[m] with my
1:9 whole heart in preaching the gospel of his Son, is
m2Ti 1:3 my witness[n] how constantly I remember you 10 in
nPhp 1:8 my prayers at all times; and I pray that now at last
by God's will the way may be opened for me to
1:10 come to you.[o]
oRo 15:32 11 I long to see you[p] so that I may impart to you
1:11 some spiritual gift to make you strong— 12 that is,
pRo 15:23 that you and I may be mutually encouraged by
each other's faith. 13 I do not want you to be
unaware, brothers, that I planned many times to
1:13 come to you (but have been prevented from doing
qRo 15:22,23 so until now)[q] in order that I might have a harvest among you, just as I have had among the oth-
1:14 er Gentiles.
r1Co 9:16 14 I am obligated[r] both to Greeks and non-
Greeks, both to the wise and the foolish. 15 That is
why I am so eager to preach the gospel also to you
1:15 who are at Rome.[s]
sRo 15:20 16 I am not ashamed of the gospel,[t] because it is
1:16 the power of God[u] for the salvation of everyone
t2Ti 1:8 u1Co 1:18 who believes: first for the Jew,[v] then for the Gen-
vAc 3:26 tile.[w] 17 For in the gospel a righteousness from God
wRo 2:9,10 is revealed,[x] a righteousness that is by faith from
1:17 first to last,[c] just as it is written: "The righteous
xRo 3:21 yHab 2:4; will live by faith."[d][y]
Gal 3:11; Heb 10:38

God's Wrath Against Mankind

1:18 18 The wrath of God[z] is being revealed from
zEph 5:6; heaven against all the godlessness and wicked-
Col 3:6 ness of men who suppress the truth by their
wickedness, 19 since what may be known about
God is plain to them, because God has made it
1:19 plain to them.[a] 20 For since the creation of the
aAc 14:17 world God's invisible qualities—his eternal pow-

[a] 4 *Or who as to his spirit* [b] 4 *Or was appointed to be the Son of God with power* [c] 17 *Or is from faith to faith* [d] 17 Hab. 2:4

A Spiritual Gift

RO 1:11–12

The spiritual gift mentioned here is not one of the spiritual gifts listed in 1 Corinthians 12:7–11. Spiritual gifts, as *they are most commonly defined, are given by the Holy Spirit to believers. Believers cannot give them to one another. The gift Paul plans to give is the strengthening of the Roman believers' faith. There is nothing prideful about this offer. As an apostle, Paul is uniquely equipped to encourage and challenge them spiritually. Everything he has suffered and accomplished for Christ gives him a firm foundation from which to draw as he helps them in their trials as well as in their spiritual growth. Yet, with humility, Paul admits he is fully aware that he needs encouragement from them as well.*

As women, we know that, like Paul, we have needs. Do you ever feel like the "Lone Ranger" in your spiritual life? Make a list of five friends who might like to join you in developing a relationship of "mutual encouragement."

No Excuse

RO 1:20

Paul's words here may seem harsh. He says no excuses will be accepted from those who fail to worship and thank God. The Lord's anger is aroused by the godless and the wicked. Those who neglect to serve him have no defense, for evidence of his existence surrounds them in the things of this world he has made. Those who are willing to accept the clear evidence of God's existence and power will then search further to discover more of this God—a God not only of creation but also of grace and love.

Go outside and revel in the God of nature. Enjoy the beauty and order of the things around you, and ask God to show you what those things reveal about him.

er and divine nature—have been clearly seen, being understood from what has been made,[b] so that men are without excuse.

21 For although they knew God, they neither glorified him as God nor gave thanks to him, but their thinking became futile and their foolish hearts were darkened.[c] 22 Although they claimed to be wise, they became fools[d] 23 and exchanged the glory of the immortal God for images[e] made to look like mortal man and birds and animals and reptiles.

24 Therefore God gave them over[f] in the sinful desires of their hearts to sexual impurity for the degrading of their bodies with one another.[g] 25 They exchanged the truth of God for a lie,[h] and worshiped and served created things[i] rather than the Creator—who is forever praised.[j] Amen.

26 Because of this, God gave them over[k] to shameful lusts.[l] Even their women exchanged natural relations for unnatural ones.[m] 27 In the same way the men also abandoned natural relations with women and were inflamed with lust for one another. Men committed indecent acts with other men, and received in themselves the due penalty for their perversion.[n]

28 Furthermore, since they did not think it worthwhile to retain the knowledge of God, he gave them over[o] to a depraved mind, to do what ought not to be done. 29 They have become filled with every kind of wickedness, evil, greed and depravity. They are full of envy, murder, strife, deceit and malice. They are gossips,[p] 30 slanderers, God-haters, insolent, arrogant and boastful; they invent ways of doing evil; they disobey their parents;[q] 31 they are senseless, faithless, heartless,[r] ruthless. 32 Although they know God's righteous decree that those who do such things deserve death,[s] they not only continue to do these very things but also approve[t] of those who practice them.

God's Righteous Judgment

2 You, therefore, have no excuse,[u] you who pass judgment on someone else, for at whatever point you judge the other, you are condemning yourself, because you who pass judgment do the same things.[v] 2 Now we know that God's judgment against those who do such things is based on truth. 3 So when you, a mere man, pass judgment on them and yet do the same things, do you think you will escape God's judgment? 4 Or do you show contempt for the riches[w] of his kindness,[x] tolerance[y] and patience,[z] not realizing that God's kindness leads you toward repentance?[a]

5 But because of your stubbornness and your unrepentant heart, you are storing up wrath against yourself for the day of God's wrath, when his righteous judgment[b] will be revealed. 6 God "will give to each person according to what he has done."[a c] 7 To those who by persistence in doing good seek glory, honor[d] and immortality,[e] he will

1:20 [b] Ps 19:1-6
1:21 [c] Jer 2:5; Eph 4:17,18
1:22 [d] 1Co 1:20,27
1:23 [e] Ps 106:20; Jer 2:11; Ac 17:29
1:24 [f] Eph 4:19 [g] 1Pe 4:3
1:25 [h] Isa 44:20 [i] Jer 10:14 [j] Ro 9:5
1:26 [k] ver 24,28 [l] 1Th 4:5 [m] Lev 18:22, 23
1:27 [n] Lev 18:22; 20:13
1:28 [o] ver 24,26
1:29 [p] 2Co 12:20
1:30 [q] 2Ti 3:2
1:31 [r] 2Ti 3:3
1:32 [s] Ro 6:23 [t] Ps 50:18; Lk 11:48; Ac 8:1; 22:20
2:1 [u] Ro 1:20 [v] 2Sa 12:5-7; Mt 7:1,2
2:4 [w] Ro 9:23; Eph 1:7,18; 2:7 [x] Ro 11:22 [y] Ro 3:25 [z] Ex 34:6 [a] 2Pe 3:9
2:5 [b] Jude 6
2:6 [c] Ps 62:12; Mt 16:27
2:7 [d] ver 10 [e] 1Co 15:53, 54

[a] 6 Psalm 62:12; Prov. 24:12

give eternal life. 8But for those who are self-seek-
2:8 f2Th 2:12 ing and who reject the truth and follow evil,[f] there
will be wrath and anger. 9There will be trouble
and distress for every human being who does evil:
2:9 g1Pe 4:17 first for the Jew, then for the Gentile;[g] 10but glory,
2:10 honor and peace for everyone who does good:
hver 9 first for the Jew, then for the Gentile.[h] 11For God
2:11 does not show favoritism.[i]
iAc 10:34 12All who sin apart from the law will also perish
apart from the law, and all who sin under the law[j]
2:12 will be judged by the law. 13For it is not those who
jRo 3:19; 1Co 9:20,21 hear the law who are righteous in God's sight, but
it is those who obey[k] the law who will be declared
2:13 kJas 1:22,23, righteous. 14(Indeed, when Gentiles, who do not
25 have the law, do by nature things required by the
2:14 law,[l] they are a law for themselves, even though
lAc 10:35 they do not have the law, 15since they show that
the requirements of the law are written on their
hearts, their consciences also bearing witness,
and their thoughts now accusing, now even
2:16 defending them.) 16This will take place on the day
mEcc 12:14 when God will judge men's secrets[m] through
nAc 10:42 oRo 16:25 Jesus Christ,[n] as my gospel[o] declares.

The Jews and the Law

17Now you, if you call yourself a Jew; if you rely
on the law and brag about your relationship to
2:17 pver 23; God;[p] 18if you know his will and approve of what
Mic 3:11; is superior because you are instructed by the law;
Ro 9:4 19if you are convinced that you are a guide for the
blind, a light for those who are in the dark, 20an
2:21 qMt 23:3,4 instructor of the foolish, a teacher of infants,
because you have in the law the embodiment of
2:22 knowledge and truth— 21you, then, who teach
rAc 19:37 others, do you not teach yourself? You who preach
2:23 against stealing, do you steal?[q] 22You who say that
sver 17 people should not commit adultery, do you commit adultery? You who abhor idols, do you rob
2:24 tIsa 52:5; temples?[r] 23You who brag about the law,[s] do you
Eze 36:22 dishonor God by breaking the law? 24As it is writ-
2:25 ten: "God's name is blasphemed among the Gen-
uGal 5:3 vJer 4:4 tiles because of you."[a][t]
25Circumcision has value if you observe the
2:26 wRo 8:4 law,[u] but if you break the law, you have become
x1Co 7:19 as though you had not been circumcised.[v] 26If
those who are not circumcised keep the law's
2:27 yMt 12:41,42 requirements,[w] will they not be regarded as
though they were circumcised?[x] 27The one who is
2:28 zMt 3:9; not circumcised physically and yet obeys the law
Jn 8:39; will condemn you[y] who, even though you have
Ro 9:6,7 aGal 6:15 the[b] written code and circumcision, are a
lawbreaker.
2:29 bPhp 3:3; 28A man is not a Jew if he is only one outward-
Col 2:11 ly,[z] nor is circumcision merely outward and phys-
cRo 7:6 dJn 5:44; ical.[a] 29No, a man is a Jew if he is one inwardly;
1Co 4:5; and circumcision is circumcision of the heart, by
2Co 10:18; 1Th 2:4; the Spirit,[b] not by the written code.[c] Such a man's
1Pe 3:4 praise is not from men, but from God.[d]

[a] *24* Isaiah 52:5; Ezek. 36:22 [b] *27* Or *who, by means of a*

Saying and Doing

RO 2:21–23

It is not enough just to know what is right. We must also do it. If there is a disparity between what comes from our lips and what is manifested in our lives, then our faith is without integrity. It is empty and ineffective. Worse, it brings dishonor to God.

Logically, the opposite is also true: When our words and actions are both in alignment with God's perfect will, when we "practice what we preach," he is wonderfully glorified—and other believers are profoundly encouraged. We also gain favor in his eyes. "For it is not those who hear the law who are righteous in God's sight, but it is those who obey the law who will be declared righteous" **(Ro 2:13).**

The Law's Effect

RO 3:20

Though we are now under a new covenant with God through Jesus Christ, the Mosaic Law, which is the foundation of the old covenant, is still important to us. Why? Because that law reveals to us that we are sinful creatures. Before the existence of the law, people also sinned against God, but their sins were not recognized as such (Rom 4:15; 7:7-11), although those sins still had their negative effect (Ro 5:13). Knowledge of our sin leads us to an acute awareness of our need for a Savior (Ro 3:10-12; 6:23), which in turn leads us to the only one who can redeem us: Jesus Christ (Ro 3:23-25).

God's Faithfulness

3 What advantage, then, is there in being a Jew,
or what value is there in circumcision? 2Much
in every way! First of all, they have been entrusted with the very words of God.[e]
3What if some did not have faith?[f] Will their
lack of faith nullify God's faithfulness?[g] 4Not at
all! Let God be true,[h] and every man a liar.[i] As it
is written:

> "So that you may be proved right when
> you speak
> and prevail when you judge."[a][j]

5But if our unrighteousness brings out God's
righteousness more clearly, what shall we say?
That God is unjust in bringing his wrath on us? (I
am using a human argument.)[k] 6Certainly not! If
that were so, how could God judge the world?[l]
7Someone might argue, "If my falsehood enhances
God's truthfulness and so increases his glory,[m]
why am I still condemned as a sinner?" 8Why not
say—as we are being slanderously reported as
saying and as some claim that we say—"Let us do
evil that good may result"?[n] Their condemnation
is deserved.

No One Is Righteous

9What shall we conclude then? Are we any better[b]? Not at all! We have already made the charge
that Jews and Gentiles alike are all under sin.[o]
10As it is written:

> "There is no one righteous, not even
> one;
> 11 there is no one who understands,
> no one who seeks God.
> 12 All have turned away,
> they have together become worthless;
> there is no one who does good,
> not even one."[c][p]
> 13 "Their throats are open graves;
> their tongues practice deceit."[d][q]
> "The poison of vipers is on their lips."[e][r]
> 14 "Their mouths are full of cursing and
> bitterness."[f][s]
> 15 "Their feet are swift to shed blood;
> 16 ruin and misery mark their ways,
> 17 and the way of peace they do not
> know."[g]
> 18 "There is no fear of God before their
> eyes."[h][t]

19Now we know that whatever the law says,[u] it
says to those who are under the law,[v] so that
every mouth may be silenced and the whole
world held accountable to God. 20Therefore no
one will be declared righteous in his sight by

3:2 [e]Dt 4:8; Ps 147:19
3:3 [f]Heb 4:2 [g]2Ti 2:13
3:4 [h]Jn 3:33 [i]Ps 116:11 [j]Ps 51:4
3:5 [k]Ro 6:19; Gal 3:15
3:6 [l]Ge 18:25
3:7 [m]ver 4
3:8 [n]Ro 6:1
3:9 [o]ver 19,23; Gal 3:22
3:12 [p]Ps 14:1-3
3:13 [q]Ps 5:9 [r]Ps 140:3
3:14 [s]Ps 10:7
3:18 [t]Ps 36:1
3:19 [u]Jn 10:34 [v]Ro 2:12

[a] *4* Psalm 51:4 [b] *9* Or *worse* [c] *12* Psalms 14:1–3; 53:1–3; Eccles. 7:20 [d] *13* Psalm 5:9 [e] *13* Psalm 140:3 [f] *14* Psalm 10:7 [g] *17* Isaiah 59:7,8 [h] *18* Psalm 36:1

3:20 [w]Ac 13:39; Gal 2:16 [x]Ro 7:7 observing the law;[w] rather, through the law we
become conscious of sin.[x]

Righteousness Through Faith

3:21 [y]Ro 1:17; 9:30 [z]Ac 10:43 21But now a righteousness from God,[y] apart
from law, has been made known, to which the
Law and the Prophets testify.[z] 22This righteous-
3:22 [a]Ro 9:30 [b]Ro 10:12; Gal 3:28; Col 3:11 ness from God comes through faith[a] in Jesus
Christ to all who believe. There is no difference,[b]
23for all have sinned and fall short of the glory of
God, 24and are justified freely by his grace[c]
3:24 [c]Ro 4:16; Eph 2:8 [d]Eph 1:7,14; Col 1:14; Heb 9:12 through the redemption[d] that came by Christ
Jesus. 25God presented him as a sacrifice of atone-
ment,[a][e] through faith in his blood.[f] He did this to
demonstrate his justice, because in his forbearance he had left the sins committed beforehand
3:25 [e]1Jn 4:10 [f]Heb 9:12,14 [g]Ac 17:30 unpunished[g]— 26he did it to demonstrate his justice at the present time, so as to be just and the
one who justifies those who have faith in Jesus.
27Where, then, is boasting?[h] It is excluded. On
3:27 [h]Ro 2:17,23; 4:2; 1Co 1:29-31; Eph 2:9 what principle? On that of observing the law? No,
but on that of faith. 28For we maintain that a man
is justified by faith apart from observing the law.[i]
29Is God the God of Jews only? Is he not the God of
3:28 [i]ver 20,21; Ac 13:39; Eph 2:9 Gentiles too? Yes, of Gentiles too,[j] 30since there is
only one God, who will justify the circumcised by
faith and the uncircumcised through that same
3:29 [j]Ro 9:24 faith.[k] 31Do we, then, nullify the law by this faith?
Not at all! Rather, we uphold the law.

3:30 [k]Gal 3:8

Abraham Justified by Faith

4 What then shall we say that Abraham, our
forefather, discovered in this matter? 2If, in fact,
Abraham was justified by works, he had some-
4:2 [l]1Co 1:31 thing to boast about—but not before God.[l] 3What
4:3 [m]ver 5,9,22; Ge 15:6; Gal 3:6; Jas 2:23 does the Scripture say? "Abraham believed God,
and it was credited to him as righteousness."[b][m]
4Now when a man works, his wages are not
credited to him as a gift,[n] but as an obligation.
5However, to the man who does not work but
4:4 [n]Ro 11:6 trusts God who justifies the wicked, his faith is
credited as righteousness. 6David says the same
thing when he speaks of the blessedness of the
man to whom God credits righteousness apart
from works:

7"Blessed are they
    whose transgressions are forgiven,
    whose sins are covered.
8Blessed is the man
4:8 [o]Ps 32:1,2; 2Co 5:19   whose sin the Lord will never count
        against him."[c][o]

4:9 [p]Ro 3:30 [q]ver 3 9Is this blessedness only for the circumcised, or
also for the uncircumcised?[p] We have been saying
that Abraham's faith was credited to him as righteousness.[q] 10Under what circumstances was it
credited? Was it after he was circumcised, or
before? It was not after, but before! 11And he

[a] 25 Or *as the one who would turn aside his wrath, taking away sin* [b] 3 Gen. 15:6; also in verse 22 [c] 8 Psalm 32:1,2

A Basic Spiritual Need

RO 3:23-24

Since no human being is inherently righteous (Ro 3:10,20), no one can enter into fellowship with God on his or her own (Ro 3:23). A person's most basic spiritual need is to be reconciled to God (Ro 6:23), to be *made right and whole before God.* The sole answer to our dilemma is found in Christ, who justifies us (makes us right) in God's sight through our faith in him (Ro 5:1-2,9-11; 2Co 5:17-19).

Benefits of Suffering

RO 5:3–5

Suffering can cause people to feel hopeless. Or it can give them greater hope. It's all in how they respond to the "joy" of suffering (Ro 5:3). Some focus on their suffering and become hopeless, despondent people. Others focus on God's work in their lives and respond as Paul describes here. Suffering teaches people to be steadfast and determined. This, in turn, builds character. And strong character produces trust in God and his plan for their future. They have hope.

Are you suffering today? Jot down five to ten positive things that have come, or could come, from your current trial. Confess to God that you don't know exactly what he's doing in your life, but that you trust him to use every detail for your ultimate good (Ro 8:28).

received the sign of circumcision, a seal of the
righteousness that he had by faith while he was
still uncircumcised.[r] So then, he is the father[s] of
all who believe[t] but have not been circumcised,
in order that righteousness might be credited to
them. 12 And he is also the father of the circumcised who not only are circumcised but who also
walk in the footsteps of the faith that our father
Abraham had before he was circumcised.
13 It was not through law that Abraham and his
offspring received the promise[u] that he would be
heir of the world,[v] but through the righteousness
that comes by faith. 14 For if those who live by law
are heirs, faith has no value and the promise is
worthless,[w] 15 because law brings wrath.[x] And
where there is no law there is no transgression.[y]
16 Therefore, the promise comes by faith, so that
it may be by grace[z] and may be guaranteed[a] to all
Abraham's offspring—not only to those who are
of the law but also to those who are of the faith of
Abraham. He is the father of us all. 17 As it is written: "I have made you a father of many nations."[a][b]
He is our father in the sight of God, in whom he
believed—the God who gives life[c] to the dead and
calls[d] things that are not[e] as though they were.
18 Against all hope, Abraham in hope believed
and so became the father of many nations,[f] just
as it had been said to him, "So shall your offspring
be."[b][g] 19 Without weakening in his faith, he faced
the fact that his body was as good as dead[h]—since
he was about a hundred years old[i]—and that Sarah's womb was also dead.[j] 20 Yet he did not waver
through unbelief regarding the promise of God,
but was strengthened in his faith and gave glory
to God,[k] 21 being fully persuaded that God had
power to do what he had promised.[l] 22 This is why
"it was credited to him as righteousness."[m] 23 The
words "it was credited to him" were written not
for him alone, 24 but also for us,[n] to whom God
will credit righteousness—for us who believe in
him[o] who raised Jesus our Lord from the dead.[p]
25 He was delivered over to death for our sins[q] and
was raised to life for our justification.

Peace and Joy

5 Therefore, since we have been justified
through faith,[r] we[c] have peace with God
through our Lord Jesus Christ, 2 through whom we
have gained access[s] by faith into this grace in
which we now stand.[t] And we[c] rejoice in the
hope[u] of the glory of God. 3 Not only so, but we[c]
also rejoice in our sufferings,[v] because we know
that suffering produces perseverance;[w] 4 perseverance, character; and character, hope. 5 And hope[x]
does not disappoint us, because God has poured
out his love into our hearts by the Holy Spirit,[y]
whom he has given us.
6 You see, at just the right time,[z] when we were
still powerless, Christ died for the ungodly.[a] 7 Very

4:11 [r]Ge 17:10,11 [s]ver 16,17; Lk 19:9 [t]Ro 3:22
4:13 [u]Gal 3:16,29 [v]Ge 17:4-6
4:14 [w]Gal 3:18
4:15 [x]Ro 7:7-25; 1Co 15:56; 2Co 3:7; Gal 3:10; Ro 7:12 [y]Ro 3:20; 7:7
4:16 [z]Ro 3:24 [a]Ro 15:8
4:17 [b]Ge 17:5 [c]Jn 5:21 [d]Isa 48:13 [e]1Co 1:28
4:18 [f]ver 17 [g]Ge 15:5
4:19 [h]Heb 11:11,12 [i]Ge 17:17 [j]Ge 18:11
4:20 [k]Mt 9:8
4:21 [l]Ge 18:14; Heb 11:19
4:22 [m]ver 3
4:24 [n]Ro 15:4; 1Co 9:10; 10:11 [o]Ro 10:9 [p]Ac 2:24
4:25 [q]Isa 53:5,6; Ro 5:6,8
5:1 [r]Ro 3:28
5:2 [s]Eph 2:18 [t]1Co 15:1 [u]Heb 3:6
5:3 [v]Mt 5:12 [w]Jas 1:2,3
5:5 [x]Php 1:20 [y]Ac 2:33
5:6 [z]Gal 4:4 [a]Ro 4:25

[a] *17* Gen. 17:5 [b] *18* Gen. 15:5 [c] *1,2,3* Or *let us*

Week 40

Peace, Joy and Hope

People are seekers. Often they're seeking the benefits of God: peace, joy, love and heaven, but they are not seeking the relationship with God required to attain those benefits. God wants people to seek *him* (Am 5:4), not just his benefits. He wants people who are looking for a relationship with him, people who are willing to sacrifice for that relationship—not because he wants to see them suffer but because he knows the benefits suffering brings. Peace, joy and hope shine most brightly in a life of suffering.

How can you have true peace (Ro 5:1)? How can you personally experience this peace (Ac 13:38-39)? Being justified means that you have been pronounced righteous, you have been reconciled to God.

What does this peace give you confidence to do (Ro 5:2)? You can have "access" to and a relationship with the Creator of the universe!

Having a relationship with God produces hope (Ro 5:2). How is this hope developed (Ro 5:3-4)? How is this hope different from the world's hope (Ro 5:5)? The Holy Spirit is the One who fills us with the love of God.

This hope produces joy (Ro 5:2). Just as Paul learned the secret of contentment (Php 4:12), you can learn the secret of joy. What is Paul's secret (Ro 15:13; Php 1:4-6)? How does this attitude allow you to view your sufferings in a new way (Ro 5:3-4; Jas 1:2-4; 1Pe 1:6-9)?

You will only gain true peace, joy and hope through having a relationship with God. That relationship can only be developed in Jesus Christ. And your experience of it can only be accomplished by the Holy Spirit. Though suffering is often a part of the Christian life people anticipate with fear, God uses it to produce deep and lasting peace, joy and hope.

Enjoying God THROUGH the Word

Read Philippians 4:4-7 (page 1945). Joy is not only an emotion to be desired, it is also a command to be obeyed. Joy is—to some degree—a choice. How can this be? Are you to simply ignore your circumstances and live outside of reality? No, but a life of joy can be learned—and suffering is most often the teacher. The Scriptures clearly point out the path toward a life of joy: accept your circumstances and be thankful in them (1Th 5:16-18), choose not to worry (Php 4:6), fix your eyes on Jesus rather than on your situation—following his example in suffering (Heb 12:2)—and put your hope in future glory (2Co 4:16-18; Col 1:5; Tit 1:2). It is through the joy and peace exhibited in suffering that God is most visible in your life. When you live a life of joy—regardless of your circumstances—others will see Jesus in you.

Enjoying God THROUGH Experience

Whatever your current circumstances, God longs to comfort you, heal you and give you his peace, joy and hope. Take your needs to him in prayer. Lay all your hurts and worries before him. Ask him to help you accept your circumstances, fix your eyes on Jesus and live life in joy and peace. "May the God of hope fill you with all joy and peace as you trust in him, so that you may overflow with hope by the power of the Holy Spirit" (Ro 15:13).

This week, try to look at your life from a new perspective. See your life on the screen of eternity: Your 70 years of life are a mere blip on the screen. It is eternity that matters. Praise God that he is your hope. He will never disappoint you (Ro 5:5).

Go to page 1882 for your next weekly study.

One for All

RO 5:12–21

Adam is the first man to sin, but he certainly isn't the last. Through him, death and sin come to the human race. That's not the end of the story however. Through another man (God clothed in human flesh), Jesus Christ, life is given to every person who believes in him (1Ti 1:16). Here, Paul compares the two, emphasizing Christ's vast superiority: Adam is the head of the old age, but Christ is the head of the new, and his gift of grace is far more powerful than the "gift" of sin that Adam gives to humanity. When Jesus gives his life, that sacrifice is enough to pay for the sins and sinfulness of every human being (1Pe 3:18). The power of that one life and one redemptive act triumphs over the power of that former life and former sinful act. Just as we become sinners through Adam, we become the redeemed through Jesus. Our sin comes through Adam but, praise God, our salvation comes through Christ.

rarely will anyone die for a righteous man, though
for a good man someone might possibly dare to die.
8But God demonstrates his own love for us in this:
While we were still sinners, Christ died for us.[b]
9Since we have now been justified by his blood,[c]
how much more shall we be saved from God's
wrath[d] through him! 10For if, when we were God's
enemies,[e] we were reconciled[f] to him through the
death of his Son, how much more, having been
reconciled, shall we be saved through his life![g]
11Not only is this so, but we also rejoice in God
through our Lord Jesus Christ, through whom we
have now received reconciliation.

Death Through Adam, Life Through Christ

12Therefore, just as sin entered the world
through one man,[h] and death through sin,[i] and in
this way death came to all men, because all
sinned— 13for before the law was given, sin was
in the world. But sin is not taken into account
when there is no law.[j] 14Nevertheless, death
reigned from the time of Adam to the time of
Moses, even over those who did not sin by breaking a command, as did Adam, who was a pattern
of the one to come.[k]
15But the gift is not like the trespass. For if the
many died by the trespass of the one man,[l] how
much more did God's grace and the gift that came
by the grace of the one man, Jesus Christ,[m] overflow to the many! 16Again, the gift of God is not
like the result of the one man's sin: The judgment
followed one sin and brought condemnation, but
the gift followed many trespasses and brought justification. 17For if, by the trespass of the one man,
death[n] reigned through that one man, how much
more will those who receive God's abundant provision of grace and of the gift of righteousness
reign in life through the one man, Jesus Christ.
18Consequently, just as the result of one trespass
was condemnation for all men,[o] so also the result
of one act of righteousness was justification[p] that
brings life for all men. 19For just as through the
disobedience of the one man[q] the many were
made sinners, so also through the obedience[r] of
the one man the many will be made righteous.
20The law was added so that the trespass might
increase.[s] But where sin increased, grace
increased all the more,[t] 21so that, just as sin
reigned in death,[u] so also grace might reign
through righteousness to bring eternal life
through Jesus Christ our Lord.

Dead to Sin, Alive in Christ

6 What shall we say, then? Shall we go on sinning so that grace may increase?[v] 2By no
means! We died to sin;[w] how can we live in it any
longer? 3Or don't you know that all of us who
were baptized[x] into Christ Jesus were baptized
into his death? 4We were therefore buried with
him through baptism into death in order that, just

5:8 [b]Jn 15:13; 1Pe 3:18
5:9 [c]Ro 3:25 [d]Ro 1:18
5:10 [e]Ro 11:28; Col 1:21 [f]2Co 5:18, 19; Col 1:20, 22 [g]Ro 8:34
5:12 [h]ver 15,16, 17; 1Co 15:21,22 [i]Ge 2:17; 3:19; Ro 6:23
5:13 [j]Ro 4:15
5:14 [k]1Co 15:22, 45
5:15 [l]ver 12,18, 19 [m]Ac 15:11
5:17 [n]ver 12
5:18 [o]ver 12 [p]Ro 4:25
5:19 [q]ver 12 [r]Php 2:8
5:20 [s]Ro 7:7,8; Gal 3:19 [t]1Ti 1:13,14
5:21 [u]ver 12,14
6:1 [v]ver 15; Ro 3:5,8
6:2 [w]Col 3:3,5; 1Pe 2:24
6:3 [x]Mt 28:19

as Christ was raised from the dead[y] through the
glory of the Father, we too may live a new life.[z]
5 If we have been united with him like this in
his death, we will certainly also be united with
him in his resurrection.[a] 6 For we know that our
old self[b] was crucified with him[c] so that the body
of sin[d] might be done away with,[a] that we should
no longer be slaves to sin— 7 because anyone who
has died has been freed from sin.
8 Now if we died with Christ, we believe that we
will also live with him. 9 For we know that since
Christ was raised from the dead,[e] he cannot die
again; death no longer has mastery over him.[f]
10 The death he died, he died to sin[g] once for all;
but the life he lives, he lives to God.
11 In the same way, count yourselves dead to sin[h]
but alive to God in Christ Jesus. 12 Therefore do not
let sin reign in your mortal body so that you obey
its evil desires. 13 Do not offer the parts of your
body to sin, as instruments of wickedness,[i] but
rather offer yourselves to God, as those who have
been brought from death to life; and offer the
parts of your body to him as instruments of righteousness.[j] 14 For sin shall not be your master,
because you are not under law,[k] but under grace.[l]

Slaves to Righteousness

15 What then? Shall we sin because we are not
under law but under grace? By no means! 16 Don't
you know that when you offer yourselves to someone to obey him as slaves, you are slaves to the one
whom you obey—whether you are slaves to sin,[m]
which leads to death,[n] or to obedience, which leads
to righteousness? 17 But thanks be to God[o] that,
though you used to be slaves to sin, you wholeheartedly obeyed the form of teaching[p] to which
you were entrusted. 18 You have been set free from
sin[q] and have become slaves to righteousness.
19 I put this in human terms[r] because you are
weak in your natural selves. Just as you used to
offer the parts of your body in slavery to impurity
and to ever-increasing wickedness, so now offer
them in slavery to righteousness[s] leading to holiness. 20 When you were slaves to sin,[t] you were free
from the control of righteousness. 21 What benefit
did you reap at that time from the things you are
now ashamed of? Those things result in death![u]
22 But now that you have been set free from sin[v]
and have become slaves to God,[w] the benefit you
reap leads to holiness, and the result is eternal life.
23 For the wages of sin is death,[x] but the gift of God
is eternal life[y] in[b] Christ Jesus our Lord.

An Illustration From Marriage

7 Do you not know, brothers[z]—for I am speaking to men who know the law—that the law
has authority over a man only as long as he lives?
2 For example, by law a married woman is bound
to her husband as long as he is alive, but if her

6:4 [y]Col 2:12 [z]Ro 7:6; Gal 6:15; Eph 4:22-24; Col 3:10
6:5 [a]2Co 4:10; Php 3:10,11
6:6 [b]Eph 4:22; Col 3:9 [c]Gal 2:20; Col 2:12,20 [d]Ro 7:24
6:9 [e]Ac 2:24 [f]Rev 1:18
6:10 [g]ver 2
6:11 [h]ver 2
6:13 [i]ver 16,19; Ro 7:5 [j]Ro 12:1; 1Pe 2:24
6:14 [k]Gal 5:18 [l]Ro 3:24
6:16 [m]Jn 8:34; 2Pe 2:19 [n]ver 23
6:17 [o]Ro 1:8; 2Co 2:14 [p]2Ti 1:13
6:18 [q]ver 7,22; Ro 8:2
6:19 [r]Ro 3:5 [s]ver 13
6:20 [t]ver 16
6:21 [u]ver 23
6:22 [v]ver 18 [w]1Co 7:22; 1Pe 2:16
6:23 [x]Ge 2:17; Ro 5:12; Gal 6:7,8; Jas 1:15 [y]Mt 25:46
7:1 [z]Ro 1:13

[a] 6 Or *be rendered powerless* [b] 23 Or *through*

Slaves of Righteousness

RO 6:14,18

Slavery is considered abhorrent today—with good reason. Throughout history, people have kept fellow human beings in bondage, often believing in an imagined superiority that supposedly justified their actions. Many of these slaves were grossly mistreated at the hands of their earthly "masters."

Naturally, this reality makes us resistant to the idea of slavery. But the fact is, on one level we are all slaves. We all have something or someone we serve and obey. The question is, who will be our master? Sin or righteousness? If we choose sin, we choose a road that leads to death (Ro 6:20-21). But if we embrace righteousness, we are given holiness and eternal life in Christ (Ro 6:20-23).

The Power of Sin

RO 7:19–20

Humans are sinful creatures. There is no getting around that fact. However, there is a part of our inner self that desires the things of God and longs to be in agreement with his good and perfect will. Despite our best intentions, however, sin often gets the upper hand. This is true even for Paul, who says, "Now if I do what I do not want to do, it is no longer I who do it, but it is sin living in me that does it" (Ro 7:20).

What possible recourse do we have against sins that are stronger than our will? In our own strength, none. But we can achieve victory over them through Jesus Christ (Ro 7:24–25) and through the Spirit of God, who mercifully frees us from the law of sin and death (Ro 8:2–7) and enables us to live holy lives.

husband dies, she is released from the law of marriage.[a] [3]So then, if she marries another man while her husband is still alive, she is called an adulteress. But if her husband dies, she is released from that law and is not an adulteress, even though she marries another man.

[4]So, my brothers, you also died to the law[b] through the body of Christ,[c] that you might belong to another, to him who was raised from the dead, in order that we might bear fruit to God. [5]For when we were controlled by the sinful nature,[a] the sinful passions aroused by the law[d] were at work in our bodies,[e] so that we bore fruit for death. [6]But now, by dying to what once bound us, we have been released from the law so that we serve in the new way of the Spirit, and not in the old way of the written code.[f]

Struggling With Sin

[7]What shall we say, then? Is the law sin? Certainly not! Indeed I would not have known what sin was except through the law.[g] For I would not have known what coveting really was if the law had not said, "Do not covet."[bh] [8]But sin, seizing the opportunity afforded by the commandment,[i] produced in me every kind of covetous desire. For apart from law, sin is dead.[j] [9]Once I was alive apart from law; but when the commandment came, sin sprang to life and I died. [10]I found that the very commandment that was intended to bring life[k] actually brought death. [11]For sin, seizing the opportunity afforded by the commandment, deceived me,[l] and through the commandment put me to death. [12]So then, the law is holy, and the commandment is holy, righteous and good.[m]

[13]Did that which is good, then, become death to me? By no means! But in order that sin might be recognized as sin, it produced death in me through what was good, so that through the commandment sin might become utterly sinful.

[14]We know that the law is spiritual; but I am unspiritual,[n] sold[o] as a slave to sin. [15]I do not understand what I do. For what I want to do I do not do, but what I hate I do.[p] [16]And if I do what I do not want to do, I agree that the law is good.[q] [17]As it is, it is no longer I myself who do it, but it is sin living in me.[r] [18]I know that nothing good lives in me, that is, in my sinful nature.[cs] For I have the desire to do what is good, but I cannot carry it out. [19]For what I do is not the good I want to do; no, the evil I do not want to do—this I keep on doing.[t] [20]Now if I do what I do not want to do, it is no longer I who do it, but it is sin living in me that does it.[u]

[21]So I find this law at work:[v] When I want to do good, evil is right there with me. [22]For in my inner being[w] I delight in God's law;[x] [23]but I see another law at work in the members of my body, waging

7:2 [a]1Co 7:39
7:4 [b]Ro 8:2; Gal 2:19 [c]Col 1:22
7:5 [d]Ro 7:7-11 [e]Ro 6:13
7:6 [f]Ro 2:29; 2Co 3:6
7:7 [g]Ro 3:20; 4:15 [h]Ex 20:17; Dt 5:21
7:8 [i]ver 11 [j]Ro 4:15; 1Co 15:56
7:10 [k]Lev 18:5; Lk 10:26-28; Ro 10:5; Gal 3:12
7:11 [l]Ge 3:13
7:12 [m]1Ti 1:8
7:14 [n]1Co 3:1 [o]1Ki 21:20, 25; 2Ki 17:17
7:15 [p]ver 19; Gal 5:17
7:16 [q]ver 12
7:17 [r]ver 20
7:18 [s]ver 25
7:19 [t]ver 15
7:20 [u]ver 17
7:21 [v]ver 23,25
7:22 [w]Eph 3:16 [x]Ps 1:2

[a] 5 Or *the flesh*; also in verse 25 [b] 7 Exodus 20:17; Deut. 5:21 [c] 18 Or *my flesh*

war[y] against the law of my mind and making me a prisoner of the law of sin at work within my members. 24What a wretched man I am! Who will rescue me from this body of death?[z] 25Thanks be to God—through Jesus Christ our Lord!

So then, I myself in my mind am a slave to God's law, but in the sinful nature a slave to the law of sin.

Life Through the Spirit

8 Therefore, there is now no condemnation[a] for those who are in Christ Jesus,[a][b] 2because through Christ Jesus the law of the Spirit of life[c] set me free[d] from the law of sin[e] and death. 3For what the law was powerless[f] to do in that it was weakened by the sinful nature,[b] God did by sending his own Son in the likeness of sinful man[g] to be a sin offering.[c][h] And so he condemned sin in sinful man,[d] 4in order that the righteous requirements of the law might be fully met in us, who do not live according to the sinful nature but according to the Spirit.[i]

5Those who live according to the sinful nature have their minds set on what that nature desires;[j] but those who live in accordance with the Spirit have their minds set on what the Spirit desires.[k] 6The mind of sinful man[e] is death, but the mind controlled by the Spirit is life[l] and peace; 7the sinful mind[f] is hostile to God.[m] It does not submit to God's law, nor can it do so. 8Those controlled by the sinful nature cannot please God.

9You, however, are controlled not by the sinful nature but by the Spirit, if the Spirit of God lives in you.[n] And if anyone does not have the Spirit of Christ,[o] he does not belong to Christ. 10But if Christ is in you,[p] your body is dead because of sin, yet your spirit is alive because of righteousness. 11And if the Spirit of him who raised Jesus from the dead[q] is living in you, he who raised Christ from the dead will also give life to your mortal bodies[r] through his Spirit, who lives in you.

12Therefore, brothers, we have an obligation—but it is not to the sinful nature, to live according to it. 13For if you live according to the sinful nature, you will die; but if by the Spirit you put to death the misdeeds of the body, you will live,[s] 14because those who are led by the Spirit of God[t] are sons of God.[u] 15For you did not receive a spirit that makes you a slave again to fear,[v] but you received the Spirit of sonship.[g] And by him we cry, *"Abba,*[h] Father."[w] 16The Spirit himself testifies with our spirit[x] that we are God's children. 17Now if we are children, then we are heirs[y]—heirs of God and co-heirs with Christ, if indeed we share in his sufferings in order that we may also share in his glory.[z]

7:23 [y]Gal 5:17; Jas 4:1; 1Pe 2:11
7:24 [z]Ro 6:6; 8:2
8:1 [a]ver 34 [b]ver 39; Ro 16:3
8:2 [c]1Co 15:45 [d]Ro 6:18 [e]Ro 7:4
8:3 [f]Ac 13:39; Heb 7:18 [g]Php 2:7 [h]Heb 2:14, 17
8:4 [i]Gal 5:16
8:5 [j]Gal 5:19-21 [k]Gal 5:22-25
8:6 [l]Gal 6:8
8:7 [m]Jas 4:4
8:9 [n]1Co 6:19; Gal 4:6 [o]Jn 14:17; 1Jn 4:13
8:10 [p]Gal 2:20; Eph 3:17; Col 1:27
8:11 [q]Ac 2:24 [r]Jn 5:21
8:13 [s]Gal 6:8
8:14 [t]Gal 5:18 [u]Jn 1:12; Rev 21:7
8:15 [v]2Ti 1:7; Heb 2:15 [w]Mk 14:36; Gal 4:5,6
8:16 [x]Eph 1:13
8:17 [y]Ac 20:32; Gal 4:7 [z]1Pe 4:13

[a] *1* Some later manuscripts *Jesus, who do not live according to the sinful nature but according to the Spirit,* [b] *3* Or *the flesh;* also in verses 4, 5, 8, 9, 12 and 13 [c] *3* Or *man, for sin* [d] *3* Or *in the flesh* [e] *6* Or *mind set on the flesh* [f] *7* Or *the mind set on the flesh* [g] *15* Or *adoption* [h] *15* Aramaic for *Father*

Children of God

RO 8:12–17

Who are the sons—and daughters—of God? They *are those who are led by the Holy* Spirit. Without the Spirit to guide *and convict of sin, they could not be a part of God's family and thus could not be heirs to the inheritance that is theirs in Christ.* Through the Holy Spirit's leadership, *they become adopted children of God.* The Spirit leads them *to* Christ and also to *become* like Christ. Yet believers also have *an active role in this process, for leadership cannot happen unless someone is willing to be led.* The battle *against the sinful nature will only* be won by those controlled by the Holy Spirit, *those who are,* there*fore, assured of their position as* children of God, with his power *backing their fight.*

For Our Good

RO 8:28

Let's be crystal clear here. God works everything in believers' lives for their "good." This doesn't mean that everything works for pleasant lifestyles, enjoyable futures and happiness. The "good" here, though it isn't defined or specified, is to be understood as a spiritual and eternal "good." God uses everything in believers' lives—and often the difficult things in their lives—to remake them, to transform them into the likeness of his Son. Everything that happens to us—the easy, the difficult, the grief, the pain, the joy—has one purpose: to make us more like Jesus.

Future Glory

18 I consider that our present sufferings are not worth comparing with the glory that will be revealed in us.[a] 19 The creation waits in eager expectation for the sons of God to be revealed. 20 For the creation was subjected to frustration, not by its own choice, but by the will of the one who subjected it,[b] in hope 21 that[a] the creation itself will be liberated from its bondage to decay[c] and brought into the glorious freedom of the children of God.

22 We know that the whole creation has been groaning[d] as in the pains of childbirth right up to the present time. 23 Not only so, but we ourselves, who have the firstfruits of the Spirit,[e] groan[f] inwardly as we wait eagerly[g] for our adoption as sons, the redemption of our bodies. 24 For in this hope we were saved.[h] But hope that is seen is no hope at all. Who hopes for what he already has? 25 But if we hope for what we do not yet have, we wait for it patiently.

26 In the same way, the Spirit helps us in our weakness. We do not know what we ought to pray for, but the Spirit himself intercedes for us[i] with groans that words cannot express. 27 And he who searches our hearts[j] knows the mind of the Spirit, because the Spirit intercedes for the saints in accordance with God's will.

More Than Conquerors

28 And we know that in all things God works for the good of those who love him,[b] who[c] have been called[k] according to his purpose. 29 For those God foreknew[l] he also predestined[m] to be conformed to the likeness of his Son,[n] that he might be the firstborn among many brothers. 30 And those he predestined,[o] he also called; those he called, he also justified;[p] those he justified, he also glorified.[q]

31 What, then, shall we say in response to this?[r] If God is for us, who can be against us?[s] 32 He who did not spare his own Son,[t] but gave him up for us all—how will he not also, along with him, graciously give us all things? 33 Who will bring any charge[u] against those whom God has chosen? It is God who justifies. 34 Who is he that condemns? Christ Jesus, who died[v]—more than that, who was raised to life—is at the right hand of God[w] and is also interceding for us.[x] 35 Who shall separate us from the love of Christ? Shall trouble or hardship or persecution or famine or nakedness or danger or sword?[y] 36 As it is written:

> "For your sake we face death all day
> long;
> we are considered as sheep to be
> slaughtered."[d][z]

[a] *20,21* Or *subjected it in hope.* [21]*For* [b] *28* Some manuscripts *And we know that all things work together for good to those who love God* [c] *28* Or *works together with those who love him to bring about what is good—with those who* [d] *36* Psalm 44:22

8:18 [a]2Co 4:17; 1Pe 4:13
8:20 [b]Ge 3:17-19
8:21 [c]Ac 3:21; 2Pe 3:13; Rev 21:1
8:22 [d]Jer 12:4
8:23 [e]2Co 5:5 [f]2Co 5:2,4 [g]Gal 5:5
8:24 [h]1Th 5:8
8:26 [i]Eph 6:18
8:27 [j]Rev 2:23
8:28 [k]1Co 1:9; 2Ti 1:9
8:29 [l]Ro 11:2 [m]Eph 1:5,11 [n]1Co 15:49; 2Co 3:18; Php 3:21; 1Jn 3:2
8:30 [o]Eph 1:5,11 [p]1Co 6:11 [q]Ro 9:23
8:31 [r]Ro 4:1 [s]Ps 118:6
8:32 [t]Jn 3:16; Ro 4:25; 5:8
8:33 [u]Isa 50:8,9
8:34 [v]Ro 5:6-8 [w]Mk 16:19 [x]Heb 7:25; 9:24; 1Jn 2:1
8:35 [y]1Co 4:11
8:36 [z]Ps 44:22; 2Co 4:11

8:37 [37]No, in all these things we are more than con-
[a]1Co 15:57 querors[a] through him who loved us.[b] [38]For I am
[b]Gal 2:20; convinced that neither death nor life, neither
Rev 1:5; 3:9 angels nor demons,[a] neither the present nor the
8:38 future, nor any powers,[c] [39]neither height nor
[c]Eph 1:21; depth, nor anything else in all creation, will be
1Pe 3:22 able to separate us from the love of God[d] that is
8:39 in Christ Jesus our Lord.

[d]Ro 5:8

God's Sovereign Choice

9:1
[e]2Co 11:10; **9** I speak the truth in Christ—I am not lying,[e]
Gal 1:20; 1Ti 2:7 my conscience confirms[f] it in the Holy Spir-
[f]Ro 1:9 it— [2]I have great sorrow and unceasing anguish
9:3 in my heart. [3]For I could wish that I myself[g] were
[g]Ex 32:32 [h]1Co 12:3; cursed[h] and cut off from Christ for the sake of my
16:22 brothers, those of my own race,[i] [4]the people of
[i]Ro 11:14 Israel. Theirs is the adoption as sons;[j] theirs the
divine glory, the covenants,[k] the receiving of the
9:4 law,[l] the temple worship[m] and the promises.[n]
[j]Ex 4:22 [k]Ge 17:2; [5]Theirs are the patriarchs, and from them is traced
Ac 3:25; Eph 2:12 the human ancestry of Christ,[o] who is God over
[l]Ps 147:19 all,[p] forever praised![b][q] Amen.
[m]Heb 9:1 [6]It is not as though God's word had failed. For
[n]Ac 13:32 not all who are descended from Israel are Israel.[r]
9:5 [7]Nor because they are his descendants are they all
[o]Mt 1:1-16 Abraham's children. On the contrary, "It is
[p]Jn 1:1 [q]Ro 1:25 through Isaac that your offspring will be reckoned."[c][s] [8]In other words, it is not the natural chil-
9:6 dren who are God's children,[t] but it is the children
[r]Ro 2:28,29; Gal 6:16 of the promise who are regarded as Abraham's
offspring. [9]For this was how the promise was stat-
9:7 [s]Ge 21:12; ed: "At the appointed time I will return, and Sar-
Heb 11:18 ah will have a son."[d][u]
9:8 [10]Not only that, but Rebekah's children had one
[t]Ro 8:14 and the same father, our father Isaac.[v] [11]Yet, before
the twins were born or had done anything good or
9:9 [u]Ge 18:10,14 bad—in order that God's purpose[w] in election
9:10 might stand: [12]not by works but by him who
[v]Ge 25:21 calls—she was told, "The older will serve the
9:11 younger."[e][x] [13]Just as it is written: "Jacob I loved,
[w]Ro 8:28 but Esau I hated."[f][y]
[14]What then shall we say? Is God unjust? Not at
9:12 [x]Ge 25:23 all![z] [15]For he says to Moses,

"I will have mercy on whom I have
9:13 mercy,
[y]Mal 1:2,3 and I will have compassion on whom
9:14 [z]2Ch 19:7 I have compassion."[g][a]

9:15 [16]It does not, therefore, depend on man's desire or
[a]Ex 33:19 effort, but on God's mercy.[b] [17]For the Scripture
9:16 says to Pharaoh: "I raised you up for this very pur-
[b]Eph 2:8 pose, that I might display my power in you and
9:17 that my name might be proclaimed in all the
[c]Ex 9:16 earth."[h][c] [18]Therefore God has mercy on whom he
9:18 wants to have mercy, and he hardens whom he
[d]Ex 4:21 wants to harden.[d]

[a] *38* Or *nor heavenly rulers* [b] *5* Or *Christ, who is over all. God be forever praised!* Or *Christ. God who is over all be forever praised!* [c] *7* Gen. 21:12 [d] *9* Gen. 18:10,14
[e] *12* Gen. 25:23 [f] *13* Mal. 1:2,3 [g] *15* Exodus 33:19
[h] *17* Exodus 9:16

Nothing Can Separate

RO 8:38–39

In this context, the idea of nothing is beautiful. Make a list, however long you want to make, of all the things that might separate you from God. Jot down whatever comes to mind: too much TV viewing, financial troubles, a busy schedule, obsession with work, conflicts with your husband, failure with your kids, alcoholism, addiction to drugs or food, divorce, sexual indiscretions, abortions, swearing, shady business deals, envy, jealousy. The list could go on and on and on . . .

***How does it look? Pretty intimidating? Now read what Paul has to say in Romans 8:38–39.** Nothing can separate you "from the love of God that is in Christ Jesus our Lord." No **thing.** No **person.** No **being.** No **hardship.** Nothing can separate from God those who are willing to follow him. Note the caveat there: The only thing that actually **can** separate you from God is your own rebellion, your own refusal to trust God completely for your salvation. What confidence that can put into the life of any true believer!*

A Sovereign God

RO 9:21

Because the God who created us is sovereign (all-powerful and independent of outside control), we can know that his purposes for his creation will be fulfilled. Like the potter who crafts each pot, bowl or cup to meet a specific objective, God forms each one of us with his plan for our lives in mind.

We have a choice in how we respond to this reality. We can take it as a threat and resent God's power. Or we can gain comfort from it, knowing that no matter what life holds, God has designed us to successfully meet each challenge and, in the process, bring him glory.

19 One of you will say to me:[e] "Then why does
God still blame us? For who resists his will?"[f]
20 But who are you, O man, to talk back to God?
"Shall what is formed say to him who formed it,[g]
'Why did you make me like this?' "[ah] 21 Does not
the potter have the right to make out of the same
lump of clay some pottery for noble purposes and
some for common use?[i]

22 What if God, choosing to show his wrath and
make his power known, bore with great patience[j]
the objects of his wrath—prepared for destruction? 23 What if he did this to make the riches of
his glory[k] known to the objects of his mercy,
whom he prepared in advance for glory[l]— 24 even
us, whom he also called,[m] not only from the Jews
but also from the Gentiles?[n] 25 As he says in Hosea:

"I will call them 'my people' who are
not my people;
and I will call her 'my loved one' who
is not my loved one,"[bo]

26 and,

"It will happen that in the very place
where it was said to them,
'You are not my people,'
they will be called 'sons of the living
God.' "[cp]

27 Isaiah cries out concerning Israel:

"Though the number of the Israelites be
like the sand by the sea,[q]
only the remnant will be saved.[r]
28 For the Lord will carry out
his sentence on earth with speed and
finality."[ds]

29 It is just as Isaiah said previously:

"Unless the Lord Almighty[t]
had left us descendants,
we would have become like Sodom,
we would have been like
Gomorrah."[eu]

Israel's Unbelief

30 What then shall we say? That the Gentiles,
who did not pursue righteousness, have obtained
it, a righteousness that is by faith;[v] 31 but Israel,
who pursued a law of righteousness,[w] has not
attained it.[x] 32 Why not? Because they pursued it
not by faith but as if it were by works. They stumbled over the "stumbling stone."[y] 33 As it is written:

"See, I lay in Zion a stone that causes
men to stumble
and a rock that makes them fall,
and the one who trusts in him will
never be put to shame."[fz]

9:19 [e]Ro 11:19 [f]2Ch 20:6; Da 4:35
9:20 [g]Isa 64:8 [h]Isa 29:16
9:21 [i]2Ti 2:20
9:22 [j]Ro 2:4
9:23 [k]Ro 2:4 [l]Ro 8:30
9:24 [m]Ro 8:28 [n]Ro 3:29
9:25 [o]Hos 2:23; 1Pe 2:10
9:26 [p]Hos 1:10
9:27 [q]Ge 22:17; Hos 1:10 [r]Ro 11:5
9:28 [s]Isa 10:22,23
9:29 [t]Jas 5:4 [u]Isa 1:9; Dt 29:23; Isa 13:19; Jer 50:40
9:30 [v]Ro 1:17; 10:6; Gal 2:16; Php 3:9; Heb 11:7
9:31 [w]Isa 51:1; Ro 10:2,3 [x]Gal 5:4
9:32 [y]1Pe 2:8
9:33 [z]Isa 28:16; Ro 10:11

[a] *20* Isaiah 29:16; 45:9 [b] *25* Hosea 2:23 [c] *26* Hosea 1:10 [d] *28* Isaiah 10:22,23 [e] *29* Isaiah 1:9 [f] *33* Isaiah 8:14; 28:16

10 Brothers, my heart's desire and prayer to God for the Israelites is that they may be saved. 2For I can testify about them that they are zealous[a] for God, but their zeal is not based on knowledge. 3Since they did not know the righteousness that comes from God and sought to establish their own, they did not submit to God's righteousness.[b] 4Christ is the end of the law[c] so that there may be righteousness for everyone who believes.[d]

5Moses describes in this way the righteousness that is by the law: "The man who does these things will live by them."[ae] 6But the righteousness that is by faith[f] says: "Do not say in your heart, 'Who will ascend into heaven?'[b]"[g] (that is, to bring Christ down) 7"or 'Who will descend into the deep?'[c]" (that is, to bring Christ up from the dead). 8But what does it say? "The word is near you; it is in your mouth and in your heart,"[dh] that is, the word of faith we are proclaiming: 9That if you confess[i] with your mouth, "Jesus is Lord," and believe in your heart that God raised him from the dead,[j] you will be saved. 10For it is with your heart that you believe and are justified, and it is with your mouth that you confess and are saved. 11As the Scripture says, "Anyone who trusts in him will never be put to shame."[ek] 12For there is no difference between Jew and Gentile[l]—the same Lord is Lord of all[m] and richly blesses all who call on him, 13for, "Everyone who calls on the name of the Lord[n] will be saved."[fo]

14How, then, can they call on the one they have not believed in? And how can they believe in the one of whom they have not heard? And how can they hear without someone preaching to them? 15And how can they preach unless they are sent? As it is written, "How beautiful are the feet of those who bring good news!"[gp]

16But not all the Israelites accepted the good news. For Isaiah says, "Lord, who has believed our message?"[hq] 17Consequently, faith comes from hearing the message,[r] and the message is heard through the word of Christ.[s] 18But I ask: Did they not hear? Of course they did:

"Their voice has gone out into all the
earth,
their words to the ends of the
world."[it]

19Again I ask: Did Israel not understand? First, Moses says,

"I will make you envious[u] by those who
are not a nation;
I will make you angry by a nation
that has no understanding."[jv]

20And Isaiah boldly says,

10:2 [a]Ac 21:20
10:3 [b]Ro 1:17
10:4 [c]Gal 3:24; Ro 7:1-4 [d]Ro 3:22
10:5 [e]Lev 18:5; Ne 9:29; Eze 20:11, 13,21; Ro 7:10
10:6 [f]Ro 9:30 [g]Dt 30:12
10:8 [h]Dt 30:14
10:9 [i]Mt 10:32; Lk 12:8 [j]Ac 2:24
10:11 [k]Isa 28:16; Ro 9:33
10:12 [l]Ro 3:22,29 [m]Ac 10:36
10:13 [n]Ac 2:21 [o]Joel 2:32
10:15 [p]Isa 52:7; Na 1:15
10:16 [q]Isa 53:1; Jn 12:38
10:17 [r]Gal 3:2,5 [s]Col 3:16
10:18 [t]Ps 19:4; Mt 24:14; Col 1:6,23; 1Th 1:8
10:19 [u]Ro 11:11,14 [v]Dt 32:21

Israel Rejects the Gospel

RO 10:2-3

During the New Testament era, God's chosen people had a lot going for them. They knew God. They knew the Scriptures. They wanted to live in a way that was pleasing to him. Unfortunately, what many of the Jewish people didn't have was an accurate understanding of the nature of righteousness (Ro 1:17). Rejecting the gospel, they persisted in their attempts to gain God's approval through their own good works, not understanding that their works would never gain them righteousness (Ro 4:4–5). Only through Christ, the whole and true manifestation of God's righteousness, can people become right with God.

The Jewish people's "zealous" (Ro 10:2) attitude for God and his laws was a barrier to full knowledge of the fulfillment of the law, Jesus Christ. Their need—and Paul thoroughly understood this because he was once as they were—was to protect Judaism from heresy, idolatry and compromise. But by zealously guarding the law, they missed the great truth of God: He has sent his son as their Savior.

[a] *5* Lev. 18:5 [b] *6* Deut. 30:12 [c] *7* Deut. 30:13
[d] *8* Deut. 30:14 [e] *11* Isaiah 28:16 [f] *13* Joel 2:32
[g] *15* Isaiah 52:7 [h] *16* Isaiah 53:1 [i] *18* Psalm 19:4
[j] *19* Deut. 32:21

The Remnant

RO 11:5

Scripture teaches that God chooses those who follow him (Jn 15:16). For centuries, great thinkers and theologians have wrestled with this dilemma: How can God's election of believers and humankind's freedom of choice coexist (see the note on Ephesians 1:4–5,11, page 1929). A clear answer to this question eludes us. Only God knows how both can occur simultaneously. Yet there is one thing about our election that Paul makes perfectly clear: We could not be chosen by God were it not for his grace.

This beautiful grace extends to both Jews and Gentiles. Paul points out that when Elijah grieved because he thought he was the only one left serving God, the Lord assured him there was still a remnant who worshiped him (1Ki 19:10,14,18; Ro 11:2–4). With this as his example, Paul reassures his listeners that God has not abandoned his people and that there is a faithful remnant of Jewish believers who are following Christ.

"I was found by those who did not seek
me;
I revealed myself to those who did not
ask for me."[a][w]

21 But concerning Israel he says,

"All day long I have held out my hands
to a disobedient and obstinate
people."[b][x]

The Remnant of Israel

11 I ask then: Did God reject his people? By no
means![y] I am an Israelite myself, a descendant of Abraham,[z] from the tribe of Benjamin.[a]
2 God did not reject his people, whom he
foreknew.[b] Don't you know what the Scripture
says in the passage about Elijah—how he
appealed to God against Israel: 3 "Lord, they have
killed your prophets and torn down your altars; I
am the only one left, and they are trying to kill
me"?[c][c] 4 And what was God's answer to him? "I
have reserved for myself seven thousand who
have not bowed the knee to Baal."[d][d] 5 So too, at the
present time there is a remnant[e] chosen by grace.
6 And if by grace, then it is no longer by works;[f] if
it were, grace would no longer be grace.[e]
7 What then? What Israel sought so earnestly it
did not obtain,[g] but the elect did. The others were
hardened,[h] 8 as it is written:

"God gave them a spirit of stupor,
eyes so that they could not see
and ears so that they could not hear,[i]
to this very day."[f][j]

9 And David says:

"May their table become a snare and a
trap,
a stumbling block and a retribution
for them.
10 May their eyes be darkened so they
cannot see,
and their backs be bent forever."[g][k]

Ingrafted Branches

11 Again I ask: Did they stumble so as to fall
beyond recovery? Not at all![l] Rather, because of
their transgression, salvation has come to the
Gentiles[m] to make Israel envious.[n] 12 But if their
transgression means riches for the world, and
their loss means riches for the Gentiles,[o] how
much greater riches will their fullness bring!
13 I am talking to you Gentiles. Inasmuch as I
am the apostle to the Gentiles,[p] I make much of
my ministry 14 in the hope that I may somehow
arouse my own people to envy[q] and save[r] some of

10:20 [w]Isa 65:1; Ro 9:30
10:21 [x]Isa 65:2
11:1 [y]1Sa 12:22; Jer 31:37 [z]2Co 11:22 [a]Php 3:5
11:2 [b]Ro 8:29
11:3 [c]1Ki 19:10, 14
11:4 [d]1Ki 19:18
11:5 [e]Ro 9:27
11:6 [f]Ro 4:4
11:7 [g]Ro 9:31 [h]ver 25; Ro 9:18
11:8 [i]Mt 13:13-15 [j]Dt 29:4; Isa 29:10
11:10 [k]Ps 69:22,23
11:11 [l]ver 1 [m]Ac 13:46 [n]Ro 10:19
11:12 [o]ver 25
11:13 [p]Ac 9:15
11:14 [q]ver 11; Ro 10:19 [r]1Co 1:21; 1Ti 2:4; Tit 3:5

[a] *20* Isaiah 65:1 [b] *21* Isaiah 65:2 [c] *3* 1 Kings 19:10,14
[d] *4* 1 Kings 19:18 [e] *6* Some manuscripts *be grace. But if by works, then it is no longer grace; if it were, work would no longer be work.* [f] *8* Deut. 29:4; Isaiah 29:10
[g] *10* Psalm 69:22,23

11:15 [s]Ro 5:10 them. [15]For if their rejection is the reconciliation[s]
[t]Lk 15:24,32 of the world, what will their acceptance be but life
from the dead?[t] [16]If the part of the dough offered
11:16 as firstfruits[u] is holy, then the whole batch is holy;
[u]Lev 23:10, 17; if the root is holy, so are the branches.
Nu 15:18-21 [17]If some of the branches have been broken off,[v]
11:17 and you, though a wild olive shoot, have been
[v]Jer 11:16; grafted in among the others[w] and now share in
Jn 15:2 [w]Ac 2:39; the nourishing sap from the olive root, [18]do not
Eph 2:11-13 boast over those branches. If you do, consider
this: You do not support the root, but the root sup-
11:18 [x]Jn 4:22 ports you.[x] [19]You will say then, "Branches were
broken off so that I could be grafted in." [20]Grant-
ed. But they were broken off because of unbelief,
11:20 [y]1Co 10:12; and you stand by faith.[y] Do not be arrogant,[z] but
2Co 1:24 [z]Ro 12:16; be afraid.[a] [21]For if God did not spare the natural
1Ti 6:17 [a]1Pe 1:17 branches, he will not spare you either.
[22]Consider therefore the kindness[b] and stern-
11:22 ness of God: sternness to those who fell, but kind-
[b]Ro 2:4 ness to you, provided that you continue[c] in his
[c]1Co 15:2; Heb 3:6 kindness. Otherwise, you also will be cut off.[d]
[d]Jn 15:2 [23]And if they do not persist in unbelief, they will
11:23 be grafted in, for God is able to graft them in
[e]2Co 3:16 again.[e] [24]After all, if you were cut out of an olive
tree that is wild by nature, and contrary to nature
were grafted into a cultivated olive tree, how
much more readily will these, the natural
branches, be grafted into their own olive tree!

All Israel Will Be Saved

11:25 [25]I do not want you to be ignorant[f] of this mys-
[f]Ro 1:13 [g]Ro 16:25 tery,[g] brothers, so that you may not be conceited:[h]
[h]Ro 12:16 [i]ver 7; Israel has experienced a hardening[i] in part until
Ro 9:18 the full number of the Gentiles has come in.[j]
[j]Lk 21:24 [26]And so all Israel will be saved, as it is written:

> "The deliverer will come from Zion;
> he will turn godlessness away from
> Jacob.
> 11:27 [27]And this is[a] my covenant with them
> [k]Isa 27:9; Heb 8:10,12 when I take away their sins."[b][k]

[28]As far as the gospel is concerned, they are
11:28 [l]Ro 5:10 enemies[l] on your account; but as far as election
[m]Dt 7:8; is concerned, they are loved on account of the
10:15; Ro 9:5 patriarchs,[m] [29]for God's gifts and his call[n] are
11:29 irrevocable.[o] [30]Just as you who were at one time
[n]Ro 8:28 disobedient[p] to God have now received mercy as a
[o]Heb 7:21 result of their disobedience, [31]so they too have
11:30 now become disobedient in order that they too
[p]Eph 2:2 may now[c] receive mercy as a result of God's mercy to you. [32]For God has bound all men over to
11:32 disobedience[q] so that he may have mercy on them
[q]Ro 3:9 all.

Doxology

> 11:33 [r]Ro 2:4 [33]Oh, the depth of the riches[r] of the
> [s]Ps 92:5 wisdom and[d] knowledge of God![s]

[a] 27 Or *will be* [b] 27 Isaiah 59:20,21; 27:9; Jer. 31:33,34
[c] 31 Some manuscripts do not have *now.* [d] 33 Or *riches and the wisdom and the*

All night had shouts
of men and cry
Of woeful women filled
His way;
Until that noon of sombre sky
On Friday, clamour and
display
Smote Him; no solitude had He.
No silence, since Gethsemane.

Public was death; but power,
but might,
But life *again*, but victory,
Were hushed within the dead
of night,
The shuttered dark, the secrecy.
And all alone, alone, alone
He rose again behind the
stone.

—*Alice Meynell* (*1847-1922*)

How unsearchable his judgments,
and his paths beyond tracing out![t]
34“Who has known the mind of the Lord?
Or who has been his counselor?”[a][u]
35“Who has ever given to God,
that God should repay him?”[b][v]
36For from him and through him and to
him are all things.[w]
To him be the glory forever! Amen.[x]

Living Sacrifices

12 Therefore, I urge you,[y] brothers, in view of
God’s mercy, to offer your bodies as living
sacrifices,[z] holy and pleasing to God—this is your
spiritual[c] act of worship. 2Do not conform[a] any
longer to the pattern of this world,[b] but be transformed by the renewing of your mind.[c] Then you
will be able to test and approve what God’s will
is[d]—his good, pleasing and perfect will.
3For by the grace given me[e] I say to every one of
you: Do not think of yourself more highly than
you ought, but rather think of yourself with sober
judgment, in accordance with the measure of faith
God has given you. 4Just as each of us has one
body with many members, and these members do
not all have the same function,[f] 5so in Christ we
who are many form one body,[g] and each member
belongs to all the others. 6We have different gifts,[h]
according to the grace given us. If a man’s gift is
prophesying, let him use it in proportion to his[d]
faith.[i] 7If it is serving, let him serve; if it is teaching, let him teach;[j] 8if it is encouraging, let him
encourage;[k] if it is contributing to the needs of
others, let him give generously;[l] if it is leadership,
let him govern diligently; if it is showing mercy,
let him do it cheerfully.

Love

9Love must be sincere.[m] Hate what is evil; cling to
what is good. 10Be devoted to one another in brotherly love.[n] Honor one another above yourselves.[o]
11Never be lacking in zeal, but keep your spiritual
fervor,[p] serving the Lord. 12Be joyful in hope,[q]
patient in affliction,[r] faithful in prayer. 13Share with
God’s people who are in need. Practice hospitality.[s]
14Bless those who persecute you;[t] bless and do
not curse. 15Rejoice with those who rejoice;
mourn with those who mourn.[u] 16Live in harmony with one another.[v] Do not be proud, but be
willing to associate with people of low position.[e]
Do not be conceited.[w]
17Do not repay anyone evil for evil.[x] Be careful
to do what is right in the eyes of everybody.[y] 18If
it is possible, as far as it depends on you, live at
peace with everyone.[z] 19Do not take revenge,[a] my
friends, but leave room for God’s wrath, for it is

11:33 [t]Job 11:7
11:34 [u]Isa 40:13, 14; Job 15:8; 36:22; 1Co 2:16
11:35 [v]Job 35:7
11:36 [w]1Co 8:6; Col 1:16; Heb 2:10 [x]Ro 16:27
12:1 [y]Eph 4:1 [z]Ro 6:13,16, 19; 1Pe 2:5
12:2 [a]1Pe 1:14 [b]1Jn 2:15 [c]Eph 4:23 [d]Eph 5:17
12:3 [e]Ro 15:15; Gal 2:9; Eph 4:7
12:4 [f]1Co 12:12-14; Eph 4:16
12:5 [g]1Co 10:17
12:6 [h]1Co 7:7; 12:4,8-10 [i]1Pe 4:10,11
12:7 [j]Eph 4:11
12:8 [k]Ac 15:32 [l]2Co 9:5-13
12:9 [m]1Ti 1:5
12:10 [n]Heb 13:1 [o]Php 2:3
12:11 [p]Ac 18:25
12:12 [q]Ro 5:2 [r]Heb 10:32, 36
12:13 [s]1Ti 3:2
12:14 [t]Mt 5:44
12:15 [u]Job 30:25
12:16 [v]Ro 15:5 [w]Jer 45:5; Ro 11:25
12:17 [x]Pr 20:22 [y]2Co 8:21
12:18 [z]Mk 9:50; Ro 14:19
12:19 [a]Lev 19:18; Pr 20:22; 24:29

[a] 34 Isaiah 40:13 [b] 35 Job 41:11 [c] 1 Or *reasonable* [d] 6 Or *in agreement with the* [e] 16 Or *willing to do menial work*

Living Sacrifices

RO 12:1

When the Jewish people offered sacrifices to God, the animals were killed and the meat was presented to God. As Christians, we are called to make sacrifices of a very different kind. God desires from us **living** ***sacrifices, and we ourselves are the sacrifices. Like the rams, goats and lambs that were once presented at the altar, we, too, become his.***

But how exactly do we act as “living sacrifices”? By dying to our own desires (Ro 8:13) and putting God first. We are living sacrifices when we choose his will over our own and we follow him instead of the world (Ro 12:2). The Bible teaches that there are many ways to worship God, including praise, prayer, thanksgiving, rejoicing, sacrifice and service. But perhaps no act more clearly demonstrates our desire to follow God than that of laying down our lives—and our desires—for him.

written: “It is mine to avenge; I will repay,”[ab] says
the Lord. 20 On the contrary:

> “If your enemy is hungry, feed him;
> if he is thirsty, give him something to drink.
> In doing this, you will heap burning coals on his head.”[bc]

21 Do not be overcome by evil, but overcome evil
with good.

Submission to the Authorities

13 Everyone must submit himself to the governing authorities,[d] for there is no authority except that which God has established.[e] The
authorities that exist have been established by
God. 2 Consequently, he who rebels against the
authority is rebelling against what God has instituted, and those who do so will bring judgment
on themselves. 3 For rulers hold no terror for those
who do right, but for those who do wrong. Do
you want to be free from fear of the one in authority? Then do what is right and he will commend
you.[f] 4 For he is God’s servant to do you good. But
if you do wrong, be afraid, for he does not bear
the sword for nothing. He is God’s servant, an
agent of wrath to bring punishment on the wrong-
doer.[g] 5 Therefore, it is necessary to submit to the
authorities, not only because of possible punishment but also because of conscience.
6 This is also why you pay taxes, for the authorities are God’s servants, who give their full time to
governing. 7 Give everyone what you owe him: If
you owe taxes, pay taxes;[h] if revenue, then revenue; if respect, then respect; if honor, then honor.

Love, for the Day Is Near

8 Let no debt remain outstanding, except the
continuing debt to love one another, for he who
loves his fellowman has fulfilled the law.[i] 9 The
commandments, “Do not commit adultery,” “Do
not murder,” “Do not steal,” “Do not covet,”[cj] and
whatever other commandment there may be, are
summed up in this one rule: “Love your neighbor
as yourself.”[dk] 10 Love does no harm to its neighbor. Therefore love is the fulfillment of the law.[l]
11 And do this, understanding the present time.
The hour has come[m] for you to wake up from your
slumber,[n] because our salvation is nearer now than
when we first believed. 12 The night is nearly over;
the day is almost here.[o] So let us put aside the
deeds of darkness[p] and put on the armor[q] of light.
13 Let us behave decently, as in the daytime, not in
orgies and drunkenness, not in sexual immorality
and debauchery, not in dissension and jealousy.[r]
14 Rather, clothe yourselves with the Lord Jesus
Christ,[s] and do not think about how to gratify the
desires of the sinful nature.[e]

12:19 [b]Dt 32:35
12:20 [c]Pr 25:21,22; Mt 5:44; Lk 6:27
13:1 [d]Tit 3:1; 1Pe 2:13,14 [e]Da 2:21; Jn 19:11
13:3 [f]1Pe 2:14
13:4 [g]1Th 4:6
13:7 [h]Mt 17:25; 22:17,21; Lk 23:2
13:8 [i]ver 10; Jn 13:34; Gal 5:14; Col 3:14
13:9 [j]Ex 20:13-15, 17; Dt 5:17-19,21 [k]Lev 19:18; Mt 19:19
13:10 [l]ver 8; Mt 22:39,40
13:11 [m]1Co 7:29-31; 10:11 [n]Eph 5:14; 1Th 5:5,6
13:12 [o]1Jn 2:8 [p]Eph 5:11 [q]Eph 6:11,13
13:13 [r]Gal 5:20,21
13:14 [s]Gal 3:27; 5:16; Eph 4:24

[a] *19* Deut. 32:35 [b] *20* Prov. 25:21,22 [c] *9* Exodus 20:13–15,17; Deut. 5:17–19,21 [d] *9* Lev. 19:18 [e] *14* Or *the flesh*

Civil Obedience

RO 13:1–7

Have you ever complained about the government? If so, you’re not alone! Christians and nonbelievers alike harbor doubt, displeasure and even anger toward local and national authorities. But regardless of our feelings, God’s expectations for Christians are clear. We are to submit to the government because it is there for our benefit and protection, and God is the one who allows all authorities to rule (see the note on Titus 3:1–2, page 1984).

Yet there are also times when civil disobedience is warranted. When a government’s actions violate the precepts of God, believers have a responsibility to act (Ac 5:29). Prayer, protests, boycotts and other campaigns all can be utilized to bring about change, but all must be couched in love (1Co 16:14).

Weak and Strong

RO 14

In living out the Christian walk, weak or immature believers can cling to relatively unimportant details about the faith. Here, Paul gives the example of Christians who are overly concerned about matters of conscience: which foods could be eaten and under what circumstances. Paul tells the believers at Rome to treat these immature Christians with dignity and exhorts them not to argue about things that, ultimately, are not of eternal significance.

That's also good advice for Christians today. All too often we get caught up in minor skirmishes at church: arguing about what color carpet should be chosen for the sanctuary or how the nursery or Sunday school or music program should be run. When such conflicts arise, refrain from arguing (Ro 14:19). Engage in thoughtful conversations and use proper channels of authority—but let God worry about the details while you focus on things like love, service and worship. In other words, focus on the things that have eternal significance (Ro 14:17–18).

The Weak and the Strong

14 Accept him whose faith is weak,[t] without
passing judgment on disputable matters.
2One man's faith allows him to eat everything, but
another man, whose faith is weak, eats only vegetables. 3The man who eats everything must not
look down on[u] him who does not, and the man
who does not eat everything must not condemn[v]
the man who does, for God has accepted him.
4Who are you to judge someone else's servant?[w]
To his own master he stands or falls. And he will
stand, for the Lord is able to make him stand.
5One man considers one day more sacred than
another;[x] another man considers every day alike.
Each one should be fully convinced in his own
mind. 6He who regards one day as special, does
so to the Lord. He who eats meat, eats to the Lord,
for he gives thanks to God;[y] and he who abstains,
does so to the Lord and gives thanks to God. 7For
none of us lives to himself alone[z] and none of us
dies to himself alone. 8If we live, we live to the
Lord; and if we die, we die to the Lord. So,
whether we live or die, we belong to the Lord.[a]
9For this very reason, Christ died and returned
to life[b] so that he might be the Lord of both the
dead and the living.[c] 10You, then, why do you
judge your brother? Or why do you look down on
your brother? For we will all stand before God's
judgment seat.[d] 11It is written:

"'As surely as I live,' says the Lord,
'every knee will bow before me;
every tongue will confess to God.'"[a][e]

12So then, each of us will give an account of himself to God.[f]
13Therefore let us stop passing judgment[g] on one
another. Instead, make up your mind not to put
any stumbling block or obstacle in your brother's
way. 14As one who is in the Lord Jesus, I am fully
convinced that no food[b] is unclean in itself.[h] But if
anyone regards something as unclean, then for him
it is unclean.[i] 15If your brother is distressed because
of what you eat, you are no longer acting in love.[j]
Do not by your eating destroy your brother for
whom Christ died.[k] 16Do not allow what you consider good to be spoken of as evil.[l] 17For the kingdom of God is not a matter of eating and drinking,[m]
but of righteousness, peace and joy in the Holy
Spirit,[n] 18because anyone who serves Christ in this
way is pleasing to God and approved by men.[o]
19Let us therefore make every effort to do what
leads to peace[p] and to mutual edification.[q] 20Do
not destroy the work of God for the sake of food.[r]
All food is clean, but it is wrong for a man to eat
anything that causes someone else to stumble.[s]
21It is better not to eat meat or drink wine or to do
anything else that will cause your brother to fall.[t]
22So whatever you believe about these things
keep between yourself and God. Blessed is the

14:1 [t]Ro 15:1; 1Co 8:9-12
14:3 [u]Lk 18:9 [v]Col 2:16
14:4 [w]Jas 4:12
14:5 [x]Gal 4:10
14:6 [y]Mt 14:19; 1Co 10:30,31; 1Ti 4:3,4
14:7 [z]2Co 5:15; Gal 2:20
14:8 [a]Php 1:20
14:9 [b]Rev 1:18 [c]2Co 5:15
14:10 [d]2Co 5:10
14:11 [e]Isa 45:23; Php 2:10,11
14:12 [f]Mt 12:36; 1Pe 4:5
14:13 [g]Mt 7:1
14:14 [h]Ac 10:15 [i]1Co 8:7
14:15 [j]Eph 5:2 [k]1Co 8:11
14:16 [l]1Co 10:30
14:17 [m]1Co 8:8 [n]Ro 15:13
14:18 [o]2Co 8:21
14:19 [p]Ps 34:14; Ro 12:18; Heb 12:14 [q]Ro 15:2; 2Co 12:19
14:20 [r]ver 15 [s]1Co 8:9-12
14:21 [t]1Co 8:13

[a] *11* Isaiah 45:23 [b] *14* Or *that nothing*

14:22 man who does not condemn[u] himself by what he
[u]1Jn 3:21 approves. [23]But the man who has doubts[v] is con-
14:23 demned if he eats, because his eating is not from
[v]ver 5 faith; and everything that does not come from
faith is sin.

15 We who are strong ought to bear with the
15:1 [w]Ro 14:1; failings of the weak[w] and not to please our-
Gal 6:1,2; selves. [2]Each of us should please his neighbor for
1Th 5:14 his good,[x] to build him up.[y] [3]For even Christ did
15:2 not please himself[z] but, as it is written: "The
[x]1Co 10:33 insults of those who insult you have fallen on
[y]Ro 14:19 me."[aa] [4]For everything that was written in the past
15:3 was written to teach us,[b] so that through
[z]2Co 8:9 endurance and the encouragement of the Scrip-
[a]Ps 69:9 tures we might have hope.
15:4 [5]May the God who gives endurance and encour-
[b]Ro 4:23,24 agement give you a spirit of unity[c] among your-
15:5 selves as you follow Christ Jesus, [6]so that with
[c]Ro 12:16; one heart and mouth you may glorify the God and
1Co 1:10 Father[d] of our Lord Jesus Christ.
15:6 [7]Accept one another,[e] then, just as Christ accept-
[d]Rev 1:6 ed you, in order to bring praise to God. [8]For I tell
15:7 you that Christ has become a servant of the Jews[bf]
[e]Ro 14:1 on behalf of God's truth, to confirm the promises[g]
15:8 made to the patriarchs [9]so that the Gentiles[h] may
[f]Mt 15:24; Ac 3:25,26 glorify God[i] for his mercy, as it is written:

[g]2Co 1:20 "Therefore I will praise you among the
15:9 [h]Ro 3:29 Gentiles;
[i]Mt 9:8 I will sing hymns to your name."[cj]

[j]2Sa 22:50; Ps 18:49 [10]Again, it says,
15:10 "Rejoice, O Gentiles, with his people."[dk]

[k]Dt 32:43 [11]And again,
"Praise the Lord, all you Gentiles,
and sing praises to him, all you
15:11 [l]Ps 117:1 peoples."[el]

[12]And again, Isaiah says,
15:12 [m]Rev 5:5 "The Root of Jesse[m] will spring up,
[n]Isa 11:10; one who will arise to rule over the
Mt 12:21 nations;
the Gentiles will hope in him."[fn]

15:13 [o]Ro 14:17 [13]May the God of hope fill you with all joy and
[p]ver 19; 1Co 2:4; peace[o] as you trust in him, so that you may over-
1Th 1:5 flow with hope by the power of the Holy Spirit.[p]

Paul the Minister to the Gentiles

15:14 [q]Eph 5:9 [14]I myself am convinced, my brothers, that you
[r]2Pe 1:12 yourselves are full of goodness,[q] complete in
15:15 [s]Ro 12:3 knowledge[r] and competent to instruct one anoth-
15:16 er. [15]I have written you quite boldly on some
[t]Ac 9:15; Ro 11:13 points, as if to remind you of them again, because
[u]Ro 1:1 of the grace God gave me[s] [16]to be a minister of
Christ Jesus to the Gentiles[t] with the priestly duty
of proclaiming the gospel of God,[u] so that the Gen-

[a] *3* Psalm 69:9 [b] *8* Greek *circumcision*
[c] *9* 2 Samuel 22:50; Psalm 18:49 [d] *10* Deut. 32:43
[e] *11* Psalm 117:1 [f] *12* Isaiah 11:10

A Spirit of Unity

RO 15:5

The church of Jesus Christ encompasses a vast community of believers, each one with a unique set of talents, background and insights. Although Christians agree on a number of key doctrinal issues, they also hold many different opinions. Thankfully, Paul is not saying that we need to be identical. He does, however, direct us to be unified (Ro 12:16; 2Co 13:11). Evidence of such unity includes "having the same love, being one in spirit and purpose" (Php 2:2), and "agree[ing] with each other in the Lord" (Php 4:2).

Ask God right now how you can be a unifying presence in your ministry or fellowship. If there is an ongoing struggle that you are privy to, consider inviting the key individuals to your home, not to rehash the matter, but to pray that God will unite the entire group in spirit and purpose.

tiles might become an offering[v] acceptable to God,
sanctified by the Holy Spirit.
[17]Therefore I glory in Christ Jesus[w] in my service to God.[x] [18]I will not venture to speak of anything except what Christ has accomplished
through me in leading the Gentiles[y] to obey God[z]
by what I have said and done— [19]by the power of
signs and miracles,[a] through the power of the
Spirit.[b] So from Jerusalem[c] all the way around to
Illyricum, I have fully proclaimed the gospel of
Christ. [20]It has always been my ambition to preach
the gospel where Christ was not known, so that I
would not be building on someone else's foundation.[d] [21]Rather, as it is written:

> "Those who were not told about him
> will see,
> and those who have not heard will
> understand."[a][e]

[22]This is why I have often been hindered from
coming to you.[f]

Paul's Plan to Visit Rome

[23]But now that there is no more place for me to
work in these regions, and since I have been longing for many years to see you,[g] [24]I plan to do so
when I go to Spain.[h] I hope to visit you while
passing through and to have you assist me on my
journey there, after I have enjoyed your company
for a while. [25]Now, however, I am on my way to
Jerusalem[i] in the service[j] of the saints there. [26]For
Macedonia[k] and Achaia[l] were pleased to make a
contribution for the poor among the saints in
Jerusalem. [27]They were pleased to do it, and
indeed they owe it to them. For if the Gentiles
have shared in the Jews' spiritual blessings, they
owe it to the Jews to share with them their material blessings.[m] [28]So after I have completed this
task and have made sure that they have received
this fruit, I will go to Spain and visit you on the
way. [29]I know that when I come to you,[n] I will
come in the full measure of the blessing of Christ.
[30]I urge you, brothers, by our Lord Jesus Christ
and by the love of the Spirit,[o] to join me in my
struggle by praying to God for me.[p] [31]Pray that I
may be rescued[q] from the unbelievers in Judea
and that my service in Jerusalem may be acceptable to the saints there, [32]so that by God's will[r] I
may come to you[s] with joy and together with you
be refreshed.[t] [33]The God of peace[u] be with you all.
Amen.

Personal Greetings

16 I commend[v] to you our sister Phoebe, a servant[b] of the church in Cenchrea.[w] [2]I ask you
to receive her in the Lord[x] in a way worthy of the
saints and to give her any help she may need from
you, for she has been a great help to many people,
including me.

15:16 [v]Isa 66:20
15:17 [w]Php 3:3 [x]Heb 2:17
15:18 [y]Ac 15:12; 21:19; Ro 1:5 [z]Ro 16:26
15:19 [a]Jn 4:48; Ac 19:11 [b]ver 13 [c]Ac 22:17-21
15:20 [d]2Co 10:15, 16
15:21 [e]Isa 52:15
15:22 [f]Ro 1:13
15:23 [g]Ac 19:21; Ro 1:10,11
15:24 [h]ver 28
15:25 [i]Ac 19:21 [j]Ac 24:17
15:26 [k]Ac 16:9; 2Co 8:1 [l]Ac 18:12
15:27 [m]1Co 9:11
15:29 [n]Ro 1:10,11
15:30 [o]Gal 5:22 [p]2Co 1:11; Col 4:12
15:31 [q]2Th 3:2
15:32 [r]Ac 18:21 [s]Ro 1:10,13 [t]1Co 16:18
15:33 [u]Ro 16:20; 2Co 13:11; Php 4:9; 1Th 5:23; Heb 13:20
16:1 [v]2Co 3:1 [w]Ac 18:18
16:2 [x]Php 2:29

[a] *21* Isaiah 52:15 [b] *1* Or *deaconess*

Elvina Hall penned this hymn on the flyleaf of her hymnbook one Sunday morning when the pastor's prayer went long and her thoughts began to wander.

Jesus Paid It All

I hear the Savior say,
"Thy strength indeed is small;
Child of weakness, watch and pray,
Find in Me thine all in all."

Jesus paid it all,
All to Him I owe;
Sin had left a crimson stain,
He washed it white as snow.

For nothing good have I
Whereby Thy grace to claim,
I'll wash my garments white
In the blood of Calvary's Lamb.

And now complete in Him
My robe His righteousness,
Close sheltered 'neath His side,
I am divinely blest.

Lord, now indeed I find
Thy power and Thine alone,
Can change the leper's spots
And melt the heart of stone.

When from my dying bed
My ransomed soul shall rise,
"Jesus paid it all,"
Shall rend the vaulted skies.

And when before the throne
I stand in Him complete,
I'll lay my trophies down
All down at Jesus' feet.

—Elvina Hall (1820-1889)

3 Greet Priscilla[a] and Aquila,[y] my fellow workers
in Christ Jesus.[z] 4 They risked their lives for
me. Not only I but all the churches of the
Gentiles are grateful to them.
5 Greet also the church that meets at their house.[a]
Greet my dear friend Epenetus, who was the
first convert[b] to Christ in the province of Asia.
6 Greet Mary, who worked very hard for you.
7 Greet Andronicus and Junias, my relatives[c] who
have been in prison with me. They are outstanding among the apostles, and they were
in Christ before I was.
8 Greet Ampliatus, whom I love in the Lord.
9 Greet Urbanus, our fellow worker in Christ,[d]
and my dear friend Stachys.
10 Greet Apelles, tested and approved in Christ.
Greet those who belong to the household of
Aristobulus.
11 Greet Herodion, my relative.[e]
Greet those in the household of Narcissus who
are in the Lord.
12 Greet Tryphena and Tryphosa, those women
who work hard in the Lord.
Greet my dear friend Persis, another woman
who has worked very hard in the Lord.
13 Greet Rufus, chosen in the Lord, and his mother, who has been a mother to me, too.
14 Greet Asyncritus, Phlegon, Hermes, Patrobas,
Hermas and the brothers with them.
15 Greet Philologus, Julia, Nereus and his sister,
and Olympas and all the saints[f] with them.[g]
16 Greet one another with a holy kiss.[h]
All the churches of Christ send greetings.

17 I urge you, brothers, to watch out for those
who cause divisions and put obstacles in your
way that are contrary to the teaching you have
learned.[i] Keep away from them.[j] 18 For such people are not serving our Lord Christ, but their
own appetites.[k] By smooth talk and flattery
they deceive[l] the minds of naive people.
19 Everyone has heard[m] about your obedience, so
I am full of joy over you; but I want you to be
wise about what is good, and innocent about
what is evil.[n]
20 The God of peace[o] will soon crush[p] Satan
under your feet.
The grace of our Lord Jesus be with you.[q]
21 Timothy,[r] my fellow worker, sends his greetings to you, as do Lucius,[s] Jason[t] and Sosipater,
my relatives.[u]
22 I, Tertius, who wrote down this letter, greet
you in the Lord.
23 Gaius, whose hospitality I and the whole
church here enjoy, sends you his greetings.
Erastus,[v] who is the city's director of public
works, and our brother Quartus send you their
greetings.[b]

16:3 [y]Ac 18:2 [z]ver 7,9,10
16:5 [a]1Co 16:19; Col 4:15; Phm 2 [b]1Co 16:15
16:7 [c]ver 11,21
16:9 [d]ver 3
16:11 [e]ver 7,21
16:15 [f]ver 2 [g]ver 14
16:16 [h]1Co 16:20; 2Co 13:12; 1Th 5:26
16:17 [i]Gal 1:8,9; 1Ti 1:3; 6:3 [j]2Th 3:6,14; 2Jn 10
16:18 [k]Php 3:19 [l]Col 2:4
16:19 [m]Ro 1:8 [n]Mt 10:16; 1Co 14:20
16:20 [o]Ro 15:33 [p]Ge 3:15 [q]1Th 5:28
16:21 [r]Ac 16:1 [s]Ac 13:1 [t]Ac 17:5 [u]ver 7,11
16:23 [v]Ac 19:22

Wisdom and Innocence

RO 16:19

The issue Paul raises here is a matter of participation. His desire is that the Roman Christians will become wise in regard to goodness. Such wisdom comes from two sources: participation (in goodness) and revelation (from God). When Solomon asked for wisdom, God was pleased to grant his request (2Ch 1:8–12). If we ask, God will do the same for us (Jas 1:5). And we will grow in wisdom as we participate in good things.

Paul also exhorts the believers to be innocent about evil. Here, innocence comes because of non-participation. It would be illogical for us to immerse ourselves in sin in order to learn how to avoid it. Thankfully, wisdom and the leading of the Spirit can help us to discern which situations and behaviors to avoid.

[a] 3 Greek *Prisca*, a variant of *Priscilla* [b] 23 Some manuscripts *their greetings.* [24]*May the grace of our Lord Jesus Christ be with all of you. Amen.*

Why Does God Wait?

RO 16:25–26

We don't know why God waited as long as he did to reveal his plan of redemption. But we do know that his timing is always perfect (Ps 18:30). Since the beginning of time, God has longed for, and made a way for, the faithful to come to him. Sacrifices reconciled the people to God (at least temporarily). Although the whole truth of the gospel wasn't yet revealed, by faith many came to a saving knowledge of God (Heb 11). But only when God knew that the time was exactly right did he send his only Son to earth and allow the gospel in all its power to unfold.

25 Now to him who is able[w] to establish you by
my gospel[x] and the proclamation of Jesus Christ,
according to the revelation of the mystery[y] hidden
for long ages past, 26 but now revealed and made
known through the prophetic writings by the
command of the eternal God, so that all nations
might believe and obey him— 27 to the only wise
God be glory forever through Jesus Christ! Amen.[z]

16:25 [w] Eph 3:20 [x] Ro 2:16 [y] Eph 1:9; Col 1:26,27

16:27 [z] Ro 11:36

1 Corinthians

Christian conduct in a sinful world.

The city of Corinth was an influential trading port in Paul's day, populated by 250,000 free persons and as many as 400,000 slaves. And, like many port cities, Corinth was filled with vile practices and loose living. Paul stops in Corinth on his second missionary journey and establishes a church there (Ac 18:1–17). Shortly thereafter, he receives disturbing reports of sexual misconduct, misunderstandings of Christian beliefs, and the abuse of spiritual gifts among some of the Corinthian believers.

In this letter filled with exhortation and correction, Paul reminds believers that the wisdom that comes from God is in direct contradiction to the ways of the world (1Co 1–2). He warns of the dangers of spiritual competition (1Co 3) and the need to refrain from sexual immorality (1Co 5). He teaches a lesson about lawsuits (1Co 6) and reviews God's principles for marriage and singleness (1Co 7). He then goes on to discuss the issue of conforming to one's culture only when it does not conflict with God's ways (1Co 9). And he informs his readers about God's plan for worship, covering roles in leadership, spiritual giftedness and worship when the believers assemble (1Co 11–14).

This pastoral guide helps us maintain a Christian lifestyle in a sinful society. With love as our aim, we can build relationships that are pure and considerate, attitudes and actions that are confident but not arrogant, and hearts that are committed to honoring God.

Quick Study

Author
The apostle Paul.

Date Written
Around A.D. 55.

Written From
Ephesus, during Paul's extended stay there.

Key Passage
1 Corinthians 13:13
"And now these three remain: faith, hope and love. But the greatest of these is love."

Outline

Paul's *greetings.*
1Co 1:1-9

Division in the church.
1Co 1:10–4:21

Moral and ethical disorder.
1Co 5:1–6:20

Lessons on marriage.
1Co 7:1-40

Lessons on questionable practices.
1Co 8:1–11:1

Lessons on worship and gifts.
1Co 11:2–12:31

Lessons on love.
1Co 13:1-13

More lessons on worship and gifts.
1Co 14:1-40

Lessons on resurrection.
1Co 15:1-58

Some personal matters.
1Co 16:1-18

Closing *greetings.*
1Co 16:19-24

The Women of 1 Corinthians

Chloe	*Members of her household reported the church's quarrels to Paul.* 1Co 1:10-11
Father's wife	*In an immoral relationship with her stepson.* 1Co 5:1-5
Believing wife	*She sanctifies her unbelieving husband.* 1Co 7:10-14
Unbelieving wife	*She is sanctified through her husband.* 1Co 7:10-14
A praying or prophesying woman	*Her head should be covered.* 1Co 11:5-6
⚘ **Priscilla**	*A church met in her home.* 1Co 16:19 (page 2047)

⚘ *Denotes a sketch written about this character*

1 Paul, called to be an apostle[a] of Christ Jesus
by the will of God,[b] and our brother Sosthenes,[c]

2To the church of God in Corinth,[d] to those sanctified in Christ Jesus and called[e] to be holy, together with all those everywhere who call on the name
of our Lord Jesus Christ—their Lord and ours:

3Grace and peace to you from God our Father
and the Lord Jesus Christ.[f]

Thanksgiving

4I always thank God for you[g] because of his grace
given you in Christ Jesus. 5For in him you have
been enriched[h] in every way—in all your speaking
and in all your knowledge[i]— 6because our testimony[j] about Christ was confirmed in you. 7There-
fore you do not lack any spiritual gift as you eagerly wait for our Lord Jesus Christ to be revealed.[k]
8He will keep you strong to the end, so that you
will be blameless[l] on the day of our Lord Jesus
Christ. 9God, who has called you into fellowship
with his Son Jesus Christ our Lord,[m] is faithful.[n]

Divisions in the Church

10I appeal to you, brothers, in the name of our
Lord Jesus Christ, that all of you agree with one
another so that there may be no divisions among
you and that you may be perfectly united in mind
and thought. 11My brothers, some from Chloe's
household have informed me that there are quarrels among you. 12What I mean is this: One of you
says, "I follow Paul";[o] another, "I follow Apollos";[p]
another, "I follow Cephas[*a*]";[q] still another, "I follow Christ."

13Is Christ divided? Was Paul crucified for you?
Were you baptized into[*b*] the name of Paul?[r] 14I am
thankful that I did not baptize any of you except
Crispus[s] and Gaius,[t] 15so no one can say that you
were baptized into my name. 16(Yes, I also baptized the household of Stephanas;[u] beyond that, I
don't remember if I baptized anyone else.) 17For
Christ did not send me to baptize,[v] but to preach
the gospel—not with words of human wisdom,[w]
lest the cross of Christ be emptied of its power.

Christ the Wisdom and Power of God

18For the message of the cross is foolishness to
those who are perishing,[x] but to us who are being
saved it is the power of God.[y] 19For it is written:

> "I will destroy the wisdom of the wise;
> the intelligence of the intelligent I will
> frustrate."[*c*z]

20Where is the wise man?[a] Where is the scholar?
Where is the philosopher of this age? Has not God
made foolish[b] the wisdom of the world? 21For since
in the wisdom of God the world through its wis-

1:1 [a]Ro 1:1; Eph 1:1 [b]2Co 1:1 [c]Ac 18:17
1:2 [d]Ac 18:1 [e]Ro 1:7
1:3 [f]Ro 1:7
1:4 [g]Ro 1:8
1:5 [h]2Co 9:11 [i]2Co 8:7
1:6 [j]Rev 1:2
1:7 [k]Php 3:20; Tit 2:13; 2Pe 3:12
1:8 [l]1Th 3:13
1:9 [m]1Jn 1:3 [n]Isa 49:7; 1Th 5:24
1:12 [o]1Co 3:4,22 [p]Ac 18:24 [q]Jn 1:42
1:13 [r]Mt 28:19
1:14 [s]Ac 18:8; Ro 16:23 [t]Ac 19:29
1:16 [u]1Co 16:15
1:17 [v]Jn 4:2 [w]1Co 2:1,4, 13
1:18 [x]2Co 2:15 [y]Ro 1:16
1:19 [z]Isa 29:14
1:20 [a]Isa 19:11,12 [b]Job 12:17; Ro 1:22

a 12 That is, Peter *b* 13 Or *in;* also in verse 15
c 19 Isaiah 29:14

The Church at Corinth

1CO 1:10-17

Paul lives in Corinth for almost two years during his second missionary journey. It is natural then that he appeals to his readers as "brothers," for he knows them well. He has strong words to say to them. The church at Corinth suffers from internal division. Leaders vie for position and control; they question Paul's authority as an apostle. Paul directs the Corinthians to the only source of unity—then and now. Only Christ and the power of his cross can bring Christians together in harmony. Where Christ—not human personality or wisdom—is central, unity in the church will be demonstrated.

The Wisdom of God

1CO 2

Paul draws a sharp distinction between the wisdom of God and the wisdom of humans, which he calls "foolishness"(1Co 3:19). The wisdom of God belongs to God alone; it is divine revelation, known by him, given for our future glory, and communicated by the Spirit of God to our spirit (1Co 2:7–10). The purpose of divine wisdom is to help us understand all that God has given us in Christ (1Co 1:23–24).

The foolishness of the world may masquerade as wisdom, but it is a state of spiritual blindness that makes people unable to comprehend the truths of God (1Co 2:14). Paul uses the rulers of Jesus' day as the supreme example of foolishness—learned men who blindly crucified the very One whom they professed to be seeking (1Co 2:8). True spiritual wisdom, in contrast, comes only from God, and it enlightens and redeems, never destroys.

dom did not know him, God was pleased through
the foolishness of what was preached to save those
who believe. 22Jews demand miraculous signs[c] and
Greeks look for wisdom, 23but we preach Christ
crucified: a stumbling block[d] to Jews and foolishness[e] to Gentiles, 24but to those whom God has
called,[f] both Jews and Greeks, Christ the power of
God and the wisdom of God.[g] 25For the foolishness[h] of God is wiser than man's wisdom, and the
weakness[i] of God is stronger than man's strength.
26Brothers, think of what you were when you
were called. Not many of you were wise by human
standards; not many were influential; not many
were of noble birth. 27But God chose[j] the foolish[k]
things of the world to shame the wise; God chose
the weak things of the world to shame the strong.
28He chose the lowly things of this world and the
despised things—and the things that are not[l]—to
nullify the things that are, 29so that no one may
boast before him.[m] 30It is because of him that you
are in Christ Jesus, who has become for us wisdom from God—that is, our righteousness,[n] holiness and redemption.[o] 31Therefore, as it is written:
"Let him who boasts boast in the Lord."[a][p]

2 When I came to you, brothers, I did not come
with eloquence or superior wisdom[q] as I proclaimed to you the testimony about God.[b] 2For I
resolved to know nothing while I was with you
except Jesus Christ and him crucified.[r] 3I came to
you[s] in weakness and fear, and with much trembling. 4My message and my preaching were not
with wise and persuasive words, but with a
demonstration of the Spirit's power,[t] 5so that your
faith might not rest on men's wisdom, but on
God's power.[u]

Wisdom From the Spirit

6We do, however, speak a message of wisdom
among the mature,[v] but not the wisdom of this
age[w] or of the rulers of this age, who are coming
to nothing. 7No, we speak of God's secret wisdom,
a wisdom that has been hidden and that God destined for our glory before time began. 8None of
the rulers of this age understood it, for if they had,
they would not have crucified the Lord of glory.[x]
9However, as it is written:

"No eye has seen,
  no ear has heard,
no mind has conceived
  what God has prepared for those who
    love him"[c][y]—

10but God has revealed[z] it to us by his Spirit.[a]
The Spirit searches all things, even the deep
things of God. 11For who among men knows the
thoughts of a man[b] except the man's spirit[c] within him? In the same way no one knows the
thoughts of God except the Spirit of God. 12We

1:22 [c]Mt 12:38
1:23 [d]Lk 2:34; Gal 5:11 [e]1Co 2:14
1:24 [f]Ro 8:28 [g]ver 30; Col 2:3
1:25 [h]ver 18 [i]2Co 13:4
1:27 [j]Jas 2:5 [k]ver 20
1:28 [l]Ro 4:17
1:29 [m]Eph 2:9
1:30 [n]Jer 23:5,6; 2Co 5:21 [o]Ro 3:24; Eph 1:7,14
1:31 [p]Jer 9:23,24; 2Co 10:17
2:1 [q]1Co 1:17
2:2 [r]Gal 6:14; 1Co 1:23
2:3 [s]Ac 18:1-18
2:4 [t]Ro 15:19
2:5 [u]2Co 4:7; 6:7
2:6 [v]Eph 4:13; Php 3:15; Heb 5:14 [w]1Co 1:20
2:8 [x]Ac 7:2; Jas 2:1
2:9 [y]Isa 64:4; 65:17
2:10 [z]Mt 13:11; Eph 3:3,5 [a]Jn 14:26
2:11 [b]Jer 17:9 [c]Pr 20:27

[a] *31* Jer. 9:24 [b] *1* Some manuscripts *as I proclaimed to you God's mystery* [c] *9* Isaiah 64:4

Crippled Woman

Straightened by Jesus' Touch

She was bent and rigid. She walked with difficulty. Some great burden seemed to weigh down her shoulders and her soul. She could not hold a child, hug or be hugged, lift her head into a breeze, look anyone in the eye or see the moon and stars without great effort. Was she married? Did she have children? Perhaps her body had twisted early in her life, depriving her of all familiar blessings others considered their due. We only know she had suffered for eighteen long years.

She hadn't come to the synagogue expecting to be healed. She hurt, but she didn't complain. Jesus singled her out. He understood the pain she had endured for so long. It was an urgent matter to him. He hated the demon who robbed her, and he commanded it to leave. Eighteen years was long enough!

She straightened up and stood tall under Jesus' touch, and she poured out praise and thanksgiving to God. Amazingly, her joy was cut short and turned to embarrassment and shame. The ruler of the synagogue disapproved, implying she was *selfish* to seek healing on the Sabbath. This poor woman was not accustomed to being the center of attention. She had known how she looked to others, even those who loved her. Now everyone was looking at her. But Jesus' answer humiliated his opponents and reassured the woman that she was certainly of value.

How could this synagogue ruler defer to rules at such a holy moment? The minions of Satan had beaten down the woman for a long time, and they now tried to reassert their control, using her very *religion* to rebuke her! Jesus knew she needed to understand her worth in the eyes of God. She was worth more—*much* more—than the beasts of burden who were still cared for on the Sabbath. God had made her in his own image and called her to spend eternity with him. There was kingdom work for her, a destiny to fulfill. What an outrage that anyone should suggest she be content to suffer even one more minute!

Watch for the downtrodden and physically disabled, and reach out to them with Jesus' love. They can often be found in corners and on the fringes. Though they may not be healed, at the least we can lighten their burdens and help them lift their eyes to heaven. They must know that they, too, have an earthly destiny from God—and an eternity to spend in a *perfect* body.

Crippled woman

Luke 13:10-17

Candid SNAPSHOT On a Sabbath Jesus was teaching in one of the synagogues, and a woman was there who had been crippled by a spirit for eighteen years. She was bent over and could not straighten up at all. When Jesus saw her, he called her forward and said to her, "Woman, you are set free from your infirmity" (Luke 13:10-12).

Salome, Mother of Zebedee's Sons

Asking Without Understanding

She kneeled at Jesus' feet and looked imploringly into his face to ask a favor. Salome was not someone who had just shown up looking for special treatment. Evidence suggests she was Jesus' mother's sister and thus his aunt. She had traveled with Jesus throughout Galilee, and she contributed to the monetary needs of Jesus and the Twelve. She witnessed both the adulation and the rejection of the crowds, as well as the Pharisees' bitter criticism. Her sons, James and John, were close to Jesus. Salome knew Jesus, but she still didn't understand who he was.

Apparently, James and John thought that it was time to ask for special assignments, so they enlisted their mother's aid. Jesus' ministry had gained much momentum. The disciples had all discussed who should be his main advisors. Somebody had to break the ice. She thought it was a natural question. Could Jesus promote James and John when he came into power? After all, their whole family had committed themselves to serving his ministry.

This was what all of Jesus' disciples were thinking! They were all jockeying for position; James and John were merely the first to ask. Jesus' disciples still did not understand what he had been telling them. He was going to *die*—not be crowned king of Israel!

When Jesus answered her, it dawned on Salome that her question had caused him pain. She regretted it, and she began to see a larger issue than her sons' desires. Jesus had spoken of suffering before, and now it was close at hand. Her sons would suffer, too. She had to be ready. She had to be and to do all she could for Jesus. He needed someone to stand with him in his ordeal.

The day came when Salome stood at the foot of Jesus' cross—one of the few who were faithful when others fled in fright. After his death and burial, she went tearfully with others to anoint his body in its tomb, where, instead of his body, they found an angel. " 'Don't be alarmed,' he said. 'You are looking for Jesus the Nazarene, who was crucified. He has risen! He is not here' " (Mk 16:6). She finally understood. The kingdom of heaven was *Jesus'* kingdom!

Sometimes we go to the Lord asking for favors without understanding what we are really saying. We may feel crushed when he says no, but he only withholds out of love. He has the wisdom of all eternity at his disposal and is a wise judge. Ask him to reveal his perspective. It will make all the difference.

Salome, Mother of James and John

(the female form of Solomon)

Matthew 20:20-24; 27:55-56

Mark 15:40-41; 16:1-8

Candid SNAPSHOT "What is it you want?" [Jesus] asked. She said, "Grant that one of these two sons of mine may sit at your right and the other at your left in your kingdom" (Matthew 20:21).

2:12 [d]Ro 8:15 [e]1Co 1:20,27 have not received the spirit[d] of the world[e] but the
Spirit who is from God, that we may understand
what God has freely given us. [13]This is what we
2:13 [f]1Co 1:17 speak, not in words taught us by human wisdom[f]
but in words taught by the Spirit, expressing spiritual truths in spiritual words.[a] [14]The man without
2:14 the Spirit does not accept the things that come
[g]1Co 1:18 from the Spirit of God, for they are foolishness[g] to
him, and he cannot understand them, because
they are spiritually discerned. [15]The spiritual man
makes judgments about all things, but he himself
is not subject to any man's judgment:

> [16]"For who has known the mind of the Lord
> 2:16 [h]Isa 40:13 that he may instruct him?"[b][h]

[i]Jn 15:15 But we have the mind of Christ.[i]

On Divisions in the Church

3:1 [j]1Co 2:15 **3** Brothers, I could not address you as spiritual[j]
[k]Ro 7:14; 1Co 2:14 but as worldly[k]—mere infants[l] in Christ. [2]I
gave you milk, not solid food,[m] for you were not
[l]Heb 5:13 yet ready for it.[n] Indeed, you are still not ready.
3:2 [3]You are still worldly. For since there is jealousy
[m]Heb 5:12-14; 1Pe 2:2 and quarreling[o] among you, are you not worldly?
[n]Jn 16:12 Are you not acting like mere men? [4]For when one
says, "I follow Paul," and another, "I follow Apol-
3:3 [o]1Co 1:11; Gal 5:20 los,"[p] are you not mere men?
[5]What, after all, is Apollos? And what is Paul?
Only servants, through whom you came to
3:4 [p]1Co 1:12 believe—as the Lord has assigned to each his task.
[6]I planted the seed,[q] Apollos watered it, but God
3:6 [q]Ac 18:4-11 made it grow. [7]So neither he who plants nor he
who waters is anything, but only God, who makes
things grow. [8]The man who plants and the man
who waters have one purpose, and each will be
3:8 [r]Ps 62:12 rewarded according to his own labor.[r] [9]For we are
God's fellow workers;[s] you are God's field,[t] God's
3:9 [s]2Co 6:1 building.[u]
[t]Isa 61:3 [10]By the grace God has given me,[v] I laid a foun-
[u]Eph 2:20-22; 1Pe 2:5 dation[w] as an expert builder, and someone else is
building on it. But each one should be careful
3:10 [v]Ro 12:3 how he builds. [11]For no one can lay any founda-
[w]Ro 15:20 tion other than the one already laid, which is
Jesus Christ.[x] [12]If any man builds on this founda-
3:11 [x]Isa 28:16; Eph 2:20 tion using gold, silver, costly stones, wood, hay or
straw, [13]his work will be shown for what it is,[y]
because the Day[z] will bring it to light. It will be
3:13 [y]1Co 4:5 revealed with fire, and the fire will test the quali-
[z]2Th 1:7-10 ty of each man's work. [14]If what he has built survives, he will receive his reward. [15]If it is burned
up, he will suffer loss; he himself will be saved,
3:15 [a]Jude 23 but only as one escaping through the flames.[a]
[16]Don't you know that you yourselves are God's
3:16 [b]1Co 6:19; 2Co 6:16 temple[b] and that God's Spirit lives in you? [17]If
anyone destroys God's temple, God will destroy
him; for God's temple is sacred, and you are that
temple.

[a] *13* Or *Spirit, interpreting spiritual truths to spiritual men*
[b] *16* Isaiah 40:13

A Spiritual Foundation

1CO 3:1-15

The Corinthian Christians can't agree on much of anything. They argue over who's the better teacher: Paul or Apollos. Their relationships are marred by jealousy and quarreling. Paul calls such behavior "worldly" (1Co 3:3). He encourages them to look at the spiritual foundation he laid among them when he was there. That foundation is Christ, the cornerstone of their salvation and the architect of their faith. To mix the wisdom of mere humans with the wisdom of God is as foolish as alternating layers of straw and marble in the erection of a temple. Nothing other than the revealed truth of Christ is solid and strong enough to form a foundation for Christian life.

Take a moment to consider this question: To whom do you give your devotion? Many people rely on the teaching of their pastor or a Christian personality as their means for spiritual nourishment. But the foundation for our spiritual walk must be rooted in our relationship with Jesus Christ (1Co 3:11).

A Bit of Sarcasm

1CO 4:8-13

Without mincing any words, Paul contrasts the supposed position of the Corinthians—rich, content, mature—with the actual position of himself and the other apostles—in need, tortured, condemned to die. While the Corinthians boast about their excellent position, Paul points out the lowliness of his. Paul plays on the word "fools," calling himself a "fool for Christ" (1Co 4:10) and commending the wisdom of being willing to suffer—in hunger, thirst, nakedness and homelessness—in order to bring others the gospel. He boldly encourages the Corinthians—and us—to imitate his example in costly obedience to Christ.

[18]Do not deceive yourselves. If any one of you thinks he is wise[c] by the standards of this age, he should become a "fool" so that he may become wise. [19]For the wisdom of this world is foolishness[d] in God's sight. As it is written: "He catches the wise in their craftiness"[a];[e] [20]and again, "The Lord knows that the thoughts of the wise are futile."[b][f] [21]So then, no more boasting about men![g] All things are yours,[h] [22]whether Paul or Apollos or Cephas[c][i] or the world or life or death or the present or the future[j]—all are yours, [23]and you are of Christ,[k] and Christ is of God.

Apostles of Christ

4 So then, men ought to regard us as servants of Christ and as those entrusted[l] with the secret things[m] of God. [2]Now it is required that those who have been given a trust must prove faithful. [3]I care very little if I am judged by you or by any human court; indeed, I do not even judge myself. [4]My conscience is clear, but that does not make me innocent.[n] It is the Lord who judges me. [5]Therefore judge nothing[o] before the appointed time; wait till the Lord comes. He will bring to light what is hidden in darkness and will expose the motives of men's hearts. At that time each will receive his praise from God.[p]

[6]Now, brothers, I have applied these things to myself and Apollos for your benefit, so that you may learn from us the meaning of the saying, "Do not go beyond what is written."[q] Then you will not take pride in one man over against another.[r] [7]For who makes you different from anyone else? What do you have that you did not receive?[s] And if you did receive it, why do you boast as though you did not?

[8]Already you have all you want! Already you have become rich![t] You have become kings—and that without us! How I wish that you really had become kings so that we might be kings with you! [9]For it seems to me that God has put us apostles on display at the end of the procession, like men condemned to die[u] in the arena. We have been made a spectacle[v] to the whole universe, to angels as well as to men. [10]We are fools for Christ,[w] but you are so wise in Christ![x] We are weak, but you are strong![y] You are honored, we are dishonored! [11]To this very hour we go hungry and thirsty, we are in rags, we are brutally treated, we are homeless.[z] [12]We work hard with our own hands.[a] When we are cursed, we bless;[b] when we are persecuted, we endure it; [13]when we are slandered, we answer kindly. Up to this moment we have become the scum of the earth, the refuse[c] of the world.

[14]I am not writing this to shame you, but to warn you, as my dear children.[d] [15]Even though you have ten thousand guardians in Christ, you do not have many fathers, for in Christ Jesus I became your father through the gospel.[e] [16]There-

3:18 [c]Isa 5:21; 1Co 8:2
3:19 [d]1Co 1:20,27 [e]Job 5:13
3:20 [f]Ps 94:11
3:21 [g]1Co 4:6 [h]Ro 8:32
3:22 [i]1Co 1:12 [j]Ro 8:38
3:23 [k]1Co 15:23; 2Co 10:7; Gal 3:29
4:1 [l]1Co 9:17; Tit 1:7 [m]Ro 16:25
4:4 [n]Ro 2:13
4:5 [o]Mt 7:1,2; Ro 2:1 [p]Ro 2:29
4:6 [q]1Co 1:19, 31; 3:19,20 [r]1Co 1:12
4:7 [s]Jn 3:27; Ro 12:3,6
4:8 [t]Rev 3:17,18
4:9 [u]Ro 8:36 [v]Heb 10:33
4:10 [w]1Co 1:18; Ac 17:18 [x]1Co 3:18 [y]1Co 2:3
4:11 [z]Ro 8:35; 2Co 11:23-27
4:12 [a]Ac 18:3 [b]1Pe 3:9
4:13 [c]La 3:45
4:14 [d]1Th 2:11
4:15 [e]1Co 9:12, 14,18,23

[a] *19* Job 5:13 [b] *20* Psalm 94:11 [c] *22* That is, Peter

4:16 [f]1Co 11:1; fore I urge you to imitate me.[f] [17]For this reason I
Php 3:17; am sending to you Timothy, my son[g] whom I love,
1Th 1:6; who is faithful in the Lord. He will remind you of
2Th 3:7,9 my way of life in Christ Jesus, which agrees with
4:17 what I teach everywhere in every church.[h]
[g]1Ti 1:2 [18]Some of you have become arrogant, as if I
[h]1Co 7:17 were not coming to you. [19]But I will come to you
4:19 very soon,[i] if the Lord is willing,[j] and then I will
[i]2Co 1:15,16 find out not only how these arrogant people are
[j]Ac 18:21 talking, but what power they have. [20]For the kingdom of God is not a matter of talk but of power.
4:21 [21]What do you prefer? Shall I come to you with a
[k]2Co 1:23; whip,[k] or in love and with a gentle spirit?
13:2,10

Expel the Immoral Brother!

5 It is actually reported that there is sexual
immorality among you, and of a kind that does
not occur even among pagans: A man has his
5:1 [l]Lev 18:8; father's wife.[l] [2]And you are proud! Shouldn't you
Dt 22:30 rather have been filled with grief[m] and have put out
of your fellowship the man who did this? [3]Even
5:2 [m]2Co 7:7-11 though I am not physically present, I am with you
in spirit.[n] And I have already passed judgment on
5:3 [n]Col 2:5 the one who did this, just as if I were present.
[4]When you are assembled in the name of our Lord
5:4 [o]2Th 3:6 Jesus[o] and I am with you in spirit, and the power of
5:5 our Lord Jesus is present, [5]hand this man over[p] to
Satan, so that the sinful nature[a] may be destroyed
[p]1Ti 1:20 and his spirit saved on the day of the Lord.
5:6 [6]Your boasting is not good.[q] Don't you know
[q]Jas 4:16 that a little yeast[r] works through the whole batch
[r]Mt 16:6,12 of dough?[s] [7]Get rid of the old yeast that you may
[s]Gal 5:9 be a new batch without yeast—as you really are.
5:7 For Christ, our Passover lamb, has been sacri-
[t]Mk 14:12; ficed.[t] [8]Therefore let us keep the Festival, not with
1Pe 1:19 the old yeast, the yeast of malice and wickedness,
5:8 but with bread without yeast,[u] the bread of sin-
[u]Ex 12:14, cerity and truth.
15; Dt 16:3 [9]I have written you in my letter not to associ-
5:9 [v]Eph 5:11; ate[v] with sexually immoral people— [10]not at all
2Th 3:6,14 meaning the people of this world[w] who are
5:10 immoral, or the greedy and swindlers, or idol-
[w]1Co 10:27 aters. In that case you would have to leave this
world. [11]But now I am writing you that you must
not associate with anyone who calls himself a
5:11 brother but is sexually immoral or greedy, an idol-
[x]1Co 10:7,14 ater[x] or a slanderer, a drunkard or a swindler.
With such a man do not even eat.
5:12 [12]What business is it of mine to judge those out-
[y]Mk 4:11 side[y] the church? Are you not to judge those
[z]ver 3-5; inside?[z] [13]God will judge those outside. "Expel the
1Co 6:1-4 wicked man from among you."[b][a]
5:13 [a]Dt 13:5

Lawsuits Among Believers

6:1 [b]Mt 18:17 **6** If any of you has a dispute with another, dare
6:2 he take it before the ungodly for judgment
[c]Mt 19:28; instead of before the saints?[b] [2]Do you not know
Lk 22:30 that the saints will judge the world?[c] And if you

[a]5 Or *that his body*; or *that the flesh* [b]13 Deut. 17:7; 19:19; 21:21; 22:21,24; 24:7

Sexual Immorality

1CO 5:1-5

Corinth was a city of culture and commerce, known for its corrupt morals and licentious behavior. Paul rebukes the church of Corinth for not confronting the immoral behavior taking place among its members. One man has married his father's wife— —most likely his stepmother. Unbelievably, the believers are "proud" (1Co 5:2)! They think they are so spiritually mature that they're beyond worrying about such ordinary, earthly matters. However, Paul disagrees: Sexual immorality must be addressed within the body of believers. He gives instruction for the exercise of judicial authority by the church among its members. Specifically regarding the man guilty of incest, Paul says, "Hand this man over to Satan" (1Co 5:5). His sinful nature will be destroyed in order that his soul will be saved. This solemn exercise of judicial power by the apostle is not meant to bring a spirit of harshness or condemnation into the church but to bring the whole church body to sincere and deep repentance.

Week 41

A Kingdom of Power

"He's all talk," people say about those who make a lot of promises and declarations but who don't have the power or the initiative to act on them. Their words mean nothing because there is nothing of substance behind them. Some people in the Corinthian church were like this. Paul says, "The kingdom of God is not a matter of talk but of power" (1Co 4:20). God's power is not just talk.

How does Jesus display his power (Mk 5:29-30; Lk 4:36)? Where does Jesus' power come from (Lk 4:14)?

Is Jesus able to heal whenever he wants to (Mt 13:58; Lk 5:17)? Do the people recognize those times when God's power is present (Lk 6:19)?

To whom does Jesus *give* power and authority (Lk 9:1-2; 10:1,9,17)? What is its purpose (Mt 28:19-20)? This includes you (Jn 14:12; 2Ti 1:7)!

All power, including temporal power, comes from God (Jn 19:10-11). But *a special, spiritual* power is at work in believers (Eph 3:20). Why has God chosen to display his power in someone like you (2Co 4:7)?

How do you receive this power (Lk 24:49; Ac 1:8)? What does this power produce within you (Ro 15:13; Col 1:11-12)?

Enjoying God through the Word

Read Ephesians 1:18-21 (pages 1929-1930). What incredible power God has placed within you—it is like the mighty power that raised Christ from the dead (Eph 1:19-20)! God's power is immediately available to you. Are you using it? You have been given an assignment: bring healing to the wounded and hurting (Mt 10:8), offer freedom to those in spiritual bondage (Isa 42:6-7) and spread the gospel, which is the power of God for salvation (Ro 1:16; 1Co 1:18). You are not capable of these things on your own; you are only able to do them in the power of God (1Co 2:1-5).

Your power and authority are limited, however, by God's will—just as Jesus' power was (Jn 5:19). The degree to which God can use you is determined by your discernment of his will. You must line up your will with his and ask according to his will (1Jn 5:14). How can you discern God's will in order to effectively use the power and authority God has given you? Do as Jesus did: develop a close, intimate relationship with the Father (Jn 5:20).

Enjoying God through Experience

Do you lack the power necessary to live out the assignment God has given you? Then follow the example of Jesus and his disciples: ask for and wait for the Holy Spirit's power (Lk 11:11-13; Ac 1:4-5), develop an intimate relationship with God in order to discern his will (Jn 5:19-20) and move out in faith, not human wisdom (1Co 2:4-5).

Your faith plays an important role in regard to power. It is God's power in you, but it is appropriated through your faith. If you don't use it, it's as if you never had it to begin with. Ask God to fill you with power through his Spirit. Pray for his wisdom. Pray for the faith to go out and be his disciple. Then, *go!*

Go to page 1903 for your next weekly study.

are to judge the world, are you not competent to
judge trivial cases? [3]Do you not know that we will
judge angels? How much more the things of this
life! [4]Therefore, if you have disputes about such
matters, appoint as judges even men of little
6:5 account in the church![a] [5]I say this to shame you.[d]
[d]1Co 4:14 Is it possible that there is nobody among you wise
[e]Ac 1:15 enough to judge a dispute between believers?[e]
6:6 [6]But instead, one brother goes to law against
[f]2Co 6:14,15 another—and this in front of unbelievers![f]

[7]The very fact that you have lawsuits among
you means you have been completely defeated
6:7 already. Why not rather be wronged? Why not
[g]Mt 5:39,40 rather be cheated?[g] [8]Instead, you yourselves cheat
6:8 and do wrong, and you do this to your brothers.[h]

[h]1Th 4:6 [9]Do you not know that the wicked will not
6:9 inherit the kingdom of God?[i] Do not be deceived:[j]
[i]Gal 5:21 Neither the sexually immoral nor idolaters nor
[j]1Co 15:33; adulterers nor male prostitutes nor homosexual
Jas 1:16 offenders [10]nor thieves nor the greedy nor drunkards nor slanderers nor swindlers will inherit the
6:11 kingdom of God. [11]And that is what some of you
[k]Eph 2:2 were.[k] But you were washed,[l] you were sancti-
[l]Ac 22:16 fied,[m] you were justified in the name of the Lord
[m]1Co 1:2 Jesus Christ and by the Spirit of our God.

Sexual Immorality

6:12 [12]"Everything is permissible for me"—but not
[n]1Co 10:23 everything is beneficial.[n] "Everything is permissible for me"—but I will not be mastered by any-
6:13 thing. [13]"Food for the stomach and the stomach
[o]Col 2:22 for food"—but God will destroy them both.[o] The
body is not meant for sexual immorality, but for
6:14 the Lord, and the Lord for the body. [14]By his pow-
[p]Ro 6:5; er God raised the Lord from the dead, and he will
Eph 1:19,20 raise us also.[p] [15]Do you not know that your bodies
6:15 are members of Christ himself?[q] Shall I then take
[q]Ro 12:5 the members of Christ and unite them with a
prostitute? Never! [16]Do you not know that he who
6:16 unites himself with a prostitute is one with her in
[r]Ge 2:24; body? For it is said, "The two will become one
Mt 19:5; flesh."[b][r] [17]But he who unites himself with the
Eph 5:31 6:17 Lord is one with him in spirit.[s]
[s]Jn 17:21-23; [18]Flee from sexual immorality.[t] All other sins a
Gal 2:20 man commits are outside his body, but he who sins
6:18 sexually sins against his own body.[u] [19]Do you not
[t]2Co 12:21; know that your body is a temple[v] of the Holy Spir-
1Th 4:3,4; Heb 13:4 it, who is in you, whom you have received from
[u]Ro 6:12 God? You are not your own;[w] [20]you were bought at
6:19 a price.[x] Therefore honor God with your body.
[v]Jn 2:21
[w]Ro 14:7,8

Marriage

6:20 [x]Ac 20:28; **7** Now for the matters you wrote about: It is
1Co 7:23; good for a man not to marry.[c][y] [2]But since there
1Pe 1:18,19; is so much immorality, each man should have his
Rev 5:9 own wife, and each woman her own husband.
7:1 [y]ver 8,26 [3]The husband should fulfill his marital duty to his

[a] 4 Or *matters, do you appoint as judges men of little account in the church?* [b] 16 Gen. 2:24 [c] 1 Or *"It is good for a man not to have sexual relations with a woman."*

Christian Liberty

1CO 6:12

The principle of Christian liberty evolves from this verse as well as from Romans 14:13-23 and 1 Corinthians 8:7-13; 10:23-33. A Christian has the freedom to participate in activities not expressly forbidden. However, Paul does give several guidelines: Is it "beneficial" (1Co 6:12)? Is it something that will overpower me (1Co 6:12)? Will the Lord who created my body find glory in it (1Co 6:13, 15)? Is it in line with the truth that my body is the Holy Spirit's temple (1Co 6:19)?

Some Corinthians believe that just as food is used to satisfy the stomach, so it is legitimate to satisfy other natural appetites. Paul uses the example of food to teach important truths about the relationship of the body and the soul. Food will be destroyed—but our bodies are members of Christ; they will be raised with him. Our bodies are temples of the Holy Spirit; God wants us to honor him with our bodies. When we participate in sexual immorality, we sin against ourselves and we sin against the Lord.

Marriage

1CO 7:1-16

The Corinthians approach Paul with questions about marriage. In this chapter he gives a variety of instructions on the topic. First, because of some crisis in Corinth (1Co 7:26), he advises against marriage for those who are unmarried. This is not, however, a general truth but is specifically related to the situation in Corinth, since in other letters (Eph 5; 1Ti 3) Paul advocates marriage.

Since the sin of sexual immorality is so prevalent in Corinth, it is the framework for Paul's instructions on marriage. Sexual abstinence in marriage should only be for a short time so that the partners are not tempted to look elsewhere for gratification (1Co 7:3–5). For men and for women, it is better to be married than to be sexually tempted (1Co 7:9). To spouses who leave a marriage, the Scripture offers two options: to remain unmarried or to work toward reconciliation (1Co 7:11). When a Christian spouse is married to an unbeliever, Paul encourages the Christian to remain in the marriage (1Co 7:12–14).

wife,[z] and likewise the wife to her husband. 4The
wife's body does not belong to her alone but also
to her husband. In the same way, the husband's
body does not belong to him alone but also to his
wife. 5Do not deprive each other except by mutual consent and for a time,[a] so that you may devote
yourselves to prayer. Then come together again so
that Satan[b] will not tempt you[c] because of your
lack of self-control. 6I say this as a concession, not
as a command.[d] 7I wish that all men were as I
am.[e] But each man has his own gift from God; one
has this gift, another has that.[f]

8Now to the unmarried and the widows I say: It
is good for them to stay unmarried, as I am.[g] 9But
if they cannot control themselves, they should
marry,[h] for it is better to marry than to burn with
passion.

10To the married I give this command (not I, but
the Lord): A wife must not separate from her husband.[i] 11But if she does, she must remain unmarried or else be reconciled to her husband. And a
husband must not divorce his wife.

12To the rest I say this (I, not the Lord):[j] If any
brother has a wife who is not a believer and she is
willing to live with him, he must not divorce her.
13And if a woman has a husband who is not a
believer and he is willing to live with her, she
must not divorce him. 14For the unbelieving husband has been sanctified through his wife, and
the unbelieving wife has been sanctified through
her believing husband. Otherwise your children
would be unclean, but as it is, they are holy.[k]

15But if the unbeliever leaves, let him do so. A
believing man or woman is not bound in such circumstances; God has called us to live in peace.[l]
16How do you know, wife, whether you will save[m]
your husband?[n] Or, how do you know, husband,
whether you will save your wife?

17Nevertheless, each one should retain the place
in life that the Lord assigned to him and to which
God has called him.[o] This is the rule I lay down in
all the churches.[p] 18Was a man already circumcised when he was called? He should not become
uncircumcised. Was a man uncircumcised when
he was called? He should not be circumcised.[q]
19Circumcision is nothing and uncircumcision is
nothing.[r] Keeping God's commands is what
counts. 20Each one should remain in the situation
which he was in when God called him.[s] 21Were
you a slave when you were called? Don't let it
trouble you—although if you can gain your freedom, do so. 22For he who was a slave when he
was called by the Lord is the Lord's freedman;[t]
similarly, he who was a free man when he was
called is Christ's slave.[u] 23You were bought at a
price;[v] do not become slaves of men. 24Brothers,
each man, as responsible to God, should remain
in the situation God called him to.[w]

25Now about virgins: I have no command from
the Lord,[x] but I give a judgment as one who by
the Lord's mercy[y] is trustworthy. 26Because of the

7:3 [z]Ex 21: 10; 1Pe 3:7
7:5 [a]Ex 19:15; 1Sa 21:4,5 [b]Mt 4:10 [c]1Th 3:5
7:6 [d]2Co 8:8
7:7 [e]ver 8; 1Co 9:5 [f]Mt 19:11,12; Ro 12:6; 1Co 12:4,11
7:8 [g]ver 1,26
7:9 [h]1Ti 5:14
7:10 [i]Mal 2:14-16; Mt 5:32; 19:3-9; Mk 10:11; Lk 16:18
7:12 [j]ver 6,10; 2Co 11:17
7:14 [k]Mal 2:15
7:15 [l]Ro 14:19; 1Co 14:33
7:16 [m]Ro 11:14 [n]1Pe 3:1
7:17 [o]Ro 12:3 [p]1Co 4:17; 14:33; 2Co 8:18; 11:28
7:18 [q]Ac 15:1,2
7:19 [r]Ro 2:25-27; Gal 5:6; 6:15; Col 3:11
7:20 [s]ver 24
7:22 [t]Jn 8:32,36; Phm 16 [u]Eph 6:6
7:23 [v]1Co 6:20
7:24 [w]ver 20
7:25 [x]ver 6; 2Co 8:8 [y]2Co 4:1; 1Ti 1:13,16

7:26 present crisis, I think that it is good for you to
[z]ver 1,8 remain as you are.[z] [27]Are you married? Do not
seek a divorce. Are you unmarried? Do not look
for a wife. [28]But if you do marry, you have not
sinned; and if a virgin marries, she has not
sinned. But those who marry will face many troubles in this life, and I want to spare you this.
[29]What I mean, brothers, is that the time is
7:29 short.[a] From now on those who have wives
[a]ver 31; Ro 13:11,12 should live as if they had none; [30]those who
mourn, as if they did not; those who are happy,
as if they were not; those who buy something, as
if it were not theirs to keep; [31]those who use the
7:31 things of the world, as if not engrossed in them.
[b]1Jn 2:17 For this world in its present form is passing away.[b]
[32]I would like you to be free from concern. An
unmarried man is concerned about the Lord's
7:32 affairs[c]—how he can please the Lord. [33]But a mar-
[c]1Ti 5:5 ried man is concerned about the affairs of this
world—how he can please his wife— [34]and his
interests are divided. An unmarried woman or virgin is concerned about the Lord's affairs: Her aim
7:34 is to be devoted to the Lord in both body and spir-
[d]Lk 2:37 it.[d] But a married woman is concerned about the
affairs of this world—how she can please her husband. [35]I am saying this for your own good, not
7:35 to restrict you, but that you may live in a right
[e]Ps 86:11 way in undivided[e] devotion to the Lord.
[36]If anyone thinks he is acting improperly
toward the virgin he is engaged to, and if she is
getting along in years and he feels he ought to
7:36 marry, he should do as he wants. He is not sin-
[f]ver 28 ning.[f] They should get married. [37]But the man who
has settled the matter in his own mind, who is
under no compulsion but has control over his own
will, and who has made up his mind not to marry
7:38 the virgin—this man also does the right thing. [38]So
[g]Heb 13:4 then, he who marries the virgin does right,[g] but
he who does not marry her does even better.[a]
7:39 [39]A woman is bound to her husband as long as
[h]Ro 7:2,3 he lives.[h] But if her husband dies, she is free to
[i]2Co 6:14 marry anyone she wishes, but he must belong to
7:40 the Lord.[i] [40]In my judgment,[j] she is happier if she
[j]ver 25 stays as she is—and I think that I too have the
Spirit of God.

Food Sacrificed to Idols

8:1 **8** Now about food sacrificed to idols:[k] We know
[k]Ac 15:20 [l]Ro 15:14 that we all possess knowledge.[b][l] Knowledge
8:2 puffs up, but love builds up. [2]The man who
[m]1Co 3:18 thinks he knows something[m] does not yet know

[a] *36–38* Or [36]*If anyone thinks he is not treating his daughter properly, and if she is getting along in years, and he feels she ought to marry, he should do as he wants. He is not sinning. He should let her get married.* [37]*But the man who has settled the matter in his own mind, who is under no compulsion but has control over his own will, and who has made up his mind to keep the virgin unmarried—this man also does the right thing.* [38]*So then, he who gives his virgin in marriage does right, but he who does not give her in marriage does even better.* [b] *1* Or *"We all possess knowledge," as you say*

Concerns of Marriage

1CO 7:32

"I would like you to be free from concern" (1Co 7:32).

Paul here gives three reasons why he wants the Christians in Corinth to consider the possibility of remaining unmarried. First, marriage in difficult times simply brings with it increased troubles (1Co 7:28). Having no family to provide for or protect in times of distress and persecution means one is less encumbered with worldly cares. Second, because time may be short before the Lord's appearing, marriage lends itself to becoming overly concerned with temporal affairs (1Co 7:29). And third, those who remain unmarried are free to devote themselves entirely to the Lord (1Co 7:32). They are able to serve the Lord with less distraction. However, Paul is clear that this is only his personal direction, not a command from God (1Co 7:25). No sin is involved for those who *do* decide to marry (1Co 7:28).

A Matter of Conscience

1CO 8

The question discussed here concerns whether a Christian, when in public, should refrain from eating meat that has been sacrificed to idols. Paul uses the occasion to give overall guidelines useful for weighing matters of conscience. He begins with the principle of truth. In this case, Christians know there is only one God; the gods before whom this meat has been sacrificed do not actually exist and therefore have no actual effect on the meat (1Co 8:4–6). The relevant matter concerns the conscience of weaker believers. If eating meat sacrificed to idols causes them to have a guilty conscience, then the law of love supercedes the law of liberty. Paul says it is better to forego the matter in question—that is, eating meat sacrificed to idols—than to wound a fellow believer (1Co 8:13). To sin against fellow believers, in weakening their conscience, is to sin against Christ. The key element in decision making should not be one's own freedom but one's love for Christian brothers and sisters.

as he ought to know.[n] 3But the man who loves
God is known by God.[o]
4So then, about eating food sacrificed to idols:[p]
We know that an idol is nothing at all in the
world[q] and that there is no God but one.[r] 5For
even if there are so-called gods,[s] whether in heav-
en or on earth (as indeed there are many "gods"
and many "lords"), 6yet for us there is but one
God, the Father,[t] from whom all things came[u] and
for whom we live; and there is but one Lord,[v]
Jesus Christ, through whom all things came[w] and
through whom we live.
7But not everyone knows this. Some people are
still so accustomed to idols that when they eat
such food they think of it as having been sacrificed to an idol, and since their conscience is
weak,[x] it is defiled. 8But food does not bring us
near to God;[y] we are no worse if we do not eat,
and no better if we do.
9Be careful, however, that the exercise of your
freedom does not become a stumbling block[z] to
the weak.[a] 10For if anyone with a weak conscience
sees you who have this knowledge eating in an
idol's temple, won't he be emboldened to eat what
has been sacrificed to idols? 11So this weak brother, for whom Christ died, is destroyed[b] by your
knowledge. 12When you sin against your brothers[c]
in this way and wound their weak conscience, you
sin against Christ. 13Therefore, if what I eat causes
my brother to fall into sin, I will never eat meat
again, so that I will not cause him to fall.[d]

The Rights of an Apostle

9 Am I not free? Am I not an apostle?[e] Have I not
seen Jesus our Lord?[f] Are you not the result of
my work in the Lord?[g] 2Even though I may not be
an apostle to others, surely I am to you! For you
are the seal[h] of my apostleship in the Lord.
3This is my defense to those who sit in judgment on me. 4Don't we have the right to food and
drink?[i] 5Don't we have the right to take a believing wife[j] along with us, as do the other apostles
and the Lord's brothers[k] and Cephas[a]? 6Or is it
only I and Barnabas[l] who must work for a living?
7Who serves as a soldier at his own expense?
Who plants a vineyard[m] and does not eat of its
grapes? Who tends a flock and does not drink of
the milk? 8Do I say this merely from a human
point of view? Doesn't the Law say the same
thing? 9For it is written in the Law of Moses: "Do
not muzzle an ox while it is treading out the
grain."[b][n] Is it about oxen that God is concerned?[o]
10Surely he says this for us, doesn't he? Yes, this
was written for us,[p] because when the plowman
plows and the thresher threshes, they ought to do
so in the hope of sharing in the harvest.[q] 11If we
have sown spiritual seed among you, is it too
much if we reap a material harvest from you?[r]

[a] 5 That is, Peter [b] 9 Deut. 25:4

8:2 [n]1Co 13:8,9, 12; 1Ti 6:4
8:3 [o]Ro 8:29; Gal 4:9
8:4 [p]ver 1,7,10 [q]1Co 10:19 [r]Dt 6:4; Eph 4:6
8:5 [s]2Th 2:4
8:6 [t]Mal 2:10 [u]Ro 11:36 [v]Eph 4:5 [w]Jn 1:3
8:7 [x]Ro 14:14; 1Co 10:28
8:8 [y]Ro 14:17
8:9 [z]Gal 5:13 [a]Ro 14:1
8:11 [b]Ro 14:15,20
8:12 [c]Mt 18:6
8:13 [d]Ro 14:21
9:1 [e]2Co 12:12 [f]1Co 15:8 [g]1Co 3:6; 4:15
9:2 [h]2Co 3:2,3
9:4 [i]1Th 2:6
9:5 [j]1Co 7:7,8 [k]Mt 12:46
9:6 [l]Ac 4:36
9:7 [m]Dt 20:6; Pr 27:18
9:9 [n]Dt 25:4; 1Ti 5:18 [o]Dt 22:1-4
9:10 [p]Ro 4:23,24 [q]2Ti 2:6
9:11 [r]Ro 15:27

12If others have this right of support from you, shouldn't we have it all the more?

But we did not use this right.[s] On the contrary, we put up with anything rather than hinder[t] the gospel of Christ. 13Don't you know that those who work in the temple get their food from the temple, and those who serve at the altar share in what is offered on the altar?[u] 14In the same way, the Lord has commanded that those who preach the gospel should receive their living from the gospel.[v]

15But I have not used any of these rights.[w] And I am not writing this in the hope that you will do such things for me. I would rather die than have anyone deprive me of this boast.[x] 16Yet when I preach the gospel, I cannot boast, for I am compelled to preach.[y] Woe to me if I do not preach the gospel! 17If I preach voluntarily, I have a reward;[z] if not voluntarily, I am simply discharging the trust committed to me.[a] 18What then is my reward? Just this: that in preaching the gospel I may offer it free of charge,[b] and so not make use of my rights in preaching it.

19Though I am free[c] and belong to no man, I make myself a slave to everyone,[d] to win as many as possible.[e] 20To the Jews I became like a Jew, to win the Jews.[f] To those under the law I became like one under the law (though I myself am not under the law), so as to win those under the law. 21To those not having the law I became like one not having the law[g] (though I am not free from God's law but am under Christ's law), so as to win those not having the law. 22To the weak I became weak, to win the weak. I have become all things to all men[h] so that by all possible means I might save some.[i] 23I do all this for the sake of the gospel, that I may share in its blessings.

24Do you not know that in a race all the runners run, but only one gets the prize? Run[j] in such a way as to get the prize. 25Everyone who competes in the games goes into strict training. They do it to get a crown that will not last; but we do it to get a crown that will last forever.[k] 26Therefore I do not run like a man running aimlessly; I do not fight like a man beating the air. 27No, I beat my body[l] and make it my slave so that after I have preached to others, I myself will not be disqualified for the prize.

Warnings From Israel's History

10 For I do not want you to be ignorant of the fact, brothers, that our forefathers were all under the cloud[m] and that they all passed through the sea.[n] 2They were all baptized into Moses in the cloud and in the sea. 3They all ate the same spiritual food 4and drank the same spiritual drink; for they drank from the spiritual rock[o] that accompanied them, and that rock was Christ. 5Nevertheless, God was not pleased with most of them; their bodies were scattered over the desert.[p]

6Now these things occurred as examples[a] to

a 6 Or *types*; also in verse 11

9:12 [s]Ac 18:3 [t]2Co 11:7-12
9:13 [u]Lev 6:16, 26; Dt 18:1
9:14 [v]Mt 10:10; 1Ti 5:18
9:15 [w]Ac 18:3 [x]2Co 11:9,10
9:16 [y]Ro 1:14; Ac 9:15
9:17 [z]1Co 3:8,14 [a]Gal 2:7; Col 1:25
9:18 [b]2Co 11:7; 12:13
9:19 [c]ver 1 [d]Gal 5:13 [e]Mt 18:15; 1Pe 3:1
9:20 [f]Ac 16:3; 21:20-26; Ro 11:14
9:21 [g]Ro 2:12,14
9:22 [h]1Co 10:33 [i]Ro 11:14
9:24 [j]Gal 2:2; 2Ti 4:7; Heb 12:1
9:25 [k]Jas 1:12; Rev 2:10
9:27 [l]Ro 8:13
10:1 [m]Ex 13:21 [n]Ex 14:22,29
10:4 [o]Ex 17:6; Nu 20:11; Ps 78:15
10:5 [p]Nu 14:29; Heb 3:17

Spiritual Discipline

1CO 9:24-27

Paul speaks here to the tendency toward self-indulgence common among Corinthians; he challenges them to consider the discipline of a Greek athlete. (Every other year Corinth hosted the Isthmian games in which athletes competed for a coveted prize. The Corinthians were, therefore, intimately acquainted with the discipline Paul was talking about.) Paul challenges the Christian to the same discipline and rigorous self-denial as a prize-winning athlete, yet not for the reward of a garland of green leaves, but for a crown that endures forever (see 1Co 9:25).

While the word "beat" (1Co 9:27) may bring to mind actual abuse of his body, Paul is not referring to actual physical beating but to the kind of tough training that athletes go through to prepare their bodies for a race. Paul says that in running his race, he works to keep his body under subjection—his body is* his *slave rather than he being a slave to his body. His goal? The glorious prize of eternal life (see 1Co 9:25).

No Temptation Too Great

1CO 10:13

Paul here records one of Scriptures' most beautiful and assuring truths: Yes, temptation will come, but God will be there, too (see the note on 1 Peter 5:8-9, page 2029). Every Christian is faced with temptation of some sort. The temptation is itself not sin (even Jesus was tempted—Mt 4:1). Yielding to temptation is the sin. Some Christians may feel they are bombarded with temptation, and they grow weary under its weight. Through Paul, God responds to those weary Christians with his kindest and most reassuring words regarding the temptations they face: He is right there with them, and if they will only look about them, they will see a way he has provided that will help them to resist.

keep us from setting our hearts on evil things as
they did. 7 Do not be idolaters,[q] as some of them
were; as it is written: "The people sat down to eat
and drink and got up to indulge in pagan revelry."[a][r] 8 We should not commit sexual immorality,
as some of them did—and in one day twenty-three
thousand of them died.[s] 9 We should not test the
Lord, as some of them did—and were killed by
snakes.[t] 10 And do not grumble, as some of them
did[u]—and were killed[v] by the destroying angel.[w]
11 These things happened to them as examples
and were written down as warnings for us, on
whom the fulfillment of the ages has come.[x] 12 So,
if you think you are standing firm,[y] be careful that
you don't fall! 13 No temptation has seized you
except what is common to man. And God is faithful;[z] he will not let you be tempted beyond what
you can bear.[a] But when you are tempted, he will
also provide a way out so that you can stand up
under it.

Idol Feasts and the Lord's Supper

14 Therefore, my dear friends, flee from idolatry.
15 I speak to sensible people; judge for yourselves
what I say. 16 Is not the cup of thanksgiving for
which we give thanks a participation in the blood
of Christ? And is not the bread that we break a
participation in the body of Christ?[b] 17 Because
there is one loaf, we, who are many, are one
body,[c] for we all partake of the one loaf.
18 Consider the people of Israel: Do not those
who eat the sacrifices[d] participate in the altar?
19 Do I mean then that a sacrifice offered to an idol
is anything, or that an idol is anything?[e] 20 No, but
the sacrifices of pagans are offered to demons,[f] not
to God, and I do not want you to be participants
with demons. 21 You cannot drink the cup of the
Lord and the cup of demons too; you cannot have
a part in both the Lord's table and the table of
demons.[g] 22 Are we trying to arouse the Lord's jealousy?[h] Are we stronger than he?[i]

The Believer's Freedom

23 "Everything is permissible"—but not everything is beneficial.[j] "Everything is permissible"—
but not everything is constructive. 24 Nobody
should seek his own good, but the good of
others.[k]
25 Eat anything sold in the meat market without
raising questions of conscience,[l] 26 for, "The earth
is the Lord's, and everything in it."[b][m]
27 If some unbeliever invites you to a meal and
you want to go, eat whatever is put before you[n]
without raising questions of conscience. 28 But if
anyone says to you, "This has been offered in sacrifice," then do not eat it, both for the sake of the
man who told you and for conscience' sake[c][o]—

10:7 [q]ver 14 [r]Ex 32:4,6, 19
10:8 [s]Nu 25:1-9
10:9 [t]Nu 21:5,6
10:10 [u]Nu 16:41 [v]Nu 16:49 [w]Ex 12:23
10:11 [x]Ro 13:11
10:12 [y]Ro 11:20
10:13 [z]1Co 1:9 [a]2Pe 2:9
10:16 [b]Mt 26:26-28
10:17 [c]Ro 12:5; 1Co 12:27
10:18 [d]Lev 7:6,14, 15
10:19 [e]1Co 8:4
10:20 [f]Dt 32:17; Ps 106:37; Rev 9:20
10:21 [g]2Co 6:15,16
10:22 [h]Dt 32:16,21 [i]Ecc 6:10; Isa 45:9
10:23 [j]1Co 6:12
10:24 [k]ver 33; Ro 15:1,2; 1Co 13:5; Php 2:4,21
10:25 [l]Ac 10:15; 1Co 8:7
10:26 [m]Ps 24:1
10:27 [n]Lk 10:7
10:28 [o]1Co 8:7,10-12

[a] *7* Exodus 32:6 [b] *26* Psalm 24:1 [c] *28* Some manuscripts *conscience' sake, for "the earth is the Lord's and everything in it"*

29the other man's conscience, I mean, not yours.
For why should my freedom[p] be judged by another's conscience? 30If I take part in the meal with
thankfulness, why am I denounced because of
something I thank God for?[q]
31So whether you eat or drink or whatever you
do, do it all for the glory of God.[r] 32Do not cause
anyone to stumble,[s] whether Jews, Greeks or the
church of God[t]— 33even as I try to please everybody in every way.[u] For I am not seeking my own
good but the good of many, so that they may be
saved.[v] 1Follow my example,[w] as I follow
11 the example of Christ.

Propriety in Worship

2I praise you[x] for remembering me in everything[y] and for holding to the teachings,[a] just as I
passed them on to you.[z]
3Now I want you to realize that the head of
every man is Christ,[a] and the head of the woman
is man,[b] and the head of Christ is God.[c] 4Every
man who prays or prophesies with his head covered dishonors his head. 5And every woman who
prays or prophesies[d] with her head uncovered dishonors her head—it is just as though her head
were shaved.[e] 6If a woman does not cover her
head, she should have her hair cut off; and if it is
a disgrace for a woman to have her hair cut or
shaved off, she should cover her head. 7A man
ought not to cover his head,[b] since he is the
image[f] and glory of God; but the woman is the
glory of man. 8For man did not come from
woman, but woman from man;[g] 9neither was man
created for woman, but woman for man.[h] 10For
this reason, and because of the angels, the woman
ought to have a sign of authority on her head.
11In the Lord, however, woman is not independent of man, nor is man independent of
woman. 12For as woman came from man, so also
man is born of woman. But everything comes
from God.[i] 13Judge for yourselves: Is it proper for
a woman to pray to God with her head uncovered?
14Does not the very nature of things teach you that
if a man has long hair, it is a disgrace to him, 15but
that if a woman has long hair, it is her glory? For
long hair is given to her as a covering. 16If anyone
wants to be contentious about this, we have no
other practice—nor do the churches of God.[j]

The Lord's Supper

17In the following directives I have no praise for
you,[k] for your meetings do more harm than good.
18In the first place, I hear that when you come

10:29 [p]Ro 14:16; 1Co 9:1,19
10:30 [q]Ro 14:6
10:31 [r]Col 3:17; 1Pe 4:11
10:32 [s]Ac 24:16 [t]Ac 20:28
10:33 [u]Ro 15:2; 1Co 9:22 [v]Ro 11:14
11:1 [w]1Co 4:16
11:2 [x]ver 17,22 [y]1Co 4:17 [z]1Co 15:2,3; 2Th 2:15
11:3 [a]Eph 1:22 [b]Ge 3:16; Eph 5:23 [c]1Co 3:23
11:5 [d]Ac 21:9 [e]Dt 21:12
11:7 [f]Ge 1:26; Jas 3:9
11:8 [g]Ge 2:21-23; 1Ti 2:13
11:9 [h]Ge 2:18
11:12 [i]Ro 11:36
11:16 [j]1Co 7:17
11:17 [k]ver 2,22

[a] 2 Or *traditions* [b] 4–7 Or *4Every man who prays or prophesies with long hair dishonors his head. 5And every woman who prays or prophesies with no covering ⌊of hair⌋ on her head dishonors her head—she is just like one of the "shorn women." 6If a woman has no covering, let her be for now with short hair, but since it is a disgrace for a woman to have her hair shorn or shaved, she should grow it again. 7A man ought not to have long hair*

An Area of Dispute

1CO 11:3–16

In this much-studied and disputed passage of Scripture, Paul gives instructions regarding worship in the family of believers (see the note on 1 Timothy 2:9–15, page 1968). In the Corinthian church at this time, women who were delighted with their new-found freedom in Christ threw aside all present cultural principles and prayed and prophesied in worship services with their heads uncovered. Proper feminine attire at the time called for a head covering because women who refused to cover their heads in public were considered loose and promiscuous.

The disputes over this passage arise, of course, when applying it to contemporary society. Are the principles given cultural or theological? All the differing views and interpretations cannot be included in this short essay; however, the underlying principle of order is relevant to any age. Paul begins his treatise by explaining the order or "flow" of creation: God the Father to Christ the Son to man to woman. Each has a specific and meaningful place. He is not implying the man is more important than the woman any more than he is implying the Father is more important than the Son. Each is equal in essence, varied in role and interdependent (1Co 11:11–12).

The Lord's Supper

1CO 11:17-34

In the early church, communion was part of regular worship. It was preceded by a "love feast," which in the Corinthian church degenerated into a party that Paul says did "more harm than good" (1Co 11:17). The meal included food brought in by the participants. However, class distinction quickly caused the time of fellowship to become a time of disunity. The rich brought more food and ate more; whereas the poor brought less and departed hungry.

Paul urges the Corinthians to take the Lord's Supper seriously and tells them that the one who does not do so, "eats and drinks judgment on himself" (1Co 11:29). Anytime other believers are excluded from the table, as was happening in Corinth, the Lord's Supper is being taken in an "unworthy manner" (1Co 11:27). When we willfully pay more attention to our own needs and wishes than to those of others in our worship community, when our worship through the Lord's Supper divides rather than draws us together, we need to carefully examine our hearts to ascertain if we are taking this sacrament seriously enough.

together as a church, there are divisions[l] among
you, and to some extent I believe it. 19No doubt
there have to be differences among you to show
which of you have God's approval.[m] 20When you
come together, it is not the Lord's Supper you eat,
21for as you eat, each of you goes ahead without
waiting for anybody else.[n] One remains hungry,
another gets drunk. 22Don't you have homes to eat
and drink in? Or do you despise the church of
God[o] and humiliate those who have nothing?[p]
What shall I say to you? Shall I praise you[q] for
this? Certainly not!

23For I received from the Lord[r] what I also
passed on to you:[s] The Lord Jesus, on the night
he was betrayed, took bread, 24and when he had
given thanks, he broke it and said, "This is my
body, which is for you; do this in remembrance
of me." 25In the same way, after supper he took
the cup, saying, "This cup is the new covenant[t] in
my blood;[u] do this, whenever you drink it, in
remembrance of me." 26For whenever you eat this
bread and drink this cup, you proclaim the Lord's
death until he comes.

27Therefore, whoever eats the bread or drinks
the cup of the Lord in an unworthy manner will
be guilty of sinning against the body and blood of
the Lord.[v] 28A man ought to examine himself[w]
before he eats of the bread and drinks of the cup.
29For anyone who eats and drinks without recognizing the body of the Lord eats and drinks judgment on himself. 30That is why many among you
are weak and sick, and a number of you have fall-
en asleep. 31But if we judged ourselves, we would
not come under judgment.[x] 32When we are judged
by the Lord, we are being disciplined[y] so that we
will not be condemned with the world.

33So then, my brothers, when you come together to eat, wait for each other. 34If anyone is hungry,[z] he should eat at home,[a] so that when you
meet together it may not result in judgment.

And when I come[b] I will give further directions.

Spiritual Gifts

12 Now about spiritual gifts,[c] brothers, I do not
want you to be ignorant. 2You know that
when you were pagans,[d] somehow or other you
were influenced and led astray to mute idols.[e]
3Therefore I tell you that no one who is speaking
by the Spirit of God says, "Jesus be cursed,"[f] and
no one can say, "Jesus is Lord,"[g] except by the
Holy Spirit.[h]

4There are different kinds of gifts, but the same
Spirit.[i] 5There are different kinds of service, but the
same Lord. 6There are different kinds of working,
but the same God[j] works all of them in all men.

7Now to each one the manifestation of the Spirit is given for the common good.[k] 8To one there is
given through the Spirit the message of wisdom,[l]
to another the message of knowledge[m] by means
of the same Spirit, 9to another faith[n] by the same
Spirit, to another gifts of healing[o] by that one Spir-

11:18 [l]1Co 1:10-12; 3:3
11:19 [m]1Jn 2:19
11:21 [n]2Pe 2:13; Jude 12
11:22 [o]1Co 10:32 [p]Jas 2:6 [q]ver 2,17
11:23 [r]Gal 1:12 [s]1Co 15:3
11:25 [t]Lk 22:20 [u]1Co 10:16
11:27 [v]Heb 10:29
11:28 [w]2Co 13:5
11:31 [x]Ps 32:5; 1Jn 1:9
11:32 [y]Ps 94:12; Heb 12:7-10; Rev 3:19
11:34 [z]ver 21 [a]ver 22 [b]1Co 4:19
12:1 [c]Ro 1:11; 1Co 14:1,37
12:2 [d]Eph 2:11, 12; 1Pe 4:3 [e]Ps 115:5; Jer 10:5; Hab 2:18,19; 1Th 1:9
12:3 [f]Ro 9:3 [g]Jn 13:13 [h]1Jn 4:2,3
12:4 [i]Ro 12:4-8; Eph 4:11; Heb 2:4
12:6 [j]Eph 4:6
12:7 [k]Eph 4:12
12:8 [l]1Co 2:6 [m]2Co 8:7
12:9 [n]Mt 17:19, 20; 2Co 4:13 [o]ver 28,30

it, [10]to another miraculous powers,[p] to another prophecy, to another distinguishing between spirits,[q] to another speaking in different kinds of tongues,[a][r] and to still another the interpretation of tongues.[a] [11]All these are the work of one and the same Spirit,[s] and he gives them to each one, just as he determines.

One Body, Many Parts

[12]The body is a unit, though it is made up of many parts; and though all its parts are many, they form one body.[t] So it is with Christ.[u] [13]For we were all baptized by[b] one Spirit[v] into one body—whether Jews or Greeks, slave or free[w]—and we were all given the one Spirit to drink.[x]

[14]Now the body is not made up of one part but of many. [15]If the foot should say, "Because I am not a hand, I do not belong to the body," it would not for that reason cease to be part of the body. [16]And if the ear should say, "Because I am not an eye, I do not belong to the body," it would not for that reason cease to be part of the body. [17]If the whole body were an eye, where would the sense of hearing be? If the whole body were an ear, where would the sense of smell be? [18]But in fact God has arranged[y] the parts in the body, every one of them, just as he wanted them to be.[z] [19]If they were all one part, where would the body be? [20]As it is, there are many parts, but one body.[a]

[21]The eye cannot say to the hand, "I don't need you!" And the head cannot say to the feet, "I don't need you!" [22]On the contrary, those parts of the body that seem to be weaker are indispensable, [23]and the parts that we think are less honorable we treat with special honor. And the parts that are unpresentable are treated with special modesty, [24]while our presentable parts need no special treatment. But God has combined the members of the body and has given greater honor to the parts that lacked it, [25]so that there should be no division in the body, but that its parts should have equal concern for each other. [26]If one part suffers, every part suffers with it; if one part is honored, every part rejoices with it.

[27]Now you are the body of Christ,[b] and each one of you is a part of it.[c] [28]And in the church[d] God has appointed first of all apostles,[e] second prophets, third teachers, then workers of miracles, also those having gifts of healing,[f] those able to help others, those with gifts of administration,[g] and those speaking in different kinds of tongues.[h] [29]Are all apostles? Are all prophets? Are all teachers? Do all work miracles? [30]Do all have gifts of healing? Do all speak in tongues[c]?[i] Do all interpret? [31]But eagerly desire[d][j] the greater gifts.

12:10 [p]Gal 3:5 [q]1Jn 4:1 [r]Mk 16:17
12:11 [s]ver 4
12:12 [t]Ro 12:5 [u]ver 27
12:13 [v]Eph 2:18 [w]Gal 3:28; Col 3:11 [x]Jn 7:37-39
12:18 [y]ver 28 [z]ver 11
12:20 [a]ver 12,14
12:27 [b]Eph 1:23; 4:12; Col 1:18,24 [c]Ro 12:5
12:28 [d]1Co 10:32 [e]Eph 4:11 [f]ver 9 [g]Ro 12:6-8 [h]ver 10
12:30 [i]ver 10
12:31 [j]1Co 14:1,39

[a] *10* Or *languages;* also in verse 28 [b] *13* Or *with;* or *in*
[c] *30* Or *other languages* [d] *31* Or *But you are eagerly desiring*

Spiritual Gifts

1CO 12

The coming of the Holy Spirit to dwell permanently in the hearts of believers takes place on the day of Pentecost (Ac 2:1–4,17–18) and is a clear fulfillment of prophecy (Joel 2:28–29). Part of the work of the Holy Spirit is to give spiritual gifts to each believer for the building up of the body (Eph 4:11–13) so that they might reflect Christ to a broken world. Though everyone has some gift(s), no one has every gift (1Co 12:18–20). No spiritual gift is rightly used if its exercise contradicts the law of love (1Co 13). The great principle of spiritual gifts is that their expression leads to interdependence among members of the body. Each gift has its own value, just as each part of the physical body is needed; none should be disdained, rather "those parts of the body that seem to be weaker are indispensable" (1Co 12:22). Paul concludes by encouraging believers to seek "the greater gifts" (1Co 12:31)—those that encourage, lift up and edify fellow believers through humility and unselfishness.

The Love Chapter

1CO 13

This passage is universally considered one of the great "jewels of Scripture." For its sheer beauty and moral force, it has been admired by believers as well as unbelievers through the ages. Paul's intent is to draw the Corinthians away from questions of who is wiser, more spiritual or more important. Love is the point. Without love, no other gift matters.

Love takes many forms, all active: patience, kindness, humility, unselfishness, forgiveness, holiness, protection, trust. The three impeccable Christian graces are faith and hope and love. But love reigns supreme.

Review the words used in this chapter, making special note of those that describe what love is and then what love is not. Over the next weeks and months, ask God to work in your life to build up loving characteristics.

Love

And now I will show you the most excellent
way.
13 If I speak in the tongues[a][k] of men and of
angels, but have not love, I am only a
resounding gong or a clanging cymbal. [2]If I have
the gift of prophecy and can fathom all mysteries[l]
and all knowledge, and if I have a faith[m] that can
move mountains,[n] but have not love, I am nothing.
[3]If I give all I possess to the poor[o] and surrender
my body to the flames,[b][p] but have not love,
I gain nothing.
[4]Love is patient,[q] love is kind. It does not envy,
it does not boast, it is not proud. [5]It is not rude, it
is not self-seeking,[r] it is not easily angered, it
keeps no record of wrongs. [6]Love does not delight
in evil[s] but rejoices with the truth.[t] [7]It always protects,
always trusts, always hopes, always
perseveres.
[8]Love never fails. But where there are prophecies,[u]
they will cease; where there are tongues,[v]
they will be stilled; where there is knowledge, it
will pass away. [9]For we know in part[w] and we
prophesy in part, [10]but when perfection comes,[x]
the imperfect disappears. [11]When I was a child, I
talked like a child, I thought like a child, I reasoned
like a child. When I became a man, I put
childish ways behind me. [12]Now we see but a poor
reflection as in a mirror; then we shall see face to
face.[y] Now I know in part; then I shall know fully,
even as I am fully known.[z]
[13]And now these three remain: faith, hope and
love.[a] But the greatest of these is love.[b]

Gifts of Prophecy and Tongues

14 Follow the way of love[c] and eagerly desire[d]
spiritual gifts,[e] especially the gift of prophecy.
[2]For anyone who speaks in a tongue[c][f] does
not speak to men but to God. Indeed, no one
understands him; he utters mysteries[g] with his
spirit.[d] [3]But everyone who prophesies speaks to
men for their strengthening,[h] encouragement and
comfort. [4]He who speaks in a tongue[i] edifies himself,
but he who prophesies[j] edifies the church. [5]I
would like every one of you to speak in tongues,[e]
but I would rather have you prophesy.[k] He who
prophesies is greater than one who speaks in
tongues,[e] unless he interprets, so that the church
may be edified.
[6]Now, brothers, if I come to you and speak in
tongues, what good will I be to you, unless I bring
you some revelation[l] or knowledge or prophecy
or word of instruction?[m] [7]Even in the case of lifeless
things that make sounds, such as the flute or
harp, how will anyone know what tune is being
played unless there is a distinction in the notes?

13:1 [k]ver 8
13:2 [l]1Co 14:2 [m]1Co 12:9 [n]Mt 17:20; 21:21
13:3 [o]Mt 6:2 [p]Da 3:28
13:4 [q]1Th 5:14
13:5 [r]1Co 10:24
13:6 [s]2Th 2:12 [t]2Jn 4; 3Jn 3,4
13:8 [u]ver 2 [v]ver 1
13:9 [w]ver 12; 1Co 8:2
13:10 [x]Php 3:12
13:12 [y]Ge 32:30; 2Co 5:7; 1Jn 3:2 [z]1Co 8:3
13:13 [a]Gal 5:5,6 [b]1Co 16:14
14:1 [c]1Co 16:14 [d]ver 39; 1Co 12:31 [e]1Co 12:1
14:2 [f]Mk 16:17 [g]1Co 13:2
14:3 [h]ver 4,5,12, 17,26; Ro 14:19
14:4 [i]Mk 16:17 [j]1Co 13:2
14:5 [k]Nu 11:29
14:6 [l]ver 26; Eph 1:17 [m]Ro 6:17

[a] *1* Or *languages* [b] *3* Some early manuscripts *body that I may boast* [c] *2* Or *another language*; also in verses 4, 13, 14, 19, 26 and 27 [d] *2* Or *by the Spirit* [e] *5* Or *other languages*; also in verses 6, 18, 22, 23 and 39

14:8 [n]Nu 10:9; Jer 4:19

8 Again, if the trumpet does not sound a clear call,
who will get ready for battle?[n] 9 So it is with you.
Unless you speak intelligible words with your
tongue, how will anyone know what you are saying? You will just be speaking into the air.
10 Undoubtedly there are all sorts of languages in
the world, yet none of them is without meaning.
11 If then I do not grasp the meaning of what someone is saying, I am a foreigner to the speaker, and
he is a foreigner to me. 12 So it is with you. Since
you are eager to have spiritual gifts, try to excel
in gifts that build up the church.
13 For this reason anyone who speaks in a
tongue should pray that he may interpret what he
says. 14 For if I pray in a tongue, my spirit prays,
but my mind is unfruitful. 15 So what shall I do? I
will pray with my spirit, but I will also pray with

14:15 [o]Eph 5:19; Col 3:16

my mind; I will sing[o] with my spirit, but I will
also sing with my mind. 16 If you are praising God
with your spirit, how can one who finds himself

14:16 [p]Dt 27:15-26; 1Ch 16:36; Ne 8:6; Ps 106:48; Rev 5:14; 7:12 [q]1Co 11:24

among those who do not understand[a] say
"Amen"[p] to your thanksgiving,[q] since he does not
know what you are saying? 17 You may be giving
thanks well enough, but the other man is not
edified.
18 I thank God that I speak in tongues more than
all of you. 19 But in the church I would rather
speak five intelligible words to instruct others
than ten thousand words in a tongue.

14:20 [r]Eph 4:14; Heb 5:12,13; 1Pe 2:2 [s]Ro 16:19

20 Brothers, stop thinking like children.[r] In
regard to evil be infants,[s] but in your thinking be
adults. 21 In the Law[t] it is written:

14:21 [t]Jn 10:34 [u]Isa 28:11,12

"Through men of strange tongues
and through the lips of foreigners
I will speak to this people,
but even then they will not listen to
me,"[b][u]
says the Lord.

14:22 [v]ver 1

22 Tongues, then, are a sign, not for believers but
for unbelievers; prophecy,[v] however, is for believers, not for unbelievers. 23 So if the whole church
comes together and everyone speaks in tongues,
and some who do not understand[c] or some unbelievers come in, will they not say that you are out

14:23 [w]Ac 2:13

of your mind?[w] 24 But if an unbeliever or someone
who does not understand[d] comes in while everybody is prophesying, he will be convinced by all
that he is a sinner and will be judged by all, 25 and
the secrets of his heart will be laid bare. So he will

14:25 [x]Isa 45:14; Zec 8:23

fall down and worship God, exclaiming, "God is
really among you!"[x]

Orderly Worship

14:26 [y]1Co 12:7-10 [z]Eph 5:19 [a]ver 6

26 What then shall we say, brothers? When you
come together, everyone[y] has a hymn,[z] or a word
of instruction,[a] a revelation, a tongue or an interpretation. All of these must be done for the

[a] *16* Or *among the inquirers* [b] *21* Isaiah 28:11,12 [c] *23* Or *some inquirers* [d] *24* Or *or some inquirer*

Use of Spiritual Gifts

1CO 14:22-25

In Paul's discussion of spiritual gifts, one primary consideration shapes the force of his *argument:* How can the use of that spiritual gift benefit others, *especially* the body of Christ? Thus, while the gift of tongues—*speaking in unintelligible speech*—benefits the individual, without an *interpreter,* no one else can profit. He commends prophecy—speaking forth truth—because others are *strengthened, encouraged* and *comforted* in the exercise of the *gift.* The Corinthians tend to magnify the gift of tongues, seeing in it a higher form of spirituality. Paul directs their attention and ours to the gifts that are a benefit to the church, those that uplift and instruct the body of Christ.

Orderly Worship

1CO 14:26–40

The worship of the early church benefits from the participation of various members who offer psalms, teachings, tongues, revelations and interpretations. Paul encourages this, but stresses two principles: All must be done for the strengthening of the body and all must be done "in a fitting and orderly way" (1Co 14:40). God is not a God of disorder but of peace (1Co 14:33).

Paul appears to expect the participation of women (see 1Co 11:5, where women pray and prophesy). Various interpretations have been offered then regarding his exhortation that women should "remain silent" (1Co 14:34). At one end of the spectrum are those who think Paul is disallowing all speech by women in worship. Others think Corinthian women were asking questions about the meaning of particular prophecies and messages in tongues in a disruptive manner and should have been quiet. Others consider that since the main subject of discussion is tongues, the prohibition here is that women should refrain from ecstatic utterance during worship. It is instructive to note that Paul discourages speech by other worship participants in two other instances in this passage (1Co 14:28,30). His instructions on silence then are not aimed only at women and are intended primarily to bring respect and order into the church's worship experience.

strengthening[b] of the church. 27If anyone speaks
in a tongue, two—or at the most three—should
speak, one at a time, and someone must interpret.
28If there is no interpreter, the speaker should keep
quiet in the church and speak to himself and God.
29Two or three prophets should speak, and the
others should weigh carefully what is said.[c] 30And
if a revelation comes to someone who is sitting
down, the first speaker should stop. 31For you can
all prophesy in turn so that everyone may be
instructed and encouraged. 32The spirits of prophets are subject to the control of prophets.[d] 33For
God is not a God of disorder[e] but of peace.
As in all the congregations of the saints,[f]
34women should remain silent in the churches.
They are not allowed to speak, but must be in
submission,[g] as the Law[h] says. 35If they want to
inquire about something, they should ask their
own husbands at home; for it is disgraceful for a
woman to speak in the church.
36Did the word of God originate with you? Or
are you the only people it has reached? 37If anybody thinks he is a prophet[i] or spiritually gifted,
let him acknowledge that what I am writing to
you is the Lord's command.[j] 38If he ignores this,
he himself will be ignored.[a]
39Therefore, my brothers, be eager[k] to prophesy,
and do not forbid speaking in tongues. 40But
everything should be done in a fitting and orderly[l] way.

The Resurrection of Christ

15 Now, brothers, I want to remind you of the
gospel[m] I preached to you, which you
received and on which you have taken your stand.
2By this gospel you are saved,[n] if you hold firmly[o]
to the word I preached to you. Otherwise, you
have believed in vain.
3For what I received[p] I passed on to you[q] as of
first importance[b]: that Christ died for our sins[r]
according to the Scriptures,[s] 4that he was buried,
that he was raised[t] on the third day[u] according to
the Scriptures,[v] 5and that he appeared to Peter,[c w]
and then to the Twelve.[x] 6After that, he appeared
to more than five hundred of the brothers at the
same time, most of whom are still living, though
some have fallen asleep. 7Then he appeared to
James, then to all the apostles,[y] 8and last of all he
appeared to me also,[z] as to one abnormally born.
9For I am the least of the apostles[a] and do not
even deserve to be called an apostle, because I
persecuted[b] the church of God. 10But by the grace
of God I am what I am, and his grace to me[c] was
not without effect. No, I worked harder than all
of them[d]—yet not I, but the grace of God that was
with me.[e] 11Whether, then, it was I or they, this is
what we preach, and this is what you believed.

14:26 [b]Ro 14:19
14:29 [c]1Co 12:10
14:32 [d]1Jn 4:1
14:33 [e]ver 40 [f]Ac 9:13
14:34 [g]1Ti 2:11,12 [h]Ge 3:16
14:37 [i]2Co 10:7 [j]1Jn 4:6
14:39 [k]1Co 12:31
14:40 [l]ver 33
15:1 [m]Ro 2:16
15:2 [n]Ro 1:16 [o]Ro 11:22
15:3 [p]Gal 1:12 [q]1Co 11:23 [r]Isa 53:5; 1Pe 2:24 [s]Lk 24:27; Ac 26:22,23
15:4 [t]Ac 2:24 [u]Mt 16:21 [v]Ac 2:25,30,31
15:5 [w]Lk 24:34 [x]Mk 16:14
15:7 [y]Lk 24:33,36,37; Ac 1:3,4
15:8 [z]Ac 9:3-6,17; 1Co 9:1
15:9 [a]Eph 3:8; 1Ti 1:15 [b]Ac 8:3
15:10 [c]Ro 12:3 [d]2Co 11:23 [e]Php 2:13

[a] 38 Some manuscripts *If he is ignorant of this, let him be ignorant* [b] 3 Or *you at the first* [c] 5 Greek *Cephas*

The Resurrection of the Dead

12But if it is preached that Christ has been raised
15:12 [f]Ac 17:32; 23:8; 2Ti 2:18 from the dead, how can some of you say that there
is no resurrection of the dead?[f] 13If there is no res-
urrection of the dead, then not even Christ has
been raised. 14And if Christ has not been raised,[g]
15:14 [g]1Th 4:14 our preaching is useless and so is your faith.
15More than that, we are then found to be false witnesses about God, for we have testified about God
15:15 [h]Ac 2:24 that he raised Christ from the dead.[h] But he did not
raise him if in fact the dead are not raised. 16For if
the dead are not raised, then Christ has not been
15:17 [i]Ro 4:25 raised either. 17And if Christ has not been raised,
your faith is futile; you are still in your sins.[i]
18Then those also who have fallen asleep in Christ
are lost. 19If only for this life we have hope in
15:19 [j]1Co 4:9 Christ, we are to be pitied more than all men.[j]
20But Christ has indeed been raised from the
15:20 [k]1Pe 1:3 [l]ver 23; Ac 26:23; Rev 1:5 [m]ver 6,18 dead,[k] the firstfruits[l] of those who have fallen
asleep.[m] 21For since death came through a man,[n]
the resurrection of the dead comes also through a
man. 22For as in Adam all die, so in Christ all will
be made alive.[o] 23But each in his own turn: Christ,
15:21 [n]Ro 5:12 the firstfruits;[p] then, when he comes,[q] those who
belong to him. 24Then the end will come, when he
15:22 [o]Ro 5:14-18 hands over the kingdom[r] to God the Father after he
has destroyed all dominion, authority and power.[s]
15:23 [p]ver 20 [q]ver 52 25For he must reign until he has put all his enemies
under his feet.[t] 26The last enemy to be destroyed is
death.[u] 27For he "has put everything under his
15:24 [r]Da 7:14,27 [s]Ro 8:38 feet."[a][v] Now when it says that "everything" has
been put under him, it is clear that this does not
include God himself, who put everything under
15:25 [t]Ps 110:1; Mt 22:44 Christ.[w] 28When he has done this, then the Son
himself will be made subject to him who put every-
thing under him,[x] so that God may be all in all.[y]
15:26 [u]2Ti 1:10; Rev 20:14; 21:4 29Now if there is no resurrection, what will
those do who are baptized for the dead? If the
dead are not raised at all, why are people baptized
15:27 [v]Ps 8:6 [w]Mt 28:18 for them? 30And as for us, why do we endanger
ourselves every hour?[z] 31I die every day[a]—I mean
that, brothers—just as surely as I glory over you
15:28 [x]Php 3:21 [y]1Co 3:23 in Christ Jesus our Lord. 32If I fought wild beasts[b]
in Ephesus[c] for merely human reasons, what have
I gained? If the dead are not raised,

15:30 [z]2Co 11:26 "Let us eat and drink,
for tomorrow we die."[b][d]

15:31 [a]Ro 8:36 33Do not be misled: "Bad company corrupts good
character." 34Come back to your senses as you
15:32 [b]2Co 1:8 [c]Ac 18:19 [d]Isa 22:13; Lk 12:19 ought, and stop sinning; for there are some who
are ignorant of God—I say this to your shame.

The Resurrection Body

15:35 [e]Ro 9:19 [f]Eze 37:3 35But someone may ask,[e] "How are the dead
raised? With what kind of body will they come?"[f]
15:36 [g]Lk 11:40 [h]Jn 12:24 36How foolish![g] What you sow does not come to
life unless it dies.[h] 37When you sow, you do not

[a] 27 Psalm 8:6 [b] 32 Isaiah 22:13

Death Is Defeated

1CO 15:22-28

Gnostic philosophy, which influenced the Corinthians, viewed the body as evil and the spirit as good. Thus, Paul devotes significant space in his letter to the doctrine of the resurrection of the body.

Paul says that if the resurrection is mere fable, then Christians should be pitied for basing their hope on a myth (1Co 15:19,32). *But* (1Co 15:20)—that's a wonderful word in this context—Christ's victory places all things, including death, in subjection to him. Death is our inheritance from Adam, but we inherit life eternal through Christ's victory over death on Easter morning. As we die in Adam, so we are made alive in Christ. There are many enemies, and the most powerful is death. Christ defeats even that great enemy for us and offers us the results: eternal life with him in the glorious kingdom he will deliver to his Father "so that God may be all in all" (1Co 15:28).

We Will Be Changed

1CO 15:51-54

In this prelude to Paul's glorious proclamation "Death has been swallowed up in victory" (1Co 15:54), Paul discloses a "mystery" (wisdom that would not otherwise be known). Those who are alive when Christ returns will not taste death; in an instant, they will be changed from their perishable state into their imperishable form. The last trumpet will sound, reminiscent of the trumpet at Mt. Sinai (Ex 19:16). The dead in Christ will rise first, then those who are alive will be caught up with them to meet the Lord in the air (1Th 4:17). Death itself will be an enemy that is forever conquered. The "sting" and "victory" of death are forever removed (1Co 15:55). Paul intends these words to be a beacon of hope and encouragement to the Corinthians and to us so that we will be firm in our commitment and faith.

plant the body that will be, but just a seed, perhaps of wheat or of something else. 38But God
gives it a body as he has determined, and to each
kind of seed he gives its own body.[i] 39All flesh is 15:38
not the same: Men have one kind of flesh, animals [i]Ge 1:11
have another, birds another and fish another.
40There are also heavenly bodies and there are
earthly bodies; but the splendor of the heavenly
bodies is one kind, and the splendor of the earthly bodies is another. 41The sun has one kind of
splendor, the moon another and the stars another;
and star differs from star in splendor. 15:42
42So will it be[j] with the resurrection of the dead. [j]Da 12:3;
The body that is sown is perishable, it is raised Mt 13:43
imperishable; 43it is sown in dishonor, it is raised 15:43
in glory;[k] it is sown in weakness, it is raised in [k]Php 3:21;
power; 44it is sown a natural body, it is raised a Col 3:4
spiritual body.[l] 15:44
If there is a natural body, there is also a spiritu- [l]ver 50
al body. 45So it is written: "The first man Adam 15:45
became a living being"[a];[m] the last Adam,[n] a life- [m]Ge 2:7
giving spirit.[o] 46The spiritual did not come first, [n]Ro 5:14
but the natural, and after that the spiritual. 47The [o]Jn 5:21; Ro 8:2
first man was of the dust of the earth,[p] the second 15:47
man from heaven.[q] 48As was the earthly man, so [p]Ge 2:7; 3:19
are those who are of the earth; and as is the man [q]Jn 3:13,31
from heaven, so also are those who are of heav- 15:48
en.[r] 49And just as we have borne the likeness of [r]Php 3:20,21
the earthly man,[s] so shall we[b] bear the likeness of 15:49
the man from heaven.[t] [s]Ge 5:3
50I declare to you, brothers, that flesh and [t]Ro 8:29
blood[u] cannot inherit the kingdom of God, nor 15:50
does the perishable inherit the imperishable. 51Lis- [u]Jn 3:3,5
ten, I tell you a mystery:[v] We will not all sleep, 15:51
but we will all be changed[w]— 52in a flash, in the [v]1Co 13:2
twinkling of an eye, at the last trumpet. For the [w]Php 3:21
trumpet will sound,[x] the dead[y] will be raised 15:52
imperishable, and we will be changed. 53For the [x]Mt 24:31
perishable must clothe itself with the imperish- [y]Jn 5:25
able,[z] and the mortal with immortality. 54When 15:53
the perishable has been clothed with the imper- [z]2Co 5:2,4
ishable, and the mortal with immortality, then the
saying that is written will come true: "Death has
been swallowed up in victory."[c][a] 15:54 [a]Isa 25:8;

> 55"Where, O death, is your victory? Rev 20:14
> Where, O death, is your sting?"[d][b] 15:55 [b]Hos 13:14

56The sting of death is sin,[c] and the power of sin is
the law.[d] 57But thanks be to God![e] He gives us the 15:56
victory through our Lord Jesus Christ.[f] [c]Ro 5:12 [d]Ro 4:15
58Therefore, my dear brothers, stand firm. Let 15:57
nothing move you. Always give yourselves fully [e]2Co 2:14
to the work of the Lord,[g] because you know that [f]Ro 8:37
your labor in the Lord is not in vain. 15:58 [g]1Co 16:10

The Collection for God's People

16 Now about the collection[h] for God's people:[i] 16:1 [h]Ac 24:17
Do what I told the Galatian[j] churches to do. [i]Ac 9:13 [j]Ac 16:6

[a] 45 Gen. 2:7 [b] 49 Some early manuscripts *so let us*
[c] 54 Isaiah 25:8 [d] 55 Hosea 13:14

16:2 [k]Ac 20:7 [2]On the first day of every week,[k] each one of you
[l]2Co 9:4,5 should set aside a sum of money in keeping with
his income, saving it up, so that when I come no
16:3 collections will have to be made.[l] [3]Then, when I
[m]2Co 8:18, 19 arrive, I will give letters of introduction to the men
you approve[m] and send them with your gift to
16:5 [n]1Co 4:19 Jerusalem. [4]If it seems advisable for me to go also,
[o]Ac 19:21 they will accompany me.

16:6 [p]Ro 15:24

Personal Requests

[5]After I go through Macedonia, I will come to
16:7 [q]Ac 18:21 you[n]—for I will be going through Macedonia.[o]
[6]Perhaps I will stay with you awhile, or even spend
16:8 the winter, so that you can help me on my jour-
[r]Ac 18:19 [s]Ac 2:1 ney,[p] wherever I go. [7]I do not want to see you now
and make only a passing visit; I hope to spend
16:9 [t]Ac 14:27 some time with you, if the Lord permits.[q] [8]But I
will stay on at Ephesus[r] until Pentecost,[s] [9]because
16:10 a great door for effective work has opened to me,[t]
[u]Ac 16:1 [v]1Co 15:58 and there are many who oppose me.
[10]If Timothy[u] comes, see to it that he has noth-
16:11 [w]1Ti 4:12 ing to fear while he is with you, for he is carrying
[x]Ac 15:33 on the work of the Lord,[v] just as I am. [11]No one,
then, should refuse to accept him.[w] Send him on
16:12 [y]Ac 18:24; his way in peace[x] so that he may return to me. I
1Co 1:12 am expecting him along with the brothers.
[12]Now about our brother Apollos:[y] I strongly
16:13 [z]Gal 5:1; urged him to go to you with the brothers. He was
Php 1:27; quite unwilling to go now, but he will go when
1Th 3:8; 2Th 2:15 he has the opportunity.
[a]Eph 6:10 [13]Be on your guard; stand firm[z] in the faith; be
men of courage; be strong.[a] [14]Do everything in
16:14 [b]1Co 14:1 love.[b]
[15]You know that the household of Stephanas[c]
16:15 [c]1Co 1:16 were the first converts[d] in Achaia,[e] and they have
[d]Ro 16:5 devoted themselves to the service of the saints. I
[e]Ac 18:12 urge you, brothers, [16]to submit[f] to such as these
16:16 and to everyone who joins in the work, and labors
[f]Heb 13:17 at it. [17]I was glad when Stephanas, Fortunatus and
Achaicus arrived, because they have supplied
16:17 [g]2Co 11:9; what was lacking from you.[g] [18]For they refreshed[h]
Php 2:30 my spirit and yours also. Such men deserve
16:18 [h]Phm 7 recognition.[i]

[i]Php 2:29

Final Greetings

16:19 [19]The churches in the province of Asia send you
[j]Ac 18:2 greetings. Aquila and Priscilla[a][j] greet you warmly
[k]Ro 16:5 in the Lord, and so does the church that meets at
16:20 their house.[k] [20]All the brothers here send you
[l]Ro 16:16 greetings. Greet one another with a holy kiss.[l]
16:21 [21]I, Paul, write this greeting in my own hand.[m]
[m]Gal 6:11; [22]If anyone does not love the Lord[n]—a curse[o] be
Col 4:18 on him. Come, O Lord[b]![p]
16:22 [23]The grace of the Lord Jesus be with you.[q]
[n]Eph 6:24 [24]My love to all of you in Christ Jesus. Amen.[c]
[o]Ro 9:3
[p]Rev 22:20

16:23 [q]Ro 16:20

[a] *19* Greek *Prisca,* a variant of *Priscilla* [b] *22* In Aramaic the expression *Come, O Lord* is *Marana tha.* [c] *24* Some manuscripts do not have *Amen.*

A Holy Kiss

1CO 16:20

A kiss was a common token of affection among early church members. In the East, a kiss is a sign of friendship among equals or one of reverence and submission to a superior. First-century Christians often *greeted each other with a kiss. In their worship services and after the Lord's Supper, they exchanged this token of friendship and respect. Paul seems to be requesting that, when his letter is publicly read, the members of the church give each other a kiss as an expression of respect and love.*

2 Corinthians

God's strength in our weakness.

Quick Study

Author
The apostle Paul.

Date Written
Later in A.D. 55.

Written From
Macedonia.

Key Passage
2 Corinthians 4:16–18
"Therefore we do not lose heart. Though outwardly we are wasting away, yet inwardly we are being renewed day by day. For our light and momentary troubles are achieving for us an eternal glory that far outweighs them all. So we fix our eyes not on what is seen, but on what is unseen. For what is seen is temporary, but what is unseen is eternal."

Paul's second letter to the Corinthians addresses his concerns about recurring problems in the church at Corinth. The conflicts of Christians living in a sinful society, false teaching about Paul's integrity of his claims to apostolic leadership, and disagreements among the believers plague this struggling church. With openness and compassion Paul declares the truth about his motives and actions as he seeks to restore unity among the believers and reestablish his role as their spiritual leader.

This letter is filled with autobiographical snippets about the apostle's life that convey Paul's feelings for this group of believers. Pulsating with emotion, Paul's words describe his ministry for Christ and the wonder of the gospel message (2Co 1–5). He rejoices at the Corinthians' repentance and response to the gospel (2Co 6–7). He praises their generous spirit and presents his rationale for sharing material blessings (2Co 8–9). Paul reminds believers of the divine strength available to them (2Co 10). And he speaks honestly about a difficulty he faces and the strength he is given to handle it (2Co 12).

Touching on the topics of ministry, personality conflicts, forgiveness, servanthood and generosity, the book of 2 Corinthians teaches dependence on God in every situation. Learning to accept criticism, growing despite conflicts, living a godly life and finding a hope for the future in the midst of present trouble are all found in the heart of 2 Corinthians: God's strength is sufficient—in any time and in any situation.

Outline

Paul's greetings and comfort.
2Co 1:1-11

Paul's ministry.
2Co 1:12–2:4

Restoring the sinner.
2Co 2:5-11

The new covenant.
2Co 2:12–3:18

Treasure in jars of clay.
2Co 4:1-15

Teachings on heaven.
2Co 4:16–5:10

The ministry of reconciliation.
2Co 5:11–6:2

Paul's joys and hardships.
2Co 5:11–7:16

Teachings on giving.
2Co 8:1–9:15

Paul defends his ministry.
2Co 10:1–12:10

Paul's love for the Corinthians.
2Co 12:11-21

Paul's warnings.
2Co 13:1-10

Final greetings.
2Co 13:11-14

The Women of 2 Corinthians

No women are mentioned in the book of 2 Corinthians.

Comfort From God

2CO 1:3-7

Paul writes from his own experience about the comfort of God and suffering with Christ. The "troubles" he speaks of were difficulties so severe that, while in Asia, he was not even sure he would survive (2Co 1:8). Paul maintains that suffering is the occasion for experiencing the compassion of God. Paul uses the word "comfort" nine times in 2 Corinthians 1:3–7. Its meaning is derived from the Greek word picture of a person who comes alongside to encourage when one is being severely tested. The word is also used in reference to the Holy Spirit (Jn 14:15; 16:7). To follow Christ is to follow him into suffering—but we can be encouraged that God comes beside us to comfort and console, to strengthen and to guide.

1 Paul, an apostle of Christ Jesus by the will of
God,[a] and Timothy our brother,

To the church of God[b] in Corinth, together with
all the saints throughout Achaia:[c]

2 Grace and peace to you from God our Father
and the Lord Jesus Christ.[d]

The God of All Comfort

3 Praise be to the God and Father of our Lord
Jesus Christ,[e] the Father of compassion and the
God of all comfort, 4 who comforts us[f] in all our
troubles, so that we can comfort those in any trouble with the comfort we ourselves have received
from God. 5 For just as the sufferings of Christ flow
over into our lives,[g] so also through Christ our
comfort overflows. 6 If we are distressed, it is for
your comfort and salvation;[h] if we are comforted,
it is for your comfort, which produces in you
patient endurance of the same sufferings we suffer. 7 And our hope for you is firm, because we
know that just as you share in our sufferings,[i] so
also you share in our comfort.

8 We do not want you to be uninformed, brothers, about the hardships we suffered[j] in the province of Asia. We were under great pressure, far
beyond our ability to endure, so that we despaired
even of life. 9 Indeed, in our hearts we felt the sentence of death. But this happened that we might
not rely on ourselves but on God,[k] who raises the
dead. 10 He has delivered us from such a deadly
peril,[l] and he will deliver us. On him we have set
our hope that he will continue to deliver us, 11 as
you help us by your prayers.[m] Then many will
give thanks[n] on our[a] behalf for the gracious favor
granted us in answer to the prayers of many.

Paul's Change of Plans

12 Now this is our boast: Our conscience[o] testifies that we have conducted ourselves in the
world, and especially in our relations with you,
in the holiness and sincerity[p] that are from God.
We have done so not according to worldly wisdom[q] but according to God's grace. 13 For we do
not write you anything you cannot read or understand. And I hope that, 14 as you have understood
us in part, you will come to understand fully that
you can boast of us just as we will boast of you in
the day of the Lord Jesus.[r]

15 Because I was confident of this, I planned to
visit you[s] first so that you might benefit twice.[t] 16 I
planned to visit you on my way[u] to Macedonia
and to come back to you from Macedonia, and
then to have you send me on my way to Judea.
17 When I planned this, did I do it lightly? Or do I
make my plans in a worldly manner[v] so that in
the same breath I say, "Yes, yes" and "No, no"?

18 But as surely as God is faithful,[w] our message
to you is not "Yes" and "No." 19 For the Son of God,

1:1 [a] 1Co 1:1; Eph 1:1; Col 1:1; 2Ti 1:1 [b] 1Co 10:32 [c] Ac 18:12
1:2 [d] Ro 1:7
1:3 [e] Eph 1:3; 1Pe 1:3
1:4 [f] 2Co 7:6,7, 13
1:5 [g] 2Co 4:10; Col 1:24
1:6 [h] 2Co 4:15
1:7 [i] Ro 8:17
1:8 [j] 1Co 15:32
1:9 [k] Jer 17:5,7
1:10 [l] Ro 15:31
1:11 [m] Ro 15:30; Php 1:19 [n] 2Co 4:15
1:12 [o] Ac 23:1 [p] 2Co 2:17 [q] 1Co 2:1,4, 13
1:14 [r] 1Co 1:8
1:15 [s] 1Co 4:19 [t] Ro 1:11,13; 15:29
1:16 [u] 1Co 16:5-7
1:17 [v] 2Co 10:2,3
1:18 [w] 1Co 1:9

[a] *11* Many manuscripts *your*

Jesus Christ, who was preached among you by me
1:19 and Silas[a] and Timothy, was not "Yes" and "No,"
[x]Heb 13:8 but in him it has always[x] been "Yes." 20 For no mat-
1:20 ter how many promises[y] God has made, they are
[y]Ro 15:8 "Yes" in Christ. And so through him the "Amen"[z]
[z]1Co 14:16 is spoken by us to the glory of God. 21 Now it is
1:21 God who makes both us and you stand firm in
[a]1Jn 2:20,27 Christ. He anointed[a] us, 22 set his seal of owner-
1:22 ship on us, and put his Spirit in our hearts as a
[b]2Co 5:5 deposit, guaranteeing what is to come.[b]
1:23 23 I call God as my witness[c] that it was in order
[c]Ro 1:9; to spare you[d] that I did not return to Corinth.
Gal 1:20 24 Not that we lord it over[e] your faith, but we work
[d]1Co 4:21; 2Co 2:1,3; with you for your joy, because it is by faith you
13:2,10 **2** stand firm.[f] 1 So I made up my mind that I
1:24 would not make another painful visit to you.[g]
[e]1Pe 5:3 2 For if I grieve you,[h] who is left to make me glad
[f]Ro 11:20; but you whom I have grieved? 3 I wrote as I did[i]
1Co 15:1 so that when I came I should not be distressed[j] by
2:1 those who ought to make me rejoice. I had confi-
[g]2Co 1:23 dence[k] in all of you, that you would all share my
2:2 joy. 4 For I wrote you[l] out of great distress and
[h]2Co 7:8 anguish of heart and with many tears, not to
2:3 grieve you but to let you know the depth of my
[i]2Co 7:8,12 [j]2Co 12:21 love for you.
[k]2Co 8:22; Gal 5:10

Forgiveness for the Sinner

2:4 5 If anyone has caused grief,[m] he has not so
[l]2Co 7:8,12 much grieved me as he has grieved all of you, to
2:5 some extent—not to put it too severely. 6 The pun-
[m]1Co 5:1,2 ishment[n] inflicted on him by the majority is sufficient for him. 7 Now instead, you ought to forgive
2:6 [n]1Co 5:4,5 and comfort him,[o] so that he will not be overwhelmed by excessive sorrow. 8 I urge you, there-
2:7 [o]Gal 6:1; fore, to reaffirm your love for him. 9 The reason I
Eph 4:32 wrote you was to see if you would stand the test
2:9 and be obedient in everything.[p] 10 If you forgive
[p]2Co 10:6 anyone, I also forgive him. And what I have for-
2:11 given—if there was anything to forgive—I have
[q]Mt 4:10 [r]Lk 22:31; forgiven in the sight of Christ for your sake, 11 in
2Co 4:4; order that Satan[q] might not outwit us. For we are
1Pe 5:8,9 not unaware of his schemes.[r]

Ministers of the New Covenant

2:12 [s]Ac 16:8
[t]Ro 1:1 12 Now when I went to Troas[s] to preach the gospel
[u]Ac 14:27 of Christ[t] and found that the Lord had opened a
2:13 door[u] for me, 13 I still had no peace of mind,[v]
[v]2Co 7:5 [w]2Co 7:6,13; because I did not find my brother Titus[w] there. So
12:18 I said good-by to them and went on to Macedonia.
14 But thanks be to God,[x] who always leads us
2:14 [x]Ro 6:17 in triumphal procession in Christ and through us
[y]Eph 5:2; spreads everywhere the fragrance[y] of the knowl-
Php 4:18 edge of him. 15 For we are to God the aroma of
2:15 Christ among those who are being saved and
[z]1Co 1:18 those who are perishing.[z] 16 To the one we are the
2:16 smell of death;[a] to the other, the fragrance of life.
[a]Lk 2:34 [b]2Co 3:5,6 And who is equal to such a task?[b] 17 Unlike so
many, we do not peddle the word of God for prof-

[a] 19 Greek *Silvanus,* a variant of *Silas*

The Fragrance of Christ

2CO 2:14-17

When Paul writes of how believers are led in "triumphal procession in Christ" (2Co 2:14), he is using a picture familiar to his readers. It was Roman custom for a victorious general to lead captives as a public spectacle before a crowd of onlookers. Paul's intent is to help us see that we who were God's enemies (Ro 5:10) have been overcome by his love and taken captive in his victory parade, on display before the world as a trophy of his extravagant grace. These Roman processions were accompanied by the sweet odor of burning spices in the streets. Through our lives the fragrance of Christ himself is released, an unmistakable odor that is pleasing and fragrant to those who accept Christ, but the odor of death to those who reject him.

Veiled Faces

2CO 3:13,18

The focus of this passage is the hope we have in Christ. When Moses came down from Mount Sinai, he covered his radiant face with a veil so that the glory of God shining from his face was hidden from the Israelites (Ex 34:33–35). They saw only a glimpse of the awesome glory of God. The veil also prevented them from seeing the glory fade from Moses' face, an indication of the temporary nature of that old covenant with God.

The ministry of the Spirit today, however, is not one of concealment but one of openness and invitation, an invitation to view the glory of God in Christ. As believers, we reflect this glory of Christ to the world, and in so doing we are slowly being changed into the image we reflect—the image of Christ—not fading as with Moses, but instead becoming an ever-increasing reflection of the glory of God. Our greatest joy is to anticipate the moment when that transformation will be complete—when we see Christ at his return (1Jn 3:2).

it.[c] On the contrary, in Christ we speak before God
with sincerity,[d] like men sent from God.[e]
3 Are we beginning to commend ourselves[f]
again? Or do we need, like some people, letters of recommendation[g] to you or from you? 2You
yourselves are our letter, written on our hearts,
known and read by everybody.[h] 3You show that
you are a letter from Christ, the result of our ministry, written not with ink but with the Spirit of
the living God, not on tablets of stone[i] but on
tablets of human hearts.[j]
4Such confidence[k] as this is ours through Christ
before God. 5Not that we are competent in ourselves to claim anything for ourselves, but our
competence comes from God.[l] 6He has made us
competent as ministers of a new covenant[m]—not
of the letter but of the Spirit; for the letter kills,
but the Spirit gives life.[n]

The Glory of the New Covenant

7Now if the ministry that brought death, which
was engraved in letters on stone, came with glory,
so that the Israelites could not look steadily at the
face of Moses because of its glory,[o] fading though
it was, 8will not the ministry of the Spirit be even
more glorious? 9If the ministry that condemns
men[p] is glorious, how much more glorious is the
ministry that brings righteousness![q] 10For what
was glorious has no glory now in comparison
with the surpassing glory. 11And if what was fading away came with glory, how much greater is
the glory of that which lasts!
12Therefore, since we have such a hope, we are
very bold.[r] 13We are not like Moses, who would
put a veil over his face[s] to keep the Israelites from
gazing at it while the radiance was fading away.
14But their minds were made dull,[t] for to this day
the same veil remains when the old covenant[u] is
read.[v] It has not been removed, because only in
Christ is it taken away. 15Even to this day when
Moses is read, a veil covers their hearts. 16But
whenever anyone turns to the Lord,[w] the veil is
taken away.[x] 17Now the Lord is the Spirit,[y] and
where the Spirit of the Lord is, there is freedom.[z]
18And we, who with unveiled faces all reflect[aa] the
Lord's glory,[b] are being transformed into his likeness[c] with ever-increasing glory, which comes
from the Lord, who is the Spirit.

Treasures in Jars of Clay

4 Therefore, since through God's mercy[d] we
have this ministry, we do not lose heart.
2Rather, we have renounced secret and shameful
ways;[e] we do not use deception, nor do we distort
the word of God.[f] On the contrary, by setting forth
the truth plainly we commend ourselves to every
man's conscience[g] in the sight of God. 3And even
if our gospel[h] is veiled,[i] it is veiled to those who
are perishing.[j] 4The god[k] of this age has blinded[l]

2:17 [c]2Co 4:2 [d]1Co 5:8 [e]2Co 1:12
3:1 [f]2Co 5:12; 12:11 [g]Ac 18:27
3:2 [h]1Co 9:2
3:3 [i]Ex 24:12 [j]Pr 3:3; Jer 31:33; Eze 11:19
3:4 [k]Eph 3:12
3:5 [l]1Co 15:10
3:6 [m]Lk 22:20 [n]Jn 6:63
3:7 [o]Ex 34:29-35
3:9 [p]ver 7 [q]Ro 1:17; 3:21,22
3:12 [r]Eph 6:19
3:13 [s]ver 7; Ex 34:33
3:14 [t]Ro 11:7,8 [u]Ac 13:15 [v]ver 6
3:16 [w]Ro 11:23 [x]Ex 34:34
3:17 [y]Isa 61:1,2 [z]Jn 8:32
3:18 [a]1Co 13:12 [b]2Co 4:4,6 [c]Ro 8:29
4:1 [d]1Co 7:25
4:2 [e]1Co 4:5 [f]2Co 2:17 [g]2Co 5:11
4:3 [h]2Co 2:12 [i]2Co 3:14 [j]1Co 1:18
4:4 [k]Jn 12:31 [l]2Co 3:14

[a] *18* Or *contemplate*

Week 42

Jars of Clay

Do you sometimes feel unworthy to be called God's child—you have too much baggage, too many wounds, too many scars? Or maybe you don't feel smart enough or spiritual enough to be used by God. If so, then you're not alone. There's a positive side to your feelings of inadequacy: God loves to use jars of clay to reveal his glory! When something beautiful flows from an ordinary vessel, it is both surprising and inspiring. This passage in 2 Corinthians compares the old covenant of righteousness through the law with the new covenant of righteousness through Jesus Christ.

When Moses comes down from Mount Sinai with the Ten Commandments, his face is radiant with the glory of God (Ex 34:29). What brings the radiance of God's glory to Moses' face (Ex 34:33-35)? Why does Moses put a veil over his face (2Co 3:13)?

Why is the glory of the new covenant better than the fading glory of the old covenant (2Co 3:6,9-11)?

Why do you, as a child of God, have an unveiled face (2Co 3:18)? Whose light shines in your heart, and what is the outcome (2Co 4:6)?

How can you keep the radiance of Christ shining in your heart and life (Lk 11:35-36; 2Co 3:18)? The closer you are to Jesus, the more like him you will become and the more light you will reflect.

What assurance do you have that you will some day be completely transformed into the likeness of Jesus and share in his glory (Ro 8:29-30; Eph 1:13-14; 1Jn 3:1-2)?

Why does God place the light of his glory within you (2Co 4:7)? What does your weakness accomplish (2Co 12:9)? How is God able to work through your weaknesses?

Enjoying God THROUGH the Word

Read Matthew 22:36-40 (page 1623). The Pharisees often try to trick Jesus with their technical questions. The law is their area of expertise. They believe strict compliance with the law's detailed instructions brings righteousness. But Jesus preaches a different view of the law. Jesus agrees that the law is to be obeyed; however, he says that what matters is the heart attitude, not outward behavior (1Sa 16:7). Jesus takes the Pharisees' outward rules of behavior and reveals the heart beneath the behavior (Mt 5:21-48). He takes the law and wraps it with love. According to Jesus, by loving God and your neighbor you fulfill every command (Mt 22:37-40).

You are now free from the law (Gal 5:18)! You are made righteous by faith in Christ Jesus (Ro 3:21-22). This glorious truth sheds light on your feelings of unworthiness. Your worthiness is not the issue. Jesus' righteousness is what matters; he has met every requirement of the law for you (Ro 8:1-4). As you keep in step with Jesus, you no longer need to struggle to measure up. Simply wrap yourself in the love of your Savior. As you are being transformed by his Spirit, your acts of love toward God and toward others fulfill every requirement of the law.

Enjoying God THROUGH Experience

What really matters in life? Ask God to show you what matters most: your heart or your hands. You are a clay jar, not a glittering treasure chest—by his design. You are not beautiful in yourself, but you are beautiful in him. This week, try to forget yourself and all your inadequacies and allow his glory to shine forth from you.

Go to page 1915 for your next weekly study.

Treasures in Jars of Clay

2CO 4

The "treasure in jars of clay" (2Co 4:7) that Paul is speaking of here is "the light of the knowledge of the glory of God" (2Co 4:6). With that introduction he sets up a series of contrasts. Affliction and weakness are the stark backdrop against which the brilliance of the light shines most brightly. The spectacle of a Roman military triumph is the metaphor many feel Paul has in mind. The Persians melted gold and silver taken as plunder or taxes and poured it into common clay pots; so the victorious Christ entrusts the riches of the gospel to poor earthen vessels like Paul, like us. The clear import is that human weakness presents no barrier to the purposes of God; indeed, his power is made more obvious in our inadequacy. We are not just overcomers, we are *more* than overcomers by virtue of the goodness and grace of God (Ro 8:37).

the minds of unbelievers, so that they cannot see
the light of the gospel of the glory of Christ, who
is the image of God. 5For we do not preach ourselves,[m] but Jesus Christ as Lord, and ourselves as
your servants[n] for Jesus' sake. 6For God, who said,
"Let light shine out of darkness,"[a][o] made his light
shine in our hearts[p] to give us the light of the
knowledge of the glory of God in the face of
Christ.

7But we have this treasure in jars of clay[q] to
show that this all-surpassing power is from God[r]
and not from us. 8We are hard pressed on every
side,[s] but not crushed; perplexed, but not in
despair; 9persecuted,[t] but not abandoned;[u] struck
down, but not destroyed.[v] 10We always carry
around in our body the death of Jesus, so that the
life of Jesus may also be revealed in our body.[w]
11For we who are alive are always being given over
to death for Jesus' sake,[x] so that his life may be
revealed in our mortal body. 12So then, death is at
work in us, but life is at work in you.[y]

13It is written: "I believed; therefore I have spoken."[b][z] With that same spirit of faith we also
believe and therefore speak, 14because we know
that the one who raised the Lord Jesus from the
dead will also raise us with Jesus[a] and present us
with you in his presence.[b] 15All this is for your
benefit, so that the grace that is reaching more
and more people may cause thanksgiving[c] to overflow to the glory of God.

16Therefore we do not lose heart. Though outwardly we are wasting away, yet inwardly[d] we are
being renewed[e] day by day. 17For our light and
momentary troubles are achieving for us an eternal glory that far outweighs them all.[f] 18So we fix
our eyes not on what is seen, but on what is
unseen.[g] For what is seen is temporary, but what
is unseen is eternal.

Our Heavenly Dwelling

5 Now we know that if the earthly[h] tent[i] we live
in is destroyed, we have a building from God,
an eternal house in heaven, not built by human
hands. 2Meanwhile we groan,[j] longing to be
clothed with our heavenly dwelling,[k] 3because
when we are clothed, we will not be found naked.
4For while we are in this tent, we groan and are
burdened, because we do not wish to be
unclothed but to be clothed with our heavenly
dwelling,[l] so that what is mortal may be swallowed up by life. 5Now it is God who has made us
for this very purpose and has given us the Spirit
as a deposit, guaranteeing what is to come.[m]

6Therefore we are always confident and know
that as long as we are at home in the body we are
away from the Lord. 7We live by faith, not by
sight.[n] 8We are confident, I say, and would prefer
to be away from the body and at home with the
Lord.[o] 9So we make it our goal to please him,[p]

4:5 [m]1Co 1:13 [n]1Co 9:19
4:6 [o]Ge 1:3 [p]2Pe 1:19
4:7 [q]Job 4:19; 2Co 5:1 [r]1Co 2:5
4:8 [s]2Co 7:5
4:9 [t]Jn 15:20 [u]Heb 13:5 [v]Ps 37:24
4:10 [w]Ro 6:5
4:11 [x]Ro 8:36
4:12 [y]2Co 13:9
4:13 [z]Ps 116:10
4:14 [a]1Th 4:14 [b]Eph 5:27
4:15 [c]2Co 1:11
4:16 [d]Ro 7:22 [e]Col 3:10
4:17 [f]Ro 8:18; 1Pe 1:6,7
4:18 [g]Ro 8:24; Heb 11:1
5:1 [h]1Co 15:47 [i]2Pe 1:13,14
5:2 [j]ver 4; Ro 8:23 [k]1Co 15:53, 54
5:4 [l]1Co 15:53, 54
5:5 [m]Ro 8:23; 2Co 1:22
5:7 [n]1Co 13:12
5:8 [o]Php 1:23
5:9 [p]Ro 14:18

[a] *6* Gen. 1:3 [b] *13* Psalm 116:10

whether we are at home in the body or away from
it. 10For we must all appear before the judgment
5:10 seat of Christ, that each one may receive what is
[q]Mt 16:27; due him[q] for the things done while in the body,
Ro 14:10; Eph 6:8 whether good or bad.

The Ministry of Reconciliation

11Since, then, we know what it is to fear the
5:11 [r]Heb 10:31; Lord,[r] we try to persuade men. What we are is
Jude 23 plain to God, and I hope it is also plain to your
[s]2Co 4:2 conscience.[s] 12We are not trying to commend our-
5:12 selves to you again,[t] but are giving you an oppor-
[t]2Co 3:1 tunity to take pride in us,[u] so that you can answer
[u]2Co 1:14 those who take pride in what is seen rather than
5:13 in what is in the heart. 13If we are out of our
[v]2Co 11:1, 16,17 mind,[v] it is for the sake of God; if we are in our
right mind, it is for you. 14For Christ's love com-
pels us, because we are convinced that one died
5:14 [w]Gal 2:20 for all, and therefore all died.[w] 15And he died for
all, that those who live should no longer live for
5:15 [x]Ro 14:7-9 themselves[x] but for him who died for them and
was raised again.
16So from now on we regard no one from a
5:16 [y]2Co 11:18 worldly[y] point of view. Though we once regarded
Christ in this way, we do so no longer. 17There-
5:17 [z]Gal 6:15 fore, if anyone is in Christ, he is a new creation;[z]
[a]Isa 65:17; the old has gone, the new has come![a] 18All this is
Rev 21:4,5 from God, who reconciled us to himself through
Christ[b] and gave us the ministry of reconciliation:
5:18 [b]Ro 5:10; 19that God was reconciling the world to himself in
Col 1:20 Christ, not counting men's sins against them.[c]
5:19 And he has committed to us the message of rec-
[c]Ro 4:8 onciliation. 20We are therefore Christ's ambassa-
5:20 dors,[d] as though God were making his appeal
[d]2Co 6:1; through us. We implore you on Christ's behalf: Be
Eph 6:20 reconciled to God. 21God made him who had no
5:21 sin[e] to be sin[a] for us, so that in him we might
[e]Heb 4:15; become the righteousness of God.[f]
1Pe 2:22,24; 6 As God's fellow workers[g] we urge you not to
1Jn 3:5 [f]Ro 1:17 receive God's grace in vain. 2For he says,

6:1 [g]1Co 3:9; "In the time of my favor I heard you,
2Co 5:20 and in the day of salvation I helped
you."[b][h]

6:2 [h]Isa 49:8 I tell you, now is the time of God's favor, now is
the day of salvation.

6:3 [i]Ro 14:13, *Paul's Hardships*

20; 1Co 9:12; 3We put no stumbling block in anyone's path,[i]
10:32 so that our ministry will not be discredited.
6:5 4Rather, as servants of God we commend our-
[j]2Co 11:23- selves in every way: in great endurance; in trou-
25 bles, hardships and distresses; 5in beatings,
[k]1Co 4:11 imprisonments[j] and riots; in hard work, sleepless
6:6 [l]1Th 1:5 nights and hunger;[k] 6in purity, understanding,
patience and kindness; in the Holy Spirit[l] and in
6:7 sincere love; 7in truthful speech[m] and in the pow-
[m]2Co 4:2 [n]2Co 10:4; er of God; with weapons of righteousness[n] in the
Eph 6:10-18 right hand and in the left; 8through glory and dis-

[a] 21 Or *be a sin offering* [b] 2 Isaiah 49:8

New Birth

2CO 5:16-17

These two verses provide some of the New Testament's clearest teaching concerning new birth in Christ. This "new creation" (2Co 5:17) is of such transcendent importance that our past lives of sin have no bearing on our current relationship with God in Christ. The expression "in Christ" (2Co 5:17) expresses briefly, but profoundly, the incredible significance of our redemption. It speaks of security in the One who bears God's judgment for our sin, of acceptance in the One with whom God is well pleased, of assurance of a present and future glory in him that is beyond our ability to comprehend. The miracle of new birth is the basis by which Paul pleads with others—be reconciled to God!

Holiness

2CO 7:1

Despite their treatment of him and their distressing moral lapses, Paul attempts to persuade the Corinthians in a brotherly and loving way: In light of all God has promised, pursue purity of body and soul out of reverence for God. He urges a complete break with anything that compromises or defiles the body or the spirit. "Perfecting holiness" (2Co 7:1) requires leaving behind any thought, activity, action or word that does not build us up or bring us closer to Jesus' image. These aren't only "bad" things but are also those things that are more benign, not necessarily *bad* but not *good* either. Paul's words echo the apostle John's, who says that when Christ appears, we will be like him, and that all those who have this hope will seek to purify themselves so they will be pure, "just as he is pure" (1Jn 3:3).

Spend some time evaluating your own life. What activities or relationships are benign but not necessarily beneficial in your walk with God? Ask God's direction for whether you should continue in them or not.

honor,[o] bad report and good report; genuine, yet
regarded as impostors;[p] 9known, yet regarded as
unknown; dying,[q] and yet we live on;[r] beaten,
and yet not killed; 10sorrowful, yet always rejoicing;[s] poor, yet making many rich;[t] having nothing, and yet possessing everything.[u]
11We have spoken freely to you, Corinthians,
and opened wide our hearts to you.[v] 12We are not
withholding our affection from you, but you are
withholding yours from us. 13As a fair exchange—
I speak as to my children[w]—open wide your
hearts also.

Do Not Be Yoked With Unbelievers

14Do not be yoked together[x] with unbelievers.
For what do righteousness and wickedness have
in common? Or what fellowship can light have
with darkness?[y] 15What harmony is there between
Christ and Belial[a]? What does a believer[z] have in
common with an unbeliever? 16What agreement is
there between the temple of God and idols? For we
are the temple[a] of the living God. As God has said:
"I will live with them and walk among them, and
I will be their God, and they will be my people."[b][b]

17"Therefore come out from them[c]
and be separate,
says the Lord.
Touch no unclean thing,
and I will receive you."[c][d]
18"I will be a Father to you,
and you will be my sons and
daughters,[e]
says the Lord Almighty."[d]

7 Since we have these promises,[f] dear friends,
let us purify ourselves from everything that
contaminates body and spirit, perfecting holiness
out of reverence for God.

Paul's Joy

2Make room for us in your hearts.[g] We have
wronged no one, we have corrupted no one, we
have exploited no one. 3I do not say this to condemn you; I have said before that you have such
a place in our hearts[h] that we would live or die
with you. 4I have great confidence in you; I take
great pride in you. I am greatly encouraged; in all
our troubles my joy knows no bounds.[i]
5For when we came into Macedonia,[j] this body
of ours had no rest, but we were harassed at every
turn[k]—conflicts on the outside, fears within.[l] 6But
God, who comforts the downcast,[m] comforted us
by the coming of Titus,[n] 7and not only by his coming but also by the comfort you had given him.
He told us about your longing for me, your deep
sorrow, your ardent concern for me, so that my
joy was greater than ever.

6:8 [o]1Co 4:10 [p]Mt 27:63
6:9 [q]Ro 8:36 [r]2Co 1:8-10; 4:10,11
6:10 [s]2Co 7:4 [t]2Co 8:9 [u]Ro 8:32; 1Co 3:21
6:11 [v]2Co 7:3
6:13 [w]1Co 4:14
6:14 [x]1Co 5:9,10 [y]Eph 5:7,11; 1Jn 1:6
6:15 [z]Ac 5:14
6:16 [a]1Co 3:16 [b]Lev 26:12; Jer 32:38; Eze 37:27
6:17 [c]Rev 18:4 [d]Isa 52:11
6:18 [e]Isa 43:6
7:1 [f]2Co 6:17,18
7:2 [g]2Co 6:12,13
7:3 [h]2Co 6:11,12
7:4 [i]2Co 6:10
7:5 [j]2Co 2:13 [k]2Co 4:8 [l]Dt 32:25
7:6 [m]2Co 1:3,4 [n]ver 13; 2Co 2:13

[a] *15* Greek *Beliar*, a variant of *Belial* [b] *16* Lev. 26:12; Jer. 32:38; Ezek. 37:27 [c] *17* Isaiah 52:11; Ezek. 20:34,41 [d] *18* 2 Samuel 7:14; 7:8

7:8 8Even if I caused you sorrow by my letter,[o] I do
[o]2Co 2:2,4 not regret it. Though I did regret it—I see that my
letter hurt you, but only for a little while— 9yet
now I am happy, not because you were made sorry, but because your sorrow led you to repentance. For you became sorrowful as God intended
and so were not harmed in any way by us. 10God-
ly sorrow brings repentance that leads to salva-
7:10 tion[p] and leaves no regret, but worldly sorrow
[p]Ac 11:18 brings death. 11See what this godly sorrow has
produced in you: what earnestness, what eager-
7:11 ness to clear yourselves, what indignation, what
[q]ver 7 alarm, what longing, what concern,[q] what readiness to see justice done. At every point you have
7:12 proved yourselves to be innocent in this matter.
[r]ver 8; 12So even though I wrote to you,[r] it was not on
2Co 2:3,9 [s]1Co 5:1,2 account of the one who did the wrong[s] or of the
injured party, but rather that before God you
could see for yourselves how devoted to us you
are. 13By all this we are encouraged.
In addition to our own encouragement, we
7:13 [t]ver 6; were especially delighted to see how happy Titus[t]
2Co 2:13 was, because his spirit has been refreshed by all of
7:14 you. 14I had boasted to him about you,[u] and you
[u]ver 4 [v]ver 6 have not embarrassed me. But just as everything
we said to you was true, so our boasting about
you to Titus[v] has proved to be true as well. 15And
his affection for you is all the greater when he
7:15 remembers that you were all obedient,[w] receiving
[w]2Co 2:9 [x]Php 2:12 him with fear and trembling.[x] 16I am glad I can
7:16 [y]2Co 2:3 have complete confidence in you.[y]

Generosity Encouraged

8 And now, brothers, we want you to know
about the grace that God has given the Mace-
8:1 donian[z] churches. 2Out of the most severe trial,
[z]Ac 16:9 their overflowing joy and their extreme poverty
welled up in rich generosity. 3For I testify that they
8:3 gave as much as they were able,[a] and even beyond
[a]1Co 16:2 their ability. Entirely on their own, 4they urgently
8:4 pleaded with us for the privilege of sharing in this
[b]Ac 24:17 [c]Ro 15:25; service[b] to the saints.[c] 5And they did not do as we
2Co 9:1 expected, but they gave themselves first to the
8:6 Lord and then to us in keeping with God's will.
[d]ver 17; 6So we urged[d] Titus,[e] since he had earlier made a
2Co 12:18 [e]ver 16,23 beginning, to bring also to completion[f] this act of
[f]ver 10,11 grace on your part. 7But just as you excel in every-
8:7 thing[g]—in faith, in speech, in knowledge,[h] in
[g]2Co 9:8 complete earnestness and in your love for us*[a]*—
[h]1Co 1:5 see that you also excel in this grace of giving.
8I am not commanding you,[i] but I want to test
8:8 [i]1Co 7:6 the sincerity of your love by comparing it with the
earnestness of others. 9For you know the grace of
8:9 [j]2Co 13:14 our Lord Jesus Christ,[j] that though he was rich,
[k]Mt 20:28; yet for your sakes he became poor,[k] so that you
Php 2:6-8 through his poverty might become rich.
8:10 10And here is my advice[l] about what is best for
[l]1Co 7:25,40 [m]1Co 16:2,3; you in this matter: Last year you were the first not
2Co 9:2 only to give but also to have the desire to do so.[m]

a 7 Some manuscripts *in our love for you*

Riches Not Required

2CO 8:2

The grace of giving is not dependent on the wealth of the giver, as Paul makes clear in this passage. He points to the Macedonian Christians who, though poor and distressed themselves, give generously to Christians in Jerusalem whom they have never met. Paul urges the Corinthians to follow their example. Generosity in giving is a way of following Christ, who became poor that we might become rich in God (2Co 8:9).

Financial Stewardship

2CO 8:16–24

When handling the offering for needy Christians in Jerusalem, Paul carefully discloses his plans. He does not want to give anyone cause for slander or suspicion. Modeling integrity in his financial stewardship, he arranges for Titus, whom the Corinthians love and trust, as well as two others, to collect the money and carry it to Jerusalem. Paul mentions how conscientious he has been in order to be above suspicion and to find favor in the sight of God and the people. In doing so, Paul shows us the importance of being accountable to others and rigorously faithful in our stewardship of money, among Christians and in the world at large.

11Now finish the work, so that your eager willingness[n] to do it may be matched by your completion
of it, according to your means. 12For if the willingness is there, the gift is acceptable according
to what one has,[o] not according to what he does
not have.
13Our desire is not that others might be relieved
while you are hard pressed, but that there might
be equality. 14At the present time your plenty will
supply what they need,[p] so that in turn their plenty will supply what you need. Then there will be
equality, 15as it is written: "He who gathered
much did not have too much, and he who gathered little did not have too little."[a][q]

Titus Sent to Corinth

16I thank God,[r] who put into the heart[s] of Titus[t]
the same concern I have for you. 17For Titus not
only welcomed our appeal, but he is coming to
you with much enthusiasm and on his own initiative.[u] 18And we are sending along with him the
brother[v] who is praised by all the churches[w] for
his service to the gospel.[x] 19What is more, he was
chosen by the churches to accompany us[y] as we
carry the offering, which we administer in order
to honor the Lord himself and to show our eagerness to help.[z] 20We want to avoid any criticism of
the way we administer this liberal gift. 21For we
are taking pains to do what is right, not only in
the eyes of the Lord but also in the eyes of men.[a]
22In addition, we are sending with them our
brother who has often proved to us in many ways
that he is zealous, and now even more so because
of his great confidence in you. 23As for Titus, he is
my partner[b] and fellow worker[c] among you; as for
our brothers,[d] they are representatives of the
churches and an honor to Christ. 24Therefore
show these men the proof of your love and the
reason for our pride in you,[e] so that the churches
can see it.

9 There is no need[f] for me to write to you about
this service to the saints.[g] 2For I know your
eagerness to help, and I have been boasting[h]
about it to the Macedonians, telling them that
since last year[i] you in Achaia[j] were ready to give;
and your enthusiasm has stirred most of them to
action. 3But I am sending the brothers in order
that our boasting about you in this matter should
not prove hollow, but that you may be ready, as I
said you would be.[k] 4For if any Macedonians[l]
come with me and find you unprepared, we—not
to say anything about you—would be ashamed of
having been so confident. 5So I thought it necessary to urge the brothers to visit you in advance
and finish the arrangements for the generous gift
you had promised. Then it will be ready as a generous gift,[m] not as one grudgingly given.[n]

8:11 [n]2Co 9:2
8:12 [o]Mk 12:43, 44; Lk 21:3
8:14 [p]2Co 9:12
8:15 [q]Ex 16:18
8:16 [r]2Co 2:14 [s]Rev 17:17 [t]2Co 2:13
8:17 [u]ver 6
8:18 [v]2Co 12:18 [w]1Co 7:17 [x]2Co 2:12
8:19 [y]1Co 16:3,4 [z]ver 11,12
8:21 [a]Ro 12:17; 14:18
8:23 [b]Phm 17 [c]Php 2:25 [d]ver 18,22
8:24 [e]2Co 7:4,14; 9:2
9:1 [f]1Th 4:9 [g]2Co 8:4
9:2 [h]2Co 7:4,14 [i]2Co 8:10 [j]Ac 18:12
9:3 [k]1Co 16:2
9:4 [l]Ro 15:26
9:5 [m]Php 4:17 [n]2Co 12:17, 18

[a] *15* Exodus 16:18

Sowing Generously

6Remember this: Whoever sows sparingly will
9:6 [o]Pr 11:24,25; 22:9; Gal 6:7,9 also reap sparingly, and whoever sows generously will also reap generously.[o] 7Each man should
give what he has decided in his heart to give,[p] not
reluctantly or under compulsion,[q] for God loves a
9:7 [p]Ex 25:2; 2Co 8:12 [q]Dt 15:10 [r]Ro 12:8 cheerful giver.[r] 8And God is able[s] to make all grace
abound to you, so that in all things at all times,
having all that you need,[t] you will abound in
every good work. 9As it is written:

9:8 [s]Eph 3:20 [t]Php 4:19 "He has scattered abroad his gifts to the
poor;
his righteousness endures forever."[a][u]

9:9 [u]Ps 112:9 10Now he who supplies seed to the sower and
9:10 [v]Isa 55:10 [w]Hos 10:12 bread for food[v] will also supply and increase your
store of seed and will enlarge the harvest of your
righteousness.[w] 11You will be made rich[x] in every
9:11 [x]1Co 1:5 [y]2Co 1:11 way so that you can be generous on every occasion, and through us your generosity will result
in thanksgiving to God.[y]

12This service that you perform is not only sup-
9:12 [z]2Co 8:14 [a]2Co 1:11 plying the needs[z] of God's people but is also overflowing in many expressions of thanks to God.[a]
9:13 [b]2Co 8:4 [c]Mt 9:8 [d]2Co 2:12 13Because of the service[b] by which you have
proved yourselves, men will praise God[c] for the
obedience that accompanies your confession of
the gospel of Christ,[d] and for your generosity in
sharing with them and with everyone else. 14And
in their prayers for you their hearts will go out to
you, because of the surpassing grace God has giv-
9:15 [e]2Co 2:14 [f]Ro 5:15,16 en you. 15Thanks be to God[e] for his indescribable
gift![f]

Paul's Defense of His Ministry

10:1 [g]Mt 11:29 [h]Gal 5:2 **10** By the meekness and gentleness[g] of Christ,
I appeal to you—I, Paul,[h] who am "timid"
when face to face with you, but "bold" when
10:2 [i]1Co 4:21; 2Co 13:2,10 away! 2I beg you that when I come I may not have
to be as bold[i] as I expect to be toward some peo-
ple who think that we live by the standards of this
world. 3For though we live in the world, we do
not wage war as the world does. 4The weapons
10:4 [j]2Co 6:7 [k]1Co 2:5 [l]Jer 1:10; 2Co 13:10 we fight with[j] are not the weapons of the world.
On the contrary, they have divine power[k] to
demolish strongholds.[l] 5We demolish arguments
and every pretension that sets itself up against the
10:5 [m]Isa 2:11,12; 1Co 1:19 [n]2Co 9:13 knowledge of God,[m] and we take captive every
thought to make it obedient[n] to Christ. 6And we
will be ready to punish every act of disobedience,
10:6 [o]2Co 2:9; 7:15 once your obedience is complete.[o]

7You are looking only on the surface of things.[b][p]
If anyone is confident that he belongs to Christ,[q] he
10:7 [p]Jn 7:24 [q]1Co 1:12; 3:23; 14:37 [r]2Co 11:23 should consider again that we belong to Christ just
as much as he.[r] 8For even if I boast somewhat freely
about the authority the Lord gave us for building
you up rather than pulling you down,[s] I will not be
ashamed of it. 9I do not want to seem to be trying
10:8 [s]2Co 13:10

[a] *9* Psalm 112:9 [b] *7* Or *Look at the obvious facts*

Joyful Giving

2CO 9:6–15

Paul's most concise and explicit teaching on Christian giving is contained in 2 Corinthians 9:6–15. He likens financial giving to seed, which is sown by a farmer. What we give is not lost, but rather seed is sown that will yield a harvest with potency for life and increase. The amount we sow is directly related to the bounty of the crop of blessing we reap. Also, the state of the heart of the one who gives is fully as important as the gift given (2Co 9:7). Giving should take place freely, with individuals responding as the Lord directs them. Genuine, free giving, without regret, is marked by cheerfulness, literally an "exhilarating experience." The joy of giving is an expression of thanksgiving to God, who has given us Christ, the "indescribable gift!" (2Co 9:15).

Paul's Ministry Validated

2CO 10

The entire letter of 2 Corinthians reveals the pressure on Paul to authenticate his apostleship, and nowhere more so than in 2 Corinthians 10 and 11. Though Paul is the spiritual father of the church at Corinth, false teachers have accused him of being "unimpressive," a spiritual lightweight (2Co 10:10). Paul writes with a touch of irony as he offers validation for his ministry among them: his power in the spiritual realm (2Co 10:4), his willingness to suffer to bring them the gospel (1Co 11:9,23–29), and his vision of paradise (2Co 12:3–4). Essentially, Paul appeals not to self-commendation, which should be viewed with suspicion, but to the judgment of the Lord (1Co 4:4). His goal is always the spiritual growth of the Corinthians, especially their return to the sincerity and purity of devotion to Christ (2Co 11:3).

to frighten you with my letters. 10 For some say, "His
letters are weighty and forceful, but in person he is
unimpressive[t] and his speaking amounts to nothing."[u] 11 Such people should realize that what we
are in our letters when we are absent, we will be in
our actions when we are present.
12 We do not dare to classify or compare ourselves with some who commend themselves.[v]
When they measure themselves by themselves and
compare themselves with themselves, they are not
wise. 13 We, however, will not boast beyond proper
limits, but will confine our boasting to the field
God has assigned to us,[w] a field that reaches even
to you. 14 We are not going too far in our boasting,
as would be the case if we had not come to you,
for we did get as far as you[x] with the gospel of
Christ.[y] 15 Neither do we go beyond our limits by
boasting of work done by others.[a][z] Our hope is
that, as your faith continues to grow,[a] our area of
activity among you will greatly expand, 16 so that
we can preach the gospel in the regions beyond
you.[b] For we do not want to boast about work
already done in another man's territory. 17 But, "Let
him who boasts boast in the Lord."[b][c] 18 For it is not
the one who commends himself[d] who is approved,
but the one whom the Lord commends.[e]

Paul and the False Apostles

11 I hope you will put up with[f] a little of my
foolishness;[g] but you are already doing that.
2 I am jealous for you with a godly jealousy. I
promised you to one husband,[h] to Christ, so that
I might present you[i] as a pure virgin to him. 3 But
I am afraid that just as Eve was deceived by the
serpent's cunning,[j] your minds may somehow be
led astray from your sincere and pure devotion to
Christ. 4 For if someone comes to you and preaches
a Jesus other than the Jesus we preached,[k] or if
you receive a different spirit[l] from the one you
received, or a different gospel[m] from the one you
accepted, you put up with it easily enough. 5 But I
do not think I am in the least inferior to those
"super-apostles."[n] 6 I may not be a trained speaker,[o] but I do have knowledge.[p] We have made this
perfectly clear to you in every way.
7 Was it a sin[q] for me to lower myself in order to
elevate you by preaching the gospel of God to you
free of charge?[r] 8 I robbed other churches by
receiving support from them[s] so as to serve you.
9 And when I was with you and needed something, I was not a burden to anyone, for the brothers who came from Macedonia supplied what I
needed. I have kept myself from being a burden
to you[t] in any way, and will continue to do so.
10 As surely as the truth of Christ is in me,[u] nobody

[a] 13–15 Or 13 *We, however, will not boast about things that cannot be measured, but we will boast according to the standard of measurement that the God of measure has assigned us—a measurement that relates even to you.* 14 . . . 15 *Neither do we boast about things that cannot be measured in regard to the work done by others.* [b] 17 Jer. 9:24

10:10 [t]1Co 2:3; Gal 4:13,14 [u]1Co 1:17
10:12 [v]2Co 3:1
10:13 [w]ver 15,16
10:14 [x]1Co 3:6 [y]2Co 2:12
10:15 [z]Ro 15:20 [a]2Th 1:3
10:16 [b]Ac 19:21
10:17 [c]Jer 9:24; 1Co 1:31
10:18 [d]ver 12 [e]Ro 2:29; 1Co 4:5
11:1 [f]ver 4,19,20; Mt 17:17 [g]ver 16,17, 21; 2Co 5:13
11:2 [h]Hos 2:19; Eph 5:26,27 [i]2Co 4:14
11:3 [j]Ge 3:1-6,13; Jn 8:44; 1Ti 2:14; Rev 12:9
11:4 [k]1Co 3:11 [l]Ro 8:15 [m]Gal 1:6-9
11:5 [n]2Co 12:11; Gal 2:6
11:6 [o]1Co 1:17 [p]Eph 3:4
11:7 [q]2Co 12:13 [r]1Co 9:18
11:8 [s]Php 4:15,18
11:9 [t]2Co 12:13, 14,16
11:10 [u]Ro 9:1

Widow With Two Coins

Giving Everything

She stood in the corner of the temple, fingering her last two coins. They were worth less than a penny, but she hesitated, reflecting on the last few years of her life, her husband's death, the struggle to make ends meet. Without a family to support her, she had nowhere to turn. All she had left lay in her hand. It wasn't much—perhaps she should hang on to it.

Then she remembered the goodness of the Lord and all that he had done for her. She could not withhold from the One who had sustained her and blessed her. No. She had to let go. Surely he would provide a way for her to survive.

As she dropped the coins into the box, a heavy weight fell from her shoulders. She was totally in the Lord's hands now. He had invited her to trust him far beyond the comfort zone of her faith. Her heart leapt. She felt *free*. Her struggle was over, and God was in control. She felt safer than she had ever felt in her life. She fell on her knees to worship *Jehovah-Jireh,* her provider, *Jehovah-Shalom*, her peace.

She had given her coins in secret, thinking no one saw. Unknown to her, Jesus watched and made note of her gift. "Calling his disciples to him, Jesus said, 'I tell you the truth, this poor widow has put more into the treasury than all the others' " (Mk 12:43).

He alone knew how much it had cost her. *Everything.* She gave not just her money, but her heart, her trust, her daily bread, her future. He alone knew how much she had gained—the freedom of a child of God leaning wholly on her Creator. Her act was praiseworthy in his sight.

Life is unpredictable. We never know when we might come to the end of our resources—financial, emotional, mental or spiritual. We may think ourselves alone in our struggle, but the Lord is always watching. In our time of need, we can remember this dear widow who so blessed the Lord. She brought everything she had and laid it at his feet. She left with everything she needed, her hand in his.

Widow With Two Coins

Mark 12:41-44

Luke 21:1-4

Candid SNAPSHOT Calling his disciples to him, Jesus said, "I tell you the truth, this poor widow has put more into the treasury than all the others. They all gave out of their wealth; but she, out of her poverty, put in everything—all she had to live on" (Mark 12:43-44).

Pilate's Wife

A Dream Worth Heeding

She is faceless and nameless. We know nothing of her character or gifts, only that she had a dream—a dream that caused her to suffer—a dream about Jesus that confirmed her husband's leaning when he found it impossible to decide on his own.

Pilate had full powers of life and death. He could reverse capital sentences passed by the Sanhedrin, which were submitted for his ratification. He even appointed the high priests. But Pilate lacked the courage to stand against the crowd. He was rigid and harsh by nature and did not understand the Jews. His tenure in Judea was rife with bribery, violence, pride, spiteful treatment, executions without trial and grievous brutality toward the people he governed. He was hated and disrespected. Yet the decision fell to him. Should Jesus be condemned to death?

Pilate needed the help of his wife to temper his approach. Maybe he even sought her advice. She was perhaps the one bright light in his dismal existence—someone he could trust, someone who cared about him, someone with good judgment. She sent him her message at the very moment when he sat on the judgment seat: "Don't have anything to do with that innocent man, for I have suffered a great deal today in a dream because of him" (Mt 27:19). Pilate, too, knew in his heart that Jesus was innocent and should go free.

But rather than release Jesus, Pilate washed his hands. As if that could erase his responsibility! Why didn't he listen to his wife, the one he could trust, the one who cared? When his power was threatened, he caved in to pressure. Yet he had only the power granted him from on high. His decision was foreknown: "The kings of the earth take their stand and the rulers gather together against the LORD and against his Anointed One" (Ps 2:2). The Jews had condemned Jesus and demanded his death, but the Gentiles carried out the sentence. Yet, even Pilate had his chance to take a stand for God when his wife had a dream of warning.

The Lord will often use our spouses to bring balance and perspective to our biases. We are wise to heed one another's input. A spouse's insight may the very thing needed to give us the confidence to follow God and resist the crowd.

Pilate's Wife
Matthew 27:19

Candid SNAPSHOT While Pilate was sitting on the judge's seat, his wife sent him this message: "Don't have anything to do with that innocent man, for I have suffered a great deal today in a dream because of him" (Matthew 27:19).

11:10 in the regions of Achaia[v] will stop this boasting[w]
[v]Ac 18:12 [w]1Co 9:15 of mine. 11 Why? Because I do not love you? God
knows I do![x] 12 And I will keep on doing what I
11:11 [x]2Co 12:15 am doing in order to cut the ground from under
those who want an opportunity to be considered
11:13 equal with us in the things they boast about.
[y]2Pe 2:1 13 For such men are false apostles,[y] deceitful[z]
[z]Tit 1:10 [a]Rev 2:2 workmen, masquerading as apostles of Christ.[a]
14 And no wonder, for Satan himself masquerades
as an angel of light. 15 It is not surprising, then, if
his servants masquerade as servants of righteous-
11:15 [b]Php 3:19 ness. Their end will be what their actions deserve.[b]

11:16 *Paul Boasts About His Sufferings*

[c]ver 1 16 I repeat: Let no one take me for a fool.[c] But if
you do, then receive me just as you would a fool,
11:17 so that I may do a little boasting. 17 In this self-con-
[d]1Co 7:12,25 fident boasting I am not talking as the Lord would,[d]
11:18 but as a fool. 18 Since many are boasting in the way
[e]Php 3:3,4 the world does, I too will boast.[e] 19 You gladly put
11:19 up with fools since you are so wise![f] 20 In fact, you
[f]1Co 4:10 even put up with anyone who enslaves you[g] or
11:20 exploits you or takes advantage of you or pushes
[g]Gal 2:4 himself forward or slaps you in the face. 21 To my
11:21 shame I admit that we were too weak[h] for that!
[h]2Co 10:1,10 What anyone else dares to boast about—I am
[i]Php 3:4 speaking as a fool—I also dare to boast about.[i]
11:22 22 Are they Hebrews? So am I.[j] Are they Israelites?
[j]Php 3:5 [k]Ro 9:4 So am I.[k] Are they Abraham's descendants? So am
I. 23 Are they servants of Christ? (I am out of my
11:23 mind to talk like this.) I am more. I have worked
[l]1Co 15:10 much harder,[l] been in prison more frequently,[m]
[m]Ac 16:23; been flogged more severely, and been exposed to
2Co 6:4,5 death again and again. 24 Five times I received
11:24 from the Jews the forty lashes[n] minus one. 25 Three
[n]Dt 25:3 times I was beaten with rods,[o] once I was stoned,[p]
11:25 three times I was shipwrecked, I spent a night and
[o]Ac 16:22 [p]Ac 14:19 a day in the open sea, 26 I have been constantly on
the move. I have been in danger from rivers, in
11:26 [q]Ac 9:23; danger from bandits, in danger from my own
14:5 countrymen,[q] in danger from Gentiles; in danger
[r]Ac 21:31 [s]Gal 2:4 in the city,[r] in danger in the country, in danger at
sea; and in danger from false brothers.[s] 27 I have
labored and toiled and have often gone without
sleep; I have known hunger and thirst and have
11:27 [t]1Co 4:11,12; often gone without food;[t] I have been cold and
2Co 6:5 naked. 28 Besides everything else, I face daily the
pressure of my concern for all the churches.
29 Who is weak, and I do not feel weak? Who is
led into sin, and I do not inwardly burn?
11:30 30 If I must boast, I will boast of the things that
[u]1Co 2:3 show my weakness.[u] 31 The God and Father of the
Lord Jesus, who is to be praised forever,[v] knows
11:31 [v]Ro 9:5 that I am not lying. 32 In Damascus the governor
under King Aretas had the city of the Damascenes
11:32 guarded in order to arrest me.[w] 33 But I was low-
[w]Ac 9:24 ered in a basket from a window in the wall and
11:33 [x]Ac 9:25 slipped through his hands.[x]

Paul Defends Himself

2CO 11:1-14

The church at Corinth is marked by internal splits and rival factions, with each pseudo-apostle (2Co 11:13) competing for pre-eminence. These false teachers say Paul's teaching is worth nothing to the Corinthians because they have paid nothing for it. Paul preached to them "free of charge" (2Co 11:7). (Common practice in that day required paying a teacher based on the value of his teaching.) Paul passionately affirms his love for the Corinthians (2Co 11:11), which he demonstrated by his willingness to not be a financial burden. It is distasteful to Paul, whose whole being is taken up with the person and work of Christ, to enumerate his own experiences (2Co 11:21-33); but it is also necessary in order to refute these self-inflated deceivers in the Corinthian church.

The problem with believing that God wants to heal people lies in the fact that not everybody is healed. The apostle Paul had a thorn (pain, suffering, or physical infirmity) in his flesh. He pleaded with God three times to remove it. God refused. But God *gave* him sufficient *grace* and power to live with his infirmity.

God certainly doesn't always heal in the ways we expect. Because he is sovereign, he has many options. I've seen him heal instantly; through medical procedures and processes; through death (the ultimate, most revered healing for a Christian, in my opinion). Just because we doubt, just because we haven't experienced healing, or just because we think miracles are not for this modern day doesn't stop God from doing what he promised in whatever way he chooses.

—Thelma Wells

Paul's Vision and His Thorn

12 I must go on boasting.[y] Although there is
nothing to be gained, I will go on to visions
and revelations[z] from the Lord. 2 I know a man in
Christ who fourteen years ago was caught up[a] to
the third heaven.[b] Whether it was in the body or
out of the body I do not know—God knows.[c] 3 And
I know that this man—whether in the body or
apart from the body I do not know, but God
knows— 4 was caught up to paradise.[d] He heard
inexpressible things, things that man is not permitted to tell. 5 I will boast about a man like that,
but I will not boast about myself, except about my
weaknesses. 6 Even if I should choose to boast, I
would not be a fool,[e] because I would be speaking
the truth. But I refrain, so no one will think more
of me than is warranted by what I do or say.
7 To keep me from becoming conceited because
of these surpassingly great revelations, there was
given me a thorn in my flesh,[f] a messenger of
Satan, to torment me. 8 Three times I pleaded with
the Lord to take it away from me.[g] 9 But he said to
me, "My grace is sufficient for you, for my power[h]
is made perfect in weakness." Therefore I will
boast all the more gladly about my weaknesses,
so that Christ's power may rest on me. 10 That is
why, for Christ's sake, I delight in weaknesses, in
insults, in hardships,[i] in persecutions,[j] in difficulties. For when I am weak, then I am strong.[k]

Paul's Concern for the Corinthians

11 I have made a fool of myself,[l] but you drove
me to it. I ought to have been commended by you,
for I am not in the least inferior to the "super-
apostles,"[m] even though I am nothing.[n] 12 The
things that mark an apostle—signs, wonders and
miracles[o]—were done among you with great perseverance. 13 How were you inferior to the other
churches, except that I was never a burden to
you?[p] Forgive me this wrong![q]
14 Now I am ready to visit you for the third time,[r]
and I will not be a burden to you, because what I
want is not your possessions but you. After all,
children should not have to save up for their parents,[s] but parents for their children.[t] 15 So I will
very gladly spend for you everything I have and
expend myself as well.[u] If I love you more, will
you love me less? 16 Be that as it may, I have not
been a burden to you.[v] Yet, crafty fellow that I am,
I caught you by trickery! 17 Did I exploit you
through any of the men I sent you? 18 I urged[w]
Titus to go to you and I sent our brother[x] with
him. Titus did not exploit you, did he? Did we not
act in the same spirit and follow the same course?
19 Have you been thinking all along that we have
been defending ourselves to you? We have been
speaking in the sight of God[y] as those in Christ;
and everything we do, dear friends, is for your
strengthening.[z] 20 For I am afraid that when I
come[a] I may not find you as I want you to be, and

12:1 [y]2Co 11:16, 30 [z]ver 7
12:2 [a]Ac 8:39 [b]Eph 4:10 [c]2Co 11:11
12:4 [d]Lk 23:43; Rev 2:7
12:6 [e]2Co 11:16
12:7 [f]Nu 33:55
12:8 [g]Mt 26:39,44
12:9 [h]Php 4:13
12:10 [i]2Co 6:4 [j]Ro 5:3; 2Th 1:4 [k]2Co 13:4
12:11 [l]2Co 11:1 [m]2Co 11:5 [n]1Co 15:9,10
12:12 [o]Jn 4:48
12:13 [p]1Co 9:12,18 [q]2Co 11:7
12:14 [r]2Co 13:1 [s]1Co 4:14,15 [t]Pr 19:14
12:15 [u]Php 2:17; 1Th 2:8
12:16 [v]2Co 11:9
12:18 [w]2Co 8:6,16 [x]2Co 8:18
12:19 [y]Ro 9:1 [z]2Co 10:8
12:20 [a]2Co 2:1-4

Week 43

An Experience of God

This passage is Paul's attempt to describe what many believe to have been his own experience or encounter with God. Paul relates an experience that happened 14 years before but that had not lost its mystery or its influence on his life. Some people today are uncomfortable talking about such experiences, while others spend their lives desiring them. What can you learn from this Biblical description of an actual experience with God?

What does Paul call this experience and from whom did it originate (2Cor 12:1)?

Paul's experience makes such an impression on him that 14 years later he has not forgotten it (2Cor 12:2). Is it a spiritual experience or is his body involved (2Cor 12:2–3)? Does it really seem to matter?

To what place is Paul "caught up" (2Cor 12:2)? The "third heaven" is beyond the earth's atmosphere, beyond outer space as humans know it and into God's presence. What do you think "caught up" means? Without comparing type or degree, describe an experience you have had in which you felt your spirit was somehow lifted up—a time of deep communion with God in which you experienced something beyond yourself? Did it seem too holy to share with others? Why or why not?

What things does Paul hear (2Cor 12:4)? Paul's experience with God is meant for Paul and God alone. How do you think this experience strengthened Paul's relationship with God? How do you think spiritual experiences can strengthen a person's relationship with God? What role should an experience with God play in the foundation of your faith (Jn 20:29; 2Co 5:7)?

An intimate relationship with God often brings with it an experience—one that is mysterious because God himself is mysterious.

Enjoying God THROUGH the Word

Read Isaiah 6:1–7 (page 1114). Isaiah reports on an encounter with God that takes place either in the body or out of the body. We are not told if the experience is spiritual (a vision) or physical (material, in the body). It doesn't seem to matter. What matters is that the experience is real. Isaiah's response to his encounter with God is dread—seeing God's holiness only amplifies Isaiah's perception of his own sin and unworthiness. But God provides a way for Isaiah to reach God. After a seraph touches a hot coal to Isaiah's lips, God tells him, "Your guilt is taken away and your sin atoned for" (Isa 6:7). God desires encounters with his children. He has given his own Son so that he can have an encounter with you.

Isaiah's encounter with the Holy One changes him forever. Have you had such an encounter? How has it changed you? Through Jesus, God has provided the way to intimacy with him. Your experience of God may not be as "inexpressible" as Paul's, but it can be just as real and just as life changing.

Enjoying God THROUGH Experience

God's purpose in offering his only Son for your sin is to reconcile you to himself (Ro 5:10). His intent is to have an intimate relationship with you. Go to him in prayer. Permit him to love you. Permit yourself to have a mysterious encounter with him. The type or degree of your experience is unimportant. What *is* important is that you encounter him.

Go to page 1925 for your next weekly study.

Examine Yourselves

2CO 13:5

Paul's instruction to "examine yourselves . . . test yourselves" (2Co 13:5) is issued because false teachers are demanding proof that Christ speaks through Paul (2Co 13:3). The Corinthians are influenced by the criticism of the false teachers, but Paul proves that he is who he says he is. Paul's proof comes not from himself, but from the people themselves. If they examine and test themselves, they'll discover whether they are motivated by faith and are true believers (and they would be such only because of Paul's teachings) or are motivated by their own egos and selfish aspirations (2Co 13:6). Paul wants them to turn their eyes away from the false teachers and their accusations and toward what is most important, their own relationship with Christ.

you may not find me as you want me to be.[b] I fear
that there may be quarreling,[c] jealousy, outbursts
of anger, factions,[d] slander, gossip,[e] arrogance and
disorder.[f] 21 I am afraid that when I come again my
God will humble me before you, and I will be
grieved[g] over many who have sinned earlier[h] and
have not repented of the impurity, sexual sin and
debauchery in which they have indulged.

Final Warnings

13 This will be my third visit to you.[i] "Every
matter must be established by the testimony of two or three witnesses."[aj] 2 I already gave
you a warning when I was with you the second
time. I now repeat it while absent: On my return
I will not spare[k] those who sinned earlier[l] or any
of the others, 3 since you are demanding proof that
Christ is speaking through me.[m] He is not weak
in dealing with you, but is powerful among you.
4 For to be sure, he was crucified in weakness,[n] yet
he lives by God's power.[o] Likewise, we are weak[p]
in him, yet by God's power we will live with him
to serve you.

5 Examine yourselves[q] to see whether you are in
the faith; test yourselves.[r] Do you not realize that
Christ Jesus is in you[s]—unless, of course, you fail
the test? 6 And I trust that you will discover that
we have not failed the test. 7 Now we pray to God
that you will not do anything wrong. Not that
people will see that we have stood the test but that
you will do what is right even though we may
seem to have failed. 8 For we cannot do anything
against the truth, but only for the truth. 9 We are
glad whenever we are weak but you are strong;
and our prayer is for your perfection.[t] 10 This is
why I write these things when I am absent, that
when I come I may not have to be harsh in my
use of authority—the authority the Lord gave me
for building you up, not for tearing you down.[u]

Final Greetings

11 Finally, brothers,[v] good-by. Aim for perfection,
listen to my appeal, be of one mind, live in
peace.[w] And the God of love and peace[x] will be
with you.

12 Greet one another with a holy kiss.[y] 13 All the
saints send their greetings.[z]

14 May the grace of the Lord Jesus Christ,[a] and
the love of God,[b] and the fellowship of the Holy
Spirit[c] be with you all.

12:20 [b]1Co 4:21 [c]1Co 1:11; 3:3 [d]Gal 5:20 [e]Ro 1:29 [f]1Co 14:33
12:21 [g]2Co 2:1,4 [h]2Co 13:2
13:1 [i]2Co 12:14 [j]Dt 19:15; Mt 18:16
13:2 [k]2Co 1:23 [l]2Co 12:21
13:3 [m]Mt 10:20; 1Co 5:4
13:4 [n]Php 2:7,8; 1Pe 3:18 [o]Ro 1:4; 6:4 [p]ver 9
13:5 [q]1Co 11:28 [r]Jn 6:6 [s]Ro 8:10
13:9 [t]ver 11
13:10 [u]2Co 10:8
13:11 [v]1Th 4:1; 2Th 3:1 [w]Mk 9:50 [x]Ro 15:33; Eph 6:23
13:12 [y]Ro 16:16
13:13 [z]Php 4:22
13:14 [a]Ro 16:20; 2Co 8:9 [b]Ro 5:5; Jude 21 [c]Php 2:1

[a] *1* Deut. 19:15

Galatians

Justification by faith alone.

A controversy surfaces in the church in Galatia. Some Jewish Christians insist that non-Jewish Christians need to follow Jewish laws and rituals in order to be true members of the church. The book of Galatians offers Paul's defense of the true gospel by warning against mixing legalism and religious ritual with God's gospel of grace. With a feisty, hard-hitting style, Paul reminds the believers to depend on Christ alone for salvation. He details the practical implications of living by grace and under the control of the Holy Spirit.

Paul's letter to the Galatians explains what it means to be saved by faith alone. Paul defines what the gospel is (Gal 3:22), how it is received (Gal 3:26), and how it applies to daily life (Gal 5:16—6:10). He is concerned about the temptation to please others (Gal 1). He reminds believers of their status as co-heirs with Christ through God's grace (Gal 3). Paul carefully outlines the work of the law and of grace, of bondage and freedom, using Hagar and Sarah as examples (Gal 4). And he encourages believers to reflect God's character as they allow the fruit of the Holy Spirit to take root in their lives (Gal 5).

What joy the book of Galatians brings as it makes clear that we cannot be saved by keeping laws and rules, but we find salvation through faith in Christ alone. With the Holy Spirit working in us to instruct and guide us, we can live in faith, joyfully set free by the grace of God.

Quick Study

Author
The apostle Paul.

Date Written
Probably sometime around A.D. 50.

Written From
Several cities have been proposed, including Antioch, Ephesus and Macedonia.

Key Passage
Galatians 5:22-25 "The fruit of the Spirit is love, joy, peace, patience, kindness, goodness, faithfulness, gentleness and self-control. Against such things there is no law. Those who belong to Christ Jesus have crucified the sinful nature with its passions and desires. Since we live by the Spirit, let us keep in step with the Spirit."

Outline

Paul's greetings and denunciations.
Gal 1:1-10

An authentic gospel.
Gal 1:11–2:21

Faith or law.
Gal 3:1–4:31

Freedom in Christ.
Gal 5

Doing good.
Gal 6:1-10

Final words.
Gal 6:11-18

The Women of Galatians

✡ **Hagar**	*Still enslaved.* Gal 4:24-25 (page 68)
Slave woman	*A reference to Hagar.* Gal 4:30-31
Free woman	*A reference to Sarah.* Gal 4:30-31

✡ *Denotes a sketch written about this character*

1 Paul, an apostle—sent not from men nor by
man, but by Jesus Christ[a] and God the Father,
who raised him from the dead[b]— 2 and all the
brothers with me,[c]

To the churches in Galatia:[d]

3 Grace and peace to you from God our Father
and the Lord Jesus Christ,[e] 4 who gave himself for
our sins[f] to rescue us from the present evil age,
according to the will of our God and Father,[g] 5 to
whom be glory for ever and ever. Amen.[h]

No Other Gospel

6 I am astonished that you are so quickly deserting the one who called[i] you by the grace of Christ
and are turning to a different gospel[j]— 7 which is
really no gospel at all. Evidently some people are
throwing you into confusion[k] and are trying to
pervert the gospel of Christ. 8 But even if we or an
angel from heaven should preach a gospel other
than the one we preached to you,[l] let him be eternally condemned![m] 9 As we have already said, so
now I say again: If anybody is preaching to you a
gospel other than what you accepted,[n] let him be
eternally condemned!

10 Am I now trying to win the approval of men,
or of God? Or am I trying to please men?[o] If I were
still trying to please men, I would not be a servant
of Christ.

Paul Called by God

11 I want you to know, brothers,[p] that the gospel
I preached is not something that man made up.
12 I did not receive it from any man,[q] nor was I
taught it; rather, I received it by revelation[r] from
Jesus Christ.

13 For you have heard of my previous way of life
in Judaism,[s] how intensely I persecuted the church
of God and tried to destroy it.[t] 14 I was advancing in
Judaism beyond many Jews of my own age and
was extremely zealous for the traditions of my
fathers.[u] 15 But when God, who set me apart from
birth[a][v] and called me[w] by his grace, was pleased
16 to reveal his Son in me so that I might preach him
among the Gentiles,[x] I did not consult any man,[y]
17 nor did I go up to Jerusalem to see those who
were apostles before I was, but I went immediately into Arabia and later returned to Damascus.

18 Then after three years,[z] I went up to
Jerusalem[a] to get acquainted with Peter[b] and
stayed with him fifteen days. 19 I saw none of the
other apostles—only James,[b] the Lord's brother.
20 I assure you before God that what I am writing
you is no lie.[c] 21 Later I went to Syria and Cilicia.[d]
22 I was personally unknown to the churches of
Judea[e] that are in Christ. 23 They only heard the
report: "The man who formerly persecuted us is
now preaching the faith[f] he once tried to destroy."
24 And they praised God[g] because of me.

[a] 15 Or *from my mother's womb* [b] 18 Greek *Cephas*

1:1 [a]Ac 9:15 [b]Ac 2:24
1:2 [c]Php 4:21 [d]Ac 16:6; 1Co 16:1
1:3 [e]Ro 1:7
1:4 [f]Mt 20:28; Ro 4:25; Gal 2:20 [g]Php 4:20
1:5 [h]Ro 11:36
1:6 [i]Gal 5:8 [j]2Co 11:4
1:7 [k]Ac 15:24; Gal 5:10
1:8 [l]2Co 11:4 [m]Ro 9:3
1:9 [n]Ro 16:17
1:10 [o]Ro 2:29; 1Th 2:4
1:11 [p]1Co 15:1
1:12 [q]ver 1 [r]ver 16
1:13 [s]Ac 26:4,5 [t]Ac 8:3
1:14 [u]Mt 15:2
1:15 [v]Isa 49:1,5; Jer 1:5 [w]Ac 9:15
1:16 [x]Gal 2:9 [y]Mt 16:17
1:18 [z]Ac 9:22,23 [a]Ac 9:26,27
1:19 [b]Mt 13:55
1:20 [c]Ro 9:1
1:21 [d]Ac 6:9
1:22 [e]1Th 2:14
1:23 [f]Ac 6:7
1:24 [g]Mt 9:8

The Truth

GAL 1:8,12

It's hard to imagine Paul being more certain of the truth he preaches to the Galatians. He trusts in the truth of the gospel only as much as he trusts the One who gives it to him. Paul's revelation is indisputable, for it comes, not from any human source—the writings or teaching of someone—but from Jesus Christ himself. Paul is so completely convinced of the truth that he warns the church at Galatia to reject any teaching that might appear contradictory, even if it comes from himself or an angel!

How sure are you of the gospel? Questions and doubts are a normal part of the journey of faith. Yet it is God's desire that we believe completely in him. What unspoken questions might be keeping your faith from deepening? Don't be afraid to take them to God. Go now and echo the prayer of the man who cried, "I do believe; help me overcome my unbelief!" (Mk 9:24).

Paul Rebukes Peter

GAL 2:11-17

The church has already decided that Gentile believers shouldn't be required to adopt Jewish customs (Ac 15:28-29). Peter's actions seem to undermine this decision. Until recently, Peter has associated freely with Gentiles and has even eaten meals with them. But when representatives from the church at Jerusalem arrive, a fearful Peter begins to withdraw from his Gentile friends, probably remembering that he once was rebuked for establishing similar relationships (Ac 11:1-18).

Understandably, Peter's behavior is upsetting to Paul, who is a strong advocate of Gentiles in the church. One concern is that Peter's actions will cause believers to think that Gentiles must observe Jewish traditions, a contradiction to the gospel of grace. Another danger is that two separate Christian churches might be established, one for Jews and one for Gentiles, causing division in the body of Christ. Paul also wants to halt any action that might falsely give the impression that Jews are superior to other believers (Ro 3:9).

Paul Accepted by the Apostles

2 Fourteen years later I went up again to Jerusalem,[h] this time with Barnabas. I took Titus along also. 2 I went in response to a revelation and set before them the gospel that I preach among the Gentiles.[i] But I did this privately to those who seemed to be leaders, for fear that I was running or had run my race[j] in vain. 3 Yet not even Titus,[k] who was with me, was compelled to be circumcised, even though he was a Greek.[l] 4 ⌊This matter arose⌋ because some false brothers[m] had infiltrated our ranks to spy on[n] the freedom[o] we have in Christ Jesus and to make us slaves. 5 We did not give in to them for a moment, so that the truth of the gospel[p] might remain with you.

6 As for those who seemed to be important[q]—whatever they were makes no difference to me; God does not judge by external appearance[r]—those men added nothing to my message. 7 On the contrary, they saw that I had been entrusted with the task[s] of preaching the gospel to the Gentiles,[a][t] just as Peter[u] had been to the Jews.[b] 8 For God, who was at work in the ministry of Peter as an apostle[v] to the Jews, was also at work in my ministry as an apostle to the Gentiles. 9 James, Peter[c][w] and John, those reputed to be pillars,[x] gave me and Barnabas[y] the right hand of fellowship when they recognized the grace given to me.[z] They agreed that we should go to the Gentiles, and they to the Jews. 10 All they asked was that we should continue to remember the poor,[a] the very thing I was eager to do.

Paul Opposes Peter

11 When Peter[b] came to Antioch,[c] I opposed him to his face, because he was clearly in the wrong. 12 Before certain men came from James, he used to eat with the Gentiles.[d] But when they arrived, he began to draw back and separate himself from the Gentiles because he was afraid of those who belonged to the circumcision group.[e] 13 The other Jews joined him in his hypocrisy, so that by their hypocrisy even Barnabas[f] was led astray.

14 When I saw that they were not acting in line with the truth of the gospel,[g] I said to Peter[h] in front of them all, "You are a Jew, yet you live like a Gentile and not like a Jew.[i] How is it, then, that you force Gentiles to follow Jewish customs?

15 "We who are Jews by birth[j] and not 'Gentile sinners'[k] 16 know that a man is not justified by observing the law, but by faith in Jesus Christ.[l] So we, too, have put our faith in Christ Jesus that we may be justified by faith in Christ and not by observing the law, because by observing the law no one will be justified.

17 "If, while we seek to be justified in Christ, it becomes evident that we ourselves are sinners,[m] does that mean that Christ promotes sin? Absolute-

[a] 7 Greek *uncircumcised* [b] 7 Greek *circumcised*; also in verses 8 and 9 [c] 9 Greek *Cephas*; also in verses 11 and 14

2:1 [h]Ac 15:2
2:2 [i]Ac 15:4,12 [j]1Co 9:24; Php 2:16
2:3 [k]2Co 2:13 [l]Ac 16:3; 1Co 9:21
2:4 [m]2Co 11:26 [n]Jude 4 [o]Ac 15:1; Gal 5:1,13
2:5 [p]ver 14
2:6 [q]Gal 6:3 [r]Ac 10:34
2:7 [s]1Th 2:4; 1Ti 1:11 [t]Ac 9:15 [u]ver 9,11,14
2:8 [v]Ac 1:25
2:9 [w]ver 7,11,14 [x]1Ti 3:15 [y]Ac 4:36 [z]Ro 12:3
2:10 [a]Ac 24:17
2:11 [b]ver 7,9,14 [c]Ac 11:19
2:12 [d]Ac 11:3 [e]Ac 11:2
2:13 [f]ver 1; Ac 4:36
2:14 [g]ver 5 [h]ver 7,9,11 [i]Ac 10:28
2:15 [j]Php 3:4,5 [k]1Sa 15:18
2:16 [l]Ac 13:39; Ro 9:30
2:17 [m]ver 15

ly not![n] 18If I rebuild what I destroyed, I prove that
I am a lawbreaker. 19For through the law I died to
the law[o] so that I might live for God.[p] 20I have been
crucified with Christ[q] and I no longer live, but
Christ lives in me.[r] The life I live in the body, I live
by faith in the Son of God,[s] who loved me[t] and
gave himself for me.[u] 21I do not set aside the grace
of God, for if righteousness could be gained
through the law,[v] Christ died for nothing!"[a]

Faith or Observance of the Law

3 You foolish Galatians! Who has bewitched
you?[w] Before your very eyes Jesus Christ was
clearly portrayed as crucified.[x] 2I would like to
learn just one thing from you: Did you receive the
Spirit by observing the law, or by believing what
you heard?[y] 3Are you so foolish? After beginning
with the Spirit, are you now trying to attain your
goal by human effort? 4Have you suffered so much
for nothing—if it really was for nothing? 5Does
God give you his Spirit and work miracles[z] among
you because you observe the law, or because you
believe what you heard?

6Consider Abraham: "He believed God, and it
was credited to him as righteousness."[b][a] 7Under-
stand, then, that those who believe[b] are children
of Abraham. 8The Scripture foresaw that God
would justify the Gentiles by faith, and announced the gospel in advance to Abraham: "All
nations will be blessed through you."[c][c] 9So those
who have faith[d] are blessed along with Abraham,
the man of faith.

10All who rely on observing the law are under a
curse, for it is written: "Cursed is everyone who
does not continue to do everything written in the
Book of the Law."[d][e] 11Clearly no one is justified
before God by the law, because, "The righteous
will live by faith."[e][f] 12The law is not based on
faith; on the contrary, "The man who does these
things will live by them."[f][g] 13Christ redeemed us
from the curse of the law[h] by becoming a curse
for us, for it is written: "Cursed is everyone who is
hung on a tree."[g][i] 14He redeemed us in order that
the blessing given to Abraham might come to the
Gentiles through Christ Jesus,[j] so that by faith we
might receive the promise of the Spirit.[k]

The Law and the Promise

15Brothers, let me take an example from everyday life. Just as no one can set aside or add to a
human covenant that has been duly established,
so it is in this case. 16The promises were spoken to
Abraham and to his seed.[l] The Scripture does not
say "and to seeds," meaning many people, but
"and to your seed,"[h] meaning one person, who is
Christ. 17What I mean is this: The law, introduced

2:17 [n]Gal 3:21
2:19 [o]Ro 7:4 [p]Ro 6:10,11, 14; 2Co 5:15
2:20 [q]Ro 6:6 [r]1Pe 4:2 [s]Mt 4:3 [t]Ro 8:37 [u]Gal 1:4
2:21 [v]Gal 3:21
3:1 [w]Gal 5:7 [x]1Co 1:23
3:2 [y]Ro 10:17
3:5 [z]1Co 12:10
3:6 [a]Ge 15:6; Ro 4:3
3:7 [b]ver 9
3:8 [c]Ge 12:3; Ac 3:25
3:9 [d]ver 7; Ro 4:16
3:10 [e]Dt 27:26; Jer 11:3
3:11 [f]Hab 2:4; Gal 2:16; Heb 10:38
3:12 [g]Lev 18:5; Ro 10:5
3:13 [h]Gal 4:5 [i]Dt 21:23; Ac 5:30
3:14 [j]Ro 4:9,16 [k]ver 2; Joel 2:28; Ac 2:33
3:16 [l]Lk 1:55; Ro 4:13,16

[a] *21* Some interpreters end the quotation after verse 14.
[b] *6* Gen. 15:6 [c] *8* Gen. 12:3; 18:18; 22:18 [d] *10* Deut. 27:26 [e] *11* Hab. 2:4 [f] *12* Lev. 18:5 [g] *13* Deut. 21:23
[h] *16* Gen. 12:7; 13:15; 24:7

Crucified With Christ

GAL 2:20–21

What does Paul mean when he says he has been "crucified with Christ"? Clearly, he is not talking about a literal crucifixion, for he is still alive. His death wouldn't be necessary anyway because Jesus has already made that sacrifice for him—and for us. Yet it is in that very sense that Christ's crucifixion is Paul's, just as it is ours. We, too, have been crucified with Christ. When he died on the cross, he died for *our* sins—so in a sense, we died with him (2Co 5:14).

Imagine yourself standing before Jesus just before he is nailed to the cross. Envision yourself handing over to him every sin in your past, present and future. In the future, when you hear the phrase "crucified with Christ," let that image come to mind, and remember that when Christ gave his life, he did it willingly and lovingly—for you.

Equal and Valuable

GAL 3:28

In our society many people make judgments based on gender, race or age. Most of us have encountered men who believe their gender is superior to ours; increasingly, women are making their own bold claims of superiority over men.

Throughout Jesus' ministry and the early history of the church, believers also attempted to claim superiority or favoritism. Jesus' own disciples argued over who was the greatest (Mk 9:34; Lk 9:46). Some Jews sought to elevate themselves above the Gentiles (Ac 11:1–3; 15:1–5).

Here, Paul clarifies the hierarchy of God's kingdom: There isn't one! No believer is greater than any other. In Christ, distinctions no longer exist. We are not judged on our own merits but on those of Jesus. Therefore, each one of us is valuable, every one of us great. And while equality in Christ does not mean that we are all alike, it does testify that we are all deeply valued and loved.

430 years[m] later, does not set aside the covenant
previously established by God and thus do away
with the promise. 18For if the inheritance depends
on the law, then it no longer depends on a promise;[n] but God in his grace gave it to Abraham
through a promise.
19What, then, was the purpose of the law? It
was added because of transgressions[o] until the
Seed[p] to whom the promise referred had come.
The law was put into effect through angels[q] by a
mediator.[r] 20A mediator,[s] however, does not represent just one party; but God is one.
21Is the law, therefore, opposed to the promises
of God? Absolutely not![t] For if a law had been giv-
en that could impart life, then righteousness
would certainly have come by the law.[u] 22But the
Scripture declares that the whole world is a prisoner of sin,[v] so that what was promised, being
given through faith in Jesus Christ, might be giv-
en to those who believe.
23Before this faith came, we were held prisoners[w] by the law, locked up until faith should be
revealed. 24So the law was put in charge to lead
us to Christ[a][x] that we might be justified by faith.[y]
25Now that faith has come, we are no longer under
the supervision of the law.

Sons of God

26You are all sons of God[z] through faith in Christ
Jesus, 27for all of you who were baptized into
Christ[a] have clothed yourselves with Christ.[b]
28There is neither Jew nor Greek, slave nor free,[c]
male nor female, for you are all one in Christ
Jesus.[d] 29If you belong to Christ,[e] then you are
Abraham's seed, and heirs according to the
promise.[f]

4 What I am saying is that as long as the heir is
a child, he is no different from a slave,
although he owns the whole estate. 2He is subject
to guardians and trustees until the time set by his
father. 3So also, when we were children, we were
in slavery[g] under the basic principles of the
world.[h] 4But when the time had fully come,[i] God
sent his Son, born of a woman,[j] born under law,[k]
5to redeem those under law, that we might receive
the full rights[l] of sons. 6Because you are sons, God
sent the Spirit of his Son into our hearts,[m] the
Spirit who calls out, *"Abba,*[b] Father."[n] 7So you are
no longer a slave, but a son; and since you are a
son, God has made you also an heir.[o]

Paul's Concern for the Galatians

8Formerly, when you did not know God,[p] you
were slaves to those who by nature are not gods.[q]
9But now that you know God—or rather are
known by God[r]—how is it that you are turning
back to those weak and miserable principles? Do
you wish to be enslaved[s] by them all over again?[t]
10You are observing special days and months and

3:17 [m]Ge 15:13, 14; Ex 12:40
3:18 [n]Ro 4:14
3:19 [o]Ro 5:20 [p]ver 16 [q]Ac 7:53 [r]Ex 20:19
3:20 [s]Heb 8:6; 9:15; 12:24
3:21 [t]Gal 2:17 [u]Gal 2:21
3:22 [v]Ro 3:9-19; 11:32
3:23 [w]Ro 11:32
3:24 [x]Ro 10:4 [y]Gal 2:16
3:26 [z]Ro 8:14
3:27 [a]Mt 28:19; Ro 6:3 [b]Ro 13:14
3:28 [c]Col 3:11 [d]Jn 10:16; 17:11; Eph 2:14,15
3:29 [e]1Co 3:23 [f]ver 16
4:3 [g]Gal 2:4 [h]Col 2:8,20
4:4 [i]Mk 1:15; Eph 1:10 [j]Jn 1:14 [k]Lk 2:27
4:5 [l]Jn 1:12
4:6 [m]Ro 5:5 [n]Ro 8:15,16
4:7 [o]Ro 8:17
4:8 [p]1Co 1:21; Eph 2:12; 1Th 4:5 [q]2Ch 13:9; Isa 37:19
4:9 [r]1Co 8:3 [s]ver 3 [t]Col 2:20

[a] 24 Or *charge until Christ came* [b] 6 Aramaic for *Father*

4:10 seasons and years![u] 11I fear for you, that somehow
uRo 14:5 I have wasted my efforts on you.[v]
4:11 12I plead with you, brothers,[w] become like me,
v1Th 3:5 for I became like you. You have done me no
4:12 wrong. 13As you know, it was because of an ill-
wGal 6:18 ness[x] that I first preached the gospel to you.
4:13 14Even though my illness was a trial to you, you
x1Co 2:3 did not treat me with contempt or scorn. Instead,
4:14 you welcomed me as if I were an angel of God, as
yMt 10:40 if I were Christ Jesus himself.[y] 15What has happened to all your joy? I can testify that, if you
could have done so, you would have torn out your
4:16 eyes and given them to me. 16Have I now become
zAm 5:10 your enemy by telling you the truth?[z]
17Those people are zealous to win you over, but
for no good. What they want is to alienate you ⌊from
us⌋, so that you may be zealous for them. 18It is fine
4:18 to be zealous, provided the purpose is good, and to
aver 13,14 be so always and not just when I am with you.[a]
4:19 19My dear children,[b] for whom I am again in the
b1Co 4:15 pains of childbirth until Christ is formed in you,[c]
cEph 4:13 20how I wish I could be with you now and change
my tone, because I am perplexed about you!

Hagar and Sarah

21Tell me, you who want to be under the law,
are you not aware of what the law says? 22For it is
written that Abraham had two sons, one by the
4:22 slave woman[d] and the other by the free woman.[e]
dGe 16:15 23His son by the slave woman was born in the
eGe 21:2 ordinary way;[f] but his son by the free woman was
4:23 born as the result of a promise.[g]
fRo 9:7,8 24These things may be taken figuratively, for the
gGe 18:10-14; women represent two covenants. One covenant is
Heb 11:11 from Mount Sinai and bears children who are to
be slaves: This is Hagar. 25Now Hagar stands for
Mount Sinai in Arabia and corresponds to the
present city of Jerusalem, because she is in slavery with her children. 26But the Jerusalem that is
4:26 above[h] is free, and she is our mother. 27For it is
hHeb 12:22; Rev 3:12 written:

"Be glad, O barren woman,
who bears no children;
break forth and cry aloud,
you who have no labor pains;
because more are the children of the
4:27 desolate woman
iIsa 54:1 than of her who has a husband."[a][i]

28Now you, brothers, like Isaac, are children of
promise. 29At that time the son born in the ordi-
4:29 nary way[j] persecuted the son born by the power
jver 23 kGe 21:9 of the Spirit.[k] It is the same now. 30But what does
the Scripture say? "Get rid of the slave woman and
her son, for the slave woman's son will never
4:30 share in the inheritance with the free woman's
lGe 21:10 son."[b][l] 31Therefore, brothers, we are not children
of the slave woman, but of the free woman.

[a] *27* Isaiah 54:1 [b] *30* Gen. 21:10

The only way we can fulfill the will of God in our lives is to be love-inspired, love-mastered, and love-driven. A person controlled by the Holy Spirit needs no law to cause her to live a righteous life. I imagine we've all been in situations where self-control was difficult to maintain, but we will bear the fruit of God's Spirit if we surrender to him.

—Thelma Wells

Freedom

GAL 5

The freedom Paul speaks of is not freedom to act however one desires (Gal 5:16–21); it is freedom from the law. Before Christ's sacrifice, the Jewish people attempted, unsuccessfully, to gain a right relationship with God by obeying certain laws. In Christ, however, a new relationship with God has been created. When guided by their relationship with God, believers follow the way of righteousness not because they have to, but because they want to. And therein they find freedom because the law has no bearing on their actions. Despite the vast superiority of this new covenant, some people are tempted to return to the familiar confines of the old regulations—something Paul clearly warns against.

In addition to freedom from the law's authority, believers also enjoy the freedom to participate in the work of the Spirit. As believers allow themselves to be guided, evidence of their freedom, the fruit of the Spirit (Gal 5:22–25), will appear in their lives.

Freedom in Christ

5 It is for freedom that Christ has set us free.[m]
Stand firm,[n] then, and do not let yourselves be
burdened again by a yoke of slavery.[o]
2Mark my words! I, Paul, tell you that if you let
yourselves be circumcised,[p] Christ will be of no
value to you at all. 3Again I declare to every man
who lets himself be circumcised that he is obligated to obey the whole law.[q] 4You who are trying
to be justified by law have been alienated from
Christ; you have fallen away from grace.[r] 5But by
faith we eagerly await through the Spirit the righteousness for which we hope.[s] 6For in Christ Jesus
neither circumcision nor uncircumcision has any
value.[t] The only thing that counts is faith expressing itself through love.[u]
7You were running a good race.[v] Who cut in on
you[w] and kept you from obeying the truth? 8That
kind of persuasion does not come from the one
who calls you.[x] 9"A little yeast works through the
whole batch of dough."[y] 10I am confident[z] in the
Lord that you will take no other view.[a] The one
who is throwing you into confusion[b] will pay the
penalty, whoever he may be. 11Brothers, if I am
still preaching circumcision, why am I still being
persecuted?[c] In that case the offense[d] of the cross
has been abolished. 12As for those agitators,[e] I
wish they would go the whole way and emascu-
late themselves!
13You, my brothers, were called to be free. But
do not use your freedom to indulge the sinful
nature[a];[f] rather, serve one another[g] in love. 14The
entire law is summed up in a single command:
"Love your neighbor as yourself."[b][h] 15If you keep
on biting and devouring each other, watch out or
you will be destroyed by each other.

Life by the Spirit

16So I say, live by the Spirit,[i] and you will not
gratify the desires of the sinful nature.[j] 17For the
sinful nature desires what is contrary to the Spirit, and the Spirit what is contrary to the sinful
nature.[k] They are in conflict with each other, so
that you do not do what you want.[l] 18But if you
are led by the Spirit, you are not under law.[m]
19The acts of the sinful nature are obvious: sexual immorality,[n] impurity and debauchery; 20idol-
atry and witchcraft; hatred, discord, jealousy, fits
of rage, selfish ambition, dissensions, factions
21and envy; drunkenness, orgies, and the like.[o] I
warn you, as I did before, that those who live like
this will not inherit the kingdom of God.
22But the fruit[p] of the Spirit is love,[q] joy, peace,
patience, kindness, goodness, faithfulness, 23gen-
tleness and self-control.[r] Against such things there
is no law. 24Those who belong to Christ Jesus have
crucified the sinful nature[s] with its passions and
desires.[t] 25Since we live by the Spirit, let us keep

[a] *13* Or *the flesh*; also in verses 16, 17, 19 and 24
[b] *14* Lev. 19:18

5:1 [m]Jn 8:32 [n]1Co 16:13 [o]Ac 15:10; Gal 2:4
5:2 [p]Ac 15:1
5:3 [q]Gal 3:10
5:4 [r]Heb 12:15; 2Pe 3:17
5:5 [s]Ro 8:23,24
5:6 [t]1Co 7:19 [u]1Th 1:3
5:7 [v]1Co 9:24 [w]Gal 3:1
5:8 [x]Ro 8:28; Gal 1:6
5:9 [y]1Co 5:6
5:10 [z]2Co 2:3 [a]Php 3:15 [b]Gal 1:7
5:11 [c]Gal 4:29; 6:12 [d]1Co 1:23
5:12 [e]ver 10
5:13 [f]1Co 8:9; 1Pe 2:16 [g]1Co 9:19; Eph 5:21
5:14 [h]Lev 19:18; Mt 22:39
5:16 [i]Ro 8:2,4-6, 9,14 [j]ver 24
5:17 [k]Ro 8:5-8 [l]Ro 7:15-23
5:18 [m]Ro 6:14; 1Ti 1:9
5:19 [n]1Co 6:18
5:21 [o]Ro 13:13
5:22 [p]Mt 7:16-20; Eph 5:9 [q]Col 3:12-15
5:23 [r]Ac 24:25
5:24 [s]Ro 6:6 [t]ver 16,17

Week 44

Whose Slave Are You?

Have you become a slave to your job, your home, your spouse, your children? Eventually, something or someone will run your life. Of course, there are always the independent types who say they run their own lives—Ha! They're *really* clueless. The truth is that all of us are slaves, either "slaves to sin" or "slaves to righteousness" (Ro 6:16–18). So what does Paul mean when he says, "It is for freedom that Christ has set us free" (Gal 5:1)?

How can you know if you are a slave to something (Ro 6:16; 2Pe 2:19)? In light of these Scriptures, what are you a slave to?

Who is a "slave to sin" according to Jesus (Jn 8:34)? As a Christian, how has your slave status changed (1Co 7:22–23)?

Since you are now a slave of God, what must you do (Eph 6:6)? Is your freedom from sin a freedom to do your own will (1Pe 4:2)? What should you use your freedom for (Gal 5:13; 1Pe 2:16)?

Is it possible to be burdened again by a life of slavery after having once been set free (Gal 4:8–10; 5:1)? How have you done this, to a greater or lesser extent, in your life? How can you gain freedom again in that area of your life (Ps 118:5; Jn 8:31-32; 2Co 3:17)?

What is the difference between the status of a slave and that of a son or daughter (Jn 8:34–36)? Are you, ultimately, a slave or a child (Gal 4:7)? What difference does that change in status make in your life, spiritually and practically?

Enjoying God THROUGH the Word

Read Romans 8:9–17 (page 1859). Here is wonderful news! Although you were once a slave controlled by your sinful nature, you are now free to be controlled by the Holy Spirit. Jesus no longer calls you a servant; he calls you his friend (Jn 15:14–15). But more than that—God has declared you to be his child (1Jn 3:1). Although a slave may be treated as part of the family, the slave has no rights as an heir—only children of the master are heirs. But God has called you his child, his heir (Tit 3:4–7). He has given you his Spirit, "and where the Spirit of the Lord is, there is freedom" (2Co 3:17). You now have the freedom to serve God (Eph 6:6) and to "serve one another in love" (Gal 5:13).

The freedom described in the Scriptures is not freedom to be independent. You will always have a master. Which master will you choose? If you choose sin, it will end in death, but if you choose Jesus Christ, it will lead to righteousness and life (Ro 6:16).

Enjoying God THROUGH Experience

Examine your heart. Are you living a life controlled by self, by sin or by the Spirit? Ask God to reveal areas in your life that need to be surrendered to his control. Pray for the Holy Spirit's power to choose God's way and God's will in your life. In him you will find true freedom to enjoy both God and your life.

Go to page 1931 for your next weekly study.

Dangers of Comparison

GAL 6:4–5

The practice of comparing ourselves with others is so common in today's society that it's difficult to imagine how *not* to do it. Our bodies, children, salaries, spouses and houses are all fair game. Yet our reason for comparing remains a mystery. Rarely does it bring anything but misery. If, in our minds, we dominate the subject of our comparison, we can easily be swallowed up by pride. If we don't measure up favorably, our self-esteem suffers a severe blow. Neither option brings glory to God.

Paul suggests that we focus instead on our own responsibilities. Are we faithfully living for God and fulfilling our responsibilities before him? Ask yourself now: Am I living up to my potential? Is my love for Christ as deep as it could be?

in step with the Spirit. [26]Let us not become conceited,[u] provoking and envying each other.

Doing Good to All

6 Brothers, if someone is caught in a sin, you
who are spiritual[v] should restore him gently.
But watch yourself, or you also may be tempted.
[2]Carry each other's burdens, and in this way you
will fulfill the law of Christ.[w] [3]If anyone thinks he
is something[x] when he is nothing, he deceives
himself. [4]Each one should test his own actions.
Then he can take pride in himself, without comparing himself to somebody else, [5]for each one
should carry his own load.
[6]Anyone who receives instruction in the word
must share all good things with his instructor.[y]
[7]Do not be deceived:[z] God cannot be mocked.
A man reaps what he sows.[a] [8]The one who sows
to please his sinful nature, from that nature[a] will
reap destruction;[b] the one who sows to please the
Spirit, from the Spirit will reap eternal life.[c] [9]Let us
not become weary in doing good,[d] for at the proper time we will reap a harvest if we do not give
up.[e] [10]Therefore, as we have opportunity, let us do
good[f] to all people, especially to those who belong
to the family[g] of believers.

Not Circumcision but a New Creation

[11]See what large letters I use as I write to you
with my own hand![h]
[12]Those who want to make a good impression
outwardly are trying to compel you to be circumcised.[i] The only reason they do this is to avoid
being persecuted[j] for the cross of Christ. [13]Not
even those who are circumcised obey the law,[k] yet
they want you to be circumcised that they may
boast about your flesh.[l] [14]May I never boast except
in the cross of our Lord Jesus Christ, through
which[b] the world has been crucified to me, and I
to the world.[m] [15]Neither circumcision nor uncircumcision means anything;[n] what counts is a new
creation.[o] [16]Peace and mercy to all who follow this
rule, even to the Israel of God.
[17]Finally, let no one cause me trouble, for I bear
on my body the marks[p] of Jesus.
[18]The grace of our Lord Jesus Christ[q] be with
your spirit,[r] brothers. Amen.

5:26 [u]Php 2:3
6:1 [v]1Co 2:15
6:2 [w]Ro 15:1; Jas 2:8
6:3 [x]Ro 12:3; 1Co 8:2
6:6 [y]1Co 9:11,14
6:7 [z]1Co 6:9 [a]2Co 9:6
6:8 [b]Job 4:8; Hos 8:7 [c]Jas 3:18
6:9 [d]1Co 15:58 [e]Rev 2:10
6:10 [f]Pr 3:27 [g]Eph 2:19
6:11 [h]1Co 16:21
6:12 [i]Ac 15:1 [j]Gal 5:11
6:13 [k]Ro 2:25 [l]Php 3:3
6:14 [m]Ro 6:2,6
6:15 [n]1Co 7:19 [o]2Co 5:17
6:17 [p]Isa 44:5; 2Co 1:5
6:18 [q]Ro 16:20 [r]2Ti 4:22

[a]8 Or *his flesh, from the flesh* [b]14 Or *whom*

Ephesians

A new identity in Christ.

Paul sends this personal message to the believers at Ephesus, as well as the churches in the surrounding areas, to encourage them. Reminding the Ephesians of their spiritual resources and offering many practical suggestions, he urges them to look at their relationship with God in a new way. He helps them discover what this new life "in Christ" is, how to live in Christ and how to face the struggles of life through Christ's power.

Paul develops his theme of the believers' relationship in Christ through a series of word pictures. He begins by asking God to fill his children with spiritual wisdom (Eph 1). He goes on to explain that believers are no longer dead in sin but alive in Christ and that they are a temple in which God dwells (Eph 2). Believers are not children of darkness but children of light, according to Paul (Eph 4), and are to be imitators of God in the way they live (Eph 5). Paul concludes by offering valuable lessons for nurturing a marriage and a family just as Christ does the church (Eph 5–6) and for waging spiritual warfare using the armor of God (Eph 6).

In the book of Ephesians, Paul paints a clear picture of God's love for everyone in the body of Christ. No matter what our skills or abilities may be, we are all necessary. God's family would not be complete without any one of us. Recognizing such a purpose and high calling should fill us with joy and encourage us to live each day as true children of God *in Christ*.

Quick Study

Author
The apostle Paul.

Date Written
Around A.D. 60.

Written From
Rome during Paul's imprisonment there.

Key Passage
Ephesians 1:5–8 "In love he predestined us to be adopted as his sons through Jesus Christ, in accordance with his pleasure and will—to the praise of his glorious grace, which he has freely given us in the One he loves. In him we have redemption through his blood, the forgiveness of sins, in accordance with the riches of God's grace that he lavished on us with all wisdom and understanding."

Outline

Paul's greetings.
Eph 1:1-2

In Christ.
Eph 1:3–2:22

Preacher to the Gentiles.
Eph 3

Unity in Christ.
Eph 4:1-16

Children of the light.
Eph 4:17–5:21

Lessons on various relationships.
Eph 5:22–6:9

God's armor.
Eph 6:10-20

Final greetings.
Eph 6:21-24

The Women of Ephesians

Wives — *Relationships with their husbands examined.*
Eph 5:21-33

1 Paul, an apostle[a] of Christ Jesus by the will of
God,[b]

To the saints in Ephesus,[a] the faithful[bc] in Christ
Jesus:

2 Grace and peace to you from God our Father
and the Lord Jesus Christ.[d]

Spiritual Blessings in Christ

3 Praise be to the God and Father of our Lord
Jesus Christ,[e] who has blessed us in the heavenly
realms[f] with every spiritual blessing in Christ.
4 For he chose us in him before the creation of the
world to be holy and blameless[g] in his sight. In
love[h] 5 he[c] predestined[i] us to be adopted as his
sons through Jesus Christ, in accordance with his
pleasure[j] and will— 6 to the praise of his glorious
grace, which he has freely given us in the One he
loves.[k] 7 In him we have redemption[l] through his
blood, the forgiveness of sins, in accordance with
the riches of God's grace 8 that he lavished on us
with all wisdom and understanding. 9 And he[d]
made known to us the mystery[m] of his will
according to his good pleasure, which he purposed in Christ, 10 to be put into effect when the
times will have reached their fulfillment[n]—to
bring all things in heaven and on earth together
under one head, even Christ.[o]

11 In him we were also chosen,[e] having been predestined according to the plan of him who works
out everything in conformity with the purpose[p] of
his will, 12 in order that we, who were the first to
hope in Christ, might be for the praise of his glory.[q] 13 And you also were included in Christ when
you heard the word of truth,[r] the gospel of your
salvation. Having believed, you were marked in
him with a seal,[s] the promised Holy Spirit, 14 who
is a deposit guaranteeing our inheritance[t] until the
redemption of those who are God's possession—to
the praise of his glory.

Thanksgiving and Prayer

15 For this reason, ever since I heard about your
faith in the Lord Jesus and your love for all the
saints,[u] 16 I have not stopped giving thanks for
you,[v] remembering you in my prayers. 17 I keep
asking that the God of our Lord Jesus Christ, the
glorious Father,[w] may give you the Spirit[f] of wisdom[x] and revelation, so that you may know him
better. 18 I pray also that the eyes of your heart may
be enlightened[y] in order that you may know the
hope to which he has called you, the riches of his
glorious inheritance in the saints, 19 and his
incomparably great power for us who believe.
That power[z] is like the working of his mighty
strength,[a] 20 which he exerted in Christ when he

1:1 [a]1Co 1:1 [b]2Co 1:1 [c]Col 1:2
1:2 [d]Ro 1:7
1:3 [e]2Co 1:3 [f]Eph 2:6; 3:10; 6:12
1:4 [g]Eph 5:27; Col 1:22 [h]Eph 4:2,15, 16
1:5 [i]Ro 8:29,30 [j]1Co 1:21
1:6 [k]Mt 3:17
1:7 [l]Ro 3:24
1:9 [m]Ro 16:25
1:10 [n]Gal 4:4 [o]Col 1:20
1:11 [p]Eph 3:11; Heb 6:17
1:12 [q]ver 6,14
1:13 [r]Col 1:5 [s]Eph 4:30
1:14 [t]Ac 20:32
1:15 [u]Col 1:4
1:16 [v]Ro 1:8
1:17 [w]Jn 20:17 [x]Col 1:9
1:18 [y]Ac 26:18; 2Co 4:6
1:19 [z]Col 1:29 [a]Eph 6:10

[a] 1 Some early manuscripts do not have *in Ephesus.* [b] 1 Or *believers who are* [c] 4,5 Or *sight in love.* [5]*He* [d] 8,9 Or *us. With all wisdom and understanding,* [9]*he* [e] 11 Or *were made heirs* [f] 17 Or *a spirit*

The Chosen

EPH 1:4-5,11

The doctrines of election and predestination have caused hours of discussion as well as dissension in the church. First, the doctrine of election tells us that because God is sovereign, he is in control of all things at all times. No event ever catches him by surprise. Included within his sovereignty is his selection—or election—of people who at some point in their lives will turn in faith to him. At the same time, we as humans are free to choose how we live our lives. Only God understands how it is possible for these two realities, which seem mutually exclusive, to be simultaneously true.

Second, on the doctrine of predestination, there are two primary views. The view of Arminianism, established by Dutch theologian Jacobus Arminius, emphasizes the power of a person's free will. Christ died for all people, and anyone can accept or refuse the gift of redemption. According to the Arminian view, God elects those people who would have chosen Christ anyway (called foreknowledge). In contrast, Calvinism, named for French theologian and reformer John Calvin, stresses the importance of God's election. In the Calvinist view, called "irresistible grace," God chooses those whom he will save. These predestined ones have neither the opportunity nor desire to turn away.

Life Versus Death

EPH 2:1-10

At the heart of the gospel is the message of salvation: the story of life versus death. Paul reminds the Ephesians of where they once were: spiritually dead in sin. Next, he celebrates with them the spiritual life they now have in Jesus Christ. He goes on to speak of the "heavenly realms" (Eph 2:6), where they will now live and live with Jesus in the ages to come.

It is important for all believers to be reminded of what they have been given. They have not received just the gift of goodness, they have received the gift of life *(Eph 2:4-5). Christians have, in the very truest sense, escaped death—and not through any merit of their own. Grace, not good works, is their salvation (Eph 2:8-9). Though physical bodies will perish, spirits live on with Christ. Even while we are still here on earth, Jesus gives us a new vitality, a new awareness of what it means to truly* live *when we turn our hearts toward him.*

raised him from the dead[b] and seated him at his
right hand in the heavenly realms, 21far above all
rule and authority, power and dominion, and
every title[c] that can be given, not only in the present age but also in the one to come. 22And God
placed all things under his feet[d] and appointed
him to be head[e] over everything for the church,
23which is his body, the fullness of him who fills
everything in every way.

Made Alive in Christ

2 As for you, you were dead in your transgressions and sins,[f] 2in which you used to live[g]
when you followed the ways of this world and of
the ruler of the kingdom of the air,[h] the spirit who
is now at work in those who are disobedient.[i] 3All
of us also lived among them at one time, gratify-
ing the cravings of our sinful nature[a][j] and following its desires and thoughts. Like the rest, we
were by nature objects of wrath. 4But because of
his great love for us, God, who is rich in mercy,
5made us alive with Christ even when we were
dead in transgressions[k]—it is by grace you have
been saved.[l] 6And God raised us up with Christ
and seated us with him[m] in the heavenly realms[n]
in Christ Jesus, 7in order that in the coming ages
he might show the incomparable riches of his
grace, expressed in his kindness[o] to us in Christ
Jesus. 8For it is by grace you have been saved,[p]
through faith—and this not from yourselves, it is
the gift of God— 9not by works,[q] so that no one
can boast.[r] 10For we are God's workmanship, created[s] in Christ Jesus to do good works,[t] which
God prepared in advance for us to do.

One in Christ

11Therefore, remember that formerly you who
are Gentiles by birth and called "uncircumcised"
by those who call themselves "the circumcision"
(that done in the body by the hands of men)[u]—
12remember that at that time you were separate
from Christ, excluded from citizenship in Israel
and foreigners to the covenants of the promise,[v]
without hope[w] and without God in the world.
13But now in Christ Jesus you who once were far
away have been brought near[x] through the blood
of Christ.[y]

14For he himself is our peace, who has made the
two one[z] and has destroyed the barrier, the dividing wall of hostility, 15by abolishing in his flesh[a]
the law with its commandments and regulations.[b]
His purpose was to create in himself one[c] new
man out of the two, thus making peace, 16and in
this one body to reconcile both of them to God
through the cross,[d] by which he put to death their
hostility. 17He came and preached peace to you
who were far away and peace to those who were
near.[e] 18For through him we both have access[f] to
the Father[g] by one Spirit.[h]

1:20 [b]Ac 2:24
1:21 [c]Php 2:9,10
1:22 [d]Mt 28:18 [e]Eph 4:15; 5:23
2:1 [f]ver 5; Col 2:13
2:2 [g]Col 3:7 [h]Jn 12:31; Eph 6:12 [i]Eph 5:6
2:3 [j]Gal 5:16
2:5 [k]ver 1 [l]ver 8; Ac 15:11
2:6 [m]Eph 1:20 [n]Eph 1:3
2:7 [o]Tit 3:4
2:8 [p]ver 5
2:9 [q]2Ti 1:9 [r]1Co 1:29
2:10 [s]Eph 4:24 [t]Tit 2:14
2:11 [u]Col 2:11
2:12 [v]Gal 3:17 [w]1Th 4:13
2:13 [x]ver 17; Ac 2:39 [y]Col 1:20
2:14 [z]1Co 12:13
2:15 [a]Col 1:21,22 [b]Col 2:14 [c]Gal 3:28
2:16 [d]Col 1:20,22
2:17 [e]Ps 148:14; Isa 57:19
2:18 [f]Eph 3:12 [g]Col 1:12 [h]1Co 12:13

[a] 3 Or *our flesh*

Week 45

Mercy and Grace

Most people are concerned about rights. They feel they must protect their rights even if it means infringing on someone else's. But there are two things no one has a right to expect: mercy and grace. Mercy is compassion shown to an undeserving person. If you don't deserve compassion and receive it anyway, you are receiving mercy. Grace, on the other hand, is unmerited favor and assistance. If you receive a gift or a favor without earning it or deserving it, you are receiving grace. God's love overflows in both visible and invisible expressions of grace and mercy. If you think you deserve either or both, you have yet to get a complete picture of yourself.

How does Paul describe the presalvation state of "all of us" (that means *you*) in Ephesians 2:1-3? What impact did sin have on you spiritually (Eph 2:1)?

Did you deserve salvation and freedom from sin and death (Eph 2:3)? Then why and how did you receive it (Eph 2:4-5; Col 1:19-20; Tit 3:5; 1Pe 1:18-19)?

You were once considered an "object of wrath" (Eph 2:3). What are you now called (Ro 9:23)? What is your response to God's extraordinary mercy (Mk 5:19)?

Since God is not obligated to show mercy (Ex 33:19), why does he (Ps 51:1; Mic 7:18)? How is God's mercy described (1Ch 21:13; Ps 25:6; Lk 1:78; Eph 2:4)?

Just as mercy is undeserved, grace is also a gift from God (Eph 3:7). What is the supreme expression of this gift (Jn 1:17; Ro 5:15-17)? How has God expressed his grace to you (Ro 3:23-24; Eph 2:6-7; Tit 3:7)?

How is the gospel described in Colossians 1:6? How does this description sum up God's provision for you?

What part does grace play in salvation (Ac 15:11; Ro 11:5; Eph 2:8-9)? What is your response to this amazing truth?

When you are in need of God's mercy and grace, what should you do and where should you go (Pr 28:13; Isa 55:7; Heb 4:16)? How does God's grace free you to live life without fear (2Co 9:8-9; 12:9)?

Enjoying God THROUGH the Word

Read Ephesians 1:3-10 (page 1929). This passage expresses the incredible blessings God has poured out on you by his grace. He has chosen you, adopted you as his child, redeemed you, forgiven you and made known to you the mystery of his will—righteousness by grace through Christ. All this was done to reveal "his glorious grace" (Eph 1:6).

In thanks, offer yourself and your praises to God (Ro 12:1; 1Pe 2:9-10). Allow the Holy Spirit to transform you (Ro 12:2) so that you will reflect God's glory as you become more and more like Jesus (2Co 3:18). What blessings you have in Jesus and what freedom you have in knowing that your salvation—as well as your entire Christian life—is based on God's grace, not your own efforts (2Ti 1:8-9)!

Enjoying God THROUGH Experience

Make a list of the many spiritual and material blessings God has given you. Include people on your list, too. Share your list with your family or friends, giving thanks together for who God is and what he has done for you. "And the God of all grace . . . will himself restore you and make you strong, firm and steadfast" (1Pe 5:10).

Go to page 1949 for your next weekly study.

You Are Loved

EPH 3:14–20

On some level, you probably know that you are cherished by God. The Bible is filled with verses that testify to the depth of his love for you. Most of us, though, have a hard time feeling what we know in our minds. It's a common human struggle, and Paul understands it. That's why he asks God to help the church at Ephesus reach a deeper appreciation of Jesus' love.

Now, it's your *turn to be the church at Ephesus, to better understand "how wide and long and high and deep is the love of Christ" (Eph 3:18). Read this passage every day for two weeks. Memorize it, tape it to your bathroom mirror or hang a copy in a plastic sleeve on the wall of your shower. Implore God to turn your head knowledge into a glorious heart experience. Then prepare to be changed.*

[19]Consequently, you are no longer foreigners
and aliens,[i] but fellow citizens[j] with God's people
and members of God's household,[k] [20]built on the
foundation[l] of the apostles and prophets, with
Christ Jesus himself as the chief cornerstone.[m] [21]In
him the whole building is joined together and
rises to become a holy temple[n] in the Lord. [22]And
in him you too are being built together to become
a dwelling in which God lives by his Spirit.

Paul the Preacher to the Gentiles

3 For this reason I, Paul, the prisoner[o] of Christ
Jesus for the sake of you Gentiles—
[2]Surely you have heard about the administration of God's grace that was given to me[p] for you,
[3]that is, the mystery[q] made known to me by revelation,[r] as I have already written briefly. [4]In reading this, then, you will be able to understand my
insight[s] into the mystery of Christ, [5]which was not
made known to men in other generations as it has
now been revealed by the Spirit to God's holy
apostles and prophets.[t] [6]This mystery is that
through the gospel the Gentiles are heirs[u] together with Israel, members together of one body,[v]
and sharers together in the promise in Christ
Jesus.

[7]I became a servant of this gospel[w] by the gift of
God's grace given me through the working of his
power.[x] [8]Although I am less than the least of all
God's people,[y] this grace was given me: to preach
to the Gentiles the unsearchable riches of Christ,
[9]and to make plain to everyone the administration
of this mystery,[z] which for ages past was kept hidden in God, who created all things. [10]His intent
was that now, through the church, the manifold
wisdom of God[a] should be made known[b] to the
rulers and authorities[c] in the heavenly realms,
[11]according to his eternal purpose which he
accomplished in Christ Jesus our Lord. [12]In him
and through faith in him we may approach God[d]
with freedom and confidence.[e] [13]I ask you, therefore, not to be discouraged because of my sufferings for you, which are your glory.

A Prayer for the Ephesians

[14]For this reason I kneel[f] before the Father,
[15]from whom his whole family[a] in heaven and on
earth derives its name. [16]I pray that out of his glorious riches he may strengthen you with power[g]
through his Spirit in your inner being,[h] [17]so that
Christ may dwell in your hearts[i] through faith.
And I pray that you, being rooted[j] and established
in love, [18]may have power, together with all the
saints, to grasp how wide and long and high and
deep[k] is the love of Christ, [19]and to know this love
that surpasses knowledge—that you may be filled[l]
to the measure of all the fullness of God.[m]
[20]Now to him who is able[n] to do immeasurably
more than all we ask or imagine, according to his

2:19 [i]ver 12 [j]Php 3:20 [k]Gal 6:10
2:20 [l]Mt 16:18; Rev 21:14 [m]1Pe 2:4-8
2:21 [n]1Co 3:16,17
3:1 [o]Ac 23:18; Eph 4:1
3:2 [p]Col 1:25
3:3 [q]Ro 16:25 [r]1Co 2:10
3:4 [s]2Co 11:6
3:5 [t]Ro 16:26
3:6 [u]Gal 3:29 [v]Eph 2:15,16
3:7 [w]1Co 3:5 [x]Eph 1:19
3:8 [y]1Co 15:9
3:9 [z]Ro 16:25
3:10 [a]1Co 2:7 [b]1Pe 1:12 [c]Eph 1:21
3:12 [d]Eph 2:18 [e]Heb 4:16
3:14 [f]Php 2:10
3:16 [g]Col 1:11 [h]Ro 7:22
3:17 [i]Jn 14:23 [j]Col 1:23
3:18 [k]Job 11:8,9
3:19 [l]Col 2:10 [m]Eph 1:23
3:20 [n]Ro 16:25

[a]15 Or *whom all fatherhood*

power that is at work within us, 21to him be glory
3:21 in the church and in Christ Jesus throughout all
oRo 11:36 generations, for ever and ever! Amen.[o]

Unity in the Body of Christ

4:1 pEph 3:1 **4** As a prisoner[p] for the Lord, then, I urge you
qPhp 1:27; to live a life worthy[q] of the calling you have
Col 1:10 received. 2Be completely humble and gentle; be
4:2 rCol 3:12,13 patient, bearing with one another[r] in love.[s] 3Make
sEph 1:4 every effort to keep the unity[t] of the Spirit through
the bond of peace. 4There is one body and one
4:3 tCol 3:14 Spirit[u]— just as you were called to one hope when
you were called— 5one Lord, one faith, one bap-
4:4 u1Co 12:13 tism; 6one God and Father of all, who is over all
and through all and in all.[v]
4:6 7But to each one of us[w] grace has been given[x] as
vRo 11:36 Christ apportioned it. 8This is why it[a] says:

4:7 w1Co 12:7,11 "When he ascended on high,
xRo 12:3 he led captives[y] in his train
and gave gifts to men."[b][z]

4:8 yCol 2:15 9(What does "he ascended" mean except that he
zPs 68:18 also descended to the lower, earthly regions[c]? 10He
who descended is the very one who ascended
higher than all the heavens, in order to fill the
4:11 whole universe.) 11It was he who gave some to be
a1Co 12:28 apostles,[a] some to be prophets, some to be evan-
bAc 21:8 gelists,[b] and some to be pastors and teachers, 12to
4:12 prepare God's people for works of service, so that
c1Co 12:27 the body of Christ[c] may be built up 13until we all
4:13 reach unity[d] in the faith and in the knowledge of
dver 3,5 the Son of God and become mature,[e] attaining to
eCol 1:28 the whole measure of the fullness of Christ.
4:14 14Then we will no longer be infants,[f] tossed
f1Co 14:20 gJas 1:6 back and forth by the waves,[g] and blown here and
hEph 6:11 there by every wind of teaching and by the cunning and craftiness of men in their deceitful
scheming.[h] 15Instead, speaking the truth in love,
4:15 we will in all things grow up into him who is the
iEph 1:22 Head,[i] that is, Christ. 16From him the whole body,
4:16 joined and held together by every supporting lig-
jCol 2:19 ament, grows[j] and builds itself up in love, as each
part does its work.

Living as Children of Light

4:17 17So I tell you this, and insist on it in the Lord,
kRo 1:21 that you must no longer live as the Gentiles do,
4:18 in the futility of their thinking.[k] 18They are dark-
lRo 1:21 ened in their understanding[l] and separated from
mEph 2:12 the life of God[m] because of the ignorance that is in
n2Co 3:14 them due to the hardening of their hearts.[n] 19Hav-
4:19 o1Ti 4:2 ing lost all sensitivity,[o] they have given them-
pRo 1:24 qCol 3:5 selves over[p] to sensuality[q] so as to indulge in
every kind of impurity, with a continual lust for
more.
20You, however, did not come to know Christ
that way. 21Surely you heard of him and were
taught in him in accordance with the truth that is
in Jesus. 22You were taught, with regard to your

[a] 8 Or *God* [b] 8 Psalm 68:18 [c] 9 Or *the depths of the earth*

The Fullness of Christ

EPH 4:11-16

Through the insight and direction of those God has placed in leadership over us, we reach spiritual maturity—"the fullness of Christ" (Eph 4:13). And in the process, we learn discernment. Immature believers are easily duped. They are unsure of what is true and what is untrue. With discernment, they become steady and rooted in Christ's love, no longer spiritual "lightweights" who are easily "blown here and there" (Eph 4:14) by every new notion.

How would you categorize your spiritual "age"? Are you an infant? A gangly teen? A mature parent? A seasoned elder? What age would you like to be? Make a list of two to three daily or weekly disciplines—such as Bible study, prayer, solitude, service, fasting or meeting with an accountability group—that will help push you to a new level of maturity. Now, pick one to start with and begin!

The Problem of Anger

EPH 4:26

In addressing the problem of anger, Paul offers the Ephesians an extraordinarily practical piece of advice. He first suggests that they simply not allow themselves to sin in their anger. But knowing human nature as he does, Paul counsels them, and us, to keep short accounts when such feelings arise. By resolving our differences and dealing with our emotions before nightfall, we effectively starve, rather than feed, our hostility.

Paul's recommendation can be applied to more than just anger. He goes on to talk about a wide range of sins that require repentance: stealing, gossip, crabbiness, bitterness, rage, fighting, slander and malice. Don't let the sun go down—or at least don't let your head hit the pillow—before you take each battle to the Lord, and you are reconciled in your relationships.

former way of life, to put off[r] your old self,[s] which
is being corrupted by its deceitful desires; 23 to be
made new in the attitude of your minds;[t] 24 and to
put on the new self,[u] created to be like God in true
righteousness and holiness.[v]
25 Therefore each of you must put off falsehood
and speak truthfully[w] to his neighbor, for we are
all members of one body.[x] 26 "In your anger do not
sin"[a]: Do not let the sun go down while you are
still angry, 27 and do not give the devil a foothold.
28 He who has been stealing must steal no longer,
but must work,[y] doing something useful with his
own hands,[z] that he may have something to share
with those in need.[a]
29 Do not let any unwholesome talk come out of
your mouths,[b] but only what is helpful for building others up according to their needs, that it may
benefit those who listen. 30 And do not grieve the
Holy Spirit of God,[c] with whom you were sealed
for the day of redemption.[d] 31 Get rid of all bitterness, rage and anger, brawling and slander, along
with every form of malice.[e] 32 Be kind and compassionate to one another, forgiving each other,
just as in Christ God forgave you.[f]
5 Be imitators of God,[g] therefore, as dearly loved
children 2 and live a life of love, just as Christ
loved us and gave himself up for us[h] as a fragrant
offering and sacrifice to God.[i]
3 But among you there must not be even a hint
of sexual immorality, or of any kind of impurity,
or of greed,[j] because these are improper for God's
holy people. 4 Nor should there be obscenity, foolish talk or coarse joking, which are out of place,
but rather thanksgiving.[k] 5 For of this you can be
sure: No immoral, impure or greedy person—such
a man is an idolater[l]—has any inheritance in the
kingdom of Christ and of God.[b][m] 6 Let no one
deceive you with empty words, for because of
such things God's wrath[n] comes on those who are
disobedient. 7 Therefore do not be partners with
them.
8 For you were once[o] darkness, but now you are
light in the Lord. Live as children of light[p] 9 (for
the fruit[q] of the light consists in all goodness, righteousness and truth) 10 and find out what pleases
the Lord. 11 Have nothing to do with the fruitless
deeds of darkness, but rather expose them. 12 For it
is shameful even to mention what the disobedient
do in secret. 13 But everything exposed by the light[r]
becomes visible, 14 for it is light that makes everything visible. This is why it is said:

> "Wake up, O sleeper,[s]
> rise from the dead,[t]
> and Christ will shine on you."[u]

15 Be very careful, then, how you live—not as
unwise but as wise, 16 making the most of every
opportunity,[v] because the days are evil.[w] 17 Therefore do not be foolish, but understand what the

4:22 [r]1Pe 2:1 [s]Ro 6:6
4:23 [t]Col 3:10
4:24 [u]Ro 6:4 [v]Eph 2:10
4:25 [w]Zec 8:16 [x]Ro 12:5
4:28 [y]Ac 20:35 [z]1Th 4:11 [a]Lk 3:11
4:29 [b]Col 3:8
4:30 [c]1Th 5:19 [d]Ro 8:23
4:31 [e]Col 3:8
4:32 [f]Mt 6:14,15
5:1 [g]Lk 6:36
5:2 [h]Gal 1:4 [i]2Co 2:15; Heb 7:27
5:3 [j]Col 3:5
5:4 [k]ver 20
5:5 [l]Col 3:5 [m]1Co 6:9
5:6 [n]Ro 1:18
5:8 [o]Eph 2:2 [p]Lk 16:8
5:9 [q]Gal 5:22
5:13 [r]Jn 3:20,21
5:14 [s]Ro 13:11 [t]Jn 5:25 [u]Isa 60:1
5:16 [v]Col 4:5 [w]Eph 6:13

[a] 26 Psalm 4:4 [b] 5 Or *kingdom of the Christ and God*

5:17 [x]Ro 12:2; Lord's will is.[x] 18Do not get drunk on wine,[y]
1Th 4:3 which leads to debauchery. Instead, be filled with
the Spirit.[z] 19Speak to one another with psalms,
5:18 [y]Pr 20:1 hymns and spiritual songs.[a] Sing and make music
[z]Lk 1:15 in your heart to the Lord, 20always giving thanks[b]
to God the Father for everything, in the name of
5:19 [a]Ac 16:25; our Lord Jesus Christ.
Col 3:16 21Submit to one another[c] out of reverence for
5:20 [b]Ps 34:1 Christ.

Wives and Husbands

5:21 [c]Gal 5:13 22Wives, submit to your husbands[d] as to the
Lord.[e] 23For the husband is the head of the wife as
5:22 [d]Ge 3:16; Christ is the head of the church,[f] his body, of
1Pe 3:1,5,6 which he is the Savior. 24Now as the church sub-
[e]Eph 6:5 mits to Christ, so also wives should submit to
5:23 their husbands in everything.
[f]1Co 11:3; 25Husbands, love your wives,[g] just as Christ
Eph 1:22 loved the church and gave himself up for her[h] 26to
5:25 [g]Col 3:19 make her holy, cleansing[a] her by the washing[i]
[h]ver 2 with water through the word, 27and to present her
to himself as a radiant church, without stain or
5:26 [i]Ac 22:16 wrinkle or any other blemish, but holy and
blameless.[j] 28In this same way, husbands ought to
5:27 [j]Eph 1:4; love their wives[k] as their own bodies. He who
Col 1:22 loves his wife loves himself. 29After all, no one
ever hated his own body, but he feeds and cares
5:28 [k]ver 25 for it, just as Christ does the church— 30for we are
members of his body.[l] 31"For this reason a man
5:30 [l]1Co 12:27 will leave his father and mother and be united to
his wife, and the two will become one flesh."[b][m]
5:31 [m]Ge 2:24; 32This is a profound mystery—but I am talking
Mt 19:5; about Christ and the church. 33However, each one
1Co 6:16 of you also must love his wife[n] as he loves him-
5:33 [n]ver 25 self, and the wife must respect her husband.

Children and Parents

6 Children, obey your parents in the Lord, for
6:1 [o]Col 3:20 this is right.[o] 2"Honor your father and mother"—which is the first commandment with a
promise— 3"that it may go well with you and that
6:3 [p]Ex 20:12 you may enjoy long life on the earth."[c][p]
4Fathers, do not exasperate your children;[q]
6:4 [q]Col 3:21 instead, bring them up in the training and instruc-
[r]Ge 18:19; Dt 6:7 tion of the Lord.[r]

Slaves and Masters

6:5 [s]1Ti 6:1 5Slaves, obey your earthly masters with respect[s]
[t]Col 3:22 and fear, and with sincerity of heart,[t] just as you
[u]Eph 5:22 would obey Christ.[u] 6Obey them not only to win
their favor when their eye is on you, but like
slaves of Christ, doing the will of God from your
heart. 7Serve wholeheartedly, as if you were serv-
6:7 [v]Col 3:23 ing the Lord, not men,[v] 8because you know that
the Lord will reward everyone for whatever good
6:8 [w]Col 3:24 he does,[w] whether he is slave or free.
9And masters, treat your slaves in the same
way. Do not threaten them, since you know that

Submission

EPH 5:21-33

Here it is. The passage that brings many women to a screeching halt in front of God and their husbands. Paul exhorts women to submit to their husbands. Just how does one integrate such teachings into practical, everyday, 21st century married life?

Well, first of all as women and wives, we can't ignore the passage. But if we start with the beginning of the passage, Ephesians 5:21, we see that all people are called to submit to one another for the sake of Christ—husbands, wives, children, singles . . . Christ has paid the ultimate sacrifice to save us, and we love him for it. Therefore, we willingly submit to our brothers and sisters in the Lord out of that love. We love and submit because Christ first loved us.

In the same way, in the married relationship, the beginning of the equation is not submission, but love. A husband's loving interaction with his wife will produce a willing submission to him. A wife's loving interaction with her husband will produce tender leadership on his part.

Submission doesn't mean women become wimpy, doormat wives. Submission requires an inner strength to obey God and willingly submit to one's husband. It means finding fulfillment and esteem in the godly role of a wife.

If we all willingly and lovingly put others before self, submission becomes a non-issue. What a transformation such selflessness would make in a marriage, in a home, in the church!

[a] *26* Or *having cleansed* [b] *31* Gen. 2:24 [c] *3* Deut. 5:16

he who is both their Master and yours[x] is in heav-
en, and there is no favoritism with him.

The Armor of God

10Finally, be strong in the Lord[y] and in his
mighty power.[z] 11Put on the full armor of God[a] so
that you can take your stand against the devil's
schemes. 12For our struggle is not against flesh
and blood, but against the rulers, against the
authorities,[b] against the powers[c] of this dark
world and against the spiritual forces of evil in the
heavenly realms.[d] 13Therefore put on the full
armor of God, so that when the day of evil comes,
you may be able to stand your ground, and after
you have done everything, to stand. 14Stand firm
then, with the belt of truth buckled around your
waist,[e] with the breastplate of righteousness in
place,[f] 15and with your feet fitted with the readiness that comes from the gospel of peace.[g] 16In
addition to all this, take up the shield of faith,[h]
with which you can extinguish all the flaming
arrows of the evil one. 17Take the helmet of salvation[i] and the sword of the Spirit, which is the
word of God.[j] 18And pray in the Spirit on all occasions[k] with all kinds of prayers and requests.[l]
With this in mind, be alert and always keep on
praying for all the saints.

19Pray also for me,[m] that whenever I open my
mouth, words may be given me so that I will fearlessly[n] make known the mystery of the gospel,
20for which I am an ambassador[o] in chains.[p] Pray
that I may declare it fearlessly, as I should.

Final Greetings

21Tychicus,[q] the dear brother and faithful servant in the Lord, will tell you everything, so that
you also may know how I am and what I am
doing. 22I am sending him to you for this very purpose, that you may know how we are,[r] and that
he may encourage you.

23Peace[s] to the brothers, and love with faith
from God the Father and the Lord Jesus Christ.
24Grace to all who love our Lord Jesus Christ with
an undying love.

6:9 [x]Job 31:13, 14
6:10 [y]1Co 16:13 [z]Eph 1:19
6:11 [a]Ro 13:12
6:12 [b]Eph 1:21 [c]Ro 8:38 [d]Eph 1:3
6:14 [e]Isa 11:5 [f]Isa 59:17
6:15 [g]Isa 52:7
6:16 [h]1Jn 5:4
6:17 [i]Isa 59:17 [j]Heb 4:12
6:18 [k]Lk 18:1 [l]Mt 26:41; Php 1:4
6:19 [m]1Th 5:25 [n]Ac 4:29; 2Co 3:12
6:20 [o]2Co 5:20 [p]Ac 21:33
6:21 [q]Ac 20:4
6:22 [r]Col 4:7-9
6:23 [s]Gal 6:16; 1Pe 5:14

Put Your Armor On

EPH 6:10-18

Most women have a pretty regular morning routine. **From a cup of steaming coffee to a brisk morning run, time with the newspaper's early edition to breakfast with the kids, there are patterns in our lives that add strength, vitality and purpose to our days.**

Think about routines for a moment. Clothes, hair, makeup . . . we've got the basics covered. Or do we? According to Paul, we need to be dressed in "the full armor of God" (Eph 6:11) before we are truly ready to face the world. **Look at the pieces of armor listed in this passage, and consider how each one helps you. In light of these, is there something you want to add to your routine?** ***For example, imagine that you are preparing yourself for battle as you dress in the morning. Or try setting aside time to pick up "the sword of the Spirit" (Eph 6:17) at the beginning of each day.***

Philippians

Rejoice always.

Paul's letter to the Philippians radiates with reasons to be thankful, joyful and contented. Paul writes these words to thank the Philippians for their generous gift to cover his living expenses while he awaits trial. Focusing on Jesus instead of his painful, desperate situation, Paul's warm enthusiasm and hopeful contentment encourage the Philippian believers to share Christ with others and to find joy in every situation.

Paul overflows with thankfulness for close friends and their kindness (Php 1). He encourages the Philippian believers to take on Christ's attitude of humility and self-sacrifice, becoming God's shining stars in a dark world (Php 2). He urges them to press on in a lifetime pursuit of an intimate relationship with Jesus (Php 3). Two women, Euodia and Syntyche, who are in the middle of some sort of dispute, receive Paul's entreaty that they agree "in the Lord" (Php 4). Paul ends with more words of encouragement, reminding his readers that they can disarm stress and find contentment by focusing on God's peace and on good things (Php 4).

There's always room for joy in a believer's heart. If we fill our hearts with Jesus and a desire for his attitudes of thankfulness, humility and contentment, nothing will be able to wipe out our joy. Whether chained to a Roman guard or to some other situation you can't change, a good dose of Philippians is great medicine!

Quick Study

Author
The apostle Paul.

Date Written
Around A.D. 61.

Written From
Rome during Paul's imprisonment there.

Key Passage
Philippians 1:9-11 "And this is my prayer: that your love may abound more and more in knowledge and depth of insight, so that you may be able to discern what is best and may be pure and blameless until the day of Christ, filled with the fruit of righteousness that comes through Jesus Christ—to the glory and praise of God."

Outline

Paul's *greetings.*
Php 1:1-2

Thanksgiving *and prayer.*
Php 1:3-11

Paul's *difficult situation and its consequences.*
Php 1:12-30

How *to live.*
Php 2:1-18

Paul's *messengers.*
Php 2:19-30

Teachings.
Php 3:1—4:1

Exhortations.
Php 4:2-9

Thanksgiving.
Php 4:10-20

Final *greetings.*
Php 4:21-23

The Women of Philippians

Euodia	*Part of an on-going feud.* Php 4:2 (page 2079)
Syntyche	*With Euodia, a co-worker with Paul.* Php 4:2 (page 2079)

Denotes a sketch written about this character

1

1 Paul and Timothy,[a] servants of Christ Jesus,
To all the saints[b] in Christ Jesus at Philippi,[c]
together with the overseers[ad] and deacons:[e]

2Grace and peace to you from God our Father
and the Lord Jesus Christ.[f]

Thanksgiving and Prayer

3I thank my God every time I remember you.[g] 4In
all my prayers for all of you, I always pray[h] with
joy 5because of your partnership[i] in the gospel from
the first day[j] until now, 6being confident of this,
that he who began a good work in you will carry it
on to completion until the day of Christ Jesus.[k]
7It is right[l] for me to feel this way about all of
you, since I have you in my heart;[m] for whether I
am in chains[n] or defending[o] and confirming the
gospel, all of you share in God's grace with me.
8God can testify[p] how I long for all of you with the
affection of Christ Jesus.
9And this is my prayer: that your love[q] may
abound more and more in knowledge and depth
of insight, 10so that you may be able to discern
what is best and may be pure and blameless until
the day of Christ,[r] 11filled with the fruit of righteousness[s] that comes through Jesus Christ—to
the glory and praise of God.

Paul's Chains Advance the Gospel

12Now I want you to know, brothers, that what
has happened to me has really served to advance
the gospel. 13As a result, it has become clear
throughout the whole palace guard[b] and to everyone else that I am in chains[t] for Christ. 14Because
of my chains,[u] most of the brothers in the Lord
have been encouraged to speak the word of God
more courageously and fearlessly.
15It is true that some preach Christ out of envy
and rivalry, but others out of goodwill. 16The latter do so in love, knowing that I am put here for
the defense of the gospel.[v] 17The former preach
Christ out of selfish ambition,[w] not sincerely, supposing that they can stir up trouble for me while
I am in chains.[cx] 18But what does it matter? The
important thing is that in every way, whether
from false motives or true, Christ is preached. And
because of this I rejoice.
Yes, and I will continue to rejoice, 19for I know
that through your prayers[y] and the help given by
the Spirit of Jesus Christ,[z] what has happened to
me will turn out for my deliverance.[d] 20I eagerly
expect[a] and hope that I will in no way be
ashamed, but will have sufficient courage[b] so that
now as always Christ will be exalted in my body,[c]
whether by life or by death.[d] 21For to me, to live is
Christ[e] and to die is gain. 22If I am to go on living
in the body, this will mean fruitful labor for me.

1:1 [a]Ac 16:1; 2Co 1:1 [b]Ac 9:13 [c]Ac 16:12 [d]1Ti 3:1 [e]1Ti 3:8
1:2 [f]Ro 1:7
1:3 [g]Ro 1:8
1:4 [h]Ro 1:10
1:5 [i]Ac 2:42; Php 4:15 [j]Ac 16:12-40
1:6 [k]ver 10; 1Co 1:8
1:7 [l]2Pe 1:13 [m]2Co 7:3 [n]ver 13,14, 17; Ac 21:33 [o]ver 16
1:8 [p]Ro 1:9
1:9 [q]1Th 3:12
1:10 [r]ver 6; 1Co 1:8
1:11 [s]Jas 3:18
1:13 [t]ver 7,14,17
1:14 [u]ver 7,13,17
1:16 [v]ver 7,12
1:17 [w]Php 2:3 [x]ver 7,13,14
1:19 [y]2Co 1:11 [z]Ac 16:7
1:20 [a]Ro 8:19 [b]ver 14 [c]1Co 6:20 [d]Ro 14:8
1:21 [e]Gal 2:20

[a] *1* Traditionally *bishops* [b] *13* Or *whole palace* [c] *16,17* Some late manuscripts have verses 16 and 17 in reverse order. [d] *19* Or *salvation*

Our Promise Keeper

PHP 1:6

Unfinished projects.
Unkept promises. Unfulfilled dreams. We all know the disappointment that comes with starting down a road with excitement and never seeming to reach the end. Our intentions are good at the start, but with time we lose steam.

Now comes the good news. When it comes to our spiritual life and God's plans for us, we will not end in failure. The project will be finished. The promise will be kept. The dream will be realized . . . in living color! Why? How? What is so different about this project?

Paul is confident that the work will come to completion for one reason and one reason only. It is God's work, God's project, and he will do it! A promise is only as reliable as the one who makes it. This promise in Philippians 1:6 is made by the heavenly promise keeper, God himself. He always keeps his promises. What good news!

Worthy of the Gospel

PHP 1:9–11,27

Following Christ means *accepting a new set of standards that is far beyond our reach. We could never hope to reach the pinnacle of God's calling without* his power and the indwelling of the Holy Spirit. *We are called to conduct ourselves in a manner* that is "worthy of the gospel of Christ." *What a high calling!*

What does this look like in the life of a follower of Christ? Paul's prayer (Php 1:9–11) *gives us a window through which we can see what such a life looks like:*

A heart full of love.

A mind filled with God's knowledge and deep insight.

A spirit so discerning that it *leads to purity and blamelessness.*

A life overflowing with the fruit of righteousness.

***We can gain none of these* things on our own. *Only as we pray passionately and seek the* power that only God can offer, *as* he fills us with himself, *will we inherit these attributes through* Jesus Christ. *Our lives will bring* glory and praise to God!**

Yet what shall I choose? I do not know! 23I am
torn between the two: I desire to depart[f] and be
with Christ,[g] which is better by far; 24but it is
more necessary for you that I remain in the body.
25Convinced of this, I know that I will remain, and
I will continue with all of you for your progress
and joy in the faith, 26so that through my being
with you again your joy in Christ Jesus will overflow on account of me.
27Whatever happens, conduct yourselves in a
manner worthy[h] of the gospel of Christ. Then,
whether I come and see you or only hear about
you in my absence, I will know that you stand
firm[i] in one spirit, contending[j] as one man for the
faith of the gospel 28without being frightened in
any way by those who oppose you. This is a sign
to them that they will be destroyed, but that you
will be saved—and that by God. 29For it has been
granted to you[k] on behalf of Christ not only to
believe on him, but also to suffer[l] for him, 30since
you are going through the same struggle[m] you
saw[n] I had, and now hear[o] that I still have.

Imitating Christ's Humility

2 If you have any encouragement from being
united with Christ, if any comfort from his
love, if any fellowship with the Spirit,[p] if any tenderness and compassion,[q] 2then make my joy
complete[r] by being like-minded,[s] having the same
love, being one[t] in spirit and purpose. 3Do nothing
out of selfish ambition or vain conceit,[u] but in
humility consider others better than yourselves.[v]
4Each of you should look not only to your own
interests, but also to the interests of others.
5Your attitude should be the same as that of
Christ Jesus:[w]

6Who, being in very nature[a] God,[x]
did not consider equality with God[y]
something to be grasped,
7but made himself nothing,
taking the very nature[b] of a servant,[z]
being made in human likeness.[a]
8And being found in appearance as a man,
he humbled himself
and became obedient to death[b]—
even death on a cross!
9Therefore God exalted him[c] to the highest place
and gave him the name that is above every name,[d]
10that at the name of Jesus every knee should bow,[e]
in heaven and on earth and under the earth,[f]
11and every tongue confess that Jesus Christ is Lord,[g]
to the glory of God the Father.

1:23 [f]2Ti 4:6 [g]Jn 12:26; 2Co 5:8
1:27 [h]Eph 4:1 [i]1Co 16:13 [j]Jude 3
1:29 [k]Mt 5:11,12 [l]Ac 14:22
1:30 [m]Col 2:1; 1Th 2:2 [n]Ac 16:19-40 [o]ver 13
2:1 [p]2Co 13:14 [q]Col 3:12
2:2 [r]Jn 3:29 [s]Php 4:2 [t]Ro 12:16
2:3 [u]Gal 5:26 [v]Ro 12:10; 1Pe 5:5
2:5 [w]Mt 11:29
2:6 [x]Jn 1:1 [y]Jn 5:18
2:7 [z]Mt 20:28 [a]Jn 1:14; Heb 2:17
2:8 [b]Mt 26:39; Jn 10:18; Heb 5:8
2:9 [c]Ac 2:33; Heb 2:9 [d]Eph 1:20,21
2:10 [e]Ro 14:11 [f]Mt 28:18
2:11 [g]Jn 13:13

[a]6 Or *in the form of* [b]7 Or *the form*

Women Who Followed Jesus

True Disciples

The women hurried to gather their things. The Master would leave tomorrow morning for the next town down the road. There was much to do. Jesus and his disciples would be hungry after the journey and would need a place to sleep. If the women left today, they could have things ready for the men when they arrived in the next town.

We don't know how many women traveled with Jesus and the disciples throughout Galilee. We have the names of a few: Mary, the mother of James the younger and of Joses, Mary Magdalene, and Salome, the mother of Zebedee's sons. These women were disciples in the deepest sense of the word. They followed Jesus, gave him their exclusive loyalty. They left homes, family ties and possessions, just as the Twelve had done. They had faith in Jesus and believed his message. They followed him even to his death.

The women who traveled with Jesus used their own resources to help provide for the disciples' needs—food, water, clean clothes and a place to stay (Lk 8:3). Jewish women of their time rarely had control of much money. God had chosen and prepared them especially to fill this role.

Most likely the presence of these women offended many in Israel. Jewish tradition did not allow women to study the law with a rabbi. Obviously, Jesus broke the customs of his culture when he invited women to join him and encouraged them to sit at his feet to learn from him (Lk 10:39,42).

Jesus valued women. The Father had said, "It is not good for the man to be alone. I will make a helper suitable for him" (Ge 2:18). While this principle applies most directly to marriage, it is not necessarily exclusive to it. Men need the gifts, perspective and observations of the women in their lives. Godly women complement godly men—in ministry, in work and in service. Though Jesus never married, he affirmed the worth of women by breaking down the boundaries put on women in that culture. He not only didn't ignore them—as was common in his day—he included them in his life and ministry, teaching them, listening to them, and affirming their worth as children of God.

Women Who Followed Jesus

Matthew 27:55-56,61; 28:1

Mark 15:40-41,47; 16:1

Luke 23:49,55-56; 24:10

John 19:25

Candid SNAPSHOT Some women were watching from a distance. Among them were Mary Magdalene, Mary the mother of James the younger and of Joses, and Salome. In Galilee these women had followed him and cared for his needs. Many other women who had come up with him to Jerusalem were also there (Mark 15:40-41).

Sapphira

Looking Good

If Sapphira wanted a unique place in history, she got it, but assuredly not the way she had hoped. The names of Sapphira and Ananias, her husband, are synonymous with hypocrisy, deceit and God's wrath—not a desirable legacy.

God was pouring out his grace on the newborn church in incredible ways. Rooms shook. A wind came from heaven and brought tongues of fire and languages the speakers didn't know. Healings and mass conversions were commonplace. "Everyone was filled with awe, and many wonders and miraculous signs were done by the apostles. All the believers were together and had everything in common" (Ac 2:43-44).

The rich provided for the poor among the believers. No one was in want or hungry. No one made windfall profits; no one was impoverished. Those who sold their land and surrendered the money to the apostles acted on their commitment to God and to the church. It was a holy act, inspired by the Holy Spirit. But this holy act became a mockery in the hands of Ananias and Sapphira. Their public show of "giving all" offended the Holy Spirit.

Ananias and Sapphira discussed their decision. Barnabas received a lot of attention when he gave the money he'd gotten by selling some property. If Ananias and Sapphira wanted to increase their chances for leadership in the church, they needed to increase their visibility. Why not sell some land and give some money to the church as Barnabas had? They wouldn't have to give it all up. They could keep some for a nest egg—because who could tell how long this new religion would last?—and no one would be the wiser.

Peter was astonished. How could they do this? Were they so blind, so unaffected by God's presence that they truly believed they would not be found out? If the Lord allowed such gross deception in the newborn church, it would soon be full of cynics and hypocrites. Ananias and Sapphira were tools of the devil—the enemy within—to cast doubt on the reality of God himself. God struck them dead. Theirs was no white lie. It was a scheme rising straight from hell. The dramatic public deaths of Ananias and Sapphira proved that God was very real and very much alive. The church grew faster and stronger than it had before, and no one but true believers dared to join them.

People set on impressing others never impress God. In fact, it is one of the shortest routes to his displeasure. Purity of heart is what pleases God, not appearances.

Sapphira
(beautiful)
Acts 5:1-11

Candid SNAPSHOT About three hours later his wife came in, not knowing what had happened. Peter asked her, "Tell me, is this the price you and Ananias got for the land?" "Yes," she said, "that is the price" (Acts 5:7-8).

Shining as Stars

12Therefore, my dear friends, as you have
always obeyed—not only in my presence, but now
much more in my absence—continue to work out
2:12 your salvation with fear and trembling,[h] 13for it is
h2Co 7:15 God who works in you[i] to will and to act accord-
2:13 ing to his good purpose.
iEzr 1:5 14Do everything without complaining[j] or argu-
2:14 ing, 15so that you may become blameless and pure,
j1Co 10:10; children of God[k] without fault in a crooked and
1Pe 4:9 depraved generation,[l] in which you shine like stars
2:15 in the universe 16as you hold out[a] the word of
kMt 5:45,48; life—in order that I may boast on the day of Christ
Eph 5:1 that I did not run or labor for nothing.[m] 17But even
lAc 2:40 if I am being poured out like a drink offering[n] on
2:16 the sacrifice[o] and service coming from your faith,
m1Th 2:19 I am glad and rejoice with all of you. 18So you too
2:17 should be glad and rejoice with me.
n2Ti 4:6
oRo 15:16

Timothy and Epaphroditus

19I hope in the Lord Jesus to send Timothy to
2:19 you soon,[p] that I also may be cheered when I
pver 23 receive news about you. 20I have no one else like
2:20 him,[q] who takes a genuine interest in your wel-
q1Co 16:10 fare. 21For everyone looks out for his own inter-
2:21 ests,[r] not those of Jesus Christ. 22But you know
r1Co 10:24; that Timothy has proved himself, because as a son
13:5 with his father[s] he has served with me in the
2:22 work of the gospel. 23I hope, therefore, to send
s1Co 4:17; him as soon as I see how things go with me.[t]
1Ti 1:2 24And I am confident[u] in the Lord that I myself
2:23 will come soon.
tver 19 25But I think it is necessary to send back to you
2:24 Epaphroditus, my brother, fellow worker[v] and fel-
uPhp 1:25 low soldier,[w] who is also your messenger, whom
2:25 you sent to take care of my needs.[x] 26For he longs
vPhp 4:3 for all of you[y] and is distressed because you heard
wPhm 2
xPhp 4:18 he was ill. 27Indeed he was ill, and almost died.
2:26 But God had mercy on him, and not on him only
yPhp 1:8 but also on me, to spare me sorrow upon sorrow.
28Therefore I am all the more eager to send him,
so that when you see him again you may be glad
and I may have less anxiety. 29Welcome him in the
2:29 Lord with great joy, and honor men like him,[z]
z1Co 16:18; 30because he almost died for the work of Christ,
1Ti 5:17 risking his life to make up for the help you could
2:30 not give me.[a]
a1Co 16:17

No Confidence in the Flesh

3 Finally, my brothers, rejoice in the Lord! It is
no trouble for me to write the same things to
3:2 you again, and it is a safeguard for you.
bPs 22:16,20 2Watch out for those dogs,[b] those men who do
3:3 evil, those mutilators of the flesh. 3For it is we
cRo 2:28,29; who are the circumcision,[c] we who worship by
Gal 6:15; the Spirit of God, who glory in Christ Jesus, and
Col 2:11 who put no confidence in the flesh— 4though I
myself have reasons for such confidence.

[a] 16 Or *hold on to*

Complaining

PHP 2:14

Grumbling and complaining. It is a national past time. It is a recreational activity in the foyer of many churches. **Although we know it is sin and that it breaks the heart of God, many Christians tolerate it in their own lives and in the lives of others.**

The people of Israel mastered the art of grumbling (Ex 15:24, 16:2–12, 17:3), and God disciplined them for it. Paul reminds the people of his day of the high cost their ancestors paid for grumbling (1Co 10:6–10). He lists four of the sins Israel committed as they wandered in the desert: idolatry, sexual immorality, testing God and *grumbling*. We probably wouldn't put grumbling on our list of the worst of sins. But God takes it very seriously because it is an outward indication of an inward problem. Hear God's invitation one more time: "Do everything without complaining or arguing."

The Prize

PHP 3:8–14

Throughout history followers of Christ have chosen to make sacrifices for the sake of Jesus. This should not surprise us. Jesus himself said, "If anyone would come after me, he must deny himself and take up his cross and follow me" (Mt 16:24).

The apostle Paul certainly learned this lesson. As a Jewish rabbi, a second-generation Pharisee and a leader in the Jewish community, he gave up everything when he followed Jesus. In the book of Acts we have a record of the staggering shift that occurred in Paul's life. Saul, the Jewish zealot, was a persecutor of the church and a leader in the effort to crush it (Ac 8:3). After receiving Jesus and becoming his follower, however, we see the same man, later named Paul, being chased out of town, his life in danger for preaching Jesus as savior (Ac 9:23–25). When Paul says that he has lost all things and counts them like yesterday's trash (Php 3:8), he means it. He is willing to give up everything if that is the price of knowing Jesus.

If anyone else thinks he has reasons to put confidence in the flesh, I have more: 5circumcised[d] on
the eighth day, of the people of Israel,[e] of the tribe
of Benjamin,[f] a Hebrew of Hebrews; in regard to
the law, a Pharisee;[g] 6as for zeal, persecuting the
church;[h] as for legalistic righteousness,[i] faultless.
7But whatever was to my profit I now consider
loss[j] for the sake of Christ. 8What is more, I consider everything a loss compared to the surpassing
greatness of knowing[k] Christ Jesus my Lord, for
whose sake I have lost all things. I consider them
rubbish, that I may gain Christ 9and be found in
him, not having a righteousness of my own that
comes from the law,[l] but that which is through
faith in Christ—the righteousness that comes from
God and is by faith.[m] 10I want to know Christ and
the power of his resurrection and the fellowship of
sharing in his sufferings,[n] becoming like him in
his death,[o] 11and so, somehow, to attain to the resurrection[p] from the dead.

Pressing on Toward the Goal

12Not that I have already obtained all this, or
have already been made perfect,[q] but I press on to
take hold[r] of that for which Christ Jesus took hold
of me.[s] 13Brothers, I do not consider myself yet to
have taken hold of it. But one thing I do: Forgetting what is behind[t] and straining toward what is
ahead, 14I press on[u] toward the goal to win the
prize for which God has called[v] me heavenward
in Christ Jesus.
15All of us who are mature[w] should take such a
view of things.[x] And if on some point you think
differently, that too God will make clear to you.
16Only let us live up to what we have already
attained.
17Join with others in following my example,[y]
brothers, and take note of those who live according to the pattern we gave you. 18For, as I have
often told you before and now say again even
with tears,[z] many live as enemies of the cross of
Christ.[a] 19Their destiny is destruction, their god is
their stomach,[b] and their glory is in their shame.[c]
Their mind is on earthly things.[d] 20But our citizenship[e] is in heaven.[f] And we eagerly await a
Savior from there, the Lord Jesus Christ,[g] 21who,
by the power[h] that enables him to bring everything under his control, will transform our lowly
bodies[i] so that they will be like his glorious body.[j]

4 Therefore, my brothers, you whom I love and
long for,[k] my joy and crown, that is how you
should stand firm[l] in the Lord, dear friends!

Exhortations

2I plead with Euodia and I plead with Syntyche
to agree with each other[m] in the Lord. 3Yes, and I
ask you, loyal yokefellow,[a] help these women
who have contended at my side in the cause of
the gospel, along with Clement and the rest of my

3:5 [d]Lk 1:59 [e]2Co 11:22 [f]Ro 11:1 [g]Ac 23:6
3:6 [h]Ac 8:3 [i]Ro 10:5
3:7 [j]Mt 13:44; Lk 14:33
3:8 [k]Eph 4:13; 2Pe 1:2
3:9 [l]Ro 10:5 [m]Ro 9:30
3:10 [n]Ro 8:17 [o]Ro 6:3-5
3:11 [p]Rev 20:5,6
3:12 [q]1Co 13:10 [r]1Ti 6:12 [s]Ac 9:5,6
3:13 [t]Lk 9:62
3:14 [u]Heb 6:1 [v]Ro 8:28
3:15 [w]1Co 2:6 [x]Gal 5:10
3:17 [y]1Co 4:16; 1Pe 5:3
3:18 [z]Ac 20:31 [a]Gal 6:12
3:19 [b]Ro 16:18 [c]Ro 6:21 [d]Ro 8:5,6
3:20 [e]Eph 2:19 [f]Col 3:1 [g]1Co 1:7
3:21 [h]Eph 1:19 [i]1Co 15:43-53 [j]Col 3:4
4:1 [k]Php 1:8 [l]1Co 16:13; Php 1:27
4:2 [m]Php 2:2

[a] 3 Or *loyal Syzygus*

fellow workers, whose names are in the book of
life.
4Rejoice in the Lord always. I will say it again:
Rejoice![n] 5Let your gentleness be evident to all.
The Lord is near.[o] 6Do not be anxious about anything,[p] but in everything, by prayer and petition,
with thanksgiving, present your requests to God.[q]
7And the peace of God,[r] which transcends all
understanding, will guard your hearts and your
minds in Christ Jesus.
8Finally, brothers, whatever is true, whatever is
noble, whatever is right, whatever is pure, whatever is lovely, whatever is admirable—if anything
is excellent or praiseworthy—think about such
things. 9Whatever you have learned or received or
heard from me, or seen in me—put it into practice.[s] And the God of peace[t] will be with you.

Thanks for Their Gifts

10I rejoice greatly in the Lord that at last you
have renewed your concern for me.[u] Indeed, you
have been concerned, but you had no opportunity to show it. 11I am not saying this because I am
in need, for I have learned to be content[v] whatever the circumstances. 12I know what it is to be in
need, and I know what it is to have plenty. I have
learned the secret of being content in any and
every situation, whether well fed or hungry,[w]
whether living in plenty or in want.[x] 13I can do
everything through him who gives me strength.[y]
14Yet it was good of you to share[z] in my troubles. 15Moreover, as you Philippians know, in the
early days[a] of your acquaintance with the gospel,
when I set out from Macedonia, not one church
shared with me in the matter of giving and receiving, except you only;[b] 16for even when I was in
Thessalonica,[c] you sent me aid again and again
when I was in need.[d] 17Not that I am looking for a
gift, but I am looking for what may be credited to
your account.[e] 18I have received full payment and
even more; I am amply supplied, now that I have
received from Epaphroditus[f] the gifts you sent.
They are a fragrant[g] offering, an acceptable sacrifice, pleasing to God. 19And my God will meet all
your needs[h] according to his glorious riches[i] in
Christ Jesus.
20To our God and Father[j] be glory for ever and
ever. Amen.[k]

Final Greetings

21Greet all the saints in Christ Jesus. The brothers who are with me[l] send greetings. 22All the
saints[m] send you greetings, especially those who
belong to Caesar's household.
23The grace of the Lord Jesus Christ[n] be with
your spirit. Amen.[a]

4:4 [n]Ro 12:12; Php 3:1
4:5 [o]Heb 10:37; Jas 5:8,9
4:6 [p]Mt 6:25-34 [q]Eph 6:18
4:7 [r]Isa 26:3; Jn 14:27; Col 3:15
4:9 [s]Php 3:17 [t]Ro 15:33
4:10 [u]2Co 11:9
4:11 [v]1Ti 6:6,8
4:12 [w]1Co 4:11 [x]2Co 11:9
4:13 [y]2Co 12:9
4:14 [z]Php 1:7
4:15 [a]Php 1:5 [b]2Co 11:8,9
4:16 [c]Ac 17:1 [d]1Th 2:9
4:17 [e]1Co 9:11,12
4:18 [f]Php 2:25 [g]2Co 2:14
4:19 [h]Ps 23:1; 2Co 9:8 [i]Ro 2:4
4:20 [j]Gal 1:4 [k]Ro 11:36
4:21 [l]Gal 1:2
4:22 [m]Ac 9:13
4:23 [n]Ro 16:20

[a] *23* Some manuscripts do not have *Amen*.

The words of this hymn by Madame Guyon are especially meaningful because they speak of her attitude during and after many years of imprisonment for her beliefs.

My Lord, How Full of Sweet Content

My Lord, how full of sweet content;
I pass my years of banishment!
Where'er I dwell, I dwell with Thee,
In heaven, in earth, or on the sea.

To me remains nor place nor time;
My country is in every clime;
I can be calm and free from care
On any shore, since God is there.

While place we seek, or place we
shun
The soul finds happiness in none;
But with God to guide our way,
'Tis equal joy, to go or stay.

Could I be cast where Thou are not,
That were indeed a dreadful lot:
But regions none remote I call,
Secure of finding God in all.

—Madame Guyon (1648-1717)

Colossians

Jesus Christ is all we need.

Some religious teachers insisted that they had additional knowledge that was necessary for salvation. These teachers began pressuring the believers in Colosse to incorporate Jewish and pagan beliefs into the gospel message. In this brief letter, Paul charts a course of faith for the Colossians as he shows them the dangers of mixing the gospel message with worthless beliefs, and he reminds them that Christ is Lord of all and is completely adequate for all of life's situations.

With words of warning in powerful prose, Paul's letter to the Colossians declares the fullness and freedom that can be found in Christ. Jesus Christ is God the Creator, come to earth in the flesh (Col 1). Believers are members of God's family, above reproach, holy, blameless and complete (Col 1–2). Paul admonishes believers to keep their focus on Christ (Col 3) and to remember the importance of praying for those in leadership positions in the church and in the community (Col 4).

The book of Colossians reminds us that the way we live is important. If we lack a clear understanding of our faith as revealed in God's Word, we can easily be swayed by the persuasive words of false teachers. Only by setting our minds on who Jesus is and focusing on the life we have in him can we truly find our way. Using Colossians as a roadmap, we can swerve around the potholes of false teaching, profane philosophies and worthless beliefs as we travel the road of faith.

Quick Study

Author
The apostle Paul.

Date Written
Around A.D. 60.

Written From
Rome during Paul's imprisonment there.

Key Passage
Colossians 2:13 "When you were dead in your sins and in the uncircumcision of your sinful nature, God made you alive with Christ. He forgave us all our sins."

Outline

Paul's greetings, thanksgiving and prayer.
Col 1:1–14

The supremacy of Christ.
Col 1:15–23

Paul's work in the church.
Col 1:24—2:7

Freedom in Christ.
Col 2:8–23

Guidance for living.
Col 3:1–17

Guidance for Christian households.
Col 3:18—4:1

Instructions and final greetings.
Col 4:2–18

The Women of Colossians

Wives *Submitting and being loved.* Col 3:18–19

Nympha *She had a church in her home.* Col 4:15

Christ Is Supreme

COL 1:15-20

We have all heard the same bland statements: "Jesus was just a good, moral teacher" or "Jesus was a wonderful, loving rabbi, but he was really just a person like you and me." There is one problem: These statements do not take into account the teaching of the Bible. In this first chapter of Colossians, Paul paints a picture of Jesus with vivid and powerful strokes.

Who is Jesus? The One who makes visible the invisible God. He is the One by whom and for whom everything in all of creation was made. He holds the entire universe together. He is Lord over the church. He is the first to rise from the dead to live eternally. He is supreme over all. The fullness of God the Father dwells in Jesus. His shed blood is the payment for our sins, and only he can make peace between God and us. This is Jesus. This is far more than a good, moral teacher. This is God!

1 Paul, an apostle[a] of Christ Jesus by the will of
God,[b] and Timothy our brother,

[2]To the holy and faithful[a] brothers in Christ at
Colosse:

Grace[c] and peace to you from God our Father.[bd]

Thanksgiving and Prayer

[3]We always thank God,[e] the Father of our Lord
Jesus Christ, when we pray for you, [4]because we
have heard of your faith in Christ Jesus and of the
love[f] you have for all the saints[g]— [5]the faith and
love that spring from the hope[h] that is stored up
for you in heaven[i] and that you have already heard
about in the word of truth, the gospel [6]that has
come to you. All over the world[j] this gospel is
bearing fruit[k] and growing, just as it has been
doing among you since the day you heard it and
understood God's grace in all its truth. [7]You
learned it from Epaphras,[l] our dear fellow servant,
who is a faithful minister[m] of Christ on our[c] behalf,
[8]and who also told us of your love in the Spirit.[n]

[9]For this reason, since the day we heard about
you,[o] we have not stopped praying for you and
asking God to fill you with the knowledge of his
will[p] through all spiritual wisdom and understanding.[q] [10]And we pray this in order that you
may live a life worthy[r] of the Lord and may please
him in every way: bearing fruit in every good
work, growing in the knowledge of God, [11]being
strengthened with all power[s] according to his glorious might so that you may have great endurance
and patience,[t] and joyfully [12]giving thanks to the
Father,[u] who has qualified you[d] to share in the
inheritance[v] of the saints in the kingdom of light.
[13]For he has rescued us from the dominion of
darkness[w] and brought us into the kingdom[x] of
the Son he loves,[y] [14]in whom we have redemption,[ez] the forgiveness of sins.[a]

The Supremacy of Christ

[15]He is the image[b] of the invisible God,[c] the
firstborn over all creation. [16]For by him all things
were created:[d] things in heaven and on earth, visible and invisible, whether thrones or powers or
rulers or authorities;[e] all things were created by
him and for him.[f] [17]He is before all things,[g] and
in him all things hold together. [18]And he is the
head[h] of the body, the church; he is the beginning
and the firstborn from among the dead,[i] so that in
everything he might have the supremacy. [19]For
God was pleased[j] to have all his fullness[k] dwell in
him, [20]and through him to reconcile[l] to himself all
things, whether things on earth or things in heav-
en,[m] by making peace through his blood,[n] shed
on the cross.

1:1 [a]1Co 1:1 [b]2Co 1:1
1:2 [c]Col 4:18 [d]Ro 1:7
1:3 [e]Ro 1:8
1:4 [f]Gal 5:6 [g]Eph 1:15
1:5 [h]1Th 5:8; Tit 1:2 [i]1Pe 1:4
1:6 [j]Ro 10:18 [k]Jn 15:16
1:7 [l]Phm 23 [m]Col 4:7
1:8 [n]Ro 15:30
1:9 [o]Eph 1:15 [p]Eph 5:17 [q]Eph 1:17
1:10 [r]Eph 4:1
1:11 [s]Eph 3:16 [t]Eph 4:2
1:12 [u]Eph 5:20 [v]Ac 20:32
1:13 [w]Ac 26:18 [x]Eph 6:12; 2Pe 1:11 [y]Mt 3:17
1:14 [z]Ro 3:24 [a]Eph 1:7
1:15 [b]2Co 4:4 [c]Jn 1:18
1:16 [d]Jn 1:3 [e]Eph 1:20,21 [f]Ro 11:36
1:17 [g]Jn 1:2
1:18 [h]Eph 1:22 [i]Ac 26:23; Rev 1:5
1:19 [j]Eph 1:5 [k]Jn 1:16
1:20 [l]2Co 5:18 [m]Eph 1:10 [n]Eph 2:13

[a] 2 Or *believing* [b] 2 Some manuscripts *Father and the Lord Jesus Christ* [c] 7 Some manuscripts *your* [d] 12 Some manuscripts *us* [e] 14 A few late manuscripts *redemption through his blood*

Week 46

Pleasing God

Many believers find it hard to imagine that they can actually please God. They have the notion that God is keeping score of their faults, writing down every sin and mistake. Certainly, God is not smiling and yelling, "*Yes!*" when you get it right, is he? The Scriptures make it quite clear that, indeed, God is thrilled with you at times (Zep 3:17). According to Colossians 1:10-12, there are four things that please God: bearing fruit in good works, growing in the knowledge of God, having great endurance and patience, and joyfully giving thanks to the Father.

Before you can please God, what is necessary (Col 1:9)? How is this accomplished (Eph 3:16-19)?

If you are saved by grace, not works (Eph 2:8-9), why are works so important (Eph 2:10; Jas 2:14-24)? What does a person's fruit tell you about that person (Mt 7:15-20)?

Your knowledge of God should always be in the process of growth. What does "knowledge of God" actually mean and how is it gained (Jn 5:39-40)?

Jesus told the Pharisees that they did not know him (Jn 8:19). How could they get to know Jesus (Jn 8:31-32)? It is important to remember that only through obedience can you fully experience what a relationship with God offers.

How can you have endurance and patience (Col 1:11)? The power to endure comes from God himself (2Co 1:8-10); in fact, all power comes from God (Jn 19:10-11; 2Co 4:7). How great is the power that God shares with you (Eph 1:18-20)?

Despite your situation, what can you joyfully give thanks for (Col 1:12-14)? What is God's will for you regarding giving thanks (1Th 5:16-18)? How is this possible?

The only way to please God is through a personal relationship with Jesus, which involves both your faith and your deeds. It is impossible to please God without faith (Heb 11:6), it is impossible to have faith without good deeds (Jas 2:24) and it is impossible to have either of these without Christ and his Word (Ro 10:17).

Enjoying God THROUGH the Word

Read 2 Peter 1:3-8 (page 2032). This passage gives a challenge and an encouragement. Because God has given you everything you need, by sending the Holy Spirit to dwell in you and by infusing you with his power (Jn 14:16-17; Ac 1:8), you can please him by living a godly life. A godly life includes an increasing measure of faith, goodness, knowledge, self-control, perseverance, godliness, kindness and love.

All of these qualities increase, not as you try harder or put forth more effort to be godly, but as your walk with Jesus becomes more and more intimate. The more time you spend with a person, the more you become like that person. So it is when we spend time with Jesus.

Enjoying God THROUGH Experience

As you read God's Word, expect God to speak to you through the Holy Spirit. Don't think of Bible reading as only an intellectual study, but look for ways to know God personally. He has revealed himself through his Word. As you pray, think of Jesus sitting beside you. Speak to him as you would any other friend. Allow the Holy Spirit, who is also a person, to speak to your heart in return. Remember: True Christianity is not a *religion* but a *relationship.*

Go to page 1995 for your next weekly study.

Hollow Philosophies

COL 2:8

Can Christians get side-tracked from the central concerns of the faith? Can followers of Christ get tangled up in things that distract them from what matters most in life? The answer is yes. The apostle Paul is speaking to solid believers (Col 2:6) who need to hear an urgent warning: Don't get caught up in the false philosophies and traditions of this world.

There are plenty of traditions and philosophies that became pitfalls in the apostle Paul's day, and there are just as many in our world today. From New Age spirituality to self-help to materialism to the rainbow of world religions—philosophies abound. Those who have grown up in the church know that traditions, even religious ones, can take on idolatrous proportions when they become the focus of our lives and worship. Paul calls us to carefully examine our lives to be sure that no human philosophy or tradition ever stands in the way of our relationship with Christ.

21 Once you were alienated from God and were
enemies[o] in your minds[p] because of[a] your evil
behavior. 22 But now he has reconciled you by
Christ's physical body[q] through death to present
you holy in his sight, without blemish and free
from accusation[r]— 23 if you continue in your faith,
established[s] and firm, not moved from the hope[t]
held out in the gospel. This is the gospel that you
heard and that has been proclaimed to every creature under heaven,[u] and of which I, Paul, have
become a servant.[v]

Paul's Labor for the Church

24 Now I rejoice in what was suffered for you,
and I fill up in my flesh what is still lacking in
regard to Christ's afflictions,[w] for the sake of his
body, which is the church. 25 I have become its servant[x] by the commission God gave me[y] to present
to you the word of God in its fullness— 26 the mystery[z] that has been kept hidden for ages and generations, but is now disclosed to the saints. 27 To
them God has chosen to make known[a] among the
Gentiles the glorious riches of this mystery, which
is Christ in you, the hope of glory.
28 We proclaim him, admonishing[b] and teaching
everyone with all wisdom,[c] so that we may present everyone perfect[d] in Christ. 29 To this end I
labor,[e] struggling[f] with all his energy, which so
powerfully works in me.[g]

2 I want you to know how much I am struggling[h] for you and for those at Laodicea,[i] and
for all who have not met me personally. 2 My purpose is that they may be encouraged in heart[j] and
united in love, so that they may have the full
riches of complete understanding, in order that
they may know the mystery of God, namely,
Christ, 3 in whom are hidden all the treasures of
wisdom and knowledge.[k] 4 I tell you this so that
no one may deceive you by fine-sounding arguments.[l] 5 For though I am absent from you in body,
I am present with you in spirit[m] and delight to see
how orderly[n] you are and how firm[o] your faith in
Christ is.

Freedom From Human Regulations Through Life With Christ

6 So then, just as you received Christ Jesus as
Lord,[p] continue to live in him, 7 rooted[q] and built
up in him, strengthened in the faith as you were
taught, and overflowing with thankfulness.
8 See to it that no one takes you captive through
hollow and deceptive philosophy,[r] which depends
on human tradition and the basic principles of
this world[s] rather than on Christ.
9 For in Christ all the fullness of the Deity lives
in bodily form, 10 and you have been given fullness
in Christ, who is the head[t] over every power and
authority. 11 In him you were also circumcised,[u] in
the putting off of the sinful nature,[b v] not with a

1:21 [o]Ro 5:10 [p]Eph 2:3
1:22 [q]Ro 7:4 [r]Eph 5:27
1:23 [s]Eph 3:17 [t]ver 5 [u]Ro 10:18 [v]ver 25; 1Co 3:5
1:24 [w]2Co 1:5
1:25 [x]ver 23 [y]Eph 3:2
1:26 [z]Ro 16:25
1:27 [a]Mt 13:11
1:28 [b]Col 3:16 [c]1Co 2:6,7 [d]Eph 5:27
1:29 [e]1Co 15:10 [f]Col 2:1 [g]Eph 1:19
2:1 [h]Col 1:29; 4:12 [i]Rev 1:11
2:2 [j]Col 4:8
2:3 [k]Ro 11:33; 1Co 1:24,30
2:4 [l]Ro 16:18
2:5 [m]1Th 2:17 [n]1Co 14:40 [o]1Pe 5:9
2:6 [p]Col 1:10
2:7 [q]Eph 3:17
2:8 [r]1Ti 6:20 [s]Gal 4:3
2:10 [t]Eph 1:22
2:11 [u]Ro 2:29; Php 3:3 [v]Gal 5:24

[a] *21* Or *minds, as shown by* [b] *11* Or *the flesh*

circumcision done by the hands of men but with
2:12 the circumcision done by Christ, 12having been
[w]Ro 6:5 buried with him in baptism and raised with him[w]
[x]Ac 2:24 through your faith in the power of God, who
2:13 raised him from the dead.[x]
[y]Eph 2:1,5 13When you were dead in your sins[y] and in the
uncircumcision of your sinful nature,[a] God made
you[b] alive with Christ. He forgave us all our sins,
2:14 14having canceled the written code, with its regu-
[z]Eph 2:15 lations,[z] that was against us and that stood
[a]1Pe 2:24 opposed to us; he took it away, nailing it to the
2:15 cross.[a] 15And having disarmed the powers and
[b]Eph 6:12 authorities,[b] he made a public spectacle of them,
[c]Lk 10:18 triumphing over them[c] by the cross.[c]
2:16 16Therefore do not let anyone judge you[d] by
[d]Ro 14:3,4 what you eat or drink,[e] or with regard to a reli-
[e]Ro 14:17 [f]Ro 14:5 gious festival,[f] a New Moon celebration[g] or a Sab-
[g]1Ch 23:31 [h]Gal 4:10 bath day.[h] 17These are a shadow of the things that
were to come;[i] the reality, however, is found in
2:17 Christ. 18Do not let anyone who delights in false
[i]Heb 8:5 humility[j] and the worship of angels disqualify you
2:18 [j]ver 23 for the prize.[k] Such a person goes into great detail
[k]Php 3:14 about what he has seen, and his unspiritual mind
puffs him up with idle notions. 19He has lost con-
2:19 nection with the Head,[l] from whom the whole
[l]Eph 1:22 body, supported and held together by its liga-
[m]Eph 4:16 ments and sinews, grows as God causes it to
grow.[m]
2:20 20Since you died with Christ to the basic princi-
[n]Gal 4:3,9 ples of this world,[n] why, as though you still
[o]ver 14,16 belonged to it, do you submit to its rules:[o] 21"Do
not handle! Do not taste! Do not touch!"? 22These
2:22 are all destined to perish[p] with use, because they
[p]1Co 6:13 [q]Isa 29:13; are based on human commands and teachings.[q]
Mt 15:9; 23Such regulations indeed have an appearance of
Tit 1:14 wisdom, with their self-imposed worship, their
false humility and their harsh treatment of the
3:2 body, but they lack any value in restraining sen-
[r]Php 3:19,20 sual indulgence.

3:3 [s]Ro 6:2; 2Co 5:14

Rules for Holy Living

3 Since, then, you have been raised with Christ,
3:4 [t]1Co 1:7 set your hearts on things above, where Christ
[u]1Pe 1:13; is seated at the right hand of God. 2Set your minds
1Jn 3:2 on things above, not on earthly things.[r] 3For you
3:5 died,[s] and your life is now hidden with Christ in
[v]Eph 5:3 God. 4When Christ, who is your[d] life, appears,[t]
[w]Eph 5:5 then you also will appear with him in glory.[u]
3:6 5Put to death, therefore, whatever belongs to
[x]Ro 1:18 your earthly nature: sexual immorality, impurity,
3:7 lust, evil desires and greed,[v] which is idolatry.[w]
[y]Eph 2:2 6Because of these, the wrath of God[x] is coming.[e]
3:8 7You used to walk in these ways, in the life you
[z]Eph 4:22 once lived.[y] 8But now you must rid yourselves[z] of
[a]Eph 4:31 all such things as these: anger, rage, malice, slan-
[b]Eph 4:29 der,[a] and filthy language from your lips.[b] 9Do not
3:9 [c]Eph 4:22,25 lie to each other,[c] since you have taken off your

[a] 13 Or *your flesh* [b] 13 Some manuscripts *us* [c] 15 Or *them in him* [d] 4 Some manuscripts *our* [e] 6 Some early manuscripts *coming on those who are disobedient*

No Spiritual Games

COL 2:16-19

When Paul writes to the Christians in the city of Colosse, he is clearly addressing some false teaching that is being spread throughout the congregation. A group of people claim to be followers of Christ, but they have added additional requirements to the simple gospel of faith. This group requires people to give up certain foods, observe special festivals and worship every Sabbath. They also call people to deep levels of self-denial and ascetic practices. On top of this, they advocate worship of angels, and they depreciate the place and worth of Christ. In light of the pressure from this fringe group, Paul calls the people of God to walk in freedom! Once they have Christ, they are saved. They don't need to play spiritual games to prove they are worthy. Human rules and regulations are no longer their concern; instead, their focus is a heart yielded to the Savior.

Seasoned With Salt

COL 4:5–6

Imagine you are getting out the ingredients to bake a batch of cookies, but you have unknowingly mixed up the salt and sugar. You end up putting in a dash of sugar and a cup of salt. Now picture a little child taking a big bite of one of those cookies. How long will it take the child to realize something is wrong? Do you think he or she will ask for another cookie? Of course not!

The art of seasoning is a matter of balance. Just enough salt to notice, but not too much to overwhelm. Salt creates a thirst, a desire for more.

As Christians, we sprinkle the salt of God's grace and gospel into our daily conversations. We don't saturate every conversation in a way that drives others away. The artful seasoning of God's loving grace into our conversation will create a thirst, a desire in the lives of others. They will long to know more of Jesus.

old self with its practices 10and have put on the new self, which is being renewed[d] in knowledge in the image of its Creator.[e] 11Here there is no Greek or Jew,[f] circumcised or uncircumcised,[g] barbarian, Scythian, slave or free,[h] but Christ is all,[i] and is in all.

12Therefore, as God's chosen people, holy and dearly loved, clothe yourselves with compassion, kindness, humility,[j] gentleness and patience.[k] 13Bear with each other[l] and forgive whatever grievances you may have against one another. Forgive as the Lord forgave you.[m] 14And over all these virtues put on love,[n] which binds them all together in perfect unity.[o]

15Let the peace of Christ[p] rule in your hearts, since as members of one body you were called to peace. And be thankful. 16Let the word of Christ[q] dwell in you richly as you teach and admonish one another with all wisdom,[r] and as you sing psalms, hymns and spiritual songs with gratitude in your hearts to God.[s] 17And whatever you do,[t] whether in word or deed, do it all in the name of the Lord Jesus, giving thanks[u] to God the Father through him.

Rules for Christian Households

18Wives, submit to your husbands,[v] as is fitting in the Lord.

19Husbands, love your wives and do not be harsh with them.

20Children, obey your parents in everything, for this pleases the Lord.

21Fathers, do not embitter your children, or they will become discouraged.

22Slaves, obey your earthly masters in everything; and do it, not only when their eye is on you and to win their favor, but with sincerity of heart and reverence for the Lord. 23Whatever you do, work at it with all your heart, as working for the Lord, not for men, 24since you know that you will receive an inheritance[w] from the Lord as a reward. It is the Lord Christ you are serving. 25Anyone who does wrong will be repaid for his wrong, and there is no favoritism.[x]

4 Masters, provide your slaves with what is right and fair, because you know that you also have a Master in heaven.

Further Instructions

2Devote yourselves to prayer,[y] being watchful and thankful. 3And pray for us, too, that God may open a door[z] for our message, so that we may proclaim the mystery of Christ, for which I am in chains.[a] 4Pray that I may proclaim it clearly, as I should. 5Be wise[b] in the way you act toward outsiders;[c] make the most of every opportunity.[d] 6Let your conversation be always full of grace,[e] seasoned with salt,[f] so that you may know how to answer everyone.[g]

3:10 [d]Ro 12:2; Eph 4:23 [e]Eph 2:10
3:11 [f]Ro 10:12 [g]1Co 7:19 [h]Gal 3:28 [i]Eph 1:23
3:12 [j]Php 2:3 [k]2Co 6:6; Gal 5:22,23
3:13 [l]Eph 4:2 [m]Eph 4:32
3:14 [n]1Co 13:1-13 [o]Eph 4:3
3:15 [p]Jn 14:27
3:16 [q]Ro 10:17 [r]Col 1:28 [s]Eph 5:19
3:17 [t]1Co 10:31 [u]Eph 5:20
3:18 [v]Eph 5:22
3:24 [w]Ac 20:32
3:25 [x]Ac 10:34
4:2 [y]Lk 18:1
4:3 [z]Ac 14:27 [a]Eph 6:19,20
4:5 [b]Eph 5:15 [c]Mk 4:11 [d]Eph 5:16
4:6 [e]Eph 4:29 [f]Mk 9:50 [g]1Pe 3:15

Final Greetings

7 Tychicus[h] will tell you all the news about me.
He is a dear brother, a faithful minister and fellow
servant[i] in the Lord. 8 I am sending him to you for
the express purpose that you may know about
our[a] circumstances and that he may encourage
your hearts.[j] 9 He is coming with Onesimus,[k] our
faithful and dear brother, who is one of you. They
will tell you everything that is happening here.
10 My fellow prisoner Aristarchus[l] sends you his
greetings, as does Mark, the cousin of Barnabas.[m]
(You have received instructions about him; if he
comes to you, welcome him.) 11 Jesus, who is
called Justus, also sends greetings. These are the
only Jews among my fellow workers for the kingdom of God, and they have proved a comfort to
me. 12 Epaphras,[n] who is one of you and a servant
of Christ Jesus, sends greetings. He is always
wrestling in prayer for you,[o] that you may stand
firm in all the will of God, mature[p] and fully
assured. 13 I vouch for him that he is working hard
for you and for those at Laodicea[q] and Hierapolis.
14 Our dear friend Luke,[r] the doctor, and Demas[s]
send greetings. 15 Give my greetings to the brothers
at Laodicea, and to Nympha and the church in her
house.[t]
16 After this letter has been read to you, see that
it is also read[u] in the church of the Laodiceans and
that you in turn read the letter from Laodicea.
17 Tell Archippus:[v] "See to it that you complete
the work you have received in the Lord."[w]
18 I, Paul, write this greeting in my own hand.[x]
Remember[y] my chains. Grace be with you.[z]

4:7 [h]Ac 20:4 [i]Eph 6:21,22
4:8 [j]Eph 6:21,22
4:9 [k]Phm 10
4:10 [l]Ac 19:29 [m]Ac 4:36
4:12 [n]Col 1:7; Phm 23 [o]Ro 15:30 [p]1Co 2:6
4:13 [q]Col 2:1
4:14 [r]2Ti 4:11; Phm 24 [s]2Ti 4:10
4:15 [t]Ro 16:5
4:16 [u]2Th 3:14
4:17 [v]Phm 2 [w]2Ti 4:5
4:18 [x]1Co 16:21 [y]Heb 13:3 [z]1Ti 6:21; 2Ti 4:22; Tit 3:15; Heb 13:25

In My Own Hand

COL 4:18

It was common in the first century for people to dictate their letters to a scribe. There is no question of Paul's ability to sit down and write his letters with his own hand, but it is likely that Paul followed the custom of having a scribe pen his words for him. At times Paul put his personal signature at the end of a letter he dictated (1Co 16:21; Gal 6:11; Phm 19). This was his personal seal of authenticity. In a time when there was much false teaching and debate over what was sound doctrine, Paul's signature gave apostolic authority to his letters.

[a] 8 Some manuscripts *that he may know about your*

1 Thessalonians

Facing the future with hope.

Though the believers in Thessalonica faced ridicule and persecution from their neighbors, Paul received encouraging reports of the faith evident in this small Macedonian church. He wanted to be sure the believers had the teaching they needed in order to live holy lives during a difficult time and in a pagan culture. And he wanted to be sure they understand that physical death is not the end: There is hope of life after death, and there is the surety of Christ's return. The timing may not be certain, according to Paul, but there is no uncertainty about the reality of that future event.

Paul's encouragement throughout this letter helps solidify the Thessalonians' spiritual growth. We share Paul's rejoicing and thanksgiving in the ongoing witness of the believers (1Th 1). We understand his longing to see his friends again (1Th 2). We sense the concern he expresses for their continued growth in the faith (1Th 3). We take great comfort in his words about the hope of a final resurrection (1Th 4). And we chuckle at his punchy "to-do" list for godly living because its terse style mimics the reminder lists we leave for ourselves and others on refrigerators and bulletin boards (1Th 5).

As we face our own unknown futures, we gain assurance from Paul's words to the Thessalonians. Christ will *return one day. But until he does, there is work to do and a way to live that is pleasing to God. Paul's instructions to the Thessalonians are as applicable today as when he wrote them almost two thousand years ago.*

Quick Study

Author
The apostle Paul.

Date Written
Around A.D. 51.

Written From
Corinth.

Key Passage
1 Thessalonians 4:11–12 "Make it your ambition to lead a quiet life, to mind your own business and to work with your hands, just as we told you, so that your daily life may win the respect of outsiders and so that you will not be dependent on anybody."

Outline

Paul's greetings and thanksgiving.
1Th 1:1-10

Paul's ministry and his love for the Thessalonians.
1Th 2:1–3:5

Timothy's report.
1Th 3:6-13

Living to please God.
1Th 4:1-12

The return of Christ.
1Th 4:13–5:11

Final instructions and greetings.
1Th 5:12-28

The Women of 1 Thessalonians

A mother	*The apostles' gentleness was like hers.* 1Th 2:7
A pregnant woman	*Destruction will come suddenly, like her labor pains.* 1Th 5:3

Like a Mother

1TH 2:7

Paul's ministry to the believers in Thessalonica is personal and intimate. He does not stand at a detached distance and offer nuggets of sage, but aloof, advice. While bringing them the gospel of Jesus Christ, he invests his very life in theirs. He speaks of his ministry in the most intimate way, using the image of a mother tenderly providing for her children—literally, a mother nursing her baby. Do you get the picture? As a mother gladly gives the very basic food that assures life, so Paul has given to the Thessalonian Christians life-assuring nourishment. The pure milk of the Word has been poured into their lives (1Pe 2:2), and they are growing in faith. Can you sense the tenderness Paul feels for them? Can you picture the intimacy? This kind of closeness can mark relationships in the church today, too, as we grow closer together as the family of God.

1 Paul, Silas[a] and Timothy,[a] 1:1 aAc 16:1; 2Th 1:1

To the church of the Thessalonians[b] in God the bAc 17:1
Father and the Lord Jesus Christ: cRo 1:7

Grace and peace to you.[bc]

Thanksgiving for the Thessalonians' Faith

2We always thank God for all of you,[d] mention- 1:2 dRo 1:8
ing you in our prayers. 3We continually remember before our God and Father your work pro- 1:3
duced by faith,[e] your labor prompted by love, and e2Th 1:11
your endurance inspired by hope in our Lord
Jesus Christ.
4For we know, brothers loved by God, that he 1:5
has chosen you, 5because our gospel[f] came to you f2Th 2:14
not simply with words, but also with power, with
the Holy Spirit and with deep conviction. You
know how we lived among you for your sake. 1:6
6You became imitators of us[g] and of the Lord; in g1Co 4:16
spite of severe suffering,[h] you welcomed the mes- hAc 17:5-10
sage with the joy given by the Holy Spirit.[i] 7And iAc 13:52
so you became a model to all the believers in
Macedonia and Achaia. 8The Lord's message rang
out from you not only in Macedonia and Achaia—
your faith in God has become known everywhere.[j] 1:8 jRo 1:8;
Therefore we do not need to say anything about it, 10:18
9for they themselves report what kind of reception
you gave us. They tell how you turned to God 1:9
from idols[k] to serve the living and true God, 10and k1Co 12:2;
to wait for his Son from heaven, whom he raised Gal 4:8
from the dead[l]—Jesus, who rescues us from the 1:10 lAc 2:24
coming wrath.[m] mRo 5:9

Paul's Ministry in Thessalonica

2 You know, brothers, that our visit to you[n] was 2:1 n1Th 1:5,9
not a failure. 2We had previously suffered[o] and
been insulted in Philippi, as you know, but with 2:2 oAc 16:22;
the help of our God we dared to tell you his gospel Php 1:30
in spite of strong opposition. 3For the appeal we
make does not spring from error or impure
motives,[p] nor are we trying to trick you. 4On the 2:3 p2Co 2:17
contrary, we speak as men approved by God to be
entrusted with the gospel.[q] We are not trying to 2:4 qGal 2:7
please men[r] but God, who tests our hearts. 5You rGal 1:10
know we never used flattery, nor did we put on a
mask to cover up greed[s]—God is our witness.[t] 6We 2:5 sAc 20:33
were not looking for praise from men, not from tRo 1:9
you or anyone else.
As apostles[u] of Christ we could have been a 2:6 u1Co 9:1,2
burden to you, 7but we were gentle among you,
like a mother caring for her little children.[v] 8We 2:7 vver 11
loved you so much that we were delighted to
share with you not only the gospel of God but our
lives as well,[w] because you had become so dear 2:8 w2Co 12:15;
to us. 9Surely you remember, brothers, our toil 1Jn 3:16
and hardship; we worked[x] night and day in order 2:9 xAc 18:3

[a] *1* Greek *Silvanus,* a variant of *Silas* [b] *1* Some early manuscripts *you from God our Father and the Lord Jesus Christ*

2:9 not to be a burden to anyone[y] while we preached
[y]2Th 3:8 the gospel of God to you.
2:10 10You are witnesses,[z] and so is God, of how
[z]1Th 1:5 [a]2Co 1:12 holy,[a] righteous and blameless we were among
you who believed. 11For you know that we dealt
2:11 with each of you as a father deals with his own
[b]ver 7; children,[b] 12encouraging, comforting and urging
1Co 4:14 you to live lives worthy[c] of God, who calls you
2:12 into his kingdom and glory.
[c]Eph 4:1 13And we also thank God continually[d] because,
2:13 when you received the word of God,[e] which you
[d]1Th 1:2 heard from us, you accepted it not as the word of
[e]Heb 4:12 men, but as it actually is, the word of God, which
2:14 is at work in you who believe. 14For you, broth-
[f]Gal 1:22 ers, became imitators of God's churches in Judea,[f]
[g]Ac 17:5; which are in Christ Jesus: You suffered from your
2Th 1:4 own countrymen[g] the same things those churches
suffered from the Jews, 15who killed the Lord
2:15 [h]Ac 2:23 Jesus[h] and the prophets[i] and also drove us out.
[i]Mt 5:12 They displease God and are hostile to all men 16in
2:16 their effort to keep us from speaking to the Gen-
[j]Ac 13:45,50 tiles[j] so that they may be saved. In this way they
[k]Mt 23:32 always heap up their sins to the limit.[k] The wrath
of God has come upon them at last.[a]

Paul's Longing to See the Thessalonians

2:17 17But, brothers, when we were torn away from
[l]1Co 5:3; you for a short time (in person, not in thought),[l]
Col 2:5 [m]1Th 3:10 out of our intense longing we made every effort
to see you.[m] 18For we wanted to come to you—cer-
2:18 [n]Mt 4:10 tainly I, Paul, did, again and again—but Satan[n]
[o]Ro 1:13; stopped us.[o] 19For what is our hope, our joy, or the
15:22 crown[p] in which we will glory[q] in the presence of
2:19 our Lord Jesus when he comes?[r] Is it not you?
[p]Php 4:1 20Indeed, you are our glory[s] and joy.
[q]2Co 1:14 3 So when we could stand it no longer,[t] we
[r]Mt 16:27; 1Th 3:13 thought it best to be left by ourselves in Ath-
2:20 ens.[u] 2We sent Timothy, who is our brother and
[s]2Co 1:14 God's fellow worker[b] in spreading the gospel of
Christ, to strengthen and encourage you in your
3:1 [t]ver 5 faith, 3so that no one would be unsettled by these
[u]Ac 17:15 trials. You know quite well that we were destined
for them.[v] 4In fact, when we were with you, we
3:3 [v]Ac 9:16; kept telling you that we would be persecuted. And
14:22 it turned out that way, as you well know.[w] 5For
3:4 this reason, when I could stand it no longer,[x] I
[w]1Th 2:14 sent to find out about your faith. I was afraid that
3:5 in some way the tempter[y] might have tempted
[x]ver 1 you and our efforts might have been useless.[z]
[y]Mt 4:3 [z]Gal 2:2; Php 2:16

Timothy's Encouraging Report

3:6 6But Timothy has just now come to us from
[a]Ac 18:5 you[a] and has brought good news about your faith
[b]1Th 1:3 and love.[b] He has told us that you always have
pleasant memories of us and that you long to see
us, just as we also long to see you. 7Therefore,
brothers, in all our distress and persecution we
were encouraged about you because of your faith.

[a] 16 Or *them fully* [b] 2 Some manuscripts *brother and fellow worker*; other manuscripts *brother and God's servant*

Like a Father

1TH 2:11–12

Paul's relationship with the Thessalonians is marked not only with the tenderness and gentleness of a mother (1Th 2:7), but also with the encouragement and comfort of a father (1Th 2:11–12). Paul is reminding the Thessalonian Christians that he is not afraid to call them to growth and maturity. He is committed to encouraging and challenging them onward until they become all God has called them to be.

What a beautiful balance we see in the ministry of Paul: Gentle and nurturing provision like a mother. Encouragement, challenge and discipline like a father. Through his care and concern, Paul brings a healthy and whole ministry to these believers who long to "live lives worthy of God," who loves them (1Th 2:12).

Growing and Maturing

1TH 3:10

The apostle Paul yearns to be with his friends again, so he can help them grow. He wants to supply what is yet lacking in their faith. Paul knows what every believer learns with time: The Christian life is a journey. Like the Thessalonians, we are all growing, maturing and learning to walk more intimately with the Savior.

One of Paul's greatest desires is to see believers grow into a deeper life of faith. What does this life look like? More knowledge of—and obedience to—the Word, fresher encounters with the Holy Spirit, deeper experiences in worship and prayer, more intimate relationships with the people in God's family, more radical commitments to humble service, and a purer life of holiness. The seeds of this life have been planted in the hearts of the Thessalonians and in our hearts as well. Paul's prayer is that these seeds will take root, grow and blossom.

8For now we really live, since you are standing
firm[c] in the Lord. 9How can we thank God enough
for you[d] in return for all the joy we have in the
presence of our God because of you? 10Night and
day we pray[e] most earnestly that we may see you
again[f] and supply what is lacking in your faith.
11Now may our God and Father himself and our
Lord Jesus clear the way for us to come to you.
12May the Lord make your love increase and overflow for each other[g] and for everyone else, just as
ours does for you. 13May he strengthen your
hearts so that you will be blameless[h] and holy in
the presence of our God and Father when our Lord
Jesus comes[i] with all his holy ones.

Living to Please God

4 Finally, brothers,[j] we instructed you how to
live in order to please God,[k] as in fact you are
living. Now we ask you and urge you in the Lord
Jesus to do this more and more. 2For you know
what instructions we gave you by the authority of
the Lord Jesus.
3It is God's will that you should be sanctified:
that you should avoid sexual immorality;[l] 4that
each of you should learn to control his own
body[am] in a way that is holy and honorable, 5not in
passionate lust[n] like the heathen,[o] who do not
know God; 6and that in this matter no one should
wrong his brother or take advantage of him.[p] The
Lord will punish men for all such sins,[q] as we have
already told you and warned you. 7For God did not
call us to be impure, but to live a holy life.[r] 8There-
fore, he who rejects this instruction does not reject
man but God, who gives you his Holy Spirit.[s]
9Now about brotherly love[t] we do not need to
write to you,[u] for you yourselves have been taught
by God to love each other.[v] 10And in fact, you do
love all the brothers throughout Macedonia.[w] Yet
we urge you, brothers, to do so more and more.[x]
11Make it your ambition to lead a quiet life, to
mind your own business and to work with your
hands,[y] just as we told you, 12so that your daily
life may win the respect of outsiders[z] and so that
you will not be dependent on anybody.

The Coming of the Lord

13Brothers, we do not want you to be ignorant
about those who fall asleep, or to grieve like the
rest of men, who have no hope.[a] 14We believe that
Jesus died and rose again and so we believe that
God will bring with Jesus those who have fallen
asleep in him.[b] 15According to the Lord's own
word, we tell you that we who are still alive, who
are left till the coming of the Lord, will certainly
not precede those who have fallen asleep.[c] 16For the
Lord himself will come down from heaven, with a
loud command, with the voice of the archangel and
with the trumpet call of God,[d] and the dead in
Christ will rise first.[e] 17After that, we who are still

3:8 [c]1Co 16:13
3:9 [d]1Th 1:2
3:10 [e]2Ti 1:3 [f]1Th 2:17
3:12 [g]1Th 4:9,10
3:13 [h]1Co 1:8 [i]1Th 2:19
4:1 [j]2Co 13:11 [k]2Co 5:9
4:3 [l]1Co 6:18
4:4 [m]1Co 7:2,9
4:5 [n]Ro 1:26 [o]Eph 4:17
4:6 [p]1Co 6:8 [q]Heb 13:4
4:7 [r]Lev 11:44; 1Pe 1:15
4:8 [s]Ro 5:5; Gal 4:6
4:9 [t]Ro 12:10 [u]1Th 5:1 [v]Jn 13:34
4:10 [w]1Th 1:7 [x]1Th 3:12
4:11 [y]Eph 4:28; 2Th 3:10-12
4:12 [z]Mk 4:11
4:13 [a]Eph 2:12
4:14 [b]1Co 15:18
4:15 [c]1Co 15:52
4:16 [d]Mt 24:31 [e]1Co 15:23; 2Th 2:1

[a] 4 Or *learn to live with his own wife*; or *learn to acquire a wife*

alive and are left[f] will be caught up together with
them in the clouds[g] to meet the Lord in the air. And
so we will be with the Lord[h] forever. 18Therefore
encourage each other with these words.

5 Now, brothers, about times and dates[i] we do
not need to write to you,[j] 2for you know very
well that the day of the Lord[k] will come like a
thief in the night.[l] 3While people are saying,
"Peace and safety," destruction will come on them
suddenly, as labor pains on a pregnant woman,
and they will not escape.

4But you, brothers, are not in darkness[m] so that
this day should surprise you like a thief. 5You are
all sons of the light and sons of the day. We do not
belong to the night or to the darkness. 6So then,
let us not be like others, who are asleep,[n] but let
us be alert and self-controlled. 7For those who
sleep, sleep at night, and those who get drunk, get
drunk at night.[o] 8But since we belong to the day,
let us be self-controlled, putting on faith and love
as a breastplate,[p] and the hope of salvation[q] as a
helmet.[r] 9For God did not appoint us to suffer
wrath but to receive salvation through our Lord
Jesus Christ.[s] 10He died for us so that, whether we
are awake or asleep, we may live together with
him.[t] 11Therefore encourage one another and
build each other up, just as in fact you are doing.

Final Instructions

12Now we ask you, brothers, to respect those
who work hard among you, who are over you in
the Lord[u] and who admonish you. 13Hold them in
the highest regard in love because of their work.
Live in peace with each other.[v] 14And we urge
you, brothers, warn those who are idle,[w] encourage the timid, help the weak,[x] be patient with
everyone. 15Make sure that nobody pays back
wrong for wrong,[y] but always try to be kind to
each other[z] and to everyone else.

16Be joyful always;[a] 17pray continually; 18give
thanks in all circumstances, for this is God's will
for you in Christ Jesus.

19Do not put out the Spirit's fire;[b] 20do not treat
prophecies[c] with contempt. 21Test everything.[d]
Hold on to the good. 22Avoid every kind of evil.

23May God himself, the God of peace,[e] sanctify
you through and through. May your whole spirit,
soul and body be kept blameless at the coming of
our Lord Jesus Christ. 24The one who calls you is
faithful[f] and he will do it.

25Brothers, pray for us.[g] 26Greet all the brothers
with a holy kiss.[h] 27I charge you before the Lord to
have this letter read to all the brothers.[i]

28The grace of our Lord Jesus Christ be with
you.[j]

4:17 [f]1Co 15:52 [g]Ac 1:9; Rev 11:12 [h]Jn 12:26
5:1 [i]Ac 1:7 [j]1Th 4:9
5:2 [k]1Co 1:8 [l]2Pe 3:10
5:4 [m]Ac 26:18; 1Jn 2:8
5:6 [n]Ro 13:11
5:7 [o]Ac 2:15; 2Pe 2:13
5:8 [p]Eph 6:14 [q]Ro 8:24 [r]Eph 6:17
5:9 [s]2Th 2:13,14
5:10 [t]2Co 5:15
5:12 [u]1Ti 5:17; Heb 13:17
5:13 [v]Mk 9:50
5:14 [w]2Th 3:6,7, 11 [x]Ro 14:1
5:15 [y]1Pe 3:9 [z]Gal 6:10; Eph 4:32
5:16 [a]Php 4:4
5:19 [b]Eph 4:30
5:20 [c]1Co 14:1-40
5:21 [d]1Co 14:29; 1Jn 4:1
5:23 [e]Ro 15:33
5:24 [f]1Co 1:9
5:25 [g]Eph 6:19
5:26 [h]Ro 16:16
5:27 [i]Col 4:16
5:28 [j]Ro 16:20

We all need to hear encouragement. We need our strengths to be named and appreciated. On the other hand, friends who never speak what they perceive to be true about our sin or our failures are like tightly wrapped umbrellas that are full of holes: You think you can count on them until the rain begins to fall and you find yourself soaked to the skin. We need to love each other so actively that we speak both words of challenge and words of hope.

—Sheila Walsh

2 Thessalonians

Christ is coming again! Be ready!

Commendation, correction and encouragement fill this short letter to the persecuted church of Thessalonica. Some of the Thessalonians misunderstood Paul's first letter and became lazy, believing that Christ's second coming was imminent. These believers sat and watched the sky for his return while depending on others to supply their needs and to do their work. Paul writes this second letter to encourage all the believers to be patient and to faithfully persevere in their daily responsibilities as they await Christ's return.

Paul's second letter to the Thessalonians provides a stronger dose of the same advice found in his first letter. Paul rejoices in the Thessalonian believers' commitment to Christ (2Th 1). He urges them to stand strong despite the pressures of a godless society (2Th 2). He exhorts them to mind their own business, to carefully choose their friends, and to persevere in work and service until Christ returns (2Th 3).

Paul's good advice to the Thessalonians is good advice for us also. As we wait for Christ's return, we are compelled by Paul's words to avoid apathy and to not succumb to extremes. Paul's words encourage us, as they did the Thessalonians, to do what God gives us to do for as long as God gives us time on earth, with hearts that long for Christ's coming and lives that reflect diligence, responsibility and faith.

Quick Study

Author
The apostle Paul.

Date Written
Not long after 1 Thessalonians, around A.D. 51 or 52.

Written From
Corinth.

Key Passage
2 Thessalonians 3:11-13 "We hear that some among you are idle. They are not busy; they are busybodies. Such people we command and urge in the Lord Jesus Christ to settle down and earn the bread they eat. And as for you, brothers, never tire of doing what is right."

Outline

Paul's greetings, thanksgiving and prayer.
2Th 1:1–12

The second coming.
2Th 2:1–12

Christian behavior.
2Th 2:13–17

A prayer request.
2Th 3:1–5

Warnings against idleness.
2Th 3:6–15

Final greetings.
2Th 3:16–18

The Women of 2 Thessalonians

No women are mentioned in the book of 2 Thessalonians.

Paul's Prayer

2TH 1:11

Paul lives with a piercing reality that there is a real heaven and a real hell, and real people will spend eternity in one place or the other. We can't understand Paul's passionate prayer in 2 Thessalonians 1:11 without this reality firmly in our minds. Second Thessalonians 1:5–10 sets the scene for Paul's prayer. He is deeply aware that some will suffer an eternal punishment and separation from God and that those who believe in God will be swept into his glorious presence forever. That awareness drives Paul to his knees.

Paul's prayer is an excellent model for us as we pray for those around us. He prays for two distinct things: (1) that the church in Thessalonica will fulfill God's plans for their lives; and (2) that God will fulfill every good purpose in their lives. Paul's prayer covers both inner worthiness and holiness and outer actions motivated by faith. Prayer transforms the whole person, inside and out.

1 Paul, Silas[a] and Timothy,[a]

To the church of the Thessalonians in God our
Father and the Lord Jesus Christ:

2Grace and peace to you from God the Father
and the Lord Jesus Christ.[b]

Thanksgiving and Prayer

3We ought always to thank God for you, brothers, and rightly so, because your faith is growing
more and more, and the love every one of you has
for each other is increasing.[c] 4Therefore, among
God's churches we boast[d] about your perseverance and faith[e] in all the persecutions and trials
you are enduring.[f]
5All this is evidence[g] that God's judgment is
right, and as a result you will be counted worthy
of the kingdom of God, for which you are suffering. 6God is just: He will pay back trouble to those
who trouble you[h] 7and give relief to you who are
troubled, and to us as well. This will happen when
the Lord Jesus is revealed from heaven in blazing
fire with his powerful angels.[i] 8He will punish
those who do not know God[j] and do not obey the
gospel of our Lord Jesus.[k] 9They will be punished
with everlasting destruction[l] and shut out from the
presence of the Lord and from the majesty of his
power[m] 10on the day[n] he comes to be glorified[o] in
his holy people and to be marveled at among all
those who have believed. This includes you,
because you believed our testimony to you.[p]
11With this in mind, we constantly pray for you,
that our God may count you worthy[q] of his calling, and that by his power he may fulfill every
good purpose of yours and every act prompted by
your faith.[r] 12We pray this so that the name of our
Lord Jesus may be glorified in you,[s] and you in
him, according to the grace of our God and the
Lord Jesus Christ.[b]

The Man of Lawlessness

2 Concerning the coming of our Lord Jesus
Christ and our being gathered to him,[t] we ask
you, brothers, 2not to become easily unsettled or
alarmed by some prophecy, report or letter[u] supposed to have come from us, saying that the day
of the Lord[v] has already come. 3Don't let anyone
deceive you[w] in any way, for ⌞that day will not
come⌟ until the rebellion occurs and the man of
lawlessness[c] is revealed,[x] the man doomed to
destruction. 4He will oppose and will exalt himself over everything that is called God[y] or is worshiped, so that he sets himself up in God's temple, proclaiming himself to be God.[z]
5Don't you remember that when I was with you
I used to tell you these things? 6And now you know
what is holding him back, so that he may be

1:1 [a]Ac 16:1; 1Th 1:1
1:2 [b]Ro 1:7
1:3 [c]1Th 3:12
1:4 [d]2Co 7:14 [e]1Th 1:3 [f]1Th 2:14
1:5 [g]Php 1:28
1:6 [h]Col 3:25; Rev 6:10
1:7 [i]1Th 4:16; Jude 14
1:8 [j]Gal 4:8 [k]Ro 2:8
1:9 [l]Php 3:19; 2Pe 3:7 [m]2Th 2:8
1:10 [n]1Co 3:13 [o]Jn 17:10 [p]1Co 1:6
1:11 [q]ver 5 [r]1Th 1:3
1:12 [s]Php 2:9-11
2:1 [t]Mk 13:27; 1Th 4:15-17
2:2 [u]2Th 3:17 [v]1Co 1:8
2:3 [w]Eph 5:6-8 [x]Da 7:25; 8:25; 11:36; Rev 13:5,6
2:4 [y]1Co 8:5 [z]Isa 14:13, 14; Eze 28:2

[a] *1* Greek *Silvanus,* a variant of *Silas* [b] *12* Or *God and Lord, Jesus Christ* [c] *3* Some manuscripts *sin*

revealed at the proper time. 7For the secret power of
lawlessness is already at work; but the one who
now holds it back will continue to do so till he is
taken out of the way. 8And then the lawless one
2:8 will be revealed, whom the Lord Jesus will over-
[a]Isa 11:4; throw with the breath of his mouth[a] and destroy
Rev 19:15 by the splendor of his coming. 9The coming of the
lawless one will be in accordance with the work of
2:9 Satan displayed in all kinds of counterfeit miracles,
[b]Mt 24:24; signs and wonders,[b] 10and in every sort of evil that
Jn 4:48 deceives those who are perishing.[c] They perish
2:10 because they refused to love the truth and so be
[c]1Co 1:18 saved. 11For this reason God sends them[d] a power-
2:11 ful delusion so that they will believe the lie 12and so
[d]Ro 1:28 that all will be condemned who have not believed
2:12 the truth but have delighted in wickedness.[e]
[e]Ro 1:32

Stand Firm

13But we ought always to thank God for you,
2:13 brothers loved by the Lord, because from the begin-
[f]Eph 1:4 [g]1Th 5:9 ning God chose you[a][f] to be saved[g] through the
[h]1Pe 1:2 sanctifying work of the Spirit[h] and through belief
in the truth. 14He called you to this through our
gospel, that you might share in the glory of our
2:15 Lord Jesus Christ. 15So then, brothers, stand firm[i]
[i]1Co 16:13 and hold to the teachings[b] we passed on to you,[j]
[j]1Co 11:2 whether by word of mouth or by letter.
16May our Lord Jesus Christ himself and God
2:16 our Father, who loved us[k] and by his grace gave
[k]Jn 3:16 us eternal encouragement and good hope,
2:17 17encourage[l] your hearts and strengthen[m] you in
[l]1Th 3:2 [m]2Th 3:3 every good deed and word.

Request for Prayer

3:1 [n]1Th 4:1 **3** Finally, brothers,[n] pray for us[o] that the mes-
[o]1Th 5:25 [p]1Th 1:8 sage of the Lord[p] may spread rapidly and be
honored, just as it was with you. 2And pray that
3:2 we may be delivered from wicked and evil men,[q]
[q]Ro 15:31 for not everyone has faith. 3But the Lord is faith-
3:3 ful,[r] and he will strengthen and protect you from
[r]1Co 1:9 the evil one.[s] 4We have confidence[t] in the Lord
[s]Mt 5:37 that you are doing and will continue to do the
3:4 things we command. 5May the Lord direct your
[t]2Co 2:3 hearts[u] into God's love and Christ's perseverance.
3:5 [u]1Ch 29:18

Warning Against Idleness

3:6 6In the name of the Lord Jesus Christ,[v] we com-
[v]1Co 5:4 [w]Ro 16:17 mand you, brothers, to keep away from[w] every
[x]ver 7,11 brother who is idle[x] and does not live according to
[y]1Co 11:2 the teaching[c] you received from us.[y] 7For you
3:7 yourselves know how you ought to follow our
[z]1Co 4:16 example.[z] We were not idle when we were with
3:8 you, 8nor did we eat anyone's food without pay-
[a]Ac 18:3; ing for it. On the contrary, we worked[a] night and
Eph 4:28 day, laboring and toiling so that we would not be
3:9 a burden to any of you. 9We did this, not because
[b]1Co 9:4-14 we do not have the right to such help,[b] but in
order to make ourselves a model for you to fol-

[a] 13 Some manuscripts *because God chose you as his firstfruits*
[b] 15 Or *traditions* [c] 6 Or *tradition*

The Lawless One

2TH 2:8

The title "lawless one" appears only in the book of 2 Thessalonians. This rebellious and lawless one is the antichrist. He will be the final and ultimate manifestation of evil and will lead the forces of Satan against Christ and his church. The lawless one is not Satan himself but is someone who operates in his power. The antichrist will exalt himself, demand human worship and seek to take the very place of God (2Th 2:4). Yet when we read the Word of God closely, we are made profoundly aware of the ultimate impotence of this evil one, who is "doomed to destruction" (2Th 2:3). God can hold him back with a word. Jesus will cast him down with the "breath of his mouth" (2Th 2:8). In majesty and glory, Jesus will cast out Satan and all of his workers into destruction. No matter how we might see the power of evil at work in this world, we can never forget that Christ is on the throne. Jesus rules and reigns. The ultimate victory is his!

low.[c] 10For even when we were with you,[d] we gave
you this rule: "If a man will not work,[e] he shall
not eat."
11We hear that some among you are idle. They
are not busy; they are busybodies.[f] 12Such people
we command and urge in the Lord Jesus Christ[g] to
settle down and earn the bread they eat.[h] 13And
as for you, brothers, never tire of doing what is
right.[i]
14If anyone does not obey our instruction in this
letter, take special note of him. Do not associate
with him,[j] in order that he may feel ashamed.
15Yet do not regard him as an enemy, but warn
him as a brother.[k]

Final Greetings

16Now may the Lord of peace[l] himself give you
peace at all times and in every way. The Lord be
with all of you.[m]
17I, Paul, write this greeting in my own hand,[n]
which is the distinguishing mark in all my letters.
This is how I write.
18The grace of our Lord Jesus Christ be with you
all.[o]

3:9 [c]ver 7
3:10 [d]1Th 3:4 [e]1Th 4:11
3:11 [f]ver 6,7; 1Ti 5:13
3:12 [g]1Th 4:1 [h]1Th 4:11; Eph 4:28
3:13 [i]Gal 6:9
3:14 [j]ver 6
3:15 [k]Gal 6:1; 1Th 5:14
3:16 [l]Ro 15:33 [m]Ru 2:4
3:17 [n]1Co 16:21
3:18 [o]Ro 16:20

On Laziness

2TH 3:6-13

It was a problem in ancient Thessalonica, and it is still a problem today. There are those who want a free ride. They are idle, lazy and content to live on handouts from church members. Paul uses the same word here as in 1 Thessalonians 5:14—idle, which has a connotation of being disorderly as well as lazy. Paul also cleverly says that not only are they "not busy," but they are also "busybodies" (2Th 3:11). In other words, they are meddling in other peoples' affairs.

All of Paul's counsel is aimed at one thing: getting the idlers back to work. Such people aren't to be viewed as enemies but as brothers (2Th 3:15). Their discipline should not be administered harshly or without love, but with kindness and encouragement so they will do their part to support both themselves and the gospel.

1 Timothy

Counsel for church leaders.

Timothy, an unswerving partner in Paul's missionary journeys, now follows in Paul's footsteps in leading the church at Ephesus. Though Paul and Timothy share a common goal to see the Ephesian Christians grow strong in their faith, young Timothy lacks the experience of his mentor to deal with some of the day-to-day problems that surface in Ephesus. Paul writes this letter to Timothy to warn him about false teachers, to encourage him in instructing the believers and to help him organize the church. Filled with useful principles and clear instruction about who should be chosen for church leadership, the book of 1 Timothy also offers a call to sound doctrine, advice for dealing with heretics and recommendations for leaders in handling relationships with different groups of believers.

With warm encouragement and step-by-step instructions, Paul leaves a wonderful legacy of guidance. He outlines a woman's conduct in the church and shares his sense of purpose and mission (1Ti 2). God's plan for marital faithfulness highlights women's favored status in marriage (1Ti 3). God's concern for widows and relationships between believers confirms women's worth in God's sight (1Ti 5). And the reminder to make contentment a primary goal instead of pursuing wealth reinforces the wonder of God's good gifts to us (1Ti 6).

This personal letter gives young pastor Timothy some trustworthy guidelines that we, too, can follow to keep on the right path in faith and godliness.

Quick Study

Author
The apostle Paul.

Date Written
Around A.D. 64, or at least eight years after Paul spent three years in Ephesus.

Written From
Perhaps Macedonia.

Key Passage
1 Timothy 4:12 "Don't let anyone look down on you because you are young, but set an example for the believers in speech, in life, in love, in faith and in purity."

Outline

Paul's greetings and warnings.
1Ti 1:1-11

God's grace to Paul.
1Ti 1:12-20

Teachings on worship.
1Ti 2

Teachings on leadership.
1Ti 3

Instruction for Timothy.
1Ti 4

Teachings on relationships.
1Ti 5:1–6:2

Teachings on money.
1Ti 6:3-10

Charge to Timothy.
1Ti 6:11-21

The Women of 1 Timothy

Women in the church	*Their conduct.* 1Ti 2:9-15
✿ **Eve**	*Formed after Adam and deceived.* 1Ti 2:13-14 (page 5)
Deacons' wives	*Respectable, temperate, trustworthy.* 1Ti 3:11
Older and younger women	*Treat them as mothers and sisters.* 1Ti 5:2
Widows	*Their care.* 1Ti 5:3-10
Young widows	*Paul's counsel for them.* 1Ti 5:11-14
Women who are believers	*Their responsibilities to widows.* 1Ti 5:16

✿ *Denotes a sketch written about this character*

1 Paul, an apostle of Christ Jesus by the command of God[a] our Savior and of Christ Jesus
our hope,[b]

2To Timothy[c] my true son[d] in the faith:

Grace, mercy and peace from God the Father
and Christ Jesus our Lord.

Warning Against False Teachers of the Law

3As I urged you when I went into Macedonia,
stay there in Ephesus[e] so that you may command
certain men not to teach false doctrines[f] any
longer 4nor to devote themselves to myths[g] and
endless genealogies. These promote controversies[h]
rather than God's work—which is by faith. 5The
goal of this command is love, which comes from
a pure heart[i] and a good conscience and a sincere
faith.[j] 6Some have wandered away from these and
turned to meaningless talk. 7They want to be
teachers of the law, but they do not know what
they are talking about or what they so confidently affirm.
8We know that the law is good[k] if one uses it
properly. 9We also know that law[a] is made not for
the righteous but for lawbreakers and rebels,[l] the
ungodly and sinful, the unholy and irreligious; for
those who kill their fathers or mothers, for murderers, 10for adulterers and perverts, for slave
traders and liars and perjurers—and for whatever
else is contrary to the sound doctrine[m] 11that con-
forms to the glorious gospel of the blessed God,
which he entrusted to me.[n]

The Lord's Grace to Paul

12I thank Christ Jesus our Lord, who has given
me strength,[o] that he considered me faithful,
appointing me to his service. 13Even though I was
once a blasphemer and a persecutor[p] and a violent man, I was shown mercy because I acted in
ignorance and unbelief.[q] 14The grace of our Lord
was poured out on me abundantly,[r] along with
the faith and love that are in Christ Jesus.[s]
15Here is a trustworthy saying[t] that deserves full
acceptance: Christ Jesus came into the world to
save sinners—of whom I am the worst. 16But for
that very reason I was shown mercy[u] so that in
me, the worst of sinners, Christ Jesus might display his unlimited patience as an example for
those who would believe on him and receive eternal life. 17Now to the King[v] eternal, immortal,
invisible,[w] the only God, be honor and glory for
ever and ever. Amen.[x]
18Timothy, my son, I give you this instruction
in keeping with the prophecies once made about
you,[y] so that by following them you may fight the
good fight,[z] 19holding on to faith and a good conscience. Some have rejected these and so have
shipwrecked their faith.[a] 20Among them are

[a] 9 Or *that the law*

1:1 [a]Tit 1:3 [b]Col 1:27
1:2 [c]Ac 16:1 [d]2Ti 1:2; Tit 1:4
1:3 [e]Ac 18:19 [f]Gal 1:6,7
1:4 [g]1Ti 4:7; Tit 1:14 [h]1Ti 6:4
1:5 [i]2Ti 2:22 [j]2Ti 1:5
1:8 [k]Ro 7:12
1:9 [l]Gal 3:19
1:10 [m]2Ti 4:3; Tit 1:9
1:11 [n]Gal 2:7
1:12 [o]Php 4:13
1:13 [p]Ac 8:3 [q]Ac 26:9
1:14 [r]Ro 5:20 [s]2Ti 1:13
1:15 [t]1Ti 3:1; 2Ti 2:11; Tit 3:8
1:16 [u]ver 13
1:17 [v]Rev 15:3 [w]Col 1:15 [x]Ro 11:36
1:18 [y]1Ti 4:14 [z]2Ti 2:3
1:19 [a]1Ti 6:21

God's Grace

1TI 1:16

Paul's understanding of how much he needs the grace of God has grown with time. In an earlier letter, he called himself the "least of the apostles" (1Co 15:9); later he described himself as "less than the least of all God's people" (Eph 3:8); and now, near the end of his life, he says he is the "worst of sinners" (1Ti 1:16). Paul's purpose in each of these descriptions is not so much to belittle himself as to reveal the enormity of the grace of God. Paul says that he himself—a former persecutor of the church (Gal 1:13)—is clear evidence to all of how great the grace of God is. No matter what we know about ourselves today, no matter what we might one day realize about ourselves, God's grace is still big enough to forgive and cleanse us, just as it cleansed Paul.

Rules for Women

1TI 2:9–15

Paul's comments in these verses raise many questions that students of Scripture are still debating. But the following conclusions can be drawn: (1) A woman's beauty arises from her good deeds and her character rather than from her external appearance; (2) a woman should study and learn the truths of Scripture (a revolutionary idea in a time when Greeks and Jews alike considered women to be either uneducable or not in need of an education); and (3) a woman's spirit is to be peaceful.

The word in 1 Timothy 2:12 translated "silent" is the same word translated "in quietness" in 1 Timothy 2:11. Difficulty arises when one tries to corroborate Paul's instruction regarding silence in light of other instances in his writings in which the ministries of various women are accepted and even applauded (Ac 18:26; Ro 16:1–2; Php 4:3). From Paul's reference to Adam and Eve, however, we can conclude that he also recognizes an order within the church that acknowledges the headship God gave Adam at creation (see the note on 1Co 11:3–16, page 1889).

Hymenaeus[b] and Alexander,[c] whom I have handed over to Satan[d] to be taught not to blaspheme.

Instructions on Worship

2 I urge, then, first of all, that requests, prayers, intercession and thanksgiving be made for everyone— [2]for kings and all those in authority,[e] that we may live peaceful and quiet lives in all godliness and holiness. [3]This is good, and pleases God our Savior, [4]who wants[f] all men[g] to be saved and to come to a knowledge of the truth.[h] [5]For there is one God[i] and one mediator[j] between God and men, the man Christ Jesus, [6]who gave himself as a ransom for all men—the testimony[k] given in its proper time.[l] [7]And for this purpose I was appointed a herald and an apostle—I am telling the truth, I am not lying—and a teacher[m] of the true faith to the Gentiles.[n]

[8]I want men everywhere to lift up holy hands[o] in prayer, without anger or disputing.

[9]I also want women to dress modestly, with decency and propriety, not with braided hair or gold or pearls or expensive clothes,[p] [10]but with good deeds, appropriate for women who profess to worship God.

[11]A woman should learn in quietness and full submission.[q] [12]I do not permit a woman to teach or to have authority over a man; she must be silent. [13]For Adam was formed first, then Eve.[r] [14]And Adam was not the one deceived; it was the woman who was deceived and became a sinner.[s] [15]But women[a] will be saved[b] through childbearing—if they continue in faith, love[t] and holiness with propriety.

Overseers and Deacons

3 Here is a trustworthy saying:[u] If anyone sets his heart on being an overseer,[c][v] he desires a noble task. [2]Now the overseer must be above reproach,[w] the husband of but one wife, temperate, self-controlled, respectable, hospitable,[x] able to teach,[y] [3]not given to drunkenness, not violent but gentle, not quarrelsome,[z] not a lover of money.[a] [4]He must manage his own family well and see that his children obey him with proper respect.[b] [5](If anyone does not know how to manage his own family, how can he take care of God's church?)[c] [6]He must not be a recent convert, or he may become conceited[d] and fall under the same judgment as the devil. [7]He must also have a good reputation with outsiders, so that he will not fall into disgrace and into the devil's trap.[e]

[8]Deacons,[f] likewise, are to be men worthy of respect, sincere, not indulging in much wine,[g] and not pursuing dishonest gain. [9]They must keep hold of the deep truths of the faith with a clear conscience.[h] [10]They must first be tested; and then

1:20 [b]2Ti 2:17 [c]2Ti 4:14 [d]1Co 5:5
2:2 [e]Ezr 6:10; Ro 13:1
2:4 [f]Eze 18:23, 32 [g]Tit 2:11 [h]2Ti 2:25
2:5 [i]Ro 3:29,30 [j]Gal 3:20
2:6 [k]1Co 1:6 [l]1Ti 6:15
2:7 [m]2Ti 1:11 [n]Ac 9:15; Eph 3:7,8
2:8 [o]Ps 134:2; Lk 24:50
2:9 [p]1Pe 3:3
2:11 [q]1Co 14:34
2:13 [r]Ge 2:7,22; 1Co 11:8
2:14 [s]Ge 3:1-6,13; 2Co 11:3
2:15 [t]1Ti 1:14
3:1 [u]1Ti 1:15 [v]Ac 20:28
3:2 [w]Tit 1:6-8 [x]Ro 12:13 [y]2Ti 2:24
3:3 [z]2Ti 2:24 [a]Heb 13:5; 1Pe 5:2
3:4 [b]Tit 1:6
3:5 [c]1Co 10:32
3:6 [d]1Ti 6:4
3:7 [e]2Ti 2:26
3:8 [f]Php 1:1 [g]Tit 2:3
3:9 [h]1Ti 1:19

[a] *15* Greek *she* [b] *15* Or *restored* [c] *1* Traditionally *bishop*; also in verse 2

if there is nothing against them, let them serve as
deacons.
11 In the same way, their wives[a] are to be women
3:11 [i]2Ti 3:3; worthy of respect, not malicious talkers[i] but tem-
Tit 2:3 perate and trustworthy in everything.
12 A deacon must be the husband of but one wife
3:12 and must manage his children and his household
[j]ver 4 well.[j] 13 Those who have served well gain an excellent standing and great assurance in their faith in
Christ Jesus.
14 Although I hope to come to you soon, I am
writing you these instructions so that, 15 if I am
delayed, you will know how people ought to con-
3:15 duct themselves in God's household, which is the
[k]ver 5; church[k] of the living God, the pillar and founda-
Eph 2:21 tion of the truth. 16 Beyond all question, the mys-
3:16 tery[l] of godliness is great:
[l]Ro 16:25

[m]Jn 1:14 He[b] appeared in a body,[c][m]
[n]Col 1:23 was vindicated by the Spirit,
[o]Mk 16:19 was seen by angels,
was preached among the nations,[n]
was believed on in the world,
was taken up in glory.[o]

Instructions to Timothy

4:1 [p]Jn 16:13 **4** The Spirit[p] clearly says that in later times[q]
[q]2Ti 3:1 some will abandon the faith and follow
[r]2Th 2:3 deceiving spirits[r] and things taught by demons.
2 Such teachings come through hypocritical liars,
4:2 whose consciences have been seared as with a hot
[s]Eph 4:19 iron.[s] 3 They forbid people to marry[t] and order
them to abstain from certain foods,[u] which God
4:3 [t]Heb 13:4 created[v] to be received with thanksgiving[w] by
[u]Col 2:16 those who believe and who know the truth. 4 For
[v]Ge 1:29 everything God created is good,[x] and nothing is
[w]Ro 14:6 to be rejected if it is received with thanksgiving,
4:4 5 because it is consecrated by the word of God and
[x]Ro 14:14-18 prayer.
6 If you point these things out to the brothers,
4:6 you will be a good minister of Christ Jesus,
[y]1Ti 1:10 brought up in the truths of the faith[y] and of the
good teaching that you have followed. 7 Have
4:7 nothing to do with godless myths and old wives'
[z]2Ti 2:16 tales;[z] rather, train yourself to be godly. 8 For physical training is of some value, but godliness has
4:8 value for all things,[a] holding promise for both the
[a]1Ti 6:6 [b]Ps 37:9,11; present life[b] and the life to come.
Mk 10:29,30 9 This is a trustworthy saying[c] that deserves full
4:9 acceptance 10 (and for this we labor and strive),
[c]1Ti 1:15 that we have put our hope in the living God, who
is the Savior of all men, and especially of those
who believe.
4:11 11 Command and teach these things.[d] 12 Don't let
[d]1Ti 5:7; 6:2 anyone look down on you because you are young,
4:12 but set an example[e] for the believers in speech, in
[e]Tit 2:7; life, in love, in faith[f] and in purity. 13 Until I come,
1Pe 5:3 devote yourself to the public reading of Scripture,
[f]1Ti 1:14 to preaching and to teaching. 14 Do not neglect

[a] *11* Or *way, deaconesses* [b] *16* Some manuscripts *God*
[c] *16* Or *in the flesh*

On Leadership

1TI 3:1-10

Paul gives his disciple Timothy guidelines for the type of people Timothy should designate as leaders in the church. Paul knows true leadership flows out of the spiritual quality of a person's life. Good character, conduct, involvement in service, and reputation with the unbelieving world must be clearly established before a person is selected.

In 1 Timothy 4:6, Paul turns his attention to Timothy's own growth as a leader. First, Timothy must train his heart, his spiritual life, so that his character and his godliness will be an example for all who believe (1Ti 4:7–8,11–12). Second, his commitment to the truth of God's Word must be constant and unwavering (1Ti 4:6, 11,13). Third, he must be diligent to develop the ministry and gift God has given him (1Ti 4:14). Character, truth, development of gifts—these exhortations apply not just to Timothy, but to all who lead.

Caring for Widows

1TI 5:3–16

Paul now turns his attention to a problem: The widows in the church are a group particularly at risk. In Paul's day widows without family (or a family willing to care for them) had no way to provide for themselves. They were seldom trained beyond their domestic duties, so they could not be employed.

In the Old Testament God commanded his people to take care of widows (Dt 26:12). That care continues in the New Testament church (Ac 6:1–4). Now Paul establishes guidelines for ministering to widows. The specifics of our age have changed, but principles from this passage still operate today. Families are to take care of their own. Widows should take advantage of their singleness by using their lives in service. And the church has a responsibility to care for the truly destitute.

your gift, which was given you through a prophetic message[g] when the body of elders laid their
hands on you.[h]
15 Be diligent in these matters; give yourself
wholly to them, so that everyone may see your
progress. 16 Watch your life and doctrine closely.
Persevere in them, because if you do, you will
save both yourself and your hearers.

Advice About Widows, Elders and Slaves

5 Do not rebuke an older man[i] harshly,[j] but
exhort him as if he were your father. Treat
younger men[k] as brothers, 2 older women as mothers, and younger women as sisters, with absolute
purity.
3 Give proper recognition to those widows who
are really in need.[l] 4 But if a widow has children or
grandchildren, these should learn first of all to put
their religion into practice by caring for their own
family and so repaying their parents and grand-
parents,[m] for this is pleasing to God.[n] 5 The widow
who is really in need[o] and left all alone puts her
hope in God[p] and continues night and day to
pray[q] and to ask God for help. 6 But the widow
who lives for pleasure is dead even while she
lives.[r] 7 Give the people these instructions,[s] too, so
that no one may be open to blame. 8 If anyone
does not provide for his relatives, and especially
for his immediate family, he has denied[t] the faith
and is worse than an unbeliever.
9 No widow may be put on the list of widows
unless she is over sixty, has been faithful to her
husband,[a] 10 and is well known for her good
deeds,[u] such as bringing up children, showing
hospitality, washing the feet[v] of the saints, helping
those in trouble[w] and devoting herself to all kinds
of good deeds.
11 As for younger widows, do not put them on
such a list. For when their sensual desires overcome their dedication to Christ, they want to marry. 12 Thus they bring judgment on themselves,
because they have broken their first pledge.
13 Besides, they get into the habit of being idle and
going about from house to house. And not only
do they become idlers, but also gossips and busybodies,[x] saying things they ought not to. 14 So I
counsel younger widows to marry,[y] to have children, to manage their homes and to give the enemy no opportunity for slander.[z] 15 Some have in
fact already turned away to follow Satan.[a]
16 If any woman who is a believer has widows in
her family, she should help them and not let the
church be burdened with them, so that the church
can help those widows who are really in need.[b]
17 The elders[c] who direct the affairs of the
church well are worthy of double honor,[d] especially those whose work is preaching and teaching. 18 For the Scripture says, "Do not muzzle the
ox while it is treading out the grain,"[be] and "The

4:14 [g] 1Ti 1:18 [h] Ac 6:6; 2Ti 1:6
5:1 [i] Tit 2:2 [j] Lev 19:32 [k] Tit 2:6
5:3 [l] ver 5,16
5:4 [m] Eph 6:1,2 [n] 1Ti 2:3
5:5 [o] ver 3,16 [p] 1Co 7:34; 1Pe 3:5 [q] Lk 2:37
5:6 [r] Lk 15:24
5:7 [s] 1Ti 4:11
5:8 [t] 2Pe 2:1; Jude 4; Tit 1:16
5:10 [u] Ac 9:36; 1Ti 6:18; 1Pe 2:12 [v] Lk 7:44 [w] ver 16
5:13 [x] 2Th 3:11
5:14 [y] 1Co 7:9 [z] 1Ti 6:1
5:15 [a] Mt 4:10
5:16 [b] ver 3-5
5:17 [c] Ac 11:30 [d] Php 2:29; 1Th 5:12
5:18 [e] Dt 25:4; 1Co 9:7-9

[a] 9 Or *has had but one husband* [b] 18 Deut. 25:4

worker deserves his wages."[a][f] 19 Do not entertain
an accusation against an elder[g] unless it is
brought by two or three witnesses.[h] 20 Those who
sin are to be rebuked[i] publicly, so that the others
may take warning.[j]
21 I charge you, in the sight of God and Christ
Jesus[k] and the elect angels, to keep these instructions without partiality, and to do nothing out of
favoritism.
22 Do not be hasty in the laying on of hands,[l]
and do not share in the sins of others.[m] Keep yourself pure.
23 Stop drinking only water, and use a little
wine[n] because of your stomach and your frequent
illnesses.
24 The sins of some men are obvious, reaching
the place of judgment ahead of them; the sins of
others trail behind them. 25 In the same way, good
deeds are obvious, and even those that are not
cannot be hidden.

6 All who are under the yoke of slavery should
consider their masters worthy of full respect,[o]
so that God's name and our teaching may not be
slandered.[p] 2 Those who have believing masters
are not to show less respect for them because they
are brothers.[q] Instead, they are to serve them even
better, because those who benefit from their service are believers, and dear to them. These are the
things you are to teach and urge on them.[r]

Love of Money

3 If anyone teaches false doctrines[s] and does not
agree to the sound instruction[t] of our Lord Jesus
Christ and to godly teaching, 4 he is conceited and
understands nothing. He has an unhealthy interest in controversies and quarrels about words[u]
that result in envy, strife, malicious talk, evil suspicions 5 and constant friction between men of corrupt mind, who have been robbed of the truth[v]
and who think that godliness is a means to financial gain.
6 But godliness with contentment[w] is great
gain.[x] 7 For we brought nothing into the world,
and we can take nothing out of it.[y] 8 But if we have
food and clothing, we will be content with that.[z]
9 People who want to get rich[a] fall into temptation
and a trap[b] and into many foolish and harmful
desires that plunge men into ruin and destruction.
10 For the love of money[c] is a root of all kinds of
evil. Some people, eager for money, have wandered from the faith[d] and pierced themselves with
many griefs.

Paul's Charge to Timothy

11 But you, man of God,[e] flee from all this, and
pursue righteousness, godliness, faith, love,[f]
endurance and gentleness. 12 Fight the good fight[g]
of the faith. Take hold of[h] the eternal life to which
you were called when you made your good con-

5:18 [f]Lk 10:7; Lev 19:13; Dt 24:14,15; Mt 10:10; 1Co 9:14
5:19 [g]Ac 11:30 [h]Mt 18:16
5:20 [i]2Ti 4:2; Tit 1:13 [j]Dt 13:11
5:21 [k]1Ti 6:13; 2Ti 4:1
5:22 [l]Ac 6:6 [m]Eph 5:11
5:23 [n]1Ti 3:8
6:1 [o]Eph 6:5; Tit 2:9; 1Pe 2:18 [p]Tit 2:5,8
6:2 [q]Phm 16 [r]1Ti 4:11
6:3 [s]1Ti 1:3 [t]1Ti 1:10
6:4 [u]2Ti 2:14
6:5 [v]Tit 1:15
6:6 [w]Php 4:11; Heb 13:5 [x]1Ti 4:8
6:7 [y]Job 1:21; Ecc 5:15
6:8 [z]Heb 13:5
6:9 [a]Pr 15:27 [b]1Ti 3:7
6:10 [c]1Ti 3:3 [d]Jas 5:19
6:11 [e]2Ti 3:17 [f]2Ti 2:22
6:12 [g]1Co 9:25, 26; 1Ti 1:18 [h]Php 3:12

[a] 18 Luke 10:7

The Love of Money

1TI 6:3-10

How much is enough? That question is raised more than once in Scripture. Ecclesiastes 5:10 says the one who loves money will never have enough. Paul says the well-being we long for will never come from money but from inside our souls when godliness is united with contentment (1Ti 6:6). The word he uses for **contentment** ***means "enough, an inner sufficiency" (2Co 9:8; Php 4:12). But there are enemies of that inner soul sufficiency, Paul warns. Spending our lives accumulating things is a short term, pointless goal (1Ti 6:7). Wanting to be rich opens up many avenues of temptation (1Ti 6:9). Loving money can lead to evil choices (1Ti 6:10). Contentment and godliness are the best way to guard our souls from the ruin that love of money and possessions can cause.***

Our Future

1TI 6:17-19

The future will be more real than the present, and *we can begin our investment program in that future today.* In 1 Timothy 6:6-10 Paul's concern *is for those who are not wealthy but who want more.* Now in 1 Timothy 6:17-19, *he speaks to those who are wealthy in this life. The best thing to do with earthly wealth, he says, is to trade it for treasure that cannot be taken away once this life is over.* As *incredible as it seems, it's possible to build, from this life, a foundation that will stand the test of God's judgment.* Paul says *we can build things now that will endure eternally* (1Co 3:10-15). According to 1 Timothy 6:18-19, *we build that future foundation by our good deeds and our generosity.* Discover what Jesus says about foundations that last and future treasures in Matthew 6:19-27.

fession in the presence of many witnesses. 13 In the
sight of God, who gives life to everything, and of
Christ Jesus, who while testifying before Pontius
Pilate[i] made the good confession, I charge you[j]
14 to keep this command without spot or blame
until the appearing of our Lord Jesus Christ,
15 which God will bring about in his own time—
God, the blessed[k] and only Ruler,[l] the King of
kings and Lord of lords,[m] 16 who alone is immortal[n] and who lives in unapproachable light, whom
no one has seen or can see.[o] To him be honor and
might forever. Amen.

17 Command those who are rich in this present
world not to be arrogant nor to put their hope in
wealth,[p] which is so uncertain, but to put their
hope in God,[q] who richly provides us with everything for our enjoyment.[r] 18 Command them to do
good, to be rich in good deeds,[s] and to be generous and willing to share.[t] 19 In this way they will
lay up treasure for themselves[u] as a firm foundation for the coming age, so that they may take
hold of the life that is truly life.

20 Timothy, guard what has been entrusted[v] to
your care. Turn away from godless chatter[w] and
the opposing ideas of what is falsely called knowledge, 21 which some have professed and in so
doing have wandered from the faith.[x]

Grace be with you.[y]

6:13 [i]Jn 18:33-37 [j]1Ti 5:21
6:15 [k]1Ti 1:11 [l]1Ti 1:17 [m]Rev 17:14; 19:16
6:16 [n]1Ti 1:17 [o]Jn 1:18
6:17 [p]Lk 12:20,21 [q]1Ti 4:10 [r]Ac 14:17
6:18 [s]1Ti 5:10 [t]Ro 12:8,13
6:19 [u]Mt 6:20
6:20 [v]2Ti 1:12,14 [w]2Ti 2:16
6:21 [x]2Ti 2:18 [y]Col 4:18

2 Timothy

Paul's final words.

Paul is a prisoner in Rome; there is little chance that he will be released. Probably due to the intense persecution of believers under Emperor Nero, many of his supporters have abandoned him. Sensing that the end is near, Paul writes this poignant letter to encourage his faithful young friend to stand firm in his faith. Despite Paul's difficult circumstances, his concern for Timothy and the church in Ephesus prompts him to issue passionate warnings, quiet reflections and inspirational counsel.

With deliberate care Paul shares the wisdom he has gained through the years of his ministry and service to God. Paul passionately calls for boldness (2Ti 1), and he urges Timothy to study the Scriptures as a guard against confusion and error (2Ti 2). Paul gives a distressing description of sin in the last days and rejoices that Timothy's faith is sure because it is founded in the power of God's Word (2Ti 3). Paul ends his letter with words that give a very personal glimpse of a solitary man who has suffered the loss of many of his supporters and looks forward to seeing his young friend Timothy again (2Ti 4).

Paul's eloquent letter to Timothy reminds us that despite threats to our values and beliefs, we can run the race of faith and finish well. Our lives can count for Christ if we guard our faith and continue to follow God's Word despite difficult or discouraging circumstances.

Quick Study

Author
The apostle Paul.

Date Written
Around A.D. 66.

Written From
A prison cell in Rome.

Key Passage
2 Timothy 1:8–9 "So do not be ashamed to testify about our Lord, or ashamed of me his prisoner. But join with me in suffering for the gospel, by the power of God, who has saved us and called us to a holy life—not because of anything we have done but because of his own purpose and grace."

Outline

Paul's greetings.
2Ti 1:1-2

Paul's concern for Timothy.
2Ti 1:3-14

Paul's situation.
2Ti 1:15-18

Paul's instruction for Timothy.
2Ti 2

Warning about the last days.
2Ti 3:1-9

Paul's charge to Timothy.
2Ti 3:10–4:8

Some personal remarks.
2Ti 4:9-18

Final greetings.
2Ti 4:19-22

The Women of 2 Timothy

⚘ **Lois**	*Timothy's grandmother.* 2Ti 1:5; 3:14-15 (page 2080)
⚘ **Eunice**	*Timothy's mother.* 2Ti 1:5; 3:14-15 (page 2080)
Weak-willed women	*Partners in the sin of the last days.* 2Ti 3:6
⚘ **Priscilla**	*Paul sent greetings to her and her husband.* 2Ti 4:19 (page 2047)
Claudia	*She sent greetings through Paul to Timothy.* 2Ti 4:21

⚘ *Denotes a sketch written about this character*

1 Paul, an apostle of Christ Jesus by the will of
God,[a] according to the promise of life that is
in Christ Jesus,[b]

2To Timothy,[c] my dear son:[d]

Grace, mercy and peace from God the Father
and Christ Jesus our Lord.

Encouragement to Be Faithful

3I thank God,[e] whom I serve, as my forefathers
did, with a clear conscience, as night and day I
constantly remember you in my prayers.[f] 4Recall-
ing your tears,[g] I long to see you,[h] so that I may be
filled with joy. 5I have been reminded of your sincere faith,[i] which first lived in your grandmother
Lois and in your mother Eunice[j] and, I am persuaded, now lives in you also. 6For this reason I
remind you to fan into flame the gift of God,
which is in you through the laying on of my
hands.[k] 7For God did not give us a spirit of timidity,[l] but a spirit of power, of love and of self-
discipline.

8So do not be ashamed[m] to testify about our
Lord, or ashamed of me his prisoner.[n] But join
with me in suffering for the gospel,[o] by the power of God, 9who has saved us and called[p] us to a
holy life—not because of anything we have done
but because of his own purpose and grace. This
grace was given us in Christ Jesus before the
beginning of time, 10but it has now been revealed[q]
through the appearing of our Savior, Christ Jesus,
who has destroyed death[r] and has brought life
and immortality to light through the gospel. 11And
of this gospel I was appointed a herald and an
apostle and a teacher.[s] 12That is why I am suffering as I am. Yet I am not ashamed, because I
know whom I have believed, and am convinced
that he is able to guard[t] what I have entrusted to
him for that day.[u]

13What you heard from me, keep[v] as the pattern
of sound teaching, with faith and love in Christ
Jesus.[w] 14Guard the good deposit that was entrusted to you—guard it with the help of the Holy Spirit who lives in us.[x]

15You know that everyone in the province of
Asia has deserted me,[y] including Phygelus and
Hermogenes.

16May the Lord show mercy to the household of
Onesiphorus,[z] because he often refreshed me and
was not ashamed of my chains. 17On the contrary,
when he was in Rome, he searched hard for me
until he found me. 18May the Lord grant that he
will find mercy from the Lord on that day! You
know very well in how many ways he helped me[a]
in Ephesus.

2 You then, my son, be strong[b] in the grace that
is in Christ Jesus. 2And the things you have
heard me say[c] in the presence of many witnesses[d]
entrust to reliable men who will also be qualified
to teach others. 3Endure hardship with us like a
good soldier[e] of Christ Jesus. 4No one serving as a

1:1 [a]2Co 1:1 [b]Eph 3:6; 1Ti 6:19
1:2 [c]Ac 16:1 [d]1Ti 1:2
1:3 [e]Ro 1:8 [f]Ro 1:10
1:4 [g]Ac 20:37 [h]2Ti 4:9
1:5 [i]1Ti 1:5 [j]Ac 16:1
1:6 [k]1Ti 4:14
1:7 [l]Ro 8:15
1:8 [m]Mk 8:38; Ro 1:16 [n]Eph 3:1 [o]2Ti 2:3,9; 4:5
1:9 [p]Ro 8:28
1:10 [q]Eph 1:9 [r]1Co 15:26, 54
1:11 [s]1Ti 2:7
1:12 [t]1Ti 6:20 [u]ver 18
1:13 [v]Tit 1:9 [w]1Ti 1:14
1:14 [x]Ro 8:9
1:15 [y]2Ti 4:10,11, 16
1:16 [z]2Ti 4:19
1:18 [a]Heb 6:10
2:1 [b]Eph 6:10
2:2 [c]2Ti 1:13 [d]1Ti 6:12
2:3 [e]1Ti 1:18

Timothy's Situation

2TI 1:6–7

Timothy has human reasons to be discouraged and afraid. He is pastor of the church in Ephesus, an important church in a very pagan city, and is disregarded by many because of his young age. His dear friend and mentor, Paul, is imprisoned nearly a thousand miles away. Missing Timothy and knowing Timothy needs encouragement, Paul writes to him. We could paraphrase Paul's opening exhortation (2Ti 1:6) this way: "Go ahead, Timothy, use your God-given gift with a passion." How can Timothy be bold in difficult circumstances? By using God's gifts to him (2Ti 1:7): the *power* to do right, the *love* to keep caring for people through every challenge, and the *self-discipline* to keep his own life on course with God. In our struggles and fears, in the lonely places we face, God's gifts of power, love and self-discipline are there for us as well.

A High Standard

2TI 2:15

Paul sets a high standard for ministry. Speaking of character issues, he draws images of soldiers, athletes, farmers, and clean vessels (2Ti 2:3–6,21). By way of warning, he talks of disciples who have aborted their own ministries (2Ti 2:17–18). The focal point for Timothy probably comes in 2 Timothy 2:15. Paul calls Timothy to diligence as a worker or laborer. As a laborer Timothy's primary task is to handle the Scriptures carefully and correctly. (At this point in history, the Scriptures would have included the Old Testament and what Timothy had heard and read from Paul.) To "correctly handle" means to "cut straight." Paul's admonition is clear: Be diligent to use God's Word carefully and well in your ministry; then you will not be ashamed when you one day stand before him.

soldier gets involved in civilian affairs—he wants
to please his commanding officer. 5 Similarly, if
anyone competes as an athlete, he does not
receive the victor's crown[f] unless he competes — **2:5** [f]1Co 9:25
according to the rules. 6 The hardworking farmer
should be the first to receive a share of the crops.
7 Reflect on what I am saying, for the Lord will
give you insight into all this.
8 Remember Jesus Christ, raised from the dead,[g] — **2:8** [g]Ac 2:24
descended from David.[h] This is my gospel,[i] 9 for — [h]Mt 1:1
which I am suffering[j] even to the point of being — [i]Ro 2:16
chained like a criminal. But God's word is not — **2:9**
chained. 10 Therefore I endure everything[k] for the — [j]Ac 9:16
sake of the elect, that they too may obtain the sal- — **2:10**
vation that is in Christ Jesus, with eternal glory.[l] — [k]Col 1:24
11 Here is a trustworthy saying: — [l]2Co 4:17

> If we died with him,
> we will also live with him;[m] — **2:11** [m]Ro 6:2-11
> 12 if we endure,
> we will also reign with him.[n] — **2:12** [n]Ro 8:17; 1Pe 4:13
> If we disown him,
> he will also disown us;[o] — [o]Mt 10:33
> 13 if we are faithless,
> he will remain faithful,[p] — **2:13** [p]Nu 23:19; Ro 3:3
> for he cannot disown himself.

A Workman Approved by God

14 Keep reminding them of these things. Warn
them before God against quarreling about words;[q] — **2:14** [q]1Ti 6:4
it is of no value, and only ruins those who listen.
15 Do your best to present yourself to God as one
approved, a workman who does not need to be
ashamed and who correctly handles the word of
truth.[r] 16 Avoid godless chatter,[s] because those who — **2:15** [r]Eph 1:13;
indulge in it will become more and more ungod- — Jas 1:18
ly. 17 Their teaching will spread like gangrene.
Among them are Hymenaeus[t] and Philetus, 18 who — **2:16** [s]Tit 3:9
have wandered away from the truth. They say that — **2:17**
the resurrection has already taken place, and they — [t]1Ti 1:20
destroy the faith of some.[u] 19 Nevertheless, God's
solid foundation stands firm,[v] sealed with this — **2:18** [u]1Ti 1:19
inscription: "The Lord knows those who are
his,"[a][w] and, "Everyone who confesses the name — **2:19** [v]Isa 28:16
of the Lord[x] must turn away from wickedness." — [w]Jn 10:14
20 In a large house there are articles not only of — [x]1Co 1:2
gold and silver, but also of wood and clay; some
are for noble purposes and some for ignoble.[y] 21 If — **2:20** [y]Ro 9:21
a man cleanses himself from the latter, he will be
an instrument for noble purposes, made holy, useful to the Master and prepared to do any good
work.[z] — **2:21** [z]2Ti 3:17
22 Flee the evil desires of youth, and pursue righ-
teousness, faith, love[a] and peace, along with those — **2:22** [a]1Ti 1:14; 6:11
who call on the Lord out of a pure heart.[b] 23 Don't
have anything to do with foolish and stupid argu- — [b]1Ti 1:5
ments, because you know they produce quarrels.
24 And the Lord's servant must not quarrel;
instead, he must be kind to everyone, able to

[a] *19* Num. 16:5 (see Septuagint)

Dorcas (Tabitha)

Hands That Showed Love

There are many ways to communicate love. Poets have filled volumes trying to find the perfect words. Preachers preach, teachers teach, prophets prophesy. And so love spreads, from person to person. But we are not all good with words. Many would be at a loss if it weren't for their hands—hands to caress, hands to stroke, hands to wipe away tears, hands to scratch backs and massage feet—hands to work. Dorcas used her hands to show her love. She made things. She loved the poor by sewing clothes for them.

The Jewish faith emphasized caring for the poor and the widowed. The concept was not new. But Dorcas's commitment was extraordinary. She was known throughout Joppa for her charity, and her untimely death stunned the Christian community there. They cherished Dorcas and did not want to let her go. So, in faith, they sent for Peter. Perhaps God would grant them a miracle.

Mourners crowded the room where she lay ready for burial. Few could have guessed how many Dorcas had helped until they all gathered here. Each had a story to tell about the love she had shown. And tears filled every eye. Her life had great impact.

Peter sent the mourners from the room, got on his knees and prayed, then simply told Dorcas to get up. She opened her eyes and sat up. Peter took her hand and helped her stand. Her hand. How fitting that the Lord used Dorcas's hand as a conduit of his love for her. Peter "called the believers and the widows and presented her to them alive" (Ac 9:41).

The Lord was pleased with Dorcas. He used her life to showcase his love both through her and to her. Her good works had made Jesus known in Joppa—simply because she sewed. Now all Joppa quickly learned of the miracle of her return to life, and many believed in Christ because of it.

Hands: the terminal parts of the human arms, used as grasping organs—functional body parts. But God made them for loving. Our hands can be God's saving instruments in the lives of others. Our *hands* can "preach good news to the poor . . . bind up the brokenhearted . . . proclaim freedom for the captives and release from darkness for the prisoners . . . proclaim the year of the LORD's favor and . . . comfort all who mourn" (Isa 61:1–2).

Dorcas (Tabitha)
(gazelle)
Acts 9:36-43

Candid SNAPSHOT Peter went with them, and when he arrived he was taken upstairs to the room. All the widows stood around him, crying and showing him the robes and other clothing that Dorcas had made while she was still with them (Acts 9:39).

Rhoda

Seeing Is Believing

Rhoda, the servant, was startled by a knock on the door. Her heart pounded. Who could it be? Nobody was out in the streets at this time of night. She pressed her ear against the door. It sounded like Peter's voice, but it couldn't be *Peter*. He was in prison—she'd heard someone say he was under double guard. Perhaps Herod had heard of the gathering in her mistress's home and had come to take them all to jail, too. There was another knock, and Peter's voice again asked her to open the door. It *was* Peter! The Lord had answered their prayers! She ran to the room where the others were praying to tell them the news—so excited she still didn't open the door.

When Rhoda rushed in and excitedly told the believers that Peter was at the door, they weren't convinced. They thought Rhoda was out of her mind. Though Peter was certainly in their prayers that evening, perhaps no one had even thought to pray for him to *escape* from prison. He was chained to two guards, and sentries blocked all the exits. Release maybe, at his trial tomorrow, but escape? Not this time. Herod had made sure of that. It was easier to believe that it was Peter's angel than to believe it was Peter himself.

But Rhoda was unshakable. The knocking continued, and finally they opened the door. It was Peter.

Rhoda was a servant, not a guest. She was there to do a job, not pray with the others. Yet because she was doing her job, she was the first to know of this miracle of Peter's deliverance from persecution. It was a story she probably told again and again to her children and grandchildren—and anyone else who would listen. *I* was there when Peter knocked on the door. The Lord allowed *me* the honor of being the first to know and believe.

There are many menial tasks in the body of Christ. Some may even require your attention when others are worshiping the Lord. But God knows where you are. He may use your serving place as an entry point for his glory!

Rhoda
(*rose*)
Acts 12:1–19

Candid SNAPSHOT Peter knocked at the outer entrance, and a servant girl named Rhoda came to answer the door. When she recognized Peter's voice, she was so overjoyed she ran back without opening it and exclaimed, "Peter is at the door!" (Acts 12:13–14).

2:24 teach, not resentful.[c] [25]Those who oppose him he
[c]1Ti 3:2,3 must gently instruct, in the hope that God will
grant them repentance leading them to a knowl-
2:25 [d]1Ti 2:4 edge of the truth,[d] [26]and that they will come to
2:26 their senses and escape from the trap of the devil,[e]
[e]1Ti 3:7 who has taken them captive to do his will.

Godlessness in the Last Days

3:1 **3** But mark this: There will be terrible times in
[f]1Ti 4:1 the last days.[f] [2]People will be lovers of them-
3:2 selves, lovers of money,[g] boastful, proud,[h] abu-
[g]1Ti 3:3 [h]Ro 1:30 sive, disobedient to their parents,[i] ungrateful,
[i]Ro 1:30 unholy, [3]without love, unforgiving, slanderous,
without self-control, brutal, not lovers of the good,
3:4 [4]treacherous, rash, conceited,[j] lovers of pleasure
[j]1Ti 3:6 rather than lovers of God— [5]having a form of godliness but denying its power. Have nothing to do
with them.
3:6 [k]Jude 4 [6]They are the kind who worm their way[k] into
homes and gain control over weak-willed women,
who are loaded down with sins and are swayed
by all kinds of evil desires, [7]always learning but
3:8 [l]Ex 7:11 never able to acknowledge the truth. [8]Just as Jan-
[m]Ac 13:8 nes and Jambres opposed Moses,[l] so also these
[n]1Ti 6:5 men oppose[m] the truth—men of depraved minds,[n]
3:9 who, as far as the faith is concerned, are rejected.
[o]Ex 7:12 [9]But they will not get very far because, as in the
3:10 case of those men,[o] their folly will be clear to
[p]1Ti 4:6 everyone.

3:11 [q]Ac 13:14,50 *Paul's Charge to Timothy*

[r]2Co 11:23-27 [10]You, however, know all about my teaching,[p]
[s]Ps 34:19 my way of life, my purpose, faith, patience, love,
3:12 endurance, [11]persecutions, sufferings—what kinds
[t]Ac 14:22 of things happened to me in Antioch,[q] Iconium
3:13 and Lystra, the persecutions I endured.[r] Yet the
[u]2Ti 2:16 Lord rescued me from all of them.[s] [12]In fact, everyone who wants to live a godly life in Christ Jesus
3:14 [v]2Ti 1:13 will be persecuted,[t] [13]while evil men and impostors will go from bad to worse,[u] deceiving and
3:15 [w]2Ti 1:5 being deceived. [14]But as for you, continue in what
[x]Jn 5:39 you have learned and have become convinced of,
[y]Ps 119:98, 99 because you know those from whom you learned
it,[v] [15]and how from infancy[w] you have known the
3:16 [z]2Pe 1:20,21 holy Scriptures,[x] which are able to make you
[a]Ro 4:23,24 wise[y] for salvation through faith in Christ Jesus.
[16]All Scripture is God-breathed[z] and is useful for
3:17 [b]1Ti 6:11 teaching,[a] rebuking, correcting and training in
[c]2Ti 2:21 righteousness, [17]so that the man of God[b] may be
thoroughly equipped for every good work.[c]
4:1 **4** In the presence of God and of Christ Jesus,
[d]Ac 10:42 who will judge the living and the dead,[d] and
[e]1Ti 5:21 in view of his appearing and his kingdom, I give
4:2 you this charge:[e] [2]Preach[f] the Word;[g] be prepared
[f]1Ti 4:13 [g]Gal 6:6 in season and out of season; correct, rebuke[h] and
[h]1Ti 5:20; encourage—with great patience and careful
Tit 1:13; 2:15 instruction. [3]For the time will come when men
will not put up with sound doctrine.[i] Instead, to
4:3 suit their own desires, they will gather around
[i]1Ti 1:10 them a great number of teachers to say what their

Terrible Times

2TI 3:1

"Last days" is a term used in both the Old Testament (Isa 2:2, Mic 4:1) and the New (2Ti 3:1; 2Pe 3:3). It refers to the last phase in God's dealing with the world. The work of God that began in the garden continued through his work with his chosen people and culminated in the cross and resurrection. Each day since then is part of the "last days," the time in which God through the Spirit is building his church. How long God will choose to do his work among the people and nations of the world, no one knows. The "last days" are a time of grace but will increasingly become a time of degeneration and disintegration of individuals, the physical environment, governments and culture. The exact time of Christ's second coming is known to no one, but the general nature of the term "the last days" reminds us that it could be *any* day.

Drink Offerings

2TI 4:6

Twice Paul refers to himself as a "drink offering," here and in Philippians 2:17. In the Old Testament, a drink offering was a small portion of wine poured around the base of the altar of the animal sacrifice. It was a small thing compared to the carcass of the animal that was being sacrificed, but it expressed the worshiper's thankfulness to God. Paul sees himself in the same way, particularly as he knows his life is ending. His service to God is an insignificant thing in comparison to the sacrifice of Christ, but it is freely offered to God in gratitude.

itching ears want to hear. 4 They will turn their
ears away from the truth and turn aside to myths.[j]
5 But you, keep your head in all situations, endure
hardship,[k] do the work of an evangelist,[l] discharge all the duties of your ministry.

6 For I am already being poured out like a drink
offering,[m] and the time has come for my departure.[n] 7 I have fought the good fight,[o] I have finished the race,[p] I have kept the faith. 8 Now there
is in store for me[q] the crown of righteousness,
which the Lord, the righteous Judge, will award
to me on that day[r]—and not only to me, but also
to all who have longed for his appearing.

Personal Remarks

9 Do your best to come to me quickly, 10 for
Demas,[s] because he loved this world,[t] has deserted me and has gone to Thessalonica. Crescens has
gone to Galatia,[u] and Titus to Dalmatia. 11 Only
Luke[v] is with me.[w] Get Mark[x] and bring him with
you, because he is helpful to me in my ministry.
12 I sent Tychicus[y] to Ephesus. 13 When you come,
bring the cloak that I left with Carpus at Troas,
and my scrolls, especially the parchments.

14 Alexander[z] the metalworker did me a great
deal of harm. The Lord will repay him for what
he has done.[a] 15 You too should be on your guard
against him, because he strongly opposed our
message.

16 At my first defense, no one came to my support, but everyone deserted me. May it not be held
against them.[b] 17 But the Lord stood at my side[c]
and gave me strength, so that through me the
message might be fully proclaimed and all the
Gentiles might hear it.[d] And I was delivered from
the lion's mouth. 18 The Lord will rescue me from
every evil attack[e] and will bring me safely to his
heavenly kingdom. To him be glory for ever and
ever. Amen.[f]

Final Greetings

19 Greet Priscilla[a] and Aquila[g] and the household
of Onesiphorus. 20 Erastus[h] stayed in Corinth, and
I left Trophimus[i] sick in Miletus. 21 Do your best to
get here before winter.[j] Eubulus greets you, and
so do Pudens, Linus, Claudia and all the brothers.

22 The Lord be with your spirit.[k] Grace be with
you.[l]

4:4 [j]1Ti 1:4
4:5 [k]2Ti 1:8 [l]Ac 21:8
4:6 [m]Php 2:17 [n]Php 1:23
4:7 [o]1Ti 1:18 [p]1Co 9:24
4:8 [q]Col 1:5 [r]2Ti 1:12
4:10 [s]Col 4:14 [t]1Jn 2:15 [u]Ac 16:6
4:11 [v]Col 4:14 [w]2Ti 1:15 [x]Ac 12:12
4:12 [y]Ac 20:4
4:14 [z]Ac 19:33 [a]Ro 12:19
4:16 [b]Ac 7:60
4:17 [c]Ac 23:11 [d]Ac 9:15
4:18 [e]Ps 121:7 [f]Ro 11:36
4:19 [g]Ac 18:2
4:20 [h]Ac 19:22 [i]Ac 20:4
4:21 [j]ver 9
4:22 [k]Gal 6:18; Phm 25 [l]Col 4:18

[a] 19 Greek *Prisca*, a variant of *Priscilla*

Titus

Follow what is good.

Arguments and disagreements plague the church on the island of Crete. Founded originally by Paul, this church finds itself slipping into the sinful practices of a godless society. Paul puts the church's difficulties into perspective as he gives Titus guidelines for choosing church leaders and for dealing with opposition. Paul also warns about false teachers and instructs the believers in good conduct.

Paul's letters to the young pastors of the first century provide a good handbook for church leadership and godly living. While his letters to Timothy stress the need to defend the truth of the gospel and to declare it without apology, Paul's letter to Titus stresses that believers' deeds should reflect their faith. Paul's affirms Titus as his true son in the faith and reminds him of the commission given him (Tit 1). He encourages the older women to serve as godly role models for younger women in both spiritual and practical ways (Tit 2). And he calls on the church in Crete to remember God's kindness, love and grace, and to do what is good, showing God's love to others (Tit 3).

How we relate to others is a clear reflection of our faith and beliefs. How we live in a godless society is as important as what position we hold in a church or in a corporation. How we overcome disagreements between believers will reflect our understanding of God's grace and forgiveness. This letter to Titus brings home the message that our behavior must be consistent with our beliefs, for we have been redeemed to live godly lives as a witness to a godless world.

Quick Study

Author
The apostle Paul.

Date Written
Around A.D. 64.

Written From
Possibly Macedonia.

Key Passage
Titus 3:3–5 "At one time we too were foolish, disobedient, deceived and enslaved by all kinds of passions and pleasures. We lived in malice and envy, being hated and hating one another. But when the kindness and love of God our Savior appeared, he saved us, not because of righteous things we had done, but because of his mercy."

Outline

Paul's greetings.
Tit 1:1-4

Instructions regarding elders.
Tit 1:5-9

Instruction on various groups.
Tit 2

Instruction for believers in general.
Tit 3:1-8

Instruction on responding to spiritual error.
Tit 3:9-11

Final remarks.
Tit 3:12-15

The Women of Titus

A wife	***A leader should have only one.*** Tit 1:6
Older and younger women	***Instruction on how to live.*** Tit 2:3-5

1:1 aRo 1:1 **1** Paul, a servant of God[a] and an apostle of Jesus
b1Ti 2:4 Christ for the faith of God's elect and the
knowledge of the truth[b] that leads to godliness—
1:2 2 a faith and knowledge resting on the hope of
c2Ti 1:1 eternal life,[c] which God, who does not lie, prom-
d2Ti 1:9 ised before the beginning of time,[d] 3 and at his
1:3 appointed season[e] he brought his word to light[f]
e1Ti 2:6 through the preaching entrusted to me[g] by the
f2Ti 1:10 g1Ti 1:11 command of God our Savior,[h]

hLk 1:47 4 To Titus,[i] my true son in our common faith:

1:4 i2Co 2:13 Grace and peace from God the Father and Christ
Jesus our Savior.

Titus's Task on Crete

1:5 jAc 27:7 kAc 11:30 5 The reason I left you in Crete[j] was that you
might straighten out what was left unfinished and
appoint[a] elders[k] in every town, as I directed you.
1:6 l1Ti 3:2 6 An elder must be blameless,[l] the husband of but
one wife, a man whose children believe and are
not open to the charge of being wild and disobe-
1:7 m1Ti 3:1 dient. 7 Since an overseer[bm] is entrusted with God's
n1Co 4:1 work,[n] he must be blameless—not overbearing,
o1Ti 3:3,8 not quick-tempered, not given to drunkenness,
1:8 not violent, not pursuing dishonest gain.[o] 8 Rather
p1Ti 3:2 he must be hospitable,[p] one who loves what is
q2Ti 3:3 good,[q] who is self-controlled, upright, holy and
1:9 disciplined. 9 He must hold firmly[r] to the trust-
r1Ti 1:19 s1Ti 1:10 worthy message as it has been taught, so that he
can encourage others by sound doctrine[s] and
refute those who oppose it.
1:10 10 For there are many rebellious people, mere
t1Ti 1:6 talkers[t] and deceivers, especially those of the cir-
u11:2 cumcision group.[u] 11 They must be silenced,
1:11 because they are ruining whole households[v] by
v2Ti 3:6 teaching things they ought not to teach—and that
for the sake of dishonest gain. 12 Even one of their
1:12 wAc 17:28 own prophets[w] has said, "Cretans[x] are always
xAc 2:11 liars, evil brutes, lazy gluttons." 13 This testimony
1:13 is true. Therefore, rebuke[y] them sharply, so that
y2Co 13:10 they will be sound in the faith[z] 14 and will pay no
zTit 2:2 attention to Jewish myths[a] or to the commands[b] of
1:14 those who reject the truth. 15 To the pure, all things
a1Ti 1:4 are pure, but to those who are corrupted and do
bCol 2:22 not believe, nothing is pure.[c] In fact, both their
1:15 minds and consciences are corrupted. 16 They
cRo 14:14,23 claim to know God, but by their actions they deny
1:16 him.[d] They are detestable, disobedient and unfit
d1Jn 2:4 for doing anything good.

What Must Be Taught to Various Groups

2:1 **2** You must teach what is in accord with sound
e1Ti 1:10 doctrine.[e] 2 Teach the older men to be temperate, worthy of respect, self-controlled, and sound
2:2 fTit 1:13 in faith,[f] in love and in endurance.
3 Likewise, teach the older women to be reverent
2:3 in the way they live, not to be slanderers or addict-
g1Ti 3:8 ed to much wine,[g] but to teach what is good.
4 Then they can train the younger women to love

[a] 5 Or *ordain* [b] 7 Traditionally *bishop*

Role of Older Women

TIT 2:3–4

In these verses Paul highlights the value of a woman's influence and work. Whether young or old, a woman has the potential to affect her world and church by her character and the conduct of her life. Some have seen these verses as a restriction on a woman's role, but they are not. Instead, these verses picture the opportunity available to a creative, godly woman to build a life where love and faith can flourish. As responsibilities at home decrease with time, a woman is able to use the character and wisdom she has gained to have a broader influence on the world. It is important to note that her impact comes primarily through her godly character, not through the accomplishments of domestic duties.

Good Citizens

TIT 3:1–2

We know from secular history that the people of ancient Crete were a difficult people to govern. So as Paul instructs Titus concerning his ministry there, he gives a detailed list of the ways the Cretan believers are to participate in their community as good citizens. The call to obey, to cooperate and to do good is a call that applies to every Christian. God has established governments (see the note on Ro 13:1–7, page 1867), and he is able to use them even when they do great harm. (Consider Peter's commentary on the crucifixion of Jesus, Acts 2:22–24; 1 Peter 2:13–25).

At the same time, there are times and reasons to resist an evil government. When its requirements fly in the face of God's specific will, we are to obey God rather than the government (Ac 5:27–29).

their husbands and children, 5to be self-controlled
and pure, to be busy at home, to be kind, and to
be subject to their husbands,[h] so that no one will
malign the word of God.[i]
6Similarly, encourage the young men[j] to be self-
controlled. 7In everything set them an example[k]
by doing what is good. In your teaching show
integrity, seriousness 8and soundness of speech
that cannot be condemned, so that those who
oppose you may be ashamed because they have
nothing bad to say about us.[l]
9Teach slaves to be subject to their masters in
everything,[m] to try to please them, not to talk
back to them, 10and not to steal from them, but to
show that they can be fully trusted, so that in
every way they will make the teaching about God
our Savior attractive.[n]
11For the grace of God that brings salvation has
appeared to all men.[o] 12It teaches us to say "No" to
ungodliness and worldly passions,[p] and to live
self-controlled, upright and godly lives[q] in this
present age, 13while we wait for the blessed
hope—the glorious appearing of our great God
and Savior, Jesus Christ,[r] 14who gave himself for
us to redeem us from all wickedness and to purify for himself a people that are his very own,[s]
eager to do what is good.[t]
15These, then, are the things you should teach.
Encourage and rebuke with all authority. Do not
let anyone despise you.

Doing What Is Good

3 Remind the people to be subject to rulers and
authorities,[u] to be obedient, to be ready to do
whatever is good,[v] 2to slander no one,[w] to be
peaceable and considerate, and to show true
humility toward all men.
3At one time we too were foolish, disobedient,
deceived and enslaved by all kinds of passions
and pleasures. We lived in malice and envy, being
hated and hating one another. 4But when the
kindness[x] and love of God our Savior appeared,[y]
5he saved us, not because of righteous things we
had done,[z] but because of his mercy. He saved us
through the washing of rebirth and renewal[a] by
the Holy Spirit, 6whom he poured out on us[b] generously through Jesus Christ our Savior, 7so that,
having been justified by his grace,[c] we might
become heirs[d] having the hope[e] of eternal life.[f]
8This is a trustworthy saying.[g] And I want you to
stress these things, so that those who have trusted in God may be careful to devote themselves to
doing what is good.[h] These things are excellent
and profitable for everyone.
9But avoid foolish controversies and genealogies
and arguments and quarrels[i] about the law,
because these are unprofitable and useless.
10Warn a divisive person once, and then warn him
a second time. After that, have nothing to do with
him.[j] 11You may be sure that such a man is
warped and sinful; he is self-condemned.

2:5 [h]Eph 5:22 [i]1Ti 6:1
2:6 [j]1Ti 5:1
2:7 [k]1Ti 4:12
2:8 [l]1Pe 2:12
2:9 [m]Eph 6:5
2:10 [n]Mt 5:16
2:11 [o]1Ti 2:4
2:12 [p]Tit 3:3 [q]2Ti 3:12
2:13 [r]2Pe 1:1
2:14 [s]Ex 19:5 [t]Eph 2:10
3:1 [u]Ro 13:1 [v]2Ti 2:21
3:2 [w]Eph 4:31; 2Ti 2:24
3:4 [x]Eph 2:7 [y]Tit 2:11
3:5 [z]Eph 2:9 [a]Ro 12:2
3:6 [b]Ro 5:5
3:7 [c]Ro 3:24 [d]Ro 8:17 [e]Ro 8:24 [f]Tit 1:2
3:8 [g]1Ti 1:15 [h]Tit 2:14
3:9 [i]1Ti 1:4; 2Ti 2:14
3:10 [j]Ro 16:17

Final Remarks

12 As soon as I send Artemas or Tychicus[k] to
you, do your best to come to me at Nicopolis,
because I have decided to winter there.[l] 13 Do
everything you can to help Zenas the lawyer and
Apollos[m] on their way and see that they have
everything they need. 14 Our people must learn to
devote themselves to doing what is good,[n] in
order that they may provide for daily necessities
and not live unproductive lives.
15 Everyone with me sends you greetings. Greet
those who love us in the faith.[o]
Grace be with you all.[p]

3:12 [k]Ac 20:4 [l]2Ti 4:9,21
3:13 [m]Ac 18:24
3:14 [n]ver 8
3:15 [o]1Ti 1:2 [p]Col 4:18

In one great selfless act, as he got down on his knees and washed the feet of his friends, Christ destroyed the concept of what's "appropriate." If one followed the rules of position and authority, he—the leader, the respected teacher and miracle worker—was the last person in the room who should have performed that menial task. In the final few hours with his twelve disciples—men who had been with him since the beginning of his ministry—he delivered a powerful punch to what true greatness really is.

—Sheila Walsh

Philemon

The cost of forgiveness.

During Paul's first imprisonment in Rome, he meets a runaway slave from Colosse named Onesimus. Paul shares the gospel message with him and leads this runaway slave to faith in Christ. After convincing Onesimus to return to his master, Paul writes this letter to Philemon, a Christian businessman and Onesimus's owner.

Slavery was a common practice in Paul's day, and the punishment for running away was severe. Yet Paul's briefest letter calls for grace and forgiveness rather than anger and retribution as he reminds Philemon of the forgiveness Philemon has already received from God through Christ. Recognizing the importance of restitution, Paul also offers to personally repay whatever Onesimus has stolen.

Hidden in this illustration of radical forgiveness is a reference to Apphia, a woman whose name few will recognize. Probably the wife of Philemon and hostess of the church that meets in their home, we can only speculate if Paul's message is troublesome to her (Phm 2). Perhaps Apphia understands that she, too, has run away from God through sin and disobedience. But God, in his grace, has forgiven her. Like Philemon, she is called to extend that same forgiveness to their runaway slave Onesimus.

Paul's urgent letter to Philemon emphasizes that Christian relationships must exude forgiveness and acceptance. Whether others have betrayed us, offended us or turned away from us for any reason, we can look to God for the grace to show them what Christ has shown us—gracious forgiveness, willing acceptance and abundant love.

Quick Study

Author
The apostle Paul.

Date Written
Around A.D. 60.

Written From
From prison in Rome; Paul sent it to Philemon with Onesimus.

Key Passage
Philemon 1:4–7 "I always thank my God as I remember you in my prayers, because I hear about your faith in the Lord Jesus and your love for all the saints. I pray that you may be active in sharing your faith, so that you will have a full understanding of every good thing we have in Christ. Your love has given me great joy and encouragement, because you, brother, have refreshed the hearts of the saints."

Outline

Paul's greetings and thanksgiving. Phm 1–7

Paul's plea. Phm 8–21

Personal notes and greetings. Phm 22–25

The Women of Philemon

Apphia	*Believing member of Philemon's household, perhaps his wife.* Phm 2

Forgiveness in Action

PHM 1-25

It's one thing to forgive a person; it's quite another to receive him or her back into your heart on a more intimate level than before the offense. It's one thing to release a person from some debt owed you; it's quite another to elevate him or her to the position of truly being your equal.

Paul writes to Philemon, a wealthy Christian in Colosse who has been influenced by Paul's ministry. He is urging Philemon to offer to his former slave, Onesimus, a lavish forgiveness. "Don't just release Onesimus from what he owes you," Paul says, "make him part of your family as well." Full forgiveness where it is fully undeserved is quite a challenge. Yet that is exactly the forgiveness God has offered us in Christ: lavish, undeserved, and fully and freely given.

1Paul, a prisoner[a] of Christ Jesus, and Timothy
our brother,[b]

To Philemon our dear friend and fellow worker,[c]
2to Apphia our sister, to Archippus[d] our fellow soldier[e] and to the church that meets in your home:[f]

3Grace to you and peace from God our Father
and the Lord Jesus Christ.

Thanksgiving and Prayer

4I always thank my God[g] as I remember you in
my prayers, 5because I hear about your faith in the
Lord Jesus and your love for all the saints.[h] 6I pray
that you may be active in sharing your faith, so
that you will have a full understanding of every
good thing we have in Christ. 7Your love has given
me great joy and encouragement,[i] because you,
brother, have refreshed[j] the hearts of the saints.

Paul's Plea for Onesimus

8Therefore, although in Christ I could be bold
and order you to do what you ought to do, 9yet I
appeal to you on the basis of love. I then, as
Paul—an old man and now also a prisoner[k] of
Christ Jesus— 10I appeal to you for my son[l] Onesimus,[a][m] who became my son while I was in
chains. 11Formerly he was useless to you, but now
he has become useful both to you and to me.

12I am sending him—who is my very heart—
back to you. 13I would have liked to keep him
with me so that he could take your place in helping me while I am in chains for the gospel. 14But
I did not want to do anything without your consent, so that any favor you do will be spontaneous
and not forced.[n] 15Perhaps the reason he was separated from you for a little while was that you
might have him back for good— 16no longer as a
slave, but better than a slave, as a dear brother.[o]
He is very dear to me but even dearer to you, both
as a man and as a brother in the Lord.

17So if you consider me a partner,[p] welcome
him as you would welcome me. 18If he has done
you any wrong or owes you anything, charge it to
me. 19I, Paul, am writing this with my own hand.
I will pay it back—not to mention that you owe
me your very self. 20I do wish, brother, that I may
have some benefit from you in the Lord; refresh[q]
my heart in Christ. 21Confident[r] of your obedience,
I write to you, knowing that you will do even
more than I ask.

22And one thing more: Prepare a guest room for
me, because I hope to be[s] restored to you in
answer to your prayers.[t]

23Epaphras,[u] my fellow prisoner in Christ Jesus,
sends you greetings. 24And so do Mark,[v] Aristarchus,[w] Demas[x] and Luke, my fellow workers.

25The grace of the Lord Jesus Christ be with
your spirit.[y]

1 [a]ver 9,23; Eph 3:1 [b]2Co 1:1 [c]Php 2:25
2 [d]Col 4:17 [e]Php 2:25 [f]Ro 16:5
4 [g]Ro 1:8
5 [h]Eph 1:15; Col 1:4
7 [i]2Co 7:4,13 [j]ver 20
9 [k]ver 1,23
10 [l]1Co 4:15 [m]Col 4:9
14 [n]2Co 9:7; 1Pe 5:2
16 [o]Mt 23:8; 1Ti 6:2
17 [p]2Co 8:23
20 [q]ver 7
21 [r]2Co 2:3
22 [s]Php 1:25; 2:24 [t]2Co 1:11
23 [u]Col 1:7
24 [v]Ac 12:12 [w]Ac 19:29 [x]Col 4:14
25 [y]2Ti 4:22

[a] 10 *Onesimus* means *useful.*

Hebrews

The superiority of Christ.

Persecution is a real threat to the Jewish Christians of the first century. Many find themselves torn between their newfound faith in Christ and their Old Testament way of life. By demonstrating the superiority of Christ to all of the Old Testament rituals and sacrifices, the book of Hebrews counsels these early believers to stay true to the gospel of Jesus Christ.

Because of its many references to the Old Testament, Hebrews reads like a sequel to the book of Leviticus. It can be helpful to read Hebrews and compare its difficult passages about the priestly system, covenants, sacrifices, the tabernacle design and Jewish feasts with their fuller explanations in Leviticus. Yet there are passages in Hebrews that need no further explanation. Believers are to be encouragers (Heb 3; 10). God's Word is captivating and alive, and it pierces peoples' hearts (Heb 4). Believers need to keep growing in their faith and not become complacent (Heb 5-6). God created his people to be confident and strong (Heb 10). And the hall of fame of faith includes several women whose footsteps and examples are worth following (Heb 11).

Old habits are comfortable. But settling for second best is not God's plan for the Jews of the early church or for believers today. Jesus removes our sin, guarantees our access to God and promises always to be with us. The message of Hebrews is clear: Persevere in your faith because Jesus is all you need.

Quick Study

Author
Although authorship is uncertain at best, two possibilities are Barnabas or Apollos.

Date Written
Before the destruction of Jerusalem in A.D. 70.

Written From
The author is uncertain; therefore, so is the location for writing.

Key Passage
Hebrews 4:14-16 "Let us hold firmly to the faith we profess. For we do not have a high priest who is unable to sympathize with our weaknesses, but we have one who has been tempted in every way, just as we are—yet was without sin. Let us then approach the throne of grace with confidence, so that we may receive mercy and find grace to help us in our time of need."

Outline

Christ's superior revelation.
Heb 1:1-3

Christ's superiority over angels.
Heb 1:4–2:18

Christ's superiority over Moses.
Heb 3:1–4:13

Christ's superiority over the priesthood.
Heb 4:14–7:28

Christ's superior sacrifice.
Heb 8:1–10:39

Hall of fame of the faithful.
Heb 11

God's discipline.
Heb 12

Final teachings.
Heb 13:1-21

Final greetings.
Heb 13:22-25

The Women of Hebrews

⚘ **Sarah**	*A barren woman who conceived.* Heb 11:11 (page 67)
⚘ **Moses' mother (Jochebed)**	*With his father, hid Moses and was not afraid.* Heb 11:23 (page 329)
⚘ **Pharaoh's daughter**	*She raised Moses as her own son.* Heb 11:24 (page 330)
⚘ **Rahab**	*A prostitute but one of the faithful.* Heb 11:31 (page 469)
Women of faith	*Their dead were raised to life.* Hebrews 11:35

⚘ *Denotes a sketch written about this character*

The Son Superior to Angels

1 In the past God spoke[a] to our forefathers through the prophets[b] at many times and in various ways,[c] 2 but in these last days he has spoken to us by his Son, whom he appointed heir[d] of all things, and through whom[e] he made the universe. 3 The Son is the radiance of God's glory[f] and the exact representation of his being, sustaining all things[g] by his powerful word. After he had provided purification for sins,[h] he sat down at the right hand of the Majesty in heaven.[i] 4 So he became as much superior to the angels as the name he has inherited is superior to theirs.[j]

5 For to which of the angels did God ever say,

"You are my Son;
today I have become your Father"[a][b]?[k]

Or again,

"I will be his Father,
and he will be my Son"[c]?[l]

6 And again, when God brings his firstborn into the world,[m] he says,

"Let all God's angels worship him."[d][n]

7 In speaking of the angels he says,

"He makes his angels winds,
his servants flames of fire."[e][o]

8 But about the Son he says,

"Your throne, O God, will last for ever and ever,
and righteousness will be the scepter of your kingdom.
9 You have loved righteousness and hated wickedness;
therefore God, your God, has set you above your companions[p]
by anointing you with the oil[q] of joy."[f]

10 He also says,

"In the beginning, O Lord, you laid the foundations of the earth,
and the heavens are the work of your hands.
11 They will perish, but you remain;
they will all wear out like a garment.[r]
12 You will roll them up like a robe;
like a garment they will be changed.
But you remain the same,[s]
and your years will never end."[g][t]

13 To which of the angels did God ever say,

"Sit at my right hand
until I make your enemies
a footstool[u] for your feet"[h]?[v]

[a] 5 Or *have begotten you* [b] 5 Psalm 2:7
[c] 5 2 Samuel 7:14; 1 Chron. 17:13 [d] 6 Deut. 32:43 (see Dead Sea Scrolls and Septuagint) [e] 7 Psalm 104:4
[f] 9 Psalm 45:6,7 [g] 12 Psalm 102:25–27 [h] 13 Psalm 110:1

1:1 [a]Jn 9:29; Heb 2:2,3 [b]Ac 2:30 [c]Nu 12:6,8
1:2 [d]Ps 2:8 [e]Jn 1:3
1:3 [f]Jn 1:14 [g]Col 1:17 [h]Heb 7:27 [i]Mk 16:19
1:4 [j]Eph 1:21; Php 2:9,10
1:5 [k]Ps 2:7 [l]2Sa 7:14
1:6 [m]Heb 10:5 [n]Dt 32:43 (LXX and DSS); Ps 97:7
1:7 [o]Ps 104:4
1:9 [p]Php 2:9 [q]Isa 61:1,3
1:11 [r]Isa 34:4
1:12 [s]Heb 13:8 [t]Ps 102:25-27
1:13 [u]Jos 10:24; Heb 10:13 [v]Ps 110:1

God the Son

HEB 1:1-3

These opening lines establish Jesus Christ as the One through whom God now speaks to the human race. In Old Testament times, the Jewish people relied on the prophets to tell them what God had to say. Here, the author of Hebrews states that God's most recent revelations come through his Son. The Son is made heir to all things and is the Creator of the universe. Such statements lead to the conclusion that the Son is also God and thus can speak on the Father's behalf with an authority the prophets never possessed.

14 Are not all angels ministering spirits[w] sent to
serve those who will inherit salvation?[x]

Warning to Pay Attention

2 We must pay more careful attention, therefore, to what we have heard, so that we do
not drift away. 2 For if the message spoken[y] by
angels[z] was binding, and every violation and
disobedience received its just punishment,[a]
3 how shall we escape if we ignore such a great
salvation?[b] This salvation, which was first
announced by the Lord,[c] was confirmed to us by
those who heard him.[d] 4 God also testified to it
by signs, wonders and various miracles,[e] and
gifts of the Holy Spirit[f] distributed according to
his will.[g]

Jesus Made Like His Brothers

5 It is not to angels that he has subjected the
world to come, about which we are speaking. 6 But
there is a place where someone has testified:

> "What is man that you are mindful of
> him,
> the son of man that you care for
> him?[h]
> 7 You made him a little[a] lower than the
> angels;
> you crowned him with glory and
> honor
> 8 and put everything under his feet."[b][i]

In putting everything under him, God left nothing
that is not subject to him. Yet at present we do not
see everything subject to him. 9 But we see Jesus,
who was made a little lower than the angels, now
crowned with glory and honor[j] because he suffered death,[k] so that by the grace of God he might
taste death for everyone.[l]

10 In bringing many sons to glory, it was fitting
that God, for whom and through whom everything exists,[m] should make the author of their salvation perfect through suffering.[n] 11 Both the one
who makes men holy and those who are made
holy[o] are of the same family. So Jesus is not
ashamed to call them brothers.[p] 12 He says,

> "I will declare your name to my
> brothers;
> in the presence of the congregation I
> will sing your praises."[c][q]

13 And again,

> "I will put my trust in him."[d][r]

And again he says,

> "Here am I, and the children God has
> given me."[e][s]

14 Since the children have flesh and blood, he

1:14 [w]Ps 103:20 [x]Heb 5:9
2:2 [y]Heb 1:1 [z]Dt 33:2; Ac 7:53 [a]Heb 10:28
2:3 [b]Heb 10:29 [c]Heb 1:2 [d]Lk 1:2
2:4 [e]Jn 4:48 [f]1Co 12:4 [g]Eph 1:5
2:6 [h]Job 7:17
2:8 [i]Ps 8:4-6; 1Co 15:25
2:9 [j]Ac 2:33; 3:13; Php 2:9 [k]Php 2:7-9 [l]Jn 3:16; 2Co 5:15
2:10 [m]Ro 11:36 [n]Lk 24:26; Heb 7:28
2:11 [o]Heb 10:10 [p]Mt 28:10; Jn 20:17
2:12 [q]Ps 22:22
2:13 [r]Isa 8:17 [s]Isa 8:18; Jn 10:29

[a] *7* Or *him for a little while*; also in verse 9 [b] *8* Psalm 8:4-6
[c] *12* Psalm 22:22 [d] *13* Isaiah 8:17 [e] *13* Isaiah 8:18

Angels

HEB 1:14

Angels are an order of heavenly, supernatural beings created by God for his purposes. Superior to human beings in intelligence and power, their full-time job and joy is to praise and serve God. As part of their acts of service to him, angels interact with humans, protecting, helping and delivering messages from God. But, as the author points out to the Hebrews, Jesus is far superior to these glorious creatures. For a short time, during his life as a man on earth, Christ was, in a sense, "made a little lower than the angels" (Heb 2:9). Yet he has never ceased to be God, and the angels remain subject to him.

2:14 too shared in their humanity[t] so that by his death
[t]Jn 1:14 [u]1Co 15:54– he might destroy[u] him who holds the power of
57; 2Ti 1:10 death—that is, the devil[v]— 15and free those who
[v]1Jn 3:8 all their lives were held in slavery by their fear[w] of
2:15 death. 16For surely it is not angels he helps, but
[w]2Ti 1:7 Abraham's descendants. 17For this reason he had
2:17 to be made like his brothers[x] in every way, in
[x]Php 2:7 order that he might become a merciful[y] and faith-
[y]Heb 5:2 ful high priest[z] in service to God,[a] and that he
[z]Heb 4:14, 15; 7:26,28 might make atonement for[a] the sins of the people.
[a]Heb 5:1 18Because he himself suffered when he was
tempted, he is able to help those who are being
2:18 [b]Heb 4:15 tempted.[b]

Jesus Greater Than Moses

3:1 [c]Heb 2:11 **3** Therefore, holy brothers,[c] who share in the
[d]Heb 2:17 heavenly calling, fix your thoughts on Jesus,
[e]Heb 4:14 the apostle and high priest[d] whom we confess.[e]
2He was faithful to the one who appointed him,
3:2 just as Moses was faithful in all God's house.[f]
[f]Nu 12:7 3Jesus has been found worthy of greater honor
than Moses, just as the builder of a house has
greater honor than the house itself. 4For every
3:5 house is built by someone, but God is the builder
[g]Ex 14:31 of everything. 5Moses was faithful as a servant[g] in
[h]ver 2; all God's house,[h] testifying to what would be said
Nu 12:7 in the future. 6But Christ is faithful as a son[i] over
3:6 God's house. And we are his house,[j] if we hold
[i]Heb 1:2 [j]1Co 3:16 on[k] to our courage and the hope[l] of which we
[k]Ro 11:22 boast.
[l]Ro 5:2

Warning Against Unbelief

3:7 [m]Heb 9:8 7So, as the Holy Spirit says:[m]

"Today, if you hear his voice,
8 do not harden your hearts
as you did in the rebellion,
during the time of testing in the
desert,
3:9 9where your fathers tested and tried me
[n]Ac 7:36 and for forty years saw what I did.[n]
10That is why I was angry with that
generation,
and I said, 'Their hearts are always
going astray,
and they have not known my ways.'
3:11 11So I declared on oath in my anger,
[o]Heb 4:3,5 'They shall never enter my rest.' [o]"[b][p]
[p]Ps 95:7–11

12See to it, brothers, that none of you has a sin-
3:13 ful, unbelieving heart that turns away from the
[q]Heb 10:24, 25 living God. 13But encourage one another daily,[q] as
long as it is called Today, so that none of you may
[r]Eph 4:22 be hardened by sin's deceitfulness.[r] 14We have
3:14 come to share in Christ if we hold firmly[s] till the
[s]ver 6 end the confidence we had at first. 15As has just
been said:

"Today, if you hear his voice,

[a] 17 *Or and that he might turn aside God's wrath, taking away*
[b] 11 Psalm 95:7–11

Do Not Turn Away

HEB 3:7–13

Following their exodus from Egypt, the Israelite nation rebelled against God in the desert when things didn't go according to their plans. Because of their lack of faith, they did not receive all that God had waiting for them in the promised land (Nu 14). Their experiences can be a lesson for us.

Is there an aspect in which your heart is especially hard? Are there areas of your life in which you're trying to seize control from God? Ask the Holy Spirit to make you aware of these things; then confess them in prayer. Since rebellion comes so naturally to us as humans, the writer to the Hebrews also encourages us to support each other in our journeys (Heb 3:13). We aren't on this road alone.

Rest

HEB 4:1-13

God rested on the seventh day of creation, and he intends the faithful to rest as well. There are two opinions regarding what exactly this "rest" means. One opinion is that this rest is what believers will one day experience in heaven. Another view is that this rest is immediate and becomes a believer's condition when he or she ceases striving to earn God's approval and trusts in Christ.

The writer urges his readers to "make every effort to enter that rest" (Heb 4:11), which may seem like a contradiction, since we normally think that effort involves work. However, he does not mean for us to work to enter rest but to faithfully and fully focus our eyes on the work Jesus has already accomplished for us.

do not harden your hearts
as you did in the rebellion."[a][t]

[16]Who were they who heard and rebelled? Were
they not all those Moses led out of Egypt?[u] [17]And
with whom was he angry for forty years? Was it
not with those who sinned, whose bodies fell in
the desert?[v] [18]And to whom did God swear that
they would never enter his rest[w] if not to those
who disobeyed[b]?[x] [19]So we see that they were not
able to enter, because of their unbelief.[y]

A Sabbath-Rest for the People of God

4 Therefore, since the promise of entering his
rest still stands, let us be careful that none of
you be found to have fallen short of it.[z] [2]For we
also have had the gospel preached to us, just as
they did; but the message they heard was of no
value to them, because those who heard did not
combine it with faith.[c][a] [3]Now we who have
believed enter that rest, just as God has said,

"So I declared on oath in my anger,
'They shall never enter my rest.' "[d][b]

And yet his work has been finished since the creation of the world. [4]For somewhere he has spoken about the seventh day in these words: "And
on the seventh day God rested from all his
work."[e][c] [5]And again in the passage above he says,
"They shall never enter my rest."[d]

[6]It still remains that some will enter that rest,
and those who formerly had the gospel preached
to them did not go in, because of their disobedience.[e] [7]Therefore God again set a certain day, calling it Today, when a long time later he spoke
through David, as was said before:

"Today, if you hear his voice,
do not harden your hearts."[a][f]

[8]For if Joshua had given them rest,[g] God would
not have spoken[h] later about another day. [9]There
remains, then, a Sabbath-rest for the people of
God; [10]for anyone who enters God's rest also rests
from his own work, just as God did from his.[i] [11]Let
us, therefore, make every effort to enter that rest,
so that no one will fall by following their example
of disobedience.[j]

[12]For the word of God[k] is living and active.[l]
Sharper than any double-edged sword,[m] it penetrates even to dividing soul and spirit, joints and
marrow; it judges the thoughts and attitudes of
the heart.[n] [13]Nothing in all creation is hidden from
God's sight.[o] Everything is uncovered and laid
bare before the eyes of him to whom we must give
account.

Jesus the Great High Priest

[14]Therefore, since we have a great high priest

3:15 [t]ver 7,8; Ps 95:7,8
3:16 [u]Nu 14:2
3:17 [v]Nu 14:29; Ps 106:26
3:18 [w]Nu 14:20-23 [x]Heb 4:6
3:19 [y]Jn 3:36
4:1 [z]Heb 12:15
4:2 [a]1Th 2:13
4:3 [b]Ps 95:11; Heb 3:11
4:4 [c]Ge 2:2,3; Ex 20:11
4:5 [d]Ps 95:11
4:6 [e]Heb 3:18
4:7 [f]Ps 95:7,8; Heb 3:7,8,15
4:8 [g]Jos 22:4 [h]Heb 1:1
4:10 [i]ver 4
4:11 [j]Heb 3:18
4:12 [k]1Pe 1:23 [l]Jer 23:29 [m]Eph 6:17; Rev 1:16 [n]1Co 14:24, 25
4:13 [o]Ps 33:13-15

[a] *15,7* Psalm 95:7,8 [b] *18* Or *disbelieved* [c] *2* Many manuscripts *because they did not share in the faith of those who obeyed* [d] *3* Psalm 95:11; also in verse 5 [e] *4* Gen. 2:2

Week 47

Rest in the Lord

"Busy" is becoming the universal response to "How are you?" in today's fast-paced world. People seem to rate their worth and recognition on the relentless busyness of their schedules. Who has time for a contemplative thought when every moment is filled with activity? And who would ever consider the idea of rest?

What is the first instance of rest mentioned in the Scriptures (Ge 2:2)? In what sense did God rest (Ge 2:3)?

How does God guarantee physical rest for his children (Ex 20:8-11)? In what other ways does God provide rest (Dt 12:10; Jos 21:44; Isa 32:18; Jer 30:10)? Rest is an emotional and spiritual experience as well as a physical one.

How does the Israelites' observance of the Sabbath reveal their obedience to the law and acceptance of their covenant with God (Ex 31:15-17)? When Jesus died, the new covenant of grace was instituted, and Sabbath observance was no longer a prerequisite and means of righteousness. Although the *legalism* of Sabbath rest is eclipsed by the new covenant, the *principle* of rest is still valid today.

What can prevent a person from entering God's rest (Ps 95:10-11; Heb 3:18-19; 4:1-2, 6)? How does a legalistic lifestyle prevent someone from entering God's rest (Ac 15:10-11; Gal 5:1)? God has set you free from the law (Gal 5:1); it is in repentance and rest that you will find your salvation (Isa 30:15).

What, then, should be your goal in life (Heb 4:11)?

The finished work of Jesus Christ on the cross makes it possible for you to enter his rest (Isa 11:10). There's no need to struggle, no need to fill your life with busywork. You can rest in Christ.

Enjoying God THROUGH the Word

Read Matthew 11:28-30 (page 1399). A yoke is a wooden frame placed across the necks of two animals (often oxen), so they can work together. Often a young, inexperienced ox is trained in a yoke with an experienced, older ox. The stronger ox bears most of the weight and sets the pace. If the younger ox tries to run ahead, fall behind or pull away, it gets a stiff neck, but it is still connected to the older, steady ox. Eventually the younger one will learn from the older one.

Jesus wants you to voluntarily take his yoke and learn from him (Mt 11:29). You may get a stiff neck at times from trying to go your own way, but his gentleness will continually guide you in the right direction. In him you will find rest for your weary soul.

Enjoying God THROUGH Experience

Are you looking for rest? Go to Jesus. Accept his yoke of companionship. He will carry your burdens and give you rest. Perhaps you have already accepted his yoke, but your neck is chafed from constant straining. If so, acknowledge your desire to go your own way. Ask Jesus for the rest you desire: "Oh, that I had the wings of a dove! I would fly away and be at rest—I would flee far away and stay in the desert; I would hurry to my place of shelter, far from the tempest and storm" (Ps 55:6-8). Jesus is your shelter and rest from the storms of life. Accept his rest.

Go to page 2006 for your next weekly study.

who has gone through the heavens,[a][p] Jesus the 4:14
Son of God, let us hold firmly to the faith we pro- [p]Heb 6:20
fess.[q] 15 For we do not have a high priest who is [q]Heb 3:1
unable to sympathize with our weaknesses, but
we have one who has been tempted in every way, 4:15
just as we are[r]—yet was without sin.[s] 16 Let us [r]Heb 2:18
then approach the throne of grace with confi- [s]2Co 5:21
dence, so that we may receive mercy and find
grace to help us in our time of need.

5 Every high priest is selected from among men
and is appointed to represent them in matters 5:1
related to God, to offer gifts and sacrifices[t] for [t]Heb 8:3
sins.[u] 2 He is able to deal gently with those who [u]Heb 7:27
are ignorant and are going astray,[v] since he him-
self is subject to weakness.[w] 3 This is why he has 5:2 [v]Heb 2:18
to offer sacrifices for his own sins, as well as for [w]Heb 7:28
the sins of the people.[x] 5:3
4 No one takes this honor upon himself; he must [x]Heb 7:27;
be called by God, just as Aaron was.[y] 5 So Christ 9:7
also did not take upon himself the glory[z] of 5:4
becoming a high priest. But God said[a] to him, [y]Ex 28:1

> "You are my Son; 5:5
> today I have become your Father.[b]"[c][b] [z]Jn 8:54 [a]Heb 1:1

6 And he says in another place, [b]Ps 2:7

> "You are a priest forever,
> in the order of Melchizedek."[d][c] 5:6 [c]Ps 110:4; Heb 7:17,21

7 During the days of Jesus' life on earth, he
offered up prayers and petitions with loud cries
and tears[d] to the one who could save him from 5:7 [d]Mt 27:46,50
death, and he was heard because of his reverent [e]Mk 14:36
submission.[e] 8 Although he was a son, he learned
obedience from what he suffered[f] 9 and, once 5:8 [f]Php 2:8
made perfect,[g] he became the source of eternal
salvation for all who obey him 10 and was desig- 5:9
nated by God to be high priest[h] in the order of [g]Heb 2:10
Melchizedek.[i] 5:10 [h]ver 5 [i]ver 6

Warning Against Falling Away

11 We have much to say about this, but it is hard
to explain because you are slow to learn. 12 In fact,
though by this time you ought to be teachers, you 5:12
need someone to teach you the elementary truths[j] [j]Heb 6:1
of God's word all over again. You need milk, not [k]1Co 3:2;
solid food![k] 13 Anyone who lives on milk, being 1Pe 2:2
still an infant,[l] is not acquainted with the teaching 5:13
about righteousness. 14 But solid food is for the [l]1Co 14:20
mature,[m] who by constant use have trained them- 5:14
selves to distinguish good from evil.[n] [m]1Co 2:6

6 Therefore let us leave[o] the elementary teach- [n]Isa 7:15
ings[p] about Christ and go on to maturity, not 6:1
laying again the foundation of repentance from [o]Php 3:12-14
acts that lead to death,[e][q] and of faith in God, [p]Heb 5:12
2 instruction about baptisms,[r] the laying on of [q]Heb 9:14
hands,[s] the resurrection of the dead,[t] and eternal 6:2 [r]Jn 3:25
judgment. 3 And God permitting,[u] we will do so. [s]Ac 6:6
4 It is impossible for those who have once been [t]Ac 17:18,32

6:3 [u]Ac 18:21

[a] 14 Or *gone into heaven* [b] 5 Or *have begotten you* [c] 5 Psalm 2:7 [d] 6 Psalm 110:4 [e] 1 Or *from useless rituals*

I often share that the love of God is like this little prayer: "Lord, *I have sinned and fallen away from you. I am no longer worthy to be called your child.*"

God's reply: "*My child, I know, but my Son is eternally worthy to be called your Savior.*" That's the love of God . . . *When we were sinners, God loved us so much that he sent his Son to die for us. God's love never fails, and it can heal our hurting hearts* . . . *I am absolutely convinced that life does not happen by chance. God has a plan; God's plan is full of his love for us; and God's plan will succeed!* When we are in the midst of pain it is hard to believe that, but I know it's true, and I've seen it work!

—Barbara Johnson

6:4 [v]Heb 10:32 enlightened,[v] who have tasted the heavenly gift,[w]
[w]Eph 2:8 [x]Gal 3:2 who have shared in the Holy Spirit,[x] 5who have
tasted the goodness of the word of God and the
6:6 powers of the coming age, 6if they fall away, to be
[y]2Pe 2:21; 1Jn 5:16 brought back to repentance,[y] because[a] to their loss
they are crucifying the Son of God all over again
and subjecting him to public disgrace.
7Land that drinks in the rain often falling on it
and that produces a crop useful to those for whom
it is farmed receives the blessing of God. 8But land
6:8 that produces thorns and thistles is worthless and
[z]Ge 3:17,18; is in danger of being cursed.[z] In the end it will be
Isa 5:6 burned.
6:9 9Even though we speak like this, dear friends,[a]
[a]1Co 10:14 we are confident of better things in your case—
things that accompany salvation. 10God is not
unjust; he will not forget your work and the love
6:10 you have shown him as you have helped his peo-
[b]Mt 10:40, 42; 25:40; ple and continue to help them.[b] 11We want each
1Th 1:3 of you to show this same diligence to the very
6:11 end, in order to make your hope[c] sure. 12We do
[c]Heb 3:6 not want you to become lazy, but to imitate[d] those
who through faith and patience[e] inherit what has
6:12 [d]Heb 13:7 been promised.[f]

[e]2Th 1:4; Jas 1:3;

The Certainty of God's Promise

Rev 13:10 [f]Heb 10:36 13When God made his promise to Abraham,
since there was no one greater for him to swear
6:13 [g]Ge 22:16; by, he swore by himself,[g] 14saying, "I will surely
Lk 1:73 bless you and give you many descendants."[b][h]
6:14 15And so after waiting patiently, Abraham
[h]Ge 22:17 received what was promised.[i]
16Men swear by someone greater than them-
6:15 [i]Ge 21:5 selves, and the oath confirms what is said and puts
an end to all argument.[j] 17Because God wanted to
6:16 [j]Ex 22:11 make the unchanging[k] nature of his purpose very
clear to the heirs of what was promised,[l] he con-
6:17 firmed it with an oath. 18God did this so that, by
[k]Ps 110:4 [l]Heb 11:9 two unchangeable things in which it is impossible
for God to lie,[m] we who have fled to take hold of
6:18 [m]Nu 23:19; the hope[n] offered to us may be greatly encouraged.
Tit 1:2 19We have this hope as an anchor for the soul, firm
[n]Heb 3:6 and secure. It enters the inner sanctuary behind
6:19 [o]Lev 16:2; the curtain,[o] 20where Jesus, who went before us,
Heb 9:2,3,7 has entered on our behalf.[p] He has become a high
priest[q] forever, in the order of Melchizedek.[r]

6:20 [p]Heb 4:14 [q]Heb 2:17

Melchizedek the Priest

[r]Heb 5:6 7 This Melchizedek was king of Salem and
7:1 priest of God Most High.[s] He met Abraham
[s]Mk 5:7 returning from the defeat of the kings and blessed
[t]Ge 14:18-20 him,[t] 2and Abraham gave him a tenth of everything. First, his name means "king of righteousness"; then also, "king of Salem" means "king of
7:3 peace." 3Without father or mother, without
[u]ver 6 [v]Mt 4:3 genealogy,[u] without beginning of days or end of
life, like the Son of God[v] he remains a priest
forever.
4Just think how great he was: Even the patri-

[a] 6 Or *repentance while* [b] 14 Gen. 22:17

Hope is a precious gift of our salvation. According to Hebrews 6:19, "*We have this hope as an anchor for the soul, firm and secure.*" While we can "hope" that circus performers don't fall and that our kids don't spill their soda, *we must remember that our only reliable hope is in what we cannot see or control: the outrageous faithfulness of God.* Our responsibility to him as his children is to study his character so we will know, without a doubt, that whatever way he deals with our circumstances in life, it's the right way. Even when things don't work out the way we planned or desired, he is *all-knowing, all-loving, the beginning and the ending.* Hope is acting on the conviction that despite what we see with the natural eye, God is working in the spiritual realm to accomplish his perfect will in our lives. His hope does not disappoint!

—Thelma Wells

A Priest Forever

HEB 7:11-28

A priest-king of Salem, Melchizedek, went out to meet Abraham as he returned from his victory over the kings of the East. Melchizedek gave Abraham bread and wine and then blessed him. In return, Abraham gave ten percent of the battle spoils to Melchizedek, indicating that he recognized Melchizedek as a follower of the one true God and a priest higher than he in spiritual rank (Ge 14:18–20).

Jesus, as a priest in the order of Melchizedek, is greater than the Hebrew priests, just as Melchizedek was greater than the Hebrew Abraham and the priests who descended from him. The priesthood of Jesus is vastly superior to any past priesthood because (1) Jesus' perfection doesn't need sacrificial atonement (the Levitical priests needed to sacrifice for their own sin before they could come to God on behalf of the people—Lev 16:6); (2) Jesus' complete sacrifice negates the need for daily sacrifice for sin; and (3) although the Levitical priests eventually died and required a successor, Jesus will live forever, will intercede on our behalf with God forever, and will never require a successor.

arch[w] Abraham gave him a tenth of the plunder![x]
5 Now the law requires the descendants of Levi
who become priests to collect a tenth from the
people[y]—that is, their brothers—even though
their brothers are descended from Abraham. 6 This
man, however, did not trace his descent from Levi,
yet he collected a tenth from Abraham and
blessed[z] him who had the promises.[a] 7 And without doubt the lesser person is blessed by the
greater. 8 In the one case, the tenth is collected by
men who die; but in the other case, by him who is
declared to be living.[b] 9 One might even say that
Levi, who collects the tenth, paid the tenth
through Abraham, 10 because when Melchizedek
met Abraham, Levi was still in the body of his
ancestor.

Jesus Like Melchizedek

11 If perfection could have been attained through
the Levitical priesthood (for on the basis of it the
law was given to the people),[c] why was there still
need for another priest to come[d]—one in the order
of Melchizedek,[e] not in the order of Aaron? 12 For
when there is a change of the priesthood, there
must also be a change of the law. 13 He of whom
these things are said belonged to a different tribe,[f]
and no one from that tribe has ever served at the
altar.[g] 14 For it is clear that our Lord descended
from Judah,[h] and in regard to that tribe Moses
said nothing about priests. 15 And what we have
said is even more clear if another priest like
Melchizedek appears, 16 one who has become a
priest not on the basis of a regulation as to his
ancestry but on the basis of the power of an indestructible life. 17 For it is declared:

> "You are a priest forever,
> in the order of Melchizedek."[a][i]

18 The former regulation is set aside because it
was weak and useless[j] 19 (for the law made nothing perfect),[k] and a better hope is introduced, by
which we draw near to God.[l]
20 And it was not without an oath! Others
became priests without any oath, 21 but he became
a priest with an oath when God said to him:

> "The Lord has sworn
> and will not change his mind:[m]
> 'You are a priest forever.' "[a][n]

22 Because of this oath, Jesus has become the guarantee of a better covenant.[o]
23 Now there have been many of those priests,
since death prevented them from continuing in
office; 24 but because Jesus lives forever, he has a
permanent priesthood.[p] 25 Therefore he is able to
save completely[b] those who come to God[q] through
him, because he always lives to intercede for
them.[r]
26 Such a high priest meets our need—one who

7:4 [w]Ac 2:29 [x]Ge 14:20
7:5 [y]Nu 18:21,26
7:6 [z]Ge 14:19,20 [a]Ro 4:13
7:8 [b]Heb 5:6; 6:20
7:11 [c]ver 18,19; Heb 8:7 [d]Heb 10:1 [e]ver 17
7:13 [f]ver 11 [g]ver 14
7:14 [h]Isa 11:1; Mt 1:3; Lk 3:33
7:17 [i]Ps 110:4; ver 21; Heb 5:6
7:18 [j]Ro 8:3
7:19 [k]Ac 13:39; Ro 3:20; Heb 9:9 [l]Heb 4:16
7:21 [m]1Sa 15:29 [n]Ps 110:4
7:22 [o]Heb 8:6
7:24 [p]ver 28
7:25 [q]ver 19 [r]Ro 8:34

[a] *17,21* Psalm 110:4 [b] *25* Or *forever*

is holy, blameless, pure, set apart from sinners,[s] exalted above the heavens.[t] 27 Unlike the other high priests, he does not need to offer sacrifices[u] day after day, first for his own sins,[v] and then for the sins of the people. He sacrificed for their sins once for all[w] when he offered himself.[x] 28 For the law appoints as high priests men who are weak;[y] but the oath, which came after the law, appointed the Son,[z] who has been made perfect[a] forever.

The High Priest of a New Covenant

8 The point of what we are saying is this: We do have such a high priest,[b] who sat down at the right hand of the throne of the Majesty in heaven, 2 and who serves in the sanctuary, the true tabernacle[c] set up by the Lord, not by man.

3 Every high priest is appointed to offer both gifts and sacrifices,[d] and so it was necessary for this one also to have something to offer.[e] 4 If he were on earth, he would not be a priest, for there are already men who offer the gifts prescribed by the law.[f] 5 They serve at a sanctuary that is a copy[g] and shadow[h] of what is in heaven. This is why Moses was warned[i] when he was about to build the tabernacle: "See to it that you make everything according to the pattern shown you on the mountain."[a][j] 6 But the ministry Jesus has received is as superior to theirs as the covenant[k] of which he is mediator[l] is superior to the old one, and it is founded on better promises.

7 For if there had been nothing wrong with that first covenant, no place would have been sought for another.[m] 8 But God found fault with the people and said[b]:

"The time is coming, declares the Lord,
    when I will make a new covenant[n]
with the house of Israel
    and with the house of Judah.
9 It will not be like the covenant
    I made with their forefathers[o]
when I took them by the hand
    to lead them out of Egypt,
because they did not remain faithful to
        my covenant,
    and I turned away from them,
                declares the Lord.
10 This is the covenant I will make with
        the house of Israel
    after that time, declares the Lord.
I will put my laws in their minds
    and write them on their hearts.[p]
I will be their God,
    and they will be my people.[q]
11 No longer will a man teach his
        neighbor,
    or a man his brother, saying, 'Know
        the Lord,'
because they will all know me,[r]

7:26 [s]2Co 5:21 [t]Heb 4:14
7:27 [u]Heb 5:1 [v]Heb 5:3 [w]Heb 9:12, 26,28 [x]Eph 5:2; Heb 9:14,28
7:28 [y]Heb 5:2 [z]Heb 1:2 [a]Heb 2:10
8:1 [b]Heb 2:17
8:2 [c]Heb 9:11,24
8:3 [d]Heb 5:1 [e]Heb 9:14
8:4 [f]Heb 5:1
8:5 [g]Heb 9:23 [h]Col 2:17; Heb 10:1 [i]Heb 11:7; 12:25 [j]Ex 25:40
8:6 [k]Lk 22:20 [l]Heb 7:22
8:7 [m]Heb 7:11, 18
8:8 [n]Jer 31:31
8:9 [o]Ex 19:5,6
8:10 [p]2Co 3:3; Heb 10:16 [q]Zec 8:8
8:11 [r]Isa 54:13; Jn 6:45

[a] 5 Exodus 25:40 [b] 8 Some manuscripts may be translated *fault and said to the people.*

A Shadow

HEB 8:5

After God gave the Ten Commandments to Moses at Mount Sinai, he commanded Moses to build a tabernacle for him, so that he might live among the people of Israel (Ex 25:8–9). God's true dwelling place is heaven (Dt 26:15; 2Ch 6:21), but on earth he lived in the tabernacle Moses built to his specifications. In a sense, the tabernacle was a heavenly prototype. But just as a shadow is an inferior depiction of the item it represents, so the tabernacle was only a mere copy of God's heavenly home.

The Blood of Christ

HEB 9:14

Scripture teaches that *every person is guilty of sin* (Ro 3:23) *and that the price that must be paid for sin is death* (Ro 6:23). *Under the old covenant of the law, animal sacrifices were made to God to fulfill this requirement* (Lev 17:11). *Blood was shed for the atonement of sins. Yet, although sacrifices were made daily, it was impossible to maintain a clean slate with God. No animal sacrifice could pay the total price.*

Through the shed blood of Jesus Christ, *a new covenant has been made between God and the human race* (Lk 22:20). *Under this new covenant, blood is still required for the atonement of sins, but the blood is that of the Son of God. Through his death and resurrection, Christ paid completely for our transgressions—now and forever—making it possible for us to come to God with a clean conscience and enter into relationship with him* (Ro 8:1–4).

from the least of them to the greatest.
12 For I will forgive their wickedness
and will remember their sins no
more.[s]"[a][t]

13 By calling this covenant "new," he has made
the first one obsolete;[u] and what is obsolete and
aging will soon disappear.

Worship in the Earthly Tabernacle

9 Now the first covenant had regulations for
worship and also an earthly sanctuary.[v] 2 A
tabernacle[w] was set up. In its first room were the
lampstand,[x] the table[y] and the consecrated bread;[z]
this was called the Holy Place. 3 Behind the second curtain was a room called the Most Holy
Place,[a] 4 which had the golden altar of incense[b]
and the gold-covered ark of the covenant.[c] This
ark contained the gold jar of manna,[d] Aaron's
staff that had budded,[e] and the stone tablets of the
covenant. 5 Above the ark were the cherubim of
the Glory,[f] overshadowing the atonement cover.[b]
But we cannot discuss these things in detail now.
6 When everything had been arranged like this,
the priests entered regularly[g] into the outer room
to carry on their ministry. 7 But only the high
priest entered[h] the inner room, and that only once
a year,[i] and never without blood, which he offered
for himself[j] and for the sins the people had committed in ignorance. 8 The Holy Spirit was showing[k] by this that the way[l] into the Most Holy Place
had not yet been disclosed as long as the first tabernacle was still standing. 9 This is an illustration
for the present time, indicating that the gifts and
sacrifices being offered[m] were not able to clear the
conscience of the worshiper. 10 They are only a
matter of food[n] and drink[o] and various ceremonial washings—external regulations[p] applying until
the time of the new order.

The Blood of Christ

11 When Christ came as high priest[q] of the good
things that are already here,[c][r] he went through the
greater and more perfect tabernacle[s] that is not
man-made, that is to say, not a part of this creation. 12 He did not enter by means of the blood of
goats and calves;[t] but he entered the Most Holy
Place[u] once for all[v] by his own blood, having
obtained eternal redemption. 13 The blood of goats
and bulls and the ashes of a heifer[w] sprinkled on
those who are ceremonially unclean sanctify them
so that they are outwardly clean. 14 How much
more, then, will the blood of Christ, who through
the eternal Spirit[x] offered himself unblemished to
God, cleanse our consciences[y] from acts that lead
to death,[d][z] so that we may serve the living God!
15 For this reason Christ is the mediator[a] of a
new covenant, that those who are called may

8:12 [s]Heb 10:17 [t]Ro 11:27
8:13 [u]2Co 5:17
9:1 [v]Ex 25:8
9:2 [w]Ex 25:8,9 [x]Ex 25:31-39 [y]Ex 25:23-29 [z]Lev 24:5-8
9:3 [a]Ex 26:31-33
9:4 [b]Ex 30:1-5 [c]Ex 25:10-22 [d]Ex 16:32,33 [e]Nu 17:10
9:5 [f]Ex 25:17-19
9:6 [g]Nu 28:3
9:7 [h]Lev 16:11-19 [i]Lev 16:34 [j]Heb 5:2,3
9:8 [k]Heb 3:7 [l]Jn 14:6; Heb 10:19,20
9:9 [m]Heb 5:1
9:10 [n]Lev 11:2-23 [o]Col 2:16 [p]Heb 7:16
9:11 [q]Heb 2:17 [r]Heb 10:1 [s]Heb 8:2
9:12 [t]Heb 10:4 [u]ver 24 [v]Heb 7:27
9:13 [w]Nu 19:9,17,18
9:14 [x]1Pe 3:18 [y]Tit 2:14; Heb 10:2,22 [z]Heb 6:1
9:15 [a]1Ti 2:5

[a] *12* Jer. 31:31–34 [b] *5* Traditionally *the mercy seat*
[c] *11* Some early manuscripts *are to come* [d] *14* Or *from useless rituals*

receive the promised eternal inheritance—now
9:15 that he has died as a ransom to set them free from
bHeb 7:22 the sins committed under the first covenant.[b]
16In the case of a will,[a] it is necessary to prove
the death of the one who made it, 17because a will
is in force only when somebody has died; it never takes effect while the one who made it is living.
18This is why even the first covenant was not put
9:18 into effect without blood.[c] 19When Moses had pro-
cEx 24:6-8 claimed every commandment of the law to all the
people, he took the blood of calves, together with
9:19 water, scarlet wool and branches of hyssop, and
dEx 24:6-8 sprinkled the scroll and all the people.[d] 20He said,
"This is the blood of the covenant, which God has
9:20 eEx 24:8; commanded you to keep."[b][e] 21In the same way, he
Mt 26:28 sprinkled with the blood both the tabernacle and
everything used in its ceremonies. 22In fact, the
9:22 law requires that nearly everything be cleansed
fLev 8:15 with blood,[f] and without the shedding of blood
gLev 17:11 there is no forgiveness.[g]
9:23 23It was necessary, then, for the copies[h] of the
hHeb 8:5 heavenly things to be purified with these sacrifices, but the heavenly things themselves with
better sacrifices than these. 24For Christ did not
9:24 enter a man-made sanctuary that was only a copy
iHeb 8:2 of the true one;[i] he entered heaven itself, now to
appear for us in God's presence. 25Nor did he enter
9:25 heaven to offer himself again and again, the way
jHeb 10:19 the high priest enters the Most Holy Place[j] every
kver 7,8 year with blood that is not his own.[k] 26Then Christ
would have had to suffer many times since the
9:26 creation of the world.[l] But now he has appeared
lHeb 4:3 mHeb 7:27 once for all[m] at the end of the ages to do away
with sin by the sacrifice of himself. 27Just as man
9:27 nGe 3:19 is destined to die once,[n] and after that to face judg-
o2Co 5:10 ment,[o] 28so Christ was sacrificed once to take
away the sins of many people; and he will appear
9:28 pTit 2:13 a second time,[p] not to bear sin,[q] but to bring sal-
q1Pe 2:24 r1Co 1:7 vation to those who are waiting for him.[r]

Christ's Sacrifice Once for All

10:1 10 The law is only a shadow[s] of the good
sHeb 8:5 tHeb 9:11 things[t] that are coming—not the realities
uHeb 9:23 themselves.[u] For this reason it can never, by the
vHeb 7:19 same sacrifices repeated endlessly year after year,
make perfect[v] those who draw near to worship.
2If it could, would they not have stopped being
offered? For the worshipers would have been
cleansed once for all, and would no longer have
felt guilty for their sins. 3But those sacrifices are
10:3 wHeb 9:7 an annual reminder of sins,[w] 4because it is impos-
10:4 sible for the blood of bulls and goats[x] to take away
xHeb 9:12, 13 sins.
5Therefore, when Christ came into the world,[y]
10:5 he said:

yHeb 1:6 "Sacrifice and offering you did not
z1Pe 2:24 desire,
but a body you prepared for me;[z]

[a] *16* Same Greek word as *covenant;* also in verse 17
[b] *20* Exodus 24:8

Eliza Hewitt studied and became a teacher before a serious illness made her a partial invalid. She turned to hymn writing to express her love for her Lord and her reactions to her illness.

Once My Way Was Dark and Dreary

Once my way was dark and dreary,
For my heart was full of sin,
But the sky is bright and cheery,
Since the fullness of His love
came in.

I can never tell how much I love
Him,
I can never tell His love for me,
For it passeth human measure,
Like a deep, unfathomed sea;
'Tis redeeming love in Christ my
Savior,
In my soul the heav'nly joys begin;
And I live for Jesus only,
Since the fullness of His love
came in.

There is grace for all the lowly,
Grace to keep the trusting soul:
Pow'r to cleanse and make me holy,
Jesus shall my yielded life control.

Let me spread abroad the story,
Other souls to Jesus win;
For the cross is now my glory,
Since the fullness of His love
came in.

—Eliza Edmunds Stites Hewitt (1851–1920)

On Fellowship

HEB 10:25

Followers of Christ are called to persevere in a number of areas, one of the most vital being fellowship with other believers. We are given no background information on why some believers had abandoned fellowship with other believers. Perhaps they feared persecution. Perhaps they were offended by Gentile worshipers. Perhaps they simply didn't recognize the significance and necessity of fellowship for growth in their Christian walk.

The writer stresses the importance of being together as believers in order to offer support and encouragement to each other (Heb 10:25). Believers need help from each other in order to successfully persevere in difficult times (Heb 10:36), in order to continue to do good works (Heb 10:24), and in order to hang on to hope when life gets crazy (Heb 10:23). Moving forward toward "the Day" (Heb 10:25) when Christ returns, we hold on to each other as brothers and sisters in Christ, offering the love, support and assurance each one of us needs.

6 with burnt offerings and sin offerings
you were not pleased.
7 Then I said, 'Here I am—it is written
about me in the scroll[a]—
I have come to do your will,
O God.' "[ab]

8 First he said, "Sacrifices and offerings, burnt
offerings and sin offerings you did not desire, nor
were you pleased with them"[c] (although the law
required them to be made). 9 Then he said, "Here
I am, I have come to do your will."[d] He sets aside
the first to establish the second. 10 And by that will,
we have been made holy[e] through the sacrifice of
the body[f] of Jesus Christ once for all.[g]
11 Day after day every priest stands and performs
his religious duties; again and again he offers the
same sacrifices,[h] which can never take away sins.[i]
12 But when this priest had offered for all time one
sacrifice for sins, he sat down at the right hand of
God. 13 Since that time he waits for his enemies to
be made his footstool,[j] 14 because by one sacrifice
he has made perfect[k] forever those who are being
made holy.
15 The Holy Spirit also testifies[l] to us about this.
First he says:

16 "This is the covenant I will make with
them
after that time, says the Lord.
I will put my laws in their hearts,
and I will write them on their
minds."[bm]

17 Then he adds:

"Their sins and lawless acts
I will remember no more."[cn]

18 And where these have been forgiven, there is no
longer any sacrifice for sin.

A Call to Persevere

19 Therefore, brothers, since we have confidence
to enter the Most Holy Place[o] by the blood of
Jesus, 20 by a new and living way[p] opened for us
through the curtain,[q] that is, his body, 21 and since
we have a great priest[r] over the house of God, 22 let
us draw near to God[s] with a sincere heart in full
assurance of faith, having our hearts sprinkled to
cleanse us from a guilty conscience[t] and having
our bodies washed with pure water. 23 Let us hold
unswervingly to the hope[u] we profess, for he who
promised is faithful.[v] 24 And let us consider how
we may spur one another on toward love and
good deeds. 25 Let us not give up meeting together,[w]
as some are in the habit of doing, but let us
encourage one another[x]—and all the more as you
see the Day approaching.
26 If we deliberately keep on sinning[y] after we
have received the knowledge of the truth, no sacri-

10:7 [a]Jer 36:2 [b]Ps 40:6-8
10:8 [c]ver 5,6; Mk 12:33
10:9 [d]ver 7
10:10 [e]Jn 17:19 [f]Heb 2:14; 1Pe 2:24 [g]Heb 7:27
10:11 [h]Heb 5:1 [i]ver 1,4
10:13 [j]Heb 1:13
10:14 [k]ver 1
10:15 [l]Heb 3:7
10:16 [m]Jer 31:33; Heb 8:10
10:17 [n]Heb 8:12
10:19 [o]Eph 2:18; Heb 9:8,12, 25
10:20 [p]Heb 9:8 [q]Heb 9:3
10:21 [r]Heb 2:17
10:22 [s]Heb 7:19 [t]Eze 36:25; Heb 9:14
10:23 [u]Heb 3:6 [v]1Co 1:9
10:25 [w]Ac 2:42 [x]Heb 3:13
10:26 [y]Nu 15:30; 2Pe 2:20

[a] *7* Psalm 40:6–8 (see Septuagint) [b] *16* Jer. 31:33
[c] *17* Jer. 31:34

fice for sins is left, 27but only a fearful expectation of judgment and of raging fire[z] that will consume the enemies of God. 28Anyone who rejected the law of Moses died without mercy on the testimony of two or three witnesses.[a] 29How much more severely do you think a man deserves to be punished who has trampled the Son of God under foot,[b] who has treated as an unholy thing the blood of the covenant[c] that sanctified him, and who has insulted the Spirit[d] of grace?[e] 30For we know him who said, "It is mine to avenge; I will repay,"[a][f] and again, "The Lord will judge his people."[b][g] 31It is a dreadful thing to fall into the hands of the living God.[h]

32Remember those earlier days after you had received the light,[i] when you stood your ground in a great contest in the face of suffering.[j] 33Sometimes you were publicly exposed to insult and persecution;[k] at other times you stood side by side with those who were so treated.[l] 34You sympathized with those in prison[m] and joyfully accepted the confiscation of your property, because you knew that you yourselves had better and lasting possessions.[n]

35So do not throw away your confidence; it will be richly rewarded. 36You need to persevere[o] so that when you have done the will of God, you will receive what he has promised. 37For in just a very little while,

> "He who is coming[p] will come and will
> not delay.[q]
> 38 But my righteous one[c] will live by
> faith.[r]
> And if he shrinks back,
> I will not be pleased with him."[d]

39But we are not of those who shrink back and are destroyed, but of those who believe and are saved.

By Faith

11 Now faith is being sure of what we hope for and certain of what we do not see.[s] 2This is what the ancients were commended for.[t]

3By faith we understand that the universe was formed at God's command,[u] so that what is seen was not made out of what was visible.

4By faith Abel offered God a better sacrifice than Cain did. By faith he was commended as a righteous man, when God spoke well of his offerings.[v] And by faith he still speaks, even though he is dead.[w]

5By faith Enoch was taken from this life, so that he did not experience death; he could not be found, because God had taken him away.[x] For before he was taken, he was commended as one who pleased God. 6And without faith it is impossible to please God, because anyone who comes to him[y] must believe that he exists and that he rewards those who earnestly seek him.

10:27 [z]Isa 26:11; 2Th 1:7; Heb 9:27
10:28 [a]Dt 17:6,7; Heb 2:2
10:29 [b]Heb 6:6 [c]Mt 26:28 [d]Eph 4:30; Heb 6:4 [e]Heb 2:3
10:30 [f]Dt 32:35; Ro 12:19 [g]Dt 32:36
10:31 [h]Mt 16:16
10:32 [i]Heb 6:4 [j]Php 1:29,30
10:33 [k]1Co 4:9 [l]Php 4:14; 1Th 2:14
10:34 [m]Heb 13:3 [n]Heb 11:16
10:36 [o]Lk 21:19; Heb 12:1
10:37 [p]Mt 11:3 [q]Rev 22:20
10:38 [r]Ro 1:17; Gal 3:11
11:1 [s]Ro 8:24; 2Co 4:18
11:2 [t]ver 4,39
11:3 [u]Ge 1; Jn 1:3; 2Pe 3:5
11:4 [v]Ge 4:4; 1Jn 3:12 [w]Heb 12:24
11:5 [x]Ge 5:21-24
11:6 [y]Heb 7:19

[a] *30* Deut. 32:35 [b] *30* Deut. 32:36; Psalm 135:14
[c] *38* One early manuscript *But the righteous* [d] *38* Hab. 2:3,4

Defining Faith

HEB 11:1

What is faith? Faith is believing in something we *cannot see or prove,* but which we trust to be true. The Christian *faith involves a belief both in* God (Heb 11:6) and in his Son (Heb 12:2). Our faith is instru*mental in our salvation; though our faith itself cannot save us,* it is the conduit through which God's *grace can* (Eph 2:8–9).

In Hebrews 11:1, the writer of Hebrews reveals two distinct dimensions of faith: Faith is a confidence in God's plan and provision for our future ("what we hope for") as well as an expectation that God will fulfill everything he has promised, though we haven't experienced fulfillment yet ("certain of what we do not see").

Heroes of the Faith

HEB 11

In this all-star list of heroes of the faith, two women stand out: Sarah and Rahab (Heb 11:11,31). Both strong women who trusted in God, these spiritual sisters had a profound impact on the nation of Israel. Sarah was barren when God told her husband, Abraham, that he would make her the mother of nations (Ge 17:15–19). By faith they believed, and God's promise was fulfilled when Isaac was born. Both Abraham and Isaac are listed as ancestors of Jesus (Mt 1:2).

Rahab, a prostitute who lived in the city of Jericho, helped the nation of Israel by hiding the men sent to spy out the city (Jos 2:1–14). When Jericho collapsed, Rahab and her family were spared and were embraced by God's people (Jos 6:25). Rahab, though at first a prostitute, was one of the faithful. She, too, appears in the genealogy of Christ (Mt 1:5).

The faithful also include women who received loved ones back from death (Heb 11:35). This includes the widow of Zarephath (1Ki 17:17–23) and the woman of Shunem (2Ki 4:18–37). (See the character sketch for Sarah on page 67, Rahab on page 469, the widow of Zarephath on page 1143 and the woman of Shunem on page 1211.)

7By faith Noah, when warned about things not
yet seen, in holy fear built an ark[z] to save his family.[a] By his faith he condemned the world and
became heir of the righteousness that comes by
faith.
8By faith Abraham, when called to go to a place
he would later receive as his inheritance,[b] obeyed
and went,[c] even though he did not know where
he was going. 9By faith he made his home in the
promised land[d] like a stranger in a foreign country; he lived in tents,[e] as did Isaac and Jacob, who
were heirs with him of the same promise.[f] 10For
he was looking forward to the city[g] with foundations,[h] whose architect and builder is God.
11By faith Abraham, even though he was past
age—and Sarah herself was barren[i]—was enabled
to become a father[j] because he[a] considered him
faithful who had made the promise. 12And so from
this one man, and he as good as dead,[k] came
descendants as numerous as the stars in the sky
and as countless as the sand on the seashore.[l]
13All these people were still living by faith when
they died. They did not receive the things promised;[m] they only saw them and welcomed them
from a distance.[n] And they admitted that they
were aliens and strangers on earth.[o] 14People who
say such things show that they are looking for a
country of their own. 15If they had been thinking
of the country they had left, they would have had
opportunity to return.[p] 16Instead, they were longing for a better country—a heavenly one.[q] Therefore God is not ashamed[r] to be called their God,[s]
for he has prepared a city[t] for them.
17By faith Abraham, when God tested him,
offered Isaac as a sacrifice.[u] He who had received
the promises was about to sacrifice his one and
only son, 18even though God had said to him, "It
is through Isaac that your offspring[b] will be reckoned."[c][v] 19Abraham reasoned that God could raise
the dead,[w] and figuratively speaking, he did
receive Isaac back from death.
20By faith Isaac blessed Jacob and Esau in
regard to their future.[x]
21By faith Jacob, when he was dying, blessed
each of Joseph's sons,[y] and worshiped as he
leaned on the top of his staff.
22By faith Joseph, when his end was near, spoke
about the exodus of the Israelites from Egypt and
gave instructions about his bones.[z]
23By faith Moses' parents hid him for three
months after he was born,[a] because they saw he
was no ordinary child, and they were not afraid
of the king's edict.[b]
24By faith Moses, when he had grown up,
refused to be known as the son of Pharaoh's
daughter.[c] 25He chose to be mistreated[d] along with
the people of God rather than to enjoy the plea-

[a] 11 Or *By faith even Sarah, who was past age, was enabled to bear children because she* [b] 18 Greek *seed*
[c] 18 Gen. 21:12

11:7 [z]Ge 6:13-22 [a]1Pe 3:20
11:8 [b]Ge 12:7 [c]Ge 12:1-4; Ac 7:2-4
11:9 [d]Ac 7:5 [e]Ge 12:8; 18:1,9 [f]Heb 6:17
11:10 [g]Heb 12:22; 13:14 [h]Rev 21:2,14
11:11 [i]Ge 17:17-19; 18:11-14 [j]Ge 21:2
11:12 [k]Ro 4:19 [l]Ge 22:17
11:13 [m]ver 39 [n]Mt 13:17 [o]Ge 23:4; Ps 39:12; 1Pe 1:17
11:15 [p]Ge 24:6-8
11:16 [q]2Ti 4:18 [r]Mk 8:38 [s]Ex 3:6,15 [t]Heb 13:14
11:17 [u]Ge 22:1-10; Jas 2:21
11:18 [v]Ge 21:12; Ro 9:7
11:19 [w]Ro 4:21
11:20 [x]Ge 27:27-29,39,40
11:21 [y]Ge 48:1,8-22
11:22 [z]Ge 50:24,25; Ex 13:19
11:23 [a]Ex 2:2 [b]Ex 1:16,22
11:24 [c]Ex 2:10,11
11:25 [d]ver 37

sures of sin for a short time. 26He regarded disgrace[e] for the sake of Christ as of greater value
than the treasures of Egypt, because he was looking ahead to his reward.[f] 27By faith he left Egypt,[g]
not fearing the king's anger; he persevered
because he saw him who is invisible. 28By faith
he kept the Passover and the sprinkling of blood,
so that the destroyer of the firstborn would not
touch the firstborn of Israel.[h]
29By faith the people passed through the Red
Sea[a] as on dry land; but when the Egyptians tried
to do so, they were drowned.[i]
30By faith the walls of Jericho fell, after the people had marched around them for seven days.[j]
31By faith the prostitute Rahab, because she welcomed the spies, was not killed with those who
were disobedient.[b][k]
32And what more shall I say? I do not have time
to tell about Gideon, Barak,[l] Samson, Jephthah,
David,[m] Samuel[n] and the prophets, 33who through
faith conquered kingdoms,[o] administered justice,
and gained what was promised; who shut the
mouths of lions,[p] 34quenched the fury of the
flames, and escaped the edge of the sword; whose
weakness was turned to strength;[q] and who
became powerful in battle and routed foreign
armies.[r] 35Women received back their dead, raised
to life again.[s] Others were tortured and refused to
be released, so that they might gain a better resurrection. 36Some faced jeers and flogging,[t] while
still others were chained and put in prison.[u]
37They were stoned[c];[v] they were sawed in two;
they were put to death by the sword.[w] They went
about in sheepskins and goatskins,[x] destitute, persecuted and mistreated— 38the world was not
worthy of them. They wandered in deserts and
mountains, and in caves[y] and holes in the ground.
39These were all commended[z] for their faith, yet
none of them received what had been promised.[a]
40God had planned something better for us so that
only together with us would they be made perfect.

God Disciplines His Sons

12 Therefore, since we are surrounded by such
a great cloud of witnesses, let us throw off
everything that hinders and the sin that so easily
entangles, and let us run[b] with perseverance[c] the
race marked out for us. 2Let us fix our eyes on
Jesus, the author and perfecter of our faith, who
for the joy set before him endured the cross,[d]
scorning its shame,[e] and sat down at the right
hand of the throne of God. 3Consider him who
endured such opposition from sinful men, so that
you will not grow weary[f] and lose heart.
4In your struggle against sin, you have not yet
resisted to the point of shedding your blood.[g]
5And you have forgotten that word of encouragement that addresses you as sons:

11:26 [e]Heb 13:13 [f]Heb 10:35
11:27 [g]Ex 12:50,51
11:28 [h]Ex 12:21-23
11:29 [i]Ex 14:21-31
11:30 [j]Jos 6:12-20
11:31 [k]Jos 2:1,9-14; 6:22-25; Jas 2:25
11:32 [l]Jdg 4-5 [m]1Sa 16:1,13 [n]1Sa 1:20
11:33 [o]2Sa 7:11; 8:1-3 [p]Da 6:22
11:34 [q]2Ki 20:7 [r]Jdg 15:8
11:35 [s]1Ki 17:22, 23
11:36 [t]Jer 20:2 [u]Ge 39:20
11:37 [v]2Ch 24:21 [w]1Ki 19:10 [x]2Ki 1:8
11:38 [y]1Ki 18:4
11:39 [z]ver 2,4 [a]ver 13
12:1 [b]1Co 9:24 [c]Heb 10:36
12:2 [d]Php 2:8,9 [e]Heb 13:13
12:3 [f]Gal 6:9
12:4 [g]Heb 10:32-34

A Cloud of Witnesses

HEB 12:1-3

The "great cloud of witnesses" (Heb 12:1) refers to the roll call of the faithful just given in Hebrews 11, from Abel to Samuel and the prophets. These spectators are watching the race of our lives, cheering us on as we actively live out our faith. The historical record we have of their lives—their faith even to death, their perseverance through the most difficult trials, their successful completion of the race—is like a loud shout of encouragement to us as we run our race.

Think of the passion and excitement of a crowd at a large sporting event. That's just a fraction of the power behind us. Imagine Sarah and Rahab clapping wildly. Picture Abraham, Moses and David shouting encouragement. Those who have already won the race are enthusiastically supporting us in our bid for the prize. With desire, discipline and Jesus as our "coach," there's no way we can't win.

[a] 29 That is, Sea of Reeds [b] 31 Or *unbelieving* [c] 37 Some early manuscripts *stoned; they were put to the test;*

Week 48

What Are *You* Looking At?

Have you ever watched a swimmer in a long race? Experienced swimmers have a plan: They know the speed at which they must set their pace. They know that it's not necessarily the amount of energy expended that matters; it's the stroke technique that counts. They focus on the final goal as well as the intermediate goal of the wall at each turn.

So it is with the Christian life: It's a marathon, not a sprint. False starts and breaks in the momentum cause delays. It's not the effort or the quantity of service that counts; it's the attitude of heart and the quality of the relationship that matter. The intermediate victories encourage perseverance, but it's the final victory that we strive for.

What things hinder your race? What should you do about them (Heb 12:1)?

What is necessary in order to participate in the race (Heb 12:1)? How can you acquire it (Ro 5:3-4; Jas 1:2-4)?

Perseverance is gained through suffering, just as a swimmer's strength is gained through the endurance of training (1Co 9:24-27). What painful circumstances in your life have, in retrospect, brought you spiritual growth?

Where should you fix your eyes as you persevere (Heb 12:2)? Why is Jesus a good example for you (Heb 12:2-3)?

Your race has been marked out for you (Heb 12:1). Why should this comfort you (Job 23:10)?

Why is it important to persevere (Heb 10:36)?

Enjoying God THROUGH the Word

Read Matthew 14:22-33 (pages 1606-1607). When this passage is read, a discussion often follows about Peter's lack of faith. But look at the flip side. It took enormous faith for Peter to say, "Jesus! If it's really you, tell me to come out there with you. I'd like to walk on water, too." Would you have had enough faith to step out of the boat onto the water?

Peter's faith is strong as long as he focuses on Jesus. But when he gets out in the wind and waves, concentrating on Jesus is more difficult. When Peter takes his eyes off Jesus, disaster quickly follows. Does your faith seem strong until trouble comes? Perhaps you take your eyes off Jesus and start looking too intently at your situation.

In Numbers 21, the Lord sends poisonous snakes among the Israelites to punish them for their sins. Their cure: Look up at the snake on the pole—a symbol of Christ on the cross. When the disciples doubt that Jesus has risen from the dead, Jesus says, "Look at my hands and my feet. It is I myself!" (Lk 24:39). When you are in difficult circumstances or when you doubt God, look to Jesus.

Enjoying God THROUGH Experience

One day everyone will see Jesus come again (Rev 1:7). Every eye will be on Jesus at that moment. What will go through your mind that day? Look into Jesus' eyes right now. In quiet meditation, focus on him. Letting the Holy Spirit guide you, speak to Jesus as though you were looking directly into his eyes. Listen for his response. Then go forth in faith.

Go to page 2013 for your next weekly study.

"My son, do not make light of the Lord's
discipline,
and do not lose heart when he
rebukes you,
12:6 6 because the Lord disciplines those he
[h]Ps 94:12; loves,[h]
Rev 3:19 [i]Pr 3:11,12 and he punishes everyone he accepts
12:7 as a son."[a][i]
[j]Dt 8:5 7 Endure hardship as discipline; God is treating
you as sons.[j] For what son is not disciplined by
his father? 8 If you are not disciplined (and every-
12:8 [k]1Pe 5:9 one undergoes discipline),[k] then you are illegitimate children and not true sons. 9 Moreover, we
have all had human fathers who disciplined us
and we respected them for it. How much more
12:9 [l]Nu 16:22 should we submit to the Father of our spirits[l] and
[m]Isa 38:16 live![m] 10 Our fathers disciplined us for a little while
as they thought best; but God disciplines us for
12:10 [n]2Pe 1:4 our good, that we may share in his holiness.[n] 11 No
discipline seems pleasant at the time, but painful.
Later on, however, it produces a harvest of righ-
12:11 [o]Isa 32:17; teousness and peace[o] for those who have been
Jas 3:17,18 trained by it.
12:12 12 Therefore, strengthen your feeble arms and
[p]Isa 35:3 weak knees.[p] 13 "Make level paths for your feet,"[b][q]
so that the lame may not be disabled, but rather
12:13 [q]Pr 4:26 [r]Gal 6:1 healed.[r]

Warning Against Refusing God

14 Make every effort to live in peace with all
12:14 [s]Ro 14:19 men[s] and to be holy;[t] without holiness no one will
[t]Ro 6:22 see the Lord.[u] 15 See to it that no one misses the
[u]Mt 5:8 grace of God[v] and that no bitter root grows up to
12:15 cause trouble and defile many. 16 See that no one is
[v]Gal 5:4; sexually immoral, or is godless like Esau, who for
Heb 3:12 a single meal sold his inheritance rights as the
12:16 oldest son.[w] 17 Afterward, as you know, when he
[w]Ge 25:29-34 wanted to inherit this blessing, he was rejected.
12:17 He could bring about no change of mind, though
[x]Ge 27:30-40 he sought the blessing with tears.[x]
18 You have not come to a mountain that can be
touched and that is burning with fire; to darkness,
12:18 gloom and storm;[y] 19 to a trumpet blast[z] or to such
[y]Ex 19:12-22; Dt 4:11 a voice speaking words that those who heard it
12:19 begged that no further word be spoken to them,[a]
[z]Ex 20:18 [a]Ex 20:19; 20 because they could not bear what was com-
Dt 5:5,25 manded: "If even an animal touches the mountain,
it must be stoned."[c][b] 21 The sight was so terrifying
12:20 that Moses said, "I am trembling with fear."[d]
[b]Ex 19:12,13 22 But you have come to Mount Zion, to the
12:22 heavenly Jerusalem,[c] the city[d] of the living God.
[c]Gal 4:26 You have come to thousands upon thousands of
[d]Heb 11:10 angels in joyful assembly, 23 to the church of the
12:23 firstborn, whose names are written in heaven.[e]
[e]Lk 10:20 You have come to God, the judge of all men,[f] to
[f]Ps 94:2 [g]Php 3:12 the spirits of righteous men made perfect,[g] 24 to
Jesus the mediator of a new covenant, and to the

[a] 6 Prov. 3:11,12 [b] 13 Prov. 4:26 [c] 20 Exodus 19:12,13
[d] 21 Deut. 9:19

God's Loving Discipline

HEB 12:7

Have you ever disciplined a child? If you're a parent, you've done it hundreds, maybe thousands, of times. (Some days it may even feel like *millions* of times!) Why do you reprimand your kids? Is it because you enjoy it? Do you like the feeling of power? Do you want to bring your children pain?

Of course not. Parents discipline their children because they love them. They do it because they want their children to learn and grow, because it's their job to protect them, and because discipline teaches children that rules and boundaries are there for their own good.

Our heavenly Father also disciplines his children. When it happens to you (as it does to us all), don't be too surprised. And don't be dismayed. Just remember what it means: You are God's child, and he loves you enough to give you exactly what you need.

Some Practical Concerns

HEB 13:1-8

Before closing his letter, and with a complete change of literary pace, the author quickly addresses several practical concerns. Similar to the way a loving mother might end her letter to a child at college (eat right, dress warmly, study hard), he offers a list of instructions on how to live: Love your fellow Christians like family. Help strangers. Remember prisoners and those who are suffering. Stay faithful in marriage. Don't serve money. Be happy with what you have. Respect and emulate your spiritual leaders.

This advice is as relevant today as it was centuries ago. That's because it is inspired by the teachings and character of Jesus Christ, who is "the same yesterday and today and forever" (Heb 13:8).

sprinkled blood that speaks a better word than the blood of Abel.[h]

25 See to it that you do not refuse him who speaks. If they did not escape when they refused him who warned[i] them on earth, how much less will we, if we turn away from him who warns us from heaven?[j] 26 At that time his voice shook the earth,[k] but now he has promised, "Once more I will shake not only the earth but also the heavens."[a][l] 27 The words "once more" indicate the removing of what can be shaken[m]—that is, created things—so that what cannot be shaken may remain.

28 Therefore, since we are receiving a kingdom that cannot be shaken,[n] let us be thankful, and so worship God acceptably with reverence and awe,[o] 29 for our "God is a consuming fire."[b][p]

Concluding Exhortations

13 Keep on loving each other as brothers.[q] 2 Do not forget to entertain strangers,[r] for by so doing some people have entertained angels without knowing it.[s] 3 Remember those in prison[t] as if you were their fellow prisoners, and those who are mistreated as if you yourselves were suffering.

4 Marriage should be honored by all, and the marriage bed kept pure, for God will judge the adulterer and all the sexually immoral.[u] 5 Keep your lives free from the love of money and be content with what you have,[v] because God has said,

"Never will I leave you;
never will I forsake you."[c][w]

6 So we say with confidence,

"The Lord is my helper; I will not be afraid.
What can man do to me?"[d]

7 Remember your leaders,[x] who spoke the word of God to you. Consider the outcome of their way of life and imitate[y] their faith. 8 Jesus Christ is the same yesterday and today and forever.[z]

9 Do not be carried away by all kinds of strange teachings.[a] It is good for our hearts to be strengthened[b] by grace, not by ceremonial foods,[c] which are of no value to those who eat them. 10 We have an altar from which those who minister at the tabernacle have no right to eat.[d]

11 The high priest carries the blood of animals into the Most Holy Place as a sin offering, but the bodies are burned outside the camp.[e] 12 And so Jesus also suffered outside the city gate[f] to make the people holy through his own blood. 13 Let us, then, go to him outside the camp, bearing the disgrace he bore.[g] 14 For here we do not have an enduring city, but we are looking for the city that is to come.[h]

15 Through Jesus, therefore, let us continually

12:24 [h]Ge 4:10; Heb 11:4
12:25 [i]Heb 8:5; 11:7 [j]Heb 2:2,3
12:26 [k]Ex 19:18 [l]Hag 2:6
12:27 [m]1Co 7:31; 2Pe 3:10
12:28 [n]Da 2:44 [o]Heb 13:15
12:29 [p]Dt 4:24
13:1 [q]Ro 12:10; 1Pe 1:22
13:2 [r]Mt 25:35 [s]Ge 18:1-33
13:3 [t]Mt 25:36; Col 4:18
13:4 [u]1Co 6:9
13:5 [v]Php 4:11 [w]Dt 31:6,8; Jos 1:5
13:7 [x]ver 17,24 [y]Heb 6:12
13:8 [z]Heb 1:12
13:9 [a]Eph 4:14 [b]Col 2:7 [c]Col 2:16
13:10 [d]1Co 9:13; 10:18
13:11 [e]Ex 29:14; Lev 16:27
13:12 [f]Jn 19:17
13:13 [g]Heb 11:26
13:14 [h]Php 3:20; Heb 12:22

[a] *26* Haggai 2:6 [b] *29* Deut. 4:24 [c] *5* Deut. 31:6
[d] *6* Psalm 118:6,7

offer to God a sacrifice[i] of praise—the fruit of lips[j]
that confess his name. 16 And do not forget to do
good and to share with others,[k] for with such sacrifices[l] God is pleased.
17 Obey your leaders and submit to their authority. They keep watch over you[m] as men who must
give an account. Obey them so that their work
will be a joy, not a burden, for that would be of no
advantage to you.
18 Pray for us.[n] We are sure that we have a clear
conscience[o] and desire to live honorably in every
way. 19 I particularly urge you to pray so that I may
be restored to you soon.[p]
20 May the God of peace,[q] who through the
blood of the eternal covenant[r] brought back from
the dead[s] our Lord Jesus, that great Shepherd of
the sheep,[t] 21 equip you with everything good for
doing his will, and may he work in us[u] what is
pleasing to him,[v] through Jesus Christ, to whom
be glory for ever and ever. Amen.[w]

22 Brothers, I urge you to bear with my word of
exhortation, for I have written you only a short
letter.[x]
23 I want you to know that our brother Timothy[y]
has been released. If he arrives soon, I will come
with him to see you.
24 Greet all your leaders[z] and all God's people.
Those from Italy[a] send you their greetings.
25 Grace be with you all.[b]

13:15 [i]1Pe 2:5 [j]Hos 14:2
13:16 [k]Ro 12:13 [l]Php 4:18
13:17 [m]Isa 62:6; Ac 20:28
13:18 [n]1Th 5:25 [o]Ac 23:1
13:19 [p]Phm 22
13:20 [q]Ro 15:33 [r]Isa 55:3; Eze 37:26; Zec 9:11 [s]Ac 2:24 [t]Jn 10:11
13:21 [u]Php 2:13 [v]1Jn 3:22 [w]Ro 11:36
13:22 [x]1Pe 5:12
13:23 [y]Ac 16:1
13:24 [z]ver 7,17 [a]Ac 18:2
13:25 [b]Col 4:18

The devil's most devilish when respectable.

—Elizabeth Barrett Browning (1806-1861)

Our actions matter.

James presents a strikingly direct approach to Christian living in this message to Jewish Christians scattered among the nations. Some of these believers have incorporated worldly habits into their Christian faith. They practice favoritism; they quarrel and boast. They exhibit a lack of patience and misuse their wealth. Recognizing that it is possible to believe all of the right things and still live the wrong way, James urges these believers to put their faith into action through their words and deeds.

With practical guidelines and penetrating insights, James exposes the wrong motives and shaky foundations of these confused Christians. He calls believers to live out their faith day after day, holding to God's promise to provide the wisdom to do so (Jas 1). He states matter of factly that faith without corresponding deeds is "dead" (Jas 2). He urges his readers to avoid self-centeredness and to be careful not to slip into gossip or hurtful words, recognizing that placing their own interests above others' displeases God (Jas 3). He reminds his readers that those who submit to God will come under God's care (Jas 4) and that prayer needs to be a priority in their lives (Jas 5).

According to James, if we truly believe what Jesus says, we will show it by living godly lives. To merely say we have faith is insufficient. Living in faith should pair adoration with action and supplication with service. Such a faith will make a difference to us and to others; how we live and what we do really does matter to God.

Quick Study

Author
Jesus' half-brother James probably wrote the book that bears his name.

Date Written
Two approximate dates are suggested. The first is about A.D. 60. The second, before A.D. 50, would make the book of James most likely the first New Testament book written.

Written From
Possibly Jerusalem, where James was the leader of the church.

Key Passage
James 1:22–25 "Do not merely listen to the word, and so deceive yourselves. Do what it says. Anyone who listens to the word but does not do what it says is like a man who looks at his face in a mirror and, after looking at himself, goes away and immediately forgets what he looks like. But the man who looks intently into the perfect law that gives freedom, and continues to do this, not forgetting what he has heard, but doing it—he will be blessed in what he does."

Outline

James's greetings.
Jas 1:1

Trials and temptations.
Jas 1:2-18

Listening and doing.
Jas 1:19-27

Favoritism not allowed.
Jas 2:1-13

Faith and deeds.
Jas 2:14-26

Taming the tongue.
Jas 3:1-12

Two kinds of wisdom.
Jas 3:13-18

Right behavior.
Jas 4

Warnings to the rich.
Jas 5:1-6

Various exhortations.
Jas 5:7-20

The Women of James

Widows	*The faithful look after them.* Jas 1:27
Sister in need	*True believers will care for her.* Jas 2:15-16
♀ **Rahab**	*Her faith and deeds matched.* Jas 2:25 (page 469)

♀ Denotes a sketch written about this character

Joy During Trials

JAS 1:2

How is it possible to "consider it pure joy" whenever we face trials? Each of us knows what trials are all about, and they are anything but joyous! So why would James place such a steep requirement on believers? First, it is important to note that these "trials" are afflictions, persecutions or sicknesses. These are not troubles that believers bring on themselves due to sin. They are simply the difficulties everyone faces in life. We can begin to find joy in our trials when we accept them for what they are—schools of instruction for our soul. Through this tutelage, James says, we learn perseverance. And through perseverance, we become mature and complete. Difficult times come to everyone; yet we can be glad knowing that, with God's help, precious lessons come from difficult times.

1 James,[a] a servant of God[b] and of the Lord
Jesus Christ,

To the twelve tribes[c] scattered[d] among the
nations:

Greetings.

Trials and Temptations

2 Consider it pure joy, my brothers, whenever
you face trials of many kinds,[e] 3 because you
know that the testing of your faith develops perseverance. 4 Perseverance must finish its work so
that you may be mature and complete, not lacking anything. 5 If any of you lacks wisdom, he
should ask God,[f] who gives generously to all
without finding fault, and it will be given to
him.[g] 6 But when he asks, he must believe and not
doubt,[h] because he who doubts is like a wave of
the sea, blown and tossed by the wind. 7 That
man should not think he will receive anything
from the Lord; 8 he is a double-minded man,[i]
unstable in all he does.

9 The brother in humble circumstances ought to
take pride in his high position. 10 But the one who
is rich should take pride in his low position,
because he will pass away like a wild flower.[j]
11 For the sun rises with scorching heat and withers[k] the plant; its blossom falls and its beauty is
destroyed.[l] In the same way, the rich man will
fade away even while he goes about his business.

12 Blessed is the man who perseveres under trial, because when he has stood the test, he will
receive the crown of life[m] that God has promised
to those who love him.[n]

13 When tempted, no one should say, "God is
tempting me." For God cannot be tempted by evil,
nor does he tempt anyone; 14 but each one is
tempted when, by his own evil desire, he is
dragged away and enticed. 15 Then, after desire
has conceived, it gives birth to sin;[o] and sin,
when it is full-grown, gives birth to death.[p]

16 Don't be deceived,[q] my dear brothers.[r]
17 Every good and perfect gift is from above,[s] coming down from the Father of the heavenly lights,
who does not change[t] like shifting shadows. 18 He
chose to give us birth[u] through the word of truth,
that we might be a kind of firstfruits[v] of all he
created.

Listening and Doing

19 My dear brothers, take note of this: Everyone
should be quick to listen, slow to speak[w] and
slow to become angry, 20 for man's anger does not
bring about the righteous life that God desires.
21 Therefore, get rid of[x] all moral filth and the evil
that is so prevalent and humbly accept the word
planted in you,[y] which can save you.

22 Do not merely listen to the word, and so
deceive yourselves. Do what it says. 23 Anyone
who listens to the word but does not do what it

1:1 [a]Ac 15:13 [b]Tit 1:1 [c]Ac 26:7 [d]Dt 32:26; Jn 7:35; 1Pe 1:1
1:2 [e]Mt 5:12; 1Pe 1:6
1:5 [f]1Ki 3:9,10; Pr 2:3-6 [g]Mt 7:7
1:6 [h]Mk 11:24
1:8 [i]Jas 4:8
1:10 [j]1Co 7:31; 1Pe 1:24
1:11 [k]Ps 102:4,11 [l]Isa 40:6-8
1:12 [m]1Co 9:25 [n]Jas 2:5
1:15 [o]Job 15:35; Ps 7:14 [p]Ro 6:23
1:16 [q]1Co 6:9 [r]ver 19
1:17 [s]Jn 3:27 [t]Nu 23:19; Mal 3:6
1:18 [u]Jn 1:13 [v]Eph 1:12; Rev 14:4
1:19 [w]Pr 10:19
1:21 [x]Eph 4:22 [y]Eph 1:13

Week 49

Struggling With Doubt

Doubt can be an uncertainty that produces hesitation; it can be a questioning that leads to investigation; it can be a lack of confidence that leads to distrust and unbelief. Of these three forms of doubt, only the last deserves rebuke. There is a broad spectrum of doubt: At one end is faith and at the other, unbelief (Mk 11:23; Heb 3:12,19). If not stopped, waves of doubt can build until the breakers crash over your soul, leaving your faith "shipwrecked" (1Ti 1:19). But you need not sink.

Do you ever worry about your needs financially (Mt 6:25-34), physically (Mt 8:23-26) or spiritually (Mt 17:14-21)? Jesus does not condemn you as having no faith; he says you have "little faith" (Mt 8:26; 17:20). What is the cure for this type of doubt (Mk 5:36; 9:24)?

Jesus' disciples are plagued by doubt (Mt 8:26; 14:31; 16:8; 17:20). Yet Jesus patiently teaches them, loves them and cares for them. How is Jesus acting on your behalf when you doubt (Ro 8:34; Heb 4:14-16)? How does this encourage you?

The disciples reach a point, however, when they are repeatedly confronted with truth yet continually doubt (Mk 16:9-13). Jesus then rebukes them for their lack of faith. What phrase in Mark 16:14 indicates their shift toward unbelief? A huge difference exists between mental questioning and hardness of heart.

How did God respond to Paul's unbelief (1Ti 1:13)? How does this encourage you in dealing with your own doubts?

What is the cure for doubt (Lk 17:5; 1Co 2:4-5)?

Enjoying God THROUGH the Word

Read John 20:24-29 (pages 1785-1786). Thomas is not present when Jesus appears after his resurrection to the rest of the disciples. Perhaps quite naturally, Thomas does not believe the disciples' story. He cannot accept the fact that Jesus is alive after he knew that Jesus died. Jesus responds in love and gentleness, "Put your finger here; see my hands. Reach out your hand and put it into my side." What a sweet moment. Jesus offers tangible evidence to Thomas to strengthen and build his faith, then tells him, "Stop doubting and believe."

Thomas responds with a beautiful testimony of Jesus' lordship and divinity: "My Lord and my God!" Doubt flees from Thomas's heart and mind. We so often remember Thomas as "Doubting Thomas," but tradition holds that he went on to preach the gospel in India.

Enjoying God THROUGH Experience

When doubts assail you, examine your heart. Is your doubt simply a mental questioning or testing? If so, don't berate yourself. Seek wisdom (Jas 1:5) and continue to test all things (1Th 5:21). If your doubt arises from hardness of heart, repent and ask God for greater faith. Jesus is the "perfecter of [your] faith" (Heb 12:2). It is only through your trust in him that your faith will be built up (Tit 1:1-3) and that your doubts will finally and fully be put to rest.

Go to page 2024 for your next weekly study.

Look, Study, Act

JAS 1:25

Have you ever read something exciting in God's Word, but then five minutes later you couldn't remember what it was? James tells believers they need to look intently into the ethical demands of the gospel; they need to examine them with deep concentration. When their mind and hearts are focused on God and his Word, believers are better able to live a life of obedience and faithfulness to God.

James here calls the obligations of the gospel "the perfect law that gives freedom." With this description, he paints a complete picture, joining this law (requirements from God) with freedom (liberty from guilt and sin). No longer slaves of sin, believers are now free to become everything God has planned for them to be.

says is like a man who looks at his face in a mirror 24and, after looking at himself, goes away and
immediately forgets what he looks like. 25But the
man who looks intently into the perfect law that
gives freedom,[z] and continues to do this, not forgetting what he has heard, but doing it—he will
be blessed in what he does.[a]

26If anyone considers himself religious and yet
does not keep a tight rein on his tongue,[b] he
deceives himself and his religion is worthless.
27Religion that God our Father accepts as pure
and faultless is this: to look after[c] orphans and
widows[d] in their distress and to keep oneself
from being polluted by the world.[e]

Favoritism Forbidden

2 My brothers, as believers in our glorious[f] Lord
Jesus Christ, don't show favoritism.[g] 2Sup-
pose a man comes into your meeting wearing a
gold ring and fine clothes, and a poor man in
shabby clothes also comes in. 3If you show special attention to the man wearing fine clothes and
say, "Here's a good seat for you," but say to the
poor man, "You stand there" or "Sit on the floor
by my feet," 4have you not discriminated among
yourselves and become judges[h] with evil
thoughts?

5Listen, my dear brothers:[i] Has not God chosen
those who are poor in the eyes of the world[j] to be
rich in faith[k] and to inherit the kingdom he promised those who love him?[l] 6But you have insulted
the poor.[m] Is it not the rich who are exploiting
you? Are they not the ones who are dragging you
into court?[n] 7Are they not the ones who are slan-
dering the noble name of him to whom you
belong?

8If you really keep the royal law found in Scripture, "Love your neighbor as yourself,"[a][o] you are
doing right. 9But if you show favoritism,[p] you sin
and are convicted by the law as lawbreakers.[q]
10For whoever keeps the whole law and yet stumbles at just one point is guilty of breaking all of
it.[r] 11For he who said, "Do not commit adultery,"[b][s]
also said, "Do not murder."[c][t] If you do not commit adultery but do commit murder, you have
become a lawbreaker.

12Speak and act as those who are going to be
judged by the law that gives freedom,[u] 13because
judgment without mercy will be shown to anyone who has not been merciful.[v] Mercy triumphs
over judgment!

Faith and Deeds

14What good is it, my brothers, if a man claims
to have faith but has no deeds?[w] Can such faith
save him? 15Suppose a brother or sister is without clothes and daily food.[x] 16If one of you says to
him, "Go, I wish you well; keep warm and well

1:25 [z]Jas 2:12 [a]Jn 13:17
1:26 [b]Ps 34:13; 1Pe 3:10
1:27 [c]Mt 25:36 [d]Isa 1:17,23 [e]Ro 12:2
2:1 [f]1Co 2:8 [g]Lev 19:15
2:4 [h]Jn 7:24
2:5 [i]Jas 1:16,19 [j]1Co 1:26-28 [k]Lk 12:21 [l]Jas 1:12
2:6 [m]1Co 11:22 [n]Ac 8:3
2:8 [o]Lev 19:18
2:9 [p]ver 1 [q]Dt 1:17
2:10 [r]Mt 5:19; Gal 3:10
2:11 [s]Ex 20:14; Dt 5:18 [t]Ex 20:13; Dt 5:17
2:12 [u]Jas 1:25
2:13 [v]Mt 5:7; 18:32-35
2:14 [w]Mt 7:26; Jas 1:22-25
2:15 [x]Mt 25:35,36

[a] *8* Lev. 19:18 [b] *11* Exodus 20:14; Deut. 5:18 [c] *11* Exodus 20:13; Deut. 5:17

fed," but does nothing about his physical needs, what good is it?[y] 17In the same way, faith by itself, if it is not accompanied by action, is dead.

18But someone will say, "You have faith; I have deeds."

Show me your faith without deeds,[z] and I will show you my faith by what I do.[a] 19You believe that there is one God.[b] Good! Even the demons believe that[c]—and shudder.

20You foolish man, do you want evidence that faith without deeds is useless[a]?[d] 21Was not our ancestor Abraham considered righteous for what he did when he offered his son Isaac on the altar?[e] 22You see that his faith and his actions were working together,[f] and his faith was made complete by what he did.[g] 23And the scripture was fulfilled that says, "Abraham believed God, and it was credited to him as righteousness,"[b][h] and he was called God's friend.[i] 24You see that a person is justified by what he does and not by faith alone.

25In the same way, was not even Rahab the prostitute considered righteous for what she did when she gave lodging to the spies and sent them off in a different direction?[j] 26As the body without the spirit is dead, so faith without deeds is dead.[k]

Taming the Tongue

3 Not many of you should presume to be teachers, my brothers, because you know that we who teach will be judged more strictly. 2We all stumble[l] in many ways. If anyone is never at fault in what he says,[m] he is a perfect man,[n] able to keep his whole body in check.[o]

3When we put bits into the mouths of horses to make them obey us, we can turn the whole animal.[p] 4Or take ships as an example. Although they are so large and are driven by strong winds, they are steered by a very small rudder wherever the pilot wants to go. 5Likewise the tongue is a small part of the body, but it makes great boasts.[q] Consider what a great forest is set on fire by a small spark. 6The tongue also is a fire,[r] a world of evil among the parts of the body. It corrupts the whole person,[s] sets the whole course of his life on fire, and is itself set on fire by hell.

7All kinds of animals, birds, reptiles and creatures of the sea are being tamed and have been tamed by man, 8but no man can tame the tongue. It is a restless evil, full of deadly poison.[t]

9With the tongue we praise our Lord and Father, and with it we curse men, who have been made in God's likeness.[u] 10Out of the same mouth come praise and cursing. My brothers, this should not be. 11Can both fresh water and salt[c] water flow from the same spring? 12My brothers, can a fig tree bear olives, or a grapevine bear

a 20 Some early manuscripts *dead* *b 23* Gen. 15:6
c 11 Greek *bitter* (see also verse 14)

2:16 [y]1Jn 3:17,18
2:18 [z]Ro 3:28 [a]Jas 3:13
2:19 [b]Dt 6:4 [c]Mt 8:29; Lk 4:34
2:20 [d]ver 17,26
2:21 [e]Ge 22:9,12
2:22 [f]Heb 11:17 [g]1Th 1:3
2:23 [h]Ge 15:6; Ro 4:3 [i]2Ch 20:7; Isa 41:8
2:25 [j]Heb 11:31
2:26 [k]ver 17,20
3:2 [l]1Ki 8:46; Jas 2:10 [m]1Pe 3:10 [n]Mt 12:37 [o]Jas 1:26
3:3 [p]Ps 32:9
3:5 [q]Ps 12:3,4
3:6 [r]Pr 16:27 [s]Mt 15:11, 18,19
3:8 [t]Ps 140:3; Ro 3:13
3:9 [u]Ge 1:26,27; 1Co 11:7

Taming the Tongue

JAS 3:1–12

Consider for a moment the greatest compliment you've ever received. Now think of the greatest insult. One brought such joy, the other such pain; yet the tongue achieved both. The tongue has great potential—for good as well as harm. James knows this. He also knows that our human frailty and our tendency to sin make it impossible to completely tame the tongue (Jas 3:8). Read James 3:1–12 again. Underline the tongue's deeds. Note which are commendable and which are not. The key to controlling one's tongue is to oversee the source from which words flow (Jas 3:11). What's inside will come out. If we listen closely to our own words, we're sure to find out just what our inner source is—and that, in turn, will lead to understanding how to tame our unruly, powerful tongue.

figs?[v] Neither can a salt spring produce fresh
water.

Two Kinds of Wisdom

13Who is wise and understanding among you?
Let him show it[w] by his good life, by deeds done
in the humility that comes from wisdom. 14But if
you harbor bitter envy and selfish ambition[x] in
your hearts, do not boast about it or deny the
truth.[y] 15Such "wisdom" does not come down
from heaven[z] but is earthly, unspiritual, of the
devil.[a] 16For where you have envy and selfish
ambition, there you find disorder and every evil
practice.
17But the wisdom that comes from heaven[b] is
first of all pure; then peace-loving, considerate,
submissive, full of mercy[c] and good fruit, impartial and sincere.[d] 18Peacemakers who sow in
peace raise a harvest of righteousness.[e]

Submit Yourselves to God

4 What causes fights and quarrels[f] among you?
Don't they come from your desires that battle[g] within you? 2You want something but don't
get it. You kill and covet, but you cannot have
what you want. You quarrel and fight. You do not
have, because you do not ask God. 3When you
ask, you do not receive,[h] because you ask with
wrong motives,[i] that you may spend what you
get on your pleasures.
4You adulterous people, don't you know that
friendship with the world[j] is hatred toward God?[k]
Anyone who chooses to be a friend of the world
becomes an enemy of God.[l] 5Or do you think
Scripture says without reason that the spirit he
caused to live in us envies intensely?[a] 6But he
gives us more grace. That is why Scripture says:

> "God opposes the proud
> but gives grace to the humble."[bm]

7Submit yourselves, then, to God. Resist the
devil,[n] and he will flee from you. 8Come near to
God and he will come near to you.[o] Wash your
hands,[p] you sinners, and purify your hearts, you
double-minded.[q] 9Grieve, mourn and wail.
Change your laughter to mourning and your joy
to gloom.[r] 10Humble yourselves before the Lord,
and he will lift you up.
11Brothers, do not slander one another.[s] Anyone who speaks against his brother or judges
him[t] speaks against the law and judges it. When
you judge the law, you are not keeping it,[u] but
sitting in judgment on it. 12There is only one
Lawgiver and Judge, the one who is able to save
and destroy.[v] But you—who are you to judge
your neighbor?[w]

3:12 [v]Mt 7:16
3:13 [w]Jas 2:18
3:14 [x]ver 16 [y]Jas 5:19
3:15 [z]Jas 1:17 [a]1Ti 4:1
3:17 [b]1Co 2:6 [c]Lk 6:36 [d]Ro 12:9
3:18 [e]Pr 11:18; Isa 32:17
4:1 [f]Tit 3:9 [g]Ro 7:23
4:3 [h]Ps 18:41 [i]1Jn 3:22; 5:14
4:4 [j]Jas 1:27 [k]1Jn 2:15 [l]Jn 15:19
4:6 [m]Ps 138:6; Pr 3:34; Mt 23:12
4:7 [n]Eph 4:27; 1Pe 5:6-9
4:8 [o]2Ch 15:2 [p]Isa 1:16 [q]Jas 1:8
4:9 [r]Lk 6:25
4:11 [s]1Pe 2:1 [t]Mt 7:1 [u]Jas 1:22
4:12 [v]Mt 10:28 [w]Ro 14:4

[a] 5 Or *that God jealously longs for the spirit that he made to live in us*; or *that the Spirit he caused to live in us longs jealously* [b] 6 Prov. 3:34

Two Wisdoms

JAS 3:13–18

Most people come from one of two mindsets. One group places its trust in the wisdom of human achievement. The other group places its trust in God's wisdom. James describes the first wisdom as "earthly, unspiritual, of the devil" (Jas 3:15). It harbors "envy and selfish ambition" (Jas 3:14). It also leads to disorder and depraved behavior (Jas 3:16). James says the second wisdom "comes from heaven" (Jas 3:17). Read James 3:17–18, underlining the manifestations of this wisdom.

From James's descriptions, it would appear that each type of wisdom can be easily identified. One is disorderly, the other peaceful. One is selfish, the other impartial. However, the wisdom of the world can at times cloak itself in good actions, making it more difficult to distinguish. Only concentration on the things of God will help the believer discern what is true wisdom and what is not.

Lydia

A Conduit of Blessing

Lydia did not turn to the Lord in desperation. She was in the prime of life, and things were going well. She had a successful business in the trade of purple cloth, which at that time was very valuable. Philippi was a city of sophistication, culture and affluence—the perfect place for a sophisticated, cultured and affluent woman. Lydia was at the top of her game and felt no material need that she could not satisfy herself if she put her mind to it. Nevertheless, God opened her heart, and she believed Paul's message.

Lydia was a Gentile who, though not a full convert, had accepted the Jewish faith. Apparently quite devout, she and her friends set aside a time and a place to pray, to study the Scriptures and to pursue God. Apparently, there were not enough Jews in Philippi for a synagogue to be built. In such circumstances, worshipers traditionally chose a spot under the open sky and near running water. Paul found these women at the riverside and introduced them to Christ.

Lydia was the first Christian convert reported in Europe. The first thing she did was to offer her considerable resources—money, servants and her own home—to the apostles in gratitude for Christ's gift to her.

Paul was careful with new converts. He had to be sure their faith was real. Lydia must have glowed with the Spirit of God. She not only convinced Paul of her sincerity, she also convinced him to stay in her home while he was in Philippi. The blessing was multiplied many times over as others came to Christ. Paul discipled Lydia, and he and his missionary companions were guests in her home.

Those who come to Christ with material riches have a unique opportunity to become conduits of God's provision to the church. Paul wrote to Timothy, "Command [those who are rich in this present world] to do good, to be rich in good deeds, and to be generous and willing to share. In this way they will lay up treasure for themselves as a firm foundation for the coming age, so that they may take hold of the life that is truly life" (1Ti 6:18–19).

Lydia
(bending)
Acts 16:12–15,40

Candid SNAPSHOT When [Lydia] and the members of her household were baptized, she invited us to her home. "If you consider me a believer in the Lord," she said, "come and stay at my house." And she persuaded us (Acts 16:15).

Drusilla

A Prodigal Daughter

She was Jewish, a member of the Herod family. Her road had led her away from her Jewish roots, but God was wooing her back. Would she heed his call?

Drusilla was probably a beauty, and powerful men pursued her. By the time she was fifteen, she already had been betrothed to one crown prince, but was married to Azizus, the king of Emesa. Only one year later, Felix, procurator of Judea, seduced her. She left Azizus to join Felix—as his third wife. Drusilla's life might form the script of a bad soap opera.

Drusilla's father, Herod Agrippa I, had been consumed by worms for his accepting the peoples' claim that he was "a god" (Ac 12:22), for persecuting Christians and for killing the apostle James. Her great-uncle Herod Antipas had decapitated John the Baptist, serving his head on a platter to Salome in reward for her sensual dance. Drusilla's great-grandfather Herod the Great tried to kill Jesus shortly after his birth, ordering all boys in Bethlehem two years old and under to be slaughtered. She had quite a family history. Yet the Lord had not given up on her.

She was not yet twenty when Paul appeared before her husband, Felix. She and Felix formed a private audience for Paul. God gave Drusilla the best—the most articulate speaker for her Jewish heritage as well as for the grace of God through Christ. Felix trembled when he heard Paul's words. Drusilla might have tipped the scales for both of them—but she was silent. Tragically, Drusilla and Felix chose to stay in their sin and refused the gift of God.

After two years, Felix was recalled to Rome. Known for his ferocious temper and the prevailing discontent throughout his realm, Felix was brought down when the Jews accused him of bad administration. Felix left Paul in prison to pacify those same Jews.

Heaven had been ready to welcome Drusilla home, but she didn't come. When she walked away, was it her last chance, though she was so young? How God grieved to see her go. How he grieves to see any of us turn our backs on his gift of life! But there comes an end, when the choices made are final, even those made by not choosing.

Oh, Father, soften our hearts to your call.

Drusilla
(*watered by the dew*)
Acts 24:24–27

Candid SNAPSHOT Several days later Felix came with his wife Drusilla, who was a Jewess. He sent for Paul and listened to him as he spoke about faith in Christ Jesus (Acts 24:24).

Boasting About Tomorrow

13 Now listen, you who say, "Today or tomorrow we will go to this or that city, spend a year there, carry on business and make money."[x] 14 Why, you do not even know what will happen tomorrow. What is your life? You are a mist that appears for a little while and then vanishes.[y] 15 Instead, you ought to say, "If it is the Lord's will,[z] we will live and do this or that." 16 As it is, you boast and brag. All such boasting is evil.[a] 17 Anyone, then, who knows the good he ought to do and doesn't do it, sins.[b]

Warning to Rich Oppressors

5 Now listen, you rich people,[c] weep and wail because of the misery that is coming upon you. 2 Your wealth has rotted, and moths have eaten your clothes.[d] 3 Your gold and silver are corroded. Their corrosion will testify against you and eat your flesh like fire. You have hoarded wealth in the last days.[e] 4 Look! The wages you failed to pay the workmen[f] who mowed your fields are crying out against you. The cries[g] of the harvesters have reached the ears of the Lord Almighty.[h] 5 You have lived on earth in luxury and self-indulgence. You have fattened yourselves[i] in the day of slaughter.[a][j] 6 You have condemned and murdered innocent men,[k] who were not opposing you.

Patience in Suffering

7 Be patient, then, brothers, until the Lord's coming. See how the farmer waits for the land to yield its valuable crop and how patient he is for the autumn and spring rains.[l] 8 You too, be patient and stand firm, because the Lord's coming is near.[m] 9 Don't grumble against each other, brothers,[n] or you will be judged. The Judge[o] is standing at the door![p]

10 Brothers, as an example of patience in the face of suffering, take the prophets[q] who spoke in the name of the Lord. 11 As you know, we consider blessed[r] those who have persevered. You have heard of Job's perseverance[s] and have seen what the Lord finally brought about.[t] The Lord is full of compassion and mercy.[u]

12 Above all, my brothers, do not swear—not by heaven or by earth or by anything else. Let your "Yes" be yes, and your "No," no, or you will be condemned.[v]

The Prayer of Faith

13 Is any one of you in trouble? He should pray.[w] Is anyone happy? Let him sing songs of praise.[x] 14 Is any one of you sick? He should call the elders of the church to pray over him and anoint him with oil[y] in the name of the Lord. 15 And the prayer offered in faith will make the sick person

[a] 5 Or *yourselves as in a day of feasting*

4:13 [x]Pr 27:1
4:14 [y]Job 7:7; Ps 102:3
4:15 [z]Ac 18:21
4:16 [a]1Co 5:6
4:17 [b]Lk 12:47; Jn 9:41
5:1 [c]Lk 6:24
5:2 [d]Job 13:28; Mt 6:19,20
5:3 [e]ver 7,8
5:4 [f]Lev 19:13 [g]Dt 24:15 [h]Ro 9:29
5:5 [i]Am 6:1 [j]Jer 12:3; 25:34
5:6 [k]Heb 10:38
5:7 [l]Dt 11:14; Jer 5:24
5:8 [m]Ro 13:11; 1Pe 4:7
5:9 [n]Jas 4:11 [o]1Co 4:5; 1Pe 4:5 [p]Mt 24:33
5:10 [q]Mt 5:12
5:11 [r]Mt 5:10 [s]Job 1:21,22; 2:10 [t]Job 42:10, 12-17 [u]Nu 14:18
5:12 [v]Mt 5:34-37
5:13 [w]Ps 50:15 [x]Col 3:16
5:14 [y]Mk 6:13

Guaranteed Healing

JAS 5:14–15

James encourages believers to pray for the sick (Jas 5:14). *Sick* here has the connotation of being "feeble" in any sense of the word. James is not speaking only about those sick in body but also those frail in mind and spirit. He then makes a bold statement: "The prayer offered in faith will make the sick person well" (Jas 5:15). Is James saying that healing is guaranteed? Yes, the healing James speaks of is guaranteed, for the term he uses for healing means "made whole and forgiven." Spiritual healing is the ultimate result of a "prayer offered in faith." And while God does sometimes choose to heal physically also, spiritual wholeness is the highest desire.

Reading by age four and writing verse by age seven, Frances Ridley Havergal penned these words when she "passed most of the night in praise and renewal of [her] own consecration; and these little couplets formed themselves, and chimed in [her] heart one after another."

Take My Life and Let It Be

Take my life, and let it be
consecrated, Lord, to Thee.
Take my moments and my days; let
them flow in ceaseless praise.
Take my hands, and let them move
at the impulse of Thy love.
Take my feet, and let them be swift
and beautiful for Thee.

Take my voice, and let me sing
always, only, for my King.
Take my lips, and let them be filled
with messages from Thee.
Take my silver and my gold; not a
mite would I withhold.
Take my intellect, and use every
power as Thou shalt choose.

Take my will, and make it Thine;
it shall be no longer mine.
Take my heart, it is Thine own;
it shall be Thy royal throne.
Take my love, my Lord, I pour at
Thy feet its treasure store.
Take myself, and I will be ever, only,
all for Thee.

—Frances Ridley Havergal (1836-1879)

well; the Lord will raise him up. If he has sinned,
he will be forgiven. 16Therefore confess your sins[z]
to each other and pray for each other so that you
may be healed.[a] The prayer of a righteous man is
powerful and effective.[b]

17Elijah was a man just like us.[c] He prayed
earnestly that it would not rain, and it did not
rain on the land for three and a half years.[d]
18Again he prayed, and the heavens gave rain,
and the earth produced its crops.[e]

19My brothers, if one of you should wander
from the truth[f] and someone should bring him
back,[g] 20remember this: Whoever turns a sinner
from the error of his way will save[h] him from
death and cover over a multitude of sins.[i]

5:16 [z]Mt 3:6 [a]1Pe 2:24 [b]Jn 9:31
5:17 [c]Ac 14:15 [d]1Ki 17:1; Lk 4:25
5:18 [e]1Ki 18:41-45
5:19 [f]Jas 3:14 [g]Mt 18:15
5:20 [h]Ro 11:14 [i]1Pe 4:8

1 Peter

Stand strong in your faith.

Christianity was not a popular religion in the Roman Empire under Emperor Nero. Believers faced discrimination, slander, confiscation of property and threats to their lives. These hardships caused some early Christians to wonder if God had abandoned them. Peter's letter brings encouragement to these struggling believers as he offers them grace and hope to counteract their fear and suffering. Though many feel that this is a time for despair, Peter encourages them to rejoice in their sufferings, assured of their eternal life and Christ's return.

Peter's letter becomes a survival manual for all who live in a shattered and hopeless world. Peter promises that trials are only temporary (1Pe 1). He reminds his readers of their royal identity and God's ability to redeem every situation (1Pe 2) and that they are created to be beautiful in appearance, conversation and lifestyle (1Pe 3). Peter affirms that believers can rejoice and even be hospitable to others when they face trying times (1Pe 4). His words are a cause for celebration when he says that God's plan may be painful, but it is never hopeless (1Pe 5).

Persecution, trouble, pain and suffering can rob us of our peace and tear apart our faith. Peter's words urge us to live in the confidence, patience and hope that come to all who place themselves in God's care. God can use difficulties to strengthen our faith if only we will trust him.

Quick Study

Author
The apostle Peter.

Date Written
The early A.D. 60s before Peter was martyred in 67 or 68.

Written From
First Peter 5:13 places the writing in Babylon, either the real Babylon or a symbolic Babylon as is used in the book of Revelation. It could refer to Rome, where Peter spent the latter part of his life.

Key Passage
1 Peter 1:3–4 "Praise be to the God and Father of our Lord Jesus Christ! In his great mercy he has given us new birth into a living hope through the resurrection of Jesus Christ from the dead, and into an inheritance that can never perish, spoil or fade—kept in heaven for you."

Outline

Peter's greetings.
1Pe 1:1-2

Praise God for hope.
1Pe 1:3-12

On being holy.
1Pe 1:13–2:3

Lessons on holy living.
1Pe 2:4–5:11

Final greetings.
1Pe 5:12-14

The Women of 1 Peter

Wives	*Winning unbelieving husbands.* 1Pe 3:1-7
Holy women	*Their beauty derived from their hope in God.* 1Pe 3:5
♀ **Sarah**	*Obeyed Abraham, calling him her master.* 1Pe 3:6 (page 67)
She who is in Babylon	*Sends greetings through Peter.* 1Pe 5:13

♀ *Denotes a sketch written about this character*

1:1 [a]2Pe 1:1 [b]Mt 24:22 **1** Peter, an apostle of Jesus Christ,[a]
[c]Ac 16:7 To God's elect,[b] strangers in the world, scattered
throughout Pontus, Galatia, Cappadocia, Asia and
1:2 Bithynia,[c] [2]who have been chosen according to
[d]Ro 8:29 the foreknowledge[d] of God the Father, through the
[e]2Th 2:13 [f]Heb 10:22; sanctifying work of the Spirit,[e] for obedience to
12:24 Jesus Christ and sprinkling by his blood:[f]

Grace and peace be yours in abundance.

Praise to God for a Living Hope

1:3 [3]Praise be to the God and Father of our Lord
[g]2Co 1:3; Jesus Christ![g] In his great mercy[h] he has given us
Eph 1:3 new birth into a living hope through the resur-
[h]Tit 3:5; Jas 1:18 rection of Jesus Christ from the dead,[i] [4]and into
[i]1Co 15:20 an inheritance that can never perish, spoil or
1:4 fade—kept in heaven for you,[j] [5]who through faith
[j]Col 1:5 are shielded by God's power[k] until the coming of
1:5 the salvation that is ready to be revealed in the
[k]Jn 10:28 last time. [6]In this you greatly rejoice,[l] though now
1:6 for a little while[m] you may have had to suffer grief
[l]Ro 5:2 in all kinds of trials.[n] [7]These have come so that
[m]1Pe 5:10 your faith—of greater worth than gold, which per-
[n]Jas 1:2 ishes even though refined by fire[o]—may be proved
1:7 genuine[p] and may result in praise, glory and hon-
[o]Job 23:10; or when Jesus Christ is revealed.[q] [8]Though you
Ps 66:10; Pr 17:3 have not seen him, you love him; and even
[p]Jas 1:3 though you do not see him now, you believe in
[q]Ro 2:7 him[r] and are filled with an inexpressible and glo-
1:8 rious joy, [9]for you are receiving the goal of your
[r]Jn 20:29 faith, the salvation of your souls.[s]
1:9 [10]Concerning this salvation, the prophets, who
[s]Ro 6:22 spoke[t] of the grace that was to come to you,
1:10 searched intently and with the greatest care,[u]
[t]Mt 26:24 [11]trying to find out the time and circumstances to
[u]Mt 13:17 which the Spirit of Christ[v] in them was pointing
1:11 when he predicted the sufferings of Christ and the
[v]2Pe 1:21 glories that would follow. [12]It was revealed to
them that they were not serving themselves but
you, when they spoke of the things that have now
been told you by those who have preached the
1:12 [w]ver 25 gospel to you[w] by the Holy Spirit sent from heav-
en. Even angels long to look into these things.

Be Holy

1:14 [13]Therefore, prepare your minds for action; be
[x]Ro 12:2 [y]Eph 4:18 self-controlled; set your hope fully on the grace to
be given you when Jesus Christ is revealed. [14]As
1:15 [z]2Co 7:1; obedient children, do not conform[x] to the evil
1Th 4:7 desires you had when you lived in ignorance.[y]
1:16 [15]But just as he who called you is holy, so be holy
[a]Lev 11:44, in all you do;[z] [16]for it is written: "Be holy, because
45 I am holy."[aa]
1:17 [17]Since you call on a Father who judges each
[b]Ac 10:34 [c]Heb 12:28 man's work impartially,[b] live your lives as
strangers here in reverent fear.[c] [18]For you know
1:18 that it was not with perishable things such as sil-
[d]Mt 20:28; 1Co 6:20 ver or gold that you were redeemed[d] from the

Walking in Holiness

1PE 1:15–16

Peter's call to walk in holiness is certainly not new. All the way back in Leviticus (Lev 11:44–45), God called his people to walk in holiness. In fact, Peter is simply quoting this text from the Pentateuch and reminding the people that the call to holiness still speaks to their lives. To *be* holy is to live a life separated and conformed to God and his Son. We are made holy, cleansed and saved by the grace of God through faith in Jesus Christ.

Yet we are also called to be holy in all we *do*. True holiness is not only an inward work, but it is also evidenced by outward action. Peter uses active language in describing holiness, using words like *prepare* (1Pe 1:13), *self-controlled* (1Pe 1:13) and *obedient* (1Pe 2:14). We need to strike a critical balance between what we are and what we do.

[a] *16* Lev. 11:44,45; 19:2

Week 50

A Living Hope

She is dying of cancer and the treatment options are exhausted. "I've given up hoping to get well," she says, "but my hope in the Lord will never die." Her hope to get well has been a wish, a desire, but her hope in the Lord is a firm conviction. God knows you cannot live without hope. He's not in the business of merely fulfilling wishes; he is in the business of giving "a living hope." Even facing death, Christians, though at times discouraged, have a living, eternal hope.

Where does this hope come from (Ps 62:5)? *Just as faith is a gift of God, hope is as well. It is God's sweet kiss of mercy when you are born into his family (1Pe 1:3–4).*

What is this hope based on (Ps 130:7)? *God's unfailing love and your full redemption are a sure thing. God himself guards his gift for you in heaven (1Pe 1:4).*

When trials come and doubts sweep over you, on what does your faith rest (Tit 1:2)? *Your hope is based on God's faithfulness, not on your own ability to stand.*

When you need something tangible, where can you turn (Ro 15:4)? *The Bible is God's book of promises to you, promises that are all met in Jesus (2Co 1:20).*

What are the benefits of this "living hope" (Ps 25:3; 33:18)? What does hope produce (Col 1:5)?

Enjoying God THROUGH the Word

Read Hebrews 6:13–20 (page 1997). The account of Abraham is a wonderful example to us of God's kept promises. Like Abraham, we may have to wait, which is difficult, but we can be sure we will receive what is promised (Heb 6:15). We may have to wait longer than we expect; the promise may not even be fulfilled during our lifetimes (Heb 11:39). But God *will* honor his promises. God's promises fulfilled in the past assure us that he will fulfill those in the future.

Your hope in Christ is your "anchor" (Heb 6:19–20). Hope allows God's grace and kindness to come to you (Ps 33:22). It is your link to strength and courage (Ps 31:24). But if you do not put your anchor—hope—in Jesus, if you choose to flounder in the turbulent sea of despair, there is no other hope for your rescue. "But let all who take refuge in [God] be glad; let them ever sing for joy" (Ps 5:11).

Enjoying God THROUGH Experience

If you are experiencing a lack of hope, believe that God "will make the Valley of Achor [Trouble] a door of hope" (Hos 2:15). God will take your trouble and turn it into an entry for hope and a doorway to him.

In a time of prayer, picture yourself handing your worries and despair to Jesus. See yourself walking through a doorway toward Jesus. Allow the Holy Spirit to fill you with a "living hope." Take refuge in Jesus, your guide into the safe harbor of God's arms. His love and faithfulness will never fail. "Because of the LORD's great love we are not consumed, for his compassions never fail. They are new every morning; great is your faithfulness. The LORD is good to those whose hope is in him, to the one who seeks him" (La 3:22–23,25).

Go to page 2063 for your next weekly study.

empty way of life handed down to you from your
1:19 forefathers, 19 but with the precious blood of
[e]Jn 1:29 Christ, a lamb[e] without blemish or defect.[f] 20 He
[f]Ex 12:5 was chosen before the creation of the world,[g] but
1:20 was revealed in these last times[h] for your sake.
[g]Eph 1:4 21 Through him you believe in God,[i] who raised
[h]Heb 9:26 him from the dead and glorified him, and so your
1:21 faith and hope are in God.
[i]Ro 4:24 22 Now that you have purified[j] yourselves by
1:22 obeying the truth so that you have sincere love for
[j]Jas 4:8 your brothers, love one another deeply,[k] from the
[k]Jn 13:34; heart.[a] 23 For you have been born again,[l] not of
Heb 13:1 perishable seed, but of imperishable, through the
1:23 living and enduring word of God.[m] 24 For,
[l]Jn 1:13
[m]Heb 4:12

> "All men are like grass,
> and all their glory is like the flowers
> of the field;
> the grass withers and the flowers fall,
> 25 but the word of the Lord stands
> forever."[b][n]

1:25
[n]Isa 40:6-8
2:1 And this is the word that was preached to you.
[o]Eph 4:22 **2** Therefore, rid yourselves[o] of all malice and all
[p]Jas 4:11 deceit, hypocrisy, envy, and slander[p] of every
kind. 2 Like newborn babies, crave pure spiritual
2:2 milk,[q] so that by it you may grow up[r] in your sal-
[q]1Co 3:2 vation, 3 now that you have tasted that the Lord is
[r]Eph 4:15,16 good.[s]
2:3
[s]Heb 6:5

The Living Stone and a Chosen People

2:4 4 As you come to him, the living Stone[t]—reject-
[t]ver 7 ed by men but chosen by God and precious to
him— 5 you also, like living stones, are being
2:5 built[u] into a spiritual house[v] to be a holy priest-
[u]1Co 3:9 hood,[w] offering spiritual sacrifices acceptable to
[v]1Ti 3:15 God through Jesus Christ.[x] 6 For in Scripture it
[w]Isa 61:6 says:
[x]Php 4:18;
Heb 13:15

> "See, I lay a stone in Zion,
> a chosen and precious cornerstone,[y]
> and the one who trusts in him
> will never be put to shame."[c][z]

2:6
[y]Eph 2:20
[z]Isa 28:16
7 Now to you who believe, this stone is precious.
2:7 But to those who do not believe,[a]
[a]2Co 2:16
[b]Ps 118:22

> "The stone the builders rejected
> has become the capstone,"[d][e][b]

8 and,

> "A stone that causes men to stumble
> and a rock that makes them fall."[f][c]

2:8
[c]Isa 8:14;
1Co 1:23
[d]Ro 9:22 They stumble because they disobey the message—
which is also what they were destined for.[d]
2:9 9 But you are a chosen people,[e] a royal priest-
[e]Dt 10:15 hood, a holy nation,[f] a people belonging to God,
[f]Isa 62:12 that you may declare the praises of him who
called you out of darkness into his wonderful

[a] *22* Some early manuscripts *from a pure heart*
[b] *25* Isaiah 40:6–8 [c] *6* Isaiah 28:16 [d] *7* Or *cornerstone*
[e] *7* Psalm 118:22 [f] *8* Isaiah 8:14

A Royal Priesthood

1PE 1:20; 2:9

Look closely at the language Peter uses as he points to both Jesus Christ and to us. Jesus Christ is God's chosen One (1Pe 1:20). Before the world was spoken into existence, the Father chose Jesus, his only Son, as the high priest who would offer himself as the ultimate sacrifice for the sins of lost human beings (1Pe 1:19). Now look at what Peter calls those who follow Jesus: "You are a chosen people, a royal priesthood" (1Pe 2:9). Jesus is chosen, and we are chosen. Jesus is chosen as the high priest over the house of God (Heb 4:14), and we are chosen to be God's royal priesthood. Amazing!

In this identity-deficient generation, God tells us who we are: chosen priests who make up a holy nation of people who belong to God. You are his chosen child, his beloved, a priest with access to the very throne of grace.

light.[g] 10 Once you were not a people, but now you
are the people of God;[h] once you had not received
mercy, but now you have received mercy.
11 Dear friends, I urge you, as aliens and
strangers in the world, to abstain from sinful
desires,[i] which war against your soul.[j] 12 Live such
good lives among the pagans that, though they
accuse you of doing wrong, they may see your
good deeds[k] and glorify God[l] on the day he
visits us.

Submission to Rulers and Masters

13 Submit yourselves for the Lord's sake to every
authority[m] instituted among men: whether to the
king, as the supreme authority, 14 or to governors,
who are sent by him to punish those who do
wrong[n] and to commend those who do right.[o]
15 For it is God's will[p] that by doing good you
should silence the ignorant talk of foolish men.[q]
16 Live as free men,[r] but do not use your freedom
as a cover-up for evil; live as servants of God.[s]
17 Show proper respect to everyone: Love the
brotherhood of believers,[t] fear God, honor the
king.[u]
18 Slaves, submit yourselves to your masters
with all respect,[v] not only to those who are good
and considerate,[w] but also to those who are harsh.
19 For it is commendable if a man bears up under
the pain of unjust suffering because he is conscious of God.[x] 20 But how is it to your credit if you
receive a beating for doing wrong and endure it?
But if you suffer for doing good and you endure it,
this is commendable before God.[y] 21 To this[z] you
were called, because Christ suffered for you, leaving you an example,[a] that you should follow in
his steps.

22 "He committed no sin,
and no deceit was found in his
mouth."[a][b]

23 When they hurled their insults at him, he did
not retaliate; when he suffered, he made no
threats.[c] Instead, he entrusted himself[d] to him
who judges justly. 24 He himself bore our sins[e] in
his body on the tree, so that we might die to sins[f]
and live for righteousness; by his wounds you
have been healed.[g] 25 For you were like sheep
going astray,[h] but now you have returned to the
Shepherd[i] and Overseer of your souls.

Wives and Husbands

3 Wives, in the same way be submissive[j] to your
husbands[k] so that, if any of them do not
believe the word, they may be won over[l] without
words by the behavior of their wives, 2 when they
see the purity and reverence of your lives. 3 Your
beauty should not come from outward adornment, such as braided hair and the wearing of
gold jewelry and fine clothes.[m] 4 Instead, it should

[a] *22* Isaiah 53:9

2:9 [g]Ac 26:18
2:10 [h]Hos 1:9,10
2:11 [i]Gal 5:16 [j]Jas 4:1
2:12 [k]Php 2:15; 1Pe 3:16 [l]Mt 5:16; 9:8
2:13 [m]Ro 13:1
2:14 [n]Ro 13:4 [o]Ro 13:3
2:15 [p]1Pe 3:17 [q]ver 12
2:16 [r]Jn 8:32 [s]Ro 6:22
2:17 [t]Ro 12:10 [u]Ro 13:7
2:18 [v]Eph 6:5 [w]Jas 3:17
2:19 [x]1Pe 3:14,17
2:20 [y]1Pe 3:17
2:21 [z]Ac 14:22 [a]Mt 16:24
2:22 [b]Isa 53:9
2:23 [c]Isa 53:7 [d]Lk 23:46
2:24 [e]Heb 9:28 [f]Ro 6:2 [g]Isa 53:5; Heb 12:13; Jas 5:16
2:25 [h]Isa 53:6 [i]Jn 10:11
3:1 [j]1Pe 2:18 [k]Eph 5:22 [l]1Co 7:16; 9:19
3:3 [m]Isa 3:18-23; 1Ti 2:9

If faith produce no works,
I see
That faith is not *a living tree.*
Thus faith *and works together*
grow;
No *separate life they e'er can*
know:
They're soul and body, hand
and heart:
What God hath joined, let no
man part.

***—Hannah More** (1745–1833)*

3:4 be that of your inner self,[n] the unfading beauty of
[n]Ro 7:22 a gentle and quiet spirit, which is of great worth
in God's sight. 5 For this is the way the holy
3:5 women of the past who put their hope in God[o]
[o]1Ti 5:5 used to make themselves beautiful. They were
3:6 submissive to their own husbands, 6 like Sarah,
[p]Ge 18:12 who obeyed Abraham and called him her master.[p]
You are her daughters if you do what is right and
3:7 do not give way to fear.
[q]Eph 5:25-33 7 Husbands,[q] in the same way be considerate as
you live with your wives, and treat them with
respect as the weaker partner and as heirs with
you of the gracious gift of life, so that nothing will
hinder your prayers.

Suffering for Doing Good

3:8 8 Finally, all of you, live in harmony with one
[r]Ro 12:10 another; be sympathetic, love as brothers,[r] be
[s]1Pe 5:5 compassionate and humble.[s] 9 Do not repay evil
3:9 with evil[t] or insult with insult,[u] but with blessing,
[t]Ro 12:17 [u]1Pe 2:23 because to this[v] you were called so that you may
[v]1Pe 2:21 [w]Heb 6:14 inherit a blessing.[w] 10 For,

> "Whoever would love life
> and see good days
> must keep his tongue from evil
> and his lips from deceitful speech.
> 11 He must turn from evil and do good;
> he must seek peace and pursue it.
> 12 For the eyes of the Lord are on the righteous
> 3:12 and his ears are attentive to their
> [x]Ps 34:12-16 prayer,
> 3:13 but the face of the Lord is against those
> [y]Pr 16:7 who do evil."[a][x]

3:14 13 Who is going to harm you if you are eager to
[z]1Pe 2:19, 20; 4:15,16 do good?[y] 14 But even if you should suffer for what
[a]Isa 8:12,13 is right, you are blessed.[z] "Do not fear what they
3:15 fear[b]; do not be frightened."[c][a] 15 But in your hearts
[b]Col 4:6 set apart Christ as Lord. Always be prepared to
3:16 give an answer[b] to everyone who asks you to give
[c]Heb 13:18 the reason for the hope that you have. But do this
[d]1Pe 2:12,15 with gentleness and respect, 16 keeping a clear con-
3:17 science,[c] so that those who speak maliciously
[e]1Pe 2:15 against your good behavior in Christ may be
[f]1Pe 2:20 ashamed of their slander.[d] 17 It is better, if it is
3:18 God's will,[e] to suffer for doing good[f] than for
[g]1Pe 2:21 doing evil. 18 For Christ died for sins[g] once for all,
[h]Col 1:22; 1Pe 4:1 the righteous for the unrighteous, to bring you to
[i]1Pe 4:6 God. He was put to death in the body[h] but made
3:19 alive by the Spirit,[i] 19 through whom[d] also he went
[j]1Pe 4:6 and preached to the spirits in prison[j] 20 who dis-
3:20 obeyed long ago when God waited patiently in the
[k]Ge 6:3,5, days of Noah while the ark was being built.[k] In it
13,14 only a few people, eight in all, were saved[l]
[l]Heb 11:7 through water, 21 and this water symbolizes bap-
3:21 tism that now saves you[m] also—not the removal
[m]Tit 3:5

[a] *12* Psalm 34:12–16 [b] *14* Or *not fear their threats*
[c] *14* Isaiah 8:12 [d] *18,19* Or *alive in the spirit,* [19]*through which*

A Deep Intimacy

1PE 3:1–7

Many people struggle with Scripture passages regarding women and their role in marriage. To some, these passages are countercultural. To others, they are offensive. To still others, they bring comfort by identifying the unique roles and relationships of men and women.

God has a plan for deep intimacy in husband-wife relationships. Each spouse has a part in fulfilling God's plan, working together in an inseparable partnership. When we look at Peter's teaching as well as the exhortations of the apostle Paul (Eph 5:22; see the note on page 1935), we find a divine model in this two-way relationship.

Submission is something that runs counter to our natural tendencies; however, it is an intrinsic part of the Christian life of servanthood, for both men and women (Mk 9:35; 1Co 16:15–16; Eph 5:21). Wives are called to have a submissive spirit toward their husbands even as they do toward God. At the same time, husbands are to have a considerate spirit toward their wives and serve them even as Christ served the church, in service and in humility.

The End

1PE 4:7

Peter has a crystal clear sense that Jesus could return at any time. Peter wrote this letter over 1,900 years ago. And Jesus still hasn't returned. Was he wrong? No! He was absolutely right. In his day, as in ours, the return of Jesus is at hand. The old covenant has been fulfilled, and the new covenant is in place—God is in his last stage of dealing with his people (see the note on 1Jn 2:18, page 2039). Peter also reminds us that our sense of time is very different from God's (2Pe 3:8).

Peter's concern is not that Christians begin charting fanciful time lines to figure out when Jesus will return. Rather, he wishes every follower of Christ to live in daily readiness to meet Jesus. The questions in Peter's day are the same questions we ask today: *If Jesus would return today, would I be ready to meet him? If Jesus does not return this day, week, year or decade, will I be ready to live for him tomorrow?*

of dirt from the body but the pledge[a] of a good
conscience toward God. It saves you by the resurrection of Jesus Christ,[n] 22who has gone into heav-
en and is at God's right hand[o]—with angels,
authorities and powers in submission to him.[p]

Living for God

4 Therefore, since Christ suffered in his body,
arm yourselves also with the same attitude,
because he who has suffered in his body is done
with sin. 2As a result, he does not live the rest of
his earthly life for evil human desires,[q] but rather
for the will of God. 3For you have spent enough
time in the past[r] doing what pagans choose to
do—living in debauchery, lust, drunkenness,
orgies, carousing and detestable idolatry. 4They
think it strange that you do not plunge with them
into the same flood of dissipation, and they heap
abuse on you.[s] 5But they will have to give account
to him who is ready to judge the living and the
dead.[t] 6For this is the reason the gospel was
preached even to those who are now dead,[u] so
that they might be judged according to men in
regard to the body, but live according to God in
regard to the spirit.

7The end of all things is near.[v] Therefore be
clear minded and self-controlled so that you can
pray. 8Above all, love each other deeply,[w] because
love covers over a multitude of sins.[x] 9Offer hospitality to one another without grumbling.[y] 10Each
one should use whatever gift he has received to
serve others,[z] faithfully[a] administering God's
grace in its various forms. 11If anyone speaks, he
should do it as one speaking the very words of
God. If anyone serves, he should do it with the
strength God provides,[b] so that in all things God
may be praised[c] through Jesus Christ. To him be
the glory and the power for ever and ever. Amen.

Suffering for Being a Christian

12Dear friends, do not be surprised at the painful
trial you are suffering,[d] as though something
strange were happening to you. 13But rejoice that
you participate in the sufferings of Christ, so that
you may be overjoyed when his glory is revealed.[e]
14If you are insulted because of the name of Christ,
you are blessed,[f] for the Spirit of glory and of God
rests on you. 15If you suffer, it should not be as a
murderer or thief or any other kind of criminal, or
even as a meddler. 16However, if you suffer as a
Christian, do not be ashamed, but praise God that
you bear that name.[g] 17For it is time for judgment
to begin with the family of God;[h] and if it begins
with us, what will the outcome be for those who
do not obey the gospel of God?[i] 18And,

> "If it is hard for the righteous to be saved,
> what will become of the ungodly and
> the sinner?"[b][j]

3:21 [n]1Pe 1:3
3:22 [o]Mk 16:19 [p]Ro 8:38
4:2 [q]Ro 6:2
4:3 [r]Eph 2:2
4:4 [s]1Pe 3:16
4:5 [t]Ac 10:42; 2Ti 4:1
4:6 [u]1Pe 3:19
4:7 [v]Ro 13:11
4:8 [w]1Pe 1:22 [x]Pr 10:12
4:9 [y]Php 2:14
4:10 [z]Ro 12:6,7 [a]1Co 4:2
4:11 [b]Eph 6:10 [c]1Co 10:31
4:12 [d]1Pe 1:6,7
4:13 [e]Ro 8:17
4:14 [f]Mt 5:11
4:16 [g]Ac 5:41
4:17 [h]Jer 25:29 [i]2Th 1:8
4:18 [j]Pr 11:31; Lk 23:31

[a] 21 Or *response* [b] 18 Prov. 11:31

19 So then, those who suffer according to God's
will should commit themselves to their faithful
Creator and continue to do good.

To Elders and Young Men

5 To the elders among you, I appeal as a fellow
elder,[k] a witness[l] of Christ's sufferings and one
who also will share in the glory to be revealed:[m]
2 Be shepherds of God's flock[n] that is under your
care, serving as overseers—not because you must,
but because you are willing, as God wants you to
be; not greedy for money,[o] but eager to serve; 3 not
lording it over[p] those entrusted to you, but being
examples[q] to the flock. 4 And when the Chief Shepherd appears, you will receive the crown of glory[r]
that will never fade away.
5 Young men, in the same way be submissive[s] to
those who are older. All of you, clothe yourselves
with humility toward one another, because,

"God opposes the proud
but gives grace to the humble."[a][t]

6 Humble yourselves, therefore, under God's
mighty hand, that he may lift you up in due time.[u]
7 Cast all your anxiety on him[v] because he cares
for you.[w]
8 Be self-controlled and alert. Your enemy the
devil prowls around[x] like a roaring lion looking
for someone to devour. 9 Resist him,[y] standing firm
in the faith,[z] because you know that your brothers
throughout the world are undergoing the same
kind of sufferings.[a]
10 And the God of all grace, who called you to
his eternal glory[b] in Christ, after you have suffered
a little while, will himself restore you and make
you strong,[c] firm and steadfast. 11 To him be the
power for ever and ever. Amen.[d]

Final Greetings

12 With the help of Silas,[b][e] whom I regard as a
faithful brother, I have written to you briefly,[f]
encouraging you and testifying that this is the true
grace of God. Stand fast in it.
13 She who is in Babylon, chosen together with
you, sends you her greetings, and so does my son
Mark.[g] 14 Greet one another with a kiss of love.[h]
Peace[i] to all of you who are in Christ.

5:1 [k]Ac 11:30 [l]Lk 24:48 [m]1Pe 1:5,7; Rev 1:9
5:2 [n]Jn 21:16 [o]1Ti 3:3
5:3 [p]Eze 34:4 [q]Php 3:17
5:4 [r]1Co 9:25
5:5 [s]Eph 5:21 [t]Pr 3:34; Jas 4:6
5:6 [u]Jas 4:10
5:7 [v]Ps 37:5; Mt 6:25 [w]Heb 13:5
5:8 [x]Job 1:7
5:9 [y]Jas 4:7 [z]Col 2:5 [a]Ac 14:22
5:10 [b]2Co 4:17 [c]2Th 2:17
5:11 [d]Ro 11:36
5:12 [e]2Co 1:19 [f]Heb 13:22
5:13 [g]Ac 12:12
5:14 [h]Ro 16:16 [i]Eph 6:23

Be Alert!

1PE 5:8–9

The greatest tactic a lion has is surprise. Once its prey realizes there is a lion in the thicket, there is a good chance the lion will go hungry that night. Peter posts a warning sign right in front of every follower of Christ. *There is a lion in the thicket!* His warning resounds throughout history. Satan is still alive and active. His tactics have not changed. His intentions are still as evil and destructive as they have ever been. That's the bad news.

Here comes the good news. We have power to resist. We can stand strong against the enemy and be victorious (see the note on 1Co 10:13, page 1888). James puts it this way: "Submit yourselves, then, to God. Resist the devil, and he will flee from you" (Jas 4:7). John says it like this: "The one who is in you is greater than the one who is in the world" (1Jn 4:4). There is a battle at hand—no question! But there is power for victory in Jesus Christ.

[a] 5 Prov. 3:34 [b] 12 Greek *Silvanus,* a variant of *Silas*

2 Peter

Hold on to the truth.

False teachers, promoting moral compromise and doctrinal errors, infiltrate the Christian community and dupe the believers into following their enticing words. Peter writes this letter to expose the dangers and the destructiveness of their teachings. He shares some practical guidelines for detecting false teachers and their doctrines. Encouraging the believers to stand firm in their faith, Peter reminds them of their purpose for the present and of their hope for the future.

Peter quickly comes to the point in this guide to godly living. A strong Christian character is developed as believers heed Peter's exhortation to keep following what they already know about God (2Pe 1). Peter describes the destruction awaiting false teachers (2Pe 2). Last of all, Peter calls the believers to live holy lives while focusing on the Lord's return (2Pe 3).

Our society is increasingly lawless, complacent and godless—much like the society in Peter's day. Peter reminds us that as Christians we must persevere in our faith in order to combat the influences of the world around us. Indifference and shortsightedness will only bring about a lazy faith. Peter's second letter urges us to be salt and light to a dying and darkened world by actively living godly lives as we confidently wait for Christ's return.

Quick Study

Author
The apostle Peter.

Date Written
Toward the end of Peter's life, probably between A.D. 65 and 68.

Written From
Unknown. Possibly Rome.

Key Passage
2 Peter 1:3–4 "His divine power has given us everything we need for life and godliness through our knowledge of him who called us by his own glory and goodness. Through these he has given us his very great and precious promises, so that through them you may participate in the divine nature and escape the corruption in the world caused by evil desires."

Outline

Peter's greetings.
2Pe 1:1–2

Divine confidence.
2Pe 1:3–21

False teachers.
2Pe 2

The last days.
2Pe 3

The Women of 2 Peter

No women are mentioned in the book of 2 Peter.

Healthy Growth

2PE 1:3–9

Peter gives a clear warning in 2 Peter 1:9. If you lack "these qualities" (2Pe 1:8), it will lead to spiritual nearsightedness and even blindness. This problem is so serious that Peter declares that anyone who does not have these qualities will become so darkened in their spirit that they will forget the forgiveness of sins and cleansing that comes through Jesus alone.

Peter is pointing to some of the basic building blocks of spiritual maturity. He is giving a DNA code for the healthy Christian life. Together, these qualities make believers effective in their spiritual lives and help them grow deep in their understanding of Jesus and life in his name. Look closely at these core attributes of a healthy follower of Christ; then examine your life for evidence of them: faith, goodness, knowledge, self-control, perseverance, godliness, brotherly kindness and love.

1 Simon Peter, a servant[a] and apostle of Jesus Christ,[b]

To those who through the righteousness[c] of our God and Savior Jesus Christ[d] have received a faith as precious as ours:

2 Grace and peace be yours in abundance through the knowledge of God and of Jesus our Lord.[e]

Making One's Calling and Election Sure

3 His divine power[f] has given us everything we need for life and godliness through our knowledge of him who called us[g] by his own glory and goodness. 4 Through these he has given us his very great and precious promises,[h] so that through them you may participate in the divine nature[i] and escape the corruption in the world caused by evil desires.[j]

5 For this very reason, make every effort to add to your faith goodness; and to goodness, knowledge;[k] 6 and to knowledge, self-control;[l] and to self-control, perseverance; and to perseverance, godliness;[m] 7 and to godliness, brotherly kindness; and to brotherly kindness, love.[n] 8 For if you possess these qualities in increasing measure, they will keep you from being ineffective and unproductive[o] in your knowledge of our Lord Jesus Christ. 9 But if anyone does not have them, he is nearsighted and blind,[p] and has forgotten that he has been cleansed from his past sins.[q]

10 Therefore, my brothers, be all the more eager to make your calling and election sure. For if you do these things, you will never fall,[r] 11 and you will receive a rich welcome into the eternal kingdom of our Lord and Savior Jesus Christ.

Prophecy of Scripture

12 So I will always remind you of these things,[s] even though you know them and are firmly established in the truth you now have. 13 I think it is right to refresh your memory as long as I live in the tent of this body,[t] 14 because I know that I will soon put it aside,[u] as our Lord Jesus Christ has made clear to me.[v] 15 And I will make every effort to see that after my departure[w] you will always be able to remember these things.

16 We did not follow cleverly invented stories when we told you about the power and coming of our Lord Jesus Christ, but we were eyewitnesses of his majesty.[x] 17 For he received honor and glory from God the Father when the voice came to him from the Majestic Glory, saying, "This is my Son, whom I love; with him I am well pleased."[a][y] 18 We ourselves heard this voice that came from heaven when we were with him on the sacred mountain.[z]

19 And we have the word of the prophets made more certain, and you will do well to pay attention to it, as to a light[a] shining in a dark place,

1:1 [a]Ro 1:1 [b]1Pe 1:1 [c]Ro 3:21-26 [d]Tit 2:13
1:2 [e]Php 3:8
1:3 [f]1Pe 1:5 [g]1Th 2:12
1:4 [h]2Co 7:1 [i]Eph 4:24; Heb 12:10; 1Jn 3:2 [j]2Pe 2:18-20
1:5 [k]Col 2:3
1:6 [l]Ac 24:25 [m]ver 3
1:7 [n]1Th 3:12
1:8 [o]Jn 15:2; Tit 3:14
1:9 [p]1Jn 2:11 [q]Eph 5:26
1:10 [r]2Pe 3:17
1:12 [s]Php 3:1; 1Jn 2:21
1:13 [t]2Co 5:1,4
1:14 [u]2Ti 4:6 [v]Jn 21:18,19
1:15 [w]Lk 9:31
1:16 [x]Mt 17:1-8
1:17 [y]Mt 3:17
1:18 [z]Mt 17:6
1:19 [a]Ps 119:105

[a] *17* Matt. 17:5; Mark 9:7; Luke 9:35

1:19 until the day dawns and the morning star[b] rises
[b]Rev 22:16 in your hearts. [20]Above all, you must understand
that no prophecy of Scripture came about by the
prophet's own interpretation. [21]For prophecy nev-
1:21 er had its origin in the will of man, but men spoke
[c]2Ti 3:16 from God[c] as they were carried along by the Holy
[d]2Sa 23:2; Ac 1:16; Spirit.[d]
1Pe 1:11

False Teachers and Their Destruction

2:1
[e]Dt 13:1-3 **2** But there were also false prophets[e] among the
[f]1Ti 4:1 [g]Jude 4 people, just as there will be false teachers
[h]1Co 6:20 among you.[f] They will secretly introduce destructive heresies, even denying the sovereign Lord[g]
who bought them[h]—bringing swift destruction on
themselves. [2]Many will follow their shameful
ways and will bring the way of truth into disrepute. [3]In their greed these teachers will exploit
2:3 you[i] with stories they have made up. Their con-
[i]2Co 2:17; demnation has long been hanging over them, and
1Th 2:5 their destruction has not been sleeping.
[4]For if God did not spare angels when they
sinned, but sent them to hell,[a] putting them into
2:4 gloomy dungeons[b] to be held for judgment;[j] [5]if he
[j]Jude 6; did not spare the ancient world[k] when he brought
Rev 20:1,2 the flood on its ungodly people, but protected
2:5 Noah, a preacher of righteousness, and seven oth-
[k]2Pe 3:6 [l]Heb 11:7; ers;[l] [6]if he condemned the cities of Sodom and
1Pe 3:20 Gomorrah by burning them to ashes,[m] and made
2:6 them an example[n] of what is going to happen to
[m]Ge 19:24, the ungodly; [7]and if he rescued Lot,[o] a righteous
25 man, who was distressed by the filthy lives of law-
[n]Nu 26:10; Jude 7 less men[p] [8](for that righteous man, living among
2:7 them day after day, was tormented in his righ-
[o]Ge 19:16 teous soul by the lawless deeds he saw and
[p]2Pe 3:17 heard)— [9]if this is so, then the Lord knows how to
2:9 rescue godly men from trials[q] and to hold the
[q]1Co 10:13 unrighteous for the day of judgment, while con-
2:10 tinuing their punishment.[c] [10]This is especially true
[r]2Pe 3:3 of those who follow the corrupt desire[r] of the sin-
[s]Jude 8 ful nature[d] and despise authority.
Bold and arrogant, these men are not afraid to
slander celestial beings;[s] [11]yet even angels,
although they are stronger and more powerful, do
not bring slanderous accusations against such
2:11 beings in the presence of the Lord.[t] [12]But these
[t]Jude 9 men blaspheme in matters they do not understand. They are like brute beasts, creatures of
2:12 instinct, born only to be caught and destroyed,
[u]Jude 10 and like beasts they too will perish.[u]
[13]They will be paid back with harm for the
2:13 harm they have done. Their idea of pleasure is to
[v]Ro 13:13 carouse in broad daylight.[v] They are blots and
[w]1Co 11:20, 21; Jude 12 blemishes, reveling in their pleasures while they
feast with you.[e][w] [14]With eyes full of adultery, they
2:14 [x]ver 18 never stop sinning; they seduce[x] the unstable;
[y]ver 3 they are experts in greed[y]—an accursed brood![z]
[z]Eph 2:3

[a] 4 Greek *Tartarus* [b] 4 Some manuscripts *into chains of darkness* [c] 9 Or *unrighteous for punishment until the day of judgment* [d] 10 Or *the flesh* [e] 13 Some manuscripts *in their love feasts*

False Teachers

2PE 2

As it was then, so it is now, and so it shall be until Jesus returns. Here is the simple reality: False teachers seek to lead people away from God. Peter states this with a sober intensity. They will come among you. They will teach what is destructive and deceptive. And, saddest of all, some of you will believe their lies and follow them.

In the arid and parched land of Israel, water is life. A broken cistern or a dry spring can mean death for an entire community. False teachers are portrayed as springs without water. They promise life, refreshment and living water. They deliver only death. They leave people spiritually dry, desolate and lost. Peter's warning is as powerful and necessary today as it was 2,000 years ago. False teachers still deceive. It is as important today as it was then to test everything against the unchanging truth of God's Word.

God's Timetable

2PE 3:8-10

We live in a "give it to me now" culture that is pathological about getting things on demand. With the click of a mouse, we can access information through the Internet, and in a matter of seconds, gather thousands of files of information on every topic—from a through z. We want it now, or better yet, yesterday!

In a world stuck in fast-forward mode, God wants us to know that he does not work on our timetable. To him a day is like a thousand years and a thousand years are like a day; which is to say, God's timing is very much his own. He is at work—on his schedule. Jesus is coming soon, but what is "soon" in God's timing could be very different from ours. Jesus delays for one reason only: He doesn't want anyone to die in his or her sin (2Pe 3:9), so in loving patience he gives unbelievers a few more hours, days, weeks, years.

15 They have left the straight way and wandered
off to follow the way of Balaam[a] son of Beor, who 2:15 [a]Nu 22:4-20;
loved the wages of wickedness. 16 But he was Jude 11
rebuked for his wrongdoing by a donkey—a beast
without speech—who spoke with a man's voice 2:16
and restrained the prophet's madness.[b] [b]Nu 22:21-30
17 These men are springs without water[c] and 2:17
mists driven by a storm. Blackest darkness is [c]Jude 12
reserved for them.[d] 18 For they mouth empty, [d]Jude 13
boastful words[e] and, by appealing to the lustful 2:18
desires of sinful human nature, they entice peo- [e]Jude 16
ple who are just escaping from those who live in
error. 19 They promise them freedom, while they
themselves are slaves of depravity—for a man is a 2:19
slave to whatever has mastered him.[f] 20 If they [f]Jn 8:34;
have escaped the corruption of the world by Ro 6:16
knowing[g] our Lord and Savior Jesus Christ and 2:20
are again entangled in it and overcome, they are [g]2Pe 1:2
worse off at the end than they were at the begin- [h]Mt 12:45
ning.[h] 21 It would have been better for them not to
have known the way of righteousness, than to
have known it and then to turn their backs on the 2:21
sacred command that was passed on to them.[i] 22 Of [i]Heb 6:4-6
them the proverbs are true: "A dog returns to its 2:22
vomit,"[a][j] and, "A sow that is washed goes back to [j]Pr 26:11
her wallowing in the mud."

The Day of the Lord

3 Dear friends, this is now my second letter to 3:1
you. I have written both of them as reminders[k] [k]2Pe 1:13
to stimulate you to wholesome thinking. 2 I want
you to recall the words spoken in the past by the
holy prophets and the command given by our
Lord and Savior through your apostles. 3:3
3 First of all, you must understand that in the [l]1Ti 4:1
last days[l] scoffers will come, scoffing and follow- [m]2Pe 2:10;
ing their own evil desires.[m] 4 They will say, Jude 18
"Where is this 'coming' he promised?[n] Ever since 3:4 [n]Isa 5:19;
our fathers died, everything goes on as it has since Eze 12:22; Mt 24:48
the beginning of creation."[o] 5 But they deliberate- [o]Mk 10:6
ly forget that long ago by God's word[p] the heavens 3:5
existed and the earth was formed out of water and [p]Ge 1:6,9;
by water.[q] 6 By these waters also the world of that Heb 11:3
time was deluged and destroyed.[r] 7 By the same [q]Ps 24:2
word the present heavens and earth are reserved 3:6
for fire,[s] being kept for the day of judgment and [r]Ge 7:21,22
destruction of ungodly men. 3:7
8 But do not forget this one thing, dear friends: [s]ver 10,12;
With the Lord a day is like a thousand years, and 2Th 1:7
a thousand years are like a day.[t] 9 The Lord is not 3:8
slow in keeping his promise,[u] as some understand [t]Ps 90:4
slowness. He is patient[v] with you, not wanting 3:9
anyone to perish, but everyone to come to repen- [u]Hab 2:3;
tance.[w] Heb 10:37
10 But the day of the Lord will come like a thief.[x] [v]Ro 2:4 [w]1Ti 2:4
The heavens will disappear with a roar; the ele-
ments will be destroyed by fire, and the earth and 3:10 [x]Lk 12:39;
everything in it will be laid bare.[b][y] 1Th 5:2
11 Since everything will be destroyed in this way, [y]Mt 24:35; Rev 21:1

[a] 22 Prov. 26:11 [b] 10 Some manuscripts *be burned up*

what kind of people ought you to be? You ought to
3:12 [z]1Co 1:7 live holy and godly lives [12]as you look forward[z] to
[a]Ps 50:3 the day of God and speed its coming.[a][a] That day
[b]ver 10 will bring about the destruction of the heavens by
fire, and the elements will melt in the heat.[b] [13]But
in keeping with his promise we are looking for-
3:13 [c]Isa 65:17; ward to a new heaven and a new earth,[c] the home
66:22; of righteousness.
Rev 21:1 [14]So then, dear friends, since you are looking
forward to this, make every effort to be found
3:14 spotless, blameless[d] and at peace with him. [15]Bear
[d]1Th 3:13 in mind that our Lord's patience[e] means salva-
3:15 tion,[f] just as our dear brother Paul also wrote you
[e]Ro 2:4 with the wisdom that God gave him.[g] [16]He writes
[f]ver 9 [g]Eph 3:3 the same way in all his letters, speaking in them
of these matters. His letters contain some things
3:16 that are hard to understand, which ignorant and
[h]2Pe 2:14 [i]ver 2 unstable[h] people distort, as they do the other
Scriptures,[i] to their own destruction.
3:17 [17]Therefore, dear friends, since you already
[j]1Co 10:12 know this, be on your guard[j] so that you may not
[k]2Pe 2:18 [l]Rev 2:5 be carried away by the error[k] of lawless men and
fall from your secure position.[l] [18]But grow in the
grace and knowledge of our Lord and Savior Jesus
3:18 [m]2Pe 1:11 Christ.[m] To him be glory both now and forever!
Amen.

Jesus Is Coming

2PE 3:10–14

We don't know if it is a thousand years away or tomorrow. But Jesus is coming. Peter paints a vivid and shocking picture of the consummation of time. Like a thief in the night, Jesus will return, the heavens and the earth will be consumed and a new order will begin. A new heaven and earth will replace the old. Yet this news does not seem to be the focal point of Peter's teaching.

Here is Peter's message about the end times. It comes down to seven simple words: What kind of person should you be? Peter calls us to invest our energy in living "spotless, blameless" lives (2Pe 3:14).

Our confidence that Jesus will return is not meant to draw us into complex speculations on when and where and how. Rather, it should move us into godly living that will honor him and empower us to reach those who do not yet know his grace.

[a] 12 Or *as you wait eagerly for the day of God to come*

1 John

Living in God's love.

John dispels believers' doubts about Jesus in this profound letter to early Christians. Sharing personal observations and powerful insights, John exposes false teachers and assures believers of their salvation. Instead of following a systematic progression of ideas, John simply talks about the things he wants believers to know, writing one section and then moving to a different thought that becomes the subject of the next section. These spiritual nuggets ultimately frame a common thought: We need to love as God loves.

Vivid images that contrast light and dark, truth and error, life and death, and love and hate fill the chapters of 1 John. The apostle reassures believers that God will powerfully overcome sin as they seek his forgiveness (1Jn 1). He warns them about loving "the world" and being influenced by false teachers (1Jn 2). He reminds them that obedience to God brings a love for other believers (1Jn 3) and that true love is more than a good feeling (1Jn 4). John wants his readers to enjoy the assurance of having eternal life (1Jn 5).

The spiritual gems of the book of 1 John are profound in their very simplicity. Applying them to our lives will affect our interaction with God and with others. The truth of the gospel and genuine fellowship with God will be reflected in our lives as we learn to live and walk in the light of his love.

Quick Study

Author
The apostle John, who also wrote the Gospel of John, 2 and 3 John and Revelation.

Date Written
Probably written toward the end of the first century, around A.D. 90.

Written From
Not known for certain, but possibly Ephesus.

Key Passage
1 John 3:16–18 "This is how we know what love is: Jesus Christ laid down his life for us. And we ought to lay down our lives for our brothers. If anyone has material possessions and sees his brother in need but has no pity on him, how can the love of God be in him? Dear children, let us not love with words or tongue but with actions and in truth."

Outline

The incarnation's reality.
1Jn 1:1-4

Living in the light.
1Jn 1:5–2:17

Warnings about false teachers.
1Jn 2:18-27

Children of God.
1Jn 2:28–3:10

Loving God and each other.
1Jn 3:11–4:21

Faith in Christ.
1Jn 5:1-12

Conclusion.
1Jn 5:13-21

The Women of 1 John

No women are mentioned in the book of 1 John.

The Word of Life

1 That which was from the beginning,[a] which
we have heard, which we have seen with our
eyes,[b] which we have looked at and our hands
have touched[c]—this we proclaim concerning the
Word of life. 2 The life appeared;[d] we have seen it
and testify to it, and we proclaim to you the eternal life, which was with the Father and has
appeared to us. 3 We proclaim to you what we
have seen and heard, so that you also may have
fellowship with us. And our fellowship is with the
Father and with his Son, Jesus Christ.[e] 4 We write
this[f] to make our[*a*] joy complete.[g]

Walking in the Light

5 This is the message we have heard[h] from him
and declare to you: God is light; in him there is
no darkness at all. 6 If we claim to have fellowship
with him yet walk in the darkness,[i] we lie and do
not live by the truth.[j] 7 But if we walk in the light,
as he is in the light, we have fellowship with one
another, and the blood of Jesus, his Son, purifies
us from all[*b*] sin.[k]
8 If we claim to be without sin,[l] we deceive ourselves and the truth is not in us.[m] 9 If we confess
our sins, he is faithful and just and will forgive us
our sins[n] and purify us from all unrighteousness.
10 If we claim we have not sinned, we make him out
to be a liar[o] and his word has no place in our lives.[p]

2 My dear children,[q] I write this to you so that
you will not sin. But if anybody does sin, we
have one who speaks to the Father in our
defense[r]—Jesus Christ, the Righteous One. 2 He is
the atoning sacrifice for our sins,[s] and not only for
ours but also for[*c*] the sins of the whole world.
3 We know that we have come to know him if
we obey his commands.[t] 4 The man who says, "I
know him," but does not do what he commands
is a liar, and the truth is not in him.[u] 5 But if anyone obeys his word,[v] God's love[*d*] is truly made
complete in him.[w] This is how we know we are
in him: 6 Whoever claims to live in him must walk
as Jesus did.[x]
7 Dear friends, I am not writing you a new command but an old one, which you have had since
the beginning.[y] This old command is the message
you have heard. 8 Yet I am writing you a new command;[z] its truth is seen in him and you, because
the darkness is passing[a] and the true light[b] is
already shining.[c]
9 Anyone who claims to be in the light but hates
his brother is still in the darkness. 10 Whoever
loves his brother lives in the light,[d] and there is
nothing in him[*e*] to make him stumble. 11 But whoever hates his brother is in the darkness and
walks around in the darkness; he does not know

1:1 [a]Jn 1:2 [b]Jn 1:14; 2Pe 1:16 [c]Jn 20:27
1:2 [d]Jn 1:1-4; 1Ti 3:16
1:3 [e]1Co 1:9
1:4 [f]1Jn 2:1 [g]Jn 3:29
1:5 [h]1Jn 3:11
1:6 [i]2Co 6:14 [j]Jn 3:19-21
1:7 [k]Heb 9:14; Rev 1:5
1:8 [l]Pr 20:9; Jas 3:2 [m]1Jn 2:4
1:9 [n]Ps 32:5; 51:2
1:10 [o]1Jn 5:10 [p]1Jn 2:14
2:1 [q]ver 12,13, 28 [r]Ro 8:34; Heb 7:25
2:2 [s]Ro 3:25
2:3 [t]Jn 14:15
2:4 [u]1Jn 1:6,8
2:5 [v]Jn 14:21,23 [w]1Jn 4:12
2:6 [x]Mt 11:29; 1Pe 2:21
2:7 [y]1Jn 3:11,23; 2Jn 5,6
2:8 [z]Jn 13:34 [a]Ro 13:12 [b]Jn 1:9 [c]Eph 5:8; 1Th 5:5
2:10 [d]1Jn 3:14

[*a*] 4 Some manuscripts *your* [*b*] 7 Or *every* [*c*] 2 Or *He is the one who turns aside God's wrath, taking away our sins, and not only ours but also* [*d*] 5 Or *word, love for God* [*e*] 10 Or *it*

It would be such a shame to sit in church and listen to what's being said about God but never grasp that this is a personal invitation, a homecoming, a welcome mat thrown on the ground just for you.

"If we confess our sins, he is faithful and just and will forgive us our sins and purify us from all unrighteousness" (1Jn 1:9). Isn't that great? Isn't that simple? All you have to do is pray.

—Sheila Walsh

where he is going, because the darkness has
2:11 [e]Jn 12:35 blinded him.[e]

[12]I write to you, dear children,
because your sins have been forgiven
on account of his name.
[13]I write to you, fathers,
because you have known him who is
from the beginning.
I write to you, young men,
because you have overcome the evil
2:13 [f]ver 14 one.[f]
I write to you, dear children,
because you have known the Father.
[14]I write to you, fathers,
because you have known him who is
from the beginning.
2:14 I write to you, young men,
[g]Eph 6:10 because you are strong,[g]
[h]Jn 5:38; 1Jn 1:10 and the word of God lives in you,[h]
[i]ver 13 and you have overcome the evil one.[i]

Do Not Love the World

2:15 [15]Do not love the world or anything in the
[j]Ro 12:2 world.[j] If anyone loves the world, the love of the
[k]Jas 4:4 Father is not in him.[k] [16]For everything in the
2:16 world—the cravings of sinful man,[l] the lust of his
[l]Ro 13:14 eyes[m] and the boasting of what he has and does—
[m]Pr 27:20 comes not from the Father but from the world.
2:17 [17]The world and its desires pass away,[n] but the
[n]1Co 7:31 man who does the will of God lives forever.

Warning Against Antichrists

2:18 [18]Dear children, this is the last hour; and as you
[o]ver 22; have heard that the antichrist is coming,[o] even
1Jn 4:3; now many antichrists have come.[p] This is how we
2Jn 7 know it is the last hour. [19]They went out from us,[q]
[p]1Jn 4:1 but they did not really belong to us. For if they
2:19 had belonged to us, they would have remained
[q]Ac 20:30 with us; but their going showed that none of them
[r]1Co 11:19 belonged to us.[r]
2:20 [20]But you have an anointing[s] from the Holy One,[t]
[s]2Co 1:21 [t]Mk 1:24 and all of you know the truth.[a][u] [21]I do not write to
[u]Jn 14:26 you because you do not know the truth, but
2:21 because you do know it[v] and because no lie comes
[v]2Pe 1:12; Jude 5 from the truth. [22]Who is the liar? It is the man who
denies that Jesus is the Christ. Such a man is the
2:22 antichrist—he denies the Father and the Son.[w] [23]No
[w]2Jn 7 one who denies the Son has the Father; whoever
2:23 acknowledges the Son has the Father also.[x]
[x]Jn 8:19; [24]See that what you have heard from the begin-
1Jn 4:15 ning remains in you. If it does, you also will
2:24 remain in the Son and in the Father.[y] [25]And this
[y]Jn 14:23 is what he promised us—even eternal life.
[26]I am writing these things to you about those
2:26 who are trying to lead you astray.[z] [27]As for you,
[z]2Jn 7 the anointing[a] you received from him remains in
2:27 you, and you do not need anyone to teach you.
[a]ver 20 But as his anointing teaches you about all things

The Last Hour

1JN 2:18

John declares to his readers that this is the "last hour." But we look back and see that Jesus did not return in John's lifetime. Now, 2,000 years later, should we wonder if he was right in his declaration?

The first coming of Jesus into human history marks the beginning of the last hour (see the note on 1Pe 4:7, page 2028). Once Jesus comes on the scene, lives, dies and rises again, it is the beginning of the end. When the New Testament writers speak of the last days or the final hour, they are pointing to a time in human history that began in their day and continues into ours. So that day is still today! We are in the final hour. These are the end times. It is just as accurate for us to declare this truth as it was for John and others in the first century.

[a] 20 Some manuscripts *and you know all things*

and as that anointing is real, not counterfeit—just
as it has taught you, remain in him.

Children of God

28And now, dear children,[b] continue in him, so
that when he appears[c] we may be confident[d] and
unashamed before him at his coming.[e]
29If you know that he is righteous,[f] you know
that everyone who does what is right has been
born of him.

3 How great is the love[g] the Father has lavished
on us, that we should be called children of
God![h] And that is what we are! The reason the
world does not know us is that it did not know
him.[i] 2Dear friends, now we are children of God,
and what we will be has not yet been made
known. But we know that when he appears,[a] we
shall be like him,[j] for we shall see him as he is.[k]
3Everyone who has this hope in him purifies himself,[l] just as he is pure.
4Everyone who sins breaks the law; in fact, sin
is lawlessness.[m] 5But you know that he appeared
so that he might take away our sins. And in him
is no sin.[n] 6No one who lives in him keeps on sinning.[o] No one who continues to sin has either
seen him[p] or known him.[q]
7Dear children,[r] do not let anyone lead you
astray.[s] He who does what is right is righteous,
just as he is righteous.[t] 8He who does what is sinful is of the devil,[u] because the devil has been sinning from the beginning. The reason the Son of
God appeared was to destroy the devil's work. 9No
one who is born of God[v] will continue to sin,[w]
because God's seed[x] remains in him; he cannot go
on sinning, because he has been born of God.
10This is how we know who the children of God
are and who the children of the devil are: Anyone
who does not do what is right is not a child of
God; nor is anyone who does not love[y] his
brother.

Love One Another

11This is the message you heard[z] from the
beginning: We should love one another.[a] 12Do not
be like Cain, who belonged to the evil one and
murdered his brother.[b] And why did he murder
him? Because his own actions were evil and his
brother's were righteous. 13Do not be surprised,
my brothers, if the world hates you.[c] 14We know
that we have passed from death to life,[d] because
we love our brothers. Anyone who does not love
remains in death.[e] 15Anyone who hates his brother is a murderer,[f] and you know that no murderer has eternal life in him.[g]
16This is how we know what love is: Jesus
Christ laid down his life for us. And we ought to
lay down our lives for our brothers.[h] 17If anyone
has material possessions and sees his brother in
need but has no pity on him,[i] how can the love of

2:28 [b]ver 1 [c]1Jn 3:2 [d]1Jn 4:17 [e]1Th 2:19
2:29 [f]1Jn 3:7
3:1 [g]Jn 3:16 [h]Jn 1:12 [i]Jn 16:3
3:2 [j]Ro 8:29; 2Pe 1:4 [k]2Co 3:18
3:3 [l]2Co 7:1; 2Pe 3:13,14
3:4 [m]1Jn 5:17
3:5 [n]2Co 5:21
3:6 [o]ver 9 [p]3Jn 11 [q]1Jn 2:4
3:7 [r]1Jn 2:1 [s]1Jn 2:26 [t]1Jn 2:29
3:8 [u]Jn 8:44
3:9 [v]Jn 1:13 [w]1Jn 5:18 [x]1Pe 1:23
3:10 [y]1Jn 4:8
3:11 [z]1Jn 1:5 [a]Jn 13:34, 35; 2Jn 5
3:12 [b]Ge 4:8
3:13 [c]Jn 15:18, 19; 17:14
3:14 [d]Jn 5:24 [e]1Jn 2:9
3:15 [f]Mt 5:21,22; Jn 8:44 [g]Gal 5:20,21
3:16 [h]Jn 15:13
3:17 [i]Dt 15:7,8

[a] 2 Or *when it is made known*

Lavish Love

1JN 3:1–3

John unveils a truth that is reinforced repeatedly in God's Word: We are the children of God. All who receive the grace of God through Jesus Christ are adopted as his children. He lavishly pours out on us a flood of heavenly love and acceptance.

Paul says it this way: "The Spirit himself testifies with our spirit that we are God's children" (Ro 8:16). What greater confirmation can we have than the Holy Spirit sealing this truth to our hearts? In the Gospel of John we read these words, "Yet to all who received him, to those who believed in his name, he gave the right to become children of God" (Jn 1:12). In this first letter of John we have his bold declaration: "How great is the love the Father has lavished on us, that we should be called children of God! And that is what we are!" (1Jn 3:1). Our primary identity can be securely wrapped up in the confidence of being children of God.

3:17 God be in him?[j] 18Dear children,[k] let us not love
[j]1Jn 4:20 with words or tongue but with actions and in
3:18 truth.[l] 19This then is how we know that we belong
[k]1Jn 2:1 [l]Eze 33:31; to the truth, and how we set our hearts at rest in
Ro 12:9 his presence 20whenever our hearts condemn us.
For God is greater than our hearts, and he knows
everything.
21Dear friends, if our hearts do not condemn us,
3:21 [m]1Jn 5:14 we have confidence before God[m] 22and receive
from him anything we ask,[n] because we obey his
3:22 commands and do what pleases him.[o] 23And this
[n]Mt 7:7 [o]Jn 8:29 is his command: to believe[p] in the name of his
Son, Jesus Christ, and to love one another as he
3:23 [p]Jn 6:29 commanded us.[q] 24Those who obey his com-
[q]Jn 13:34 mands live in him,[r] and he in them. And this is
how we know that he lives in us: We know it by
3:24 [r]1Jn 2:6 [s]1Jn 4:13 the Spirit he gave us.[s]

Test the Spirits

4:1 [t]2Pe 2:1; 4 Dear friends, do not believe every spirit, but
1Jn 2:18 test the spirits to see whether they are from
4:2 God, because many false prophets have gone out
[u]Jn 1:14; into the world.[t] 2This is how you can recognize
1Jn 2:23 [v]1Co 12:3 the Spirit of God: Every spirit that acknowledges
that Jesus Christ has come in the flesh[u] is from
4:3 [w]1Jn 2:22; God,[v] 3but every spirit that does not acknowledge
2Jn 7 Jesus is not from God. This is the spirit of the
antichrist,[w] which you have heard is coming and
4:4 [x]Ro 8:31 even now is already in the world.
[y]Jn 12:31 4You, dear children, are from God and have
4:5 overcome them, because the one who is in you[x] is
[z]Jn 15:19 greater than the one who is in the world.[y] 5They
are from the world[z] and therefore speak from the
4:6 [a]Jn 8:47 viewpoint of the world, and the world listens to
[b]Jn 14:17 them. 6We are from God, and whoever knows God
4:7 listens to us; but whoever is not from God does
[c]1Jn 3:11 not listen to us.[a] This is how we recognize the
[d]1Jn 2:4 Spirit[a] of truth[b] and the spirit of falsehood.

4:8 [e]ver 7,16

God's Love and Ours

4:9 7Dear friends, let us love one another,[c] for love
[f]Jn 3:16,17; comes from God. Everyone who loves has been
1Jn 5:11 born of God and knows God.[d] 8Whoever does not
4:10 love does not know God, because God is love.[e]
[g]Ro 5:8,10 9This is how God showed his love among us: He
[h]1Jn 2:2 sent his one and only Son[b] into the world that we
4:11 might live through him.[f] 10This is love: not that
[i]Jn 3:16 we loved God, but that he loved us[g] and sent his
4:12 Son as an atoning sacrifice for[c] our sins.[h] 11Dear
[j]Jn 1:18; friends, since God so loved us,[i] we also ought to
1Ti 6:16 [k]1Jn 2:5 love one another. 12No one has ever seen God;[j] but
if we love one another, God lives in us and his
4:13 love is made complete in us.[k]
[l]1Jn 3:24 13We know that we live in him and he in us,
4:14 because he has given us of his Spirit.[l] 14And we
[m]Jn 15:27 [n]Jn 3:17 have seen and testify[m] that the Father has sent his
Son to be the Savior of the world.[n] 15If anyone
4:15 [o]Ro 10:9 acknowledges that Jesus is the Son of God,[o] God

[a]6 Or *spirit* [b]9 Or *his only begotten Son* [c]10 Or *as the one who would turn aside his wrath, taking away*

Test the Spirits

1JN 4:1

John is addressing a very specific situation. When a person is teaching or prophesying, others in the church are expected to "test the spirits" to be sure that the person is speaking by the Holy Spirit and not by a false spirit. False teachers were speaking lies in the church of John's day, even as they do in the church today. John does not give us the details of this testing process but simply calls us to "test the spirits."

Here are some questions that can help us test the spirits:

1. Is this teaching consistent with the Word of God? If it is contrary to the Scriptures, it is not of God, for God will never contradict his Word.

2. Does the teacher acknowledge that Jesus Christ is the Son of God? If not, no matter what else he or she says, the truth of God is not in that teacher.

3. Will this teaching edify Jesus and his church? When a teacher is edifying self rather than Jesus, it is often false teaching.

4. Does the Holy Spirit who dwells within us confirm that this teaching is of God? Although we can't put all our trust in our own spiritual discernment, the Holy Spirit will often convict us when we hear false teaching. We should be responsive to his still, small voice.

The Truth About Love

1JN 4:16–21

These six brief verses paint a picture so vivid that it encompasses the heart of both divine and human love. The starting point: God is love. Without this, nothing else makes sense. God loves us first. He is the One who initiates a love relationship with us and then pursues us with his love. When we have been apprehended by his powerful love, we are changed. We have a new address, a new residence; it is called the love of God. This becomes our primary dwelling place. We live in God and his love, and he lives in us!

Next, we have a new heart. Bold! Confident! Fearless! The love of God drives out all fear. The culmination of this love relationship is a transformed life.

Now, we begin to love each other. We can't help it. God has so loved us that we begin to relate to others in a similar manner. God loves us, we love him, and that love flows into loving our brothers and sisters.

lives in him and he in God. 16 And so we know and
rely on the love God has for us.
God is love.[p] Whoever lives in love lives in God,
and God in him.[q] 17 In this way, love is made complete[r] among us so that we will have confidence
on the day of judgment, because in this world we
are like him. 18 There is no fear in love. But perfect love drives out fear,[s] because fear has to do
with punishment. The one who fears is not made
perfect in love.
19 We love because he first loved us.[t] 20 If anyone
says, "I love God," yet hates his brother,[u] he is a
liar.[v] For anyone who does not love his brother,
whom he has seen,[w] cannot love God, whom he
has not seen.[x] 21 And he has given us this command: Whoever loves God must also love his
brother.[y]

Faith in the Son of God

5 Everyone who believes that Jesus is the Christ[z]
is born of God,[a] and everyone who loves the
father loves his child as well.[b] 2 This is how we
know that we love the children of God: by loving
God and carrying out his commands. 3 This is love
for God: to obey his commands.[c] And his commands are not burdensome,[d] 4 for everyone born
of God overcomes[e] the world. This is the victory
that has overcome the world, even our faith.
5 Who is it that overcomes the world? Only he who
believes that Jesus is the Son of God.
6 This is the one who came by water and
blood[f]—Jesus Christ. He did not come by water
only, but by water and blood. And it is the Spirit
who testifies, because the Spirit is the truth.[g] 7 For
there are three[h] that testify: 8 the[a] Spirit, the water
and the blood; and the three are in agreement.
9 We accept man's testimony,[i] but God's testimony is greater because it is the testimony of God,[j]
which he has given about his Son. 10 Anyone who
believes in the Son of God has this testimony in
his heart.[k] Anyone who does not believe God has
made him out to be a liar,[l] because he has not
believed the testimony God has given about his
Son. 11 And this is the testimony: God has given us
eternal life, and this life is in his Son.[m] 12 He who
has the Son has life; he who does not have the
Son of God does not have life.[n]

Concluding Remarks

13 I write these things to you who believe in the
name of the Son of God[o] so that you may know
that you have eternal life.[p] 14 This is the confidence[q] we have in approaching God: that if we
ask anything according to his will, he hears us.[r]
15 And if we know that he hears us—whatever we

4:16 [p] ver 8 [q] 1Jn 3:24
4:17 [r] 1Jn 2:5
4:18 [s] Ro 8:15
4:19 [t] ver 10
4:20 [u] 1Jn 2:9 [v] 1Jn 2:4 [w] 1Jn 3:17 [x] ver 12
4:21 [y] Mt 5:43
5:1 [z] 1Jn 2:22 [a] Jn 1:13; 1Jn 2:23 [b] Jn 8:42
5:3 [c] Jn 14:15; 2Jn 6 [d] Mt 11:30
5:4 [e] Jn 16:33
5:6 [f] Jn 19:34 [g] Jn 14:17
5:7 [h] Mt 18:16
5:9 [i] Jn 5:34 [j] Mt 3:16,17; Jn 8:17,18
5:10 [k] Ro 8:16; Gal 4:6 [l] Jn 3:33
5:11 [m] Jn 1:4; 1Jn 2:25
5:12 [n] Jn 3:15,16, 36
5:13 [o] 1Jn 3:23 [p] Jn 20:31; 1Jn 1:1,2
5:14 [q] 1Jn 3:21 [r] Mt 7:7

[a] 7,8 Late manuscripts of the Vulgate *testify in heaven: the Father, the Word and the Holy Spirit, and these three are one.* 8 *And there are three that testify on earth: the* (not found in any Greek manuscript before the fourteenth century)

5:15 ask—we know[s] that we have what we asked of
[s]ver 18,19, 20 him.
[16]If anyone sees his brother commit a sin that
5:16 does not lead to death, he should pray and God
[t]Jas 5:15 [u]Heb 6:4-6; will give him life.[t] I refer to those whose sin does
10:26 not lead to death. There is a sin that leads to
[v]Jer 7:16 death.[u] I am not saying that he should pray about
5:17 that.[v] [17]All wrongdoing is sin,[w] and there is sin
[w]1Jn 3:4 [x]1Jn 2:1 that does not lead to death.[x]
[18]We know that anyone born of God does not
5:18 continue to sin; the one who was born of God
[y]Jn 14:30 keeps him safe, and the evil one cannot harm
5:19 him.[y] [19]We know that we are children of God,[z]
[z]1Jn 4:6 and that the whole world is under the control of
[a]Gal 1:4 the evil one.[a] [20]We know also that the Son of God
5:20 has come and has given us understanding,[b] so
[b]Lk 24:45 that we may know him who is true.[c] And we are
[c]Jn 17:3 [d]ver 11 in him who is true—even in his Son Jesus Christ.
He is the true God and eternal life.[d]
5:21 [21]Dear children, keep yourselves from idols.[e]
[e]1Co 10:14; 1Th 1:9

Sin That Leads to Death

1JN 5:16

We cannot be certain what John means when he speaks of the "sin that leads to death." Yet in the context of this book and the prevailing false teaching in the church, there is a high level of probability that John is pointing to Gnostic teaching, which denies the incarnation of Jesus Christ and the grace that comes through his death and resurrection. This denial of the core of the Christian faith, and the brazen, immoral behavior that comes with this false belief system, might very well be the "sin that leads to death" about which John is writing.

False teachers perpetuated the Gnostic heresy and called others to do the same. This persistent denial of the person of Christ became self-condemning. John is telling the church to pray for those who find themselves trapped in sin. But those who repeatedly and forcefully deny Christ are condemned. They are denying the very One who could give them life.

2 John

Discernment in hospitality.

Several religious teachers add their own philosophies and false beliefs to the gospel message. These teachers travel throughout the area using the homes of their hosts as meeting places to teach their false doctrines. John writes this letter to expose these erroneous teachings and the ungodly conduct that can result from them and to warn believers to withdraw from all contact with these teachers. Though God encourages his children to practice hospitality, John wants the believers to know when to close their doors.

The letter of 2 John is directed to a "chosen lady and her children" (2Jn 1). While some scholars suggest that this may refer to a church, other students of Scripture suggest that 2 John is a personal letter to a devoted Christian woman. In either case, John rejoices as he finds these believers "walking in the truth" (2Jn 4), knowing that a firm grasp of God's truth is the mark of a strong, growing faith. He reminds his listeners to walk in love (2Jn 6). John's spiritual yardstick to guard against teachings that run contrary to Biblical truth is found in 2 John 7. And he strongly warns his readers to guard against such teachings and such teachers (2Jn 9–11).

The best way for us to keep on target spiritually is to follow John's call to truth, love and obedience. To be certain of what we believe and to walk in it in love and without faltering is the hallmark of true Christianity.

Quick Study

Author
The apostle John, who also wrote the Gospel of John, 1 and 3 John and Revelation.

Date Written
Probably about the same time as John's first letter, around A.D. 90.

Written From
Not known for certain, but possibly Ephesus.

Key Passage
2 John 5–6 "I am not writing you a new command but one we have had from the beginning. I ask that we love one another. And this is love: that we walk in obedience to his commands. As you have heard from the beginning, his command is that you walk in love."

Outline

John's greetings.
2Jn 1-3
Commendation.
2Jn 4
Warning.
2Jn 5-11
Conclusion.
2Jn 12-13

The Women of 2 John

The chosen lady	*She lived in the truth.* 2Jn 1-5
The chosen sister	*Her children sent their greetings through John.* 2Jn 13

Face to Face

2JN 12

In John's day, there were really only two ways to communicate: face to face or through a letter (or a messenger). In our day and age the options continue to multiply: cell phones, e-mail, chat rooms and faxes are just a few of the new wave of communication options. Yet John captures a truth that speaks to us even today. He lets his dear friends know that he could write a great deal more, but what he really wants is to see them face to face.

In our high-tech age, we need to cling to the great value of communicating with fellow believers face to face. We can echo the heart of John, getting back to the basics of gathering with other followers of Christ and connecting on the deepest levels. To hold hands for prayer, to lift our voices together in worship, to share our lives together in an Acts 2:42–47 type of fellowship—this is the cry of John's heart—and ours.

1 The elder,[a]

To the chosen[b] lady and her children, whom I
love in the truth—and not I only, but also all who
know the truth[c]— 2 because of the truth,[d] which
lives in us[e] and will be with us forever:

3 Grace, mercy and peace from God the Father
and from Jesus Christ,[f] the Father's Son, will be
with us in truth and love.

4 It has given me great joy to find some of your
children walking in the truth,[g] just as the Father
commanded us. 5 And now, dear lady, I am not
writing you a new command but one we have had
from the beginning.[h] I ask that we love one another. 6 And this is love:[i] that we walk in obedience to
his commands. As you have heard from the beginning, his command is that you walk in love.
7 Many deceivers, who do not acknowledge
Jesus Christ[j] as coming in the flesh, have gone out
into the world.[k] Any such person is the deceiver
and the antichrist.[l] 8 Watch out that you do not
lose what you have worked for, but that you may
be rewarded fully.[m] 9 Anyone who runs ahead and
does not continue in the teaching of Christ does
not have God; whoever continues in the teaching
has both the Father and the Son.[n] 10 If anyone
comes to you and does not bring this teaching, do
not take him into your house or welcome him.[o]
11 Anyone who welcomes him shares[p] in his
wicked work.
12 I have much to write to you, but I do not want
to use paper and ink. Instead, I hope to visit you
and talk with you face to face,[q] so that our joy
may be complete.

13 The children of your chosen[r] sister send their
greetings.

1:1 [a]3Jn 1 [b]Ro 16:13 [c]Jn 8:32
1:2 [d]2Pe 1:12 [e]1Jn 1:8
1:3 [f]Ro 1:7
1:4 [g]3Jn 3,4
1:5 [h]1Jn 2:7; 3:11
1:6 [i]1Jn 2:5
1:7 [j]1Jn 2:22; 4:2,3 [k]1Jn 4:1 [l]1Jn 2:18
1:8 [m]1Co 3:8
1:9 [n]1Jn 2:23
1:10 [o]Ro 16:17
1:11 [p]1Ti 5:22
1:12 [q]3Jn 13,14
1:13 [r]ver 1

Priscilla

Pass It On

Priscilla enjoyed having people in their home, so it was no inconvenience when Aquila showed up one day with the apostle Paul. Paul was a tentmaker like they were. But Paul was also an apostle of Jesus Christ. Priscilla and Aquila's lives were about to change forever. They were already Christians, but they had never met anyone quite like Paul.

They had come to Corinth from Rome when the emperor ordered all Jews to leave that city. They were flexible—there was a demand for their tents wherever they lived. Flexibility proved an important asset. Although most people of the time lived and died where they were born, Priscilla and Aquila moved several times, for the Lord had chosen them not only as Paul's hosts in Corinth, but as his lifelong friends and his co-workers in the church.

Priscilla was passionate for Christ and eager to draw others to him. She and Aquila are mentioned seven times in the New Testament, never one without the other. They were an extraordinary husband-wife ministry team. Their home became a meeting place for the new Christians to soak up Scripture and Paul's teaching. Priscilla and Aquila became experts in the faith. Paul trusted them to answer difficult questions and to settle disputes in the growing community of believers.

When Paul left Corinth for Ephesus, the couple went with him. Once again, their home became a meeting place. When Paul moved on, he left them in charge. Priscilla had an eye for what the Father was doing. She also had tact and sensitivity. When a new evangelist, Apollos, arrived on the scene, Priscilla recognized his gift but spotted holes in his theology. Between them, Priscilla and Aquila equipped Apollos with the full gospel, and Apollos was greatly used by the Lord in Corinth.

Priscilla was not a dead end, a woman focused on her own needs and growth. Her love for the Lord was a conduit of life for others. As soon as she mastered something, she passed it on. Some consider the churches at Corinth and Ephesus to be Paul's most successful churches. Undoubtedly, Priscilla and Aquila deserve some of the credit.

Church planting did not end with Paul's time. God assigns missionaries to places all over the world, including our own backyards, neighborhoods and nearby cities. The skills are simple: love God and his people, study his Word, be *available*. Could you be God's Priscilla for the twenty-first century?

Priscilla
(ancient)
Acts 18:2–3,18–19,26
Romans 16:3–4
1 Corinthians 16:19
2 Timothy 4:19

Candid SNAPSHOT [Apollos] began to speak boldly in the synagogue. When Priscilla and Aquila heard him, they invited him to their home and explained to him the way of God more adequately (Acts 18:26).

Phoebe, Mary, Tryphena, Tryphosa and Persis

Women Who Worked Hard

There are certain things to love about life—homemade cookies and potlucks and clean houses and new clothes and fresh bread. There's beautiful needlework, well-kept ledgers, flower gardens and hundreds of other things, too. These things have value, but we will not take *any* of them to heaven with us. The only thing that will go is *people*. The women in the early church worked for eternal bounty. Everything else was secondary.

Paul did not need to explain to his readers what Phoebe, Mary, Tryphena, Tryphosa, and Persis did. Everyone knew who these women were, for they were in the very center of ministry. They labored to exhaustion. They "worked very hard in the Lord." Phoebe even delivered a letter from Paul to the Roman church and served as his representative.

This prominence of women was something definitely new to Jewish culture. Jewish gatherings had separated men and women and assigned them different roles. By contrast, Jesus had raised the women who followed him to new levels of visibility and responsibility. They formed a unified group of dedicated followers: They were *disciples,* fellow workers (Ro 16:3), even apostles (Ro 16:7). Jesus was their model. They believed that God intended all of them to be his witnesses on earth.

So what was "working very hard in the Lord"? They prayed (Ac 1:14). They received the Spirit (Ac 2:17). They met regularly and hosted churches in their homes (Ac 2:46–47; Col 4:15). They were thrown in prison (Ac 8:3). They traveled with Paul (Ac 18:18). They taught (Ac 18:26). They proclaimed the gospel (Php 4:3), and they provided for Paul and his companions (Ac 16:15). They sewed and otherwise cared for the poor (Ac 9:39). They carried letters that became part of the New Testament (Ro 16:1). This list merely touches the surface of the parts women played in the ministry of the early church.

Phoebe, Mary, Tryphena, Tryphosa and Persis
Romans 16:1,6,12

Though Paul regarded them so much as to mention them by name, none of these women is well known to us. There are lots of "Marys" around, and a few "Phoebes," though probably they are not named after these women. But we don't often hear of anyone naming a daughter Tryphena, Tryphosa or Persis. Like these women, you may work for the Lord in relative obscurity, but your name is known where it matters, and the work you do makes a difference.

Candid SNAPSHOT Greet Tryphena and Tryphosa, those women who work hard in the Lord. Greet my dear friend Persis, another woman who has worked very hard in the Lord (Romans 16:12).

Faithfulness to the truth.

John's third letter gives us a look at three different people in the early church. Gaius is John's friend, to whom the letter is written. John encourages him to continue to offer hospitality to those who are faithful to the gospel. Diotrephes is a leader in a local church, perhaps in Gaius's church. John condemns Diotrephes's misuse of his position, promising, if he comes, to present the matter to the church. Then, he commends Demetrius, who may have been carrying this letter, to Gaius.

John opens his letter with joy and thanksgiving to Gaius for his faithful hospitality and support of traveling missionaries (3Jn 5). Hospitality for such people is taking part in their ministry (3Jn 8). John condemns in no uncertain terms Diotrephes' domineering ways (3Jn 9–10). Demetrius, however, gets praise and affirmation for his excellent reputation (3Jn 12).

John admonishes his friend not to imitate evil but to continue to do good (3Jn 11). The book of third John encourages us to do what's right even in the face of opposition.

Quick Study

Author
The apostle John, who also wrote the Gospel of John, 1 and 2 John and Revelation.

Date Written
Probably around the same time as John's first and second letters, around A.D. 90.

Written From
Not known for certain, but possibly Ephesus.

Key Passage
3 John 11 "Dear friend, do not imitate what is evil but what is good. Anyone who does what is good is from God. Anyone who does what is evil has not seen God."

Outline

John's greetings.
3Jn 1–2

Commendation of Gaius.
3Jn 3–8

Condemnation of Diotrephes.
3Jn 9–10

Exhortation to Gaius.
3Jn 11

Commendation of Demetrius.
3Jn 12

Conclusion.
3Jn 13–14

The Women of 3 John

No women are mentioned in the book of 3 John.

3 JOHN

1 [a]2Jn 1 1The elder,[a]

To my dear friend Gaius, whom I love in the
truth.

2Dear friend, I pray that you may enjoy good
health and that all may go well with you, even as
3 your soul is getting along well. 3It gave me great
[b]ver 5,10 joy to have some brothers[b] come and tell about
[c]2Jn 4 your faithfulness to the truth and how you con-
4 tinue to walk in the truth.[c] 4I have no greater joy
[d]1Co 4:15; than to hear that my children[d] are walking in the
1Jn 2:1 truth.
5Dear friend, you are faithful in what you are
doing for the brothers, even though they are
5 strangers to you.[e] 6They have told the church
[e]Ro 12:13; Heb 13:2 about your love. You will do well to send them on
their way in a manner worthy of God. 7It was for
7 [f]Jn 15:21 the sake of the Name[f] that they went out, receiv-
[g]Ac 20:33,35 ing no help from the pagans.[g] 8We ought therefore
to show hospitality to such men so that we may
work together for the truth.
9I wrote to the church, but Diotrephes, who
10 loves to be first, will have nothing to do with us.
[h]2Jn 12 10So if I come,[h] I will call attention to what he is
[i]ver 5 doing, gossiping maliciously about us. Not satis-
[j]Jn 9:22,34 fied with that, he refuses to welcome the brothers.[i] He also stops those who want to do so and
puts them out of the church.[j]
11 11Dear friend, do not imitate what is evil but
[k]Ps 37:27 what is good.[k] Anyone who does what is good is
[l]1Jn 2:29 [m]1Jn 3:6,9, from God.[l] Anyone who does what is evil has not
10 seen God.[m] 12Demetrius is well spoken of by
12 everyone[n]—and even by the truth itself. We also
[n]1Ti 3:7 speak well of him, and you know that our testi-
[o]Jn 21:24 mony is true.[o]
13I have much to write you, but I do not want to
do so with pen and ink. 14I hope to see you soon,
14 and we will talk face to face.[p]
[p]2Jn 12 [q]Jn 10:3

Peace to you. The friends here send their greetings. Greet the friends there by name.[q]

Hospitality

3JN 8

John is affirming his friend Gaius for Gaius's hospitality in caring for brothers in Christ. It is right for Gaius to offer hospitality to these men who come to proclaim the truth of Jesus Christ.

Hospitality is applauded and encouraged throughout Scripture. Paul ties the practice of hospitality to the assistance of those in need (Ro 12:13) and tells Timothy to motivate leaders and widows to be hospitable (1Ti 3:2; 5:10). Peter tells his listeners to practice hospitality "without grumbling" (1Pe 4:9).

True hospitality welcomes guests not only when it's planned and convenient for you, but also when it's hard or when you don't feel like you have it all together. True hospitality welcomes those people who need you, not just those you need. True hospitality welcomes those whose lifestyle or income or social graces may not be up to "par." True hospitality welcomes the messy youngster, the annoying teenager and the graceless adult. True hospitality is "being Jesus" to all those you meet.

Jude

Contend for the faith.

Some religious teachers in the first century claimed that anything that is made of matter is evil but anything that is spiritual or intellectual is good. Other religious teachers claimed that believers can sin if they want, since their spirits are already saved by grace. Jude writes this brief letter as a direct warning against these teachings, challenging believers to stand firm in their faith. Though he originally planned to write a letter about salvation, he says, Jude writes this cautionary letter to strengthen believers who might be drawn away from the gospel by the persuasive words of these misguided philosophers.

With colorful imagery, direct warnings and forceful promises, Jude's 25 verses give a clear encouragement to contend for the true faith. Jude is alarmed to hear of the infiltration of false teachers into the church (Jude 1–13). He reminds believers of the consequences of ungodly lives (Jude 14–16), and he encourages them to stand firm in a faithful commitment to Christ (Jude 17–21). Jude crowns his letter with a powerfully reassuring benediction of God's majesty and glory (Jude 24–25).

Jude's powerful words urge us to stand firm in the faith. Persuasive teachers of false religion still abound. If we overlook our sin or bend the principles God has given us to live by, our faith rests on shaky foundations. "Build yourselves up in your most holy faith and pray in the Holy Spirit," says Jude (Jude 20). "Keep yourselves in God's love" (Jude 21). Only by these can we stand firm against the false teachings and philosophies that abound in our society today.

Quick Study

Author
Probably Jesus' half-brother Jude (Jude 1).

Date Written
Most likely around A.D. 65.

Written From
Unknown.

Key Passage
Jude 20–22 "Dear friends, build yourselves up in your most holy faith and pray in the Holy Spirit. Keep yourselves in God's love as you wait for the mercy of our Lord Jesus Christ to bring you to eternal life. Be merciful to those who doubt."

Outline

Jude's greeting.
Jude 1-2

Reason for the letter.
Jude 3-4

Warnings against false teachers.
Jude 5-16

Encouraging believers.
Jude 17-23

Closing praise.
Jude 24-25

The Women of Jude

No women are mentioned in the book of Jude.

Arrogance

JUDE 8-10

The book of Jude sounds a passionate warning to believers whose faith is under attack, not from the world, but from immoral and rebellious elements within the church. The warning is directed toward those who have become arrogant, especially in regard to the spiritual realm. They "slander," or curse, angels. The example Jude uses in Jude 9 is not found in the Biblical account of Moses' death (Dt 34:5-6) but is recorded in another ancient writing, the Assumption of Moses, and is part of Jewish tradition. Even Michael, an important archangel, isn't so arrogant as to curse other angelic beings. Jude's point is an essential one for believers: We are to conduct ourselves with humility in the spiritual realm. Our responsibility is to submit to the authority of God himself, not to usurp his authority by taking it on ourselves.

1 Jude,[a] a servant of Jesus Christ and a brother of
James,

To those who have been called,[b] who are loved
by God the Father and kept by[a] Jesus Christ:[c]

2 Mercy, peace and love be yours in abundance.[d]

The Sin and Doom of Godless Men

3 Dear friends, although I was very eager to
write to you about the salvation we share,[e] I felt I
had to write and urge you to contend[f] for the faith
that was once for all entrusted to the saints. 4 For
certain men whose condemnation was written
about[b] long ago have secretly slipped in among
you.[g] They are godless men, who change the
grace of our God into a license for immorality and
deny Jesus Christ our only Sovereign and Lord.[h]
5 Though you already know all this, I want to
remind you that the Lord[c] delivered his people out
of Egypt, but later destroyed those who did not
believe.[i] 6 And the angels who did not keep their
positions of authority but abandoned their own
home—these he has kept in darkness, bound with
everlasting chains for judgment on the great Day.[j]
7 In a similar way, Sodom and Gomorrah and the
surrounding towns[k] gave themselves up to sexual
immorality and perversion. They serve as an
example of those who suffer the punishment of
eternal fire.[l]
8 In the very same way, these dreamers pollute
their own bodies, reject authority and slander
celestial beings.[m] 9 But even the archangel Michael,[n] when he was disputing with the devil about
the body of Moses, did not dare to bring a slanderous accusation against him, but said, "The
Lord rebuke you!"[o] 10 Yet these men speak abusively against whatever they do not understand;
and what things they do understand by instinct,
like unreasoning animals—these are the very
things that destroy them.[p]
11 Woe to them! They have taken the way of
Cain;[q] they have rushed for profit into Balaam's
error;[r] they have been destroyed in Korah's
rebellion.[s]
12 These men are blemishes at your love feasts,[t]
eating with you without the slightest qualm—
shepherds who feed only themselves. They are
clouds without rain,[u] blown along by the wind;[v]
autumn trees, without fruit and uprooted[w]—twice
dead. 13 They are wild waves of the sea,[x] foaming
up their shame;[y] wandering stars, for whom
blackest darkness has been reserved forever.[z]
14 Enoch,[a] the seventh from Adam, prophesied
about these men: "See, the Lord is coming with
thousands upon thousands of his holy ones[b] 15 to
judge[c] everyone, and to convict all the ungodly of
all the ungodly acts they have done in the ungodly way, and of all the harsh words ungodly sin-

1 [a]Mt 13:55; Ac 1:13 [b]Ro 1:6,7 [c]Jn 17:12
2 [d]2Pe 1:2
3 [e]Tit 1:4 [f]1Ti 6:12
4 [g]Gal 2:4 [h]Tit 1:16; 2Pe 2:1
5 [i]Nu 14:29; Ps 106:26
6 [j]2Pe 2:4,9
7 [k]Dt 29:23 [l]2Pe 2:6
8 [m]2Pe 2:10
9 [n]Da 10:13,21 [o]Zec 3:2
10 [p]2Pe 2:12
11 [q]Ge 4:3-8; 1Jn 3:12 [r]2Pe 2:15 [s]Nu 16:1-3, 31-35
12 [t]2Pe 2:13; 1Co 11:20-22 [u]Pr 25:14; 2Pe 2:17 [v]Eph 4:14 [w]Mt 15:13
13 [x]Isa 57:20 [y]Php 3:19 [z]2Pe 2:17
14 [a]Ge 5:18,21-24 [b]Dt 33:2; Da 7:10
15 [c]2Pe 2:6-9

[a] 1 Or *for*; or *in condemnation* [b] 4 Or *men who were marked out for* [c] 5 Some early manuscripts *Jesus*

15 ners have spoken against him."[d] 16These men are
[d]1Ti 1:9 grumblers and faultfinders; they follow their own
16 evil desires; they boast[e] about themselves and flat-
[e]2Pe 2:18 ter others for their own advantage.

A Call to Persevere

17 [f]2Pe 3:2 17But, dear friends, remember what the apostles
of our Lord Jesus Christ foretold.[f] 18They said to
18 [g]1Ti 4:1 you, "In the last times[g] there will be scoffers who
[h]2Pe 2:1 will follow their own ungodly desires."[h] 19These
are the men who divide you, who follow mere
19 [i]1Co 2:14,15 natural instincts and do not have the Spirit.[i]
20But you, dear friends, build yourselves up[j] in
20 [j]Col 2:7 your most holy faith and pray in the Holy Spirit.[k]
[k]Eph 6:18 21Keep yourselves in God's love as you wait[l] for
the mercy of our Lord Jesus Christ to bring you to
21 [l]Tit 2:13; eternal life.
2Pe 3:12 22Be merciful to those who doubt; 23snatch others from the fire and save them;[m] to others show
23 [m]Am 4:11; mercy, mixed with fear—hating even the clothing
Zec 3:2-5 stained by corrupted flesh.[n]
[n]Rev 3:4

Doxology

24 [o]Ro 16:25 24To him who is able[o] to keep you from falling
[p]2Co 4:14 and to present you before his glorious presence[p]
[q]Col 1:22 without fault[q] and with great joy— 25to the only
25 [r]Jn 5:44; God[r] our Savior be glory, majesty, power and
1Ti 1:17 authority, through Jesus Christ our Lord, before
[s]Heb 13:8 all ages, now and forevermore![s] Amen.[t]
[t]Ro 11:36

Be Merciful.

JUDE 22-23

As believers, we are always called to be people of mercy (Mt 5:7). But that mercy is to be mixed with wisdom so that tenderness, truthfulness and humility mark our ministry to those who are struggling with their faith and to those who still do not believe. We must be especially careful as we approach those caught up in moral sins. Immorality produces a pervasive corruption, much like death. Even the clothes on a dead body will be destroyed by the decay of that body. Therefore, we must take care that we guard our own lives. Galatians 6:1 makes a similar point: Our involvement with those in sin must be conducted with a cautious humility. We are all "temptable" people and can never assume we are safe from sinful choices.

Revelation

Jesus is the victor!

John's vision in the book of Revelation gives us a glimpse of Jesus Christ as the returning King of kings. John, exiled by the Romans to the island of Patmos as a result of his proclamation of the gospel, receives a vision from God that reveals the hidden happenings of the future. Filled with bizarre images and supernatural beings, the vision affirms God's control over history and proclaims Jesus' ultimate victory over Satan.

John's warnings to the seven churches of the Roman province of Asia (Rev 2–3) reminds us that our attitudes and actions are important to God. We are awed as we glimpse the throne of heaven (Rev 4–5), and we shudder as we watch the devastation of God's judgment (Rev 6–11). Yet we also find great comfort as we see God's protection for the woman and her child (Rev 12). We read the *hallelujahs* of Revelation 19 and shout our own joy and relief at Jesus' victory. The picture John paints through his vision is one of initial horror and judgment but ultimate beauty and rest and victory for our God. We rejoice in the wonder of John's description of the new Jerusalem (Rev 21–22)—a place with no more death, no more crying, no more pain.

Though scholars differ on the exact interpretation and timetable of events in John's vision, the book of Revelation deserves careful study because of its powerful promise of Jesus Christ as the coming King and glorified Lord. Sin and evil will not last forever. God, who holds the future firmly in his hands, promises that good will triumph. Jesus Christ will overcome!

Quick Study

Author
The apostle John, who also wrote the Gospel of John and the letters of John.

Date Written
Around A.D. 95.

Written From
The island of Patmos, which was probably a Roman penal settlement.

Key Passage
Revelation 21:2–4 "I saw the Holy City, the new Jerusalem, coming down out of heaven from God, prepared as a bride beautifully dressed for her husband. And I heard a loud voice from the throne saying, 'Now the dwelling of God is with men, and he will live with them. They will be his people, and God himself will be with them and be their God. He will wipe every tear from their eyes. There will be no more death or mourning or crying or pain, for the old order of things has passed away.' "

Outline

Prologue and John's greetings. Rev 1:1-8

Jesus among the seven churches. Rev 1:9-20

Letters to the seven churches. Rev 2:1—3:22

The throne, the scroll and the Lamb. Rev 4:1—5:14

The seven seals. Rev 6:1—8:1

The seven trumpets. Rev 8:2—11:19

The woman and the dragon. Rev 12:1—13:1

The beast out of the sea. Rev 13:2-10

The beast out of the earth. Rev 13:11-18

The Lamb and the 144,000. Rev 14:1-5

Three angels and a harvest. Rev 14:6-20

Seven angels and seven plagues. Rev 15

The seven bowls. Rev 16

Babylon, the great prostitute. Rev 17:1—19:5

The wedding of the Lamb. Rev 19:6-10

The return of Christ. Rev 19:11-21

The thousand years. Rev 20:1-6

Satan's doom. Rev 20:7-10

The great white throne judgment. Rev 20:11-15

New heaven, new earth and new Jerusalem. Rev 21:1—22:5

Coming soon. Rev 22:6-21

The Women of Revelation

Jezebel	*She misled God's people.* Rev 2:20-23
The woman clothed with the sun	*She gave birth to a son.* Rev 12:1-17
The great prostitute	*Intoxicating to the people of earth.* Rev 17:1—18:24
The bride of the Lamb	*Dressed in fine linen, bright and clean.* Rev 19:7-8; 21:2,9; 22:17

Alpha and Omega

REV 1:8

Alpha, the first letter of the Greek alphabet, and omega, the last, are used in Revelation 1:8 to signify God's authority over all creation and history. From the beginning to the end, first to last, he is the ruler of all—the One "who is, and who was, and who is to come" (Rev 1:4). Everything that we know of, and all that we do not know, exist "from him and through him and to him" (Ro 11:36).

What are you most thankful for? Your children? Your spouse? Health? Home? Work? Friends? Ultimately, God created and controls all that you treasure. Make a list of five to ten things for which you are grateful. Then acknowledge to God that he is the source of each one. Tell him that you know he is in charge at this moment, that he always has been and that he always will be. Now praise him! Give him glory for his mighty works that you are enjoying in your life today.

Prologue

1 The revelation of Jesus Christ, which God gave
him to show his servants what must soon take
place. He made it known by sending his angel[a] to
his servant John, 2who testifies to everything he
saw—that is, the word of God and the testimony
of Jesus Christ.[b] 3Blessed is the one who reads the
words of this prophecy, and blessed are those who
hear it and take to heart what is written in it,[c]
because the time is near.

Greetings and Doxology

4John,

To the seven churches in the province of Asia:

Grace and peace to you from him who is, and
who was, and who is to come, and from the sev-
en spirits[a][d] before his throne, 5and from Jesus
Christ, who is the faithful witness,[e] the firstborn
from the dead,[f] and the ruler of the kings of the
earth.[g]

To him who loves us and has freed us from our
sins by his blood, 6and has made us to be a kingdom and priests[h] to serve his God and Father—to
him be glory and power for ever and ever! Amen.[i]

7Look, he is coming with the clouds,[j]
and every eye will see him,
even those who pierced him;
and all the peoples of the earth will
mourn[k] because of him.
So shall it be! Amen.

8"I am the Alpha and the Omega,"[l] says the
Lord God, "who is, and who was, and who is to
come, the Almighty."[m]

One Like a Son of Man

9I, John, your brother and companion in the
suffering[n] and kingdom and patient endurance[o]
that are ours in Jesus, was on the island of Patmos because of the word of God and the testimony of Jesus. 10On the Lord's Day I was in the Spirit,[p] and I heard behind me a loud voice like a
trumpet,[q] 11which said: "Write on a scroll what
you see and send it to the seven churches:[r] to Ephesus, Smyrna, Pergamum, Thyatira, Sardis,[s] Philadelphia and Laodicea."

12I turned around to see the voice that was
speaking to me. And when I turned I saw seven
golden lampstands,[t] 13and among the lampstands
was someone "like a son of man,"[b][u] dressed in a
robe reaching down to his feet and with a golden
sash around his chest.[v] 14His head and hair were
white like wool, as white as snow, and his eyes
were like blazing fire.[w] 15His feet were like bronze
glowing in a furnace,[x] and his voice was like the
sound of rushing waters.[y] 16In his right hand he

1:1 [a]Rev 22:16
1:2 [b]1Co 1:6; Rev 12:17
1:3 [c]Lk 11:28
1:4 [d]Rev 3:1; 4:5
1:5 [e]Rev 3:14 [f]Col 1:18 [g]Rev 17:14
1:6 [h]1Pe 2:5 [i]Ro 11:36
1:7 [j]Da 7:13 [k]Zec 12:10
1:8 [l]Rev 21:6 [m]Rev 4:8
1:9 [n]Php 4:14 [o]2Ti 2:12
1:10 [p]Rev 4:2 [q]Rev 4:1
1:11 [r]ver 4,20 [s]Rev 3:1
1:12 [t]Ex 25:31-40; Zec 4:2
1:13 [u]Eze 1:26; Da 7:13; 10:16 [v]Da 10:5; Rev 15:6
1:14 [w]Da 7:9; 10:6; Rev 19:12
1:15 [x]Da 10:6 [y]Eze 43:2; Rev 14:2

[a] 4 Or *the sevenfold Spirit* [b] 13 Daniel 7:13

held seven stars,[z] and out of his mouth came a sharp double-edged sword.[a] His face was like the sun shining in all its brilliance.

[17]When I saw him, I fell at his feet[b] as though dead. Then he placed his right hand on me and said: "Do not be afraid. I am the First and the Last.[c] [18]I am the Living One; I was dead,[d] and behold I am alive for ever and ever![e] And I hold the keys of death and Hades.[f]

[19]"Write, therefore, what you have seen, what is now and what will take place later. [20]The mystery of the seven stars that you saw in my right hand and of the seven golden lampstands[g] is this: The seven stars are the angels[a] of the seven churches,[h] and the seven lampstands are the seven churches.[i]

To the Church in Ephesus

2 "To the angel[b] of the church in Ephesus write:

These are the words of him who holds the seven stars in his right hand[j] and walks among the seven golden lampstands:[k] [2]I know your deeds,[l] your hard work and your perseverance. I know that you cannot tolerate wicked men, that you have tested[m] those who claim to be apostles but are not, and have found them false.[n] [3]You have persevered and have endured hardships for my name,[o] and have not grown weary.

[4]Yet I hold this against you: You have forsaken your first love.[p] [5]Remember the height from which you have fallen! Repent[q] and do the things you did at first. If you do not repent, I will come to you and remove your lampstand[r] from its place. [6]But you have this in your favor: You hate the practices of the Nicolaitans,[s] which I also hate.

[7]He who has an ear, let him hear[t] what the Spirit says to the churches. To him who overcomes, I will give the right to eat from the tree of life,[u] which is in the paradise[v] of God.

To the Church in Smyrna

[8]"To the angel of the church in Smyrna[w] write:

These are the words of him who is the First and the Last,[x] who died and came to life again.[y] [9]I know your afflictions and your poverty—yet you are rich![z] I know the slander of those who say they are Jews and are not,[a] but are a synagogue of Satan.[b] [10]Do not be afraid of what you are about to suffer. I tell you, the devil will put some of you in prison to test you,[c] and you will suffer persecution for ten days.[d] Be faithful,[e] even to the point of death, and I will give you the crown of life.

[11]He who has an ear, let him hear what the

[a] 20 Or *messengers* [b] 1 Or *messenger*; also in verses 8, 12 and 18

Ephesus and Smyrna

REV 2:1-11

Located at the mouth of the Cayster River, on the western coast of Asia Minor, Ephesus was home to one of the Roman Empire's major harbors. *A center of trade on the primary route from Rome to the East, this large city served as a meeting point for Western and Eastern religions and cultures.* It was also well known for its temple to the Greek goddess Artemis (Ac 19:35). Though the church at Ephesus *excelled at resisting false teaching and in persevering through adversity, it focused too much on fighting error and fell short in one vital area: love.*

One of the richest Asian trading centers of its time, the beautiful port city of Smyrna served as a center for culture and claimed to be the birthplace of the Greek poet Homer. The believers at Smyrna *appear to have found favor in the eyes of the risen Christ, who testified that although they faced persecution and poverty, they remained truly wealthy in the spiritual realm.*

See Map 13: Paul's Missionary Journeys at the back of this Bible for the location of Ephesus and Smyrna.

1:16 [z]Rev 2:1; 3:1 [a]Isa 49:2; Heb 4:12; Rev 2:12,16
1:17 [b]Eze 1:28; Da 8:17,18 [c]Isa 41:4; 44:6; 48:12; Rev 22:13
1:18 [d]Ro 6:9 [e]Rev 4:9,10 [f]Rev 20:1
1:20 [g]Zec 4:2 [h]ver 4,11 [i]Mt 5:14,15
2:1 [j]Rev 1:16 [k]Rev 1:12,13
2:2 [l]Rev 3:1,8, 15 [m]1Jn 4:1 [n]2Co 11:13
2:3 [o]Jn 15:21
2:4 [p]Mt 24:12
2:5 [q]ver 16,22 [r]Rev 1:20
2:6 [s]ver 15
2:7 [t]Mt 11:15; Rev 3:6,13, 22 [u]Ge 2:9; Rev 22:2,14, 19 [v]Lk 23:43
2:8 [w]Rev 1:11 [x]Rev 1:17 [y]Rev 1:18
2:9 [z]Jas 2:5 [a]Rev 3:9 [b]Mt 4:10
2:10 [c]Rev 3:10 [d]Da 1:12,14 [e]ver 13

Pergamum and Thyatira

REV 2:12–29

Found in the Caicus River Valley of northwestern Asia Minor, approximately 15 miles from the Aegean Sea, Pergamum served as the seat of an independent kingdom before becoming the capital of the Roman province of Asia in 133 B.C., despite the fact that it was not located on any major trade routes. Worship of the Roman emperor was considered a test of loyalty in Pergamum, and Antipas (Rev 2:13) became the first martyr of Asia. Yet the Christian church held firm through persecution. Though Jesus commended the church in Pergamum for their faithfulness, he also noted that he had "a few things against" them (Rev 2:14), things for which he called them to repentance (Rev 2:16).

The city of Thyatira was located in the province of Lydia, in western Asia Minor, along the route between Pergamum and Sardis. Though not a large city, Thyatira was a thriving manufacturing and commercial center and was home to many trade guilds. Members of these guilds were often required to participate in pagan practices. In this letter, the Christian church is warned against paganism and sexual immorality; the believers, however, are praised for their love, faithfulness, service and perseverance.

See Map 13: Paul's Missionary Journeys at the back of this Bible for the location of Pergamum and Thyatira.

Spirit says to the churches. He who overcomes will not be hurt at all by the second
death.[f]

To the Church in Pergamum

12"To the angel of the church in Pergamum[g] write:

These are the words of him who has the
sharp, double-edged sword.[h] 13I know where
you live—where Satan has his throne. Yet
you remain true to my name. You did not
renounce your faith in me,[i] even in the days
of Antipas, my faithful witness, who was put
to death in your city—where Satan lives.[j]
14Nevertheless, I have a few things against
you:[k] You have people there who hold to the
teaching of Balaam,[l] who taught Balak to
entice the Israelites to sin by eating food sacrificed to idols and by committing sexual
immorality.[m] 15Likewise you also have those
who hold to the teaching of the Nicolaitans.[n]
16Repent therefore! Otherwise, I will soon
come to you and will fight against them with
the sword of my mouth.[o]
17He who has an ear, let him hear what the
Spirit says to the churches. To him who overcomes, I will give some of the hidden manna.[p] I will also give him a white stone with a
new name[q] written on it, known only to him
who receives it.[r]

To the Church in Thyatira

18"To the angel of the church in Thyatira[s] write:

These are the words of the Son of God,
whose eyes are like blazing fire and whose
feet are like burnished bronze.[t] 19I know your
deeds,[u] your love and faith, your service and
perseverance, and that you are now doing
more than you did at first.
20Nevertheless, I have this against you: You
tolerate that woman Jezebel,[v] who calls herself a prophetess. By her teaching she misleads my servants into sexual immorality and
the eating of food sacrificed to idols. 21I have
given her time[w] to repent of her immorality,
but she is unwilling.[x] 22So I will cast her on a
bed of suffering, and I will make those who
commit adultery[y] with her suffer intensely,
unless they repent of her ways. 23I will strike
her children dead. Then all the churches will
know that I am he who searches hearts and
minds,[z] and I will repay each of you according to your deeds. 24Now I say to the rest of
you in Thyatira, to you who do not hold to
her teaching and have not learned Satan's so-
called deep secrets (I will not impose any other burden on you):[a] 25Only hold on to what
you have[b] until I come.
26To him who overcomes and does my will

2:11 [f]Rev 20:6,14; 21:8
2:12 [g]Rev 1:11 [h]Rev 1:16
2:13 [i]Rev 14:12 [j]ver 9,24
2:14 [k]ver 20 [l]2Pe 2:15 [m]1Co 6:13
2:15 [n]ver 6
2:16 [o]2Th 2:8; Rev 1:16
2:17 [p]Jn 6:49,50 [q]Isa 62:2 [r]Rev 19:12
2:18 [s]Rev 1:11 [t]Rev 1:14,15
2:19 [u]ver 2
2:20 [v]1Ki 16:31; 21:25; 2Ki 9:7
2:21 [w]Ro 2:4 [x]Rev 9:20
2:22 [y]Rev 17:2; 18:9
2:23 [z]1Sa 16:7; Jer 11:20; Ac 1:24; Ro 8:27
2:24 [a]Ac 15:28
2:25 [b]Rev 3:11

to the end, I will give authority over the nations[c]—

27 'He will rule them with an iron scepter;[d]
he will dash them to pieces like
pottery'[a][e]—

just as I have received authority from my Father. 28 I will also give him the morning star.[f] 29 He who has an ear, let him hear[g] what the Spirit says to the churches.

To the Church in Sardis

3 "To the angel[b] of the church in Sardis write:

These are the words of him who holds the seven spirits[c][h] of God and the seven stars.[i] I know your deeds;[j] you have a reputation of being alive, but you are dead.[k] 2 Wake up! Strengthen what remains and is about to die, for I have not found your deeds complete in the sight of my God. 3 Remember, therefore, what you have received and heard; obey it, and repent.[l] But if you do not wake up, I will come like a thief,[m] and you will not know at what time I will come to you.

4 Yet you have a few people in Sardis who have not soiled their clothes.[n] They will walk with me, dressed in white,[o] for they are worthy. 5 He who overcomes will, like them, be dressed in white. I will never blot out his name from the book of life,[p] but will acknowledge his name before my Father[q] and his angels. 6 He who has an ear, let him hear[r] what the Spirit says to the churches.

To the Church in Philadelphia

7 "To the angel of the church in Philadelphia[s] write:

These are the words of him who is holy and true,[t] who holds the key of David.[u] What he opens no one can shut, and what he shuts no one can open. 8 I know your deeds. See, I have placed before you an open door[v] that no one can shut. I know that you have little strength, yet you have kept my word and have not denied my name.[w] 9 I will make those who are of the synagogue of Satan,[x] who claim to be Jews though they are not, but are liars—I will make them come and fall down at your feet[y] and acknowledge that I have loved you.[z] 10 Since you have kept my command to endure patiently, I will also keep you[a] from the hour of trial that is going to come upon the whole world to test[b] those who live on the earth.[c]

11 I am coming soon. Hold on to what you have,[d] so that no one will take your crown.[e]

2:26 [c]Ps 2:8; Rev 3:21
2:27 [d]Rev 12:5 [e]Isa 30:14; Jer 19:11
2:28 [f]Rev 22:16
2:29 [g]ver 7
3:1 [h]Rev 1:4 [i]Rev 1:16 [j]Rev 2:2 [k]1Ti 5:6
3:3 [l]Rev 2:5 [m]2Pe 3:10
3:4 [n]Jude 23 [o]Rev 4:4; 6:11; 7:9,13, 14
3:5 [p]Rev 20:12 [q]Mt 10:32
3:6 [r]Rev 2:7
3:7 [s]Rev 1:11 [t]1Jn 5:20 [u]Isa 22:22; Mt 16:19
3:8 [v]Ac 14:27 [w]Rev 2:13
3:9 [x]Rev 2:9 [y]Isa 49:23 [z]Isa 43:4
3:10 [a]2Pe 2:9 [b]Rev 2:10 [c]Rev 6:10; 17:8
3:11 [d]Rev 2:25 [e]Rev 2:10

[a] *27* Psalm 2:9 [b] *1* Or *messenger*; also in verses 7 and 14
[c] *1* Or *the sevenfold Spirit*

Sardis and Philadelphia

REV 3:1–13

The capital of the ancient kingdom of Lydia, located on the western coast of Asia Minor, Sardis was at one time one of the most powerful cities of the world. Well fortified and easy to defend, this city was eventually controlled by several different ancient empires—Persia, Greece and Rome. Under Roman rule, Sardis served as a vital center for the Christian church. Yet this success may have been due more to the city's past reputation than to an ongoing vitality (Rev 3:1).

The city of Philadelphia was located 28 miles southeast of Sardis. Once a major center of Greek culture, Philadelphia suffered from an earthquake in A.D. 17 and much rebuilding was required. The church at Philadelphia had "little strength" (Rev 3:8), probably meaning its numbers were small. Yet the risen Lord promised that the believers would be rewarded richly for the faithfulness they had demonstrated.

See Map 13: Paul's Missionary Journeys at the back of this Bible for the location of Sardis and Philadelphia.

12 Him who overcomes I will make a pillar[f] in the temple of my God. Never again will he leave it. I will write on him the name of my God[g] and the name of the city of my God, the new Jerusalem,[h] which is coming down out of heaven from my God; and I will also write on him my new name. 13 He who has an ear, let him hear what the Spirit says to the churches.

To the Church in Laodicea

14 "To the angel of the church in Laodicea write:

These are the words of the Amen, the faithful and true witness, the ruler of God's creation.[i] 15 I know your deeds, that you are neither cold nor hot.[j] I wish you were either one or the other! 16 So, because you are lukewarm—neither hot nor cold—I am about to spit you out of my mouth. 17 You say, 'I am rich; I have acquired wealth and do not need a thing.'[k] But you do not realize that you are wretched, pitiful, poor, blind and naked. 18 I counsel you to buy from me gold refined in the fire, so you can become rich; and white clothes to wear, so you can cover your shameful nakedness;[l] and salve to put on your eyes, so you can see.

19 Those whom I love I rebuke and discipline.[m] So be earnest, and repent.[n] 20 Here I am! I stand at the door[o] and knock. If anyone hears my voice and opens the door,[p] I will come in[q] and eat with him, and he with me.

21 To him who overcomes, I will give the right to sit with me on my throne,[r] just as I overcame[s] and sat down with my Father on his throne. 22 He who has an ear, let him hear[t] what the Spirit says to the churches."

The Throne in Heaven

4 After this I looked, and there before me was a door standing open in heaven. And the voice I had first heard speaking to me like a trumpet[u] said, "Come up here,[v] and I will show you what must take place after this."[w] 2 At once I was in the Spirit,[x] and there before me was a throne in heaven[y] with someone sitting on it. 3 And the one who sat there had the appearance of jasper and carnelian. A rainbow,[z] resembling an emerald, encircled the throne. 4 Surrounding the throne were twenty-four other thrones, and seated on them were twenty-four elders.[a] They were dressed in white[b] and had crowns of gold on their heads. 5 From the throne came flashes of lightning, rumblings and peals of thunder.[c] Before the throne, seven lamps[d] were blazing. These are the seven spirits[a][e] of God. 6 Also before the throne there was what looked like a sea of glass,[f] clear as crystal.

In the center, around the throne, were four living creatures,[g] and they were covered with eyes, in

3:12 [f]Gal 2:9 [g]Rev 14:1; 22:4 [h]Rev 21:2,10
3:14 [i]Col 1:16,18
3:15 [j]Ro 12:11
3:17 [k]Hos 12:8; 1Co 4:8
3:18 [l]Rev 16:15
3:19 [m]Pr 3:12; Heb 12:5,6 [n]Rev 2:5
3:20 [o]Mt 24:33 [p]Lk 12:36 [q]Jn 14:23
3:21 [r]Mt 19:28 [s]Rev 5:5
3:22 [t]Rev 2:7
4:1 [u]Rev 1:10 [v]Rev 11:12 [w]Rev 1:19
4:2 [x]Rev 1:10 [y]Isa 6:1; Eze 1:26-28; Da 7:9
4:3 [z]Eze 1:28
4:4 [a]Rev 11:16 [b]Rev 3:4,5
4:5 [c]Rev 8:5; 16:18 [d]Zec 4:2 [e]Rev 1:4
4:6 [f]Rev 15:2 [g]Eze 1:5

Laodicea

REV 3:14-22

Named after Laodice, wife of its founder (Antiochus II), the city of Laodicea was built on the banks of the Lycus River in the district of Phrygia around the middle of the third century B.C. *Located on a major trade route to the West, Laodicea thrived under Roman rule and became a strong agricultural and marketing center. After being damaged severely by an earthquake in* A.D. *60, wealthy Laodicea was able to rebuild without financial assistance from Rome. While Jesus does not cite specific reasons for his displeasure with the Laodicean church, his language indicates that their transgressions—which seemingly include apathy, complacency and excessive self-sufficiency—were severe.*

See Map 13: Paul's Missionary Journeys at the back of this Bible for the location of Laodicea.

[a] 5 Or *the sevenfold Spirit*

Week 51

Are You Coping or Conquering?

Life is hard, and most people get through it simply by coping. If people are unhappy in marriage, parenthood, career or friendships, they mostly do the best they can. They cope. But is this the way God wants believers to live?

Paul once referred to life as a race (1Co 9:24-27). The goal is not merely to finish the race, but to *win*, to *conquer*. Paul says in Romans 8:37, "We are more than conquerors through him who loved us." Is your goal in life simply to cope, to get through? Or do you want to be a conqueror, an overcomer? How can you be an overcomer, and what does overcoming require?

Jesus says, "Take heart! I have overcome the world" (Jn 16:33). And John assures us, "The one who is in you is greater than the one who is in the world" (1Jn 4:4). What is the imperative to enjoy Jesus' victory over the world and over Satan (Rev 2:3)? What will be your reward if you overcome (Rev 2:7)?

Although believers must continue their struggle with sin and Satan in this life, there is a finish line in the distance. What must you do in order to gain the crown of life at the end of your race (Rev 2:10)? What will be your reward if you overcome (Rev 2:11)?

Spiritual battles are being fought around you every moment (Eph 6:12). How can you stand against the enemy (Rev 2:13)? What will be your reward if you overcome (Rev 2:17)?

Spiritual deceptions abound in the world. What can you do to stand against them (Rev 2:24-25)? What will be your reward if you overcome (Rev 2:26)?

How can you prevent apathy in your Christian life (Rev 3:2-3)? What will be your reward if you overcome (Rev 3:5)?

What is the key to overcoming (Rev 3:8)? What will be your reward if you overcome (Rev 3:12)?

Enjoying God THROUGH the Word

Read Romans 8:35-39 (pages 1860-1861) and allow these beautiful words of hope to flood your soul. You are an overcomer because of Jesus Christ. "Who is it that overcomes the world? Only he who believes that Jesus is the Son of God" (1Jn 5:5); and, "The one who is in you is greater than the one who is in the world" (1 Jn 4:4). Praise God!

When trials, troubles, persecutions, disasters or attacks come, don't give in to fear. God will supply the strength you need to overcome in your adversity. Notice that little word "in." God does not usually deliver you out of adversity; he gives you the strength to overcome in (or through) the adversity.

Enjoying God THROUGH Experience

Think about some of the things in which you're experiencing difficulty right now. Are you merely coping in these areas instead of overcoming? Express your thanks to God in prayer for his love and the power he makes available to you so that you can do more than cope—you can overcome. If you feel weak, ask him for his strength. He is able to supply all your needs (Php 4:19).

Go to page 2084 for your next weekly study.

front and in back. 7 The first living creature was like
a lion, the second was like an ox, the third had a
face like a man, the fourth was like a flying eagle.[h]
8 Each of the four living creatures had six wings[i]
and was covered with eyes all around, even under
his wings. Day and night they never stop saying:

> "Holy, holy, holy
> is the Lord God Almighty,[j]
> who was, and is, and is to come."[k]

9 Whenever the living creatures give glory, honor
and thanks to him who sits on the throne[l] and
who lives for ever and ever, 10 the twenty-four elders[m] fall down before him[n] who sits on the
throne,[o] and worship him who lives for ever and
ever. They lay their crowns before the throne and
say:

> 11 "You are worthy, our Lord and God,
> to receive glory and honor and
> power,[p]
> for you created all things,
> and by your will they were created
> and have their being."[q]

The Scroll and the Lamb

5 Then I saw in the right hand of him who sat
on the throne[r] a scroll with writing on both
sides[s] and sealed[t] with seven seals. 2 And I saw a
mighty angel proclaiming in a loud voice, "Who is
worthy to break the seals and open the scroll?"
3 But no one in heaven or on earth or under the
earth could open the scroll or even look inside it.
4 I wept and wept because no one was found who
was worthy to open the scroll or look inside.
5 Then one of the elders said to me, "Do not weep!
See, the Lion[u] of the tribe of Judah, the Root of
David,[v] has triumphed. He is able to open the
scroll and its seven seals."
6 Then I saw a Lamb,[w] looking as if it had been
slain, standing in the center of the throne, encircled by the four living creatures and the elders.
He had seven horns and seven eyes,[x] which are
the seven spirits[a] of God sent out into all the
earth. 7 He came and took the scroll from the right
hand of him who sat on the throne.[y] 8 And when
he had taken it, the four living creatures and the
twenty-four elders fell down before the Lamb.
Each one had a harp[z] and they were holding gold-
en bowls full of incense, which are the prayers[a] of
the saints. 9 And they sang a new song:[b]

> "You are worthy[c] to take the scroll
> and to open its seals,
> because you were slain,
> and with your blood[d] you purchased[e]
> men for God
> from every tribe and language and
> people and nation.

4:7 [h]Eze 1:10; 10:14
4:8 [i]Isa 6:2 [j]Isa 6:3; Rev 1:8 [k]Rev 1:4
4:9 [l]Ps 47:8
4:10 [m]ver 4 [n]Rev 5:8,14 [o]ver 2
4:11 [p]Rev 5:12 [q]Rev 10:6
5:1 [r]ver 7,13 [s]Eze 2:9,10 [t]Isa 29:11; Da 12:4
5:5 [u]Ge 49:9 [v]Isa 11:1,10; Ro 15:12; Rev 22:16
5:6 [w]Jn 1:29 [x]Zec 4:10
5:7 [y]ver 1
5:8 [z]Rev 14:2 [a]Ps 141:2
5:9 [b]Ps 40:3 [c]Rev 4:11 [d]Heb 9:12 [e]1Co 6:20

R*unning to hide our faces in God is not like seeking the comfort and familiarity of a childhood blanket that allows us to tune out the realities of our lives. God is a mighty lion, whose roar is heard in every corner of the world. Still, when you are in trouble, you can hide your face from him or run to him and let him hide you . . . There you will find strength to live your life.*

—Sheila Walsh

[a] 6 Or *the sevenfold Spirit*

> 10 You have made them to be a kingdom
> and priests[f] to serve our God,
> and they will reign on the earth."

11 Then I looked and heard the voice of many angels, numbering thousands upon thousands, and ten thousand times ten thousand.[g] They encircled the throne and the living creatures and the elders. 12 In a loud voice they sang:

> "Worthy is the Lamb, who was slain,
> to receive power and wealth and
> wisdom and strength
> and honor and glory and praise!"[h]

13 Then I heard every creature in heaven and on earth and under the earth[i] and on the sea, and all that is in them, singing:

> "To him who sits on the throne and to
> the Lamb[j]
> be praise and honor and glory and
> power,
> for ever and ever!"[k]

14 The four living creatures said, "Amen,"[l] and the elders fell down and worshiped.[m]

The Seals

6 I watched as the Lamb[n] opened the first of the seven seals.[o] Then I heard one of the four living creatures[p] say in a voice like thunder,[q] "Come!" 2 I looked, and there before me was a white horse![r] Its rider held a bow, and he was given a crown,[s] and he rode out as a conqueror bent on conquest.[t]

3 When the Lamb opened the second seal, I heard the second living creature[u] say, "Come!" 4 Then another horse came out, a fiery red one.[v] Its rider was given power to take peace from the earth[w] and to make men slay each other. To him was given a large sword.

5 When the Lamb opened the third seal, I heard the third living creature[x] say, "Come!" I looked, and there before me was a black horse![y] Its rider was holding a pair of scales in his hand. 6 Then I heard what sounded like a voice among the four living creatures,[z] saying, "A quart[a] of wheat for a day's wages,[b] and three quarts of barley for a day's wages,[b] and do not damage[a] the oil and the wine!"

7 When the Lamb opened the fourth seal, I heard the voice of the fourth living creature[b] say, "Come!" 8 I looked, and there before me was a pale horse![c] Its rider was named Death, and Hades[d] was following close behind him. They were given power over a fourth of the earth to kill by sword, famine and plague, and by the wild beasts of the earth.[e]

9 When he opened the fifth seal, I saw under the altar[f] the souls of those who had been slain[g] because of the word of God and the testimony they had maintained. 10 They called out in a loud

[a] 6 Greek *a choinix* (probably about a liter) [b] 6 Greek *a denarius*

5:10 f1Pe 2:5
5:11 gDa 7:10; Heb 12:22
5:12 hRev 4:11
5:13 iver 3; Php 2:10 jRev 6:16 k1Ch 29:11
5:14 lRev 4:9 mRev 4:10; 19:4
6:1 nRev 5:6 oRev 5:1 pRev 4:6,7 qRev 14:2; 19:6
6:2 rZec 6:3; Rev 19:11 sZec 6:11; Rev 14:14 tPs 45:4
6:3 uRev 4:7
6:4 vZec 6:2 wMt 10:34
6:5 xRev 4:7 yZec 6:2
6:6 zRev 4:6,7 aRev 9:4
6:7 bRev 4:7
6:8 cZec 6:3 dHos 13:14 eJer 15:2,3; Eze 5:12,17
6:9 fRev 14:18; 16:7 gRev 20:4

Seals

REV 6:1-10

Though we do not know specifically what information these seals contain, scholars believe that the scene depicted by the seals tells of future events, including God's judgment and the end of the world. The prospect of these two occurrences is in many ways frightening. Yet we can find tremendous assurance in knowing that nothing will happen that is out of the control of the God who created us and loves us. Just as a seal—a stamped wax impression—is used historically to prove the authenticity and authority of a letter or document, so do these seals testify that the events described are under the authority of God and will happen only with his permission.

144,000

REV 7:1–8

Many scholars believe that the "144,000 from all the tribes of Israel" (Rev 7:4) represent the Christian church. This is a perfectly reasonable explanation, for in the book of Revelation it is common to see Christians described in language generally associated with Jews (Rev 1:6). Other scholars prefer a literal interpretation, viewing the 144,000 as a remnant of believers in the nation of Israel. Whoever they are, we know that God's judgment on the earth will not begin until they receive the seal that will assure them divine protection from his wrath.

voice, "How long,[h] Sovereign Lord, holy and true,[i]
until you judge the inhabitants of the earth and
avenge our blood?"[j] 11Then each of them was giv-
en a white robe,[k] and they were told to wait a little longer, until the number of their fellow servants and brothers who were to be killed as they
had been was completed.[l]
12I watched as he opened the sixth seal. There
was a great earthquake.[m] The sun turned black[n]
like sackcloth made of goat hair, the whole moon
turned blood red, 13and the stars in the sky fell to
earth,[o] as late figs drop from a fig tree[p] when
shaken by a strong wind. 14The sky receded like a
scroll, rolling up, and every mountain and island
was removed from its place.[q]
15Then the kings of the earth, the princes, the
generals, the rich, the mighty, and every slave and
every free man hid in caves and among the rocks
of the mountains.[r] 16They called to the mountains
and the rocks, "Fall on us[s] and hide us from the
face of him who sits on the throne and from the
wrath of the Lamb! 17For the great day[t] of their
wrath has come, and who can stand?"[u]

144,000 Sealed

7 After this I saw four angels standing at the
four corners of the earth, holding back the
four winds[v] of the earth to prevent any wind from
blowing on the land or on the sea or on any tree.
2Then I saw another angel coming up from the
east, having the seal of the living God. He called
out in a loud voice to the four angels who had
been given power to harm the land and the sea:
3"Do not harm[w] the land or the sea or the trees
until we put a seal on the foreheads[x] of the servants of our God." 4Then I heard the number[y] of
those who were sealed: 144,000[z] from all the
tribes of Israel.

5From the tribe of Judah 12,000 were sealed,
from the tribe of Reuben 12,000,
from the tribe of Gad 12,000,
6from the tribe of Asher 12,000,
from the tribe of Naphtali 12,000,
from the tribe of Manasseh 12,000,
7from the tribe of Simeon 12,000,
from the tribe of Levi 12,000,
from the tribe of Issachar 12,000,
8from the tribe of Zebulun 12,000,
from the tribe of Joseph 12,000,
from the tribe of Benjamin 12,000.

The Great Multitude in White Robes

9After this I looked and there before me was a
great multitude that no one could count, from
every nation, tribe, people and language,[a] standing before the throne[b] and in front of the Lamb.
They were wearing white robes and were holding
palm branches in their hands. 10And they cried
out in a loud voice:

6:10 [h]Zec 1:12 [i]Rev 3:7 [j]Rev 19:2
6:11 [k]Rev 3:4 [l]Heb 11:40
6:12 [m]Rev 16:18 [n]Mt 24:29
6:13 [o]Mt 24:29; Rev 8:10; 9:1 [p]Isa 34:4
6:14 [q]Jer 4:24; Rev 16:20
6:15 [r]Isa 2:10,19, 21
6:16 [s]Hos 10:8; Lk 23:30
6:17 [t]Zep 1:14, 15; Rev 16:14 [u]Ps 76:7
7:1 [v]Da 7:2
7:3 [w]Rev 6:6 [x]Eze 9:4; Rev 22:4
7:4 [y]Rev 9:16 [z]Rev 14:1,3
7:9 [a]Rev 5:9 [b]ver 15

"Salvation belongs to our God,[c]
who sits on the throne,
and to the Lamb."

11 All the angels were standing around the throne
and around the elders[d] and the four living creatures.[e] They fell down on their faces[f] before the
throne and worshiped God, 12 saying:

"Amen!
Praise and glory
and wisdom and thanks and honor
and power and strength
be to our God for ever and ever.
Amen!"[g]

13 Then one of the elders asked me, "These in
white robes—who are they, and where did they
come from?"

14 I answered, "Sir, you know."

And he said, "These are they who have come
out of the great tribulation; they have washed
their robes[h] and made them white in the blood of
the Lamb.[i] 15 Therefore,

"they are before the throne of God[j]
and serve him[k] day and night in his
temple;[l]
and he who sits on the throne will
spread his tent over them.[m]
16 Never again will they hunger;
never again will they thirst.
The sun will not beat upon them,
nor any scorching heat.[n]
17 For the Lamb at the center of the throne
will be their shepherd;[o]
he will lead them to springs of living
water.
And God will wipe away every tear from
their eyes."[p]

The Seventh Seal and the Golden Censer

8 When he opened the seventh seal,[q] there was
silence in heaven for about half an hour.

2 And I saw the seven angels[r] who stand before
God, and to them were given seven trumpets.

3 Another angel,[s] who had a golden censer,
came and stood at the altar. He was given much
incense to offer, with the prayers of all the
saints,[t] on the golden altar[u] before the throne.
4 The smoke of the incense, together with the
prayers of the saints, went up before God[v] from
the angel's hand. 5 Then the angel took the
censer, filled it with fire from the altar,[w] and
hurled it on the earth; and there came peals of
thunder,[x] rumblings, flashes of lightning and an
earthquake.[y]

The Trumpets

6 Then the seven angels who had the seven
trumpets[z] prepared to sound them.

7 The first angel sounded his trumpet, and there

7:10 [c]Ps 3:8; Rev 12:10; 19:1
7:11 [d]Rev 4:4 [e]Rev 4:6 [f]Rev 4:10
7:12 [g]Rev 5:12-14
7:14 [h]Rev 22:14 [i]Heb 9:14; 1Jn 1:7
7:15 [j]ver 9 [k]Rev 22:3 [l]Rev 11:19 [m]Isa 4:5,6; Rev 21:3
7:16 [n]Isa 49:10
7:17 [o]Ps 23:1; Jn 10:11 [p]Isa 25:8; Rev 21:4
8:1 [q]Rev 6:1
8:2 [r]ver 6-13; Rev 9:1,13; 11:15
8:3 [s]Rev 7:2 [t]Rev 5:8 [u]Ex 30:1-6; Heb 9:4; Rev 9:13
8:4 [v]Ps 141:2
8:5 [w]Lev 16:12,13 [x]Rev 4:5 [y]Rev 6:12
8:6 [z]ver 2

The Great Tribulation

REV 7:14

While it is quite possible that Revelation speaks of the *beginning* of the great tribulation being experienced by John's readers through the present, "the great tribulation" proper refers to a definite period of extreme suffering and persecution before Christ's return.

Believers today should not focus their thoughts and energy on attempting to predict, or somehow avoid, the great tribulation. As believers, we are certain to experience difficulty and suffering (2Ti 3:12; 1Pe 4:12–16). Jesus himself warned his disciples of this very thing: "If they presecuted me, they will persecute you also" (Jn 15:20; see also Jn 16:33). As believers, we, too, can find assurance in the knowledge that Christ—the One who claims us as his own—will be victorious in every battle, affliction and event described in the book of Revelation.

The Trumpets

REV 8:6—9:21

After a period of glorious praise, joyfully sung by all the creatures of heaven (Rev 7), John is witness to a dramatic silence (Rev 8:1) that is eventually—in God's perfect timing—broken by a blast of thunder, lightning and an earthquake, followed by the sounding of seven trumpets. The significance of their music is great, for the events they call forth will bring destruction to a full third of the earth. The trumpets are the second of three judgments of Revelation, each of which is sevenfold: seven seals (Rev 6; 8:1-5), seven trumpets (Rev 8-9; 11:15-19) and seven bowls (Rev 16).

came hail and fire[a] mixed with blood, and it was
hurled down upon the earth. A third[b] of the earth
was burned up, a third of the trees were burned
up, and all the green grass was burned up.[c]
8 The second angel sounded his trumpet, and
something like a huge mountain,[d] all ablaze, was
thrown into the sea. A third[e] of the sea turned into
blood,[f] 9 a third[g] of the living creatures in the sea
died, and a third of the ships were destroyed.
10 The third angel sounded his trumpet, and a
great star, blazing like a torch, fell from the sky[h]
on a third of the rivers and on the springs of
water[i]— 11 the name of the star is Wormwood.[a] A
third[j] of the waters turned bitter, and many people
died from the waters that had become bitter.[k]
12 The fourth angel sounded his trumpet, and a
third of the sun was struck, a third of the moon,
and a third of the stars, so that a third[l] of them
turned dark.[m] A third of the day was without
light, and also a third of the night.
13 As I watched, I heard an eagle that was flying
in midair[n] call out in a loud voice: "Woe! Woe!
Woe[o] to the inhabitants of the earth, because of
the trumpet blasts about to be sounded by the
other three angels!"

9 The fifth angel sounded his trumpet, and I saw
a star that had fallen from the sky to the
earth.[p] The star was given the key to the shaft of
the Abyss.[q] 2 When he opened the Abyss, smoke
rose from it like the smoke from a gigantic furnace.[r] The sun and sky were darkened[s] by the
smoke from the Abyss. 3 And out of the smoke
locusts[t] came down upon the earth and were giv-
en power like that of scorpions[u] of the earth.
4 They were told not to harm[v] the grass of the earth
or any plant or tree,[w] but only those people who
did not have the seal of God on their foreheads.[x]
5 They were not given power to kill them, but only
to torture them for five months.[y] And the agony
they suffered was like that of the sting of a scorpion[z] when it strikes a man. 6 During those days
men will seek death, but will not find it; they will
long to die, but death will elude them.[a]
7 The locusts looked like horses prepared for battle.[b] On their heads they wore something like
crowns of gold, and their faces resembled human
faces.[c] 8 Their hair was like women's hair, and
their teeth were like lions' teeth.[d] 9 They had
breastplates like breastplates of iron, and the
sound of their wings was like the thundering of
many horses and chariots rushing into battle.[e]
10 They had tails and stings like scorpions, and in
their tails they had power to torment people for
five months.[f] 11 They had as king over them the
angel of the Abyss,[g] whose name in Hebrew is
Abaddon, and in Greek, Apollyon.[b]
12 The first woe is past; two other woes are yet to
come.[h]

a *11* That is, Bitterness *b* *11* *Abaddon* and *Apollyon* mean *Destroyer.*

8:7 [a]Eze 38:22 [b]ver 7-12; Rev 9:15,18; 12:4 [c]Rev 9:4
8:8 [d]Jer 51:25 [e]ver 7 [f]Rev 16:3
8:9 [g]ver 7
8:10 [h]Isa 14:12; Rev 6:13; 9:1 [i]Rev 14:7; 16:4
8:11 [j]ver 7 [k]Jer 9:15; 23:15
8:12 [l]ver 7 [m]Ex 10:21-23; Rev 6:12, 13
8:13 [n]Rev 14:6; 19:17 [o]Rev 9:12; 11:14
9:1 [p]Rev 8:10 [q]ver 2,11; Lk 8:31
9:2 [r]Ge 19:28; Ex 19:18 [s]Joel 2:2,10
9:3 [t]Ex 10:12-15 [u]ver 5,10
9:4 [v]Rev 6:6 [w]Rev 8:7 [x]Rev 7:2,3
9:5 [y]ver 10 [z]ver 3
9:6 [a]Job 3:21; Jer 8:3; Rev 6:16
9:7 [b]Joel 2:4 [c]Da 7:8
9:8 [d]Joel 1:6
9:9 [e]Joel 2:5
9:10 [f]ver 3,5,19
9:11 [g]ver 1,2
9:12 [h]Rev 8:13

13 The sixth angel sounded his trumpet, and I
heard a voice coming from the horns[a][i] of the gold-
en altar that is before God.[j] 14 It said to the sixth
angel who had the trumpet, "Release the four
angels who are bound at the great river Euphrates."[k] 15 And the four angels who had been kept
ready for this very hour and day and month and
year were released to kill a third of mankind.[l]
16 The number of the mounted troops was two
hundred million. I heard their number.[m]
17 The horses and riders I saw in my vision
looked like this: Their breastplates were fiery red,
dark blue, and yellow as sulfur. The heads of the
horses resembled the heads of lions, and out of
their mouths[n] came fire, smoke and sulfur.[o] 18 A
third of mankind was killed[p] by the three plagues
of fire, smoke and sulfur[q] that came out of their
mouths. 19 The power of the horses was in their
mouths and in their tails; for their tails were like
snakes, having heads with which they inflict
injury.
20 The rest of mankind that were not killed by
these plagues still did not repent of the work of
their hands;[r] they did not stop worshiping
demons,[s] and idols of gold, silver, bronze, stone
and wood—idols that cannot see or hear or walk.[t]
21 Nor did they repent[u] of their murders, their magic arts,[v] their sexual immorality[w] or their thefts.

The Angel and the Little Scroll

10 Then I saw another mighty angel[x] coming
down from heaven. He was robed in a
cloud, with a rainbow above his head; his face
was like the sun,[y] and his legs were like fiery pillars.[z] 2 He was holding a little scroll, which lay
open in his hand. He planted his right foot on the
sea and his left foot on the land, 3 and he gave a
loud shout like the roar of a lion. When he shouted, the voices of the seven thunders[a] spoke. 4 And
when the seven thunders spoke, I was about to
write; but I heard a voice from heaven say, "Seal
up what the seven thunders have said and do not
write it down."[b]
5 Then the angel I had seen standing on the sea
and on the land raised his right hand to heaven.[c]
6 And he swore by him who lives for ever and ever,
who created the heavens and all that is in them,
the earth and all that is in it, and the sea and all
that is in it,[d] and said, "There will be no more
delay![e] 7 But in the days when the seventh angel is
about to sound his trumpet, the mystery[f] of God
will be accomplished, just as he announced to his
servants the prophets."
8 Then the voice that I had heard from heaven[g]
spoke to me once more: "Go, take the scroll that
lies open in the hand of the angel who is standing
on the sea and on the land."
9 So I went to the angel and asked him to give
me the little scroll. He said to me, "Take it and eat

9:13 [i]Ex 30:1-3 [j]Rev 8:3
9:14 [k]Rev 16:12
9:15 [l]ver 18
9:16 [m]Rev 5:11; 7:4
9:17 [n]Rev 11:5 [o]ver 18
9:18 [p]ver 15 [q]ver 17
9:20 [r]Dt 31:29 [s]1Co 10:20 [t]Ps 115:4-7; 135:15-17; Da 5:23
9:21 [u]Rev 2:21 [v]Rev 18:23 [w]Rev 17:2,5
10:1 [x]Rev 5:2 [y]Mt 17:2; Rev 1:16 [z]Rev 1:15
10:3 [a]Rev 4:5
10:4 [b]Da 8:26; 12:4,9; Rev 22:10
10:5 [c]Da 12:7
10:6 [d]Rev 4:11; 14:7 [e]Rev 16:17
10:7 [f]Ro 16:25
10:8 [g]ver 4

[a] *13* That is, projections

A Little Scroll

REV 10

We do not know what information or instruction is contained on the little scroll, but, in swallowing it, John symbolically accepts its message (see Ezekiel's similar experience with a scroll in Eze 2:9–3:3). The scroll tastes sweet to John because it is from God, but it also tastes bitter because it concerns severe judgments and suffering. It may include insights into future revelations and visions that John is about to receive, for directly after consuming it he is informed of his responsibility to prophesy again (Rev 10:11).

it. It will turn your stomach sour, but in your mouth it will be as sweet as honey."[h] 10 I took the little scroll from the angel's hand and ate it. It tasted as sweet as honey in my mouth, but when I had eaten it, my stomach turned sour. 11 Then I was told, "You must prophesy[i] again about many peoples, nations, languages and kings."

The Two Witnesses

11 I was given a reed like a measuring rod[j] and was told, "Go and measure the temple of God and the altar, and count the worshipers there. 2 But exclude the outer court;[k] do not measure it, because it has been given to the Gentiles.[l] They will trample on the holy city[m] for 42 months.[n] 3 And I will give power to my two witnesses,[o] and they will prophesy for 1,260 days, clothed in sackcloth."[p] 4 These are the two olive trees[q] and the two lampstands that stand before the Lord of the earth.[r] 5 If anyone tries to harm them, fire comes from their mouths and devours their enemies.[s] This is how anyone who wants to harm them must die.[t] 6 These men have power to shut up the sky so that it will not rain during the time they are prophesying; and they have power to turn the waters into blood[u] and to strike the earth with every kind of plague as often as they want.

7 Now when they have finished their testimony, the beast[v] that comes up from the Abyss will attack them,[w] and overpower and kill them. 8 Their bodies will lie in the street of the great city, which is figuratively called Sodom[x] and Egypt, where also their Lord was crucified.[y] 9 For three and a half days men from every people, tribe, language and nation will gaze on their bodies and refuse them burial.[z] 10 The inhabitants of the earth[a] will gloat over them and will celebrate by sending each other gifts,[b] because these two prophets had tormented those who live on the earth.

11 But after the three and a half days a breath of life from God entered them,[c] and they stood on their feet, and terror struck those who saw them. 12 Then they heard a loud voice from heaven saying to them, "Come up here."[d] And they went up to heaven in a cloud,[e] while their enemies looked on.

13 At that very hour there was a severe earthquake[f] and a tenth of the city collapsed. Seven thousand people were killed in the earthquake, and the survivors were terrified and gave glory[g] to the God of heaven.[h]

14 The second woe has passed; the third woe is coming soon.[i]

The Seventh Trumpet

15 The seventh angel sounded his trumpet,[j] and there were loud voices[k] in heaven, which said:

> "The kingdom of the world has become
> the kingdom of our Lord and of
> his Christ,[l]

10:9 [h]Jer 15:16; Eze 2:8-3:3
10:11 [i]Eze 37:4,9
11:1 [j]Eze 40:3; Rev 21:15
11:2 [k]Eze 40:17, 20 [l]Lk 21:24 [m]Rev 21:2 [n]Da 7:25; Rev 13:5
11:3 [o]Rev 1:5 [p]Ge 37:34
11:4 [q]Ps 52:8; Jer 11:16; Zec 4:3,11 [r]Zec 4:14
11:5 [s]2Ki 1:10; Jer 5:14 [t]Nu 16:29,35
11:6 [u]Ex 7:17,19
11:7 [v]Rev 13:1-4 [w]Da 7:21
11:8 [x]Isa 1:9 [y]Heb 13:12
11:9 [z]Ps 79:2,3
11:10 [a]Rev 3:10 [b]Est 9:19,22
11:11 [c]Eze 37:5,9, 10,14
11:12 [d]Rev 4:1 [e]2Ki 2:11; Ac 1:9
11:13 [f]Rev 6:12 [g]Rev 14:7 [h]Rev 16:11
11:14 [i]Rev 8:13
11:15 [j]Rev 10:7 [k]Rev 16:17; 19:1 [l]Rev 12:10

Two Witnesses

REV 11:1-14

In Biblical times, a minimum of two witnesses was required for legal testimony to be valid. Many theories have been formed concerning the two witnesses John speaks of here. Some scholars claim that they are Moses and Elijah, who also could call on fire to devour their enemies (2Ki 1:10), cause droughts (1Ki 17:1), and turn water into blood (Ex 7:17,20). Some scholars think these are two actual men who will prophesy during the last days and be martyred for their faith. Others suggest that the witnesses are Enoch and Elijah; still others have viewed the figures as representative of faithful Christian believers, the Old and New Testaments, or Israel and the Word of God. Though we do not know which, if any, of these assessments is correct, we do know that these witnesses are sent by God and, thus, possess great power and authority.

and he will reign for ever and ever."[m]

16 And the twenty-four elders,[n] who were seated
on their thrones before God, fell on their faces and
worshiped God, 17 saying:

"We give thanks to you, Lord God
Almighty,[o]
the One who is and who was,
because you have taken your great
power
and have begun to reign.[p]
18 The nations were angry;[q]
and your wrath has come.
The time has come for judging the dead,
and for rewarding your servants the
prophets[r]
and your saints and those who
reverence your name,
both small and great[s]—
and for destroying those who destroy
the earth."

19 Then God's temple[t] in heaven was opened,
and within his temple was seen the ark of his covenant. And there came flashes of lightning, rumblings, peals of thunder, an earthquake and a
great hailstorm.[u]

The Woman and the Dragon

12 A great and wondrous sign appeared in
heaven: a woman clothed with the sun,
with the moon under her feet and a crown of
twelve stars on her head. 2 She was pregnant and
cried out in pain[v] as she was about to give birth.
3 Then another sign appeared in heaven: an enormous red dragon with seven heads and ten horns[w]
and seven crowns[x] on his heads. 4 His tail swept a
third[y] of the stars out of the sky and flung them to
the earth.[z] The dragon stood in front of the
woman who was about to give birth, so that he
might devour her child[a] the moment it was born.
5 She gave birth to a son, a male child, who will
rule all the nations with an iron scepter.[b] And her
child was snatched up to God and to his throne.
6 The woman fled into the desert to a place prepared for her by God, where she might be taken
care of for 1,260 days.[c]

7 And there was war in heaven. Michael and his
angels fought against the dragon,[d] and the dragon
and his angels fought back. 8 But he was not
strong enough, and they lost their place in heav-
en. 9 The great dragon was hurled down—that
ancient serpent[e] called the devil,[f] or Satan, who
leads the whole world astray.[g] He was hurled to
the earth,[h] and his angels with him.

10 Then I heard a loud voice in heaven[i] say:

"Now have come the salvation and the
power and the kingdom of our
God,
and the authority of his Christ.
For the accuser of our brothers,[j]

11:15 [m]Da 2:44; 7:14,27
11:16 [n]Rev 4:4
11:17 [o]Rev 1:8 [p]Rev 19:6
11:18 [q]Ps 2:1 [r]Rev 10:7 [s]Rev 19:5
11:19 [t]Rev 15:5,8 [u]Rev 16:21
12:2 [v]Gal 4:19
12:3 [w]Da 7:7,20; Rev 13:1 [x]Rev 19:12
12:4 [y]Rev 8:7 [z]Da 8:10 [a]Mt 2:16
12:5 [b]Ps 2:9; Rev 2:27
12:6 [c]Rev 11:2
12:7 [d]ver 3
12:9 [e]Ge 3:1-7 [f]Mt 25:41 [g]Rev 20:3,8,10 [h]Lk 10:18; Jn 12:31
12:10 [i]Rev 11:15 [j]Job 1:9-11; Zec 3:1

Anytime we feel diminished or accused of being unworthy, those are Satan's words. Jesus said in Revelation 12:10 that Satan is "the accuser of our brothers." We can recognize his creepy voice anytime we feel accused. The Holy Spirit woos us, loves us, and moves us to a place of understanding. He never undermines us, his children, with derogatory messages that make us feel worthless. We are worth the price of Jesus on the cross, which makes us acceptable to a holy God just as we are.

—Marilyn Meberg

Leila Naylor Morris wrote more than 1,000 hymns during her lifetime. She wrote the words and music to this hymn when she was 50 years old. As her eyes began to fail with age, her son built her a 28-foot blackboard so that she could continue writing and composing.

Sweeter as the Years Go By

Of Jesus' love that sought me,
when I was lost in sin;
Of wondrous grace that brought me
back to His fold again;
Of heights and depths of mercy,
far deeper than the sea,
And higher than the heavens,
my theme shall ever be.

Sweeter as the years go by, sweeter
as the years go by,
Richer, fuller, deeper, Jesus' love is
sweeter,
Sweeter as the years go by.

He trod in old Judea, life's pathway
long ago;
The people thronged about Him,
His saving grace to know;
He healed the brokenhearted, and
caused the blind to see;
And still His great heart yearneth
in love for even me.

'Twas wondrous love which led Him
for us to suffer loss,
To bear without a murmur
the anguish of the cross;
With saints redeemed in glory,
let us our voices raise,
Till heav'n and earth re-echo with
our Redeemer's praise.

–Leila Naylor Morris (1862–1929)

who accuses them before our God day
and night,
has been hurled down.
11 They overcame him
by the blood of the Lamb[k]
and by the word of their testimony;[l]
they did not love their lives so much
as to shrink from death.[m]
12 Therefore rejoice, you heavens[n]
and you who dwell in them!
But woe[o] to the earth and the sea,[p]
because the devil has gone down to
you!
He is filled with fury,
because he knows that his time is
short."

13 When the dragon[q] saw that he had been
hurled to the earth, he pursued the woman who
had given birth to the male child.[r] 14 The woman
was given the two wings of a great eagle,[s] so that
she might fly to the place prepared for her in the
desert, where she would be taken care of for a
time, times and half a time,[t] out of the serpent's
reach. 15 Then from his mouth the serpent spewed
water like a river, to overtake the woman and
sweep her away with the torrent. 16 But the earth
helped the woman by opening its mouth and swallowing the river that the dragon had spewed out
of his mouth. 17 Then the dragon was enraged at
the woman and went off to make war[u] against the
rest of her offspring[v]—those who obey God's commandments[w] and hold to the testimony of Jesus.[x]

13 1 And the dragon[a] stood on the shore of the
sea.

The Beast out of the Sea

And I saw a beast coming out of the sea.[y] He
had ten horns and seven heads,[z] with ten crowns
on his horns, and on each head a blasphemous
name.[a] 2 The beast I saw resembled a leopard,[b] but
had feet like those of a bear[c] and a mouth like that
of a lion.[d] The dragon gave the beast his power
and his throne and great authority.[e] 3 One of the
heads of the beast seemed to have had a fatal
wound, but the fatal wound had been healed.[f]
The whole world was astonished[g] and followed
the beast. 4 Men worshiped the dragon because he
had given authority to the beast, and they also
worshiped the beast and asked, "Who is like[h] the
beast? Who can make war against him?"
5 The beast was given a mouth to utter proud
words and blasphemies[i] and to exercise his
authority for forty-two months.[j] 6 He opened his
mouth to blaspheme God, and to slander his
name and his dwelling place and those who live
in heaven.[k] 7 He was given power to make war[l]
against the saints and to conquer them. And he
was given authority over every tribe, people, lan-

[a] 1 Some late manuscripts *And I*

12:11 [k]Rev 7:14 [l]Rev 6:9 [m]Lk 14:26
12:12 [n]Ps 96:11; Isa 49:13; Rev 18:20 [o]Rev 8:13 [p]Rev 10:6
12:13 [q]ver 3 [r]ver 5
12:14 [s]Ex 19:4 [t]Da 7:25
12:17 [u]Rev 11:7 [v]Ge 3:15 [w]Rev 14:12 [x]Rev 1:2
13:1 [y]Da 7:1-6; Rev 15:2 [z]Rev 12:3 [a]Da 11:36; Rev 17:3
13:2 [b]Da 7:6 [c]Da 7:5 [d]Da 7:4 [e]Rev 16:10
13:3 [f]ver 12,14 [g]Rev 17:8
13:4 [h]Ex 15:11
13:5 [i]Da 7:8,11, 20,25; 11:36; 2Th 2:4 [j]Rev 11:2
13:6 [k]Rev 12:12
13:7 [l]Da 7:21; Rev 11:7

13:7 [m]Rev 5:9 guage and nation.[m] [8]All inhabitants of the earth[n]
will worship the beast—all whose names have not
13:8 been written in the book of life[o] belonging to the
[n]Rev 3:10 Lamb that was slain from the creation of the
[o]Rev 3:5; 20:12 world.[a][p]
[p]Mt 25:34 [9]He who has an ear, let him hear.[q]

13:9 [q]Rev 2:7 [10]If anyone is to go into captivity,
into captivity he will go.
If anyone is to be killed[b] with the sword,
13:10 [r]Jer 15:2; with the sword he will be killed.[r]
43:11 This calls for patient endurance and faithfulness[s]
[s]Heb 6:12 [t]Rev 14:12 on the part of the saints.[t]

The Beast out of the Earth

[11]Then I saw another beast, coming out of the
13:12 earth. He had two horns like a lamb, but he spoke
[u]ver 4 [v]ver 14 like a dragon. [12]He exercised all the authority[u] of
[w]Rev 14:9,11 the first beast on his behalf,[v] and made the earth
[x]ver 3 and its inhabitants worship the first beast,[w] whose
13:13 fatal wound had been healed.[x] [13]And he per-
[y]Mt 24:24 formed great and miraculous signs,[y] even causing
[z]1Ki 18:38; Rev 20:9 fire to come down from heaven[z] to earth in full
view of men. [14]Because of the signs[a] he was given
13:14 power to do on behalf of the first beast, he
[a]2Th 2:9,10 [b]Rev 12:9 deceived[b] the inhabitants of the earth. He ordered
them to set up an image in honor of the beast who
was wounded by the sword and yet lived. [15]He
was given power to give breath to the image of the
first beast, so that it could speak and cause all
13:15 [c]Da 3:3-6 who refused to worship the image to be killed.[c]
[16]He also forced everyone, small and great,[d] rich
13:16 and poor, free and slave, to receive a mark on his
[d]Rev 19:5 [e]Rev 14:9 right hand or on his forehead,[e] [17]so that no one
could buy or sell unless he had the mark,[f] which
13:17 [f]Rev 14:9 is the name of the beast or the number of his
[g]Rev 14:11; 15:2 name.[g]
[18]This calls for wisdom.[h] If anyone has insight,
13:18 let him calculate the number of the beast, for it is
[h]Rev 17:9 [i]Rev 15:2; 21:17 man's number.[i] His number is 666.

The Lamb and the 144,000

14:1 **14** Then I looked, and there before me was the
[j]Rev 5:6 Lamb,[j] standing on Mount Zion,[k] and with
[k]Ps 2:6 him 144,000[l] who had his name and his Father's
[l]Rev 7:4 [m]Rev 3:12 name[m] written on their foreheads. [2]And I heard a
sound from heaven like the roar of rushing
14:2 [n]Rev 1:15 waters[n] and like a loud peal of thunder. The
[o]Rev 5:8 sound I heard was like that of harpists playing
their harps.[o] [3]And they sang a new song[p] before
14:3 [p]Rev 5:9 the throne and before the four living creatures and
[q]ver 1 the elders. No one could learn the song except the
144,000[q] who had been redeemed from the earth.
14:4 [4]These are those who did not defile themselves
[r]2Co 11:2; Rev 3:4 with women, for they kept themselves pure.[r] They
[s]Rev 5:9 follow the Lamb wherever he goes. They were
purchased from among men[s] and offered as first-

[a] 8 Or *written from the creation of the world in the book of life belonging to the Lamb that was slain* [b] 10 Some manuscripts *anyone kills*

The Book of Life

REV 13:8

A common picture in Jewish literature and tradition, the concept of the book of life first appears in Scripture in Exodus 32:31–33 when Moses offered to have his own name removed from it in order to shield the people of Israel from God's righteous wrath. In Psalm 69:28 the psalmist asks God to remove his enemies' names from the book of life. Daniel mentions this book in his prophecies (Da 12:1), and Paul mentions that his fellow workers already have their names written in it (Php 4:3).

The book of life is filled with the names of all who accept Jesus Christ as Savior. It is a divine record of the identities of those who will enter eternal life. Just as the Hebrews registered their citizens, so, too, citizens of heaven are registered in this book. If you have been saved by faith in Christ, your name is already on the list.

The Beast

REV 14:9-10

The beast will attempt to force all humans to receive his mark on the forehead or right hand; this will be a requirement for all buying and selling (Rev 13:16–17). *The temptation for people to accept the mark will be great, but the angel warns that torment will come to all who do so* (Rev 14:11). *The angel, however, also offers assurance that "the saints" will refuse the mark* (Rev 14:12).

If you were told that you must accept such a mark in order to buy food for your family, what would you do? Would you struggle with the decision? If so, you're not alone. God created people with a strong survival instinct, and women in particular have a great passion to protect their children. Even if you never face this particular decision, the future does hold tough choices with eternal ramifications. Take some time today to talk with God about your desire to remain faithful to him no matter what—and ask him to give you the strength to face whatever life brings.

fruits[t] to God and the Lamb. 5 No lie was found in
their mouths;[u] they are blameless.[v]

The Three Angels

6 Then I saw another angel flying in midair,[w]
and he had the eternal gospel to proclaim to those
who live on the earth[x]—to every nation, tribe, language and people.[y] 7 He said in a loud voice, "Fear
God[z] and give him glory,[a] because the hour of his
judgment has come. Worship him who made the
heavens, the earth, the sea and the springs of
water."[b]

8 A second angel followed and said, "Fallen!
Fallen is Babylon the Great,[c] which made all the
nations drink the maddening wine of her adulteries."[d]

9 A third angel followed them and said in a loud
voice: "If anyone worships the beast and his
image[e] and receives his mark on the forehead or
on the hand, 10 he, too, will drink of the wine of
God's fury,[f] which has been poured full strength
into the cup of his wrath.[g] He will be tormented
with burning sulfur in the presence of the holy
angels and of the Lamb. 11 And the smoke of their
torment rises for ever and ever.[h] There is no rest
day or night for those who worship the beast and
his image, or for anyone who receives the mark
of his name." 12 This calls for patient endurance on
the part of the saints[i] who obey God's commandments and remain faithful to Jesus.

13 Then I heard a voice from heaven say, "Write:
Blessed are the dead who die in the Lord[j] from
now on."

"Yes," says the Spirit, "they will rest from their labor, for their deeds will follow them."

The Harvest of the Earth

14 I looked, and there before me was a white
cloud, and seated on the cloud was one "like a son
of man"[a][k] with a crown[l] of gold on his head and
a sharp sickle in his hand. 15 Then another angel
came out of the temple and called in a loud voice
to him who was sitting on the cloud, "Take your
sickle[m] and reap, because the time to reap has
come, for the harvest[n] of the earth is ripe." 16 So he
who was seated on the cloud swung his sickle
over the earth, and the earth was harvested.

17 Another angel came out of the temple in heaven, and he too had a sharp sickle. 18 Still another
angel, who had charge of the fire, came from the
altar and called in a loud voice to him who had
the sharp sickle, "Take your sharp sickle and gather the clusters of grapes from the earth's vine,
because its grapes are ripe." 19 The angel swung
his sickle on the earth, gathered its grapes and
threw them into the great winepress of God's
wrath.[o] 20 They were trampled in the winepress[p]
outside the city,[q] and blood flowed out of the

14:4 [t]Jas 1:18
14:5 [u]Ps 32:2; Zep 3:13 [v]Eph 5:27
14:6 [w]Rev 8:13 [x]Rev 3:10 [y]Rev 13:7
14:7 [z]Rev 15:4 [a]Rev 11:13 [b]Rev 8:10
14:8 [c]Isa 21:9; Jer 51:8 [d]Rev 17:2,4; 18:3,9
14:9 [e]Rev 13:14
14:10 [f]Isa 51:17; Jer 25:15 [g]Rev 18:6
14:11 [h]Isa 34:10; Rev 19:3
14:12 [i]Rev 13:10
14:13 [j]1Co 15:18; 1Th 4:16
14:14 [k]Da 7:13; Rev 1:13 [l]Rev 6:2
14:15 [m]Joel 3:13 [n]Jer 51:33
14:19 [o]Rev 19:15
14:20 [p]Isa 63:3 [q]Heb 13:12; Rev 11:8

[a] 14 Daniel 7:13

press, rising as high as the horses' bridles for a
distance of 1,600 stadia.[a]

Seven Angels With Seven Plagues

15:1 **15** I saw in heaven another great and mar-
[r]Rev 12:1,3 [s]Rev 16:1 velous sign:[r] seven angels[s] with the seven
[t]Lev 26:21 last plagues[t]—last, because with them God's
15:2 wrath is completed. 2And I saw what looked like
[u]Rev 4:6 a sea of glass[u] mixed with fire and, standing
[v]Rev 13:14 beside the sea, those who had been victorious
over the beast and his image[v] and over the num-
15:3 ber of his name. They held harps given them by
[w]Ex 15:1; God 3and sang the song of Moses[w] the servant of
Dt 32:4 [x]Ps 111:2 God and the song of the Lamb:
[y]Ps 145:17

"Great and marvelous are your deeds,[x]
Lord God Almighty.
Just and true are your ways,[y]
15:4 King of the ages.
[z]Jer 10:7 4Who will not fear you, O Lord,[z]
[a]Isa 66:23 and bring glory to your name?
For you alone are holy.
All nations will come
and worship before you,[a]
for your righteous acts have been
revealed."

15:5 5After this I looked and in heaven the temple,[b]
[b]Rev 11:19 [c]Nu 1:50 that is, the tabernacle of the Testimony,[c] was
15:6 opened. 6Out of the temple[d] came the seven angels
[d]Rev 14:15 with the seven plagues.[e] They were dressed in
[e]ver 1 [f]Rev 1:13 clean, shining linen and wore golden sashes
around their chests.[f] 7Then one of the four living
15:7 creatures[g] gave to the seven angels seven golden
[g]Rev 4:6 bowls filled with the wrath of God, who lives for
ever and ever. 8And the temple was filled with
15:8 smoke[h] from the glory of God and from his power,
[h]Isa 6:4 [i]Ex 40:34, and no one could enter the temple[i] until the seven
35; 1Ki 8:10, 11; 2Ch 5:13, 14 plagues of the seven angels were completed.

The Seven Bowls of God's Wrath

16:1 **16** Then I heard a loud voice from the temple
[j]Rev 15:1 saying to the seven angels,[j] "Go, pour out
the seven bowls of God's wrath on the earth."
16:2 2The first angel went and poured out his bowl
[k]Rev 8:7 [l]Ex 9:9-11 on the land,[k] and ugly and painful sores[l] broke
[m]Rev 13:15-17 out on the people who had the mark of the beast
and worshiped his image.[m]
3The second angel poured out his bowl on the
16:3 sea, and it turned into blood like that of a dead
[n]Ex 7:17-21; Rev 8:8,9 man, and every living thing in the sea died.[n]
4The third angel poured out his bowl on the
16:4 rivers and springs of water,[o] and they became
[o]Rev 8:10 [p]Ex 7:17-21 blood.[p] 5Then I heard the angel in charge of the
waters say:

16:5 "You are just in these judgments,[q]
[q]Rev 15:3 [r]Rev 1:4 you who are and who were,[r] the Holy
[s]Rev 15:4 One,[s]
because you have so judged;

[a] *20* That is, about 180 miles (about 300 kilometers)

Seven **REV 15-16**

The number seven appears frequently in Scripture, beginning with the creation account in Genesis (Ge 2:2-3). Many sacred Old Testament rituals, such as the sprinkling of blood in the sanctuary, were performed seven times (Lev 4:6). Units of time were frequently calculated in multiples of seven (Da 9:25), and the number often appeared as a sign in dreams (Ge 41:1-7). Jesus cast seven demons from Mary Magdalene (Mk 16:9) and fed more than 4,000 people at the Sea of Galilee with just seven loaves and some fish (Mt 15:32-38).

To the ancient Hebrews, this sacred number represented fullness and completion (see the note on Jdg 16:7, page 398). The number seven appears 52 times throughout the book of Revelation (for example, seven churches—Rev 1:4; seven lampstands—Rev 1:12; seven stars—Rev 1:16; seven seals—Rev 5:1; seven trumpets—Rev 8:2; seven crowns—Rev 12:3; seven bowls—Rev 15:7; and seven kings—Rev 17:10). The frequent use of this number is one of the distinctive features of the book of Revelation.

Armageddon

REV 16:16

When the kings of earth assemble to wage war against God, they will gather at a place called Armageddon, literally, "mountain of Megiddo." The city of Megiddo (see Map 5: Kingdom of David and Solomon at the back of this Bible) is found at the head of the Valley of Esdraelon, called the Valley of Jezreel in the Old Testament. It was the location of many battles, including the battle between Gideon and the Midianites (Jdg 6:33—7:25), King Saul's fight to the death against the Philistines (1Sa 31; Mount Gilboa overlooks the Valley of Jezreel) and King Josiah's fatal battle against Egypt (2Ki 23:29).

From our limited human perspective, we cannot grasp why God allows evil to exist in the world. But we do know that he will not permit it to continue forever. One day God will crush his enemies completely. At Armageddon, the last battle of our present age (whether a physical, literal battle or a spiritual one—scholars disagree), God's wrath will be poured out on Satan and his armies. Eventually, Satan himself will be cast into the lake of burning sulfur (Rev 20:10), and all the forces of evil will be forever destroyed.

6 for they have shed the blood of your
saints and prophets,
and you have given them blood to
drink[t] as they deserve."

7 And I heard the altar[u] respond:

"Yes, Lord God Almighty,
true and just are your judgments."[v]

8 The fourth angel[w] poured out his bowl on the sun, and the sun was given power to scorch people with fire.[x] 9 They were seared by the intense heat and they cursed the name of God,[y] who had control over these plagues, but they refused to repent[z] and glorify him.[a]

10 The fifth angel poured out his bowl on the throne of the beast,[b] and his kingdom was plunged into darkness.[c] Men gnawed their tongues in agony 11 and cursed[d] the God of heaven[e] because of their pains and their sores,[f] but they refused to repent of what they had done.[g]

12 The sixth angel poured out his bowl on the great river Euphrates,[h] and its water was dried up to prepare the way for the kings from the East.[i] 13 Then I saw three evil[a] spirits that looked like frogs; they came out of the mouth of the dragon,[j] out of the mouth of the beast[k] and out of the mouth of the false prophet.[l] 14 They are spirits of demons[m] performing miraculous signs, and they go out to the kings of the whole world, to gather them for the battle[n] on the great day of God Almighty.

15 "Behold, I come like a thief! Blessed is he who stays awake[o] and keeps his clothes with him, so that he may not go naked and be shamefully exposed."

16 Then they gathered the kings together to the place that in Hebrew[p] is called Armageddon.[q]

17 The seventh angel poured out his bowl into the air,[r] and out of the temple[s] came a loud voice[t] from the throne, saying, "It is done!"[u] 18 Then there came flashes of lightning, rumblings, peals of thunder[v] and a severe earthquake.[w] No earthquake like it has ever occurred since man has been on earth,[x] so tremendous was the quake. 19 The great city[y] split into three parts, and the cities of the nations collapsed. God remembered[z] Babylon the Great[a] and gave her the cup filled with the wine of the fury of his wrath.[b] 20 Every island fled away and the mountains could not be found.[c] 21 From the sky huge hailstones[d] of about a hundred pounds each fell upon men. And they cursed God on account of the plague of hail,[e] because the plague was so terrible.

The Woman on the Beast

17 One of the seven angels[f] who had the seven bowls[g] came and said to me, "Come, I will show you the punishment[h] of the great prostitute,[i]

16:6 [t]Isa 49:26; Rev 17:6
16:7 [u]Rev 6:9 [v]Rev 15:3; 19:2
16:8 [w]Rev 8:12 [x]Rev 14:18
16:9 [y]ver 11,21 [z]Rev 2:21 [a]Rev 11:13
16:10 [b]Rev 13:2 [c]Rev 9:2
16:11 [d]ver 9,21 [e]Rev 11:13 [f]ver 2 [g]Rev 2:21
16:12 [h]Rev 9:14 [i]Isa 41:2
16:13 [j]Rev 12:3 [k]Rev 13:1 [l]Rev 19:20
16:14 [m]1Ti 4:1 [n]Rev 17:14
16:15 [o]Lk 12:37
16:16 [p]Rev 9:11 [q]2Ki 23:29, 30
16:17 [r]Eph 2:2 [s]Rev 14:15 [t]Rev 11:15 [u]Rev 21:6
16:18 [v]Rev 4:5 [w]Rev 6:12 [x]Da 12:1
16:19 [y]Rev 17:18 [z]Rev 18:5 [a]Rev 14:8 [b]Rev 14:10
16:20 [c]Rev 6:14
16:21 [d]Rev 11:19 [e]Ex 9:23-25
17:1 [f]Rev 15:1 [g]Rev 21:9 [h]Rev 16:19 [i]Rev 19:2

[a] *13* Greek *unclean*

17:1 who sits on many waters.[j] 2With her the kings of
[j]Jer 51:13 the earth committed adultery and the inhabitants
17:2 of the earth were intoxicated with the wine of her
[k]Rev 14:8; 18:3 adulteries."[k]
3Then the angel carried me away in the Spirit
17:3 [l]Rev 12:6,14 into a desert.[l] There I saw a woman sitting on a
[m]Rev 13:1 scarlet beast that was covered with blasphemous
[n]Rev 12:3 names[m] and had seven heads and ten horns.[n]
4The woman was dressed in purple and scarlet,
and was glittering with gold, precious stones and
17:4 [o]Rev 18:16 pearls.[o] She held a golden cup[p] in her hand, filled
[p]Jer 51:7; with abominable things and the filth of her adul-
Rev 18:6 teries. 5This title was written on her forehead:

MYSTERY
17:5 [q]Rev 14:8 BABYLON THE GREAT[q]
THE MOTHER OF PROSTITUTES
AND OF THE ABOMINATIONS OF THE EARTH.

6I saw that the woman was drunk with the blood
17:6 of the saints,[r] the blood of those who bore testi-
[r]Rev 18:24 mony to Jesus.
When I saw her, I was greatly astonished. 7Then
the angel said to me: "Why are you astonished? I
17:7 [s]ver 5 will explain to you the mystery[s] of the woman and
[t]ver 3 of the beast she rides, which has the seven heads
and ten horns.[t] 8The beast, which you saw, once
was, now is not, and will come up out of the Abyss
17:8 [u]Rev 13:10 and go to his destruction.[u] The inhabitants of the
[v]Rev 3:10 earth[v] whose names have not been written in the
[w]Rev 13:8 book of life[w] from the creation of the world will be
[x]Rev 13:3 astonished[x] when they see the beast, because he
once was, now is not, and yet will come.
17:9 9"This calls for a mind with wisdom.[y] The sev-
[y]Rev 13:18 en heads are seven hills on which the woman sits.
10They are also seven kings. Five have fallen, one
17:11 is, the other has not yet come; but when he does
[z]ver 8 come, he must remain for a little while. 11The
beast who once was, and now is not,[z] is an eighth
17:12 [a]Rev 12:3 king. He belongs to the seven and is going to his
[b]Rev 18:10, 17,19 destruction.
12"The ten horns[a] you saw are ten kings who
17:13 have not yet received a kingdom, but who for one
[c]ver 17 hour[b] will receive authority as kings along with
17:14 the beast. 13They have one purpose and will give
[d]Rev 16:14 their power and authority to the beast.[c] 14They
[e]1Ti 6:15; will make war[d] against the Lamb, but the Lamb
Rev 19:16 will overcome them because he is Lord of lords
[f]Mt 22:14 and King of kings[e]—and with him will be his
17:15 [g]Isa 8:7 called, chosen[f] and faithful followers."
[h]Rev 13:7 15Then the angel said to me, "The waters[g] you
17:16 saw, where the prostitute sits, are peoples, multi-
[i]Rev 18:17, 19 tudes, nations and languages.[h] 16The beast and the
[j]Eze 16:37, 39 ten horns you saw will hate the prostitute. They
will bring her to ruin[i] and leave her naked;[j] they
[k]Rev 19:18 will eat her flesh[k] and burn her with fire.[l] 17For
[l]Rev 18:8 God has put it into their hearts to accomplish his
17:17 purpose by agreeing to give the beast their power
[m]Rev 10:7 to rule, until God's words are fulfilled.[m] 18The
17:18 woman you saw is the great city[n] that rules over
[n]Rev 16:19 the kings of the earth."

Babylon the Great

REV 17:5

The woman on the beast is identified by one of the seven angels as "the great prostitute" (Rev 17:1). On her forehead is written the title "BABYLON THE GREAT THE MOTHER OF PROSTITUTES."

Throughout the book of Revelation, the city of Babylon represents a rebellious world that rejects God. The name comes from the capital of ancient Babylon, which was known for its decadence, idolatry and opposition to God's people. Some scholars see the Babylon of Revelation as a symbol of Rome, built on seven hills (Rev 17:9) and a persecutor of early Christians. Yet Rome is not the only "Babylon" to have pitted itself against believers. Many of the faithful have suffered at the hands of other nations and cultures who have opposed God and his followers. Whatever its exact identity, Revelation clearly teaches that Babylon's coming destruction is certain.

The title "MOTHER OF PROSTITUTES" is appropriate as well, for in ancient times those who practiced idolatry were said to have "prostituted themselves to other gods" (Jdg 2:17).

Interpretation

REV 18

The book of Revelation is one of the most fascinating accounts in the Bible. It is also one of the most difficult to understand. While it is always important to use care when interpreting Scripture, it is best to employ an extra dose of caution when studying this mysterious, apocalyptic book.

Students of the book of Revelation fall into one of four basic categories in their approaches to its interpretation: (1) those who see the events as already mostly fulfilled; (2) those who see the book as a record of events of the church until the end of history; (3) those who see the book's fulfillment during the end times; and (4) those who see the book's fulfillment as spiritual rather than literal. Whatever approach is taken, however, the basic truths of the book remain valid: A battle has been fought, is now ongoing, and will continue to be fought between the forces of good and evil. The forces of good—in the person of Jesus Christ—will eventually be victorious over evil.

The Fall of Babylon

18 After this I saw another angel[o] coming
down from heaven.[p] He had great authority,
and the earth was illuminated by his splendor.[q]
2 With a mighty voice he shouted:

"Fallen! Fallen is Babylon the Great![r]
She has become a home for demons
and a haunt for every evil[a] spirit,
a haunt for every unclean and
detestable bird.[s]
3 For all the nations have drunk
the maddening wine of her adulteries.[t]
The kings of the earth committed
adultery with her,[u]
and the merchants of the earth grew
rich[v] from her excessive
luxuries."[w]

4 Then I heard another voice from heaven say:

"Come out of her, my people,[x]
so that you will not share in her sins,
so that you will not receive any of her
plagues;
5 for her sins are piled up to heaven,[y]
and God has remembered[z] her crimes.
6 Give back to her as she has given;
pay her back[a] double for what she has
done.
Mix her a double portion from her
own cup.[b]
7 Give her as much torture and grief
as the glory and luxury she gave
herself.[c]
In her heart she boasts,
'I sit as queen; I am not a widow,
and I will never mourn.'[d]
8 Therefore in one day[e] her plagues will
overtake her:
death, mourning and famine.
She will be consumed by fire,[f]
for mighty is the Lord God who
judges her.

9 "When the kings of the earth who committed
adultery with her[g] and shared her luxury see the
smoke of her burning,[h] they will weep and mourn
over her.[i] 10 Terrified at her torment, they will
stand far off[j] and cry:

" 'Woe! Woe, O great city,[k]
O Babylon, city of power!
In one hour[l] your doom has come!'

11 "The merchants[m] of the earth will weep and
mourn over her because no one buys their cargoes
any more[n]— 12 cargoes of gold, silver, precious
stones and pearls; fine linen, purple, silk and scarlet cloth; every sort of citron wood, and articles of
every kind made of ivory, costly wood, bronze,
iron and marble;[o] 13 cargoes of cinnamon and

18:1 [o]Rev 17:1 [p]Rev 10:1 [q]Eze 43:2
18:2 [r]Rev 14:8 [s]Isa 13:21, 22; Jer 50:39
18:3 [t]Rev 14:8 [u]Rev 17:2 [v]Eze 27:9-25 [w]ver 7,9
18:4 [x]Isa 48:20; Jer 50:8; 2Co 6:17
18:5 [y]Jer 51:9 [z]Rev 16:19
18:6 [a]Ps 137:8; Jer 50:15,29 [b]Rev 14:10; 16:19
18:7 [c]Eze 28:2-8 [d]Isa 47:7,8; Zep 2:15
18:8 [e]ver 10; Isa 47:9; Jer 50:31,32 [f]Rev 17:16
18:9 [g]Rev 17:2,4 [h]ver 18; Rev 19:3 [i]Eze 26:17, 18
18:10 [j]ver 15,17 [k]ver 16,19 [l]Rev 17:12
18:11 [m]Eze 27:27 [n]ver 3
18:12 [o]Rev 17:4

[a] 2 Greek *unclean*

Euodia and Syntyche

Talk of the Town

Have you ever struggled to fall asleep on a hot summer evening only to be jarred awake by the screams of a territorial cat fight? And nobody but the cats can appreciate where and why they battle. Unfortunately, that's how conflict in the church can appear to the world. Those outside the circle can't even figure out what it's about. They just shrug their shoulders and think, *That's Christians for you.*

Christians are sinners like everyone else on the planet, but what sets us apart from the world is Christ's challenge to us to sincerely love one another. Euodia and Syntyche had "contended"—fought at Paul's side—in the cause of the gospel. But some conflict had arisen between the two women, and they could not resolve their differences. These women were leaders, and their behavior threatened to divide the fledgling church in Philippi and to discredit its witness of love and unity.

Euodia and Syntyche's disagreement had erupted into a public squabble so serious that Paul learned of it even though he was in prison. In response, Paul was direct but kind. He did not boot them out of the church. Nor did he dismiss their concerns. Instead, he commended them to the care of their brothers and sisters to work it out. Paul wanted reconciliation not censure, forgiveness not retribution.

It must have been a great relief for Euodia and Syntyche to read Paul's letter. After time spent in disagreement and stress, they could rest in the knowledge that their brothers and sisters were available to help them. They didn't have to fight the battle alone, trying (unsuccessfully) to hide discord from the eyes of the world. They could be open and honest, and the church would grow stronger as they worked through the difficulty together.

A sister in the church is never an enemy—the Enemy is our enemy (1Pe 5:8). When we allow him to separate and divide us, we weaken our growth in Christ and our outreach to the lost. The church is a family. There are squabbles even in the best of families. The goal is learning to love one another through them.

Euodia and Syntyche
(fragrant; with fate)
Philippians 4:2-3

Candid SNAPSHOT I plead with Euodia and I plead with Syntyche to agree with each other in the Lord (Philippians 4:2).

Lois and Eunice

Women of Sincere Faith

The Roman Empire traveled by Paul was a confluence of cultures—Paul himself was a Jew and a Roman citizen, with a Greek education. The repeated conquests of the Jewish homeland beginning with the Assyrians in 722 B.C. and finally the Romans in 63 B.C. dispersed the Jews throughout the Mediterranean area. These Jews freely mingled with other peoples, and they adopted the Greek language and elements of Greek culture, though in most places they formed communities that maintained their distinct beliefs in one God, in the Scriptures and in honoring the Sabbath.

Lois was a Jewish woman who had married a Greek man. It must have seemed so exciting to her to be a part of the Greek culture, for the Greeks were the undisputed masters in the art, literature and philosophy of the age. However, Lois's faith set her at odds with the culture of the city of Lystra and perhaps the faith of her husband. Lois was a Jewish Christian and lived out her faith in all areas of her life. Her faith was so obvious and firm that her daughter, Eunice, also became a Christian and lived a life devoted to Christ.

The Apostle Paul met these two women while he was on one of his missionary journeys. He was impressed by their faith. What Paul saw in these two women caused him to characterize their faith as "sincere"—genuine, with no hypocrisy, no pretending, no fake exaggeration or embellishment. And Lois and Eunice were together committed to passing this faith on to their grandson and son, Timothy.

It is possible that Lois and Eunice were both widowed, for no mention is made of the spiritual influences of their husbands, and Paul credits Eunice herself for her son's maturity. The lives Lois and Eunice lived in their home—in Timothy's sight—was the real influence that led to Timothy's spiritual growth. It helped him become a believer and the kind of person he grew to be, a deeply trusted co-worker and friend to Paul. Whatever the obstacles he faced, Timothy saw in them that the Lord Jesus Christ was up to the job—that Christ was enough to deal with the internal and external struggles of real life. Lois and Eunice had that kind of faith, and Timothy learned it from them. As a woman, as a mother, as a grandmother, you have the greatest influence possible on those around you. Your life speaks volumes, whether you open your mouth or not. What message are you communicating?

Lois and Eunice
(agreeable; conquering well)

Acts 16:1
2 Timothy 1:5

Candid SNAPSHOT I have been reminded of your sincere faith, which first lived in your grandmother Lois and in your mother Eunice and, I am persuaded, now lives in you also (2 Timothy 1:5).

spice, of incense, myrrh and frankincense, of wine
and olive oil, of fine flour and wheat; cattle and
18:13 sheep; horses and carriages; and bodies and souls
[p]Eze 27:13; 1Ti 1:10 of men.[p]
14 "They will say, 'The fruit you longed for is
gone from you. All your riches and splendor have
vanished, never to be recovered.' 15 The merchants
who sold these things and gained their wealth
18:15 [q]ver 3 from her[q] will stand far off, terrified at her tor-
[r]Eze 27:31 ment. They will weep and mourn[r] 16 and cry out:

" 'Woe! Woe, O great city,
dressed in fine linen, purple and
scarlet,
and glittering with gold, precious
18:16 [s]Rev 17:4 stones and pearls![s]
17 In one hour[t] such great wealth has been
18:17 [t]ver 10 brought to ruin!'[u]

[u]Rev 17:16 [v]Eze 27:28-30 "Every sea captain, and all who travel by ship,
the sailors, and all who earn their living from the
sea,[v] will stand far off. 18 When they see the smoke
of her burning, they will exclaim, 'Was there ever
18:18 [w]Eze 27:32; Rev 13:4 a city like this great city?'[w] 19 They will throw dust
on their heads,[x] and with weeping and mourning
18:19 [x]Jos 7:6; Eze 27:30 cry out:

" 'Woe! Woe, O great city,
[y]Rev 17:16 where all who had ships on the sea
became rich through her wealth!
In one hour she has been brought to
ruin![y]
18:20 [z]Jer 51:48; Rev 12:12 20 Rejoice over her, O heaven![z]
[a]Rev 19:2 Rejoice, saints and apostles and
prophets!
God has judged her for the way she
treated you.' "[a]

18:21 [b]Rev 5:2 21 Then a mighty angel[b] picked up a boulder the
[c]Jer 51:63 size of a large millstone and threw it into the sea,[c]
and said:

"With such violence
the great city of Babylon will be
thrown down,
never to be found again.
22 The music of harpists and musicians,
18:22 flute players and trumpeters,
[d]Isa 24:8; Eze 26:13 will never be heard in you again.[d]
[e]Jer 25:10 No workman of any trade
will ever be found in you again.
The sound of a millstone
will never be heard in you again.[e]
23 The light of a lamp
will never shine in you again.
The voice of bridegroom and bride
18:23 [f]Jer 7:34; 16:9; 25:10 will never be heard in you again.[f]
Your merchants were the world's great
[g]Isa 23:8 men.[g]
[h]Na 3:4 By your magic spell[h] all the nations
were led astray.
18:24 [i]Rev 16:6; 17:6 24 In her was found the blood of prophets
and of the saints,[i]

Mourning Babylon

REV 18:9-24

Following the ruin of the great prostitute, three groups lament her demise: the kings of the earth (Rev 18:9-10), the merchants of the earth (Rev 18:11-17), and those who trade on the sea (Rev 18:17-20). The kings represent those leaders of the earth who have resisted the authority of God and have caused those they influence to do the same. The merchants, or the "world's great men" (Rev 18:23), are those who gain great riches because of Babylon's decadence. The sea captains (Rev 18:17) also acquire great wealth from trade with this wicked city. The focus of the mourning by all three groups is the destruction of Babylon's great wealth and power and the direct effect it has on their own wealth and power.

The Bride of the Lamb

REV 19:7–8

In the Old Testament, God's relationship with his chosen people is described in terms of a marriage, with God as the bridegroom and Israel as his bride (Isa 62:5). That characterization continues in the New Testament, with Christ as the groom and we, the Christian church, as his betrothed (Eph 5:25–27). While Babylon is dressed in purple and scarlet (Rev 17:4), the church is given bright and clean linen—that is, "righteous acts"—to wear.

In our modern society, we as women—arguably more than men—are driven to pay constant attention to our outward appearance. Far too often, our inner "attire," our godly behavior, can suffer as a result. Take a few minutes to clean out your spiritual wardrobe. Picture yourself as a bride getting ready for her wedding. What fine clothing—good deeds—will you put on for your groom? What less-than-beautiful clothing—sins—will you remove?

and of all who have been killed on
the earth."[j]

Hallelujah!

19 After this I heard what sounded like the
roar of a great multitude[k] in heaven
shouting:

"Hallelujah!
Salvation[l] and glory and power[m] belong
to our God,
2 for true and just are his judgments.
He has condemned the great prostitute
who corrupted the earth by her
adulteries.
He has avenged on her the blood of his
servants."[n]

3 And again they shouted:

"Hallelujah!
The smoke from her goes up for ever
and ever."[o]

4 The twenty-four elders[p] and the four living
creatures[q] fell down[r] and worshiped God, who
was seated on the throne. And they cried:

"Amen, Hallelujah!"

5 Then a voice came from the throne, saying:

"Praise our God,
all you his servants,[s]
you who fear him,
both small and great!"[t]

6 Then I heard what sounded like a great multitude,[u] like the roar of rushing waters and like loud
peals of thunder, shouting:

"Hallelujah!
For our Lord God Almighty reigns.
7 Let us rejoice and be glad
and give him glory!
For the wedding of the Lamb[v] has come,
and his bride[w] has made herself
ready.
8 Fine linen, bright and clean,
was given her to wear."

(Fine linen stands for the righteous acts[x] of the
saints.)

9 Then the angel said to me,[y] "Write:[z] 'Blessed
are those who are invited to the wedding supper
of the Lamb!' "[a] And he added, "These are the
true words of God."[b]

10 At this I fell at his feet to worship him.[c] But
he said to me, "Do not do it! I am a fellow servant
with you and with your brothers who hold to the
testimony of Jesus. Worship God![d] For the testimony of Jesus[e] is the spirit of prophecy."

The Rider on the White Horse

11 I saw heaven standing open and there before

18:24 [j]Jer 51:49
19:1 [k]Rev 11:15 [l]Rev 7:10 [m]Rev 4:11
19:2 [n]Dt 32:43; Rev 6:10
19:3 [o]Isa 34:10; Rev 14:11
19:4 [p]Rev 4:4 [q]Rev 4:6 [r]Rev 5:14
19:5 [s]Ps 134:1 [t]Rev 11:18; 20:12
19:6 [u]Rev 11:15
19:7 [v]Mt 22:2; 25:10; Eph 5:32 [w]Rev 21:2,9
19:8 [x]Rev 15:4
19:9 [y]ver 10 [z]Rev 1:19 [a]Lk 14:15 [b]Rev 21:5; 22:6
19:10 [c]Rev 22:8 [d]Ac 10:25,26; Rev 22:9 [e]Rev 12:17

me was a white horse, whose rider[f] is called Faithful and True.[g] With justice he judges and makes
war.[h] 12 His eyes are like blazing fire,[i] and on his
head are many crowns.[j] He has a name written on
him that no one knows but he himself.[k] 13 He is
dressed in a robe dipped in blood,[l] and his name
is the Word of God.[m] 14 The armies of heaven were
following him, riding on white horses and dressed
in fine linen,[n] white and clean. 15 Out of his mouth
comes a sharp sword[o] with which to strike down[p]
the nations. "He will rule them with an iron
scepter."[a][q] He treads the winepress[r] of the fury of
the wrath of God Almighty. 16 On his robe and on
his thigh he has this name written:[s]

KING OF KINGS AND LORD OF LORDS.[t]

17 And I saw an angel standing in the sun, who
cried in a loud voice to all the birds[u] flying in
midair,[v] "Come,[w] gather together for the great supper of God, 18 so that you may eat the flesh of
kings, generals, and mighty men, of horses and
their riders, and the flesh of all people,[x] free and
slave, small and great."

19 Then I saw the beast and the kings of the
earth[y] and their armies gathered together to make
war against the rider on the horse and his army.
20 But the beast was captured, and with him the
false prophet[z] who had performed the miraculous
signs on his behalf.[a] With these signs he had
deluded those who had received the mark of the
beast and worshiped his image. The two of them
were thrown alive into the fiery lake[b] of burning
sulfur.[c] 21 The rest of them were killed with the
sword[d] that came out of the mouth of the rider on
the horse,[e] and all the birds[f] gorged themselves on
their flesh.

The Thousand Years

20 And I saw an angel coming down out of
heaven,[g] having the key[h] to the Abyss and
holding in his hand a great chain. 2 He seized the
dragon, that ancient serpent, who is the devil, or
Satan,[i] and bound him for a thousand years.[j] 3 He
threw him into the Abyss, and locked and sealed[k]
it over him, to keep him from deceiving the
nations[l] anymore until the thousand years were
ended. After that, he must be set free for a short
time.

4 I saw thrones[m] on which were seated those
who had been given authority to judge. And I saw
the souls of those who had been beheaded[n]
because of their testimony for Jesus and because
of the word of God. They had not worshiped the
beast[o] or his image and had not received his mark
on their foreheads or their hands.[p] They came to
life and reigned with Christ a thousand years.
5 (The rest of the dead did not come to life until
the thousand years were ended.) This is the first
resurrection.[q] 6 Blessed[r] and holy are those who

a 15 Psalm 2:9

19:11 [f]Rev 6:2 [g]Rev 3:14 [h]Isa 11:4
19:12 [i]Rev 1:14 [j]Rev 6:2 [k]Rev 2:17
19:13 [l]Isa 63:2,3 [m]Jn 1:1
19:14 [n]ver 8
19:15 [o]Rev 1:16 [p]Isa 11:4; 2Th 2:8 [q]Ps 2:9; Rev 2:27 [r]Rev 14:20
19:16 [s]ver 12 [t]Rev 17:14
19:17 [u]ver 21 [v]Rev 8:13 [w]Eze 39:17
19:18 [x]Eze 39:18-20
19:19 [y]Rev 16:14,16
19:20 [z]Rev 16:13 [a]Rev 13:12 [b]Da 7:11; Rev 20:10,14,15; 21:8 [c]Rev 14:10
19:21 [d]ver 15 [e]ver 11,19 [f]ver 17
20:1 [g]Rev 10:1 [h]Rev 1:18
20:2 [i]Rev 12:9 [j]2Pe 2:4
20:3 [k]Da 6:17 [l]Rev 12:9
20:4 [m]Da 7:9 [n]Rev 6:9 [o]Rev 13:12 [p]Rev 13:16
20:5 [q]Lk 14:14; Php 3:11
20:6 [r]Rev 14:13

A Rider on a White Horse

REV 19:11-16

At last, Christ's return to earth is accomplished in a burst of glory! As heaven opens, he appears astride a white horse, his eyes flashing and his head adorned with crowns. Behind him are the armies of heaven, pure and clean and prepared to ride into battle. Many believe this passage to be the high point of the book of Revelation, as well as the most important moment of time in all history.

Christ is given the title "Faithful and True," words used earlier to describe him (Rev 1:5; 3:7,14). He is also identified as the "Word of God" (Rev 19:13). Long ago, the Word of God created the world and became flesh to live among us (Jn 1:1-3,14). Now, he returns in righteousness to judge his creation, and he is given his final, glorious and well-deserved title: **KING OF KINGS AND LORD OF LORDS.**

Week 52

Jesus Is Faithful and True

Betrayal. It is ugly and has devastation as its constant companion. It produces shock, then questioning, anger, numbness and, finally, deep and excruciating pain. Betrayal causes such pain because it is the act of someone trusted and loved. Usually the relationship between the betrayer and the betrayed is forever damaged because betrayal results in the loss of faith and trust.

Have you been betrayed? If so, you need to know that there is, indeed, someone who is faithful, someone you can always count on. Meet Jesus, who is also called "Faithful and True" (Rev 19:11).

God himself is faithful (1Co 1:9). In what ways is God faithful (Ps 25:10; 145:13; 1Th 5:23-24)? How does this give you confidence?

How great is God's faithfulness (Ps 108:4; Isa 25:1)? How long will it last (Ps 146:6)?

How does God deal with his children's unfaithfulness (Ps 89:30-33)? How does this give you peace?

What is the companion of faithfulness (Ps 85:10; 89:14)? How does this give you a greater understanding of the Father's heart?

How can God's faithfulness benefit you in times of trouble (Ps 61:7; 91:4)? How does this give you hope (Heb 10:23)?

How should you respond to God's faithfulness (Ps 89:5; 138:2)?

God's love for you is so great and his faithfulness so unswerving that you never need to fear. "Because of the LORD's great love we are not consumed, for his compassions never fail. They are new every morning; great is [his] faithfulness" (La 3:22-23).

Enjoying God THROUGH the Word

Read John 13:21-30 (page 1771). Jesus, deeply saddened by the knowledge that Judas will betray him (Jn 6:64), shares his hurt with his friends.

What kind of pain do you think Jesus feels? If you have been betrayed, you may feel that no one truly understands your pain. But Jesus does. He is betrayed by one of his closest friends. Judas's betrayal is no minor event in the gospel story. A final tearing of the tenuous relationship between Judas and Jesus occurs that night. Although Judas has never believed (Jn 6:64-65) and is, therefore, not in spiritual fellowship with Jesus, their earthly relationship is one of companionship.

If you are in that dark place of betrayal, know that Jesus understands. You can share your pain, confusion and doubts with him. His arms are open wide, waiting to embrace you and ease your pain.

Enjoying God THROUGH Experience

Betrayal is painful, and your memory of it may always be with you (though time does lessen the pain). There is no easy formula for healing—especially if your betrayer has not changed or sought your forgiveness. Although Jesus cannot change the past or wipe out your memory, he can take your pain, bring truth to the situation and provide healing to your heart.

Sit with Jesus awhile, conscious that he's with you. You are safe with him. Share your pain with him. He understands it, and though you may feel unable to trust even him, he will reveal himself to you as Faithful and True. "A bruised reed he will not break, and a smoldering wick he will not snuff out" (Isa 42:3).

Go to page 9 for your next weekly study.

have part in the first resurrection. The second
20:6 sRev 2:11 death[s] has no power over them, but they will be
tRev 1:6 priests[t] of God and of Christ and will reign with
uver 4 him[u] for a thousand years.

Satan's Doom

20:7 vver 2 7 When the thousand years are over,[v] Satan will
be released from his prison 8 and will go out to
20:8 wver 3,10 deceive the nations[w] in the four corners of the
xEze 38:2; earth—Gog and Magog[x]—to gather them for bat-
39:1 tle.[y] In number they are like the sand on the
yRev 16:14 zHeb 11:12 seashore.[z] 9 They marched across the breadth of
the earth and surrounded[a] the camp of God's peo-
20:9 aEze 38:9,16 ple, the city he loves. But fire came down from
bEze 38:22; heaven[b] and devoured them. 10 And the devil, who
39:6 deceived them,[c] was thrown into the lake of burn-
20:10 ing sulfur, where the beast and the false prophet
cRev 19:20 had been thrown. They will be tormented day and
dRev 14:10, 11 night for ever and ever.[d]

The Dead Are Judged

20:11 eRev 4:2 11 Then I saw a great white throne[e] and him who
was seated on it. Earth and sky fled from his presence, and there was no place for them. 12 And I
20:12 saw the dead, great and small, standing before the
fDa 7:10 gRev 3:5 throne, and books were opened.[f] Another book
hJer 17:10; was opened, which is the book of life.[g] The dead
Mt 16:27; Rev 2:23 were judged according to what they had done[h] as
recorded in the books. 13 The sea gave up the dead
20:13 that were in it, and death and Hades[i] gave up the
iRev 6:8 dead[j] that were in them, and each person was
jIsa 26:19 judged according to what he had done. 14 Then
20:14 death[k] and Hades were thrown into the lake of
k1Co 15:26 fire. The lake of fire is the second death. 15 If any-
20:15 one's name was not found written in the book of
lver 12 life,[l] he was thrown into the lake of fire.

The New Jerusalem

21:1 mIsa 65:17; 21 Then I saw a new heaven and a new earth,[m]
2Pe 3:13 for the first heaven and the first earth had
21:2 passed away, and there was no longer any sea. 2 I
nHeb 11:10; saw the Holy City, the new Jerusalem, coming
12:22; Rev 3:12 down out of heaven from God,[n] prepared as a
bride beautifully dressed for her husband. 3 And I
21:3 o2Co 6:16 heard a loud voice from the throne saying, "Now
the dwelling of God is with men, and he will live
21:4 pRev 7:17 with them. They will be his people, and God him-
q1Co 15:26; self will be with them and be their God.[o] 4 He will
Rev 20:14 wipe every tear from their eyes.[p] There will be no
rIsa 35:10; 65:19 more death[q] or mourning or crying or pain,[r] for
the old order of things has passed away."
21:5 5 He who was seated on the throne[s] said, "I am
sRev 4:9; 20:11 making everything new!" Then he said, "Write this
tRev 19:9 down, for these words are trustworthy and true."[t]
6 He said to me: "It is done.[u] I am the Alpha and
21:6 uRev 16:17 the Omega,[v] the Beginning and the End. To him
vRev 1:8; 22:13 who is thirsty I will give to drink without cost
wJn 4:10 from the spring of the water of life.[w] 7 He who
overcomes will inherit all this, and I will be his
God and he will be my son. 8 But the cowardly, the

The New Jerusalem

REV 21:1-5

From the first words in Genesis, the Scriptures have been leading up to this climactic description of the new Jerusalem: the city of God, Zion, our magnificent heavenly home. This glorious city stands in sharp contrast to the idolatrous and worldly Babylon described in earlier chapters. The inhabitants of the new Jerusalem will not worship any false gods. They will only worship the Lord God and the Lamb, who are themselves the city's temple (Rev 21:22).

Just as the historical Jerusalem was home to God and his people, so the new Jerusalem will be the home of the true God, Christ and his bride, the church. And as the old Jerusalem is identified as "the Holy City," so, too, is the new. Holiness itself will permeate the city, and righteousness will be ours as we live and rule throughout eternity with the One who loves us and makes us holy.

God's Light

REV 21:22-27

In the new Jerusalem the sun and the moon will no longer be needed for light; the glory of God himself will provide every bit of light his people need! This does not necessarily mean that the sun and moon will not exist. It is very possible that they will continue to shine; if so, however, their light will be eclipsed by the great light flowing from God himself. We will quickly become accustomed to the glorious radiance and brilliance of the God who is our light and life (Jn 1:4), and we will be freed of nighttime and darkness—symbols of evil—forever.

unbelieving, the vile, the murderers, the sexually
immoral, those who practice magic arts, the idolaters and all liars[x]—their place will be in the fiery
lake of burning sulfur. This is the second death."[y]
9One of the seven angels who had the seven
bowls full of the seven last plagues[z] came and said
to me, "Come, I will show you the bride,[a] the wife
of the Lamb." 10And he carried me away[b] in the
Spirit[c] to a mountain great and high, and showed
me the Holy City, Jerusalem, coming down out of
heaven from God. 11It shone with the glory of
God,[d] and its brilliance was like that of a very precious jewel, like a jasper, clear as crystal.[e] 12It had
a great, high wall with twelve gates, and with
twelve angels at the gates. On the gates were written the names of the twelve tribes of Israel.[f]
13There were three gates on the east, three on the
north, three on the south and three on the west.
14The wall of the city had twelve foundations, and
on them were the names of the twelve apostles of
the Lamb.
15The angel who talked with me had a measuring rod[g] of gold to measure the city, its gates and
its walls. 16The city was laid out like a square, as
long as it was wide. He measured the city with the
rod and found it to be 12,000 stadia[a] in length,
and as wide and high as it is long. 17He measured
its wall and it was 144 cubits[b] thick,[c] by man's
measurement, which the angel was using. 18The
wall was made of jasper,[h] and the city of pure
gold, as pure as glass.[i] 19The foundations of the
city walls were decorated with every kind of precious stone.[j] The first foundation was jasper, the
second sapphire, the third chalcedony, the fourth
emerald, 20the fifth sardonyx, the sixth carnelian,[k]
the seventh chrysolite, the eighth beryl, the ninth
topaz, the tenth chrysoprase, the eleventh jacinth,
and the twelfth amethyst.[d] 21The twelve gates
were twelve pearls, each gate made of a single
pearl. The great street of the city was of pure gold,
like transparent glass.[l]
22I did not see a temple[m] in the city, because the
Lord God Almighty[n] and the Lamb[o] are its temple.
23The city does not need the sun or the moon to
shine on it, for the glory of God gives it light,[p] and
the Lamb is its lamp. 24The nations will walk by
its light, and the kings of the earth will bring their
splendor into it.[q] 25On no day will its gates ever
be shut,[r] for there will be no night there.[s] 26The
glory and honor of the nations will be brought
into it. 27Nothing impure will ever enter it, nor
will anyone who does what is shameful or deceitful,[t] but only those whose names are written in
the Lamb's book of life.

21:8 [x]1Co 6:9 [y]Rev 2:11
21:9 [z]Rev 15:1,6,7 [a]Rev 19:7
21:10 [b]Rev 17:3 [c]Rev 1:10
21:11 [d]Rev 15:8; 22:5 [e]Rev 4:6
21:12 [f]Eze 48:30-34
21:15 [g]Rev 11:1
21:18 [h]ver 11 [i]ver 21
21:19 [j]Isa 54:11,12
21:20 [k]Rev 4:3
21:21 [l]ver 18
21:22 [m]Jn 4:21,23 [n]Rev 1:8 [o]Rev 5:6
21:23 [p]Isa 24:23; 60:19,20; Rev 22:5
21:24 [q]Isa 60:3,5
21:25 [r]Isa 60:11 [s]Zec 14:7; Rev 22:5
21:27 [t]Isa 52:1; Joel 3:17; Rev 22:14,15

[a] *16* That is, about 1,400 miles (about 2,200 kilometers)
[b] *17* That is, about 200 feet (about 65 meters) [c] *17* Or *high*
[d] *20* The precise identification of some of these precious stones is uncertain.

The River of Life

22 Then the angel showed me the river of the water of life, as clear as crystal,[u] flowing[v] from the throne of God and of the Lamb 2down the middle of the great street of the city. On each side of the river stood the tree of life,[w] bearing twelve crops of fruit, yielding its fruit every month. And the leaves of the tree are for the healing of the nations.[x] 3No longer will there be any curse.[y] The throne of God and of the Lamb will be in the city, and his servants will serve him.[z] 4They will see his face,[a] and his name will be on their foreheads.[b] 5There will be no more night.[c] They will not need the light of a lamp or the light of the sun, for the Lord God will give them light.[d] And they will reign for ever and ever.[e]

6The angel said to me,[f] "These words are trustworthy and true.[g] The Lord, the God of the spirits of the prophets,[h] sent his angel[i] to show his servants the things that must soon take place."

Jesus Is Coming

7"Behold, I am coming soon![j] Blessed[k] is he who keeps the words of the prophecy in this book."

8I, John, am the one who heard and saw these things.[l] And when I had heard and seen them, I fell down to worship at the feet[m] of the angel who had been showing them to me. 9But he said to me, "Do not do it! I am a fellow servant with you and with your brothers the prophets and of all who keep the words of this book.[n] Worship God!"[o]

10Then he told me, "Do not seal up[p] the words of the prophecy of this book, because the time is near.[q] 11Let him who does wrong continue to do wrong; let him who is vile continue to be vile; let him who does right continue to do right; and let him who is holy continue to be holy."[r]

12"Behold, I am coming soon![s] My reward is with me,[t] and I will give to everyone according to what he has done. 13I am the Alpha and the Omega,[u] the First and the Last,[v] the Beginning and the End.[w]

14"Blessed are those who wash their robes, that they may have the right to the tree of life[x] and may go through the gates[y] into the city.[z] 15Outside[a] are the dogs,[b] those who practice magic arts, the sexually immoral, the murderers, the idolaters and everyone who loves and practices falsehood.

16"I, Jesus,[c] have sent my angel to give you[a] this testimony for the churches.[d] I am the Root[e] and the Offspring of David, and the bright Morning Star."[f]

17The Spirit[g] and the bride say, "Come!" And let him who hears say, "Come!" Whoever is thirsty,

22:1 [u]Rev 4:6 [v]Eze 47:1; Zec 14:8
22:2 [w]Rev 2:7 [x]Eze 47:12
22:3 [y]Zec 14:11 [z]Rev 7:15
22:4 [a]Mt 5:8 [b]Rev 14:1
22:5 [c]Rev 21:25 [d]Rev 21:23 [e]Da 7:27; Rev 20:4
22:6 [f]Rev 1:1 [g]Rev 19:9; 21:5 [h]Heb 12:9 [i]ver 16
22:7 [j]Rev 3:11 [k]Rev 1:3
22:8 [l]Rev 1:1 [m]Rev 19:10
22:9 [n]ver 10,18, 19 [o]Rev 19:10
22:10 [p]Da 8:26; Rev 10:4 [q]Rev 1:3
22:11 [r]Eze 3:27; Da 12:10
22:12 [s]ver 7,20 [t]Isa 40:10
22:13 [u]Rev 1:8 [v]Rev 1:17 [w]Rev 21:6
22:14 [x]Rev 2:7 [y]Rev 21:12 [z]Rev 21:27
22:15 [a]1Co 6:9,10; Gal 5:19-21; Col 3:5,6 [b]Php 3:2
22:16 [c]Rev 1:1 [d]Rev 1:4 [e]Rev 5:5 [f]2Pe 1:19; Rev 2:28
22:17 [g]Rev 2:7

a 16 The Greek is plural.

The River of Life

REV 22:1-6

The water flowing from the throne of God may represent the Holy Sprit, the promise of eternal life or the abundance of life given to God's people—or it may very well symbolize all three.

Spend a few moments reviewing the descriptions of the new Jerusalem in Revelation 21 and 22. Which word pictures impress you the most? What do you think it will be like to experience God wiping the tears from your eyes (Rev 21:4)? Why do you think God wants his people to live together with him in one city (Rev 21:2-5)? How might we serve God in the new Jerusalem (Rev 22:3)? How do you think it will affect you to see the Lord face to face (Rev 22:4)? You may not know the answers to all your questions until you get to heaven, but considering the possibilities can help you to grasp more fully the reality of heaven's existence and the truth that if you are a believer in Christ, one day you will live in this glorious home.

"I Am Coming Soon"

REV 22:18–21

The events depicted in the book of Revelation are astounding—some would even call them fantastic. Yet they are completely real and true. Symbolism has played a key role throughout the text. But at the book's conclusion, the bottom line is stated clearly and succinctly in Jesus' own words: "Yes, I am coming soon" (Rev 22:20). The author of Revelation responds: "Amen," or "So be it."

The hope of the world is coming. Are you ready? God commands his people to remain completely faithful to him. In our human strength, we could never achieve such a goal. But, thankfully, believers can live in a manner that is pleasing to him—not just in the future, but this very day—because the power of the Spirit and the grace of the Lord Jesus are with us.

We are an Easter people living in a Good Friday world, not Good Friday people living in an Easter world. That means we are destined for joy no matter how difficult our daily life.

—Barbara Johnson

let him come; and whoever wishes, let him take
the free gift of the water of life.

18 I warn everyone who hears the words of the
prophecy of this book: If anyone adds anything to
them,[h] God will add to him the plagues described
in this book.[i] 19 And if anyone takes words away[j]
from this book of prophecy, God will take away
from him his share in the tree of life and in the
holy city, which are described in this book.
20 He who testifies to these things[k] says, "Yes, I
am coming soon."
Amen. Come, Lord Jesus.[l]
21 The grace of the Lord Jesus be with God's people.[m] Amen.

22:18 [h]Dt 4:2; Pr 30:6 [i]Rev 15:6-16:21

22:19 [j]Dt 4:2

22:20 [k]Rev 1:2 [l]1Co 16:22

22:21 [m]Ro 16:20

Weights and Measures

	BIBLICAL UNIT	APPROXIMATE AMERICAN EQUIVALENT	APPROXIMATE METRIC EQUIVALENT
WEIGHTS	talent (60 minas)	75 pounds	34 kilograms
	mina (50 shekels)	1 1/4 pounds	0.6 kilogram
	shekel (2 bekas)	2/5 ounce	11.5 grams
	pim ($^{2}1/4_{3}$ shekel)	1/3 ounce	7.6 grams
	beka (10 gerahs)	1/5 ounce	5.5 grams
	gerah	1/50 ounce	0.6 gram
LENGTH	cubit	18 inches	0.5 meter
	span	9 inches	23 centimeters
	handbreadth	3 inches	8 centimeters
CAPACITY			
Dry Measure	cor [homer] (10 ephahs)	6 bushels	220 liters
	lethek (5 ephahs)	3 bushels	110 liters
	ephah (10 omers)	3/5 bushel	22 liters
	seah (1/3 ephah)	7 quarts	7.3 liters
	omer (1/10 ephah)	2 quarts	2 liters
	cab (1/18 ephah)	1 quart	1 liter
Liquid Measure	bath (1 ephah)	6 gallons	22 liters
	hin (1/6 bath)	4 quarts	4 liters
	log (1/72 bath)	1/3 quart	0.3 liter

The figures of the table are calculated on the basis of a shekel equaling 11.5 grams, a cubit equaling 18 inches and an ephah equaling 22 liters. The quart referred to is either a dry quart (slightly larger than a liter) or a liquid quart (slightly smaller than a liter), whichever is applicable. The ton referred to in the footnotes is the American ton of 2,000 pounds.

This table is based upon the best available information, but it is not intended to be mathematically precise; like the measurement equivalents in the footnotes, it merely gives approximate amounts and distances. Weights and measures differed somewhat at various times and places in the ancient world. There is uncertainty particularly about the ephah and the bath; further discoveries may shed more light on these units of capacity.

Study Helps

Timeline of Women in the Bible

B.C. | 2000 | 1500 | 1000 | 500 | 1 A.D. | 500

Eve
Noah's Wife
Sarah
Hagar
Rebekah
Leah
Rachel
Moses' mother
Miriam
Rahab
Deborah
Hannah
Samson's Mother
Delilah
Naomi
Ruth
Michal
Abigail
Bathsheba
Queen of Sheba
Jezebel
Widow of Zarephath
Athaliah
Woman of Shunem
Gomer
Ezekiel's Wife
Vashti
Esther
Anna
Elizabeth
Mary
Mary Magdalene
Mary of Bethany
Martha
Woman at the Well
Woman Caught in Adultery
Sapphira
Dorcas
Rhoda
Lydia
Priscilla
Lois
Eunice

The Genealogy of Jesus
(*according to Matthew*)

Abraham (Sarah)
Isaac (Rebekah)
Jacob (Leah)
Judah (Tamar)
Perez (unknown)
Hezron (unknown)
Ram (unknown)
Amminadab (unknown)
Nahshon (unknown)
Salmon (Rahab)
Boaz (Ruth)
Obed (unknown)
Jesse (unknown)
David (Bathsheba)
Solomon (Naamah)
Rehoboam (Maacah)
Abijah (unknown)
Asa (Azubah)
Jehoshaphat (unknown)
Jehoram (Athaliah)
Uzziah (Jerusha)
Jotham (unknown)
Ahaz (Abijah)
Hezekiah (Hephzibah)
Manasseh (unknown)
Amon (Jedidah)
Josiah (Zebidah)
Jehoiachin (unknown)
Shealtiel (unknown)
Zerubbabel (unknown)
Abiud (unknown)
Eliakim (unknown)
Azor (unknown)
Zadok (unknown)
Akim (unknown)
Eliud (unknown)
Eleazar (unknown)
Matthan (unknown)
Jacob (unknown)
Joseph (Mary)

JESUS

Jesus and New Testament Women

Jesus Meets . . .	What Happens	Scripture
Mary, his mother	*She loves him as her son and Savior.*	Mt 1–2; 12:46-50 Mk 3:31-35 Lk 1–2; 8:19-21 Jn 2:1-11; 19:25 Ac 1:14
Elizabeth	*She gives birth to Jesus' forerunner.*	Lk 1:5-80
Anna	*She praises God for the baby Jesus.*	Lk 2:36-38
Woman at the Well	*She believes Jesus is the Messiah.*	Jn 4:1-42
Peter's Mother-in-law	*Jesus heals her.*	Mt 8:14-15 Mk 1:29-31 Lk 4:38-39
Widow of Nain	*Jesus raises her son from death.*	Lk 7:11-17
Sinful Woman at Simon's House	*She washes Jesus' feet with her tears.*	Lk 7:36-50
Joanna	*She supports Jesus financially.*	Lk 8:1-3; 23:55; 24:10
Susanna	*She helps Jesus in his ministry.*	Lk 8:1-3
Woman Subject to Bleeding	*She is healed when she touches Jesus.*	Mt 9:20-22 Mk 5:25-34 Lk 8:43-48
Jairus's Daughter	*Jesus raises her from death.*	Mt 9:18-26 Mk 5:21-43 Lk 8:41-56
Syrophoenician Woman	*Jesus responds to her plea.*	Mt 15:21-28 Mk 7:24-30
Woman Caught in Adultery	*Jesus saves her and tells her to sin no more.*	Jn 8:1-11
Mary of Bethany	*She sits at Jesus' feet.*	Lk 10:38-42 Jn 11; 12:1-8
Martha	*Jesus sets her priorities straight.*	Lk 10:38-42 Jn 11; 12:1-2
A Woman in the Crowd	*She calls out a blessing on Jesus' mother.*	Lk 11:27-28
Crippled Woman	*Jesus heals her.*	Lk 13:10-13
Mother of James and John	*She asks Jesus a favor, and he admonishes her.*	Mt 20:20-28; 27:56 Mk 15:40-41; 16:1-2
Widow with Two Coins	*She models a lesson on giving for the disciples.*	Mk 12:41-44 Lk 21:1-4
Daughters of Jerusalem	*They weep as Jesus walks to his death.*	Lk 23:27-31
Women at Calvary	*They mourn as Jesus dies.*	Mt 27:55
Mary, the mother of James and Joses	*She helps take care of Jesus.*	Mt 27:56,61; 28:1 Mk 15:40-41,47: 16:1 Lk 24:10; Jn 19:25
Mary Magdalene	*She faithfully follows Jesus.*	Mt 27:56,61; 28:1 Mk 15:40-47; 16:1-11; Lk 8:1-2; 24:10 Jn 19:25; 20:1-18

Dictionary of NIV Terms

This dictionary will give you a better understanding of many of the names, words, phrases and place names found in The Women of Faith Study Bible.

Abba
An Aramaic word best translated *Daddy* (Mark 14:36). *Abba* was a deeply personal and affectionate word, that most of Jesus' contemporaries would have considered disrespectful to use in addressing God.

Abomination
That which is repugnant or detestable to God or his people, such as idolatry or immorality (Isaiah 66:3).

Abyss
A bottomless pit where, at the end of the age, Satan will be banished for a time (Rev. 20:3). The Greeks used this word to describe the underworld of spirits, suggesting a place so deep it is unfathomable (Luke 8:31).

Acacia
A durable wood readily available in the Sinai Desert and used in the Old Testament tabernacle. Today the gum of the acacia tree is used for commercial and medicinal uses.

Afflict
See *Affliction*.

Affliction
Hardships, calamities and suffering, often lasting a long time. Sometimes imposed by others, sometimes self-imposed and at other times divinely imposed.

Alien
In the Old Testament, a non-Israelite living in Israel, typically in poverty. Later, a stranger away from home.

Anoint
The symbolic act of pouring oil on objects or individuals as a sign of consecration. The name *Messiah* means *the Anointed One*.

Antichrist
Anyone who opposes or rejects God has, to some degree, the spirit of antichrist (1 John 2:18). Also, at the end of the age, the figure who will embody the worst of the spirit of antichrist but who will finally be defeated.

Apostle
Someone sent to represent another; in the New Testament someone who had seen Jesus and been commissioned by him to teach others about him.

Aramaic
The common language in Palestine at the time of Jesus and the early church.

Asherah poles
See *Poles, Asherah*.

Ashtoreth
Female consort of the chief Canaanite god, Baal. The goddess of love, fertility and war. Also known as Ishtar to Babylonians, Aphrodite to Greeks and Venus to Romans. Also called Asherah.

Assembly, Sacred
The gathering of the entire Israelite community for common worship, celebration or repentance.

Atonement
Act by which sinners are made "at one" with God—when barriers of sin between God and sinners are removed. The Day of Atonement was an Old Testament annual fast when the high priest entered the Most Holy Place to atone for the sins of the people (Lev. 16). Sacrifices on the Day of Atonement cleansed the whole nation of sin—even unknown transgressions. Later Christ's death made the final atonement for believers, making further sacrifices unnecessary (Heb. 9:23-28).

Avenge
To get back at or punish someone who has done wrong.

Baal
The Canaanite fertility god believed to be responsible for germinating crops, increasing flocks and adding children to the community. Best known of the Canaanite gods.

Backsliding
To turn or move away from a relationship with God.

Baptism
A Christian rite symbolizing cleansing from sin and identification with Jesus. Sprinkling, immersion and pouring are three ways Christians today practice water baptism.

Beelzebub
Satan, the prince of demons. In the Old Testament, Baal was a Canaanite deity, whose name was expanded to Beelzebul (meaning *Exalted* or *Prince Baal*).

Birthright
In the Old Testament, special rights given to the firstborn son, including the authority as leader of the family.

Blaspheme
To speak about God or holy things in a careless, false or insulting way.

Blasphemy
See *Blaspheme*.

Block, Stumbling
Anything or anyone that causes someone to sin.

Bloodguilt
The verdict on a person for crimes deserving death.

Breastpiece
A colorful pouch nine inches square, attached to the attire of the Old Testament high priest. Twelve precious

stones on the pouch represented the 12 tribes of Israel—so when it hung around the priest's neck, the people could be close to his heart. Inside the breastpiece were the Urim and Thummim (Exodus 28:15,30; See *Urim;* See *Thummim*).

Burnt offering
See *Offering, Burnt*.

Byword
An object of scorn and ridicule, a term of verbal abuse (Job 17:6).

Calamus
An aromatic spice cane; its juice was an ingredient in incense offerings (Isaiah 43:24).

Capstone
Either the bottom corner of a building (a foundation stone) or the keystone of an archway (Mark 12:10). It can cause a person to stumble (1 Peter 2:8), or it can fall on someone (Matt. 21:44).

Censer
A container used for burning incense (Rev. 8:3).

Centurion
A Roman army officer in charge of 100 soldiers.

Chaff
(1) After wheat was harvested, the chaff (the seed covering, straw and dust) was blown away from the grain in a process called winnowing. See *Fork, Winnowing*. (2) A word used to describe the wicked who would be separated from the righteous at judgment (Psalm 1:4).

Cherub
A winged, angelic being who exists primarily to glorify God and to vindicate God's holiness against the presumptuous pride of fallen humans. Symbolic attendant marking the place of God's enthronement in his earthly kingdom (Exodus 25:18). The plural of *cherub* is *cherubim*.

Circumcise
See *Circumcision*.

Circumcision
Cutting off the foreskin of the penis—usually on the eighth day after birth (Gen. 17:10-14). It was a physical reminder of the special, spiritual relationship between God and his chosen people.

Cistern
Covered pits cut into rock or clay to catch and store rainwater (Jer. 14:3). Critical to life in an arid climate, cisterns symbolize security.

Citadel
A tower or building equipped for war, especially one in a city, often thought of as the city's final defense unit.

Collectors, Tax
Those employed by Roman authorities to collect taxes for them. They were notorious for imposing more taxes than were required, skimming off the top to line their own pockets. They were despised by the Jews for collaborating with the Roman government that ruled over them.

Concubine
A woman who belonged to a man in a relationship inferior to that of a wife. Commonly found in ancient cultures where polygamy was practiced, a concubine was often one of the spoils of war—with the primary purpose of bearing children for the man.

Consecrate
To set aside or dedicate for God's use (Exodus 13:2).

Covenant
A mutually binding agreement between two parties. In the Old Testament, God entered into a covenant with Israel. But God alone set the conditions to the agreement. In return for their loyalty and obedience, God promised to protect and love Israel and to give them his presence. The *new covenant* (Heb. 8:7) brought salvation to God's people through the shedding of Jesus' blood.

Cows, Sea
Dugongs (see NIV text note on Exodus 25:5)—marine animals abounding on the coral banks of the Red Sea and in other tropical waters. A dugong can grow to be 11 feet long, with a round head, fish-like tail and flippers for forelimbs. Their appearance is similar to seals.

Cubit
A unit of measurement 18 to 21 inches in length—from the elbow to the tip of the middle finger.

Cyrus
The founder of the Persian empire, Cyrus the Great ruled Persia from 559 to 530 B.C.

Day of the Lord
An Old Testament concept describing the time when God would intervene to vindicate the righteous and judge the wicked (Isaiah 2:12). The New Testament links it more specifically to Jesus' second coming (1 Cor. 1:8). The *Day of the Lord* was both a time of salvation and of judgment.

Death
The end of physical life. Spiritual death means separation from God (Eph. 2:1-5). Other uses of the word include: the end of a sinful way of life (Romans 6:4-8) and the final and irreversible separation from God after judgment (Rev. 20:11-15).

Decapolis
The name of the confederation of ten Gentile cities wrenched from Jewish control by the Roman general Pompey in 63 B.C. All but one were east of the Jordan River. See *Map 9* at the back of this Bible.

Desecrate
To treat without respect or reverence (Lev. 21:12).

Disciple
A student or follower; an adherent to the teachings of a particular teacher or school of thought. In the New Testament, *disciple* usually refers to a follower of Jesus.

Dissipation
Living only for your own pleasure; wasting your life on foolish or evil pleasures.

Divination
Using a human intermediary or inanimate objects, such as the examination of animal entrails, to receive messages from the spirit world.

Dregs
Sediment that forms during the fermentation of wine. When not separated from the wine, dregs caused bitter tasting wine. Used as a picture of undesirable characteristics and the bitterness of God's wrath on the wicked (Psalm 75:8).

Drink offering
See *Offering, Drink*.

Dross
The worthless by-product left over and thrown out after refining precious metals like gold or silver ore. A

picture of how those who stray are treated (Psalm 119:119).

Edict
An order made by someone with power to enforce it.

Edom
The nation of descendants of Esau, the twin brother of Jacob (Gen. 25:23-28). Located south of the Dead Sea amid the reddish sandstone of the Rift Valley (see *Map 6* at the back of this Bible), Edom was often hostile to Israel (Obad. v. 1).

Elect
Those chosen for a particular relationship or function. The people of God chosen in Christ before the foundation of the world (Eph. 1:4).

Ephod
One of six articles of clothing specified for Israelite priests' uniforms (Exodus 28:4-8), the ephod consisted of a sleeveless garment made of finely twisted linen. In some instances in the Old Testament, the word is used to describe an object of worship (Judges 8:27).

Eternal life
See *Life, Eternal*.

Eunuch
A castrated male who in the ancient Near East was often employed in a governmental position. The term came to designate an officer, whether physically a eunuch or not.

Exile
One who is banished from his or her own country and taken captive to a foreign land. One of the means God used in the Old Testament to punish his people, purging them of their sinful and rebellious ways.

Extol
To praise highly, to glorify, to laud (Psalm 34:1).

Extortion
Gaining something from someone by force or by some other illegal means.

Fear of the Lord
See *Lord, Fear of the*.

Fellowship offering
See *Offering, Fellowship*.

Festival, New Moon
Both a religious and a civil Old Testament festival (1 Samuel 20:5), the New Moon festival was celebrated at the beginning of each month and is often mentioned in the Old Testament together with the Sabbath (Isaiah 1:13).

Firstborn
Oldest son and the possessor of special privileges. In the Old Testament the term often described the privilege and favor God granted to Israel (Exodus 4:22). In the New Testament, Jesus is called the *firstborn* of the Father, the one who rules over all (Heb. 1:6).

Firstfruits
The first crops of the season that ripened. The offering of the firstfruits was a gift of the first and best part of the harvest, signifying that all of Israel's sustenance came from God (Exodus 23:19). In the New Testament, the term is applied to Jesus (1 Cor. 15:20) and to believers (James 1:18).

Footstool
A stool for supporting the feet of someone sitting on a throne (2 Chron. 9:18). The Bible depicts God's *footstool* as (1) the earth (Isaiah 66:1), (2) the ark of the covenant (which in the Old Testament represented God's presence among the Israelites (1 Chron. 28:2), (3) the temple (Psalm 99:5) and (4) the defeated enemies of the Messiah (Psalm 110:1).

Fork, Winnowing
A large, wooden fork used in Bible times to toss the threshed grain into the air so the wind would blow away the lighter chaff while the heavier grain dropped back to the ground.

Gabriel
An angel whose name means *man of God* or *God is powerful*. He heralded the coming births of John the Baptist (Luke 1:11-20) and Jesus (Luke 1:26-28).

Genealogy
A list of a person's ancestors or descendants.

Gentile
A term for anyone who is not an Israelite. Jews and Gentiles have been reconciled to God and to each other through Christ (Eph. 2:11-22).

Glory
An essential quality of God's character (Psalm 63:2), his glory is his worthiness. Everything about him testifies that he is worthy to receive praise, honor and respect. In the New Testament, Jesus is revealed to be the *Lord of glory* (1 Cor. 2:8). In the Bible, glory is often associated with brightness or splendor (Luke 2:9).

Glutton
A person who habitually eats too much.

God, Kingdom of
God's rule on earth. Both present and still future. Began with the arrival of Christ and will be consummated when Christ comes back to earth for the second time.

Gospel
Good news—specifically, the good news of salvation through Jesus Christ, who died for our sins and rose again. *Gospel* describes the message of Christianity, as well as the first four books of the New Testament (Matthew, Mark, Luke and John) in which the record of Jesus' life and teaching is found.

Grace
Unmerited favor, unearned benefit, undeserved kindness. God's amazing gift of forgiveness of sins and power to live with dignity in the present and with hope for the future.

Grain offering
See *Offering, Grain*.

Guilt offering
See *Offering, Guilt*.

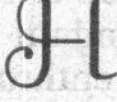

Hades
Greek word referring to the place of the dead, akin to the Hebrew *Sheol*.

Hallelujah
Occurring only four times in the New Testament, *hallelujah* comes from two Hebrew words that mean *praise the* LORD (Rev. 19:1).

Hebrew
(1) The language in which most of

the Old Testament was written. (2) Another name for an Israelite; a descendant of Abraham. (3) Sometimes refers to a broader group, including non-Israelites descended from Eber (Gen. 10:21-32)—such as Arameans (descendants of Nahor) and Moabites and Ammonites (descendants of Lot).

Hell
Place of final punishment for the wicked. In the New Testament, the word *hell* typically translates the Greek word *ge[h]enna.* and is used as a metaphor to picture hell. *Ge[h]enna* comes from a Hebrew expression meaning *the Valley of Ben Hinnom,* a deep ravine outside Jerusalem where human sacrifices had at one time been offered to the pagan god, Molech (2 Kings 23:10). See ***Topheth.***

Herodians
A group of Jews who opposed Jesus and supported the Herods, a line of Judean kings during Jesus' lifetime. They were supporters of Rome, from which the Herods received their authority.

High places
See *Places, High.*

Holy kiss
See *Kiss, Holy.*

Holy Place
See *Place, Holy.*

Hosts, Starry
The stars and other heavenly bodies, the worship of which is warned against in the Bible (Deut. 4:19).

Hyssop
A plant used in a ritual cleansing ceremony. Its hairy branches were dipped in sacrificial blood, which was then brushed or sprinkled on the object or person being cleansed (Exodus 12:22), symbolizing spiritual cleansing from sin.

Idol
Image of a god (Exodus 20:3-4). Anything that takes the place of God or steals our affections from him—often things like our relationships, work or hobbies.

Idolatry
The worship of false gods, sometimes by means of images. Anything that takes us away from the worship of the one true God (Romans 1:18-25).

Incense
Aromatic substances such as frankincense and myrrh burned to make a fragrant smoke. Used as an offering in worship. Can symbolize either prayers (Psalm 141:2) or the presence of God (Exodus 30:1-10).

Intercede
To pray for another person, usually to obtain God's help.

Jericho
An ancient city situated several miles west of the Jordan River and north of the Dead Sea. See *Map 4* at the back of this Bible.

Jerusalem
(1) The capital of Israel before it split into two kingdoms in 930 B.C. After the split, it was the capital of the southern kingdom of Judah. (2) The place where Solomon built the temple. (3) Captured by the Babylonians in 597 B.C. and then destroyed by them in 586 B.C., Jerusalem was rebuilt between 538 and 445 B.C. (4) Jewish center of worship during the time of Jesus. See ***Zion.***

Jew
Derived from *Judah,* the term originally denoted one belonging to the tribe of Judah and later was applied to all the descendants of Abraham. Other names: Israelites and Hebrews.

Joppa
A seaport located about 35 miles northwest of Jerusalem, known today as Jaffa. See *Map 6* at the back of this Bible.

Jubilee
An Old Testament celebration held every 50 years (Lev. 25:10). During the 49th and 50th years, the land would have lain idle for two consecutive years (Isaiah 37:30), enslaved Israelites were freed and property was returned to its original owners.

Justification
That act of God whereby he places us in a right relationship with him (Romans 5:16); a declaration of innocence or righteousness, a freeing from guilt or blame.

Justify
To erase someone's sins; to declare righteous.

Kidron Valley
See *Valley, Kidron.*

Kingdom of God
See *God, Kingdom of.*

Kiss, Holy
A sign of mutual respect and trust; the equivalent of a handshake or hug (2 Cor. 13:12).

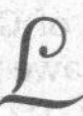

Lament
A musical or poetic dirge—a song of sorrow, a cry of grief (often a recognition of judgment). The Bible book of Lamentations is composed of five laments.

Legion
A very large number (Mark 5:9). The name of a Roman army division of 6,000 soldiers.

Leprosy
Known today as "Hansen's disease," although the Biblical term included other types of skin diseases as well. Can cause paralysis, deformity and gangrene.

Leviathan
(1) A great marine mammal—possibly a crocodile (see NIV text note on Job 41:1) or a sea serpent. (2) Thought by some to be an ancient mythological dragon that caused eclipses by twisting itself around the sun (Job 3:8). (3) A creature said by ancient mythology to represent the chaotic waters overcome by God at creation (Psalm 74:14; 89:10; See ***Rahab).***

Levite
The name given to the descendants of Levi. Given a place of privilege and responsibility among God's people in overseeing worship and in caring for the tabernacle. Only Levites could become priests, but not all Levites were priests.

Life, Eternal
A quality of life that begins the moment someone trusts in Jesus for salvation (John 3:36) and continues after physical death through fellow-

ship with God in life that will never end (Jude v. 21).

Line, Measuring
(1) A rope, string or cord of a specific length used for measuring. (2) Sometimes used to picture God's thorough and calculated punishment of Judah and other nations (2 Kings 21:13), but also used as a symbol of restoration (Zech. 1:16).

Locust
An insect similar to the grasshopper but more aggressive. An army of these insects can devastate entire fields of crops within minutes.

Lord, Fear of the
An attitude of reverence or worship in the presence of God—an attitude of humility and awe more than dread and fright (Prov. 1:7).

Lyre
A harplike instrument made of wood and distinguished by its number of strings (historians say the lyre had about ten strings). Lyres typically had a sound board over which the vibrating strings could resonate.

M

Magicians
Ancient wise men who were expected to foretell the future and influence such events as harvests, droughts and battles (Daniel 2:2). Many claimed to possess occult knowledge.

Man, Son of
An expression found in the Old Testament and used as a self-description of Jesus in the New Testament. Over 90 times Ezekiel is called *son of man* to emphasize his humanity in the presence of Almighty God (Ezek. 2:1). Jesus used this name to show he was the Messiah prophesied by Daniel (Daniel 7:13).

Mandrake
A fragrant flowering plant that grew wild in desert areas. Thought by ancients to possess magical powers, it was used for medicinal purposes and as a charm against evil spirits; it was also credited with aphrodisiac qualities.

Manna
The food God miraculously supplied during the Israelites' 40 years of wilderness wandering (the manna stopped at the time of their first Passover in Canaan). Israelites described its appearance as *white like coriander seed* and its taste as *wafers made with honey* (Exodus 16:31).

Measuring line
See *Line, Measuring*.

Medium
Someone believed to be able to consult with ghosts or spirits; a person through whom the spirit of a dead person would communicate with the living (Isaiah 8:19). The practice was condemned and prohibited in the Old Testament (Deut. 18:10-11).

Meeting, Tent of
Another name for the tabernacle, for it was the place where God showed his presence and met with his people.

Mercy
Compassion or kindness shown to someone instead of severity, especially to someone who doesn't deserve it.

Midwife
A person who helps with the birth of a baby (Gen. 35:17).

Millstone
One of a pair of stones used to crush grain for flour.

Molech
Traditionally understood as the name of a pagan god to whom children were burned in sacrifice (Lev. 18:21).

Most Holy Place
See *Place, Most Holy*.

Myrrh
A fragrant gum extracted from a small tree growing in certain areas of the Middle East. Its oil was used as a spice, as a medicine and as a cosmetic; myrrh was applied to Jesus' body after his burial (John 19:39-40). One of the gifts of the Magi to Jesus after his birth (Matt. 2:11).

Mystery
Among the Greeks, a secret imparted only to the initiated. For Paul in the New Testament, a divine truth once hidden but now revealed in the gospel. The Christian mystery is God's strategy to redeem people through Christ (Eph. 3:2-9)—Jews and Gentiles united in Christ.

Nazirite
One who demonstrated total consecration to the Lord by taking a vow of separation and abstinence for the purpose of some special service; the three standard prohibitions were abstaining from grape products, from haircuts and from contact with dead bodies (Num. 6:2-8).

Negev
The area stretching southward from Beersheba in southern Palestine (see *Map 2* at the back of this Bible). It is usually desertlike, but at times there are seasons of rain that leave pools of water (Psalm 126:4).

New Moon festival
See *Festival, New Moon*.

New wine
See *Wine, New*.

Offal
The entrails of an animal burned as part of a sin offering (Exodus 29:14).

Offering, Burnt
The most frequent of the sacrifices at the Old Testament sanctuary—offered morning and evening of every day. To make payment for sins, a worshiper voluntarily brought an unblemished animal to the priest and laid his hand on the animal's head to express identification. The priest then killed it and burned it up completely, symbolizing the person's total devotion to God (Lev. 1).

Offering, Drink
Usually a wine or oil poured out as a sacrifice of dedication to God—part of the regular offerings made every day in connection with the grain offering (Exodus 29:38-41). In the New Testament, it is a picture of expending one's life for the cause of Christ (Phil. 2:17).

Offering, Fellowship
To express gratitude to God, a worshiper sacrificed an unblemished animal on the altar. Part of it was burned, and a portion of it was eaten by the worshiper, symbolizing peace and fellowship with God (Lev. 3). Traditionally called *peace offerings*.

Offering, Grain
An offering presented as an act of worship (Lev. 2). It was intended simply to remember God's favor and, by remembering, to please him. The worshiper who offered the sacrifice brought prepared loaves of bread,

wafers or small cakes to the sanctuary; a portion was consumed by fire and the rest of the offering was eaten by the priests.

Offering, Guilt
An offering that absolved the worshiper in instances where restitution was required—in cases of theft or cheating, for example. A ram was offered (no substitutes allowed), and complete restitution plus 20 percent was to be paid, satisfying both God and the person wronged. Only guilt offerings eased guilty consciences with restitution for sin.

Offering, Sin
The Old Testament blood sacrifice required for unintentional sins (Lev. 4:1-35). Sin offerings were made for the whole congregation on all feast days and especially on the Day of Atonement, and they were prescribed for individuals in a number of instances that demanded payment of the penalty for sins.

Offering, Thank
A type of fellowship offering, the thank offering expressed gratitude to God for deliverance from trouble, healing of sickness, answers to prayer or some other blessing received (Lev. 7:12).

Offering, Wave
A ceremony whereby offerings are dedicated to the Lord—most likely by lifting the object up before the Lord. A number of objects could be the subject of the wave offering, including the breast portion of the fellowship offering (Lev. 7:30).

Oracle
An announcement or message from God. The word often suggests unwelcome news or judgment.

Ordination
An Old Testament ritual signifying the responsibilities and privileges of the Levitical priesthood (Lev. 8:22). The Hebrew word translated *ordination* literally meant *to fill the hand* and probably referred to offerings placed in their hands. Ordination of ministers today has its roots in this Old Testament practice.

Parable
A saying or story that drives home a point using illustrations from everyday life; a comparison of two objects for the purpose of teaching. Jesus told many parables during the course of his life on earth.

Patriarch
The father of a family or head of a tribe or race; a forefather of the Israelites (Heb. 7:4).

Peace
The Biblical concept of peace has at its root the meaning of "totality," or "completeness." Important nuances of meaning include such things as "fulfillment," "maturity," "soundness," "wholeness," "harmony," "security," "well-being" and "prosperity." Also connotes absence of war and freedom from disturbance.

Pharisees
A powerful branch of the Jewish religious community during Jesus' time. Considered to be religious experts, this group believed that the oral law of the Jewish faith was as equally authoritative and inspired by God as the Torah, or written law. Consequently, they obeyed very strictly God's laws and all the tradition of interpretation they had established. Jesus reserved some of his harshest criticism for them (Matt. 23).

Place, Holy
Part of the Israelite sanctuaries (tabernacle and temple), located just outside the Most Holy Place. Contained the altar of incense, the table for the bread of the Presence and the lampstand.

Place, Most Holy
The inner sanctuary of both the Old Testament tabernacle and the temple, containing the ark of the covenant, the symbol of God's presence. The high priest alone was allowed to enter it once each year on the Day of Atonement (Lev. 16).

Places, High
Places of worship often associated with pagan religious practices, immorality and human sacrifice. Religious objects were placed on the tops of hills to appease pagan gods (Num. 33:52). Generally, Israelites were forbidden to worship God there, and God commanded them to destroy these areas.

Plunder
To rob or loot as an act of war. Used as a noun, plunder refers to the spoils gained through the act of looting.

Poles, Asherah
Wooden poles, perhaps carved in the image of Asherah, Canaanite goddess of love and war, set up in her honor and placed near the altars in Canaanite worship.

Precepts
Commands, usually divine injunctions setting forth human obligations.

Priest
The person appointed to act on behalf of men and women in relation to God. The Old Testament group of male leaders descended from Aaron, who performed religious duties in the temple. The New Testament calls Jesus the great high priest (Heb. 4:14) and the body of Christ a holy priesthood (1 Peter 2:5).

Profane
To make a holy thing impure or defiled by treating it with disrespect or irreverence.

Prophecy
The message of a prophet. Also, a spiritual gift, a supernatural empowering to build up God's family. Those with this gift either proclaimed to God's people new truth from God or challenged them with existing Scriptural truths (1 Cor. 14:1–5).

Prophet
A mouthpiece for God, one who receives a message from God and proclaims it to a specific audience.

Prophetess
A female prophet (Exodus 15:20).

Prostitute, Shrine
A special class of ancient Middle Eastern prostitutes (male and female) used in the fertility cults. They performed sexual acts in the temple of their god as acts of religious devotion (Deut. 23:17).

Purify
To make clean or pure. To be ceremonially pure means to be free from defects that would disqualify someone or something from holy uses or holy acts. To be ethically pure means to show oneself, in thought and conduct, to be a person chosen by God.

Purple
A symbol of wealth and royalty. The most highly prized dye in the ancient world, purple dye was obtained from various shellfish common to Phoenicia (a name that means *land of purple*).

Quail
A small spotted bird similar to the partridge; quail migrated from North Africa through Egypt, Sinai and Palestine. God provided quail along with manna (See ***Manna***) as food to sustain the Israelites in their desert wanderings (Exodus 16:13).

Rabbi
A title of respect meaning *my master* or *my teacher,* given to teachers of the law (Matt. 23:2–7). Jesus was also addressed as *Rabbi* (Mark 9:5).

Rahab
(1) Old Testament prostitute from Jericho who hid two Hebrew spies and helped them escape danger (Joshua 2:1). (2) A name symbolizing a mythical sea monster that allegedly ruled over the chaos at the time of creation (Psalm 89:10; Isaiah 51:9). See ***Leviathan.*** (3) A nickname for Egypt (Psalm 87:4; Isaiah 30:7). (4) A symbol of hostility toward God's people.

Redeem
To obtain release by paying a price, to buy back.

Redeemer
One who delivers from bondage or trouble. Applied to family situations where a *kinsman-redeemer* was responsible to protect the interests of needy members of the extended family (Ruth 3:9). Applied to God as the protector and deliverer of Israel (Isaiah 41:14). Though Jesus is not specifically called "Redeemer" in the New Testament, he is the one in whom believers have redemption (Eph. 1:7).

Redemption
Deliverance and freedom—described in the New Testament as freedom from the penalty of sin by payment of a ransom. Through his death on the cross Jesus paid the ransom for us (Romans 3:24) and set us free.

Remnant
(1) The remaining part or group after destruction or dispersal (2 Kings 19:30–31). (2) Those who escape God's judgment because of God's grace (Romans 11:5). (3) A symbol of hope pointing toward the great multitude that one day will stand saved before God (Rev. 7).

Repent
To consciously turn from sin to God; to be sorry for what you have done and to resolve not to do it again.

Repentance
A profound change of mind from sin-centeredness to God-centeredness. Though repentance may represent only regret or remorse over a past thought or action, in its fullest sense it connotes a change of orientation involving a deliberate redirection for the future (Acts 26:20).

Reproach
To rebuke or chide, to blame or accuse. Used as a noun, a source of disgrace or shame, an expression of disapproval or rebuke (Psalm 79:4).

Resurrection
The act of coming back to life after being dead. Described as applying to both the righteous and the wicked (Daniel 12:2). Jesus' resurrection (Matt. 28:1–10), along with his death, is considered essential to the salvation of believers (Romans 4:25) and guarantees our resurrection (1 Cor. 15:12–19).

Retribution
Deserved punishment for doing wrong, but also deserved reward for doing good.

Revelation
The act of disclosure or making known; more particularly, God's self-unveiling, his deliberate disclosure of true knowledge of himself and his purposes and actions on our behalf (Eph. 1:17).

Revere
See *Reverence.*

Reverence
An attitude of deep respect, honor and deference. Our worthy response to God's majesty and holiness. From an attitude of reverence naturally flow obedient actions (2 Cor. 7:1). See ***Lord, Fear of the.***

Righteous
See *Righteousness.*

Righteousness
The fulfillment of the demands of a relationship. God brings believers into a right relation with him, erasing their guilt and crediting righteousness to them (Romans 3:21–22) and helping them to be devoted to the service of what God says is right (Romans 6:11–13).

Ring, Signet
A ring containing a design or a name of someone in authority and used to make an impression in soft clay or wax. Used to authorize official documents. A symbol of authority (Gen. 41:42).

Sabbath
The Hebrew weekly day of rest and worship observed on the seventh day of the week. It began at sunset on Friday and ended at sunset on Saturday.

Sackcloth
A coarse material, dark in color, usually made of goat's hair. Worn especially during times of mourning or social protest. A symbol of grief and mourning.

Sacred assembly
See *Assembly, Sacred.*

Sacred stones
See *Stones, Sacred.*

Sacrifice
A gift or offering to God (Exodus 12:27). Something offered to God to atone for sin. Jesus is the ultimate sacrifice, which satisfies God's wrath toward humankind (1 John 4:10). Believers are to live in such a way that they offer themselves to God as *living sacrifices* (Romans 12:1).

Sadducees
A group of leaders in the Jewish religious community opposed to the teachings of both the Pharisees and Jesus. During the first century A.D. they held considerable political power and controlled the highest Jewish court in the land, the Sanhedrin. They denied the doctrine of the resurrection of the body (Mark 12:18) and the existence of angels and spirits (Acts 23:8).

Saints
Those dedicated to God and set apart for his service (Phil. 1:1). All who believe in Jesus, regardless of their character or spiritual maturity.

Salvation
Deliverance from danger or death; especially deliverance from all that separates people from God (Titus 2:12).

Sanctification
Act of God by which believers become more and more conformed to Christ's image (1 Thessalonians 4:3).

Sanctify
To make holy; to set apart (John 17:17).

Sanhedrin
The highest Jewish authority in Palestine prior to A.D. 70. This court, composed of 70 members and the high priest as president, had complete control over the religious affairs of Israel and had the final say-so in the interpretation of Mosaic Law. It also governed civil affairs and tried certain criminal cases under the authority of the Romans; it could not, however, impose capital punishment (John 18:31).

Satrap
An official who ruled over a major division of the Persian empire (Ezra 8:36).

Scepter
A staff or pole the king held as a symbol of his royal authority.

Sea Cows
See *Cows, Sea.*

Seer
A person who prophesies future events. A prophet. One who speaks the word of God (1 Samuel 9:9). See ***Prophet.***

Selah
Generally believed to be a musical cue or instruction for the performer. Some think it may have been a call for a pause or interlude or for a brief liturgical response by the congregation.

Shekel
The basic weight used in ancient Semitic systems of measurement. The exact weight of a shekel is not known. Some estimate it weighed between 11.3 and 11.47 grams.

Shrine prostitute
See *Prostitute, Shrine.*

Siege works
See *Works, Siege.*

Signet ring
See *Ring, Signet.*

Sin offering
See *Offering, Sin.*

Son of man
See *Man, Son of.*

Sorcery
The use of means believed to have supernatural power to produce or prevent a particular result; the craft of controlling or using such means of supernatural powers. Included in the list of magical arts condemned and prohibited in the Old Testament (Deut. 18:10).

Soul
Represents primarily the life force of the person; also the inner life, encompassing desires and emotions. The part of a person that does not die (Rev. 6:9).

Starry hosts
See *Hosts, starry.*

Stones, Sacred
Stone monuments used in idol worship, often engraved with writing and likely intended to be representations of the pagan deity (2 Kings 3:2). Explicitly forbidden to the Israelites (Lev. 26:1-2).

Stronghold
A place of refuge or defense, such as a tower, fortress or fortified hilltop from which an enemy could be resisted. A metaphor for refuge and security (Psalm 27:1).

Stumbling block
See *Block, Stumbling.*

Tabernacle
A tent used by the Israelites as a place of worship while they were on the move in the desert (Exodus 25:9). Its basic structure was 15 feet wide by 45 feet long by 15 feet high, a space about half the size of a football field. The holy place of God's presence among his people, the tabernacle was also called the *Tent of Meeting* (See ***Meeting, Tent of***).

Tax collectors
See *Collectors, Tax.*

Tent of Meeting
See *Meeting, Tent of.*

Tetrarch
Originally a ruler over a fourth of a region; later used of a number of rulers (lower in rank than kings) who depended on Rome for power to govern land conquered by the Romans.

Thank offering
See *Offering, Thank.*

Thummim
Together with Urim, some sort of devices by which an Old Testament priest could discern God's will (Exodus 28:30). They were possibly sacred lots or stones cast like dice to determine a yes or no answer from God.

Tithe
One-tenth of one's income. The dedication of a tenth of agricultural products, livestock or other goods to the worship of a deity or to the persons who served in the worship of the deity. In the Old Testament, the Israelites devoted a tithe to support the Levites (Num. 18:21), freeing them to serve the Lord. Some suggest that the New Testament standard for giving for the Lord's work is an amount proportionate to one's income (1 Cor. 16:2).

Topheth
A place in the Valley of Ben Hinnom just outside Jerusalem, where apostate Israelites sacrificed children to the pagan god, Molech (Jer. 7:31). Used as a trash dump with perpetual fires that symbolized judgment. Topheth may derive from the Aramaic word for *fireplace.* See ***Hell.***

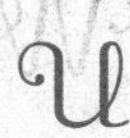

Uncircumcised
(1) Males who have not had a circle of skin cut off at the front end of the penis (Gen. 17:14). See ***Circumcision.*** (2) Figuratively, a heart that is unresponsive is said to be *uncircumcised* (Acts 7:51), that is, not consecrated to the Lord. (3) Gentiles were called *uncircumcised* (Eph. 2:11), but Paul said real circumcision is *circumcision of the heart* (Romans 2:29).

Unclean
Ritually defiled or polluted, for which various rituals of cleansing were prescribed (Lev. 5:2). By the blood of Jesus, *unclean* sinners are cleansed (Heb. 10:22) and enabled to live a fruitful Christian life (2 Peter 1:5-9).

Uncleanness
See *Unclean.*

Urim
Together with Thummim, some sort of devices by which an Old Testament priest could discern God's will

(Exodus 28:30). They were possibly sacred lots or stones cast like dice to determine a yes or no answer from God.

Usury
Interest, often excessive, charged on money lent (Psalm 15:5).

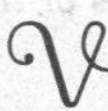

Valley, Kidron
Just east of Jerusalem, between the city and the Mount of Olives (see *Map 8* at the back of this Bible). Pagan relics were destroyed there under Asa, Hezekiah and Josiah (2 Kings 23:4–6).

Vision
A supernatural revelation, message or insight communicated through images seen only within a person's mind or spirit. The pictures seen in a vision may illustrate spiritual truths or future events (Isaiah 1:1).

Vow
A solemn, voluntary promise made to God to perform some action or refrain from performing some action in return for some hoped-for benefits (Judges 11:30–31).

Watchman
Someone on a tower or a high point entrusted to watch for approaching messengers or enemies (Ezek. 3:17).

Watchtower
A tower where guards could watch for danger or where a group of people could find protection from invaders.

Wave offering
See *Offering, Wave.*

Wine, New
The newly pressed juice of the grape. It contains less flavor and less alcohol because of the short aging process.

Winepress
A large vat or trough where several people could work together stomping on grapes to squeeze out the juice so it could be drained off and collected.

Wineskin
A leather container used to store wine (Matt. 9:17).

Winnowing fork
See *Fork, Winnowing.*

Witchcraft
A title linked with the practice of predicting the future by interpreting omens, examining livers of sacrificed animals, and contacting the dead—among other techniques. The Old Testament law prohibited these occultic and magical practices (Deut. 18:9-12).

Works, Siege
Military equipment used in capturing a walled city. Assyrian art shows wheeled battering rams and huge, wheeled towers packed with archers. Soldiers pushed these towers against the wall and used them as protected ladders.

Yeast
(1) A substance that causes bread to rise—often by putting a bit of dough from an earlier batch in the flour, which fermented the entire loaf of bread. (2) A symbol of the pervasiveness of the kingdom of heaven (Matt. 13:33). (3) A symbol of undesirable teaching (Matt. 16:6). (4) A symbol of the pervasiveness of evil (1 Cor. 5:6–7).

Yoke
(1) A piece of timber or a heavy wooden pole formed to fit over the necks of animals (often two oxen) and connected to a plow or cart. (2) A figurative description of slavery and oppression (1 Kings 12:4); in contrast to the heavy "yoke" of the law (Gal. 5:1), the *yoke* of Jesus is easy to bear (Matt. 11:29–30).

Zeal
Impassioned devotion to a person or a cause.

Zion
One of the hills on which Jerusalem stood. Often used to refer to the temple or Jerusalem as a whole (Psalm 48).

Concordance

AARON

Priesthood of (Ex 28:1; Nu 17; Heb 5:1-4; 7), garments (Ex 28; 39), consecration (Ex 29), ordination (Lev 8).

Spokesman for Moses (Ex 4:14-16, 27-31; 7:1-2). Supported Moses' hands in battle (Ex 17:8-13). Built golden calf (Ex 32; Dt 9:20). Talked against Moses (Nu 12). Priesthood opposed (Nu 16); staff budded (Nu 17). Forbidden to enter land (Nu 20:1-12). Death (Nu 20:22-29; 33:38-39).

ABANDON

Dt 4:31 he will not *a* or destroy you
1Ti 4:1 in later times some will *a* the faith

ABBA

Ro 8:15 And by him we cry, "*A*, Father."
Gal 4:6 the Spirit who calls out, "*A*, Father

ABEL

Second son of Adam (Ge 4:2). Offered proper sacrifice (Ge 4:4; Heb 11:4). Murdered by Cain (Ge 4:8; Mt 23:35; Lk 11:51; 1Jn 3:12).

ABHORS

Pr 11:1 The LORD *a* dishonest scales,

ABIGAIL

Wife of Nabal (1Sa 25:30); pled for his life with David (1Sa 25:14-35). Became David's wife (1Sa 25:36-42).

ABIJAH

Son of Rehoboam; king of Judah (1Ki 14:31-15:8; 2Ch 12:16-14:1).

ABILITY (ABLE)

Ezr 2:69 According to their *a* they gave
2Co 1:8 far beyond our *a* to endure,
8:3 were able, and even beyond their *a*.

ABIMELECH

1. King of Gerar who took Abraham's wife Sarah, believing her to be his sister (Ge 20). Later made a covenant with Abraham (Ge 21:22-33).

2. King of Gerar who took Isaac's wife Rebekah, believing her to be his sister (Ge 26:1-11). Later made a covenant with Isaac (Ge 26:12-31).

ABLE (ABILITY ENABLE ENABLED ENABLES)

Eze 7:19 and gold will not be *a* to save them
Da 3:17 the God we serve is *a* to save us
Ro 8:39 will be *a* to separate us
14:4 for the Lord is *a* to make him stand
16:25 to him who is *a* to establish you
2Co 9:8 God is *a* to make all grace abound
Eph 3:20 him who is *a* to do immeasurably
2Ti 1:12 and am convinced that he is *a*
3:15 which are *a* to make you wise
Heb 7:25 he is *a* to save completely
Jude :24 To him who is *a* to keep you
Rev 5:5 He is *a* to open the scroll

ABOLISH

Mt 5:17 that I have come to *a* the Law

ABOMINATION

Da 11:31 set up the *a* that causes desolation.

ABOUND (ABOUNDING)

2Co 9:8 able to make all grace *a* to you,
Php 1:9 that your love may *a* more

ABOUNDING (ABOUND)

Ex 34:6 slow to anger, *a* in love
Ps 86:5 *a* in love to all who call to you.

ABRAHAM

Covenant relation with the LORD (Ge 12:1-3; 13:14-17; 15; 17; 22:15-18; Ex 2:24; Ne 9:8; Ps 105; Mic 7:20; Lk 1:68-75; Ro 4; Heb 6:13-15).

Called from Ur, via Haran, to Canaan (Ge 12:1; Ac 7:2-4; Heb 11:8-10). Moved to Egypt, nearly lost Sarah to Pharoah (Ge 12:10-20). Divided the land with Lot (Ge 13). Saved Lot from four kings (Ge 14:1-16); blessed by Melchizedek (Ge 14:17-20; Heb 7:1-20). Declared righteous by faith (Ge 15:6; Ro 4:3; Gal 3:6-9). Fathered Ishmael by Hagar (Ge 16).

Name changed from Abram (Ge 17:5; Ne 9:7). Circumcised (Ge 17; Ro 4:9-12). Entertained three visitors (Ge 18); promised a son by Sarah (Ge 18:9-15; 17:16). Moved to Gerar; nearly lost Sarah to Abimelech (Ge 20). Fathered Isaac by Sarah (Ge 21:1-7; Ac 7:8; Heb 11:11-12); sent away Hagar and Ishmael (Ge 21:8-21; Gal 4:22-30). Tested by offering Isaac (Ge 22; Heb 11:17-19; Jas 2:21-24). Sarah died; bought field of Ephron for burial (Ge 23). Secured wife for Isaac (Ge 24). Death (Ge 25:7-11).

ABSALOM

Son of David by Maacah (2Sa 3:3; 1Ch 3:2). Killed Amnon for rape of his sister Tamar; banished by David (2Sa 13). Returned to Jerusalem; received by David (2Sa 14). Rebelled against David; seized kingdom (2Sa 15-17). Killed (2Sa 18).

ABSTAIN (ABSTAINS)

1Pe 2:11 to *a* from sinful desires,

ABSTAINS* (ABSTAIN)

Ro 14:6 thanks to God; and he who *a*,

ABUNDANCE (ABUNDANT)

Lk 12:15 consist in the *a* of his possessions."
Jude :2 peace and love be yours in *a*.

ABUNDANT (ABUNDANCE)

Dt 28:11 will grant you *a* prosperity—
Ps 145:7 will celebrate your *a* goodness
Pr 28:19 works his land will have *a* food,
Ro 5:17 who receive God's *a* provision

ACCEPT (ACCEPTED ACCEPTS)

Ex 23:8 "Do not *a* a bribe,
Pr 10:8 The wise in heart *a* commands,
19:20 Listen to advice and *a* instruction,
Ro 15:7 *A* one another, then, just
Jas 1:21 humbly *a* the word planted in you,

ACCEPTED (ACCEPT)

Lk 4:24 "no prophet is *a* in his hometown.

ACCEPTS (ACCEPT)

Ps 6:9 the LORD *a* my prayer.
Jn 13:20 whoever *a* anyone I send *a* me;

ACCOMPANY

Mk 16:17 these signs will *a* those who believe
Heb 6:9 your case—things that *a* salvation.

ACCOMPLISH

Isa 55:11 but will *a* what I desire

ACCORD

Nu 24:13 not do anything of my own *a*,
Jn 10:18 but I lay it down of my own *a*.
12:49 For I did not speak of my own *a*,

ACCOUNT (ACCOUNTABLE)

Mt 12:36 to give *a* on the day of judgment
Ro 14:12 each of us will give an *a* of himself
Heb 4:13 of him to whom we must give *a*.

ACCOUNTABLE (ACCOUNT)

Eze 33:6 but I will hold the watchman *a*
Ro 3:19 and the whole world held *a* to God.

ACCUSATION (ACCUSE)

1Ti 5:19 Do not entertain an *a*

ACCUSATIONS (ACCUSE)

2Pe 2:11 do not bring slanderous *a*

ACCUSE (ACCUSATION ACCUSATIONS)

Pr 3:30 Do not *a* a man for no reason—
Lk 3:14 and don't *a* people falsely—

ACHAN*

Sin at Jericho caused defeat at Ai; stoned (Jos 7; 22:20; 1Ch 2:7).

ACHE*

Pr 14:13 Even in laughter the heart may *a*,

ACKNOWLEDGE

Mt 10:32 *a* him before my Father in heaven.
1Jn 4:3 spirit that does not *a* Jesus is not

ACQUIT

Ex 23:7 to death, for I will not *a* the guilty.

ACTION (ACTIONS ACTIVE ACTS)
Jas 2:17 if it is not accompanied by *a,*
1Pe 1:13 minds for *a;* be self-controlled;

ACTIONS (ACTION)
Mt 11:19 wisdom is proved right by her *a.*"
Gal 6: 4 Each one should test his own *a.*
Tit 1:16 but by their *a* they deny him.

ACTIVE (ACTION)
Heb 4:12 For the word of God is living and *a*

ACTS (ACTION)
Ps 145:12 all men may know of your mighty *a*
150: 2 Praise him for his *a* of power;
Isa 64: 6 all our righteous *a* are like filthy
Mt 6: 1 not to do your '*a* of righteousness'

ADAM
First man (Ge 1:26-2:25; Ro 5:14; 1Ti 2:13). Sin of (Ge 3; Hos 6:7; Ro 5:12-21). Children of (Ge 4:1-5:5). Death of (Ge 5:5; Ro 5:12-21; 1Co 15:22).

ADD
Dt 12:32 do not *a* to it or take away from it.
Pr 30: 6 Do not *a* to his words,
Lk 12:25 by worrying can *a* a single hour
Rev 22:18 God will *a* to him the plagues

ADMIRABLE*
Php 4: 8 whatever is lovely, whatever is *a*—

ADMONISH
Col 3:16 and *a* one another with all wisdom,

ADOPTED (ADOPTION)
Eph 1: 5 In love he predestined us to be *a*

ADOPTION (ADOPTED)
Ro 8:23 as we wait eagerly for our *a* as sons,

ADORE*
SS 1: 4 How right they are to *a* you!

ADORNMENT* (ADORNS)
1Pe 3: 3 should not come from outward *a,*

ADORNS (ADORNMENT)
Ps 93: 5 holiness *a* your house

ADULTERY
Ex 20:14 "You shall not commit *a.*
Mt 5:27 that it was said, 'Do not commit *a.*'
5:28 lustfully has already committed *a*
5:32 the divorced woman commits *a.*
15:19 murder, *a,* sexual immorality, theft

ADULTS*
1Co 14:20 but in your thinking be *a.*

ADVANCED
Job 32: 7 *a* years should teach wisdom.'

ADVANTAGE
Ex 22:22 "Do not take *a* of a widow
Dt 24:14 Do not take *a* of a hired man who is
1Th 4: 6 should wrong his brother or take *a*

ADVERSITY
Pr 17:17 and a brother is born for *a.*

ADVICE
1Ki 12: 8 rejected the *a* the elders
1Ki 12:14 he followed the *a* of the young men
Pr 12: 5 but the *a* of the wicked is deceitful.
12:15 but a wise man listens to *a.*
19:20 Listen to *a* and accept instruction,
20:18 Make plans by seeking *a;*

AFFLICTION
Ro 12:12 patient in *a,* faithful in prayer.

AFRAID (FEAR)
Ge 26:24 Do not be *a,* for I am with you;
Ex 3: 6 because he was *a* to look at God.
Ps 27: 1 of whom shall I be *a?*
56: 3 When I am *a,* / I will trust in you.
Pr 3:24 lie down, you will not be *a;*
Jer 1: 8 Do not be *a* of them, for I am
Mt 8:26 You of little faith, why are you so *a*
10:28 be *a* of the One who can destroy
10:31 So don't be *a;* you are worth more
Mk 5:36 "Don't be *a;* just believe."
Jn 14:27 hearts be troubled and do not be *a.*
Heb 13: 6 Lord is my helper; I will not be *a.*

AGED
Job 12:12 Is not wisdom found among the *a?*
Pr 17: 6 children are a crown to the *a,*

AGREE
Mt 18:19 on earth *a* about anything you ask
Ro 7:16 want to do, I *a* that the law is good.
Php 4: 2 with Syntyche to *a* with each other

AHAB
Son of Omri; king of Israel (1Ki 16:28-22:40), husband of Jezebel (1Ki 16:31). Promoted Baal worship (1Ki 16:31-33); opposed by Elijah (1Ki 17:1; 18; 21), a prophet (1Ki 20:35-43), Micaiah (1Ki 22:1-28). Defeated Ben-Hadad (1Ki 20). Killed for failing to kill Ben-Hadad and for murder of Naboth (1Ki 20:35-21:40).

AHAZ
Son of Jotham; king of Judah, (2Ki 16; 2Ch 28; Isa 7).

AHAZIAH
1. Son of Ahab; king of Israel (1Ki 22:51-2Ki 1:18; 2Ch 20:35-37).
2. Son of Jehoram; king of Judah (2Ki 8:25-29; 9:14-29), also called Jehoahaz (2Ch 21:17-22:9; 25:23).

AIM
1Co 7:34 Her *a* is to be devoted to the Lord
2Co 13:11 *A* for perfection, listen

AIR
Mt 8:20 and birds of the *a* have nests,
1Co 9:26 not fight like a man beating the *a.*
Eph 2: 2 of the ruler of the kingdom of the *a,*
1Th 4:17 clouds to meet the Lord in the *a.*

ALABASTER
Mt 26: 7 came to him with an *a* jar

ALERT
Jos 8: 4 All of you be on the *a.*
Mk 13:33 Be *a!* You do not know
Eph 6:18 be *a* and always keep on praying
1Th 5: 6 but let us be *a* and self-controlled.

ALIEN (ALIENATED)
Ex 22:21 "Do not mistreat an *a*

ALIENATED (ALIEN)
Gal 5: 4 by law have been *a* from Christ;

ALIVE (LIVE)
Ac 1: 3 convincing proofs that he was *a.*
Ro 6:11 but *a* to God in Christ Jesus.
1Co 15:22 so in Christ all will be made *a.*

ALMIGHTY (MIGHT)
Ge 17: 1 "I am God *A;* walk before me
Job 11: 7 Can you probe the limits of the *A?*
33: 4 the breath of the *A* gives me life.
Ps 91: 1 will rest in the shadow of the *A.*
Isa 6: 3 "Holy, holy, holy is the LORD *A;*

ALTAR
Ge 22: 9 his son Isaac and laid him on the *a,*
Ex 27: 1 "Build an *a* of acacia wood,
1Ki 18:30 and he repaired the *a* of the LORD
2Ch 4: 1 made a bronze *a* twenty cubits
4:19 the golden *a;* the tables

ALWAYS
Ps 16: 8 I have set the LORD *a* before me.
51: 3 and my sin is *a* before me.
Mt 26:11 The poor you will *a* have with you,
28:20 And surely I will be with you *a,*
1Co 13: 7 *a* protects, *a* trusts, *a* hopes, *a*
Php 4: 4 Rejoice in the Lord *a.*
1Pe 3:15 *A* be prepared to give an answer

AMAZIAH
Son of Joash; king of Judah (2Ki 14; 2Ch 25).

AMBASSADORS
2Co 5:20 We are therefore Christ's *a,*

AMBITION
Ro 15:20 It has always been my *a*
1Th 4:11 Make it your *a* to lead a quiet life,

AMON
Son of Manasseh; king of Judah (2Ki 21:18-26; 1Ch 3:14; 2Ch 33:21-25).

ANANIAS
1. Husband of Sapphira; died for lying to God (Ac 5:1-11).
2. Disciple who baptized Saul (Ac 9:10-19).
3. High priest at Paul's arrest (Ac 22:30-24:1).

ANCHOR
Heb 6:19 We have this hope as an *a*

ANCIENT
Da 7: 9 and the *A* of Days took his seat.

ANDREW*
Apostle; brother of Simon Peter (Mt 4:18; 10:2; Mk 1:16-18, 29; 3:18; 13:3; Lk 6:14; Jn 1:35-44; 6:8-9; 12:22; Ac 1:13).

ANGEL (ANGELS ARCHANGEL)
Ps 34: 7 The *a* of the LORD encamps
Ac 6:15 his face was like the face of an *a.*
2Co 11:14 Satan himself masquerades as an *a*
Gal 1: 8 or an *a* from heaven should preach

ANGELS (ANGEL)
Ps 91:11 command his *a* concerning you
Mt 18:10 For I tell you that their *a*
25:41 prepared for the devil and his *a.*
Lk 20:36 for they are like the *a.*
1Co 6: 3 you not know that we will judge *a?*
Heb 1: 4 as much superior to the *a*

Mt 9: 6 the Son of Man has *a* on earth
28:18 "All *a* in heaven and on earth has
Ro 13: 1 for there is no *a* except that which
13: 2 rebels against the *a* is rebelling
1Co 11:10 to have a sign of *a* on her head.
1Ti 2: 2 for kings and all those in *a,*
2:12 to teach or to have *a* over a man;
Heb 13:17 your leaders and submit to their *a.*

AVENGE (VENGEANCE)
Dt 32:35 It is mine to *a;* I will repay.

AVOID
Pr 20: 3 It is to a man's honor to *a* strife,
20:19 so *a* a man who talks too much.
1Th 4: 3 you should *a* sexual immorality;
5:22 *A* every kind of evil.
2Ti 2:16 *A* godless chatter, because those
Tit 3: 9 But *a* foolish controversies

AWAKE
Ps 17:15 when I *a,* I will be satisfied

AWE (AWESOME)
Job 25: 2 "Dominion and *a* belong to God;
Ps 119:120 I stand in *a* of your laws.
Ecc 5: 7 Therefore stand in *a* of God.
Isa 29:23 will stand in *a* of the God of Israel.
Jer 33: 9 they will be in *a* and will tremble
Hab 3: 2 I stand in *a* of your deeds,
Mal 2: 5 and stood in *a* of my name.
Mt 9: 8 they were filled with *a;*
Lk 7:16 They were all filled with *a*
Ac 2:43 Everyone was filled with *a,*
Heb 12:28 acceptably with reverence and *a,*

AWESOME (AWE)
Ge 28:17 and said, "How *a* is this place!
Ex 15:11 *a* in glory,
Dt 7:21 is among you, is a great and *a* God.
10:17 the great God, mighty and *a,*
28:58 revere this glorious and *a* name—
Jdg 13: 6 like an angel of God, very *a.*
Ne 1: 5 of heaven, the great and *a* God,
9:32 the great, mighty and *a* God,
Job 10:16 again display your *a* power
37:22 God comes in *a* majesty.
Ps 45: 4 let your right hand display *a* deeds.
47: 2 How *a* is the LORD Most High,
66: 5 how *a* his works in man's behalf!
68:35 You are *a,* O God,
89: 7 he is more *a* than all who surround
99: 3 praise your great and *a* name—
111: 9 holy and *a* is his name.
145: 6 of the power of your *a* works,
Da 9: 4 "O Lord, the great and *a* God,

BAAL
1Ki 18:25 Elijah said to the prophets of *B,*

BAASHA
King of Israel (1Ki 15:16-16:7; 2Ch 16:1-6).

BABIES (BABY)
Lk 18:15 also bringing *b* to Jesus
1Pe 2: 2 Like newborn *b,* crave pure

BABY (BABIES)
Isa 49:15 "Can a mother forget the *b*
Lk 1:44 the *b* in my womb leaped for joy.
2:12 You will find a *b* wrapped in strips
Jn 16:21 but when her *b* is born she forgets

BABYLON
Ps 137: 1 By the rivers of *B* we sat and wept

BACKSLIDING
Jer 3:22 I will cure you of *b.*"
Jer 14: 7 For our *b* is great;
Eze 37:23 them from all their sinful *b,*

BALAAM
Prophet who attempted to curse Israel (Nu 22-24; Dt 23:4-5; 2Pe 2:15; Jude 11). Killed (Nu 31:8; Jos 13:22).

BALM
Jer 8:22 Is there no *b* in Gilead?

BANISH
Jer 25:10 I will *b* from them the sounds of joy

BANQUET
SS 2: 4 He has taken me to the *b* hall,
Lk 14:13 when you give a *b,* invite the poor,

BAPTIZE (BAPTIZED)
Mt 3:11 He will *b* you with the Holy Spirit
Mk 1: 8 he will *b* you with the Holy Spirit."
1Co 1:17 For Christ did not send me to *b,*

BAPTIZED (BAPTIZE)
Mt 3: 6 they were *b* by him in the Jordan
Mk 1: 9 and was *b* by John in the Jordan.
10:38 or be *b* with the baptism I am
16:16 believes and is *b* will be saved,
Jn 4: 2 in fact it was not Jesus who *b,*
Ac 1: 5 but in a few days you will be *b*

BARABBAS
Mt 27:26 Then he released *B* to them.

BARBS*
Nu 33:55 allow to remain will become *b*

BARE
Heb 4:13 and laid *b* before the eyes of him

BARNABAS*
Disciple, originally Joseph (Ac 4:36), prophet (Ac 13:1), apostle (Ac 14:14). Brought Paul to apostles (Ac 9:27), Antioch (Ac 11:22-29; Gal 2:1-13), on the first missionary journey (Ac 13-14). Together at Jerusalem Council, they separated over John Mark (Ac 15). Later co-workers (1Co 9:6; Col 4:10).

BARREN
Ps 113: 9 He settles the *b* woman

BARTHOLOMEW*
Apostle (Mt 10:3; Mk 3:18; Lk 6:14; Ac 1:13). Possibly also known as Nathanael (Jn 1:45-49; 21:2).

BATH
Jn 13:10 person who has had a *b* needs only

BATHSHEBA
Wife of Uriah who committed adultery with and became wife of David (2Sa 11), mother of Solomon (2Sa 12:24; 1Ki 1-2; 1Ch 3:5).

BATTLE
2Ch 20:15 For the *b* is not yours, but God's.
Ps 24: 8 the LORD mighty in *b.*
Ecc 9:11 or the *b* to the strong,

BEAR (BEARING BIRTH BIRTHRIGHT BORN FIRSTBORN NEWBORN)
Ge 4:13 punishment is more than I can *b.*
Ps 38: 4 like a burden too heavy to *b.*
Isa 53:11 and he will *b* their iniquities.
Da 7: 5 beast, which looked like a *b.*
Mt 7:18 A good tree cannot *b* bad fruit,
Jn 15: 2 branch that does *b* fruit he prunes
15:16 and appointed you to go and *b* fruit—
Ro 15: 1 ought to *b* with the failings
1Co 10:13 tempted beyond what you can *b.*
Col 3:13 *B* with each other and forgive

BEARING (BEAR)
Eph 4: 2 *b* with one another in love.
Col 1:10 *b* fruit in every good work,

BEAST
Rev 13:18 him calculate the number of the *b,*

BEAT (BEATING)
Isa 2: 4 They will *b* their swords
Joel 3:10 *B* your plowshares into swords
1Co 9:27 I *b* my body and make it my slave

BEATING (BEAT)
1Co 9:26 I do not fight like a man *b* the air.
1Pe 2:20 if you receive a *b* for doing wrong

BEAUTIFUL (BEAUTY)
Ge 6: 2 that the daughters of men were *b,*
12:11 "I know what a *b* woman you are.
12:14 saw that she was a very *b* woman.
24:16 The girl was very *b,* a virgin;
26: 7 of Rebekah, because she is *b.*"
29:17 Rachel was lovely in form, and *b.*
Job 38:31 "Can you bind the *b* Pleiades?
Pr 11:22 is a *b* woman who shows no
Ecc 3:11 He has made everything *b*
Isa 4: 2 of the LORD will be *b*
52: 7 How *b* on the mountains
Eze 20: 6 and honey, the most *b* of all lands.
Zec 9:17 How attractive and *b* they will be!
Mt 23:27 which look *b* on the outside
26:10 She has done a *b* thing to me.
Ro 10:15 "How *b* are the feet
1Pe 3: 5 in God used to make themselves *b.*

BEAUTY (BEAUTIFUL)
Ps 27: 4 to gaze upon the *b* of the LORD
45:11 The king is enthralled by your *b;*
Pr 31:30 is deceptive, and *b* is fleeting;
Isa 33:17 Your eyes will see the king in his *b*
53: 2 He had no *b* or majesty
61: 3 to bestow on them a crown of *b*
Eze 28:12 full of wisdom and perfect in *b.*
1Pe 3: 4 the unfading *b* of a gentle

BED
Heb 13: 4 and the marriage *b* kept pure,

BEELZEBUB
Lk 11:15 "By *B,* the prince of demons,

BEER
Pr 20: 1 Wine is a mocker and *b* a brawler;

BEERSHEBA
Jdg 20: 1 all the Israelites from Dan to *B*

BEGINNING
Ge 1: 1 In the *b* God created the heavens
Ps 102:25 In the *b* you laid the foundations
111:10 of the LORD is the *b* of wisdom;
Pr 1: 7 of the LORD is the *b* of knowledge
Jn 1: 1 In the *b* was the Word,
1Jn 1: 1 That which was from the *b,*
Rev 21: 6 and the Omega, the *B* and the End.

BEHAVE
Ro 13:13 Let us *b* decently, as in the daytime

BELIEVE (BELIEVED BELIEVER BELIEVERS BELIEVES BELIEVING)
Mt 18: 6 one of these little ones who *b* in me
21:22 If you *b*, you will receive whatever
Mk 1:15 Repent and *b* the good news!"
9:24 "I do *b*; help me overcome my
16:17 signs will accompany those who *b*:
Lk 8:50 just *b*, and she will be healed."
24:25 to *b* all that the prophets have
Jn 1: 7 that through him all men might *b*.
3:18 does not *b* stands condemned
6:29 to *b* in the one he has sent."
10:38 you do not *b* me, *b* the miracles,
11:27 "I *b* that you are the Christ,
14:11 *B* me when I say that I am
16:30 This makes us *b* that you came
16:31 "You *b* at last!" Jesus answered.
17:21 that the world may *b* that you have
20:27 Stop doubting and *b*."
20:31 written that you may *b* that Jesus is
Ac 16:31 They replied, "*B* in the Lord Jesus,
24:14 I *b* everything that agrees
Ro 3:22 faith in Jesus Christ to all who *b*.
4:11 he is the father of all who *b*
10: 9 *b* in your heart that God raised him
10:14 And how can they *b* in the one
16:26 so that all nations might *b*
1Th 4:14 We *b* that Jesus died and rose again
2Th 2:11 delusion so that they will *b* the lie
1Ti 4:10 and especially of those who *b*.
Tit 1: 6 a man whose children *b*
Heb 11: 6 comes to him must *b* that he exists
Jas 2:19 Even the demons *b* that—
1Jn 4: 1 Dear friends, do not *b* every spirit,

BELIEVED (BELIEVE)
Ge 15: 6 Abram *b* the LORD, and he
Jnh 3: 5 The Ninevites *b* God.
Jn 1:12 to those who *b* in his name,
2:22 Then they *b* the Scripture
3:18 because he has not *b* in the name
20: 8 He saw and *b*.
20:29 who have not seen and yet have *b*."
Ac 13:48 were appointed for eternal life *b*.
Ro 4: 3 Scripture say? "Abraham *b* God,
10:14 call on the one they have not *b* in?
1Co 15: 2 Otherwise, you have *b* in vain.
Gal 3: 6 Consider Abraham: "He *b* God,
2Ti 1:12 because I know whom I have *b*,
Jas 2:23 that says, "Abraham *b* God,

BELIEVER (BELIEVE)
1Co 7:12 brother has a wife who is not a *b*
2Co 6:15 What does a *b* have in common

BELIEVERS (BELIEVE)
Ac 4:32 All the *b* were one in heart
5:12 And all the *b* used to meet together
1Co 6: 5 to judge a dispute between *b*?
1Ti 4:12 set an example for the *b* in speech,
1Pe 2:17 Love the brotherhood of *b*,

BELIEVES (BELIEVE)
Pr 14:15 A simple man *b* anything,
Mk 9:23 is possible for him who *b*."
11:23 *b* that what he says will happen,
16:16 Whoever *b* and is baptized will be
Jn 3:16 that whoever *b* in him shall not
3:36 Whoever *b* in the Son has eternal
5:24 *b* him who sent me has eternal life
6:35 and he who *b* in me will never be
Jn 6:40 and *b* in him shall have eternal life,
6:47 he who *b* has everlasting life.
7:38 Whoever *b* in me, as the Scripture
11:26 and *b* in me will never die.
Ro 1:16 for the salvation of everyone who *b*
10: 4 righteousness for everyone who *b*.
1Jn 5: 1 Everyone who *b* that Jesus is
5: 5 Only he who *b* that Jesus is the Son

BELIEVING (BELIEVE)
Jn 20:31 and that by *b* you may have life

BELONG (BELONGS)
Dt 29:29 The secret things *b*
Job 25: 2 "Dominion and awe *b* to God;
Ps 47: 9 for the kings of the earth *b* to God;
95: 4 and the mountain peaks *b* to him.
Jn 8:44 You *b* to your father, the devil,
15:19 As it is, you do not *b* to the world,
Ro 1: 6 called to *b* to Jesus Christ.
7: 4 that you might *b* to another,
14: 8 we live or die, we *b* to the Lord.
Gal 5:24 Those who *b* to Christ Jesus have
1Th 5: 8 But since we *b* to the day, let us be

BELONGS (BELONG)
Job 41:11 Everything under heaven *b* to me.
Ps 111:10 To him *b* eternal praise.
Eze 18: 4 For every living soul *b* to me,
Jn 8:47 He who *b* to God hears what God
Ro 12: 5 each member *b* to all the others.

BELOVED (LOVE)
Dt 33:12 "Let the *b* of the LORD rest secure

BELT
Isa 11: 5 Righteousness will be his *b*
Eph 6:14 with the *b* of truth buckled

BENEFIT (BENEFITS)
Ro 6:22 the *b* you reap leads to holiness,
2Co 4:15 All this is for your *b*,

BENEFITS (BENEFIT)
Ps 103: 2 and forget not all his *b*.
Jn 4:38 you have reaped the *b* of their labor

BENJAMIN
Twelfth son of Jacob by Rachel (Ge 35:16-24; 46:19-21; 1Ch 2:2). Jacob refused to send him to Egypt, but relented (Ge 42-45).

BEREANS*
Ac 17:11 the *B* were of more noble character

BESTOWS
Ps 84:11 the LORD *b* favor and honor;

BETHLEHEM
Mt 2: 1 After Jesus was born in *B* in Judea,

BETRAY
Pr 25: 9 do not *b* another man's confidence,

BIND (BINDS)
Dt 6: 8 and *b* them on your foreheads.
Pr 6:21 *B* them upon your heart forever;
Isa 61: 1 me to *b* up the brokenhearted,
Mt 16:19 whatever you *b* on earth will be

BINDS (BIND)
Ps 147: 3 and *b* up their wounds.
Isa 30:26 when the LORD *b* up the bruises

BIRDS
Mt 8:20 and *b* of the air have nests,

BIRTH (BEAR)
Ps 58: 3 Even from *b* the wicked go astray;
Mt 1:18 This is how the *b* of Jesus Christ
1Pe 1: 3 great mercy he has given us new *b*

BIRTHRIGHT (BEAR)
Ge 25:34 So Esau despised his *b*.

BLAMELESS
Ge 17: 1 walk before me and be *b*.
Job 1: 1 This man was *b* and upright;
Ps 84:11 from those whose walk is *b*.
119: 1 Blessed are they whose ways are *b*,
Pr 19: 1 Better a poor man whose walk is *b*
1Co 1: 8 so that you will be *b* on the day
Eph 5:27 any other blemish, but holy and *b*.
Php 2:15 so that you may become *b* and pure
1Th 3:13 hearts so that you will be *b*
5:23 and body be kept *b* at the coming
Tit 1: 6 An elder must be *b*, the husband of
Heb 7:26 *b*, pure, set apart from sinners,
2Pe 3:14 effort to be found spotless, *b*

BLASPHEMES
Mk 3:29 whoever *b* against the Holy Spirit

BLEMISH
1Pe 1:19 a lamb without *b* or defect.

BLESS (BLESSED BLESSING BLESSINGS)
Ge 12: 3 I will *b* those who *b* you,
Ro 12:14 Bless those who persecute you; *b*

BLESSED (BLESS)
Ge 1:22 God *b* them and said, "Be fruitful
2: 3 And God *b* the seventh day
22:18 nations on earth will be *b*,
Ps 1: 1 *B* is the man
2:12 *B* are all who take refuge in him.
33:12 *B* is the nation whose God is
41: 1 *B* is he who has regard for the weak
84: 5 *B* are those whose strength is
106: 3 *B* are they who maintain justice,
112: 1 *B* is the man who fears the LORD,
118:26 *B* is he who comes in the name
Pr 29:18 but *b* is he who keeps the law.
31:28 Her children arise and call her *b*;
Mt 5: 3 saying: "*B* are the poor in spirit,
5: 4 *B* are those who mourn,
5: 5 *B* are the meek,
5: 6 *B* are those who hunger
5: 7 *B* are the merciful,
5: 8 *B* are the pure in heart,
5: 9 *B* are the peacemakers,
5:10 *B* are those who are persecuted
5:11 "*B* are you when people insult you,
Lk 1:48 on all generations will call me *b*,
Jn 12:13 "*B* is he who comes in the name
Ac 20:35 'It is more *b* to give than to receive
Tit 2:13 while we wait for the *b* hope—
Jas 1:12 *B* is the man who perseveres
Rev 1: 3 *B* is the one who reads the words
22:14 "*B* are those who wash their robes,

BLESSING (BLESS)
Eze 34:26 there will be showers of *b*.

BLESSINGS (BLESS)
Pr 10: 6 *B* crown the head of the righteous,

BLIND
Mt 15:14 a *b* man leads a *b* man, both will fall
23:16 "Woe to you, *b* guides! You say,
Jn 9:25 I was *b* but now I see!"

BLOOD
Ge 9: 6 "Whoever sheds the *b* of man,
Ex 12:13 and when I see the *b,* I will pass
24: 8 "This is the *b* of the covenant that
Lev 17: 11 For the life of a creature is in the *b,*
Ps 72:14 for precious is their *b* in his sight.
Pr 6:17 hands that shed innocent *b,*
Mt 26:28 This is my *b* of the covenant,
Ro 3:25 of atonement, through faith in his *b*
5: 9 have now been justified by his *b,*
1Co 11:25 cup is the new covenant in my *b;*
Eph 1: 7 we have redemption through his *b,*
2:13 near through the *b* of Christ.
Col 1:20 by making peace through his *b,*
Heb 9:12 once for all by his own *b,*
9:22 of *b* there is no forgiveness.
1Pe 1:19 but with the precious *b* of Christ,
1Jn 1: 7 and the *b* of Jesus, his Son,
Rev 1: 5 has freed us from our sins by his *b,*
5: 9 with your *b* you purchased men
7:14 white in the *b* of the Lamb.
12: 11 him by the *b* of the Lamb

BLOT (BLOTS)
Ex 32:32 then *b* me out of the book you have
Ps 51: 1 *b* out my transgressions.
Rev 3: 5 I will never *b* out his name

BLOTS (BLOT)
Isa 43:25 "I, even I, am he who *b* out

BLOWN
Eph 4:14 and *b* here and there by every wind
Jas 1: 6 doubts is like a wave of the sea, *b*

BOAST
1Ki 20: 11 armor should not *b* like one who
Ps 34: 2 My soul will *b* in the LORD;
44: 8 In God we make our *b* all day long,
Pr 27: 1 Do not *b* about tomorrow,
1Co 1:31 Let him who boasts *b* in the Lord."
Gal 6:14 May I never *b* except in the cross
Eph 2: 9 not by works, so that no one can *b.*

BOAZ
Wealthy Bethlehemite who showed favor to Ruth (Ru 2), married her (Ru 4). Ancestor of David (Ru 4:18-22; 1Ch 2:12-15), Jesus (Mt 1:5-16; Lk 3:23-32).

BODIES (BODY)
Ro 12: 1 to offer your *b* as living sacrifices,
1Co 6:15 not know that your *b* are members
Eph 5:28 to love their wives as their own *b.*

BODY (BODIES)
Zec 13: 6 What are these wounds on your *b?*
Mt 10:28 afraid of those who kill the *b*
26:26 saying, "Take and eat; this is my *b*
26:41 spirit is willing, but the *b* is weak."
Jn 13:10 wash his feet; his whole *b* is clean.
Ro 6:13 Do not offer the parts of your *b*
12: 4 us has one *b* with many members,
1Co 6:19 not know that your *b* is a temple
11:24 "This is my *b,* which is for you;
1Co 12:12 The *b* is a unit, though it is made up
Eph 5:30 for we are members of his *b.*

BOLD (BOLDNESS)
Ps 138: 3 you made me *b* and stouthearted.
Pr 21:29 A wicked man puts up a *b* front,
28: 1 but the righteous are as *b* as a lion.

BOLDNESS* (BOLD)
Ac 4:29 to speak your word with great *b.*

BONDAGE
Ezr 9: 9 God has not deserted us in our *b.*

BOOK (BOOKS)
Jos 1: 8 Do not let this *B* of the Law depart
Ne 8: 8 They read from the *B* of the Law
Jn 20:30 which are not recorded in this *b.*
Php 4: 3 whose names are in the *b* of life.
Rev 21:27 written in the Lamb's *b* of life.

BOOKS (BOOK)
Ecc 12:12 Of making many *b* there is no end,

BORN (BEAR)
Isa 9: 6 For to us a child is *b,*
Jn 3: 7 at my saying, 'You must be *b* again
1Pe 1:23 For you have been *b* again,
1Jn 4: 7 Everyone who loves has been *b*
5: 1 believes that Jesus is the Christ is *b*

BORROWER
Pr 22: 7 and the *b* is servant to the lender.

BOUGHT
Ac 20:28 which he *b* with his own blood.
1Co 6:20 You are not your own; you were *b*
7:23 You were *b* at a price; do not
2Pe 2: 1 the sovereign Lord who *b* them—

BOW
Ps 95: 6 Come, let us *b* down in worship,
Isa 45:23 Before me every knee will *b;*
Ro 14: 11 'every knee will *b* before me;
Php 2:10 name of Jesus every knee should *b,*

BRANCH (BRANCHES)
Isa 4: 2 In that day the *B* of the LORD will
Jer 33:15 I will make a righteous *B* sprout

BRANCHES (BRANCH)
Jn 15: 5 "I am the vine; you are the *b.*

BRAVE
2Sa 2: 7 Now then, be strong and *b,*

BREAD
Dt 8: 3 that man does not live on *b* alone
Pr 30: 8 but give me only my daily *b.*
Ecc 11: 1 Cast your *b* upon the waters,
Isa 55: 2 Why spend money on what is not *b*
Mt 4: 4 'Man does not live on *b* alone,
6: 11 Give us today our daily *b.*
Jn 6:35 Jesus declared, "I am the *b* of life.
21:13 took the *b* and gave it to them,
1Co 11:23 took *b,* and when he had given

BREAK (BREAKING BROKEN)
Nu 30: 2 he must not *b* his word
Jdg 2: 1 'I will never *b* my covenant
Isa 42: 3 A bruised reed he will not *b,*
Mt 12:20 A bruised reed he will not *b,*

BREAKING (BREAK)
Jas 2:10 at just one point is guilty of *b* all

BREASTPIECE (BREASTPLATE)
Ex 28:15 Fashion a *b* for making decisions—

BREASTPLATE* (BREASTPIECE)
Isa 59:17 He put on righteousness as his *b,*
Eph 6:14 with the *b* of righteousness in place
1Th 5: 8 putting on faith and love as a *b,*

BREATHED (GOD-BREATHED)
Ge 2: 7 *b* into his nostrils the breath of life,
Jn 20:22 And with that he *b* on them

BREEDS*
Pr 13:10 Pride only *b* quarrels,

BRIBE
Ex 23: 8 "Do not accept a *b,*
Pr 6:35 will refuse the *b,* however great it

BRIDE
Rev 19: 7 and his *b* has made herself ready,

BRIGHTER (BRIGHTNESS)
Pr 4:18 shining ever *b* till the full light

BRIGHTNESS (BRIGHTER)
2Sa 22:13 Out of the *b* of his presence
Da 12: 3 who are wise will shine like the *b*

BROAD
Mt 7:13 and *b* is the road that leads

BROKEN (BREAK)
Ps 51:17 The sacrifices of God are a *b* spirit;
Ecc 4:12 of three strands is not quickly *b.*
Jn 10:35 and the Scripture cannot be *b*—

BROKENHEARTED* (HEART)
Ps 34:18 The LORD is close to the *b*
109:16 and the needy and the *b.*
147: 3 He heals the *b*
Isa 61: 1 He has sent me to bind up the *b,*

BROTHER (BROTHER'S BROTHERS)
Pr 17:17 and a *b* is born for adversity.
18:24 a friend who sticks closer than a *b.*
27:10 neighbor nearby than a *b* far away.
Mt 5:24 and be reconciled to your *b;*
18:15 "If your *b* sins against you,
Mk 3:35 Whoever does God's will is my *b*
Lk 17: 3 "If your *b* sins, rebuke him,
1Co 8:13 if what I eat causes my *b* to fall
1Jn 2:10 Whoever loves his *b* lives
4:21 loves God must also love his *b.*

BROTHER'S (BROTHER)
Ge 4: 9 "Am I my *b* keeper?" The LORD

BROTHERS (BROTHER)
Ps 133: 1 is when *b* live together in unity!
Pr 6:19 who stirs up dissension among *b.*
Mt 25:40 one of the least of these *b* of mine,
Mk 10:29 or *b* or sisters or mother or father
Heb 13: 1 Keep on loving each other as *b.*
1Pe 3: 8 be sympathetic, love as *b,*
1Jn 3:14 death to life, because we love our *b.*

BUILD (BUILDING BUILDS BUILT)
Mt 16:18 and on this rock I will *b* my church,
Ac 20:32 which can *b* you up and give you
1Co 14:12 excel in gifts that *b* up the church.
1Th 5: 11 one another and *b* each other up,

BUILDING (BUILD)
1Co 3: 9 you are God's field, God's *b.*

2Co 10: 8 us for *b* you up rather
Eph 4:29 helpful for *b* others up according

BUILDS (BUILD)
Ps 127: 1 Unless the LORD *b* the house,
1Co 3:10 one should be careful how he *b.*
8: 1 Knowledge puffs up, but love *b* up.

BUILT (BUILD)
Mt 7:24 is like a wise man who *b* his house
Eph 2:20 *b* on the foundation of the apostles
4:12 the body of Christ may be *b* up

BURDEN (BURDENED BURDENS)
Ps 38: 4 like a *b* too heavy to bear.
Mt 11:30 my yoke is easy and my *b* is light."

BURDENED (BURDEN)
Gal 5: 1 do not let yourselves be *b* again

BURDENS (BURDEN)
Ps 68:19 who daily bears our *b.*
Gal 6: 2 Carry each other's *b,*

BURIED
Ro 6: 4 *b* with him through baptism
1Co15: 4 that he was *b,* that he was raised

BURNING
Lev 6: 9 the fire must be kept *b* on the altar.
Ro 12:20 you will heap *b* coals on his head."

BUSINESS
Da 8:27 and went about the king's *b.*
1Th 4:11 to mind your own *b* and to work

BUSY
1Ki 20:40 While your servant was *b* here
2Th 3:11 They are not *b;* they are
Tit 2: 5 to be *b* at home, to be kind,

CAESAR
Mt 22:21 "Give to *C* what is Caesar's,

CAIN
Firstborn of Adam (Ge 4:1), murdered brother Abel (Ge 4:1-16; 1Jn 3:12).

CALEB
Judahite who spied out Canaan (Nu 13:6); allowed to enter land because of faith (Nu 13:30-14:38; Dt 1:36). Possessed Hebron (Jos 14:6-15:19).

CALF
Ex 32: 4 into an idol cast in the shape of a *c,*
Lk 15:23 Bring the fattened *c* and kill it.

CALL (CALLED CALLING CALLS)
Ps 105: 1 to the LORD, *c* on his name;
145:18 near to all who *c* on him,
Pr 31:28 children arise and *c* her blessed;
Isa 5:20 Woe to those who *c* evil good
55: 6 *c* on him while he is near.
65:24 Before they *c* I will answer;
Jer 33: 3 '*C* to me and I will answer you
Mt 9:13 come to *c* the righteous,
Ro 10:12 and richly blesses all who *c* on him,
11:29 gifts and his *c* are irrevocable.
1Th 4: 7 For God did not *c* us to be impure,

CALLED (CALL)
1Sa 3: 5 and said, "Here I am; you *c* me."
2Ch 7:14 if my people, who are *c*
Ps 34: 6 This poor man *c,* and the LORD
Mt 21:13 " 'My house will be *c* a house
Ro 8:30 And those he predestined, he also *c*
1Co 7:15 God has *c* us to live in peace.
Gal 5:13 You, my brothers, were *c* to be free
1Pe 2: 9 of him who *c* you out of darkness

CALLING (CALL)
Jn 1:23 I am the voice of one *c* in the desert
Ac 22:16 wash your sins away, *c* on his name
Eph 4: 1 worthy of the *c* you have received.
2Pe 1:10 all the more eager to make your *c*

CALLS (CALL)
Joel 2:32 And everyone who *c*
Jn 10: 3 He *c* his own sheep by name
Ro 10:13 "Everyone who *c* on the name

CAMEL
Mt 19:24 it is easier for a *c* to go
23:24 strain out a gnat but swallow a *c.*

CANAAN
1Ch16:18 "To you I will give the land of *C*

CANCELED
Lk 7:42 so he *c* the debts of both.
Col 2:14 having *c* the written code,

CAPITAL
Dt 21:22 guilty of a *c* offense is put to death

CAPSTONE (STONE)
Ps 118:22 has become the *c;*
1Pe 2: 7 has become the *c,*"

CARE (CAREFUL CARES CARING)
Ps 8: 4 the son of man that you *c* for him?
Pr 29: 7 The righteous *c* about justice
Lk 10:34 him to an inn and took *c* of him.
Jn 21:16 Jesus said, "Take *c* of my sheep."
Heb 2: 6 the son of man that you *c* for him?
1Pe 5: 2 of God's flock that is under your *c,*

CAREFUL (CARE)
Ex 23:13 "Be *c* to do everything I have said
Dt 6: 3 be *c* to obey so that it may go well
Jos 23: 6 be *c* to obey all that is written
23:11 be very *c* to love the LORD your
Pr 13:24 he who loves him is *c*
Mt 6: 1 "Be *c* not to do your 'acts
Ro 12:17 Be *c* to do what is right in the eyes
1Co 3:10 each one should be *c* how he builds
8: 9 Be *c,* however, that the exercise
Eph 5:15 Be very *c,* then, how you live—

CARELESS
Mt 12:36 for every *c* word they have spoken.

CARES (CARE)
Ps 55:22 Cast your *c* on the LORD
Na 1: 7 He *c* for those who trust in him,
Eph 5:29 but he feeds and *c* for it, just
1Pe 5: 7 on him because he *c* for you.

CARING* (CARE)
1Th 2: 7 like a mother *c* for her little
1Ti 5: 4 practice by *c* for their own family

CARRIED (CARRY)
Ex 19: 4 and how I *c* you on eagles' wings
Isa 53: 4 and *c* our sorrows,
Heb13: 9 Do not be *c* away by all kinds
2Pe 1:21 as they were *c* along by the Holy

CARRIES (CARRY)
Dt 32:11 and *c* them on its pinions.
Isa 40:11 and *c* them close to his heart;

CARRY (CARRIED CARRIES)
Lk 14:27 anyone who does not *c* his cross
Gal 6: 2 *C* each other's burdens,
6: 5 for each one should *c* his own load.

CAST
Ps 22:18 and *c* lots for my clothing.
55:22 *C* your cares on the LORD
Ecc 11: 1 *C* your bread upon the waters,
Jn 19:24 and *c* lots for my clothing."
1Pe 5: 7 *C* all your anxiety on him

CATCH (CAUGHT)
Lk 5:10 from now on you will *c* men."

CATTLE
Ps 50:10 and the *c* on a thousand hills.

CAUGHT (CATCH)
1Th 4:17 and are left will be *c* up together

CAUSE (CAUSES)
Pr 24:28 against your neighbor without *c,*
Ecc 8: 3 Do not stand up for a bad *c,*
Mt 18: 7 of the things that *c* people to sin!
Ro 14:21 else that will *c* your brother
1Co 10:32 Do not *c* anyone to stumble,

CAUSES (CAUSE)
Isa 8:14 a stone that *c* men to stumble
Mt 18: 6 if anyone *c* one of these little ones

CAUTIOUS*
Pr 12:26 A righteous man is *c* in friendship,

CEASE
Ps 46: 9 He makes wars *c* to the ends

CENSER
Lev 16:12 is to take a *c* full of burning coals

CENTURION
Mt 8: 5 had entered Capernaum, a *c* came

CERTAIN (CERTAINTY)
2Pe 1:19 word of the prophets made more *c,*

CERTAINTY* (CERTAIN)
Lk 1: 4 so that you may know the *c*
Jn 17: 8 They knew with *c* that I came

CHAFF
Ps 1: 4 They are like *c*

CHAINED
2Ti 2: 9 But God's word is not *c.*

CHAMPION
Ps 19: 5 like a *c* rejoicing to run his course.

CHANGE (CHANGED)
1Sa 15:29 of Israel does not lie or *c* his mind;
Ps 110: 4 and will not *c* his mind:
Jer 7: 5 If you really *c* your ways
Mal 3: 6 "I the LORD do not *c.*
Mt 18: 3 unless you *c* and become like little
Heb 7:21 and will not *c* his mind:
Jas 1:17 who does not *c* like shifting

CHANGED (CHANGE)
1Co15:51 but we will all be *c*— in a flash,

CHARACTER
Ru 3:11 that you are a woman of noble *c.*
Pr 31:10 A wife of noble *c* who can find?
Ro 5: 4 perseverance, *c;* and *c,* hope.
1Co15:33 "Bad company corrupts good *c.*"

CHARGE
Ro 8:33 Who will bring any *c*

2Co 11: 7 the gospel of God to you free of *c?*
2Ti 4: 1 I give you this *c:* Preach the Word;

CHARIOTS
2Ki 6:17 and *c* of fire all around Elisha.
Ps 20: 7 Some trust in *c* and some in horses,

CHARM
Pr 31:30 *C* is deceptive, and beauty is

CHASES
Pr 12: 11 he who *c* fantasies lacks judgment.

CHATTER* (CHATTERING)
1Ti 6:20 Turn away from godless *c*
2Ti 2:16 Avoid godless *c,* because those

CHATTERING* (CHATTER)
Pr 10: 8 but a *c* fool comes to ruin.
10: 10 and a *c* fool comes to ruin.

CHEAT* (CHEATED)
Mal 1:14 "Cursed is the *c* who has
1Co 6: 8 you yourselves *c* and do wrong,

CHEATED (CHEAT)
Lk 19: 8 if I have *c* anybody out of anything,
1Co 6: 7 Why not rather be *c?* Instead,

CHEEK
Mt 5:39 someone strikes you on the right *c,*

CHEERFUL* (CHEERS)
Pr 15:13 A happy heart makes the face *c,*
15:15 but the *c* heart has a continual feast
15:30 A *c* look brings joy to the heart,
17:22 A *c* heart is good medicine,
2Co 9: 7 for God loves a *c* giver.

CHEERS (CHEERFUL)
Pr 12:25 but a kind word *c* him up.

CHILD (CHILDISH CHILDREN)
Pr 20: 11 Even a *c* is known by his actions,
22: 6 Train a *c* in the way he should go,
22:15 Folly is bound up in the heart of a *c*
23:13 not withhold discipline from a *c;*
29:15 *c* left to himself disgraces his mother.
Isa 7:14 The virgin will be with *c*
9: 6 For to us a *c* is born,
11: 6 and a little *c* will lead them.
66:13 As a mother comforts her *c,*
Mt 1:23 "The virgin will be with *c*
18: 2 He called a little *c* and had him
Lk 1:42 and blessed is the *c* you will bear!
1:80 And the *c* grew and became strong
1Co 13: 11 When I was a *c,* I talked like a *c,*
1Jn 5: 1 who loves the father loves his *c*

CHILDISH* (CHILD)
1Co 13: 11 When I became a man, I put *c* ways

CHILDREN (CHILD)
Dt 4: 9 Teach them to your *c*
11:19 them to your *c,* talking about them
Ps 8: 2 From the lips of *c* and infants
Pr 17: 6 Children's *c* are a crown
31:28 Her *c* arise and call her blessed;
Mt 7: 11 how to give good gifts to your *c,*
11:25 and revealed them to little *c.*
18: 3 you change and become like little *c*
19:14 "Let the little *c* come to me,
21:16 " 'From the lips of *c* and infants
Mk 9:37 one of these little *c* in my name
10:14 "Let the little *c* come to me,
10:16 And he took the *c* in his arms,
13:12 *C* will rebel against their parents
Lk 10: 21 and revealed them to little *c.*
18:16 "Let the little *c* come to me,
Ro 8:16 with our spirit that we are God's *c.*
2Co 12:14 parents, but parents for their *c.*
Eph 6: 1 *C,* obey your parents in the Lord,
6: 4 do not exasperate your *c;* instead,
Col 3:20 *C,* obey your parents in everything,
3: 21 Fathers, do not embitter your *c,*
1Ti 3: 4 and see that his *c* obey him
3:12 and must manage his *c* and his
5: 10 bringing up *c,* showing hospitality,
1Jn 3: 1 that we should be called *c* of God!

CHOOSE (CHOOSES CHOSE CHOSEN)
Dt 30:19 Now *c* life, so that you
Jos 24:15 then *c* for yourselves this day
Pr 8: 10 *C* my instruction instead of silver,
16:16 to *c* understanding rather
Jn 15:16 You did not *c* me, but I chose you

CHOOSES (CHOOSE)
Jn 7:17 If anyone *c* to do God's will,

CHOSE (CHOOSE)
Ge 13: 11 So Lot *c* for himself the whole plain
Ps 33:12 the people he *c* for his inheritance.
Jn 15:16 but I *c* you and appointed you to go
1Co 1:27 But God *c* the foolish things
Eph 1: 4 he *c* us in him before the creation
2Th 2:13 from the beginning God *c* you

CHOSEN (CHOOSE)
Isa 41: 8 Jacob, whom I have *c,*
Mt 22:14 For many are invited, but few are *c*
Lk 10:42 Mary has *c* what is better,
23:35 the Christ of God, the *C* One."
Jn 15:19 but I have *c* you out of the world.
1Pe 1:20 He was *c* before the creation
2: 9 But you are a *c* people, a royal

CHRIST (CHRIST'S CHRISTIAN CHRISTS)
Mt 1:16 was born Jesus, who is called *C.*
16:16 Peter answered, "You are the *C,*
22:42 "What do you think about the *C?*
Jn 1:41 found the Messiah" (that is, the *C).*
20: 31 you may believe that Jesus is the *C,*
Ac 2:36 you crucified, both Lord and *C."*
5:42 the good news that Jesus is the *C.*
9:22 by proving that Jesus is the *C.*
17: 3 proving that the *C* had to suffer
18:28 the Scriptures that Jesus was the *C.*
26:23 that the *C* would suffer and,
Ro 3:22 comes through faith in Jesus *C*
5: 6 we were still powerless, *C* died
5: 8 While we were still sinners, *C* died
5:17 life through the one man, Jesus *C.*
6: 4 as *C* was raised from the dead
8: 1 for those who are in *C* Jesus,
8: 9 Spirit of *C,* he does not belong to *C.*
8:35 us from the love of *C?*
10: 4 *C* is the end of the law
14: 9 *C* died and returned to life
15: 3 For even *C* did not please himself
1Co 1:23 but we preach *C* crucified:
2: 2 except Jesus *C* and him crucified.
3: 11 one already laid, which is Jesus *C.*
5: 7 For *C,* our Passover lamb,
8: 6 and there is but one Lord, Jesus *C,*
1Co 10: 4 them, and that rock was *C.*
11: 1 as I follow the example of *C.*
11: 3 the head of every man is *C,*
12:27 Now you are the body of *C,*
15: 3 that *C* died for our sins according
15:14 And if *C* has not been raised,
15:22 so in *C* all will be made alive.
15:57 victory through our Lord Jesus *C.*
2Co 3: 3 show that you are a letter from *C,*
4: 5 not preach ourselves, but Jesus *C*
5: 10 before the judgment seat of *C,*
5:17 Therefore, if anyone is in *C,*
11: 2 you to one husband, to *C,*
Gal 2:20 I have been crucified with *C*
3:13 *C* redeemed us from the curse
6:14 in the cross of our Lord Jesus *C,*
Eph 1: 3 with every spiritual blessing in *C.*
3: 8 the unsearchable riches of *C,*
4:13 measure of the fullness of *C.*
5: 2 as *C* loved us and gave himself up
5:23 as *C* is the head of the church,
5:25 just as *C* loved the church
Php 1: 21 to live is *C* and to die is gain.
1:27 worthy of the gospel of *C.*
4:19 to his glorious riches in *C* Jesus.
Col 1:27 which is *C* in you, the hope of glory
1:28 may present everyone perfect in *C.*
2: 6 as you received *C* Jesus as Lord,
2:17 the reality, however, is found in *C.*
3:15 Let the peace of *C* rule
2Th 2: 1 the coming of our Lord Jesus *C*
1Ti 1:15 *C* Jesus came into the world
2: 5 the man *C* Jesus, who gave himself
2Ti 2: 3 us like a good soldier of *C* Jesus.
3:15 salvation through faith in *C* Jesus.
Tit 2:13 our great God and Savior, Jesus *C,*
Heb 3:14 to share in *C* if we hold firmly
9:14 more, then, will the blood of *C,*
9:15 For this reason *C* is the mediator
9:28 so *C* was sacrificed once
10: 10 of the body of Jesus *C* once for all.
13: 8 Jesus *C* is the same yesterday
1Pe 1:19 but with the precious blood of *C,*
2: 21 because *C* suffered for you,
3:18 For *C* died for sins once for all,
4:14 insulted because of the name of *C,*
1Jn 2:22 man who denies that Jesus is the *C.*
3:16 Jesus *C* laid down his life for us.
5: 1 believes that Jesus is the *C* is born
Rev 20: 4 reigned with *C* a thousand years.

CHRIST'S (CHRIST)
2Co 5:14 For *C* love compels us,
5:20 We are therefore *C* ambassadors,
12: 9 so that *C* power may rest on me.

CHRISTIAN (CHRIST)
1Pe 4:16 as a *C,* do not be ashamed,

CHRISTS (CHRIST)
Mt 24:24 For false *C* and false prophets will

CHURCH
Mt 16:18 and on this rock I will build my *c,*
18:17 if he refuses to listen even to the *c,*
Ac 20:28 Be shepherds of the *c* of God,
1Co 5:12 of mine to judge those outside the *c*
14: 4 but he who prophesies edifies the *c.*
14:12 to excel in gifts that build up the *c.*
14:26 done for the strengthening of the *c.*
Eph 5:23 as Christ is the head of the *c,*
Col 1:24 the sake of his body, which is the *c.*

CIRCUMCISED
Ge 17:10 Every male among you shall be *c.*

CIRCUMSTANCES
Php 4:11 to be content whatever the *c.*
1Th 5:18 continually; give thanks in all *c,*

CITIZENS (CITIZENSHIP)
Eph 2:19 but fellow *c* with God's people

CITIZENSHIP (CITIZENS)
Php 3:20 But our *c* is in heaven.

CITY
Mt 5:14 A *c* on a hill cannot be hidden.
Heb 13:14 here we do not have an enduring *c,*

CIVILIAN*
2Ti 2:4 a soldier gets involved in *c* affairs—

CLAIM (CLAIMS)
Pr 25:6 do not *c* a place among great men;
1Jn 1:6 If we *c* to have fellowship
1:8 If we *c* to be without sin, we
1:10 If we *c* we have not sinned,

CLAIMS (CLAIM)
Jas 2:14 if a man *c* to have faith
1Jn 2:6 Whoever *c* to live in him must walk
2:9 Anyone who *c* to be in the light

CLAP
Ps 47:1 *C* your hands, all you nations;
Isa 55:12 will *c* their hands.

CLAY
Isa 45:9 Does the *c* say to the potter,
64:8 We are the *c,* you are the potter;
Jer 18:6 "Like *c* in the hand of the potter,
La 4:2 are now considered as pots of *c,*
Da 2:33 partly of iron and partly of baked *c.*
Ro 9:21 of the same lump of *c* some pottery
2Co 4:7 we have this treasure in jars of *c*
2Ti 2:20 and *c;* some are for noble purposes

CLEAN
Lev 16:30 you will be *c* from all your sins.
Ps 24:4 He who has *c* hands and a pure
Mt 12:44 the house unoccupied, swept *c*
23:25 You *c* the outside of the cup
Mk 7:19 Jesus declared all foods *"c.")*
Jn 13:10 to wash his feet; his whole body is *c*
15:3 are already *c* because of the word
Ac 10:15 impure that God has made *c."*
Ro 14:20 All food is *c,* but it is wrong

CLING (CLINGS)
Ro 12:9 Hate what is evil; *c* to what is good.

CLINGS (CLING)
Ps 63:8 My soul *c* to you;

CLOAK
2Ki 4:29 "Tuck your *c* into your belt,

CLOSE (CLOSER)
Ps 34:18 LORD is *c* to the brokenhearted
Isa 40:11 and carries them *c* to his heart;
Jer 30:21 himself to be *c* to me?'

CLOSER (CLOSE)
Ex 3:5 "Do not come any *c,"* God said.
Pr 18:24 there is a friend who sticks *c*

CLOTHE (CLOTHED CLOTHES CLOTHING)
Ps 45:3 *c* yourself with splendor
Isa 52:1 *c* yourself with strength.
Ro 13:14 *c* yourselves with the Lord Jesus
Col 3:12 *c* yourselves with compassion,
1Pe 5:5 *c* yourselves with humility

CLOTHED (CLOTHE)
Ps 30:11 removed my sackcloth and *c* me
Pr 31:25 She is *c* with strength and dignity;
Lk 24:49 until you have been *c* with power

CLOTHES (CLOTHE)
Mt 6:25 the body more important than *c?*
6:28 "And why do you worry about *c?*
Jn 11:44 Take off the grave *c* and let him go

CLOTHING (CLOTHE)
Dt 22:5 A woman must not wear men's *c,*
Mt 7:15 They come to you in sheep's *c,*

CLOUD (CLOUDS)
Ex 13:21 them in a pillar of *c* to guide them
Isa 19:1 See, the LORD rides on a swift *c*
Lk 21:27 of Man coming in a *c* with power
Heb 12:1 by such a great *c* of witnesses,

CLOUDS (CLOUD)
Ps 104:3 He makes the *c* his chariot
Da 7:13 coming with the *c* of heaven.
Mk 13:26 coming in *c* with great power
1Th 4:17 with them in the *c* to meet the Lord

CO-HEIRS* (INHERIT)
Ro 8:17 heirs of God and *c* with Christ,

COALS
Pr 25:22 you will heap burning *c* on his head
Ro 12:20 you will heap burning *c* on his head

COLD
Pr 25:25 Like *c* water to a weary soul
Mt 10:42 if anyone gives even a cup of *c* water
24:12 the love of most will grow *c,*

COMFORT (COMFORTED COMFORTS)
Ps 23:4 rod and your staff, they *c* me.
119:52 and I find *c* in them.
119:76 May your unfailing love be my *c,*
Zec 1:17 and the LORD will again *c* Zion
1Co 14:3 encouragement and *c.*
2Co 1:4 so that we can *c* those
2:7 you ought to forgive and *c* him,

COMFORTED (COMFORT)
Mt 5:4 for they will be *c.*

COMFORTS* (COMFORT)
Job 29:25 I was like one who *c* mourners.
Isa 49:13 For the LORD *c* his people
51:12 "I, even I, am he who *c* you.
66:13 As a mother *c* her child,
2Co 1:4 who *c* us in all our troubles,
7:6 But God, who *c* the downcast,

COMMAND (COMMANDED COMMANDING COMMANDMENT COMMANDMENTS COMMANDS)
Ex 7:2 You are to say everything I *c* you,
Nu 24:13 to go beyond the *c* of the LORD—
Dt 4:2 Do not add to what I *c* you
30:16 For I *c* you today to love
32:46 so that you may *c* your children
Ps 91:11 For he will *c* his angels concerning
Pr 13:13 but he who respects a *c* is rewarded
Ecc 8:2 Obey the king's *c,* I say,
Joel 2:11 mighty are those who obey his *c.*
Jn 14:15 love me, you will obey what I *c.*
15:12 My *c* is this: Love each other
1Co 14:37 writing to you is the Lord's *c.*
Gal 5:14 law is summed up in a single *c:*
1Ti 1:5 goal of this *c* is love, which comes
Heb 11:3 universe was formed at God's *c,*
1Jn 3:23 this is his *c:* to believe in the name
2Jn :6 his *c* is that you walk in love.

COMMANDED (COMMAND)
Ps 33:9 he *c,* and it stood firm.
148:5 for he *c* and they were created.
Mt 28:20 to obey everything I have *c* you.
1Co 9:14 Lord has *c* that those who preach
1Jn 3:23 and to love one another as he *c* us.

COMMANDING (COMMAND)
2Ti 2:4 he wants to please his *c* officer.

COMMANDMENT (COMMAND)
Jos 22:5 But be very careful to keep the *c*
Mt 22:38 This is the first and greatest *c.*
Jn 13:34 "A new *c* I give you: Love one
Ro 7:12 and the *c* is holy, righteous
Eph 6:2 which is the first *c* with a promise

COMMANDMENTS (COMMAND)
Ex 20:6 who love me and keep my *c.*
34:28 of the covenant—the Ten *C.*
Ecc 12:13 Fear God and keep his *c,*
Mt 5:19 one of the least of these *c*
22:40 the Prophets hang on these two *c."*

COMMANDS (COMMAND)
Dt 7:9 those who love him and keep his *c.*
11:27 the blessing if you obey the *c*
Ps 112:1 who finds great delight in his *c.*
119:47 for I delight in your *c*
119:86 All your *c* are trustworthy;
119:98 Your *c* make me wiser
119:127 Because I love your *c*
119:143 but your *c* are my delight.
119:172 for all your *c* are righteous.
Pr 3:1 but keep my *c* in your heart,
6:23 For these *c* are a lamp,
10:8 The wise in heart accept *c,*
Da 9:4 all who love him and obey his *c,*
Mt 5:19 teaches these *c* will be called great
Jn 14:21 Whoever has my *c* and obeys them,
Ac 17:30 but now he *c* all people everywhere
1Co 7:19 Keeping God's *c* is what counts.
1Jn 5:3 And his *c* are not burdensome,
5:3 This is love for God: to obey his *c.*

COMMEND (COMMENDED COMMENDS)
Ecc 8:15 So I *c* the enjoyment of life,
Ro 13:3 do what is right and he will *c* you.
1Pe 2:14 and to *c* those who do right.

COMMENDED (COMMEND)
Heb 11:39 These were all *c* for their faith,

COMMENDS (COMMEND)
2Co 10:18 not the one who *c* himself who is

COMMIT (COMMITS COMMITTED)
Ex 20:14 "You shall not *c* adultery.
Ps 37:5 *C* your way to the LORD;
Mt 5:27 that it was said, 'Do not *c* adultery.'
Lk 23:46 into your hands I *c* my spirit."
Ac 20:32 I *c* you to God and to the word
1Co 10:8 We should not *c* sexual immorality,

1Pe 4:19 to God's will should *c* themselves

COMMITS (COMMIT)
Pr 6:32 man who *c* adultery lacks
29:22 a hot-tempered one *c* many sins.
Mt 19: 9 marries another woman *c* adultery

COMMITTED (COMMIT)
Nu 5: 7 and must confess the sin he has *c.*
1Ki 8:61 But your hearts must be fully *c*
2Ch 16: 9 those whose hearts are fully *c*
Mt 5:28 lustfully has already *c* adultery
2Co 5:19 And he has *c* to us the message
1Pe 2:22 "He *c* no sin,

COMMON
Pr 22: 2 Rich and poor have this in *c:*
1Co 10:13 has seized you except what is *c*
2Co 6:14 and wickedness have in *c?*

COMPANION (COMPANIONS)
Pr 13:20 but a *c* of fools suffers harm.
28: 7 a *c* of gluttons disgraces his father.
29: 3 *c* of prostitutes squanders his

COMPANIONS (COMPANION)
Pr 18:24 A man of many *c* may come to ruin

COMPANY
Pr 24: 1 do not desire their *c;*
Jer 15:17 I never sat in the *c* of revelers,
1Co 15:33 "Bad *c* corrupts good character."

COMPARED (COMPARING)
Eze 31: 2 Who can be *c* with you in majesty?
Php 3: 8 I consider everything a loss *c*

COMPARING* (COMPARED)
Ro 8:18 present sufferings are not worth *c*
2Co 8: 8 the sincerity of your love by *c* it
Gal 6: 4 without *c* himself to somebody else

COMPASSION (COMPASSIONATE COMPASSIONS)
Ex 33:19 I will have *c* on whom I will have *c.*
Ne 9:19 of your great *c* you did not
9:28 in your *c* you delivered them time
Ps 51: 1 according to your great *c*
103: 4 and crowns you with love and *c.*
103:13 As a father has *c* on his children,
145: 9 he has *c* on all he has made.
Isa 49:13 and will have *c* on his afflicted ones
49:15 and have no *c* on the child she has
Hos 2:19 in love and *c.*
11: 8 all my *c* is aroused.
Jnh 3: 9 with *c* turn from his fierce anger
Mt 9:36 When he saw the crowds, he had *c*
Mk 8: 2 "I have *c* for these people;
Ro 9:15 and I will have *c* on whom I have *c*
Col 3:12 clothe yourselves with *c,* kindness,
Jas 5:11 The Lord is full of *c* and mercy.

COMPASSIONATE (COMPASSION)
Ne 9:17 gracious and *c,* slow to anger
Ps 103: 8 The LORD is *c* and gracious,
112: 4 the gracious and *c* and righteous
Eph 4:32 Be kind and *c* to one another,
1Pe 3: 8 love as brothers, be *c* and humble.

COMPASSIONS* (COMPASSION)
La 3:22 for his *c* never fail.

COMPELLED (COMPELS)
Ac 20:22 "And now, *c* by the Spirit,
1Co 9:16 I cannot boast, for I am *c* to preach.

COMPELS (COMPELLED)
2Co 5:14 For Christ's love *c* us, because we

COMPETENCE* (COMPETENT)
2Co 3: 5 but our *c* comes from God.

COMPETENT* (COMPETENCE)
Ro 15:14 and *c* to instruct one another.
1Co 6: 2 are you not *c* to judge trivial cases?
2Co 3: 5 Not that we are *c* in ourselves
3: 6 He has made us *c* as ministers

COMPETES*
1Co 9:25 Everyone who *c* in the games goes
2Ti 2: 5 Similarly, if anyone *c* as an athlete,
2: 5 unless he *c* according to the rules.

COMPLACENT
Am 6: 1 Woe to you who are *c* in Zion,

COMPLAINING*
Php 2:14 Do everything without *c* or arguing

COMPLETE
Jn 15:11 and that your joy may be *c.*
16:24 will receive, and your joy will be *c.*
17:23 May they be brought to *c* unity
Ac 20:24 *c* the task the Lord Jesus has given
Php 2: 2 then make my joy *c*
Col 4:17 to it that you *c* the work you have
Jas 1: 4 so that you may be mature and *c,*
2:22 his faith was made *c* by what he did

CONCEAL (CONCEALED CONCEALS)
Ps 40:10 I do not *c* your love and your truth
Pr 25: 2 It is the glory of God to *c* a matter;

CONCEALED (CONCEAL)
Jer 16:17 nor is their sin *c* from my eyes.
Mt 10:26 There is nothing *c* that will not be
Mk 4:22 and whatever is *c* is meant

CONCEALS (CONCEAL)
Pr 28:13 He who *c* his sins does not prosper,

CONCEITED
Ro 12:16 Do not be *c.*
Gal 5:26 Let us not become *c,* provoking
1Ti 6: 4 he is *c* and understands nothing.

CONCEIVED
Mt 1:20 what is *c* in her is from the Holy
1Co 2: 9 no mind has *c*

CONCERN (CONCERNED)
Eze 36:21 I had *c* for my holy name, which
1Co 7:32 I would like you to be free from *c.*
12:25 that its parts should have equal *c*
2Co 11:28 of my *c* for all the churches.

CONCERNED (CONCERN)
Jnh 4:10 "You have been *c* about this vine,
1Co 7:32 An unmarried man is *c* about

CONDEMN (CONDEMNATION CONDEMNED CONDEMNING CONDEMNS)
Job 40: 8 Would you *c* me to justify yourself?
Isa 50: 9 Who is he that will *c* me?
Lk 6:37 Do not *c,* and you will not be
Jn 3:17 Son into the world to *c* the world,
12:48 very word which I spoke will *c* him
Ro 2:27 yet obeys the law will *c* you who,
1Jn 3:20 presence whenever our hearts *c* us.

CONDEMNATION (CONDEMN)
Ro 5:18 of one trespass was *c* for all men,
8: 1 there is now no *c* for those who are

CONDEMNED (CONDEMN)
Ps 34:22 no one will be *c* who takes refuge
Mt 12:37 and by your words you will be *c."*
23:33 How will you escape being *c* to hell
Jn 3:18 Whoever believes in him is not *c,*
5:24 has eternal life and will not be *c;*
16:11 prince of this world now stands *c.*
Ro 14:23 But the man who has doubts is *c*
1Co 11:32 disciplined so that we will not be *c*
Heb 11: 7 By his faith he *c* the world

CONDEMNING (CONDEMN)
Pr 17:15 the guilty and *c* the innocent—
Ro 2: 1 judge the other, you are *c* yourself,

CONDEMNS (CONDEMN)
Ro 8:34 Who is he that *c?* Christ Jesus,
2Co 3: 9 the ministry that *c* men is glorious,

CONDUCT
Pr 10:23 A fool finds pleasure in evil *c,*
20:11 by whether his *c* is pure and right.
21: 8 but the *c* of the innocent is upright.
Ecc 6: 8 how to *c* himself before others?
Jer 4:18 "Your own *c* and actions
17:10 to reward a man according to his *c,*
Eze 7: 3 I will judge you according to your *c*
Php 1:27 *c* yourselves in a manner worthy
1Ti 3:15 to *c* themselves in God's household

CONFESS (CONFESSION)
Lev 16:21 and *c* over it all the wickedness
26:40 " 'But if they will *c* their sins
Nu 5: 7 must *c* the sin he has committed.
Ps 38:18 I *c* my iniquity;
Ro 10: 9 That if you *c* with your mouth,
Php 2:11 every tongue *c* that Jesus Christ is
Jas 5:16 Therefore *c* your sins to each other
1Jn 1: 9 If we *c* our sins, he is faithful

CONFESSION (CONFESS)
Ezr 10:11 Now make *c* to the LORD,
2Co 9:13 obedience that accompanies your *c*

CONFIDENCE
Ps 71: 5 my *c* since my youth.
Pr 3:26 for the LORD will be your *c*
11:13 A gossip betrays a *c,*
25: 9 do not betray another man's *c,*
31:11 Her husband has full *c* in her
Isa 32:17 will be quietness and *c* forever.
Jer 17: 7 whose *c* is in him.
Php 3: 3 and who put no *c* in the flesh—
Heb 3:14 till the end the *c* we had at first.
4:16 the throne of grace with *c,*
10:19 since we have *c* to enter the Most
10:35 So do not throw away your *c;*
1Jn 5:14 This is the *c* we have

CONFORM* (CONFORMED)
Ro 12: 2 Do not *c* any longer to the pattern
1Pe 1:14 do not *c* to the evil desires you had

CONFORMED (CONFORM)
Ro 8:29 predestined to be *c* to the likeness

CONQUERORS
Ro 8:37 than *c* through him who loved us.

CONSCIENCE (CONSCIENCES)
Ro 13: 5 punishment but also because of *c.*
1Co 8: 7 since their *c* is weak, it is defiled.
8:12 in this way and wound their weak *c*
10:25 without raising questions of *c,*
10:29 freedom be judged by another's *c?*
Heb 10:22 to cleanse us from a guilty *c*
1Pe 3:16 and respect, keeping a clear *c,*

CONSCIENCES* (CONSCIENCE)
Ro 2:15 their *c* also bearing witness,
1Ti 4: 2 whose *c* have been seared
Tit 1:15 their minds and *c* are corrupted.
Heb 9:14 cleanse our *c* from acts that lead

CONSCIOUS*
Ro 3:20 through the law we become *c* of sin
1Pe 2:19 of unjust suffering because he is *c*

CONSECRATE (CONSECRATED)
Ex 13: 2 "*C* to me every firstborn male.
Lev 20: 7 " '*C* yourselves and be holy,

CONSECRATED (CONSECRATE)
Ex 29:43 and the place will be *c* by my glory.
1Ti 4: 5 because it is *c* by the word of God

CONSIDER (CONSIDERATE CONSIDERED CONSIDERS)
1Sa 12:24 *c* what great things he has done
Job 37:14 stop and *c* God's wonders.
Ps 8: 3 When I *c* your heavens,
107:43 and *c* the great love of the LORD.
143: 5 and *c* what your hands have done.
Lk 12:24 *C* the ravens: They do not sow
12:27 about the rest? "*C* how the lilies
Php 2: 3 but in humility *c* others better
3: 8 I *c* everything a loss compared
Heb 10:24 And let us *c* how we may spur one
Jas 1: 2 *C* it pure joy, my brothers,

CONSIDERATE* (CONSIDER)
Tit 3: 2 to be peaceable and *c,*
Jas 3:17 then peace-loving, *c,* submissive,
1Pe 2:18 only to those who are good and *c,*
3: 7 in the same way be *c* as you live

CONSIDERED (CONSIDER)
Job 1: 8 "Have you *c* my servant Job?
2: 3 "Have you *c* my servant Job?
Ps 44:22 we are *c* as sheep to be slaughtered.
Isa 53: 4 yet we *c* him stricken by God,
Ro 8:36 we are *c* as sheep to be slaughtered

CONSIDERS (CONSIDER)
Pr 31:16 She *c* a field and buys it;
Ro 14: 5 One man *c* one day more sacred
Jas 1:26 If anyone *c* himself religious

CONSIST
Lk 12:15 a man's life does not *c*

CONSOLATION
Ps 94:19 your *c* brought joy to my soul.

CONSTRUCTIVE*
1Co 10:23 but not everything is *c.*

CONSUME (CONSUMING)
Jn 2:17 "Zeal for your house will *c* me."

CONSUMING (CONSUME)
Dt 4:24 For the LORD your God is a *c* fire,
Heb 12:29 and awe, for our "God is a *c* fire."

CONTAIN
1Ki 8:27 the highest heaven, cannot *c* you.
2Pe 3:16 His letters *c* some things that are

CONTAMINATES*
2Co 7: 1 from everything that *c* body

CONTEMPT
Pr 14:31 He who oppresses the poor shows *c*
17: 5 He who mocks the poor shows *c*
18: 3 When wickedness comes, so does *c*
Da 12: 2 others to shame and everlasting *c.*
Ro 2: 4 Or do you show *c* for the riches
Gal 4:14 you did not treat me with *c*
1Th 5:20 do not treat prophecies with *c.*

CONTEND (CONTENDING)
Jude : 3 you to *c* for the faith that was once

CONTENDING* (CONTEND)
Php 1:27 *c* as one man for the faith

CONTENT (CONTENTMENT)
Pr 13:25 The righteous eat to their hearts' *c,*
Php 4:11 to be *c* whatever the circumstances
4:12 I have learned the secret of being *c*
1Ti 6: 8 and clothing, we will be *c* with that.
Heb 13: 5 and be *c* with what you have,

CONTENTMENT (CONTENT)
1Ti 6: 6 But godliness with *c* is great gain.

CONTINUAL (CONTINUE)
Pr 15:15 but the cheerful heart has a *c* feast.

CONTINUE (CONTINUAL)
Php 2:12 *c* to work out your salvation
2Ti 3:14 *c* in what you have learned
1Jn 5:18 born of God does not *c* to sin;
Rev 22:11 and let him who is holy *c* to be holy
22:11 let him who does right *c* to do right;

CONTRITE*
Ps 51:17 a broken and *c* heart,
Isa 57:15 also with him who is *c* and lowly
57:15 and to revive the heart of the *c.*
66: 2 he who is humble and *c* in spirit,

CONTROL (CONTROLLED SELF-CONTROL SELF-CONTROLLED)
Pr 29:11 a wise man keeps himself under *c.*
1Co 7: 9 But if they cannot *c* themselves,
7:37 but has *c* over his own will,
1Th 4: 4 you should learn to *c* his own body

CONTROLLED (CONTROL)
Ps 32: 9 but must be *c* by bit and bridle
Ro 8: 6 but the mind *c* by the Spirit is life
8: 8 Those *c* by the sinful nature cannot

CONTROVERSIES
Tit 3: 9 But avoid foolish *c* and genealogies

CONVERSATION
Col 4: 6 Let your *c* be always full of grace,

CONVERT
1Ti 3: 6 He must not be a recent *c,*

CONVICT
Jn 16: 8 he will *c* the world of guilt in regard

CONVINCED (CONVINCING)
Ro 8:38 For I am *c* that neither death
2Ti 1:12 and am *c* that he is able
3:14 have learned and have become *c*

CONVINCING* (CONVINCED)
Ac 1: 3 and gave many *c* proofs that he was

CORNELIUS*
Roman to whom Peter preached; first Gentile Christian (Ac 10).

CORNERSTONE (STONE)
Isa 28:16 a precious *c* for a sure foundation;
Eph 2:20 Christ Jesus himself as the chief *c.*
1Pe 2: 6 a chosen and precious *c,*

CORRECT (CORRECTING CORRECTION CORRECTS)
2Ti 4: 2 *c,* rebuke and encourage—

CORRECTING* (CORRECT)
2Ti 3:16 *c* and training in righteousness,

CORRECTION (CORRECT)
Pr 10:17 whoever ignores *c* leads others
12: 1 but he who hates *c* is stupid.
15: 5 whoever heeds *c* shows prudence.
15:10 he who hates *c* will die.
29:15 The rod of *c* imparts wisdom,

CORRECTS* (CORRECT)
Job 5:17 "Blessed is the man whom God *c;*
Pr 9: 7 Whoever *c* a mocker invites insult;

CORRUPT (CORRUPTS)
Ge 6:11 Now the earth was *c* in God's sight

CORRUPTS*(CORRUPT)
Ecc 7: 7 and a bribe *c* the heart.
1Co 15:33 "Bad company *c* good character."
Jas 3: 6 It *c* the whole person, sets

COST
Pr 4: 7 Though it *c* all you have, get
Isa 55: 1 milk without money and without *c.*
Rev 21: 6 to drink without *c* from the spring

COUNSEL (COUNSELOR)
1Ki 22: 5 "First seek the *c* of the LORD."
Pr 15:22 Plans fail for lack of *c,*
Rev 3:18 I *c* you to buy from me gold refined

COUNSELOR (COUNSEL)
Isa 9: 6 Wonderful *C,* Mighty God,
Jn 14:16 he will give you another *C* to be
14:26 But the *C,* the Holy Spirit,

COUNT (COUNTING COUNTS)
Ro 4: 8 whose sin the Lord will never *c*
6:11 *c* yourselves dead to sin

COUNTING (COUNT)
2Co 5:19 not *c* men's sins against them.

COUNTRY
Jn 4:44 prophet has no honor in his own *c.*)

COUNTS (COUNT)
Jn 6:63 The Spirit gives life; the flesh *c*
1Co 7:19 God's commands is what *c.*

Gal 5: 6 only thing that *c* is faith expressing

COURAGE (COURAGEOUS)
Ac 23: 11 "Take *c!* As you have testified
1Co 16: 13 stand firm in the faith; be men of *c;*

COURAGEOUS (COURAGE)
Dt 31: 6 Be strong and *c.*
Jos 1: 6 and *c,* because you will lead these

COURSE
Ps 19: 5 a champion rejoicing to run his *c.*
Pr 15: 21 of understanding keeps a straight *c.*

COURTS
Ps 84: 10 Better is one day in your *c*
100: 4 and his *c* with praise;

COVENANT (COVENANTS)
Ge 9: 9 "I now establish my *c* with you
Ex 19: 5 if you obey me fully and keep my *c,*
1Ch 16: 15 He remembers his *c* forever,
Job 31: 1 "I made a *c* with my eyes
Jer 31: 31 "when I will make a new *c*
1Co 11: 25 "This cup is the new *c* in my blood;
Gal 4: 24 One *c* is from Mount Sinai
Heb 9: 15 Christ is the mediator of a new *c,*

COVENANTS (COVENANT)
Ro 9: 4 theirs the divine glory, the *c,*
Gal 4: 24 for the women represent two *c.*

COVER (COVER-UP COVERED COVERS)
Ps 91: 4 He will *c* you with his feathers,
Jas 5: 20 and *c* over a multitude of sins.

COVER-UP (COVER)
1Pe 2: 16 but do not use your freedom as a *c*

COVERED (COVER)
Ps 32: 1 whose sins are *c.*
Isa 6: 2 With two wings they *c* their faces,
Ro 4: 7 whose sins are *c.*
1Co 11: 4 with his head *c* dishonors his head.

COVERS (COVER)
Pr 10: 12 but love *c* over all wrongs.
1Pe 4: 8 love *c* over a multitude of sins.

COVET
Ex 20: 17 You shall not *c* your neighbor's
Ro 13: 9 "Do not steal," "Do not *c,*"

COWARDLY*
Rev 21: 8 But the *c,* the unbelieving, the vile,

CRAFTINESS (CRAFTY)
1Co 3: 19 "He catches the wise in their *c*";

CRAFTY (CRAFTINESS)
Ge 3: 1 the serpent was more *c* than any
2Co 12: 16 *c* fellow that I am, I caught you

CRAVE
Pr 23: 3 Do not *c* his delicacies,
1Pe 2: 2 newborn babies, *c* pure spiritual

CREATE (CREATED CREATION CREATOR)
Ps 51: 10 *C* in me a pure heart, O God,
Isa 45: 18 he did not *c* it to be empty,

CREATED (CREATE)
Ge 1: 1 In the beginning God *c* the heavens
1: 21 God *c* the great creatures of the sea
1: 27 So God *c* man in his own image,
Ps 148: 5 for he commanded and they were *c*
Isa 42: 5 he who *c* the heavens and stretched
Ro 1: 25 and served *c* things rather
1Co 11: 9 neither was man *c* for woman,
Col 1: 16 For by him all things were *c:*
1Ti 4: 4 For everything God *c* is good,
Rev 10: 6 who *c* the heavens and all that is

CREATION (CREATE)
Mk 16: 15 and preach the good news to all *c.*
Jn 17: 24 me before the *c* of the world.
Ro 8: 19 The *c* waits in eager expectation
8: 39 depth, nor anything else in all *c,*
2Co 5: 17 he is a new *c;* the old has gone,
Col 1: 15 God, the firstborn over all *c.*
1Pe 1: 20 chosen before the *c* of the world,
Rev 13: 8 slain from the *c* of the world.

CREATOR (CREATE)
Ge 14: 22 God Most High, *C* of heaven
Ro 1: 25 created things rather than the *C*—

CREATURE (CREATURES)
Lev 17: 11 For the life of a *c* is in the blood,

CREATURES (CREATURE)
Ge 6: 19 bring into the ark two of all living *c,*
Ps 104: 24 the earth is full of your *c.*

CREDIT (CREDITED)
Ro 4: 24 to whom God will *c* righteousness
1Pe 2: 20 it to your *c* if you receive a beating

CREDITED (CREDIT)
Ge 15: 6 and he *c* it to him as righteousness.
Ro 4: 5 his faith is *c* as righteousness.
Gal 3: 6 and it was *c* to him as righteousness
Jas 2: 23 and it was *c* to him as righteousness

CRIED (CRY)
Ps 18: 6 I *c* to my God for help.

CRIMSON
Isa 1: 18 though they are red as *c,*

CRIPPLED
Mk 9: 45 better for you to enter life *c*

CRITICISM
2Co 8: 20 We want to avoid any *c*

CROOKED
Pr 10: 9 he who takes *c* paths will be found
Php 2: 15 children of God without fault in a *c*

CROSS
Mt 10: 38 and anyone who does not take his *c*
Lk 9: 23 take up his *c* daily and follow me.
Ac 2: 23 to death by nailing him to the *c.*
1Co 1: 17 lest the *c* of Christ be emptied
Gal 6: 14 in the *c* of our Lord Jesus Christ,
Php 2: 8 even death on a *c!*
Col 1: 20 through his blood, shed on the *c.*
2: 14 he took it away, nailing it to the *c.*
2: 15 triumphing over them by the *c.*
Heb 12: 2 set before him endured the *c,*

CROWD
Ex 23: 2 Do not follow the *c* in doing wrong.

CROWN (CROWNED CROWNS)
Pr 4: 9 present you with a *c* of splendor."
10: 6 Blessings *c* the head
12: 4 noble character is her husband's *c,*
17: 6 Children's children are a *c*
Isa 61: 3 to bestow on them a *c* of beauty
Zec 9: 16 like jewels in a *c.*
Mt 27: 29 then twisted together a *c* of thorns
1Co 9: 25 it to get a *c* that will last forever.
2Ti 4: 8 store for me the *c* of righteousness,
Rev 2: 10 and I will give you the *c* of life.

CROWNED (CROWN)
Ps 8: 5 and *c* him with glory and honor.
Pr 14: 18 the prudent are *c* with knowledge.
Heb 2: 7 you *c* him with glory and honor

CROWNS (CROWN)
Rev 4: 10 They lay their *c* before the throne
19: 12 and on his head are many *c.*

CRUCIFIED (CRUCIFY)
Mt 20: 19 to be mocked and flogged and *c.*
27: 38 Two robbers were *c* with him,
Lk 24: 7 be *c* and on the third day be raised
Jn 19: 18 Here they *c* him, and with him two
Ac 2: 36 whom you *c,* both Lord and Christ
Ro 6: 6 For we know that our old self was *c*
1Co 1: 23 but we preach Christ *c:* a stumbling
2: 2 except Jesus Christ and him *c.*
Gal 2: 20 I have been *c* with Christ
5: 24 Christ Jesus have *c* the sinful

CRUCIFY (CRUCIFIED CRUCIFYING)
Mt 27: 22 They all answered, "*C* him!" "Why
27: 31 Then they led him away to *c* him.

CRUCIFYING* (CRUCIFY)
Heb 6: 6 to their loss they are *c* the Son

CRUSH (CRUSHED)
Ge 3: 15 he will *c* your head,
Isa 53: 10 it was the LORD's will to *c* him
Ro 16: 20 The God of peace will soon *c* Satan

CRUSHED (CRUSH)
Ps 34: 18 and saves those who are *c* in spirit.
Isa 53: 5 he was *c* for our iniquities;
2Co 4: 8 not *c;* perplexed, but not in despair;

CRY (CRIED)
Ps 34: 15 and his ears are attentive to their *c;*
40: 1 he turned to me and heard my *c.*
130: 1 Out of the depths I *c* to you,

CUP
Ps 23: 5 my *c* overflows.
Mt 10: 42 if anyone gives even a *c* of cold water
23: 25 You clean the outside of the *c*
26: 39 may this *c* be taken from me.
1Co 11: 25 after supper he took the *c,* saying,

CURSE (CURSED)
Dt 11: 26 before you today a blessing and a *c*
21: 23 hung on a tree is under God's *c.*
Lk 6: 28 bless those who *c* you, pray
Gal 3: 13 of the law by becoming a *c* for us,
Rev 22: 3 No longer will there be any *c.*

CURSED (CURSE)
Ge 3: 17 "*C* is the ground because of you;
Dt 27: 15 "*C* is the man who carves an image

Dt 27:16 "*C* is the man who dishonors his
27:17 "*C* is the man who moves his
27:18 "*C* is the man who leads the blind
27:19 *C* is the man who withholds justice
27:20 "*C* is the man who sleeps
27:21 "*C* is the man who has sexual
27:22 "*C* is the man who sleeps
27:23 "*C* is the man who sleeps
27:24 "*C* is the man who kills his
27:25 "*C* is the man who accepts a bribe
27:26 "*C* is the man who does not uphold
Ro 9: 3 I could wish that I myself were *c*
Gal 3:10 "*C* is everyone who does not

CURTAIN
Ex 26:33 The *c* will separate the Holy Place
Lk 23:45 the *c* of the temple was torn in two.
Heb 10:20 opened for us through the *c*,

CYMBAL*
1Co 13: 1 a resounding gong or a clanging *c*.

DANCE (DANCING)
Ecc 3: 4 a time to mourn and a time to *d*,
Mt 11:17 and you did not *d*;

DANCING (DANCE)
Ps 30:11 You turned my wailing into *d*;
149: 3 Let them praise his name with *d*

DANGER
Pr 27:12 The prudent see *d* and take refuge,
Ro 8:35 famine or nakedness or *d* or sword?

DANIEL
Hebrew exile to Babylon, name changed to Belteshazzar (Da 1:6-7). Refused to eat unclean food (Da 1:8-21). Interpreted Nebuchadnezzar's dreams (Da 2; 4), writing on the wall (Da 5). Thrown into lion's den (Da 6). Visions of (Da 7-12).

DARK (DARKNESS)
Job 34:22 There is no *d* place, no deep
Pr 31:15 She gets up while it is still *d*;
Ro 2:19 a light for those who are in the *d*,
2Pe 1:19 as to a light shining in a *d* place,

DARKNESS (DARK)
Ge 1: 4 he separated the light from the *d*.
2Sa 22:29 the LORD turns my *d* into light.
Jn 3:19 but men loved *d* instead of light
2Co 6:14 fellowship can light have with *d*?
Eph 5: 8 For you were once *d*, but now you
1Pe 2: 9 out of *d* into his wonderful light.
1Jn 1: 5 in him there is no *d* at all.
2: 9 but hates his brother is still in the *d*.

DAUGHTERS
Joel 2:28 sons and *d* will prophesy,

DAVID
Son of Jesse (Ru 4:17-22; 1Ch 2:13-15), ancestor of Jesus (Mt 1:1-17; Lk 3:31).
Anointed king by Samuel (1Sa 16:1-13). Musician to Saul (1Sa 16:14-23; 18:10). Killed Goliath (1Sa 17). Relation with Jonathan (1Sa 18:1-4; 19-20; 23:16-18; 2Sa 1). Disfavor of Saul (1Sa 18:6-23:29). Spared Saul's life (1Sa 24; 26). Among Philistines (1Sa 21:10-14; 27-30). Lament for Saul and Jonathan (2Sa 1).
Anointed king of Judah (2Sa 2:1-11); of Israel (2Sa 5:1-4; 1Ch 11:1-3). Promised eternal dynasty (2Sa 7; 1Ch 17; Ps 132). Adultery with Bathsheba (2Sa 11-12). Absalom's revolt (2Sa 14-18). Last words (2Sa 23:1-7). Death (1Ki 2:10-12; 1Ch 29:28).

DAWN
Ps 37: 6 your righteousness shine like the *d*,
Pr 4:18 is like the first gleam of *d*,

DAY (DAYS)
Ge 1: 5 God called the light "*d*,"
Ex 20: 8 "Remember the Sabbath *d*
Lev 23:28 because it is the *D* of Atonement,
Nu 14:14 before them in a pillar of cloud by *d*
Jos 1: 8 meditate on it *d* and night,
Ps 84:10 Better is one *d* in your courts
96: 2 proclaim his salvation *d* after *d*.
118:24 This is the *d* the LORD has made;
Pr 27: 1 not know what a *d* may bring forth.
Joel 2:31 and dreadful *d* of the LORD.
Ob :15 The *d* of the LORD is near
Lk 11: 3 Give us each *d* our daily bread.
Ac 17:11 examined the Scriptures every *d*
2Co 4:16 we are being renewed *d* by *d*.
1Th 5: 2 for you know very well that the *d*
2Pe 3: 8 With the Lord a *d* is like

DAYS (DAY)
Dt 17:19 he is to read it all the *d*, of his life
Ps 23: 6 all the *d* of my life,
90:10 The length of our *d* is seventy years
Ecc 12: 1 Creator in the *d* of your youth,
Joel 2:29 I will pour out my Spirit in those *d*.
Mic 4: 1 In the last *d*
Heb 1: 2 in these last *d* he has spoken to us
2Pe 3: 3 that in the last *d* scoffers will come,

DEACONS
1Ti 3: 8 *D*, likewise, are to be men worthy

DEAD (DIE)
Dt 18:11 or spiritist or who consults the *d*.
Mt 28: 7 'He has risen from the *d*
Ro 6:11 count yourselves *d* to sin
Eph 2: 1 you were *d* in your transgressions
1Th 4:16 and the *d* in Christ will rise first.
Jas 2:17 is not accompanied by action, is *d*.
2:26 so faith without deeds is *d*.

DEATH (DIE)
Nu 35:16 the murderer shall be put to *d*.
Ps 23: 4 the valley of the shadow of *d*,
116:15 is the *d* of his saints.
Pr 8:36 all who hate me love *d*."
14:12 but in the end it leads to *d*.
Ecc 7: 2 for *d* is the destiny of every man;
Isa 25: 8 he will swallow up *d* forever.
53:12 he poured out his life unto *d*,
Jn 5:24 he has crossed over from *d* to life.
Ro 5:12 and in this way *d* came to all men,
6:23 For the wages of sin is *d*,
8:13 put to *d* the misdeeds of the body,
1Co 15:21 For since *d* came through a man,
15:55 Where, O *d*, is your sting?"
Rev 1:18 And I hold the keys of *d* and Hades
20: 6 The second *d* has no power
20:14 The lake of fire is the second *d*.
21: 4 There will be no more *d*

DEBAUCHERY
Ro 13:13 not in sexual immorality and *d*,
Eph 5:18 drunk on wine, which leads to *d*.

DEBORAH
Prophetess who led Israel to victory over Canaanites (Jdg 4-5).

DEBT (DEBTORS DEBTS)
Ro 13: 8 Let no *d* remain outstanding,
13: 8 continuing *d* to love one another,

DEBTORS (DEBT)
Mt 6:12 as we also have forgiven our *d*.

DEBTS (DEBT)
Dt 15: 1 seven years you must cancel *d*.
Mt 6:12 Forgive us our *d*,

DECAY
Ps 16:10 will you let your Holy One see *d*.
Ac 2:27 will you let your Holy One see *d*.

DECEIT (DECEIVE)
Mk 7:22 greed, malice, *d*, lewdness, envy,
1Pe 2: 1 yourselves of all malice and all *d*,
2:22 and no *d* was found in his mouth."

DECEITFUL (DECEIVE)
Jer 17: 9 The heart is *d* above all things
2Co 11:13 men are false apostles, *d* workmen,

DECEITFULNESS (DECEIVE)
Mk 4:19 the *d* of wealth and the desires
Heb 3:13 of you may be hardened by sin's *d*.

DECEIVE (DECEIT DECEITFUL DECEITFULNESS DECEIVED DECEIVES DECEPTIVE)
Lev 19:11 " 'Do not *d* one another.
Pr 14: 5 A truthful witness does not *d*,
Mt 24: 5 'I am the Christ,' and will *d* many.
Ro 16:18 and flattery they *d* the minds
1Co 3:18 Do not *d* yourselves.
Eph 5: 6 Let no one *d* you with empty words
Jas 1:22 to the word, and so *d* yourselves.
1Jn 1: 8 we *d* ourselves and the truth is not

DECEIVED (DECEIVE)
Ge 3:13 "The serpent *d* me, and I ate."
Gal 6: 7 Do not be *d*: God cannot be
1Ti 2:14 And Adam was not the one *d*;
2Ti 3:13 to worse, deceiving and being *d*.
Jas 1:16 Don't be *d*, my dear brothers.

DECEIVES (DECEIVE)
Gal 6: 3 when he is nothing, he *d* himself.
Jas 1:26 he *d* himself and his religion is

DECENCY*
1Ti 2: 9 women to dress modestly, with *d*

DECEPTIVE (DECEIVE)
Pr 31:30 Charm is *d*, and beauty is fleeting;
Col 2: 8 through hollow and *d* philosophy,

DECLARE (DECLARED DECLARING)
1Ch 16:24 *D* his glory among the nations,
Ps 19: 1 The heavens *d* the glory of God;
96: 3 *D* his glory among the nations,
Isa 42: 9 and new things I *d*;

DECLARED (DECLARE)
Mk 7:19 Jesus *d* all foods "clean.")
Ro 2:13 the law who will be *d* righteous.
3:20 no one will be *d* righteous

DECLARING (DECLARE)
Ps 71: 8 *d* your splendor all day long.
Ac 2:11 we hear them *d* the wonders

DECREED (DECREES)
La 3:37 happen if the Lord has not *d* it?
Lk 22:22 Son of Man will go as it has been *d*,

DECREES (DECREED)
Lev 10:11 Israelites all the *d* the LORD has
Ps 119:112 My heart is set on keeping your *d*

DEDICATE (DEDICATION)
Nu 6:12 He must *d* himself to the LORD
Pr 20:25 for a man to *d* something rashly

DEDICATION (DEDICATE)
1Ti 5:11 sensual desires overcome their *d*

DEED (DEEDS)
Col 3:17 you do, whether in word or *d*,

DEEDS (DEED)
1Sa 2: 3 and by him *d* are weighed.
Ps 65: 5 with awesome *d* of righteousness,
66: 3 "How awesome are your *d!*
78: 4 the praiseworthy *d* of the LORD,
86:10 you are great and do marvelous *d;*
92: 4 For you make me glad by your *d,*
111: 3 Glorious and majestic are his *d,*
Hab 3: 2 I stand in awe of your *d,* O LORD.
Mt 5:16 that they may see your good *d*
Ac 26:20 prove their repentance by their *d.*
Jas 2:14 claims to have faith but has no *d?*
2:20 faith without *d* is useless?
1Pe 2:12 they may see your good *d*

DEEP (DEPTH)
1Co 2:10 all things, even the *d* things
1Ti 3: 9 hold of the *d* truths of the faith

DEER
Ps 42: 1 As the *d* pants for streams of water,

DEFEND (DEFENSE)
Ps 74:22 Rise up, O God, and *d* your cause;
Pr 31: 9 *d* the rights of the poor and needy
Jer 50:34 He will vigorously *d* their cause

DEFENSE (DEFEND)
Ps 35:23 Awake, and rise to my *d!*
Php 1:16 here for the *d* of the gospel.
1Jn 2: 1 speaks to the Father in our *d*—

DEFERRED*
Pr 13:12 Hope *d* makes the heart sick,

DEFILE (DEFILED)
Da 1: 8 Daniel resolved not to *d* himself

DEFILED (DEFILE)
Isa 24: 5 The earth is *d* by its people;

DEFRAUD
Lev 19:13 Do not *d* your neighbor or rob him.

DEITY*
Col 2: 9 of the *D* lives in bodily form,

DELIGHT (DELIGHTS)
1Sa 15:22 "Does the LORD *d*
Ps 1: 2 But his *d* is in the law of the LORD
16: 3 in whom is all my *d.*
35: 9 and *d* in his salvation.
37: 4 *D* yourself in the LORD
43: 4 to God, my joy and my *d.*
51:16 You do not *d* in sacrifice,
119:77 for your law is my *d.*
Pr 29:17 he will bring *d* to your soul.
Isa 42: 1 my chosen one in whom I *d;*
55: 2 and your soul will *d* in the richest
61:10 I *d* greatly in the LORD;
Jer 9:24 for in these I *d,"*
15:16 they were my joy and my heart's *d,*
Mic 7:18 but *d* to show mercy.
Zep 3:17 He will take great *d* in you,
Mt 12:18 the one I love, in whom I *d;*
1Co 13: 6 Love does not *d* in evil
2Co 12:10 for Christ's sake, I *d* in weaknesses,

DELIGHTS (DELIGHT)
Ps 22: 8 since he *d* in him."
35:27 who *d* in the well-being
36: 8 from your river of *d.*
37:23 if the LORD *d* in a man's way,
Pr 3:12 as a father the son he *d* in.
12:22 but he *d* in men who are truthful.
23:24 he who has a wise son *d* in him.

DELILAH*
Woman who betrayed Samson (Jdg 16:4-22).

DELIVER (DELIVERANCE DELIVERED DELIVERER DELIVERS)
Ps 72:12 For he will *d* the needy who cry out
79: 9 *d* us and forgive our sins
Mt 6:13 but *d* us from the evil one.'
2Co 1:10 hope that he will continue to *d* us,

DELIVERANCE (DELIVER)
Ps 3: 8 From the LORD comes *d.*
32: 7 and surround me with songs of *d.*
33:17 A horse is a vain hope for *d;*

DELIVERED (DELIVER)
Ps 34: 4 he *d* me from all my fears.
Ro 4:25 He was *d* over to death for our sins

DELIVERER (DELIVER)
Ps 18: 2 is my rock, my fortress and my *d;*
40:17 You are my help and my *d;*
140: 7 O Sovereign LORD, my strong *d,*
144: 2 my stronghold and my *d,*

DELIVERS (DELIVER)
Ps 34:17 he *d* them from all their troubles.
34:19 but the LORD *d* him from them all
37:40 The LORD helps them and *d* them
37:40 he *d* them from the wicked

DEMANDED
Lk 12:20 This very night your life will be *d*
12:48 been given much, much will be *d;*

DEMONS
Mt 12:27 And if I drive out *d* by Beelzebub,
Mk 5:15 possessed by the legion of *d,*
Ro 8:38 neither angels nor *d,* neither
Jas 2:19 Good! Even the *d* believe that—

DEMONSTRATE (DEMONSTRATES)
Ro 3:26 he did it to *d* his justice

DEMONSTRATES* (DEMONSTRATE)
Ro 5: 8 God *d* his own love for us in this:

DEN
Da 6:16 and threw him into the lions' *d.*
Mt 21:13 you are making it a '*d* of robbers.' "

DENARIUS
Mk 12:15 Bring me a *d* and let me look at it."

DENIED (DENY)
1Ti 5: 8 he has *d* the faith and is worse

DENIES (DENY)
1Jn 2:23 No one who *d* the Son has

DENY (DENIED DENIES DENYING)
Ex 23: 6 "Do not *d* justice to your poor
Job 27: 5 till I die, I will not *d* my integrity.
La 3:35 to *d* a man his rights
Lk 9:23 he must *d* himself and take up his
Tit 1:16 but by their actions they *d* him.

DENYING* (DENY)
Eze 22:29 mistreat the alien, *d* them justice.
2Ti 3: 5 a form of godliness but *d* its power.
2Pe 2: 1 *d* the sovereign Lord who bought

DEPART (DEPARTED)
Ge 49:10 The scepter will not *d* from Judah,
Job 1:21 and naked I will *d.*
Mt 25:41 '*D* from me, you who are cursed,
Php 1:23 I desire to *d* and be with Christ,

DEPARTED (DEPART)
1Sa 4:21 "The glory has *d* from Israel"—
Ps 119:102 I have not *d* from your laws,

DEPOSIT
2Co 1:22 put his Spirit in our hearts as a *d,*
5: 5 and has given us the Spirit as a *d,*
Eph 1:14 who is a *d* guaranteeing our
2Ti 1:14 Guard the good *d* that was

DEPRAVED (DEPRAVITY)
Ro 1:28 he gave them over to a *d* mind,
Php 2:15 fault in a crooked and *d* generation,

DEPRAVITY (DEPRAVED)
Ro 1:29 of wickedness, evil, greed and *d.*

DEPRIVE
Dt 24:17 Do not *d* the alien or the fatherless
Pr 18: 5 or to *d* the innocent of justice.
Isa 10: 2 to *d* the poor of their rights
29:21 with false testimony *d* the innocent
1Co 7: 5 Do not *d* each other

DEPTH (DEEP)
Ro 8:39 any powers, neither height nor *d,*
11:33 the *d* of the riches of the wisdom

DESERT
Nu 32:13 wander in the *d* forty years,
Ne 9:19 you did not abandon them in the *d.*
Ps 78:19 "Can God spread a table in the *d?*
78:52 led them like sheep through the *d.*
Mk 1:13 and he was in the *d* forty days,

DESERTED (DESERTS)
Ezr 9: 9 our God has not *d* us
Mt 26:56 all the disciples *d* him and fled.
2Ti 1:15 in the province of Asia has *d* me,

DESERTING (DESERTS)
Gal 1: 6 are so quickly *d* the one who called

DESERTS (DESERTED DESERTING)
Zec 11:17 who *d* the flock!

DESERVE (DESERVES)
Ps 103:10 he does not treat us as our sins *d*
Jer 21:14 I will punish you as your deeds *d,*
Mt 22: 8 those I invited did not *d* to come.
Ro 1:32 those who do such things *d* death,

DESERVES (DESERVE)
2Sa 12: 5 the man who did this *d* to die!
Lk 10: 7 for the worker *d* his wages.
1Ti 5:18 and "The worker *d* his wages."

DESIRABLE (DESIRE)
Pr 22: 1 A good name is more *d*

DESIRE (DESIRABLE DESIRES)
Ge 3:16 Your *d* will be for your husband,
Dt 5:21 You shall not set your *d*
1Ch 29:18 keep this *d* in the hearts
Ps 40: 6 Sacrifice and offering you did not *d*

Ps 40: 8 I *d* to do your will, O my God;
73:25 earth has nothing I *d* besides you
Pr 3:15 nothing you *d* can compare
10:24 what the righteous *d* will be
11:23 The *d* of the righteous ends only
Isa 26: 8 are the *d* of our hearts.
53: 2 appearance that we should *d* him.
55:11 but will accomplish what I *d*
Hos 6: 6 For I *d* mercy, not sacrifice,
Mt 9:13 learn what this means: 'I *d* mercy,
Ro 7:18 For I have the *d* to do what is good,
1Co 12:31 But eagerly *d* the greater gifts.
14: 1 and eagerly *d* spiritual gifts,
Php 1:23 I *d* to depart and be with Christ,
Heb 13:18 *d* to live honorably in every way.
Jas 1:15 Then, after *d* has conceived,

DESIRES (DESIRE)
Ge 4: 7 at your door; it *d* to have you,
Ps 34:12 and *d* to see many good days,
37: 4 he will give you the *d* of your heart.
103: 5 satisfies your *d* with good things,
145:19 He fulfills the *d* of those who fear
Pr 11: 6 the unfaithful are trapped by evil *d*.
19:22 What a man *d* is unfailing love;
Mk 4:19 and the *d* for other things come in
Ro 8: 5 set on what that nature *d;*
13:14 to gratify the *d* of the sinful nature.
Gal 5:16 and you will not gratify the *d*
5:17 the sinful nature *d* what is contrary
1Ti 3: 1 an overseer, he *d* a noble task.
6: 9 and harmful *d* that plunge men
2Ti 2:22 Flee the evil *d* of youth,
Jas 1:20 about the righteous life that God *d*.
4: 1 from your *d* that battle within you?
1Pe 2:11 to abstain from sinful *d*, which war
1Jn 2:17 The world and its *d* pass away,

DESOLATE
Isa 54: 1 are the children of the *d* woman

DESPAIR
Isa 61: 3 instead of a spirit of *d*.
2Co 4: 8 perplexed, but not in *d;* persecuted,

DESPISE (DESPISED DESPISES)
Job 42: 6 Therefore I *d* myself
Pr 1: 7 but fools *d* wisdom and discipline.
3:11 do not *d* the LORD's discipline
23:22 do not *d* your mother
Lk 16:13 devoted to the one and *d* the other.
Tit 2:15 Do not let anyone *d* you.

DESPISED (DESPISE)
Ge 25:34 So Esau *d* his birthright.
Isa 53: 3 He was *d* and rejected by men,
1Co 1:28 of this world and the *d* things—

DESPISES (DESPISE)
Pr 14:21 He who *d* his neighbor sins,
15:20 but a foolish man *d* his mother.
15:32 who ignores discipline *d* himself,
Zec 4:10 "Who *d* the day of small things?

DESTINED (DESTINY)
Lk 2:34 "This child is *d* to cause the falling

DESTINY (DESTINED PREDESTINED)
Ps 73:17 then I understood their final *d*.
Ecc 7: 2 for death is the *d* of every man;

DESTITUTE
Pr 31: 8 for the rights of all who are *d*.
Heb 11:37 *d*, persecuted and mistreated—

DESTROY (DESTROYED DESTROYS DESTRUCTION)
Pr 1:32 complacency of fools will *d* them;
Mt 10:28 of the One who can *d* both soul

DESTROYED (DESTROY)
Job 19:26 And after my skin has been *d*,
Isa 55:13 which will not be *d*."
1Co 8:11 for whom Christ died, is *d*
15:26 The last enemy to be *d* is death.
2Co 5: 1 if the earthly tent we live in is *d*,
Heb 10:39 of those who shrink back and are *d*,
2Pe 3:10 the elements will be *d* by fire,

DESTROYS (DESTROY)
Pr 6:32 whoever does so *d* himself.
11: 9 mouth the godless *d* his neighbor,
18: 9 is brother to one who *d*.
28:24 he is partner to him who *d*.
Ecc 9:18 but one sinner *d* much good.
1Co 3:17 If anyone *d* God's temple,

DESTRUCTION (DESTROY)
Pr 16:18 Pride goes before *d*,
Hos 13:14 Where, O grave, is your *d*?
Mt 7:13 broad is the road that leads to *d*,
Gal 6: 8 from that nature will reap *d;*
2Th 1: 9 punished with everlasting *d*
1Ti 6: 9 that plunge men into ruin and *d*.
2Pe 2: 1 bringing swift *d* on themselves.
3:16 other Scriptures, to their own *d*.

DETERMINED (DETERMINES)
Job 14: 5 Man's days are *d;*
Isa 14:26 This is the plan *d* for the whole
Da 11:36 for what has been *d* must take place
Ac 17:26 and he *d* the times set for them

DETERMINES* (DETERMINED)
Ps 147: 4 He *d* the number of the stars
Pr 16: 9 but the LORD *d* his steps.
1Co 12:11 them to each one, just as he *d*.

DETESTABLE (DETESTS)
Pr 21:27 The sacrifice of the wicked is *d*—
28: 9 even his prayers are *d*.
Isa 1:13 Your incense is *d* to me.
Lk 16:15 among men is *d* in God's sight.
Tit 1:16 They are *d*, disobedient

DETESTS (DETESTABLE)
Dt 22: 5 LORD your God *d* anyone who
23:18 the LORD your God *d* them both.
25:16 LORD your God *d* anyone who
Pr 12:22 The LORD *d* lying lips,
15: 8 The LORD *d* the sacrifice
15: 9 The LORD *d* the way
15:26 The LORD *d* the thoughts
16: 5 The LORD *d* all the proud of heart
17:15 the LORD *d* them both.
20:23 The LORD *d* differing weights,

DEVIL (DEVIL'S)
Mt 13:39 the enemy who sows them is the *d*.
25:41 the eternal fire prepared for the *d*
Lk 4: 2 forty days he was tempted by the *d*.
8:12 then the *d* comes and takes away
Eph 4:27 and do not give the *d* a foothold.
2Ti 2:26 and escape from the trap of the *d*,
Jas 4: 7 Resist the *d*, and he will flee
1Pe 5: 8 Your enemy the *d* prowls
1Jn 3: 8 who does what is sinful is of the *d*,
Rev 12: 9 that ancient serpent called the *d*

DEVIL'S* (DEVIL)
Eph 6:11 stand against the *d* schemes.
1Ti 3: 7 into disgrace and into the *d* trap.
1Jn 3: 8 was to destroy the *d* work.

DEVOTE (DEVOTED DEVOTING DEVOTION DEVOUT)
Job 11:13 "Yet if you *d* your heart to him
Jer 30:21 for who is he who will *d* himself
Col 4: 2 *D* yourselves to prayer, being
1Ti 4:13 *d* yourself to the public reading
Tit 3: 8 may be careful to *d* themselves

DEVOTED (DEVOTE)
Ezr 7:10 For Ezra had *d* himself to the study
Ac 2:42 They *d* themselves
Ro 12:10 Be *d* to one another
1Co 7:34 Her aim is to be *d* to the Lord

DEVOTING (DEVOTE)
1Ti 5:10 *d* herself to all kinds of good deeds.

DEVOTION (DEVOTE)
1Ch 28: 9 and serve him with wholehearted *d*
Eze 33:31 With their mouths they express *d*,
1Co 7:35 way in undivided *d* to the Lord.
2Co 11: 3 from your sincere and pure *d*

DEVOUR
2Sa 2:26 "Must the sword *d* forever?
Mk 12:40 They *d* widows' houses
1Pe 5: 8 lion looking for someone to *d*.

DEVOUT (DEVOTE)
Lk 2:25 Simeon, who was righteous and *d*.

DIE (DEAD DEATH DIED DIES)
Ge 2:17 when you eat of it you will surely *d*
Ex 11: 5 Every firstborn son in Egypt will *d*,
Ru 1:17 Where you *d* I will *d*, and there I
2Ki 14: 6 each is to *d* for his own sins."
Pr 5:23 He will *d* for lack of discipline,
10:21 but fools *d* for lack of judgment.
15:10 he who hates correction will *d*.
23:13 with the rod, he will not *d*.
Ecc 3: 2 a time to be born and a time to *d*,
Isa 66:24 their worm will not *d*, nor will their
Eze 3:18 that wicked man will *d* for his sin,
18: 4 soul who sins is the one who will *d*.
33: 8 'O wicked man, you will surely *d*,'
Mt 26:52 "for all who draw the sword will *d*
Jn 11:26 and believes in me will never *d*.
Ro 5: 7 Very rarely will anyone *d*
14: 8 and if we *d*, we *d* to the Lord.
1Co 15:22 in Adam all *d*, so in Christ all will
15:31 I *d* every day—I mean that,
Php 1:21 to live is Christ and to *d* is gain.
Heb 9:27 Just as man is destined to *d* once,
Rev 14:13 Blessed are the dead who *d*

DIED (DIE)
Ro 5: 6 we were still powerless, Christ *d*
6: 2 By no means! We *d* to sin;
6: 8 if we *d* with Christ, we believe that
14:15 brother for whom Christ *d*.
1Co 8:11 for whom Christ *d*, is destroyed
15: 3 that Christ *d* for our sins according
2Co 5:14 *d* for all, and therefore all *d*.
Col 3: 3 For you *d*, and your life is now
1Th 5:10 He *d* for us so that, whether we are
2Ti 2:11 If we *d* with him,
Heb 9:15 now that he has *d* as a ransom
1Pe 3:18 For Christ *d* for sins once for all,

Rev 2: 8 who *d* and came to life again.

DIES (DIE)
Job 14:14 If a man *d,* will he live again?
Pr 11: 7 a wicked man *d,* his hope perishes;
Jn 11:25 in me will live, even though he *d;*
1Co 15:36 does not come to life unless it *d.*

DIFFERENCE (DIFFERENT)
Ro 10:12 For there is no *d* between Jew

DIFFERENT (DIFFERENCE)
1Co 12: 4 There are *d* kinds of gifts,
2Co 11: 4 or a *d* gospel from the one you

DIGNITY
Pr 31:25 She is clothed with strength and *d;*

DIGS
Pr 26:27 If a man *d* a pit, he will fall into it;

DILIGENCE (DILIGENT)
Heb 6:11 to show this same *d* to the very end

DILIGENT (DILIGENCE)
Pr 21: 5 The plans of the *d* lead to profit
1Ti 4:15 Be *d* in these matters; give yourself

DIRECT (DIRECTS)
Ps 119:35 *D* me in the path of your
119:133 *D* my footsteps according
Jer 10:23 it is not for man to *d* his steps.
2Th 3: 5 May the Lord *d* your hearts

DIRECTS (DIRECT)
Ps 42: 8 By day the LORD *d* his love,
Isa 48:17 who *d* you in the way you should

DIRGE
Mt 11:17 we sang a *d,*

DISAPPEAR
Mt 5:18 will by any means *d* from the Law
Lk 16:17 earth to *d* than for the least stroke

DISAPPOINT* (DISAPPOINTED)
Ro 5: 5 And hope does not *d* us,

DISAPPOINTED (DISAPPOINT)
Ps 22: 5 in you they trusted and were not *d.*

DISASTER
Ps 57: 1 wings until the *d* has passed.
Pr 3:25 Have no fear of sudden *d*
17: 5 over *d* will not go unpunished.
Isa 45: 7 I bring prosperity and create *d;*
Eze 7: 5 An unheard-of *d* is coming.

DISCERN (DISCERNING DISCERNMENT)
Ps 19:12 Who can *d* his errors?
139: 3 You *d* my going out and my lying
Php 1:10 you may be able to *d* what is best

DISCERNING (DISCERN)
Pr 14: 6 knowledge comes easily to the *d.*
15:14 The *d* heart seeks knowledge,
17:24 A *d* man keeps wisdom in view,
17:28 and *d* if he holds his tongue.
19:25 rebuke a *d* man, and he will gain

DISCERNMENT (DISCERN)
Pr 17:10 A rebuke impresses a man of *d*
28:11 a poor man who has *d* sees

DISCIPLE (DISCIPLES)
Mt 10:42 these little ones because he is my *d,*
Lk 14:27 and follow me cannot be my *d.*

DISCIPLES (DISCIPLE)
Mt 28:19 Therefore go and make *d*
Jn 8:31 to my teaching, you are really my *d*
13:35 men will know that you are my *d*
Ac 11:26 The *d* were called Christians first

DISCIPLINE (DISCIPLINED DISCIPLINES)
Ps 38: 1 or *d* me in your wrath.
39:11 You rebuke and *d* men for their sin;
94:12 Blessed is the man you *d,* O LORD
Pr 1: 7 but fools despise wisdom and *d.*
3:11 do not despise the LORD's *d*
5:12 You will say, "How I hated *d!*
5:23 He will die for lack of *d,*
6:23 and the corrections of *d*
10:17 He who heeds *d* shows the way
12: 1 Whoever loves *d* loves knowledge,
13:18 He who ignores *d* comes to poverty
13:24 who loves him is careful to *d* him.
15: 5 A fool spurns his father's *d,*
15:32 He who ignores *d* despises himself,
19:18 *D* your son, for in that there is hope
22:15 the rod of *d* will drive it far
23:13 Do not withhold *d* from a child;
29:17 *D* your son, and he will give you
Heb 12: 5 do not make light of the Lord's *d,*
12: 7 as *d;* God is treating you
12:11 No *d* seems pleasant at the time,
Rev 3:19 Those whom I love I rebuke and *d.*

DISCIPLINED (DISCIPLINE)
Pr 1: 3 for acquiring a *d* and prudent life,
Jer 31:18 'You *d* me like an unruly calf,
1Co 11:32 we are being *d* so that we will not
Tit 1: 8 upright, holy and *d.*
Heb 12: 7 For what son is not *d* by his father?

DISCIPLINES (DISCIPLINE)
Dt 8: 5 your heart that as a man *d* his son,
Pr 3:12 the LORD *d* those he loves,
Heb 12: 6 because the Lord *d* those he loves,
12:10 but God *d* us for our good,

DISCLOSED
Lk 8:17 is nothing hidden that will not be *d,*

DISCOURAGED
Jos 1: 9 Do not be terrified; do not be *d,*
10:25 "Do not be afraid; do not be *d.*
1Ch 28:20 or *d,* for the LORD God,
Isa 42: 4 he will not falter or be *d*
Col 3:21 children, or they will become *d.*

DISCREDITED
2Co 6: 3 so that our ministry will not be *d.*

DISCRETION*
1Ch 22:12 May the LORD give you *d*
Pr 1: 4 knowledge and *d* to the young—
2:11 *D* will protect you,
5: 2 that you may maintain *d*
8:12 I possess knowledge and *d.*
11:22 a beautiful woman who shows no *d.*

DISCRIMINATED*
Jas 2: 4 have you not *d* among yourselves

DISFIGURED
Isa 52:14 his appearance was so *d*

DISGRACE (DISGRACEFUL DISGRACES)
Pr 11: 2 When pride comes, then comes *d,*
14:34 but sin is a *d* to any people.
19:26 is a son who brings shame and *d.*
Ac 5:41 of suffering *d* for the Name.
Heb 13:13 the camp, bearing the *d* he bore.

DISGRACEFUL (DISGRACE)
Pr 10: 5 during harvest is a *d* son.
17: 2 wise servant will rule over a *d* son,

DISGRACES (DISGRACE)
Pr 28: 7 of gluttons *d* his father.
29:15 but a child left to itself *d* his mother

DISHONEST
Pr 11: 1 The LORD abhors *d* scales,
29:27 The righteous detest the *d;*
Lk 16:10 whoever is *d* with very little will
1Ti 3: 8 wine, and not pursuing *d* gain.

DISHONOR (DISHONORS)
Lev 18: 7 " 'Do not *d* your father
Pr 30: 9 and so *d* the name of my God.
1Co 15:43 it is sown in *d,* it is raised in glory;

DISHONORS (DISHONOR)
Dt 27:16 Cursed is the man who *d* his father

DISMAYED
Isa 28:16 the one who trusts will never be *d.*
41:10 do not be *d,* for I am your God.

DISOBEDIENCE (DISOBEY)
Ro 5:19 as through the *d* of the one man
11:32 to *d* so that he may have mercy
Heb 2: 2 and *d* received its just punishment,
4: 6 go in, because of their *d.*
4:11 fall by following their example of *d.*

DISOBEDIENT (DISOBEY)
2Ti 3: 2 proud, abusive, *d* to their parents,
Tit 1: 6 to the charge of being wild and *d.*
1:16 *d* and unfit for doing anything

DISOBEY (DISOBEDIENCE DISOBEDIENT)
Dt 11:28 the curse if you *d* the commands
2Ch 24:20 'Why do you *d* the LORD's
Ro 1:30 they *d* their parents; they are

DISORDER
1Co 14:33 For God is not a God of *d*
2Co 12:20 slander, gossip, arrogance and *d.*
Jas 3:16 there you find *d* and every evil

DISOWN
Pr 30: 9 I may have too much and *d* you
Mt 10:33 I will *d* him before my Father
26:35 to die with you, I will never *d* you."
2Ti 2:12 If we *d* him,

DISPLAY (DISPLAYS)
Eze 39:21 I will *d* my glory among the nations
1Ti 1:16 Christ Jesus might *d* his unlimited

DISPLAYS (DISPLAY)
Isa 44:23 he *d* his glory in Israel.

DISPUTE (DISPUTES)
Pr 17:14 before a *d* breaks out.
1Co 6: 1 If any of you has a *d* with another,

DISPUTES (DISPUTE)
Pr 18:18 Casting the lot settles *d*

DISQUALIFIED
1Co 9:27 I myself will not be *d* for the prize.

DISREPUTE*
2Pe 2: 2 will bring the way of truth into *d.*

DISSENSION*
Pr 6:14 he always stirs up *d.*
6:19 and a man who stirs up *d*
10:12 Hatred stirs up *d,*
15:18 A hot-tempered man stirs up *d,*
16:28 A perverse man stirs up *d,*
28:25 A greedy man stirs up *d,*
29:22 An angry man stirs up *d,*
Ro 13:13 debauchery, not in *d* and jealousy.

DISSIPATION*
Lk 21:34 will be weighed down with *d,*
1Pe 4: 4 with them into the same flood of *d,*

DISTINGUISH
1Ki 3: 9 and to *d* between right and wrong.
Heb 5:14 themselves to *d* good from evil.

DISTORT
2Co 4: 2 nor do we *d* the word of God.
2Pe 3:16 ignorant and unstable people *d,*

DISTRESS (DISTRESSED)
Ps 18: 6 In my *d* I called to the LORD;
Jnh 2: 2 "In my *d* I called to the LORD,
Jas 1:27 after orphans and widows in their *d*

DISTRESSED (DISTRESS)
Ro 14:15 If your brother is *d*

DIVIDED (DIVISION)
Mt 12:25 household *d* against itself will not
Lk 23:34 they *d* up his clothes by casting lots
1Co 1:13 Is Christ *d?* Was Paul crucified

DIVINATION
Lev 19:26 " 'Do not practice *d* or sorcery.

DIVINE
Ro 1:20 his eternal power and *d* nature—
2Co 10: 4 they have *d* power
2Pe 1: 4 you may participate in the *d* nature

DIVISION (DIVIDED DIVISIONS DIVISIVE)
Lk 12:51 on earth? No, I tell you, but *d.*
1Co 12:25 so that there should be no *d*

DIVISIONS (DIVISION)
Ro 16:17 to watch out for those who cause *d*
1Co 1:10 another so that there may be no *d*
11:18 there are *d* among you,

DIVISIVE* (DIVISION)
Tit 3:10 Warn a *d* person once,

DIVORCE
Mal 2:16 "I hate *d,*" says the LORD God
Mt 19: 3 for a man to *d* his wife for any
1Co 7:11 And a husband must not *d* his wife.
7:27 Are you married? Do not seek a *d.*

DOCTOR
Mt 9:12 "It is not the healthy who need a *d,*

DOCTRINE
1Ti 4:16 Watch your life and *d* closely.
Tit 2: 1 is in accord with sound *d.*

DOMINION
Ps 22:28 for *d* belongs to the LORD

DOOR
Ps 141: 3 keep watch over the *d* of my lips.
Mt 6: 6 close the *d* and pray to your Father
7: 7 and the *d* will be opened to you.
Rev 3:20 I stand at the *d* and knock.

DOORKEEPER
Ps 84:10 I would rather be a *d* in the house

DOUBLE-EDGED
Heb 4:12 Sharper than any *d* sword,
Rev 1:16 of his mouth came a sharp *d* sword.
2:12 of him who has the sharp, *d* sword.

DOUBLE-MINDED (MIND)
Ps119:113 I hate *d* men,
Jas 1: 8 he is a *d* man, unstable

DOUBT
Mt 14:31 he said, "why did you *d?*"
21:21 if you have faith and do not *d,*
Mk 11:23 and does not *d* in his heart
Jas 1: 6 he must believe and not *d,*
Jude :22 Be merciful to those who *d;*

DOWNCAST
Ps 42: 5 Why are you *d,* O my soul?
2Co 7: 6 But God, who comforts the *d,*

DRAW (DRAWING DRAWS)
Mt 26:52 "for all who *d* the sword will die
Jn 12:32 up from the earth, will *d* all men
Heb 10:22 let us *d* near to God

DRAWING (DRAW)
Lk 21:28 because your redemption is *d* near

DRAWS (DRAW)
Jn 6:44 the Father who sent me *d* him,

DREADFUL
Heb 10:31 It is a *d* thing to fall into the hands

DRESS
1Ti 2: 9 I also want women to *d* modestly,

DRINK (DRUNK DRUNKARDS DRUNKENNESS)
Pr 5:15 *D* water from your own cistern,
Lk 12:19 Take life easy; eat, *d* and be merry
Jn 7:37 let him come to me and *d.*
1Co 12:13 were all given the one Spirit to *d.*
Rev 21: 6 to *d* without cost from the spring

DRIVES
1Jn 4:18 But perfect love *d* out fear,

DROP
Pr 17:14 so *d* the matter before a dispute
Isa 40:15 Surely the nations are like a *d*

DRUNK (DRINK)
Eph 5:18 Do not get *d* on wine, which leads

DRUNKARDS (DRINK)
Pr 23:21 for *d* and gluttons become poor,
1Co 6:10 nor the greedy nor *d* nor slanderers

DRUNKENNESS (DRINK)
Lk 21:34 weighed down with dissipation, *d*
Ro 13:13 and *d,* not in sexual immorality
Gal 5:21 factions and envy; *d,* orgies,
1Pe 4: 3 living in debauchery, lust, *d,* orgies,

DRY
Isa 53: 2 and like a root out of *d* ground.
Eze 37: 4 '*D* bones, hear the word

DUST
Ge 2: 7 man from the *d* of the ground
Ps 103:14 he remembers that we are *d.*
Ecc 3:20 all come from *d,* and to *d* all return.

DUTY
Ecc 12:13 for this is the whole *d* of man.
Ac 23: 1 I have fulfilled my *d* to God
1Co 7: 3 husband should fulfill his marital *d*

DWELL (DWELLING)
1Ki 8:27 "But will God really *d* on earth?
Ps 23: 6 I will *d* in the house of the LORD
Isa 43:18 do not *d* on the past.
Eph 3:17 so that Christ may *d* in your hearts
Col 1:19 to have all his fullness *d* in him,
3:16 the word of Christ *d* in you richly

DWELLING (DWELL)
Eph 2:22 to become a *d* in which God lives

EAGER
Pr 31:13 and works with *e* hands.
1Pe 5: 2 greedy for money, but *e* to serve;

EAGLE'S (EAGLES)
Ps 103: 5 your youth is renewed like the *e.*

EAGLES (EAGLE'S)
Isa 40:31 They will soar on wings like *e;*

EAR (EARS)
1Co 2: 9 no *e* has heard,
12:16 if the *e* should say, "Because I am

EARNED
Pr 31:31 Give her the reward she has *e,*

EARS (EAR)
Job 42: 5 My *e* had heard of you
Ps 34:15 and his *e* are attentive to their cry;
Pr 21:13 If a man shuts his *e* to the cry
2Ti 4: 3 to say what their itching *e* want

EARTH (EARTHLY)
Ge 1: 1 God created the heavens and the *e.*
Ps 24: 1 *e* is the LORD's, and everything
108: 5 and let your glory be over all the *e.*
Isa 6: 3 the whole *e* is full of his glory."
51: 6 the *e* will wear out like a garment
55: 9 the heavens are higher than the *e,*
66: 1 and the *e* is my footstool.
Jer 23:24 "Do not I fill heaven and *e?*"
Hab 2:20 let all the *e* be silent before him."
Mt 6:10 done on *e* as it is in heaven.
16:19 bind on *e* will be bound
24:35 Heaven and *e* will pass away,
28:18 and on *e* has been given to me.
Lk 2:14 on *e* peace to men
1Co 10:26 The *e* is the Lord's, and everything
Php 2:10 in heaven and on *e* and under the *e,*
2Pe 3:13 to a new heaven and a new *e,*

EARTHLY (EARTH)
Php 3:19 Their mind is on *e* things.
Col 3: 2 on things above, not on *e* things.

EAST
Ps 103:12 as far as the *e* is from the west,

EASY
Mt 11:30 For my yoke is *e* and my burden is

EAT (EATING)
Ge 2:17 but you must not *e* from the tree
Isa 55: 1 come, buy and *e!*
65:25 and the lion will *e* straw like the ox,
Mt 26:26 "Take and *e;* this is my body."
Ro 14: 2 faith allows him to *e* everything,
1Co 8:13 if what I *e* causes my brother to fall
10:31 So whether you *e* or drink
2Th 3:10 man will not work, he shall not *e."*

EATING (EAT)
Ro 14:17 kingdom of God is not a matter of *e*

EDICT
Heb 11:23 they were not afraid of the king's *e.*

EDIFIES
1Co 14: 4 but he who prophesies *e* the church

EFFECT
Isa 32:17 *e* of righteousness will be quietness
Heb 9:18 put into *e* without blood.

EFFORT
Lk 13:24 "Make every *e* to enter
Ro 9:16 depend on man's desire or *e,*
14:19 make every *e* to do what leads
Eph 4: 3 Make every *e* to keep the unity
Heb 4:11 make every *e* to enter that rest,
12:14 Make every *e* to live in peace
2Pe 1: 5 make every *e* to add
3:14 make every *e* to be found spotless,

ELAH
Son of Baasha; king of Israel (1Ki 16:6-14).

ELDERLY* (ELDERS)
Lev 19:32 show respect for the *e*

ELDERS (ELDERLY)
1Ti 5:17 The *e* who direct the affairs

ELECTION
Ro 9:11 God's purpose in *e* might stand:
2Pe 1:10 to make your calling and *e* sure.

ELI
High priest in youth of Samuel (1Sa 1-4). Blessed Hannah (1Sa 1:12-18); raised Samuel (1Sa 2:11-26).

ELIJAH
Prophet; predicted famine in Israel (1Ki 17:1; Jas 5:17). Fed by ravens (1Ki 17:2-6). Raised Sidonian widow's son (1Ki 17:7-24). Defeated prophets of Baal at Carmel (1Ki 18:16-46). Ran from Jezebel (1Ki 19:1-9). Prophesied death of Azariah (2Ki 1). Succeeded by Elishah (1Ki 19:19-21; 2Ki 2:1-18). Taken to heaven in whirlwind (2Ki 2:11-12).
Return prophesied (Mal 4:5-6); equated with John the Baptist (Mt 17:9-13; Mk 9:9-13; Lk 1:17). Appeared with Moses in transfiguration of Jesus (Mt 17:1-8; Mk 9:1-8).

ELISHA
Prophet; successor of Elijah (1Ki 19:16-21); inherited his cloak (2Ki 2:1-18). Miracles of (2Ki 2-6).

ELIZABETH*
Mother of John the Baptist, relative of Mary (Lk 1:5-58).

EMBITTER*
Col 3:21 Fathers, do not *e* your children,

EMPTY
Eph 5: 6 no one deceive you with *e* words,
1Pe 1:18 from the *e* way of life handed

ENABLE (ABLE)
Lk 1:74 to *e* us to serve him without fear
Ac 4:29 *e* your servants to speak your word

ENABLED (ABLE)
Lev 26:13 *e* you to walk with heads held high.
Jn 6:65 unless the Father has *e* him."

ENABLES (ABLE)
Php 3:21 by the power that *e* him

ENCAMPS*
Ps 34: 7 The angel of the LORD *e*

ENCOURAGE (ENCOURAGEMENT)
Ps 10:17 you *e* them, and you listen
Isa 1:17 *e* the oppressed.
Ac 15:32 to *e* and strengthen the brothers.
Ro 12: 8 if it is encouraging, let him *e;*
1Th 4:18 Therefore *e* each other
2Ti 4: 2 rebuke and *e*— with great patience
Tit 2: 6 *e* the young men to be
Heb 3:13 But *e* one another daily, as long
10:25 but let us *e* one another—

ENCOURAGEMENT (ENCOURAGE)
Ac 4:36 Barnabas (which means Son of *E),*
Ro 15: 4 *e* of the Scriptures we might have
15: 5 and *e* give you a spirit of unity
1Co 14: 3 to men for their strengthening, *e*
Heb 12: 5 word of *e* that addresses you

END
Ps 119:33 then I will keep them to the *e.*
Pr 14:12 but in the *e* it leads to death.
19:20 and in the *e* you will be wise.
23:32 In the *e* it bites like a snake
Ecc 12:12 making many books there is no *e,*
Mt 10:22 firm to the *e* will be saved.
Lk 21: 9 but the *e* will not come right away
Ro 10: 4 Christ is the *e* of the law
1Co 15:24 the *e* will come, when he hands

ENDURANCE (ENDURE)
Ro 15: 4 through *e* and the encouragement
15: 5 May the God who gives *e*
2Co 1: 6 which produces in you patient *e*
Col 1:11 might so that you may have great *e*
1Ti 6:11 faith, love, *e* and gentleness.
Tit 2: 2 and sound in faith, in love and in *e.*

ENDURE (ENDURANCE ENDURES)
Ps 72:17 May his name *e* forever;
Pr 12:19 Truthful lips *e* forever,
27:24 for riches do not *e* forever,
Ecc 3:14 everything God does will *e* forever;
Mal 3: 2 who can *e* the day of his coming?
2Ti 2: 3 *E* hardship with us like a good
2:12 if we *e,* / we will also reign
Heb 12: 7 *E* hardship as discipline; God is
Rev 3:10 kept my command to *e* patiently,

ENDURES (ENDURE)
Ps 112: 9 his righteousness *e* forever;
136: 1 *His love e forever.*
Da 9:15 made for yourself a name that *e*

ENEMIES (ENEMY)
Ps 23: 5 in the presence of my *e.*
Mic 7: 6 a man's *e* are the members
Mt 5:44 Love your *e* and pray
Lk 20:43 hand until I make your *e*

ENEMY (ENEMIES ENMITY)
Pr 24:17 Do not gloat when your *e* falls;
25:21 If your *e* is hungry, give him food
27: 6 but an *e* multiplies kisses.
1Co 15:26 The last *e* to be destroyed is death.
1Ti 5:14 and to give the *e* no opportunity

ENJOY (JOY)
Dt 6: 2 and so that you may *e* long life.
Eph 6: 3 and that you may *e* long life
Heb 11:25 rather than to *e* the pleasures of sin

ENJOYMENT (JOY)
Ecc 4: 8 and why am I depriving myself of *e*
1Ti 6:17 us with everything for our *e.*

ENLIGHTENED* (LIGHT)
Eph 1:18 that the eyes of your heart may be *e*
Heb 6: 4 for those who have once been *e,*

ENMITY* (ENEMY)
Ge 3:15 And I will put *e*

ENOCH
Walked with God and taken by him (Ge 5:18-24; Heb 11:5). Prophet (Jude 14).

ENTANGLED (ENTANGLES)
2Pe 2:20 and are again *e* in it and overcome,

ENTANGLES* (ENTANGLED)
Heb 12: 1 and the sin that so easily *e,*

ENTER (ENTERED ENTERS ENTRANCE)
Ps 100: 4 *E* his gates with thanksgiving
Mt 5:20 will certainly not *e* the kingdom
7:13 *"E* through the narrow gate.
18: 8 It is better for you to *e* life maimed
Mk 10:15 like a little child will never *e* it."
10:23 is for the rich to *e* the kingdom

ENTERED (ENTER)
Ro 5:12 as sin *e* the world through one man,
Heb 9:12 but he *e* the Most Holy Place once

ENTERS (ENTER)
Mk 7:18 you see that nothing that *e* a man
Jn 10: 2 The man who *e* by the gate is

ENTERTAIN
1Ti 5:19 Do not *e* an accusation
Heb 13: 2 Do not forget to *e* strangers,

ENTHRALLED*
Ps 45:11 The king is *e* by your beauty;

ENTHRONED (THRONE)
1Sa 4: 4 who is *e* between the cherubim.
Ps 2: 4 The One *e* in heaven laughs;
102:12 But you, O LORD, sit *e* forever;
Isa 40:22 He sits *e* above the circle

ENTICE
Pr 1:10 My son, if sinners *e* you,
2Pe 2:18 they *e* people who are just escaping

ENTIRE
Gal 5:14 The *e* law is summed up

ENTRUSTED (TRUST)
1Ti 6:20 guard what has been *e* to your care.
2Ti 1:12 able to guard what I have *e* to him
1:14 Guard the good deposit that was *e*
Jude :3 once for all *e* to the saints.

ENVY
Pr 3:31 Do not *e* a violent man
14:30 but *e* rots the bones.
1Co 13:4 It does not *e,* it does not boast,

EPHRAIM
1. Second son of Joseph (Ge 41:52; 46:20). Blessed as firstborn by Jacob (Ge 48).
2. Synonymous with Northern Kingdom (Isa 7:17; Hos 5).

EQUAL
Isa 40:25 who is my *e?"* says the Holy One.
Jn 5:18 making himself *e* with God.
1Co 12:25 that its parts should have *e* concern

EQUIP* (EQUIPPED)
Heb 13:21 *e* you with everything good

EQUIPPED (EQUIP)
2Ti 3:17 man of God may be thoroughly *e*

ERROR
Jas 5:20 Whoever turns a sinner from the *e*

ESAU
Firstborn of Isaac, twin of Jacob (Ge 25:21-26). Also called Edom (Ge 25:30). Sold Jacob his birthright (Ge 25:29-34); lost blessing (Ge 27). Reconciled to Jacob (Gen 33).

ESCAPE (ESCAPING)
Ro 2:3 think you will *e* God's judgment?
Heb 2:3 how shall we *e* if we ignore such

ESCAPING (ESCAPE)
1Co 3:15 only as one *e* through the flames.

ESTABLISH
Ge 6:18 But I will *e* my covenant with you,
1Ch 28:7 I will *e* his kingdom forever
Ro 10:3 God and sought to *e* their own,

ESTEEMED
Pr 22:1 to be *e* is better than silver or gold.
Isa 53:3 he was despised, and we *e* him not.

ESTHER
Jewess who lived in Persia; cousin of Mordecai (Est 2:7). Chosen queen of Xerxes (Est 2:8-18). Foiled Haman's plan to exterminate the Jews (Est 3-4; 7-9).

ETERNAL (ETERNALLY ETERNITY)
Ps 16:11 with *e* pleasures at your right hand.
111:10 To him belongs *e* praise.
119:89 Your word, O LORD, is *e;*
Isa 26:4 LORD, the LORD, is the Rock *e.*
Mt 19:16 good thing must I do to get *e* life?"
25:41 into the *e* fire prepared for the devil
25:46 they will go away to *e* punishment,
Jn 3:15 believes in him may have *e* life.
3:16 him shall not perish but have *e* life.
3:36 believes in the Son has *e* life,
4:14 spring of water welling up to *e* life."
5:24 believes him who sent me has *e* life
Jn 6:68 You have the words of *e* life.
10:28 I give them *e* life, and they shall
17:3 this is *e* life: that they may know
Ro 1:20 his *e* power and divine nature—
6:23 but the gift of God is *e* life
2Co 4:17 for us an *e* glory that far outweighs
4:18 temporary, but what is unseen is *e.*
1Ti 1:16 believe on him and receive *e* life.
1:17 Now to the King *e,* immortal,
Heb 9:12 having obtained *e* redemption.
1Jn 5:11 God has given us *e* life,
5:13 you may know that you have *e* life.

ETERNALLY (ETERNAL)
Gal 1:8 let him be *e* condemned! As we

ETERNITY (ETERNAL)
Ps 93:2 you are from all *e.*
Ecc 3:11 also set *e* in the hearts of men;

ETHIOPIAN
Jer 13:23 Can the *E* change his skin

EUNUCHS
Mt 19:12 For some are *e* because they were

EVANGELIST (EVANGELISTS)
2Ti 4:5 hardship, do the work of an *e,*

EVANGELISTS* (EVANGELIST)
Eph 4:11 some to be prophets, some to be *e,*

EVE
2Co 11:3 as *E* was deceived by the serpent's
1Ti 2:13 For Adam was formed first, then *E*

EVEN-TEMPERED*
Pr 17:27 and a man of understanding is *e.*

EVER (EVERLASTING FOREVER)
Ex 15:18 LORD will reign for *e* and *e."*
Dt 8:19 If you *e* forget the LORD your
Ps 5:11 let them *e* sing for joy.
10:16 The LORD is King for *e* and *e;*
25:3 will *e* be put to shame,
26:3 for your love is *e* before me,
45:6 O God, will last for *e* and *e;*
52:8 God's unfailing love for *e* and *e.*
89:33 nor will I *e* betray my faithfulness.
145:1 I will praise your name for *e* and *e.*
Pr 4:18 shining *e* brighter till the full light
5:19 may you *e* be captivated
Isa 66:8 Who has *e* heard of such a thing?
Jer 31:36 the descendants of Israel *e* cease
Da 7:18 it forever—yes, for *e* and *e.'*
12:3 like the stars for *e* and *e.*
Mk 4:12 *e* hearing but never understanding;
Jn 1:18 No one has *e* seen God,
Rev 1:18 and behold I am alive for *e* and *e!*
22:5 And they will reign for *e* and *e.*

EVER-INCREASING* (INCREASE)
Ro 6:19 to impurity and to *e* wickedness,
2Co 3:18 into his likeness with *e* glory,

EVERLASTING (EVER)
Dt 33:27 and underneath are the *e* arms.
Ne 9:5 your God, who is from *e* to *e."*
Ps 90:2 from *e* to *e* you are God.
139:24 and lead me in the way *e.*
Isa 9:6 *E* Father, Prince of Peace.
33:14 Who of us can dwell with *e* burning
35:10 *e* joy will crown their heads.
45:17 the LORD with an *e* salvation;
54:8 but with *e* kindness
55:3 I will make an *e* covenant with you,
Isa 63:12 to gain for himself *e* renown,
Jer 31:3 "I have loved you with an *e* love;
Da 9:24 to bring in *e* righteousness,
12:2 some to *e* life, others to shame
Jn 6:47 the truth, he who believes has *e* life.
2Th 1:9 punished with *e* destruction
Jude :6 bound with *e* chains for judgment

EVER-PRESENT*
Ps 46:1 an *e* help in trouble

EVIDENCE (EVIDENT)
Jn 14:11 on the *e* of the miracles themselves.

EVIDENT (EVIDENCE)
Php 4:5 Let your gentleness be *e* to all.

EVIL
Ge 2:9 of the knowledge of good and *e.*
Job 1:1 he feared God and shunned *e.*
1:8 a man who fears God and shuns *e."*
34:10 Far be it from God to do *e,*
Ps 23:4 I will fear no *e,*
34:14 Turn from *e* and do good;
51:4 and done what is *e* in your sight,
97:10 those who love the LORD hate *e,*
101:4 I will have nothing to do with *e.*
Pr 8:13 To fear the LORD is to hate *e;*
10:23 A fool finds pleasure in *e* conduct,
11:27 *e* comes to him who searches for it.
24:19 Do not fret because of *e* men
24:20 for the *e* man has no future hope,
Isa 5:20 Woe to those who call *e* good
13:11 I will punish the world for its *e,*
55:7 and the *e* man his thoughts.
Hab 1:13 Your eyes are too pure to look on *e;*
Mt 5:45 He causes his sun to rise on the *e*
6:13 but deliver us from the *e* one.'
7:11 If you, then, though you are *e,*
12:35 and the *e* man brings *e* things out
Jn 17:15 you protect them from the *e* one.
Ro 2:9 for every human being who does *e:*
12:9 Hate what is *e;* cling
12:17 Do not repay anyone *e* for *e.*
16:19 and innocent about what is *e.*
1Co 13:6 Love does not delight in *e*
14:20 In regard to *e* be infants,
Eph 6:16 all the flaming arrows of the *e* one.
1Th 5:22 Avoid every kind of *e.*
1Ti 6:10 of money is a root of all kinds of *e.*
2Ti 2:22 Flee the *e* desires of youth,
Jas 1:13 For God cannot be tempted by *e,*
1Pe 2:16 your freedom as a cover-up for *e;*
3:9 Do not repay *e* with *e* or insult

EXACT
Heb 1:3 the *e* representation of his being,

EXALT (EXALTED EXALTS)
Ps 30:1 I will *e* you, O LORD,
34:3 let us *e* his name together.
118:28 you are my God, and I will *e* you.
Isa 24:15 *e* the name of the LORD, the God

EXALTED (EXALT)
2Sa 22:47 *E* be God, the Rock, my Savior!
1Ch 29:11 you are *e* as head over all.
Ne 9:5 and may it be *e* above all blessing
Ps 21:13 Be *e,* O LORD, in your strength;
46:10 I will be *e* among the nations,
57:5 Be *e,* O God, above the heavens;
97:9 you are *e* far above all gods.
99:2 he is *e* over all the nations.
108:5 Be *e,* O God, above the heavens,
148:13 for his name alone is *e;*

Isa 6: 1 *e,* and the train of his robe filled
12: 4 and proclaim that his name is *e.*
33: 5 The LORD is *e,* for he dwells
Eze 21:26 The lowly will be *e* and the *e* will be
Mt 23:12 whoever humbles himself will be *e.*
Php 1:20 always Christ will be *e* in my body,
2: 9 Therefore God *e* him

EXALTS (EXALT)
Ps 75: 7 He brings one down, he *e* another.
Pr 14:34 Righteousness *e* a nation,
Mt 23:12 For whoever *e* himself will be

EXAMINE (EXAMINED)
Ps 26: 2 *e* my heart and my mind;
Jer 17:10 and *e* the mind,
La 3:40 Let us *e* our ways and test them,
1Co 11:28 A man ought to *e* himself
2Co 13: 5 *E* yourselves to see whether you

EXAMINED (EXAMINE)
Ac 17: 11 *e* the Scriptures every day to see

EXAMPLE (EXAMPLES)
Jn 13:15 have set you an *e* that you should
1Co 11: 1 Follow my *e,* as I follow
1Ti 4:12 set an *e* for the believers in speech,
Tit 2: 7 In everything set them an *e*
1Pe 2:21 leaving you an *e,* that you should

EXAMPLES* (EXAMPLE)
1Co 10: 6 Now these things occurred as *e*
10: 11 as *e* and were written down
1Pe 5: 3 to you, but being *e* to the flock.

EXASPERATE*
Eph 6: 4 Fathers, do not *e* your children;

EXCEL (EXCELLENT)
1Co 14:12 to *e* in gifts that build up the church
2Co 8: 7 But just as you *e* in everything—

EXCELLENT (EXCEL)
1Co 12:31 now I will show you the most *e* way
Php 4: 8 if anything is *e* or praiseworthy—
1Ti 3:13 have served well gain an *e* standing
Tit 3: 8 These things are *e* and profitable

EXCHANGED
Ro 1:23 *e* the glory of the immortal God
1:25 They *e* the truth of God for a lie,

EXCUSE (EXCUSES)
Jn 15:22 they have no *e* for their sin.
Ro 1:20 so that men are without *e.*

EXCUSES* (EXCUSE)
Lk 14:18 "But they all alike began to make *e.*

EXISTS
Heb 2:10 and through whom everything *e,*
11: 6 to him must believe that he *e*

EXPECT (EXPECTATION)
Mt 24:44 at an hour when you do not *e* him.

EXPECTATION (EXPECT)
Ro 8:19 waits in eager *e* for the sons
Heb 10:27 but only a fearful *e* of judgment

EXPEL*
1Co 5:13 *E* the wicked man from among you

EXPENSIVE
1Ti 2: 9 or gold or pearls or *e* clothes,

EXPLOIT
Pr 22:22 Do not *e* the poor because they are
2Co 12:17 Did I *e* you through any

EXPOSE
1Co 4: 5 will *e* the motives of men's hearts.
Eph 5: 11 of darkness, but rather *e* them.

EXTENDS
Pr 31:20 and *e* her hands to the needy.
Lk 1:50 His mercy *e* to those who fear him,

EXTINGUISHED
2Sa 21:17 the lamp of Israel will not be *e.*"

EXTOL*
Job 36:24 Remember to *e* his work,
Ps 34: 1 I will *e* the LORD at all times;
68: 4 *e* him who rides on the clouds—
95: 2 and *e* him with music and song.
109:30 mouth I will greatly *e* the LORD;
111: 1 I will *e* the LORD with all my heart
115:18 it is we who *e* the LORD,
117: 1 *e* him, all you peoples.
145: 2 and *e* your name for ever and ever.
145:10 your saints will *e* you.
147:12 *E* the LORD, O Jerusalem;

EXTORT*
Lk 3:14 "Don't *e* money and don't accuse

EYE (EYES)
Ex 21:24 you are to take life for life, *e* for *e,*
Ps 94: 9 Does he who formed the *e* not see?
Mt 5:29 If your right *e* causes you to sin,
5:38 *'E* for *e,* and tooth for tooth.'
7: 3 of sawdust in your brother's *e*
1Co 2: 9 "No *e* has seen,
Col 3:22 not only when their *e* is on you
Rev 1: 7 and every *e* will see him,

EYES (EYE)
Nu 33:55 remain will become barbs in your *e*
Jos 23:13 on your backs and thorns in your *e,*
2Ch 16: 9 For the *e* of the LORD range
Job 31: 1 "I made a covenant with my *e*
36: 7 He does not take his *e*
Ps 119:18 Open my *e* that I may see
121: 1 I lift up my *e* to the hills—
141: 8 But my *e* are fixed on you,
Pr 3: 7 Do not be wise in your own *e;*
4:25 Let your *e* look straight ahead,
15: 3 The *e* of the LORD are everywhere
Isa 6: 5 and my *e* have seen the King,
Hab 1:13 Your *e* are too pure to look on evil;
Jn 4:35 open your *e* and look at the fields!
2Co 4:18 So we fix our *e* not on what is seen,
Heb 12: 2 Let us fix our *e* on Jesus, the author
Jas 2: 5 poor in the *e* of the world to be rich
1Pe 3:12 For the *e* of the Lord are
Rev 7:17 wipe away every tear from their *e.*"
21: 4 He will wipe every tear from their *e*

EZEKIEL
Priest called to be prophet to the exiles (Eze 1-3).

EZRA
Priest and teacher of the Law who led a return of exiles to Israel to reestablish temple and worship (Ezr 7-8). Corrected intermarriage of priests (Ezr 9-10). Read Law at celebration of Feast of Tabernacles (Neh 8).

FACE (FACES)
Ge 32:30 "It is because I saw God *f* to *f,*
Ex 34:29 was not aware that his *f* was radiant
Nu 6:25 the LORD make his *f* shine
1Ch 16: 11 seek his *f* always.
2Ch 7:14 and seek my *f* and turn
Ps 4: 6 Let the light of your *f* shine upon us
27: 8 Your *f,* LORD, I will seek.
31:16 Let your *f* shine on your servant;
105: 4 seek his *f* always.
119:135 Make your *f* shine
Isa 50: 7 Therefore have I set my *f* like flint,
Mt 17: 2 His *f* shone like the sun,
1Co 13:12 mirror; then we shall see *f* to *f.*
2Co 4: 6 the glory of God in the *f* of Christ.
1Pe 3:12 but the *f* of the Lord is
Rev 1:16 His *f* was like the sun shining

FACES (FACE)
2Co 3:18 who with unveiled *f* all reflect

FACTIONS
Gal 5:20 selfish ambition, dissensions, *f*

FADE
1Pe 5: 4 of glory that will never *f* away.

FAIL (FAILING FAILINGS FAILS)
1Ch 28:20 He will not *f* you or forsake you
2Ch 34:33 they did not *f* to follow the LORD,
Ps 89:28 my covenant with him will never *f.*
Pr 15:22 Plans *f* for lack of counsel,
Isa 51: 6 my righteousness will never *f.*
La 3:22 for his compassions never *f.*
2Co 13: 5 unless, of course, you *f* the test?

FAILING (FAIL)
1Sa 12:23 sin against the LORD by *f* to pray

FAILINGS (FAIL)
Ro 15: 1 ought to bear with the *f* of the weak

FAILS (FAIL)
1Co 13: 8 Love never *f.*

FAINT
Isa 40:31 they will walk and not be *f.*

FAIR
Pr 1: 3 doing what is right and just and *f;*
Col 4: 1 slaves with what is right and *f,*

FAITH (FAITHFUL FAITHFULLY FAITHFULNESS FAITHLESS)
2Ch 20:20 Have *f* in the LORD your God
Hab 2: 4 but the righteous will live by his *f*—
Mt 9:29 According to your *f* will it be done
17:20 if you have *f* as small as a mustard
24:10 many will turn away from the *f*
Mk 11:22 "Have *f* in God," Jesus answered.
Lk 7: 9 I have not found such great *f*
12:28 will he clothe you, O you of little *f!*
17: 5 "Increase our *f!*" He replied,
18: 8 will he find *f* on the earth?"
Ac 14: 9 saw that he had *f* to be healed
14:27 the door of *f* to the Gentiles.
Ro 1:12 encouraged by each other's *f.*
1:17 is by *f* from first to last,
1:17 "The righteous will live by *f.*"
3: 3 What if some did not have *f?*

Ro 3:22 comes through *f* in Jesus Christ
3:25 a sacrifice of atonement, through *f*
4: 5 his *f* is credited as righteousness.
5: 1 we have been justified through *f*,
10:17 *f* comes from hearing the message,
14: 1 Accept him whose *f* is weak,
14:23 that does not come from *f* is sin.
1Co 13: 2 and if I have a *f* that can move
13:13 And now these three remain: *f*,
16:13 stand firm in the *f*; be men
2Co 5: 7 We live by *f*, not by sight.
13: 5 to see whether you are in the *f*;
Gal 2:16 Jesus that we may be justified by *f*
2:20 I live by *f* in the Son of God,
3: 11 "The righteous will live by *f*."
3:24 that we might be justified by *f*.
Eph 2: 8 through *f*— and this not
4: 5 one Lord, one *f*, one baptism;
6:16 to all this, take up the shield of *f*,
Col 1:23 continue in your *f*, established
1Th 5: 8 on *f* and love as a breastplate,
1Ti 2:15 if they continue in *f*, love
4: 1 later times some will abandon the *f*
5: 8 he has denied the *f* and is worse
6:12 Fight the good fight of the *f*.
2Ti 3:15 wise for salvation through *f*
4: 7 finished the race, I have kept the *f*.
Phm : 6 may be active in sharing your *f*,
Heb 10:38 But my righteous one will live by *f*.
11: 1 *f* is being sure of what we hope for
11: 3 By *f* we understand that
11: 5 By *f* Enoch was taken from this life
11: 6 And without *f* it is impossible
11: 7 By *f* Noah, when warned about
11: 8 By *f* Abraham, when called to go
11:17 By *f* Abraham, when God tested
11:20 By *f* Isaac blessed Jacob
11:21 By *f* Jacob, when he was dying,
11:22 By *f* Joseph, when his end was near
11:24 By *f* Moses, when he had grown up
11:31 By *f* the prostitute Rahab,
12: 2 the author and perfecter of our *f*,
Jas 2:14 if a man claims to have *f*
2:17 In the same way, *f* by itself,
2:26 so *f* without deeds is dead.
2Pe 1: 5 effort to add to your *f* goodness;
1Jn 5: 4 overcome the world, even our *f*.
Jude : 3 to contend for the *f* that was once

FAITHFUL (FAITH)
Nu 12: 7 he is *f* in all my house.
Dt 7: 9 your God is God; he is the *f* God,
32: 4 A *f* God who does no wrong,
2Sa 22:26 "To the *f* you show yourself *f*,
Ps 25:10 of the LORD are loving and *f*
31:23 The LORD preserves the *f*,
33: 4 he is *f* in all he does.
37:28 and will not forsake his *f* ones.
97:10 for he guards the lives of his *f* ones
145:13 The LORD is *f* to all his promises
146: 6 the LORD, who remains *f* forever.
Pr 31:26 and *f* instruction is on her tongue.
Mt 25:21 'Well done, good and *f* servant!
Ro 12:12 patient in affliction, *f* in prayer.
1Co 4: 2 been given a trust must prove *f*.
10:13 And God is *f*; he will not let you be
1Th 5:24 The one who calls you is *f*
2Ti 2:13 he will remain *f*,
Heb 3: 6 But Christ is *f* as a son
10:23 for he who promised is *f*.
1Pe 4:19 themselves to their *f* Creator
1Jn 1: 9 he is *f* and just and will forgive us
Rev 1: 5 who is the *f* witness, the firstborn
2:10 Be *f*, even to the point of death,
19: 11 whose rider is called *F* and True.

FAITHFULLY (FAITH)
Dt 11:13 if you *f* obey the commands I am
1Sa 12:24 and serve him *f* with all your heart;
1Ki 2: 4 and if they walk *f* before me
1Pe 4:10 *f* administering God's grace

FAITHFULNESS (FAITH)
Ps 57:10 your *f* reaches to the skies.
85:10 Love and *f* meet together;
86:15 to anger, abounding in love and *f*.
89: 1 mouth I will make your *f* known
89:14 love and *f* go before you.
91: 4 his *f* will be your shield
117: 2 the *f* of the LORD endures forever.
119:75 and in *f* you have afflicted me.
Pr 3: 3 Let love and *f* never leave you;
Isa 11: 5 and *f* the sash around his waist.
La 3:23 great is your *f*.
Ro 3: 3 lack of faith nullify God's *f*?
Gal 5:22 patience, kindness, goodness, *f*,

FAITHLESS (FAITH)
Ps 119:158 I look on the *f* with loathing,
Jer 3:22 "Return, *f* people;
Ro 1:31 they are senseless, *f*, heartless,
2Ti 2:13 if we are *f*,

FALL (FALLEN FALLING FALLS)
Ps 37:24 though he stumble, he will not *f*,
55:22 he will never let the righteous *f*.
69: 9 of those who insult you *f* on me.
Pr 11:28 Whoever trusts in his riches will *f*,
Lk 11:17 a house divided against itself will *f*.
Ro 3:23 and *f* short of the glory of God,
Heb 6: 6 if they *f* away, to be brought back

FALLEN (FALL)
2Sa 1:19 How the mighty have *f*!
Isa 14:12 How you have *f* from heaven,
1Co 15:20 of those who have *f* asleep.
Gal 5: 4 you have *f* away from grace.
1Th 4:15 precede those who have *f* asleep.

FALLING (FALL)
Jude :24 able to keep you from *f*

FALLS (FALL)
Pr 24:17 Do not gloat when your enemy *f*;
Jn 12:24 a kernel of wheat *f* to the ground
Ro 14: 4 To his own master he stands or *f*.

FALSE (FALSEHOOD FALSELY)
Ex 20:16 "You shall not give *f* testimony
23: 1 "Do not spread *f* reports.
Pr 13: 5 The righteous hate what is *f*,
19: 5 A *f* witness will not go unpunished,
Mt 7:15 "Watch out for *f* prophets.
19:18 not steal, do not give *f* testimony,
24: 11 and many *f* prophets will appear
Php 1:18 whether from *f* motives or true,
1Ti 1: 3 not to teach *f* doctrines any longer
2Pe 2: 1 there will be *f* teachers among you.

FALSEHOOD (FALSE)
Ps 119:163 I hate and abhor *f*
Pr 30: 8 Keep *f* and lies far from me;
Eph 4:25 each of you must put off *f*

FALSELY (FALSE)
Lev 19:12 " 'Do not swear *f* by my name
Lk 3:14 and don't accuse people *f*—
1Ti 6:20 ideas of what is *f* called knowledge,

FALTER*
Pr 24:10 If you *f* in times of trouble,
Isa 42: 4 he will not *f* or be discouraged

FAMILIES (FAMILY)
Ps 68: 6 God sets the lonely in *f*,

FAMILY (FAMILIES)
Pr 15:27 greedy man brings trouble to his *f*,
31:15 she provides food for her *f*
Lk 9:61 go back and say good-by to my *f*."
12:52 in one *f* divided against each other,
1Ti 3: 4 He must manage his own *f* well
3: 5 how to manage his own *f*,
5: 4 practice by caring for their own *f*
5: 8 and especially for his immediate *f*,

FAMINE
Ge 41:30 seven years of *f* will follow them.
Am 8: 11 but a *f* of hearing the words
Ro 8:35 or persecution or *f* or nakedness

FAN*
2Ti 1: 6 you to *f* into flame the gift of God,

FAST
Dt 13: 4 serve him and hold *f* to him.
Jos 22: 5 to hold *f* to him and to serve him
23: 8 to hold *f* to the LORD your God,
Ps 119:31 I hold *f* to your statutes, O LORD;
139:10 your right hand will hold me *f*.
Mt 6:16 "When you *f*, do not look somber
1Pe 5:12 Stand *f* in it.

FATHER (FATHER'S FATHERLESS FATHERS FOREFATHERS)
Ge 2:24 this reason a man will leave his *f*
17: 4 You will be the *f* of many nations.
Ex 20:12 "Honor your *f* and your mother,
21:15 "Anyone who attacks his *f*
21:17 "Anyone who curses his *f*
Lev 18: 7 " 'Do not dishonor your *f*
19: 3 you must respect his mother and *f*,
Dt 5:16 "Honor your *f* and your mother,
21:18 son who does not obey his *f*
Ps 27:10 Though my *f* and mother forsake
68: 5 A *f* to the fatherless, a defender
Pr 10: 1 A wise son brings joy to his *f*,
17:21 there is no joy for the *f* of a fool.
23:22 Listen to your *f*, who gave you life,
23:24 *f* of a righteous man has great joy;
28: 7 of gluttons disgraces his *f*.
29: 3 loves wisdom brings joy to his *f*,
Isa 9: 6 Everlasting *F*, Prince of Peace.
Mt 6: 9 " 'Our *F* in heaven,
10:37 "Anyone who loves his *f*
15: 4 'Honor your *f* and mother'
19: 5 this reason a man will leave his *f*
Lk 12:53 *f* against son and son against *f*,
23:34 Jesus said, "*F*, forgive them,
Jn 6:44 the *F* who sent me draws him,
6:46 No one has seen the *F*
8:44 You belong to your *f*, the devil,
10:30 I and the *F* are one."
14: 6 No one comes to the *F*
14: 9 who has seen me has seen the *F*.
Ro 4: 11 he is the *f* of all who believe
2Co 6:18 "I will be a *F* to you,
Eph 6: 2 "Honor your *f* and mother"—
Heb 12: 7 what son is not disciplined by his *f*?

FATHER'S (FATHER)
Pr 13: 1 A wise son heeds his *f* instruction,
15: 5 A fool spurns his *f* discipline,
19:13 A foolish son is his *f* ruin,
Lk 2:49 had to be in my *F* house?"
Jn 2:16 How dare you turn my *F* house
10:29 can snatch them out of my *F* hand.
14: 2 In my *F* house are many rooms;

FATHERLESS (FATHER)
Dt 10:18 He defends the cause of the *f*

Dt 24:17 Do not deprive the alien or the *f*
24:19 Leave it for the alien, the *f*
Ps 68: 5 A father to the *f*, a defender
Pr 23:10 or encroach on the fields of the *f*,

FATHERS (FATHER)
Ex 20: 5 for the sin of the *f* to the third
Lk 11:11 "Which of you *f*, if your son asks
Eph 6: 4 *F*, do not exasperate your children;
Col 3:21 *F*, do not embitter your children,

FATHOM*
Job 11: 7 "Can you *f* the mysteries of God?
Ps 145: 3 his greatness no one can *f*.
Ecc 3:11 yet they cannot *f* what God has
Isa 40:28 and his understanding no one can *f*
1Co 13: 2 and can *f* all mysteries and all

FAULT (FAULTS)
Mt 18:15 and show him his *f*, just
Php 2:15 of God without *f* in a crooked
Jas 1: 5 generously to all without finding *f*,
Jude :24 his glorious presence without *f*

FAULTFINDERS*
Jude :16 These men are grumblers and *f*;

FAULTS (FAULT)
Ps 19:12 Forgive my hidden *f*.

FAVORITISM*
Ex 23: 3 and do not show *f* to a poor man
Lev 19:15 to the poor or *f* to the great,
Ac 10:34 true it is that God does not show *f*
Ro 2:11 For God does not show *f*.
Eph 6: 9 and there is no *f* with him.
Col 3:25 for his wrong, and there is no *f*.
1Ti 5:21 and to do nothing out of *f*.
Jas 2: 1 Lord Jesus Christ, don't show *f*.
2: 9 But if you show *f*, you sin

FEAR (AFRAID FEARS)
Dt 6:13 *F* the LORD your God, serve him
10:12 but to *f* the LORD your God,
31:12 and learn to *f* the LORD your God
Ps 19: 9 The *f* of the LORD is pure,
23: 4 I will *f* no evil,
27: 1 whom shall I *f*?
91: 5 You will not *f* the terror of night,
111:10 *f* of the LORD is the beginning
Pr 8:13 To *f* the LORD is to hate evil;
9:10 *f* of the LORD is the beginning
10:27 The *f* of the LORD adds length
14:27 The *f* of the LORD is a fountain
15:33 *f* of the LORD teaches a man
16: 6 through the *f* of the LORD a man
19:23 The *f* of the LORD leads to life:
29:25 *F* of man will prove to be a snare,
Isa 11: 3 delight in the *f* of the LORD.
41:10 So do not *f*, for I am with you;
Lk 12: 5 I will show you whom you should *f*:
Php 2:12 to work out your salvation with *f*
1Jn 4:18 But perfect love drives out *f*,

FEARS (FEAR)
Job 1: 8 a man who *f* God and shuns evil."
Ps 34: 4 he delivered me from all my *f*.
Pr 31:30 a woman who *f* the LORD is
1Jn 4:18 The one who *f* is not made perfect

FEED
Jn 21:15 Jesus said, "*F* my lambs."
21:17 Jesus said, "*F* my sheep.
Ro 12:20 "If your enemy is hungry, *f* him;
Jude :12 shepherds who *f* only themselves.

FEET (FOOT)
Ps 8: 6 you put everything under his *f*:
22:16 have pierced my hands and my *f*.
40: 2 he set my *f* on a rock
Ps 110: 1 a footstool for your *f*."
119:105 Your word is a lamp to my *f*
Ro 10:15 "How beautiful are the *f*
1Co 12:21 And the head cannot say to the *f*,
15:25 has put all his enemies under his *f*.
Heb 12:13 "Make level paths for your *f*,"

FELLOWSHIP
2Co 6:14 what *f* can light have with darkness
13:14 and the *f* of the Holy Spirit be
Php 3:10 the *f* of sharing in his sufferings,
1Jn 1: 6 claim to have *f* with him yet walk
1: 7 we have *f* with one another,

FEMALE
Ge 1:27 male and *f* he created them.
Gal 3:28 *f*, for you are all one in Christ Jesus

FERVOR
Ro 12:11 but keep your spiritual *f*, serving

FIELD (FIELDS)
Mt 6:28 See how the lilies of the *f* grow.
13:38 *f* is the world, and the good seed
1Co 3: 9 you are God's *f*, God's building.

FIELDS (FIELD)
Lk 2: 8 were shepherds living out in the *f*
Jn 4:35 open your eyes and look at the *f*!

FIG (FIGS)
Ge 3: 7 so they sewed *f* leaves together

FIGHT (FOUGHT)
Ex 14:14 The LORD will *f* for you; you need
Dt 1:30 going before you, will *f* for you,
3:22 the LORD your God himself will *f*
Ne 4:20 Our God will *f* for us!"
Ps 35: 1 *f* against those who *f* against me.
Jn 18:36 my servants would *f*
1Co 9:26 I do not *f* like a man beating the air.
2Co 10: 4 The weapons we *f*
1Ti 1:18 them you may *f* the good *f*,
6:12 Fight the good *f* of the faith.
2Ti 4: 7 fought the good *f*, I have finished

FIGS (FIG)
Lk 6:44 People do not pick *f*

FILL (FILLED FILLS FULL FULLNESS FULLY)
Ge 1:28 and increase in number; *f* the earth
Ps 16:11 you will *f* me with joy
81:10 wide your mouth and I will *f* it.
Pr 28:19 who chases fantasies will have his *f*
Hag 2: 7 and I will *f* this house with glory,'
Jn 6:26 you ate the loaves and had your *f*.
Ac 2:28 you will *f* me with joy
Ro 15:13 the God of hope *f* you with all joy

FILLED (FILL)
Ps 72:19 may the whole earth be *f*
119:64 The earth is *f* with your love,
Eze 43: 5 the glory of the LORD *f* the temple
Hab 2:14 For the earth will be *f*
Lk 1:15 and he will be *f* with the Holy Spirit
1:41 and Elizabeth was *f* with the Holy
Jn 12: 3 the house was *f* with the fragrance
Ac 2: 4 All of them were *f*
4: 8 Then Peter, *f* with the Holy Spirit,
9:17 and be *f* with the Holy Spirit."
13: 9 called Paul, *f* with the Holy Spirit,
Eph 5:18 Instead, be *f* with the Spirit.
Php 1:11 *f* with the fruit of righteousness

FILLS (FILL)
Nu 14:21 of the LORD *f* the whole earth,
Ps 107: 9 and *f* the hungry with good things.
Eph 1:23 fullness of him who *f* everything

FILTHY
Isa 64: 6 all our righteous acts are like *f* rags;
Col 3: 8 and *f* language from your lips.
2Pe 2: 7 by the *f* lives of lawless men

FIND (FINDS FOUND)
Nu 32:23 be sure that your sin will *f* you out.
Dt 4:29 you will *f* him if you look for him
1Sa 23:16 and helped him *f* strength in God.
Ps 36: 7 *f* refuge in the shadow
91: 4 under his wings you will *f* refuge;
Pr 14:22 those who plan what is good *f* love
31:10 A wife of noble character who can *f*
Jer 6:16 and you will *f* rest for your souls.
Mt 7: 7 seek and you will *f*; knock
11:29 and you will *f* rest for your souls.
16:25 loses his life for me will *f* it.
Lk 18: 8 will he *f* faith on the earth?"
Jn 10: 9 come in and go out, and *f* pasture.

FINDS (FIND)
Ps 62: 1 My soul *f* rest in God alone;
112: 1 who *f* great delight
119:162 like one who *f* great spoil.
Pr 18:22 He who *f* a wife *f* what is good
Mt 7: 8 he who seeks *f*; and to him who
10:39 Whoever *f* his life will lose it,
Lk 12:37 whose master *f* them watching
15: 4 go after the lost sheep until he *f* it?

FINISH (FINISHED)
Jn 4:34 him who sent me and to *f* his work.
5:36 that the Father has given me to *f*,
Ac 20:24 if only I may *f* the race
2Co 8:11 Now *f* the work, so that your eager
Jas 1: 4 Perseverance must *f* its work

FINISHED (FINISH)
Ge 2: 2 seventh day God had *f* the work he
Jn 19:30 the drink, Jesus said, "It is *f*."
2Ti 4: 7 I have *f* the race, I have kept

FIRE
Ex 13:21 in a pillar of *f* to give them light,
Lev 6:12 *f* on the altar must be kept burning;
Isa 30:27 and his tongue is a consuming *f*.
Jer 23:29 my word like *f*," declares
Mt 3:11 you with the Holy Spirit and with *f*.
5:22 will be in danger of the *f* of hell.
25:41 into the eternal *f* prepared
Mk 9:43 where the *f* never goes out.
Ac 2: 3 to be tongues of *f* that separated
1Co 3:13 It will be revealed with *f*,
1Th 5:19 Do not put out the Spirit's *f*;
Heb 12:29 for our "God is a consuming *f*."
Jas 3: 5 set on *f* by a small spark.
2Pe 3:10 the elements will be destroyed by *f*,
Jude :23 snatch others from the *f*
Rev 20:14 The lake of *f* is the second death.

FIRM
Ex 14:13 Stand *f* and you will see
2Ch 20:17 stand *f* and see the deliverance
Ps 33:11 of the LORD stand *f* forever,
37:23 he makes his steps *f*;
40: 2 and gave me a *f* place to stand.

Ps 89: 2 that your love stands *f* forever,
119:89 it stands *f* in the heavens.
Pr 4:26 and take only ways that are *f*.
Zec 8:23 nations will take *f* hold of one Jew
Mk 13:13 he who stands *f* to the end will be
1Co 16:13 on your guard; stand *f* in the faith;
2Co 1:24 because it is by faith you stand *f*.
Eph 6:14 Stand *f* then, with the belt
Col 4:12 that you may stand *f* in all the will
2Th 2:15 stand *f* and hold to the teachings
2Ti 2:19 God's solid foundation stands *f*,
Heb 6:19 an anchor for the soul, *f* and secure
1Pe 5: 9 Resist him, standing *f* in the faith,

FIRST
Isa 44: 6 I am the *f* and I am the last;
48:12 I am the *f* and I am the last.
Mt 5:24 *F* go and be reconciled
6:33 But seek *f* his kingdom
7: 5 *f* take the plank out
20:27 wants to be *f* must be your slave—
22:38 This is the *f* and greatest
23:26 *F* clean the inside of the cup
Mk 13:10 And the gospel must *f* be preached
Ac 11:26 disciples were called Christians *f*
Ro 1:16 *f* for the Jew, then for the Gentile.
1Co 12:28 in the church God has appointed *f*
2Co 8: 5 they gave themselves *f* to the Lord
1Ti 2:13 For Adam was formed *f*, then Eve.
Jas 3:17 comes from heaven is *f* of all pure;
1Jn 4:19 We love because he *f* loved us.
3Jn : 9 but Diotrephes, who loves to be *f*,
Rev 1:17 I am the *F* and the Last.
2: 4 You have forsaken your *f* love.

FIRSTBORN (BEAR)
Ex 11: 5 Every *f* son in Egypt will die,

FIRSTFRUITS
Ex 23:19 "Bring the best of the *f* of your soil

FISHERS
Mk 1:17 "and I will make you *f* of men."

FITTING*
Ps 33: 1 it is *f* for the upright to praise him.
147: 1 how pleasant and *f* to praise him!
Pr 10:32 of the righteous know what is *f*,
19:10 It is not *f* for a fool to live in luxury
26: 1 honor is not *f* for a fool.
1Co 14:40 everything should be done in a *f*
Col 3:18 to your husbands, as is *f* in the Lord
Heb 2:10 sons to glory, it was *f* that God,

FIX
Dt 11:18 *F* these words of mine
Pr 4:25 *f* your gaze directly before you.
2Co 4:18 we *f* our eyes not on what is seen,
Heb 3: 1 heavenly calling, *f* your thoughts
12: 2 Let us *f* our eyes on Jesus,

FLAME (FLAMES FLAMING)
2Ti 1: 6 you to fan into *f* the gift of God,

FLAMES (FLAME)
1Co 3:15 only as one escaping through the *f*.
13: 3 and surrender my body to the *f*,

FLAMING (FLAME)
Eph 6:16 you can extinguish all the *f* arrows

FLASH
1Co 15:52 in a *f*, in the twinkling of an eye,

FLATTER (FLATTERING FLATTERY)
Job 32:21 nor will I *f* any man;
Jude :16 *f* others for their own advantage.

FLATTERING (FLATTER)
Ps 12: 2 their *f* lips speak with deception.
12: 3 May the LORD cut off all *f* lips
Pr 26:28 and a *f* mouth works ruin.

FLATTERY (FLATTER)
Ro 16:18 and *f* they deceive the minds
1Th 2: 5 You know we never used *f*,

FLAWLESS*
2Sa 22:31 the word of the LORD is *f*.
Job 11: 4 You say to God, 'My beliefs are *f*
Ps 12: 6 And the words of the LORD are *f*,
18:30 the word of the LORD is *f*.
Pr 30: 5 "Every word of God is *f*;
SS 5: 2 my dove, my *f* one.

FLEE
Ps 139: 7 Where can I *f* from your presence?
1Co 6:18 *F* from sexual immorality.
10:14 my dear friends, *f* from idolatry.
1Ti 6:11 But you, man of God, *f* from all this
2Ti 2:22 *F* the evil desires of youth,
Jas 4: 7 Resist the devil, and he will *f*

FLEETING
Ps 89:47 Remember how *f* is my life.
Pr 31:30 Charm is deceptive, and beauty is *f*

FLESH
Ge 2:23 and *f* of my *f*;
2:24 and they will become one *f*.
Job 19:26 yet in my *f* I will see God;
Eze 11:19 of stone and give them a heart of *f*.
36:26 of stone and give you a heart of *f*.
Mk 10: 8 and the two will become one *f*.'
Jn 1:14 The Word became *f* and made his
6:51 This bread is my *f*, which I will give
1Co 6:16 "The two will become one *f*."
Eph 5:31 and the two will become one *f*."
6:12 For our struggle is not against *f*

FLOCK (FLOCKS)
Isa 40:11 He tends his *f* like a shepherd:
Eze 34: 2 not shepherds take care of the *f*?
Zec 11:17 who deserts the *f*!
Mt 26:31 the sheep of the *f* will be scattered.'
Ac 20:28 all the *f* of which the Holy Spirit
1Pe 5: 2 Be shepherds of God's *f* that is

FLOCKS (FLOCK)
Lk 2: 8 keeping watch over their *f* at night.

FLOG
Ac 22:25 to *f* a Roman citizen who hasn't

FLOODGATES
Mal 3:10 see if I will not throw open the *f*

FLOURISHING
Ps 52: 8 *f* in the house of God;

FLOW (FLOWING)
Nu 13:27 and it does *f* with milk and honey!
Jn 7:38 streams of living water will *f*

FLOWERS
Isa 40: 7 The grass withers and the *f* fall,

FLOWING (FLOW)
Ex 3: 8 a land *f* with milk and honey—

FOLDING
Pr 6:10 a little *f* of the hands to rest—

FOLLOW (FOLLOWING FOLLOWS)
Ex 23: 2 Do not *f* the crowd in doing wrong.
Lev 18: 4 and be careful to *f* my decrees.
Dt 5: 1 Learn them and be sure to *f* them.
Ps 23: 6 Surely goodness and love will *f* me
Mt 16:24 and take up his cross and *f* me.
Jn 10: 4 his sheep *f* him because they know
1Co 14: 1 *F* the way of love and eagerly
Rev 14: 4 They *f* the Lamb wherever he goes.

FOLLOWING (FOLLOW)
1Ti 1:18 by *f* them you may fight the good

FOLLOWS (FOLLOW)
Jn 8:12 Whoever *f* me will never walk

FOOD (FOODS)
Pr 20:13 you will have *f* to spare.
22: 9 for he shares his *f* with the poor.
25:21 If your enemy is hungry, give him *f*
31:15 she provides *f* for her family
Da 1: 8 to defile himself with the royal *f*
Jn 6:27 Do not work for *f* that spoils,
Ro 14:14 fully convinced that no *f* is unclean
1Co 8: 8 But *f* does not bring us near to God
1Ti 6: 8 But if we have *f* and clothing,
Jas 2:15 sister is without clothes and daily *f*.

FOODS (FOOD)
Mk 7:19 Jesus declared all *f* "clean.")

FOOL (FOOLISH FOOLISHNESS FOOLS)
Ps 14: 1 The *f* says in his heart,
Pr 15: 5 A *f* spurns his father's discipline,
17:28 Even a *f* is thought wise
18: 2 A *f* finds no pleasure
26: 5 Answer a *f* according to his folly,
28:26 He who trusts in himself is a *f*,
Mt 5:22 But anyone who says, 'You *f*!'

FOOLISH (FOOL)
Pr 10: 1 but a *f* son grief to his mother.
17:25 A *f* son brings grief to his father
Mt 7:26 practice is like a *f* man who built
25: 2 of them were *f* and five were wise.
1Co 1:27 God chose the *f* things of the world

FOOLISHNESS (FOOL)
1Co 1:18 of the cross is *f* to those who are
1:25 For the *f* of God is wiser
2:14 for they are *f* to him, and he cannot
3:19 of this world is *f* in God's sight.

FOOLS (FOOL)
Pr 14: 9 *F* mock at making amends for sin,
1Co 4:10 We are *f* for Christ, but you are

FOOT (FEET FOOTHOLD)
Jos 1: 3 every place where you set your *f*,
Isa 1: 6 From the sole of your *f* to the top
1Co 12:15 If the *f* should say, "Because I am

FOOTHOLD (FOOT)
Eph 4:27 and do not give the devil a *f*.

FORBEARANCE*
Ro 3:25 because in his *f* he had left the sins

FORBID
1Co 14:39 and do not *f* speaking in tongues.

FOREFATHERS (FATHER)
Heb 1: 1 spoke to our *f* through the prophets

FOREKNEW* (KNOW)
Ro 8:29 For those God *f* he
11: 2 not reject his people, whom he *f*.

FOREVER (EVER)
1Ch 16:15 He remembers his covenant *f*,
16:34 his love endures *f*.
Ps 9: 7 The LORD reigns *f*;
23: 6 dwell in the house of the LORD *f*.
33: 11 the plans of the LORD stand firm *f*
86:12 I will glorify your name *f*.
92: 8 But you, O LORD, are exalted *f*.
110: 4 "You are a priest *f*,
119: 111 Your statutes are my heritage *f*;
Jn 6:51 eats of this bread, he will live *f*.
14:16 Counselor to be with you *f*—
1Co 9:25 it to get a crown that will last *f*.
1Th 4:17 And so we will be with the Lord *f*.
Heb 13: 8 same yesterday and today and *f*.
1Pe 1:25 but the word of the Lord stands *f*."
1Jn 2:17 who does the will of God lives *f*.

FORFEIT
Lk 9:25 and yet lose or *f* his very self?

FORGAVE (FORGIVE)
Ps 32: 5 and you *f*
Eph 4:32 just as in Christ God *f* you.
Col 2:13 He *f* us all our sins, having
3:13 Forgive as the Lord *f* you.

FORGET (FORGETS FORGETTING)
Dt 6:12 that you do not *f* the LORD,
Ps 103: 2 and *f* not all his benefits.
137: 5 may my right hand *f* its skill.
Isa 49:15 "Can a mother *f* the baby
Heb 6:10 he will not *f* your work

FORGETS (FORGET)
Jn 16:21 her baby is born she *f* the anguish
Jas 1:24 immediately *f* what he looks like.

FORGETTING (FORGET)
Php 3:13 *F* what is behind and straining

FORGIVE (FORGAVE FORGIVENESS FORGIVING)
2Ch 7:14 will *f* their sin and will heal their
Ps 19:12 *F* my hidden faults.
Mt 6:12 *F* us our debts,
6:14 For if you *f* men when they sin
18:21 many times shall I *f* my brother
Mk 11:25 in heaven may *f* you your sins."
Lk 11: 4 *F* us our sins,
23:34 Jesus said, "Father, *f* them,
Col 3:13 *F* as the Lord forgave you.
1Jn 1: 9 and just and will *f* us our sins

FORGIVENESS (FORGIVE)
Ps 130: 4 But with you there is *f*;
Ac 10:43 believes in him receives *f* of sins
Eph 1: 7 through his blood, the *f* of sins,
Col 1:14 in whom we have redemption, the *f*
Heb 9:22 the shedding of blood there is no *f*.

FORGIVING (FORGIVE)
Ne 9:17 But you are a *f* God, gracious
Eph 4:32 to one another, *f* each other,

FORMED
Ge 2: 7 And the LORD God *f* man
Ps 103:14 for he knows how we are *f*,
Isa 45:18 but *f* it to be inhabited—

Ro 9:20 "Shall what is *f* say to him who *f* it,
1Ti 2:13 For Adam was *f* first, then Eve.
Heb 11: 3 understand that the universe was *f*

FORSAKE (FORSAKEN)
Jos 1: 5 I will never leave you nor *f* you.
24:16 "Far be it from us to *f* the LORD
2Ch 15: 2 but if you *f* him, he will *f* you.
Ps 27:10 Though my father and mother *f* me
Isa 55: 7 Let the wicked *f* his way
Heb 13: 5 never will I *f* you."

FORSAKEN (FORSAKE)
Ps 22: 1 my God, why have you *f* me?
37:25 I have never seen the righteous *f*
Mt 27:46 my God, why have you *f* me?"
Rev 2: 4 You have *f* your first love.

FORTRESS
Ps 18: 2 The LORD is my rock, my *f*
71: 3 for you are my rock and my *f*.

FOUGHT (FIGHT)
2Ti 4: 7 I have *f* the good fight, I have

FOUND (FIND)
1Ch 28: 9 If you seek him, he will be *f* by you;
Isa 55: 6 Seek the LORD while he may be *f*;
Da 5:27 on the scales and *f* wanting.
Lk 15: 6 with me; I have *f* my lost sheep.'
15: 9 with me; I have *f* my lost coin.'
Ac 4:12 Salvation is *f* in no one else,

FOUNDATION
Isa 28:16 a precious cornerstone for a sure *f*;
1Co 3:11 For no one can lay any *f* other
Eph 2:20 built on the *f* of the apostles
2Ti 2:19 God's solid *f* stands firm,

FOXES
Mt 8:20 "*F* have holes and birds

FRAGRANCE
2Co 2:16 of death; to the other, the *f* of life.

FREE (FREED FREEDOM FREELY)
Ps 146: 7 The LORD sets prisoners *f*,
Jn 8:32 and the truth will set you *f*."
Ro 6:18 You have been set *f* from sin
Gal 3:28 slave nor *f*, male nor female,
1Pe 2:16 *f* men, but do not use your freedom

FREED (FREE)
Rev 1: 5 has *f* us from our sins by his blood,

FREEDOM (FREE)
Ro 8:21 into the glorious *f* of the children
2Co 3:17 the Spirit of the Lord is, there is *f*.
Gal 5:13 But do not use your *f* to indulge
1Pe 2:16 but do not use your *f* as a cover-up

FREELY (FREE)
Isa 55: 7 and to our God, for he will *f* pardon
Mt 10: 8 Freely you have received, *f* give.
Ro 3:24 and are justified *f* by his grace
Eph 1: 6 which he has *f* given us

FRIEND (FRIENDS)
Ex 33:11 as a man speaks with his *f*.
Pr 17:17 A *f* loves at all times,
18:24 there is a *f* who sticks closer
27: 6 Wounds from a *f* can be trusted,
27:10 Do not forsake your *f* and the *f*
Jas 4: 4 Anyone who chooses to be a *f*

FRIENDS (FRIEND)
Pr 16:28 and a gossip separates close *f*.
Zec 13: 6 given at the house of my *f*.'
Jn 15:13 that he lay down his life for his *f*.

FRUIT (FRUITFUL)
Ps 1: 3 which yields its *f* in season
Pr 11:30 The *f* of the righteous is a tree
Mt 7:16 By their *f* you will recognize them.
Jn 15: 2 branch in me that bears no *f*,
Gal 5:22 But the *f* of the Spirit is love, joy,
Rev 22: 2 of *f*, yielding its *f* every month.

FRUITFUL (FRUIT)
Ge 1:22 "Be *f* and increase in number
Ps 128: 3 Your wife will be like a *f* vine
Jn 15: 2 prunes so that it will be even more *f*.

FULFILL (FULFILLED FULFILLMENT)
Ps 116:14 I will *f* my vows to the LORD
Mt 5:17 come to abolish them but to *f* them.
1Co 7: 3 husband should *f* his marital duty

FULFILLED (FULFILL)
Pr 13:19 A longing *f* is sweet to the soul,
Mk 14:49 But the Scriptures must be *f*."
Ro 13: 8 loves his fellowman has *f* the law.

FULFILLMENT (FULFILL)
Ro 13:10 Therefore love is the *f* of the law.

FULL (FILL)
Ps 127: 5 whose quiver is *f* of them.
Pr 31:11 Her husband has *f* confidence
Isa 6: 3 the whole earth is *f* of his glory."
11: 9 for the earth will be *f*
Jn 10:10 may have life, and have it to the *f*.
Ac 6: 3 known to be *f* of the Spirit

FULLNESS (FILL)
Col 1:19 to have all his *f* dwell in him,
2: 9 in Christ all the *f* of the Deity lives

FULLY (FILL)
1Ki 8:61 your hearts must be *f* committed
2Ch 16: 9 whose hearts are *f* committed
Ps 119: 4 that are to be *f* obeyed.
119:138 they are *f* trustworthy.
1Co 15:58 Always give yourselves *f*

FUTURE
Ps 37:37 there is a *f* for the man of peace.
Pr 23:18 There is surely a *f* hope for you,
Ro 8:38 neither the present nor the *f*,

GABRIEL*
Angel who interpreted Daniel's visions (Da 8:16-26; 9:20-27); announced births of John (Lk 1:11-20), Jesus (Lk 1:26-38).

GAIN (GAINED)
Ps 60:12 With God we will *g* the victory,
Mk 8:36 it for a man to *g* the whole world,
1Co 13: 3 but have not love, I *g* nothing.
Php 1:21 to live is Christ and to die is *g*.
3: 8 that I may *g* Christ and be found
1Ti 6: 6 with contentment is great *g*.

GAINED (GAIN)
Ro 5: 2 through whom we have *g* access

GALILEE
Isa 9: 1 but in the future he will honor *G*

GALL
Mt 27:34 mixed with *g*; but after tasting it,

GAP
Eze 22:30 stand before me in the *g* on behalf

GARDENER
Jn 15: 1 true vine, and my Father is the g.

GARMENT (GARMENTS)
Ps 102:26 they will all wear out like a g.
Mt 9:16 of unshrunk cloth on an old g,
Jn 19:23 This g was seamless, woven

GARMENTS (GARMENT)
Ge 3:21 The LORD God made g of skin
Isa 61:10 me with g of salvation
63: 1 with his g stained crimson?
Jn 19:24 "They divided my g among them

GATE (GATES)
Mt 7:13 For wide is the g and broad is
Jn 10: 9 I am the g; whoever enters

GATES (GATE)
Ps 100: 4 Enter his g with thanksgiving
Mt 16:18 the g of Hades will not overcome it.

GATHER (GATHERS)
Zec 14: 2 I will g all the nations to Jerusalem
Mt 12:30 he who does not g with me scatters
23:37 longed to g your children together,

GATHERS (GATHER)
Isa 40:11 He g the lambs in his arms
Mt 23:37 a hen g her chicks under her wings,

GAVE (GIVE)
Ezr 2:69 According to their ability they g
Job 1:21 LORD g and the LORD has taken
Jn 3:16 so loved the world that he g his one
2Co 8: 5 they g themselves first to the Lord
Gal 2:20 who loved me and g himself for me
1Ti 2: 6 who g himself as a ransom

GAZE
Ps 27: 4 to g upon the beauty of the LORD
Pr 4:25 fix your g directly before you.

GENEALOGIES
1Ti 1: 4 themselves to myths and endless g.

GENERATIONS
Ps 22:30 future g will be told about the Lord
102:12 your renown endures through all g.
145:13 dominion endures through all g.
Lk 1:48 now on all g will call me blessed,
Eph 3: 5 not made known to men in other g

GENEROUS
Ps 112: 5 Good will come to him who is g
Pr 22: 9 A g man will himself be blessed,
2Co 9: 5 Then it will be ready as a g gift,
1Ti 6:18 and to be g and willing to share.

GENTILE (GENTILES)
Ro 1:16 first for the Jew, then for the G.
10:12 difference between Jew and G—

GENTILES (GENTILE)
Isa 42: 6 and a light for the G,
Ro 3: 9 and G alike are all under sin.
11:13 as I am the apostle to the G,
1Co 1:23 block to Jews and foolishness to G,

GENTLE (GENTLENESS)
Pr 15: 1 A g answer turns away wrath,
Zec 9: 9 g and riding on a donkey,
Mt 11:29 for I am g and humble in heart,
21: 5 g and riding on a donkey,
1Co 4:21 or in love and with a g spirit?
1Pe 3: 4 the unfading beauty of a g

GENTLENESS* (GENTLE)
2Co 10: 1 By the meekness and g of Christ,
Gal 5:23 faithfulness, g and self-control.
Php 4: 5 Let your g be evident to all.
Col 3:12 kindness, humility, g and patience.
1Ti 6:11 faith, love, endurance and g.
1Pe 3:15 But do this with g and respect,

GETHSEMANE
Mt 26:36 disciples to a place called G,

GIDEON*
Judge, also called Jerub-Baal; freed Israel from Midianites (Jdg 6-8; Heb 11:32). Given sign of fleece (Jdg 6:36-40).

GIFT (GIFTS)
Pr 21:14 A g given in secret soothes anger,
Mt 5:23 if you are offering your g
Ac 2:38 And you will receive the g
Ro 6:23 but the g of God is eternal life
1Co 7: 7 each man has his own g from God;
2Co 8:12 the g is acceptable according
9:15 be to God for his indescribable g!
Eph 2: 8 it is the g of God—not by works,
1Ti 4:14 not neglect your g, which was
2Ti 1: 6 you to fan into flame the g of God,
Jas 1:17 and perfect g is from above,
1Pe 4:10 should use whatever g he has

GIFTS (GIFT)
Ro 11:29 for God's g and his call are
12: 6 We have different g, according
1Co 12: 4 There are different kinds of g,
12:31 But eagerly desire the greater g.
14: 1 and eagerly desire spiritual g,
14:12 excel in g that build up the church.

GILEAD
Jer 8:22 Is there no balm in G?

GIVE (GAVE GIVEN GIVER GIVES GIVING)
Nu 6:26 and g you peace." '
1Sa 1:11 then I will g him to the LORD
2Ch 15: 7 be strong and do not g up,
Pr 21:26 but the righteous g without sparing
23:26 My son, g me your heart
30: 8 but g me only my daily bread.
31:31 G her the reward she has earned,
Isa 42: 8 I will not g my glory to another
Eze 36:26 I will g you a new heart
Mt 6:11 G us today our daily bread.
10: 8 Freely you have received, freely g.
22:21 "G to Caesar what is Caesar's,
Mk 8:37 Or what can a man g in exchange
Lk 6:38 G, and it will be given to you.
11:13 Father in heaven g the Holy Spirit
Jn 10:28 I g them eternal life, and they shall
13:34 "A new commandment I g you:
Ac 20:35 blessed to g than to receive.' "
Ro 12: 8 let him g generously;
13: 7 G everyone what you owe him:
14:12 each of us will g an account
2Co 9: 7 Each man should g what he has
Rev 14: 7 "Fear God and g him glory,

GIVEN (GIVE)
Nu 8:16 are to be g wholly to me.
Ps 115:16 but the earth he has g to man.
Isa 9: 6 to us a son is g,
Mt 6:33 and all these things will be g to you
7: 7 "Ask and it will be g to you;
Lk 22:19 saying, "This is my body g for you;
Jn 3:27 man can receive only what is g him
Ro 5: 5 the Holy Spirit, whom he has g us.
1Co 4: 2 those who have been g a trust must
12:13 we were all g the one Spirit to drink
Eph 4: 7 to each one of us grace has been g

GIVER* (GIVE)
Pr 18:16 A gift opens the way for the g
2Co 9: 7 for God loves a cheerful g.

GIVES (GIVE)
Ps 119:130 The unfolding of your words g light;
Pr 14:30 A heart at peace g life to the body,
15:30 good news g health to the bones.
28:27 He who g to the poor will lack
Isa 40:29 He g strength to the weary
Mt 10:42 if anyone g even a cup of cold water
Jn 6:63 The Spirit g life; the flesh counts
1Co 15:57 He g us the victory
2Co 3: 6 the letter kills, but the Spirit g life.

GIVING (GIVE)
Ne 8: 8 g the meaning so that the people
Ps 19: 8 g joy to the heart.
Mt 6: 4 so that your g may be in secret.
2Co 8: 7 also excel in this grace of g.

GLAD (GLADNESS)
Ps 31: 7 I will be g and rejoice in your love,
46: 4 whose streams make g the city
97: 1 LORD reigns, let the earth be g;
118:24 let us rejoice and be g in it.
Pr 23:25 May your father and mother be g;
Zec 2:10 and be g, O Daughter of Zion.
Mt 5:12 be g, because great is your reward

GLADNESS (GLAD)
Ps 45:15 They are led in with joy and g;
51: 8 Let me hear joy and g;
100: 2 Serve the LORD with g;
Jer 31:13 I will turn their mourning into g;

GLORIFIED (GLORY)
Jn 13:31 Son of Man g and God is g in him.
Ro 8:30 those he justified, he also g.
2Th 1:10 comes to be g in his holy people

GLORIFY (GLORY)
Ps 34: 3 G the LORD with me;
86:12 I will g your name forever.
Jn 13:32 God will g the Son in himself,
17: 1 G your Son, that your Son may

GLORIOUS (GLORY)
Ps 45:13 All g is the princess
111: 3 G and majestic are his deeds,
145: 5 of the g splendor of your majesty,
Isa 4: 2 the LORD will be beautiful and g,
12: 5 for he has done g things;
42:21 to make his law great and g.
63:15 from your lofty throne, holy and g.
Mt 19:28 the Son of Man sits on his g throne,
Lk 9:31 appeared in g splendor, talking
Ac 2:20 of the great and g day of the Lord.
2Co 3: 8 of the Spirit be even more g?
Php 3:21 so that they will be like his g body.
4:19 to his g riches in Christ Jesus.
Tit 2:13 the g appearing of our great God
Jude :24 before his g presence without fault

GLORY (GLORIFIED GLORIFY GLORIOUS)
Ex 15: 11 awesome in g,
33: 18 Moses said, "Now show me your g
1Sa 4: 21 "The g has departed from Israel"—
1Ch 16: 24 Declare his g among the nations,
16: 28 ascribe to the LORD g
29: 11 and the g and the majesty
Ps 8: 5 and crowned him with g and honor
19: 1 The heavens declare the g of God;
24: 7 that the King of g may come in.
29: 1 ascribe to the LORD g
72: 19 the whole earth be filled with his g.
96: 3 Declare his g among the nations,
Pr 19: 11 it is to his g to overlook an offense.
25: 2 It is the g of God to conceal
Isa 6: 3 the whole earth is full of his g."
48: 11 I will not yield my g to another.
Eze 43: 2 and the land was radiant with his g.
Mt 24: 30 of the sky, with power and great g.
25: 31 the Son of Man comes in his g,
Mk 8: 38 in his Father's g with the holy
13: 26 in clouds with great power and g.
Lk 2: 9 and the g of the Lord shone
2: 14 saying, "G to God in the highest,
Jn 1: 14 We have seen his g, the g of the One
17: 5 presence with the g I had with you
17: 24 to see my g, the g you have given
Ac 7: 2 The God of g appeared
Ro 1: 23 exchanged the g of the immortal
3: 23 and fall short of the g of God,
8: 18 with the g that will be revealed
9: 4 theirs the divine g, the covenants,
1Co 10: 31 whatever you do, do it all for the g
11: 7 but the woman is the g of man.
15: 43 it is raised in g; it is sown
2Co 3: 10 comparison with the surpassing g.
3: 18 faces all reflect the Lord's g,
4: 17 us an eternal g that far outweighs
Col 1: 27 Christ in you, the hope of g.
3: 4 also will appear with him in g.
1Ti 3: 16 was taken up in g.
Heb 1: 3 The Son is the radiance of God's g
2: 7 you crowned him with g and honor
1Pe 1: 24 and all their g is like the flowers
Rev 4: 11 to receive g and honor and power,
21: 23 for the g of God gives it light,

GLUTTONS
Tit 1: 12 always liars, evil brutes, lazy g."

GNASHING
Mt 8: 12 where there will be weeping and g

GNAT*
Mt 23: 24 You strain out a g but swallow

GOAL
2Co 5: 9 So we make it our g to please him,
Gal 3: 3 to attain your g by human effort?
Php 3: 14 on toward the g to win the prize

GOAT (GOATS SCAPEGOAT)
Isa 11: 6 the leopard will lie down with the g

GOATS (GOAT)
Nu 7: 17 five male g and five male lambs

GOD (GOD'S GODLINESS GODLY GODS)
Ge 1: 1 In the beginning G created
1: 2 and the Spirit of G was hovering
Ge 1: 26 Then G said, "Let us make man
1: 27 So G created man in his own image
1: 31 G saw all that he had made,
2: 3 And G blessed the seventh day
2: 22 Then the LORD G made a woman
3: 21 The LORD G made garments
3: 23 So the LORD G banished him
5: 22 Enoch walked with G 300 years
6: 2 sons of G saw that the daughters
9: 16 everlasting covenant between G
17: 1 "I am G Almighty; walk before me
21: 33 name of the LORD, the Eternal G.
22: 8 "G himself will provide the lamb
28: 12 and the angels of G were ascending
32: 28 because you have struggled with G
32: 30 "It is because I saw G face to face,
35: 10 G said to him, "Your name is Jacob
41: 51 G has made me forget all my
50: 20 but G intended it for good
Ex 2: 24 G heard their groaning
3: 6 because he was afraid to look at G.
6: 7 own people, and I will be your G.
8: 10 is no one like the LORD our G.
13: 18 So G led the people
15: 2 He is my G, and I will praise him,
17: 9 with the staff of G in my hands."
19: 3 Then Moses went up to G,
20: 2 the LORD your G, who brought
20: 5 the LORD your G, am a jealous G,
20: 19 But do not have G speak to us
22: 28 "Do not blaspheme G
31: 18 inscribed by the finger of G.
34: 6 the compassionate and gracious G,
34: 14 name is Jealous, is a jealous G.
Lev 18: 21 not profane the name of your G.
19: 2 the LORD your G, am holy.
26: 12 walk among you and be your G,
Nu 22: 38 I must speak only what G puts
23: 19 G is not a man, that he should lie,
Dt 1: 17 for judgment belongs to G.
3: 22 LORD your G himself will fight
3: 24 For what g is there in heaven
4: 24 is a consuming fire, a jealous G.
4: 31 the LORD your G is a merciful G;
4: 39 heart this day that the LORD is G
5: 11 the name of the LORD your G,
5: 14 a Sabbath to the LORD your G.
5: 26 of the living G speaking out of fire,
6: 4 LORD our G, the LORD is one.
6: 5 Love the LORD your G
6: 13 the LORD your G, serve him only
6: 16 Do not test the LORD your G
7: 9 your G is G; he is the faithful G,
7: 12 the LORD your G will keep his
7: 21 is a great and awesome G.
8: 5 the LORD your G disciplines you.
10: 12 but to fear the LORD your G,
10: 14 the LORD your G belong
10: 17 For the LORD your G is G of gods
11: 13 to love the LORD your G
13: 3 The LORD your G is testing you
13: 4 the LORD your G you must
15: 6 the LORD your G will bless you
19: 9 to love the LORD your G
25: 16 the LORD your G detests anyone
29: 29 belong to the LORD our G,
30: 2 return to the LORD your G
30: 16 today to love the LORD your G,
30: 20 you may love the LORD your G,
31: 6 for the LORD your G goes
32: 3 Oh, praise the greatness of our G!
32: 4 A faithful G who does no wrong,
33: 27 The eternal G is your refuge,
Jos 1: 9 for the LORD your G will be
14: 8 the LORD my G wholeheartedly.
22: 5 to love the LORD your G,
22: 34 Between Us that the LORD is G.
Jos 23: 11 careful to love the LORD your G.
23: 14 the LORD your G gave you has
Jdg 16: 28 O G, please strengthen me just
Ru 1: 16 be my people and your G my G.
1Sa 2: 2 there is no Rock like our G.
2: 3 for the LORD is a G who knows,
2: 25 another man, G may mediate
10: 26 men whose hearts G had touched.
12: 12 the LORD your G was your king.
17: 26 defy the armies of the living G?"
17: 46 world will know that there is a G
30: 6 strength in the LORD his G.
2Sa 14: 14 But G does not take away life;
22: 3 my G is my rock, in whom I take
22: 31 "As for G, his way is perfect;
1Ki 4: 29 G gave Solomon wisdom
8: 23 there is no G like you in heaven
8: 27 "But will G really dwell on earth?
8: 61 committed to the LORD our G,
18: 21 If the LORD is G, follow him;
18: 37 are G, and that you are turning
20: 28 a g of the hills and not a g
2Ki 19: 15 G of Israel, enthroned
1Ch 16: 35 Cry out, "Save us, O G our Savior;
28: 2 for the footstool of our G,
28: 9 acknowledge the G of your father,
29: 10 G of our father Israel,
29: 17 my G, that you test the heart
2Ch 2: 4 for the Name of the LORD my G
5: 14 of the LORD filled the temple of G
6: 18 "But will G really dwell on earth
18: 13 I can tell him only what my G says
20: 6 are you not the G who is in heaven?
25: 8 for G has the power to help
30: 9 for the LORD your G is gracious
33: 12 the favor of the LORD his G
Ezr 8: 22 "The good hand of our G is
9: 6 "O my G, I am too ashamed
9: 13 our G, you have punished us less
Ne 1: 5 the great and awesome G,
8: 8 from the Book of the Law of G,
9: 17 But you are a forgiving G,
9: 32 the great, mighty and awesome G,
Job 1: 1 he feared G and shunned evil.
2: 10 Shall we accept good from G,
4: 17 a mortal be more righteous than G?
5: 17 is the man whom G corrects;
11: 7 Can you fathom the mysteries of G
19: 26 yet in my flesh I will see G;
22: 13 Yet you say, 'What does G know?
25: 4 can a man be righteous before G?
33: 14 For G does speak—now one way,
34: 12 is unthinkable that G would do
36: 26 is G— beyond our understanding!
37: 22 G comes in awesome majesty.
Ps 18: 2 my G is my rock, in whom I take
18: 28 my G turns my darkness into light.
19: 1 The heavens declare the glory of G;
22: 1 G, my G, why have you forsaken
29: 3 the G of glory thunders,
31: 14 I say, "You are my G."
40: 3 a hymn of praise to our G.
40: 8 I desire to do your will, O my G;
42: 2 thirsts for G, for the living G.
42: 11 Put your hope in G,
45: 6 O G, will last for ever and ever;
46: 1 G is our refuge and strength,
46: 10 "Be still, and know that I am G;
47: 7 For G is the King of all the earth;
50: 3 Our G comes and will not be silent;
51: 1 Have mercy on me, O G,
51: 10 Create in me a pure heart, O G,
51: 17 O G, you will not despise.
62: 7 my honor depend on G;
65: 5 O G our Savior,
66: 1 Shout with joy to G, all the earth!
66: 16 listen, all you who fear G;

Ps 68: 6 G sets the lonely in families,
71:17 my youth, O G, you have taught
71:19 reaches to the skies, O G,
71:22 harp for your faithfulness, O my G;
73:26 but G is the strength of my heart
77:13 What g is so great as our God?
78:19 Can G spread a table in the desert?
81: 1 Sing for joy to G our strength;
84: 2 out for the living G.
84:10 a doorkeeper in the house of my G
86:12 O Lord my G, with all my heart;
89: 7 of the holy ones G is greatly feared;
90: 2 to everlasting you are G.
91: 2 my G, in whom I trust."
95: 7 for he is our G
100: 3 Know that the LORD is G.
108: 1 My heart is steadfast, O G;
113: 5 Who is like the LORD our G,
139:23 Search me, O G, and know my
Pr 3: 4 in the sight of G and man.
25: 2 of G to conceal a matter;
30: 5 "Every word of G is flawless;
Ecc 3:11 cannot fathom what G has done
11: 5 cannot understand the work of G,
12:13 Fear G and keep his
Isa 9: 6 Wonderful Counselor, Mighty G,
37:16 you alone are G over all
40: 3 a highway for our G.
40: 8 the word of our G stands forever."
40:28 The LORD is the everlasting G,
41:10 not be dismayed, for I am your G.
44: 6 apart from me there is no G.
52: 7 "Your G reigns!"
55: 7 to our G, for he will freely pardon.
57:21 says my G, "for the wicked."
59: 2 you from your G;
61:10 my soul rejoices in my G.
62: 5 so will your G rejoice over you.
Jer 23:23 "Am I only a G nearby,"
31:33 I will be their G,
32:27 "I am the LORD, the G
Eze 28:13 the garden of G;
Da 3:17 the G we serve is able to save us
9: 4 O Lord, the great and awesome G,
Hos 12: 6 and wait for your G always.
Joel 2:13 Return to the LORD your G,
Am 4:12 prepare to meet your G, O Israel."
Mic 6: 8 and to walk humbly with your G.
Na 1: 2 LORD is a jealous and avenging G;
Zec 14: 5 Then the LORD my G will come,
Mal 3: 8 Will a man rob G? Yet you rob me.
Mt 1:23 which means, "G with us."
5: 8 for they will see G.
6:24 You cannot serve both G
19: 6 Therefore what G has joined
19:26 but with G all things are possible."
22:21 and to G what is God's."
22:37 " 'Love the Lord your G
27:46 which means, "My G, my G,
Mk 12:29 the Lord our G, the Lord is one.
16:19 and he sat at the right hand of G.
Lk 1:37 For nothing is impossible with G."
1:47 my spirit rejoices in G my Savior,
10: 9 'The kingdom of G is near you.'
10:27 " 'Love the Lord your G
18:19 "No one is good—except G alone.
Jn 1: 1 was with G, and the Word was G.
1:18 seen G, but G the One and Only,
3:16 "For G so loved the world that he
4:24 G is spirit, and his worshipers must
14: 1 Trust in G; trust also in me.
20:28 "My Lord and my G!"
Ac 2:24 But G raised him from the dead,
5: 4 You have not lied to men but to G
5:29 "We must obey G rather than men!
7:55 to heaven and saw the glory of G,
17:23 TO AN UNKNOWN G.
20:27 to you the whole will of G.
20:32 "Now I commit you to G
Ro 1:17 a righteousness from G is revealed,
2:11 For G does not show favoritism.
3: 4 Let G be true, and every man a liar.
3:23 and fall short of the glory of G,
4:24 to whom G will credit
5: 8 G demonstrates his own love for us
6:23 but the gift of G is eternal life
8:28 in all things G works for the good
11:22 the kindness and sternness of G:
14:12 give an account of himself to G.
1Co 1:20 Has not G made foolish
2: 9 what G has prepared
3: 6 watered it, but G made it grow.
6:20 Therefore honor G with your body.
7:24 each man, as responsible to G,
8: 8 food does not bring us near to G;
10:13 G is faithful; he will not let you be
10:31 do it all for the glory of G.
14:33 For G is not a G of disorder
15:28 so that G may be all in all.
2Co 1: 9 rely on ourselves but on G,
2:14 be to G, who always leads us
3: 5 but our competence comes from G.
4: 7 this all-surpassing power is from G
5:19 that G was reconciling the world
5:21 G made him who had no sin
6:16 we are the temple of the living G.
9: 7 for G loves a cheerful giver.
9: 8 G is able to make all grace abound
Gal 2: 6 G does not judge by external
6: 7 not be deceived: G cannot be
Eph 2:10 which G prepared in advance for us
4: 6 one baptism; one G and Father
5: 1 Be imitators of G, therefore,
Php 2: 6 Who, being in very nature G,
4:19 And my G will meet all your needs
1Th 2: 4 trying to please men but G,
4: 7 For G did not call us to be impure,
4: 9 taught by G to love each other.
5: 9 For G did not appoint us
1Ti 2: 5 one mediator between G and men,
4: 4 For everything G created is good,
5: 4 for this is pleasing to G.
Tit 2:13 glorious appearing of our great G
Heb 1: 1 In the past G spoke
4:12 For the word of G is living
6:10 G is not unjust; he will not forget
10:31 to fall into the hands of the living G
11: 6 faith it is impossible to please G,
12:10 but G disciplines us for our good,
12:29 for our "G is a consuming fire."
13:15 offer to G a sacrifice of praise—
Jas 1:13 For G cannot be tempted by evil,
2:19 You believe that there is one G.
2:23 "Abraham believed G,
4: 4 the world becomes an enemy of G.
4: 8 Come near to G and he will come
1Pe 4:11 it with the strength G provides,
2Pe 1:21 but men spoke from G
1Jn 1: 5 G is light; in him there is no
3:20 For G is greater than our hearts,
4: 7 for love comes from G.
4: 9 This is how G showed his love
4:11 Dear friends, since G so loved us,
4:12 No one has ever seen G;
4:16 G is love.
Rev 4: 8 holy is the Lord G Almighty,
7:17 G will wipe away every tear
19: 6 For our Lord G Almighty reigns.

GOD-BREATHED* (BREATHED)
2Ti 3:16 All Scripture is G and is useful

GOD'S (GOD)
2Ch 20:15 For the battle is not yours, but G.
Job 37:14 stop and consider G wonders.
Ps 52: 8 I trust in G unfailing love
69:30 I will praise G name in song
Mk 3:35 Whoever does G will is my brother
Jn 7:17 If anyone chooses to do G will,
10:36 'I am G Son'? Do not believe me
Ro 2: 3 think you will escape G judgment?
2: 4 not realizing that G kindness leads
3: 3 lack of faith nullify G faithfulness?
7:22 in my inner being I delight in G law
9:16 or effort, but on G mercy.
11:29 for G gifts and his call are
12: 2 and approve what G will is—
12:13 Share with G people who are
13: 6 for the authorities are G servants,
1Co 7:19 Keeping G commands is what
2Co 6: 2 now is the time of G favor,
Eph 1: 7 riches of G grace that he lavished
1Th 4: 3 It is G will that you should be
5:18 for this is G will for you
1Ti 6: 1 so that G name and our teaching
2Ti 2:19 G solid foundation stands firm,
Tit 1: 7 overseer is entrusted with G work,
Heb 1: 3 The Son is the radiance of G glory
9:24 now to appear for us in G presence.
11: 3 was formed at G command,
1Pe 2:15 For it is G will that
3: 4 which is of great worth in G sight.
1Jn 2: 5 G love is truly made complete

GODLINESS (GOD)
1Ti 2: 2 and quiet lives in all g and holiness.
4: 8 but g has value for all things,
6: 6 g with contentment is great gain.
6:11 and pursue righteousness, g, faith,

GODLY (GOD)
Ps 4: 3 that the LORD has set apart the g
2Co 7:10 G sorrow brings repentance that
11: 2 jealous for you with a g jealousy.
2Ti 3:12 everyone who wants to live a g life
2Pe 3:11 You ought to live holy and g lives

GODS (GOD)
Ex 20: 3 "You shall have no other g
Ac 19:26 He says that man-made g are no g

GOLD
Job 23:10 tested me, I will come forth as g.
Ps 19:10 They are more precious than g,
119:127 more than g, more than pure g,
Pr 22: 1 esteemed is better than silver or g.

GOLGOTHA
Jn 19:17 (which in Aramaic is called G).

GOLIATH
Philistine giant killed by David (1Sa 17; 21:9).

GOOD
Ge 1: 4 God saw that the light was g,
1:31 he had made, and it was very g.
2:18 "It is not g for the man to be alone.
50:20 but God intended it for g
Job 2:10 Shall we accept g from God,
Ps 14: 1 there is no one who does g.
34: 8 Taste and see that the LORD is g;
37: 3 Trust in the LORD and do g;
84:11 no g thing does he withhold
86: 5 You are forgiving and g, O Lord
103: 5 satisfies your desires with g things,
119:68 You are g, and what you do is g;
133: 1 How g and pleasant it is

Ps 147: 1 How *g* it is to sing praises
Pr 3: 4 you will win favor and a *g* name
11:27 He who seeks *g* finds *g* will,
17:22 A cheerful heart is *g* medicine,
18:22 He who finds a wife finds what is *g*
22: 1 A *g* name is more desirable
31:12 She brings him *g*, not harm,
Isa 5:20 Woe to those who call evil *g*
52: 7 the feet of those who bring *g* news,
Jer 6:16 ask where the *g* way is,
32:39 the *g* of their children after them.
Mic 6: 8 has showed you, O man, what is *g*.
Mt 5:45 sun to rise on the evil and the *g*,
7:17 Likewise every *g* tree bears *g* fruit,
12:35 The *g* man brings *g* things out
19:17 "There is only One who is *g*.
25:21 'Well done, *g* and faithful servant!
Mk 3: 4 lawful on the Sabbath: to do *g*
8:36 What *g* is it for a man
Lk 6:27 do *g* to those who hate you,
Jn 10:11 "I am the *g* shepherd.
Ro 8:28 for the *g* of those who love him,
10:15 feet of those who bring *g* news!"
12: 9 Hate what is evil; cling to what is *g*.
1Co 10:24 should seek his own *g*, but the *g*
15:33 Bad company corrupts *g* character
2Co 9: 8 you will abound in every *g* work.
Gal 6: 9 us not become weary in doing *g*,
6:10 as we have opportunity, let us do *g*
Eph 2:10 in Christ Jesus to do *g* works,
Php 1: 6 that he who began a *g* work
1Th 5:21 Hold on to the *g*.
1Ti 3: 7 have a *g* reputation with outsiders,
4: 4 For everything God created is *g*,
6:12 Fight the *g* fight of the faith.
6:18 them to do *g*, to be rich in *g* deeds,
2Ti 3:17 equipped for every *g* work.
4: 7 I have fought the *g* fight, I have
Heb 12:10 but God disciplines us for our *g*,
1Pe 2: 3 you have tasted that the Lord is *g*.
2:12 Live such *g* lives among the pagans

GOSPEL
Ro 1:16 I am not ashamed of the *g*,
15:16 duty of proclaiming the *g* of God,
1Co 1:17 to preach the *g*— not with words
9:16 Woe to me if I do not preach the *g*!
15: 1 you of the *g* I preached to you,
Gal 1: 7 a different *g*— which is really no *g*
Php 1:27 in a manner worthy of the *g*

GOSSIP
Pr 11:13 A *g* betrays a confidence,
16:28 and a *g* separates close friends.
18: 8 of a *g* are like choice morsels;
26:20 without *g* a quarrel dies down.
2Co 12:20 slander, *g*, arrogance and disorder.

GRACE (GRACIOUS)
Ps 45: 2 lips have been anointed with *g*,
Jn 1:17 *g* and truth came through Jesus
Ac 20:32 to God and to the word of his *g*,
Ro 3:24 and are justified freely by his *g*
5:15 came by the *g* of the one man,
5:17 God's abundant provision of *g*
5:20 where sin increased, *g* increased all
6:14 you are not under law, but under *g*.
11: 6 if by *g*, then it is no longer by works
2Co 6: 1 not to receive God's *g* in vain.
8: 9 For you know the *g*
9: 8 able to make all *g* abound to you,
12: 9 "My *g* is sufficient for you,
Gal 2:21 I do not set aside the *g* of God,
5: 4 you have fallen away from *g*.
Eph 1: 7 riches of God's *g* that he lavished
2: 5 it is by *g* you have been saved.
2: 7 the incomparable riches of his *g*,
2: 8 For it is by *g* you have been saved,
Php 1: 7 all of you share in God's *g* with me.
Col 4: 6 conversation be always full of *g*,
2Th 2:16 and by his *g* gave us eternal
2Ti 2: 1 be strong in the *g* that is
Tit 2:11 For the *g* of God that brings
3: 7 having been justified by his *g*,
Heb 2: 9 that by the *g* of God he might taste
4:16 find *g* to help us in our time of need
4:16 the throne of *g* with confidence,
Jas 4: 6 but gives *g* to the humble."
2Pe 3:18 But grow in the *g* and knowledge

GRACIOUS (GRACE)
Nu 6:25 and be *g* to you;
Pr 22:11 a pure heart and whose speech is *g*
Isa 30:18 Yet the LORD longs to be *g* to you

GRAIN
1Co 9: 9 ox while it is treading out the *g*."

GRANTED
Php 1:29 For it has been *g* to you on behalf

GRASS
Ps 103:15 As for man, his days are like *g*,
1Pe 1:24 "All men are like *g*,

GRAVE (GRAVES)
Pr 7:27 Her house is a highway to the *g*,
Hos 13:14 Where, O *g*, is your destruction?

GRAVES (GRAVE)
Jn 5:28 are in their *g* will hear his voice
Ro 3:13 "Their throats are open *g*;

GREAT (GREATER GREATEST GREATNESS)
Ge 12: 2 "I will make you into a *g* nation
Dt 10:17 the *g* God, mighty and awesome,
2Sa 22:36 you stoop down to make me *g*.
Ps 19:11 in keeping them there is *g* reward.
89: 1 of the LORD's *g* love forever;
103:11 so *g* is his love for those who fear
107:43 consider the *g* love of the LORD.
108: 4 For *g* is your love, higher
119:165 *G* peace have they who love your
145: 3 *G* is the LORD and most worthy
Pr 23:24 of a righteous man has *g* joy;
Isa 42:21 to make his law *g* and glorious.
La 3:23 *g* is your faithfulness.
Mk 10:43 whoever wants to become *g*
Lk 21:27 in a cloud with power and *g* glory.
1Ti 6: 6 with contentment is *g* gain.
Tit 2:13 glorious appearing of our *g* God
Heb 2: 3 if we ignore such a *g* salvation?
1Jn 3: 1 How *g* is the love the Father has

GREATER (GREAT)
Mk 12:31 There is no commandment *g*
Jn 1:50 You shall see *g* things than that."
15:13 *G* love has no one than this,
1Co 12:31 But eagerly desire the *g* gifts.
Heb 11:26 as of *g* value than the treasures
1Jn 3:20 For God is *g* than our hearts,
4: 4 is in you is *g* than the one who is

GREATEST (GREAT)
Mt 22:38 is the first and *g* commandment.
Lk 9:48 least among you all—he is the *g*."
1Co 13:13 But the *g* of these is love.

GREATNESS (GREAT)
Ps 145: 3 his *g* no one can fathom.
Ps 150: 2 praise him for his surpassing *g*.
Isa 63: 1 forward in the *g* of his strength?
Php 3: 8 compared to the surpassing *g*

GREED (GREEDY)
Lk 12:15 on your guard against all kinds of *g*
Ro 1:29 kind of wickedness, evil, *g*
Eph 5: 3 or of any kind of impurity, or of *g*,
Col 3: 5 evil desires and *g*, which is idolatry
2Pe 2:14 experts in *g*— an accursed brood!

GREEDY (GREED)
Pr 15:27 A *g* man brings trouble
1Co 6:10 nor thieves nor the *g* nor drunkards
Eph 5: 5 No immoral, impure or *g* person—
1Pe 5: 2 not *g* for money, but eager to serve;

GREEN
Ps 23: 2 makes me lie down in *g* pastures,

GREW (GROW)
Lk 2:52 And Jesus *g* in wisdom and stature,
Ac 16: 5 in the faith and *g* daily in numbers.

GRIEF (GRIEVE)
Ps 10:14 O God, do see trouble and *g*;
Pr 14:13 and joy may end in *g*.
La 3:32 Though he brings *g*, he will show
Jn 16:20 but your *g* will turn to joy.
1Pe 1: 6 had to suffer *g* in all kinds of trials.

GRIEVE (GRIEF)
Eph 4:30 do not *g* the Holy Spirit of God,
1Th 4:13 or to *g* like the rest of men,

GROUND
Ge 3:17 "Cursed is the *g* because of you;
Ex 3: 5 where you are standing is holy *g*."
Eph 6:13 you may be able to stand your *g*,

GROW (GREW)
Pr 13:11 by little makes it *g*.
1Co 3: 6 watered it, but God made it *g*.
2Pe 3:18 But *g* in the grace and knowledge

GRUMBLE (GRUMBLING)
1Co 10:10 And do not *g*, as some of them did
Jas 5: 9 Don't *g* against each other,

GRUMBLING (GRUMBLE)
Jn 6:43 "Stop *g* among yourselves,"
1Pe 4: 9 to one another without *g*.

GUARANTEE (GUARANTEEING)
Heb 7:22 Jesus has become the *g*

GUARANTEEING (GUARANTEE)
2Co 1:22 as a deposit, *g* what is to come.
Eph 1:14 who is a deposit *g* our inheritance

GUARD (GUARDS)
Ps 141: 3 Set a *g* over my mouth, O LORD;
Pr 4:23 Above all else, *g* your heart,
Isa 52:12 the God of Israel will be your rear *g*
Mk 13:33 Be on *g*! Be alert! You do not know
1Co 16:13 Be on your *g*; stand firm in the faith
Php 4: 7 will *g* your hearts and your minds
1Ti 6:20 *g* what has been entrusted

GUARDS (GUARD)
Pr 13: 3 He who *g* his lips *g* his life,
19:16 who obeys instructions *g* his life,

Pr 21:23 He who *g* his mouth and his tongue
22: 5 he who *g* his soul stays far

GUIDE
Ex 13:21 of cloud to *g* them on their way
15:13 In your strength you will *g* them
Ne 9:19 cease to *g* them on their path,
Ps 25: 5 *g* me in your truth and teach me,
43: 3 let them *g* me;
48:14 he will be our *g* even to the end.
67: 4 and *g* the nations of the earth.
73:24 You *g* me with your counsel,
139:10 even there your hand will *g* me,
Pr 4:11 I *g* you in the way of wisdom
6:22 When you walk, they will *g* you;
Isa 58:11 The LORD will *g* you always;
Jn 16:13 comes, he will *g* you into all truth.

GUILTY
Ex 34: 7 does not leave the *g* unpunished;
Jn 8:46 Can any of you prove me *g* of sin?
Heb 10:22 to cleanse us from a *g* conscience
Jas 2:10 at just one point is *g* of breaking all

HADES
Mt 16:18 the gates of *H* will not overcome it.

HAGAR
Servant of Sarah, wife of Abraham, mother of Ishmael (Ge 16:1-6; 25:12). Driven away by Sarah while pregnant (Ge 16:5-16); after birth of Isaac (Ge 21:9-21; Gal 4:21-31).

HAGGAI*
Post-exilic prophet who encouraged rebuilding of the temple (Ezr 5:1; 6:14; Hag 1-2).

HAIR (HAIRS)
Lk 21:18 But not a *h* of your head will perish
1Co 11: 6 for a woman to have her *h* cut

HAIRS (HAIR)
Mt 10:30 even the very *h* of your head are all

HALLELUJAH*
Rev 19: 1, 3, 4, 6

HALLOWED (HOLY)
Mt 6: 9 *h* be your name,

HAND (HANDS)
Ps 16: 8 Because he is at my right *h*,
37:24 the LORD upholds him with his *h*.
139:10 even there your *h* will guide me,
Ecc 9:10 Whatever your *h* finds to do,
Mt 6: 3 know what your right *h* is doing,
Jn 10:28 one can snatch them out of my *h*.
1Co 12:15 I am not a *h*, I do not belong

HANDS (HAND)
Ps 22:16 they have pierced my *h*
24: 4 He who has clean *h* and a pure
31: 5 Into your *h* I commit my spirit;
31:15 My times are in your *h*;
Pr 10: 4 Lazy *h* make a man poor,
31:20 and extends her *h* to the needy.
Isa 55:12 will clap their *h*.
65: 2 All day long I have held out my *h*
Lk 23:46 into your *h* I commit my spirit."
1Th 4:11 and to work with your *h*,
1Ti 2: 8 to lift up holy *h* in prayer,
5:22 hasty in the laying on of *h*,

HANNAH*
Wife of Elkanah, mother of Samuel (1Sa 1). Prayer at dedication of Samuel (1Sa 2:1-10). Blessed (1Sa 2:18-21).

HAPPY
Ps 68: 3 may they be *h* and joyful.
Pr 15:13 A *h* heart makes the face cheerful,
Ecc 3:12 better for men than to be *h*
Jas 5:13 Is anyone *h*? Let him sing songs

HARD (HARDEN HARDSHIP)
Ge 18:14 Is anything too *h* for the LORD?
Mt 19:23 it is *h* for a rich man
1Co 4:12 We work *h* with our own hands.
1Th 5:12 to respect those who work *h*

HARDEN (HARD)
Ro 9:18 he hardens whom he wants to *h*.
Heb 3: 8 do not *h* your hearts

HARDHEARTED* (HEART)
Dt 15: 7 do not be *h* or tightfisted

HARDSHIP (HARD)
Ro 8:35 Shall trouble or *h* or persecution
2Ti 2: 3 Endure *h* with us like a good
4: 5 endure *h*, do the work
Heb 12: 7 Endure *h* as discipline; God is

HARM
Ps 121: 6 the sun will not *h* you by day,
Pr 3:29 not plot *h* against your neighbor,
31:12 She brings him good, not *h*,
Ro 13:10 Love does no *h* to its neighbor.
1Jn 5:18 and the evil one cannot *h* him.

HARMONY
Ro 12:16 Live in *h* with one another.
2Co 6:15 What *h* is there between Christ
1Pe 3: 8 live in *h* with one another;

HARVEST
Mt 9:37 *h* is plentiful but the workers are
Jn 4:35 at the fields! They are ripe for *h*.
Gal 6: 9 at the proper time we will reap a *h*
Heb 12:11 it produces a *h* of righteousness

HASTE (HASTY)
Pr 21: 5 as surely as *h* leads to poverty.
29:20 Do you see a man who speaks in *h*?

HASTY* (HASTE)
Pr 19: 2 nor to be *h* and miss the way.
Ecc 5: 2 do not be *h* in your heart
1Ti 5:22 Do not be *h* in the laying

HATE (HATED HATES HATRED)
Lev 19:17 " 'Do not *h* your brother
Ps 5: 5 you *h* all who do wrong.
45: 7 righteousness and *h* wickedness;
97:10 those who love the LORD *h* evil,
139:21 Do I not *h* those who *h* you,
Pr 8:13 To fear the LORD is to *h* evil;
Am 5:15 *H* evil, love good;
Mal 2:16 "I *h* divorce," says the LORD God
Mt 5:43 your neighbor and *h* your enemy.'
10:22 All men will *h* you because of me,
Lk 6:27 do good to those who *h* you,
Ro 12: 9 *H* what is evil; cling to what is good

HATED (HATE)
Ro 9:13 "Jacob I loved, but Esau I *h*."
Eph 5:29 no one ever *h* his own body,
Heb 1: 9 righteousness and *h* wickedness;

HATES (HATE)
Pr 6:16 There are six things the LORD *h*,
13:24 He who spares the rod *h* his son,
Jn 3:20 Everyone who does evil *h* the light,
1Jn 2: 9 *h* his brother is still in the darkness.

HATRED (HATE)
Pr 10:12 *H* stirs up dissension,
Jas 4: 4 with the world is *h* toward God?

HAUGHTY
Pr 16:18 a *h* spirit before a fall.

HAY
1Co 3:12 costly stones, wood, *h* or straw,

HEAD (HEADS HOTHEADED)
Ge 3:15 he will crush your *h*,
Ps 23: 5 You anoint my *h* with oil;
Pr 25:22 will heap burning coals on his *h*,
Isa 59:17 and the helmet of salvation on his *h*
Mt 8:20 of Man has no place to lay his *h*."
Ro 12:20 will heap burning coals on his *h*."
1Co 11: 3 and the *h* of Christ is God.
12:21 And the *h* cannot say to the feet,
Eph 5:23 For the husband is the *h* of the wife
2Ti 4: 5 keep your *h* in all situations,
Rev 19:12 and on his *h* are many crowns.

HEADS (HEAD)
Lev 26:13 you to walk with *h* held high.
Isa 35:10 everlasting joy will crown their *h*.

HEAL (HEALED HEALING HEALS)
2Ch 7:14 their sin and will *h* their land.
Ps 41: 4 *h* me, for I have sinned against you
Mt 10: 8 *H* the sick, raise the dead,
Lk 4:23 to me: 'Physician, *h* yourself!
5:17 present for him to *h* the sick.

HEALED (HEAL)
Isa 53: 5 and by his wounds we are *h*.
Mt 9:22 he said, "your faith has *h* you."
14:36 and all who touched him were *h*.
Ac 4:10 this man stands before you *h*.
14: 9 saw that he had faith to be *h*
Jas 5:16 for each other so that you may be *h*
1Pe 2:24 by his wounds you have been *h*.

HEALING (HEAL)
Eze 47:12 for food and their leaves for *h*."
Mal 4: 2 rise with *h* in its wings.
1Co 12: 9 to another gifts of *h*
12:30 Do all have gifts of *h*? Do all speak
Rev 22: 2 are for the *h* of the nations.

HEALS (HEAL)
Ex 15:26 for I am the LORD, who *h* you."
Ps 103: 3 and *h* all your diseases;
147: 3 He *h* the brokenhearted

HEALTH (HEALTHY)
Pr 3: 8 This will bring *h* to your body
15:30 and good news gives *h* to the bones

HEALTHY (HEALTH)
Mk 2:17 "It is not the *h* who need a doctor,

HEAR (HEARD HEARING HEARS)
Dt 6: 4 *H*, O Israel: The LORD our God,
31:13 must *h* it and learn
2Ch 7:14 then will I *h* from heaven
Ps 94: 9 he who implanted the ear not *h*?
Isa 29:18 that day the deaf will *h* the words
65:24 while they are still speaking I will *h*
Mt 11:15 He who has ears, let him *h*.
Jn 8:47 reason you do not *h* is that you do
2Ti 4: 3 what their itching ears want to *h*.

HEARD (HEAR)
Job 42: 5 My ears had *h* of you
Isa 66: 8 Who has ever *h* of such a thing?
Mt 5:21 "You have *h* that it was said

Mt 5:27 "You have *h* that it was said,
5:33 you have *h* that it was said
5:38 "You have *h* that it was said,
5:43 "You have *h* that it was said,
1Co 2: 9 no ear has *h,*
1Th 2:13 word of God, which you *h* from us,
2Ti 1:13 What you *h* from me, keep
Jas 1:25 not forgetting what he has *h,*

HEARING (HEAR)
Ro 10:17 faith comes from *h* the message,

HEARS (HEAR)
Jn 5:24 whoever *h* my word and believes
1Jn 5:14 according to his will, he *h* us.
Rev 3:20 If anyone *h* my voice and opens

HEART (BROKENHEARTED HARDHEARTED HEARTS WHOLEHEARTEDLY)
Ex 25: 2 each man whose *h* prompts him
Lev 19:17 Do not hate your brother in your *h.*
Dt 4:29 if you look for him with all your *h*
6: 5 LORD your God with all your *h*
10:12 LORD your God with all your *h*
15:10 and do so without a grudging *h;*
30: 6 you may love him with all your *h*
30:10 LORD your God with all your *h*
Jos 22: 5 and to serve him with all your *h*
1Sa 13:14 sought out a man after his own *h*
16: 7 but the LORD looks at the *h."*
2Ki 23: 3 with all his *h* and all his soul,
1Ch 28: 9 for the LORD searches every *h*
2Ch 7:16 and my *h* will always be there.
Job 22:22 and lay up his words in your *h.*
37: 1 "At this my *h* pounds
Ps 14: 1 The fool says in his *h,*
19:14 and the meditation of my *h*
37: 4 will give you the desires of your *h.*
45: 1 My *h* is stirred by a noble theme
51:10 Create in me a pure *h,* O God,
51:17 a broken and contrite *h,*
66:18 If I had cherished sin in my *h,*
86:11 give me an undivided *h,*
119:11 I have hidden your word in my *h*
119:32 for you have set my *h* free.
139:23 Search me, O God, and know my *h*
Pr 3: 5 Trust in the LORD with all your *h*
4:21 keep them within your *h;*
4:23 Above all else, guard your *h,*
7: 3 write them on the tablet of your *h.*
13:12 Hope deferred makes the *h* sick,
14:13 Even in laughter the *h* may ache,
15:30 A cheerful look brings joy to the *h,*
17:22 A cheerful *h* is good medicine,
24:17 stumbles, do not let your *h* rejoice,
27:19 so a man's *h* reflects the man.
Ecc 8: 5 wise *h* will know the proper time
SS 4: 9 You have stolen my *h,* my sister,
Isa 40:11 and carries them close to his *h;*
57:15 and to revive the *h* of the contrite.
Jer 17: 9 The *h* is deceitful above all things
29:13 when you seek me with all your *h.*
Eze 36:26 I will give you a new *h*
Mt 5: 8 Blessed are the pure in *h,*
6:21 treasure is, there your *h* will be
12:34 of the *h* the mouth speaks.
22:37 the Lord your God with all your *h*
Lk 6:45 overflow of his *h* his mouth speaks.
Ro 2:29 is circumcision of the *h,*
10:10 is with your *h* that you believe
1Co 14:25 the secrets of his *h* will be laid bare.
Eph 5:19 make music in your *h* to the Lord,
6: 6 doing the will of God from your *h.*
Col 3:23 work at it with all your *h,*
1Pe 1:22 one another deeply, from the *h.*

HEARTS (HEART)
Dt 11:18 Fix these words of mine in your *h*
1Ki 8:39 for you alone know the *h* of all men
8:61 your *h* must be fully committed
Ps 62: 8 pour out your *h* to him,
Ecc 3:11 also set eternity in the *h* of men;
Jer 31:33 and write it on their *h.*
Lk 16:15 of men, but God knows your *h.*
24:32 "Were not our *h* burning within us
Jn 14: 1 "Do not let your *h* be troubled.
Ac 15: 9 for he purified their *h* by faith.
Ro 2:15 of the law are written on their *h,*
2Co 3: 2 written on our *h,* known
3: 3 but on tablets of human *h.*
4: 6 shine in our *h* to give us the light
Eph 3:17 dwell in your *h* through faith.
Col 3: 1 set your *h* on things above,
Heb 3: 8 do not harden your *h*
10:16 I will put my laws in their *h,*
1Jn 3:20 For God is greater than our *h,*

HEAT
2Pe 3:12 and the elements will melt in the *h.*

HEAVEN (HEAVENLY HEAVENS)
Ge 14:19 Creator of *h* and earth.
1Ki 8:27 the highest *h,* cannot contain you.
2Ki 2: 1 up to *h* in a whirlwind,
2Ch 7:14 then will I hear from *h*
Isa 14:12 How you have fallen from *h,*
66: 1 "*H* is my throne,
Da 7:13 coming with the clouds of *h.*
Mt 6: 9 " 'Our Father in *h,*
6:20 up for yourselves treasures in *h,*
16:19 bind on earth will be bound in *h,*
19:23 man to enter the kingdom of *h.*
24:35 *H* and earth will pass away,
26:64 and coming on the clouds of *h."*
28:18 "All authority in *h*
Mk 16:19 he was taken up into *h*
Lk 15: 7 in *h* over one sinner who repents
18:22 and you will have treasure in *h.*
Ro 10: 6 'Who will ascend into *h?*' " (that is,
2Co 5: 1 an eternal house in *h,* not built
12: 2 ago was caught up to the third *h.*
Php 2:10 *h* and on earth and under the earth,
3:20 But our citizenship is in *h.*
1Th 1:10 and to wait for his Son from *h,*
Heb 8: 5 and shadow of what is in *h.*
9:24 he entered *h* itself, now to appear
2Pe 3:13 we are looking forward to a new *h*
Rev 21: 1 Then I saw a new *h* and a new earth

HEAVENLY (HEAVEN)
Ps 8: 5 him a little lower than the *h* beings
2Co 5: 2 to be clothed with our *h* dwelling,
Eph 1: 3 in the *h* realms with every spiritual
1:20 at his right hand in the *h* realms,
2Ti 4:18 bring me safely to his *h* kingdom.
Heb 12:22 to the *h* Jerusalem, the city

HEAVENS (HEAVEN)
Ge 1: 1 In the beginning God created the *h*
1Ki 8:27 The *h,* even the highest heaven,
2Ch 2: 6 since the *h,* even the highest
Ps 8: 3 When I consider your *h,*
19: 1 The *h* declare the glory of God;
102:25 the *h* are the work of your hands.
108: 4 is your love, higher than the *h;*
119:89 it stands firm in the *h.*
139: 8 If I go up to the *h,* you are there;
Isa 51: 6 Lift up your eyes to the *h,*
55: 9 "As the *h* are higher than the earth,
65:17 new *h* and a new earth.
Joel 2:30 I will show wonders in the *h*
Eph 4:10 who ascended higher than all the *h,*
2Pe 3:10 The *h* will disappear with a roar;

HEBREW
Ge 14:13 and reported this to Abram the *H.*

HEEDS
Pr 13: 1 wise son *h* his father's instruction,
13:18 whoever *h* correction is honored.
15: 5 whoever *h* correction shows
15:32 whoever *h* correction gains

HEEL
Ge 3:15 and you will strike his *h."*

HEIRS (INHERIT)
Ro 8:17 then we are *h*— *h* of God
Gal 3:29 and *h* according to the promise.
Eph 3: 6 gospel the Gentiles are *h* together
1Pe 3: 7 as *h* with you of the gracious gift

HELL
Mt 5:22 will be in danger of the fire of *h.*
Lk 16:23 In *h,* where he was in torment,
2Pe 2: 4 but sent them to *h,* putting them

HELMET
Isa 59:17 and the *h* of salvation on his head;
Eph 6:17 Take the *h* of salvation
1Th 5: 8 and the hope of salvation as a *h.*

HELP (HELPED HELPER HELPING HELPS)
Ps 18: 6 I cried to my God for *h.*
30: 2 my God, I called to you for *h*
46: 1 an ever-present *h* in trouble.
79: 9 *H* us, O God our Savior,
121: 1 where does my *h* come from?
Isa 41:10 I will strengthen you and *h* you;
Jnh 2: 2 depths of the grave I called for *h,*
Mk 9:24 *h* me overcome my unbelief!"
Ac 16: 9 Come over to Macedonia and *h* us
1Co 12:28 those able to *h* others, those

HELPED (HELP)
1Sa 7:12 "Thus far has the LORD *h* us."

HELPER (HELP)
Ge 2:18 I will make a *h* suitable for him."
Ps 10:14 you are the *h* of the fatherless.
Heb 13: 6 Lord is my *h;* I will not be afraid.

HELPING (HELP)
Ac 9:36 always doing good and *h* the poor.
1Ti 5:10 *h* those in trouble and devoting

HELPS (HELP)
Ro 8:26 the Spirit *h* us in our weakness.

HEN
Mt 23:37 as a *h* gathers her chicks

HERITAGE (INHERIT)
Ps 127: 3 Sons are a *h* from the LORD,

HEROD
1. King of Judea who tried to kill Jesus (Mt 2; Lk 1:5).
2. Son of 1. Tetrarch of Galilee who arrested and beheaded John the Baptist (Mt 14:1-12; Mk 6:14-29; Lk 3:1, 19-20; 9:7-9); tried Jesus (Lk 23:6-15).
3. Grandson of 1. King of Judea who killed James (Ac 12:2); arrested Peter (Ac 12:3-19). Death (Ac 12:19-23).

HERODIAS

Wife of Herod the Tetrarch who persuaded her daughter to ask for John the Baptist's head (Mt 14:1-12; Mk 6:14-29).

HEZEKIAH

King of Judah. Restored the temple and worship (2Ch 29-31). Sought the LORD for help against Assyria (2Ki 18-19; 2Ch 32:1-23; Isa 36-37). Illness healed (2Ki 20:1-11; 2Ch 32:24-26; Isa 38). Judged for showing Babylonians his treasures (2Ki 20:12-21; 2Ch 32:31; Isa 39).

HID (HIDE)

Ge 3: 8 and they *h* from the LORD God
Ex 2: 2 she *h* him for three months.
Jos 6:17 because she *h* the spies we sent.
Heb 11:23 By faith Moses' parents *h* him

HIDDEN (HIDE)

Ps 19:12 Forgive my *h* faults.
119:11 I have *h* your word in my heart
Pr 2: 4 and search for it as for *h* treasure,
Isa 59: 2 your sins have *h* his face from you,
Mt 5:14 A city on a hill cannot be *h*.
13:44 of heaven is like treasure *h*
Col 1:26 the mystery that has been kept *h*
2: 3 in whom are *h* all the treasures
3: 3 and your life is now *h* with Christ

HIDE (HID HIDDEN)

Ps 17: 8 *h* me in the shadow of your wings
143: 9 for I *h* myself in you.

HILL (HILLS)

Mt 5:14 A city on a *h* cannot be hidden.

HILLS (HILL)

Ps 50:10 and the cattle on a thousand *h*.
121: 1 I lift up my eyes to the *h*—

HINDER (HINDERS)

1Sa 14: 6 Nothing can *h* the LORD
Mt 19:14 come to me, and do not *h* them,
1Co 9:12 anything rather than *h* the gospel
1Pe 3: 7 so that nothing will *h* your prayers.

HINDERS (HINDER)

Heb 12: 1 let us throw off everything that *h*

HINT*

Eph 5: 3 even a *h* of sexual immorality,

HOLD

Ex 20: 7 LORD will not *h* anyone guiltless
Lev 19:13 " 'Do not *h* back the wages
Jos 22: 5 to *h* fast to him and to serve him
Ps 73:23 you *h* me by my right hand.
Pr 4: 4 "Lay *h* of my words
Isa 54: 2 do not *h* back;
Mk 11:25 if you *h* anything against anyone,
Php 2:16 as you *h* out the word of life—
3:12 but I press on to take *h* of that
Col 1:17 and in him all things *h* together.
1Th 5:21 *H* on to the good.
1Ti 6:12 Take *h* of the eternal life
Heb 10:23 Let us *h* unswervingly

HOLINESS (HOLY)

Ex 15:11 majestic in *h*,
Ps 29: 2 in the splendor of his *h*.
96: 9 in the splendor of his *h;*
Ro 6:19 to righteousness leading to *h*.
2Co 7: 1 perfecting *h* out of reverence
Eph 4:24 God in true righteousness and *h*.
Heb 12:10 that we may share in his *h*.
12:14 without *h* no one will see the Lord.

HOLY (HALLOWED HOLINESS)

Ex 19: 6 kingdom of priests and a *h* nation.'
20: 8 the Sabbath day by keeping it *h*.
Lev 11:44 and be *h*, because I am *h*.
20: 7 " 'Consecrate yourselves and be *h*,
20:26 You are to be *h* to me because I,
21: 8 Consider them *h*, because I
22:32 Do not profane my *h* name.
Ps 16:10 will you let your *H* One see decay.
24: 3 Who may stand in his *h* place?
77:13 Your ways, O God, are *h*.
99: 3 he is *h*.
99: 5 he is *h*.
99: 9 for the LORD our God is *h*.
111: 9 *h* and awesome is his name.
Isa 5:16 the *h* God will show himself *h*
6: 3 *H*, *h*, *h* is the LORD Almighty;
40:25 who is my equal?" says the *H* One.
57:15 who lives forever, whose name is *h*:
Eze 28:25 I will show myself *h* among them
Da 9:24 prophecy and to anoint the most *h*.
Hab 2:20 But the LORD is in his *h* temple;
Ac 2:27 will you let your *H* One see decay.
Ro 7:12 and the commandment is *h*,
12: 1 as living sacrifices, *h* and pleasing
Eph 5: 3 improper for God's *h* people.
2Th 1:10 to be glorified in his *h* people
2Ti 1: 9 saved us and called us to a *h* life—
3:15 you have known the *h* Scriptures,
Tit 1: 8 upright, *h* and disciplined.
1Pe 1:15 But just as he who called you is *h*,
1:16 is written: "Be *h*, because I am *h*."
2: 9 a royal priesthood, a *h* nation,
2Pe 3:11 You ought to live *h* and godly lives
Rev 4: 8 "*H*, *h*, *h* is the Lord God

HOME (HOMES)

Dt 6: 7 Talk about them when you sit at *h*
Ps 84: 3 Even the sparrow has found a *h*,
Pr 3:33 but he blesses the *h* of the righteous
Mk 10:29 "no one who has left *h* or brothers
Jn 14:23 to him and make our *h* with him.
Tit 2: 5 to be busy at *h*, to be kind,

HOMES (HOME)

Ne 4:14 daughters, your wives and your *h*."
1Ti 5:14 to manage their *h* and to give

HOMOSEXUAL*

1Co 6: 9 male prostitutes nor *h* offenders

HONEST

Lev 19:36 Use *h* scales and *h* weights,
Dt 25:15 and *h* weights and measures,
Job 31: 6 let God weigh me in *h* scales
Pr 12:17 truthful witness gives *h* testimony,

HONEY

Ex 3: 8 a land flowing with milk and *h*—
Ps 19:10 than *h* from the comb.
119:103 sweeter than *h* to my mouth!

HONOR (HONORABLE HONORABLY HONORED HONORS)

Ex 20:12 "*H* your father and your mother,
Nu 25:13 he was zealous for the *h* of his God
Dt 5:16 "*H* your father and your mother,
1Sa 2:30 Those who *h* me I will *h*,
Ps 8: 5 and crowned him with glory and *h*.
Pr 3: 9 *H* the LORD with your wealth,
15:33 and humility comes before *h*.
20: 3 It is to a man's *h* to avoid strife,
Mt 15: 4 '*H* your father and mother'
Ro 12:10 *H* one another above yourselves.
1Co 6:20 Therefore *h* God with your body.
Eph 6: 2 "*H* your father and mother"—
1Ti 5:17 well are worthy of double *h*,
Heb 2: 7 you crowned him with glory and *h*
Rev 4: 9 *h* and thanks to him who sits

HONORABLE (HONOR)

1Th 4: 4 body in a way that is holy and *h*,

HONORABLY (HONOR)

Heb 13:18 and desire to live *h* in every way.

HONORED (HONOR)

Ps 12: 8 when what is vile is *h* among men.
Pr 13:18 but whoever heeds correction is *h*.
1Co 12:26 if one part is *h*, every part rejoices
Heb 13: 4 Marriage should be *h* by all,

HONORS (HONOR)

Ps 15: 4 but *h* those who fear the LORD,
Pr 14:31 to the needy *h* God.

HOOKS

Isa 2: 4 and their spears into pruning *h*.
Joel 3:10 and your pruning *h* into spears.

HOPE (HOPES)

Job 13:15 Though he slay me, yet will I *h*
Ps 42: 5 Put your *h* in God,
62: 5 my *h* comes from him.
119:74 for I have put my *h* in your word.
130: 7 O Israel, put your *h* in the LORD,
147:11 who put their *h* in his unfailing love
Pr 13:12 *H* deferred makes the heart sick,
Isa 40:31 but those who *h* in the LORD
Ro 5: 4 character; and character, *h*.
8:24 But *h* that is seen is no *h* at all.
12:12 Be joyful in *h*, patient in affliction,
15: 4 of the Scriptures we might have *h*.
1Co 13:13 now these three remain: faith, *h*
15:19 for this life we have *h* in Christ,
Col 1:27 Christ in you, the *h* of glory.
1Th 5: 8 and the *h* of salvation as a helmet.
1Ti 6:17 but to put their *h* in God,
Tit 2:13 while we wait for the blessed *h*—
Heb 6:19 We have this *h* as an anchor
11: 1 faith is being sure of what we *h* for
1Jn 3: 3 Everyone who has this *h*

HOPES (HOPE)

1Co 13: 7 always *h*, always perseveres.

HORSE

Ps 147:10 not in the strength of the *h*,
Pr 26: 3 A whip for the *h*, a halter
Zec 1: 8 before me was a man riding a red *h*
Rev 6: 2 and there before me was a white *h!*
6: 4 Come!" Then another *h* came out,
6: 5 and there before me was a black *h!*
6: 8 and there before me was a pale *h!*
19:11 and there before me was a white *h*,

HOSANNA

Mt 21: 9 "*H* in the highest!"

HOSHEA

Last king of Israel (2Ki 15:30; 17:1-6).

HOSPITABLE* (HOSPITALITY)

1Ti 3: 2 self-controlled, respectable, *h*,
Tit 1: 8 Rather he must be *h*, one who loves

HOSPITALITY (HOSPITABLE)

Ro 12:13 Practice *h*.

1Ti 5:10 as bringing up children, showing *h,*
1Pe 4: 9 Offer *h* to one another

HOSTILE
Ro 8: 7 the sinful mind is *h* to God.

HOT
1Ti 4: 2 have been seared as with a *h* iron.
Rev 3:15 that you are neither cold nor *h.*

HOT-TEMPERED
Pr 15:18 A *h* man stirs up dissension,
19:19 A *h* man must pay the penalty;
22:24 Do not make friends with a *h* man,
29:22 and a *h* one commits many sins.

HOTHEADED (HEAD)
Pr 14:16 but a fool is *h* and reckless.

HOUR
Ecc 9:12 knows when his *h* will come:
Mt 6:27 you by worrying can add a single *h*
Lk 12:40 the Son of Man will come at an *h*
Jn 12:23 The *h* has come for the Son of Man
12:27 for this very reason I came to this *h*

HOUSE (HOUSEHOLD STOREHOUSE)
Ex 20:17 shall not covet your neighbor's *h.*
Ps 23: 6 I will dwell in the *h* of the LORD
84:10 a doorkeeper in the *h* of my God
122: 1 "Let us go to the *h* of the LORD."
127: 1 Unless the LORD builds the *h,*
Pr 7:27 Her *h* is a highway to the grave,
21: 9 than share a *h* with a quarrelsome
Isa 56: 7 a *h* of prayer for all nations."
Zec 13: 6 given at the *h* of my friends.'
Mt 7:24 is like a wise man who built his *h*
12:29 can anyone enter a strong man's *h*
21:13 My *h* will be called a *h* of prayer,'
Mk 3:25 If a *h* is divided against itself,
Lk 11:17 a *h* divided against itself will fall.
Jn 2:16 How dare you turn my Father's *h*
12: 3 the *h* was filled with the fragrance
14: 2 In my Father's *h* are many rooms;
Heb 3: 3 the builder of a *h* has greater honor

HOUSEHOLD (HOUSE)
Jos 24:15 my *h,* we will serve the LORD."
Mic 7: 6 are the members of his own *h.*
Mt 10:36 will be the members of his own *h.*'
12:25 or *h* divided against itself will not
1Ti 3:12 manage his children and his *h* well.
3:15 to conduct themselves in God's *h,*

HUMAN (HUMANITY)
Gal 3: 3 to attain your goal by *h* effort?

HUMANITY* (HUMAN)
Heb 2:14 he too shared in their *h* so that

HUMBLE (HUMBLED HUMBLES HUMILIATE HUMILITY)
2Ch 7:14 will *h* themselves and pray
Ps 25: 9 He guides the *h* in what is right
Pr 3:34 but gives grace to the *h.*
Isa 66: 2 he who is *h* and contrite in spirit,
Mt 11:29 for I am gentle and *h* in heart,
Eph 4: 2 Be completely *h* and gentle;
Jas 4:10 *H* yourselves before the Lord,
1Pe 5: 6 *H* yourselves,

HUMBLED (HUMBLE)
Mt 23:12 whoever exalts himself will be *h,*
Php 2: 8 he *h* himself

HUMBLES (HUMBLE)
Mt 18: 4 whoever *h* himself like this child is
23:12 whoever *h* himself will be exalted.

HUMILIATE* (HUMBLE)
Pr 25: 7 than for him to *h* you
1Co 11:22 and *h* those who have nothing?

HUMILITY (HUMBLE)
Pr 11: 2 but with *h* comes wisdom.
15:33 and *h* comes before honor.
Php 2: 3 but in *h* consider others better
Tit 3: 2 and to show true *h* toward all men.
1Pe 5: 5 clothe yourselves with *h*

HUNGRY
Ps 107: 9 and fills the *h* with good things.
146: 7 and gives food to the *h.*
Pr 25:21 If your enemy is *h,* give him food
Eze 18: 7 but gives his food to the *h*
Mt 25:35 For I was *h* and you gave me
Lk 1:53 He has filled the *h* with good things
Jn 6:35 comes to me will never go *h,*
Ro 12:20 "If your enemy is *h,* feed him;

HURT (HURTS)
Ecc 8: 9 it over others to his own *h.*
Mk 16:18 deadly poison, it will not *h* them
Rev 2:11 He who overcomes will not be *h*

HURTS* (HURT)
Ps 15: 4 even when it *h,*
Pr 26:28 A lying tongue hates those it *h,*

HUSBAND (HUSBAND'S HUSBANDS)
1Co 7: 3 The *h* should fulfill his marital duty
7:10 wife must not separate from her *h.*
7:11 And a *h* must not divorce his wife.
7:13 And if a woman has a *h* who is not
7:39 A woman is bound to her *h* as long
2Co 11: 2 I promised you to one *h,* to Christ,
Eph 5:23 For the *h* is the head of the wife
5:33 and the wife must respect her *h.*
1Ti 3: 2 the *h* of but one wife, temperate,

HUSBAND'S (HUSBAND)
Pr 12: 4 of noble character is her *h* crown,
1Co 7: 4 the *h* body does not belong

HUSBANDS (HUSBAND)
Eph 5:22 submit to your *h* as to the Lord.
5:25 *H,* love your wives, just
Tit 2: 4 the younger women to love their *h*
1Pe 3: 1 same way be submissive to your *h*
3: 7 *H,* in the same way be considerate

HYMN
1Co 14:26 everyone has a *h,* or a word

HYPOCRISY (HYPOCRITE HYPOCRITES)
Mt 23:28 but on the inside you are full of *h*
1Pe 2: 1 *h,* envy, and slander of every kind.

HYPOCRITE (HYPOCRISY)
Mt 7: 5 You *h,* first take the plank out

HYPOCRITES (HYPOCRISY)
Ps 26: 4 nor do I consort with *h;*
Mt 6: 5 when you pray, do not be like the *h*

HYSSOP
Ps 51: 7 with *h,* and I will be clean;

IDLE (IDLENESS)
1Th 5:14 those who are *i,* encourage
2Th 3: 6 away from every brother who is *i*
1Ti 5:13 they get into the habit of being *i*

IDLENESS* (IDLE)
Pr 31:27 and does not eat the bread of *i.*

IDOL (IDOLATRY IDOLS)
Isa 44:17 From the rest he makes a god, his *i;*
1Co 8: 4 We know that an *i* is nothing at all

IDOLATRY (IDOL)
Col 3: 5 evil desires and greed, which is *i.*

IDOLS (IDOL)
1Co 8: 1 Now about food sacrificed to *i:*

IGNORANT (IGNORE)
1Co 15:34 for there are some who are *i* of God
Heb 5: 2 to deal gently with those who are *i*
1Pe 2:15 good you should silence the *i* talk
2Pe 3:16 which *i* and unstable people distort

IGNORE (IGNORANT IGNORES)
Dt 22: 1 do not *i* it but be sure
Ps 9:12 he does not *i* the cry of the afflicted
Heb 2: 3 if we *i* such a great salvation?

IGNORES (IGNORE)
Pr 10:17 whoever *i* correction leads others
15:32 He who *i* discipline despises

ILLUMINATED*
Rev 18: 1 and the earth was *i* by his splendor.

IMAGE
Ge 1:26 "Let us make man in our *i,*
1:27 So God created man in his own *i,*
1Co 11: 7 since he is the *i* and glory of God;
Col 1:15 He is the *i* of the invisible God,
3:10 in knowledge in the *i* of its Creator.

IMAGINE
Eph 3:20 more than all we ask or *i,*

IMITATE (IMITATORS)
1Co 4:16 Therefore I urge you to *i* me.
Heb 6:12 but to *i* those who through faith
13: 7 of their way of life and *i* their faith.
3Jn :11 do not *i* what is evil but what is

IMITATORS* (IMITATE)
Eph 5: 1 Be *i* of God, therefore,
1Th 1: 6 You became *i* of us and of the Lord
2:14 became *i* of God's churches

IMMANUEL
Isa 7:14 birth to a son, and will call him *I.*
Mt 1:23 and they will call him *I*"—

IMMORAL* (IMMORALITY)
Pr 6:24 keeping you from the *i* woman,
1Co 5: 9 to associate with sexually *i* people
5:10 the people of this world who are *i,*
5:11 but is sexually *i* or greedy,
6: 9 Neither the sexually *i* nor idolaters
Eph 5: 5 No *i,* impure or greedy person—
Heb 12:16 See that no one is sexually *i,*
13: 4 the adulterer and all the sexually *i.*
Rev 21: 8 the murderers, the sexually *i,*
22:15 the sexually *i,* the murderers,

INVESTIGATED
Lk 1: 3 I myself have carefully *i* everything

INVISIBLE
Ro 1:20 of the world God's *i* qualities—
Col 1:15 He is the image of the *i* God,
1Ti 1:17 immortal, *i*, the only God,

INVITE (INVITED INVITES)
Lk 14:13 you give a banquet, *i* the poor,

INVITED (INVITE)
Mt 22:14 For many are *i*, but few are chosen
25:35 I was a stranger and you *i* me in,

INVITES (INVITE)
1Co 10:27 If some unbeliever *i* you to a meal

INVOLVED
2Ti 2: 4 a soldier gets *i* in civilian affairs—

IRON
1Ti 4: 2 have been seared as with a hot *i*.
Rev 2:27 He will rule them with an *i* scepter;

IRREVOCABLE*
Ro 11:29 for God's gifts and his call are *i*.

ISAAC
Son of Abraham by Sarah (Ge 17:19; 21:1-7; 1Ch 1:28). Offered up by Abraham (Ge 22; Heb 11:17-19). Rebekah taken as wife (Ge 24). Fathered Esau and Jacob (Ge 25:19-26; 1Ch 1:34). Tricked into blessing Jacob (Ge 27). Father of Israel (Ex 3:6; Dt 29:13; Ro 9:10).

ISAIAH
Prophet to Judah (Isa 1:1). Called by the LORD (Isa 6).

ISHMAEL
Son of Abraham by Hagar (Ge 16; 1Ch 1:28). Blessed, but not son of covenant (Ge 17:18-21; Gal 4:21-31). Sent away by Sarah (Ge 21:8-21).

ISRAEL (ISRAELITES)
1. Name given to Jacob (see JACOB).
2. Corporate name of Jacob's descendants; often specifically Northern Kingdom.
Dt 6: 4 Hear, O *I*: The LORD our God,
1Sa 4:21 "The glory has departed from *I*"—
Isa 27: 6 *I* will bud and blossom
Jer 31:10 'He who scattered *I* will gather
Eze 39:23 of *I* went into exile for their sin,
Mk 12:29 'Hear, O *I*, the Lord our God,
Lk 22:30 judging the twelve tribes of *I*.
Ro 9: 6 all who are descended from *I* are *I*.
11:26 And so all *I* will be saved,
Eph 3: 6 Gentiles are heirs together with *I*,

ISRAELITES (ISRAEL)
Ex 14:22 and the *I* went through the sea
16:35 The *I* ate manna forty years,
Hos 1:10 "Yet the *I* will be like the sand
Ro 9:27 the number of the *I* be like the sand

ITCHING*
2Ti 4: 3 to say what their *i* ears want to hear

JACOB
Second son of Isaac, twin of Esau (Ge 26:21-26; 1Ch 1:34). Bought Esau's birthright (Ge 26:29-34); tricked Isaac into blessing him (Ge 27:1-37). Abrahamic covenant perpetuated through (Ge 28:13-15; Mal 1:2). Vision at Bethel (Ge 28:10-22). Wives and children (Ge 29:1-30:24; 35:16-26; 1Ch 2-9). Wrestled with God; name changed to Israel (Ge 32:22-32). Sent sons to Egypt during famine (Ge 42-43). Settled in Egypt (Ge 46). Blessed Ephraim and Manasseh (Ge 48). Blessed sons (Ge 49:1-28; Heb 11:21). Death (Ge 49:29-33). Burial (Ge 50:1-14).

JAMES
1. Apostle; brother of John (Mt 4:21-22; 10:2; Mk 3:17; Lk 5:1-10). At transfiguration (Mt 17:1-13; Mk 9:1-13; Lk 9:28-36). Killed by Herod (Ac 12:2).
2. Apostle; son of Alphaeus (Mt 10:3; Mk 3:18; Lk 6:15).
3. Brother of Jesus (Mt 13:55; Mk 6:3; Lk 24:10; Gal 1:19) and Judas (Jude 1). With believers before Pentecost (Ac 1:13). Leader of church at Jerusalem (Ac 12:17; 15; 21:18; Gal 2:9, 12). Author of epistle (Jas 1:1).

JAPHETH
Son of Noah (Ge 5:32; 1Ch 1:4-5). Blessed (Ge 9:18-28).

JARS
2Co 4: 7 we have this treasure in *j* of clay

JEALOUS (JEALOUSY)
Ex 20: 5 the LORD your God, am a *j* God,
34:14 whose name is Jealous, is a *j* God.
Dt 4:24 God is a consuming fire, a *j* God.
Joel 2:18 the LORD will be *j* for his land
Zec 1:14 I am very *j* for Jerusalem and Zion,
2Co 11: 2 I am *j* for you with a godly jealousy

JEALOUSY (JEALOUS)
1Co 3: 3 For since there is *j* and quarreling
2Co 11: 2 I am jealous for you with a godly *j*.
Gal 5:20 hatred, discord, *j*, fits of rage,

JEHOAHAZ
1. Son of Jehu; king of Israel (2Ki 13:1-9).
2. Son of Josiah; king of Judah (2Ki 23:31-34; 2Ch 36:1-4).

JEHOASH
Son of Jehoahaz; king of Israel (2Ki 13-14; 2Ch 25).

JEHOIACHIN
Son of Jehoiakim; king of Judah exiled by Nebuchadnezzar (2Ki 24:8-17; 2Ch 36:8-10; Jer 22:24-30; 24:1). Raised from prisoner status (2Ki 25:27-30; Jer 52:31-34).

JEHOIAKIM
Son of Josiah; king of Judah (2Ki 23:34-24:6; 2Ch 36:4-8; Jer 22:18-23; 36).

JEHORAM
Son of Jehoshaphat; king of Judah (2Ki 8:16-24).

JEHOSHAPHAT
Son of Asa; king of Judah (1Ki 22:41-50; 2Ki 3; 2Ch 17-20).

JEHU
King of Israel (1Ki 19:16-19; 2Ki 9-10).

JEPHTHAH
Judge from Gilead who delivered Israel from Ammon (Jdg 10:6-12:7). Made rash vow concerning his daughter (Jdg 11:30-40).

JEREMIAH
Prophet to Judah (Jer 1:1-3). Called by the LORD (Jer 1). Put in stocks (Jer 20:1-3). Threatened for prophesying (Jer 11:18-23; 26). Opposed by Hananiah (Jer 28). Scroll burned (Jer 36). Imprisoned (Jer 37). Thrown into cistern (Jer 38). Forced to Egypt with those fleeing Babylonians (Jer 43).

JEROBOAM
1. Official of Solomon; rebelled to become first king of Israel (1Ki 11:26-40; 12:1-20; 2Ch 10). Idolatry (1Ki 12:25-33); judgment for (1Ki 13-14; 2Ch 13).
2. Son of Jehoash; king of Israel (1Ki 14:23-29).

JERUSALEM
2Ki 23:27 and I will reject *J*, the city I chose,
2Ch 6: 6 now I have chosen *J* for my Name
Ne 2:17 Come, let us rebuild the wall of *J*,
Ps 122: 6 Pray for the peace of *J*:
125: 2 As the mountains surround *J*,
137: 5 If I forget you, O *J*,
Isa 40: 9 You who bring good tidings to *J*,
65:18 for I will create *J* to be a delight
Joel 3:17 *J* will be holy;
Zep 3:16 On that day they will say to *J*,
Zec 2: 4 '*J* will be a city without walls
8: 8 I will bring them back to live in *J*;
14: 8 living water will flow out from *J*,
Mt 23:37 "O *J*, *J*, you who kill the prophets
Lk 13:34 die outside *J*! "O *J*, *J*,
21:24 *J* will be trampled
Jn 4:20 where we must worship is in *J*."
Ac 1: 8 and you will be my witnesses in *J*,
Gal 4:25 corresponds to the present city of *J*
Rev 21: 2 I saw the Holy City, the new *J*,

JESUS
LIFE: Genealogy (Mt 1:1-17; Lk 3:21-37). Birth announced (Mt 1:18-25; Lk 1:26-45). Birth (Mt 2:1-12; Lk 2:1-40). Escape to Egypt (Mt 2:13-23). As a boy in the temple (Lk 2:41-52). Baptism (Mt 3:13-17; Mk 1:9-11; Lk 3:21-22; Jn 1:32-34). Temptation (Mt 4:1-11; Mk 1:12-13; Lk 4:1-13). Ministry in Galilee (Mt 4:12-18:35; Mk 1:14-9:50; Lk 4:14-13:9; Jn 1:35-2:11; 4; 6), Transfiguration (Mt 17:1-8; Mk 9:2-8; Lk 9:28-36), on the way to Jerusalem (Mt 19-20; Mk 10; Lk 13:10-19:27), in Jerusalem (Mt 21-25; Mk 11-13; Lk 19:28-21:38; Jn 2:12-3:36; 5; 7-12). Last supper (Mt 26:17-35; Mk 14:12-31; Lk 22:1-38; Jn 13-17). Arrest and trial (Mt 26:36-27:31; Mk 14:43-15:20; Lk 22:39-23:25; Jn 18:1-19:16). Crucifixion (Mt 27:32-66; Mk 15:21-47; Lk 23:26-55; Jn 19:28-42). Resurrection and appearances (Mt 28; Mk 16; Lk 24; Jn 20-21; Ac 1:1-11; 7:56; 9:3-6; 1Co 15:1-8; Rev 1:1-20).

MIRACLES. Healings: official's son (Jn 4:43-54), demoniac in Capernaum (Mk 1:23-26; Lk 4:33-35), Peter's mother-in-law (Mt 8:14-17; Mk 1:29-31; Lk 4:38-39), leper (Mt 8:2-4; Mk 1:40-45; Lk 5:12-16), paralytic (Mt 9:1-8; Mk 2:1-12; Lk 5:17-26), cripple (Jn 5:1-9), shriveled hand (Mt 12:10-13; Mk 3:1-5; Lk 6:6-11), centurion's servant (Mt 8:5-13; Lk 7:1-10), widow's son raised (Lk 7:11-17), demoniac (Mt 12:22-23; Lk 11:14), Gadarene demoniacs (Mt 8:28-34; Mk 5:1-20; Lk 8:26-39), woman's bleeding and Jairus' daughter (Mt 9:18-26; Mk 5:21-43; Lk 8:40-56), blind man (Mt 9:27-31), mute man (Mt 9:32-33), Canaanite woman's daughter (Mt 15:21-28; Mk 7:24-30), deaf man (Mk 7:31-37), blind man (Mk 8:22-26), demoniac boy (Mt 17:14-18; Mk 9:14-29; Lk 9:37-43), ten lepers (Lk 17:11-19), man born blind (Jn 9:1-7), Lazarus raised (Jn 11), crippled woman (Lk 13:11-17), man with dropsy (Lk 14:1-6), two blind men (Mt 20:29-34; Mk 10:46-52; Lk 18:35-43), Malchus' ear (Lk 22:50-51). Other

Miracles: water to wine (Jn 2:1-11), catch of fish (Lk 5:1-11), storm stilled (Mt 8:23-27; Mk 4:37-41; Lk 8:22-25), 5,000 fed (Mt 14:15-21; Mk 6:35-44; Lk 9:10-17; Jn 6:1-14), walking on water (Mt 14:25-33; Mk 6:48-52; Jn 6:15-21), 4,000 fed (Mt 15:32-39; Mk 8:1-9), money from fish (Mt 17:24-27), fig tree cursed (Mt 21:18-22; Mk 11:12-14), catch of fish (Jn 21:1-14).

MAJOR TEACHING: Sermon on the Mount (Mt 5-7; Lk 6:17-49), to Nicodemus (Jn 3), to Samaritan woman (Jn 4), Bread of Life (Jn 6:22-59), at Feast of Tabernacles (Jn 7-8), woes to Pharisees (Mt 23; Lk 11:37-54), Good Shepherd (Jn 10:1-18), Olivet Discourse (Mt 24-25; Mk 13; Lk 21:5-36), Upper Room Discourse (Jn 13-16).

PARABLES: Sower (Mt 13:3-23; Mk 4:3-25; Lk 8:5-18), seed's growth (Mk 4:26-29), wheat and weeds (Mt 13:24-30, 36-43), mustard seed (Mt 13:31-32; Mk 4:30-32), yeast (Mt 13:33; Lk 13:20-21), hidden treasure (Mt 13:44), valuable pearl (Mt 13:45-46), net (Mt 13:47-51), house owner (Mt 13:52), good Samaritan (Lk 10:25-37), unmerciful servant (Mt 18:15-35), lost sheep (Mt 18:10-14; Lk 15:4-7), lost coin (Lk 15:8-10), prodigal son (Lk 15:11-32), dishonest manager (Lk 16:1-13), rich man and Lazarus (Lk 16:19-31), persistent widow (Lk 18:1-8), Pharisee and tax collector (Lk 18:9-14), payment of workers (Mt 20:1-16), tenants and the vineyard (Mt 21:28-46; Mk 12:1-12; Lk 20:9-19), wedding banquet (Mt 22:1-14), faithful servant (Mt 24:45-51), ten virgins (Mt 25:1-13), talents (Mt 25:14-30; Lk 19:12-27).

DISCIPLES see APOSTLES. Call of (Jn 1:35-51; Mt 4:18-22; 9:9; Mk 1:16-20; 2:13-14; Lk 5:1-11, 27-28). Named Apostles (Mk 3:13-19; Lk 6:12-16). Twelve sent out (Mt 10; Mk 6:7-11; Lk 9:1-5). Seventy sent out (Lk 10:1-24). Defection of (Jn 6:60-71; Mt 26:56; Mk 14:50-52). Final commission (Mt 28:16-20; Jn 21:15-23; Ac 1:3-8).

Ac 2:32 God has raised this *J* to life,
9: 5 "I am *J*, whom you are persecuting
15: 11 of our Lord *J* that we are saved,
16: 31 "Believe in the Lord *J*,
Ro 3:24 redemption that came by Christ *J*.
5:17 life through the one man, *J* Christ,
8: 1 for those who are in Christ *J*,
1Co 2: 2 except *J* Christ and him crucified.
8: 6 and there is but one Lord, *J* Christ,
12: 3 and no one can say, "*J* is Lord,"
2Co 4: 5 not preach ourselves, but *J* Christ
Gal 2:16 but by faith in *J* Christ.
3:28 for you are all one in Christ *J*.
5: 6 in Christ *J* neither circumcision
Eph 2:10 created in Christ *J*
2:20 with Christ *J* himself as the chief
Php 1: 6 until the day of Christ *J*.
2: 5 be the same as that of Christ *J*:
2:10 name of *J* every knee should bow,
Col 3:17 do it all in the name of the Lord *J*,
2Th 2: 1 the coming of our Lord *J* Christ
1Ti 1:15 Christ *J* came into the world
2Ti 3:12 life in Christ *J* will be persecuted,
Tit 2:13 our great God and Savior, *J* Christ,
Heb 2: 9 But we see *J*, who was made a little
3: 1 fix your thoughts on *J*, the apostle
4:14 through the heavens, *J* the Son
7:22 *J* has become the guarantee
7:24 but because *J* lives forever,
12: 2 Let us fix our eyes on *J*, the author
2Pe 1:16 and coming of our Lord *J* Christ,
1Jn 1: 7 and the blood of *J*, his Son,
2: 1 *J* Christ, the Righteous One.
2: 6 to live in him must walk as *J* did.
4:15 anyone acknowledges that *J* is
Rev 22:20 Come, Lord *J*.

JEW (JEWS JUDAISM)
Zec 8:23 of one *J* by the edge of his robe
Ro 1:16 first for the *J*, then for the Gentile.
10:12 there is no difference between *J*
1Co 9:20 To the Jews I became like a *J*,
Gal 3:28 There is neither *J* nor Greek,

JEWELRY (JEWELS)
1Pe 3: 3 wearing of gold *j* and fine clothes.

JEWELS (JEWELRY)
Isa 61:10 as a bride adorns herself with her *j*.
Zec 9:16 like *j* in a crown.

JEWS (JEW)
Mt 2: 2 who has been born king of the *J*?
27: 11 "Are you the king of the *J*?" "Yes,
Jn 4:22 for salvation is from the *J*.
Ro 3:29 Is God the God of *J* only?
1Co 1:22 *J* demand miraculous signs
9:20 To the *J* I became like a Jew,
12:13 whether *J* or Greeks, slave or free
Gal 2: 8 of Peter as an apostle to the *J*,
Rev 3: 9 claim to be *J* though they are not,

JEZEBEL
Sidonian wife of Ahab (1Ki 16:31). Promoted Baal worship (1Ki 16:32-33). Killed prophets of the LORD (1Ki 18:4, 13). Opposed Elijah (1Ki 19:1-2). Had Naboth killed (1Ki 21). Death prophesied (1Ki 21:17-24). Killed by Jehu (2Ki 9:30-37).

JOASH
Son of Ahaziah; king of Judah. Sheltered from Athaliah by Jehoiada (2Ki 11; 2Ch 22:10-23:21). Repaired temple (2Ki 12; 2Ch 24).

JOB
Wealthy man from Uz; feared God (Job 1:1-5). Righteousness tested by disaster (Job 1:6-22), personal affliction (Job 2). Maintained innocence in debate with three friends (Job 3-31), Elihu (Job 32-37). Rebuked by the LORD (Job 38-41). Vindicated and restored to greater stature by the LORD (Job 42). Example of righteousness (Eze 14:14, 20).

JOHN
1. Son of Zechariah and Elizabeth (Lk 1). Called the Baptist (Mt 3:1-12; Mk 1:2-8). Witness to Jesus (Mt 3:11-12; Mk 1:7-8; Lk 3:15-18; Jn 1:6-35; 3:27-30; 5:33-36). Doubts about Jesus (Mt 11:2-6; Lk 7:18-23). Arrest (Mt 4:12; Mk 1:14). Execution (Mt 14:1-12; Mk 6:14-29; Lk 9:7-9). Ministry compared to Elijah (Mt 11:7-19; Mk 9:11-13; Lk 7:24-35).

2. Apostle; brother of James (Mt 4:21-22; 10:2; Mk 3:17; Lk 5:1-10). At transfiguration (Mt 17:1-13; Mk 9:1-13; Lk 9:28-36). Desire to be greatest (Mk 10:35-45). Leader of church at Jerusalem (Ac 4:1-3; Gal 2:9). Elder who wrote epistles (2Jn 1; 3Jn 1). Prophet who wrote Revelation (Rev 1:1; 22:8).

3. Cousin of Barnabas, co-worker with Paul, (Ac 12:12-13:13; 15:37), see MARK.

JOIN (JOINED)
Pr 23:20 Do not *j* those who drink too much
24:21 and do not *j* with the rebellious,
Ro 15:30 to *j* me in my struggle by praying
2Ti 1: 8 *j* with me in suffering for the gospel

JOINED (JOIN)
Mt 19: 6 Therefore what God has *j* together,
Mk 10: 9 Therefore what God has *j* together,
Eph 2:21 him the whole building is *j* together
4:16 *j* and held together

JOINTS
Heb 4:12 even to dividing soul and spirit, *j*

JOKING
Eph 5: 4 or coarse *j*, which are out of place,

JONAH
Prophet in days of Jeroboam II (2Ki 14:25). Called to Nineveh; fled to Tarshish (Jnh 1:1-3). Cause of storm; thrown into sea (Jnh 1:4-16). Swallowed by fish (Jnh 1:17). Prayer (Jnh 2). Preached to Nineveh (Jnh 3). Attitude reproved by the LORD (Jnh 4). Sign of (Mt 12:39-41; Lk 11:29-32).

JONATHAN
Son of Saul (1Sa 13:16; 1Ch 8:33). Valiant warrior (1Sa 13-14). Relation to David (1Sa 18:1-4; 19-20; 23:16-18). Killed at Gilboa (1Sa 31). Mourned by David (2Sa 1).

JORAM
1. Son of Ahab; king of Israel (2Ki 3; 8-9; 2Ch 22).

JORDAN
Nu 34:12 boundary will go down along the *J*
Jos 4:22 Israel crossed the *J* on dry ground.'
Mt 3: 6 baptized by him in the *J* River.

JOSEPH
1. Son of Jacob by Rachel (Ge 30:24; 1Ch 2:2). Favored by Jacob, hated by brothers (Ge 37:3-4). Dreams (Ge 37:5-11). Sold by brothers (Ge 37:12-36). Served Potiphar; imprisoned by false accusation (Ge 39). Interpreted dreams of Pharaoh's servants (Ge 40), of Pharaoh (Ge 41:4-40). Made greatest in Egypt (Ge 41:41-57). Sold grain to brothers (Ge 42-45). Brought Jacob and sons to Egypt (Ge 46-47). Sons Ephraim and Manasseh blessed (Ge 48). Blessed (Ge 49:22-26; Dt 33:13-17). Death (Ge 50:22-26; Ex 13:19; Heb 11:22). 12,000 from (Rev 7:8).

2. Husband of Mary, mother of Jesus (Mt 1:16-24; 2:13-19; Lk 1:27; 2; Jn 1:45).

3. Disciple from Arimathea, who gave his tomb for Jesus' burial (Mt 27:57-61; Mk 15:43-47; Lk 24:50-52).

4. Original name of Barnabas (Ac 4:36).

JOSHUA
1. Son of Nun; name changed from Hoshea (Nu 13:8, 16; 1Ch 7:27). Fought Amalekites under Moses (Ex 17:9-14). Servant of Moses on Sinai (Ex 24:13; 32:17). Spied Canaan (Nu 13). With Caleb, allowed to enter land (Nu 14:6, 30). Succeeded Moses (Dt 1:38; 31:1-8; 34:9).

Charged Israel to conquer Canaan (Jos 1). Crossed Jordan (Jos 3-4). Circumcised sons of wilderness wanderings (Jos 5). Conquered Jericho (Jos 6), Ai (Jos 7-8), five kings at Gibeon (Jos 10:1-28), southern Canaan (Jos 10:29-43), northern Canaan (Jos 11-12). Defeated at Ai (Jos 7). Deceived by Gibeonites (Jos 9). Renewed covenant (Jos 8:30-35; 24:1-27). Divided land among tribes (Jos 13-22). Last words (Jos 23). Death (Jos 24:28-31).

2. High priest during rebuilding of temple (Hag 1-2; Zec 3:1-9; 6:11).

JOSIAH
Son of Amon; king of Judah (2Ki 22-23; 2Ch 34-35).

JOTHAM
Son of Azariah (Uzziah); king of Judah (2Ki 15:32-38; 2Ch 26:21-27:9).

JOY (ENJOY ENJOYMENT JOYFUL OVERJOYED REJOICE REJOICES REJOICING)
Dt 16:15 and your *j* will be complete.
1Ch 16:27 strength and *j* in his dwelling place.
Ne 8:10 for the *j* of the LORD is your
Est 9:22 their sorrow was turned into *j*
Job 38: 7 and all the angels shouted for *j*?
Ps 4: 7 have filled my heart with greater *j*
21: 6 with the *j* of your presence.
30: 11 sackcloth and clothed me with *j*,
43: 4 to God, my *j* and my delight.
51:12 to me the *j* of your salvation
66: 1 Shout with *j* to God, all the earth!
96:12 the trees of the forest will sing for *j*;
107:22 and tell of his works with songs of *j*
119: 111 they are the *j* of my heart.
Pr 10: 1 A wise son brings *j* to his father,
10:28 The prospect of the righteous is *j*,
12:20 but *j* for those who promote peace.
Isa 35:10 everlasting *j* will crown their heads
51: 11 Gladness and *j* will overtake them,
55:12 You will go out in *j*
Lk 1:44 the baby in my womb leaped for *j*.
2: 10 news of great *j* that will be
Jn 15: 11 and that your *j* may be complete.
16:20 but your grief will turn to *j*.
2Co 8: 2 their overflowing *j* and their
Php 2: 2 then make my *j* complete
4: 1 and long for, my *j* and crown,
1Th 2:19 For what is our hope, our *j*,
Phm : 7 Your love has given me great *j*
Heb 12: 2 for the *j* set before him endured
Jas 1: 2 Consider it pure *j*, my brothers,
1Pe 1: 8 with an inexpressible and glorious *j*
2Jn : 4 It has given me great *j* to find some
3Jn : 4 I have no greater *j*

JOYFUL (JOY)
Ps 100: 2 come before him with *j* songs.
Hab 3:18 I will be *j* in God my Savior.
1Th 5:16 Be *j* always; pray continually;

JUDAH
1. Son of Jacob by Leah (Ge 29:35; 35:23; 1Ch 2:1). Tribe of blessed as ruling tribe (Ge 49:8-12; Dt 33:7).
2. Name used for people and land of Southern Kingdom.
Jer 13:19 All *J* will be carried into exile,
Zec 10: 4 From *J* will come the cornerstone,
Heb 7:14 that our Lord descended from *J*,

JUDAISM (JEW)
Gal 1:13 of my previous way of life in *J*,

JUDAS
1. Apostle (Lk 6:16; Jn 14:22; Ac 1:13). Probably also called Thaddaeus (Mt 10:3; Mk 3:18).
2. Brother of James and Jesus (Mt 13:55; Mk 6:3), also called Jude (Jude 1).
3. Apostle, also called Iscariot, who betrayed Jesus (Mt 10:4; 26:14-56; Mk 3:19; 14:10-50; Lk 6:16; 22:3-53; Jn 6:71; 12:4; 13:2-30; 18:2-11). Suicide of (Mt 27:3-5; Ac 1:16-25).

JUDGE (JUDGED JUDGES JUDGING JUDGMENT)
Ge 18:25 Will not the *J* of all the earth do
1Ch 16:33 for he comes to *j* the earth.
Ps 9: 8 He will *j* the world in righteousness
Joel 3:12 sit to *j* all the nations on every side.
Mt 7: 1 Do not *j*, or you too will be judged.
Jn 12:47 For I did not come to *j* the world,
Ac 17:31 a day when he will *j* the world
Ro 2:16 day when God will *j* men's secrets
1Co 4: 3 indeed, I do not even *j* myself.
6: 2 that the saints will *j* the world?
Gal 2: 6 not *j* by external appearance—
2Ti 4: 1 who will *j* the living and the dead,
4: 8 which the Lord, the righteous *J*,
Jas 4:12 There is only one Lawgiver and *J*,
4:12 who are you to *j* your neighbor?
Rev 20: 4 who had been given authority to *j*.

JUDGED (JUDGE)
Mt 7: 1 "Do not judge, or you too will be *j*.
1Co 11:31 But if we *j* ourselves, we would not
Jas 3: 1 who teach will be *j* more strictly.
Rev 20:12 The dead were *j* according

JUDGES (JUDGE)
Jdg 2:16 Then the LORD raised up *j*,
Ps 58: 11 there is a God who *j* the earth."
Heb 4:12 it *j* the thoughts and attitudes
Rev 19: 11 With justice he *j* and makes war.

JUDGING (JUDGE)
Mt 19:28 *j* the twelve tribes of Israel.
Jn 7:24 Stop *j* by mere appearances,

JUDGMENT (JUDGE)
Dt 1:17 of any man, for *j* belongs to God.
Ps 1: 5 the wicked will not stand in the *j*,
119:66 Teach me knowledge and good *j*,
Pr 6:32 man who commits adultery lacks *j*;
12: 11 but he who chases fantasies lacks *j*.
Ecc 12:14 God will bring every deed into *j*,
Isa 66:16 the LORD will execute *j*
Mt 5:21 who murders will be subject to *j*.'
10:15 on the day of *j* than for that town.
12:36 have to give account on the day of *j*
Jn 5:22 but has entrusted all *j* to the Son,
7:24 appearances, and make a right *j*."
16: 8 to sin and righteousness and *j*:
Ro 14:10 stand before God's *j* seat.
14:13 Therefore let us stop passing *j*
1Co 11:29 body of the Lord eats and drinks *j*
2Co 5:10 appear before the *j* seat of Christ,
Heb 9:27 to die once, and after that to face *j*,
10:27 but only a fearful expectation of *j*
1Pe 4:17 For it is time for *j* to begin
Jude : 6 bound with everlasting chains for *j*

JUST (JUSTICE JUSTIFICATION JUSTIFIED JUSTIFY JUSTLY)
Dt 32: 4 and all his ways are *j*.
Ps 37:28 For the LORD loves the *j*
111: 7 of his hands are faithful and *j*;
Pr 1: 3 doing what is right and *j* and fair;
2: 8 for he guards the course of the *j*
Da 4:37 does is right and all his ways are *j*.
Ro 3:26 as to be *j* and the one who justifies
Heb 2: 2 received its *j* punishment,
1Jn 1: 9 and *j* and will forgive us our sins
Rev 16: 7 true and *j* are your judgments."

JUSTICE (JUST)
Ex 23: 2 do not pervert *j* by siding
23: 6 "Do not deny *j* to your poor people
Job 37:23 in his *j* and great righteousness,
Ps 9: 8 he will govern the peoples with *j*.
9:16 The LORD is known by his *j*;
11: 7 he loves *j*;
45: 6 a scepter of *j* will be the scepter
101: 1 I will sing of your love and *j*;
106: 3 Blessed are they who maintain *j*,
Pr 21:15 When *j* is done, it brings joy
28: 5 Evil men do not understand *j*,
29: 4 By *j* a king gives a country stability
29:26 from the LORD that man gets *j*.
Isa 9: 7 it with *j* and righteousness
28:17 I will make *j* the measuring line
30:18 For the LORD is a God of *j*.
42: 1 and he will bring *j* to the nations.
42: 4 till he establishes *j* on earth.
56: 1 "Maintain *j*
61: 8 "For I, the LORD, love *j*;
Jer 30: 11 I will discipline you but only with *j*;
Eze 34:16 I will shepherd the flock with *j*.
Am 5:15 maintain *j* in the courts.
5:24 But let *j* roll on like a river,
Zec 7: 9 'Administer true *j*; show mercy
Lk 11:42 you neglect *j* and the love of God.
Ro 3:25 He did this to demonstrate his *j*,

JUSTIFICATION (JUST)
Ro 4:25 and was raised to life for our *j*.
5:18 of righteousness was *j* that brings

JUSTIFIED (JUST)
Ac 13:39 him everyone who believes is *j*
Ro 3:24 and are *j* freely by his grace
3:28 For we maintain that a man is *j*
5: 1 since we have been *j* through faith,
5: 9 Since we have now been *j*
8:30 those he called, he also *j*; those he *j*,
1Co 6: 11 you were *j* in the name
Gal 2:16 observing the law no one will be *j*.
3: 11 Clearly no one is *j* before God
3:24 to Christ that we might be *j* by faith
Jas 2:24 You see that a person is *j*

JUSTIFY (JUST)
Gal 3: 8 that God would *j* the Gentiles

JUSTLY (JUST)
Mic 6: 8 To act *j* and to love mercy

KEEP (KEEPER KEEPING KEEPS KEPT)
Ge 31:49 "May the LORD *k* watch
Ex 20: 6 and *k* my commandments.
Nu 6:24 and *k* you;
Ps 18:28 You, O LORD, *k* my lamp burning
19:13 *K* your servant also from willful
119: 9 can a young man *k* his way pure?
121: 7 The LORD will *k* you
141: 3 *k* watch over the door of my lips.
Pr 4:24 *k* corrupt talk far from your lips.
Isa 26: 3 You will *k* in perfect peace
Mt 10:10 for the worker is worth his *k*.
Lk 12:35 and *k* your lamps burning,
Gal 5:25 let us *k* in step with the Spirit.
Eph 4: 3 Make every effort to *k* the unity
1Ti 5:22 *K* yourself pure.
2Ti 4: 5 *k* your head in all situations,
Heb 13: 5 *K* your lives free from the love
Jas 1:26 and yet does not *k* a tight rein
2: 8 If you really *k* the royal law found
Jude :24 able to *k* you from falling

KEEPER (KEEP)
Ge 4: 9 I my brother's *k*?" The LORD

KEEPING (KEEP)
Ex 20: 8 the Sabbath day by *k* it holy.

Ps 19: 11 in *k* them there is great reward.
Mt 3: 8 Produce fruit in *k* with repentance.
Lk 2: 8 *k* watch over their flocks at night.
1Co 7:19 *K* God's commands is what counts.
2Pe 3: 9 Lord is not slow in *k* his promise,

KEEPS (KEEP)
Pr 17:28 a fool is thought wise if he *k* silent,
Am 5:13 Therefore the prudent man *k* quiet
1Co 13: 5 is not easily angered, it *k* no record
Jas 2: 10 For whoever *k* the whole law

KEPT (KEEP)
Ps 130: 3 If you, O LORD, *k* a record of sins,
2Ti 4: 7 finished the race, I have *k* the faith.
1Pe 1: 4 spoil or fade—*k* in heaven for you,

KEYS
Mt 16:19 I will give you the *k* of the kingdom

KILL (KILLS)
Mt 17:23 They will *k* him, and on the third

KILLS (KILL)
Lev 24:21 but whoever *k* a man must be put
2Co 3: 6 for the letter *k*, but the Spirit gives

KIND (KINDNESS KINDS)
Ge 1:24 animals, each according to its *k*."
2Ch 10: 7 "If you will be *k* to these people
Pr 11:17 A *k* man benefits himself,
12:25 but a *k* word cheers him up.
14:21 blessed is he who is *k* to the needy.
14:31 whoever is *k* to the needy honors
19:17 He who is *k* to the poor lends
Da 4:27 by being *k* to the oppressed.
Lk 6:35 because he is *k* to the ungrateful
1Co 13: 4 Love is patient, love is *k*.
15:35 With what *k* of body will they
Eph 4:32 Be *k* and compassionate
1Th 5:15 but always try to be *k* to each other
2Ti 2:24 instead, he must be *k* to everyone,
Tit 2: 5 to be busy at home, to be *k*,

KINDNESS (KIND)
Ac 14:17 He has shown *k* by giving you rain
Ro 11:22 Consider therefore the *k*
Gal 5:22 peace, patience, *k*, goodness,
Eph 2: 7 expressed in his *k* to us
2Pe 1: 7 brotherly *k*; and to brotherly *k*,

KINDS (KIND)
1Co 12: 4 There are different *k* of gifts,
1Ti 6:10 of money is a root of all *k* of evil.

KING (KINGDOM KINGS)
1. Kings of Judah and Israel: see Saul, David, Solomon.
2. Kings of Judah: see Rehoboam, Abijah, Asa, Jehoshaphat, Jehoram, Ahaziah, Athaliah (Queen), Joash, Amaziah, Uzziah, Jotham, Ahaz, Hezekiah, Manasseh, Amon, Josiah, Jehoahaz, Jehoiakim, Jehoiachin, Zedekiah.
3. Kings of Israel: see Jeroboam I, Nadab, Baasha, Elah, Zimri, Tibni, Omri, Ahab, Ahaziah, Joram, Jehu, Jehoahaz, Jehoash, Jeroboam II, Zechariah, Shallum, Menahem, Pekah, Pekahiah, Hoshea.
Jdg 17: 6 In those days Israel had no *k*;
1Sa 12:12 the LORD your God was your *k*.
Ps 24: 7 that the *K* of glory may come in.
Isa 32: 1 See, a *k* will reign in righteousness
Zec 9: 9 See, your *k* comes to you,
1Ti 6:15 the *K* of kings and Lord of lords,
1Pe 2:17 of believers, fear God, honor the *k*.
Rev 19:16 *K* OF KINGS AND LORD

KINGDOM (KING)
Ex 19: 6 you will be for me a *k* of priests
1Ch 29: 11 Yours, O LORD, is the *k*;
Ps 45: 6 justice will be the scepter of your *k*.
Da 4: 3 His *k* is an eternal *k*;
Mt 3: 2 Repent, for the *k* of heaven is near
5: 3 for theirs is the *k* of heaven.
6:10 your *k* come,
6:33 But seek first his *k* and his
7:21 Lord,' will enter the *k* of heaven,
11: 11 least in the *k* of heaven is greater
13:24 "The *k* of heaven is like a man who
13:31 *k* of heaven is like a mustard seed,
13:33 "The *k* of heaven is like yeast that
13:44 *k* of heaven is like treasure hidden
13:45 the *k* of heaven is like a merchant
13:47 *k* of heaven is like a net that was let
16:19 the keys of the *k* of heaven;
18:23 the *k* of heaven is like a king who
19:24 for a rich man to enter the *k* of God
24: 7 rise against nation, and *k* against *k*.
24:14 gospel of the *k* will be preached
25:34 the *k* prepared for you
Mk 9:47 better for you to enter the *k* of God
10:14 for the *k* of God belongs to such
10:23 for the rich to enter the *k* of God!"
Lk 10: 9 'The *k* of God is near you.'
12:31 seek his *k*, and these things will be
17:21 because the *k* of God is within you
Jn 3: 5 no one can enter the *k* of God
18:36 "My *k* is not of this world.
1Co 6: 9 the wicked will not inherit the *k*
15:24 hands over the *k* to God the Father
Rev 1: 6 has made us to be a *k* and priests
11:15 of the world has become the *k*

KINGS (KING)
Ps 2: 2 The *k* of the earth take their stand
72: 11 All *k* will bow down to him
Da 7:24 ten horns are ten *k* who will come
1Ti 2: 2 for *k* and all those in authority,
Rev 1: 5 and the ruler of the *k* of the earth.

KINSMAN-REDEEMER (REDEEM)
Ru 3: 9 over me, since you are a *k*."

KISS
Ps 2:12 *K* the Son, lest he be angry
Pr 24:26 is like a *k* on the lips.
Lk 22:48 the Son of Man with a *k*?"

KNEE (KNEES)
Isa 45:23 Before me every *k* will bow;
Ro 14: 11 'every *k* will bow before me;
Php 2:10 name of Jesus every *k* should bow,

KNEES (KNEE)
Isa 35: 3 steady the *k* that give way;
Heb 12:12 your feeble arms and weak *k*.

KNEW (KNOW)
Job 23: 3 If only I *k* where to find him;
Jnh 4: 2 I *k* that you are a gracious
Mt 7:23 tell them plainly, 'I never *k* you.

KNOCK
Mt 7: 7 *k* and the door will be opened
Rev 3:20 I am! I stand at the door and *k*.

KNOW (FOREKNEW KNEW KNOWING KNOWLEDGE KNOWN KNOWS)
Dt 18:21 "How can we *k* when a message
Job 19:25 I *k* that my Redeemer lives,
42: 3 things too wonderful for me to *k*.
Ps 46:10 "Be still, and *k* that I am God;
139: 1 and you *k* me.
139:23 Search me, O God, and *k* my heart;
Pr 27: 1 for you do not *k* what a day may
Jer 24: 7 I will give them a heart to *k* me,
31:34 his brother, saying, '*K* the LORD,'
Mt 6: 3 let your left hand *k* what your right
24:42 you do not *k* on what day your
Lk 1: 4 so that you may *k* the certainty
Jn 3: 11 we speak of what we *k*,
4:22 we worship what we do *k*,
9:25 One thing I do *k*.
10:14 I *k* my sheep and my sheep *k* me—
17: 3 that they may *k* you, the only true
21:24 We *k* that his testimony is true.
Ac 1: 7 "It is not for you to *k* the times
Ro 6: 6 For we *k* that our old self was
7:18 I *k* that nothing good lives in me,
8:28 we *k* that in all things God works
1Co 2: 2 For I resolved to *k* nothing
6:15 Do you not *k* that your bodies are
6:19 Do you not *k* that your body is
13:12 Now I *k* in part; then I shall *k* fully,
15:58 because you *k* that your labor
Php 3:10 I want to *k* Christ and the power
2Ti 1:12 because I *k* whom I have believed,
Jas 4:14 *k* what will happen tomorrow.
1Jn 2: 4 The man who says, "I *k* him,"
3:14 We *k* that we have passed
3:16 This is how we *k* what love is:
5: 2 This is how we *k* that we love
5:13 so that you may *k* that you have

KNOWING (KNOW)
Ge 3: 5 and you will be like God, *k* good
Php 3: 8 of *k* Christ Jesus my Lord,

KNOWLEDGE (KNOW)
Ge 2: 9 the tree of the *k* of good and evil.
Job 42: 3 obscures my counsel without *k*?'
Ps 19: 2 night after night they display *k*.
73: 11 Does the Most High have *k*?"
139: 6 Such *k* is too wonderful for me,
Pr 1: 7 of the LORD is the beginning of *k*,
10:14 Wise men store up *k*,
12: 1 Whoever loves discipline loves *k*,
13:16 Every prudent man acts out of *k*,
19: 2 to have zeal without *k*,
Isa 11: 9 full of the *k* of the LORD
Hab 2:14 filled with the *k* of the glory
Ro 11:33 riches of the wisdom and *k* of God!
1Co 8: 1 *K* puffs up, but love builds up.
8: 11 Christ died, is destroyed by your *k*.
13: 2 can fathom all mysteries and all *k*,
2Co 2:14 everywhere the fragrance of the *k*
4: 6 light of the *k* of the glory of God
Eph 3:19 to know this love that surpasses *k*
Col 2: 3 all the treasures of wisdom and *k*
1Ti 6:20 ideas of what is falsely called *k*,
2Pe 3:18 grow in the grace and *k* of our Lord

KNOWN (KNOW)
Ps 16: 11 You have made *k* to me the path
105: 1 make *k* among the nations what he
Isa 46:10 *k* the end from the beginning,
Mt 10:26 or hidden that will not be made *k*.
Ro 1:19 since what may be *k* about God is
11:34 "Who has *k* the mind of the Lord?
15:20 the gospel where Christ was not *k*,

2Co 3: 2 written on our hearts, *k*
2Pe 2:21 than to have *k* it and then

KNOWS (KNOW)
1Sa 2: 3 for the LORD is a God who *k*,
Job 23:10 But he *k* the way that I take;
Ps 44:21 since he *k* the secrets of the heart?
94:11 The LORD *k* the thoughts of man;
Ecc 8: 7 Since no man *k* the future,
Mt 6: 8 for your Father *k* what you need
24:36 "No one *k* about that day or hour,
Ro 8:27 who searches our hearts *k* the mind
1Co 8: 2 who thinks he *k* something does
2Ti 2:19 The Lord *k* those who are his," and

LABAN
Brother of Rebekah (Ge 24:29-51), father of Rachel and Leah (Ge 29-31).

LABOR
Ex 20: 9 Six days you shall *l* and do all your
Isa 55: 2 and your *l* on what does not satisfy
Mt 6:28 They do not *l* or spin.
1Co 3: 8 rewarded according to his own *l*.
15:58 because you know that your *l*

LACK (LACKING LACKS)
Pr 15:22 Plans fail for *l* of counsel,
Ro 3: 3 Will their *l* of faith nullify God's
Col 2:23 *l* any value in restraining sensual

LACKING (LACK)
Ro 12:11 Never be *l* in zeal, but keep your
Jas 1: 4 and complete, not *l* anything.

LACKS (LACK)
Pr 6:32 who commits adultery *l* judgment;
12:11 he who chases fantasies *l* judgment
Jas 1: 5 any of you *l* wisdom, he should ask

LAID (LAY)
Isa 53: 6 and the LORD has *l* on him
1Co 3:11 other than the one already *l*,
1Jn 3:16 Jesus Christ *l* down his life for us.

LAKE
Rev 19:20 into the fiery *l* of burning sulfur.
20:14 The *l* of fire is the second death.

LAMB (LAMB'S LAMBS)
Ge 22: 8 "God himself will provide the *l*
Ex 12:21 and slaughter the Passover *l*.
Isa 11: 6 The wolf will live with the *l*,
53: 7 he was led like a *l* to the slaughter,
Jn 1:29 *L* of God, who takes away the sin
1Co 5: 7 our Passover *l*, has been sacrificed.
1Pe 1:19 a *l* without blemish or defect.
Rev 5: 6 Then I saw a *L*, looking
5:12 "Worthy is the *L*, who was slain,
14: 4 They follow the *L* wherever he

LAMB'S (LAMB)
Rev 21:27 written in the *L* book of life.

LAMBS (LAMB)
Lk 10: 3 I am sending you out like *l*
Jn 21:15 Jesus said, "Feed my *l*."

LAMENT
2Sa 1:17 took up this *l* concerning Saul

LAMP (LAMPS)
2Sa 22:29 You are my *l*, O LORD;
Ps 18:28 You, O LORD, keep my *l* burning;
119:105 Your word is a *l* to my feet
Pr 31:18 and her *l* does not go out at night.
Lk 8:16 "No one lights a *l* and hides it
Rev 21:23 gives it light, and the Lamb is its *l*.

LAMPS (LAMP)
Mt 25: 1 be like ten virgins who took their *l*
Lk 12:35 for service and keep your *l* burning,

LAND
Ge 1:10 God called the dry ground "*l*,"
1:11 "Let the *l* produce vegetation:
12: 7 To your offspring I will give this *l*."
Ex 3: 8 a *l* flowing with milk and honey—
Nu 35:33 Do not pollute the *l* where you are.
Dt 34: 1 LORD showed him the whole *l*—
Jos 13: 2 "This is the *l* that remains:
14: 4 Levites received no share of the *l*
2Ch 7:14 their sin and will heal their *l*.
7:20 then I will uproot Israel from my *l*,
Eze 36:24 and bring you back into your own *l*.

LANGUAGE
Ge 11: 1 Now the whole world had one *l*
Ps 19: 3 There is no speech or *l*
Jn 8:44 When he lies, he speaks his native *l*
Ac 2: 6 heard them speaking in his own *l*.
Col 3: 8 slander, and filthy *l* from your lips.
Rev 5: 9 from every tribe and *l* and people

LAST (LASTING LASTS LATTER)
2Sa 23: 1 These are the *l* words of David:
Isa 44: 6 I am the first and I am the *l*;
Mt 19:30 But many who are first will be *l*,
Mk 10:31 are first will be *l*, and the *l* first."
Jn 15:16 and bear fruit—fruit that will *l*.
Ro 1:17 is by faith from first to *l*,
2Ti 3: 1 will be terrible times in the *l* days.
2Pe 3: 3 in the *l* days scoffers will come,
Rev 1:17 I am the First and the *L*.
22:13 the First and the *L*, the Beginning

LASTING (LAST)
Ex 12:14 to the LORD—a *l* ordinance.
Lev 24: 8 of the Israelites, as a *l* covenant.
Nu 25:13 have a covenant of a *l* priesthood,
Heb 10:34 had better and *l* possessions.

LASTS (LAST)
Ps 30: 5 For his anger *l* only a moment,
2Co 3:11 greater is the glory of that which *l*!

LATTER (LAST)
Job 42:12 The LORD blessed the *l* part

LAUGH (LAUGHS)
Ecc 3: 4 a time to weep and a time to *l*,

LAUGHS (LAUGH)
Ps 2: 4 The One enthroned in heaven *l*;
37:13 but the Lord *l* at the wicked,

LAVISHED
Eph 1: 8 of God's grace that he *l* on us
1Jn 3: 1 great is the love the Father has *l*

LAW (LAWS)
Dt 31:11 you shall read this *l* before them
31:26 "Take this Book of the *L*
Jos 1: 8 of the *L* depart from your mouth;
Ne 8: 8 from the Book of the *L* of God,
Ps 1: 2 and on his *l* he meditates day
19: 7 The *l* of the LORD is perfect,
119:18 wonderful things in your *l*.
Ps 119:72 *l* from your mouth is more precious
119:97 Oh, how I love your *l*!
119:165 peace have they who love your *l*,
Isa 8:20 To the *l* and to the testimony!
Jer 31:33 "I will put my *l* in their minds
Mt 5:17 that I have come to abolish the *L*
7:12 sums up the *L* and the Prophets.
22:40 All the *L* and the Prophets hang
Lk 16:17 stroke of a pen to drop out of the *L*.
Jn 1:17 For the *l* was given through Moses;
Ro 2:12 All who sin apart from the *l* will
2:15 of the *l* are written on their hearts,
5:13 for before the *l* was given,
5:20 *l* was added so that the trespass
6:14 because you are not under *l*,
7: 6 released from the *l* so that we serve
7:12 *l* is holy, and the commandment is
8: 3 For what the *l* was powerless to do
10: 4 Christ is the end of the *l*
13:10 love is the fulfillment of the *l*.
Gal 3:13 curse of the *l* by becoming a curse
3:24 So the *l* was put in charge to lead us
5: 3 obligated to obey the whole *l*.
5: 4 justified by *l* have been alienated
5:14 The entire *l* is summed up
Heb 7:19 (for the *l* made nothing perfect),
10: 1 The *l* is only a shadow
Jas 1:25 intently into the perfect *l* that gives
2:10 For whoever keeps the whole *l*

LAWLESSNESS*
2Th 2: 3 and the man of *l* is revealed,
2: 7 power of *l* is already at work;
1Jn 3: 4 sins breaks the law; in fact, sin is *l*.

LAWS (LAW)
Lev 25:18 and be careful to obey my *l*,
Ps 119:30 I have set my heart on your *l*.
119:120 I stand in awe of your *l*.
Heb 8:10 I will put my *l* in their minds
10:16 I will put my *l* in their hearts,

LAY (LAID LAYING)
Job 22:22 and *l* up his words in your heart.
Isa 28:16 "See, I *l* a stone in Zion,
Mt 8:20 of Man has no place to *l* his head."
Jn 10:15 and I *l* down my life for the sheep.
15:13 that he *l* down his life
1Co 3:11 no one can *l* any foundation other
1Jn 3:16 And we ought to *l* down our lives
Rev 4:10 They *l* their crowns

LAYING (LAY)
1Ti 5:22 Do not be hasty in the *l* on of hands
Heb 6: 1 not *l* again the foundation

LAZARUS
1. Poor man in Jesus' parable (Lk 16:19-31).
2. Brother of Mary and Martha whom Jesus raised from the dead (Jn 11:1-12:19).

LAZY
Pr 10: 4 *L* hands make a man poor,
Heb 6:12 We do not want you to become *l*,

LEAD (LEADERS LEADERSHIP LEADS LED)
Ex 15:13 "In your unfailing love you will *l*
Ps 27:11 *l* me in a straight path
61: 2 *l* me to the rock that is higher
139:24 and *l* me in the way everlasting.

Ps 143:10 *l* me on level ground.
Ecc 5: 6 Do not let your mouth *l* you
Isa 11: 6 and a little child will *l* them.
Da 12: 3 those who *l* many to righteousness,
Mt 6:13 And *l* us not into temptation,
1Jn 3: 7 do not let anyone *l* you astray.

LEADERS (LEAD)
Heb 13: 7 Remember your *l*, who spoke
13:17 Obey your *l* and submit

LEADERSHIP (LEAD)
Ro 12: 8 if it is *l*, let him govern diligently;

LEADS (LEAD)
Ps 23: 2 he *l* me beside quiet waters,
Pr 19:23 The fear of the LORD *l* to life:
Isa 40:11 he gently *l* those that have young.
Mt 7:13 and broad is the road that *l*
15:14 If a blind man *l* a blind man,
Jn 10: 3 sheep by name and *l* them out.
Ro 14:19 effort to do what *l* to peace
2Co 2:14 always *l* us in triumphal procession

LEAH
Wife of Jacob (Ge 29:16-30); bore six sons and one daughter (Ge 29:31-30:21; 34:1; 35:23).

LEAN
Pr 3: 5 *l* not on your own understanding;

LEARN (LEARNED LEARNING)
Isa 1:17 *l* to do right!
Mt 11:29 yoke upon you and *l* from me,

LEARNED (LEARN)
Php 4:11 for I have *l* to be content whatever
2Ti 3:14 continue in what you have *l*

LEARNING (LEARN)
Pr 1: 5 let the wise listen and add to their *l*,
2Ti 3: 7 always *l* but never able

LED (LEAD)
Ps 68:18 you *l* captives in your train;
Isa 53: 7 he was *l* like a lamb to the slaughter
Am 2:10 and I *l* you forty years in the desert
Ro 8:14 those who are *l* by the Spirit
Eph 4: 8 he *l* captives in his train

LEFT
Jos 1: 7 turn from it to the right or to the *l*,
Pr 4:27 Do not swerve to the right or the *l*;
Mt 6: 3 do not let your *l* hand know what
25:33 on his right and the goats on his *l*.

LEGION
Mk 5: 9 "My name is *L*," he replied,

LEND (LENDS)
Dt 15: 8 freely *l* him whatever he needs.
Ps 37:26 are always generous and *l* freely;
Lk 6:34 if you *l* to those from whom you

LENDS (LEND)
Pr 19:17 to the poor *l* to the LORD,

LENGTH (LONG)
Ps 90:10 The *l* of our days is seventy years—
Pr 10:27 The fear of the LORD adds *l* to life

LEPROSY
2Ki 7: 3 men with *l* at the entrance

LETTER (LETTERS)
Mt 5:18 not the smallest *l*, not the least
2Co 3: 2 You yourselves are our *l*, written
3: 6 for the *l* kills, but the Spirit gives
2Th 3:14 not obey our instruction in this *l*,

LETTERS (LETTER)
2Co 3: 7 which was engraved in *l* on stone,
10:10 "His *l* are weighty and forceful,
2Pe 3:16 His *l* contain some things that are

LEVEL
Ps 143:10 lead me on *l* ground.
Pr 4:26 Make *l* paths for your feet
Isa 26: 7 The path of the righteous is *l*;
Heb 12:13 "Make *l* paths for your feet,"

LEVI (LEVITES)
1. Son of Jacob by Leah (Ge 29:34; 46:11; 1Ch 2:1). Tribe of blessed (Ge 49:5-7; Dt 33:8-11), chosen as priests (Nu 3-4), numbered (Nu 3:39; 26:62), allotted cities, but not land (Nu 18; 35; Dt 10:9; Jos 13:14; 21), land (Eze 48:8-22), 12,000 from (Rev 7:7).
2. See MATTHEW.

LEVITES (LEVI)
Nu 1:53 The *L* are to be responsible
8: 6 "Take the *L* from among the other
18:21 I give to the *L* all the tithes in Israel

LEWDNESS
Mk 7:22 malice, deceit, *l*, envy, slander,

LIAR (LIE)
Pr 19:22 better to be poor than a *l*.
Jn 8:44 for he is a *l* and the father of lies.
Ro 3: 4 Let God be true, and every man a *l*.

LIBERATED*
Ro 8:21 that the creation itself will be *l*

LIE (LIAR LIED LIES LYING)
Lev 19:11 " 'Do not *l*.
Nu 23:19 God is not a man, that he should *l*,
Dt 6: 7 when you *l* down and when you get
Ps 23: 2 me *l* down in green pastures,
Isa 11: 6 leopard will *l* down with the goat,
Eze 34:14 they will *l* down in good grazing
Ro 1:25 exchanged the truth of God for a *l*,
Col 3: 9 Do not *l* to each other,
Heb 6:18 which it is impossible for God to *l*,

LIED (LIE)
Ac 5: 4 You have not *l* to men but to God."

LIES (LIE)
Ps 34:13 and your lips from speaking *l*.
Jn 8:44 for he is a liar and the father of *l*.

LIFE (LIVE)
Ge 2: 7 into his nostrils the breath of *l*,
2: 9 of the garden were the tree of *l*
9:11 Never again will all *l* be cut
Ex 21:23 you are to take *l* for *l*, eye for eye,
Lev 17:14 the *l* of every creature is its blood.
24:18 must make restitution—*l* for *l*.
Dt 30:19 Now choose *l*, so that you
Ps 16:11 known to me the path of *l*;
23: 6 all the days of my *l*,
34:12 Whoever of you loves *l*
39: 4 let me know how fleeting is my *l*.
49: 7 No man can redeem the *l*
104:33 I will sing to the LORD all my *l*;
Pr 1: 3 a disciplined and prudent *l*,
6:23 are the way to *l*,
7:23 little knowing it will cost him his *l*.
8:35 For whoever finds me finds *l*
11:30 of the righteous is a tree of *l*,
21:21 finds *l*, prosperity and honor.
Jer 10:23 that a man's *l* is not his own;
Eze 37: 5 enter you, and you will come to *l*.
Da 12: 2 some to everlasting *l*, others
Mt 6:25 Is not *l* more important than food,
7:14 and narrow the road that leads to *l*,
10:39 Whoever finds his *l* will lose it,
16:25 wants to save his *l* will lose it,
20:28 to give his *l* as a ransom for many."
Mk 10:45 to give his *l* as a ransom for many."
Lk 12:15 a man's *l* does not consist
12:22 do not worry about your *l*,
14:26 even his own *l*— he cannot be my
Jn 1: 4 In him was *l*, and that *l* was
3:15 believes in him may have eternal *l*.
3:36 believes in the Son has eternal *l*,
4:14 of water welling up to eternal *l*."
5:24 him who sent me has eternal *l*
6:35 Jesus declared, "I am the bread of *l*
6:47 he who believes has everlasting *l*.
6:68 You have the words of eternal *l*.
10:10 I have come that they may have *l*,
10:15 and I lay down my *l* for the sheep.
10:28 I give them eternal *l*, and they shall
11:25 "I am the resurrection and the *l*.
14: 6 am the way and the truth and the *l*.
15:13 lay down his *l* for his friends.
20:31 that by believing you may have *l*
Ac 13:48 appointed for eternal *l* believed.
Ro 4:25 was raised to *l* for our justification.
6:13 have been brought from death to *l*;
6:23 but the gift of God is eternal *l*
8:38 convinced that neither death nor *l*,
1Co 15:19 If only for this *l* we have hope
2Co 3: 6 letter kills, but the Spirit gives *l*.
Gal 2:20 The *l* I live in the body, I live
Eph 4: 1 I urge you to live a *l* worthy
Php 2:16 as you hold out the word of *l*—
Col 1:10 order that you may live a *l* worthy
1Th 4:12 so that your daily *l* may win
1Ti 4: 8 for both the present *l* and the *l*
4:16 Watch your *l* and doctrine closely.
6:19 hold of the *l* that is truly *l*.
2Ti 3:12 to live a godly *l* in Christ Jesus will
Jas 1:12 crown of *l* that God has promised
3:13 Let him show it by his good *l*,
1Pe 3:10 "Whoever would love *l*
2Pe 1: 3 given us everything we need for *l*
1Jn 3:14 we have passed from death to *l*,
5:11 has given us eternal *l*, and this *l* is
Rev 13: 8 written in the book of *l* belonging
20:12 was opened, which is the book of *l*.
21:27 written in the Lamb's book of *l*.
22: 2 side of the river stood the tree of *l*,

LIFT (LIFTED)
Ps 121: 1 I *l* up my eyes to the hills—
134: 2 *L* up your hands in the sanctuary
La 3:41 Let us *l* up our hearts and our
1Ti 2: 8 everywhere to *l* up holy hands

LIFTED (LIFT)
Ps 40: 2 He *l* me out of the slimy pit,
Jn 3:14 Moses *l* up the snake in the desert,
12:32 when I am *l* up from the earth,

LIGHT (ENLIGHTENED)
Ge 1: 3 "Let there be *l*," and there was *l*.
2Sa 22:29 LORD turns my darkness into *l*.

Job 38:19 "What is the way to the abode of *l*?
Ps 4: 6 Let the *l* of your face shine upon us
19: 8 giving *l* to the eyes.
27: 1 Lord is my *l* and my salvation—
56:13 God in the *l* of life.
76: 4 You are resplendent with *l*,
104: 2 He wraps himself in *l*
119:105 and a *l* for my path.
119:130 The unfolding of your words gives *l*;
Isa 2: 5 let us walk in the *l* of the Lord.
9: 2 have seen a great *l*;
49: 6 also make you a *l* for the Gentiles,
Mt 4:16 have seen a great *l*;
5:16 let your *l* shine before men,
11:30 yoke is easy and my burden is *l*."
Jn 3:19 but men loved darkness instead of *l*
8:12 he said, "I am the *l* of the world.
2Co 4: 6 made his *l* shine in our hearts
6:14 Or what fellowship can *l* have
11:14 masquerades as an angel of *l*.
1Ti 6:16 and who lives in unapproachable *l*,
1Pe 2: 9 of darkness into his wonderful *l*.
1Jn 1: 5 God is *l*; in him there is no
1: 7 But if we walk in the *l*,
Rev 21:23 for the glory of God gives it *l*,

LIGHTNING
Da 10: 6 his face like *l*, his eyes like flaming
Mt 24:27 For as the *l* that comes from the east
28: 3 His appearance was like *l*,

LIKENESS
Ge 1:26 man in our image, in our *l*,
Ps 17:15 I will be satisfied with seeing your *l*
Isa 52:14 his form marred beyond human *l*—
Ro 8: 3 Son in the *l* of sinful man
8:29 to be conformed to the *l* of his Son,
2Co 3:18 his *l* with ever-increasing glory,
Php 2: 7 being made in human *l*.
Jas 3: 9 who have been made in God's *l*.

LILIES
Lk 12:27 "Consider how the *l* grow.

LION
Isa 11: 7 and the *l* will eat straw like the ox.
1Pe 5: 8 around like a roaring *l* looking
Rev 5: 5 See, the *L* of the tribe of Judah,

LIPS
Ps 8: 2 From the *l* of children and infants
34: 1 his praise will always be on my *l*.
119:171 May my *l* overflow with praise,
Pr 13: 3 He who guards his *l* guards his life,
27: 2 someone else, and not your own *l*.
Isa 6: 5 For I am a man of unclean *l*,
Mt 21:16 " 'From the *l* of children
Col 3: 8 and filthy language from your *l*.

LISTEN (LISTENING LISTENS)
Dt 30:20 *l* to his voice, and hold fast to him.
Pr 1: 5 let the wise *l* and add
Jn 10:27 My sheep *l* to my voice; I know
Jas 1:19 Everyone should be quick to *l*,
1:22 Do not merely *l* to the word,

LISTENING (LISTEN)
1Sa 3: 9 Speak, Lord, for your servant is *l*
Pr 18:13 He who answers before *l*—

LISTENS (LISTEN)
Pr 12:15 but a wise man *l* to advice.

LIVE (ALIVE LIFE LIVES LIVING)
Ex 20:12 so that you may *l* long
33:20 for no one may see me and *l*."
Dt 8: 3 to teach you that man does not *l*
Job 14:14 If a man dies, will he *l* again?
Ps119:175 Let me *l* that I may praise you,
Isa 55: 3 hear me, that your soul may *l*.
Eze 37: 3 can these bones *l*?" I said,
Hab 2: 4 but the righteous will *l* by his faith
Mt 4: 4 'Man does not *l* on bread alone,
Ac 17:24 does not *l* in temples built by hands
17:28 'For in him we *l* and move
Ro 1:17 "The righteous will *l* by faith."
2Co 5: 7 We *l* by faith, not by sight.
Gal 2:20 The life I *l* in the body, I *l* by faith
5:25 Since we *l* by the Spirit, let us keep
Php 1:21 to *l* is Christ and to die is gain.
1Th 5:13 *L* in peace with each other.
2Ti 3:12 who wants to *l* a godly life
Heb12:14 Make every effort to *l* in peace
1Pe 1:17 *l* your lives as strangers here

LIVES (LIVE)
Job 19:25 I know that my Redeemer *l*,
Isa 57:15 he who *l* forever, whose name is
Da 3:28 to give up their *l* rather than serve
Jn 14:17 for he *l* with you and will be in you.
Ro 7:18 I know that nothing good *l* in me,
14: 7 For none of us *l* to himself alone
1Co 3:16 and that God's Spirit *l* in you?
Gal 2:20 I no longer live, but Christ *l* in me.
Heb13: 5 Keep your *l* free from the love
2Pe 3:11 You ought to live holy and godly *l*
1Jn 3:16 to lay down our *l* for our brothers.
4:16 Whoever *l* in love *l* in God,

LIVING (LIVE)
Ge 2: 7 and man became a *l* being.
Jer 2:13 the spring of *l* water,
Mt 22:32 the God of the dead but of the *l*."
Jn 7:38 streams of *l* water will flow
Ro 12: 1 to offer your bodies as *l* sacrifices,
Heb 4:12 For the word of God is *l* and active.
10:31 to fall into the hands of the *l* God.
Rev 1:18 I am the *L* One; I was dead,

LOAD
Gal 6: 5 for each one should carry his own *l*.

LOCUSTS
Mt 3: 4 His food was *l* and wild honey.

LOFTY
Ps 139: 6 too *l* for me to attain.
Isa 57:15 is what the high and *l* One says—

LONELY
Ps 68: 6 God sets the *l* in families,

LONG (LENGTH LONGED LONGING LONGS)
1Ki 18:21 "How *l* will you waver
Jn 9: 4 As *l* as it is day, we must do
Eph 3:18 to grasp how wide and *l* and high
1Pe 1:12 Even angels *l* to look

LONGED (LONG)
Mt 13:17 righteous men *l* to see what you see
23:37 how often I have *l*
2Ti 4: 8 to all who have *l* for his appearing.

LONGING (LONG)
Pr 13:19 A *l* fulfilled is sweet to the soul,
2Co 5: 2 *l* to be clothed with our heavenly

LONGS (LONG)
Isa 30:18 Yet the Lord *l* to be gracious

LOOK (LOOKING LOOKS)
Dt 4:29 you will find him if you *l* for him
Job 31: 1 not to *l* lustfully at a girl.
Ps 34: 5 Those who *l* to him are radiant;
Pr 4:25 Let your eyes *l* straight ahead,
Isa 60: 5 Then you will *l* and be radiant,
Hab 1:13 Your eyes are too pure to *l* on evil;
Zec 12:10 They will *l* on me, the one they
Mk 13:21 '*L*, here is the Christ!' or, '*L*,
Lk 24:39 *L* at my hands and my feet.
Jn 1:36 he said, "*L*, the Lamb of God!"
4:35 open your eyes and *l* at the fields!
19:37 "They will *l* on the one they have
Jas 1:27 to *l* after orphans and widows
1Pe 1:12 long to *l* into these things.

LOOKING (LOOK)
2Co 10: 7 You are *l* only on the surface
Rev 5: 6 I saw a Lamb, *l* as if it had been

LOOKS (LOOK)
1Sa 16: 7 Man *l* at the outward appearance,
Lk 9:62 and *l* back is fit for service
Php 2:21 For everyone *l* out

LORD† (LORD'S† LORDING)
Ne 4:14 Remember the *L*, who is great
Job 28:28 'The fear of the *L*— that is wisdom,
Ps 54: 4 the *L* is the one who sustains me.
62:12 and that you, O *L*, are loving.
86: 5 You are forgiving and good, O *L*,
110: 1 The Lord says to my *L*:
147: 5 Great is our *L* and mighty in power
Isa 6: 1 I saw the *L* seated on a throne,
Da 9: 4 "O *L*, the great and awesome God,
Mt 3: 3 'Prepare the way for the *L*,
4: 7 'Do not put the *L* your God
7:21 "Not everyone who says to me, '*L*,
22:37 " 'Love the *L* your God
22:44 For he says, " 'The *L* said to my *L*:
Mk 12:11 the *L* has done this,
12:29 the *L* our God, the *L* is one.
Lk 2: 9 glory of the *L* shone around them,
6:46 "Why do you call me, '*L*, *L*,'
10:27 " 'Love the *L* your God
Ac 2:21 on the name of the *L* will be saved.'
16:31 replied, "Believe in the *L* Jesus,
Ro 10: 9 with your mouth, "Jesus is *L*,"
10:13 on the name of the *L* will be saved
12:11 your spiritual fervor, serving the *L*.
14: 8 we live to the *L*; and if we die,
1Co 1:31 Let him who boasts boast in the *L*."
3: 5 the *L* has assigned to each his task.
7:34 to be devoted to the *L* in both body
10: 9 We should not test the *L*,
11:23 For I received from the *L* what I
12: 3 "Jesus is *L*," except by the Holy
15:57 victory through our *L* Jesus Christ.
16:22 If anyone does not love the *L*—
2Co 3:17 Now the *L* is the Spirit,
8: 5 they gave themselves first to the *L*
10:17 Let him who boasts boast in the *L*."
Gal 6:14 in the cross of our *L* Jesus Christ,
Eph 4: 5 one *L*, one faith, one baptism;
5:10 and find out what pleases the *L*.
5:19 make music in your heart to the *L*,
Php 2:11 confess that Jesus Christ is *L*,

Php 3: 1 my brothers, rejoice in the *L*!
4: 4 Rejoice in the *L* always.
Col 2: 6 as you received Christ Jesus as *L*,
3:17 do it all in the name of the *L* Jesus,
3:23 as working for the *L*, not for men,
4:17 work you have received in the *L*."
1Th 3:12 May the *L* make your love increase
5: 2 day of the *L* will come like a thief
5:23 at the coming of our *L* Jesus Christ.
2Th 2: 1 the coming of our *L* Jesus Christ
2Ti 2:19 "The *L* knows those who are his,"
Heb 12:14 holiness no one will see the *L*.
13: 6 *L* is my helper; I will not be afraid.
Jas 4:10 Humble yourselves before the *L*,
1Pe 1:25 the word of the *L* stands forever."
2: 3 you have tasted that the *L* is good.
3:15 in your hearts set apart Christ as *L*.
2Pe 1:16 and coming of our *L* Jesus Christ,
2: 1 the sovereign *L* who bought
3: 9 The *L* is not slow in keeping his
Jude :14 the *L* is coming with thousands
Rev 4: 8 holy, holy is the *L* God Almighty,
4:11 "You are worthy, our *L* and God,
17:14 he is *L* of lords and King of kings—
22:20 Come, *L* Jesus.

LORD'S† (LORD†)

Ac 21:14 and said, "The *L* will be done."
1Co 10:26 "The earth is the *L*, and everything
11:26 you proclaim the *L* death
2Co 3:18 faces all reflect the *L* glory,
2Ti 2:24 And the *L* servant must not quarrel
Jas 4:15 you ought to say, "If it is the *L* will,

LORDING* (LORD†)

1Pe 5: 3 not *l* it over those entrusted to you,

LORD‡ (LORD'S‡)

Ge 2: 4 When the *L* God made the earth
2: 7 the *L* God formed the man
3:21 The *L* God made garments of skin
7:16 Then the *L* shut him in.
15: 6 Abram believed the *L*,
18:14 Is anything too hard for the *L*?
31:49 "May the *L* keep watch
Ex 3: 2 the angel of the *L* appeared to him
9:12 the *L* hardened Pharaoh's heart
14:30 That day the *L* saved Israel
20: 2 "I am the *L* your God, who
33:11 The *L* would speak to Moses face
40:34 glory of the *L* filled the tabernacle.
Lev 19: 2 'Be holy because I, the *L* your God,
Nu 8: 5 *L* said to Moses: "Take the Levites
14:21 glory of the *L* fills the whole earth,
Dt 2: 7 forty years the *L* your God has
5: 9 the *L* your God, am a jealous God,
6: 4 The *L* our God, the *L* is one.
6: 5 Love the *L* your God
6:16 Do not test the *L* your God
10:14 To the *L* your God belong
10:17 For the *L* your God is God of gods
11: 1 Love the *L* your God and keep his
28: 1 If you fully obey the *L* your God
30:16 today to love the *L* your God,
30:20 For the *L* is your life, and he will
31: 6 for the *L* your God goes with you;
Jos 22: 5 to love the *L* your God, to walk
24:15 my household, we will serve the *L*
1Sa 1:28 So now I give him to the *L*.
2: 2 "There is no one holy like the *L*;
7:12 "Thus far has the *L* helped us."
1Sa 12:22 his great name the *L* will not reject
15:22 "Does the *L* delight
2Sa 22: 2 "The *L* is my rock, my fortress
1Ki 2: 3 and observe what the *L* your God
8:11 the glory of the *L* filled his temple.
8:61 fully committed to the *L* our God,
18:21 If the *L* is God, follow him;
2Ki 13:23 But the *L* was gracious to them
1Ch 16: 8 Give thanks to the *L*, call
16:23 Sing to the *L*, all the earth;
28: 9 for the *L* searches every heart
29:11 O *L*, is the greatness and the power
2Ch 5:14 the glory of the *L* filled the temple
16: 9 of the *L* range throughout the earth
19: 6 judging for man but for the *L*,
30: 9 for the *L* your God is gracious
Ne 1: 5 Then I said: "O *L*, God of heaven,
Job 1:21 *L* gave and the *L* has taken away;
38: 1 the *L* answered Job out
42: 9 and the *L* accepted Job's prayer.
Ps 1: 2 But his delight is in the law of the *L*
9: 9 The *L* is a refuge for the oppressed,
12: 6 And the words of the *L* are flawless
16: 8 I have set the *L* always before me.
18:30 the word of the *L* is flawless.
19: 7 The law of the *L* is perfect,
19:14 O *L*, my Rock and my Redeemer.
23: 1 The *L* is my shepherd, I shall not be
23: 6 I will dwell in the house of the *L*
27: 1 The *L* is my light and my salvation
27: 4 to gaze upon the beauty of the *L*
29: 1 Ascribe to the *L*, O mighty ones,
32: 2 whose sin the *L* does not count
33:12 is the nation whose God is the *L*,
33:18 But the eyes of the *L* are
34: 3 Glorify the *L* with me;
34: 7 The angel of the *L* encamps
34: 8 Taste and see that the *L* is good;
34:18 The *L* is close to the brokenhearted
37: 4 Delight yourself in the *L*
40: 1 I waited patiently for the *L*;
47: 2 How awesome is the *L* Most High,
48: 1 Great is the *L*, and most worthy
55:22 Cast your cares on the *L*
75: 8 In the hand of the *L* is a cup
84:11 For the *L* God is a sun and shield;
86:11 Teach me your way, O *L*,
89: 5 heavens praise your wonders, O *L*,
91: 2 I will say of the *L*, "He is my refuge
95: 1 Come, let us sing for joy to the *L*;
96: 1 Sing to the *L* a new song;
98: 4 Shout for joy to the *L*, all the earth,
100: 1 Shout for joy to the *L*, all the earth.
103: 1 Praise the *L*, O my soul;
103: 8 The *L* is compassionate
104: 1 O *L* my God, you are very great;
107: 8 to the *L* for his unfailing love
110: 1 The *L* says to my Lord:
113: 4 *L* is exalted over all the nations,
115: 1 Not to us, O *L*, not to us
116:15 Precious in the sight of the *L*
118: 1 Give thanks to the *L*, for he is good
118:24 This is the day the *L* has made;
121: 2 My help comes from the *L*,
121: 5 The *L* watches over you—
125: 2 so the *L* surrounds his people
127: 1 Unless the *L* builds the house,
127: 3 Sons are a heritage from the *L*,
130: 3 If you, O *L*, kept a record of sins,
135: 6 The *L* does whatever pleases him,
Ps 136: 1 Give thanks to the *L*, for he is good
139: 1 O *L*, you have searched me
144: 3 O *L*, what is man that you care
145: 3 Great is the *L* and most worthy
145:18 The *L* is near to all who call on him
Pr 1: 7 The fear of the *L* is the beginning
3: 5 Trust in the *L* with all your heart
3: 9 Honor the *L* with your wealth,
3:12 the *L* disciplines those he loves,
3:19 By wisdom the *L* laid the earth's
5:21 are in full view of the *L*,
6:16 There are six things the *L* hates,
10:27 The fear of the *L* adds length to life
11: 1 The *L* abhors dishonest scales,
12:22 The *L* detests lying lips,
14:26 He who fears the *L* has a secure
15: 3 The eyes of the *L* are everywhere,
16: 2 but motives are weighed by the *L*.
16: 4 The *L* works out everything
16: 9 but the *L* determines his steps.
16:33 but its every decision is from the *L*.
18:10 The name of the *L* is a strong tower
18:22 and receives favor from the *L*.
19:14 but a prudent wife is from the *L*.
19:17 to the poor lends to the *L*,
21: 3 to the *L* than sacrifice.
21:30 that can succeed against the *L*.
21:31 but victory rests with the *L*.
22: 2 The *L* is the Maker of them all.
24:18 or the *L* will see and disapprove
31:30 a woman who fears the *L* is
Isa 6: 3 holy, holy is the *L* Almighty;
11: 2 The Spirit of the *L* will rest on him
11: 9 full of the knowledge of the *L*
12: 2 The *L*, the *L*, is my strength
24: 1 the *L* is going to lay waste the earth
25: 8 The Sovereign *L* will wipe away
29:15 to hide their plans from the *L*,
33: 6 the fear of the *L* is the key
35:10 the ransomed of the *L* will return.
40: 5 the glory of the *L* will be revealed,
40: 7 the breath of the *L* blows on them.
40:10 the Sovereign *L* comes with power,
40:28 The *L* is the everlasting God,
40:31 but those who hope in the *L*
42: 8 "I am the *L*; that is my name!
43:11 I, even I, am the *L*,
44:24 I am the *L*,
45: 5 I am the *L*, and there is no other;
45:21 Was it not I, the *L*?
51:11 The ransomed of the *L* will return.
53: 6 and the *L* has laid on him
53:10 and the will of the *L* will prosper
55: 6 Seek the *L* while he may be found;
58: 8 of the *L* will be your rear guard.
58:11 The *L* will guide you always;
59: 1 the arm of the *L* is not too short
61: 3 a planting of the *L*
61:10 I delight greatly in the *L*;
Jer 1: 9 Then the *L* reached out his hand
9:24 I am the *L*, who exercises kindness,
16:19 O *L*, my strength and my fortress,
17: 7 is the man who trusts in the *L*,
La 3:40 and let us return to the *L*.
Eze 1:28 of the likeness of the glory of the *L*.
Hos 1: 7 horsemen, but by the *L* their God."
3: 5 They will come trembling to the *L*
6: 1 "Come, let us return to the *L*.
Joel 2: 1 for the day of the *L* is coming.
2:11 The day of the *L* is great;
3:14 For the day of the *L* is near

Am 5:18 long for the day of the *L?*
Jnh 1: 3 But Jonah ran away from the *L*
Mic 4: 2 up to the mountain of the *L,*
6: 8 And what does the *L* require of you
Na 1: 2 The *L* takes vengeance on his foes
1: 3 The *L* is slow to anger
Hab 2:14 knowledge of the glory of the *L,*
2:20 But the *L* is in his holy temple;
Zep 3:17 The *L* your God is with you,
Zec 1:17 and the *L* will again comfort Zion
9:16 The *L* their God will save them
14: 5 Then the *L* my God will come,
14: 9 The *L* will be king
Mal 4: 5 and dreadful day of the *L* comes.

LORD'S‡ (LORD‡)
Ex 34:34 he entered the *L* presence
Nu 14:41 you disobeying the *L* command?
Dt 6:18 is right and good in the *L* sight,
32: 9 For the *L* portion is his people,
Jos 21:45 Not one of all the *L* good promises
Ps 24: 1 The earth is the *L,* and everything
32:10 but the *L* unfailing love
89: 1 of the *L* great love forever;
103:17 *L* love is with those who fear him,
Pr 3:11 do not despise the *L* discipline
Isa 24:14 west they acclaim the *L* majesty.
62: 3 of splendor in the *L* hand,
Jer 48:10 lax in doing the *L* work!
La 3:22 of the *L* great love we are not
Mic 4: 1 of the *L* temple will be established

LOSE (LOSES LOSS LOST)
1Sa 17:32 "Let no one *l* heart on account
Mt 10:39 Whoever finds his life will *l* it,
Lk 9:25 and yet *l* or forfeit his very self?
Jn 6:39 that I shall *l* none of all that he has
Heb 12: 3 will not grow weary and *l* heart.
12: 5 do not *l* heart when he rebukes you

LOSES (LOSE)
Mt 5:13 But if the salt *l* its saltiness,
Lk 15: 4 you has a hundred sheep and *l* one
15: 8 has ten silver coins and *l* one.

LOSS (LOSE)
Ro 11:12 and their *l* means riches
1Co 3:15 he will suffer *l;* he himself will be
Php 3: 8 I consider everything a *l* compared

LOST (LOSE)
Ps 73: 2 I had nearly *l* my foothold.
Jer 50: 6 "My people have been *l* sheep;
Eze 34: 4 the strays or searched for the *l.*
34:16 for the *l* and bring back the strays.
Mt 18:14 any of these little ones should be *l.*
Lk 15: 4 go after the *l* sheep until he finds it?
15: 6 with me; I have found my *l* sheep.'
15: 9 with me; I have found my *l* coin.'
15:24 is alive again; he was *l* and is found
19:10 to seek and to save what was *l.*"
Php 3: 8 for whose sake I have *l* all things.

LOT (LOTS)
Nephew of Abraham (Ge 11:27; 12:5). Chose to live in Sodom (Ge 13). Rescued from four kings (Ge 14). Rescued from Sodom (Ge 19:1-29; 2Pe 2:7). Fathered Moab and Ammon by his daughters (Ge 19:30-38).
Est 3: 7 the *l*) in the presence of Haman
9:24 the *l*) for their ruin and destruction.
Pr 16:33 The *l* is cast into the lap,
18:18 Casting the *l* settles disputes
Ecc 3:22 his work, because that is his *l.*
Ac 1:26 Then they drew lots, and the *l* fell

LOTS (LOT)
Ps 22:18 and cast *l* for my clothing.
Mt 27:35 divided up his clothes by casting *l.*

LOVE (BELOVED LOVED LOVELY LOVER LOVERS LOVES LOVING)
Ge 22: 2 your only son, Isaac, whom you *l,*
Ex 15:13 "In your unfailing *l* you will lead
20: 6 showing *l* to a thousand generations
20: 6 of those who *l* me
34: 6 abounding in *l* and faithfulness,
Lev 19:18 but *l* your neighbor as yourself.
19:34 *L* him as yourself,
Nu 14:18 abounding in *l* and forgiving sin
Dt 5:10 showing *l* to a thousand generations
5:10 of those who *l* me
6: 5 *L* the LORD your God
7:13 He will *l* you and bless you
10:12 to walk in all his ways, to *l* him,
11:13 to *l* the LORD your God
13: 6 wife you *l,* or your closest friend
30: 6 so that you may *l* him
Jos 22: 5 to *l* the LORD your God, to walk
1Ki 3: 3 Solomon showed his *l*
8:23 you who keep your covenant of *l*
2Ch 5:13 his *l* endures forever."
Ne 1: 5 covenant of *l* with those who *l* him
Ps 18: 1 I *l* you, O LORD, my strength.
23: 6 Surely goodness and *l* will follow
25: 6 O LORD, your great mercy and *l,*
31:16 save me in your unfailing *l.*
32:10 but the LORD's unfailing *l*
33: 5 the earth is full of his unfailing *l.*
33:18 whose hope is in his unfailing *l,*
36: 5 Your *l,* O LORD, reaches
36: 7 How priceless is your unfailing *l!*
45: 7 You *l* righteousness and hate
51: 1 according to your unfailing *l;*
57:10 For great is your *l,* reaching
63: 3 Because your *l* is better than life,
66:20 or withheld his *l* from me!
70: 4 may those who *l* your salvation
77: 8 Has his unfailing *l* vanished forever
85: 7 Show us your unfailing *l,* O LORD
85:10 *L* and faithfulness meet together;
86:13 For great is your *l* toward me;
89: 1 of the LORD's great *l* forever;
89:33 but I will not take my *l* from him,
92: 2 to proclaim your *l* in the morning
94:18 your *l,* O LORD, supported me.
100: 5 is good and his *l* endures forever;
101: 1 I will sing of your *l* and justice;
103: 4 crowns you with *l* and compassion.
103: 8 slow to anger, abounding in *l.*
103:11 so great is his *l* for those who fear
107: 8 to the LORD for his unfailing *l*
108: 4 For great is your *l,* higher
116: 1 I *l* the LORD, for he heard my
118: 1 his *l* endures forever.
119:47 because I *l* them.
119:64 The earth is filled with your *l,*
119:76 May your unfailing *l* be my
119:97 Oh, how I *l* your law!
119:119 therefore I *l* your statutes.
119:124 your servant according to your *l*
119:132 to those who *l* your name.
119:159 O LORD, according to your *l.*
119:163 but I *l* your law.
119:165 peace have they who *l* your law,
122: 6 "May those who *l* you be secure.
130: 7 for with the LORD is unfailing *l*
136: 1 *His l endures forever.*
143: 8 of your unfailing *l,*
145: 8 slow to anger and rich in *l.*
145:20 over all who *l* him,
147:11 who put their hope in his unfailing *l*
Pr 3: 3 Let *l* and faithfulness never leave
4: 6 *l* her, and she will watch over you.
5:19 you ever be captivated by her *l.*
8:17 I *l* those who *l* me,
9: 8 rebuke a wise man and he will *l* you
10:12 but *l* covers over all wrongs.
14:22 those who plan what is good find *l*
15:17 of vegetables where there is *l*
17: 9 over an offense promotes *l,*
19:22 What a man desires is unfailing *l;*
20: 6 claims to have unfailing *l,*
20:13 Do not *l* sleep or you will grow
20:28 through *l* his throne is made secure
21:21 who pursues righteousness and *l*
27: 5 rebuke than hidden *l.*
Ecc 9: 6 Their *l,* their hate
9: 9 life with your wife, whom you *l,*
SS 2: 4 and his banner over me is *l.*
8: 6 for *l* is as strong as death,
8: 7 Many waters cannot quench *l;*
8: 7 all the wealth of his house for *l,*
Isa 5: 1 I will sing for the one I *l*
16: 5 In *l* a throne will be established;
38:17 In your *l* you kept me
54:10 yet my unfailing *l* for you will not
55: 3 my faithful *l* promised to David.
61: 8 "For I, the LORD, *l* justice;
63: 9 In his *l* and mercy he redeemed
Jer 5:31 and my people *l* it this way.
31: 3 you with an everlasting *l;*
32:18 You show *l* to thousands
33:11 his *l* endures forever."
La 3:22 of the LORD's great *l* we are not
3:32 so great is his unfailing *l.*
Eze 33:32 more than one who sings *l* songs
Da 9: 4 covenant of *l* with all who *l* him
Hos 2:19 in *l* and compassion.
3: 1 Go, show your *l* to your wife again,
11: 4 with ties of *l;*
12: 6 maintain *l* and justice,
Joel 2:13 slow to anger and abounding in *l,*
Am 5:15 Hate evil, *l* good;
Mic 3: 2 you who hate good and *l* evil;
6: 8 To act justly and to *l* mercy
Zep 3:17 he will quiet you with his *l,*
Zec 8:19 Therefore *l* truth and peace."
Mt 3:17 "This is my Son, whom I *l;*
5:44 *L* your enemies and pray
6:24 he will hate the one and *l* the other,
17: 5 "This is my Son, whom I *l;*
19:19 and '*l* your neighbor as yourself.' "
22:37 " '*L* the Lord your God
Lk 6:32 Even 'sinners' *l* those who *l* them.
7:42 which of them will *l* him more?"
20:13 whom I *l;* perhaps they will respect
Jn 13:34 I give you: *L* one another.
13:35 disciples, if you *l* one another."
14:15 "If you *l* me, you will obey what I
15:13 Greater *l* has no one than this,
15:17 This is my command: *L* each other.
21:15 do you truly *l* me more than these
Ro 5: 5 because God has poured out his *l*
5: 8 God demonstrates his own *l* for us
8:28 for the good of those who *l* him,
8:35 us from the *l* of Christ?
8:39 us from the *l* of God that is
12: 9 *L* must be sincere.
12:10 to one another in brotherly *l.*
13: 8 continuing debt to *l* one another,
13: 9 "*L* your neighbor as yourself."
13:10 Therefore *l* is the fulfillment
13:10 *L* does no harm to its neighbor.
1Co 2: 9 prepared for those who *l* him"—

1Co 8: 1 Knowledge puffs up, but *l* builds up
13: 1 have not *l*, I am only a resounding
13: 2 but have not *l*, I am nothing.
13: 3 but have not *l*, I gain nothing.
13: 4 Love is patient, *l* is kind.
13: 4 *L* is patient, love is kind.
13: 6 *L* does not delight in evil
13: 8 *L* never fails.
13:13 But the greatest of these is *l*.
13:13 three remain: faith, hope and *l*.
14: 1 way of *l* and eagerly desire spiritual
16:14 Do everything in *l*.
2Co 5:14 For Christ's *l* compels us,
8: 8 sincerity of your *l* by comparing it
8:24 show these men the proof of your *l*
Gal 5: 6 is faith expressing itself through *l*.
5:13 rather, serve one another in *l*.
5:22 But the fruit of the Spirit is *l*, joy,
Eph 1: 4 In *l* he predestined us
2: 4 But because of his great *l* for us,
3:17 being rooted and established in *l*,
3:18 and high and deep is the *l* of Christ,
3:19 and to know this *l* that surpasses
4: 2 bearing with one another in *l*.
4:15 Instead, speaking the truth in *l*,
5: 2 loved children and live a life of *l*,
5:25 *l* your wives, just as Christ loved
5:28 husbands ought to *l* their wives
5:33 each one of you also must *l* his wife
Php 1: 9 that your *l* may abound more
2: 2 having the same *l*, being one
Col 1: 5 *l* that spring from the hope that is
2: 2 in heart and united in *l*,
3:14 And over all these virtues put on *l*,
3:19 *l* your wives and do not be harsh
1Th 1: 3 your labor prompted by *l*,
4: 9 taught by God to *l* each other.
5: 8 on faith and *l* as a breastplate,
2Th 3: 5 direct your hearts into God's *l*
1Ti 1: 5 The goal of this command is *l*,
2:15 *l* and holiness with propriety.
4:12 in life, in *l*, in faith and in purity.
6:10 For the *l* of money is a root
6:11 faith, *l*, endurance and gentleness.
2Ti 1: 7 of power, of *l* and of self-discipline.
2:22 and pursue righteousness, faith, *l*
3:10 faith, patience, *l*, endurance,
Tit 2: 4 women to *l* their husbands
Phm : 9 yet I appeal to you on the basis of *l*.
Heb 6:10 and the *l* you have shown him
10:24 may spur one another on toward *l*
13: 5 free from the *l* of money
Jas 1:12 promised to those who *l* him.
2: 5 he promised those who *l* him?
2: 8 "*L* your neighbor as yourself,"
1Pe 1:22 the truth so that you have sincere *l*
1:22 *l* one another deeply,
2:17 *L* the brotherhood of believers,
3: 8 be sympathetic, *l* as brothers,
3:10 "Whoever would *l* life
4: 8 Above all, *l* each other deeply,
4: 8 *l* covers over a multitude of sins.
5:14 Greet one another with a kiss of *l*.
2Pe 1: 7 and to brotherly kindness, *l*.
1:17 "This is my Son, whom I *l*;
1Jn 2: 5 God's *l* is truly made complete
2:15 Do not *l* the world or anything
3: 1 How great is the *l* the Father has
3:10 anyone who does not *l* his brother.
3:11 We should *l* one another.
3:14 Anyone who does not *l* remains
3:16 This is how we know what *l* is:
3:18 let us not *l* with words or tongue
1Jn 3:23 to *l* one another as he commanded
4: 7 Dear friends, let us *l* one another,
4: 7 for *l* comes from God.
4: 8 Whoever does not *l* does not know
4: 9 This is how God showed his *l*
4:10 This is *l*: not that we loved God,
4:11 we also ought to *l* one another.
4:12 and his *l* is made complete in us.
4:16 God is *l*.
4:16 Whoever lives in *l* lives in God,
4:17 *l* is made complete among us
4:18 But perfect *l* drives out fear,
4:19 We *l* because he first loved us.
4:20 If anyone says, "I *l* God,"
4:21 loves God must also *l* his brother.
5: 2 we know that we *l* the children
5: 3 This is *l* for God: to obey his
2Jn : 5 I ask that we *l* one another.
: 6 his command is that you walk in *l*.
: 6 this is *l*: that we walk in obedience
Jude :12 men are blemishes at your *l* feasts,
:21 Keep yourselves in God's *l*
Rev 2: 4 You have forsaken your first *l*.
3:19 Those whom I *l* I rebuke
12:11 they did not *l* their lives so much

LOVED (LOVE)

Ge 24:67 she became his wife, and he *l* her;
29:30 and he *l* Rachel more than Leah.
37: 3 Now Israel *l* Joseph more than any
Dt 7: 8 But it was because the LORD *l* you
1Sa 1: 5 a double portion because he *l* her,
20:17 because he *l* him as he *l* himself.
Ps 44: 3 light of your face, for you *l* them.
Jer 2: 2 how as a bride you *l* me
31: 3 "I have *l* you with an everlasting
Hos 2:23 to the one I called 'Not my *l* one.'
3: 1 though she is *l* by another
9:10 became as vile as the thing they *l*.
11: 1 "When Israel was a child, I *l* him,
Mal 1: 2 "But you ask, 'How have you *l* us?'
Mk 12: 6 left to send, a son, whom he *l*.
Jn 3:16 so *l* the world that he gave his one
3:19 but men *l* darkness instead of light
11: 5 Jesus *l* Martha and her sister
12:43 for they *l* praise from men more
13: 1 Having *l* his own who were
13:23 the disciple whom Jesus *l*,
13:34 As I have *l* you, so you must love
14:21 He who loves me will be *l*
15: 9 the Father has *l* me, so have I *l* you.
15:12 Love each other as I have *l* you.
19:26 the disciple whom he *l* standing
Ro 8:37 conquerors through him who *l* us.
9:13 "Jacob I *l*, but Esau I hated."
9:25 her 'my *l* one' who is not my *l* one,"
11:28 they are *l* on account
Gal 2:20 who *l* me and gave himself for me.
Eph 5: 2 as Christ *l* us and gave himself up
5:25 just as Christ *l* the church
2Th 2:16 who *l* us and by his grace gave us
2Ti 4:10 for Demas, because he *l* this world,
Heb 1: 9 You have *l* righteousness
1Jn 4:10 This is love: not that we *l* God,
4:11 Dear friends, since God so *l* us,
4:19 We love because he first *l* us.

LOVELY (LOVE)

Ps 84: 1 How *l* is your dwelling place,
SS 2:14 and your face is *l*.
5:16 he is altogether *l*.
Php 4: 8 whatever is *l*, whatever is

LOVER (LOVE)

SS 2:16 *Beloved* My *l* is mine and I am his;
7:10 I belong to my *l*,
1Ti 3: 3 not quarrelsome, not a *l* of money.

LOVERS (LOVE)

2Ti 3: 2 People will be *l* of themselves,
3: 3 without self-control, brutal, not *l*
3: 4 *l* of pleasure rather than *l* of God—

LOVES (LOVE)

Ps 11: 7 he *l* justice;
33: 5 The LORD *l* righteousness
34:12 Whoever of you *l* life
91:14 Because he *l* me," says the LORD,
127: 2 for he grants sleep to those he *l*.
Pr 3:12 the LORD disciplines those he *l*,
12: 1 Whoever *l* discipline *l* knowledge,
13:24 he who *l* him is careful
17:17 A friend *l* at all times,
17:19 He who *l* a quarrel *l* sin;
22:11 He who *l* a pure heart and whose
Ecc 5:10 whoever *l* wealth is never satisfied
Mt 10:37 anyone who *l* his son or daughter
Lk 7:47 has been forgiven little *l* little."
Jn 3:35 Father *l* the Son and has placed
10:17 reason my Father *l* me is that I lay
12:25 The man who *l* his life will lose it,
14:21 obeys them, he is the one who *l* me.
14:23 Jesus replied, "If anyone *l* me,
Ro 13: 8 for he who *l* his fellowman has
2Co 9: 7 for God *l* a cheerful giver.
Eph 5:28 He who *l* his wife *l* himself.
5:33 must love his wife as he *l* himself,
Heb 12: 6 the Lord disciplines those he *l*,
1Jn 2:10 Whoever *l* his brother lives
2:15 If anyone *l* the world, the love
4: 7 Everyone who *l* has been born
4:21 Whoever *l* God must also love his
5: 1 who *l* the father *l* his child
3Jn : 9 but Diotrephes, who *l* to be first,
Rev 1: 5 To him who *l* us and has freed us

LOVING (LOVE)

Ps 25:10 All the ways of the LORD are *l*
62:12 and that you, O Lord, are *l*.
145:17 and *l* toward all he has made.
Heb 13: 1 Keep on *l* each other as brothers.
1Jn 5: 2 by *l* God and carrying out his

LOWLY

Job 5:11 The *l* he sets on high,
Pr 29:23 but a man of *l* spirit gains honor.
Isa 57:15 also with him who is contrite and *l*
Eze 21:26 *l* will be exalted and the exalted
1Co 1:28 He chose the *l* things of this world

LUKE*

Co-worker with Paul (Col 4:14; 2Ti 4:11; Phm 24).

LUKEWARM*

Rev 3:16 So, because you are *l*— neither hot

LUST

Pr 6:25 Do not *l* in your heart
Col 3: 5 sexual immorality, impurity, *l*,
1Th 4: 5 not in passionate *l* like the heathen,
1Jn 2:16 the *l* of his eyes and the boasting

LYING (LIE)

Pr 6:17 a *l* tongue,
26:28 A *l* tongue hates those it hurts,

MACEDONIA

Ac 16: 9 "Come over to *M* and help us."

MADE (MAKE)
Ge 1:16 He also *m* the stars.
1:25 God *m* the wild animals according
2:22 Then the LORD God *m* a woman
2Ki 19:15 You have *m* heaven and earth.
Ps 95: 5 The sea is his, for he *m* it,
100: 3 It is he who *m* us, and we are his;
118:24 This is the day the LORD has *m;*
139:14 I am fearfully and wonderfully *m;*
Ecc 3:11 He has *m* everything beautiful
Mk 2:27 "The Sabbath was *m* for man,
Jn 1: 3 Through him all things were *m;*
Ac 17:24 "The God who *m* the world
Heb 1: 2 through whom he *m* the universe.
Rev 14: 7 Worship him who *m* the heavens,

MAGI
Mt 2: 1 *M* from the east came to Jerusalem

MAGOG
Eze 38: 2 of the land of *M,* the chief prince
39: 6 I will send fire on *M*
Rev 20: 8 and *M*— to gather them for battle.

MAIDEN
Pr 30:19 and the way of a man with a *m.*
Isa 62: 5 As a young man marries a *m,*
Jer 2:32 Does a *m* forget her jewelry,

MAIMED
Mt 18: 8 It is better for you to enter life *m*

MAJESTIC (MAJESTY)
Ex 15: 6 was *m* in power.
15:11 *m* in holiness,
Ps 8: 1 how *m* is your name in all the earth
29: 4 the voice of the LORD is *m.*
111: 3 Glorious and *m* are his deeds,
SS 6:10 *m* as the stars in procession?
2Pe 1:17 came to him from the *M* Glory,

MAJESTY (MAJESTIC)
Ex 15: 7 In the greatness of your *m*
Dt 33:26 and on the clouds in his *m.*
1Ch 16:27 Splendor and *m* are before him;
Est 1: 4 the splendor and glory of his *m.*
Job 37:22 God comes in awesome *m.*
40:10 and clothe yourself in honor and *m*
Ps 45: 4 In your *m* ride forth victoriously
93: 1 The LORD reigns, he is robed in *m*
110: 3 Arrayed in holy *m,*
145: 5 of the glorious splendor of your *m,*
Isa 53: 2 or *m* to attract us to him,
Eze 31: 2 can be compared with you in *m?*
2Pe 1:16 but we were eyewitnesses of his *m.*
Jude :25 only God our Savior be glory, *m,*

MAKE (MADE MAKER MAKES MAKING)
Ge 1:26 "Let us *m* man in our image,
2:18 I will *m* a helper suitable for him."
12: 2 "I will *m* you into a great nation
Ex 22: 3 thief must certainly *m* restitution,
Nu 6:25 the LORD *m* his face shine
Ps 108: 1 *m* music with all my soul.
Isa 14:14 I will *m* myself like the Most High
29:16 "He did not *m* me"?
Jer 31:31 "when I will *m* a new covenant
Mt 3: 3 *m* straight paths for him.' "
28:19 and *m* disciples of all nations,
Mk 1:17 "and I will *m* you fishers of men."
Lk 13:24 "*M* every effort to enter
14:23 country lanes and *m* them come in,
Ro 14:19 *m* every effort to do what leads
2Co 5: 9 So we *m* it our goal to please him,
Eph 4: 3 *M* every effort to keep the unity
Col 4: 5 *m* the most of every opportunity.
1Th 4:11 *M* it your ambition
Heb 4:11 *m* every effort to enter that rest,
12:14 *M* every effort to live in peace
2Pe 1: 5 *m* every effort to add
3:14 *m* every effort to be found spotless,

MAKER (MAKE)
Job 4:17 Can a man be more pure than his *M*
36: 3 I will ascribe justice to my *M.*
Ps 95: 6 kneel before the LORD our *M;*
Pr 22: 2 The LORD is the *M* of them all.
Isa 45: 9 to him who quarrels with his *M,*
54: 5 For your *M* is your husband—
Jer 10:16 for he is the *M* of all things,

MAKES (MAKE)
1Co 3: 7 but only God, who *m* things grow.

MAKING (MAKE)
Ps 19: 7 *m* wise the simple.
Ecc 12:12 Of *m* many books there is no end,
Jn 5:18 *m* himself equal with God.
Eph 5:16 *m* the most of every opportunity,

MALE
Ge 1:27 *m* and female he created them.
Gal 3:28 slave nor free, *m* nor female,

MALICE (MALICIOUS)
Ro 1:29 murder, strife, deceit and *m.*
Col 3: 8 *m,* slander, and filthy language
1Pe 2: 1 rid yourselves of all *m*

MALICIOUS (MALICE)
Pr 26:24 A *m* man disguises himself
1Ti 3:11 not *m* talkers but temperate
6: 4 *m* talk, evil suspicions

MAN (MEN WOMAN WOMEN)
Ge 1:26 "Let us make *m* in our image,
2: 7 God formed the *m* from the dust
2:18 for the *m* to be alone
2:23 she was taken out of *m.*
9: 6 Whoever sheds the blood of *m,*
Dt 8: 3 *m* does not live on bread
1Sa 13:14 a *m* after his own heart
15:29 he is not a *m* that he
Job 14: 1 *M* born of woman is of few
14:14 If a *m* dies, will he live
Ps 1: 1 Blessed is the *m* who does
8: 4 what is *m* that you are
119: 9 can a young *m* keep his
127: 5 Blessed is the *m* whose quiver
Pr 14:12 that seems right to a *m,*
30:19 way of a *m* with a maiden.
Isa 53: 3 a *m* of sorrows,
Mt 19: 5 a *m* will leave his father
Mk 8:36 What good is it for a *m*
Lk 4: 4 '*M* does not live on bread
Ro 5:12 entered the world through one *m*
1Co 7: 2 each *m* should have his own
11: 3 head of every *m* is Christ,
11: 3 head of woman is *m*
13:11 When I became a *m,*
Php 2: 8 found in appearance as a *m,*
1Ti 2: 5 the *m* Christ Jesus,
2:12 have authority over a *m;*
Heb 9:27 as *m* is destined to die

MANAGE
Jer 12: 5 how will you *m* in the thickets
1Ti 3: 4 He must *m* his own family well
3:12 one wife and must *m* his children
5:14 to *m* their homes and to give

MANASSEH
1. Firstborn of Joseph (Ge 41:51; 46:20). Blessed (Ge 48).
2. Son of Hezekiah; king of Judah (2Ki 21:1-18; 2Ch 33:1-20).

MANGER
Lk 2:12 in strips of cloth and lying in a *m.*"

MANNA
Ex 16:31 people of Israel called the bread *m.*
Dt 8:16 He gave you *m* to eat in the desert,
Jn 6:49 Your forefathers ate the *m*
Rev 2:17 I will give some of the hidden *m.*

MANNER
1Co 11:27 in an unworthy *m* will be guilty
Php 1:27 conduct yourselves in a *m* worthy

MARITAL* (MARRY)
Ex 21:10 of her food, clothing and *m* rights.
Mt 5:32 except for *m* unfaithfulness,
19: 9 except for *m* unfaithfulness,
1Co 7: 3 husband should fulfill his *m* duty

MARK (MARKS)
Cousin of Barnabas (Col 4:10; 2Ti 4:11; Phm 24; 1Pe 5:13), see JOHN.
Ge 4:15 Then the LORD put a *m* on Cain
Rev 13:16 to receive a *m* on his right hand

MARKS (MARK)
Jn 20:25 Unless I see the nail *m* in his hands
Gal 6:17 bear on my body the *m* of Jesus.

MARRED
Isa 52:14 his form *m* beyond human likeness

MARRIAGE (MARRY)
Mt 22:30 neither marry nor be given in *m;*
24:38 marrying and giving in *m,*
Ro 7: 2 she is released from the law of *m.*
Heb 13: 4 by all, and the *m* bed kept pure,

MARRIED (MARRY)
Ro 7: 2 by law a *m* woman is bound
1Co 7:27 Are you *m?* Do not seek a divorce.
7:33 But a *m* man is concerned about
7:36 They should get *m.*

MARRIES (MARRY)
Mt 5:32 and anyone who *m* the divorced
19: 9 and *m* another woman commits
Lk 16:18 the man who *m* a divorced woman

MARRY (INTERMARRY MARITAL MARRIAGE MARRIED MARRIES)
Mt 22:30 resurrection people will neither *m*
1Co 7: 1 It is good for a man not to *m.*
7: 9 control themselves, they should *m,*
1Ti 5:14 So I counsel younger widows to *m,*

MARTHA*
Sister of Mary and Lazarus (Lk 10:38-42; Jn 11; 12:2).

MARVELED
Lk 2:33 mother *m* at what was said about

MARY
1. Mother of Jesus (Mt 1:16-25; Lk 1:27-56; 2:1-40). With Jesus at temple (Lk 2:41-52), at the wedding in Cana (Jn 2:1-5), questioning his sanity (Mk 3:21), at the cross (Jn 19:25-27). Among disciples after Ascension (Ac 1:14).
2. Magdalene; former demoniac (Lk 8:2). Helped support Jesus' ministry (Lk 8:1-3). At the cross (Mt 27:56; Mk 15:40; Jn 19:25), burial (Mt 27:61; Mk 15:47). Saw angel after

resurrection (Mt 28:1-10; Mk 16:1-9; Lk 24:1-12); also Jesus (Jn 20:1-18).
3. Sister of Martha and Lazarus (Jn 11). Washed Jesus' feet (Jn 12:1-8).

MASQUERADES*
2Co 11:14 for Satan himself *m* as an angel

MASTER (MASTERED MASTERS)
Mt 10:24 nor a servant above his *m*.
23: 8 for you have only one *M*
24:46 that servant whose *m* finds him
25:21 "His *m* replied, 'Well done,
Ro 6:14 For sin shall not be your *m*,
14: 4 To his own *m* he stands or falls.
2Ti 2:21 useful to the *M* and prepared

MASTERED* (MASTER)
1Co 6:12 but I will not be *m* by anything.
2Pe 2:19 a slave to whatever has *m* him.

MASTERS (MASTER)
Mt 6:24 "No one can serve two *m*.
Eph 6: 5 obey your earthly *m* with respect
6: 9 And *m*, treat your slaves
Tit 2: 9 subject to their *m* in everything,

MATTHEW*
Apostle; former tax collector (Mt 9:9-13; 10:3; Mk 3:18; Lk 6:15; Ac 1:13). Also called Levi (Mk 2:14-17; Lk 5:27-32).

MATURE (MATURITY)
Eph 4:13 of the Son of God and become *m*,
Php 3:15 of us who are *m* should take such
Heb 5:14 But solid food is for the *m*,
Jas 1: 4 work so that you may be *m*

MATURITY* (MATURE)
Heb 6: 1 about Christ and go on to *m*,

MEAL
Pr 15:17 Better a *m* of vegetables where
1Co 10:27 some unbeliever invites you to a *m*
Heb 12:16 for a single *m* sold his inheritance

MEANING
Ne 8: 8 and giving the *m* so that the people

MEANS
1Co 9:22 by all possible *m* I might save some

MEAT
Ro 14: 6 He who eats *m*, eats to the Lord,
14:21 It is better not to eat *m*

MEDIATOR
1Ti 2: 5 and one *m* between God and men,
Heb 8: 6 of which he is *m* is superior
9:15 For this reason Christ is the *m*
12:24 to Jesus the *m* of a new covenant,

MEDICINE*
Pr 17:22 A cheerful heart is good *m*,

MEDITATE (MEDITATES MEDITATION)
Jos 1: 8 from your mouth; *m* on it day
Ps 119:15 I *m* on your precepts
119:78 but I will *m* on your precepts.
119:97 I *m* on it all day long.
145: 5 I will *m* on your wonderful works.

MEDITATES* (MEDITATE)
Ps 1: 2 and on his law he *m* day and night.

MEDITATION* (MEDITATE)
Ps 19:14 of my mouth and the *m* of my heart

Ps 104:34 May my *m* be pleasing to him,

MEDIUM
Lev 20:27 " 'A man or woman who is a *m*

MEEK (MEEKNESS)
Ps 37:11 But the *m* will inherit the land
Mt 5: 5 Blessed are the *m*,

MEEKNESS* (MEEK)
2Co 10: 1 By the *m* and gentleness of Christ,

MEET (MEETING)
Ps 85:10 Love and faithfulness *m* together;
Am 4:12 prepare to *m* your God, O Israel."
1Th 4:17 them in the clouds to *m* the Lord

MEETING (MEET)
Heb 10:25 Let us not give up *m* together,

MELCHIZEDEK
Ge 14:18 *M* king of Salem brought out bread
Ps 110: 4 in the order of *M*."
Heb 7:11 in the order of *M*, not in the order

MELT
2Pe 3:12 and the elements will *m* in the heat.

MEMBERS
Mic 7: 6 a man's enemies are the *m*
Ro 7:23 law at work in the *m* of my body,
12: 4 of us has one body with many *m*,
1Co 6:15 not know that your bodies are *m*
12:24 But God has combined the *m*
Eph 4:25 for we are all *m* of one body.
Col 3:15 as *m* of one body you were called

MEN (MAN)
Mt 4:19 will make you fishers of *m*
5:16 your light shine before *m*
12:36 *m* will have to give account
Jn 12:32 will draw all *m* to myself
Ac 5:29 obey God rather than *m*!
Ro 1:27 indecent acts with other *m*,
5:12 death came to all *m*,
1Co 9:22 all things to all *m*
2Co 5:11 we try to persuade *m*.
1Ti 2: 4 wants all *m* to be saved
2Ti 2: 2 entrust to reliable *m*
2Pe 1:21 but *m* spoke from God

MENAHEM
King of Israel (2Ki 15:17-22).

MERCIFUL (MERCY)
Dt 4:31 the LORD your God is a *m* God;
Ne 9:31 for you are a gracious and *m* God.
Mt 5: 7 Blessed are the *m*,
Lk 6:36 Be *m*, just as your Father is *m*.
Heb 2:17 in order that he might become a *m*
Jude :22 Be *m* to those who doubt; snatch

MERCY (MERCIFUL)
Ex 33:19 *m* on whom I will have *m*,
Ps 25: 6 O LORD, your great *m* and love,
Isa 63: 9 and *m* he redeemed them;
Hos 6: 6 For I desire *m*, not sacrifice,
Mic 6: 8 To act justly and to love *m*
Hab 3: 2 in wrath remember *m*.
Mt 12: 7 'I desire *m*, not sacrifice,' you
23:23 justice, *m* and faithfulness.
Ro 9:15 "I will have *m* on whom I have *m*,
Eph 2: 4 who is rich in *m*, made us alive
Jas 2:13 *M* triumphs over judgment!
1Pe 1: 3 In his great *m* he has given us new

MESSAGE
Isa 53: 1 Who has believed our *m*
Jn 12:38 "Lord, who has believed our *m*

Ro 10:17 faith comes from hearing the *m*,
1Co 1:18 For the *m* of the cross is
2Co 5:19 to us the *m* of reconciliation.

MESSIAH*
Jn 1:41 "We have found the *M*" (that is,
4:25 "I know that *M*" (called Christ) "is

METHUSELAH
Ge 5:27 Altogether, *M* lived 969 years,

MICHAEL
Archangel (Jude 9); warrior in angelic realm, protector of Israel (Da 10:13, 21; 12:1; Rev 12:7).

MIDWIVES
Ex 1:17 The *m*, however, feared God

MIGHT (ALMIGHTY MIGHTY)
Jdg 16:30 Then he pushed with all his *m*,
2Sa 6:14 before the LORD with all his *m*,
Ps 21:13 we will sing and praise your *m*.
Zec 4: 6 'Not by *m* nor by power,
1Ti 6:16 To him be honor and *m* forever.

MIGHTY (MIGHT)
Ex 6: 1 of my *m* hand he will drive them
Dt 7: 8 he brought you out with a *m* hand
2Sa 1:19 How the *m* have fallen!
23: 8 the names of David's *m* men:
Ps 24: 8 The LORD strong and *m*,
50: 1 The *M* One, God, the LORD,
89: 8 You are *m*, O LORD,
136:12 with a *m* hand and outstretched
147: 5 Great is our Lord and *m* in power;
Isa 9: 6 Wonderful Counselor, *M* God,
Zep 3:17 he is *m* to save.
Eph 6:10 in the Lord and in his *m* power.

MILE*
Mt 5:41 If someone forces you to go one *m*,

MILK
Ex 3: 8 a land flowing with *m* and honey—
Isa 55: 1 Come, buy wine and *m*
1Co 3: 2 I gave you *m*, not solid food,
Heb 5:12 You need *m*, not solid food!
1Pe 2: 2 babies, crave pure spiritual *m*,

MILLSTONE (STONE)
Lk 17: 2 sea with a *m* tied around his neck

MIND (DOUBLE-MINDED MINDFUL MINDS)
1Sa 15:29 Israel does not lie or change his *m*;
1Ch 28: 9 devotion and with a willing *m*,
Ps 26: 2 examine my heart and my *m*;
Isa 26: 3 him whose *m* is steadfast,
Mt 22:37 all your soul and with all your *m*.'
Ac 4:32 believers were one in heart and *m*.
Ro 7:25 I myself in my *m* am a slave
8: 7 the sinful *m* is hostile to God.
12: 2 by the renewing of your *m*.
1Co 2: 9 no *m* has conceived
14:14 spirit prays, but my *m* is unfruitful.
2Co 13:11 be of one *m*, live in peace.
Php 3:19 Their *m* is on earthly things.
1Th 4:11 to *m* your own business
Heb 7:21 and will not change his *m*:

MINDFUL* (MIND)
Ps 8: 4 what is man that you are *m* of him,
Lk 1:48 God my Savior, for he has been *m*
Heb 2: 6 What is man that you are *m* of him,

MINDS (MIND)
Ps 7: 9 who searches *m* and hearts,
Jer 31:33 "I will put my law in their *m*
Eph 4:23 new in the attitude of your *m;*
Col 3: 2 Set your *m* on things above,
Heb 8:10 I will put my laws in their *m*
Rev 2:23 I am he who searches hearts and *m,*

MINISTERING (MINISTRY)
Heb 1:14 Are not all angels *m* spirits sent

MINISTRY (MINISTERING)
Ac 6: 4 to prayer and the *m* of the word."
2Co 5:18 gave us the *m* of reconciliation:
2Ti 4: 5 discharge all the duties of your *m.*

MIRACLES (MIRACULOUS)
1Ch 16:12 his *m,* and the judgments he
Ps 77:14 You are the God who performs *m;*
Mt 11:20 most of his *m* had been performed,
11:21 If the *m* that were performed
24:24 and perform great signs and *m*
Mk 6: 2 does *m!* Isn't this the carpenter?
Jn 10:32 "I have shown you many great *m*
14:11 the evidence of the *m* themselves.
Ac 2:22 accredited by God to you by *m,*
19:11 God did extraordinary *m*
1Co 12:28 third teachers, then workers of *m,*
Heb 2: 4 it by signs, wonders and various *m,*

MIRACULOUS (MIRACLES)
Jn 3: 2 could perform the *m* signs you are
9:16 "How can a sinner do such *m* signs
20:30 Jesus did many other *m* signs
1Co 1:22 Jews demand *m* signs and Greeks

MIRE
Ps 40: 2 out of the mud and *m;*
Isa 57:20 whose waves cast up *m* and mud.

MIRIAM
Sister of Moses and Aaron (Nu 26:59). Led dancing at Red Sea (Ex 15:20-21). Struck with leprosy for criticizing Moses (Nu 12). Death (Nu 20:1).

MIRROR
Jas 1:23 a man who looks at his face in a *m*

MISERY
Ex 3: 7 "I have indeed seen the *m*
Jdg 10:16 he could bear Israel's *m* no longer.
Hos 5:15 in their *m* they will earnestly seek
Ro 3:16 ruin and *m* mark their ways,
Jas 5: 1 of the *m* that is coming upon you.

MISLED
1Co 15:33 Do not be *m:* "Bad company

MISS
Pr 19: 2 nor to be hasty and *m* the way.

MIST
Hos 6: 4 Your love is like the morning *m,*
Jas 4:14 You are a *m* that appears for a little

MISUSE*
Ex 20: 7 "You shall not *m* the name
Dt 5:11 "You shall not *m* the name
Ps 139:20 your adversaries *m* your name.

MOCK (MOCKED MOCKER MOCKERS MOCKING)
Ps 22: 7 All who see me *m* me;
Pr 14: 9 Fools *m* at making amends for sin,
Mk 10:34 who will *m* him and spit on him,

MOCKED (MOCK)
Mt 27:29 knelt in front of him and *m* him.
27:41 of the law and the elders *m* him.
Gal 6: 7 not be deceived: God cannot be *m.*

MOCKER (MOCK)
Pr 9: 7 corrects a *m* invites insult;
9:12 if you are a *m,* you alone will suffer
20: 1 Wine is a *m* and beer a brawler;
22:10 Drive out the *m,* and out goes strife

MOCKERS (MOCK)
Ps 1: 1 or sit in the seat of *m.*

MOCKING (MOCK)
Isa 50: 6 face from *m* and spitting.

MODEL*
Eze 28:12 " 'You were the *m* of perfection,
1Th 1: 7 And so you became a *m*
2Th 3: 9 to make ourselves a *m* for you

MOMENT
Job 20: 5 the joy of the godless lasts but a *m.*
Ps 30: 5 For his anger lasts only a *m,*
Isa 66: 8 or a nation be brought forth in a *m?*
Gal 2: 5 We did not give in to them for a *m,*

MONEY
Ecc 5:10 Whoever loves *m* never has *m*
Isa 55: 1 and you who have no *m,*
Mt 6:24 You cannot serve both God and *M.*
Lk 9: 3 no bread, no *m,* no extra tunic.
1Co 16: 2 set aside a sum of *m* in keeping
1Ti 3: 3 not quarrelsome, not a lover of *m.*
6:10 For the love of *m* is a root
2Ti 3: 2 lovers of *m,* boastful, proud,
Heb 13: 5 free from the love of *m*
1Pe 5: 2 not greedy for *m,* but eager to serve

MOON
Ps 121: 6 nor the *m* by night.
Joel 2:31 and the *m* to blood
1Co 15:41 *m* another and the stars another;

MORNING
Ge 1: 5 and there was *m*— the first day.
Dt 28:67 In the *m* you will say, "If only it
Ps 5: 3 In the *m,* O LORD,
2Pe 1:19 and the *m* star rises in your hearts.
Rev 22:16 of David, and the bright *M* Star."

MORTAL
1Co 15:53 and the *m* with immortality.

MOSES
Levite; brother of Aaron (Ex 6:20; 1Ch 6:3). Put in basket into Nile; discovered and raised by Pharaoh's daughter (Ex 2:1-10). Fled to Midian after killing Egyptian (Ex 2:11-15). Married to Zipporah, fathered Gershom (Ex 2:16-22).
Called by the LORD to deliver Israel (Ex 3-4). Pharaoh's resistance (Ex 5). Ten plagues (Ex 7-11). Passover and Exodus (Ex 12-13). Led Israel through Red Sea (Ex 14). Song of deliverance (Ex 15:1-21). Brought water from rock (Ex 17:1-7). Raised hands to defeat Amalekites (Ex 17:8-16). Delegated judges (Ex 18; Dt 1:9-18).
Received Law at Sinai (Ex 19-23; 25-31; Jn 1:17). Announced Law to Israel (Ex 19:7-8; 24; 35). Broke tablets because of golden calf (Ex 32; Dt 9). Saw glory of the LORD (Ex 33-34). Supervised building of tabernacle (Ex 36-40). Set apart Aaron and priests (Lev 8-9). Numbered tribes (Nu 1-4; 26). Opposed by Aaron and Miriam (Nu 12). Sent spies into Canaan (Nu 13). Announced forty years of wandering for failure to enter land (Nu 14). Opposed by Korah (Nu 16). Forbidden to enter land for striking rock (Nu 20:1-13; Dt 1:37). Lifted bronze snake for healing (Nu 21:4-9; Jn 3:14). Final address to Israel (Dt 1-33). Succeeded by Joshua (Nu 27:12-23; Dt 34). Death (Dt 34:5-12).
"Law of Moses" (1Ki 2:3; Ezr 3:2; Mk 12:26; Lk 24:44). "Book of Moses" (2Ch 25:12; Ne 13:1). "Song of Moses" (Ex 15:1-21; Rev 15:3). "Prayer of Moses" (Ps 90).

MOTH
Mt 6:19 where *m* and rust destroy,

MOTHER (MOTHER'S)
Ge 2:24 and *m* and be united to his wife,
3:20 because she would become the *m*
Ex 20:12 "Honor your father and your *m,*
Lev 20: 9 " 'If anyone curses his father or *m,*
Dt 5:16 "Honor your father and your *m,*
21:18 who does not obey his father and *m*
27:16 who dishonors his father or his *m."*
1Sa 2:19 Each year his *m* made him a little
Ps 113: 9 as a happy *m* of children.
Pr 23:25 May your father and *m* be glad;
29:15 child left to himself disgraces his *m.*
31: 1 an oracle his *m* taught him:
Isa 49:15 "Can a *m* forget the baby
66:13 As a *m* comforts her child,
Mt 10:37 or *m* more than me is not worthy
15: 4 'Honor your father and *m'*
19: 5 and *m* and be united to his wife,
Mk 7:10 'Honor your father and your *m,'*
10:19 honor your father and *m.'* "
Jn 19:27 to the disciple, "Here is your *m."*

MOTHER'S (MOTHER)
Job 1:21 "Naked I came from my *m* womb,
Pr 1: 8 and do not forsake your *m* teaching

MOTIVES*
Pr 16: 2 but *m* are weighed by the LORD.
1Co 4: 5 will expose the *m* of men's hearts.
Php 1:18 whether from false *m* or true,
1Th 2: 3 spring from error or impure *m,*
Jas 4: 3 because you ask with wrong *m,*

MOUNTAIN (MOUNTAINS)
Mic 4: 2 let us go up to the *m* of the LORD,
Mt 17:20 say to this *m,* 'Move from here

MOUNTAINS (MOUNTAIN)
Isa 52: 7 How beautiful on the *m*
55:12 the *m* and hills
1Co 13: 2 if I have a faith that can move *m,*

MOURN (MOURNING)
Ecc 3: 4 a time to *m* and a time to dance,
Isa 61: 2 to comfort all who *m,*
Mt 5: 4 Blessed are those who *m,*
Ro 12:15 *m* with those who *m.*

MOURNING (MOURN)
Jer 31:13 I will turn their *m* into gladness;
Rev 21: 4 There will be no more death or *m*

MOUTH
Jos 1: 8 of the Law depart from your *m;*
Ps 19:14 May the words of my *m*
40: 3 He put a new song in my *m,*
119:103 sweeter than honey to my *m!*
Pr 16:23 A wise man's heart guides his *m,*
27: 2 praise you, and not your own *m;*
Isa 51:16 I have put my words in your *m*

NEW
Ps 40: 3 He put a *n* song in my mouth,
Ecc 1: 9 there is nothing *n* under the sun.
Isa 65:17 *n* heavens and a *n* earth.
Jer 31:31 "when I will make a *n* covenant
Eze 36:26 give you a *n* heart and put a *n* spirit
Mt 9:17 Neither do men pour *n* wine
Lk 22:20 "This cup is the *n* covenant
2Co 5:17 he is a *n* creation; the old has gone,
Eph 4:24 and to put on the *n* self, created
2Pe 3:13 to a *n* heaven and a *n* earth,
1Jn 2: 8 Yet I am writing you a *n* command;

NEWBORN (BEAR)
1Pe 2: 2 Like *n* babies, crave pure spiritual

NEWS
Isa 52: 7 the feet of those who bring good *n,*
Mk 1:15 Repent and believe the good *n!"*
16:15 preach the good *n* to all creation.
Lk 2:10 I bring you good *n*
Ac 5:42 proclaiming the good *n* that Jesus
17:18 preaching the good *n* about Jesus
Ro 10:15 feet of those who bring good *n!"*

NICODEMUS*
Pharisee who visited Jesus at night (Jn 3). Argued fair treatment of Jesus (Jn 7:50-52). With Joseph, prepared Jesus for burial (Jn 19:38-42).

NIGHT
Job 35:10 who gives songs in the *n,*
Ps 1: 2 on his law he meditates day and *n.*
91: 5 You will not fear the terror of *n,*
Jn 3: 2 He came to Jesus at *n* and said,
1Th 5: 2 Lord will come like a thief in the *n.*
5: 5 We do not belong to the *n*
Rev 21:25 for there will be no *n* there.

NOAH
Righteous man (Eze 14:14, 20) called to build ark (Ge 6-8; Heb 11:7; 1Pe 3:20; 2Pe 2:5). God's covenant with (Ge 9:1-17). Drunkenness of (Ge 9:18-23). Blessed sons, cursed Canaan (Ge 9:24-27).

NOBLE
Ru 3:11 you are a woman of *n* character.
Ps 45: 1 My heart is stirred by a *n* theme
Pr 12: 4 of *n* character is her husband's
31:10 A wife of *n* character who can find?
31:29 "Many women do *n* things,
Isa 32: 8 But the *n* man makes *n* plans,
Lk 8:15 good soil stands for those with a *n*
Ro 9:21 of clay some pottery for *n* purposes
Php 4: 8 whatever is *n,* whatever is right,
2Ti 2:20 some are for *n* purposes

NOTHING
Ne 9:21 in the desert; they lacked *n,*
Jer 32:17 *N* is too hard for you
Jn 15: 5 apart from me you can do *n.*

NULLIFY
Ro 3:31 Do we, then, *n* the law by this faith

OATH
Dt 7: 8 and kept the *o* he swore

OBEDIENCE (OBEY)
2Ch 31:21 in *o* to the law and the commands,
Pr 30:17 that scorns *o* to a mother,
Ro 1: 5 to the *o* that comes from faith.
6:16 to *o,* which leads to righteousness?
2Jn : 6 that we walk in *o* to his commands.

OBEDIENT (OBEY)
Lk 2:51 with them and was *o* to them.
Php 2: 8 and became *o* to death—
1Pe 1:14 As *o* children, do not conform

OBEY (OBEDIENCE OBEDIENT OBEYED)
Ex 12:24 "*O* these instructions as a lasting
Dt 6: 3 careful to *o* so that it may go well
13: 4 Keep his commands and *o* him;
21:18 son who does not *o* his father
30: 2 and *o* him with all your heart
32:46 children to *o* carefully all the words
1Sa 15:22 To *o* is better than sacrifice,
Ps 119:34 and *o* it with all my heart.
Mt 28:20 to *o* everything I have commanded
Jn 14:23 loves me, he will *o* my teaching.
Ac 5:29 "We must *o* God rather than men!
Ro 6:16 slaves to the one whom you *o*—
Gal 5: 3 obligated to *o* the whole law.
Eph 6: 1 *o* your parents in the Lord,
6: 5 *o* your earthly masters with respect
Col 3:20 *o* your parents in everything,
1Ti 3: 4 and see that his children *o* him
Heb 13:17 *O* your leaders and submit
1Jn 5: 3 love for God: to *o* his commands.

OBEYED (OBEY)
Ps 119: 4 that are to be fully *o.*
Jnh 3: 3 Jonah *o* the word of the LORD
Jn 17: 6 and they have *o* your word.
Ro 6:17 you wholeheartedly *o* the form
Heb 11: 8 *o* and went, even though he did not
1Pe 3: 6 who *o* Abraham and called him her

OBLIGATED
Ro 1:14 I am *o* both to Greeks
Gal 5: 3 himself be circumcised that he is *o*

OBSCENITY
Eph 5: 4 Nor should there be *o,* foolish talk

OBSOLETE
Heb 8:13 he has made the first one *o;*

OBTAINED
Ro 9:30 not pursue righteousness, have *o* it,
Php 3:12 Not that I have already *o* all this,
Heb 9:12 having *o* eternal redemption.

OFFENDED (OFFENSE)
Pr 18:19 An *o* brother is more unyielding

OFFENSE (OFFENDED OFFENSIVE)
Pr 17: 9 over an *o* promotes love,
19:11 it is to his glory to overlook an *o.*

OFFENSIVE (OFFENSE)
Ps 139:24 See if there is any *o* way in me,

OFFER (OFFERED OFFERING OFFERINGS)
Ro 12: 1 to *o* your bodies as living sacrifices,
Heb 13:15 therefore, let us continually *o*

OFFERED (OFFER)
Heb 7:27 once for all when he *o* himself.
11: 4 By faith Abel *o* God a better

OFFERING (OFFER)
Ge 22: 8 provide the lamb for the burnt *o,*
Ps 40: 6 Sacrifice and *o* you did not desire,
Isa 53:10 the LORD makes his life a guilt *o,*
Mt 5:23 if you are *o* your gift at the altar
Eph 5: 2 as a fragrant *o* and sacrifice to God.
Heb 10: 5 "Sacrifice and *o* you did not desire,

OFFERINGS (OFFER)
Mal 3: 8 do we rob you?' "In tithes and *o.*
Mk 12:33 is more important than all burnt *o*

OFFICER
2Ti 2: 4 wants to please his commanding *o.*

OFFSPRING
Ge 3:15 and between your *o* and hers;
12: 7 "To your *o* I will give this land."

OIL
Ps 23: 5 You anoint my head with *o;*
Isa 61: 3 the *o* of gladness
Heb 1: 9 by anointing you with the *o* of joy."

OLIVE (OLIVES)
Zec 4: 3 Also there are two *o* trees by it,
Ro 11:17 and you, though a wild *o* shoot,
Rev 11: 4 These are the two *o* trees

OLIVES (OLIVE)
Jas 3:12 a fig tree bear *o,* or a grapevine bear

OMEGA
Rev 1: 8 "I am the Alpha and the *O,"*

OMRI
King of Israel (1Ki 16:21-26).

OPINIONS*
1Ki 18:21 will you waver between two *o?*
Pr 18: 2 but delights in airing his own *o.*

OPPORTUNITY
Ro 7:11 seizing the *o* afforded
Gal 6:10 as we have *o,* let us do good
Eph 5:16 making the most of every *o,*
Col 4: 5 make the most of every *o.*
1Ti 5:14 to give the enemy no *o* for slander.

OPPOSES
Jas 4: 6 "God *o* the proud
1Pe 5: 5 because, "God *o* the proud

OPPRESS (OPPRESSED)
Ex 22:21 "Do not mistreat an alien or *o* him,
Zec 7:10 Do not *o* the widow

OPPRESSED (OPPRESS)
Ps 9: 9 The LORD is a refuge for the *o,*
Isa 53: 7 He was *o* and afflicted,
Zec 10: 2 *o* for lack of a shepherd.

ORDAINED
Ps 8: 2 you have *o* praise

ORDERLY
1Co 14:40 done in a fitting and *o* way.
Col 2: 5 and delight to see how *o* you are

ORGIES*
Ro 13:13 not in *o* and drunkenness,
Gal 5:21 drunkenness, *o,* and the like.
1Pe 4: 3 *o,* carousing and detestable

ORIGIN
2Pe 1:21 For prophecy never had its *o*

ORPHANS
Jn 14:18 will not leave you as *o;* I will come
Jas 1:27 to look after *o* and widows

OUTCOME
Heb13: 7 Consider the *o* of their way of life
1Pe 4:17 what will the *o* be for those who do

OUTSIDERS*
Col 4: 5 wise in the way you act toward *o;*
1Th 4:12 daily life may win the respect of *o*
1Ti 3: 7 also have a good reputation with *o,*

OUTSTANDING
SS 5:10 *o* among ten thousand.
Ro 13: 8 no debt remain *o,*

OUTSTRETCHED
Ex 6: 6 and will redeem you with an *o* arm
Jer 27: 5 and *o* arm I made the earth
Eze 20:33 an *o* arm and with outpoured wrath

OUTWEIGHS
2Co 4:17 an eternal glory that far *o* them all.

OVERCOME (OVERCOMES)
Mt 16:18 and the gates of Hades will not *o* it.
Mk 9:24 I do believe; help me *o* my unbelief
Jn 16:33 But take heart! I have *o* the world."
Ro 12:21 Do not be *o* by evil, but *o* evil
1Jn 5: 4 is the victory that has *o* the world,
Rev 17:14 but the Lamb will *o* them

OVERCOMES* (OVERCOME)
1Jn 5: 4 born of God *o* the world.
5: 5 Who is it that *o* the world?
Rev 2: 7 To him who *o,* I will give the right
2:11 He who *o* will not be hurt at all
2:17 To him who *o,* I will give some
2:26 To him who *o* and does my will
3: 5 He who *o* will, like them, be
3:12 Him who *o* I will make a pillar
3:21 To him who *o,* I will give the right
21: 7 He who *o* will inherit all this,

OVERFLOW (OVERFLOWS)
Ps119:171 May my lips *o* with praise,
Lk 6:45 out of the *o* of his heart his mouth
Ro 15:13 so that you may *o* with hope
2Co 4:15 to *o* to the glory of God.
1Th 3:12 *o* for each other and for everyone

OVERFLOWS* (OVERFLOW)
Ps 23: 5 my cup *o.*
2Co 1: 5 also through Christ our comfort *o.*

OVERJOYED* (JOY)
Da 6:23 The king was *o* and gave orders
Mt 2:10 they saw the star, they were *o.*
Jn 20:20 The disciples were *o*
Ac 12:14 she was so *o* she ran back
1Pe 4:13 so that you may be *o*

OVERSEER (OVERSEERS)
1Ti 3: 1 anyone sets his heart on being an *o,*
3: 2 Now the *o* must be above reproach,
Tit 1: 7 Since an *o* is entrusted

OVERSEERS* (OVERSEER)
Ac 20:28 the Holy Spirit has made you *o.*
Php 1: 1 together with the *o* and deacons:
1Pe 5: 2 as *o*— not because you must,

OVERWHELMED
Ps 38: 4 My guilt has *o* me
65: 3 When we were *o* by sins,
Mt 26:38 "My soul is *o* with sorrow
Mk 7:37 People were *o* with amazement.

OWE
Ro 13: 7 If you *o* taxes, pay taxes; if revenue
Phm :19 to mention that you *o* me your very

OX
Dt 25: 4 Do not muzzle an *o*
Isa 11: 7 and the lion will eat straw like the *o*
1Co 9: 9 "Do not muzzle an *o*

PAGANS
Mt 5:47 Do not even *p* do that? Be perfect,
1Pe 2:12 such good lives among the *p* that,

PAIN (PAINFUL)
Ge 3:16 with *p* you will give birth
Job 33:19 may be chastened on a bed of *p*
Jn 16:21 woman giving birth to a child has *p*

PAINFUL (PAIN)
Ge 3:17 through *p* toil you will eat of it
Heb12:11 seems pleasant at the time, but *p.*
1Pe 4:12 at the *p* trial you are suffering,

PALMS
Isa 49:16 you on the *p* of my hands;

PANTS
Ps 42: 1 As the deer *p* for streams of water,

PARADISE*
Lk 23:43 today you will be with me in *p.*"
2Co 12: 4 God knows—was caught up to *p.*
Rev 2: 7 of life, which is in the *p* of God.

PARALYTIC
Mk 2: 3 bringing to him a *p,* carried by four

PARDON (PARDONS)
Isa 55: 7 and to our God, for he will freely *p.*

PARDONS* (PARDON)
Mic 7:18 who *p* sin and forgives

PARENTS
Pr 17: 6 and *p* are the pride of their children
Lk 18:29 left home or wife or brothers or *p*
21:16 You will be betrayed even by *p,*
Ro 1:30 they disobey their *p;* they are
2Co 12:14 for their *p,* but *p* for their children.
Eph 6: 1 Children, obey your *p* in the Lord,
Col 3:20 obey your *p* in everything,
2Ti 3: 2 disobedient to their *p,* ungrateful,

PARTIALITY
Dt 10:17 who shows no *p* and accepts no
2Ch 19: 7 our God there is no injustice or *p*
Lk 20:21 and that you do not show *p*

PARTICIPATION
1Co 10:16 is not the bread that we break a *p*

PASS
Ex 12:13 and when I see the blood, I will *p*
La 1:12 to you, all you who *p* by?
Lk 21:33 Heaven and earth will *p* away,
1Co 13: 8 there is knowledge, it will *p* away.

PASSION (PASSIONS)
1Co 7: 9 better to marry than to burn with *p.*

PASSIONS (PASSION)
Gal 5:24 crucified the sinful nature with its *p*
Tit 2:12 to ungodliness and worldly *p,*

PASSOVER
Ex 12:11 Eat it in haste; it is the LORD's *P.*
Dt 16: 1 celebrate the *P* of the LORD your
1Co 5: 7 our *P* lamb, has been sacrificed.

PAST
Isa 43:18 do not dwell on the *p.*
Ro 15: 4 in the *p* was written to teach us,
Heb 1: 1 In the *p* God spoke

PASTORS*
Eph 4:11 and some to be *p* and teachers,

PASTURE (PASTURES)
Ps 37: 3 dwell in the land and enjoy safe *p.*
100: 3 we are his people, the sheep of his *p*
Jer 50: 7 against the LORD, their true *p,*
Eze 34:13 I will *p* them on the mountains
Jn 10: 9 come in and go out, and find *p.*

PASTURES (PASTURE)
Ps 23: 2 He makes me lie down in green *p,*

PATCH
Mt 9:16 No one sews a *p* of unshrunk cloth

PATH (PATHS)
Ps 27:11 lead me in a straight *p*
119:105 and a light for my *p.*
Pr 15:19 the *p* of the upright is a highway.
15:24 The *p* of life leads upward
Isa 26: 7 The *p* of the righteous is level;
Lk 1:79 to guide our feet into the *p* of peace
2Co 6: 3 no stumbling block in anyone's *p,*

PATHS (PATH)
Ps 23: 3 He guides me in *p* of righteousness
25: 4 teach me your *p;*
Pr 3: 6 and he will make your *p* straight.
Ro 11:33 and his *p* beyond tracing out!
Heb12:13 "Make level *p* for your feet,"

PATIENCE (PATIENT)
Pr 19:11 A man's wisdom gives him *p;*
2Co 6: 6 understanding, *p* and kindness;
Gal 5:22 joy, peace, *p,* kindness, goodness,
Col 1:11 may have great endurance and *p,*
3:12 humility, gentleness and *p.*

PATIENT (PATIENCE PATIENTLY)
Pr 15:18 but a *p* man calms a quarrel.
Ro 12:12 Be joyful in hope, *p* in affliction,
1Co 13: 4 Love is *p,* love is kind.
Eph 4: 2 humble and gentle; be *p,*
1Th 5:14 help the weak, be *p* with everyone.

PATIENTLY (PATIENT)
Ps 40: 1 I waited *p* for the LORD;
Ro 8:25 we do not yet have, we wait for it *p.*

PATTERN
Ro 5:14 who was a *p* of the one to come.
12: 2 longer to the *p* of this world,
2Ti 1:13 keep as the *p* of sound teaching,

PAUL
Also called Saul (Ac 13:9). Pharisee from Tarsus (Ac 9:11; Php 3:5). Apostle (Gal 1). At

stoning of Stephen (Ac 8:1). Persecuted Church (Ac 9:1-2; Gal 1:13). Vision of Jesus on road to Damascus (Ac 9:4-9; 26:12-18). In Arabia (Gal 1:17). Preached in Damascus; escaped death through the wall in a basket (Ac 9:19-25). In Jerusalem; sent back to Tarsus (Ac 9:26-30).

Brought to Antioch by Barnabas (Ac 11:22-26). First missionary journey to Cyprus and Galatia (Ac 13-14). Stoned at Lystra (Ac 14:19-20). At Jerusalem council (Ac 15). Split with Barnabas over Mark (Ac 15:36-41).

Second missionary journey with Silas (Ac 16-20). Called to Macedonia (Ac 16:6-10). Freed from prison in Philippi (Ac 16:16-40). In Thessalonica (Ac 17:1-9). Speech in Athens (Ac 17:16-33). In Corinth (Ac 18). In Ephesus (Ac 19). Return to Jerusalem (Ac 20). Farewell to Ephesian elders (Ac 20:13-38). Arrival in Jerusalem (Ac 21:1-26). Arrested (Ac 21:27-36). Addressed crowds (Ac 22), Sanhedrin (Ac 23:1-11). Transferred to Caesarea (Ac 23:12-35). Trial before Felix (Ac 24), Festus (Ac 25:1-12). Before Agrippa (Ac 25:13-26:32). Voyage to Rome; shipwreck (Ac 27). Arrival in Rome (Ac 28).

PAY (REPAID REPAY)
Lev 26:43 They will *p* for their sins
Pr 22:17 *P* attention and listen
Mt 22:17 Is it right to *p* taxes to Caesar
Ro 13: 6 This is also why you *p* taxes,
2Pe 1:19 you will do well to *p* attention to it,

PEACE (PEACEMAKERS)
Nu 6:26 and give you *p*." '
Ps 34:14 seek *p* and pursue it.
85:10 righteousness and *p* kiss each other
119:165 Great *p* have they who love your
122: 6 Pray for the *p* of Jerusalem:
Pr 14:30 A heart at *p* gives life to the body,
17: 1 Better a dry crust with *p* and quiet
Isa 9: 6 Everlasting Father, Prince of *P*.
26: 3 You will keep in perfect *p*
48:22 "There is no *p*," says the LORD,
Zec 9:10 He will proclaim *p* to the nations.
Mt 10:34 I did not come to bring *p*,
Lk 2:14 on earth *p* to men on whom his
Jn 14:27 *P* I leave with you; my *p*
16:33 so that in me you may have *p*.
Ro 5: 1 we have *p* with God
1Co 7:15 God has called us to live in *p*.
14:33 a God of disorder but of *p*.
Gal 5:22 joy, *p*, patience, kindness,
Eph 2:14 he himself is our *p*, who has made
Php 4: 7 the *p* of God, which transcends all
Col 1:20 by making *p* through his blood,
3:15 Let the *p* of Christ rule
1Th 5: 3 While people are saying, "*P*
2Th 3:16 the Lord of *p* himself give you *p*
2Ti 2:22 righteousness, faith, love and *p*,
1Pe 3:11 he must seek *p* and pursue it.
Rev 6: 4 power to take *p* from the earth

PEACEMAKERS* (PEACE)
Mt 5: 9 Blessed are the *p*,
Jas 3:18 *P* who sow in peace raise a harvest

PEARL* (PEARLS)
Rev 21:21 each gate made of a single *p*.

PEARLS (PEARL)
Mt 7: 6 do not throw your *p* to pigs.
13:45 like a merchant looking for fine *p*.
1Ti 2: 9 or gold or *p* or expensive clothes,
Rev 21:21 The twelve gates were twelve *p*,

PEKAH
King of Israel (2Ki 15:25-31; Isa 7:1).

PEKAHIAH*
Son of Menahem; king of Israel (2Ki 15:22-26).

PEN
Mt 5:18 letter, not the least stroke of a *p*,

PENTECOST
Ac 2: 1 of *P* came, they were all together

PEOPLE (PEOPLES)
Dt 32: 9 the LORD's portion is his *p*,
Ru 1:16 Your *p* will be my *p*
2Ch 7:14 if my *p*, who are called
Jer 24: 7 They will be my *p*,
Zec 2:11 and will become my *p*.
Lk 2:10 joy that will be for all the *p*.
Ac 15:14 from the Gentiles a *p*.
2Co 6:16 and they will be my *p*."
Tit 2:14 a *p* that are his very own,
1Pe 2: 9 you are a chosen *p*,
Rev 21: 3 They will be his *p*,

PEOPLES (PEOPLE)
Da 7:14 all *p*, nations and men
Mic 4: 1 and *p* will stream to it.

PERCEIVING
Isa 6: 9 be ever seeing, but never *p*.'

PERFECT (PERFECTER PERFECTION)
SS 6: 9 but my dove, my *p* one, is unique,
Isa 26: 3 You will keep in *p* peace
Mt 5:48 as your heavenly Father is *p*.
Ro 12: 2 his good, pleasing and *p* will.
2Co 12: 9 for my power is made *p*
Col 1:28 so that we may present everyone *p*
3:14 binds them all together in *p* unity.
Heb 9:11 and more *p* tabernacle that is not
10:14 he has made *p* forever those who
Jas 1:17 Every good and *p* gift is from above
1:25 into the *p* law that gives freedom,
3: 2 he is a *p* man, able
1Jn 4:18 But *p* love drives out fear,

PERFECTER* (PERFECT)
Heb 12: 2 the author and *p* of our faith,

PERFECTION (PERFECT)
Ps 119:96 To all *p* I see a limit;
2Co 13:11 Aim for *p*, listen to my appeal,
Heb 7:11 If *p* could have been attained

PERFORMS
Ps 77:14 You are the God who *p* miracles;

PERISH (PERISHABLE)
Ps 1: 6 but the way of the wicked will *p*.
102:26 They will *p*, but you remain;
Lk 13: 3 unless you repent, you too will all *p*
Jn 10:28 eternal life, and they shall never *p*;
Col 2:22 These are all destined to *p* with use,
Heb 1:11 They will *p*, but you remain;
2Pe 3: 9 not wanting anyone to *p*,

PERISHABLE (PERISH)
1Co 15:42 The body that is sown is *p*,

PERJURERS
1Ti 1:10 for slave traders and liars and *p*—

PERMISSIBLE (PERMIT)
1Co 10:23 "Everything is *p*"— but not

PERMIT (PERMISSIBLE)
1Ti 2:12 I do not *p* a woman to teach

PERSECUTE (PERSECUTED PERSECUTION)
Mt 5:11 *p* you and falsely say all kinds
Jn 15:20 they persecuted me, they will *p* you
Ac 9: 4 why do you *p* me?" "Who are you,
Ro 12:14 Bless those who *p* you; bless

PERSECUTED (PERSECUTE)
1Co 4:12 when we are *p*, we endure it;
2Ti 3:12 life in Christ Jesus will be *p*,

PERSECUTION (PERSECUTE)
Ro 8:35 or hardship or *p* or famine

PERSEVERANCE (PERSEVERE)
Ro 5: 3 we know that suffering produces *p*;
5: 4 *p*, character; and character, hope.
Heb 12: 1 run with *p* the race marked out
Jas 1: 3 the testing of your faith develops *p*.
2Pe 1: 6 *p*; and to *p*, godliness;

PERSEVERE* (PERSEVERANCE PERSEVERED PERSEVERES)
1Ti 4:16 *P* in them, because if you do,
Heb 10:36 You need to *p* so that

PERSEVERED* (PERSEVERE)
Heb 11:27 he *p* because he saw him who is
Jas 5:11 consider blessed those who have *p*.
Rev 2: 3 You have *p* and have endured

PERSEVERES* (PERSEVERE)
1Co 13: 7 trusts, always hopes, always *p*.
Jas 1:12 Blessed is the man who *p*

PERSUADE
2Co 5:11 is to fear the Lord, we try to *p* men.

PERVERSION (PERVERT)
Lev 18:23 sexual relations with it; that is a *p*.
Jude : 7 up to sexual immorality and *p*.

PERVERT (PERVERSION PERVERTS)
Gal 1: 7 are trying to *p* the gospel of Christ.

PERVERTS* (PERVERT)
1Ti 1:10 for murderers, for adulterers and *p*,

PESTILENCE
Ps 91: 6 nor the *p* that stalks in the darkness

PETER
Apostle, brother of Andrew, also called Simon (Mt 10:2; Mk 3:16; Lk 6:14; Ac 1:13), and Cephas (Jn 1:42). Confession of Christ (Mt 16:13-20; Mk 8:27-30; Lk 9:18-27). At transfiguration (Mt 17:1-8; Mk 9:2-8; Lk 9:28-36; 2Pe 1:16-18). Caught fish with coin (Mt 17:24-27). Denial of Jesus predicted (Mt 26:31-35; Mk 14:27-31; Lk 22:31-34; Jn 13:31-38). Denied Jesus (Mt 26:69-75; Mk 14:66-72; Lk 22:54-62; Jn 18:15-27). Commissioned by Jesus to shepherd his flock (Jn 21:15-23).

Speech at Pentecost (Ac 2). Healed beggar (Ac 3:1-10). Speech at temple (Ac 3:11-26), before Sanhedrin (Ac 4:1-22). In Samaria (Ac 8:14-25). Sent by vision to Cornelius (Ac 10). Announced salvation of Gentiles in Jerusalem (Ac 11; 15). Freed from prison (Ac 12). Inconsistency at Antioch (Gal 2:11-21). At Jerusalem Council (Ac 15).

POSSESS (POSSESSING POSSESSION POSSESSIONS)
Nu 33:53 for I have given you the land to *p.*
Jn 5:39 that by them you *p* eternal life.

POSSESSING* (POSSESS)
2Co 6:10 nothing, and yet *p* everything.

POSSESSION (POSSESS)
Ge 15: 7 to give you this land to take *p* of it
Nu 13:30 "We should go up and take *p*
Eph 1:14 of those who are God's *p*—

POSSESSIONS (POSSESS)
Lk 12:15 consist in the abundance of his *p.*"
2Co 12:14 what I want is not your *p* but you.
1Jn 3:17 If anyone has material *p*

POSSIBLE
Mt 19:26 but with God all things are *p.*"
Mk 9:23 "Everything is *p* for him who
10:27 all things are *p* with God."
Ro 12:18 If it is *p,* as far as it depends on you,
1Co 9:22 by all *p* means I might save some.

POT (POTSHERD POTTER POTTERY)
2Ki 4:40 there is death in the *p!*"
Jer 18: 4 But the *p* he was shaping

POTSHERD (POT)
Isa 45: 9 a *p* among the potsherds

POTTER (POT)
Isa 29:16 Can the pot say of the *p,*
45: 9 Does the clay say to the *p,*
64: 8 We are the clay, you are the *p;*
Jer 18: 6 "Like clay in the hand of the *p,*
Ro 9:21 Does not the *p* have the right

POTTERY (POT)
Ro 9:21 of clay some *p* for noble purposes

POUR (POURED)
Ps 62: 8 *p* out your hearts to him,
Joel 2:28 I will *p* out my Spirit on all people.
Mal 3:10 *p* out so much blessing that you
Ac 2:17 I will *p* out my Spirit on all people.

POURED (POUR)
Ac 10:45 of the Holy Spirit had been *p* out
Ro 5: 5 because God has *p* out his love

POVERTY (POOR)
Pr 14:23 but mere talk leads only to *p.*
21: 5 as surely as haste leads to *p.*
30: 8 give me neither *p* nor riches,
Mk 12:44 out of her *p,* put in everything—
2Co 8: 2 and their extreme *p* welled up
8: 9 through his *p* might become rich.

POWER (POWERFUL POWERS)
1Ch 29:11 LORD, is the greatness and the *p*
2Ch 32: 7 for there is a greater *p* with us
Job 36:22 "God is exalted in his *p.*
Ps 63: 2 and beheld your *p* and your glory.
68:34 Proclaim the *p* of God,
147: 5 Great is our Lord and mighty in *p;*
Pr 24: 5 A wise man has great *p,*
Isa 40:10 the Sovereign LORD comes with *p*
Zec 4: 6 nor by *p,* but by my Spirit,'
Mt 22:29 do not know the Scriptures or the *p*
24:30 on the clouds of the sky, with *p*
Ac 1: 8 you will receive *p* when the Holy
4:33 With great *p* the apostles
10:38 with the Holy Spirit and *p,*
Ro 1:16 it is the *p* of God for the salvation
1Co 1:18 to us who are being saved it is the *p*
15:56 of death is sin, and the *p*
2Co 12: 9 for my *p* is made perfect
Eph 1:19 and his incomparably great *p*
Php 3:10 and the *p* of his resurrection
Col 1:11 strengthened with all *p* according
2Ti 1: 7 but a spirit of *p,* of love
Heb 7:16 of the *p* of an indestructible life.
Rev 4:11 to receive glory and honor and *p,*
19: 1 and glory and *p* belong to our God,
20: 6 The second death has no *p*

POWERFUL (POWER)
Ps 29: 4 The voice of the LORD is *p;*
Lk 24:19 *p* in word and deed before God
2Th 1: 7 in blazing fire with his *p* angels.
Heb 1: 3 sustaining all things by his *p* word.
Jas 5:16 The prayer of a righteous man is *p*

POWERLESS
Ro 5: 6 when we were still *p,* Christ died
8: 3 For what the law was *p* to do

POWERS (POWER)
Ro 8:38 nor any *p,* neither height nor depth
1Co 12:10 to another miraculous *p,*
Col 1:16 whether thrones or *p* or rulers
2:15 And having disarmed the *p*

PRACTICE
Lev 19:26 " 'Do not *p* divination or sorcery.
Mt 23: 3 for they do not *p* what they preach.
Lk 8:21 hear God's word and put it into *p.*"
Ro 12:13 *P* hospitality.
1Ti 5: 4 to put their religion into *p* by caring

PRAISE (PRAISED PRAISES PRAISING)
Ex 15: 2 He is my God, and I will *p* him,
Dt 32: 3 Oh, *p* the greatness of our God!
Ru 4:14 said to Naomi: "*P* be to the LORD,
2Sa 22:47 The LORD lives! *P* be to my Rock
1Ch 16:25 is the LORD and most worthy of *p;*
2Ch 20:21 and to *p* him for the splendor
Ps 8: 2 you have ordained *p*
33: 1 it is fitting for the upright to *p* him.
34: 1 his *p* will always be on my lips.
40: 3 a hymn of *p* to our God.
48: 1 the LORD, and most worthy of *p,*
68:19 *P* be to the Lord, to God our Savior
89: 5 The heavens *p* your wonders,
100: 4 and his courts with *p;*
105: 2 Sing to him, sing *p* to him;
106: 1 *P* the LORD.
119:175 Let me live that I may *p* you,
139:14 I *p* you because I am fearfully
145:21 Let every creature *p* his holy name
146: 1 *P* the LORD, O my soul.
150: 2 *p* him for his surpassing greatness.
150: 6 that has breath *p* the LORD.
Pr 27: 2 Let another *p* you, and not your
27:21 man is tested by the *p* he receives.
31:31 let her works bring her *p*
Mt 5:16 and *p* your Father in heaven.
21:16 you have ordained *p*'?"
Jn 12:43 for they loved *p* from men more
Eph 1: 6 to the *p* of his glorious grace,
1:12 might be for the *p* of his glory.
1:14 to the *p* of his glory.
Heb 13:15 offer to God a sacrifice of *p*—
Jas 5:13 happy? Let him sing songs of *p.*

PRAISED (PRAISE)
1Ch 29:10 David *p* the LORD in the presence
Ne 8: 6 Ezra *p* the LORD, the great God;
Da 2:19 Then Daniel *p* the God of heaven
Ro 9: 5 who is God over all, forever *p!*
1Pe 4:11 that in all things God may be *p*

PRAISES (PRAISE)
2Sa 22:50 I will sing *p* to your name.
Ps 47: 6 Sing *p* to God, sing *p;*
147: 1 How good it is to sing *p* to our God,
Pr 31:28 her husband also, and he *p* her:

PRAISING (PRAISE)
Ac 10:46 speaking in tongues and *p* God.
1Co 14:16 If you are *p* God with your spirit,

PRAY (PRAYED PRAYER PRAYERS PRAYING)
Dt 4: 7 is near us whenever we *p* to him?
1Sa 12:23 the LORD by failing to *p* for you.
2Ch 7:14 will humble themselves and *p*
Job 42: 8 My servant Job will *p* for you,
Ps 122: 6 *P* for the peace of Jerusalem:
Mt 5:44 and *p* for those who persecute you,
6: 5 "And when you *p,* do not be like
6: 9 "This, then, is how you should *p:*
26:36 Sit here while I go over there and *p*
Lk 6:28 *p* for those who mistreat you.
18: 1 them that they should always *p*
22:40 "*P* that you will not fall
Ro 8:26 do not know what we ought to *p,*
1Co 14:13 in a tongue should *p* that he may
1Th 5:17 Be joyful always; *p* continually;
Jas 5:13 one of you in trouble? He should *p.*
5:16 *p* for each other so that you may be

PRAYED (PRAY)
1Sa 1:27 I *p* for this child, and the LORD
Jnh 2: 1 From inside the fish Jonah *p*
Mk 14:35 *p* that if possible the hour might

PRAYER (PRAY)
2Ch 30:27 for their *p* reached heaven,
Ezr 8:23 about this, and he answered our *p.*
Ps 6: 9 the LORD accepts my *p.*
86: 6 Hear my *p,* O LORD;
Pr 15: 8 but the *p* of the upright pleases him
Isa 56: 7 a house of *p* for all nations."
Mt 21:13 house will be called a house of *p,*'
Mk 11:24 whatever you ask for in *p,*
Jn 17:15 My *p* is not that you take them out
Ac 6: 4 and will give our attention to *p*
Php 4: 6 but in everything, by *p* and petition
Jas 5:15 *p* offered in faith will make the sick
1Pe 3:12 and his ears are attentive to their *p,*

PRAYERS (PRAY)
1Ch 5:20 He answered their *p,* because they
Mk 12:40 and for a show make lengthy *p.*
1Pe 3: 7 so that nothing will hinder your *p.*
Rev 5: 8 which are the *p* of the saints.

PRAYING (PRAY)
Mk 11:25 And when you stand *p,*
Jn 17: 9 I am not *p* for the world,
Ac 16:25 and Silas were *p* and singing hymns
Eph 6:18 always keep on *p* for all the saints.

PREACH (PREACHED PREACHING)
Mt 23: 3 they do not practice what they *p.*
Mk 16:15 and *p* the good news to all creation.
Ac 9:20 At once he began to *p*
Ro 10:15 how can they *p* unless they are sent

Ro 15:20 to *p* the gospel where Christ was
1Co 1:17 to *p* the gospel—not with words
1:23 wisdom, but we *p* Christ crucified:
9:14 that those who *p* the gospel should
9:16 Woe to me if I do not *p* the gospel!
2Co 10:16 so that we can *p* the gospel
Gal 1: 8 from heaven should *p* a gospel
2Ti 4: 2 I give you this charge: *P* the Word;

PREACHED (PREACH)
Mk 13:10 And the gospel must first be *p*
Ac 8: 4 had been scattered *p* the word
1Co 9:27 so that after I have *p* to others,
15: 1 you of the gospel I *p* to you,
2Co 11: 4 other than the Jesus we *p*,
Gal 1: 8 other than the one we *p* to you,
Php 1:18 false motives or true, Christ is *p*.
1Ti 3:16 was *p* among the nations,

PREACHING (PREACH)
Ro 10:14 hear without someone *p* to them?
1Co 9:18 in *p* the gospel I may offer it free
1Ti 4:13 the public reading of Scripture, to *p*
5:17 especially those whose work is *p*

PRECEPTS
Ps 19: 8 The *p* of the LORD are right,
111: 7 all his *p* are trustworthy.
111:10 who follow his *p* have good
119:40 How I long for your *p*!
119:69 I keep your *p* with all my heart.
119:104 I gain understanding from your *p*;
119:159 See how I love your *p*;

PRECIOUS
Ps 19:10 They are more *p* than gold,
116:15 *P* in the sight of the LORD
Pr 8:11 for wisdom is more *p* than rubies,
Isa 28:16 a *p* cornerstone for a sure
1Pe 1:19 but with the *p* blood of Christ,
2: 6 a chosen and *p* cornerstone,
2Pe 1: 4 us his very great and *p* promises,

PREDESTINED* (DESTINY)
Ro 8:29 *p* to be conformed to the likeness
8:30 And those he *p*, he also called;
Eph 1: 5 In love he *p* us to be adopted
1:11 having been *p* according

PREDICTION*
Jer 28: 9 only if his *p* comes true."

PREPARE (PREPARED)
Ps 23: 5 You *p* a table before me
Am 4:12 *p* to meet your God, O Israel."
Jn 14: 2 there to *p* a place for you.
Eph 4:12 to *p* God's people for works

PREPARED (PREPARE)
Mt 25:34 the kingdom *p* for you
1Co 2: 9 what God has *p* for those who love
Eph 2:10 which God *p* in advance for us
2Ti 4: 2 be *p* in season and out of season;
1Pe 3:15 Always be *p* to give an answer

PRESENCE (PRESENT)
Ex 25:30 Put the bread of the *P* on this table
Ezr 9:15 one of us can stand in your *p*."
Ps 31:20 the shelter of your *p* you hide them
89:15 who walk in the light of your *p*,
90: 8 our secret sins in the light of your *p*
139: 7 Where can I flee from your *p*?
Jer 5:22 "Should you not tremble in my *p*?
Heb 9:24 now to appear for us in God's *p*.
Jude :24 before his glorious *p* without fault

PRESENT (PRESENCE)
2Co 11: 2 so that I might *p* you as a pure
Eph 5:27 and to *p* her to himself
2Ti 2:15 Do your best to *p* yourself to God

PRESERVES
Ps 119:50 Your promise *p* my life.

PRESS (PRESSED PRESSURE)
Php 3:14 I *p* on toward the goal

PRESSED (PRESS)
Lk 6:38 *p* down, shaken together

PRESSURE (PRESS)
2Co 1: 8 We were under great *p*, far
11:28 I face daily the *p* of my concern

PREVAILS
1Sa 2: 9 "It is not by strength that one *p*;

PRICE
Job 28:18 the *p* of wisdom is beyond rubies.
1Co 6:20 your own; you were bought at a *p*.
7:23 bought at a *p*; do not become slaves

PRIDE (PROUD)
Pr 8:13 I hate *p* and arrogance,
16:18 *P* goes before destruction,
Da 4:37 And those who walk in *p* he is able
Gal 6: 4 Then he can take *p* in himself,
Jas 1: 9 ought to take *p* in his high position.

PRIEST (PRIESTHOOD PRIESTS)
Heb 4:14 have a great high *p* who has gone
4:15 do not have a high *p* who is unable
7:26 Such a high *p* meets our need—
8: 1 We do have such a high *p*,

PRIESTHOOD (PRIEST)
Heb 7:24 lives forever, he has a permanent *p*.
1Pe 2: 5 into a spiritual house to be a holy *p*,
2: 9 you are a chosen people, a royal *p*,

PRIESTS (PRIEST)
Ex 19: 6 you will be for me a kingdom of *p*
Rev 5:10 to be a kingdom and *p*

PRINCE
Isa 9: 6 Everlasting Father, *P* of Peace.
Jn 12:31 now the *p* of this world will be
Ac 5:31 as *P* and Savior that he might give

PRISON (PRISONER)
Isa 42: 7 to free captives from *p*
Mt 25:36 I was in *p* and you came to visit me
1Pe 3:19 spirits in *p* who disobeyed long ago
Rev 20: 7 Satan will be released from his *p*

PRISONER (PRISON)
Ro 7:23 and making me a *p* of the law of sin
Gal 3:22 declares that the whole world is a *p*
Eph 3: 1 the *p* of Christ Jesus for the sake

PRIVILEGE*
2Co 8: 4 pleaded with us for the *p* of sharing

PRIZE
1Co 9:24 Run in such a way as to get the *p*.
Php 3:14 on toward the goal to win the *p*

PROCLAIM (PROCLAIMED PROCLAIMING)
1Ch 16:23 *p* his salvation day after day.
Ps 19: 1 the skies *p* the work of his hands.
50: 6 the heavens *p* his righteousness,
68:34 *P* the power of God,
118:17 will *p* what the LORD has done.
Zec 9:10 He will *p* peace to the nations.
Ac 20:27 hesitated to *p* to you the whole will
1Co 11:26 you *p* the Lord's death

PROCLAIMED (PROCLAIM)
Ro 15:19 I have fully *p* the gospel of Christ.
Col 1:23 that has been *p* to every creature

PROCLAIMING (PROCLAIM)
Ro 10: 8 the word of faith we are *p*:

PRODUCE (PRODUCES)
Mt 3: 8 *P* fruit in keeping with repentance.
3:10 tree that does not *p* good fruit will

PRODUCES (PRODUCE)
Pr 30:33 so stirring up anger *p* strife."
Ro 5: 3 that suffering *p* perseverance;
Heb 12:11 it *p* a harvest of righteousness

PROFANE
Lev 22:32 Do not *p* my holy name.

PROFESS*
1Ti 2:10 for women who *p* to worship God.
Heb 4:14 let us hold firmly to the faith we *p*.
10:23 unswervingly to the hope we *p*,

PROMISE (PROMISED PROMISES)
1Ki 8:20 The LORD has kept the *p* he made
Ac 2:39 The *p* is for you and your children
Gal 3:14 that by faith we might receive the *p*
1Ti 4: 8 holding *p* for both the present life
2Pe 3: 9 Lord is not slow in keeping his *p*,

PROMISED (PROMISE)
Ex 3:17 And I have *p* to bring you up out
Dt 26:18 his treasured possession as he *p*,
Ps 119:57 I have *p* to obey your words.
Ro 4:21 power to do what he had *p*.
Heb 10:23 for he who *p* is faithful.
2Pe 3: 4 "Where is this 'coming' he *p*?

PROMISES (PROMISE)
Jos 21:45 one of all the LORD's good *p*
Ro 9: 4 the temple worship and the *p*.
2Pe 1: 4 us his very great and precious *p*,

PROMPTED
1Th 1: 3 your labor *p* by love, and your
2Th 1:11 and every act *p* by your faith.

PROPHECIES (PROPHESY)
1Co 13: 8 where there are *p*, they will cease;
1Th 5:20 do not treat *p* with contempt.

PROPHECY (PROPHESY)
1Co 14: 1 gifts, especially the gift of *p*.
2Pe 1:20 you must understand that no *p*

PROPHESY (PROPHECIES PROPHECY PROPHESYING PROPHET PROPHETS)
Joel 2:28 Your sons and daughters will *p*,
Mt 7:22 Lord, did we not *p* in your name,
1Co 14:39 my brothers, be eager to *p*,

PROPHESYING (PROPHESY)
Ro 12: 6 If a man's gift is *p*, let him use it

PROPHET (PROPHESY)
Dt 18:18 up for them a *p* like you
Am 7:14 "I was neither a *p* nor a prophet's

Mt 10:41 Anyone who receives a *p*
Lk 4:24 "no *p* is accepted in his hometown.

PROPHETS (PROPHESY)
Ps 105:15 do my *p* no harm."
Mt 5:17 come to abolish the Law or the *P;*
7:12 for this sums up the Law and the *P.*
24:24 false Christs and false *p* will appear
Lk 24:25 believe all that the *p* have spoken!
Ac 10:43 All the *p* testify about him that
1Co 12:28 second *p,* third teachers, then
14:32 The spirits of *p* are subject
Eph 2:20 foundation of the apostles and *p,*
Heb 1: 1 through the *p* at many times
1Pe 1:10 Concerning this salvation, the *p,*
2Pe 1:19 word of the *p* made more certain,

PROSPER (PROSPERITY PROSPERS)
Pr 28:25 he who trusts in the LORD will *p.*

PROSPERITY (PROSPER)
Ps 73: 3 when I saw the *p* of the wicked.
Pr 13:21 but *p* is the reward of the righteous.

PROSPERS (PROSPER)
Ps 1: 3 Whatever he does *p.*

PROSTITUTE (PROSTITUTES)
1Co 6:15 of Christ and unite them with a *p?*

PROSTITUTES (PROSTITUTE)
Lk 15:30 property with *p* comes home,
1Co 6: 9 male *p* nor homosexual offenders

PROSTRATE
Dt 9:18 again I fell *p* before the LORD

PROTECT (PROTECTS)
Ps 32: 7 you will *p* me from trouble
Pr 2:11 Discretion will *p* you,
Jn 17:11 *p* them by the power of your name

PROTECTS (PROTECT)
1Co 13: 7 It always *p,* always trusts,

PROUD (PRIDE)
Pr 16: 5 The LORD detests all the *p*
Ro 12:16 Do not be *p,* but be willing
1Co 13: 4 it does not boast, it is not *p.*

PROVE
Ac 26:20 *p* their repentance by their deeds.
1Co 4: 2 been given a trust must *p* faithful.

PROVIDE (PROVIDED PROVIDES)
Ge 22: 8 "God himself will *p* the lamb
Isa 43:20 because I *p* water in the desert
1Ti 5: 8 If anyone does not *p*

PROVIDED (PROVIDE)
Jnh 1:17 But the LORD *p* a great fish
4: 6 Then the LORD God *p* a vine
4: 7 dawn the next day God *p* a worm,
4: 8 God *p* a scorching east wind,

PROVIDES (PROVIDE)
1Ti 6:17 who richly *p* us with everything
1Pe 4:11 it with the strength God *p,*

PROVOKED
Ecc 7: 9 Do not be quickly *p* in your spirit,

PRUDENT
Pr 14:15 a *p* man gives thought to his steps.
19:14 but a *p* wife is from the LORD.
Am 5:13 Therefore the *p* man keeps quiet

PRUNING
Isa 2: 4 and their spears into *p* hooks.
Joel 3:10 and your *p* hooks into spears.

PSALMS
Eph 5:19 Speak to one another with *p,*
Col 3:16 and as you sing *p,* hymns

PUBLICLY
Ac 20:20 have taught you *p* and from house
1Ti 5:20 Those who sin are to be rebuked *p,*

PUFFS
1Co 8: 1 Knowledge *p* up, but love builds up

PULLING
2Co 10: 8 building you up rather than *p* you

PUNISH (PUNISHED PUNISHES)
Ex 32:34 I will *p* them for their sin."
Pr 23:13 if you *p* him with the rod, he will
Isa 13:11 I will *p* the world for its evil,
1Pe 2:14 by him to *p* those who do wrong

PUNISHED (PUNISH)
La 3:39 complain when *p* for his sins?
2Th 1: 9 be *p* with everlasting destruction
Heb 10:29 to be *p* who has trampled the Son

PUNISHES (PUNISH)
Heb 12: 6 and he *p* everyone he accepts

PURE (PURIFIES PURIFY PURITY)
2Sa 22:27 to the *p* you show yourself *p,*
Ps 24: 4 who has clean hands and a *p* heart,
51:10 Create in me a *p* heart, O God,
119: 9 can a young man keep his way *p?*
Pr 20: 9 can say, "I have kept my heart *p;*
Isa 52:11 Come out from it and be *p,*
Hab 1:13 Your eyes are too *p* to look on evil;
Mt 5: 8 Blessed are the *p* in heart,
2Co 11: 2 I might present you as a *p* virgin
Php 4: 8 whatever is *p,* whatever is lovely,
1Ti 5:22 Keep yourself *p.*
Tit 1:15 To the *p,* all things are *p,*
2: 5 to be self-controlled and *p,*
Heb 13: 4 and the marriage bed kept *p,*
1Jn 3: 3 him purifies himself, just as he is *p.*

PURGE
Pr 20:30 and beatings *p* the inmost being.

PURIFIES* (PURE)
1Jn 1: 7 of Jesus, his Son, *p* us from all sin.
3: 3 who has this hope in him *p* himself,

PURIFY (PURE)
Tit 2:14 to *p* for himself a people that are
1Jn 1: 9 and *p* us from all unrighteousness.

PURITY (PURE)
2Co 6: 6 in *p,* understanding, patience
1Ti 4:12 in life, in love, in faith and in *p.*

PURPOSE
Pr 19:21 but it is the LORD's *p* that prevails
Isa 55:11 and achieve the *p* for which I sent it
Ro 8:28 have been called according to his *p.*
Php 2: 2 love, being one in spirit and *p.*

PURSES
Lk 12:33 Provide *p* for yourselves that will

PURSUE
Ps 34:14 seek peace and *p* it.
2Ti 2:22 and *p* righteousness, faith,
1Pe 3:11 he must seek peace and *p* it.

QUALITIES (QUALITY)
2Pe 1: 8 For if you possess these *q*

QUALITY (QUALITIES)
1Co 3:13 and the fire will test the *q*

QUARREL (QUARRELSOME)
Pr 15:18 but a patient man calms a *q.*
17:14 Starting a *q* is like breaching a dam;
17:19 He who loves a *q* loves sin;
2Ti 2:24 And the Lord's servant must not *q;*

QUARRELSOME (QUARREL)
Pr 19:13 a *q* wife is like a constant dripping.
1Ti 3: 3 not violent but gentle, not *q,*

QUICK-TEMPERED
Tit 1: 7 not *q,* not given to drunkenness,

QUIET (QUIETNESS)
Ps 23: 2 he leads me beside *q* waters,
Zep 3:17 he will *q* you with his love,
Lk 19:40 he replied, "if they keep *q,*
1Ti 2: 2 we may live peaceful and *q* lives
1Pe 3: 4 beauty of a gentle and *q* spirit,

QUIETNESS (QUIET)
Isa 30:15 in *q* and trust is your strength,
32:17 the effect of righteousness will be *q*
1Ti 2:11 A woman should learn in *q*

QUIVER
Ps 127: 5 whose *q* is full of them.

RACE
Ecc 9:11 The *r* is not to the swift
1Co 9:24 that in a *r* all the runners run,
2Ti 4: 7 I have finished the *r,* I have kept
Heb 12: 1 perseverance the *r* marked out

RACHEL
Daughter of Laban (Ge 29:16); wife of Jacob (Ge 29:28); bore two sons (Ge 30:22-24; 35:16-24; 46:19).

RADIANCE (RADIANT)
Heb 1: 3 The Son is the *r* of God's glory

RADIANT (RADIANCE)
Ex 34:29 he was not aware that his face was *r*
Ps 34: 5 Those who look to him are *r;*
SS 5:10 *Beloved* My lover is *r* and ruddy,
Isa 60: 5 Then you will look and be *r,*
Eph 5:27 her to himself as a *r* church,

RAIN (RAINBOW)
Mt 5:45 and sends *r* on the righteous

RAINBOW (RAIN)
Ge 9:13 I have set my *r* in the clouds,

RAISED (RISE)
Ro 4:25 was *r* to life for our justification.
10: 9 in your heart that God *r* him
1Co 15: 4 that he was *r* on the third day

RAN (RUN)
Jnh 1: 3 But Jonah *r* away from the LORD

RANSOM
Mt 20:28 and to give his life as a *r* for many."
Heb 9:15 as a *r* to set them free

RAVENS
1Ki 17: 6 The *r* brought him bread
Lk 12:24 Consider the *r:* They do not sow

READ (READS)
Jos 8:34 Joshua *r* all the words of the law—
Ne 8: 8 They *r* from the Book of the Law
2Co 3: 2 known and *r* by everybody.

READS (READ)
Rev 1: 3 Blessed is the one who *r* the words

REAL (REALITY)
Jn 6:55 is *r* food and my blood is *r* drink.

REALITY* (REAL)
Col 2:17 the *r,* however, is found in Christ.

REAP (REAPS)
Job 4: 8 and those who sow trouble *r* it.
2Co 9: 6 generously will also *r* generously.

REAPS (REAP)
Gal 6: 7 A man *r* what he sows.

REASON
Isa 1:18 "Come now, let us *r* together,"
1Pe 3:15 to give the *r* for the hope that you

REBEKAH
Sister of Laban, secured as bride for Isaac (Ge 24). Mother of Esau and Jacob (Ge 25:19-26). Taken by Abimelech as sister of Isaac; returned (Ge 26:1-11). Encouraged Jacob to trick Isaac out of blessing (Ge 27:1-17).

REBEL
Mt 10:21 children will *r* against their parents

REBUKE (REBUKED REBUKING)
Pr 9: 8 *r* a wise man and he will love you.
27: 5 Better is open *r*
Lk 17: 3 "If your brother sins, *r* him,
2Ti 4: 2 correct, *r* and encourage—
Rev 3:19 Those whom I love I *r*

REBUKED (REBUKE)
1Ti 5:20 Those who sin are to be *r* publicly,

REBUKING (REBUKE)
2Ti 3:16 *r,* correcting and training

RECEIVE (RECEIVED RECEIVES)
Ac 1: 8 you will *r* power when the Holy
20:35 'It is more blessed to give than to *r*
2Co 6:17 and I will *r* you."
Rev 4:11 to *r* glory and honor and power,

RECEIVED (RECEIVE)
Mt 6: 2 they have *r* their reward in full.
10: 8 Freely you have *r,* freely give.
1Co 11:23 For I *r* from the Lord what I
Col 2: 6 just as you *r* Christ Jesus as Lord,
1Pe 4:10 should use whatever gift he has *r*

RECEIVES (RECEIVE)
Mt 7: 8 everyone who asks *r;* he who seeks
10:40 he who *r* me *r* the one who sent me.
Ac 10:43 believes in him *r* forgiveness of sins

RECKONING
Isa 10: 3 What will you do on the day of *r,*

RECOGNIZE (RECOGNIZED)
Mt 7:16 By their fruit you will *r* them.

RECOGNIZED (RECOGNIZE)
Mt 12:33 for a tree is *r* by its fruit.
Ro 7:13 in order that sin might be *r* as sin,

RECOMPENSE
Isa 40:10 and his *r* accompanies him.

RECONCILE (RECONCILED RECONCILIATION)
Eph 2:16 in this one body to *r* both of them

RECONCILED (RECONCILE)
Mt 5:24 First go and be *r* to your brother;
Ro 5:10 we were *r* to him through the death
2Co 5:18 who *r* us to himself through Christ

RECONCILIATION* (RECONCILE)
Ro 5:11 whom we have now received *r.*
11:15 For if their rejection is the *r*
2Co 5:18 and gave us the ministry of *r:*
5:19 committed to us the message of *r.*

RECORD
Ps 130: 3 If you, O LORD, kept a *r* of sins,

RED
Isa 1:18 though they are *r* as crimson,

REDEEM (KINSMAN-REDEEMER REDEEMED REDEEMER REDEMPTION)
2Sa 7:23 on earth that God went out to *r*
Ps 49: 7 No man can *r* the life of another
Gal 4: 5 under law, to *r* those under law,

REDEEMED (REDEEM)
Gal 3:13 Christ *r* us from the curse
1Pe 1:18 or gold that you were *r*

REDEEMER (REDEEM)
Job 19:25 I know that my *R* lives,

REDEMPTION (REDEEM)
Ps 130: 7 and with him is full *r.*
Lk 21:28 because your *r* is drawing near."
Ro 8:23 as sons, the *r* of our bodies.
Eph 1: 7 In him we have *r* through his blood
Col 1:14 in whom we have *r,* the forgiveness
Heb 9:12 having obtained eternal *r.*

REFLECT
2Co 3:18 unveiled faces all *r* the Lord's

REFUGE
Nu 35:11 towns to be your cities of *r,*
Dt 33:27 The eternal God is your *r,*
Ru 2:12 wings you have come to take *r.*"
Ps 46: 1 God is our *r* and strength,
91: 2 "He is my *r* and my fortress,

REHOBOAM
Son of Solomon (1Ki 11:43; 1Ch 3:10). Harsh treatment of subjects caused divided kingdom (1Ki 12:1-24; 14:21-31; 2Ch 10-12).

REIGN
Ex 15:18 The LORD will *r*
Ro 6:12 Therefore do not let sin *r*
1Co 15:25 For he must *r* until he has put all
2Ti 2:12 we will also *r* with him.
Rev 20: 6 will *r* with him for a thousand years

REJECTED (REJECTS)
Ps 118:22 The stone the builders *r*
Isa 53: 3 He was despised and *r* by men,
1Ti 4: 4 nothing is to be *r* if it is received
1Pe 2: 4 *r* by men but chosen by God
2: 7 "The stone the builders *r*

REJECTS (REJECTED)
Lk 10:16 but he who *r* me *r* him who sent me
Jn 3:36 whoever *r* the Son will not see life,

REJOICE (JOY)
Ps 2:11 and *r* with trembling.
66: 6 come, let us *r* in him.
118:24 let us *r* and be glad in it.
Pr 5:18 may you *r* in the wife of your youth
Lk 10:20 but *r* that your names are written
15: 6 '*R* with me; I have found my lost
Ro 12:15 Rejoice with those who *r;* mourn
Php 4: 4 *R* in the Lord always.

REJOICES (JOY)
Isa 61:10 my soul *r* in my God.
Lk 1:47 and my spirit *r* in God my Savior,
1Co 12:26 if one part is honored, every part *r*
13: 6 delight in evil but *r* with the truth.

REJOICING (JOY)
Ps 30: 5 but *r* comes in the morning.
Lk 15: 7 in the same way there will be more *r*
Ac 5:41 *r* because they had been counted

RELIABLE
2Ti 2: 2 witnesses entrust to *r* men who will

RELIGION
1Ti 5: 4 all to put their *r* into practice
Jas 1:27 *R* that God our Father accepts

REMAIN (REMAINS)
Nu 33:55 allow to *r* will become barbs
Jn 15: 7 If you *r* in me and my words
Ro 13: 8 Let no debt *r* outstanding,
1Co 13:13 And now these three *r:* faith,
2Ti 2:13 he will *r* faithful,

REMAINS (REMAIN)
Ps 146: 6 the LORD, who *r* faithful forever.
Heb 7: 3 Son of God he *r* a priest forever.

REMEMBER (REMEMBERS REMEMBRANCE)
Ex 20: 8 "*R* the Sabbath day
1Ch 16:12 *R* the wonders he has done,
Ecc 12: 1 *R* your Creator
Jer 31:34 and will *r* their sins no more."
Gal 2:10 we should continue to *r* the poor,
Php 1: 3 I thank my God every time I *r* you.
Heb 8:12 and will *r* their sins no more."

REMEMBERS (REMEMBER)
Ps 103:14 he *r* that we are dust.
111: 5 he *r* his covenant forever.
Isa 43:25 and *r* your sins no more.

REMEMBRANCE (REMEMBER)
1Co 11:24 which is for you; do this in *r* of me

REMIND
Jn 14:26 will *r* you of everything I have said

REMOVED
Ps 30:11 you *r* my sackcloth and clothed me
103:12 so far has he *r* our transgressions
Jn 20: 1 and saw that the stone had been *r*

RENEW (RENEWED RENEWING)
Ps 51:10 and *r* a steadfast spirit within me.

Isa 40:31 will *r* their strength.

RENEWED (RENEW)
Ps 103: 5 that your youth is *r* like the eagle's.
2Co 4:16 yet inwardly we are being *r* day

RENEWING (RENEW)
Ro 12: 2 transformed by the *r* of your mind.

RENOUNCE (RENOUNCES)
Da 4:27 *R* your sins by doing what is right,

RENOUNCES (RENOUNCE)
Pr 28:13 confesses and *r* them finds

RENOWN
Isa 63:12 to gain for himself everlasting *r*,
Jer 32:20 have gained the *r* that is still yours.

REPAID (PAY)
Lk 14:14 you will be *r* at the resurrection
Col 3:25 Anyone who does wrong will be *r*

REPAY (PAY)
Dt 32:35 It is mine to avenge; I will *r*.
Ru 2:12 May the LORD *r* you
Ps 116:12 How can I *r* the LORD
Ro 12:19 "It is mine to avenge; I will *r*,"
1Pe 3: 9 Do not *r* evil with evil

REPENT (REPENTANCE REPENTS)
Job 42: 6 and *r* in dust and ashes."
Jer 15:19 "If you *r*, I will restore you
Mt 4:17 "*R*, for the kingdom of heaven is
Lk 13: 3 unless you *r*, you too will all perish.
Ac 2:38 Peter replied, "*R* and be baptized,
17:30 all people everywhere to *r*.

REPENTANCE (REPENT)
Lk 3: 8 Produce fruit in keeping with *r*.
5:32 call the righteous, but sinners to *r*."
Ac 26:20 and prove their *r* by their deeds.
2Co 7:10 Godly sorrow brings *r* that leads

REPENTS (REPENT)
Lk 15:10 of God over one sinner who *r*."
17: 3 rebuke him, and if he *r*, forgive him

REPROACH
1Ti 3: 2 Now the overseer must be above *r*,

REPUTATION
1Ti 3: 7 also have a good *r* with outsiders,

REQUESTS
Ps 20: 5 May the LORD grant all your *r*.
Php 4: 6 with thanksgiving, present your *r*

REQUIRE
Mic 6: 8 And what does the LORD *r* of you

RESCUE (RESCUES)
Da 6:20 been able to *r* you from the lions?"
2Pe 2: 9 how to *r* godly men from trials

RESCUES (RESCUE)
1Th 1:10 who *r* us from the coming wrath.

RESIST
Jas 4: 7 *R* the devil, and he will flee
1Pe 5: 9 *R* him, standing firm in the faith,

RESOLVED
Ps 17: 3 I have *r* that my mouth will not sin.
Da 1: 8 But Daniel *r* not to defile himself
1Co 2: 2 For I *r* to know nothing while I was

RESPECT (RESPECTABLE)
Lev 19: 3 " 'Each of you must *r* his mother
19:32 show *r* for the elderly and revere
Pr 11:16 A kindhearted woman gains *r*,
Mal 1: 6 where is the *r* due me?" says
1Th 4:12 so that your daily life may win the *r*
5:12 to *r* those who work hard
1Ti 3: 4 children obey him with proper *r*.
1Pe 2:17 Show proper *r* to everyone:
3: 7 them with *r* as the weaker partner

RESPECTABLE* (RESPECT)
1Ti 3: 2 self-controlled, *r*, hospitable,

REST
Ex 31:15 the seventh day is a Sabbath of *r*,
Ps 91: 1 will *r* in the shadow
Jer 6:16 and you will find *r* for your souls.
Mt 11:28 and burdened, and I will give you *r*.

RESTITUTION
Ex 22: 3 "A thief must certainly make *r*,
Lev 6: 5 He must make *r* in full, add a fifth

RESTORE (RESTORES)
Ps 51:12 *R* to me the joy of your salvation
Gal 6: 1 are spiritual should *r* him gently.

RESTORES (RESTORE)
Ps 23: 3 he *r* my soul.

RESURRECTION
Mt 22:30 At the *r* people will neither marry
Lk 14:14 repaid at the *r* of the righteous."
Jn 11:25 Jesus said to her, "I am the *r*
Ro 1: 4 Son of God by his *r* from the dead:
1Co 15:12 some of you say that there is no *r*
Php 3:10 power of his *r* and the fellowship
Rev 20: 5 This is the first *r*.

RETRIBUTION
Jer 51:56 For the LORD is a God of *r*;

RETURN
2Ch 30: 9 If you *r* to the LORD, then your
Ne 1: 9 but if you *r* to me and obey my
Isa 55:11 It will not *r* to me empty,
Hos 6: 1 "Come, let us *r* to the LORD.
Joel 2:12 "*r* to me with all your heart,

REVEALED (REVELATION)
Dt 29:29 but the things *r* belong to us
Isa 40: 5 the glory of the LORD will be *r*,
Mt 11:25 and *r* them to little children.
Ro 1:17 a righteousness from God is *r*,
8:18 with the glory that will be *r* in us.

REVELATION (REVEALED)
Gal 1:12 I received it by *r* from Jesus Christ.
Rev 1: 1 *r* of Jesus Christ, which God gave

REVENGE (VENGEANCE)
Lev 19:18 " 'Do not seek *r* or bear a grudge
Ro 12:19 Do not take *r*, my friends,

REVERE (REVERENCE)
Ps 33: 8 let all the people of the world *r* him

REVERENCE (REVERE)
Lev 19:30 and have *r* for my sanctuary.
Ps 5: 7 in *r* will I bow down
Col 3:22 of heart and *r* for the Lord.
1Pe 3: 2 when they see the purity and *r*

REVIVE (REVIVING)
Ps 85: 6 Will you not *r* us again,
Isa 57:15 to *r* the spirit of the lowly

REVIVING (REVIVE)
Ps 19: 7 *r* the soul.

REWARD (REWARDED)
Ps 19:11 in keeping them there is great *r*.
127: 3 children a *r* from him.
Pr 19:17 he will *r* him for what he has done.
25:22 and the LORD will *r* you.
31:31 Give her the *r* she has earned,
Jer 17:10 to *r* a man according to his conduct
Mt 5:12 because great is your *r* in heaven,
6: 5 they have received their *r* in full.
16:27 and then he will *r* each person
1Co 3:14 built survives, he will receive his *r*.
Rev 22:12 I am coming soon! My *r* is with me

REWARDED (REWARD)
Ru 2:12 May you be richly *r* by the LORD,
Ps 18:24 The LORD has *r* me according
Pr 14:14 and the good man *r* for his.
1Co 3: 8 and each will be *r* according

RICH (RICHES)
Pr 23: 4 Do not wear yourself out to get *r*;
Jer 9:23 or the *r* man boast of his riches,
Mt 19:23 it is hard for a *r* man
2Co 6:10 yet making many *r*; having nothing
8: 9 he was *r*, yet for your sakes he
1Ti 6:17 Command those who are *r*

RICHES (RICH)
Ps 119:14 as one rejoices in great *r*.
Pr 30: 8 give me neither poverty nor *r*,
Isa 10: 3 Where will you leave your *r*?
Ro 9:23 to make the *r* of his glory known
11:33 the depth of the *r* of the wisdom
Eph 2: 7 he might show the incomparable *r*
3: 8 to the Gentiles the unsearchable *r*
Col 1:27 among the Gentiles the glorious *r*

RID
Ge 21:10 "Get *r* of that slave woman
1Co 5: 7 Get *r* of the old yeast that you may
Gal 4:30 "Get *r* of the slave woman

RIGHT (RIGHTS)
Ge 18:25 the Judge of all the earth do *r*?"
Ex 15:26 and do what is *r* in his eyes,
Dt 5:32 do not turn aside to the *r*
Ps 16: 8 Because he is at my *r* hand,
19: 8 The precepts of the LORD are *r*,
63: 8 your *r* hand upholds me.
110: 1 "Sit at my *r* hand
Pr 4:27 Do not swerve to the *r* or the left;
14:12 There is a way that seems *r*
Isa 1:17 learn to do *r*!
Jer 23: 5 and do what is just and *r* in the land
Hos 14: 9 The ways of the LORD are *r*;
Mt 6: 3 know what your *r* hand is doing,
Jn 1:12 he gave the *r* to become children
Ro 9:21 Does not the potter have the *r*
12:17 careful to do what is *r* in the eyes
Eph 1:20 and seated him at his *r* hand
Php 4: 8 whatever is *r*, whatever is pure,
2Th 3:13 never tire of doing what is *r*.

RIGHTEOUS (RIGHTEOUSNESS)
Ps 34:15 The eyes of the LORD are on the *r*
37:25 yet I have never seen the *r* forsaken
119:137 *R* are you, O LORD,
143: 2 for no one living is *r* before you.
Pr 3:33 but he blesses the home of the *r*.
11:30 The fruit of the *r* is a tree of life,

Pr 18:10 the *r* run to it and are safe.
Isa 64: 6 and all our *r* acts are like filthy rags
Hab 2: 4 but the *r* will live by his faith—
Mt 5:45 rain on the *r* and the unrighteous.
9:13 For I have not come to call the *r*,
13:49 and separate the wicked from the *r*
25:46 to eternal punishment, but the *r*
Ro 1:17 as it is written: "The *r* will live
3:10 "There is no one *r*, not even one;
1Ti 1: 9 that law is made not for the *r*
1Pe 3:18 the *r* for the unrighteous,
1Jn 3: 7 does what is right is *r*, just as he is *r*.
Rev 19: 8 stands for the *r* acts of the saints.)

RIGHTEOUSNESS (RIGHTEOUS)
Ge 15: 6 and he credited it to him as *r*.
1Sa 26:23 LORD rewards every man for his *r*
Ps 9: 8 He will judge the world in *r*;
23: 3 He guides me in paths of *r*
45: 7 You love *r* and hate wickedness;
85:10 *r* and peace kiss each other.
89:14 *R* and justice are the foundation
111: 3 and his *r* endures forever.
Pr 14:34 *R* exalts a nation,
21:21 He who pursues *r* and love
Isa 5:16 will show himself holy by his *r*.
59:17 He put on *r* as his breastplate,
Eze 18:20 The *r* of the righteous man will be
Da 9:24 to bring in everlasting *r*,
12: 3 and those who lead many to *r*,
Mal 4: 2 the sun of *r* will rise with healing
Mt 5: 6 those who hunger and thirst for *r*,
5:20 unless your *r* surpasses that
6:33 But seek first his kingdom and his *r*
Ro 4: 3 and it was credited to him as *r*."
4: 9 faith was credited to him as *r*.
6:13 body to him as instruments of *r*.
2Co 5:21 that in him we might become the *r*
Gal 2:21 for if *r* could be gained
3: 6 and it was credited to him as *r*."
Eph 6:14 with the breastplate of *r* in place,
Php 3: 9 not having a *r* of my own that
2Ti 3:16 correcting and training in *r*,
4: 8 is in store for me the crown of *r*,
Heb 11: 7 became heir of the *r* that comes
2Pe 2:21 not to have known the way of *r*,

RIGHTS (RIGHT)
La 3:35 to deny a man his *r*
Gal 4: 5 that we might receive the full *r*

RISE (RAISED)
Isa 26:19 their bodies will *r*.
Mt 27:63 'After three days I will *r* again.'
Jn 5:29 those who have done good will *r*
1Th 4:16 and the dead in Christ will *r* first.

ROAD
Mt 7:13 and broad is the *r* that leads

ROBBERS
Jer 7:11 become a den of *r* to you?
Mk 15:27 They crucified two *r* with him,
Lk 19:46 but you have made it 'a den of *r*.'"
Jn 10: 8 came before me were thieves and *r*,

ROCK
Ps 18: 2 The LORD is my *r*, my fortress
40: 2 he set my feet on a *r*
Mt 7:24 man who built his house on the *r*.
16:18 and on this *r* I will build my church
Ro 9:33 and a *r* that makes them fall,
1Co 10: 4 the spiritual *r* that accompanied

ROD
Ps 23: 4 your *r* and your staff,
Pr 13:24 He who spares the *r* hates his son,
23:13 if you punish him with the *r*,

ROOM (ROOMS)
Mt 6: 6 But when you pray, go into your *r*,
Lk 2: 7 there was no *r* for them in the inn.
Jn 21:25 the whole world would not have *r*

ROOMS (ROOM)
Jn 14: 2 In my Father's house are many *r*;

ROOT
Isa 53: 2 and like a *r* out of dry ground.
1Ti 6:10 of money is a *r* of all kinds of evil.

ROYAL
Jas 2: 8 If you really keep the *r* law found
1Pe 2: 9 a *r* priesthood, a holy nation,

RUBBISH*
Php 3: 8 I consider them *r*, that I may gain

RUDE*
1Co 13: 5 It is not *r*, it is not self-seeking,

RUIN (RUINS)
Pr 18:24 many companions may come to *r*,
1Ti 6: 9 desires that plunge men into *r*

RUINS (RUIN)
Pr 19: 3 A man's own folly *r* his life,
2Ti 2:14 and only *r* those who listen.

RULE (RULER RULERS RULES)
1Sa 12:12 'No, we want a king to *r* over us'—
Ps 2: 9 You will *r* them with an iron
119:133 let no sin *r* over me.
Zec 9:10 His *r* will extend from sea to sea
Col 3:15 the peace of Christ *r* in your hearts,
Rev 2:27 He will *r* them with an iron scepter;

RULER (RULE)
Ps 8: 6 You made him *r* over the works
Eph 2: 2 of the *r* of the kingdom of the air,
1Ti 6:15 God, the blessed and only *R*,

RULERS (RULE)
Ps 2: 2 and the *r* gather together
Col 1:16 or powers or *r* or authorities;

RULES (RULE)
Ps 103:19 and his kingdom *r* over all.
Lk 22:26 one who *r* like the one who serves.
2Ti 2: 5 he competes according to the *r*.

RUMORS
Mt 24: 6 You will hear of wars and *r* of wars,

RUN (RAN)
Isa 40:31 they will *r* and not grow weary,
1Co 9:24 *R* in such a way as to get the prize.
Heb 12: 1 let us *r* with perseverance the race

RUST
Mt 6:19 where moth and *r* destroy,

RUTH*
Moabitess; widow who went to Bethlehem with mother-in-law Naomi (Ru 1). Gleaned in field of Boaz; shown favor (Ru 2). Proposed marriage to Boaz (Ru 3). Married (Ru 4:1-12); bore Obed, ancestor of David (Ru 4:13-22), Jesus (Mt 1:5).

SABBATH
Ex 20: 8 "Remember the *S* day
Dt 5:12 "Observe the *S* day
Col 2:16 a New Moon celebration or a *S* day

SACKCLOTH
Mt 11:21 would have repented long ago in *s*

SACRED
Mt 7: 6 "Do not give dogs what is *s*;
1Co 3:17 for God's temple is *s*, and you are

SACRIFICE (SACRIFICED SACRIFICES)
Ge 22: 2 *S* him there as a burnt offering
Ex 12:27 'It is the Passover *s* to the LORD,
1Sa 15:22 To obey is better than *s*,
Hos 6: 6 For I desire mercy, not *s*,
Mt 9:13 this means: 'I desire mercy, not *s*.'
Heb 9:26 away with sin by the *s* of himself.
13:15 offer to God a *s* of praise—
1Jn 2: 2 He is the atoning *s* for our sins,

SACRIFICED (SACRIFICE)
1Co 5: 7 our Passover lamb, has been *s*.
8: 1 Now about food *s* to idols:
Heb 9:28 so Christ was *s* once

SACRIFICES (SACRIFICE)
Ps 51:17 The *s* of God are a broken spirit;
Ro 12: 1 to offer your bodies as living *s*,

SADDUCEES
Mk 12:18 *S*, who say there is no resurrection,

SAFE (SAVE)
Ps 37: 3 in the land and enjoy *s* pasture.
Pr 18:10 the righteous run to it and are *s*.

SAFETY (SAVE)
Ps 4: 8 make me dwell in *s*.
1Th 5: 3 people are saying, "Peace and *s*,"

SAINTS
Ps 116:15 is the death of his *s*.
Ro 8:27 intercedes for the *s* in accordance
Eph 1:18 of his glorious inheritance in the *s*,
6:18 always keep on praying for all the *s*
Rev 5: 8 which are the prayers of the *s*.
19: 8 for the righteous acts of the *s*.)

SAKE
Ps 44:22 Yet for your *s* we face death all day
Php 3: 7 loss for the *s* of Christ.
Heb 11:26 He regarded disgrace for the *s*

SALT
Ge 19:26 and she became a pillar of *s*.
Mt 5:13 "You are the *s* of the earth.

SALVATION (SAVE)
Ex 15: 2 he has become my *s*.
1Ch 16:23 proclaim his *s* day after day.
Ps 27: 1 The LORD is my light and my *s*—
51:12 Restore to me the joy of your *s*
62: 2 He alone is my rock and my *s*;
85: 9 Surely his *s* is near those who fear
96: 2 proclaim his *s* day after day.
Isa 25: 9 let us rejoice and be glad in his *s*."
45:17 the LORD with an everlasting *s*;
51: 6 But my *s* will last forever,
59:17 and the helmet of *s* on his head;
61:10 me with garments of *s*
Jnh 2: 9 *S* comes from the LORD."
Zec 9: 9 righteous and having *s*,
Lk 2:30 For my eyes have seen your *s*,
Jn 4:22 for *s* is from the Jews.
Ac 4:12 *S* is found in no one else,
13:47 that you may bring *s* to the ends
Ro 11:11 *s* has come to the Gentiles

2Co 7:10 brings repentance that leads to *s*
Eph 6:17 Take the helmet of *s* and the sword
Php 2:12 to work out your *s* with fear
1Th 5:8 and the hope of *s* as a helmet.
2Ti 3:15 wise for *s* through faith
Heb 2:3 escape if we ignore such a great *s*?
6:9 case—things that accompany *s*.
1Pe 1:10 Concerning this *s*, the prophets,
2:2 by it you may grow up in your *s*,

SAMARITAN
Lk 10:33 But a *S*, as he traveled, came where

SAMSON
Danite judge. Birth promised (Jdg 13). Married to Philistine (Jdg 14). Vengeance on Philistines (Jdg 15). Betrayed by Delilah (Jdg 16:1-22). Death (Jdg 16:23-31). Feats of strength: killed lion (Jdg 14:6), 30 Philistines (Jdg 14:19), 1,000 Philistines with jawbone (Jdg 15:13-17), carried off gates of Gaza (Jdg 16:3), pushed down temple of Dagon (Jdg 16:25-30).

SAMUEL
Ephraimite judge and prophet (Heb 11:32). Birth prayed for (1Sa 1:10-18). Dedicated to temple by Hannah (1Sa 1:21-28). Raised by Eli (1Sa 2:11, 18-26). Called as prophet (1Sa 3). Led Israel to victory over Philistines (1Sa 7). Asked by Israel for a king (1Sa 8). Anointed Saul as king (1Sa 9-10). Farewell speech (1Sa 12). Rebuked Saul for sacrifice (1Sa 13). Announced rejection of Saul (1Sa 15). Anointed David as king (1Sa 16). Protected David from Saul (1Sa 19:18-24). Death (1Sa 25:1). Returned from dead to condemn Saul (1Sa 28).

SANCTIFIED (SANCTIFY)
Ac 20:32 among all those who are *s*.
Ro 15:16 to God, *s* by the Holy Spirit.
1Co 6:11 But you were washed, you were *s*,
7:14 and the unbelieving wife has been *s*
Heb 10:29 blood of the covenant that *s* him,

SANCTIFY (SANCTIFIED SANCTIFYING)
1Th 5:23 *s* you through and through.

SANCTIFYING (SANCTIFY)
2Th 2:13 through the *s* work of the Spirit

SANCTUARY
Ex 25:8 "Then have them make a *s* for me,

SAND
Ge 22:17 and as the *s* on the seashore.
Mt 7:26 man who built his house on *s*.

SANDALS
Ex 3:5 off your *s*, for the place where you
Jos 5:15 off your *s*, for the place where you

SANG (SING)
Job 38:7 while the morning stars *s* together
Rev 5:9 And they *s* a new song:

SARAH
Wife of Abraham, originally named Sarai; barren (Ge 11:29-31; 1Pe 3:6). Taken by Pharaoh as Abraham's sister; returned (Ge 12:10-20). Gave Hagar to Abraham; sent her away in pregnancy (Ge 16). Name changed; Isaac promised (Ge 17:15-21; 18:10-15; Heb 11:11). Taken by Abimelech as Abraham's sister; returned (Ge 20). Isaac born; Hagar and Ishmael sent away (Ge 21:1-21; Gal 4:21-31). Death (Ge 23).

SATAN
Job 1:6 and *S* also came with them.
Zec 3:2 said to *S*, "The LORD rebuke you,
Mk 4:15 *S* comes and takes away the word
2Co 11:14 for *S* himself masquerades
12:7 a messenger of *S*, to torment me.
Rev 12:9 serpent called the devil, or *S*,
20:2 or *S*, and bound him for a thousand
20:7 *S* will be released from his prison

SATISFIED (SATISFY)
Isa 53:11 he will see the light ⌞of life⌟ and be *s*

SATISFIES (SATISFY)
Ps 103:5 who *s* your desires with good things,

SATISFY (SATISFIED SATISFIES)
Isa 55:2 and your labor on what does not *s*?

SAUL
1. Benjamite; anointed by Samuel as first king of Israel (1Sa 9-10). Defeated Ammonites (1Sa 11). Rebuked for offering sacrifice (1Sa 13:1-15). Defeated Philistines (1Sa 14). Rejected as king for failing to annihilate Amalekites (1Sa 15). Soothed from evil spirit by David (1Sa 16:14-23). Sent David against Goliath (1Sa 17). Jealousy and attempted murder of David (1Sa 18:1-11). Gave David Michal as wife (1Sa 18:12-30). Second attempt to kill David (1Sa 19). Anger at Jonathan (1Sa 20:26-34). Pursued David: killed priests at Nob (1Sa 22), went to Keilah and Ziph (1Sa 23), life spared by David at En Gedi (1Sa 24) and in his tent (1Sa 26). Rebuked by Samuel's spirit for consulting witch at Endor (1Sa 28). Wounded by Philistines; took his own life (1Sa 31; 1Ch 10).
2. See PAUL

SAVE (SAFE SAFETY SALVATION SAVED SAVIOR)
Isa 63:1 mighty to *s*."
Da 3:17 the God we serve is able to *s* us
Zep 3:17 he is mighty to *s*.
Mt 1:21 he will *s* his people from their sins
16:25 wants to *s* his life will lose it,
Lk 19:10 to seek and to *s* what was lost."
Jn 3:17 but to *s* the world through him.
1Ti 1:15 came into the world to *s* sinners—
Jas 5:20 of his way will *s* him from death

SAVED (SAVE)
Ps 34:6 he *s* him out of all his troubles.
Isa 45:22 "Turn to me and be *s*,
Joel 2:32 on the name of the LORD will be *s*;
Mk 13:13 firm to the end will be *s*.
16:16 believes and is baptized will be *s*,
Jn 10:9 enters through me will be *s*.
Ac 4:12 to men by which we must be *s*."
16:30 do to be *s*?" They replied,
Ro 9:27 only the remnant will be *s*.
10:9 him from the dead, you will be *s*.
1Co 3:15 will suffer loss; he himself will be *s*,
15:2 By this gospel you are *s*,
Eph 2:5 it is by grace you have been *s*.
2:8 For it is by grace you have been *s*,
1Ti 2:4 who wants all men to be *s*

SAVIOR (SAVE)
Ps 89:26 my God, the Rock my *S*.'
Isa 43:11 and apart from me there is no *s*.
Hos 13:4 no *S* except me.
Lk 1:47 and my spirit rejoices in God my *S*,
2:11 of David a *S* has been born to you;
Jn 4:42 know that this man really is the *S*
Eph 5:23 his body, of which he is the *S*.
1Ti 4:10 who is the *S* of all men,
Tit 2:10 about God our *S* attractive.
2:13 appearing of our great God and *S*,
3:4 and love of God our *S* appeared,
1Jn 4:14 Son to be the *S* of the world.
Jude :25 to the only God our *S* be glory,

SCALES
Lev 19:36 Use honest *s* and honest weights,
Da 5:27 You have been weighed on the *s*

SCAPEGOAT (GOAT)
Lev 16:10 by sending it into the desert as a *s*.

SCARLET
Isa 1:18 "Though your sins are like *s*,

SCATTERED
Jer 31:10 'He who *s* Israel will gather them
Ac 8:4 who had been *s* preached the word

SCEPTER
Rev 19:15 "He will rule them with an iron *s*."

SCHEMES
2Co 2:11 For we are not unaware of his *s*.
Eph 6:11 stand against the devil's *s*.

SCOFFERS
2Pe 3:3 that in the last days *s* will come,

SCORPION
Rev 9:5 sting of a *s* when it strikes a man.

SCRIPTURE (SCRIPTURES)
Jn 10:35 and the *S* cannot be broken—
1Ti 4:13 yourself to the public reading of *S*,
2Ti 3:16 All *S* is God-breathed
2Pe 1:20 that no prophecy of *S* came about

SCRIPTURES (SCRIPTURE)
Lk 24:27 said in all the *S* concerning himself.
Jn 5:39 These are the *S* that testify about
Ac 17:11 examined the *S* every day to see

SCROLL
Eze 3:1 eat what is before you, eat this *s*;

SEA
Ex 14:16 go through the *s* on dry ground.
Isa 57:20 the wicked are like the tossing *s*,
Mic 7:19 iniquities into the depths of the *s*.
Jas 1:6 who doubts is like a wave of the *s*,
Rev 13:1 I saw a beast coming out of the *s*.

SEAL (SEALS)
Jn 6:27 God the Father has placed his *s*
2Co 1:22 set his *s* of ownership on us,
Eph 1:13 you were marked in him with a *s*,

SEALS (SEAL)
Rev 5:2 "Who is worthy to break the *s*
6:1 opened the first of the seven *s*.

SEARCH (SEARCHED SEARCHES SEARCHING)
Ps 4:4 *s* your hearts and be silent.
139:23 *S* me, O God, and know my heart;
Pr 2:4 and *s* for it as for hidden treasure,
Jer 17:10 "I the LORD *s* the heart
Eze 34:16 I will *s* for the lost and bring back
Lk 15:8 and *s* carefully until she finds it?

SEARCHED (SEARCH)
Ps 139:1 O LORD, you have *s* me

SEARCHES (SEARCH)
Ro 8:27 And he who *s* our hearts knows
1Co 2:10 The Spirit *s* all things,

SEARCHING (SEARCH)
Am 8:12 *s* for the word of the LORD,

SEARED
1Ti 4: 2 whose consciences have been *s*

SEASON
2Ti 4: 2 be prepared in *s* and out of *s;*

SEAT (SEATED SEATS)
Ps 1: 1 or sit in the *s* of mockers.
Da 7: 9 and the Ancient of Days took his *s.*
2Co 5:10 before the judgment *s* of Christ,

SEATED (SEAT)
Ps 47: 8 God is *s* on his holy throne.
Isa 6: 1 I saw the Lord *s* on a throne,
Col 3: 1 where Christ is *s* at the right hand

SEATS (SEAT)
Lk 11:43 you love the most important *s*

SECRET (SECRETS)
Dt 29:29 The *s* things belong
Jdg 16: 6 Tell me the *s* of your great strength
Ps 90: 8 our *s* sins in the light
Pr 11:13 but a trustworthy man keeps a *s.*
Mt 6: 4 so that your giving may be in *s.*
2Co 4: 2 we have renounced *s* and shameful
Php 4:12 I have learned the *s*

SECRETS (SECRET)
Ps 44:21 since he knows the *s* of the heart?
1Co 14:25 the *s* of his heart will be laid bare.

SECURE (SECURITY)
Ps 112: 8 His heart is *s,* he will have no fear;
Heb 6:19 an anchor for the soul, firm and *s.*

SECURITY (SECURE)
Job 31:24 or said to pure gold, 'You are my *s,*'

SEED (SEEDS)
Lk 8:11 of the parable: The *s* is the word
1Co 3: 6 I planted the *s,* Apollos watered it,
2Co 9:10 he who supplies *s* to the sower
Gal 3:29 then you are Abraham's *s,*
1Pe 1:23 not of perishable *s,*

SEEDS (SEED)
Jn 12:24 But if it dies, it produces many *s.*
Gal 3:16 Scripture does not say "and to *s,*"

SEEK (SEEKS SELF-SEEKING)
Dt 4:29 if from there you *s* the LORD your
1Ch 28: 9 If you *s* him, he will be found
2Ch 7:14 themselves and pray and *s* my face
Ps 119:10 I *s* you with all my heart;
Isa 55: 6 *S* the LORD while he may be
65: 1 found by those who did not *s* me.
Mt 6:33 But *s* first his kingdom
Lk 19:10 For the Son of Man came to *s*
Ro 10:20 found by those who did not *s* me;
1Co 7:27 you married? Do not *s* a divorce.

SEEKS (SEEK)
Jn 4:23 the kind of worshipers the Father *s.*

SEER
1Sa 9: 9 of today used to be called a *s.*)

SELF-CONTROL (CONTROL)
1Co 7: 5 you because of your lack of *s.*
Gal 5:23 faithfulness, gentleness and *s.*
2Pe 1: 6 and to knowledge, *s;* and to *s,*

SELF-CONTROLLED* (CONTROL)
1Th 5: 6 are asleep, but let us be alert and *s.*
5: 8 let us be *s,* putting on faith and love
1Ti 3: 2 *s,* respectable, hospitable,
Tit 1: 8 who is *s,* upright, holy
2: 2 worthy of respect, *s,* and sound
2: 5 to be *s* and pure, to be busy at home
2: 6 encourage the young men to be *s.*
2:12 to live *s,* upright and godly lives
1Pe 1:13 prepare your minds for action; be *s;*
4: 7 and *s* so that you can pray.
5: 8 Be *s* and alert.

SELF-INDULGENCE
Mt 23:25 inside they are full of greed and *s.*

SELF-SEEKING (SEEK)
1Co 13: 5 it is not *s,* it is not easily angered,

SELFISH*
Ps 119:36 and not toward *s* gain.
Pr 18: 1 An unfriendly man pursues *s* ends;
Gal 5:20 fits of rage, *s* ambition, dissensions,
Php 1:17 preach Christ out of *s* ambition,
2: 3 Do nothing out of *s* ambition
Jas 3:14 and *s* ambition in your hearts,
3:16 you have envy and *s* ambition,

SEND (SENDING SENT)
Isa 6: 8 *S* me!" He said, "Go and tell this
Mt 9:38 to *s* out workers into his harvest
Jn 16: 7 but if I go, I will *s* him to you.

SENDING (SEND)
Jn 20:21 Father has sent me, I am *s* you."

SENSES*
Lk 15:17 "When he came to his *s,* he said,
1Co 15:34 Come back to your *s* as you ought,
2Ti 2:26 and that they will come to their *s*

SENSUAL
Col 2:23 value in restraining *s* indulgence.

SENT (SEND)
Isa 55:11 achieve the purpose for which I *s* it.
Mt 10:40 me receives the one who *s* me.
Jn 4:34 "is to do the will of him who *s* me
Ro 10:15 can they preach unless they are *s?*
1Jn 4:10 but that he loved us and *s* his Son

SEPARATE (SEPARATED SEPARATES)
Mt 19: 6 has joined together, let man not *s.*"
Ro 8:35 Who shall *s* us from the love
1Co 7:10 wife must not *s* from her husband.
2Co 6:17 and be *s,* says the Lord.

SEPARATED (SEPARATE)
Isa 59: 2 But your iniquities have *s*

SEPARATES (SEPARATE)
Pr 16:28 and a gossip *s* close friends.

SERPENT
Ge 3: 1 the *s* was more crafty than any
Rev 12: 9 that ancient *s* called the devil

SERVANT (SERVANTS)
1Sa 3:10 "Speak, for your *s* is listening."
Mt 20:26 great among you must be your *s,*
25:21 'Well done, good and faithful *s!*
Lk 16:13 "No *s* can serve two masters.
Php 2: 7 taking the very nature of a *s,*
2Ti 2:24 And the Lord's *s* must not quarrel;

SERVANTS (SERVANT)
Lk 17:10 should say, 'We are unworthy *s;*
Jn 15:15 longer call you *s,* because a servant

SERVE (SERVICE SERVING)
Dt 10:12 to *s* the LORD your God
Jos 22: 5 and to *s* him with all your heart
24:15 this day whom you will *s,*
Mt 4:10 Lord your God, and *s* him only.' "
6:24 "No one can *s* two masters.
20:28 but to *s,* and to give his life
Eph 6: 7 *S* wholeheartedly,

SERVICE (SERVE)
1Co 12: 5 There are different kinds of *s,*
Eph 4:12 God's people for works of *s,*

SERVING (SERVE)
Ro 12:11 your spiritual fervor, *s* the Lord.
Eph 6: 7 as if you were *s* the Lord, not men,
Col 3:24 It is the Lord Christ you are *s.*
2Ti 2: 4 No one *s* as a soldier gets involved

SEVEN (SEVENTH)
Ge 7: 2 Take with you *s* of every kind
Jos 6: 4 march around the city *s* times,
1Ki 19:18 Yet I reserve *s* thousand in Israel—
Pr 6:16 *s* that are detestable to him:
24:16 a righteous man falls *s* times,
Isa 4: 1 In that day *s* women
Da 9:25 comes, there will be *s* 'sevens,'
Mt 18:21 Up to *s* times?" Jesus answered,
Lk 11:26 takes *s* other spirits more wicked
Ro 11: 4 for myself *s* thousand who have not
Rev 1: 4 To the *s* churches in the province
6: 1 opened the first of the *s* seals.
8: 2 and to them were given *s* trumpets.
10: 4 And when the *s* thunders spoke,
15: 7 to the *s* angels *s* golden bowls filled

SEVENTH (SEVEN)
Ge 2: 2 By the *s* day God had finished
Ex 23:12 but on the *s* day do not work,

SEXUAL (SEXUALLY)
1Co 6:13 body is not meant for *s* immorality,
6:18 Flee from *s* immorality.
10: 8 should not commit *s* immorality,
Eph 5: 3 even a hint of *s* immorality,
1Th 4: 3 that you should avoid *s* immorality

SEXUALLY (SEXUAL)
1Co 5: 9 to associate with *s* immoral people
6:18 he who sins *s* sins against his own

SHADOW
Ps 23: 4 through the valley of the *s* of death,
36: 7 find refuge in the *s* of your wings.
Heb 10: 1 The law is only a *s*

SHALLUM
King of Israel (2Ki 15:10-16).

SHAME (ASHAMED)
Ps 34: 5 their faces are never covered with *s*
Pr 13:18 discipline comes to povertv
Heb 12: 2 endured the cross, scorn

SHARE (SHARED)
Ge 21:10 that slave woma
never *s*

Lk 3:11 "The man with two tunics should *s*
Gal 4:30 the slave woman's son will never *s*
6: 6 in the word must *s* all good things
Eph 4:28 something to *s* with those in need.
1Ti 6:18 and to be generous and willing to *s*.
Heb 12:10 that we may *s* in his holiness.
13:16 to do good and to *s* with others,

SHARED (SHARE)
Heb 2:14 he too *s* in their humanity so that

SHARON
SS 2: 1 I am a rose of *S*,

SHARPER*
Heb 4:12 *S* than any double-edged sword,

SHED (SHEDDING)
Ge 9: 6 by man shall his blood be *s*;
Col 1:20 through his blood, *s* on the cross.

SHEDDING (SHED)
Heb 9:22 without the *s* of blood there is no

SHEEP
Ps 100: 3 we are his people, the *s*
119:176 I have strayed like a lost *s*.
Isa 53: 6 We all, like *s*, have gone astray,
Jer 50: 6 "My people have been lost *s*;
Eze 34:11 I myself will search for my *s*
Mt 9:36 helpless, like *s* without a shepherd.
Jn 10: 3 He calls his own *s* by name
10:15 and I lay down my life for the *s*.
10:27 My *s* listen to my voice; I know
21:17 Jesus said, "Feed my *s*.
1Pe 2:25 For you were like *s* going astray,

SHELTER
Ps 61: 4 take refuge in the *s* of your wings.
91: 1 in the *s* of the Most High

SHEM
Son of Noah (Ge 5:32; 6:10). Blessed (Ge 9:26). Descendants (Ge 10:21-31; 11:10-32).

SHEPHERD (SHEPHERDS)
Ps 23: 1 LORD is my *s*, I shall not be in want.
Isa 40:11 He tends his flock like a *s*:
Jer 31:10 will watch over his flock like a *s*.'
Eze 34:12 As a *s* looks after his scattered
Zec 11:17 "Woe to the worthless *s*,
Mt 9:36 and helpless, like sheep without a *s*.
Jn 10:11 The good *s* lays down his life
10:16 there shall be one flock and one *s*.
1Pe 5: 4 And when the Chief *S* appears,

SHEPHERDS (SHEPHERD)
Jer 23: 1 "Woe to the *s* who are destroying
Lk 2: 8 there were *s* living out in the fields
Ac 20:28 Be *s* of the church of God,
1Pe 5: 2 Be *s* of God's flock that is

SHIELD
Ps 28: 7 LORD is my strength and my *s*;
Eph 6:16 to all this, take up the *s* of faith,

[illegible]INE (SHONE)
Is[illegible]6 Let the light of your face *s* upon
Da [illegible]s,
Mt [illegible]een the cherubim, *s* forth
13:[illegible] 6 for your light has come,
2Co 4: [illegible] *s* like the brightness
Eph 5:14 [illegible]before men,
[illegible]like the sun
[illegible]hearts
[illegible]"

SHIPWRECKED*
2Co 11:25 I was stoned, three times I was *s*,
1Ti 1:19 and so have *s* their faith.

SHONE (SHINE)
Mt 17: 2 His face *s* like the sun,
Lk 2: 9 glory of the Lord *s* around them,
Rev 21:11 It *s* with the glory of God,

SHORT
Isa 59: 1 of the LORD is not too *s* to save,
Ro 3:23 and fall *s* of the glory of God,

SHOULDERS
Isa 9: 6 and the government will be on his *s*
Lk 15: 5 he joyfully puts it on his *s*

SHOWED
1Jn 4: 9 This is how God *s* his love

SHREWD
Mt 10:16 Therefore be as *s* as snakes and

SHUN*
Job 28:28 and to *s* evil is understanding.' "
Pr 3: 7 fear the LORD and *s* evil.

SICK
Pr 13:12 Hope deferred makes the heart *s*,
Mt 9:12 who need a doctor, but the *s*.
25:36 I was *s* and you looked after me,
Jas 5:14 of you *s*? He should call the elders

SICKLE
Joel 3:13 Swing the *s*,

SIDE
Ps 91: 7 A thousand may fall at your *s*,
124: 1 If the LORD had not been on our *s*
2Ti 4:17 But the Lord stood at my *s*

SIGHT
Ps 90: 4 For a thousand years in your *s*
116:15 Precious in the *s* of the LORD
2Co 5: 7 We live by faith, not by *s*.
1Pe 3: 4 which is of great worth in God's *s*.

SIGN (SIGNS)
Isa 7:14 the Lord himself will give you a *s*:

SIGNS (SIGN)
Mk 16:17 these *s* will accompany those who
Jn 20:30 Jesus did many other miraculous *s*

SILENT
Pr 17:28 a fool is thought wise if he keeps *s*,
Isa 53: 7 as a sheep before her shearers is *s*,
Hab 2:20 let all the earth be *s* before him."
1Co 14:34 women should remain *s*
1Ti 2:12 over a man; she must be *s*.

SILVER
Pr 25:11 is like apples of gold in settings of *s*.
Hag 2: 8 'The *s* is mine and the gold is mine,'
1Co 3:12 *s*, costly stones, wood, hay or straw

SIMON
1. See PETER.
2. Apostle, called the Zealot (Mt 10:4; Mk 3:18; Lk 6:15; Ac 1:13).
3. Samaritan sorcerer (Ac 8:9-24).

SIN (SINFUL SINNED SINNER SINNERS SINNING SINS)
Nu 5: 7 and must confess the *s* he has
32:23 be sure that your *s* will find you
Dt 24:16 each is to die for his own *s*.
1Ki 8:46 for there is no one who does not *s*
2Ch 7:14 and will forgive their *s* and will heal
Ps 4: 4 In your anger do not *s*;
32: 2 whose *s* the LORD does not count
32: 5 Then I acknowledged my *s* to you
51: 2 and cleanse me from my *s*.
66:18 If I had cherished *s* in my heart,
119:11 that I might not *s* against you.
119:133 let no *s* rule over me.
Isa 6: 7 is taken away and your *s* atoned
Mic 7:18 who pardons *s* and forgives
Mt 18: 6 little ones who believe in me to *s*,
Jn 1:29 who takes away the *s* of the world!
8:34 everyone who sins is a slave to *s*.
Ro 5:12 as *s* entered the world
5:20 where *s* increased, grace increased
6:11 count yourselves dead to *s*
6:23 For the wages of *s* is death,
14:23 that does not come from faith is *s*.
2Co 5:21 God made him who had no *s* to be *s*
Gal 6: 1 if someone is caught in a *s*,
Heb 9:26 to do away with *s* by the sacrifice
11:25 the pleasures of *s* for a short time.
12: 1 and the *s* that so easily entangles,
1Pe 2:22 "He committed no *s*,
1Jn 1: 8 If we claim to be without *s*,
3: 4 in fact, *s* is lawlessness.
3: 5 And in him is no *s*.
3: 9 born of God will continue to *s*,
5:18 born of God does not continue to *s*;

SINCERE
Ro 12: 9 Love must be *s*.
Heb 10:22 near to God with a *s* heart

SINFUL (SIN)
Ps 51: 5 Surely I was *s* at birth
51: 5 *s* from the time my mother
Ro 7: 5 we were controlled by the *s* nature,
8: 4 not live according to the *s* nature
8: 9 are controlled not by the *s* nature
Gal 5:19 The acts of the *s* nature are obvious
5:24 Jesus have crucified the *s* nature
1Pe 2:11 abstain from *s* desires, which war

SING (SANG SINGING SONG SONGS)
Ps 30: 4 *S* to the LORD, you saints of his;
47: 6 *S* praises to God, *s* praises;
59:16 But I will *s* of your strength,
89: 1 I will *s* of the LORD's great love
101: 1 I will *s* of your love and justice;
Eph 5:19 *S* and make music in your heart

SINGING (SING)
Ps 63: 5 with *s* lips my mouth will praise
Ac 16:25 Silas were praying and *s* hymns

SINNED (SIN)
2Sa 12:13 "I have *s* against the LORD."
Job 1: 5 "Perhaps my children have *s*
Ps 51: 4 Against you, you only, have I *s*
Da 9: 5 we have *s* and done wrong.
Mic 7: 9 Because I have *s* against him,
Lk 15:18 I have *s* against heaven
Ro 3:23 for all have *s* and fall short
1Jn 1:10 claim we have not *s*, we make him

SINNER (SIN)
Ecc 9:18 but one *s* destroys much good.
Lk 15: 7 in heaven over one *s* who repents
18:13 'God, have mercy on me, a *s*.'
1Co 14:24 convinced by all that he is a *s*
Jas 5:20 Whoever turns a *s* from the error
1Pe 4:18 become of the ungodly and the *s*?"

SINNERS (SIN)
Ps 1: 1 or stand in the way of *s*
Pr 23:17 Do not let your heart envy *s*,
Mt 9:13 come to call the righteous, but *s*."
Ro 5: 8 While we were still *s*, Christ died
1Ti 1:15 came into the world to save *s*—

SINNING (SIN)
Ex 20:20 be with you to keep you from *s*."
1Co 15:34 stop *s*; for there are some who are
Heb 10:26 If we deliberately keep on *s*
1Jn 3: 6 No one who lives in him keeps on *s*
3: 9 go on *s*, because he has been born

SINS (SIN)
2Ki 14: 6 each is to die for his own *s*."
Ezr 9: 6 our *s* are higher than our heads
Ps 19:13 your servant also from willful *s*;
32: 1 whose *s* are covered.
103: 3 who forgives all your *s*
130: 3 O LORD, kept a record of *s*,
Pr 28:13 who conceals his *s* does not
Isa 1:18 "Though your *s* are like scarlet,
43:25 and remembers your *s* no more.
59: 2 your *s* have hidden his face
Eze 18: 4 soul who *s* is the one who will die.
Mt 1:21 he will save his people from their *s*
18:15 "If your brother *s* against you,
Lk 11: 4 Forgive us our *s*,
17: 3 "If your brother *s*, rebuke him,
Ac 22:16 be baptized and wash your *s* away,
1Co 15: 3 died for our *s* according
Eph 2: 1 dead in your transgressions and *s*,
Col 2:13 us all our *s*, having canceled
Heb 1: 3 he had provided purification for *s*,
7:27 He sacrificed for their *s* once for all
8:12 and will remember their *s* no more
10:12 for all time one sacrifice for *s*,
Jas 4:17 ought to do and doesn't do it, *s*.
5:16 Therefore confess your *s*
5:20 and cover over a multitude of *s*.
1Pe 2:24 He himself bore our *s* in his body
3:18 For Christ died for *s* once for all,
1Jn 1: 9 If we confess our *s*, he is faithful
Rev 1: 5 has freed us from our *s* by his blood

SITS
Ps 99: 1 *s* enthroned between the cherubim,
Isa 40:22 He *s* enthroned above the circle
Mt 19:28 of Man *s* on his glorious throne,
Rev 4: 9 thanks to him who *s* on the throne

SKIN
Job 19:20 with only the *s* of my teeth.
19:26 And after my *s* has been destroyed,
Jer 13:23 Can the Ethiopian change his *s*

SLAIN (SLAY)
Rev 5:12 "Worthy is the Lamb, who was *s*,

SLANDER (SLANDERED SLANDERERS)
Lev 19:16 " 'Do not go about spreading *s*
1Ti 5:14 the enemy no opportunity for *s*.
Tit 3: 2 to *s* no one, to be peaceable

SLANDERED (SLANDER)
1Co 4:13 when we are *s*, we answer kindly.

SLANDERERS (SLANDER)
Ro 1:30 They are gossips, *s*, God-haters,
1Co 6:10 nor the greedy nor drunkards nor *s*
Tit 2: 3 not to be *s* or addicted

SLAUGHTER
Isa 53: 7 he was led like a lamb to the *s*,

SLAVE (SLAVERY SLAVES)
Ge 21:10 "Get rid of that *s* woman
Mt 20:27 wants to be first must be your *s*—
Jn 8:34 everyone who sins is a *s* to sin.
1Co 12:13 whether Jews or Greeks, *s* or free
Gal 3:28 *s* nor free, male nor female,
4:30 Get rid of the *s* woman and her son
2Pe 2:19 a man is a *s* to whatever has

SLAVERY (SLAVE)
Ro 6:19 parts of your body in *s* to impurity
Gal 4: 3 were in *s* under the basic principles

SLAVES (SLAVE)
Ro 6: 6 that we should no longer be *s* to sin
6:22 and have become *s* to God,

SLAY (SLAIN)
Job 13:15 Though he *s* me, yet will I hope

SLEEP (SLEEPING)
Ps 121: 4 will neither slumber nor *s*.
1Co 15:51 We will not all *s*, but we will all be

SLEEPING (SLEEP)
Mk 13:36 suddenly, do not let him find you *s*.

SLOW
Ex 34: 6 and gracious God, *s* to anger,
Jas 1:19 *s* to speak and *s* to become angry,
2Pe 3: 9 The Lord is not *s* in keeping his

SLUGGARD
Pr 6: 6 Go to the ant, you *s*;
20: 4 A *s* does not plow in season;

SLUMBER
Ps 121: 3 he who watches over you will not *s*;
Pr 6:10 A little sleep, a little *s*,
Ro 13:11 for you to wake up from your *s*,

SNAKE (SNAKES)
Nu 21: 8 "Make a *s* and put it up on a pole;
Pr 23:32 In the end it bites like a *s*
Jn 3:14 Moses lifted up the *s* in the desert,

SNAKES (SNAKE)
Mt 10:16 as shrewd as *s* and as innocent
Mk 16:18 they will pick up *s* with their hands;

SNATCH
Jn 10:28 no one can *s* them out of my hand.
Jude :23 *s* others from the fire and save

SNOW
Ps 51: 7 and I will be whiter than *s*.

SOAR
Isa 40:31 They will *s* on wings like eagles;

SODOM
Ge 19:24 rained down burning sulfur on *S*
Ro 9:29 we would have become like *S*,

SOIL
Ge 4: 2 kept flocks, and Cain worked the *s*.
Mt 13:23 on good *s* is the man who hears

SOLDIER
1Co 9: 7 as a *s* at his own expense?
2Ti 2: 3 with us like a good *s* of Christ Jesus

SOLE
Dt 28:65 place for the *s* of your foot.
Isa 1: 6 From the *s* of your foot to the top

SOLID
2Ti 2:19 God's *s* foundation stands firm,
Heb 5:12 You need milk, not *s* food!

SOLOMON
Son of David by Bathsheba; king of Judah (2Sa 12:24; 1Ch 3:5, 10). Appointed king by David (1Ki 1); adversaries Adonijah, Joab, Shimei killed by Benaiah (1Ki 2). Asked for wisdom (1Ki 3; 2Ch 1). Judged between two prostitutes (1Ki 3:16-28). Built temple (1Ki 5-7; 2Ch 2-5); prayer of dedication (1Ki 8; 2Ch 6). Visited by Queen of Sheba (1Ki 10; 2Ch 9). Wives turned his heart from God (1Ki 11:1-13). Jeroboam rebelled against (1Ki 11:26-40). Death (1Ki 11:41-43; 2Ch 9:29-31).
Proverbs of (1Ki 4:32; Pr 1:1; 10:1; 25:1); psalms of (Ps 72; 127); song of (SS 1:1).

SON (SONS)
Ge 22: 2 "Take your *s*, your only *s*, Isaac,
Ex 11: 5 Every firstborn *s* in Egypt will die,
Dt 21:18 rebellious *s* who does not obey his
Ps 2: 7 He said to me, "You are my *S*;
2:12 Kiss the *S*, lest he be angry
Pr 10: 1 A wise *s* brings joy to his father,
13:24 He who spares the rod hates his *s*,
29:17 Discipline your *s*, and he will give
Isa 7:14 with child and will give birth to a *s*,
Hos 11: 1 and out of Egypt I called my *s*.
Mt 2:15 "Out of Egypt I called my *s*."
3:17 "This is my *S*, whom I love;
11:27 one knows the *S* except the Father,
16:16 "You are the Christ, the *S*
17: 5 "This is my *S*, whom I love;
20:18 and the *S* of Man will be betrayed
24:30 They will see the *S* of Man coming
24:44 the *S* of Man will come at an hour
27:54 "Surely he was the *S* of God!"
28:19 and of the *S* and of the Holy Spirit,
Mk 10:45 even the *S* of Man did not come
14:62 you will see the *S* of Man sitting
Lk 9:58 but the *S* of Man has no place
18: 8 when the *S* of Man comes,
19:10 For the *S* of Man came to seek
Jn 3:14 so the *S* of Man must be lifted up,
3:16 that he gave his one and only *S*,
17: 1 Glorify your *S*, that your *S* may
Ro 8:29 conformed to the likeness of his *S*,
8:32 He who did not spare his own *S*,
1Co 15:28 then the *S* himself will be made
Gal 4:30 rid of the slave woman and her *s*,
1Th 1:10 and to wait for his *S* from heaven,
Heb 1: 2 days he has spoken to us by his *S*,
10:29 punished who has trampled the *S*
1Jn 1: 7 his *S*, purifies us from all sin.
4: 9 only *S* into the world that we might
5: 5 he who believes that Jesus is the *S*
5:11 eternal life, and this life is in his *S*.

SONG (SING)
Ps 40: 3 He put a new *s* in my mouth,
96: 1 Sing to the LORD a new *s*;
149: 1 Sing to the LORD a new *s*,
Isa 49:13 burst into *s*, O mountains!
55:12 will burst into *s* before you,
Rev 5: 9 And they sang a new *s*:
15: 3 and sang the *s* of Moses the servant

SONGS (SING)
Job 35:10 who gives *s* in the night,
Ps 100: 2 come before him with joyful *s.*
Eph 5:19 with psalms, hymns and spiritual *s.*
Jas 5:13 Is anyone happy? Let him sing *s*

SONS (SON)
Joel 2:28 Your *s* and daughters will prophesy
Jn 12:36 so that you may become *s* of light."
Ro 8:14 by the Spirit of God are *s* of God.
2Co 6:18 and you will be my *s* and daughters
Gal 4: 5 we might receive the full rights of *s.*
Heb 12: 7 discipline; God is treating you as *s.*

SORROW (SORROWS)
Jer 31:12 and they will *s* no more.
Ro 9: 2 I have great *s* and unceasing
2Co 7:10 Godly *s* brings repentance that

SORROWS (SORROW)
Isa 53: 3 a man of *s,* and familiar

SOUL (SOULS)
Dt 6: 5 with all your *s* and with all your
10:12 all your heart and with all your *s,*
Jos 22: 5 with all your heart and all your *s."*
Ps 23: 3 he restores my *s.*
42: 1 so my *s* pants for you, O God.
42:11 Why are you downcast, O my *s?*
103: 1 Praise the LORD, O my *s;*
Pr 13:19 A longing fulfilled is sweet to the *s,*
Isa 55: 2 your *s* will delight in the richest
Mt 10:28 kill the body but cannot kill the *s.*
16:26 yet forfeits his *s?* Or what can
22:37 with all your *s* and with all your
Heb 4:12 even to dividing *s* and spirit,

SOULS (SOUL)
Pr 11:30 and he who wins *s* is wise.
Jer 6:16 and you will find rest for your *s.*
Mt 11:29 and you will find rest for your *s.*

SOUND
1Co 14: 8 if the trumpet does not *s* a clear call
15:52 the trumpet will *s,* the dead will
2Ti 4: 3 men will not put up with *s* doctrine.

SOVEREIGN
Da 4:25 that the Most High is *s*

SOW (SOWS)
Job 4: 8 and those who *s* trouble reap it.
Mt 6:26 they do not *s* or reap or store away
2Pe 2:22 and, "A *s* that is washed goes back

SOWS (SOW)
Pr 11:18 he who *s* righteousness reaps a sure
22: 8 He who *s* wickedness reaps trouble
2Co 9: 6 Whoever *s* sparingly will
Gal 6: 7 A man reaps what he *s.*

SPARE (SPARES)
Ro 8:32 He who did not *s* his own Son,
11:21 natural branches, he will not *s* you

SPARES (SPARE)
Pr 13:24 He who *s* the rod hates his son,

SPEARS
Isa 2: 4 and their *s* into pruning hooks.
Joel 3:10 and your pruning hooks into *s.*
Mic 4: 3 and their *s* into pruning hooks.

SPECTACLE
1Co 4: 9 We have been made a *s*
Col 2:15 he made a public *s* of them,

SPIN
Mt 6:28 They do not labor or *s.*

SPIRIT (SPIRIT'S SPIRITS SPIRITUAL SPIRITUALLY)
Ge 1: 2 and the *S* of God was hovering
6: 3 "My *S* will not contend
2Ki 2: 9 inherit a double portion of your *s,"*
Job 33: 4 The *S* of God has made me;
Ps 31: 5 Into your hands I commit my *s;*
51:10 and renew a steadfast *s* within me.
51:11 or take your Holy *S* from me.
51:17 sacrifices of God are a broken *s;*
139: 7 Where can I go from your *S?*
Isa 57:15 him who is contrite and lowly in *s,*
63:10 and grieved his Holy *S.*
Eze 11:19 an undivided heart and put a new *s*
36:26 you a new heart and put a new *s*
Joel 2:28 I will pour out my *S* on all people.
Zec 4: 6 but by my *S,'* says the LORD
Mt 1:18 to be with child through the Holy *S*
3:11 will baptize you with the Holy *S*
3:16 he saw the *S* of God descending
4: 1 led by the *S* into the desert
5: 3 saying: "Blessed are the poor in *s,*
26:41 *s* is willing, but the body is weak."
28:19 and of the Son and of the Holy *S,*
Lk 1:80 child grew and became strong in *s;*
11:13 Father in heaven give the Holy *S*
Jn 4:24 God is *s,* and his worshipers must
7:39 Up to that time the *S* had not been
14:26 But the Counselor, the Holy *S,*
16:13 But when he, the *S* of truth, comes,
20:22 and said, "Receive the Holy *S.*
Ac 1: 5 will be baptized with the Holy *S."*
2: 4 of them were filled with the Holy *S*
2:38 will receive the gift of the Holy *S.*
6: 3 who are known to be full of the *S*
19: 2 "Did you receive the Holy *S*
Ro 8: 9 And if anyone does not have the *S*
8:26 the *S* helps us in our weakness.
1Co 2:10 God has revealed it to us by his *S.*
2:14 man without the *S* does not accept
6:19 body is a temple of the Holy *S,*
12:13 baptized by one *S* into one body—
2Co 3: 6 the letter kills, but the *S* gives life.
5: 5 and has given us the *S* as a deposit,
Gal 5:16 by the *S,* and you will not gratify
5:22 But the fruit of the *S* is love, joy,
5:25 let us keep in step with the *S.*
Eph 1:13 with a seal, the promised Holy *S,*
4:30 do not grieve the Holy *S* of God,
5:18 Instead, be filled with the *S.*
6:17 of salvation and the sword of the *S,*
2Th 2:13 the sanctifying work of the *S*
Heb 4:12 even to dividing soul and *s,*
1Pe 3: 4 beauty of a gentle and quiet *s,*
2Pe 1:21 carried along by the Holy *S.*
1Jn 4: 1 Dear friends, do not believe every *s*

SPIRIT'S (SPIRIT)
1Th 5:19 not put out the *S* fire; do not treat

SPIRITS (SPIRIT)
1Co 12:10 to another distinguishing between *s,*
14:32 The *s* of prophets are subject
1Jn 4: 1 test the *s* to see whether they are

SPIRITUAL (SPIRIT)
Ro 12: 1 this is your *s* act of worship.
12:11 but keep your *s* fervor, serving
1Co 2:13 expressing *s* truths in *s* words.
3: 1 I could not address you as *s* but
12: 1 Now about *s* gifts, brothers,
14: 1 of love and eagerly desire *s* gifts,
15:44 a natural body, it is raised a *s* body.
Gal 6: 1 you who are *s* should restore him
Eph 1: 3 with every *s* blessing in Christ.
5:19 with psalms, hymns and *s* songs.
6:12 and against the *s* forces of evil
1Pe 2: 2 newborn babies, crave pure *s* milk,
2: 5 are being built into a *s* house

SPIRITUALLY (SPIRIT)
1Co 2:14 because they are *s* discerned.

SPLENDOR
1Ch 16:29 the LORD in the *s* of his holiness.
29:11 the glory and the majesty and the *s,*
Job 37:22 of the north he comes in golden *s;*
Ps 29: 2 in the *s* of his holiness.
45: 3 clothe yourself with *s* and majesty.
96: 6 *S* and majesty are before him;
96: 9 in the *s* of his holiness;
104: 1 you are clothed with *s* and majesty.
145: 5 of the glorious *s* of your majesty,
Isa 61: 3 the LORD for the display of his *s.*
63: 1 Who is this, robed in *s,*
Lk 9:31 appeared in glorious *s,* talking
2Th 2: 8 and destroy by the *s* of his coming.

SPOIL
Ps 119:162 like one who finds great *s.*

SPOTLESS
2Pe 3:14 make every effort to be found *s,*

SPREAD (SPREADING)
Ac 12:24 of God continued to increase and *s.*
19:20 the word of the Lord *s* widely

SPREADING (SPREAD)
1Th 3: 2 God's fellow worker in *s* the gospel

SPRING
Jer 2:13 the *s* of living water,
Jn 4:14 in him a *s* of water welling up
Jas 3:12 can a salt *s* produce fresh water.

SPUR*
Heb 10:24 how we may *s* one another

SPURNS*
Pr 15: 5 A fool *s* his father's discipline,

STAFF
Ps 23: 4 your rod and your *s,*

STAKES
Isa 54: 2 strengthen your *s.*

STAND (STANDING STANDS)
Ex 14:13 *S* firm and you will see
2Ch 20:17 *s* firm and see the deliverance
Ps 1: 5 Therefore the wicked will not *s*
40: 2 and gave me a firm place to *s.*
119:120 I *s* in awe of your laws.
Eze 22:30 *s* before me in the gap on behalf

Zec 14: 4 On that day his feet will *s*
Mt 12:25 divided against itself will not *s*.
Ro 14:10 we will all *s* before God's judgment
1Co 10:13 out so that you can *s* up under it.
15:58 Therefore, my dear brothers, *s* firm
Eph 6:14 *S* firm then, with the belt
2Th 2:15 *s* firm and hold to the teachings we
Jas 5: 8 You too, be patient and *s* firm,
Rev 3:20 Here I am! I *s* at the door

STANDING (STAND)
Ex 3: 5 where you are *s* is holy ground."
Jos 5:15 the place where you are *s* is holy."
1Pe 5: 9 Resist him, *s* firm in the faith,

STANDS (STAND)
Ps 89: 2 that your love *s* firm forever,
119:89 it *s* firm in the heavens.
Mt 10:22 but he who *s* firm to the end will be
2Ti 2:19 God's solid foundation *s* firm,
1Pe 1:25 but the word of the Lord *s* forever

STAR (STARS)
Nu 24:17 A *s* will come out of Jacob;
Rev 22:16 and the bright Morning *S*."

STARS (STAR)
Da 12: 3 like the *s* for ever and ever.
Php 2:15 in which you shine like *s*

STATURE
Lk 2:52 And Jesus grew in wisdom and *s*,

STEADFAST
Ps 51:10 and renew a *s* spirit within me.
Isa 26: 3 him whose mind is *s*,
1Pe 5:10 and make you strong, firm and *s*.

STEAL
Ex 20:15 "You shall not *s*.
Mt 19:18 do not *s*, do not give false
Eph 4:28 has been stealing must *s* no longer,

STEP (STEPS)
Gal 5:25 let us keep in *s* with the Spirit.

STEPS (STEP)
Pr 16: 9 but the LORD determines his *s*.
Jer 10:23 it is not for man to direct his *s*.
1Pe 2:21 that you should follow in his *s*.

STICKS
Pr 18:24 there is a friend who *s* closer

STIFF-NECKED
Ex 34: 9 Although this is a *s* people,

STILL
Ps 46:10 "Be *s*, and know that I am God;
Zec 2:13 Be *s* before the LORD, all mankind

STIRS
Pr 6:19 and a man who *s* up dissension
10:12 Hatred *s* up dissension,
15: 1 but a harsh word *s* up anger.
15:18 hot-tempered man *s* up dissension,
16:28 A perverse man *s* up dissension,
28:25 A greedy man *s* up dissension,
29:22 An angry man *s* up dissension,

STONE (CAPSTONE CORNERSTONE MILLSTONE)
1Sa 17:50 the Philistine with a sling and a *s*;
Isa 8:14 a *s* that causes men to stumble
Eze 11:19 remove from them their heart of *s*
Mk 16: 3 "Who will roll the *s* away
Lk 4: 3 tell this *s* to become bread."
Jn 8: 7 the first to throw a *s* at her."
2Co 3: 3 not on tablets of *s* but on tablets

STOOP
2Sa 22:36 you *s* down to make me great.

STORE
Pr 10:14 Wise men *s* up knowledge,
Mt 6:19 not *s* up for yourselves treasures

STOREHOUSE (HOUSE)
Mal 3:10 Bring the whole tithe into the *s*,

STRAIGHT
Pr 3: 6 and he will make your paths *s*.
4:25 Let your eyes look *s* ahead,
15:21 of understanding keeps a *s* course.
Jn 1:23 'Make *s* the way for the Lord.'"

STRAIN
Mt 23:24 You *s* out a gnat but swallow

STRANGER (STRANGERS)
Mt 25:35 I was a *s* and you invited me in,
Jn 10: 5 But they will never follow a *s*;

STRANGERS (STRANGER)
1Pe 2:11 as aliens and *s* in the world,

STREAMS
Ps 1: 3 He is like a tree planted by *s*
46: 4 is a river whose *s* make glad
Ecc 1: 7 All *s* flow into the sea,
Jn 7:38 *s* of living water will flow

STRENGTH (STRONG)
Ex 15: 2 The LORD is my *s* and my song;
Dt 6: 5 all your soul and with all your *s*.
2Sa 22:33 It is God who arms me with *s*
Ne 8:10 for the joy of the LORD is your *s*."
Ps 28: 7 The LORD is my *s* and my shield;
46: 1 God is our refuge and *s*,
96: 7 ascribe to the LORD glory and *s*.
118:14 The LORD is my *s* and my song;
147:10 not in the *s* of the horse,
Isa 40:31 will renew their *s*.
Mk 12:30 all your mind and with all your *s*.'
1Co 1:25 of God is stronger than man's *s*.
Php 4:13 through him who gives me *s*.
1Pe 4:11 it with the *s* God provides,

STRENGTHEN (STRONG)
2Ch 16: 9 to *s* those whose hearts are fully
Ps 119:28 *s* me according to your word.
Isa 35: 3 *S* the feeble hands,
41:10 I will *s* you and help you;
Eph 3:16 of his glorious riches he may *s* you
2Th 2:17 and *s* you in every good deed
Heb 12:12 *s* your feeble arms and weak knees.

STRENGTHENING (STRONG)
1Co 14:26 done for the *s* of the church.

STRIFE
Pr 20: 3 It is to a man's honor to avoid *s*,
22:10 out the mocker, and out goes *s*;

STRIKE (STRIKES)
Ge 3:15 and you will *s* his heel."
Zec 13: 7 "*S* the shepherd,
Mt 26:31 "'I will *s* the shepherd,

STRIKES (STRIKE)
Mt 5:39 If someone *s* you on the right

STRONG (STRENGTH STRENGTHEN STRENGTHENING)
Dt 31: 6 Be *s* and courageous.
1Ki 2: 2 "So be *s*, show yourself a man,
Pr 18:10 The name of the LORD is a *s* tower
31:17 her arms are *s* for her tasks.
SS 8: 6 for love is as *s* as death,
Lk 2:40 And the child grew and became *s*;
Ro 15: 1 We who are *s* ought to bear
1Co 1:27 things of the world to shame the *s*.
16:13 in the faith; be men of courage; be *s*
2Co 12:10 For when I am weak, then I am *s*.
Eph 6:10 be *s* in the Lord and in his mighty

STRUGGLE
Ro 15:30 me in my *s* by praying to God
Eph 6:12 For our *s* is not against flesh
Heb 12: 4 In your *s* against sin, you have not

STUDY
Ezr 7:10 Ezra had devoted himself to the *s*
Ecc 12:12 and much *s* wearies the body.
Jn 5:39 You diligently *s* the Scriptures

STUMBLE (STUMBLING)
Ps 37:24 though he *s*, he will not fall,
119:165 and nothing can make them *s*.
Isa 8:14 a stone that causes men to *s*
Jer 31: 9 a level path where they will not *s*,
Eze 7:19 for it has made them *s* into sin.
1Co 10:32 Do not cause anyone to *s*,
1Pe 2: 8 and, "A stone that causes men to *s*

STUMBLING (STUMBLE)
Ro 14:13 up your mind not to put any *s* block
1Co 8: 9 freedom does not become a *s* block
2Co 6: 3 We put no *s* block in anyone's path,

SUBDUE
Ge 1:28 in number; fill the earth and *s* it.

SUBJECT (SUBJECTED)
1Co 14:32 of prophets are *s* to the control
15:28 then the Son himself will be made *s*
Tit 2: 5 and to be *s* to their husbands,
2: 9 slaves to be *s* to their masters
3: 1 Remind the people to be *s* to rulers

SUBJECTED (SUBJECT)
Ro 8:20 For the creation was *s*

SUBMISSION (SUBMIT)
1Co 14:34 but must be in *s*, as the Law says.
1Ti 2:11 learn in quietness and full *s*.

SUBMISSIVE (SUBMIT)
Jas 3:17 then peace-loving, considerate, *s*,
1Pe 3: 1 in the same way be *s*
5: 5 in the same way be *s*

SUBMIT (SUBMISSION SUBMISSIVE SUBMITS)
Ro 13: 1 Everyone must *s* himself
13: 5 necessary to *s* to the authorities,
1Co 16:16 to *s* to such as these
Eph 5:21 *S* to one another out of reverence
Col 3:18 Wives, *s* to your husbands,
Heb 12: 9 How much more should we *s*
13:17 Obey your leaders and *s*
Jas 4: 7 *S* yourselves, then, to God.
1Pe 2:18 *s* yourselves to your masters

SUBMITS* (SUBMIT)
Eph 5:24 Now as the church *s* to Christ,

SUCCESSFUL
Jos 1: 7 that you may be *s* wherever you go.
2Ki 18: 7 he was *s* in whatever he undertook.
2Ch 20:20 in his prophets and you will be *s*."

SUFFER (SUFFERED SUFFERING SUFFERINGS SUFFERS)
Isa 53:10 to crush him and cause him to *s*,
Mk 8:31 the Son of Man must *s* many things
Lk 24:26 the Christ have to *s* these things
24:46 The Christ will *s* and rise
Php 1:29 to *s* for him, since you are going
1Pe 4:16 However, if you *s* as a Christian,

SUFFERED (SUFFER)
Heb 2:9 and honor because he *s* death,
2:18 Because he himself *s*
1Pe 2:21 Christ *s* for you, leaving you

SUFFERING (SUFFER)
Isa 53:3 of sorrows, and familiar with *s*.
Ac 5:41 worthy of *s* disgrace for the Name.
2Ti 1:8 But join with me in *s* for the gospel,
Heb 2:10 of their salvation perfect through *s*.

SUFFERINGS (SUFFER)
Ro 8:17 share in his *s* in order that we may
8:18 that our present *s* are not worth
2Co 1:5 as the *s* of Christ flow
Php 3:10 the fellowship of sharing in his *s*,

SUFFERS (SUFFER)
Pr 13:20 but a companion of fools *s* harm.
1Co 12:26 If one part *s*, every part *s* with it;

SUFFICIENT
2Co 12:9 said to me, "My grace is *s* for you,

SUITABLE
Ge 2:18 I will make a helper *s* for him."

SUN
Ecc 1:9 there is nothing new under the *s*.
Mal 4:2 the *s* of righteousness will rise
Mt 5:45 He causes his *s* to rise on the evil
17:2 His face shone like the *s*,
Rev 1:16 His face was like the *s* shining
21:23 The city does not need the *s*

SUPERIOR
Heb 1:4 he became as much *s* to the angels
8:6 ministry Jesus has received is as *s*

SUPERVISION
Gal 3:25 longer under the *s* of the law.

SUPREMACY* (SUPREME)
Col 1:18 in everything he might have the *s*.

SUPREME (SUPREMACY)
Pr 4:7 Wisdom is *s*; therefore get wisdom.

SURE
Nu 32:23 you may be *s* that your sin will find
Dt 6:17 Be *s* to keep the commands
14:22 Be *s* to set aside a tenth
Isa 28:16 cornerstone for a *s* foundation;
Heb 11:1 faith is being *s* of what we hope for
2Pe 1:10 to make your calling and election *s*.

SURPASS* (SURPASSES SURPASSING)
Pr 31:29 but you *s* them all."

SURPASSES (SURPASS)
Mt 5:20 unless your righteousness *s* that
Eph 3:19 to know this love that *s* knowledge

SURPASSING* (SURPASS)
Ps 150:2 praise him for his *s* greatness.
2Co 3:10 in comparison with the *s* glory.
9:14 of the *s* grace God has given you.
Php 3:8 the *s* greatness of knowing Christ

SURROUNDED
Heb 12:1 since we are *s* by such a great cloud

SUSPENDS*
Job 26:7 he *s* the earth over nothing.

SUSTAINING* (SUSTAINS)
Heb 1:3 *s* all things by his powerful word.

SUSTAINS (SUSTAINING)
Ps 18:35 and your right hand *s* me;
146:9 and *s* the fatherless and the widow,
147:6 The LORD *s* the humble
Isa 50:4 to know the word that *s* the weary.

SWALLOWED
1Co 15:54 "Death has been *s* up in victory."
2Co 5:4 so that what is mortal may be *s* up

SWEAR
Mt 5:34 Do not *s* at all: either by heaven,

SWORD (SWORDS)
Ps 45:3 Gird your *s* upon your side,
Pr 12:18 Reckless words pierce like a *s*,
Mt 10:34 come to bring peace, but a *s*.
26:52 all who draw the *s* will die by the *s*.
Lk 2:35 a *s* will pierce your own soul too."
Ro 13:4 for he does not bear the *s*
Eph 6:17 of salvation and the *s* of the Spirit,
Heb 4:12 Sharper than any double-edged *s*,
Rev 1:16 came a sharp double-edged *s*.

SWORDS (SWORD)
Isa 2:4 They will beat their *s*
Joel 3:10 Beat your plowshares into *s*

SYMPATHETIC*
1Pe 3:8 in harmony with one another; be *s*,

SYNAGOGUE
Lk 4:16 the Sabbath day he went into the *s*,
Ac 17:2 custom was, Paul went into the *s*,

TABERNACLE
Ex 40:34 the glory of the LORD filled the *t*.

TABLE (TABLES)
Ps 23:5 You prepare a *t* before me

TABLES (TABLE)
Ac 6:2 word of God in order to wait on *t*.

TABLET (TABLETS)
Pr 3:3 write them on the *t* of your heart.
7:3 write them on the *t* of your heart.

TABLETS (TABLET)
Ex 31:18 he gave him the two *t*
Dt 10:5 and put the *t* in the ark I had made,
2Co 3:3 not on *t* of stone but on *t*

TAKE (TAKEN TAKES TAKING TOOK)
Dt 12:32 do not add to it or *t* away from it.
31:26 "*T* this Book of the Law
Job 23:10 But he knows the way that I *t*;
Ps 49:17 for he will *t* nothing with him
51:11 or *t* your Holy Spirit from me.
Mt 10:38 anyone who does not *t* his cross
11:29 *T* my yoke upon you and learn
16:24 deny himself and *t* up his cross

TAKEN (TAKE)
Lev 6:4 must return what he has stolen or *t*
Isa 6:7 your guilt is *t* away and your sin
Mt 24:40 one will be *t* and the other left.
Mk 16:19 he was *t* up into heaven
1Ti 3:16 was *t* up in glory.

TAKES (TAKE)
1Ki 20:11 should not boast like one who *t* it
Ps 5:4 You are not a God who *t* pleasure
Jn 1:29 who *t* away the sin of the world!
Rev 22:19 And if anyone *t* words away

TAKING (TAKE)
Ac 15:14 by *t* from the Gentiles a people
Php 2:7 *t* the very nature of a servant,

TALENT
Mt 25:15 to another one *t*, each according

TAME*
Jas 3:8 but no man can *t* the tongue.

TASK
Mk 13:34 each with his assigned *t*,
Ac 20:24 complete the *t* the Lord Jesus has
1Co 3:5 the Lord has assigned to each his *t*.
2Co 2:16 And who is equal to such a *t*?

TASTE (TASTED)
Ps 34:8 *T* and see that the LORD is good;
Col 2:21 Do not *t*! Do not touch!"?
Heb 2:9 the grace of God he might *t* death

TASTED (TASTE)
1Pe 2:3 now that you have *t* that the Lord

TAUGHT (TEACH)
Mt 7:29 he *t* as one who had authority,
1Co 2:13 but in words *t* by the Spirit,
Gal 1:12 nor was I *t* it; rather, I received it

TAXES
Mt 22:17 Is it right to pay *t* to Caesar or not
Ro 13:7 If you owe *t*, pay *t*; if revenue,

TEACH (TAUGHT TEACHER TEACHERS TEACHES TEACHING)
Ex 33:13 *t* me your ways so I may know you
Dt 4:9 *T* them to your children
8:3 to *t* you that man does not live
11:19 *T* them to your children, talking
1Sa 12:23 I will *t* you the way that is good
Ps 32:8 *t* you in the way you should go;
51:13 I will *t* transgressors your ways,
90:12 *T* us to number our days aright,
143:10 *T* me to do your will,
Jer 31:34 No longer will a man *t* his neighbor
Lk 11:1 said to him, "Lord, *t* us to pray,
Jn 14:26 will *t* you all things and will remind
1Ti 2:12 I do not permit a woman to *t*
3:2 respectable, hospitable, able to *t*,
Tit 2:1 You must *t* what is in accord
Heb 8:11 No longer will a man *t* his neighbor
Jas 3:1 know that we who *t* will be judged
1Jn 2:27 you do not need anyone to *t* you.

TEACHER (TEACH)
Mt 10:24 "A student is not above his *t*,
Jn 13:14 and *T*, have washed your feet,

TEACHERS (TEACH)
1Co 12:28 third *t,* then workers of miracles,
Eph 4:11 and some to be pastors and *t,*
Heb 5:12 by this time you ought to be *t,*

TEACHES (TEACH)
1Ti 6:3 If anyone *t* false doctrines

TEACHING (TEACH)
Pr 1:8 and do not forsake your mother's *t.*
Mt 28:20 *t* them to obey everything I have
Jn 7:17 whether my *t* comes from God or
14:23 loves me, he will obey my *t.*
1Ti 4:13 of Scripture, to preaching and to *t.*
2Ti 3:16 is God-breathed and is useful for *t,*
Tit 2:7 In your *t* show integrity,

TEAR (TEARS)
Rev 7:17 God will wipe away every *t*

TEARS (TEAR)
Ps 126:5 Those who sow in *t*
Php 3:18 and now say again even with *t,*

TEETH (TOOTH)
Mt 8:12 will be weeping and gnashing of *t."*

TEMPERATE*
1Ti 3:2 *t,* self-controlled, respectable,
3:11 not malicious talkers but *t*
Tit 2:2 Teach the older men to be *t,*

TEMPEST
Ps 55:8 far from the *t* and storm."

TEMPLE (TEMPLES)
1Ki 8:27 How much less this *t* I have built!
Hab 2:20 But the LORD is in his holy *t;*
1Co 3:16 that you yourselves are God's *t*
6:19 you not know that your body is a *t*
2Co 6:16 For we are the *t* of the living God.

TEMPLES (TEMPLE)
Ac 17:24 does not live in *t* built by hands.

TEMPT (TEMPTATION TEMPTED)
1Co 7:5 again so that Satan will not *t* you

TEMPTATION (TEMPT)
Mt 6:13 And lead us not into *t,*
26:41 pray so that you will not fall into *t.*
1Co 10:13 No *t* has seized you except what is

TEMPTED (TEMPT)
Mt 4:1 into the desert to be *t* by the devil.
1Co 10:13 he will not let you be *t*
Heb 2:18 he himself suffered when he was *t,*
4:15 but we have one who has been *t*
Jas 1:13 For God cannot be *t* by evil,

TEN (TENTH TITHE TITHES)
Ex 34:28 covenant—the *T* Commandments.
Ps 91:7 *t* thousand at your right hand,
Mt 25:28 it to the one who has the *t* talents.
Lk 15:8 suppose a woman has *t* silver coins

TENTH (TEN)
Dt 14:22 Be sure to set aside a *t*

TERRIBLE (TERROR)
2Ti 3:1 There will be *t* times

TERROR (TERRIBLE)
Ps 91:5 You will not fear the *t* of night,
Lk 21:26 Men will faint from *t,* apprehensive
Ro 13:3 For rulers hold no *t*

TEST (TESTED TESTS)
Dt 6:16 Do not *t* the LORD your God
Ps 139:23 *t* me and know my anxious
Ro 12:2 Then you will be able to *t*
1Co 3:13 and the fire will *t* the quality
1Jn 4:1 *t* the spirits to see whether they are

TESTED (TEST)
Ge 22:1 Some time later God *t* Abraham.
Job 23:10 when he has *t* me, I will come forth
Pr 27:21 man is *t* by the praise he receives.
1Ti 3:10 They must first be *t;* and then

TESTIFY (TESTIMONY)
Jn 5:39 are the Scriptures that *t* about me,
2Ti 1:8 ashamed to *t* about our Lord,

TESTIMONY (TESTIFY)
Isa 8:20 and to the *t!* If they do not speak
Lk 18:20 not give false *t,* honor your father

TESTS (TEST)
Pr 17:3 but the LORD *t* the heart.
1Th 2:4 but God, who *t* our hearts.

THADDAEUS
Apostle (Mt 10:3; Mk 3:18); probably also known as Judas son of James (Lk 6:16; Ac 1:13).

THANKFUL (THANKS)
Heb 12:28 let us be *t,* and so worship God

THANKS (THANKFUL THANKSGIVING)
1Ch 16:8 Give *t* to the LORD, call
Ne 12:31 assigned two large choirs to give *t.*
Ps 100:4 give *t* to him and praise his name.
1Co 15:57 *t* be to God! He gives us the victory
2Co 2:14 *t* be to God, who always leads us
9:15 *T* be to God for his indescribable
1Th 5:18 give *t* in all circumstances,

THANKSGIVING (THANKS)
Ps 95:2 Let us come before him with *t*
100:4 Enter his gates with *t*
Php 4:6 by prayer and petition, with *t,*
1Ti 4:3 created to be received with *t*

THIEF (THIEVES)
Ex 22:3 A *t* must certainly make restitution
1Th 5:2 day of the Lord will come like a *t*
Rev 16:15 I come like a *t!* Blessed is he who

THIEVES (THIEF)
1Co 6:10 nor homosexual offenders nor *t*

THINK (THOUGHT THOUGHTS)
Ro 12:3 Do not *t* of yourself more highly
Php 4:8 praiseworthy—*t* about such things

THIRST (THIRSTY)
Ps 69:21 and gave me vinegar for my *t.*
Mt 5:6 Blessed are those who hunger and *t*
Jn 4:14 the water I give him will never *t.*

THIRSTY (THIRST)
Isa 55:1 "Come, all you who are *t,*
Jn 7:37 "If anyone is *t,* let him come to me
Rev 22:17 Whoever is *t,* let him come;

THOMAS
Apostle (Mt 10:3; Mk 3:18; Lk 6:15; Jn 11:16; 14:5; 21:2; Ac 1:13). Doubted resurrection (Jn 20:24-28).

THONGS
Mk 1:7 *t* of whose sandals I am not worthy

THORN (THORNS)
2Co 12:7 there was given me a *t* in my flesh,

THORNS (THORN)
Nu 33:55 in your eyes and *t* in your sides.
Mt 27:29 then twisted together a crown of *t*
Heb 6:8 But land that produces *t*

THOUGHT (THINK)
Pr 14:15 a prudent man gives *t* to his steps.
1Co 13:11 I talked like a child, I *t* like a child,

THOUGHTS (THINK)
Ps 94:11 The LORD knows the *t* of man;
139:23 test me and know my anxious *t.*
Isa 55:8 "For my *t* are not your *t,*
Heb 4:12 it judges the *t* and attitudes

THREE
Ecc 4:12 of *t* strands is not quickly broken.
Mt 12:40 *t* nights in the belly of a huge fish,
18:20 or *t* come together in my name,
27:63 'After *t* days I will rise again.'
1Co 13:13 And now these *t* remain: faith,
14:27 or at the most *t*— should speak,
2Co 13:1 testimony of two or *t* witnesses."

THRESHING
2Sa 24:18 an altar to the LORD on the *t* floor

THRONE (ENTHRONED)
2Sa 7:16 your *t* will be established forever
Ps 45:6 Your *t,* O God, will last for ever
47:8 God is seated on his holy *t.*
Isa 6:1 I saw the Lord seated on a *t,*
66:1 "Heaven is my *t*
Heb 4:16 Let us then approach the *t* of grace
12:2 at the right hand of the *t* of God.
Rev 4:10 They lay their crowns before the *t*
20:11 Then I saw a great white *t*
22:3 *t* of God and of the Lamb will be

THROW
Jn 8:7 the first to *t* a stone at her."
Heb 10:35 So do not *t* away your confidence;
12:1 let us *t* off everything that hinders

THWART*
Isa 14:27 has purposed, and who can *t* him?

TIBNI
King of Israel (1Ki 16:21-22).

TIME (TIMES)
Est 4:14 come to royal position for such a *t*
Da 7:25 to him for a *t,* times and half a *t.*
Hos 10:12 for it is *t* to seek the LORD,
Ro 9:9 "At the appointed *t* I will return,
Heb 9:28 and he will appear a second *t,*
10:12 for all *t* one sacrifice for sins,
1Pe 4:17 For it is *t* for judgment to begin

TIMES (TIME)
Ps 9:9 a stronghold in *t* of trouble.
31:15 My *t* are in your hands;
62:8 Trust in him at all *t,* O people;
Pr 17:17 A friend loves at all *t,*
Am 5:13 for the *t* are evil.
Mt 18:21 how many *t* shall I forgive my
Ac 1:7 "It is not for you to know the *t*
Rev 12:14 *t* and half a time, out

TIMIDITY*
2Ti 1:7 For God did not give us a spirit of *t*

TIMOTHY
Believer from Lystra (Ac 16:1). Joined Paul on second missionary journey (Ac 16-20). Sent to settle problems at Corinth (1Co 4:17; 16:10). Led church at Ephesus (1Ti 1:3). Co-writer with Paul (1Th 1:1; 2Th 1:1; Phm 1).

TIRE (TIRED)
2Th 3:13 never *t* of doing what is right.

TIRED (TIRE)
Ex 17:12 When Moses' hands grew *t,*
Isa 40:28 He will not grow *t* or weary,

TITHE (TEN)
Lev 27:30 " 'A *t* of everything from the land,
Dt 12:17 eat in your own towns the *t*
Mal 3:10 the whole *t* into the storehouse,

TITHES (TEN)
Mal 3: 8 'How do we rob you?' "In *t*

TITUS
Gentile co-worker of Paul (Gal 2:1-3; 2Ti 4:10); sent to Corinth (2Co 2:13; 7-8; 12:18), Crete (Tit 1:4-5).

TODAY
Mt 6:11 Give us *t* our daily bread.
Lk 23:43 *t* you will be with me in paradise."
Heb 3:13 daily, as long as it is called *T,*
13: 8 Christ is the same yesterday and *t*

TOIL
Ge 3:17 through painful *t* you will eat of it

TOLERATE
Hab 1:13 you cannot *t* wrong.
Rev 2: 2 that you cannot *t* wicked men,

TOMB
Mt 27:65 make the *t* as secure as you know
Lk 24: 2 the stone rolled away from the *t,*

TOMORROW
Pr 27: 1 Do not boast about *t,*
Isa 22:13 "for *t* we die!"
Mt 6:34 Therefore do not worry about *t,*
Jas 4:13 "Today or *t* we will go to this

TONGUE (TONGUES)
Ps 39: 1 and keep my *t* from sin;
Pr 12:18 but the *t* of the wise brings healing.
1Co 14: 2 speaks in a *t* does not speak to men
14: 4 He who speaks in a *t* edifies himself
14:13 in a *t* should pray that he may
14:19 than ten thousand words in a *t.*
Php 2:11 every *t* confess that Jesus Christ is
Jas 1:26 does not keep a tight rein on his *t,*
3: 8 but no man can tame the *t.*

TONGUES (TONGUE)
Isa 28:11 with foreign lips and strange *t*
66:18 and gather all nations and *t,*
Mk 16:17 in new *t;* they will pick up snakes
Ac 2: 4 and began to speak in other *t*
10:46 For they heard them speaking in *t*
19: 6 and they spoke in *t* and prophesied
1Co 12:30 Do all speak in *t?* Do all interpret?
14:18 speak in *t* more than all of you.
14:39 and do not forbid speaking in *t.*

TOOK (TAKE)
1Co 11:23 the night he was betrayed, *t* bread,
Php 3:12 for which Christ Jesus *t* hold of me.

TOOTH (TEETH)
Ex 21:24 eye for eye, *t* for *t,* hand for hand,
Mt 5:38 'Eye for eye, and *t* for *t.*'

TORMENTED
Rev 20:10 They will be *t* day and night

TORN
Gal 4:15 you would have *t* out your eyes
Php 1:23 I do not know! I am *t*

TOUCH (TOUCHED)
Ps 105:15 "Do not *t* my anointed ones;
Lk 24:39 It is I myself! *T* me and see;
2Co 6:17 *T* no unclean thing,
Col 2:21 Do not taste! Do not *t!*"?

TOUCHED (TOUCH)
1Sa 10:26 men whose hearts God had *t.*
Mt 14:36 and all who *t* him were healed.

TOWER
Ge 11: 4 with a *t* that reaches to the heavens
Pr 18:10 of the LORD is a strong *t;*

TOWNS
Nu 35: 2 to give the Levites *t* to live
35:15 These six *t* will be a place of refuge

TRACING*
Ro 11:33 and his paths beyond *t* out!

TRADITION
Mt 15: 6 word of God for the sake of your *t.*
Col 2: 8 which depends on human *t*

TRAIN (TRAINING)
Pr 22: 6 *T* a child in the way he should go,
Eph 4: 8 he led captives in his *t*

TRAINING (TRAIN)
1Co 9:25 in the games goes into strict *t.*
2Ti 3:16 correcting and *t* in righteousness,

TRAMPLED
Lk 21:24 Jerusalem will be *t*
Heb 10:29 to be punished who has *t* the Son

TRANCE
Ac 10:10 was being prepared, he fell into a *t.*

TRANSCENDS*
Php 4: 7 which *t* all understanding,

TRANSFIGURED
Mt 17: 2 There he was *t* before them.

TRANSFORM* (TRANSFORMED)
Php 3:21 will *t* our lowly bodies

TRANSFORMED (TRANSFORM)
Ro 12: 2 be *t* by the renewing of your mind.
2Co 3:18 are being *t* into his likeness

TRANSGRESSION (TRANSGRESSIONS TRANSGRESSORS)
Isa 53: 8 for the *t* of my people he was
Ro 4:15 where there is no law there is no *t.*

TRANSGRESSIONS (TRANSGRESSION)
Ps 32: 1 whose *t* are forgiven,
51: 1 blot out my *t.*
103:12 so far has he removed our *t* from us
Isa 53: 5 But he was pierced for our *t,*
Eph 2: 1 you were dead in your *t* and sins,

TRANSGRESSORS (TRANSGRESSION)
Ps 51:13 Then I will teach *t* your ways,
Isa 53:12 and made intercession for the *t.*
53:12 and was numbered with the *t.*

TREADING
Dt 25: 4 an ox while it is *t* out the grain.
1Co 9: 9 an ox while it is *t* out the grain."

TREASURE (TREASURED TREASURES)
Isa 33: 6 of the LORD is the key to this *t.*
Mt 6:21 For where your *t* is, there your
2Co 4: 7 But we have this *t* in jars of clay

TREASURED (TREASURE)
Dt 7: 6 to be his people, his *t* possession.
Lk 2:19 But Mary *t* up all these things

TREASURES (TREASURE)
Mt 6:19 up for yourselves *t* on earth,
Col 2: 3 in whom are hidden all the *t*
Heb 11:26 of greater value than the *t* of Egypt,

TREAT
Lev 22: 2 sons to *t* with respect the sacred
1Ti 5: 1 *T* younger men as brothers,
1Pe 3: 7 and *t* them with respect

TREATY
Dt 7: 2 Make no *t* with them, and show

TREE
Ge 2: 9 and the *t* of the knowledge of good
2: 9 of the garden were the *t* of life
Dt 21:23 hung on a *t* is under God's curse.
Ps 1: 3 He is like a *t* planted by streams
Mt 3:10 every *t* that does not produce good
12:33 for a *t* is recognized by its fruit.
Gal 3:13 is everyone who is hung on a *t.*"
Rev 22:14 they may have the right to the *t*

TREMBLE (TREMBLING)
1Ch 16:30 *T* before him, all the earth!
Ps 114: 7 *T,* O earth, at the presence

TREMBLING (TREMBLE)
Ps 2:11 and rejoice with *t.*
Php 2:12 out your salvation with fear and *t,*

TRESPASS
Ro 5:17 For if, by the *t* of the one man,

TRIALS
1Th 3: 3 one would be unsettled by these *t.*
Jas 1: 2 whenever you face *t* of many kinds,
2Pe 2: 9 how to rescue godly men from *t*

TRIBES
Ge 49:28 All these are the twelve *t* of Israel,
Mt 19:28 judging the twelve *t* of Israel.

TRIBULATION*
Rev 7:14 who have come out of the great *t;*

TRIUMPHAL* (TRIUMPHING)
Isa 60:11 their kings led in *t* procession.
2Co 2:14 us in *t* procession in Christ

TRIUMPHING* (TRIUMPHAL)
Col 2:15 of them, *t* over them by the cross.

TROUBLE (TROUBLED TROUBLES)
Job 14: 1 is of few days and full of *t.*
Ps 46: 1 an ever-present help in *t.*
107:13 they cried to the LORD in their *t,*
Pr 11:29 He who brings *t* on his family will

Eze 11:19 I will give them an *u* heart
1Co 7:35 way in *u* devotion to the Lord.

UNDOING
Pr 18: 7 A fool's mouth is his *u*,

UNDYING*
Eph 6:24 Lord Jesus Christ with an *u* love.

UNFADING*
1Pe 3: 4 the *u* beauty of a gentle

UNFAILING
Ps 33: 5 the earth is full of his *u* love.
119:76 May your *u* love be my comfort,
143: 8 bring me word of your *u* love,
Pr 19:22 What a man desires is *u* love;
La 3:32 so great is his *u* love.

UNFAITHFUL (UNFAITHFULNESS)
Lev 6: 2 is *u* to the LORD by deceiving his
1Ch 10:13 because he was *u* to the LORD;
Pr 13:15 but the way of the *u* is hard.

UNFAITHFULNESS (UNFAITHFUL)
Mt 5:32 except for marital *u*, causes her
19: 9 for marital *u*, and marries another

UNFOLDING
Ps119:130 the *u* of your words gives light;

UNGODLINESS
Tit 2:12 It teaches us to say "No" to *u*

UNIT
1Co 12:12 body is a *u*, though it is made up

UNITED (UNITY)
Ro 6: 5 If we have been *u* with him
Php 2: 1 from being *u* with Christ,
Col 2: 2 encouraged in heart and *u* in love,

UNITY (UNITED)
Ps 133: 1 is when brothers live together in *u*!
Ro 15: 5 a spirit of *u* among yourselves
Eph 4: 3 effort to keep the *u* of the Spirit
4:13 up until we all reach *u* in the faith
Col 3:14 them all together in perfect *u*.

UNIVERSE
Php 2:15 which you shine like stars in the *u*
Heb 1: 2 and through whom he made the *u*.

UNKNOWN
Ac 17:23 TO AN *U* GOD.

UNLEAVENED
Ex 12:17 "Celebrate the Feast of *U* Bread,

UNPROFITABLE
Tit 3: 9 because these are *u* and useless.

UNPUNISHED
Ex 34: 7 Yet he does not leave the guilty *u*;
Pr 19: 5 A false witness will not go *u*,

UNREPENTANT*
Ro 2: 5 stubbornness and your *u* heart,

UNRIGHTEOUS*
Zep 3: 5 yet the *u* know no shame.
Mt 5:45 rain on the righteous and the *u*.
1Pe 3:18 the righteous for the *u*, to bring you
2Pe 2: 9 and to hold the *u* for the day

UNSEARCHABLE
Ro 11:33 How *u* his judgments,
Eph 3: 8 preach to the Gentiles the *u* riches

UNSEEN
2Co 4:18 on what is seen, but on what is *u*.
4:18 temporary, but what is *u* is eternal.

UNSTABLE*
Jas 1: 8 he is a double-minded man, *u*
2Pe 2:14 they seduce the *u*; they are experts
3:16 ignorant and *u* people distort,

UNTHINKABLE*
Job 34:12 It is *u* that God would do wrong,

UNVEILED*
2Co 3:18 with *u* faces all reflect the Lord's

UNWORTHY
Job 40: 4 "I am *u*— how can I reply to you?
Lk 17:10 should say, 'We are *u* servants;

UPRIGHT
Job 1: 1 This man was blameless and *u*;
Pr 2: 7 He holds victory in store for the *u*,
15: 8 but the prayer of the *u* pleases him.
Tit 1: 8 who is self-controlled, *u*, holy
2:12 *u* and godly lives in this present

UPROOTED
Jude :12 without fruit and *u*— twice dead.

USEFUL
2Ti 2:21 *u* to the Master and prepared
3:16 Scripture is God-breathed and is *u*

USELESS
1Co 15:14 our preaching is *u*
Jas 2:20 faith without deeds is *u*?

USURY
Ne 5:10 But let the exacting of *u* stop!

UTTER
Ps 78: 2 I will *u* hidden things, things from of

UZZIAH
Son of Amaziah; king of Judah also known as Azariah (2Ki 15:1-7; 1Ch 6:24; 2Ch 26).

VAIN
Ps 33:17 A horse is a *v* hope for deliverance;
Isa 65:23 They will not toil in *v*
1Co 15: 2 Otherwise, you have believed in *v*.
15:58 labor in the Lord is not in *v*.
2Co 6: 1 not to receive God's grace in *v*.

VALLEY
Ps 23: 4 walk through the *v* of the shadow
Isa 40: 4 Every *v* shall be raised up,
Joel 3:14 multitudes in the *v* of decision!

VALUABLE (VALUE)
Lk 12:24 And how much more *v* you are

VALUE (VALUABLE)
Mt 13:46 When he found one of great *v*,
1Ti 4: 8 For physical training is of some *v*,
Heb 11:26 as of greater *v* than the treasures

VEIL
Ex 34:33 to them, he put a *v* over his face.
2Co 3:14 for to this day the same *v* remains

VENGEANCE (AVENGE REVENGE)
Isa 34: 8 For the LORD has a day of *v*,

VICTORIES (VICTORY)
Ps 18:50 He gives his king great *v*;
21: 1 great is his joy in the *v* you give!

VICTORIOUSLY* (VICTORY)
Ps 45: 4 In your majesty ride forth *v*

VICTORY (VICTORIES VICTORIOUSLY)
Ps 60:12 With God we will gain the *v*,
1Co 15:54 "Death has been swallowed up in *v*
15:57 He gives us the *v* through our Lord
1Jn 5: 4 This is the *v* that has overcome

VINDICATED
1Ti 3:16 was *v* by the Spirit,

VINE
Jn 15: 1 "I am the true *v*, and my Father is

VINEGAR
Mk 15:36 filled a sponge with wine *v*,

VIOLATION
Heb 2: 2 every *v* and disobedience received

VIOLENCE
Isa 60:18 No longer will *v* be heard
Eze 45: 9 Give up your *v* and oppression

VIPERS
Ro 3:13 "The poison of *v* is on their lips."

VIRGIN
Isa 7:14 The *v* will be with child
Mt 1:23 "The *v* will be with child
2Co 11: 2 that I might present you as a pure *v*

VIRTUES*
Col 3:14 And over all these *v* put on love,

VISION
Ac 26:19 disobedient to the *v* from heaven.

VOICE
Ps 95: 7 Today, if you hear his *v*,
Isa 30:21 your ears will hear a *v* behind you,
Jn 5:28 are in their graves will hear his *v*
10: 3 and the sheep listen to his *v*.
Heb 3: 7 "Today, if you hear his *v*,
Rev 3:20 If anyone hears my *v* and opens

VOMIT
Pr 26:11 As a dog returns to its *v*,
2Pe 2:22 "A dog returns to its *v*," and,

VOW
Nu 30: 2 When a man makes a *v*

WAGES
Lk 10: 7 for the worker deserves his *w*.
Ro 4: 4 his *w* are not credited to him
6:23 For the *w* of sin is death,

WAILING
Ps 30:11 You turned my *w* into dancing;

WAIST
2Ki 1: 8 with a leather belt around his *w*."
Mt 3: 4 he had a leather belt around his *w*.

WAIT (WAITED WAITS)
Ps 27:14 *W* for the LORD;
130: 5 I *w* for the LORD, my soul waits,
Isa 30:18 Blessed are all who *w* for him!
Ac 1: 4 *w* for the gift my Father promised,
Ro 8:23 as we *w* eagerly for our adoption
1Th 1:10 and to *w* for his Son from heaven,
Tit 2:13 while we *w* for the blessed hope—

WAITED (WAIT)
Ps 40: 1 I *w* patiently for the LORD;

WAITS (WAIT)
Ro 8:19 creation *w* in eager expectation

WALK (WALKED WALKS)
Dt 11:19 and when you *w* along the road,
Ps 1: 1 who does not *w* in the counsel
23: 4 Even though I *w*
89:15 who *w* in the light of your presence
Isa 2: 5 let us *w* in the light of the LORD.
30:21 saying, "This is the way; *w* in it."
40:31 they will *w* and not be faint.
Jer 6:16 ask where the good way is, and *w*
Da 4:37 And those who *w* in pride he is able
Am 3: 3 Do two *w* together
Mic 6: 8 and to *w* humbly with your God.
Mk 2: 9 'Get up, take your mat and *w*'?
Jn 8:12 Whoever follows me will never *w*
1Jn 1: 7 But if we *w* in the light,
2Jn : 6 his command is that you *w* in love.

WALKED (WALK)
Ge 5:24 Enoch *w* with God; then he was no
Jos 14: 9 which your feet have *w* will be your
Mt 14:29 *w* on the water and came toward

WALKS (WALK)
Pr 13:20 He who *w* with the wise grows wise

WALL
Jos 6:20 *w* collapsed; so every man charged
Ne 2:17 let us rebuild the *w* of Jerusalem,
Rev 21:12 It had a great, high *w*

WALLOWING
2Pe 2:22 back to her *w* in the mud."

WANT (WANTED WANTING WANTS)
1Sa 8:19 "We *w* a king over us.
Ps 23: 1 is my shepherd, I shall not be in *w*.
Lk 19:14 'We don't *w* this man to be our king
Ro 7:15 For what I *w* to do I do not do,
Php 3:10 I *w* to know Christ and the power

WANTED (WANT)
1Co 12:18 of them, just as he *w* them to be.

WANTING (WANT)
Da 5:27 weighed on the scales and found *w*.
2Pe 3: 9 with you, not *w* anyone to perish,

WANTS (WANT)
Mt 20:26 whoever *w* to become great
Mk 8:35 For whoever *w* to save his life will
Ro 9:18 he hardens whom he *w* to harden.
1Ti 2: 4 who *w* all men to be saved

WAR (WARS)
Isa 2: 4 nor will they train for *w* anymore.
Da 9:26 *W* will continue until the end,
2Co 10: 3 we do not wage *w* as the world does
Rev 19:11 With justice he judges and makes *w*

WARN (WARNED WARNINGS)
Eze 3:19 But if you do *w* the wicked man
33: 9 if you do *w* the wicked man to turn

WARNED (WARN)
Ps 19:11 By them is your servant *w*;

WARNINGS (WARN)
1Co 10:11 and were written down as *w* for us,

WARS (WAR)
Ps 46: 9 He makes *w* cease to the ends
Mt 24: 6 You will hear of *w* and rumors of *w*,

WASH (WASHED WASHING)
Ps 51: 7 *w* me, and I will be whiter
Jn 13: 5 and began to *w* his disciples' feet,
Ac 22:16 be baptized and *w* your sins away,
Rev 22:14 Blessed are those who *w* their robes

WASHED (WASH)
1Co 6:11 you were *w*, you were sanctified,
Rev 7:14 they have *w* their robes

WASHING (WASH)
Eph 5:26 cleansing her by the *w* with water
Tit 3: 5 us through the *w* of rebirth

WATCH (WATCHES WATCHING WATCHMAN)
Ge 31:49 "May the LORD keep *w*
Jer 31:10 will *w* over his flock like a shepherd
Mt 24:42 "Therefore keep *w*, because you do
26:41 *W* and pray so that you will not fall
Lk 2: 8 keeping *w* over their flocks at night
1Ti 4:16 *W* your life and doctrine closely.

WATCHES (WATCH)
Ps 1: 6 For the LORD *w* over the way
121: 3 he who *w* over you will not slumber

WATCHING (WATCH)
Lk 12:37 whose master finds them *w*

WATCHMAN (WATCH)
Eze 3:17 I have made you a *w* for the house

WATER (WATERED WATERS)
Ps 1: 3 like a tree planted by streams of *w*,
22:14 I am poured out like *w*,
Pr 25:21 if he is thirsty, give him *w* to drink.
Isa 49:10 and lead them beside springs of *w*.
Jer 2:13 broken cisterns that cannot hold *w*.
Zec 14: 8 On that day living *w* will flow out
Mk 9:41 anyone who gives you a cup of *w*
Jn 4:10 he would have given you living *w*."
7:38 streams of living *w* will flow
Eph 5:26 washing with *w* through the word,
1Pe 3:21 this *w* symbolizes baptism that now
Rev 21: 6 cost from the spring of the *w* of life.

WATERED (WATER)
1Co 3: 6 I planted the seed, Apollos *w* it,

WATERS (WATER)
Ps 23: 2 he leads me beside quiet *w*,
Ecc 11: 1 Cast your bread upon the *w*,
Isa 58:11 like a spring whose *w* never fail.
1Co 3: 7 plants nor he who *w* is anything,

WAVE (WAVES)
Jas 1: 6 he who doubts is like a *w* of the sea,

WAVES (WAVE)
Isa 57:20 whose *w* cast up mire and mud.
Mt 8:27 Even the winds and the *w* obey him
Eph 4:14 tossed back and forth by the *w*,

WAY (WAYS)
Dt 1:33 to show you the *w* you should go.
2Sa 22:31 "As for God, his *w* is perfect;
Job 23:10 But he knows the *w* that I take;
Ps 1: 1 or stand in the *w* of sinners
37: 5 Commit your *w* to the LORD;
119: 9 can a young man keep his *w* pure?
139:24 See if there is any offensive *w* in me
Pr 14:12 There is a *w* that seems right
16:17 he who guards his *w* guards his life.
22: 6 Train a child in the *w* he should go,
Isa 30:21 saying, "This is the *w*; walk in it."
53: 6 each of us has turned to his own *w*;
55: 7 Let the wicked forsake his *w*
Mt 3: 3 'Prepare the *w* for the Lord,
Jn 14: 6 "I am the *w* and the truth
1Co 10:13 also provide a *w* out so that you can
12:31 will show you the most excellent *w*.
Heb 4:15 who has been tempted in every *w*,
9: 8 was showing by this that the *w*
10:20 and living *w* opened for us

WAYS (WAY)
Ex 33:13 teach me your *w* so I may know
Ps 25:10 All the *w* of the LORD are loving
51:13 I will teach transgressors your *w*,
Pr 3: 6 in all your *w* acknowledge him,
Isa 55: 8 neither are your *w* my *w*,"
Jas 3: 2 We all stumble in many *w*.

WEAK (WEAKER WEAKNESS)
Mt 26:41 spirit is willing, but the body is *w*."
Ro 14: 1 Accept him whose faith is *w*,
1Co 1:27 God chose the *w* things
8: 9 become a stumbling block to the *w*.
9:22 To the *w* I became *w*, to win the *w*.
2Co 12:10 For when I am *w*, then I am strong.
Heb 12:12 your feeble arms and *w* knees.

WEAKER (WEAK)
1Co 12:22 seem to be *w* are indispensable,
1Pe 3: 7 them with respect as the *w* partner

WEAKNESS (WEAK)
Ro 8:26 the Spirit helps us in our *w*.
1Co 1:25 and the *w* of God is stronger
2Co 12: 9 for my power is made perfect in *w*
Heb 5: 2 since he himself is subject to *w*.

WEALTH
Pr 3: 9 Honor the LORD with your *w*,
Mk 10:22 away sad, because he had great *w*.
Lk 15:13 and there squandered his *w*

WEAPONS
2Co 10: 4 The *w* we fight with are not

WEARIES (WEARY)
Ecc 12:12 and much study *w* the body.

WEARY (WEARIES)
Isa 40:31 they will run and not grow *w*,
Mt 11:28 all you who are *w* and burdened,
Gal 6: 9 Let us not become *w* in doing good,

WEDDING
Mt 22:11 who was not wearing *w* clothes.

Rev 19: 7 For the *w* of the Lamb has come,

WEEP (WEEPING WEPT)
Ecc 3: 4 a time to *w* and a time to laugh,
Lk 6: 21 Blessed are you who *w* now,

WEEPING (WEEP)
Ps 30: 5 *w* may remain for a night,
126: 6 He who goes out *w*,
Mt 8: 12 where there will be *w* and gnashing

WELCOMES
Mt 18: 5 whoever *w* a little child like this
2Jn : 11 Anyone who *w* him shares

WELL
Lk 17: 19 your faith has made you *w*."
Jas 5: 15 in faith will make the sick person *w*

WEPT (WEEP)
Ps 137: 1 of Babylon we sat and *w*
Jn 11: 35 Jesus *w*.

WEST
Ps 103: 12 as far as the east is from the *w*,

WHIRLWIND (WIND)
2Ki 2: 1 to take Elijah up to heaven in a *w*,
Hos 8: 7 and reap the *w*.
Na 1: 3 His way is in the *w* and the storm,

WHITE (WHITER)
Isa 1: 18 they shall be as *w* as snow;
Da 7: 9 His clothing was as *w* as snow;
Rev 1: 14 hair were *w* like wool, as *w* as snow,
3: 4 dressed in *w*, for they are worthy.
20: 11 Then I saw a great *w* throne

WHITER (WHITE)
Ps 51: 7 and I will be *w* than snow.

WHOLE
Mt 16: 26 for a man if he gains the *w* world,
24: 14 will be preached in the *w* world
Jn 13: 10 to wash his feet; his *w* body is clean
21: 25 the *w* world would not have room
Ac 20: 27 proclaim to you the *w* will of God.
Ro 3: 19 and the *w* world held accountable
8: 22 know that the *w* creation has been
Gal 3: 22 declares that the *w* world is
5: 3 obligated to obey the *w* law.
Eph 4: 13 attaining to the *w* measure
Jas 2: 10 For whoever keeps the *w* law
1Jn 2: 2 but also for the sins of the *w* world.

WHOLEHEARTEDLY (HEART)
Dt 1: 36 because he followed the LORD *w*
Eph 6: 7 Serve *w*, as if you were serving

WICKED (WICKEDNESS)
Ps 1: 1 walk in the counsel of the *w*
1: 5 Therefore the *w* will not stand
73: 3 when I saw the prosperity of the *w*.
Pr 10: 20 the heart of the *w* is of little value.
11: 21 The *w* will not go unpunished,
Isa 53: 9 He was assigned a grave with the *w*
55: 7 Let the *w* forsake his way
57: 20 But the *w* are like the tossing sea,
Eze 3: 18 that *w* man will die for his sin,
18: 23 pleasure in the death of the *w*?
33: 14 to the *w* man, 'You will surely die,'

WICKEDNESS (WICKED)
Eze 28: 15 created till *w* was found in you.

WIDE
Isa 54: 2 stretch your tent curtains *w*,
Mt 7: 13 For *w* is the gate and broad is
Eph 3: 18 to grasp how *w* and long and high

WIDOW (WIDOWS)
Dt 10: 18 cause of the fatherless and the *w*,
Lk 21: 2 saw a poor *w* put in two very small

WIDOWS (WIDOW)
Jas 1: 27 look after orphans and *w*

WIFE (WIVES)
Ge 2: 24 and mother and be united to his *w*,
24: 67 she became his *w*, and he loved her;
Ex 20: 17 shall not covet your neighbor's *w*,
Dt 5: 21 shall not covet your neighbor's *w*.
Pr 5: 18 in the *w* of your youth.
12: 4 *w* of noble character is her
18: 22 He who finds a *w* finds what is
19: 13 quarrelsome *w* is like a constant
31: 10 *w* of noble character who can find?
Mt 19: 3 for a man to divorce his *w* for any
1Co 7: 2 each man should have his own *w*,
7: 33 how he can please his *w*—
Eph 5: 23 the husband is the head of the *w*
5: 33 must love his *w* as he loves himself,
1Ti 3: 2 husband of but one *w*, temperate,
Rev 21: 9 I will show you the bride, the *w*

WILD
Lk 15: 13 squandered his wealth in *w* living.
Ro 11: 17 and you, though a *w* olive shoot,

WILL (WILLING WILLINGNESS)
Ps 40: 8 I desire to do your *w*, O my God;
143: 10 Teach me to do your *w*,
Isa 53: 10 Yet it was the LORD's *w*
Mt 6: 10 your *w* be done
26: 39 Yet not as I *w*, but as you *w*."
Jn 7: 17 If anyone chooses to do God's *w*,
Ac 20: 27 to you the whole *w* of God.
Ro 12: 2 and approve what God's *w* is—
1Co 7: 37 but has control over his own *w*,
Eph 5: 17 understand what the Lord's *w* is.
Php 2: 13 for it is God who works in you to *w*
1Th 4: 3 God's *w* that you should be
5: 18 for this is God's *w* for you
Heb 9: 16 In the case of a *w*, it is necessary
10: 7 I have come to do your *w*, O God
Jas 4: 15 "If it is the Lord's *w*,
1Jn 5: 14 we ask anything according to his *w*,
Rev 4: 11 and by your *w* they were created

WILLING (WILL)
Ps 51: 12 grant me a *w* spirit, to sustain me.
Da 3: 28 were *w* to give up their lives rather
Mt 18: 14 Father in heaven is not *w* that any
23: 37 her wings, but you were not *w*.
26: 41 The spirit is *w*, but the body is weak

WILLINGNESS (WILL)
2Co 8: 12 For if the *w* is there, the gift is

WIN (WINS)
Php 3: 14 on toward the goal to *w* the prize
1Th 4: 12 your daily life may *w* the respect

WIND (WHIRLWIND)
Jas 1: 6 blown and tossed by the *w*.

WINE
Pr 20: 1 *W* is a mocker and beer a brawler;
Isa 55: 1 Come, buy *w* and milk
Mt 9: 17 Neither do men pour new *w*
Lk 23: 36 They offered him *w* vinegar
Ro 14: 21 not to eat meat or drink *w*
Eph 5: 18 on *w*, which leads to debauchery.

WINESKINS
Mt 9: 17 do men pour new wine into old *w*.

WINGS
Ru 2: 12 under whose *w* you have come
Ps 17: 8 hide me in the shadow of your *w*
Isa 40: 31 They will soar on *w* like eagles;
Mal 4: 2 rise with healing in its *w*.
Lk 13: 34 hen gathers her chicks under her *w*,

WINS (WIN)
Pr 11: 30 and he who *w* souls is wise.

WIPE
Rev 7: 17 God will *w* away every tear

WISDOM (WISE)
1Ki 4: 29 God gave Solomon *w* and very
Ps 111: 10 of the LORD is the beginning of *w*;
Pr 31: 26 She speaks with *w*,
Jer 10: 12 he founded the world by his *w*
Mt 11: 19 But *w* is proved right by her actions
Lk 2: 52 And Jesus grew in *w* and stature,
Ro 11: 33 the depth of the riches of the *w*
Col 2: 3 are hidden all the treasures of *w*
Jas 1: 5 of you lacks *w*, he should ask God,

WISE (WISDOM WISER)
1Ki 3: 12 give you a *w* and discerning heart,
Job 5: 13 He catches the *w* in their craftiness
Ps 19: 7 making *w* the simple.
Pr 3: 7 Do not be *w* in your own eyes;
9: 8 rebuke a *w* man and he will love
10: 1 A *w* son brings joy to his father,
11: 30 and he who wins souls is *w*.
13: 20 He who walks with the *w* grows *w*,
17: 28 Even a fool is thought *w*
Da 12: 3 Those who are *w* will shine like
Mt 11: 25 hidden these things from the *w*
1Co 1: 27 things of the world to shame the *w*;
2Ti 3: 15 able to make you *w* for salvation

WISER (WISE)
1Co 1: 25 of God is *w* than man's wisdom,

WITHER (WITHERS)
Ps 1: 3 and whose leaf does not *w*.

WITHERS (WITHER)
Isa 40: 7 The grass *w* and the flowers fall,
1Pe 1: 24 the grass *w* and the flowers fall,

WITHHOLD
Ps 84: 11 no good thing does he *w*
Pr 23: 13 Do not *w* discipline from a child;

WITNESS (WITNESSES)
Jn 1: 8 he came only as a *w* to the light.

WITNESSES (WITNESS)
Dt 19: 15 by the testimony of two or three *w*.
Ac 1: 8 and you will be my *w* in Jerusalem,

WIVES (WIFE)
Eph 5: 22 *W*, submit to your husbands
5: 25 love your *w*, just as Christ loved
1Pe 3: 1 words by the behavior of their *w*,

WOE
Isa 6: 5 "*W* to me!" I cried.

WOLF
Isa 65:25 *w* and the lamb will feed together,

WOMAN (MAN)
Ge 2:22 God made a *w* from
3:15 between you and the *w*,
Lev 20:13 as one lies with a *w*,
Dt 22:5 *w* must not wear men's
Ru 3:11 a *w* of noble character
Pr 31:30 a *w* who fears the LORD
Mt 5:28 looks at a *w* lustfully
Jn 8:3 a *w* caught in adultery.
Ro 7:2 a married *w* is bound to
1Co 11:3 the head of the *w* is man,
11:13 a *w* to pray to God with
1Ti 2:11 A *w* should learn in

WOMEN (MAN)
Lk 1:42 Blessed are you among *w*,
1Co 14:34 *w* should remain silent in
1Ti 2:9 want *w* to dress modestly
Tit 2:3 teach the older *w* to be
1Pe 3:5 the holy *w* of the past

WOMB
Job 1:21 Naked I came from my mother's *w*,
Jer 1:5 you in the *w* I knew you,
Lk 1:44 the baby in my *w* leaped for joy.

WONDER (WONDERFUL WONDERS)
Ps 17:7 Show the *w* of your great love,

WONDERFUL (WONDER)
Job 42:3 things too *w* for me to know.
Ps 31:21 for he showed his *w* love to me
119:18 *w* things in your law.
119:129 Your statutes are *w*;
139:6 Such knowledge is too *w* for me,
Isa 9:6 *W* Counselor, Mighty God,
1Pe 2:9 out of darkness into his *w* light.

WONDERS (WONDER)
Job 37:14 stop and consider God's *w*.
Ps 119:27 then I will meditate on your *w*.
Joel 2:30 I will show *w* in the heavens
Ac 2:19 I will show *w* in the heaven above

WOOD
Isa 44:19 Shall I bow down to a block of *w*?"
1Co 3:12 costly stones, *w*, hay or straw,

WORD (WORDS)
Dt 8:3 but on every *w* that comes
2Sa 22:31 the *w* of the LORD is flawless.
Ps 119:9 By living according to your *w*.
119:11 I have hidden your *w* in my heart
119:105 Your *w* is a lamp to my feet
Pr 12:25 but a kind *w* cheers him up.
25:11 A *w* aptly spoken
30:5 "Every *w* of God is flawless;
Isa 55:11 so is my *w* that goes out
Jn 1:1 was the *W*, and the *W* was
1:14 The *W* became flesh and made his
2Co 2:17 we do not peddle the *w* of God
4:2 nor do we distort the *w* of God.
Eph 6:17 of the Spirit, which is the *w* of God.
Php 2:16 as you hold out the *w* of life—
Col 3:16 Let the *w* of Christ dwell
2Ti 2:15 and who correctly handles the *w*
Heb 4:12 For the *w* of God is living
Jas 1:22 Do not merely listen to the *w*,
2Pe 1:19 And we have the *w* of the prophets

WORDS (WORD)
Dt 11:18 Fix these *w* of mine in your hearts
Ps 119:103 How sweet are your *w* to my taste
119:130 The unfolding of your *w* gives light;
Ps 119:160 All your *w* are true;
Pr 30:6 Do not add to his *w*,
Jer 15:16 When your *w* came, I ate them;
Mt 24:35 but my *w* will never pass away.
Jn 6:68 You have the *w* of eternal life.
15:7 in me and my *w* remain in you,
1Co 14:19 rather speak five intelligible *w*
Rev 22:19 And if anyone takes *w* away

WORK (WORKER WORKERS WORKING WORKMAN WORKMANSHIP WORKS)
Ex 23:12 "Six days do your *w*,
Nu 8:11 ready to do the *w* of the LORD.
Dt 5:14 On it you shall not do any *w*,
Ecc 5:19 his lot and be happy in his *w*—
Jer 48:10 lax in doing the LORD's *w*!
Jn 6:27 Do not *w* for food that spoils,
9:4 we must do the *w* of him who sent
1Co 3:13 test the quality of each man's *w*.
Php 1:6 that he who began a good *w*
2:12 continue to *w* out your salvation
Col 3:23 Whatever you do, *w* at it
1Th 5:12 to respect those who *w* hard
2Th 3:10 If a man will not *w*, he shall not eat
2Ti 3:17 equipped for every good *w*.
Heb 6:10 he will not forget your *w*

WORKER (WORK)
Lk 10:7 for the *w* deserves his wages.
1Ti 5:18 and "The *w* deserves his wages."

WORKERS (WORK)
Mt 9:37 is plentiful but the *w* are few.
1Co 3:9 For we are God's fellow *w*;

WORKING (WORK)
Col 3:23 as *w* for the Lord, not for men,

WORKMAN (WORK)
2Ti 2:15 a *w* who does not need

WORKMANSHIP* (WORK)
Eph 2:10 For we are God's *w*, created

WORKS (WORK)
Pr 31:31 let her *w* bring her praise
Ro 8:28 in all things God *w* for the good
Eph 2:9 not by *w*, so that no one can boast.
4:12 to prepare God's people for *w*

WORLD (WORLDLY)
Ps 50:12 for the *w* is mine, and all that is in it
Isa 13:11 I will punish the *w* for its evil,
Mt 5:14 "You are the light of the *w*.
16:26 for a man if he gains the whole *w*,
Mk 16:15 into all the *w* and preach the good
Jn 1:29 who takes away the sin of the *w*!
3:16 so loved the *w* that he gave his one
8:12 he said, "I am the light of the *w*.
15:19 As it is, you do not belong to the *w*,
16:33 In this *w* you will have trouble.
18:36 "My kingdom is not of this *w*.
Ro 3:19 and the whole *w* held accountable
1Co 3:19 the wisdom of this *w* is foolishness
2Co 5:19 that God was reconciling the *w*
10:3 For though we live in the *w*,
1Ti 6:7 For we brought nothing into the *w*,
1Jn 2:2 but also for the sins of the whole *w*.
2:15 not love the *w* or anything in the *w*.
Rev 13:8 slain from the creation of the *w*.

WORLDLY (WORLD)
Tit 2:12 to ungodliness and *w* passions,

WORM
Mk 9:48 " 'their *w* does not die,

WORRY (WORRYING)
Mt 6:25 I tell you, do not *w* about your life,
10:19 do not *w* about what to say

WORRYING (WORRY)
Mt 6:27 of you by *w* can add a single hour

WORSHIP
1Ch 16:29 *w* the LORD in the splendor
Ps 95:6 Come, let us bow down in *w*,
Mt 2:2 and have come to *w* him."
Jn 4:24 and his worshipers must *w* in spirit
Ro 12:1 this is your spiritual act of *w*.

WORTH (WORTHY)
Job 28:13 Man does not comprehend its *w*;
Pr 31:10 She is *w* far more than rubies.
Mt 10:31 are *w* more than many sparrows.
Ro 8:18 sufferings are not *w* comparing
1Pe 1:7 of greater *w* than gold,
3:4 which is of great *w* in God's sight.

WORTHLESS
Pr 11:4 Wealth is *w* in the day of wrath,
Jas 1:26 himself and his religion is *w*.

WORTHY (WORTH)
1Ch 16:25 For great is the LORD and most *w*
Eph 4:1 to live a life *w* of the calling you
Php 1:27 in a manner *w* of the gospel
3Jn :6 on their way in a manner *w* of God.
Rev 5:2 "Who is *w* to break the seals

WOUNDS
Pr 27:6 *W* from a friend can be trusted,
Isa 53:5 and by his *w* we are healed.
Zec 13:6 'What are these *w* on your body?'
1Pe 2:24 by his *w* you have been healed.

WRATH
2Ch 36:16 scoffed at his prophets until the *w*
Ps 2:5 and terrifies them in his *w*, saying,
76:10 Surely your *w* against men brings
Pr 15:1 A gentle answer turns away *w*,
Jer 25:15 filled with the wine of my *w*
Ro 1:18 The *w* of God is being revealed
5:9 saved from God's *w* through him!
1Th 5:9 God did not appoint us to suffer *w*
Rev 6:16 and from the *w* of the Lamb!

WRESTLED
Ge 32:24 and a man *w* with him till daybreak

WRITE (WRITING WRITTEN)
Dt 6:9 *W* them on the doorframes
Pr 7:3 *w* them on the tablet of your heart.
Heb 8:10 and *w* them on their hearts.

WRITING (WRITE)
1Co 14:37 him acknowledge that what I am *w*

WRITTEN (WRITE)
Jos 1:8 careful to do everything *w* in it.
Da 12:1 everyone whose name is found *w*
Lk 10:20 but rejoice that your names are *w*
Jn 20:31 these are *w* that you may believe
1Co 4:6 "Do not go beyond what is *w*."
2Co 3:3 *w* not with ink but with the Spirit
Col 2:14 having canceled the *w* code,
Heb 12:23 whose names are *w* in heaven.

WRONG (WRONGDOING WRONGED WRONGS)
Ex 23: 2 Do not follow the crowd in doing *w*
Nu 5: 7 must make full restitution for his *w*,
Job 34:12 unthinkable that God would do *w*,
1Th 5:15 that nobody pays back *w* for *w*,

WRONGDOING (WRONG)
Job 1:22 sin by charging God with *w*.

WRONGED (WRONG)
1Co 6: 7 not rather be *w*? Why not rather

WRONGS (WRONG)
Pr 10:12 but love covers over all *w*.
1Co 13: 5 angered, it keeps no record of *w*.

YEARS
Ps 90: 4 For a thousand *y* in your sight
90:10 The length of our days is seventy *y*
2Pe 3: 8 the Lord a day is like a thousand *y*,
Rev 20: 2 and bound him for a thousand *y*.

YESTERDAY
Heb 13: 8 Jesus Christ is the same *y*

YOKE (YOKED)
Mt 11:29 Take my *y* upon you and learn

YOKED (YOKE)
2Co 6:14 Do not be *y* together

YOUNG (YOUTH)
Ps 119: 9 How can a *y* man keep his way
1Ti 4:12 down on you because you are *y*,

YOUTH (YOUNG)
Ps 103: 5 so that your *y* is renewed like
Ecc 12: 1 Creator in the days of your *y*,
2Ti 2:22 Flee the evil desires of *y*,

ZEAL
Pr 19: 2 to have *z* without knowledge,
Ro 12:11 Never be lacking in *z*,

ZECHARIAH
1. Son of Jeroboam II; king of Israel (2Ki 15:8-12).
2. Post-exilic prophet who encouraged rebuilding of temple (Ezr 5:1; 6:14; Zec 1:1).
3. Father of John the Baptist (Lk 1:13; 3:2).

ZEDEKIAH
Mattaniah, son of Josiah (1Ch 3:15), made king of Judah by Nebuchadnezzar (2Ki 24:17-25:7; 2Ch 36:10-14; Jer 37-39; 52:1-11).

ZERUBBABEL
Descendant of David (1Ch 3:19; Mt 1:3). Led return from exile (Ezr 2-3; Ne 7:7; Hag 1-2; Zec 4).

ZIMRI
King of Israel (1Ki 16:9-20).

ZION
Ps 137: 3 "Sing us one of the songs of *Z*!"
Jer 50: 5 They will ask the way to *Z*
Ro 9:33 I lay in *Z* a stone that causes men
11:26 "The deliverer will come from *Z*;

Acknowledgments for Permissions

12 Sheila Walsh, *Gifts for Your Soul,* Zondervan, © 1997, p. 36. Used by permission.

14 Patsy Clairmont, Barbara Johnson, Marilyn Meberg, Luci Swindoll, Sheila Walsh, Thelma Wells, *Outrageous Joy*, Zondervan, ©1999, p. 66. Used by permission.

18 Marilyn Meberg, *I'd Rather Be Laughing,* Word Publishing, © 1998, pp. 55,57. Used by permission.

31 Emily Brontë, from "Last Lines" in *12,000 Religious Quotations*, compiled by Frank S. Mead, Baker Book House, ©1989, p. 415.

33 Patsy Clairmont, Barbara Johnson, Marilyn Meberg, Luci Swindoll, *Joy Breaks*, Zondervan, © 1997, p. 273. Used by permission.

44 Teresa of Avila, *Interior Castle,* 1577, Wheaton Christian Classics Ethereal Library, www.ccel.org.

46 Sarah Fuller Flower Adams, "Nearer My God to Thee," http://tch.simplenet.com.

60 Nicole Johnson, *Fresh-Brewed Life*, Nelson Publishing House, © 1999, p.9. Used by permission.

74 Marilyn Meberg, *I'd Rather Be Laughing,* Word Publishing, © 1998, p. 54. Used by permission.

79 Luci Swindoll, *You Bring the Confetti, God Brings the Joy,* Word, © 1986, p. 101. Used by permission.

81 Annie Sherwood Hawks, "I Need Thee Every Hour," http://tch.simplenet.com/.

84 Patsy Clairmont, Barbara Johnson, Marilyn Meberg, Luci Swindoll, *Joy Breaks*, Zondervan, © 1997, pp. 28–29. Used by permission.

97 Dinah Maria Mulock Craik, in *12,000 Religious Quotations*, compiled by Frank S. Mead, Baker Book House, ©1989, p. 2.

110 Thelma Wells, *God Will Make a Way*, Nelson, © 1998, p. 80. Used by permission.

Madame Guyon, *The French of Madame de la Mothe Guion,* Wheaton Christian Classics Ethereal Library, www.ccel.org.

132 Catherine of Siena, *Dialog of St. Catherine of Siena*, 1370, Wheaton Christian Classics Ethereal Library, www.ccel.org.

151 Barbara Johnson, *Boomerang Joy,* Zondervan, © 1998. p. 143. Used by permission.

153 Sheila Walsh, *Life Is Tough but God Is Faithful*, Nelson, © 1999, p.22. Used by permission.

154 Patsy Clairmont, Barbara Johnson, Marilyn Meberg, Luci Swindoll, *Joy Breaks*, Zondervan, © 1997, p. 268. Used by permission.

160 Kathy Troccoli, *My Life Is in Your Hands,* Zondervan, © 1997, p. 139. Used by permission.

167 Christina Georgina Rossetti, in *12,000 Religious Quotations*, compiled by Frank S. Mead, Baker Book House, ©1989, p. 440.

168 Patsy Clairmont, Barbara Johnson, Marilyn Meberg, Luci Swindoll, *Joy Breaks*, Zondervan, © 1997, p. 15. Used by permission.

171 Luci Swindoll, *You Bring the Confetti, God Brings the Joy,* Word, © 1986, p. 147. Used by permission.

177 Harriet Beecher Stowe, in *12,000 Religious Quotations*, compiled by Frank S. Mead, Baker Book House, ©1989, p. 414.

190 Luci Swindoll, *Wide My World, Narrow My Bed,* Multnomah Press, ©1982, p. 82. Used by permission.

Teresa of Avila, in *12,000 Religious Quotations*, compiled by Frank S. Mead, Baker Book House, ©1989, p. 409.

198 Dickinson, Emily, *Poems,* 1896, http://www.bartleby.com/.

206 Catherine of Siena, *Dialog of St. Catherine of Siena*, 1370, Wheaton Christian Classics Ethereal Library, www.ccel.org.

210 Teresa of Avila, *Interior Castle,* 1577, Wheaton Christian Classics Ethereal Library, www.ccel.org.

218 Madame Guyon, *The French of Madame de la Mothe Guion,* Wheaton Christian Classics Ethereal Library, www.ccel.org.

219 Emily Brontë, from "Last Lines" in *12,000 Religious Quotations*, compiled by Frank S. Mead, Baker Book House, ©1989, p. 415.

233 Luci Swindoll, *You Bring the Confetti, God Brings the Joy,* Word, © 1986, p. 101. Used by permission.

249 Catherine of Siena, *Dialog of St. Catherine of Siena*, 1370, Wheaton Christian Classics Ethereal Library, www.ccel.org.

256 Teresa of Avila, *Interior Castle,* 1577, Wheaton Christian Classics Ethereal Library, www.ccel.org.

257 Catherine of Genoa, from Christian Quote of the Day, http://www.gospelcom.net/cqod.

258 Hannah Whitall Smith, *The Christian's Secret of a Happy Life*, Wheaton Christian Classics Ethereal Library, www.ccel.org.

262 Lady Jane Grey, http://ladyjane.iinet.net.au/execution.html.

278 Barbara Johnson, *Fresh Elastic for Stretched Out Moms*, Fleming H. Revell, © 1986, p. 36. Used by permission.

282 Catherine of Siena, *Dialog of St. Catherine of Siena*, 1370, Wheaton Christian Classics Ethereal Library, www.ccel.org.

284 Madame Guyon, *The French of Madame de la Mothe Guion*, Wheaton Christian Classics Ethereal Library, www.ccel.org.

290 Mary Wortley Montagu, from "Letter to the Countess of Bute" in *12,000 Religious Quotations*, compiled by Frank S. Mead, Baker Book House, ©1989, p. 371.

298 Mary Elizabeth Coleridge, from Christian Quote of the Day, http://www.gospelcom.net/cqod.

306 Nicole Johnson, *Fresh-Brewed Life*, Nelson Publishing House, © 1999, pp. 2–4. Used by permission.

312 Edna St. Vincent Millay, *Renascence and Other Poems*, 1917, http://www.bartleby.com/.

324 Patsy Clairmont, Barbara Johnson, Marilyn Meberg, Luci Swindoll, Sheila Walsh, Thelma Wells, *Outrageous Joy*, Zondervan, ©1999, pp. 27–28. Used by permission.

328 Nicole Johnson, *Fresh-Brewed Life*, Nelson Publishing House, © 1999, p.xiii. Used by permission.

340 Phoebe Cary, from "A Legend of the Northland" in *12,000 Religious Quotations*, compiled by Frank S. Mead, Baker Book House, ©1989, p.160.

344 Mary Gardiner Brainard, from "Not Knowing" in *12,000 Religious Quotations*, compiled by Frank S. Mead, Baker Book House, ©1989, p.167.

353 Kathy Troccoli, *My Life Is in Your Hands*, Zondervan, © 1997, p. 183. Used by permission.

362 Elizabeth Barrett Browning, from "Rhyme of the Duchess May" in *12,000 Religious Quotations*, compiled by Frank S. Mead, Baker Book House, ©1989, p.205

367 Nicole Johnson, *Fresh-Brewed Life*, Nelson Publishing House, © 1999, pp. 2–4. Used by permission.

377 Catherine of Siena, *Dialog of St. Catherine of Siena*, 1370, Wheaton Christian Classics Ethereal Library, www.ccel.org.

380 Mary Artemesia Lathbury, "Day Is Dying in the West," http://tch.simplenet.com/.

388 Anna Laetitia Barbauld, "Life," http://www.bibliomania.com/.

389 Thelma Wells, *God Will Make a Way*, Nelson, © 1998, p. 18. Used by permission.

392 Patsy Clairmont, Barbara Johnson, Marilyn Meberg, Luci Swindoll, *Joy Breaks*, Zondervan, © 1997, p. 93. Used by permission.

409 Madame Guyon, *The French of Madame de la Mothe Guion*, Wheaton Christian Classics Ethereal Library, www.ccel.org.

416 Louisa May Alcott, "A Little Kingdom I Possess," http://tch.simplenet.com.

417 Patsy Clairmont, *Under His Wings*, Tyndale, © 1994, p. 25. Used by permission.

428 Catherine of Siena, *Dialog of St. Catherine of Siena*, 1370, Wheaton Christian Classics Ethereal Library, www.ccel.org.

440 Nicole Johnson, *Fresh-Brewed Life*, Nelson Publishing House, © 1999, pp. 24. Used by permission.

448 Mary Wortley Montagu, from "Letter to the Countess of Bute" in *12,000 Religious Quotations*, compiled by Frank S. Mead, Baker Book House, ©1989, p. 371.

452 Mary Gardiner Brainard, from "Not Knowing" in *12,000 Religious Quotations*, compiled by Frank S. Mead, Baker Book House, ©1989, p. 446

468 Hannah More, from "Reflections of King Hezekiah" in *12,000 Religious Quotations*, compiled by Frank S. Mead, Baker Book House, ©1989, p. 420.

486 Teresa of Avila, *Interior Castle*, 1577, Wheaton Christian Classics Ethereal Library, www.ccel.org.

495 Thelma Wells, *What's Going On, Lord?* Nelson Publishing House, © 1999, pp.5–6. Used by permission.

503 Barbara Johnson, *Fresh Elastic for Stretched Out Moms*, Fleming H. Revell, © 1986, p. 185. Used by permission.

506 Thelma Wells, *God Will Make a Way*, Nelson, © 1998, p. 124. Used by permission.

511 Christina Georgina Rossetti, "None Other Land," http://tch.simplenet.com..

514 Catherine of Siena, *Dialog of St. Catherine of Siena*, 1370, Wheaton Christian Classics Ethereal Library, www.ccel.org.

522 Madame Guyon, *The French of Madame de la Mothe Guion*, Wheaton Christian Classics Ethereal Library, www.ccel.org.

537 Patsy Clairmont, Barbara Johnson, Marilyn Meberg, Luci Swindoll, Sheila Walsh, Thelma Wells, *We Brake for Joy!* Zondervan, © 1998, p. 76. Used by permission.

542 Elizabeth Barrett Browning, from "The Cry of the Human" in *12,000 Religious Quotations*, compiled by Frank S. Mead, Baker Book House, ©1989, p. 456.

550 Patsy Clairmont, Barbara Johnson, Marilyn Meberg, Luci Swindoll, *Joy Breaks*, Zondervan, © 1997, p. 116–117. Used by permission.

555 Luci Swindoll, *Wide My World, Narrow My Bed*, Multnomah Press, ©1982, p. 119. Used by permission.

564 Mary Frances Butts, from "Trust" in *12,000 Religious Quotations*, compiled by Frank S. Mead, Baker Book House, ©1989, p. 448.

573 Catherine of Siena, *Dialog of St. Catherine of Siena*, 1370, Wheaton Christian Classics Ethereal Library, www.ccel.org.

589 Patsy Clairmont, Barbara Johnson, Marilyn Meberg, Luci Swindoll, *Joy Breaks*, Zondervan, © 1997, p. 220. Used by permission.

596 Kathy Troccoli, *My Life Is in Your Hands*, Zondervan, © 1997, p. 144. Used by permission.

609 Patsy Clairmont, Barbara Johnson, Marilyn Meberg, Luci Swindoll, *Joy Breaks*, Zondervan, © 1997, p. 239. Used by permission.

610 Catherine of Genoa, *The Life and Dialog of St. Catherine of Genoa*, Wheaton Christian Classics Ethereal Library, www.ccel.org.

614 Hannah Whitall Smith, *The Christian's Secret of a Happy Life*, Wheaton Christian Classics Ethereal Library, www.ccel.org.

626 Luci Swindoll, *Wide My World, Narrow My Bed*, Multnomah Press, ©1982, p. 123. Used by permission.

627 Catherine of Siena, *Dialog of St. Catherine of Siena*, 1370, Wheaton Christian Classics Ethereal Library, www.ccel.org.

630 Patsy Clairmont, Barbara Johnson, Marilyn Meberg, Luci Swindoll, *Joy Breaks*, Zondervan, © 1997, p. 271. Used by permission.

633 Catherine of Genoa, *The Life and Dialog of St. Catherine of Genoa*, Wheaton Christian Classics Ethereal Library, www.ccel.org.

635 Madame Guyon, *The French of Madame de la Mothe Guion*, Wheaton Christian Classics Ethereal Library, www.ccel.org.

638 Sheila Walsh, *Honestly*, Zondervan, © 1996, p. 80. Used by permission.

643 Madame Guyon, *The French of Madame de la Mothe Guion*, Wheaton Christian Classics Ethereal Library, www.ccel.org.

652 Hannah Whitall Smith, *The Christian's Secret of a Happy Life*, Wheaton Christian Classics Ethereal Library, www.ccel.org.

654 Felicia Dorothea Hemans, "Dirge," http://www.bibliomania.com/.

658 Teresa of Avila, *Interior Castle*, 1577, Wheaton Christian Classics Ethereal Library, www.ccel.org.

662 Lucy Larcom, "Draw Thou My Soul, O Christ," http://tch.simplenet.com/.

664 Dinah Maria Mulock Craik, "A Lacashire Doxology," http://prod.library.utoronto.ca.

666 Maria McIntosh, in *12,000 Religious Quotations*, compiled by Frank S. Mead, Baker Book House, ©1989, p.10.

668 Sarah Fuller Flower Adams, from "He Sendeth Sun, He Sendeth Shower" in *12,000 Religious Quotations*, compiled by Frank S. Mead, Baker Book House, ©1989, p.164.

682 Nicole Johnson, *Fresh-Brewed Life*, Nelson Publishing House, © 1999, pp. 60. Used by permission.

692 Elizabeth Barrett Browning, from "Aurora Leigh" in *12,000 Religious Quotations*, compiled by Frank S. Mead, Baker Book House, ©1989, p.167.

693 Alice Cary, in *12,000 Religious Quotations*, compiled by Frank S. Mead, Baker Book House, ©1989, p. 208.

707 Dorothy Frances Gurney, from "God's Garden" in *12,000 Religious Quotations*, compiled by Frank S. Mead, Baker Book House, ©1989, p. 212

714 Kathy Troccoli, *My Life Is in Your Hands*, Zondervan, © 1997, p. 113. Used by permission.

717 Barbara Johnson, *Fresh Elastic for Stretched Out Moms*, Fleming H. Revell, © 1986, pp. 44–45. Used by permission.

722 Luci Swindoll, *Wide My World, Narrow My Bed*, Multnomah Press, ©1982, p. 56. Used by permission.

725 Madame Anne Germaine de Staël, in *12,000 Religious Quotations*, compiled by Frank S. Mead, Baker Book House, ©1989, p. 254.

730 Luci Swindoll, *Wide My World, Narrow My Bed*, Multnomah Press, ©1982, pp. 70–71. Used by permission.

741 Patsy Clairmont, *Under His Wings*, Tyndale, © 1994, p. 109. Used by permission.

747 Patsy Clairmont, Barbara Johnson, Marilyn Meberg, Luci Swindoll, Sheila Walsh, Thelma Wells, *Outrageous Joy*, Zondervan, © 1999, pp. 152. Used by permission.

750 Patsy Clairmont, Barbara Johnson, Marilyn Meberg, Luci Swindoll, *Joy Breaks*, Zondervan, © 1997, p. 8. Used by permission.

768 Patsy Clairmont, Barbara Johnson, Marilyn Meberg, Luci Swindoll, Sheila Walsh, Thelma Wells, *We Brake for Joy!* Zondervan, © 1998, pp. 71, 73. Used by permission.

775 Patsy Clairmont, Barbara Johnson, Marilyn Meberg, Luci Swindoll, Sheila Walsh, Thelma Wells, *We Brake for Joy!* Zondervan, © 1998, pp. 71, 73. Used by permission.

779 Adelaide Ann Procter, from "Friend Sorrow" in *12,000 Religious Quotations*, compiled by Frank S. Mead, Baker Book House, ©1989, p. 414.

792 Marilyn Meberg, *I'd Rather Be Laughing*, Word Publishing, © 1998, pp. 146–147. Used by permission.

811 Teresa of Avila, *Interior Castle*, 1577, Wheaton Christian Classics Ethereal Library, www.ccel.org.

778 Sheila Walsh, *Gifts for Your Soul,* Zondervan, © 1997, p. 182. Used by permission.

816 Marilyn Meberg, *I'd Rather Be Laughing,* Word Publishing, © 1998, p. 11. Used by permission.

825 Julia Harriet Johnson, "Marvelous Grace," http://tch.simplenet.com/.

833 Sheila Walsh, *Gifts for Your Soul,* Zondervan, © 1997, p. 63. Used by permission.

839 Barbara Johnson, *I'm So Glad You Told Me What I Didn't Wanna Hear,* Word, © 1996, p. 38. Used by permission.

842 Sheila Walsh, *Life Is Tough but God Is Faithful,* Nelson, © 1999, pp. 56–57. Used by permission.

844 Sheila Walsh, *Gifts for Your Soul,* Zondervan, © 1997, pp. 48–49. Used by permission.

845 Sheila Walsh, *Honestly,* Zondervan, © 1996, pp. 114–115. Used by permission.

846 Anne Bradstreet, "By Night When Others Soundly Slept," http://www.emule.com/.

869 Marilyn Meberg, *Choosing the Amusing,* Word Publishing, © 1999, pp. 34–35. Used by permission.

871 Sheila Walsh, *Gifts for Your Soul,* Zondervan, © 1997, p. 149. Used by permission.

875 Frances Whitmarsh Wile, "All the Beautiful March of the Days," http://tch.simplenet.com/.

880 Patsy Clairmont, Barbara Johnson, Marilyn Meberg, Luci Swindoll, *Joy Breaks,* Zondervan, © 1997, p. 22. Used by permission.

884 Sheila Walsh, *Gifts for Your Soul,* Zondervan, © 1997, p. 176. Used by permission.

895 Thelma Wells, *God Will Make a Way,* Nelson, © 1998, p. 10. Used by permission.

902 Clara Tear Williams, "Satisfied," http://tch.simplenet.com/.

903 Adelaide Anne Procter, "I Do Not Ask, O Lord," http://tch.simplenet.com/.

906 Thelma Wells, *What's Going On, Lord?* Nelson Publishing House, © 1999. pp. 53–54. Used by permission.

911 Kathy Troccoli, *My Life Is in Your Hands,* Zondervan, © 1997, p. 129. Used by permission.

915 Luci Swindoll, *You Bring the Confetti, God Brings the Joy,* Word, © 1986, p. 164. Used by permission.

925 Thelma Wells, *God Will Make a Way,* Nelson Publishing House, © 1998, pp. 66–67. Used by permission.

932 Thelma Wells, *What's Going On, Lord?* Nelson Publishing House, © 1999, pp. 15–16. Used by permission.

934 Sheila Walsh, *Honestly,* Zondervan, © 1996, p. 118. Used by permission.

936 Marilyn Meberg, *I'd Rather Be Laughing,* Word Publishing, © 1998, p. 36. Used by permission.

938 Catherine of Siena, *Dialog of St. Catherine of Siena,* 1370, Wheaton Christian Classics Ethereal Library, www.ccel.org.

942 Patsy Clairmont, Barbara Johnson, Marilyn Meberg, Luci Swindoll, *Joy Breaks,* Zondervan, © 1997, p. 17. Used by permission.

947 Barbara Johnson, *I'm So Glad You Told Me What I Didn't Wanna Hear,* Word, © 1996, p. 69. Used by permission.

954 Anne Steele, "Father, Whate'er of Earthly Bliss," http://tch.simplenet.com/.

965 Marilyn Meberg, *Choosing the Amusing,* Word Publishing, © 1999, pp. 91–92. Used by permission.

971 Madame Guyon, *The French of Madame de la Mothe Guion,* Wheaton Christian Classics Ethereal Library, www.ccel.org.

980 Sheila Walsh, *Life Is Tough but God Is Faithful,* Nelson, © 1999, pp. 122–123. Used by permission.

990 Hannah Whitall Smith, *The Christian's Secret of a Happy Life,* Wheaton Christian Classics Ethereal Library, www.ccel.org.

991 Thelma Wells, *God Will Make a Way,* Nelson, © 1998, p. 35. Used by permission.

992 Teresa of Avila, *Interior Castle,* 1577, Wheaton Christian Classics Ethereal Library, www.ccel.org.

1001 Patsy Clairmont, Barbara Johnson, Marilyn Meberg, Luci Swindoll, *Joy Breaks,* Zondervan, © 1997, p. 200. Used by permission.

1005 Sheila Walsh, *Gifts for Your Soul,* Zondervan, © 1997, pp. 51–52. Used by permission.

1021 Patsy Clairmont, Barbara Johnson, Marilyn Meberg, Luci Swindoll, Sheila Walsh, Thelma Wells, *We Brake for Joy!* Zondervan, © 1998, pp. 236–237. Used by permission.

1029 Emily Dickinson, "I Never Saw a Moor," http://www.emule.com/.

1046 Mary Ann Vincent, in *12,000 Religious Quotations,* compiled by Frank S. Mead, Baker Book House, ©1989, p.13.

1048 Patsy Clairmont, Barbara Johnson, Marilyn Meberg, Luci Swindoll, Sheila Walsh, Thelma Wells, *We Brake for Joy!* Zondervan, © 1998, p. 113. Used by permission.

1069 Patsy Clairmont, Barbara Johnson, Marilyn Meberg, Luci Swindoll, Sheila Walsh, Thelma Wells, *Outrageous Joy,* Zondervan, ©1999, pp. 119–120,125–126. Used by permission.

1078 Patsy Clairmont, Barbara Johnson, Marilyn Meberg, Luci Swindoll, *The Joyful Journey,* Zondervan, © 1997, p.199. Used by permission.

1079 Patsy Clairmont, Barbara Johnson, Marilyn Meberg, Luci Swindoll, *Joy Breaks,* Zondervan, © 1997, pp. 189–191. Used by permission.

1081 Marilyn Meberg, *Choosing the Amusing,* Word Publishing, © 1999, pp. 122–123. Used by permission.

1096 Sheila Walsh, *Life Is Tough but God Is Faithful,* Nelson, © 1999, p.38. Used by permission.

1101 Dorothy Gurney, "O Perfect Love," http://tch.simplenet.com/.

1111 Patsy Clairmont, *Under His Wings*, Tyndale, © 1994, pp. 8–9. Used by permission.

1132 Hannah More, in *12,000 Religious Quotations*, compiled by Frank S. Mead, Baker Book House, ©1989, p. 257.

1147 Patsy Clairmont, *Under His Wings*, Tyndale, © 1994, p. 40. Used by permission.

1154 Katharina von Schlege, "Be Still My Soul," http://tch.simplenet.com/.

1156 Marilyn Meberg, *Choosing the Amusing*, Lydia Maria Child, in *12,000 Religious Quotations*, compiled by Frank S. Mead, Baker Book House, ©1989, p. 278.

1160 Barbara Johnson, *Boomerang Joy*, Zondervan, © 1998, p. 35. Used by permission.

1163 Maria Mitchell, in *12,000 Religious Quotations*, compiled by Frank S. Mead, Baker Book House, ©1989, p. 317.

1164 Christina Georgina Rossetti, from "From House to House" in *12,000 Religious Quotations*, compiled by Frank S. Mead, Baker Book House, ©1989, p. 323.

1175 Catherine of Siena, from Christian Quote of the Day, http://www.gospelcom.net/cqod.

1179 Marilyn Meberg, *I'd Rather Be Laughing*, Word Publishing, © 1998, pp. 128–129. Used by permission.

1188 Christina Rossetti, from Christian Quote of the Day, http://www.gospelcom.net/cqod

1191 Patsy Clairmont, Barbara Johnson, Marilyn Meberg, Luci Swindoll, Sheila Walsh, Thelma Wells, *We Brake for Joy!* Zondervan, © 1998, p. 133. Used by permission.

1205 Nicole Johnson, *Fresh-Brewed Life*, Nelson Publishing House, © 1999, pp.58–59. Used by permission.

1215 Patsy Clairmont, Barbara Johnson, Marilyn Meberg, Luci Swindoll, Sheila Walsh, Thelma Wells, *We Brake for Joy!* Zondervan, © 1998, p.114. Used by permission.

1218 Barbara Johnson, *Boomerang Joy*, Zondervan, © 1998, p. 60. Used by permission.

1228 Lady Jane Grey, in *12,000 Religious Quotations*, compiled by Frank S. Mead, Baker Book House, ©1989, p.28.

1236 Sheila Walsh, *Gifts for Your Soul*, Zondervan, © 1997, p. 120. Used by permission.

1251 Elizabeth Barrett Browning, from "Content in Service" in *12,000 Religious Quotations*, compiled by Frank S. Mead, Baker Book House, ©1989, p.87.

1257 Harriet Beecher Stowe, "Abide in Me," http://tch.simplenet.com/.

1262 May Louise Riley Smith, from "Sometime" in *12,000 Religious Quotations*, compiled by Frank S. Mead, Baker Book House, ©1989, p.88.

1274 Barbara Johnson, *Boomerang Joy*, Zondervan, © 1998, p. 67. Used by permission.

1280 Thelma Wells, *God Will Make a Way*, Nelson, © 1998, pp. 40–41. Used by permission.

1301 Patsy Clairmont, Barbara Johnson, Marilyn Meberg, Luci Swindoll, Sheila Walsh, Thelma Wells, *We Brake for Joy!* Zondervan, © 1998, p. 257. Used by permission.

1303 Patsy Clairmont, *Under His Wings*, Tyndale, © 1994, pp. 82–83. Used by permission.

1307 Alice Cary, in *12,000 Religious Quotations*, compiled by Frank S. Mead, Baker Book House, ©1989, p.146.

1313 Hannah More, from "Moses in the Bulrushes" in *12,000 Religious Quotations*, compiled by Frank S. Mead, Baker Book House, ©1989, p. 344.

1315 Barbara Johnson, *Boomerang Joy*, Zondervan, © 1998, p. 192. Used by permission.

1320 Madame Ann Germaine de Staël, from "Corinne" in *12,000 Religious Quotations*, compiled by Frank S. Mead, Baker Book House, ©1989, p.347.

1326 Sheila Walsh, *Honestly*, Zondervan, © 1996, pp. 201–202. Used by permission.

1327 Anna Laetitia Waring, "In Heavenly Love Abiding," http://tch.simplenet.com/.

Barbara Johnson, *I'm So Glad You Told Me What I Didn't Wanna Hear*, Word, © 1996, p. 37. Used by permission.

1345 Kathy Troccoli, *My Life Is in Your Hands*, Zondervan, © 1997, p. 121. Used by permission.

1354 Barbara Johnson, *Boomerang Joy*, Zondervan, © 1998, p. 46. Used by permission.

1361 Kathy Troccoli, *My Life Is in Your Hands*, Zondervan, © 1997, p. 15. Used by permission.

1364 Christina Georgina Rossetti, "Saints and Angels," in *12,000 Religious Quotations*, compiled by Frank S. Mead, Baker Book House, ©1989, p. 252.

1366 Patsy Clairmont, *Normal Is Just a Setting on Your Dryer*, Tyndale, © 1993, p. 118. Used by permission.

1369 Luci Swindoll, *You Bring the Confetti, God Brings the Joy*, Word, © 1986, p. 126. Used by permission.

1374 Thelma Wells, *What's Going On, Lord?* Nelson Publishing House, © 1999, pp. 127–128. Used by permission.

1378 Patsy Clairmont, Barbara Johnson, Marilyn Meberg, Luci Swindoll, Sheila Walsh, Thelma Wells, *We Brake for Joy!* Zondervan, © 1998, pp. 148,150. Used by permission.

1379 Elizabeth Lloyd Howell, "Milton's Prayer of Patience," http://www.bartleby.com/.

1386 Patsy Clairmont, Barbara Johnson, Marilyn Meberg, Luci Swindoll, Sheila Walsh, Thelma Wells, *We Brake for Joy!* Zondervan, © 1998, p. 151. Used by permission.

1389 Nancy Priest Wakefield, "Over the River," http://www.bartleby.com/.

1393 Katharine Tynan Hinkson, "Sheep and Lambs," http://www.bartleby.com/.

1396 Queen Elizabeth I, in *12,000 Religious Quotations*, compiled by Frank S. Mead, Baker Book House, ©1989, p. 443.

1404 Patsy Clairmont, Barbara Johnson, Marilyn Meberg, Luci Swindoll, Sheila Walsh, Thelma Wells, *We Brake for Joy!* Zondervan, © 1998, p. 170. Used by permission.

1409 Patsy Clairmont, Barbara Johnson, Marilyn Meberg, Luci Swindoll, Sheila Walsh, Thelma Wells, *Outrageous Joy*, Zondervan, ©1999, pp. 109–111. Used by permission.

1415 Patsy Clairmont, Barbara Johnson, Marilyn Meberg, Luci Swindoll, Sheila Walsh, Thelma Wells, *Outrageous Joy*, Zondervan, ©1999, pp. 84–85. Used by permission.

1420 Lady Dufferin, "Lament of the Irish Emigrant," http://www.bartleby.com/.

1427 Julia A. Fletcher, "Little Things," http://www.bartleby.com/.

1428 Barbara Johnson, *I'm So Glad You Told Me What I Didn't Wanna Hear,* Word, © 1996, p. 4. Used by permission.

1439 Patsy Clairmont, Barbara Johnson, Marilyn Meberg, Luci Swindoll, Sheila Walsh, Thelma Wells, *Outrageous Joy*, Zondervan, ©1999, pp. 11–12. Used by permission.

1448 Phoebe Hinsdale Brown, "I Love to Steal Away," http://tch.simplenet.com/.

1453 Emily Dickinson, from "Belshazzar Had a Letter" in *12,000 Religious Quotations*, compiled by Frank S. Mead, Baker Book House, ©1989, p. 381.

1454 Hannah More, in *12,000 Religious Quotations*, compiled by Frank S. Mead, Baker Book House, ©1989, p.148.

1461 Patsy Clairmont, Barbara Johnson, Marilyn Meberg, Luci Swindoll, Sheila Walsh, Thelma Wells, *Outrageous Joy*, Zondervan, ©1999, pp. 37–38. Used by permission.

1472 Emma Willard, "Rocked in the Cradle of the Deep," http://www.bartleby.com/.

1473 Hannah Whitall Smith, *The Christian's Secret of a Happy Life,* Wheaton Christian Classics Ethereal Library, www.ccel.org.

1484 Hannah Whitall Smith, *The Christian's Secret of a Happy Life,* Wheaton Christian Classics Ethereal Library, www.ccel.org.

1492 Patsy Clairmont, *Normal Is Just a Setting on Your Dryer*, Tyndale, © 1993, p. 105. Used by permission.

1499 Patsy Clairmont, Barbara Johnson, Marilyn Meberg, Luci Swindoll, Sheila Walsh, Thelma Wells, *We Brake for Joy!* Zondervan, © 1998, p. 225. Used by permission.

1500 Annie Johnson Flint, in *12,000 Religious Quotations*, compiled by Frank S. Mead, Baker Book House, ©1989, p. 439

1502 Patsy Clairmont, Barbara Johnson, Marilyn Meberg, Luci Swindoll, Sheila Walsh, Thelma Wells, *We Brake for Joy!* Zondervan, © 1998, p. 173. Used by permission.

1512 Adelaide Addison Pollard, "Have Thine Own Way," http://tch.simplenet.com/.

1515 Hilda W. Smith, from "The Carpenter of Galilee" in *12,000 Religious Quotations*, compiled by Frank S. Mead, Baker Book House, ©1989, p.58.

1518 Elizabeth Barrett Browning, "Conclusion," http://www.bartleby.com/.

1522 Julia A. Fletcher Carney, "Little Things," http://www.bartleby.com/.

1529 Helen Maria Williams, "Trust in Providence," http://www.bartleby.com/.

1534 Jane Taylor, "For a Very Little Child," http://www.bartleby.com/.

1536 Patsy Clairmont, *Under His Wings*, Tyndale, © 1994, p. 122. Used by permission.

1538 Anna Laetitia Aiken Barbauld, "Praise to God, Immortal Praise," http://tch.simplenet.com/.

1543 Thelma Wells, *What's Going On, Lord?* Nelson Publishing House, © 1999, p. 137. Used by permission.

1562 Jane Taylor, "A Child's Hymn of Praise," http://www.bartleby.com/.

1565 Patsy Clairmont, Barbara Johnson, Marilyn Meberg, Luci Swindoll, *Joy Breaks*, Zondervan, © 1997, p. 177. Used by permission.

1573 Edith Gilling Cherry, from Christian Quote of the day, http://www.gospelcom.net/cqod/.

1581 Anne Brontë, "Music on a Christmas Morning," http://tch.simplenet.com/.

1589 Barbara Johnson, *Boomerang Joy,* Zondervan, © 1998, p. 105. Used by permission.

Cecil Frances Humphreys Alexander, "Jesus Calls Us," http://tch.simplenet.com/.

1603 Kathy Troccoli, *My Life Is in Your Hands,* Zondervan, © 1997, p. 39.

1610 Sheila Walsh, *Honestly*, Zondervan, ©1996, pp. 45,47. Used by permission.

1611 Charlotte Elliot, "Just As I Am," http://tch.simplenet.com/, *My Life and the Story of the Gospel Hymns*, Ira D. Sankey, The Sunday School Times Company, Philadelphia: 1907.

1616 Karolina Wilhelmina Sandell-Berg, "Children of the Heavenly Father," http://tch.simplenet.com/.

1619 Luci Swindoll, *You Bring the Confetti, God Brings the Joy,* Word, © 1986, p. 131. Used by permission.

1625 Fanny Crosby, "I Long to See My Savior Most of All," http://tch.simplenet.com/.

1647 Alice Meynell, from Christian Quote of the Day, http://www.gospelcom.net/cqod.

1661 Marilyn Meberg, *Choosing the Amusing,* Word Publishing, © 1999, pp. 131–132. Used by permission.

1665 Jesse Brown Pounds, "Anywhere With Jesus," http://tch.simplenet.com/.

1679 Patsy Clairmont, Barbara Johnson, Marilyn Meberg, Luci Swindoll, *Joy Breaks*, Zondervan, © 1997, pp. 109–110. Used by permission.

1681 Mary Macdougall Macdonald, "Child in the Manger," http://tch.simplenet.com/.

1684 Patsy Clairmont, Barbara Johnson, Marilyn Meberg, Luci Swindoll, *The Joyful Journey,* Zondervan, © 1997, p.18. Used by permission.

1692 Anna Bartlett Warner, "Jesus Loves Me," http://tch.simplenet.com/.

1695 Marilyn Meberg, *Choosing the Amusing,* Word Publishing, © 1999, pp. 55–56. Used by permission.

1701 Patsy Clairmont, *Under His Wings*, Tyndale, © 1994, p. 101. Used by permission.

1705 Thelma Wells, *What's Going On, Lord?* Nelson Publishing House, © 1999, p. 32. Used by permission.

1711 Civilla Durfee Martin, "His Eye Is on the Sparrow," http://tch.simplenet.com/.

1719 Patsy Clairmont, Barbara Johnson, Marilyn Meberg, Luci Swindoll, Sheila Walsh, Thelma Wells, *Outrageous Joy*, Zondervan, ©1999, pp. 69–71. Used by permission.

1724 Luci Swindoll, *You Bring the Confetti, God Brings the Joy,* Word, © 1986, pp. 142–143. Used by permission.

1732 Edith Gilling Cherry, "We Rest on Thee," http://tch.simplenet.com/.

1735 Barbara Johnson, *Boomerang Joy,* Zondervan, © 1998, p. 21. Used by permission.

1749 Lucy J. Rider, "Ho, Everyone That Is Thirsty," http://tch.simplenet.com/.

1751 Sheila Walsh, *Honestly,* Zondervan, ©1996, pp. 43–44. Used by permission.

1759 Patsy Clairmont, Barbara Johnson, Marilyn Meberg, Luci Swindoll, *The Joyful Journey,* Zondervan, © 1997, p.107. Used by permission.

1760 Sheila Walsh, *Gifts for Your Soul,* Zondervan, © 1997, p.108. Used by permission.

1762 Thelma Wells, *God Will Make a Way*, Nelson, © 1998, p. 68. Used by permission.

1774 Sheila Walsh, *Gifts for Your Soul,* Zondervan, © 1997, pp. 116–117. Used by permission.

1778 Barbara Johnson, *I'm So Glad You Told Me What I Didn't Wanna Hear,* Word, © 1996, p. 4. Used by permission.

1781 Elizabeth Cecelia Douglas Clephane, "Beneath the Cross of Jesus," http://tch.simplenet.com/.

1796 Madame Guyon, *The French of Madame de la Mothe Guion,* Wheaton Christian Classics Ethereal Library, www.ccel.org.

1801 Sheila Walsh, *Gifts for Your Soul,* Zondervan, © 1997, p. 122. Used by permission.

1810 Charlotte Brontë, "The Missionary," http://www.emule.com/.

1829 Elizabeth Payson Prentiss, "More Love to Thee," http://tch.simplenet.com/.

1832 Thelma Wells, *What's Going On, Lord?* Nelson Publishing House, © 1999, p. 97. Used by permission.

1865 Alice Meynell, from Christian Quote of the Day, http://www.gospelcom.net/cqod.

1870 Elvina Hall, "Jesus Paid It All," http://tch.simplenet.com/.

1914 Thelma Wells, *What's Going On, Lord?* Nelson Publishing House, © 1999, p. 90. Used by permission.

1923 Thelma Wells, *God Will Make a Way*, Nelson, © 1998, p. 62. Used by permission.

1945 Madame Guyon, "My Lord, How Full of Sweet Content," http://tch.simplenet.com/.

1959 Sheila Walsh, *Honestly*, Zondervan, © 1996, pp. 174–175. Used by permission.

1985 Sheila Walsh, *Gifts for Your Soul,* Zondervan, © 1997, p. 112. Used by permission.

1996 Barbara Johnson, *Fresh Elastic for Stretched Out Moms,* Fleming H. Revell, © 1986, p. 36. Used by permission.

1997 Patsy Clairmont, Barbara Johnson, Marilyn Meberg, Luci Swindoll, Sheila Walsh, Thelma Wells, *Outrageous Joy*, Zondervan, ©1999, p. 156. Used by permission.

2001 Eliza Edmunds Stites Hewitt, "Once My Way Was Dark and Dreary," http://tch.simplenet.com/.

2009 Elizabeth Barrett Browning, in "Aurora Leigh," in *12,000 Religious Quotations*, compiled by Frank S. Mead, Baker Book House, ©1989, p. 108.

2020 Frances Ridley Havergal, "Take My Life and Let It Be," http://tch.simplenet.com/.

2026 Hannah More, "Dan and Jane," in *12,000 Religious Quotations*, compiled by Frank S. Mead, Baker Book House, ©1989, p. 135.

2038 Patsy Clairmont, Barbara Johnson, Marilyn Meberg, Luci Swindoll, Sheila Walsh, Thelma Wells, *We Brake for Joy!* Zondervan, © 1998, p. 278. Used by permission.

2064 Sheila Walsh, *Honestly,* Zondervan, © 1996, pp. 72–73. Used by permission.

2071 Marilyn Meberg, *I'd Rather Be Laughing,* Word Publishing, © 1998, p. 70. Used by permission.

2072 Leila Naylor Morris, "Sweeter as the Years Go By," http://tch.simplenet.com/.

2088 Barbara Johnson, *Boomerang Joy,* Zondervan, © 1998, p. 181. Used by permission.

Every effort has been made to give proper credit for each quotation used. If any error or inaccuracy is noted, please inform the publishers.

Index to Color Maps

The Index to Color Maps will lead you to place-names found on the color maps in the back of this Bible. References are to the map number and the map margin markings.

NIV Women of Faith Study Bible

Project Management and Editorial: Catherine DeVries, Shari TeSlaa

Editorial Assistance: Natalie Block, Ruth DeJager, Donna Huisjen, Diana Wallis

Theological Review: Michael J. Klassen, M.Div., Fuller Theological Seminary; and Andrew Sloan, M.Div., Oral Roberts University

Interior Proofreading: Peachtree Editorial and Proofreading Service, Peachtree City, GA

Interior Typesetting: Blue Heron Bookcraft, Battle Ground, WA

Interior Design: Sharon Wright, Belmont, MI

Cover Design: Jamie K. DeBruyn

Interior Illustration © Laurie Lafrance / i2i Art

Production Management: Phil Herich

Printing and Binding: R.R. Donnelley and Sons, Inc., Crawfordsville, IN

Literary Agency: Alive Communications, Colorado Springs, CO

Guarantee

Zondervan guarantees leather Bibles unconditionally against manufacturing defects for a lifetime and hardcover, softcover and Leather Look™ Bibles for four years. This guarantee does not apply to normal wear. Contact Zondervan Customer Service, 800-727-1309, for replacement instructions.

Care

We suggest loosening the binding of your new Bible by gently pressing on a small section of pages at a time from the center. To ensure against breakage of the spine, it is best not to bend the cover backward around the spine or to carry study notes, church bulletins, pens, etc., inside the cover. Because a felt-tipped marker will "bleed" through the pages, we recommend use of a ball-point pen or pencil to underline favorite passages. Your Bible should not be exposed to excessive heat, cold, or humidity.

Map 1: **WORLD OF THE PATRIARCHS**

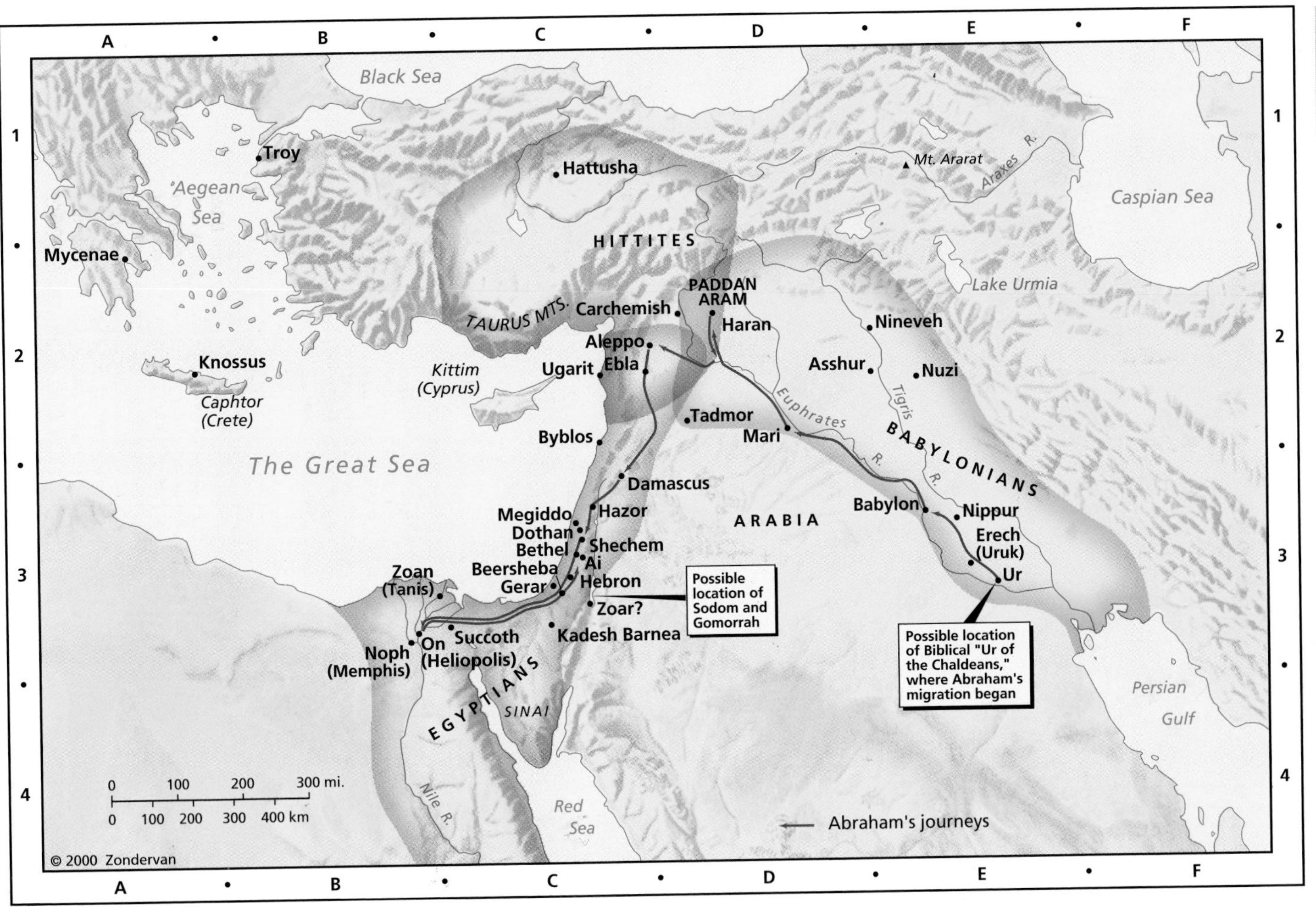

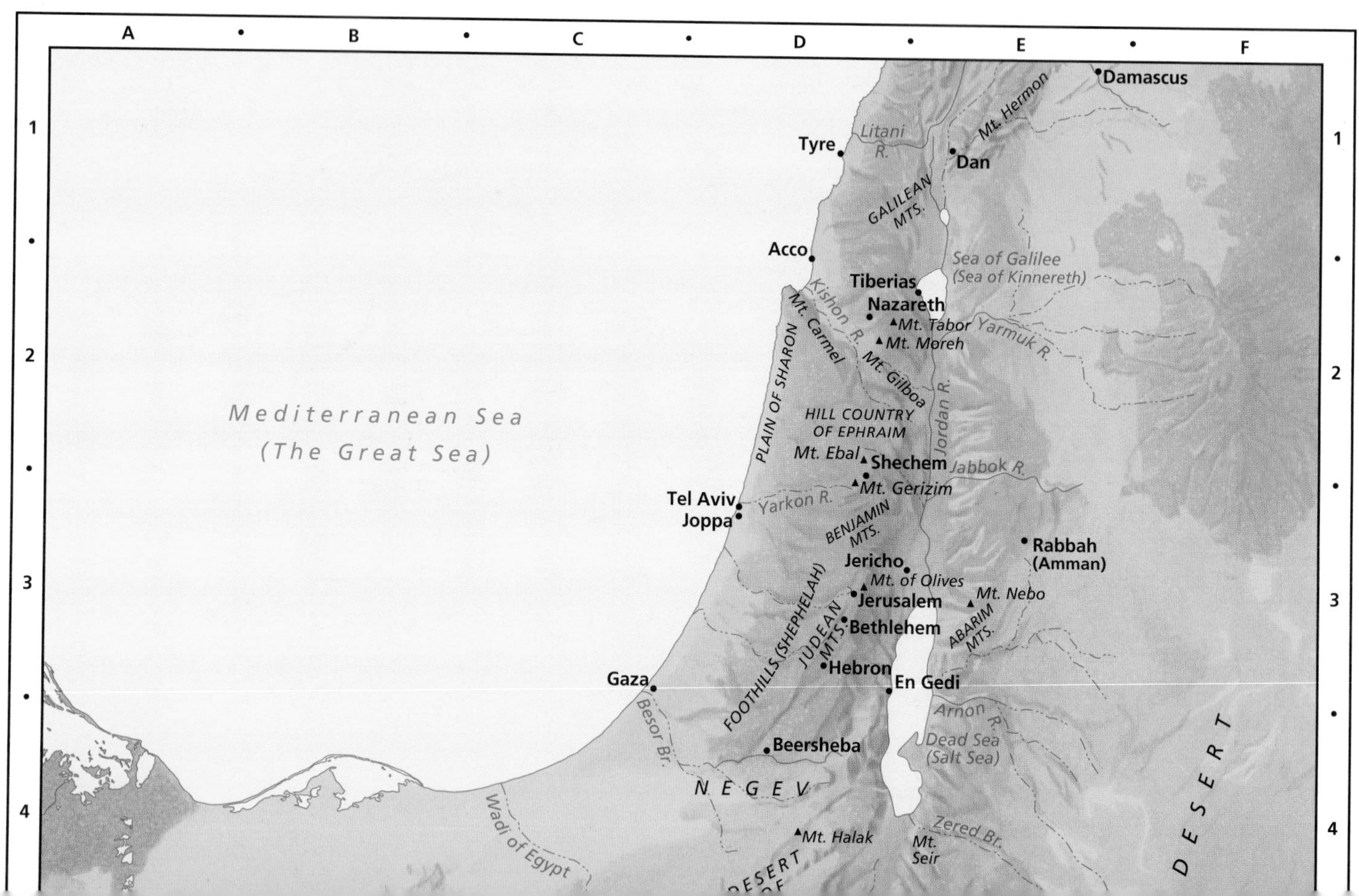

A
B
C
D
E
F
1
2
3
4
Damascus
Mt. Hermon
Tyre
Litani R.
Dan
GALILEAN MTS.
Acco
Sea of Galilee
(Sea of Kinnereth)
Tiberias
Nazareth
Kishon R.
Mt. Carmel
Mt. Tabor
Mt. Moreh
Yarmuk R.
Mt. Gilboa
PLAIN OF SHARON
Mediterranean Sea
(The Great Sea)
HILL COUNTRY
OF EPHRAIM
Jordan R.
Mt. Ebal
Shechem
Jabbok R.
Mt. Gerizim
Tel Aviv
Joppa
Yarkon R.
BENJAMIN
MTS.
Rabbah
(Amman)
Jericho
Mt. of Olives
Jerusalem
Mt. Nebo
FOOTHILLS (SHEPHELAH)
JUDEAN
MTS.
Bethlehem
ABARIM
MTS.
Hebron
En Gedi
Gaza
Besor Br.
Arnon R.
Beersheba
Dead Sea
(Salt Sea)
N E G E V
D E S E R T
Wadi of Egypt
Mt. Halak
Zered Br.
Mt.
Seir

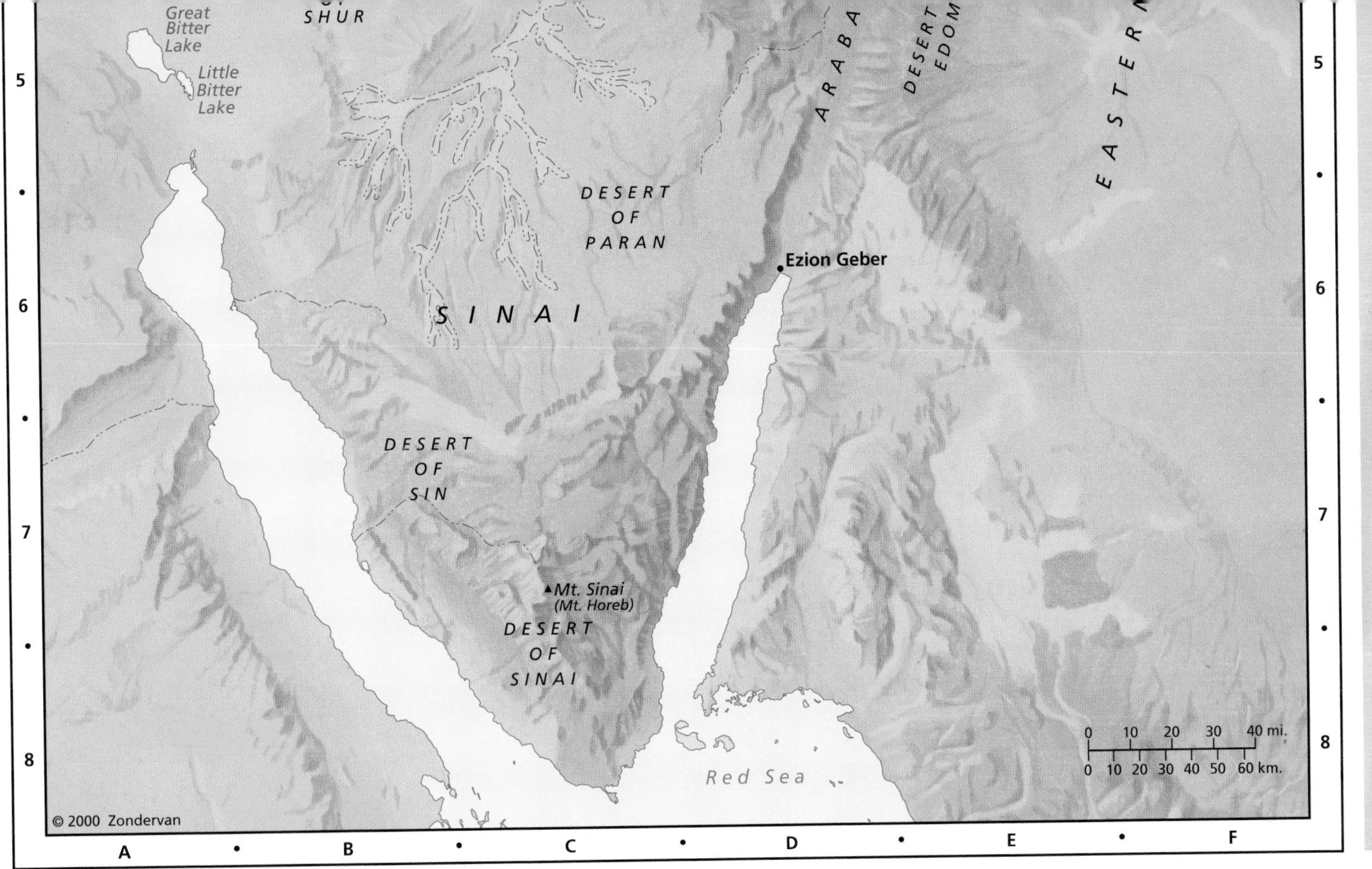

Great Bitter Lake
Little Bitter Lake
SHUR
DESERT OF PARAN
SINAI
Ezion Geber
ARABA
DESERT EDOM
EASTERN
DESERT OF SIN
Mt. Sinai (Mt. Horeb)
DESERT OF SINAI
Red Sea
0 10 20 30 40 mi.
0 10 20 30 40 50 60 km.
A B C D E F
5 6 7 8

Map 3: **EXODUS AND CONQUEST OF CANAAN**

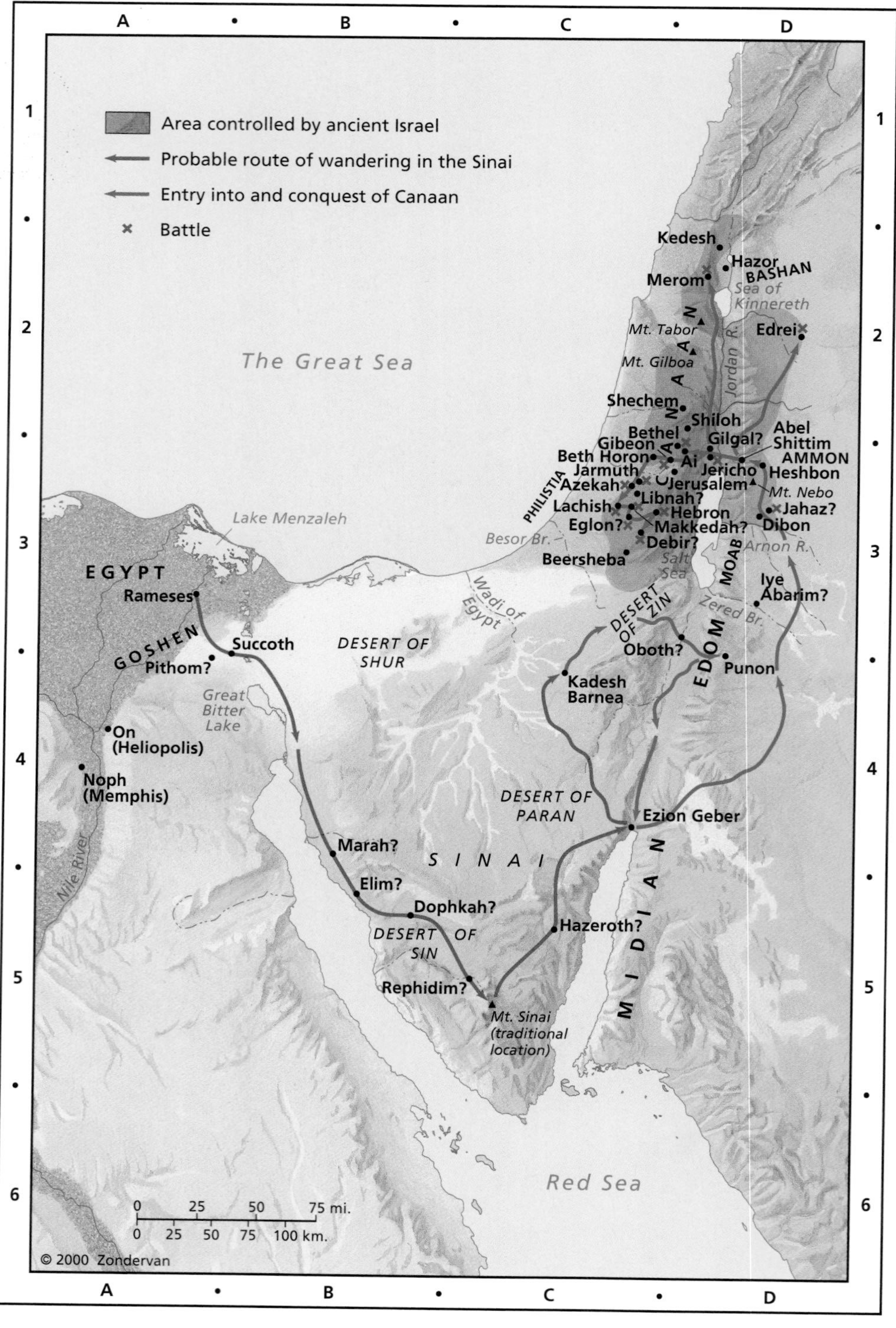

A
B
C
D
1
2
3
4
5
6
Area controlled by ancient Israel
Probable route of wandering in the Sinai
Entry into and conquest of Canaan
Battle
Kedesh
Hazor
BASHAN
Merom
Sea of Kinnereth
Mt. Tabor
Edrei
Mt. Gilboa
Jordan R.
CANAAN
The Great Sea
Shechem
Shiloh
Bethel
Abel Shittim
Gibeon
Gilgal?
Beth Horon
Ai
AMMON
Jarmuth
Jericho
Heshbon
Azekah
Jerusalem
Mt. Nebo
PHILISTIA
Libnah?
Lachish
Hebron
Jahaz?
Eglon?
Makkedah?
Dibon
Lake Menzaleh
Besor Br.
Debir?
Arnon R.
Beersheba
Salt Sea
MOAB
EGYPT
Rameses
Wadi of Egypt
DESERT OF ZIN
Iye Abarim?
Zered Br.
GOSHEN
Succoth
DESERT OF SHUR
Oboth?
EDOM
Punon
Pithom?
Kadesh Barnea
Great Bitter Lake
On (Heliopolis)
Noph (Memphis)
DESERT OF PARAN
Ezion Geber
Nile River
Marah?
SINAI
MIDIAN
Elim?
Dophkah?
DESERT OF SIN
Hazeroth?
Rephidim?
Mt. Sinai (traditional location)
Red Sea
0 25 50 75 mi.
0 25 50 75 100 km.
© 2000 Zondervan

Map 4: **LAND OF THE TWELVE TRIBES**

Map 5: KINGDOM OF DAVID AND SOLOMON

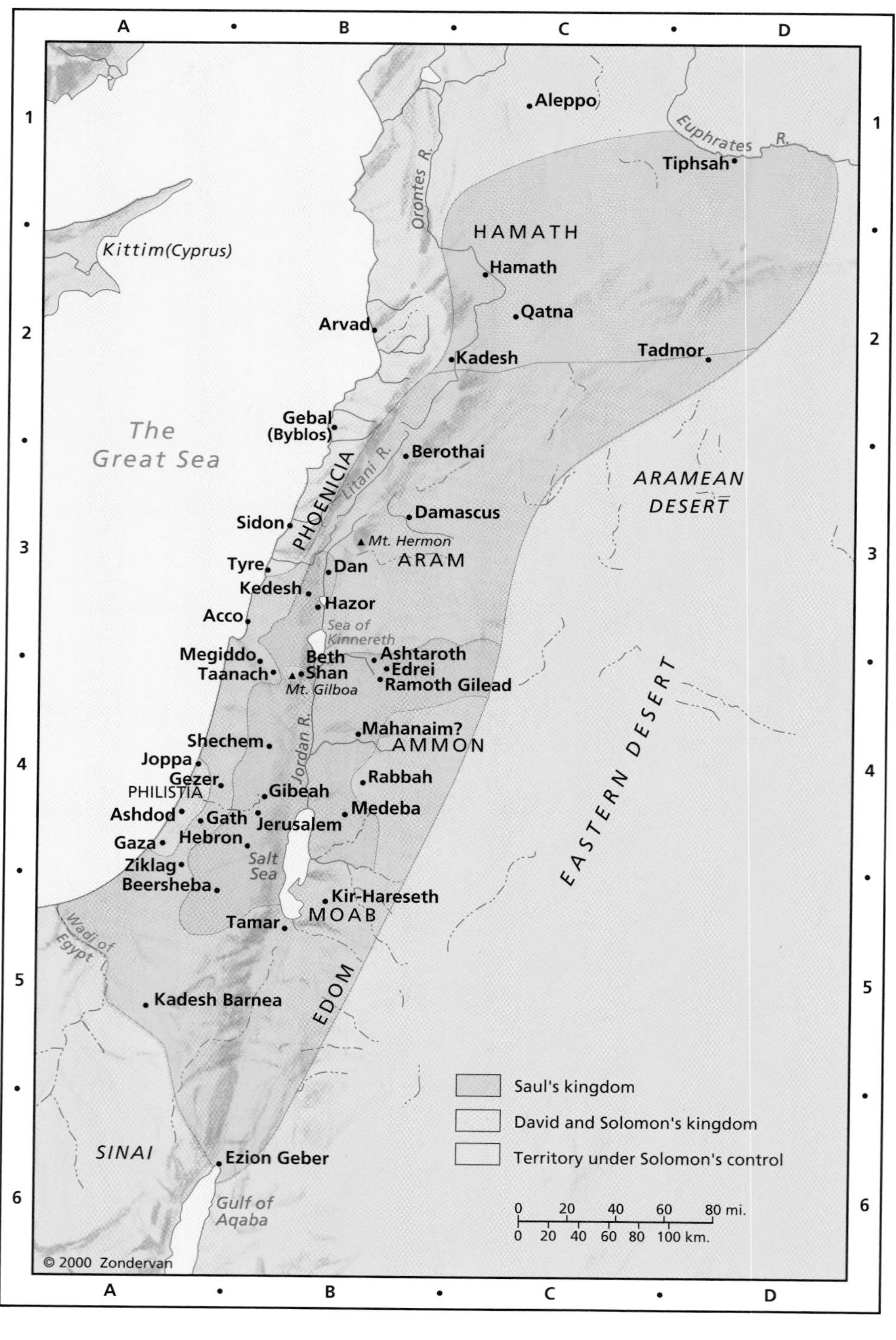
A
B
C
D
1
2
3
4
5
6
Aleppo
Euphrates R.
Tiphsah
Orontes R.
HAMATH
Hamath
Kittim (Cyprus)
Qatna
Arvad
Tadmor
Kadesh
Gebal (Byblos)
The Great Sea
Berothai
Litani R.
PHOENICIA
ARAMEAN DESERT
Damascus
Sidon
Mt. Hermon
Tyre
Dan
ARAM
Kedesh
Hazor
Acco
Sea of Kinnereth
Megiddo
Beth Shan
Ashtaroth
Taanach
Edrei
Ramoth Gilead
Mt. Gilboa
Jordan R.
Mahanaim?
Shechem
AMMON
EASTERN DESERT
Joppa
Gezer
Rabbah
PHILISTIA
Gibeah
Ashdod
Gath
Medeba
Jerusalem
Gaza
Hebron
Salt Sea
Ziklag
Beersheba
Kir-Hareseth
MOAB
Tamar
Wadi of Egypt
EDOM
Kadesh Barnea
Saul's kingdom
David and Solomon's kingdom
Territory under Solomon's control
SINAI
Ezion Geber
Gulf of Aqaba
0 20 40 60 80 mi.
0 20 40 60 80 100 km.
© 2000 Zondervan

A
B
C
D
1
2
3
4
5
6
0 10 20 30 mi.
0 10 20 30 40 km.
Beirut
Sidon
Tyre
PHOENICIA
Litani R.
Abana R.
Damascus
Mt. Hermon
Pharpar R.
Dan
ARAM
Kedesh
Hazor
J. Jarmuk
Acco
Sea of Kinnereth
Ashtaroth
Mt. Carmel
Mt. Tabor
Kishon R.
Yarmuk R.
Edrei
The Great Sea
Megiddo
Mt. Moreh
Beth Shan
Ramoth Gilead
Taanach
Mt. Gilboa
Ibleam
Jordan R.
Jabesh Gilead?
Tirzah
Samaria
Mt. Ebal
Succoth?
Penuel?
Mahanaim?
Yarkon R.
Shechem
Jabbok R.
Mt. Gerizim
Aphek
Joppa
Shiloh
ISRAEL
Rabbah (Amman)
AMMON
Bethel
Jericho
Gezer
Aijalon
Mt. Nebo
Heshbon
Ashdod
Jerusalem
Medeba
Gath
Bethlehem
Ashkelon
Mareshah
Hebron
Dibon
Gaza
Salt Sea
Arnon R.
Besor Br.
Gerar
JUDAH
Raphia
Beersheba
MOAB
Kir Hareseth
PHILISTIA
Zered Br.
WILDERNESS
W. el-Arish
Region periodically contested by Judah and Edom
Bozrah
EDOM
Kadesh Barnea
WILDERNESS

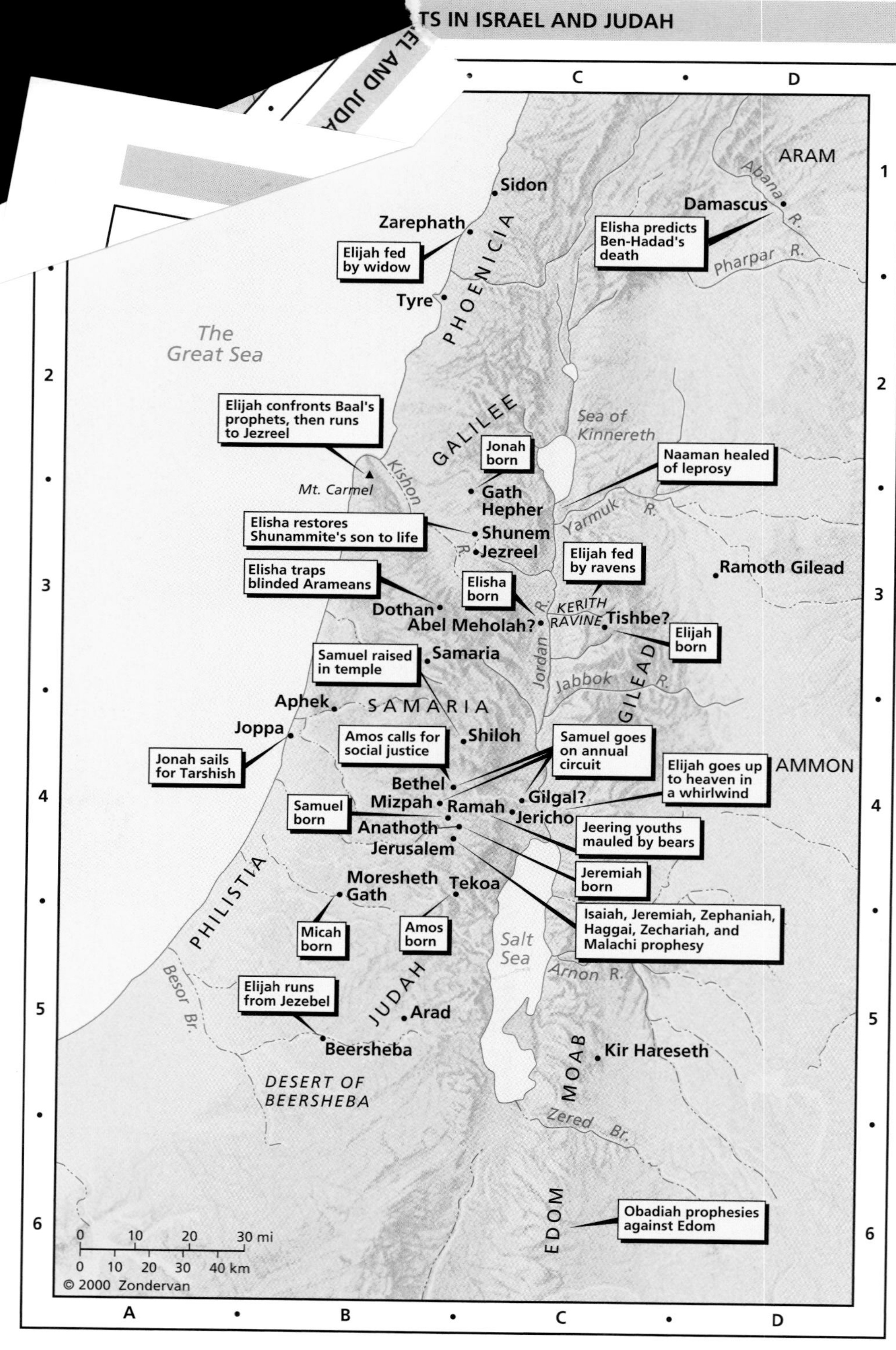

EL AND JUDA
ARAM
Abana R.
Damascus
Elisha predicts Ben-Hadad's death
Pharpar R.
Sidon
Zarephath
Elijah fed by widow
PHOENICIA
Tyre
The Great Sea
Elijah confronts Baal's prophets, then runs to Jezreel
Mt. Carmel
Kishon
GALILEE
Jonah born
Gath Hepher
Sea of Kinnereth
Naaman healed of leprosy
Yarmuk R.
Elisha restores Shunammite's son to life
Shunem
Jezreel
Elijah fed by ravens
Ramoth Gilead
Elisha traps blinded Arameans
Elisha born
KERITH RAVINE
Tishbe?
Dothan
Abel Meholah?
Elijah born
Samuel raised in temple
Samaria
Jordan R.
Jabbok R.
GILEAD
Aphek
SAMARIA
Joppa
Shiloh
Amos calls for social justice
Samuel goes on annual circuit
Jonah sails for Tarshish
Elijah goes up to heaven in a whirlwind
AMMON
Bethel
Gilgal?
Mizpah
Ramah
Jericho
Samuel born
Anathoth
Jeering youths mauled by bears
Jerusalem
Jeremiah born
PHILISTIA
Moresheth Gath
Tekoa
Isaiah, Jeremiah, Zephaniah, Haggai, Zechariah, and Malachi prophesy
Micah born
Amos born
Salt Sea
Arnon R.
Besor Br.
Elijah runs from Jezebel
JUDAH
Arad
Beersheba
MOAB
Kir Hareseth
DESERT OF BEERSHEBA
Zered Br.
EDOM
Obadiah prophesies against Edom
0 10 20 30 mi
0 10 20 30 40 km
A B C D
1 2 3 4 5 6

Map 8: **ASSYRIAN AND BABYLONIAN EMPIRES**

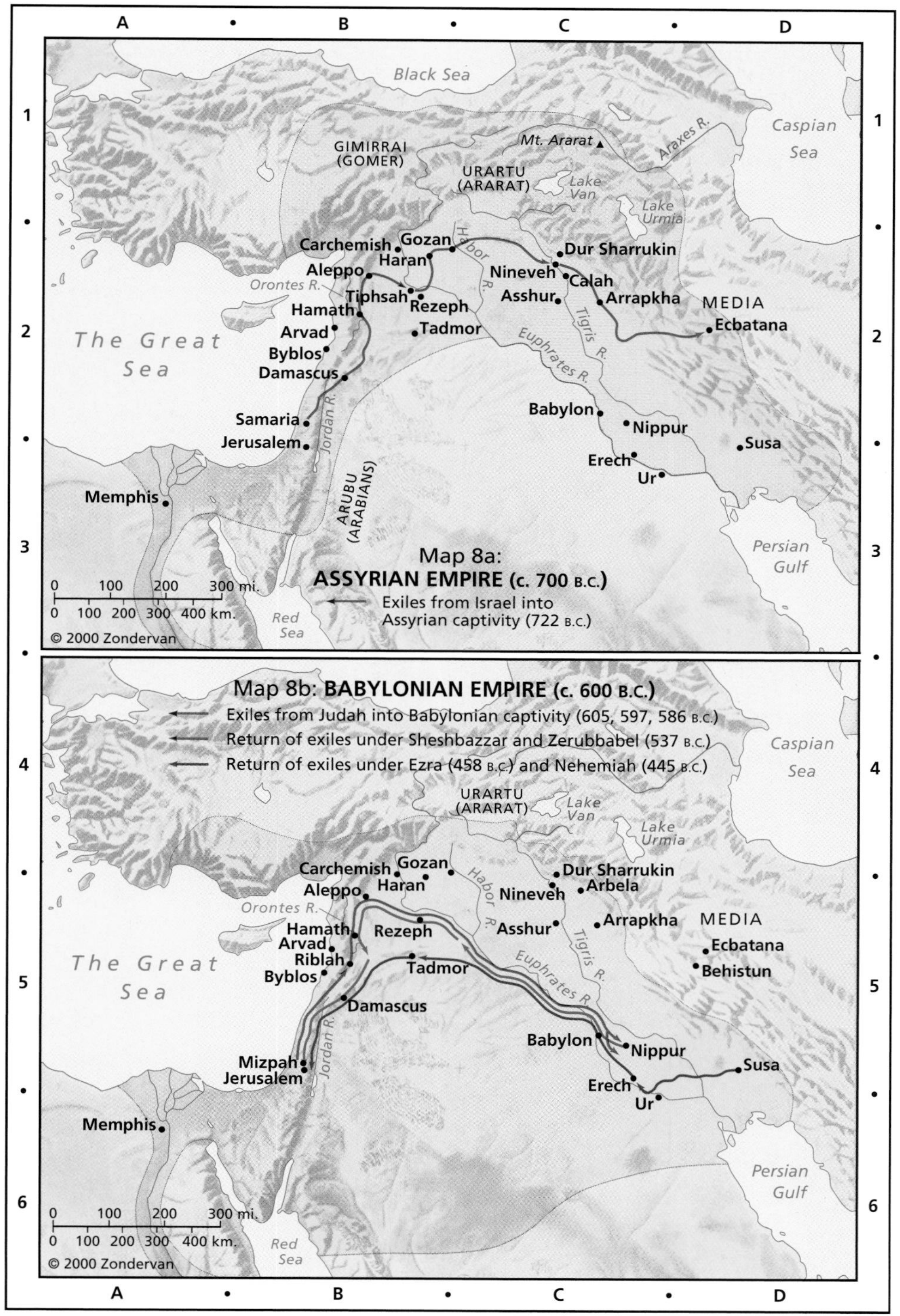

Map 9: HOLY LAND IN THE TIME OF JESUS

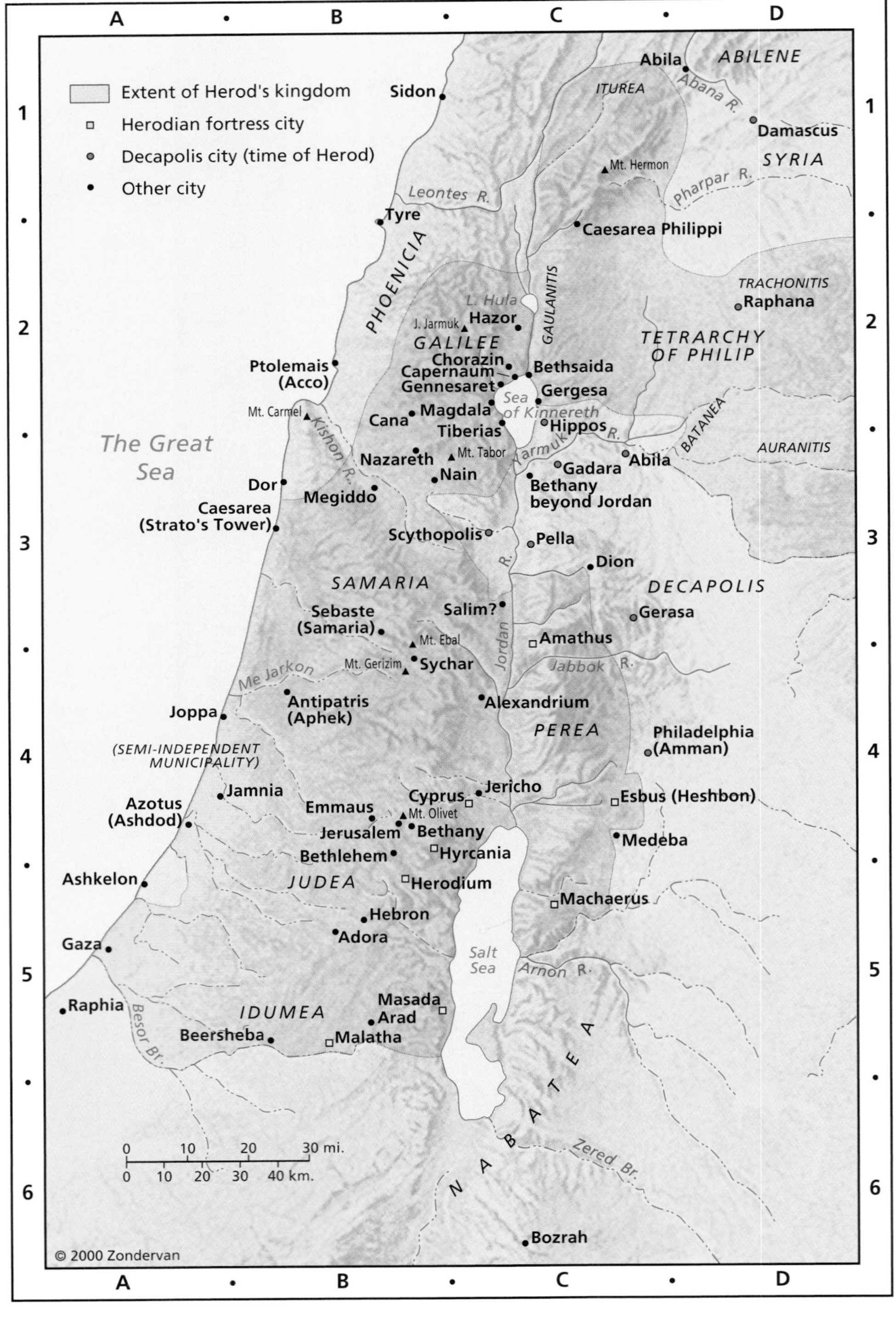

A
B
C
D
1
2
3
4
5
6
Extent of Herod's kingdom
Herodian fortress city
Decapolis city (time of Herod)
Other city
Sidon
Abila
ABILENE
ITUREA
Abana R.
Damascus
SYRIA
Mt. Hermon
Pharpar R.
Leontes R.
Tyre
Caesarea Philippi
PHOENICIA
GAULANITIS
TRACHONITIS
Raphana
L. Hula
J. Jarmuk
Hazor
GALILEE
TETRARCHY OF PHILIP
Ptolemais (Acco)
Chorazin
Capernaum
Bethsaida
Gennesaret
Gergesa
Sea of Kinnereth
Mt. Carmel
Cana
Magdala
Tiberias
Hippos
BATANEA
Kishon R.
The Great Sea
Nazareth
Mt. Tabor
Yarmuk R.
AURANITIS
Gadara
Abila
Nain
Dor
Megiddo
Bethany beyond Jordan
Caesarea (Strato's Tower)
Scythopolis
Pella
Dion
SAMARIA
DECAPOLIS
Salim?
Sebaste (Samaria)
Gerasa
Mt. Ebal
Amathus
Jordan R.
Mt. Gerizim
Sychar
Me Jarkon
Jabbok R.
Antipatris (Aphek)
Alexandrium
Joppa
PEREA
Philadelphia (Amman)
(SEMI-INDEPENDENT MUNICIPALITY)
Jamnia
Jericho
Cyprus
Esbus (Heshbon)
Azotus (Ashdod)
Emmaus
Mt. Olivet
Jerusalem
Bethany
Medeba
Bethlehem
Hyrcania
Ashkelon
JUDEA
Herodium
Machaerus
Hebron
Adora
Gaza
Salt Sea
Arnon R.
Raphia
Besor Br.
IDUMEA
Masada
Arad
Beersheba
Malatha
NABATEA
Zered Br.
0 10 20 30 mi.
0 10 20 30 40 km.
Bozrah
© 2000 Zondervan

Map 10: **JERUSALEM IN THE TIME OF JESUS**

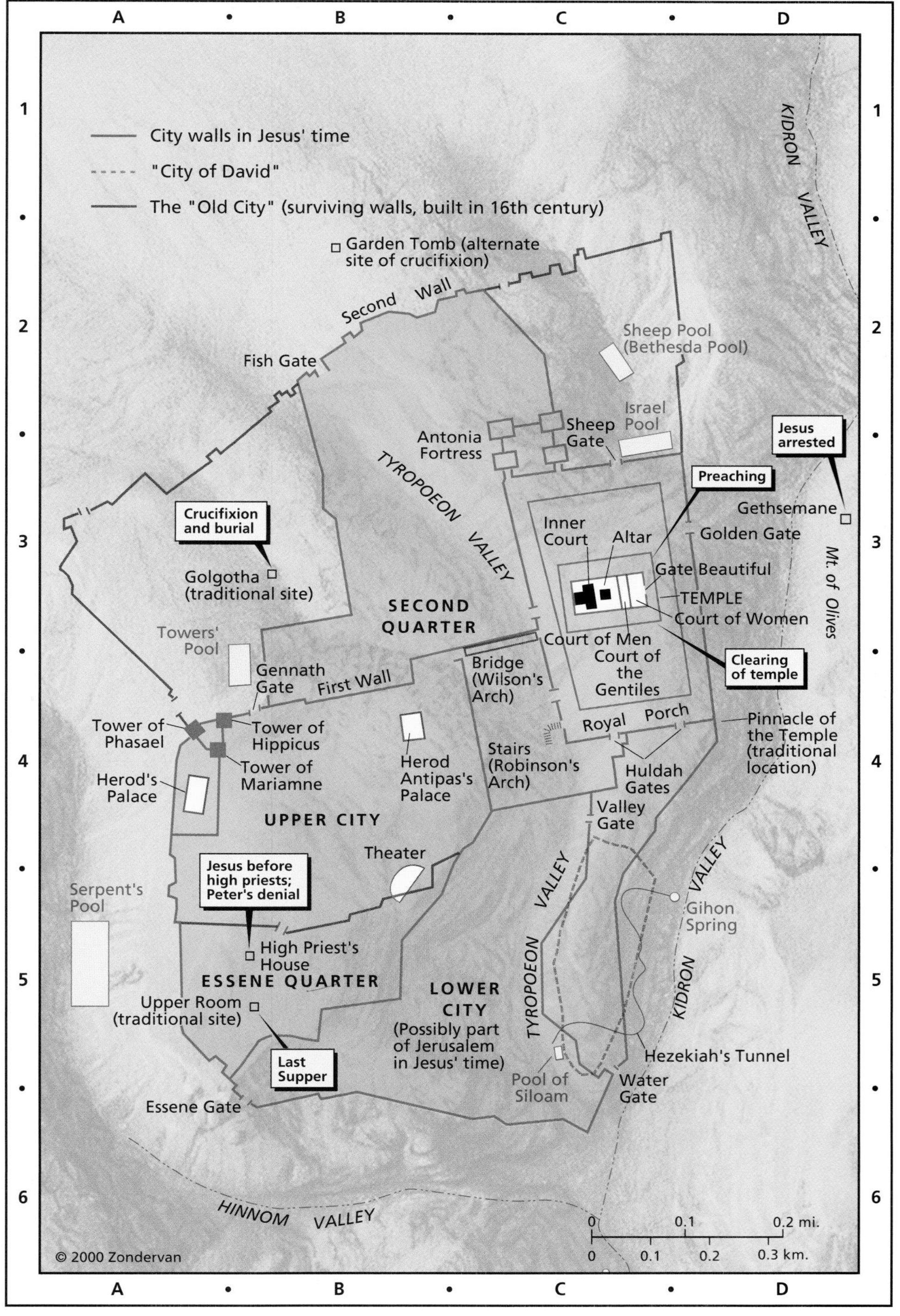

A
B
C
D
1
2
3
4
5
6
City walls in Jesus' time
"City of David"
The "Old City" (surviving walls, built in 16th century)
Garden Tomb (alternate site of crucifixion)
Second Wall
Fish Gate
Sheep Pool (Bethesda Pool)
Israel Pool
Sheep Gate
Antonia Fortress
Jesus arrested
Preaching
Gethsemane
Golden Gate
KIDRON VALLEY
Mt. of Olives
TYROPOEON VALLEY
Crucifixion and burial
Golgotha (traditional site)
Inner Court
Altar
Gate Beautiful
TEMPLE
Court of Women
SECOND QUARTER
Towers' Pool
Court of Men
Court of the Gentiles
Clearing of temple
Gennath Gate
First Wall
Bridge (Wilson's Arch)
Royal Porch
Pinnacle of the Temple (traditional location)
Tower of Phasael
Tower of Hippicus
Tower of Mariamne
Herod's Palace
Herod Antipas's Palace
Stairs (Robinson's Arch)
Huldah Gates
Valley Gate
UPPER CITY
Theater
Jesus before high priests; Peter's denial
Serpent's Pool
Gihon Spring
High Priest's House
ESSENE QUARTER
LOWER CITY (Possibly part of Jerusalem in Jesus' time)
Upper Room (traditional site)
Last Supper
Hezekiah's Tunnel
Pool of Siloam
Water Gate
Essene Gate
HINNOM VALLEY
0 0.1 0.2 mi.
0 0.1 0.2 0.3 km.

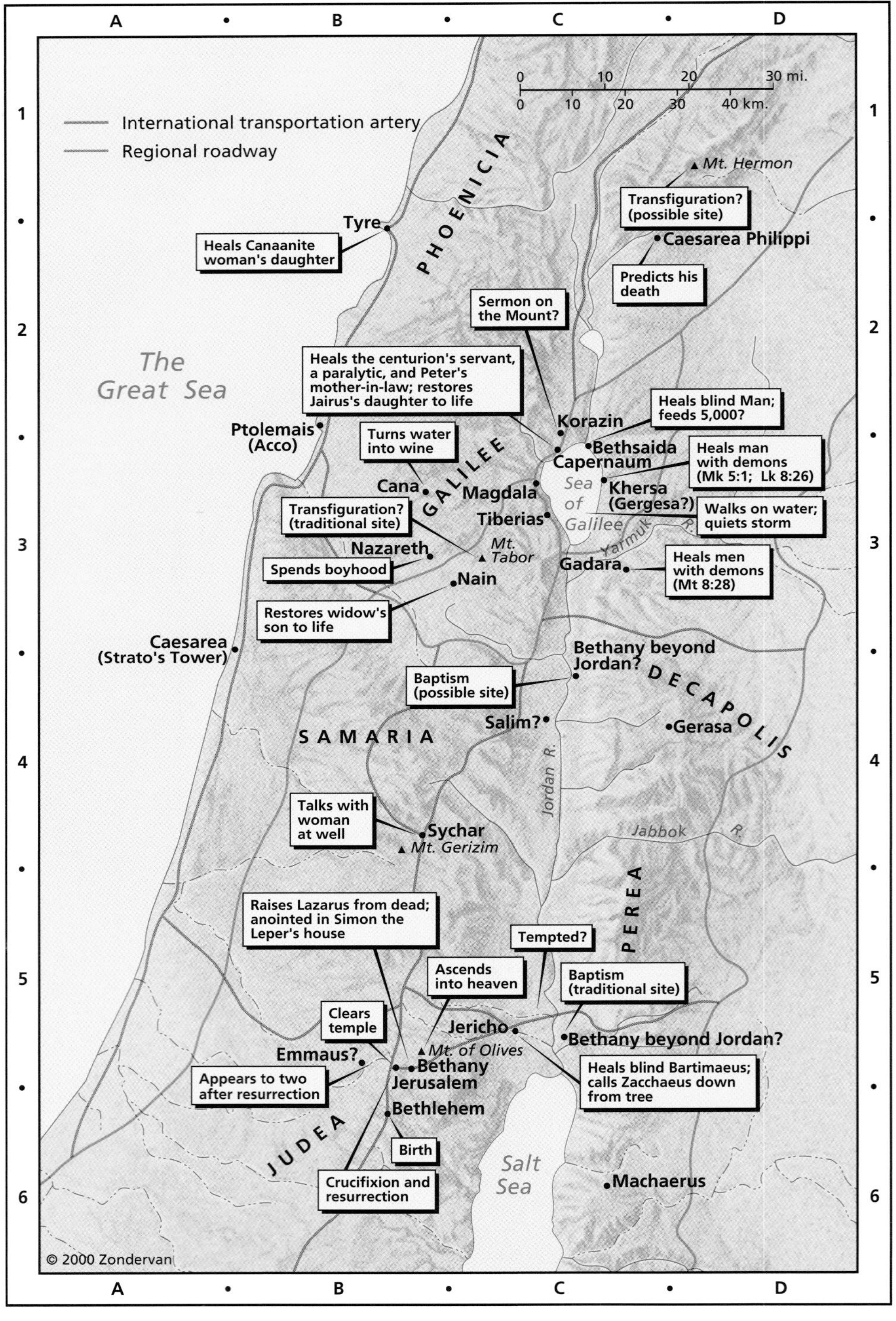

A
B
C
D
1
2
3
4
5
6
0
10
20
30 mi.
0
10
20
30
40 km.
International transportation artery
Regional roadway
The Great Sea
PHOENICIA
Mt. Hermon
Transfiguration? (possible site)
Caesarea Philippi
Predicts his death
Tyre
Heals Canaanite woman's daughter
Sermon on the Mount?
Heals the centurion's servant, a paralytic, and Peter's mother-in-law; restores Jairus's daughter to life
Heals blind Man; feeds 5,000?
Korazin
Ptolemais (Acco)
Turns water into wine
Bethsaida
Capernaum
Heals man with demons (Mk 5:1; Lk 8:26)
GALILEE
Cana
Magdala
Sea of Galilee
Khersa (Gergesa?)
Walks on water; quiets storm
Transfiguration? (traditional site)
Tiberias
Yarmuk R.
Mt. Tabor
Nazareth
Spends boyhood
Gadara
Heals men with demons (Mt 8:28)
Nain
Restores widow's son to life
Caesarea (Strato's Tower)
Bethany beyond Jordan?
Baptism (possible site)
DECAPOLIS
Salim?
Gerasa
SAMARIA
Jordan R.
Talks with woman at well
Sychar
Mt. Gerizim
Jabbok R.
PEREA
Raises Lazarus from dead; anointed in Simon the Leper's house
Tempted?
Ascends into heaven
Baptism (traditional site)
Clears temple
Jericho
Bethany beyond Jordan?
Mt. of Olives
Emmaus?
Appears to two after resurrection
Bethany
Jerusalem
Heals blind Bartimaeus; calls Zacchaeus down from tree
Bethlehem
JUDEA
Birth
Salt Sea
Machaerus
Crucifixion and resurrection

Map 12: **APOSTLES' EARLY TRAVELS**

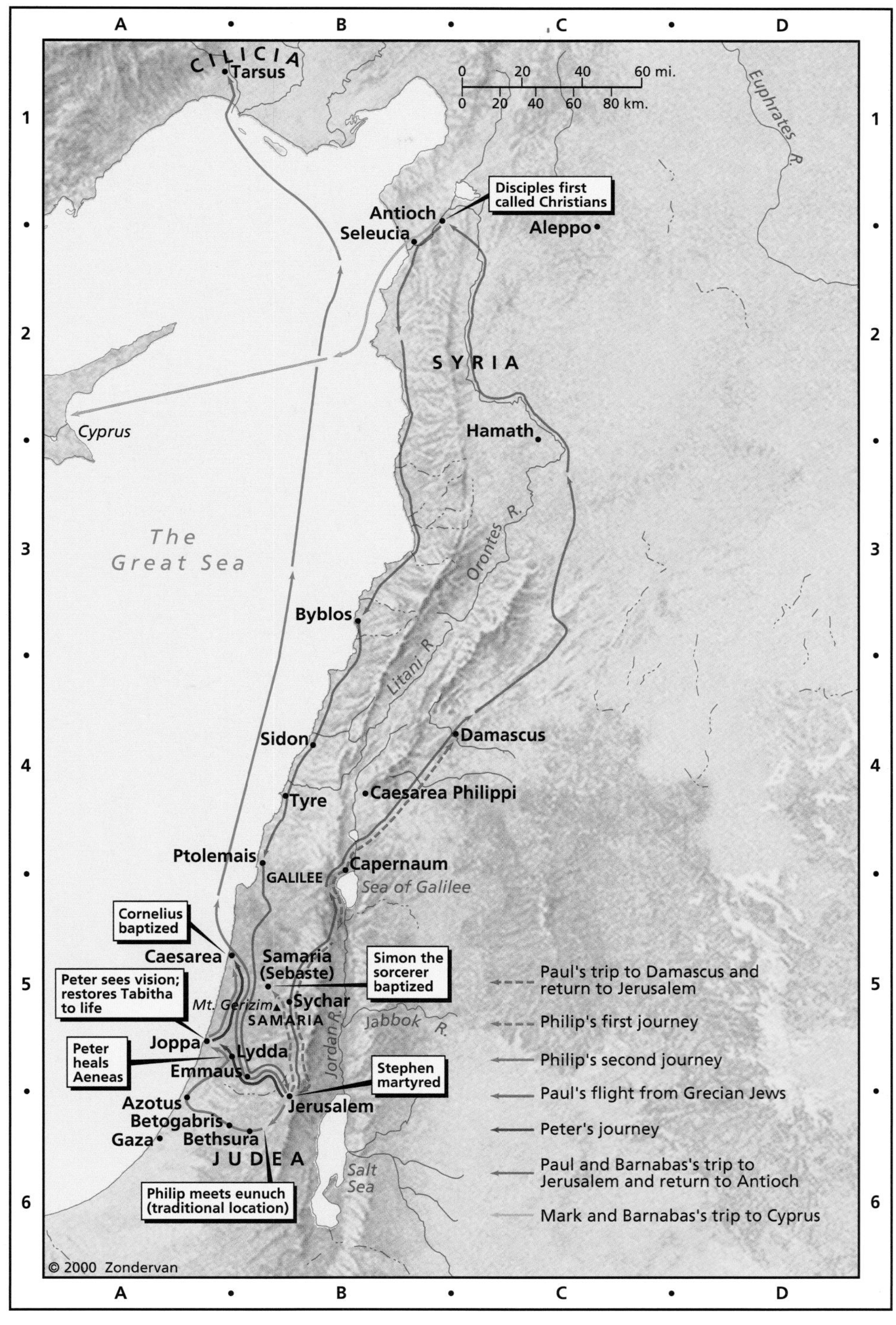

A
B
C
D
1
2
3
4
5
6
CILICIA
Tarsus
0 20 40 60 mi.
0 20 40 60 80 km.
Euphrates R.
Disciples first called Christians
Antioch
Seleucia
Aleppo
SYRIA
Cyprus
Hamath
The Great Sea
Orontes R.
Byblos
Litani R.
Sidon
Damascus
Tyre
Caesarea Philippi
Ptolemais
Capernaum
GALILEE
Sea of Galilee
Cornelius baptized
Caesarea
Samaria (Sebaste)
Simon the sorcerer baptized
Peter sees vision; restores Tabitha to life
Mt. Gerizim
Sychar
SAMARIA
Jabbok R.
Jordan R.
Joppa
Lydda
Peter heals Aeneas
Emmaus
Stephen martyred
Azotus
Jerusalem
Betogabris
Gaza
Bethsura
JUDEA
Salt Sea
Philip meets eunuch (traditional location)
Paul's trip to Damascus and return to Jerusalem
Philip's first journey
Philip's second journey
Paul's flight from Grecian Jews
Peter's journey
Paul and Barnabas's trip to Jerusalem and return to Antioch
Mark and Barnabas's trip to Cyprus

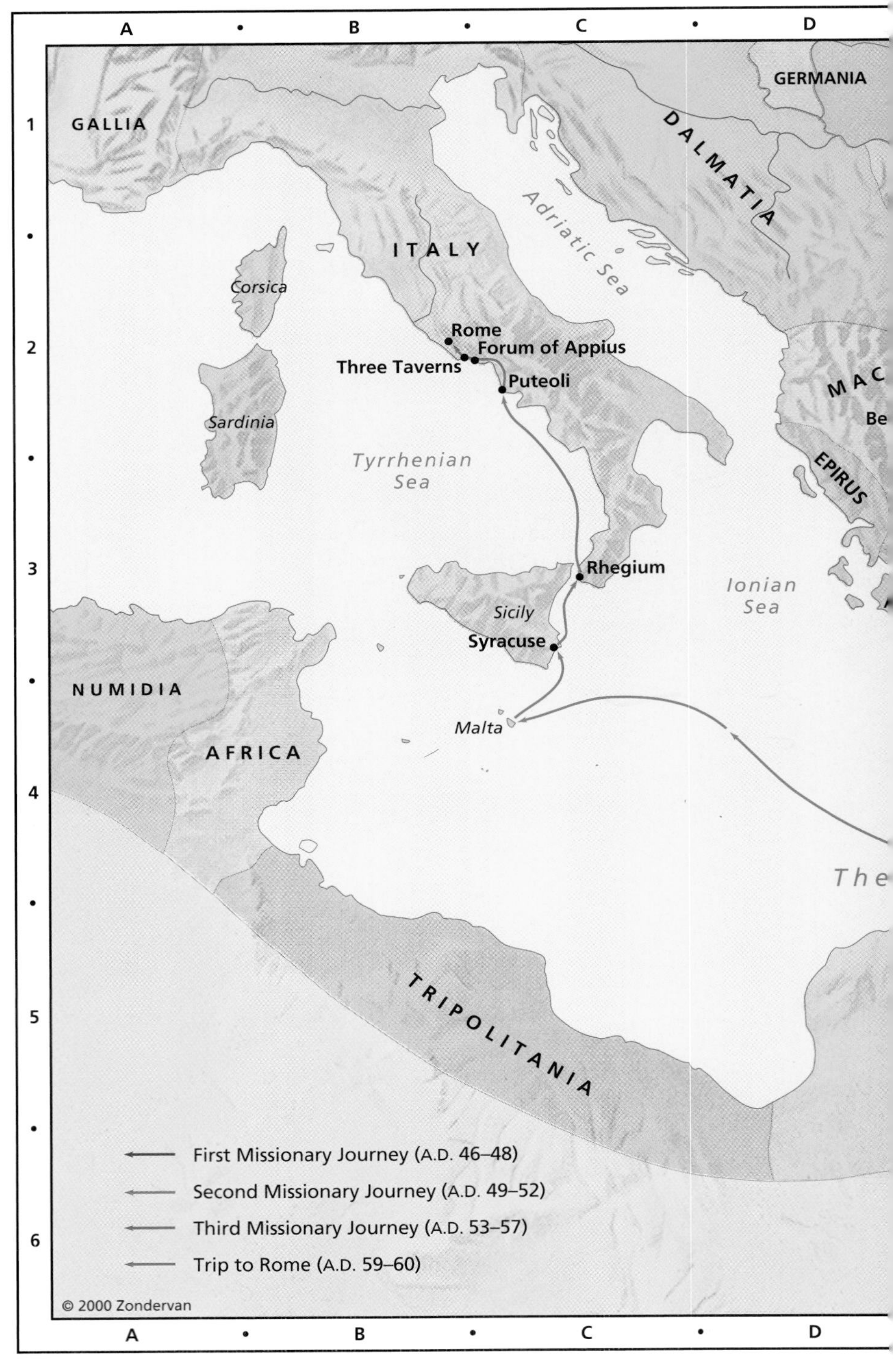
A
B
C
D
1
2
3
4
5
6
GALLIA
GERMANIA
DALMATIA
ITALY
Adriatic Sea
Corsica
Sardinia
Rome
Forum of Appius
Three Taverns
Puteoli
Tyrrhenian Sea
Rhegium
Ionian Sea
Sicily
Syracuse
Malta
EPIRUS
MAC
Be
NUMIDIA
AFRICA
TRIPOLITANIA
The
First Missionary Journey (A.D. 46–48)
Second Missionary Journey (A.D. 49–52)
Third Missionary Journey (A.D. 53–57)
Trip to Rome (A.D. 59–60)
© 2000 Zondervan

E
F
G
H
1
2
3
4
5
6
DACIA
MOESIA
THRACE
Black Sea
BITHYNIA AND PONTUS
GALATIA
Philippi
Neapolis
Apollonia
Samothrace
hessalonica
Troas
Assos
Mitylene
Aegean Sea
MYSIA
Pergamum
Thyatira
ASIA
Sardis
Philadelphia
Kios
Smyrna
LYDIA
Ephesus
Samos
Athens
PHRYGIA
Laodicea
Colosse
Miletus
Patmos
Cos
Cnidus
Rhodes
Pisidian Antioch
LYCAONIA
Iconium
Lystra
Derbe
PISIDIA
PAMPHYLIA
Attalia
Perga
LYCIA
Patara
Myra
CAPPADOCIA
COMMAGENE
CILICIA
Tarsus
Issus
Euphrates R.
Antioch
Aleppo
Seleucia
SYRIA
Cyprus
Salamis
Paphos
Crete
Lasea
Fair Havens
Salmone
Great Sea
PHOENICIA
ABILENE
Sidon
Damascus
Tyre
Ptolemais
Caesarea
JUDEA
Jordan R.
Jerusalem
Salt Sea
ARABIA
RENAICA
EGYPT
Nile R.
Red Sea
0
100
200 mi.
0
100
200
300 km.

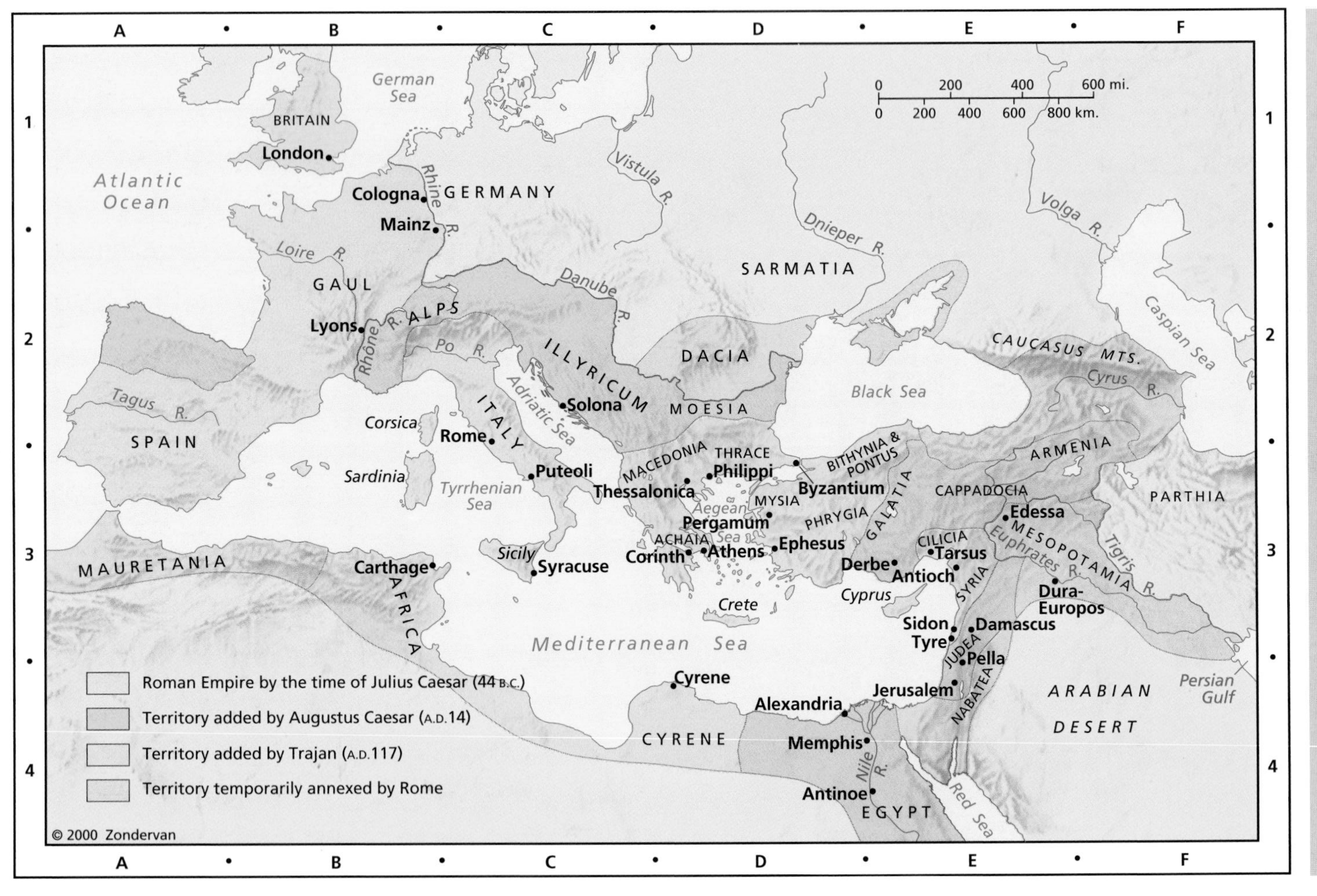
0 200 400 600 mi.
0 200 400 600 800 km.
A B C D E F
1 2 3 4
German Sea
BRITAIN
London
Atlantic Ocean
Cologna
Rhine R.
GERMANY
Mainz
Vistula R.
Volga R.
Dnieper R.
Loire R.
SARMATIA
GAUL
Danube R.
Caspian Sea
Lyons
Rhône R.
ALPS
Po R.
DACIA
CAUCASUS MTS.
Cyrus R.
ILLYRICUM
Tagus R.
Solona
MOESIA
Black Sea
ITALY
Adriatic Sea
Corsica
Rome
SPAIN
BITHYNIA & PONTUS
ARMENIA
MACEDONIA
THRACE
Sardinia
Puteoli
Philippi
Tyrrhenian Sea
Thessalonica
Byzantium
CAPPADOCIA
PARTHIA
Aegean Sea
MYSIA
GALATIA
Pergamum
PHRYGIA
Edessa
ACHAIA
CILICIA
MESOPOTAMIA
Euphrates R.
Tigris R.
Sicily
Corinth
Athens
Ephesus
Tarsus
MAURETANIA
Syracuse
Carthage
Derbe
Antioch
SYRIA
AFRICA
Dura-Europos
Cyprus
Crete
Sidon
Damascus
Tyre
Mediterranean Sea
JUDEA
Pella
Roman Empire by the time of Julius Caesar (44 B.C.)
Cyrene
Jerusalem
ARABIAN
Persian Gulf
NABATEA
Alexandria
Territory added by Augustus Caesar (A.D.14)
DESERT
CYRENE
Memphis
Territory added by Trajan (A.D.117)
Nile R.
Territory temporarily annexed by Rome
Antinoe
Red Sea
EGYPT